Who's Who in Religion

Biographical Titles Currently Published by Marquis Who's Who

Who's Who in America
Who's Who in America derivatives:
    Who's Who in America Junior & Senior High School Version
    Geographic/Professional Index
    Supplement to Who's Who in America
    Who's Who in America Classroom Project Book
Who Was Who in America
    Historical Volume (1607-1896)
    Volume I (1897-1942)
    Volume II (1943-1950)
    Volume III (1951-1960)
    Volume IV (1961-1968)
    Volume V (1969-1973)
    Volume VI (1974-1976)
    Volume VII (1977-1981)
    Volume VIII (1982-1985)
    Volume IX (1985-1989)
    Index Volume (1607-1989)
Who's Who in the World
Who's Who in the East
Who's Who in the Midwest
Who's Who in the South and Southwest
Who's Who in the West
Who's Who in Advertising
Who's Who in American Law
Who's Who of American Women
Who's Who of Emerging Leaders in America
Who's Who in Entertainment
Who's Who in Finance and Industry
Who's Who in Religion
Who's Who in Science and Engineering
Index to Who's Who Books
Directory of Medical Specialists
Supplement to Directory of Medical Specialists

Who's Who
in Religion

**4th edition
1992-1993**

**MARQUIS
Who'sWho**

A Reed Reference Publishing Company
3002 Glenview Road
Wilmette, Illinois 60091 U.S.A.

Sandra S. Barnes—President
Sallie A. Lambert—Senior Product Manager
William H. Hamblin—Director of Production
John L. Daniels—Product Manager
Julia C. DeGraf—Operations Manager
Frederick M. Marks—Manager, Biographical Research
Samuel C. Moore—Publication Manager
Renee R. Bagg—Researcher

WHO'S WHO IN RELIGION is a registered trademark of
Reed Publishing (Nederland) b.v., used under license.

Library of Congress Catalog Card Number 76-25357
International Standard Book Number 0-8379-1604-6
Product Code Number 030662

Manufactured in the United States of America

Table of Contents

Preface vi

Board of Advisors vii

Standards of Admission viii

Key to Information ix

Table of Abbreviations x

Alphabetical Practices xvi

Biographies 1

Preface

As the world advances in all areas of science and technology at a faster and faster pace, the role of religion in the life of modern woman and man seems more crucial than ever. Our outer lives are changed almost daily, it seems, by the remarkable work of modern scientists and engineers, but inwardly, we continue to grapple with the questions and problems religion has always addressed, in addition to the new challenges modern society presents. Rather than causing a flight from questions of religion, it seems our advancing society, for many, is causing a re-evaluation of and a renewed interest in questions of conscience, morality, and virtue. Here near the end of the twentieth century, religion is more important than ever.

Marquis Who's Who offers, in this fourth edition of *Who's Who in Religion*, a volume that chronicles the lives of today's religious leaders. Here are profiled more than 15,600 religious men and women from throughout the world. These individuals represent the following general categories:

Church officials—national and regional, both lay and clergy of all denominations, and heads of orders;

Clergy—priests, rabbis, ministers, and other clergy, selected for their contributions to the various activities of their faith;

Religious educators—professors of religion, theology, or divinity at theological seminaries, denominational colleges, and other colleges and universities with schools of religion or theology;

Lay Leaders—founders or directors of religious charities, lay organizations, lay writers and editors of religious publications, and many other professionals working on every aspect of religious endeavor.

The names recorded in *Who's Who in Religion* reflect the culmination of a two-year process of research, writing, and editing by the Marquis Who's Who staff. In addition to careful examination of literature, communications media, and other available data sources, the editors worked with a distinguished Board of Advisors, whose members nominated outstanding individuals in their own denominations for inclusion in this volume.

As with all Marquis Who's Who directories, final selection of names rests on one principle: reference value. Significant work and achievement in the area of religion was the sole criterion for inclusion in the book. An individual's desire to be listed was not sufficient reason for inclusion.

In the majority of cases, the men and women listed in *Who's Who in Religion* supplied their own data, thus assuring a high degree of accuracy. As in previous editions, biographees were given the opportunity to review prepublication proofs of their sketches. In some instances where individuals failed to furnish data, the Marquis editorial staff compiled the information through careful, independent research. Sketches compiled in this manner are denoted by an asterisk.

Each biographical sketch provides the following information: name, religious and/or secular occupation, denomination, vital statistics, parents' names, marriage information and children's names (where applicable), education history, ordination and certification background, as well as career history. In addition, each sketch profiles religious activities, creative works, civic and political activities, awards received, memberships, political affiliation, and address information. Finally, many of these sketches conclude with the biographee's Thoughts on Life—a statement of personal philosophy.

Marquis Who's Who exercises the greatest care in preparing each sketch for publication. Occasionally, however, errors do occur. Users of this directory are requested to report such errors to the publisher so that corrections can be made in a later edition.

Board of Advisors

Marquis Who's Who gratefully acknowledges the following distinguished individuals who have made themselves available for review, evaluation, and general comment with regard to the publication of the fourth edition of *Who's Who in Religion*. The advisors have enhanced the reference value of this edition by the nomination of outstanding individuals for inclusion. However, the Board of Advisors, either collectively or individually, is in no way responsible for the final selection of names appearing in this volume, nor does the Board of Advisors bear responsibility for the accuracy or comprehensiveness of the biographical information or other material contained herein.

Standards of Admission

The foremost consideration in selecting biographees for *Who's Who in Religion* is the extent of an individual's reference interest. Such reference interest is based on either of two factors: (1) the position of responsibility held, or (2) the level of significant achievement attained.

Admission based on the factor of position includes:

Presiding clergy of organized religious groups in North America

U.S. and Canadian bishops of all churches

Executive directors or heads of major religious agencies or organizations

Leaders of religious orders

Presidents and deans of major theological seminaries and schools

Leading publishers of religious books and periodicals

Religion editors of major daily newspapers

Admission based on individual achievement is based on objective qualitative criteria. To be selected, a person must have attained conspicuous achievement.

Key to Information

[1] JAMIESON, BURTON CARTER, [2] minister; [3] b. Chgo., Jan. 20, 1930; [4] s.William and Elizabeth (Donne) J.; [5] m. Janice Deanne Clark, May 11, 1954; [6] children: Elizabeth, Carter, Monica. [7] AB in Theology, Southeastern Bible Coll., 1952; MDiv, Harvard U., 1955. [8] Ordained to ministry Chs. of Christ, 1952. [9] Chaplain USNR, 1955-57; pastor chs., Minn. and Wis., 1957-62; pastor First Ch. of Christ, Mundelein, Ill., 1962-68, Main St. Christian Ch., Danville, Ill., 1968-70; exec. sec. Midwestern region Chs. of Christ, Chgo., 1970-73; sr. pastor First Christian Ch., Elmhurst, Ill., 1973—; [10] bd. dirs. Christian Home for the Aged, Monroeville, Wis., 1981—. [11] Contbr. articles to religious jours. [12] Area capt. Crusade of Mercy, Elmhurst, 1980-84. [13] With USNR, 1955-59. [14] Recipient Award of Honor Danville Ministerial Assn. [15] Mem. Assn. Pastoral Counselors, Am. Bible Rsch. Assn. [16] Republican. [17] Home: 1345 Grove Ave Elmhurst IL 60126 [18] Office: 1352 Forest Ave Elmhurst IL 60126 [19] *Do unto others as you would have them do unto you.*

KEY

[1]	Name
[2]	Occupation
[3]	Vital statistics
[4]	Parents
[5]	Marriage
[6]	Children
[7]	Education
[8]	Professional certifications
[9]	Career
[10]	Career Related
[11]	Writings and creative works
[12]	Civic and political activities
[13]	Military
[14]	Awards and fellowships
[15]	Professional and association memberships Clubs and Lodges
[16]	Political affiliation
[17]	Home address
[18]	Office address
[19]	Thoughts on Life

Table of Abbreviations

The following abbreviations and symbols are frequently used in this book.

*An asterisk following a sketch indicates that it was researched by the Marquis Who's Who editorial staff and has not been verified by the biographee.

AA, A.A. Associate in Arts, Associate of Arts
AAAL American Academy of Arts and Letters
AAAS American Association for the Advancement of Science
AACD American Association for Counseling and Development
AACN American Association of Critical Care Nurses
AAHA American Academy of Health Administrators
AAHP American Association of Hospital Planners
AAHPER Alliance for Health, Physical Education and Recreation
AASL American Association of School Librarians
AASPA American Association of School Personnel Administrators
AAU Amateur Athletic Union
AAUP American Association of University Professors
AAUW American Association of University Women
AB, A.B. Arts, Bachelor of
AB Alberta
ABA American Bar Association
ABC American Broadcasting Company
AC Air Corps
acad. academy, academic
acct. accountant
acctg. accounting
ACDA Arms Control and Disarmament Agency
ACHA American College of Hospital Administrators
ACLS Advanced Cardiac Life Support
ACLU American Civil Liberties Union
ACP American College of Physicians
ACS American College of Surgeons
ADA American Dental Association
a.d.c. aide-de-camp
adj. adjunct, adjutant
adj. gen. adjutant general
adm. admiral
adminstr. administrator
adminstrn. administration
adminstrv. administrative
ADN Associate's Degree in Nursing
ADP Automatic Data Processing
adv. advocate, advisory
advt. advertising
AE, A.E. Agricultural Engineer
A.E. and P. Ambassador Extraordinary and Plenipotentiary
AEC Atomic Energy Commission

aero. aeronautical, aeronautic
aerodyn. aerodynamic
AFB Air Force Base
AFL-CIO American Federation of Labor and Congress of Industrial Organizations
AFTRA American Federation of TV and Radio Artists
AFSCME American Federation of State, County and Municipal Employees
agr. agriculture
agrl. agricultural
agt. agent
AGVA American Guild of Variety Artists
agy. agency
A&I Agricultural and Industrial
AIA American Institute of Architects
AIAA American Institute of Aeronautics and Astronautics
AICPA American Institute of Certified Public Accountants
AID Agency for International Development
AIDS Acquired Immune Deficiency Syndrome
AIEE American Institute of Electrical Engineers
AIM American Institute of Management
AIME American Institute of Mining, Metallurgy, and Petroleum Engineers
AK Alaska
AL Alabama
ALA American Library Association
Ala. Alabama
alt. alternate
Alta. Alberta
A&M Agricultural and Mechanical
AM, A.M. Arts, Master of
Am. American, America
AMA American Medical Association
amb. ambassador
A.M.E. African Methodist Episcopal
Amtrak National Railroad Passenger Corporation
AMVETS American Veterans of World War II, Korea, Vietnam
ANA American Nurses Association
anat. anatomical
ann. annual
ANTA American National Theatre and Academy
anthrop. anthropological
AP Associated Press
APA American Psychological Association
APGA American Personnel Guidance Association
APHA American Public Health Association
APO Army Post Office
apptd. appointed
Apr. April
apt. apartment

AR Arkansas
ARC American Red Cross
archeol. archeological
archtl. architectural
Ariz. Arizona
Ark. Arkansas
ArtsD, ArtsD. Arts, Doctor of
arty. artillery
AS American Samoa
AS Associate in Science, Associate of Applied Science
ASCAP American Society of Composers, Authors and Publishers
ASCD Association for Supervision and Curriculum Development
ASCE American Society of Civil Engineers
ASHRAE American Society of Heating, Refrigeration, and Air Conditioning Engineers
ASME American Society of Mechanical Engineers
ASNSA American Society for Nursing Service Administrators
ASPA American Society for Public Administration
ASPCA American Society for the Prevention of Cruelty to Animals
assn. association
assoc. associate
asst. assistant
ASTD American Society for Training and Development
ASTM American Society for Testing and Materials
astron. astronomical
astrophys. astrophysical
ATSC Air Technical Service Command
AT&T American Telephone & Telegraph Company
atty. attorney
Aug. August
AUS Army of the United States
aux. auxiliary
Ave. Avenue
AVMA American Veterinary Medical Association
AZ Arizona

B. Bachelor
b. born
BA, B.A. Bachelor of Arts
BAgr, B.Agr. Bachelor of Agriculture
Balt. Baltimore
Bapt. Baptist
BArch, B.Arch. Bachelor of Architecture
BAS, B.A.S. Bachelor of Agricultural Science
BBA, B.B.A. Bachelor of Business Administration

BBC British Broadcasting Corporation
BC, B.C. British Columbia
BCE, B.C.E. Bachelor of Civil Engineering
BChir, B.Chir. Bachelor of Surgery
BCL, B.C.L. Bachelor of Civil Law
BCLS Basic Cardiac Life Support
BCS, B.C.S. Bachelor of Commercial
   Science
BD, B.D. Bachelor of Divinity
bd. board
BE, B.E. Bachelor of Education
BEE, B.E.E. Bachelor of Electrical
   Engineering
BFA, B.F.A. Bachelor of Fine Arts
bibl. biblical
bibliog. bibliographical
biog. biographical
biol. biological
BJ, B.J. Bachelor of Journalism
Bklyn. Brooklyn
BL, B.L. Bachelor of Letters
bldg. building
BLS, B.L.S. Bachelor of Library Science
BLS Basic Life Support
Blvd. Boulevard
BMW Bavarian Motor Works (Bayerische
   Motoren Werke)
bn. battalion
B.& O.R.R. Baltimore & Ohio Railroad
bot. botanical
BPE, B.P.E. Bachelor of Physical
   Education
BPhil, B.Phil. Bachelor of Philosophy
br. branch
BRE, B.R.E. Bachelor of Religious
   Education
brig. gen. brigadier general
Brit. British, Brittanica
Bros. Brothers
BS, B.S. Bachelor of Science
BSA, B.S.A. Bachelor of Agricultural
   Science
BSBA Bachelor of Science in Business
   Administration
BSChemE Bachelor of Science in Chemical
   Engineering
BSD, B.S.D. Bachelor of Didactic Science
BSN Bachelor of Science in Nursing
BST, B.S.T. Bachelor of Sacred Theology
BTh, B.Th. Bachelor of Theology
bull. bulletin
bur. bureau
bus. business
B.W.I. British West Indies

CA California
CAA Civil Aeronautics Administration
CAB Civil Aeronautics Board
CAD-CAM Computer Aided Design-
   Computer Aided Model
Calif. California
C.Am. Central America
Can. Canada, Canadian
CAP Civil Air Patrol
capt. captain
CARE Cooperative American Relief
   Everywhere
Cath. Catholic

cav. cavalry
CBC Canadian Broadcasting Company
CBI China, Burma, India Theatre of
   Operations
CBS Columbia Broadcasting Company
CCC Commodity Credit Corporation
CCNY City College of New York
CCU Cardiac Care Unit
CD Civil Defense
CE, C.E. Corps of Engineers, Civil
   Engineer
cen. central
CEN Certified Emergency Nurse
CENTO Central Treaty Organization
CERN European Organization of
   Nuclear Research
cert. certificate, certification, certified
CETA Comprehensive Employment
   Training Act
CFL Canadian Football League
ch. church
ChD, Ch.D. Doctor of Chemistry
chem. chemical
ChemE, Chem.E. Chemical Engineer
Chgo. Chicago
chirurg. chirurgical
chmn. chairman
chpt. chapter
CIA Central Intelligence Agency
Cin. Cincinnati
cir. circuit
Cleve. Cleveland
climatol. climatological
clin. clinical
clk. clerk
C.L.U. Chartered Life Underwriter
CM, C.M. Master in Surgery
CM Northern Mariana Islands
CMA Certified Medical Assistant
CNA Certified Nurse's Aide
CNOR Certified Nurse (Operating Room)
C.&N.W.Ry. Chicago & North Western
   Railway
CO Colorado
Co. Company
COF Catholic Order of Foresters
C. of C. Chamber of Commerce
col. colonel
coll. college
Colo. Colorado
com. committee
comd. commanded
comdg. commanding
comdr. commander
comdt. commandant
commd. commissioned
comml. commercial
commn. commission
commr. commissioner
compt. comptroller
condr. conductor
Conf. Conference
Congl. Congregational, Congressional
Conglist. Congregationalist
Conn. Connecticut
cons. consultant, consulting
consol. consolidated
constl. constitutional
constn. constitution

constrn. construction
contbd. contributed
contbg. contributing
contbn. contribution
contbr. contributor
contr. controller
Conv. Convention
coop. cooperative
coord. coordinator
CORDS Civil Operations and
   Revolutionary Development Support
CORE Congress of Racial Equality
corp. corporation, corporate
corr. correspondent, corresponding,
   correspondence
C.&O.Ry. Chesapeake & Ohio Railway
coun. council
C.P.A. Certified Public Accountant
C.P.C.U. Chartered Property and Casualty
   Underwriter
CPH, C.P.H. Certificate of Public Health
cpl. corporal
C.P.R. Cardio-Pulmonary Resuscitation
C.P.Ry. Canadian Pacific Railway
CRT Cathode Ray Terminal
C.S. Christian Science
CSB, C.S.B. Bachelor of Christian Science
C.S.C. Civil Service Commission
CT Connecticut
ct. court
ctr. center
CWS Chemical Warfare Service
C.Z. Canal Zone

D. Doctor
d. daughter
DAgr, D.Agr. Doctor of Agriculture
DAR Daughters of the American Revolution
dau. daughter
DAV Disabled American Veterans
DC, D.C. District of Columbia
DCL, D.C.L. Doctor of Civil Law
DCS, D.C.S. Doctor of Commercial Science
DD, D.D. Doctor of Divinity
DDS, D.D.S. Doctor of Dental Surgery
DE Delaware
Dec. December
dec. deceased
def. defense
Del. Delaware
del. delegate, delegation
Dem. Democrat, Democratic
DEng, D.Eng. Doctor of Engineering
denom. denomination, denominational
dep. deputy
dept. department
dermatol. dermatological
desc. descendant
devel. development, developmental
DFA, D.F.A. Doctor of Fine Arts
D.F.C. Distinguished Flying Cross
DHL, D.H.L. Doctor of Hebrew Literature
dir. director
dist. district
distbg. distributing
distbn. distribution
distbr. distributor
disting. distinguished
div. division, divinity, divorce

DLitt, D.Litt. Doctor of Literature
DMD, D.M.D. Doctor of Dental Medicine
DMS, D.M.S. Doctor of Medical Science
DO, D.O. Doctor of Osteopathy
DON Director of Nursing
DPH, D.P.H. Diploma in Public Health
DPhil, D.Phil. Doctor of Philosophy
D.R. Daughters of the Revolution
Dr. Drive, Doctor
DRE, D.R.E. Doctor of Religious Education
DrPH, Dr.P.H. Doctor of Public Health,
    Doctor of Public Hygiene
D.S.C. Distinguished Service Cross
DSc, D.Sc. Doctor of Science
D.S.M. Distinguished Service Medal
DST, D.S.T. Doctor of Sacred Theology
DTM, D.T.M. Doctor of Tropical Medicine
DVM, D.V.M. Doctor of Veterinary
    Medicine
DVS, D.V.S. Doctor of Veterinary Surgery

E, E. East
ea. eastern
E. and P. Extraordinary and
    Plenipotentiary
Eccles. Ecclesiastical
ecol. ecological
econ. economic
ECOSOC Economic and Social Council (of
    the UN)
ED, E.D. Doctor of Engineering
ed. educated
EdB, Ed.B. Bachelor of Education
EdD, Ed.D. Doctor of Education
edit. edition
EdM, Ed.M. Master of Education
edn. education
ednl. educational
EDP Electronic Data Processing
EdS, Ed.S. Specialist in Education
EE, E.E. Electrical Engineer
E.E. and M.P. Envoy Extraordinary and
    Minister Plenipotentiary
EEC European Economic Community
EEG Electroencephalogram
EEO Equal Employment Opportunity
EEOC Equal Employment Opportunity
    Commission
E.Ger. German Democratic Republic
EKG Electrocardiogram
elec. electrical
electrochem. electrochemical
electrophys. electrophysical
elem. elementary
EM, E.M. Engineer of Mines
EMT Emergency Medical Technician
ency. encyclopedia
Eng. England
engr. engineer
engring. engineering
entomol. entomological
environ. environmental
EPA Environmental Protection Agency
epidemiol. epidemiological
Episc. Episcopalian
ERA Equal Rights Amendment
ERDA Energy Research and Development
    Administration
ESEA Elementary and Secondary Education
    Act

ESL English as Second Language
ESPN Entertainment and Sports
    Programming Network
ESSA Environmental Science Services
    Administration
ethnol. ethnological
ETO European Theatre of Operations
Evang. Evangelical
exam. examination, examining
Exch. Exchange
exec. executive
exhbn. exhibition
expdn. expedition
expn. exposition
expt. experiment
exptl. experimental
Expwy. Expressway

F.A. Field Artillery
FAA Federal Aviation Administration
FAO Food and Agriculture Organization (of
    the UN)
FBI Federal Bureau of Investigation
FCA Farm Credit Administration
FCC Federal Communications Commission
FCDA Federal Civil Defense
    Administration
FDA Food and Drug Administration
FDIA Federal Deposit Insurance
    Administration
FDIC Federal Deposit Insurance
    Corporation
FE, F.E. Forest Engineer
FEA Federal Energy Administration
Feb. February
fed. federal
fedn. federation
FERC Federal Energy Regulatory
    Commission
fgn. foreign
FHA Federal Housing Administration
fin. financial, finance
FL Florida
Fl. Floor
Fla. Florida
FMC Federal Maritime Commission
FNP Family Nurse Practitioner
FOA Foreign Operations Administration
found. foundation
FPC Federal Power Commission
FPO Fleet Post Office
frat. fraternity
FRS Federal Reserve System
Frwy. Freeway
FSA Federal Security Agency
Ft. Fort
FTC Federal Trade Commission

G-1 (or other number) Division of General
    Staff
GA, Ga. Georgia
GAO General Accounting Office
gastroent. gastroenterological
GATE Gifted and Talented Educators
GATT General Agreement of Tariff and
    Trades
GE General Electric Company
gen. general
geneal. genealogical

geod. geodetic
geog. geographic, geographical
geol. geological
geophys. geophysical
gerontol. gerontological
G.H.Q. General Headquarters
GM General Motors Corporation
GMAC General Motors Acceptance
    Corporation
G.N.Ry. Great Northern Railway
gov. governor
govt. government
govtl. governmental
GPO Government Printing Office
grad. graduate, graduated
GSA General Services Administration
Gt. Great
GTE General Telephone and Electric
    Company
GU Guam
gynecol. gynecological

HBO Home Box Office
hdqrs. headquarters
HEW Department of Health, Education
    and Welfare
HHD, H.H.D. Doctor of Humanities
HHFA Housing and Home Finance
    Agency
HHS Department of Health and Human
    Services
HI Hawaii
hist. historical, historic
HM, H.M. Master of Humanics
HMO Health Maintenance Organization
homeo. homeopathic
hon. honorary, honorable
Ho. of Dels. House of Delegates
Ho. of Reps. House of Representatives
hort. horticultural
hosp. hospital
HUD Department of Housing and Urban
    Development
Hwy. Highway
hydrog. hydrographic

IA Iowa
IAEA International Atomic Energy Agency
IBM International Business Machines
    Corporation
IBRD International Bank for Reconstruction
    and Development
ICA International Cooperation
    Administration
ICC Interstate Commerce Commission
ICCE International Council for Computers
    in Education
ICU Intensive Care Unit
ID Idaho
IEEE Institute of Electrical and
    Electronics Engineers
IFC International Finance Corporation
IGY International Geophysical Year
IL Illinois
Ill. Illinois
illus. illustrated
ILO International Labor Organization
IMF International Monetary Fund
IN Indiana

Inc. Incorporated
Ind. Indiana
ind. independent
Indpls. Indianapolis
indsl. industrial
inf. infantry
info. information
ins. insurance
insp. inspector
insp. gen. inspector general
inst. institute
instl. institutional
instn. institution
instr. instructor
instrn. instruction
internat. international
intro. introduction
IRE Institute of Radio Engineers
IRS Internal Revenue Service
ITT International Telephone &
    Telegraph Corporation

JAG Judge Advocate General
JAGC Judge Advocate General Corps
Jan. January
Jaycees Junior Chamber of Commerce
JB, J.B. Jurum Baccalaureus
JCB, J.C.B. Juris Canoni Baccalaureus
JCD, J.C.D. Juris Canonici Doctor, Juris
    Civilis Doctor
JCL, J.C.L. Juris Canonici Licentiatus
JD, J.D. Juris Doctor
jg. junior grade
jour. journal
jr. junior
JSD, J.S.D. Juris Scientiae Doctor
JUD, J.U.D. Juris Utriusque Doctor
jud. judicial

Kans. Kansas
K.C. Knights of Columbus
K.P. Knights of Pythias
KS Kansas
K.T. Knight Templar
KY, Ky. Kentucky

LA, La. Louisiana
L.A. Los Angeles
lab. laboratory
lang. language
laryngol. laryngological
LB Labrador
LDS Church Church of Jesus Christ of
    Latter Day Saints
lectr. lecturer
legis. legislation, legislative
LHD, L.H.D. Doctor of Humane Letters
L.I. Long Island
libr. librarian, library
lic. licensed, license
L.I.R.R. Long Island Railroad
lit. literature
LittB, Litt.B. Bachelor of Letters
LittD, Litt.D. Doctor of Letters
LLB, LL.B. Bachelor of Laws
LLD, L.L.D. Doctor of Laws
LLM, L.L.M. Master of Laws
Ln. Lane
L.&N.R.R. Louisville & Nashville Railroad
LPGA Ladies Professional Golf Association

LS, L.S. Library Science (in degree)
lt. lieutenant
Ltd. Limited
Luth. Lutheran
LWV League of Women Voters

M. Master
m. married
MA, M.A. Master of Arts
MA Massachusetts
MADD Mothers Against Drunk Driving
mag. magazine
MAgr, M.Agr. Master of Agriculture
maj. major
Man. Manitoba
Mar. March
MArch, M.Arch. Master in Architecture
Mass. Massachusetts
math. mathematics, mathematical
MATS Military Air Transport Service
MB, M.B. Bachelor of Medicine
MB Manitoba
MBA, M.B.A. Master of Business
    Administration
MBS Mutual Broadcasting System
M.C. Medical Corps
MCE, M.C.E. Master of Civil Engineering
mcht. merchant
mcpl. municipal
MCS, M.C.S. Master of Commercial
    Science
MD, M.D. Doctor of Medicine
MD, Md. Maryland
MDiv Master of Divinity
MDip, M.Dip. Master in Diplomacy
mdse. merchandise.
MDV, M.D.V. Doctor of Veterinary
    Medicine
ME, M.E. Mechanical Engineer
ME Maine
M.E.Ch. Methodist Episcopal Church
mech. mechanical
MEd., M.Ed. Master of Education
med. medical
MEE, M.E.E. Master of Electrical
    Engineering
mem. member
meml. memorial
merc. mercantile
met. metropolitan
metall. metallurgical
MetE, Met.E. Metallurgical Engineer
meteorol. meteorological
Meth. Methodist
Mex. Mexico
MF, M.F. Master of Forestry
MFA, M.F.A. Master of Fine Arts
mfg. manufacturing
mfr. manufacturer
mgmt. management
mgr. manager
MHA, M.H.A. Master of Hospital
    Administration
M.I. Military Intelligence
MI Michigan
Mich. Michigan
micros. microscopic, microscopical
mid. middle
mil. military

Milw. Milwaukee
Min. Minister
mineral. mineralogical
Minn. Minnesota
MIS Management Information Systems
Miss. Mississippi
MIT Massachusetts Institute of Technology
mktg. marketing
ML, M.L. Master of Laws
MLA Modern Language Association
M.L.D. Magister Legnum Diplomatic
MLitt, M.Litt. Master of Literature,
    Master of Letters
MLS, M.L.S. Master of Library Science
MME, M.M.E. Master of Mechanical
    Engineering
MN Minnesota
mng. managing
MO, Mo. Missouri
moblzn. mobilization
Mont. Montana
MP Northern Mariana Islands
M.P. Member of Parliament
MPA Master of Public Administration
MPE, M.P.E. Master of Physical Education
MPH, M.P.H. Master of Public Health
MPhil, M.Phil. Master of Philosophy
MPL, M.P.L. Master of Patent Law
Mpls. Minneapolis
MRE, M.R.E. Master of Religious
    Education
MS, M.S. Master of Science
MS, Ms. Mississippi
MSc, M.Sc. Master of Science
MSChemE Master of Science in Chemical
    Engineering
MSF, M.S.F. Master of Science of Forestry
MST, M.S.T. Master of Sacred Theology
MSW, M.S.W. Master of Social Work
MT Montana
Mt. Mount
MTO Mediterranean Theatre of Operation
MTV Music Television
mus. museum, musical
MusB, Mus.B. Bachelor of Music
MusD, Mus.D. Doctor of Music
MusM, Mus.M. Master of Music
mut. mutual
mycol. mycological

N. North
NAACOG Nurses Association of the
    American Association of Ob-Gyn
NAACP National Association for the
    Advancement of Colored People
NACA National Advisory Committee for
    Aeronautics
NACU National Association of Colleges
    and Universities
NAD National Academy of Design
NAE National Academy of Engineering,
    National Association of Educators
NAESP National Association of Elementary
    School Principals
NAFE National Association of Female
    Executives
N.Am. North America
NAM National Association of
    Manufacturers
NAMH National Association for Mental

Health
NAPA National Association of Performing
    Artists
NARAS National Academy of Recording
    Arts and Sciences
NAREB National Association of Real
    Estate Boards
NARS National Archives and Record
    Service
NAS National Academy of Sciences
NASA National Aeronautics and Space
    Administration
NASP National Association of School
    Psychologists
NASW National Association of Social
    Workers
nat. national
NATAS National Academy of Television
    Arts and Sciences
NATO North Atlantic Treaty Organization
NATOUSA North African Theatre of
    Operations
nav. navigation
NB, N.B. New Brunswick
NBA National Basketball Association
NBC National Broadcasting Company
NC, N.C. North Carolina
NCAA National College Athletic
    Association
NCCJ National Conference of Christians
    and Jews
ND, N.D. North Dakota
NDEA National Defense Education Act
NE Nebraska
NE, N.E. Northeast
NEA National Education Association
Nebr. Nebraska
NEH National Endowment for Humanities
neurol. neurological
Nev. Nevada
NF Newfoundland
NFL National Football League
Nfld. Newfoundland
NG National Guard
NH, N.H. New Hampshire
NHL National Hockey League
NIH National Institutes of Health
NIMH National Institute of Mental Health
NJ, N.J. New Jersey
NLRB National Labor Relations Board
NM New Mexico
N.Mex. New Mexico
No. Northern
NOAA National Oceanographic and
    Atmospheric Administration
NORAD North America Air Defense
Nov. November
NOW National Organization for Women
N.P.Ry. Northern Pacific Railway
nr. near
NRA National Rifle Association
NRC National Research Council
NS, N.S. Nova Scotia
NSC National Security Council
NSF National Science Foundation
NSTA National Science Teachers
    Association
NSW New South Wales
N.T. New Testament

NT Northwest Territories
numis. numismatic
NV Nevada
NW, N.W. Northwest
N.W.T. Northwest Territories
NY, N.Y. New York
N.Y.C. New York City
NYU New York University
N.Z. New Zealand

OAS Organization of American States
ob-gyn obstetrics-gynecology
obs. observatory
obstet. obstetrical
Oct. October
OD, O.D. Doctor of Optometry
OECD Organization of European
    Cooperation and Development
OEEC Organization of European Economic
    Cooperation
OEO Office of Economic Opportunity
ofcl. official
OH Ohio
OK Oklahoma
Okla. Oklahoma
ON Ontario
Ont. Ontario
oper. operating
ophthal. ophthalmological
ops. operations
OR Oregon
orch. orchestra
Oreg. Oregon
orgn. organization
ornithol. ornithological
OSHA Occupational Safety and Health
    Administration
OSRD Office of Scientific Research and
    Development
OSS Office of Strategic Services
osteo. osteopathic
otol. otological
otolaryn. otolaryngological

PA, Pa. Pennsylvania
P.A. Professional Association
paleontol. paleontological
path. pathological
PBS Public Broadcasting System
P.C. Professional Corporation
PE Prince Edward Island
P.E.I. Prince Edward Island
PEN Poets, Playwrights, Editors, Essayists
    and Novelists (international association)
penol. penological
P.E.O. women's organization (full name
    not disclosed)
pers. personnel
pfc. private first class
PGA Professional Golfers' Association of
    America
PHA Public Housing Administration
pharm. pharmaceutical
PharmD, Pharm.D. Doctor of Pharmacy
PharmM, Pharm.M. Master of Pharmacy
PhB, Ph.B. Bachelor of Philosophy
PhD, Ph.D. Doctor of Philosophy
PhDChemE Doctor of Science in
    Chemical Engineering

PhM, Ph.M. Master of Philosophy
Phila. Philadelphia
philharm. philharmonic
philol. philological
philos. philosophical
photog. photographic
phys. physical
physiol. physiological
Pitts. Pittsburgh
Pk. Park
Pkwy. Parkway
Pl. Place
Pla. Plaza
P.&L.E.R.R. Pittsburgh & Lake Erie
    Railroad
PNP Pediatric Nurse Practitioner
P.O. Post Office
PO Box Post Office Box
polit. political
poly. polytechnic, polytechnical
PQ Province of Quebec
PR, P.R. Puerto Rico
prep. preparatory
pres. president
Presbyn. Presbyterian
presdl. presidential
prin. principal
proc. proceedings
prod. produced (play production)
prodn. production
prof. professor
profl. professional
prog. progressive
propr. proprietor
pros. atty. prosecuting attorney
pro tem pro tempore
PSRO Professional Services Review
    Organization
psychiat. psychiatric
psychol. psychological
PTA Parent-Teachers Association
ptnr. partner
PTO Pacific Theatre of Operations, Parent
    Teacher Organization
pub. publisher, publishing, published
pub. public
publ. publication
pvt. private

quar. quarterly
qm. quartermaster
Q.M.C. Quartermaster Corps
Que. Quebec

radiol. radiological
RAF Royal Air Force
RCA Radio Corporation of America
RCAF Royal Canadian Air Force
RD Rural Delivery
Rd. Road
R&D Research & Development
REA Rural Electrification Administration
rec. recording
ref. reformed
regt. regiment
regtl. regimental
rehab. rehabilitation
rels. relations
Rep. Republican

rep. representative
Res. Reserve
ret. retired
Rev. Reverend
rev. review, revised
RFC Reconstruction Finance Corporation
RFD Rural Free Delivery
rhinol. rhinological
RI, R.I. Rhode Island
RISD Rhode Island School of Design
Rm. Room
RN, R.N. Registered Nurse
roentgenol. roentgenological
ROTC Reserve Officers Training Corps
RR Rural Route
R.R. Railroad
rsch. research
Rte. Route
Ry. Railway

S. South
s. son
SAC Strategic Air Command
SAG Screen Actors Guild
SALT Strategic Arms Limitation Talks
S.Am. South America
san. sanitary
SAR Sons of the American Revolution
Sask. Saskatchewan
savs. savings
SB, S.B. Bachelor of Science
SBA Small Business Administration
SC, S.C. South Carolina
SCAP Supreme Command Allies Pacific
ScB, Sc.B. Bachelor of Science
SCD, S.C.D. Doctor of Commercial Science
ScD, Sc.D. Doctor of Science
sch. school
sci. science, scientific
SCLC Southern Christian Leadership
    Conference
SCV Sons of Confederate Veterans
SD, S.D. South Dakota
SE, S.E. Southeast
SEATO Southeast Asia Treaty Organization
SEC Securities and Exchange Commission
sec. secretary
sect. section
seismol. seismological
sem. seminary
Sept. September
s.g. senior grade
sgt. sergeant
SHAEF Supreme Headquarters Allied
    Expeditionary Forces
SHAPE Supreme Headquarters Allied
    Powers in Europe
S.I. Staten Island
S.J. Society of Jesus (Jesuit)
SJD Scientiae Juridicae Doctor
SK Saskatchewan
SM, S.M. Master of Science
SNP Society of Nursing Professionals
So. Southern
soc. society
sociol. sociological
S.P. Co. Southern Pacific Company
spl. special
splty. specialty

Sq. Square
S.R. Sons of the Revolution
sr. senior
SS Steamship
SSS Selective Service System
St. Saint, Street
sta. station
stats. statistics
statis. statistical
STB, S.T.B. Bachelor of Sacred Theology
stblzn. stabilization
STD, S.T.D. Doctor of Sacred Theology
Ste. Suite
subs. subsidiary
SUNY State University of New York
supr. supervisor
supt. superintendent
surg. surgical
svc. service
SW, S.W. Southwest

TAPPI Technical Association of the Pulp
    and Paper Industry
Tb. Tuberculosis
tchr. teacher
tech. technical, technology
technol. technological
Tel. & Tel. Telephone & Telegraph
temp. temporary
Tenn. Tennessee
Ter. Territory
Terr. Terrace
Tex. Texas
ThD, Th.D. Doctor of Theology
theol. theological
ThM, Th.M. Master of Theology
TN Tennessee
tng. training
topog. topographical
trans. transaction, transferred
transl. translation, translated
transp. transportation
treas. treasurer
TT Trust Territory
TV television
TVA Tennessee Valley Authority
TWA Trans World Airlines
twp. township
TX Texas
typog. typographical

U. University
UAW United Auto Workers
UCLA University of California at Los
    Angeles
UDC United Daughters of the Confederacy
U.K. United Kingdom
UN United Nations
UNESCO United Nations Educational,
    Scientific and Cultural Organization
UNICEF United Nations International
    Children's Emergency Fund
univ. university
UNRRA United Nations Relief and
    Rehabilitation Administration
UPI United Press International
U.P.R.R. United Pacific Railroad
urol. urological
U.S. United States

U.S.A. United States of America
USAAF United States Army Air Force
USAF United States Air Force
USAFR United States Air Force Reserve
USAR United States Army Reserve
USCG United States Coast Guard
USCGR United States Coast Guard Reserve
USES United States Employment Service
USIA United States Information Agency
USMC United States Marine Corps
USMCR United States Marine Corps
    Reserve
USN United States Navy
USNG United States National Guard
USNR United States Naval Reserve
USO United Service Organizations
USPHS United States Public Health Service
USS United States Ship
USSR Union of the Soviet Socialist
    Republics
USTA United States Tennis Association
USV United States Volunteers
UT Utah

VA Veterans Administration
VA, Va. Virginia
vet. veteran, veterinary
VFW Veterans of Foreign Wars
VI, V.I. Virgin Islands
vice pres. vice president
vis. visiting
VISTA Volunteers in Service to America
VITA Volunteers in Technical Service
vocat. vocational
vol. volunteer, volume
v.p. vice president
vs. versus
VT, Vt. Vermont

W, W. West
WA Washington (state)
WAC Women's Army Corps
Wash. Washington (state)
WAVES Women's Reserve, US Naval
    Reserve
WCTU Women's Christian Temperance
    Union
we. western
W. Ger. Germany, Federal Republic of
WHO World Health Organization
WI Wisconsin
W.I. West Indies
Wis. Wisconsin
WSB Wage Stabilization Board
WV West Virginia
W.Va. West Virginia
WY Wyoming
Wyo. Wyoming

YK Yukon Territory
YMCA Young Men's Christian Association
YMHA Young Men's Hebrew Association
YM & YWHA Young Men's and Young
    Women's Hebrew Association
yr. year
YT, Y.T. Yukon Territory
YWCA Young Women's Christian
    Association

zool. zoological

Alphabetical Practices

Names are arranged alphabetically according to the surnames, and under identical surnames according to the first given name. If both surname and first given name are identical, names are arranged alphabetically according to the second given name. Where full names are identical, they are arranged in order of age—with the elder listed first.

Surnames beginning with De, Des, Du, however capitalized or spaced, are recorded with the prefix preceding the surname and arranged alphabetically under the letter D.

Surnames beginning with Mac and Mc are arranged alphabetically under M.

Surnames beginning with Saint or St. appear after names that begin Sains, and are arranged according to the second part of the name, e.g. St. Clair before Saint Dennis.

Surnames beginning with Van, Von or von are arranged alphabetically under letter V.

Compound hyphenated surnames are arranged according to the first member of the compound. Compound unhyphenated surnames are treated as hyphenated names.

Parentheses used in connection with a name indicate which part of the full name is usually deleted in common usage. Hence Abbott, W(illiam) Lewis indicates that the usual form of the given name is W. Lewis. In such a case, the parentheses are ignored in alphabetizing and the name would be arranged as Abbott, William Lewis. However, if the name is recorded Abbott, (William) Lewis, signifying that the entire name William is not commonly used, the alphabetizing would be arranged as though the name were Abbott, Lewis. If an entire middle or last name is enclosed in parentheses, that portion of the name is used in the alphabetical arrangement. Hence Abbott, William (Lewis) would be arranged as Abbott, William Lewis.

Who'sWho in Religion

AADLAND, THOMAS VERNON, minister; b. Mpls., Dec. 24, 1950; s. Otto Sidney and Dorothy Jean (Holmquist) A.; m. Mary Joanne Pratt, June 27, 1981; children: Evangeline Faith, Brigitta Hope, Andrew Paul, Marian Joy. AB in Philosophy, Wheaton Coll., 1973; MDiv, Luther Theol. Sem., 1980. Ordained to ministry Am. Luth. Ch., 1980. Assoc. pastor Christ Luth. Ch., Duluth, Minn., 1980-91, sr. pastor, 1991—; sec. Am. Assn. Luth. Chs., Mpls., 1987—. Pres., bd. dirs. Lake Superior Life Care Ctr., Duluth, Minn., 1987-90. Home: 2409 Ensign St Duluth MN 55811 Office: Christ Luth Ch 2415 Ensign St Duluth MN 55811 *I believe Americans are inescapably religious. The enjoyment of our freedoms—in some vitally important sense—depends upon a humble and grateful recognition that the source of our fundamental rights to life, liberty and property is transcendent: they derive not from the generosity of the State but from the magnanimity of God, in Whose image we are created.*

ABATA, RUSSELL JAMES, priest, author; b. North East, Pa., May 30, 1930; s. Joseph and Josephine (Cuccia) A. Licentiae, Academia Alfonsiana, Rome, 1959; D in Moral Guidance, Angelicum, Rome, 1962. Joined Order Redemptorist Fathers; ordained priest Roman Cath. Ch., 1957. Preacher Eastern seacoast missions, 1962; tchr. Mt. St. Alphonsus Sem., Esopus, N.Y., 1963-85; counselor mental health Our Lady of Perpetual Help, N.Y.C., 1966—; prof. comparative religions Fordham U., N.Y.C., 1969. Author: Love Is a Rainbow, 1971, Double Dare To Be You, 1972, Sex Sanity in the Modern World, 1975, Helps for the Scrupulous, 1976, You and the Ten Commandments, 1976, How to Develop a Better Self-Image, 1980, Unlocking the Doors of Your Heart, 1984, Is Love In and Sin Out, 1985, (with W. Weir) Dealing with Depression, 1982, A Book of Poetry, 1984; contbg. author: All Things to All Men, 1967. Home: 323 E 61st St New York NY 10021

ABATIE, RODGER PAUL, minister, radio executive; b. La Jolla, Calif., May 16, 1951; s. John Robert and Margaret Jane (Moore) A.; m. Robin Ruth York, Aug. 4, 1973; children: Kristen Michelle, Justin Paul. AA, Concordia Coll., Ann Arbor, Mich., 1971; BA, Concordia Coll., Ft. Wayne, Ind., 1973, MDiv, 1977; MA in Communications, Sangamon State U., 1975. Ordained to ministry Luth. Ch.-Mo. Synod, 1977. Pastor St. Mark Ch., Muskegon, Mo., 1977-82; gen. mgr., exec. sec. Radio Sta. KFUO, St. Louis, 1982-86; pastor Prince of Peace Luth. Ch., Coralville, Iowa, 1986-90; adminstrv. pastor Trinity Luth. Ch., Pekin, Ill., 1990—; pres. Mo. Fedn./Aid Assn. for Luths., St. Louis, 1983-84; chmn. Word of Life Sch. Assn., 1983-84; dir. communications for Iowa Dist. E. of Luth. Ch.-Mo. Synod, 1987-90; chmn. communications com. Cen. Ill. dist. Luth. Ch.-Mo. Synod, 1991—. Recipient Cert. of Merit Boy Scouts Am., Pottawatomie Coun., 1971. Mem. Nat. Assn. Broadcasters, Mo.Broadcasters Assn., St. Louis Radio Assn. Office: Trinity Luth Ch 700 S Fourth St Pekin IL 61554

ABBEY, MERRILL RAY, retired religion educator; b. Luverne, Minn., Apr. 19, 1905; s. Ray Schuyler and Harriet L. (Henton) A.; m. Lucy Marie Robinson, Sept. 9, 1927 (dec. Sept. 1987); children: Mary Ruth, Stuart Gilbert; m. Bessmary Doty Torgerson, Aug. 22, 1988. BA, Hamline U., 1929; MDiv, Garrett Theol. Sem., 1930; DD (hon.), Hamline U., 1942. Ordained to ministry United Meth. Ch., 1930. Pastor First Meth. Ch., Milw., 1941-46; pastor First Univ. Meth. Ch., Madison, Wis., 1946-53, First United Meth. Ch., Ann Arbor, Mich., 1953-58; prof. Preaching Garrett Theol. Sem., Evanston, Ill., 1959-73; ret. Garrett Theol. Sem., Evanston, 1973; vis. prof. So. Meth. U., 1976-77; pres. Wis. Coun. Chs., 1949-52; trustee Meth. Hosp., Madison, 1946-53; pres. Ann Arbor-Washtenaw Coun. Chs., 1954-57; del. Gen. Conf. Meth. Ch., San Francisco, 1954. Author: Creed of Our Hope, 1954, Encounter With Christ, 1960, Preaching to the Contemporary Mind, 1962, Living Doctrine in a Vital Pulpit, 1964, The Word Interprets Us, 1967, Man, Media and the Message, 1970, The Shape of the Gospel, 1970, Communication in Pulpit and Parish, 1973, (with O.C. Edwards) Proclamation, Series A, 1974, Day Dawns in Fire, 1976, The Epic of United Methodist Preaching, 1984. Pres. Wis. Temperance Fedn., 1948-52. Named Outstanding Sr. Citizen by Gov. of Minn., 1984. Mem. Rotary, Masons. Democrat. Home: 1113 Elm Cove Luverne MN 56156

ABBOT, WILLIAM BRIMBERRY, retired minister and social worker; b. Augusta, Ga., Sept. 4, 1923; s. Gardner Phillips and Frances Marion (Brimberry) A.; m. Marguerite Robb Cooper, June 30, 1949 (div. Dec. 1967); children: Katherine Abbot Troxel, Marguerite Abbot Auclair; m. Betty Doreen, May 24, 1968; stepchildren: Donald A. Gast, Michael K. Gast, Thomas J. Gast, David R. Gast. BA, Davidson Coll., 1947; BD, Princeton U., 1950; postgrad., U. Zurich, Switzerland, 1955-56. Ordained to ministry Presbyn. Ch. (U.S.A.), 1950. Pastor chs., N.C., Va., 1950-57, Oakdale Presbyn. Ch., Norfolk, Va., 1957-63, 1st Presbyn. Ch., Anaheim, Calif., 1963-65, Westminster Presbyn. Ch., L.A., 1986-88; social worker Los Angeles County, L.A., 1965-80; Presbyn. interim pastor, 1981-85; pastor 1st Presbyn. Ch., 1989-91; ret., 1991; dir. Commn. on Religion and Race, Presbyn. Ch. (U.S.A.), Cordele, Ga., summer 1964. Co-founder, leader CORE, Norfolk, 1958-60; dir. voter registration project Am. Friends Svc. Com., Jackson, Tenn., 1962; co-founder Anaheim Coun. on Human Rels., 1963. Lt. (j.g.) USNR, 1943-46. Democrat. Home: 120 2d St Manhattan Beach CA 90266 *It appears to me that one of the greatest needs of humanity today is to bring as many opposing groups together as possible and to engage in genuine dialogue over differences that we may learn how to live together in peace and harmony. In resolving conflict we can learn how to build a better world without resorting constantly to war and violence.*

ABBOTT, ALVIN RICHARD, minister; b. Chgo., May 12, 1929; s. Richard Thomas and Lauretta Mary (Lieser) A.; m. Donna Jean Bailey, Dec. 16, 1956; children: Alvin Richard, Bradley Roy, Chrystal Jean. Student, Wright Jr. Coll., Chgo., 1947-48; BA, Park Coll., 1952; diploma, McCormick Theol. Sem., 1957, MDiv, 1974, D Ministry, 1980; postgrad., Bethany Theol. Sem., 1973-74. Ordained to ministry United Presbyn. Ch. in U.S.A., 1957. Intern, then pastor Green Valley (Ill.) Ch., 1954-62; pastor Clinton (Ill.) Ch., 1963-68, Westminster Ch., Joliet, Ill., 1969—; moderator Blackhawk Presbytery, Oregon, Ill., 1976, chmn. coun., 1978-83; mem. Gen. Assembly Vocation Agy., 1977-83, Gen. Assembly Bd. of Pension, 1980-83; active in camps, conf., youth work, communications recreation, adminstrn.; mem. numerous coun. chs. Chmn. Joliet Renewal Task Force; active Boy Scouts Am., Mental Health and Drugs, ARC, YMCA, PTA. Mem. Joliet Ecumenical Clergy Assn. (pres. 1983—), Alpha Phi Omega, Mu Sigma. Home: 417 Tana Ln Joliet IL 60435 Office: Westminster Presbyn Ch Clara and Larkin Aves Joliet IL 60435

ABBOTT, GARY LOUIS, SR., minister; b. Millen, Ga., Sept. 26, 1947; s. Albert Louis and Viola Rose (Kingston) A.; m. Billie Avalie Uselton, July 26, 1969; children: Louis, Russell. BA, Mercer U., 1969; MDiv, Southwestern Seminary, Ft. Worth, 1972; postgrad., Columbia Seminary, Decatur, Ga., 1974-76; D of Ministry, New Orleans Seminary, 1978. Ordained to ministry Bapt. Ch., 1968. Minister Fairview (Tex.) Bapt. Ch., 1970-72; assoc. pastor First Bapt. Ch., Washington, Ga., 1972-73; minister First Bapt. Ch., Hoganville, Ga., 1973-77, Harlem (Ga.) Bapt. Ch., 1978-82, First Bapt. Ch., Hawkinsville, Ga., 1982—; mem. exec. com. Ga. Bapt. Conv., 1977, 89—; bd. dirs. The Christian Index, 1991—; mem. pastoral leadership com. Bapt. World Alliance, 1986-90, sec. Bapt. worship study commn., 1991—, mem. study/rsch. exec. com., 1991—. Contbr. articles to religious publs. Bd. dirs. Nat. Kidney Found. of Ga., Atlanta, 1977-79, Hawkinsville/Pulaski County C. of C., 1987-89, pres. United Way of Pulaski County, Hawkinsville, 1989-90. Named Citizen of Yr., Hawkinsville/Pulaski County C. of C., 1988. Mem. Rotary. Home: 500 Clark Dr Hawkinsville GA 31036 Office: 1st Bapt Ch Broad St at McCormick Ave PO Box 216 Hawkinsville GA 31036-0216

ABBOTT, JOE BOONE, minister, pastoral counselor; b. Tuscaloosa, Ala., Feb. 24, 1932; s. Charles E. and Frances R. (Boone) A.; m. Margaret A. Burks, Apr. 13, 1954; children: Margaret, Joe Boone, James. BA, Baylor U., 1954; MDiv, So. Bapt. Theol. Sem., 1957; D Ministry, Columbia Theol. Sem., 1989. Ordained to ministry So. Bapt. Conv., 1956. Pastor chs. Ind., 1952-54, Ala., 1957-62; intern pastoral care N.C. Bapt. Hosp., 1962-63, resident, 1962-63, chaplain, 1962-64; corp. v.p. pastoral care and counseling Bapt. Med. Ctrs., Birmingham, Ala., 1964—. Fellow Coll. Chaplains, Am. Assn. Pastoral Counselors (diplomate), Am. Protestant Hosp. Assn., Am. Assn. Marriage and Family Therapy (approved supr.); mem. Internat. Transactional Analysis Assn., Assn. Clin. Pastoral Edn. (supr.). Home: 4221 Shiloh Dr Mountain Brook AL 35213 Office: 750 Montclair Rd Birmingham AL 35213

ABBOTT, JOHN DAVID, clergyman, church official; b. Wyoming, Del., Sept. 29, 1922; s. John Wesley and Mary Mabel (Boggs) A.; m. Gladys Irene Kirkendall, July 22, 1943; children: John David, Kenneth Wayne. Th.B., United Wesleyan Coll., 1943; D.D. (hon.), Houghton Coll., 1969. Ordained to ministry The Wesleyan Ch., 1944; pastor in Chestertown, Md., 1943, Richeyville and Bentleyville, Pa., 1944, Warren, Pa., 1945-49, Cambridge, Md., 1949-53; dist. supt. Delmarva dist. The Wesleyan Ch., Denton, Md., 1953-60; gen. sec. Sunday schs. and youth The Wesleyan Ch., Indpls., 1960-62; pres. Wesleyan Ch. Corp., Indpls., 1984—; exec. dir. Pilgrim Pension Plan, 1960-62, gen. sec.-treas., 1962-66, gen. supt., 1966—, mem. bd. pensions, 1960-80; Mem. exec. com. World Methodist Council, 1971—, 1st vice chmn. Am. sect., 1977-82, sec. Am. sect., 1971-76, 82-86, v.p. N.Am. sect., 1986—; v.p. Wesleyan World Fellowship, 1976—, The Wesleyan Ch. Corp., 1976-80; mem. exec. bd. Gen. Commn. Chaplains and Armed Forces Personnel, 1977-80; trustee United Wesleyan Coll. Editor: Sunday Sch. Advance, 1960, Pilgrim Youth News, 1960-62. Mem. Christian Holiness Assn. (pres. 1976-78), Nat. Assn. Evangelicals, Delta Epsilon Chi. Office: Wesleyan Ch Corp Box 50434 Indianapolis IN 46250-0434

ABDALLAH, BASSAM JOSEPH, minister; b. Jerusalem, Palestine, July 7, 1950; came to U.S., 1970; s. Joseph and Fadwa (Barham) A.; m. Katy Saleh, Nov. 16, 1977; 1 child, Joseph. BS, U. Louisville, 1973; MDiv, Luth. Sch. of Theol., Chgo., 1976; grad. studies, United Theol. Sem., Dayton, Ohio, 1979-81; DDiv, Calif. Grad. Sch. Theol., 1987. Ordained to ministry Luth. Ch., 1977. Pastor Redeemer Luth. Ch., Bryant, Ind., 1977-89, First United Evangelical Luth. Ch., Hammond, Ind., 1989—; Bd. dirs. Union Iron & Metal, Inc., Berne, Ind., 1986—. Contbr. articles to profl. magazine. Pres. Jay County Mental Health Assn., Portland, Ind., 1986-89. Named Ky. Col., Ky. Cols., Frankfurt, Ky., 1975; Vol. of Yr., Mental Health Assn., Portland, Ind., 1988; recipient Gold Cross medal Justinian I, Patriarch of Ruomania, 1977, Gold Cross medal, Venadecktos I, Patriarch of Jerusalem, 1980, Silver medal, Terra Sancta order, 1981. Home: 6630 Hohman Ave Hammond IN 46324 Office: First United Evang Luth Ch 6705 Hohman Ave Hammond IN 46324

ABDI, PETRUS SUHADI, priest; b. Sragen-Solo-Java, Indonesia, June 16, 1934; s. Stephanus and Theresia (Rasminah) Harjosukatmo; Fac.Theol.Licentiatus, Gregorian U., Rome, 1962, Canon Law Licentiate, 1964. Ordained priest, Roman Catholic Ch., 1961; tchr. St. Paul Sem., Palembang, Indonesia, 1964-65, mem. diocesan tribunal, 1965—; parish priest Baturaja, S. Sumatra, 1965-72; gen. vicar and parish priest Cathedral parish, Palembang and diocesan social del, 1973-78; vicar, gen., dir. diocesan office for human devel., Sumatra, Indonesia, 1973—; dir. regional/inter-diocesan office for human devel. apostolate, 1979—; parish prist St. Paulus' parish, Plaju and Pasangsurut, 1983—; dir. diocesan office for Cath. family welfare, 1974—. Exec. dir. Assn. Voluntary Health Services Indonesia, 1976-83; pres. Inst. Family Welfare, 1979—; v.p. nat. com. human devel. Indonesian Bishops' Conf., 1985—. Home: Pastoran katolik, Pintu Gereja Pertamina Plaju Indonesia Office: 52 Jlm Kol Atmo, Palembang Indonesia

ABDUR-RAZZAQ, MUHAMMAD See **MILLER, F(REDERICK) RICHARD, JR.**

ABE, MASAO, religion educator; b. Osaka, Japan, Feb. 9, 1915; came to U.S., 1980; d. Yoshio and Risa Tomomatsu; m. Ikuko Abe, Oct. 20, 1979. Shogakushi, Osaka U., 1936; Bungakushi, Kyoto U., 1944, LLD, 1985. Vis. prof. dept. philosophy Purdue U., West Lafayette, Ind., 1991—; bd. dirs. Buddhist-Christian Theol. Encounter Meeting, 1982—. Author: Zen and Western Thought, 1985 (Am. Acad. Religion award); editor: A Zen Life: D.T. Suzuki, 1986; translator: An Inquiry into the Good (Kitaro Nishida), 1990; contbr. to The Emptying God. A Buddhist-Jewish-Christian Conversation, 1990; mem. editorial bd. Ea. Buddhist, 1970—. Rockefeller Found. fellow, 1955-57; recipient Rising Sun decoration Govt. of Japan, 1987. Fellow Soc. Arts, Religion and Contemporary Culture; mem. Internat. Assn. History of Religion (v.p. 1975-80), Soc. Buddhist Christian Studies (bd. dirs. 1989—), Am. Acad. Religion, FAS Soc. (bd. dirs.), Japanese Assn. Religious Studies (trustee), Theta Chi Beta. Home: 400 N River Rd Apt 1411 West Lafayette IN 47906 Office: Purdue U Dept Philosophy West Lafayette IN 47907

ABEJO, SISTER MARIA ROSALINA, nun; b. Tagoloan, Philippines, July 13, 1922; came to U.S., 1977, 1985; d. Don Pedro Abejo y Villegas and Dona Beatriz Zamarro de Abejo. AA in Music, St. Scholastica's Coll., Manila, 1949; MusB, Philippine Womens U., 1956, MusM, 1958; postgrad., Cath. U. Am., 1962-64; postrad. studies in theory and composition, Eastman Sch. Music, 1962; studies with, Fritz Mahler, N.Y.C., summers 1964, 65, 68, Maestro Franco Ferrara, Rome, 1972-75. Dean Lourdes Coll., Manila, 1958-61, Immaculate Coll., Manila, 1961-62, St. Mary's Coll., Manila, 1964-76; music dir. Holy Spirit Ch., Fremont, Calif., 1978-82, St. Leonard's Ch., Fremont, 1982—; sec. Nat. Liturgical Commn. Sacred Music, Manila, 1964-76; rep. Cath. ch. Ecumenical Council Chs., Manila, 1966-76; founder, dir., conductor Nuns Concerts For Charities, 1967-76; lectr. music Kans. U., Lawrence, 1977-79, Consular Wives and All Nations Group, San Francisco, 1980-82; faculty dir. Schola Cantroum & Seminarians Glee Club St. Pius X Sem., Covington, Ky., 1978-79; founder, dir., conductor Ars Nova Symphony Orchestra and Ars Nova Concert Chorus, Fremont, 1979—; cultural officer U.N. Assn., Manila, 1967-77, Dr. J.P. Rizal Found., MacArthur Found.; del. music convs., assemblies to Russia, Poland, Hungary, Czechoslovakia, Europe, U.S.A. omposer: Why Should We Weep So, 1968, First Oratorio in Pilipino, 1969, Ode to the Statesmen, 1971, Guerilla Symphony, 1971, Onward Ye Women, 1975, Death and Victory, 1976, Loops Circles & Squares, 1979, Five Wedding Songs, 1983, Surge of the Fair Sex, 1984, Explosion of the Pyramids, 1985, Brotherhood Symphony and Muslim Diver, 1986, The Mutiny and The Woman: Bloodless Revolution, 1987, Story of Was for Orchestra, 1991, Easts Meets West in Dance, 1991, over 500 others; commd. works include: The Conversion of King Humabon, 1967, Panahon, 1969, Fanfare For 8 Instruments, 1970, Overture 1081, 1972, (ballet) The Ritual, 1976, Eternal Memory, 1978, Strings on the Dignity of Man, 1980, Jubilee Cantata, 1984, The Absent Baritone, 1985; various compositions recorded on discs and tapes; author: (textbooks) Learning To Read and Write Music, Music for Philippine High Schools, Kantahin Pilipino, Our Own Choruses; commd compositions: Iberian Promenade, 1980, Hold High The Torch, 1981, Dithyrambic Strings for Gen. C.P. Romulo, 1982, Jubilee Symphoney, 1984, Symphony of Psalms, 1988, Genesis, 1986, World Premiere the Mutiny and the Woman, 1987, Symphony of Life, 1988, Dance of Adam and Eve, 1989, The Bridges of Fremont, 1989, Symphony of Fortitude and Sudden Spring, 1989; other works include Vespers in a Convent Garden, 1957, Advent Cantata, 1957, Thirteen Variations for Two Pianos, 1957, Three String Quartets, 1958, Piano Pieces, 1959-60, Band Marches for World Pres., 1961-62, Pope VI Pontifical March, 1964, Lut Us Play The Piano, 1965, Recuerdos De Manila, Blood Compact, 1966, The Conversion of King Humabon, (Philippine Rep. Cultural Heritage award), 1967, Why Shouls We Weep, 1968, Filipiniana, 1969, (poem) Beautiful Cities (Merit award), 1991. Recipient numerous awards including: Republic Cultural Heritage award, Govt. of Manila, 1967, U.N. award, 1970, 76, Pontifical Plaque of Recognition, 1972, Plaque of Recognition Zonta, 1973, Dr. J.P. Rizal-MacArthur award, 1974, Internat. Womens award In Womens Yr., 1975, Bay Area Recognition plaque, 1984, Philippine Consulate Gen. Recognition Plaque, 1984, Life Achievement award, 1990, two Trophys for Svc. Role Model Internat. Eye Pub., 1990, Outstanding Filipino-American in Northern Calif. award, 1990; Contbg.-Activities-Participating-Achievement Internat. award Philippine Women's Univ. Centennial Celebration, 1986. Mem. Conductors Assn. (v.p.), League of Filipino Composers (sec.-treas. 1966-77), Internat. Music Council (bd. dirs.), Internat. Soc. Music Edn., League of Asian Composers. Avocations: reading, composing. Home and Office: 37950 #62 Fremont Blvd Fremont CA 94536

ABEL, RICHARD FRANCIS, government official, air force officer; b. Akron, Ohio, Oct. 28, 1933; s. Frank William and Cecelia Marie (Kleinhenz) A.; m. Shirley Ann Voelcker, Nov. 10, 1956; children: Tamara D. Abel Mattson, Teresa M., Katrina L., Timothy L. B.S., U. Detroit, 1956; postgrad., Boston U., 1962. Commd. 2d lt. U.S. Air Force, 1956, advanced through grades to brig. gen., 1981; served chief combat news div. 7th Air Force, Republic of Vietnam, 1968-69; pub. affairs officer for commander-in-chief U.S. Pacific Command, 7th Air Force, Hawaii, 1969-72; dir. admissions liason office U.S. Air Force Acad., Colorado Springs, Colo., 1972-75; dir. pub. affairs Pacific Command, 1975-78; spl. asst. to Chmn. Joint Chief of Staff U.S. Air Force Acad., Washington, 1978-80; dir. pub. affairs Office Sec. of Air Force, Washington, 1980—. Contbr. articles to publs. Vice chmn. nat. bd. dirs. Fellowship of Christian Athletes, 1980; mem. Nat. Pub. Info. Com. USO, 1980. Decorated Bronze Star; decorated Meritorious Service Medal with oak leaf cluster, Def. Superior Service Medal, Def. Meritorious Service Medal. Mem. Air Force Assn., Nat. Aero. Assn. (dir. 1980), Order of Daedalians. Office: Sec of Air Force Office Public Affairs Room 4D922 Pentagon Washington DC 20330

ABERNATHY, RALPH DAVID, clergyman; b. Linden, Ala., Mar. 11, 1926; s. W.L. and Louivery (Bell) A.; m. Juanita Odessa Jones, Aug. 31, 1952; children: Juandalynn Ralpheda, Donzaleigh Avis, Ralph David III, Kwame Luthuli. B.S., Ala. State Coll., 1950; M.A. in Sociology, Atlanta U., 1951; LL.D., Allen U., S.C., 1960, Southampton Coll., L.I. U., 1969, Ala. State U., Montgomery, 1974; D.D. (hon.), Morehouse Coll., 1971, Kalamazoo Coll., 1978. Personnel counselor, instr. social sci. Ala. State Coll., 1951; ordained to ministry Bapt. Ch., 1948; pastor First Bapt. Ch., Montgomery, Ala., 1951-61, West Hunter St. Bapt. Ch., Atlanta, 1961—. Author: And The Walls Came Tumbling Down, 1989. Organizer Montgomery Improvement Assn., 1955, initiator bus. boycott, Montgomery, 1955, an organizer, 1957; since financial sec.-treas. So. Christian Leadership Conf., v.p. at large, then pres., 1968-77; leader Poor People's Campaign, Resurrection City, Washington, 1968; chmn. Commn. on Racism and Apartheid; addressed UN, 1971; mem. Atlanta Ministers Union; organizer, chmn. Operation Breadbasket, Atlanta; mem. adv. com. Congress of Racial Equality; participant World Peace Council Presdl. Com. Meeting, Santiago, Chile, 1972; active local ARC, Am. Cancer Soc., YMCA. Recipient Peace medal German Democratic Republic, 1971. Mem. NAACP, Kappa Alpha Psi, Phi Delta Kappa. Club: Mason (32 deg.). Home and church dynamited, 1957. Office: 1040 Gordon St SW Atlanta GA 30310

ABESAMIS, GIL S., minister; b. Penaranda, Philippines, Oct. 1, 1937; came to U.S., 1985; s. Angel A. Abesamis and Alodia P. Serrano; m. Rosalina V. Arquiza, Aug. 3, 1963; children: Gilyn Gay, Nympha Nini, Urania Ulla Lani. BS in Commerce, Far Eastern U., Philippines, 1960; BD, Union Theol. Sem., Philippines, 1965; MST, Andover Newton Theol. Sem., 1967; MBA, City U. Manila (Philippines), 1980. Ordained to ministry Meth. Ch. Treas. Philippine Bible Soc., Manila, 1979-81; chmn. commn. on theol. edn. Union Theol. Sem., Philippines, 1981-82; gen. sec. Evang. Meth. Ch. in the Philippines, 1982-86; pastor 1st East Coast Congregation, Evang. Meth. Ch. in N.J., Jersey City, 1986—. Pres. Philippine Found. for Pub. Adminstrn., Manila, 1984-85; auditor Manila Family Planning Orgn., 1980-84. Ecumenical scholar World Coun. Chs., 1966-67. Mem. Jersey City Religious Profls. Assn. Home: PO Box 16015 Jersey City NJ 07306

ABINGTON, JAMES WILLIAM, minister; b. Memphis, Sept. 27, 1933; s. Ephraim Butler and Mary (James) A.; m. Doris Elaine Adams, Aug. 16, 1955; children: William Brian, Lisa Kay, Susan Elaine, Sheri Lea. BA, La. Coll., 1955; MDiv, Southwestern Bapt. Theol. Sem., Ft. Worth, 1958. Ordained to ministry So. Bapt. Conv., 1958. Asst. pastor North Ft. Worth Bapt. Ch., 1958-60; pastor 1st Bapt. Ch., League City, Tex., 1960-69, Woodlawn Bapt. Ch., Austin, Tex., 1969-73, Bannockburn Bapt. Ch., Austin, 1973—; Chmn. Galveston Bapt. Exec. Bd., Texas City, Tex., 1966-67; dir. Teen Liberators, Houston, 1967-69; mem. Austin Bapt. Exec. Bd., 1970-91; chmn. evangelism com. Bapt. Student Union, Austin, 1982-84. Contbr. articles to religious jours. Nen. Austin Traffic Safety Commn., 1978. Office: Bannockburn Bapt Ch 7100 Brodie Ln Austin TX 78745

ABNEY, RICHARD JOHN, minister; b. Franklin, Ohio, July 27, 1943; s. Clelan R. and Mercile L. (Winslow) A.; m. Florence Ann Jones, Nov. 3, 1965; children: Ralph Gayle, Paul Jason. B in Religious Edn., Midwestern Bapt., 1973. Ordained to ministry Bapt. Ch., 1973. Pastor Bible Bapt., Belva, W.Va., 1973-75, Faith Bapt., Knoxville, Tenn., 1975-77; missionary to Philippines Hillcrest Bapt., Richmond, Ind., 1977-86; pastor Community Bapt., Franklin, Ohio, 1986-91; alumni missions field rep., missions fund raiser Midwestern Bapt. Coll., Pontiac, Mich., 1977—. Author: Another World, 1988. With USAFA, 1960-63. Named Missionary of Yr. Midwestern Bapt. Coll., 1983.

ABRAHAM, ABRAM KENNETH, pastor, author; b. Indiana, Pa., Sept. 3, 1951; s. Howard George and Minnie Bryce (Clayton) A.; m. Angela Reneé Koppelberger, Sept. 25, 1982; children: Ashleigh Anne, Alyssa Reneé. BA, Asbury Coll., 1973. Ordained to ministry Christian Fellowship Ctr., 1985. V.p. Watchmen Ministries, Clymer, Pa., 1976-85, pres., 1991—; sr. pastor Christian Fellowship Ctr., Greensburg, Pa., 1985-90; bd. dirs. Doorkeepers Christian Outreach, Spring Creek, Pa., 1980—. Author: Don't Bite the Apple Til You Check for Worms, 1985, Designer Genes, 1986, Hot Trax for Guys, Hot Trax for Girls, 1987, Positive Holiness, 1988, Promises of the Messiah, 1989, Unmasking the Myths of Marriage, 1990, The Disillusioned Christian, 1991, This Isn't the Trip I Signed Up For, 1991, Armed and Dangerous, 1991, The King and the Beast, 1991; contbr. to Contemporary English Version of New Testament, 1991. Mem. ASCAP, Nat. Speakers Assn., Christian Holiness Assn., Wesleyan Theol. Soc., Country Music Assn. Republican. Home: 6153 Firelight Trail Antioch TN 37013 Office:

Watchmen Ministries P O Box 218 Clymer PA 15728 *The one principle that guides my every decision is the question: "What would Jesus do?" As a follower of Christ, I seek to represent Him in a manner that reflects positively on His love, His character, and His Holiness.*

ABRAHAM, MICHAEL LEWIS, rabbi; b. N.Y.C., Aug. 7, 1938; s. Arthur and Mina (Simon) A.; m. Sandra Faust, Dec. 26, 1962; children: Joel, Daniel. BA in Physics and Math., Johns Hopkins U., 1959; BA in Hebrew Letters, Hebrew Union Coll., 1962, MA in Hebrew Letters, 1965, DD (hon.), 1990. Ordained rabbi, 1965. Rabbi Temple Beth-El, Somerville, N.J., 1968-86, Congregation Beth Or, Spring House, Pa., 1986-88, Temple Shalom, Norwalk, Conn., 1989—; mem. faculty Sch. Edn., Hebrew Union Coll., N.J., 1970-71; dir. Jewish Family Svc., Somerville, 1980-86; mem. Pa. Assn. Reform Rabbis, 1986-88; pres. Norwalk Counseling Ctr., 1991—. Contbr. articles to profl. jours. Pres. Somerset (N.J.) Community Action Program, 1968-72, Somerville Area Ministerial Assn.; bd. dirs. Family Counseling Svcs., Somerset, 1968-73. Capt. U.S. Army, 1965-68. Recipient Hannah Solomon award Nat. Coun. Jewish Women, 1971. Mem. Cen. Conf. Am. Rabbis, N.J. Assn. Reform Rabbis (pres. 1981-83), New Eng. Reform Rabbis, Norwalk Clergy Assn. (pres. 1989-91), Nat. Fedn. Temple Youth (life). Home: 19 Grey Hollow Rd Norwalk CT 06850 Office: Temple Shalom 259 Richards Ave Norwalk CT 06850 *"Observe the Sabbath Day to make it holy." It is our actions that make the Sabbath a special day. In effect, to make the Sabbath holy is to make our lives holy.*

ABRAHAM, REUBEN ISRAEL, rabbi; b. Rockford, Ill., Nov. 4, 1951; m. Patricia Carole Hayward, Sept. 1, 1973 (div.); 1 child, Aaron David Jones; m. Jennifer Stamm Gabriel, July 1, 1988; stepchildren: Daniel Avraham Gabriel, Adeena Michal Gabriel. BA in Econs., Rockford Coll., 1973; postgrad., U. South Fla. and Reconstructionist Rabbinical Coll., 1985—. Rabbi Adath Tikvah-Montefiore, Phila., 1988—; instr. Adult Edn. Inst. N.E., Phila., 1990—. Lt. comdr. USN, 1976-87. Recipient Navy Achievement medal USN, 1984. Mem. Reconstructionist Rabbinical Assn. Democrat. Office: Adath Tikvah-Montefiore Hoffnagle & Summerdale Philadelphia PA 19152

ABRAHAMSEN, SAMUEL, retired Judaic studies educator; b. Trondheim, Norway, Oct. 28, 1917; came to U.S., 1940, naturalized, 1948; s. Solomon and Miriam (Fischer) A.; m. Minerva S. Passman, June 8, 1947; children: Joy S. Abrahamsen Land, Judith (dec.). AB, U. Oslo, 1939; postgrad., U. Calif., Berkeley, 1940-41, Cambridge U., 1943; PhD (Agnes Brown Leach fellow), New Sch., N.Y.C., 1955; PhD prin. cert., Hebrew Union Coll., 1957; postgrad. (Univ. fellow), Cornell U., 1962. U.S. coord. of info. Short Wave Research, Inc., N.Y.C., 1941-42; with Royal Norwegian Free Forces in Can., U.K. and Norway, 1942-45; instr. Trondheim Katedralskole, Norway, 1945-46; instr. Norwegian and social studies Bay Ridge High Sch., Bklyn., 1951-63; asst. prof. edn. Bklyn. Coll., 1963-69, assoc. prof., 1970-73, prof. Judaic studies, 1973-84, resident prof., 1984-87, prof. emeritus, 1987—, acting chmn. dept. Judaic studies, 1971-72, dep. chmn., 1972-75, chmn., 1975-80, faculty coordinator Judaic studies program, 1970-71; instr. Norwegian CCNY, 1954-58, Internat. Summer Sch., U. Oslo, 1959; instr. contemporary civilization and econs. Bronx Community Coll., 1960-63; vis. assoc. prof. Cornell U., summer 1967, NYU, 1967-68; adj. prof. Norwegian CUNY Continuing Edn. Sch., 1985—; dir. grad. travel seminar in comparative and internat. edn. Queens Coll., summers 1969, 70; mem. faculty seminar Leo Baeck Inst., N.Y.C., 1976-80, sec., 1977-82, adv. bd., 1978—; participant Ibsen Sesquicentennial Symposium, N.Y.C., 1977-78; mem. nominating com. Acad. for Humanities and Scis., Grad. Ctr., CUNY, 1987-88. Author: Sweden's Foreign Policy, 1957, Say It in Norwegian, 1957 ; assoc. editor: Western European Education, 1968-72; contbg. editor: Edn. News and Notes, 1968-71, The Rescue of Denmark's Jews, 1988, Norway's Response to the Holocaust, 1991; contbr. articles to scholarly jours. Mem. nat. gov. council Am. Jewish Congress, 1973—, v.p. Bklyn. div., 1975—, chmn. commn. Jewish affairs, 1977-80, co-chmn. com. on Jewish life and culture, 1980—; mem. acad. com. World Jewish Congress, 1979—; mem. adv. bd. Met. N.Y. Commn. on Tchr. Edn. and Profl. Standards, 1966-70; mem. staff religious sch. Temple Beth Emeth, 1952-57; mem. faculty Congregation Beth Elohim, Bklyn., 1956-61; sec. Center for Migratory Studies, Bklyn. Coll., 1965-76; mem. com. on planning and ednl. policy, 1972-74; sec. Tribute to Danes, Inc., 1968-72, Norwegian Immigration Sesquicentennial Commn., 1973-75; mem. adv. bd. study-abroad program CUNY, 1968-70; chmn. adv. council Scandinavian Seminars, 1981—, Ctr. European Studies; chmn. acad. com. Scandinavia Today, Am.-Scandinavian Found., 1981-83; trustee Conservative Synagogue Fifth Ave., N.Y.C., 1967-80; dir. Bklyn. Coll. Summer Inst. in Israel, 1971-72, 73-74; adviser to academic council Am. Colls. Jerusalem, 1967-72; participant Ann. Am. Israeli Dialogue, Jerusalem, 1973, 77, 80; chmn. Kallah session Hillel Found., Bklyn. Coll., 1978-81, found. bd. dirs., 1972—. Decorated King Haakon VII Meml. medal, 1942, Royal Norwegian St. Olav medal, Norway, 1968; recipient award Thanks to Scandinavia, Inc., 1987, Nat. Hillel Gold Key, 1970; hon. citation Alumni Assn. New Sch., 1971; scroll of honor State of Israel Bonds, 1975; award Ind. Jewish Student Union, Bklyn. Coll., 1978; honoree Salute to Scholars CUNY, 1982, 83, United Jewish Appeal, Bklyn. Coll., 1984, citation Bklyn. Coll. Faculty Coun., 1988; Jewish Commn. on Edn. fellow Israel, summer 1964; CUNY research award, 1975-76; fellow Meml. Found. for Jewish Culture, 1975-76, 81-82; Am. Council Learned Socs. grantee, 1981; Royal Norwegian Ministry grantee, 1981; NEH research grantee, 1982-83; N.Y. Council Humanities grantee, 1982-83. Mem. MLA, AAUP, NEA, Norseman's League (advisory bd. 1954-60, dir. 1968-77, v.p. 1978-80), Am. Scandinavian Found. (chmn. library and info. com. 1965-76, pres. N.Y. chpt. 1979-81), Doctorate Assn. N.Y. Educators (editor Lux et Veritas 1959-61), Soc. for Advancement Scandinavian Study, Ibsen Soc. Am. (sec. 1978-80), Faculty Hillel Assn. (past pres.), Comparative Edn. Soc., History Edn. Soc., N.Y. Soc. Exptl. Study Edn., Norwegian-Am. Hist. Assn. (exec. bd. 1981—), Am.-Jewish Hist. Soc., Assn. Jewish Studies, Am. Acad. Jewish Research, Univ. Centers for Rational Alternatives (chpt. pres. 1969-70), World Union Jewish Studies, Conf. Jewish Social Studies, Am. Acad. Com. for Peace in Middle East, Nat. Council Jewish Edn., Am. Friends Hebrew U. Home: 4 Washington Square Village New York NY 10012 Office: Bklyn Coll Dept Judaic Studies Brooklyn NY 11210

ABRAMOWICZ, ALFRED L., bishop; b. Chgo., Jan. 27, 1919. Ed., St. Mary Sem., Mundelein, Ill.; J.C.L., Gregorian U., Rome. Ordained priest Roman Cath. Ch., 1943; papal chamberlain, very rev. msgr. and officialis Chgo. Archdiocesan Ct. when named titular bishop of paestum and aux. of Chgo., 1968, consecrated bishop, 1968. Home: 6101 S 75th Ave Box 40 Summit IL 60501-1628

ABRAMS, ARTHUR JAY, rabbi; b. N.Y.C., Apr. 2, 1934; s. Leo and Blanche Abrams; m. Claire Rosenberg, Dec. 25, 1955; children: Naomi, Rachel. BA, Calif. State U., L.A., 1955; MA in Hebrew Letters, rabbi, Hebrew Union Coll., 1961; MS, Nova U., 1975; LLD (hon.), Kans. Newman Coll., 1985; DD (hon.), Hebrew Union Coll., 1986. Ordained rabbi, 1961. Rabbi Beth Ohr, Inglewood, Calif., 1961-63; rabbi Temple Emanu-El, Beverly Hills, Calif., 1963-65, Berkeley, Calif., 1965-70, Ft. Lauderdale, Calif., 1970-75, Wichita, Kans., 1975-88; rabbi Temple Adath B'nai Israel, Evansville, Ind., 1989—; civilian chaplain USAF, Wichita, Kans., 1976-88; chmn. Religious Coalition for Social Action, Wichita, 1984-86, Interreligious Inst., Wichita, 1984-86. Contbr. regular column to Evansville Courier. Adv. mem. Midwest region U.S. Civil Rights Commn., 1986-88. Recipient Disting. Merit cert. NCCJ, 1988. Mem. Cen. Conf. Am. Rabbis (exec. com.), S.E. Assn. Reform Rabbis (v.p.), Midwest Assn. Reform Rabbis (pres.). Home: 915 N Nottingham Ct Evansville IN 47715 Office: Temple Adath B'nai Israel 3600 Washington Ave Evansville IN 47714

ABRAMS, SYLVIA FLECK, religion educator; b. Buffalo, Apr. 5, 1942; d. Abraham and Ann (Hanf) Fleck; m. Ronald M. Abrams, June 30, 1963; children—Ruth, Sharon. BA magna cum laude, Western Res. U., 1963, MA, 1964, PhD, 1988; BHL, Cleve. Coll. Jewish Studies, 1976, MHL, 1983; postgrad. U. Haifa, 1975, Yad Va Shem Summer Inst., Hebrew U., 1983. Hebrew tchr. The Temple, 1959-77, Hebrew coord., 1973-77; tchr. Beachwood High Sch., 1964-66; tchr. Hebrew and social studies Agnon Sch., Cleve., 1975-77, social studies resource tchr., 1976-77; ednl. dir. Temple Emanu El, Cleve., 1977-85; asst. dir. Cleve. Bur. Jewish Edn., 1985—; chmn. ednl. dirs. coun. Cleve. Bd. Jewish Edn., 1982-85. Appointed to Ohio Coun. Holocaust Edn., 1986. Recipient Elbert J. Benton award Western Res. U., 1963; Fred and Rose Rosenwasser Bible award Coll. Jewish Studies, 1974; Emmanuel Gamoran Meml. Curriculum award Nat. Assn. Temple Educator, 1978; Samuel Lipson Meml. award Coll. Jewish Studies, 1981 Bingham fellow Case Western Res. U., 1984-86. Mem. ASCD, Nat. Assn. Temple Educators (bd. dirs. 1984-88), Coun. Jewish Edn. (bd. dirs. 1991—), Coalition for Alternative in Jewish Edn. (bd. mem. at large 1989—), Union Am. Hebrew Congregations (Israel curriculum task force), Cleve. Bur. Jewish Edn. (chmn. ednl. dirs. coun. 1982-85), Nat. Coun. Jewish Women (life), Phi Beta Kappa. Jewish. Club: Hadassah (life). Editor: You and Your Schools, 1972. Office: Cleve Bur Jewish Edn 2030 S Taylor Rd Cleveland OH 44118

ABSHIRE, BRIAN MARSHALL, minister; b. Clarke Island, Maine, May 14, 1954; s. Jack Marshall and Marjorie (YaHaw) A.; m. Elaine Robinson, Apr. 22, 1978; children: Jonathan Calvin Edwards, Elizabeth Anne, Matthew Robinson. Student, Bethel Sem., St. Paul, 1980-81; BA., Bethel Coll., St. Paul, 1981; postgrad., Talbot Sem., La Mirada, Calif., 1983; ThM, Internat. Sem., Plymouth, Fla., 1989; PhD, Greenwich U., Hilo, Hawaii, 1991. Lic. to ministry Ref. Bapt. Ch., 1980, ordained, 1986. Asst. pastor Grove Bapt. Ch., Mpls., 1980-81, Grace Ch. Roseville, Minn., 1981-83; dir. Beck House Trust, Beck Row, Eng., 1984-89; pastor Littlefield Meml. Bapt. Ch., Rockland, Maine, 1989—; lectr., seminar condr., 1984—. Author: Get More from Your Bible, 1988; contbr. articles to profl. jours. and mags. Staff sgt. USAF, 1973-78. Recipient Josephine Butler award, Liverpool, Eng., 1984. Mem. Assn. Bibl. Counsellors (instr. London 1985-89, chmn. credentials 1986-88, editor jour. 1987-89). Home: 47 Acadia Dr Rockland ME 04841 Office: Littlefield Meml Bapt Ch 1 Waldo Ave Rockland ME 04841

ABSTEIN, WILLIAM ROBERT, II, minister; b. Jacksonville, Fla., Aug. 21, 1940; s. William Russell and Edith Virginia (Sanders) A.; m. Roberta Joy Warren, July 1, 1966; children: William Robert III, Roberta Chandler. BA, Fla. State U., 1962; MDiv, U. of the South, 1965, D Ministry, 1978. Ordained to ministry Episcopal Ch. as deacon, 1965. Vicar St. Cyprian's Ch. and St. Monica's Ch., Fla., 1965-67; asst. rector Holy Trinity Episcopal Ch., Decatur, Ga., 1967-70; rector St. Jude's Episcopal Ch., Smyrna, Ga., 1970-84, St. John's Episcopal Ch., Tallahassee, Fla., 1984—; del. Gen. Convention Episcopal Ch., Detroit, 1988, Phoenix, 1991; chmn. Episcopal Found. of Tallahassee, 1984—; rep. Ecumenical Dialogue with Lutherans, Diocese of Fla., 1990—, chmn. Div. Social Ministries, 1991—. Bd. dirs. Friends of Leon County Libr., Tallahassee, 1989—; pres., treas. Literacy Vols. of Leon County, Tallahassee, 1989—; mem. adv. bd. for religious news Tallahassee Democrat newspaper, Tallahassee, 1988—; mem. adv. bd. Ctr. for Profl. Devel., Fla. State U., Tallahassee, 1990—. Mem. Associated Parishes for Liturgy and Mission, Downtown Episcopal Rectors of New South, Rotary. Office: St John's Episcopal Ch 211 N Monroe St Tallahassee FL 32301 *I believe there is today a hunger for meaning stemming from the loss of awareness of the transcendent God. I have chosen to live my life committed to proclaiming by word and actions the relevance of that power to fill this void. I have found a profound sense of fulfillment from this ministry in the world.*

ACKER, RAYMOND ABIJAH, minister; b. Hartford, Conn., Jan. 4, 1932; s. Abijah F. and Mary Esther (Willys) A.; m. Ann Hamm, June 14, 1958 (dec. Sept. 1959); 1 child, Marianne (dec.); m. D. Jean Rineer, Sept. 3, 1960; children: Thomas R., Douglas B. BS in Bible, Phila. Coll. Bible, 1959; MDiv, Phila. Theol. Sem., 1962; ThM, Dallas Theol. Sem., 1964; MS in Guidance and Counseling, L.I. U., 1973. Ordained to ministry, Ind. Fundamental Chs. Am. Enlisted U.S. Army, 1953-55, commd. 2d lt., 1963, advanced through grades to lt. col., 1978, chaplain, 1965-83; dir. alumni affairs Phila. Coll. Bible, Langhorne, Pa., 1983-84; asst. to gen. dir. Bibl. Ministries Worldwide, Lawrenceville, Ga., 1984-89; dir. World Wide Bible Insts., South Gibson, Pa., 1990—; mem. chaplains commn. Ind. Fundamental Chs. Am., 1977—, v.p. Delmarva Regional, 1981-83. Author: History of the Theological Seminary of the Reformed Episcopal Church, 1965. Pres. PTA, Aberdeen, Md., 1971-72, Giesson, Fed. Republic Germany, 1975-76; mem. com. Boy Scouts Am., Copperas Cove, Tex., 1976-79; mem. centennial com. Phila. Theol. Sem., 1983-87. Decorated Bronze Star. Mem. N.E. Regional Assn. N.Am. Missions (chmn. 1991—). Republican. Home and Office: Grace & Truth Evang Assn PO Box 64 Camp Rd South Gibson PA 18842-0064 *The Psalmist said "Commit thy way unto the Lord; trust also in Him; and He shall bring it to pass." The Lord meets special needs before, during and after the need occurs in our lives. It is great to trust and not to fret!.*

ACKERMAN, ELIZABETH DAVIS, lay church worker; b. Oaklyn, N.J., Oct. 14, 1940; d. Albert Pflomm and Margaret Ludlow (McCullough) Davis; m. Richard LeRoy Ackerman, June 14, 1961; children: David Andrew, Timothy Richard, Anne Rachel, Jonathan Michael. BA, Hood Coll., Frederick, Md., 1962; MusM, U. Utah, 1965. Choir dir., asst. organist Good Shepherd Luth. Ch., Claremont, Calif., 1967; sr. choir dir., counselor Luther League, 1968-69; choir mem., asst. organist Christ the King Luth. Ch., Tigard, Oreg., 1970; dir. sr. choir Calvin Presbyn. Ch., Tigard, 1971; dir. music Zoar Luth. Ch., Canby, Oreg., 1972-77; dir. chamber orch. St. Luke's Luth. Ch., Portland, Oreg., 1978-82; sr. choir dir. Augustana Luth. Ch., Portland, Oreg., 1987-88; owner, exec. dir. Small World Music Sch., Tigard, 1988-91. Active mem. choir ascension Luth. Ch., Haddon Heights, N.J., 1948-58; Sunday sch. accompanist, 1952-58, vacation ch. sch. accompanist, 1954-58; Luther League accompanist, 1954-58; organizer, leader girl's quartet; ch. pianist Noway (Maine) Ctr. Ch., 1958-61; mem. choir Hood Coll., 1958-62; asst. organist, mem. choir Zion Luth. Ch., Salt Lake City, 1962-66; accompanist St. Anthony's Boys' Choir, 1981-85; dir. summer Music Camp, St. Anthony's, Tigard, Oreg., 1983; asst. organist Christ the King Luth. Ch., Tigard, 1989-91, pvt. piano tchr., 1960-91; accompianist Glee Club, St. Anthony's Boys Choir, 1979-84. Mem. Nat. Guild Piano Tchrs., Am. Choral Dirs. Assn., Music Tchrs. Nat. Assn., Choristers Guild. Home: 10905 SW Mira Ct Tigard OR 97223

ACKERMAN, SCOTT FULTON, priest; b. New Orleans, La., Apr. 10, 1944; s. Stephen Wilson and Helen (Bennet) A.; m. Suzanne Kittles, Aug. 17, 1968. AB, U. N.C., 1966; MDiv, Episcopal Divinity Sch., Cambridge, Mass., 1970. Asst. minister Grace Episcopal Ch., Bklyn.; rector St. Gabriels Ch., Bklyn., 1973-78, Atlanta, 1978-83, Holy Comforter, Atlanta, 1982—; chaplain Atlanta, 1978-79; adj. prof. Ga. State U., 1983—; prof., 1983—; chmn. dept. pastor care N.Y. City Coun. Chs., 1972-78; founder Bklyn. Clergy Assn., 1974; chaplain Westminister Schs., Atlanta, 1978-79; contbg. founder The Phoenix (News), Bklyn. Author numerous poems; writer Ga. Dem. Asst. campaign mgr. Sam Nunn for Senate, 1986. Mem. Ga. Assn. Realtors, Atlanta City Club, Harvard Club. Avocations: camping, sailing, chess. Home: 28 W Belle Isle Rd NE Atlanta GA 30342

ACKERSON, CHARLES STANLEY, minister, social worker; b. St. Louis, June 19, 1935; s. Charles Albert and Glenda Mae (Brown) A.; m. Carol Jean Stehlick, Aug. 18, 1957; children: Debra Lynn, Charles Mark, Heather Sue. AB, William Jewell Coll., 1957; MDiv, Colgate Rochester Div. Sch., 1961. Ordained to ministry Am. Bapt. Ch., 1961. Pastor, Glens Falls (N.Y.) Friends Meeting, 1961-65; assoc. pastor Delmar Bapt. Ch., St. Louis, 1965-68; resource dir. Block Ptnrship., St. Louis, 1968-71; group home dir. North Side YMCA, St. Louis, 1971-72; group home supr. St. Louis Juvenile Ct., 1973-74; program dir. Youth Opportunities Unltd., casework supr. St. Louis County Juvenile Ct., 1974-83; youth svcs. specialist St. Louis County Dept. Human Svcs., 1985—; instr. adminstrn. of justice Mo. Bapt. Coll., St. Louis, 1980—; asst. pastor St. Jordan's and St. John's United Chs. of Christ, 1976—; exhibit coord. Dog Mus., 1989—; cons. Am. Youth Found., 1990—; mem. ordination coun. area V, Great Rivers region Am. Bapt. Chs. U.S.A., 1982-84; chmn. youth focus group Interfaith Ptnrship. Met. St. Louis, 1985-88; chmn. St. Louis Area Youth Svcs. Network, 1987-89. Chmn. group home com. Mo. Coun. on Criminal Justice, 1973-75; chmn. cts. and instns. sub-com. Juvenile Delinquency Task Force for Gov. Mo. Action Plan for Pub. Safety, 1976. Mem. Nat. Coun. Juvenile and Family Ct. Judges, Mo. Juvenile Justice Assn. (v.p., chmn. tng. com.), Am. Correctional Assn., Nat. Audobon Soc., Smithsonian Instn. Assn., Cairn Terrier Club Am., Three Rivers Kennel Club of Mo. (past pres.), Mo. Conservation Fedn., Lambda Chi Alpha. Democrat. Baptist. Home: 1221 Havenhurst Rd Manchester MO 63011 *Every birth is a miracle birth; every child is a child of God. We are responsible for the memories we leave with our children. Our primary conversation should be about values and priorities because that which is important to each of us shapes the choices we make and the actions we take.*

ACKLIN, THOMAS PATRICK, priest, seminary rector; b. Sewickley, Pa., Jan. 6, 1950; s. Thomas and Doris Lenore (Hallisey) A. BA in Philosophy, Duquesne U., 1971, MA, 1975; MDiv, St. Vincent Sem., 1978; Licentiate of Sacred Theology, U. Louvain, 1980, PhD, 1982, STD, 1983; postgrad., Belgian Sch. Psychoanalysis, 1980-82; diploma, Pitts. Psychoanalytic Ctr., 1985; postgrad., Pitts. Psychoanalytic Inst., 1985—. Ordained priest Roman Cath. Ch., 1980. Tchr. Seton High Sch., Balt., 1972-74, St. Mary of the Mt. High Sch., Pitts., 1974-75; lectr. St. Vincent Coll., Latrobe, Pa., 1976-78; asst. prof. St. Vincent Sem. and St. Vincent Coll., Latrobe, 1982-87, assoc. prof., 1987—; acting rector St. Vincent Sem., Latrobe, 1987-88, rector, 1989—; staff announcer, engr. Sta. WBJC-FM, Sta. WITH-AM-FM, Balt., 1973-74, host program Sta. WEDO-AM, 1988—, Sta. WTAE-TV, 1991—; grad. asst. Louvain U., 1980-82; pvt. practice, 1982—; psychotherapist Pitts. Psychoanalytic Ctr., 1983-85, Latrobe Psychotherapy Assocs. Inc., 1990—; dir. formation for jr.-professed monks St. Vincent Archabbey, 1983-87; psychoanalytic psychotherapist Latrobe Psychotherapy Assocs. Inc., 1991—. Contbr. articles to religious jours. Mem. Belgian Sch. Psychoanalysis (corr.), Nat. Assn. for Advancement Psychoanalysis (cert.), European Soc. for Psychology of Religion, Pitts. Psychoanalytic Soc. (assoc.), Soc. for Sci. Study of Religion, Menninger Found., Cath. Theol. Soc. Am., Ea. Conf. Maj. Sem. Rectors, Internat. Psychoanalytical Studies Orgn. Democrat. Home: St Vincent Archabbey Latrobe PA 15650 Office: St Vincent Sem Rector's Office Latrobe PA 15650 also: Latrobe Psychotherapy Assocs Inc PO Box QQ Fraser Purchase Rd Latrobe PA 15650

ACREE, FLORENCE HORNBECK, preschool provider; b. Poughkeepsie, N.Y., Jan. 6, 1954; d. William Lee and Adele (Olson) Hornbeck; m. Malcolm Taylor, June 4, 1975; children: Jennifer, Allison. BA in Psychology, Mt. St. Mary Coll., Newburgh, N.Y., 1976; MEd, U. Alaska, 1979. Cert. tchr., N.Y. Dir. Wee Care Christian Preschool & Daycare, Monterey, Calif., 1990—. Active Christian life bd. Ch. of Nazarene, Monterey, 1990—. Mem. Assn. Christian Schs. Internat. Home: 1430 Augusta Pl Monterey CA 93940 Office: Wee Care Christian Presch 1375 Josselyn Canyon Rd Monterey CA 93940

ACTON, THOMAS RAYMOND, minister; b. Elmhurst, Ill., Sept. 5, 1953; s. Raymond E. and Margaret L. (Bell) A.; m. Carol L. Jevne, Aug. 17, 1974; children: John, Mark, Kimberly. BA, No. Ill. U., 1975, MEd, 1987, postgrad., 1987—; MDiv, Concordia Theol. Sem., Ft. Wayne, Ind., 1979. Ordained to ministry Luth. Ch.-Mo. Synod, 1979. Missionary Luth. Ch. in The Philippines, 1979-82; campus pastor Concordia U., River Forest, Ill., 1982-87; counselor Trinity Ch., Lombard, Ill., 1987-88; sr. pastor Zion Luth. Ch., McHenry, Ill., 1988—; prin. Zion Luth. Sch., 1990—; advisor to Helpmates Ministry, Lisle, Ill., 1990—. Mem. Strategic Task Force Sch. Dist. #15, McHenry, 1991. Recipient Weibi Mission grant Weibi Fellowship, 1987-90. Mem. Kappa Delta Pi. Home: 3900 Kane McHenry IL 60050 Office: Zion Luth Ch 4206 W Elm Mc Henry IL 60050

ADAIR, JAMES ROBERT, JR., minister; b. San Antonio, Aug. 12, 1960; s. James Robert and Vela Marie (Keefer) A.; m. Rosa Magali Sierra, July 28, 1984; 1 child, Danielle Marie. BS, Trinity U., San Antonio, 1980; MDiv, Southwestern Bapt. Theol. Sem., 1985; B.A. (honors), U. Stellenbosch (S. Africa), 1989; postgrad., Southwestern Bapt. Theol. Sem. Ordained to ministry So. Bapt. Ch., 1986. Minister of youth and music Univ. Bapt. Ch., San Antonio, 1981-82; assoc. pastor Primera Iglesia Bautista, Ft. Worth, 1985-88, 90—; instr. Bapt. Theol. Coll., Cape Town, South Africa, 1988-89; teaching fellow Southwestern Bapt. Theol. Sem., Ft. Worth, 1986—; free-lance computer programmer, Ft. Worth, 1982—; rsch. asst. Qumran Database Project, 1988-89. Mem. Soc. Biblical Lit. Home: 4722 McCart Fort Worth TX 76115 Office: Primera Iglesia Bautista 1519 Circle Park PO Box 4338 Fort Worth TX 76106

ADAIR, TOBY WARREN, JR., minister; b. Beaumont, Tex., Sept. 8, 1922; s. Toby Warren and Mildred Lee (Muldrow) A.; m. Ann Ivareese Redden, May 8, 1943; 1 child, Robin Lee Adair Fleming. BS, Centenary Coll., 1947; MDiv, Golden Gate Bapt. Theol. Sem., 1973, MA, 1974; ThD, Internat. Sem., 1990. Ordained to ministry So. Bapt. Conv., 1973. Commd. 2d lt. USAF, 1944, advanced through grades to maj., 1959, command pilot, 1967-70, ret., 1967; pastor South Reno (Nev.) Bapt. Ch., 1973-77, Bancroft Bapt. Ch., Spring Valley, Calif., 1977-81, Mt. Zion Bapt. Ch., Praireville, La., 1982-85, Forrest Park Bapt. Ch., Pine Bluff, Ark., 1986—; pres. pastor's conf. San Diego (Calif.) So. Bapt. Assn., 1981, Ascension So. Bapt. Assn., Prairieville, 1984, Harmony So. Bapt. Assn., Pine Bluff, 1988. Prayer-time host Radio Sta. KNIS, Reno-Carson City, Nev., 1974-76. Dir. Jefferson County Mus. Guild, Pine Bluff, 1990—. Decorated Army Commendation medal USAF, Japan, 1950, DFC Air Medal with 2 oak leaf clusters USAF, Korea, 1951, USAF Commendation medal, USAF, USA, 1959. Named Boss of the Yr., Am. Bus. Women Assn., Reno, 1975. Mem. Jefferson County Clergy Conf. (treas.), Confedn. Air Forces (chaplain Razor Base wing), Kemper Mil. Sch. and Coll. Assn. (bd. dirs. 1991—), Rotary (Pine Bluff, bd. dirs. 1988-91, pres. 1991—). Republican. Home: 803 W 12th Ave Pine Bluff AR 71601 Office: Forrest Park Bapt Ch 3706 Cherry St Pine Bluff AR 71603

ADAMEC, JOSEPH VICTOR, bishop; b. Bannister, Mich., Aug. 13, 1935. Ed., Mich. State U., Nepomucene Coll., Lateran U., Rome. Ordained priest Roman Cath. Ch. (for Nita diocese, Czech and Slovak Federative Republic), 1960, ordained bishop of Altoona-Johnstown, Pa., 1987. Asst. pastor Diocese of Saginaw, Mich., 1960-65, notary, 1965-69, sec. to bishop, master of ceremonies, 1969-72, chancellor, 1972-77; pastor St. Hyacinth Ch., All Saints Cath. High Sch., Bay City, Mich., 1977-84, Sts. Peter and Paul Parish, Bay City, 1984-87; bishop Altoona-Johnstown, Pa., 1987—. Mem. Nat. Conf. Cath. Bishops (joint com. Orthodox and Roman Cath. Bishops, ad hoc com. for aid to the Ch. in Cen. and Ea. Europe and USSR). Avocations: photography, sailing, writing. Address: Logan Blvd Box 126 Hollidaysburg PA 16648

ADAMS, BERESFORD, minister; b. Colon, Panama, Jan. 16, 1940; s. Cyril Da Costa and Etta Gwendolyn (Golding) A.; m. Gloria Elena Maxwell, Feb. 20, 1962; children: Patricio, Natasha, Derick, Darnell. Student, Princeton Theol. Sem., 1989—. Ordained to ministry Bapt. Ch., 1965. Religious educator Faith Bapt. Ch., Coram, N.Y., 1982-85, asst. pastor, 1985-87, pastor, 1987—; pres. Middle Island Alliance, N.Y., 1988—; bd. dirs. The Ministries, Coram, 1987—. Mem. Ea. Suffolk Minority Bus. Adv. Coun., Riverhead, N.Y., 1991—; advisor Sagamore Psychiat. Hosp., Melville, 1990—. Recipient Humanitarian award, Nat. Assn. Negro Bus. and Profl. Clubs, 1990. Mem. NAACP, Ea. Bapt. Assn., Assn. Black Seminarians. Home: 23 Wilmont Turn Coram NY 11727 *I try to live by the principle that the best expression of love is to love people for the sake of love itself.*

ADAMS, CAROL ANN, early childhood director; b. Abilene, Tex., Jan. 18, 1946; d. Taylor and Mary Nell (Baker) Paul; m. Gary Milton Adams, June 10, 1967; children: Rob, Krista. BA in Elem. Edn., Sam Houston U., 1967. Cert. elem. edn. tchr., Tex. Asst. dir. Green Acres Early Edn. Ctr., Tyler, Tex., 1974-76, dir., 1976—; tchr. children's choirs and presch. Sunday Sch., Ft. Worth and Tyler, 1971—; adv. bd. Bapt. Gen. Conv. of Tex., Dallas, 1975—. Mem. Nat. Assn. Edn. for the Young Children, Tex. Assn. Edn. for the Young Children, Delta Kappa Gamma (1st v.p. 1990—). Office: Green Acres Bapt Ch 1612 Leo Lynn Tyler TX 75701

ADAMS, CHARLES JOSEPH, Islamic studies educator; b. Houston, Apr. 24, 1924; s. Joseph Edward Adams and Viola Jane (Terry) Robinson; m. Joanna Zofia Teslar, Aug. 1964. BA, Baylor U., 1947; PhD, U. Chgo., 1956. Prof. McGill U., Montreal, Can., 1957—. Editor: Readers' Guide to the Great Religions, 1965; editor Ency. of Religion, 1986. With USAAF, 1942-45. Fellowship Ford Found., 1954-57, Rockefeller Found., 1960, Can. Coun., 1968, 81. Mem. Am. Soc. for the Study of Religion (treas., pres.), Am. Oriental Soc., Am. Acad. Religion, Middle East Studies Assn. (founder, v.p.). Home: 123 Rang des 25 Ouest, Saint Bruno de Montarville, PQ Canada J3V 4P6 Office: Inst Islamic Studies, 3485 McTavish St, Montreal, PQ Canada H3A 1Y1

ADAMS, DENNIS ADAMS, minister; b. Albany, Mo., Aug. 31, 1949; s. Robert Lee and Alice Margaret (Browning) A.; m. Cindy Marcella Gabaldon, June 22, 1971; children: Joshua Wood, Nathan Martinez. BA, Grand Canyon U., 1972; MDiv, Southwestern Bapt. Theol. Sem., 1975.

Ordained to ministry So. Bapt. Conv., 1974. Pastor Ward's Chapel Bapt. Ch., Atoka, Okla., 1973-75, Scottsdale Rd. Bapt. Mission, Tempe, Ariz., 1975-77, 1st Bapt. Ch., Show Low, Ariz., 1977-91, North Phoenix Bapt. Ch. West, Glendale, Ariz., 1991—; 1st v.p. Ariz. So. Bapt. Convention, Phoenix, 1988-89, pres., 1990-91; pres. Ariz. Bapt. Children's Svcs., Phoenix, 1986-88; chmn. White Mountain Ministerial Alliance, Show Low, 1982-90. Regional rep. No. Ariz. Child Devel. Adv. Bd., 1982-83; bd. dirs. Transient Aid Program, Show Low, 1986-89. Mem. Bapt. Found. of Ariz. (bd. dirs. 1989—). Office: North Phoenix Bapt Ch West 5341 W Greenway Rd Glendale AZ 85306

ADAMS, DOUGLAS GLENN, Christianity and arts educator; b. DeKalb, Ill., Apr. 12, 1945; s. Glenn Hammer and Harriet Foote (Engstrom) A.; m. Margo Alice Miller, June 7, 1968. BA, Duke U., 1967; MA, Pacific Sch. of Religion, 1970, MDiv, 1970; ThD, Grd. Theol. Union, 1974. Ordained United Ch. of Christ, 1970. Asst. pastor Arlington Community Ch., Kensington, Calif., 1968-70; pastor Coll. Heights Ch., San Mateo, Calif., 1970-72; asst. prof. religion dept. U. Mont., Missoula, 1975-76; asst. prof. Pacific Sch. Religion & Grad. Theol. Union, Berkeley, Calif., 1976-79; assoc. prof. Pacific Sch. Religion & Grad. Theol. Union, Berkeley, 1979-84, prof., 1984—; editorial bd. mem. Modern Liturgy, San Jose, Calif., 1977—, Church Teachers, Durham, N.C., 1986—. Author: Humor in the American Pulpit, 1975, Meeting House to Camp Meeting, 1981, Transcendence with the Body in Art, 1991; editor: Art as Religious Studies, 1987, Dance as Religious Studies, 1990. Pres. Internat. Sacred Dance Guild, N.Y., 1977-79. Named Overseas Fellow Third Internat. Congress of Religion Art & Architecture, Jerusalem, 1973, Vis. Theologian, The Rockwell Found., Univ. Houston, Tex., 1986; recipient of Post-doctoral Fellowship in Art History, Nat. Mus. Am. Art, Smithsonian Instn., Washington, 1974-75. Fellow Soc. for the Arts, Religion and Contemporary Culture, N. Am. Acad. of Liturgy (chmn. fine arts com.); mem. Am. Acad. Religion (chmn. arts sect. 1984-86), Am. Acad. Homiletics, Coll. Art Assn. Democrat. Home: 6226 Bernhard Richmond CA 94805 Office: Pacific Sch Religion 1798 Scenic Ave Berkeley CA 94709

ADAMS, EDWARD JOHN, lay worker; b. Hoosick Falls, N.Y., Jan. 4, 1946; s. Edward John Adams and Elizabeth June (Cunningham) Goff; m. Shirley Ruth Johnson, Jan. 14, 1972. Cert. electronics tech., Trenton (N.J.) Tech. Inst., 1971. Electronic technician N.J. Bell, Hamilton, 1973—; ch. clk. Hamilton Square Bapt. Ch., Trenton, N.J., 1986-88, adminstr., 1988-89, treas., 1989—.

ADAMS, FRANK CLIFTON, minister, counselor; b. Roanoke, Va., Jan. 10, 1934; s. John Louis and Nora Mae (Chockett) A.; m. Jeanette Mae Crenshaw, June 12, 1958; children: Daniel, Jean Lynn, Betsy. AA, Bluefield (Va.) Coll., 1956; BA, U. Richmond, Va., 1958; MDiv, So. Bapt. Sem., 1962; MS in Social Work, U. Louisville, 1968. Lic. social worker, N.Y. Dir. boys residential care Ormsby Village Treatment Ctr., Anchorage, Ky., 1960-70; dir. social svcs. Elmcrest Children's Ctr., Syracuse, N.Y., 1970-75; pvt. practice counseling Fayetteville, N.Y., 1975-80, 80-85; dir. treatment Cayuga Home for Children, Auburn, 1985; pvt. practice, 1985-88; with Evang. Adoption & Family Svc., North Syracuse, N.Y., 1988; pastor United Bapt. Ch., Oswego, N.Y., 1988—. Dir. counseling follow-up Cen. N.Y. Billy Graham Crusade, Syracuse, 1989. Mem. NASW, Phi Kappa Phi. Baptist. Avocation: organic gardening. Office: United Bapt Ch of Scriba RR 2 Box 140 Oswego NY 13126

ADAMS, HOPE HOWLETT, minister; b. Wilmington, Del., May 30, 1942; d. Harold H. and Helen (Hope) Howlett; children: Daniel, Bryan G., Bruce H. BS, Northwestern U., Evanston, Ill., 1963; MS, Sarah Lawrence Coll., Bronxville, N.Y., 1971; MDiv, Yale U., 1989. Ordained to ministry Episcopal Ch., 1989. Assoc. rector Trinity Episcopal Ch., Hartford, Conn., 1989—; sec. Hartford Deanery, 1990—. Author: A Textbook of Physiology, 1989; contbr. articles to profl. jours. Home: 54 Garfield Rd West Hartford CT 06107 Office: Trinity Episcopal Ch 120 Sigourney St Hartford CT 06105

ADAMS, JAMES HOMER, minister; b. Oklahoma City, Sept. 6, 1939; s. James Homer Jr. and Harriette Elizabeth (Maine) A.; m. Margaret E. Grimes, July 6, 1963 (div. June 1986); children: Charles, Lisa, Michael, Heather; m. Marilyn Johnson, July 8, 1989. BA cum laude, Princeton U., 1961; BD, Union Sem., N.Y.C., 1965; STD, San Francisco Sem., San Anselmo, Calif., 1981. Ordained to ministry Presbyn. Ch. (U.S.A.), 1965. Assoc. pastor 1st Presbyn. Ch., Youngstown, Ohio, 1967-69; pastor Union Presbyn. Ch., Wilmerding, Pa., 1965-67, Trinity Presbyn. Ch., Independence, Mo., 1969-74; pastor/co-pastor Rockville (Md.) Presbyn. Ch., 1975—; curriculum writer Presbyn. Ch. (U.S.A.), 1974-91. Columnist Gazette Newspapers, 1989—; creator The Game of Future Shock, 1973. Fellow Found. for Theol. Edn., 1974-75. Mem. Jesus Seminar, Rotary (officer 1971—). Home: 836 New Mark Esplanade Rockville MD 20850 Office: Rockville Presbyn Ch 215 W Montgomery Ave Rockville MD 20850

ADAMS, JAMES JAY, minister, district youth director; b. Encino, Calif., July 9, 1955; s. John Gordon and Georgina Alfreda (Copeland) A.; m. Lori Tuttle Adams, Nov. 4, 1978; children: Alissa Marie, Amanda Reneé. BA, Life Bible Coll., 1977. Ordained to ministry Internat. Ch. of Foursquare Gospel, 1977. Youth pastor Burbank (Calif.) Foursquare Ch., 1977-79; tchr. Heritage Jr./Sr. High Sch., Glendale, Calif., 1979-81; ch. adminstr., youth pastor Valley View Foursquare Ch., Canoga Park, Calif., 1981-90; dist. youth dir. Western Dist. Foursquare Chs., Modesto, Calif., 1990—; camp dir. Old Oak Ranch, Sonora, Calif., 1990—; mem. camp staff, coord. Camp Cedar Crest, So. CAlif., 1981—; cons., speaker in field. Res. officer, chaplain West Valley div. L.A. Police Dept., Canoga Park, 1985-90. Recipient Cert. of Recognition, County of L.A., 1989, City of L.A., 1989, Calif. State Assembly, 1989, Calif. State Senate, 1989. Republican. Avocations: computers, writing, consulting. Office: Youthwest/Western Dist Foursquare Chs PO Box 3008 Modesto CA 95353

ADAMS, JAMES KENNETH, music minister; b. Kosciusko, Miss., July 6, 1953; s. Herbert Wilson and Doris Elizabeth (Arnold) A.; m. Betty Joyce Brooks, July 17, 1976; children: Brooke Elizabeth, Rebecca Ann. AA, Holmes Jr. Coll., 1973; MusB in Edn., Miss. Coll., 1975, MusM in Edn., 1977. Cert. music educator. Min. of music Noxapater (Miss.) Bapt. Ch., 1976-77; mini. of music First Bapt. Ch., Itta Bena, Miss., 1977-80; min. of music First Bapt. Ch., Bruce, Miss., 1980—; pres. Miss. Singing Churchmen, Miss., 1990—; dir. youth Winston County (Miss.) Bapt. Assn., 1976-77; dir. music Holmes-Leflore Assn., 1977-80. Composer choral anthems including Just a Little While, 1988, I've Heard My Shepherd's Voice, 1990, Hush, Be Still, 1990, There's a Great Day Comin' Some Day, 1990. Bulletin editor Bruce Rotary Club, 1983—, sec., 1989-90, v.p., 1990—. Mem. Calhoun County Bapt. Assn. (dir. music 1981—). Home: Bryant St Bruce MS 38915 Office: First Bapt Ch Countiss and Johnson Bruce MS 38915 *True happiness in life comes from loving God and your fellow man. A natural outgrowth of such love is service.*

ADAMS, JAMES LUTHER, theologian; b. Ritzville, Wash., Nov. 12, 1901; s. James Carey and Lella May (Barnett) A.; m. Margaret Ann Young, Sept. 21, 1927; children—Eloise, Elaine Adams Miller, Barbara Adams Thompson. A.B., U.Minn., 1924; S.T.B., Harvard U., 1927, A.M., 1930; Ph.D., U. Chgo., 1945; D.D., Meadville Theol. Sch., Chgo., 1958; Theol. D., Marburg U., W. Ger., 1960; D.H.L., Middlebury Coll., 1979. Ordained to ministry Unitarian Ch., 1927. Minister Second Ch., Salem, Mass., 1927-34; instr. English dept. Boston U., 1929-32; minister 1st Unitarian Soc., Wellesley Hills, Mass., 1934-35; prof. religious ethics Meadville Theol. Sch., also Div. Sch., U. Chgo., 1936-56; prof. Christian ethics Div. Sch., Harvard U., Cambridge, Mass., 1956-68; now prof. emeritus Div. Sch., Harvard U.; Disting. prof. social ethics Andover Newton Theol. Sch., Newton Centre, Mass., 1968-72; Disting. scholar in residence Meadville-Lombard Theol. Sch., 1972-73; prof. theology and religious ethics Div. Sch., 1972-76; minister adult edn. Arlington Street Ch., Boston, 1971—; Noble lectr. Harvard U., 1953; lectr. Albert Schweitzer Coll., 1952, Internat. Assn. History of Religion, Tokyo, 1958, World Ctr. for Buddhistic Studies, Rangoon, 1958, Theol. Coll., Bangalore, 1958; Hibbert lectr. Oxford, Manchester, Liverpool univs., Eng., 1963. Author: Irving Babbitt: Man and Teacher, 1941; The Changing Reputation of Human Nature, 1943; Taking Time Seriously, 1956; Paul Tillich's Philosophy of Culture, Science and Religion, 1965; On Being Human Religiously, 1976; (with others) New Perspective on Peace, 1944, Together We Advance, 1946, Voices of Liberalism II, 1947, Orientation in Religious Education, 1950, Religion in the State University, 1950, The Theology of Paul Tillich, 1952, rev. edit., 1984, Authority and Freedom, 1952, The Meaning of Love, 1953, Man's Faith and Freedom: The Theological Influence of Jacobus Arminius, 1962, Interpreters of Luther, 1968, Political and Legal Obligation, 1970, Religion of the Republic, 1971, Festschrift for Erich Fromm, In the Name of Life, 1971, Festschrift for W. Alvin Pitcher, Ethics and Belief, 1978, Democracy and Mediating Structures: A Theological Inquiry, 1980, Readings on Professionalism, 1980; author: (with others) Pastoral Care in the Liberal Churches, 1970; editor: (with others) Christian Register, 1932, The Directive in History (H.N. Wieman), 1949, What Did Luther Understand by Religion ? (Karl Holl), 1977, Taking Times Seriously (John R. Wilcox), 1978, The Reconstruction of Morality, 1979, (with Roger L. Shinn) The Thought of Paul Tillich, 1985, The Prophethood of All Believers, 1986, Voluntary Associations, 1986, Festschrift for Harold Berman, The Weightier Matters of the Law, 1988, An Examined Faith, 1991; editor (with others) Phoenix series of vols. on sociology of politics and religion; editor, translator: (with others) What Is Religion? (Paul Tillich), 1969; Political Expectation, 1971; editor Jour. Liberal Religion, 1939-49; assoc. editor Faith and Freedom, 1950—, Jour. Liberal Ministry, 1979; co-editor Jour. Religion, 1951-56; mem. editorial bd. Jour. Religious Ethics, 1973—; translator: Dogma of Christ (Erich Fromm), 1963, Religion in History, Essays by Ernst Troelstch, 1991; transl. and introductory essay on Paul Tillich, The Protestant Era, 1948; contbr. to profl. publs. Chmn. adv. com. dept. social responsibility Unitarian-Universalist Assn., 1965-69; bd. dirs. Ctr. for Vol. Soc., F.I.R.S.T., Inc., Mass. chpt. ACLU, Ctr. Applied Ethics, Mass. chpt. Ams. for Dem. Action; chmn. bd. dirs. Fellowship Racial and Econ. Equality; mem. adv. bd. Americans United for Separation of Ch. and State. Fulbright research scholar U. Marburg, 1963; hon. fellow Manchester Coll., Oxford. Fellow Am. Acad. Arts and Sci.; mem. Soc. Sci. Study of Religion (pres. 1957-59), Am. Soc. Christian Ethics (pres. 1967-68), Am. Theol. Soc. (pres. 1972-73), Am. Sociol. Soc., Societe Europeenne de Culture (internat. council), Soc. Art Religion and Contemporary Culture (chmn. bd. 1971-73, pres. 1984-85, pres. emeritus 1986—), Council Religion and Law (bd. dirs.), Assn. for Vol. Action Scholars (v.p. 1971—), Soc. Polit. and Legal Philosophy. Home: 60 Francis Ave Cambridge MA 02138 *Hosea said it rightly, that new beginnings are always possible, liberating us from imprisonment in the past, our past, or in the present.*

ADAMS, JAMES WILLIAM LEMUEL, minister; b. Temple, Tex., Sept. 5, 1929; s. J. W. Lemuel and Mary Ellen (Green) A.; m. Geraldyne Seymour, Mar. 18, 1950; children: Jim, Beth, David, Julie. BA, Baylor U., 1952, postgrad., 1959; BD, S.W. Bapt. Theol. Sem., 1956, MDiv, 1973, DMin, 1977. Ordained to ministry So. Bapt. Conv., 1949. Pastor 1st Bapt. Ch., South Houston, Tex., 1960-63, Victoria, Tex., 1963-73; pastor Beech St. 1st Bapt. Ch., Texarkana, Ark., 1973-86; pres. Internat. Bapt. Ministries, Inc., Madisonville, Tex., 1980—; pastor 1st Bapt. Ch., Madisonville, 1986—; mem. exec. bd. Bapt. Gen. Conv. Tex., 1990—; coord. Australian Partnership Fgn. Mission Bd., So. Bapt. Conv., Richmond, Va., 1991. Contbr. articles to profl. jours. Chmn. Victoria County Child Welfare Bd., 1970-72, Miller County (Ark.) Health Bd., 1981-85; mem. Vol. Svcs. Bur. Bd., Texarkana, Ark., Tex., 1975-78; mem., vice-chmn. Cen. Sch. Bd., Miller County, 1981-85. Office: 1st Bapt Ch Trinity at Elm PO Box 159 Madisonville TX 77864

ADAMS, JOE DALE, minister; b. Louisville, Feb. 10, 1946; s. Waid T. Adams and Charlene (Harris) Linker; m. Saundra Patterson, Oct. 10, 1965; children: Alesha, Paul, Andrea. BS, Western Ky. U., 1976; DD (hon.), Faith Evang. Christian Coll., Morgantown, Ky., 1984; D Sacred Laws, Great Plains Bible Coll., Sioux Falls, S.D., 1987. Ordained to ministry Ind. Bapt. Ch., 1973. Pastor Fairview Bapt. Chapel, Franklin, Ky., 1973-78, Faith Bapt. Ch., Franklin, 1978-80, LaRue County Bapt. Ch., Hodgenville, Ky., 1980-82; missionary, chaplain Nelson County Bapt. Ch., Bardstown, Ky., 1983—; chaplain Ky. State Govt., Frankfort, 1983—; bd. dirs. Christian Home Educator Ky. (chmn.). Sgt. USAF, 1966-70, Vietnam. Democrat. Home and Office: PO Box 220 Bardstown KY 40004 *Life is not what we can add to humanity but what we can do for Christ.*

ADAMS, JOHN HURST, bishop; b. Columbia, S.C., Nov. 27, 1929; s. Eugene Avery and Charity A. (Nash) A.; m. Dolly Desselle, Aug. 25, 1956; children: Gaye Desselle, Jann Hurst, Madelyn Rose. AB, Johnson C. Smith Coll., 1948; STB, Boston U., 1951, STM, 1953; DD, Wilberforce U., 1956, Paul Quinn Coll., 1972. Ordained to ministry A.M.E. Ch. as deacon, 1948, elder, 1952, bishop, 1972. Pastor Bethel A.M.E. Ch., Lynn, Mass., 1950-52; prof. Wilberforce (Ohio) U., 1952-56; pres. Paul Quinn Coll., Waco, Tex., 1956-62, chmn. bd., 1972—; pastor 1st A.M.E. Ch., Seattle, 1962-68, Grant A.M.E. ch., L.A., 1968-72; 87th A.M.E. bishop 10th Dist. Tex. councils chs., from 1972; bishop 2d Dist., 1986-89; sr. bishop Atlanta, 1989—. Author: Ethnic Education in Black Church, 1970. Bd. dirs. Nat., Tex. couns. chs., Nat. Conf. Black Churchmen, Nat. Bd. Black United Funds, Nat. Coun. Chs., PUSH (People United to Save Humanity). Named Man of Yr., B'nai B'rith, 1964, Urban League, Seattle, 1965. Mem. Boulé, Alpha Phi Alpha. Office: AME Ch 208 Auburn Ave NE Atlanta GA 30303

ADAMS, JOHN RODGER, hydrologist, deacon; b. Milw., Apr. 15, 1937; s. John Henry and Frances Agnes (Rodger) A.; m. Barbara Ruth Froehlich, July 28, 1962; children—Catherine Marie, Robert Rodger. BCE, Marquette U., 1959; MCE, Mich. State U., 1961, PhD, 1966. Ordained to ministry Roman Cath. Ch. as deacon, 1976. Asst. St. Patrick's Ch, Urbana, Ill, 1976—; asst. prof. Lehigh U., Bethlehem, Pa., 1965-70; rsch.hydrologist Ill. State Water Survey, Champaign, 1970—. Coop. Grad. fellow NSF, 1962. Mem. ASCE (sec., treas. sect. 1973-75, div. news corr. 1981-85), Am. Geophys. Union, Upper Mississippi River Research Consortium, Internat. Water Resources Assn., Internat. Assn. Hydraulic Research. Roman Catholic. Avocations: camping, model railroading. Home: 406 W Nevada St Urbana IL 61801 Office: Illinois Water Survey 2204 Griffith Dr Champaign IL 61820

ADAMS, KATHRYN GRACE, religious organization administrator, educator; b. Ravenna, Ohio, Oct. 8, 1958; d. Robert K. and Mary Kathryn (Henderson) Davis; m. Craig A. Adams, Aug. 1, 1981; children: Russell, Robert, Ross. BS in Edn., Ohio U., 1981. cert. spl. edn. tchr., Ohio. Dir. Christian edn. Macedonia (Ohio) United Meth. Ch., 1991—; tchr. Meth. Youth Fellowship, counselor United Meth. Ch., Sugarland, Tex., 1981-83, tchr., Arlington, Tex., 1983-85, tchr., Sunday sch. supt., mem. edn. com., Bedford, Ohio, 1985-91; bd. dirs. Walton Hills (Ohio) Coop. Sch. Mem. Nat. Arbor Soc., Nat. Wildlife Fedn. (Backyard Wildlife Habitat award 1990). Democrat. Office: Macedonia United Meth Ch PO Box 155 Macedonia OH 44056 *Today I see constant changes in family structure, morality and societal acceptance of values that are not within the Biblical teachings of Christ. I must remember, and am called to share with others, the one constant in our lives - the Lord Jesus Christ and His love. The Lord is my ever present source of strength in troubled times, Who offers joy that knows no bounds.*

ADAMS, MARK REGINALD, pastor, administrator; b. Las Vegas, Nev., Oct. 3, 1963; s. Reginald Burton Avey and Laura Belle (Graham) Adams; m. Kerrie Anne Carpenter, Dec. 1, 1984; children: Lars Christopher, Jacob David. BA in Psychology, Judson Coll., 1986; postgrad., Trinity Divinity Sch., Deerfield, Ill., 1987—. Ordained minister, Free Meth. Ch. Youth dir. Parkside Ch., Streamwood, Ill., 1985-86, sr. pastor, 1988—; asst. pastor Evanston (Ill.) Free Meth. Ch., 1986-88; asst. supr. Ray Graham Assn., Elmhurst, Ill., 1985-86, mgr., 1986-87, behavior specialist, 1987-90, resident living coord., 1988-89, adminstr., 1990—; cons. behavioral specialist, Evanston & Streamwood, 1987-90. Creator, presenter seminars, 1987, 89. Mem. Am. Assn. Counseling and Devel., Am. Assn. Mental Health Counselors. Avocations: computer science, cross-country skiing, existentialism. Home: 315 Field Ln Streamwood IL 60107 Office: Ray Graham Assn 420 W Madison Elmhurst IL 60126

ADAMS, MENDLE EUGENE, minister; b. Bath County, Va., July 1, 1938; s. Earl and Margaret M. (Godsey) A.; m. N. Ruth Williams, Feb. 2, 1957; children: David Mendle, Brian Richard, Josef Wayne, Vicki Ruth. AB, Ind. Wesleyan U., 1967; MA in Religion, Christian Theol. Sem., 1969; postgrad., Aquinas Coll., 1977, Harvard U., 1978. Ordained to ministry Meth. Ch. as deacon, 1968, as min., United Ch. of Christ, 1981. Pastor Windfall (Ind.) Pilgrim Ch., 1960-63, Mt. Olive Meth. Ch., Marion, Ind., 1963-67, Mt. Comfort United meth. Ch., Indpls., 1967-69, United Meth. Cir., Donnybrook, Maxbass, Lansford, N.D., 1979, Hope Congl. United Ch. of Christ, Granville, N.D., 1980-82, 1st Congl. United Ch. of Christ, McPherson, Kans., 1982-87; chaplain ecumenical campus Okla. State U., Stillwater, 1987-91; interim pastor Peace United Ch. of Christ, Loyal, Okla., 1988, 1st Christian Ch. (Disciples of Christ), Stillwater, 1990, Bethel Congl. Ch., Edmond, Okla., 1991; organizing min. Boone County (Ky.) United Ch. of Christ, 1991—; ednl. trips to Israel-Palestine, 1980, Nicaragua, 1983, The Philippines, 1985. Co-author: Touching Center Adventures in Christ Consciousness, 1990. Mem. Ind. Ho. of Reps., 1975-76, Ind. Solid Waste Com., 1976; mem. Ind. and Okla. group for Equal Rights Ammendment to U.S. Constn., 1977, 81; bd. dirs. McPherson Family Life Ctr., 1983-84; chmn. com. McPherson Community Nursing Home, 1984; mem. Gov.'s Task Force on AIDS, Okla., 1987-88, Gov.'s Cabinet on Children's Issues, 1988-91, Ecumenical Coun. on Maternal and Infant Health, So. Gov.'s Leadership Coun., 1989-91; cert. mediator Okla. Dispute Resolution, Supreme Ct. Okla., 1991. Recipient Honored Legislator citation Ind. Coun. Chs., 1976. Democrat. Home: 7706 Walnut Creek Dr Florence KY 41042 *Upon being ordained Deacon, Bishop Richard Raines counseled, "The Divine call is where your abilities intersect human needs." I have sought to discern that call and respond in Christ's name; trusting in Providence for a spiritual legacy.*

ADAMS, MICHAEL LEE, minister; b. Indpls., Feb. 28, 1951; s. Robert Lee and Betty (Magauthlin) A.; m. Jane Hinton Goodrich, Aug. 18, 1972; children: Jed Allen, Matthew Benjamin. BA, Union U., Jackson, Tenn., 1972; MDiv, So. Sem., Louisville, 1976, DMin, 1980. Ordained to ministry So. Bapt. Conv., 1971. Pastor Spring Hill Bapt. Ch., Trenton, Tenn., 1971-76; Pastor First Bapt. Ch., Grand Junction, Tenn., 1976-81, Fulton, Ky., 1981-83, Union City, Tenn., 1983-88, Jasper, Ala., 1988—. Contbr. articles to profl. jours. Active Union City Leadership Sch. Mem. Union City C. of C., Rotary. Home: 1503 Valley Rd Jasper AL 35501 Office: First Bapt Ch PO Box 210 Jasper AL 35501

ADAMS, NICK DWAYNE, youth minister; b. Kingsport, Tenn., June 18, 1963. Diploma, Shekinah Bible Inst., 1986; BS, E. Tenn. State U., 1990. Ordained to ministry Shekinah Ministries, 1991. With short term missions Mana Ministries, Hyderbad, India, 1983; educator Shekinah Christian Acad., Blountville, Tenn., 1985-90; mission trips to Cuernavaca, Mex., 1991, Kiev, USSR, 1991. dir. edn. Kingsport Boys Club, 1988; intern Tenn. Gen. Assembly, Nashville, 1989. Mem. Phi Kappa Phi, Pi Gamma Mu. Home: 595 Rocky Branch Rd Blountville TN 37617 Office: Shekinah Ministries 394 Glory Rd Blountville TN 37617

ADAMS, PENNY SUE, minister; b. Franklin, Pa., Sept. 11, 1953; d. Dean Plummer and Shirley Alice (Crawford) A. BS in Spl. Edn., Clarion State Coll., 1976; MDiv, United Theol. Sem., 1985. Ordained to ministry United Meth. Ch., as deacon, 1986, as elder, 1988. Min. Mt. Lebanon and Glenwood United Meth. Chs., Tarrs, Pa., 1985-88; min. of congl. life Christ United Meth. Ch., Bethel Park, Pa., 1988—; tchr. Disciple Bible Study; trained John Savage Calling and Caring Ministries; rep. N.E. Jurisdiction single adult ministries nat. task force United Meth. Ch., Nashville, 1990—, clergy rep. com. on episcopacy Western Pa. Conf., Pitts., 1987—. Mem. United Meth. Single Adult Ministries, Western Pa. Conf. Singles Coun. (dist. rep. 1990—), Pitts. Ecumenical Singles Network (rep. 1990—). Home: 5708 Glen Hill Dr Bethel Park PA 15102 Office: Christ United Meth Ch 44 Highland Rd Bethel Park PA 15102 *Now, more than ever before in history, is the time to be actively involved in Single Adult Ministries. By the year 2000, over 53% of the adult population will be single. Reaching out to single adults in a couple-oriented society is both challenging and very rewarding.*

ADAMS, ROBERT LAZENBY, minister; b. Rochester, N.Y., May 23, 1929; s. Benjamin Hedges and Georgia (Lazenby) A.; m. Judith Carol McLellan, July 30, 1960; children: Elizabeth, Margaret, Carrie, Charles. AB, U. Pa., 1951; MDiv, Harvard U., 1959. Ordained to ministry Congl. Ch., 1960. Organizing minister United Ch. of Christ in Bayberry, Liverpool, N.Y., 1960-65; univ. minister U. S.D., Vermillion, 1965-67, adminstr., lectr. astronomy, 1967-83, adj. prof. astronomy, lectr., 1983-91; interim minister United Ch. of Christ, Vermillion, 1982-83; minister 1st Congregational Ch. United Ch. of Christ, Algona, Iowa, 1983—; bd. dirs. Iowa Conf. United Ch. of Christ, Des Moines, 1988-90, moderator, 1989-90; organizer Workshop on Creativity, NW Assn., Lake Okaboji, Iowa, 1990; pres. Algona (Iowa) Ministerial Assn., 1987-89. Contbr. articles to Des Moines Register. Pres. trustees Algona Pub. Libr., 1988-89, bd. dirs., 1985-89; pres. Algona Arts Coun., 1984-86; co-chmn. Task Force on Ednl. Improvement, Algona Pub. Schs., 1988-91. Staff sgt. USAF, 1951-55. Grantee State Legis., S.D., 1983. Mem. Ames Area Amateur Astronomers, Rotary. Republican. Home: 321 S Moore St Algona IA 50511 Office: 1st Congregational Ch UCC 315 S Moore St Box 641 Algona IA 50511

ADAMS, ROBERT MERRIHEW, minister, philosophy educator; b. Phila., Sept. 8, 1937; s. Arthur Merrihew and Margaret (Baker) A.; m. Marilyn Ann McCord, June 10, 1966. AB, Princeton U., 1959; BA, Oxford U., 1961, MA, 1965; BD, Princeton Theol. Sem., 1962; MA, Cornell U., 1967, PhD, 1969. Ordained to ministry Presbyn. Ch., 1962. Pastor Montauk (N.Y.) Com. Ch., 1962-65; prof. Philosophy UCLA, L.A., 1976—. Author: The Virtue of Faith, 1987; contbr. articles to profl. jours. Younger Humanist Fellow NEH, 1974, 75; recipient Pres.'s Faculty Rsch. Fellowship in the Humanities UCLA, 1988-89. Mem. AAUP, Am. Acad. Arts and Scis., Soc. Christian Ethics, Am. Acad. Religion, Am. Philos. Assn., Soc. Christian Philosophers. Office: UCLA Dept Philosophy 405 Hilgard Ave Los Angeles CA 90024-1451

ADAMS, SANDRA L., preschool director; b. Phila., Oct. 29, 1955; d. Thomas J. and Dorothy (March) A. BS in Bible, Phila. Coll. of Bible, Phila., 1977. Dir. Rainbow Child Care, Folcroft, Pa., 1981—. Fellow Mem. Assn. for Childhood Ed. Internat., Del. County Early Childhood Educator Assn. Republican. Avocations; traveling, swimming, church girls club. Office: Rainbow Child Care Primos and Virginia Ave Folcroft PA 19032

ADAMS, THURMAN LEON, JR., minister; b. Jackson, Miss., Dec. 21, 1945; s. Thurman Leon Adams Sr. and Erma Frances (Evans) Lemser; m. Mary Eloise Hardwick, Nov. 24, 1965; children: Stephanie Renee, Lori Marie. BA, Miss. Coll., 1969; postgrad., New Orleans Bapt. Theol. Sem., 1977-79, 81-82. Ordained to ministry So. Bapt. Conv., 1968. Pastor Salem Bapt. Ch., Preston, Miss., 1970-72, Mashulaville Bapt. Ch., Macon, Miss., 1972-73, Macedonia Bapt. Ch., Louisville, Miss., 1973-76, Arkadelphia Bapt. Ch., Bailey, Miss., 1976-80, Oak Grove Bapt. Ch., Meridian, Miss., 1980—; chaplain Meridian Police Dept., 1981—; mem. Meridian/Lauderdale County ACTS Bd., 1983—, chmn., 1986-88; assoc. moderator Lauderdale Bapt. Assn., Meridian, 1989-90. Mem. Internat. Conf. Police Chaplains (cert. sr. chaplain, regional dir., bd. dirs. 1990—), Miss. Bapt. Chaplains Assn. (pres. 1987). Home: 805 Oak Grove Dr Meridian MS 39301-4653 Office: Oak Grove Bapt Ch 801 Oak Grove Dr Meridian MS 39301-4653

ADAMS, VERNON GERARD, religion educator; b. Balt., Aug. 8, 1959; s. Vernon George and Geraldine Lucille (Phillips) A. BA summa cum laude, St. Hyacinth Coll., Granby, Mass., 1983; STB summa cum laude, Seraphicum, Rome, Italy, 1989. Joined Order of Friars Minor Conventual, Roman Cath. Ch., ordained priest, 1990. Dir. religious edn. St. Adalbert Parish, Elmhurst, N.Y., 1989—. Republican. Office: St Adalbert Ch 52-29 83d St Elmhurst NY 11373

ADAMS, WILLIAM JAMES, JR., lay worker; b. Cin., May 14, 1938; s. William J. Sr. and Eleanor Sarah (Burley) A.; m. Florence Ann Yokum, Dec. 13, 1963; children: Cynthia, BethAnn, Jared, Thomas. BS, Brigham Young U., 1964; MA, Hebrew Union Coll., 1971; PhD, U. Utah, 1987. Missionary East Cen. States Mission, Luisville, Ky., 1960-62; dist. councilman W.Va. North Dist., Morgantown, 1974-80; pres. Sunday sch. Sandy Utah North Stake, 1982-85, priesthood instr., 1986—; edn. coord. Utah Opportunities Industrialization Ctr., Salt Lake City, 1986—; instr. ancient scripture Brigham Young U., Provo, Utah, 1970-73; lectr. in lang. Davis and Elkins (W.Va.) Coll., 1974-80. Recipient Eagle Scout, Boy Scouts Am., 1953; rsch. fellow U. Utah, 1982-83. Mem. Soc. Bibl. Lit., Nat. Assn. of Profs. of Hebrew, Soc. Early Hist. Archaeology (bd. trustees 1983—). Home: 1412

Sudbury Ave Sandy UT 84093 Office: Hawthorne U 155 E 3300 S Salt Lake City UT 84115 *For generations my family has served the American public as firemen, policemen, newspaper editors and medical practitioners. I am glad that I have been able to continue this tradition as a father, layworker and successful adult educator.*

ADAMSHICK, ELIZABETH THERESE, pastoral associate; b. Columbus, Ohio, Sept. 26, 1962; d. Donald Raymond and Carolyn Marie (VandeKerkhoff) A. BA in Theology/Philosophy, Walsh Coll., 1984; postgrad., Pontifical Coll. Josephinum, 1985-87, 90—. Religion tchr., campus min. Bishop Watterson High Sch., Columbus, 1986-87; dir. campus ministry Bishop Ready High Sch., Columbus, 1987-90; pastoral assoc. St. Thomas More Newman Ctr., Ohio State Univ., Columbus, 1990—. Del. Witness for Peace, Nicaragua, 1988. Named Outstanding Young Women of Am., 1985, 87-89. Mem. Campus Ministry Assn. Ohio State U., Cath. Campus Ministry Assn., Habitat for Humanity, Amnesty Internat. USA (mem. Group 87 1986-90, group coord. 1989-90). Office: St Thomas More Newman Ctr 64 W Lane Ave Columbus OH 43201

ADAMSON, RANDOLPH J., minister; b. Greeley, Colo., Feb. 7, 1954; s. Reed Phillips and Tina (Syrost) A.; m. Zoe Adamson, Aug. 28, 1977; children: Rebecca, Emily, Anna. BA, U. North Colo., 1978. Dir. ministry Youth for Christ, Greeley, 1978-80; English tchr. Weld Cen. High Sch., Hudson, Colo., 1980-81; pharm. rep. Squibb Pharms., Greeley, 1981-84; area dir. Youth For Christ, Denver, 1984-86; exec. dir. Youth For Christ, Greeley, 1986—; cons. Youth For Christ, 1986-90; bd. dirs. Home Educator's Fellowship, Greeley, 1987-89; editor Frontline Report Newsletter, Greeley, 1986—. Deacon 1st United Presbyn. Ch., Greeley, 1982-84, elder, 1988-91; precinct chmn. Reb. Party, Greeley, 1990-92; bd. dirs. Union Calory Forum, Greeley, 1988-89; guest editorial local newspaper, 1987-98. Mem. Nat. Assn. Evangelicals, Weld Assn. Evangelicals, Network. Republican. Avocations: reading, biking, various athletic endeavors. Office: No Colo Youth For Christ 1231 12th Ave Greeley CO 80631

ADAMSON, WILLIAM ROBERT, academic administrator, minister; b. Maclean, Sask., Can., Dec. 14, 1927; s. Joseph and Edith Sarah (Miller) A.; m. Louise Kruger, July 3, 1951; children: Bruce, Shelley, Susan, Michael. BA, U. Sask., Saskatoon, Can., 1948; BD, St. Andrew's Coll., Saskatoon, 1953; STM magna cum laude, Pacific Sch. of Religion, 1955, ThD, 1960; MEd, U. Toronto, Ont., Can., 1975. Ordained to ministry United Ch. Can., 1951. Min. Esterhazy (Sask.) United Ch., 1951-54, 55-57, Broadway United Ch., Regina, Sask., Can., 1959-64; staff assoc. Naramata (B.C.) Ctr. for Contining Edn., 1964-67; assoc. sec. leadership devel. Nat. Office United Ch. Can., Toronto, 1968-73; prof. christian ministry St. Andrew's Coll., Sask., 1973-84, pres., 1985—; commr. Gen. Coun. United Ch., Sudbury, Ont., 1986; mem. Nat. Com. Theol. Edn. for Ministry, Toronto, 1977-83, 89—, Continuing Edn. Com. Sask. Conf., 1971-80; convener Christian Edn. Commn., Sask. Conf., 1964-65. Author: Bushell Rediscovered, 1966, Empowering Disciples, 1990. Bd. dirs. Family Svc. Bur., Sask., 1975-77. Mem. Assn. Theol. Field Educators. Home: 805 Acadia Dr, Saskatoon, SK Canada S7H 3W2 Office: St Andrew's Coll, 1121 College Dr, Saskatoon, SK Canada S7N 0W3

ADAY, CARLA RENEE, minister; b. Ft. Worth, May 25, 1963; d. Roman Harrison and Glenda Rae (Dortch) A. BJ, U. Tex., 1985; MDiv, Yale U., 1988. Ordained to ministry Christian Ch. (Disciples of Christ), 1988. Intern East Dallas Christian Ch., summer 1985, Univ. Christian Ch., Ft. Worth, summers 1982, 86, 87; parish assoc. 1st Congl. Ch., Guilford, Conn., 1986-87; asst. pastor Darien (Conn.) United Meth. Ch., 1987-88; min. singles County Club Christian Ch., Kansas City, Mo., 1988—; chair Young Adult Com. Kansas City region, 1989-91; co-chair Task Force on Clergywomen, Kansas City, 1989—; mem. Disciples Peace Fellowship, Kansas City, 1990. Vis. resource Marillac Ctr. for Children, Kansas City, 1988-91. Fiers Cook scholar Yale U., 1986-88, DuPont scholar, 1985-86, Granville Walker scholar Walker Found., 1985-88. Mem. Disciples Mins. Assn. Office: Country Club Christian Club 6101 Ward Pkwy Kansas City MO 64113

ADDISON, CARL VERNON, JR., minister; b. Welch, W.Va., Mar. 19, 1957; s. Carl Vernon and Jo Anne (Gammon) A.; m. Valerie Ann Hartshorn, July 28, 1979; children: Matthew Paul, Steven Andrew, Sarah Elizabeth. BA, Anderson U., 1978; MDiv, Anderson Sch. Theology, 1981. Ordained to ministry Ch. of God (Anderson, Ind.), 1982. Assoc. pastor Evanswood Ch. of God, Troy, Mich., 1980-82; pastor 1st Ch. of God, West Chester, Ohio, 1983-90; sr. pastor Tanner St. Ch. of God, Sikeston, Mo., 1990—; chmn. bd. Christian edn. S.W. Ohio Assembly, Hamilton, 1983-85, mem. exec. com., 1984-90, chmn. bd. pastoral and ch. rels., 1987-90; treas. Ohio State Bd. Christian Edn., Columbus, 1984-86; mem. Mo. Bd. of Ch. Extension, Ch. of God; instr. Towne Bible Inst., Middletown, Ohio, 1985-89. Mem. Sikeston Ministerial Alliance. Republican. Home: 927 Hawthorne Sikeston MO 63801

ADDISON, DUANE LEROY, minister, educator; b. Tracy, Minn., Dec. 27, 1930; s. Virtis Charles and Frances Lillian (Swanson) A.; m. Carol Lynne Alberts, June 4, 1960; children: Richard, Roy, Linnea. BA, U. Minn., 1953; BD, Luther Theol. Sem., 1960; MA, Yale U., 1962, PhD, 1965. Ordained to ministry Am. Luth. Ch., 1963. Luth. campus min. U. Iowa, 1963-67; prof. religion Augustana Coll., Sioux Falls, S.D., 1967—. Mem. NAACP, World Future Soc., Soc. Christian Ethics, Am. Acad. Religion. Democrat. Home: 2404 S Sherman Ave Sioux Falls SD 57105 Office: Augustana Coll Sioux Falls SD 57197

ADDISON, HOWARD ALAN, rabbi; b. Chgo., Sept. 26, 1950; s. Henry and Lorraine (Goldblatt) A.; m. Ethel Miller, Aug. 27, 1972 (div. Aug. 1983); children: Mara, Leora; m. Adina S. Gutstein, Mar. 6, 1986; children: Arona, Eliasaf. BA, U. Ill., 1971; MA, Hunter Coll., 1974, Jewish Theol. Sem., 1974; D Ministry, Chgo. Theol. Sem., 1982. Ordained rabbi, 1976. Counselor Hillel Found., Cleve. State U.; dir. Hillel Found., Wayne State U., Detroit, 1976-78; spiritual leader Congregation Shaare Tikvah, Chgo., 1978-86, Temple Beth Israel, Sunrise, Fla., 1986—; adj. prof. Broward County Community Coll., Ft. Lauderdale, Fla., 1989—; v.p. Nat. Labor Zionist Alliance, N.Y.C., 1981-86; mem. chancallor's cabinet Jewish Theol. Sem., N.Y.C., 1990—; mem. Ideological Commn. of Conservative Judaism, N.Y.C., 1985—; mem. exec. com. Nat. Jewish Community Rels. Adv. Bd., N.Y.C.; mem. rabbinic cabinet United Jewish Appeal. Contbr.: The Seminary at 100, 1987, Emet Ve-Emunah, 1988; contbr. column to mag. Chgo. Jewish Sentinel, 1983-86, articles to Anglo Jewish jours. Chmn. Ft. Lauderdale Community Rels. Com., 1988-91; v.p. North River Commn., Chgo., 1982-86; mem. Community Adv. Com. on Sch. Desegregation, Chgo., 1981-84; mem. Interfaith Coun. of Urban Affairs, Chgo., 1983. Mem. Rabbinical Assembly (regional v.p. 1990—), North Broward Bd. Rabbis (pres. 1989-90), Chgo. Bd. Rabbis (bd. dirs. 1981-86). Office: Temple Beth Israel 7100 W Oakland Park Blvd Sunrise FL 33313 *To be truly human is to act as God's partner in the task of perfecting creation.*

ADDISON, LESLIE WAYNE, clergyman; b. Balt., Sept. 6, 1954; s. Raleigh Evans and Margaret Evelyn (Whitt) A.; m. Lora Kay Carr, May 18, 1974; children: Hannah Kay, Rachel Lynne, Deborah Leigh, Miriam Jeanette. BA, Graham Bible Coll., 1976. Ordained to ministry So. Bapt. Conv., 1974. Pastor Pleasant Home Bapt. Ch., Laurel Bloomery, Tenn., 1974-83; assoc. pastor lst Bapt. Ch., Mountain City, Tenn., 1983-84; pastor Beulah Bapt. Ch., Kingsport, Tenn., 1984—; tchr. S.W. Va. Christian Acad., 1978-79. Mem. Holston Bapt. Assn. Home and Office: 491 Beulah Ch Rd Kingsport TN 37663 *No decision, no experience and no achievement can compare with the joy of knowing Jesus Christ as your personal friend.*

ADDY, LOWELL DAVID, religious organization administrator, consultant; b. Mobile, Ala., Jan. 3, 1951; s. Alton James and Margaret (Glass) A.; m. Judith Ann Thomason, July 10, 1976; children: Mason Lowell, Lucas David. BA, U. South Ala., 1973. Adminstrv. asst. City of Mobile, 1974-78; rsch. systems analyst Design Rsch., Inc., Mobile, 1978-83; ch. adminstr. Cottage Hill Bapt. Ch., Mobile, 1983—; cons. Ch. Growth Design, Nashville, 1983—; deacon Cottage Hill Bapt. Ch., Mobile, 1977—. Chmn. Hist. Preservation Authority, Mobile, 1979-84; bd. dirs., treas. Sav-A-Life, Mobile, 1984-86; vice chmn. bd. So. Bapt. Christian Broadcast Network of Mobile, 1984-88; mem. So. Bapt. Network Mobile, 1984—. Mem. Nat. Assn. Ch. Bus. Adminstrs. (chmn., pres. Mobile Bay chpt.), Nat. Assn. Ch. Bus. Adminstrn., Christian Ministries Assn., Pi Sigma Alpha. Office: Cottage Hill Bapt Ch PO Box 9129 Mobile AL 36691

ADELMAN, LUCILLE MARIE, nun; b. Rosen, Minn., Dec. 13, 1933; d. Andrew Anton and Susan Marie (Vonderharr) A. BA, U. N.D., 1969; postgrad., Moorhead State Coll., 1969, McGill U., Can., 1970, St. Louis U., 1973-74, St. John's U., Collegeville, Minn., 1982-83; MA, Loyola U., Chgo., 1990. Joined Order Sisters of St. Benedict, Roman Cath. Ch., 1951. Tchr. St. Joseph Sch., Moorhead, Minn., 1952-61; mem. faculty Corbett Coll., Crookston, Minn., 1969-71; novitiate dir. St. Benedict's Noviatiate, Crookston, 1970-76, juniorate dir., 1971-76, spiritual dir., dir. retreats, 1974—, pastoral assoc., 1985-89, pastoral adminstr., 1989—; pvt. tchr. music, Moorhead and Crookston, 1952-71. Mem. Minn. Music Tchrs. Assn. (dist. chmn. 1967-70), Sister Formation Conf., Phi Beta Kappa. Home and Office: St Joseph's Ch Box 97 Oslo MN 56744

ADKINS, JOHNIE KEMPER, minister; b. Oxford, Miss., May 1, 1961; s. Edmond James and Sanra Lillian (Berry) A.; m. Teri Lynn Doyle, May 21, 1983; children: Kyle James, Cody Lee. BTh, Ozark Christian Coll., Joplin, Mo., 1985; postgrad., Cin. Christian Seminary, 1987, Kans. State U., 1986. Ordained to ministry Christian Ch., 1982. Minister Waco (Mo.) Christian Ch., 1983-85, Center Christian Ch., Columbus, Ks., 1985—; grounds crew chief, Ozark Christian Coll., 1981-85; trustee Hidden Haven Christian Camp, Thayer, Kans., 1991, Collegiates for Christ, Miami, Okla., 1990-91; pres. Ministerial Alliance, Columbus, Kans., 1986-89. Named Outstanding Young Minister, Standard Pub. Co., Cin., 1989, Outstanding Young Man in Am., 1988, 89. Home: Rte 4 PO Box 48 Columbus KS 66725

ADKISSON, RANDALL LYNN, minister; b. Atlanta, May 28, 1957; s. John Earl and Mearl (Cox) A.; m. Salee Robin Smith, Nov. 7, 1981; 1 child, Katheryn Lynsey. BA in Journalism, U. Ga., 1979; MDiv, Southwestern Bapt. Theol. Sem., Ft. Worth, 1985; PhD, New Orleans Bapt. Theol. Sem., 1990. Licensed to ministry So. Bapt. Conv., 1974; ordained, 1979. Min. of youth Bethel Bapt. Ch., Good Hope, Ga., 1976-79; assoc. pastor Orange Hill Bapt. Ch., Austell, Ga., 1979-82; pastor Shifalo Bapt. Ch., Kiln, Miss., 1985-88, Foxworth (Miss.) 1st Bapt. Ch., 1988-91, 1st Bapt. Ch., Monroeville, Ala., 1991—; teaching fellow New Orleans Bapt. Theol. Sem., 1985-86. Mem. Marion Bapt. Assn. (pastoral ministries dir. 1990-91, pres. min.'s conf. 1990-91), Nat. Assn. of Bapt. Profs. Religion, Soc. of Bibl. Lit. Office: 1st Bapt Ch 420 Pineville Rd Monroeville AL 36460 *Christian faith is not a faith that can be separated from action and ethic. To be a "believer" must by necessity impact every area of conduct as well as attitude.*

AEBI, CHARLES JERRY, minister, educator; b. Webster, Pa., Feb. 15, 1931; s. Jerry and Madeline (Stipes) A.; m. Imogene D. McDonough, Aug. 5, 1955; children: Ruth, Joy, Mark, Mary. BS, Pa. State U., 1952; MA, Abilene Christian U., 1959; PhD, Ohio U., 1972. Part-time minister Ch. of Christ, Vanceville, Pa., 1954-55; minister Ch. of Christ, Coraopolis, Pa., 1956-61, Sistersville, W.Va., 1962-64, Vienna, W.Va., 1971-82, Parkersburg, W.Va., 1964-70, 82—; chmn. Bible Dept. Ohio Valley Coll., Parkersburg, W.Va., 1964-70, v.p., acad. dean, 1970-85; prof. Bible and religion Ohio Valley Coll., Parkersburg, 1985—; cons., evaluator North Cen. Assn. Colls. and Schs. Author: Old Testament Survey, 1964; Herzberg's Job Satisfaction Theory, 1972; Lamp to My Feet, A Thorough Study of the Bible, 1978; New Testament Survey, 1984; editor: The New Birth and Its Implications, 1980; Educating to Service, OVC Self Study, 1977, 2d edit, 1982, New Testament Thought, 1990. Mem. Am. Assn. Higher Edn., W.Va. Coun. Acad. Deans, Phi Delta Kappa, Kiwanis. Home: Rt 1 Vincent OH 45784 Office: Ohio Valley Coll College Pkwy Parkersburg WV 26101

AGA KHAN, HIS HIGHNESS PRINCE KARIM, IV, spiritual leader and Imam of the Ismaili Muslims; b. Geneva, Dec. 13, 1936; s. Prince Aly Salomon and Viscountess Camrose; m. Sarah Frances Croker Poole , 1969; children: Zahra, Rahim, Hussein. Student, Le Rosey, Switzerland; BA with honors, Harvard U.; LLD (hon.), Peshawar U., 1967, U. Sind, 1970, McGill U., 1983; DLitt (hon.), U. London, 1989. Became Aga Khan on death of grandfather Sir Sultan Mohamed Shah, Aga Khan III, 1957; granted title of His Highness by Queen Elizabeth II, 1957, His Royal Highness by the Shah of Iran, 1959; founder chancellor Aga Khan U., Karachi, Pakistan, 1983—; head Aga Khan Found., Switzerland, 1967—, Banglash, Can., India, Kenya, Pakistan, U.K., U.S. and Portugal, Aga Khan Fund for Econ. Devel., Geneva, 1984—, Aga Khan Award for Arch., 1976—, Inst. Ismaili Studies, 1977—, Aga Khan Trust for Cluture, Geneva, 1988. Decorated comdr. Ordre du Merite Mauritanien, 1960; Gran Crox de l'Ordre du Prince Henry du Gouvernement Portuis, 1960; grand croix Order Nat. de la Cote d'Ivoire, 1965; Ordre Nat. de la Haute-Volta, 1965; Ordre Nat. Malgache, 1966; Ordre du Croissant Vert des Comores, 1966; grand cordon Ordre du Tadj Iran, 1967; Nishan-i-Imtiaz, Pakistan, 1970; cavaliere di Gran Croce (Italy), 1977; Gran Officier de l'Ordre Nat. du Lion, Senegal, 1982; Nishan-e-Pakistan, 1983, Grand Gordon of Quissam-al Arch Morocco, 1986, Cavaliere del Lavoro, 1988; Commdr. de la Lé d'Honneur, France, 1990; recipient Thomas Jefferson award in arch. U. Va., 1984, honor award AIA, 1984, La Medalla de Oro del Consejo Superior de Colegios de Arquitectos, Spain, 1987. Home: Aiglemont, 60270 Gouvieux France

AGBEJA, TIMOTHY OMOLAYO, minister; b. Ilesha, Nigeria, Mar. 27, 1954; came to U.S., 1986; s. Abraham Olayiwola and Lydia 'Funso (Folorunso) A.; m. Agnes Adebomi Adeniji, Jan. 31, 1981; children: Gabriel 'Bukola, Victor Oluwabunmi, Timothy Bolade, Lydia Adebisi. Diploma in theology, Assemblies of God Bible Coll., Eng., 1983; BS, Somerset U., 1984; ThM, Internat. Sem., Plymouth, Fla., 1987, LittD (hon.), 1988; PhD, Internat. Sem., Plymouth, 1991. Ordained to ministry Christ Apostolic Ch. Am., 1984. Asst. pastor Christ Apostolic Ch., 1974-84; head dept. Christian edn. Evang. Tng. Coll., Akure, Nigeria, 1984-86; pastor Christ Apostolic Ch., Miami, Fla., 1986-88, N.Y.C., 1988-90, L.A., 1990—. Author: Christianity: Life Not Religion, 1990. Home: 4101 Palmwood Dr #3 Los Angeles CA 90008 Office: Christ Apostolic Ch 3016 W Slauson Ave Los Angeles CA 90043 *No conquest is so important as victory over self.*

AGEE, KEVIN JEROME, minister; b. Washington, Dec. 20, 1960; s. Charles Henry Jr. and Emma Abbie (Light) A. BA, U. Md., 1982; MDiv, Wesley Theol. Sem., 1990; postgrad., Hartford Sem., 1991—. Lic. to ministry Christian Meth. Episcopal Ch., 1987; deacon, 1988; elder, 1989. Asst. pastor Israel Met. Christian Meth. Episcopal Ch., Washington, 1987-89; fellow Nat. Fellowship Program for Black Pastors Congress Nat. Black Chs., Washington, 1988-89; pastor St. Paul and Williams Temple Christian Meth. Episcopal Chs., Halifax, Va., 1989-90; dir. youth ctr. Good Shepherd Ministries, Washington, 1989-90; pastor Christ Christian Meth. Episcopal Ch., Waterbury, Conn., 1990—; subs. tchr. City of Waterbury Dept. Edn., 1990—; mem. inter-ch. rels. task force Christian Conf. Conn., Hartford, 1990-91, Commn. on Social Concerns, 1991—; bd. dirs., mem. pub. rels. com. Waterbury Area Coun. Chs., 1991—; bd. dirs. Christian Conf. Conn., 1991—. Mem. adv. bd. Pride Inc., Waterbury, 1991; bd. dirs. Green Community Svcs., 1991—. Delaplain scholar Wesley Theol. Sem., 1990. Mem. NAACP, Interfaith Clergy Assn., Toastmasters Internat. (Competent Toastmaster award 1986, pres. 1985-87). Democrat. Home: 40 Maple St Waterbury CT 06702 Office: Christ Christian Meth Episcopal Ch 32 Maple St Waterbury CT 06702 *One who truly loves the Lord loves his/her neighbor as well. If we all loved our neighbors, racism, sexism, classism, war, violence, poverty, homelessness and other societal ills would be non existent.*

AGEE, ROBIN DIANE, camp director; b. Berkeley, Calif., Sept. 27, 1958; d. James William and Audrey Jane (Sumner) A. BA, U. Calif., Davis, 1980; MA in Christian Edn., Talbot Sem., 1982. Intern Ponderosa Lodge Mt. Hermon (Calif.) Assn., 1982-83, dir., 1984—; dir. high sch., intern Menlo Park (Calif.) Presbyn. Ch., 1983-84; dir. day camp Oakland (Calif.) Covenant Ch., 1978; seasonal counselor Mt. Hermon Assn., 1979, staff counselor, 1981, 82; leader seminars Nat. Youth Workers Conv., 1990. Contbr. articles to profl. jours. Vol. high sch. counselor U. Bapt. Ch., Santa Cruz, Calif., 1988—. Mem. Kappa Tau Epsilon. Baptist. Office: Mt Hermon Assn PO Box 413 Mount Hermon CA 95041

AGHIORGOUSSIS, MAXIMOS DEMETRIOS See MAXIMOS, BISHOP

AGNEW, CHRISTOPHER MACK, minister; b. Santa Barbara, Calif., Aug. 7, 1944; s. Jack and Agnes Emma (Mack) A.; m. Suzanne Marie Souder, June 1, 1974. AB, Bucknell U., Lewisburg, Pa., 1967; MA, U. Del., Newark, 1975, PhD, 1980; STM, Gen. Theol. Sem., N.Y.C., 1991. Ordained to ministry Episcopal Ch. as deacon, 1991. Registrar Diocese of Del., Wilmington, 1985-89; assoc. ecumenical officer Episcopal Ch., N.Y.C., 1989—; staff Anglican-Roman Cath. Dialogue, 1989—; mem. NCC Interfaith Working Group, 1990—, Planning Com., Na.t Workshop on Chritian Unity, 1990—. Editor: The Ecumenical Bull., 1989—; author: God With Us, 1986; contbr. articles to profl. jours. Mem. Nat. Episcopal Historians Assn., Hist. Soc. of Episcopal Ch., Orgn. Am. Historians, Am. Hist. Assn., Can. Hist. Assn. Home: 605 Delaware St New Castle DE 19720 Office: The Episcopal Ch Ctr 815 Second Ave New York NY 10017

AGUIRRE, ROBERTA PAULINE, nun; b. Temple, Tex., Apr. 29, 1946; d. Eugenio and Maria (Quinteros) A. AA, McClennan Community Coll., 1971; BA, Baylor U., 1973; M. Religious Edn., St. Thomas U., Houston, 1985. Joined Franciscan Sisters Daus. of Mercy, 1968; cert. tchr., Tex. With Franciscan Sisters Daug. of Mercy, Palma de Mallorca, Baleares, Spain, 1965—; superior Franciscan Sisters Daug. of Mercy, Waco, Tex., 1983—, del. regional coun., 1990; tchr. St. Francis Nursery and Kindergarten, Waco, 1975—; dir. religious edn. St. Francis Ch., Waco, 1975—, vol. immigration office, 1986—; rep. No. Deanery, Austin (Tex.) Diocese Roman Cath. Ch., 1990—, del. diocese synod, 1989—. Home: 612 N 3d St Waco TX 76701 Office: Franciscan Daus of Mercy 612 N 3d St Waco TX 76701 *We must do our best to take advantage of those "once-in-a-lifetime" opportunities offered to us by God to help our fellowman.*

AHERN, PATRICK V., bishop; b. N.Y.C., Mar. 8, 1919. Student, Manhattan Coll., Cathedral Coll., N.Y.C., St. Joseph's Sem., N.Y., St. Louis U., Notre Dame U. Ordained priest Roman Cath. Ch., 1945; ordained titular bishop of Naiera and aux. bishop N.Y.C., 1970—. Office: Chancery Office 1011 1st Ave New York NY 10022

AHL, EDWIN EUGENE, minister; b. Everett, Wash., Sept. 23, 1950; s. Edwin Earl Ahl and Barbara Jean (Hebert) Guffie; m. Kay Jean Allen, Aug. 7, 1971 (div. July 1984); children: Erin Christine, David Curtis, Joy Marie; m. Jane Louise Belcher, June 14, 1986. BA, Humboldt State U., 1977; MDiv, Oral Roberts U., 1986. Ordained to ministry So. Bapt. Conv. Youth pastor Sunny Brae Bapt. Ch., Arcata, Calif., 1978-80, drug/alcohol counselor, 1980-81; evangelist Full Gospel Ch., Tulsa, 1983-86; chaplain U.S. Army, Fulda, Fed. Republic Germany, 1988—. Capt. U.S. Army, 1988—. Democrat. Office: 4th Squadron 11th Cav Reg APO New York NY 09146

AHLBORN, MARVIN JAMES, clergyman; b. Chgo., May 22, 1945; s. Marvin Clairday and Florence Ruth (Ahlborn) Griffin; m. Helen Marie Hanson, July 2, 1966; children: Nathan, Matthew, Timothy. Student, Northwestern Coll., Watertown, Wis., 1963-66, Bethany Luth. Coll., Mankato, Minn., 1967-68; MDiv, Wis. Luth. Sem., Mequon, Wis., 1973. Ordained to ministry Luth Ch., 1973. Pastor Grace Luth. Ch., Muskegon, Mich., 1973-75, Beautiful Savior Luth. Ch., Grove City, Ohio, 1975-83; sr. adminstrv. pastor Emmaus Luth. Ch., Milw., 1984—. Republican. Home and Office: 2811 N 23d St Milwaukee WI 53206 *If it is not a challenge it is not worth doing.*

AHLBORN, MICHAEL WESLEY, minister, editor; b. Orange, Calif., Sept. 11, 1956; s. David Wesley Ahlborn and Shirley Faye (Pentecost) Rockland; m. Linda Jean Rhodes, June 14, 1978; 1 child, Steven. AA in Music Performance, Coll. Idaho, 1977; BRE, Berean Bible Coll., 1982; AB in Acctg., Link's Sch. Bus., 1984. Ordained to ministry Ch. of God, 7th Day. Assoc. pastor First Full Gospel Ch., Caldwell, Idaho, 1984-88; pastor Assembly in Christ Jesus, Homedale, Idaho, 1988—; editor Ch. of God Pub. House, Meridian, Idaho, 1989—; sec. Ministerial Orgn. Ch. of God, 7th Day, Meridian, 1989—; chmn. licensing Ch. of God, 7th Day, Meridian, 1990-91, evangelical min., 1990—. Author: (booklets) Biblical Studies, 1988—; editor Fellowship Herald, 1988—, Advocating Christ the Savior, 1988—. opera soloist Coll. Idaho, Caldwell, 1974-77, choral singer, 1982-84; opera soloist Boise (Idaho) Opera, 1976-77; counselor Crisis Pregnancy Ctr., Nampa, Idaho, 1986. Mem. Internat. Ministerial Assn. (sec., treas. Rocky Mountain dist. 1985-87). Republican. Home: 502 Everett Caldwell ID 83605 Office: Assembly in Christ Jesus 711 W Idaho Homedale ID 83642

AHLSCHWEDE, ARTHUR MARTIN, church educational official; b. Seward, Nebr., Dec. 5, 1914; s. Herman F. and Elizabeth (Birky) A.; m. Marie S. Spomer, Nov. 27, 1942; children—Carol, Kathleen, Nancy. B.S. in Edn, Concordia Tchrs. Coll., Seward, 1941, Litt.D., 1962; M.A., U. Minn., 1949; L.H.D., Concordia, Bronxville, 1980; LL.D., Concordia, River Forest, 1980. Prin. Luth. elementary schs., Hepler, Kans., 1935-37, Gillett, Ark., 1937-40, Mpls., 1942-49; prin. Concordia High Sch., St. Paul, 1949-53; acad. dean Concordia Coll., St. Paul, 1953-56; asst. exec. sec. bd. higher edn. Luth. Ch.-Mo. Synod, St. Louis, 1956-61; exec. sec. Luth. Ch.-Mo. Synod, 1961—, chmn. div. higher edn., 1962-80; with Concordia, Austin, 1981—; mem. div. edn. Luth. Council U.S., 1966—. Recipient Christus Primus award Concordia Coll., Ann Arbor, Mich., 1965. Mem. Minn. Pvt. Sch. League, Luth. Edn. Assn., Internat. Walther League, Luth. Laymen's League, Gamma Sigma Delta, Phi Delta Kappa. Democrat. Home: 10105 Willfield Dr Austin TX 78753 Office: 3400 Interstate 35 North Austin TX 78705

AHN, PETER PYUNG-CHOO, dean; b. Chor-won, Korea, May 21, 1917; came to U.S., 1948; s. Kyung-sam and Ok-bong (Lee) A.; m. Grace Chung, June 10, 1950; children: David Kyu-young and John Avery (twins). Diploma, St. Paul's U., Tokyo, 1944; BD, Garrett Theol. Sem., 1949; MA, Northwestern U., 1951; PhD, Boston U., 1962. Ordained to ministry United Meth. Ch., 1954. Pastor San Francisco Korean Meth. Ch., 1953-60, various United Meth. Chs., Calif., 1965-82; asst. prof. L.A. Pacific Coll., 1963-65; dean Korean Christian Acad., Oakland, Calif., 1986—; trustee Calif.-Nev. annual conf. United Meth. Ch., San Francisco, 1970-73, chair div. higher edn., 1973-76. Compiler: English-Korean and Koran-English dictionaries, 1947-48; translator: New American Standard Bible, 1965-70; chmn. translation project: New Korean Standard Bible, 1989—; rsch. dir. New Am. Standard Bible Exhaustive Concordance, 1970-76. Recipient Outstanding Contbn. award Lockman Found., 1973, Korean-Eng. Bible pub., 1990. Mem. Soc. Biblical Lit. Republican. Home: 608 Princeton Dr Sunnyvale CA 94087 Office: Lockman Found 900 S Euclud St La Habra CA 90631 *Our joy of life should be shared with others in service with compassion and understanding. Our Christian journey has worth when we remember our responsibility to witness our love amid the world's materialistic temptation.*

AHNE, JOSEPH JOO-YOUNG, minister; b. Korea, May 2, 1943; came to U.S. 1970; m. Angie Jung Kim, Aug. 30, 1969; children: Andrew, Herbert, Philip. BA in English, Hankuk U., Seoul, Korea, 1968; MA in Polit. Sci., U. Ill., Chgo., 1972; MDiv, Garett Evang. Theol. Sem., Evanston, Ill., 1983. Ordained to ministry United Meth. Ch., 1984. Youth pastor First Korean United Meth. Ch., Chgo., 1981-82; interim pastor, staff Peoples Ch. of Chgo., 1982-84; pastor Vincent United Meth. Ch., Chgo., 1984-85, Wesley United Meth. Ch., Mt. Prospect, Ill., 1985-90, Faith United Meth. Ch., Elmhurst, Ill., 1990—; chmn. Asian edn. com. Urban Acad. of Chgo., 1982-84. Bd. dirs. Nat. Rainbow Coalition, Washington, 1986—. Recipient Ann. Human Rels. award, Chgo. Commn. on Human Rels., 1986. Democrat. Home: 621 Colfax Ave Elmhurst IL 60126 Office: Faith United Meth Ch 111 W North Ave Elmhurst IL 60126 *American culture today emphasizes too much on family values. The irony is that there are more broken families in our society, because too many Americans idol family as a god to avoid God on Sunday.*

AIGNER, EMILY BURKE, lay worker; b. Henrico, Va., Oct. 28, 1920; d. William Lyne and Susie Emily (Willson) Burke; m. Louis Cottrell Aigner, Nov. 27, 1936; children: Lyne, Betty, D. Muriel (dec.), Willson, Norman, William, Randolph, Dorothy. Cert. in Bible, U. Richmond, 1969; postgrad., So. Bapt. Seminary Extension, Nashville, 1987, Va. Commonwealth U., 1981, Liberty Home Bible Inst., 1991—. Deacon Four Mile Creek Bapt. Ch., Richmond, Va., 1972—, trustee, 1991—, WMU dir., 1986—, treas., 1984-89, dir. Sunday sch., 1969-78, 84-85, 1989—; acctg. tech., 1959-80. Producer Dial-A-Devotion for pub. by tel. Solicitor ARC, Henrico County, 1947-49, United Givers' Fund, Henrico County, 1945-48; sec.-treas. Varina Sch.,

1946-49; singer Bellwood Choir, Chesterfield County, Va., 1965-70; telephone counselor Richmond Contact, 1980-82, Am. Cancer Soc., Richmond, 1980-82; program chmn. Varina (Va.) Home Demonstration Club, 1950-53; vol. worker Vol. Visitor Program Capital Area on Aging, 1983—; jail min. Richmond City Jail, 1973-90. Mem. Gideons Internat. (sec. aux. Va. 1977-80, 82-84, new mem. plan rep. 1981, 85, zone leader 1988-89, 90-91, state cabinet rep. 1989-90, pres. Richmond N.E. Camp 1976-78, sec. treas. 1980-82, scripture sec. 1973-75, 87-89), Alpha Phi Sigma. Home: 9717 Varina Rd Richmond VA 23231 *Forgive or not to forgive. I choose to forgive that I may not become bitter and cynical within but have peace and love to share with others with whom I encounter.*

AIKEN, CURTIS DALE, minister; b. Benton, Ill., Feb. 10, 1935; s. Terry and Tena (Thompson) A. Student, St. Louis Coll., 1964-67. Ordained to ministry Bapt. Ch., 1958. Pastor Old Dutch Community Ch., Elletsville, Ind., 1958—; sr. record clk. Ind. U., Bloomington; mgr., dir. Monroe County Sr. Citizens Kitchen. Condr., mgr., dir. Monroe County Sr. Citizens Kitchen Band. Mem. Monroe County Hist. Soc., Ind. State Hist. Soc., Nat. Hist. Soc. (Washington). Home: 1206 S Lincoln St Bloomington IN 47401

AIKEN, JEFFERSON KIRKSEY, JR., minister; b. Baton Rouge, Nov. 7, 1941; s. Jefferson Kirksey Sr. and Jane (Henderson) A.; m. Elizabeth Monroe, June 2, 1966; children: Stephen Kirk, Cameron James. BS, La. State U., 1963; MDiv., Columbia Seminary, Decatur, Ga., 1969; D of Ministry, McCormick Seminary, Chgo., 1975. Ordained to ministry Presbyn. Ch., 1969. Tv announcer, newscaster KALB-TV, Alexandria, La., 1963; minister First Presbyn. Ch., Dallas, N.C., 1969-73; sr. minister Paw Creek Presbyn. Ch., Charlotte, N.C., 1973-80, First Presbyn. Ch., Sumter, S.C., 1980—; chmn. presbyterey council Harmony Presbytery, S.C., 1984-86, chmn. transition com. for merger of four presbyteries, S.C., 1984-86; moderator New Harmony Presbytery, S.C., 1987-88. Co-author: Models of Metropolitan Ministry, 1979; newspaper columnist, Sumter Daily Item, 1987—. Bd. dirs., mem. exec. com., v.p. United Way Sumter, Lee and Clarendon Counties, S.C., 1987-90, pres., 1990-91; bd. visitors Presbyn. Coll., Clinton, S.C., 1987—; trustee L. Arthur O'Neill Found., 1986—; mem. Leadership S.C.; bd. dirs. Leadership Sumter, mem. exec. com., 1988, v.p., 1990. Recipient S.C. Govs. award for svc., 1983, S.C. Govs. Ann. Vol. award 1986. Mem. Greater Sumter C. of C. (bd. dirs., exec. com., pres. 1988—), Rotary (pres. Sumter 1986-87, area rep. 1987—, Presdl. citation 1986, Paul Harris fellow 1988, Rotarian of Yr. award 1991). Avocations: fine arts, music, golf, tennis, photography. Home: 2799 Powhatan Dr Sumter SC 29150 Office: First Presbyn Ch 9 West Calhoun St Sumter SC 29150 *So often the course of least resistance leads one to take too few risks and to accept too few challenges. A life of faithfulness requires one to constantly demonstrate courage and to take risks. This is not an appeal for impulsive recklessness. Responsible risk takers will always be guided by logical thinking and common sense. However, when we are convinced we should act, there is no need to be tenative.*

AINSWORTH, GORDON ROBERT, theology and Bible educator; b. Westerly, R.I., Mar. 31, 1947; s. Gordon and Arlene (McFarland) A.; m. Tamara Mansfield Ainsworth, Sept. 9, 1972. BS in Aerospace Engring., U. Okla., 1970; ThM in Christian Edn., Dallas Theol. Sem., 1978, ThD in Bible Exposition, 1988. Ordained to ministry Woodhaven Bible Ch., 1984. City dir. high sch. ministry Campus Crusade for Christ, Baton Rouge, 1971-73; staff mem. Campus Crusade for Christ, Birmingham, Ala., 1970-71; stockrm. clk. Direction One, Inc., Dallas, 1973-80; asst. bookkeeper Drs. Binion, Hosford, Thomas, Allday, Dallas, 1980-82; assoc. prof., chmn. dept. Christian studies William Tyndale Coll., Farmington Hills, Mich., 1982—; instr. Walk Thru the Bible Ministries, Atlanta, 1987-91; singles pastor Highland Park Bapt. Ch., Southfield, Mich., 1991—. Mem. Highland Park Bapt. Ch., Southfield, Mich. Mem. Evang. Theol. Soc. Avocations: music, reading, baseball, playing piano. Office: William Tyndale Coll 35700 W 12 Mile Rd Farmington Hills MI 48331

AINSWORTH, MICHAEL SCOTT, pastor; b. Pitts., Nov. 17, 1962; s. Thomas Holden and Judith Carolyn (Knepshield) A.; m. Patricia Ruth Joyce Ainsworth, June 30, 1984; children: Heather Lynn, Michael Scott Jr. AA in Religion, Emmanuel Coll., Franklin Springs, Ga., 1982; BS in Religion, Sch. Christian Ministries, Franklin Springs, Ga., 1984. Lic. to ministry Pentecostal Holiness Ch., 1983, ordained, 1985. Asst. pastor Goldmine Pentecostal Holiness Ch., Franklin Springs, 1982-84; pastor Hillsborough (N.C.) Pentecostal Holiness Ch., 1986-87; intern pastor Burlington (N.C.) Pentecostal Holiness Ch., summer 1983, asst. pastor, 1984-86, assoc. pastor, 1987—; adj. staff pastoral care chapliancy Alamance Health Svcs., Burlington, 1988—; mem. Conf. Christian Edn. Bd., Greensboro, 1990-94. mem. Alamance Coalition Against Drug Abuse, 1990—. Mem. Burlington-Alamance Min. Orgn. (v.p. 1990-91, pres. 1991—), Emmanuel Coll. Alumni Orgn. (conf. coord. western N.C. 1989—). Home: 1108 N Mebane St Burlington NC 27216 Office: 1st Pentecostal Holiness Ch PO Box 1321 Burlington NC 27216

AIREY, CHRISTIAN G., clergyman; b. Port-au-Prince, Haiti, W.I., Sept. 14, 1938; came to U.S., 1963; s. George and Luciana (Antonio) A.; m. Marnelle Pluviose, June 27, 1981; children—Chrisner, Emmanuel Pluviose, Marnelle-Anastasie. B.A., Va. Union U., 1967; M.Div., Howard U., 1970; Th.M., Harvard U., 1972; Ph.D., U. Paris, 1974. Ordained minister Lutheran Ch. French lab. dir. Howard U., Washington, 1968-70; pastor Zion Luth. Ch., Bklyn., 1974-78, St. Stephen Luth. Ch., Chgo., 1978—; refugee resettlement program dir. Luth. Child and Family Services, Chgo., 1980-82; exec. dir. Haitian Christian Alliance for Progress, Chgo., 1979—. Democrat. Home and Office: 8500 S Maryland Ave Chicago IL 60619

AKERS, BOWDEN CLARENCE, JR., minister; b. Atlanta, Sept. 28, 1934; s. Bowden Clarence and Lucille (Glenn) A.; m. Frances Harper, June 8, 1956 (dec. Oct. 21, 1982); children: Mary Alice Florey, Laura L. Mueller, Gary A.; m. Mary Lee Hoy, Aug. 2, 1987; children: Sherrie L. Pence, David E. Cupp, Jamie, Carla. AB, Stetson U., 1957; MDiv, Southeastern Bapt. Sem., 1963. Ordained to ministry So. Bapt. Conv., 1963. Pastor Connaritsa Bapt. Ch., Aulander, N.C., 1963-65, Western Br. Bapt. Ch., Suffolk, Va., 1965-72, Shenandoah Heights Bapt. Ch., Waynesboro, Va., 1972—. Contbr. articles to various mags. Mem. Waynesboro Ministerial Assn. (pres. 1990-91), Augusta Bapt. Assn. (moderator 1984, 85, chmn. ch. minister rels. com. 1989—), Va. Bapt. Assn. (bd. dirs. 1990—), Ruritan Club, Widowed Persons Svc. (pres. 1984-85). Home: 345 Walnut Ave Waynesboro VA 22980 Office: Shenandoah Heights Bapt Ch 901 Shenandoah Ave Waynesboro VA 22980

AKERS, JOHN NANCE, clergyman; b. Colorado Springs, Colo., Apr. 10, 1940; s. Byron Lionel and Lois Parke (Nance) A.; m. Anne Kathryn Wolfenden, June 15, 1968; 1 child, John Timothy. B.A., U. Colo., 1962; B.D., Columbia Theol. Sem., 1965, Th.M., 1968; Ph.D., U. Edinburgh, Scotland, 1973. Ordained to ministry Presbyn. Ch., 1965. Instr. of Bible, Belhaven Coll., Jackson, Miss., 1965-70; prof. Bible Montreat-Anderson Coll., Montreat, N.C., 1972-73, dean of coll., 1973-77; spl. asst. to Dr. Billy Graham, Billy Graham Evangelistic Assn., Montreat, 1977—; mem. exec. com., dir. Christianity Today, Inc., Carol Stream, Ill. Boettcher Found. scholar, 1958-62, Alumni scholar Columbia Theol. Sem., 1965. Sr. editor Christianity Today Mag., 1987-89. Mem. Conf. Faith and History, Presbyn. Hist. Soc., Evangelical Theol. Soc. (pres. Southeastern region 1976-77). Republican. Avocations: antiques; mineralogy. Home: Box 1089 Montreat NC 28757 Office: Billy Graham Evangelistic Assn Box 937 Montreat NC 28757

AKERS, JOHN REYNOLDS, pastor, religious organization administrator; b. Sayre, Pa., July 12, 1950; s. Reynolds and Louise (Fletcher) A.; m. Eileen Gloria Kaplan, Mar. 28, 1973 (div. 1985); children: John R. Jr., Rhett Andrew. BA in Computer Sci., U. Wis., 1978; MA in Theology, Emmaus Bible Sch., 1985. Ordained to ministry Ch. of God, 1983. Chief exec. officer, founder Friends of Paul & Silas Soc., Morristown, Pa., 1982—; assoc. pastor Fountain Life Community Ch., Morristown, 1987—; chief exec. officer J.R.A. Assoc., Ltd., Warrington, Pa., 1976—; dir. F.O.P.S., Norristown, 1982—. Contbr. articles to profl. jours. With U.S. Army, 1968-71, Vietnam. Decorated Purple Heart, Bronze Star with oak leaf cluster. Mem. Assn. Pastoral Counselors, Assn. for Cert. Data Processing Profls. (cert.). Republican. Home: 410 E Oak St Norristown PA 19406 Office: Friends of Paul & Silas Soc 60 Eagleville Rd Norristown PA 19403

AKERS, ROGER LEE, evangelist, clergyman; b. Whitby, W.Va., Feb. 2, 1950; s. William Grayson and Arvilla Angeline (Keffer) A.; m. Aldetta Fern Wallace, Aug. 3, 1968; children: Michelle Lee, Roger Lee II, James Wesley. Student, Beckley Coll., 1968-70. Lic. radio operator FCC. Evangelist Ch. of God, Beckley, W.Va., 1970-72, pastor, 1972-86, evangelist, 1986-88; pastor Calvary Pentecostal Tabernacle, Beckley, 1988-89; missionary evangelist Calvary Pentecostal Tabernacle, Ashland, Va., 1989—; account exec., on-air personality for Sta. WPES Calvary Communications, Inc., Ashland, 1989—; communications dir. Calvary Communications, Calvary Pentecostal Tabernacle, Ashland, 1989—; counsellor Ch. of God Youth Camps, Beckley, 1975-85; dist. youth dir. Ch. of God, Beckley, 1975-85; minister of music Beckley Ch. of God, 1985-86. Community dir. United Way, Pennsboro, W.Va., 1978; umpire Ritchie County Tee-Bau Assn., Pennsboro, 1977-79; pres. parts of svc. guild Chrysler Corp., Oak Hill, W.Va., 1985-87. Republican. Home: Rte 1 Box 365 Ashland VA 23005-9707 Office: Sta WPES Radio PO Box 148 Ashland VA 23005-0148

AKINS, CLINTON MILES, religion educator; b. Augsburg, Fed. Republic Germany, Nov. 2, 1952; arrived in Madagascar, 1983; s. Kossie Carlyle and Fay (Stevens) A.; m. Kathy Ann Piquard, Nov. 25, 1972; children: Jennifer Lea, Kimberly Anne, Heather Ruth. BA, Tenn. Temple Coll., 1977; MDiv, Mid-Am. Bapt. Sem., 1980; D in Ministry, So. Bapt. Sem., 1990. Pastor Bethel Bapt. Mission, Ringgold, Ga., 1976-77, First Bapt. Ch., Cardwell, Mo., 1977-80; missionary sem. tchr. Conservative Bapt. Fgn. Mission Soc., Fianarantsoa, Madagascar, 1980—; field chairperson Conservative Bapt. Fgn. Mission Soc., Tananarive, 1989—; sem. tchr. Malagasy Bapt. Sem., Antsirabs, Madagascar, 1990—; dir. Extension Sem., Fianarantsoa, 1990—. With U.S. Army, 1970-73, Vietnam. Recipient Youth Leadership in Religion award Kiwanis, 1969; named one of Outstanding Young Men of Am., Jaycees, 1981. Home: B.P. 1191, Fianarantsoa 301, Madagascar Office: Conservative Bapt Fgn Mission Soc PO Box 5 Wheaton IL 60189-0005

AKINS, GLENN LEE, minister; b. Bartlesville, Okla., Sept. 4, 1952; s. Herbert Glenn Akins and Dorothy (Harris) Lee; m. Elizabeth Anne Cantrell, Oct. 25, 1980; children: Andrew Lee, Holly Elizabeth. AA, Mo. Bapt. Coll., 1972, BA, 1975; MDiv, MRE, So. Bapt. Theol. Sem., 1981. Ordained to ministry Bapt. Ch., 1980. Min. of youth Third Bapt. Ch., St. Louis, 1974-77; ch. planter Mecklenburg Bapt. Assn., Charlotte, N.C., 1981-83, adminstrv. assoc., 1983-85; ch. starter, strategist S.C. Bapt. Conv., Columbia, 1985-88, dir. missions devel., 1988—; treas. Master Design Assocs., Inc., Columbia, 1990—; mega focus cities cons. Home Mission Bd., Atlanta, 1987—. Mem. New Work Fellowship, Dir. Missions Fellowship, So. Bapt. Rsch. Fellowship. Office: SC Bapt Conv 907 Richland St Columbia SC 29201

AKWUE, FRANCIS AMAECHI, pastor, religion educator; b. Ogidi, Anambra, Nigeria, Feb. 14, 1938; came to U.S., 1990; s. Akwue Ogbuaku and Maria (Nwude) Akwue. BTh., Urban U., 1971; MA, St. John's U., 1976; PhD, U. Ottawa, 1980; DTh., St. Paul U., Ottawa, 1988. Assoc. pastor St. Finbarr's Ch., Nigeria, 1971; sem. rector Sons of Mercy, Nigeria, 1972-75, Holy Ghost Novitiate, Nigeria, 1980-88; assoc. pastor Ch. of the Little Flower, Coral Gables, Fla., 1990, Dir. of Christian Formation, Coral Gables, 1990—; deputy pastor Sch. Adv. Bd., Coral Gables, 1990—, Home and Sch. Bd., Coral Gables, 1990—; chaplain St. Theresa Sch., Coral Gables, 1990—; dir. Religious Edn., Coral Gables, 1990—. Roman Catholic. Home: 1270 Anastasia Ave Coral Gables FL 33134 *We may talk about and attempt to solve the moral and ethical problems in our societies today. Nevertheless, a true understanding of the preacher's statement that nothing is new under the sun leads those who are gravely disturbed toward achieving peace of heart while the struggle continues.*

AL-AZMEH, AZIZ, religious studies educator; b. Damascus, Syria, July 23, 1947; s. Malak and Salma (Nabulsi) Al-A.; m. Kasturi Sen; 1 child, Omar. License-ès-lettres, Beirut Arab U., 1971; MA, Eberhard-Karls U., Tübingen, 1973; D. of Philosophy, U. Oxford, 1978. Lectr. U. Kuwait, 1981-83; fellow dept. Arabic and Islamic studies U. Exeter, Eng., 1983-84, Sharjah prof. Islamic studies, 1985—; cons. BBC TV, BBC Svc., various univs., project for translation of Arabic lits. UNESCO, ALESCO, UNITAR; bd. dirs. Arts Worldwide, London. Author: Ibn Khaldun in Modern Scholarship, 1981, Ibn Khaldun: An Essay in Reinterpretation, 1982, Historical Writing and Historical Culture (in Arabic), 1983, Arabic Thought and Islamic Societies, 1986, The Politics and History of Heritage (in Arabic), 1987; gen. editor Arabic and Islamic Studies; mem. editorial bd. Review of Middle East Studies. Chmn. Arab Orgn. for Human Rights, London, 1986. Fellow British Soc. for Middle East Studies; mem. Nat. Conf. of Univ. Profs., Arabic Club Gt. Britain, Arabic Philos. Soc., Arabic Writer's Union. Office: U Exeter, Prince of Wales Rd, Exeter EA4 4QJ, England

ALBERS, JAMES WILLIAM, theology educator, dean; b. Plymouth, Wis., Nov. 17, 1937; s. Waldemar H. and Alyda I. Albers; m. Joanne Helen Graf, Aug. 12, 1961; children: Laura L., Andrew R., Stephen M. BA, Concordia Sr. Coll., Ft. Wayne, Ind., 1959; BDiv, Concordia Sem., St. Louis, 1963, MST, 1964, ThD, 1972. Ordained to ministry Luth. Ch., 1968. Instr. Valparaiso (Ind.) U., 1965-69, asst. prof., 1969-76; dir. Study Ctr. Valparaiso U., Beutlingen, Fed. Rep. of Germany, 1972-74; assoc. prof. Valparaiso (Ind.) U., 1976-85, prof., 1986—, assoc. dean Coll. Arts and Scis., 1983-86, v.p. admissions and fin. aid, 1986-90, dean Grad. Studies and Continuing Edn., 1990—; pres. Luth. Hist. Conf., St. Louis, 1978-82, 86-90. Author: From Centennial to Golden Anniversary-History of Valparaiso University, 1974; contbr. articles to profl. jours. Lutheran. Home: 303 Highland Dr Valparaiso IN 46383 Office: Valparaiso U Theology Dept Valparaiso IN 46383

ALBERS, ROBERT HERBERT, seminary educator; b. Kiester, Minn., Sept. 28, 1940; s. Herbert Frederick and Helena Marie (Beckmann) A.; m. Sonia Ann Syverson, Aug. 12, 1962; children: Joyce Lynette, Stephen Mark, Joel David. BA, Wartburg Coll., 1962; MDiv, Wartburg Sem., 1966; PhD, So. Calif. Sch. Theology, 1982. Ordained to ministry Luth. Ch., 1968. Pastor St. Paul's Luth. Ch., Corby, Northants, Eng., 1966-67; asst. pastor First Luth. Ch., Blair, Nebr., 1968-69, sr. pastor, 1969-78; asst. prof. Luth. Northwestern Sem., St. Paul, 1981-83, assoc. prof., 1983-91, prof., 1991—; dir. ThD program pastoral counseling Luth. Northwestern Sem., St. Paul, 1987, dir. MTh program in pastoral care, 1985—. Author: A Life of Prayer, 1984, Healing the Hurts: Separation and Loss, 1991; contbg. author: Handbook for Basic Types of Pastoral Care, 1990; editor Jour. Ministry in Addiction and Recovery, 1990; also articles. Bd. trustees Good Shepherd Luth. Home, Blair, 1979-88; bd. mem. Washington County Mental Health Assn., Blair, 1980-88, Region VI, Mental/Health and Alcohol Commn., Omaha, 1982-88. Mem. Nat. Interfaith Network on Alcohol and Drugs, Pastoral Care Network for Social Responsibility. Democrat. Avocations: fishing, reading, playing the piano. Home: 2890 Arthur Pl Roseville MN 55113 Office: Luther Northwestern Sem 2481 Como Ave Saint Paul MN 55108

ALBERS, THOMAS LEO, priest, religious order administrator; b. Minster, Ohio, May 4, 1940; s. Leo Anthony and Onnolee Rosemary (Makley) A. BA, U. Dayton, 1963, MA, 1987. Ordained priest Roman Cath. Ch., joined Soc. Precious Blood. Assoc. chaplain Little Co. of Mary Hosp., Evergreen Park, Ill., 1967-69, dir. pastoral svcs., 1973-79; chaplain intern St. Elizabeth's Hosp., NIMH, Washington, 1969-70, Anna (Ill.) State Hosp., 1970-71; chaplain VA Hosp., Milw., 1971-73, Christ Hosp., Oak Lawn, Ill., 1979-84; dir. formation Soc. Precious Blood, Kansas City, Mo., 1984-87; provincial dir. Soc. Precious Blood, Liberty, Mo., 1987—. Columnist Kansas City Province newsletter, 1984—. Mem. Nat. Assn. Cath. Chaplains (pres. 1982-84), Conf. Maj. Superiors of Men (rep. to midwest region Assn. Vicars for Religious). Home: PO Box 339 Liberty MO 64068 Office: Soc Precious Blood 2130 Hughes Rd Liberty MO 64068

ALBERT, ROBERT LAWRENCE, minister; b. Far Rockaway, N.Y., May 19, 1945; s. William Otto and Anna May (Janzen) A.; m. Cheryl Kay Lyberger, Nov. 11, 1967; children: Kimberley Marie, Patricia Lynn. AS, Community Coll. of Air Force, 1983; BA in Pastoral Ministries, Trevecca Nazarene Coll., 1989. Ordained to ministry Ch. of the Nazarene, 1989. Enlisted USAF, 1965, advanced through ranks to sr. master sgt., 1987; ret.; pastor Myrtle Beach (S.C.) Ch. of the Nazarene, 1981-84, 89—; assoc. pastor Melwood Ch. of the Nazarene, Upper Marlboro, Md., 1984-86; assoc. pastor Palmer (Tenn.) Ch. of the Nazarene, 1987; assoc. pastor Trinity Ch. of the Nazarene, Nashville, 1987-89. Bd. dirs. Grand Strand Citizens for Life, Myrtle Beach, 1990-91; chaplain CAP , Myrtle Beach, 1989-91. Mem. Phi Delta Lambda. Home: 612 4th Ave N Myrtle Beach SC 29577 Office: Ch of the Nazarene 612 4th Ave N Myrtle Beach SC 29577

ALBRECHT, ARDON DU WAYNE, minister; b. Burlington, Wis., Sept. 2, 1936; s. Franklin William and Esther Maria (Braatz) A.; m. Edith Elizabeth Spillner, Aug. 21, 1960; children: Kim, Rebekah, Suzanne, Matthew, Marc. AA, Concordia Coll., Milw., 1956; BD, MDiv, Concordia Sem., St. Louis, 1962; MS, Syracuse U., 1969; LittD (hon.), Christ Coll., Calif., 1987. Ordained to ministry Luth. Ch.-Mo. Synod, 1962. Missionary Taiwan, 1962-71; mem. bd. control Joint Luth. TV, Taiwan, 1968-70, asst. exec. sec., 1970-71; program dir. Luth. TV Luth. Ch.-Mo. Synod, 1971-77, exec. producer, 1977-88; pastor Pilgrim Luth. Ch., Santa Monica, Calif., 1988—; v.p. Taiwan Christian Audio Visual Assn., 1970-71; trustee Luth. Film Assn., 1975-87. Author: Essential Christian Doctrines (Chinese Mandarin and Taiwanese transls.), 1966; translator: Taiwanese Customs and Superstitution, 1965. Recipient Gold and Silver awards for This Is The Life, Yeshua, Three Days, The Little Troll Princes Internat. Film and TV Festival N.Y. Mem. Writers Guild of Am. Home: 2016 Alscot Ave Simi CA 93063

ALBRECHT, BRIAN MICHAEL, minister; b. Casper, Wyo., Sept. 10, 1944; s. John Walter and Dorcas (Ferree) A.; m. Patricia Maloy, Apr. 22, 1967; children: Brian Michael II, Timothy John. BS, York Coll. Pa., 1972; MTh, Dallas Theol. Sem., 1982. Ordained to ministry Bapt. Ch., 1988. Internat. comptroller Global Outreach Mission, London, Ont., Can., 1972-78; bd. mem. Global Outreach Mission, Buffalo, 1986—; elder Lake Ridge Bible Ch., Garland, Tex., 1983-88; pastor Second Cape May Bapt. Ch., Marmora, N.J., 1988—. With U.S. Army, 1965-69. Mem. Nat. Right to Life, Nat. Rifle Assn. Republican. Office: Second Cape May Bapt Ch 600 S Shore Rd Marmora NJ 08223 *It is my desire to serve the Lord Jesus Christ with my whole being. To put Him first in my life and to see what can be accomplished by allowing Him to live through me.*

ALBRIGHT, JIMMY LEE, minister, educator; b. Lubbock, Tex., Nov. 25, 1942; s. Jimmie W. and Margie M. (Tew) A.; m. Janice Jeanne Lain, Aug. 24, 1962; children: Jana Lynn, Jennifer Lee. AB, Stephen Austin U., 1965; BD, N.Am. Theol. Sem., 1968; MDiv, Southwestern Sem., 1976, PhD, 1980. Ordained to ministry Bapt. Ch., 1964. Pastor First Bapt. Ch., Mount Selman, Tex., 1963-65, Davis St. Bapt. Ch., Sulphur Spings, Tex., 1968-75; interim pastor First Bapt. Ch., Lipan, Tex., 1976-77; youth min. First Bapt. Ch., Burleson, Tex., 1978-79; pastor Wyatt Park Bapt. Ch., St. Jospeh, Mo., 1980—; 1st v.p. Mo. Bapt. Conv., Jefferson City, Mo., 1983—, mem. nominating and Christian Life coms., 1982-84, exec. bd., 1983—; prof. Mo. Western State Coll., St. Joseph, 1981—; adj. prof. Southwestern Theol. Sem., Ft. Worth, 1978-80, Midwestern Theol. Sem., Kansas City, Mo., 1983-84. Contbr. articles and photographs to profl. publs. Div. dir. United Fund, Sulphur Springs, 1972-73; bd. dirs. Am. Cancer Soc., St. Joseph, 1982—; city chmn. tax levy campaign St. Joseph Sch. Systems, 1984; supr. Tel Batash Archaeol. Expedition, 1978-79, Tel 'Uza Archaeol. Expdn., 1981-84. Recipient David Meier Internat. Study League award Southwestern Sem., 1979. Mem. Am. Schs. Oriental Rsch., Soc. Bibl. Lit., Alpha Chi, Lions, Kiwanis. Home: 2209 Elephant Trail Saint Joseph MO 64507 Office: Wyatt Park Bapt Ch 2739 Mitchell Saint Joseph MO 64507

ALBRIGHT, THOMAS HUBERT, minister, religious organization administrator; b. Sedro-Voolley, Wash., Aug. 10, 1946; s. Hubert Wilbur Albright and Reda Edith Albright Nachtrieb; m. Carol Jean Hicks, June 16, 1972; children: Joshua, Seth, Geoffrey. BA, U. Puget Sound, 1968; D Religion, Sch. Theology at Claremont, 1972. Ordained to ministry United Meth. Ch. Pastor Winlock-Pe Ell (Wash.) United Meth. Ch., 1972-76, Cheney (Wash.) Ch., 1976-79, Cen. United Meth. Ch., Spokane, Wash., 1979-83, Aidersgate United Meth. Ch., Bellevue, Wash., 1983-88; supt. Vancouver (Wash.) Dist., United Meth. Ch., 1988—. Office: United Meth Ch Vancouver Dist 2904 Main St Ste 100 Vancouver WA 98663 *The loss of soul in Western culture is directly connected to our pre-occupation with measuring human value only in economic terms.*

ALBRITTON, WALTER MATTHEW, JR., minister; b. Wetumpka, Ala., Mar. 24, 1932; m. Dean Brown, June 1, 1952; children: David (dec.), Matthew, Mark, Timothy, Stephen. BS in English, Auburn U., 1954; MDiv, Emory U., 1958. Ordained to ministry Meth. Ch., 1958. Pastor LaPlace Cir., Tuskegee, Ala., 1953-54, Midway (Ala.) Charge, 1956-58, Pine Forest United Meth., Pensacola, Fla., 1958-63, Government St. United Meth Ch., Mobile, Ala., 1972-75, 1st United Meth. Ch., Demopolis, Ala., 1975-80, Whitfield Meml. United Meth. Ch., Montgomery, Ala., 1980-82, Richards Meml. United Meth. Ch., Pensacola, Fla., 1982-89; sr. pastor Trinity United Meth. Ch., Opelika, Ala., 1989—; assoc. dir. Ala.-West Fla. Conf., Coun., Andalusia, Ala., 1963-68; mem. staff Gen. Bd. Evangelism, United Meth. Ch., Nashville, 1968-72. Author: If You Want to Walk on Water, You've Got to Get Out of the Boat, 1978; contbr. articles to profl. jours. Mem. Meth. Hour Internat. (bd. dirs.), Mission Soc. for United Meths. (advising coun.). Office: Trinity United Meth Ch 800 2d Ave Opelika AL 36801

ALBY, JAMES FRANCIS PAUL, priest, educator; b. Milw., July 16, 1936; s. Francis Joseph and Sarah Sophie (Hansen) A.; B.A., Gallaudet U., 1963, M.S. in Edn., 1964; M.Div., Va. Theol. Sem., 1971; m. Jan Lorraine Peplinski, Aug. 2, 1980; 1 child. Ordained priest Episcopal Ch., 1971; priest to the deaf St. James Mission of the Deaf, Milw., 1971-76; priest assoc. St. Peter's Ch., West Allis, Wis., 1972-83; asst. to rector: Ministry of the Deaf, St. James Parish, Milw., 1983-88; assoc. priest St. Edmund's Ch., Elm Grove, Wis., 1990—; affiliated with Episcopal Diocese of Fond Du Lac, 1988—; tchr. high sch. hearing impaired Milw. Pub. Schs., 1972—; priest assoc. Holy House of Our Lady of Walsingham, Norfolk, Eng., 1984—; instr. interpreting for deaf U. Wis., Milw., 1975-77; sr. high sch. boys dorm supr.-counselor St. John's Sch. for the Deaf, St. Francis, Wis., 1971-72; tchr. lang. of signs Milw. Area Tech. Coll., 1974-75; mem. adv. com. continuing edn. deaf adults, Milw., 1976-84, mem. adv. com. on edn. hearing impaired Milw. Pub. Schs., 1977-85; mem. sect. 504 com. Southeastern Wis. Disabilities Coalition, 1979-81, mem. adult edn. adv. com. Milw. Hearing Soc., 1976-83. Contbr. articles to profl. jours. Mem. Nashotah House Sem. Alumni Assn. (assoc.), Nat. Fraternal Soc. Deaf, Nat. Assn. of Deaf, Wis. Assn. Deaf, Danish Brotherhood in Am., Greater Milw. Lions Club (charter pres.), Lioness (liaison 1980-84), Gallaudet U. Alumni Assn., Milw. Fire Hist. Soc. (charter), Soc. for the Preservation and Appreciation of Antique Motor Fire Apparatus in Am., Ahrens-Fox Fire Buffs Assn., Alpha Sigma Pi. Avocations: collecting Danish blue plates and firematic collectibles.

ALCANTARA, MIGUEL BACCAY, priest; b. Atimonan, Quezon, The Philippines, Sept. 26, 1940; came to U.S., 1970; naturalized, 1984; BS in Philosophy, Ateneo de Manila U., 1960; BST magna cum laude, Lateran U., Rome, 1965; MA in Philosophy Edn., Loyola U., Chgo., 1971; MA in Sociology, De Paul U., 1973; LittD (hon.), Colegio Estadual de Jandaia do Sul, Brazil, 1980. Ordained priest Roman Cath. Ch., 1965. Curate St. Isidore Ch., Cuenca, Batangas, The Philippines, 1966-67, Cathedral St. Sebastian, Lipa City, The Philippines, 1966-68; dean studies Major Sem. Bauan, The Philippines, 1968-70, also curate of city parish; resident St. John Berchmans Ch., Chgo., 1970-74; assoc. pastor St. Rocco's Ch., Pittston, Pa., 1974-78; missionary Brazil, 1978-81; assoc. pastor St. Sebastian Parish, Middletown, Conn., 1981, St. Andrew's Parish, Calumet City, Ill., 1982—; incardinated Archdiocese of Chgo., 1988—. Religious editor, columnist Via Times. Named Cidadao Benemerito, City Coun. of Jandaia do Sul, 1981, Outstanding New Citizen Chgo. Met. Coun. for Citizenship, 1984. Address: 768 Lincoln Ave Calumet City IL 60409 *I pray the Lord daily to bless me according to my thanklessness, lest He bless me according to my thankfulness, and I starve. I believe joy is really the simplest form of gratitude. One cannot be sad and moody and at the same time say he is grateful.*

ALCARAZ FIGUEROA, ESTANISLAO, clergyman; b. Patzcuaro, Michoacan, Mex., Oct. 23, 1918; s. Estanislao Alcaraz and Rafaela (Figueroa). Humanidades, Morelia Sem., 1937; Filosofía y Teología, Montezuma Sem., N.Mex., 1943. Ordained priest Roman Catholic Ch., 1942, consecrated bishop, 1959; bishop of Matamoros Tamaulipas, 1959-68, San Luis Potosí, 1968-72, Morelia, Michoacan; archbishop of Morelia, 1972—. Office: Archbishop of Morelia, Apartado 17, Morelia Michoacan, Mexico

ALCORN, RANDY CRAIG, minister; b. Portland, Oreg., June 23, 1954; s. Arthur Loren and Lucille Vivian (Tovrea) A.; m. Nanci Annette Noren, May 31, 1975; children: Karina Elizabeth, Angela Marie. ThB, Multnomah Sch. of the Bible, 1975; MA in Biblical Studies, Western Bapt. Sem., 1979. Ordained to ministry, 1977. Youth pastor Powell Valley Covenant Ch., Gresham, Oreg., 1975-77; pastor Good Shepherd Community Ch., Gresham, 1977-90; dir. Eternal Perspective Ministries, Gresham, 1990—; bd. dirs. Crisis Pregnancy Ctrs., Portland, 1983-84; sec. Internat. Inst. for Christian Communication, Portland, 1989—; mem. part-time faculty Multnomah Sch. Bible, 1980-82, Western Bapt. Sem., Portland, 1985-86. Author: Christians in the Wake of the Sexual Revolution, 1985, Women under Stress, 1986, Sexual Temptation, 1988, Money, Possessions and Eternity, 1989, Is Rescuing Right?, 1990, Pro-Life Answers to Pro-Choice Arguments, 1991; contbr. articles to religious jours. Republican. Home: 5430 SE Chase Gresham OR 97080 Office: Eternal Perspective Ministries 2229 E Burnside Ste 23 Gresham OR 97030 *If our treasures are on earth, every day we are moving away from them. If our treasures are in heaven, every day we are moving toward them. He who is always moving away from his treasures has reason to despair. He who is always moving toward his treasures has reason to rejoice.*

ALCORN, STEPHEN KENNETH, minister; b. Kansas City, Mo., Aug. 14, 1961; s. Kenneth MacCallum and Dorothy Leora (Roberts) A.; m. Linda Lou Bodine, July 23, 1983; children: Kenneth, Kristen, Robert. BA, Eas. Nazarene Coll., 1983; completion cert., New Eng. Sch. Broadcasting, Bangor, Maine, 1986; postgrad., Nazarene Theol. Sem., Kansas City, Mo., 1991—. Dir. youth ministries 1st Ch. of the Nazarene, Bangor, Maine, 1985-88; assoc. min. youth Trinity Ch. of the Nazarene, Rochester, N.Y., 1988-91, Dundee Hills Ch. of the Nazarene, Gladstone, Mo., 1991—; Rochester zone youth pres. Ch. of the Nazarene, 1988-91, mem. Upstate N.Y. Dist. Youth Coun., Rochester, 1988-91; dir. N.Y.C. Congress, Upstate N.Y. Dist. Regional Nazarene Youth Internat., Orlando, Fla., 1991; del. to Nazarene gen. conv. Upstate N.Y. Dist. Nazarene Youth Internat., 1989; mem. Kansas City Dist. Youth Coun., 1991—. Contbg. author: (with others) The Evolution of Christian Music, 1989. Mem. Nazarene Multiple Staff Assn., Nat. Assn. Religious Broadcasters, Greece Youth Pastors Assn. (co-founder), Rochester Youthworkers Roundtable. *What our world today needs is a people who have given themselves to Jesus Christ, living by biblical principles and lead by the Holy Spirit. These are the people who have found what everyone else is looking for.*

ALCORN, TROY GENE, minister; b. Sulphur Springs, Tex., Aug. 4, 1930; s. Mahlon Winifield and Quincy Blanche (Shrode) A.; m. Bobbie Yvonne McCrady, Sept. 1, 1950; children: Karen L. Havens, Chris Alan Alcorn, Gayle M. Haggard, Cynthia J. Morris. BA, East Tex. State U., 1952; postgrad. Indsl. Coll. Armed Forces, 1972-73. Commd. U.S. Air Force, 1952, advanced through grades to col., 1971, ret., 1976; ordained to ministry, Christian Assembly, 1974; asst. pastor Christian Assembly, Vienna, Va., 1976-77, pastor, Colorado Springs, Colo., 1977-87. Decorated Legion of Merit with oak leaf cluster, Meritorious Svc. medal, Air Force Commendation medal with oak leaf cluster. Home: 3812 Templeton Gap Rd Colorado Springs CO 80907

ALCORN, WALLACE ARTHUR, minister; b. Milw., Aug. 29, 1930; s. William Keith and Dora Mildred (Brazee) A.; m. Ann Margaret Carmichael, June 5, 1958; children: John Mark, Allison Alcorn-Oppedahl, Stephen Paul. Student, Marquette U., 1950; AB, Wheaton Coll., 1952; MDiv, Grand Rapids Bapt. Theol. Sem., 1959; AM, Wheaton Grad. Sch. Theology, 1959; postgrad., Mich. State U., 1959-60, U. Mich., 1960-61; ThM, Princeton Theol. Sem., 1965; PhD, NYU, 1974; cert. in clin. pastoral edn., Fitzsimons Army Med. Ctr., 1975; postgrad., U. Minn., 1980-81. Ordained to ministry Gen. Assn. Regular Bapt. Chs., 1957. Pastor Caddy Vista Bapt. Ch., Caldonia, Wis., 1955-57, Bloomfield Hills (Mich.) Bapt. Ch., 1960-61, Community Bapt. Ch. Shark River Hills, Neptune, N.J., 1961-67, 1st Bapt. Ch., Austin, Minn., 1976-83; prof. bible Moody Bible Inst., Chgo., 1967-73; assoc. prof. N.T. N.W. Bapt. Sem., Tacoma, 1974-76; affiliate chaplain Madigan Army Med. Ctr., Tacoma, 1974-76; police chaplain Tacoma, 1974-76, Austin, Minn., 1976—; prin. Wallace Alcorn Assocs., Austin, 1983—; pastoral counselor New Life Family Svcs., Rochester, Minn., 1987—; radio tchr. Moody Radio Network, 1968-74; radio commentator Sta. KTIS and Northwestern Coll. Network, 1987—; chmn. Minn. Assn. Regular Bapt. Chs., 1980-83; pres. Faith Acad., Fridley, Minn., 1986. Author: The Bible as Literature, 1965, Elijah, Prophet of God, 1972, The Life of Christ Visualized, 1973, Knowing and Using the Bible, 1975, Momentum, 1986; nat. editor Christian Life, 1956-59, Mil. Life, 1983-86; N.T. editor Living Bible Commentary, 1974-76; contbr. Wycliffe Bible Ency., 1974, Tyndale Family Bible Ency., 1976, New Commentary on the Whole Bible, 1990; contbr. numerous articles to profl. jours. Mem. citizen's adv. coun. Neptune (N.J.) Bd. Edn., 1965-67, Austin Human Rights Commn., 1989—; mem. profl. adv. coun. Pub. Edn. Religion Studies Ctr., Wright State U., 1972-76; dir. The Good News Hour, Austin, 1976-83. With USNR, 1947-52; U.S. Army, 1952-54; USAR, 1954-57, chaplain, col., 1957-90. Mem. Evang. Theol. Soc., Evang. Press Assn., Nat. Assn. Religious Broadcasters, Mil. Chaplains Assn. (pres. Chgo. chpt. 1970-74), hist. socs. Wis., Ohio, S.C. Home: 1010 7th Ave NW Austin MN 55912 Office: PO Box 733 Austin MN 55912-0773 *If the fruit of the Spirit is growing in one's life, everything else is in place.*

ALDEN, ROBERT LESLIE, religion educator; b. Brockton, Mass., Dec. 10, 1937; s. Allen Nathan and Lona Eva (Simon) A.; m. Mary Jane Emilie Hauck, June 4, 1966; children: John Simon, Grace Ann Byrd. BA, Barrington (R.I.) Coll., 1959; MDiv, Westminster Theol. Sem., 1962; PhD, Hebrew Union Coll., 1966. Prof. old testament Denver Sem., 1966—. Named Alumnus of Yr., Barrington Coll., 1984. Mem. Evang. Theol. Soc., Soc. of Bibl. Lit., Cath. Bibl. Soc., Near East Archaeol. Soc., Colo. Mountain Club, Near East Archaeol. Soc. (bd. dirs. 1986—). Office: Denver Sem Box 10,000 Denver CO 80210

ALDEN, WILLIAM LEWIS, film producer; b. Springfield, Mass., May 17, 1926; s. Milton and Florence (Eldridge) A.; m. Judith Grose, June 23, 1951; children: Wendy, Lincoln, Polly, Luther, Jonathan. BA, Harvard U., 1950, MBA, 1952. Gen. ptnr. Alden Film Assocs. Ltd., Westboro, Mass., 1987—; pres. Pilgrim Prodns. Ltd., Westboro, 1989—; presenter at confs. Producer: A Touch of the Times, 1949, also miscellaneous indsl. films, Behind God's Back; patentee self-transit rail and road car. Pres., bd. dirs. Packyrd Manse, Stoughton, Mass., 1955-70; trustee Andover Newton Theol. Sch., Newton Centre, Mass., 1982—; bd. dirs. Ctr. for Ministry of Laity, Newton Centre, 1982—; charter bd. dirs. Facing History and Ourselves, Brooklin, Mass., 1983-87. Co-recipient Brotherhood award NCCJ, 1969. Mem. Bus. Execs. for Nat. Security (charter bd. dirs.). Office: Pilgrim Prodns Ltd PO Box 721 Westboro MA 01581 *The pendulum is swinging back toward the spiritual—and none too soon. We should enhance and guide this movement.*

ALDERMAN, MINNIS AMELIA, psychologist, educator, small business owner; b. Douglas, Ga., Oct. 14, 1928; d. Louis Cleveland Sr. and Minnis Amelia (Wooten) A. AB in Music, Speech and Drama, Ga. State Coll., Milledgeville, 1949; MA in Supervision and Counseling Psychology, Murray State U., 1960; postgrad. Columbia Pacific U., 1987—. Tchr. music Lake County Sch. Dist., Umatilla, Fla., 1949-50; instr. vocal and instrumental music, dir. band, orch. and choral Fulton County Sch. Dist., Atlanta, 1950-54; instr. English, speech, debate, vocal and instrumental music, dir. drama, band, choral and orch. Elko County Sch. Dist., Wells, Nev., 1954-59; tchr. English and social studies Christian County Sch. Dist., Hopkinsville, Ky., 1960; instr. psychology, guidance counselor Murray (Ky.) State U., 1961-63, U. Nev., Reno, 1963-67; owner Minisizer Exercising Salon, Ely, Nev., 1969-71, Knit Knook, Ely, 1969—, Minimimeo, Ely, 1969—, Gift Gamut, Ely, 1977—; prof. dept. fine arts Wassuk Coll., Ely, 1986-91, assoc. dean, 1986-87, dean, 1987-90; counselor White Pine County Sch. Dist., Ely, 1960-68; dir. Child and Family Ctr., Ely Indian Colony, 1988—, Family and Community Ctr., Ely Shoshone Indian Tribe, 1989—; supr. testing Ednl. Testing Svc., Princeton, N.J., 1960-68, Am. Coll. Testing Program, Iowa, 1960-68, U. Nev., Reno, 1960-68; chmn. bd. White Pine Sch. Dist. Employees Fed. Credit Union, Ely, 1961-69; psychologist mental hygiene div. Nev. Pers., Ely, 1969-75, dept. employment security, 1975-80; sec.-treas. bd. dirs. Gt. Basin Enterprises, Ely, 1969-71; pvt. instr. piano, violin, voice and organ, Ely, 1981—; bd. dir. band Sacred Heart Sch., Ely, 1982—; dir. Family and Community Ctr. Ely Shoshone Indian Tribe, 1989—. Author various news articles, feature stories, pamphlets, handbooks and grants in field. Pres. White Pine County Mental Health Assn., 1960-63, 78—; mem. Gov.'s Mental Health State Commn., 1963-65; bd. dirs. White Pine County Sch. Employees Fed. Credit Union, 1961-68, pres., 1963-68; 2d v.p. White Pine Community Concert Assn., 1965-67, pres., 1967, 85—, treas., 1975-79, dr. chmn., 1981-85; chmn. of bd., 1984; bd. dirs. White Pine chpt. ARC, 1978-82; mem. Nev. Hwy. Safety Leaders Bd., 1979-82; mem. Gov.'s Commn. on Status Women, 1968-74; sec.-treas. White Pine Rehab. Tng. Ctr. for Retarded Persons, 1973-75; mem. Gov.'s Commn. on Hwy. Safety, 1979-81; dir. Ret. Sr. Vol. Program, 1973-74; vice chmn. Gt. Basin Health Coun., 1973-75, Home Extension Adv. Bd., 1977-80; sec.-treas. Great Basin chpt. Nev. Employees Assn.; bd. dirs. United Way, 1970-76; vice chmn. White Pine Coun. on Alcoholism and Drug Abuse, 1975-76, chmn., 1976-77; grants author 3 yrs. Indian Child Welfare Act, originator Community Tng. Ctr. for Retarded People, 1972, Ret. Sr. Vol. Program, 1974, Nutrition Program for Sr. Citizens, 1974, Sr. Citizens Ctr., 1974, Home Repairs for Sr. Citizens, 1974, Sr. Citizens Home Assistance Program, 1977, Creative Crafters Assns., 1976, Inst. Current World Affairs, 1989, Victims of Crime, 1990; bd. dirs. Family /coalition, 1990—, Sacred Heart Parochial Sch., 1982—, dir. band, 1982—; candidate for diaconal ministry, 1982—; dir. White Pine Community Choir, 1962—, Ely Meth. Ch. Choir, 1960-84; choir dir., organist Sacred Heart Ch., 1984—. Precinct reporter ABC News 1966. Fellow Am. Coll. Musicians, Nat. Guild Piano Tchrs.; mem. NEA (life), Nat. Fedn. Ind. Bus. (dist. chair 1971-85, nat. guardian coun. 1985—, state guardian coun. 1987—), AAUW (pres. Wells br. 1957-58, pres. White Pine br. 1965-66, 86-87, 89-91, bd. dirs. 1965-87, rep. edn. 1965-67, implementation chair 1967-69, area advisor 1969-73, 89-91), Nat. Fedn. Bus. and Profl. Women (1st v.p. Ely chpt. 1965-66, pres. Ely chpt. 1966-68, 74-76, 85—, bd. dirs. Nev. chpt. 1966—, 1st v.p. Nev. Fedn. 1970-71, pres. Nev. chpt. 1972-73, nat. bd. dirs. 1972-73), Mensa (supr. testing 1965—), Delta Kappa Gamma (br. pres. 1968-72, state bd. 1967—, chpt. parliamentarian 1974-78, state 1st v.p. 19671, nat. bd. 1969-71, state parliamentarian 1971-73), White Pine Knife and Fork Club (1st v.p. 1969-70, pres. 1970-71, bd. dirs. 1979—). Home: 1280 Ave F PO Box 150457 East Ely NV 89315-0457 Office: Ely Shoshone Tribe 16 Shoshone Circle Ely NV 89301 also: 1280 Ave F East Ely NV 89315 *My mission in this life: To use to the fullest good, the talents and abilities that have been given me in order to productively help whenever and wherever the opportunity arises.*

ALDRIDGE, MARION DOUGLAS, minister; b. Savannah, Ga., Feb. 11, 1947; s. E. Carlton and Allene H. A.; m. Sarah M. Craig, Dec. 22, 1972; children: Jenna Elizabeth, Julie Rebecca. BA, Clemson (S.C.) U., 1976; MDiv, So. Bapt. Theol. Sem., Louisville, 1976, DMin, 1979. Ordained to ministry, So. Bapt. Conv., 1973. Area dir. Young Life Campaign, Ga., S.C., 1969-73; family minister First Bapt. Ch., Columbia, S.C., 1973-75; pastor Lake Dreamland Bapt. Ch., Louisville, 1975-77, First Bapt. Ch., Batesburg, S.C., 1977-84, Greenlawn Bapt. Ch., Columbia, S.C., 1984—; pres. S.C Christian Action Coun., 1990—; exec. com. Bapt. Committed to the So. Bapt. Conv., 1988-91, S.C. Bapt. Conv., 1981-84. Cons. editor Bapt. Peacemaker, 1985-89; author: The Pastor's Guidebook: A Manual for Worship, 1984, The Pastor's Guidebook: A Manual for Special Occasions, 1989; contbr. over 100 articles to religious publs. Home: 6518 Christie Rd Colubia SC 29209 Office: Greenlawn Bapt Ch 6612 Garners Ferry Rd Columbia SC 29209

ALDWORTH, THOMAS PATRICK, priest; b. Chgo., Nov. 4, 1947; s. Patrick Henry and Margaret (Shinners) A. BA in Philosophy, Quincy Coll., 1970; MDiv, Cath. Theol. Union, Chgo., 1974; MA in Counseling, La. Tech. U., 1988. Ordained priest Roman Cath. Ch., 1974. Parochial vicar St. Francis Ch., Quincy, Ill., 1974-76, St. Peter's Ch., Chgo., 1976-77, 81-83; instr. Marian Coll., Indpls., 1977; retreat dir. Alverna Retreat House, Indpls., 1977-78; campus minister Ind. U.-Purdue U., Indpls., 1978, La. Tech. U., Ruston, 1983-86; pastor St. Benedict the Black, Gramblin, La., 1986—; campus minister Grambling State U., 1986—; religious superior Franciscan Friars, Ruston, 1984-87, regional coord. La., 1986-88; chmn. Franciscan Justice and Peace Com., 1987—; vice chmn. Franciscan Pastoral Ministries Com., 1987—. Author: Shaping a Healthy Religion 1985 (Thomas More medal 1985); contbr. articles to Markings. Mem. Am. Assn. Counseling and Devel., Diocesan Dirs. Campus Ministry, Cath. Campus Ministry Assn., Nat. Fedn. Cath. Seminarians (midwest coord. 1971-72), U.S. Taekwondo Assn. Democrat. Avocation: taekwondo (2d degree black belt). Home and Office: St Benedict the Black 101 S Main St Grambling LA 71245

ALESSI, JOSEPH GABRIEL, JR., religious organization administrator; b. Phila., Nov. 6, 1946; s. Joseph Gabriel and Columbia Florida (Mancini) A.; m. Vicki Anne Smith, Dec. 22, 1973; children: Natalie Nicole, Jacqueline Gabrielle. BA in Bibl. Edn., Fla. Bible Coll., 1974. Pres., dir. Eternity, Inc., Austin, Tex., 1973—. Republican. Baptist. Avocations: motorcycling, boating, flying. Office: Eternity Inc PO Box 10998 #400 Austin TX 78766

ALEXANDER, CAMERON MADISON, minister; b. Atlanta, Feb. 12, 1932; s. Homer M. and Augusta (Hutchins) A.; m. Barbara Jackson, Nov. 25, 1954; children: Cameron Eric, Gregory Madison, Kenneth Lamont, Barbara Maria Alexander Mansfield. BA, Morehouse Coll., Atlanta, MDiv, DD (hon.), 1990; DD (hon.), United Theol. Sem., Monroe, La., 1978. Pastor Flagg Chapel Bapt. Ch., Milledgeville, Ga., New Pleasant Grove Ch., Macon, Ga., 1958-65, St. John Bapt. Ch., Savannah, Ga., 1965-69, Antioch Bapt. Ch. North, Atlanta, 1969—; chmn. bd. trustees Morehouse Sch. of Religion; bd. trustees Morehouse Sch. of Medicine, ITC; pres. Gen. Missionary Bapt. Conv. Mem. NAACP, Atlanta, 1991. Mem. SCLS. Home: 1163 Lynhurst Dr Atlanta GA 30311 Office: Antioch Bapt Ch North 540 Kennedy St NW Atlanta GA 30318

ALEXANDER, GEORGE VALENTINE, minister; b. Lancaster, Pa., July 12, 1936; s. George Ashworth and Miriam Lenia (Clark) A.; m. Carol Ann Murphy, May 24, 1958; 1 child, James Mark. BS, Millersville State Coll., 1960; MDiv., United Theol. Sem., 1963; MA, NYU, 1979; M of Sacred Theology, Lancaster Theol. Sem., 1980. Ordained minister Am. Bapt. Chs., 1963. Pastor Grace E.U.B. Ch., Cressona, Pa., 1963-69, 1st Bapt. Ch., Freeport, N.Y., 1969-72, North Fork Bapt. Ch., Mattituck, N.Y., 1972-78; assoc. pastor 1st Bapt. Ch., Lancaster, Pa., 1978-80; pastor 1st Bapt. Ch., Scottdale, Pa., 1980-84, Salem, Ohio, 1984-88; pastor United Ch. of Penacook, N.H., 1990—; chaplain Freeport (N.Y.) Fire Dept., 1971-72, Salem (Ohio) Fire Dept., 1986-90, Penacook Resque Squad, 1991—; bd. mgrs. Camp Carmel, 1981-84. Leadership positions Boy Scouts of Am., 1946—. Comdr. USNR, 1971—. Recipient Good Shepherd award Assn. Bapts. for Scouting, 1983. Mem. Mins. Coun. Am. Bapt. Chs. Republican. Home: 10 Eel St Penacook NH 03303 Office: United Church of Penacook 21 Merrimack St Penacook NH 03303

ALEXANDER, HENRY ALAN, academic affairs dean; b. Berkeley, Calif., Aug. 24, 1953; s. Ernest and Frances (Connelley) A.; m. Shelley Tornheim, Aug. 24, 1975; children: Aliza, Yonina, Yehuda. AB in Philosophy summa cum laude, UCLA, 1976; BA in Philosophies of Judaism, U. Judaism, 1977; MA in Judaic Studies, The Jewish Theol. Sem. Am., 1982; EdS in Evaluation Studies, Stanford U., 1982, PhD in Edn. and Humanities, 1985. Ordained rabbi, 1982. Instr. philosophy and edn. U. Judaism, L.A., 1983-85, asst. prof., 1985-88, assoc. prof. philosophy and edn., 1988—, from acad. coord. to dean Lee Coll., 1984—, dean acad. affairs, 1990—; program dir. Camp Young Judaea, St. Helena, Calif., summer 1973; ednl. activities coord. Hashachar/Young Judaea, L.A., 1972-74; dir. informal edn. Herzl High Sch., L.A., 1976-77; day camp dir. Encino, Calif., summer 1976; staff tng. coord. Camp Ramah in the Berkshires, summer 1981; dir. leadership devel. The Jewish Theol. Sem. Am., 1980-82; prof. edn. in residence, dir. Mador Leadership Tng. Program Camp Ramah in Calif., summers 1984, 85, prof. in residence, summers 1986, 87; vis. scholar The Hebrew U. of Jerusalem, 1982-83; vis. scholar, lectr. Sch. Edn. UCLA, 1989—; dir. Lee Coll. U. Judaism, 1986-89; editor: Religious Education, 1991—. Reviewer jour. Curriculum Inquiry, 1989, The Jour. of Moral Edn., 1987-88; editor Religious Edn., 1991—; contbr. chpts. to books and articles to profl. jours. Rsch. cons. Commn. on Jewish Edn. in N.Am., 1989, Commn. Jewish Future Jewish Fedn. Coun., L.A., 1988-89; curriculum cons. Wexner Found. Project Stanford U., 1989; trustee Jewish Educators Assembly, 1989—; ednl. dir. Congregation Beth Sholom, San Francisco, 1978-80; chair leadership devel. program Temple Beth Am. L.A., 1986—; evaluation cons. Hollywood Temple Beth El, L.A., 1985, Bur. Jewish Edn., Sacramento, 1985. Mem. ASCD, Am. Conf. Acad. Deans, Am. Ednl. Rsch. Assn., Am. Assn. Higher Edn., Am. Phils. Assn., Assn. Philosophy Education, Assn. Jewish Studies, Calif. Assn. Philosophy Edn. (pres. 1989-91), Farwestern Philosophy Edn. Soc., Moral Edn. Assn., Coalition for Advancement of Jewish Edn., Jewish Edn. Rsch. Network, Jewish Educators Assembly, Nat. Soc. for Study of Edn., Philosophy Edn. Soc. (program chair 1991—), Rabbinical Assembly. Office: U Judaism 15600 Mulholland Dr Los Angeles CA 90077

ALEXANDER, SISTER IRENE, minister; b. Washington, July 24, 1925; d. Stanford Tamlage and Martha Naomi (Beattie) A. BEd, Duquesne U., Pitts., 1967; MRE, LaSalle Coll., Phila., 1974; postgrad., Va. Communwealth U., Richmond, 1980. Joined Benedictine Sisters, Roman Cath. Ch. Founder Pax Christi No. Va., Arlington, 1984—; minister religious edn. and social minister Our Lady Queen of Peace, Arlington, 1989—; vol. Hospice, Arlington, 1987-91; mem. Global Horizon Team, Arlington, 1990—; bd. dirs. Cath. for Housing, Arlington, 1989-91; coord. Peace Camp for Children, Arlington, 1990, Pax Christi, Bristou, Va., 1987; mem. N.Am. Bd. for East-West Dialogue, 1989-91. Recipient Social Justice award Cath. Charities, Arlington, 1991. Office: Our Lady Queen of Peace Ch 2700 S 19th St Arlington VA 22204

ALEXANDER, JOSEPH JOHN MURPHY, priest, educator; b. Lafayette, La., Aug. 20, 1933; s. Frederick O. and Elizabeth (Rubin) A. BL in Music, St. John U., Collegeville, Minn., 1957; BA, Western Ky. U., 1968; MDiv, St. Meinrad (Ind.) Sem., 1974; MA, Ind. U., 1977, PhD in Speech Communication, 1980; postgrad., Cath. U. Am., 1983-84. Joined Order St. Benedict, 1955, ordained priest, 1973. Choir master, organist St. Mark's Monastery, South Union, Ky., 1955—, infirmarian, 1955—, trustee, 1958—; mem. faculty St. Maur Sem. and High Sch., 1955-66; asst. chaplain St. Thomas Aquinas Newman Ctr., Western Ky. U., 1966-70, faculty dept. speech communication, 1984; asst. chaplain Bowling Green, Ky., 1974; prof. homiletics, liturgy and liturgical law and music St. Mark's Sch. Theology, South Union, 1974-83, dean students and student affairs, vice rector, 1975-77, vice rector, 1975-77; sub-prior St. Mark's Priory, South Union, 1975-77, prior, 1977-83; adminstr. Wisdom Cath. Studies Ctr. U. Southwestern La., Lafayette, 1984—; assoc. St. Anthony Padua Ch., Eunice, La., 1988—; tchr. religion and music edn. St. Edmund High Sch., Eunice, 1988—; mem. area ministry Barren River Area Cath. Enterprise, Diocese Owensboro, Ky., 1974—, Diocese Lafayette, 1987; tchr. Confrat. Christian Doctrine secondary and elem. schs., Russellville, Ky.-Bowling Green area, Religious Edn. St. Thomas More High Sch., Lafayetter, 1985-86, 1988—; prin., adminstr. Holy Rosary Inst., Lafayette, 1986-88; mem. Lafayette Diocese Vocation Team; asst. in campus ministry La. State U., Eunice, 1988—. Active Shaker Pageant Festival, 1966-72, dir., 1967; trustee Order St. Benedict; mem. Ky. Humanities Coun., 1982-84. Mem. St. Meinrad Sch. Theology, Western Ky. U., Ind. U. alumni assns., Speech Communication Assn., So. Speech Communication Assn., Liturgical Conf., Black Cath. Clergy Caucus, Nat. Cath. Music Assn., Ky. Music Educators Assn., Ky. Bluegrass Music Assn. Address: St Anthony of Padua Ch PO Box 31 Eunice LA 70535

ALEXANDER, PAUL HARRISON, minister; b. Carolyn, N.Y., Jan. 29, 1933; s. Fred Augustus and Anne Elizabeth (Shattuck) A.; m. Lorraine Mae Johnson, Aug. 24, 1956; children: Junia, Charysse, Deann, Gregory. BA, Bob Jones U., 1955; BD, Covenant Theol. Sem., St. Louis, 1958. Ordained to ministry Presbyn. Ch. in Am., 1958. Sr. pastor Westminster Presbyn. Ch., Huntsville, Ala., 1958—; trustee Covenant Theol. Sem., 1965-82; moderator Nat. Synod Ref. Presbyn. Ch., 1975; trustee, mem. Christian edn. com. and publs. com. Presbyn. Ch. in Am., Atlanta, 1984-88; founder Westminster Christian Acad. Republican. Office: Westminster Presbyn Ch 1400 Evangel Dr Huntsville AL 35816

ALEXANDER, RALPH HOLLAND, religion educator, author; b. Tyler, Tex., Sept. 3, 1936; s. Joe Barkley and Virginia Louise (Kinard) A.; m. Myrna Jean Campbell, June 20, 1964; children—David Campbell, Christina Louise, Jonathan Barkley. A.B., Rice U., 1959; Th.M., Dallas Theol. Sem., 1963, Th.D., 1968. Ordained to ministry Conservative Baptist Ch., 1963. Instr. So. Bible Sch., Dallas, 1963-64, 65-66; asst. prof. Wheaton Coll., Ill., 1966-72; prof. Hebrew scriptures Western Conservative Bapt. Sem., Portland, Oreg., 1972—. Author: Ezekiel, 1986, articles in field. Active David Douglas Citizens' Adv. Com., Portland, 1979-82. Served to 1st lt., chaplain, U.S. Army, 1959-67. Recipient Henry C. Theissen award, Dallas Theol. Sem., 1963; Fulbright grantee, Israel, 1964-65; Israel govt. scholar, 1964-65. Mem. Archaeol. Inst. Am., Am. Schs. Oriental Research, Soc. Bibl. Lit., Nat. Assn. Hebrew Profs., Evang. Theol. Soc., Near East Archaeol. Soc. (dir. Chgo. 1974—). Republican. Home: 4815 SE 140th Ave Portland OR 97236 Office: Western Conservative Bapt Sem 5511 SE Hawthorne Blvd Portland OR 97215

ALEXANDER, ROBERT WILLIAM, lay worker; b. Phila., May 1, 1967; s. William Joseph and Carolyn Welch A.; m. Rebecca Wagner, Aug. 4, 1990. BS in Mech. Engring., U. Del., 1989. Engr. in tng., Del. Dir. youth Union Chapel by the Sea, Ocean City, N.J., 1985, 86; mem. staff Penn Grad. Fellowship, Intervarsity Christian Fellowship, Phila., 1991—; mech. engr. United Engrs. & Constructors, Phila., 1989—. Author: AIDS - A Christian Response, 1987; author mus. play: Luke: Encounters with the Master, 1991; inventor blanket, 1991.

ALEXANDER, THOMAS CRAIG, minister, religion educator; b. Selmer, Tenn., Dec. 15, 1947; s. Thomas Russell and Mary Louoise (Carothers) A.; m. Phyllis Marlene Smith; children: Rachel Elizabeth, Isaac Thomas, Hannah Carol. AA, Freed-Hardeman Coll., 1967; BA, David-Lipscomb Coll., 1969; MA, ThM, Harding Grad. Sch., 1971, 73; PhD, Emory U., 1990. Ordained to ministry Ch. of Christ. Youth min. Getwell Ch. of Christ, Memphis, 1969-72; pulpit min. Providence Rd. Ch. of Christ, Charlotte, N.C., 1972-78; assoc. prof. Bible Harding U., Searcy, Ark., 1978—. Home: 8 Baker Dr Searcy AR 72143 Office: Harding U Sta A Searcy AR 72143

ALEXANDER, TIMOTHY L., minister; b. Knoxville, Sept. 4, 1944; s. Irwin and Edna Opal (Brown) A.; m. George Ann Chesney, Dec. 21, 1962; children: Aminda Ann, Julianna, Timothy Edwin, Molly Suzanna. BA, S.W. Bapt. Coll., 1975; DDiv, Internat. Bible Inst. & Sem., Orlando, Fla., 1984. Ordained to ministry, So. Bapt. Conv. Pastor Colomokee Bapt. Ch., Blakely, Ga., 1971-72, First Bapt. Ch., Crocker, Mo., 1973-74; sr. pastor Towering Oaks Bapt. Ch., Greenville, Tenn., 1975-85, Florence (Ky.) Bapt. Ch., 1985—; mem. pastoral adv. com. Cumberland Coll., Williamsburg, Ky., 1990—; bd. dirs. Bapt. Convalescent Ctr., Newport, Ky., 1990-91; com. on nominations Ky. Bapt. Conv., Louisville, 1989-91. Contbr. articles to profl. jours. Gov.'s rep. Group Study Exchange with Tanzania, E. Africa, 1991. Republican. Home: 11069 Paddock Dr Walton KY 41094 Office: Florence Bapt Ch 283 Main St Florence KY 41042

ALEXANDER, VERNELL, minister; b. Jacksonville, Tex., Aug. 20, 1940; s. Charlie and Nommie (Kennedy) A.; m. Sue Johnson, Apr. 25, 1962; children: Gregory, Ramona, Norman Craig. Ordained to ministry Christian Ch. (Disciples of Christ), 1967. Machine operator Trance C.A.C., Tyler, Tex., 1966—; deacon Christian Ch. (Disciples of Christ), Jacksonville, 1967-70, elder, 1971-78, min., 1978—; with Evangelistic Field, 1985-88; pastor Christian Ch., Kilgore, TEx., 1988—. Coord. Title I Jacksonville Sch. System, 198-83; pres. Jacksonville Sch. Reunion Com., 1985-88; mem. United Way Com., 1980-90 (plaque). Home: Rte 6 1009 Pierce Ln Jacksonville TX 75766

ALEXIOU, MARGARET BEATRICE, Greek studies educator; b. Birmingham, Eng., Mar. 25, 1939; d. George Derwent and Katharine Fraser (Stewart) Thomson; m. Christos Dimitriou Alexiou, July 14, 1961 (div. 1981); children: Dimitris George, Pavlos Michael. BA with honors, U. Cambridge, Eng., 1961, MA, 1964, PhD, 1967. Lectr. in Byzantine and Modern Greek U. Birmingham, 1964-76, sr. lectr., 1976-85; George Seferis prof. Modern Greek Studies Harvard U., Cambridge, Mass., 1986—. Author: The Ritual Lament, 1974; editor: (book) The Text and Its Margins, 1985; mem. editorial bd. Byzantine and Modern Greek Studies, 1976-85, Jour. Modern Greek Studies, 1986—; contbr. articles to profl. jours. Mem. Modern Greek Studies Assn. (mem. exec. com. 1986—), Newnham Coll. Alumni (assoc.). Avocations: walking, cooking, reading, swimming. Office:

Harvard U Dept Modern Greek Studies 319 Boylston Hall Cambridge MA 02138

ALFORD, KENNETH LEON, minister; b. Newport, Wash., Feb. 12, 1959; s. Calvin Leon and Ellen Kay (Lauzon) A.; m. Debra Kay Taylor, Dec. 20, 1980; children: Kimberly, David, Kelli. BA in Comprehensive Bible, Cedarville (Ohio) Coll., 1984; MA in Bibl. Studies, N.W. Bapt. Sem., Tacoma, Wash., 1989. Ordained to ministry Bapt. Ch., 1989. Min. evangelism Puyallup (Wash.) Regular Bapt. Ch., 1980-81; itinerant min. Ohio, Ind., 1981-84; 1st asst. pastor Community Bapt. Ch., Puyallup, 1984-91; sr. pastor 1st Bapt. Ch., Othello, Wash., 1991—; vice chmn. bd. Tacoma Bapt. Schs., 1985-87, chmn. bd., 1987-90; exec. sec. Tacoma Area Fellowhsip of Youth, 1984-86. Wrestling coach Puyallup High Sch., 1985-91. With U.S. Army, 1977-80. Jimmy O'Quin Evang. grantee Cedarville Coll., 1984, Alumni scholar, 1983. Republican. Office: 1st Bapt Ch 705 E Larch Othello WA 99344

ALFORD, PAUL LEGARE, college and religious foundation administrator; b. Tampa, Fla., Mar. 16, 1930; s. Louis Emerson and Mary (Alderman) A.; m. Grace Alford, Dec. 29,1951; children: Rebecca Grace, Sharon Ann. Student, U. Fla., 1947; diploma, Nyack Coll., 1948-51; DD (hon.), Trinity Coll., 1964, Asbury Coll., 1978; LLD (hon.), Toccoa Falls Coll., 1976. Supt. Ind. Life, Columbus, Ga., 1951-53; founding pastor Christian & Missionary Alliance, Columbus, 1951-56; missionary Ecuador, 1956-60; dir. Spanish ministries Christian Missionary Alliance, Nyack, N.Y., 1960-70; dist. supt. Christian & Missionary Alliance, Orlando, Fla., 1970-79, v.p., 1976-86; pres. Toccoa Falls (Ga.) Coll., 1979—; chmn. DeLand (Fla.) Retirement Bd., 1970-79; bd. mgrs. Christian & Missionary Alliance, Nyack, N.Y., 1973—, v.p., 1976-86; trustee Asbury Coll., Wilmore, Ky.; chmn. bd. dirs. Lake Swan Conf. Grounds, Melrose, Fla.; bd. dirs. Shell Point Village, Ft. Myers, Fla.; del. Congress on Edn., 1971, 86. Mem. editorial bd. New King James Bible; producer daily radio broadcast, 1975—. Mem. leadership council Stephens County, Toccoa, 1982—; bd. dirs. Salvation Army, Toccoa, 1986—. Served with USNR, 1947-54. Mem. Am. Assn. Bible Colls. (bd. dirs. 1987—), So. Assn. Colls. and Schs. (evaluation com.), Rotary. Republican. Avocations: golf, tennis. Home: 380 Carlyle Circle Toccoa Falls GA 30598 Office: Toccoa Falls Coll Chapel Dr Toccoa Falls GA 30598

ALGER, DAVID TOWNLEY, religious organization director; b. Warsaw, N.Y., June 4, 1945; s. Clifton and Dorothy (Townley) A.; m. Sarah Ileene Alger, Aug. 17, 1968; 1 child, Hannah Ileene. BA, Coll. of Wooster, 1967; MSW, U. Ill., Chgo., 1971; MDiv, McCormick Theol. Sem., Chgo., 1971. Ordained to ministry Presbyn. Ch. (U.S.A.). Assoc. pastor 1st Presbyn. Ch., Grand Forks, N.D., 1971-75; pastor Riverside Presbyn. Ch., Clinton, Iowa, 1975-79; exec. dir. Associated Ministries, Tacoma, 1980—; mem. Adv. Coun. on Ch. and Soc., United Presbyn. Ch. in U.S.A., 1976-82, mem. Coun. on Ch. and Race, 1981-82; chair mission strategy and evangelism com. Olympia (Wash.) Presbytery, 1982-88; accredited visitor World Coun. of Chs., 1983; del., planner Pacific Ecumenical Forum, Hilo, Hawaii, 1990. Mem. Clinton City Coun., 1978-80; pres. Tacoma Community House Bd., 1980-88; vice-chair Tacoma Housing Com., 1991—. Recipient key to city City of Clinton, 1979, St. Francis award Franciscan Found., 1989, Disting. Citizen award Tacoma chpt. Rotary, 1989. Mem. Presbyn. Health, Edn. and Welfare Assn., Nat. Assn. Ecumenical Staff, Wash. Assn. Chs. (bd. dirs. 1980—, treas. 1991—). Democrat. Home: 4510 N Defiance Tacoma WA 98407 Office: Associated Ministries 1224 South I St Tacoma WA 98405

ALHO, SISTER BONNIE KATHLEEN, religion educator; b. Superior, Wis., Feb. 6, 1942; d. Jack Wayne and Agnes (Osman) A. BS in Elem. Edn., Mt. Senario Coll., Ladysmith, Wis., 1970; MRE, St. Thomas U., Houston, 1978. Joined Order Servants of Mary, Roman Cath. Ch., 1959. Kindergarten tchr. St. Domitilla's Sch., Hillside, Ill., 1961-62; 3rd grade tchr. Annunciata, Chgo., 1962-67; 2nd grade tchr. St. Rose of Lima Sch., St. Paul, 1967-71; 1st grade tchr. St. Joseph's Sch., Carteret, N.J., 1971-72; mem. staff Diocese of Superior, Cameron, Wis., 1972-81; dir. religious edn. Our Lady of Sorrows, Ladysmith, 1981—; mem. steering com. Wis. Dirs. of Religious Edn., State of Wis., 1979, bd. com. mem. 1987-90; bd. dirs. deacons com. Diocese of Superior, 1983-89, chair. Summit Bd., 1986-89, initiated Marriage Encounter; active in formation of retreat programs for teens; co-chair., treas. Area Clergy Assn., Ladysmith, 1991—. Recipient Outstanding Leadership in Catechetical Ministry award Diocese of Superior, Mt. Telemark, Wis., 1988. Mem. Wis. Dirs. Religious Edn. (bd. dirs. 1987-89). Home: 500 E 2nd St S Ladysmith WI 54848 Office: Our Lady of Sorrows 105 Washington Ladysmith WI 54848 *It has been said "For all that has been Thanks...For all that will be Yes." It is important to me to approach life in this way.*

ALI, H. A. MUKTI, religion consultant; b. Central Java, 1923; married; 3 children. Studied in Indonesia, Pakistan, Can. Vice-chancellor IAIN Sunan Kalijaga, Yogjakarta, 1964-71; minister of religious affairs Govt. Indonesia, 1971-78; mem. Sup. Adv. Council, Jakarta, Indonesia, 1978-83; mem. sci. com. on Islamic culture UNESCO, 1979—; mem. Akademi Jakarta, 1979—; mem. adv. bd. Hijra coun. on writing 100 books on Islam Govt. Pakistan, 1985—. Mem. Nat. Rsch. Coun. Author: Modernization of Islamic Schools; Comparative Religion, its Method and System; Religian and Development in Indonesia, others. Home: Sagan GKI/100, Yogyakarta Indonesia Office: Iain Sunan Kalijaga, Yogyakarta Indonesia

ALLABY, STANLEY REYNOLDS, clergyman; b. Providence, Dec. 28, 1931; s. Edwin T. and Hope (Swift) A.; m. Marion Arlene Johnson, Dec. 18, 1954; children—Norman R., Darlene R., Kimberly A., Stephen R. A.B., Gordon Coll., 1953; M.Div., Gordon Conwell Sem., 1956; D.D., Barrington (R.I.) Coll., 1977; D.Min., Westminster Theol. Sem., 1978. Ordained to ministry, 1956; pastor Black Rock Conglist. Ch., Fairfield, Conn., 1956—; dir. Sudan Interior Mission, N.J., 1970—; chmn. bd. Sudan Interior Mission, 1985—, vice chmn. internat. bd. govs., 1985-90; vice chmn. Billy Graham New Haven Crusade, 1982; exec. com. Billy Graham Hartford Crusade, 1985; Ockenga lectr. Gordon-Conway Sem., 1983. Bd. dirs. United Neighbors for Self Devel., Bridgeport, Conn., 1963-64, Christian Freedom Found., 1960-70, Operation Hope, Fairfield, 1986—; trustee Gordon Coll., Wenham, Mass., 1965-69, 77-81, Gordon Div. Sch., 1965-69. Recipient George Washington honor medal Freedoms Found., 1968, 69; Alumnus-of-Year award Gordon Coll., 1976. Mem. Gordon Coll. Alumni Assn. (past pres.), Nat. Assn. Evangelicals (dir. 1974—, exec. com. 1980-82, nat. conv. coordinator 1981-82, (chmn. resolutions com. 1982-83), Bridgeport Pastors Assn. (past pres.), Greater Bridgeport Fellowship Evangelicals (past pres.). Home: 1371 Bronson Rd Fairfield CT 06430 Office: Black Rock Conglist Ch 3685 Black Rock Turnpike Fairfield CT 06430

ALLAIN, LEON GREGORY, architect; b. New Orleans, Nov. 17, 1924; s. George Augustine and Cecile (Warnick) A.; m. Gloria Grace Dinvaut, Sept. 4, 1952; children: Reneé, Diane. BArch, U. Mich., 1949. Ordained to ministry Roman Cath. Ch. as deacon, 1982; registered architect, Ga., Ala., La., Tex., N.C., S.C., N.Y., Mich. Pvt. practice New Orleans, 1949-53; architect Parsons, Brinkerhoff, Hall & MacDonald, N.Y.C., 1953-56, Mayer, Whittlesey & Glass, N.Y.C., 1956-57, Skidmore, Owings & Merrill, N.Y.C., 1957-58, Edward C. Miller, Architect, Atlanta, 1958-60; ptnr. Miller & Allain, Architects, Atlanta, 1960-67; prin., owner Allain and Assocs., Inc., Atlanta, 1967—. 1st lt. U.S. Army, 1943-46, PTO. Recipient Atlanta Urban Design Commn. award of excellence for restoration of Graves Hall, Morehouse Coll., 1983. Mem. AIA, NAACP (life), Nat. Orgn. Minority Architects, Nat. Coun. Archtl. Registration Bds. (cert.). Avocations: traveling, aviation. *Family is the foundation of human life and the development of morals and character to enrich our spiritual life.*

ALLAN, BRIAN SHANE, religious organization official, minister, youth director; b. Muncie, Ind., Sept. 27, 1967; s. Geoffrey and Marian (Botu) A.; m. Laura Ann Nourse, Aug. 5, 1989. Student, Wayne State U., 1985-87, Coll. of Du Page, 1987-88, U. Ill., Chgo., 1988-89. Songster chaplain, bandsman Salvation Army, Detroit, 1983-87; summer day camp leader Salvation Army, Norridge, Ill., 1988; dir. Salvation Army, Oakbrook, Ill., 1989, youth chorus leader, 1987-88; youth dir. Salvation Army, Rockford, Ill., 1989—; bandsman staff band Salvation Army, Chgo., 1987—. Contbr. articles to profl. jours. Phillip McCraten scholar Wayne State U., 1985-86. Mem. Amnesty Internat., Rotary Internat. Home: 246 Evelyn Ave # 4 Loves Park IL 61111 Office: The Salvation Army 500 S Rockford Ave Rockford IL 61104

ALLAN, HUGH JAMES PEARSON, bishop; b. Winnipeg, Man., Can., Aug. 7, 1928; s. Hugh Blomfield and Agnes Dorothy (Pearson) A.; m. Beverley Edith Baker, Sept. 10, 1955; children: Douglas, Mary, Barbara, Jennifer. L.Th., St. John's Coll., Winnipeg, 1956, D.D. (hon.), 1974; B.A., U. Man., 1957. Ordained to ministry Anglican Ch., as deacon, 1954, as priest, 1955. Asst. St. Aidan's Ch., Winnipeg, 1954, All Saints Ch., Winnipeg, 1955; incumbent Peguis Indian Res., Man., 1956-59; rector St. Mark's Ch., Winnipeg, 1960-68, St. Stephen's Ch., Swift Current, Sask., 1968-70, St. Paul's Cathedral, Regina, Sask.; dean Diocese of Qu'Appelle, Regina, 1970-74; bishop Diocese of Keewatin, Kenora, Ont., Can., 1974—. Office: Box 118, Kenora, ON Canada P9N 3X1

ALLBRITTON, CLIFF, editor; b. Aransas Pass, Tex., Aug. 19, 1931. Editor family ministry dept. Bapt. Sunday Sch. Bd., Nashville, 1979—; pres. Successful Living Inst., Nashville, 1991—. Address: 500 Plantation Ct S-2 Nashville TN 37221

ALLEE, C. RAMON, theologian, educator, clergyman; b. San Francisco, Jan. 12, 1931; s. Clyde Irvin Allee and Daisy Maeree Gifford. B.A., San Francisco State Coll. Ordained to ministry Eastern Catholic Apostolic Ch., 1960. Pastor Eastern Catholic Apostolic Ch., Los Angeles, 1960-76; pastor, theologian, educator James the Just Eastern Catholic Apostolic Ch, Long Beach, Calif., 1977—. Author jour. Spiritual Outlook, 1977-82. Mem. Am. Acad. Religion, Soc. Bibl. Lit. Democrat. Office: James the Just Eastern Cath Apostolic Ch 1542 E 7th St Long Beach CA 90813

ALLEN, BRADFORD JON, music minister, administrator; b. Ellsworth AFB, S.D., May 30, 1960; s. Howell Franklin and Ola J. (Davis) A.; m. Allyson Jane Andreone, Jun. 18, 1988. MusB, Baylor U., 1984; MusM, Southwestern Bapt. Theol. Sem., 1987. Youth min. Willow Park Bapt. Ch., Houston, Tex., 1980; assc. youth min. First Bapt. Ch., Houston, Tex., 1981; music min. First Bapt. Ch., Crawford, Tex., 1982-84; assc. music min. First Bapt. Ch., Waco, Tex., 1986-87; music min. First Bapt. Ch., Windermere, Fla., 1988—. Composer religious mus. Behold the Lamb. Mem. Tex. Bapt. Music Conf., Fla. Bapt. Ch. Music Conf., Natl. Assc. Ch. Bus. Adminstrn. Baptist. Home: PO Box 1602 Windermere FL 34786 Office: First Baptist Ch Windermere PO Box 250 300 N Main Windermere FL 34786

ALLEN, CRAWFORD LEONARD, religion educator; b. Manhatten, Kans., June 19, 1952; s. Crawford William and Carolyn (Odom) A.; m. Holly Jeanene Catterton, Apr. 7, 1972; children: David, Daniel, Bethany. BA, Harding U., 1973; MA in Religion, Harding Grad. Sch. Religion, 1975; PhD, U. Iowa, 1984. Asst. prof. Abilene (Tex.) Christian U., 1982-89, assoc. prof., 1989—; lectr., Europe, Japan. Co-author: Illusions of Innocence, 1988, The Worldly Church, 1988, Discovering Out Roots, 1988; author: The Cruciform Church, 1990; also articles; assoc. editor Restoration Quar., 1988—. Pres. bd. dirs. Pregnancy Counseling Svc., Abilene, 1986—. Named Honors Prof. of Yr. Abilene Christian U., 1987-88; grantee Cullen Found., 1984-90. Mem. Am. Acad. Religion, Am. Soc. Ch. History, Disciples of Christ Hist. Soc. Democrat. Mem. Chs. of Christ. Avocations: writing, gardening. Office: Abilene Christian U Box 8401 Abilene TX 79699

ALLEN, DANIEL ROSS, rabbi, religious organization administrator; b. Reno, Nev., Feb. 13, 1949; s. Harry Samuel and Anna (Arbitman) A.; m. Mary Lou Frishberg, June 15, 1972; children: Sarah, Uri, Noah. BA, U. Nebr., 1972; M Hebrew Letters, Hebrew Union Coll., 1974. Ordained rabbi, 1976. Exec. dir. Mich. State U. Hillel, 1976-84, Atlanta Hillel, 1981-84; rabbi Shaare Zion, Sioux City, Iowa, 1984-86; dir. young leadership United Jewish Appeal, N.Y.C., 1986-88; asst. exec. vice chmn. United Israel Appeal, N.Y.C., 1988—. Bd. dirs. Hospitality House, Atlanta, 1981-84; chmn. Prairie Pac, Sioux City, 1984-86. Mem. Rabbinical Assembly, Cen. Conf. Am. Rabbis, Assn. Jewish Community Orgnl. Profls. Home: 406 Lenox Pl South Orange NJ 07079 Office: United Israel Appeal 110 E 59th St New York NY 10022

ALLEN, DAVID SEARLES, clergyman; b. Phila., Apr. 11, 1934; s. Ralph Ethan and Anna Jessine (Olsen) A.; m. Wilma Irene Gifford, Aug. 9, 1957; children—Wilma Lee, David, Donna, John, Timothy, Daniel Mark. Student Phila. Coll. Bible, 1969-70, Wis. State U., 1970-71, Maranatha Baptist Bible Coll., 1971-74, Prim Methodist Sch. Theology, summers 1970-74, Evang. Ch. Alliance, 1975—. Ordained to ministry Evang. Ch. Alliance. Pastor Prim Meth. Ch., Ridgeway, Wis., 1970-75, Wesleyan Chapel, Dodgeville, Wis., 1978-81, Pilgrim Wesleyan Ch., Hannibal, Mo., 1981-84, Bethel Wesleyan Ch., Harrisburg, Pa., 1984—. Served to sgt. USMC, 1957-59. Republican. Home: 3633 N 2d St Harrisburg PA 17110 Office: Bethel Wesleyan Ch 4100 N 6th St Harrisburg PA 17110

ALLEN, DAVID WATSON, pastor; b. Shreveport, La., July 14, 1956; s. Walter Leroy and Anna Jean (Watson) A.; m. Debbie Lynn Parkes, Mar. 3, 1984; children: Jonathan Parkes, Joshua David. BA, Blue Mountain Coll., 1978; Mdiv., S.W. Bapt. Theol. Sem., 1981. Assoc. pastor 1st Bapt. Ch., Edgewood, Tex., 1980-81, 2d Bapt. Ch., Indianolla, Mo., 1981; pastor Moss Hill Bapt. Mission, New Albany, Mo., 1981-84, Shuqualak (Mo.) Bapt. Ch., 1984-87, Shilo Bapt. Ch., Ralph, Ala., 1987—. Chair Tuscaloosa (Ala.) County Prolife Coalition, 1990-91; mem. Tuscaloosa Rep. exec. com., 1990-91. 1st lt. Ala. Army N.G., 1990—. Home: Rte 1 Box 191 Ralph AL 35480 Office: Shiloh Bapt Ch Rte 1 Box 191 Ralph AL 35480

ALLEN, DEBORAH LEAH, minister; b. Ft. Wayne, Ind., Aug. 3, 1953; d. Ronnell L. and Virginia (Young) A. B of Religious Edn., Great Lakes Bible Coll., Lansing, Mich., 1976; M of Religious Edn., Cin. Bible Seminary, 1987. Ordained to ministry Ch. of Christ, 1985. Dir. Christian edn. North Highlands Ch. of Christ, Ft. Wayne, 1976-80, Meadow Park Ch. of Christ, Rochester, Minn., 1980-83, First Christian Ch., Columbus, Ind., 1984-88, Worthington (Ohio) Christian Ch., 1988—; speaker retreats and tchr. tng. seminars. Contbr. articles to profl. jours. Mem. Nat. Right to Life, 1980—; vol./tutor kindergarten classroom, Tree of Life Christian Sch., Columbus. Recipient Estral award scholarship Eastern Star, Ind., 1983-86. Mem. Fellowship of Christian Educators, Profl. Assn. Christian Educators, Great Lakes Bible Coll. Alumni Assn. (sec. 1977-80). Office: Worthington Christian Ch 8145 North High St Worthington OH 43235 *God's gift of children is a priceless treasure that deserves the secular and spiritual world's finest. I am committed to excellence for our children's spiritual needs.*

ALLEN, DESI WAYNE, clergyman; b. London, Ky., June 13, 1954; s. Ellis and Marion Belle (Turner) A.; m. Virginia Sue Kidd, Oct. 6, 1973 (dec. July 1978); 1 child, Heather; m. Joanne Lentz, Nov. 25, 1978; children: Desha, Paige. Student, Tide Water Community Coll., 1990, Lee Coll., 1990-91. Ordained to ministry Pentecostal Ch., 1989. Evangelist Ind. Pentecostal Ch., 1973-75; pastor Ind. Pentecostal Ch., Couch, Mo., 1975-77, Ind. Holiness Ch., Willits, Calif., 1978-79; missionary evangelist Ind. Pentecostal Ch., U.S.A., Mexico, India, 1979-89; pastor Internat. Pentecostal Ch. of Christ, Virginia Beach, Va., 1989—, dist. bd. mem., 1990-91; bd. mem. Nat. Com. Evangelism and Edn., London, Ohio, 1990-91. Editor New Life Challenge, 1976; contbg. editor Theology in Thought, 1979-81. Mem. Lakewood Civic League, Virginia Beach, 1991. Republican. Office: Pentecostal Ch of Christ 501 15th St Virginia Beach VA 23451

ALLEN, DIOGENES, clergyman, philosophy educator; b. Lexington, Ky., Oct. 17, 1932; m. Jane Mary Billing, Sept. 8, 1958; children: Mary, George, John, Timothy. B.A. with high distinction, U. Ky., 1954; postgrad., Princeton U., 1954-55; B.A. with honors, Oxford U., 1957, M.A., 1961; B.D., Yale U., 1959, Ph.D., 1965. Ordained to ministry Presbyterian Ch., 1959. Minister Windham Presbyn. Ch., N.H., 1958-61; asst. prof. York U., Toronto, Ont., Can., 1964-66, assoc. prof. philosophy, 1966-67; assoc. prof. Princeton Theol. Sem., N.J., 1967-74, prof., 1974—, Stuart prof. philosophy, 1981—. Author: The Reasonableness of Faith, 1968, Finding Our Father, 1974, reissued under title The Path to Perfect Love, 1992, Between Two Worlds, 1978, reissued under title Temptation, 1985, Traces of God, 1981, Three Outsiders: Pascal, Kierkegaard and S. Weil, 1983, Mechanical Explanations and Their Relation to the Ultimate Origin of the Universe According to Leibniz, 1983, Philosophy for Understanding Theology, 1985, Love, 1987, Christian Belief in a Postmodern World, 1989, Quest, 1990; editor: Theodicy (Leibniz), 1966. Rhodes scholar, 1955-57, 63-64; fellow Rockefeller, 1962-64, Ctr. Theol. Inquiry, Princeton, 1985-88, Adv. Bd. Ctr. Theol. Inquiry, 1988—. Mem. Soc. Christian Philosophers (bd. dirs.), Am. Weil Soc. (bd. dirs.), Leibniz Gellschaft, N.J. Com. for the Humanities, Phi Beta Kappa. Home: 133 Cedar Ln Princeton NJ 08542 Office: Princeton Theol Seminary Princeton NJ 08542 *In my life I have found there are many people who are glad to encourage and help another person in the pursuit of worthwhile tasks.*

ALLEN, EDGAR FREDRICK, minister; b. Lewis, Ind., Oct. 22, 1927; s. Walter Glen and Mary Elizabeth (Clark) A.; m. Phyllis Elaine Feltz, May 15, 1949; children: Judith Lorraine Allen Lund, Karen Elaine Allen Curtis. Student, Notre Dame Coll., 1947-50, Berean Bible Coll., Springfield, Mo., 1953-58. Ordained to ministry Assemblies of God, 1957. Pastor 1st Assembly of God, Bremen, Ind., 1952, Logansport, Ind., 1955-60, Covington, Ind., 1960-91; assoc. pastor 1st Assembly of God, Franklin, Ind., 1991—; presbyter Ind. dist. Assemblies of God, 1973-91; mem. bd. dirs. Christians in Action, Purdue U., West Lafayette, Ind., 1988-91. Vice pres. PTO, Covington, 1963, pres., 1964. With U.S. Army, 1952-54. Home: 200 West St Whiteland IN 46184 Office: 1st Assembly of God PO Box 447 Franklin IN 46131 *Life has been good to me: joy and peace in knowing Christ blessings and fullfillment in the people I have been privileged to know and contentment in the ministry. There is so much living in life.*

ALLEN, EDWIN RUSSELL, JR., religious organization administrator; b. Huntington, W.Va., Aug. 7, 1949; s. Edwin Russell and Suzzane (Conner) A.; m. Sandy Lee Grieser, April 19, 1980; children: Aaron, Krista, Adam. AA, Vincennes U., 1970; BA, Ball State U., 1972; postgrad., Tex. Christian U. Cert. Fund Raising Exec. Sr. min. Fayette (Ohio) Christian Ch.; organizing min. New Hope Christian Ch., Toledo, Ohio; devel. cons. Christian Ch. Found., Indpls.; dir. devel. Nat. Benevolent Assn., St. Louis. Active Greater Kans. City Coun. Philanthropy, Planned Giving Coun., Kans. City. Mem. Nat. Soc. Fundraising Execs. Office: Foxwood Springs 1500 W Foxwood Raymore MO 64083

ALLEN, GEORGE PAUL, minister; b. Scranton, Pa., June 1, 1930; s. William Howard Allen and Martha (Waldmann) Last; m. Marguerite Lillian Malko, July 28, 1956; children: James, Virginia Hopkins, Laurel Devino, Daniel, Georgia Wrinkle, Kristen. BA, Catawba Coll., 1951; BD, Lancaster (Pa.) Sem., 1954. Ordained to ministry United Ch. of Christ, 1954. Pastor Zoar Evang. and Reformed Ch., Buffalo, 1954-57; assoc. pastor Trinity United Ch. of Christ, Canton, Ohio, 1957-59; pastor Ringtown (Pa.) Charge United Ch. of Christ, 1959-62, St. Paul's United Ch. of Christ, Cherryville, Pa., 1962-82; sr. pastor Peace United Ch. of Christ, Detroit, 1982—; dir. Christian Communication Coun., Detroit, 1983—; moderator Detroit Met. Assn., United Ch. of Christ, 1989-91, bd. dirs., trustee, 1983—. Chairperson Bows Lake Retreat Ctr., Vanderbilt, Mich., 1986—. Mem. Rotary (pres. Northampton, Pa. chpt. 1970-71), Masons. Republican. Home: 14009 Huff Dr Warren MI 48093 Office: Peace United Ch of Christ 15325 Gratiot Ave Detroit MI 48205

ALLEN, JACK BRADLEY, lay worker, retired secondary education educator; b. Norwich, Conn., Sept. 25, 1925; s. Louis Bradley and Lila Evelyn (Phillips) A.; m. Elizabeth Valerie Phillips, Oct. 28, 1950; 1 child, Mark Steven. BA in Edn., Butler U., 1951; postgrad., Wesleyan U., 1950s; BEd, John Herron Art Inst., 1951; postgrad., Ea. Conn. State Coll., 1960s. Cert. permanent tchr., Conn. Deacon First Bapt. Ch., Willimantic, Conn., 1972—; supt. Sunday sch. First Bapt. Ch., Willimantic, 1982-83, trustee 1987—. Prin. works include working miniature circus, ceramic murals, various cover designs. Petty officer 3d class USN, 1944-46. Art scholar John Herron Inst., 1944; recipient Blue Ribbon award Nat. Grange, 1990. Mem. Grangers (asst. steward local chpt. 1991). Home: Box 78 40 Sanitarium Rd South Windham CT 06266 *Wait the day, for darkness presses close for men blinded by worldly things, prisoners behind the walls they've built. But look, a light is seen. A Son is born, and men are freed.*

ALLEN, JAMES HAROLD, lay worker; b. Lubbock, Tex., Jan. 15, 1935; s. John Clifton and Mary Ola (Wiley) A.; m. Delta Mae Rogers, Feb. 14, 1958; children: Debra Elaine, Roger Dean. BA in Bus., So. Nazarene U., Bethany, Okla., 1957. Lic. real estate broker, Mo.; lic. real estate assoc., Kans. Adminstrv. asst., loan coord. dept. home mission Ch. Nazarene Internat. Hdqrs., Kansas City, Mo, 1969-83, property mgr. Planned Giving, 1986—; bd. mem. 1st Ch. Nazarene, Kansas City, 1990-91. With U.S. Army, 1958-60. Office: Ch Nazarene Planned Giving 6401 The Paseo Kansas City MO 64131

ALLEN, JOHN CARLTON, minister; b. Galveston, Tex., Dec. 7, 1943; s. F.A. and A.V. (Spiller) A.; m. Alice M. Geters, July 8, 1966; children: Renard D., John Carlton Jr., Joel C. BA, Bishop Coll., 1965; LLD (hon.), Guadalupe Coll., Union Bapt. Coll. Ordained to ministry Nat. Bapt. Conv. Am., 1961. Pastor St. Matthew Bapt. Ch., 1965-67, New Mt. Pleasant Bapt. Ch., San Antonio, 1967—; auditor Nat. Bapt. Conv. Am., 1986—, Missionary Bapt. Gen. Conv. Tex., 1975—. Mem. Bapt. Mins. Union San Antonio (pres. 1976-78). Home: 12507 La Bahia San Antonio TX 78233 Office: New Mt Pleasant Bapt Ch 1639 Hays St San Antonio TX 78202

ALLEN, JOHN EUGENE, minister; b. Borger, Tex., July 27, 1939; s. Harry Eugene and Grace E. (Bostwick) A.; m. Mary Alyce Hibbard, Aug. 25, 1957; children: John Eugene Jr., Russell Wayne, Timothy Lee, Stephen Lynn. Student, Okla. Bapt. U., 1960-61, Cen. State U., Edmond, Okla., 1963-64, Southwestern Bapt. Theol. Sem., Ft. Worth, 1975-78, Okla. State U., 1980. Ordained to ministry So. Bapt. Conv. Pastor Witcher Bapt. Ch., Oklahoma City, 1962-64, Crutcho Bapt. Ch., Midwest City, Okla., 1964-67, 40th Street Bapt. Ch., Oklahoma City, 1967-71, Oak Avenue Bapt. Ch., Ada, Okla., 1971-79, 1st Bapt. Ch., Noble, Okla., 1979—; moderator Banner Bapt. Assn., Ada, 1972-74, Union Bapt. Assn., Norman, Okla., 1981-82; v.p. Okla. Pastors Conf., Oklahoma City, 1974-75; bd. dirs. Bapt. Gen. Conv. Okla., Oklahoma City, 1975-79. Pres. All-Sports Club, Noble, 1984. Mem. Kiwanis (pres. Noble 1981). Home: 201 Skyridge Trail Noble OK 73068 Office: 1st Bapt Ch 120 S 4th St Noble OK 73068

ALLEN, JOSEPH LAND, educator, minister; b. Burlington, N.C., Nov. 17, 1928; s. Louis Carr and Bess (Land) A.; m. Mary David Ritter, Aug. 5, 1953; children: Robert Bruce, Joyce Leigh. BA, Duke U., 1950; MDiv, Yale Div. Sch., 1953; PhD, Yale U., 1958. Ordained to ministry United Meth. Ch., 1952. Instr. Perkins Sch. Theology, So. Meth. U., Dallas, 1957-58, asst. prof., 1958-63, assoc. prof., 1963-70, prof. Christian ethics, 1970—. Author: Love and Conflict: A Covenantal Model of Christian Ethics, 1984, War: A Primer for Christians, 1991; contbr. articles to profl. jours. Kent fellow, 1956, Assn. Theol. Schs. fellow, 1970-71. Mem. Soc. Christian Ethics (exec. sec. 1980-84, v.p. 1991-92, pres.-elect 1992—), Phi Beta Kappa. Office: So Meth U Perkins Sch Theology Dallas TX 75275

ALLEN, JOSEPH LEE, librarian; b. Indpls., Oct. 28, 1944; s. Roy Lee and June B. (Goodrum) A.; m. Jo Ann Martin, June 24, 1966; children: Joseph Jr., Jonathan, Jeannie. BA, Bob Jones U., 1967, MA, 1970; MLS, U. S.C., 1974. Asst. libr. dir. Bob Jones U., Greenville, S.C., 1976-86, libr. dir., 1987—. Chmn. Boy Scouts Am. Troop 519, Bob Jones U., Greenville, 1987—. Mem. S.C. Libr. Assn. (chmn. constn. com. 1988, 89). Baptist. Home: 103 Stadium View Dr Greenville SC 29609 Office: Bob Jones U Mack Libr Greenville SC 29614

ALLEN, LESLIE CHRISTOPHER, religion educator; b. Bristol, Eng., Dec. 25, 1935; came to U.S., 1983; s. Bertie and Dorothy (Harp) A.; m. Elizabeth Ruth Gulliver, Aug. 21, 1965; children: Jeremy Lawrence, Miriam Ismahanna. BA, Cambridge (Eng.) U., 1959, MA, 1961; PhD, London U., 1968. Lectr. Old Testament and lit. London Bible Coll., 1960-83; prof. Old Testament Fuller Theol. Sem., Pasadena, Calif., 1983—. Author: The Greek Chronicles, 1974, The Books of Joel, Obadiah, Jonah and Micah, 1976, Psalms 101-150, 1983, Chronicles, 1987, Ezekiel 20-48, 1990; contbr. articles to theol. jours. Recipient award NEH, 1988. Mem. Soc. O.T. Study, Soc. Bibl. Lit., Inst. Bibl. Religion. Office: Fuller Theol Sem 135 N Oakland Ave Pasadena CA 91182

ALLEN, LISA MICHELLE, community service director; b. Louisville, Aug. 4, 1963; d. James Edward Jr. and Dorris Louise (Minor) Starkey; children: Clyde M. Jr., Dominique N. Student, Miami U. Bible worker

Emmanual Seventh-Day Adventist Ch., Cin., summer 1990, community svc. dir., bd. dirs., 1989—, video team leader, 1990. Recipient Extra Spl. Parent award Miami Valley Child Devel. Ctrs., Hamilton, Ohio. Mem. United Black Assn. Office: Emmanuel Seventh-Day Adventist Ch 5100 Whetsel Dr Cincinnati OH 45227 *Time and time again people have told me life is what you make of it. However, through my trials and tribulations, I have found that to be false; life is what you allow God to make of you.*

ALLEN, MARY ELIZABETH, religious organization administrator; b. Cleburne, Tex., Mar. 29, 1931; d. Earl D. and Elsie E. (Miller) A. Assoc. in religious edn., Southwestern Sem., Ft. Worth, 1953. Sec., youth dir. Avenue J Bapt. Ch., Ft. Worth, 1950, Cherokee Bapt. Ch., Memphis, 1953-58; youth dir. 1st Bapt. Ch., West Monroe, La., 1958-64; dir. youth work discipleship tng. dept. Tenn. Bapt. Conv., Nashville, 1964—; associational youth leader Discipleship Tng., Ft. Worth, Memphis, West Monroe, 1953-64; tchr. Ridgecrest, Glorieta, 1964—; sec. and treas. Tenn. Religious Edn. Assn., Nashville. Author: 127 Ideas to Promote Church Training, 1973; contbr. articles to profl. jours. Home: 5105 Briarwood Dr Nashville TN 37211 Office: Tenn Bapt Conv PO Box 728 Brentwood TN 37024

ALLEN, PETER JOHN, youth minister, broadcasting executive; b. N.Y.C., June 2, 1956; s. Freeman Edward and Doris Jean (Negedly) A.; m. Eileen Mary Hornlein, July 14, 1979; children: Becky, Betsy, Bonnie, Bethany, Brittany, Belinda, Benjamin. B Religious Edn., Prairie Bible Inst., Three Hills, Alta., Can., 1979. Dir. Christian Edn. Arlington Bapt. Ch., Balt., 1979-84, youth minister, 1979—; sales rep. Peter & John Radio Fellowship, Balt., 1985-87; dir. engring. WRBS-FM Radio, Balt., 1987—; dir. Awana Clubs, Balt., 1985—. Republican. Home: 10101 Marriottsville Rd Randallstown MD 21133 Office: Sta WRBS-FM 3600 Georgetown Rd Baltimore MD 21227

ALLEN, RAYMOND FULTON, minister; b. Amherst, Va., Apr. 13, 1938; m. Ann Carter Cobb, July 13, 1957; children: Ann Elizabeth, Ray, Kathleen Johnson. BA, U. Richmond, 1962; BD, So. Bapt. Theol. Sem., Louisville, Ky., 1965; D of Min., Southeastern Bapt. Theol. Sem., Wake Forest, N.C., 1976; DD (hon.), U. Richmond, 1974; Clin. Pastoral Edn., Med. Coll. Va., 1974. Ordained to ministry Bapt. Ch., 1960. Pastor Wise (Va.) Bapt. Ch., 1965-70, Cosby Meml. Bapt. Ch., Richmond, Va., 1970-74, Blacksburg (Va.) Bapt. Ch., 1974—; mem. exec. com. Va. Bapt. Gen. Bd., Richmond, 1968-74, 90—; first v.p. Bapt. Gen. Assn. Va., Richmond, 1970; trustee U. Richmond, 1975-80, 86-90, Bluefield (Va.) Coll., 1983-85. Author: How to Be a Christian Happy and Successful, 1978, Our Common Faith, 1990. With U.S. Army, 1956-59. Mem. Kiwanis Club (dir.). Office: Blacksburg Bapt Ch 550 N Main St Blacksburg VA 24060

ALLENDER, PETER JOHN (SIR PETER), archbishop; b. Somerset, Eng., Sept. 15, 1921; s. Alfred John and Dorothy (Thomas) A.; m. Marjorie Edith Tomkins, Nov. 6, 1955. BS, U. London, 1950, PhD, 1955; MA, U. Reading, 1960; DD, Lambeth Coll., London, 1988. Ordained to ministry Ch. of Eng., 1946, Apostolic Free Ch. 1986, consecrated bishop, 1990, archbishop, 1991. Rsch. technician Hardy Spicer Group, 1940=46; rsch. engr. Valor Co. Ltd., Birmingham, Eng., 1946-48, Brit. Thomson Houston Ltd., Rugby, Eng., 1954-58; devel. engr. Birmingham Small Arms Ltd., 1948-54; materials engr. Metro-Cammen Ltd., Birmingham, 1958-84; cons. John Allen Assocs., Birmingham, 1984; min. Apostolic Free Ch., London, 1986—; provost Bedfont Theol. Sem., London, 1988—; prior, provost Order of St. Luke, London, 1989—. Author: (monograph) Passenger Train Fire Safety, 1979, Fire Safety Engineering, 1982, Railway Passenger Rolling Stock, 1986, Systems Engineering, 1988. Advisor Dept. Transport, London, 1979. Decorated Knight, 1990. Fellow Soc. Co. and Comml. Accts., Instn. Diagnostic Engrs. Avocations: writing, travel. Home: 9 Jeremy Grove, Solihull B92 8JH, England Office: Bedfont Theol Sem, London England

ALLIK, TIINA KATRIN, religious studies educator; b. Mpls., June 13, 1951; d. Erich Johannes and Anadie (Saluste) A. BS, MIT, 1972; MAR, Westminster Theol. Sem., 1974; PhD, Yale U., 1982. Asst. prof. theology Loyola Marymount U., Los Angeles, 1982—. Douglas Clyde Macintosh fellow for Theology and Philosophy of Religion, 1979-80;Kanzer fellow Kanzer Fund for Psychoanalysis and the Humanities, 1980-81; Deutsche Akademische Austauschdienst grantee, 1982; Loyola Marymount U. Summer Research grantee, 1985. Mem. Am. Acad. Religion (Narrative Theology Group, Person, Culture and Religion Group). Lutheran. Office: Loyola Marymount U Theology Dept Loyola Blvd at W 80th St Los Angeles CA 90045

ALLIN, JOHN MAURY, bishop; b. Helena, Ark., Apr. 22, 1921; s. Richard and Dora (Harper) A.; m. Frances Ann Kelly, Oct. 18, 1949; children: Martha May, Kelly Ann and John Maury (twins), Frances Elizabeth. BA, U. of South, 1943, MDiv, 1945, DD, 1962; MEd, Miss. Coll., 1960. Ordained to ministry Episcopal Ch., 1944; vicar St. Peter's Ch., Conway, Ark., 1945-49; curate St. Andrew's Ch., New Orleans, 1950-51; chaplain to Episcopal students and insts. New Orleans, 1950-52; rector Grace Ch., Monroe, La., 1952-58; rector, pres. All Saints Jr. Coll., Vicksburg, Miss., 1958-61; bishop coadjutor Diocese of Miss., P.E. Ch., Jackson, 1961-66; bishop Diocese of Miss., P.E. Ch., 1966-73; 23d presiding bishop Episcopal Ch. in U.S.A., 1974-86; chaplin Christ Meml. Chapel, Hobe Sound, Fla., 1986—, St. Ann's Summer Chapel, Kennebunkport, Maine, 1991—; mem. Joint Commn. on Ecumenical Rels., 1964-73; mem. Anglican-Roman Cath.Consultation, 1967-73; mem. exec. coun. Episcopal Ch., 1970-85; mem. Miss. Religious Leadership Conf., 1969-73, chmn., 1972-73. Trustee All Saints Episcopal Sch., Vicksburg, 1961—; trustee U. of South, 1961—, bd. regents, 1965-71, 79-85, chancellor, 1973-79. Home: 2015 Douglas Dr Jackson MS 39211 Office: Christ Meml Chapel 57 S Beach Rd Hobe Sound FL 33455

ALLIN, LEWIS FREDERICK, clergyman; b. Grand Rapids, Minn., Apr. 2, 1923; s. Frederick William and Frances Lenora (Larson) A.; m. Joyce Carolyn Carter, Sept. 3, 1950; children: David, Kevin, Carol. AA, Itasca Jr. Coll., 1942; B Chem. Engring., U. Minn., 1948; B Div., Drew U., 1952. Ordained to ministry, United Meth. Ch., 1952. Petroleum engr. Creole Petroleum Co., San Joaquin, Venezuela, 1948-49; pastor various congregations United Meth. Ch., Minn., 1952-76; missionary, nat. div. Bd. Global Ministries, Red Bird Mission United Meth. Ch., Roark, Ky., 1976-79; pastor United Meth. Ch., Wells, Minn., 1979-88; ret., 1988; chmn. nominating com., Minn. Meth. Conf., Mpls., 1962-65; mem. conf., Bd. Global Ministries, Mpls., 1979-87. 1st lt. USAAF, 1943-46, CBI, ETO. Mem.Meth. Philatelic Soc., Am. Philatelic Soc., Kiwanis (pres. Wells chpt. 1984-85). Democrat. Avocations: stamp collecting, bicycling, tennis, skiing. Home: Rte 2 Box 287A Park Rapids MN 56470 *Illnesses to loved ones come unbidden and test us in many ways. May how we react strengthen others in their trials.*

ALLIS, ANDREW PARKER B., priest; b. Mansfield, Pa., Feb. 27, 1938; s. Leo Joseph and Evelyn Norton (Bateman) A.; m. Pauline Ann Middleton, Oct. 13, 1979; children: Andrew, Ryan. EdB, Mansfield U., 1960; cert. of study, Va. Theol. Sem., 1963; M in Liberal Studies, Duquesne U., 1983; D in Ministry, Pitts. Theol. Sem., 1986; postgrad., U.S. Navy Chaplains Sch. Ordained priest Episcopal Ch., 1964. Canon pastor Christ Ch. Cathedral, Houston, 1966-69; rector St. Mark's Ch., Johnstown, Pa., 1969-76; min., dir. Wilkinsburg (Pa.) Community Ministry, 1976-79; rector St. Peter's Ch., Pitts., 1979-86, St. James Ch., Woonsocket, R.I., 1986—; dean Blackstone Valley Deanery, Providence, 1988—; alt. dep. Gen. Conv., N.Y.C., 1989—; chair diocesan Pastoral Care of Clergy Family, Providence, 1990—; bd. govs. Sch. for Ministries, Providence, 1990—. Com. mem. Woonsocket City Coun. adv. bd., 1987, Woonsocket Sch. Bd., 1990—. With USNR, 1962-64. Evang. Edn. Soc. Phila. scholar, 1961-62; Soc. for Increase of Ministry scholar, 1961-63; Am. Zionist Fedn., N.Y.C., 1973; Ministry for Higher Edn. grantee, N.Y.C., 1971. Mem. NCCJ, Ch. and City Cconf., Episcopal Urban Caucus, Nightingale Home Found. (pres. 1986—), Rotary (pres. Pitts. club 1984-84, chaplain Woonsocket club 1987-89). Democrat. Home: 28 Hamlet Ave Woonsocket RI 02895 Office: St James Ch 24 Hamlet Ave Woonsocket RI 02895

ALLISON, CHRISTOPHER FITZSIMONS, bishop; b. Columbia, S.C., Mar. 5, 1927; s. James Richard and Susan Milliken (FitzSimons) A.; m. Martha Allston Parker, June 10, 1950. B.A., U. of South, 1949, D.D., 1978; M.Div., Va. Theol. Sem., 1952, D.D., 1981; D.Phil., Oxford U., 1956; D.D., Episcopal Theol. Sem. Ky., 1981. Asst. Trinity, Columbia, 1952-54; assoc. prof. ch. history U. of South, Sewanee, Tenn., 1956-67; prof. ch. history Va. Theol. Sem., Alexandria, 1967-75; rector Grace Ch., N.Y.C., 1975-80; bishop of S.C. Episcopal Ch., Charleston, S.C., 1980-90, ret., 1990. Author: Fear, Love & Worship; Rise of Moralism; Guilt, Anger & God. Served as sgt. U.S. Army, 1945-47. Democrat. Home: 1081 Indigo Ave Georgetown SC 29440

ALLISON, DALE CLIFFORD, JR., writer; b. Wichita, Kans., Nov. 25, 1955; s. Dale Clifford and Virginia Francis (Hudson) A.; m. Kristine Alison Yates, May 28, 1983; children: Emily Melissa, Andrew William, John Matthew. BA, Wichita State U., 1977; MA, Duke U., 1979, PhD, 1982. Rsch. fellow Friends U., Wichita, 1989—. Author: The End of the Ages Has Come, 1985; (with W.D. Davies) A Critical and Exegetical Commentary on the Gospel According to St. Matthew (3 vols.), 1988, 91; contbr. articles to profl. jours. Scholarship Duke U., 1978-82. Mem. Soc. Bibl. Lit., Internat. Soc. Neoplatonic Studies, Nat. Assn. Bapt. Profs. of Religion, Phi Beta Kappa, Phi Kappa Phi. Republican. Home: 1633 Porter Wichita KS 67203 Office: Friends Univ 2100 University Wichita KS 67213

ALLISON, DENNIS RAY, minister; b. Kansas City, Mo., July 24, 1953; s. Raymond Emmett and Edith Eleanor (Kistler) A.; m. Rebecca Jane Durham, May 27, 1953; children: Monica Michelle, Lauren Megan. AB, Ottawa U., 1980; MDiv, Princeton U., 1984. Ordained to ministry in Presbyn. Ch., 1984. Pastor White Oak Springs Presbyn. Ch., Butler, Pa., 1984-88, Northminster Presbyn. Ch., Pitts., 1988—. Home: 70 S Harrison Ave Pittsburgh PA 15202 Office: Northminster Presbyn Ch 45 N Fremont Ave Pittsburgh PA 15202

ALLISON, JAMES ABNER, JR., retired minister; b. Richlands, Va., Aug. 20, 1924; s. James Abner and Margaret Louise (Brown) A.; m. Margaret Tuthill Anderson, Dec. 30, 1950; children: Susan, James Craig, Judith Louise. BA, Va. Mil. Inst., 1948; BD, Princeton Sem., 1951; DD (hon.), Hampden-Sydney (Va.) Coll., 1974. Pastor Augusta Stone Presbyn. Ch., Ft. Defiance, Va., 1952-59; pastor Raleigh Ct. Presbyn. Ch., Roanoke, Va., 1960-90, ret., 1990. Lt. U.S. Army, 1943-46, chaplain, 1951-52. Home: 1869 Greenwood Rd Roanoke VA 24015

ALLISON, WILLIAM HUGH, biology educator, botanist; b. Harrison Twp., Pa., Nov. 25, 1934; s. Wesley Leroy and Elizabeth Martha (Hazlett) A.; m. Evelyn Frear, Aug. 31, 1958; children: Patricia Ruth, Timothy Daniel, James David. BS, Pa. State U., 1956, MS, 1957, PhD, 1963. Grad. asst. Pa. State U., University Park, Pa., 1956-60; plant pathologist U.S. Army Biol. Labs., Frederick, Md., 1960-63; dir. rsch. Brandywine Mushroom Co., West Chester, Pa., 1963-66; mgr. Great Lakes Spawn Co., Utica, N.Y., 1966-68; prof. biology Delaware Valley Coll., Doylestown, Pa., 1968—, chair biology dept., 1990—. Contbr. articles to publs. Com. mem. pack 170, troop 175 Boy Scouts Am., Danboro, Pa., 1972—, scoutmaster troop 175, 1976-80; lay worker Deer Creek United Presbyn. Ch., Gibsonia, Pa., 1946-63, 1st Presbyn. Ch., West Chester, Pa., 1963-66; elder Doylestown (Pa.) Presbyn. Ch., 1974—. Capt. U.S. Army, 1960-63. Mem. AAAS, Am. Inst. Biol. Sci., Am. Phytopathological Soc., Bot. Soc. Am., Am. Soc. Plant Taxonomists, Mycological Soc. Am., Mid Atlantic Assn. Coll. Biologists, Sigma Xi, Phi Epsilon Phi, Phi Sigma, Gamma Sigma Delta. Republican. Presbyn. Home: 4581 Landesville Rd Doylestown PA 18901 Office: Delaware Valley Coll Doylestown PA 18901

ALLPORT, DAVID BRUCE, minister; b. Pulaski, N.Y., Sept. 7, 1954; s. Edward Adelbert Allport and Betty Arline (Kling) Goodsell; m. Catherine Mary Stento, June 7, 1980; children: Rachel Ann, Bethany Grace. BS, SUNY, Oswego, 1981. Ordained to ministry, 1986. Assoc. dir. B.A.S.I.C Cen./Elim Fellowship, Lima, N.Y., 1983-86, dir., 1986—. Author: The BASIC Plan for Bible Memorization, 1989. With USN, 1972-76. Home: 7264 Kober Dr Lima NY 14485 Office: Elim Fellowship 7245 College St Lima NY 14485

ALLREAD, ARDITH, minister; b. Salt Lake City, June 30, 1943; d. Arvel Victor and Grace Jr. (Casale) A.; m. David Allen Coolidge, July 1, 1967 (div. Aug. 1983); children: Joshua, Peter; m. Gregg Theodore Atkins, May 12, 1990; 1 stepchild, Jocelyn. BA, Calif. State U., Chico, 1965; MDiv, Pacific Sch. of Religion, Berkeley, Calif., 1984. Cert. tchr. K-8, Calif.; ordained to ministry Meth. Ch., 1984, as elder, 1986. Assoc. pastor Concord (Calif.) United Meth. Ch., 1984-87; pastor St. Paul United Meth. Ch., Fremont, Calif., 1987—. Mem. AAUW. Democrat. Office: St Paul United Methodist Ch PO Box 183 Newark CA 94560

ALLRED, GARLAND HOWARD, minister; b. Greensboro, N.C., May 28, 1922; s. William Fletcher and Etta Gertrude (Ritter) A.; m. Florence Lee Oakley, June 8, 1941; children: Donald Howard, Susan Ann Allred Singletary, Laura Etta Allred Allred. AB, Guilford Coll., 1949; MDiv, Duke U., 1952; DD (hon.), High Point Coll., 1990. Ordained to ministry Meth. Ch. as deacon, 1951, as elder, 1952. Pastor Pelham (N.C.)/Hickory Grove United Meth. Chs., 1948-53, 1st United Meth. Ch., Eden, N.C., 1953-56, Maylo United Meth. Ch., Gastonia, N.C., 1956-64, Epworth United Meth. Ch., Concord, N.C., 1964-72, Cen. United Meth. Ch., Asheboro, N.C., 1972-78, Meml. United Meth. Ch., Thomasville, N.C., 1978-82; dist. supt. Western N.C. Conf., 1982-87; pastor 1st United Meth. Ch., High Point, N.C., 1987-91; del. World Meth. Conf., Kenya, 1986, Gen. Conf. United Meth. Balt., 1984, St. Louis, 1988, southeastern jurisdiction United Meth., Lake Junaluska, N.C., 1980, 84, 88. Chmn. United Way, Eden, N.C., 1955; bd. dirs. Mental Health Assn., Concord, N.C., 1960-62, Drug Action Coun., High Point, 1989-91; mem. bd. visitors High Point Coll., 1989-91. 1st lt. U.S. Army, 1942-45, MTO. Mem. Optimist Internat. (charter pres. Gastonia, N.C. 1959), Rotary, Masons, Shriners. Home: 2111 Adams Farm Pkwy Greensboro NC 27407-5401 Office: First United Meth Ch 512 N Main St High Point NC 27260 *I believe that the power of love is greater than the love of power, and that whoever lives by the power of love will share in the victory that will overcome the world.*

ALLRED, JEFFREY ALLEN, minister; b. Nashville, May 12, 1965; s. Gerald Hobson and Nancy Marie (Bates) A.; m. Lisa Dawn Simmons, July 30, 1988; 1 child, Brandon Mikell Lewis. AA, Brewton-Parker Coll., 1985; BA, Mercer U., 1987. Min. music and youth Leslie (Ga.) Bapt. Ch., 1984; min. youth 1st Bapt. Ch., Hazlehurst, Ga., 1985-90; min. music and youth Reidsville (Ga.) Bapt. Ch., 1990—. Mem. Tattnall Band Boosters, Reidsville, 1990—. Mem. Ga. Bapt. Ch. Music Conf., Ga. Bapt. Youth Mins. Fellowship, Tattnall-Evans Assn. (dir. music 1990), Jubal Brass, Lions Club. Office: Reidsville Bapt Ch 146 E Brazell St Reidsville GA 30453

ALLSHOUSE, JOHN, minister, educator, principal; b. Struthers, Ohio, Jan. 13, 1951; s. John and Marilyn Joan (Maggianetti) A. Student, N.Y. Christian Inst., 1968; BA, Youngstown State U., 1974; MS, Westminster Coll., 1978; postgrad. in Biblical Langs., Hebrew Union, 1978-80; MRE, Cin. Christian Sem., 1980, DRE, 1983; ThD, Christian Bible Coll., Rocky Mountain, N.C., 1984; postgrad., Trinity Evang. Div. Sch., 1980-90. Ordained minister So. Bapt. Conv., 1968; cert. Christian pastoral counsellor; cert. tchr., adminstr., guidance counselor, Ohio, Pa., Ky., Ind., Md., Mich. Substitute tchr. Youngstown (Ohio) Bd. of Edn., 1968-79; intern Higginsport (Ohio) Bapt. Ch., 1978-79, Moscow (Ohio) Bapt. Ch., 1979-80; tchr., prin. Lighthouse Christian Sch., Columbiana, Ohio, 1979-86; interim pastor Butler (Ind.) Bapt. Ch., 1980-81, Boonesboro (Ky.) Bapt. Ch., 1981-82; substitute tchr. Mahoning and Columbiana County Sch. Bds., Youngstown and Columbiana, Ohio, 1986-89; guidance counselor Dayton (Ohio) Pub. Schs., 1988-90; pastor Stillwater Community Ch., Covington, Ohio, 1989-90; group leader Habitat for Humanity Internat., Inc., Americus, Ga., 1990-91. Author: Bible Commentary, The Living Word Commentary, 1978-80, also religious articles. Mem. Young Reps., Ohio, 1968—, Ohio Right to Life; instr. Laubach (Adult Literacy), So. Ohio, Youngstown, 1968-90. Mem. Christian Counseling Assn., NEA, Ohio Edn. Assn., Nat. Assn. Christian Educators (cert.), C.C.E., Menninger Found. Republican. Baptist. Avocations: coins, writing articles and poetry, reading, gardening, collecting video films. Home: 491 W Wilson St Struthers OH 44471-1209 *We live in a complex and changing society. We must not only know what we believe but we must be cognizant of the issues of today's world.*

ALMEIDA MERINO, ADALBERTO, archbishop; b. Chihuahua, Mex., June 5, 1916; s. Luis Almeida Aldrete and Maria Merino Saenz. Grad. in philosophy, theology and canon law, Gregorian U., Rome, 1945. Ordained to Roman Catholic Ch., as priest. Prof. theology, 1946-56; archbishop State of Chihuahua; mem. Episcopal Conf. Mex., Commn. Medros de Comuncacron Social; founder, past pres. Commn. Episcopal de Pastoral Social. Pres. Commn. Sacred Music and Arts. Office: State of Chihuahua, Apartado Postal No 7, CP 31000 Chihuahua Mexico

ALMEN, LOWELL GORDON, church official; b. Grafton, N.D., Sept. 25, 1941; s. Paul Orville and Helen Eunice (Johnson) A.; m. Sally Arlyn Clark, Aug. 14, 1965; children: Paul Simon, Cassandra Gabrielle. BA, Concordia Coll., Moorhead, Minn., 1963; MDiv, Luther Theol. Sem., St. Paul, 1967; LittD (hon.), Capital U., 1981; DD (hon.), Carthage Coll., 1989. Ordained to ministry Luth. Ch., 1967. Pastor St. Peter's Luth. Ch., Dresser, Wis., 1967-69; asso. campus pastor, dir. communications Concordia Coll., Moorhead, Minn., 1969-74; mng. editor Luth. Standard ofcl. publ. Am. Luth. Ch., Mpls., 1974-78; editor Am. Luth. Ch., 1979-87; sec., officer Evangelical Luth. Ch. Am., Chgo., 1987—. Author: Old Songs for a New Journey, 1990; author, co-editor: The Many Faces of Pastoral Ministry, 1989; editor: World Religions and Christian Mission, 1967, Our Neighbor's Faith, 1968. Recipient Disting. Alumnus award Concordia Coll., 1982; Bush Found. grantee, 1972. Office: Evang Luth Ch 8765 W Higgins Rd Chicago IL 60631

ALMOND, JOHNNY RUSSELL, minister; b. Little Rock, Dec. 16, 1944; s. Russell Ray and Mildred Geneva (Johnson) A.; m. Beverly Ann McCullough, June 17, 1967; children: Brent, Bradley, Bryan, Brandon. BA, Henderson U., 1965; MTh, Bapt. Seminary, Little Rock, 1968, DTh, 1976; D of Ministry, Drew Univ., 1980. Pastor Wood River (Ill.) Bapt. Ch., 1969-71, Lakeview Bapt. Ch., Spiro, Okla., 1971, Cen. Bapt. Ch., Fayetteville, Ark., 1971-76; chaplain U.S. Army/Fort Stewart, Hinesville, Ga., 1977-79; chpalain USAF/Chanute AFB, Rantoul, Ill., 1980-82, USAF/Kadena AFB, Okinawa, Japan, 1983-85, USAF/Brooks AFB, San Antonio, 1986-88, USAF Acad., Colorado Springs, Colo., 1989—. Author Sunday Sch. quarterly, 1976—. Named to Outstanding Young Men of Am., 1976. Home: 3515 Fair Dawn Dr Colorado Springs CO 80920-4223 Office: USAFA/HCD USAF Academy Colorado Springs CO 80840-5081

ALMY, LEE ANDRADE, JR., pastor; b. Milledgeville, Ga., Aug. 30, 1955; m. Lee Andrade Sr. and Mary Patty (Carpenter) A.; m. Renée Frances Engel, Sept. 16, 1989. BS in Edn., West Ga. Coll., 1976, MEd in Spl. Edn., 1977; MDiv, Emory U., 1985. Ordained elder United Meth. Ch., 1986. Pastor Glenn (Ga.) Cir. United Meth. Ch., 1980-82, Warm Springs (Ga.) United Meth. Ch., 1982-85; min. of program Hartwell (Ga.) First United Meth. Ch., 1985-87; pastor Warren County Charge Camak United Meth. Ch., Thomson, Ga., 1987-90, Shiloh United Meth. Ch., Appling, Ga., 1990—; ministerial rep. Hydra (Aart County's Youth Program), Hartwell, 1985-87; town and country ministries coord. North Ga. Ann. Conf., Augusta Dist. United Meth. Ch., Atlanta, 1990—. Home: Star Rte Box 44 Appling GA 30802 Office: Shiloh United Meth Ch Rte 5 Box 879 Thomson GA 30824

ALONSO SCHOKEL, LUIS, biblical studies educator; b. Madrid, Feb. 15, 1920; s. Adalberto Alonso de Ylera and Maria Schokel. Grad. in classics Jesuits Sch., Salamanca, Spain, 1940; Philosophy Licence, Faculty of Philosophy, Ona, Spain, 1943; Theology Licence, Faculty of Theology, Comillas, Spain, 1950; D. Holy Scripture, Pontifical Bibl. Inst., Rome, 1957. Prof. Pontifical Bibl. Inst., Rome, 1957; vice rector, 1969-78, dean bibl. faculty, 1975-81, prof., 1983—; pres. Internat. Orgn. Study O.T., Cambridge, 1980-83; guest prof. Grad. Theol. Union, Berkeley, Calif., 1973, U. San Francisco, 1970, 76, 79, 81, 85; guest lectr. in U.S.A., Latin Am., Tokyo, Seoul, others. Author: The Inspired World, 1965; (with others) Nueva Biblia Española, 1975; Profetas Comentario, 1980; Job Comentario, 1983; Proverbios Comentario, 1984; Textos de fraternidad en el Génesis, 1985, Manual de Poética Hebrea, 1987, Diccionario Biblico Hebreo Español, 1990-92. Home: via Pilotta 25, 00187 Rome Italy

ALPERIN, IRWIN EPHRAIM, clothing company executive; b. Scranton, Pa., Apr. 29, 1925; s. Louis I. and Bessie (Wickner) A.; m. Francine Leah Friedman, Dec. 5, 1948; children: Barbara Joy, Jane Leslie. Cert. Mech. Engring., Pa. State U., 1945; BS in Indsl. Engring., Lehigh U., 1947; DHL (hon.), U. Scranton, Pa., 1991. Mgmt. trainee Mayflower Mfg. Co., Scranton, 1947-49, sec., 1952-79, pres., 1980—; with Triple A. Trouser Mfg. Co., Inc., Scranton, 1952, v.p., treas., 1958-79, prs., 1980—; with Gold Star Mfg. Co., Inc., Scranton, 1956, pres., 1956-91; sec. Astro Warehousing Inc., Scranton, 1962—; sec.-treas. Bondeal, Inc., Scranton, 1978-89, pres., 1989—; v.p. RCO, Inc., 1989—; vice chmn. Montage Inc., 1979—; sec. Alperin Inc., 1982—, All Star Industries, Inc., 1989—; bd. dirs. Sacquoit Industries, Inc., Scranton, 1980—. Bd. dirs. Econ. Devel. Council N.E. Pa., Avoca, 1974—, v.p., 1978-83; bd. dirs. ARC, Scranton, 1968-88, pres. spl. adv. bd., 1988—; bd. dirs. Jewish Home Eastern Pa., Scranton, 1970—, treas., 1981—; bd. dirs. Jewish Community Ctr., Scranton, 1971-86, now life mem.; bd. dirs. Pa. United Way, Harrisburg, Pa., 1973-78, Scranton Mental Health-Mental Retardation Ctr., 1975-78, trustee, 1979—; pres. Planning Council Social Svcs. Lackawanna County, 1972-74, now life mem.; pres. Jewish Family Svc. of Lackawanna County, 1967-70, now life bd. mem.; v.p. United Way Lackawanna County, 1974-78, exec. com., 1978-86; pres. Alperin Found., Scranton, 1962—; treas. Scranton-Lackawanna Jewish Fedn., 1973-75, life mem. bd. dirs.; trustee Amos Lodge Found., 1982—, v.p., 1989—, Found. Jewish Elderly, 1984—, v.p. 1985—; trustee Pocono N.E. Devel. Fund, 1983-86, sec. 1986—; pres. Temple Hesed, 1969-71, life mem., bd. dirs., Scranton, Pa.; mem. Lackawanna County Libr. Bd., 1983-85; treas. Lackawanna Regional Cultural Coun., 1988-91; bd. dirs. Broadway Theatre League Lackawanna County, 1989—, Masonic Temple Civic Ctr. Found., 1989—; trustee U. Scranton, 1991—. Served with C.E., AUS, 1944-46. Recipient Americanism award, 1982; named Man of Year, Jewish Community Ctr., 1973, Disting. Pennsylvanian, Phila. C. of C., 1982. Mem. Am. Inst. Indsl. Engrs. (sr.), Glen Oak Country Club (Clarks Summit, Pa.), Wave Oak Realty (Clarks Summit) (v.p. 1989-91), Masons, Shriners, Elks, B'nai B'rith (trustee, Man of Yr. 1982). Home: 1010 Victoria Ln Clarks Summit PA 18411 Office: P O Box 3627 Scranton PA 18505 *To know your god—know yourself.*

ALPERN, ROBERT ZELLMAN, religious organization administrator; b. New Haven, Conn., May 13, 1928; s. Harry and Charlotte (Fields) A.; m. Carolyn Montgomery, Nov. 17, 1936; 1 child, Steven P. BS, N.Y.U., 1951; postgrad., Columbia U., 1952-53. Dir. Credit Svc., Inc., Balt., 1962-69; adminstrv. dir. Sane - Nat. Com. For a Sane Nuclear Policy, N.Y.C. and Washington, 1969-75; dir. Unitarian Universalist Assn. of Congregations, Washington, 1975—; chair Chs. for Mid. East Peace; bd. dirs. Interfaith/Impact, Washington, Pax World Found., Bethesda, Md. Chmn. Nuclear Free Takoma Park (Md.) Com., 1985-91; numerous peace missions to India, Bangladesh, Northern Ireland, Cuba, Mid. East, others. Sgt. U.S. Army, 1946-48. Avocations: wood carving, gardening, wild mushroom hunting, gourmet cooking. Home: 316 Elm Ave Takoma Park MD 20912 Office: Unitarian Universalist Assn 100 Maryland Ave NE Washington DC 20002

ALPERT, ROBERT LAWRENCE, rabbi; b. N.Y.C., Aug. 30, 1955; s. Meyer and Caroline (Spalter) A. BA, Columbia U., 1978; B in Hebrew Lit., Jewish Theol. Sem., 1978, MA, 1982. Ordained rabbi, 1983. Rabbi Temple Sholom, Medford, mass., 1983-85, Congregation Beth El, Edison, N.J., 1985-89; asst. rabbi Beth Sholom Congregation, Elkins Park, 1989—. Mem. Rabbinical Assembly, Phila. Bd. Rabbis, N.Y. Bd. Rabbis, Assn. Jewish Studies. Democrat. Office: Beth Sholom Congregation Old York and Foxcroft Rds Enkins Park PA 19117 *I am looking to create a deeper appreciation of the spiritual aspects of Judaism through study and prayer in those I work with. I hope to create an authentic committed lay community that shares these values with their leadership.*

ALQUIST, GEORGE HERMAN, JR., pastor; b. New Kensington, Pa., Apr. 11, 1952; s. George Herman and Myrna Jane (Thomas) A.; m. Melva Lee Harkins, July 31, 1952; children: Aubrae Ann, Brenda Lee. B Bibl. Studies, Commonwealth Bapt. Coll., Louisville, 1986; M Christian Counseling, Bethany Theol. Sem., Dothan, Ala., 1990; diploma, Prin.'s Clinic, 1985. Ordained to ministry Bapt. Ch., 1984; cert. dactylology. Vice chmn. Bethal Christian Sch., Erie, Pa., 1977-83, tchr. Bible, 1981-82; founder, pastor Grace of Calvary Bapt. Ch., Erie, 1983—; founder, pres. Erie Christian Libr., 1978—; founder Wonderful tracts Ministry, Erie, 1985—; mem. adv. bd. Dave Arnold Evangelistic Assn., Chambersburg, Pa., 1985, Camp Faith Unltd., Smethport, Pa., 1987. Author: (booklet) Spiritual Growth, 1985, series 12 Gospel tracts Who, How, Why, When Series, 1984. Recipient Contending for Faith award Walnut Creek Bapt. Ch., Fairview, Pa., 1983, Grace of Calvary Bapt. Ch., 1984. Mem. Internat. Assn. Christian Librs. (founder). Republican. Office: Grace of Calvary Bapt Ch 806 Parade St Erie PA 16510

ALSTON, BETTYE JO, clergywoman, nurse; b. Memphis, Dec. 17, 1938; d. Thomas L. and Bettie Marie (Golden) Harris; m. Neasbie Alston, Nov. 29, 1980; children: Donna, Robin, Bernetta, Lissa, Karen, Nataline, Rebecca, Neasbie Jr. AA, Memphis State U., 1969; MDiv cum laude, Memphis Theol. Sem., 1984; D Ministry, St. Paul Sch. Theology, Kansas City, Mo., 1986; PhD in Counseling Psychology, Emmanuel Bapt. U., 1990. RN, Tenn. Nursing supr. John Gaston Hosp., Memphis, 1969-78; nurse recruiter W.F. Bowld Hosp., U. Tenn. Coll. Health Scis., Memphis, 1978-81; dir. nursing Collins Chapel Health Care Ctr., Memphis, 1981-82; asst. adminstr. North Memphis Home Health Agy., 1982-84; pastor Brown Chapel A.M.E. Ch., Memphis, 1977-88; pastor, founder New Beginning Ch., Memphis, 1988—; staff adviser, counselor Regional Med. Ctr., Memphis, 1987-89; dir. nursing spl. svcs. Regional Med. Ctr., 1989—; with West Tenn. Audit Conf., Memphis, 1974-78. Author poetry and devotionals. Mem. Leadership Memphis, 1990-91. Named Outstanding Pastor Memphis A.M.E. Ch., 1982, Disting. African Am. Alumnae, Memphis Theol. Sem., 1990. Mem. Tenn. Nurses Assn., Exec. Female, Interdenominational Women Ministerial Alliance (pres. 1989—), Alston Family Evangelistic Assn. (v.p., exec. dir. 1981—), Nat. Coun. Negro Women, Ch. Women United, Toastmasters. Democrat. Avocations: writing, swimming, reading. Office: Regional Med Ctr 877 Jefferson Memphis TN 38103

ALT, MARTHA S. (MARTI ALT), religious studies librarian; b. Jelloway, Ohio, Jan. 10, 1943; d. Robert John and Mildred (Patterson) Stratton; m. Richard F. Alt, May 12, 1973; children: Stratton, LeAnne, Leslie. BA, cert. in teaching, Ind. Wesleyan U., 1964; MLS, Ind. U., Bloomington, 1967. Tchr. English Mt. Gilead (Ohio) High Sch., 1964-66; libr. Briarwood High Sch., East Point, Ga., 1967-70, Asbury (Ky.) Coll., 1970-71; libr. acquisitions dept. Ohio State U. Librs., Columbus, 1971-84, libr. for religious studies, 1984—. Editor: Encyclopedia of Ohio Associations, 1978, 88, 50-yr. Index OLA Bulletin, 1980; contbr. articles to profl. jours. Mem. ALA, Am. Theol. Libr. Assn., Ohio Theol. Librs. Assn. (program chair 1988-91), Ohio Libr. Assn. (bull. editor 1985-87), Ohio Acad. Religion, Midwest Acad. Religion, Assn. Coll. and Rsch. Librs. Mem. Grace Brethren Ch. Office: Ohio State U Librs 1858 Neil Ave Mall Columbus OH 43210-1286

ALTMAN, JANICE MARY, religious organization administrator, educator; b. Columbus, Ohio, Apr. 13, 1938; d. Norman John and Nettie Mae (Sullivan) A. BA, Ohio Dominican Coll., 1962; MEd, Marygrove Coll., 1969; ThM, Trinity Coll., 1978; EdD, George Washington U., 1985. Tchr. St. Andrew Sch., Flushing, N.Y., 1969-72, St. Thomas Sch., Zanesville, Ohio, 1972-74; dir. Holy Family & St. Aloysius, Columbus, 1974-76; chaplain intern Children's Hosp. Nat. Med. Ctr., Washington, 1977-80; intern Pastoral Counseling Ctr., Washington, 1979-81; dir. Pastoral Counseling Ctr., Suitland, Md., 1981-88; pres., counselor Alta-Vista Pastoral Counseling Ctr., Inc., Bowie, Md., 1988—; supr. Prince George Pastoral Counseling Ctr., Lanham, Md., 1987—; mem. adj. faculty Howard U. Sch. Divinity, Washington, 1988—. Author: Library of Congress, 1986. Fellow Am. Assn. Pastoral Counselors (chmn. 1983-87), Md. Mental Health Counselors (pres.-elect 1989-90, pres. 1990-91), Greater Bowie C. of C. (women in bus. com. 1989—). Democrat. Roman Catholic. Avocations: swimming, tennis, walking. Office: Alta Vista Pastoral Ctr PO Box 876 Bowie MD 20718

ALURI, RAJARATHNAM SUDARSHANAM, lay worker; b. Suryapet, India, June 28, 1952; came to U.S., 1976; s. Sudarashanam J. and Rathnamma (Jattoth) A.; m. Katherine G. Huschilt, May 18, 1985; children: Lydia R., James T. MA, Osmania U., Hyderabad, India, 1976, U. S.C., 1979; M in Media Arts, U. S.C., 1981, EdD, 1987. Youth leader Bapt. Youth Fellowship, Deccan Region, India, 1970-76; founder, pres., dir. Internat. Friendship Ministries, Columbia, S.C., 1981—; del. Asian Bapt. Youth Fellowship, Colombo, Sri Lanka, 1976. Office: Internat Friendship Ministries 610 Pickens St PO Box 12504 Columbia SC 29211

ALVAREZ, EDUARDO JORGE, religion educator; b. LaHabana, Cuba, Aug. 29; came to U.S., 1991; s. Eduardo and Rosa J. (Hidalgo) A. Lic. Philosophy, U. Pontificia Quito (Ecuador), 1968; MDiv, St. Mary's U., Halafax, N.S., Can., 1973; MA in Theology, St. Michael's Coll., Toronto, Ont., Can., 1977; MS in Counseling, Barry U., 1979. Joined Soc. of Jesus. Theology dept. chmn., campus ministry dir., chaplain Belen Jesuit Prep. Sch., Miami, Fla., 1974—; dir. summer missionary work in Dominican Republic, Beler Jesuit Prep. Sch., Miami, 1976-91.

ALVAREZ TENA, VICTORINO, clergyman; b. Puruándiro, Mex., Mar. 10, 1920; s. Joaquín Alvarez Parra and Concepción Tena. Ed., Colegio Morelos de Puruándiro, Sem. de Morelia, Sem. de Montezuma. Ordained priest Roman Catholic Ch. Bishop Celaya, Mex. Home: Altamirano 404 en Celya, Guanajuato Mexico Office: Manuel Doblado 110 En Celaya, Guanajuato Mexico

ALVES, JOSEPH THOMAS, priest, mental health clinic executive; b. Boston, Oct. 4, 1921; s. Joseph Francis and Mary (McDermott) A.; A.B., Boston Coll., 1944, M.S.W., 1948; M.A., St. John's Sem., 1953, M.Div., 1977; Dr. Social Work, Catholic U. Am., 1959. Diplomate in Clin. Social Work; ordained priest Roman Cath. Ch., 1953. Assoc. dir. Pittsfield (Mass.) Community Chest and Berkshire County Council Social Agys., 1948-49; parish priest, Everett, Mass., 1953-56; elevated to domestic prelate by Pope, 1965; exec. dir. Family Counseling and Guidance Centers Inc., Boston, 1958-86; pastor St. Philip Neri Ch., Newton, Mass., 1986—; pres. Samaritans, Inc., 1977-84, dir., 1971—. Bd. dirs., exec. com. Nat. Council on Aging, 1969—, chmn. membership com., 1974-77, v.p., 1978-79; treas. Family Counseling Endowment Fund, Inc., 1980—; bd. dirs. Pastoral Service Commn., Mass. Council Chs., 1971-75; del. White House Conf. on Aging, 1961, 81; mem. adv. com. on services Mass. Dept. Pub. Welfare; mem. Health Planning Council for Greater Boston; chmn. adv. council for Community Mental Health Center Constrn.; mem. Beth Israel Hosp. com. on pub. responsibility in medicine and research, pres.'s coun. St. Margaret's Hosp.; trustee Third Century Found., Archdiocese Boston; bd. dirs. Assn. Psychiat. Outpatient Centers Am., 1978—, sec., 1979—, pres.-elect 1980; bd. dirs. Nat. Conf. Cath. Charities, 1959—; mem. affiliates council United Way Mass. Bay; mem. Gov.'s Com. on Children and the Family, 1979-82. Served as 1st lt., pilot USAAF, 1942-45. Decorated D.F.C., Air medal with oak leaf clusters. Mem. Nat. Assn. Social Workers (chmn. social policy and action com. Eastern Mass. chpt. 1967—), Acad. Religion and Mental Health, Gerontol. Soc. Inc., Nat. Council on Family Relations, Mass. Conf. on Social Welfare, Council Social Work Edn., Nat. Conf. Social Welfare, Nat. Conf. Catholic Charities, Am. Acad. Clin. Sociologists, Inst. Soc., Ethics and Life Scis., Internat. Council Social Welfare (U.S. com.), Am. Sociol. Assn., Acad. Polit. and Social Sci., Boston Soc. Gerontol. Psychiatry, Citizens for Decent Housing, Soc. Family Therapy and Research, Internat. Soc. Existential Psychology and Psychiatry, AAAS, Mass. Pub. Welfare Council, Am. Acad. Psychotherapists, Am. Arbitration Assn. (nat. panel arbitrators), AAAS, Mass. Assn. to Advance Human Scis., Am. Acad. Arts and Scis., Boston Latin Sch. Assn., South Shore C. of C., New Directions, Common Cause, World Federalist Assn., 73d Bomb Wing Assn. U.S. Air Force. Clubs: St. Botolph (Boston); Windsor (Newton). Author: Confidentiality in Social Work, 1959. Contbr. articles to profl. and popular jours. and mags. Home: 229 Adams St Milton MA 02186 Office: 1518 Beacon St Newton MA 02168

ALVIS, JOEL LAWRENCE, JR., minister; b. Memphis, Nov. 12, 1955; s. Joel Lawrence Sr. and Martha Jean (Lowe) A.; m. Vicki Lynn Welch, Aug. 12, 1978; children: Joel Lawrence III, Mark Thomas. BA, Samford U., 1977; MA, U. Miss., 1980; PhD, Auburn U., 1985; MDiv, Louisville Presbyn. Theol. Sem, 1989. Ordained to ministry Presbyn. Ch. (U.S.A.), 1989. Local ch. history and records adminstr. Presbyn. Hist. Found., Montreat, N.C., 1982-86; rsch. assoc. Louisville Presbyn. Sem., 1986-89; pastor St. Pauls (N.C.) Presbyn. Ch., 1989—; mem. com. on ministry Coastal Carolina Presbytery, Fayetteville, 1990—. Author: (with others) Diversity of Discipleship, 1991. Mem. Com. on Disabled, St. Pauls, 1991, John Walker Meml. Fund, St. Pauls, 1990. Recipient Nelson R. Burr prize Hist. Soc. of Episcopal Ch., 1981; Univ. fellow U. Miss., 1977-78, Anderson fellow Louisville Presbyn. Theol. Sem., 1991. Office: St Pauls Presbyn Ch 200 N Old Stage Rd Saint Pauls NC 28384

AMANO, KOEI HIROFUSA, religious philosophy educator; b. Yanai, Japan, June 30, 1931; s. Shunei Toshifusa and Tazuko A.; m. Noriko Amano, May 28, 1967; children: Takafusa, Tomofusa. BA, Ryukoku U., Kyoto, Japan, 1954; MA, Tohoku Grad. Sch., Sendai, Japan, 1956; post-grad., Tohoku Grad. Sch., 1956-59. Lectr. Tohoku U., 1963-66, Hijiyama Women's Jr. Coll., Hiroshima City, Japan, 1966-68; asst. prof. Hijiyama Women's Jr. Coll., 1968-77, prof., 1977-84; prof. Buddhist philosophy Shimane U., Matsue City, Japan, 1984—. Author: A Study on the Abhisamayālamkāra-kārikā-sāstra-vrtti, 1975. Mem. Soc. Indian and Buddhist Studies in Japan (award 1970), Japanese Assn. Religious Studies. Buddhist. Home: 1875 Yota, Yanai City 742, Japan Office: Shimane U, 1060 Nishikawatsu cho, Matsue 690, Japan

AMBROZIC, ALOYSIUS MATTHEW, archbishop; b. Gabrje, Slovenia, Yugoslavia, Jan. 27, 1930; s. Aloysius and Helen (Pecar) A. Student, St. Augustine Sem., 1955; S.T.L., U. San Tommaso, Rome, 1958, Sacrae Scripturae Licentiatus, Biblicum, Rome, 1960; Th.D., U. Wurzburg, 1970. Ordained priest Roman Cath. Ch., 1955; ordained aux. bishop of Roman Cath. Ch., Toronto, 1976; appointed Coadjutor Archbishop of Toronto, 1986-90, Archbishop of Toronto, 1990—; parish work Port Colborne, Ont., Can., 1955-56; faculty St. Augustines Sem., Scarborough, Ont., Can., 1956-76, dean studies, 1971-76; prof. N.T. exegesis Toronto Sch. Theology, 1970-76; apptd. to Pontifical Coun. for Pastoral Care of Migrants and Itinerant People, 1990, Vatican Congregation for Clergy, 1991; rep. Synod on the Formation of Priests, Rome, 1990. Author: The Hidden Kingdom: A Redaction-Critical Study of the References to the Kingdom of God in Mark's Gospel, 1972, Remarks on the Canadian Catechism, 1974; columnist The Cath. Register. Office: 355 Church St, Toronto, ON Canada M5B 1Z8

AMES, GUY CHETWOOD, III, minister; b. Oklahoma City, July 1, 1951; s. Guy C. Jr. and Mabel Jeanne (Cooper) A.; m. Margaret Theresa Gorham, May 19, 1978; children: Chet, Micah J., Aaron C. Student, Bacone Coll., 1969-70; BA in Psychology, Oral Roberts U., 1973; MDiv., Asbury Theol. Sem., 1978; D in Ministry, Phillips Grad. Sem., 1987. Ordained to ministry United Meth. Ch., deacon, 1971, elder, 1979. Min. Spencer Meml. United Meth. Ch., Muskogee, Okla., 1970, Asbury & Francis United Meth. Chs., Ada, Okla., 1978-83, Mustang (Okla.) United Meth. Ch., 1983-88, Wesley United Meth. Ch., El Reno, Okla., 1988—; disaster response coord. Okla. United Meth. Disaster Com., 1982-90; disaster response cons. United Meth. Com. on Relief, N.Y.C., 1988—; chair, post-grad. program Bd. Ordained Ministry, Okla. Conf., 1988—; reserve del. United Meth. Jurisdictional Conf., 1988. Mem. Child Abuse Task Force, Canadian County, Okla., 1990—. Mem. C. of C. (El Reno), Kiwanis (El Reno spiritual dir. 1989, 90). Democrat. Home: 100 S Macomb El Reno OK 73036 Office: Wesley United Meth Ch PO Box 216 El Reno OK 73036

AMES, JOHN COOPER, minister; b. Oklahoma City, June 14, 1961; s. Guy Chetwood and Mabel Jeanne (Cooper) A.; m. Deborah Lee Prescott, Aug. 12, 1989. BA in Psychology, Okla. State U., 1985; MDiv, So. Meth. U., 1989. Ordained to ministry United Meth. Ch., 1987. Dir., coord. Lake Texoma United Ministries, Inc., Texoma Lake, Okla./Tex., 1986-87; prog. coord. Cookson (Okla.) Hills United Meth. Mission, 1987-88; minister Okla. United Meth. Conf., Springer, Gene Autry, Okla., 1988-89, British Meth. Conf., Mansfield, Eng., 1989-90; min., dir. Wesley Found., Campus Ministry, U. Cen. Okla., Edmond, 1990—; pres. Perkins Evang. Fellowship, Dallas, 1986-87. Mem. Oklahomans-for-Life, 1982-91, Nat. Right to Life, Washington, 1984-88, Soc. for Protection of Unborn, London, 1990, SANE, Washington, 1984-88. Mem. Lions, Toastmasters. Home: 777 E 15th #159 Edmond OK 73013 Office: Wesley Found Campus Ministry 311 E Hurd Edmond OK 73034 *Peace will come not when conflict is absent, but when we face conflict, through the creative diversity of God's eternal faces; redeeming the dysfunctional and evil images that we constantly try and cosmetically paint on the face of God. The first place for peace must be in the Church universal.*

AMES, MARY JANE, religion educator; b. West Paris, Maine, Aug. 21, 1939; d. Lawrence Parker and Florence Nellie (Hart) Abbott; m. John Lyndon Ames, May 24, 1969; children: Alice Victoria, Lois Marie. Diploma in Christian Edn., Trinity Coll., 1966, BA, 1968. Tchr., treas. missions North Paris Bapt. Ch., West Paris, Maine, 1952-68; tchr. Sunday sch. Community Bapt. Ch., Gorham, N.H., 1972—, mem. missions com., 1980—; tchr. Community Bapt. Ch. Christian Sch., Gorham, 1976-88, sch. counselor, asst. dir., 1988—; mission sec., correspondent Community Bapt. Ch., Gorham, 1977—; del., supr. Accelerated Christian Edn., Gorham, 1987-90. Author: (poem) Winter, 1957 (Nat. Recognition award 1957). Del. Girls' State Am. Legion Aux., West Paris, Maine, 1956, Rep. Party State Conv., West Paris, 1961. Named to Pres.'s List Trinity Coll., 1968. Mem. H.O.P.E. Republican. Home: 12 School St Gorham NH 03581-1641 Office: Community Bapt Ch 108 Main St Gorham NH 03581-1645 *The joy of my life is knowing the Lord Jesus Christ as my personal Saviour and having a personal relationship with Him on a daily basis. I find this gives me a positive attitude in every area of my life, and greatly influences our family life as well as my social involvement, for the better.*

AMICO, SISTER GINA MARIA, nun, religious order councilor; b. Farrell, Pa., Mar. 4, 1936; d. Joseph and Josephine (Scarmack) A. RN, St. Michael Med. Ctr., Newark, 1960; BA, Goddard Coll., 1976. Joined Franciscan Sisters of St. Elizabeth, Roman Cath. Ch. 1952; cert. early childhood edn., handicapped and elem. tchr., N.J., Montessori tchr. Prin., dir. Franciscan Sisters St. Elizabeth Child Care Ctr., Jersey City, 1955-64; adminstr., prin. St. Elizabeth's Montessori Nursery Sch., Parsippany, N.J., 1970-84; dir. novices Franciscan Sisters St. Elizabeth, Parsippany, 1965-70; superior, prin., 1st councilor Franciscan Sisters St. Elizabeth, Jersey City, 1984—; tutor Sons of Italy Orphanage, Nutley, N.J., 1965-66; cons. Bldg. Blocks Nursery Sch., Wharton, N.J., 1978-81, co-pioneer, founder St. Elizabeth Convent Trichur Dt. Kerala, S. India. Democrat. Avocations: filmmaking, slide presentations. Home and Office: Franciscan Sisters 129 Garrison Ave Jersey City NJ 07306

AMIS, JOAN SKAGGS, lay worker; b. Stanton, Ky., June 14, 1934; d. Martin H. and Hazel (Walden) Skaggs; m. Robert Edward Amis, July 7, 1957 (dec. Apr. 1989); children: Jeanne Amis Jorash, Jonathan Edward, Amanda Martine, Evelyn Carol, Christopher Martin. MusB, U. Ky., 1956, MusM, 1957. Ch. organist 1st Bapt., Taylorsville, Ky., 1951-52; appointed missionary to Nigeria So. Bapt. Conv., Nigeria, 1965-73; dir. Sta. WNKJ Christian Radio, Penneyrile Christian Community, Hopkinsville, Ky., 1989—; pres. Penneyrile Christian Community, Hopkinsville, 1989—; weekly broadcaster Sta. WNKJ,. Hopkinsville, tchr. ladies' Bible study, 1973—. Soprano soloist at various chs. and pub. gatherings; recitals in Ky. and Nigeria; rec. vocal albums: The Glory of His Presence, 1969, To Encourage You, 1984. Republican. Home: 1524 E 7th St Hopkinsville KY 42240 *It is my desire to walk in the Spirit of my Lord Jesus Christ and to encourage others along the way.*

AMISSAH, JOHN KODWO, archbishop; b. Elmina, Ghana, Nov. 27, 1922; s. John Bentil and Mary Efua (Busumafi) A. JCD, Pontifical Urban U., Rome, 1954; DD honoris causa, LLD honoris causa, U. Cape Coast, Ghana, 1972. Asst. priest Sekondi (Ghana) Parish, 1950; tchr. St. Teresa's Minor Sem., Amisano, Elmina, Ghana, 1950-51, sr. Latin master, lectr. in canon law, 1954-57; aux. bishop Archdiocese of Cape Coast, Cen. Region, Ghana, 1957-59, archbishop, 1959—. Author: Fante Funeral Eulogy. Mem. Council of State, Accra, Ghana, 1969-72, Ghana Edn., Service Council, Accra, 1973-77. Recipient Grand medal Govt. of Ghana, 1975. Mem. Canon Law Soc. Am. Avocation: music. Address: care Archbishop's House, PO Box 112, 52A/2 Elmina Rd, Cape Coast Central, Ghana *Died Sept. 22, 1991.*

AMMONS, BRUCE CARL, minister; b. Spearman, Tex., Aug. 31, 1961; s. Darryl Carl and Dorothy Nell (Pitts) A.; m. Ruth Elaine Fortune, Nov. 9, 1959. BA in Theology, Wayland Bapt. U., 1985. Ordained to ministry Bapt. Ch., 1985. Youth minister 1st Bapt. Ch., Dimmitt, Tex., 1982-84, Hale Ctr., Tex., 1984-85; youth minister Monterey Bapt. Ch., Lubbock, Tex., 1985—. Named one of Outstanding Young Men in Am., 1985. Avocations: golf, snow skiing, camping, guitar playing, tennis. Office: Monterey Bapt Ch 3601-50th St Lubbock TX 79413

AMMONS, EDSEL ALBERT, bishop; b. Chgo., Feb. 17, 1924; s. Albert Clifton and Lila Kay (Sherrod) A.; m. June Billingsley, Aug. 18, 1951; children—Marilyn, Edsel, Carol, Kenneth, Carlton, Lila. B.A., Roosevelt U., 1948; B.D., Garrett Theol. Sem., 1956; D.Min., Chgo. Theol. Sem., 1975; D.D. (hon.), Westmar Coll., 1975. Social case worker Dept. Welfare Cook County, Chgo., 1951-56; ordained to ministry Meth. Ch., 1949; pastor Whitfield Meth. Ch., Chgo., 1957-60, Ingleside-Whitfield Meth. Ch., Chgo., 1960-63; dist. dir. urban work Rockford dist. No. Ill. Conf. United Meth. Ch., 1963-66; council staff ann. conf. No. Ill. Conf., 1966-68; urban ch. cons., prof. ch. and soc., dir. basic degree studies Garrett Evang. Theol. Sem., Evanston, Ill., 1968-76; bishop United Meth. Ch., Mich. area, 1976-84; bishop United Meth. Ch., West Ohio area, 1984—; exec. dir. Ednl. and Cultural Inst. Black Clergy, Chgo., 1972-73. V.p. Chatham-Avalon Community Council, Chgo., 1958-61; pres. W. Avalon Community Council, 1959-60. With U.S. Army, 1943-46. Mem. Alpha Phi Alpha. Office: United Meth Ch 471 Broad St Ste 1106 Columbus OH 43215

AMOS, JAMES LARRY, minister; b. Spartanburg, S.C., Feb. 3, 1938; s. Cedric DeFoix and Canzada Jane (Coggins) A.; m. Elizabeth Annette Westmoreland, Aug. 16, 1959; children: Carl, Warren, Dennis, Laura. AB, Wofford, 1959; MDiv, Emory U., 1962; D of Ministry, McCormick, 1988. Ordained to ministry Meth. Ch., 1961. Pastor Bethany United Meth. Ch., Fairburn, Ga., 1973-77, Social Circle United Meth. Ch., Social Circle, Ga., 1977-81, Franklin (Ga.) United Meth. Ch., 1981-84, Collins Meml. United Meth. Ch., Atlanta, 1984-89, Winterville (Ga.) United Meth. Ch., 1989—; chairperson Athens Urban Ministries, 1991—. Chaplain Winterville Civitan Club, 1990—; pres. Social Circle (Ga.) Lions Club, 1979. Home: PO Box 30 Winterville GA 30683 Office: Winterville United Meth Ch PO Box 30 Winterville GA 30068-3000

AMOS, STANLEY EDD, minister; b. Jackson, Miss., Dec. 18, 1956; m. Gladys Anes; m. Arlinda Staley, Aug. 15, 1987; 1 child, Preston Charles. BA in Polit. Sci. and Sociology, Tougaloo (Miss.) Coll., 1985; MDiv, Andover Newton Theol. Sch., Boston, 1988. Ordained to ministry Nat. Bapt. and Am. Bapt. Chs., 1983. Asst. pastor Zion Travelers Missionary Bapt. Ch., Jackson, Miss., 1983-85; chaplain Boston City Hosp., 1986; instl. chaplain Southeastern Correctional Ctr., Bridgewater, Mass., 1987-89; interim pastor Ebenezer Bapt. Ch., Boston, 1988-89; pastor Trinity Missionary Bapt. Ch., Honolulu, 1989—. Founder, exec. dir. The Hawaii African-Am. Unity Orgn., Honolulu, 1990—; advisor Martin Luther King Jr. Commn., 1990-91, apptd. chmn., 1991—. Fellow Afro-Am. Ministerial Alliance, The Afro-Am. Assn. of Hawaii; mem. NAACP, Hawaii Assn. Am. Bapt. Chs. (exec. bd. 1989—), African Am. C. of C. Hawaii (exec. bd.), Afro-Am. C. of C. (fellow mem.). Home: 3950 Paine Cir Honolulu HI 96818 Office: Trinity Missionary Bapt Ch PO Box 31182 Honolulu HI 96820

AMRICH, DELORES ELAINE, religion educator; b. Morrisville, Pa., June 6, 1936; d. Frederick A. and Viola Mildred (Kuhl) Nirshl; m. Richard E. Amrich, Aug. 17, 1957; children: Denise Marie, Daniel Edward. Student, Mercer County Community Coll., Trenton, N.J., 1989-91. Tchr. religion Incarnation Parish, Trenton, 1980—; bookkeeper N.J. Mfrs. Ins. Co., Trenton. Sec. Mercer County 4-H Adv. Bd., Trenton, 1970-71, leader, tchr. 4-H Club, camp counselor, Stokes Forest, N.J.; v.p. Cath. Adopt Mothers Club, Trenton, 1974, pres., 1975. Home: 1 Aaron Ave Trenton NJ 08618 *My thoughts are: Take one day and live it to its fullness, making sure to make someone smile. I have made my hobby making people happy. The old rule I try to live by is: Do unto others what you would want done unto you.*

AMSLER, LAURA LYNN, lay minister; b. Cedar Rapids, Iowa, Aug. 19, 1963; d. Raymond Harold and Judith Arlene (Vlcko) A.; m. James Stephen Cain, Aug. 13, 1988. BS in Social Work, Iowa State U., 1986. Ordained to ministry Roman Cath. Ch. Peer min. St. Thomas Aquinas Ch. and Student Ctr., Ames, Iowa, 1983-84; migrant min. Diocese of New Ulm, Olivia and Bird Island, Minn., summers 1985, 86; dir. youth ministry Christian Family Sch. Religion, Calmar, Iowa, 1986-88, St. James Ch., Cin., 1988—. Fellow Cath. Youth Min.'s Assn. (svc. team 1989-90). Home: 3585 Epley Ln #1 Cincinnati OH 45247 Office: St James Ch 3565 Hubble Rd Cincinnati OH 45247

AMSTUTZ, JAMES LOUIS, minister; b. Lima, Ohio, Jan. 9, 1960; s. John Francis and Edna Lavonne (Scheele) A.; m. Joyce Elaine Thorp, Aug. 23, 1987. B of Religion, Great Lakes Bible Coll., Lansing, Mich., 1987; post-grad., Emmanuel Sch. of Religion, Johnson City, Tenn. Youth minister Macomb Christian Ch., Sterling Heights, Mich., 1986-87; assoc. minister 1st Christian Ch., Kingsport, Tenn., 1987-91. Sgt. USAF, 1978-82. Home: 1108 Jay St Johnson City TN 37601

ANANTHASOUTHONE, THONG KHOUNE, religious organization executive; b. Ban Lopadi Khong, Champasak, Laos, Dec. 31, 1923; s. Phahn and Kong A. Student secondary sch., 1933-39. Monk, Nalom Temple, 1943-46; with Lao Buddhist Fellowship Orgn., Vientiane, Laos, 1946—, sec., 1976-79, pres., 1979—; leader Lao Buddhist del. Internat. Conf. on Buddhism and Nat. Cultures, 1984. Author: The Buddhism, 1946 (medal of ABCP in Mongolia 1982). Active in internat. peace movements, 1976—. Office: That Luang Neua Temple, Xaysetha, Vientiane Lao People's Democratic Republic

ANDERSEN, FRANCES ELIZABETH GOLD, religious leadership educator; b. Hot Springs, Ark., Feb. 11, 1916; d. Benjamin Knox and Pearl Scott (Smith) Gold; m. Robert Thomas Andersen, June 27, 1942; children: Nancy Ruth (Mrs. Bernd Neumann), Robert Thomas. BA, UCLA, 1936, sec. teaching credential, 1937. Tchr. math. L.A. City Schs., 1937-42, 46-48; faculty Ariz. State Coll., Tempe, 1943-45; mem. nat. bd. missions United Meth. Ch., 1940-44; dir. Christian edn. 1st Presbyn. Ch., Phoenix, 1943-45, Trinity Meth. ch., L.A., 1953-55, 1st Bapt. Ch., Lakewood, Calif., 1955-57; dir. Christian edn. Grace Bapt. Ch., Riverside, 1958-83, chmn. nursery sch. bd., 1969-83; mem. nat. bd. Bible sch. and youth Bapt. Gen. Conf., 1966-71; coord. leadership tng. insts. Greater L.A. Sunday Sch. Assn., 1956-80; exec. dir. San Bernardino-Riverside Sunday Sch. Assn., 1959—; prin. Riverside Christian Sch., 1985-87, bd. dirs., 1985—; mem. Christian edn. bd. S.W. Bapt. Conf., 1956-59, 63-66, 72-75, 80-83; bd. dirs. GLASS, 1956—; dir. Women's guild, Calif. Bapt. Coll., Riverside, 1983—. Author: How to Organize Area Leadership Training Institutes, 1964. Pres. Univ. Jr. High Sch., PTA, Riverside, 1963-64, Poly High Sch., PTA, 1965-67; life mem. PTA. Named Grace Bapt. Mother of Yr., 1981. Mem. Sons of Norway, Alpha Delta Chi (nat. pres. 1950-51, exec. sec. 1952-54), Pi Mu Epsilon. Avocations: travel, entertaining, music. Home: 1787 Prince Albert Dr Riverside CA 92507 *Serving the Lord brings joy and fulfillment—working together with God's dedicated servants; witnesssing lives transformed by the power of the Holy Spirit; seeing children, youth and adults grow in grace and in the knowledge of God as they are taught God's Word.*

ANDERSEN, FRANCIS IAN, minister, educator; b. Warwick, Australia, July 28, 1925; came to U.S., 1958; s. Rasmus Ludwig Emil and Hilda Fanny (Holmes) A.; m. Lois Clarissa Garrett, Dec. 5, 1952; children: John, David, Martin, Nedra, Kathryn. BS (with honors), U. Queensland, Australia, 1947; MS, U. Melbourne, Australia, 1951, BA, 1955; BD (with honors), U. London, 1956; MA, Johns Hopkins U., 1958, PhD, 1960; DD (hon.), Ch. Div. Sch. of the Pacific, 1972. Ordained to ministry Anglican Ch., 1958. V.p. Ridley Coll., Melbourne, 1960-62; prof. Old Testament Ch. Div. Sch. of the Pacific, Berkeley, Calif., 1963-72; warden St. John's Coll., Auckland, New Zealand, 1973; mission chaplain Fellowship of St. John, Brisbane, Australia, 1981-88; chaplain New Coll. for Advanced Christian Studies, Berkeley, 1988—. Author: Verbless Clause, 1970, The Sentence, 1974; co-author: (commentaries) Job, 1976, Hosea, 1980, Amos, 1989. Fulbright scholar, 1958; Rayner fellow Johns Hopkins U., 1959; grantee NEH, 1972, Australian Rsch. Coun., 1979-89. Office: New Coll for Advanced Christian Studies 2600 Dwight Way Berkeley CA 94704

ANDERSEN, JOHN PRINZING, minister; b. Decatur, Ill., Mar. 19, 1965; s. Elward Dean and R. Whanola (Deal) A. ; m. Carrie S. Aaron, Dec. 21, 1985; 1 child, John Prinzing Jr. AA in Religion, Brewton-Parker Coll., 1985, BMin., 1987; MDiv., So. Bapt. Theol. Sem., 1990. Ordained to ministry So. Bapt. Conv. Min. youth Meml. Bapt. Ch., Jesup, Ga., 1985; min. children Southside Bapt. Ch., Hazelhurst, Ga., 1986; pastor Blockhouse Bapt. Ch., Jacksonville, Ga., 1986-87; min. youth Mt. Tabor United Meth. Ch., Crestwood, Ky., 1987-88; pastor First Bapt. Ch., Loogootee, Ind., 1988-90, Georgetown (Ind.) So. Bapt. Ch., 1990—; mem. assist team S.E. Assn., Jeffersonville, Ind., 1991. Mem. Ams. United for Separation of Ch. and State, Georgetown Ministerial Assn., Brewton-Parker Coll. Alumni Assn. (pres. 1990—). Republican. Home: 8585 State Rd 64 Georgetown IN 47122

ANDERSEN, RICHARD, minister; b. Kansas City, Kans., Aug. 23, 1931; s. Marius Thevdor and Ellen Kjestine (Christensen) A.; m. Lois Jeanette Petersen, June 9, 1957; children: Kristyn, Deryk, Jennifer. BA, Dana Coll., 1953; MDiv, Trinity Theol. Sem., 1960; PhD, Calif. Grad. Sch. Theology, 1972. Ordained to ministry Luth. Ch., 1960. Intern pastor St. Andrew Ch., Whittier, Calif., 1958-69; assoc. pastor Valley Luth. Ch., North Hollywood, Calif., 1960-62; founding pastor Luth. Ch. of the Holy Cross, Ojai, Calif., 1962-64; pastor Grace Luth. Ch., Rancho Cordova, Calif., 1964-68; sr. pastor Luth. Ch. of the Master, La Habra, Calif., 1968-73; founding pastor Community Ch. of Joy, Glendale, Ariz., 1964-78; sr. pastor Our Saviour's Luth. Ch., Long Beach, Calif., 1978-87, St. Timothy's Luth. Ch., San Jose, Calif., 1987—. Author: Devotions Along the Way, 1972, Loving in Forgiveness, 1973, Your Keys to the Executive Suite, 1973, Flights of Devotion, 1973, The Love Formula, 1974, Roads to Recovery, 1974, Now the Good Wine, 1974, For Those Who Mourn, 1974, The Joy of Easter, 1975, Highways to Health, 1975, The Bread of Christmas, 1975, For Grieving Friends, 1975, Living Lenten Portraits, 1975, Grace and the Rest of Life, 1976, Devotions for Church School Teachers, 1976, (with Roy Barlag) They Were There, 1977, (with Donald L. Deffner) For Example, 1977, Inspirational Meditations for Sunday School Teachers, 1980, Sermon Illustrations for the Gospel Lessons, 1980, 82, Devotional Guidebook for Board and Committee Chairpersons, 1982, The Positive Power of Christian Partnership, 1982, Every Child is a Greening Valley, 1991; contbr. to 9 sermon anthologies and articles to jours. and newspapers. Recipient Disting. Merit citation NCCJ, 1987, Medal of Honor DAR, 1985. Mem. Sierra Pacific Synod Communications Commn., Concern for the Poor Inc. (sec.). Home: 372 Colville Dr San Jose CA 95123 Office: 5100 Camden Ave San Jose CA 95124 *Of all life's needs, faith is major and joy follows. It is in Christ that we find the source of faith and the cause for joy, because both stretch beyond the immediate to the eternal. For that reason, though it is popular today to put it aside, I opt for a buoyant faith that is never drowned by life's waves.*

ANDERSEN, VICTOR EUGENE, minister; b. Smith Center, Kans., Jan. 27, 1956; s. Victor Carsten Einar and Helen Olena (Aase) A.; m. Sue Karen Peterson, Aug. 19, 1978; children: Eric Jens, Rebecca Lis. BA, Tex. Luth. Coll., 1978; MDiv, Wartburg Theol. Sem., 1982. Ordained to ministry Evang. Luth. Ch., 1983. Lay min. Faith in Christ Luth. Ch., Daingerfield, Tex., 1982-83; pastor Faith Luth Ch., Meridian, Tex., 1983-85, Trinity Luth. Ch., Haskell, Tex., 1985-89, Christ Luth. Ch., Stamford, Tex., 1985-89, First Luth. Ch., Floresville, Tex., 1989—; pres. Haskell Ministerial Alliance, 1987-88; treas. Big Country Luths., Abilene, Tex., 1985-89; mem. San Antonio Conf. Exec. Com., S.W Tex. Synod, 1990—; mem. Floresville Ministerial Alliance, Floresville, 1990—. Coach Floresville Little League, 1990; mem. Village Band, Floresville, 1990—. Mem. Floresville Lions Club (1st v.p. 1991—), Haskell Lions Club (pres. 1987-88). Office: First Luth Ch 1406 Sixth St Floresville TX 78114

ANDERSON, ALAN BRAUER, religion educator, administrator; b. Oklahoma City, Dec. 4, 1934; s. Homer Spaulding and Margaret Frances (Brauer) A.; m. Deborah H. Nelson, Aug. 11, 1956 (div. 1976); children: Amy Elizabeth, Margaret Hunt; m. Gwyneth B. Davis, Apr. 22, 1978 (dec. 1988). BA, Knox Coll., 1956; BD, U. Chgo., 1959, MA, 1966, PhD, 1975. Ordained to ministry United Meth. Ch., 1961. Instr., then asst. prof. Div. Sch., U. Chgo., 1966-75; prof. interdisciplinary studies Wilberforce (Ohio) U., 1976-78; head dept. religious studies U. N.C., Greensboro, 1978-83; head dept. philosophy and religion Western Ky. U., Bowling Green, 1985—. Author: Confronting the Color Line, 1986; editor: Desegregation and Chicago Public Schools, 1976. Rockefeller Bros. Theology fellow, 1956-57, Danforth Grad. fellow, 1957-59, 62-66. Mem. Am. Acad. Religion (chmn. ethics sect. 1983-86, bd. dirs. 1983-88), Southeastern Am. Acad. Religion (sec.-treas. 1983-88), Soc. Christian Ethics (bd. dirs. 1984-86, editor ann. 1985-86), Phi Beta Kappa. Office: Western Ky U Dept Philosophy & Religion Bowling Green KY 42101

ANDERSON, BERT AXEL, minister; b. L.A., Feb. 18, 1929; s. Bert Axel and Alma Louise (Tucker) A.; m. Valdene Vanote, 1951 (div. 1971); children: Bert III, Michael, John; m. Nancy Lou Daniels, Dec. 3, 1973. BA, Calif. State U., L.A., 1956; MDiv, Ch. Div. Sch., Berkeley, Calif., 1959; PhD, Sierra U., Costa Mesa, Calif., 1988. Ordained to ministry, Episcopal Ch. Chaplain Episcopal Community Svc., San Diego, 1954-60; rector St Andrews by the Sea Episcopal Ch., San Diego, 1960-67; vicar Holy Spirit Episcopal Ch., Bullhead City, Ariz., 1979-82; pastoral assoc. Trinity Episcopal Ch., Redlands, Calif., 1988—; marriage and family therapist Redlands, Calif., 1967—; cons. on ch. conflict, Redlands, 1990—. Contbr. articles to profl. jours. Mem. Calif. Assn. Marriage and Family Therapists, Alban Inst., Am. Assn. of Applied Psychophysiology and Biofeedback. Republican.

ANDERSON, CARL AUGUST, educational administrator; b. Anoka, Minn., July 12, 1929; s. August and Grace Edith (Waddell) A.; m. Verna Mary Getter, June 3, 1949; children—Gary Dean, Linda Jean Anderson Peterson. B.A., Minn. Bible Coll., 1951; B.D., Butler U., 1956; M.Ed. U. Ariz., 1969. Ordained to ministry Church of Christ, 1951. Minister, Ch. of Christ, Canno Falls, Minn., 1950-51, Campbellsburg, Ind., 1951-52, Lexington, Ind., 1952-56; minister Christian Ch., Casa Grande, Ariz., 1956-61, Ch. of Christ, Tucson, 1961-77; prof., acad. dean Boise Bible Coll., Idaho, 1977—; tchr. Dist. #1, Tucson, 1962-71; pres., v.p. Ariz. Christian Conv., Phoenix, 1960; dir. Ariz. Evang. Assn., Phoenix, 1968-77; mem. adv. council San Jose Bible Coll., Calif., El Paso Christian Coll., Tex., 1974-77. Mem. Ariz. Edn. Assn., Tucson Edn. Assn. (rep. 1964-71), NEA, Phi Delta Kappa. Republican. Home: 3662 Pepperwood Dr Boise ID 83704 Office: Boise Bible Coll 8695 Marigold St Boise ID 83714

ANDERSON, CLIFTON EINAR, editor, writer; b. Frederic, Wis., Dec. 17, 1923; s. Andrew John and Ida Louise (Johnson) A.; m. Phyllis Mary Nolan, Oct. 5, 1943; children: Kristine, Craig. BS, U. Wis., 1947; MA, U. Calif., Berkeley, 1954. News editor Chgo. Daily Drover's Jour., 1943-45; asst. editor The Progressive, Madison, Wis., 1946-47; dir. publs. Am. Press, Beirut, 1948-53; mgr. rural programs Houston C. of C., 1957-62; faculty Tex. A&M U., College Station, 1962-65; rsch. fellow U. Tex., Austin, 1965-68; faculty Southwestern Okla. U., Weatherford, 1968-72; extension editor U. Idaho, Moscow, 1972—; speaker John Macmurray Centennial Conf., Marquette U., 1991. Editor: The Horse Interlude, 1976; author: (with others) Ways Out: The Book of Changes for Peace, 1988, The Future: Opportunity Not Destiny, 1989; contbr. articles to profl. jours. and mags. Chmn. ch. and soc. com. 1st Presbyn. Ch., Moscow, 1982-86; treas. Moscow Sister City Assn., 1986—; sec.-treas. Latah Task Force on Human Rights, Moscow, 1989-91; founding mem. Coalition for Cen. Am., Moscow, 1986; chmn. U. Idaho Affirmative Action Com., 1990; writer campaign staff Senator R.M. La Follette, Jr., Madison, Wis., 1946, on the senatorial campaign staff of Hubert H. Humphrey, Mpls., 1948; chmn. Borah Found. for the Outlawry of War, U. Idaho, 1986-87, chmn. Borah Symposium, 1986-87. Recipient Rsch. award The Fund for Adult Edn., 1954-55, U.S. Office Edn., 1965-68, 1st prize in newswriting competition Assn. Am. Agrl. Coll. Editors, 1976. Mem. World Future Soc. (speaker 6th gen. assembly 1989), Agr., Food and Social Values Soc., Agrl. Communicators in Edn., Am. Acad. Religion, Profs. World Peace Acad., Martin Peace Inst. (Moscow, adv. com.). Democrat. Avocations: gardening, photography, writing poetry. Home: 234 N Washington St Moscow ID 83843 Office: U Idaho Agrl Communications Ctr Moscow ID 83843

ANDERSON, CRAIG BARRY, bishop; b. Glendale, Calif., Feb. 12, 1942. BA, Valparaiso U., 1963; grad., U. of South Sch. Theology; MA, Vanderbilt U., 1981, PhD, 1985. Ordained priest, Episcopal Ch., 1975. With mktg. div. Procter and Gamble, 1965-71; faculty U. of the South Sch. of Theology, Sewanee, Tenn.; bishop Diocese of S.D., Rapid City, 1984—. Served with AUS, 1963-65. Office: Diocese of SD 200 W 18th St PO Box 517 Sioux Falls SD 57101

ANDERSON, DANITA RUTH, minister; b. Chgo., Nov. 5, 1956; d. Walter and Doris E. (Terrell) A. BSBA, Chgo. State U., 1978; MDiv, Gammon Theol. Sem., Atlanta, 1983. Ordained deacon United Meth. Ch., 1983, elder, 1985. Ch. sec. Grace-Calvary Ch., Chgo., 1976-78; parish sec. Ingleside-Whitfield Meth. Ch., Chgo., 1978-79; computer programmer trainee Sears, Roebuck & Co., Chgo., 1979-80; ch. sec. Gorham United Meth. Ch., Chgo., 1980; asst. pastor Cascade United Meth. Ch., Atlanta, 1980-83; assoc. minister St. Mark Ch., Chgo., 1983-86; pastor Neighborhood United Meth. Ch., Maywood Ill., 1986-90; pastor Ingleside-Whitfield United Meth. Ch., Chgo., 1990—; pres. coun. on fin. and adminstrn. No. Ill. Conf.; sec. Clergy Fellowship; chairperson Black Meths. for Ch. Renewal, Chgo., 1979; mem. Acad. for Preaching of the Gen. Bd. of Discipleship of United Meth. Ch. Bd. Global Ministries Crusade scholar, 1981-83; Women's Div. United Meth. Ch. grantee, 1982; recipient Joseph W. Queen award Gammon Sem., 1982, James and Emma Todd award, 1983. Mem. Delta Sigma Theta. Home: 7144 S Jeffery Blvd Apt #10B Chicago IL 60649 Office: 929 E 76th St Chicago IL 60619

ANDERSON, DAVID LAWRENCE, college official, minister; b. Onawa, Iowa, July 31, 1934; s. Oscar Britanius and Nina Christina (Olson) A. BA, St. Olaf Coll., 1956; MDiv, Luther Theol. Sem., 1960. Ordained minister, Luth. Ch., 1960. Pastor youth and edn. Hill Ave Grace Luth. Ch., Pasadena, Calif., 1960-63; asst. dean men St. Olaf Coll., Northfield, Minn., 1963-66; pastor youth & edn. Cen. Luth. Ch., Mpls., 1967-72; dean students Golden Valley Luth. Coll., Mpls., 1972-73; sr. pastor Trinity Luth. Ch., Moorhead, 1973-85; exec. v.p. Ebenezer Soc., Mpls., 1986-88; v.p. sem. relations Luther Northwestern Sem., St. Paul, 1988-90; v.p. coll. rels. St. Olaf Coll., Northfield, Minn., 1990—; instr. Luther Theological Sem., St. Paul, Minn., 1972-73, Fargo/Moorhead Communiversity Concordia Coll., Moorhead, Minn., 1977. Contbr. Book of Sermons, Augsburg Book of Sermons, 1984, 85; composer: Sunday School Christmans Songs, 1972. Mem. Nat. Soc. Fund Raising Execs., Assn. Luth. Devel. Execs. Office: St Olaf Coll Northfield MN 55057

ANDERSON, DAVID RICHARD, film producer; b. Pasadena, Calif., Feb. 25, 1943; s. Arthur David and Mabel Marion (Lundin) A.; m. Carol Belle Kelley, Aug. 31, 1963; children: Arlene, Laura, Rebecca. BA, Calif. State U., L.A., 1965; MDiv, Fuller Sem., 1968. Assoc. producer Johnson-Nyquist Films, Northridge, Calif., 1964-72; v.p. Cathedral Films, Burbank, Calif., 1973-79; bd. dirs. Bd. Publs. Covenant Ch., Chgo. Author: Vixualize, Live-Laugh-Love. Set designer Muskegen (Mich.) Civic Theatre, 1989—; assoc. producer Miss Mich. Pageant, Muskegen. Mem. Christian Mgmt. Asn., Fuller Theol. Sem. Alumni (chmn.). Republican. Office: Gospel Films 2735 E Apple Ave Muskegon MI 49443

ANDERSON, DENNIS ALBIN, bishop; b. Glenwood, Minn., July 8, 1937; s. Albin G. and Florence Elizabeth (Larson) A.; m. Barbara Ann Forse, Dec. 30, 1960; children: Kristin, Charles. B.A., Gustavus Adolphus Coll., 1959; M.Div., Luth. Sch. Theology, Chgo., 1963; D.Div. hon., Gustavus Adolphus Coll., 1978; D.H.L. (hon.), Midland Luth. Coll., Fremont, Nebr., 1980. Ordained to ministry Lutheran Ch. Am., 1963. Mission developer Luth. Ch. in Am., Austin, Tex., 1963-64; pastor Holy Cross Luth. Ch., Austin, 1964-66, Luth. Ch. Good Shepherd, Prospect Heights, Ill., 1966-71, St. Paul Luth. Ch., Grand Island, Nebr., 1973-78; bishop Nebr. synod Luth. Ch. in Am., Omaha, 1978—, mem. exec. council, 1976-84; pres. Trinity Luth. Sem., Columbus, Ohio, 1990—. Author: Searching for Faith, 1975, Baptism and ..., 1976, Jesus My Brother in Suffering, 1977. Office: Trinity Luth Sem 2199 E Main St Columbus OH 43209

ANDERSON, DONALD WHIMBEY, priest, council executive; b. Ottawa, Ont., Can., Oct. 14, 1931; arrived in Eng., 1988; s. Roland Kumpf and Florence Catharine (Whimbey) A.; m. Veronica Agnes Ryan, Sept. 11, 1954; children: Hilary Mary, Mark Ryan. BA, U. Toronto, Ont., Can., 1954; MA, U. Toronto, 1958; STB, U. Trinity Coll., Toronto, 1957; ThD, Toronto Sch. Theology, 1971; postgrad., Harvard U., 1959-60. Ordained priest Anglican Ch. of Can., 1957. Priest asst. St. James Cathedral, Toronto, 1957-59; lectr. Cen. Theol. Coll., Tokyo, 1960-61; rector Ch. of the Holy Wisdom, Japan, 1961-64; prof. Cen. Theol. Coll, St. Paul's U., Tokyo, 1964-73, St. Andrew's Sem., Manila, Philippines, 1974-75; gen,. sec. Can. Coun. Chs., Toronto, 1975-88; ecumenical officer Anglican Consultative Coun., London, 1988—. Sidney Childs fellow, 1969-71. Office: Anglican Consultative Coun, 157 Waterloo Rd, London SE1 8UT, England

ANDERSON, ELDON THURLOW, minister; b. Tennessee Ridge, Tenn., Aug. 24, 1935; s. James Daniel and Thula Idel (Barnes) A; m. Naomi Francise Wilson, Dec. 26, 1959; children: Mark Allen, Dale Edward, Douglas Duane, Beth Yvonne. Student, So. Ill. U., Edwardsville, 1957-59, Cen. Bible Coll., Springfield, Mo., 1967-75. Ordained to ministry Assemblies of God. Sunday sch. tchr. Washington Park Assembly of God Ch., East St. Louis, Ill., 1957—, deacon, 1968-79, assoc. min., 1987—; field engr. NCR Corp., St. Louis, 1960—; dir. sectional men's ministry Ill. dist. coun. Assemblies of God, Carlinville, 1977-85. With U.S. Army, 1959-66. Home: 205 Julia St Collinsville IL 62234

ANDERSON, GENE RAY, minister; b. Independence, Mo., Oct. 28, 1934; s. Lewis Pendleton Anderson and Naomi Esther (Porter) Sutton; m. Doris Carolyn Wright, May 1, 1961 (div. June 1974); m. Susan Lee Johnson, Mar. 1, 1975; children: Lisa, Amy, Laura. BS, Cen. Mo. State U., 1956; MDiv, Episc. Theol. Sem. of SW, 1964. Ordained to ministry Episc. Ch. as priest, 1965; cert. pastoral counseling. Rector St. Andrew's Episcopal Ch., Leonardtown, Md., 1964-68, St. Mark's Episcopal Ch., Highland, Md., 1968-75; vicar St. Luke's Episcopal Chapel, Annapolis, Md., 1976-78; rector St. John's Episcopal Ch., Marcellus, N.Y., 1978—; sec., asst. Diocesan Conv., Diocese of Cen. N.Y., Syracuse, 1986—, chair cons. commn., 1982—, mem. diocesan personnel com., 1982-86. Mem. Institutional Rev. Bd. for Rsch. on Human Subjects SUNY, Syracuse, 1989—. With U.S. Army, 1956-59. Home: 11 Orange St Marcellus NY 13108 Office: St Johns Episcopal Ch 15 Orange St Marcellus NY 13108

ANDERSON, GERALD HARRY, religious organization administrator, educator; b. New Castle, Pa., June 9, 1930; s. Elmer Arthur and Dorothy Emma (Miller) A.; m. Joanne Marie Pemberton, July 9, 1960; children: Brooks Arthur, Allison Hope. BS in Commerce, Grove City Coll., 1952; MDiv, Boston U., 1955; cert., U. Geneva, 1957; postgrad., U. Edinburgh, Scotland, 1957; PhD, Boston U., 1960. Ordained to ministry United Meth. Ch., 1955. Assoc. minister Trinity United Meth. Ch., Providence, 1957-60; prof. ch. history and ecumenics Union Theol. Sem., Manila, Philippines, 1961-70; pres. Scarritt Coll., Nashville, 1970-73; sr. research assoc. S.E. Asia program Cornell U., Ithaca, N.Y., 1973-74; assoc. dir. Overseas Ministries Study Ctr., Ventnor, N.J., 1974-76, dir., 1976-87; dir. Overseas Ministries Study Ctr., New Haven, 1987—; Beamer lectr. DePauw U., Greencastle, Ind., 1971; Hester lectr. Edn. Commn., So. Bapt. Conv., 1979; Belk lectr. Wesleyan Coll., Macon, Ga., 1980; Van Dyke lectr. Calvin Sem., Grand Rapids, Mich., 1984; Ingram lectr. Memphis Theol. Sem., 1989; E. Stanley Jones lectr. Boston U. Sch. Theology, 1989; Isaac Hecker lectr. St. Paul's Coll., Washington, 1990. Co-author, editor: The Theology of the Christian Mission, 1961, Christ and Crisis in Southeast Asia, 1968, Studies in Philippine Church History, 1969, Asian Voices in Christian Theology, 1976; co-editor: Concise Dictionary of the Christian World Mission, 1971, Christ's Lordship and Religious Pluralism, 1981, Mission Trends, 5 vols., 1976, Mission in the 1990s, 1991; editor Internat. Bull. Missionary Rsch., 1977—. Mem. Fellowship of Reconciliation, Nyack, N.Y., 1966—; trustee Found. Theol. Edn. SE Asia, N.Y.C., 1975—, U.S. Cath. Mission Assn., 1983-90, Mission Soc. United Meths., Decatur, Ga., 1984—. Recipient Disting. Alumnus award Boston U. Sch. Theology, 1971; Fulbright scholar Marburg U., Fed. Republic Germany, 1955-56. Mem. Internt. Assn. Mission Studies (pres. 1982-85), Am. Soc. Missiology (pres. 1973-75, sec.-treas. 1976-79), Am. Soc. Ch. History, Assn. Profs. Mission, Deutsche Gesellschaft für Missionswissenschaft. Office: Overseas Ministries Study Ctr 490 Prospect St New Haven CT 06511

ANDERSON, GERSHON FREDDIE, minister; b. Freetown, Sierra Leone, Nov. 28, 1930; s. Geroge and Mary-Weather (Ward) A.; m. Beatrice Gershon Thomas, Oct. 7, 1961; children: Gershon Ward, Beatrice Ward. Student, U. Durham, Freetown, 1953-56, Swansea U. Coll., Wales, Eng., 1958-61. Cir. probationer min. Meth. Ch. Sierra Leone, Freetown, 1956-63, cir. supt., 1964-80, chmn. western dist., 1980-86, pres. conf., 1987—. Author: Speaking in Verse, 1983, 8 Years in The Wilberforce Circuit, 1986. Fellow Victoria Coll. Music; mem. Lodge Harmony 1448 S.C. Master Mason Date. Office: Meth Ch Sierra Leone, 4 George St, Western Area Sierra Leone

ANDERSON, GLENN ALLEN, minister; b. Forest Lake, Minn., May 29, 1948; s. August and Grace (Waddell) A.; m. Linda Mae Feece, Aug. 16, 1969; children: Jena Marie, Jeremy Paul, Jolynda Sue. BS in Ministry, Minn. Bible Coll., 1971; postgrad., Lincoln (Ill.) Christian Sem., 1971-72. Ordained to ministry Christian Ch./Chs. of Christ. Pastor/minister First Christian Ch., Sciota, Ill., 1971-73, Lane, Ill., 1973-76, Bushnell, Ill., 1977-78, Francesville, Ind., 1979-84; pastor/minister Southside Christian Ch., Ottawa, Ill., 1984—; bd. dirs., sec. Rock River Christian Camp, Polo, Ill., 1989—. Office: Southside Christian Ch 1180 Catherine St Ottawa IL 61350

ANDERSON, GORDON LOUIS, foundation executive, educator; b. St. Croix Falls, Wis., Nov. 16, 1947; s. Erwin Louis and Eunice Arlene (Johnson) A.; m. Mary Jane Evenson, July 1, 1982; children: Tamara, Jayna, Greta, Evan. BME, U. Minn., 1975; MDiv in Ethics, Union Theol. Sem., N.Y.C., 1980; MA in Religion, Claremont Grad. Sch., 1985, PhD Philosophy Religion, 1986. Engr. Gull Engring. Inc., Mpls., 1974-80, now bd. dirs.; owner, mgr. Aerograph Aerial Photography, Claremont, Calif., 1981-84; sec. gen. Profs. World Peace Acad., N.Y.C., 1984—; sec., gen., bd. dirs. Internat. Cultural Found., N.Y.C., 1986—; lectr. Unification Theol. Sem., Barrytown, N.Y., 1987—, bd. dirs., 1988—. Assoc. editor Internat. Jour. on World Peace, 1985—; contbr. articles and book revs. to profl. jours., chpts. to books. Mem. Citizens for Better N.J., 1986—. With U.S. Army, 1969-72, Vietnam. Mem. Am. Acad. Religion, Am. Polit. Sci. Assn., Internat. Studies Assn., Consortium on Peace Rsch. Mem. Unification Ch. Office: Internat Cultural Found 4 W 43d St New York NY 10036 *Religion or culture has always defined manhood, womanhood, the relation to our neighbor, the government, the spiritual world and God. This has yet to take place in a normative way for the modern world.*

ANDERSON, GREGG WINSTON, evangelist; b. Cin., Oct. 11, 1953; s. William M. and Julia J. Anderson. AA in Liberal Arts, St. Catharine Jr. Coll., Springfield, Ky., 1972; BS in Psychology and Communications, Trevecca Nazarene Coll., Nashville, 1976; cert. in pastoral counseling, Assemblies of God Theol. Sem., Springfield, Mo., 1989. Ordained to ministry Evang. Ch., 1990. Dir. no. Ky. region Fellowship Christian Athletes, Highland Heights, 1984-86; dir. pub. rels. Christian Leaders and Sunday Sch., Cin., 1990—; dir. publicity Full Gospel Bus. Men's, Covington, Ky., 1990—; exec. dir. 70x7 Evangelistic Ministry, Highland Heights, 1990—; exec. bd. Jesus 1990's, Cin., 1991—; vis. instr. Cin. Christian Coll., 1990—; bd. dirs. Action Unltd. News Svc., Hightland Heights, Ky. Mem. No. Ky. Teen Com., Covington, 1987, Highland Heights Planning and Zoning, 1990. Named Ky. Col., Gov. of Ky., 1989; Gregg Anderson Day established in his honor Mayor of Cin., 1987. Office: 70x7 Evangelistic Ministry PO Box 151 Highland Heights KY 41076-0151 *After spending 15 years as a radio or TV news reporter God has given me a new "News Assignment." He wants me to report the good news of Jesus Christ.*

ANDERSON, GREGORY MARTIN, minister; b. Colorado Springs, Colo., June 22, 1955; s. Ellsworth Lee and Mary Lou (Sand) A.; m. Holly Ann Pierce, Aug. 11, 1984; children: Lindsey Elizabeth, Andrew David, James Alexander. BA, Wheaton Coll., 1976; MDiv, Princeton Theol. Sem., 1980; STM, Yale U., 1985; postgrad., U. Minn., 1989—. Ordained to ministry, Presby. Ch., 1981. Assoc. min. Kirkmont Presby. Ch., Beavercreek, Ohio, 1981-86; min. Westminster Presby. Ch., Rapid City, S.D., 1986—; coun. Presbytery of S.D., Sioux Falls, 1990. Bd. dirs. Habitat for Humanity, Rapid City, 1990—, Beavercreek YMCA, 1985-86. Mem. Am. Acad. Religion, Soc. Bibl. Lit., Internat. Soc. History Rhetoric, Speech Communication Assn., Religious Speech Communication Assn., Lions. Republican. Home: 924 Fulton St Rapid City SD 57701 Office: Westminster Presbyn Ch 1012 Soo San Dr Rapid City SD 57702

ANDERSON, H. MICHAEL, minister; b. Parkersburg, W.Va., June 5, 1957; s. Harold Richard and Pebble Jean (Starcher) A.; m. Marie Dool, June 10, 1978; children: Angela Marie, Holly Elizabeth. ThB, Tex. Bible Coll., 1978. Ordained to ministry United Pentecostal Ch. Internat., 1987. Evangelist in ea. and so. U.S., United Pentecostal Ch., 1978-80; asst. pastor Lakeview United Pentecostal Ch., Chgo., 1980-83; sch. adminstr. Westgate United Pentecostal Ch., Austin, Tex., 1983-85; pastor United Pentecostal Ch., Burkesville, Ky., 1985—; instr. Dale Carnegie Courses, Ky., 1984—; Sunday sch. sec. Ky. dist. United Pentecostal Ch. Internat., 1988-89, dist. sec.-treas., 1989—. Writer adult Sunday sch. lit. and elective series, 1988—; editor., contbg. writer Ky. Dist. News, 1987—. Del. Williamson County Rep. Com., 1984; mem. Cumberland County emergency food and shelter nat. bd. program Fed. Emergency Mgmt. Adminstr., 1989-90; bd. dirs. Tupelo (Miss.) Children's Mansion, 1989—. Named Dir. of Yr., Ky. Sunday Sch. Dept., 1987. Mem. Cumberland County Ministerial Assn. (pres. 1988-89). Home and Office: 9832 Smith Grove Rd Burkesville KY 42717

ANDERSON, HAROLD JAMES, minister; b. Jonesboro, Ark., Dec. 9, 1934; s. Harmon Benjamin and Ruby Macie (Wood) A.; m. Shirley Ann Grant, June 19, 1954; children: Melody Ann, Michael Andrew. AA, Salisbury State U., 1955; BBA, Ga. State U., 1975. Gen. sec. N.C. S.C. div. The Salvation Army, Charlotte, N.C., 1977-81; gen. sec. for nat. capital and Va., div. dir. The Salvation Army, Washington, 1981-83; prin. for sch. for officers tng. The Salvation Army, Palos Verdes, Calif., 1983-86; territorial youth sec. for so. territory The Salvation Army, 1986-89; div. comdr., Ark. and Okla. div. The Salvation Army, Oklahoma City, 1989—; del. Salvation Army Internat. Coll., London, 1978; chaplain Boy Scouts of Am., Atlanta, 1968-90. Del. White House Conf. on Families, Washington, 1979. Mem. Blue Ridge Inst. for Non-Profit Agy. Execs., Rotary (Oklahoma City). Home: 4028 NW 61st St Oklahoma City OK 73157 Office: The Salvation ARmy A-OK DHQ 5101 N Pennsylvania Ave Oklahoma City OK 73157

ANDERSON, HERBERT E., clergyman; b. Madrid, Iowa, Mar. 1, 1916; s. Oscar Albim and Ellen (Peterson) A.; m. Alice Elizabeth Johnson, Sept. 28, 1942; children: Mark, Karen, Stephen, Timothy, James, Peter. B.A., Wheaton (Ill.) Coll., 1941; B.D., Princeton Theol. Sem., 1947; D.D. (hon.), Western Baptist Theol. Sem., Portland, Oreg., 1962. Ordained to ministry Bapt. Ch., 1948; dir. Salem (Oreg.) Youth Center, 1947-48; pastor in Gladstone, Oreg., 1948-52; pastor in The Dalles, Oreg., 1952-58, Lebanon, Oreg., 1958-62; gen. dir. Conservative Bapt. Fgn. Mission Soc., Wheaton, Ill., 1967-71; pastor Hinson Meml. Bapt. Ch., Portland, Oreg., 1963-67, 71-73; pastor First Bapt. Ch., Corvallis, Oreg., 1973-78, Monmouth, Oreg., 1978-82; pres., chmn. dept. Bible and philosophy Judson Bapt. Coll., The Dalles, 1980-83; Mem. bd. Conservative Bapt. Assn. Am., 1958-63, pres., 1963-67; moderator Conservative Bapt. Assn. Oreg., 1961-62; part-time instr. Western Bapt. Coll.; interim pastor succession of 7 Bapt. chs. Bd. dirs. Western Bapt. Theol. Sem., Judson Bapt. Coll., Portland. also: Cath Theol Union 5401 S Cornell Ave Chicago IL 60615

ANDERSON, HERMAN LEROY, bishop; b. Wilmington, N.C.; s. Felix Sylvester and Bessie Bernice (Bizzell) A.; m. Ruth Rosetta Rogers, July 6, 1946; children: Deborah Anderson Kareem, Herman L., Derrick R. B.S., Tuskegee Inst., 1943; B.Div., Hood Theol. Sem., Salisbury, N.C., 1959; D.Div. (hon.), Livingstone Coll., Salisbury, 1980. Pastor, St. James A.M.E. Zion Ch., Ithaca, N.Y., 1959-62, Soldiers Meml. A.M.E. Zion Ch., Salisbury, N.C., 1962-72, Broadway Temple A.M.E. Zion Ch., Louisville, 1972-76; gen. sec. A.M.E. Zion Ch., Charlotte, N.C., 1976-80, bishop, 1980—. Co-author: Churches and Church Membership, 1980. Bd. dirs. World Meth. Council; trustee Livingstone Coll. Served with USNR, 1944-46. Mem. Congress Nat. Black Churchmen (dir. 1984—). Address: AME Zion Ch 7031 Toby St Charlotte NC 28213

ANDERSON, HOMER LYNN, clergyman; b. Anson, Tex., June 5, 1935; s. James Homer and Inez (Newton) A.; m. Elna Maxine Whitehead, Sept. 2, 1955; children: Brad Lyndon, Gregory Mark, Kim Denise Funkhouser, Lane

Randal. BA, Abilene Christian U., 1958. Ordained to ministry Ch. of Christ. Min. Ft. Davis (Tex.) Ch. of Christ, 1958-59, Rush Springs (Okla.) Ch. of Christ, 1959-62, Garriott Rd. Ch. of Christ, Enid, Okla., 1962-67; missionary Canberra (Australia) Ch. of Christ, 1967-72; min. Pittman Creek Ch. of Christ, Plano, Tex., 1972-73, Stafford (Tex.) Ch. of Christ, 1973-77, Lake Jackson (Tex.) Ch. of Christ, 1977-91, 37th St. Ch. of Christ, Snyder, Tex., 1991—; mem. alumni bd. Abilene (Tex.) Christian U., 1979—; dir. Roman Nose Christian Youth Camp, Watonga, Okla., 1962-67; asst. dir. Bandina Christian Youth Camp, Bandera, Tex., 1977—. Mem. Canberra City Lions (dir. 1967-72), Brazosport Rotary (bull. editor 1977-85). Republican. Home: 3500 Ave W Snyder TX 79549

ANDERSON, HUGH DAVID, minister; b. Youngstown, Ohio, Nov. 23, 1951; s. David Dalton and June Florence (Larson) A.; m. Teena Donna Jolly, Jul. 14, 1973; children: David Donald, James Axel, Benjamin John. BA cum laude, Westminster Coll., 1973; DMin, Union Theol. Sem., 1977. Ordained to ministry Presbyn. Ch. (U.S.A.), 1977. Pastor Rich Hill Presbyn. Ch., Volant, Pa., 1977-81, First Presbyn. Ch., Willard, Ohio, 1981-88; assoc. First Presbyn. Ch., Manitowoc, Wis., 1988—; assoc. exec. presbyter Winnebago Presbytery, Wis., 1988—; co-dir. Mid-East Coun. Chs. Travel/Study, 1980; mem. summer staff Correymeela Community, No. Ireland, 1986; participant Internat. Designs for Econ. Awareness, Cuba, Jamaica, 1990; speaker in field. Pres. United Way, Willard, Ohio, 1986-89; bd. dirs. Willard Libr. Bd., 1986-89, Habitat for Humanity, Manitowoc, 1990—. Recipient E.T. George award, 1974. Mem. Assn. Presbyn. Ch. Educators. Office: First Presbyn Ch 502 N 8th St Manitowoc WI 54220

ANDERSON, JAMES ALBIN, minister; b. Jackson, Minn., Apr. 13, 1936; s. Hans Albin and Phylinda Anine (Madsen) A.; m. Corrine Joyce Lyon, Aug. 22, 1958; children: Phylinda, Laurie, Allen. BS, Mankato (Minn.) State U., 1958; BD, U. Dubuque, 1961, STM, 1970. Pastor 1st Presbyn. Ch., Rochester, Minn., 1961-68; fellow Menninger Found., Topeka, Kans., 1968-70; chaplain supr. Hennepin County Med. Ctr., Mpls., 1970-77; Dir. Clin. Pastoral Edn. Met. Med. Ctr., Mpls., 1977—; stated clk. Sheldon Jackson Presbytery, Rochester, 1963-68. Fellow Am. Assn. Pastoral Counselors, Assn. Mental Health Clergy; mem Assn. Clin. Pastoral Edn. (supr., Researcher of Yr. 1981). Democrat. Presbyterian. Avocations: cooking, baking, poetry. Home: 1913 Dupont Ave S #5 Minneapolis MN 55403 Office: Met Med Ctr 900 S Eight St Minneapolis MN 55404

ANDERSON, JAMES FREDERICK, clergyman; b. Elizabeth, N.J., Aug. 23, 1927; s. Fred and Hazel Minerva (Brown) A.; m. Bette Dillensnyder, Sept. 8, 1951; children: Judith (Mrs. Wayne Westbury), James Frederick, Mark, Rebecca. BA, Princeton, 1949; BD, Princeton Theol. Sem., 1952; DD, Alma Coll., 1974. Ordained to ministry Presbyn. Ch., 1952; chaplain Hun Sch. for Boys, Princeton, 1953; instr. religion Lafayette Coll., Easton, Pa., 1954-55; pastor Presbyn. chs., Catasauqua, Pa., 1956-61, Narberth, Pa., 1961-66; pastor Second Presbyn. Ch., Richmond, Va., 1966-72, Kirk in the Hills, Bloomfield Hills, Mich., 1972—; Trustee emeritus Alma (Mich.) Coll., William Beaumont Hosp., Royal Oak, Mich. With USNR, 1945-46. Home: 1420 W Long Lake Rd Bloomfield Hills MI 48302 Office: 1340 W Long Lake Rd Bloomfield Hills MI 48302

ANDERSON, JEANNIE ELLEN, religion educator; b. Saginaw, Mich., July 25, 1959; d. Roscoe Roy and Dolores Marie (Endstrasser) A. BS, U. Ark., 1983, MS, 1989; MA, Presbyn. Sch. Christian Edn., Richmond, Va., 1991. Tchr. Fayetteville (Ark.) Pub. Sch. System, 1985-86, 89-90, U. Ark., Fayetteville, 1987-88; youth dir. First United Presbyn. Ch., Fayetteville, 1989-90. Mem. AAUW, Assn. Presbyn. Ch. Educators, NAFE, N.W. Ark. Audubon Soc., Scottish Soc. N.W. Ark., Toastmasters, Rep. Women's Club, LWV, Phi Epsilon Omicron. Avocations: tennis, coin collecting, guitar, paino, painting. Home: 2312 Lawson St Fayetteville AR 72703

ANDERSON, JEROME MURPHY, music and education minister; b. Charlotte, N.C., Nov. 26, 1957; s. Carl Dewitt and Lena Jerome (Brittain) A.; m. Julie Dawn Bailey, June 18, 1988. Mus B, Mars Hill Coll., 1981. Music dir. First Bapt. Ch., Glen Alpine, N.C., 1975-76; minister music/youth GreenLee Bapt. Ch., Old Fort, N.C., 1978-83, First Bapt. Ch., Icard, N.C., 1983-86; minister music/edn. Alexis (N.C.) Bapt. Ch., 1986—; founder, dir. New Beginning Singers, Mars Hill, 1978-81; music dir. Burke Chorale Community Choir, Morganton, N.C., 1981-83. Supporter Unifour Citizens for Decency, Burke County, 1983-86; counselor, trainee Crisis Pregnancy Ctrs., Mecklenburg County, N.C., 1991. Republican. Home: PO Box 64 Alexis NC 28006 Office: PO Box 39 Alexis Church Rd Alexis NC 28006-0039 *Of all the practical and achievable goals in life, it is imperative to make an impact upon the spiritual life, growth and maturity of those to whom God has granted us the privilege of relationship.*

ANDERSON, JOHN FIRTH, church administrator, librarian; b. Saginaw, Mich., Oct. 5, 1928; s. Harlan Firth and Irene Martha (Bowser) A.; m. Patricia Ann Goble, June 18, 1950; children: Douglas Firth, Elizabeth Ann. B.A., Mich. State U., 1949; M.S. in L.S, U. Ill., 1950. Young people's librarian Enoch Pratt Free Library, Balt., 1950-52; with Balt. County Pub. Library, 1952-58, supr. adult work, 1955- 56, asst. county librarian, 1956-58; dir. Knoxville (Tenn.) Pub. Library System, 1958-62, Tucson Pub. Library, 1962-68, 73-82; city librarian San Francisco Pub. library, 1968-73; exec. presbyter, stated clk. Presbytery of Santa Barbara (Calif.), 1982-91; ret., 1991; mem. Presbyn. Churchwide Adminstrv. Coordinating Cabinet, 1987-89; cons. on library bldgs., devel. and mgmt. Contbr. articles to profl. publs. Bd. dirs. Amigos Bibliographic Council, 1977-81, vice-chmn., 1977-79, sec., 1980-81; mem. Ariz. Library Adv. Council, 1975-81; charter mem. Freedom to Read Found.; bd. dirs. Ariz. Theatre Co., 1978-82. Recipient Disting. Citizen award U. Ariz., 1981. Mem. ALA (mem. at large coun. 1961-65, 66-70, bd. dirs. pub. libr. assn. 1961-65, bd. dirs. libr. adminstrn. div. 1964-65, chmn. libr. orgn. and mgmt. sect. 1964-65, pres. libr. adminstrn. div. 1968-69), Calif. Libr. Assn. (coun. 1970-71), Southwestern Libr. Assn. (pres. 1976-78), Ariz. Libr. Assn. (pres. pub. librs. div. 1964-65, pres. 1967-68, Libr. of Year 1968, Rosenzweig award 1981), Ariz. Assn. County Librs. (pres. 1979-80), Ariz. China Coun. (pres. 1979-80), World Alliance Reformed Chs. (mem. Caribbean and N.Am. Area Coun. 1991-93), Beta Phi Mu. Presbyterian (elder).

ANDERSON, JOHN KERBY, communications media executive, columnist, radio talk show host; b. Berkeley, Calif., Dec. 7, 1951; s. John Albert and Mary Lorraine (Allen) A.; m. Susanne Elise Pardey, Aug. 3, 1974; children: Amy, Jonathan, Catherine. BS, Oreg. State U., 1974; MFS, Yale U., 1976; MA, Georgetown U., 1981. V.p. Probe Ministries, Dallas, 1976-81; host news talk radio talk show Probe radio program, Richardson, Tex., 1983—; host Lost News Talk, 1989; guest host Point of View radio talk show, Dallas. Author: Life, Death and Beyond, 1980, Genetic Engineering, 1982, Origin Science, 1987, Living Ethically in the 90s, 1990. Republican. Evangelical Christian. Avocations: writing, basketball, tennis. Office: Probe 1900 Firman Dr Richardson TX 75081

ANDERSON, JOHN ROGER, bishop; m. Beverly Anderson; children: Craig, Laurel, Mark. BA cum laude, Gustavus Adolphus Coll., 1957; MDiv magna cum laude, Luth. Sch. Theology, Chgo., 1961; DD, Calif. Luth. U., 1987; postgrad., Bishop's Acad., 1990, 91. Ordained to ministry Evang. Luth. Ch. in Am., 1961. Intern Angelica Luth. Ch., L.A., 1959-60; pastor Sunset Luth. Ch., San Francisco, 1961-67, Holy Trinity Luth. Ch., Thousand Oaks, Calif., 1967-78; asst. to bishop Pacific S.W. synod Luth. Ch. in Am., L.A., 1978-87, bishop So. Calif. West synod, 1987—. Chaplain San Francisco Youth Guidance Ctr.; active C.Am. Refugee Com., 1990. Calif. Luth. U. fellow. Mem. Optimists (life). Avocations: music, travel, photography, horseback riding, gardening. Office: Synod of So Calif W 1340 S Bonnie Brae St Los Angeles CA 90006

ANDERSON, JOLORENE MILLER PARKER, minister; b. Chgo., Feb. 7, 1916; d. John Meredith and Dorothea Emeline (Hauk) Miller; m. Clarence Hanley Parker, Oct. 29, 1961 (dec. 1981); m. Paul Anderson, July 30, 1989. MusB, Am. Conservatory Music, 1933; AA, Kendall Coll., 1952; BA in Religion, Syracuse U., 1955; STB, Boston U., 1958. Ordained to ministry United Meth. Ch., 1958. Summer pastor Vesper (N.Y.) United Meth. Ch., 1955; pastor chs. in Georgetown, Sheds and Otselic N.Y., 1957-61; pastor Perryville (N.Y.) United Meth. Ch., 1961-62, Otselic United Meth. Ch., 1967-81, 83—; pastor United Meth. Ch., Georgetown, 1981—, Sheds, 1982-83. Address: PO Box 134 Georgetown NY 13072

ANDERSON, JONATHAN WILLIAM (JON ANDERSON), pastor; b. Seattle, June 16, 1955; s. Carl William and Marion Christine (Luche) A.; m. Laura Lee Micheli: childen: Marshal, Nicollette. BA, Azusa (Calif.) Pacific Coll., 1977; MDiv, Fuller Theol. Sem., 1981. Ordained to ministry Evang. Luth. Ch. in Am., 1985. Pastor Zion's Luth. Ch., 1985—; chmn. Campus Ministry, Trinidad Colo., 1987-89, stewardship rep., S.E. Colo. Cong, Southern Colo., 1987. Chmn. Advocates Against Domestic Assault, Trinidad, 1988-91. Mem. Rotary Club (sec.-treas. Trinidad, 1987—, zone rep. dist. 547, Trinidad, 1988-89), Trinidad Ministerial Assn. (v.p. 1988-90, pres. 1990—). Home: 613 Prospect Trinidad CO 81082 Office: Zion's Luth Ch 613 Prospect Trinidad CO 81082 *The good news that God forgives and accepts us becomes real when we, in turn, forgive and accept each other.*

ANDERSON, JONPATRICK SCHUYLER, minister, financial consultant, archivist; b. Chgo., July 20, 1951; s. Ralph Anderson and Helena Hilda (Robinson) Hardy; children: André, Mary, David. AA, L.A. Trade Tech. Coll., 1978; BA, UCLA, 1979; postgrad., SUNY, Albany, 1983, Govs. State U., 1985; MRE, DMin., PhD, Internat. Sem. (in coop. with Unification Theol. Sem. N.Y.), 1989. Clerical supr. VA, L.A., 1976-80; fin. adminstr. Antioch Primitive Bapt. Ch., L.A., 1979-80; pres., exec. dir. All-Around Prodns., L.A., 1980-83; assoc. minister St. Stephen Ch., San Diego, Calif., 1983-87; stadium mgr. San Diego Jack Murphy Stadium, 1985-87; exec. dir. Christ-Immanuel Ministerial Assn., San Diego, 1983—; cons. pvt. practice mgmt., cons. comptr., San Diego, 1981-82; cons. writer All-Around Music div. Broadcast Music, Inc., San Diego, 1980—; instr. San Diego Community Coll. Dist., 1984; lib. asst. San Diego State U., 1982-83; archives technician Nat. Archives & Records Adminstrn., Laguna Niguel, Calif., 1988; mem. Nat. Conf. Ministry Armed Forces. Mem. Am. Freedom Coalition, Washington, 1988, Causa, USA, Washington, 1985-87. With USAR, 1979-80. Grammy nominee NARAS, 1980; recipient Personal award former Pres. Ronald Reagan, L.A., 1988. Mem. NAACP (life), NARAS, AFTRA, AGVA, Assn. MBA Execs. (bus. award 1980), UCLA Alumni Assn. (life), Res. Officers Assn. of the U.S. (life), UCLA Black Alumni Assn. (life), Nat. Guard Assn. Calif. (life), Nat. Conf. on Ministry to the Armed Forces, VFW (life), Am. Legion, AMVETS, Ret. Officers Assn. Of U.S., Am. Assn. Religious Counselors. Democrat. Mem. Ch. of God. Avocations: reading, writing, gospel music, outdoor recreation. Office: Christ-Immanuel Ministries PO Box 1202 San Diego CA 92112

ANDERSON, KENNETH ARTHUR, minister; b. Worcester, Mass., June 1, 1942; s. John Henry Arnold and Ruth Otellia (Johnson) A.; m. Barbara Michael Prolesky, Apr. 16, 1962 (div. Feb. 1979); children: Kathryn, Kenneth; m. Lisa Gay Goodkowsky, June 14, 1980. BA, Defiance Coll., 1964; MDiv, Pitts. Theol. Sem., 1986, postgrad., 1991—. Ordained to ministry Presbyn. Ch. (U.S.A.), 1986. Pastor Forest Grove Presbyn. Ch., Coraopolis, Pa., 1985—; chmn. Pitts. Presbyn. Div. on Serving, 1989-90; vice chair communication unit Mission Interpretation Stewardship, 1991; chair communication com. Pitts. Presbytery, 1991. Sec. Parkway West Rotary, Pitts., 1988, v.p., 1989, pres. 1990; del. Mayor's Task Force on Hunger, Pitts., 1987-89. Mem. Robinson Assn. Chs. (pres., moderator 1988—). Republican. Home: 108 Williams Dr Coraopolis PA 15108 Office: Forest Grove Presbyn Church Williams Dr Coraopolis PA 15108 *I believe that as pastors, we must remember that we are not healers but rather are journeying with those who God has entrusted to us, representative of God's care. In this way we assist them in recognizing that God's Spirit is working withing their spirit creating new life and opportunities.*

ANDERSON, LACOUNT (LOUIS), III, minister; b. Jacksonville, Fla., Apr. 7, 1952; s. LaCount Louis Jr. and Agatha (Neville) A.; m. Anna Clyde Daniels, June 21, 1980; 1 child, Leah Cannady. BA, Gardner-Webb Coll., 1977; MRE, Southeastern Sem., 1980. Minister of music and youth Spring Creek Rd. Bapt. Ch., Chattanooga, 1980-82; minister of edn. and youth First Bapt. Ch., Weaverville, N.C., 1982-84; minister of edn. First Bapt. Ch., Forest City, N.C., 1984-87; assoc. minister Oakmont Bapt. Ch., Greenville, N.C., 1987—; trustee Gardner-Webb Coll., Boiling Springs, N.C., 1986-89; Sunday sch. dir. South Roanoke Bapt. Assn., Greenville, 1988—. Bd. dirs. Community Homeless Shelter, Greenville, 1990—; Sunday sch. dir. Buncombe County Bapt. Assn., Asheville, N.C., 1982-84. With USN, 1972-76. Mem. So. Bapt. Religious Educators Conf., N.C. Bapt. Religious Edn. Conf. Office: Oakmont Bapt Ch 1100 Red Banks Rd Greenville NC 27858

ANDERSON, LAURENCE ERNEST, retired minister; b. Fir Mountain, Sask., Can., Feb. 4, 1914; s. Leonard Elvin and Mary Aquina (Price) A.; m. Edna Fern Gladys Haverfield, June 15, 1937; children: Karlene, Lornel, Starla, Dalton, Cheryl, Vickie. BA, U. Sask., 1934; BD, St. Andrew's, Saskatoon, Sask., 1940; MEd, U. Mont., 1959; PhD, U. W.I., Kingston, Jamaica, 1973. Ordained to ministry United Ch. Can., 1937, United Ch. Christ, 1947. Min. United Ch., Glendive, Mont., 1947-54, Minto United Ch., Moose Jaw, Sask., 1954-60; tutor Ch. Tchrs. Coll., Kingston, 1968-72; supply pastor United Ch., Empress, Alta., Can., 1974-87; pvt. practice in psychology Medicine Hat, Alta., 1979-91; cons. Medicine Hat Community Counseling Ctr., 1985-90; senator St. Andrew's Coll., 1955; chmn. Presbytery Moose Jaw, 1957-58; chmn. Christian edn. So. Alta. Presbytery, 1973074. Teaching fellow U. Mont., 1960; Bursary grantee Govt. Sask., 1961. Mem. Alta. Psychol. Assn., Can. Psychol. Assn., Am. Psychol. Assn., Can. Hypnosis Soc., Soc. for Study of Multiple Personality Disorders, Kiwanis (lt. gov. So. Alta. 1982-83), Masons (past grand chaplain Mont., past master). Address: 1390 24th St SE, Medicine Hat, AB Canada T1A 2E6 *As a religious psychologist I pray I may administer these antidotes: faith for anxiety, hope for depression and love for hostility.*

ANDERSON, LEIF DAVID, minister; b. Menomonie, Wis., Oct. 6, 1963; s. David Lawrence Anderson and Karen Lorraine (Gray) Webb; m. Jean Elaine Johnson, June 6, 1987; 1 child, Linnea Jean. BA in Phys. Edn., Bethel Coll., St. Paul, 1986. Youth paster Missionary Ch., Gurnee, Ill., 1990—. Mem. Nat. Youth Orgn. Home and Office: 1319 N Hunt Club Rd Gurnee IL 60031-2442

ANDERSON, LEITH CHARLES, minister; b. Glen Ridge, N.J., Oct. 11, 1944; s. Charles William and Margery Sanley (Freeman) A.; m. Charleen Lillian Alles, June 18, 1965; children: Jill, Gregrey, Brian, Jeffrey. Diploma, Moody Bible Inst., Chgo., 1965; BA, Bradley U., Peoria, Ill., 1967; MDiv, Denver Sem., 1969; D of Ministry, Fuller Sem., Pasadena, Calif., 1978. Ordained to ministry Conservative Bapt. Assn. Am., 1969. Pastor Calvary Ch., Longmont, Colo., 1967-76, Wooddale Ch., Eden Prairie, Minn., 1977—; adj. prof. Denver Sem., 1973-76, Bethel Sem., St. Paul, 1980—; mem. adv. bd. Your Ch. mag., Carol Stream, Ill., 1990—. Author: Making Happiness Happen, 1986, Dying For Change, 1990; co-author: Mastering Church Management, 1990; contbr. articles to profl. jours. Mem. Evang. Theol. Soc. Baptist. Office: Wooddale Ch 6630 Shady Oak Rd Eden Prairie MN 55344

ANDERSON, LUKE, priest, monk; b. N.Y.C., Sept. 16, 1927; s. John William and Nora M. (Conway) A. PhL, Pontifical Angelicum, Rome, Italy, 1958; PhD, Pontifical Angelicum, 1965; ThM, Princeton Theol. Sem., 1988. Cert. clin. pastoral educator. Asst. novice master St. Joseph's Abbey, Spencer, Mass., 1951-53; prior St. Joseph's Abbey, Spencer, 1962-64, St. Mary's Cistercian Prior, New Ringgold, Pa., 1964—; bd. editors Cistercian Publs., Kalamazoo, Mich., 1973—, bd. dirs., 1982—. Contbr. articles to profl. jours. Mem. U.S. Conf. Major Superiors, Calvin Studies Soc. Republican. Home and Office: Saint Mary's Monastery Box 206 New Ringgold PA 17961

ANDERSON, MARBURY EARL, minister; b. Ogilvie, Minn., Aug. 4, 1923; s. Hilding J. and Ellen C. (Johnson) A.; m. Sylvia L. Anderson, June 13, 1948; children: Bradbury, Marston, Lynnette. BA, Gustavus Adolphus Coll., 1945; MD, Augustana Coll., Rock Island, Ill., 1948; DD (hon.), Bethany Coll., Lindsborg, Kans., 1972. Ordained to ministry Evang. Luth. Ch. in Am., 1945. Pastor Trinity Luth. Ch., Sheridan, Wyo., 1948-52, St. Luke's Luth. Ch., Buffalo, Wyo., 1948-52, Grace Luth. Ch., Ft. Worth, 1952-55, Messiah Luth. Ch., Mpls., 1956-69, Augustana Luth. Ch., Denver, 1969-79, Grace Luth. Ch., Mankato, Minn., 1979-91; ret., 1991; del. to Assembly Bd. Social Ministry, St. Paul, 1989-91. Author: I Believe in Jesus Christ, 1962. Mem. City Charter Commn., Mankato, 1986—. Mem. Ministerial Assn. (pres. 1982-83), Rotary.

ANDERSON, MARGARET CAUGHMAN (MICKEY ANDERSON), religious association executive; b. Wagener, S.C., Mar. 14, 1936; d. Carl Davis and Iola (Gantt) Caughman; m. Hal Cecil Anderson, June 8, 1958; children: Elizabeth Caughman Anderson Gruber, Jonathan Hal. AB in Edn., U. S.C., 1958. Tchr. North Charleston High Sch., S.C., 1958-60; sec. to dean Coll. Charleston, S.C., 1960-61; ch. sec. Grace Lutheran Ch., Rock Hill, S.C., 1969—, numerous activities include sec. ch. council, 1976-79, lay asst., 1980-84, lector, 1980—, mem. altar guild, 1982—, mem. com. on ministries, 1983—; active S.C. synod Luth. Ch. in Am., including co-lay vice-chairperson camping and conf. ministries appeal, 1979-83, mem. mgmt. com., sec. pers. subcom. and chairperson Lutheridge satellite com., 1979-84, and S.C. del. to Luth. Ch. Am. Biennial Conv., 1980; active Luth. Ch. Women, including circle leader and sec., mem. S.C. exec. bd., 1977-78, conv. del., 1977, 80, co-chmn. family enrichment seminar, 1978, chmn. learning resources com., 1978, and mem. constn. com., 1977; v.p. Ebinport PTA, Rock Hill, 1972-74; treas. York County Multi-Disciplinary Com., Rock Hill, 1973-79; active York County Med. Assn. Aux., Rock Hill, including pres., 1974; chmn. ch. scout com. Boy Scouts Am., 1979-83; pres. Accolade Garden Club, Rock Hill, 1982, scrapbook chmn. 1984-86). Mem. S.C. Med. Assn. Aux. (corr. sec. 1979).

ANDERSON, MARJO ELIZABETH, minister; b. Keyser, W.Va., Apr. 4, 1954; d. Donald David and Lorna Jo (Douglass) A.; m. Mark Roland Dollhopf, Aug. 14, 1977; 1 child, Johann Roland Anderson-Dollhopf. B of Music Edn., Wittenberg U., 1976; MDiv, Yale U., 1980. Ordained to ministry Luth. Ch. in Am., 1983. Dir. music St. James Luth. Ch., Southbury, Conn., 1977-80; pastoral assoc. St. Paul's Evang. Luth. Ch., Bridgeport, Conn., 1980-82; adminstrv. asst. Inst. Sacred Music Yale U., New Haven, 1983; asst. pastor Emmanuel Luth. Ch., Norwood, Mass., 1983-86; pastor St. John's Evang. Luth. Ch., New Britain, Conn., 1986—; chairperson Bd. for Congregational Life, New Eng. Synod, Worcester, Mass., 1988—. Mem. New Eng. Synod Coun. Evang. Luth. Ch. in Am., 1988—. Democrat. Avocations: running, weight lifting, piano, organ, voice. Home: 507 Whitney Ave New Haven CT 06511 Office: St Johns Evang Luth Ch 295-303 Arch St New Britain CT 06051

ANDERSON, MARK ALLEN, pastor; b. La Crosse, Wis., Oct. 21, 1962; s. James A. and Ruth L. (Aas) A.; m. Beverly Sue Anderson, June 1, 1985. BA, Luther Coll., Decorah, Iowaa, 1985; MDiv, Luth. Sch. Theol. at Chgo., 1989. Ordained to ministry Evang. Luth. Ch. in Am., 1989. Assoc. pastor Prince of Peace Luth. Ch., La Crescent, Minn., 1989—; bd. dirs. Sugar Creek Bible Camp, Ferryville, Wis., 1990—; mem. Luth. Hosp. Corp., La Crosse, 1990—. Bd. dirs. La Crescent Pub. Libr., 1990—, Sr. Nutrition Site, La Crescent, 1990—. Mem. La Crosse Clergy Assn., La Crescent Clergy Assn., La Crescent Area C. of C., Lions (sec. La Crescent 1990—). Office: Prince of Peace Luth Ch Hill and Main Sts La Crescent MN 55947

ANDERSON, MARK MAGNUS, clergyman; b. Neenah, Wis., Dec. 13, 1933; s. Fridtjof B. and Lavinia M. (Larsen) A.; m. Donna Mae Aga, Aug. 26, 1956; children: Scott, Nathan, Karn. BA, St. Olaf Coll., 1955; BD, Luther Theol. Sem., 1959, ThM, 1965. Ordained to ministry Am. Luth. Ch., 1959. Pastor Grace Luth. Ch., Ukiah, Calif., 1959-63; chaplain resident Fairview Hosp., Mpls., 1963-66; dir. chaplaincy svcs., clin. pastoral edn. Met. Med. Ctr., Mpls., 1966—. Fellow Am. Assn. Pastoral Counselors; mem. Assn. Mental Health Chaplains. Home: 5341 Clinton Ave S Minneapolis MN 55419 Office: 900 S 8th St Minneapolis MN 55404

ANDERSON, MARY MARGARET, minister; b. Kewanee, Ill., Feb. 22, 1944; d. William Jonathan and Theodora Blanche (Anderson) Curtis; m. George Edmund Anderson, Sept. 13, 1964 (div. 1979); children: Thomas William, Teresa Lynn, Timothy Wilson. AA, Carl Sandberg Coll., Galesburg, Ill., 1984; MDiv, Luth. Sch. Theology, Chgo., 1988. Ordained to ministry, Evang. Luth. Ch. Am., 1989. Pastor Zion Luth. Ch., Streator, Ill., 1989—, Bethany Luth. Ch., Wenona, Ill., 1989—; pres. Night Chaplains St. Marys Assoc. Hosp., Streator, 1990—, mem. adv. coun., 1990—; mem. nominating com. No. Ill. Synod of Evang. Luth. Ch. in Am., Rockford, 1991, mem. subcom. #3 of communication of Soc. Min. Com., 1991. Bd. dirs. LaSalle County Coun. on Alcohol and Drug Abuse, Ottawa, 1990—. Mem. C. of C. of Wenona, HANDS. Home: PO Box 176 Wenona IL 61377 Office: Bethany Luth Ch PO Box 176 Wenona IL 61377

ANDERSON, BROTHER MEL, academic administrator; b. Oakland, Calif., Sept. 28, 1928. BA, St. Mary's Coll., Moraga, Calif., 1952; DLitt, St. Albert's Coll., 1976; LHD, Lewis U., 1979. Tchr. Sacred Heart High Sch., San Francisco, 1952-56; vice prin. La Salle High Sch., Pasadena, Calif., 1956-62; prin. San Joaquin Meml. High Sch., Fresno, Calif., 1962-64; prin., superior St Mary's High Sch., Residence Sch., Grammar Sch., Berkeley, Calif., 1964-69; pres. St. Mary's Coll. of Calif., Moraga, 1969—. Trustee St. Mary's Coll., Moraga., 1968—. Named Alumnus of Yr. St. Mary's Coll., 1987; inducted Contra Costa County Hall of Fame, 1988. Mem. Assn. Ind. Calif. Colls. and Univs. (exec. com. 1973—, chmn. 1988, 89), Regional Assn. East Bay Colls. and Univs. (chmn. 1979-81, 90-91), Fratres Scholarum Christianarum. Democrat. Roman Catholic. Lodge: Rotary Internat. Avocations: photography, woodworking, travel, drama, music. Office: St Mary's Coll Calif PO Box 3005 Moraga CA 94575-3005

ANDERSON, MELVIN ROBERT (ANDY), retired minister; b. Orlando, Fla., Dec. 20, 1925; s. Paul Raymond and Edith Regina (Schock) A.; m. Carolyn Clift, Oct. 17, 1947; children: Roy Wesley, Thomas Paul, David Robert. BEE, Ga. Inst. Tech., 1947; M in Religious Edn., New Orleans Bapt. Theol. Sem., 1955. Ordained minister Bapt. ch., Fla., 1969. Jr. engr. So. Bell Telephone & Telephone Co., Atlanta, 1947-49, Jacksonville, Fla., 1949-51; minister of edn. First Bapt. Ch., Oxford, Miss., 1955-58, Dothan, Ala., 1958-62, Mobile, Ala., 1962-65; minister of edn. Southside Bapt. Ch., Jacksonville, 1965-69, Univ. Bapt. Ch., Coral Gables, Fla., 1969-74; minster of edn. Forest Hills Bapt. Ch., Raleigh, N.C., 1974-88, ret., 1988; spl. worker Sun. sch. dept. Fla. Bapt. Conv., Coral Gables, 1972-73, Sun. sch. dept. Bapt. State Conv., Raleigh, 1974-84; reg. v.p. Primerica Fins. Svcs., 1989-91. Author: Handbook: Leading the Adult Class, 1982, Workbook: Adult Workers Preparing for the 1987-88 Sunday School Challenge, 1987; contbr. articles to profl. jours. Served to lt. USNR, 1943-46, 1951-53. Mem. Eastern Bapt. Religious Edn. (pres. 1981-82), So. Bapt. Religious Edn. Assn., Religious Edn. Workers Ala. (pres. 1961), Raleigh Bapt. Assn. (sr. adult coord. 1988-91), Civitan Club (bd. dirs. Mobile chpt. 1964-65, chaplain Raleigh chpt. 1991). Democrat. Lodge: Civitan (bd. dirs. Mobile chpt. 1964-65). Avocations: amateur radio, gardening. *Life goals written and reviewed daily help one maintain a positive outlook on life, accomplish what one considers important and enjoy the process. How blessed we humans are for the availability of divine direction and strength for every aspect of life!.*

ANDERSON, MORRIS LYNN, minister; b. Metropolis, Ill., May 13, 1951; s. Lyndall and Edith (Mizell) A.; m. Darlenia Rea Galloway, Aug. 14, 1970; children: Angela Lynn, Sarah Rachel. BS, So. Ill. U., 1976; MDiv, So. Bapt. Theol. Sem., 1982; DMin., So. Bapt. Ctr., 1985. Ordained to ministry So. Bapt. Conv., 1975. Pastor New Salem Bapt. Ch., Creal Springs, Ill., 1975, College Heights Bapt. Ch., Eldorado, Ill., 1975-78, Grace Bapt. Ch., Granite City, Ill., 1978-81, Dotson Meml. Bapt. Ch., Maryville, Tenn., 1981—; trustee New Orleans Theol. Sem., 1989—. Author: Wise Ways to Win the World, 1985. Mem. Concerned Citizens of Blount County, Maryville, 1987. Mem. Chilhowee Bapt. Assn. (mem. evangelism com. 1986-90, chmn. camp com. 1990—). Home: 220 Amy Dr Maryville TN 37801 Office: Dotson Meml Bapt Ch 814 Dotson Meml Rd Maryville TN 37801

ANDERSON, MOSES B., bishop; b. Selma, Ala., Sept. 9, 1928. Student, St. Michael's Coll., St. Edmunds Sem., U. Legon, Ghana. Ordained priest Roman Cath. Ch., 1958. Ordained aux. bisop Detroit; titular bishop of Vatarba, 1983. Office: 1234 Washington Blvd Detroit MI 48226

ANDERSON, NEIL FREEMAN, minister; b. Colfax, Wash., Apr. 19, 1954; s. Donald Dean and Manon (Freeman) A.; m. Debra Sue Moss, June 24, 1982; children: Amber, Marie, Marcus Alan. BA in Religion, Warner Pacific Coll., 1979. Ordained to ministry Ch. of God, 1985. Min. edn.

Garfield (Wash.) Christian Ch.; pastor Hillcrest Community Ch. of God, Moses Lake, Wash., 1981-82, First Ch. of God, Eureka, Mont., 1982-85; intern Grace Chapel Community Ch. of God, Worland, Wyo., 1986; assoc. min. First Ch. of God, Bellefontaine, 1986-91; pastor Sea-Tac Ch. of God, Seattle, 1991—; facilities dir. Associated Students of Warner Pacific Coll., Portland, Oreg., 1976-78, spiritual life dir., 1978-79; mem. Moses Lake Ministerial Assn., 1981-82. Mem. Tobacco Valley Improvement Assn., Eureka, 1982, Lincoln County Parks and Recreation Bd., Libby, Mont., 1984-85; bd. dirs. Mercy Substance Abuse Program, Bellefontaine, 1987. Office: Sea-Tac Ch of God 18435 42d Ave S Seattle WA 98185

ANDERSON, OTIS LEE, JR., clergyman; b. Crossett, Ark., Apr. 16, 1933; s. Otis Lee and Geneva (Harris) A.; m. Lois Jean Samuels, Jan. 12, 1954; children: Dawna B., Brian Scott, Geoffrey C. Student, U. Ill., 1949-50, Wilson Jr. Coll., Chgo., 1960; AA, Chgo. Bapt. Inst., 1961; DD (hon.), Universal Bapt. Inst., 1973. Ordained to ministry Progressive Nat. Bapt. Conv., 1960. Assoc. min. Greater New Morning Star Ch., L.A., 1960-61; asst. pastor Greater Mt. Olive Ch., Chgo., 1961-63; adminstrv. asst. Monumental Bapt. Ch., Chgo., 1963-69; pastor Broadview (Ill.) Bapt. Ch., 1969-72, Old Ship of Zion Missionary Bapt. Ch., Chgo., 1972-75, Cathedral Bapt. Ch., Chgo., 1975—; 3d v.p. Progressive State Conv. Mem. aux. adv. bd. Mantoya Coll. Recipient svc. award Manteno Mental Hosp., 1973. Mem. Mins. Alliance (sec. 1970), SCLC, NAACP. Home: 35 Timberlane Rd Matteson IL 60443 Office: Cathedral Bapt Ch 4821 S Wabash Ave Chicago IL 60615

ANDERSON, RICHARD SANFORD, minister; b. Monte Vista, Colo., Mar. 2, 1929; s. Axel Theodore and Leila Belle (Mount) A.; m. Shirley Ann Becker, June 17, 1952; children: Mark, Dale, Dana. AB, Hanover Coll., 1951; BD, Louisville Presbyn. Seminary, 1954. Missionary Dept. Sunday Sch. Missions United Presbyn. Ch. USA, Reserve, N.Mex., 1954-58; pastor Community Presbyn. Ch., Stanfield, Ariz., 1958-62, Trinity United Presbyn. Ch., Prescott, Ariz., 1962-72, First Presbyn. Ch., Salaida, Colo., 1973-75, Wayside Chapel, Sedona (Ariz.) Community Ch., 1975—; moderator Grand Canyon Presbytery, Ariz., 1962; chaplain Fort Whipple VA Hosp., Prescott, 1963-67. Chmn. Coordination Com., Prescott, 1965-69, Minister's Assn., Prescott, 1969; treas. Minister's Assn., Sedona, 1977—. Mem. Kiwanis. Office: Wayside Chapel PO Box M Sedona AZ 86336

ANDERSON, ROBERT JEFFRIES, JR., minister; b. Harrisburg, Pa., Aug. 15, 1954; s. Robert J. Sr. and Icie Lee (Carter) A.; m. Jacqueline Sullivan, July 7, 1979; children: Shani Charissa, Robert J. III, Nia Joy. B in Bible Edn., Carver Bible Inst. and Coll., 1977; MDiv, Grace Theol. Sem., 1982. Ordained to ministry Bapt. Ch., 1983. Interim pastor Whipporwill Community Ch., Rochester, Ind., 1981-82; pastor Trinity Bapt. Ch., Indpls., 1982—; prof. Bible and urban ministries Bapt. Bible Coll., Indpls., 1991—. Mem. Fundamental Bapt. Fellowship Assn. (pub. rels. dir. 1984-88, 1st v.p. 1988—). Republican. Home: 3615 N Illinois St Indianapolis IN 46208 Office: Trinity Bapt Ch 3162 N Baltimore Ave Indianapolis IN 46218

ANDERSON, ROBERT LAZELLE, minister; b. Chgo., May 29, 1932; s. Claude H. and Leona (Sherman) A.; m. Elizabeth Anne Ward, Aug. 22, 1952; children—Claudia Anne, Robert Briggs, Lawrence LaZelle, Mary Elizabeth. A.A., Graceland Coll., 1954; B.A., Calif. State U., San Jose, 1956; diploma in religion Sch. of Restoration, 1970; M.Ed., Lewis and Clark Coll., 1976. Ordained to ministry Reorganized Ch. Jesus Christ of Latter Day Saints, 1952. Account mgr. Pillsbury Co., San Mateo, Calif., 1956-61; asst. dist. sales mgr. J. Nelson Prewitt, Inc., San Francisco, 1961-62; sales supr. Joseph Howard and Co., San Francisco, 1961-64; min., Independence, Mo., 1964—; adminstr. cen. Pacific region, pres. Sacramenton dist. Reorganized Ch. of Jesus Christ of Latter-Day Saints. Author: Establishing New Congregation, 1984; contbg. author: Personal Responsibility in Daily Evangelism, 1980; contbr. articles to ch. publs. Mayor, Spartan City (San Jose State married housing), 1954-56; vol. counselor Clark County Family Ct. and Evergreen High Sch., 1975-76; pres., bd. dirs. San Pablo, Calif. Boys Club, 1956-57; bd. dirs. West Contra Costa Community Chest, 1956-57, Calif. Coun. on Alcohol Problem, Cabinet Chancellors Sacramento Interfaith Svc. Bur. Served with U.S. Army, 1950-52. Decorated Combat Inf. badge; recipient Appreciation award for services to ch. youth San Francisco Bay Dist., 1961. Mem. PTA (hon. life Calif.). Republican. Home: 8235 Majestic Oak Way Citrus Heights CA 95610

ANDERSON, ROBERT MARSHALL, bishop; b. S.I., N.Y., Dec. 18, 1933; s. Arthur Harold and Hazel Schneider A.; m. Mary Artemis Evans, Aug. 24, 1960; children: Martha, Elizabeth, Catherine, Thomas. BA, Colgate U., 1955; STB, Berkeley Div. Sch., 1961, DD (hon.), 1977; DD (hon.), Seabury Western Sem., 1978, Yale U., 1977. Ordained priest Episcopal Ch. Curate St. John's Ch., Stamford, Conn., 1961-63, vicar, 1963-67, assoc. rector, 1968-72; priest in charge Middle Haddan, Conn., 1963-67, rector, 1967-68; dean St. Mark's Cathedral, Salt Lake City, 1972-78; bishop Episcopal Diocese of Minn., Mpls., 1978—. Served with U.S. Army. Danforth fellow, 1959-60. Mem. Berkeley Alumni Assn. (pres. 1972-76). Democrat. Clubs: Mpls, Minikahda. Office: Diocese of Minn 430 Oak Grove St #306 Minneapolis MN 55403

ANDERSON, ROGER GORDON, minister; b. Milw., Feb. 1, 1937; s. Arthur Gordon and Dorothy R. (Junger) A.; m. Margery V. Burleson; children: Jonathan P., Nancy L., Leslie J., Kristi A. BA, Grace Bible Coll., Grand Rapids, Mich., 1958; postgrad., Purdue U., U. Minn. Ordained to ministry Grace Gospel Fellowship, 1960. Pastor Grace Bible Ch., Lafayette, Ind., 1958-60, Preakness Bible Ch., Wayne, N.J., 1960-69, Bethesda Free Ch., Mpls., 1969-86, Grace Community Ch., Salinas, Calif., 1986-91; pres. Grace Gospel Fellowship, Grand Rapids, Mich., 1991—; pres. Evang. Ministers' Fellowship, Mpls., 1972-85; trainer Evangelism Explosion, Mpls., 1980-89. Bd. dirs. Goodwill Home and Rescue Mission, Newark, 1962-69; bd. dirs. Grace Bible Coll., Grand Rapids, 1975—, chmn. bd., 1984-91; bd. dirs. Grace Missions Inc., Grand Rapids, 1966-75; chaplain Police Dept., Mpls., 1975-80. Recipient Meritorious Svc. award City of Mpls., 1977. Mem. Grace Gospel Fellowship (bd. dirs. 1966-68). Republican. Home: 18423 Vierra Canyon Rd Salinas CA 93907 Office: Grace Gospel Fellowship 2125 Martindale SW Grand Rapids MI 49509 *Life is a constant series of choices, the best of which are always those made with God and His will as the central factor. All are spokes from that hub.*

ANDERSON, ROGER WILLIAM, JR., religion educator; b. Centralia, Wash., Dec. 1, 1948; s. Roger William and Elva Vida (Hammonds) A.; m. Arletta Jean Prestbye, Aug. 30, 1970; 1 child, Brita Catherine. BA, Pac. Luth. U., 1971; MDiv, Luth. Sch. Theology, 1975; PhD, U. Chgo., 1985. Instr. St. Xavier Coll., Chgo., 1977, Augustana Coll., Rock Island, Ill., 1978-79, Loyola U., Chgo., 1988-89; lectr. in Old Testament United Theol. Coll., Harare, Zimbabwe, 1989—, U. Zimbabwe, Harare, 1989—; bd. dirs. Joint Archeol. Expedition to Tell el-Hesi. Mem. Soc. of Bibl. Lit., Cath. Bibl. Assn., Israel Exploration Soc., Chgo. Soc. Bibl. Rsch., Am. Schs. of Oriental Rsch. Office: U Zimbabwe, Dept Religious Studies, PO Box MP 167, Harare Zimbabwe

ANDERSON, ROSS JERROLD, minister; b. Salt Lake City, June 6, 1955; s. LeRay J. and Alice Grace (McCormick) A.; m. Nancy Louise Hammond, Aug. 25, 1979; children: Daniel Mark, Heather Michelle. AA, Santa Ana (Calif.) Coll., 1976; BA, U. Calif. San Diego, 1979; MDiv, Trinity Evang. Div. Sch., Deerfield, Ill., 1983. Ordained to ministry Evang. Free Ch. Am., 1987. Founding pastor Wasatch Evang. Free Ch., Ogden, Utah, 1983—; tchr. Utah Inst. for Bibl. Studies, Salt Lake City, 1988; chmn. Intermountain WEst Region, Evang. Free Ch. Am., Ogden, 1987-88. Contbr. articles to profl. jours.; columnist in Ogden Std. Examiner, 1988—. Chmn. bd. dirs. Crisis Pregnancy Ctr. No. Utah, 1988—. Recipient Arne Hansen Meml. award, Trinity Evang. Div. Sch., Deerfield, 1983. Mem. Ogden Ministerial Assn. (treas. 1990-91), Evang. Free Ch. Ministerial Assn. Home: 1148 5th St Ogden UT 84404 Office: Wasatch Evang Free Ch 3701 Washington Blvd Ogden UT 84403

ANDERSON, SHIRLEY ANNE, minister; b. Birmingham, Ala., Dec. 14, 1950; d. Floyd J. and Eddie Mae (Shelton) Jemison; m. Hosea Anderson, June 21, 1969; children: Clarence, Chandria, Kennyth, Cherryl, Kevin, Celeste, Kraig, Candace, Cynthia, Crystal. Diploma in Programming Tech., Control Data Inst., Chgo., 1973; student, Marilyn Hickey Bible Encounter, Chgo., 1987. Youth dir. God's House of Prayer, Chgo., 1974-88, Heavenly Places Outreach Ministries, Kankakee, Ill., 1989—, Youth for Jesus Outreach Ministries, 1990—. Home: 10217 S State St Chicago IL 60628 Office: Youth for Jesus Outreach Ministries PO Box 289239 Chicago IL 60628 *In my life I've found that true happiness is receiving Jesus as my Lord; then going on to know Him as my personal Savior. I've found total happiness is finding and knowing His perfect and divine will for my life.*

ANDERSON, VINTON RANDOLPH, bishop; b. Somerset, Bermuda; came to U.S., 1947; m. Vivienne Louise Cholmondeley, 1952; children: Vinton Jr., Jeffrey, Carlton, Kenneth. BA, Wilberforce U., HHD (hon.), 1973; MDiv, Payne Theol. Sem., 1952; MA in Philosophy, Kans. U., 1962; postgrad., Yale U. Div. Sch.; DD (hon.), Paul Quinn Coll., Payne Theol. Sem., Temple Bible Coll.; LHD (hon.), Morris Brown Coll. Ordained to ministry A.M.E. Ch., 1952, bishop, 1972. Pastor various chs. in Kans. and Mo., 1952-72; presiding bishop A.M.E. Ch., Ala., 1972-76; presiding bishop, chief pastor A.M.E. Ch., Ohio, W.Va., Western Pa., 1976-84; dir. Office of Ecumenical Rels. and Devel. A.M.E. Ch., 1984-88, presiding bishop 5th Episcopal dist., 1988—; chmn. bd. dirs. Payne Theol. Sem., Xenia, Ohio; preacher, lectr. in Caribbean, Republic of South and West Africa, Middle East, Europe, South Pacific; del. World Meth. conf., Nairobi, Kenya, 1986; mem. exec. com. World Meth. Coun., 1981—, 1st v.p. N.Am. region; v.p. Consultation on Ch. Union; mem. Gen. Commn. Christian Unity and Interreligious Concern, United Meth. Ch.; pres. World Coun. Chs., 1991—, del. 7th assembly, moderator liaison com. of hist. black chs.; mem. governing bd., faith and order Nat. Coun. Chs.; charter mem., v.p. Congress Nat. Black Chs. Founder, editor Connector, info. publ.; editor A Syllabus for Celebrating the Bicentennial; contbr. articles to profl. jours. Mem. nat. adv. com. on the black population 1990 U.S. Census; mem. Nat. Commn. on Sch./Community Role in Improving Adolescent Health; mem. nat. adv. bd. Schomburg Ctr. for Rsch. in Black Culture; immediate past chairperson bd. trustees Wilberforce U.; chairperson bd. dirs. Payne Theol. Sem. Recipient Ann. Religion award Ebony mag., 1988, Disting. Alumni Honoree award Nat. Assn. for Equal Opportunity in Higher Edn., 1991. Home: 7748 Peachtree Ln University City MO 63130 Office: AME Ch 5th Episcopal Dist AMEC 4144 Lindell #222 Saint Louis MO 63108

ANDERSON, WESLEY BAXTER, minister; b. Bellepoint, W.Va., Sept. 27, 1932; s. Walter Herman and Pearl Elizabeth (Wiley) A.; m. Shirley Jeanne Dyer, Aug. 15, 1968; children: Mark Kevin, Kirk Loren, Kari Lynne. ThB, No. Bapt. Theol. Sem., Chgo., 1955. Minister Christian Edn. Judson Meml. Bapt. Ch., Lansing, Mich., 1955-57, First Bapt. Ch., St. Paul, 1957-61; pastor First Bapt. Ch., Battle Lake, Minn., 1961-66; minister of Christian Edn. Emerson Ave. Bapt. Ch., Indpls., 1966-74; pastor Gauley Bridge Bapt. Ch., W.Va., 1974-82; pastor First Bapt. Ch., Berwick, Pa., 1982-86, Princeton, Ill., 1986—; chmn. Christian Edn. com. Great Rivers Region, Am. Bapt. Ch. USA, ARea I, 1989— mem. Christian Edn. task force W. Va. Bapt. Conv., 1979-82. Recipient Christian Svc. award, Alderson-Broaddus Coll., Philippi, W.Va., 1981. Mem. Princeton Ministerial Assn. (sec. 1987-88). Avocations: camping, photography. Home: 208 N Main St Princeton IL 61356 Office: First Baptist Church 1719 S Euclid Ave Princeton IL 61356

ANDERSON, WILLIAM BURKE, minister; b. Bluff City, Tenn., Mar. 19, 1936; s. George Rhea and Hessie Lee (Burke) A.; m. Linda Sue Dotson, Sept. 6, 1964; children: Todd Alan, Mark Steven. BA, Milligan Coll., 1958; postgrad., Christian Theol. Sem., Indpls., 1959-61; MA, Lincoln Christian Sem., Ill., 1968, MDiv, 1970; postgrad., Emmanuel Sch. Religion, 1974-76. Ordained to ministry Christian Ch., 1957. Min. New Whiteland (Ind.) Christian Ch., 1958-62, Henning (Ill.) Ch. of Christ, 1962-66, The Christian Ch., Heyworth, Ill., 1966-70, Franklin (Ind.) Meml. Christian Ch., 1970-73, East Unaka Ch. of Christ, Johnson City, Tenn., 1973-78, 1st Christian Ch., Erwin, Tenn., 1978—; organizer, dir. ann. elders' and deacons' clinic Milligan Coll., 1976-83; pres. 150th ann. conv. Christian Chs. of East Tenn., 1979. Mem. bd. advisors Milligan Coll., Tenn., 1974—; bd. dirs. Unicoi County chpt. Am. Cancer Soc., Erwin, 1987—; active Com. for Troubled Youth and Adults, Unicoi County, 1987-89; mem. planning and evaluation com. for cancer residency for clergy Johnson City Med. Ctr., 1989. Recipient cert. local chpt. Modern Woodmen Am., 1991. Mem. Unicoi County Ministerial Assn. (chmn. vol. hosp. chaplaincy 1980—), Kiwanis (pres. local chpt. 1988-89, lt. gov. div. 7 1990-91, Kiwanian of Yr. Erwin chpt. 1985). Avocations: woodworking, wood refinishing, collecting books. Home: 635 Cedar Erwin TN 37650 Office: First Christian Ch 307 S Main St Erwin TN 37650

ANDERSSON, ANNE RESPOL, lay worker, theologian, tax consultant; b. N.Y.C., Aug. 15, 1943; d. John J. and Lillian (Mannello) Respol; m. Bruno Andersson, July 23, 1966; children: Christopher, Michael, David. BA, Hunter Coll., 1965, MS, 1969; MA in Systematic Theology, Fordham U., 1991. Cert. tchr., N.Y.; lic. IRS Enrolled Agent. Co-founder, co-dir. Micromatic Programming Co., Weston, 1979-85; co-planner, panel moderator for confs. on women Women's Com., Office of the Laity, Diocese of Bridgeport (Conn.) Cath. Ch., 1984-89; co-founder, dir. Christian Women: Quo Vadis?, Weston, Conn., 1983—. Author poetry; co-author: Computer Income Tax Software, 1980, 81; creator, editor, pub. Christian Women: Quo Vadis? quar. newsletter, 1983—; designer adult edn. course in women's studies, 1976-77. Bd. dirs. NOW, Huntington chpt., 1974-77, chairperson edn. com., 1974-77, co-convener edn. coll. L.I. chpts., 1975; advisor Regents External Degree Program, SUNY, Albany, 1975-77. Mem. Am. Acad. Religion, Nat. Soc. Pub. Accts., Nat. Assn. Enrolled Agents, Coll. Theology Soc. Home: 24 Old Farm Rd Weston CT 06883 *The greatest challenge to humanity today is to transform its focus on domination/subordination to that of emphasis on partnership—a partnership which would be incorporated into all levels of relationship—human to human, human to plant/animal, to earth with human understood as part of the cosmos. This form of partnership recognizes a linking of spirit and matter, eliminates dualistic thinking, recognizes the divine in nature and in experience, values all of creation. The first change must occur in the male-female relationship precisely because it is upon this relationship, as primordial base, which all others rest and derive their pattern.*

ANDERT, DAVID AUGUST, minister; b. Morris, Minn., Aug. 8, 1946; s. Audrew Bach and Bertha Clara (Huebner) A.; m. Anne Lee Graupner, July 31, 1982; children: Elizabeth, Katherine, Rebecca. Grad., Calif. Luth. Bible Sch., L.A., 1967; BA, U. Minn., 1970; MDiv, Luth. Northwestern Theol. Sem., St. Paul, 1974. Ordained to ministry, Evang. Luth. Ch. in Am. Assoc. pastor Normandale Luth. Ch., Edina, Minn., 1974-79; pastor Bethesda & Elim Luth. Chs., Carlton, Minn., 1979-88; sr. pastor Luth. Ch. of Good Shepherd, Duluth, Minn., 1988—; chmn., mem. ref. and counsel com. N.E. Minn. Synod, Duluth, 1987-91; mem. ch. coun. Evang. Luth. Ch. in Am., 1991—. Author newspaper col. The Village Times "Weekly Messenger", 1986-88. Participant Leadership Duluth, 1990—. Mem. Acad. of Preachers. Office: Luth Ch Good Shepherd 45th Ave E & Colorado St Duluth MN 55804

ANDES, LARRY DALE, minister; b. Warrenton, Va., June 7, 1947; s. William Christian and Hilda Elizabeth (Beech) A.; m. Bobbi E. Stephens, July 16, 1966; 1 child, Joshua Dale. Student, North Cen. Bible Coll., 1966-70, U. Richmond, 1970. Assoc. pastor Calvary Assembly of God, Staunton, Va., 1971-72; youth min. Arlington (Va.) Assembly of God, 1972-75; assoc. pastor West End Assembly of God, Richmond, Va., 1975-76; founder, pres., festival dir. Fishnet Ministries Inc., Richmond, Front Royal, Va., 1976—; sr. pastor People's Ch., Manassas, Va., 1987—. Named one of Outstanding Young Men of Am., 1984. Office: Fishnet Ministries Inc PO Box 1919 Front Royal VA 22630

ANDRE, PAUL REVERE, minister; b. Nesbit, Nebr., Oct. 25, 1935; s. George Martin and Iva Elsie (Cassens) A.; m. Anna Katherine Jones, June 7, 1953; children: Paul, Georgia, Iva, Katherine. AA, Cen. Coll., McPherson, Kans., 1957; BA, Greenville (Ill.) Coll., 1959; MDiv, Ashbury Sem., Wilmore, Ky., 1962. Ordained to ministry Free Meth. Ch., 1962. Pastor Free Meth. Ch., Amelia, Nebr., 1962-64, Kearney, Nebr., 1964-66, Colville, Wash., 1966-70, Bellevue, Nebr., 1970-85; pastor MacArthur Free Meth. Ch., Oklahoma City, 1985-90, Cornwall Ave. Free Meth. Ch., Waterloo, Iowa, 1990—; asst. supt. Nebr. Conf. Free Meth. Ch. N. Am., 1977-79, supt., 1979-83, gen conf. del., 1979, 85. Mem. mayor's commn. on preservation of historic sites City of Bellevue, 1984—. Recipient Outstanding Citizen of Omaha award, 1976. Mem. Nebr. Assn. Evang. (v.p. 1976), Met. Assn. Evangs. Omaha (pres. 1973-76), Greater Omaha Christian Edn. Assn. (pres. 1976-77), Bellevue Ministerial Assn. (v.p. 1971-73, pres. 1973-75, 84—, sec. 1982-83), Rotary (pres. Bellevue 1978-79, Paul Harris fellow, 1981). Office: Cornwall Ave Free Meth Ch 1725 Cornwall Ave Waterloo IA 50702-2638 *Too often in our pursuit of ministry we forget the little people. Ministry to children is touching the world one child at a time.*

ANDREA, FREDERICK WILHELM, III, clergyman; b. Greenville, S.C., Feb. 21, 1952; s. Fred W. Jr. and Jean (Wilson) A.; m. Dawn H. Hull, July 10, 1976; children: Margaret E., Sarah K. BA, Clemson U., 1973; MDiv, So. Sem., Louisville, 1976, PhD, 1982. Ordained to ministry Bapt. Ch., 1976. Assoc. pastor Bethany Bapt. Ch., Louisville, 1974-76; adminstrv. asst. Ministry Tng. Ctr. Bethany Bapt. Ch., 1977-81, adj. prof., 1987-88; pastor Rock Creek Bapt. Ch., Westport, Ind., 1978-83, Augusta Heights Bapt. Ch., Greenville, 1983-89; sr. minister 1st Bapt. Ch., Savannah, Ga., 1989—; bd. dirs. So. Bapt. Alliance, Washington, 1987-89. Compiler: Shooting the Rapids, 1989; contbg. author: The Ministers' Manual, 1984-86; contbr. articles to profl. jours. Grad. Leadership Greenville, 1984; bd. dirs. Greenville United Ministries, 1987-89, Grace House. Mem. S.C. Bapt. Hist. Soc. (pres. 1988-89), Lions (1st v.p. Greenville 1988-89). Avocations: jogging, racquetball, spectator sports, reading. Home: 302 Gloucester Rd Savannah GA 31410 Office: 1st Bapt Ch 102 W McDonough St Savannah GA 31401

ANDREASEN, NIELS-ERIK ALBINNS, religious educator; b. Asminderod, Denmark, May 14, 1941; came to U.S., 1963; s. Caleb A. and Erna E. (Pedersen) A.; m. Demetra Lougani, Sept. 5, 1965; 1 child, Michael. BA, Newbold Coll., England, 1963; MA, Andrews U., Mich., 1965, BD, 1966; PhD, Vanderbilt U., 1971. From asst. to assoc. prof. Pacific Union Coll., Calif., 1970-75; vis. lectr. Avondale Coll., Australia, 1975-77; prof., dean of religion Loma Linda (Calif.) U., 1977-90; pres. Walla Walla (Wash.) Coll., 1990—. Author: The Old Testament Sabbath, 1972, Rest and Redemption, 1978, The Christian Use of Time, 1978. Mem. Soc. Bibl. Lit. Seventh Day Adventist. Office: Walla Walla Coll College Place WA 99324

ANDREASEN, PHILL E., minister; b. Carroll, Iowa, May 14, 1949; s. Holger Christian and Norene Grace (Fett) A.; m. Monica Louise Aho, Apr. 15,1 973; children: Jeffrey, Jeremy, Jill, Janay, Jordon, Jonathon, Joy. AA, Concordia Coll., 1969, BA, 1971; MDiv, Concordia Theol. Sem., 1975. Pastor St. Mark Luth. Ch., Garrison, Iowa, 1975-79; pastor St. Paul Luth. Ch., Milford Center, Ohio, 1979-84, Williamsburg, Iowa, 1984—; dist. pastoral advisor Bible Trans., Milford Center, 1980-84. Mem. care rev. com. Williamsburg Care Ctr., 1986—; bd. dirs. Luth. Home for Aged of Iowa, Garrison, 1977-79. Republican. Office: St Paul Luth Ch 500 Clark St Williamsburg IA 52361

ANDREASEN, SAMUEL GENE, minister; b. Kearney, Nebr., May 7, 1927; s. Fred and Esther Elizabeth Andreasen; m. Rachel Mae Poe, May 29, 1959; children: Paul S., Cathye Elizabeth. BA, Sterling Coll., 1951; MDiv, Columbia Theol., 1954; Th.M., Chgo. Grad. Sch., 1968; EdD, Ariz. State U., 1976. Ordained minister in Presbyn. Ch., 1954; lic. profl. counselor, Ala. Pastor Grace Presbyn. Ch., Aiken, S.C., 1956-60; enlisted USAF, 1960, advanced through grades to col., chaplain, 1963-71, retired, 1987; coord. religious svcs. Partlow Devel. Ctr., Tuscaloosa, 1976—. Pres. Community Svc. Network, Tuscaloosa, 1990-91; mem., lt. col. Civil Air Patrol, Tuscaloosa, 1980—. Republican. Office: Box 1730 Tuscaloosa AL 35401

ANDREWS, CHESTER W., minister; b. Minters, Ala., Aug. 16, 1936; s. Jesse and Edna (Boxdale) A.; m. Doris Glenn, Sept. 13, 1959; chester W. II, Dareell Lamar, Kenneth Anthony, Dana Nicole, Heather Lyn. Student, Spokane Falls Community Coll., 1983. Ordained to ministry Am. Bapt. Chs. Pastor Calvary Bapt. Ch., Spokane, 1974—; ind. mktg. rep. U.S. Sprint 2000, Spokane, 1991—; pres. ednl. ministries Am. Bapt. Chs., Spokane, 1990—, del., Spokane, 1985—; 2d v.p. North Pacific Bapt. Conv., Spokane, 1985—. V.p. Spokane Police Dept., 1991; mem. Spokane Human Svc. Adv. Bd., 1987-91; chaplain Deaconess Hosp., Spokane, 1988. Staff sgt. U.S. Army, 1959-67. Named Outstanding Citizen City of Spokane, 1987. Mem. NAACP (membership com. 1990-91), Mins. Fellowship Union (pres. Spokane 1984-86 1989-91), Tel. Pioneers Am. (life), Masons (chaplain Prince Hall chpt. 1980-86). Democrat. Office: Calvary Bapt Ch 203 E Third Ave Spokane WA 99202

ANDREWS, JAMES EDGAR, church official, minister; b. Whittenburg, Tex., Dec. 29, 1928; s. Bryan McEvrie and Rose Ellen (Simpson) A.; m. Sarah Elizabeth Crouch, Sept. 16, 1962; children: Charis Megan, Bryan Hugh. BA, Austin Coll., 1952, MA, 1953, DD, 1974; BD, Austin Presbyn. Theol. Sem., 1956. Ordained to ministry Presbyn. Ch. U.S., 1956. Asst. minister St. Andrews Presbyn. Ch., Houston, 1956-58; info. officer World Alliance of Ref. Chs., Geneva, 1958-60; dir. pub. relations and asst. to pres. Princeton (N.J.) Theol. Sem., 1960-71; asst. to stated clk. Presbyn. Ch. U.S., 1971-73, stated clk., 1973-83; interim co-stated clk. Presbyn. Ch. (U.S.A.), 1983-84, stated clk., 1984—. Office: Presbyterian Church (USA) 100 Witherspoon St Louisville KY 40202

ANDREWS, MARTHA WILMOTH, broadcasting executive, radio disc jockey; b. Alexandria, Va., July 21, 1960; d. Kathleen Ramona (McGuire) Wilmoth. Student, Liberty U., Lynchburg, Va., 1989—. News announcer Armed Forces Radio and TV, Elmendorf Air Force Base, Alaska, 1981-84; morning disc journey, news-music dir. Sta. WDCT-AM, Marsh Broadcasting, Washington, 1987—; intern program The Insiders with Jack Anderson Sta. UPI-TV, Washington, 1990-91; news dir. Mash Broadcasting Network, Washington, 1987—; producer, host radio talk show Capital Mag., 1990. Vol. Republican Party of Alaska, Anchorage, 1984. With USAF, 1981-84. Mem. The Conservative Network. Republican. Presbyterian. Office: Sta WDCT-AM Box 1310 3909 Oak St Fairfax VA 22030

ANDREWS, ROBERT FREDERICK, religious organization administrator, retired bishop; b. Sedalia, Mo., Nov. 26, 1927; s. Milton Paul and Lydia Allen (Newberry) A.; m. Genevieve Arlene Hendricks, June 25, 1949; children—Robert F., Mary Louise, Melva Arlene, Vondria Beth. A.A., Central Coll., 1946; B.A., Greenville Coll., 1949; B.D., Asbury Theol. Sem., 1952; D.D. (hon.), Western Evang. Sem., 1977. Ordained to ministry Free Meth. Ch., 1953. Pastor Free Meth. Ch., Caldwell, Kans., 1952-55; no. regional dir. Free Meth. Youth, Winona Lake, Ind., 1955-60; pres. Wessington Springs Coll., S.D., 1960-65; speaker and dir. Light and Life Hour Internat. (radio broadcast), 1965-79; exec. dir. Light and Life Men Internat., Winona Lake, 1968-71; gen. dir. Evang. Outreach Free Meth. Ch. N.Am., 1971-79; bishop Free Meth. Ch. N.Am., Indpls., 1979-91, ret., 1991; supt. Okla. Conf. Free Meth. Ch., Oklahoma City, 1991—. Author: When You Need a Friend, 1979; contbg. editor Light and Life mag., 1979-91; editor Light and Life Transmitter, 1966-79. Served with U.S. Army, 1946-47. Acad. Achievers fellow. Republican. Address: Okla Conf Free Meth Ch Office of Supt 5008 N Warren Oklahoma City OK 73112

ANDREWS, WILLIAM HENRY, clergyman, school psychologist; b. Decatur, Ga., May 4, 1929; s. John Edward and Semite Rebecca (Hall) A. B.S., U. Ga., 1953, M.Ed., 1969, Ed.S., 1972; A.B., Ga. State U., 1963; M.S. in Edn., Baylor U., 1968; B.D., So. Baptist Sem., 1956, M.Div., 1969; Th.M., Luther Rice Sem., 1971, Th.D., 1973, D.Ministry, 1982. Ordained to ministry Bapt. Ch., 1956. Pastor 1st Bapt. Ch., Danielsville, Ga., 1956-61, County Line Bapt. Ch., Douglasville, Ga., 1962-67, 71-75, New Ga. Bapt. Ch., Dallas, 1968-71, 1st Bapt. Ch., Damascus, Ga., 1984—; evangelist Bill Andrews Assocs., Blakely, Ga., 1976-84; sch. psychologist Early County Bd. Edn., Blakely, 1977-85, 89—; moderator Tallapoos Bapt. Assn., Dallas, 1969-71. Mem. Am. Assn. Pastoral Counselors, So. Bapt. Religious Edn. Soc. Republican. Lodge: Masons (sr. deacon 1959-60). Avocations: hunting; fishing; stamp collecting. Home: PO Box 227 Blakely GA 31723 Office: First Bapt Ch of Damascus PO Box 227 Blakely GA 31723

ANDREWS, WILLIAM JOSEPH, lay worker; b. Troy, Ala., May 27, 1950; s. William Cullen and Lula Bell (Bastin) A.; m. Sheila Lynn Newman, Dec. 29, 1977. Grad. high sch., Enterprise, Ala. Rte. salesman Coca Cola Bottling Co., Speedway, Ind., 1981—; tchr. Ind. Boys Sch., Plainfield, 1987—; youth leader Cathedral of Prayer Bapt. Ch., Plainfield, 1988-90, bus. dir., 1988-89, supt. Sunday Sch., trustee, 1988—. Pres. Christ Is the Answer

Prison Ministeries, Indpls., 1990—. Home: RR 1 Box 552 Camby IN 46113 Office: Cathedral Prayer Bapt Ch 2238 E Camby Rd Plainfield IN 46168

ANDRINGA, ROBERT CHARLES, management consultant; b. Grand Rapids, Mich., Dec. 30, 1940; B.A. with honors, Mich. State U., 1963, M.A., 1964, Ph.D. in Higher Edn. Adminstrn., 1967. Asst. dir. Honors Coll., Mich. State U., East Lansing, 1965-67; mem. faculty and research staff Indsl. Coll. Armed Forces, Washington, 1967-69; minority staff dir. U.S. Ho. of Reps. Com. Edn. and Labor, Washington, 1969-77; campaign mgr. Al Quie for Gov. of Minn., 1977-78; dir. policy research Office of Gov. Minn., 1978-80; exec. dir. Edn. Commn. of the States, Denver, 1980-84, Conant sr. fellow, 1984-85; pres. Discovery Network, Inc., 1984—, pres. Creative Solutions div. of Discovery Network, Inc., 1986—; mem. Sec. Navy's Adv. Bd. on Edn. and Tng., 1981—; alt./cons. Nat. Commn. on Financing Postsecondary Edn., 1972-73; mem. Newman Task Force on Higher Edn., 1971-73; mem. governance study adv. panel Carnegie Found., 1983-84; chmn. nat. adv. bd. Life Insts., 1982-84. Contbr. articles to profl. jours. Bd. dirs. Inst. Ednl. Leadership; trustee Trinity Coll., Internat. Sch. Law (now George Mason U.), Ucross Found. Served to capt. USAR, 1967-69. Recipient Disting. Alumni award Coll. Edn., Mich. State U., 1978. Mem. Am. Assn. Higher Edn. (life), Am. Soc. Assn. Execs., Forum for Edn. Orgn. Leaders, Phi Kappa Phi, Omicron Delta Kappa (charter pres.), Blue Key, Beta Gamma Sigma, Phi Delta Kappa, Mich. State U. Alumni Assn. (bd. dirs.). Presbyterian. Office: 7412 S Monaco Englewood CO 80112

ANDRON, ALEXANDER, educator; b. N.Y.C., Nov. 6, 1938; s. David S. and Hortense (Schlang) A.; m. Goldie Fishman, Nov. 12, 1959; children: Jonathan, Vicki, Beth. BA, U. Miami, Coral Gables, Fla., 1962; MEd, Clemson U., 1974; EdD, Nova U., 1980. Lic. Jewish educator/prin., Fla. Hebrew tchr. Beth Torah, North Miami Beach, Fla., 1961-69; dir. youth program Cen. Agy. for Jewish Edn., Miami, 1976—; lay rabbi Meals on Wheels for Aged, Hallandale, Fla., 1976—. Author: (serial) Gift Rapping, 1976, (tour guides) In-Quest, 1980, Clutivating Cult-Evading, 1980. Mem. Cult Awareness Network (v.p. 1988—, Leo J. Ryan award 1984), Jewish Educator's Alliance, Coun. Exceptional Children, Am. Family Found., Internat. Brotherhood Magicians, Soc. Am. Magicians, Mensa. Home: 21400 NE 20th Ave North Miami Beach FL 33179 Office: Cen Agy Jewish Edn 4200 Biscayne Blvd Miami FL 33137

ANDRYS, DAVID PAUL, principal; b. Grand Forks, N.D., Apr. 3, 1956; s. George Alfred Jr. and Mary Ann (Logan) A.; m. Bonita Marie Bridgeford, Aug. 8, 1982; 1 child, Simon Kenneth. BS in Social Studies, U. N.D., 1979. Cert. secondary education tchr., N.D. Prin. Sacred Heart Grade Sch., East Grand Forks, Minn., 1979—. Mem. com. City Centennial Book, East Grand Forks, 1987-88. Roman Catholic. Office: Sacred Heart Schs 131 4th St NW East Grand Forks MN 56721

ANGELINI, FIORENZO CARDINAL, archbishop; b. Rome, Aug. 1, 1916. ordained priest, Roman Catholic Ch. Feb. 3, 1940, bishop (titular see of Messene) July 29, 1956. Archbishop, 1985—; pres. Curia agy. for health care workers; deacon Holy Spirit (in Sassio); Pres. Pontifical Coun. for Pastoral Assistance to Health Care Workers, 1985; elevated to Sacred College of Cardinals, 1991. Office: Pontifical Council, for Health Care, Vatican City Vatican*

ANGELL, JOHN WILLIAM, theology educator; b. Mocksville, N.C., Feb. 29, 1920; s. John Tilden and Juanita (Hanes) A.; m. Marjorie Sutterlin, June 6, 1944; children: John William Jr., George Sutterlin. AA, Mars Hill Coll., 1939; BA, Wake Forest U., 1941; MST, Andover Newton Theol. Sem., 1948; ThM, PhD, So. Bapt. Theol. Sem., 1945, 1949. Ordained to ministry Bapt. Ch., 1945. Pastor, chaplain Campbell Coll., Buies Creek, N.C., 1949-52; assoc. prof. Stetson U., Deland, Fla., 1952-55; from assoc. prof. to Easley prof. theology Wake Forest U., Winston-Salem, N.C., 1955-90, emeritus, 1990—; cons., chmn. bd. Ecumenical Inst. N.C., Winston Salem, 1974—. Author: Can The Church Be Saved?, 1967; co-author: Images of Man, 1984, Meaning and Value in Wester Thought, 1981, 2d vol., 1988, A Controversy on Baptism, 1977, To Understand Each Other, 1988; Editor: Seminar on Authority, 1974, A Convocation of Jews and Baptists, 1971; contbr., editor: Catholics and Baptists, 1974; contbr. articles to profl. jours. Recipient Ecumenism medal Pope Paul VI, Vatican, Rome, 1973; Cuthbert Allen award Belmont Abbey, N.C., 1986. Mem. Am. Acad. Religion (pres. 1978), Soc. Biblical Literature, Internat. Soc. Neoplatonic Studies, Internat. Torch Club, Omicron Delta Kappa. Democrat. Baptist. Avocations: travel, gardening. Home: 108 Belle Vista Ct Winston-Salem NC 27106 Office: Wake Forest Univ Winston-Salem NC 27109

ANGELL, KENNETH ANTHONY, bishop; b. Providence, Aug. 3, 1930; s. Henry L. and Mae T. (Cooney) A. AB in Philosophy, St. Mary's Sem., Balt., 1950, STB, 1955; STD (hon.), Our Lady of Providence Sem., 1975; JCD (hon.), Providence Coll., 1975. Ordained priest Roman Catholic Ch., 1956, consecrated bishop, 1974. Assoc. pastor St. Mark Ch., Jamestown, R.I., 1956; assoc. pastor Sacred Heart Ch., Pawtucket, R.I., 1956-60, St. Mary Ch., Newport, R.I., 1960-68; asst. chancellor and sec. to bishop Diocese of Providence, 1968-72, chancellor, 1972-74, aux. bishop, vicar gen., 1974—; pastor St. John Ch., Providence, 1975-81. Mem. Nat. Conf. Cath. Bishops, U.S. Cath. Conf. Office: Diocese of Providence 1 Cathedral Sq Providence RI 02903

ANGERS, JOANN MARIE, religious education director, nurse; b. Bay City, Mich., May 19, 1944; d. Virgil H. and Marie Veronica (Nowak) Goyett; m. Theodore Leibert Angers, Feb. 6, 1965; children: Theodore Allen, Toni Marie, Terry Michael, Troy, Theresa, Tammy, Timothy. Grad., Bay City Sch. Nursing, 1964; postgrad., St. Mary's Coll., Orchard Lake, Mich., Lansing (Mich.) Community Coll. Lic. nurse, Mich.; cert. catechist, Mich., 1977. Nurse Bay Osteopathic Hosp., Bay City, 1964-65, physician's office, Lansing, 1966, nursing home, Lansing, 1968; coord. religious edn. Immaculate Heart of Mary, Lansing, 1968-84, dir. religious edn., 1984—; master catechist, speaker Diocese Lansing, 1968—; mem. diocesan team determining AIDS policy, Lansing, 1990. Author: My Beginning Mass Book, 1978, Meeting the Forgiving Jesus, 1984; (filmstrip) Celebrating Sunday with God's Family, 1981, (video) Amanda Goes to Mass, 1991; contbr. articles to religious publs. Recipient Dedicated Svc. award Diocese of Lansing, 1969-89, Pastor's Religious Edn. Award Immaculate Heart of Mary Parish, 1982, Pius X award Diocese of Lansing, 1983, Vol. Svc. award Lansing Sch. Dist., 1985-90, Children's Reading Round Table award, 1985. Mem. Profl. Pastoral Mins. Assn., Nat. Cath. Ednl. Assn. Home: 310 E Miller Rd Lansing MI 48911

ANGLIN, WALTER MICHAEL, evangelist, law enforcement professional; b. Cheverly, Md., Jan. 10, 1958; s. Lawrence Tilmon and Margaret Lorraine (Thrash) A.; m. Meloene Alene Williams, Mar. 1, 1980; children: Walter Michael Jr., Mary Elizabeth. A in Practical Theology, Christ For The Nations Inst., 1979; BA in Pastoral Ministry, S.W. Assemblies of God Coll., 1991. Ordained to ministry Am. Bapt. Assn., 1978; lic. to ministry Assemblies of God, 1980. Evangelist Assemblies of God, Duncanville, Tex., 1980—; police officer Duncanville Police Dept., 1986—, chaplain, 1990—, high sch. liaison officer, 1990—; youth sponsor Meml. Assembly of God., Duncanville, 1989-91; youth care leader Ch. on the Rock S., Duncanville, 1991—; youth evangelist SWAT Youth Ministries, Duncanville, 1989—; del. South Dallas sect. coun. Assemblies of God, Dallas, 1989, 90, Am. Bapt. Assn., Plain Dealing, La., 1974. Exec. advisor local post Duncanville Law Enforcement Post, 1990-91; asst. coach Best S.W. Soccer Assn., Duncanville, 1989-91, YMCA Youth Baseball, Dallas, 1990; assoc. coord. Duncanville Citizen Police Acad., 1990-91. Fellow Fraternal Order Police (chaplain local chpt. 1989—); mem. Tex. Peace Officers Assn. (cert. advanced peace officer), Duncanville Youth Pastor's Assn. Office: Duncanville Police Dept PO Box 380280 Duncanville TX 75138-0280

ANGLINE, ROBERT ALDEN, minister; b. Burnsville, N.C., June 30, 1915; s. William Thomas and Maude Mae (Wilson) A.; m. Mabyn Wilson, July 20, 1941; 1 child, Pamela Louise Angline Bowman. Grad., U. N.C., 1938; postgrad., S.W. Bapt. Theol. Sem., 1950. Min. religious edn. 1st Bapt. Ch., Asheville, N.C., 1950-80, min. to sr. adults, 1980-90; leader workshops in religious edn. adminstrn., teaching; bd. dirs. Bibl. Recorder, 1959-67. Contbr. articles to religious jours. Mem. com. Golden Care Club St. Joseph Hosp., Asheville; mem. steering com. Bapt. Children Homes N.C., Capital Fund Dr. With U.S. Army, 1942-45, ETO. Recipient 5 Campaign Battle Stars. Mem. N.C. Bapt. Religious Edn. Assn. (pres. 1954, 58), S.E. Bapt. Religious Edn. Assn. (v.p. 1962), Lions. Republican. Home: 34 Forest View Dr Ashveville NC 28804 Office: 5 Oak St Asheville NC 28801 *Being involved in church leadership development, I am impressed with the inate goodness of people to respond favorably to clearly defined and worthily orientated challenges for ministry and participation.*

ANKERBERG, WILLIAM C., minister; b. Chgo., Dec. 8, 1950; s. Daniel C. and Joyce (Dahlberg) A.; m. Arlie P. DeWitt, Nov. 23, 1973; children: Elisabeth, Rebekah, Peter. BA, Bethel Coll., St. Paul, 1972; MDiv, Bethel Sem., St. Paul, 1976; postgrad., Trinity Evang. Div. Sch., Deerfield, Ill., 1985—. Ordained to ministry, Bapt. Gen. Conf. Pastor Calvary Bapt. Ch., Kewanee, Ill., 1976-80; sr. pastor Trinity Bapt. Ch., Palos Hills, Ill., 1980-84, Homewood (Ill.) Ch., 1984—; chmn. exec. com. Midwest Bapt. Conf., Park Ridge, Ill., 1989—; dir. Fairview Bapt. Home, Downers Grove, Ill., 1989—; adv. bd. Southside Christian Counseling Ctr., Orland Park, Ill., 1985—; nominating com. sec. Bapt. Gen. Conf., Arlington Hts., 1982-85. Contbr. articles to profl. jours. Human rights commr. Village of Kewanee, 1978-80; adv. bd. Black Hawk Coll. E., Kewanee, 1978-80. Anna Anderson scholar, Bethel Coll., 1971; recipient Community Svc. award, S. Suburban Hosp., Hazel Crest, 1984-91. Mem. Christian Mgmt. Assn. Office: Homewood Ch 183rd & Governors Hwy Homewood IL 60430 *Blessed are the balanced.*

ANKROM, ROBERT LYNN, artist manager; b. Youngstown, Ohio, Sept. 2, 1959; s. Alonzo Everett and Edith Ann (Moore) A. Student, Youngstown Coll., 1977-79. Exec. dir. Anchor Artist Mgmt., Austintown, Ohio, 1983—; machine operator Namaco Industries, Youngstown, 1980—; pres. Omega Sonship Music Ministries, Inc., Niles, Ohio, 1985-88; bd. dirs. Y'Shua Ministries, Inc., Carrollton, Ohio, 1986-88; mem. adv. bd. Am. Biog. Inst., 1987—; mem. Penn-Ohio Christian Arts Coun., Hubbard, Ohio, 1987—. Mem. Christian Mgmt. Assn. Republican. Office: Anchor Artist Mgmt 2509 Bainbridge St Austintown OH 44511-1972

ANNAND, JAMES EARLE, university dean, minister, educator; b. Glendale, Calif., May 23, 1929; s. David Earle and Wilma (Aver) A.; m. Connie Lou Cousins, Aug. 22, 1953; children: David, Paul, Priscilla. BA, Occidental Coll., 1951; BD, Berkeley Div. Sch., Yale U., 1954, STM, 1956; DD (hon.), Yale U., 1975. Ordained to ministry Episc. Ch., 1954. Vicar Ch. Holy Spirit, Monterey Park, Calif., 1956-58; rector Christ Ch., Westerly, R.I., 1958-69, St. Paul's Ch., Greenwich, Conn., 1969-74; interim rector St. Luke's Ch., Darien, Conn., 1975-77, St. Peter's Ch., Narragansett, R.I., 1978, St. Paul's Ch., Fairfield, Conn., 1979-80; lectr. Berkeley Divinity Sch., Yale U., New Haven, 1981-82, acting dean, 1982, dean, 1983-91; canon Christ Ch. Cathedral, Hartford, Conn., 1985—. Fellow Coll. Preachers.

ANSELL, FRED ASHER, minister; b. Bradford, Pa., June 6, 1945; s. Wilbert Kenneth and Harriet Sarah (Acker) A.; m. Ann Maria Augusta Abrams, July 2, 1966; children: Jennifer Leslie, Aaron Paul. BA in Sociology, Eastern Coll., St. Davids, Pa., 1967; MDiv in Ministry, Am. Bapt. Sem. of West, Covina, Calif., 1971, DMin in Family Therapy, 1974. Ordained to ministry Am. Bapt. Ch., 1971. Youth minister Atwater Park Bapt. Ch., L.A., 1970-71; campus, resource minister Ft. Hays (Kans.) State U./Kans. Bapt. Conv., 1972-77; area minister Am. Bapt. Chs. of Cen. Region, Pittsburg, Kans., 1977-85; assoc. exec. minister Am. Bapt. Chs. of Cen. Region, Topeka, Kans., 1985—; bd. dirs., officer Am. Bapt. Ch. of Cen. Region, Topeka, 1986—. Contbg. author: Call for Christian Action, 1976, Friendship Evangelism, 1983, Respond, Vol. 5, 1977, Christian Parenting, 1985. Trustee Bacone Coll., Muskogee, Okla., 1989—; bd. dirs. Murrow Indian Children's Home, Muskogee, 1981-91. Mem. Kans. Ecumenical Ministries (bd. dirs. 1985—, pres. 1985-89), Alban Inst., Mins. Coun. of Am. Bapt. Chs. Office: Am Bapt Chs of Cen Region PO Box 4105 Topeka KS 66604-4105 *The amount of pain people carry constantly amazes me. The ability to cope with this must only be possible because the strongest force in the world is love.*

ANTHONY, BISHOP (ANTHONY EMMANUEL GERGIANNAKIS), bishop; b. Heraklion, Crete, Mar. 2, 1935. Degree in theology, Theol. Sch., Halki, Constantinople, 1960; MDiv, Yale U., 1964; postgrad., U. Chgo., U. Wis. Ordained deacon Greek Orthodox Ch., 1958, ordained priest, 1960. Priest Holy Trinity Ch., Ansonia, Conn., 1961-64; priest Assumption Ch., Chicago Heights, Ill., 1964-69, Madison, Wis., 1969-73; dean St. George Cathedral, Montreal, 1974-78; elevated to bishop, 1978; titular bishop Ammissos, Denver, 1978-79; bishop San Francisco, 1979—; pres. Archdiocesan Council of Dept. of Edn.; founder St. Nicholas Ranch and Retreat Ctr., Dunlop Calif., northwest Orthodox Found. Retreat Facilities, Tacoma, Wash. Office: Greek Orthodox Diocese 372 Santa Clara Ave San Francisco CA 94127

ANTHONY, HOMER BRUCE, minister, educator; b. Avalon, Calif., May 4, 1934; s. Homer Ira and Irma Frances (Bruce) A.; m. Lorraine Iris Bartha; children: Laura, Mary Beth , Sharon Rose, Janet Marie. BA, Grand Canyon Coll., 1957; MA, LaSierra Coll., 1976; PhD, Ariz. State U. cert. elementary, secondary tchr, adminstr. Pastor First Southern Bapt. Ch., Tempe, Ariz., 1954-57, Arlington Ave., Bapt. Ch., Riverside, Calif., 1957-59, Pleasantview Bapt. Ch., Phoenix, 1970-71; pub. relations cons. Cartwright Sch. Dist., Phoenix, 1971-72; dir. language arts Wichita (Kans.) Pub. Schs., 1972-73; pastor U. Bapt. Ch., Wichita, 1973-77, First Bapt. Ch. of Urbondale, Dallas, 1977-80; assoc. pastor First Bapt. Ch., Tulsa, Okla., 1980-83; pastor Southern Bapt. Ch., Greensboro, N.C., 1984—; mem. Gen. Bd. N.C. Bapt. Conv., Cary, N.C., 1987—, exec. com., 1988—; chmn. State Budget Com. N.C. Bapt. Conv., Cary, N.C., 1989—. Chaplain Calif. Young Repubs., Sacramento, 1969. Mem. Lions Club, Alumni Assn. Grand Canyon Coll. (pres. 1971-72), Phi Delta Kappa. Avocations: reading, gardening. Home: 4704 Middleton Greensboro NC 27406 Office: Southeast Bapt Ch Greensboro NC 27406

ANTHONY, KENNETH CHRISTOPHER, priest; b. Syracuse, N.Y., Sept. 29, 1960; s. Peter Anthony and Christine (Christ) A.; m. Nancy Jane Blakowski, May 28, 1988. BBA, St. Bonventure U., 1982; MDiv, Holy Cross Sch. Theology, 1990. Ordained priest Greek Orthodox Ch., 1990; CPA, N.Y. Asst. pastor Annunciation Greek Orthodox Cathedral, Houston, 1990—; fin. dir. Young Life, Buffalo, 1984-85; program dir. Greek Orthodox Youth Am., 1990—. Mem. N.Y. State Soc. CPAs, Houston Orthodox Clergy Assn., Houston Area Apple Users Group. Office: Annunciation Greek Orthodox Cathedral 3522 Yoakum Blvd Houston TX 77006

ANTHONY, RHONDA LEA, youth minister; b. Greenville, S.C., July 25, 1962; d. Fulton Howard and Doris Elizabeth (Smith) A. MusB, Furman U., 1984; MA, So. Bapt. Sem., 1986. Campus min. Anderson (S.C.) Coll., 1986-87; min. youth Berea 1st Bapt. Ch., Greenville, 1987-91, Lee Rd. United Meth. Ch., Taylors, S.C., 1991—; specialist Sch. Intervention Program, S.C. Drug and Alcohol Commn., 1991—. Del. Miss S.C. Delegation, Greenville, 1990. Mem. So. Bapt. Sem. Alumni (edn. adv. bd.). Home: 129 Club Circle Greenville SC 29611 Office: Lee Rd United Meth Ch 1377 E Lee Rd Taylors SC 29687

ANTHONY, YANCEY LAMAR, minister; b. Cordova, Ala., Feb. 13, 1922; s. Clifford Elmo and Tula (Barton) A.; m. Betty Pratt. B.A., Samford U., 1944; B.Th., So. Baptist Theol. Sem., 1947; Dr. è s scis., Paris; D.Th., Pioneer Theol. Sem., Rockford, Ill., Vanderbilt U., 1956, Galileo U., Italy; D.Ph., Accademia Universitaria Internazionale, Rome, 1957; D.D., Ministerial Tng. Coll., Sheffield, Eng., 1973; Ph.D. in History, Gt. China World U., Hong Kong. Ordained to ministry Baptist Ch., 1942; pastor Valley Grove Bapt. Ch., Tuscumbia, Ala., 1942-44, Walnut Grove Bapt. Ch., Lodiburg, Ky., 1945-47, First Bapt. Ch., Fort Walton Beach, Fla., 1947-53, Harsh Chapel Bapt. Ch., Nashville, 1953-56, Central Bapt. Ch., Fort Walton Beach, 1957-67; ambassador to all the Americas, Republik Danizig in Exile, N.Y.C., 1973—; moderator Okaloosa County Bapt. Assn., 1949-50; pres. Fort Walton Beach Ministerial Assn., 1952-55; mem. exec. bd. Fla. Bapt. Conv., 1948-56; pres. The Albert Schweitzer Internat. Open U., El Salvadore, 1989—. Pres. Okaloosa County Better Govt. League, 1950-52; mem. Fla. Bd. Social Welfare, 1959-68, chmn., 1960-64; dir. Ch. Missions Fund Bapt. Found., 1947—; dir. Ch. Devel. Found. Fla., 1962—; lt. col. and a.d.c. Gov. Ala.; a.d.c. Gov. Miss., 1976. Decorated Knights of Malta, 1973, knight Ordre dela Courtoisie Francais; Ordine Internazionale della Legion d'Onore de l'Immacolata (Italy); Gold medal of Labour (Netherlands), 1975; grand officier Ordre du Merite Africain; d'Honneur de l'Institut des Relations Diplomatiques, Brussels; Lit. award Belgian High Fidelity Inst., 1976; Legion of Honor, Chapel of Four Chaplains, Phila., 1981; numerous others; hon. academician W.A. Mozart (Germany), French Acad. Golden Letters. Fellow Brit. Inst. Adv. Cons.'s; mem. Accademia Delle Scienze di Roma (life), Inst. Diplomatic Relations Brussels (hon.), Royal Acad. Golden Letters (hon.), Accademia Gentium Populorum Progressie, Accademia Gentium Pro Pace, Nobility Acad. of Kaspis, Nat. Soc. Univ. Profs. (pres. 1981), Albert Schweitzer Soc. Internat. (pres. 1982-85, 90—), Internat. Assn. Educators for World Peace (v.p. fin. affairs 1989—), Mt. Kenya Safari Club (exec. com.), Masons. Bd. editors Study Centre for Am. Indians, Antwerp, Belgium, 1989—. Democrat. Home: 1913 Stanford Rd Jacksonville FL 32207

ANTHONY PETER, HIS BEATITUDE See KHORAICHE, ANTOINE PIERRE CARDINAL

ANTLEY, BARRY THOMAS, minister; b. Orangeburg, S.C., Feb. 12, 1954; s. Thomas Elsworth and Louise (Bedenbaugh) A.; m. Deborah Denise Tanner, Nov. 20, 1976; children: Jennifer Anne, Jason Thomas. BS in Math., Clemson U., 1976; MDiv, Luth. Theol. So. Sem., 1980. Pastor Mt. Hebron Luth. Ch., Leesville, S.C., 1980-85, St. James Luth. Ch., Graniteville, S.C., 1985--; Dean Peach Cluster-S.C. Synod, Aiken-Saluda 1989--, pres. CSRA Luth., Inc., Augusta, GA 1987-88, 1990--, chmn. S.C. Synod Youth Min. Cabinet, Columbia, trustee Luth. Conf. & Retreat Centers, Inc., Leesville, S.C. Mem. Gregg Pk. Adv. Bd., Aiken Co. Adult Edn. Adv. Com., coach Gregg Pk. baseball, football. Mem. Graniteville Ministerium (convener), Valley Ministerial Alliance, CSRA Luth. Pasters Assc., Western Conf. S.C. Synod Pastors. Evangelical Lutheran Church in Am. Office: St James Lutheran Church 200 Laurel Dr PO Box 98 Graniteville SC 29829

ANTLEY, EUGENE BREVARD, sociology and religion educator; b. Brownwood, Tex., Aug. 2, 1929; s. George Brewton and Frances Nell (Brevard) A.; m. Dolores Stephan, July 12, 1953; children: Barbara, Corinne, Bruce. BA, Millsaps Coll., 1955; M Social Studies, U. Miss., 1956. Instr. Spartanburg (S.C.) Jr. Coll., 1957-58; asst. prof. Coll. of Ozarks, Clarksville, Ark., 1967-69; instr. history So. Oreg. Coll./Coll. of Siskiyous, Calif., 1958-67; assoc. prof. sociology Edinboro (Pa.) U. Pa., 1969—, also. instr. sociology of religion course. Author: Southern Families, 1988; co-editor Social Problems, 1990. Mem. Pa. Sociol. Soc., Assn. Pa. Schs., Colls. and Univ. Faculties, Fellowship of Reconciliation. Democrat. Home: 12241 Lakeview Dr Edinboro PA 16412 Office: Edinboro U Pa 218 Hendricks Hall Edinboro PA 16444

ANTOLI GUARCH, MIGUEL, theology educator; b. Portell, Spain, Jan. 11, 1934; s. José Antoli and Roberta Guarch. Degree, U. Gregoriana, Rome, 1961; doctorate in theology, U. Comillas, Madrid, 1976. Ordained to ministry, Nov., 1957. Prof. Sem. Mater Dei, Castellón, Spain, 1961-69; vicar Episcopalian Diocese of Castellón, 1966-70; rector Teologado Mater Dei, Castellón, 1969-73; prof. Centro Estudios Teologic, Valencia, Spain, 1970-73, Facultad de Teologia, Valencia, 1973—. Author books; contbr. articles to profl. jours. Roman Catholic. Avocation: tennis. Home: Marco Merenciano 47, 12A, 46025 Valencia Spain

ANTONELLI, FERDINANDO GIUSEPPE, Italian ecclesiastic; b. Subbiano, Italy, July 14, 1896. Joined Order of Friars Minor, Roman Cath. Ch., 1914, ordained priest, 1922; tchr. ch. history Antonianum, 1928-32, instr. Christian archeology, 1932-65, rector magnificus, 1937-43, 53-59; definator gen. Friars Minor, 1939-45; various offices Roman Curia, sec. Congregation of Rites, 1965-69, Congregation for Causes of Saints, 1969-73; consecrated titular archbishop of Idicra, 1966; elevated to Sacred Coll. of Cardinals, 1973. Address: Vatican City Vatican City

ANTONIO, VICTOR, minister; b. Porterville, Calif., Apr. 6, 1960; s. Manuel and Frances (Ponce) Camarena; m. Rebecca R. Garcia, May 16, 1987; children: Julian Ryan, Devon Gabriel. BA in Social Sci., Bethany Bible Coll., Scotts Valley, Calif., 1983. Ordained to ministry Assemblies of God Ch., 1983. Youth pastor Templo Calvario Ch., Bakersfield, Calif., 1983-84, Templo Betania, Fremont, Calif., 1984-87, City Team Ministries, San Jose, Calif., 1984; sr. pastor Christian Community Ch., Fresno, Calif., 1987—; instr. Latin Am. Bible Inst., Fremont, 1986-87; presbyter Pacific Latin Am. Dist. Coun., Assemblies of God, La Puente, Calif., 1988—; mem. ad hoc com. Ctr. for Hispanic Ministries, Bethany Bible Coll., 1986-87. Recipient appreciation award Youth Ministries Pacific Latin Am. Dist., 1986, 87, Pacific Latin Am. Dist. Coun., 1990. Republican. Office: Christian Community Ch 4677 E Harvey Ave Fresno CA 93702 *If there is one thing that this world is desperately in need of, it is to see Christians who are annointed with the spirit of God in such a way that all that say and do testifies to the power of God working in and through their lives. (from V. Antonio's sermon The Annointig of the Spirit of the Lord).*

ANTONSEN, CONRAD (ROBERT MICHAEL ANTONSEN), priest, educator; b. Vallejo, Calif., May 24, 1937; s. R. Wallace and Zaira (Castagnini) A. BS, U. San Francisco, 1959; BPh, St. Albert's Coll., Oakland, Calif., 1962, MA in Philosophy, 1963, MA in Theology, 1965; Lectorate, Licentiate in Sacred Theology, Le Saulchoir-Etiolles, France, 1969; Peritus in Sacred Liturgy, Institut Catholique de Paris, 1971. Joined Dominican Order, 1960, ordained priest Roman Cath. Ch., 1966. Campus minister, instr. Dominican Coll., San Rafael, Calif., 1974-78; pastor Blessed Sacrament Parish, Seattle, 1979-85, St. Mary Magdalen Parish, Berkeley, Calif., 1987—; instr. Dominican Sch. Philosophy and Theology, grad. Theo. Union, Berkeley, 1975—, St. Thomas U., Rome, 1986, St. Mary's Coll., Moraga, Calif., 1987; dir., preacher retreats for Dominican Sisters New Zealand, 1976; facilitator for group dynamics Religious Women in Phoenix, 1973. Mem. N.Am. Acad. Liturgy, Am. Dominican Liturgical Commn., Pastoral Coun. Archdiocese Seattle, Western Dominican Planning and Ministry Commn, Alcuin. Democrat. Home and Office: 2005 Berryman St Berkeley CA 94709 *Faith, family and friends are the foundations of my life, and I am happiest when I am able to combine learning and teaching.*

ANTONSON, NEWMAN NEIL, minister; b. Waco, Tex., Aug. 8, 1926; s. Toby and Iva Myrtle (McNiel) A.; m. Dorothy Lee Cox, Mar. 4, 1948; children: Deborah Lee Mai, Roberta Lynn Jenkins, Peggy Sue Burns. BA, Baylor U., 1949; BD, Southwestern Bapt. Theol. Sem., 1953. Ordained to ministry So. Bapt. Conv., 1947. Pastor First Bapt. Ch., Davis, Okla., 1955-60, Carnegie, Okla., 1960-61; Pastor Dumas Ave. Bapt. Ch., Oklahoma City, 1961-63, Trinity Bapt. Ch., Lawton, Okla., 1963-78, Tyler Rd. So. Bapt. Ch., Wichita, Kans., 1978—; mem. Brotherhood Commn., So. Bapt. Ch., Memphis, 1965-71; v.p. KNCSB, Topeka, 1990—; pres. KNCSB Found., 1983-84, others. With USN, 1944-46. Democrat. Office: Tyler Rd So Bapt Ch 571 S Tyler Rd Wichita KS 67209

APONTE MARTINEZ, LUIS, archbishop; b. Lajas, P.R., Aug. 4, 1922; s. Santiago E. Aponte and Rosa Martinez. Student, San Ildefonso Sem., San Juan, P.R., 1944, St. John's Sem., Boston, 1950; LL.D. (hon.), Fordham U., 1965. Ordained priest Roman Cath. Ch., 1950; asst. in Patillas, P.R.; pastor in Maricao, P.R., Sta. Isabel, P.R., 1953-55; sec. to bishop of Ponce, P.R., 1955-57; pastor in Aibonito, P.R., 1957-60; aux. bishop of Ponce, 1960-63, bishop, 1963-64; archbishop of San Juan, 1964—; elevated to cardinal, 1973; Chancellor Cath. U. P.R., Ponce, 1963—; pres. Puerto Rican Episcopal Conf. Served as chaplain P.R. N.G., 1957-60. Mem. Lions. Address: Calle San Jorge 201 Santurce PR 00912 also: PO Box S-1967 San Juan PR 00903

APPELL, KEITH DOUGLAS, school principal; b. Cooperstown, N.Y., Apr. 7, 1941; s. Virgil Luther and Ruth (Hawver) A.; m. Sarah Ruth Tangen, Jan. 15, 1966; children: Breck, Grant, Neil, Jed, Mark. BS, N.Y. State Sch. of Forestry, 1964; BA, Syracuse U., 1964. Supr., tchr. Faith Bible Acad., Sprakers, N.Y., 1974-79, prin., 1979—. Home: PO Box 624 Ames NY 13317 *Of all the varied pursuits in life, I find that one of highest value to be declared by the Lord Jesus Christ in Matthew 6:33, "But seek ye first the kingdom of God, and His righteousness, and all these things shall be added unto you."*

APPELQUIST, ALBIN RAY, church executive; b. Kewanee, Ill., June 17, 1918; s. Albin Emanuel and Nan (Lundberg) A.; m. Carol Jane Engwall,

June 19, 1943; children—Nancy, Janet, John, MaryLou, Carla. B.Th., Bethel Theol. Sem., St. Paul, 1943; B.A., Roosevelt U., Chgo., 1948; D.Div. (hon.), Judson Coll., Elgin, Ill., 1968. Ordained to ministry, 1943. Exec. sec. Gen. Commn. on Chaplains, Washington, 1962-75; staff and exec. sec. Congl. Christian Chs., Oak Creek, Wis., 1975-85, Congl. Ch., Mount Dora, Fla., 1985—. Editor and compiler: Church State and Chaplaincy, 1969; editor The Chaplain mag., 1962-75. Served to capt. U.S. Army, 1945-46, 51-58. Recipient Freedoms Found. medal, 1957. Home: Box 875 Mount Dora FL 32754 Office: Congl Church PO Box 944 Mount Dora FL 32757

APPLE, DOUGLAS MERLE, radio station executive; b. Shelbyville, Ill., Aug. 5, 1963; s. Donald Merle and Judith Joanne (Cook) A.; m. Michele Celine Marren, June 7, 1986; children: Ashlyn Ariél, Andrew Douglas, Bethany Julia. BA, Ea. Ill. U., 1985. Music dir. Sta. WXAN Christian Radio, Ava, Ill., 1986-90, program dir., 1989-90, gen. mgr., 1990—; Sunday sch. supt. 1st Assembly of God, Murphysboro, Ill., 1987—; radio-TV advisor So. Gospetality Promotions, Ava, 1989—; tchr. John A. Logan Community Coll., Carterville, Ill., 1991—. Editor So. Gospetality News, 1991—. Named one of Top 10 So. Gospel DJs, Singing News Mag., 1988, 90, 91; Sta. WXAN voted # 1 Gospel radio sta. in Am., 1991. Republican. Office: Sta WXAN Rte 2 Box 213A Ava IL 62907 *The moments of life are roses. They are worthless if ignored, precious if considered.*

APPLEBAUM, ELIZABETH LILIANE, editor; b. Columbus, Ohio, Apr. 2, 1958; d. Michael F. Kaplan and Claudia L. Mandelbaum; m. Phillip A. Applebaum, July 2, 1989. B, Stephens Coll., 1980; postgrad., Hebrew U., Jerusalem, 1982—. Asst. dir. Henry S. Jacobs Camp, Utica, Miss., 1982-83; outreach worker Tulane U. B'nai Brith Hillel Found., New Orleans, 1983-84; assoc. editor Kansas City (Mo.) Jewish Chronicle, 1984-88; asst. editor Detroit Jewish News, Southfield, Mich., 1988—. Author: Saying Kaddish, 1980. Recipient 1st pl. awards Coun. Jewish Fedns., 1989-90. Mem. Am. Jewish Press Assn. (1st pl. awards 1988-89, 1989-90). Jewish. Office: care Detroit Jewish News 27676 Franklin Rd Southfield MI 48034

APPLEBAUM, EMANUEL, educator; b. N.Y.C., Jan. 14, 1922; s. Litman Eliezer and Sarah Rachel (Korobchinsky) A.; m. Jacqueline Rhoda Goodman, Mar. 21, 1949; children—David Leslie, Avrom Michael, Geela Beth. B.A., Bklyn. Coll., 1945; M.A., NYU, 1950; Ph.D., Yeshiva U., 1953, M.Sc., 1982; Litt.D., Mich. Luth. U., Detroit, 1956; grad. cert. Wayne State U., 1963. Ordained rabbi, 1945; cert. tchr., adminstr., Ohio, Man., Can. Tchr., social worker N.Y.C. schs., 1946-53; supr., prin. United Hebrew Schs., Detroit, 1953-62; headmaster Hillel Day Sch., Detroit, 1962-65; prof. Israeli Ministry Edn., Jerusalem 1965-66; dir. secondary edn. Bd. Jewish Edn., Cleve., 1966-69; ednl. dir. Community Day Schs., Cin., 1969-72; prin. Hillel Acad., Dayton, Ohio, 1972-75, Winnipeg Hebrew Day Sch., Man., Can., Joseph Wolinsky Collegiate, Winnipeg, 1975-78, Yeshiva Manhattan Beach, Bklyn., 1978-81; ret., 1981; lectr. Coll. Jewish Studies, Detroit, 1953-65; prof. Gt. Lakes Coll., Detroit, 1955-65. Author: Curriculum: Elementary Instructional Program, 1965; Hebrew Day School Curriculum, 1977. Editor: Mich. Jewish History, 1960-63. Contbr. articles to profl. jours. Mem. Nat. Council Jewish Edn. (bd. dirs.), Nat. Assn. Profs. Hebrew (bd. dirs. 1955-75), Rabbinical Alliance Am., Nat. Conf. Day Sch. Prins. (bd. dirs. 1970—), Educators Council Am. (bd. dirs. 1969—), Mizrachi Orgn., Phi Delta Kappa, Republican. Office: Ha Rav Chen 7, Jerusalem 92514, Israel

APPLEBAUM, MORTON M., rabbi; b. Toronto, Ont., Can., Aug. 25, 1911; s. Joseph and Sarah (Levit) A.; m. Eleanor Wides, June 9, 1940; children: Lois Jean Podolny, Bruce Jay (dec.). BA, U. Toronto; MHL, Hebrew Union Coll., Cin., 1940; DDiv honoris cause, Hebrew Union Coll., 1965. Ordained rabbi, 1940. Rabbi Congregation Shaarey Zedek, Lansing, Mich., 1940-43, Temple Beth El, Fint, Mich., 1943-53, Temple Israel, Akron, Ohio, 1953-79; ret.; counselor B'nai B'rith Hillel Extension, Mich. State U., 1940-43; faculty U. Akron Spl. Programs, 1969-79; tchr. adult edn. St. Paul's Episcopal Ch., Akron, 1979—; bd. trustees Union Am. Hebrew Congregations; bd. govs. Hebrew Union Coll.-Jewish Inst. Religion; exec. bd. Cen. Conf. Am. Rabbis; hon. vice chmn. Rabbinical Pension Bd.; mem. various coms. Cen. Conf. Am. Rabbis. Author: What Everyone Should Know About Judaism, 4th edit.; co-author (with Rabbi Samuel M. Silver) Sermonettes for Young People, Speak to the Children of Israel. Active in past Jewish Family Svcs., Police Pub. Rels., Child Welfare Bd. Summit County Citizens Com., Goodwill Industries, ARC, many others;;mem. Commn. on Internat. Community Concerns. Mem. Rotary. Home: 6668 Burning Wood Dr #166 Boca Raton FL 33433

APPLEBY, JERRY LEE, minister; b. St. Louis, Aug. 17, 1942; s. Ralph Hallett and Myrtle Jane (Doerle) A.; m. Pauline McBryant, Dec. 14, 1963; children: Loren, Julie, Gregory, Syndi. BA, Trevecca Nazarene Coll., 1964; MDiv, Nazarene Theol. Sem., 1967; postgrad., Fuller Theol. Sem., 1989—. Ordained to ministry Ch. of the Nazarene, 1969. Field supr., coll. pres. Samoa Dist. Ch. of the Nazarene, Apia, Western Samoa, 1968-76; sr. pastor Honolulu First Ch. of the Nazarene, Honolulu, 1976-81; ethnic, urban coord. Ch. of the Nazarene Hdqrs., Kansas City, Mo., 1981-84; sr. pastor Bresee Ch. of the Nazarene, Pasadena, Calif., 1984-91; exec. v.p. Frontline Outreach, Orlando, Fla., 1991—; founding bd. Assn. Nazarenes in Social Work, Kansas City, 1982-84; bd. trustee, sec. Armenian Bible Coll., Pasadena, 1984-90; dist. adv. bd. Hawaii Dist. Ch. of the Nazarene, 1977-81, L.A. Dist. Ch. of the Nazarene, Pasadena, 1984-91. Author: Missions Have Come Home to America, 1986, The Church Is In a Stew, 1990. Home: PO Box 608034 Orlando FL 32860 Office: Frontline Outreach 3000 W Carter Orlando FL 32855 *By conserving immigrating Christians, evangelizing and training ethnic America, a launching pad can be established whereby the entire world can be reached with the gospel of Jesus Christ. We must think globally while we act locally.*

APPLEBY, WILLIAM FRANKLIN, SR., minister; b. Drew, Miss., June 20, 1928; s. James Chester Appleby and Zelma Evelyn (Taylor) McCorkle; m. Betty Sue Smith, June 7, 1953 (dec. Dec. 1985); children: William Franklin Jr., Elizabeth Ann; m. Minna Sue Hayes, Nov. 15, 1986. BA, Millsaps Coll., 1950; BDiv, Emory U., 1952; D in Ministry, Meth. Theol. Sch., 1978. Pastor United Meth. Ch., Tishomingo, Miss., 1953-56; United Meth. Ch., Burnsville, Miss., 1956-58, Guntown (Miss.)-Saltillo United Meth. Ch., 1958-62; program counselor No. Miss. Conf. Inter Bd. Council, Grenada, Miss., 1962-66; pastor First United Meth. Ch., Corinth, Miss., 1966-71; dist. supt. Tupelo (Miss.) Dist., 1971-76; pastor First United Meth. Ch., Louisville, 1976-81, Clarksdale, Miss., 1981-86; council dir. No. Miss. Conf. on Ministries, Grenada, Miss., 1986-89, Miss. Conf. on Ministries, Jackson, Miss., 1989—; mem. S.E. Jurisdiction Adminstrv. Council, Lake Junaluska, N.C., 1986—. Named Rural Minister of the Year for Miss. Progressive Farmer, 1959. Mem. United Meth. Rural Fellowship (life, v.p. 1972-80, pres. 1980-84, exec. com. 1984—), United Meth. Men (life), Miss. Christian Community Fellowship, Miss. Religious Leadership Conf. Methodist. Avocation: golf. Home: 49 Northtown Circle Jackson MS 39211 Office: Miss Conf Coun on Ministry PO Box 1147 Jackson MS 39215

APPLEGATE, KENNETH IRA, minister; b. Arkansas City, Kans., Oct. 3, 1958; s. Loyd Uel and Caroline Sue (Hinsey) A.; m. Hollis Anne Kelly, May 2, 1987; stepchildren: Larissa Anne Robel, Emmie Suzanne Robel. BA, Okla. State U., 1980; MDiv, Princeton Theol. Sem., 1983. Ordained to ministry Presbyn. Ch., 1984. Interim pastor Westminster Presbyn. Ch., Trenton, N.J., 1984, Milford (N.J.) Presbyn. Ch., 1985-87; pastor Bethany Presbyn. Ch., Menands, N.Y., 1987—; active mem. Presbyn. of Albany, N.Y., 1987—; del. Synod of the N.E., Syracu. Bd. mem. Habitat for Humanity, Albany, 1988-91. Democrat. Presbyterian. Home: 21 N Lyon Ave Menands NY 12204 Office: Bethany Presbyn Ch 21 1/2 Lyon Ave Menands NY 12204

APPLEMAN, MORRIS, rabbi; b. Yonivel, Poland, Mar. 30, 1922; came to U.S., 1922; s. Dov Berr and Esther Appleman; m. Vivienne Kippelman, Oct. 30, 1949; children: Gaylr, Solomon, Rena Beth, Stuart, Ezra Mordechai. BA, Yeshiva U., 1945; MA, Hofstra U., 1956. Ordained rabbi, 1947. Chaplain Lakehurst Naval Air Sta., Washington, 1949-53; rabbi Toms River, N.J., 1949-53, East Nassau Hebrew Congregation, Syosset, N.Y., 1954—. Author: Isaac Mayer Wise, 1956. Mem. Am. Israel Polit. Action Com. Mem. Rabbinical Coun. Am., L.I. Commn. Rabbis, N.Y. Bd. Rabbis, Nassau Bd. Rabbis, AIPAC. Home: 1 Dover Ln Syosset NY 11791 Office: East Nassau Hebrew Cong 310A S Oyster Rd Syosset NY 11791

APPOLD, MARK LEONARD, pastor, religion educator; b. Chgo., Aug. 8, 1936; s. Theodore George and Hertha Mina (Guettler) A.; m. Rosemarie Baerbel Lehmann, Apr. 11, 1964; children: Kenneth, Martin, Kevin, Kirsten. BA, Concordia Sem., 1958, BD, 1961; ThD, Tuebingen U., Federal Republic Germany, 1973; student, Washington U., St. Louis, 1957-59, 61-62. Pastor Faith Luth. Ch., Kirksville, Mo., 1967—; adj. assoc. prof. N.E. Mo. State U., Kirksville, 1976—; vis. prof. U. Iowa, Iowa City, 1976-77, Christ Sem., St. Louis, 1982, Luth. Sch. Theology, Chgo., 1986; chmn. Kirksville Hosp. Chaplaincy Inc., Kirksville, 1989—; bd. dirs. Kirksville Osteopathic Med. Ctr.; pres. Kirksville Interchurch Ministries, Kirksville, 1985. Author: The Oneness Motif in the Fourth Gospel, 1976; contbr. articles to profl jours. Luth. World Fedn. grantee, Geneva, 1962, 65, 66. Mem. Soc. Bibl. Lit., Am. Acad. Religion, Park Ridge Ctr. for Study of Health, Faith and Ethics (assoc.). Office: Faith Luth Ch 1820 S Baltimore St Kirksville MO 63501

APURON, ANTHONY SABLAN, archbishop; b. Agana, Guam, Nov. 1, 1945; s. Manuel Taijito and Ana Santos (Sablan) P. BA, St. Anthony Coll., 1969; MDiv, Maryknoll Sem., 1972, M Theology, 1973; MA in Liturgy, Notre Dame U., 1974. Ordained priest Roman Catholic ch., 1972, ordained bishop, 1984, installed archbishop, 1986. Chmn. Diocesan Liturgical Commn., Agana, 1974-86; vice chmn. Chamorro Lang. Commn., Agana, 1984-86; aux. bishop Archdiocese of Agana, 1984-85, archbishop, 1986—; chmn. Interfaith Vols. Caregivers, Agana, 1984—; mem. Civilian Adv. com., Agana, 1986—; pres. Cath. Bishops' Conf. of Pacific, 1990—; v.p. Cath. Bishops' Conf. of Aceania, 1990—. Author: A Structural Analysis of the Content of Myth in the Thought of Mircea Eliade, 1973. Chmn. Cath. Ednl. Radio. Named Most Outstanding Young Man, Jaycees of Guam, 1984. Avocations: jogging, walking, swimming. Office: Archbishop's Office Cuesta San Ramon Agana GU 96910

AQUILA, VINCENT SALVADOR, religious youth coordinator; b. Huntsville, Ala., June 3, 1963; s. Vincent Salvador and Dolores (Intile) A. BSBA, U. Ala., Huntsville, 1986. Drafter Intergraph Corp., Huntsville, 1982-84; Cath. youth coord. Lees-Haley Inc., Huntsville, 1986—; religious edn. tchr. St. Joseph's Cath. Community, Huntsville, 1980—; fin. mgr., Huntsville, 1985—. Mem. Nat. Assn. Accts., Acctg. Club (U. Ala. Huntsville). Democrat. Avocations: music, sports. Home: 1117 Tyler Rd Huntsville AL 35816

ARAMBURU, JUAN CARLOS CARDINAL, archbishop of Buenos Aires; b. Reduccion, Argentina, Feb. 11, 1912; Ordained priest Roman Catholic Ch., 1934; ordained titular bishop of Plataea and aux. of Tucuman, Argentina, 1946, bishop, 1953, 1st archbishop, 1957; titular archbishop of Torri di Bizacena and coadjutor archbishop of Buenos Aires, 1967, archbishop of Buenos Aires, 1975, elevated to cardinal, 1976; titular ch., St. John the Baptist of Florentines; ordinary for Eastern Rite Catholics in Brazil without ordinaries of their own rites. Mem. of Congregations: Oriental Chs., Cath. Edn. Office: Arzobispado, Suipacha 1034, Buenos Aires 1008, Argentina

ARAPASU, TEOCTIST, patriarch of Romanian Orthodox Church; b. Tocileni, Moldowa, Romania, Feb. 7, 1915; s. Marghioala (Dumitru) A. Student, Theol. Sem., Cernica Monastery, Romania, 1932-40; Diploma in Theology, Theol. Sem., Bucharest, Romania, 1940, ThM, 1945. Ordained to ministry Romanian Orthodox Ch. Patriarchal bishop Romanian Orthodox Ch., Bucharest, 1950-62; bishop of Arad Romania, 1962-73; archbishop and met. of Oltenia Craiova, Romania, 1973-77; archbishop of Iasi, met. of Moldova, 1977-86; patriarch Romanian Orthodox Ch., Bucharest, 1986—. Author: Metropolitan Iacob Putneanul, 1978, Christian Diaconia. Decorated commodore Order of Sts. Apostles Peter and Paul, Patriarchate of Antioch, 1950, 74, gt. officer, 1958; officer Order of St. Vladimir, Alexey-The Patriarch of Moscow and All Russia, 1962; Commemorative medal Athenogoras I-Ecumenical Patriarch, 1967; officer Order of The Holy Lamb, Paavali-Archbishop of Karelia and All Finland, 1971; gt. crusader Order of Orthodox Crusaders of the Holy Tomb, Diodoros-Patriarch of Jerusalem, 1986; officer Order Sts. Methodios and Kirilos, Dorothey-Met. of Prague and All Czechoslovakia, 1986; officer The Golden Cross of the Holy Monastery of Pathmos, Dimitrios I-Ecumenical Patriarch, 1988. Address: Romanian Orthodox Ch, Dealul Mitropoliei No 2, 70526 Bucharest Romania

ARAUJO, DENIS, priest; b. Alleppey, India, Feb. 6, 1917; came to U.S., 1956; naturalized, 1976; s. John-Chrysostom Thomas Arasarkadavil and Christina Denis Therath. BA with honors, U. Madras, India, 1950, MA, 1951, BE, 1952; MA, U. San Francisco, 1958; PhD, U. Calif., Berkeley, 1961. Ordained priest Roman Cath. Ch., 1944. Tchr. St. Francis Assisi High Sch., Alleppey, 1950-56, head master, 1961-67; supt. schs. Roman Cath. Diocese, Alleppey, 1950-56, dir. social svc., 1961-69, insp. schs., 1961-69; pastor St. Francis Assisi Ch., Thykal and Alleppey, 1964; vice prin., dean dept. econs. St. Michael's Coll., Alleppey, 1967-69; assoc. pastor St. Agnes Ch., Concord, Calif., 1970-74, St. Michael's Ch., Livermore, Calif., 1974-77; pastor St. John the Baptist Ch., El Cerrito, Calif., 1977-82, Our Lady of Mercy Ch., Point Richmond, Calif., 1982-89; ret., 1990; dean West Contra Costa County of Diocese of Oakland, Calif., 1981-84; senator Diocese of Oakland, 1981-84; consultor to bishop of Oakland, 1984—; chaplain Cath. Daus. Am., Ct. De La Salle, Italian Cath. Fedn. of Contra Costa County. Author: Secondary School Leaving Examination in India, 1963. Founder Fish. Indsl. Coop. Soc., Shertallay, India, 1953, St. Sebastians Hosp., Arathinkal, Alleppey, 1965. Mem. Phi Delta Kappa. Address: 445 La Gonda Way Danville CA 94526 *The impacts I have made were very significant. My example, dedication to duty and to my calling changed human lives. My students achieved some of the higher pinacles of life. Workers were organized to move huge hurdles. My guileless intentions were well known. So people supported me and stood by me. I was vulnerable. So some cheated me. I received joy in giving and rejoiced in the fruits my giving produced. My father used to say: the story of Fr. Denis is the story of changing water into wine.*

ARCE-MARTINEZ, SERGIO SAMUEL, educator; b. Caibarien, Villa Clara, Cuba, Feb. 21, 1924; s. Sergio Rogelio Arce-Ojeda and Esther Justa Martinez-Diaz; m. Dora Encarnacion Valentin Morales, May 29, 1945; children: Reinerio Miguel, Dora Ester. BA, La Progresiva, Cardenas, Cuba, 1940; BTh., Sem. Evangelico, Rio Peidras, P.R., 1945; ThM, Princeton Sem., 1956, postgrad., 1959-61; PhD, U. Havana, Cuba, 1963; ThD, Sem. Comenius, Praha, Czechoslovakia, 1978. Guest prof. Sem. Evangelico, Matanzas, Cuba, 1947-59, prof. dogmatics, 1961-84, pres., 1969-84, emeritus prof., 1985—; guest prof. Union Theol. Sem., N.Y.C., 1985-86; pres. Christian Movement for Peace in Latin Am. and the Caribbean, Matanzas, 1991—; guest prof. Pacific Sch. Religion, Berkeley, Calif., 1979, San Francisco Theol. Sem., San Anselmo, Calif., 1982; moderator Presbyn. Ch., Cuba, 1957-58, 61-62; gen. sec. Presbyn. Reformed Ch., Cuba, 1965-84. Author: Hacia Una Teologia de Liberacion, 1970, Latin America Hinterhoef des North America, 1970, Teologié en Revolucion, 1985, Church and Socialism, 1985; also articles. Pres. Ctr. de Accion Social, Nueva Paz, Cuba, 1946-50, Ateneo Cultural Jose Marti, Nueva Paz, 1947-50; bd. dirs. Evang. Youth Cuba, 1948-50, Ecumenical Study Ctr., Havana, 1973-85; v.p. Christian Peace Conf., Praha, 1968-69; emeritus pres. Ctr. Informacion ecumenica, Matanzas, 1989. Recipient Order Frank Pais Cuban Ministerio Edn., 1965, Order San Sergio Russian Orthodox Ch., 1978. Mem. Assn. Teologos del 3d Mundo, Assn. Teologos de Cuba (pres. 1969-71), Assn. Teologos en Contexto Global. Office: Movimiento Xno por la Paz, en America Latina y El Caribe, Matanzas 42100, Cuba

ARCENEAUX, JULES MENOU, II, priest; b. Lafayette, La., Dec. 18, 1953; s. Jules Menou and Patrica Josephine Miller A. BFA, U. Southwestern La., Lafayette, 1979; BA, Brooks Inst., Santa Barbara, Calif., 1982; STB, Gregorian U., Rome, 1989, ThM, 1990. Ordained priest Roman Cath. Ch., 1990. Assoc. pastor Our Lady of Sacred Heart Ch., Church Point, La., 1990-92; pastor St. Thomas More Ch., Eunice, La., 1992—; asst. curator Live Oaks Art Gallery, Lafayette, 1974-76; shop foreman Gammaloy, Ltd., Lafayette, 1976-78; prodn. asst. Flemings Prodn. Co., Santa Barbara, 1979-80, Crystal Films Prodn. Co., Santa Barbara, 1980-82; producer, dir. Ind. Agt., L.A., 1982-83; dir. mktg. John E. Chance & Assocs., Inc., Lafayette, 1983-85; ind. film producer Rome, 1986—; cons. N.Am. Coll., Rome, 1983—; bd. dirs., New Iberia Rental Tools, Inc., Lafayette; cons., Griffin Photography, N.Y.C., 1983—, John E. Chance & Assocs., Inc., Lafayette, 1985—. Mem. Profl. Photographers Am., Amnesty Internat., Pax Christi, KC. Address: PO Box 403 Church Point LA 70525 *A faith which does not affect and change the culture we live in is a faith which has not been fully received, not thoroughly thought through, not fully lived out.*

ARCHBOLD, PHIL CARLOS, minister; b. Colón, Panamá, Mar. 22, 1936; s. Jaroth and Sophronia (Stevens) A. BTh., Northwestern Coll., 1973; M in Relegious Edn., Clarksville Sch. Theol., 1976, D in Religious Edn., 1980. Ordained minister Ch. of the Brethren. Pers. interviewer Wyckoff Heights Hosp., Bklyn., 1968-69, pers. asst., 1969-70, employment mgr., 1970, asst. pers. dir., 1970-72; dir. pers. and community rels. Prospect Hosp., Bronx, 1972-74; adminstr. community bd. Harlem Hosp. Ctr., N.Y.C., 1974-82; assoc. pastor First Ch. of the Brethren, Bklyn., 1982—; mem. dist. bd. Atlantic N.E. Dist. Ch. of the Brethren, Harrisburg, Pa.; evangelist Ch. of the Brethren, Harrisburg, 1984—. Vol. ARC, 1988—. Sgt. U.S. Army, 1961-68, Vietnam. Recipient Appreciation award Police Athletic League, 1973, Youth Pastor of Yr. award Group Mag., 1991; named to Men Achievement, Cambridge, Eng., 1983. Mem. Am. Cancer Soc., Nat. Assn. Dirs. Christian Educators, Evang. Tchr. Tng. Assn. (instr. 1988—), Greater N.Y. Sunday Sch. Assn. (bd. mem.). Democrat. Avocations: reading, worldwide traveling, tennis, bowling. Home: 318 60th St Brooklyn NY 11220 Office: First Ch Brethren 352-6 60th St Brooklyn NY 11220

ARCHER, C. RUSSELL, minister, church administrator, former college president; b. Sarahsville, Ohio, Dec. 6, 1918; s. Harry Lee and Mary Ruth (Leisure) A.; m. Lavonne A. Surls, Jan. 18, 1941; 1 child, Calvin R. Diploma, Bethany Bible Coll., 1937; DD (hon.), Fla. Beacon Coll. and Sem., 1970. Ordained to ministry Open Bible Standard Chs., 1940. Pastor various chs. Open Bible Standard Chs., Des Moines, 1943-53; pres. Open Bible Coll., Tacoma, Wash., 1953-60; pastor Faith Temple, Des Moines, 1960-77; regional supt. Open Bible Standard Chs., Vandalia, Ohio, 1977—; pres. Dayton (Ohio) Bible Coll., 1970-86; nat. bd. dirs. Open Bible Standard Chs., Des Moines; gen. overseer Open Bible Standard Chs. Can., Toronto, Ont., 1980—; prof. Colo. Sch. Bible, Tacoma Bible Inst., Abbott Loop Sch. Bible; del. to World Pentecostal Conf., Zurich, Switzerland. Author: What We Believe, 1991. Bd. dirs. Eugene (Oreg.) Bible Coll., 1960-75. Recipient plaque of honor Ea. div. Open Bible Standard Chs., 1985; named to Hon. Order of Ky. Col., 1978. Home: 950 Rayberta Dr Vandalia OH 45377 Office: Open Bible Standard Chs Easter Region PO Box 518 Vandalia OH 45377

ARCHIBALD, CLAUDIA JANE, parapsychologist; b. Atlanta, Nov. 14, 1939; d. Claud Bernard and Doris Evelyn (Linch) A. B in Psychology, Georgia State U., 1962; BTh., Emory U., 1964; DD, Stanton Coll., 1969. Pvt. practice psycho-spiritual counselor Atlanta, 1960—; minister Nat. Spiritualist Assn., Atlanta, 1969-72; parapsychologist Ctr. for Life, Atlanta, 1985-86; parapsychologist Inst. of Metaphysical Inquiry, Atlanta, 1980—, also bd. dirs., founder, 1980—. Author: (book) Quantitative Symbolism, 1980; dir. Phoenix Dance Unltd., 1984—; choregrapher (dance) Phoenix Rising, 1985. Vol. Aid Atlanta, 1987—. Recipient City Grant award Bur. Cultural Affairs, Atlanta, 1985, 86. Mem. Am. Psychical Research Assn., Soc. Metaphysicians (corr. Eng. chpt.), Am. Assn. Parapsychology, Nat. Assn. Alcoholism and Drug Abuse Counselors, Ga. Addiction Counselors' Assn., N.Am. Ballet Assn. Avocation: writing. Home: 2638 Valmar Dr Atlanta GA 30340

ARENA, MARY HELEN, lay worker; b. Pensacola, Fla., Dec. 12, 1951; d. Richard Joseph and Mary Eileen (Adams) Owens; m. Augustine Anthony Arena, Aug. 23, 1975; children: Andrew, Philip, Thomas, Katherine. Diploma, Berkeley Bus. Sch., White Plains, N.Y., 1971; student, Westchester Community Coll., White Plains, N.Y., 1975-76. Catechist St. Columbanus Parish, Peekskill, N.Y., 1979—; founder, facilitator Parish Mothers and Preschoolers Group, Peekskill, 1981-90; coord. St. Columbanus N.Y. Archdiocesan Synod Efforts, Peekskill; mem. N.Y. Archdiocesan Pastoral Coun., N.Y.C., 1985-90, No. Westchester/Putnam Vicariate Coun., Mahopac, N.Y., 1983-90; chmn. St. Colombanus Parish Coun., 1990—, catechist/coord. RCIA prog. 1990—, mem. St. Columbanus choir, 1983-89, Bible study group, 1983—. Leader Taconic Girl Scout Coun., Mahopac, 1970-73. Republican. Home: 14 Mountain View Rd Putnam Valley NY 10579 *I once read, "When we deal with each other we should do so with the sense of awe that arises in the presence of something holy and sacred. For...we are created in the image and likeness of God." How wonderful it is when we meet people who live this.*

ARENSMAN, KEVIN KEITH, minister; b. Denver, Mar. 14, 1959; s. Elton Eugene and Marilynn June (Russell) A. BS in Packaging Engring., Mich. State U., 1981; MDiv cum laude, Phillips U., 1987. Ordained to ministry Christian Ch. (Disciples of Christ), 1987. Coord. youth program St. Paul's United Meth. Ch., Ponca City, Okla., 1983-84; interim assoc. min. 1st Christian Ch., Garden City, Kans., 1984; assoc. min. 1st Christian Ch., Broken Arrow, Okla., 1985-87; min. youth and edn. Cen. Christian Ch., Enid, Okla., 1987—; dist. rep. regional edn. com. Christian Ch. in Okla., 1987—, youth sponsor dist. 2 youth coordinating coun., 1991—. Bd. dirs. Sooner Health Svcs., Enid, 1990—; mem. activities com. Big Bros. and Sisters, Enid, 1991. Mem. Assn. Christian Ch. Educators, Disciples Youth Ministry Fellowship (founder), Okla. Christian Educators Fellowship, Phi Kappa Gamma. Home: 1117 E Park Enid OK 73701 Office: Cen Christian Ch 1111 W Broadway Enid OK 73703 *In any given situation, whether good or bad circumstances, I try to remember that God has a vision and a use for everything which happens. In God there is always hope.*

ARGUE, DON HARVEY, college president, minister; b. Winnipeg, Man., Can., July 12, 1939; came to U.S., 1948; s. Andrew Watson and Hazel Bell (May) A.; m. Patricia Jean Opheim, Sept. 23, 1961; children: Laurie, Lee, Jonathan. BA, Cen. Bible Coll., Springfield, Mo., 1961; MA, Santa Clara U., 1967; EdD, U. of the Pacific, 1969; postdoctoral study, Gordon-Conwell Theol. Sem., 1990, Regent Coll., Vancouver, Can., 1990. Ordained to ministry Assemblies of God, 1964. Pastor 1st Assembly of God, Morganville, Calif., 1965-67; dean of students/men Bethany Coll., Santa Cruz, Calif., 1967-69; asst. prof., dean of student life, dean of students Evangel Coll., Springfield, 1969-74; dean, v.p. North Cen. Bible Coll., Mpls., 1974-79, pres., 1979—; gen. presbyter Assemblies of God, Springfield. Recipient Decade of Growth award Christianity Today, 1990. Mem. Nat. Assn. Evangs. (1st v.p.), Soc. for Pentecostal Studies (pres.), Rotary. Home: 7198 Arbor Glen Dr Minneapolis MN 55346 Office: North Cen Bible Coll 910 Elliot Ave S Minneapolis MN 55404

ARIAN, CHARLES LAWRENCE, rabbi; b. Bklyn., Feb. 9, 1960; s. Elliott and Audrey (Beal) A. BSFS, Georgetown U., 1981; MA in Hebrew Letters, Hebrew Union Coll., 1985. Ordained rabbi, 1986. Rabbi-in-residence Kibbutz Yahel, Israel, 1986-88; rabbi, dir. B'nai Brith Hillel Found., U. Va., Charlottesville, 1988-91; chaplain, Hillel dir. Am. Univ., Washington, 1991—; mem. youth com. Mid-Atlantic Union of Am. Hebrew Congregations Coll., 1989—. Contbr. articles to profl. publs. Coolidge fellow Assn. for Religious and Intellectual Life, 1989. Coolidge fellow Assn. for Religious and Int. Life, 1989. Mem. Cen. Conf. of Am. Rabbis, Rabbinical Assembly (assoc.), Assn. Hillel and Jewish Campus Profls., B'nai Brith. Democrat. Office: Key Spiritual Life Ctr American University Washington DC 20016

ARIARAJAH, WESLEY SEEVARATNAM, clergyman, church administrator; b. Jaffna, Sri Lanka, Dec. 2, 1941; s. Ponniah David and Grace Annalukshimi (Sinnappu) S.; m. Christine Shyamala Chinniah, Dec. 7, 1953; children: Sudharshini, Niroshini, Anushini. BSc, Madras Christian Coll., India, 1963; BD, United Theol. Coll., Bangalore, India, 1966; ThM, Princeton (N.J.) Seminary, 1972; M. Phil., U. London, 1974, PhD, 1987. Ordained to ministry Methodist Ch. Minister Meth. Ch. of Sri Lanka, Jaffna, 1966-68; lectr. Theol. Coll. Lanka, Pilimatalawa, Sri Lanka, 1969-71; chmn. North and East Dist. Meth. Ch., Jaffna, 1974-81; program staff WCC program on Dialogue with People of Living Faiths, Geneva, 1981-83; dir. World Council Chs. program on Dialogue with People of Living Faiths, Geneva, 1983—. Author: Dialogue, 1980, The Bible and People of Other Faiths, 1986, Hindus and Christians: A Century of Protestant Ecumenical Thought, Currents of Encounter Series, Vol. 5, 1991; contbr. articles to profl. jours. Home: Avenue des Amazones 16, 1224 Chene Bougeries, Geneva Switzerland Office: World Coun Chs Dialogue, PO Box 2100, CH-1211 Geneva 2, Switzerland

ARIAS, DAVID, bishop; b. Mataluenga, Leon, Spain, July 22, 1929; came to U.S., 1958; s. Atanasio and Magdalena (Perez) A. Grad., St. Rita's Coll., San Sebastian, Spain, 1948, Good Counsel Theolgate, Granada, Spain, 1952, Teresianum, Rome, 1964. Ordained priest Roman Catholic Ch., 1952, aux. bishop of Newark, 1983. Tchr. St. Rita Coll., San Sebastian, Spain, 1953; tchr., prefect St. Augustine Sem., Kansas City, 1964-66; assoc. pastor Lourdes Parish, Mexico City, 1958-63; dir. Spanish Apostolate Archdiocese of N.Y., N.Y.C., 1978-83; vicar provincial Augustinian Recollects, West Orange, N.J., 1981-83; aux. bishop Archdiocese of Newark, 1983—; dir. Cursillo Movement, N.Y.C., 1966-78. Author: Luz y Vida, 1979. Mem. Nat. Conf. Cath. Bishops, U.S. Cath. Conf. Avocations: reading; music; golfing. Address: 502 Palisade Ave Union City NJ 07087

ARIAS, MORTIMER, seminary president, theology educator, bishop emeritus; b. Durazno, Uruguay, Jan. 7, 1924; came to U.S., 1980; m. Esther Leguizamon, Jan. 3, 1948 (dec. 1984); children: Eunice Esther, Ruben Daniel; m. Ana Beatriz Ferrari, Jan. 1986. B.Th., Union Theol. Sem., Buenos Aires, 1946, M.Th., 1957; B.Pre-Medicine, Montevideo U., 1948; D.Min., Perkins Sch. Theology, Dallas, 1977; L.H.D., De Pauw U., Ind., 1985. Ordained to ministry Meth. Ch., 1947; deacon, elder, and bishop orders; exec. pastor Meth. Ch., Uruguay, 1947-56, 58-61; pastor, dist. supt. Meth. Ch., Bolivia, 1962-67, nat. exec. sec., 1668-69; bishop Evang. Meth. Ch., Bolivia, 1969-76; vis. prof. Perkins Sch. Theology, Boston U., 1976-78, Sch. Theology, Claremont, Calif., 1981-85; E. Stanley Jones prof. mission and evangelization Sch. Theology, 1985—; pres. Latin Am. Sem., San José, Costa Rica, 1986-89; pres. mission and evangelism Iliff Sch. Theology, 1989-91; exec. sec. Latin Am. Meth. Council, 1978-80; sec. of mission Latin Am. Council of Chs., 1979-80; mem. Com. on World Mission World Council Chs., Geneva, 1973-83, Intenat. Assn. Missiology (Amsterdam), Holland, 1980—. Author: Salvation is Liberation (Spanish and Portuguese), 1973, Your Kingdom Come (Spanish), 1980, Announcing the Reign of God (English), 1983; co-author: The Cry of My People (English and Spanish), 1980, The Great Commission: Biblical Models for Evangelism, 1991. Active Assembly of Human Rights, Bolivia, 1975—; active Justice and Peace Commn., 1970-75, Meth. Fedn. for Social Action, U.S., 1981—, Central Am. Task Force, 1981—. Mem. Assn. Profs. of Mission U.S., Acad. of Evangelism U.S. Address: Mi Amor, Colon and Nandu, 15100 Salinas Uruguay

ARINZE, FRANCIS CARDINAL, cardinal; b. Eziowelle, Anambra, Nigeria, Nov. 1, 1932; s. Joseph Nwankwu and Bernadette (Ekwoanya) A. BD, Urban U., Rome, 1957, MDiv, 1959, DD, 1960; diploma in edn., U. London, 1964; DLitt (hon.), U. Nigeria, Nsukka, 1986. Ordained priest Roman Cath. Ch., 1958. Lectr. in philosophy, logic Bigard Meml. Sem., Enugu, Nigeria, 1961-62; ednl. sec. Cath. Ch. Ea. Nigeria, Enugu, 1962-65; aux. bishop of Onitsha Nigeria, 1965-67, archbishop of Onitsha, 1967-85; pres. Cath. Bishops Conf. Nigeria, Lagos, 1979-84, Pontifical Coun. for Inter-religious Dialogue, Vatican City, 1984—; created cardinal Vatican City, 1985—. Author: Sacrifice in Ibo Religion, 1980, Answering God's Call, 1982, Living Our Faith, 1983, Alone with God, 1987. Patron Soc. for Promotion of Ibo Language and Culture, Onitsha, 1979; v.p. Africa United Bible Socs., Stuttgart, Fed. Republic Germany, 1980. Roman Catholic. Avocation: lawn tennis. Office: Pontifical Coun Inter-relig, Via Dell' Erba 1, 00120 Vatican City Vatican City

ARISTODOMOU, CHRYSTOFOROS See **CHRYSOSTOMOS, ARCHBISHOP**

ARKIN, JEAN MARIE, religion educator; b. Seattle, Oct. 14, 1932; d. Wilbur Thomas and Ruth Edith (Scott) Bond; m. George Hudson Fox, Apr. 21, 1954 (div. Aug. 1984); children: David Fox, Alice Smith, Ruth Fink, Richard Fox, George Hudson Fox Jr., Joyce Anne Fox; m. Steve I. Arkin, Sept. 7, 1984. BA, Prairie, Alberta, Can., 1954. Cert. Accelerated Christian Edn. tchr. Missionary Regions Beyond Missionary Union, India, 1956-62; tchr. women and children Bapt. Chs., Calif., Idaho, 1962—; writer, sec. The Friendship Ministry, 1974-79; Vacation Bible Sch. dir., pres. women's ministry Bethel Bapt. Ch., Coeur d'Alene, Idaho, 1986—; area rep. women's team Columbia Conf., Bapt. Gen. Conf., Bellingham, 1989—; del. Columbia Bapt. Conf., Coeur d'Alene, 1987, Tacoma, 1989, Bellingham, 1990; pres. Bapt. Women's Retreats, L.A., 1979-80. Counselor Lambda Theta Chi, L.A., 1975-84. Mem. VFW Aux. (v.p., del.). Home and Office: E 4396 Woodland Dr Post Falls ID 83854 *We are responsible to our Creator God, who has provided the means for us to personally know, love and serve Him through the death of His Son, Jesus Christ. The resurrection power of Jesus enables me to experience and share His life with others.*

ARLE, EDWARD J., clergyman, counselor; b. Spokane, Wash., Feb. 19, 1944; s. Edward Charles and Stella (Hausmann) A.; m. Judith Lynn (Wells) Arle, Apr. 25, 1976; children: Scott Christopher, Grant Edward. MDiv, Concordia Sem., St. Louis, Mo., 1970. Pastor Trinity Lutheran Ch., Paola, Kans., 1970-78; assoc. pastor Immanuel Lutheran Ch., Sebewaing, Mich., 1978-85; sr. pastor Our Savior Lutheran Ch., St. Charles, Mo., 1985--; counselor Care and Counseling, St. Louis, 1987--. Pres. Paola Assn. for Ch. Action, Paola, Kans., 1974. Mem. Kiwanis (com. mem.). Democrat. Office: Our Savior Luth Ch 2800 W Elm Saint Charles MO 63301

ARLEDGE, PATRICIA O'BRIEN, minister; b. Pitts., Oct. 14, 1934; d. Raymond F. and Anna C. (Hoffman) O'Brien; d. James A. Arledge, Mar. 22, 1958 (dec. Nov. 1989); 1 child, Zeta Ann Turner; m. Frank Benko, Sept. 22, 1990. Diploma in Bible, Gt. Work Sch. Ministry, Monroeville, Pa., 1983; ThB, Internat. Sem., Plymouth, Fla., 1985, ThM, 1987, MA, 1987. Ordained to ministry Full Gospel Ch., 1982, Bapt. Ch., 1987. Interim pastor, dir. Christian edn. Shiloh Bapt. Ch., Apollo, Pa. Leader Eastmont coun. Girl Scouts U.S.A., 1964, troup organizer, 1965-66; camping leader, 1967, neighborhood chmmn., 1968-74; vol. chaplain Presbyn. U. Eye and Ear and Children's hosps., Pitts., 1983-88; vol. nursing homes and hosps. Mem. Nat. Women's Ministerial Alliance, Pitts. Regional Assn. Internat. Assn. Women Ministers (charter), Chaplains Soc., Church Women United (pres. Apollo chpt. 1991-92), Kiski Valley Union Chs., NAFE, Allegheny Pekingese Kennel Club (pres. 1974-80), Order Ea. Star (matron 1967). Avocations: showing dogs, sewing, computers, gardening, reading. Office: Shiloh Bapt Ch 719 N Warren Ave Apollo PA 15613

ARMAGOST, LESA ANN, minister; b. St. Joseph, Mo., Jan. 8, 1957; d. Maurice and Alice Jane (Schildknecht) A. BA, William Jewell Coll., Liberty, Mo., 1979; postgrad., Cen. Mo. State U., Warrensburg, 1979-81; MRE, Midwestern Bapt. Theol. Sem., Kansas City, Mo., 1984. Youth minister First Bapt. Ch., Sweet Springs, Mo., 1980-81; dir. youth bus ministries First Bapt. Ch., Warrensburg, 1981-83; minister youth/sr. adults First Bapt. Ch., North Kansas City, Mo., 1986-90; minister youth and students Crescent Hill Bapt. Ch., Louisville, 1990—; asst. team mem. Johnson Bapt. Assn., Warrensburg, 1981-83; discipleship team mem. Blue River Kansas City Bapt. Assn., 1988-90. Mem. Nat. Network of Youth Ministers, Ea. Bapt. Religious Edn. Assn. Office: Crescent Hill Bapt Ch 2800 Frankfort Ave Louisville KY 40206

ARMBRISTER, DAVID MASON, minister, religion educator; b. Bluefield, W.Va., Aug. 2, 1934; s. George Stuart and Stella Prince (Bailey) A.; m. Catherine Elizabeth Blair, Aug. 3, 1957; children: Blair, Kenneth, Glenn (dec.), Craig (dec). AA, Bluefield (Va.) Coll., 1954; BA, U. Richmond, 1956, MA, 1958; MDiv, So. Bapt. Theol. Sem., Louisville, 1961. Ordained to ministry So. Bapt. Conv., 1959. Pastor Immanuel Bapt. Mission, Blairtown, Ky., 1961-64, Mt. Plain Bapt. Ch., Charlottesville, Va., 1964-68; tchr. Albemarle County (Va.) pub. schs., Crozet, 1964-68; youth dir. Graham Christian Ch., Bluefield, 1971-72, Trinity United Meth. Ch., Bluefield, 1969-71; assoc. prof. Bluefield Coll., 1968—, acting chmn. Div. Social Scis.; mem. 1st Bapt. Ch., Bluefield. Co-author: Dr. Charlie, 1986; author booklet: History of Bluefield College, 1972. Trustee Oak Hill Acad., 1989—. Recipient S.C. Mitchell History award, U. Richmond, 1956, Jefferson Davis History award, United Daus. of Confederacy, 1989, Disting. Prof. award, Bluefield Coll., 1986. Mem. Lions (past pres.), Phi Theta Kappa, Phi Beta Kappa, Kappa Delta Pi. Avocations: drawing, walking, reading. Office: Bluefield College 3000 College Dr Bluefield VA 24605 *In the midst of a world where one still hears sounds of conflict—verbal, physical, mental, or otherwise—and these sounds are deafening and disturbing, it is good and comforting to hear rising above it all, the "still small voice of God" directing the affairs of men.*

ARMENTROUT, DONALD SMITH, religion educator, minister; b. Harrisonburg, Va., Apr. 22, 1939; s. Louis Smith and Edith Irene (Moomaw) A.; m. Sue Ellen Gray, Mar. 26, 1967; children: Emily Gray, Ellen Scherer, Philip Donald. BA, Roanoke Coll., 1961; BD, Luth. Theol. Sem., 1964; PhD, Vanderbilt U., 1970. Ordained to ministry Evang. Luth. Ch. in Am., 1972. Prof. ch. history. Sch. Theology, Sewanee, Tenn., 1967—; mem. examining com. Southeastern Synod, Luth. Ch. in Am., 1972—, chmn. subcom. on continuing edn., 1973—; mem. Commn. on Publs., Luth Hist. Conf., 1973-74; bd. dirs. joint D Ministry program Vanderbilt U.-Sewanee, 1975—, dir. Advanced Degrees Program, 1984—, assoc. dean acad. affairs, 1989, interim dean, 1985-86, 90-91, Quintartd prof. theology, 1991—. Mem. AAUP, Am. Ch. History Soc., Luth. Hist. Conf., Concordia Hist. Inst., Luth. Peace Fellowship, Episcopal Peace Fellowship, ACLU, Common Cause. Democrat. Home: Alabama Ave Sewanee TN 37375 Office: Sch Theology Sewanee TN 37375

ARMEY, DOUGLAS RICHARD, minister; b. Fresno, Calif., Oct. 23, 1948; s. Wilbur Rutter and Mildred (Broadbent) A.; m. Jennifer Louise Armey, Sept. 23, 1972; children: Laura Elizabeth, Andrew Douglas. AA, Fresno (Calif.) City Coll., 1969; Bs summa cum laude, Calif. State U., Fresno, 1971; MA, Mennonite Brethren Sem., Fresno, 1976. Ordained to ministry, Ch. of Brethren, 1973. Intern pastor The Peoples Ch. of Fresno, 1972-73; founding chaplain Fresno County Juvenile Hall, 1973; pres. Precision Parts Distbrs., Inc., Fresno, 1973-80, Rutter Armey Engine Co., Inc., Bakersfield, Calif., 1980-88; sr. pastor Fresno Ch. of the Brethren, 1988—; radio broadcaster Fresno Youth for Christ/KIRV Radio, 1987—. Contbr articles to profl. jours. Bd. dirs. Fresno Youth for Christ, 1985-87. With Calif. Air N.G., 1968-74. Mem. Nat. Assn. Evangelicals, Sigma Alpha Epsilon, Sunnyside Country Club. Republican. Ch. of the Brethren. Avocations: golf, snow skiing, tennis. Office: 3901 E Clinton Ave Fresno CA 93703

ARMOUR, CLIFFORD ARNETT, JR., minister; b. Elkton, Md., Jan. 16, 1941; s. Clifford Arnett Sr. and Dorothy Elizabeth (Goodnow) A.; m. Miriam Jeanette Amick, Dec. 21, 1969; 1 child, Randall Crawford. AB, Duke U., 1963; MDiv, Wesley Theol. Sem., 1966, grad., 1971. Assoc. minister Elkton United Meth. Ch., 1966-68, Asbury United Meth. Ch., Salisbury, Md., 1971-75; sr. minister Ocean City (Md.) Charge, 1975-79, Unite Meth. Ch. of the Atonement, Claymond, Del., 1979-85, Newark (Del.) United Meth. Ch., 1985—; trustee Wesley Theol. Sem., Washington, 1975—, Wesley Coll., Dover, Del., 1984—; bd. dirs., pres. Pacem in Terris, Wilmington, 1986—. Bd. dirs. Network Symphony Orch., 1990—, East Coast Opera Co., 1989—; chair Del. County Papayo Partnership, 1990—. Mem. Am. Acad. of Religion, Nat. Assn. United Meth.'s in Music, Worship and Other Arts, Soc. Bib. Lit., Christian Educators Fellowship, World Meth. Coun. (del. Lake Juna Luska, N.C. chpt. 1985—). Office: Newark United Meth Ch 69 E Main St Newark DE 19711

ARMSTRONG, BENJAMIN LEIGHTON, association executive; b. Newark, Oct. 18, 1923; s. Benjamin L. and Margaret D. (Denison) A.; m. Ruth Freed, Apr. 11, 1946; children: Robert, Bonnie, Debbie. B.S., NYU, 1948, M.A., 1950, Ph.D., 1968; M.Div., Union Theol. Sem., N.Y.C., 1955. Ordained to ministry Presbyn. Ch. U.S.A., U.S.A., 1949; pastor Central Presbyn. Ch., Paterson, N.J., 1950-54; dir. radio Trans World Radio, 1958-67; exec. dir. Nat. Religious Broadcasters, Morristown, N.J., 1967-89; pres. Chinese Am. Christian Friendship Alliance, Taipei, Republic of China, 1985—, Highland Christian Mission, Washington, 1990—, Madison Broadcasting Group, Inc., Madison, N.J., 1990—; chmn. communications commn. World Evang. Fellowship, 1974-81; co-chmn. 11th Internat. Christian Prayer Breakfast in Honor of Israel, Jerusalem, 1992. Author: The Electric Church, 1979; editor: Ann. Directory Religious Broadcasting, 1986, Religious Broadcasting Sourcebook II. Recipient Founders Day award NYU, 1968, Faith and Freedom award Religious Heritage of Am., 1982. Mem. Kappa Delta Pi.

ARMSTRONG, ERNEST WALTER, religious organization administrator, accountant; b. San Diego, Oct. 29, 1955; s. John Francis and Marianne (Zingerle) A.; m. Frances Clair, Sept. 14, 1985; children: Eli, Alois. BS in Acctg., San Diego State U., 1979. CPA, Colo. Parish adminstr. St. Joseph's Ch., Ft. Collins, Colo., 1982-85, Most Precious Blood Ch., Denver, 1985-91; parish acctg. mgr. Archdiocese of Denver, 1991—; presenter, speaker workshop Successful Ch., 1989. Bd. dirs. Discovery: Job Network, Englewood, Colo., 1989-91. Pres.'s grantee, San Diego State U., 1979. Mem. Nat. Assn. Ch. Bus. Adminstrn. (bd. dirs. region 13, Colo., N.Mex. 1990-91, chpt. pres. 1988-89), Archdiocese of Denver Bus. Adminstrs. Group (founder 1988). Mem. Christian Cath. Ch. Home: 2840 S Dexter Way Denver CO 80222 Office: Archdiocese of Denver 200 Josephine Denver CO 80206

ARMSTRONG, FRANK WILBUR, minister; b. Duluth, Minn., Oct. 29, 1940; s. Ralph Leonard and Hannah margret (Granning) A.; m. Meredith Ellen Hanson, June 5, 1965; children: Amy, Brenda. Diploma missions and Bible, Moody Bible Inst., 1961; BA in History, U. Minn., 1964; MDiv, Trinity Evang. Div. Sch., 1967. Ordained to ministry Bapt. Ch., 1972. Pastor Mountain View Evang. Free Ch., Greeley, Colo., 1967-70; youth pastor Temple Bapt. Ch., Duluth, Minn., 1970-73; pastor 1st Bapt. Ch., Thief River Falls, Minn., 1973-82; sr. pastor Calvary Bapt. Ch., Albert Lea, Minn., 1982—; chmn. InterVarsity Christian Fellowship, Duluth, Minn., 1970-73. Mem. Freeborn County Ministerial Assn. (pres. 1984-85), Kiwanis, Rotary. Home: 608 Fountain Albert Lea MN 56007 Office: Calvary Bapt Ch 2016 N Brige Ave Albert Lea MN 56007

ARMSTRONG, GARY MURRAY, minister; b. St. John, N.B., Can., Aug. 24, 1943; s. Murray Jamieson and Evelyn Doris (Stanley) A.; m. Sandra Louise Denton, May 22, 1971; 1 child, Alisa Ann. BA, Gordon Coll., 1967; MDiv, Ea. Bapt. Theol. Sem., 1970; ThM, Cen. Bapt. Theol. Sem., 1982. Ordained to ministry Ind. Bapt. Ch., 1970. Pastor Bass River Community Bapt. Ch., South Yarmouth, Mass., 1970-72; pastor, founder New Testament Bapt. Ch., West Yarmouth, Mass., 1972-77, St. Paul, 1977-87; pastor New Testament Bapt. Ch., West Yarmouth, 1987—; dir., founder New Testament Bible Inst., St. Paul, 1983-87, Cape Cod Bible Inst., West Yarmouth, 1987-91. Office: New Testament Bapt Ch 491 Higgins Crowell Rd West Yarmouth MA 02673

ARMSTRONG, GREGORY TIMON, religion educator, minister; b. Evanston, Ill, Dec. 23, 1933; s. John Robert and Clara Joanna (Carlson) A.; m. Edna Louise Stagg, May 11, 1957; children: Edna Louise Armstrong Montague, Elizabeth S. Armstrong Roncace. B.A. with honors, Wesleyan U., 1955; B.D. with highest honors, McCormick Theol. Sem., 1958; Th.D. magna cum laude, U. Heidelberg, 1961. Ordained to ministry United Presbyterian Ch., 1961; instr. ch. history McCormick Theol. Sem., Chgo., 1961-62; asst. prof. ch. history Vanderbilt U. Div. Sch., Nashville, 1962-68; assoc. prof. religion Sweet Briar (Va.) Coll., 1968-75, prof., 1975-81, Charles A. Dana prof. religion, 1981—, chmn. dept. religion, 1972-74, 78-81, 83-88; research fellow U. Goettingen, Fed. Republic Germany, 1974-75; vis. prof. hist. studies Union Theol. Sem., Richmond, 1983. Author: Die Genesis in der Alten Kirche, 1962; contbr.: articles and book revs. on ch. history and art to scholary jours. and encys. Mem. Nashville United Givers Fund, 1966-68; pres. local PTA, Amherst, Va., 1971-72; mem. Wesleyan U. Alumni Fund, 1971-74; mem. bd. suprs. Amherst County, Va., 1988-91, vice chmn., 1990, chmn., 1991; mem. Cen. Va. Community Svcs. Bd., 1988-91, sec., 1990-91. Rotary Internat. fellow, 1958-59; Rockefeller doctoral fellow, 1959-61; Nettie F. McCormick fellow, 1959-61; Presbyn. Grad. fellow, 1960-61; Am. Council Learned Soc. Study fellow, 1965-66; NEH grantee, 1971; Fulbright Hays sr. research fellow, 1974-75; Sweet Briar faculty fellow, 1981-82; Vanderbilt U. Research Council grantee, 1966-68; Am. Philos. Soc. grantee, 1981; Am. Council Learned Socs. grantee, 1985. Mem. Am. Hist. Assn., Am. Soc. Ch. History (membership chmn. 1972-74, coun. 1985-87), AAUP (pres. chpt. 1976, state exec. com. 1984-86, pres VA conf. 1986-87), N.Am. Patristics Soc., Rotary, Phi Beta Kappa (chpt. pres. 1976-78). Address: PO Box AY Sweet Briar VA 24595

ARMSTRONG, HARRY E., minister, counselor; b. Enterprise, Ala., Aug. 26, 1945; s. Ralph Sr. and Ruby Elizabeth (Aycock) A.; m. Judith Hill, Mar. 6, 1965; children: Leah Anne, Mary Joyce. AA, Polk Community Coll., 1974; BA, Stetson U., 1976; MDiv, Southeastern Bapt. Theol. Sem., Lake Forest, N.C., 1979; D Ministry in Pastoral Counseling, Grad. Theol. Found., Notre Dame, Ind., 1989. Ordained to ministry So. Bapt. Conv. Assoc. pastor Stetson Bapt. Ch., Deland, Fla., 1979-81; pastor 1st Bapt. Ch., Pierson, Fla., 1981-87, Louisville, 1987—; counselor St. Joseph's Hospice, Augusta, Ga., 1989—; mem. State Bd. Missions, Fla. Bapt. Conv., 1982-87; staff chaplain Univ. Hosp., Louisville, 1988-91. Counselor I Can Cope, Deland, 1982-87, Jefferson Clunty Project Desert/Shield, Louisville, 1990-91; chaplain Lions Club, Pierson, 1982-87; coord. The Chem. People, Pierson, 1982; chmn. N.W. Volusia County Ministerial Assn., Pierson, 1986-87. With USN, 1964-68. Fellow Grad. Theol. Found.; mem. Acad. Parish Clergy, Albin Inst., Kiwanis, Rotary (founding Louisville club). Home: 825 Walnut St Louisville GA 30434 Office: 1st Bapt Ch 101 E 9th St Louisville GA 30434

ARMSTRONG, HART REID, minister, editor, publisher; b. St. Louis, May 11, 1912; s. Hart Champlin and Zora Lillian (Reid) A.; m. Iona Rhoda Mehl, Feb. 21, 1932; 1 son, Hart Reed. Grad. Life Bible Coll., 1931; A.B., Christian Temples U., 1936; Litt.D., Geneva Theol. Coll., 1967; D.D. (hon.) Central Sch. Religion, Surrey, Eng., 1972; Th.M., Central Christian Coll., 1968, Th.D., 1970; Ph.D. in Religion, Berean Christian Coll., 1980. Ordained to ministry Assembly of God, 1932; pastor, 1932-34; dean Bible Standard Coll., Eugene, Oreg., 1935-40; missionary, Indonesia, 1941-42; editor Open Bible Pubs., Des Moines, 1944-46, Gospel Pub. House, Springfield, Mo., 1947-53, Gospel Light Pubs., Glendale, Calif., 1954; crusade adminstr. Oral Roberts Assn., Tulsa, 1955-62; exec. dir. Assembly Homes, Inc., Glenwood, Minn., 1963-66; pres. Defenders Christian Faith, Kansas City, Mo., 1967-80; founder, pres., editor Christian Communications, Inc., Wichita, Kans., 1981—; editor Communicare mag. Fellow London Royal Soc. Arts; mem. Nat. Sunday Sch. Assn., Pope County Hist. Soc., Sigma Delta Chi. Lodge: Rotary (past charter pres. Glenwood, Minn.). Author: To Those Who Are Left, 1950; You Should Know, 1951; The Rebel, 1967; The Beast, 1967; How Do I Pray, 1968; All Things for Life, 1969; What Will Happen to the United States, 1969; Impossible Events of Bible Prophecy, 1979; All You Need to Know about Bible Prophecy, 1980; Thoughts at Three Score and Ten, 1981; The A-B-C of Last Day Events, 1982. Home: 6436 N Hillside Ave Wichita KS 67219 Office: 6450 N Hillside Ave Wichita KS 67219

ARMSTRONG, (ARTHUR) JAMES, minister, religion educator, religious organization executive, consultant; b. Marion, Ind., Sept. 17, 1924; s. Arthur J. and Frances (Green) A.; m. Sue Peterson, Dec. 10, 1988; children: Eve Marie, Allison Peterson; children from previous marriage: James, Teresa Armstrong Etchison, John, Rebecca Armstrong Putens, Leslye Armstrong Hope. A.B., Fla. So. Coll., 1948; B.D., Candler Sch. Theology, Emory U., 1952; D.D., Fla. So. U., 1960, DePauw U., 1965; L.H.D., Ill. Wesleyan U., 1970, Dakota Wesleyan U., 1970, Westmar Coll., 1971, Ind. Central U., 1982, Emory U., 1982. Ordained to ministry Meth. Ch., 1948; minister in Fla., 1945-58; sr. minister Broadway Meth. Ch., Indpls., 1958-68; bishop United Meth. Ch., Dakotas area, 1968-80, Ind. area, Indpls., 1980-83; vis. prof. preaching and social ministries Iliff Sch. Theology, Denver, 1985-91; sr. min. 1st Congl. Ch., Winter Park, Fla., 1991—; exec. dir. Ctr. on Dialogue and Devel., Denver, 1984—; instr. Christian Theol. Sem., Indpls., 1961-68; del. 4th Gen. Assembly World Council Chs., 1968, 6th Gen. Assembly World Council Chs., 1983; pres. Nat. Council Chs., 1982-83; pres. bd. ch. and society United Meth. Ch., 1972-76, chmn. com. for peace and self-devel. of peoples, 1972-76, pres. commn. on religion and race, from 1976-83; exec. v.p. Pagan Internat., 1985-87. Author: The Journey That Men Make, 1969, The Urgent Now, 1970, Mission: Middle America, 1971, The Pastor and the Public Servant, 1972, United Methodist Primer, 1973, 77, Wilderness Voices, 1974, The Nation Yet To Be, 1975, Telling Truth: The Foolishness of Preaching in a Real World, 1977, From the Underside, 1981; contbg. author: The Pulpit Speaks on Race, 1966, War Crimes and the American Conscience, 1970, Rethinking Evangelism, 1971, What's a Nice Church Like You Doing in a Place Like This?, 1972, The Miracle of Easter, 1980, Preaching on Peace, 1982, Ethics and the Multi-National Enterprise, 1986, The Best of the Circuit Rider, 1987. Vice-chmn. Hoosiers for Peace, 1968; mem. Ind. State Platform Com. Democratic Party, 1968, Nat. Coalition for a Responsible Congress, 1970. Served with USNR, 1942. Recipient distinguished service award Indpls. Jr. C. of C., 1959. Office: 1st Congl Ch 225 S Interlachen Ave Winter Park FL 32789

ARMSTRONG, JAMES FRANKLIN, religion educator. Registrar Princeton Theol. Sem., N.J., until 1987, chief libr., 1987—, now also Helena prof. Old Testament. Office: Princeton Theol Sem Speer Libr PO Box 110 Mercer St & Libr Pl Princeton NJ 08540

ARMSTRONG, KENNY BRYAN, minister; b. Covington, Ky., Jan. 27, 1953; s. Jack Walls and Mary Katherine (Shields) A.; m. Tonja Sue Geist, Aug. 6, 1983; children: Bryan Ray, Michael David, Angela Joyce. Student, No. Ky. Coll., 1971-72, Nazarene Bible Coll., 1982-84, Nazarene Bible Coll., 199—. Lic. to ministry Ch. of the Nazarene, 1988. Assoc. pastor Burlington (Ky.) Ch. of the Nazarene, 1988-90; pastor Hanover Community Ch., Colorado Springs, Colo., 1990—; locksmith Allied Locksmiths, Colorado Springs, 1990—; supt. Sunday sch. Burlington Ch. of the Nazarene, 1979-82, 84-90, tchr. adults, 1984-90, tchr. teens, 1990; del. E. Ky. Dist. Ch. of the Nazarene, Ashland, 1988, 89, 90; bd. dirs. 1st Ch. of the Nazarene, Covington, Ky., 1977-79. Mem. PTA, Burlington, 1990. Democrat. Home and Office: 17480 Peyton Hwy Colorado Springs CO 80928 *There is no greater institution on earth ordained of God than that of the family. There is no greater need of society today than a return to the family as God intended it to be.*

ARMSTRONG, LEROY ROBERT, JR., minister, electrical engineer; b. Kansas City, Mo., Apr. 2, 1961; s. Leroy Robert Sr. and Eloise Jean (Canton) A.; m. Cynthia Hawthorne, Feb. 11, 1989. BSEE, U. Kans., 1984; postgrad., Dallas Theol. Sem., 1989—. Lic. to ministry Bapt. Ch., 1985, ordained, 1991. Dir. young adults Met. Missionary Bapt. Ch., Kansas City, Mo., 1985-88, youth min., 1987-88, asst. pastor, 1988-89; pastor singles Concord Missionary Bapt. Ch., Dallas, 1990-91, assoc. pastor Christian edn., 1991—; tech. contracts writer pvt. practice, Dallas, 1990—; mem. Dallas Theol. Sem. Leadership Group, 1990—; pres. Black Student Fellowship, 1991-92; guest speaker E. K. Bailey Ministries Inst. for Ch. Growth, Dallas, 1991—. Mem. Soc. Tech. Communication. Home: 2301 Seminole Dr # 704 Arlington TX 76010 *True success in the Christian life is measured by how well you understand and do (obey) the will of God for your life.*

ARMSTRONG, LOREN DOYLE, pastor; b. Enid, Okla., Nov. 10, 1947; s. Loren Ray and Veda Marcine (West) A.; m. Donna Marie Badger, June 30, 1966; children: Denny, Tammy. Student, Clark Coll., 1966-67; BTh., Bethany Bible Coll.; MTh., Internat. Bible Inst. and Seminary, 1988; ThD, Faith Theol. Sem., 1989. Cert. electric engr. Electronics technician Am. Music, Vancouver, Wash., 1966-67, Armstrong Enterprises, Palmer, Ak., 1968-71; electronics engr. Internat. Tools Co., Newark, Ohio, 1974-75; pastor The Ch. of God, Bradford, Ark., 1972-73, Dayton, Ohio, 1975-91; group leader Cambridge Sales Orgn., San Francisco, 1981-83; tchr. Sword and Trumpet Library, West Carrollton, Ohio, 1975-91; owner/operator Sky-Vision, 1984-81; adminstr. Bible Study Acad., 1988-91. Author 49 Bible study books and booklets; contbr. articles to profl. jours. Clark Coll. scholar, 1966. Mem. Quill and Scroll. Club: Photo (Anchorage) (pres. 1964-65). Avocations: music, building houses, hunting, farming, boating, writing. Home: Box 1 Irvine KY 40336 Office: Bible Study Ctr 33 Eades Dr White Oak Rd Irvine KY 40336

ARMSTRONG, MARK STEVEN, minister; b. Ft. Wayne, Ind., May 6, 1951; s. Charles Ray and Ellen May (Osborn) A.; m. Teresa Marlene Wood, Apr. 9, 1972; children: Elizabeth Ann, Laura Elaine. BS in Bus. Mgmt. and Adminstrn., Ind. U., 1979; MDiv, Nazarene Theol. Sem., 1989; postgrad., Trinity Theol. Sem. Ordained to ministry Ch. of the Nazarene, 1990. Minister Mirabile Community Ch., Kingston, Mo., 1986-89, First Ch. of the Nazarene, Perry, Fla., 1989—; adult ministries dir. north Fla. dist. Ch. of the Nazarene, 1990—; sec. Taylor County Ministerial Assn., Perry, Fla., 1989—; zone chmn. north Fla. dist. Ch. of the Nazarene, 1990—. Mem. Community of Friends, Perry, 1989-91; organizer Habitat for Humanity, Perry, 1991, Love Inc., Perry, 1991. With U.S. Army, 1969-71, Vietnam. Mem. Wesleyan Theol. Soc. Republican. Home: 804 W Ash St Perry FL 32347 Office: First Ch of the Nazarene 900 W Ash St Perry FL 32347 *When I exit the sanctuary I enter the harvest field of God. I must choose either to trample the fruit of His labor or to harvest it.*

ARMSTRONG, RICHARD STOLL, minister, ministry and evangelism educator; b. Balt., Mar. 29, 1924; s. Herbert Eustace and Elsie Davis (Stoll) A.; m. Margaret Childs, Jan. 31, 1948; children: Ellen, Richard, Andrew, William, Elsie. BA, Princeton U., 1947; MDiv, Princeton Theol. Sem., 1958; DMin, Christian Theol. Sem.-Indpls., 1978; doctoral, Temple U., 1962-68. Ordained to ministry Presbyn. Ch., 1958. Pastor Oak Lane Presbyn. Ch., Phila., 1958-68; dir. devel. Princeton (N.J.) Theol. Sem., 1968-71, v.p. devel., 1971-74, prof. ministry and evangelism, 1980—; pastor 2d Presbyn. Ch., Indpls., 1974-80; life trustee Fellowship Christian Athletes, Inc., Kansas City, Mo., 1979—; mem. ch. mins. adv. bd. Christian Theol. Sem., 1975-80; bd. dirs. Nat. Conf. Christians and Jews, Ind., 1975-80, Ind. Inter-Religious Commn. on Human Equality, 1975-80. Author: The Oak Lane Story, 1971, Service Evangelism, 1979, The Pastor as Evangelist, 1984, The Pastor-Evangelist in Worship, 1986, Faithful Witnesses, 1987, The Pastor-Evangelist in the Parish, 1990; contbg. author: Westminster Dictionary of Christian Theology, 1983. Bd. dirs. Indpls. Symphony Orch., 1978-80; trustee Am. Boychoir Sch., 1980—, McDonogh Sch., Md., 1980—; mem. adv. bd. Surveyors Ministry, 1972—. Lt. (j.g.) USN, 1942-46. Recipient Disting. Svc. award Fellowship of Christian Athletes, 1965, Branch Rickey Meml. award, 1974, Alumni Svc. award Princeton Theol. Sem., 1974, Outstanding Svc. award Nat. Conf. Christians and Jews, 1980, Robert L. Peters award Princeton U., 1990; named Man of Week, Princeton Town Topics, 1957, 68. Mem. Presbytery of New Brunswick (v.p.), Acad. for Evangelism Theol. Edn. (pres. 1989—), Presbyn. Writers' Guild. Home: 3620 Lawrenceville Rd Princeton NJ 08540 Office: Princeton Theol Sem CN821 Princeton NJ 08542

ARMSTRONG, ROBERT LAURENCE, philosophy educator; b. Bayonne, N.J., Apr. 6, 1926; s. Robert L. and Mary Agnes (Klein) A.; m. Betty Burnett, Sept. 14, 1960; children—Benjamin, Marianne. B.A., Antioch Coll., 1951; M.A., Roosevelt U., 1954; Ph.D., U. Calif.-Berkeley, 1962. Instr. U. Nev., 1962-64, asst. prof. 1964-67; assoc. prof., chmn. philosophy and religious studies, U. West Fla., 1967-70, prof., chmn., 1970-76, prof., chmn. dept. art, philosophy, and religious studies, 1976-87, prof., chmn. dept. philosophy and religious studies, 1987—. Served with USN, 1944-46. Mem. Am. Philos. Assn., So. Soc. Philosophy and Psychology, Fla. Philos. Assn., Phi Kappa Phi. Democrat. Author: Metaphysics and British Empiricism, 1970; contbr. articles to profl. jours. Home: 6118 Bougainvilla Circle Pensacola FL 32504 Office: U West Fla Dept Philosophy & Religion Pensacola FL 32514

ARNETT, GREGORY SCOTT, clergyman; b. Kalamazoo, Mich., Oct. 31, 1965; s. David Owen and Ruth Betty (Marlatt) A.; m. Catherine Louise Beagle, Sept. 26, 1987. AA, Kalamazoo Valley Coll., 1985; BA, Concordia Coll., 1987, Dir. Christian Edn. Cert., 1988. Commd. to ministry Luth. Ch., 1988. Intern St. John's Luth. Ch., Green Valley, Ill., 1987-88; dir. youth and young adult ministries St. John's Luth. Ch., Lombard, Ill., 1988—; fin. counselor Christian Fin. Concepts, Gainesville, Ga., 1990—; instr. Leadership Edn. and Devel., Reynoldsburg, Ohio, 1989—; speaker Luth. Youth Encounter, Chgo., 1991. Mem. Luth. Educators Assn. Home: 454 Crescent Lombard IL 60148 Office: St Johns Luth Ch 215 S Lincoln Lombard IL 60148

ARNOLD, CHARLES HARVEY, minister; b. Atlanta, May 25, 1920; s. Charles Hill and Ida (Ashley) A.; m. Patricia Arnold, June 18, 1945; children: Erick, Jan, Lauren, Gregory, Lael, Jonathan, Lisa Plorkin. BD, U. Chgo., 1950, MA, 1961. Ordained to ministry Christian Chs. (Disciples of Christ), 1944. Evangelist Ga. and Pa., 1937-44; min. Ill., 1944—; rsch. historian Disciples Divinity Home, U. Chgo., 1980—; centennial historian University Ch. of Disciples, Chgo., 1986—. Contbr. articles to profl. jours. Mem. Am. Acad. Regilion.

ARNOLD, CHARLES RYAN, JR., minister; b. Greenville, S.C., Aug. 4, 1960; s. Charles Ryan and Betsy Dale (Callahan) A.; m. Erika Lee Nebel, June 11, 1983; 1 child, Charles Ryan III. BA in Religion, Wofford Coll., 1978; MDiv, Southwestern Bapt. Theol. Sem., 1986; postgrad., Luther Rice Seminar, Jacksonville, Fla. Ordained to ministry So. Bapt. Conv. Indsl. chaplain Casa Bonita Resturant, Ft. Worth, 1983-85; dir. apt. ministries Bapt. Gen. Conv. Tex., Ft. Worth, 1985-86; pastor Cityview Bapt. Ch. (formerly Southwestern Ft. Worth Bapt. Ch.), 1985-86, The Island Bapt. Ch., South Padre Island, Tex., 1986-90, Seaside Bapt. Ch., Galveston, Tex., 1991—. Contbr. articles to religious jours.; producer maj. outdoor Christian concerts. V.p. South Padre Island Mchts. Assn., 1988-89. Mem. Rio Grande Valley Bapt. Assn. (dir. Christian life commn. 1988-90, lower valley Bapt. student union 1989-90, pastor ministries dir. 1987-88), Bapt. Gen. Conv. Tex. (dir. resort ministry 1991—), Port Isabel/South Padre Island C. of C. (1s v.p. 1988-89). Home: 16547 Jamaica Inn Rd Galveston TX 77554

ARNOLD, DORIS FOLTZ, minister, former health care administrator; b. Hagerstown, Md., May 2, 1926; d. Xenia James and Elton Irene (Kline) Foltz; m. Raymond Merton Arnold, Apr. 1, 1953. AB, Lynchburg Coll., 1948; MRE, Lexington Theol. Sem., 1951; MA, Columbua U., 1964; postgrad., So. Ill. U., 1968—. Ordained to ministry Disciples of Christ (Christian Ch.), 1948; cert. spl. edn. tchr., N.Y. Asst. chaplain Lynchburg (Va.) Sch. for Retarded, 1944-48; chaplain Va. Indsl. Sch. for Delinquent Girls, Bon Air, 1948-51; assoc. min. Paris (Ky.) Christian Ch., 1951-55; psychologist Harlem Valley Psychiat. Hosp., Wingdale, N.Y., 1955-56, Cleve. Mental Hosp., 1956; edn. supr. Wassaic Developmental Ctr. for the Retarded, 1956-83; min. Dover Plains United Meth. Ch. and South Dover United Meth. Ch., 1978-90; min. part time Gallatin (N.Y.) Reformed Ch., 1989—; dir. music Ky. Reform Sch., 1951; owner Past Times Gifts and Antiques Shop, Dover Plains, N.Y; speaker in field; organist Dover Plains United Meth. Ch., South Dover United Meth. Ch., Gallatin Reformed Ch. Author 4 books. Trustee Lynchburg Coll., 1979-80; mem. com. Dutchess County Battered Women, Boys Scouts Am., also Cub Scouts, Explorers; active various civic and community orgns. Mem. Mentally Retared Educators (sec. 1957-83), Am. Assn. for Mentally Defective, Order of Ea. Star (matron local lodge). Republican. Avocation: collecting antiques; restoring Greek Revival mansion. Home: Rte 22 PO Box 316 Dover Plains NY 12522 *It is with a grateful living pattern that I feel I have been sent to this world by a Power of Creativity and ability to produce with my fellow travelers in this world. With the Lord Jesus Christ as my inspiration and director of my ways, my stewardship to my Creator will be a system filled with love, understanding and compassion. May each moment allow me to be accountable unto the Shepherd who allows me to work with His sheep.*

ARNOLD, DUANE WADE-HAMPTON, minister, educator; b. Ft. Wayne, Ind., Aug. 5, 1953; s. Herman Wade-Hampton and Louise Elizabeth (Hensley) A.; m. Janet Lee Drew, Nov. 1, 1980. BA magna cum laude, SUNY, Albany, 1979; MA in Religion summa cum laude, Concordia Theol. Sem., Ft. Wayne, Ind., 1981; Diploma in Theology, Cambridge U., 1984; STh Lambeth diploma, 1985; PhD in Patristics, U. Durham (Eng.), 1989. Ordained to ministry Congl. Ch.; ordained priest Episcopal Ch., 1987. Rsch. asst. in hist. theology Concordia Theol. Sem., 1980-82; minister Shildon (Eng.) Congl. Ch., 1983-85; interim minister 1st Congl. Ch. Detroit, 1985-87; Episc. chaplain Wayne State U., Detroit, 1987-91; precentor Cathedral Ch. of St. Paul, Detroit, 1988-90; sr. asst. St. Thomas Ch., N.Y.C., 1991—; tutor St. Chad's Coll., U. Durham, 1983-85; lectr. religious studies U. Detroit, 1985-88; adj. lectr. ch. history Ashland Theol. Sem., Detroit, 1987-91; tutor Gen. Theol. Sem., 1991—; sr. rsch. fellow Ctr. for Reformation Studies, U. Sheffield, Eng., 1987; mem. Congl. Chs. Internat. Christian Rels. Commn., 1985-88, mem. Ecumenical Commn., Diocese of Mich., 1988-91, mem. Evangelism Commn., 1991; mem. Mich. Ecumenical Commn., 1986-91, N.Y. Ecumenical Commn., 1991—. Author: (with C. George Fry) The Way, The Truth and The Life, 1982, A Lutheran Reader, 1983, In Dire Straits, 1987, Francis: A Call to Conversion, 1988, Prayers of the Martyrs, 1990, The Early Career of Athanasius of Alexandria, 1991, Praying with Donne and Herbert, 1992; contbr. to Ency. World Faiths, 1987; contbr. numerous articles to profl. jours. Alumni trustee, pres. SUNY, 1985-90, bd. overseers, 1988-90; mem. Presdl. Commn. on Substance Abuse Edn., 1989; mem. Grosberg Religious Found., 1987-91, treas., 1990-91; mem. Ewald B. Nyquist Found., 1989—; trustee St. Xenia'a Hosp. Found., Leningrad, USSR, 1991—. Decorated caplain Most Venerable Order Hosp. St. John of Jerusalem (Eng.); recipient Mich. Gov.'s award, 1988, Detroit Disting. Svc. award, 1988. Fellow Coll. Preachers, Coll. Preceptors; mem. St. John's Club (London), Detroit Athletic Club. Home: 202 W 58th St New York NY 10019 Office: 1 W 53d St New York NY 10019

ARNOLD, ERNEST WOODROW, minister; b. White Springs, Fla., Mar. 20, 1914; s. Turner Benjamin and Francis Essie (Wise) A.; m. Mildred Virginia Thomas, Jan. 26, 1945; children: Ernest Woodrow Jr., Cheryl Ruth Arnold Daves. BA magna cum laude, Furman U., 1943; BD, New Orleans Bapt. Theol. Sem., 1948; ThD, Luther Rice Sem., 1965. Ordained to ministry So. Bapt. Conv., 1942. Pastor East Pk. Bapt. Ch., Greenville, S.C., 1950-54, Brentwood Bapt. Ch., Charleston, S.C., 1955-58, Bethel Bapt. Ch., Shelby, N.C., 1958-72, Catawba Bapt. Ch., Rock Hill, S.C., 1972-75, 1st Bapt. Ch., Bostic, N.C., 1975-81, Lily Meml. Bapt. Ch., Shelby, 1987—; mem. faculty Luther Rice Sem., 1968-76. With USMC, 1934-38. Recipient commendation USMC, 1935; New Orleans Bapt. Theol. Sem. fellow, 1948-50. Democrat. Home: 117 Ken Daves Rd Box 715 Boiling Springs NC 28017 *Life can be a circle or it can be a line of movement to never ending joy and peace, accompanied by achievement, fulfillment and faith in God, the Eternal One.*

ARNOLD, JANET DREW, church administrator; b. St. Louis, Dec. 12, 1951; d. George Dunlop and Barbara Lee (Millner) Drew; m. Duane Wade-Hampton Arnold, Nov. 1, 1980. BA, Hillsdale Coll., 1974; MBA, U. Durham, Eng., 1985. Dir. sales Marriott Corp., Ft. Wayne, Ind., 1974-77; dir. adminstrn. Ft. Wayne Ballet, Inc., 1979-82; researcher Sch. Edn., U. Durham, 1983-85; dir. annual fund Mich. Opera Theatre, Detroit, 1986-87; dir. devel. Cathedral Ch. St. Paul, Detroit, 1988-90; cons. Diocese of Mich., Detroit, 1991—. Sec. Fine Arts Found., Ft. Wayne, 1977-80; advisor Northern Arts, Newcastle, Eng., 1984-85; trustee Cathedral Found., Detroit, 1986—; mem. com. Gen. Dirs. Cirlic Mich. Opera, Detroit, 1987; trustee St. Xenia's Hosp. Found., Leningrad, USSR, 1991—, St. Hilda & St. Hugh Episcopal Sch., N.Y., 1991—. Decorated Officer of the Order of St. John (Eng.), 1991. Mem. Nat. Soc. Fund Raising Execs., St. John's Club (London), Univ. Club. Democrat. Mem. Ch. of England. Avocations: oil painting, travel. Home: 202 W 58th St New York NY 10019

ARNOLD, LARRY ROBERT, minister; b. Sherman, Tex., Sept. 18, 1958; s. Donald Ray and Mary (Atnip) A.; m. Paula Lynette Cunningham, Jan. 17, 1987; children: Andra Lee, Shiloh Michelle. BA in Religion, Baylor U., 1982; MDiv, Southwestern Bapt. Theol. Sem., 1986. Ordained to ministry So. Bapt. Conv., 1986. Min. of youth 1st Bapt. Ch., Whitesboro, Tex., 1982-89; min. of youth, edn. Calvary Bapt. Ch., Dumas, Tex., 1989—. Home: 901 Bruce Dumas TX 79029 Office: Calvary Bapt Ch 1315 Zauk Dumas TX 79029 *In all of life our greatest struggle is to be honest: honest with ourself, honest with others and honest with God.*

ARNOLD, LOUIS WALKER, minister; b. Garrard County, Ky., Jan. 17, 1914; s. Edward Lawrence and Texie Bell (Agee) A.; m. Jessie Arnold; children—June Louise Arnold Parker, Sue Ann Arnold True. Student So. Baptist Sem., Louisville, 1942; D.D., Pioneer Theol. Sem., 1953; student U. Ky., 1955; D.Litt., Colonial Acad., 1956. Ordained to ministry Baptist Ch., 1933; pastor Fellowship Bapt. Ch., Lexington, Ky., 1950-57, Central Bapt. Ch., Cin., 1945-47; flying pastor, preaching from airplane over powerful PA system; fgn. missionary; radio preacher on network stas.; evangelist; owner Arnold Publs., Nicholasville, Ky., 1965—; past pres. Blue Grass Bible Inst., Internat. Fellowship Fundamentalists. Ky. Col., Hon. Commr. Agr., Ky., Hon. Dep. Sheriff, Jessamine County, Adm., Cherry River Navy (W.Va.). Author: Way of Revival, 1947, God's Message for This Hour, 1944, Israel: Countdown to Eternity, 1985, The Legend of Old Faithful, 1986, Beyond the Rapture, 1986, Out of the Night, 1987, Fathoms Deep, 1988, Riverman, 1990, Sunshine Valley, 1991; composer numerous gospel songs; contbr. articles to religious publs. Home and Office: 2440 Bethel Rd Nicholasville KY 40356

ARNOLD, MARIA, nun; b. Marietta, Ohio, Mar. 16, 1915; d. John H. and Virginia Mary (Schilling) A. BS in Edn., St. Mary of the Springs, Columbus, Ohio, 1947; MLS, Duquesne U., 1959. Joined Sisters of St. Dominic, 1933. Tchr. St. Clare Sch., Grosse Pointe, Mich., 1945-49, 60-62, Holy Name Sch., Steubenville, Ohio, 1949-54, St. Lawrence Sch., Pitts., 1937-45, 54-60, St. Francis Sch., Newark, Ohio, 1964, St. James the Less, Columbus, 1965; libr. Northwest Cath. High Sch., West Hartford, Conn., 1965-77, Newark Cath. High Sch., 1977—. Recipient Libr. Sci. award NDEA, 1967. Mem. Nat. Coun. English. Address: 1 Green Wave Dr Newark OH 43055

ARNOLD, MORRIS FAIRCHILD, bishop; b. Mpls., Jan. 5, 1915; s. LeRoy and Kate (Fairchild) A.; m. Harriet Borda Schmidgall, Jan. 1978; children by previous marriage: Jaqueline Fairchild (Mrs. Arnold Crocker), William Morris. B.A. magna cum laude, Williams Coll., 1936; M.Div. cum laude, Episcopal Theol. Sch., 1940; D.D., Kenyon Coll., 1961, Williams Coll., 1972. Ordained priest Episcopal Ch., 1940; priest-in-charge St. John's Ch., Saugus, Mass., 1940-43; chaplain U.S. Army, 1943-45; rector Grace Ch., Medford, Mass., 1945-50; Episcopal students chaplain Tufts Coll., Boston, 1945-50; rector Christ Ch., Cin., 1950-72; consecrated suffragan bishop, 1972; suffragan bishop Episcopal Diocese of Mass., 1972—. Del. to Anglican Congress from So. Ohio, 1954; dep. to 7 Gen. Convs. of Episcopal Ch., 1958-70; co-founder U.S. Ch. and City Conf., 1959, pres., 1964-66; mem. Joint Commn. on Edn. for Holy Orders, 1961-68; program and budget com. of Episcopal Ch., 1961-70, 77-80; pres. Council of Chs. of Greater Cin., 1961-63; treas. Cin. Met. Area Religious Coalition, 1968-72; trustee ARC, 1957-63, Family Service, 1962-71, Better Housing League, 1951-72; mem. Cathedral Deans Assn., 1955-72; mem. steering com. Urban Bishop's Coalition, 1977-82. Mem. Soc. for the Relief of Aged or Disabled Clergymen (v.p. 1972-82), Alumni Assn. Episcopal Theol. Sch. (pres. 1969-72), Phi Beta Kappa, Delta Phi.

ARNOLD, ROBERT EDWIN, chaplain, marriage and family therapist; b. Ages, Ky., Feb. 19, 1948; s. Jasper E. and Zenna I. (Greer) A.; m. Karen Ann Villafarra, July 28, 1979; 1 child, Julie Ann. AA, Sinclair Community Coll., 1968; BS in Edn., Wright State U., 1971; MA, Southwestern Bapt. Theol. Sem., 1973; EdD, New Orleans Bapt. Theol. Sem., 1982. Ordained to ministry Bapt. Ch., 1972; lic. marriage and family therapist, Iowa; cert. secondary edn. tchr., N.J.; diplomate Am. Bd. Sexology. Youth minister First Bapt. Ch., Englewood, Ohio, 1972, Madison (N.J.) Bapt. Ch., 1973-75; assoc. pastor Lakeland Bapt. Chapel, Sparta, N.J., 1974-77; minister of edn. United Meth. Ch., Kenner, La., 1979-80; family therapist De Paul Hosp., New Orleans, 1980-82; clin. social worker Assn. Cath. Charities, New Orleans, 1982; chaplain VA Med. Ctr., Knoxville, Iowa, 1983—; cons. marriage and family therapy Iowa State U., 1987; supr./instr. Clin. Pastoral Tng., 1989—. Trustee First So. Bapt. Ch., Newton, Iowa, 1986. Fellow Am. Orthopsychiat. Assn.; mem. Am. Assn. Marriage and Family Therapists (clin., approved supr.), N.Am. Assn. Christians in Social Work, Am. Assn. Sex Educators, Counselors and Therapists (life., cert.). Home: Rural Rt 2 Box 586 Bittersweet Estates Newton IA 50208

ARNOTT, JACOB WILLARD, retired administrator; b. Rensselaer, Ind., Sept. 6, 1918; s. Fred E. and Mary Irene (Lutz) A.; m. Mary Louise McGee, Oct. 25, 1942; 1 child, Marilyn Sue. Student, Ball State U., 1938-39. Chmn. USAF Chapel Bd., Yakota, Japan, 1954-56, Trinity Meth. Ch. Bd., Austin, Tex., 1962-64; bus. adminstr. University United Meth. Ch., Austin, Tex., 1964-74; chmn. Air Force Village Protestant Ch., San Antonio, 1985-86, Air Force Village II High Flight Chapel Policy Com., Air Force Village II Protestant Ch., San Antonio, 1987-88. Lt. col. USAF, 1939-63, WWII, Korea. Republican. Home: 5100 John D Ryan Blvd San Antonio TX 78245

ARNS, PAULO EVARISTO CARDINAL, archbishop of São Paulo; b. Criciuma, Brazil, Sept. 14, 1921; s. Gabriel and Helena (Steiner) A.; ed. U. Parana, Sorbonne, 1952; LL.D. (hon.), U. Notre Dame (Ind.), 1977, Siena Coll., Albany, N.Y., 1981; Fordham U., N.Y.C., 1981, Seton Hall U., South Orange, N.J., 1982, LL.D (hon.) U. Münster, Fed. Republic Germany, 1983, St. Francis Xavier U., Antigonish, Can., 1986, U. Dubuque, 1988, U. S. Francisco, São Paulo, 1989, Piracicaba, SP, 1990; LHD (hon.), Manhattanville Coll., 1991. Ordained priest Roman Cath. Ch.; prof. patrology and didatics Cath. U. Petropolis; pastor, 1956-66; aux. bishop of São Paulo, 1966-70, archbishop, 1970—; created cardinal of São Paulo, 1973; chancellor Pontifical Cath. U., São Paulo, 1970—. Recipient Nansen medal for def. of human rights in Latin Am., U.N., 1985. Author 48 books. Office: Caixa Postal 916, 01000 São Paulo Brazil

ARONOVITCH, ROBERTA GAIL, religious organization administrator; b. Winnipeg, Man., Can., Apr. 9, 1949; d. Geroge and Helen (Stolback) Miles; m. Sheldon Lyle Aronovitch, June 18, 1970; children: Jorelle, Todd, Blaine. BA, U. Winnipeg; MBA, U. Man., Winnipeg. Ind. acct., mgmt. cons. Winnipeg, 1974-83; exec. dir. Shaarey Zedek Synagogue, Winnipeg, 1983-87, Temple Emanu El of Houston, 1987-88, Temple Beth El of Great Neck, N.Y., 1988—. Mem. NAFE, Nat. Assn. Synagogue Adminstrs., Nat. Assn. Temple Adminstrs. (profl. ethics com. 1988-89, convs. planning task force 1989—). Avocation: reading. Home: 4612 Concord Ave Great Neck NY 11020 Office: Temple Beth El Great Neck 5 Old Mill Rd Great Neck NY 11023

ARONS, JOHN CLARK, lay worker; b. Washington, Feb. 14, 1952; s. Henry Carroll and Jo Anna (Parsons) A.; m. Linda Sue Wingo, Dec. 22, 1972; children: Amanda Michaelle, Carrie Diane. Dipl., Cedarhill (Tex.) High Sch., 1970. Ch. adminstr. St. Paul Luth. Ch., Davenport, Iowa, 1989—; adminstr. Camp Shalom, Maquoketa, Iowa, 1988—; del. Evang. Luth. Ch. in Am. Nat. Conv., Chgo., 1989. Bd. dirs. Youth Alternative Program, Davenport, 1990—, Elim Project (Housing for Under Priviledged), Davenport, 1991; treas. Cen. High Sch. After Prom Party, Davenport, 1991; pres. Davenport Chs. Disaster Relief, 1990. Mem. Nat. Assn. Ch. Bus. Adminstrs. Republican. Office: St Paul Luth Ch 2136 Brady St Davenport IA 52803

ARP, ROBERT KELLEY, clergyman; b. Bremen, Ga., Dec. 23, 1962; s. George Marion Arp and Janelle (Robinson) Benton; m. Robbin Carole Patterson, May 9, 1984; children: Emily Elizabeth, Robert Charles. BA in Theology, Lee Coll., 1984; MDiv, Columbia Sem., 1988. Ordained to ministry, Living Faith Fellowship, 1988. Chaplain Alpha Gamma Chi, Cleveland, Tenn., 1983-84; youth pastor Hairston Rd. Ch. of God, Stone Mountain, Ga., 1984-86; missionary St. John, V.I., 1986-87; pastor to single adults Living Faith Fellowship, Athens, Ga., 1987—. Contbg. author: Single to Single, 1991. Mem. Nat. Single Adult Leaders, Nat. Christian Counselors Assn. (assoc.), Campus Ministry Assn. (assoc.), Alpha Gamma Chi (chaplain 1983-84), Sigma Nu Sigma (Big Bro. 1983-84). Home: 1081 Hancock Ct Watkinsville GA 30677 Office: Living Faith Fellowship 8780 Macon Hwy Athens GA 30606

ARRIETA, ROMAN, archbishop; b. Belen, Heredia, Costa Rica, Nov. 13, 1924; s. Carlos Arrieta and Francisca Villalobos. Bachiller, Colegio Seminario, San José, Costa Rica, 1942; MA, Cath. U. Am., 1952. Ordained priest Roman Cath. Ch., 1948. Bishop of Tilarán Costa Rica, 1961-79; archbishop of San José, 1979—; mem. Pontifical Commn. for Revision of Canon Law, 1966-83; pres. Episcopal Conf. Costa Rica, 1970—; v.p. CELAM, 1980-83; commentator radio show. Address: Arzobispado de San José, Aptdo. 497, San Jose 1000, Costa Rica

ARRINGTON, TERESA ROSS, religion educator, language educator; b. Detroit, July 2, 1949; d. Arthur Peter and Mary Stella (McRae) Ross; m. Melvin Slay Arrington, Jr., Aug. 10, 1973; children: Linda Diane, Debra Anne. AB, U. Detroit, 1971; MA, U. Ky., 1973, PhD, 1977. Cert. secondary tchr., Mich., Miss. Tchr. confrat. Christian doctrine St. John Cath. Ch., Oxford, Miss., 1983-87, coord., 1987—; asst. prof. modern langs. U. Miss., University, 1982—. Contbg. author: Escitoras hispanoamericanas, 1991, Dictionary Mexican Literature, 1991. Troop leader Girl Scouts U.S.A., Knoxville, Tenn., 1981-82, Oxford, 1984-88, com. mem., Oxford, 1982-84, chmn., 1985-90. Grad. fellow NDEA, 1972-74, U. Ky., 1974-75; scholar Ford Motor Co. Fund, 1967-71. Mem. MLA, Am. Assn. Tchrs. Spanish and Portuguese, Southeastern Coun. on Latin Am. Studies, Miss. Fgn. Lang. Assn. (exec. sec.-treas. 1988—). Office: St John Cath Ch 403 University Ave Oxford MS 38655

ARROYO, NELSON, minister; b. Bklyn., Apr. 12, 1959; s. Martin Arroyo and Milagros (Diaz) Guzman; m. Wanda Ivette Vazquez, June 16, 1984; children: Elias Nelson, Gabriel Victor. BA, Nyack Coll., 1981; MDiv, Eastern Bapt. Theol. Seminary, Phila., 1986. Ordained deacon United Meth. Ch., 1986; elder 1989. Short-term missionary Operation Mobilization, Huesca, Spain, 1981; pastoral intern 1st United Meth. Ch., Haddon Hgts., N.J., 1983-86, El Redentor United Meth. Ch., Camden, N.J., 1983-86; pastor Broad St. United Meth. Ch., Millvills, N.J., 1986-87, Trinity United Meth. Ch., Bridgeton, N.J., 1987-89; assoc. pastor First United Meth. Ch., Toms River, N.J., 1989—; mem. conf. commn. on religion and race, So. N.J. Conf., United Meth. Ch., 1988—, hispanic com. Conf. Bd. of Global Ministries, 1986—. Named to Outstanding Young Men of Am., 1988. Home: 101 Walchest Dr Toms River NJ 08753 Office: First Untied Methodist Ch 129 Chestnut St Toms River NJ 08753 *For I am not ashamed of the gospel, for it is the power of God for salvation to everyone who believes... (Rom. 8:16).*

ARTERBURN, STEPHEN FORREST, health care company executive; b. Ranger, Tex., June 18, 1953; s. Walter James and Clara Faye (Russell) A.; m. Sandy Simonian, Feb. 7, 1982. Student, Tex. A&M U., 1972, Southwest Bapt. Theol. Sem., 1977; BS, Baylor U., 1976; MEd, U. N. Tex., 1979. Alcoholism counselor Trinity Oaks Hosp., CompCare, Ft. Worth, 1979-80, program dir., 1980-81; asst. adminstr. CareUnit Hosp. Orange (Calif.), CompCare, 1981-82; dir. life style ctr. Comprehensive Care Corp., Santa Ana, Calif., 1982-83; dir. ops. Comprehensive Care Corp., Irvine, Calif., 1983-84, v.p. ops., 1984-85; exec. v.p. Westworld Community Healthcare, Lake Forest, Calif., 1985-86, chmn., pres., chief exec. officer, 1987-88; chmn. New Life Treatment Ctrs., 1988; owner Beach Front Property Swimwear, Laguna Beach, Calif., 1983—, bd. dirs. Author: Hooked on Life, 1984, Growing Up Addicted, 1987; co-author: How Will I Tell My Mother?, 1988, When Someone You Love is Someone You Hate, 1988, Drug Proof Your Kids, 1989, 52 Simple Ways to Say I Love You, 1990, Toxic Faith, 1990, Answers to Children's Questions About War, 1991, The Angry Man, 1991, Addicted to Love, 1991. Mem. bd. elders Coast Hills Community Ch., Dana Point, Calif., 1987; bd. dirs. South Coast Ctr. for Personal Growth, Irvine, 1982—, Mariposa Women's Ctr., Orange, 1982-83. Mem. Overcomers Outreach (bd. dirs.), Naaman's Fellowship (bd. dirs.), Nat. Coun. on Sexual Addiction (bd. dirs.), Nat. Assn. for Christian Recovery (adv. bd.). Republican. Mem. Christian Evangelical Ch. Club: Balboa Bay (Newport Beach, Calif.). Avocations: marathon running, skiing, writing, painting, singing. Home: 905 Canyon View Laguna Beach CA 92651 Office: 570 Glenneyre Ste 170 Laguna Beach CA 92651

ARVEDSON, PETER FREDRICK, clergyman; b. Peoria, Ill., Apr. 15, 1937; s. Fredrick St. Clair and Dorothy Evelyn (Young) A.; m. Joan Carol Swiggum, Aug. 17, 1963; children: Stephen, Mark. BS, U. Ill., 1959; PhD, U. Wis., 1964; MDiv., Gen. Theol. Sem., N.Y.C., 1967. Ordained priest Episcopal Ch., 1967. Vicar St. Laurence's Ch., Effingham, Ill., 1967-72; rector All Souls' Ch., Okinawa, Japan, 1972-78, St. Andrew's Ch., Madison, Wis., 1978—; dir. Inst. For Christian Studies, Milw., 1984—. V.p. Assn. of Attending Clergy, Madison Gen. Hosp., 1983-86. Avocation: running. Home: 9 Rye Circle Madison WI 53717 Office: St Andrew's Episcopal Ch 1833 Regent St Madison WI 53705

ARZUBE, JUAN ALFREDO, bishop; b. Guayaquil, Ecuador, June 1, 1918; came to U.S., 1944, naturalized, 1961; s. Juan Bautista and Maria (Jaramillo) A. B.S. in Civil Engring, Rensselaer Poly. Inst., 1942; B.A., St. John's Sem., 1954. Ordained priest Roman Catholic Ch., 1954; asso. pastor St. Agnes Ch., Los Angeles, Resurrection Ch., Los Angeles, Ascension Ch., Los Angeles, Our Lady of Guadalupe Ch., El Monte, Calif.; aux. bishop of Los Angeles, 1971—, episcopal vicar for Spanish speaking, 1973—; mem. nat. bishops coms. Ad Hoc Com. for Spanish Speaking; chmn. Com. for Latin Am. Recipient Humanitarian award Mexican Am. Opportunity Found., 1978, John Anson Ford award Los Angeles County Commn. Human Relations, 1979. Address: 3149 Sunset Hill Dr West Covina CA 91791

ASARE, SETH OHENE, theology educator; b. Nkawkaw, Ghana, West Africa, Aug. 31, 1946; came to U.S., 1984; s. Edmund Bediako and Ami (Dokuyo) A.; m. Dorothy Yaa Adomako, Feb. 15, 1975; children: Kwaku, Ohene, Abena, Amma. BSc with honors, U. Ghana, Legon, 1971, MSc, 1973; PhD, U. R.I., Kingston, 1979; MDiv, Boston U., 1988. Teaching asst. U. Ghana, Legon, 1971-73; lectr. U. Cape Coast (Ghana), 1973-83, sr. lectr., 1983-85, dean, hall warden, 1980-83; pastor Cochesett United Meth. Ch., West Bridgewater, Mass., 1985—; lectr. Boston U., 1989, prof. evangelism, 1989—; lectr. U. Ghana, Legon, 1979-83; vis. lectr. U. Sierra Leone, Freetown, 1983-84; cons. third world evangelism United Meth. Ch., Boston,

1984-85; cons. Growth Plus, Bd. Discipleship Conf., Nashville, 1989—. Mem. Acad. for Evangelism in Theol. Edn. Home: 517 W Center St West Bridgewater MA 02379 Office: Boston U Sch Theology 745 Commonwealth Ave Boston MA 02215

ASAY, CARLOS EGAN, church association administrator; b. Southerland, Utah, June 12, 1926; s. Aaron Elias Lyle and Elsie (Egan) A.; m. Colleen Webb, Oct. 20, 1947; children—Carlos (dec.), Marcianne, James, Marcus, Brent, Clair, Tim, Carleen. B.S. in Social Sci. with distinction, U. Utah, 1953, Ed.D. with honors in Secondary Edn. Adminstrn., 1967; M.A., Long Beach State U., 1958. Tchr. Schs., Salt Lake City, 1953-56, Long Beach, Calif., 1956-59; supr. social studies Granite Sch. Dist., Salt Lake City, 1959-66, dir. secondary edn., 1966-67; asst. supt. Jordon Sch. Dist., Sandy, Utah, 1967-69; prof. edn. Brigham Young U., Provo, Utah, 1969-70, 73-74, asst. dean, Hawaii Campus Laie, 1974-75; mission pres. Tex. North Mission, 1970-73; exec. asst. to presiding bishopric Ch. Jesus Christ Latter-day Saints, Salt Lake City, 1975-76, gen. authority, 1976—. Contbr. articles to profl. jours. Served with U.S. Army, 1944-46. Mem. Nat. Council Tchrs. Social Studies, Phi Delta Kappa. Office: Ch Jesus Christ LDS Presidency of the 70 47 East South Temple Salt Lake City UT 84150

ASBURY, MARY RUTH, religious program administrator; b. Asheveille, N.C., Sept. 6, 1954; d. Mary Ruth (Nance) Clodfelter; m. Samuel Jennings Asbury IV, June 3, 1978; 1 child, Andrew Jennings. Student, Pfeiffer Coll. Intern 1st United Meth. Ch., Mt. Holly, N.C., 1973, Maylo United Meth. Ch., Gastonia, N.C., 1974, 1sr United Meth. Ch., Charlotte, N.C., 1975; dir. program ministries Matthews (N.C.) United Meth. Ch., 1977—; bd. dirs., Pfeiffer Coll. Alumni Assn.,dist. youth coord., Charlotte Dist. Pres. PTA, Piney Grove Elem. Sch., 1989. Named Outstanding Career Woman, Assn. Bus. Profl. Women, 1978. Mem. Nat. Christian Educators Assn., Christian Educator's Fellowship, Conf. Christian Educators Assn. Office: Matthews United Meth Ch PO Box 518 Matthews NC 28106

ASCHMANN, MOTHER MARY FRANCIS See FRANCIS, MOTHER MARY

ASEKOFF, STANLEY LOUIS, rabbi; b. Cambridge, Mass., Apr. 19, 1944; s. Max and Esther (Gold) A.; m. Cecille Judith Allman, Sept. 7, 1969; children: Sarah Gila, Shira Leah. BJ, Hebrew Coll., 1965; BA in Edn., Brandeis U., 1967; M in Hebrew Letters, Jewish Theol. Sem., 1970. Ordained rabbi, 1972. Rabbi B'nai Shalom, The Jewish Ctr. of West Orange (N.J.), 1972—. Mem. Rabbinical Assembly (pres. N.J. region 1979-81). Home: 18 Stevens Terr West Orange NJ 07052 Office: B'Nai Shalom Jewish Ctr West Orange 300 Pleasant Valley Way West Orange NJ 07052

ASH, ERIC DUANE, minister; b. Balt., Aug. 1, 1959; s. James Franklin and Shirley Grace (Warthen) A.; m. Melanie Napfel, Feb. 14, 1982; children: Eric Duane Jr., Miranda Elizabeth. BA in Psychology, U. Md., Catonsville, 1981; MDiv, Luth. Theol. Sem., Gettysburg, Pa., 1989. Ordained to ministry, Luth. Ch., 1989. Med. tech. U. Of Md. Cancer Ctr., Balt., 1981-85; assoc. pastor St. Mark's Luth. Ch., Springfield, Va., 1989—; bd. dirs. Luth. House of Studies, Washington, 1988-89. Contbr. articles to religious jours. Vol. chaplain Alexandria Hosp., 1990—; chmn. Chrysalis, 1991. Mem. Psi Chi. Home: 5804 Craig St Springfield VA 22150 Office: St Mark's Luth Ch 5800 Backlick Rd Springfield VA 22150

ASH, JAMES LEE, JR., academic administrator; b. Palestine, Tex., Mar. 29, 1945; s. James Lee and Ruth Agnes (Walling) A.; m. Patricia Bryan, Aug. 24, 1969; children: Erin Patricia, Eleanor Ruth. BA, Abilene Christian Coll., 1968; ThM, So. Meth. U., 1972; MA, U. Chgo., 1974, PhD, 1976. Ordained to ministry Presbyn. Ch., 1978. Asst. prof. religious studies Oreg. State U., Corvallis, 1975-77; asst. prof. religious studies U. Miami, Fla., 1977-81, assoc. prof., 1981-89, chmn. dept., 1979-81, assoc. dean, Coll. Arts and Scis., 1981-83, dir. Honors and Privileged Studies, 1981-83, assoc. provost, Honors and Undergrad. Studies, 1983-87, vice provost, 1987-89; pres. Whittier (Calif.) Coll., Calif., 1989—. Author: Protestantism and the American University, 1982; contbr. articles to profl. jours. Named Outstanding Tchr. Humanities, Premed. Student Soc., U. Miami, 1980, Prof. of Yr. Undergrad. Student Body, U. Miami, 1981, Prof. of Yr. Honors Student Assn., U. Miami, 1985. Mem. Am. Acad. Religion, Am. Soc. Ch. History. Democrat. Avocations: racquetball, gardening. Office: Whittier Coll Office of President 13406 E Philadelphia Whittier CA 90608

ASHBECK, DAVID KILIAN, priest; b. Blenker, Wis., Apr. 12, 1942; s. Kilian Louis and Caroline Margaret (Grassel) A. BA, St. Mary Sem., Crown Point, Ind., 1965; MDiv, St. Anthony Sem., Marathon, Wis., 1969; PhD, Aquinas Inst., 1972; MSW, U. Wis., Milw., 1981. Ordained priest Roman Cath. Ch., 1968. Prof. St. Mary Sem., 1973-74, Sacred Heart Sch. Theology, Hales Corners, Wis., 1974-82; pastor St. Benedict Ch., Milw., 1981-82, St. Sebastian Ch., Seymour, Wis., 1987—; co-pastor St. Elizabeth Ch., Milw., 1974-81; assoc. dir., clin. social worker Am. Found. Counseling Svcs., Green Bay, Wis., 1986—. Contbr. articles to profl. publs. Mem. Am. Acad. Religion, Cath. Biblical Assn., Cath. Theol. Soc. Am., Nat. Assn. Social Workers, Acad. Family Mediators, Alpha Delta Mu. Home: St Sebastian Ch N 9269 Isaar Rd Seymour WI 54165 Office: Am Found Counseling Svcs 130 E Walnut St Green Bay WI 54301

ASHBROOK, JAMES BARBOUR, theology educator; b. Adrian, Mich., Nov. 1, 1925; s. Milan Forest and Elizabeth (Barbour) A.; m. Patricia Jane Cober, Aug. 14, 1948; children: Peter, Susan, Martha, Karen. A.B. with honors, Denison U., 1947, LL.D., 1976; B.D., Colgate Rochester Div. Sch., 1950; M.A., Ohio State U., 1962, Ph.D., 1964; postdoctoral fellow, U. Rochester, 1971-73; postgrad., Union Theol. Sem., 1954-55. Diplomate: Am. Assn. Pastoral Counselors, Am. Bd. Profl. Psychology (subsplty. clin. psychology). Ordained to ministry Am. Bapt. Ch., 1950; asst. chaplain U. Rochester, 1948-50; pastor South Congl. Ch., Rochester, N.Y., 1950-54, First Baptist Ch., Granville, Ohio, 1955-60; asso. prof. pastoral theology Colgate Rochester Div. Sch., 1960-65, prof., 1965-69, prof. psychology and theology, 1969-81; prof. religion and personality Garrett-Evang. Sem., 1981—; adv. mem. Grad. Faculty Northwestern U., 1982—; vis. lectr. Denison U., 1958-60; vis. asso. prof. Ohio State U., 1966; vis. prof. Princeton Theol. Sem., 1970-71; pastoral counselor Merit Recognition, Am. Bapt. Chs., 1991—. Author: Become Community, 1971, In Human Presence-Hope, 1971, Humanitas, 1973, The Old Me and A New i, 1974, Responding to Human Pain, 1975; co-author: Christianity for Pious Skeptics, 1977; The Human Mind and the Mind of God, 1984; editor with introduction: Paul Tillich in Conversation, 1988, The Brain and Belief, 1988; editor with contbns.: Faith and Ministry in Light of the Double Brain, 1989; co-editor: At the Point of Need: Essays in Honor of Carroll A. Wise, 1988; contbr. chpts. to Religion and Medicine, 1967, Psychological Testing for Ministerial Selection, 1970, Explorations in Ministry, 1971, Religious and Ethical Factors in Psychiatric Practice, 1990. Bd. mgrs. ministers and missionaries benefit bd. Am. Bapt. Chs., 1962-71, 72-80. Recipient W.C. and J.V. Stone Found. grants, 1969-72, Alumni citation Denison U., 1972; Past Counselor Merit Recognition award Am. Bapt. Chs., 1991; faculty fellow Am. Assn. Theol. Schs., 1963-64, 71-72. Mem. Am. Psychol. Assn., Am. Assn. Pastoral Counselors (recognized pioneer in pastoral therapy, 1987, Disting. Contbn. award 1990), Soc. Sci. Study Religion, Am. Acad. Religion, Phi Beta Kappa. Home: 1205 Wesley Ave Evanston IL 60202 Office: 2121 Sheridan Rd Evanston IL 60201

ASHBY, BERNADETTE EVALLE, youth worker; b. Manila, Philippines, Feb. 12, 1963; d. Juanito Fabay and Ligaya (Arcinas) Evalle; m. Myron Hollon Ashby, May 29, 1989. BS in Health Sci., San Jose State U., 1986, teaching cert., 1988. Curriculum, tng. coord. City Team Ministries, San Jose, Calif., 1988—. Office: City Team Ministries PO Box 143 San Jose CA 95103 *Discipleship takes a long time. Start early-invest in children.*

ASHBY, JOHN FORSYTHE, bishop; b. Tulsa, Mar. 26, 1929; s. Thomas Albert and Margaret (Mote) A.; m. Mary Carver, Aug. 12, 1954; children: Anne Carver Ashby Ghostbear, Elizabeth Ashby McBride. B.A., Okla. State U., 1952; M.Div., Episcopal Theol. Sem. Southwest, Austin, Tex., 1955, D.D. hon., 1981; M.A., Cambridge U., Eng., 1967. Ordained to ministry Episcopal Ch., 1955. Vicar St. John's Episcopal Ch., Durant, Okla., 1955-59; rector St. Luke's Episcopal Ch., Ada, Okla., 1959-81; bishop Episcopal Diocese of Western Kans., Salina, 1981—. Served to lt. col. USNG, 1960-81. Home: 512 Sunset Dr Salina KS 67401 Office: Diocese of Western Kans PO Box 1383 142 S 8th St Salina KS 67401

ASHJIAN, MESROB, archbishop; b. Beirut, Jan. 3, 1941; s. Nerces and Martha (Kassabian) A. Student, Armenian Theol. Sem., Antelias, Lebanon, 1957-61, Ecumenical Inst., Bossey, Switzerland, 1962-63; BA, Princeton Theol. Sem., 1964, postgrad., 1970-74, ThM, 1990. Ordained priest Armenian Apostolic Ch., 1961. Mem. faculty Armenian Theol. Sem., Antelias, Lebanon, 1961-62, 64, 65, 66-70; vice dean Armenian Theol. Sem., 1964-65, dean, 1966-70; instr. Karen Jeppe Coll., Aleppo, Syria, 1965-66; preacher St. Gregory Ch., Aleppo, 1965-66; prelate Diocese of Armenians in Iran and India, Isfahan, Iran, 1974-77; consecrated bishop, 1977, consecrated archbishop, 1983; prelate Armenian Apostolic Ch. of Am., Eastern States and Can., N.Y.C., 1978—; pres. Armenian Diocese, U.S., Can., 1978. Editor: Hask monthly, 1966-70, Deghegadou, 1976-77, The Holy Week in the Armenian Church Tradition, 1978, Unpublished Papers and Works of Mesrob Taliatine, 1979. Pres. Land and Culture Orgn., N.Y.C., 1980—. Decorated grand protector Order Hospitallers St. George of Carinthea. Mem. Asia Soc., World Coun. Chs., Princeton Club, Icomos Club. Office: 138 E 39th St New York NY 10016

ASHLEY, WILLARD WALDEN C., SR., minister; b. N.Y.C., Nov. 16, 1953; s. Will and Clara (Peterkin) A.; m. Veronica Lamb, June, 1975 (div. Sept., 1976); 1 child, Willard W. C. Ashley, Jr.; m. Diane Theresa Manning, Sept. 29, 1979. AAS, Fashion Inst. Tech., N.Y.C., 1974; BA, Montclair (N.J.) State Coll., 1981; MDiv, Andover Newton Sch. Theol., 1984, postgrad. studies, 1989—. Ordained to ministry Am. Bapt. Ch., 1982. Seminarian First Bapt. Ch., Tewksbury, Mass., 1981-82; pastor New Hope Bapt. Ch., Portsmouth, N.H., 1982-84; asst. dean students, dir. recruitment Andover Newton Theol. Sch., Newton, Mass., 1984-86; pastor Monumental Bapt. Ch., Jersey City, N.J., 1986—; mem. Am. Bapt. Statement of Concerns Com., 1988-90, North N.J. Missionary Bapt. Assn., 1988—; co-chmn. Interfaith Community Orgn., Jersey City, strategy team, 1988—, Indsl. Areas Found., Nat. Leaders Team, 1991—. Preacher weekly radio program WNJR, Hillside, N.J., 1987—. Bd. dirs. Visiting Homemakers of Hudson, Jersey City, 1988—, YMCA of Jersey City, 1989. Recipient Montclair State Coll. award, 1981, H. Otherman Smith Preaching award, 1984, Citation, Phi Delta Kapppa, 1989, Appreciation award, Alpha Kappa Alpha, 1990, Humanitarian award, Nat. Conf. Christians and Jews. Mem. Clin. Pastoral Edn., Ministers Coun. Am. Bapt. Ch. Home: 16 Krueger Ct Society Hill at University Hts Newark NJ 07103 Office: Monumental Bapt Ch 121-127 Lafayette St Jersey City NJ 07304

ASHLOCK, BRUCE E., minister; b. Phila., July 18, 1948; s. Charles Edward and Ruth (Leber) A. BS in Bible, Phila. Coll. Bible, 1971. Ordained to ministry United Ch. of Christ. Mem. staff Highlands Youth for Christ, Elkins, W.Va., 1972-73; dir. Butler County Youth for Christ, Hamilton, Ohio, 1973-79; pastor Fairview United Ch. of Christ, Georgetown, Ohio, 1987—. Home and Office: 10888 US Hwy 68 Georgetown OH 45121

ASHLOCK, JAMES ALLEN, minister; b. Flint, Mich., Aug. 10, 1955; s. James Andrew and Lowanda June (Proctor) A.; m. Mary Beth Wood, Aug. 20, 1977; children—Sarah Elizabeth, Jason Ashlock. B.S., Freed-Hardeman Coll. Ordained minister Church of Christ, 1977. Minister, Church of Christ, Bay, Ark., 1977-87, Collinsville, Ill., 1987-88, minister Main St. Ch. of Christ, Walnut Ridge, Ark., 1988—; tchr. Ch. of Christ Coll., Paragould, Arks., 1984; radio and TV speaker Northeast Ark.; lectr. in field. Author publs. in field; editor weekly religious jours. Dir. Craighead Country Youth Orgn. Named Outstanding Young Men Am., 1981, 83, 86; recipient Cert. Appreciation Freed-Hardeman Coll., 1977, Outstanding Service award, 1977; Appreciation award Soc. Disting. High Sch. Students, 1985, 86. Mem. Crowleys Ridge Acad. (plaque 1983), Am. Philatelic Soc. Republican. Avocations: stamp collecting; hiking; swimming; fishing. Home: 123 Fontaine Walnut Ridge AR 72476 *The whole purpose of life is to glorify God. The more we glorify God, the better our life will be.*

ASHLOCK, KEN, religious organization administrator. V.p. Am. Bapt. Assn., Garland, Tex., then pres., 1988—. Office: Am Bapt Assn 333 W Centerville Rd Garland TX 75041

ASHMAN, CHARLES HENRY, minister; b. Johnstown, Pa., June 1, 1924; s. Charles H. Sr. and Flora (Brown) A.; m. Frances Marie Bradley, July 12, 1946; children: Kenneth W., Judy Ashman Fairman, Karl W. BA cum laude, Westmont Coll., 1947; MDiv magna cum laude, Grace Theol. Seminary, Winona Lake, Ind., 1950. Ordained to ministry Ch. of Brethren. Sr. pastor Grace Brethren Ch., Rittman, Ohio, 1950-55, Phoenix, 1955-62, Winona Lake, Ind., 1962-89; fellowship coord. Fellowship of Grace Brethren Chs., Winona Lake, 1979—; prof. Grace Theol. Seminary, 1969-89.; bd. dirs. Grace Village, Winona Lake. Mem. Nat. Fellowship Grace Brethren Ministers (pres. 1984, Pastor of Yr. 1989, moderator nat. conf. 1973-74), Kiwanis (pres. 1991-92). Home: 1531 S Cherry Creek Ln Winona Lake IN 46580 Office: Fellowship Grace Brethren Churches PO Box 386 Winona Lake IN 46590

ASHMAN, JOYCE ELAINE, lay church worker; b. Peru, Ind., June 17, 1939; d. Robert Allen and Bernice (Miller) A. Student, Internat. Bus. Sch., Ft. Wayne, Ind., 1957-58. Mem. ch. choir Winona Lake Grace Brethren Ch., 1959—, mem. Sunday sch. secretarial staff, 1965—; nat. pres. Sisterhood of Mary and Martha, Nat. Fellowship Bretheran Chs., 1960-64, fin. sec.-treas., 1964-68, fin. sec.-treas. Women's Missionary Coun., 1971—; bookkeeper Grace Schs., Winona Lake, Ind., 1961-90; sec. Jefferson Elem. Sch., Winona Lake, 1991—. Mem. Christian Bus. and Profl. Women (chmn. name tag and prayer favor 1968-69, 76-77, treas. 1970-71, 80-81, telephone chmn. 1972-73, 78-79, 90-91, chmn. decorations 1974-75, ticket chmn. 1982, music chmn. 1983, contact adviser 1984). Home: 602 Chestnut Ave Winona Lake IN 46590

ASHPOLE, WILLIAM EMORY, minister; b. Buffalo Center, Iowa, June 3, 1929; s. Harold Lester and Emily Jane (Hays) A.; m. Bonnie Lou Mundale, Oct. 16, 1950; children: Bryan Lee, Brenda Kay, Bradley Chris, Brent Harold. BA in Theology, N. Cen. Bible Coll., Mpls., 1971; student, Ark. Stte Coll. Lic. to ministry Assemblies of God, 1950, ordained, 1956. Pastor Horatio (Ark.) Assembly of God, 1950-51, Montevideo (Minn.) Assembly of God, 1954-59, Redwood Falls (Minn.) Assembly of God, 1959-60, Portia (Ark.) Assembly of God, 1960-62, Bay Village (Ark.) Assembly of God, 1962-64, Montevideo Assembly of God, 1964-67, Aloha Assembly of God, Lihue, Hawaii, 1967-78, Faith Assembly of God, Mililani, Hawaii, 1978—; dir., teen challenge pres. Home Mission, Mililani, 1978—; asst. supt. Hawaii Assemblies of God, Honolulu, 1978—, Christian Edn. dir., 1969-78, presbyter (Kauai), 1967-69; evangelist, dir. Youth with a Mission, 1964-65; short-term missionary evangelist Philippines, Guam, P.R., Tonga, Samoa, Ponape; coord. Hawaii Coll. Fund, 1978—; contact pastor Mil. Ministry, 1978—. Chaplain (Maj.) Civil Air Patrol, 1969-74; precinct chmn. Rep. Party, Wahiawa, 1988. Mem. Chi Alpha (com. mem. 1978—). Home: 57 Ilima St Wahiawa HI 96786 Office: Faith Assembly of God 95-121 Waimakua Dr Mililani HI 96789 *Forty-one years of my ministry have come and gone, but what I count most dear to my life is what I have done for Jesus, my Lord.*

ASKEW, MICHAEL EUGENE, SR., minister; b. Dayton, Ohio, Aug. 14, 1957; s. Jake L. and Delores (Askew) Whelchel; m. Renee Taylor, Aug. 18, 1977 (div. Mar. 1984); children: Dewayne L., Donte L.; m. Gloria Walker, Nov. 27, 1987; children: Michael Jr., Marcus. BA, Lane Coll., 1980; MDiv, McCormick Theol. Sem., Chgo., 1985. Ordained to ministry Presbyn. Ch. (U.S.A.), 1988. Student min. 6th Grace Presbyn. Ch., Chgo., 1982-83, Bellwood (Ill.) Presbyn. Ch., 1983-84; intern min. 7th Presbyn. Ch., Chgo., 1984-85; supply pastor United Ch. Atgeld Gardens, Chgo., 1986-88; pastor Reid Meml. Presbyn. Ch., Mooresville, N.C., 1988—. V.p., mem. edn. com. NAACP, Mooresville, 1991; bd. dirs. Mooresville/Lake Norman Habitat for Humanity. Recipient Religious Affairs award Las Amous, 1991. Mem. Mooresville Ministerial Assn. (chaplain 1989-90), Salem-Presbytery Assn., Gamma Phi Psi. Democrat. Home: 270 E Mclelland Ave Mooresville NC 28115

ASMA, LAWRENCE FRANCIS, priest; b. Waukegan, Ill., Oct. 21, 1947; s. Francis Victor and Isabelle Amelia (Recktenwald) A. BA in English, U. Wis., Whitewater, 1969; MA in English, Ill. State U., 1974; MA in Scripture magna cum laude, De Andreis Sem., 1982, MDiv, 1983. Ordained priest Roman Cath. Chr., 1983. Dir. spritual formation Cardinal Glennon Coll., St. Louis, 1983-85, instr. theology dept., 1983-85; chaplain St. Vincent's Div. DePaul Health Ctr., St. Louis, 1985—; Bd. dirs. Rosati Stabilization Ctr., St. Louis, 1988—; v-chmn. Rosati Stabilization Ctr., 1990—. with USNR, 1970-72, Vietnam. Mem. Assn. Mental Health Clergy, Cath. Biblical Assn., Congregation of Mission, Sigma Tau Delta. Avocations: ornithology, photography, drawing. Office: DePaul Health Center 12303 DePaul Dr Bridgeton MO 63044

ASONSKY, GEORGE (BISHOP GREGORY OF SITKA), bishop; Bishop Orthodox Ch. Am., Sitka, Alaska. Office: Orthodox Church in Am St Michael's Cathedral Box 697 Sitka AK 99835

ASTRACHAN, GEORGE JULES, rabbi; b. Rochester, N.Y., Oct. 16, 1939; s. Louis And Esther T. (Beckler) A.; m. Rita Faye Yamin, Dec. 23, 1962; children: Bruce, Jeffrey. BA, Miami U., 1961; B. Hebrew Letters, Hebrew Union Coll., 1965, MA Hebrew Letters, 1969. Ordained rabbi, 1967. Rabbi Temple Beth El, Glens Falls, N.Y., 1969-72, Temple B'nai Israel, Elmont, N.Y., 1972-79, Temple Sinai, Cranston, R.I., 1979—; treas. R.I. Religious Coalition for Abortion Rights, 1990—; mem. AIDS task force R.I. Coun. Chs., Providence, 1988—; pres. Cranston (R.I.) Clergy Assn., 1985-87. Sec. R.I. Mental Health Svcs., Johnston, 1990—. Mem. Cen. Conf. Am. Rabbis (com. on retirement 1990-91), R.I. Bd. Rabbis (pres. 1988—), Masons. Office: Temple Sinai 30 Hagen Ave Cranston RI 02920

ATEN, GARY JON, minister; b. Ragan, Nebr., Sept. 4, 1938; s. Roy Wallace and Elizabeth (Bielefeld) A.; m. Caroline Jane Skopec, Aug. 13, 1961. BSc, U. Nebr., 1960; BD, Garrett Sch. Theology, 1963. Ordained to ministry United Meth. Ch., 1965. Minister Meth. Ch., Lodgepole, Nebr., 1963-67, various Meth. chs., 1967-78, Columbus Parish, Silver Creek, Nebr., 1978-83, Custer Parish, Merna, Nebr., 1983-86, Christ Meml. United Meth. Ch., Bloomfield, Nebr., 1986—; Mem. Conf. Coun. on Ministries, Lincoln, Nebr., 1988—; mem. Dist. Com. of Ordained MInistry, Norfolk, Nebr., 1988—; pres. Lewis & Clark Lake Ministries, Nebr., 1989—; mem. Conf. Com. on Planning and Rsch., Nebr., 1988—. Author ch. sch. materials. Bd. dirs. Bloomfield City Libr., 1990—, County Extension Svc., Knox County, Nebr., 1990—, Extension Program Unit, Knox, Holt and Keha Paha Counties, 1990—. Mem. Christian Educator's Fellowship, Nebr. Christian Educator's Fellowship (past pres.), Nebr. Assn. County Extension Bd. Mems., Ruritan. Home: PO Box 130 Bloomfield NE 68718 Office: Christ Meml United Meth Ch PO Box 130 Bloomfield NE 68718 *My goal is to be the best I can be with God's help so that I can help others be the best they can be.*

ATHANASSOULAS, SOTIRIOS (BISHOP SOTIRIOS OF TORONTO), bishop; b. Epirus, Greece, Feb. 19, 1936; s. George and Anastasia A. B.D., U. Athens, 1961; M.A., U. Montreal Scis. Religieuses, 1971. Ordained priest Greek Orthodox Ch., 1962; priest St. George Ch., Edmonton, Alta., Can., 1962-65, St. George Cathedral, Montreal, Que., Can., 1965-73; consecrated bishop, 1973; bishop of Toronto, Ont., Can., 1979—; head Greek Orthodox Ch. of Can., 1979—; mem. archdiocese council Greek Orthodox Archdiocese, 1968—, pres. diocesan council, 1974, mem. holy synod, 1977—, mem. archdiocese council, 1968, pres. diocesan council, 1974—; mem. exec. com. Can. Council Chs., 1974—; hon. pres. Thalassemia Found., 1975—; mem. Presbyters Council, 1970-73. Vice pres. Christian Pavilion, Expo 67; mem. governing council U. Toronto, 1975-78. Recipient Centennial medal of Can., 1967. Address: Greek Orthodox Diocese, 27 Teddington Park Ave, Toronto, ON Canada M4N 2C4

ATHANS, SISTER MARY CHRISTINE, church history educator; b. Joliet, Ill., Apr. 7, 1932; d. Christophil Nicholas and Mary Elizabeth (Anderson) A. BS in Humanities, Loyola U., Chgo., 1954; MA in History, Cath. U. Am., 1966; MA in Theology, U. San Francisco, 1975; Licentiate in Sacred Theology, Jesuit Sch. Theology, Berkeley, Calif., 1982; PhD in Hist. Theology, Grad. Theol. Union, Berkeley, Calif., 1982. Joined Sisters of Charity of Blessed Virgin Mary, Roman Cath. Ch., 1955. Exec. dir. N. Phoenix Corp. Ministry, 1970-76; asst. acad. dean/dean students Sch. Theology, Claremont, Calif., 1979-80; adj. faculty U. San Francisco and U. Santa Clara, 1980-82; asst. prof. religious studies U. Ill., Urbana-Champaign, 1982-84; assoc. prof. ch. history The St. Paul Sem. Sch. of Div., U. St. Thomas, St. Paul, 1984—; mem. numerous religious and civic bds. and commns. Author: The Coughlin-Fahey Connection: Father Charles E. Coughlin, Father Denis Fahey C.S.Sp., and Religious Anti-Semitism in the United States, 1938-54, 1991; contbr. articles to profl. jours. bd. dirs. Minn. Interreligious Com., Mpls.; mem. Com. on Cath.-Jewish Rels., Archdiocese of St. Paul and Mpls., 1987—; trustee Mundelein Coll., Chgo., 1984-87, Grad. Theol. Union, Berkeley, 1978-79. Recipient Humanitarian of Yr. award B'nai B'rith, Phoenix, 1974; Inst. for Ecumenical and Cultural Rsch. fellow, 1990. Mem. Am. Acad. Religion, Am. Cath. Hist. Assn., Cath. Theol. Soc. Am., U.S. Cath. Hist. Soc., Phi Alpha Theta. Democrat. Office: U St Thomas Sch Div 2260 Summit Ave Saint Paul MN 55105

ATHAS, ROBERT THOMAS, priest; b. N.Y.C., Oct. 22, 1946; s. Louis and Joy Julia (Alt) A.; m. Anthe Joy Demeter, June 3, 1972; children Zoe, Anastasios. BA, Hellenic Coll., 1968; postgrad., Holy Cross U., Boston, 1968-69, N.Y. Theol. Sem., 1969-70; MDiv., St. Vladimir's, 1974. Ordained Deacon Greek Orthodox Ch., 1972, Priest, 1974. Priest St. Spyridon Ch., Newport, R.I., 1974-76, St. Peter Ch., Danville, Va., 1976-80, St. Nicholas Ch., Babylon, N.Y., 1980-81, St. George Ch., Albuquerque, 1981-83, Holy Trinity Ch., Tulsa, 1983—; Deacon St. Michaels Home, Yonkers, N.Y., 1972-74; mem. task force on energy and ecology Va. Council of Chs., 1976-80, task force on faith and order N.Mex. council on Chs., Albuquerque, 1981-83; bd. dirs. Tulsa Met. Ministry, 1984—. Vol., chmn. bd. Helpline, Danville, Va., 1977-80; bd. dirs. Domestic Violence Emergency Services, Danville, 1979-80.

ATHENS, ANDREW A., steel company executive. Chmn., pres., chief exec. officer Matron Steel Corp., Chgo.; pres. archdiocesan coun. Greek Orthodox Archdiocese of N. and S.Am., 1987&. Office: Metron Steel Corp 12900 S Metron Dr Chicago IL 60633 also: Greek Orthodox Archdiocese North & South Am 8-10 E 79th St New York NY 10021

ATKINS, CHRIS ALAN, pastor, educator; b. Redbud, Ill., Sept. 19, 1954; s. Robert Atkins and Bettie Jean (Hawkins) Cave; m. Eunice Laura Thorup, Aug. 3, 1979; children: Christopher Ryan, Jonathan Scott, Andrew Michael, Jennifer Lauren. Student, Cen. Mo. State U., 1972-73; BA, Calvary Bible Coll., Kansas City, Mo., 1979; ThM, Dallas Theol. Seminary, 1985; postgrad., Pensacola Christian Coll., 1989—. Ordained to ministry Gen. Conf. Mennonite Ch., 1988. Intern Grace Community Ch., L.A., 1979; tchr. 1st Bapt. Ch., Dallas, 1981-85; sr. pastor 1st Mennonite Ch., Clinton, Okla., 1985—; founder Western Okla. Christian Sch., Clinton, 1987—, chmn. bd.; del. Congress on Bible, San Diego, 1982, Congress on Bibl. Exposition, Anaheim, Calif., 1986; assoc. Mennonite Bibl. Sem., 1988. Chaplain Clinton Regional Hosp.; active Custer County Rep. Exec. Com., Clinton. Named one of Outstanding Young Men Am., 1987. Mem. Evangel. Theol. Soc. Home: 432 S 7th St Clinton OK 73601 Office: 1st Mennonite Ch 700 S 19th St Clinton OK 73601 *The grace and glory of God are undoubtedly the supreme themes of the biblical revelation. It is in the ineffable person and work of Jesus Christ this self-motived, active, stooping grace finds its highest manifestation. Accordingly the writer to Hebrews states that Jesus Christ is the "radiance of His glory." To know by experience the riches of His grace is to live life unto His glory.*

ATKINS, ROBERT ALAN, JR., pastor; b. Dallas, Oct. 7, 1949; s. Robert Alan and Dorothy (Bradley) A.; m. Marlene Fredette Atkins, Nov. 20, 1971; children: Christina Lynn, Matthew William. BA in Philosophy, Elmhurst (Ill.) Coll., 1971; MA in Theatre, Northwestern U., 1973; MDiv, Garrett Evang. Seminary, Evanston, Ill., 1977, PhD in Bible, 1987. Ordained elder, 1982. Pastor Malden (Ill.) United Meth. Ch., 1980-84, Christ United Meth. Ch., Rockford, Ill., 1984—; chair bd. evangelism No. Ill. Conf., 1986-88. Contbr. articles to profl. jours. Chair Coun. Community Svcs., Princeton, Ill., 1983-84, Rockford Area Substance Abuse Coun., 1989. Mem. Soc. Bibl.

Lit., Cath. Bibl. Assn., Lions (dir. Malden chpt. 1983-84). Office: Christ United Meth Ch 4509 Highcrest Rd Rockford IL 61107

ATKINS, THOMAS KENT, foundation executive, minister; b. Tyler, Tex., Apr. 21, 1947; s. Priscilla Dean (More) A.; m. Mary Helen White, Dec. 21, 1974; 1 child, Amy Elizabeth. BA, Dallas Bapt. U., 1974; MDiv, Southwestern Bapt. Theol. Sem., 1976; PhD, U. Tex., Dallas, 1981; D Ministry (hon.), Bapt. Sem. Rio de Janeiro, 1990. Ordained to ministry So. Bapt. Conv., 1974. Asst. prof. Dallas Bapt. U., 1976-80, v.p., 1984-86; pastor Univ. Bapt. Ch., Lake Charles, La., 1980-84; pres. S.W. Ednl. Media Found., Dallas, 1984—; trustee Caprock Ednl. Broadcasting, Amarillo, Tex., 1987-90. Author: In The Eye Of The Storm, 1981; contbr. articles to various jours. Mem. Soc. Broadcast Engrs. Office: SW Ednl Media Found 2921 Brown Trail Ste 140 Bedford TX 76021

ATKINSON, KATHLEEN LOIS, nun; b. Bismarck, N.D., Dec. 4, 1955; d. Myron and Marjorie Lois (Barth) A. BS in Edn., U. Mary, Bismarck, 1977; MA in Religious Edn., St. John's U., Collegeville, Minn., 1990. Joined Order of St. Benedict, Roman Cath. Ch., 1979. Tchr. St. Mary's Grade Sch., Bismarck, 1978-81, St. Mary's High Sch., Bismarck, 1981-85, Ryan High Sch., Minot, N.D., 1985-86, Trinity High Sch., Dickinson, N.D., 1986-87; dir. campus ministry U. Mary, Bismarck, 1987—; pres. Diocesan Sister's Coun., N.D., 1986-90; mem. Diocesan Youth Commn., N.D., 1984-90. Mem. CROP Walk for Hunger, Bismarck, 1989—; mem. Martin Luther King Meml. Bd., Bismarck, 1988-89. Named Outstanding Adminstr., Student Body of U. Mary, 1989-90. Mem. Cath. Campus Ministry Assn., Toastmasters. Republican. Office: Univ of Mary 7500 University Dr Bismarck ND 58504

ATKINSON, ROBERT POLAND, bishop; b. Washington, Nov. 16, 1927; s. William Henry and Anna P. Atkinson; m. Rosemary Clemence, Aug. 8, 1953. BA, U. Va., 1950; BD, Va. Theol. Sem., 1953, DD, 1973. Ordained to ministry Episcopal Ch. Rector, Ch. of Fairmont, 1955-58, Trinity Ch., Huntington, W.Va., 1958-64, W.Va. Bd. Examining Chaplains, 1958-62; chmn. BEC, 1958-64; rector Calvary of Memphis, 1964-73; bishop, co-adjutor, W. Va., 1973-76; bishop of W. Va., Charleston, 1976-89; asst. bishop of Va., 1989—. Chmn. bd. trustees Va. Theol. Sem., 1985—; pres. W.Va. Coun. Chs., 1985-87. Address: Diocese of Va 51 Cantenbury Rd Charlottesville VA 22901

ATTER, GORDON FRANCIS, minister; b. Abingdon, Ont., Can., Nov. 13, 1905; s. Arthur Manley and Jessie Mernelva (Snyder) A.; m. Margaret Hope McKinney, Apr. 2, 1940; 1 child, Arthur James. Student, Can. Pentecostal Bible Coll., Winnipeg, Man., 1928; D Sacred Lit., Trinity So. Bible Coll. and Sem., 1963. Ordained to ministry Pentecostal Assemblies Can., 1929. Pastor chs. Ont., 1925-26, 33-56, Sask., Can., 1928-29, Alta., Can., 1930-32; prof. Ea. Pentecostal Bible Coll., Petersborough, Ont., 1956-72; asst. dist. supt. Western Ont. Conf. Pentecostal Assemblies Can., 1942-54, mem. gen. exec. com., 1946-54. Author: Messages for the Last Days, 1954, Rivers of Blessing, 1960, The Students' Handbook on Divine Healing, 1960, Friendship, Courtship and Marriage, 1961, The Third Force, 1962, God's Financial Plan, 1962, Cults and Heresies, 1963, Interpreting the Scriptures, 1964, Rethinking Bible Prophecy, 1967, Down Memory's Lane, 1974; editor Full Gospel Adv., 1945-54, Glad Tidings Messenger, 1955-57. Mem. Nat. Geog. Soc., Can. Wild Life Fedn. Home: 6042 Murray St Ste 210, Niagara Falls, ON Canada L2G 2K3 Office: Pentecostal Assemblies Can, 6745 Century Ave, Mississauga, ON Canada L5N 6P7 *In these changing and sometimes unsettled times of human history it is important to know the God of the Bible and to uphold the basic standards of Christian faith as expressed in the "Ten Commandments" and in the " Sermon on the Mount."*

AU, LAWRENCE, minister; b. Nanjing, Peoples Republic of China, Jan. 14, 1938; came to U.S., 1967; s. Kaying and Waichun (Lee) A.; married; 1 child, Lorenzo. BTh, Hong Kong Bapt. Theol., Seminary, 1963; BS, U. San Francisco, 1979; MA, MDiv, Golden Gate Bapt. Theol., Seminary, Mill Valley, Calif., 1969, 1972, D of Ministry, 1975. Cert. counselor, adminstr., Calif.; ordained to ministry Chinese Bapt. Ch., 1967. Pastor First Bapt. Ch., Macao, 1963-65, Ipoh, Malaysia, 1965-67; pastor First Chinese So. Bapt. Ch., San Francisco, 1967-84; pres. Christian Witness Theol. Seminary, Berkeley, Calif., 1984-88; pastor San Bruno (Calif.) Chinese Bapt. Ch., 1988—; adv. pastor San Francisco Mandarin Bapt. Ch., 1984-88; moderator San Francisco So. Bapt. Assn, 1978-80; com. chmn. Calif. So. Bapt. State Conv., Fresno, 1979-82, teller, L.A., 1981; trustee/chmn. San Francisco Chinese Childrens Choir, 1984-90; commd. chaplain San Francisco Police Dept., 1983—. Author/translator: Baptist Church Manual, 1982; translator Calif. Bar, 1991. Charter mem. Rep. Presdl. Task Force, Washington, 1982, mem. Rep. Nat. Com., 1990, Rep. Senatorical Inner Circle, Washington, 1990; com. chmn. Calif. State Ednl. Dept., Sacramento; co-chmn. Pete Wilson for Gov., San Francisco, 1990; diplomate World Jewish Congress, 1990—; leader San Francisco Internat. Airport Aircrash Team, 1989—. Recipient certs. Appreciation, Fgn. Mission Bd./So. Bapt. Conv., Richmond, Va., 1970, 81, Civil Air Patrol/USAF, San Francisco, 1978, Calif. State Edn. Dept., Sacramento, 1988, San Francisco So. Bapt. Assn., 1990, medal of Merit Rep. Presdl. Task Force, 1986, 89. Mem. Internat. Conf. Police Chaplains, Am. Assn. Christian Counselors, San Francisco Assn. Evangelicals, World Affairs Coun., others. Home: 639 38th Ave San Francisco CA 94121-2617 Office: San Bruno Chinese Bapt Church 250 Courtland Dr San Bruno CA 94066 *There are two kinds of builders: some are wall builders and the others are bridge builders.*

AU, WILLIAM AUGUST, III, priest, public relations director; b. Phillipsburg, N.J., Jan. 12, 1949; s. William August Au and Annabell Agnes (Lawler) Penyak. BA in Philosophy, St. Mary's Seminary, Balt., 1971; STM, St. Mary's Sch. Theology, Balt., 1975; PhD in Ch. History, The Cath. U. Am., 1983. Assoc. pastor SS Philip & James Ch., Balt., 1975-78; doctoral student The Catholic U. Am., Washington, 1978-83; resident asst. St Dominic's Ch., Balt., 1978-80; chaplain Cardinal Shehan Ctr. for the Aging, Balt., 1980-83; assoc. pastor Most Precious Blood Ch., Balt., 1983-84, St. Clare Ch., Balt., 1984-86; cons. justice and peace commn. Archdiocese of Balt., 1983-84, asst. chancellor, 1984-86, dir. pub. rels., 1986—; mem. editorial bd. The U.S. Cath. Historian. Author: (book) The Cross, The Flag and the Bomb, 1984; author:(with others) Papal Teaching on War and Peace, 1985. Recipient Thomas Shahan award The Catholic Univ. Am., Washington, 1983. Mem. Am. Cath. Hist. Soc., Pub. Relations Soc. Am., Balt. Pub. Relations Soc. Democrat. Roman Catholic. Avocations: reading, hiking. Home: 1402 Bolton St Baltimore MD 21217 Office: Office of Pub Rels The Cath Ctr 320 Cathedral St Baltimore MD 21201

AUDET, LEONARD, theologian; b. Maria, Que., Can., Nov. 26, 1932; s. Ernest and Emilie (Loubert) A. DTh, U. Montreal, 1964; Licence en Ecriture Sainte, Pontificium Institutum Biblicum, Rome, 1964. Prof. Scolasticat de Theologie de Joliette, Que., Can., 1965-67; prof. Bible, Faculty of Theology U. Montreal, 1967-77, 85—, dean Faculty of Theology, 1977-85; superior gen. Clerics of St. Viator, 1988—. Author: Résurrection: Espérance humaine et don de Dieu, 1971, Jésus? de l'histoire à la foi, 1974, Neuve est ta Parole, 1974, Apres Jesus, Autorite et Liberte dans le peuple de Dieu, 1977, A Companion to Paul, 1975, Vivante est ta parole, 1975, Je crois en Dieu, 1989. Mem. Can. Cath. Soc. of the Bible, Can. Soc. Theology, Cath. Assn. Bibl. Study of Can. (treas. 1968-77). Home: Chierici di San Viatore, Casella Postale 10793, 00144 Rome Italy

AUDET, RENE, bishop; b. Montreal, Que., Can., Jan. 18, 1920; s. Louis Napoleon and Marie-Louise (Blais) A. Student, St. Ignace Coll., 1936-41, Brebeuf Coll., 1941-43; B.A., Montreal U., 1943; postgrad., Immaculate Conception Scolasticate, 1943-48; B.Sc. in Sociology, St. Louis U., 1953, M.A., 1955. Ordained priest Roman Catholic Ch., 1948; curate St. Joseph's Ch., Rouyn, Que., 1948-51; chaplain Syndicates, 1948-51, Youville Hosp., Noranda, Que., 1951-52; curate Kirkland Lake, Ont., 1952-55; diocesan procurator Bishop's House, Timmins, Ont., 1955-63; chaplain St. Mary's Acad., Haileybury, Ont., 1955-63; aux. bishop of Ottawa, Ont., Can., 1963; consecrated bishop, 1963; vicar gen. of Ottawa, 1963-68; bishop of Joliette, Que., 1968-90; ret., 1990. Lodges: Optimists, K.C. Home: 2 St Charles Borromeo N, Joliette, PQ Canada J6E 6H6 Office: Bishop's House, Joliette, PQ Canada J6E 6H6

AUDLIN, JAMES DAVID (DISTANT EAGLE), minister, writer; b. Alexandria Bay, N.Y., Sept. 19, 1954; s. David John Sr. and Eleanor May (Vock) A.; m. Lisa Manthei, Dec. 27, 1975; children: Katharine Manthei Audlin, John William Manthei Audlin. BA magna cum laude, Eisenhower Coll., 1975; MDiv, Andover Newton (Mass.) Theol., 1978. Asst. pastor Union United Ch. of Christ, Newton, 1975-78; pastor East Congl. United Ch. of Christ, Concord, N.H., 1978-82; sr. pastor North Madison Cong. United Ch. of Christ, Madison, Conn., 1982—; del. Gen. Synod United Ch. of Christ, 1989—; worship leader Free Cherokee Nation, Mechanicsville, Md., 1989—, area chief New Eng./N.Y. region, 1990—; Dharma tchr. Kwan Um Zen Sch. Author: Moths the Seek the Moon, and Other Dreams, 1990, (novels) A Stitch in Time, 1990, A Mirror Filled with Light, 1990, The Productions of Time, 1990, The Wings of the Morning, 1990, The Voice of Day, 1990; author poetry; contbr. numerous articles to profl. jours. Mem. Conn. Assn. for Jungian Psychology, Sci. Fiction Writers Am., Sci. Fiction Poetry Assn., Free Cherokee Nation, Conn. Conf. Dept. Ch. and Soc., Shoreline Interfaith Coun. Office: 1271 Durham Rd Madison CT 06443 *Human beings, like spokes on a wheel, begin from many different beginnings, but seek the same ineffable goal. In my involvement with many religious faiths, I seek to encourage others to find value in them all. In my creative writings, I try to enliven indescribable truth in the sanctity of archetypal stories.*

AUE, CRAIG S., minister; b. Detroit, Dec. 10, 1954; s. Arnold E. and Shirley J. (Gibson) A.; m. Pamela Jean Willwerth, Aug. 12, 1978; children: J. Taylor, Ashley E. BS, Cen. Mich. U., 1978; MDiv, Louisville Presbyn. Theol., 1982. Ordained to ministry Presbyn. Ch. (USA). Pastor Blue Ball Presbyn. Ch., Middletown, Ohio, 1982-89, Starr Presbyn. Ch., Royal Oak, Mich., 1989—. Trustee Middletown Pastoral Counseling, 1985-89. Office: Starr Presbyn Ch 1717 W 13 Mile Rd Royal Oak MI 48073

AUER, ALFONS, theology educator; b. Schönebürg, Baden-Württemberg, Germany, Feb. 12, 1915; s. Gustav Jakob and Ursula (Münst) A. Diploma in Theology, U. Tübingen, Germany, 1938, D in Theology, 1947; habilitation, U. Tuebingen, 1953. Curate Diocese Rottenburg-Stuttgart, Stuttgart-Bad Cannstatt, Germany, 1939-44, dir. Cath. acad., 1953-55; asst. Theologenkonvikt, Tübingen, 1944-45; studentenpfarrer U Tübingen, 1945-53, prof., 1966-81, prof. emeritus, 1981—; prof. U. Würzburg, 1955-66; cons. Bundesfamilienministerium, Bonn, Fed. Republic Germany, 1960-63, Papal Comm. for Family Planning, Rome, 1964-66, German Conf. Bishops, Bonn, 1978-83, Wissenschaftsministerium, Stuttgart, 1972—. Author 7 books; editor 4 books; contbr. articles to profl. jours. lectr. ethical theology varius European countries and Jerusalem. Recipient Verdienstorden award Land Baden-Württemberg, 1984. Avocations: traveling, reading. Home: Paul Lechler Strasse 8, D-7400 Tübingen Federal Republic of Germany Office: Kath Theology Seminar, Liebermeisterstrasse 12, D-7400 Tübingen Federal Republic of Germany *Wer ein erfülltes Alter erreichen will, muss im kontreten Alltag die ihm verbleibenden Chancen wahrnemhen, die ihm auferlegten Zumutungen ertragen und die ihm geschenkten Erfüllungen auskosten.*

AUERBACH, DAVID HILLEL, rabbi; b. Montreal, Que., Can., May 26, 1938; came to U.S., 1959; s. Jack and Jennie (Freeman) A.; m. Gloria Rita Bassel, June 30, 1963 (dec. Mar. 1978); children: Lianne, Jonathan, Jennifer. BA, McGill U., 1959; M. Hebrew Lit., Jewish Theol. Sem., 1963, DD, 1991. Ordained rabbi, 1965. Rabbi Shaar Shalom Congregation, Chomedey, Que., 1965-70; assoc. rabbi Ahavath Achim Synagogue, Atlanta, 1970-81; rabbi Beth David Congregation, Miami, Fla., 1981-85, Bet Shira Congregation, Miami, 1985—. Recipient Reunited Jerusalem award State of Israel Bonds, 1977. Mem. Rabbinical Assembly (exec. coun. 1983—, pres. S.E. region 1982-84), Greater Miami Rabbinical Assn. Democrat. Office: Bet Shira Congregation 7500 SW 120th St Miami FL 33156

AUGSBURGER, AARON DONALD, clergyman; b. Elida, Ohio, Dec. 21, 1925; s. C.A. and Estella R. (Shenk) A.; m. Martha L. Kling, June 5, 1948; children: Phyllis Augsburger Ressler, Patricia Augsburger Blum, Don Richard. BA, Mennonite Coll., 1949; M in Religion Edn., Ea. Bapt. Sem., 1956; DEd, Temple U., 1963. Ordained to ministry Mennonite Ch., 1951. Mem. pers. and student svcs. coms. Mennonite Bd. Missions and Charities, 1954-70; pastor students, tchr. Christian edn. Ea. Mennonite Coll., Harrisonburg, Va., 1958-64; asst. dean Goshen (Ind.) Sem., 1964-65; pastor, bishop North Goshen (Ind.) Mennonite Ch., 1965-70; tchr. psychology Goshen (Ind.) Coll., 1965-67; pastor Park View Mennonite Ch., Harrisonburg, 1974-80; prof. Ea. Mennonite Sem., 1980-89; pastor Bahia Vista Mennonite Ch., Sarasota, Fla., 1989—. Author: Creating Christian Personality, 1966; editor: Marriages That Work, 1984. Guidance counsellor Bethany Christian High Sch., Goshen, 1966-68, supt., 1968-70; mem. Mennonite Comm. for Christian Edn.; moderator Gen. Assembly of Mennonite Chs., 1971-73. Home: 1304 Oak View Dr Sarasota FL 34232 Office: Bahia Vista Mennonite Ch 4041 Bahia Vista St Sarasota FL 34232

AULL, JAMES STROUD, bishop; b. Winnsboro, S.C., Mar. 3, 1931; s. Luther Bachman and Ruth (Bull) A.; m. Virginal Kloeppel, Aug. 9, 1958; children: Diane, James Jr. (dec.), Virginia Ruth. AB magna cum laude, Newberry Coll., 1953; MDiv cum laude, Luth. Theol. So. Sem., Columbia, S.C., 1960; M in Systematic Theology, Luth. Sch. Theology, Chgo., 1970; PhD, Duke U., 1971; DD (hon.), Newberry Coll., 1988. Pastor St. Timothy Luth. Ch., Camden, S.C., 1961-62; instr., staff mem. Luth. Theol. So. Sem., Columbia, S.C., 1962-79; sec. S.C. Synod, Luth. Ch. in Am., Columbia, 1979-87, bishop, 1988—; trustee Newberry Coll., 1972—, sec. 1977-82; trustee Luth. Home, White Rock, S.C.; bd. dirs. Div. for Edn. Evang. Luth. Ch. Am., Chgo., 1988-91. Author: Obey My Voice: a Form Critical Study of Selected Prose in the Book of Jeremiah", 1971. With U.S. Army, 1954-56, Korea. Mem. Soc. Bibl. Lit., Rotary (bd. dirs. 1987-90). Home: 413 Challedon Dr Columbia SC 29212 Office: SC Synod Evang Luth Ch Am PO Box 43 1003 Richland St Columbia SC 29202

AULT, JAMES MASE, bishop; b. Sayre, Pa., Aug. 24, 1918; s. Tracey Everett and Bessie (Mase) A.; m. Dorothy Mae Barnhart, Dec. 22, 1943; children: James Mase, Kathryn Louise, Elizabeth Ann, Christopher John (dec.). A.B. magna cum laude, Colgate U., 1949; B.D. magna cum laude, Union Theol. Sem., N.Y.C., 1952, S.T.M., 1964; postgrad., St. Andrews U., Scotland, 1966; D.D., Am. U., Washington, 1968; LL.D., Albright Coll., 1973, Ohio Wesleyan U., 1973; D.H.L., Drew U., 1986; L.H.D., Allegheny Coll., 1987. Ordained to ministry Meth. Ch. as deacon, 1951, as elder, 1952. Tool engr. Ingersoll-Rand Co., 1936-42; pastor Meth. Ch., Preston, N.Y., 1946-49, Carlton Hill Meth. Ch., East Rutherford, N.J., 1951-53, Meth. Ch., Leonia, N.J., 1953-58, First Meth. Ch., Pittsfield, Mass., 1958-61; dean students, asso. prof. practical theology Union Theol. Sem., N.Y.C., 1961-64; prof. practical theology, dir. field edn. Union Theol. Sem., 1964-68; dean, prof. pastoral theology Theol. Sch., Drew U., Madison, N.J., 1968-72; bishop Phila. area United Meth. Ch., 1972-80, bishop Pitts. area, 1980-88, bishop Wyo. conf., 1990; prof. contemporary ministries Theol. Sch., Drew U., Madison, N.J., 1988—; interim dean Theol. Sch. Drew U., Madison, N.J., 1990-91; sec. council of bishops United Meth. Ch., 1980-84, pres. council bishops, 1986-87; mem. governing bd. Nat. Coun. Chs. of Christ in U.S.A., 1981-84; mem. central com. World Coun. Chs., 1981-91; mem. exec. com. World Meth. Coun., 1981-88. Author: Responsible Adults for Tomorrow's World, 1962. Served to 1st lt. AUS, 1942-46. Faculty fellow Am. Assn. Theol. Schs., 1965-66. Mem. AAUP, Acad. Polit. and Social Sci., Phi Beta Kappa. Home: 7912 Blossom Heights Fogelsville PA 18051

AULT, JEFFREY MICHAEL, minister, educator, evangelist, religious organization administrator; b. Norfolk, Va., Jan. 20, 1947; s. Frank Willis and Helen Blake (Hamner) A.; m. Martha E. Giles, July 1972 (div. 1974); m. Vera Eileen Saunders, Dec. 19, 1975; children: Jeffrey Franklin, Jeannette Sharlene, Katrina Anne. BA, U. Calif., San Diego, 1974, postgrad., 1975-84; postgrad., World of Faith Bible Inst., Dallas. Ordained to ministry Fedn. Gen. Assemblies Internat., 1988. Sr. pastor Jubilee Christian Ch., Tampa, Fla., 1988—; pres. Maranatha Vision Ministries, Inc., Tampa, 1988—; dir. new bus. devel. San Diego Van and Storage Co., 1970-75; dir. nat. accounts Smith's Aero-Mayflower Transit Co., Alexandria, Va., 1976-78; v.p. Merchants Mgmt. Co., Washington, 1976-78; v.p. mktg. Stevens Van Lines, Saginaw, Mich., 1978-80; exec. v.p. Fla. Am. Van Lines Inc., Tampa, 1980-84; sr. v.p. Victory Van Corp., Washington, 1984-85; pres. Victory World Trade Corp., Washington, 1984-85; chmn., chief exec. officer Maranatha Van Lines, Inc., Tampa, 1984-90. Mem. U.S. Senate Trust, U.S. Senate Inner Circle, Republican Congl. Circle, Hillsborough County Republican Party; sustaining mem. Republican Nat. Com. Sgt. USMC, 1966-72, Vietnam. Mem. Aircraft Owners and Pilots Assn., Nat. Running and Fitness Assn., U. Calif. at San Diego Alumni Assn., First U.S. Marine Div. Assn., USMC Combat Corrs. Assn., Mensa. Home: 18336 Wayne Rd Odessa FL 33556 Office: Jubilee Ch PO Box 262587 Tampa FL 33685-2587 *Faith in God gets things done: because God is able to accomplish those things that are impossible for us to do. However, many people have removed themselves from this dynamic of faith, from the ability that God has given injected into their hearts. Some of us cannot understand why we are such "faith failures". The reason we fail to live a successful spiritual life is because we are trying to do so without being spiritual.*

AUNE, DAVID EDWARD, educator; b. Mpls., Nov. 8, 1939; s. Edward Marius and Anna Belle (Skar) A.; m. Mary Louise Lundberg, Sept. 11, 1965; children: Karl, Kristofer, Kurt, Karen. BA, Wheaton (Ill.) Coll., 1961, MA, 1963; MA, U. Minn., 1965; PhD, U. Chgo., 1970. Asst. prof. St. Xavier Coll., Chgo., 1968-72, assoc. prof., 1972-75, prof., 1975-90; prof. Loyola U., Chgo., 1990—. Author: (books) Prophecy in Early Christianity, 1983, The New Testament in It's Literary Environment, 1987. Mem. Chgo. Soc. Bibl. Research (pres. 1984-85), Studiorum Novi Testamenti Societas, Soc. Bibl. Lit., Cath. Bibl. Assn., Am. Philol. Assn. Home: 9410 S Hamilton Chicago IL 60620 Office: Loyola U Dept Theology 6525 N Sheridan Rd Chicago IL 60626

AUS, ROGER DAVID, minister; b. Jamestown, N.D., Sept. 26, 1940; s. Adrian Clarence and Dagny Hannah (Brevig) A.; m. Anneliese Malsch, Mar. 5, 1966 (div.); children—Martin, Christopher, Jonathan. B.A., St. Olaf Coll., 1962; postgrad., Harvard Div. Sch., 1964; B.D., Luther Theol. Sem., 1967; M.A., Yale U., 1969, Ph.D., 1971. Ordained to ministry Evang. Luth. Ch. in Am., 1972. Pastor Protestant Ch., Berlin, 1971—. Author 3 books; co-author 1 book; contbr. articles to profl. jours. Mem. Jour. Bibl. Lit., Soc. N.T. Studies. Home: Winterthurstr 7, 1000 Berlin 51, Federal Republic of Germany *One of my main endeavors in recent years has been to further the Jewish-Christian dialog by interpreting New Testament texts in the light of their Jewish background. This hopefully will bear fruit.*

AUSTIN, ARTHUR CONVERSE, clergyman, missionary; b. N.Y.C., June 9, 1911; s. Alva Carlos and Ada Florence (Stevens) A.; m. Esther Naoma Plank, Jan. 1, 1933; children—Dorothy Orilla, Edith Nell, Ada Marie, Arthur Converse, Isabelle Joan. Student Moody Bible Inst., summer 1955, U. Md., 1963-64. Archtl. designer, Zephyrhills, Fla., 1945-53; ordained to ministry Apostolic Meth. Ch., Christian and Missionary Alliance; ofcl. worker, evangelist S.E. dist. Christian and Missionary Alliance, 1951-53; missionary Far East Broadcasting Co., Okinawa, Korea, 1957-72, Eastern U.S. rep., 1973-83, semi-ret., Zephyrhills, 1983—; vol. mission svc. Greater Europe Mission, France, 1984-88. Charter mem. Republican Presdl. Task Force. Designed and built radio stas. in Far East; designed rec. studio in Bolivia. Address: PO Box 576 Zephyrhills FL 33539 *In the totality of my being I must be for the praise of Jesus Christ; nothing less than this, and nothing more. This, and this only, must be my reason for being.*

AUSTIN, CHARLES MARSHALL, minister; b. Sioux City, Iowa, May 17, 1941; s. Wilbur T. and Anna C. (Swanson) A.; m. Janet J. Singer, Aug. 17, 1963; children: Adam Paul, Glenda Marie. BA, Midland Coll., Fremont, Nebr., 1963; MDiv, Luth. Sch. Theology, Chgo.; 1967; MTh, Aquinas Inst., Dubuque, Iowa, 1970. Ordained to ministry Luth. Ch., 1967. Pastor St. Mark's Ch., Dubuque, 1967-70; reporter Religious News Svc., N.Y.C., 1970-71; editor Luth. Coun. U.S.A., N.Y.C., 1972-76; English editor Luth. World Fedn., Geneva, 1976-79; reporter Bergen Record, Hackensack, N.J., 1979-81; religion writer N.Y. Times, N.Y.C., 1981-84; news dir. Luth. Ch. in Am., N.Y.C., 1984-88; editor Hearst News Svc., N.Y.C., 1988-89; pastor Christ Luth. Ch., Ridgefield Park, N.J., 1989—. Author: Let the People Know, 1975, Desktop Publishing for Congregations, 1988; contbr. numerous articles to newspapers and mags. Mem. Am. Soc. Journalists and Authors, Religion Newswriters Assn. (newsletter editor 1986—). Office: Christ Luth Ch 90 Mt Vernon Ridgefield Park NJ 07660

AUSTIN, DAVID LEONARD, II, bishop; b. Tampa, Fla., Nov. 19, 1928; s. David Leonard Sr. and Lula (Thompson) A.; m. Elnora Sanders, Sept. 22, 1956; children: Susan, David Leonard III, Kathy, Bernadett. Student, CCNY, 1948-49; D in Evangelism, Fuller Theol. Sem., 1960. Mem. dept. Evangelism Gen. Ch., 1950, exec. sec., 1950-65, 1st conv. chmn. Evangelism dept., 1969—, 1st v.p.; founder Maranatha Ch., L.A., 1976—, Assemblies of God in Christ, L.A., 1989—; founder 12 other chs. and missions, 1953—; bishop Cen. Ky. Chs. of God in Christ, 1966-71. Author: Doing the Work of an Evangelism; contbr. articles to profl. jours.; composer ch. music. Home: 2064 Cullivan St Los Angeles CA 90047

AUSTIN, JACK SPENCER, minister; b. Sayre, Okla., Dec. 21, 1936; s. Spencer Peter and Margaret Ellen (Wolfinger) A.; m. Patricia Ann Steuart, June 6, 1956; children: Pamela Jane Austin Findley, Michel Roy (dec.), DeAnna Ruth Austin McCoy, Kae Ellen Austin Bruch. BA with honors, Phillips U., 1959; BDiv with honors, The Coll. of the Bible, 1962. Minister First Congl. Ch., Anthony, Kans., 1958-59, Point Pleasant Christian Ch., Eminence, Ky., 1959-62, Glen Oak Christian Ch., Peoria, Ill., 1962-71; minister First Christian Ch., Falls Church, Va., 1971-82; assoc. regional minister Christian Ch. (Disciples of Christ) in Va., Roanoke, 1982-85; regional minister Christian Ch. (Disciples of Christ) in Va., Lynchburg, 1985-91; mem. gen. bd. Christian Ch. (Disciples of Christ), 1971-75. Trustee Eureka (Ill.) Coll., 1969-73, Lexington Theol. Sem., Lexington, 1977—, Lynchburg (Va.) Coll., 1985-91; bd. dirs. Met. Peoria Coun. Chs., 1966-71; mem. Mayor's Human Rels. Coun., Peoria, 1967-71; counselor Op. Drug Alert, Peoria, 1967-71; bd. dirs. Pastoral Counselling and Consultation Ctrs., Washington, 1978-82. Mem. Va. Council Chs. (mem. exec. com., mem. conf. regional ministers and moderators, ex-officio mem. gen. bd.). Lodge: Kiwanis. Avocations: camping, hiking, fishing, skiing. Office: The Christian Ch in Va 5024 Harvest Ridge Rd Roanoke VA 24019

AUSTIN, JAMES RAY, minister; b. St. Petersburg, Fla., July 25, 1952; s. Estel and Edith Mae (Wilkerson) A.; m. Linda, Apr. 4, 1974; children: Jamie Lynn, Joy Marie, Jennifer Mae. BA in Bibl. Edn. and Theology, Fla. Bible Coll., 1974; postgrad., New Orleans Bapt. Seminary, 1990—. Tchr., trainer Evangelism Explosion Internat. III. Minister of music/youth Six Mile (S.C.) Bapt. Ch., 1976-78; minister of edn. Arlington Heights Bapt. Ch., Pascagoula, Miss., 1978-80; pastor First Bapt. Ch., Elfers, Fla., 1980-86, Holiday, Fla., 1987—. Mem. Nat. Assn. Ch. Bus. Adminstrs., Suncoast Bapt. Assn. (new work com. 1988-90, Moon Lake assembly com. 1985-87), West Pasco Pilots Assn. Republican. Home: 4225 Hillsdale Dr New Port Richey FL 34652 Office: First Baptist Ch/Holiday PO Box 3645 1210 Dixie Hwy Holiday FL 34690

AUSTIN, KENT ARLON, religious school administrator; b. Ft. Morgan, Colo., June 14, 1940; s. Kenneth Judd and Marian Julia (Graeber) A.; m. Patricia Mae Hodge, Aug. 12, 1962; children: Brian, Mark. AS, Mesa Jr. Coll., Grand Junction, Colo., 1961; BS, Colo. State U., 1964; MA, U. No. Colo., 1978. Adminstr. Victory Christian Acad., Emporia, Kans., 1985—; freelance photographer. Contbr. articles to religious jours. Pres. Pregnancy Crisis Ctr., Family Life Svcs., Emporia, 1988-90; mem. Christian Coalition, Virginia Beach, Va., 1990—. Mem. Fellowship Christian Sch. Adminstrs., Am. Speech and Hearing Assn. (cert. of clin. competence in speech). Republican. Home: 2520 Coronado Ct Emporia KS 66801 Office: Victory Christian Acad 2929 Americus Rd Emporia KS 66801-9137

AUSTIN, PATRICIA MAE, religion educator; b. Forest, Va., Feb. 4, 1953; d. Walter Sr. and Emma Louise (Ross) A. BA, Lynchburg Coll., 1974; postgrad., U. Va., Bedford, 1986-90. Tchr. Bible sch. Community Outreach, Bedford, 1986-90, choir dir., 1990—; tchr. Bedford County schs., 1975—. Organizer NAACP, Bedford, 1986-89. Mem. NEA, Va. Edn. Assn. Home: Rte 1 Box 191 Bedford VA 24523-9724

AUSTIN, SPENCER PETER, minister; b. Lone Wolf, Okla., Dec. 15, 1909; s. Otis Frank and Bertha Ethel (Sinclair) A.; m. Margaret Ellen Wolfinger, Dec. 15, 1932 (dec. Apr. 1968); children—Roy Frank, Jack Spencer, Margaret Anna; m. Kathleen B. Bailey, Dec. 30, 1969 (dec. June 1981); m.

Kathleen B. Havens, Dec. 28, 1982. A.B., Phillips U., 1931, M.A., 1932, B.D., 1933, D.D., 1957; student, Boston U. Sch. Theology, 1943-45. Ordained to ministry Christian Ch. (Disciples of Christ), 1931; pastor in Cedardale and Tangier, Okla., 1929-33, Sayre, Okla., 1933-36, Mangum, Okla., 1937, Duncan, Okla., 1937-43, Everett, Mass., 1943-45; nat. dir. evangelism United Christian Missionary Soc., 1945-50, exec. resources dept., 1950-56; exec. Unified Promotion Christian Chs., 1957-74, chmn. com. relief appeals, 1957-63, adminstrv. sec. com. fraternal aid to Brit. chs., 1954-70; chmn. Week of Compassion com., 1963-76; pres. Christian Ch. Found., 1961-69; Trustee Nat. Christian Missionary Conv., 1957-69; exec. com. Council Christian Unity, 1957-82; mem. grad. sem. council Phillips U., 1962-70; denomination rep. Nat. Council Chs., 1950-72; also mem. exec. com. dept. stewardship and chmn. benevolence promotion com.; mem. exec. com. Ch. World Service, chmn., 1966-70; interim com. Council Agencies Christian Chs., 1952-68; pres. Ch. Finance Council, 1974-76; dir. spl. resources Christian Theol. Sem., 1976-82. Author: Evangelism, 1947. Mem. Disciples of Christ Hist. Soc. (life). Lodges: Rotary, Kiwanis (pres. Sayre 1936), Odd Fellow. Home: 6426 Chapelwood Ct Indianapolis IN 46268 *Most of our own advantages were a gift from others beyond what we deserve. Simple justice demands that we provide similar opportunities for other human beings.*

AUSTIN, WILLIAM BOULDIN, priest; b. Abilene, Tex., Aug. 31, 1949; s. William Thomas Jr. and Johnnie Ellen (Bouldin) A.; m. Robin Dahlstrom, Nov. 1, 1975; 1 child, William Robinson. BA in Psychology, U. of the South, Sewanee, Tenn., 1971; MDiv, Seabury Western Theol. Sem., Evanston, Ill., 1975. Ordained priest Episcopal Ch. Vicar Diocese of Nassau, The Bahamas, 1975-79; rector Ch. of Redeemer, Avon Park, Fla., 1981-87; fellow in clin. pastoral edn. Emory U. Hosp., Atlanta, 1987-90; pastoral assoc. Cathedral St. Philip, Atlanta, 1990—; chaplain Avon Park police and fire depts., 1981-87; assoc. Order of Holy Cross, West Park, N.Y., 1982—; mem. Order St. Luke, San Antonio, 1987—. Mem. Assn. Clin. Pastorate Edn. Home: 1936 K Johnson Ferry Rd Atlanta GA 30319 Office: Cathedral St Philip 2744 Peachtree St Atlanta GA 30363

AUSTIN-LUCAS, BARBARA ETTA, minister; b. Boston, Nov. 9, 1951; d. Robert James and Etta Lee (Amos) Austin; m. Frederick Aloyisious Lucas, Jr., Dec. 24, 1972; children: Kemba Jarena, Hakim Jabez, Kareem Mandela. BA, Tufts U., Meford, Mass., 1973; MA, Boston U., 1975; MDiv, Colgate Rochester Div. Sch., N.Y., 1982; postgrad., Columbia U., 1990—. Ordained to ministry A.M.E. Ch. as elder, 1984. Tchr. Monrovia (Liberia) Coll., 1974; instr. U. Liberia, Monrovia, 1974-75; tchr. Henry Buckner Sch., Cambridge, Mass., 1975-76; substitute tchr. Phila. Pub. Sch., 1977; minister missions and outreach Agape A.M.E. Ch., Buffalo, 1979-82; minister to families Bridge St. A.M.E. Ch., Bklyn., 1982-86, dir., organizer After Sch. Tutorial Ctr., 1983-84; asst. pastor Bridge St. A.M.E. Ch., 1986—; ednl. counselor Bklyn. Coll., CUNY, 1984-86; chmn. bd. trustees Bridge St. Prep. Sch., Bklyn., 1988—; mem. A.M.E. Ch. N.Y. Bd. Christian Edn., N.Y.C., 1983—. Bd. dirs. Bklyn. Hist. Soc., 1990. Recipient Sister Sharing award Agape A.M.E. Ch., Buffalo, 1982, Community Svc. awards Kings County Bus. and Profl. Women, Bklyn., 1988, Men's Caucus for Congressman Edolphus Towns, Bklyn., 1990. Mem. AAUW, Religious Edn. Assn., Key Women of Am. (Ch. Woman of Yr. 1984), Ch. Women United, N.Y. Assn. Black Sch. Educators. Avocations: creative writing, poetry, drama. Office: Bridge St AME Ch 277 Stuyvesant Ave Brooklyn NY 11221 *I have attempted to live my life believing that with God I can do all things. (Philipians 4:13). It is important to learn early in life that nothing and/or no one can withhold from you what God has already ordained for you. Never give up, rather, live up to your potential.*

AUTERINEN, OLLI, retired church official; b. Helsinki, Finland, Sept. 13, 1921; s. Lauri Hendell and Mathilde Louise (Donner) A.; B. Forestry, U. Helsinki, 1949; m. Victoria Schauman, Oct. 27, 1963; 1 son, Lassi Johan. Sec., Student Christian Movement Finland, 1948-49, 50-51; forest officer State Forest Adminstrn., also tchr. State Forest Inst., 1949-50, 54-56; research asst. U. Helsinki, 1951-54; worker Finnish Seamen's Mission, Hamburg, W. Ger., 1956-60; youth sec. Diocese Helsinki, Lutheran Ch. Finland, 1961-63, gen. sec. council on youthwork Luth. Ch. Finland, 1963-74, dir. Conf. Center, 1974-84; 1st pres. Del. Youth Orgns. Finland, 1962-64. Chmn. youth com. Finnish Red Cross, 1962-69. Served as officer Finnish Army, 1940-44. Decorated Knight of Finnish White Rose 1st class, Cross of Freedom 4th class with swords; recipient Finnish Red Cross medal, 1967; Boy Scouts Silver medal, 1967. Mem. Assn. Foresters Finland, Finnish-W. German Soc. Liberal. Club: Helsinki-Hietalahti Lions (past pres.). Home: Professorintie 4A6, SF 00330 Helsinki 33, Finland

AUXENTIOS, BISHOP, clergyman; b. June 28, 1953. BA in Religion, Princeton U., 1976; Lic. Theol., Ctr. for Traditionalist Orthodox Studies, 1986; postgrad., Grad. Theol. Union, Berkeley, Calif., 1986—. Ordained as rasophore monk, then hierodeacon Greek Orthodox Ch., 1976, hieromonk, 1977, great schema, 1986, oikonomos, 1989, archimandrite, 1989, titular bishop of Photiki, 1991. Co-dir. Ctr. for Traditionalist Orthodox Studies, 1987—. Author: (with Chrysostomos and Akakios) Contemporary Eastern Orthodox Thought: The Traditionalist Voice, 1982, (with Chrysostomos and Ambrosios) Scripture and Tradition, 1982, (with Chrysostomos) The Roman West and the Byzantine East, 1988, The Holy Fire, 1991; translator: (with Chrysostomos) The Future Life According to Orthodox Teaching (Constantine Cavarnos), 1988, The Monastic Life (Met. Cyprian of Oropos and Fili), 1988; (with others) The Evergetinos: A Complete Text, Vol. I of the First Book, 1988, Vol. II, 1990; editor Orthodox Tradition, 1989—; contbr. articles to profl. jours. Address: St Gregory Palamas Monastery Etna CA 96027-0398

AUYEUNG, KENNETH, clergyman; b. Canton, Kwang Tong, China, Sept. 12, 1941; s. Hong T. and Laiyung (Young) A.; m. Esther T. Hsia, July 6, 1968; children: John Christina. BA, Chung Hsing U., Taipei, Taiwan, 1965; MS, Calif. State U., Hayward, 1972; MA in Bibl. Sci., Dallas Theol. Sem., 1983. Ordained to ministry. Sr. pastor Cleve. Chinese Christian Ch., 1982-85, South Bay Chinese Alliance Ch., Manhattan Beach, Calif., 1985-88, Riverside (Calif.) Chinese Alliance Ch., 1988-90, Chinese Evang. Free Ch., Santa Barbara, Calif., 1991—; sch. counselor Sacramento City Unified Sch. Dist., 1974-81. Republican. Home: 4710 Dexter Dr Apt 12 Santa Barbara CA 93110 Office: Chinese Evang Free Ch 400 Puente Dr Santa Barbara CA 93110

AVALONE, RONNIE (ROMUALDO AVALLONE), minister, singer; b. Bronx, N.Y., Sept. 24, 1922; s. Romeo and Mary Elizabeth (Giacco) A.; m. Anita Filocco, Apr. 22, 1950; 1 child, Delia. Student, Juilliard Sch. Music, N.Y., 1945-47; MusD, Ea. Nebr. Christian Coll., Valley, 1972. Ordained to Bapt. ministry, 1963. With Metro Studios, 1929-30, Met. Opera Co., N.Y.C., 1945-48; founder, pres. Ronnie Avalone Evangelistic Assoc., Inc., 1954—; with stage and radio, lead soloist in Europe, chorus singer; soloist Radio City Music Hall/Carnegie Hall, Word Records, Inc., Waco, Tex., 1955—, Zondervan Records, Grand Rapids, Mich., Supreme Records, Hollywood, Calif., 1980, Bibletown, Boca Raton, Fla., 1953-73, Gospel Assn. for the Blind; owner radio program Pathway to Heaven; taught voice in Delray Beach, West Palm Beach, and Boca Raton, Fla. Writer, composer 14 religious songs, lyricist; author of numerous poems. With U.S. Army, 1941. Decorated Bronze Star, Combat Infantry medal, others; recipient Best Male Vocalist Oscar award, 1959, 64, 4 Star awards Secular B'way Billboard News. Mem. DAV, Am. Legion. Republican. Avocations: photography, religious theology, travel. Home and Office: 4712 Barrett St Delray Beach FL 33445 *Only one life, twill soon be past, only what's done for Christ will last.*

AVERA, ALAN JAMES, minister; b. Atlanta, Ga., Mar. 11, 1955; s. Woodrow Wilson and Willie (Edwards) A.; m. Eileen Elizabeth Merlie, May 30, 1981; children: Kimberly Lynne, Mark Wesley, Bethany Noel. BA in Econs., U. N.C., 1977; MDiv cum laude, Trinity Evang. Div. Sch., Deerfield, Ill., 1984; postgrad., U. Md., 1985-87. Ordained to ministry Assoc. Reformed Presbyn. Ch. (Gen. Synod), 1986. Coll. dir. Carter-Westminster Presbyn. Ch., Skokie, Ill., 1983-84; assoc. pastor Christian edn. Atonement Presbyn. Ch., Silver Spring, Md., 1984-88; pastor, mission developer Faith Presbyn. Ch., Olney, Md., 1988—; bd. dirs., sec. Synod Bd. Christian Edn., Greenville, S.C., 1985-90; chmn. Presbytery Christian Edn. Com., 1986-90. Newsletter editor Olney Boys and Girls Club, 1991. Lt. USN, 1977-81, USNR (chaplain), 1986—. NROTC scholar, 1973-77. Mem. Greater Washington Christian Edn. Assn. (bd. dirs. 1985-88), Olney C. of C. (scholarship chmn. 1990—). Home and Office: 3913 Shallow Brook Ln Olney MD 20832

AVERILL, LLOYD JAMES, JR., religion educator; b. Warrenville, Ill., Apr. 23, 1923; s. Lloyd James and Dorothy Mae (Rogers) A.; m. Shirley Mae Karr, Feb. 9, 1944 (div. June 1968); children: Shelley Ann, Leslie Jean, Scott Alan; m. Carol Anne White, July 13, 1968 (div. Dec. 1989). Student, Beloit Coll., 1942-43; B.A. with honors, U. Wis.,, 1947; M.Div., Colgate Rochester Div. Sch., 1950, Th.M., 1966; M.A. in Sociology,, U. Rochester,, 1952; sr. mem., Fitzwilliam Coll., Cambridge U.,, 1965-66; assoc. mem., Westminster Coll.,, Cambridge U.,, 1965-66; L.H.D.,, Lewis and Clark Coll., , 1962, Coll. of Idaho,, 1975, Sienna Heights Coll.,, 1984; LL.D.,, Carroll Coll.,, 1967, William Jewell Coll.,, 1967; Litt.D.,, Augustana (Ill.) Coll.,, 1968; D.D.,, Tusculum Coll.,, 1968. Ordained to ministry Baptist Ch., 1949; transferred to United Ch. of Christ, 1986; assoc. dir. field work, instr. practical theology Colgate Rochester Div. Sch., 1951-54; dean chapel Kalamazoo Coll., 1954-67, asst. prof. religion, then assoc. prof., 1954-62, prof., 1962-67, asst. to pres., 1957-63, v.p. coll., 1963-67; pres. Council Protestant Colls. and Univs., 1967-68; vis. disting. prof. Ottawa U., mem. faculty, 1968-70; v.p., dean of faculty Davis and Elkins Coll., Elkins, W.Va., 1970-72; pres. Kansas City Regional Council for Higher Edn., 1972-79; v.p. acad. affairs, prof. religious studies Barat Coll., 1979-80; cons. coll. curriculum and adminstrn., 1980-84; dir. continuing edn., devel., community relations, sr. lectr. social work Sch. Social Work, U. Wash., Seattle, 1984—; adj. prof. religion Graceland Coll., 1972-78; adj. prof. Northwest Theol. Union, Seattle, 1984-90; frequent speaker, lectr.; adj. prof. San Francisco Theol. Sem., 1965-71, Central Bapt. Theol. Sem., 1979; cons. assoc. Assn. Am. Colls., 1967-68; cons. commn. on fed. relations Am. Council on Edn., 1967-68; mem. adv. council on campus ministry programs Danforth Found. Author: A Strategy for the Protestant College, 1966; American Theology in the Liberal Tradition, 1967; Between Faith and Unfaith, 1968; The Problem of Being Human, 1974; Learning to Be Human: A Vision for the Liberal Arts, 1983, Religious Right, Religious Wrong: A Critique of the Fundamentalist Phenomenon, 1989; also articles, book revs.; editor: Leadership in Colleges and Universities: Assessment and Search, 1977; co-editor: Colleges and Commitments, 1971; cons. editor: Jour. Higher Edn., 1974-77. Served with USAAF, 1943-46. Recipient Campus Ministry grant Danforth Found., 1958-59; grad. fellow Colgate Rochester Div. Sch., 1950. Fellow Soc. Values in Higher Edn.; mem. Native Am. Art Studies Assn., Can. Native Art Studies Assn. Democrat. Home: 1001 NW Richmond Beach Rd Seattle WA 98177 Office: U Wash Sch Social Work JH-30 Seattle WA 98195

AVERY, CARL GERSHOM, minister; b. Fairgrove, Mich., Feb. 8, 1935; s. Irving Harry and Mary Ellen (Putnam) A.; children: Gershom Lawrence, Ruth Ann Avery Tallman, Michael Patrick; m. Marilyn Martha Lauber, July 27, 1968; children: Peter John, Phillip Carl, Jonathan Adam. Student, Helfrecht Machine Com. Tng., Bay Christian Fellowship, Bay Med. Ctr., 1985. Bakery dough mixer Rainbow Bread, Saginaw, Mich., 1948-52; tool, die maker Helfrecht Machine Co., Saginaw, Mich., 1952-62, estimating, drafting, 1952-62; tool makerSaginaw div. GM, 1962-85; minister Liberty Fellowship, Bay City, Mich., 1986-; chaplain Bay Med. Ctr., 1983—. v.p. Internat. Soc. Skilled Trades, Saginaw 1976-78, treas. Full Gospel Businessmen's Fellowship, Caro 1978-80, election com. Norm Hughes For Congress, Saginaw 1976; counselor Bay County Jail, 1986-87; mem. Boys Scouts Am., Liberty Fellowship Ch., 1986—. Mem. Bay County Ministerial Assn., Bay Clergy Assn., United Auto Workers Local 699, Bay County Firefighters Assn. (chaplain 1987—), Mariners Club. Republican. Avocations: vol. in field ministerial needs. Office: Liberty Fellowship Ch 1008 N Farragut St Bay City MI 48708

AVERY, MARK DOUGLAS, minister; b. Ann Arbor, Mich., Mar. 18, 1957; s. Arthur H. and Marjory Ann (Riggs) A.; m. Carol Fay McGehee, Aug. 2, 1980; children: Michael Douglas, Michelle Diane. BA in Religion, Kansas City Coll. & Bible Sch., Overland Park, Kans., 1982. Ordaind to min. Ch. of God, 1989. Pastor Ch. of God (Holiness), Appleton City, Mo., 1982-88; Pastor Kinser Chapel, Springfield, Mo., 1988—; bd. dirs. Herriman Chapel Camp, El Dorado Springs, Mo., 1982-88, Ch. of God Home Mission Dept., Overland Park, 1987—; asst. chmn. Rogersville (Mo.) Camp, 1988-90, camp chmn. 1990—. writer The Way, Truth and Life, 1983—. Mem. Appleton City Head Start Policy Coun., 1984-87, pres. 1987; bd. dirs. Mount Zion Bible Sch., 1989—, sec. 1990; bd. dirs. Ch. of God Home Mission, 1990—, asst. sec., 1990—. Recipient Outstanding Svc. award Head Start Policy Coun., 1987. Mem. Gen. Camp Com. (publicity chmn. 1987), Conv. Role Com. (asst. sec.-treas. 1985—), Kansas City Coll. and Bible Sch. Coun. Republican. Avocations: hunting, boating, photography. Office: Kinser Chapel Rte 18 Box 266 Springfield MO 65809

AVERY-PECK, ALAN JEFFERY, Judaic studies educator; b. Chgo., June 26, 1953; s. Richard W. and Eileen Sardra (Chibnik) Peck; m. Lisa Joy Avery-Peck, June 21, 1981; 1 child, Gabrielle Sophia Avery-Peck. BA, U. Ill., 1975; PhD, Brown U., 1981. Dir. Jewish studies program, assoc. prof. classics Tulane U., New Orleans, 1981—. Author: The Priestly Life in Mishnah, 1981, Mishnah's Division of Agriculture, 1985; translator: The Talmud of Babylonia: Vol. 7. Tractate Besah, 1986, The Talmud of the Land of Israel: Vol. 6. Tractate Terumot, 1988, The Talmud of the Land of Israel Vol. 5. Tractatate Shebiit, 1991; contbr. articles to profl. jours. Mem. Am. Acad. Religion, Soc. Bibl. Lit. Assn. for Jewish Studies, European Assn. for Jewish Studies. Home: 46 W Park Pl New Orleans LA 70124 Office: Tulane U Coll Arts and Scis New Orleans LA 70118-5698

AVIDANO, RAYMOND ANTHONY, minister; b. Flushing, N.Y., Aug. 12, 1938; s. Attilio Anthony and Madeline (Pettenati) A.; m. Mary L. Hanke, Apr. 5, 1975; children: Yolanda, Raymond, Jennifer, John, Carl. BA, St. Pius X Sem. Graymoor, Garrison, N.Y., 1963; ThD, Cath. U., 1967. Asst. pastor SAõ Sebastiaõ, Rio Verde, Goias, Brazil, 1967-68; pastor Saõ Sebastiaõ, Jatai, Goias, Brazil, 1968-70, Saõ Joaõ, Itaja, Goias, Brazil, 1970-73, Albion (Nebr.) United Ch. Christ, 1985-90, United Meth. Ch., Elgin, Nebr., 1990—, Park United Ch. Christ, Elgin, 1990—; founder, dir. Homes for Christ, Jatai, 1968-73. Home: Box J Elgin NE 68636

AVIGDOR, ISAAC CHAIM, rabbi; b. Nowy Sacz, Poland, Dec. 2, 1920; came to U.S., 1947; s. Jacob and Rachael (Horowitz) A.; m. Esther Horowitz, June 14, 1949; children: David, Morton, Merrill, Jacob. Docent, U. Lwow, Poland, 1939. Ordained rabbi, 1939. Rabbi Jewish Community, Borislaw, Poland, 1938-40, Milano (Italy) Kibutz Torah 'V' Avoda, 1945-46, Bachad House, Antwerp, Belgium, 1946-47; prin. dir. Yeshiva Religion Sch., Kluger, N.Y., 1948-49; exec. dir. Religious Zionist Movement, N.Y., 1949-50; rabbi United Synagogues Greater Hartford, Conn., 1950—; pres. Rabbinical Coun. Conn., Hartford, 1965-67, Mizrachi Conn., Hartford, 1967-70. Author: (poems) Treren Nisht Fartrikente; Ten for Two, 1960, One of the Holy Cast, Emuna Hanotzrit L'or Halacha, Six Reasons Why You Should Keep Kosher, Hakol B'Seder, From Prison to Pulpit; also articles. Active in various civic and ednl. orgns. of Hartford community. Recipient Lit. award Jiddish Writers of Mexico, 1980. Mem. Rabbinical Coun. Am., Religious Zionists Am. Home: 25 Overhill Rd West Hartford CT 06117 Office: United Synagogues 840 N Main St West Hartford CT 06117

AVIS, PAUL DAVID LOUP, clergyman, theologian; b. Essex, Eng., July 21, 1947; s. Peter George Hobden and Diana Joan (Loup) A.; m. Susan Janet Haywood, July 11, 1970; children: Edward, Jonathan, Daniel. Student, London Bible Coll., 1967-70; BD with honors, U. London, 1970, PhD, 1976; postgrad., Wescott House Cambridge U., 1973-75. Ordained to ministry Anglican Ch., 1975. Asst. curate South Molton Group Parishes, Devon, Eng., 1975-80; vicar Stoke Canon, Devon, 1980—; mem. Ch. of Eng.-Gen. Synod, 1990—. Author: The Church in the Theology of the Reformers, 1982, Ecumenical Theology--Truth Beyond Words, 1986, Foundations of Modern Historical Thought, 1986, The Methods of Modern Theology, 1986, Gore: Construction and Conflict, 1988, Anglicanism and the Christian Church, 1989, Eros and the Sacred, 1989, Christians in Communion, 1990, Authority, Leadership and Conflict, 1991. Mem. Soc. for Study Theology, Ch. of Eng. Doctrine Commn., Faith and Order Adv. Group. Office: Stoke Canon Vicarage, Exeter EX5 4AS, England

AWUME, minister. Acting moderator Directorate Protestant Chs., Lome, Tago. Office: Directorate Protestant Chs, 1 rue Marechal Foch, BP 378, Lome Togo*

AXFORD, WARREN SCOTT, minister; b. Plymouth, Mass., Nov. 27, 1956; s. Warren Morton and Arlene Beatrice (Christie) A. AB, Dartmouth Coll., 1978; DivM, Harvard U., 1988. Ordained minister Unitarian Universalist Chs. and Congl. Christian Ch. Market adminstr. New Eng. Telephone Co., Burlington, Vt., 1978-81; sr. programmer New Eng. Telephone Co., Boston, 1981-84; user asst. Harvard Computer Ctr., Cambridge, Mass., 1984-89; proctor Divinity Hall Harvard Divinity Sch., Cambridge, 1985-86; ministerial intern Unitarian Ch. of Montpelier (Vt.), 1986-87; pastor, tchr. Walpole (N.H.) Unitarian Ch., 1989-91; extension min. First Universalist Ch., Providence, 1992—; student chaplain N.H. Hosp., Concord, summer 1986; pub. tchr. of piety, religion and morality Walpole Town Congl. Soc., 1988-92—; scribe Coun. of Christian Chs. within Unitarian Universalist Assn.; active Walpole Players. Active Walpole Players. Mem. Am. Congl. Assn., Victorian Soc., Clan MacRae Soc. N.Am., Belfast Hist. Soc., Unitarian Universalist Ministers Assn., The First Parish Ch., Pilgrim Soc. (life), Unitarian Universalist Christian Fellowship (bd. dirs. 1989—), Nat. Assn. Congl. Christian Chs., Mass. Convention Congl. Ministers (Karl Barth group), Dartmouth Alumni Assn. Eastern Mass. (continuing edn. officer 1981-87, newsletter editor 1980-84, 88-90), Walpole Hist. Soc., Walpole Players, Wolfe Pack, Vt. and Conn. Sherlock Holmes Soc., Dartmouth Club S.W. N.H. Republican. Office: First Universalist Ch 250 Washington St Providence RI 02903-0087

AYER, G. W., bishop. Assoc. bishop Apostolic Overcoming Holy Ch. of God, Inc., El Cerrito, Calif. Office: Apostolic Overcoming Holy Ch of God Inc 1717 Arlington Blvd El Cerrito CA 94530*

AYERS, CHERYL S., lay worker; b. Miami, Fla., July 5, 1957; d. Donald James and Ellen (Boyles) Schile; m. Robert C. Ayers; children: Nichole Lynn Rose, Rebecca Leigh Rose. ADRN, Pensacola Jr. Coll., Niceville, Fla., 1989. RN, Fla. Dir. religious edn. St Andrews Episcopal Ch., Destin, Fla., 1989-91; sec. N.O.E.L. St. Andrews, Destin, Fla., 1990—; staff nurse Fort Walton Beach Care Ctr., Fla., 1990—. Leader Girl Scouts Am., Destin, 1986-88; coach Odessy of the Mind, Okaloosa County, 1989-90; mem. Emerald Coast Right to Life, 1989—. Pensacola Jr. Coll. scholar, 1990. Mem. Altar Guild St. Andrews, Fort Walton Beach Jr. League. Republican. Home: 626 Pelican Dr Fort Walton Beach FL 32548

AYERS, JULE, minister; b. Detroit, Mar. 12, 1911; s. Jule C. and Camilla (Chalmers) A.; m. Faith Ralph, Aug. 31, 1934 (dec. Apr. 1945); children: David, Joanne; m. Alice Howorth, June 12, 1946; 1 child, Camilla Alice. AB, U. Mich., 1933; BA, Union Theol. Sem., 1936; MS in Edn., Temple U., 1969. Ordained to ministry Presbyn. Ch., 1936. Asst. min. Cen. Presbyn. Ch., N.Y.C., 1936-39; min. 1st Presbyn. Ch., Ossining, N.Y., 1939-43; chaplain U.S. Army, USAF, 1943-44; min. 1st Presbyn. Ch., Wilkes-Barre, Pa., 1944-83, pastor emeritus, 1983—; chmn., bd. dirs. Ecumenical Enterprises, Inc., Dallas, 1968—; dir. family svc. Family Svc. Assn., Wilkes-Barre, 1950—; dir. Sordoni Found., Wilkes-Barre, 1960—, Osterhout Free Libr., Wilkes-Barre, 1944—; chaplain Irem Temple Shrine, 1970—; instr. social ethics Wilkes U., 1984—. Author: Jewels, 1982. Pres. Kiwanis, Wilkes-Barre, 1960; chmn. citizens com. adv. City Mgr. Govt., Wilkes-Barre, 1965; chmn. Martin Luther King Com. for Social Justice, Wilkes-Barre, 1979—. 1st lt. USAF, 1943-44. Recipient Young Man of Yr. award Jr. C. of C., Wilkes Barre, 1946, Jewish War Vet., 1947, Labor award AFL-CIO Labor Coun., 1965, Interfaith award Interfaith Coun., 1983. Mem. Torch Club (pres. 1985-87), Westmoreland Club, Radium Lodge, Shekinah Royal Arch chpt. # 182, Dieu Le Veut Commandery # 45, Inem Temple, Caldwell Conistory. Republican. Home: 361 Ridge Ave Kingston PA 18704

AYLOR, GARY LEON, minister; b. Oklahoma City, Okla., Mar. 8, 1947; s. Leon P. and Ruth (Degraffenreid) A.; m. Joyce Hardgraves, May 26, 1968; children: Bradley, Steven, Amy. BA, Okla. Bapt. U., 1969. Cert. tchr. Okla., 1969. Youth min. Meadowood Bapt. Ch., Midwest City, Okla., 1969-76; assoc. pastor, adminstrn. 1st. Southern Bapt. Ch., Phoenix, 1976-79; assoc. pastor, adminstrn. and evangelism Champion Forest Bapt. Ch., Houston, 1979—; clinic tchr. Evangelism Explosion III, Ft. Lauderdale, Fla., 1985—. V.p. Klein Forest High Sch. Baseball Club, Houston, 1989-90, pres. 1990-91. Mem. Nat. Assn. Ch. Bus. Adminstrn. Home: 4715 Theall Houston TX 77066 Office: Champion Forest Bapt Ch 12501 Champion Forest Dr Houston TX 77066

AYLWARD, CHRISTOPHER PAUL, minister; b. Mass., Dec. 9, 1967; s. Arthur Walter and Lillian Anne (Smith) A. Gen. Dipl. Missions, Faith Sch. Theology, Charleston, Maine, 1991, Evang. Tchr. Tng. Assoc. Dipls., 1991. Ordained to ministry, Assemblies of God. Resource dir. World Missions Outreach Group, Charleston, 1989-91; dir. Teen Challenge, Syracuse, N.Y., 1991—. Home: 124 Furman St Syracuse NY 13205

AYMOND, GREGORY M., academic administrator. Pres. Grad. Sch. Theology, Notre Dame Sem., New Orleans. Office: Notre Dame Sem Grad Sch Theol Office of Pres New Orleans LA 70118*

AZ-ZAWI, SHEIKH TAHER AHMAD, Islamic leader. Chief mufti of Libya Tripoli. Office: Chief Mufti of Libya, Tripoli Libya*

BAAK, DAVID P., religious organization administrator. Exec. dir. Grand Rapids (Mich.) Area Ctr. for Ecumenism. Office: Grand Rapids Area Ctr for Ecumenism 38 W Fulton Grand Rapids MI 49503*

BAAR, KENNETH DONALD, minister; b. Oshkosh, Wis., Aug. 21, 1926; s. Edward F. and Eleanor (Timmerman) B.; m. Louise Marie Siedman, JUne 13, 1953; childen: Ruth Marie, David Allen, James Arthur. BBA, U. Wis., 1950; BDiv, Evangelical Luth. Theol. Sem., Columbus, Ohio, 1955. Ordained to ministry Evang. Luth. Ch. Am., 1955. Intern St Paul Luth. Ch., Massilon, Ohio, 1953-54; asst. pastor Zion Luth. Ch., Pitts., 1955-56; pastor Grace Luth. Ch., New Orleans, La., 1956-63, Redeemer Luth. Ch., Bradenton, Fla., 1963—; statistician Fla. Synod Evangelical Luth. Ch. Am. , Tampa, Fla. 1988—; dean Mid Gulf Conf., Fla. Synod, Tampa, Fla., 1988—. Chmn. bd. Meals on Wheels Plus, Manatee County, Bradenton, Fla., 1970, Exec. com. ARC Manatee chpt., Bradenton, 1979-84. With US Army 1944-46, PTO. Named Citizen for Edn., Phi Delta Kappa, Bradenton, 1974. Mem. Kiwanis (Kiwanian of Yr. 1975). Office: Redeemer Luth Ch 6311 Third Ave W Bradenton FL 34209

BAARDA, TJITZE, religious studies educator; b. Vogelenzang, The Netherlands, July 8, 1932; s. Reinder and Huberta Jacoba (Guyt) B.; m. Hilda Juliana Giliam, Feb. 23, 1958; children: Reint Menno, Fokke Bert, Martin Johan, Eelco Pieter, Maria Elizabeth. B in Sem. Studies, Vrije U., Amsterdam, 1958, BTh, 1961, DTM, 1962; DTM, Vrije U., Amsterdam, 1975. Asst. prof. Faculty of Theology Vrije U., 1958-67, lectr. new testament, 1967-75, prof. new testament, 1975-83; prof. new testament Rijksuniversiteit, Utrecht, 1981-83, prof. N.T. and early Judaism, 1983-90; prof. N.Y. Vrye U., 1990—; vis. lectr. St. Mary's Coll., St. Andrews, Scotland, 1967; vis. prof. new testament and early ch. history Harvard Div. Sch., Cambridge, Mass., 1989. Author: The Gospel Quotations of Aphrahat the Persian Sage, 1975, Early Transmission of Words of Jesus, Thomas, Tatian and the Text of the New Testament, 1983; contbr. articles to profl. jours. Mem. Koninklijke Nederlandse Academie Van Wetenschappen, Gebiedsraad voor de geesteswetenschappen NWo, The Netherlands, Netherlands Inst. for Advanced Studies (selection com.). Home: Troskerslaan 27, 1185BV Amstelveen The Netherlands Office: Vrye U, De Boelelaan 1105 PO Box 80105, 1081 HB Amsterdam 3508TC, The Netherlands

BABB, WYLIE SHERRILL, college president; b. Greenville, S.C., Aug. 20, 1940; s. J. Wylie and Sally P. B.; m. Linda Witmer, June 30, 1963; children: Corinne, Michelle, David. B.A. in History, Post Coll., 1963; Th.M., Dallas Theol. Sem., 1967; Ph.D. in Ednl. Adminstrn, U. Pitts., 1979. Ordained to ministry Scottsdale, Ariz., 1967; pastor Bible Ch., 1967-71; dean acad. affairs Lancaster (Pa.) Bible Coll., 1971-76; dean faculty Moody Bible Inst., Chgo.,

1976-79; pres. Phila. Coll. Bible, 1979—; speaker, cons. in field. Mem. Am. Assn. Higher Edn., Doctoral Assn. Educators, Am. Assn. Bible Colls. (pres.), Fellowship Ind. Missions (bd. mem.), Am. Scripture Gift Mission, Lower Bucks County C. of C., Phi Delta Kappa. Home: 161 Andrew Dr Newtown PA 18940 Office: Phila Coll Bible Langhorne Manor 200 Manor Ave Langhorne PA 19047

BABCOCK, JOHN MONTRAN, army chaplain; b. L.A., Aug. 19, 1949; s. Montran Benson and Doris Agnes B.; m. Corinne Suzanne McWilliams, Mar. 18, 1972; children: Robert, Matthew. BA, The Principia Coll., 1971; MDiv, Andover Newton Theol. Sch., Newton Ctr., Mass., 1977; ThM, Duke U., 1988; diploma, Command and Gen. Staff Coll., Ft. Leavenworth, Kans., 1989. Commd. capt. U.S. Army, 1977, advanced through grades to maj., 1986; bn. chaplain U.S. Army, Ft. Benning, Ga., 1977-79; community life chaplain U.S. Army, Ft. Benning, 1979-80; bn. chaplain U.S. Army, Nuernberg, Fed. Republic of Germany, 1980-83; brigade chaplain U.S. Army, Ft. Leonard Wood, Mo., 1983-87; instr. World Religions Defense Lang. Inst., Presidio of Monterey, Calif., 1988-91; brigade chaplain U.S. Army, Fed. Republic Germany, 1991—. Asst. Scoutmaster, Boy Scouts of Am., Ft. Leonard Wood, Mo., 1984-88; scoutmaster Boy Scouts Am., Ft. Ord., Calif., 1989, '90. Decorated Meritorious Svc. medal, Army Commendation medal with oak leaf cluster. Recipient Wood Badge award Boy Scouts Am., 1989, Scouters Key, 1990. Mem. Am. Acad. Religion, Assn. of the U.S. Army. Mem. Ch. of Christ Scientist.

BABCOCK, WENDELL KEITH, religion educator; b. Mt. Morris, Mich., Nov. 21, 1925; s. George Dewey and Nettie (Miller) B.; m. Esther Marie Winger, Aug. 23, 1951; children: Timothy, Stephen. BA, Bob Jones U., Greenville, S.C., 1967; MA, PhD, Columbia Pacific U., San Rafael, Calif., 1984; PhD, World U., Benson, Ariz., 1987; LLD, London Inst. Applied Rsch., 1989; PhD, Australian Inst. Coord. Rsch., 1991. Cert. minister, S.C., Mich., Tenn. Pastor Free Bapt. Ch., Timmonsville, S.C., 1951-53; prof. Free Bapt. Coll., Nashville, Tenn., 1953-55, Grand Rapids (Mich.) Sch. Bible & Music, 1955—; chmn. gen. ministries Grand Rapids Sch. Bible, 1978—; chmn. Grand Rapids Correspondence Sch., 1986—. Composer Songs in the Heavenlies 1957, vol. 2, 1958, Everywhere You Go It's Christmas, 1970; arranger keyboard duets Favorite Hymn Duets, 1964; keyboard artist WFUR Radio, 1956-57, Sound Assocs., 1962, 66, 70; author Portraits of a Changing World, 1987, (poems) Glimpses of Worship, 1990; editor Grand Rapids Sch. Bible, 1960—. Organist religious stage prodns. Grand Rapids Civic Ctr., 1960-70, Gull Lake Conf., 1986—; dir. libr., Grand Rapids Sch., 1989-90. Mem. N.Y. Acad. Scis., World Wildlife Assn. Republican. Avocations: horticulture, fishing. Home: 3455 Williamson NE Grand Rapids MI 49505 Office: Grand Rapids Sch Bible 1331 Franklin SE Grand Rapids MI 49506 *Coping with the vicissitudes of life can be a successful venture if one's focus is kept on the Sovereign Ruler of the universe and of mankind.*

BACALIS, NICHOLAS GEORGE, priest; b. Norfolk, Va., Aug. 19, 1942; s. George Nicholas and Katherine (Gretakis) B.; m. Vivian Couchell, May 24, 1970; children: Katrina Nicole, Anastasia Dawn. BA in English, U. Va., 1964; BD in Theology, St. Vladimir's Sem., 1968; cert., The Ecumenical Inst., Geneva, 1969. Ordained deacon Greek Orthodox Archdiocese of North and South Am., 1971; ordained priest, 1972. Dir. youth ministry Greek Orthodox Cathedral, Charlotte, N.C., 1969-71; parish priest St. Nicholas Ch., Jamestown, N.Y., 1972-76, Holy Trinity Ch., Roanoke, Va., 1976—; assoc. chaplain VA Med. Ctr., Salem, Va., 1976—; mem. faith and order com. Va. Coun. Chs., Richmond, 1980—; state youth dir. Diocese of New Jersey, Va., 1984—. Rep. Multiple Sclerosis Soc., Roanoke, 1980, cen. coun. PTA, Roanoke, 1982. Mem. NCCJ (steering com. 1980-88, Brotherhood citation 1981), Nat. Presbyters Conf., Roanoke Valley Ministerial Assn. (pres. 1978-79, exec. bd. 1988—), Va. Coun. Greek Orthodox Chs. (pres. 1981-83), Philo Soc., U. Va. Alumni Assn. (bd. dirs. Roanoke chpt. 1987). Office: Holy Trinity Greek Orthodox Ch 30 Huntington Blvd Roanoke VA 24012

BACHA, HABIB, archbishop. Archbishop of Beirut and Gibail Zouk-Mikael, Lebanon. Office: Archeveche Grec-Melkite-, Catholique, POB 58, Zouk-Mikael Lebanon*

BACHELDER, ROBERT STEPHEN, minister; b. Middletown, N.Y., Nov. 2, 1951; s. Stephen and Dorothy Esther (Gunderson) B.; m. Beverly June Brandt, Sept. 17, 1977; children: Stephen, Elizabeth. AB, Dartmouth Coll., 1973; MDiv, Yale U., 1978. Ordained to ministry United Ch. of Christ, 1978. Pastor United Ref. Ch., Pangbourne, Eng., 1978-79; min. 1st Congl. Ch., Shrewsbury, Mass., 1980-84; min. for mission and svc. Worcester (Mass.) Area Missionary Soc., 1984—; bd. dirs. Cen. Assn. Mass. Conf., United Ch. of Christ, 1983—. Author: Mystery and Miracle, 1983, Between Dying and Birth, 1983; contbr. articles to profl. jours. Pres. Habitat Worcester, 1984-86, Worcester Community Loan Fund, 1986-90, Worcester Com. on Homelessness and Housing, 1988-91; mem. City Mgr.'s Housing Task Force, 1990—; v.p. Worcester Housing Partnership, 1991—. Mem. St. Wulstan Soc., Worcester Com. on Fgn. Rels., Worcester Econ. Club, Dartmouth Club of Cen. Mass. (pres.). Home: PO Box 67 North Oxford MA 01537 Office: Worcester Area Missionary Soc 128 Central St Auburn MA 01501

BACHERT, ALAN HAROLD, minister; b. Aurora, Ill., Apr. 24, 1942; s. Harold C. L. and Esther E. (Holtz) B.; m. Judith Ann Sweatman, Aug. 21, 1965; children: Kristianna, Jennifer, Jason. BA, Aurora Coll., 1965; BD, Concordia Theol. Sem., Springfield, Ill., 1969, MDiv, 1971; D of Ministry, Concordia Theol. Sem., 1989. Ordained to ministry Luth. Ch.-Mo. Synod, 1969. Pastor St. Paul Luth. Ch., Steelville, Ill., 1969-72, Good Shepherd Chapel, Cape Girardeau, Mo., 1972-74; mission developer, campus pastor Murfreesboro, Tenn., 1974-77; min. discipleship St. Peter Luth. Ch., Arlington Heights, Ill., 1978-81; sr. pastor Trinity Luth. Ch., Tinley Park, Ill., 1981-87, King of Kings Luth. Ch., Chesterfield, Mo., 1987—; chaplain Howe Devel. Ctr., Tinley Park, 1981—; sec. Mo. dist. Luth. Ch.-Mo. Synod, 1991—. Pres. Bellwood PTA, Murfreesboro, 1979, Carl Sandburg High Sch. Music Parents, Orland Park, Ill., 1984. Named Outstanding PTA Pres., Tenn. PTA, 1979. Mem. Luth. Ch.-Mo. Synod Edn. Assn. (bd. evangelism 1982—), Chesterfield Ministerial Assn, Rotary (sec. local chpt. 1970-72, pres. 1991-92). Home: 1133 Quails Nest Run Ellisville MO 63021 Office: King of Kings Luth Ch Chesterfield MO 63017

BACHERT, SHARON KAY, lay worker; b. Columbia, Pa., Nov. 6, 1969; d. William Webster and Sandra Kay (Deitzel) B. BS in Ch. Youth Ministries and Bible, Pillsbury Bapt. Bible Coll., 1991. Pianist Columbia (Pa.) Bible Ch., 198-84; pianist, tchr. Word of Life Chapel, Elizabethtown, Pa., 1984-88; worker Camp Victory, Samson, Ala., 1986-87, Ponderosa Bible Camp, Mentone, Ala., 1986-87; mgr. food svc. Pillsbury Co., Owatonna, Minn., 1988-91; camp counselor Trails End Ranch, Ekalaka, Mont., 1990; youth leader Bryant Ave Bapt. Ch., Mpls., 1990-91; pianist Grace Bapt. ch., Owatonna, Minn., 1990-91; coord., counselor Home Missionary, Trails End Ranch, Ekalaka, Mont., 1991—. Pell grantee Fed. Govt., 1988-91, Harriet Bratrude scholar, 1990-91. Home: PO Box 271 Ekalaka MT 59324

BACHLE, ANNE ELIZABETH, lay worker, lawyer; b. Portsmouth, Va., Feb. 8, 1956; d. Carl and Patricia Bachle. BA, St. Mary's Coll., Notre Dame, Ind., 1978; JD, U. Mich., 1983. Bar: Mich. 1983. Instr. Lansing Community Coll., 1986-87, 89—; exec. dir. Christian Conciliation Svc. Cen. Mich., Lansing, 1987—. Contbr. articles to profl. jours. Bd. dirs. Habitat for Humanity, Lansing, 1991—. Internat. fellow Rotary, Berne, Switzerland, 1979-80. Mem. Assn. Christian Conciliation Svcs. (bd. dirs. 1989—), Mich. Community Dispute Resolution Program (adv. coun. 1989-91), Evang. Women's Caucus. Office: Christian Conciliation Svc 1710 E Michigan Ave Lansing MI 48912

BACHMAN, A. A., academic administrator. Head Berean Christian Coll., Long Beach, Calif. Office: Berean Christian Coll 6801 Milkmark Ave Long Beach CA 90805*

BACHMAN, JAMES VERNON, minister, educator; b. Council Bluffs, Iowa, June 14, 1946; s. Merle Edward and Louise Clara (Meyermann) B.; m. Susan Happel Ortmeyer, June 14, 1969; children: Henry Nathaniel, Katherine Jeanne, Joshua Karl. BS in Math. and Philosophy, Valparaiso U., 1968; BA with honors, Cambridge (Eng.) U., 1970, MA in Theology, 1974; MDiv, Concordia Sem., St. Louis, 1972; PhD, Fla. State U., 1986. Ordained to ministry Luth. Ch.-Mo. Synod, 1972. Pastor Our Redeemer Luth. Ch., Lake City, Fla., 1971-81; pastor, dir. Univ. Luth. Ctr., Tallahassee, 1981-89; instr. philosophy and world religions Lake City (Fla.) Community Coll., 1971-81, chmn. dept., 1978-81; asst. prof. philosophy Fla. State U., Tallahassee, 1985-89; prof. philosophy, John R. Eckrich chair in religion and healing arts Valparaiso (Ind.) U., 1989—; chmn. com. to restructure Fla.-Ga. dist. Luth. Ch.-Mo. Synod, Orlando, Fla., 1974-78, sec. coun. on ministry in higher edn., 1974-80, chmn., 1981-89, dist. coord. campus ministry Fla.-Ga., 1981-89; treas. campus ministries Fla. State U., 1981-89. Co-author: (with Jaakko Hintikka) What If...? Toward Excellence in Reasoning, 1991; contbr. articles to profl. jours. Mem. Lake City Community Choir, 1975-80, Tallahassee Bach Parley, 1981-91. Fulbright grantee, 1968-70; Fla. State U. fellow, 1982-83, Univ. fellow Fla. State U., 1983-86. Mem. Am. Philos. Assn., Inst. for Theol. Encounter with Sci. and Tech., Inst. for Religion and Democracy, Phi Kappa Phi. Republican. Home: 1452 Beargrass Ct Valparaiso IN 46383 Office: Valparaiso U Dept Philosophy Valparaiso IN 46383 *I consider my continuing task to be to discover how simultaneously to affirm the significance of my community's convictions about life and to keep open the dialog with other communities that makes for a genuine pluralism of choice in modern society.*

BACHMEIER, ADAM BERNARD, priest; b. Balfour, N.D., Aug. 21, 1938; s. Ignatius and Ethel (Lauinger) B. BA in Journalism, U. N.D., 1961; BD, St. John's Sem., 1968. Ordained priest Roman Cath. Ch., 1968. Assoc. pastor St. Mary's Cathedral, Fargo, N.D., 1968-73, St. Alphonsus Ch., Langdon, N.D., 1973-74; pastor St. Francis Ch., Marion, N.D., 1974-79, Assumption Ch., Dickey, N.D., 1974-79, Holy Family Ch., Grand Forks, N.D., 1979—; active Liturgy Commn., 1970-75, 1989—, Communivesity Bd., Grand Forks, 1981—. Democrat. Home and Office: Holy Family Church 1122 18th Ave S Grand Forks ND 58201

BACK, JERRY LEE, evangelist; b. Middletown, Ohio, Oct. 17, 1933; s. William Daniel and Dorothy Isabell (Sherrotts) B.; m. Margaret Ann Sloan, Jan. 28, 1952; children: Jerry Lee Jr., Deborah Ann, Michael David, Robyn Suzanne. Student, U. Bucharest, 1986. Ordained to ministry Pentecostal Ch., 1967. Evangelist Pentecostal Ministerial Assn. Am., Dayton, Ohio, 1956-65, chmn., pres., 1970-74; pastor Glendell Ch. of God, Franklin, Ohio, 1965-78; missionary, evangelist, missions dir. various places in 43 countries, 1978—; dir. missions East European Mission, 1991—. With U.S. Army, 1952-54, Korea. Republican. Office: East European Mission PO Box 7 Franklin OH 45005

BACKHUUS, TROY ALAN, religious education administrator; b. Omaha, Jan. 25, 1966; s. Thomas Gilmore and Dora Mae (Miller) B.; m. Roma Jean Oder, May 21, 1988. BS in Christian Edn., Neb. Christian Coll., 1989. Ordained to ministry Ch. of Christ, 1990. Intern 1st Christian Ch., Rapid City, S,D,, 1986; coord., jr high sch. retreat Neb. Christian Coll., Norfolk, 1987-88; min. Ch. of Christ, Ewing, Neb., 1988-89; min. Christian edn. Christview Christian Ch., Tulsa, 1990—. Office: Christview Christian Ch 2525 S Garnett Tulsa OK 74129 *Life is like a college exam: you have to have good notes to pass it.*

BACKUS, KEVIN MICHAEL, minister, school administrator; b. Holyoke, Mass., Oct. 27, 1956; m. Sharon Diane Marshall, Aug. 16, 1980. BA in Bibl. Lit., Shelton Coll., Cape Canaveral, Fla., 1978; MDiv, Faith Theol. Seminary, Elkins Park, Pa., 1982. Cert. tchr. Bible, history, and langs; ordained to ministry Bible Presbyn. Ch., 1982. Asst. pastor Armor Bible Presbyn. Ch., Orchard Park, N.Y., 1977; asst. pastor Bible Presbyn. Ch., Grand Island, N.Y., 1978-80, assoc. pastor, 1982—; stated supply pastor Calvary Bible Presbyn. Ch., Trenton, N.J., 1980-82; dir. devel. Faith Christian Sch., Collingswood, N.J., 1981-82; adminstr. Grand Island Christian Sch., 1986—; pres. Internat. Christian Youth, Collingswood, 1982-86; stated clk. Bible Presbyn. Ch.-Gen. Synod, Grand Island, 1989—, chmn. interchurch rels., 1989—. Contbr. articles to profl. jours. Mem. Internat. Fellowship Christian Sch. Adminstrs., ASCD, Presbyn. Missionary Union (coun. mem. 1989—, exec. mem. 1989—, v.p. 1991—). Office: Bible Presbyn Ch 1650 Love Rd Grand Island NY 14072 *Two things I constantly underestimate in life: the depravity of man, and the grace of God. Thankfully sovereign grace is greater.*

BACON, ARTHUR DENNIS, religious educator; b. Ft. Wayne, Ind., Oct. 31, 1948; s. Arthur Edward and Frances Helen (Gallagher) B.; m. Susan Eileen Hopkins, Dec. 18, 1971; children: Matthew Micah, Rebekah Sue, Benjamin Jon Kim. BS, Concordia Tchrs. Coll., 1970; MDiv, Concordia Theol. Sem., 1976; MA in Teaching, Saginaw Valley State U., 1983; PhD, Mich. State U., 1988; MS in Edn., No. Ill. U., 1990. Pastor Triune Luth. Ch., Sharon, Wis., 1976-80, St. John Luth. Ch., Bay City, Mich., 1980-84; asst. prof. Concordia U., River Forest, Ill., 1984-88, St. Louis, 1988—. Major USAR, 1976. Decorated Meritorious Svc. medal. Lutheran. Home: 910 Esic Dr Edwardsville IL 62025

BACON, DARWIN DEE, minister, church growth consultant; b. Scroggins, Tex., Aug. 27, 1947; s. Alton Lee and Minnie Sarah (Castle) B.; m. Gloria Jane Haire; children: David Timothy, Joel Andrew, Benjamin Paul. BS in Religion, East Tex. Bapt. U., Marshall, 1972; MDiv, Golden Gate Sem., Mill Valley, Calif., 1975; MBA, Rutgers U., 1990. Ordained to ministry So. Bapt. Conv., 1969. Systems analyst GYM-Dandy Inc., Bossier City, La., 1970-72; Pastor First Bapt. Ch., Pacheco, Calif., 1972-75, Farmingdale (N.Y.) Bapt. Ch., 1975-81; exec. dir. Syracuse (N.Y.) Bapt. Assn., 1981-84; Pastor Colts Neck (N.Y.) Bapt. Ch., 1984—; pres. pastors conf. Metro N.Y. Bapt. Assn., N.Y.C., 1979-81, exec. dir. search com., 1988—, chmn. mission coun., 1985—. Contbr. articles to profl. jours. Bd. dirs. Citizens Adv. Bd., Red Bank, N.J., 1988—, Coalition for Excellence, Colts Neck, 1986-88. With U.S. Army, 1968-70. Named Citizen of the Yr. Farmingdale Civic Orgn., 1980-81; Ch. Planter award Bapt. Home Mission Bd., Atlanta, 1987-88. Office: Colts Neck Bapt Ch PO Box 177 Colts Neck NY 07722

BACON, PATRICIA S., religious educator; b. Milw., Oct. 11, 1942; d. Kenneth Morrow and Lorraine Christine (Fritzke) Kenney; m. Arthur Williston Bacon, Sept. 18, 1965; children: Chet Arthur, Lee Kenneth, Rex Terrence, Tricia Lorraine. BA, Ohio Wesleyan U., Delaware, 1964; MA, John Carroll U., 1987. Dir. young adult ministry United Meth. Ch. of So. Euclid (Ohio), 1979-82; dir. Christian edn. Mentor (Ohio) Plains United Meth. Ch., 1982-86, Lyndhurst (Ohio) Community Presbyn. Ch., 1987-88, Willoughby (Ohio) Hills United Meth. Ch., 1987-88; program asst. Painesville (Ohio) Dist. United Meth. Ch., 1988—; mem. Ch. Edn. and Leader Devel. com. Interch. Coun. Greater Cleve., 1990-91; peace advocate United Meth. Ch., 1984—. Contbr. articles to profl. jours. Mem. Christian Educators Fellowship. Home: 5249 Ashwood Dr Lyndhurst OH 44124 Office: Painesville Dist United Met 153 E Erie St #401 Painesville OH 44077

BACON, PAUL ERWIN, minister; b. Oak Park, Ill., Mar. 5, 1942; s. Herman Erwin Greifendorf and Lydia Marie (Geiseman) B.; m. Annette Louise Voth, June 5, 1965; children: Paul M., Dean M., Elizabeth. BA, Concordia Coll., Ft. Wayne, Ind., 1963; MDiv, Concordia Sem., St. Louis, 1967; MST, Luth. Sch. Theology, Chgo., 1976. Ordained to ministry Luth. Ch.-Mo. Synod, 1967. Pastor St. John Luth. Ch., 1967-70, St. Paul Luth. Ch., Glenwood City, Wis., 1967-70, Good Shepherd Luth. Ch., Mayawood, Ill., 1970-76, Trinity Luth. Ch., New Lenox, Ill., 1976—; sec. English Dist. Luth. Ch. Mo. Synod, Detroit, 1976-88, v.p. 1988-91, cir. counselor, 1991—; bd. dirs. Luth. Child and Family Svcs., River Forest, Ill., 1974-86; bd. dirs. Luth. Family Svcs. Joliet, 1985—. Mem. Rotary (pres. 1973-74). Home: 515 N Cedar Rd New Lenox IL 60451 Office: Trinity Luth Ch N Cedar and Elm Sts New Lenox IL 60451 *Being a Cub fan prepares a person for living the Christian life in this world, for one knows what suffering is about and the full rewards are always, "Wait 'til next year."*

BACON, RALPH GORDON, minister; b. Colgate, N.D., Aug. 11, 1923; s. Ralph Paul and Violet Mae (Orser) B.; m. Phyllis Marie Reisenburg, June 2, 1944; children: Ronald James, Joel Francis, Robert Paul, Barbara Elaine. BS, Vennard Coll., 1945; BA, Bethel Coll., Mishawaka, Ind., 1949, DD, 1977. Ordained to ministry Missionary Ch., 1949. Pastor Bremen (Ind.) Missionary Ch., 1946-49, West Eckford Missionary Ch., Marshall, Mich., 1949-52, Beulah Missionary Ch., Elkhart, Ind., 1952-63; dist. supt. Ind. Dist./Missionary Ch., Elkhart, 1963-69; dir. of field svcs. Nat. Assn. Evangelicals, Wheaton, Ill., 1969-89; v.p. for coll. rels. Bethel Coll., Mishawaka, 1989—; trustee Vennard Coll., Univ. Park, Iowa, 1980—, Bethel Coll., 1963-87, Evangel. Child and Family Agy., Wheaton, 1970-91. Contbr. articles to profl. jours. Named Alumnus of Yr. Bethel Coll., 1967; recipient Disting. Alumnus award Vennard Coll., 1979. Mem. Delta Epsilon Chi. Home: 1471 Hampton Circle Goshen IN 46526 Office: Bethel Coll 1001 W McKinley Ave Mishawaka IN 46545

BADALEWSKI, BARBARA ANN, minister, educator, social worker; b. Berwyn, Ill., Nov. 29, 1953; d. Frank Joseph Jr. and Gloria Virginia (Smith) B. BA in Social Work, Coll. of St. Francis, 1985. Cert. tchr., Ill. Social worker St. Mary's Hosp., Centralia, Ill., 1984-86; tchr. 3d grade St. Mary's Sch., Plainfield, Ill., 1987-89; youth minister Divine Savior Parish/Joliet (Ill.) Diocese, Downers Grove, Ill., 1989—; tchr. 2d grade Rex Bell Sch., Las Vegas, Nev.; religious sister Felician Sisters, Chgo., 1981-87. *"Wait and be calm, rest in quiet and peace". This statement has helped me through many an experience. I pray that it will help to guide others on their journey to the everlasting peace.*

BADAMI, ROSE MARY RITA, lay worker; b. Denison, Tex., Nov. 13, 1929; d. Frank Anthony and Josephine Theresa (Burriesci) B. BA, U. St. Thomas, Houston, 1954; DHL, U. St. Thomas, 1986. Foundress Magnificat Houses, Houston, 1968—, Sancta Maria Hostel for Women, Houston, 1964-67. Recipient 1st Alumni of the Yr., St. Thomas Alumni Assn., 1968, Outstanding Woman award, AAUW, 1976, Woman of Valor award, Jewish Nat. Fund, 1983. Office: Magnificat House 3300 Caroline Houston TX 77265

BADAMO, THOMAS JOHN, religion educator, accountant; b. Freeport, N.Y., Aug. 6, 1965; s. Joseph and Mary Anne (Timmes) B. BBA, Hofstra U., 1987. CPA, N.Y. Tchr. confrat. Christian doctrine Viacom Internat., N.Y.C., 1990—; sr. auditor Viacom Internat., N.Y.C., 1990—. Republican. Roman Catholic. Home: 2390 Spruce St Seaford NY 11783

BADERMAN, ALFRED CARL, chaplain; b. Henderson Harbor, N.Y., July 25, 1927; s. Arthur G. and Ethel (Cook) B.; m. Dorothy Ann Erickson, Oct. 12, 1957; children: Daniel Kent, Lori Ann, Kari Sue. Student, U. Chgo., 1946-47, Miss. Tng. Inst., 1949-50; BA, AS in Psychology, Syracuse (N.Y.) U., 1953; BTh, Am. Bible Coll., 1955; postgrad., Luth. Brethren Sem., 1959. Ordained to ministry Luth. Ch., 1964. Pastor Stockholm (Wis.) Moravian Ch., 1959-61; pastor Elim Luth. Brethren Ch., Westby, Wis., 1961-66, Frontier, Sask., Can., 1966-70; pastor Salem Luth. Brethren Ch., Grand Rapids, Minn., 1970-79, Ebenezer Luth. Brethren Ch., Mayville, N.D., 1979-86, Elim Luth. Ch., Osakis, Minn., 1986-87; chaplain Mesa (Ariz.) Christian Care Ctr., 1987—. Contbr. articles to profl. jours. Avocations: outdoor activities, woodworking. Home: 222 W Brown Rd Mesa AZ 85201 Office: Mesa Christian Care Ctr 255 W Brown Rd Mesa AZ 85201

BADGER, BRYANT D., minister; b. Council Bluffs, Iowa, Oct. 7, 1938; s. Thomas E. and Ruth Badger;m. Kathryn A. Chlumsky, June 1964; children: Jennifer Rene, Julie Ruthe. BS in Religious Edn., Phillips U., 1961, BD, 1965, DMin, 1978. Ordained to ministry Christian Ch. (Disciples of Christ), 1965. Youth dir. Cen. Christian Ch., Wichita, Kans., 1960-63; student pastor First Christian Ch., Perkins, Okla., 1964-69; pastor First Christian Ch. (Disciples), Stroud, Okla., 1969-74, Meml. Christian Ch. (Disciples), Oklahoma City, 1974-83; sr. minister First Christian Ch. (Disciples), Casper, Wyo., 1983—; past sec. Wyo. Ministries in Higher Edn.; past. chmn. com. on the ministry Christian Ch., Wyo., Colo.; past pres. Casper Clergy Assn.; past dist. pres. 2 dists., Okla.; rel. del. Gen. Ch. Bd. Christian Ch., 1990-94. Author: (pamphlet) History of the Christian Church (Disciples of Christ) in Wyoming, 1991. Bd. pres. Cen. Wyo. Counseling Ctr., Casper, 1990—1; vol. Wyo. Law Enforcement Chaplain, Natrona County, Wyo., 1987—. Mem. Cen. Mountain Region of Christian Ch. (Disciples of Christ, clergy), Casper Clergy, Wyo. Law Enforcement Chaplains Assn., Lions (v.p. and program chmn. 1990-91). Home: 2105 S Poplar Casper WY 82601 Office: First Christian Ch 520 Cy Ave Casper WY 82601

BADIA-BATALLA, FRANCESC, veguer episcopal; b. Montblanc, Spain, Jan. 10, 1923; s. Francesc Badia-Anguela and Angela Batalla-Pinas; m. Maria Gomis-Dominguez, 1955; children: Francesc, Mariona, Montserrat. Grad. in law, U. Barcelona, Spain, 1945. Fis. atty., Barcelona, 1947-71; veguer episcopal of Andorra, 1972—. Author: Law of the Registers of Birth, Marriages, and Deaths, 1959; contbr. articles on family law and land registry law to Revista Juridica de Catalunya. Roman Catholic. Office: Veguer Episcopal, Andorra la Vella Andorra

BAEHR, THEODORE, religious organization administrator, communications executive; b. May 31, 1946; student in French lit. U. Bordeaux and Toulouse (France), 1967; student English lit. Cambridge (Eng.) U., 1967; student German lit. U. Munich (W. Ger.), 1968; m. Liliana Milani, 1975; children: Thedore Peirce, James Stuart Castiglioni, Robert Gallatin, Evelyn Noelle. BA in Comparative Lit. with high distinction (Rufus Choate scholar), Dartmouth Coll., 1969; JD, NYU, 1972; postgrad. Inst. Theology, Cathedral St. John the Divine, N.Y.C., 1978-80. Rsch. engr. Precision Sci. Co., Chgo., 1964-65; legal cons. firm Dandeub, Fleissig & Assocs., N.Y.C., 1970-71; law student asst. U.S. Atty.'s Office, So. Dist. N.Y., 1971-72; pres. Agape Prodns., N.Y.C., 1972-79, chmn. bd., 1979-82; exec. dir. Good News Communications, Inc., N.Y.C., 1978-80, chmn. bd., 1980—; pres., chmn. bd. Christian Film and TV Commn., 1990—; pres. Episc. Radio-TV Found., Inc., Atlanta, 1981-82, Trinity Concepts, 1982; cons. media; dir. TV Center, CUNY at Bklyn. Coll., 1979-80, 82—; AT&T, Cocoa, Fla., 1979-80, Episc. Communicators, 1981-84; exec. producer Ch.'s Presence at World's Fair, Knoxville, Tenn., 1982; dir. Am. Theater Actors, Episcipal Communications. Vice pres. Ctr. for TV in Humanities, 1982; bd. dirs. Christian Conciliation Service, Dorsey Theatre, SUP, Inc., Coalition on Revival, Habitat for Humanity. Mem. Soc. Motion Picture and TV Engrs., Nat. Religious Broadcasters (dir., sec. TV com.), Bishop in Ind. Christian Chs. Internat., Seawanhaka Corinthian Yacht Club., Nat. Press Club. Editor, Commentator, NYU Law Sch. newspaper, 1969-72, Contemporary Drug Problems, 1971-72, Atlanta Area Christian News; creator, coordinator Communicate Workshops, 1979; creator, writer, editor Episc. Ch. Video Resource Guide and Episcopal Video/TV Newsletter, 1979; producer, dir., writer various TV and radio programs including Movieguide, Joy of Music, Perspectives, PBS, 1981-82, Religionwise on WGST, CBS, 1981—(Religion in Media award), Searching, 1978-80, others; editor, writer various books, including TV and Reality, Asking the Right Question, Tangled Christian Communications, Getting the Word Out (Wilbur award), Movie and Video Guide for Christian Families (Religion in Media award); dir. Runaways (Chgo. Intercom Gold Plaque and Religion in Media award 1989), Hollywood's Reel of Fortune, 1991; producer In Their Own Words, Was It Love (Religion in Media award).

BAER, AGNES MARIE, nun; b. St. Louis, Nov. 6, 1921; d. Oliver Lewis and Agnes Carrie (Robineau) B. AB, Fontbonne Coll., St. Louis, 1943; AM, St. Louis U., 1952; postgrad., Regina Mundi, Rome, 1961-62. Joined Sisters of St. Joseph of Carondelet, Roman Cath. Ch., 1944—. Tchr. Our Lady of Lourdes Grade Sch., St. Louis, 1946-51, St. Teresa's Grade Sch., St. Louis, 1951-52, St. Francis de Sales High Sch., Denver, 1952-61; postulant dir. Sisters of St. Joseph, St. Louis Province, 1962-68; asst. prin. Acad. of Our Lady, Peoria, Ill., 1968-72, St. Thomas Aquinas High Sch., Florissant, Mo., 1972-74; tchr. Rosati-Kain High Sch., St. Louis, 1974-79; founder, dir. New Life Style Prog., St. Louis, 1979—. Adv. bd. Adult Basic Edn., St. Louis, 1989—, Our Lady's Inn, St. Louis, 1988—. Recipient Page One Civic Award, St. Louis Newspaper Guild, 1983, Woman of Achievement award, 1985. Mem. Mo. Assn. Social Workers, Soroptimist. Democrat. Roman Catholic. Home: 2307 S Lindbergh Saint Louis MO 63131 Office: New Life Style Program 4219 Laclede Saint Louis MO 63108

BAER, SISTER BARBARA, nun; b. Wichita, Kans., July 18, 1936; d. Howard LeRoy and Geneva (Langford) B. BS, St. Mary of the Plains, Dodge City, Kans., 1964; MA, Marquette U., Milw., 1971, PhD, 1976. Cert. tchr., Kans. Elem. tchr. Cath. Diocese Wichita, 1958-71; asst. prof. St. Mary of the Plains Coll., Dodge City, 1976-80, v.p. acad. affairs, 1980-84; asst. gen. superior Sisters of St. Joseph of Wichita, 1984—, dir. ministry, dir. planning, 1984—, dir. ongoing formation, mem. congl. leadership team,

1984—; mem. fedn. rsch. team Sisters of St. Joseph, 1975-80. Bd. trustees Pratt (Kans.) Regional Med. Ctr., 1982-87, Halstead (Kans.) Hosp., 1984—, The St. Mary Hosp., Manhattan, Kans., 1988—; bd. regents St. Mary of the Plains Coll., Dodge City, 1984—; bd. dirs. CSJ Health System Wichita, Inc., 1984—. Roman Catholic. Avocations: needlework, crafts. Home and Office: 3700 E Lincoln Wichita KS 67218

BAER, MAX FRANK, consultant; b. Frankfurt, Germany, Nov. 10, 1912; came to U.S., 1921; s. Bernard Baer and Erna (Pollak) Hoelzel; m. Gertrude Smith, Feb. 14, 1967; children: Richard Rosenbaum, Randye Low. Student, U. Notre Dame, 1930-34; LLB, JD, Creighton U., 1937; MA, Columbia U., 1942; EdD, George Washington U., 1947. Typist Assoc. Investment Co., South Bend, Ind., 1931-34; acting exec. sec. AZA B'nai B'rith, Omaha, 1934-38; nat. dir. Vocat. Svc. B'nai Brith, Washington, 1938-54, internat. dir. Youth Orgn., 1948-77; cons. planning and rsch. Washington, 1977-91, sesquicentennial historian, 1991—. Author: Occupational Information, 1951, 3d edit., 1967, Dealing in Futures, 1983; editor: Playing Around With Words, 1990. Mem. fed. adv. coun. Bur. Employment Security, Washington, 1948-58, bd. mgrs. Adas Israel Congregation, Washington, 1954—. Recipient Bisno award Profl. Excellence J & C Spitzer, 1988; Max. F. Baer Lodge named in his honor, Mukwonago, Wis., 1980, Baer Cultural Ctr. named in his honor, Ossifiya, Israel, 1975. Mem. APA, AACD, Acad. Cert. Social Workers (charter), Nat. Career Devel. Assn. (past pres.), Conf. Jewish Communal Svc., Phi Delta Kappa. Avocations: writing, reading, rsch., ballroom dancing. Home: 4201 Cathedral Ave NW Washington DC 20016 Office: 1640 Rhode Island NW Washington DC 20036

BAER, MICHAEL LEE, minister; b. Wabash, Ind., Mar. 31, 1954; s. John Everett and Lois Ann (Tyner) B.; m. Kim Mickelson, Dec. 18, 1982; 1 child, Christian Taylor. BSE, Ind. U., 1976; postgrad., Warnborough Coll., 1981, Boston U., 1987, Ball State U., 1990—. Youth coord. White River Christian Ch., Noblesville, Ind., 1984-86; youth min. Converse (Ind.) Ch. of Christ, 1989—. Vol. asst. Fellowship of Christian Athletes, North Cen. Ind., 1989—, Youth for Christ/Campus Life, Marion, Ind., 1989—. Mem. Oak Hill Min. Assn. (sec.-treas. 1990-91). Office: Converse Ch of Christ 301 E Wabash St Converse IN 46919

BAFILE, CORRADO CARDINAL, clergyman; b. L'Aquila, Italy, July, 1903; s. Vincenzo and Maddalena (Tedeschini) B.; LL.D., U. Rome, 1926, D.C.L., Lateran U., Rome, 1939. Ordained priest, Roman Cath. Ch., 1936, consecrated bishop, 1960, elevated to cardinal, 1976; officer Sec. of State, Vatican, 1939-58; privy chamberlain of the Pope, 1958-60; apostolic nuncio, Germany, 1960-75; prefect Sacred Congregation for the Causes of Saints, 1976-80; cardinal Roman Curia, Rome, 1976—. Home: 10 Via P Pancrazio Pfeiffer, 00193 Rome Italy

BAGBY, DANIEL GORDON, minister; b. Porto Alegre, Brazil, May 30, 1941; (parents Am. citizens); s. Albert Ian and Thelma (Frith) B.; m. Janet Glee Pitman, June 12, 1965; children: Douglas Ian, Meredith Bryn. BA, Baylor U., 1962, MS, 1964; B.D., So. Bapt. Theol. Sem., 1967, PhD, 1973. Ordained to ministry Bapt. Ch., 1968. Chaplain Louisville Detention Ctr., 1964-68; assoc. pastor Ravensworth Bapt. Ch., Annandale, Va., 1968-71; chaplain Ky. Correctional Instn. for Women, Pewee Valley, 1971-74; marriage and family counselor Jeffersonville Personal Counseling Ctr., Clarksville, Ind., 1971-74; instr. psychology of religion So. Bapt. Theol. Sem., Louisville, 1973-74, state alumni pres., 1975-76; pastor Calvary Bapt. Ch., West Lafayette, Ind., 1973-79, Seventh & James Bapt. Ch., Waco, Tex., 1979—. Author: Understanding Anger in the Church, Transition and Newness, Before You Marry, The Church: The Power to Help and to Hurt; contbr. articles to religious publs. Pres. Tippecanoe County Ministerial Assn.; trustee Midwestern Bapt. Theol. Sem., Kansas City, Mo., Baylor U., 1980-88; active Ind. InterReligious Commn. on Human Equality, United Way McLennan County; chmn. bd. Food and Emergency Shelter Bd. McClennan County. Mem. Am. Assn. Marriage and Family Counselors (clin.), Omicron Delta Kappa. Home: 927 Deer Ridge Waco TX 76712 Office: Seventh and James Bapt Ch 602 James St PO Box 6398 Waco TX 76706

BAGGER, RALPH WILLIAM, minister; b. Butler, Pa., June 12, 1923; s. Henry Horneman and Margaret (Finck) B.; m. Elizabeth Louise Hodges, Aug. 26, 1950;. AB, Muhlenberg Coll., 1948; BD, Luth. Theol. Sem., Phila., 1951; AM, U. Pa., 1951. Ordained to ministry United Luth. Ch. in Am. (now Evang. Luth. Ch. in Am.), 1951. Pastor St. Mark's Luth. Ch., Allentown, Pa., 1951-55, Immanuel Luth. Ch., East Lansdowne, Pa., 1955-59, Friedens Luth. Ch., Hegins, Pa., 1959-68; periodicals editor Luth. Ch. Am., Phila., 1968-88; dir. Luth. Theol. Sem., Phila., 1981—. Author: (with Elizabeth H. Bagger) Official Summary of Biennial Conventions of United Lutheran Church in America, 1954-60, Official Summary of Biennial Conventions of Lutheran Church in America, 1964-84; editor: Light for Today, 1968-88, The Lessons, 1991. Charter mem. East Lansdowne (Pa.) Civic Assn., 1956-59. Sgt. AUS, 1943-46, ETO, PTO. Mem. Hymn Soc. Am., Omicron Delta Kappa. Home: 9 Terrace Rd Norristown PA 19401-2617

BAGGETT, LOUIS BURNEY, minister; b. Clarksville, Tenn., Nov. 1, 1949; s. Edward Burney and Eileen Mae (Bruce) B.; m. Mary Dell Blackwell, June 3, 1971; 1 child, Brittyne Anne. BS, Austin Peay State U., 1971; MS, Purdue U., 1973; postgrad., Harding Grad. Sch., 1975, Marshall U., 1981-83. Registered environ. profl., environ. chemist. Campus min. Purdue Univ., Elmwood Ave Ch. of Christ, 1973-74, Austin Peay State Univ., Madison St. Ch. of Christ, 1974-80, Marshall Univ., Norway Ave Ch. of Christ, 1980-86; min. Charbo & Karen St. Ch. of Christ, St. Charles, Mo., 1986—; environ. chemist Am. Car and Foundry Industries, Inc., Earth City, Mo., 1988—; min. Ch. of Christ, St. Charles, 1986-91; deacon, 1990-91. Contbr. articles to profl. jours. Promoter Red Cross, Huntington, W.Va., 1982-85; bd. Kiwanis Club Circle K, Huntington, 1984-85; v.p. PTO Gallaher Sch., Huntington, 1985. Named Outstanding Young Man of Am., 1984, 86. Mem. Am. Assn. Christian Counselors, Registry Environ. Profls. Republican. Home: 432 Willow Wood Ct Saint Charles MO 63303

BAGGIO, SEBASTIANO CARDINAL, archbishop; b. Rosà, Italy, May 16, 1913; s. Giovanni Battista and Pierina B. Ed., Seminario Vescovile di Vicenza, Pontificia Universita Gregoriana, Pontificia Accademia Ecclesiastica and Scuola di Paleografia e Biblioteconomia in Vaticano. Ordained priest Roman Catholic Ch., 1935. Sec. Nunciatures in El Salvador, Bolivia, Venezuela, 1938-46, with sec. state, 1946-48; chargé d'Affaires Colombia, 1948-50, Sacra Congregazione Concistoriale, 1950-53; titular archbishop of Ephesus, 1953—; apostolic nuncio, Chile, 1953-59; Apostolic del., Can., 1959-64; Apostolic Nuncio, Brazil, 1964-69; elevated to Cardinal, 1969; archbishop of Cagliari, 1969-73; head Sacred Congregation for Bishops of Roman Cath. Ch., 1973-84; pres. Pontifical Commn. for Latin Am., 1973, for Vatican City's State, 1984; Chamber of the Roman Ch., 1985; cardinal patron Sovereign Mil. Order of Malta, 1984. Decorated orders from Bolivia, Brazil, Chile, Colombia, Ecuador, Venezuela, Portugal; Bailli Great Cross Order of Malta. Address: Piazza della Città Leonina 9, 00193 Rome Italy

BAGLEY, GARY J., priest; b. Buffalo, Dec. 16, 1946; s. Howard Henry and Beatrice Elizabeth (Westfield) B. BA, St. John Vianney Sem., East Aurora, N.Y., 1966, MDiv, 1972; postgrad., Fordham U., 1968; MRE, Notre Dame Sem., New Orleans, 1975. Ordained priest Roman Cath. Ch., 1972. Assoc. pastor St. Christopher's Ch., Tonawanda, N.Y., 1972-76; tchr. Bishop Turner High Sch., Buffalo, 1976; assoc. dir. Youth Dept., Diocese of Buffalo, 1976-86, dir. dept., 1986—; chaplain Sacred Heart Acad., Buffalo, 1977—, Franciscan Missionary Sisters, Williamsville, N.Y., 1979—. Contbr. articles to religious jours. Active Ellicott Creek Vol. Fire Co., Amherst, N.Y., 1972-76; bd. dirs. Our Lady of Victory Infant Home, Lackawanna, N.Y., 1980-86, Hopevale Inc., Hamburg, N.Y., 1989—. Mem. Nat. Fedn. for Cath. Youth (chairperson com.). Democrat. Office: Diocese of Buffalo Youth Dept 795 Main St Buffalo NY 14203

BAGLEY, RONALD MICHAEL, priest; b. Buffalo, July 14, 1950; s. Raymond and Doreen Frances (Nold) B. BA, St. John Vianney Sem., 1972; BTh, U. Ottawa, Ont., Can., 1973; ThM, St. Paul U., 1974; DMin, Andover Newton Theol. Sch., 1989. Ordained priest Roman Cath. Ch., 1977. Campus min. Cardinal Dougherty High Sch., Buffalo, 1976-79; dir. Office of Young Adult Ministry, Buffalo, 1979-85; assoc. pastor St. Christopher Parish, Tonawanda, N.Y., 1986-90; dir. St. John Eudes Ctr., Buffalo, 1990—; mem. adj. staff Ctr. for Youth Ministry Devel., Naugatuck, Conn., 1983—. Author: Young Adults and Families, 1991; editor: Young Adult Ministry: A Book of Readings, 1987. Mem. Nat. Cath. Young Adult Ministry Assn. (treas. 1982-85, bd. dirs.). Home and Office: St John Eudes Ctr 71 Burke Dr Buffalo NY 14215 *Life in this world has meaning to the extent that we are able to move beyond ourselves and reach out to others. Human life can only be lived in relationship.*

BAGWELL, GERALD EZRA, minister; b. Buford, Ga., Feb. 20, 1936; s. Cecil E. and Ola (Roberts) B.; m. Betty Tanner, Sept. 2, 1955; children: Gregory Charles, Jeffery Gerald, Philip Edward. BS, Piedmont Coll., Demorest, Ga., 1963; MDiv, Southeastern Bapt. Theol. Sem., Wake Forest, N.C., 1966; ThM, Luther Rice Sem., Jacksonville, Fla., 1968, ThD, 1969. Ordained to ministry So. Bapt. Conv., 1961. Pastor Mountain Park 1st Bapt. Ch., Stone Mountain, Ga., 1970-77, 1st Bapt. Ch., Lakeland, Fla., 1978-86, Bethany Bapt. Ch., Snellville, Ga., 1986—; pres. Gwinnett Metro Pastor's Conf., Lawrenceville, Ga., 1970-71; tchr. nationwide seminar on ch. growth, Republic of Korea, 1978; chmn. evangelism South Fla. Bapt. Assn., Lakeland, 1979-80; trustee Fla. Bapt. Theol. Coll., Graceville, 1984-86; speaker Someone Cares program Sta. WONN, Lakeland, 1982-85. Columnist Lakeland Ledger, 1984-86, Lakeland Consumer Shopping News, 1985. Home: 2346 Bethany Rd Snellville GA 30278 *In the daily walk called life, I have found that "people don't care what you know, unless they know you care."*

BAGWELL, SARA RUTH, religious organization official; b. Gray Court, S.C., Nov. 20, 1919; d. Luther and Janie Sue (Weathers) Bagwell. B.A., Furman U., 1947; postgrad. So. Baptist Theol. Sem., 1958. Sch. tchr., China Grove, N.C., 1947-48; dir. associational missions Baptist Ch., Murphy, N.C., 1948-51, Salisbury, N.C., 1951-56; dir. religious edn. Eglin AFB, Ft. Walton, Fla., 1958-64; assoc. dir. Woman's Missionary Union, Fla. Bapt. Conv., Jacksonville, 1964—. Office: Florida Baptist Convention 1230 Hendricks Ave Jacksonville FL 32207

BAHMANN, MANFRED KURT, minister, educator; b. Dresden, Saxony, Germany, Jan. 19, 1930; s. Kurt Richard and Norma (Führer) B.; m. Marianne Eloise Schneider, Aug. 28, 1958; children: Andrea, Christoph. B.D., United Theol Sem., 1954; first Theol. Exam, Gottingen, Heidelberg and Bonn, W.Ger., 1955, second Theol. Exam, 1958; Ph.D., Hartford Sem. Found., 1965. Ordained to ministry Church of the Palatine, 1955, mem. Luth. Ch. in Am., Evang. Luth. Ch. in Am., 1959—. Chaplain NATO, Kaiserslautern, Ramstein, Fed. Republic Germany, 1955-59; pastor St. Pauls Luth. Ch., Grafton, W.Va., 1959-62; prof. ch. history Facultad Luterana de Teologia, Jose C. Paz, Argentina, 1966-70; pastor First Luth. Ch., Parkersburg, W.Va., 1971-73; campus pastor Stanford U., Palo Alto, Calif., 1973-82; pastor Univ. Luth. Ch., Palo Alto, 1973-82, St. Thomas Ch., West Berlin, Germany, 1982-86, Zion-St. Mark's Ch., N.Y.C., 1986—; mem. ordination examining com. Landeskirche Berlin, 1983-86; lectr. Goethe Inst., Mexico City, 1983. Author: Obras De Martin Luthero, Volume 1, 1967, Volume 5, 1971. Contbr. articles to profl. jours. Bd. dirs. Stattbau, West Berlin, 1983-86. Recipient Cert. award Adult Ctr. Retarded 1973; Cert. award Mid-Peninsula Peace Community 1983. Democrat.. Home and Office: 424 E 84th St New York NY 10028 *My philosophy of life is expressed in a couplet I wrote when as a German teenager in 1945 I discovered the extent of the collapse of the German culture: "Halt im Gedächtnis Jesus Christ, weil alles andere grosser Scheissdreck ist."*

BAHN, DAVID LOUIS, pastor; b. Cape Girardeau, Mo., Dec. 1, 1951; s. Louis William and Lynne (Dodson) B.; m. Diane Lee Dolan, June 21, 1975; children: Matthew David, Timothy Robert, Aaron William, Stephen Paul. B in Gen. Studies, SE Mo. State U., 1974; MDiv, Concordia Theol. Sem., 1979; D of Ministry, Fuller Theol. Sem. Pastor Our Savior Lutheran Ch., Vernal, Vt., 1979-83, Trinity Luth. Ch., Rangely, Colo., 1979-81, Faith Lutheran Ch., Roosevelt, Utah, 1981-83, Trinity Luth. Ch., Pine Bluff, Ark., 1983—; sec. Circuit Pastor's Conf., Utah, Ark., 1979, 83; action group dir. Forward-In- Remembrance Conf., Vernal, 1980-81; continuing edn. coordinator Mid-South Dist. The Luth. Ch., Mo. Synod, Pine Bluff, 1986—, cir. counselor Stuttgart Cir., 1986—. Bd. dirs. The Shepards Ctr., Pine Bluff, 1986-87. Avocations: computers, stereos, photography. Office: Trinity Luth Ch 4200 Old Warren Rd Pine Bluff AR 71603 *The greatest single discovery that one can make about oneself is to find that God has gifted him or her with unique, valuable and strategic gifts to be shared in Jesus' name.*

BAHNER, GEORGE WASHINGTON, clergyman; b. Dalmatia, Pa., Feb. 22, 1937; s. Ralph Eston and Lottie Miriam (Bingaman) B.; m. Shirley Jean Latsha, June 18, 1960; children: Jean Marie, Linda Kay. AB, Franklin and Marshall Coll., 1959; MDiv, Union Theol. Sem., N.Y.C., 1963; MS, U. Wis., Madison, 1975; postgrad. Pa. State U., 1973-77. Intern Campus Ministry, Ohio State U., Columbus, 1961-62; ordained to ministry United Ch. of Christ, 1963; min. North Congl. Ch., Columbus, 1963-66; Salem United Ch. of Christ, Verona, Wis., 1966-73; adminstrv. asst. Pa. State U., 1976; adminstr. Homewood Retirement Ctr. and Thornwald Home, Carlisle, Pa., 1977-83; cons. health care mgmt.; min. St. John's United Ch. of Christ, Harrisburg, Pa., 1983-86, St. Matthew's United Ch. of Christ, Carlisle, Pa., Salem Stone United Ch. of Christ, Carlisle, 1989-90; pastor Trinity United Ch. of Christ, Coplay, Pa., 1990—; pres. Whitehall-Coplay Ministerium, 1991; cons. parish ministry United Ch. of Christ, Orlando, 1991; mem. Evangelism Task Force, Pa. N.E. Conf., 1990-91; fund raising program Fund Raising Sch., San Rafael, Calif., 1984; fund raising cons. The Carlisle Group, 1986—, Bahner Assocs., 1987; mem. Pa. White House Conf. on Aging, 1981; mem. faculty 6th N. Am. Symposium on Long-Term Care Adminstrn., 1980. Pres. trustees Campus Ministry United Ch. Christ, Ohio State U., 1965-66. Mem. Am. Coll. Health Care Adminstrs. (cert. fellow, del. to visit health facilities China and USSR 1983), Nat. Soc. Fund Raising Execs., Soc. Preservation and Encouragement Barbershop Quartet Singing Am., Phi Alpha Theta, Pi Gamma Mu. Home: 7918 Woodsbluff Run Fogelsville PA 18051 Office: 11 N Third St Coplay PA 18037

BAIL, CAROLINE, minister; b. Brockton, Mass., Apr. 22, 1953; d. Richard Nelson and Vivian Mae (Gibbs) B.; m. Darius Kenyi Jonathan, Aug. 17, 1986; 1 child, Jonah Iyeli Jonathan. BA in Anthropology, Yale U., 1975; Diploma, Women's Theol. Ctr., Boston, 1984; MDiv, Pacific Sch. of Religion, Berkeley, Calif., 1986. Ordained to ministry United Ch. of Christ, 1987. Student intern Woodside (Calif.) Village Ch., 1985-86; supply pastor Waianae (Hawaii) Protestant Ch., 1986; minister Ka Hana O Ke Akua United Ch. Christ, Waianae, 1987—; bd. dirs. Oahu Assn. Hawaii Conf. United Ch. Christ, Honolulu, 1987-90, commn. on women's concerns, 1986—, chaplain for annual mtg., 1991; del. to nat. assembly Coordinating Ctr. for Women, United Ch. Christ, 1988, 90. Author articles for newsletter. Bd. dirs. Waianae Coast Community Mental Health Ctr., 1989—. Democrat. Office: Ka Hana O Ke Akua United Church of Christ 85-256 Farrington Hwy Waianae HI 96792 *God calls us to be the body of Christ. In this mobile, acquisitive, individualistic culture it is the task of the Church to be a community, a colony, which acts as the hands and the heart of Jesus Christ.*

BAILEY, A. V., minister; b. Calhoun County, Miss., Jan. 1, 1921; s. Archie Lee and Cully Viola (Dye) B.; m. Rosa Alice Raper, July 12, 1941; children: Barbara Ann, Grady Howard. Student, Blue Mt. (Miss.) Coll., 1964-68. Ordained to ministry, So. Bapt. Conv. Minister Palestine Bapt. Ch., Lee County, Miss., 1964-68, Chesterville Bapt. Ch., Lee County, Miss., 1968-73, Cumberland Bapt. Ch., Webster County, Miss., 1973-74, Chesterville Calvary Bapt. Ch., Pontotoc County, Miss., 1974-79, Cumberland Bapt. Ch., 197982, Indian Hills Bapt. Ch., Lee County, Miss., 1982-85, Clarkson Bapt. Ch., Webster County, Miss., 1985-87, Chesterville Calvary Bapt. Ch., 1987—. With U.S. Army, 1942-45. Home: Route 7 Box 109 Tupelo MS 38801

BAILEY, AMOS PURNELL, clergyman, journalist; b. Grotons, Va., May 2, 1918; s. Louis William and Evelyn (Charnock) B.; m. Ruth Martin Hill, Aug. 22, 1942; children: Eleanor Carol Bailey Harriman, Anne Ruth Bailey Page, Joyce Elizabeth Bailey Richardson, Jeanne Bailey Dodge-Allen. BA, Randolph-Macon Coll., 1942, DD, 1956; BD, Duke U., 1948; ThM, Union Theol. Sem., 1957. Ordained to ministry United Meth. Ch., 1942; pastor Emporia, Va., 1938, Beulah UMC Ch., Richmond, Va., 1938-43; pastor New Kent circuit, 1943-44, Norfolk, 1948-50, Newport News, Va., 1950-54; pastor Centenary Ch., Richmond, 1954-61; supt. Richmond dist. United Meth. Ch., 1961-67; sr. minister Reveille Ch., Richmond, 1967-70; assoc. gen. sec., div. chaplains Bd. Higher Edn. and Ministry United Meth. Ch., Washington, 1970-79; v.p. Nat. Meth. Found., 1979-82; interim minister Herndon Ch., 1985-86; pres. Nat. Temple Ministries, Inc., 1981—; pres. S.E.J. and S.C.U. Communications, 1968-76; dir. Reeves-Parvin Co., 1978-85; v.p. Va. Conf. Bd. Missions, 1955-61, Meth. Commn. Town and Country Work, 1956-67; mem. Meth. Commn. on Higher Edn., 1960-70, Meth. Interbd. Council, 1960-70; del. Southeastern Jurisdictional Conf., 1964, 68, Gen. Conf., 1964, 66, 68, 70, World Meth. Conf., London, 1966, Denver, 1970, Dublin, 1976; exec. com., Congress, 1987-88; fin. com. Nat. Ch. Growth Research Ctr., 1986—; frequent chaplain U.S. Senate, U.S. Ho. of Reps., Va. Gen. Assembly; mem. council, exec. com., pres. communications com. Southeastern Jurisdiction, 1968-76; pres. Joint Communications Com., 1968-76; vice chmn. Ministry to Service Personnel in East Asia, 1972-79; mem. Commn. on Interpretation, Va. Conf.; participant Ednl. Study Mission to Eng., 1988. Writer: syndicated column Daily Bread, 1945—; syndicated radio devotional, 1945-69; condr.: weekly radio counseling program The Night Pastor, 1955-690, Sunshine and Shadows, 1967-70; contbr. articles to profl. jours. Mem. exec. com. Va. Conf. Bd. Edn., 1968-72; mem. World Meth. Council.; Mem. Va. Commn. Aging; pres. adv. bd. Richmond Welfare Dept., 1956-68; group chmn. industry div. Richmond United Givers Fund, 1961; mem. Va. Conf. Bd. Ministry, Richmond Pub. Assistance Com., Richmond Council on Alcoholism; chmn. chaplains adv. council VA, Washington; bd. mgrs. Richmond YMCA, 1961-69; Bd. dirs. Va. Meth. Advisers; trustee Randolph-Macon Coll., 1960-82, trustee emeritus, 1986; bd. visitors Duke Div. Sch., 1964-70; trustee So. Sem., 1961-76. Served with Chaplains Corps AUS, 1945-47. Mem. Meth. Hist. Soc., Duke Div. Alumni Assn. (pres.). Club: Kiwanis. Home: 7815 Falstaff Rd McLean VA 22102 Office: 1835 N Nash St Arlington VA 22209 *Life for me is rich and meaningful in a Christian commitment which allows a free and unfettered search for truth. Discipline of time and resources, the love of persons in my sphere of activity, a devoted family —all are part of the life I cherish daily.*

BAILEY, BETTY JANE, minister; b. East Orange, N.J., Jan. 16, 1931; d. Edward George and Lillian Anna (Poeter) Wenzel; m. J. Martin Bailey, June 5, 1954; children: Kristine Elizabeth Bailey Leffel, Susan Ruth Bailey Razzaz. BA, Drew U., 1952, MDiv magna cum laude, 1976; MA, Eden Theol. Sem., 1954; D Ministry, McCormick Theol. Sem., Chgo., 1987. Ordained to minstry United Ch. of Christ, 1977. Assoc. min. Union Congl. Ch., Upper Montclair, N.J., 1976—; founder, dir. Watchung Ch. Nursery Sch., Upper Montclair, 1967-73; cons. edn. St. Luke's Episcopal Ch., Montclair, N.J., 1973-75; cons. Bishop Anand Resource Ctr., Episcopal Diocese of Newark, 1976, St. Louis Presbytery, 1961; moderator Cen. Atlantic Conf., United Ch. of Christ, 1980-81; chair ch. and ministry com. N.J. Assn., United Ch. of Christ, 1981-84; mem. exec. com. N.J. Coun. Chs., East Orange, 1988—, chair commn. on theology and interreligious rels., 1988—. Author: Worship with Youth, 1962, Youth Plan Worship, 1987; co-author: (with Constance Tarasar) Eyes to See, Ears to Hear, 1987; contbr. numerous articles to profl. jours. Past v.p. Montclair YWCA; trustee N.E. Career Ctr., Princeton, N.J., 1983-85; mem. adv. bd. Bridge Program of Montclair Bd. Edn., 1988-90; coord. Montclair CROP Walk, 1990-91; mem. Civil Rights Commn., Montclair, 1991—. Mem. Religious Edn. Assn., Assn. United Ch. Educators, Montclair Clergy Assn. Home: 45 Watchung Ave Upper Montclair NJ 07043 Office: Union Congl Ch 176 Cooper Ave Upper Montclair NJ 07043

BAILEY, CLOVER THOMASSON, minister; b. Tyler, Tex., Aug. 25, 1952; d. Lacy S. and Clover (Riggs) Thomasson; m. Glenn E. Bailey, July 16, 1982; children: Virginia Clover, Lee Edward. BS in Edn., Stephen F. Austin State U., 1975; MDiv., Austin Presbyn. Sem., 1984; ThM, Fullr Theological Grad. Sch., 1984. Ordained to ministry Presbyn. Ch. , 1984. With Young Life Youth Ministry, Dallas, 1976-79; assoc. min. 1st Presbyn. Ch., Temple, Tex., 1983-86; chaplain VA Hosp., Ann Arbor, Mich., 1988-90, chief chaplain, 1990—; bd. dirs. Synod Mgmt. Unit, Detroit, chmn. 1991—; co-chair Local Ch. Devel., Detroit, 1990—; founding bd. dirs. Habitat for Humanity, Waco, Tex., 1983-85. Home: 2256 Delaware Ann Arbor MI 48103 Office: VA Med Center Fuller Rd Ann Arbor MI 48105

BAILEY, DORIS ADELINE, lay worker; b. Eureka, Calif., Mar. 15, 1924; d. John Gustoff and Adelaide (Zeigler) Strand; m. Barton J. Higginbotham (div. Oct. 1950); children: Gerald, Candice; m. Mar. 29, 1951 (dec.); children: Kenneth, Howard, Kirk. RN, Children's Hosp., 1945; CMA, Shasta Coll., 1982. Supt. Sunday Sch. Ch. of the Nazarene, Casa Grade, Ariz., 1949-80; mem. bd. dirs. Nazarene Ch., Redding, Calif., 1979-81, 89-90; Support svc. asst. Calif. Vocat. Rehab., Redding, 1982—; del. Dist. Assembly Nazarene, Sacremento, Calif., 1979, 85. Republican. Home: 18400 Keeper Way PO Box 314 Cottonwood CA 96022 Office: 1900 Churn Creek Rd Ste 100 Redding CA 96002

BAILEY, EARL EUGENE, religion educator; b. Shreveport, La., Apr. 16, 1927; s. William Henry and Essie Belle (Crowell) B.; m. Doris Josephine Fox, June 1, 1946; children: Marilyn Elizabeth Bailey Lewis, Margaret Cecilia Bailey Gill. BA, La. Coll., Pineville, Ark., 1948; MusM Edn., Ouachita U., 1964; postgrad., U. West Fla., 1972. Min. music and edn. First Bapt. Ch., Hope, Ark., 1953-54, Marshall, Tex., 1955-56; min. music and edn. Sunset Acres Bapt. Ch., Shreveport, 1956-57; min. edn. Cen. Bapt. Ch., Magnolia, Ark., 1958-66, First Bapt. Ch., Panama City, Fla., 1966-71; prof. religion Gulf Coast Community Coll., Panama City, 1971—; lectr. Holy Land Tours, 1983—; mem. faculty Ridgecrest Bapt. Assembly, Black Mountain, N.C., 1969; bd. dirs. Bailey Tours, Inc., Panama City. Host, producer weekly TV program This Believing World, Panama City, 1983—; columnist Panama City News Herald, 1970—; contbr. articles to various jours. Pres. Rotary Club, Magnolia, Ark., 1966, program chmn., Panama City, 1970, chaplain, 1972; vice chmn. State Bd. Missions, Jacksonville, Fla., 1969. Named Outstanding Prof. Yr., Gulf Coast Community Coll., 1986; Paul Harris fellow Rotary Club, 1987. Mem. Ark. Bapt. Religious Edn. Assn. (pres.), Bibl. Archael. Soc., Fla. Assn. Community Colls. Democrat. Home: 799 Wood Ave Panama City FL 32401 Office: Gulf Coast Community Coll 5230 W Hwy 98 Panama City FL 32401 *A person who makes a mistake and doesn't correct it is making an even greater mistake. We must learn from our shortcomings if we are to be productive human beings.*

BAILEY, EMMANUEL FRANKLIN, minister; b. Monrovia, Liberia, Nov. 30, 1954; came to U.S., 1977; s. Mackerson and Harriett (Madison) B.; m. Taylorie Major, May 28, 1977; children: Carmina, Norris, Emmanuel. BS, Wayne State U., 1980; MDiv, Meth. Theol. Sch., 1983; D. Ministry, St. Mary's U., Balt., 1988; MA, Eastern Mich. U., 1990. Ordained to ministry United Meth. Ch., 1982. Pastor Lee Ave. United Meth. Ch., Columbus, Ohio, 1981-83, Flint (Mich.) Park United Meth. Ch., 1983-88, Charity United Meth. Ch., Flint, 1988—; mem. program com. Detroit Conf. United Meth. Ch., 1987—, mem. urban ministry com., 1986—; mem. Flint dist. Coun. of Ministry, 1988—. Recipient award Flint African Am. Festival, 1986, Liberian Assn. Mich., 1989, Flint Urban Youth, 1990. Mem. Flint Coun. of Chs. (bd. dirs. 1989—), NAACP, Am. Assn. Counselors, Nat. Assn. Christian Counselors, Concern Pastor Assn. Mich., African Assn. Mich. (pres. 1986-91), Masons, Eurica Lodge. Home: 5048 Wilshire Dr Flint MI 48504 Office: Charity United Meth Ch 4601 Clio Rd Flint MI 48504 *Black men and women are on every ship in the world except the ship of partnership.*

BAILEY, GLENN E., wholesale distribution executive; b. Scranton, Pa., July 17, 1954; s. Harry E. and Naomi K. (Lee) B.; m. Karan Clover Thomasson, July 16, 1982; children: Virginia, Lee. BSBA, Oral Roberts, 1976; MBA, Harvard U., 1978. Chief fin. officer Spring Arbor Distributors, Belleville, Mich., 1986-87, chief exec. officer, 1987—, also bd. dirs.; v.p. planning Word, Inc., Waco, Tex., 1978-82, chief fin. officer, Waco, 1982-86; bd. advisors M Bank, Waco, 1984-86. Founding bd. mem. Habitat for Humanity of Waco, 1985-86. Mem. Am. Wholesale Booksellers Assn. (bd. trustees 1990—). Office: Spring Arbor Distbrs 10885 Textile Rd Belleville MI 48111

BAILEY, GLENN ROSS, minister; b. Kansas City, Mo., Sept. 10, 1929; s. Glenn Plater and Clara Geneva (Brady) B.; m. Marian Jean Egner, Aug. 20, 1950; (div. 1974); m. Willie Janice McCormick, Aug. 4, 1974; children: Timothy, Janice, Robin, Geoffrey. BS, U. Mo., 1966; BA, U. Ozarks, 1984; MDiv, U. Dubuque, 1987. Ordained to ministry Bapt. Ch.; cert. pastoral counselor. Pastoral intern Lamar (Ariz.)-Mt. Olive United Meth. Ch., 1979-82, Sherrill (Iowa) United Ch. Christ, 1982-85, Faith United Meth. Ch., Monmouth, Iowa, 1985-87; sr. pastor First Bapt. Ch., Rolla, Kans., 1987—; vice moderator Pioneer Assn. Am. Bapt., S.W. Kans., 1989—; treas. Ministerial Alliance, Rolla, 1989—; chaplain Morton County Hosp. ethics com., Elkhart, Kans., 1990—, del. county Ministerial Alliance, 1991—. Author: (manual) Electronic Field Interrogation, 1967, (books) The Wankel RC Engine, 1968, Rotary Piston Machines, 1969 (awarded medal and cash 1969). Councilman City of Rolla, 1989; police chaplain Morton County Law Enforcement Ctr., Elkhart, 1990; active Rolla Devel. Assn., 1990, Santa Fe Trail Coun. BSA (v.p. 1988—). With U.S. Army, 1956-60, Korea. Recipient Innovataor award Sony Corp., N.Y. and Tokyo, 1970; Named Outstanding Vol. gov. State of Ark., 1981, gov. State of Kans., 1990. Fellow Illumination Engring. Soc. (v.p. 1972-74, nat. 1st place award 1961); mem. USCG aux., Fire Fighters Hall Fame (life, v.p. bd. dirs. 1971—), Tribe of MIC-O-SAY. Home: 408 Taylor Rolla KS 67954

BAILEY, H. BARRY, minister; b. Hampton, Ark., Sept. 30, 1926; s. Lamar and Marguerite B.; m. Joan Kessler, May 4, 1950; children: Barry Kessler, Janice Bailey Robinson. BA, Hendrix Coll., 1947; MTh., Perkins Sch. Theology, Dallas, 1951; DD, Centenary Coll., 1970; LittD, HHD, Southwestern U., Tex. Wesleyan, 1978, 89. Ordained to ministry United Meth. Ch. Minister First United Meth. Ch., Rison, Ark., 1951-53, Lewisville, Ark., 1953-56; assoc. minister First United Meth. Ch., Shreveport, La., 1956-62; sr. minister Broadmoore United Meth. Ch., Baton Rouge, 1962-72; sr. minister First United Meth. Ch., Richardson, Tex., 1972-76, Fort Worth, Tex., 1976—; guest minister numerous annual confs., United Meth. Ch.; pres. South Ark. Telephone Co. Author: Especially For You, 1978, We Are Not Alone, 1979, Living With Your Feelings, 1980, With Best Wishes, 1982, Living With The Unexpected, 1984, Come, Join The Family, 1986; speaker weekly TV program, KTVT. Trustee So. Meth. U., Dallas, Tex. Wesleyan U., Ft. Worth; pres. Tarrant Area Community of Chs., 1982-83; mem. The Arts Coun. of Ft. Worth and Tarrant County, Cen. Bus. Dist. Planning Coun., Ft. Worth; del. Gen. Conf. of United Meth. Ch. Mem. The World Meth. Coun., Rotary, Exch. Club. Office: First United Methodist Ch 800 W Fifth St Fort Worth TX 76102

BAILEY, HOWARD ROBERT, pastor; b. St. Louis, Mar. 16, 1932; s. Theodore Jennings and Dorothy Mae (Rickard) B.; m. Kay McCastlain, June 30, 1957; 1 child, Kevin Glenn. Student, Ark. State Coll., Jonesboro, 1949-50; BA in Psychology, Hendrix Coll., 1957; ThM in Theology, Iliff Sch. Theology, Denver, 1960, ThD in Philosophy of Religion, 1963. Ordained to ministry Meth. Ch., 1961. Acad. dean John J. Pershing Coll., Beatrice, Nebr., 1970-71; exec. minister First United Meth. Ch., Omaha, 1971-79; dir. ministries Nebr. Annual Conf., United Meth. Ch., Lincoln, Nebr., 1979-80, exec. dir. ministries, 1980-85; sr. pastor First United Meth. Ch., Blair, Nebr., 1985—; chmn. Conf. Bd. Discipleship, Lincoln, 1976-79; rep. south cen. jurisdiction Coun. on Ministries, Dallas, 1980-86. Bd. dirs. Crowell Meml. Home, Blair, Nebr., 1985—; sec. Neb. Conf. Bd. Pensions, Lincoln, 1986—. Mem. United Meth. Ch. Bus. Adminstrs., Rotary. Office: First United Meth Ch 1656 Colfax St Blair NE 68008

BAILEY, JAMES MARTIN, minister, ecumenical executive, public relations consultant; b. Emmetsburg, Iowa, July 28, 1929; s. Allen Ransom and Kathryn (Ausl) B.; m. Betty Jane Wenzel, June 5, 1954; children: Kristine Elizabeth, Susan Ruth. BA in Journalism, State U. Iowa, 1951; BD, Eden Theol. Sem., 1954, DD, 1966; MS in Journalism, Northwestern U., 1956; DD, Lakeland Coll., 1967. Ordained to ministry United Ch. Christ, 1954. Mem. staff Nat. Coun. Chs., N.Y.C., 1954-60, mem. news and information dept., 1974-83; assoc. gen. sec. for media, mem. svcs. Nat. Coun. Chs. of Christ, 1985-90, unit dir. for edn., communication and discipleship, 1991—; bus. mgr. Internat. Jour. Religious Edn., N.Y.C., 1954-60; dir. circulation, advt. and promotion United Ch. Herald, St. Louis, 1960-63; editor United Ch. Herald, N.Y.C., 1963-72, A.D. Mag., N.Y.C., 1973-83, CWS Connections, 1983-85; bd. dirs. Overseas Ministries Study Ctr., 1984—, pres., 1988—, trustee; bd. dirs. United Ch. Christ Office of Communication, 1985. Author: Windbreaks, 1959, Youth in the Town and Country Church, 1959, From Wrecks to Reconciliation, 1969; (with Mrs. Bailey) Worship with Youth, 1962, Youth Plan Worship, 1987, (with Douglas Gilbert) The Steps of Bonhoeffer, 1969, One Thousand Years, 1987, The Spring of Nations, 1991; contbg. editor Reformed World, Geneva, Switzerland. Mem. Associated Ch. Press (pres. 1979-81), Interchurch Features (chmn. 1969-73), Religious Pub. Rels. Coun. (bd. dirs. 1987-91). Home: 45 Watchung Ave Upper Montclair NJ 07043 Office: 475 Riverside Dr Rm 852 New York NY 10115

BAILEY, JON NELSON, minister; b. Edinburg, Tex., Apr. 16, 1954; s. George Nelson and Boyde (Chasteen) B.; m. Peggy DeAnn Wooten, Mar. 8, 1975; children: Joel Nathan, Jessica Ann. MA, Abilene Christian U., 1985, MDiv, 1986; MA, U. Notre Dame, 1989, postgrad., 1986—. Min. Grandview Ch. of Christ, Des Moines, 1978-79, Rising Star (Tex.) Ch. of Christ, 1979, Lawn (Tex.) Ch. of Christ, 1984-86, Eleventh and WIllis Ch. of Christ, Abilene, Tex., 1989—; asst. prof. coll. Bibl. studies Abilene Christian U., 1989—. Mem. Soc. Bibl. Lit., North Am. Patristic Soc., Seminar on Devel. Early Cath. Christianity, Southwest Regional Bibl. Studies Seminar. Home: 1722 Bent Tree Dr Abilene TX 79602 Office: Abilene Christian U ACU Station Box 8429 Abilene TX 79699

BAILEY, KEELS DALE, minister, psychologist; b. Belvedere, S.C., May 10, 1936; s. Samuel Keels and Emma Murral (Thompson) B.; m. Gwendolyn McKeithen, Apr. 4, 1964 (div. Oct. 1972); children, Brenda Susan, Phillip Oliver; m. Phyllis Kay Bekemeyer, June 23, 1984. BA, Coll. Wooster, 1958; Cert., U. Oxford, Eng., 1960; STB, Harvard U., 1961; ThD, Sch. Theology at Claremont, Calif., 1967. Lic. psychologist, Calif. Min. counseling 1st Meth. Ch., Pasadena, Calif., 1963-64; pvt. practice in psychology Albany, Calif., 1964—; parish assoc. Montclair Presbyn. Ch., Oakland, Calif., 1988—; clin. coord. Samaritan Counseling Ctr., Walnut Creek, Calif., 1990—. Mem. APA, San Francisco Presbytery, Internat. Ctr. for Integrative Studies. Home: 1250 Washington Ave Albany CA 94706 Office: Albany CA 94706

BAILEY, MARCIA BARNES, minister; b. Utica, N.Y., Jan. 29, 1961; d. Norman Stafford and Janet Lloyd Barnes; m. Richard Curtis Bailey, June 9, 1984; children: Sarah Elizabeth, Adam James. BA, Alderson-Broaddus Coll., 1983; MDiv, Eastern Bapt. Theol. Sem., 1986. Ordained to ministry Am. Bapt. Ch., 1986. Pastor Mayfair Coun. Meml. Bapt. Ch., Phila., 1986—; chair Phila. Bapt. Adv. Com., 1987—; vice chair adv. bd. Mayfair Pastoral Counseling Ctr., Phila., 1990-91. Mem. Phila. Bapt. Assn. (bd. dirs. 1989—), Am. Bapt. Minister's Coun. Office: Mayfair Conwell Meml Bapt Ch Rowland and Tyson Aves Philadelphia PA 19149

BAILEY, MARK LEROY, educator, minister; b. Monte Vista, Colo., Sept. 28, 1950; s. Arthur Charles and Martha Virginia (Jones) B.; m. Barbara Kay Green, June 23, 1972; children—Joshua, Jeremy. A.A., Maricopa Tech. Coll., 1970; B.A., Southwestern Coll., 1972; M.Div., Western Sem., 1975, Th.M., 1977; postgrad., Dallas Theol. Sem., 1984—. Registered radiol. technician, Ariz., Oreg. X-ray technician Meml. Hosp., Phoenix, 1968-72, Adventist Hosp., Portland, Oreg., 1972-76, Mesquite Community Hosp., Dallas, 1979-80; Southwestern Coll., Phoenix, 1976-79, prof. Bible, acad. dean, 1980-85; assoc. pastor Palmcroft Bapt. Ch., Phoenix, 1980-85; prof. Bible Dallas Theol. Sem., 1985—. Bd. dirs. Valley Bible Inst., 1982—; mem. nominating com. Mission Soc., Phoenix, 1983—. Recipient Homiletics award Western Sem., 1975, Scholarship award, 1977. Mem. Am. Registry of Radiol. Technicians, Creation Research Soc., Bibl. Archaeol. Soc., Evang. Theol. Soc., Delta Epsilon Chi. Republican. Home: 2219 Havenwood Dr Arlington TX 76018 Office: 3909 Swiss Ave Dallas TX 75214 *The number one goal of life is to live my life for the only one God who both created me and redeemed me.*

BAILEY, R. RICHARD, minister; b. Washington, Oct. 4, 1953; s. V. Gilbert and J. June (Altier) B.; m. Karen Edwina Graham, May 24, 1975; children: Heather Melaine, Christopher Richard. BA, Carson-Newman Coll., 1976; MDiv, Southeastern Seminary, Wake Forest, N.C., 1983. Minister of music/youth Cen. Bapt. Ch., Lenoir, N.C., 1976-78; minister of music, youth and Christian edn. Mt. Home Bapt. Ch., Morganton, N.C., 1978-81; minister of music/youth Fall Creek Bapt., Bennett, N.C., 1981-83; minister of Christian edn./youth The Meml. Bapt. Ch., Greenville, N.C., 1983—. Named to Outstanding Young Men of Am., 1985; recipient Svc. award Jaycees, Jefferson City, Tenn., 1976. Mem. N.C. Youth Ministers Assn. (editor 1984-86, v.p. 1986-87, pres. 1987-88, sec./treas. 1990—), N.C. Religion Educators Assn., Civitan (chaplain 1987-89, bd. dirs. 1988-89), Phi Mu Alpha. Office: The Memorial Baptist Ch 1510 Greenville Blvd SE Greenville NC 27858

BAILEY, RAYMOND H., religion educator, minister; m. Patricia Lawson; children: Ramona Holland, Sarah Elizabeth. BA in Religion, Drama, Baylor U., 1959; MA in Speech, Tex. Tech U., 1964; postgrad., Northwestern U., 1965, 66; MDiv, So. Bapt. Theol. Sem., 1970, PhD in History-Philosophy, 1973; postdoctoral studies, U. Chgo. Div. Sch., 1984-85. Ordained to ministry Bapt. Ch. Tchr. pub. schs. Orange, Tex., 1960-63; instr. Sul Ross State Coll., 1964-65; asst. prof. Hardin-Simmons U., 1965-67; assoc. prof., chmn. dept. Bellarmine Coll., 1967-74, trustee, 1972-74, dir. Ctr. for Community Edn., 1973-74; pastor 1st Bapt. Ch., Newport, Ky., 1974-77, Plantation, Fla., 1977-79; prof. Christian preaching So. Bapt. Theol. Sem., 1979—; bd. dirs. Nat. Ctr. for Christian Preaching. Author: Thomas Merton on Mysticism, 1975, Destiny and Disappointment: Religion in America, 1990-1950, 1977, Jesus the Preacher, 1990, Paul the Preacher, 1991; also articles; (with others) Preaching in American History, 1969, Sermons in American History, 1979, Illustrating the Gospel of Matthew, 1982, Illustrating Paul's Letter to the Romans, 1984, Preach the Word in Love and Power, 1986; co-author: (with James Blevins) The Bible Alive: The Dramatic Monologue Sermon, 1990. Trustee St. Meinrad Sem. and Sch. Theology, 1971-72. Recipient Teilhard de Chardin award Bellarmine Coll., 1971, William T. Miles Faculty award Bellarmine Coll., 1971. Mem. Acad. Homiletics, N.Am. Acad. Liturgy. Office: So Bapt Theol Sem 2825 Lexington Rd Louisville KY 40280

BAILEY, ROBERT DAVID, minister; b. Florence, S.C., Dec. 17, 1951; s. Robert James and Emily (Williamson) B.; m. Mary Ellen Putnam, Aug. 24, 1974; 1 child, Megan Alexandra. BS, Frances Marion Coll., 1974; MDiv, Southern Sem., 1983, postgrad., 1987—. Ordained to ministry So. Bapt. Conv., 1983. Minister Double Branch Bapt. Ch., Orangeburg, S.C., 1983-88, Maple Bapt. Ch., Conway, S.C., 1988—; mem. ministers adv. coun. Charleston (S.C.) So. U., 1991—. Mem. S.C. Bapt. Conv., Waccamaw Bapt. Assn. (assoc. discipleship tng. dir. 1988-90, Christian life and pub. affairs dir. 1990—), Waccamaw Bapt. Assn. Pastor's Conf. Democrat. Home: 4511 Hwy 65 Conway SC 29526 Office: Maple Bapt Ch 4500 Hwy 65 Conway SC 29526

BAILEY, ROBERT LESLIE, minister; b. Detroit, May 26, 1945; s. Robert and Dorothy (Hollis) B.; m. Connie J. Gaddy, Nov. 20, 1966; children: Kerissa Michelle, Robert L. Jr. BA, Lee Coll., 1978; grad., Ch. of God Sch. Theology, 1991. Ordained to ministry Ch. of God (Cleveland, Tenn.), 1970. State evangelist Ch. of God, Atlanta, 1964-66, 74-78; pastor Atlanta, 1966-68; sr. pastor Rockmart (Ga.) Ch. of God, 1968-70; pastor Bremen (Ga.) Ch. of God, 1970-72; sr. pastor Ch. of God, Toledo-Sylvania, Ohio, 1972-74; nat. evangelist Ch. of God, Cleveland, Tenn., 1978-81; sr. pastor Woodlawn Hills Ch. of God, Canton, Ohio, 1981-87, South Cleveland (Tenn.) Ch. of God, 1987—; chmn. Ordain Ministerial Examining Bd., Chattannoga, Evangelism Bd. Akron, State Youth Bd., Atlanta; dist. overseer Ch. of God, Canton, 1982-87, Cleve., 1987—; mem. Family and Social Concerns Commn., Ch. of God Internat. Office, 1988—, state coun., Akron, Ohio, 1984-87; mem. study com. No. Ohio state office Ch. of God;dist. youth dir. Rome, Ga., 1968-70. Named one of Outstanding Young Men of Am., 1976. Home: 430 26th St NW Cleveland TN 37312 Office: S Cleve Ch of God 940 S Ocoee St Cleveland TN 37311

BAILEY, RUTH HILL (MRS. A. PURNELL BAILEY), foundation executive; b. Roanoke, Va., Sept. 17, 1916; d. Henry Palmer and Carolyn Ruffin (Andrews) Hill, m. Amos Purnell Bailey, Aug. 22, 1942; children: Eleanor Carol Bailey Harriman, Anne Ruth Bailey Page, Joyce Elizabeth Bailey Richardson, Jeanne Purnell Bailey Allen. AA Va. Intermont Coll., 1936; student Hollins Coll., 1936-38; BS in Edn., Longwood Coll., Farmville, Va., 1939; postgrad. Ecumenical Inst., Jerusalem, 1979. High sch. tchr. in Va., 1939-48; tour dir. to Europe and Mid. East, 1963-73; participant ednl. study mission to Eng., 1988; syndicated columnist family newspapers, 1954-70; exec. sec. Nat. Meth. Found., Arlington, Va., 1979-82; pres. Va. Conf. Bishop Cabinet Wives, United Meth. Ch., 1963-64; pres. Richmond (Va.) Ministers Wives, 1965-66; chmn. bd. missions Trinity United Meth. Ch., McLean, Va., 1975-79, adminstrv. bd., 1971-79; life mem. United Meth. Women. Div. sec. United Givers Fund, 1964-65; sec. bd. dirs. N.T.M., Inc., 1981—. Recipient Staff award Bd. Higher Edn. and Ministry, United Meth. Ch., 1976, Chaplain Ministry award, 1981. Clubs: Country of Va., Jefferson Woman's. Home: 7815 Falstaff Rd McLean VA 22102 Office: PO Box 5646 Washington DC 20016-1246

BAILEY, SCOTT FIELD, retired bishop; b. Houston, Oct. 7, 1916; s. William Stuart and Tallulah (Smith) B.; m. Evelyn Williams, Dec. 11, 1943; children—Louise (Mrs. Allen C. Taylor), Nicholas, Scott Field, Sarah (Mrs. Hugh A. Fitzsimons III). BA, Rice U., 1938; postgrad., U. Tex. Law Sch., 1938-39; MDiv, Va. Theol. Sem., 1942, DD, 1965; STM, U. of South, 1953, DD, 1965; DD, Episcopal Seminary of Southwest, 1987. Ordained to ministry Episcopal Ch., 1942; pastor in Waco, Lampasas, San Augustine, Nacogdoches, Austin, Tex., 1942-51; asst. to bishop of Tex., 1961-64, suffragan bishop of, 1964-75; coadjutor bishop of West Tex., 1976-77, bishop of, 1977-87; Sec. ho. of bishops Episcopal Ch., 1967-86, exec. officer Gen. Conv., 1973-77; chmn. bd. archives Episcopal Ch., 1982—. Served as chaplain USNR, World War II. Fellow Coll. of Preachers; mem. Phi Delta Theta. Home: 1 Towers Park Ln # 2116 San Antonio TX 78209

BAILEY, SHELBY JEAN, lay worker; b. Gary, W.Va., July 21, 1947; d. Irvin and Hannah (Kennedy) Roberts; m. Garry Lee Bailey, Nov. 9, 1963 (wid. May 1982); children: Patricia Lynn, Larry Lee, Melissa Pauline. BA, Bluefield State Coll., 1986; MA, U. W.Va., 1990. Cert. elem. edn. tchr., K-8, specific learning disabilities tchr./spl. edn. K-12, W.Va. Sec./treas. Bethel Assembly of God, Kimball, W.Va., 1965-78, youth dir., 1968-78; youth dir. Rolfe Pentecostal Holiness Ch., Northfork, W.Va., 1990; tchr. Sunday sch. Bethel Assembly of God and Rolfe Pentecostal Holiness Chs., 1965-91; sch. tchr. McDowell County Bd. of Edn., Welch, W.Va., 1986—. Sponsor Fellowship of Christian Students Club, Elkhorn Jr. High, Northfork, W.Va., 1989-91. Democrat. Home: Po Box 556 Keystone WV 24852 *Although life offered many challenges, along with the challenges come opportunities to rise higher in life and become a better person. Facing life with a positive attitude and faith in God will allow life's rocks to become stepping stones to our success.*

BAIN, CLINTON DWIGHT, marriage and family therapist; b. Pineville, Ky., Aug. 2, 1960; s. Clinton and May (Valentine) B.; m. Sheila Joanne Campbell, Aug. 3, 1985. AA, Valencia Community Coll., Orlando, Fla., 1981; BS, Heritage Coll., 1981; postgrad., Liberty U., 1982-84, MA, 1984. Cert. marriage and family therapist. Crisis counselor Old Time Gospel Hour, Lynchburg, Va., 1982-84; high sch. tchr. Heritage Preparatory Sch., Orlando, 1978-82; dir. therapy Orlando Counseling Ctr., 1984—; program dir. Park Place Hosp., Kissimmee, Fla., 1988-89; cons. The First Acad., Orlando, 1988—; cons. Univ. Behavioral Ctr., Orlando Spiritual Group Therapy, Children & Adolescent Units; talk show host Sta. WTLN AM/FM, Orlando, 1987—; seminar leader Sta. WTGL-TV 52, Orlando, 1988—; workshop leader Orange County Schs., Orlando, 1985-88, Christian Educators Assn., Orlando, 1987—. Contbr. articles to profl. jours. Mem. exec. bd. dirs. Christian Media Assn., Orlando, 1986-88; bd. dirs. Additions-Sch. Vols., Orlando, 1985-88, New Beginnings Home, Orlando, 1985-89, Christian Counseling Assn., Kissimmee, 1986-88. Named Vol. of Yr., Additions-Orange County Schs., 1987. Mem. Am. Assn. Counseling & Devel., Assn. Religious Values in Counseling, Menniger Found. for Mental Health, Am. Assn. for Marriage & Family Therapists, Toastmasters Internat. (Best Speaker, Orlando chpt. 1987, 88). Republican. Baptist. Office: Orlando Counseling Ctr 826 N John St 200 Orlando FL 32808 *The best advice I was ever given as a teenager was from my science teacher, Mary Hillyard, simply put, "The world will stand aside to let any man pass who knows where he is going." She was right and this insight made a difference in my developmental years; and now I share her advice with hundreds of other teenagers. Thanks Mary, for touching my life.*

BAIN, DOUGLAS COGBURN, JR., religious educator; b. Pearl River County, Miss., Nov. 30, 1940; s. Douglas Cogburn and Audrey (Smith) B.; children: Sherwood Kent, Stewart Kevin. Student, Miss. State U., Starkville, 1958-60; BA, Miss. Coll., Clinton, 1962; MDiv, Southwestern Sem., Ft. Worth, Tex., 1967; ThD, Southwestern Sem., 1973. Prof. religion and psychology Blue Mt. (Miss.) Coll., 1975—; bd. ministerial edn. pres. Miss. Bapt. Conv., 1983-84. Contbr. articles to Christian Single mag., 1987-89, Mercer Dictionary of the Bible, 1990. Mem. Nat. Assn. Bapt. Profs. of Religion. Baptist. Avocations: house plants, tennis, photography, backpacking, motorbiking. Office: Blue Mountain Coll Box 337 Blue Mountain MS 38610-0337 *Truth, from a functional and dynamic perspective, whether referencing philosophical, psychological, theological or gender issues, is found in a balance between two distinctive postures.*

BAIN, PATRICIA MONEY, church official; b. Wilmington, N.C., Oct. 19, 1942; d. Hilary Branscom and Nannie Ruth (Ratcliff) Money; m. Robert Tucker Bain, Jr., Aug. 13, 1966 (div. Nov. 1990); children: Elisabeth Michelle, Michael Christopher, Catherine Reneé. BA, Radford (Va.) U., 1965; MALS, Hollins Coll., Roanoke, Va., 1980; postgrad., Wesley theol. Sem., 1991—. Grad. profl. cert., Va. Tchr. Woodbridge, Roanoke, Giles County, Norfolk city schs., Va., 1965-73; dir. Christian edn. Larchmont United Meth. Ch., Norfolk, 1980-82; dir. program ministries 1st United Meth. Ch., Hampton, Va., 1982-87, Monumental United Meth. Ch., Portsmouth, Va., 1987-89; dir. ednl. ministries Trinity United Meth. Ch., Newport News, Va., 1989-91, Bethel charge, Cokesbury charge, United Meth. ch., 1991—; cons. Christian Ministry Resources, Virginia Beach and Front Royal, Va. 1989—; dir. Cancer & Our Spiritual Journey, Virginia Beach, 1989-91.—. Mem. Christian Educator's Fellowship (dist. rep. 1985-87), United Meth. Women, Indsl. and Comml. Ministries (chaplain). Avocations: fishing, crafts, drama, mission projects, youth minister. Home: 530 Villa Ave Front Royal VA 22630 Office: Parsonage 530 Villa Ave Front Royal VA 22630

BAIR, DALE LEROY, retired minister; b. Sharon, Pa., July 11, 1926; s. John and Sarah M. (Reuff) B.; m. Blanche Lauffer, Dec. 30, 1950; children: David W., Darrell L., Duane R., Dale W. Grad., Allentown (Pa.) Bible Inst., 1951. Ordained to ministry Pilgrim Holiness Ch., 1954. Youth leader Pilgrim Holiness Ch., Pitts., 1951-64, dist. treas., 1962-64; conf. del. Pilgrim Holiness Ch., Mt. Pleasant, Pa., 1951-72; desk clk. YMCA, 1981-86. Chaplain Aux. Police, Titusville, Pa., 1953-58; active war cry ministry collection Salvation Army, Titusville, 1977-91. Home: 714 Jones St Titusville PA 16354 *Do not set around hoping for everything to come to you. Open your eyes and help others out who are needy. "Do unto others as ye would have them do unto you."*

BAIRD, ALBERT WASHINGTON, III, minister; b. Beaumont, Tex., June 21, 1940; s. Albert W. and Daisy (West) B.; m. Gloria Elaine Treat, Sept. 11, 1961; children—Staci, Kristi, Keri. B.A., Abilene Christian U., 1963; B.S. in Elec. Engring., U. Tex., 1963, Ph.D., 1968. Ordained to ministry Ch. of Christ, 1984; research scientist Sperry Research Ctr., Sudbury, Mass., 1968-83; elder Boston Ch. of Christ, 1983—. Contbr. articles to sci. jours. Patentee in field. Mem. IEEE (sr.), Tau Beta Pi, Eta Kappa Nu. Fellow Tex. Atomic Energy Research Found., 1964, NASA, 1965-68. Home: 5 Brantwood Ln Burlington MA 01803

BAIRD, DONALD GEORGE, minister; b. Phoenix, Mar. 15, 1946; s. Homer V. and Alberta Charlotte (Bealey) B.; m. Leslie J. Reinman, June 29, 1974; children: Joshua Thomas, Zachary Edward, Micah William, Noelle Lynn. BA, U. of Redlands, 1968; MDiv, Vanderbilt U., 1971, D of Ministry, 1972. Ordained to ministry Christian Ch. (Disciples of Christ), 1971. Assoc. pastor Eastwood Christian Ch., 1971-72, Cen. Christian Ch., Youngstown, Ohio, 1972-77; pastor Northwest Christian Ch., Dayton, Ohio, 1977-84; sr. pastor 1st Christian Ch., Cuyahoga Falls, Ohio, 1984—; mem. exec. bd. Disciples Peace Fellowship, Indpls., 1971-83; bd. dirs. Ecumenical Campus Ministry, Youngstown, 1972-77, Met. Chs. United, Dayton, 1980-84; mem. New Ch. Establishment Com., Cleve., 1984-91; min.-in-residence Vanderbilt Div. Sch., Nashville, 1989; keynote speaker Conf. on Successful Aging, Akron, Ohio, 1990. Chmn., fundraiser Youngstown Area CROP/Ch. World Svc., Youngstown, 1975-77; mem. Citizen's Adv. Coun. Black Grant Dispersement, Youngstown, 1975-77, v.p. Pastoral Counseling Ctr., Akron, Ohio, 1991. Democrat. Office: 1st Christian Ch 2253 Third St Cuyahoga Falls OH 44221

BAIRD, HARRY RUSSELL, minister, educator; b. Las Animas, Colo., Apr. 6, 1918; s. Harry Simon and Tennie Mae (Russell) B.; m. Margaret Lucile Mills, July 23, 1941; children: Marilyn Patrice, Douglas Lynn, Thomas Michael, Joel Edward. BTh, Northwest Christian Coll., 1941; MDiv, Butler Sch. Religion, 1947, MA, 1958; D Missiology, Fuller Theol. Sem., 1979. Pastor various chs., Oreg., Ind., 1941-47, Wash., Kans., 1947-69; missionary Brazil, 1970-80; prof. missiology Manhattan (Kans.) Christian Coll., 1980-87; instr. anthropology, missions Trinity Western Univ., Langley, B.C., Can., 1988—. Mem. Health and Safety Through Edn. (v.p. 1991—), Statewide Drug and Alcohol Edn. in Pub. Schs., Theta Phi. Home and Office: 3801 Lakeway Dr Bellingham WA 98226

BAIRD, JOSEPH ARTHUR, religion educator; b. Boise, Idaho, June 17, 1922; s. Jesse H. and Susanna (Bragstad) B.; m. Mary Harriet Chapman, June 10, 1947; children: Andrew Arthur, Paul Chapman. B.A., Occidental Coll., 1943; B.D., San Francisco Theol. Sem., 1949; Ph.D., U. Edinburgh, 1953; student, U. Basel, Switzerland, 1951, U. Marburg, Germany, 1962. Ordained to ministry Presbyn. Ch., 1949; asst. pastor San Francisco, 1946-47; Western field rep. Intersem. Movement, 1947-48; music tchr. Marin County (Calif.) schs., 1948-49; pastor White Sulphur Springs, Mont., 1948-49; asst. pastor Edinburgh, 1949-51; pastor Burney, Calif., 1952-54; prof. religion Coll. Wooster, Ohio, 1954-86; chmn. dept. Coll. Wooster, 1967-71, Synod chair religion, 1972; researcher, writer, lectr., 1986—; adj. prof. San Francisco Theol. Sem., 1964-69; Rep. theol. edn. Am. Acad. Religion, 1956-66; chmn. Lilly Endowment study presem. edn., 1958-64, mem. internat. com. computer Bib. studies, 1968-71; chmn. (Pella Archaeol. Bd.), 1965-67; mem. dept. campus Christian life Synod Ohio, 1966-69. Author: Justice of God in the Teachings of Jesus, 1963, Audience Criticism and the Historical Jesus, 1969, A Critical Concordance to the Synoptic Gospels, 1971, Rediscovering the Power of the Gospel, 1982, The Greed Syndrome, 1990; also articles.; editor: The Computer Bible, Internat. Concordance Library, Iona Press. Pres. Bibl. Research Assos.; Mem. Wooster Symphony Bd., 1960-64. Served to lt. (j.g.) USNR, 1943-46. Mem. Am. Acad. Religion, Soc. Bib. Lit., Studiorum Novi Testamenti Societas, Phi Beta Kappa. Club: Rotarian (chmn. com. internat. service Wooster 196869). Pioneer use computers for content research Greek N.T., devel. audience criticism for N.T. research. Home: 1435 Gasche St Wooster OH 44691 *The guiding raison d'etre of my life is a sense of God's calling to the work I am doing. I find this most adequately expressed in the life and teachings of Jesus Christ, who has been the subject of my research, writing and lecturing through the years.*

BAIRD, LARRY DON, minister, nurse; b. Abilene, Tex., Sept. 23, 1949; s. Delmar Lee baird and Frances Elizabeth Weathers; m. Mary Margaret Ledbetter, Dec. 22, 1970; 1 child, Shannon Kirk; 1 adopted child, Walter Dale. Student, San Diego State U., 1971-72, Cisco Jr. Coll., Clyde, Tex., 1977-78; diploma in nursing, Hendrick Meml. Hosp., Abilene, 1972-73. Ordained to ministry United Pentecostal Ch. Internat., 1973-84, Assemblies of Lord Jesus Christ, 1984. Evangelist United Pentecostal Ch., 1973-78; pastor United Pentecostal Ch., Hamlin, Tex., 1979-82; residential dir. Tupelo (Miss.) Children's Mansion, 1982-84, campus dean, 1983-84; co-pastor 1st Pentecostal Ch., Abilene, 1984; dir. nurses Valley View Care Ctr., Anson, Tex., 1990-91; asst. choir dir., musician, dir. and interpreter for deaf United Pentecostal Ch., Abilene, 1984—; dir. Spirit of Freedom Alcoholic Ministries, 1984—; pvt. nurse coord. Health Care Svcs., Abilene, 1984—; sr. pastor Abundant Life Apostolic Ministries, Abilene, 1984—; dir. home missions Tex.-N.Mex. Distr. for Assemblies of Lord Jesus Christ, 1986-91; bd. dirs. Blue Mountain (Miss.) Childrens Home. Active various health support groups, Abilene, 1984—; chmn., mem. exec. bd. Abilene Coord. Coun., 1984—. With USNR, 1970-76. Fellow Ministerial Alliance (pres. 1980-82). Republican. Home: 1918 Sayles Blvd Abilene TX 79605 Office: First Pentecostal Ch 741 S 11th St Abilene TX 79603 *Life is like jig saw puzzle. Many pieces seem unnecessary, however, the true beauty is only seen at* *the time of completion, when all pieces fit perfectly together. It is finished—so also is a finished life in Christ.*

BAIRD, RANDY MICHAEL, minister; b. Norman, Okla., Apr. 22, 1955; s. Billie Maurice and Eileen (Wegener) B.; m. Kimberly Susan Jordan, June 23, 1979; 1 child, Cassandra Marie. BA, Christ Coll., Irvine, Calif., 1980; MDiv, Concordia Theol. Seminary, Ft. Wayne, Ind., 1988. Ordained to ministry Luth. Ch., 1988. Pastor St. John Luth. Ch., Nashville, Kans., 1988-91, Pryor, Okla., 1991—. Mem. Okla. Dist. Luth. Ch. Mo. Synod. Republican. Home: 109 Bryan Pryor OK 74361 Office: St John Lutheran Church 607 SE Ninth St Pryor OK 74361

BAIRD, ROBERT DAHLEN, religious educator; b. Phila., June 29, 1933; s. Jesse Dahlen and Clara (Sonntag) B.; m. Patty Jo Lutz, Dec. 18, 1954; children: Linda Sue, Stephen Robert, David Bryan, Janna Ann. BA, Houghton Coll., 1954; BD, Fuller Theol. Sem., 1957; STM, So. Meth. U., 1959; PhD, U. Iowa, 1964. Instr. philosophy and religion U. Omaha, 1962-65; fellow Asian religions Soc. for Religion in Higher Edn., 1965-66; asst. prof. religion U. Iowa, Iowa City, 1966-69, assoc. prof., 1969-74, prof., 1974-88, 89—, acting dir. Sch. Religion, 1985; Leonard S. Florsheim Sr. Eminent Scholar's chair New Coll., U. South Fla., Sarasota, 1988-89; faculty fellow Am. Inst. Indian Studies, India, 1972, sr. fellow, 1992; vis. prof. Grinnell Coll., 1983. Author: Category Formation and the History of Religions, 1971, 2d paperback edit., 1991, (with W.R. Comstock et al) Religion and Man: An Introduction, 1971, Indian and Far Eastern Religious Traditions, 1972; editor, contbr.: Methodological Issues in Religious Studies, 1975, Religion in Modern India, 1981, 2d edit., 1988, Essays in the History of Religion, 1991; book rev. editor: Jour. Am. Acad. Religion, 1979-84; contbr. articles to profl. jours. Ford Found. fellow, 1965-66; U. Iowa Faculty Devel. grantee, 1979, 86, 92; Am. Inst. Indian studies sr. fellow, spring 1992. Mem. Am. Acad. Religion, Assn. Asian Studies, N.Am. Assn. for the Study Religion. Democrat. Presbyterian. Office: U Iowa Sch of Religion Iowa City IA 52242

BAIRD, ROBERT DEAN, mission director; b. Hereford, Tex., Aug. 12, 1933; s. Kay and Maybelle (Witherspoon) B.; m. Margaret Ann Roberts, Aug. 27, 1953; children: Sandy, Deana Young. AA, Amarillo Jr. Coll., 1953; BTh., Bapt. Bible Coll., 1970, DD (hon.), 1986; DD (hon.), Atlantic Bapt. Bible Coll., 1986. Asst. pastor High St. Bapt. Ch., Springfield, Mo., 1969-72; missionary Bapt. Bible Fellowship Internat., Springfield, 1972-77, asst. mission dir., 1977-81; pastor Hallmark Bapt. Ch., Fort Worth, 1981-86; mission dir. Bapt. Bible Fellowship Internat., Springfield, 1986—. Mem. Internat. Conf. on World Evangelism (steering com. 1990—). Office: Bapt Bible Fellowship Inter 720 E Kearney St Springfield MO 65803

BAIRD, WILLIAM ROBB, theologian, educator; b. Santa Cruz, Calif., Feb. 27, 1924; s. William Robb and Martha (Watson) B.; m. Shirley Elizabeth Bauman, June 2l, 1946; children: Elisabeth Baird Parks, Eric Robb. BTh, N.W. Christian Coll., Eugene, Oreg., 1946; BA, U. Oreg., 1947; BD, Yale U., 1950, MA, 1952, PhD, 1955. Ordained to ministry Christian Ch. (Disciples of Christ). Assoc. prof. grad. sem. Phillips U., Enid, Okla., 1952-56; prof. Lexington (Ky.) Theol. Sem., 1956-67; prof. Brite Div. Sch. Tex. Christian U., Ft. Worth, 1967—; sr. fellow Inst. for Advanced Study of Religion, U. Chgo., 1989-90. Author: Paul's Message and Mission, 1960, The Corinthian Church, 1964 (Religious Book Club award), The Quest of the Christ of Faith, 1977, 1 and 2 Corinthians, 1980. Recipient Chancellor's award Tex. Christian U., 1985; Two Brothers fellow Yale U., 1950-51. Mem. Soc. Bibl. Lit. (regional pres. 1970), Studiorum Novi Testamenti Societas, Assn. of Disciples for Theol. Discussion, Phi Beta Kappa. Mem. Christian Ch. (Disciples of Christ). Home: 3824 Winifred Dr Fort Worth TX 76133 Office: Tex Christian U Brite Div Sch Fort Worth TX 76129

BAK, MICHAEL JOE, minister; b. Prosser, Wash., Oct. 31, 1962; s. Mike and Florence Mary (Wilhelm) B.; m. Mona Lee Kennedy, June 21, 1986. BA, Eugene Bible Coll., 1990; diploma, Evang. Tchr. Tng., 1990. Asst. pastor Open Bible Standard, Elmira, Oreg., 1989-90, Spokane, Wash., 1990—. Mem. Home & Family Life Adv. Com., Greenacres, Wash., 1991. Home: 905 N McDonald Spokane WA 99216 Office: Open Bible Standard Ch 905 N McDonald Spokane WA 99216

BAKELY, DONALD CARLISLE, minister; b. Elwood, N.J., Aug. 23, 1928; s. Edwin Paul and Margaret Catherine (Decker) B.; m. Jeanne Flagg; children: Paul, Stephen, Claudia, Peter, Matthew, Lois, Bethany. BS in Edn., Temple U., 1952, MDiv, 1955; HHD, Rockhurst Coll., 1990. Ordained to ministry, 1955. Assoc. pastor Centenary Tabernacle Meth. Ch., Camden, N.J., 1949-50, pastor, 1958-65; pastor Fairview Meth. Ch., Camden, 1950-53, Brooklawn (Pa.) Meth. Ch., 1953-58; exec. dir. Cross-Lines Coop. Coun., Kansas City, Kans., 1965—; chmn. Cross Lines Towers, 1980—, Commn. on Vol. Svc. & Action, N.Y.C., 1983-86. Author: If--A Big Word With the Poor, 1976, Bethy and the Mouse, 1984. With U.S. Army, 1946-48. Recipient Liberty Bell award, 1969, Bicentennial award Pres. Gerald Ford, 1976, Svc. to Mankind award Sertoma, 1978, Appreciation award Nat. Community Action, 1981, Community Svc. awards Jr. League, bd. of Global Ministries and Project Equality, 1990, letter of commendation, Pres. George Bush, 1990; named Kans. Pub. Citizen of Yr., 1990. Mem. Nat. Assn. Ecumenical Staff, Kans. East Conf. United Meth. Ch. Home: 3109 Shearer Rd Kansas City KS 66106 Office: Cross Lines Coop Coun 1620 S 37th St Kansas City KS 66106 *In the 40 years that I have worked with the poor, people have told me that the way to eliminate poverty is to get the poor to change their ways. I have found that the way to diminish poverty is to get the rest of us to change OUR ways.*

BAKER, ANDREW ELIOT, rabbi; b. Worcester, Mass., Nov. 23, 1949; s. Louis and Barbara (Gordon) B.; m. Christine Richardson, Oct. 24, 1982; children: Johanna, Gabriel, Jesse, Emma. BA, Wesleyan U., Middletown, Conn., 1971; MAHL, Hebrew Union Coll., N.Y.C., 1972. Rabbi, 1977. Area dir. Am. Jewish Com., Washington, 1980—; pres. Interfaith Conf. Metro. Washington, 1990—, Washington Bd. Rabbis, 1989-91. Office: 2027 Massachusetts Ave NW Washington DC 20136

BAKER, BILLY ROSS, minister; b. Trumann, Ark., Aug. 30, 1937; s. Ross Earl and Elsie Lorene (Banks) B.; m. Beverly Jane Monroe, Apr. 20, 1956; child: Bradley Paul. Bible diploma, Central Bible Coll., 1959. Pastor First Assembly of God, Lebanon, Mo., 1959-62; dist. youth dir. So. Mo. Dist. Council of Assemblies of God, Springfield, Mo., 1962-65; pastor Blue Ridge Assemblies of God, Kansas City, Mo., 1965-70, Parc-way Assembly of God, Indianapolis, Ind., 1970-75, Belton Assembly of God, Belton, Mo., 1978--; exec. presbyter So. Mo. Dist. Non Region, 1978-- and So. Mo. Dist. Assemblies of God, Springfield 1985--; bd. Teen Challenge, Indpls. 1970-75; dir. Christian edn. Ind. Dist. Assemblies of God, Indpls. 1973-75 and So. Mo. Dist., Springfield 1982-85. Mem. Chamber of Commerce, Belton, Mo. Assemblies of God. Office: Belton Assembly of God Ch 613 E North Ave Belton MO 64012

BAKER, BRUCE LEE, pastor; b. Pasadena, Tex., Sept. 10, 1958; s. Jimmie Carl and Marcy Ann (Carlisle) B.; m. Penny Jeanne Hendricks, Nov. 28, 1981; children: Christopher James, Stephanie Kathleen. BA, East Tex. Bapt. U., Marshall, 1982; MDiv., S.W. Bapt. Theol. Sem., Fort Worth, 1985, Doctor of Min., 1989. Min. to youth Mem. Bapt. Ch., Gladewater, Tex., 1980-82; assoc. pastor First Bapt Ch., Lake Jackson, Tex., 1982; pastor First Bapt Ch., Tioga, Tex., 1982-85; sr. pastor Second Bapt. Ch., Baytown, Tex., 1985—; evangelism cons. Bapt. Gen. Conv. Tex., Dallas, 1987— (stewardship cons. 1990—). Bd. mem. Sheltering Arms, Baytown, Tex., 1989-91, Love In the Name of Christ, 1990—; active mem. C. of C., 1988—. Recipient H.C. Brown Preaching award S.W. Sem., Fort Worth, 1985 (Press. award 1982). Home: 805 W Murrill Baytown TX 77520 Office: Second Baptist Church 500 E James Baytown TX 77520

BAKER, COSETTE MARLYN, religious writer, editor; b. Miami, Fla., Sept. 22, 1933; d. Juel Marlyn and Corene Frances (Emery) Baker; B.B.A., U. Miami, Fla., 1955; M.R.E., So. Bapt. Theol. Sem., 1959. Dir. childhood edn. First Bapt. Ch., Knoxville, Tenn., 1959-63; minister to children South Main Bapt. Ch., Houston, 1964-73; asst. to minister of edn. Central Bapt. Ch., Miami, Fla., 1973-74; cons. in Sunday Sch. Dept., Bapt. Sunday Sch. Bd., Nashville, 1974—, children's program editor, 1974—, cons., children's program editor, 1985—. Recipient YWCA award outstanding woman in religious work U. Miami, 1955, cert. achievement award for Bible Study Resource Kit for Children's Worship, 1991.. Mem. Tenn. Assn. for Edn. Young Children, Gamma Alpha Chi. Baptist. Author: God's Outdoors, 1967; writer children's teaching tapes for Broadman Press, 1979-81; writer, on-camera person Bapt. Telecommunication Network, 1984—; editor Children's Leadership, 1985-91, design editor, 1991—; design team shairperson The Sunday Sch. Leader Smaller Ch. Edit. Home: 100 Longwood Pl Nashville TN 37215 Office: 127 9th Ave N Nashville TN 37234

BAKER, DAVID E., minister; b. St. Paul, Mar. 30, 1934; s. E.H. and Aurora (Tengblad) B.; m. Nancy Helena Tolin, Aug. 18, 1957 (div. 1984); children: Karla, Peter, Lee, Andrea; m. Gloria Edith Skinner, Oct. 20, 1984. BA, Augustana Coll., 1956; BD, Augustana Theol. Sem., Rock Island, Ill., 1960; MDiv, Luth. Sch. Theology, Chgo., 1972; DMin, San Francisco Theol. Sem., 1985. Ordained to ministry Luth. Ch., 1960. Pastor Christ Luth. Ch., Edmonton, Alta., 1960-65, Cen. Luth. Ch., Yakima, Wash., 1965-72, Grace Luth. Ch., Corvallis, Oreg., 1972-83; staff Holden Village, Chelan, Wash., 1985-86; pastor Immanuel Luth. Ch., San Jose, 1986—; pres. Ecumenical Ministries of Oreg., 1977-80; dean So. Dist. Pacific N.W. Synod, Luth. Ch. Am., 1974-77; mem. bd. trustees Luth. Bible Inst., 1966-72; exec. bd. Pacific N.W. Synod, Luth. Ch. Am., 1967-70, 74-77; bd. dirs. Wash. Coun. Ch., 1969-72. Bd. dirs. Emanuel Hosp., Portland, Oreg., 1974-77. Office: Immanuel Luth Ch 1710 Moorpark San Jose CA 95128

BAKER, DENNIS NEWTON, minister; b. Portland, Oreg., Feb. 22, 1944; s. Orville Newton and Ethel Gladys (Rogers) B.; m. Lynette Elizabeth Dick, June 18, 1966; children: Rachelle Lynn, Suzanne Lynn, Meredith Anne. BA, Biola U., LaMirada, Calif., 1968; MDiv, Western Sem., Portland, Oreg., 1970; MA, Denver Sem., 1974. Ordained to ministry, Judson Meml. Bapt. Ch., 1972. Dir. pub. rels. Western Sem., Portland, 1974-75; assoc. pastor South Shore Bapt. Ch., Hingham, Mass., 1976-77; sr. pastor First Bapt. Ch., St. Cloud, Minn., 1977-82, Colony Park Bapt. Ch., Edina, Minn., 1982-87; gen. dir. Conservative Bapt. Assn. So. Calif., Anaheim, 1987—; bd. dirs. Ch. Resource Ministries, Fullerton, Calif., 1990—; bd. dirs., sec. Charis Found., Diamond Bar, 1990—; bd. dirs. Mission: Moving Mountains, Burnsville, Minn., 1985-87, Conservative Bapt. Fgn. Mission Soc., Wheaton, Ill., 1979-85. Bd. dirs. Love L.A., Van Nuys, 1988—. Republican. Office: Conservative Bapt Assn 2528 W LaPalma Anaheim CA 92801

BAKER, DOUGLAS WAYNE, minister; b. Halls, Tenn., Feb. 8, 1948; s. James Walter and Leota (Pounds) B.; m. Bettye Louise Hooper, Aug. 15, 1971; children: Jeffery Wayne, Amy Elizabeth, Michael Douglas. BA, Union U., Jackson, Tenn., 1972; MA, Southwestern Bapt. Theol. Sem., 1974. Ordained to ministry So. Bapt. Conv. Youth dir. Park Temple Bapt. Ch., Ft. Worth, 1972-73, Grace Temple Bapt. Ch., Denton, Tex., 1973-74; pastor New Madrid (Mo.) Bapt. Ch., 1974-76; dir. edn., assoc. pastor 1st Bapt. Ch., Collierville, Tenn., 1976-78; pastor Parrans Chapel Bapt. Ch., Bolivar, Tenn., 1978—; mem. exec. bd. Tenn. Bapt. Conv., Brentwood, 1988—. Bd. dirs. United Tenn. League, Nashville, 1988. Named Chaplain of the Day, Tenn. Ho. of Reps., Nashville, 1991. Mem. Hardeman County Bapt. Assn. (moderator 1989—).

BAKER, GARY DWAIN, minister; b. Grand Junction, Colo., Jan. 1, 1951; s. Alvin Lee and Mary Louise (Raber) B.; m. Patricia Lynn Miracle, June 20, 1981; 1 child, James Matthew. BA summa cum laude, Howard Payne U., 1986. Ordained to ministry So. Bapt. Conv., 1986. Pastor South Leon Bapt. Ch., Comanche, Tex., 1984-90; interim pastor South Side Bapt. Ch., Brownwood, Tex., 1990-91; coord. Prayer Ministries Southside Bapt. Ch., Brownwood, 1991—; dir. ch. tng. South Side Bapt. Ch., Brownwood, Tex., 1984; dir. Sunday sch. Melwood Bapt. Ch., Brownwood; mem. exec. bd. Comanche Bapt. Assn., 1984-90. Liaison Brown County Child Welfare Bd., Brownwood, 1989—; mem. Region 4 Foster Adoptive Adv. Coun., Abilene, Tex., 1990-91; v.p. Brownwood Cen. Tex. Foster Parent Assn., 1990, mem. pub. rels. com., 1991. Mem. Brown County Bapt. Assn. (mem. exec. com. 1990-91), Child Protective Svcs. (Austin adv. bd. 1991—). Republican. Home: 202 Park Dr Early TX 76801 *In the midst of the precious and good things of my life and during the many times of sorrow and encounters with the possibility of death God has been my life and strength and the love of my family has been an anchor.*

BAKER, JAMES DONALD, religion educator, minister; b. Brownbranch, Mo., Nov. 7, 1930; s. John C. and Riffie (Ashwell) B.; m. Pat A. Hoffmeister, June 22, 1952; children—Pamela Bultmann, Dana Harrigan, Beth Grabowski. A.A.A.S., S.W. Bapt. Coll., 1950; A.B., William Jewell Coll., 1953; B.D., Central Bapt. Theol. Sem., 1957, M.Div., 1968; Th.D., New Orleans Bapt. Theol. Sem., 1970. Pub. relations dir. S.W. Bapt. Coll., Bolivar, Mo., 1957-66; pub. relations asst. New Orleans Bapt. Theol. Sem., 1967-70; pastor Bapt. chs., Ark., La., Mo., 1967-76; dir. in-service tng. S.W. Bapt. U., Bolivar, 1976—, acting dean Redford Sch. Theology, 1983—. Author: Mr. Baptist Hour, 1974. Editor: SWBC Newsletter, 1957-66. Contbr. articles to profl. jours. Bd. dirs. ARC, Bolivar, 1963-65. Recipient Life Beautiful award, S.W. Bapt. Coll., 1950. Mem. Assn. Bapt. Tchrs. Religion, In-Service Guidance Conf. (sec.), Redford Curators (founding chmn. 1964-65), C. of C. Lodge: Kiwanis. Avocations: Woodworking; canoeing; antique autos; fishing; hunting. Office: Southwest Bapt Univ Bolivar MO 65613

BAKER, JOE BENNY, minister; b. Corinth, Miss., Sept. 18, 1948; s. Irvin Larvis and Mary Jewel (Wilson) B.; m. Donna Lee Wood, Dec. 21, 1974; children: Andrew, Jonathan, Cathy, Tiffany. BA, Lubbock Christian Coll., 1974; MA, Pepperdine U., 1979; postgrad., Abilene Christian U.-Dallas, 1982. Minister of youth Ch. of Christ, Swartz Creek, Mich., 1974-75; asst. to pres. Mich. Christian Coll., Rockester, 1975; minister of youth Central Ch. of Christ, Tulia, Tex., 1975-77, Bayshore Ch. of Christ, Seabrook, Tex., 1977-78, Meadowbrook Ch. of Christ, Jackson, Miss., 1978-80, Saturn Rd. Ch. of Christ, Garland, Tex., 1980-83; v.p. His Enterprises, Garland, 1979-83; minister Utica Ch. of Christ (N.Y.), 1983-88, Alberta Ch. Christ, Tuscaloosa, Ala., 1988-90, 4th Bedford Ch. of Christ, Dimmitt, Tex., 1990—; host radio program Life Source, 1983-88; producer 60 Seconds; tchr. Shelton State Community Coll., Tuscaloosa, 1990. Chmn., Garland Mayor's Citizen's Youth Com., 1982, Utica Youth Com., 1984-88. Served with USN, 1968-71. Regional finalist speech contest Toastmaster Internat., 1985. Mem. West Ala. Soccer Assn. (officer 1989). Office: Bedford Ch Christ 101 SW 4th Dimmitt TX 79027

BAKER, JOSEPHINE L. REDENIUS (MRS. MILTON G. BAKER), minister, civic leader, retired U.S. Army officer, former public relations company executive; b. Oceanville, N.J., Aug. 31, 1920; d. Jacob and Josephine (Palmer) Redenius. Student, Columbia U., 1948-49, L.I. U., 1957-58, George Washington U., 1947-48; MA in Journalism, Am. U., 1963; LHD, Temple U., 1964; MA in Religious Studies, St. Charles Sem., 1981; MDiv., Eastern Baptist Theol. Sem., 1984; D Ministry, Ea. Bapt. Theol. Sem., 1990. Ordained Deacon Episcopal Ch. Enlisted as pvt. WAAC, 1943; advanced through grades to lt. col. U.S. Army, 1963; col. Pa. N.G., 1967; intelligence officer atomic installations throughout U.S. and Can., 1943-53; asst. office chief of staff Army Forces Far East, Japan, 1954-56; pub. info. officer Office Chief of Info., Washington, 1958-61; chief Women's Army Corps recruiting U.S. Army, 1962-66, info liaison officer, 1966-67, ret., 1967; dir. pub. rels. and devel. Valley Forge Mil. Acad. and Jr. Coll., Wayne, Pa., 1967-71; dir. Valley Forge Mil. Acad. and Jr. Coll., Wayne, 1970-79; pres. Potential Inc., Ardmore, Pa., 1979-83, Intercounty Trading Co., Inc., Surfside, Fla., 1976-80. Deacon All Souls' Episcopal Ch., Miami Beach, Fla.; bd. dirs. Valley Forge Freedom Valley dist. Girl Scouts Am., Republican Women of Pa., Opera Guild of Miami; pres. bd. dirs. St. Cornelius the Centurian Found., 1976—; dir. St. Anne's Home for Women, Phila.; v.p. Episcopal Ch. Women, Diocese of Pa., 1984-86; pres. Episcopal Ch. Women, Diocese of S.E. Fla., 1990—. Decorated Legion of Merit, Pa. Meritorious Service medal; U.S. Army Commendation medal with oak leaf cluster; recipient Order Golden Sword Valley Forge Mil. Acad., 1986, Martha Washington medal S.R., 1990; named Disting. Alumnus Am. U., 1969. Mem. Pub. Rels. Soc. Am., Am. Personnel and Guidance Assn., Am. Coll. Personnel Assn., Nat. Vocat. Guidance Assn., Am. Sch. Counselors Assn., Pa. Med. Missionary Soc. (dir. 1983-89), Am. Legion Aux., Ret. Officers Assn., Assn. U.S. Army (Anthony J. Drexel Biddle medal 1968), Army-Navy Union, Assn. Measurement and Evaluation in Guidance, Am. Legion, La Boutique Des Hult Chapeaux et Quarante Femmes, Emergency Aid of Pa., Women in Communications, Soc. of St. Francis, Mil. Order World Wars, Miami Heart Inst. Aux., Surf Club, Bald Peak Colony Club, Women's Club, Miami Beach Garden Club (chaplain), St. David's Golf Club, Acorn Club, Soroptimists.

BAKER, KENRICK MARTIN, JR., minister; b. Brockton, Mass., Apr. 25, 1923; s. Kenrick Martin and Elinor (Furber) B.; m. Marion Anna Aschaffenburg, Apr. 24, 1954; children—Christoph Martin, Katerina Lois, Nicole Anita. A.B., Bowdoin Coll., 1941-43; B.D., Yale Div. Sch., 1948; cert., Grad. Sch. Ecumenical Studies (Switzerland), 1953. Ordained to ministry United Church of Christ, 1948. Instr. Am. U. Cairo, 1945-47; asst. chaplain, assoc. minister Amherst Coll., First Congl. Ch., Amherst, Mass., 1948-50; pastor First Congl. Ch., Hinsdale, Mass., 1950-52; asst. to gen. sec. World Council Chs., Geneva, 1953-55; interim pastor Trinity Fellowship, Shelburne Falls, Mass., 1955-56; dir. Fellowship Ctr., United Ch. Bd. World Ministries, le Chambon-sur-Lignon, France, 1956-63; sec. personnel, teams and fraternal workers Commn. Inter-Ch. Aid, Refugee and World Service, World Council Chs., Geneva, 1963-72; sect. dir. Dienste in Uebersee, Stuttgart, Germany, 1972-76; dir. Schiller Coll., Strasbourg, France, 1976-80; dir. World Council Chs. Service to Refugees, Rome, 1980-88.

BAKER, LARRY CURTIS, minister; b. L.A., Sept. 19, 1945; s. Charles Leonard and Genevee (Becker) B.; m. Mary Callicoat, Oct. 23, 1964; children: Christopher Daniel, Sarah Morgan. BA, Hardin-Simmons U., 1970; MDiv, Golden Gate Sem., 1975. Ordained to ministry So. Bapt. Conv., 1969. Pastor First Bapt. Ch., Maryneal, Tex., 1968-69, Cen. Bapt. Ch., Stamford, Tex., 1969-71, DeAnza Bapt. Ch., Cupertino, Calif., 1971-73; pub. rels. assoc. Golden Gate Bapt. Sem., Mill Valley, Calif., 1973-75; pastor First So. Bapt. Ch., Lodi, Calif., 1975-77, Ventura, Calif., 1977-81; v.p. communications Golden Gate Sem., Mill Valley, 1981-83; pastor Bethel Bapt. Ch., Concord, Calif., 1983—. Editor newspaper the HSU Brand, 1968-70; asst. pubr. newspaper Stamford Am., 1970-71. With USAF, 1963-67. Republican. Avocations: writing, tennis, racquetball, gardening. Office: Bethel Bapt Ch 3578 Clayton Rd Concord CA 94519

BAKER, LARRY NEAL, minister; b. Ft. Worth, Tex., Apr. 17, 1950; s. Cornelius Bunyan and Mary Leona (Sisk) B.; m. Kathleen Marie Peters, May 31, 1974; children: Joshua, Peter. BA in Physics, U. Tex., 1972; MDiv, Southwestern Bapt. Theol. Sem., Ft. Worth, Tex., 1975. Ordained to ministry So. Bapt. Conv., 1975. Minister of edn. Calvary Bapt. Ch., Lawton, Okla., 1982-83; tchr. Moore (Okla.) Christian Acad., 1983-84; pastor Franklin Rd. Bapt. Ch., Norman, 1984-86, Agnew Ave. Bapt. Ch., Oklahoma City, 1986—; mem. spl. ministries com. Capitol Bapt. Assn., Oklahoma City, 1990-91. Author: Study Guide in 1 and 2 Peter, 1984. Com. mem. Habitat for Humanity, Oklahoma City, 1991, Action, Bartlesville, Okla., 1978. Republican. Home: 625 N Dallas Moore OK 73160 Office: Agnew Ave Bapt Ch 2401 SW 32nd St Oklahoma City OK 73119 *1. Be it for children or adults, moral values need to be determined by someone higher and transcendent than those living by them, hence the importance of religion in public and private life. 2. If people are told they came from animals, don't be surprise when they act like them.*

BAKER, LAUREN CHARLES, minister; b. Champaign, Ill., Mar. 22, 1939; s. Frank Wesley and Marjorie Eloise (Curtis) B.; m. Judith Anne Smith, Oct. 12, 1959; children: Sharon Kae, Carolyn Sue, Barbara Ann. Student, Parkland Jr. Coll., 1970. Lic. to ministry Meth. Ch., 1969, ordained Gospel Crusade Inc., 1976. Minister United Meth. Ch., Sadorus, Ill., 1969-71, West Frankfort, Ill., 1971; assoc. minister Bethesda Chapel, West Frankfort, 1971-72; minister New Testament Ch., Summerville, S.C., 1976-78; itenerant tchr. Gospel Crusade, Inc., Bradenton, Fla., 1978-79; minister Christian Assembly of Portage, Ind., 1979-80, Portage Christian Fellowship, 1980—; area committeeman Gospel Crusade Ministerial Assn., Bradenton, Fla., 1988—. Committeeman Citizens Against Pornography, Portage, 1989. Mem. Lions. Avocation; camping. Home and Office: PO Box 605 Portage IN 46368

BAKER, MARY EVELYN, church librarian, retired academic librarian; b. Columbus, Ohio, May 8, 1912; d. Abram Jackson and Martha Maria (Dailey) Shoemaker; m. Richard Heinley Baker, Sept. 18, 1937; children: Richard Shoemaker, David Guy. BA, Ohio State U., 1934; M.S. in Libr. Sci., Western Res. U., Cleve., 1935. Mem. staff libr. Ohio State U., Columbus, 1935-37, 38-44, 1955-74, part-time libr., 1955-66, adminstrv. asst., 1958, serial cataloger, 1958-67, asst. reviser, sr. cataloger, 1967-68, head serial div. catalog dept., 1968-71, head catalog dept., 1971-74; libr. com. First Congl. Ch., Columbus, 1950—, libr. co-chmn., 1962-65, 74-75, libr. chmn., 1976—; past mem. ALA, sec. serials sect., resources and tech. div., 1970-73. Den mother Boy Scouts Am., Columbus, 1953-58; libr. co-chmn. Friendship Village, Dublin, Ohio, 1981—. Mem. Ohio Libr. Assn., Ohioana Libr. Assn. (past chmn. various coms.), Ohio Valley Group Tech. Svc. Librarians, PEO, Phi Mu, Univ. Women's (past pres.), Agrl. Circle (past pres.). Republican. Home: 6000 Riverside Dr Apt A233 Dublin OH 43017

BAKER, MICHAEL LYNDON, minister; b. Lancaster, S.C., June 25, 1949; s. Robert Lynn and Ruby Arretta (Shelton) B.; m. Sharon Elaine Sibbett, Apr. 9, 1971; 1 child, Kysha Lyn. B in Music Edn., Lee Coll., 1971; MusM, U. N.C., Greensboro, 1978, postgrad., 1979-84. Ordained to ministry Ch. of God (Cleveland, Tenn.), 1971; cert. elem., high sch. tchr., N.C. Min. Randleman (N.C.) Ch. of God, 1971-80, sr. pastor, 1989—; prof. East Coast Bible Coll., Charlotte, N.C., 1980-84; adminstrv. asst. media dept. internat. offices Ch. of God, Cleveland, Tenn., 1984-88; mem. ch. music com. Ch. of God, Cleve., 1984—; bd. dirs. Gen. Assembly, Ch. of God., 1991. Contbr. articles to religious publs.; author various musical works to Pathway Music, 1978—. Chmn. March of Dimes, Randleman, 1978; chmn. bd. dirs. Randleman Housing Authority, 1991—. Republican. Home: 215 E Brown St Randleman NC 27317 Office: Randleman Ch of God 305 E Brown St Randleman NC 27317

BAKER, NATHAN LARRY, minister; b. Frierson, La., Oct. 31, 1937; s. Nathan Forrest and Anner Lara (Looper) B.; m. Wanda Marie Campbell, June 16, 1959; children: Anne Elisabeth, Angela Eileen, Andrew Nathan. BS, East Tex. Bapt. Coll., 1959; BD, Southwestern Bapt. Theol. Sem., Ft. Worth, 1963, ThM, 1966, ThD, 1974. Ordained to ministry So. Bapt. Conv., 1953. Pastor Doddridge (Ark.) Bapt. Ch., 1957-59, Dial Bapt. Ch., Honey Grove, Tex., 1960-63, 1st Bapt. Ch., Hamilton, Tex., 1967-70, Parkview Bapt. Ch., Monroe, La., 1970-73, 1st Bapt. Ch., Fayetteville, Ark., 1975-78; assoc. pastor Grace Temple Bapt. Ch., Denton, Tex., 1965-67; asst. prof. Christian ethics and pastoral ministry Southwestern Bapt. Theol. Sem., 1973-75; assoc. prof., prof., acad. dean, v.p. acad. affairs Midwestern Bapt. Theol. Sem., Kansas City, Mo., 1978-87; exec. dir., treas. Christian Life Commn., So. Bapt. Conv., Nashville, 1987-88; pastor 1st Bapt. Ch., Pineville, La., 1988—; interim pastor various chs., Tex., La., Mo.; dir. Bapt. Student Union, instr. Bible, Tex. Woman's U., Denton, 1963-65; prof. Bible, Ouachita Bapt. U. Extension Ctr., Fayetteville, 1976; prof. Boyce Bible Sch., Little Rock, 1977, 78, 80; vis. prof. preaching So. Bapt. Theol. Sem., Louisville, 1989, Midwestern Bapt. Theol. Sem., 1991; mem. com. on moral and social concerns La. Bapt. Conv.; mem. steering com. associational strategy planning North Rapides Bapt. Assn.; speaker, lectr. in field. Contbr. to books; author curriculum materials; contbr. articles and book revs. to religious publs. Mem. adv. com. La. Moral and Civic Found.; mem. citizens rev. panel United Way Cen. La.; pres. bd. dirs. ACTS of Cen. La. Recipient J. Wesley Smith Outstanding Alumnus award East Tex. Bapt. U., 1987; named hon. alumnus Midwestern Bapt. Theol. Sem., 1988. Mem. North Rapides Bapt. Mins. Assn. (pres.), Cen. La. C. of C., Rotary. Home: 104 Rose Ct Pineville LA 71360 Office: 1st Bapt Ch 901 Main St Pineville LA 71360

BAKER, PHILLIP, minister; b. Monterey Park, Calif., Feb. 13, 1938; s. Lawrence Aloysius and Edna Beatrice (Cockrell) B.; m. Myra Kay Meyer, June 10, 1967; children: Janel Renee, Ria Kristine. AB, Chico State U., 1964; MDiv, Wartburg Sem., 1968; PhD, Aquinas Inst. Theology, 1976. Ordained to ministry Evang. Luth. Ch. Am., 1968. Asst. pastor Holy Trinity Luth. Ch., Dubuque, Iowa, 1968-70; pastor Zion Evang. Luth. Ch., La Porte City, Iowa, 1970-72, Shepherd of the Valley Luth. Ch., Council Bluffs, Iowa, 1972-78, Sychar Luth. Ch., Silver Bay, Minn., 1978-81, Shepherd of the Valley Luth. Ch., Orinda, Calif., 1987—; missionary Am. Luth. Ch., Nigeria, 1981-87; chair Synod Com. on Global Mission, Oakland,

Calif., 1990—; bd. dirs. Pacific S.W. Conf. on World Christian Mission, 1990; adj. prof. Pacific Luth. Theol. Sem., Berkeley, Calif., 1987—; Lavik lectr. Luth. Bible Inst., Issaquah, Wash., 1989. Author: (essays) Lutheran Church and Growth and Missions, 1990. With USAF, 1956-59. Named Outstanding Young Religious Leader, Council Bluffs Jaycees, 1973. Mem. Pacific Coast Theol. Soc. Democrat. Home: 119 Ascot Ct #7 Moraga CA 94556 Office: Shepherd of Valley Luth Ch 433 Moraga Way Orinda CA 94563

BAKER, RONNIE, minister; b. Seymour, Ind., June 5, 1967; s. Hubert Baker and Wanda Kay (Barrett) Bexley; m. Denise Lynn Peters, Mar. 11, 1989; children: Ronald Corey, Corbin Ray. Student, Cin. Bible Coll., 1988-89. Ordained to ministry Ch. of God, 1988. Assoc. min., evangelist Wooster New Hope Ch. of God, Scottsburg, Ind., 1983-87, youth leader, 1985-86; min. Jennings Ch. of Christ, North Vernon, Ind., 1988-90, Manville Christian Ch., Madison, Ind., 1991—; vesper speaker Camp Illianna, Washington, Ind., 1986. Asst. Children's Christmas, Dive Christian Ch., 1986-87; fund raiser speaker Ronald McDonald House Fund Raisers, North Vernon, Ind., 1989. Named Missionary of Yr. Community Christian Ch., 1987-88; recipient scholarship Kiamichi Mens Clinic, Okla., 1986, Cin. Bible Coll., 1988. Republican. Home: 12485 S Hillview Estates Columbus IN 45201 *Life is filled with good and bad times. When bad times arise we may choose to be stumbling blocks or stepping stones to others. I have chosen to be a stepping stone.*

BAKER, THOMAS BRENT, minister; b. Louisville, Ky., Oct. 29, 1960; s. Tommy and Mary Evelyn (Holt) B.; m. Lisa Jo Earnest, July 11, 1987. BS, U. Ky., 1982, Ky. Christian Coll., 1987. Youth min. Minorsville Christian Ch., Stamping Ground, Ky., 1985-86; intern Kingsway Christian Ch., Indpls., 1986; youth min. 1st Ch. Christ, Grayson, Ky., 1986-87; assoc. min. Cen. Christian Ch., Ironton, Ohio, 1987—. Asst. Teen Child Assault Prevention, Ironton, 1989—. Mem. Tri State Mins. Orgn. (v.p. 1990—), Tri State Bible Bowl Round (bd. dirs. 1987-90), Hon. Order Ky. Cols. Home: 1306 S 8th St Ironton OH 45638 Office: Cen Christian Ch 1541 S 7th St Ironton OH 45638

BAKER, VENETTA DENISE, minister; b. Charlotte, N.C., June 7, 1955; d. William H. and Ida (Scott) B. BA in Sociology, Meredith Coll., 1977; MDiv, Louisville Presbyn. Theol. Sem., 1983. Ordained to ministry Presbyn. Ch., 1984. Christian educator Menaul Sch., Albuquerque, 1983-84; mem. pulpit supply Catawba Presbytery, Charlotte, 1986-88; staff chaplain W.C. Ctr., Morganton, N.C., 1988—; mem. gen. assembly com. on representation Presbyn. Ch., 1986-88, also mem. senate justice for women com., presbytery level com., examinations com., self devel. of the people com. Vol. Peace Corps, Columbia, Hospice of Burke County, 1988—. Mem. Am. Coun. Blind, Delta Sigma Theta. Democrat. Home: 102 Stephens Morganton NC 28655

BAKLE, JOHN LEWIS, priest, school administrator, researcher; b. Hicksville, Ohio, Jan. 7, 1937; s. George William and Marie Jett (Hoff) B. BSEd, U. Dayton, 1960; STB, U. Fribourgh, Switzerland, 1965, STL, 1967; PhD, Ohio State U., 1989. Tchr. Chaminade High Sch., Dayton, Ohio, 1957-60; tchr., adminstr. Purcell High Sch., Cin., 1960-62; tchr. Assumption High Sch., East St. Louis, Ill., 1962-63; conf. dir., exec. dir. Bergamo Conf. Ctr., Dayton, Ohio, 1967-69; exec. dir. Bergamo/East Conf. Ctr., Marcy, N.Y., 1969-71; chaplain U.S. Army, 1971, advanced through grades to maj., 1983; counselor, adminstr. North Cath. High Sch., Pitts., 1983-85; exec. dir. Hackett High Sch., Kalamazoo, Mich., 1987-88; researcher Ohio State U., Columbus, 1989—. Mem. Kalamazoo Area AIDS Task Force, 1988. Mem. Nat. Cath. Edn. Assn., Am. Edn. Rsch. Assn., Assn. Supervision and Curriculum Devel., Phi Delta Kappa, Nat. Exchange, KC. Democrat. Roman Catholic. Avocations: music, skiing. Home: 167 Orchard Ln Columbus OH 43214 Office: Ohio State U 240-M W 8th Ave Columbus OH 43201

BALANZA, VIRGILIO DOMINE, clergyman; b. Sagada, Mt. Province, Philippines, Aug. 8, 1930; s. Fidel and Isabel (Domine) B.; m. Erlinda Busacay, May 10, 1951; children—Michael, Rebecca, Virgilio, Paul, Walter, Francis, Frederick, Erlinda, Jane. Th.B., St. Andrew's Theol. Sem., 1957. Ordained to ministry Episcopal Ch., 1957. Tchr., Philippine Episcopal Ch., Baguio, 1957-59; dir. Good Shepherd Mission Sch., Zamboanga, 1959-61; dean Cathedral of St. Mary and St. John, Manila, 1972-74; archdeacon Diocese of Central Philippines, Baguio, 1974-77; chaplain Brent Sch., Baguio, 1982—; coordinator Cordillera Schs. Group, Baguio, 1979-82, Brent Sch. outreach program; chmn. bd. Easter Weaving Room, Inc., Baguio City, 1982-86; del. Internat. Council on Social Welfare, Manila, 1970. Founding mem. Urban Indsl. Mission, NCCP, Manila, 1968; mem. Manila Community Services, Inc., 1972-77. Recipient Unawaan award Assn. Barangay Councils, Baguio, 1984; Appreciation award Philippine Tuberculosis Soc., 1972; Plaque of Appreciation, Manila Community Services, 1978. Address: Brent Sch, PO Box 35, Baguio City The Philippines

BALAS, JOHN PAUL, III, religion educator, minister; b. Charleroi, Pa., June 5, 1940; s. John. P. Jr. and Mary (Mihovich) B.; m. Karen Ann Schall, Nov. 24, 1962; children: John Paul IV, James Andrew, Michael Thomas. BA, Thiel Coll., 1962; BD, Luth. Sem., Gettysburg, Pa., 1966; MEd, U. Pitts., 1971, PhD, 1980. Ordained to ministry Luth. Ch. Am. (now Evang. Luth. Ch. in Am.), 1966. Pastor Ascension Luth. Ch., McKees Rocks, Pa., 1966-69; campus pastor Luth. Student Found., Pitts., 1969-74; pastor Prince of Peace Luth. Ch., Pleasant Hills, Pa., 1974-78; coll. pastor Thiel Coll., Greenville, Pa., 1978-89; assoc. prof. Luth. Theol. Sem., Gettysburg, 1989—. Mem. Am. Acad. Religion, Assn. for Clin. Pastoral Edn. Republican. Office: Luth Theol Sem 61 NW Confederate Ave Gettysburg PA 17325

BALCH, GLENN MCCLAIN, JR., administrator, minister, former university president, author; b. Shattuck, Okla., Nov. 1, 1937; s. Glenn McClain and Marjorie (Daily) B.; student Panhandle State U., 1958-60, So. Meth. U., summers 1962-64; BA, S.W. State U. Okla., 1962; B.D., Phillips U., 1965; MA, Chapman Coll., 1973, MA in Edn., 1975, M.A. in Psychology, 1975; PhD, U.S. Internat. U., 1978; postgrad. Claremont Grad. Sch., 1968-70, U. Okla., 1965-66; m. Diana Gale Seeley, Oct. 15, 1970; children: Bryan, Gayle, Wesley, Johnny. Ordained to ministry Methodist Ch., 1962; sr. minister First Meth. Ch., Eakly, Okla., 1960-63, First Meth. Ch., Calumet, Okla., 1963-65, Goodrich Meml. Ch., Norman, Okla., 1965-66, First Meth. Ch., Barstow, Calif., 1966-70; asst. dean Chapman Coll., Orange, Calif., 1970-76; v.p. Pacific Christian Coll., Fullerton, Calif., 1976-79; pres. Newport U., Newport Beach, Calif., 1979-82; sr. pastor Brea United Meth. Ch., 1978-89; pres., chief exec. officer So. Calif. Inst., 1988—; edn. cons. USAF, 1974-75; mental health cons. U.S. Army, 1969. Mem. Community Adv. Bd. Minority Problems; Mayor's rep. to County Dependency Prevention Commn.; mem. Brea Econ. Devel. Com. With USMC, 1956-57. Recipient Eastern Star Religious Tng. award, 1963, 64; named Man of Year, Jr. C. of C., Barstow, 1969; Broadhurst fellow, 1963-65. Mem. Calif. Assn. Marriage and Family Therapists, Am. Assn. Marriage and Family Therapist, Rotary (pres. 1969-70, 83-84, dist. gov. 1987-88, 88-89), Masons, Shriners, Elks. Home: 1016 Steele Dr Brea CA 92621 Office: So Calif Inst 401 S Brea Blvd Brea CA 92621

BALCOMB, RAYMOND EVERETT, retired minister; b. San Bernardino, Calif., Feb. 8, 1923; s. Jean Bart and Rose (Gibbs) B.; m. Hazel F. Schlosser, June 18, 1944; children: Bernice, Rosemary, Joanne, Gene, Scott. AB, San Jose State Coll., 1944; STB, Boston U., 1947, PhD, 1951. Ordained deacon Meth. Ch., 1946, elder, 1948. Pastor Holbrook, Mass., 1945-49, Federated Ch., Ashland, Mass., 1949-51, Sellwood Meth. Ch., Portland, Oreg., 1951-54, Medford (Oreg.) 1st Meth. Ch., 1954-57, Corvallis (Oreg.) 1st Meth. Ch., 1957-63, 1st United Meth. Ch., Portland, 1963-82; dist. supt. United Meth. Ch., Portland, 1982-88; ret., 1988. Author: Stir What You've Got!, 1967, Try Reading the Bible, 1970, also articles. Republican. Home: 868 SW Troy Portland OR 97219

BALDERMANN, INGO HERBERT, theology educator; b. Berlin, Germany, May 2, 1929; s. Herbert and Elsa (Hornke) B.; m. Renate Fricke; 1 child, Ulrike. ThD, U. Hamburg, Fed. Republic Germany, 1962. Pfarrer Evangelisch-Lutherische Landeskirche Hannovers, Loccum, Fed. Republic Germany, 1957-63; dozent Pädagogisches Inst., U. Hamburg, Fed. Republic Germany, 1963-65; prof. U. Gesamthochschule-Siegen, Fed. Republic Germany, 1965—. Author: Biblische Didaktik, 1962, Der Biblische Unterricht, 1969, Einführung in die Bibel, 1989, Der Gott des Friedens, 1983, Wer hört mein Weinen, 1986, Psalmen als Gebrauchstexte, 1989; editor Jahrbuch für bibl. Theologie. Chmn. Gustav-Heinemann-Friedensgesellschaft e.V., Siegen, 1986—. Named hon. prof. U. Freiburg, 1971; recipient medal of merit Baden-Württemberg State Govt., 1989. Mem. SPD Party. Evangelisch. Home: Laaspher StraBe 26, D-7802 Merzhausen/Freiburg Federal Republic of Germany Office: U Gesamthochschule Siegn, Adolf-Reichwein-StraBe 2, D-5900 Siegen Federal Republic of Germany

BALDWIN, BARBARA GEARLDINE, church lay worker, counselor; b. Louisville, Ky., Jan. 24, 1935; d. Paul Gordon and Alice Elizabeth (Hash) Thompson; m. Harold Bernard Baldwin, Dec. 27, 1952; children—Brian Gordon, Cheryl Lynn Baldwin Rodgers, Robin Thomas. Counselor, His House Ministry, Campbellsville, Ky., 1970—. Author: Boycott Hell, 1972. Den mother Old Ky. Home council Boy Scouts Am., 1964; Sunday Sch. tchr. Campbellsville Baptist Ch., 1964-66; pres. Taylor County PTA, 1968; campaign worker local circuit judge campaign, Campbellsville, 1968. Republican. Avocations: collecting and creating silk flower arrangements; collecting ceramic angels; writing. Home: 304 Summit Dr Campbellsville KY 42718

BALDWIN, DANA CLARK, minister; b. Mayfield, Ky., Oct. 31, 1959; s. John Walter and Donna Joye (Mays) B.; m. Barbara Elaine Oakes, July 10, 1981; children: Spenser Thomas, Maria Ann. BA, David Lipscomb U., Nashville, 1981; MAR, Harding Grad. Sch. Religion, Memphis, 1986. Ordained to ministry, Ch. of Christ. Bus minister Cen. Ch. of Christ, Nashville, 1979-81; minister Park Ave. Ch. of Christ, Memphis, 1982—. Author booklet: Power for Today. Reader W. Tenn. Talking Libr. for the Blind, Memphis, 1990—. Office: Park Ave Ch of Christ 5295 Park Ave Memphis TN 38119

BALDWIN, FREDERICK STEPHEN, priest; b. Syracuse, N.Y., Aug. 11, 1946; s. Robert Frederick and Elizabeth (Thompson) B.; m. Elizabeth Carter, July 14, 1972 (div.); 1 child, Elizabeth Thompson. AB, Georgetown U., 1968; MDiv, Episcopal Div. Sch., 1976. Ordained as priest Episcopal Ch., 1977. Curate Holy Trinity Ch., N.Y.C., 1976-79; dir. pub. rels. Assn. Episcopal Colls., Nat. Hdqrs. Episcopal Ch., N.Y.C., 1979-82; assoc. rector St. James' Ch., N.Y.C., 1982-85; rector St. Bernard's Ch., Bernardsville, N.J., 1985—; chaplain Ch. Ctr. of UN, N.Y.C., 1979—, Episcopal cons., 1978—; pres. St. Martin's Retreat House, Bernardsville, 1985—. Bd. dirs. YMCA, Somerset Hills, 1987—, Harlem Sch. of Arts, N.Y.C., 1976-85, Lead Poison Control, Onondaga County, N.Y., 1971-73; mem. staff Office of Senator Robert F. Kennedy, Washington and Syracuse, 1965-68. Lt. USN, 1968-73. Mem. Coll. of Preachers, Holland Lodge (chaplain). Home: The Rectory 29 Stevens St Bernardsville NJ 07924 Office: St Bernard's Ch Claremont Rd Bernardsville NJ 07924 *The deepest human longing is to know I am not alone in the universe and the most lethal pathology is to mask that longing with rigid individualism. Community filled with the grace of God is the only hope for the human race.*

BALDWIN, GARRY WAYNE, minister; b. Burlington, N.C., Aug. 13, 1954; s. Gaston Solomon and Peggy (Burke) B.; m. Cheryl Tucker, June 19, 1976; children: Jeremiah, Anna Grace, Caleb. BA in History, The Citadel, 1976; MDiv, MRE, Southeastern Bapt. Theol. Sem., 1981; DMin, Bethany Theol. Sem., 1987. Ordained to ministry So. Bapt. Conv. Min. music/edn. Hampton Pk. Bapt. Ch., Charleston, S.C., 1973-76; min. edn./youth Grove Pk. Bapt. Ch., Burlington, N.C., 1976-83; pastor Westport Bapt. Ch., Denver, N.C., 1983-91, Brookwood Bapt. Ch., Burlington, N.C., 1991—; Chaplain East Lincoln Rescue Squad, Denver, 1991. Mem. edn. coun. Lincolnton/Lincoln County Human Rels. Commn., 1988—; trustee Christian Action League N.C., Raleigh, 1990—. Mem. East Lincoln Clergy Assn. (pres. 1990—), Fellowship Christian Athletes (bd. dirs. 1988—). Office: 1606 W Davis Burlington NC 27215

BALDWIN, JACK OKEY, minister; b. Winchester, Ind., Dec. 29, 1949; s. George Robert and Mary Lucille (Peters) B.; m. Martha Rosetta Ekstrand, May 21, 1972; children: Jack Robert, Alethea Faith, Marta Joellen. AB, Johnson Bible Coll., Knoxville, Tenn., 1972; MDiv, Lexington (Ky.) Theol. Sem., 1979. Ordained to ministry Christian Ch. (Disciples of Christ), 1972. Min. Walshville (Ill.) Christian Ch., 1972-73, Cen. Christian Ch., Sumner, Ill., 1973-75, Ravanna (Ky.) Christian Ch. (Disciples of Christ), 1975-84, First Christian Ch. (Disciples of Christ), Athens, Ala., 1984—; pres. Lawrence Co. Ministerial Assn., Sumner, 1974-75, dist. 4 Christian Chs. Ky., Lexington, 1983-84, dist. 1 chs. Christian Ch., Ala.-N.W. Fla., Birmingham, 1987-89, Christians in Prison Ministry, Athens, Ala., 1988-90, Chs. Involved, Athens, 1991—; treas. Estill County Ministerial Assn., Irvine, Ky., 1977-80; dir. Jr. Camp Christian Chs. Ky., Lexington, 1984, Ala.-N.W. Fla., Birmingham, 1986-90; bd. dirs. Regional Bd. Christian Ch. Ala.-N.W. Fla., Birmingham, 1987-88, chair. Com. on Ministry, 1988—; chaplain Athens-Limestone Hosp., 1989—. Bd. dirs. Sr. Citizen Project Coun., Sumner, 1974-75, Ret. Sr. Vol. Program, Irvine, 1975-78, Coun. on Aging, Athens, 1984—; v.p. Mental Health Bd., Irvine, 1982-84; chmn. Wilderness Rd. svc. unit Girl Scouts U.S., Lexington, 1982-84, co-chmn. svc. unit cookie, North Ala., Huntsville, 1990-91; chaplain Estill County Jaycees, Irvine, 1983. Recipient Outstanding Young Man of Am. award U.S. Jaycees, 1983, 1st pl. Close-up Magic award World of Wizards, Murfreesboro, Tenn., 1987. Mem. Internat. Brotherhood Magicians, Huntsville, Ala. Ring #194 (sec. 1988). Office: First Christian Ch W Market St Athens AL 35611

BALDWIN, JAMES MARK, minister; b. Lima, Ohio, Sept. 12, 1949; s. John M. and Helen R. (Adkins) B.; m. Sheila Maureen Dorley, June 2, 1973; children: Mara, Elyse, John, Emily, Sarah, Leigh Ellen, Rebekah, Rachel. Student, Mich. State. U., 1967-70, Melodyland Sch. Theol., 1974-75; BA in English, Ga. Southwestern, 1977. Reference libr. Melodyland Sch. Theol., Anaheim, Calif., 1974-75; headmaster Christian Covenant Sch., Albany, Ga., 1977-87; pastor Cornerstone Ch., Americus, Ga., 1987—; bd. dirs. Rainbow Ministries, Christian Rebuilders. Bd. dirs. Ga. Right to Life, Albany, 1985-87, pres. Albany Right to Life, 1983-87. Recipient Merit scholar, 1967. Mem. Fellowship Covenant Minstries and Chs. Office: Cornerstone Ch 702 S Lee St Americus GA 31709

BALDWIN, LEROY FRANKLIN, minister; b. Marion, Va., May 21, 1934; s. Charles Lee and Florence Lorene (Parks) B.; m. Betty Lou Mason, Feb. 24, 1953; children: Dennis Ray, Sandra Kay. BA, Wade Hampton Coll., 1962, M of Ministry, 1964; DD, Am. Bible Inst., 1973. Ordained to ministry Ch. of God, 1963. Evangelist Ch. of God, 1964-69; pastor Ch. of God, Va., N.C., S.C., 1969-90, Orangeburg, S.C., 1990-91; chaplain CAP, 1971-81; chmn., tchr. Ch. of God Ministerial Enrichment for Advancement of Mins.' Edn.; state chmn. World Missions Bd., Ch. of God., N.C., 1980-85; mem. Ministerial Examining-Licensing Bd. for Ch. of God, S.C., 1986-91; guest speaker orgns. and schs.; tchr. coll. extension courses. Capt. Aux. USAF, CAP. Home: 1640 Spring Valley Circle NE Orangeburg SC 29115 Office: Ch of God 1640 Spring Valley Circle NE Orangeburg SC 29115

BALDWIN, WILLIAM RAY, pastor; b. Jefferson, N.C., Feb. 8, 1956; s. William Garland and Lura Dean (Fowler) B.; m. Kathy Diane McLain, June 18, 1977; children: Joshua Aaron, Carmen Elizabeth. BA, Catawba Coll., 1978; MDiv, Emory U., 1981; postgrad., U. Bibl. Studies. Pastor 1st Assembly of God, Albemarle, N.C., 1982-87, 90—, Life Ch., Charlotte, N.C., 1987-90. Author: Care Group Manual, 1984. Republican. Home: PO Box 516 Albemarle NC 28002-0516 Office: 1st Assembly 1501 24/27 W Albemarle NC 28002-0516

BALES, BRADLEY R., broadcasting executive; b. Olympia, Wash., Nov. 4, 1959; s. Harlow and Lois (Ford) B.; m. Marcella Faye, Nov. 27, 1981; children: Brittany, Colin. Grad. high sch., Bismarck, N.D., 1978. Staff announcer Sta. KNDR FM, Mandan, N.D., 1977-86, sta. mgr., 1986—; tchr.-trainer Evangelism Explosion III. Mem. Bismarck Reformed Ch.

BALES, NORMAN LANE, minister; b. Hico, Tex., June 21, 1935; s. Burl and Ruby Lois (Lane) B.; m. Sarah Ann Williams, Dec. 26, 1959; children: William Elliott, James Charles, Ruby Francis, Gary Len. BS, Abilene Christian Coll., 1957; postgrad., Abilene Christian U., 1959-60, 62, 89. Ordained to ministry Ch. of Christ, 1957. Minister Ch. of Christ, Rosebud, Tex., 1957-59; assoc. minister Ch. of Christ, Belton, Tex., 1960-62; minister Ch. of Christ, Jamestown, N.Y., 1964-69, Argentine Ch. of Christ, Kansas City, Kans., 1969-73, Cen. Ch. of Christ, Cedar Rapids, Iowa, 1977—; bd. dirs. Christian Youth Enterprises, Inc., Buffalo, 1965-69, Americall Inc., Love Inc., Cedar Rapids, 1991—. Author: How Do I Know I'm Saved, 1989, A Sense of Belonging, 1989; contbr. articles to Image mag. Devotional chmn. PTA, Kansas City, 1973; bd. dirs. Camp Sunset Inc., Groesbeck, Tex., 1961-63, Partons of the Performing Arts, Cedar Rapids, 1984-87; hon. life mem. Turner (Kans.) PTA, 1973. Republican. Home: 401 35th St SE Cedar Rapids IA 52403 Office: Cen Ch of Christ 1500 1st NW Ave Cedar Rapids IA 52405 *Too much of life is spent anticipating future success. While I regard myself as a goal-oriented person, I refuse to become so preoccupied with tomorrow's dreams that I'm unable to appreciate the joy that's in my life today.*

BALINT, DANIEL LYNN, lay worker; b. Montgomery, Ala., July 10, 1961; s. John Steve and Mattie Lee (Duggar) B.; m. Karen Kay Wilkinson, Jan. 21, 1984; children: Daniel Allen, Luke Andrew. BS, Auburn U., Montgomery, Ala., 1984. Cert. phys. edn. tchr., Ala. Tchr., coach, athletic dir. Ind. Meth. Sch., Mobile, Ala., 1985-88; dir. youth and children Orchard Bapt. Ch., Mobile, Ala., 1989—; vol. leader Young Life-Montgomery, 1977-81; del. So. Bapt. Conv., Mobile, 1990; instr. Spring Hill Coll. Basketball Camp, Mobile, 1986-88, Mark Gottfried All star Baksetball Camp, Mobile, 1987-88. Mem. Mobile Youth Ministers Assn., Fellowship Christian Students, Phy. Edn. Club (parliamentarian 1983-84).

BALJON, JOHANNES MARINUS SIMON, Islamologist, writer, researcher; b. Modjowarno, East Java, Indonesia, July 18, 1919; arrived in The Netherlands, 1932; s. Johannes Marinus Simon and Maria Cornelia L. (Ossewaarde) B.; m. Krijna Petronella van den Ende, Aug. 14, 1947; children: Marijke, Kees, Christophoor, Maarten, Theo. Cand. philology, Utrecht U., The Netherlands, 1948, DD, 1949; student Urdu, Sch. Oriental Studies, London, 1946-48; student Arabic, Leiden U., The Netherlands, 1948-49. Ordained minister Dutch Ref. Ch., 1950. Minister Dutch Ref. Ch., Blankenham, The Netherlands, 1950-57, Loppersum, The Netherlands, 1957-60; asst. prof. Faculty Theology and Arts, Groningen (The Netherlands) U., 1961-71, prof., 1971-84; writer on Islamic subjects, Leiden, 1984—; mem. Gen. Synod Ref. Ch., Kampen, The Netherlands, 1955-57; mem. adv. com. Netherlands Orgn. for Pure Rsch., The Hague, 1974-80. Author: Reforms and Religious Ideas of Sir Sayyid Ahmad Khan, 1949, reprinted, 1958, 64, Modern Muslim Koran Interpretation, 1961, Religion and Thought of Shah Wali Allah, 1986, Full Moon Appearing on the Horizon, 1988. Gen. pres. Netherlands-Arab Circle, The Hague, 1986-89. Mem. Soc. for Study History Religions, Oriental Soc. Netherlands. Avocations: tennis, chess, bridge. Home: Plantsoen 73, 2311 KK Leiden The Netherlands *The most satisfactory research result a Christian Islamologist can imagine is the acknowledgement of a Muslim colleague: "You are working for us. You are one of us".*

BALKE, VICTOR H., bishop; b. Meppen, Ill., Sept. 29, 1931; s. Bernard H. and Elizabeth A. (Knese) B. B.A. in Philosophy, St. Mary of Lake Sem., Mundelein, Ill., 1954, S.T.B. in Theology, 1956, M.A. in Religion, 1957, S.T.L. in Theology, 1958; M.A. in English, St. Louis U., 1964, Ph.D., 1973. Ordained priest Roman Catholic Ch., 1958; asst. pastor Springfield, Ill., 1958-62; chaplain St. Joseph Home Aged, Springfield, 1962-63; procurator, instr. Diocesan Sem., Springfield, 1963-70; rector, instr. Diocesan Sem., 1970-76; ordained, installed 6th bishop of Crookston, Minn., 1976—. Clubs: K.C, Lions. Office: Chancery Office 1200 Memorial Dr PO Box 610 Crookston MN 56716

BALL, EARL ELLSWORTH, pastor; b. Wayne, Okla., June 22, 1930; s. Charles Otis and Dorothea Ieula (Crawford) B.; m. Betty Elwanda Wanda Herrin, Jan. 14, 1949; children: Diana Rodman, Belinda Richey, Dacia Lust. BA, Ea. N.Mex. U., 1956; ThM, So. Meth. U., 1963. Ordained to ministry United Meth. Ch., 1958. Pastor United Meth. Ch., Okla., N.Mex., Tex., 1950-87, 91, St. Mark's United Meth. Ch., Midland, Tex., 1987-91. With U.S. Army, 1947. Home: 1401 S 4th Raton NM 87740 Office: 1st United Meth Ch 1501 S 4th St Raton NM 87740

BALL, ERIC GREAHAM, youth pastor; b. Orlando, Fla., Mar. 13, 1955; s. Eric G. Sr. and Redetha May (Jackson) B.; m. Linda Anne Patzke, July 12, 1980; children: Rachael Elizabeth, Rebekah JoyLynn, Amyleigh Christine. BS in Acctg., Troy State U., 1978; postgrad., Columbia Bible Sem., 1989-90. Ordained to ministry Bapt. Ch., 1984. Campus pres. Fellowship of Christian Athletes, Troy, Ala., 1977-78; counselor Christians in Action, Titusville, Fla., 1978-79; youth lay worker Park Ave. Bapt. Ch., Titusville, Fla., 1979-82, youth pastor, 1982—. Football, track coach Titusville High Sch., 1986, 87; speaker Astronaut High Sch., Titusville, 1989-90. Mem. Nat. Network of Youth Ministry (state coord. 1989-91), Omicron Delta Kappa (Leadership award 1978), Gamma Beta Phi. Office: Park Ave Bapt Ch 2600 Park Ave Titusville FL 32780

BALL, JOHN NELSON, minister; b. Mexico, Mo., Aug. 30, 1938; s. Lebbius Mac and Elizabeth Sue (Field) B.; m. Joyce Jeanne Beatty, May 31, 1959; children: John Anthony, Jeanne Alice, Jane Ann (dec.). BA in Bible Studies, Cen. Christian Coll. of Bible, 1967. Ordained to ministry Christian Ch., 1967. Minister Union (Iowa) Ch. Christ, 1967-68, Waterloo (Iowa) Ch. Christ, 1968-69, W. Eminence (Mo.) Christian Ch., 1969-73, S. Telegraph Christian Ch., St. Louis, 1973-74, Oak Grove (Mo.) Christian Ch., 1974-78, Callao (Mo.) Christian Ch., 1978-83, Lakeview Christian Ch., House Springs, Mo., 1983-91; supply preacher, interim minister, writer Fenton, Mo., 1991—; Co-founder, dean Iowa Sch. Missions, Liscomb, 1968-70; dean curriculum Rock Garden Christian Service Camp, Eminence, 1970-72; treas. N.E. Iowa Christian Service Camp, Bristow, 1968-69, Rock Garden Christian Service Camp, Eminence, 1971-73. Bd. dirs. Show Me Christian Youth Home, LaMonte, Mo., 1970-73, 75-79; bd. dirs. High Hill (Mo.) Christian Service Camp, 1973-74, chmn. bd. 1986-90; bd. dirs. Christian Campus Fellowship, Kirksville, Mo., 1980-82, sec. 1981-82; chmn. bd. Mid-Western Camp Leaders Conf. Com., 1980-81; pres. PTA, Eminence, 1971-72; mem. Community Betterment Orgn., Callao, 1979-83; bd. dirs. High Hill (Mo.) Christian Assembly., v.p., 1984-85, pres. 1986-90. Recipient Sandy Ninanger award Mexico (Mo.) High Sch., 1956, Appreciation award Soc. Dist. High Sch. Students, Birmingham, Ala., 1977-86, Vol. award Normandy Osteo. Hosps., St. Louis, 1983-89. Mem. Ministerial Alliance (Oak Grove chpt. 1973-78, pres. 1977-78). Republican. Office: 5 Chism Trails Fenton MO 63026 *"For me to live is Christ." (Phil. 1:21). It is my desire that my life exhalts Christ and draws others to Him.*

BALL, ROBERT JAMES, minister; b. Mammoth Spring, Ark., July 2, 1949; s. George Gray Sr. and Ruth Lyle (Charlton) B.; m. Kathy Sharlene Haney, June 1, 1967; children: Kath Michelle, Carolyn Jean. BA, Internat. Bible Coll., 1983; MA, Alabama Christian Coll., 1985, MDiv, 1989; postgrad., Drew U., 1988—. Ordained to ministry Ch. of Christ. Min. Priceville Ch. of Christ, Decatur, Ala., 1981-86, North Main St. Ch. of Christ, Mocksville, N.C., 1986-89, Old Hickory (Tenn.) Ch. of Christ, 1989—. Home: 407 Jones St Old Hickory TN 37138 Office: Old Hickory Ch of Christ 1001 Hadley Ave Old Hickory TN 37138

BALL, THOMAS ERIC, minister; b. Lansing, Mich., Aug. 31, 1956; s. Cecil Melvin and Mary Ann (Hartel) B.; m. Sept. 22, 1990. BA, Albion (Mich.) Coll., 1979; MDiv, Drew Theol. Sem., Madison, N.J., 1984. Ordained to ministry, United Meth. Ch., as deacon, 1982, as elder, 1986. Youth pastor Franklin Lakes United Meth. Ch., N.J., 1981-83; pastor Girard and Ellis Corners United Meth. Chs., 1984-88, Climax and Scotts (Mich.) United Meth. Chs., 1988—; dist. youth coord. W. Mich. Conf. United Meth. Ch., Albion Dist., 1985-89. Office: 270 Snapdragon Ln Climax MI 49034

BALLARD, CHARLES JOSEPH, minister; b. Memphis, Feb. 19, 1943; s. Charles J. and Ruby Jane (Williams) B.; m. Beverly Ann Marshall; 1 child, Krista Leigh. BS, Memphis State U., 1966; MRE, Southwestern Bapt. Theol. Sem., 1967. Ordained to ministry So. Bapt. Conv., 1973. Min. edn. Liberty Bapt. Ch., Hampton, Va., 1967-71, Edgewood Bapt. Ch., Columbus, Ga., 1971-76; assoc. pastor Terry Parker Bapt. Ch., Jacksonville, Fla., 1976-79, 1st Bapt. Ch., Brandon, Fla., 1979-89; min. edn. 1st Bapt. Ch., Maryville, Tenn., 1989—. Contbr. articles to religious jours. Bd. dirs. Crisis Pregnancy Ctr., Brandon, Fla., 1987-89, Pregnancy Testing Resource Ctr., Maryville, 1990—. Mem. So. Bapt. Religious Edn. Assn. (v.p. 1991—), Fla. Bapt. Religious Edn. Assn. (past pres.), Fla. Bapt. Religious Edn. Roundtable (past chmn.). Office: First Bapt Ch 202 W Lamar Alexander Pkwy Maryville TN 37801 *In the world today it is easy to lose your sense of awe and awareness of all the wonderful things that the Lord has created and that are going on around you. It is easy to overlook the sound of a bird singing, to not see the delicate flowers growing at your feet and not notice the smell of a new mown lawn in the spring. We should never be too busy to be aware of the wonder of God's glorious creation.*

BALLARD, GERALD PORTER (JERRY BALLARD), humanitarian organization executive; b. Asheville, N.C., Oct. 16, 1936; s. Loy E. and Gertrude (Oakley) B.; m. Winnie Underwood, Aug. 31, 1958; children: Kimberly Michelle, Keri Melynn. BBE, Columbia (S.C.) Bible Coll., 1960; postgrad., East Carolina U., N.C. State U., Vanderbilt U.; MA in Communications, Syracuse U., 1969; LLD, Geneva Coll., 1991. Dir. communications World Vision Internat., Monrovia, Calif., 1970-72; prof. communications Columbia Grad. Sch., 1972-75; founder, pres. Ballard and Puckett, Inc., advt., pub. rels., mgmt. cons., Atlanta and Chgo., 1975-78; bd. dirs. World Relief Corp. of Nat. Assn. Evangs., Carol Stream, Ill., 1968-70, exec. dir., chief exec. officer, 1978-91; cons. to internat. orgns., 1972-78, 91—; lectr., condr. communications and mgmt. seminars, adminstr. communication projects in over 40 countries; cons. Congress World Evangelism, Pattaya, Thailand, 1980; lectr. evangelistic writing Internat. Congress on World Evangelization, Lausanne, Switzerland, 1974; featured speaker Missionary Info. Bur. Conf., Brazil, 1975. Author 6 books; writer, producer, dir. over 30 films. Active Christian humanitarian concerns, Caribbean, Africa, India, SE Asia, 1965—. Recipient numerous nat. awards for excellence in creative writing and graphic design, 1961-72, hon. recognition for contbn. to humanitarian assistance from C.Am., India, Korea, The Philippines, Vietnam, West Africa. Mem. Nat. Assn. Evangs. (bd. adminstrn. 1973-78). Office: World Relief Corp 450 Gundersen Dr Carol Stream IL 60188 also: 2821 Emerywood Blvd Richmond VA 23229

BALLARD, MELVIN RUSSELL, JR., church official; b. Salt Lake City, Oct. 8, 1928; s. Melvin Russell and Geraldine (Smith) B.; student U. Utah, 1946, 1950-52; m. Barbara Bowen, Aug. 28, 1951; children—Clark, Holly, Meleea, Tamara, Stacey, Brynn, Craig. Sales mgr. Ballard Motor Co., Salt Lake City, 1950-54; investment counselor, Salt Lake City, 1954-56; founder, owner, mgr. Russ Ballard Auto, Inc., Salt Lake City, 1956-58, Ballard-Wade Co., 1958-67; owner, mgr. Ballard & Co., Salt Lake City, 1962-72; gen. authority Ch. of Jesus Christ of Latter-day Saints, Salt Lake City, 1976—, now pres. 1st Quorum of the 70; dir. Foothill Thrift & Loan, Nate-Wade, Inc., Silver King Mines, Inc. (all Salt Lake City); gen. partner N & R Investment, Salt Lake City, 1958—, Ballard Investment Co., Salt Lake City, 1955—. Mem. bd. Salt Lake Jr. Achievement, 1978-80; bd. dirs. Freedoms Found., 1978—, David O. McKay Inst. Edn., 1979—; Served to 1st lt. USAR, 1950-57. Mem. Salt Lake Area C. of C. (gov. 1979—). Republican. Office: LDS Church Quorum of the Twelve 50 E N Temple St Salt Lake City UT 84150

BALLARD, MICHAEL ALAN, minister; b. Indpls., July 31, 1960; s. Donald Louis and Barbara Lee (Runyan) B.; m. Denise L. Huffman, July 5, 1986; 1 child, Bryce. BA in Bible Studies, Harding U., 1985; grad., Inst. Practical Religion, Dallas, 1988. Ordained to ministry Ch. of Christ, 1985. Jr. high min. Highland Oak Ch. of Christ, Dallas, 1986-88; youth min. West Houston Ch. of Christ, Houston, Tex., 1988-90; pro-teen leader Weinberger, Hall & Assocs., P.C., Houston, 1988-90; youth and family min. Poplar Ave. Ch. Christ, Wichita, Kans., 1990—. Author: Teenage Behavior from The Book of James, 1988. Republican. Home: 4618 S Ellis Wichita KS 67216 Office: Poplar Ave Ch Christ 600 S Poplar Ave Wichita KS 67211

BALLESTEROS, JUVENTINO RAY, JR., minister; b. L.A., June 27, 1953; s. Juventino Ray and Esther Marie (Mendoza) B.; m. Rebecca Ann Williamson, Dec. 30, 1978. BA, Birmingham South Coll., 1977; MA, Presbyn. Sch. Christian Edn., 1979; D Ministry, Union Theol. Sem., 1982. Intern minister Crystal Cathedral, Garden Grove, Calif., 1978, Philippi Presbyn. Ch., Raeford, N.C., 1980-81; assoc. minister 1st Presbyn. Ch., Fayetteville, N.C., 1982-84, Orlando, Fla., 1984—; chmn. Div. Edn., Fayetteville, 1982-84, Nat. Tchr. Edn. Program, Fayetteville, 1983-84. Bd. dirs. Cumberland County Clean Community Council, Fayetteville, 1982-84, Nat. Tchr. Ednl. Program, Durham, N.C.; bd. advisors Jr. League, Fayetteville, 1983-84; v.p. Spouse Abuse Inc., Orlando, 1984-86. Named one of Outstanding Young Men of Am., 1985, one of Men of Achievement, 1989, Internat. Dir. of Disting. Leadership, 1989. Mem. Religious Educators Assn., Assn. Presbyn. Ch. Educators. Republican. Avocation: all sports. Office: 1st Presbyn Ch 106 E Church St Orlando FL 32801

BALLESTRERO, ANASTASIO ALBERTO CARDINAL, archbishop of Turin; b. Genoa, Italy, Oct. 3, 1913; Professed in Order of Discalced Carmelites, 1929; ordained priest Roman Catholic Ch., 1936; provincial, 1948-54; superior gen., 1955-67, of Carmelites; ordained archbishop of Bari, Italy, 1974; archbishop of Turin, Italy, 1977—; elevated to cardinal, 1979; titular ch. S. Maria sopra Minerva; pres. Italian Episcopal Conf., 1979-86. Mem. Consiglio per gli Affari Pubblici della Chiesa. Mem. Congregation Religious and Secular Insts., S. Congregazione per i Vescovi. Author of many books. Office: Via Arcivescovado 12, 10121 Turin Italy

BALLEW, ROYCE AVERY, minister; b. Dallas, May 17, 1935; s. Roy Ernest and Ouida Olivia (Lyles) B.; m. Anne Joy Feezor, Aug. 1, 1958; children: David Brian, Christopher Brent. BA, Baylor U., 1957; BD, Southwestern Bapt. Theol. Sem., Ft. Worth, 1962, MDiv, 1973. Ordained to ministry So. Bapt. Conv. Pioneer missionary Bapt. Gen. Conv. Tex., Sheboygan, Wis., 1962; deacon Wilshire Bapt. Ch., Dallas, 1970-72; pastor Calvary Bapt. Ch., San Juan, P.R., 1972-77, Waco (N.C.) Bapt. Ch., 1977—; treas. Bapt. Assn. P.R., San Juan, 1975-77; Sunday sch. dir. Kings Mountain Bapt. Assn., Shelby, N.C., 1977-90; dir. Christian Svc. Orgn., Gardner-Webb Coll., Boiling Springs, N.C., 1988-91, Conservative Carolina Bapts., Charlotte, N.C., 1991—. Author Sunday sch. lessons, 1985—. Bd. dirs. Am. Diabetes Assn., N.Y.C., 1968-72, pres., Shelby, 1978; trustee Christian Action League, Raleigh, N.C., 1981—; asst. chief Waco Vol. Fire Dept., 1987-89. Recipient Homenaje de Vejez, State Assn. for Aging in P.R., 1977, gov.'s cert. of appreciation State of N.C., 1979. Mem. Ruritan (sec. Waco 1987-89, 91). Home: 236 N Main St PO Box 297 Waco NC 19169 Office: Waco Bapt Ch 262 N Main St PO Box 297 Waco NC 28169 *When we break God's rules for living, seeking short-term pleasure, we find that we receive long-term pain and trouble—not only for ourselves but for people around us.*

BALLINGER, LAURA, minister; b. Miami, Fla., June 14, 1957; d. L. Clifford and Florence (Scarborough) Jordan; m. David Leon Ballinger, June 9, 1989. AA, Miami-Dade Community Coll., 1977; BS, U. Fla., 1985; MRE, Asbury Theol. Sem., 1990. Ordained to ministry United Meth. Ch., 1991. Coord. youth ministry United Meth. Ch. Switzerland/Ohio Counties, 1990—. Diaconal Ministry Div. Switzerland/Ohio Counties grantee, 1990-91. Home: RR 1 Box 135 Bennington IN 47011

BALL-KILBOURNE, DEBRA GAYLE, minister; b. Slayton, Minn., Apr. 6, 1951; d. Alvin and Leona (DeVine) Ball;m. Gary Lee Kilbourne, Sept. 5, 1976; 1 child, Matthew. BA, Buena Vista Coll., 1972; M. Christian Edn., Garrett-Evang. Theol. Sem., 1976, MDiv, 1978. Ordained to ministry Meth. Ch., 1976. Pastor Asbury United Meth. Ch., Charles Town, W.Va., 1978-80; ednl. cons. United Meth. Pub. House, Nashville, 1980-83; pastor Mo. Valley Parish, Washburn, N.D., 1983-85; dist. supt. Western dist. N.D. Annual Conf., Bismarck, N.D., 1985-87; pastor 1st United Meth. Ch., Jamestown, N.D., 1987—; del. North Cen. Jurisdiction Conf., 1988; res. del. Gen. Conf., 1988. Conbr. articles to profl. jours. Home: PO Box 1347 Jamestown ND 58402 Office: 1st United Meth Ch 115 3d St SE Jamestown ND 58401

BALL-KILBOURNE, GARY LEE, minister; b. Washington, Feb. 14, 1953; s. George J. and Ernestelle (Loffler) Kilbourne; m. Debra G. Ball, Sept. 5, 1976; children: Matthew, Zachary. BA, Western Md. Coll., 1974; MDiv, Garrett-Evang. Theol. Sem., 1978; MA, Vanderbilt U., 1983, PhD, 1988. Ordained to ministry United Meth. Ch., 1976. Pastor Harper's Ferry (W.Va.) United Meth. Parish, 1978-80, Missouri Valley Parish, Washburn, N.D., 1983-85, Center (N.D.) United Meth. Ch., 1985-87, First United Meth. Ch., Jamestown, N.D., 1987-91; editor Adult Publs. United Meth. Pub. House, Nashville, 1991—; conf. sec. N.D. Annual Conf., 1985-91. Coauthor: (study guide) In Defense of Creation, 1986; contbr. articles to profl. jours. Dempster fellow Gen. Bd. of Higher Edn. and Ministry of the United Meth. Ch., 1983; Harold Stirling Vanderbilt scholar Vanderbilt U., 1980. Mem. Am. Acad. Religion, Soc. Christian Ethics, Christian Educators Fellowship. Home: 8207 Sawyer Brown Rd H-3 Nashville TN 37221 Office: PO Box 801 Nashville TN 37202

BALM-DEMMEL, DARLINE DAWN MILLER, minister; b. Marshall, Minn., Dec. 16, 1933; d. Russell Neil and Laura Esther (Seiler) M.; m. Thomas Ree Balm, Apr. 15, 1954 (div. Dec. 1981); children—Stephen Paul, Jonathon Mark, Brian Scott, Michelle Dawn; m. Gary H. Demmel, June 28, 1987. BA, Westmar Coll., 1954; MA, U. North Iowa, 1968; postgrad., State U. Iowa, 1977-79; MDiv, U. Dubuque, 1987. Ordained to ministry United Meth. Ch. as deacon, 1987, as elder, 1990; cert. tchr., Iowa. Tchr. Pub. Sch., Lisle, Ill., 1954-55, Allamakee High Sch., Lansing, Iowa, 1961-63, Dysart-Geneseo Sch., Dysart, Iowa, 1964-69; English instr. Westmar Coll., LeMars, Iowa, 1970-76; sec. Wesley Found., Iowa City, 1978-79; promotion adminstr. Control-o-fax- Corp., Waterloo, Iowa, 1980-81, promotion coord., 1981-86; pastor United Meth. Ch., 1986—; vice chmn. Dist. Coun. on Ministries, United Meth. Ch., Waterloo, 1984-86, chmn. nominating com. Iowa conf., 1984-86. Mem. AAUW, LWV (pres. Black Haw-Bremer counties 1983-85, pres. Dubuque chpt. 1990—). Democrat. Avocations: reading, piano, biking, travel, theater. Home and Office: 5498 S Mound Rd Sherrill IA 52073

BALNICKY, ROBERT GABRIEL, minister; b. Elizabeth, N.J., Apr. 18, 1922; s. Harry and Irene (Sawicky) B.; m. Annette Virginia Hawkins, Dec. 24, 1977; children by previous marriage: Richard Ozzie, Barbara Gail. Student Pensacola Jr. Coll., 1949, Emory U., 1950, Columbia Theol. Sem., Decatur, Ga., 1952; B Ministry, M Ministry, Internat. Sem., Plymouth, Fla., 1979, DD, 1980, D Ministry, 1985. With Merck & Co., Rahway, N.J., 1939-42; pastor Troy (N.C.) Presbyn. Ch., 1952-55, 1st Presbyn. Ch., Ocean Dr. Beach, S.C., 1955-56, McCutchen Meml. Ch., Union, S.C., 1956-60, Fairfield Presbyn. Ch., Pensacola, Fla., 1960-64; founder, pastor Trinity Bible Ch., Pensacola, 1964-70; pastor Inskip Presbyn. Ch., Knoxville, Tenn., 1970-72; chaplain Pay Cash Wholesale Grocery, 1972-74; founding pastor Grace Presbyn. Ch., Knoxville, 1973-74; counseling ctr. dir. Christian Broadcasting Network, Inc., Knoxville, 1975-76; pastor Handsboro Presbyn. Ch., Gulfport, Miss., 1979-81; interim pastor Berean Presbyn. Ch., New Orleans, 1982-83; chmn. Ch. Devel. Commn., Evang. Presbyn. Ch., 1982-85; dir. communications, dir. family svcs. Salvation Army, New Orleans, 1983-85; chaplain coord. La. World Expn., 1984; coord. chaplaincy New Orleans Fire Dept., 1985-88; chaplain New Orleans Fire Fighters Assn. and New Orleans Fire chief's Assn., 1985-88; pres. Robert G. Balnicky Evang. Assn., Inc.; pres. Union County (S.C.) Ministers Assn., 1957; chmn. Enoree Presbytery Com. Evangelism, 1956-60; mem. com. evangelism S.C. Synod, 1956-60; chmn. bd. dirs. Pensacola Youth for Christ; bd. dirs. Fla. Alcohol-Narcotics, Inc., Fla. United Christian Action, Inc.; mem. adv. bd. Community Action Program, Am. Security Council. Lt. col., chaplain Fla. CAP, 1965-70; dep. wing chaplain Tenn. CAP, 1970-74, dep. chaplain S.E. Region CAP, 1974-82, 91—; chaplain S.W. regional staff CAP, 1982-91; asst. mgr. VIP transp. Rep. Nat. Conv., New Orleans, 1988; mem. Bd. Elections Pinellas County, 1989-90; mem. U.S. Census Bur., 1990. Served flight engr. 1st class USN, 1942-49. Recipient Four Chaplains citation Chapel Four Chaplains, Phila., 1960, Meritorious Svc. award CAP 1973, Exceptional Svc. award, 1982, Grover Loening Aerospace award, 1974, Paul E. Garber award 1981, Gill Robb Wilson award, 1989, Vol. of Yr. award New Orleans City Welfare Dept. Emergency Svcs., 1984, citation of appreciation Fla. Coop. Svc., 1989; named Master Gardener, U. Fla/Pinellas County Coop. Extension Svc., 1989. Mem. DAV (life), Am. Legion (state chaplain S.C. 1956-58, post comdr. 1953-54; grad. Am. Legion Coll., Indpls. 1954; mem. nat. press assn.; chmn. S.C. religious emphasis com. 1956-58, mem. nat. comdr.'s flying squadron; mem. Century Club 1954-55), 40 and 8 (grand aumonier S.C.; state chaplain 1957-59, aumonier nat., nat. chaplain 1959-60; local chaplain 1961-70, life), Navy League, World Ministry Fellowship (pres. 1966-68), Mil. Chaplains Assn. (life), Nat. Assn. Evangs., Fellowship of Fire Chaplains, Firefighters for Christ, Fellowship of Christian Fighters, Internat. Order St. Luke the Physician. Address: 14080 Marguerite Dr Madeira Beach FL 33708

BALS, JERRY JOHN, media specialist, clergyman; b. Cleve., Jan. 8, 1941; s. Frank and Eleanor (Zack) B.; m. Renée Marie Montesanto, Aug. 17, 1963; children: Kimberely, Michelle, Vincent, Kristine, Renée, Jill, Jerry, Sarah. BS in Edn., Kent State U., 1964; student, St. John U., 1973, John Carroll U., 1969-73. Ordained as minister Roman Catholic Ch., 1973. Tchr., coach North High Sch., Eastlake, Ohio, 1967-71; chaplain, wrestling coach Lake Catholic High Sch., Mentor, Ohio, 1971-85; minister St. Justin Catholic Ch., Eastlake, Ohio, 1973—; counselor Willowridge Hosp., Willoughby, Ohio, 1985; campus minister St. Ignatius High Sch., Cleve., 1986-88; media specialist Willoughby Eastlake (Ohio) Schs., 1988—; pvt. practice, Eastlake, 1985—. Bd. dirs. Zoning Appeals Bd., Eastlake. Mem. NEA, Ohio Edn. Assn., KC. Home: 352 E Overlook Dr Eastlake OH 44095

BALSIGER, DAVID WAYNE, publisher, author, film video executive; b. Monroe, Wis., Dec. 14, 1945; s. Leon C. and Dorothy May (Meythaler) B.; m. Nancy Marie Dixon, Oct. 12, 1991; children from previous marriages: Jennifer Anne, Lisa Atalie, Lori Faith. Student, Pepperdine U., Malibu, Calif., 1964-66, Cypress Jr. Coll., 1966, Chapman Coll. World Campus Afloat, Orange, Calif., 1967-68, Internat. Coll., Copenhagen, 1968; BA, Nat. U., San Diego, 1977; LHD (hon.), Lincoln Meml. U., Harrogate, Tenn., 1978. Chief photographer, feature writer Anaheim (Calif.) Bull., 1968-69; pub., editor Money Doctor, consumer mag., Anaheim, 1969-70; media dir. World Evangelism, San Diego, 1970-72; dir. mktg. Logos Internat. Christian Book Pubs., Plainfield, N.J., 1972-73; pres., dir. Master Media, advt. agy., Costa Mesa, Calif., 1973-75; pres. Balsiger Lit. Svc., Costa Mesa, 1973-78; v.p. communications Donald S. Smith Assocs., Anaheim, Calif., 1975-78; assoc. producer, dir. creative devel. Sunn Classic Pictures, L.A., Salt Lake City, 1976-78; owner Writeway Lit. Assocs., Costa Mesa, 1978—, Balsiger Enterprises, Costa Mesa, 1978—, Writeway Lit. Assocs., Bibl. News Svc., 1980—; v.p. Donald S. Smith Assocs., Anaheim, 1982-86; owner BNS Publs., 1986—; v.p. Am. Portrait Films Internat., 1990-91; vis. prof. Nat. U., San Diego, 1977-80. Author: The Satan Seller, 1972, The Back Side of Satan, 1973, Noah's Ark: I Touched It, 1974, One More Time, 1974, It's Good to Know, 1975, In Search of Noah's Ark, 1976, The Lincoln Conspiracy, 1977, Beyond Defeat, 1978, On the Other Side, 1978, Mistah Abe, 1992, 8 Mini Guide Books (travel series), 1979, Presidential Biblical Scoreboard, 1980, 84, 88, Family Protection Scoreboard, 1987, 88, 89, Candidates Biblical Scoreboard, 1986, Scoreboard Alert, 1989; writer, researcher: TV and motion pictures including Operation Thanks, 1965, The Life and Times of Grizzly Adams, 1976-77, In Search of Noah's Ark, 1976, The Lincoln Conspiracy, 1977, The Bermuda Triangle, 1977, In God We Trust: The Impact of Prayer on America, 1991, Mistah Abe, 1991; pub.-editor Christian Singles Connection, 1991—; frequent debate page columnist USA Today, 1987—; author numerous law enforcement publs. Press agt. John G. Schmitz congl. campaign, 1972, Gordon Bishop supr. campaign, Orange County, 1970; press agt. asst. Ronald Reagan for Gov., statewide, 1966; statewide campaign mgr. James E. Johnson for U.S. Senate, 1974; campaign mgr. Dave Gubler Congl. campaign, 1974; candidate Costa Mesa City Coun., 1980; Rep. candidate for Congress from 38th Dist. Calif., 1978; mem. Calif. Rep. Assembly, 1975-78, 81-84, Rep. Assocs. Orange County, 1977-79; mem. World Affairs Coun. Orange County and San Diego, 1969-70; assoc. mem. Calif. Rep. Cen. Com., 1969-70; bd. dirs. Chapman Coll. World Campus Afloat, 1967, Chrisma Ministries, Orange, Calif., 1969-73; founder Ban the Soviets Coalition, 1983-84; exec. com. Anatole Fellowship, 1983-87; founder, pres. Nat. Citizens Action Network, 1984—; bd. dirs. Internat. Ch. Relief Fund, 1987—. Recipient Vietnam appreciation citation Am. Soldiers in Vietnam, 1966, George Washington Honor medal Freedoms Found., 1978, 79, Religion in Media Angel trophy, 1981, 85, 87, 88, 89; named Writer of Month Calif. Writer, 1967; grand winner Mercury award for Pub. Affairs, 1987, Gold Mercury award for Pub. Affairs Mag., 1987, Silver Mercury award for affairs video script, 1988; named to Lit. Hall of Fame, 1977; hon. tourism amb. Republic of South Africa, 1991. Mem. Nat. Univ. Pres. Assocs., Coun. on Nat. Policy, Prayer In Action Convocation (co-chmn.), Campus Crusade for Christ (com. on reference), Internat. Bible Reading Assn. (adv. bd.), Evang. Press Assn., Christian Action Network (adv. bd.). Address: PO Box 10428 Costa Mesa CA 92627 *I believe successful people have a God given purpose strong enough to make them form the habit of doing things they don't like to do in order to accomplish their purpose. Every single qualification for success is acquired through habit. People form habits and habits form futures.*

BALTAKIS, PAUL ANTANAS, bishop; b. Troškunai, Panevezys, Lithuania, Jan. 1, 1925; s. Juozas and Apolonia (Lauzikaite) B. PhD, Franciscan Sem., Rekem, Belgium, 1949; ThD, Franciscan Sem., St. Truidem, Belgium, 1955. Assoc. pastor Roman Cath. Parish of Resurrection, Toronto, Ont., Can., 1953-69; councilman Lithuanian Franciscan Vicariate, Kennebunkport, Maine, 1967-79, provincial superior, 1979-84; Roman Cath. bishop Lithuanian Catholics, Bklyn., 1984—. Spiritual adviser Lithuanian Boy Scouts Assn., Bklyn., 1964-84, Lithuanian Vets., Bklyn., 1970-79. Recipient For the Merits award Lithuanian Boy Scouts Assn., 1988, For the Merits award Lithuanian Vets., 1977. Mem. Knights of Lithuania (hon.), Nat. Conf. Bishops & U.S. Cath. Conf. Home and Office: 361 Highland Blvd Brooklyn NY 11207

BALYO, JOHN GABRIEL, minister, theology educator; b. Greenville, S.C., Jan. 18, 1920; s. John Gabor and Etta (Groce) B.; m. Betty Louise Lindstrand, Oct. 14, 1945; 1 son, John Michael. Student, Atlanta Law Sch., 1937-40; LL.B., Valparaiso U., 1945; student, Goshen Coll., 1945-46; A.B., Grace Theol. Sem., 1944, MDiv. magna cum laude, 1946; D.D., Grand Rapids Theol. Sem., 1960. Ordained to ministry Bible Bapt. Ch., 1950. Pastor Three Oaks, Mich., 1942-45, Elkhart, Ind., 1945-46, Kokomo, Ind., 1946-53; pastor Cedar Hill Bapt. Ch., Cleve., 1953-72; prof. Bible and practical theology Grand Rapids (Mich.) Bapt. Theol. Sem., 1972-80; chmn. council of ten Sunshine State Fellowship of Regular Bapt. Chs., Fla., 1980-81; pastor Sun Coast Bapt. Ch., New Port Richey, Fla., 1980-81; prof. theology and Bible Bapt. Bible Coll. and Sch. Theology, Clarks Summit, Pa., 1981-83; pres. Western Bapt. Coll., Salem, Oreg., 1983-91, chancellor, 1991—; mem. gen. council Bapt. Mid-Mission, 1954—, adminstrv. com., 1962-73, trustee, 1963-75, chmn. bd. trustees, 1968-75, chmn. council, 1966-68; mem. council 14 Gen. Assn. Regular Bapt. Chs., 1955-59, 60-64, sec. council, 1957-58, chmn. publs. com., 1956-60, 63-66, chmn. council 14, 1966-68, mem. finance com., 1968-69, publs. com., 1968-69, chmn. program com., 1968-69, chmn. edn. com., 1960-62, vice chmn. council, 1962-64, chmn., 1970-72, chmn. publs. com., 1972-73, chmn. council of 18, 1973-74, vice chmn. council of 18, 1983-86, chmn., 1986-87; exec. bd. dirs. Grand Rapids Bapt. Bible Coll. and Sem., 1961-72, chmn. curriculum com., 1963-66; missionary survey trips to, Europe and Africa, 1957-58, Ecuador, 1962, Peru, 1969, Brazil, 1975; Bd. dirs. Hebrew Christian Soc., 1956-64. Author: Sunday sch. material for Regular Bapt. Press; also booklet Creation and Evolution. Mem. Oreg. Ind. Colls. Assn. (exec. com. Portland chpt. 1990-91). Home: 5515 Springwood Ave SE Salem OR 97306 Office: Western Bapt Coll 5000 Deer Park Dr SE Salem OR 97301 *Memory can be a closet of skeletons or a storehouse of treasures. If we are kind to our memories our memories will be kind to us.*

BALZER, JOEL, minister; b. Bimidji, Minn., June 14, 1956; s. Reuben James and Jean Caroline (Harlow) B.; m. Lisa Marion Hannigan, Aug. 13, 1983. BA in Bibl. Lit. Urban Studies, Simpson Coll., 1982, ThM, 1988; postgrad., Golden Gate Sem., 1982-84. Ordained to ministry Christian and Missionary Alliance, 1987. Asst. recruiter M-2 Sponsors, Hayward, Calif., 1981; asst. dir. Lifeline Brethren in Christ Mission, San Francisco, 1981; interim pastor San Francisco Neighborhood Ch., 1985, pastor, 1986—; carpenter The Floorworks, San Francisco, 1982—. Contbr. articles to profl. publs. Position statement draftee San Francisco Christian AIDS Coun., 1989. Mem. Evang. Theol. Soc., Sierra Club, Delta Epsilon Chi. Democrat. Home: 302 Jules Ave San Francisco CA 94112 Office: San Francisco Neighborhood Ch 302 Jules Ave San Francisco CA 94112

BAMBERGER, HENRY, rabbi; b. Albany, N.Y., June 1, 1935; s. Bernard and Ethel (Kraus) B.; m. Sheila Lister, June 21, 1959; children: Judith G., Miriam R. AB, Columbia U., 1956; MAHL, Hebrew Union Coll., N.Y.C., 1961, DHL, 1971, DD, 1986. Ordained rabbi 1961. Rabbi Temple Sinai, Sharon, Mass., 1961-66, Vassar Temple, Poughkeepsie, N.Y., 1966-75, Temple Emanuel, Birmingham, Ala., 1975-79; rabbi Temple Ohev Shalom, Harrisburg, Pa., 1979-81, Temple Emanu-El, Utica, N.Y., 1982—; dir. Munson-Williams-Proctor Inst., Utica, 1989—; pres. Dutchess Interfaith Coun., Poughkeepsie, 1966; instr. dept. religion Colgate U., Hamilton, N.Y., 1985-91. Contbr. articles to profl. jours. Founding advisor Inst. of Applied Ethics at Utica Coll., 1988—; dir., past pres. Utica Community Food Bank, 1983—. Mem. Cen. Conf. Am. Rabbis (editorial bd.). Office: Temple Emanu-El 2710 Genesee St Utica NY 13502

BANDEL, EHUD, rabbi; b. Jerusalem, Apr. 4, 1956; s. Menachem and Azgad (Amira) B.; 1 child, Naama. BA, Hebrew U., Jerusalem, 1982. Ordained rabbi, 1988. Nat. dir. youth Masorti Movement, Jerusalem, 1983-88, dir. edn. and outreach, 1988—. Exec. dir. Rabbis for Human Rights, Israel. Mem. Internat. Coun. Christians and Jews (exec. com.). Office: Masorti Movement, PO Box 7559, Jerusalem Israel

BANES, JACKIE KYLE, youth minister; b. Hazlehurst, Miss., Aug. 19, 1964; s. Joel Webster and Rita (Huffman) B.; m. Tammy Barton, Aug. 9, 1985. AA, Copiah-Lincoln Jr. Coll., Wesson, Miss., 1984; BA, William Carey Coll., 1987; MRE, New Orleans Bapt. Theol Sem., 1989. Min. of youth Harmony Bapt. Ch., Crystal Springs, Miss., 1984-86; interim pastor New Providence Bapt. Ch., Hazlehurst, 1989; min. of youth, children, and recreation Indian Lake Bapt. Ch., Northport, Ala., 1989—. Home: 2506 27th Ave Northport AL 35476 Office: Indian Lake Bapt Ch 3815 Watermelon Rd Northport AL 35476

BANGERTER, WILLIAM GRANT, religious organization executive; b. Granger, Utah, June 8, 1918; s. William Henry and Isabelle (Bawden) B.; m. Mildred Lee Schwantes, Mar. 8, 1944 (dec. Aug. 1952); children: Lee Ann, Cory William, Glenda, Mildred Elizabeth; m. Geraldine Hamblin, Oct. 14, 1953; children: Julie, Grant Hamblin, Howard Kent, Peggy, Glenn, Layne, Duella. BA with honors, U. Utah, 1948. Farmer Granger, 1937-42, carpenter, 1942-74, bldg. contractor, 1948-74, real estate broker, 1966—; gen. authority LDS Ch., Salt Lake City, 1975—; Pres. Jordan River LDS Temple, 1990—. Bd. dirs. LDS Hosp., Salt Lake City, U. Utah Alumni Bd.; pres. Magna (Utah) and Granger Sem. Bds.; councilman City of Alpine, Utah; mem. Salt Lake coun. Boy Scouts Am.; pres. ch. missions for Brazil, Portugal, Mideast, Chile, LDS Ch., exec. dir. ch. temples, 1980-89, mem. presidency of Salt Lake City Quorum, 1978-89. 1st lt. USAF, 1942-46. Office: LDS Ch 1st Quorum of the 70 50 E North Temple St Salt Lake City UT 84150

BANGS, CARL OLIVER, retired theology educator; b. Seattle, Apr. 5, 1922; s. Carl Oliver and Méry (Dupertuis) B.; m. Marjorie Evlynn Friesen, Sept. 6, 1942; children: Carl Oliver, Jeremy Dupertuis, Jeanne Elise Bangs Kasten. AB magna cum laude, Pasadena Coll., 1945; BD, Nazarene Theol. Sem., 1949; PhD, U. Chgo., 1958. Prof. philosophy and religion Olivet Nazarene U., Kankakee, Ill., 1953-61; prof. hist. theology St. Paul Sch. Theology, Kansas City, Mo., 1961-89; guest prof. theology U. Leiden (The Netherlands), 1968-69, 75; guest prof. history of Christianity Ariz. State U., Tempe, 1985; lectr. in field. Author: The Communist Encounter, 1963, Arminius: A Study in the Dutch Reformation, 1971, The Auction Catalogue of J. Arminius, 1985; editor: The Works of James Arminius, 3 vols., 1986. Mem. Am. Soc. Ch. History (pres. 1972), Am. Theol. Soc. (pres. midwest div. 1966), Kerkhistorisch Gezelschap, Am. Hist. Assn., Am. Soc. Reformation Rsch. Democrat. Home: 7205 Canterbury St Prairie Village KS 66208 *In every situation of life there are people who are quietly confident that life has meaning. That is why human inquiry is not complete without theology.*

BANGURA, T. S., bishop. Presiding bishop United Meth. Ch., Freetown, Sierra Leone. Office: United Meth Ch, PO Box 523, Freetown Sierra Leone*

BANISZEWSKI, DAVID EDMUND, religious school administrator; b. Erie, Pa., Feb. 15, 1954; s. Edmund Joseph and Dorothy Stanislawa (Gorczycki) B.; m. Heidi Jo Tofel, Apr. 28, 1979; children: Carrie Jean, Casimir Edmund. BA in English, Gannon U., 1977; MRE in Christian Sch. Adminstrn., Grand Rapids Bapt. Sem., Mich., 1991. Cert. tchr. secondary English, Pa. Prin. Erie Christian Acad., 1980-83; acad. prin. Heritage Christian Acad., Erie, 1983-84; prin., adminstr. North East (Pa.) Christian Acad., 1984—; dir. educational div. Christian Minutemen, Erie, 1981-83; lectr. Ch. of God Christian Schs., Cleve., Tenn., 1989-91. Author: (collection short stories) Vapors & Wisps, 1977, various stage plays, 1984-91. Mem. ASCD, Men's Fellowship Club, North East (sec.-treas. 1987-91), Internat. Fellowship Christian Sch. Adminstrs. Republican. Home: 5297 Station Rd

North East PA 16428 Office: North East Christian Acad 5335 Station Rd North East PA 16428 *The focus of education should be the life-changing integration of knowledge with wisdom. And the source of all knowledge and wisdom is Jesus Christ.*

BANKS, DEIRDRE MARGARET, church organization administrator; b. Melbourne, Australia, May 9, 1934; came to U.S., 1975; d. Haldane Stuart and Vera Avice (Fisher) B. MA, Simpson Coll., 1980. Missionary nurse Leprosy Mission, Kathmandu, Nepal, 1960-69; dean of women Melbourne Bible Inst., 1970-75; asst. to dir. Bible Study Fellowship, Oakland, Calif., 1975-79; dir. adult ministries First Covenant Ch., Oakland, 1980-87; assoc. pastor for adults, First Covenant Ch., St. Paul, 1987-89; exec. sec. Covenant Women Ministries, Chgo., 1989—. Chairperson ch. edn. bd. Pacific S.W. Conf. Evang. Ch., 1985-87, Gilead Group, Oakland, 1985-87, bd. Barnabas Project for Abused and Homeless Women and Children, 1990—; mem. bd. of world mission Evang. Covenant Ch., 1987-89. Mem. Evangel. Covenant Ch. Office: Evang Covenant Ch 5101 N Francisco Ave Chicago IL 60625

BANKS, JAMES R., II, clergyman; b. Albany, N.Y., June 28, 1955; s. James R. Sr. and Joyce L. (Jackson) B.; m. Judy C. Shaw, July 3, 1976; children: Bekesica K., Janine R., Jamye R. BA, Am. Bapt. Coll., 1978. Ordained to ministry Bapt. Ch. Mem. faculty Nat. Bapt. Congress Christian Edn., 1982—, Empire State Congress Christian Edn., 1981—, St. John Bapt. Ch. Inst., Buffalo, 1984—, We. Bapt. Assn. Christian Edn., Buffalo, 1987—; pastor Faith Bapt. Ch., Buffalo, 1981—; sr. chaplain Wende Correctional Facility, Alden, N.Y., 1985-87; sec. Empire State Conv. N.Y. State, 1984-90; vice-moderator Great Lakes Bapt. Assn., Western N.Y., 1985-90. Mem. NAACP. Office: Faith Missionary Bapt Ch 626 Humboldt Pkwy Buffalo NY 14211

BANKS, ROBERT J., bishop; b. Winthrop, Mass., Feb. 26, 1928; s. Robert Joseph and Rita Katherine (Sullivan) B. AB, St. John's Sem., Brighton, Mass., 1949; STL, Gregorian U., Rome, 1953; JCD, Lateran U., Rome, 1957. Ordained priest Roman Cath. Ch., 1952, ordained titular bishop of Taraqua, 1985. Prof. canon laaw St. John Sem., Brighton, Mass., 1959-71, acad. dean, 1967-71; rector St. John's Sem., 1971-81; vicar gen. Boston Archdiocese, 1984; aux. bishop Boston, 1985—; bishop Diocese of Green Bay, Wis., 1990—. Address: Diocese of Green Bay PO Box 23066 Green Bay WI 54305

BANKS, ROBERT JOHN, religion educator; b. Sydney, N.S.W., Australia, Aug. 6, 1939; came to U.S., 1989; s. John and Evelyn Muriel (Dyke) B.; m. Julia Lonsdale Johnson, Nov. 25, 1962; children: Mark Robert, Simon. BA, U. Sydney, 1958; BD, U. London, 1962, MTh, 1965; PhD, U. Cambridge, 1969. Rsch. fellow Inst. Advanced Studies, Australian Nat. U., Canberra, A.C.T., Australia, 1969-74; lectr., sr. lectr. history, philosophy and politics Macqarie U., Sydney, 1974-79; theol. cons. Inst. for Christianity and Soc., Zadok Centre, Canberra, 1979-83, fellow, 1983-89; Homer L. Goddard prof. ministry of laity Fuller Theol. Sem., Pasadena, 1989—; mem. adv. bd. Helmers & Howard Pub., Colorado Springs, Colo., 1989—, Marketplace Ministries, Madison. Author: Jesus and the Law, 1975, Paul's Idea of Commmunity, 1979, The Tyranny of Time, 1983 (Christian Book of Yr. 1984), All the Business of Life, 1987; editorial assoc. Interchange, 1975—. Tyndale fellow Bibl. rsch., Cambridge, 1966-68, Bethune-Baker/Burney grantee Cambridge U., 1968. Mem. Soc. N.T. Studies, Australian and New Zealand Soc. Theol. Studies, Tyndale Fellowship Bibl. Rsch., Assn. Christian Scholarship, Soc. Bibl. Lit. Office: Fuller Theol Sem 135 N Oakland Pasadena CA 91182

BANKS, ROBERT THOMAS, religious organization administrator; b. Griffin, Ga., Apr. 13, 1931; m. Martha Banks, Aug. 27, 1952; children: Sibyl Ann, Brenda Lee Benson, Brian Nelson. BA, Baylor U., 1953; MRE, Southwestern Bapt. Theol. Sem., 1956. Dir. RA work Bapt. Gen. Conv. Okla., Oklahoma City, 1954-68; dir. brotherhood Bapt. Gen. Conv. Okla., 1968-74; exec. asst. to exec. dir. Brotherhood Commn., Memphis, 1974-76; dir. program sect. Brotherhood Commn., 1977-80, dir. RA div., 1980-81; assoc. to pres. Home Mission Bd., Atlanta, 1981-82; v.p. for adminstrn. Home Mission Bd., 1982-85, exec. v.p., 1985—, interim chief exec. officer, 1986-87. Co-author: Royal Ambassador Camp Craft, 1981, From Sea to Shining Sea, 1986; contbr. articles to Ch. Adminstrn., Open Windows, Ch. Recreation. Mem. Baylor U. Devel. Coun., Waco, Tex., 1984—; bd. dirs. Sooner Alcohol-Narcotics, Oklahoma City, 1969-70. Mem. Atlanta Midtown Bus. Assn. Office: Home Mission Bd 1350 Spring St NW Atlanta GA 30367-5601

BANKS, TREVOR ALBERT, lay worker, medical practitioner; b. Geelong, Victoria, Australia, July 9, 1934; s. Russel Albert and Edna May (Lunn) B.; m. Helen Rae Cracknell, Jan. 8, 1958; children; Lisbeth, Kelvin, Lyle, Rohan. MB, BS, U. Melbourne, Australia, 1957. Pres. Chs. of Christ, Victoria, Tasmania, 1977-78; chmn. Fed. Dept. Christian Union, Chs. of Christ, Australia, 1983; v.p. World Conv. Chs. of Christ, 1984-88; moderator Disciples Ecumenical Consultative Coun., 1985—; regional palliative care med. officer Health Dept., Victoria, 1989—. Mem. Australian Med. Assn., Royal Australian Coll. Gen. Practitioners. Home: 13 Eton Rd, Belmont Victoria 3216, Australia Office: Regional Palliative Care, 269 Pakington St, Newtown Victoria 3215, Australia

BANNISTER, GEORGE BENJAMIN, pastor; b. Baton Rouge, Sept. 3, 1957; s. George Washington and Joyce (Held) B.; m. Lisa Lucile Thibodeaux, July 15, 1977; children: Ben, Dan, Bob. BRE, La. Coll., 1981; MDiv, So. Bapt. Ctr. Bibl. Studies, Jacksonville, Fla., 1990. Ordained to ministry So. Bapt. Conv. Pastor Bethany Bapt. Ch., Oakdale, La., 1980-82, Redwood Bapt. Ch., Ethel, La., 1982-85, Wallace Ridge Bapt. Ch., Jonesville, La., 1986-88, Emmanuel Bapt. Ch., Mansfield, La., 1988-91, Beech Springs Bapt. Ch., Minden, La., 1991—. Mem. DeSoto Bapt. Assn. (pres. pastor's conf. 1989-91, coord. world missions conf. 1990-91), Ouachita Bapt. Assn. (pres. pastor's conf. 1987-88, dir. Sunday sch. 1987-88), DeSoto Assn. Against Legalizing Lottery (chmn. fin. com. 1990), Lions. Democrat. Home and Office: Beech Springs Bapt Ch Rte 2 Box 506 Minden LA 71055

BANQUER, SISTER MYRA, school system administrator. Supt. schs. Lafayette, La. Office: Office Supt Schs PO Box E Lafayette LA 70502*

BANSE, PERRY RAY, educational administrator; b. Cedar Rapids, Iowa, Feb. 19, 1958; s. Jack Albert Banse and Beverly Lavanne (Tyler) Johansen; m. Cynthia G. Poe, Dec. 31, 1977; children: Joel David, Jill Suzanne. BS in Speech Communication Edn. and English, Grace Coll., 1987; MA in Christian Sch. Adminstrn., Grace Theol. Sem., 1987; BA in Elem. Edn. and English, Upper Iowa U., 1990. Cert. tchr., Iowa, Alaska. Youth leader 1st Conservative Bapt. Ch., 1979-80; with missionary Frontiers of Faith Ministries, Cooper Landing, Alaska, 1980-83; tchr. Anchorage Christian Sch., 1986-88, Cedar Rapids Christian Sch., 1988-89; edn. adminstr. Sunnyside Temple Christian Sch., Waterloo, Iowa, 1989—; deacon Resurrection Bible Chapel, Cooper Landing, 1980-83. Del. Rep. County Conv., Vinton, Iowa, 1976; sec., treas. Cooper Landing Vol. Fire Dept., 1980-83. Mem. Internat. Fellowship Christian Sch. Adminstrs., Alpha Omega. Home: 1027 Langley Rd Waterloo IA 50702 Office: Sunnyside Temple Christian Sch 3520 Ansborough Ave Waterloo IA 50701

BANSEMER, RICHARD FREDERICK, bishop; b. Oswego, N.Y., May 26, 1940; s. Reinhold Mathias and Oralee Ann (Brierly) B.; m. Barbara Anne Gallmeier, June 9, 1962 (dec. Feb. 1968); 1 child, John David.; m. Mary Ann Troutman, July 18, 1971; children: Aaron Richard, Andrew Christopher. BA, Newberry (S.C.) Coll., 1962; BD, Luth. Theol. So. Sem., 1966; DD (hon.), Newberry Coll., 1988, Roanoke Coll., 1988. Ordained to ministry Evang. Luth. Ch. in Am., 1966. Assoc. pastor Univ. Luth. Ch., Gainesville, Fla., 1966-68; pastor St. John Luth. Ch., Roanoke, 1968-73, Lord of the Mountains Luth. Ch., Dillon, Colo., 1973-78, Rural Retreat (Va.) Luth. Parish, 1978-87; bishop Va. Synod Evang. Luth. Ch. in Am., Salem, 1988—. Author: People Prayers, 1976, The Chosen and the Changed, 1977, Grace and the Grave, 1981, Risen Indeed, 1982, In Plain Sight, 1982, Day Full of Grace, 1987. trustee Roanoke Coll., 1988—, Luth. Theol. So. Sem., 1988—. Office: Evang Luth Ch in Am Va Synod PO Drawer 70 Salem VA 24153

BANTHER, BARRY, academic administrator. Head Trinity Coll. Fla., Holiday. Office: Trinity Coll Fla PO Box 9000 Holiday FL 34690*

BANWART, KEITH GARY, JR., religion educator; b. Sioux City, Iowa, Aug. 13, 1965; s. Keith Gary and Michele (Rihner) B. BS in Edn., Concordia Coll., Seward, Nebr., 1986, M.Parish Edn., 1990; MA in Religion, Concordia Sem., Ft. Wayne, Ind., 1991. Tchr. Benet Learning Ctr., Ft. Wayne, Ind., 1986; vicar Good Shepherd Luth. Ch., Ft. Dodge, Iowa, 1988-89; substitute tchr. Winnebago (Nebr.) Pub. Sch., 1990-91; tchr. Trinity High Sch., Las Vegas, Nev., 1991—; mem. Clin. Pastoral Edn., St. Luke's Regional Med. Ctr., Sioux City, 1991. Regional coord. Woody Harrelson Ednl. Tours, 1991. Mem. Luth. Edn. Assn., Luth. Bible Translators, Luth. Assn. Missionaries and Pilots, Religious Speech Communication Assn., Am. Assn. Christian Counselors, Am. Assn. Family Counselors, Luth. Liturgical Renewal, Speech Communication Assn., Internat. Luth. Laymen's League, Nat. Right To Live Com. Republican. Home: 8600 Starboard # 2060 Las Vegas NV 89117

BANYARD, ALFRED LOTHIAN, bishop; b. Merchantville, N.J., July 31, 1908; s. Lothian Rupert and Emma May (Irwin) B.; m. Sarah Alice Hammer, Sept. 1, 1938; 1 son, Richard David. A.B., U. Pa., 1929; student, Gen. Theol. Sem., 1929-31, S.T.B., 1933, S.T.D., 1946; postgrad., Phila. Div. Sch., 1932, D.D., 1947. Ordained to ministry Episcopal Ch., N.J., 1931; pastor St. Lukes Ch., Westville, N.J., 1932-36; rector Christ Ch., Bordentown, N.J., 1936-43; archdeacon Episcopal Diocese N.J., 1943-55; suffragan bishop, 1945-55, bishop of N.J., 1955-73, ret., 1973; Mem. Bd. Examining Chaplains, 1938-55, chmn., 1941-55; dep. to provincial synod, 1940-46; sec. Ho. of Bishops, 2d Province, 1945-48; trustee Diocesan Found., 1941-43, ex-officio, 1945—, pres., 1955—; pres. Procter Found., 1955—; master of Young Men's Conf., 1936-37, dean, 1941; mem. Bd. Religious Edn., 1939-41, 43-46, Bd. Social Service, 1940-42, 44-46; field, publicity dept., 1943-45; trustee Burlington Coll., 1945-53, v.p., 1946-53; Bd. mgrs. St. Martins Ho. of Retreats, Bernardsville, N.J., 1948—; trustee, Evergreens, Moorestown, pres., 1955; v.p. Corp. for Relief Widows and Orphans of Clergymen, 1945—; pres. Mission Advancement, 1955—; trustee Phila. Div. Sch. Mem. Newcomen Soc., Philomathean Soc. of U. Pa. (scriba 1929), Phi Beta Kappa, Eta Sigma Phi. Republican. Home: The Evergreens Moorestown NJ 08057

BANZ, CLINT JAMES, educator; b. Freeport, Ill., Oct. 4, 1958; s. Anton Stephen Banz and JoAnn (Bray) Fisher; m. Gail Elaine Reemtsma, Aug. 6, 1983; children: Jared Sammuel, Geneva Rosalie. BA, Pillsbury Coll., 1982; MDiv, Calvary Sem., 1986; MS, Drexel U., 1989. Pastor, educator Calvary Bapt. Ch., Lansdale, Pa., 1987—; libr. Calvary Bapt. Theol. Sem., Lansdale, Pa., 1987—. Mem. Am. Theol. Libr. Assn., Southeastern Pa. Theol. Libr. Assn. Home: 703 Green St Lansdale PA 19446 Office: Calvary Bapt Theol Sem 1380 Valley Forge Rd Lansdale PA 19446

BAPTISTE, CLARENCE BOYSIE, minister; b. Scarborough, Tobago, Trinidad and Tobago, June 8, 1941; came to Can., 1969; s. George and Marjorie Enid (James) B.; m. Beryl Joan Durant, June 13, 1965; children: David J., Peter L., Philip P. AA, Kingsway Coll., Oshawa, Ont., Can., 1971; BA, Andrews U., 1973, MA, 1975, MDiv., 1977. Ordained to ministry Seventh-day Adventist Ch., 1981. Lit. evangelist South Caribbean Conf. Seventh-day Adventsits Ch., Port of Spain, Trinidad and Tobago, 1962-67; pub. dir. Port of Spain, Trinidad and Tobago, 1967-69; minister Man. and Sask. Conf. of Seventh-day Adventists Ch., Saskatoon, 1977-86; pastor, evangelist Yorkton (Sask.) Seventh-day Adventist Ch., 1983-86; pastor West Edmonton (Alta.) Seventh-day Adventist Ch., 1986—; lectr. Brandon (Man., Can.) U., 1979-80. Mem. Edmonton Coralwood Jr. Acad. Sch. Bd.; dir. human relations dept. Alta. Conf. Seventh-day Adventist Chs., chmn. human relations com. Mem. Yorkton Ministerial Assn., Dauphin Ministerial Assn., Saskatoon Ministerial Assn., Edmonton Chs. Ministeral Assn. (pres.), Can. Union Conf. of Seventh Day Adventist Ch. (human relations com.). Home: 11712-135 B St, Edmonton, AB Canada T5M IL7 Office: W Edmonton Seventh-day Adventist Ch, Box 9049 Sta E, Edmonton, AB Canada T5P 4K1

BARAJAS, FELIPE LARA, deacon; b. Poncitlan, Jalisco, Mexico, May 1, 1938; came to U.S., 1973; s. Filiberto Escoto and Antonia Velazquez (Lara) B.; m. Teresa Margarita Hernandez, Apr. 7, 1973; children: Felipe de Jesus, Alfred Joseph. BA, Instituto America, 1963; Physical Edn. degree, Educacion Audiovisual, 1964; Ednl. Puppetry degree, Secretaria E. Publica, 1971. Elem. tchr. Escuela Cervantes, Guadalajara, Mex., 1961-64; instr. puppetry Dirección de Edn. Audiovisual, Guadalajara, 1964-65; elem. tchr. Jalisco State Penitentiary, 1965-67; prin. parochial sch. San Joaquín, Mex., 1967-68, Las Fuentes Zapopan, Mex., 1969-71; tchr. physical edn. Colegio Augustín de Iturbide, Tamazula, Mex., 1971-72; vol. tchr. San Antonio Literacy Coun., 1976-77; instr. puppetry Mex. Cultural Inst., San Antonio, 1982; sec. Permanent Diaconal Community, San Antonio, 1986-90; deacon Holy Rosary Cath. Ch., San Antonio, 1986—; elem. tchr. Circle Sch., San Antonio, 1986—; instr. in field; promotor Small Christian Communities, 1986—. Tchr. San Antonio Literacy Coun., Inc., 1976-77; puppetry tchr. Mexican Cultural Inst., San Antonio, 1982. Democrat. Home: 247 Havana San Antonio TX 78228 Office: Holy Rosary Cath Ch 159 Camino Santa Maria San Antonio TX 78228

BARBER, DAVID GILMER, principal; b. Salisbury, N.C., Aug. 31, 1953; s. Clarence Gilmer and Alma Lucille (Waddle) B.; m. Nancy Ann Williams, Aug. 9, 1974; children: Jessica Deanne, Jonathan David. BS in Bibl. Edn., Columbia Bible Coll., 1976; MS in Elem. Edn., Pensacola Christian Coll., 1982; postgrad., Ga. State U. Tchr. Columbia (S.C.) Christian Sch., 1976-77; supr., tchr. Columbus Christian Acad., Whiteville, N.C., 1977-79; tchr. Colonial Hills Christian Sch., East Point, Ga., 1979-82; asst. prin. Old Nat. Christian Acad., College Park, Ga., 1982-86, prin., 1986—; choral dir. Old Nat. Christian Acad., College Park, 1983—, bd. dirs., 1988—; min. of music Atlanta Bapt. Ch., College Park, 1983-87; counselor, arts and crafts dir. Ambassdor Camp, Lake Waccamaw, N.C., 1968-79. Mem. Internat. Fellowship Christian Sch. Adminstrs., Assn. Christian Schs. Internat. (conv. planning com. 1990—). Republican. Home: 8920 Peppertree Dr Jonesboro GA 30236 Office: Old Nat Christian Acad 2601 Flat Shoals Rd College Park GA 30349

BARBER, GARY FRANK, minister; b. Evanston, Ill., Dec. 21, 1953; s. Frank Joseph and Josephine (Holubek) B.; m. Kimberly Lisanby, Aug. 6, 1977; children: Kati Jean, Kari Elizabeth. BA, North Cen. Coll., Naperville, Ill., 1976; MDiv, Garrett-Evang. Theol. Sem., 1986. Ordained to ministry United Meth. Ch. as elder, 1990. Pastor Ohio (Ill.) and Red Oak United Meth. Chs., Walnut, Ill., 1986-89, Fenton (Ill.) United Meth. Ch., 1989—; mem. Ohio-Walnut Ministerium, 1986-89, Erie (Ill.) Ministerium, 1989—; sec. on ch. and society com. DeKalb Dist., 1987-88; sec. No. Ill. Conf. Bd. of Ch./Soc., United Meth. Ch., Chgo., 1988—; dist. young adult coord. mission trip to The Philippines, 1989, to Holy Land, 1990. Mem. Synapses, Cuanes-Philippines orgns. Democrat. Home: 10009 Main St PO Box 17 Fenton IL 61251 Office: Fenton United Meth Ch 10019 Main St Fenton IL 61251 *Our universal call to servants of Christ Jesus means we look beyond ourselves in open and loving compassion for all our neighbors, and do it without prejudice or condemnation. That is true discipleship.*

BARBER, JANET KATHERYNE, music minister; b. Shreveport, La., Dec. 31, 1949; d. Olen Cleon and Helen Teeple (Wilson) B. B.S., Southwestern Assemblies of God Coll., Waxahachie, Tex., 1972. Minister of music First Assembly of God, New Orleans, 1972-76, Baton Rouge, 1976-79, Honolulu, 1979—; dist. music dir. Hawaii Assemblies of God, Honolulu, 1980—; speaker Church Growth Hawaii, Honolulu, 1981-83, cons., speaker Choral Clinics, Hawaii, mainland U.S., Singapore, 1980-82. Producer, dir. music prodn. The Witness, 1980-81, The Singing Christmas Tree, 1980—; producer TV prodns. He is the Music, Celebrate Life, 1980-81; contbr. articles in field to profl. publs. Coordinator Family Court Services, Baton Rouge, 1978-79. Recipient Certificate Spl. Achievement Hawaii State Legis., 1986. Mem. Concerned Women of Am., Assemblies of God Music Dirs. Fellowship, Fellowship Christian Musicians and Dirs. (co-founder). Republican. Club: Capitol Hill Women's. Office: First Assembly of God 930 Lunalilo St Honolulu HI 96822

BARBER, NATHAN LEWIS, minister; b. Meridian, Miss., June 24, 1945; s. William Alonzo and Josie Laura (Giles) B.; m. Patricia Anne Clements, Mar. 26, 1967; children: Nathan Lewis Jr., Christopher Todd, Patrick Regan. BA, William Carey Coll., 1967; ThM, New Orleans Bapt. Theol. Sem., 1971, D Ministry, 1979. Ordained to ministry So. Bapt. Conv., 1967. Mus. dir. Edna Bapt. Ch., Columbia, Miss., 1963-64; youth dir. 1st Bapt. Ch., Wiggins, Miss., 1965-67; pastor West Side Bapt. Mission, 1st Bapt. Ch., Picayune, Miss., 1967-70, Calvary Bapt. Ch., Hattiesburg, Miss., 1970-74, 1st Bapt. Ch., Bay St. Louis, Miss., 1974—; tchr., preacher Internat. Bapt. Theol. Sem., Kenya, Africa, 1982, 86, 89, 90; bd. dirs. Miss. Bapt. Conv., 1982-87; commr. Christian Action Commn. Miss. Bapts., 1988—; trustee Miss. Bapt. Sem.,1985-88. Founder Worship Ministry for Campers, Buccaneer State Pk., 1978—. Mem. Gulf Coast Bapt. Assn. (chmn. order of bus.). Home: 506 Felicity St Bay Saint Louis MS 39520 Office: 1st Bapt Ch 141 Main St Bay Saint Louis MS 39520

BARBOUR, HUGH REVELL, publisher; b. N.Y.C., Nov. 6, 1929; s. William Rinehart and Mary Alice (McKelvey) B.; m. Eva Marie Cox, May 30, 1953; children—Deborah Faith (Mrs. Frank Dietrich), Steven Cox, Constance Revell (Mrs. Steven Morton). Student, Stevens Inst. Tech., 1949-50. Pres. Barbour & Co., Book Pubs.; pres. Barbour Realty Co., Eva and Hugh Barbour Found. Served with USAF, 1950-53. Bd. dirs. Walter Hoving Home for Girls. Mem. Evang. Christian Pubs. Assn. (past pres.), Hackensack Golf Club, The Dunes Golf and Racquet Club. Home: 15501 Shell Point Blvd Fort Myers FL 33908 also: Island Beach Club 2265 W Gulf Dr Sanibel Island FL 33957 also: 164 Mill St Westwood NJ 07675

BARBOUR, IAN GRAEME, physics and religion educator; b. Peking, China, Oct. 5, 1923; s. George Brown and Dorothy (Dickinson) B.; m. Deane Kern, Nov. 29, 1947; children: John Dickinson, Blair Winn, David Freeland, Heather Deane. B.A., Swarthmore Coll., 1943; M.A., Duke U., 1946; Ph.D., U. Chgo., 1950; B.D., Yale U., 1956. Asst. prof. physics Kalamazoo Coll., 1949-51, assoc. prof., chmn. dept., 1951-53; mem. faculty Carleton Coll., Northfield, Minn., 1955-86, prof. emeritus, 1986—; chmn. dept. religion Carleton Coll., 1956-71, prof. religion and physics, 1965-81, Winifred and Atherton Bean prof. sci., tech. and soc., 1981-86; Lilly vis. prof. sci., theology and human values Purdue U., 1973-74; Gifford lectr. Aberdeen, Scotland, 1989-91. Author: Christianity and the Scientist, 1960, Issues in Science and Religion, 1966, Science and Religion: New Perspectives on the Dialogue, 1968, Science and Secularity: The Ethics of Technology, 1970, Earth Might Be Fair, 1972, Western Man and Environmental Ethics, 1973, Myths, Models and Paradigms, 1974, Finite Resources and the Human Future, 1976, Technology, Environment and Human Values, 1980, Energy and American Values, 1982, Religion in an Age of Science, 1990; mem. editorial bd. Process Studies, Zygon, Research in Philosophy and Technology; author numerous articles. Ford Faculty fellow, 1953-54; Kent fellow, 1954-55; recipient Harbison award for disting. teaching Danforth Found., 1963; Am. Council Learned Socs. fellow, 1963-64; Guggenheim and Fulbright fellow, 1967-78; Nat. Endowment Humanities fellow, 1976-77; Nat. Humanities Center fellow, 1980-81. Mem. Phi Beta Kappa, Sigma Xi. Home: 106 Winona St Northfield MN 55057

BARBOUR, JOHN DICKINSON, religion educator; b. Kalamazoo, Mich., Aug. 8, 1951; s. Ian G. and Deane (Kern) B.; m. Margaret Ann Ojala, Aug. 26, 1978; children: Graham, Reed. BA, Oberlin Coll., 1973; MA, U. Chgo., 1975, PhD, 1981. Assoc. prof. religion St. Olaf Coll., Northfield, Minn., 1984—. Author: Tragedy as a Critique of Virtue, 1984, The Conscience of the Autobiographer, 1992; contbr. articles to profl. jours. Mem. Am. Acad. Religion. Mem. United Ch. of Christ. Office: St Olaf Coll Northfield MN 55057

BARBOUR, KENNETH O., minister. Supervising elder Kodesh Ch. of Immanuel, Bethel Park, Pa. Office: Kodesh Chs of Immanuel 932 Logan Rd Bethel Park PA 15102*

BARCROFT, DOUGLAS MORGAN, minister; b. Memphis, May 10, 1958; s. Ben Douglas and Dorothy Nell (Birchett) B.; m. Derenda Lynn Hosse, Aug. 8, 1981; 1 child, Benjamin Douglas Kim. BS in Agr., U. Tenn., Martin, 1980; MDiv, Mid-Am. Bapt. Theol. Sem., Memphis, 1987. Ordained to ministry So. Bapt. Conv. Pastor Belen (Miss.) Bapt. Ch., 1984-85, Fellowship Bapt. Ch., Batesville, Ark., 1987-88, Covington Pike Bapt. Ch., Memphis, 1988—. Home: 4185 Lansdowne Memphis TN 38128 Office: Covington Pike Bapt Ch 3411 Covington Pike Memphis TN 38128

BARD, TERRY ROSS, rabbi; b. Chgo., Jan. 17, 1944; s. Bernard David and Lillian (Terry) B.; m. Kay Elsa Bard, Aug. 6, 1966 (dec. 1974); children: Michael Aaron, Amy Shira; m. Linda Faye Bard, Dec. 18, 1975; 1 child, Rachel Joy. AB with distinction, Brown U., 1966; MAHL, Hebrew Union Coll., Cin., 1971; postgrad., Harvard U., 1975. Ordained rabbi, 1971. Asst./assoc. rabbi Temple Shalom, Newton, Mass., 1971-76; rabbi Congregation Shalom, Chelmsford, Mass., 1976—; clin. instr. pastoral counseling Dept. Psychiatry, Harvard Med. Sch., 1984—; dir. pastoral svcs. Beth Israel Hosp., Boston, 1984—; dir. Dept. Pastoral Care and Edn., Mass. Mental Health Ctr., Boston, 1976—; v.p. Interfaith Counseling Svcs., Inc., Newton, Mass., 1988—; dir., psychotherapist Rabbinic Counseling Ctr., Chestnut Hill, Mass., 1976-85; mem. bd. dirs. Jewish Community Coun., Boston, 1976-84; lectr., cons. in field. Author: Medical Ethics in Practice, 1990; editor, Cura Animarum, 1987—; editorial adv. com. Jour. Health Care, 1987—, Jour. Pastoral Care, 1984—, bd. mgrs., 1991—; abstract and book rev. editor Jour. of Assn. Mental Health Clergy, 1980-87; contbr. articles to profl. jours. Adv. bd. Health Decisions USA, The Boston Experience, 1990—, Mass. Health Decision, 1990—, New Eng. Organ Bank, 1990; mem. devel. com. Beth Israel Hosp., 1986—, pub. affairs com., 1985—, originator ethics adv. grp., coord. clin. ethics prog., 1984—, others; mem. Cath.-Jewish Com., Archdiocese of Boston, 1973—. Recipient Nat. Conf. Christians and Jews, spl. recognition, 1971, Farband Labor Zionist award for excellence in field of religious studies, 1966. Mem. Am. Psychiatric Assn. (ex-officio mem. com. on religion and psychiatry), Assn. Mental Health Clergy (pres. 1982-84), Mass. Bd. Rabbis (pres. 1980-82), Cen. Conf. Am. Rabbis, Chelmsford Clergy Assn., Assn. Clin. Pastoral Edn., Nat. Assn. Jewish Chaplains. Office: Beth Israel Hosp 330 Brookline Ave Boston MA 02215

BARDEN, KARL ALVIN, minister, dentist; b. Spokane, Wash., Feb. 14, 1940; s. Carl Methner and Hilda Marion (Tessendorf) B.; m. Sherrillann Talbot, Sept. 13, 1958; children: Tamara Karlynne, Karianne Danita, Julianne Victoria. DDS, U. Wash., 1962; D. in Ministry, Christian Internat. U., 1986. Gen. practice dentistry Spokane, 1962-64, Pullman, Wash., 1964-84; co-founder Living Faith Fellowship, Pullman, 1971—, sr. pastor, 1975—; founder, pres. bd. dirs. Living Faith Fellowship Coll. Ministry Tng., 1987—; pres. Living Faith Ednl. Ministries, 1987—; lectr. various nat. and internat. seminars and churches. Author: Basic Guidelines to Greater Blessings, 1978; Catechism Training for New Covenant Christian Found., 1980, Going for the Gold, 1989, Founded on the Solid Rock, 1989, The Secret Servant: Releasing the Church's Full Potential, 1992. ALCOA Scholar U. Wash., 1957. Bd. dirs. Pullman Federated Fund, 1966-67, officer, 1968; vestryman Episcopal Ch., 1966-69, diocesan del., 1970; community chmn. Salvation Army, 1974; mem. exec. council Revival Fellowship, 1989—, governing bd. Internat. Congress of Local Ch., 1989—; bd. regents Liberty U., 1990—. Recipient Sword of the Spirit Accelerated Christian Edn., 1984, Reformers award Accelerated Christian Edn., 1991. Mem. Spokane Dist. Dental Soc., Network of Christian Ministries, Wash. State Dental Assn., ADA, Pullman Ministerial Assn., U. Wash. Alumni Assn., Rotary (pres. 1970-71), Psi Omega. Republican. Home: SW 700 Fountain Pullman WA 99163 Office: Living Faith Fellowship SW 345 Kimball Pullman WA 99163

BARGE, JEAN MARIE, minister; b. Milw., Nov. 23, 1927; d. Charles B. and Genevieve (Schul) Wright; divorced; children: Lynn, Marc (dec.), Karl. BA, U. Rochester, 1949; MA, SUNY, Albany, 1953; MDiv, Luth. Sch. Theology, Phila., 1981. Ordained to ministry Luth. Ch., 1981. Pastor Holy Cross Luth. Ch., Farnham, N.Y., 1981—. 1st v.p. local chpt. LWV, Princeton, N.J., 1958-62; bd. dirs. Community Concern, Derby, N.Y., 1981—, Luth. Theol. Sem., Phila., 1983-86. Home: 556 Commercial St Farnham NY 14061 Address: 10633 Church St Farnham NY 14061

BARGER, LOUISE BALDWIN, religious organization administrator; b. Mexia, Tex., Nov. 7, 1938; d. Curtis Arthur and Vada Irene (Barker)

Baldwin; m. Billy Joe Barger, June 15, 1957; children: Kenneth Gene, Keith Dean, Kimberly Ann Barger Moeller. BS, Tex. Woman's U., 1961; MS in Nursing, St. Louis U., 1974, PhD in Higher Edn., 1981; MRE, So. Bapt. Theol. Sem., 1982. Ordained to ministry Am. Bapt. Chs. in U.S.A., 1986. Faculty Mo. Bapt. Hosp. Sch. Nursing, 1973, St. Louis U., 1974-80; min. Christian edn., mem. pastoral staff 3d Bapt. Ch., St. Louis, 1980-86; dir. leader devel. Am. Bapt. Chs. Pa. and Del., Valley Forge, Pa., 1986—; interim dir. evangelism and social concern Am. Bapt. Chs. Pa. and Del., Valley Forge, 1989-91; mem. Christian edn. com., Area V, Gt. Rivers region, Am. Bapt. Chs. Mo., and Am. Bapt. Chs. U.S.A., 1981-86; Handicapped Ministry, Home Mission Bd. So. Bapt. Conv., 1983; mem. Mins. Coun., Am. Bapt. Conv., U.S.A. Author: Growing through the Sunday School: A Sourcebook for Sunday School Growth, 1988; co-author: New and Renewed Churches: A Time of Prayer and Preparation for Invitation to New Life, 1991; contbr. Bapt. Leader. Mem. Handicapped Ministry Home Mission Bd., So. Bapt. Conv., 1983. Recipient Richard Hoiland citation Am. Bapt. Chs. U.S.A.; grantee Fund of Renewal Am. Bapt. Chs. U.S.A., 1980, Hazle Fund, 1984. Mem. Religious Edn. Assn., Assn. Profs. and Researchers in Religious Edn. Office: Am Bapt Chs Pa and Del PO Box 851 Valley Forge PA 19482-0851 *As Christians we are called first to BE the persons we were intended to become. All of our DOING is to be an expression of our BEING.*

BARILLA, ANITA WHITE, lay worker; b. Princeton, W.Va., Dec. 28, 1952; d. Grover Lewis and Vida May (Brookman) White; m. Bruce William Barilla, Mar. 17, 1983; children: Christi Michele, Christopher Mark. Student, Roanoke Bible Coll., 1970-72; A Sacred Lit., Bluefield (W.Va.) Coll. Evangelism, 1989. Tchr. youth group 1st Christian Ch., Chgo., 1977-85, deaconess, 1980-85; vacation Bible sch. dir. Pettrey (W.Va.) Ch. Christ, 1987; tchr., counselor Christian Acres, Bluewell, W.Va., 1986-90; Appalachian Bible Bowl sponsor Willowton (W.Va.) Christian Ch., 1988-91; sec. Concord Coll. Tourism Ctr., Athens, W.Va., 1990-91. Mem. Am. Assn. Med. Transcriptionists (Outstanding award Mercer County chpt. 1990). Home: Rte 3 Box 133-C Princeton WV 24740

BARKER, DAVID ALAN, music and youth minister; b. Castlewood, Va., Mar. 9, 1957; s. William Barry Jr. and Alice Elvira (Grizzle) B.; m. Angela Carol Frink, Aug. 14, 1980. B of Ch. Music, Shorter Coll., 1984; MusM, Southwestern Bapt. Theol. Sem., Ft. Worth, 1987. Min. youth, youth music dept. 1st Bapt. Ch., St. Paul, Va., 1980; min. music Desoto Pk. Bapt. Ch., Rome, Ga., 1982-84; dir. adult handbells Univ. Bapt. Ch., Ft. Worth, 1987-88; min. music - youth div. Harrisonburg (Va.) Bapt. Ch., 1987—; condr. bank Bapt. Youth Music Week, Lynchburg, Va., 1990—; vocal judge high sch. level Va. Regional and State Choir, 1990-91; condr. handbell festivals, Va., 1990-91; mem. Associational Youth Com., Augusta Bapt. Ch., Staunton, Va., 1990-91. Mem. Am. Choral Dirs. Assn., Am. Guild English Handbell Ringers, Choristers Guild, Music Educators Nat. Conf., Phi Mu Alpha. Home: 1046 Sherwood Ctr Harrisonburg VA 22801 Office: Harrisonburg Bapt Ch PO Box 281 Harrisonburg VA 22801

BARKER, JO ANN, minister; b. La Porte, Ind., Oct. 8, 1948; d. Rudolph Bohmil and Helen Theresa (Jagoda) Dolezal; m. Charles Lawrence Barker, July 13, 1974; children: Joseph, Michael, Amanda. AA, Ancilla Coll., Donaldson, Ind., 1969; BS in Chemistry, St. Francis Coll., Ft. Wayne, Ind., 1971; postgrad., U. of South, 1986-90. Min. for program and edn. St. Mark's Episcopal Ch., Jonesboro, Ark., 1988-90; mem. task force for Christian edn. Episcopal Diocese of Ark., 1988-90; sec. devotional life for Ark., Episcopal Ch. Women, 1988—. Violist string ensemble Ark. State U.; bd. dirs. Abilities Unltd., Jonesboro, 1988-90. Rsch. grantee Argonne Nat. Lab., 1971. Home: 2514 Rosewood Circle Jonesboro AR 72401 *We are not asked to change the world but to challenge the world. This can only be done by accepting grace and being faithful to God.*

BARKER, LAWRENCE EDWARD, pastor; b. Marion, Ind., Aug. 13, 1938; s. Ray H. and Ruth E. (Lloyd) B.; m. Sarah Elizabeth Heavilin, June 24, 1962; children—Bartholomew E., Daniel L. A.B., Earlham Coll., 1960, M.A. in Religion, 1963. Pastor, Friends Meeting, W. Milton, Ohio, 1959-65, assoc. pastor, 1965-67, pastor, 1967-84, trustee Friends Extension Corp., Richmond, Ind., 1981, Wilmington Yearly Meeting (Ohio), 1982—; v.p. Quality Quaker Mgmt. Inc, Wilmington, 1978. Mem. City Planning Commn. Wilmington, 1976—, Bd. Zoning Appeals Wilmington, 1981—; chmn. Clinton County Bd. Mental Retardation, 1967-82. Mem. Wilmington Area Ministrial Assn. Democrat. Contbr. articles to profl. jours. Lodge: Rotary. Home: 1334 Ridge Rd Wilmington OH 45177

BARKER, LEE CHARLES, minister; b. Mpls., Aug. 26, 1952; s. Lionel Charles and Beverly Arlene (Olson) B.; m. Marsha Susan Alekno, July 12, 1980. BA in Elective Studies, U. Minn., 1974; MDiv, U. Chgo., 1976; DMin, Meadville/Lombard Theol. Sch., 1978. Minister Unitarian Ch. Harrisburg, Pa., 1978-83, Unitarian Ch. Montclair, N.J., 1983—; chmn. Unitarian Universalist Panel Theol. Edn., Boston, 1986—; faculty Unitarian Universalist Preaching Seminar, Chgo., 1986. Contbr. articles to profl. jours. and pop. newspapers. Pres. Pa. Religious Coalition for Abortion Rights, Harrisburg, 1979-83; convenor Dauphin County Prison Soc., Harrisburg, 1979-83; pres. Essex County Meml. Soc., Montclair, 1985—; chmn. Homeless Shelter Fundraising, Montclair, 1988. Mem. Unitarian Universalist Ministers Assn., Montclair Clergy Assn., Unitarian Universalist Assn. (com. on excellence in ministry 1991—). Avocations: travel, reading, film, theater. Office: Unitarian Ch 67 Church St Montclair NJ 07042

BARKER, MASON CLEMENT, JR., minister; b. Cin., July 29, 1944; s. Mason Clement Sr. and Dema Caroline (Barnett) B.; M. Merry Barbara Workman, July 10, 1965; children: Anthony Mason, Johnny Edward. Received gen. high sch. diploma. Ordained Storehouse Ministries. Pastor Storehouse Ministries, Covington, Ky., 1983—. With USN 1960-63. Office: Storehouse Ministries Word Faith Chapel Covington KY 41011-2322

BARKER, VERLYN LLOYD, minister; b. Auburn, Nebr., July 25, 1931; s. Jack Lloyd and Olive Clara (Bollman) B. AB, Doane Coll., 1952, DD, 1977; BD, Yale U., 1956, STM, 1960; postgrad., U. Chgo., 1960-61; PhD, St. Louis U., 1970. Ordained to ministry United Ch. of Christ, 1956. Instr. history, chaplain Doane Coll., Crete, Nebr., 1954-55; pastor U. Nebr., 1956-59; sec. ministry higher edn. United Ch. Bd. Homeland Ministries, N.Y.C., 1961-90, Cleve., 1991—. Author: Health and Human Values: A Ministry of Theological Inquiry and Moral Discourse, 1987; editor: The Church and the Public School, 1980, Science, Technology and the Christian Faith, 1990; contbg. author: Campus Ministry, 1964; mem. editorial adv. com. Jour. Current Social Issues; contbr. articles to various publs. Pres. United Ministries in Higher Edn., N.Y.C., 1971-77. Mem. AAAS, ACLU, Am. Assn. Higher Edn., Am. Studies Assn., Acad. Polit. Sci., Am. Acad. Polit. and Social Sci., Soc. Health and Human Values, Doane Coll. Alumni Assn. (pres. 1957-58), Nat. Assn. for Sci., Tech. and Soc., Yale Club. Office: United Ch Bd for Homeland Ministries 700 Prospect St Cleveland OH 44115-1100

BARKER, WILLIAM SHIRMER, II, educator, minister; b. St. Louis, Dec. 15, 1934; s. Theodore Roosevelt and Nancy (Edwards) B.; m. Gail Kern, Dec. 28, 1957: children: Anne Kathryn, Matthew Woods. AB, Princeton U., 1956; MA, Cornell U., 1959; BD, Covenant Theol. Sem., 1960; PhD, Vanderbilt U., 1970. Pastor Hazelwood (Mo.) Presbyn. Ch., 1960-64; asst. prof. history Covenant Coll., Lookout Mountain, Ga., 1964-69, assoc. prof. history, dean faculty, 1969-72; assoc. prof. ch. history, dean faculty Covenant Theol. Sem., St. Louis, 1972-77, assoc. prof. ch. history, pres., 1977-84; editor, pub. The Presbyn. Jour., Asheville, N.C., 1984-87; prof. ch. history Westminster Theol. Sem., Phila., 1987—, acad. dean, 1991—. Co-editor: Theonomy: A Reformed Critique, 1990; contbr. articles to profl. jours. Trustee Covenant Coll., Lookout Mountain, 1973—. Mem. Am. Soc. Ch. History, Conf. on Faith and History, Evang. Theol. Soc. (membership com. 1987—), Nat. Assn. Evangs. (theology com. 1989—), Phi Beta Kappa. Presbyterian. Home: 163 Lismore Ave Glenside PA 19038 Office: Westminster Theol Sem PO Box 27009 Philadelphia PA 19118

BARKLEY, BRONSON LEE, minister; b. Austin, Tex., July 30, 1949; s. Junius Paul and Ellie Montgomery (Neal) B.; m. Darlene Lynette Hickman, July 21, 1972; children: John Paul, Jared Patrick. BA, Lamar U., 1971, MA, 1974. Ordained to ministry Assemblies of God, 1977. Assoc. pastor 1st Assembly of God, Tyler, Tex., 1972-74; pastor Faith Assembly of God, Alvin, Tex., 1974-76, Golden Acres Assembly of God, Pasadena, Tex., 1979-82, Chapel in the Forest Assembly of God, Kingwood, Tex., 1983—; revivalist Assemblies of God, Port Arthur, Tex., 1976-78, 83; pres. WZZJ Radio, Pascagoula, Miss., 1991—. Author play: The Lady and the Middle Cross, 1989; composer various songs. Bd. dirs. Birthright of Humble (Tex.), 1990—, Leadership Tng. Internat., Inc., Springdale, Ark., 1991—; precinct chmn. Rep. Party of Harris County, 1988-90. Mem. Kingwood Area Clergy Assn., Christian Coalition, Phi Eta Sigma. Office: Chapel in the Forest 4032 North Park Dr Kingwood TX 77345 *I owe everything that I am to the personally-transforming power I have experienced in Jesus Christ. Remember—Jesus loves you—and so do I!.*

BARLEY, BARRON PHILIP, minister; b. York, Pa., July 31, 1961; s. Joseph Rodney and Lois Catherine (Householder) B.; m. Cynthia Ellen Hoffman, Sept. 1, 1985; 1 child, Daniel. BS in Behavioral Sci., York Coll., 1983; MDiv, Lancaster Theol. Sem., 1986. Ordained to ministry United Ch. of Christ. Pastor McConnellsburg (Pa.)-Ft. London Charge United Ch. of Christ, 1986—; pres. Gowan's Gap Chaplaincy, Fort London, 1989-91, McConnellsburg Ministerium, 1989-91. Pres. Fulton County Food Basket, McConnellsburg, 1990—. Home: 203 E Walnut St McConnellsburg PA 17233

BARLEY, MICHAEL STEVEN, pastor; b. Winchester, Ky., Sept. 5, 1961; s. Gilbert Raymond and Anne Edwine (Fike) B. BA, U. Louisville, 1985. Sonshare player Ky. Bapt. Conv., Ky., 1980; min. youth Forest Blvd. Bapt. Ch., Jacksonville, Fla., 1987; pastor Riverbend Bapt. Chapel, St. Louis, Mich., 1988-89, Bradley (Ill.) Bapt. Ch., 1990—. Home: 1100 W Jeffery Apt 55 Kankakee IL 60901 Office: Bradley Bapt Ch 171 N Wabash Ave Bradley IL 60915

BARLOK, S. M. ELECTA, sister, pastoral associate; b. Cementon, Pa., Nov. 2, 1931; d. John Stephen and Mary Elizabeth (Makovsky) B. BS, Seton Hall; MLS, Villanova U.; MRS, St. Charles Sem., Phila. Joined Order St. Francis, Roman Cath. Ch.; cert. secondary tchr., libr., Pa. Tchr. St. Francis Acad., Bethlehem, Pa.; dir. religious edn. St. Anne Parish, Emmaus, Pa.; pastoral assoc. Blessed Sacrament Parish, Westfield, Mass.; elem. prin. Sts. Cyril and Methodius Sch., Bethlehem; pastoral assoc. St. Gabriel Parish, Hazleton, Pa.; officer Commn. Women Religious, Diocese of Allentown; mem. Diocesan Vocation Recruitment Com., Allentown. Dir. video Seed Planted, Seed Nourished, Seed Harvested.

BARLOW, AUGUST RALPH, JR., minister; b. Sewickley, Pa., Oct. 9, 1934; s. August Ralph and Kathryn Viola (Adams) B.; m. Elizabeth Evone Anderson, Aug. 27, 1960; children: Paul Martin, Andrew Ralph, Ann Kathryn. BA, Haverford Coll., 1956; BD, Yale U., 1959, STM, 1964. Ordained to ministry Meth. Ch., 1959. Pastor Fox Chapel Meth. Ch., Pitts., 1959-60; pastor Butler St. Meth. Ch., Pitts., 1961-62, Lawrenceville Community Ch., Pitts., 1962-63; intern Cleve. Inner City Protestant Parish, 1960-61; teaching min. Beneficent Congl. Ch., Providence, 1964-70, pastor, 1970—; mem. bd. govs. Beneficent House; bd. dirs. Pastoral Counseling Ctr. Greater Providence, v.p., 1984-86; bd. dirs. Steere House, Providence, 1980-86, pres., 1983-86; bd. dirs. Home Health Svcs. of R.I., 1986—; chmn. ch. in soc. com., 1985-86; mem. R.I. Conf., United Ch. of Christ, 1964—, mem. com. on ministry, 1981-83; mem. urban div. R.I. Council Chs., 1979-82. Contbr. articles to Christian Century, editorials, commentaries to Providence Jour.-Bull., Religious Broadcasting Sta. WEAN, 1964-87. Mem. adv. coun. Providence Pub. Libr., 1968-71; bd. dirs. Mouthpiece Coffee House, Providence, 1969-75, pres., 1974-75. Rsch. fellow Yale U. Div. Sch., 1979. Mem. Providence Intown Chs. Assn., Mins. Assn. R.I. Conf. United Ch. of Christ., Rotary (trustee Rotary Charities Found. 1977-82, Paul Harris fellow), Beneficent Order of Spike, Phi Beta Kappa. Democrat. Home: 95 Cole Ave Providence RI 02906 Office: 300 Weybosset St Providence RI 02903

BARLOW, BECKY ANN, ministry administrator; b. Hickory, N.C., Aug. 15, 1949; d. Adrian Arthur and Geneva (Drum) Bolick; m. Larry Moore Barlow, Jan. 3, 1968; children: David Arthur, Lisa Renae. Student, Caldwell Community Coll., Hudson, N.C., 1968-70. Bus driver Granite Falls (N.C.) Elem. Sch., 1974-87, substitute tchr., 1978-81; exec. dir. South Caldwell Christian Ministries, Granite Falls, 1982—. V.p. Caldwell Com. for Healthy Families, Lenoir, N.C., 1986-87; past sec. Bd. Adjustments, Granite Falls, 1984-85, bd. dirs., 1984—; past v.p. Community Devel. Adv., Granite Falls, 1985, bd. dirs., 1984; bd. dirs. Blue Ridge Community Action, Lenoir, 1987—, Caldwell County Health Dept. Adv. Bd., Lenoir, 1987, Caldwell Community Coll. Adv. Council, Hudson, 1987. Recipient Vol. Adminstr. Coordinator award Office of Gov., 1984, Individual Community Service award, 1987. Mem. N.W. Ministry Team (v.p. 1984-85, sec. 1985-86, bd. dirs. 1987). Democrat. Lutheran. Avocations: card games, sports. Home: 53 Forest Ave Granite Falls NC 28630 Office: South Caldwell Christian Ministries 44 Duke St Granite Falls NC 28630

BARLOWE, WILLIAM TERRY, pastor, educator; b. Birmingham, Ala., July 25, 1953; s. William Claude and V. Nell (McLain) B.; m. Vickie Lynn Simpson, Jan. 22, 1971; children: Victoria, Tara, Kristy, Landon. BTh, Internat. Bible Inst. and Sem., 1988. Ordained to ministry Ch. of God, 1984. Youth pastor Ch. of God, LaGrange, Ga., 1976-77, Bessemer, Ala., 1977-78; pastor Ch. of God, West Blocton, Ala., 1978-79, Madison, Ala., 1979-87; sr. pastor Spirit Life Family Worship Ctr., Madison, Ala., 1987—; trustee Selah Youth Ministries, Huntsville, Ala., 1985-86; dir. Ontrack Youth Ministries, Madison, 1986-90, Spiritlife Ministries, Madison, 1987—; chaplain Madison Civitan, 1979-82; support pastor Ministers Against Abortion, Huntsville, 1982—, Madison White Ribbon, 1990-91. Contbr. Proclaiming Victory, 1980-82. Republican. Office: Spiritlife Ministries PO Box 612 1469 Brownsferry Rd Madison AL 35758

BARNARD, DOROTHY GASKILL, retired church moderator, religious organization administrator; b. St. Louis, Feb. 28, 1925; d. John Edward and Lucille Anna (Zerweck) Gaskill; m. Eugene R. Barnard, June 10, 1948; children: Susan, Lynn, Cynthia. BS in Edn., Washington U., 1946, AB magna cum laude, 1946; DD (hon.), Westminster Coll., 1982. Ordained elder Presbyn. Ch. (U.S.A.), 1975. Chairperson Bd. of Women's Work, Presbyn. Ch. U.S., Atlanta, 1969-71; vice-chairperson Gen. Exec. Bd., Presbyn. Ch. U.S., Atlanta, 1972-74; v.p. Ch. Women United, N.Y.C., 1978-81; moderator Gen. Assembly Presbyn. Ch. U.S., Atlanta, 1981-82, mem. Gen. Assembly Coun., 1983-84; trustee Gen. Commn. on Unity and Interreligious Concerns, United Meth. Ch., N.Y., 1985-89; co-chmn. Strategy Commn., Consultation on Ch. Unity, Princeton, N.J, 1983; vice-chmn., chair bd. trustees Presbyn. Sch. of Christian Edn., Richmond, Va., 1983—; chair bd. trustees Presbyn. Children's Services, Farmington, Mo., 1986—. Author: Devotionals for Women, 1966; contbr. articles on ecumenism, women's issues, internat. missions. Trustee St. Luke's Hosp., St. Louis, 1987—; v.p. bd. trustees, mem. ch. and health com. Thompson Ecumenical Ctr., St. Louis; v.p. sponsors com. Presbyn. Sch. Ch. Edn., Richmond, 1991—. Recipient Valiant Woman award Ch. Women United, St. Louis, N.Y.C., 1982. Mem. Phi Beta Kappa, Kappa Delta Pi, Pi Beta Phi (v.p. 1945-46). Home: 2410 Fairoyal Dr Saint Louis MO 63131

BARNES, BILL LLOYD, religious organization administrator; b. Kansas City, Mo., July 16, 1926; s. William Lloyd and Augusta (Moore) B; BA, Drake U., 1948; MDiv, Christian Theol. Sem., 1952; MS, Butler U., 1957; m. Shirley Nadine Malone, Oct. 9, 1945; children: Judith Diane (Mrs. Robert Stall), Janis Caryl (Mrs. Kent Barnard). Student minister in Kellogg, Iowa, 1946-48, Indpls., 1948-52; ordained to ministry Christian Ch. (Disciples of Christ), 1947; minister in St. Louis, 1952-60; dir. devel. Christian Theol. Sem., Indpls., 1960-67, v.p. devel., 1967-87, v.p. devel. spl. projects Disciples of Christ Ch., 1987—. Mem. home and state missions planning coun. Disciples of Christ 1956-60; sec. Mo. Disciples State Conv., 1954; evangelism rep. St. Louis Met. Ch. Fedn., 1956; pres. St. Louis Ministers, 1957, Disciple Ministers, 1959; substitute tchr. TV program Lessons for Living, Sta. WTTV, Indpls., 1962-65; ministerial enlistment chmn. St. Louis Counseling Ctr., 1959; mem. Indpls. Ch. Fedn. New Direction Com., 1973, 74. Mem. bd. higher edn. Disciples of Christ, 1961-79, chmn. Ind. inter agy. com., 1971-75, chmn. askings commn., 1972-73, mem. theol. commn. Div. Higher Edn., 1979-87; chmn. time/place com. Ind. Christian Ch. Conv., 1964-66. Community rels. rep. YMCA, St. Louis, 1955; institutional rep. Boy Scouts Am., St, Louis, 1955-60; mem. Indpls. Urban Forum Series Com., 1969-70. Served with USAAF, 1945. A Seminarian of Year Sermon contest winner Pulpit mag., 1951, 52; recipient Disting. Alumnus award Christian Theol. Sem., 1975. Mem. Sem. Mgmt. Assn. (pres. 1972-74), Hoosier Power Squadron (chaplain 1971—), Riviera Club, Indpls. Athletic Club, Kiwanis, Theta Phi. Author Planning for the Planned Gift; contbr. articles and Sunday Sch. lessons to religious publs. Home: 411 Braeside South Dr Indianapolis IN 46260 Office: 436 Indiana Ave Indianapolis IN 46202

BARNES, ERNEST LEON, minister; b. Vernon, Ala., Sept. 16, 1946; s. Roy Hindman and Maggie Lee (Elliott) B.; m. Linda Lou Randolph, Sept. 19, 1964; children: Tammy Renee Beck, Tracie Carol Shannon, Leigh Ann Hankins. Student, Freed-Hardeman U., Henderson, Tenn., 1965-67. Min. Christian Chapel Ch. of Christ, Amory, Miss., 1967-73, Levy Ch. of Christ, North Little Rock, Ark., 1973-89, Germantown (Tenn.) Ch. of Christ, 1990—; adv. bd. mem. Freed-Hardeman U., 1985—. Author: My Place In The Body, 1981, When A Loved One Dies, 1988, The Model of Leadership, 1989, I'm Not Hungry Anymore, 1991. Pres. mintor Toast Masters, North Little Rock, 1985-87; dir. Rotary Internat., 1986-89; pres. North Little Rock Sch. Bd., 1982-87. Republican. Home: 7085 Neshoba Rd Germantown TN 38138 Office: Church of Christ 7007 Poplar Ave Germantown TN 38138 *Life is seldom fair. But with God's blessings every disppointment can become a tool for greater service to God and humanity. Our challenge is to live on God's appointments instead of our own.*

BARNES, JACK LEONARD, minister; b. Kansas City, Mo., Aug. 30, 1935; s. William Lloyd and Augusta B. (Moore) B.; m. Mildred Lucille Champion, June 14, 1957; children: Evan Lee, Edward Lloyd (dec.). BA, Culver-Stockton Coll., 1957; BD, Christian Theol. Sem., 1961; MA, Butler U., 1961; D of Ministry, Vanderbilt U., 1978. Ordained to ministry Christian Ch., 1957. Min. First Christian Ch., Macon, Mo., 1961-67; dist. min. Dist. Three Mo., Canton, 1967-74; assoc. prof. religion Culver-Stockton Coll., Canton, 1967-74; sr. min. East Side Christian Ch., Evansville, Ind., 1974-81, Cen. Christian Ch., Jacksonville, Ill., 1981-89; min. devel. Christain Ch. in Fla., Orlando, 1989—; adv. bd., dir. The Compassionate Friends, Orlando, 1989—; chmn. fin. com. Fla. Coun. Chs., 1991—. Active Planned Giving Coun., Orlando, 1990—. Fla. Ministerial fellow. Mem. Nat. Soc. Fund Raising Exec., Rotary (dir. 1966-67), Theta Phi. Democrat. Home: 811 Glen Arden Way Altamonte Springs FL 32701 Office: Christian Ch in Fla 924 N Magnolia Ste 248 Orlando FL 32803 *The value of an individual's life will ultimately be determined not by the accumulation of things or position, but by the degree of the activity of giving whatever one has to others. The meaning of life comes into clear focus in the basic force of sharing as it permeates all of existence.*

BARNES, JAMES MARK, minister; b. Carrollton, Ga., Jan. 18, 1956; s. James Morris and Sarah Nell (Marlow) B.; m. Cynthia Lynn Eddins, Jul. 7, 1979; children: Daniel Zebadiah, Rachel Lynn. MusB, West Ga. Coll., 1983; MusM, Southwestern Bapt. Theol. Sem., 1988. Min. music Oak Grove Bapt. Ch., Carrollton, Ga., 1981-83; min. music and youth Ensley 1st Bapt. Ch., Pensacola, Fla., 1983-85; min. music Ridgecrest Bapt. Ch., Ft. Worth, 1985-89, 1st Bapt. Ch., Carrollton, Ga., 1990—; band dir. 1st Bapt. Ch., Carrollton, 1989—; assoc. dir. music Carrollton Bapt. Assn., 1989—; band dir. Ranburne (Ala.) High Sch., 1989. Precint capt. Escambia Cty., Pensacola, Fla. 1984-86. Mem. Chorister's Guild, Georgia Bapt. Music Conf., Sons of Jubal. Republican. Southern Baptist. Office: 1st Bapt Ch 102 Dixie St Carrollton GA 30117

BARNES, MICHAEL HORACE, religious studies educator; b. Bovey, Minn., Aug. 8, 1937; s. Horace C. and Corlin M. (Wethern) B. BA, St. Louis U., 1961, PhL, 1962; PhD, Marquette U., 1976. Prof. U. Dayton, Ohio, 1968—. Author: In The Presence of Mystery, 1984, 90; editor: An Ecological Spirit, 1992. Mem. Am. Acad. Religion, N.Am. Assn. for Study of Religion (bd. dirs. 1989—), Cath. Theol. Soc., Ohio Acad. of Religion (pres. 1987-88), Coll. Theology Soc. (bd. dirs. 1987-89). Office: U Dayton Religious Studies Dept Dayton OH 45469-1480

BARNES, RONALD B., ecumenical agency administrator. Exec. dir. North Hills Youth Ministry, Pitts. Office: North Hills Youth Ministry 1566 Northway Mall Pittsburgh PA 15237*

BARNES, ROSEMARY LOIS, minister; b. Grand Rapids, Mich., Sept. 17, 1946; d. Floyd Herman and Cora Agnes (Beukema) Herms; m. Louis Herbert Adams, Feb. 22, 1969 (div. Oct. 1976); 1 child, Louis Herbert Jr.; m. Robert Jearold Barnes, Oct. 8, 1976. BA, Calvin Coll., 1968. Ordained to ministry Home Ministry Fellowship, 1980; cert. social worker. Group worker Kent County Juvenile Ct., Grand Rapids, Mich., 1966-68; tchr. Sheldon Elem. Sch., Grand Rapids, 1968-69; social worker Kent Dept. Social Services, Grand Rapids, 1969-75, 75-84; tchr., mission worker Emmanuel House, San Diego, 1975; co-pastor, founder River of Life Ministries, Grand Rapids, 1980—; instr. Gt. Lakes Inst. Bible Studies, Grand Rapids, 1988; tchr., founder River of Life Sch. Christian Leadership, Grand Rapids, 1981—; v.p. Aglow, Grand Rapids, 1982-83; sec., treas. Western Mich. Full Gospel Ministers Fellowship, Grand Rapids, 1984-85; mem. bd. chaplains Dunes Correctional Facility, Saugatuck, Mich., 1986-91; coord. 1988 Washington for Jesus March, One Nation Under God, Inc.; co-pastor Gun Lake River of Life, 1988; prof. Great Lakes Inst., 1988; county coord. Grand Rapids Full Gospel Ministers Fellowship, 1990—. Bd. dirs. Alcohol Incentive Ladder, Grand Rapids, 1979. Mem. Women in Leadership. Democrat. Mem. Ind. Charismatic Ch. Avocations: computers, trumpet, reading, swimming, Scrabble. Home: 2143 S Division Grand Rapids MI 49507 *My passion to see the Lord's church grow into Him, mature and spotless, is the force that motivates me to teach the Word of God. I believe that when His Bride is fully mature He will come to her and together they will rule and reign forever.*

BARNES, WILLIAM MATTISON, JR., minister; b. Gadsden, Ala., Aug. 19, 1954; s. William Mattison Sr. and Annette (Dial) B.; m. Joan Little, Feb. 6, 1975; children: April E., William Mattison III. BA, Samford U., 1975; MDiv, New Orleans Bapt. Seminary, 1975-78; D of Ministry, So. Bapt. Ctr., Jacksonville, Fla., 1984; postgrad., Jacksonville State U. Ordained to ministry So. Bapt. Conv., 1972. Pastor Highland Bapt. Ch., Fort Payne, Ala., 1978-80, Fairview Bapt. Ch., Gadsden, 1980-83, First Bapt. Ch. of Saks, Anniston, Ala., 1983—; psychologist asst./counselor, Robert Summerlin and Assocs., Anniston, 1991—; bd. dirs. Sav-A-Life Orgn., Anniston. Author various sermon booklets; contbr. articles to profl. jours. Named to Outstanding Young Men of Am., 1988-89. Mem. Alpha Kappa Omega. Home: 21 Timbercrest Cir Anniston AL 36206 Office: Robert Summerlin and Assocs 1113 Christine Ave Anniston AL 36201

BARNES, WILLIAM SHAFER, minister; b. Pitts., Apr. 16, 1951; s. Wilbur Pyle and Jean Alma (Shafer) B.; m. Kim Rosena Houser, June 30, 1978; children: Kristin Diane, Meredith Alissa. BBA summa cum laude, Emory U., 1973, MDiv magna cum laude, 1976. Ordained to ministry United Meth. Ch. as deacon, 1974, as elder, 1979. Asst. minister Trinity United Meth. Ch., Atlanta, 1970-75; pastor Haddock (Ga.) United Meth. Ch., 1975-77; assoc. pastor Christ Ch., United Meth., Ft. Lauderdale, Fla., 1977-81; chaplain of coll. Fla. Southern Coll., Lakeland, 1981-84; sr. minister 1st United Meth. Ch. of Miami (Fla.), 1985—; bd. dirs. Miami Campus Ministries, 1985—, Miami Urban Ministries, 1986-90; chair Dist. Com. on Ordained Ministry, Miami, 1990; mem. clergy adv. com. Bethune-Cookman Coll., 1988—. Bd. dirs. Epworth Village Retirement Ctr., Hialeah, Fla., 1985—, United Protestant Appeal, 1987—; bd. dirs. Met. YMCA, 1988—, also chair pers. com.; mem. Refugee Assistance Adv. Com., 1987—; founding mem. P.A.c.T., Miami, 1989; trustee Bayfront Park Mgmt. Trust, Miami, 1988-89; bd. dirs. Agape Acad. Enrichment Ctr., Miami, 1989—. Mem. Greater Miami C. of C., Miami Religious Leader's Coalition, Rotary (bd. dirs. Micmi chpt. 1989—), Kiwanis (pres. Lauderdale by the Sea chpt. 1978-79), Theta Chi Beta, Psi Chi. Home: 498 NE 55th Terr Miami FL 33137 Office: 1st United Meth Ch Miami 400 Biscayne Blvd Miami FL 33132

BARNET, VERN, minister; b. Omaha, May 25, 1942; s. Walker Barnet and Lucille (Dabbs) Dahmer; m. Carole A. Wilson, June 6, 1970; 1 child, B. Benjamin B. Barnet. BA, U. Nebr., 1965, postgrad., 1965-66; postgrad., U. Chgo., 1966-70, Meadville Theol. Sch., Chgo., 1970. Interim minister The Unitarian Ch., Rockford, Ill., 1970-71; minister The Unitarian Ch.,

Meadville, Pa., 1971-75, Shawnee Mission Unitarian Soc., Overland Park, Kans., 1975-84; minister in residence World Faiths Ctr. for Religious Experience and Study, Overland Park, 1984—; adj. prof. Park Coll., Parkville, 1988, Ottawa U. Kansas City Campus, Overland Park 1980—, St. Paul Sch. Theol., Kansas City, 1978-79; exec. sec. Congregation Abraxas, Overland Park, 1979-81; convenor Kansas City Interfaith Coun., 1989—; coord. Christian-Jewish-Muslim Dialogue Group, 1988—. Co-author: (curriculum) Unitarian Universalist Identity, 1979; author: (curriculum) Coming of Age, 1981; editor: (book anthology) Worship Reader, 1980. Bd. dirs. Western Mo. Affiliate ACLU, Kansas City, 1977-78, Ctr. for All Men, 1990—, Coalition for the Environment, 1990—; v.p. Kansas City Tomorrow Alumni, 1991—; chmn. Com. for Acad. and Religious Liberty, Overland Park, 1978-79. Mem. Unitarian Universalist Ministers Assn., (chpt. pres. 1973-74, good offices person 1977-78), Internat. Assn. for Religious Freedom, Rotary (Paul Harris fellow). Avocations: photography, computers, swimming, singing. Office: World Faiths Ctr for Religion Box 4165 Overland Park KS 66204 *In three realms of faith—the person, the community, and the environment—we are challenged as never before. Yet the encounter of the world's diverse religions today, in mutual purification, makes possible a new revelation of the sacred as we ask, "What is it on which our lives depend?" and behold infinite personhood, planetary community, and ecological interdependence.*

BARNETT, DOUGLAS EUGENE, minister; b. Fontana, Calif., Apr. 30, 1961; s. Leroy Barnett and Diane Louise Anderson Dodson; m. Dianna Lynn Jones, May 15, 1982; 1 child, Joshua. A.Bible, Springfield (Oreg.) Sch.Bible, 1988. Ordained to ministry Missionary Bapt. Ch., 1988—. Pastor Owghee Bapt. Ch., Homedale, Idaho, 1987-88, Landmark Missionary Bapt. Ch., Vancouver, Wash., 1988—; counselor, svc. dir. Union Rogue Bapt. Camp, Prospect, Oreg., 1979—. With USMC, 1979-83. Home and Office: Landmark Missionary Bapt Ch 7119 NE 133d Ave Vancouver WA 98682-4838

BARNETT, EDWARD, lay worker; b. Washington, Apr. 13, 1960; s. Edward and Mary Helen (Brooks) B.; m. Adreinne Hamlin, July 18, 1987; children: Donnell, Emmanuell. Student, Norfolk State U., Cleve. Inst. Electronics, Denver Sch. Fin., D.C. Bible Inst. Chmn., founder Little Upperroom Prayer Ministries, 1987—. Author: Junior Deacons Ministry, 1986, What God Expects from Men of God, 1991. Counselor Edgemeade Detention Ctr., Upper Marlboro, Md., 1987-89; counselor-treas. D.C. Kenya Exch. Program, Washington, 1990-91. Home: 5165 Clacton Ave Suitland MD 20746

BARNETT, JAMES MONROE, rector, author; b. Baton Rouge, La., Oct. 21, 1925; s. James Monroe Sr. and Egeria Overton (Brooks) B.; m. Marian Jean Scofield, Aug. 15, 1956; children: James Mark, John Michael, Thomas Overton, Paul Winston. BA, La. State U., 1946; MDiv., Seabury-Western Theol. Sem., 1951; D Ministry, U. of South, 1979. Ordained priest Episcopal Ch., 1952. lectr. theol. seminaries, U.S. and Eng. Author: The Diaconate: A Full and Equal Order, 1979. Chmn. Nebr. Liturgical Commn., Omaha, 1970—; mem. exec. council Diocese of Nebr., Omaha, 1980—; mem. Commn. on Ministry, Omaha, 1982-86. Mem. N.Am. Assn. for Diaconate (bd. trustees), Associated Parishes, Assn. of Liturgy and Music Commns. Avocations: woodworking, antique furniture restoration, swimming. Office: Trinity Episcopal Ch 111 S 9th St Norfolk NE 68701

BARNETT, MURPHY EUGENE, clergyman, educator, counselor; b. Carbon Hill, Ala., Nov. 28, 1935; s. Grady and Beatrice (Jennings) B.; m. Irene May, May 7, 1956; children: Curtis Allen, James Kevin, Christopher Lynn, Kimberly Elaine. BA, U. Ala., 1978, MA, 1982, EdD, 1990. Nat. cert. counselor, Ala. Adj. prof. U. Ala., Shelton State Community Coll.; pastor Ch. of God of Prophecy, Cottondale, Ala. With USN, 1953-61. Mem. Kappa Delta Pi, Chi Sigma Iota. Home: PO Box 192 Cottondale AL 35453

BARNETT, PHILLIP CHARLES, organist/choral director; b. Evanston, Ill., June 21, 1963; s. Charles Gayle and Charlotte (Booth) B.; m. Debbi Joy Bowman, Oct. 20, 1990. BME, Ill. State U., 1985; M. Ch. Music, Concordia Coll., River Forest, Ill., 1989. Cert. tchr. Organist Community Ch. LaGrange Highlands, LaGrange, Ill., 1985, Glen Oak Christian Ch., Peoria, Ill., 1986; organist/choir dir. Elmwood Pk. Presbyn. Ch., Elmwood Park, Ill., 1988-89; dir. music, organist 1st United Meth. Ch., Tullahoma, Tenn., 1989—. Condr. Tullahoma Civic Choir, 1990. Named Outstanding Young Men of America, 1986; recipient Florence Runyon scholarship, 1984, Mary Bilyeu Mem. award 1985. Mem. Am. Guild Organists, Am. Choral Dirs. Assn., Am. Guild English Handbell Ringers, Fellowship of United Meths. in Worship,Music and Other Arts, Golden Key, Pi Kappa Lambda. United Methodist. Home: 1300 Cedar Ln N4 Tullahoma TN 37388 Office: 1st United Meth Ch 208 W Lauderdale St Tullahoma TN 37388

BARNETT, TOMMY JOE, minister; b. Electra, Tex., Oct. 4, 1937; s. H. W. and Orlena (Graves) B.; m. Marja Kaarina Holmstrom, Dec. 11, 1964; children: Kristie Barnett Sexton, Luke, Matthew. DD, Oral Roberts U., Tulsa, 1985; DHL, So. Calif. Theol. Sem., Fresno, 1986; DD, Southwestern Coll., Waxahachie, Tex., 1988. Lic. to ministry Assemblies of God, 1956; ordained, 1976. Assoc. pastor Victoria Tabernacle, Kansas City, Kans.; sr. pastor Westside Assembly of God, Davenport, Iowa, 1971-79, Phoenix First Assembly, 1979—; evangelist 6 world-wide tours; trustee Oral Roberts U., 1986—; bd. dirs. James Robison Evangelistic Assn., Ft. Worth, 1989—. Author: Portraits of Vision, 1990; contbr. to numerous church growth tapes and books. Bd. dirs. Coun. for Nat. Policy, Washington, 1985—. Office: Phoenix First Assembly 13613 N Cave Creek Rd Phoenix AZ 85022

BARNEY, JOHN A., religious organization administrator; b. Rumney, N.H., Nov. 1, 1929; s. Earl Martin and Elva (Clough) B.; m. Jessie Bennett, Dec. 24, 1927; children: Paul Andrew, Janice Barney Syvertsen, Eunice Barney Paulson. BA, United Coll. Gordon & Barrington, Wenham, Mass., 1952. Ch. planter Africa Inland Mission, Napopo, Zaire, Africa, 1954-56; sch. activity dir. Africa Inland Mission, Rethy, Zaire, 1957-59; ch. planter Africa Inland Mission, Niangara, Zaire, 1960-61; constrn. engr. Africa Inland Mission, Kijabe, Kenya, Africa, 1961-72; dir. mobile film ministry Africa Inland Mission, Kijabe, 1973-77; dir. stewardship Africa Inland Mission, Pearl River, N.Y., 1978—; bd. dirs. Christian Stewardship Council, Daytona Beach, Fla., 1986—, Radio Sta. WIHS, Middletown, Conn., 1980-87. Deacon Calvary Ch., West Hartford, 1987—; alumni coun. Gordon Coll., Wenham, 1979-88. Avocations: basketball. Home: 130 Clubhouse Rd Windsor CT 06095

BARNHART, STEPHEN PAUL, music director; b. Fargo, N.D., Jan. 17, 1947; s. Arthur C. and Martha Kate (Miller) B.; m. Paula R. Barnhart, June 23, 1979; children: Matthew, Jessica, Jennifer. BA, Macalester Coll., 1969. Assoc. organist Ch. of the Messiah, Gwynedd, Pa., 1963-65; dir. of music St. Nicholas Episcopal, Richfield, Minn., 1966—; sales and svc.rep. The Reuter Organ Co., Richfield, 1985—. Mem. Am. Guild Organists. Office: St Nicholas Episcopal Ch 7227 Penn Ave S Richfield MN 55423

BARNHILL, DONALD CLAYTON, minister; b. Denver, Colo., Jan. 7, 1932; s. Lloyd K. and Lola (Morris) B.; m. Pauline Elizabeth Gustafson, Dec. 27, 1952; children: Deborah, Rebecca, Gregory, Rachel. BA, Rockmont Coll., Denver, 1957; MDiv, Denver Conservative Bapt. Sem., 1965; D Ministry, Western Conservative Bapt. Sem., Portland, Oreg., 1977. Ordained to ministry Conservative Bapt. Assn. Am., 1959. Pastor Grace Bapt. Ch., Commerce City, Colo., 1957-59, Columbine Hill Bapt. Ch., 1959-65, Grace Bapt. Ch., Des Moines, 1965-72, 1st Bapt. Ch., Worthington, Minn., 1972-82, Calvary Bapt. Ch., Longmont, Colo., 1982-86, Clinton (N.J.) Bapt. Ch., 1986—; pres. Conservative Bapt. Assn. Am., Wheaton, Ill., 1982-86. Author: A Lay Theology, 1977. Office: Clinton Bapt Ch 15 Pittstown Rd Clinton NJ 08809 *One of the great needs of man is a relentless pursuit of integrity and inner strength. It's what the old divines called character. It's the deep water stuff of honesty, purity, self-control, courage, love and faith. They are worth pursuing. Worth working at. It is what determines who you really are.*

BARNHILL, KENNETH SMALTZ, JR., lay worker; b. Mesilla, N.Mex., Aug. 2, 1928; s. Kenneth S. and Rega (Ragan) B.; m. Patricia Jean Boney, Aug. 10, 1950; children: Jane Ann, Martha Jean Barnhill-Martin. BS in Engring., N.Mex. Coll. Agrl. and Mech. Arts, 1952. Exec. dir. Episcopal Charities of the Rio Grande, Albuquerque, 1987—; adminstr./treas. Cathedral Ch. of St. John, Albuquerque, 1988—; bd. dirs. United Episcopal Charities, N.Y.C.; regional chair Diocesan Stewardship Commn., Albuquerque, 1983—; mem. Companion Diocese Commn., Albuquerque, 1983—; dir. Camp Stoney (Episcopal), Santa Fe, 1977-83. Holder 2 mineral process patents. Bd. Dirs. New Heart of Albuquerque, 1989—, N.Mex. Mining Assn., Santa Fe, 1976-83, Cibola County C . of C., 1976-82; advisor N.Mex. Sch. Mines Mining Dept., Socorro, 1977-83. With U.S. Army, 1946-48, Korea. Mem. AIME, Am. Inst. Chem. Engrs., Can. Inst. Mining and Metallurgy, Nat. Assn. Christian Bus. Adminstrs., Masons (master 1984, 87), Shriners. Home: 7223 Chickadee Ln NE Albuquerque NM 87109 Office: Cathedral Ch of St John 318 Silver Ave SW Albuquerque NM 87102

BARNHOUSE, RUTH TIFFANY, priest, psychiatrist; b. La Mur, Isere, France; d. Donald Grey Barnhouse; m. Francis G. Edmonds Jr. (div.); children: Francis, Ruth; m. William F. Beuscher (div. 1968); children: Robert, William, Christopher, Thomas, John. Student, Vassar Coll.; BA, Barnard Coll., Columbia U.; MD, Columbia U., 1950; postgrad., Boston Psychoanalytic Inst., 1966-67, Episcopal Theological Sch., 1969-70; ThM, Weston Coll. Sch. Theology, 1974. Diplomate Am. Bd. Psychiatry and Neurology; ordained to ministry Episcopal Ch., 1980. Intern Monmouth Meml. Hosp., Long Branch, N.J., 1950-51; resident in psychiatry McLean Hosp., Waverly, Mass., 1953-55, staff psychiatrist, 1958-78; fellow in psychiatry Mass. Gen. Hosp., Boston, 1955-56; pvt. practice, 1956—; prof. psychiatry and pastoral care Perkins Sch. Theology So. Meth. U., Dallas, 1980-89, prof. emerita, 1989—; staff psychiatrist Mass. Mental health Ctr., 1958-59; clin. asst. Harvard U., 1959-78; vis. lectr in pastoral theology Weston Coll. Theology, 1971-76; adj. prof. pastoral theology Va. Theol. Sem., 1978-80, Loyola Coll., Columbia, Md., 1978-80; with courtesy staff Sibley Hosp., 1979-80; lectr., workshop leader in field. Asst. editor: Anglican Theol. Rev.; co-editor: Male and Female: Christian Approaches to Sexuality; author: Identity, 1984, Clergy and the Sexual Revolution, 1987, Homosexuality: A Symbolic Confusion, 1977; contbr. numerous articles to profl. jours. Pres. Peacemakers, Inc., 1989-90, Isthmus Inst., 1989—. Recipient Maura award Women's Ctr. of Dallas, 1987. Fellow Am. Psychiat. Assn. (life, vice chair com. on religion); mem. AAAS, AAUP, Am. med. women's Assn., Am. Acad. Psychoanalysis (sci. assoc.), Am. Acad. Religion, Assn. Women Psychiatrists (pres. 1991—), Analytical Psychology Assn. of Dallas, Conf. Anglican Theologians (past pres.), Dallas Area Women Psychiatrists, Hermetic Acad., Internat. Physicians for Prevention of Nuclear War, Mass. Med. Soc., N.Y. Acad. Sci., N. Tex. Psychiat. Soc., Physicians for Social Responsibility, others. Office: 5956 Sherry Ln Ste 1221 Dallas TX 75225 *The human family needs to learn three things: the neighbor we are to love as we love ourselves includes every man, woman and child alive, all our ancestors, and all our descendants; how to balance the rights and duties of the individual with the rights and duties of the community; and how to achieve a true balance between masculine and feminine values.*

BARNWELL, RAY ERVIN, SR., church administrator; b. Greenville, S.C., Sept. 11, 1945; s. Uless Lee and Ruby (Gaines) B.; m. Rebecca Sue Duke, Dec. 23, 1966; children: Candace Angela, Ray Ervin Jr. BA, Cen. Wesleyan Coll., Central, S.C., 1968. Ordained to ministry Wesleyan Ch., 1968. Sr. pastor Wesleyan Ch., Salem, Seneca and Greenville, S.C., 1966-81; gen. dir. Sunday schs. Wesleyan Ch., Marion, Ind., 1981-84; dir. ministry advancement The Wesleyan Hour, Marion, 1984-85; sr. pastor Westview Wesleyan Ch., Jonesboro, Ind., 1985-88; dist. supt. Atlantic dist. Wesleyan Ch., Sussex, N.B., Can., 1988—; pres. youth dept. S.C. dist. Wesleyan Ch., 1971-77, mem. dist. bds. adminstrn., S.C., Ind., N.B., 1972-81, 87-88, 88—, del. to gen. confs., N.Am., 1976, 80, 88. Author Sunday sch. curricula. Bd. dirs. Oconee (S.C.) chpt. ARC, 1976-77; dir. relief fund Toccoa (Ga.) Falls Bible Coll., 1977; mem. pres.' coun. Cen. Wesleyan Coll., Central, 1980-81; chmn. bd. Bethany Bible Coll., Sussex, 1990. Recipient awards local Wesleyan chs., 1977, 81, 86, Outstanding Svc. award Gideons Internat., 1979. Mem. Can. Bible Soc. (bd. dirs. 1989—). Home and Office: Box 20, Sussex, NB Canada E0E 1P0

BARR, DAVID LAWRENCE, religion educator; b. Belding, Mich., Apr. 24, 1942; s. Fred and Henrietta Marie (Enbody) B.; m. Judith Kay Dunlap, July 2, 1966; children: Elizabeth Kay, Nathaniel David. BA in Bible and Theology, Ft. Wayne (Ind.) Bible Coll., 1965; MA in Religion, Fla. State U., 1969, PhD in Religion, 1974. Prof. religion Wright State U., Dayton, Ohio, 1975—, chair dept., 1980-86, dir. univ. honors program, 1987—; co-dir. Pub. Edn. Religion Studies Ctr., Dayton, 1978-85. Author: The Bible in American Education, 1982, New Testament Story: An Introduction, 1987, The Bible Reader's Guide, 1970; contbr. articles to profl. jours.; reader Ohio Jour. Religion, 1975-80. Wright State U. Rsch. Coun. grantee, 1986, Fla. State U. fellow, 1968-69, 71-72. Mem. Soc. Bibl. Lit. (chair seminar 1989—), Cath. Bibl. Assn., Am. Acad. Religion, Soc. for Study Narrative, Dayton N.T. Seminar, Eastern Great Lakes Bibl. Soc. (pres. 1985-86). Democrat. Presbyterian. Home: 206 Cambria Dr Dayton OH 45440 Office: Wright State U Honors Program 179 Millett Dayton OH 45435

BARR, JAMES, educator; b. Mar. 20, 1924; s. Allan B.; student Daniel Stewart's Coll., Edinburgh, Scotland; MA, Edinburgh U., 1948, BD, 1951; MA, Oxford (Eng.) U., 1976 DD, 1981; DD (hon.), Knox Coll., Toronto, Ont., Can., 1964, U. Dubuque, 1974, U. St. Andrews, 1974, U. Edinburgh, 1983, U. South Africa, 1986, Victoria U., Toronto, Ont., Can., 1988, Faculté de Théologie Protestante, Paris, 1988, U. Oslo, 1991; MA (hon.), U. Manchester, 1969; m. Jane J. S. Hepburn, 1950; 3 children. Minister of Ch. of Scotland, Tiberias, Israel, 1951-53; prof. N.T. lit. and exegesis Presbyn. Coll., Montreal, Que., Can., 1953-55; prof. Old Testament lit. and theology Edinburgh U., 1955-61, Princeton Theol. Sem., 1961-65; prof. Semitic langs. and lits. Manchester (Eng.) U., 1965-76; Oriel prof. interpretation Holy Scripture, and fellow Oriel Coll., Oxford U., 1976-78, hon. fellow, 1980; Regius prof. Hebrew, Oxford U. and student Christ Ch., 1978-89; prof. Hebrew bible, Vanderbilt U., Nashville, 1989—; vis. prof. Hebrew U., Jerusalem, 1973, U. Chgo., 1975, 81, Strasbourg U., 1975-76, Brown U., Providence, R.I., 1985, U. Otago, New Zealand, 1986, U. South Africa, 1986, Vanderbilt U., 1987-88; lectr. Princeton U., 1962-63, Union Theol. Sem., 1963; Currie lectr. Austin Theol. Sem., 1964; Guggenheim Meml. fellow for study Biblical semantics, 1965; Cadbury lectr. Birmingham U., 1969; Croall lectr. Edinburgh U., 1970; Grinfield lectr. on Septuagint, Oxford U., 1974-78; Firth lectr. Nottingham U., 1978; Sprunt lectr. Union Theol. Sem., Richmond, Va., 1982; Schweich lectr., Brit. Acad., 1986; Cole lectr. Vanderbilt U., 1988; Sarum lectr. Oxford U., 1989; Read-Tuckwell lectr. Bristol U., Eng., 1990; Gifford lectr. Edinburgh U., 1991. Served as pilot RNVR (Fleet Air Arm), 1942-45. Fellow Brit. Acad., RAS, SOAS (hon.; mem. governing body 1980-85); mem. Soc. O.T. Studies (pres. 1973), Brit. Assn. Jewish Studies (pres. 1978), Göttingen Acad. Scis. (corr.), Soc. Biblical Lit. U.S.A. (hon.), Norwegian Acad. Sci. and Letters, Swedish Roayl Acad. Sci. Author: The Semantics of Biblical Language, 1961; Biblical Words for Time, 1962; Old and New in Interpretation, 1966; Comparative Philology and the Text of the Old Testament, 1968; The Bible in the Modern World, 1973; Fundamentalism, 1977; The Typology of Literalism, 1979; Explorations in Theology 7: The Scope and Authority of the Bible, 1980; Holy Scripture; Canon, Authority, Criticism, 1983; Beyond Fundamentalism, 1984, Variable Spellings of the Hebrew Bible, 1989; editor Jour. Semitic Studies, 1965-76, Oxford Hebrew Dictionary, 1974-80; contbr. articles to profl. jours. Office: Vanderbilt Div Sch Nashville TN 37240

BARR, ROBERT, theological education administrator. With San Francisco Theol. Sem.; pres. Grad. Theol. Union, Berkeley, Calif., 1988—. Office: Graduate Theol Union 2400 Ridge Rd Berkeley CA 94709

BARR, TERENCE DAVID, clergyman; b. Bristol, Eng., July 17, 1945; s. Reginald William and Doris Lilian (Hand) B.; married, 1969; children: Paul, John, Simon, Ruth, Hannah. Diploma in Mgmt. Studies, Bristol Poly., 1971; MS in Bus. Adminstrn., Bath (Eng.) U., 1980. Ordained Ch. of Eng., 1974. Exec. officer Brit. Civil Service, London and Bristol, 1963-69; higher exec. officer Post Office Corp., Bristol, 1969-76; warden, youth chaplain Legge House Youth Ctr., Swindon, Eng., 1976-79; vicar of Locklease Parish Ch. of St. Mary Magdalane with St. Francis, Bristol, 1979—; vicar St. Andrew's and Bishop's Indsl. Chaplain, Avonmouth, Bristol, 1988—. Mem. governing body Romney Avenue Infant and Jr. Schs., Filton Avenue Jr. Sch., Lockleaze Comprehensive Sch.; chmn. Lockleaze Youth Club, Scout Assn., Bristol, 1980—, Bristol Scout group, 1980—. Fellow Brit. Inst. Mgmt. Mem. Conservative Party. Club: Redwood Lodge Country (Bristol). Lodge: Ind. Order Forresters. Office: St Andrew's Vicarage, St Andrew's Rd, Avonmouth Bristol BS11 9ES, England

BARR, WILLIAM RICHARD, theology educator; b. Enid, Okla., Dec. 12, 1934; s. Robert Lincoln and Barbara Lucile (Will) B.; m. Donna Yvonne Hadwiger, June 8, 1958; children: Gregory Scott, Jennifer Lynn. BA, Okla. State U., 1958; BD, Lexington Theol. Sem., 1961; MA, Yale U., 1963, PhD, 1969. Prof. theology Lexington (Ky.) Theol. Sem., 1964—; pres. Assn. Disciples for Theol. Discussion, 1984-85. Editor Lexington Theol. Quar., 1985—; contbg. author: Classic Themes of Disciples Theology, 1988, Harper's Encyclopedia Religious Education, 1990; contbr. articles to religious jours. Fellow Am. Assn. Theol. Schs.; mem. Am. Acad. Religion, Am. Theol. Soc. Democrat. Mem. Christian Ch. (Disciples of Christ). Office: Lexington Theol Sem 631 S Limestone St Lexington KY 40508

BARRAGAN, LINDA DIANE, religious organization administrator; b. Oct. 14, 1950. BA summa cum laude, Bklyn. Coll., 1974. Ordained to ministry Ch. of Scientology, 1980. Pub. rels. dir. Ch. of Scientology N.Y., N.Y.C., 1974-82, pres., 1980-87, dir. spl. affairs, 1982—, corp. dir., 1980-88. Dir. Task Force on Mental Retardation, N.Y. chpt., N.Y.C., 1974-76; vol. Narconon, N.Y.C., 1977; dir. Am. Citizens for Honesty in Govt., N.Y.C. chpt., 1979-82, Nat. Commn. on Law Enforcement and Social Justice, N.Y.C. chpt., 1976-79. Mem. Internat. Assn. Scientologists. Avocations: walking, reading, cooking, biking, movies. Office: Ch of Scientology NY 227 W 46th St New York NY 10036

BARRENTINE, JIMMY LLOYD, clergyman, missions administrator; b. MaGee, Miss., Oct. 4, 1946; s. Jim David and Mary Christine (Nations) B.; m. Joan Winifred Turnage, Sept. 8, 1967; children—Daniel Wayne, Jenifer Renee. B.A., Miss. Coll., Clinton, 1969; M. Divinity, Southwestern Bapt. Theol. Sem., Ft. Worth, 1972. Ordained clergyman Southern Baptist Ch., 1966. Pastor, Myrtle Springs Bapt. Ch., Hooks, Tex., 1972-75; pastor Fgn. Mission Bd., So. Bapt. Conv., Paraguay, 1975-82; dir. missions Ouachita Baptist Assn., Polk and Sevier counties, Ark., 1982-84; exec. dir. Bowie Bapt. Assn., New Boston, Tex., 1984—. Home: 103 Meadow Dr New Boston TX 75570 Office: Bowie Baptist Assn 412 Hwy 8 N New Boston TX 75570

BARRETT, BRIAN LEE, minister, evangelist; b. Huntington, W.Va., Mar. 30, 1959; s. Stanford Lee and Elizabeth Jean (Price) B.; m. Nina Lynn Dimitroff, May 8, 1982. BTh, Internat. Sem., Plymouth, Fla., 1988; postgrad., Internat. Sem., 1988—. Ordained to ministry Ch. of Christ, 1981. Evangelist Ch. of Christ, West Hamlin, W.Va., 1978-79, Buffalo, 1980-81; pulpit min., evangelist Ch. of Christ, Hamlin, W.Va., 1981—; officer in charge U.S. P.O., Woodville, W.Va., 1989—. Editor Sword of the Spirit jour., 1981-86. Vol. fireman Hamlin Fire Dept., 1976-83; emergency med. technician Lincoln Vol. Ambulance Svc., Hamlin, 1978-80; fund raiser Ohio Valley Coll., Parkersburg, W.Va., 1989-90, Lincoln Primary Care Ctr., Hamlin, 1989-90. Home: 516 May St Hamlin WV 25523 Office: Ch of Christ 8041 Vine Ave Hamlin WV 25523 *Each day our world seems to become smaller, while at the same time more complex. It should be the goal of each of us to find the path that leads to eternal perfection for ourselves and those we meet. Together we can overcome the shortcomings that plague our world. If we let God lead.*

BARRETT, CHARLES D., religion educator, minister; b. Ninety-Six, S.C., June 24, 1933; s. James Anderson and Helen Mae (Reid) B.; m. Sally Gay Cross, Aug. 20, 1966; children: Sandra Cross, Robert Christopher. AB, Wofford Coll., 1955; BD, Emory U., 1959; PhD, Drew U., 1968. Ordained to ministry United Meth. Ch. Pastor Epworth United Meth. Ch., Rock Hill, S.C., 1954-56, Malden United Meth. Charge, Malden-on-Hudson, N.Y., 1962-63, Catawba-Van Wyck (S.C.) United Meth. Charge, 1963-66; prof. religion Wofford Coll., Spartanburg, S.C., 1966—, Peter Hendrix chair, 1989; mem. bd. edn. S.C. conf. United Meth. Ch., 1990—. Author: Understanding the Christian Faith, 1980. Cubmaster local chpt. Cub Scouts div. Boy Scouts Am.; chair bd. dirs. Spartanburg Pastoral Counseling Ctr., 1988-90. Dempster fellow United Meth. Bd. Edn., 1959-62, Lilly fellow, 1959-62. Mem. S.C. Acad. Religion (past pres.), Alston Wilkes Soc. (past pres. Spartanburg County chpt.). Office: Wofford Coll N Church St Spartanburg SC 29303

BARRETT, JOHN CHARLES ALLANSON, minister; b. King's Lynn, Norfolk, Eng., June 8, 1943; s. Leonard W. A. and Marjorie J. (Hares) B.; m. Sally Elisabeth Hatley, Aug. 12, 1967; children: James, Rachel. BA in Econs. with honors, U. Newcastle Upon Tyne, Eng., 1965; BA in Theol. with honors, Fitzwilliam Coll., Cambridge, Eng., 1967, MA, 1969. Ordained to ministry Meth. Ch., 1970. Chaplain, lectr. Westminster Coll., Oxford, Eng., 1968-69; asst. tutor Wesley Coll., Bristol, Eng., 1969-71; pastor Werrington Meth. Ch., Stoke on Trent, Eng., 1971-73; chaplain, head of religious studies Kingswood Sch., Bath, Eng., 1973-83; headmaster Kent Coll., Pembury, Eng., 1983-90; leadmaster The Leys Sch., Cambridge, Eng., 1990—; trustee Epworth Old Rectory, 1986—. Author: Family Worship, 1982, Methodist Education in Britian, 1989, co-author: A New Collection of Prayers, 1983; contbr. articles to profl. jours. Mem. World Meth. Coun. (exec. com. 1981—, sec. British com. 1986—, chmn. edn. com. 1991—), Rotary. Home and Office: The Leys Sch, Cambridge CB2 2AD, England

BARRETT, JOHN VICTOR, minister, soloist, music educator; b. Long Beach, Calif., Sept. 16, 1952; s. Charles Wayne Barrett and Elizabeth Jeanette (Lewis) Egan; m. Sue Michele Simcox, July 10, 1976; 1 child, Jonathan Isaiah. AA in Music, Cerritos Coll., 1973; MusB, Calif. State U., Long Beach, 1976, MA in Music, 1983; MDiv, Fuller Theol. Sem., 1988. Ordained to ministry Ch. of the Nazarene, 1991. Assoc. pastor Ventura (Calif.) 1st Bapt. Ch., 1976-77; min. music 1st. Bapt. Ch., Novato, Calif., 1977-78, Cedar Hill, Tex., 1978-79; intern 1st. Bapt. Ch., Downey, Calif., 1979-81; min. music Puyallup (Wash.) Ch. of the Nazarene, 1984-88; assoc. pastor Highlands Community Ch., Renton, Wash., 1988-89; min. music Nazarene Ch., Port Orchard, Wash., 1990-91, Cen. Nazarene Ch., Dallas, 1991—; spl. svcs. adminstr. Assn. Lexicon Music, Inc., Newberry Park, Calif., 1981-84; ch. growth cons. Barrett Growth Enterprises, Stanwood, Wash., 1989-90. Republican. Avocations: softball, computers, baseball, composing. Home: 4729 Chilton Dr Dallas TX 75227

BARRETT, LOIS YVONNE, minister; b. Enid, Okla., Nov. 9, 1947; d. Hugh Preston and Audrey Lucille (Wilson) B.; m. Thomas Bruce Mierau, June 26, 1977; children: Barbara, Susanna, John. BA, U. Okla., 1969; MDiv, Mennonite Bibl. Sem., 1983; postgrad., Union Grad. Sch., Cin., 1989—. Ordained to Christian ministry, 1985. Assoc. editor The Mennonite, Newton, Kans., 1971-77; editor The House Ch. newsletter, Wichita, Kans., 1978-80, 83-85; instr. Great Plains Sem. Edn. Prog., North Newton, Kans., 1985, 90; co-pastor Mennonite Ch. of the Servant, Wichita, Kans., 1983—; mem. exec. coun. Inst. Mennonite Studies, Elkhart, Ind., 1983—; mem. ecumenical peace theology working group Mennonite Cen. Com., Akron, Pa., 1988—; writer Inter-Mennonite Confession of Faith com., Elkhart, 1988—; editorial com. Mennonite Ency. V, 1985-87. Author: The Vision and the Reality, 1983, Building the House Church, 1986, The Way God Fights, 1987, Doing What is Right, 1989. Convener Chs. United for Peacemaking, Wichita, 1986, 88-89, bd. dirs., 1983-90; pres. Midtown Citizens Assn., 1977-78; mem. Citizens Participation Orgn., 1977-80. Recipient Am. Bible Soc. award, 1983. Mem. Phi Beta Kappa. Home: 1508 Fairview Wichita KS 67203 Office: Mennonite Ch of the Servant 1505 Fairview Wichita KS 67203

BARRETT, ROBERT DULANEY, minister; b. Hamilton County, Tex., Jan. 29, 1935; s. J.B. and Mary Oleta (Geeslin) B.; m. Cora Joan Arnold, Sept. 4, 1954 (div. Dec. 1979); children: Lydia, Robert, Suzanna; m. Susan Elizabeth Daley, Feb. 15, 1980; 1 child, Cari Elizabeth. BA, McMurry U., Abilene, Tex., 1956; ThM, So. Meth. U., 1959, MST, 1960, D of Ministry, 1975. Ordained to ministry United Meth. Ch. as elder, 1959. Campus min., univ. chaplain, pastor various chs., 1954-83; pastor Travis St. United Meth. Ch., LaGrange, Tex., 1983-85; pastor 1st United Meth. Ch., Goldthwaite, Tex., 1985-88, Lockhart, Tex., 1988-90; exec. dir. Sacramento (N.Mex.) Meth. Assembly, 1991—; dir. cons. and edn. Pecan Valley Mental Health-Mental Retardation Region, Stephenville, Tex., 1980-82. Contbr. articles to mags. and newsletters. Del. county Dem. caucus, N.Mex., Okla.; active numerous civic orgns. Recipient Appreciation award Dona Ana County

Counseling Program. Mem. Am. Camping Assn., Christian Camping Internat., Coun. on Ch. Revitalization (cert. lay pastoral care tng.), Johnson Inst. (cert. chem. dependency). Home and Office: PO Box 8 Sacramento NM 88347-0008

BARRON, EDWARD CARROLL, minister; b. Parkersburg, W.Va., Dec. 6, 1939; s. Edward Carroll and Elsie Irene (Noland) B.; m. Sue Wright, Jan. 19, 1963; children: Scott Edward, Carroll Sue, Tracie Gayle. BA, Mars Hill (N.C.) Coll., 1972; postgrad., Southeastern Bapt. Theol. Sem., Wake Forest, N.C., 1972-75. Ordained to ministry, Bapt. Ch. Youth/edn. minister Beverly Hill Bapt. Ch., Asheville, N.C., 1970-72, Tabernacle Bapt. Ch., Raleigh, N.C., 1972-75; pastor Emanuel Bapt. Ch., Kinston, N.C., 1975-78; minister youth North Trenholm Bapt. Ch., Columbia, S.C., 1978-84; pastor Edgewood Bapt. Ch., Candler, N.C., 1984—; counselor in pvt. practice, Asheville; substitute tchr. Buncombe County Schs.; ch. tng. dir. Buncombe Assn., Asheville. Foster parent trainer Luth. Family Svcs. Mem. Southeastern Child Care Assn. Home: 789 1/2 Sand Hill Rd Asheville NC 28856 Office: Edgewood Bapt Ch Route 6 Box 115 Candler NC 28715-9806

BARRON, EUGENE CLYDE, minister; b. St. Louis, Aug. 23, 1952; s. Clyde Eugene and Marjorie Eileen (Adkins) B.; m. Karen Marie Deppe, May 26, 1973; children: Michael Joel, Jonathan Luke. Student, Southwest Mo. Bapt. U., Bolivar, 1970-71, U. Mo., 1971-73, Ozark Christian Coll., Joplin, Mo., 1973-79. Minister Wyandotte (Okla.) Christian Ch., 1973-74, North Joplin Christian Ch., 1974-79; sr. pastor Littleton (Colo.) Christian Ch., 1979—; pres. Front Range Evangelizers, Golden, Colo., 1982-86, Colo. Ch. Builders Club, Colorado Springs, 1990-93, Denver Area Christian Ministers, Thornton, Colo., 1990-91; bd. dirs. Colo. Christian Campus Ministries, Ft. Collins and Greely, Colo. Author: (study guide) The Lamp, 1986; contbg. author: The Mind of Christ, 1982; contbr. articles to religious jours. Coach/mgr. Little League Baseball, Littleton, 1984-91; referee-soccer Littleton Soccer Assn., 1990-91; follow-up coord. Mile Hi Billy Graham Crusade, Denver, 1986; assoc. Am. Rehab. Ministries, Joplin, 1976—. Avocations: softball, basketball, snow skiing, reading.

BARRON, GROVER CLEVELAND, III, bishop; b. Birmingham, Ala., Apr. 17, 1948; s. Grover Cleveland Jr. and Annie Francies (Wilkinson) B.; m. Deborah Kay Falknor, June 6, 1967; children: Gary Gurnade, Dawn Desiree. AS in Law, So. Ill. U., 1981, BSBA, 1982. Ordained minister, 1975. Chief of police Village of Energy, Ill., 1979-82; cons. security, law enforcement Pacific Intelligence, Costa Mesa, Calif., 1982-84; corp. office mgr. Ft. Lauderdale (Fla.) Rescue Tabernacle, Inc., 1984-88; pres. Wings of Love Ministries, Phoenix, 1986—; pastor Calvary Apostolic Ch., Decatur, Ill., 1988-89; acct. Pace Setters Seminars, 1990-91; bishop River of Live Tabernacle, Phoenix, 1991—; dist. sec., treas. Internat. Ministerial Assn., Ft. Lauderdale, 1985-88; acct. Pace Setters Seminars, 1990-91; evangelist, tchr. Author: Becoming a Builder for God, 1988, Love Must be Shown, 1989. Trustee Village of Energy, Ill., 1984. With U.S. Army, 1973-79. Mem. Internat. Ministerial Assn., Apostolic World Christian Fellowship. Republican. Home: 4520 E Baseline #1062 # 1062 Phoenix AZ 85040

BARROS, ANTHONY EUGENE, minister; b. Trinidad, Colo., June 5, 1950; s. Tony Eugene and Josephine (Garcia) B.; m. Jeanette Lynn Clark; children: Bryan Micahel, Ashlie Dawn, Jeffrey Scott. BA in Polit. Sci., Adams State Coll., 1972; postgrad., U. Colorado Springs, 1972-76, U. Colo., 1978-79; MA in Adminstrn., U. Wyo., 1981. Ordained to ministry So. Bapt. Conv., 1981. Tchr. Harrison Sch. Dist., Colorado Springs, Colo., 1972-73; dean of students Harrison Sch. Dist., Colorado Springs, 1973-82; assoc. pastor Circle Dr. Bapt. Ch., Colorado Springs, 1982-83, First Bapt. Ch., Woodward, Okla., 1983—; cons., speaker in field. Author: Inter Disciplinary Schooling, 1978. Medic Walk for Mankind, Colorado Springs, 1979. Mem. Am. Assn. Counselors, Mat. Assn. Ch. Adminstrs, So. Bapt. Conv. Assn. Ch. Adminstrs. Republican. Avocations: running, aerobics. Home: PO 5005 Woodward CO 73803 Office: First Bapt-Woodward 202 E Hanks Trail Woodward CO 73801

BARROW, DAME RUTH NITA, governor-general. Educated, Columbia U., U. Toronto, Edinburgh U. Mem. various staff, teaching and adminstrv. posts in nursing and pub. health Barbados and Jamaica, 1940-56; prin. nursing officer Jamaica, 1956-62; nursing advisor Pan Am. Health Orgn., 1967-71; assoc. dir. Christian med. commn. WCC, Geneva, 1971-75, dir., 1975-80; health cons. WHO, 1981-86; perm. rep. UN, 1986-90; gov.-gen. of Barbados, 1990—. Pres. World YWCA, 1975-83, Internat. Coun. for Adult Edn., 1982, WCC, 1983; participant numerous internat. confs. on population, health and women; mem. Commonwealth Group Eminent Persons on S.A., 1986. Office: Office of Gov Gen, Bridgetown Barbados

BARRY, COLMAN JAMES, religious educator; b. Lake City, Minn., May 29, 1921; s. John and Frances (O'Brien) B. B.A., St. John's U., 1942; M.A., Cath. U. Am., 1950, Ph.D., 1953. Joined Order St. Benedict, 1942; ordained priest Roman Cath. Ch., 1947. Sec. Am. Benedictine Rev.; mem. faculty St. John's U., 1953—, prof. history, 1953-64, pres., 1964-71; exec. dir. Inst. Spirituality, 1977-82; pres. Hill Monastic Manuscript Library, 1982; summer tchr. San Raphael (Calif.) Coll., 1956-59, Cath. U. Am., 1959-64, dean religious studies, 1973-77; vis. prof. ch. history Yale U., 1973; Commn. Jours. Acad. and Profl., 1958; chmn. Nat. Com. Edn. for Ecumenism, 1965; commr. N. Central Assn. Colls., 1966; pres. Assn. Minn. Colls., 1967; Penfield fellow in, Germany, 1950, Soc. Religion in Higher Edn. fellow, 1972. Author: The Catholic Church and German Americans, 1953, The Catholic University of America, IV, 1950, Worship and Work, 1956, Catholic Minnesota, 1958, Readings in Church History, 3 vols., 1959-65, American Nuncio: Cardinal Aloisius Muench, 1969, Upon These Rocks: Catholics in the Bahamas, 1973, Readings in Church History, 1985, A Sense of Place: Saint John's of Collegeville, 1987, A Sense of Place II: Benedictines of Collegeville, 1990; editor: Benedictine Studies, 1958—; contbr. numerous articles to profl. and religious publs. Mem. Am. Cath. Hist. Assn. (pres. 1976). Home: St John's Abbey Collegeville MN 56321

BARSAMIAN, KHAJAG SARKIS, primate; b. Arapkir, Turkey, July 4, 1951; came to U.S., 1977; s. Ohannes and Bulbul Borsumoglu. Student, Sem. of Armenian Patriarchate, Jerusalem, 1971; MDiv, Gen. Theol. Sem., N.Y., 1980, DD (hon.), 1991; MA, Oriental Inst. of Gregorian U., Rome, 1984, postgrad., 1984—. Ordained to ministry Armenian Ch. Asst. dean Sem. of Patriarchate of Jerusalem, 1971-74; canon sacrist Diocese of Armenian Ch., N.Y.C., 1977-80, vicar gen., dir. ecumenical office, 1984-90, o,ate, 1990—; mem. N.C.C. Governing Bd., N.Y.C. Contbr. articles to ednl. and scholarly jours. Mem. Internat. Soc. Liturgical Studies, Religion in Am. Life (bd. dirs., v.p.), Appeal of Conscience Found. (bd. dirs.), Am. Bible Soc. (bd. dirs.). Office: Diocese of the Armenian Ch 630 Second Ave New York NY 10016-4885

BARSKY, BERNARD, religious organization executive. Exec. dir. World Coun. Synagogues, N.Y.C. Office: World Coun Synagogues 155 Fifth Ave New York NY 10010*

BARTA, JAMES OMER, priest, psychology educator, academic administrator; b. Fairfax, Iowa, Oct. 22, 1931; s. Omer J. and Bertha (Brecht) B. BA, Loras Coll., 1952; Sacrae Theologiae Licentiatus, Gregorian U., Rome, 1956; PhD, Fordham U., 1962. Ordained priest Roman Cath. Ch., 1955. Prof. psychology Loras Coll., Dubuque, Iowa, 1957—, v.p. acad. affairs, 1977-87, pres., 1987—. Mem. Am. Psychol. Assn., Iowa Psychol. Assn. Office: Loras Coll Office of Pres Dubuque IA 52004-0178

BARTA, KAREN ANN, theology educator; b. Two Rivers, Wis., Sept. 1, 1939; d. Joseph Frank Barta and Sylvia Olive (Jacobosky) Siehr. BS in Edn., Marian Coll., Fond du Lac, Wis., 1964; MA in Theology, Marquette U., Milw., 1972, PhD in N.T., 1979. Asst. prof. St. Francis Coll., Loretto, Pa., 1978-81; vis. asst. prof. Sacred Heart Sch. Theology, Hales Corners, Wis., 1981-82, U. Dubuque (Iowa) Theol. Sem., 1983; assoc. prof. dept. theology Seattle U., 1983—; teaching asst. Marquette U., Milw., 1970-75. Author: The Gospel of Mark, 1988; contbr. articles to profl. jours. NEH grantee, St. Paul, 1965. Mem. Cath. Bibl. Assn., Soc. Bibl. Lit. (mem. coun. 1989-92), Pacific Northwest AAR/SBL (prs. 1987-88, sec.-treas. 1988-91). Democrat. Home: 701 N 72d St Seattle WA 98103 Office: Seattle U Seattle WA 98122

BARTEE, RUSSELL FLOYD, minister; b. Austin, Tex., Nov. 22, 1954; s. Malcolm Levere and Peggy Jeanne (Page) B.; m. Ellen Elaine Elliott, Aug. 16, 1975; children: Kristin, Jonathan, Erin. BS, Okla. Christian Univ., 1976; MEd, Univ. North Tex., 1988. Minister Lackland Ch. of Christ, San Antonio, 1976-78, Pleasant Ridge Ch. of Christ, Arlington, Tex., 1980-84, Prestoncrest Ch. of Christ, Dallas, 1984-88, Fairfax (Va.) Ch. of Christ 1988—. Office: Fairfax Church of Christ 3901 Rugby Rd Fairfax VA 22033

BARTELL, LEE, entrepreneur, lawyer; b. Milw., 1910; s. Benjamin and Lena (Beznor) B.; m. Ina Berginn, Jan. 13, 1934; children: Michael, Rusti, Richard. Student, Milw. State Tchrs. Coll., 1932, Marquette U., 1933; LLB, U. Wis., 1936. Bar: Wis. 1936, Calif. 1960. With Wis. Atty. Gen. Office; counsel Wis. Devel. Authority; trial atty. U.S. Govt.; founder Bartell Broadcasting Corp.; former pres. Bartell Media Corp., Sta. KCBQ, Inc.; sec., bd. dirs. Bartell Broadcasters, Inc., Bartell Broadcasters N.Y., Inc.; pres. McDodd Corp., Interstate 8 Hotel, Inc.; gen. ptnr. Bartell Hotels; sec. Sta. KMJC, San Diego. Editor Wis. Law Rev. Lt. (j.g.) USNR, 1943-44. Mem. Am. Legion (past post comdr.), Order of Coif. Address: 4875 N Harbor Dr San Diego CA 92106

BARTH, EUGENE HOWARD, minister, educator; b. Phila., Feb. 10, 1913; s. John Benedict and Pauline Marie (Reuber) B.; A.B., Albright Coll., 1937; B.D., Oberlin U., 1940, S.T.M., 1941; A.M., Princeton U., 1953, Ph.D., 1956; postgrad. Yale Divinity Sch., summer 1937, Union Theol. Sem., summer 1938; m. Eleanor Richards, July 14, 1939; children—Lenore, Karen, Frederic, George, Margaret. Ordained to ministry Methodist Ch., 1941; pastor Sullivan (Ohio) Congl. Ch., 1939-41, Pearl St. Evang. Ch., Lancaster, Pa., 1941-46; asst. prof. Albright Coll., Reading, Pa., 1946-49, asso. prof., 1949-56, prof. religion and philosophy, 1956—, chmn. dept. religion, 1965-78, Pfeiffer chair Religion, 1949—, faculty chmn., 1967-76; scholar in residence Jewish Community Center, Reading. Recipient Lindback Found. award, 1965; Danforth fellow, 1956-59; Woodrow Wilson scholar, 1955-56. Mem. Soc. Bibl., Lit. and Exegesis, Am. Oriental Soc., Am. Soc. of Christian Ethics. Club: Torch. Author: History of Albright Coll., 1956, The Ethics of F.D. Maurice, 1965, Festschrift to Honor Dr. F.W. Gingrich, 1972, Discovery and Promise, 1989. Home: 2122 Highland West Lawn PA 19609 Office: Albright Coll Reading PA 19604

BARTH, KARL LUTHER, seminary president; b. Milw., Nov. 7, 1924; s. G. Christian and Louise A. (Schneeman) B.; m. Jean L. Kelly, June 8, 1947; children: Linda, Karl, Laurel, Kurt, Lisa. B.A., Concordia Sem., 1945, M.Div., 1947; D.D. (hon.), Concordia Theol. Sem., 1975. Ordained to minstry, Lutheran Ch., 1947. Asst. pastor First English Lutheran Ch., New Orleans, 1947-50; pastor Trinity Evan. Lutheran Ch., Centralia, Ill., 1950-52, St. Paul's Lutheran Ch., West Allis, Wis., 1956-70; pres. So. Wis. Dist. Lutheran Ch. Mo. Synod, 1970-82, Concordia Sem., St. Louis, 1982—. Contbr. articles to profl. jours. Vice pres. So. Wis. dist. Lutheran Ch., Mo. Synod, 1966-70; chmn. Com. on Theology and Ch. Relations, St. Louis, 1974-82; denominational rep. Div. Theol. Studies Lutheran Council U.S.A., N.Y.C., 1975-81; mem. adv. bd. Wis. Citizens Concerned for Life, 1976-82. Republican. Home: 1 N Seminary Terr Clayton MO 63105 Office: 801 De Mun Ave Clayton MO 63105

BARTH, MARKUS KARL, theology educator; b. Safenwil, Aargau, Switzerland, Oct. 6, 1915; came to U.S., 1953; s. Karl and Nelly B. (Hoffmann) B.; m. Rose Marie Oswald, May 15, 1940; children: Peter, Anna, Ruth, Lukas, Rose Marie. Verbi Divini Minister, U. Basel, Switzerland, 1939; Dr.Theol., U. Gottingen, Germany, 1947. Ordained to ministry , 1940. Minister, Evangelical Reformed Ch., Baselland, 1940-53; guest prof. U. Dubuque, Iowa, 1953-55; assoc. prof. U. Chgo., 1956-63; prof. Pitts. Theol. Sem., 1963-72; prof. N.T., U. Basel, 1973-85. Author: Der Augenzeuge, 1947, Die Taufe - ein Sakrament?, 1951, The Broken Wall, 1959, Conversation with the Bible, 1964; Ephesians, 2 vols., 1974, Jesus the Jew, Israel and the Palestinians, 1978, The People of God, 1983, Rediscovering the Lord's Supper, 1988; co-editor religious jours., Chgo., Phila., Richmond, Va., 1956-73. Mem. ch. adv. bds. in U.S. and Switzerland. Served in inf. Swiss Army, 1936-39. Mem. Soc. Bibl. Lit., Soc. N.T. Studies, Karl-Barth-Stiftung. Evangelical Reformed Ch. Home: Inzlinger Strasse 275, BS CH 4125 Riehen Switzerland

BARTHELL, RONALD LEWIS, religious organization administrator; b. Spokane, Wash., Feb. 25, 1935; s. Robert Lewis Barthell; m. Marlys Cathrine Frank, Aug. 4, 1957; children: Robin Lou, Randy Lee. BA in Religion, Whitworth Coll., 1985; postgrad., Calif. Theol., Fresno, 1986. Elder (tchr.) Open Bible Standard Chs., Spokane, 1975-81, First A.G., Spokane, 1981-88; dir. Full Gospel Bus. Men's Fellowship Internat. Wash.-Idaho, Cheney, Wash., 1988—; owner, mgr. Hacienda Rentals, Cheney, 1986—; pres. Gideons Internat. Cen. Camp, Spokane, 1987; missionary Philippines Full Gospel Bus. Men's Fellowship Internat., 1990. Staff sgt. USAF, 1952-56. Mem. Soc. for Pentecostal Studies, Rotary. Republican. Home: Hacienda Motel Apt Mobile & Mini Storage W 304 1st Cheney WA 99004

BARTHOLD, LAUREN SWAYNE, lay worker; b. Wilmington, Del., Aug. 30, 1965; d. John Bancroft III and Ann (Carroll) Swayne; m. Stephen Gregory Barthold, July 8, 1989. BA in Polit. Communication cum laude, George Washington U., 1987; postgrad., Regent Coll., Vancouver, B.C., Can., 1990—. Counselor, adminstrv. asst. Crisis Pregnancy Ctr., Washington, 1987-88; Am. U., No. Va. Community Coll. campus staff min. Inter Varsity, Madison, Wis., 1987-90. Mem. Phi Beta Kappa. Avocations: acoustic guitar, cycling. Home: 3670 Oak St, Vancouver, BC Canada V6H 2M2

BARTHOLOMEW, CARROLL EUGENE, minister; b. Brookford, N.C., Feb. 10, 1935; s. Gerald Fredrick and Clarissa (Cloninger) B.; m. Jane Harriet Young, June 25, 1961; children: Gerald Lee, Nathaniel Thomas. BS in Physics and Math., Lenoir-Rhyne Coll., 1960; BD (with honors), Lancaster Theol. Sem., 1963, MDiv, 1975, D of Ministry, 1982. Ordained to ministry United Ch. of Christ, 1963. Pastor Brick United Ch. of Christ, Whitsett, N.C., 1963-66; commd. lt. (j.g.) USN, 1966, advanced through grades to comdr., 1978; detailed to Field Med. Sch., USMC Base, Camp Pendleton, Calif., 1966, 3d Marine Div., Republic of Vietnam, 1966-67, Naval Air Sta., Cecil Field, Fla., 1967-69; various assignments, 1969-1977; detailed to 2d Marine Div., Camp Lejeune, N.C., 1977-79, Naval Dist. Washington, 1979-81, Naval Mil. Personnel Command, 1981-83; served on USS Mt. Whitney, 1983-85; detailed to Naval Air Sta., Oceana, Virginia Beach, Va., 1985-87, 88-90, COMSERVGRU 2, 1987-88; ret., 1990; pastor St. Luke's United Ch. of Christ, Salisbury, N.C., 1990—; Mem. So. Conf. United Ch. of Christ Christian Edn. Commn.; bd. dirs. Franklinton Ctr. at Bricks Inc. Author: A Program of Training and a Training Manual for Religious Lay Leaders Within the United States Marine Corps, 1982. Vol. chaplain Rowan Meml. Hosp. Sgt. USMC, 1953-56. Decorated Vietnam Svc. Medal with Bronze Star, Combat Action Ribbon; Gallantry Cross (Republic of Vietnam). Mem. Rowan Ministerium, Salisbury Rowan Ministerium, Civitan. Democrat. Office: St Luke's United Ch of Christ PO Box 496 Granite Quarry NC 28072

BARTHOLOMEW, DAVID CLEAVER, minister; b. Beloit, Wis., May 17, 1960; s. Robert Marling and Barbara Katherine (Melvin) B.; m. Dena Cleaver, Aug. 22, 1987. BA, So. Meth. U., 1982; M of Pub. Affairs, U. Tex., 1984; MDiv, Yale U., 1988. Intern office of chaplain Yale U., New Haven, 1985-86, Congl. Ch. Austin, Tex., 1986-87; chaplain Mt. San Antonio Gardens Retirement Ctr., Claremont, Calif., 1990; transcriber works of Jonathon Edwards Yale U., 1987-89; leader adult Christian edn. Button-Gwinnette United Ch. of Christ, Atlanta, 1988-89; coord. coll. fellowship Claremont United Ch. of Christ, 1989-91. Mem. Soc. Bibl. Lit. Home: 106 N Crossing Way Decatur GA 30033

BARTHOLOMEW, WILLIAM LEE, minister; b. Akron, Ohio, July 29, 1950; s. Richard Ray and Polly Ann (Campbell) B.; m. Karen Marie Corbitt, Aug. 2, 1969; children: Laura Marie Bartholomew Stimmel, Virginia Lee. BA, Mt. Vernon Nazarene Coll., 1982; Master, Methodist Theological Sch., Delaware, 1986. Ordained to ministry United Meth. Ch. Pastor United Meth. Ch., Warsaw, Ohio, 1977-86, Cleve., 1986-89, Sunbury, Ohio, 1989—. Author: The True Vine, 1988, Charting My Faith Journey, 1990. Councilman Village of Nellie, 1979-83; Trustee Old Bklyn Devel. Corp., Cleve., 1987-88. Recipient Peace award Meth. Theol. Sch. in Ohio, Delaware, 1985; Rescue Efforts award Mexican Red Cross, Mexico City, 1985. Republican. Avocations: physical fitness, backpacking, swimming, woodworking. Office: Sunbury United Meth Ch PO Box 248 Sunbury OH 43074

BARTKOWIAK, DANIEL JAMES, minister; b. Stevens Point, Wis., Dec. 4, 1950; s. Edmund Albert and Olga Collette (Van de Loop) B.; m. Kathleen Ann Cosgrove, June 9, 1973; children: Jennifer, Kara, Luke. BA, North Cen. Bible Coll., 1979; MA, Ashland Theol. Sem., 1988. Ordained to ministry Assemblies of God, 1980, Ch. of Saviour, 1989. Christian edn. dir., youth dir. Assembly of God, Apple Valley, Minn., 1976-78; assoc. pastor, youth Assembly of God, Stevens Point, 1979-83, Worthington, Minn., 1983-86; assoc. pastor, youth Ch. of the Saviour, Wooster, Ohio, 1986—; free counseling practice, singles support group & min. coord Ch. of the Saviour, Wooster, 1986—. Office: Church of the Saviour 480 Fry Rd Wooster OH 44691

BARTLETT, ALLEN LYMAN, JR., bishop; b. Birmingham, Ala., Sept. 22, 1929; s. Allen Lyman and Edith Buell (West) B.; m. Jerriette L. Kohlmeier, Dec. 28, 1957; children: Christopher, Stephen, Catherine. BA, U. of South, 1951, D.D. (hon.), 1988; M.Div., Va. Theol. Sem., 1958, D.Min., 1980, D.D. (hon.), 1986. Ordained to ministry Episcopal Ch. 1958, ordained priest 1959. Vicar St. James' Ch., Alexander City, Ala., 1958-61, St. Barnabas Ch., Roanoke, Ala., 1958-61; rector Zion Ch., Charles Town, W.Va., 1961-70; dean Christ Ch. Cathedral, Louisville, 1970-85; ordained bishop, 1986; bishop coadjutor Diocese of Pa., Phila., 1986-87, bishop, 1987—; dep. Episcopal Gen. Convention, 1964-67, 73-85; mem. exec. coun. Episcopal Ch., 1979-85. Lt. (j.g.) USN, 1952-55. Mem. Racquet Club, Downtown Club, Phi Beta Kappa. Democrat. Avocations: tennis, hiking. Home: 316 S 10th St Philadelphia PA 19107 Office: Episcopal Diocese Pa 240 S 4th St Philadelphia PA 19106

BARTLETT, WILLIAM CLAIR, minister; b. Mpls., May 2, 1950; s. William M. and Shirley A. (Ness) B.; m. Cynthia A. Hinsdale, May 18, 1975; children: Kari, Derek. BA magna cum laude, St. Olaf Coll., 1972; MDiv, Northwestern Luth. Theol. Sem., St. Paul, 1976; DMin, Luth. Sch. Theology, Chgo., 1988. Ordained to ministry Luth. Ch., 1976. Pastor Arlington Hills Luth. Ch., St. Paul, 1976-78, Living Lord Luth. Ch., Bartlett, Ill., 1978-82, All Saints Luth. Ch., Phoenix, 1982-90, Luth. Ch. of the Cross, Laguna Hills, Calif., 1990—; task force mem. Evangelism Task Force, Pacifica Synod, 1990—. Office: Luth Ch of the Cross 24231 El Toro Rd Laguna Hills CA 92653

BARTLETT, WILLIAM DONALD, JR., religion educator; b. Clarksburg, W.VA., Oct. 12, 1950; s. William Donald Sr. and Mary Louvina (Shawhan) B.; m. Gloria Ann Cole, June 4, 1972; children: Angela Marie, William Derek, William Brandon. Diploma, Appalachian Bible Coll., 1971; BA, Cedarville Coll., 1973; MA, W.Va. Coll. Grad. Studies, Institute, 1984; postgrad., Va. Poly. and State U., 1990—. Pastor First Bapt. Ch., Mantua, N.J., 1973-77; pastor Bethany Bapt. Ch., St. Albans, W.Va., 1977-78; adminstr. instr. Appalachian Bible Coll., Bradley, W.Va., 1978-83; field edn. dir./asst. prof. Appalachian Bible Coll., Bradley, 1983—; pres. Appalachian Bible Coll., 1977-79. Chmn. Greater Beckley Christian Sch. Bd., Prosperity, W.Va., 1988-89. With USNG, 1980-87, USAR, 1987-90. Mem. Am. Assn. for Counseling and Devel., Nat. Career Devel. Assn., Assn. for Religious and Value Issues in Counseling, Assn. for Christian Svc. Pers., Delta Epsilon Chi. Republican. Avocations: reading, water skiing, hunting, fishing. Office: Appalachian Bible Coll Box ABC Bradley WV 25818

BARTLEY, KURT DOUGLAS, lay worker; b. Jasper, Ind., Mar. 16, 1958; s. Theodore Joseph and Dorothy Mae (Hopf) B.; m. Catherine Anne Eck, June 30, 1990. BS in Indsl. Engring., Purdue U., 1981; MA in Christian Community Devel., Regis Coll., 1984. youth ministry trainer Jesuit Internat. Vols., Belize, 1986-88; diocesan dir. for youth ministry devel. Mem. Nat. Fedn. Catholic Youth Ministry. Office: Cath Community Svcs 29 W Kiowa St Colorado Springs CO 80903

BARTON, CHARLES ANDREWS, JR., clergyman; b. Memphis, Apr. 25, 1916; s. Charles Andrews and Martha Lee (Stewart) B.; m. Jane Irby Teague, Aug. 19, 1950; children: Martha, Carol, Stewart, Susan Lee. BS, Rhodes Coll., Memphis, 1937, DD, 1964; MS, NYU, 1939; MDiv, Union Theol. Sem., N.Y.C., 1952. Ordained to ministery United Meth. Ch., 1952. Chief sales engr., wire and cable dept. U.S. Rubber Co., N.Y.C., 1939-47; pastor City Island Ch., N.Y.C., 1952-54, Crawford Meml. Ch., N.Y.C., 1954-56, 1st Ch. Jamaica, N.Y.C., 1956-67, Mt. Kisco Ch., N.Y.C., 1967-73; assoc. exec. dir. United Meth. City Soc., N.Y.C., 1973-84, ret., 1984; v.p. East Calvary Nursery, 1973-84; pres. bd. missions N.Y. Conf. United Meth. Ch., 1968-72, pres. bd. evangelism, 1962-68; pres., bd. dirs. Bklyn. Deaconess Fund, 1973-78, Five Points Mission, 1973-84; bd. dirs., v.p. N.Y. Deaconess Assn., 1973-84. pres., bd. dirs. Chinese Meth. Community Ctr., 1977-84, Anchor House, 1973-84, Harlem Interfaith Counseling Service, 1975-84. Sec. ethics com. Mt. Kisco, 1971-74; chmn. Mt. Kisco Narcotics Guidance Council, 1970-73; mem. Mt. Kisco Park Commn., 1970-73; treas. Religious Com. on N.Y.C. Health Crisis, 1982-84, Capitol Area Ministries, Atlanta, 1984-90; bd. dirs. Habitat for Humanity, Atlanta, 1984—, Wesley Community Ctrs., Atlanta, 1984-90, CALC, Atlanta, 1984—. Served as 1st lt., Signal Corps, U.S. Army, 1942-46. Named Disting. Citizen Mt. Kisco, 1972, Man of Yr., Chinese Meth. Community Center, 1982; Edn. Bldg. at 1st Ch., Jamaica named in his honor, 1982, hall at Wakefield-Grace United Meth. Ch., 1981, swimming pool at Camp Olmsted, Cornwall-on-Hudson, N.Y., 1984. Mem. St. Andrews Soc. (life), Omicron Delta Kappa, Pi Kappa Alpha, Tau Kappa Alpha, Rotary. Democrat. Home: 3945 Back Trails Clarkston GA 30021 *We are plagued with epidemics of drugs, threats of war and a loss of values. The reason is our being out of touch with the transcendent in life, the mysterious other, the realm of spirit.*

BARTON, CHARLES DAVID, religious educator; b. Austin, Tex., Jan. 28, 1954; s. Charles Grady and Hilda Rose (Seely) B.; m. Cheryl Edith Little, Mar. 18, 1978; children: Damaris Ann, Timothy David, Stephen Daniel. Degree in religious edn., Oral Roberts U., 1976. Dir. youth Aledo (Tex.) Christian Ctr., 1974-75, dir. Christian edn., dir. youth, 1977-87, dir. Christian edn., elder, 1987—; dir. youth Jenks (Okla.) 1st Assembly, 1975-76; dir. Christian edn., dir. youth Sheridan Christian Ctr., Tulsa, Okla., 1976-77; pres. Splty. Rsch. Assocs., Inc./Wallbuilders, Aledo, 1987-90. Author: America: To Pray or Not to Pray, 1987, The Myth of Separation, 1988, What Happened in Education?, 1989, The Bulletproof George Washington, 1990. Bd. dirs. Youth Leadership Coun., Cin., 1990; bd. advisors Released Time, Sacramento, Calif., 1987, Nat. Prayer Embassy, Washington, 1988; chmn. Legis. Found., 1991. Recipient Writing award Amy Found., 1989. Republican. Office: Wallbuilders PO Box 397 Aledo TX 76008

BARTON, J. S., religious organization administrator. Dir. World Mission, Anglican Ch. Can., Toronto, Ont. Office: Anglican Ch Can, 600 Jarvis St, Toronto, ON Canada M4Y 2J6*

BARTOW, CHARLES LOUIS, speech educator, minister; b. Somerville, N.J., Nov. 3, 1937; s. Ernest Henry and Elida (Abel) B.; m. Ruth Paula Goetschius, Aug. 22, 1964; children: Emma, Paula Sue, Rebecca. BA, Mich. State U., 1958, MA, 1964; BD, Princeton Theol. Sem., 1963; PhD, NYU, 1971. Ordained to ministry Presbyn. Ch. (U.S.A.), 1963. Asst. in speech Princeton (N.J.) Theol. Sem., 1963-71, Egner prof. speech, 1991—; pastor Presbyn. Ch. Deep Run, Perkasie, Pa., 1974-80; prof. speech and homiletics San Francisco Theol. Sem., San Anselmo, Calif., 1980-91, Grad. Theol. Union, Berkeley, Calif., 1980-91. Author: The Preaching Moment, 1980 (named Book of Yr. Religious Speech Communication Assn. 1980), Effective Speech Communication in Leading Worship, 1988; mem. editorial bd. Homiletic jour., 1975-78; co-founder, mem. editorial bd. Jour. Communication and Religion, 1978-87. Bd. dirs. Mansfield (Pa.) State U. chpt. United Fund, 1973, Bucks County unit Am. Cancer Soc., Doylestown, Pa., 1978-79, Ridge Crest Home for Profoundly Retarded, Perkasie, 1979-80; consumer rep. Health Systems Agy., Pa., 1978-79; trustee San Anselmo Organ Festival, 1984, 87. Mem. Religious Speech Communication Assn. (pres. 1986-87), Acad. Homiletics, Speech Communication Assn., Assn Practical Theology. Office: Princeton Theol Sem Princeton NJ 08542

BARTOW, DAVID WINFIELD, clergyman; b. Goshen, Ind., May 25, 1939; s. Homer English and Mary Elizabeth (Brunk) B.; m. Rebecca Jane Grossnickle, Dec. 24, 1966; children: Christine Kay, Kara Sue. BA in Math. and Physics, Goshen Coll., 1961; BD, Mennonite Bibl. Sem., Elkhart, Ind., 1967, MDiv, 1984. Ordained to ministry Gen. Conf. Mennonite Ch., 1971. Dir. Community Orientation Ctr., Phila., 1967-70; pastor Upper Milford Mennonite Ch., Zionsville, Pa., 1970—; mem. peace and social concerns com. Eastern Dist. Conf. Mennonite Ch., 1970-76, 88—, v.p., 1982-84, pres., 1984-86, call to kingdom commitment's com. Gen. Conf., 1986-89. Contbr articles and book revs. to profl. jours. Home: PO Box 36 Zionsville PA 18092 Office: Upper Milford Mennonite Ch PO Box 36 Zionsville PA 18092

BARTRUFF, BRYCE DUANE, religion educator; b. Lebanon, Oreg., Aug. 24, 1950; s. Bryce Oliver and Harriet Alice (Snyder) B.; m. Katherine Ann Brennan, Aug. 8, 1981; children: Bryce Kevin, Kerri Ann. BS, Warner Pacific Coll., 1974, M of Religion, 1976; PhD, Calif. Grad. Sch. Theology, 1980; MBA, St. Joseph's U., 1985. Dir. of youth Columbia Bible Ch., Portland, Oreg., 1971-73, Moreland Bible Ch., Portland, 1974-76; co-founder, dir. Youth In Action, Portland, 1976-77; admissions counselor Judson Bapt. Coll., Portland, 1978-80; mgr. edn. and tng. Am. Missionary Fellowship, Villanova, Pa., 1980—; deacon Tenth Presbyn. Ch., Phila., 1987—; bd. dirs. Mission to N.Am. Phila. Presbyn. Author: (series) Jesus: Living In My World, 1976, Jesus: Helping Me, 1978, Jesus: Caring for Me, 1979; Insight: Uncommon Sense for Common People, 1974, A Pocket Guide to the Sayings of Jesus, 1976, Personal Prayer and Bible Study Notebook, 1978, also, numerous study guides for employer. Mem. Am. Soc. Tng. and Devel., Am. Soc. Performance and Instrn., Christian Mgmt. Assn., Assn. N.Am. Missions. Home: 13 Creek Rd Sewell NJ 08080 Office: Am Missionary Fellowship 672 Conestoga Rd Box 368 Villanova PA 19085 *It is today's performance that counts. Not past successes or failures. Who am I now and what am I doing today?.*

BARTZ, RICHARD EARL, lay worker, accountant; b. St. Paul, Oct. 2, 1936; s. Michael Nicholas and Florence Viola (Bly) B.; m. Judith Ellen Anderson, June 6, 1961; children: Brenda Ruth, Karla Michelle. Student, St. Paul Bible Coll., 1958-60; BA, Bethel Coll., 1963; grad. diploma, Inst. Fin. Edn. Acct. West Pub. Co., St. Paul, 1981—; treas., sec. Elim Covenant Ch., St. Paul, 1989-91, chmn., 1991—. Mem. Bd. Edn. Minnehaha Acad., Mpls., 1991—. Mem. DBS Upper Midwest User Group (software leader 1989), Minn. Terr. Pioneers, Minn. Hist. Soc. Mem. Evang. Covenant Ch. Home: 1528 Huron St Saint Paul MN 55108-2318 Office: West Pub Co 610 Opperman Dr Eagan MN 55123 *It is amazing how God leads in a person's life. Especially when a person looks back on what appeared to be a dark period and sees that he is much better now because of the apparent trial.*

BARUCH, IZAK ZACHARIAS, religious organization executive, physician; b. Amsterdam, The Netherlands, Nov. 3, 1917; s. Baruch Israel and Morpurgo (Milka) B.; m. Louise Huysman, Sept. 13, 1954 (dec. May 1959); 1 child, Daniel Zecharja; m. Hanny Birnbaum, May 27, 1960; 1 child, Ilya. Degree in medicine, U. Amsterdam, 1946, MD, 1958. Intern Acad. Hosp. Wilhelmina Gasthuis, U. Amsterdam, 1945-46; physician in gen. practice, from 1946; head social dept. Amsterdam Centre for Rheumatic Disease, 1948-73; specialist for phys. medicine and rehab., 1950, specialist in social medicine and pub. health, 1973—; pres. Portugees-Israelietisch Kerkgenootschap, Amsterdam, 1983—; v.p. Ets Haim Libr., Amsterdam, 1980—, Portuguese-Israeli Sem., Amsterdam, 1980—; bd. dirs. Ojec, Amsterdam, 1981—. Author: Medicine in Ancient Israel, 1960, Life of Vesalius, 1962, Guillaume de Baillou, 1965. City councillor of Amsterdam, 1953-70, sr. adv. coun., 1991; M.P. (Dem. Socialist), The Hague, 1971. Decorated Medaille de la reconnaissance française; officer Orange-Nassau (The Netherlands), 1975, resistance-cross, 1981. Home: Gerrit van der Veenstraat 141, 1077 DX Amsterdam The Netherlands Office: Portuguese-Israelite Fedn, Mr Visserplein, 1011 RD Amsterdam The Netherlands

BARWIG, REGIS NORBERT JAMES, priest; b. Chgo., Jan. 16, 1932; s. Ladislas-Joseph and Josepha Agnes (Neugebauer) B. AB, St. Procopius Coll., 1954; postgrad., Georgetown U., 1957, Pontifical Lateran U., Rome, 1959-61. Ordained priest Roman Cath. Ch., 1959. Sec. to abbot of Lisle, 1955-61; sec. gen. Christian Unity Apostolate, 1961-64; founding prior Claremont Priory, Cedarburg, Wis., 1964-67; prior Community of Our Lady, Oshkosh, Wis., 1968—; co-chmn. 1st Festival Faith, Milw., 1966; chmn. Ecumenical Conf. Spiritual and Liturgical Renewal Religious Life, 1969—; mem. Green Bay Diocese Ecumenical Commn., 1970-73; theol. cons. Consortium Perfectae Caritatis, 1974—; preacher, U.S. and Europe; U.S. liaison for beatification of Pope Pius IX, 1975—; assoc. Wanda Landowska Music Ctr., Lakeville, Conn., 1969; bd. dirs. Inter-Cath. Press Agy., N.Y., 1967-72. Author: Changing Habits, 1971, Waiting for Rain, 1975, Reflections on Spiritual Life for Order of Malta, 1982; translator: His Will Alone, 1971, Wanda Landowska Diaries, 1971, Pius XI-A Close-up, 1975, Pius IX-More than a Prophet, 1977, Writings of Blessed Maximilian Maria Kolbe, 1977, Evaluations of the Possibility of Constructing a Christian Ethic on the Assumptions of the Philosophy of Max Scheler, 1982; editor: Conferences of Mother Mary of Jesus, 1968; contbr. articles to religious publs. Decorated bruderschaft Collegio Teutonico, Vatican City, knight comdr. Order Isabel la Catolica, Spain, cross of merit Sovereign Mil. Order of Malta, magistral chaplain, conventual chaplain of honor, prelatial councillor, chief of chaplains Polish Assn., Sovereign Mil. Order of Malta, knight comdr. ecclesiastical grace, Sacred Mil. Constantinian Order of St. George-Bourbon Two Sicilies, chaplain Am. Del. Mem. Selden Soc., Queen Mary Coll., Polish-Am. Assn. Wis. (chaplain 1979—), Polish Arts Club. Home and Office: 2804 Oakwood Ln Oshkosh WI 54904 *From my Roman Catholic faith and my Polish heritage I imbibed early a sense of the importance of Divine Providence in one's life. In this context, then, regret and disappointment are both futile and destructive emotions. Everything can be redeemed. Radical eternalism makes one look Above and Beyond.*

BASEY, GLEN ROBERT, college president, minister; b. Caldwell, Idaho, Dec. 9, 1942; s. Charles Howard and Lois Jean (Hutchison) B.; m. Judith Jo Mc Farland, Aug. 9, 1965; children: Michelle Carol, Sharon Lynn, Jenine Marie. Student, San Jose Bible Coll., 1961-65; BA, NW Nazarene Coll., 1967; M Religious Edn., Emmanuel Sch. Religion, 1970; D Ministry, San Francisco Theol. Sem., 1975. Ordained minister Christian Ch., 1967. Minister Ardmore Ch. of Christ, Winston-Salem, N.C., 1967-70; instr. Winston-Salem Bible Coll., 1967-70; prof. Christian edn. Puget Sound Coll. the Bible, Edmonds, Wash., 1971-85; dir. Christian Edn. Seminars, Edmonds, 1972—; pvt. practice counseling Edmonds, 1972-81; interim minister Everett Cen. Christian Ch., Everett, Wash., 1980-81; preaching minister Shoreline Christian Ch., Seattle, 1981-84; acting pres. Puget Sound Coll. the Bible, 1983-84; pres. Puget Sound Christian Coll., Edmonds, 1985—. Mem. Assn. Profs. and Researchers in Christian Edn., Coll. Pres. Assn. Ind. Christian Ch. Colls. (mem. exec. com. 1988), Pioneer Bible Translators (bd. dirs. 1985—). Republican. Avocations: backpacking, photography, woodworking. Home: 1109 3d Ave S Edmonds WA 98020 Office: Puget Sound Christian Coll 410 4th Ave N Edmonds WA 98020

BASHORE, GEORGE WILLIS, bishop; b. Lancaster, Pa., Jan. 21, 1934; m. Carolyn Ruth Baumgartner, Sept. 20, 1957; children: Wanda Bashore Allison, John, Barbara Bashore Heagy. BA, Princeton U., 1955; MDiv, United Theol. Sem., Dayton, Ohio, 1958, D.Ministry, 1976; DD, Albright Coll., 1974. Ordained elder Evang. United Brethren Ch., 1958. Pastor Cen. Pk. Ch., Reading, Pa., 1959-73; supt. Lebanon-Reading Dist., Ea. Pa. Conf., 1973-79; sr. pastor 1st United Meth. Ch., Lancaster, Pa., 1979-80; elected bishop United Meth. Ch., Boston, 1980-88, bishop, Pitts., 1988—. Office: United Meth Ctr 1204 Freedom Rd Mars PA 16046

BASINGER, EARL, bishop. Bishop Ref. Mennonite Ch., Ephrata, Pa. Office: Reformed Mennonite Ch 1036 Lincoln Heights Ave Ephrata PA 17522*

BASRI, HASAN, religious organization leader. Chmn. Indonesian Ulama Coun., Jakarta. Office: Indonesian Ulama Coun, Cen Muslim Orgn, Jakarta Indonesia*

BASS, CHARLES DANIEL, minister; b. Deweyville, Tex., July 14, 1934; s. Charles Bernard and Doris Louise (Center) B.; m. Martha Latham, Aug. 19, 1958; children: C. Daniel, Elizabeth Lee Bass Richards. BA, Baylor U., 1955; postgrad., Southwestern Bapt. Theol. Sem., Ft. Worth, 1955-58; MDiv, Golden Gate Bapt. Sem., Berkeley, Calif., 1959; MS, L.I. U., 1973; D of Ministry, San Francisco Theol. Sem., San Anselmo, Calif., 1980. Ordained to ministry So. Bapt. Conv., 1952. Pastor Denning (Tex.) Bapt. Ch., 1952-53, 1st So. Bapt. Ch., Loveland, Colo., 1959-61, Bethany Bapt. Ch., Milam, Tex., 1962-63, NW Bapt. Ch., Vidor, Tex., 1963-66; commd. 1st lt. U.S. Army, 1963, advanced through grades to lt. col., 1978; dir. support U.S. Army Chaplain Sch., Ft. Monmouth, N.J., 1983-85; ret., 1985; dir. Buckner Retirement Village, El Paso, Tex., 1986-87; pastor Elm Avenue So. Bapt. Ch., Canon City, Colo., 1990—; retreat speaker, N.Mex., Fed. Republic Germany, Switzerland. Author: Banishing Fear from Your Life, 1986. Decorated Bronze Star, Air medal. Mem. Nansemond Indian Tribal Assn., Pi Gamma Mu, Alpha Chi. Home: 1106 Dixon Ct Canon City CO 81212 Office: Elm Avenue So Bapt Ch 1007 Elm Ave Canon City CO 81212

BASS, GEORGE HAROLD, religious organization administrator; b. Nashville, Feb. 23, 1936; s. Harold G. and Marjorie (Owens) B.; m. Lorena Johnson, June 7, 1957; children: Patricia Jo Bass Pulley, Janet Gail Bass Drake. BSCE, Tenn. Tech. U., 1958; Cert. Mgmt., U. Tenn., 1979. Profl. engr., Tenn. Youth dir. Waverly Place United Meth. Ch., Nashville, 1961-69, Blakemore United Meth. Ch., Nashville, 1969-77; exec. dir. Mountain Top/Tenn. Outreach Project, Nashville, 1974—; owner, cons. George Bass & Assocs., Nashville, 1987—; dist. youth coord. Tenn. Conf. United Meth. Ch., Nashville, 1971-73; chmn. coun. on ministries, Blakemore United Meth. Ch., Nashville, 1983-85; bd. global ministries, Tenn. Conf. United Meth. Ch., Nashville, 1987—. 1st. lt. artillery U.S. Army, 1958-66. Mem. Am. Soc. Tng. and Devel. (Torch award 1977), Christian Camping Internat. Office: Mountain TOP 2704 12th Ave South Nashville TN 37204

BASS, JAMES EDWIN, minister; b. Merced, Calif., Feb. 7, 1953; s. J.E. and Nellie Grace (Rudy) B.; m. Leah Gayle Surface, May 27, 1977; children: Rachel Amanda Arwen, Jonathan Jared Elrond. BS in Forestry, Stephen F. Austin State U., Nacogdoches, Tex., 1975. Ordained to ministry Assemblies of God Ch., 1981. Campus minister XA Ministries, Nacogdoches, 1977-82; pastor Woodland Park Assembly of God Ch., Conroe, Tex., 1983—; com. person N. Tex. dist. Assemblies of God, Hurst, 1980, S. Tex. Dist., Houston, 1983; assoc. chaplain Woodlands Community Hosp., 1988—, Conroe (Tex.) Med. Ctr., 1990—. Author newspaper column in Conroe Courier, 1988—; contbr. articles to profl. jours. Pres. Fox Run Homeowners Assn., Spring, Tex., 1989—, bd. dirs., 1988. Mem. Quill and Scroll. Home: 2502 Leichester Spring TX 77386 Office: Woodland Pk Assembly of God 5050 Needham Rd Conroe TX 77385

BASS, JOSEPH OSCAR, minister; b. Vicksburg, Miss., Jan. 23, 1933; s. Sylvester and Jeanette (Sims) B.; m. Charline Delores Sanders, June 5, 1955; children: Karen Sue, Julie Yvette. BRE, Western Bapt. Coll., Kansas City, Mo., 1956; BA, Nat. Coll., Kansas City, 1958; MRE, Cen. Bapt. Sem., Kansas City, Kans., 1959; MA, U. Mo., 1969, postgrad., 1975-76; MDiv, Mo. Sch. Religion, Columbia, 1971; LHD (hon.), Va. Coll., Lynchburg, 1974; PhD, Walden U., Naples, Fla., 1976. Ordained to ministry Am. Bapt. Chs. in U.S.A., 1954. Pastor chs., Kans., Mo., 1955-62; indsl. missionary to Thailand Am. Bapt. Conv., 1962-69, assoc. exec. dir. world mission support, 1969-72; nat. dir. fund of renewal Progressive Nat. Bapt. Conv., Am. Bapt. Conv., Valley Forge, Pa., 1972-74; exec. dir. home mission bd. Progressive Bapts.; pastor, founder Alpha Bapt. Ch., Alpha Acad. Christian Growth, Willingboro, N.J., 1977—; mem. adv. coun. internat. affairs Nat. Coun. Chs., Washington, 1974-81; mem. exec. coun. Am. Bapt. Chs. Author: These Are They, 1970, The History of the Progressive National Baptist Convention, 1976; co-author: One in Nine Americans Is Black, 1973, The Black American Experience, 1974. Mem. men's com. Japan Internat. Christian U., 1972; sec. Burlington County (N.J.) Community Action Program, 1972-73, pres. 1973—; bd. dirs. Burlington County United Way Campaign; vice-chmn. N.J. Chaplaincy Cons. Com.; founder Ptnrs. in Edn. Mem. Am. Sociol. Assn., Nat. Doctoral Assn. Educators, World Wide Acad. Scholars., Willingboro Clergy Assn. (pres. 1987—). Home: 2 Normont Ln Willingboro NJ 08046 Office: 175 Somerset Dr Willingboro NJ 08046 *Since nothing in this life is forever, I have made a quality decision to accept every moment of life I have left as an unearned gift from God the Creator-giver and translate it into service to humanity.*

BASS, RICHARD O., SR., bishop. Bishop 5th dist. Christian Meth. Episcopal Ch., Birmingham, Ala. Office: Christian Meth Episcopal Ch 308 10th Ave W Birmingham AL 35204*

BASSETT, HURLEY, bishop. Bishop Ch. of God in Christ, Cedar Rapids, Iowa. Office: Ch of God in Christ 1730 4th Ave SE Cedar Rapids IA 52403*

BASSETT, PAUL MERRITT, educator; b. Lima, Ohio, May 28, 1935; s. Paul Gardner and Ruth Abbott (Wiess) B.; B.A., Olivet Nazarene Coll., 1957; B.D., Duke U. Div. Sch., 1960; postgrad. Ohio State U., 1960-62; Ph.D., Duke U., 1967; m. Pearl Ann Householter, Aug. 8, 1958; children—Emilie Ruth, Paul Stephan, Anita Suzanne. Tchr., Southeastern High Sch., Ross County, Ohio, 1961-62; asso. prof. Greek and history Trevecca Nazarene Coll., Nashville, 1965-66; asst. prof. religious studies W. Va. U., Morgantown, 1966-69; asso. prof. history of Christianity, Nazarene Theol. Sem., Kansas City, Mo., 1969-76, prof., 1976—, dir. MDiv program, 1981-86, dir. Mex. Extension program, 1981-88; vis. prof. Point Loma Coll., San Diego, 1969-72, Seminario Nazareno Centroamericana, San Jose, Costa Rica, 1972-76; lectr. U. Mo., Kansas City, others. Mem. Oxford Inst. Meth. Theol. Studies, 1982, 87. Rockefeller fellow in religion, 1964-65, Wesleyan/Holiness Project fellow, 1987-90; Assn. of Theol. Schs. in U.S. and Can. grantee, 1976-77. Mem. Am. Soc. Ch. History, Am. Hist. Assn., Am. Cath. Hist. Soc., Mediaeval Acad. Am., Acad. Religion, Soc. Bibl. Lit., Wesleyan Theol. Soc. (pres. elect 1980-81, pres. 1981-82, editor Wesleyan Theol. Jour. 1987—), Kansas City Soc. for Theol. Studies (sec.-treas. 1981-86), Acad. of Research Historians in Medieval Spain. Mem. Ch. of the Nazarene. Author: Keep the Wonder, 1979, Exploring Christian Holiness, vol. II; contbr. articles to profl. jours. Home: 9930 Linden Ln Overland Park KS 66207 Office: 1700 E Meyer Blvd Kansas City MO 64131

BASTIAN, DONALD NOEL, bishop; b. Estevan, Sask., Can., Dec. 25, 1925; s. Josiah and Esther Jane (Millington) B.; m. Kathleen Grace Swallow, Dec. 20, 1947; children: Carolyn Dawn, Donald Gregory, Robert Wilfrid, John David. BA, Greenville Coll., 1953, STD (hon.), 1974; BD, Asbury Theol. Sem., 1956, DD (hon.), 1991; DD (hon.), Seattle Pacific U., 1965; DHL (hon.), Roberts Wesleyan Coll., 1990. Ordained to ministry Free Meth. Ch. N.Am., 1954; pastor chs. Lexington, Ky., 1953-56, New Westminster, B.C., Can., 1956-61; pastor College Free Meth. Ch., Greenville, Ill., 1961-74; bishop Free Meth. Ch. N.Am., Toronto, 1974-90, mem. bd. adminstrn., 1984-90; exec. editor Light and Life mag. Free Meth. Ch. N.Am., 1974-84, chmn. editorial adv. com. Light and Life mag., 1986—; bishop Free Meth. Ch. in Can., 1990—. Author: The Mature Church Member, 1960, Along the Way, 1974, Belonging, 1974; editor: The Joy of Christian Fathering: Five First Person Accounts, 1979, Counterfeit: The Lie of Living Together Unmarried, 1988. Recipient Disting. Service award Asbury Theol. Sem., 1974; Presdl. award Greenville Coll., 1972. Mem. Meth. Hist. Soc., Can. Holiness Fedn. (pres. 1977, 78), Christian Holiness Assn. (v.p. 1977-78), Evang. Fellowship of Can. (pres. 1989-91). Home: 96 Elmbrook Crescent, Etobicoke, ON Canada M9C 5E2 Office: 4315 Village Centre Ct, Mississauga, ON Canada L4Z 1S2 *I live by the conviction that, however durable it may seem, evil is by nature unstable. Righteousness, by contrast, gives stability to life in the long pull.*

BASTIAN, DWIGHT RALPH, minister; b. KauKauna, Wis., Apr. 7, 1942; s. Ralph Carl and Alice Kay (Wall) B. BA, Carroll Coll., 1964; S.T.B., Harvard U., 1968; S.T.D., Garret-Evang., 1975; MPA, U. Wis., Kenosha, 1982. Ordained minister in United Meth. Ch., 1969. Chaplain-on-call St. Luke's Meml. Hosp., Racine, Wis., 1979-80; sr. protestant chaplain Philmont Scout Ranch, Cimarron, N.Mex., 1973-74; residence dir. for men Nat. Coll. Edn., Evanston, Ill., 1971-74; minister Bethany United Meth. Ch., Racine, Wis., 1976-83, Federated Ch., Green Lake, Wis., 1983-90; sr. min. United Meth. Ch., Platteville, Wis., 1990—. Editor: Who Are the Blessed?, 1979; contbr. articles to profl. jours. Bd. dirs. Hospice Caring, Inc., Ripon, Wis., 1984-86, Wis. Conf. Bd. Ordained Ministry, 1988—, Wis. Conf. Chs. AIDS Task Force, 1988—; Clergy Assn., Racine, 1979-81; chmn. Forest County Brotherhood Week, Crandon, Wis., 1968-70, Cystic Fibrosis Drive, Crandon, Wis., 1969; pres. Forest County Assn. for Mental health, Crandon, 1968; mem. Gov.'s Regional Health Planning Coun., Rhinelander, Wis., 1970; sec.-treas. Housing Authority, Crandon, 1970. Mem. Ripon (Wis.) Area Clergy Assn. (pres. 1985-86), Berlin Area Ministerial Assn., Green Lake Commn. on Aging. Office: United Meth Ch 1065 Lancaster Platteville WI 53818

BATCHELDER, BRUCE ANDERSON, publishing executive; b. Bridgeport, Conn., Nov. 7, 1942; s. Charles L. and Marion (Anderson) B.; m. Marie Paule Clerissy, July 28, 1968 (div. May 1982); children: Darin, Stephan. Founder Singles Group Bibletown, Boca Raton, Fla., 1984; founder, leader Fairfield (Conn.) County Christian Singles, 1986-87; founder, pres. Sunday's Singles, Ft. Lauderdale, Fla., 1988—, Single Profile Mag., Ft. Lauderdale, 1989—; vol. Black Rock Congl. Ch., Fairfield, 1985-87, 1st Bapt. Ch., Ft. Lauderdale, 1988-90. Bd. dirs. Danbury (Conn.) Hosp., 1975-81, Easter Seals, Bridgeport, 1978-81, University Bridgeport, 1975-80. Staff sgt. USAF, 1963-67. Republican. Office: Single Profile Mag PO Box 6098 Delray Beach FL 33484

BATCHELDER, KENNETH ATHERTON, minister, communications executive; b. Nashua, N.H., July 12, 1927; s. Charles John and Nellie May (Bugbee) B.; m. Ruth Lucile Hamilton, Dec. 17, 1949; children: Joyce, Sharon, Douglas, Donald. AB in Theology, Gordon Coll., 1950; M Ministry, Trinity Theol. Sem., 1978. Ordained to ministry Conservative Bapt. Assn. Am., 1951. Pastor br. work Cen. Bapt. Ch., Quincy, Mass., 1951-55; pastor 1st Bapt. Ch., Revere, Mass., 1955-60, Sturtevant Chapel, Keene, N.H., 1960-80, Calvary Bible Ch., Derry, N.H., 1980-89; area rep. Trans World Radio, Cary, N.C., 1988—; pres. Christian Counseling and Communications Ctr., Troy, N.H., 1982—; chaplain Keene Fire and Police depts., 1970-80. Del. N.H. Rep. Conv., Concord, 1979. Recipient Galantry award Keene Fire Dept., 1977. Home: Bigelow Hill Rd PO Box 5 Troy NH 03465 Office: Trans World Radio 300 Gregson Dr PO Box 700 Cary NC 27511

BATEMAN, ANN CREIGHTON, minister; b. Blythe, Calif., June 7, 1943; d. William Stanley and Lucille Mildred (Beem) Creighton; m. Thomas Herbert Bateman, June 19, 1966; children: Mark Eric, Dale Kirk. BA, Whittier Coll., 1964; MAV, San Francisco Theol. Sem., 1981. Ordained to ministry United Meth. Ch. as deacon. Dir. Christian edn. Ch. of the Good Shepherd, Arcadia, Calif., 1965-67, Arlington United Meth. Ch., Riverside, Calif., 1970-74, First Unted Meth. Ch., Roseburg, Oreg., 1974-77; cons. Christian edn. Ch. Edn. Cons. Service, Salem, Oreg., 1977—; chairperson bd. diaconal ministry Oreg.-Idaho Ann. Conf., 1985-87; del. Western Jurisdictional Conf. United Meth. Ch., 1980, 84, 88, 92; mem. gen. bd. higher edn. and ministry United Meth. Ch., Nashville, Tenn., 1988—. Author: Sermon Simulations, 1977, Doing the Bible, 1984; contbr. newsletter Teacher Training Topics, 1983-86. Project leader 4-H, Salem, 1979-90, mem. state recognition and awards com., Corvallis, Oreg., 1985. Mem. United Meth. Women (life), Oreg./Idho Christian Educators Fellowship. Democrat. Avocations: photography, volleyball. Office: Church Edn Cons Svc 595 Oregon Ave NE Salem OR 97301

BATES, DAVID VLIET, religious school administrator, minister; b. Cleve., Sept. 30, 1938; s. George Axford and Freda (Haines) B.; m. Charm Ann Kinney, June 10, 1960; children: Mark Kenneth, David Paul, Peter Jonathan. BTh, Bapt. Bible Sem., Clark's Summit, Pa., 1962; MS in Edn., So. Ill. U., 1970; cert. advanced studies in edn., No. Ill. U., 1977. Lic. to ministry Evang. Free Ch. Am., 1988; cert. tchr., supr., adminstr., Ill. Min. various chs. Evang. Free Ch. Am. chs., 1970-90; min. Rock Valley Chapel, Beloit, Wis., 1990—; adminstr. Rockford (Ill.) Christian Elem. Sch., 1977—; interim pastor Maywood Free Ch., Rockford, 1985-87, Forest Hills Free Ch., Rockford, 1987-88, Congl. Christian Ch., Stillman Valley, Ill., 1988-90; bd. dirs. Christian Life Ctr. Sch., Rockford, 1990—. Mem. Assn. Christian Sch. Internat. (regional com., state rep. 1988—). Republican. Office: Rockford Christian Elem Sch 220 Hemlock Ln Rockford IL 61107

BATES, GEORGE EDMONDS, bishop; b. Binghampton, N.Y., Aug. 11, 1933; m. Sue Onstott; children: Richard Howard, Katherine Bates Schey. BA in Sociology and English, Dartmouth Coll., 1955; MDiv, Episcopal Theol. Sem., 1958. ordained deacon, The Episcopal Ch., 1958, priest, 1959. Parish priest Ithaca and Syracuse, N.Y.; rector Ch. of the Redeemer, Pendleton, Oreg., 1970-83, St. Mark's-on-the-Mesa, Albuquerque, 1983-86; consecrated bishop Diocese of Utah, 1986. Chmn. bd. dirs. St. Mark's Hosp.; bd. dirs. Westminster Coll., Rowland Hall-St. Mark's Sch.; mem. Gov.'s Task Force on Health Care Costs, Utah Econ. Devel. Office: Diocese of Utah 231 E 1st St S Salt Lake City UT 84111

BATES, GERALD EARL, bishop; b. Caldwell, Ohio, Sept. 12, 1933; s. Earl and Lillian Inez (Merritt) B.; m. Marlene Rachel Parsons, Aug. 21, 1954; children: David Earl. William Randall, Elizabeth Ann. AA, Spring Arbor Coll., 1953; AB, Greenville Coll., 1955; MDiv, Asbury Theol. Sem., 1958; ThM, Western Theol. Sem., 1964; PhD, Mich. State U., 1975; DD (hon.), Roberts Wesleyan Coll., 1986. Missionary with Gen. Missionary Bd. Free Meth. Ch. of N.Am., Winona Lake, Ind., 1957-85; area adminstrv. asst. for Cen. Africa Free Meth. Ch. of N.Am., 1973-85; bishop Free Meth. Ch. of N.Am., Winona Lake, 1985—; mem. Accrediting Coun. for Theol. Edn. in Africa, Kaduna, Nigeria, 1978—. Author: Soul Afire, 1981; chmn. bd. editors: Book of Discipline, 1985. Recipient Alumnus of Yr. award Spring Arbor Coll., 1974, Goodwill Amb. award Noble County C. of C., 1988, Alumnus of Yr. award Asbury Theol. Sem., 1991. Mem. Victoria Inst. or Philos. Soc. of Gt. Britain, Rotary, Phi Kappa Phi. Republican. Avocations: reading, travel, photography. Home: 6715 Oak Lake Dr Indianapolis IN 46214 Office: PO Box 535002 Indianapolis IN 46253-5002

BATES, JOHN NORMAN, minister; b. Kewanee, Ill., May 11, 1954; s. Norman Louis and Helen Dorothy (Prusator) B.; m. Pamela Ann Speer, June 10, 1989; stepchildren: Kerra, Chad. BA, Augustana Coll., Rock Island, Ill., 1976; MDiv, Luth. Sch. Theology Chgo., 1981. Ordained to ministry Luth. Ch. Am., 1981. Assoc. pastor Salem Luth. Ch., Peoria, Ill., 1981—. Bd. dirs. Luth. Nursing Home, Peoria, 1987—.

BATHKE, WARREN E., academic administrator. Head Grace Coll. Bible, Omaha. Office: Grace Coll Bible Office of Pres 1515 S 10th St Omaha NE 68108*

BATSON, WILLIAM CLEVELAND, III, minister; b. Wilmington, N.C., Sept. 26, 1951; s. William Cleveland Jr. and Allie Morris (Gurganus) B.; m. Cynthia Lynne Carter, Aug. 19, 1972; children: Courtney Elizabeth, Cammie Joy. BA in Theology, Berkshire Christian Coll., Lenox, Mass., 1973; postgrad., Gordon-Conwell Theol. Sem., Hamilton, Mass., 1984-85, 90—. Ordained to ministry, Advent Christian Ch., 1973. Minister of edn., youth Grace Advent Christian Ch., Walterboro, S.C., 1973-77; pastor Advent Christian Ch., Torrington, Conn., 1977-83, Portsmouth (N.H.) Advent Christian Ch., 1983—; founder, exec. dir. The Family Builder Seminars, Portsmouth, 1987—; bd. dirs. Ken Fernald Music Ministries, Portsmouth, 1986-89; pres. N.H. Advent Christian Conf., 1987-88; Christian edn. trainer Advent Christian Gen. Conf., Charlotte, 1986-90. Author, contbr.: Super Sunday School Ideas, 1989, family column Advent Christian Witness, 1988—. Pres. Dondero PTA, Portsmouth, 1989-90. Republican. Home: 211 Hillside Dr Portsmouth NH 03801

BATTEN, PATTI SUE, lay worker; b. Caribou, Maine, May 10, 1961; d. Lynwood Earl and ARlene Avis (Ketch) Monteith; m. George Edward Batten, Sept. 17, 1983; children: Jeremy John, Jason Jeffrey, Josiah James. Student, New Brunswick Bible Inst., Victoria, N.B., 1979-80; AS, U. Maine, Presque Isle, 1983. Sun. sch. tchr. Woodland Bapt. Ch., Caribou, Maine, 1976-79; camp counselor Bapt. Park, Mapleton, Maine, 1977-79 summers; youth leader, Sun. sch. supt. Full Gospel Ch. of the Good Shepherd, Old Town, Maine, 1984-86; youth dir., Sun. sch. supt., ch. sec., kid's crusade dir. Littleton Full Gospel Assembly, Houlton, Maine, 1986—; staff nurse ob/gyn. Houlton Reg. Hosp., 1991—. Mem. Maine Christian Civic League, Augusta, 1987—, Nat. Right to Life, Maine Right to Life, Maine Homeschoolers Assn., 1990—; founder, dir. Friend to the Fatherless Program, 1988. Named Family of Yr., Maine WCTU,1989. Republican.

BATTISTON, DONALD LINO, deacon; b. Hartford, Conn., Nov. 26, 1941; s. Lind J. and Helen (Daikille) B.; m. Pamela Ann Stewart, Oct. 26, 1963; children: Jeffrey, Rebecca, Hannah, Gregory, Jacob. Ordained deacon Roman Cath. Ch., 1976. With CIA, Washington; pres. Batco Inc., West Hartford, Conn., 1983-91; deacon St. Ann's Cath. Ch., Avon, Conn.; speaker dry cleaning industry convs.; participant Varsity Internat. Conf. Cleaners (5 times); bd. dirs. Alleluia House, Avon. Bd. dirs. Conn. Spl. Olympics, YMCA, Pro Life Coun., Alleluia Players, Domus Amoris House, Greater Hartford Better Bus. Bur., Madaket Conservation Trus, Nantucket Island. Mem. Nat. Inst. Drycleaning Alumni Assn., Avon C. of C. (past pres.P, Conn. Launderers and Cleaners Assn., Greater Hartford Better Bus. Bur., New Eng. Fabric Care Assn., Rotary (past pres.). Republican. Home: 62 Stony Corners Circle Avon CT 06001-2619 Office: St Ann's Roman Cath Ch 289 Arch Rd Avon CT 06001

BATTLE, GEORGE EDWARD, JR., minister; b. Rocky Mount, N.C., May 14, 1947; s. George Edward and Mary C. Battle; m. Iris Miller; children: George Edward III, LaChandra Nickole. AA magma cum laude, Clinton Jr. Coll., Rock Hill, S.C., 1967; BA in Sociology, Livingstone Coll., 1969, MDiv magna cum laude, 1972, DD (hon.), 1982; DMin, Howard U., 1990. Ordained to ministry A.M.E. Zion Ch. Min. Center Grove, Emmanuel Mt. Vernon Cir. and Found., and Tabernacle Cir., A.M.E. Zion Ch., 1966-72, Mt. Zion A.M.E. Zion Ch., Lancaster, S.C., 1972-74; housing coord. City of Rock Hill, 1971-73; min. Greater Gethsemane A.M.E. Zion Ch., Charlotte, N.C., 1974—; cons. on social concerns, 1975—; bd. dirs. 1st Union Nat. Bank, Charlotte; mem. internat. overseas mission bd. A.M.E. Zion Ch., 1974—, mem. bd. stats. and records, 1976-84, fin. chmn., 1976—, chmn. bd. Camp Dorothy Walls, 1981—, fin. chmn. Western N.C. Conf., 1976—; founder Gethsemane Enrichment Program, 1975; co-founder Gethsemane Hot Lunch Program, 1976; del. World Meth. Coun., 1981, A.M.E. Zion Gen. Conf., 1987. Mem. Charlotte-Mecklenburg County Bd. Edn., 1978—, chmn., 1990—; bd. visitors U. N.C., Charlotte, 1987; chmn. Charlotte-Mecklenburg Urban League, 1982-83; co-founder, organizer Biddleville Housing Corp., Charlotte, 1982; organizer, pres. emeritus Five Points Community Orgn., Charlotte, 1975; bd. dirs. N.C. Day Care Commn., Livingstone Coll., Salisbury, N.C.; trustee Clinton Jr. Coll.; chmn. adv. bd. Double Oaks Community Ctr., Charlotte; mem. Charlotte Bd. Performing Arts; numerous others. Recipient mission award Soldiers Meml. A.M.E. Ch., 1969, Ch. Evangelist award 1972, Humanitarian award Nat. Assn. Negro Bus. and Profl. Women's Club, 1983, Order of Long Leaf Pine N.C. Gov.'s Office, 1984, Man of Yr. award Charlotte Post, 1986, award for outstanding community svcs. Charlotte-Mecklenburg County Urban League, 1986, Excellence in Pub. Svc. award N.C. Social Svc. Commn., 1987, award NCCJ, 1988, award for achievement in edn. Charlotte dist. A.M.E. Ch., 1990; numerous others. Mem. Alpha Phi Alpha. Home: 8233 Charles Crawford Ln Charlotte NC 28213 Office: Greater Gethsemane AME Zion Ch 531 Campus St Charlotte NC 28216

BATTLE, VANN DUWAYNE, minister; b. Washington, Aug. 15, 1957; s. Thomas Oscar and Lenora (Thomas) B.; m. Edith L. Sumner, May 19, 1979; children: Thomas Oscar, Mary Elizabeth. Student, Howard U., Wesleyan Coll., Rocky Mountain, N.C., Oxford U., Eng.; BA, Barton Coll., 1979; MDiv, S.E. Bapt. Theol. Sem., Wake Forest, N.C., 1982, D of Ministry, 1985. Ordained to ministry Nat. Bapt. Conv. U.S.A., Inc., 1979. Pastor Smith Chapel Bapt. Ch., Enfield, N.C., 1979-89, St. Paul's Bapt. Ch., Montclair, N.J., 1989—; adj. prof. Shaw U. Div. Sch., Raleigh, N.C., 1986-89; guest lectr. 43d Nat. Bapt. Student Union Retreat, Baton Rouge, 1987; lectr., guest preacher, Senegal, The Gambia, 1988, Guyana Missionary Bapt. Conv., Georgetown, 1988, 90; mem. exec. bd. Hampton (Va.) Univ. Mins. Conf., 1988—; preacher ann. conv. Union Evang. Bapt. Haiti, 1991; trustee Homes of Montclair Corp., 1989-91; mem. urban ministry com. Am. Bapt. Chs. N.J., East Orange, 1990—; mem. exec. com. mins. coun. Am. Bapt. Chs. N.J., 1991—, exec. bd. Met. Youth for Christ, 1991—. Contbr. articles to religious jours. Mem. NAACP. Democrat. Office: St Paul's Bapt Ch 119 Elm St Montclair NJ 07042

BATTLE, WILLA LEE GRANT, clergywoman, educational administrator; b. Webb, Miss., Sept. 30, 1924; d. James Carlton and Aslean (Young) Grant; m. Walter Leroy Battle, July 4, 1941. Diploma, Northwestern Coll., Mpls., 1956; B.A. cum laude, U. Minn., 1975, M.A., 1979; Ph.D. summa cum laude, Trinity Sem., 1982. Ordained to ministry, 1959. Founder, pastor Grace Temple Del. Ctr., Mpls., 1958—; founder, pres., Willa Grant Battle Ctr., Mpls., 1980—; founder House of Refuge Mission, Haiti, W.I., 1957—; adminstr., dir. Kiddie Haven Pre-Sch., Mpls., 1982—. Mem. Interdenominational Ministerial Alliance (sec. 1986—), Mpls. Ministerial Assn., AAUW, AAUP, U. Minn. Alumni Assn. (life), NAACP, Nat. Council Negro Women, Christian Educators, Nat. Assn. Female Execs. Home: 220 E 42d St Minneapolis MN 55409 Office: Willa Grant Battle Ctr 1816 Fourth Ave South Minneapolis MN 55404

BATTLES, ROBERT WINFIELD, JR., minister; b. Greensburg, Pa., Oct. 31, 1938; s. Robert Winfield and Olive Blanche (McGarvey) B.; m. Ruth Bach, Aug. 26, 1961; 1 child, Stephanie Elizabeth. BS, Nyack Coll., 1959; MA, Stetson U., 1960; MDiv, Westminster Sem., 1963; MTh, Princeton Sem., 1964, DMin, 1980. Ordained to ministry Presbyn. Ch. (U.S.A.), 1964. Asst. pastor 1st Presbyn. Ch., West Palm Beach, Fla., 1964-66; pastor Presbyn. Ch., Bridgehampton, N.Y., 1966-75, Germonds Presbyn. Ch., New City, N.Y., 1975-80; pastor 1st Presbyn. Ch., Mt. Clemens, Mich., 1980-81, Gainesville, Fla., 1991—; mem. exec. com. Presbyn. Villages of Detroit, 1981—; chair Macomb Jail Ministry, Mt. Clemens, 1983-87; mem. Teaching Ch., Princeton Sem., New City, 1975-80. Mem. exec. com. Choral Soc. Of Hamptons, Bridgehampton, 1966-75; chair Southampton (N.Y.) Bd. Ethics, 1973-75; v.p. Macomb Arts Coun., Mt. Clemens, 1987-90; mem. nation at risk com. Mt. Clemens Schs., 1985. Recipient Outstanding Svc. to Handicapped award Camp Venture-Venture Inn, 1979, Libr. Svc. award Mt. Clemens Pub. Libr., 1990. Mem. Princeton Sem. Alumnae Assn. (pres. 1983-91), Presbyn. Health and Welfare Orgn., Rotary. Office: 1st Presbyn Ch 106 SW 3d St Gainesville FL 32601

BATYE, CLIFFORD WAYNE, lay worker, counselor; b. Marceline, Mo., Jan. 1, 1947; s. John Clifford and Martha Lea (Dorrell) B.; m. Nina Kathleen Kneedler, Sept. 1, 1967; children: James Doyle, Rhonda Darlene. Cert., Ch. of God Sch. Theology, Cleveland, Tenn., Assembly of God, Springfield, Mo. Dir. youth Ch. of God, Kansas City, Mo., 1972-76; assoc. min. Ch. of God, Arch and Valdez, Alaska, 1976-79, Assembly of God, Valdez, 1979-82; lay min. Fairbanks, Alaska, 1986—; van driver, counselor Fairbanks Native Assn. Ctr. for Alcohol and Other Addictions, 1989—; vol. lay leader Prison Ministries of Alaska, Fairbanks, 1989-91. Home: 825 Badger Rd North Pole AK 99705

BAUDER, KEVIN THOMAS, minister, educator; b. Midland, Mich., Aug. 30, 1955; s. Thomas Doane and Dolores Elaine (Neeb) B.; m. Debra Sue Wright, Dec. 20, 1975; children: Rachel Anna, Joshua Caleb. BA, Faith Bapt. Bible Coll., 1979; MDiv, Denver Bapt. Theol. Sem., 1982, MTh, 1983; D Ministry, Trinity Evang. Div. Sch., 1990; ThD in Studies, Dallas Theol. Sem., 1991. Asst. prof. Denver Bapt. Bible Coll., 1983-85; pastor Immanuel Bapt. Ch., Newton, Iowa, 1985-90, Bapt. Ch., Dallas, 1990—. Author: (monograph) How Firm a Foundation, 1982, Oliver W. VanOsdel's Biography, 1983, The Evangelical Spectrum, 1983. Home and Office: 2112 El Capitan Dallas TX 75228

BAUER, BETTY LEE, hospital chaplain; b. Belleville, Ill., Dec. 18, 1945; d. Weldon Richard and Marjorie Martha (Reinhardt) Heinke; m. Paul Henry Bauer, Jan. 21, 1967; children: David Richard (dec.), Regina Marie, Michelle Lee, Catherine Ann. AAS, Belleville Area Coll., 1981; student, St. Louis U., 1989-91. Hosp. chaplain assoc. Luth. Med. Ctr., St. Louis, 1990—; resident St. John Mercy Hosp., 1991—; lay pastoral minister, Belleville Diocese Ministry to Sick and Aged, 1986-90; eucharistic minister, Belleville Diocese, 1982—; prayer leader Renew Core group St. Luke Cath. Ch., Belleville, 1984-86, communion svc. leader, 1988-90. Organizer blood drive Am. Red Cross, St. Luke's Ch., 1988-90; leader 4-H Club, Belleville, 1979-83, Girl Scouts U.S., Belleville, 1978-79. Mem. Wives of the Ill. Assn. of Hwy. Engrs. (pres. Belleville chpt. 1972-73), St. Luke's Perpetual Help Sodality. Home: 501 North Charles St Belleville IL 62220

BAUER, CATHERINE MARIE, nun, social worker; b. Cin., Aug. 3, 1954; d. John Wendle and Catherine Ann (Krantz) B. AAS, U. Cin., 1979; BA in Social Work, Thomas More Coll., 1984; postgrad., Cath. U. Cashier Parkview Market, Owensville, Ohio, 197-74; ins. agt., office mgr. John Bauer & Assoc., Owensville, 1974-79; vol. coord. Covington (Ky.) Community Ctr., 1979-80, housing cons., 1985-86; child's guidance worker Cath. Social Svc., Latonia, Ky., 1980-81; community organizer Working in Neighborhoods, Cin., 1982-83; community garden coord. No. Ky. Community Ctr., Covington, 1984-85; coord. of payee program Welcome House, Covington, 1986—; mentor Thomas More Coll., Crestview Hills, Ky., 1986—. Local chairperson Benedictine for Peace, Villa Hills, Ky., 1980—; bd. dirs. Parish Kitchen, 1988-90, Diocese Justice and Peace Office, 1986-90; chairperson For an Inclusive Ch., 1988—; coord. Benedictine Assocs. Program, 1990—; mem. Benedictine Vocation Ministry Team, 1990—. Recipient Social Work Student of Yr. No. Ky. Social Workers, 1984, Baron Community Svc. award mental Health Assn. of No. Ky., 1988. Mem. Mental Health Assn. (advocacy com. 1988—). Roman Catholic. Avocations: hiking, gardening, refinishing furniture. Home: 2500 Amsterdam Rd Villa Hills KY 41017 Office: Welcome House No Ky 141 Pike St Covington KY 41011

BAUER, JUDY MARIE, minister; b. South Bend, Ind., Aug. 24, 1947; d. Ernest Camiel and Marjorie Ann (Williams) Derho; m. Gary Dwane Bauer, Apr. 28, 1966; children—Christine Ann, Steven Dwane. Ordained to ministry Christian Ch., 1979. Sec. adminstrv. asst. Bethel Christian Ctr., Riverside, Calif., 1975-79; founder, pres. Kingdom Advancement Ministry, San Diego, 1979-89, trainer, mgr. cons., Tex., Ariz., Calif., Oreg., Washington, Ala., Okla., Idaho and Republic of South Africa, Guam, Egypt, The Philippines, Australia, Can., Mozambique, Malarwie, Mex., Zimbabwe, Guatemala, Japan, Eng., 1979—; founder, co-pastor Bernardo Christian Ctr., San Diego, 1981-91; evangelism dir. Bethel Christian Ctr., 1978-81, undershepherd minister, 1975-79, adult tchr., 1973-81; pres., founder Bethel Christian Ctr. of Rancho Bernardo, Calif., 1991—; condr. leadership tng. clinics, internat. speaker, lectr. in field. Author syllabus, booklet, tng. material packets. Mem. Internat. Conv. Faith Ministries, Inc. (area bd. dirs. 1983-88). *It's only in selling out to a cause worth dying for that we truly come alive and experience life to the fullest.*

BAUER, RICHARD H., clergyman; b. Cin., May 19, 1913; s. Samuel B. and Alice (Helck) B.; m. Eleanor Nye, July 3, 1941. Comml. Engr., U. Cin., 1936; M.Div., Garrett Theol. Sem., 1947; D.D., Ohio No. U., 1962. With Proctor & Gamble Co., 1932-44; ordained to ministry Methodist Ch., 1948; pastor in Cin., 1942-44, Ashley, Ind., 1944-47, North College Hill, Cin., 1947-53, Bellefontaine, Ohio, 1953-56; dist. supt. (Portsmouth (Ohio) dist. Meth. Ch.), 1956-60; exec. sec. interboard com. enlistment for ch. occupations United Meth. Ch., 1960-72, exec. sec. office personnel services, 1973-76; dir. devel. loans and scholarships United Meth. Ch. (Office of Personnel), 1976-78; nat. field rep. World Hunger Edn./Action Together, United Meth. Ch., 1978—; Del. World Meth. Conf., 1961, 66, 71, 81; mem. World Meth. Council, 1966-71; mem. assembly Nat. Council Chs., 1963-66, 66-69, 70-73, chmn. commn. vocation and enlistment, 1963-76, vice chmn. dept. ministry, 1966-76; sec. Meth. Council Secs., 1964-68; trustee Meth. Home Aged, 1956-60; bd. dirs., pres. Mid-South Career Devel. Center, 1974-78; chmn. Commn. on Vocation and Religion, Nat. Vocat. Guidance Assn., 1980-85; chmn. Commn. on Work and Spiritual Values, Nat. Assn. Career Devel., 1985—. Contbr. articles to ch. publs. Mem. Metro/Nashville Human Rights Commn., 1983—. Mem. Am. Personnel and Guidance Assn., Ch. Career Devel. Council (sec. 1974-78), UN Assn. U.S.A. (pres. Nashville chpt. 1982-87), Common Cause, Sigma Chi, Omicron Delta Kappa. Home: 3809 Brighton Ave Nashville TN 37205

BAUGH, C. DON, ecumenical agency executive. Exec. dir. San Antonio Community Chs. Office: San Antonio Community Chs 1101 W Woodlawn San Antonio TX 78201*

BAUGH, MARK ANTHONY, minister; b. North Reislip, Slough, Eng, Jan. 29, 1958; came to U.S. 1958; s. Oscar T. and DeLois Edith (Parker) B.; m. Holly Faye Wheeler, June 30, 1990. BBA in Fin., U. Okla., 1982; MDiv, Southwestern Bapt. Theol. Sem., 1985. Ordained to ministry, So. Bapt. Conv. Minister of youth First Bapt. Ch. of Coleman (Tex.), 1985; minister of edn. and youth First Bapt. Ch. of St. Charles, Waldorf, Md., 1986-88, Gregory Meml. Bapt. Ch., Balt., 1989-91; chmn. Potomac Bapt. Assn. Youth Com., Waldorf, 1986-88, Balt., 1989-91; lectr. in field. Editor Christian Edn. for the Blind mag., 1984-85. Coach Towson Recreation Dept., Balt., 1989. Republican. Home: 82 Chapel Towne Cir Baltimore MD 21236 Office: Gregory Meml Bapt Ch 5701 York Rd Baltimore MD 21212

BAUM, WILLIAM WAKEFIELD CARDINAL, former church official; b. Dallas, Nov. 21, 1926; s. Harold E. and Mary Leona (Hayes) W. Student, Kenrick Sem., St. Louis, 1947-51, U. St. Thomas Aquinas, Rome, 1956-58; STD, U. St. Thomas Aquinas, Rome, 1958; STL, Muhlenberg Coll., Allentown, Pa., 1957, DD, 1967; LLD, Georgetown U., St. John's U., Bklyn. Ordained priest Roman Cath. Ch., 1951. Elevated to cardinal Roman Cath. Ch., 1976; assoc. pastor St. Aloysius Parish, St. Therese's Parish and St. Peter's Parish, Kansas City, Mo., 1951-56, 61-64, 67-68; adminstr. St. Cyril's Parish, Sugar Creek, Mo., 1960-61; pastor St. James Parish, Kansas City, 1968-70; chancellor Diocese Kansas City-St. Joseph, 1967-70; bishop of Springfield-Cape Girardeau, Mo., 1970-73; archbishop of Washington, 1973-80; prefect Sacred Congregation for Cath. Edn., Rome, 1980—; instr., then prof. Avila Coll., Kansas City, Mo., 1954-56, 58-63; Hon. chaplain of the Pope, 1961; peritus 2d Vatican Council, 1962-65; hon. prelate of the Pope, 1968; 1st exec. dir. Bishops' Commn. Ecumenical and Inter-religious Affairs, 1964-67; mem. Joint Working Group; reps. Cath. Ch. and World Council Chs., 1965-69; mem. Mixed Commn.; reps. Cath. Ch. and Lutheran World Fedn., 1965-66; mem. Vatican's Congregations Cath. Edn., Doctrine of Faith and Secretariat for Non Christians, Bishop's Welfare Emergency Relief Com. Author: The Teaching of Cardinal Cajetan on the Sacrifice of the Mass, 1958, Considerations Toward the Theology on the Presbyterate, 1961. Trustee, chancellor Cath. U. Am.; chmn. bd. trustees Nat. Shrine Immaculate Conception. Mem. Nat. Conf. Cath. Bishops (adminstrv. com.). Address: Piazza della Citta, Leonina 9, 00193 Rome Italy

BAUMAN, DAVID BENJAMIN, minister; b. Angol, Araucania, Chile, Aug. 28, 1919; (parents Am. citizens); s. Ezra and Florence (Carhart) B.; m. Faith Erma Weber, Dec. 9, 1955; children: Mark Stephen, Philip David. AB, U. Denver, 1941; STB, Boston U., 1945. Ordained deacon United Meth. Ch., 1945, elder, 1947. Pastor United Meth. Ch., Gardiner, Oreg., 1944-49; missionary Bd. Global Ministries, served in tchr. children's Christian edn., dir. summer camps, dist. supt. Gujarat Conf. Meth. Ch. in India, 1951-86; pastor Zion United Meth. Ch., Elyria, Ohio, 1987—; del. Gen. Conf. Meth. Ch. in India. Mem. Grange, Sr. Fellowship Club. Home: 43550 Middle Ridge Rd Lorain OH 44053 Office: Zion United Meth Ch 43770 Telegraph Rd Elyria OH 44035

BAUMAN, MICHAEL EDWARD, theology educator, Christian studies director; b. Moline, Ill., Feb. 14, 1950; s. Edward Paul and Edith Jeanette (Pulver) B.; m. Sharon Louise Brummitt, June 9, 1973. BA, Trinity Coll., 1977; M.A.T.S., McCormick Theol. Sem., 1979; PhD, Fordham U., 1983. Dir. gen. edn. Northeastern Bible Coll., Essex Fells, N.J., 1983-88; dir. Christian studies Hillsdale (Mich.) Coll., 1988—; assoc. dean summer sch. Centre for Medieval and Renaissance Studies, Oxford, Eng., 1989—. Author: Roundtable: Conversation with European Theologians, 1990, A Scripture Index to John Milton's De Doctrina Christiana, 1989, Milton's Arianism, 1987, The Best of the Manion Forum: A Conservative and Free Market Sourcebook, 1991; book rev. editor Jour. of the Evang. Theol. Soc., 1987—; editorial asst. Newsweek, 1982-84; contbr. articles to profl. jours. Mem. Right to Life of Hillsdale County, Hillsdale, Mich., 1990. NEH rsch. fellow Princeton U., 1988. Mem. Evang. Theol. Soc. (editorial com. 1987—), Swiss-Am. Hist. Soc., Milton Soc. Am., Charles Lamb Soc. Republican. Mem. Evangelical Free Church. Home: 4202 W Hallett Rd Hillsdale MI 49242 Office: Hillsdale Coll Hillsdale MI 49242

BAUMER, MARTHA ANN, minister; b. Cleve., Sept. 12, 1938; d. Harry William and Olga Erna (Zenk) B. BA, Lakeland Coll., 1960; MA, U. Wyo., 1963; MDiv, United Theol. Sem., 1973; D Ministry, Eden Theol. Sem., 1990. Parish minister Congl. United Ch. of Christ, Amery, Wis., 1973-79; organizing minister United Ch. of Santa Fe (N.Mex.), 1979-85; conf. minister Ill. South Conf. United Ch. of Christ, Highland, Ill., 1985—; trustee pension bds. United Ch. of Christ, N.Y.C., 1983—, mem., chair exec. coun., 1977-83; del. World Coun. Chs., 1961, 83; trustee Eden Theol. Sem., St. Louis, 1990—. Contbr. articles to profl. publs. Mem. Coun. of Conf. Ministers United Ch. of Christ (sec.-treas. 1989—). Office: Ill S Conf United Ch Christ 1312 Broadway Highland IL 62249

BAUTISTA, LIBERATO DE LA CRUZ, church executive; b. Sanchez Mira, Cagayan, Philippines, Oct. 8, 1959; s. Ambrosio Bautista and Natalia (De la Cruz) B.; m. Adora Angeles; children: Arvin Louis, Aiena Laya. BA in Social Sci., U. Philippines, Manila, 1982; M.Internat. Studies, U. Philippines, Diliman, Quezon City, 1989—. Del. World Meth. Coun., Hawaii Conf., 1981, World Coun. Chs., Vancouver, B.C., Can., 1983, Luth. World Fedn. Pre-Assembly Youth Gathering, Budapest, Hungary, 1984; del. Christian Conf. Asia Assembly, Seoul, S. Korea, 1985, Quezon City, S. Korea, 1990; coord. Program Unit on Human Rights, Nat. Council Chs. in the Philippines, Quezon City, 1985—; chmn. bd. dirs. Photobank Philippines, Quezon City; participant human rights and humanitarian law course John Knox Reformed Ctr., Geneva, 1987, summer course on bibl.-theol. perspectives on power Bossey Ecumenical Inst.; mem. drafting group, World Meth. Social Creed, Geneva, 1987; participant European Ecumenical Assembly on justice and peace, Basel, Switzerland, 1989; faculty mem. St. Andrew's Theol. Sem. Quezon City, 1989-90; lectr. in field. Editor: Human Rights Readings, 1988, Religion and Society-Towards a Theology of Struggle, 1988, And She Said No: Human Rights, Women's Identities and Struggles, 1990, Human Rights Reader for Filipinos, 1990; co-editor Resistance: Esssays in Militarism and Militarization, 1991; assoc. editor Tugon Jour., 1983—; editor series: Human Rights Occasional Papers, 1987, 88; contbr. articles to profl. jours. Mem. Nuclear Free Philippines Coalition, Manila, 1985-86 (bd. dirs.); gen. com. mem. Christian Conf. of Asia, 1985-90. internat. affairs com., 1990—; vice chmn. Philippine Alliance of Human Rights Advocates, Quezon City, 1986-90; cen. conf. sec. United Meth. Ch., 1988—. Avocations: writing, reading, traveling. Office: Nat Coun Chs, 879 EDSA, Quezon City The Philippines

BAVLINKA, BARBARA JEAN CLARK, church organist; b. Holyoke, Colo., Mar. 18, 1930; d. Hulbert Royal and Ollie Gertrude (Wolfe) Clark; m. Earl Anton Bavlinka, Oct. 7, 1950; children: Carol Jean Hawkins, Mary Jane Alvis. Student, Stevens Point U., 1948-50, U. Wis. Coll. of the Air, 1950-75. Organist St. John's Luth. Ch., Mosinee, Wis., 1955-59, Our Savior's Nat. Cath. Ch., Mosinee, 1971-75; choir dir., organist Meth. Ch., Mosinee, 1978-89; organist, carollineur Wesley Meth. Ch., Wausau, Wis., 1989—; pres. Gen. Women's Meth., Mosinee, 1980; sec. Twilight Circle Meth., Mosinee, 1979-89. Pres. Hosp. Aux., Mosinee, 1957. Mem. Am. Guild Organists. Republican. *Of paramount importance are America's privileges: the right to life and its precious freedoms: of speech, of press, from fear, want or persecution, of religion and the right to assemble.*

BAXLEY, WILLIAM DUANE, religion educator; b. Dothan, Ala., Aug. 5, 1952; s. Harold and Evie Louise (Bell) B.; m. Margaret Lynn Adkison, June 9, 1972; children: Jason, Travis. BS in Animal Sci., Auburn U., 1978; MDiv, Southwestern Bapt. Theol. Sem., 1985; postgrad., Fuller Theol. Sem., 1989—. Home: 100 Harbour View Rd Brandon MS 39042-6131

BAXTER, WILLIAM MACNEIL, priest; b. Halifax, N.S., Can., Oct. 5, 1923; s. William John and Mary Ellen (MacNeil) B.; m. Jean Marlin Taylor, Oct. 25, 1946; children: Nancy Graeme, Gary MacNeil, Rebecca Roberts, Anne Marlin. BA, Amherst Coll., 1946; MDiv, Va. Theol. Sem., 1951. Advt. salesman Reuben H. Donnelley, Inc., 1947-49; ordained to ministry Episcopal Ch., 1951; curate, asst. minister St. Louis, 1951-54; rector Washington, 1954-66; dir. career info. service, also dir. public affairs Peace Corps, 1966-68; pres. Baxter Assos. (cons. edn. and tng.), 1969-70; pres., exec. dir. Marriage and Family Inst. (counseling and ednl. center), Washington, 1971-85; rector Trinity Episcopal Ch., Lewiston, Maine, 1990—; spl. cons. to State Dept. on refugee problems in Vietnam; vis. lectr. pastoral theology Va. Theol. Sem., 1960-66, Wesley Theol. Sem., 1979; Luccock lectr. Yale Div. Sch., 1965; mem. faculty field tng. colloquium Chgo. Div. Sch., 1960-64; lectr. Am. U. Law Sch., 1980-81; P.E. del. Nat. Conf. Radiation and Social Ethics, 1963; pres. Diocese of Washington Clergy, 1960-62; candidate for suffragan bishop, Washington, 1963, 1986; sr. cons. Diocese of Maine, 1987—; bd. dirs. Gen. Theol. Ctr. Maine, 1989-91. Contbr. articles to profl. jours. Mem. planning com. White House Conf. to Secure These Rights, 1964; bd. dirs. Capital Hill Community Council, Friendship Settlement House, Washington Area Council on Alcoholism, Neighborhood Service Com., Health and Welfare Council, Advocates for Children, 1991—. Served with Merchant Marine, 1946. Mem. Am. Assn. for Marriage and Family Therapy (pres. Midatlantic div. 1975-78), Cosmos Club, Chi Psi. Democrat. Home: 364 Spring St Portland ME 04102 Office: Trinity Episcopal Ch Lewiston ME 04243-0216

BAYER, KAREL, geography and religion educator; b. Náchod, Bohemia, Czechoslovakia, May 8, 1931; came to U.S., 1968; s. Václav and Karla (Novotná) B.; m. Vera Andrlíková, Feb. 6, 1954. MS, Charles U., Prague, Czechoslovakia, 1954, RNDr., 1966, PhD, 1960. Assoc. prof. U. Wis., Milw., 1968—. Roman Catholic. Office: U Wis Milwaukee WI 53201 *Awareness of the multitude of nations of the world, past and present, makes me a member of a countless host of sisters and brothers longing for love and truth and happiness and gathered in silence in a limitless cathedral still dark and chilly before the midnight mass of Christmas of humanity.*

BAYLER, LAVON, religious organization administrator; b. Sandusky, Ohio, Jan. 17, 1933; d. Emil J. Burrichter and Elsie L. (Dickel) B.; m. Robert L. Bayler, June 26, 1958; children: David Allen, Jonathan Robert, Timothy Norris. BA, Iowa State Tchrs. Coll., 1955; M in Divinity, Eden Theo. Seminary, St. Louis, 1959; postgrad., Lancaster Theo. Seminary, 1956-57, 1975-77. Nat. youth assoc. Evangelical and Reformed Ch., Phila., 1955-56; co-pastor Glenford (Ohio) Charge, 1959-63; pastor St. Paul United Ch. Christ, Hinckley, Ill., 1964-68; assoc. pastor St. Paul United Ch. Christ, Barrington, Ill., 1968-72; pastor First Congregational U.C.C., Carpentersville, Ill., 1973-79; area conf. minister United Ch. Christ, Ill., 1979—; founding dir. pres. Carpentersville Council for Child Devel., 1975-79, dir. continuing edn. v.p. Profl. Assn. Clergy Ill., 1976-80. Contbr. author: Bread for the Journey, 1983; Flames of the Spirit, 1985; author: Fresh Winds of the Spirit, 1986; Whispers of God, 1987; Refreshing Rains of the Living Word, 1988. Mem. League Women Voters. Mem. Internat. Assn. Women Ministers, Women in Mission U.C.C. Democrat. Home: 2251 Tara Dr Elgin IL 60123-4933 Office: No Assn Ill Conf 617 N First St De Kalb IL 60115 *Relationships are at the heart of life. Interacting with one another and the whole creation, we can recognize both our uniqueness and our interdependence. At our best, we value and fully employ the special gifts we have received for the common good and we respect and appreciate the contributions of our sisters and brothers.*

BAYLEY, RAY WALDO GUSTAVUS, minister; b. Beaver Dam, Wis., May 28, 1919; s. Ray Waldo and Fannie Quanita (Groling) B.; m. Hazel Jean Christoph, June 30, 1944. AA, Wayland Jr. Coll., 1939; BS in Edn., U. Wis., 1942; diploma, McCormick Theol. Sem., 1945. Pastor First Presbyn. Ch., Rosedale Presbyn. Ch., Pardeeville, Wis., 1945-48, First Presbyn. Ch., Prairie du Sac, Wis., 1949-53, 1st Presbyn. Ch., Waunakee, Wis., 1949-51, Badger Christian Fellowship, Prairie du Sac, Wis., 1951-53; field sec., dir. edn., exec. dir. Alcohol Problems Coun. of Wis., Madison, 1953-73; interim pastor part time 8 Chs., 1973-83, ret.; resort operator Pleasant View Park, Lodi, Wis., 1974—; actor KC Talent, Madison, 1988—; vol. night chaplain Meriter Hosp., Madison, 1971-91. Writer weekly column Sauk Prairie Star; contbr. articles to profl. jours. Bd. dirs. Sauk Prairie Meml. Hosp., Prairie du Sac, Wis., 1984—, Cen. Wis. Community Action Coun., Lake Delton, Wis., 1980—. Named Silver Beaver Boys Scouts Am., 1964. Mem. Internat. Platform Assn., Wis. Hosp. Assn., Optimist (pres., lt. gov.). Republican. Home: 229 Park Ave Prairie du Sac WI 53578 Office: Pleasant View Park W12763 Pleasant View Park Lodi WI 53555

BAYNE, JAMES THOMAS, JR., minister; b. Roanoke, Va., Apr. 15, 1934; s. James Thomas Sr. and Margaret Blanche (Mauk) B.; m. Phyllis Jannette Witt, May 19, 1956; children: Angela Lynn, James Kent, Christina Marie. BA, Atlanta Christian Coll., 1960; postgrad., Harding Sch. Religion, 1963-64, Emmanuel Sch. Religion, 1971-72; M of Ministry, Ky. Christian

Coll., 1985. Min. Friendship Christian Ch., River View, Ala., 1960-62, Weiner (Ark.) Christian Ch., 1962-64, Lindale Ch. Christ, Chesapeake, Va., 1964-69, New Castle (Va.) Christian Ch., 1969-81, Belmont Christian Ch., Christiansburg, Va., 1981—; trustee, sec. bd. dirs. Memphis Christian Coll., Memphis, 1962-64; editor Va. Evangelizing Fellowship News, Richmond, Va., 1967-68, bd. dirs.; dir. Blue Ridge Christian Camp, McCoy, Va., 1991—; conv. dir. So. Christian Youth Conv., Roanoke, 1975. Active Lions Club, New Castle, 1969-81; sec. Ruritan, Christiansburg, 1988-89. Home: 80 Meadow Dr NW Christiansburg VA 24073 Office: Belmont Christian Church 2149 Dominion Dr Christiansburg VA 24073 *With so much in our world decided by force and power, there is a tremendous need for the gentle touch of love extended to hurting people. But only those who are truly strong can afford to be gentle.*

BAYNE, ROBERT DONALD, JR., minister; b. Dothan, Ala., Dec. 15, 1953; s. Robert Donald Sr. and Edna Earl (Bolton) B.; m. Alyne Hermoine Walker, June 18, 1977; 1 child, Heather Leigh. Student, Enterprise State Jr. Coll., 1972-74; BA, Mobile Coll., 1977; MDiv, New Orleans Bapt. Theol. Sem., 1984. Ordained to ministry So. Bapt. Conv., 1974. Pastor Victoria Bapt. Ch., Jack, Ala., 1973-74; assoc. pastor Travis Rd. Bapt. Ch., Mobile, Ala., 1975-76; pastor Mt. Carmel Bapt. Ch., Maplesville, Ala., 1977-79, Friendship Bapt. Ch., Grady, Ala., 1980-86, Lee St. Bapt. Ch., Enterprise, Ala., 1986—. Vol. chaplain Humana Hosp., Enterprise, 1986-88. Mem. Enterprise Ministerial Assn., Coffe Bapt. Assn. (planning com. 1989-91, adult dir. Sunday Sch. ASSISTeam 1989-91, evangelism coun., 1987-91). Home: 104 Brooks Circle Enterprise AL 36330 Office: So Star 428 Andrews Ozark AL 36360

BAYS, ERIC, bishop; b. Portage La Prairie, Manitoba, Can., Aug. 10, 1932; s. Percy Clarence and Hilda (Harper) B.; m. Patricia Ann Earle, Dec. 28, 1967; children: Jonathan Edmund, Rebecca Jane. BS, U. Man., Winnipeg, Can., 1955; BA, U. Sask., Saskatoon, Can., 1959; L in Theology, U. Emmanuel Coll., Saskatoon, 1959, DD (hon.), 1987; M in Ministry, Christian Theol. Sem., Indpls., 1974. Ordained to ministry Anglican Ch., 1959. Asst. curate All Saints' Anglican Ch., Winnipeg, 1959-61; lectr. Emmanuel Coll., Saskatoon, 1961-62; mission priest Diocese Caledonia, B.C., 1962-64; novice in religion Community of the Resurrection, Mirfield, Eng., 1964-65; vicar St. Saviour's with St. Catherine Parish, Winnipeg, 1965-67; rector All Saints' Parish, Winnipeg, 1968-76; prof. Coll. Emmanuel/St. Chad, Saskatoon, 1976-81; vice-prin. Coll. of Emmanuel/St. Chad, Saskatoon, 1981-86; bishop Diocese Qu'Appelle, Regina, Sask., 1986—. With RCAF, 1955-59. Avocations: golf, curling. Office: Diocese of Qu'Appelle, 1501 College Ave, Regina, SK Canada S4P 1B8

BAYUSIK, ROBERT EDWARD, priest, builder, designer; b. Bridgeport, Conn., Mar. 1, 1927; s. John Joseph and Susan (Churma) B. Student, St. Procopius Coll., 1943-46, SS. Cyril & Methodius Sem., 1952-58, Pa. State U., Altoona, 1967-68. Ordained priest Roman Cath. Ch., 1958. Founder St. Nicholas Parish, Anchorage, 1958-62; administrator St. John's Ch., Barnesboro, Pa., 1963-66; adminstr. Sts. Peter and Paul Ch., Portage, Pa., 1966—, St. Michael's Ch., South Fork, Pa., 1966—; bd. dirs. Archdiocesan Bldg. Commn., Pitts., 1965—; trustee Magdeline Coll., Manchester, N.H., life mem.; founder St. Joseph's Apostolate, Portage, 1980—, St. Joseph's Retirement Ctr., 1980—, St. Joseph's Radio Ministry, 1982—; dir. Cen. Pa. Byzantine Communications, Portage, 1982—; dir. historic Restoration St. Michael's Ch., 1967—; supr., designer, builder SS. Peter & Paul's Ch., 1971—; designer (fabrication) Mosaic Baldachino, 1977. Co-founder Portage Ambulance Assn., 1970; interdiocesan coord. Prolife, Pitts., 1975—. 1st sgt. U.S. Army, 1947-51. Named Outstanding Young Priest Archdiocese of Pitts., 1960; recipient BaldachinoHighest Praise award Ferrari Bacci Studio, Pietrasanta, Italy, 1989. Mem. Marian Movement of Priests, Greek Cath. Union, Confraternity Cath. Clergy, Apostolatus Uniti, KC (co-founder Anchorage br., life, charter Portage br.1988-89), Judaic Heritage Soc. Democrat. Avocations: experimental horticulture, architectural design. Home and Office: 605 Prospect St Portage PA 15946

BAZEMORE, DENNIS NEAL, minister; b. Ahoskie, N.C., Oct. 10, 1955; s. Henry Lyon and Iris Verle (White) B.; m. Linda Rae Callis, July 23, 1977; children: Stephen Neal, Hannah Rae. BA, Campbell U., 1977; MDiv, Southeastern Bapt. Theol. Sem., 1982. Ordained to ministry Bapt. Ch., 1982. Min. youth Murfreesboro (N.C.) Bapt. Ch., 1975-77; asst. to the pastor Lillington (N.C.) Bapt. Ch., 1977-82; pastor Chadbourn (N.C.) Bapt. Ch., 1982-89, First Bapt. Ch., Wallace, N.C., 1989—; mem. com. on coms. Bapt. State Conv. N.C., Raleigh, 1989, trustee orientation com., 1991-93. Trustee Chowan Coll., Murfreesboro, 1985-89, 91—; mem. recreation com. Chadbourn (N.C.) Town Coun., 1984-88, mem. planning and zoning bd., 1989, N.C. Strawberry Festival, 1983-89. Office: First Bapt Ch 408 W Main St Wallace NC 28466

BAZIGA, DAVID, minister, religious organization executive. Pres. Eglise Baptiste, Butare, Rwanda. Office: Eglise Baptiste, Nyantanga, BP 59, Butare Rwanda*

BEACH, DANIEL RAYMOND, parochial school educator; b. Buffalo, N.Y., Dec. 27, 1946; s. Norman Leroy and Marian Hannah (Bartlett) B.; m. Michele Jean Burke, June 19, 1976; children: Jessica Faith, Nathaniel Stewart. BA, Roberts Wesleyan Coll., Nichili, N.Y., 1969; MRE, Grand Rapids Bapt. Seminary, 1982. Tchr. North Fla. Christian Sch., Tallahassee, 1970-72; tchr., adminstr. Univ. Christian Sch., Jacksonville, Fla., 1972-74; youth pastor 1st Bapt. Ch., Clarkston, Mich., 1974-76; tchr. Oakland Christian Sch., Pontiac, Mich., 1976-81; adminstr., tchr. Fellowship Bapt. Acad., Carson City, Mich., 1981-90, Mt. Pleasant (Mich.) Bapt. Acad., 1990—; founder local chpt. Prison Fellowship, Carson City, 1989-90. Bd. dirs. Montcalm County Mental Health, Stanton, Mich., 1990; active Prison-Community Liaison Com., Carson City, 1989-90. With U.S. Army, 1971. Home: 2531 N Mission Rd Rosebush MI 48878 Office: Mount Pleasant Bapt Acad 1802 E High Mount Pleasant MI 48858

BEACH, GEORGE KIMMICH, minister; b. Richmond, Va., June 6, 1935; s. Stephen Holbrook and Virginia (Kimmich) B.; m. Barbara Kres, June 21, 1958; children: Geoffrey K., Eric K. AB, Oberlin Coll., 1957; STB, Harvard U., 1960, ThM, 1965; D in Ministry, Wesley Theol. Sem., 1985; DD (hon.), Meadville/Lombard Theol. Sch., 1989. Ordained to ministry Unitarian Universalist Assn., 1961. Min. First Unitarian Ch., Austin, Tex., 1972-78; sr. min. Unitarian Ch. of Arlington, Va., 1978—; chmn. Collegium Assn. for Liberal Religious Studies, Chgo., 1976—; pres. Greater Washington Assn. of Unitarian Universalist Chs., 1985-86. Editor: (essays of James Luther Adams) The Prophethood of All Believers, 1986, An Examined Faith, 1991. Pres., trustee Arlingtonian Ministering to Emergency Needs (AMEN), Arlington, 1984—; adv. bd. Salvadoran Refugee Com., Washington, 1991. Mem. Unitarian Universalist Mins. Assn., Internat. Assn. for Religious Freedom. Office: Unitarian Ch of Arlington 4444 Arlington Rd Arlington VA 22204

BEACHAM, BILLY, JR. (WILLIAM E. BEACHAM), religious organization administrator, speaker, writer; b. Tuba, Okla., Aug. 29, 1954; s. William E. and Dorris Jean (Tucker) B.; m. Tracye Beacham, Dec. 11, 1982; children: Billy, Brooke. AS, Tyler (Tex.) Jr. Coll., 1975; BS in Bus. Adminstrn., U. Tex., Tyler, 1977; M in Religious Edn., Southwestern Bapt. Theol. Sem., Ft. Worth, 1980. V.p. Internat. Evang. Assn., Ft. Worth, 1977-89; pres. Student Discipleship Ministries, Ft. Worth, 1987—; bd. dirs. Nat. Network Youth Ministries, San Diego, 1982—, Student Mission Impact, Columbia, S.C., 1986—, Gabriel Ministries, Arlington, Tex., 1986—, Illusions & Reality Ministry, Crowley, Tex., 1986—. Author: Back to the Basics, 1981, Growing in Godliness, 1988, The True Test, 1989, Paul/Timothy Discipleship, 1989, Everyone Everywhere, 1990; author tract The Answer (3 million sold since 1988). Home: 237 Gatewood Circle W Burleson TX 76028 Office: Student Discipleship Ministries PO Box 6747 Fort Worth TX 76115

BEACHUM, CHRISTOPHER MARK, producer; b. Tupelo, Miss., June 4, 1966; s. James Mark and Jencie Carolyn (Moore) B. BBA, Miss. State U., 1987; postgrad., U. Ala. Ops. dir. Sta. WCFB Radio, Tupelo, 1987-89; announcer Stas. WESE/WTUP Radio, Tupelo, 1989-90, Sta. WFFX Radio, Tuscaloosa, Ala., 1990—; assoc. producer U. Ala., Tuscaloosa, 1990-91, segment producer, 1991—. Mem. Broadcast Edn. Assn. Baptist. Avocation: golf. Home: 1601 Mimosa Park # 64 Tuscaloosa AL 35405 Office: U Ala CCET PO Box 870167 Tuscaloosa AL 35487

BEAGLE, WILLIAM GERHARDT, pastor; b. Glenesta, Ohio, Mar. 21, 1946; s. Louis Gerhardt and Ann Billie (Nutick) B.; m. Stell May Good, Sept. 23, 1967; children: Kelly, Mary, Deborah. BA, Bapt. Christian Ch., 1979. Ordained to ministry Bapt. Ch., 1976. Pastor Cheshire (Ohio) United Meth. Ch., 1971-79, Dover (Ill.) Congl. Ch., 1979-82, Beecher (Ill.) Community Ch., 1982—; evangelist, pres. Rock Solid Ministries, Beecher, 1985—. Mem. Charismatic Bible Ministries, Assn. Christian Truckers (bd. dirs. 1985-86). Home: 539 Country Ln Beecher IL 60401 Office: Beecher Community Ch Rock Solid Ministries PO Box 757 Beecher IL 60401

BEAL, WINONA ROARK, religion educator; b. Birchwood, Tenn., Aug. 11, 1924; d. Thomas Jefferson and Minnie Belle (Price) Roark; m. Charles Hugh Beal, Aug. 6, 1949; children: Jeremy Lawrence, Eric David. BA in Bus., Tenn. Tech. U., 1948; postgrad., So. Bapt. Theol. Sem., 1950-54, U. Louisville, 1951-53, Manatee Community Coll., 1958-60. Tchr. Washington (Ga.) High Sch., 1948-50; asst. to treas. So. Bapt. Theol. Sem., Louisville, Ky., 1951-54; asst. to bus. mgr. Agnes Scott Coll., Decatur, Ga., 1968-71; religious edn. dir. Bay Haven Bapt. Ch., Sarasota, Fla., 1976-84, office program dir., 1985-89; ret., 1989; spritual guide dir. Bay Haven Elem. Sch., Sarasota, 1965-68; mem. Sapphire Shores Indian Beach Assn., Sarasota, 1985-90. Mem. S.W. Fla. Bapt. Assn. (exec. com. 1976-89, dir. Vacation Bible Sch. 1976-89, student work 1976-80), S.W. Manatee Assn. (pres. 1972, 80, 84-89), Fla. Pastors' Wives Conf. (v.p. 1975, program chair 1979, sec.-treas. 1983). Democrat. Home: 638 Beverly Dr Sarasota FL 34234 *I believe that the greatest profanity is not of the lips but of the life.*

BEALE, LAWRENCE L., clergyman; b. Boykins, Va., Nov. 17, 1932; s. Charlie and Nettie (Phillips) B.; m. Tessie, June 31, 1976; children: Lawrence L., John Wayne, Shelia Hardy. BA, Va. Theol. Sem. and Coll., 1973, MDiv, 1976, DMin., 1977; MA in Counseling/Student Personnel Work, W.Va. Coll. Grad. Studies, 1986. Dir. testing, counselor Bluefield (W.Va.) State Coll.; past. Mt. Zion Bapt. Ch., Bluefield. Mem. Am. Assn. for Counseling and Devel. Home: 323 N Mercer St Bluefield WV 24701

BEALE, NANCY LEE, church secretary, music teacher; b. Phila., Jan. 9, 1956; d. Robert and Lois Jean (McCullough) Alexander; m. Keith Edward Beale, July 30, 1977; children: Robert, Scott. BS in Music Edn., West Chester U., 1977. Cert. elem. tchr., Pa. Clk. Robert Morris Assocs., Phila., 1972-77; piano tchr. Fort Washington, Pa., 1973—; order processor Digital Equipment Corp., Blue Bell, Pa., 1977-78; music tchr. K-5 Tredyffrin/Easttown Sch. Dist., Strafford and Paoli, Pa., 1978-79; pianist Ch. of the Open Door, Fort Washington, 1977—; sec. Jarrettown United Meth. Ch., Dresher, Pa., 1987—; substitute tchr. Upper Dublin Sch. Dist., Fort Washington, 1991—; accompanist various vocalists and instrumentalists, 1977—, ACCENT traveling group, 1989—; dir. mus. Jarrettown United Meth. Bible Sch., 1987—, AWANA youth program, Fort Washington, 1987—; mem. adv. bd. Phila. Coll. of the Bible, Langhorne, Pa., 1990—. Mem. Fort Washington PTA (sec. 1988-89, pres. 1989-91), United Meth. Women, Dresher (cir. leader 1986-87). Republican. Avocations: tennis, walking, piano. Home: 1367 Cinnamon Dr Fort Washington PA 19034

BEALS, DUANE J., academic administrator. Head Western Evang. Sem., Portland, Oreg. Office: Western Evang Sem 4200 SE Jennings Ave Portland OR 97267*

BEALS, KENNETH ALBERT, minister; b. Findlay, Ohio, Apr. 26, 1946; s. Raymond Kenneth and Mary Elizabeth (Parks) B.; m. Jaquelyn Kaye Whitaker, June 22, 1968; children: Eve Elisabeth, Kurt Andrew. BA, Wittenberg U., 1968; ThM, Boston U., 1971, ThD, 1982. Ordained to ministry United Meth. Ch., 1969. Pastor Comml. Point (Ohio) Ch., 1973-76; assoc. pastor Ch. of the Master, Westerville, Ohio, 1976-81; pastor Northridge United Meth. Ch., Springfield, Ohio, 1981—, Mt. Olivet United Meth. Ch., Buchanan, Va., 1988; dir. program ministries Cen. United Meth. Ch., Staunton, Va., 1988—; sec. Staunton Area Ministerial Assn. Mem. Bethesda Sunday Com., Dist. Com. on Superintendency, Springfield, 1984-87; Dist. Com. on Ordained Ministry, Springfield, 1985; marshal United Meth. Ch. Gen. Conf., Balt., 1984; pres. bd. dirs. Metro Ministries, Springfield, 1984—, bd. dirs. Staunton br. ARC, Staunton Community Rels. Bd. Jacob Sleeper fellow Boston U., 1971. Mem. Clark County Ministerial Fellow, Westerville (Ohio) Ministerial Assn. (pres. 1979). Democrat. Lodge: Sertoma (treas. 1980). Home: 613 Alleghany Ave Staunton VA 24401

BEALS, PAUL ARCHER, religious educator; b. Russell, Iowa, Feb. 18, 1924; s. Archer Edwin and Myrtle Mae (Kelsey) B.; m. Vivian Brown, Sept. 29, 1945; children: Lois Ruth, Stephen Paul, Samuel Archer, Timothy Joel. AB, Wheaton (Ill.) Coll., 1945; diploma, Moody Bible Inst., Chgo., 1948; ThM with high honors, Dallas Theol. Seminary, 1952, ThD, 1964. Missionary in Cen. African Republic Bapt. Mid-Missions, Cleve., 1952-64; prof. of missiology Grand Rapids (Mich.) Bapt. Seminary, 1964—, dir. continuing edn., 1977-90; theol. cons. Bapt. Mid-Missions, 1969—; conf. speaker. Author: A People For His Name, 1985; contbr. articles to profl. jours. Mem. Evang. Theol. Soc., Evang. Missiological Soc. (pres. 1990—), Midwest Fellowship Professors, Missions, Am. Soc. Missiology, Pi Gamma Mu. Home: 2111 Audley Dr NE Grand Rapids MI 49505

BEAM, STEVEN GERALD, religious organization administrator; b. Mpls., Aug. 4, 1956; s. Donald Samuel and Joan Stephenie (Lauzon) B.; m. Nancy Sheryl Husselton, Dec. 27, 1975; children: Scott Paul, Jayne Marie. BA, Anderson U., 1977; MDiv, Anderson Sch. of Theology, 1980. Minister Ch. of God, Anderson, Ind., 1975-81, United Methodist, Fla., 1981-86; missionary, adminstr. Missionary Ventures, Inc., Orlando, Fla., 1983—; cons. Missionary Ventures, Inc., Orlando, 1985—. Author: Complete Manual for Youth Ministry, 1986. Recipient Falls scholarship, Anderson U., 1975. Republican. United Methodist. Avocations: tennis, basketball, swimming, history, anthropology. Office: Missionary Ventures Inc 6019 S Orange Ave Orlando FL 32809

BEAMER, CHARLES CHRISTIAN, minister; b. Baton Rouge, La., Nov. 21, 1950; s. Clifford Myron and Marilyn Jean (Beatty) B.; m. Pamela Jo Harter, Feb. 14, 1986; 1 child, Jason. BA in Music, Calif. Inst. of Arts, Valencia, Calif., 1973; MA in Ministry, Pacific Christian Coll., 1985. Ordained to ministry Christian Ch., 1985. Pastor First Christian Ch., Glendale, Calif., 1986-88; assoc. minister Cornerstone Christian Ch., Northridge, Calif., 1988-89, Victory Center Ch. of Christ, North Hollywood, Calif., 1984-86; church rels. specialist Every Home for Christ, Chatsworth, Calif., 1989—. Office: Every Home for Christ 20232 Sunburst St Chatsworth CA 91311 *The most important things in life are not things, for what shall a man give in exchange for his soul?.*

BEAN, DAVID IRA MITCHELL, youth minister; b. Sturgis, Ky., Jan. 25, 1954; s. Ben Ray and Eva Iris (Wallace) B.; m. Marsha Kaye Giesler, May 17, 1975; children: Gabrielle Christine, Aaron Benjamin Edward. BA, St. Louis Christian Coll., 1976. Youth minister Crestwood (Mo.) Christian Ch., 1975-84, N.W. Ave. Ch. of Christ, Tallmadge, Ohio, 1984—; dir. wilderness camping program High Hill Christian Assembly, 1975-84; staff mem. Summer in the Son, Grayson, Ky., 1988—; mem. planning com. Ohio Teens for Christ Conv., Worthington, Ohio, 1985—; mem. Akron and Canton Youth Mins., 1984—; dean, staff worker Round Lake Christian Assembly, Lakeville, Ohio, 1984—. Commr. Tallmadge Ch. Softball League, 1987, 88; mem. scholarship com. Tallmadge High Sch., 1985; mem. North Akron Bd. Trade, 1988—; chaplain, coord. Boy Scouts Am., Akron, 1986—. Mem. Fellowship Christian Educators, U.S. Slo-Pitch Softball Assn. Home: 1086 Northeast Ave Tallmadge OH 44278 Office: Northwest Ave Ch of Christ 737 Northwest Ave Tallmadge OH 44278

BEAN, MARION TALPEY, lay worker; b. Sidney, Maine, Oct. 24, 1926; d. Harold T. and Mabelle (Freeman) B. BA, Barrington Coll., 1950; MEd, Boston U., 1959, EdD, 1974. Treas. Barrington (R.I.) Bapt. Ch., 1963—; Sunday sch. tchr. Barrington Bapt. Ch., 1953-86; prof. edn. and bus. Gordon Coll., Wenham, Mass., 1956—. Mem. Area #5 Cable Adv. Bd., R.I., 1979-87. Mem. New Eng. Bus. Educators (pres. 1969), Delta Pi Epsilon (pres. 1984). Home: 176 Washington Rd Barrington RI 02806 Office: Barrington Bapt Ch 25 Old County Rd Barrington RI 02806-1601

BEAN, MARVIN DAY, clergyman; b. Tampa, Fla., Sept. 8, 1921; s. Marvin Day and Lillian (Howell) B.; AB, Fla. So. Coll., 1946, MS in Social Work, Vanderbilt U., 1948; postgrad. Ohio State U., 1951-52, Northwestern U., 1950; B.D., Garrett Theol. Sem., 1950; children: Bethany Louise, Thomas Holmes, Carol Sue. Ordained to ministry Methodist Ch., 1950; pastor, Lena Vista, Fla., 1946; assoc. pastor San Marcos Meth. Ch., Tampa, 1947; pastor Cedar Lake (Ind.) Meth. Ch., 1948-50, Shepard Meth. Ch., Columbus, Ohio, 1951-68, Stonybrook Meth. Ch., Gahanna, Ohio, 1960-65, Obetz (Ohio) Meth. Ch., 1968-73, Neil Ave. Ch., Columbus, 1973-79, St. Andrew Ch., Columbus, 1979—. Asst. to exec. sec. Meth. Union in Ch. Extension, Columbus, 1965-74; v.p. com. info. and pub. rels. Ohio Conf. Meth. Ch., 1964-68, vice chmn. health and welfare ministries, 1968-72, chmn. urban life com. Bd. Missions, 1968-70, asso. sec. Bd. Missions, 1968-72, chmn. Svcs. to Children and Youth, 1962-72; chmn. rsch. Ohio Area Study on Aging, Ohio area Meth. Ch., 1959-64; sec. Columbus dist. conf. Meth. Ch., 1960-68; chmn. sch. religion Columbus area Council Chs., 1953; sec. United Meth. Hist. Soc. of Ohio, 1984; trustee Meth. Retirement Ctr. Central Ohio, Columbus; trustee United Meth. Children's Home, Worthington, Ohio, 1973-74; chmn. bd. trustees Neil Ave. Found., 1973-79; chmn. W. Ohio Commn. Archives and History, 1984-88; conf. historian West Ohio Conf. United Meth. Ch., 1988—; pres. United Meth. Hist. Soc. Ohio. Served with AUS, 1943-46. Recipient Wolfley Found. recognition award for inner city work, 1961, Outstanding Human Svc. Dir. of Yr. award Nat. Health and Welfare Ministries, 1990. Mem. Columbus Meth. Ministerial Assn. (pres. 1960-61), Ohio Council Chs. (rep. com. strategy and planning 1965-68). Nat. Assn. Social Workers, Acad. Cert. Social Workers. Author: A Guide to United Methodist Building, 1973; You Are on the District Board, 1974; Unto the Least of These, 1981; contbr. articles to profl. jours. Home: 122 W Henderson Rd Columbus OH 43214

BEANE, MARK CHRISTOPHER, minister; b. Asheboro, N.C., Dec. 4, 1956; s. Walter Robert and Helen (Cox) B.; m. Bette Theilig, Dec. 28, 1985; 1 child, Joshua Matthew. BS, East Carolina U., 1979; MDiv, Asbury Theol. Sem., 1985; postgrad., U. N.C., 1983, N.C. Bapt. Hosp., 1990. Ordained to ministry Wesleyan Ch. as elder, 1986. Youth pastor Providence Christian Ch., Lexington, Ky., 1983-85; asst. pastor 1st Wesleyan Ch., Eden, N.C., 1985-87; asst. pastor Christ Wesleyan Ch., Winston-Salem, N.C., 1987-90, Greensboro, N.C., 1990—; adj. chaplain Moses-Cone Hosp., Greensboro, 1990—; chaplain assoc. Forsyth Meml. Hosp., Winston-Salem, 1987-90; vol. chaplain Eden Morehead Hosp., 1985-87. Named Outstanding Young Men Am., 1986. Republican. Home: 2506 Argonne Blvd Greensboro NC 27407 Office: Christ Wesleyan Ch 2400 S Holden Rd Greensboro NC 27407

BEANE, WENDELL CHARLES, educator, clergyman; b. Hamilton, Bermuda, Oct. 21, 1935; came to U.S., 1952; s. Sydney Inkle Bean and Olive Louise Ebbin; m. DeAnna Easily Banks, June 6, 1959 (div. Feb. 1987); children: Songhai Marie, Mark Wendell; m. Margaret Ann Van Deraa, Nov. 11, 1989. BA, Howard U., 1958, BD cum laude, 1961; MA, U. Chgo., 1966, PhD, 1971. Ordained to ministry United Meth. Ch. as elder, 1961. Pastor Calloway United Meth. Ch., Arlington, Va., 1959-63; instr. Rutgers U., New Brunswick, N.J., 1969-79; assoc. prof. history of religions, phenomenology of religion U. Wis., Oshkosh, 1979—, chair dept., 1989—. Author: Myth, Cult and Symbols in Sakta Hinduism, 1977; co-editor: Myths, Rites, Symbols, 1976; also articles. U. Chgo. scholar, 1963-68. Fellow Am. Inst. Indian Studies; mem. Am. Acad. Religion, Assn. for Asian Studies, Assn. for Rsch. and Enlightenment, Alpha Phi Alpha. Democrat. Methodist. Avocations: books, travelling, movies, swimming, volleyball. Office: U Wis Dept Religious Studies A&C Bldg Rm 319 800 Algoma Blvd Oshkosh WI 54901

BEARD, MICHAEL CARL, consultant, writer; b. Cambridge, Eng., Sept. 27, 1956; came to U.S., 1959; s. William Arthur Jr. and Barbara Lee (Cathey) Appleton; m. Barbara Loraine Gipson, May 6, 1978; children: Elaine Denise, Pamela Jean. BS, Southwestern Coll., 1979; MA, Western Sem., Oreg., 1982. Ordained to Ministry, Baptist Ch. Pastor Sacramento St. Bapt. Ch., Portland, 1981-82, Haley Bapt. Ch., Boring, Oreg., 1983-84; adminstr. Golf Links Acad., Tucson, 1984-86; cons., speaker Profl. Strategies Group, Inkster, Mich., 1986, Profl. Resume Service, Sterling Heights, Mich., 1986-88; corp. communications officer Genesis Internat. Corp., Farmington Hills, Mich., 1988—. Republican.

BEARD, RANDALL EVERET, minister; b. Louisville, Oct. 23, 1957; s. Jerry Lynn and Janet Carolyn (McDonald) B.; m. Rhonda Gayle Nelson, Jan. 4, 1980; children: Ryan, Rayanne. BA, Cin. Bible Coll., 1979; MDiv, So. Bapt. Theol. Seminary, Louisville, 1988. Assoc. minister Clifton Heights Christian Ch., Louisville, 1976-78; interim minister Fairdale (Ky.) Christian Ch., 1979; assoc. minister First Christian Ch., Scottsburg, Ind., 1983-89; minister River Drive Christian Ch., Irvine, Ky., 1989—; chaplain U.S. Army Res., Jeffersonville, Ind., 1990—; camp dean Wonder Valley Christian Assembly, Salem, Ind., 1987-88. Named Outstanding Young Minister North Am. Christian Conv., Cin., 1989; named to Outstanding Young Men of Am., 1986, 89. Mem. Estill County Ministerial Assn. (treas. 1991—), Greater Richmond Ministerial Assn. (v.p. 1991—), So. Ind. Christian Ministerial Assn. (sec./treas. 1989). Republican. *We like to appear as islands in the sea of life. But in our pride that often spurns the help of others, none can refuse the genuine concern of another.*

BEARDEN, ALFRED DOUGLAS, pastor; b. Newnan, Ga., Feb. 18, 1954; s. William Robert Bearden and Nellie Ruth (Weaver) Bailey; m. Susan Gail Bass, Feb. 25, 1972; children: Katherine Leigh, Douglas Bruce. Student, Moody Bible Coll., 1975-77. Pastor Providence Bapt. Ch., Roosville, Ga., 1974-77, Antioch Bapt. Ch., Whitesburg, Ga., 1977-87, Centrall Bapt. Ch., Carrollton, Ga., 1987—. Home: 15 Black Oak Dr Newnan GA 30263

BEARDSLEE, ANN NESMITH, religious organization administrator; b. Jacksonville, FLa., Apr. 3, 1929; d. Ellie W. and Pauline (Mercer) Nesmith; m. Howard M. Beardslee, June 10, 1948; children: Keith E., Beth Romano. BA summa cum laude, Upsala Coll., 1975. Asst. Ecumenical Devel. Coop. Soc., N.Y.C.; acting exec. dir. Church World Svcs., Nat. Coun. Chs., N.Y.C.; dir. Presbyn. Hunger Program, N.Y.C.; pres. Interfaith Hunger Appeal. Home: 475 Riverside Dr New York NY 10115

BEARDSLEE, WILLIAM ARMITAGE, religious organization administrator, educator; b. Holland, Mich., Mar. 25, 1916; s. John Walter Jr. and Frances Eunice (Davis) B.; m. Kathryn Quinby Walker, June 11, 1941 (dec. Nov. 1982); children—Joy Walker (dec.), William Rigby; m. Cynthia Ann Meckel, Sept. 24, 1988. AB, Harvard U., 1937; BD, New Brunswick Theol. Sem., 1941; M.A., Columbia U., 1948; Ph.D., U. Chgo., 1951. Ordained to ministry Ref. Ch. in Am., 1941. Minister Ref. Church in Am., Queens Village, N.Y., 1941-45; asst. prof. Bible studies Emory U., Atlanta, 1947-52, assoc. prof., 1952-56, prof. religion, 1956-80, Charles Howard Candler prof., 1980-84, prof. emeritus, 1984—, dir. Grad. Inst. Liberal Arts, 1957-61, acting dean Coll. Arts and Scis., 1958; dir. faith and process Ctr. for Process Studies, Claremont, Calif., 1984—; mem. rev. com. Standard Version Bible, Nat. Coun. Chs.; vis. prof. N.T. Columbia Theol. Sem., Decatur, Ga., 1990. Author: (with E. H. Rece) Reading Bible: A Guide, 1952, 2d edit., 1964, Human Achievement and Divine Vocation in The Message of Paul, 1961, (with J. Boozer) Faith to Act, 1967, Literary Criticism of the New Testament, 1970, House for Hope, 1972, (with David R. Griffin and Joe Holland) Types of Postmodern Theology, 1989, (with others) Biblical Preaching on the Death of Jesus, 1989, Margins of Belonging, 1991; editor: America and the Future of Theology, 1967, The Poetics of Faith (Semeia 12 and 13), 1978. Fulbright Sr. Research grant U. Bonn. Germany, 1961-62; vis. prof. Pomona Coll., spring 1969; fellow Center Bibl. Research, Soc. Bibl. Lit., Claremont, Calif., 1976-77; Honored by Festschrift Orientation by Disorientation (Richard A. Spencer, editor), 1980; recipient Meth. Scholar-Tchr. award Emory U., 1981. Mem. Am. Acad. Religion (asso. editor 1961-69), Soc. Bibl. Lit. (pres. So. sect. 1957-58, editor Semeia Supplements 1974-79, assoc. editor 1979-82), Archeol. Inst. Am., AAUP, Phi Beta Kappa. Home: 747 Plymouth Rd Claremont CA 91711

BEARY, SHIRLEY LORRAINE, music educator; b. New Albany, Kans., Feb. 4, 1928; d. Howard Warren and Bertha Adelia (Wilcox) Fogelsanger; children: Stephanie Beary Johnson, Susan Beary Maloney. BA, Andrews U.,

1949; MusM, U. Redlands, 1967; D Mus. Arts, Southwestern Bapt. Theol. Sem., 1977. Tchr. music Nevada, Iowa, 1949-50; prof. music Southwestern Adventist Coll., Keene, Tex., 1959-84, lectr. Christian ethics, 1978-84; prof. music Oakwood Coll., Huntsville, Ala., 1984—; ch. organist Seventh-day Adventist Ch., Kalamazoo, 1951-59, Keene, 1959-90, min. music, 1980-82. Mem. bd. advisors Am. Biog. Inst., Raleigh, N.C. Mem. Coll. Music Soc., Am. Hymn Soc., Internat. Adventist Music Assn. Democrat. Avocations: travel, flower gardening, stamps and records collecting, gospel singing. Home: 1030 Sandy Springs Rd Huntsville AL 35806 Office: Oakwood Coll Oakwood Rd Huntsville AL 35896

BEASLEY, DOUGLAS KENT, music minister; b. Ft. Smith, Ark., Sept. 28, 1954; s. Estil Cloyse and Billie Britt (Cox) B.; m. Nancy Jolene Rankin, July 10, 1982. AA, Westark Community Coll., 1975; B. Music Edn., U. Cen. Ark., 1979. Ordained minister in Bapt. Ch., 1988. Minister music First So. Bapt. Cen., Lavaca, Ark., 1980-82; minister music/media Haven Heights Bapt., Ft. Smith, 1982-85; assoc pastor music Adamsville Bapt. Ch., Goldsboro, N.C., 1985—; music coord. Bailey Smith Crusade, Ft. Smith, 1985, Freddy Gage "Go Tell" Crusade, Kinston, N.C., 1988; music evangelist, 1982—; coord.-dir. Living Christmas Tree musical drama Adamsville Bapt. Ch., Goldsboro, 1988—. Music coord./vol. minister Wayne Correctional Ctr., Goldsboro, 1985—; active mem. Wayne County Young Republicans, Goldsboro, 1988—. Mem. Neuse Bapt. Assn. (music dir. 1986-87, 91), Phi Mu Alpha (past chaplain 1976-78), Pi Kappa Phi (past chaplain 1979-80). Home: 103 William Ct Goldsboro NC 27530 Office: Adamsville Bapt Ch 1302 N Berkeley Blvd Goldsboro NC 27534

BEATY, JAMES RALPH, minister; b. Evansville, Ind., May 16, 1929; s. James Clifford and Amanda Ann (Apgar) B.; m. Emma Jean Galloway, June 13, 1950; children—Ralph Norman, James Robert, Ann Lynn, Jerri Elizabeth, William Clifford. B.A., Franklin Coll. Ind., 1951, D.D., 1979. M.Div., So. Bapt. Theol. Sem., 1954; D.D., Judson Coll., 1970. Ordained to ministry Am. Baptist Chs. U.S.A., 1952. Asst. to pastor 1st Bapt. Ch., Evansville, 1948; pastor Exeter Ave. Bapt. Ch., Indpls., 1949-52, Veale Creek Bapt. Ch., Washington, Ind., 1952-54, 1st Bapt. Ch., Salem, Ind., 1954-57; field counselor Div. World Mission Support, Am. Bapt. Conv., 1958-66; exec. minister Indpls. Bapt. Assn., 1966-67; regional minister Am. Bapt. Chs. of the Great Rivers Region, 1977—; assoc. gen. sec. Am. Bapt. Chs. in U.S.A., 1989—. Mem. alumni coun. Franklin Coll., 1960-70; mem. Ch. Fedn. Greater Indpls., 1966-67; mem. Ill. Conf. Chs., 1977—, Mo. Coun. of Chs., 1977—; bd. dirs. Shurtleff Fund, 1977—; trustee No. Bapt. Theol. Sem., 1977—, Franklin Coll., 1982—, Judson Coll., 1971; mem. Midwest commn. on ministry Am. Bapt. Conv., 1966—, mem. Regional Exec. Ministers Coun., 1966—, mem. Gen. Staff Coun., 1972—. Recipient citations Christian Higher Edn. Challenge, Am. Bapt. Conv., 1960, Franklin Coll. Alumni Council, 1971, Ch. Fedn. Greater Indpls., 1975, Ind. Bapt. Conv., 1976, Indpls. Bapt. Assn., 1977; Alumni of Yr. citation So. Bapt. Theol. Sem., 1981; Certificate of Appreciation, World Mission Campaign of Am. Bapt. Conv., 1968. Mem. Lambda Chi Alpha. Address: 6242 E Welham Dr Indianapolis IN 46220

BEAUCHAMP, E(DWARD) WILLIAM, priest, lawyer, management educator, university administrator; b. Detroit, May 17, 1942; s. Edward F. and Marion K. Beauchamp. BS in Acctg., U. Detroit, 1964, MBA, 1966; postgrad., Mich. State U., 1966-71; JD, U. Notre Dame, 1975, MDiv, 1981. Bar: Mich. 1975; ordained priest Roman Cath. Ch., 1982. Tchr., assoc. dir. admissions Alma (Mich.) Coll., 1966-71; ptnr. Goggin, Baker and Beauchamp, Alma, 1975-77; asst. prof. mgmt., adminstrv. asst. to exec. v.p. U. Notre Dame, South Bend, Ind., 1980-84, exec. asst. to pres., 1984-87, exec. v.p., 1987—. Recipient Wall St. Jour. award, 1964, Bernstein, Bernstein, Wile and Gordon award, 1963. Office: U Notre Dame Office of Exec VP Notre Dame IN 46556

BEAUCHAMP, FINIS PIERRE, minister; b. Wichita Falls, Tex., Oct. 1, 1956; s. Oluff Dudley and Isabel Louise (Bernet) B.; m. Ann Paris Leavell, May 24, 1980; children: Finis Leavell, Andrew Leavell, JoAnn Leavell, David Leavell. BA, Baylor U., 1978; MDiv, New Orleans Bapt. Theol. Sem., 1981, ThD, 1987. Ordained to ministry So. Bapt. Conv., 1980. Pastor First Bapt. Ch., Port Allen, La., 1981-91, Cameron, Tex., 1991—. Mem. La. Bapt. Conv. (ch. growth cons., exec. bd. mem. 1989-91), Judson Bapt. Assn. (dir. evangelism 1989-91), Rotary Club Port Allen (pres. 1987). Republican. Home: 502 W Main Cameron TX 76520 Office: First Bapt Ch 400 W Main Cameron TX 76520

BEAUCHAMP, ROLLIN ODELL, minister; b. Greensburg, Ky., June 11, 1950; s. Rollin Beauchamp and Anna Margie Milby; m. Laurine Wayne, June 19, 1970; children: Dena Lynn, Gregory Shawn. BTh, Clear Creek Bible Coll., Pineville, Ky., 1984; postgrad., So. Seminary, Louisville, 1984-89, Luther Rice Seminary, Jacksonville, Fla., 1990—. Ordained to ministry So. Bapt. Ch., 1975. Minister Stonega (Va.) Calvary Bapt. Ch., 1975-77; minister First Bapt. Ch., Nickelsville, Va., 1977-83, Hindman, Ky., 1983-87; minister Pleasant Grove Bapt. Church, Owensboro, Ky., 1987—; mission com. chmn. Clinch Valley Assn., Gate City, Va., 1981-82; evangelism chmn. Three Forks Bapt. Assn., Hazard, Ky., 1984-85; moderator Daviees/McLean Assn., Owensboro, Ky., 1990-91. Chmn. RADA, Gate City, 1982, 83. Recipient church growth award Home Missions Bd., Atlanta, 1982. Home: 3829 Garden Terrace Owensboro KY 42301 Office: Pleasant Grove Bapt Church PO Box 5664 Hwy 56 Owensboro KY 42301

BEAUCHANE, JUDITH ANN ORRBEN, religious organization administrator, educator; b. Mpls., July 6, 1941; d. Clarence George Orrben and Mariam Luella (Johnson) Ferschweiler; m. Robert Anthony Beauchane, June 10, 1967; children: Natalie Jeane, Monica Sarah. BA, Coll. of St. Catherine, St. Paul, Minn., 1965; postgrad., Loyola U., 1987-91. Catechist Ascension Parish, Mpls., 1966-70, St. Mary's Basilica, Lincoln, Nebr., 1970-73, Holy Cross Parish, Sparks, Nev., 1973-75, St. Louise Parish, Bellevue, Wash., 1975-77, St. John Vianney Ch., Utica, Mich., 1977-78; catechist, founder liturgical dance, dir., coord. Bible sch. St. Jerome Parish, Kenner, La., 1978-81, mem. parish coun., 1980, 81; catechist, mem. parish coun. St. Elizabeth Ann Seton Parish, Kenner, 1981-82, team founder liturgical dance, dir., 1981—, dir. religious edn., 1982—; cons. Our Sunday Visitor, Huntington, Ind., 1985-91, Benziger Pub. Co., Mission Hills, Calif., 1991—. Leader Girl Scouts U.S., Kenner, 1978-83; cons. Cath. Com. on Girl Scouting, Archdiocese of New Orleans, 1989-91, mem. 1st Eucharist and reconciliation guideline com., 1988, cons., speaker, 1986. Home: 109 Yellowstone St Kenner LA 70065 Office: St Elizabeth Ann Seton Parish 4121 Saint Elizabeth Dr PO Box 641000 Kenner LA 70064-1000

BEAVON, JOSEPH CHARLES, health and education association administrator; b. Wheeling, W.Va., Nov. 18, 1943; s. Joseph C. and Anna Martha (Marx) B.; m. Jane Ann Hutsell, Nov. 1, 1986; children: Clark, Kevin, Brian, Jason, Stephanie. BS, Union Coll., Barbourville, Ky., 1966; MDiv, Meth. Theol. Sch., 1969. Pastor Lockwood United Meth. Ch., Youngstown, Ohio, 1969-73; social worker Ohio Youth Comm. Riverview Sch., Powell, Ohio, 1973-78; pastor Hyatts United Meth. Ch., Delaware, Ohio, 1977-78, Hyatts-Powell United Meth. Ch., Delaware, 1978, 79; assoc. pastor Normandy United Meth. Ch., Dayton, 1979-84; dir. communications & community rels. Luth. Social Svcs., Dayton, 1984-88; pastor Drexel Park United Meth. Ch., Dayton, 1985-88; exec. dir. Am. Lung Assn. Miami Valley, Dayton, 1988—; part time instr. communications U. Dayton. Charter pres. Miami Valley chpt. Religious Pub. Rels. Coun., 1988-89; mem. United Meth. Assn. Communicators. Mem. Associated Photographers Internat., Hon. Order Ky. Cols. Democrat. Avocations: writing, photography. Home: 9040 Mandel Dr Centerville OH 45458

BECK, EDWARD NELSON, minister; b. Washington, Aug. 19, 1949; s. Edward and Joyce Jacqueline (Wood) B.; m. Mona Faye Gandy, Jan 1, 1971; children: Rebecca Joyce, Jonathan Edward. BA, BTh, Gulf Coast Bible Coll., Houston, 1972; ThM, Fredericksburg Bible Inst., Va., 1985, ThD, 1986. Ordained to ministry. Pastor Hillcrest Ch. of God, Cody, Wyo., 1972-74; assoc. pastor Dunn Loring (Va.) Community Ch. of God, 1975-77; pastor Arwood Ch. of God, Fredericksburg, 1977-88, Taylortown Community Ch., Shelby, Ohio, 1988—; dir. sr. high youth camp Ministerial Coun. the Ch. of God, Dunn Loring, Utica, Pa., 1975-79, Burnside, Pa., 1989—; second v.p. Lighthouse Bible Inst., Dunn Loring, 1977—; mem. exec. com. Billy Graham Evangelistic Assn. Ralph Bell Greater Fredericksburg Crusade, 1984; v.p. Ministerial Coun. Ch. of God, 1986; trustee The World Missionary Fellowship the Ch. of God, Can., 1986—; dir. community Christmas program Shelby Ministerial Assn., 1990—. Author and editor booklet The Gift of Tongues and Other Tongues, 1984. Office: Taylortown Community Ch 2656 Taylortown Rd Shelby OH 44875 *By the Grace of God I seek to implement the Apostle Paul's philosophy on life: Becoming all things to all men that I might by all means save some.*

BECK, GREG DUDLEY, minister; b. Lancaster, Pa., Oct. 2, 1948; s. Mervin Reamer and Fay Lorraine (Schlemm) B.; m. Sandra Lee Krout, Aug. 22, 1970; children—Matthew Herbert, Heather Dawn. B.A., Franklin and Marshall Coll., 1970; M. Div., Lancaster Theol. Sem., 1974. Ordained to ministry United Ch. of Christ, 1974. Pastor McConnellsburg Fort Loudon Charge, Pa., 1974-78, St. Paul's Dubs Union Ch., Hanover, Pa., 1978-82; supply pastor Mt. Zion United Ch., Spring Grove, Pa., 1982-83; pastor Uniting Ch., Bairnsdale, Victoria, Australia, 1983—; del. Synod Uniting Ch. Australia, Melbourne, 1984; mem. Bd. World Missions, N.Y., 1982—, East Gippsland Presbytery, Sale-Morwell, Victoria, 1983—; resource advisor Lakes Youth Ministry, Lakes Entrance, Victoria. Author: Understanding Hindu Astrology, 1974, Computer Selection Guide, 1987. Writer asst. Understanding the Hindu Religious Tradition, 1970. Sch. council pres. Bairnsdale West Sch., Victoria, 1984-86; Bairnsdale West Primary Sch. Council, 1983-86, Computers in State Pub. Schs., Bairnsdale, 1983-86, East Gippsland People Against Nuclear Armanent, 1984-87. Mem. Ministers Fraternal East Gippsland, United Ch. Bd. World Ministries (assoc.), Gettysburg Assn., Div. of Community Services , Div. of Computer Services of Synod, Melbourne. United Ch. Christ. Home and Office: 48 Doherty St, Bairnsdale Victoria 3875, Australia

BECK, HENRY SANFORD, III (SANDY BECK), minister, educator; b. Dublin, Ga., June 24, 1945; m. Anne Owens; children: Melodie, Bubba. AA, North Greenville Coll., 1966; cert. introduction to supervision, U. S.C., Union, 1966; B in Sociology, Ohio Christian Coll., 1973; postgrad., Ga. So. Coll., 1977-79, Shorter Coll., 1980; MEd, Augusta (Ga.) Coll., 1981; postgrad., Luther Rice Sem., Jacksonville, Fla., 1982; cert. in Christian edn., Dallas Theol. Sem., 1984; postgrad., New Orleans Bapt. Theol. Sem., 1984-86; cert. in gerontology, Ga. State U., 1989. Ordained to ministry So. Bapt. Conv., 1981. Min. music and youth Piney Grove Bapt. Ch., Augusta, 1979-82; youth pastor, dir. athletic Christian sch. One Way Bapt. Ch., Martinez, Ga., 1982-83; min. edn. 1st Bapt. Ch., Kennesaw, Ga., 1983—; instr. Bible Inst., dir. athletic, tchr. Augusta Christian Schs., Inc., Martinez, 1973-76; dir. athletic, tchr. social scis., Bible Glenn Hills Bapt. Ch. Sch., Augusta, 1976-79; vol., leader music and youth Bethel Chapel, Charlotte, N.C., 1967-70, Savannah (Ga.) Gospel Chapel, 1970-73; part-time min. music Bayvale Bapt. Ch., Augusta, 1978. Chaplain City of Kennesaw. Mem. United Assn. Christian Counselors, So. Bapt. Religious Educators Assn., Ga. Bapt. Religious Educators Assn. (regional v.p.), Metro Atlanta Bapt. Religious Educators Assn., Internat. Religious Educators Assn., Kennestone Hosp. Chaplains Assn., Phi Delta Kappa. Avocations: camping, spectator sports, reading, writing. Home: 2551 Due West Circle Kennesaw GA 30144 Office: 1st Bapt Ch 2958 N Main St Kennesaw GA 30144

BECK, NORMAN ARTHUR, theology educator; b. Oak Harbor, Ohio, Feb. 27, 1933; m. Esther Hansen, Aug. 15, 1959; children: Matthew, David, Laura. BA, Capital U., 1958; BD, Luth. Theol. Sem., Columbus, Ohio, 1962; PhD, Princeton Theol. Sem., 1967; DD (hon.), Trinity Luth. Sem., Columbus, 1990. Ordained to ministry Evang. Luth. Ch. in Am., 1966. Instr. in Greek lang. Capital U., Columbus, 1958-60, 61-62; instr. in N.T. Princeton (N.J.) Theol. Sem., 1965-66; pastor Good Shepherd Luth. Ch., Monroe, Mich., 1966-70, King of Kings Luth. Ch., Ann Arbor, Mich., 1970-75; prof. theology Tex. Luth. Coll., Seguin, 1975—. Author: Scripture Notes B, 1984, Mature Christianity, 1985, Scripture Notes C, 1985, Scripture Notes (Series A), 1986. Recipient Disting. Faculty award Tex. Luth. Coll. Alumni Assn., 1982. Mem. Soc. Bibl. Lit., Am. Acad. Religion, Am. Schs. Oriental Rsch., Christian Study Group on Jews and Judaism, Assn. Ch. Tchrs. Democrat. Office: Tex Luth Coll 1000 W Court St Seguin TX 78155

BECK, ROBERT RAYMOND, priest; b. Waterloo, Iowa, Aug. 28, 1940; s. Paul Clayton and Mildred Anne (Klein) B. BA, Loras Coll., Dubuque, Iowa, 1962; ThM, Aquinas Inst. Theology, Dubuque, 1965; cert. of study, Ecole Biblique, Jerusalem, 1978; DMin, Cath. U., 1983. Assoc. pastor St. Columbkille Parish, Dubuque, 1966-71; with campus ministry U. No. Iowa, Cedar Falls, 1971-73; instr. of Scripture Aquinas Inst. Theology, 1973-81; assoc. prof. religious studies Loras Coll., 1981—; co-founder, bd. dirs. Cath. Worker, Dubuque; co-founder, pastor Anawim Faith Community, Dubuque, 1981—; founder, dir. Roy Herman Peace Ctr., Dubuque, 1983-86. Composer: (rock opera) Mark, A Rock Gospel, 1975, 87, Our Father, 1968; columnist: Sunday's Word, 1982-87; editor: Loras Faculty Review, 1989—; contbr. articles to profl. jours. Mem. Soc. Bibl. Lit., Am. Acad. Religion. Democrat. Home and Office: Loras Coll 1450 Alta Vista Dubuque IA 52001

BECKER, ANTHONY JOSEPH, priest, psychologist; b. Amboy, Ill., Jan. 5, 1922; s. Anton Francis and Margaret Ann (Meister) B. BA, Josephinum Coll., 1943; MA, Ohio State U., 1950; PhD, Loyola U., 1962; postgrad., St. Mary U. Lic. psychologist, Ill. Prof. Josephinum Coll., Worthington, Ohio, 1947-58; prin., supt. Boylan High Sch., Rockford, Ill., 1960-63; prof., counselor St. Dominic Coll., St. Charles, Ill., 1963-67; pastor St. mary Ch., Elgin, Ill., 1967-73; clin. psychologist Insight Ctr., Elgin, 1973-76; pastor St. Mary Ch., Oregon, Ill., 1976-84, St. Patrick Ch., Amboy, 1984—; counselor Insight Ctr., Elgin, Oregon and Amboy, 1973—; instr. Elgin Community Coll., 1967-76, Kishwaukee Coll., Malta, Ill., 1984—; chaplain Elgin Police Dept., 1967-76, Amboy Police Dept., 1984—. Author: Biography of a Country Town: USA, 1954, Sublette, Illinoiw: Our Bit of USA, 1957. Mem. KC. Republican. Home: 32 N Jones Ave Amboy IL 61310 Office: Saint Patrick Ch Insight Ctr 32 N Jones Ave Amboy IL 61310

BECKER, BECKY LYNNE, minister; b. Binghamton, N.Y., Jan. 15, 1955; d. Lynn Elmo and Marietta Clara (Howard) Snedaker; m. Jeffery Lee, May 17, 1976 (div. Feb. 1981); children: Russell Lee, Janis Lynne. AAS, Tompkins Cortland Community, Coll., Dryden, N.Y., 1985; BA in Speech Communication, SUNY, Cortland, 1988; student, United Theol. Seminary, Dayton, Ohio, 1990—. Church sec. Bethany United Ch. of Christ, Oshkosh, Wis., 1980-81; church sec./youth leader Newark Valley (N.Y.) United Meth., 1988-90; student assoc. pastor Grace United Meth., Blanchester, Ohio, 1990—; videographer Wyoming Annual Conf., Binghamton, 1989-90. Producer: (video) Called by God, 1990, God in This Place, 1990. With USN, 1974-78.

BECKER, CARL KLINE, religion educator, academic administrator; b. Boyertown, Pa., Sept. 25, 1926; s. Carl K. Sr. and Marie L. (Bodey) B.; m. Gladys Isabel MacDonald, Sept. 22, 1951; children: Carl Robert, Peggy Marie, John David. BA cum laude, Houghton (N.Y.) Coll., 1947; BD, Ea. Bapt. Theol. Sem., 1951; MA, U. Pa., 1952; D Ministry, Ea. Bapt. Theol. Sem., 1984. Pastor Delavan (Ill.) Bapt. Ch., 1951-53; missionary educator Africa Inland Mission, Zaire, 1954-79; prof. missions, v.p. bus. affairs Evang. Sch. of Theology, Myerstown, Pa., 1980—. Mem. Am. Soc. Missiology and Assoc. Prof. of Missions, Rotary (v.p. Myerstown chpt. 1991—). Office: Evang Sch of Theology 121 S College St Myerstown PA 17067

BECKER, DAVID MICHAEL, minister; b. Stephenville, Tex., Dec. 14, 1955; s. Emil Victor and Illa Faye (Clark) B.; m. Melissa Roberts, Aug. 8, 1981; children: Kristen Michelle, Tyler Andrew, Kelsey Suzanne. BS, Baylor U., 1978; MDiv, Southwestern Bapt. Theol. Sem., 1981. Ordained to ministry So. Bapt. Conv., 1978. Pastor Arnett Bapt. Ch., Gatesville, Tex., 1977-80, Selden Bapt. Ch., Stephenville, Tex., 1980-83, Pineview Bapt. Ch., Hattiesburg, Miss., 1983-86, Univ. Hts. Bapt. Ch., Huntsville, 1986—; bd. dirs. Christian Life Commn., Bapt. Gen. Conv. Tex., Dallas, 1990—; sec.-treas. Tex. Bapt. Prison Family Ministry Bd., Huntsville, 1988—; pres. Huntsville Ministerial Alliance, 1986—. Bd. dirs. Huntsville Family YMCA, 1988—; coord. Texans Who Care, 1987. Home: 227 Parkhill Huntsville TX 77340 Office: Univ Hts Bapt Ch 2400 Sycamore Huntsville TX 77340

BECKER, EILEEN, ecumenical agency administrator. Exec. dir. Ecumenical Conf. Greater Altoona, Pa. Office: Ecumenical Conf 1208 13th St PO Box 305 Altoona PA 16603*

BECKER, KEVIN DALE, youth coordinator; b. Longbranch, N.J., Jan. 1, 1958; s. Wallace Eleazer and Viola Ruth (Bahrke) B. BS in Acctg., Stockton State Coll., 1981; audio recording (hon.), Shore Fire Recording, 1989. Youth adv. Christ Ch. United Meth Ch., FairHaven, N.J., 1980-88, auditor, 1988—, adminstrv. coun., 1988—, youth coord., 1988—; acct. Standard-Keil Tap Rite, Allenwood, N.J., 1986—. Home: 260 Dartmouth Ave Fair Haven NJ 07704

BECKER, RANDOLPH WILLIAM, minister; b. Utica, N.Y., Dec. 11, 1946; s. William Howard and Gladys Marion (Burdick) B.; m. G. Katherine Lehman, Mar. 21, 1970 (div. 1991); children: Lee Lehman-Becker, Suki Lehman-Becker; m. Elissa Bishop, 1991; 1 stepchild, Ericka Bishop. AB, Brandeis U., 1968; DMin, Meadville/Lombard Sem., Chgo., 1972; PhD, NYU, 1981—. Ordained to ministry Unitarian Universalist Assn., 1972; cert. religious educator. Minister Unitarian Ch. N., Mequon, Wis., 1970-72; assoc. minister First Unitarian Ch., Providence, 1972-75; minister Unitarian Universalist Ch., Andover, Mass., 1975-80; religious edn. cons. L.I. Area Coun., Shoreham, N.Y., 1980—; sec. Unirondack, Lowville, N.Y., 1988—. Editor Liberal Religious Edn. jour., 1988-89. Chmn. Child Advocacy Group, NCC, 1987-90. Mem. Liberal Religious Educators Assn. Home: 633 Sixth St East Northport NY 11731 Office: L I Area Coun PO Box 37 East Northport NY 11731 *I feel challenged daily to live with and accept the reality that amiguity and choas are natural foundations of existence. I rejoice that from such foundations I can make and discover meaning.*

BECKER, ROBERT CLARENCE, clergyman; b. N.Y.C., June 19, 1927; s. Clarence Henry and Lillian (Butler) B.; m. Harriet Louise Egland, June 23, 1951; children: John, Ruth, Paul, Carol, Joel. Student, Providence Bible Inst., 1944-47, Gordon Coll. Theology and Missions, 1947-48; B.A., Upsala Coll., 1951. Ordained to ministry Baptist Ch., 1951; pastor First Bapt. Ch., Sedgwick, Maine, 1952-54, Ticonderoga, N.Y., 1954-58; pastor Garden View Bapt. Ch., Williamsport, Pa., 1958-67, First Bapt. Ch., Clayton, N.J., 1967-73; sr. minister First Bapt. Ch., Bloomfield, N.J., 1973—; pres. Conservative Bapt. Assn. Am., 1979-82; chmn. Am. Council, Africa Evangelical Fellowship, 1981-86. Bd. dirs. Denver Conservative Bapt. Theol. Sem., 1972-84; bd. dirs. Eastern Conservative Bapt. Sem., 1982-84, Northeastern Bible Coll., 1983-86, Conservative Bapt. Fgn. Mission Soc., 1988—. Mem. Nat. Assn. Evangelicals, Conservative Bapt. Fgn. Mission Soc., Conservative Bapt. Home Mission Soc., Conservative Bapt. Assn. (eastern v.p. 1984). Home: 81 Beach St Bloomfield NJ 07003 Office: 1 Washington St Bloomfield NJ 07003

BECKER, ROLF-WALTER, theology educator; b. Hamm, Westphalia, Germany, Oct. 23, 1935; s. Juergen Echter and Erika (Kochs) B.; m. Jean Virginia Wissing, Mar. 16, 1963; 1 child, Jan Peter. Grad., Evang. Ch. of Westphalia, 1961, Evang. Ch. of Westphalia, 1965; ThD, U. Muenster, Fed. Republic Germany, 1966. Pastor Evang. Ch. Marl, Westphalia, 1965-74; docent Predigerseminar Evang. Ch. Westphalia, Soest, 1974-82, prin., 1982—. Author: Religion in Zahlen, 1968, Leben mit Terminen, 1981. Chgo. Theol. Sem. fellow, 1961-62.

BECKER, WILLIAM HARTSHORNE, religion educator; b. Ridgewood, N.J., July 8, 1935; s. Albert Oliver and Ethel Ruth (Forshay) B.; m. Judith Clare Wells, Aug. 22, 1959; children: Matthew Hartshorne, Daniel Wells, Anne Clare. AB, Colgate U., 1957; STB, Harvard U., 1960, PhD, 1964. Asst. prof. religion Bucknell U., Lewisburg, Pa., 1964-70, assoc. prof., 1971-80, prof., 1981—, chmn. dept. religion, 1974-77, 82—. Contbr. articles to religious jours. Fellow Danforth Found., 1957-64, 70-71, Am. Coun. on Edn., 1978-79; Pitcairn-Crabbe Found. grantee, 1977; Lindback award Bucknell U., 1990. Mem. Soc. for Values in Higher Edn., West Br. Chorus (pres. 1987-88), Phi Beta Kappa. Democrat. Mem. United Ch. of Christ. Office: Bucknell U Dept Religion Lewisburg PA 17837

BECKETT, JAMES ANTHONY, minister; b. Portsmouth, Ohio, Oct. 4, 1951; s. Raymond Allen and Ann (Ehrlich) B.; m. Joan Lucille Sinzinger, July 7, 1973; children: Kathryn, Rebekah, Lauren. BA, Bob Jones U., 1973; MDiv, Bibl. Theol. Sem, Hatfield, Pa., 1977. Ordained to ministry Gen. Assn. Regular Bapt. Chs., 1977. Pastor Corydon (Iowa) Bible Ch., 1977-83, Faith Bapt. Ch., Streetsboro, Ohio, 1983-91, Heritage Bapt. Ch., Clarks Summit, Pa., 1991—. Columnist Faith Life newspaper, 1984-91; radio broadcaster, 1978-83. Trustee Camp Patmos, Kelley's Island, Ohio, 1988-91. Mem. Bapts. for Israel Inst. (bd. dirs. 1986-91), Ohio Assn. Regular Bapt. Chs. (Coun. of Twelve 1986-91). Office: Heritage Bapt Ch 415 Venard Rd Clarks Summit PA 18411

BECKETT, SANFORD RAY, clergyman; b. Bonne Terre, Mo., Feb. 28, 1946; s. Sidney Russell and Ruth Iona (Bolden) B.; m. Hazel Diane Keller, May 17, 1969; children: Andrew, Rachel. BA, William Jewell Coll., 1968; MDiv, Midwestern Bapt. Theol. Sem., 1972; MRE, Midwestern Bapt. Theol. Sem., Kansas City, Mo., 1972; D Ministry, Theol. Sem., Kansas City, Mo., 1977. Ordained to ministry Bapt. Ch., 1968. Pastor Heath's Creek Bapt. Ch., Nelson, Mo., 1968-72; assoc. pastor U. Bapt. Ch., Hattiesburg, Miss., 1972-80; mini. Christian edn. 1st Bapt. Ch., Clemson, S.C., 1980-86; pastor Christian edn. Englewood Bapt. Ch., Kansas City, Mo., 1986—; specialist worker S.C. Bapt. Conv., Columbia, 1984-86; adult specialist Southern Bapt. Conv., Nashville, 1985; adj. prof. Midwestern Bapt. Theol. Sem., Kansas City, 1987—. Contbr. articles to profl. jours. Chmn. Hattiesburg (Miss.) Pub. Libr. Systems, 1976, S.E. Miss. Community Action Agy., Hattiesburg, 1979, Clay-Platte Bapt. Ministers Fellowship, Kansas City, 1990, Northland Ministerial Alliance; mem. task force on AIDS, Mo. Bapt. Conv., Jefferson City, 1988—; bd. dir. Northland Partnership, Kansas City, 1990; chmn. Northland Health Care Access, 1991—. Named Outstanding Men Hattiesburg, Ministerial Alliance, 1975, Hon. Chaplain, Miss. State Senate, 1975. Office: Englewood Bapt Ch 1900 NE Englewood Rd Kansas City MO 64118

BECKHAM, JANICE LOUISE, lay worker; b. Salina, Kans., Aug. 3, 1950; m. Robert D. Beckham, Aug. 20, 1971; children: Timothy, Phillip. Student, Cloud County Community Coll., 1968-70, Brown Mackie Sch. of Bus., Salina, 1980. Sec. Christian Ch., Fredonia, Kans., 1989—; v.p. Christian Women's Fellowship, 1989-91, pres., 1991-93; deaconess, choir mem. Mem. Fredonia Music Appreciation Club (v.p.). Office: 1st Christian Ch-Disciples 303 N 7th Fredonia KS 66736

BECKHAM, WILLIAM ARTHUR, bishop; b. Columbia, S.C., Apr. 29, 1927; s. Francis Morgan and Maud Elizabeth (Guthrie) B.; m. Harriet Louise Wingate, Dec. 17, 1948. B.S., U. S.C., 1951; M.Div., Va. Theol. Sem., 1954, D.D. (hon.), 1980; D.D. (hon.), U. of South, 1985; D.H.L. (hon.), U. S.C., 1989. Ordained to ministry Episcopal Ch. Rector, Trinity Edgefield, S.C., 1954-56; asst. sec. Conv. of Our Savior Ch., Trenton, S.C., 1956-63; priest-in-charge Union & Calvary, Glenn Springs, 1957-58; rector, Resurrection, Greenwood, S.C., 1958-64; archdeacon Upper S.C., 1964-79; bishop of Upper S.C., 1979—; mem. Ch. Pension Fund and Affiliates Bd., 1984—. Trustee U. of South, 1963-69, 79—, Voorhees Coll., 1979—. Office: Episcopal Ch PO Box 1789 Columbia SC 29202

BECKLEY, ROBERT HOWARD, minister; b. Lebanon, Pa., Nov. 17, 1920; s. Joseph Franklin and Ada May (Koons) B.; m. Doris Eleanor Luckenbill, June 29, 1945; children: Drew Robert, Susan Eleanor, Dean Paul. PhB, Dickinson Coll., 1943; MDiv, Drew U., 1946. Ordained to ministry Meth. Ch., 1946. Minister Hummelstown (Pa.) Meth. Ch., 1940-43, Geigertown (Pa.) & Harmony Meth. Ch., 1943-46, First Meth. Ch., Germantown, Pa., 1946-48, Wayne (Pa.) Meth. Ch., 1948-52; chaplain USAF, 1952-80; minister First United Meth. Ch., Montgomery, Ala., 1980-83; chaplain, faculty Huntingdon Coll., Montgomery, 1983—. Author: The Seven Last Words of Christ From the Cross, 1952. Pres. Wayne (Pa.) Coun. of Chs., 1952. Col. USAF. Recipient Heston Wiley Prize for Preaching Drew U., 1946, Legion of Merit award USAF, 1979, Bronze Star Medal USAF, 1979. Mem. Ala. Hist. Soc., New Eng. Hist. Soc., Houghton Meml. Library Patrons, Rotary Internat., Masonic Lodge. Methodist. Avocations: books, golf, hist. rsch., biblical studies, book collecting. Home: 429 Paddock Ln Montgomery AL 36109 *After having worked with young people for more than 50 years, I believe that perhaps the greatest thrill one can experience is to help someone else discover the thrill of thinking positively, caring lovingly, sharing unselfishly and loving patiently.*

BECKMAN, SISTER PATRICIA, school system administrator. Supt. Cath. schs. Diocese of Denver. Office: Office Supt Cath Schs 200 Josephine St Denver CO 80206*

BECKMANN, DONALD MCELLIGOTT, priest; b. N.Y.C., Oct. 5, 1944; s. Rudolf Robert and Veronica Kathleen (McElligott) B. BA, Cathedral Coll., Bklyn., 1966; STB, Cath. U. Am., 1970; postgrad., Immaculate Conception Sem., Huntington, N.Y., 1991—. Ordained priest Roman Cath. Ch., 1970. Assoc. pastor St. Agnes Cathedral, Rockville Centre, N.Y., 1970-78, St. Patrick Ch., Huntington, 1978-81; spiritual dir. St. Pius X Sem., Uniondale, N.Y., 1981-84; chaplain Hofstra U., Hempstead, N.Y., 1984—; pastor, dir. campus ministry Campus Parish of L.I. Diocesan, Rockville Centre, 1989—; dir. ecumenical and interreligious affairs Rockville Centre Diocese, 1988—; hon. prelate Roman Cath. Ch.; Cath. del. Interfaith Assn. Religious Leaders, Nassau-Rockville Centre, 1988—, Roman Cath.-Orthodox Interchurch Dialogue, N.Y.C., 1988—; mem. L.I. Study Group on No. Ireland, Rockville Centre, 1990—. Co-chmn. edn. com. L.I. Holocaust Meml. Ctr., Mineola, N.Y., 1988—. Recipient award Coun. Jewish Orgns. of Nassau County, 1990. Mem. Nat. Assn. Diocesan Ecumenical Dirs., Nat. Assn. Dirs. Campus Ministry. Home: 456 Greengrove Ave Uniondale NY 11553 Office: Diocese of Rockville Centre 50 N Park Ave Rockville Centre NY 11570

BECKMANN, WILLIAM CARL, librarian; b. N.Y.C., Mar. 30, 1934; s. William Carl and Dorothy Elsa (Wallendorf) B.; m. Beverly A. Bublitz, Aug. 22, 1959; children: Peter, Mark. MA, Columbia U., 1960; MDiv, Concordia Sem., St. Louis, 1958. Ordained to ministry Luth. Ch.-Mo. Synod, 1958. Tchr. Luther High Sch. North, Chgo., 1958-60, guidance dir., 1960-67; counselor, adminstrv. asst. Concordia Luth. High Sch., Ft. Wayne, Ind., 1967-69, vice prin., 1969-78; vice prin. Valley Luth. High Sch., St. Charles, Ill., 1978-81, prin., 1981-90, media dir., curriculum specialist, 1990—; site evaluator U.S. Dept. Edn., Washington, 1984-90. Mem. ASCD, Nat. Assn. Secondary Sch. Prins., Luth. Edn. Assn. (editor, pub. rels. com. 1977-85), Assn. Luth. Secondary Schs. (editor newsletter 1989—), Nat. Coun. for Social Studies, Nat. Cath. Edn. Assn. Home: 1531 Jewel Ave Saint Charles IL 60174 Office: Valley Luth High Sch 701 Geneva Rd Saint Charles IL 60174

BECKWITH, WILLIAM HUNTER, clergyman; b. Noank, Conn., Oct. 8, 1896; s. Walter Howard and Annie Elizabeth (Keddy) B. Mus.B. magna cum laude, N.Y. U., 1929, A.M., 1931, Ph.D., 1936; postgrad., U. Poitiers, France. Organist and choir master Ch. of the Transfiguration, N.Y.C., 1917-18, Trinity Ch., Lenox, Mass., 1918-19, Trinity Chapel (Trinity Parish), N.Y.C., 1919-43; instr. French Washington Sq. Coll., N.Y. U., 1931-36; instr. French Hofstra Coll., 1936-38, asst. prof., 1938-39, assoc. prof., 1939-40; prof. French and dean of Coll., 1941-48; prof., past dir. div. gen. studies Coll. Agr. and Mechanic Arts, Universidad de Puerto Rico, Mayaguez, P.R.; ordained priest Protestant Episcopal Ch. of U.S., 1954; asst. San Andrés Episcopal Mission, Mayaguez; ordained priest Antiochian Orthodox Christian Ch., 1981. Author: The Formation of the Esthetic of Romain Rolland, 1935. Served in U.S. Navy, 1918. Fellow Am. Guild Organists; mem. MLA, AAUP, Eastern Assn. Deans, Phi Beta Kappa. Republican. Home: Highland Terrace 1520 Jefford St Clearwater FL 34616

BEDELL, GAYNELL PACK, minister; b. Paintsville, Ky.; d. William Reaves and Iuka D. (Welch) Pack; grad. W.Va. Bus. Coll.; m. Charles T. Skeer, 1921 (dec. 1949); children: William Thom, Zoe (Mrs. A. G. Vecchione); m. Frederick Haller, July 25, 1953 (dec. Apr. 1957). Mgr. fashion shops, 1942-46; star Claire Angrist radio fashion show, Huntington, W.Va., 1942-46; fashion cons., resident rep. Goode-Bridgeman, Inc., N.Y.C., 1946-54; mem. Christian Sci. Ch., registered practitioner, 1955—. Pres., 1st Ch. of Christ Scientist, Huntington, reader, Flushing, N.Y., 1951-53. Mem. Nat. Fedn. Bus. and Profl. Women's Clubs (pres. Huntington). Home: 52 Otter Rd Hilton Head Island SC 29928 Office: 5 Beaver Ln Hilton Head Island SC 29928

BEDELL, KENNETH BERKLEY, computer specialist, educator; b. Oct. 16, 1947; m. Kathryn Hale; children: Charity, Sarah. BA in Chemistry, Cornell U., 1969; postgrad., Princeton Theol. Sem., 1969-70; MDiv. in Theology, Colgate/Rochester Div. Sch., 1973; MA in Religious Edn., NYU, 1973; PhD in Sociology, Temple U., 1991. Ordained to ministry United Meth. Ch., 1971. Min. Newfield United Meth. Ch., 1973-76, Seneca Castle (N.Y.) United Meth. Ch., 1978-79, Preston Parish, 1979-84; computer specialist Temple U., 1984-86; dir. computer ministries United Theol. Sem., Dayton, Ohio, 1986-91; exec. dir. EPIC, Inc., Gahanna, Ohio, 1991—; mem. software standards task force United Meth. Ch.; past sec., mem. conf. publs. com. Elmira Dist. Coun.; vol. tchr., lay preacher Mennonite Cen. Com., Luyengo, Swaziland, 1976-78; interim coord. Coalition for Whole Gospel; adv. com. Parish Devel. Ctr.; cons. in field. Author: The Role of Computers in Religious Education, 1986, Worship in the Methodist Tradition, 1987 (with others) Changing Channels, 1990; past weekly columnist Preston News and Farmer; contbr. articles to profl. jours. Past chairplanning com. Caroline County Health; past vice-chair Peninsula Conf. Div. Human Rels. Recipient Richard Wynan award. Mem. Soc. Sci. Study Religion, Religious Pub. Rels. Coun., Ch. Computer Users Network. Home: 4341 Reevis Ct Dayton OH 45415

BEDENBAUGH, MARY EVELYN, church administrator; b. Ottawa, Ont., Can., Aug. 5, 1935; d. Arthur Michael and Evelyn Mary (Kumpf) Doepp; m. William Howard Bedenbaugh, Aug. 19, 1967; 1 child, Benjamin Robert. BS, State Tchrs. Coll., Salisbury, Md., 1959. Ch. sec. Sixth Presbyn. Ch., Washington, 1984-91, ch. adminstr., 1991—; deacon St. Mark Presbyn. Ch., Rockville, Md., 1982-84, elder, clk. of session, 1984-90; mem. com. on lay employees Presbyn. Ch. (USA), Louisville, 1989—, adminstrn. and personnel com. Nat. Capital Presbytery, 1988—. Author handbooks: Session Handbook, 1989, Organizing the Church Office, 1990, Clerk of Session, 1988. Mem. Adminstrv. Personnel Assn. Presbyn. Ch. USA (nat. pres. 1990—), Presbyn. Ch. Bus. Adminstrs. Assn. Home: 5318 Crestedge Ln Rockville MD 20853 Office: Sixth Presbyn Ch 5413 Sixteenth St NW Washington DC 20011

BEDNAROWSKI, MARY FARRELL, religion educator; b. Green Bay, Wis., Apr. 17, 1942; d. Richard John and Irene Emily (Westphal) F.; m. Keith Paul Bednarowski, Aug. 29, 1964; children: Elizabeth Irene, K. Paul. BA, Marquette U., 1964; MA, Duquesne U., 1969; PhD, U. Minn., 1973. Lectr. history U. Wis., Milw., 1974-76; asst. prof. religious studies United Theol. Sem. of the Twin Cities, New Brighton, Minn., 1976-84, acting acad. v.p., 1983, assoc. prof. religious studies, 1984-89, prof. religious studies, 1989—; bd. dirs. Greater Mpls. Coun. of Chs., 1984-90. Author: New Religions and the Theological Imagination in America, 1989, American Religion, 1984; contbr. articles to profl. jours. Bd. dirs. Minn. Humanities Commn., St. Paul, 1989-92. Rsch. grantee Assn. Theol. Schs., 1979, 85. Mem. Am. Acad. Religion, Am. Studies Assn. (nat. program com. 1983), Am. Soc. Ch. History (rsch. com. 1990—), Am. Cath. Hist. Assn., Soc. for the Sci. Study of Religion. Roman Catholic. Home: 4748 Thomas Ave S Minneapolis MN 55410 Office: United Theol Sem of the Twin Cities 3000 5th St NW New Brighton MN 55112 *To my surprise, it has been the multiplicity rather than the unity of the religious views I have encountered in ecumenical settings that convinces me of religion's capacity to offer meaning and hope to a world in need of both.*

BEEBE, DAVID LEWIS, minister; b. Nady, Ark., Sept. 7, 1931; s. Clifford Averril and Clara Gertrude (Lewis) B.; m. Judy Johanne Corfitsen, Oct. 22, 1960; children: Karen Elisa Beebe Broyles, Heather Marie. AB, Salem Coll., 1953; BD, Alfred U., 1956; ThD, Pacific Sch. of Religion, Berkeley, Calif., 1966. Ordained to ministry United Ch. of Christ, 1959. Pastor San Lorenzo (Calif.) Community Ch., 1958-63; grad. fellow Homiletics Pacific Sch. Religion, Berkeley, Calif., 1963-65; assoc. pastor Petaluma (Calif.) United Ch. of Christ, 1965-66; chaplain, assoc. prof. Berry Coll., Mt. Berry, Ga., 1966-72; pastor Pilgrim Congregational Ch., Chattanooga, 1972-88; nat. assoc. for stewardship edn. Stewardship Coun. United Ch. of Christ, St. Louis, 1988—; mem. nat. commn. on worship United Ch. of Christ, N.Y.C., 1965-68; bd. dirs. Southeast Conf. United Ch. of Christ, Atlanta, 1971-87, Tenn. Assn. of Chs., Nashville, 1982-85; moderator Southeast Conf. United Ch. of Christ, Atlanta, 1977-79. Author poems. Bd. dirs. Fortwood Psychiatric Ctr., Chattanooga, 1982-87; v.p. Habitat for Humanity, Chattanooga, 1986-87; mem. Task Force on Human Relations, Chattanooga, 1986-87, Constitutional Bicentennial Commn., Chattanooga, 1987; chmn. City of Chattanooga Commn. on Human Rights and Human Relations, 1987. Named Humanitarian of Yr. The Unity Group, Chattanooga, 1986. Mem. United Ch. of Christ Network for Environ. and Econ. Responsibility, (steering com. 1988—), Ecumenical Ctr. for Stewardship Studies (chmn. advanced degree com.), Clan Ross Assn. (chaplain 1974—), Torch Club (pres. Chattanooga chpt. 1986-87). Avocations: sailing, writing poetry. Office: Stewardship Coun United Ch of Christ 800 N Third St Ste 202 Saint Louis MO 63102 *Life is about becoming humane. Life is about opening our eyes, our hearts and our hands. In the course of growing more humane, the challenge of our time is not to lose the touch in our fingertips.*

BEEBER, ALLAN HOWARD, missionary; b. New Brunswick, N.J., Oct. 25, 1951; s. Allan Robert and Elsie Coral (Powers) B.; m. Patricia Lynn Murphy, May 24, 1980; children: Christina, Joshua, Daniel. BS, Muhlenberg Coll., 1972; MS, PhD, U. Mass., 1977; MA in Bibl. Studies, Internat. Sch. Theology, San Bernardino, Calif., 1986; MA in Interdisciplinary Studies, Calif. State U., San Bernadino, 1991. MIT campus dir. Campus Crusade for Christ, San Bernardino, 1979-86, dir. Student LINC, 1987—, chmn. U.S. Ministry Evangelism Task Force, 1987—. Author, editor: Resource Manual, 1989. Office: Campus Crusade for Christ Inc 100 Sunport Ln Orlando FL 32809 *There is more politics within Christian organizations than leadership wants to admit. The key to perservering is to remember the One you should be working for.*

BEEGLE, EUGENE S., minister; b. Bedford, Pa.; s. Glenn S. and Mary E. (Kegg) B.; m. Patricia Beegle, May 30, 1950; children: Vicki, Gwen, Bryan. Grad., Christ for the Nations, Dallas, 1985. Home: Po Box 26 Enville TN 38332-0026

BEEKE, JOEL ROBERT, minister, theology educator, writer; b. Kalamazoo, Dec. 9, 1952; s. John and Johanna Lucy (Van Strein) B; m. Mary Ann Kamp, Aug. 21, 1989; 1 child, Calvin James. Student, Western Mich. U., 1971-73; BA, Thomas A. Edison Coll.; MDiv, Netherlands Reformed Theol. Sch., St. Catharines, Ont., Can., 1978; PhD in Reformation and Post-Reformation Theology, Westminster Theol. Sem., 1988. Ordained to ministry The Netherlands Ref. Congregations, 1978. Pastor The Netherlands Ref. Congregation, Sioux Center, Iowa, 1978-81, Ebenezer Netherlands Ref. Ch., Franklin Lakes, N.J., 1981-86, 1st Netherlands Ref. Congregation, Grand Rapids, Mich., 1986—; instr. theology Netherlands Ref. Theol. Sch., 1986—; clk. The Netherlands Ref. Synod, 1980—; v.p. The Netherlands Ref. Gen. Mission, 1980-82; pres. The Netherlands Ref. Book and Pub., 1980—; v.p. The Netherlands Ref. Synodical Edn., 1986—; lectr. Ctr. for Urban Theol. Studies, 1984-86, Westminster Theol. Sem., Phila., 1985-86. Author: Jehovah Shepherding His Sheep, 1982, Backsliding: Disease and Cure, 1982, Student Workbook on the Reformed Faith: Based on Rev. Hellenbroek's "A Specimen of Divine Truths", Vol. 1, 1985, Verachtering in de Genade: Kwaal en Genezing, 1989, Assurance of Faith: Calvin, English Puritanism, and the Dutch Second Reformation, 1991; also numerous articles; co-author: (with J. W. Beeke) Bible Doctrine Student Workbook, 1982; (with James W. Beeke and Diana Kleyn) Building on the Rock, Book 1, 1989, Building on the Rock, Book 2, 1990; co-translator: (with J. C. Weststrate) Reformed Dogmatics, Vol. 1, 1980, Vol. 2, 1983; editor: Religious Stories for Young and Old, Vol. 4, 1983, The Twenty-fifth Mission Day, 1984, Sovereign Grace in Life and Ministry, 1984, Experiential Grace in Dutch Biography, 1985, Collected Writings of Reverend William C. Lamain, Vol. 1, 1986; editor Banner of Truth, 1985—, Banner of Paul, 1984—. With U.S. Army, 1971-74. Mem. Evang. Theol. Soc., Soc. for Reformation Rsch., Calvin Studies Soc., 16th Century Studies Conf. Soc., Am. Soc. Ch. History, Colloquium on Calvin Studies, Conf. on Faith and History. Republican. Home and Office: 2115 Romence NE Grand Rapids MI 49503

BEELER, JAMES MARIO, Christian radio announcer; b. Pasadena, Calif., Sept. 13, 1954; s. Frank McHarry and Mary Elizabeth (Kernel) B.; m. Heidi Beth Mauer, May 11, 1979; children: Christian James, Aaron Michael, Heather Marie. Student, U. No. Colo., 1975-78. Announcer Sta. KFKZ Radio, Greeley, Colo., 1977-80; sta. mgr., announcer Sta. KUYO Radio, Casper, Wyo., 1985-86; program dir., announcer Sta. KKCM Radio, Shakopee, Minn., 1987-88, Sta. WQFL Radio, Rockford, Ill., 1988—. Republican. Mem. Assemblies of God. Office: Sta WQFL Radio 5375 Pebble Creek Trail Rockford IL 61111

BEEMAN, BOB JOE, minister; b. Billings, Mont., Nov. 3, 1952; s. Marvin Joe and Bonnie Berteen (Boegler) B. CE, Mont. Inst. of the Bible, 1972. Ordained to ministry, 1980. Dir. Acts Alive! Ministries, Billings, 1976-80, Bob Beeman Evangelistic Assn., Calif., 1980-85; pastor, founder Sanctuary Chs. Inc., Redondo Beach, Calif., 1985—. Office: Sanctuary South Bay PO Box 4130 Redondo Beach CA 90278-8330

BEERS, V(ICTOR) GILBERT, publishing executive; b. Sidell, Ill., May 6, 1928; s. Ernest S. and Jean (Bloomer) B.; m. Arlisle Felten, Aug. 26, 1950; children: Kathleen, Douglas, Ronald, Janice, Cynthia. A.B., Wheaton Coll., 1950; M.R.E., No. Baptist Sem., 1953, M.Div., 1954, Th.M., 1955, Th.D., 1960; Ph.D., Northwestern U., 1963. Prof. No. Baptist Sem., Chgo., 1954-57; editor Sr. High Pubs., David C. Cook Pub. Co., Elgin, Ill., 1957-59, exec. editor, 1959-61, editorial dir., 1961-67; pres. Books for Living Inc., Elgin, 1967—; editor Christianity Today, 1982-85, sr. editor, 1985-87; pres. Scripture Press Publs. Inc., Elgin, 1990—. Author: 85 books, including: Family Bible Libr., 10 vols., 1971, The Book of Life, 23 vols., 1980. Bd. dirs. Wheaton (Ill.) Youth Symphony, 1961-63, pres., 1962-63; bd. trustees Wheaton Coll., 1975—, Scripture Press Inc., 1975—; bd. dirs. Christian Camps Inc., N.Y., 1972—. Home: Rte 1 Box 321 Elgin IL 60120 *True strength for success or adversity is the practice of the presence of God daily.*

BEERY, NEIL L., minister; b. Wadsworth, Ohio, Sept. 18, 1926; s. Ernest E. and Marvel Viola (Marken) B.; m. Thelma E. Beichler, Jan. 1, 1947; children: Mary Lou, Martha Ann, Miriam Sue, Mark L. Grad., Akron Bible Inst., 1950. Ordained to ministry, Ind. Fundamental Chs. Am. West coast rep. Greater Europe Mission, Wheaton, Ill., 1973-76; sr. pastor The Little Ch. in the Hills, Mariposa, Calif., 1976-83, Community Bible Ch., Cave Junction, Oreg., 1983-88; speaker Tell and Teach Bible Conf., Mariposa, Calif., 1988-90; sr. pastor Calvary Bapt. Ch., Susanville, Calif., 1990—. With U.S. Army, 1944-46. Mem. Kiwanis (pres. 1988). Republican. Office: Calvary Bapt Ch 995 Paiute Ln Susanville CA 96130

BEESLEY, R. A., minister, religious organization administrator. Dist. supt. United Pentecostal Ch. in Can., Sussex, N.B. Office: United Pentecostal Ch, Box 965, Sussex, NB Canada E0E 1P0*

BEESON, RACHEL, nun, educator; b. Des Moines, Feb. 7, 1932; d. Earl Jerome and Johanna Aida (Olmstead) B. AA, Ottumwa (Iowa) Coll., 1953; BA, Marycrest Coll., Davenport, Iowa, 1963; MA, S.E. Mo. State U., 1972; Cert. Ministry, St. Louis U., 1988. Joined Sisters of Humility, Roman Cath. Ch., 1950. Tchr. St. Denis Sch., Benton, Mo., 1970-72; prin. St. Albert Elem. Sch., Council Bluffs, Iowa, 1972-77, St. Anthony Grad Sch., Des Moines, 1977-82, North Cath. Sch., Clinton, Iowa, 1984-87, Hayes Cath. Elem. Sch., Muscatine, Iowa, 1987—; pres. Davenport Diocesan Sisters Coun., 1989—; chmn. adv. com. on new membership Sisters of Humility, Davenport, 1984—, senator, 1977-84, 86-91, co-chmn. Five Yr. Plan, 1987—. Mem. Nat. Cath. Edn. Assn., Internat. Reading Assn., Assn. for Supervision and Curriculum devel. Democrat. Home: PO Box 559 Muscatine IA 52761 Office: Hayes Cath Elem Sch 2407 Cedar St Muscatine IA 52761 *The Lord is my shepherd; there is nothing I shall want. When hardships befall us the Lord is there to guide to the light that lies ahead bringing joy and hope to those who believe.*

BEGAYE, HELEN CHRISTINE, editor, religious organization official; b. Ardmore, Okla., Oct. 24, 1943; d. Winston Coleman and Delia (Cooper) Shoemaker; m. Russell Begaye, Aug. 14, 1975; 1 child, Karis Nizhoni. BA, Dallas Bapt. U., 1970; MRE, Southwestern Bapt. Theol. Sem., Ft. Worth, 1972. Missionary So. Bapt. Conv., Albuquerque, 1973-75; co-dir. Bapt. Indian Ctr., Santa Fe, 1978-80; editor Bapt. Sunday Sch. Bd., Nashville, 1988—; mem. adv. bd. Women in Evangelism, Atlanta, 1982-88; mission chmn. Fielder Road Bapt. Ch., Arlington, Tex., 1987-89; mission chmn. Woman's Missionary Union, Tarrant Bapt. Sch., 1989—; trustee Am. Bible Soc., N.Y.C., 1990—. Editor Am. Indian Bible Study quar. jours., 1988-91. Home and Office: 4114 Celtic Dr Arlington TX 76017 *My people, the American Indians, have always emphasized living a balanced life. This life is achieved through Jesus Christ.*

BEGGIANI, SEELY, religious organization administrator, educator; b. Youngstown, Ohio, June 23, 1935; s. Joseph Aaron and Sada Seely (Beggiani) B. AB, Borromeo Sem., Wickliffe, Ohio, 1956; student, John Carroll U., Cleve., 1952-54, 57-58; STL, Cath. U., Washington, 1961, STD, 1963. Tchr. St. John Coll., Cleve., 1962-67, John Carroll U., Cleve., 1964-67; rector Our Lady of Lebanon Sem., Washington, 1968—; adj. assoc. prof. Cath. U. Am., Washington, 1967—; chmn. Commn. for Lebanon, Diocese St. Maron, Washington, 1985—; consultor Diocese of St. Maron, Bklyn., 1968—. Recipient title of Monsignor from Pope Paul VI, 1975, rank of Chor-Bishop from Archbishop Francis Zayek, 1986; decorated Order of the Cedar, Govt. Lebanon, 1988. Mem. Am. Cath. Hist. Assn., Cath. Theol. Soc. Am., Cath. Bibl. Assn., Coll. Theology Soc. Avocations: travel, chess, tennis, crossword puzzles. Home and Office: 7164 Alaska Ave NW Washington DC 20012 *There must be a relationship between the moral quality of life we live now on earth and the existence that awaits us after death. I believe that we are called to be loving, gracious, and humane.*

BEGIN, GERARD HENRY, minister; b. Lewiston, Maine, June 6, 1949; s. Henry and Alberta Noella (Beaulieu) B.; m. Monique Jeanne D'Arc Pelletier, July 25, 1970; children: Scott-Henry, Avril, Wayne, Keith, Aaron, Gregory. PhD, San Antonio Theol. Sem., Mpls., 1988, D.Christian Counseling, 1988, MDiv, 1989. Ordained to ministry Ministerial Fellowship U.S.A. 1984; lic. therapist, Minn. Pres., pastor Spirit of Fire Evangelistic Ministry, Lewiston, Maine, 1984—; v.p. Ministerial Fellowship of U.S.A., Kennewick, 1991; bd. dirs. Good Shepherd Food Box Program, Lewiston, 1987—. Author: Motivational Gifts, 1987, Mobilizing the Church, 1987, Marriage Through Biblical Principles, 1988, Food/Clothing Agency, 1987. Mem. Am. Assn. Marriage and Family Therapy (cert. clin. therapist), Am. Orthopsychiat. Assn., Ministerial Fellowship of U.S.A. (bd. dirs. 1988), United Assn. Christian Counselors, Internat. Assn. Christian Pastoral Counselors (diplomate). Office: Spirit of Fire Evang PO Box 2166 Lewiston ME 04241-2166

BEGIN, ROBERT T., ecumenical agency head. Exec. dir. West Side Ecumenical Ministry, Cleve. Office: West Side Ecumenical Ministry 4315 Bridge Ave Cleveland OH 44113*

BEHL, RICHARD ALLEN, mission director, priest; b. New Brunswick, N.J., June 5, 1941; s. Harold Richard and Mae Lillian (Homall) B. AB, St. Mary U., 1963; STB, Gregorian U., 1967; D in Ministry, Princeton (N.J.) Theol. Sem., 1975. Ordained priest Roman Cath. Ch. Tchr., chaplain Red Bank (N.J.) Cath. High Sch., 1968-70; mission dir. Dioceses of Trenton/Metuchen, N.J., 1968—; pastor Our Lady of the Mount Ch., Warren, N.J., 1977-85; vicar Charities & Social Ministry, Metuchen, 1982-85; pastor Our Lady of Perpetual Help Ch., Bernardsville, N.J., 1985—; mem. Pastoral Coun./Priests Senate, Metuchen, 1982—, Sem. Bd., Metuchen, 1990—; cons. Holy Childhood Assn., Washington, 1975—; chmn. bd. trustees Cath. Charities, Metuchen, 1982—. Member Borough Sr. Citizens Commn., Bernardsville, 1989—. Named Chaplain to His Holiness, Pope Paul VI, 1977; recipient Prelate of Honor award Pope John Paul II, 1991. Mem. Consolata Missionary Soc. (Ann. honoree), Damian-Dutton Soc. (trustee 1972-81), N.Am. Coll. Alumni Assn., K.C. (chaplain 1977-80). Office: Diocese of Metuchen PO Box 191 Metuchen NJ 08840

BEHR, TED ARTHUR, religious organization administrator; b. L.A., May 28, 1934; s. Arthur William and Veta Felcia (Turner) B.; m. Barbara Jean Prevol, June 8, 1963; children: Robert Arthur, John William. AA, Santa Monica City Coll., 1954. Fellow in ch. bus. adminstrn., 1979. Exec. producer Lloyd Ogilvie Ministries, Hollywood, Calif., 1978-86; ch. adminstr. First Presbyn. Ch., Hollywood, 1975—; chmn. bd. advs. Templeton prize, Nassau, Bahamas, 1985; vice-chmn. So. Calif. Presbyn. Homes, Glendale, 1984—. Bd. dirs. Hollywood YMCA, 1972-73; deacon First Presbyn. Ch., Hollywood, 1969-71, elder, 1973-75. Quartermaster USCG, 1954-56. Mem. Nat. Assn. Ch. Bus. Adminstrs. (pres. So. Calif. chpt. 1979-80), Christian Ministry Mgmt. Assn. (bd. dirs. 1984-85), Jaycees (pres. Hollywood chpt. 1963), Rotary (pres. Hollywood chpt. 1970), Hollywood C. of C. (bd. dirs. 1975-78). Republican. Home: 1015 Alcalde Way Glendale CA 91207 Office: First Presbyterian Church 1760 N Gower St Hollywood CA 90028

BEHRENDT, TIMOTHY HUME, minister, counselor; b. Ashtabula, Ohio, Aug. 3, 1937; s. Wayne Franklin and Mary Willard (Hume) B.; m. Roberta Lanese, Dec. 31, 1959 (div. 1972); children: David, Jennifer, Rebekah, Heidi; m. Peggy Jean Spencer, Feb. 14, 1974. Student, Denison U., 1955-56; BS in Edn., Ohio U., 1959; MDiv, Garrett Theol. Sem., 1962; MS in Edn., Ind. U., 1963; counseling cert., Colgate U., 1966. Ordained to ministry Unitarian Universalist Ch., 1961; cert. counselor, N.Y. Asst. min. youth Glenview (N.Y.) Community Ch., 1960-61; asst. min. Northbrook (N.Y.) Meth. Ch., 1961-62; min. Unitarian Ch., Castine, Maine, 1963-65, Unitarian Ch. of Barneveld, N.Y., 1965-74, Unitarian Universalist Ch., Utica, N.Y., 1971—. Author: With a Village Church, 1971, The Parables of Timothy, 1973, Dawning of Human Consciousness, 1977, From the Forest, 1990. Co-founder, co-adminstr. Shawangunk Nature Preserve, 1974—; bd. dirs. Planned parenthood Mohawk Valley, Utica, 1989—; v.p. UN Assn. Mohawk Valley, Utica, 1989-90, pres., 1991. Recipient 15 Yr. Civic Svc. award City of Utica, 1985. Mem. Mohawk Valley Meml. Soc. (co-founder, v.p. 1991, pres. 1992), Unitarian Universalist Ministerial Group, Ministry for Population Concerns (nat. adv. bd. 1991—). Home: RD 1 Box 651 Cold Brook NY 13324 Office: Unitarian Universalist Ch 10 Higby Rd Utica NY 13501 *"A good leader is a follower of great principles" and "Do to all that is, was and will be as you would have it do to you, " is the consensus core of all the major world religions.*

BEITER, PHYLLIS ELIZABETH, missionary; b. Lansing, Mich., Jan. 10, 1937; d. Henry Albert and Inez Marion (LeRoy) Griffith; m. Don Reginald Beiter, Aug. 6, 1962; children: Carol Grace Beiter Hennings, Paul Russell, Jean Elizabeth, John Alan. Diploma, Moody Bible Inst., 1958; BA, Wheaton (Ill.) Coll., 1959; MA, Fuller Sem. Sch. World Mission, 1986. Linguist Evang. Alliance Mission, Irian Jaya, Indonesia, 1959-62; with field svc. flight programs ground support Mission Aviation Fellowship, Irian Jaya, 1962-69, 80-83; cross cultural trainer Mission Aviation Fellowship, Redlands, Calif., 1977-80, 83-87, mgr. ministry partnership, 1986—; dir. field svc. flight programs ground support Internat. Assistance Mission, Kabul, Afghanistan, 1970-74; sr. rsch. asst. unreached peoples World Vision Internat., Monrovia, Calif., 1984-86. Office: 1849 Wabash Redlands CA 92373

BELANGER, A. KENNETH, deacon, pension plan administrator, consultant; b. Escanaba, Mich., Nov. 11, 1942; s. Arnold Kenneth and Virginia (Olive) B.; m. Jo-Ann Irene Lyford, Jan. 16, 1965; 1 child, A. Kenneth III. Student, Rutgers U., 1967-69. CLU. Sales profl., broker various ins. cos. N.J. and Pa., 1967-73; pres. Belanger & Assocs., Spring House, Pa., 1973-79; pres. Belanger & Co., Inc., Conshohocken, Pa., 1979-86, Blue Bell, Pa., 1986—; permanent deacon St. Genevieve Roman Cath. Ch., Flourtown, Pa., 1988—, also chmn. bd. dirs. With USAF, 1961-65. Mem. Union League, Kiwanis (pres. Ambler, Pa. club 1971-83). Home: 924 Longfield Rd Erdenheim PA 19118 Office: Belanger & Co Inc 1 Valley Sq Blue Bell PA 19422

BELCH, KENNETH JAMES, minister; b. Stirling, Ont., Can., June 5, 1944; s. William Elmer and Kathleen Winnifred (Hayward) B.; m. Carol Ann Reeves, June 27, 1970; children: Ruth-Anne Louise, Janice Elaine, Heather Lynn. BA, Brock U., St. Catharine's, Ont., 1985. Ordained to ministry Plymouth Brethren Ch., 1966. Active Youth For Christ Outreach Ministry, Belleville, Ont., 1960-64; Youth dir. Bethel Chapel, Belleville, 1963-66; itinerent youth minister various, Can., 1966-70; sr. pastor Arkona (Ont.) Bible Chapel, 1970-75, Grace Chapel, Stirling, Ont., 1975-79, Grimsby (Ont.) Bible Ch., 1979-88, Lake Pointe Bible Chapel, Plymouth, Mich., 1988—; bd. dirs. Joy Bible Camp, Bancroft, Ont., 1969—. Home: 45745 Bryn Mawr Rd Canton MI 48187 Office: Lake Pointe Bible Chapel 42150 Schoolcraft Rd Plymouth MI 48170

BELDEN, JERRY LEE, minister; b. Winfield, Kans., Sept. 20, 1935; s. Leslie Francis and Vera Catherine (Workman) B.; m. Hazel Elaine Hayden Belden, Aug. 7, 1960; children: Sandra Elaine Belden Curran, Scott Alan. BA, S.E. Coll., 1957; MDiv., Cen. Bapt. Theol. Sem., 1969. Ordained to ministry Am. Bapt. Chs. in the U.S.A., 1960. Pastor S.W. Bapt. Ch., Topeka, 1967-69, 1st Bapt. Ch., Wood River, Ill., 1969-78, 1st Bapt. Ch. of Turner, Kansas City, Kans., 1978-79, South Broadway Bapt. Ch., Pitts., Kans., 1979-86, 1st Bapt. Ch., Carrollton, Ill., 1986—; mem. com. on evangelism Am. Bapt. Chs., Springfield, Ill., 1986-90, com. on ordination, 1987-90, dept. of ministry, 1987—, chair AIDS task force, 1991—; chair of chaplains Wood River Twp. Hosp., 1973-77; chaplain City Coun. City of Pitts., 1984-86. Mem. com. Tri-County AIDS Task Force, Ill., 1989—. Recipient Evangelism award Am. Bapt. Chs. Great River Regions, St. Louis, 1989. Mem. Mins. Coun. Am. Bapt. Chs. USA, Carrollton Ministerial Alliance (sec.-treas. 1987), Lions. Home: 133 Sixth St PO Box 288 Carrollton IL 62016 Office: 1st Bapt Ch 203 Fifth St PO Box 288 Carrollton IL 62016 *Self-giving relationships are the key to life. Such relationships are possible through a religious faith and in sharing in a community of faith as well as in sharing in the home/family and the community. As a clergyperson, I believe the Good News of the gospel is the only hope for a hurting world.*

BELFIORE, SISTER EVELINA, religious education director. Head religious edn. Beaumont, Tex. Office: Office Religious Edn 703 Archie St PO Box 3948 Beaumont TX 77704*

BELFORD, VIRGINIA HELEN WISDOM, free-lance writer; b. Waynesville, Mo., Oct. 20, 1948; d. David Glen and Beverly Jean (Prescott) Wisdom; m. Scott Lee Belford, Oct. 14, 1974; children: Scott J., Elizabeth (dec.). BA with honors, U. Ill., Chgo., 1972; postgrad., Garrett-Evang. Theol. Sem., 1988—. Primary teaching cert. Am. Montessori Soc. Tchr. Chatham County Schs., Savannah, Ga., 1973-74, Montessori Sch., Crown Point, Ind., 1974-75, Will County (Ill.) Pub. Schs., 1978-80; juvenile writer Pioneer Press, Wheaton, Ill., 1984-85; freelance writer Naperville, Ill., 1985-89; with Garrett Evang. Theol. Sem., Evanston, Ill., 1989—; camp dir. Opportunity Ctr., Teutopolis, Ill., summer 1976; instr. Learning Exchange, Evanston, Ill., 1975-76; adult edn. tutor Coll. of DuPage, Glen Ellyn, Ill., 1985-87. Organizer Chgo. Peace Coun., 1969-72; newsletter Women's Club, 1980-85; workshop leader Heifer Project Internat., Chgo., 1986-88; co-chmn. Women in Ministry, Garrett-Evang. Theol. Sem., 1989—. Recipient 1st place for poetry Ill. Federated Women's Club, 1982; Hoosier scholar, 1966, James scholar, 1969-72, Ga. Harkness scholar, 1991. Mem. Global Educators No. Ill. (charter, bd. dirs. 1988—), AAUW (internat. chmn. Naperville 1986-88, R & P grantee 1989-90), Ducks Unltd. Methodist. Avocation: grief crisis counseling. Home: 1517 Marquette Ave Naperville IL 60565

BELHORN, PAUL CHRISTY, deacon, federal agency administrator; b. Columbus, Ohio, Sept. 3, 1941; s. Leroy William and Louise (Thissen) B.; m. Patricia Marie MacDougall, July 15, 1972; children: Scott, Matthew, Tara, Elizabeth. BS, Ohio State U., 1964. Dir. N.Y. field office Comptr. of the Currency, Newark, 1983-91; nat. bank examiner Columbus, Ohio, 1991—; deacon St. Mary's Parish, New Monmouth, N.J., 1990-91, St. Edward's Parish, Granville, Ohio, 1991—; mem. adv. com. Congl. Youth Award. Chaplain Boy Scouts Am., New Monmouth, 1990-91. 1st lt. F.A., U.S. Army, 1963-69. Cert. of Merit Boy Scouts Am., 1991. Mem. Am. Legion, Ruffed Grouse Soc. (N.J. chpt.), N.J. Audubon Soc., Germania Sport and Singing Soc., Buckeye Game Club, Granville Conservation Club, K.C. Republican. Roman Catholic. Home: 4672 Granview Rd Granville OH 43023 Office: Comptr of the Currency 2727 Tuller Pkwy Ste 100 Ste 1675 Dublin OH 43017

BELINSKE, SISTER BARBARA, academic administrator. Adminstr. Silver Lake Coll., Manitowoc, Wis. Office: Silver Lake Coll 2406 S Alverno Rd Manitowoc WI 54220-9319*

BELISLE, GILLES, bishop; b. Clarence Creek, Ont., Can., Oct. 7, 1923; s. Hermile and Clara (Charlebois) B. Ordained priest Roman Cath. Ch., 1950; diocesan pastoral coord., aux. bishop Archdiocese of Ottawa, 1977—. Office: 1247 Kilborn, Ottawa, ON Canada K1H 6K9

BELISLE, SAMUEL DARREL, minister; b. Bradenton, Fla., Oct. 29, 1954; s. Kenneth Franklin and Katye Marjorie (McGriff) B.; m. Diane Hamilton, Aug. 16, 1975; children: Christopher Josh, Jennifer Nicole. BS, Lee Coll., 1976. Ordained to ministry Ch. of God, 1984. Youth minister Ch. of God, Jesup, Ga., 1976-78, Valdosta, Ga., 1978, Chattanooga, 1978-80, Doraville, Ga., 1980-87, Charlotte, N.C., 1987-89; sr. pastor Ch. of God, Waynesboro, Va., 1989—; dist. pastor Ch. of God, Va., 1989-90, mem. state youth bd., 1990—; bd. dirs. weekday religous edn. Ch. of God, Waynesboro, 1990—; advisor Aglow, Waynesboro, 1990—. Mem. Christians United (bd. dirs. 1991—), Waynesboro Ministers' Assn. (v.p. 1990—), Pentecostal Ministers (v.p. 1990—), Lee Coll. Alumni Assn. (v.p. 1990—), Nat. Youth Leaders (bd. dirs. 1988, pres. 1989). Republican. Home: 291 Hopeman Pkwy Waynesboro VA 22980 Office: Ch of God 291 Hopeman Pkwy Waynesboro VA 22980

BÉLIVEAU, JULES, editor; b. Longueuil, Que., Can., Mar. 9, 1942; s. Rosaire Béliveau and Marguerite Trudel; m. Diane Martin, May 7, 1966; children: Martin, Simon, Véronique, Annie. Student, Sem. St-Antoine, Trois Rivières, Que., 1956-61, Sem. Philosophie, Montreal, Que., 1962-63. Editor religion sect. La Presse, Montreal, Que., 1977—. Office: La Presse, 7 St-Jacques St, Montreal, PQ Canada H2Y 1K9

BELK, SAMUEL ELLISON, III, cultural activist, former government foreign policy officer; b. Monroe, N.C., June 9, 1920; s. James Patrick and Sarah (Nisbet) B.; m. Joanne Hebb, Sept. 8, 1949 (div. 1964); 1 child, Samuel Ellison IV. BA, U. N.C., 1949; MA, U. Calif., 1952; postgrad., U. London, 1949-50, London Sch. of Econs., 1949-50. Fgn. policy officer U.S. Govt., Washington, 1952-59, Nat. Security Council, The White House, Washington, 1959-65; UN affairs officer U.S. Dept. of State, Washington, 1965-67, asst. dir. internat. edn. program, 1967-79; patron, founder The Canterbury Cathedral Trust In Am., Washington, 1987—. Mem. Council of Friends, Folger Shakespeare Library, Washington, 1977-80; trustee Am. U. of Rome, Washington, 1979-80; founding trustee Friends of English Heritage, Washington, 1987; officer Order of St. John of Jerusalem, 1987—. Served as capt. U.S. Army, 1942-46, ETO. Decorated Bronze Star; recipient Presdl. Commendation, 1965. Club: F Street. Avocations: Anglophile studies and pursuits, music, swimming, travel. Home: 510 N Street SW Washington DC 20024 Office: Canterbury Cathedral Trust in Am 2300 Catherdral Ave NW Washington DC 20008

BELKHODJA, SIR MUHAMMAD HABIR, religious leader. Grand mufti Tunis, Tunisia. Office: Office of Grand Mufti, Tunis Tunisia*

BELL, DAVID S., minister; b. Lakewood, Ohio, June 11, 1964; s. Kerril E. and Barbara J. (Ramage) B.; m. Ethel Lynn Adams, Aug. 3, 1990. BA in Religious Studies, The Coll. of Wooster, 1986; MDiv, Drew Theol. Sch., 1990. Ordained to ministry Meth. Ch. as deacon, 1991. cert. secondary tchr., clin. pastoral tchr. Youth worker Wooster (Ohio) United Meth. Ch., 1982-84; chaplain College Hills Retirement Village, Wooster, 1983-84; youth counselor Westminster Presbyn. Ch., Wooster, 1985-86; min. youth United Meth. Ch. Summit, N.J., 1987-90; asst. to dean Drew Theol. Sch., Madison, N.J., 1989; min. Christian edn. and youth ministry Rocky River (Ohio) United Meth. Ch., 1990—. Author: A Study and Critique of the Ernest Angley Healing and Salvation Crusade, 1985, The Amish Way of Life: A Study of Amish Separation and Accommodation in American Society, 1986. Trustee Rocky River Community Challenge, 1990; cons. Rocky River High Sch. Baccalaureate Com., 1990. Mem. Christian Educators Fellowship, Rocky River Clergy Assn., Alban Inst., Clergy/Sch. Adminstrs. Coun., East Ohio Ann. Conf. United Meth. Ch., Coll. Wooster Alumni Admissions, Rotary. Office: Rocky River United Meth Ch 19414 Detroit Rd Rocky River OH 44116

BELL, J(AMES) D(AVID), educator; b. Chgo., Nov. 25, 1932; s. Mary (Jansco) B.; m. Janette McKenna, Aug. 21, 1962 (div. Oct. 1976); children: David, Marianne, Stephen. BA, De Paul U., 1967, MA, 1968. Asst. prof. Chgo. City Coll., 1968—. Author: Dialogue, 1973; contbr. articles to profl. jours. Mem. Chgo. Psychol. Assn., Free Inquiry Network, Mensa. Home: 1100 Wisconsin Ave Oak Park IL 60304 Office: Chgo City Coll 7500 N Pulaski Chicago IL 60652 *Virtually all of the tragedy that occurs in the world could be avoided if people would give up their pointless ceremonies and meaningless rituals and live by the words of the Carpenter of Nazareth: "Love one another."*

BELL, JAMES M., SR., minister; b. Hickory Grove, S.C., Apr. 5, 1928; s. Robert Murphy and Elinor Ann (Henry) B.; m. Lois Bell Alexander, June 10, 1952; children: James M. Jr., Robert W., Ann Marie, Sharon E., John Paul, Lois Allyson. BA, Erskine Coll., Due West, S.C., 1948; BD, Erskine Sem., Due West, S.C., 1952; DD, Erskin Coll., 1979. Min. Sandy Plains Assoc. Reformed Presbyn. Ch., Tryon, N.C., 1952-55, Tirzah Assoc. Reformed Presbyn. Ch., York, S.C., 1955-65, Old Providence Assoc. Reformed Presbyn. Ch., Spottswood, Va., 1965-82, Due West Assoc. Reformed Presbyn. Ch., 1982—; chaplain Erskine Coll., 1985-90; moderator Gen. Synod Assoc. Reformed Presbyn. Ch., Greenville, S.C., 1987-88. Avocations: hunting, fishing, woodwork, mechanics, softball. Office: Assoc Reformed Presbyn Ch PO Box 397 Due West SC 29639

BELL, JOHN PERRY, minister; b. Columbia, La., Feb. 8, 1948; s. John Dixon and Laverne (Beck) B.; m. Gwendolyn Jean McKay, Dec. 18, 1971; children: Felicia, Peter, Rachel. BA, N.E. La. U., 1970, MA, 1971; ThM, Southern Meth. U., 1973; DMin, Garrett Evang. Sem., 1989. Ordained to ministry United Meth. Ch., 1974. Min. youth United Meth. Ch., Athens, Tex., 1972; pastor United Meth. Ch., Argyle, Wis., 1973-76, Sheboygan Falls, Wis., 1976-84, Waupaca, Wis., 1984—; bd. dirs. Bell Press, Waupaca, 1990—; sec. Coun. on Fin. Adminstrn., Sun Prairie, Wis., 1984—; del. World Meth. Conf., Honolulu, 1981, Nairobi, 1986, New World Mission, Bangalore, India, 1989. Pres. Am. Cancer Soc., Waupaca, 1988-90, Mental Health Assn., Waupaca, 1988—. Recipient Superior award Am. Cancer Soc., 1989-90. Mem. Chain of Lakes Ministerial Assn. (pres. 1986-88), World Future Soc., Kiwanis (local pres. 1983). Democrat. Home: 505 Park Ave Waupaca WI 54981 Office: United Meth Ch 720 Demerest St Waupaca WI 54981 *Life is both internal and external. We have to place equal emphasis on both. Our internal life needs as much care as any other part of life. How we think and feel will determine what we do and say. Faith, then, is the foundation for life.*

BELL, KINITH JOHN, minister; b. Ridgeley, Tenn., Sept. 2, 1951; s. Connel and Lela Lee (Arnold) B.; m. Linda Joy Rohde, Aug. 12, 1972; children: Jacqulyn, Joshua, Joanna, Jennifer. ThB, Bapt. Bible Coll., 1973; postgrad., S.W. Mo. State U., 1973-75. Ordained to ministry Bapt. Ch., 1976. Instr. Bapt. Bible Coll., Springfield, Mo., 1974-76; missionary Chosen People Ministry, Chgo., 1976-79, regional dir., 1979-85; nat. ministry dir. Chosen People Ministry, N.Y.C. and Charlotte, N.C., 1985-89; sr. pastor Naperville (Ill.) Bible Ch., 1989—; cons. various ch. and mission agys., 1985—. Author: How to Be Like the Messiah, 1985; editor: A Response for Messianic Churches, 1986. Dem. judge, Brookfield, Ill., 1983-85. Office: Naperville Bible Ch 25 W 361 Maple Ave Naperville IL 60540

BELL, L. M., bishop. Assoc. bishop Apostolic Overcoming Holy Ch. of God, Inc., Macon, Ga. Office: Apostolic Overcoming Holy Ch of God Inc 2000 Pio Nono Ave Macon GA 31206*

BELL, ORION HANCOCK, III, minister; b. Louisville, Dec. 5, 1936; s. Orion Hancock J. and India C. (Smith) B.; m. Barbara Ellen Evans, May 31, 1958; children: Orion H. IV, Daniel Clayton, Rodney Dean. BA, Georgetown Coll., 1958; MDiv, So. Bapt. Theol. Seminary, Louisville, 1961. Ordained to ministry So. Bapt. Conv., 1959; cert. field edn. supr. Pastor Ballard Bapt. Ch., Bondville, Ky., 1959-60, Second Twelve Mile Bapt. Ch., Butler, Ky., 1960-63, First Bapt. Ch., LaCenter, Ky., 1963-69, Minors Lane Bapt. Ch., Louisville, 1969-77, Immanuel Bapt. Ch., Louisville, 1978—; exec. bd. Ky. Bapt. Conv., Louisville, 1968-69, 87-90; moderator West Union Bapt. Assn., Paducah, Ky., 1968; trustee Temperance League of Ky., Louisville, 1982—. Author: (devotionals) The Carbide Kentuckian, 1967, Western Recorder, 1974. Bd. dirs. Shelby Park Neighborhood Assn., Louisville, 1979—; chmn. Ballard County Coun. on Alcoholism, LaCenter, Ky., 1967-69; vol. fireman, LaCenter, 1964-69; active human rights com., Wendell Foster Ctr., Owensboro, Ky., 1990. Named Duke of Paducah, City of Paducah, 1967, Outstanding Parent, Thomas Jefferson High Sch., Louisville, 1980, Distinctive Citizen, Louisville, 1981, Ky. Col., 1982. Mem. Long Run Bapt. Ministers' Conf. (pres. 1971-72), Ballard County Saddle Club, Civitan. Home: 5010 Mile of Sunshine Dr Louisville KY 40219 Office: Immanuel Baptist Church 1121 S Clay St Louisville KY 40203 *As I have travelled through life there have been many things that I have not been able to understand. I have learned that I can find happiness in most situations when I know that I am in the center of God's will for my life. He continually gives me the strength to enjoy life.*

BELL, RANDALL, educational association administrator; b. Van Wert, Ohio, Aug. 17, 1943; s. Clifford Eugene and Kathryn Jean (Biery) B.; m. Carolyn Ruth Mostert, Apr. 10, 1947; children: Jeffrey Douglas, James David, Jeni Kathryn. Diploma, Moody Bible Inst., 1965; BS, Purdue U., Ft. Wayne, Ind., 1969; MBA, Calif. Luth. U., Thousand Oaks, Calif., 1973; EdD, U. Ark., 1986. Broadcast engr. WKJG Inc., Ft. Wayne, 1965-70; asst. to exec. dir. Am. Assn. Bible Colls., Wheaton, Ill., 1973-76; asst. dir. Am. Assn. Bible Colls., Wheaton, Fayetteville, Ark., 1976-81; assoc. dir. Am. Assn. Bible Colls., Fayetteville, 1981-82, exec. dir., 1982—; vice-chmn. Internat. Coun. Accrediting Agys. Evang. Theol. Edn., Wheaton, 1985-87, chmn., 1987-89; sec. Assembly Inst. Accrediting Bodies, Coun. on Post-Secondary Accreditation, Washington, 1985-88, 91—, mem. com. recognition, 1987-91. With USN, 1970-73. Named Outstanding Young Men Am., 1974. Mem. Nat. Assn. Evang. (sec., treas. commn. on higher edn. 1989—). Republican. Baptist. Office: Am Assn Bible Colls PO Box 1523 130 F N College Fayetteville AR 72702

BELL, RANDALL KEITH, minister; b. Lawton, Okla., Jan. 30, 1962; s. Louie Frank and Syble Ophelia (Kiem) B.; m. Joan Susan Kehr, May 12, 1985; 1 child, Bethany Shea. BBA, Eastern N.Mex. U., 1985. Ordained to ministry So. Bapt. Ch. Youth and music dir. New Testament Bapt. Ch., Portales, N.Mex., 1982-83, 1st Bapt. Ch., Sudan, Tex., 1984-85; youth and edn. dir. 1st Bapt. Ch., Portales, 1985-88; jyourneyman youth dir. Calvary Bapt. Ch., Bangkok, Thailand, 1988-90; youth minister 1st Bapt. Ch., Mineral Wells, Tex., 1990—; associational youth dir. Portales Bapt. Assn., 1985-88; prison ministry leader Thailand Bapt. Assn., Bangkok, 1988-90; conf. leader state convention, Albuquerque. Mem. Delta Sigma Pi. Home: 2012 SE 21st St Mineral Wells TX 76067 Office: 1st Bapt Ch 100 SW 4th Ave Mineral Wells TX 76067

BELL, RICHARD EUGENE, clergyman; b. Cumberland, Md., Oct. 1, 1947; s. Oscar Nimrod and Dorothy Viola (Daniels) B.; m. Nancy Elaine Hall, June 12, 1970; children: David Jonathan, Deborah Joy. BA in History, Grace Coll., Winona Lake, Ind., 1969, MDiv, 1973. Ordained to ministry Fellowship of Grace Brethren Chs., 1976. Assoc. pastor 1st Brethren Ch., Ft. Wayne, Ind., 1973-74; pastor North Kokomo (Ind.) Grace Brethren Ch., 1974-77, Grace Brethren Ch., Dallas Center, Iowa, 1977-83; sr. pastor Ellet Grace Brethren Ch., Akron, Ohio, 1983-86, Grace Brethren Ch., Winchester, Va., 1986—. Producer, speaker religious radio broadcast Faith of Our Fathers, WINC, 92.5 FM, , Winchester, 1986—. Home: 1425 William Dr Winchester VA 22601 Office: Grace Brethren Ch 645 Berryville Ave Winchester VA 22601 *When my life comes to an end I would like to look back and be able to say that I had made a difference, first, in the lives of others and second, in the world around me.*

BELL, SCOTT LEE, pastor; b. Madison, Wis., Mar. 5, 1954; s. LeRoy Joseph and Joyce (Johnson) B.; m. Kathleen D. Wade, July 21, 1979; children: Major, Cody, Gabriel. Degree, Inst. of Christian Studies, 1978-80; BA, Rollins Coll., 1985. Youth min. Good Shephard Episcopal, Maitland, Fla., 1977-83; dir. pastoral care Orlando (Fla.) Christian Ctr., 1984-88; pastor Restoration Christian Ctr., Bedford and Seymour, Ind., 1988—. Host: (radio show) Battle Belongs to the Lord, 1989—. Mem. Orgn. Bd. for Habitat for Humanity, Bedford, 1991; candidate for city councilman Dem. Party, Bedford, 1991; mem. Leadership Lawrence County, Bedford, 1991—. Mem. Bedford-North Lawrence Ministerial Assn. (v.p., pres. elect 1990—, pres. 1991—).

BELL, TENOLIAN RODNEY, SR., minister; b. St. Louis, Dec. 9, 1949; s. James Yarbra and Arvella Josephine (Bailey) B.; m. Janice Lavern Lester, Mar. 25, 1981; children: Tenolian Rodney Jr., Londia Iver. BA in Sociology, So. Ill. U., 1974; MSW, Washington U., St. Louis, 1976; MDiv, Eden Theol. Sem., 1984. Ordained to ministry Am. Bapt. Chs. U.S.A., 1985. Asst. pastor 1st Shiloh Bapt. Ch., Houston, 1985-86; pastor Mt. Zion Bapt. Ch., Madison, Wis., 1986-90; coord. African Am. pastors project Columbus, 1990—; mem. commn. on ministry Am. Bapt. Chs., Madison, 1988-90, mem. nat. continuing edn. commn., 1987-90. Bd. dirs. United Way Dane County, Madison, 1987—, Hospice Care, Madison, 1988, Wayland Found., Madison, 1988; v.p. bd. dirs. Mental Health Ctr., Madison, 1987-90. Named to 10 Who Made a Difference, Wis. State Jour., 1987; recipient award for advancing women's rights Women's Issues Com., 1989. Mem. Ministers Coun., Black Ministers Dane County (pres. 1987-90), Madison Assn. (pres. 1988-90). Home: 2610 Agawam Circle Columbus OH 43224-3701 *My basic view of life is that it is better to do something and fail, than do nothing and succeed. God calls us to be faithful not successful.*

BELL, WALLACE EDWARD, minister; b. Jackson, Tenn., Feb. 23, 1950; s. William and Marvelyne Eugenia (Wallace) B.; m. Johnnie Mae Mitchell, Sept. 12, 1974; children: Jonathan Edward, Candace Michelle. Student, Lambuth Coll., 1970; BS, Union U., 1972; postgrad., Calif. State U., L.A., 1973-74, Midwestern Sem., 1990—. Lic. to ministry Ch. of Christ (Holiness) U.S.A., 1973; ordained, 1979. Assoc. pastor Good News Ch., Pasadena, Calif., 1973-78; assoc. pastor Christ Temple Ch., Jackson, Tenn., 1978-79, pastor, 1979-87; pastor Greater Peace Ch., Aurora, Colo., 1987-88, Christ Temple Ch., Kansas City, Kans., 1988—; trustee C. M. & I. Coll. Nat. Bd., Jackson, 1980—; sec. Northcentral Diocese, St. Louis, 1982-90; dir. communications Nat. S.S. Congress CoCHUSA, Jackson, 1989—. Bd. dirs. Aspell Manor, Jackson, 1985-87. Recipient E.M. Wills award Tenn.-Ky. Dist., 1986. Mem. Jaycees (chaplain 1984-85). Home: 801 N 17th St Kansas City KS 66102 Office: Christ Temple Ch of Christ 801 N 17th St Kansas City KS 66102

BELL, WALLACE WILLIAM, educational administrator; b. Webster Springs, W.Va., Apr. 8, 1953; s. Burton Elmer and Goldie Geraldine (Harrison) B.; m. Frances Lynn Taylor, May 21, 1981; children: Angela Frances, Geoffrey Burton, Stephanie Rebecca. BS in Econs., Fairmont State Coll., 1978, BS in Bus. Adminstrn., 1978; MDiv, Southern Bapt. Theol. Sem., 1983; MBA, U. Louisville, 1989. Staff acct. Region VI Planning & Devel. Coun., Fairmont, W.Va., 1978-80; supr. of acctg. svcs Southern Bapt. Theol. Sem., Louisville, Ky., 1983-85; supr. of purchasing svcs. Southern Bapt. Theol. Sem., Louisville, 1985-90, dir. adminstrv. svcs., 1990—. With U.S. Army, 1973-76. Mem. Nat. Assn. Ednl. Buyers (v.p. Ky. region, 1988-89, pres. 89-90), Ky. Sq. Dance Assn. Democrat. Avocations: woodworking, juggling, square dancing, roller skating.

BELLAH, MICHAEL DEAN, pastor; b. Canyon, Tex., Feb. 22, 1949; s. Robert A. and Cecilia (Staples) B.; m. Charlotte June Ransom, Nov. 28, 1968; children: Janet, Jonathan, Joshua, Joan, Jeremy. BTh, Dallas Bible Coll., 1973. Ordained to ministry Evang. Ch. Camp dir. Wildwood Christian Retreat, Gillette, Wyo., 1973-74; assoc. pastor Paramount Community Ch., Amarillo, Tex., 1975-76; exec. dir. Hidden Falls Ranch, Wayside, Tex., 1976-80; sr. pastor The Evang. Fellowship, Amarillo, 1980—. Author: Baby Boom Believers, 1989 (Finalist for Gold Medallion award 1989); contbr. articles to profl. publs. Mem. Ministerial Assn. of Evang. Free Ch. of Am. Office: The Evang Fellowship PO Box 50504 Amarillo TX 79159

BELLAH, ROBERT NEELLY, sociologist, educator; b. Altus, Okla., Feb. 23, 1927; s. Luther Hutton and Lillian Lucille (Neelly); m. Melanie Hyman, Aug. 17, 1949; children: Jennifer, Harriet. B.A., Harvard U., 1950, Ph.D., 1955. Research assoc. Inst. Islamic Studies, McGill U., Montreal, Can., 1955-57; with Harvard U., Cambridge, Mass., 1957-67; prof. Harvard U., 1966-67; Elliott prof. sociology U. Calif., Berkeley, 1967—. Author: Tokugawa Religion, 1957, Beyond Belief, 1970, The Broken Covenant, 1975 (Sorokin award Am. Sociol. Assn. 1976), (with Charles Y. Glock) The New Religious Consciousness, 1976, (with Phillip E. Hammond) Varieties of Civil Religion, 1980, (with others) Habits of the Heart, 1985. Served with U.S. Army, 1945-46. Fulbright fellow, 1960-61; recipient Harbison award Danforth Found., 1971. Mem. Am. Acad. Arts and Scis., Assn. for Asian Studies, Am. Acad. Religion. Office: U Calif Dept Sociology Berkeley CA 94720

BELLENGER, DOMINIC AIDAN, historian, educator, monk; b. London, July 21, 1950; s. Gerald and Kathleen Patricia (O'Donnell) B. BA, Jesus Coll., Cambridge, Eng., 1972; MA, Cambridge (Eng.) U., 1975, PhD, 1978. Research historian U. Cambridge, 1972-78; asst. master Downside Sch., Bath, Eng., 1978-82; housemaster Downside Sch., Bath, 1989-91, headmaster, 1991—; monk of Order of St. Benedict Downside Abbey, Bath, 1982—; mem. com. Benedictine History Symposium and Commn., Eng., 1980; resident, Rome, 1987-88. Author: English and Welsh Priests 1558-1800, 1984, The French Exiled Clergy, 1986, Opening the Scrolls: Essays in Catholic History, 1987, Letters of Bede Jarrett, 1989; editor Western Catholic History, 1983—; contbr. articles to profl. jours. Leverhulme Trust grantee, 1986. Fellow Royal Hist. Soc., Royal Soc. Arts, The Huguenot Soc.; mem. Ecclesiastical History Soc. Eng. (com. 1982-85), The Cath. Record Soc. (coun. 1990—). Roman Catholic. Avocations: speaking, journalism, travel. Home and Office: Downside Abbey, Stratton-on-the Fosse, Bath Somerset BA3 4RH, England

BELLINGER, ELIZABETH SMITH, clergywoman; b. Lexington, N.C., Jan. 27, 1948; d. Hale Maxwell and Faye (Earnhardt) Smith; m. William H. Bellinger, Jr., Sept. 7, 1975; children: Gillian Kathleen, Charles Raymond. BA, Atlantic Christian Coll., 1970; MDiv, Southeastern Sem., 1973; D Ministry, Southwestern Sem., 1976. Ordained to ministry Bapt. Ch., 1975. Bapt. campus minister N.C. State U., Raleigh, 1972-74; adminstrv. asst. Bethel Coll., St. Paul, Minn., 1978-79; adj. prof. Bethel Coll., St. Paul, 1980; assoc. minister Spring Lake Park Bapt. Ch., Mpls., 1979-81; chaplain Inner City Ministry, Waco, Tex., 1984-86; asst. dir. Cen. Tex. Sr. Ministry, Waco, 1986—. Bd. dirs. Community Cancer Assn., Waco, 1988-89; deacon Lake Shore Bapt. Ch., Waco, 1985-88, 90—. Recipient Pathfinders award YWCA/State of Tex., Waco, 1985. Mem. So. Bapt. Women in Ministry (pres. 1987-88), So. Bapt. Alliance (dir. 1987-88), Waco Ministerial Alliance (pres. 1988-89), Waco Conf. Christians and Jews. Democrat. Avocations: reading, music, art. Office: Cen Tex Sr Ministry Box 85 1625 Herring Ave Waco TX 76708

BELLINGER, WILLIAM HAGOOD, JR., religion educator; b. Bennettsville, S.C., Dec. 28, 1949; s. William Hagood Sr. and Lavicie Rachel (Walters) B.; m. Elizabeth Faye Smith, Sept. 7, 1975; children: Gillian Kathleen, Charles Raymond. BA, Furman U., 1972; MDiv, Southeastern Bapt. Sem., 1975; PhD, U. Cambridge, 1981; postgrad., U. Notre Dame, 1983, U. Cambridge, Eng., 1989. Pastor Union Bapt. Ch., Kinston, N.C., 1972-75; asst. prof. Bethel Theol. Sem., St. Paul, 1978-81, Southwestern Bapt. Theol. Sem., Ft. Worth, 1981-84; assoc. prof., dir. grad. studies in religion Baylor U., Waco, Tex., 1984—; summer assoc. pastor Screven Bapt. Ch., Georgetown, S.C., 1969, 71; faculty S.C. Bapt. Conv. Youth Conf., 1972-74. Author: Psalmody and Prophecy, 1984, Psalms: Reading adn Studying the Book of Praises, 1990. Mem. Soc. for Bibl. Lit., Soc. for Old Testament Study, S.W. Regional Bible Studies Sem., Nat. Assn. Baptist Profs. of Religion, Am. Schs. of Oriental Research (corp. rep., 1979-81). Democrat. Avocations: sports, music, art. Home: 9210 Acorn Dr Waco TX 76712 Office: Baylor U Dept Religion PO Box 97284 Waco TX 76798-7284

BELLO RUIZ, RAFAEL, archbishop; b. Terpan de Galeana, Mex., Mar. 7, 1926. Ordained priest Roman Cath. Ch., 1950. Named titular bishop of Segia; bishop City of Acapulco, Mex., 1976-83, archbishop, 1983—. Address: Diocese of Acapulco, Apartado 201, Acapulco Mexico

BELSHAW, GEORGE PHELPS MELLICK, bishop; b. Plainfield, N.J., July 14, 1928; s. Harold and Edith (Mellick) B.; m. Elizabeth Wheeler, June 12, 1954; children: Richard, Elizabeth, George. B.A., U. of South, 1951;

S.T.B., Gen. Theol. Sem., N.Y.C., 1954, S.T.M., 1959, D.D. hon., 1975. Ordained to ministry, Episcopal Ch., consecrated bishop. Vicar St. Matthew's Ch., Hawaii, 1954-57; fellow, tutor Gen. Theol. Sem., N.Y.C., 1957-59; rector Christ Ch., Dover, Del., 1959-65, St. George's Ch., Rumson, N.J., 1965-75; suffragan bishop Diocese of N.J., Trenton, 1975-83, bishop, 1983—; vis. lectr. Gen. Theol. Sem., 1969, 70, Ctr. Continuing Edn., Princeton Theol. Sem., 1983; governing bd. Episc. Urban Caucus, 1982—, pres., 1986-89; mem. Commn. Peace of Episc. Ch., 1979-85, Econ. Justice Implementation Com., Episc. Ch., 1988—. Editor: Lent with Evelyn Underhill, 1964, Lent with William Temple, 1966; bd. dirs. The Episcopalian, 1987—; contbr. articles to theol. jours. Trustee Gen. Theol. Sem., 1975—; trustee Westminister Choir Coll., 1976-82. Mem. Am. Teilhard de Chardin Assn. (dir.), N.J. Coalition Religious Leaders (pres. 1986). Office: Diocese of NJ 808 W State St Trenton NJ 08618

BELTRAN, EUSEBIUS JOSEPH, bishop; b. Ashley, Pa., Aug. 31, 1934; s. Joseph C. and Helen Rita (Kozlowski) B. Ed., St. Charles Sem., Overbrook, Pa. Ordained priest Roman Cath. Ch., 1960. Consecrated bishop, 1978; pastor chs. in Atlanta and Decatur, Ga., 1960; notary, then vice officialis Atlanta Diocesan Tribunal, 1960-62; vice chancellor Archdiocese Atlanta, 1962; officialis Archdiocesan Tribunal, 1963-74; pastor chs. in Atlanta and Rome, Ga., 1963-66; vicar gen. Archdiocese of Atlanta, 1971-78; pastor St. Anthony's Ch., Atlanta, 1972-78; bishop of Tulsa, 1978—; mem. com. liturgy Nat. Conf. Cath. Bishops; also com. for Am. Coll., Louvain, Belgium; bd. regents Conception Sem.; bd. dirs. St. Gregory's Coll., Shawnee, Okla. Mem. Equestrian Order Holy Sepulchre, NCCJ. Club: K.C. Home: 2151 N Vancouver St Tulsa OK 74127 Office: 820 S Boulder St PO Box 2009 Tulsa OK 74101

BELZ, JOEL, religious publisher; b. Marshalltown, Iowa, Aug. 10, 1941; s. Max Victor and Jean (Franzenburg) B.; m. Diana Lynn Ewing, June 15, 1967 (div. 1974); m. Carol Esther Jackson, Jan. 11, 1975; children: Jenny, Katrina, Alice, Elizabeth, Esther. BA, Covenant Coll., 1962; MA, U. Iowa, 1971. Headmaster Lookout Mountain (Ga.) Christian Sch., 1973-77; exec. editor, pub. God's World Publs., Inc., Asheville, N.C., 1977—; chmn. bd. dirs. Covenant Coll., Lookout Mountain, Asheville Christian Acad. Named Alumnus of Yr., Covenant Coll., 1977. Presbyterian. Republican. Home: 392 Old Haw Creek Rd Asheville NC 28805 Office: God's World Publs Inc 85 Tunnel Rd Box 2330 Asheville NC 28802

BENCE, CLARENCE LUTHER, academic administrator; b. Corning, N.Y., Nov. 22, 1944; s. James Edwards and Florence Lavernia (Lytle) B.; m. Carol Jean Backenstoe, Aug. 31, 1968; children: Tamara Jill, Aimee Karis, James Ryan. BA, Houghton Coll., 1966; MDiv, Asbury Seminary, 1969; PhD, Emory U., 1981. Ordained to ministry Wesleyan Ch., 1970. Sr. pastor Penfield (N.Y.) Wesleyan Ch., 1969-74; tchr. United Wesleyan Coll., Allentown, Pa., 1978-82; prof. Marion (Ind.) Coll., 1982-87; coll. adminstr. Houghton (N.Y.) Coll., 1987—, acting pres., 1989. Pres. alumni assn Asbury Theol. Soc., Wilmore, Ky., 1983. Mem. Wesleyan Theol. Soc. (mem. coun. 1987-89). Avocations: beekeeping, reading, hiking. Office: Houghton College Houghton NY 14744

BENDER, ROBERT FRANK, JR., minister; b. Massillon, Ohio, Mar. 20, 1951; s. Robert Frank and Mary Jane (Tanzie) B.; m. Carol Jane Bliffen, June 16, 1973; children: Mari, Marshall, Melissa, Martin, Morgan. BA magna cum laude, Ky. Christian Coll., Grayson. Ordained to ministry Christian Ch. Minister Dry Run Christian Ch., Portsmouth, Ohio, 1973-75, Meadowood Ch. of Christ, Newark, 1975-78, Norwin Christian Ch., Irwin, Pa., 1978-88, Danville (Ohio) Ch. of Christ, 1988-91, Parkway Christian Ch., Sarasota, Fla., 1991—; dir. Camp Christian, Mill Run, Pa., 1985-88; v.p. Cen. Ohio Preachers Assn., Mt. Vernon, 1990; founder 5th Sunday Sing, Knox County, Ohio. Vice-pres. Acad. Boosters, Danville, 1990. Mem. Danville Area Ministers, Cen. Ohio Preachers Assn., Delta Epsilon Chi. Republican. Home: 210 Magellan Dr Sarasota FL 34243 Office: Parkway Christian Ch 6960 Prospect Rd Sarasota FL 34243

BENDER, ROSS THOMAS, minister; b. Tavistock, Ont., Can., June 25, 1929; came to U.S., 1960, naturalized, 1965; s. Christian and Katie (Bender) B.; m. Ruth Eileen Steinmann, Dec. 22, 1950; children: Ross Lynn, Elizabeth, Michael, Deborah, Anne. BA, Goshen Coll., 1954, BD, 1956; MA, Yale U., 1961, PhD, 1962. Ordained to ministry Mennonite Ch., 1958. Prin. Rockway Mennonite sch., Kitchener, Ont., 1956-60; prof. Christian edn. Goshen Bibl. Sem., Ind., 1962—; dean Assoc. Mennonite Bibl. Sems., Elkhart, Ind., 1964-79; pres. Mennonite World Conf., 1984-90. Author: The People of God, 1969, Christians in Families, 1982. Rockefeller fellow, 1960-61; Am. Assn. Theol. Schs. fellow, 1961-62; NIMH postdoctoral fellow U. Pa., 1970-71. Mem. Am. Assn. Marriage and Family Therapists. Office: Goshen Bibl Sem 3003 Benham Ave Elkhart IN 46517

BENEDEK, WILLIAM CLARK, evangelist; b. New Castle, Pa., Mar. 2, 1957; s. Joseph and Virginia Elanor (Murphy) B. BS, Geneva Coll., 1979, BSBA, 1979. Analyst Wis. Bell, Inc., Milw., 1979-84, computer staff analyst, 1984-86, staff analyst end user computing, 1986-87, staff mgr. Info. Ctr., 1987-88, tech. mgr. end user computing support, 1988-89; tech. mgr. end user data access support Ameritech Applied Techs., Milw., 1989-90; missionary The Evang. Alliance Mission, Wheaton, Ill., 1990—. Mem. missions com. Elmbrook Ch., Waukesha, Wis., 1986-89; charter mem. Rep. Presdl. Task Force. Avocations: stamp collection, missions work in Venezuela and Brazil, real estate. Home: 1153 Kerry Ln Erie PA 16505 Office: The Evang Alliance Mission PO Box 969 Wheaton IL 60189-0969

BENEDETTO, ROBERT JOSEPH, librarian, archivist; b. San Francisco, Aug. 28, 1950; s. Dominic Joseph and Frances (Coscarelli) B.; m. Linda Ann Davenport, May 13, 1978; 1 child, Christa Renée. BA, San Francisco State U., 1972; MA, Pitts. Theol. Sem., 1977; MLS, U. Hawaii, 1982. Archivist Hist. Found. of the Presbyn. and Reformed Chs., Montreat, N.C., 1984-88; dep. dir., archivist dept. of history Presbyn. Ch. (U.S.A.), Montreat, 1988-91; assoc. libr. Union Theol. Sem. in Va., Richmond, 1991—; bd. trustees Moravian Music Found., Winston-Salem, N.C., 1986-89. Author: The Hawaii Journals of the New England Missionaries, 1813-1894, 1983, Guide to the Manuscript Collections of the Presbyterian Church, U.S., 1990; contbr. articles to profl. jours. Mem. Am. Theol. Libr. Assn., Soc. Am. Archivists, Soc. N.C. Archivists (v.p., pres. 1987-89). Office: 3401 Brook Rd Richmond VA 23227

BENEDICT, MONSEIGNEUR FRIAR (MAR BENEDICT), priest, religious researcher; b. Bay City, Mich., Dec. 29, 1917. BA in Psychology, Chapman Coll., 1971; postgrad., U. So. Calif., U. Calif., Long Beach, 1972-80. Ordained priest Ch. of Antioch, 1971, consecrated monsignor, 1991. Pastor, minister Chapel of the Chimes, Orange, Calif., 1972-81; researcher Apostle Thomas Gnostics, Malabar Rite, Thousand Oaks, Calif., 1981—. Research on the cosmological connection, synaptology and brain waves, gnostic cybernetics, altered states of consciousness and varieties of religious experiences. Home and Office: 887 Saint Charles Dr Apt 16 Thousand Oaks CA 91360

BENFIELD, WILLIAM FLOYD, SR., minister; b. Valmead, N.C., May 12, 1940; s. William Howard and Lillie Mae (Dellinger) B.; m. Martha Sue Capps, July 5, 1958; children: William Floyd Jr., Timothy Paul. AA, Gardner Webb Coll., 1963; BA, Lenoir Rhyne Coll., 1965; MDiv, Southeastern Bapt. Theol. Sem., 1970. Ordained to ministry So. Bapt. Conv., 1960. Pastor Phila. Bapt. Ch., Connelly Springs, N.C., 1960-63, Mull's Chapel Bapt. Ch, Connelly Springs, 1963-66, Flat Rock Bapt. Ch., Louisburg, N.C., 1966-73, Cedar Falls Bapt. Ch., Fayetteville, N.C., 1973—. Office: Cedar Falls Bapt Ch 6181 Ramsey St Fayetteville NC 28311

BENGSTON-BRUE, DEBRA, minister; b. Morris, Ill., Nov. 5, 1956; d. Robert George and Dorothy Rose (Cater) Bengston; m. Mr. Brue, Jan. 11, 1986 (dec. Oct., 1986). BA, Concordia Coll., Moorhead, Minn., 1979; MDiv, Luther Northwestern Theol. Sem, St. Paul, Minn., 1987. Cert. tchr., Iowa. Assoc. pastor Morningside Luth. Ch., Sioux City, Iowa, 1987—; mem. Candidacy Com., Storm Lake, Iowa, 1988—. Mem. Clin. Rsch. Com., St. Luke's Hosp., Sioux City, Iowa, 1988—, Human Rights Com., Parkview, Sioux City, Iowa, 1989—. Home: 2935 S. Martha Sioux City IA 51106 Office: Morningside Luth Ch 700 S Martha Sioux City IA 51106

BENGTSON, FELIX JAN, minister; b. Galesburg, Ill., Jan. 7, 1927; s. Carl Felix and Ruth Mildred (Dahlberg) B.; m. Sarah Jean House, Sept. 9, 1950 (div.); children: Kristin, Sarah Bengtson Martin; m. Darlene Rae Worman Secrest, Jan. 7, 1984; 1 stepchild, Steven Secrest. AB, U. Ill., 1950; BD, Augustana Theol. Sem., Rock Island, Ill., 1953; MST, Union Theol. Sem., N.Y.C., 1959. Ordained to ministry Evang. Luth Ch. Am., 1954. Pastor Emmanuel Luth. Ch., Boston, 1954-60, Bethlehem Luth. Ch., Gary, Ind., 1960-68, St. Luke Luth. Ch., Sioux City, Iowa, 1968-77, Luth. Meml. Ch., Quincy, Ill., 1977-84, St. Mark Luth. Ch., Cape Girardeau, Mo., 1984-86, Faith Luth. Ch., Wataga, Ill., 1986—; tchr. Confirmation Camp, Andover Cluster, Augustana Coll., 1988-91. Author: Towards an Inclusive Lutheran Parish in an Interracial Neighborhood, 1960. Bd. dirs. Augustana Coll., 1985-90, Care at Home, Galesburg, 1989—; bd. dirs., vol. chaplain Cottage Hosp., Galesburg, 1986-91. With USN, 1945-46. Recipient appreciation St. Francis Hosp., Cape Girardeau, 1986, Svcs. Rendered award Augustana Coll., 1990. Mem. S.W. Conf. Mins., Ministerial Assn., Galesburg Ministerial Assn., Lake Bracken Country Club, Lions. Republican. Avocations: swimming, boating, carpentry, reading, travel.

BENÍTEZ, FELIPE SANTIAGO, archbishop; b. Piribebuy, Paraguay, May 10, 1926; s. Angel Benítez and Juana Avalas. Grad., Seminario Metropolitano y Facultad Teológica Pontificia de Buenos Aires. Ordained priest Roman Cath. Ch., 1952. Priest Asunción, Paraguay, 1952-61; prof. theology Instituto Superior Teología, Buenos Aires, 1955-56, Instituto de Ciencias Contables y Administrativas, Univ. Católica, 1960; bishop of Villarrica de Espíritu Santo, 1965-89, archbishop of Asunción, 1989—; with Movimiento Obrero Católico, 1960. Office: Arzobispado de Asunción, Casilla de Correo 654, Asunción Paraguay

BENITEZ, MAURICE MANUEL, bishop; b. Washington, Jan. 23, 1928; s. Enrique M. and Blossom (Compton) B.; m. Joanne Dossett, Dec. 18, 1949. B.S., U.S. Mil. Acad., 1949; B.D., U. of South, 1958, D.D., 1973. Ordained to ministry Episcopal Ch. Priest-in-charge St. James Ch., Lake City, Fla., 1958-61; canon resident St. John's Cathedral, Jacksonville, Fla., 1961-62; rector Grace Ch., Ocala, Fla., 1962-68; rector ch., San Antonio, 1968-74; exec. bd. fin. dept., trustee U. of South, 1969; dep. Gen. Conv. Episc. Ch., 1970-73, 79; regent U. of South, 1973-79; bishop of Tex., 1980—. Served to capt. USAF, 1949-55. Address: 520 San Jacinto St Houston TX 77002

BENJAMIN, DON C., JR., religion educator; b. Barksdale AFB, La., Mar. 14, 1942; s. Don C. and Edith M. (Beltz) B. BA, St. Bonaventure U., 1964; MA, Cath. U. Am., 1969; PhD, Claremont Grad. Sch., 1981. Tchr. counselor Salpointe Cath. High Sch., Tucson, 1968-69; tchr., dept. chmn. Mt. Carmel High Sch., Los Angeles, 1969-72; lectr. theology Mt. St. Mary Coll., Los Angeles, 1975-76; acting dir. Carmelite Retreat and Edn. Ctr., Los Angeles, 1976-78; lectr. Grad. Sch. Theology, U. St. Thomas, Houston, 1980-83; lectr. religious studies Rice U., Houston, 1978—; Scanlon vis. scholar in religious studies U. Houston, 1986, 88. Mem. Soc. Bibl. Lit., Cath. Bibl. Assn. Author: Deuteronomy and City Life, 1983, Old Testament Parellels, 1991; contbr. articles to profl. jours. Office: Rice U Dept Religious Studies PO Box 1892 Houston TX 77251

BENJAMIN, GARY DUANE, clergyman, fire chief; b. Garnett, Kans., Mar. 29, 1941; s. Ralph Eugene and Iva Pauline (Bailey) B.; m. Linda Sue Brown, July 30, 1959; 1 son, Stanley Eugene. B.Th., Ozark Bible Coll., 1964. Ordained to ministry Christian Ch., 1964; cert. arson investigator, Kans. Minister, Christ's Ch., Urich, Mo., 1960-62, Filley Christian Ch., El Dorado Springs, Mo., 1962-64, Ch. of Christ, Rockwell City, Iowa, 1964-69; Chaplain coordinator Iowa Women's Reformatory, Rockwell City, 1967; minister Wall Street Christian Ch. and Mound City Federated Ch., Mound City, Kans., 1970—; funeral dir. Farris-Feuerborn Meml. Chapel, Garnett, 1984—; fire chief City of Garnett, 1981—; civil defense dir. Anderson County (Kans.), 1982—, rural fire coordinator, 1982—. Adminstr. Anderson County Planning Commn., 1982—. Recipient Regional Speak Up award Kans. Jaycees, 1972. Mem. Anderson County Firefighters Relief Assn. (sec.-treas. 1984—). Avocations: camping, snow skiing, photography. Home: 315 Orange St Garnett KS 66032 Office: Fire Dept 131 W 5th St Garnett KS 66032

BENJAMIN, JERRY DEAN, clergyman; b. Pekin, Ill., Nov. 2, 1937; s. Alvin Everett and Lucille Stella (Garlish) B.; m. Barbara E. Manchester, Oct. 20, 1962; children: Steven M., James M. BS, Bradley U., 1964; MDiv, McCormick Theol., 1967; D. Ministry, Iliff Sch. Theol., 1981. Ordained to ministry Presbyn. Ch., 1967. Pastor Grace Presbyn. Ch., Winona, Minn., 1967-71, Westminster Presbyn. Ch., Keokuk, Iowa, 1971-75; pres. Emphasis, Inc., Boulder, Colo., 1975-76; pastor United Presbyn. Ch., Broomfield, Colo., 1976—; adj. instr. Chapman Coll., 1990—, U. Colo., 1990—; del. to the chs. of USSR, 1983, 87, 88; mem. Presbytery of Boulder. Author: For Freedom, 1990; translator: Eutropius: Sanctuary and the Folly of Wealth, 1990. Bd. dirs., pres. Emergency Family Assistance Assn., Boulder, 1982-88, vol. social worker, 1983-88. Mem. Am. Acad. Religion, Soc. for Bibl. Lit. Democrat. Office: United Presbyn Ch 350 Main St Broomfield CO 80020

BENNER, WILBUR WAYNE, minister, evangelist; b. Mifflintown, Pa., Feb. 15, 1929; s. Samuel M. and Mary (Adams) B.; m. Jane Book, APR. 16, 1949; children: Loreen, Kevin P. Student, Shippensburg (Pa.) U., 1947, Messiah Coll., 1962. Ordained to ministry Brethren in Christ Ch. Pastor Brethren in Christ Ch., Mifflintown, Pa., 1951-55, Columbia, Ky., 1955-59, Chambersburg, Pa., 1959-64, St. Petersburg, Fla., 1964-67, Stevensville, Ont., Can., 1967-74, Knifley, Ky., 1974-76, Greencastle, Pa., 1976—; evangelist in over 150 revivals, camp meetings; supt. missions, pastor, Ky., 1955-59; tchr. Ekuphelni Bible Inst., Bulawayo, Zimbabwe, 1988; chmn. bd. evangelism and ch. growth Allegheny Conf., Brethren in Christ Ch., 1990-91; keynote speaker Gen. Conf. Brethren in Christ Ch., Bulawango, Zimbabwe, 1991, also condr. pastoral seminars. Home and Office: Brethren in Christ Ch 9740 Antrim Church Rd Greencastle PA 17225 *"Life is a sacred trust. We live only once here on earth. We should live it to the full in Jesus Christ". Galations 2:20.*

BENNETT, ANNA DELL, minister, religion educator, retired elementary school educator; b. Cobb Hill, Ky., Jan. 11, 1935; d. James Edison Shoemaker and Chrystal (Abney) Shoemaker-Hurst; m. Stanley Bennett, Oct. 7, 1950 (dec. Jan. 1987); children: Eddie Wayne, James Lloyd, Kathryn Melissa. BS, U. Dayton, 1966; MS in Elem. Classroom Teaching, Wright State U., 1974, M in Gifted Teaching, 1980; Assoc. Bibl., Centerville Bible Coll., 1985, degree in theology, 1987. Cert. elem. tchr., Ohio. Tchr. West Carrollton (Ohio) Bd. Edn., 1966-86; dir. Christian edn., Way of the Cross Ch., Dayton, Ohio, 1989—; adj. prof. St. Joseph Coll., Cin., 1981-85. Recipient plaque Mt. St. Joseph Coll., Cin., 1985. Republican. Home: 215 E Franklin St Centerville OH 45459 Office: Open Bible Way of the Cross Ch 612 Beatrice Ave Dayton OH 45404

BENNETT, BILLY JOE, minister; b. Ft. Campbell, Ky., Aug. 18, 1953; s. Joseph Donald and Billie Jean (Sepich) B.; m. Nancy Carol Stegall, July 26, 1974; children: Joshua (dec.), Jessica, Justin, Jaime. BA, Miss. Coll., Clinton, Miss., 1978; MDiv, New Orleans Bapt. Theol. Sem., 1982, ThD, 1988. Ordained to ministry So. Bapt. Conv., 1977. Pastor Eden Bapt. Ch., Yazoo City, Miss., 1977-80, Knox Bapt. Ch., Tylertown, Miss., 1980-84; sr. pastor First Bapt. Ch., Greensburg, La., 1984-89; adj. prof. Mid-Continent Bapt. Coll., Mayfield, Ky., 1990—; sr. pastor First Bapt. Ch., Clinton, Ky., 1989—; dir. evangelism Two Rivers Bapt. Assn., Amite, La., 1987-89, West Ky. Bapt. Assn., Clinton, 1989—; fellow New Orleans Bapt. Theol. Sem., 1981-83; cons. Home Mission Bd., So. Bapt. Conv., 1990—. Office: First Bapt Ch 320 Mayfield Rd Clinton KY 42031-1445

BENNETT, CHAD DANIEL, minister; b. Ft. Worth, May 9, 1967; s. David Leo and Tige (McKinney) B.; m. Darla Sue Molen, Jan. 6, 1989. Student, S.W. Bapt. U., 1990. Ordained to ministry Bapt. Ch. Min. youth and music Tatum Chapel Bapt. Ch., Springfield, Mo., 1987—. Office: Tatum Chapel Bapt Ch Rte 4 Box 862 Springfield MO 65802

BENNETT, CHARLES O'BRIEN, clergyman, educator; b. Williamson, N.Y., Apr. 28, 1927; s. Donald Augustus and Marion (O'Brien) B.; m. June Louise Jenkins, Sept. 18, 1927; children: Brenda G., John C., Susan D., Barbara J. BA, So. Meth. Coll., 1976; MA, Columbia Bible Coll. and Sem., 1983; M Bible Studies, So. Meth. Coll., 1985. Ordained deacon Meth. Ch., 1966, elder, 1975. Pastor So. Meth. Ch., Port Salerno, Fla., 1960-66; missionary S. Meth. bd. Missions, Orangeburg, S.C., 1966-75; prof. missiology So. Meth. Coll., Orangeburg, 1975-83, pres., 1983—; field dir. Mex. ops. So. Meth. Bd. Missions, 1970-81; chmn. Child Evangelism Fellowship S.C., Columbia, 1982-90. With USN, 1944-46, PTO. Mem. Evangel. Theol. Soc., Wesleyan Theol. Soc., Evangel. Missiological Soc., Am. Legion. Republican. Avocations: travel, refinishing antiques. Office: So Meth Coll PO Box 1027 Orangeburg SC 29116

BENNETT, DAVID WILLIAM, minister; b. Muskegon, Mich., Mar. 31, 1948; s. Richard Henry and Verta Irene (Campbell) B.; m. Phyllis Roberta Houck, May 16, 1975; children: Raymond, Jonathan. BS, MIT, 1969; MDiv, Fuller Theol. Sem., 1973, D Ministry, 1974, PhD, 1990. Ordained to ministry Congl. Ch., 1974, Am. Bapt. Chs., 1991. Assoc. pastor Mariners Ch., Newport Beach, Calif., 1974-78; sr. pastor Voyagers Bible Ch., Irvine, Calif., 1978-88; min. at large Voyagers Bible Ch., Irvine, 1988-90; sr. pastor Mountain Park Ch., Lake Oswego, Oreg., 1990—; bd. dirs. Tyrannus Halls Internat., Torrance, Calif., 1st Fruit, Inc., Newport Beach, Strategic Ventures Network, Pasadena, Calif. Trustee Fuller Theol. Sem., 1978-81; bd. dirs. Irvine Med. Ctr., 1982-88, Lasor Found. for Bibl. Rsch., Altadena, Calif., 1980-90. Republican. Office: Mountain Park Ch 40 McNary Pkwy Lake Oswego OR 97035

BENNETT, EDITH LILLIAN, lay church worker, radio personality; b. Livermore, Ky., June 21, 1931; d. Dorsey Slade and Isa Carey (Taylor) B. AS, Owensboro (Ky.) Bus. Coll., 1950; student, Mid Continent Bible Coll., Owensboro, Ky., 1991—. Various positions including sec., office mgr., writer-dir. Sta. WOMI, Owensboro, 1950—; fin. sec. Third Bapt. Ch., Owensboro, 1981—. Personality weekly religious program on 4-VOC, Haiti; author, compiler, editor numerous publs. on Livermore history, genealogy and slavery. Sunday sch. tchr. Third Bapt. Ch. Named to Honorable Order of Ky. Colonels, 1969, Someone Spl., Owensboro, 1984. Mem. Owensboro Choral Soc. (co-chmn., presenter MESSIAH benefits 1940—), DAR (local and state officer 1989—). Home: 715 Princeton Pkwy Apt 15 Owensboro KY 42301 Office: Third Bapt Ch 527 Allen St Owensboro KY 42301

BENNETT, GEORGE WILLIS, minister, educator, retired academic administrator; b. Candler, N.C., July 26, 1919; s. John C. and Allie (Fisher) B.; m. Caroline Dillard, June 11, 1942; children: Susanne, Jane Stelling, Mary Shean. Student, Mars Hill Coll., 1937-39; AB, Wake Forest Coll., 1941; MDiv, So. Bapt. Theol. Sem., Louisville, 1946, ThM, 1947, PhD, 1954; MSW, U. Louisville, 1964. Pastor Olive Chapel Bapt. ch., Apex, N.C., 1950-54, 1st Bapt. Ch., Red Springs, N.C., 1954-59; assoc. prof. Christian ethics So. Bapt. Theol. Sem., 1959-69, prof. church and community, 1969-91, dir. field edn., 1969-75, dir. advanced profl. studies, 1975-80, dir. grad. studies, 1980-83, dean sch. theology, 1983-88, provost, 1987-91, sr. prof. ch. and community, 1991—; founder Urban Studies Coop., Atlanta, 1968; chmn. Ctr. Urban Ch. Studies, Nashville, Ky., 1980-86. Author: Confronting a Crisis, 1967, Mission Action in Resort Areas, 1969, Effective Urban Church Ministry, 1983, A Study of Tennessee Baptist Adult Homes, 1986. V.p. Metro United Way, Louisville, 1972-75; bd. dirs. Ky. Coun. Community Devel., Frankfort, 1960s, Family and Children's Agy., Louisville, 1976-82. Recipient Disting. Svc. award Christian Life Commn. So. Bapt. Conv., 1980, Ann. Recognition award Urban Tng. Coop., 1985. Mem. Religious Rsch. Assn., Soc., Sci. Study Religion, So. Bapt. Hist. Soc., So. Bapt. Rsch. Fellowship (v.p. 1988-90, pres. 1990-92). Democrat. Avocations: travel, walking, drama, the arts. Home: 3423 Hycliffe Ave Louisville KY 40207 Office: So Bapt Theol Sem 2825 Lexington Rd Louisville KY 40280

BENNETT, HAROLD CLARK, clergyman, religious organization administrator; b. Asheville, N.C., July 30, 1924; s. Charles C. and Emily H. (Clark) B.; m. Phyllis Jean Metz, Aug. 17, 1947; children: Jeffery Clark, John Scott, Cynthia Ann Bennett Howard. Student, Asheville Biltmore Jr. Coll., 1946, Mars Hill Coll., 1946-47; B.A., Wake Forest U., 1949; postgrad., Duke U. Div. Sch., 1949-51; M.Div., So. Bapt. Theol. Sem., 1953; LL.D. (hon.), Stetson U., 1968; D.D. (hon.), Campbell U., 1982, Wake Forest U., 1985; STD (hon.), Southwest Bapt. U., 1991. Clk. FBI, Washington, 1942-43; ordained to ministry Baptist Ch., 1948; pastor Glen Royal Bapt. Ch., Wake Forest, N.C., 1948-51; chaplain Ky. State Reformatory, LaGrange, 1951-53, Ky. Woman's Prison, 1951-53; pastor Westpoint (Ky.) Bapt. Ch., 1952; asst. pastor First Bapt. Ch., Shreveport, La., 1953-55; pastor Beech St. Bapt. Ch., Texarkana, Ark., 1955-60; supt. new work Sunday Sch. Dept., Sunday Sch. bd. So. Bapt. Conv., Nashville, Tenn., 1960-62; interim pastor Little West Fork Bapt. Ch., Hopkinsville, Ky., 1960, Two Rivers Bapt. Ch., Nashville, 1962; sec. met. missions home mission bd. So. Bapt. Conv., Atlanta, Ga., 1962-65; dir. missions div. Bapt. Gen. Conv. Tex., Dallas, 1965-67; exec. sec., treas. Fla. Bapt. Conv., Jacksonville, 1967-79; pres., treas., mem. exec. com. So. Bapt. Conv., Nashville, 1979—; Bd. dirs., vice chmn. Religion in Am. Life; bd. dirs. Bapt. Life Ins. Co., 1st Am. Nat. Bank, Nashville; chmn. U.S. Ch. Leaders, 1987-89; mem. Bapt. Joint Com. on Pub. Affairs, Washington, 1979—, Internat. Adv. Com. for World Evangelization, 1986—. Compiler: God's Awesome Challenge, 1980; Contbr. numerous articles to religious publs.; author: Reflections of Faith, 1983—. Mem. adv. council Fla. State Alcoholism, 1973-78; trustee Fla. Meml. Coll., Miami, 1967-74; mem. Nashville Literagy Task Force. Served with A.C. USN, 1942-45. Named Ky. Col.; recipient Good Shepherd award Boy Scouts Am., 1986. Mem. Assn. Bapt. State Exec. Secs. (pres. 1978-79), Assn. Bapt. State Conv. Ch. Bond Plans (pres. 1978-79), Fla. Bapt. State Bd. Missions (sec. 1967-79), Am. Bible Soc. (bd. govs. 1979—), Bapt. World Alliance (mem. gen. council, 1979—, v.p. 1990—), Nashville C. of C. (mem. law and justice com. 1984—). Lodge: Rotary. Home: 202 Long Valley Rd Brentwood TN 37027 Office: 901 Commerce St Nashville TN 37203 *In my life, with the variety of conflicts and demands thrust my way, I have discovered that a personal relationship with Jesus Christ is the only way to maintain an inner peace. It is a joy to be a Christian and to have the privilege of serving as an ambassador for Him. I long for others to come to have a similar peace with God.*

BENNETT, JOE, bishop. Assoc. bishop Apostolic Overcoming Holy Ch. of God, Inc., Dalton, Ill. Office: Apostolic Overcoming Holy Ch of God Inc 15718 Drexel Ave Dalton IL 60419*

BENNETT, ROGER SPURGEON, minister; b. Augusta, Ga., Dec. 8, 1954; s. Spurgeon Addie and Louise (Blanchard) B. BA, Columbia Bible Coll., 1977; MDiv, Southwestern Theol. Bapt. Sem., 1981; MEd, Ga. State U., 1984; cert., Psycholog. Studies Inst., 1984; postgrad., Luther Rice Sem. Ordained to ministry Bapt. Ch., 1977. Asst. tchr. Ga. State U., Atlanta, 1983-84; pastoral psychotherapist Pastoral Care Assocs., Martinez, Ga., 1984; interim pastor Goshen Bapt. Ch., Lincolnton, Ga., 1984; assoc. pastor of family ministry and evangelism Martinez Bapt. Ch., 1985—; vol. youth pastor Damascus Bapt. Ch., Leah, Ga., 1970-71; vol. chaplin Ga. Regional Hosp. Augusta, 1980; mem. clergy staff Univ. Hosp. Augusta, 1985—. Vol. tchr. Midland Ctr. for Mentally Retarded Children, Columbia, S.C., 1974-75; vol. worker Servicemen Ctr., Columbia, 1975-76. Named one of Outstanding Young Men Am., 1985. Mem. Augusta Assn. Ministers, Kappa Delta Pi. Avocations: reading, tennis, hunting. Office: Martinez Bapt Ch 3632 Old Petersburg Rd Martinez GA 30907

BENNETT, T. JAMES, bishop. V.p. Ch. of God of Prophecy in Can., Brampton, Ont. Office: Ch of God of Prophecy in Can, PO Box 457, Brampton, ON Canada L6V 1A1*

BENNETT, WILLIAM LEFFIS, minister; b. Shallotte, N.C., June 26, 1924; s. Samuel Luther and Emma Margaret Bennett; m. Doris Faye Palmer, July 19, 1952; children: Bill Jr., Philip, David. BA summa cum laude, Wake Forest U., 1948; MA, Duke U., 1950, MDiv, 1953; ThD, New Orleans Bapt. Theol. Sem., 1965. Ordained to ministry So. Bapt. Conv., 1950. Pastor Calvary Bapt. Ch., Durham, N.C., 1950-54, 16th St. Bapt. Ch., Greensboro, N.C., 1954-61, Clifton (La.) Bapt. Ch., 1961-63, Speedway Terrace Bapt. Ch., Memphis, 1963-67, Ft. Smith (Ark.) Bapt. Ch., 1967-86, Houston NW Bapt. Ch., 1988—; mem. Sunday sch. bd. So. Bapt. Convention, 1972-80, 90—; state chmn. evangelism N.C. Bapt. Convention, 1959-61; founder God and Country svcs. So. Bapt. Convention; pres. Ark. Bapt. Pastors' Conf., 1971; trustee Ouschita Bapt. U., 1968-69; speaker in field. Named one of 10 Outstanding Citizens of Ft. Wmith, 1978. Mem. Phi Beta Kappa. Republican. Home: 8310 Pheasant Glen Spring TX 77379 Office: Houston NW Bapt Ch 19911 Tomball Pkwy Houston TX 77070

BENNISON, CHARLES ELLSWORTH, JR., priest; b. Mpls., Nov. 30, 1943; s. Charles Ellsworth and Marjorie Elizabeth (Haglun) B.; m. Joan Kathryn Reahard, June 17, 1967; children: Sarah, Kathryn. BA summa cum laude, Lawrence U., 1965; BD, Harvard U., 1968, ThM, 1970; MA, Claremont Grad. Sch., 1977. Ordained to ministry Episcopal Ch. as priest, 1968. Priest St. Mark's Episcopal Ch., Upland, Calif., 1971-88, St. Clare's Episcopal Ch., Rancho Cucamonga, Calif., 1986-88, St. Luke's Episcopal Ch., Atlanta, 1988-91; chmn. Diocesan Social Rels. Commn., L.A., 1972-80; pres. Diocesan Standing Com., 1985-86; pres. corp. Diocese of L.A., 1987-88. Founder Community Appeal for Homeless, Atlanta, 1990. Recipient Kilgore award for creative ministry Sch. Theology, Claremont, 1985, Ecumenical Svc. award Pomona Valley Coun. Chs., 1986. Home: 3990 Parian Ridge Rd Atlanta GA 30327 Office: 435 Peachtree St NE Atlanta GA 30327

BENSEN, CRAIG LEE, minister; b. Keene, N.H., Aug. 11, 1948; s. Harold Bernhard and Eleanor (Brugge) B.; m. Deborah Lee Robertson, Oct. 13, 1974; children: Benjamin, Amanda. BA, U. Vt., 1970; MDiv, Gordon-Conwell Theol. Sem., S. Hamilton, Mass., 1973, postgrad. Ordained to ministry, United Ch. of Christ, 1979. Pastor Cambridge (Vt.) United Ch., 1976—; chmn. Greater Burlington Evangelicals, 1979—; vice chmn. Vt. Billy Graham Crusade, Burlington, 1982—; dir. Focus Renewal Ministries, United Ch. Christ, 1987—; pres. Vt. Bible Witness Fellowship, 1986—. Contbr. articles to profl. jours. Chmn. Vt. Life Chain, 1989—. Mem. Vt. Bible Soc. (chmn. 1977-87). Republican. Home and Office: PO Box 2 Cambridge VT 05444

BENSON, DAVID ERNEST, minister, educator; b. Homestead, Fla., Apr. 12, 1944; s. Benjamin Paul and Edith Marie (Haufler) B.; m. Sharon Lynn Ingram, Aug. 23, 1964; children: David Jr., Elisabeth. BA, Mid-Am. Nazarene Coll., Olathe, Kans., 1970; MRE, Nazarene Theo. Sem., Kansas City, Mo., 1972. Ordained to ministry Nazarene Ch., 1972. Pastor Ch. Nazarene, Walnut Ridge, Ark., 1972-73, Mountain Home, Ark., 1973-75, Oxford, Ohio, 1975-81, Lanett, Ala.; minister edn. Nazarene Christian Sch. 1st Ch. Nazarene, Xenia, Ohio, 1984--. Co-author: pilot project (book) Team Teaching Adults, 1971. Mem. Assn. Supervision Curriculum Devel., Assn. Childhood Edn. Internat., Nazarene Internat. Edn. Assn., Nat. Assn. For Edn. Young Children, Am. Mgmt. Assn., Assn. Christian Sch. Internat. Adminstr. Fellowship, Kiwanis. Avocations: golf, photography, cycling. Home: 38 High St Xenia OH 45385 Office: Nazarene Christian Sch 1204 W 2d St Xenia OH 45385

BENSON, EZRA TAFT, church executive, former secretary of agriculture; b. Whitney, Idaho, Aug. 4, 1899; s. George Taft and Sarah (Dunkley) B.; m. Flora Smith Amussen, Sept. 10, 1926; children: Reed, Mark, Barbara, Beverly, Bonnie, Flora Beth. Student, Utah State Agrl. Coll., Logan, 1918-21; BS, Brigham Young U., 1926, Dr. Pub. Service (hon.), 1955; MS in Agrl. Econs., Iowa State Coll., 1927, D Agrl. (hon.), 1953; postgrad., U. Calif., 1937-38; HHD, Coll. Osteo. Physicians and Surgeons, 1951; LLD, U. Utah, 1953, Bowdoin Coll., 1955, U. Maine, 1956; D Agr. (hon.), Mich. State Coll., 1955; DSc (hon.), Rutgers U., 1955. Mission Ch. Jesus Christ Latter-day Saints, Brit. Isles and Europe; pres. Newcastle dist. Ch. Jesus Christ Latter-day Saints, 1921-23; farm operator, 1923-30; county agrl. agt. U. Idaho Extension Service, Preston, 1929-30; extension economist and mktg. specialist in charge econ. and mktg. work State of Idaho, 1930-38; organizer, sec. Idaho Coop. Council, 1933-38; exec. sec. Nat. Council Farmer Coops., 1939-44; mem. exec. com., bd. trustees Am. Inst. Co-op, 1942-52, vice chmn. bd. trustees, 1942-49, chmn., 1952; sec. agr. U.S., Washington, 1953-61; dir. Olson Bros., Inc.; bd. dirs. Farm Found., 1946-50; mem. Nat. Agrl. Adv. Com., World War II; mem. Nat. Farm Credit Com., 1940-43; U.S. del. 1st Internat. Conf. of Farm Orgns., London, 1946. Contbr. to agrl., coop. and church jours. Mem. nat. exec. bd. Boy Scouts Am., 1948-66, awarded Silver Antelope, 1951, Silver Buffalo award, 1954; mem. Boise Stake Presidency, Ch. of Jesus Christ of Latter-day Saints, Idaho, 1935-39, pres. Boise Stake, 1938-39; pres. Wash. Dist. Council, Eastern States Mission, 1939-40, Washington Stake, 1940-44; ordained apostle of Ch., mem. Council of Twelve, 1943, pres. European Mission, 1946, 63-65, mem. Gen. Ch. Bd. Edn.; pres. Ch. Jesus Christ Latter-day Saints, Salt Lake City, 1985—; br. trustees Brigham Young U. Recipient testimonial for disting. service to agr. U. Wis., 1952; scholarship Gamma Sigma Delta, hon. soc. agr. Iowa State Coll.; fellow U. Calif., Berkeley. Mem. Am. Mktg. Assn., Farm Econs. Assn., Delta Nu, Alpha Zeta. Office: LDS Ch 50 E North Temple St Salt Lake City UT 84150

BENSON, GEORGE MICHAEL, clergyman, evangelist; b. Dayton, Ohio, Dec. 9, 1960; s. George C. and Charlotte (Hurst) B.; m. Molly Lanore, Dec. 18, 1983. BA, Freed-Hardeman, 1983. Youth minister Hartsville Pike Ch. of Christ, Gallatin, Tenn., 1981, Abilene Ch. of Christ, Statesville, N.C., 1982; personnel work dir. Ch. of Christ, Stuart, Fla., 1983-85; minister Ch. of Christ, Waverly, Tenn., 1985-89; evangelist Ch. of Christ, Adairsville, Ga., 1989—. Named one of Outstanding Young Men Am., 1985. Home: 100 McKenzie St Adairsville GA 30103 Office: Ch of Christ PO Box 346 Adairsville GA 30103

BENSON, M(ARVIN) WAYNE, minister; b. Hannibal, Mo., Oct. 28, 1946; s. Marvin Elon and Dorothy Lee (Burditt) B.; m. Mary Kathleen Williams, Mar. 22, 1967; children: Tamara Kathleen Benson McElhenny, Marcus Wayne. AB in Edn., U. Mich., 1968. Ordained to ministry Assemblies of God, 1966. Evangelist Assembly of God, Belleville, Mich., 1964-69; assoc. pastor Brightmoor Tabernacle, Detroit, 1969-74; sr. pastor 1st Assembly of God, Grand Rapids, Mich., 1974—; presbyter West Cen. sect. Mich. dist. Assemblies of God, Dearborn, 1976-78, exec. presbyter Mich. dist., 1983-88, asst. supt., 1988-90; bd. dirs. dept. fgn. missions Assemblies of God, Springfield, Mo., 1984-87, bd. edn., 1986-89; gen. presbyter Gen. Coun. Assemblies of God, Springfield, 1986—. Founder Lamb Light mag., 1976—; composer numerous songs and mus. arrangements; contbr. articles to profl. jours. Speaker, supporter Right to Life, Grand Rapids, 1975—; founder Citizens Against Pornography, Grand Rapids, 1985. M. Wayne Benson Day established in his honor Wyoming City Coun., 1985. Office: 1st Assembly of God 2100 44th St SW Grand Rapids MI 49509

BENSON, ROBERT C., II, retired religious organization adminstrator; b. Pender, Nebr., Aug. 24, 1914; s. Robert C. and Minnie Mae (Combs) B.; m. Pollie Pollard, Aug. 24, 1935 (div. 1954); children: Bette Rae, Robert C. III; m. Margaret J. Benson, July 10, 1955; children: Judy Eby, Joyce Anderson, Amy Cogdill. Student, Western Bible Inst., Denver, 1934-35; BS, U. Nebr., 1937; student, U. Omaha, 1965. Blockman Deere & Co., Omaha, 1937-47; owner, operator Benson Implement, Bankcroft, Nebr., 1947-57, Lyons, Nebr., 1957-62; v.p. fin. Western Bible Inst., 1963-70; dir. stewardship, estate planning Berean Fundamental Ch. Council, North Platte, 1970-88, ret., 1988. Mem. Rep. Nat. Com., 1981—. Mem. Nat. Stewardship Coun., Christian Bus. Men's Club, Masons, Sigma Phi Epsilon. Home: 1707 Alpha North Platte NE 69101

BENSON, WARREN STEN, seminary administrator, religion educator; b. Chgo., Aug. 23, 1929; s. Sten Walter and Evelyn Gladys (Arneson) B.; m. Lenore Evelyn Ellis, Aug. 22, 1953; children—Scott Warren, Bruce Ellis. B.A., Northwestern Coll., Roseville, Minn., 1952; Th.M., Dallas Theol. Sem., 1956; M.R.E., Southwestern Bapt. Theol. Sem., 1957; Ph.D., Loyola U., Chgo., 1975. Asst. prof. Christian edn. Trinity Evang. Div. Sch., Deerfield, Ill., 1970-74, prof. Christian edn., assoc. dean, 1978, prof., acting dean, 1979, v.p. adminstrn., prof. Christian edn., 1980, v.p. profl. doctoral programs, prof. Christian edn., 1990—; assoc. prof. Christian edn., Dallas Theol. Sem., 1974-78; minister edn. Winnetka Bible Ch., Ill., 1957-62; minister youth and edn. First Covenant Ch., Mpls., 1962-65, minister edn. Lake Ave. Congl. Ch., Pasadena, Calif., 1965-69; central regional dir. Gospel Light Pubs., Ventura, Calif., 1969-72. Co-author: Christian Education: Its History and Philosophy, 1983; co-editor: Youth Education in the Church, 1978, The Complete Book of Youth Ministry, 1987. Mem. Evang. Theol. Soc., Nat. Assn. Profs. Christian Edn., Religious Edn. Assn., Midwest History of Edn. Soc., Assn. Profs. and Researchers in Religious Edn., Am. Assn. Higher Edn. Republican. Mem. Evang. Free Ch. Am. Avocations: reading; golf. Home: 714 Arthur Ct Libertyville IL 60048 Office: Trinity Evang Div Sch 2056 Half Day Rd Deerfield IL 60015

BEN-SOREK, ESOR WINER, rabbi; b. Boston, Mar. 22, 1933; s. Leonard Jacob and Fayne (Salloway) W.; m. Rahel Hershfinkel, Jan. 24, 1960; children: Sharona, Ethan Samuel, Liora Miriam. BS, NYU, 1954, MA, 1955; PhD, U. de Poitiers, France, 1957. Ordained rabbi, 1972. Rabbi Seaford (N.Y.) Jewish Ctr., 1973—; dir. pastoral counseling svcs. Margaret Tietz Ctr., Jamaica, N.Y., 1981—; chaplain Grace Plaza Nursing Home, Great Neck, N.Y., 1977—, Mary Immaculate Hosp., Jamaica, 1988—; pres. L.I. Bd. Rabbis, 1987-89; bd. govs. N.Y. Bd. Rabbis; bd. dirs. NCCJ; lectr. in field. Author: Poems and Poets of Israel: Selected Masterpieces, 1967; contbr. articles to profl. jours. Mem. AAUP, Reconstructionist Rabbinical Assn., N.Y. Bd. Rabbis, United Zionists Revisionists of Am., Nat. Assn. Profs. of Hebrew, Educators Assembly of United Synagogue, Soc. Bible. Lit. and Exegesis, Am. Acad. Religion, Gesellschaft fur Christlich-Judische Zusammenarbeit of W. Germany. Home: 1 Wooleys Ln Great Neck NY 11023 Office: Seaford Jewish Ctr 2343 S Seamans Neck Rd Seaford NY 11783

BENSOUSSAN, ABRAHAM, rabbi; b. Agadire, Morocco, July 21, 1948; came to U.S., 1961; s. Elias Eliyahou and Esther Bensoussan; m. Linda E. Rabinsky, Aug. 23, 1973; children: Haim, Yudit. B. Religious Edn., Kaminetz Yeshiva, 1970; MA, Y. Detroit, 1974; EdS, Wayne State U., 1976. Ordained rabbi, 1972. Dir. Jafo Sch., Yafo, Israel, 1971-72; tchr. religious studies Akiva Day Sch., Detroit, 1973-76; guidance counselor Akiva Day Sch., Southfield, Mich., 1974-76; prof. advanced studies Medrasha Coll., Southfield, 1976—; rabbi Rinat Israel Congregation, Cleve., 1976—; exec. dir. Yabi, Multi Program Torah Inst., Cleve., 1976—; tchr. of Jewish law Rinat Israel, Cleve., 1989—; spiritual leader Rose Nursing Home, Cleve., 1976-80; youth, religious dir. Nat. Conference of Synagogue Youth, University Heights, Ohio, 1976—; mem. orthodox rabbinical coun., trustee Merkaz Harabonim, Cleve., 1978—; ednl. adviser Betsefer Mizrachi, 1980-85, 80-91; rabbinical adviser Coll. Jewish Studies, 1980-83; speaker in field. Contbr. articles to profl. publs. Mem. campaign cabinet United Way, Cleve., 1989, Cleve. Jewish Community Fedn., 1990-91; rabbinical cons. University Heights City Hall, 1989-91. Mem. Orthodox Rabbinical Coun. (sec. 1978-91), Jewish Educators Coun. (pres. 1987-88). *In order for an individual to acquire a closeness to G-d, he must be sincere with his fellow man. In order for one to be sincere with fellow man, one must be honest with himself. This would eventually bring the individual close to G-D.*

BENTALL, SHIRLEY FRANKLYN, author, lay church leader; b. Regina, Sask., Can., July 28, 1926; d. Frank and Viola Louise (Thom) May; m. Charles Howard Bentall, June 15, 1946; children: Edna Louise, Kathleen Margaret, Joan Elizabeth, Barnard Franklin. BA, McMaster U., Hamilton, Ont., 1946; DD (hon.), McMaster U., 1989. Retreat leader The Bapt. Union Western Can., 1971—; lectr. Bapt. Leadership Tng. Sch., Calgary, Alta., 1975-85; pres. The Bapt. Union of Western Can., 1976-77; pres. Can. Bapt. Fedn., 1985-88, chmn. pub. affairs com., 1989-91; mem. coun. The Bapt. World Alliance, 1985-88, v.p., 1990—; mem. Human Rights Commn., 1985-90, chair Christian Ethics Study Commn., 1990—. Writer Musings column for The Can. Bapt., 1965-88; author: Buckboard to Brotherhood, 1975, Amusings, 1980, The Charles Bentall Story, 1986, Discovering the Deep Places, 1988. Recipient Merit award The Bapt. Union of Western Can., 1982. Avocations: photography, travel. Home: 500 Eau Claire Ave SW, Apt H 202, Calgary, AB Canada T2P 3R8

BENTLEY, KENNETH PERSHING, minister; b. Jefferstown, Ky., Mar. 12, 1940; m. Barbara Carnes; children: Kirt, Lori. BA, Oakland City Coll., 1962; MDiv, So. Bapt. Theol. Sem., 1972, DMin, 1974. Ordained to ministry So. Bapt. Conv., 1961. Pastor various Bapt. chs., Bicknell, Ind., Mt. Vernon, Ind., Clay, Ky. and Louisville, 1961-73, Boyles Bapt. Ch., Birmingham, Ala., 1973-76, Fairfield (Ala.) First Bapt. Ch., 1976-82, Mt. Pisgah Bapt. Ch., Cropwell, Ala., 1982—; fin. advisor Ala. Bapt. Conv., Montgomery, 1974—. Contbr. articles to religious jours., sermons in field. V.p., pres. local high sch. PTA, Fairfield, 1969-72; probation officer local cts., Ind., 1962-66; vol. Little League, Ind., Ky., 1967-68, 73-74; trustee Birmingham Bapt. Hosps., 1978-82; bd. dirs. Rotary Club, Pell City, Ala., 1984. Mem. Birmingham Bapt. Assn. (vice-moderator 1978-79, moderator 1980-82), St. Clair Bapt. Assn. (chmn. pers. com. 1990-91), Alpha Psi Omega. Home: Rte 1 Box 405A Vincent AL 35178 Office: Mt Pisgah Bapt Ch Rte 1 Box 612A Cropwell AL 35054

BENTLEY, PHILIP JAY, rabbi; b. N.Y.C., May 29, 1945; s. Saul P. Barrett and June Miriam (Feldman) Bentley; adopted s. Robert R. Bentley; m. Phyllis Beth Edelman, Sept. 1, 1968; children: Shanan Dana, Aron Joshua. AB, Shimer Coll., 1966; postgrad., U. Man., Winipeg, Can., 1966-67; B. Hebrew Letters, Hebrew Union Coll., 1972, MA in Hebrew Letters, 1973. Ordained rabbi, 1973. Dir. B'nai B'rith Hillel at U. Denver, 1973-75; rabbi Congregation Mikve Israel-Emanu-el, Curaçao, Netherlands Antilles, 1975-78, Temple Or-Elohim, Jericho, N.Y., 1978-91, Temple Beth Shalom, Santa Fe, 1991—; pres. Jewish Peace Fellowship, 1987—; mem. Commn. on Social Action of Reform Movement, 1985—. Contbr. articles to profl. jours. and mags. Bd. dirs. Health and Welfare Coun. of Nassau County, N.Y., 1986-91. Mem. L.I. Assn. Reform Rabbis (pres. 1985-87), Cen. Conf. Am. Rabbis (chair social action com. N.Y. Met. Region 1986-91). Office: Temple Beth Shalom PO Box 358 Santa Fe NM 87504

BENTON, GORDON NANCE, minister; b. Charlotte, N.C., Mar. 12, 1952; s. Thurman Nance and Moretha L. (Almond) B.; m. Cynthia Ann Rickenbaker, May 15, 1976; 1 child, Luke Andrew. AA, CPCC, 1975; BA in Religion, U. N.C., 1976; MDiv, So. Bapt. Theol. Sem., 1979. Assoc. pastor First Bapt. Ch., Prospect, Ky., 1976-79; pastor Clear Creek Bapt. Ch., Charlotte, 1979-82; pastor, sr. minister Elkhardt Bapt. Ch., Richmond, Va., 1982—. Member Chesterfield County Gifted Children's Program, 1987-90; counselor Boy Scouts Am., 1990—. Mem. Mid. Dist. Bapt. Assn. (dir. evangelism Midlothian, Va. chpt. 1984-88, chair assoc. adminstrv. com. 1989—, pres.), Minister's Conf. (pres. 1991—). Republican. Home: 6715 Hull St Rd Richmond VA 23224 Office: Elkhardt Bapt Ch 6715 Hull St Rd Richmond VA 23224

BENTON, ROBERT WILMER, educational administrator; b. Guthrie County, Iowa, Aug. 28, 1931; s. Howard Jasper and Nellie Mae (Gustin) B.; m. Beryl Edna Anderson, Aug. 20, 1955; children: Gregory R., Steven S., Sharon Coram, Linda Tomaio. BA, Northwestern Coll., 1955; ThM, Dallas Theol. Sem., 1959; ThD, Grace Theol. Sem., 1968; PhD, U. Nebr., 1983. Ordained to ministry Bapt. Ch., 1959. Pastor Martensdale (Iowa) Community Ch., 1959-64, Tippecanoe (Ind.) Community Ch., 1964-67; mem. faculty Grace Bible Inst. (now Grace Coll. of Bible), Omaha, 1967-71, pres., 1971-84; pres. Northeastern Bible Coll., Essex Falls, N.J., 1984-87; dir. devel. Northwestern Coll., St. Paul, 1988-89; pres. Ariz. Coll. of the Bible, Phoenix, 1989—. Contbr. articles to religious pubs. Mem. Nat. Soc. Fund Raising Execs., Rotary Club. Republican. Baptist. Avocations: fishing, travel, gardening. Home: 4020 W Griswold Rd Phoenix AZ 85051 Office: Ariz Coll of Bible 2045 W Northern Ave Phoenix AZ 85021

BENZAQUEN, MOISES, rabbi; b. Melilla, Spain, Mar. 31, 1952; came to U.S., 1981; s. Jacob and Sultana (Sultan) B.; m. Yafa, Mar. 14, 1979; children: Tanya, Shlomo, Miriam, Ariel, Jacob, Tamar. BA in Jewish Studies, London U., 1977. Ordained rabbi, 1980. Min. religion Spanish and Portugese Synagogue, Holland Park, Eng., 1975-81; rabbi Kahal Joseph Congregation, L.A., 1981—; ednl. advisor Sephardic Edn. Ctr., L.A., 1989. Mem. Bd. Rabbis (exec. mem. 1989), Sepharad '92 (exec. bd. 1990—). Office: Kahal Joseph Congregation 10505 Santa Monica Blvd Los Angeles CA 90025

BERALL, ERIK DUSTIN (MU RYANG SUNIM), monk; b. N.Y.C., Sept. 7, 1959; s. Frank Stewart and Christiana Mary (Johnson) B. BS in Geology and Geophysics, Yale U., 1981. Cert. Buddhist dharma tchr., Bodhisatva precepts, Bhikkhu precepts. Housemaster New Haven Zen Ctr., 1980-81; fin. mgr. Providence Zen Ctr., Cumberland, R.I., 1981-83; dir. Dharma Sah Zen Ctr., L.A., 1983-85; sec. to zen master Seung Sahn at Hwa Gye Sah Temple, Seoul Internat. Zen Ctr., 1985-89; with Abbot Dharma Sah Zen Ctr., L.A., 1990—; sr. dharma tchr. Kwan Um Zen Sch., Cumberland, 1985—. Mem. Kwan Um Zen Sch., Chogye Order Korean Buddhism, Bodhi Dharma Sangha West. Avocations: walking, meditation, bowing. Home: Dharma Sah Zen Ctr 1025 S Cloverdale Ave Los Angeles CA 90019 Office: Kwan Um Zen Sch 528 Pound Rd RFD 5 Cumberland RI 02864

BERCHMAN, ROBERT MICHAEL, religious educator; b. Newport, R.I., Feb. 13, 1951; s. John Joseph and Stella Mary (Gordon) B. AB, Kenyon Coll., Gambier, Ohio, 1975; PhD, Brown U., 1984. Asst. prof. Mich. State U., East Lansing, 1984-85, 87-90; Mellon rsch. fellow U. Va., Charlottesville, 1985-87; asst. prof. Ind. U., Bloomington, 1990—. Author: From Philo to Origen, 1984; contbr. articles to profl. jours. Rsch. fellow in classics SUNY, 1984-85. Mem. Internat. Soc. for Neoplatonic Studies (v.p. 1990-91, pres 1991—), Am. Acad. Religion (chair platonism and neoplatonism group 1987—), Soc. Bibl. Lit. Office: Ind U Dept Religious Studie Sycamore Hall 230 Bloomington IN 47405

BEREN, SHELDON, educational association executive. Pres. Torah Umesorah-Nat. Soc. for Hebrew Day Schs. Office: Torah Umesorah- Nat Soc for Hebrew Day Schs 160 Broadway New York NY 10038

BERES, KENNETH DAVID, pastor, educator; b. Torrington, Conn., Mar. 12, 1931; s. Gus Geza and Ruth Alice (Geer) B.; m. Eftychia (Effie) Zika, June 21, 1961; 1 child, Kenneth Philotheos. BA in Behavioural Scis., Hartford U., 1960; M of Div., Hartford Sem. Found., 1970; PhD cum laude, Trinity Theol. Sem., 1979; BS in Nutripathy, 1984. Ordained to ministry Congl. Ch., 1970. Missionary social worker Thrace/Macedonia, Greece, 1965-67; student pastor Colebrook (Conn.) Congl. Ch., 1967-68; pastor, tchr. Mohegan Congl. Ch., Uncasville, Conn., 1969-70, Montville Ctr. Congl. Ch., Oakdale, Conn., 1968-78, Goshen Congl. Ch., 1968-78; squadron chaplain USAF CAP, Moodus, Conn., 1977-79; advanced through grades to chaplain maj. USAF CAP, 1980; squadron chaplain USAF CAP, Alton, Ill., 1979-84, dep. wing chaplain, 1982-84; chaplain So. Ill. Group 19 unit USAF CAP, Scott AFB, Ill., 1981-84; advanced through grades to chaplain lt. col. USAF CAP, 1991; pastor, tchr. Alton First Congl. Ch., 1983-84; interim pastor Darlington (Ind.) Christian Congl. Ch., 1984; prof. Greek, librarian Muncie (Ind.) Bible Coll., 1984-85; pres. Kenefil Assocs., Uxbridge, Mass., 1980—; sqdn. chpl. USAF CAP, Southbridge, Mass., 1985-86; cmdr. Webster Composite Sqdr., 1985-87; pastor, tchr. Holland (Mass.) Congl. Ch., 1985—; owner, cons. Health Hut, Webster, 1986—; chief exec. officer Nutripathic Health Orgn., 1990—; pres. High Mountain Health Ctr., 1991—; mem. Conn. Fellowship C.C.C., 1974-78, chmn. religious edn. com., 1976-77, moderator, 1977-78, Northeast region 1978-79, Midwest, 1982-83. Author: Shroud, 1979; ghost editor: Love Never Fails, 1st edit., 1979, 2d edit., 1988. Mem. Civil Air Patrol, Conn. Wing, Ill. Wing, Mass. Wing. Served with USN, 1951-55. Mem. Nat. Assn. Congl. Christian Chs., Conservative Congl. Christian Conf., Nat. Assn. Profl. Cons. Avocations: guitar, vocal music, boating, bicycling, hiking, flying. Home and Office: 932 Aldrich St Uxbridge MA 01569 *God and the world require of all mankind full personal self-responsibility and maturity. We will be fully responsible either out of fear of what the world will do, or out of respect and love for God. Jesus Christ is Lord and Savior, God's own Son, sent to reconcile sinners back to God by the blood He shed on the Cross and by His body broken for each person.*

BERG, JEAN STEWART, consultant; b. Vancouver, B.C., Feb. 16, 1934; d. Campbell and Grace (Callander) Stewart; m. B. Richard Berg, Apr. 7, 1956; children: Scott Richard, Gregory Stewart. BA, U. So. Calif., 1955; MA, Eden Theol. Seminary, St. Louis, 1983. Program dir. YMCA, South Pasadena, Calif., 1955-56, 60-63, YWCA, Lowell, Mass., 1956-57; exec. dir. YWCA County Br., St. Louis, 1969-71; asst. dir. St. Louis County Housing Authority, 1977-81; assoc. dir. Bus. Devel. Ctr. U. Mo., St. Louis, 1981-82; exec. dir. Joint Community Ministries, St. Louis, 1982-84; minister for parish life 1st Presbyn. Ch., Ferguson, Mo., 1984-90; cons. various orgns., Mo., 1990—; Outreach dir. Religious Coalition Abortion Rights, 1991; chair Mo. State Coord. Com. Internat. Women's Yr., 1977-78. Author: The Justice Church, 1986, God & Caesar: One Loyalty or Two, 1990; producer, host (TV program) Steeple and People, 1987—. Candidate U.S. Congr. 9th Dist., Mo., 1976; bd. dirs. St. Louis/Georgetown, Guyana Sister City Orgn., 1990, UN Assn., St. Louis, 1988-91, Wellspring Found., St. Louis, 1989—; bd. dirs., past pres. Friends of Peace Studies, U. Mo., Columbia, 1985—; leader Nat. Coun. Chs. ecumenical study tour, USSR, 1988; mem. Leadership St. Louis, 1978. Recipient Advancement of Women's Equality award Mo. Women's Network, 1988, Sentinel Signal award St. Louis Sentinel newspaper, 1989. Mem. Nat. Conf. Christians & Jews, Confluence St. Louis (co-chair task force). Democrat. Home: 7103 Waterman Ave Saint Louis MO 63130

BERG, LINDA LEE, religious association administrator; b. Daggett, Mich., Feb. 20, 1955; d. Arnold August and Violet Anita (Bartels) Berg; m. Peter Jonathan Luton, Dec. 30, 1989. BA, U. Wis., Green Bay, 1977. Spl. activities coordinator Whitney Elem. Sch., Green Bay, 1978; tchr. Eliot (Maine) Elem. Sch., 1979-81; dir. membership Greater Portsmouth (N.H.) C. of C., 1982-85; dir. mktg. Beacon Health, Inc., Greenland, N.H., 1985-87; dir. bldg. programs Unitarian Universalist Assn., Boston, 1987—; speaker Sacred Trusts Conf., Phila., 1988-90. Recipient Achievement award Nat. Assn. Membership Dirs., 1983. Mem. Seacoast Women's Network. Unitarian Universalist.

BERG, SISTER MARIE MAJELLA, university president; b. Bklyn., July 7, 1916; d. Peter Gustav and Mary Josephine (McAuliff) B. BA, Marymount Coll., 1938; MA, Fordham U., 1948; DHL (hon.), Georgetown U., 1970, Marymount Manhattan Coll., 1983. Registrar Marymount Sch., N.Y.C., 1943-48; prof. classics, registrar Marymount Coll., N.Y.C., 1949-57; registrar Marymount Coll. of Va., Arlington, 1957-58, Marymount Coll., Tarrytown, N.Y., 1958-60; pres. Marymount U., Arlington, Va., 1960—; pres. Consortium for Continuing Higher Edn. in Va., 1987-88; com. mem. Consortium of Univs. Washington Met. Area, 1987—. Contbr. five biographies to One Hundred Great Thinkers, 1965; editor Otherwords column of N.Va. Sun, Arlington. Bd. dirs. Internat. Hospice, 1984—, HOPE, 1983—, 10th Dist. Congrl. Award Council, No. Va. Recipient commendation Va. Gen. Assembly, Richmond, 1990, Elizabeth Ann Seton award, 1991. Mem. Council of Ind. Colls. (pres. 1986-87), Nat. Assn. Ind. Colls. and Univs., Nat. Assn. of Catholic Colls. and Univs., Arlington C. of C. (bd. dirs. 1978-83). Roman Catholic. Avocations: sewing, crocheting, reading. Home and Office: Marymount U Office Pres 2807 N Glebe Rd Arlington VA 22207-4299

BERG, RICHARD ROLAND, library director, educator; b. Lakewood, Ohio, Mar. 22, 1947; s. Herbert Herman and Dorothy Jean (Bode) B.; m. Judy Christina Smith, Aug. 16, 1969; children: Rebecca Ellen, Brian Richard. BA, Heidelberg Coll., 1969; MDiv, Andover-Newton Theol. Sch., Newton Centre, Mass., 1972; MLS, Case-Western Res. U., 1978. Ordained to ministry United Ch. Christ, 1972. Min. Parkman and Huntsburg (Ohio) Congrl. United Ch. Christ, 1972-75; dir. Geauga County Hist. Soc., Burton, Ohio, 1976-79; asst. libr. United Theol. Sem., Dayton, 1979-88; asst. prof., dir. libr. svcs. Lancaster (Pa.) Theol. Sem., 1988—; mem. ch. and ministry dept. S.W. Ohio Assn. United Ch. Christ, Dayton, 1979-88; coord. ministry of presence to the aging, Ch. of the Apostles, Lancaster, 1989—. Mem. Am. Theol. Libr. Assn., S.E. Pa. Theol. Libr. Assn., Soc. Am. Archivists. Democrat. Office: Lancaster Theol Sem 555 W James Lancaster PA 17603

BERG, ROBERT WARREN, JR., clergyman; b. Houston, Feb. 7, 1954; s. Robert Warren and S. Mae (Lowe) B.; m. Phyllis Ann Parker, July 14, 1979; children: Christopher Neal, Stephanie Nicole. Student, Hardin-Simmons U., 1972-75. Ordained to ministry, Bapt. Ch., 1985. Minister of music and youth Bethel Bapt. Ch., New Caney, Tex., 1976-78, Fairview Bapt. Ch., Levelland, Tex., 1978-79, First Bapt. Ch., McLean, Tex., 1983-85, Fairlanes Bapt. Ch., Borger, Tex., 1985—; minister of music. Manger Bapt. Ch., Tulsa, 1979-82; fin. counselor dept. city devel. City of Tulsa, 1980-82; associational clk., Pan Fork Bapt. Assn., 1984-85; associational music dir., Palo Duro Bapt. Assn., 1985—; conf. music coord. Top of Tex. Area Evang. Conf., Borger, 1984, Pampa, 1990, Top of Tex. Area Bible Conf., Borger, 1987, Panhandle Pastors' and Laymen's Conf., Plainview, Tex., 1989; musician Mission to N.W., 1988, Mission to Pa., 1990; pvt. voice instr. Frank Phillips Coll., 1991—. Soloist, Pampa (Tex.) Community Chorus, 1984; co-chmn. Miss Borger Scholarship Pageant, 1986—; mem. Houston Symphony Chorale, 1976-78, Tulsa Opera Chorus, 1979-80. Mem. Singing Men West Tex., Lions (pres. Borger Noon club 1990-91), Alpha Phi Omega. Republican. Avocations: photography, bowling. Home: PO Box 461 Borger TX 79008 Office: Fairlanes Bapt Ch 3000 Fairlanes Blvd Borger TX 79007

BERGEN, ROBERT DALE, religion educator; b. Lawrence, Kans., May 18, 1954; s. Delmar W. and Avis M. (Malan) B.; m. Martha Jane Steagall, Dec. 28, 1979. BA, Hardin-Simmons U., 1976; MDiv, Southwestern Sem., 1980, PhD, 1986. Asst. prof. Old Testament Hannibal-LaGrange Coll., Hannibal, Mo., 1986—; dir. Ctr. for the Study of Tech. in Ministry, Hannibal, 1987—; adj. asst. prof. linguistics U. Tex., Arlington, 1982—. Contbr. articles to profl. jours.; author (computer software) Discourse Analysis Program, 1988. Mem. Soc. Bibl. Lit., Evang. Theol. Soc. (sec.-treas. SW region 1985-86), Nat. Assn. Bapt. Profs. Religion, Mo. Acad. Sci. (chair linguistic sect. 1990-91). Office: Hannibal LaGrange Coll 2800 Palmyra Rd Hannibal MO 63401 *In a world mad with ambition and materialism, I have found sanity in Christ.*

BERGENDOFF, CONRAD JOHN IMMANUEL, clergyman; b. Shickley, Nebr., Dec. 3, 1895; s. Carl August and Emma Mathilda (Fahlberg) B.; m. Gertrude Carlson, June 28, 1922; children—Conrad Luther, Beatrice Gertrude, Elizabeth Ann. BA, Augustana Coll., Rock Island, Ill., 1915, BD, 1921; MA, U. Pa., 1916; postgrad., Columbia U., 1918-19, Luth. Theol. Sem., Phila., 1918-19; PhD, U. Chgo., 1928; postgrad., Upsala U., Sweden, 1926-27, U. Berlin, 1926-27; ThD (hon.), U. Upsala, Sweden, 1938; LLD (hon.), Upsala (N.J.) Coll., 1943; LittD (hon.), Rockford Coll., Ill., 1958; DD (hon.), Concordia Theol. Sem., 1967; LHD (hon.), Nat. Coll. Edn., 1968, Marycrest Coll., 1968. Ordained to ministry Augustana Synod Lutheran Ch., 1921. Asst. prof. English, prof. edn. Augustana Coll., 1916-17; asst. pastor Gustavus Adolphus Luth. Ch., N.Y.C., 1917-19; pastor Evang. Luth. Salem Ch., Chgo., 1921-31; prof. systematic theology, dean Augustana Theol. Sem., 1931; pres. Augustana Coll. and Theol. Sem., 1935-48, Augustana Coll., 1948-62; exec. sec. bd. theol. edn. Luth. Ch. in Am., 1962-64; Dudleian lectr. Harvard U., 1948; cons. Am. Mil. Occupation, Germany, 1949; mem. several coms. and bd. of ch. on ednl. matters; mem. commns. on liturgy Augustana Synod, Luth. World Fedn.; del. Nat. Council of Chs. to Russian Orthodox Ch., 1962. Author books including: One Holy Catholic Apostolic Church, 1954; The Doctrine of the Church in American Lutheranism, 1956; The Church of the Lutheran Reformation, 1967; History of Augustana College 1860-1935, 1969, The Augustana Ministerium, 1850-1962, 1980, One Hundred Years of Oratorio and Augustana, 1981, History of the Augustana Library, 1860-1990, The Church of Sweden on the Delaware 1638-1831, 1988; editor: Luther League Manual; Daily Devotions for Luth. Youth; The Luth. Quar., 1949-53; co-editor Augustana Quar. Translator vol. 40 Luther's Works, 1958, Pioneer Swedish Settlements in U.S.A. 1845-60 (Erik Norelius), 1985; contbr. articles to profl. jours. Mem. Ill. Bd. Higher Edn., 1962-69, Ill. Arts Council, 1965-68; mem. spl. coms. of Am. Council Edn., North Central Assn. Colls. and Secondary Schs.; chpt. chmn. ARC, Rock Island and Moline, 1964-66; bd. dirs. Assn. Am. Colls., 1940-41; pres. Augustana Inst. Swedish Culture, 1940-67; trustee Am. Scandinavian Found., 1943-70; pres. Am. Assn. Theol. Schs., 1947-49. Decorated comdr. Order North Star 1st Class (Sweden); hon. mem. Pro Fide et Christianismo (Stockholm), 1941; recipient Carl Sandburg medal Swedish Pioneer Hist. Soc., 1978, Disting. Service award Luth. Hist. Conf. 1978; award Swedish Council in Am., 1980. Mem. Phi Beta Kappa. Clubs: Black Hawk Hiking (Rock Island); Contemporary (Davenport, Iowa); University (Chgo.). Lodge: Rotary (Paul Harris fellow). Home: 1209-21 Ave Rock Island IL 61201

BERGER, ALAN LEWIS, educator; b. New Brunswick, N.J., Nov. 16, 1939; s. Michael and Ruth (Baum) B.; m. Naomi Berger, Aug. 1971; 3 sons. AB, Upsala Coll., 1962; AM, U. Chgo. Div. Sch., 1970; PhD, Syracuse U., 1976. Faculty dept. religion Syracuse (N.Y.) U., 1973—, dir. Jewish studies program, 1980—; bd. dirs. Inst. for Study of Genocide, 1988—. Author: Crisis and Covenant: The Holocaust in American Jewish Fiction, 1985; assoc. editor: Methodology in the Academic Teaching of the Holocaust, 1988; editor Bearing Witness, 1939-89; contbr. articles to Contemporary Jewish Thinkers and other profl. jours., to ency. Brit., 1975—. Mem. Am. Acad. Religion, Nat. Assn. Holocaust Educators, Assn. for Sociology of Religion, Assoc. Jewish Studies, Am. Jewish Hist. Soc. (bd. dirs. acad. coun. 1989), Theta Alpha Kappa. Office: Syracuse U 510 H L Religion Dept Syracuse NY 13244-1170

BERGER, DAVID G., ecumenical agency executive. Exec. dir. Interfaith Community Svcs., St. Joseph, Mo. Office: Interfaith Community Svcs 200 Cherokee St Saint Joseph MO 64504*

BERGER, FREDERICKA NOLDE, drama educator; b. Phila., May 9, 1932; d. O. Frederick and Ellen Margheretta (Jarden) N.; m. Bruce Sutton Berger, Mar. 14, 1958; children: Eric Sutton, Conrad Jarden. BA, Swarthmore Coll., 1954; MAT, Harvard U., 1957. Adj. prof. Wesley Sem., Washington, 1988—; dir. Side Door Players, University Park, Md., 1978—. Author handbook; contbr. articles to various jours. Mem. Religious Drama Soc. Gt. Britain. Presbyterian. Home: 4209 Sheridan St University Park MD 20782

BERGER, PETER LUDWIG, sociologist; b. Vienna, Austria, Mar. 17, 1929; s. George and Jelka B.; m. Brigitte Kellner, Sept. 28, 1959; children: Thomas, Michael. B.A., Wagner Coll., 1949; M.A., New Sch. Social Research, 1950, Ph.D., 1954; LL.D., Loyola U., 1970; L.H.D., Wagner Coll., 1973. Mem. faculty Women's Coll., U. N.C., 1956-58, Hartford Theol. Sem., 1958-63, New Sch. Social Research, 1963-70, Rutgers U., 1970-79, Boston Coll., 1979-81; Univ. prof. Boston U., 1981—; cons. in field. Author: 12 books including The Social Construction of Reality, 1966, Pyramids of Sacrifice, 1975, The Heretical Imperative, 1979, The Capitalist Revolution, 1986. Served with U.S. Army, 1953-55. Lutheran. Office: Boston U ISEC 10 Lenox St Brookline MA 02446

BERGER, PHILMORE, rabbi; b. Cleve., Apr. 10, 1927; s. Harry W. and Rose (Reich) B.; m. Anita Silberstein, Nov. 21, 1951; children: Debra, Daniel, David, Diane. BA, U. Cin., 1950; M Hebrew Lit., Hebrew Union Coll., 1953; diploma in pastoral counseling, Postgrad. Ctr. Mental Health, N.Y.C., 1967. Ordained rabbi, 1953. Rabbi Temple Avodah, Oceanside, N.Y., 1963—, now life tenure; pres. N.Y. Assn. Reform Rabbis, 1976-78; rabinnic dir., counselor N.Y. Fedn. Reform Synagogues, 1970—; chmn. family life com. Cen. Conf. Am. Rabbis, 1973-75; chaplain South Nassau Communities Hosp., L.I., 1972—. Mem. B'nai B'rith. Home: 333 Niles St Oceanside NY 11572 Office: Temple Avodah 3050 Oceanside Rd Oceanside NY 11572

BERGESON, DEBRA JOANN, minister; b. Moline, Ill., Aug. 12, 1951; d. Fred C. and Florence Irene (Lance) B. BA, St. Ambrose Coll., 1974; MDiv, McCormick Theol. Sem., 1983. House parent Handicap Devel. Ctr., Davenport, Iowa, 1974-75; social rehab. dir. Applegate East Retirement Ctr., Galesburg, Ill., 1975; swim instr. YWCA, Rock Island, Ill., 1976; adminstrv. sec. Marquette U., Milw., 1977-80; pastor Community Presbyn. Ch., Terry, Mont., 1983-87; assoc. pastor Southminster United Presbyn. Ch., Boise, Idaho, 1987—; moderator Com. on Preparation Yellowstone Presbytery, Billings, Mont., 1984-87; mem. Ch. and Soc. Com., Boise Presbytery, 1987—. Leader Girls Scouts USA, Boise, 1987-88; bd. mem. Prairie County Library, Terry, Mont., 1984-87. Mem. Boise Ministerial Assn., Boise Peace Fellowship. Democrat. Presbyterian. Avocations: cross stitching, reading, swimming, biking, traveling. Home: 6030 Dorian Ct Boise ID 83709 Office: Southminster United Presbyn 6500 Overland Rd Boise ID 83709

BERGESON, JOHN HENNING, denominational executive, theological educator; b. Ashland, Wis., May 10, 1919; s. Henning John and Lydia Roberta (Johnson) B.; m. Gladys Victoria Peterson, June 10, 1944; children: John Joel, Jane Ellen, Ruth Ann, Peter Lowell, Daniel Roger. BA, U. N.D., Grand Forks, 1943; BD, Bethel Theol. Sem., St. Paul, Minn., 1944. Ordination by Baptist Gen. Conf. Pastor Alma Baptist Ch., Argyle, Minn., 1941-43, Eagle Point Baptist Ch., Stepen, Minn., 1941-43, Opstead Baptist Ch., Isle, Minn., 1944-53; exec. min. Platte Valley Baptist Conf., Gothenburg, Nebr., 1953-56, Rocky Mountain Baptist Conf., Denver, 1956-59; missions dir. Minn. Baptist Conf., St. Paul, Minn., 1959-70; exec. min. Columbia Baptist Conf., Seattle, 1970-85, British Columbia Bapt. Conf., Surrey, BC, Can., 1985-87; dir. of field edn. Bethel Theol. Sem., San Diego, 1987—. Author: Churches Everywhere, 1978, Fourth Quarter, 1989. Named Moderator, Baptist Gen. Conf. Annual Meeting, Wheaton, Ill., 1973. Baptist. Home: 720 N 193 Place Seattle WA 98133 Office: Bethel Theol Seminary West 6116 Arosa St San Diego CA 92115

BERGGREN, PAUL WALTER, minister; b. Runnels, Iowa, Aug. 22, 1922; s. Walter Carl and Fern (Temple) B.; m. Dorothea F. Bierma, July 14, 1943; children: Nancy Ann, Susan Elaine, Jane Marie. BA, Kletzing Coll., 1944; student, Trinity Evang. Div. Sch., Deerfield, Ill., 1967-69. Ordained to ministry Evang. Free Ch. Am., 1942. Pastor ch. Madric, Iowa, 1944-46, Keene, Nebr., 1947-49, Mpls., 1950-55, Wayzata, Minn., 1955-63, Kenosha, Wis., 1963-66; pastor ch. 1st Evang. Free Ch., Moline Ill., 1966-76; ch. extension dir., evangelist N. Cen. dist. Evang. Free Ch. Am., Mpls., 1976-79; evangelist, Bible tchr. (nat.), 1979—; traveling evangelist, 1947—; treas. Free Ch. Internat. Ministerial Assn., 1958-60; pres. Miss. Valley Nat. Assn. Evangelicals, 1968-69; sec. overseas mission bd. Evang. Free Ch., 1971-76, chmn. Great Lakes dist., 1975-76; bd. dirs. Ozark Bible Inst., 1964-76. Home: 585 Old Crystal Bay Rd Long Lake MN 55356 Office: 901 E 78th St Minneapolis MN 55420 *I have written on the first page of my yearly appointment book for many years this quote: "Be kind, for everyone you meet is fighting a battle." I want to put kindness into practice.*

BERGMAN, JOHN, religious organization administrator. Head Edmonton and Dist Coun. Chs., Alta., Can. Office: Edmonton and Dist Coun Chs, 13340-96th St, Edmonton, AB Canada T5E 4B3*

BERGOFFEN, DEBRA BETH, philosophy educator; b. Albany, N.Y., June 21, 1941; d. Abraham and Lillian (Chersonsky) Hantman; m. Gene Bergoffen, 1961 (div. 1976); children: Jodi Bergoffen Coviello, Janice, Juli; m. Robert B. Lanman, May 20, 1978. BA, Syracuse U., 1962; MA, Georgetown U., 1966, PhD, 1974. Lectr. Georgetown U., Washington, 1967-68, Montgomery Coll., Takoma Park, Md., 1971; lectr. George Mason U., Fairfax, Va., 1971-73, asst. prof. philosophy, 1973-79, assoc. prof., 1979-86, prof., 1986—, chmn. dept., 1981-87, chmn. gen. edn. task force, 1988—; grant reviewer AAUW, 1986-90. Mem. editorial bd. Founds., 1989—; contbr. articles to profl. jours., chpt. to book. Mem. adv. bd. Georgetown Health Plan, Reston, Va., 1974; chmn. Fairfax County Student Rights and Responsibilities, 1974, Reston Symposium Program Com., 1984-85; co-pres. Shoreshim, Reston, 1990. Recipient Disting. Faculty award George Mason U., 1989; grantee NEH, 1976, 79, Woodrow Wilson Found., 1986. Mem. Am. Philos. Assn., Nietzsche Soc. (program com. 1989—), Soc. Phenomenology and Existential Philosophy, Internat. Assn. Philosophy and Lit., Sartre Soc., N.Am. Nietzsche Soc., Soc. for Philosophy of Unconscious, Washington Philosophy Club (exec. com. 1981-83, 86-90). Office: George Mason U 4400 University Dr Fairfax VA 22030

BERGSMA, DERKE PETER, religion educator, minister; b. Racine, Wis., Aug. 29, 1927; s. John Sietze and Johanna Jacoba (Vlaardingerbroek) B.; m. Doris Elaine Bielema, Oct. 28, 1950; children: Deborah, Derk, Diann, Danette. AB, Calvin Coll., 1951; BD, Calvin Sem., 1954; MA, Northwestern U., 1962; DTh, Free-U.-Amsterdam, 1964; D Religion, Chgo. Theol. Sem., 1968. Ordained to ministry Christian Reformed Ch. in Am., 1954. Instr. Calvin Coll., Grand Rapids, Mich., 1950-52; pastor Christian Reformed Ch., Grand Rapids, 1954-62; prof. Trinity Christian Coll., Palos Heights, Ill., 1968-81, Westminster Theol. Sem., Escondido, Calif., 1981—; co-founder Christian Counseling Ctr., Palos Heights, 1974-76; trustee Bd. Publs., Christian Reformed Ch., Grand Rapids, 1970-76. Author: Voices, 1976, Predestination: Islam and Calvinism, 1984, Redemption: The Triumph of God's Great Plan, 1988; contbr. articles to profl. jours. Trustee Calvin Theol. Sem., 1989—. Capt. USN. (Ret.). Chgo. Ch. Fedn. grantee, 1977. Mem. Evang. Theol. Soc., DAV, Lions. Home: 2751 Crownpoint Pl Escondido CA 92027 Office: Westminster Theol Sem 1725 Bear Valley Pkwy Escondido CA 92027

BERGSTEDT, ALAN W., religious organization administrator, consultant; b. Chgo., May 10, 1936; s. Edwin Benjamin and Gladys Lillian (Larson) B.; m. Beverly Jeanne Hope, Sept. 6, 1958; children: Robert B., Donald B., Randall B. BS, Ind. U., 1958; MBA, Pepperdine U., 1984. CPA, Ill. Treas. Youth for Christ, Arlington Heights, Ill., 1962-65, Wycliffe Bible Translators, Manila, 1966-71; chief fin. officer World Vision, Monrovia, Calif., 1975-84; pres. Visionary Mgmt. Group, Covina, Calif., 1985—; bd. dirs. Jaars, Inc., Waxhaw, N.C. Contbr. articles to profl. jours. Mem. Christian Mgmt. Assn. (founder 1976, pres. 1976-77, bd. dirs. 1976—). Republican. Baptist. Avocations: travel, bicycling.

BERGSTRAESSER, EDWARD WILLIAM, minister; b. Milw., June 13, 1935; s. Edward Karl and Florence Marie (Howe) B.; m. Carole Thora Heisel, June 11, 1960; children: Edward Mark, Paul. BA, Elmhurst (Ill.) Coll., 1956; MDiv, Union Theol. Sem., 1960; D in Ministry, Vanderbilt U., 1974. Ordained to ministry United Ch. of Christ. Assoc. minister Barrington (R.I.) Congl. Ch., 1960-63; minister St. Mark United Ch. of Christ, Cleve., 1963-68, Galewood Community Ch., Chgo., 1968-73, Bethel United Ch. of Christ, Elmhurst, 1973-80; sr. minister 1st United Ch. of Oak Pk., Ill., 1980—; researcher Ctr. for the Sci. Study of Religion, U. Chgo., 1973-78; bd. dirs. Community Renewal Soc., Chgo., Evang. Health Systems, Oakbrook, Ill. Bd. dirs. Com. Against Soviet Anti-Semitism, Cleve., 1965-67, United Way, Elmhurst, 1978-80. Union Theol. Sem. fellow, 1959-60. Mem. Profl. Clergy Assn., Chgo. Met. Assn. (moderator 1972, 82), Shalom Awards for Peacemaking (founder 1987). Democrat. Avocations: golf, roller coasters. Home: 312 N Kenilworth Oak Park IL 60302 Office: 1st United Ch of Oak Park 848 Lake St Oak Park IL 60301

BERGSTRAND, WILTON EVERET, minister; b. Bloomington, Ill., July 16, 1909; s. John Ivard and Esther (Jernberg) B.; m. Dolores Youngren, Oct. 17, 1953; children—John Wilton, Paul William, Lori Esther. B.A., Gustavus Adolphus Coll., 1930, D.D., 1949; B.D., Augustana Theol. Sem., 1935. Ordained to ministry Lutheran Ch., 1935; prof. English, speech Gustavus Adolphus Coll., 1930-32; pastor Gloria Dei Luth. Ch., Duluth, 1935-38; youth dir. Augustana Luth. Ch., Mpls., 1938-63; chaplain hdqrs. Augustana Luth. Ch., 1942-63, lectr., tchr. Bible, camp program dir., 1963-64; pastor Luth. Ch. of Holy Trinity, Jamestown, N.Y.; dir. internat. youth confs., leadership schs., Bible camps; chaplain Chautauqua Instn. Luth. House, 1984—. Producer filmstrip series; author: Stitch in Time, 1940, Luther League Scrapbook, 1942, All Smiles, 1943, Centennial Programs, 1945, The Bugles are Calling, 1946, God's Outstretched Hand, 1947, Good Counsel for Counselors, 1956, Leadership, 1956, Youth Round the World, 1958, Youth's Favorite Chuckles, 1958, Christ Unites Us; co-author: Public Speaking Question-ette, 1942, To Light A Candle, 1946, Open Doors, 1949, Who Will Go?, 1947, Luther League Handbook, 1950, A Leaders Guide, 1950, Dynamic District Leagues, 1950, Living High in High School, 1953, Banquet Lore, 1954, Adventuring with Christ in Church Staff Vocations, 1955, Bible Camp Check List, 1956, Bible Study Notes, 1956; Co-editor: The Bible and the Devotional Life, 1972, Home Altar, 1972, 75—, Counsels of Faith and Courage, 1973, Our Flag Speaks, 1973, Independence—Dependence—Interdependence, 1974, Keep the Freedom Bells Ringing, 1975, Disciplined Christian Living, 1976, Studies in Matthew, 1980, John Still Speaks, 1985, A Christian Under Construction, 1986, Roses in December, 1987, The Eagle Speaks, 1988, On Being Young a Long Time, 1988, also numerous mag. articles. Chmn. commn. young peoples work Am. Luth Conf., 1943-48; del. World Conf. Christian Youth, Oslo, Norway, 1947; Augustana rep. orgn. meeting Luth. World Fedn., Lund, Sweden, 1947. Recipient Our Flag Speaks award Freedoms Found., 1974. Mem. Bd. College Edn., Luth. Church in Am., Greater Gustavus Assn. (pres.), Am. Scandinavian Found., World Council Christian Edn., World Council Chs. (youth dept.). Address: 10655 Ironword Dr Chisago City MN 55013

BERKENPAS, DARLIS ANN, minister; b. LeMars, Iowa, Oct. 31, 1949; d. Donald and Martha Darlene (French) Berkenpas; m. Boyd Bristow, May 29, 1971. BA, Morningside Coll., 1971; MDiv., Vanderbilt U., 1985. Newspaper reporter, advt. sales rep. Various bus., Sioux Falls, S.D., 1974-78; counselor Luth. Social Services, Sioux Falls, 1978-79; pub. relations cons. Self Employed, Sioux Falls, 1978-82; pastor United Meth. Ch., Yankton, S.D., 1985--. Bd. dirs. United Way, Yankton, S. D.; chmn. Conf. Communications. Mem. Civic Dance Assn., AAUW. Avocations:gardening, listening to music, dancing. Office: United Meth Ch 207 W 11th Yankton SD 57078

BERKOWITZ, PHILIP, rabbi; b. Boston, Aug. 22, 1938; s. Louis and Ethel (Goldman) B.; m. Nancy Segel, Feb. 12, 1965; children: Jeffrey S., Judith M. AB, Boston U., 1960, BJEd, 1959; MHC, Hebrew Coll., Boston, 1962; EdM, Boston U., 1962; BHL, Hebrew Union Coll., Cin., 1963, MA in Hebrew Letters, 1966, DD, 1991. Ordained rabbi, 1966. Rabbi Temple Beth Jacob, Pontiac, Mich., 1966-75, Temple Beth Or, Washington Twp., N.J., 1975—. Sec.-treas. Interreligious Fellowship for the Homeless, Bergen County, 1988—. Mem. Cen. Conf. Am. Rabbis. Office: Temple Beth Or 56 Ridgewood Rd Washington Township NJ 07675

BERLIN, DONALD ROBERT, rabbi; b. Montreal, Que., Can., June 30, 1936; s. Saul Schnair and Isabel (Riven) B.; m. Norma Brass, Nov. 26, 1959; children: Seth Daniel, Sharon Leah. BA, U. Toronto, Ont., Can., U. Cin., 1961; B in Hebrew Lit., Hebrew Union Coll., 1963, MA in Hebrew Lit., 1969, DD, 1990. Rabbi Temple Emanuel, Roanoke, Va., 1965-71, Congregation Keneseth Israel, Allentown, Pa., 1971-76; sr. rabbi Temple Oheb Shalom, Balt., 1976—; chaplain VA Hosp., Salem, Va., 1965-71; instr. Va. Western Community Coll., Roanoke, 1968-71, Northampton (Pa.) Sem., 1972-73, Goucher Coll., 1977—, Ecumenical Inst., St. Mary's Sem. and U., 1978—; mem. nat. rabbinic cabinets United Jewish Appeal, State of Israel Bonds, World Union for Prog. Judaism; mem. nat. Jewish edn. com. Am. Jewish Com.; mem. Rabbinical Placement Commn., 1990—. Pres. Roanoke Valley Assn. Mental Health, 1968-70, rep. Mental Retardation Svcs. Bd., 1968-71; 2d v.p. Family Svc. Travelers Aid, Roanoke Valley, 1969-71; chmn. Drug Abuse Coordinating Com. Roanoke Valley, 1969-71; bd. dirs. Jewish Fedn. Allentown, 1971-76, Jewish Community Rels. Coun., 1971-76, Lehigh County Mental Health-Mental Retardation Svcs. Program, 1972-76, Greater Balt. Assn. Mental Health, 1977-81; adviser Allentown Coun. Youth, 1974-76, vice chmn. commn., 1975-76; chmn. pastoral care com. Allentown-Sacred Heart Hosp., 1975-76; chmn. coun. of clergy Md. div. corrections Dept. Health and Mental Hygiene, 1983-86; pres. Balt. BL-EWS (Blacks and Jews in Dialogue), 1984. Mem. Cen. Conf. Am. Rabbis (exec. com., pres. Mid-Atlantic region 1984-86, chair nominating com. 1989-90), Balt. Jewish Coun. (pres. 1986-88), Balt. Bd. Rabbis (pres. 1983-85), Inst. Christian Jewish Studies (founding bd. dirs.), B'nai B'rith.

BERLING, JUDITH ANN, religion educator; b. Sept. 8, 1945. BA magna cum laude, Carleton Coll., Northfield, Minn., 1967; MPhil, Columbia U., 1974, PhD, 1976. Lectr. dept. religious studies Ind. U., Bloomington, 1975-76, asst. prof., 1976-79, assoc. prof., 1979-87; dean, v.p. acad. affairs, prof. history religions Grad. Theol. Union, Berkeley, Calif., 1987—; vis. asst. prof. Stanford U., Palo Alto, Calif., 1978-79; chair planning com. 2d Internat. Confucian-Christian Dialogue, 1989-91; mem. accrediting commn. Assn. Theol. Schs., 1988; mem. adv. com. Univ.-Related Div. Sch. Project of Lilly Endowment, 1988—. Author: The Syncretic Religion of Lin Chao-en, 1980. Woodrow Wilson Found. fellow, 1967-68, Danforth Found. Kent fellow, 1971-74, Am. Coun. Learned Soc. fellow, 1978; recipient Herman Bachman Lieber Disting. Teaching award Ind. U., Bloomington, 1986. Mem. Am. Acad. Religion (pres. elect 1989—), Am. Soc. Study of Religion (sec. 1990-93), Am. Coun. Learned Socs. (chairperson 1988—). Office: Grad Theol Union 2400 Ridge Rd Berkeley CA 94709

BERMAN, HAROLD JESSE, rabbi; b. Paterson, N.J., June 8, 1948; s. Oscar and Beatrice (Charney) B.; m. Beth Shapiro; children: Micah Louis, David Asher, Jordan Samuel, Adam Barnett. BA, Rutgers U., 1969; MA, Jewish Theol. Sem., N.Y.C., 1973. Rabbi, 1975. Editor United Synagogue of Am., N.Y.C., 1970-75; rabbi Temple Emanuel, Ridgefield Park, N.J., 1974-75, Temple B'nai Shalom, Benton Harbor, Mich., 1975-79, Congregation Tifereth Israel, Columbus, Ohio, 1979—; pres. Columbus Bd. Rabbis, 1990—, Jewish Family Svcs., Columbus, 1989-90; trustee Columbus Jewish Fedn., 1983—. Chmn. Community Rels. Coun., Columbus, 1984-85; rabbinic advisor St. Anthony Hosp., Columbus, 1986—; mem. ethics com. Children's Hosp., Columbus, 1985—; Jewish chaplain Ohio Reformatory for Women, 1982—. Recipient Rabbinic Leadership award, Columbus Jewish Fedn., 1984. Mem. Rabbinical Assembly, United Jewish Appeal Rabbinic Cabinet (exec. com.), Rabbinic Cabinet of State of Israel Bonds. Home: 136 S Roosevelt Ave Columbus OH 43209 Office: Congregation Tifereth 1354 E Broad St Columbus OH 43205

BERMAN, HOWARD ALLEN, rabbi; b. Paterson, N.J., June 21, 1949; s. Bernard and Elaine (Geller) B. BA, U. Cin., 1972; BA in Hebrew Letters, Hebrew Union Coll., 1973, MA in Hebrew Letters, 1974. Ordained rabbi, 1974. Asst. rabbi Temple Emanu-El, N.Y.C., 1974-79; assoc. rabbi Temple Beth Israel, Hartford, Conn., 1979-81; sr. rabbi Chgo. Sinai Congregation, 1982—; vis. prof. Luth. Sch. Theology, Chgo., 1988—. Contbr. to World Book Ency. Year Book, 1984—. Vice pres. Hyde Park Interfaith Coun., Chgo., 1988—; mem. Chgo. Nuclear Free Zone City Commn., 1987—; mem. adv. coun. Ctr. for Ethics and Corp. Policy, 1987—. Mem. Central Conf. Am. Rabbis, Chgo. Assn. Reform Rabbis, Caxton Club, Pilgrim Soc. Avocations: collecting rare books, Pilgrim memorabilia. Home: 1366 N Dearborn Pkwy Chicago IL 60610 Office: Sinai Temple 5350 South Shore Dr Chicago IL 60615

BERMAN, PATRICIA DONDANVILLE, lawyer, religious foundation executive; b. Anchorage, Mar. 21, 1956; d. Leo J. and Ann L. (Mosey) Dondanville; m. James F. Berman, June 20, 1987; 1 child, Emily Grace. BA, U. Notre Dame, 1978; JD, U. Va., 1981. Bar: Ill. 1981. Assoc. Schiff Hardin & Waite, Chgo., 1981-86, ptnr., 1987—; v.p. Nat. Ctr. for Laity, Chgo., 1990—. Bd. govs. Notre Dame Club Chgo. Scholarship Found., 1988—. Mem. ABA, Chgo. Bar Assn., Chgo. Coun. Lawyers, Notre Dame Club Chgo. (former bd. dirs.). Democrat. Roman Catholic.

BERMOY, EMILIANO SIMACIO, minister, church planter; b. Bohol, The Philippines, June 30, 1946; came to U.S., 1985; s. Roman and Antonia (Simacio) B.; m. Amelia Gomez, July 5, 1975; children: Emil II, Jerusalem, Kathrine, Greg. BS in Edn., U. Philippines, 1972, MEd, 1975; Ma in Missiology, Fuller Theol. Sem., 1988, postgrad. Ordained to ministry Christian Cath. Ch. of The Philippines, 1985. Dean acad. affairs Febias Coll. Bible, The Philippines, 1982-83; founding pastor U. The Philippines Bliss Christian Fellowship, 1982-85; dir. crusades and counseling Asian Christian Outreach, The Philippines, 1983-85; founding pres. Christian Fellowship Ministries, The Philippines, 1985—; founding pastor Bible Christian Fellowship, L.A., 1986—; founding pres. Igniting Light Around the World, Pasadena, 1987—; bd. dirs. Christian Fellowship Found. for Mindanao, Sunnyvale, Calif. Home: 270 N Oakland Ave Pasadena CA 91101 Office: Bible Christian Fellowship 2701 W Beverly Blvd Los Angeles CA 90054

BERNADICOU, PAUL JOSEPH, priest, educator; b. Stockton, Calif., Feb. 18, 1933; s. Paul and Anna (Lucq) B. A.B., U. Santa Clara, 1958; M.A., Gonzaga U., 1961; M.A., St. Mary's U., 1966; S.T.D., P. Gregorian U., Rome, 1970. Joined Soc. of Jesus, 1952; ordained priest Roman Catholic Ch., 1965. Assoc. prof. dept. theology and religious studies U. San Francisco, 1970—. Contbr. articles to profl. jours. Mem. Coll. Theology Soc., Am. Acad. Religion, Cath. Theol. Soc. Am. Roman Catholic. Office: U San Francisco 2130 Fulton St San Francisco CA 94117

BERNAL VARGAS, JORGE, bishop; b. Apizaco, Mex., Feb. 28, 1929; s. Vadillo Justino Bernal and Calderon Emma Galdina Vargas. Lic. filosofia y teologia, Seminario Apostolica, Seminario-Universidad, 1957; student Seminario Apostolica, Gregorian U., Rome. Ordained priest Roman Catholic Ch. Asst. in humanities Legionarios de Cristo, Rome, 1957-58; rector Escuela Apostolica, Mexico City, 1958-70; bishop, prelate Prelatura of Chetumal, Quintana Roo, Mex., 1970—. Home: Casa Prelaticia, 77000 Chetumal Quintana Roo, Mexico Office: Parroquia del Sagrado Corazon, Othon P Blanco 150, 77000 Chetumal Quintana Roo, Mexico

BERNARD, EDWIN YOUNG, religion educator, minister; b. Braddock Twp., Pa., Jan. 30, 1936; s. Harry Morgan and Margaret (Thomas) B.; m. Susan Elisabeth Miller, Feb. 26, 1965; children: Melanie, Stephanie, Annette, Brent. BS in Theology, Nyack Coll., 1961; MA, Wheaton (Ill.) Coll., 1981; D of Missiology, Trinity Evang. Div. Sch., Deerfield, Ill., 1988. Ordained to ministry Christian and Missionary Alliance, 1962. Missionary Christian and Missionary Alliance, Irian Jaya, Indonesia, 1962-82; minister Christian and Missionary Alliance, Bartlett, Ill., 1982-86, Galilee Bapt. Ch., Chgo., 1988—; prof. Moody Bible Inst., Chgo., 1987—; mem. sch. bd. Wheaton Christian Grammer Sch., 1986-89. With U.S. Army, 1954-57. Mem. Evang. Missiological Soc. Home: 2192 Rockne Ct Schaumburg IL 60194 Office: Moody Bible Inst 820 N LaSalle Dr Chicago IL 60610

BERNARD, JERRY WAYNE, clergyman, evangelist; b. Piolot Point, Tex., Jan. 18, 1937; s. Floyd and Alice Lavada (Sexton) B.; m. Gaylon Fussell; children: Robyn Reneé, Crystal Lynn, Scarlet Lane, Angelique. BMus, Baylor U., 1959. Ordained to ministry Bapt. Ch., 1958. Dir. music ministry Valley View Bapt. Ch., Longview, Tex., 1958, Miller Road Bapt. Ch., Garland, Tex., 1959; evangelist JWB Evangelism, Inc., Houston, 1960—; co-founder, dir. Teen Liberators and Pulpit in Shadows, Houston, 1963; assoc. pastor, music dir. Broadway Bapt. Ch., Houston, 1967; tour dir. Ambs. for Christ and Country, Houston, 1969-71, exec. bd. dirs., 1971-74; concert tour dir. Fgn. Mission Bd., So. Bapt. Conv., Nashville, 1970; guest soloist, Dallas, Houston, St. Louis. Author: The Human Side of Deity, 1989; editor The Believer's Hope, 1981; rec. artist 17 albums, 1962-88; played part of a preacher Roger Cameras Prdn. of Another Chance, Hollywood, Calif., 1987. Trustee Broadway Bapt. Sch., Houston; guest artist Jimmy Carter Presdl. Prayer Breakfast, Washington, 1978. Republican.

BERNARDIN, JOSEPH LOUIS CARDINAL, archbishop; b. Columbia, S.C., Apr. 2, 1928; s. Joseph and Maria M. (Simion) B. AB in Philosophy, St. Mary's Sem., Balt., 1948; MA in Edn., Cath. U. Am., 1952. Ordained priest Roman Catholic Ch., 1952; asst. pastor Diocese of Charleston, S.C., 1952-54; vice chancellor Diocese of Charleston, 1954-56, chancellor, 1956-66, vicar gen., 1962-66, diocesan consultor, 1962-66, adminstr., 1964-65; aux. bishop Atlanta, 1966-68; pastor Christ the King Cathedral, 1966-68; sec., mem. exec. com. Nat. Conf. Cath. Bishops-U.S. Cath. Conf., gen. sec., 1968-72, pres., 1974-77; archbishop of Cin., 1972-82, Chgo., 1982—; mem. Sacred Congregation Bishops, 1973-78; del., mem. permanent coun. World Synod of Bishops, 1974, 77, 80, 83, 87, 90; mem. Sacred Coll. Cardinals, 1983—, Pontifical Commn. for Revision Code Canon Law, 1983, Congregation for Evangelization of Peoples, 1983-88, Congregation for Sacraments and Divine Worship, 1984—; sec. Coun. for Promoting Christian Unity, 1984—. Author: Prayer in Our Time, 1973, Let the Children Come to Me: A Guide for the Religious Education of Children, 1976, Called to Serve, Called to Lead: Reflections on the Ministerial Priesthood, 1981, It Is Christ We Preach, 1982, Our Communion, Our Peace, Our Promise, 1984, Christ Lives in Me, 1985, In Service of One Another, 1985, The Challenges We Face Together: Reflections on Selected Questions for Archiocesan Religious Educators, 1986, A Challenge and a Responsibility: A Pastoral Statement on the Church's Response to the AIDS Crisis, 1986, Growing in Wisdom, Age and Grace: A Guide for Parents in the Religious Education of Their Children, 1988, The Consistent Ethic of Life, 1988, The Family Gathered Here Before You: A Pastoral Letter on the Church, 1989. Mem. adv. coun. Am. Revolution Bicentennial, 1975-76, Pres.'s Adv. Com. Refugees, 1975, pres.'s nat. adv. coun. U. S.C., 1979—; mem. bd. trustees Cath. U. Am., 1973-81, 89—, chmn. bd. 1985-88; chmn. ad hoc com. on war and peace Nat. Conf. Cath. Bishops, 1983, chmn. ad hoc Com. to Assess the Moral Status of Deterrence, 1985-88; chmn. Nat. Conf. Cath. Bishops Com. for Pro-Life Activities, 1983-89. Recipient Albert Einstein Internat. Peace prize, 1983; named to S.C. Hall of Fame, 1988. Mem. Nat. Cath. Edn. Assn. (chmn. bd. 1978-81), Nat. Conf. Cath. Bishops (chmn. com. for marriage and family life 1990—). Home: 1555 N State Pkwy Chicago IL 60610 Office: Archdiocese of Chgo PO Box 1979 Chicago IL 60690

BERNARDS, SOLOMON SCHNAIR, clergyman, interfaith consultant; b. Chgo., May 14, 1914; s. Abraham Jacob and Margaret (Yevselman) B.; m. Ruth Segal, Dec. 26, 1948; children—Joel Abba (dec.), Reena Miriam; 1 child from previous marriage, Ezra Bud Brown. B.A.S., Lewis Inst., 1938; LL.B., J.D., John Marshall Law Sch., 1937; rabbi, M.H.L., Jewish Theol. Sem., 1942, D.H.L., 1950, D.D. (hon.), 1972; D.H.L. (hon.), Susquehanna U., 1981. Bar: Ill. bar 1937. Rabbi, 1942; served Kesher Zion, Reading, Pa., 1942-44; Midwest regional dir. United Palestine Appeal, 1946-48; rabbi Phila., 1949-50, Schenectady, 1950-61; dir. interfaith affairs dept. Anti-Defamation League of B'nai B'rith, N.Y.C., 1961-82, cons. interfaith affairs, 1982-84; pres. Friends of Congregation Mevakshei Derech of Jerusalem, N.Y.C., 1982—; lectr. Wagner Coll., 1971, B'nai B'rith Wildacres Inst., 1981; vis. lectr. Phila. Luth. Sem., Gen. Theol. Sem., N.Y.C., St. Peter's Luth. Ch., N.Y.C., Tex. Luth. Coll., 1982—; dir., originator Acad. Seminars on Jews and Judaism, Princeton Theol. Sem., 1961-88, Vanderbilt Div. Sch., 1969-79, Emory U., Trinity Sem., Columbus, Ohio, others; founder ann. lectureship on Jews, Judaism and Jewish-Christian rels., Town and Village Synagogue, N.Y.C., 1987—; leader High Holy Day Svcs., Marblehead, Mass., Washington, Manhattan, N.Y., Bklyn., Queens, N.Y.C., Stroudsberg, Pa., 1961—; founder, leader the Village Chavurah, N.Y.C., 1977—. Author, editor: Living Heritage of Passover, 1963, Living Heritage of High Holy Days, 1965, Living Heritage of Hannukah, 1968, Who is a Jew—A Reader, 1969; Contbr. articles to mags. Served as chaplain with USNR, 1944-46. Recipient citation disting. service Congregation Mevakshei Derech, Jerusalem Mem. Rabbinical Assembly, Am. Acad. Religion, Soc. Bibl. Lit., Assn. Jewish Studies, Religious Edn. Assn., Am. Jewish Hist. Soc., New Jewish Agenda Lodge: B'nai B'rith. Office: 27 W 20th St 9th Fl Ste 1 New York NY 10011 *Be of the disciples of Aaron—love peace and pursue peace; love your fellow beings and bring them near to the Torah. (Hillel the Elder).*

BERNEY, JAMES E., religious organization administrator. Gen. dir. Inter-Varsity Christian Fellowship of Can., Scarborough, Ont. Office: Inter-Varsity Christian, Fellowship/1840 Lawrence Ave, Scarborough, ON Canada M1R 2Y4*

BERNSTEIN, LOUIS, clergyman; b. N.Y.C., Apr. 2, 1927; s. Sam and Anna (Richman) B.; m. Pearl Moshel, Mar. 13, 1955; children: Sara, David, Sima, Avraham. BA, Yeshiva Coll., 1947; Hebrew Tchrs. degree, Tchrs. Inst., 1947, PhD, 1977; rabbi, Isaac Elchanan Theol. Sem., 1950. Ordained rabbi, 1950. Rabbi Glenwood (N.Y.) Jewish Center, 1950-52, Kissena Jewish Center, Flushing, N.Y., 1954-55, Young Israel of Windsor Park, Bayside, N.Y., 1955—; prof. Yeshiva U., 1955; mem. edn. staff Camp Massad, N.Y.C., 1946-81, camp dir., 1957-71; pres. Rabbinical Council Am., 1972-74, 84-86; chmn. Israel schs., 1960—; mem. exec. com. Queens Jewish Community Council, 1971—; sec. Hapoel Mizrachi Am., 1954-55; v.p. Religious Zionists Am., 1972-75, pres., 1975-81, 88—, chmn. exec. bd., 1981-88; exec. World Zionist Orgn., 1978—. Editor RCA Rec., 1954-90. Served as chaplain AUS, 1952-54, ETO. Mem. Yeshiva Coll. Alumni Assn. (pres.). Home: 64-52 Bell Blvd Bayside NY 11364 Office: Young Israel of Windsor Pk 67-45 215 St Bayside NY 11364

BERNSTEIN, NORMAN XAVIER, priest; b. Phila., Dec. 9, 1930; s. Abraham and Jennie (Geak) B. BA, La Salle U., 1958; MEd, Temple U., 1960; PhD, St. John's U., N.Y.C., 1970; MDiv, Sacred Heart Sch. Theology, Hales Corners, Wis., 1983. Ordained priest Roman Cath. Ch., 1986. Instr. in philosophy SUNY, Buffalo, 1962-64; asst. prof. philosophy of edn. St. John's U., N.Y.C., 1965-72; assoc. prof. philosophy of edn. Mt. St. Mary's Coll., Emmitsburg, Md., 1972-76; assoc. prof. catechetics Gannon U., Erie, Pa., 1976-78; equal employment opportunity officer Dept. of the Army, Ft. Drum, N.Y., 1978-80; parochial vicar Cath. Diocese of El Paso (Tex.), 1986—; dir. religious edn. St. Leo's Cath. Ch., Fairfax, Va., 1972-74. With U.S. Army, 1953-55. Fellow Philosophy of Edn. Soc.; mem. Cath. Theol. Soc. Am., Am. Acad. Religion, Am. Philos. Assn., Am. Cath. Philos. Assn., KC, Phi Delta Kappa. Home and Office: St Josephs Church 1315 Travis St El Paso TX 79903

BERQUIST, JON LAURENCE, religion educator; b. Oxnard, Calif., Dec. 19, 1963; s. Richard J. and Mary Beth (Entrekin) B.; m. Terry L. LeRud, Aug. 10, 1985. BA, Northwest Christian Coll., Eugene, Oreg., 1985; MA, Vanderbilt U., 1988, PhD, 1989. Ordained to ministry Christian Ch., 1989. Asst. prof. Old Testament Phillips Grad. Seminary, Tulsa, 1989—. Mem. Soc. Bibl. Lit. Home: 820 S Gary Pl Tulsa OK 74104 Office: Phillips Grad Seminary 600 S College Tulsa OK 74104

BERRETT, LAMAR CECIL, religion educator; b. Riveron, Utah, Mar. 28, 1926; s. John Harold and Stella (Wright) B.; m. Darlene Hamilton, Aug. 3, 1950; children: Marla, Kim, Michael, Susan, LeAnn, Nathan, Evan, Ellen, Jared. BS, U. Utah, 1952; MS, Brigham Young U., 1960, EdD, 1963. Prof. religion Brigham Young U., Provo, chmn. dept. religion, 1968-76, dir. Religious Study Ctr., 1976-82; dir. worldwide tours. Author: The Wilford Wood Collection Vol. 1, 1971, Discovering the World of the Bible, 1973; (family genealogy) Down Berrett Lane 2 Vols., 1980. Served with U.S. Army, 1944-46. Mem. Utah Hist. Soc. (pres. Utah Valley chpt. 1971-72), Sons of Utah Pioneers, Mormon History Assn. Republican. Mem. LDS Ch. Avocations: racquetball, pigeon raising, orchardist. Home: 1032 E 400 S Orem UT 84058 Office: Brigham Young U Dept Religion Office 73JSB Provo UT 84602

BERRIDGE, PAUL THOMAS, minister; b. Marion, Ohio, July 1, 1937; s. John Howard and Bertha Jane (Dulaney) B.; m. Marguerite Lucille Sheeks, Mar. 16, 1957; children: Pamela Rae, Janice Elaine, Valerie Kaye. AA, Ministerial Inst., 1968; postgrad., Wesleyan Ch., Indpls., 1972—. Ordained to ministry Wesleyan Ch., 1967. Pastor Pilgrim Holiness Ch., Lima, Ohio, 1967-69; sr. pastor Wesleyan Ch., Sandusky, Ohio, 1969-70, Springfield, Ohio, 1970—; v.p. Western Ohio Youth, Leesburg, 1962-68; dir., mem. coun. Wesleyan Ch., Vandalia, Ohio, 1972—; sec. Bd. Ministerial Standing, Westerville, Ohio, 1974—; dir. Holy Land/Greece Tour, 1971. Fellow Clark Ministerial Assn. Republican. Home: 411 N Shaffer St Springfield OH 45504-2429 *An investment with unlimited potential to achieve established goals, to be an inspiration to those persons facing devastating circumstances, and with Divine enablement I shall be a "Beacon Light" to offer hope in a troubled world.*

BERRY, DONALD KENT, religion educator, clergyman; b. Gary, Ind., Apr. 29, 1953; s. Dixie Claude and Opal Marie (Petty) B.; m. Sally Ann Howard, Aug. 11, 1972; children: Donald Elijah, Noel Evan. BA in Religion, Ky. Wesleyan Coll., 1975; MDiv, So. Bapt. Theol. Sem., 1978, PhD, 1987. Ordained to ministry Bapt. Ch., 1972. Pastor Zion Bapt. Ch., Reynolds Station, Ky., 1978-83; asst. prof. religion Mobile (Ala.) Coll., 1987—; interim pastor various churches in Washington County, Ala. Contbr. to profl. publs. Mem. AAUP, Soc. Bibl. Lit., Nat. Assn. Bapt. Profs. Religion, Christus Theol. Inst. (program com. 1989, adv. bd. 1990, worship com. 1990). Democrat. Avocations: wilderness sports, recreation. Home: 218 Tavares Dr Saraland AL 36571 Office: Mobile Coll PO Box 13220 Mobile AL 36613

BERRY, JAMES LEE, minister; b. Encino, Calif., Jan. 19, 1961; s. John Thomas and Catherine (Losino) B. Student, Fla. Bible Coll., 1981-82; BA in Christian Edn., Bryan Coll., 1984. Ordained to ministry Bapt. Ch., 1985. Intern, min. youth Bibletown Community Ch., Boca Raton, Fla., 1979-81; min. youth Fellowship Bapt. Ch., Ocala, Fla., 1983-85; min. youth West Marion Bapt. Ch., Morriston, Fla., 1987-91, min. coll., career and single adults, 1991—; group leader Fellowship Christian Athletes, Ocala, 1987—; youth pastor Youth Alive, Morriston, 1987—. Baseball coach Williston High Sch., 1990—. Home: 4125 N W 70th Ave Ocala FL 32675 Office: West Marion Bapt Ch 6001 N W 135th Ave Morriston FL 32688 *Jesus Christ, the Word of God, has spoken and speaks in answers to all of life's questions. My effort in ministry is to stand by listening to what He has to say and to be as faithful as I can be to communicate the Scriptures in a contemporary way, to all people who seek Him.*

BERRY, KEITH THOMAS, minister; b. Lincoln, Mo., Nov. 14, 1936; s. Ralph Shumate and Viola (Rouse) B.; m. Marcia Lubbers, Apr. 10, 1960; children: Jean Elizabeth, Karen Jennifer, David Thomas. BA, Cen. Meth. Coll., Fayette, Mo., 1958; STB, Boston U., 1961, ThD, 1969. Ordained to ministry United Meth. Ch. as deacon, 1959, as elder, 1962. Pastor King Hill and DeKalb United Meth. Chs., St. Joseph, Mo., 1972-76, Marshfield (Mo.) United Meth. Ch., 1976-79, 80-87, Keswick-Cockermouth Meth. Cir., Cockermouth, Eng., 1979-80; dist. supt. North Cen. Dist., Chillicothe, Mo., 1987-89; coun. dir. Mo. West Conf., Kansas City, Mo., 1989—; mem. South Cen. Jurisdictional Coun. on Ministries, 1976-79, 89—, World Meth. Coun., 1986—; process cons. Mo. Christian Leadership Forum, 1981—; chair Mo. Area Office Creative Ministries, 1984-88. Contbr. articles to profl. jours. Mem. Christian-Jewish-Muslim Dialogue Group, Nat. Assn. Conf. Coun. Dirs., Rotary (pres. Marshfield club 1985-86, Paul Harris fellow, 1987). Office: United Meth Conf Ctr 1512 Van Brunt Blvd Kansas City MO 64127

BERRY, MARY ALICE, religious organization administrator; b. Gainesville, Tex., Jan. 8, 1951; d. Travis S. and Bernice Elizabeth (Hayles) B. BA, Baylor U., 1974; MRE, Southwestern Bapt. Theol. Sem., 1982. Prodn. crew Sta. KTVT-TV, Ft. Worth, 1974-76; evangelism coordinator div. student work, Bapt. Gen. Conv. Tex., Dallas, 1976-77; asst. dir. student work Stephen F. Austin State U. Baptist Gen. Conv. Tex., Nacogdoches, 1977-80; min. youth Capital Heights Bapt. Ch., Montgomery, Ala., 1980-83; min. preschool children and youth First Bapt. Ch., Hereford, Tex., 1983-85; dir. media services First Bapt. Ch., Amarillo, Tex., 1985—. Mem. pub. relations adv. com. Bapt. Gen. Conv. Tex. Avocations: racquetball, tennis, reading, water skiing, bicycling. Home: 2832 Mays Amarillo TX 79109 Office: First Bapt Ch Tyler and 13th Amarillo TX 79101

BERRY, MICHELLE, minister; b. Virgin Island, Md., May 30, 1932; d. George and Cora (Bakerville) Day; m. Noel J. Berry, Aug. 20, 1989; children: Emmanuel Day, Desline Day, Victoria Michelle Berry. BS, St. Augustine Bay Coll., St. Louis, Miss., 1953; MA, U. Md., Balt., 1964; BD, Chaplain Assoc. Coll. of D.C., 1979; PhD, Grace Christian Coll., Phila., 1985. Chief adminstr. Psychology Assocs., Inc., Bklyn.; asst. gen. supr. Faith Restoration Ctr., Inc., Bklyn.; bishop N.Y. and The Philippines Dist. Col. WAC, 1950-53. Recipient Psychologist Achievement award, Nat. Chaplains Merit award, Nat. U.S. Chaplains Promotion Honor award, Pres.'s award for svc. beyond the call of duty, African Merit award, Blackglama award. Mem. World Wide Spiritual Ministers Assn., Internat. Clergy Assn., U.S. Chaplains Assn., Am. Guild Hypnotherapists, Religious Sci. Doctrine Inst., Writers, Students and Truthseekers Assn., Personal Counseling Svc., Inc. Home: 4001 Foster Ave Brooklyn NY 11203

BERRY, ROBERT COURTLAND, religious organization administrator; b. Moncton, N.B., Can., Apr. 3, 1931; s. Harry Allison and Bernice Catherine (Steeves) B.; m. Grace Ethel Lambert, May 23, 1953; children: Richard, Donald, Paul, Glen. BA in Theology, Gordon Coll., 1954; BDiv, Gordon Div. Sch., 1958; ThM, Fuller Theol. Sem., 1984; DD (hon.), Acadia U., 1988. Ordained to ministry Bapt. Fedn. Can., 1958. Pastor chs., Grand Falls, N.B., 1958-62, Calvary Bapt. Ch., North Sydney, N.S., Can., 1962-67, Forest Hills Bapt. Ch., St. John, N.B., 1967-70; assoc. sec. Can. Bapt. Overseas Mission Bd., Toronto, Ont., 1970-80; gen. sec. Can. Bapt. Internat. Ministries, Mississauga, Ont., 1980—. Assoc. editor The Enterprise, 1973—; contbr. articles to religious jours. Mem. Bapt. Mins. Fellowship Ont. and Que. Office: Can Bapt Internat, Ministries, 7185 Millcreek Dr, Mississauga, ON Canada L5N 5R4

BERRY, ROBERT EDWARD FRASER, retired bishop; b. Ottawa, Ont., Can., Jan. 21, 1926; s. Samuel and Clara (Hartley) B.; m. Margaret Joan Trevorrow Baillie, May 12, 1951; children: Christopher Fraser, Elisabeth Joan. B.A., Sir George Williams Coll., 1950; B.D., McGill U., 1953; LTh, Montreal Diocesan Theol. Coll., 1953, D.D. (hon.), 1972. Ordained deacon Anglican Ch. Can., 1953, ordained priest, 1954. Asst. curate Christ Ch. Cathedral, Victoria, B.C., Can., 1953-55; Priest St. Margaret's Ch., Hamilton, Ont., 1955-61; priest St. Mark's Ch., Orangeville, Ont., 1961-63, St. Luke's Ch., Winnipeg, Man., Can., 1963-67, St. Michael and All Angels Ch., Kelowna, B.C., 1967; supr. pastor Central Okanagan Region Diocese of Kootenay, Kelowna, 1967-71, bishop, 1971-89. Served with RCAF, 1943-45. Mem. Vancouver Club, Kelowna Yacht Club. Avocations: boating; fishing. Home: 1857 Maple St, Kelowna, BC Canada V1Y 1H4

BERRY, ROBERT WILLIAM, minister; b. Lock Haven, Pa., Jan. 1, 1944; s. Clifford Nelson and Mae Ellen (Noian) B.; m. Donna Sue Gerkin, May 29, 1965; children: Cynthia Lou, Timothy Robert. BA, Johnson Bible Coll., 1965; M Ministry, Ky. Christian Coll., 1985. Ordained to ministry Ch. of Christ, 1963. Min. Old Union Ch., Poseyville, Ind., 1965-67, 1st Ch. of Christ, Wilkes-Barre, Pa., 1968-70, Ch. of Christ of Hemfield Twp., Greensburg, Pa., 1971-76, Christ's Ch., Topeka, 1976-81; sr. min. Seymour (Tenn.) Hts. Christian Ch., 1981—; pres. Ea. Christian Conv., Wilkes-Barre, 1970, Alumni Assn. Johnson Bible Coll., Knoxville, Tenn., 1988; v.p. Coun. of Seventy, Johnson Bible Coll., Knoxville, 1972; dir. Mission Svcs., Knoxville, 1984—; missionary, New Zealand, Australia, Papua New Guinea, 1988, Poland, 1991; music dir. Christian Srs. Fellowship Convs., Fla., 1990-91. Performer 4 record albums of religious music, 1968, 78, 81, 91; contbr. articles to profl. jours. Republican. Home: 1828 Treetops Ln Seymour TN 37865 Office: Seymour Hts Chritian Ch 122 Boyds Creek Hwy Seymour TN 37865

BERRY, STEPHEN PRESSLEY, minister, librarian; b. Sedalia, Mo., Nov. 5, 1951; s. Karl John and Alberta Jean (Stanfield) B. BA, S.W. Mo. State U., Springfield, 1973; MLS, U. Mo., 1975; MDiv, Phillips Grad. Sem., 1979; D in Ministry, San Francisco Theol. Sem., 1985. Ordained to ministry Christian Ch., 1979. Minister Montgomery City (Mo.) Christian Ch., 1979-82; asst. libr. Disciples of Christ Hist. Soc., Nashville, 1982-84; minister Elkton (Ky.) Christian Ch., 1984-89, First Christian Ch., Weiner, Ark., 1989—; part-time libr. aide Ark. State U., State University, 1990—; mem. com. on ministry Christian Ch. of Ky., 1985-87, v.p. Dist. 15 Christian Ch. in Ky., 1985-87, pres., 1987-89; mem. dept. evangelism and membership Christian Ch. in Ark., 1990—; v.p. N.E. Dist. Christian Men's Fellowship, Ark., 1990—. Mem. Am. Theol. Libr. Assn. (assoc.), Ark. Libr. Assn., Lions (sec. Weiner club 1990—). Home: PO Box 297 Weiner AR 72479 Office: First Christian Ch PO Box 297 Weiner AR 72479

BERRYMAN, JAMES CLEO, religion and philosophy educator; b. Russellville, Ark., Sept. 28, 1935; s. Henry Cleo and Corrine (Swearengen) B.; m. Mary Anne Pierce, Aug. 5, 1961; children: James Andrew, Cathryn Anne. BA, Ouachita Bapt. U., 1957; BD, Southwestern Bapt. Sem., 1960, ThD, 1964. V.p. Book Nook Inc., Ft. Worth, 1958-63; dir. extension Southwestern Seminary, Ft. Worth, 1959-62; prof. religion and philosophy Ouachita Bapt. U., Arkadelphia, Ark., 1964—; prof. Boyce Bible Sch., 1986—; pastor Antoine (Ark.) Bapt. Ch., 1987-88; vis. prof. St. Johns Seminary, Little Rock, 1967, Henderson State U., Arkadelphia, So. Bapt. Sem., Louisville, 1984; adj. prof. med. humanities U. Ark. for Med. Scis., 1986—. Chmn. Cen. Ark. Devel. Council, Benton, 1970-80; treas., producer Arkadelphia Community Theatre, 1978-85; founder, chmn. Festival Two Rivers, Arkadelphia, 1975-84. Mem. Am. Acad. Religion, Assn. Nat. Assn. Bapt. Profs. Religion (sec., treas. 1972-82, pres. S.W. sect. 1987-88), Ark. Philos. Assn. (pres. 1984-85), Civitan Internat. (pres. 1982-83, Internat. Honor Key award 1979, 83, fellow). Democrat. Avocations: needlepoint, reading.

BERTELSEN, OLE, bishop. Bishop of Copenhagen, Evang. Luth. Ch. Office: Evang Luth Ch, Norregade 11, 1165 Copenhagen K, Denmark*

BERTHOLD, FRED, JR., educator, clergyman; b. St. Louis, Dec. 9, 1922; s. Fred and Myrtle Bernice (Williams) B.; m. Laura Bell McKusick, Dec. 27, 1945; children—Marjorie Chase, Daniel S., Timothy M., Sarah M. A.B., Dartmouth, 1944; B.D., U. Chgo., 1947, Ph.D., 1954; D.D., Middlebury Coll., 1959, Concord Coll., 1960, U. Vt., 1961. Instr. philosophy Utica Coll. of Syracuse U., 1948-49; ordained to ministry Congl.-Christian Ch., 1949; instr. philosophy Dartmouth, 1949-50, instr. religion, 1950-51, asst. prof. religion, 1951-56, prof., 1956—, chmn. dept., 1951-58, 62—; dean William Jewett Tucker Found., 1957-62, dean for humanities, 1976-80. Author: The Fear of God, 1959; Editor: Basic Sources of the Judaeo-Christian Tradition, 1962; Contbr. to The Future of Empirical Theology, 1969, The Dialogue between Psychology and Theology, 1969. Bd. dirs. Dartmouth Inst., 1985—. Mem. Soc. for Values in Higher Edn., Am. Acad. Religion, Am. Theol. Soc., Phi Beta Kappa. Home: RR 2 Box 115 Norwich VT 05055

BERTHOLD, GEORGE CHARLES, priest, theology educator; b. Lawrence, Mass., Mar. 1, 1935; s. Joseph Rudolph and Laura (Fluet) B. BA, St. John's Sem., Brighton, Mass., 1959, MA, 1963; STD, Inst. Cath., Paris, 1975. Ordained priest Roman Cath. Ch. Asst. pastor St. Joseph Ch., Salem, Mass., 1963-68, St. Matthew Ch., Dorchester, Mass., 1972-73, St. Joseph Ch., Woburn, Mass., 1973-78, Sacred Heart Ch., Amesbury, Mass., 1980-85, St. Louis de-Gonzaque Ch., Newbury Port, Mass., 1985—; prof. theology St. Anselm Coll., Manchester, N.H., 1976—. Editor, translator: Maximus the Confessor: Selected Treatises, 1985; editor: Faith Seeking Understanding: Learning and the Catholic Tradition, 1991. Mem. Cath. Theol. Soc. Am., Orthodox/Cath. Consultation. Office: St Anselm Coll 87 St Anselm's Dr Manchester NH 03102

BERTOLI, PAOLO CARDINAL, clergyman; b. Poggio, Lucca, Italy, Feb. 1, 1908; s. Carlo and Aride (Poli) B. Ordained priest Roman Cath. Ch., 1930; sec. Apostolic Nunciature, Belgrade, 1933-38, France, 1938-42; chargé d'affaires, Apostolic Nunciature, Port-au-Prince, Haiti and Netherlands Antilles, 1942-46; counsellor Apostolic Nunciature, Berne, 1946-52; chargé mission for emigration to S. Am., 1947; titular archbishop Nicomedia, 1952; apostolic del., Turkey, 1952-53; apostolic nuncio, Colombia, 1953-59, Lebanon, 1959-60, France, 1960-69; prefect Congregation for Causes of Saints, 1969-73; elevated Sacred Coll. of Cardinals, 1969—; now titular bishop of Frascati; named Camerlingue of H.R.C., 1979-85; Suburbicarian bishop of Frascati, 1979. Address: Piazza della Città, Leonina 1, 00193 Rome Italy

BERTRAND, TERRY DALE, minister; b. Eunice, La., Apr. 19, 1951; s. Elrick and Selise (Manuel) B.; m. Deborah Lynn Hooper, June 15, 1973; children: Christi Lynn, Eric Dale. B in Music Edn., Sam Houston State U., 1973; MRE, Southwestern Bapt. Theol. Sem., Ft. Worth, 1977. Ordained to ministry So. Bapt. Conv., 1978. Min. music and youth 1st Bapt. Ch., Shepherd, Tex., 1970-71, Cedar Hill, Tex., 1974-78; min. youth and activities Uvalde Bapt. Ch., Houston, 1971-74; min. edn. and adminstrn. Fairview Bapt. Ch., Grand Prairie, Tex., 1978-81; min. adminstrn. Forest Cove Bapt. Ch., Kingwood, Tex., 1981—; ch. tng. dir. Union Bapt. Assn., Houston, 1981-83, dir. Sunday sch., 1986-89; dir. ch. tng. Dallas Bapt. Assn., 1979-81. Chaplain NE Med. Ctr. Hosp., Humble, Tex., 1982—. Mem. Nat. Assn. Ch. Bus. Adminstrs., So. Bapt. Assn. Ch. Bus. Adminstrs., So. Bapt. Religious Edn. Assn. (membership sec. 1983-84), Southwestern Bapt. Religious Edn. Assn. Home: 1006 Masters Way Kingwood TX 77339 Office: Forest Cove Bapt Ch 1711 Hamblen Rd Kingwood TX 77339

BERTSCH, AUDREY, ecumenical agency administrator. Exec. dir. Greater Bethlehem (Pa.) Area Coun. Chs. Office: Greater Bethlehem Area Coun Chs 520 E Broad St Bethlehem PA 18018*

BESEL, KARL WILLIAM, lay worker; b. Lakewood, Ohio, Apr. 14, 1968; s. Ronald Robert Besel and Patricia Ann (Andersen) Johnson. BA in Social Work, Valparaiso U., 1990. Youth and family min. King of Glory Luth. Ch., Carmel, Ind., 1990—; camp counselor Outdoor Ministries, Howe, Ind., 1986-89; youth counselor Our Savior Luth. Ch., Valparaiso, Ind., 1987-88. Mem. NASW. Democrat. Home: 9259 A Yale Dr Indianapolis IN 46200 Office: King of Glory Luth Ch 2201 E 106th St Carmel IN 46032

BESHEARS, WILLIAM JOSEPH, minister; b. Albertville, Ala., June 9, 1930; s. Charlie Albert and Mary Alice (Griffie) B.; m. Grace Lee Hall, Dec. 31, 1953; children: Jill Dee Beshears Fant, Jan Elyce Beshears Hurd, John Charles. BA, William Jewell Coll., 1957; postgrad., Midwestern Bapt. Theol. Sem., 1959-62. Ordained to ministry So. Bapt. Conv., 1956. Minister edn. Wyatt Park Bapt. Ch., St. Joseph, Mo., 1963-67; minister edn. and youth Univ. Heights Bapt. Ch., Springfield, Mo., 1967-71; with Cen. Bapt. Ch., Warner Robins, Ga., 1971-77; chaplain Prison Fellowship (Charles Colson), Washington, 1977-81; minister edn./adminstrn. First Bapt. Ch., Winder, Ga., 1982-90; minister programs First So. Bapt. Ch., Phoenix, 1990—; staff devel. State of Ohio, 1957-59; mem., pres. Mo. Bapt. Religious Edn. Assn., Jefferson City, Mo., 1956-71. Contbr. articles to publs. Del. White House Conf. on Children, 1960's, 70's, mem. mass media forum; chmn. bd. dirs. Project Alcohol and Drug Abuse Ministry. With U.S. Army, 1951-53. Recipient cert. of recognition City of Winder, 1990, Congl. citation 93d Congress. Mem. So. Bapt. Religious Edn. Assn. (charter mem.), Ga. Bapt. Religious Edn. Assn. (pres.), Rotary (chaplain St. Joseph, Mo. chpt. 1964-67), Optimist Club (program v.p. Warner Robins 1971-77), Kiwanis Club (membership chmn. Winder chpt. 1982-86). Office: First Southern Bapt Ch 3100 W Camelback Rd Phoenix AZ 85017 *Someone asked me on a television talk show one time, knowing I was a minister, "What does the World need more than anything else?" Without hesitation I said, "A good belly laugh." As I have rethought it through the years, I haven't been able to improve on that. It may not be literally true, but it does make a very important point.*

BEST, CARLTON EUGENE, minister; b. La Grange, N.C., Aug. 26, 1929; s. Silas Sheetz and Mildred Bernice (Driver) B.; m. Deborah Harrison Allen,

June 18, 1946; children: Elizabeth Weisberg, Jacquelyn Snodgrass, Wesley S. BA, Atlantic Christian Coll., 1960; MDiv, Duke U., 1963; DMin, Southeastern Bapt. Theol. Sem., Wake Forest, N.C., 1977. Ordained to ministry Christian Ch. (Disciples of Christ), 1960. Student minister Eden Christian Ch., Snow Hill, N.C., 1958-62, Arthur Christian Ch., Bellarthur, N.C., 1958-62; minister Front St. Christian Ch., Burlington, N.C., 1962-64, Hood Meml. Christian Ch., Dunn, N.C., 1964-72, Pfafftown (N.C.) Christian Ch., 1972-84; sr. minister Meml. Christian Ch., Lynchburg, Va., 1984-91; pres. Chrisitan Ch. in N.C., Wilson, 1973-75, Christmount Christian Assembly, Black Mountain, N.C., 1975-80; trustee Atlantic Christian Coll., Wilson, 1983-84; mem. regional bd. Christian Ch. in Va., Lynchburg, 1985-86. Pres. Rotary Club, Dunn, 1972, Exchange Club, Winston-Salem, N.C., 1979-80; chmn. blood svcs. ARC Forsyth County, Winston-Salem, 1978-84; pres. Greater Lynchburg Habitat for Humanity, Lynchburg, 1990-91. Named Man of Yr. Dunn Area C. of C., 1970, Exchangite of Yr. Greater Winston-Salem Exch., 1981. Democrat. Home: 350 Simpson Rd Mount Airy NC 27030

BEST, ROGER DONALD, minister; b. Downing, Wis., Apr. 15, 1934; s. Donald Wallace and Olive Helen (Pickard) B.; m. Bertha Catherine White, Dec. 24, 1955; chldren: Mark Roger, Stephen Paul, Timothy John. Student, Moody Bible Inst., 1952-54; B in Religious Edn., Grand Rapids Bapt. Col., 1971. Ordained to ministry Bapt. Ch., 1971. Pastor Mich. Bapt. Chs., 1969-80, Calvary Bapt. Ch., Anaheim, Calif., 1980-87, First Bapt. Ch., Zeeland, Mich., 1987-91; field evangelist Zion's Hope, Orlando, Fla., 1991—; exec. com. Mich. Assn. Regular Bapt., 1976-80; trustee Grand Rapids Bapt. Coll., 1976-80, The Master's Coll. & Sem., Santa Clarita, Calif., 1981—; bd. dirs. Zion's Hope, Orlando, 1990—. With U.S. Army, 1955-58. Republican. Home: 1240 Creek Wood Cir Saint Cloud FL 34772 Office: Zion's Hope PO Box 690909 Orlando FL 32869-0909

BETHEA, JOSEPH BENJAMIN, bishop; b. Dillion, S.C., Sept. 9, 1932; s. Rufus E. and Ella (Johnson) B.; m. Shirley Cundiff, June 7, 1958; 1 dau., Josefa Elizabeth. BA, Claflin Coll., Orangeburg, S.C., 1953, DH (hon.), 1988; MDiv, Gammon Theol. Sem., Atlanta, 1956, DD (hon.), 1974; DD (hon.), N.C. Wesleyan Coll., Rocky Mount, 1988; DH (hon.), Columbia (S.C.) Coll., 1989. Ordained to ministry United Meth. Ch. as deacon, 1954, as elder, 1956. Pastor St. Paul Meth. Ch., Reidsville, N.C., 1961-65; dist. supt. Va. Conf., Richmond, 1965-68; pastor St. Matthews United Meth. Ch., Greensboro, N.C., 1968-72; dir. Black Studies Duke Divinity Sch., Durham, N.C., 1972-77; dist. supt. N.C. Conf. United Meth. Ch., Rockingham, 1977-83; adminstrv. asst. to bishop N.C. Conf. United Meth. Ch., Raleigh, 1983-86, dist. supt., 1986-88; resident bishop United Meth. Ch., Columbia, S.C., 1988—; lectr. Duke Div. Sch., Durham, N.C., 1980-81; mem. com. relational concerns Coun. Bishops, 1988; mem. exec. com. World Meth. Coun., 1981-88. Author: The Duke Divinity Sch. Re., 1975, 78; contbr. articles to Meth. jours. Vice chmn. Gen. Commn. Religion & Race, 1988. Mem. NAACP, Black Methodists for Ch. Renewal, Rotary Internat., Alpha Phi Alpha. Avocations: reading, sports. Office: United Meth Ch 4908 Colonial Dr Ste 108 Columbia SC 29203

BETHEL, LANDER LOUIS, JR., minister; b. Ft. Smith, Ark., June 12, 1957; s. Lander Louis Sr. and Shelba Jean (Henry) B.; m. Genna Marie Mitchell, May 25, 1985; 1 child, Lander Louis III. BA in Psychology, U. Okla., 1979; MDiv, McCormick Theol. Sem., 1984, postgrad., 1984—. Assoc. pastor St. Mark Presbyn. Ch., Boerne, Tex., 1984-87; min. First Presbyn. Ch., Laredo, Tex., 1987—; organizing moderator Laredos Unidos Border Ministry, 1988-90, Refugee Assistance Coun., Laredo, 1988-90. Member com. Mi Laredo Goals for the 90's, 1989—; mem. Leadership Laredo, 1989-90, Laredo Proud Com., 1990—; mem. Mid. East task force for peace Mission Presbytery, San Antonio, 1987—. Mem. Assn. Laredo Mins. (pres. 1989—), Beorne Ministerial Alliance (pres. 1986-87), Rotary. Office: First Presbyn Ch 2520 Lane Laredo TX 78043-2798

BETO, GEORGE JOHN, minister, educator; b. Hysham, Mont., Jan. 19, 1916; s. Louis H. and Margaret (Witsma) B.; m. Marilynn Knippa, Mar. 5, 1943; children—Dan, Lynn, Mark, Beth. Student, Concordia Coll., Milw., 1930-35, Concordia Sem., St. Louis, 1935-37, 38-39; B.A., Valparaiso U., 1938; M.A., U. Tex., 1944, Ph.D., 1955. Ordained to ministry Luth. Ch., 1943. Instr. Concordia Coll., Austin, Tex., 1939-49, pres., 1949-59; vis. instr. U. Tex., 1944; pres. Concordia Theol. Sem., Springfield, Ill., 1959-62; dir. Tex. Dept. Corrections, Huntsville, 1962-72; Disting. prof. Sam Houston State U., Huntsville, 1972-91; dir. 1st Nat. Bank, Palestine. Sec. Tex. Bd. Corrections, 1953-59; mem. Ill. Parole and Pardon Bd., 1961-62, Tex. Youth Council, 1975-88; Am. del. UN Conf. on Prevention Crime and Treatment Offender, Kyoto, Japan, 1970, Geneva, 1975, Milan, 1985; mem. commn. on correctional facilities and services Am. Bar Assn.; mem. Tex. Constl. Revision Commn., 1973-74. Recipient medal for devel. ednl. system Tex. prison system Tex. Heritage Found., 1958, Disting. Alumnus award U. Tex., 1971; Takeuchi fellow, Japan, 1990. Mem. Am. Correctional Assn. (past pres., E.R. Cass award 1972), Phi Delta Kappa, Alpha Delta Kappa. Lutheran. Home: 8203 Summer Place Dr Austin TX 78759 Office: Sam Houston State U Criminal Justice Ctr Huntsville TX 77341

BETSWORTH, ROGER G., religion educator; b. Sioux City, Iowa, Mar. 26, 1933; s. Walter Errol and Georgia Ruth (Scherrer) B.; m. Joan Carol Kleinfelter, June 16, 1960; children: David, Deborah, Sharon. BS, U.S. Naval Acad., 1955; MDiv magna cum laude, Drew U., 1962; PhD, U. So. Calif., L.A., 1973. Ordained minister in Meth. Ch. Sr. pastor Community United Meth. Ch., Huntington Beach, Calif., 1962-69, St. Paul's United Meth. Ch., San Bernardino, Calif., 1969-71; prof. religion Simpson Coll., Indianola, Iowa, 1973—; chair dept. religion Simpson Coll., Indianola, 1988—, dir. sr. colloquium, 1989—; pres. Ministerial Assn., Huntington Beach, 1967-68, San Bernardino, 1970-71. Author: The Radical Movement of the 1960's, 1980, Social Ethics, 1990. Chairperson Community Coordinating Com., Huntington Beach, 1968; chair citizens adv. com. Huntington Beach Sch. Dist., 1967. Lt. USN, 1955-59. USDA fellow U. So. Calif., L.A., 1971-73. Mem. Soc. Christian Ethics, Am. Acad. Religion, Am. Assn. Marriage and Family Therapy (clin.), Project on Religion and the Life of the Nation, Rotary. Democrat. Office: Simpson Coll 701 North C St Indianola IA 50125

BETTENDORF, JAMES BERNARD, minister, church association administrator; b. Jackson, Mich., Oct. 22, 1933; s. Bernard Anthony and Kathryn Marie (Vaughan) B. BA, Sacred Heart Sem., 1955; postgrad. U. Detroit, 1956, U. Notre Dame, 1957, Cath. U. of Am., 1958; STB, St. John Sem., 1959; MA, Western Mich. U., 1970; D Ministry, St. Mary Coll., Balt., 1989. Assoc. pastor Holy Trinity Ch., Fowler, Mich., 1959-60, St. Phillip Ch., Battle Creek, Mich., 1960-63, Sacred Heart Ch., Flint, 1963-66; dir. Flint Newman Ctr., Flint Cath. Info. Ctr., Mich., 1966—; pastor Good Shepherd Ch., Montrose, Mich., 1983-91, St. Leo Ch., Flint, Mich, 1991—. Mem. Urban Coalition, Flint, 1968—; exec. bd. Tall Pine coun. Boy Scouts Am.; mem. exec. bd. ARC, 1991—; trustee C.S. Mott Community Coll., 1987—, chmn., 1989-91; pres. Flint Neighborhood Improvement and Preservation Project. Mem. Lansing Cath. Campus Ministry Assn. (diocesan bd. dirs. 1971-86), Mich. Cath. Campus Ministry Assn., Cath. Campus Ministry Assn. (recipient Charles Forsyth award 1983). Home: 1802 E Court St Flint MI 48503 Office: Flint Newman Ctr 609 E 5th Ave Flint MI 48503

BETTENHAUSEN, ELIZABETH ANN, theology educator; b. Mobridge, S.D., July 31, 1942; d. Elmer W. and Dorothy M. (Zwicker) B. Student, Yankton Coll., 1960-61; B.A., U. Iowa, 1964; postgrad., U. Chgo., 1965-66; Ph.D., U. Iowa, 1971. Asst. prof. U. Wis.-Eau Claire, 1971-73; sec. social concerns Luth. Ch. Am., N.Y.C., 1974-79; assoc., prof. theology Boston U., 1979-88; theologian in residence Walker Ecumenical Exchange, Auburndale, Mass., 1988-89; lectr. theology Women's Theol. Ctr., Boston, 1989—; mem. exec. coun. Luth. Ch. Am, 1980-87; mem. Commn. for an New Luth. Ch., 1982-86, Luth. and Orthodox Joint Commn., 1978-85, Faith & Order Nat. Council Chs., 1976-80. Author: The Equal Rights Amendment, 1979; contbg. editor Christianity and Crisis, 1985—. Mem. Am. Acad. Religion, Soc. Christian Ethics, N.Am. Acad. Ecumenists. Lutheran. Office: Women's Theol Ctr 555 Amory St Jamaica Plain MA 02130

BETTIS, ARTILLA ELIZABETH, minister; b. Blue Mountain, Miss., June 7, 1906; d. Toney C. and Anna (Spight) Kinney; m. Albrt L. McClenton, June 1940 (dec. 1974); children: Tillie Marie. DDiv, Universal Bible Inst., Birmingham, Ala., 1976. Elder AME Ch. Pastor House of Prayer Community Ch., Cassopolis, Mich., 1961-66, Gregg AME Ch., Detroit, 1970-72; asst. pastor Ebenezer AME Ch., Detroit, 1972-88; ret.; counselor, minister of visitation, 1972-88. Recipient Spirit of Detroit award, City Council Detroit. Mem. Nat. Council Negro Women. Address: 3320 Spinnaker Ln #2E Detroit MI 48207

BETTIS, JOSEPH DABNEY, religion educator, clergyman; b. Graham, Tex., Sept. 19, 1936; s. Jack and Jo (Dabney) B.; children: David Joseph, Mark Dabney, Daniel Lee; m. Sharon Holmes, May 31, 1986. BA in Philosophy, So. Meth. U., 1958; BD cum laude, Drew U., 1961; MA in Theology, Princeton U., 1963, PhD in Theology, 1964. Ordained to ministry Meth. Ch., 1964. Instr. religion Douglass Coll., Rutgers U., 1962-64; asst. prof. religion U. Ala., 1964-66, assoc. prof., chair dept. religious studies, 1966-72; Disting. prof. humanities, scholar in residence Coll. Pub. Affairs and Community Svc., U. Nebr., Omaha, 1972-73, assoc. dean, prof. in residence, 1973-75; dean, prof. Fairhaven Coll., Western Wash. U., Bellingham, 1975-78, prof. religious studies, 1978—; cons. on prisons and corrections Nebr. Com. on the Humanities, 1974, on equal employment opportunities Omaha Nat. Bank, 1974, on human rels. Omaha C. of C., 1974, on sch. desegregation Omaha YMCA, 1974, cons. Coun. for the Advancement of Experiential Learning, 1977, Law Enforcement and the New Religions, San Francisco, 1982; tech. assistance panel cons. Southern region Office of Econ. Opportunity/Community Action Program, 1966-72; mem. Wash. Com. on Religious Liberty, 1981. Editor: Phenomenology of Religion, 1969; co-editor: (with Stanley Johannesen) The Return of the Millenium, 1984; contbr. articles and revs. to profl. jours.; editorial bd. Rev. of Applied Urban Rsch., 1973. Edn. program specialist EEO program Office of Edn. HEW, Washington, 1966; mem. at large exec. bd. Ala. Coun. on Human Rels., 1966-70; chmn. Tuscaloosa Coun. on Human Rels., 1966-67; mem. adv. bd. Tuscaloosa Head Start, 1967; regional selection com. Danforth Assoc. Program, 1968-70; bd. dirs. The New Sch., Omaha, 1973, Inst. for Social Encounters, 1974; bd. of judges outstanding young educator Omaha Jaycees, 1974; mem. acad. coun. Nat. Inst. on the Holocaust, 1977. Tipple scholar Drew U., 1958, 59, 60; fellow in religious studies Princeton U., 1961, 62, 63, fellow NEH, 1970, grad. faculty fellow U. Nebr., 1974; U. Ala. rsch. grantee 1965, 66, 68, 69, 70, 71, U. Ala. Internat. Studies grantee, 1970, Met. Life Ednl. grantee, 1977, Consultants Program grantee NEH, 1978; named Danforth Assoc., Danforth Found., 1966-75. Mem. Omicron Delta Kappa. Home: Box 4261 Bellingham WA 98225 Office: Western Wash U Bellingham WA 98225

BETTIS, ROBERT ALLEN, minister; b. Topeka, Kans., Apr. 8, 1955; s. Robert Eugene and Sylvia Jean (Crawford) B.; m. Adrea W. Bay, Jul. 30, 1973; children: James Allen, Rachel Renae. BA in bible, Cen. Bible Coll., 1983. Pastor Hazard Assembly of God, Hazard, Ky., 1983-84, North Oak Chapel Assembly of God, Kansas City, Mo., 1987--; min. Assemblies of God, Springfield, Mo. 1972--; rep. Men's Ministries Sect. 1 No. Mo. Dist. Assemblies of God, Kansas City, 1989--. Named Delta Epsilon Chi Am. Assn. Bible Coll., 1983. Assemblies of God. Home: 8607 N Holmes Kansas City MO 64155 Office: N Oak Chapel Assembly God 8641 N Oak Trafficway Kansas City MO 64155 *The first ministers of the Church were Jesus Christ's ambassadors. All that they said or did was said or done in Jesus' name. They refused, when told that they could no longer publicly mention Jesus' name. May today's ministers, as Christ's ambassadors, have the same tenacity as our predecessors.*

BETTON, JOE STEWART, minister; b. L.A., July 12, 1952; s. William Rudolph Betton and Lydia Mae (Hamilton) Coleá; m. Sharon Joyce Black, June 15, 1978; children: Tina, Marcia, Aaron. Ordained to ministry Bapt. Ch., 1988. Mem. choir Atherton Bapt. Ch., Inglewood, Calif., 1981-88, coord. youth dept., 1987; deacon, youth pastor and coord. Rubidoux (Calif.) Missionary Bapt. Ch., 1888—; dispatcher Northrop Corp., Hawthorne, Calif., 1985—. Vol. Youth Motivation Task Force, 1987, High Sch. Involvement Program, 1987. Home: 12291 Baltimore Ave Moreno Valley CA 92557-7729 Office: Rubidoux Missionary Bapt Ch 2890 Rubidoux Blvd Rubidoux CA 92509

BETTY, LEWIS STAFFORD, religious studies educator, writer; b. Mobile, Ala., Dec. 31, 1942; s. Samuel Marks and Margaret Lillian; m. Lynette Anne Doyle, Aug. 15, 1981; children: Samuel DeWestfelt, Sage Campbell, Southey Faye Lewy, Louis Robert, Samuel Stafford. BS in Math. and English, Spring Hill Coll., 1964; MA in English, U. Detroit, 1966; PhD in Theology, Fordham U., 1975. From lectr. to prof. religious studies Calif. State U., Bakersfield, 1972—. Author: (scholarly) Vadiraja's Refutation of Sankara's Non-Dualism, 1978, (novel) The Rich Man, 1984, (adult fables) Sing Like the Whippoorwill, 1987, Sunlit Waters, 1990; contbr. articles to profl. jours. Bd. dirs. Mental Health Assn. Kern County, Bakersfield, 1982-84. 1st lt. U.S. Army, 1966-68. Recipient Clean Air award Kern County Lung Assn., 1990. Democrat. Episcopalian. Office: Calif State U Stockdale Hwy Bakersfield CA 93311

BETZ, HANS DIETER, theology educator; b. Lemgo, Lippe, Germany, May 21, 1931; came to U.S., 1963, naturalized, 1973; s. Ludwig and Gertrude (Vietor) B.; m. Christel Hella Wagner, Nov. 10, 1958; children: Martin, Ludwig, Arnold. Student, Kirchliche Hochschule, Bethel, Fed. Republic Germany, 1951-52, U. Mainz, Fed. Republic Germany, 1952-55, 56-58, Westminster Coll, Cambridge, Eng., 1955-56; Doctor Theologiae, U. Mainz, Fed. Republic Germany, 1957; Habilitation, U. Mainz, 1966. Pastor Evangelical Ch., Rhineland, Fed. Republic Germany, 1961-63; from asst. prof. to prof. Sch. Theology, Claremont Grad. Sch., Calif., 1963-78; prof. N.T. and early Christian lit. U. Chgo., 1978—, Shailer Mathews prof., 1989—, chmn. dept. N.T. and early Christian lit., 1985—. Author, editor numerous books and articles in German and English, 1959—. Rsch. grantee NEH, 1970-83, Am. Assn. Theol. Schs., 1977, 84; recipient Humboldt Rsch. prize, 1986. Mem. Soc. Bibl. Lit., Studiorum Novi Testamenti Societas, Chgo. Soc. Bibl. Rsch. (pres. 1983-84), Wissenschaftliche Gesellschaft für Theologie. Office: U Chgo 1025 E 58th St Chicago IL 60637

BETZ, OTTO WILHELM, retired theology educator; b. Herrentier-Bach, Germany, June 8, 1917; s. Wilhelm and Agnes (Dierlamm) B.; m. Isolde Anna Schnabel, Feb. 14, 1958; children: Cornelia, Dorothea, Martin, Matthias. STM, Grad. Sch. Theology, Oberlin, Ohio, 1953; ThD, U. Tübingen, 1959, D Habil., 196l. With Evangelisches Stift, Tübingen, Fed. Republic Germany, 1953-56; assoc. prof. Chgo. Theol. Sem., 1962-63, prof., 1963-67; asst. U. Tübingen, 1956-6l, dozent, 196l-62, prof., sci. advisor, 1968-83; ret., 1983. Author: Offenbarung-Qumran, 1960, Der Paraklet, 1963, Was wissen wir von Jesus?, 1965, Jesus, der Messias Israels, 1987, Jesus, der Herr der Kirche, 1990, numerous others. Mem. Studiorum Novi Testamenti Soc., Soc. Bibl. Lit., World Council Jewish Studies, Gesellschaft für Wissenschaftliche Theologie. Lutheran. Avocation: music. Home: Il Rappenberghalde, D-7400 Tübingen Federal Republic of Germany Office: U Tübingen, Wilhelmstrasse 7, D-7400 Tübingen Federal Republic of Germany

BEUTEL, EUGENE WILLIAM, minister; b. Sanborn, N.Y., July 27, 1927; s. Edwin William and Alice Ruth Berniece (Williams) B.; m. Dolores Mae Hanson, June 24, 1950; children: David Lee, Paul Christian, Jonathan Andrew. BA, Capital U., 1949; BD, Evang. Luth. Theol. Sem., 1952; ThM, Princeton Theol. Sem., 1970, D. of Ministry, 1975. Ordained to ministry Luth. Ch., 1952. Pastor-developer Holy Trinity Luth. Ch., Balt., 1955-61, Redeemer Luth. Ch., Neptune, N.J., 1961-74; dir. svc. mission northeastern area Am. Luth. Ch., N.Y.C., 1974-81; dir. svc. mission eastern dist.-south area Am. Luth. Ch., Marlboro and Farmingdale, N.J., 1981-87; coord. region 8, Evang. Luth. Ch. Am., Harrisburg, Pa., 1987—; pres. Am. Luth. Ch. confs., Balt., 1958-61, N.J., 1964-70; chmn. com. on hosps. and instns. Shore Area Coun. of Chs., Asbury Park, N.J., 1970-74; v.p., trustee Luth. Social Svcs. N.J., Trenton, 1968-74; mem. task force on D. Ministry standards Am. Assn. Theol. Schs., Vandalia, Ohio, 1975-76; del. Am. Luth. Ch. Convention, Omaha, 1968. Author various devotional articles. Chaplain Hamilton Fire Co. and Aid Squad, Neptune, 1961-74; vice chmn. N.J. Juvenile Conf. Com., Neptune, 1967-74; trustee Shore Area YMCA, Asbury Park, 1961-68; cons., advisor Hope Community Counseling Ctr., Freehold, N.J., 1980-87. Served to col. U.S. Army, 1946-47, 52-55, Korea; ret. Decorated Bronze Star, Legion of Merit; named Man of Yr. Shore Area YMCA, 1968; recipient Honor cert. Freedoms Found., 1977. Mem. Res. Officers' Assn., Mil. Chaplains' Assn., Town and Country Ch. Inst. (mem. adv. coun. 1988—), VFW (chaplain 1968-74). Republican. Office: Evang Luth Ch Am Region 8 900 S Arlington Ave #210 Harrisburg PA 17109 *The most significant part of each Christian's ministry is the telling of his/her life's faith journey. What keeps me going when negative criticism strikes is this motto, " I like my way of doing it better than your way of not doing it."*

BEUTLER, STEPHEN ALBERT, minister; b. Mishawaka, Ind., Aug. 30, 1952; s. Albert Jacob and Barbara Jean (Heeter) B.; m. Jayna Diane Ringer, Aug. 14, 1976; children: Jason Richard, Sara Jayne, Stephanie Janae. BA, Bethel Coll., Mishawaka, 1974; postgrad., Inst. Holy Land Studies, Jerusalem, 1974-75; MDiv, Asbury Theol. Sem., 1978. Ordained deacon United Meth. Ch., 1981, elder, 1983. Pastor Faith Missionary Ch., Flint, Mich., 1978-79, United Meth. Ch., Mishawaka, 1979-83, Fairmount (Ind.) United Meth. Ch., 1983-85, Upland (Ind.) United Meth. Ch., 1985-89, United Meth. Ch., Lafayette, Ind., 1989—; registrar Bd. Ordained Ministry, Ind. Conf., 1986—; gen. chmn. Good News Nat. Convocation, Wilmore, Ky., 1986-87; mem. dist. bd. ministry, Marion, Ind., 1985—; dir. youth South Bend (Ind.) Dist. United Meth. Ch., 1982-83; adj. prof. dept. religion, philosophy and bibl. langs. Taylor U., Upland, 1987—. Sec., chmn. Grant County ARC, Marion, Ind., 1988-89; chmn. St. Joseph County Am. Cancer Soc., South Bend, 1982-83; bd. dirs. Am. Cancer Soc. Barrett Merit scholar Asbury Theol. Sem., 1976-78; named Outstanding Vol. ARC, 1989. Mem. Ministerial Assn. (v.p. 1984-85), Kiwanis. Avocations: magic tricks (TOPS award for Magician of the Month presentation 1967), music, stamp collecting, travel. Office: Congress St United Meth Ch 2010 Congress St Lafayette IN 47905

BEVAN, CHARLES ALBERT, JR., minister; b. Camden, N.J., Dec. 12, 1944; s. Charles Albert and Dorothy (Pape) B.; m. Virginia Flick, Oct. 14, 1972; children—Charles Albert III, Andrew Layng, George Carter, Jonathan Tatum. B.A., Rider Coll, 1967; M.Div., Phila. Div. Sch., 1970; postgrad., Princeton Theol. Sem., 1973-75; D.Min., Grad. Theol. Found., U. Notre Dame, 1986. Ordained to ministry Episcopal Ch. 1970. Seminarian St. Asaph's Episcopal Ch., Bala Cynwyd, Pa., 1967-68; chaplain to Bishop of China, 1968-70; curate Grace Episcopal Ch., Plainfield, N.J., 1970-72; assoc. rector Christ Episcopal Ch., Bloomfield-Glen Ridge, N.J., 1972-74; asst. rector Galilee Episcopal Ch., Virginia Beach, Va., 1974-79; rector St. John's Episcopal Ch., Salisbury, Conn., 1979—; dean, Convocation II, Diocese of So. Va., 1977-79, mem. exec. council, 1977-79; mem. exec. council Diocese of Conn., 1983-86, mem. Ecumenical Commn., 1983—, mem. Commn. on Ministry, 1982-84, sub-dean, Litchfield Deanery, 1980-81, dean, 1990—; mem. chpt. Christ Ch. Cathedral, Hartford, Conn., 1981-84; chaplain the Most Venerable Order of the Hosp. of St. John of Jerusalem, 1984—. Author Christian Edn. Program for Deaf, Va. Sem., 1978; Editor Christian Edn. Program, Diocese of N.J., 1970-72. Trustee Sharon Hosp., Conn., 1982-87, Northwest Conn. Hospice, Inc., Sharon, 1979-87, Salisbury Vis. Nurse Assn., Conn., 1982-86, Salisbury Prep. Sch., 1985—; bd. dirs. Inst. of World Affairs, 1984—; mem. com. on Christian and Muslim rels., Nat. Coun. Chs., 1990—, nat. adv. com. Youth Devel. Internat., 1990—; pres. Habitat for Humanity of N.W. Conn., 1990—. Fellow Va. Theol. Sem., 1976-84, Yale Div. Sch., 1983-84. Mem. English Speaking Union, Univ. Club of Conn., Chebecque Island (Maine) Yacht Club. Republican. Home: The Rectory Main St Salisbury CT 06068 Office: Saint John's Episcopal Ch 12 Main St Salisbury CT 06068

BEVAN, THOMAS ROY, priest; b. Balt., July 17, 1936; s. Leroy E. and Catherine Irene (Smith) B. BA in Philosophy and English Lit., Loyola Coll., Balt., 1958; postgrad., Mt. St. Mary's Sem., Emmitsburg, Md.; MA in Liturgy, Cath. U. Am. Ordained priest Roman Cath. Ch., 1963. Priest Our Lady of Mt. Carmel Parish, 1963-74, Ch. St. John the Evangelist, Frederick, Md., 1974-79; pastor Young Parish of St. Mark, Fallston, Md., 1979-91; chmn. archdiocesan clergy edn. com. Archdiocese of Balt., 1976-91, dir. ministry edn.; adminstr. Parish of St. Mary's, Cumberland, Md., 1991—; tchr. liturgy Mt. St. Mary's Sem., Emmitsburg, 1977-79. Author: 220 Years—A History of the Catholic Church in the Frederick Valley, 1978. Mem. Nat. Orgn. for Continuing Edn. of Roman Cath. Clergy (dir. continuing clergy formation, bd. dirs., sec. exec. com.), Soc. for Advancement Continuing Edn. for Ministry, Acad. Parish Clergy. Home: 300 Oldtown Rd Cumberland MD 21502

BEVERLY, URIAS HARRISON, minister; b. Indpls., Nov. 20, 1941; s. Roy Winston and Rosa Miller (Robinson) B.; m. Diana Marie Beverly, Dec. 30, 1966 (div. Dec. 1977); 1 adopted child, Dycus; m. Gladys Elizabeth Johnson, Apr. 6, 1985. BA in Psychology, Ind. Cen. Coll. (now U. Indpls.), 1973; MS in Edn., Butler U., 1974; MDiv., Christian Theol. Sem., Indpls., 1978; postgrad., Ind. U., Indpls., 1980-84. Pastor Trinity Bapt. Ch., Indpls., 1967-69; asst. pastor Unity Bapt. Ch., Indpls., 1970-73; co-pastor Zion Unity Ch., Indpls., 1973-76; pastoral care resident Ind. U. Hosp., Indpls., 1976-77; asst. pastor Mt. Zion Bapt. Ch., Indpls., 1976-87; staff chaplain Meth. Hosp., Indpls., 1987—; pastor Riverside Park United Meth. Ch., 1987—; Pastoral counselor Buchanan Counseling Ctr., Meth. Hosp., Indpls., 1978-84, chaplain, 1977—; field edn. cons. Christian Theol. Sem., 1985—; parish counseling educator Congress of Nat. Black Chs., Washington, 1986-89. Copyright music and poems; contbr. articles to profl. jours. Midwest community workshop leader, 1976-84; mem. steering com. Staying Healthy After 50 chpt. ARC; chmn. bd. Mt. Zion Geriatric Ctr., 1984-87, One-to-One Prison Visitation Program, 1984-88. Served with U.S. Army, 1959-62. Fellow Coll. Chaplains (council mem. 1983-86), Am. Protestant Hosp. Assn.; mem. NAACP (life), Urban League (supporting), AGAPE Soc. (founder, bd. dirs. 1978-87), Am. Assn. Pastoral Counselors, Assn. Clin. Pastoral Edn. (full supr., chairperson East cen. region 1984-87, bd. reps. 1987-91, pres.-elect 1992), Christian Theol. Sem. Alumni Assn. (bd. dirs. 1986-90, chmn. bd. 1986-89). Democrat. Avocations: piano, organ, tennis, long distance running, long distance swimming. Home: 4260 Springwood Trail Indianapolis IN 46208 Office: Meth Hosp of Ind Inc 1701 N Senate Boulevard Indianapolis IN 46202

BEVILACQUA, ANTHONY JOSEPH CARDINAL, cardinal; b. Bklyn., June 17, 1923; s. Louis and Maria (Codella) B. Student, Cathedral Coll., Bklyn., 1941-43, Sem. of Immaculate Conception, Huntington, N.Y., 1943-49; JCD, Gregorian U., Rome, Italy, 1956; MA in Polit. Sci, Columbia U., 1962; JD, St. John's U. Sch. Law, 1975. Ordained priest Roman Cath. Ch., 1949; ordained bishop, 1980. Bar: N.Y. 1976, Pa. 1988, U.S. Dist. Ct. (we. dist.) Pa. 1984, U.S. Dist. Ct. (ea. dist.) Pa. 1988, U.S. Supreme Ct., 1989. Asst. pastor Sacred Heart, St. Stephen's Ch., St. Mary's Ch., 1949-50; prof. history Cathedral Prep. Sem., Bklyn., 1950-53; prof. canon law Sem. of Immaculate Conception, Huntington, N.Y., 1968-80; adj. prof. law St. John's U. Sch. Law, Queens, N.Y., 1976-80; successively asst. chancellor, vice-chancellor, chancellor Diocese of Bklyn., 1965-83, dir. Cath. migration and refugee office, 1971-83, ordained aux. bishop, 1980; bishop Diocese of Pitts., 1983-88; archbishop Archdiocese of Phila., 1988—; created cardinal, 1991; chmn. com. on canonical affairs Nat. Conf. Cath. Bishops, 1981-84, com. on migration and tourism, 1981-86, mem. com. Pro-Life, 1989—; cons. Pontifical Commn. on Migrants and Itinerants, 1981-86; mem. Pontifical Congregation for Religious, 1989—; mem. Pontifical Congregation for Causes of Saints; mem. Pontifical Coun. Cor Unum, 1991—. Contbr. articles to profl. jours. Bd. dirs. Mercy Home for Children; chmn. Nat. Coalition for Haitian Refugees. Mem. Canon Law Soc. Am., Cath. Theol. Soc. Am., ABA, Pa. Bar Assn., Fellowship of Am. Cath. Scholars. Address: Archdiocese Phila 222 N 17th St Philadelphia PA 19103-1299

BEX, CRAIG ALAN, evangelist; b. Cedar Rapids, Iowa, Sept. 29, 1953; s. Norman Roy and Stella Grace (Oliphant) B.; m. Olga Solis Flores, Dec. 2, 1972; children: Angela Joy, Bradley James. BS, Cin. Bible Coll., 1981; MA, Ind. Christian U., 1984, DD, 1988. Ordained to ministry Evang. Ch. Alliance, 1979. Pres. Discipleship Ministries, Inc., Kamrar, Iowa, 1979—; assoc. prof. Ind. Christian Univ., Indpls., 1983-85; sr. pastor The Community Ch., Kamrar, 1985—. Author: (books) The Cross, Resurrection, Our Hope, 1986, The Ministry Planning Aid, 1988; contbr. articles to profl. jours. Founding bd. chmn. Harvest Acres Youth Ctr., Rockwell City, Iowa, 1988. With USAF, 1971-73. Mem. Internat. Assn. Christian Pastoral Counselors, United Assn. Christian Counselors, Iowa Sunday Sch. Assn. (bd. mem. 1990-91, pres. 1991—). Home: 2355 280th St Kamrar IA 50132 Office: 2351 280th St Kamrar IA 50132

BEYER, BALDWIN MARTIN, clergyman, counselor; b. Chgo., Apr. 30, 1926; s. Casimir and Helen (Wozniak) B.; B.A., Mary Immaculate Coll., Garrison, N.Y., 1950; M.A. in Theology, St. Anthony Sem., 1954. Joined Capuchin-Franciscan order Roman Catholic Ch., 1945, ordained priest, 1953; asst. pastor chs., Milw., 1954-58, Appleton, Wis., 1959-61; prof. theology Victory Noll Coll., Huntington, Ind., 1961-65, St. Francis Bros. Sch., Mt. Calvary, Wis., 1967-69; hosp. chaplain, Detroit, 1969-73; alcoholism counselor Sacred Heart Ch., Detroit and Friendship House, Bay City, Mich., 1973-74; dir. Human Aid, Inc., Gladwin, Mich., 1974-85; mem. Mich. Credentialing Bd. Addiction Profls.; cons. Saginaw Diocesan Health Panel. Cert. hosp. chaplain, addictions counselor, social worker, Mich. Mem. Mich. Assn. Alcoholism and Drug Abuse Counselors, Nat. Alcohol and Drug Problems Assn., Nat. Assn. Alcoholism Counselors, Cath. Hosp. Chaplains.

BEZANSON, RONALD SCOTT, JR., clergyman, army chaplain; b. Laconia, N.H., Oct. 28, 1936; s. Ronald Scott and Avis Maria (Preble) B.; m. Mary Joan Arthur, June 28, 1958; children: Deborah K. Rebecca K., Timothy S., Angela L. BA, Aurora (Ill.) Coll., 1958, BTh, 1959; MDiv, Evangel. Theol. Sem., Naperville, Ill., 1962; MBA, U. Tex., Austin, 1975. Ordained to ministry, Advent Christian Ch., 1962. Commd. 1st lt. U.S. Army, 1962, advanced through grades to col., 1982; chaplain, chief adminstrn. and mgmt. U.S. Army, Vietnam, 1970; staff chaplain Army Air Def. Command U.S. Army, Colorado Springs, Colo., 1971-73; instr. Chaplain Sch. U.S. Army, Ft. Wadsworth, N.Y., 1974-77; dep. chaplain materiel command U.S. Army, Alexandria, Va., 1977-81; chaplain 2d inf. div. U.S. Army, Camp Casey, Korea, 1981-82; dir. adminstrn., office chief chaplain, Pentagon U.S. Army, Washington, 1982-85; command chaplain hdqrs. Western command U.S. Army, Ft. Shafter, Hawaii, 1985-89; chief dept. of ministry and pastoral care Tripler Army Med. Ctr., Hawaii, 1989—; pastor Ft. DeRussy Chapel, Honolulu, 1985—; treas. 1st United Presbyn. Ch., Woodbridge, Va., 1982-85; bd. dirs. Dept. Army Coun. Chaplain Cols., Washington, 1982-89. Pub., Westcom Chaplain newsletter, 1985-89; columnist, Hawaii Army Weekly, 1988—. Mem. steering com., Gov.'s and Mayor's Prayer Breakfast, Honolulu, 1986-89. Decorated Legion of Merit, 3 Bronze Star medals, 9 Air Medals. Mem. Mil Chaplains Assn., Officers Club, Army Golf Assn. Republican. Avocations: computers, photography, golf. Home: 46-381 Kumoo Loop Kaneohe HI 96744-3532 Office: Tripler Army Med Ctr Attn HSHK-CH Tripler Army Medical Center HI 96859-5000 *Each new day for me is a clean page; what's written there, for good or for evil, is up to me.*

BEZOU, HENRY CHARLES, clergyman, educator; b. New Orleans, Apr. 28, 1913; s. André Ralph and Lydia Marie (Bouligny) B. Ed., St. Aloysius Coll., 1929, St. Joseph Sem., St. Benedict, La., 1932, Notre Dame Sem., New Orleans, 1932-38; A.M., Cath. U. Am., 1947; Litt.D. (honoris causa), Loyola U. of South, 1952. Ordained priest Roman Cath. Ch., 1938; with Sacred Heart Ch., Montegut, La., 1938-42, St. Charles Ch., Lafourche, La., 1942-43; head Normal Sch., Houma, La., 1940-42; archdiocesan supt. schs. New Orleans, 1943-68; named Papal Chamberlain with title Very Reverend Monsignor, 1949, domestic prelate with title Rt. Rev. Monsignor, 1954; dir. Cath. Com. S. Summer Sch., Loyola U.; pastor St. Patrick's Ch., New Orleans, 1951-65, Our Lady Star of the Sea Ch., 1965- 67; pastor St. Francis Xavier, Metairie, La., 1967-83, pastor emeritus, 1983—; spiritual dir. Ozanam Inn, 1955-65; Mem. Archdiocesan Central Council, Soc. St. Vincent de Paul, 1956-66; archdiocesan cons., 1962-77; sec. elementary div. Nat. Cath. Ednl. Assn.; mem. Gov.'s Safety Com. (also other state coms.); co-chmn. Archdiocesan Bicentennial Commn., 1975; chmn. Jefferson Parish Hist. Commn., 1976-78; mem. Archdiocesan Bldg. Commn.; co-chmn. Jefferson Parish Sesquicentennial Commn., 1974-75; chmn. La. Cath. Conf. ad hoc com., Acadian Odyssey Bicentennial, 1985; mem. Council Devel. French in La., 1981-85. Author: articles, pamphlets, monographs and brochures including Metairie: A Tongue of Land to Pasture, 1973, Jefferson Parish Historical Markers, 1977, Lourdes on Napoleon Avenue, 1980, Tent to Temple, 1985, Random Readings, 1986, Recollections and Reflections, 1988. Mem. Mayor's Adv. Coms.; bd. dirs. New Orleans Symphony Soc., New Orleans Tb League, La. Soc. Crippled Children, Community Chest; bd. dirs. United Fund, mem schs. com.; mem. adv. com. Juvenile Ct.; cons. supts.' div., dept. edn. Nat. Cath. Welfare Conf.; mem. coms. State Dept. Edn.; trustee Greater New Orleans Ednl. TV Found.; mem. White House Conf. on Edn., 1955; regional adv. bd. ARC; adv. bd. Cath. Ency. Sch. and Home; dir. Info. Council of Ams. Decorated chevalier Legion of Honor; recipient Palmes Académiques and title Officier d'Académie, 1949. Mem. Am. Cath. Hist. Assn., Fgn. Policy Assn., Nat. Cath. Edn. Assn. (pres. supts. dept.), Jefferson Hist. Soc. La. (dir. 1977—), Am. Soc. Legion of Honor. Address: 202 Betz Pl Metairie LA 70005

BIAL, MORRISON DAVID, rabbi; b. N.Y.C., Aug. 29, 1917; s. Jacob and Carrie Bial; m. Dorothy Berman, 1954; children: Anne Bial Ehrenkranz, Daniel. Grad., CUNY; M Hebrew Letters, Jewish Inst. Religion, 1946; postgrad., Princeton Theol. Sem.; DD, Hebrew Union Coll., 1970. Ordained rabbi, 1945. Rabbi Temple Sinai, Summit, N.J., 1953-85, Temple Beth Shalom, Ocala, Fla., 1985—; past tchr. Sch. Edn. Hebrew Union Coll.; leader group tours, Israel; tchr. Torah, Cen. Coll. Am. Rabbis; lectr. in field; vis. scholar at various synagogues and chs., worldwide. Author: (with Solomon Simon) The Rabbis' Bible, Vol. I, 1966, Vol. II, 1969; Liberal Judaism at Home, 1971, The Questions You Asked, 1972, Your Jewish Child, 1978. Home: 1812 SE 38 Ct Ocala FL 32671

BIALKOWSKI, DIANA, school system administrator. Supt. Cath. schs. Richmond, Va. Office: Office Supt Cath Schs 811 Cathedral Pl Ste C Richmond VA 23220*

BIALLAS, LEONARD JOHN, religion educator; b. Pontiac, Mich., May 3, 1939; s. Leonard John and Elizabeth (Mansfield) B.; m. Martha Susan Weedman, June 15, 1974. A.B., U. Notre Dame, 1961; M.A., Holy Cross Coll., 1965; S.T.D., Inst. Catholique,-Paris, 1970. Asst. prof. U. Notre Dame, Ind., 1970-73; faculty Quincy Coll. Ill., 1973—, prof. dept. theology, 1982—. Author: Myths: Gods, Heroes, and Saviors, 1986, World Religions: A Story Approach, 1991; contbr. articles to profl. jours. Editor, Bulletin of Council on Study of Religion, 1977-85. Mem. Am. Acad. Religion, Coll. Theology Soc., Cath. Theol. Soc. Am. Roman Catholic. Home: 20 Spring Lake Quincy IL 62301 Office: Quincy Coll Dept Theology and Religious Studies 1800 College Ave Quincy IL 62301

BIAS, STEVEN EUGENE, chaplain; b. Pomona, Calif., Sept. 3, 1953; s. Roderick Eugene Bias and Elsie Glennette (Bonds) Joplin; m Jerlene Sue Weil, Aug. 6, 1977; children: Douglas Glen, Bryan Michael. BA in Bible, Cen. Bible Coll., Springfield, Mo., 1975; MDiv, Assemblies of God Theol. Sem., Springfield, 1981; D of Ministry, United Theol. Sem., Dayton, Ohio, 1991. Ordained to ministry Assemblies of God, 1981. Pastor First Assembly of God Ch., Campbellsville, Ky., 1982-84; chaplain, commd. capt. USAF, Keesler AFB, Miss., 1985-87; chaplain USAF, Osan AFB, Republic of Korea, 1987-88, Wright-Patterson AFB, Ohio, 1988—. Contbr. articles to mil. publs. Mem. Air Force Assn. Home: 5120 Cobb Dr Dayton OH 45431 Office: 2750 ABW/HC Wright-Patterson AFB OH 45433

BICHOTTE, RODRIGUE BEN, minister. Min. Luth. Ch., Port-au-Prince, Haiti. Office: Luth Ch, BP 13147, Petite Pl Cuzean, Delmas, Port-au-Prince Haiti*

BICKEL, KENNETH ROBERT, minister; b. Lancaster, Pa., Dec. 28, 1952; s. George Washington and Mary Helen (Long) B.; m. Nancy Anne Nelson, Aug. 16, 1975; children: Jennie Jean, Julia Beth. BA, Lebanon Valley Coll., 1974; teaching cert., Princeton U., 1976; MDiv, Princeton Theol. Sem., 1977; postgrad. studies toward doctorate, Lancaster (Pa.) Theol. Sem., 1988—. Ordained to ministry United Ch. of Christ, 1977. Minister Blue Ridge Ch. of United Ch. of Christ, Wapwallopen, Pa., 1977-90; sr. minister First Congl. United Ch. of Christ, Dubuque, Iowa, 1990—; del. Gen. Synod United Ch. of Christ, 1971, '73. '85, '87; chmn. Evangel. Task Force Pa. N. E. Conf. United Ch. of Christ, Palmerton, 1985-90; convenor SWAP Coun. 1985-90; bd. dirs. Pa. N.E. Conf. United Ch. Christ, 1979-82. Pres. Student Coun. Lebanon Valley Coll., Annville, Pa., 1973-74, trustee, '73-74; mem. Dorrance Twp. Recreation Bd. Wapwallopen, Pa., 1977-90. Mem. Key City Rotary Club. Home: 75 Fremont Ave Dubuque IA 52003 Office: First Congl United Ch 255 W Tenth St Dubuque IA 52001

BICKERTON, THOMAS JAMES, clergyman; b. Glendale, W.Va., July 2, 1958; s. James Ronald and Shirley Marlene (Cassis) B.; m. Rebecca Jo Bodenheimer, Mar. 29, 1980; children: Elizabeth Anne, Thomas James II. BA, W.Va. Wesleyan Coll., Buckhannon, 1980; MDiv, Duke Div. Sch., Durham, 1983. Ordained to ministry United Meth. Ch., 1985. Youth min. Duff St. United Meth. Ch., Clarksburg, W.Va., 1977-79; pastor Adrian (W.Va.) United Meth. Ch., 1979-80, Perry Meml. United Meth. Ch., Shady Spring, W.Va., 1983-89, Forrest Burdette Meml. United Meth. Ch., Hurricane, W.Va., 1989—; del. Northeastern Jurisdictional Conf., 1988; bd. dirs. Beckley (W.Va.) Child Care Ctr., 1985, chmn., 1988—. Mem. W.Va. Wesleyan Alumni Coun., 1988—. Named Min. of Yr. W.Va. Ann. Conf., Buckhannon, 1987. Mem. Lions Club (chmn. Shady Spring chpt. 1987-88), Ruritan Club. Democrat. Home: 2863 Virginia Ave Hurricane WV 25526 Office: Forrest Burdette Meml United Meth Ch 2848 Putnam Ave Hurricane WV 25526

BICKES, PAUL FRANK, minister; b. Maroa, Ill., May 20, 1926; s. George Lincoln and Mildred Leon (Andrews) B.; m. Mary Anna Barrett, July 7, 1947; 1 child, Cynthia. AB in Philosophy & Religion, Asbury Coll., 1954. Pastor Ch. of the Nazarene, Winter Haven, Fla., 1966-69, So. Fla. Heights Ch. of the Nazarene, Lakeland, Fla., 1969-75; sr. pastor Cen. Ch. of the Nazarene, Orlando, Fla., 1975-76; sr. pastor First Ch. of the Nazarene, Tulsa, 1976-80, Lake Worth, Fla., 1980—; chmn. So. Fla. Dist. Sunday Sch. Ministries, 1980—. With USN, 1944-46, PTO. Republican. Office: First Ch of the Nazarene 1422 Lucerne Ave Lake Worth FL 33460

BICKET, ZENAS JOHAN, college administrator; b. Hartford, Ill., Oct. 14, 1932; s. Paul James and Marie Kamila (Johansen) B.; m. Rhoda Mae Price, Aug. 28, 1954; children: Deborah, Daniel, David. BEd, Wis. State U., 1954; BA, Cen. Bible Coll., 1956, ThB, 1957; MA, U. Ark., 1963, PhD, 1965. Acad. dean Evang. Coll., Springfield, Mo., 1966-70, 73-85, prof. English, 1970-73; dean Berean Coll., Springfield, 1985-88, pres., 1988—. Author: The Effective Pastor, 1973, Walking in the Spirit, 1988, We Hold These Truths, 1978; editor: And He Gave Pastors, 1979. Fellow Nat. Edn. Act, 1961-64. Mem. Pi Omega Pi, Delta Epsilon Chi. Mem. Assemblies of God. Home: 1434 S Essex Rd Springfield MO 65809-2123 Office: Berean Coll 1445 Boonville Ave Springfield MO 65802 *Life is too short to waste on trivia. Every moment must count for eternity.*

BICKETT, DIANNE LESLIE, youth director; b. Onida, S.D., Apr. 2, 1965; d. Kenneth Edward and Sandra Sue (Glaser) B. BA, Augustana Coll., 1989. Fin. coord. A Christian Ministry in the Nat. Parks, N.Y.C., 1986-87; dir. youth First United Meth. Ch., New Ulm, MN, 1989—; mem. steering com. Parents Communication Network, New Ulm, 1989-90. Democrat. Office: First United Meth Ch PO Box 364 New Ulm MN 56073-0364 *Let us cherish the people in our lives. The only time we can guarantee with others is now. We are fools to think otherwise.*

BIDAWID, RAPHAEL I., religious leader. Patriarch of Babylon of Chaldeans Baghdad, Iraq. Office: Patriarcat Chaldeen Catholique, Baghdad Iraq*

BIDDELMAN, MARK JAY, cantor; b. Newark, June 7, 1943; s. Meyer A. and Miriam (Bierman) B.; m. Bette Sue, Nov. 30, 1967; 1 child, Tara. BSM, Hebrew Union Coll., N.Y.C., 1967. Cert. cantor. Cantor Temple Sharey Shalom, Springfield, N.J., 1961-66, Temple Emanuel, Woodcliff Lake, N.J., 1967—; sec. N.J. Region Cantors Assembly, 1989-91, chmn. N.J. region, 1991—. Composer: Sing a New Song, 1971, B'Manginot Alizot, 1991. Named Man of the Yr., B'nai Brith, 1990, Sh'ma Yisrael, N.J. Israel Bonds, 1988. Mem. Cantors Assy., Am. Conf. Cantors, Am. Guild Variety Artists. Home: 568 Hillsdale Ave Hillsdale NJ 07642 Office: Temple Emanuel 87 Overlook Dr Woodcliff Lake NJ 07642

BIDDLE, ALLEN ALEXANDER, principal; b. Sandusky, Ohio, Oct. 23, 1939; s. Raymond A. and Rowena (Misner) B.; m. Marilyn Smith, June 2, 1962; 1 child, Amanda Alene. BA, Cedarville (Ohio) Coll., 1963; BS, North Park Coll., Chgo., 1970; MEd, No. Ill. U., 1974; Cert. Adv. Studies, U. Ala., 1979. Asst. registrar Moody Bible Inst., Chgo., 1964-69; prin., athletic dir. Wheaton Christian Acad., West Chicago, Ill., 1970-74; dept. chmn. edn. Southeastern Bible Coll., Birmingham, Ala., 1974-83; fund raising staff Moody Bible Inst., 1985-89; prin. Covenant Christian Sch., St. Louis, 1989—. Editor: Competent Teaching, 1980. Pres. Southland Christian Athletic Conf., 1982. Mem. Mo. Ednl. Leadership, St. Louis Prin. Acad., Assn. Christian Sch. Adminstrs., Assn. for Supervision and Curriculum Devel., St. Louis Basketball Ofcls. Assn. Home: 239 Clarkson Pines Ln Ellisville MO 63011 Office: Twin Oaks Christian Sch 1230 Big Bend Twin Oaks MO 63021 *Education is a life long activity that God uses to equip man to minister for him. May my life be his completely.*

BIERMAN, CHARLES JOHN, evangelist, alumni affairs director; b. Middletown, Ohio, Nov. 13, 1938; s. Charles Edward and Helen Ruth (Riddle) B.; m. Joyce Mae Lawson, Dec. 24, 1963; children: Kimberly, Krista, Robert, Karin. BA, Bob Jones U., 1961, MA, 1963, MDiv, 1965; DD, San Francisco Bapt. Theol., Seminary, 1979. Pastor First Bapt. Ch., Westfield, N.Y., 1965-71; evangelist Greenville, S.C., 1972—; dir. of alumni Bob Jones U., Greenville, 1972—; trustee Bethany Fellowship Ind. Bapt., Western N.Y., 1967-71, youth rally dir., 1968-71; bd. dirs. Evangelism, Inc., Taylors, S.C., 1990—. Contbr. articles to profl. jours. Vol. adv. coun., Greenville, 1990—, exec. com. 1991. Recipient Disting. Ministry award Lucerne (Calif.) Christian Conf. Ctr., 1982, Charles Haddon Spurgeon award Maranatha Bapt. Bible Coll., Elkton, Md., 1984. Mem. Bob Jones Alumni Assn. Office: Bob Jones Univ Alumni Assn 1700 Wade Hampton Blvd Greenville SC 29614 *Time is brief and eternity is forever. Yet most men make their choices and live with only time in view and give no thought to eternity and that they must one day face God.*

BIERMANN, TODD ALLEN, minister; b. Lethbridge, Alta., Can., Aug. 15, 1964; came to U.S., 1965; s. Herbert Lewis and Karen Kay (Quinn) B. BA, Concordia Tchrs. Coll., Seward, Nebr., 1986; MDiv, Concordia Sem., St. Louis, 1990. Ordained to ministry Luth. Ch.-Mo.Synod, 1990. Vicar Trinity Luth. Ch., Palo Alto, Calif., 1988-89; pastor Grace Luth. Ch., Brooklyn Park, Minn., 1990—. Youth counselor City of Brooklyn Park, 1990—. Republican. Home: 7890 83d Ct N Brooklyn Park MN 55445 Office: Grace Luth Ch 6810 Winnetka Ave N Brooklyn Park MN 55428 *The most profound and hopeful thought on life that can ever be expressed is that which can be stated in these three simple words, "He is risen!".*

BIFFI, GIACOMO CARDINAL, archbishop; b. Milan, June 13, 1928. Ordained priest Roman Cah. Ch., 1950. Consecrated bishop of Fidene and aux. of Milan, 1975; archbishop of Bologna, Italy, 1984; created cardinal, 1985. Office: Via Altabella 6, I-40126 Bologna Italy

BIGELOW, SISTER JANE, nun, educator; b. Phila., Jan. 30, 1933; d. Samuel Irvin and Helen A. (Walsh) B. BS, Villanova U., 1961; MA, U. Portland, 1966; cert. in adminstrn., U. Oreg., 1973. Joined Soc. of Holy Child Jesus, 1950. Tchr. Archdiocese of Phila., 1953-62; tchr. Archdiocese of Portland (Oreg.), 1962-70, elem. prin., 1970-79; coord. social ministry St. Elizabeth's Parish, N.Y.C., 1979-80; mem. edn. devel. team Archdiocese of Boston, 1980-84; elem. prin. St. Rose of Lima Sch., Short Hills, N.J., 1984-88, Annunciation Sch., Washington, 1988—; mem. Oreg. State Adv. Commn. Title II, Salem, 1970-73; mem. edn. planning com. Sisters of the Holy CHild, Rosemont, Pa., 1975-76. Trustee Sch. of the Holy Child, Rye, N.Y., 1985-88, Connelly Sch. of the Holy Child, Potomac, Md., 1991—. NSF grantee, 1973. Fellow Nat. Cath. Edn. Assn., Nat. Assn. Supervision and Curriculum Devel., Elem. Sch. Prins. Assn. (chairperson 1989-90, sec. 1990—); mem. N.W. Washington Area Prins. (chairperson 1989—). Avocations: reading, walking. Office: Annunciation Sch 3825 Klingle Place N W Washington DC 20016

BIGELOW, MICHAEL ALLAN, minister; b. Bryn Moore, Pa., Apr. 26, 1959; s. Ralph Paul and Loudonna M. (Fletcher) B.; m. Debra Ellen Brooke, Dec. 31, 1983. BS in Bible Ministries, Manhattan Christian Coll., 1987; postgrad., Emmanuel Sch. Religion, 1987—. Ordained to ministry Christian Chs. and Chs. of Christ, 1987. Min. youth Coun. Grove (Kans.) Christian Ch. of Christ, 1985-87, 1st Christian Ch., Erwin, Tenn., 1989-90; dir. youth and edn. Wataugau Ave Presbyn. Ch., Johnson City, Tenn., 1987-88; med. records clk. Johnson City (Tenn.) Med. Ctr., 1990—. With USN, 1977-83. Recipient Tng. award for religious leadership Order of Eastern Star, 1987. Mem. Delta Epsilon Chi. Republican.

BIGGERS, HOWARD DAVID, minister, contractor; b. Ocilla, Ga., Apr. 13, 1950; s. Benjamin Howard and Betty Ruth (Laminack) B.; m. Donna Jean Anderson, June 6, 1970; children: James David, Donna Rebecca. Student, Albany (Ga.) Vocat. Tech. Sch., 1968, Extension Edn. of Ga. Bapt., 1982-88. Ordained to ministry So. Bapt. Conv., 1981; lic. electrician, 1981. Pastor Dorminy's Mill Bapt. Ch., Fitzgerald, Ga., 1981-89; interim pastor Seville (Ga.) Bapt. Ch., 1990; pastor Pine Grove Bapt. Ch., Lenox, Ga., 1990—; prin. David Biggers Constrn. Co., Fitzgerald, 1975—; del. Ga. Bapt. Conv., 1981—, participant Ga.-Liberia Partnership. Mem. Ben Hill-Irwin Bapt. Assn. (v.p. 1984, mem. nominating com. 1985, chmn. mission com. 1986-87, Ga. Licensed Plumbers. Home: Rte 4 Hwy 129S Fitzgerald GA 31750 Office: Pine Grove Bapt Ch Rte 1 Lenox Hwy Lenox GA 31637

BIGGS, ERVIE GLENN, minister; b. Elk City, Okla., Feb. 23, 1930; s. Bonnie Ervin and Viola Amanda (Cordle) B.; m. Viola Ruth Prewett, Aug. 8, 1953; children: Stephen, Douglas, Timothy, Kevin, David. Diploma, Biola U., 1953; postgrad., San Jose (Calif.) State Coll., 1953-56; cert. in counseling, Narramore Found., Rosemead, Calif., 1971; cert. in emergency med. tech., Coll. Redwoods, 1974. Ordained to ministry Conservative Bapt. Assn. Am., 1961. Pastor Grace Bapt. Ch., Ft. Bragg, Calif., 1961-75, Bethany Bapt. Ch., Stockton, Calif., 1975-77; assoc. pastor Calvary Bapt. Ch., Stockton, 1977-82; pastor Community Bapt. Ch., Summit City, Calif., 1982—; chaplain Calif. Dept. Corrections, Willits, 1962-75. Chmn. Toys for Tots, Ft. Bragg, 1969. Recipient recognition plaque Staff and Men at Chamberlain Creek Facility, 1974. Mem. Conservative Bapt. Assn. No. Calif. (bd. dirs. 1965-77, 88—, rec. sec. 1968-77), Shasta Dam Area Mins. Assn. (pres. 1987-90), Shasta County Evang. Mins. Assn. (pres. 1986-87), Kiwanis (sec. Shasta Dam club 1986-87, pres. 1988-89, chmn. scholarship com. 1987-91, recognition plaque 1989). Home: 3779 Pancake Hill Dr Central Valley CA 96019 Office: Community Bapt Ch 13834 Lake Blvd PO Box 428 Summit City CA 96089 *A person of character will be morally and spiritually strong and pure in the quality of his life. He needs few outside controls because he has learned to guide himself from within.*

BIGGS, LUTHER C., pastor; b. New Orleans, May 15, 1958; s. Clark and Carolyn (Scroggin) B.; m. Anne Marie Madler, May 31, 1981; children: Faith Catherine, Matthew Paul. BA, Concordia Coll., 1980; MDiv, Concordia Sem., St. Louis, 1984. Ordained to ministry Luth. Ch. Assoc. pastor 1st Immanuel Luth. Ch., Cedarburg, Wis., 1984-88; sr. pastor, dir. ministries Messiah Luth. Ch., Lincoln, Nebr., 1988—; dir. Pastor's Prayer Group, Lincoln, 1990—. Author: The Fisherman's N.E.T., 1987, Hey God-Help Me Remember, 1988. Home: 8211 N Hazelwood Lincoln NE 68510 Office: Messiah Luth Ch 1800 S 84th Lincoln NE 68506

BIGLIARDI, MATTHEW PAUL, bishop; b. Charleroi, Pa., Sept. 14, 1920; s. Achille and Regina (Bonaccinni) B.; m. Jeanne C. Gross, Feb. 19, 1949; 1 child, Aidan. B.S., U. Calif., Berkeley, 1950; M.Div., Ch. Div. Sch. of Pacific, 1953, D.D., 1974. Ordained priest Protestant Episcopal Ch., 1954; curate Trinity Ch., Seattle, 1953-55; vicar Emmanuel Ch., Mercer Island, Wash., 1955-60, rector, 1960-74; bishop Diocese of Oreg., Lake Oswego, 1974-86; bishop in charge Convocation of Am. Chs. in Europe, 1988—; Chmn. bd. trustees Good Samaritan Hosp., Portland, Oreg., from 1974, Oreg. Episc. Schs., from 1974. Trustee Columbia council Boy Scouts Am., Portland; trustee Oreg. Heart Assn., Ch. Div. Sch. of Pacific, Berkeley, Calif., all 1977-80, Presiding Bishop's Fund for World Relief. Mem. Sigma Xi, Phi Beta Kappa. Home: PO Box 4783 Carmel CA 93921-4783 Office: The American Cathedral, 23, Ave George V, 75008 Paris France

BIGLIARDI, PATRICIA ANN, minister; b. Jackson, Mich., Aug. 1, 1943; d. Samuel Francis and Mary Cathrine (Tiano) Loria; m. Achille Mathew III, July 31, 1965 (div. Aug. 1977); 1 child, Achille Mathew IV. Communications dir. South Valley Community Ch., Gilroy, Calif., 1989—. Bd. dirs. Vols. Am., San Jose, Calif., 1978-80, Peninsula Women in Advt.. San Jose, 1977-80. Office: South Valley Community Ch 8027 Kern Ave Gilroy CA 95020

BILBO, HAL ANDREW, minister; b. Birmingham, Ala., Jan. 19, 1955; s. Hoyt Helton and Betty Jo (Swint) B.; m. Karen Melinda Aaron, Aug. 27, 1977; children: Ginya Ruth, Sarah Katherine. BBA in Mgmt., Mercer U., Atlanta, 1980; MDiv, Southeastern Bapt. Theol. Sem., 1985, DMin, 1991. Ordained to ministry So. Bapt. Conv., 1983. Assoc. pastor Poston Bapt. Ch., Wallace, N.C., 1982-86; pastor Mt. Holly Bapt. Ch., Burgaw, N.C., 1986—; ch. growth multiplier Bapt. State Conv., Cary, N.C., 1989—; chmn. Wallace/Burgaw Easter Sunrise Svc., Watha, N.C., 1987—. Mem. Wilmington Bapt. Pastors Assn. (pres. 1990—), Pender County Ministers Assn. (pres. 1989-90). Republican. Home: Hwy 117 N Rt 1 Box 1500 Burgaw NC 28425

BILECKI, SISTER MARY LYDIA, nun; b. Chgo., Jan. 24, 1929; d. Albert Alfonse and Marie (Rzepnicki) B. BS in Bus., Quincy Coll., 1963; MA in Econs., Purdue U., 1968; postgrad., various univs. Lic. tchr., Ind., Ill.; joined Sisters of St. Joseph, 1946. Tchr. various schs., Ill. and Colo., 1949-63; tchr. Lourdes High Sch., Chgo., 1963-66, St. Barbara High Sch., Chgo., 1966-67; instr. econs. and acctg. Immaculata Coll., Bartlett, Ill., 1968-69; provincial treas. religious community Immaculata Convent, Bartlett, 1968-71; prin. tchr. St. Thomas Aquinas Sch., Knox, Ind., 1971-83; exec. sec. to cen. bd. Sisters St. Joseph, South Bend, Ind., 1984-86; asst. provincial Sisters St. Joseph, Chgo., 1986-90; dir. mgmt. team, personnel coord. Immaculta Convent, Congl. Home, Bartlett, 1990—; bd. dirs. Ill. Coun. Econ. Edn., 1968-71; adv. bd. Coun. Archdiocesan Social Studies Tchrs., 1967-69; sec. Chgo. Coun. Social Studies, 1971; co-chmn. Devel. Econ. Edn. Program Diocese Gary (Ind.) Schs., 1971-73, co-chmn. social studies edn. curriculum com., 1971-72, chmn. DEEP program, 1973-75, chmn. social studies curriculum com., 1973-76; mem. State Ind. Adoption Com. for Social Studies Textbooks, 1973-74; adv. bd. Social Studies Mag., Nat. Coun. Social Studies, 1975-78. Grantee NSF, 1965,66,67, Ind. Coun. Econ. Edn., 1973, Robert R. Taft Inst. Govt., 1975, 76; U.S. Office Edn. fellow, 1967-68. Mem. Nat. Coun. Social Studies, Nat. Cath. Edn. Assn., Social Studies Suprs. Assn., Nat. Assn. Ch. Personnel Adminstrs., Nat. Assn. Religious Treas., Canon Law Soc. (assoc.), Ind. Coun. Econ. Edn.

BILINSKI, STANLEY MICHAEL, priest; b. Detroit, July 11, 1953; s. Stanley Michael and Clara Emilia (Kronen) B.; m. Deborah Joan Petrosky, Sept. 26, 1986; 1 child, Joshua Mark. BA in Physics, Wayne State U., 1976; MS in Edn., Coll. of St. Rose, 1985. Ordained priest Polish Nat. Cath. Ch., 1979. Deacon Polish Nat. Cath. Ch., Scranton, Pa., 1978-79; pastor Polish Nat. Cath. Ch., St. Francis Parish, Washington, 1979-81, Polish Nat. Cath. Ch., Blessed Virgin Mary Parish, Albany, N.Y., 1981—; nat. chaplain United Youth Assn., Albany, 1982—; prof. Polish Nat. Cath. Ch. Theol. Sem., Scranton, 1987—. Recipient Student award Am. Legion, Detroit, 1968. Home and Office: Polish Nat Cath Ch 359 Clinton Ave Albany NY 12206

BILL, LESTER HENRY, retired minister; b. Wilton Junction, Iowa, Aug. 14, 1910; s. Henry Avery and Mae (Hasbrook) B.; m. Jane Elizabeth Barber, June 1, 1940; children: Carolyn West, Anita Jane, Eileen Marie, Douglas Fremont. BA, Iowa Wesleyan coll., 1937; BST, Boston U., 1940. Pastor Newburyport People's Ch. Meth., Newburyport, Mass., 1939-40; pastor Methodist Ch., Crawfordsville, Iowa, 1940-43, Methodist Circuit, Columbus Junction, Iowa, 1943-45, Methodist Ch., West Liberty, Iowa, 1945-49, Sante Fe Methodist Ch., Ft. Madison, Iowa, 1949-53; minister of outreach Broadway Meth. Ch., Indpls., 1953-63; minister of outreach First Meth. Ch., South Bend, Ind., 1963-67, East Chicago, Ind., 1967-71; pastor Good Shepherd Meth. Ch., Elkhart, Ind., 1971-76; minister of visitation Grace United Meth. Ch., South Bend, 1977-89. Mem. Mayor's Commn. on Human Rights, Indpls., 1955-60, East Chicago, 1968-71, UN Assn., South Bend, 1946—, Pledge of Resistance on Cen. Am., South Bend, 1983—. Recipient Ecumenical Leadership citation Ind. Coun. Churches, 1983-84, Pub. Svc. award UN Assn., 1984, Peace and Justice award John P. Adams Award, 1985, Svc. and Leadership award Human Rights Commn., East Chicago, 1971. Mem. Fellowship of Reconciliation, UN Assn. (pres. 1982-84), Witness for Peace, ACLU, World Fed. Assn., Rotary, Kiwanis. Avocation: world travel. Home: 1015 White Oak Dr South Bend IN 46617

BILLERBECK, JEFFREY GEORGE, clergyman; b. Milw., Oct. 3, 1954; s. James Erwin and Mary June (Wolfe) B.;m. Janet Anderson, Aug. 12, 1979; children: Peter James, Krista Joy. BS, U. Wis., 1980; M Div, Gordon-Conwell Theol. Sem., South Hamilton, Mass., 1983. Protestant chaplain Taunton State Hosp., Dept. Mental Health Mass., 1983-89; dir. pastoral svcs. Meriter Retirement Svcs., Madison, Wis., 1989—; pres., founder Taunton chpt. Alliance for the Mentally Ill, 1985-88. Mem. Assn. for Clin. Pastoral Edn. Office: Meriter Retirement Svcs 110 S Henry St Madison WI 53703

BILLINGS, PEGGY MARIE, religious organization administrator, educator; b. McComb, Miss., Sept. 10, 1928; d. Clement David and Eynes Melissa (Dickerson) B. BS, Millsaps Coll., 1950; MA, Columbia U., 1957; D in Liberal Arts (hon.), Ewha Woman's U., 1986. Clk. Ill. Cen. R.R., McComb, 1947; instr. tennis YWCA, Jackson, Miss., 1950; missionary Republic of Korea, 1952-63; ch. exec. Global Ministries of the United Meth. Ch., N.Y.C., 1963—; vis. prof. religion and society Chandler Sch. Theology, 1972-73; lectr. in world christianity Yale Divinity Sch., 1989. Author: The Waiting People, In No One's Pocket, Paradox and Promise in Human Rights, Fire Beneath the Frost: Korea. Chairperson N.Am. Coalition for Human Rights in Republic of Korea, 1979-; mem. adv. bd. Ctr. for Internat. Policy, 1984-, Global Edn. Assocs., 1989-; bd. dirs. Ctr. Constitutional Rights, 1979-89. Recipient Human Rights award Korean Christina Scholars Assn. N.Am., Pub. Welfare medal Republic of Korea, 1963, Ball award Methodist Fedn. for Social Action, 1989. Democrat. Methodist. Avocations: tennis, reading. Home: Rt 1 Box 381 Trumansburg NY 14886

BILLMAN, FRANK HENRY, minister; b. Phila., Aug. 18, 1952; s. Walter Emil and Mabel Evelyn (Beegle) B.; m. Margaret Anne Montgomery, June 7, 1975; children: Luke Jason, Nicholas Shawn. BA magna cum laude, Houghton Coll., 1975; MDiv cum laude, Trinity Evangel. Divinity Sch., Deerfield, Ill., 1978, ThM, 1979; D of Ministry, Eastern Bapt. Theol. Seminary, Phila., 1988. Ordained to ministry United Meth. Ch. as deacon, 1976, as elder, 1980. Pastor Tabor United Meth. Ch., Woxall, Pa., 1979—; adv. coun. Manna Ministries, Nashville, 1983—. Office: Tabor United Meth Church 2209 Hendricks Station Rd Woxall PA 18979

BILLY, DENNIS JOSEPH, priest; b. N.Y.C., Aug. 26, 1953; s. Michael and Lillian (Miano) B. AB, Dartmouth Coll., 1975; MRE, 1979; MDiv, Mt. St. Alphonsus Sem., 1981; ThD, Harvard U., 1985; MA, U. Toronto, Ont., Can., 1987; MMRSc, U. Louvain, 1988. Ordained to ministry Roman Cath. Ch., 1980. Adj. prof. Coll. Notre Dame, Balt., 1985-86, Loyola Coll., Balt., 1986; prof. Accademia Alfonsiana, Rome, 1988—. Contbr. articles to theol. publs. Mem. Cath. Theol. Soc. Am., Am. Cath. Hist. Soc., Am. Soc. Ch. History, Medieval Acad. Am., Am. Hist. Assn. Avocations: reading, music, jogging, sports. Home: Via Merulana 31, CP 2458, 00100 Rome Italy Office: Acad Alfonsiana, Via Merulana 31, CP 2458, 00100 Rome Italy

BILOCK, JOHN M., bishop; b. McAdoo, Pa., June 20, 1916. Grad., St. Procopius Coll. and Sem., Ill. Ordained priest Roman Catholic Ch., 1946. Vicar gen. Byzantine archdiocese of Munhall, 1969; ordained titular bishop of Pergamum and Munhall Pitts., from 1973; aux. bishop Pitts. Byzantine Diocese, 1977—. Office: Chancery Office 54 Riverview Ave Pittsburgh PA 15214

BIMLER, RICHARD WILLIAM, religious organization administrator; b. Hillside, Ill., Aug. 28, 1940; m. Hazel Reichmann, June 10, 1961; children: Diane Bimler Cillick, Bob, Mike. BA in Theology, Valparaiso U., 1963; MA in Counseling and Guidance, U. Mo., 1972; postgrad., Concordia Coll., U. Houston; LittD, Christ Coll., Irvine, Calif., 1988. Youth dir. St. Andrew Luth. Ch., Houston, 1963-68; dir. edn. Trinity Luth. Ch., Mission, Kans., 1968-73; asst. exec. sec. dist. svcs. Luth. Ch.-Mo. Synod, St. Louis, 1977-79, exec. dir. youth svcs., 1979-89; exec. dir. for planning coun. for mission and ministry, 1989-91; pres. Wheat Ridge Found., Chgo., 1991—; instr. Parent Effectiveness Tng., Youth Effectiveness Tng.; various positions youth gatherings; cons. seminar leader Luth. Ch. Australia, 1985, United Bible Soc., Budapest, 1988; youth cons. Author: Pray, Praise and Hooray, 1972, 77 Ways to Involve in the Church, 1976, Lord I Want To Celebrate, 1980, The New You, 1983, Grand Opening: Prayers From the Empty Tomb, 1983, Celebrating Saints, 1986; Youth Meeting Guide (series) 1984 (Gold Medallion 1985); contbr. articles to profl. jours. Mem. pres.'s coun. Valparaiso U. Mem. Luth. Edn. Assn. (instr., former pres.), Religious Conf. Mgmt. Assn., Am. Bible Soc. (hon. lifetime bd. mem.). Office: 104 S Michigan Ave Chicago IL 60603

BINDER, JOHN, minister, religious organization executive; b. Can., Nov. 10, 1930; s. Henry Binder and Katherine B.; m. Barbara Weisser, Aug. 30, 1960; children: Laurette, Douglas, Brian. Student, Sioux Falls Coll., 1952-54; B.A., Augustana Coll., 1956; B.D., N.Am. Bapt. Sem., 1959; postgrad., No. Ill. U., 1967-69. Ordained to ministry N.Am. Conf.,1959. Pastor Emmanuel Bapt. Ch., Morris, Man., Can., 1959-60; youth dir. N.Am. Bapt. Conf., Forest Park, Ill., 1960-66, editor Bapt. Herald Monthly mag., 1967-71, stewardship and communications sec., 1971-79; exec. dir. N.Am. Bapt. Conf., Villa Park, Ill., 1979—. Mem. Religious Pub. Relations Council, Chgo. Fund Raising Soc. Office: NAm Bapt Conf 1 S 210 Summit Ave Oakbrook Terrace IL 60181

BINDER, PAUL JULIUS, minister; b. Seattle, Dec. 3, 1928; s. August Edward Sr. and Amanda Dorothea (Horstmann) B.; m. Margaret Louise Harding, Oct. 13, 1956; children: Paul H., Carol A., Steven E. BSEE, Purdue U., 1950; MDiv, Eden Theol. Sem., St. Louis, 1967, D of Ministry, 1989; postgrad., Webster U., 1981-82. Ordained to ministry United Ch. of Christ, 1967. Pastor 1st Congl. United Ch. of Christ, Iowa Falls, Iowa, 1967-73, Clinton, Iowa, 1973-80; supt. Emmaus Home, St. Charles, Mo., 1980-82; sr. pastor St. Andrew United Ch. of Christ, Sarasota, Fla., 1982—; vice moderator Iowa conf. United Ch. of Christ, Des Moines, 1973-74, moderator, 1974-75. Pres. Redstone Group Home, Clinton, 1985-90. Mem. Acad. Parish Clergy. Home: 2249 Florinda St Sarasota FL 34231 Office: St Andrew United Ch of Christ 6908 Beneva Rd Sarasota FL 34238

BINGHAM, MICHAEL LEE, radio station manager; b. El Paso, Tex., Sept. 15, 1957; s. Arles L. and Ann (Hicks) B.; m. T. Rene Wilson, Dec. 21, 1980; children: Paul Michael, James Daniel. BA, Palm Beach Atlantic Coll., 1979. Announcer Sta. WLIZ, Lake Worth, Fla., 1976-78; staff announcer Sta. WRMB, Moody Bible Inst., Boynton Beach, Fla., 1979-83, asst. mgr., 1983-88, station dir., 1988—. Mem. Nat. Assn. Broadcasters, Nat. Religious Broadcasters (treas. S.E. chpt. 1988-90, pres. 1990—). Office: Sta WRMB 1511 W Boynton Beach Blvd Boynton Beach FL 33436

BINGHAM, WALTER D., clergyman; b. Memphis, June 3, 1921; s. Willie and Lena (Allen) B.; m. Rebecca T. Bingham; stepchild, Gail Elaine Bingham. BA, Talladega (Ala.) Coll., 1945; MDiv, Howard U., 1948, postgrad., 1948-49; DD, Christian Theol. Sem., Indpls., 1969; LHD, Drury Coll., Springfield, Mo., 1972; LLD, Transylvania U., Lexington, Ky., 1973. Ordained to ministry Disciples of Christ Ch., 1947. Campus minister, instr. religion Jarvis Christian Coll., Hawkins, Tex., 1949-57; minister Pine St. Christian Ch., Tulsa, 1957-61, 3d Christian Ch., Louisville, 1961—; v.p. Christian Ch. Commn. Jefferson County, Ky., 1965-66; pres. Christian Ch. Commn. Jefferson County, 1978-81; mem. gen. bd. Christian Ch., 1979-87, chair coun. on Christian unity, 1981-85; pastor ecumenical Third Christian Ch., Louisville, 1986—; pres. Christian Ch. Ky., 1966-67; moderator Disciples of Christ Ch., U.S. and Can., 1971-73; mem. gov. bd. Nat. Council Ch., 1969-73; Christian Ch. del. Consultation on Ch. Union, 1968—; mem. nat. steering com. on covenant Christian Ch.-United Ch. of Christ, 1982-85; fraternal visitor for Christian Ch. to Japan, Hong Kong, Thailand, India, 1972; del. 5th Assembly, World Council Chs., Nairobi, Kenya, 1975, 6th Assembly, World Coun. Chs., Vancouver, B.C., Can., 1983. Mem. Louisville and Jefferson Air Bd. Citizens Com., 1971-74; bd. dirs. Vols. Am., 1965-71; trustee Jarvis Christian Coll., 1971-75, Lexington Theol. Sem., 1969-89, elected emeritus, 1990. Recipient Outstanding Community Leadership award Phi Beta Sigma, 1969; named Ky. Col., 1967, Pastor of Yr. Sta. WLOU, 1970, Disting. Citizen Louisville, 1971, Patron of Christian Unity, Disciples of Christ Coun. on Christian Unity; The Walter D. Bingham Leadership award Scholarship named in his honor Lexington Theol. Sem., 1990. Mem. NAACP, Urban League, Omega Psi Phi. Home: 3608 Domesnil St Louisville KY 40211 Office: 3900 W Broadway Louisville KY 40211

BINGHAM, WILLIAM ALLEN, minister; b. Washington, Mar. 22, 1962; s. William L. and Annette P. (Patton) B.; m. Cynthia Lee, Aug. 12, 1989. BS in Engring., N.C. State U., 1988; MDiv, Drew U., 1991. Ordained to ministry Meth. Ch. as deacon, 1990. Project dir. Inst. Cultural Affairs, Nairobi, Kenya, 1983-84; rsch. asst. analytical instrument facility N.C. State U., Raleigh, 1986-88; student asst. min. Bloomingdale (N.J.) United Meth. Ch., 1988-90; asst. to dir. Drew Inst. for Archeol. Rsch., Madison, N.J., 1990-91; pastor Rehoboth-Harris Chapel United Meth. Ch., Henderson, N.C., 1991—; coord. statewide student conf.-N.C. Campus Ministries, Raleigh, 1987-88; mem. univ. planning com. Drew U., Madison, N.J., 1988-90, univ. senate, 1988-90, dean's search com., 1990-91). Recipient Elaine Welker Willis award Mu Beta Psi-Alpha chpt., 1988; Ezra Squier Tipple scholar, Drew U., 1988-90, George R. Warren scholar, 1991, William S. Pilling traveling fellow, 1991. Mem. United Meth. Rural Fellowship, Order St. Luke. Office: Rte 8 Box 279 Henderson NC 27536

BINKLEY, CHARLOTTE KAY, radio station official; b. Lima, Ohio, Dec. 7, 1942; d. Gerald Chester and June Eileen (Mertz) Miller; m. Stephen Binkley, Aug. 18, 1962; children: Angela, Andrew. BS in Edn., Ft. Wayne Bible Coll., 1965; MS in Edn., Ind. U., Ft. Wayne, 1973. Lic. tchr., Ind. Tchr. DeKalb County Schs., Auburn, Ind., 1965-67, Ft. Wayne Community Coll., 1968-73; prof. Ft. Wayne Bible Coll., 1973-76; mgr., on-air personality Sta. WBCL, Ft. Wayne, 1976—. Mem. Nat. Religious Broadcasters (bd. dirs.). Republican. Office: Sta WBCL 1025 W Rudisill Blvd Fort Wayne IN 46807

BINKLEY, OLIN TRIVETTE, clergyman, seminary president emeritus; b. Harmony, N.C., Aug. 4, 1908; s. Joseph and Minnie (Trivette) B.; m. Pauline Eichmann, Aug. 24, 1933; children—Pauline Edith, Janet Margaret. A.B. magna cum laude, Wake Forest Coll., 1928; Th.B., So. Baptist Theol. Sem., 1930; D.D., Wake Forest (N.C.) Coll., 1951, U.N.C., 1964; B.D., Yale, 1931, Ph.D., 1933; D.Humanities, Campbell Coll., 1973. Ordained to ministry Bapt. Ch., 1928; asso. pastor Calvary Bapt. Ch., New Haven, 1931-33; pastor Chapel Hill (N.C.) Bapt. Ch., 1933-38; lectr. sociology U. N.C., 1937-38; head dept. religion Wake Forest Coll., 1938-44; asso. prof., acting head dept. ethics and sociology So. Bapt. Theol. Sem., 1944-46, prof., head dept., 1946-52; prof. Christian sociology and ethics Southeastern Bapt. Theol. Sem., 1952—, dean, 1958-63, pres., 1963-74, pres. emeritus, 1974—; vis. fellow Yale Divinity Sch., New Haven, 1951; Dir. Central Carolina Bank.; Pres. N.C. Com. Social Service, 1957-58, recipient Social Service award, 1967; Pres. bd. mgrs. Louisville Children's Agy., 1948-50; trustee Ministry Studies Bd., Children's Homes Soc. N.C., Bapt. Children's Homes N.C., Keesee Ednl. Fund, Davis Hosp. Author: Frontiers for Christian Youth, 1942, From Victory Unto Victory, 1945, The Churches and the Social Conscience, 1948, How to Study the Bible, 1969. Mem. Am. Assn. Theol. Schs. (pres.; commn. rsch. and counsel), Am. Sociol. Soc., So Bapt. Conv. (Christian life and social svc. commns.), Louisville Torch Club, Rotary (past pres.), Phi Beta Kappa. Home: 415 Durham Rd PO Box 311 Wake Forest NC 27587

BIONDI, LAWRENCE, university administrator, priest; b. Chgo., Dec. 15, 1938; s. Hugo and Albertina (Marchetti) B. B.A., Loyola U., Chgo., 1962, Ph.L., 1964, M.Div., 1971, S.T.L., 1971; M.S., Georgetown U., 1966, Ph.D. in Sociolinguistics, 1975. Ordained priest Roman Cath. Ch., 1970. Joined Soc. Jesus; asst. prof. sociolinguistics Loyola U., Chgo., 1974-79, assoc. prof., 1979-81, prof., 1982-87, dean Coll. Arts and Scis., 1980-87; pres. St. Louis U., 1987—. Author: The Italian-American Child: His Sociolinguistic Acculturation, 1975, Poland's Solidarity Movement, 1984; editor: Poland's Church-State Relations in the 1980s, 1980, Spain's Church-State Relations, 1982. Trustee Xavier U., 1981-87, Loyola Coll., Balt., 1988—, Santa Clara U., 1988—, Kenrick-Glennon Sem., 1988—, St. Louis U., 1982—, Loyola U., Chgo., 1988—; bd. dirs. Epilepsy Found. Am., 1985—, Civic Progress, St. Louis, 1987—, Regional Commerce and Growth Assn., 1987—, Mo. Bot. Garden, 1987—, Harry S Truman Inst. for Nat. and Internat. Affairs, 1987—. Mellon grantee, 1974, 75, 76, 82. Mem. Linguistic Soc. Am., MLA, Am. Anthrop. Assn. Democrat. Office: St Louis U 221 N Grand Blvd Saint Louis MO 63103

BIRD, ANDREW REID, JR., retired minister; b. Laurel, Md., July 14, 1909; s. Andrew Reid and Lisette Fries (Moore) B.; m. Ellen Augusta Leech, Sept. 12, 1942; children: Ellen Fries, Andrew III, James Russell, Timothy Edgeworth, Pamelia Brooke Sanderlin, John Fielding. AB, Davidson Coll., 1931; BD, Union Theol. Sem., 1938; DD (hon.), Davis and Elkins (W.Va.) Coll., 1946; LLD, Marshall U., 1964. Ordained to ministry Presbyn. Ch. (U.S.A.), 1938. Pastor Wytheville (Va.) Presbyn. Ch., 1939-43; pastor 1st Presbyn. Ch., Huntington, W.Va., 1943-63; pastor 1st Presbyn. Ch., Norfolk, Va., 1963-79, ret., 1979; interim pastor Blacksburg (Va.) Presbyn. Ch., 1980, First Presbyn. Ch., Nashville, 1981, St. Johns Presbyn. Ch., Jacksonville, Fla., 1982-83; pastor advisor Nat. Men's Coun. Presbyn. Ch. USA, Louisville, 1986-87; mem. Bd. of Christian Edn., Richmond, 1951-60; chmn. bd. trustees Union Sem., Richmond, 1955-61, Davis and Elkins Coll., 1954-62, also hon. trustee, 1962—; mem. permanent judicial com. gen. assembly Presbyn. Ch. (USA), Atlanta, 1972-78; mem. exec. com. Assembly Mens Coun./Ch. U.S., Atlanta, 1954-62; mem. steering com. Presbyn. Men's Assembly, Louisville, 1991. Bd. dirs. YMCA, Huntington, 1957-60; mem. Community Welfare Coun., Huntington, 1956-59, mem. exec. com. Billy Graham Crusade, Norfolk, 1974. With U.S. Army, 1927-31. Home: 23 Butternut Way Sterling VA 22170

BIRD, CHARLES MARK, music and youth minister; b. Dumas, Tex., May 14, 1955; s. Charles Virgil and Della May (Bowling) B.; m. Donna Jean Waldrop, Sept. 4, 1976; children: Melinda May, Charles Jacob. BA in Religious Edn., Hardin-Simmons, 1981. Music dir. Tyrrell Park Bapt. Ch., Beaumont, Tex., 1976-79; music, youth dir. East Cisco Bapt. Ch., Cisco, Tex., 1980-83, First Bapt. Ch., Raymondville, Tex., 1983—. Home: 682 W Riggs Raymondville TX 78580 *Even though the world is rapidly changing the best way to approach life is still the same as it has always been: Live your life following God's law, all to the glory of His Son, Jesus.*

BIRELEY, MARLENE KAY, educator, psychologist, consultant; b. Edgerton, Ohio, Mar. 11, 1936; d. Forest William and Pauline May (Faber) Bergman; m. Michael Ewing Bireley, Nov. 21, 1959 (div. Feb. 1981); children: Laura Jo Weaver, Christina. BS in Elem. Edn., Bowling Green State U., 1957; MA in Spl. Edn., The Ohio State U., 1961, PhD in Psychology of Exceptional Children, 1966. Lic. psychologist, Ohio. Elem. and learning disabilities tchr. Worthington (Ohio) Pub. Schs., 1957-60; spl. edn. tchr. Columbus (Ohio) Pub. Schs., 1960-61; instr., then assist. prof. The Ohio State U., Columbus, 1962-63, 68-69; sch. psychologist Franklin County Schs., Columbus, 1963-68; assoc. prof., assoc. dean. Wright State U., Dayton, Ohio, 1969-76, 78-82, prof. coll. edn. and human services, 1976—; psychologist, pvt. cons., State of Ohio, 1974—. Co-producer: I Can Learn; contbr. articles to profl. jours. Mem. Ohio Assn. for Learning Disabilities (Talisman award 1976), Nat. Assn. Sch. Psychologists (charter, sec. 1971-72), Ohio Sch. Psychologists Assn. (Clyde Bartlett award 1983), Ohio Assn. Gifted Children (disting. service award 1986). Avocations: travel, theater. Office: Wright State U 373 Millett Hall Dayton OH 45435

BIRKENFELD, SISTER ROSE MARIA, religion educator, nun; b. Amarillo, Tex., Sept. 13, 1931; d. John Simon and Dora Elizabeth (Moore) B. BS in Edn., U. Mo., 1974; BA in Religious Studies, Coll. St. Scholastica, 1976; MA in Theology, St. Mary's U., 1985. Religion coord. St. Joseph Ch., Pilot Grove, Mo., 1969-73; parish min. St. Mary's Ch., Shelbina, Mo., 1976-87; dir. religious edn. St. Peter's Ch., Marshall, Mo., 1987-89; religion coord. St. Joseph Ch., Pilot Grove, Mo., 1989—; sub-prioress Our Lady of Peace Convent, Columbia, Mo., 1987—. Home: 1511 Wilson Ave Columbia MO 65201-5992 Office: St Joseph Ch 403 Harris Rt 2 Pilot Grove MO 65276-9500

BIRKHEAD, THOMAS LARRY, minister; b. Owensboro, Ky., Nov. 20, 1941; s. Thomas Butler and Ollie Mae (Brown) B.; m. Melva Jean Young, Oct. 18, 1968; 1 child, David. AB, Western Ky. U., 1963; MDiv, So. Bapt. Theol. Sem., 1968. Ordained to ministry So. Bapt. Conv., 1966. Pastor Mt. Vernon Bapt. Ch., Calhoun, Ky., 1966-69, Sorgho Bapt. Ch., Owensboro, 1969-73, Spottsville (Ky.) Bapt. Ch., 1973-82, Yelvington Bapt. Ch., Maceo, Ky., 1982-86, Ghent (Ky.) Bapt. Ch., 1986—; mem. exec. bd. Ky. Bapt. Conv., Middletown, 1988-91. Co-author: Ghent Baptist Church History 1800-1990, 1990. Mem. Carroll County Mins. Assn. (treas. 1989—). Democrat. Home: 201 Ferry St Ghent KY 41045 Office: Ghent Bapt Ch PO Box 457 Ghent KY 41045

BIRKITT, JAMES NELSON, JR., minister, school administrator; b. Petersburg, Va., May 8, 1956; s. James Nelson Sr. and Carol Jean (Keener) B. BA, Washington Bible Coll., 1979; postgrad., Capitol Bible Sem., Lanham, Md., 1980. Ordained to ministry So. Bapt. Conv., 1981. Sr. min. Carmel Bapt. Ch., Ruther Glen, Va., 1983—; adminstr. Carmel Christian Sch., Ruther Glen, 1986—; pres. The Birkitt Group, Inc., Ruther Glen, 1990—; v.p. Christian Enterprises, Inc., Ashland, Va., 1979—; mgr. Christian radio Sta. WIVE, Ashland, 1980-83. Mem. Hanover Rep. Party, Ashland, 1973-83, Caroline County (Va.) ARC, 1989-91, Napoleon Hill Found.; bd. dirs. Carmel Day Care Ctr., Caroline, 1985—. Mem. NAACP (life), Nat. Assn. Ind. Paralegals, Assn. Christian Schs. Internat., Caroline C. of C. Home: PO Box 370 Ruther Glen VA 22546 Office: Carmel Bapt Ch Rte 1 Box 237-E Ruther Glen VA 22546

BIRKNER, HANS-JOACHIM, theology educator; b. Altenburg, Germany, May 9, 1931; s. Walter and Marie (Brambach) B.; m. Erika Lorenz, Mar. 13, 1954; children: Hans-Michael, Thomas, Dorothea, Daniel. ThD, U. Göttingen, 1959. Lectr. U. Göttingen (Fed. Republic Germany), 1962-69; prof. systematic theology U. Kiel (Fed. Republic Germany), 1969—, dir. Inst. for Systematic Theology, 1969-91, dir. Schleiermacher-Forschungsstelle, 1969—. Author: Spekulation und Heilsgeschichte, 1959, Schleiermachers Christliche Sittenlehre, 1964, Protestantismus in Wandel, 1971, Theologie und Philosophie, 1974;editor: Schleiermacher, Kritische Gesamtausgabe, 1980—. Lutheran. Home: Goethestrasse 8, D-2300 Kiel Federal Republic of Germany Office: U Kiel, Theol Inst, Olshausenstrasse 40, D-2300 Kiel Federal Republic of Germany

BIRKS, MICHAEL LYNN, minister; b. Larkspur, Calif., Mar. 9, 1958; s. Robert Lynn and Marilyn June (Petrie) B.; m. Nancy Delores Asquith, Jan. 5, 1991. BA, Christian Heritage Coll., 1981; MDiv., Western Conservative Bapt Sem., 1985. Missionary pastor N.W. Conservative Bapt. Assn., Vancouver, Wash., 1985-89; sr. pastor First Bapt. Ch., Dayton, Oreg., 1989—; summer missionary to Ea. Europe, Slavic Gospel Assn., Wheaton, Ill., summer 1979. Fire dept. chaplain Dist. 5 Clark County, Wash., 1988-89, Dayton (Oreg.) Rural Fire Dist., 1990— (named Fireman of Yr. 1990). Mem. Conservative Bapt. Assn. Am. Office: First Bapt Ch 301 Main Dayton OR 97114 *As Christian leaders of the 1990s, our greatest challenge is communicating the unchangeable word of God to a changing world. To accomplish this task, we need first to convincingly live what we preach, then preach convincingly God's truth in love.*

BIRNBAUM, JOAN WELKER, religious foundation executive; b. Oil City, Pa., Apr. 26, 1923; d. George Ernest and Josephine Wilson (Powell) Welker; m. Theodore Birnbaum, Jan. 8, 1949 (div. 1977); children: Lyuba, Margaret Jane, L. Crispin. B.A. in Econs., Wellesley Coll., 1945; postgrad. Northwestern U. Grad. Sch. Bus. Adminstrn., summer 1945, Nat. Planned Giving Inst., 1979, Philanthropy Tax Inst. Jr. acct. Price, Waterhouse and Co., N.Y.C., 1945-50; sec. to asst. treas. Rockefeller Found., N.Y.C., 1950; acct. Rye Youth Coun., N.Y., 1976-84; exec. dir. Mamaroneck/Larchmont LIFE Ctr., N.Y., 1973; assoc. dir. vols. United Hosp., Port Chester, N.Y., 1974; bus. mgr. Burke Rehab. Ctr. Day Hosp., White Plains, N.Y., 1974-78; planned giving officer Save the Children Fedn., Inc., Westport, Conn., 1979-82; exec. dir. N.Y.-Conn. Found. of United Meth. Ch., White Plains, 1982—. Bd. dirs. Rye United Fund, sec., mem. nominating com.; elder, deacon pres. Women's Assn. Rye Presbyterian Ch.; chmn. maj. reunion fund campaign Wellesley Coll. Class, 1980-85, chmn. reunion, 1975, 90, class historian, 1965—, admissions chmn. for Wellesley in Westchester Club; bd. dirs., pres. Planned Parenthood of Eastern Westchester; pres. Rye Family Svc.; telephone listener and source of referral Rye/Larchmont/Mamaroneck Hot Line; treas., exec. com. Rye Youth Coun.; sec., treas., v.p., pres. 15th Twig of United Hosp., also bd. dirs.; past pres. Rye High Sch. Mothers' Guild, chmn. 1st direct solicitation fund drive; bd. dirs. Woman's Club of Rye, pres. jr. sect.; membership chmn., bd. dirs. Midland Sch. of Rye (voted Parent of Yr.). Mem. Nat. Assn. United Meth. Founds. (treas. 1983-87), Planned Giving Group of Greater N.Y. (v.p. 1983-84, pres. 1984-85), Internat. Assn. Fin. Planners, Devel. Assn. of So. Conn. (chmn. program com. 1983-84), Nat. Soc. Fund Raising Execs., Assn. Westchester Devel. Officers. Republican. Presbyterian. Clubs: Wellesley (South Conn.), Wellesley Fairfield Villages. Avocations: silversmithing, handweaving, piano, guitar, Great Books.

BIRNBAUM, LUCIA CHIAVOLA, historian, educator; b. Kansas City, Mo., Jan. 3, 1924; d. Salvatore and Kate (Cipolla) Chiavola; m. Wallace Birnbaum, Feb. 3, 1946; children—Naury, Marc, Stefan. AB, U. Calif., Berkeley, 1948, MA, 1950, PhD, 1964. Lectr., U. Calif., Berkeley, 1963-64, rsch. assoc., 1982-83, 86; asst. prof. history San Francisco State U., 1964-69; adj. prof. San Francisco State U., 1976-78; mem. faculty Feminist Inst., Berkeley, 1981—; vis. scholar Grad. Theol. Union, 1984-85. Soroptimist fellow, 1955; affiliated scholar Inst. for Research on Women and Gender, Stanford U., 1986—; Disting. woman scholar U. Calif., Davis, 1987; guest lectr. U. Sydney, Australia, 1989, U. Melbourne, Australia, 1989, U. di Padua, 1990; lectr. Calif. Coll. Arts and Crafts, Oakland, 1991. Recipient Anniversary award San Francisco State U., 1988. Mem. PEN Am. Ctr., Orgn. Am. Historians, Am. Italian Hist. Assn. (pres. Western Regional Chpt. 1978-82), Nat. Women's Studies Assn., Center for Women and Religion of Grad. Theol. Union, Women's Party for Survival. Author: La Religione e le Donne Siculo Americane, 1981, Liberazione della Donna: Feminism in Italy, 1986 (Am. Book award 1987), also articles. Home: 349 Gravatt Dr Berkeley CA 94705 *We are living in times of great peril and extraordinary possibility. The most hopeful variable, perhaps, is that the silent of the earth--women-- have begun to speak aloud, to stop careening madness, and to turn the earth towards life.*

BIRNBROOK, LEROY ALLAN, minister, small business owner; b. Lincoln, Nebr., Mar. 2, 1940; s. Bertram Leroy and Phariaba Bernice (Evans) B.; m. Norma Jean Vining, June 14, 1963; children: Roy Dean, Matthew Lee, André Allan. Student, Biola U., 1957-58, Am. Bible Coll., 1959-60, Bartlesville Wesleyan Coll., 1961-62, 62-63, Del Mar Coll., 1965-66; DD (hon.), Coll. of the Rockies, 1969. Ordained to ministry Wesleyan Ch., 1968. Pastor Christian Bible Ch., Lincoln, Nebr., 1958-60; pianoist, singer pub. rels. Ambs. Quartet, Bartlesville, 1961-62, 62-63; pastor Borger (Tex.) Pilgrim Ch., 1963, 1st Pilgrim Ch., Corpus Christi, Tex., 1963-66, First Wesleyan Ch., Yakima, Wash., 1966-68, The Wesleyan Ch., Stratton, Nebr., 1968-69; evangelist The Wesleyan Ch., Marion, Ind., 1969-70, gen. evangelist, 1975-78; pastor The Wesleyan Ch. and Congl. Christian Ch., Lincoln, Kans., 1970-75, Emmanuel Ch., Vesper, Kans, 1970-75; interim pastor Wesleyan Ch. of the Comforter, Dalhart, Tex., 1978; tchr., adminstr. Miracle Life Acad., Dalhart, 1979; pastor First Nazarene Ch., Lafayette, La., 1979-80, Miracle Life Ctr. Fellowship, Lafayette, 1983-84; tchr., adminstr. Miracle Life Christian Sch., New Orleans and Terrytown, La., 1985-89; pastor, evangelist Miracle Life Lighthouse, Westwego, La., 1990—; radio preacher, singer Miracle Life Hour, 1960-70; piano technician, acting store mgr. Korten Music Co., Yakima, 1966-67; piano technician A1 Piano Tech., Yakima, 1967-68, Birnbrook Piano Svc., Stratton, 1968-69, Vaughan Music Co., Holdredge, Nebr., 1968-70, Birnbrook Piano Tuning Svc., Lincoln, 1970-75, Piano Tech./Birnbrook Piano Svc., Mulvane, Kans., 1975-77, Piano Tech., Ullyses, Kans., 1977-78, Dalhart, 1979, Crowley and Lafayette, 1980-84; piano technician and computer svcs. profl. A1 Piano Tech. and Electronics, Harvey, La., 1985—; dispatcher Minuteman Temporary Svcs., Lafayette, 1979-80; disk jockey, news dir., AM stas. ops. mgr., pub. affairs dir. Sta. KAJN-FM, Crowley, 1980-84; tchr., supr. Assembly Christian Sch., Lafayette, 1981-82; disk jockey, sales mgr., radio sta. ops. mgr., news and pub. affairs dir. Sta. KAGY-AM, Port Sulphur, La., 1984-85; ins. salesman Terry Gardner & Assocs., Gretna, La., 1987-88. Recs. include albums Volunteer for Jesus, 1961, I Feel Good!, The Miracles on Tour, 1979; songs include How Long Will It Be?, He Came, It's Pouring Down!, (with others Quicken Me!, Jesus Cares; author numerous cassette sermons. Active Operation Rescue, United for Life, Heartbeat; trustee Coll of the Rockies,

Denver, 1965-75. Mem. Miracle Life Ch. Soc., Miracle Life Evang. Assn. (exec. dir. 1963—), Wesleyan-Holiness Renewal Fellowship. Republican. Home: 204 Dale Ave PO Box 696 Harvey LA 70059 Office: 605 Lapalco Blvd Ste D-417 Terrytown LA 70056-7306 *If I never preach another sermon or sing another song, God, let me do something that will really make a difference for good and for You in this world!.*

BIRNEY, DAVID BELL, IV, clergyman; b. New Orleans, Nov. 26, 1929; s. David Bell Birney III and Stella (Walshe) B.; m. Virginia F. Knorr, July 28, 1968; 2 children; BA, Franklin & Marshall Coll., 1955; M Div, Va. Theol. Sem., 1955. Ordained priest, The Episc. Ch., 1955. Priest-in-charge, St. John Ch., York, Pa., 1955-57; vicar All Saints Ch., Hanover, Pa., 1957-63; rector, Mediator Ch., Allentown, Pa., 1963-69; teacher, Bishop Tucker Coll., Mukono, Uganda, 1969-72; tng., planning coord., Botswana, 1973-75; coord., Overseas Ministries, Exec. Council ot The Episc. Ch., 1976-82; bishop, Diocese of Idaho, Boise, from 1982, now assisting bishop, Diocese of Mass., Boston. Office: Episc Diocese of Mass 138 Tremont St Boston MA 02111

BIRNEY, LEROY, minister; b. Dodge City, Kans., Jan. 13, 1942; s. Ralph David and Margaret (McColm) B.; m. Norma Campbell Kew, May 23, 1964; children: Steven, Susana, Sara. BA, U. Kans., 1964; cert., Emmaus Bible Sch., Oak Park, Ill., 1965; MA in New Testament, Trinity Evang. Divinity Sch., 1968, MDiv, 1969; ThD, Internat. Sem., 1987. Ordained to ministry, 1969. Missionary Medellin, Colombia, 1970-74; missionary, founder Hermanos en Cristo Ch., Cartagena, Colombia, 1975-82, also bd. dirs.; missionary, founder Missionary Action, Inc., Cartagena, 1982-84; pres. Missionary Action, Inc., Bradenton, Fla., 1985—; missions pastor Covenant Life Assembly, Bradenton, 1986-88; pres., dir. Facultad Bíblica Bet-el, Tegucigalpa, Honduras, 1987—; bd. dirs. Amistad en Acción, Tegucigalpa; pres. Acción Misionera en Nicaragua, Diriamba, 1988—. Contbr. articles to religious jours. Faculty scholar Trinity Evang. Divinity Sch., 1968, 69; Internat. Harvester ministerial fellow. Mem. Fellowship Christian Assemblies, Assn. Evang. Chs., Am. Soc. Missiology, Phi Beta Kappa. Evangelical. Office: Missionary Action Inc PO Box 1027 Bradenton FL 34206-1027 *The measure of a man's life is not how much he gains, but how much he gives.*

BIRNHOLZ, RICHARD JOSEPH, rabbi; b. Dallas, Feb. 16, 1945; s. Samuel Hans and Elly (Levy) B.; m. Donna Linda Schneider, Dec. 22, 1968; children: Steven, Michael. BA with honors, U. Tex., 1966; B in Hebrew Letters, Hebrew Union Coll.-Jewish Inst. Religion, 1969, MA in Hebrew Lit., 1971. Ordained rabbi, 1971. Asst. rabbi Temple Israel, Memphis, 1971-73; rabbi Beth Israel Congregation, Jackson, Miss., 1973-86; sr. rabbi Congregation Schaarai Zedek, Tampa, Fla., 1986—; bd. dirs. Nat. Assn. Temple Educators, N.Y.C., 1977-81; chmn. Miss. Religious Leadership Conf., Memphis, 1978-80. Contbr. articles to profl. jours. Recipient Samuel Kaminker Meml. award Nat. Assn. Temple Educators/Hebrew Union Coll./Commn. on Jewish Edn., 1977, Nat. Rabbinic award United Jewish Appeal, 1989. Mem. Cen. Conf. Am. Rabbis (chmn. com. on cults and proselytization 1981-88), S.E. Assn. of Cen. Conf. Am. Rabbis, Tampa Rabbinical Assn. (pres. 1988-90), Tampa Jewish Fedn. (bd. dirs. 1986—), Rotary (bd. dirs. Jackson club 1984-85). Office: Congregation Schaarai Zedek 3303 W Swann Ave Tampa FL 33609-4699

BISHOP, BRUCE WILLIAM, minister; b. Quantico, Va., Oct. 8, 1948; s. Albert Harrison and Selma (Benson) B; m. Linda King, July 20, 1968; children: Jeffrey H., Sara L. BA, North Cen. Bible Coll., 1975. Ordained to ministry Assemblies of God, 1979. Pastor First Assembly of God Ch., Sauk Centre, Minn., 1975-76, Rogers, Ohio, 1977-81, Carrollton, Ohio, 1981-84, Tiffin, Ohio, 1985-91; comdr. Royal Ranger Outpost, Tiffin, 1985—; treas. Impact, 1990—. Sgt. USAF, 1968-72. Republican. Home: 388 W Perry St Tiffin OH 44883 Office: First Assembly of God 366 Wentz St Tiffin OH 44883 *To do God's Will is one of the most fulfilling and rewarding blessings in life. Seeing the Miracle of His loving plan unfold is exciting beyond measure.*

BISHOP, CECIL, bishop. Bishop 8th Episcopal dist. A.M.E. Zion Ch., Temple Hill, Md. Office: AME Zion Ch 5401 Broadwater st Temple Hills MD 20748*

BISHOP, DAVID STEWART, clergyman; b. Thunder Hawk, S.D., May 13, 1933; s. Joel Lewis and Grace Miriam (Peterson) B.; m. Shirley Yvonne Orndorff, July 15, 1941 (dec. Nov. 1964); children: Sheryl Ann Bishop Walker, Mellanie Kay Bishop Hunt; m. Sandra Alyn Reasy, Mar. 20, 1967; children: Shannon Dee, David Stewart. AA, Lee Coll., Cleveland, Tenn., 1955; BA magna cum laude, Birmingham So. Coll., 1958; MA, Calif. Grad. Sch. Theology, 1976, PhD, 1978. Ordained to ministry Ch. of God, 1960. Tchr. West Coast Bible Coll., Fresno, Calif., 1958-59, dean coll., 1960-62, supt., 1962-65; coord./tchr. Bible Inst. for Ministry/Lay Enrichment, L.A., 1971-73, Yakima and Pasco, Wash., 1975-77, 79; founder, dir., tchr. Yakima Sch. Christian Ministries, 1977—; chaplain's staff St. Joseph's Hosp., Burbank, Calif., 1970-72; pastor North Hollywood (Calif.) Ch. of God, 1969-73; sr. pastor Christian Life Ctr. Ch. of God, Yakima, 1973—; sec. Yakima Pentecostal Fellowship N.Am ., 1975-76, pres., 1975-77; v.p. Yakima Full Gospel Minister's Fellowship, 1982; mem. Mayor's Prayer Breakfast Com., Yakima, 1986, 88, Pentecostal Fellowship N.Am.; dist. overseer Ch. of God, Yakima dist., 1983—, mem. Wash. state coun., 1974-78, 80-84, 86-90, trustee Wash. state, 1974—, chmn. Wash. state edn. bd., 1978-79, mem. state ministers' examining bd., 1984-886, gen. exec. coun., 1986-90, com. for internationalization of ch., 1986-90, motions com. gen. assembly, 1990; com. of rev. Northwest Bible Coll., 1986; mem. task force on edn. Ch. of God, 1991—. Author: Effective Communication, 1977, Into His Presence, 1988; contbr. articles to profl. jours., chpts. to books; chalk artist in ministry and fine art in several media; composer several songs; producer teaching tapes and Bible study outlines and materials; founder, minister Alive Through the Word, daily radio broadcast, 1974-87, Alive in the Spirit, weekly TV ministry, 1979—. Bd. dirs. West Coast Christian Coll., 1960-69, 87—; bd. govs. Calif. Theol. Sem., Fresno, Calif., 1984-86. Recipient Vision Found. Golde Mike award Ch. of God, 1980. Mem. Phi Beta Kappa. Home: 4708 Cowden Pl Yakima WA 98908 Office: Christian Life Ctr Ch God 716 N 40th Ave Yakima WA 98908

BISHOP, DONALD HAROLD, philosophy educator; b. Fulton, N.Y., Sept. 9, 1920; s. Harold and Vivian (Butts) B.;m. Margarete L., 1951; children: Michael, Karen, David. BS, Cornell U., 1947; MDiv, Yale U., 1950; PhD, U. Edinburgh (Scotland), 1953. Chaplain Hampton (Va.) Coll., 1953-55; dir. Wesley Found., Berkeley, Calif., 1955-57; chaplain Iowa Wesleyan Coll., Mt. Pleasant, 1957-59; prof. philosophy dept. Wash. State U., Pullman, 1959—. Editor, author (with others): Indian Thought--An Introduction, 1975, Thinkers of the Indian Renaissance, 1982, reprinted, 1990, Chinese Though--An Introduction, 1985. Fulbright award U.S. Govt., 1964, Rsch. award Soc. for Religion in Higher Edn. India, 1967, Indian Coun. for Cultural Rels., 1978, Pacific Cultural Found., Republic of China, 1982. Mem. Am. Acad. Religion. Methodist. Home: 1600 Gaines Rd Pullman WA 99163 Office: Wash State U Philosophy Dept Pullman WA 99164

BISHOP, EDWIN LYMAN, priest, educator; b. Seattle, Feb. 24, 1930; s. Edwin and Velma Marie (Spencer) B.; m. Joan Gail Avery, Aug. 11, 1956; children: Victoria Elizabeth, Antoinette Avery Bishop Rennie, Matthew Frederick Francis. BA, U. Wash., 1952; STB, Gen. Theol. Sem., 1955; MEd, Va. Commonwealth U., 1977; MA, Presbyn. Sch. Christ Edn., 1978. Cert. tchr., Va. Curate St. Luke's Episcopal Ch., Vancouver, Wash., 1955-58; vicar St. Mark's Episcopal Ch., Tonopah, Nev., 1958-60; rector All Sts. Episcopal Ch., Hillsboro, Oreg., 1960-66; chaplain, instr. Oreg. Episc. Schs., Portland, 1966-68; chaplain USN, 1968-72, St. Margaret's Sch., Tappahannock, Va., 1972-76; interim pastoral specialist Diocese of So. Va., Norfolk, Va., 1976—. Dist. commr. Boy Scouts Am., Nev., 1959, tng. chmn., Oreg., 1962-66; mem. tng. com. Mental Health Assn., Oreg., 1964. Capt. USNR, 1968-90. Fellow Coll. of Preachers; mem. Naval Res. Assn. (chaplain), Res. Officers Assn., Hospitaler Order of St. John of Jerusalem, Ret. Officers Assn., Interim Ministry Network (cert.). Avocations: gardening, jogging. Home: 1407 Westshire Ln Richmond VA 23233

BISHOP, LEO KENNETH, clergyman, educator; b. Britton, Okla., Oct. 11, 1911; s. Luther and Edith (Scovill) B.; m. Pauline T. Shamburg, Sept. 15, 1935; 1 dau., Linda Paulette. A.B., Phillips U., 1932; L.H.D., 1958; M.A., Columbia U., 1944; M.B.A., U. Chgo., 1957; Litt.D., Kansas City Coll. Osteopathy and Surgery, 1964. Ordained to ministry Christian Ch., 1932; asso. minister Univ. Place Ch., Oklahoma City, 1932-35; minister First Ch., Paducah, Ky., 1935-41, Central Ch., Des Moines, 1941-45; dir. St. Louis office NCCJ, 1945-48; v.p., dir. central div. NCCJ, Chgo., 1949-63; dir. pub. affairs People-to-People, Kansas City, Mo., 1963-66; v.p. Chgo. Coll. Osteopathy, 1966-72; pres. Bishop Enterprises, Colorado Springs, Colo., 1972—; also lectr. Contbr. religious and ednl. jours.; Developed: radio series Storm Warning; TV series The Other Guy, 1954. Cons. Community Social Planning Council, Mayor's Race Relations Com., YMCA, St. Louis; Am. del. Conf. World Brotherhood, Paris, 1950; bd. dirs. Am. Heritage Found. Recipient Paducah Jr. C. of C. Most Useful Citizen award, 1937, Distinguished Service award Dore Miller Found., 1958, Freedom Found. of Valley Forge award, 1961; named Chicagoan of Year, 1960. Clubs: Rotary, Union League, Winter Night. Home: 107 W Cheyenne Rd Colorado Springs CO 80906 Office: PO Box 843 Colorado Springs CO 80901

BISHOP, WILLIAM F., minister; b. Charleston, S.C., July 25, 1936; s. William F. and Harriette (Ashley) B.; m. Ann Sanders, June 29, 1958; 1 child, William Paul. AA, North Greenville (S.C.), Jr. Coll., 1956; BA, Furman U., 1958; MDiv, New Orleans Bapt. Theol., Seminary, 1961; DD, Bapt. Coll. of Charleston, 1980. Assoc. pastor Broadway Bapt. Ch., Columbia, S.C., summer 1957; pastor Parkway Bapt. Ch., Chester, S.C., 1957-58, Macedonia Bapt. Ch., Brookhaven, Miss., 1959-65, First Bapt. Ch., Kingstree, S.C., 1966-73; exec. dir. of missions Charleston Bapt. Assn., 1973-77; dir. teaching/tng. ministries Dept. S.C. Bapt. Conv., Columbia, 1977-84, dir. Ch. Devel. Div., 1984—; trustee S.C. Bapt. Hosp.; bd. dirs. Minister's Growth Conf., Columbia, 1981-84; vis. lectr. Southeastern Bapt. Theol. Seminary, Wake Forest, N.C.; chmn. Ch. Crisis Task Force, S.C. Bapt. Conv., 1989-90, Ch. Growth Coun., Columbia, 1989-90. Editor: Aurora, 1956; mem. journalism staff, North Greenville Jr. Coll., 1956. Chmn. Bi-Racial Com., Kingstree, S.C. Recipient Citizenship award Am. Legion, 1956. Mem. Optimist Club (pres. Kingstree chpt., Outstanding Club Pres. award 1967-68), S.C. Soc. for Autistic Children (pres.). Home: 113 Loch Rd Columbia SC 29210 Office: SC Bapt Convention 907 Richland St Columbia SC 29201

BISSET, SUZANNE See FOX, SELENA MARIE

BITNER, DENVER WILLIAM, minister; b. Greeneville, Tenn., July 30, 1947; s. William Dwight Bitner and Hilda Jean (Dayton) Green; m. Pamela Fairhurst Baker, Aug. 31, 1968; children: Elizabeth, Sara, David. BA in Sociology, Wittenberg U., 1970; MST, Hamma Sch. Theology, 1972; MDiv, Wartburg Theol. Sem., 1979. Ordained to ministry Evang. Luth. Ch. in Am., 1979. From dir. youth ministry to co-pastor Zion Luth. Ch., Rockford, Ill., 1972-88; sr. pastor Zion Luth. Ch., Rockford, 1988—. Chair Mayor's Task Force on Hunger, Rockford, 1989; trustee William Howard Found., Rockford. Mem. Northern Ill. Synod (dean north conf. 1988—), Zion Devel. Corp. (pres. 1982—), Rock River Valley Epilepsy Assn. (bd. dirs., pres. 1987-88), Indochinese Svc. Ctr. (bd. dirs. v.p. 1989—). Home: 3523 Northview Rd Rockford IL 61107 Office: Zion Luth Ch 925 5th Ave Rockford IL 61104

BITTINGER, DAVID LOWELL, minister; b. Barberton, Ohio, Sept. 22, 1952; s. Albert S. and Mildred A. (Hadley) B.; m. Elizabeth Ann Peel, June 9, 1973; children: James, Stephen, Jennifer. BA in Edn., Evangel. Coll., Springfield, Mo., 1974; MA in Pastoral Psychology, Ashland (Ohio) Seminary, 1983. Music evangelist Assembly of God Ch., Akron, Ohio, 1980-82; sr. pastor Christian Life Ctr. Ch., Kent, Ohio, 1982—. Columnist; Ask the Pastor, 1988-90. Bd. dirs. Portage County Mental Health Assn., 1989-90; mem. bldg. com. Kent (Ohio) Pub. Schs., 1989-90. Mem. Kent Ministerial Assn. (pres. 1987-89), Kent Rotary Club. Office: Christian Life Ctr Ch 5931 Rhodes Rd Kent OH 44240

BITTKER, DAVID, religious organization administrator. Chmn. B'Nai B'Rith Hillel Commn., Washington, D.C. Office: B'nai Brith Hillel Founds 1640 Rhode Island Ave NW Washington DC 20036*

BITZER, WARREN W., religious organization administrator. Pres. Met. Ch. Assn., Inc., Lake Geneva, Wis. Office: Met Ch Assn Inc 323 Broad St Lake Geneva WI 53147*

BJORLING, JOEL VICTOR, minister, writer; b. Galesburg, Ill., May 26, 1952; s. Maurice Ivan and Patricia Jean (Moffett) B. AA, Robert Morris Coll., 1972; BA, Oral Roberts U., 1975; Master of Arts in Theol. Studies, McCormick Theol. Sem., 1980. Interim min. First Congl. Ch., Toulon, Ill., 1988-89. Author: The Baha'i Faith, 1985, The Church of God Seventh Day, 1987, Channeling: A Bibliography; contbr. articles to profl. jours. Mem. Phi Theta Kappa. Avocations: genealogy, song writing, nursing home ministry, cult resch. Home: Rt 2 Gilson IL 61436 Office: 228 E Main St Knoxville IL

BJORNSTAD, JAMES, religion educator; b. Bklyn., Dec. 23, 1940; s. Thomas Mikal and Gerda Amalia (Anderson) B.; m. Rebecca Ann Leonard, July 23, 1966; children: Christine Lynn, Karen Ann. BA, Northeastern Bible Coll., 1967, THB, 1967; MRE, N.Y. Theol. Sem., 1969; PhD, NYU, 1976. exec. dir. Inst. Contemporary Christianity, Oakland, N.J., 1972—; trustee New Eng. Fellowship Evangs., Rumney, N.H., 1988—; pres. Evang. Ministries to New Religions, Denver, 1990—. Dir. rsch. Christian Rsch. Inst., Wayne, N.J., 1967-72; prof. philosophy and theology Northeastern Bible Coll., Essex Fells, N.J., 1972-90, v.p. acad. affairs, 1983-88, pres., 1988-90; prof. religion and philosophy The King's Coll., Briarcliff Manor, N.Y., 1991—; exec. dir. Inst. Contemporary Christianity, Oakland, N.J., 1972; trustee New Eng. Fellowship Evangs., Rumney, N.H., 1988—; pres. Evang. Ministries to New Religions, Denver, 1990—. Author: Twentieth Century Prophecy, 1969, Stars, Signs and Salvation in the Age of Aquarius, 1971, The Transcendental Mirage, 1976, The Moon Is Not the Son, 1976, Counterfeits at Your Door, 1979, Playing with Fire, 1984. Mem. Manchester Regional High Sch. Bd. Edn., Haledon, N.J., 1974-81. Recipient Disting. scholar, lectr. award Thomas F. Staley Found., 1982—. Mem. Evang. Theol. Soc., Evang. Philos. Soc. Office: The King's Coll Briarcliff Manor NY 10510

BLACK, BOBBY C., chaplain; b. Hartford, Ky., Apr. 27, 1933; s. Clifton Cornelius and Margaret Ruth (Smith) B.; m. Marybel Davis, Aug. 26, 1956; children: Lori Elizabeth, Brian Davis. BA, Ky. Wesleyan Coll., 1955; BD, Duke Div. Sch., 1959, MDiv, 1973; cert., Duke Med. Sch., 1959. Commd. 1st lt. USAF, 1959, advanced through grades to col., chaplain, 1959-83; space command chaplain USAF, Colorado Springs, Colo., 1983-87; ret. USAF, 1987; chaplain The Village Chapel, Pinehust, N.C., 1987—; dir. USAF Christian Encounter Conf., Va., Calif., N.C., 1970-79, Christian Leadership Conf., Spearfish, S.D., 1985; pres. Sr. USAF Chaplain Sch., Montgomery, Ala., 1973; preacher Outstanding Clergy Series, USAF Acad., 1984; dir. chaplaincy Moore Regional Hosp., 1987—. Decorated Def. Superior Svc. medal, Meritorious Svc. medal with three oak leaf clusters. Mem. N.C. Chaplain's Assn., Sandhill's Retired Officer's Assn. (chaplain 1989), N.C. Conf. U. Meth. Ch., Sandhill's Fellowship of Chs., Sandhills Men's Fellowship (bd. dirs. 1990—). Republican. Home: 15 Gray Fox Run Pinehurst NC 28374 Office: The Village Chapel Village Green PO Box 1060 Pinehurst NC 28374

BLACK, CARL CLIFTON, II, minister, religion educator; b. High Point, N.C., May 5, 1955; s. Carl Clifton and Iris Rebecca (Hill) B.; m. Harriet Susan Fesperman, Aug. 5, 1978; 1 child, Caroline Elizabeth. BA, Wake Forest U., 1977; MA, U. Bristol, Eng., 1980; MDiv, Emory U., 1981; PhD, Duke U., 1986. Ordained to ministry United Meth. Ch. as elder, 1988. Instr. theology Duke U., Durham, N.C., 1984-85; asst. prof. religion U. Rochester, N.Y., 1986-89; asst. prof. New Testament Perkins Sch. Theology, So. Meth. U., Dallas, 1989—; Westminster theol. lectr. St. John's Coll., Annapolis, Md., 1990. Author: The Disciples According to Mark, 1989; assoc. editor: Ventures in Religion series, 1989—; contbr. articles and religion revs. to profl. jours. Rotary Found. fellow, 1978-79, Dempster fellow, 1984-86, Mellon fellow, 1988-89. Mem. Am. Acad. Religion, Soc. Bibl. Lit. (reviewer dissertation series 1987—), Cath. Bibl. Assn. Am., Phi Beta Kappa. Democrat. Avocations: reading, music, jogging. Home: 1601 Idyllwild Ct Plano TX 75075-2124 Office: So Meth U Perkins Sch Theology Dallas TX 75275-0133

BLACK, DAVID ALAN, religious educator; b. Kailua, Hawaii, June 9, 1952; s. John Leland and Elvera (Arsu) B.; m. Becky Lynn Lapsley, Sept. 11, 1976; children: Nathan Alan, Matthew David. BA, Biola U., La Mirada, Calif., 1975; MDiv, Talbot Sch. Theology, La Mirada, 1980; D.Theol., U. Basel, Switzerland, 1983. Lectr. in Greek and Bibl. studies Biola U., 1976-84, asst. prof. Bibl. studies, 1984-85; acad. dean Grace Grad. Sch., Long Beach, Calif., 1985-87; prof. N.T. and Greek Grace Theol. Seminary, 1987-90; scholar in residence Lockman Found., La Habra, Calif., 1990—. Author: Paul, Apostle of Weakness, 1984, Linguistics for Students of New Testament Greek, 1988; contbr. articles to profl. jours. Fellow Inst. for Bibl. Rsch.; mem. Soc. Bibl. Lit., Evang. Theol. Soc. (pres. far-west region), Cath. Bibl. Assn. Baptist. Home and Office: 11849 Stamy Rd La Mirada CA 90638

BLACK, DONALD I., religious organization administrator. 1st v.p. World Conv. Chs. of Christ, Richardson, Tex. Office: World Conv Chs Christ 100 N Central Expwy Ste 804 Richardson TX 75080*

BLACK, GARY EUGENE, minister; b. Louisville, Ky., Dec. 5, 1953; s. Charles E. Black and Edna L. (Weisenberger) Gregory; m. Linda Jean Wesner, July 27, 1974; children: John Stewart, Julie Kristin. BA cum laude, Ky. Christian Coll., 1975; MA in Communications, Morehead State U., 1977. Ordained to ministry Christian Ch., 1978. Pastor Woodford Christian Ch, Versailles, Ky., 1978—. Author: (book) Eight Weeks to a Better Marriage, 1990; contbr. numerous articles to mags. and profl. jours. Vol. various civic and community activities. Mem. Christian Writers Guild, Christian Ch. Pension Fund (bd. govs.), Cen. Ky. Christian Ministers Assn., Woodford County Ministers Assn. Democrat. Home: 404 Versailles Rd Versailles OH 40383 Office: Woodford Christian Ch Lexington Rd at Paddock Dr Versailles KY 40383

BLACK, JACOB LESLIE, minister; b. Newark, N.J., Feb. 11, 1921; s. Jacob Leslie Sr. and Alice May (Shortman) B. Student, Moody Bible Inst., 1942-43. Ordained to ministry Bapt. Ch., 1939. Asst. pastor Clinton Hill Bapt. Ch., Newark, 1944-45, Pollard Bapt. Ch., Ashland, Ky., 1945-46; field rep. High Sch. Evangelism Fellowship, Inc., N.Y.C., 1947-63; pastor Ontario Bapt. Ch., Ames, Iowa, 1963-69; v.p. Boone (Iowa) Bibl. Ministries, Inc., 1969-86, pres., 1986—; pres. N.Y./N.J. chpts. Moody Alumni Assn., N.Y.C., 1957-60, cen. Iowa chpt., Des Moines, 1971-74; trustee Joy of Living Ministry, Boone, 1986—. Author, composer: Joyful Choruses, 1988. Mem. Boone Bibl. Ch. Republican. Home: 107 State St Boone IA 50036 Office: Boone Bibl Ministries Inc 924 W 2d St Boone IA 50036 *As the natural heart beat is the center of one's physical life, so Jesus Christ will become the heart beat of one's spiritual life, when He is given the central place therein.*

BLACK, L. ALEXANDER, bishop. Bishop Evang. Luth. Ch. in Am., Fairmont, W.Va. Office: Evang Luth Ch in Am 503 Morgantown Ave Fairmont WV 26554*

BLACK, ROBERT DURWARD, producer; b. Flint, Mich., June 6, 1952; s. Joseph Perrin and Lois Jane (Hamilton) B. BA, Wheaton (Ill.) Coll., 1974. Exec. dir., producer weekly ecumenical TV broadcast Chgo. Sunday Evening Club, 1987—. Office: Chgo Sunday Evening Club 332 S Michigan Ave Chicago IL 60604

BLACK, ROBERT L., JR., retired judge; b. Cin., Dec. 11, 1917; s. Robert L. and Anna M. (Smith) B.; m. Helen Charfield, July 27, 1946; children: William C., Stephen L., Luther F. AB, Yale U., 1939; LLB, Harvard U., 1942. Bar: Ohio 1946, U.S. Ct. Appeals (6th cir.) 1947, U.S. Supreme Ct. 1955. Sole practice, Cin., 1946-53; ptnr. Graydon, Head & Ritchey, Cin., 1953-72; judge Ct. Common Pleas, Cin., 1973-77, Ct. Appeals, Cin., 1977-89, vis. and assigned judge, 1989—; chmn. jury instrns. com. Ohio Jud. Conf. 1973-86 (chmn. 1986—). Councilman Village Indian Hill (Ohio), 1953-65, mayor, 1959-65; mem. standing com. Diocese of So. Ohio, Episcopal Ch., 1958-64, lay del. to gen. assembly, 1966, 69; vestryman, warden Indian Hill Episcopal Ch.; chmn. Cin. Human Rels. Commn., 1967-70. Served to capt. U.S. Army, 1942-45. Decorated Bronze Star. Mem. Cin. Bar Assn., Ohio Bar Assn., ABA, Am. Judicature Soc., Nat. Legal Aid and Defender Assn., Ohio Cts. of Appeals Judges Assn. Republican. Episcopalian. Clubs: Queen City, Camargo, Commonwealth (Cin.). Contbr. articles on law to profl. jours. Home: 5900 Drake Rd Cincinnati OH 45243

BLACK, RONNIE DELANE, religious organization administrator, mayor; b. Poplar Bluff, Mo., Oct. 26, 1947; s. Clyde Olen and Leona Christine Black; m. Sandra Elaine Hulett, Aug. 27, 1966; 1 child, Stephanie. BA, Oakland City (Ind.) Coll., 1969; M Div, So. Bapt. Theol. Sem., 1972. Ordained to ministry Gen. Assn. of Gen. Bapts., 1967. Pastor Gen. Bapt. Ch., Fort Branch, Ind., 1972-78; stewardship dir. Gen. Bapt. Hdqrs., Poplar Bluff, Mo., 1978-91; councilman City of Poplar Bluff, 1985-91, mayor, 1986-87, 90-91. Office: Gen Bapts 100 Stinson Dr Poplar Bluff MO 63901

BLACK, THOMAS DONALD, retired religious organization administrator; b. Mercer, Pa., Feb. 7, 1920; s. Harry Alexander and Bessie (Gilkey) B.; m. Frances Anna Greenan, Mar. 1, 1923; children: David Alan, Donald Francis, Joseph Harry, Timothy John (dec.). BA, Grove City Coll., 1942, DD, 1955; MDiv, Pitts.-Xenia Theol. Sch., 1945; M of Sacred Theology, Temple U., 1954. Ordained to ministry United Presbyn. Ch. N.Am., 1945. Founding pastor Creston Hills United Presbyn. Ch., Oklahoma City, 1945-50; pastor Blvd. United Presbyn. Ch., Phila., 1950-54, Am. Ch. in London, 1973-76; exec. sec. United Presbyn. Bd. Fgn. Mission, Phila., 1954-58; assoc. gen. sec. Commn. on Ecumenical Mission and Relations United Presbyn. Ch.-U.S.A., N.Y.C., 1958-70, gen. sec. Commn. on Ecumenical Mission and Relations, 1970-72, assoc. gen. dir. Program Agy., 1977-84; exec. dir. Gen. Assembly Council Presbyn. Ch. (USA), N.Y.C. and Atlanta, 1985-87; acting assoc. gen. sec. Nat. Coun. Chs. in U.S.A., 1989-90; interim dir. U.S. Office World Coun. Chs., N.Y.C., 1991; chmn. bd. dirs. Christian Lit. Fund, Geneva, 1964-69, Ravemcco, Lit-Lit, N.Y.C., 1962-66. Author: Merging Mission and Unity, 1986; contbr. articles and pamphlets to mission and ch. publs. Home: 770 Anderson Ave Cliffside Park NJ 07010 *We want to be appreciated for what we are, but uncertain of being accepted, we try to justify our lives by what we have accomplished. God accepts us for what we are.*

BLACK, WILLIAM GRANT, bishop; b. Muncie, Ind., Apr. 18, 1920; s. Joseph Charles and Verna Dell (Grimes) B; m. June Mathewson, Dec. 3, 1942; children—Gregory, Janis, David. A.B., Greenville Coll., 1941; M.A., U. Ill., 1950; B.D., U. Chgo. Div. Sch., 1955; D.D. (hon.), Kenyon Coll., 1980, Episcopal Theol. Sem., Lexington, Ky., 1980. Ordained to ministry Episcopal Ch., 1961. Mem. program staff U. Ill. YMCA, Chgo., 1950-52; prin. Cen. Adult High Sch., Chgo., 1960-62; rector Good Sheperd Episcopal Ch., Athens, Ohio, 1962-73, Ch. of Our Saviour, Cin., 1973-79; bishop Episcopal Diocese of So. Ohio, Cin., 1980—. Trustee Kenyon Coll., Gambier, Ohio, Children's Hosp., Cin., Bexley Hall, Rochester, N.Y. Served to capt. U.S. Army, 1942-46. Decorated Purple Heart, Silver Star. Avocations: reading; music; photography. Address: Episcopal Diocese So Ohio 82 Twin Lakes Dr Fairfield OH 45014

BLACKBURN, GROVER KELLY, JR., minister, educator; b. Hope Mills, N.C., Sept. 10, 1956; s. Grover Kelly Sr. and Addie (Pilkington) B.; m. Rebecca Long, Aug. 19, 1977; children: Jonathan Levi, Hunter Long, Lauren Kelly. BA in Religion, Campbell U., 1978; MDiv, Southeastern Sem., 1981; postgrad., Duke U., 1984. Assoc. pastor Rosemary Bapt. Ch., Roanoke Rapids, N.C., 1977-83; pastor 1st Bapt. Ch., Mayodan, N.C., 1983-87; dir. religious activities Campbell U., Bules Creek, N.C., 1987—; mem. gen. bd. N.C. Bapt. State Conv., Cary, N.C., 1984-86. Chmn. St. Jude Bike-A-Thon, Roanoke Rapids, 1982; trustee United Way, Roanoke Rapids, 1980. Recipient Disting. Service Young Man of Yr. award Roanoke Rapids Jaycees, 1982. Mem. Dan Valley Assn. (chmn. missions com. 1983-86, chmn. nominating com. 1986-87). Lodges: Lions (pres. Mayodan club 1985-87, Lion of Yr. 1985), Kiwanis (sec. Roanoke Rapids club 1982). Avocations: golf, basketball, yard work. Home: Duvall St Buies Creek NC 27506 Office: Campbell U Buies Creek NC 27506

BLACKBURN, ROBERT MCGRADY, retired bishop; b. Bartow, Fla., Sept. 12, 1919; s. Charles Fred and Effie Frances (Forsythe) B.; m. Mary Jeanne Everett, Nov. 16, 1943 (dec. May 1977); children: Jeanne Marie (Mrs. Ramon Cox), Robert M., Frances Lucille; m. Jewell Haddock, Sept. 9, 1978. B.A., Fla. So. Coll., 1941; M.Div., Emory U., 1943, LL.D., 1973; D.D. (hon.), LaGrange Coll., 1961. Ordained to ministry Methodist Ch., 1943; pastor United Methodist Ch., Boca Grande, Fla., 1943-44; asso. pastor First Methodist Ch., Orlando, Fla., 1946-48, Mt. Dora, Fla., 1948-53, DeLand, Fla., 1953-60, Jacksonville, Fla., 1960-68; sr. pastor First Methodist Ch., Orlando, 1968-72; bishop United Meth. Ch., Raleigh, N.C., 1972-80, Va. Conf., 1980-88; Mem. program council United Methodist Ch., 1963-72; del. to Meth. Gen. Confs., 1968, 70, 72. Trustee Randolph-Macon Coll., Randolph-Macon Woman's Coll., Randolph-Macon Acad., Va. Wesleyan, Shenandoah Coll. and Conservatory of Music, Ferrum Coll. Served as chaplain U.S. Army, 1944-46. Home: 8431 Mizner Circle E Jacksonville FL 32217

BLACKBURN, STEVEN PETER, minister; b. Oak Park, Ill., Oct. 14, 1952; s. James Frederick Jr. and Gisele F. (Vilanova) B.; m. Susan Elizabeth Wyman, Aug. 23, 1980; children: Averill Elizabeth Wyman, Steven James Wyman. Cert., Bourguiba Inst., Tunis, Tunisia, 1972, Am. U. Cairo, 1973; BS cum laude, Georgetown U., 1974, MS, 1977; BD with honors, U. St. Andrews, Scotland, 1980. Ordained to ministry Congl. Christian Chs., 1982. Adminstrv. aide Ctr. for Applied Linguistics, Arlington, Va., 1974-77; pers. dir. Ctr. for Applied Linguistics, Washington, 1980-81; asst. minister Dunino and Boarhills Parishes, Fife, Scotland, 1977-80; sr. minister 1st Congl. Ch., Barkhamsted, Conn., 1981-89; exec. sec. Conn. Congrl. Chs., Hartford, 1989—; sec. Conn. Congl. Chs., Hartford, 1984-86, moderator, 1986-87; bd. dirs. World Christian Rels. Commn., Oak Creek Wis., 1987—, chmn., 1989-90, 91—; Arabic manuscript researcher Hartford Sem., 1989—, instr. Arabic lang., 1990—, adj. faculty, 1991—. Pres. Barkhamsted Hist. Soc., 1984-86; chmn. svc. unit Salvation Army, Barkhamsted, 1984-90; treas. Barkhamsted Fire Dist., 1986-90. Mem. Nat. Coun. Chs. of Christ (assoc., office on Christian-Muslim rels. 1983—), Internat. Congl. Fellowship, Phi Beta Kappa, Phi Alpha Theta, Alpha Sigma Nu. Republican. Avocations: collecting stamps and coins, renaissance choral and instrumental music. Home: Aberwyburn House 21 W River Rd Pleasant Valley CT 06063-0546 Office: 277 Main St Hartford CT 06106

BLACKER, IAN T., minister; b. Woking, Surrey, Eng., Sept. 29, 1954; s. Alan James and Althea Cochrane (Reid) B.; m. Lori Louise Maertens, July 5, 1983; children: Aanna Marie, Marah Ruth. BA in Pastoral Ministries, Nebr. Christian Coll., 1984. Mgr. House of Fraser, Glasgow, Scotland, 1974-77, Fine Fare, Bearsden, Scotland, 1977-80; youth, edn. minister Grinnell (Iowa) Christian Ch., 1984-88; minister Morrowville (Kans.) Christian Ch., 1988—; coll. soccer coach and referee Grinnell Coll., 1984-88; sec. bd. dirs. Solomon Camp, 1990—; v.p. Washington County Mins. Assn., 1991—. Chmn. Grinnell Substance Abuse Action Com., 1987-88. Avocations: reading, speaking, music, skiing, soccer. Home: 210 W Oak Morrowville KS 66958 Office: Morrowville Ch of Christ Elm and Miller Sts Morrowville KS 66958 *That I have found and met and enjoy a personal saving relationship with God after years of searchings is awesome and challenging. My life is to lead fellow desert dwellers to the calm oasis to take deep draughts and find satisfaction for life.*

BLACKETOR, PAUL GARBER, minister; b. Birmingham, Ala., Feb. 10, 1927; s. Everly B. and Marie (Scokel) B.; children: A. Wade, Paula. BS, Samford U., Birmingham, Ala., 1953; MS, Auburn U., 1954, MA, 1955, EdD, 1956. Ordained to ministry, Bapt. Ch. Pastor Heidrick (Ky.) Bapt. Ch., 1962-63, Clarks Summit (Pa.) Bapt. Ch., 1963-64, Dalton (Pa.) Bapt. Ch., 1963-65, Wilmington (Vt.) Bapt. Ch., 1969-88, Fitzwilliam (N.H.) Bapt. Ch., 1990—; commr. Christian McAuliffe Planters Com., Concord, 1988—. Mem. N.H. Gen. Ct., 1984-90. Capt. U.S. Army, 1987. Democrat. Home: PO Box 16 Keene NH 03431

BLACKFORD, THOMAS EARL, minister; b. Mt. Vernon, Ohio, Dec. 7, 1961; s. Robert Neil and Joyce Elaine (Burgholder) B.; m. Lisa Ann Latham, Dec. 19, 1981; children: Terry Robert, Rachelle Lanae, Kyle Thomas. Ordained to ministry, Ch. of God (Anderson), 1987. Sr. pastor Rocky Fork First Ch. of God, Newark, Ohio, 1983-87, Marion (Ohio) First Ch. of God, 1987—; trustee Warsaw (Ohio) Camp Meeting Assocs., 1984-87; state bd. Ohio State Bd. Youth, Marengo, 1985-87; sec. Cen. Dist. Ministers of Ohio, 1990—. Fundraiser D.A.R.E., Marion, 1989. Fellow Marion Ministerial Assn., Mid-Ohio Ofcls. Republican. Home: 637 Girard Ave Marion OH 43302 Office: First Ch of God 921 Woodrow Ave Marion OH 43302

BLACKMAN, MURRAY, rabbi; b. N.Y.C., Nov. 18, 1920; s. Maxwell and Sarah (Levy) B.; B.S.S., Coll. City N.Y., 1940; B.H.L., Hebrew Union Coll., 1945, M.H.L., 1949, D.D., 1974; Ph.D., Walden U., 1975; m. Martha Dora Mecklenburger, Aug. 31, 1947; children—Michael Simon, Margaret Jo, Barbara Sarah. Ordained rabbi, 1949. Asst. rabbi Temple B'nai Jeshurun, Newark, 1949-50; rabbi Temple Concord, Binghamton, N.Y., 1950-51, Barnert Temple, Paterson, N.J., 1953-56; sr. rabbi Rockdale Temple, Cin., 1956-67; rabbi St. Thomas (V.I.) Synagogue, 1967-70, Temple Sinai, New Orleans, 1970—. Spl. lectr. edn. Hebrew Union Coll., Cin., 1962-67; instr. comparative religion Coll. of V.I., 1967-70; spl. lectr. history La. State U., Baton Rouge, 1971-75; assoc. prof. U. New Orleans, 1974-79, Loyola U., New Orleans, 1980—. Chmn. Cin. Jewish Community Relations Com., 1966-67; interfaith chmn. Greater New Orleans United Fund, 1971; mem. adv. council New Orleans council Boy Scouts Am., 1971-73; mem. Mayor's Job Force for Vets. Com., 1970-72; mem. Am. Jewish Com., Central Conf. Am. Rabbis; chmn. community relations com. Jewish Welfare Fedn., New Orleans, 1971-79; pres. New Orleans Rabbinical Council, 1973-78; mem. exec. bd. Central Conf. Am. Rabbis, 1978-82; mem. exec. bd. Nat. Jewish Community Relations Adv. Council, N.Y.C., 1975-81, vice chmn., 1976-81; exec. bd. La. State Com. for Humanities, 1975-80, Willowood Home for Jewish Aged, 1977-82, La. Renaissance, Religion and the Arts, 1977-82; nat. chmn. Joint Commn. on Jewish Edn., Union Am. Hebrew Congregations-Central Conf. Am. Rabbis, 1982-89; trustee Union Am. Hebrew Congregations, 1982-89, exec. bd. S.W. Council, 1982-89. Served with USNR, 1951-53. Mem. Adult Edn. Assn. U.S., Soc. Israel Philatelists, Southwest Assn. Reform Rabbis (pres. 1978-80), Phi Delta Kappa. Author: A Guide to Jewish Themes in American Fiction 1940-80, 1981. Home: 300 Lake Marina Dr # 8A New Orleans LA 70124 Office: 6227 St Charles Ave New Orleans LA 70118

BLACKMAN, RANDELL DEAN, minister; b. Effingham, S.C., Dec. 13, 1940; s. Arnis McKinley and Grace Lenora (Fraley) B.; m. Patricia Ann Staley, Oct. 28, 1961; children: Randell Dean Jr., Ryan Jeffrey. BA, Bapt. Coll., Charleston, S.C., 1979; MDiv, Southeastern Bapt. Sem., 1982. Pastor Jamestown (S.C.) Bapt. Ch., 1975-85; pastor Kingstree (S.C.) 2d Bapt. Ch., 1985—; instr. Williamsburg Tech. Coll., Kingstree, 1989—; Sunday Sch., Vacation Bible Schmn., Williamsburg Bapt. Assn., Hemingway, S.C., 1987-90, stewardship chmn., 1988-90; chaplain Williamsburg Meml. Hosp., Kingstree, S.C., 1987—. Writer Kingstree News, 1990—. Mem. Williamsburg Community/Sch. Durg Task Force, Kingstree, 1988-91. Mem. Masons. Home: 900 Dennis Ave Kingstree SC 29556 Office: Kingstree 2d Bapt Ch 912 Dennis Ave Kingstree SC 29556

BLACKMON, LARRY TERRY, minister; b. Sulphur Springs, Tex., Jan. 18, 1946; s. Morgan Sim and Hazel Mae (Smith) B.; m. Carolyn Dianne Bingham, Jan. 28, 1967; children: Larry Wayne, Karla Lynn. BA, La. Coll., 1967; MDiv, Southwestern Bapt. Theol. Sem., 1970. Ordained to ministry So. Bapt. Conv., 1970. Pastor Northside Bapt. Ch., Sulphur Springs, Tex., 1970-73, Baugh Chapel Bapt. Ch., Austin, Ark., 1973-78, Enon Bapt. Ch., Monticello, Ark., 1978-81, Good Shepherd Bapt. Ch., Silsbee, Tex., 1981-86, 1st Bapt. Ch., Malakoff, Tex., 1986—. Founder, pres. Magness Vol. Fire Dept., Baugh Chapel, Ark., 1975. Mem. Cabot Mins. Alliance (treas. 1974-76, pres. 1976-78), Drew County Mins. Alliance (treas. 1979-81), Malakoff Mins. Assn. (pres. 1989—), Henderson Bapt. Assn. (vice moderator, treas. 1989-90), Lions (pres. Malakoff chpt. 1989-90, Man of Yr. 1990). Democrat. Home: 306 W Mitcham Malakoff TX 75148 Office: 1st Bapt Ch PO Box 408 220 W Mitcham Malakoff TX 75148 *We have duties to God, to man and to self. It is only when we are true to our duties that we can live in peace. We are to love God with all our heart, mind, and soul, and our neighbor as ourselves.*

BLACKMON, MICHAEL DALE, minister; b. Elizabeth City, July 12, 1958; s. Donald Dabney and Savilla Joyce (Gambrell) B.; m. Elizabeth Ann Cook, Mar. 14, 1981 (div. Feb. 1991); children: James Matthew, Aaron Michael. MusB, Okla. Bapt. U., 1981; MDiv, Midwestern Bapt. Theol. Sem., 1991. Ordained to ministry Bapt. Ch., 1982. Dir. music Woods Bapt. Ch., Choctaw, Okla., 1980-81; asst. mgr. Arby's, Inc., Louisville, 1981-82; dir. music and youth Highland Bapt. Ch., Edwardsville, Ind., 1982-83, Calvary Bapt. Ch., Jefferson City, Mo., 1984-85; pastor Jamestown (Mo.) Bapt. Ch., 1985-86; dir. ch. program devel. Clay-Platte Bapt. Assn., Kans. City, Mo., 1986-88; assoc. pastor Liberty (Mo.) Manor Bapt. Ch., 1988-90; dir. music North Woods Ch., Parkville, Mo., 1990—. Bd. dirs., pres. Liberty (Mo.) Alliance for Youth, Inc., 1989-91. Named Outstanding Young Man Outstanding Ams., Montgomery, Ala., 1987, 1988. Mem. Liberty Ministerial Alliance, Clay-Platte Mins. Fellowship (sec. 1988-89, v.p. 1989-90), Phi Mu Alpha (treas. Pi Tau chpt. 1980-81). Avocations: golf, water sports, snow skiing, flying. Home: 210 Melrose #103 Liberty MO 64068-2852

BLACKMON, TERRELL DAVID, minister; b. Tignall, Ga., Aug. 8, 1933; s. Druid Jackson and Julia (David) B.; m. Jackie Guin (dec. Jan. 1990); children: Marianne Blackmon Jones, David. Student, Richmond Acad., Augusta, Ga., 1949-53. Ordained to ministry So. Bapt. Conv., 1975. Pastor Loco Bapt. Ch., Lincolnton, Ga., 1974—; owner, mgr. Blackmon's Welding & Machine Shop, Lincolnton, 1979—; vice moderator Ga. Bapt. Assn., 1980-82. Pres. Jaycees, 1969; bd. dirs. Ga. YMCA Y Clubs, 1985—. Sgt. U.S. Army, 1954-57. Democrat. Home and Office: Rte 3 Box 63 Lincolnton GA 30817

BLACKSHEAR, L. T., SR., bishop. Bishop Ch. of God in Christ, New Castle, Del. Office: Ch of God in Christ 17 S Booth Dr Peen Acres New Castle DE 19720*

BLACKWELL, G. L., education administrator. Sec. dept. Christian edn. A.M.E. Zion Ch., Chgo. Office: AME Zion Ch 128 E 58th St Chicago IL 60637*

BLACKWELL, GUS RAY, minister; b. Wichita, Kans., Nov. 4, 1955; s. Carl Raymond and Myrl Kathryn (O'Dell) B.; m. Joanna Jett, May 12, 1990. BA, Okla. Bapt. U., 1976; M in Div., Southwestern Bapt. Theol. Sem., 1981; postgrad., Rose State Coll., 1983. Lic. to ministry Bapt. Ch., 1974. Youth worker Navigators, Amherst, Mass., 1976-78; asst. wrestling coach U. Mass., Amherst, 1976-78; chaplain Children's Hosp., Oklahoma City, 1979-82; asst. wrestling coach Midwest City (Okla.) Wrestling, 1981-83; writer Okla. Pub. Co., Oklahoma City, 1982-83; youth dir. Soldier Creek Bapt. Ch., Midwest City, 1982-83; campus minister Okla. Bapt. Gen. Conv., Sayre, 1983-87; prof. Sayre Jr. Coll., 1983-87; campus minister Panhandle State U., Okla., 1987—; speaker seminars in field. Coach Spl. Olympics, Oklahoma City, 1985; commnr. Kiwanis Little League, 1987; tchr. First Bapt. Ch., Sayre, 1984-87; bd. dirs. Ventilator Dependent Quadraphlegics Assn., 1983, 86. Named one of Outstanding Young Men of Am., 1985, one of Outstanding Community Leaders of Am., 1989. Mem. Okla. Sec. Sch. Activities Assn., U.S. Wrestling Assn., Am. Softball Assn., Community Leaders of Am., Internat. Register of Profiles, Phi Eta Sigma. Republican. Clubs: Sayre Wrestling (pres. 1985-86); Hobie Fleet 131 (Oklahoma City) (rep. 1986, 87). Home: 414 Aggie Ave Goodwell OK 73939 Office: Panhandle State U Box 70 Goodwell OK 73939

BLACKWELL, (JAMES) NATHAN, JR., minister; b. Slater-Marietta, S.C., Aug. 27, 1951; s. James Nathan Sr. and Nell (Carroll) B.; m. Trisha Bell, June 17, 1972; children: Ashley Elizabeth, William Adrian. AA, North Greenville Coll., 1971; BA, William Carey Coll., 1974; MDiv, Mid-Am. Bapt. Theol. Sem., 1979. Ordained to ministry, 1978. Adminstr. Westside Chrisian Sch., Abbeville, S.C., 1974-76; min. edn. and youth LaBelle Haven Bapt. Ch., Memphis, 1976-80; sr. pastor 1st Bapt. ch., East Flat Rock, N.C., 1981-86, Bethlehem Bapt. Ch., Roebuck, S.C., 1986-88, Cornerstone Bapt. Ch., St. Cloud, Fla., 1988—; asst. moderator Carolina Bapt. Assn., Hendersonville, 1982-84; v.p. Spartanburg (S.C.) Bapt. Assn. Pastors' Conf., 1986-87. Vol. chaplain Orlando Regional Med. Hosp., 1990—. Recipient 1st Pl. Ch. Growth award Greater Orlando Bapt. Assn., 1991. Mem. St. Cloud Mins. Assn. (v.p. 1990—), Christian Coalition, Osceola Mins. for Community Values, William Carey Coll. Leadership Fraternity, Omicron Delta Kappa. Home: 400 Chancellor Ct Saint Cloud FL 34769

BLACKWOOD, ROY, JR., minister; b. New Concord, Ohio, Feb. 7, 1925; s. Roy Samuel and Lena M. (Shipe) B.; m. Margaret Elizabeth Graham, Nov. 20, 1948; children: William Andrew, Elizabeth May, Robert Roy. BS, Geneva Coll., 1948; postgrad., Reformed Presbyn. Theol. Sem., 1958-51; PhD, U. Edinburgh, Scotland, 1963. Ordained to ministry Reformed Presbyn. Ch. N.Am., 1954. Pastor Reformed Presbyn. Congregation, Bloomington, Ind., 1954-61, 2d Reformed Presbyn. Ch., Indpls., 1963—; prof. Reformed Presbyn. Extension Sem., 1985—; speaker retreats, seminars, tng. programs. Contbr. articles to religious jours. Trustee Geneva Coll., 1963—; bd. corporators Inter Varsity, Madison, Wis., 1964—; bd. dirs. Inst. in Basic Life Principles, Oak Brook, Ill., 1980— (sec. 1980). Ensign USN, 1942-56, PTO. Recipient Disting. Svc. award Geneva Coll., 1981; named Hon. Sec. State, Sec. State of Ind., 1982. Mem. Christian Bus. Men. Republican. Home and Office: 1175 Princeton Pl Zionsville IN 46077

BLADE, ROBERT ERIC, minister; b. Phila., Oct. 31, 1923; s. John Emil and Henrietta Evelyn (Nessen) B.; m. Alice Elizabeth Ott, Feb. 18, 1956. BA, Temple U., 1951; BD, Princeton Sem., 1954; MA, Temple U., 1959. Ordained to ministry Presbyn. Ch., 1954. Student pastor Bd. Nat. Missions Presbyn. Ch. (U.S.A.)., Alaska, 1952-53; pastor James Evans Mem. Presbyn. Ch., Phila., 1954-59, Hamptonburgh Presbyn. Ch., Campbell Hall, N.Y., 1969-82; chaplain Otterkill Engine Co., Campbell Hall, N.Y., 1969-82; historian Presbyn. Hist. Soc., Phila., 1982—; editorial asst. Am. Presbyns., Phila., 1990—. Author: Pioneer Presbyterian Congs., 1989, Hudson River Presbyterian History, 1980; contbr. articles to profl. jours. Mem. South Phila. Planning Commn., 1955-59. With U.S. Army, 1942-45, Lt comdr. USN, 1959-68. Mem. Mil. Chaplains Assn., Canterbury Cleric, Presbyn. Hist. Soc., Hamptonburgh Hist. Soc. (founder). Office: Dept History Presbyn Ch 425 Lombard St Philadelphia PA 19147

BLAHUT, ERIC RONALD, minister; b. Teaneck, N.J., Aug. 19, 1943; s. Edwin Robert and Edythe Victoria (Erickson) B.; m. Carol Ann Bird, June 15, 1968 (dec. Dec. 1989); children: Michelle Lee, Eric Brian. AB, Hope Coll., 1968; MDiv, Princeton Sem., 1971; D of Ministry, McCormick Sem., Chgo., 1985. Ordained to ministry Ref. Ch. in Am., 1971. Pastor Glen Reformed Ch., N.Y., 1971-77, Ghent (N.Y.) Reformed Ch., 1977—; treas. Columbia-Greene Classics, Claverack, N.Y., 1985—. Fellow Acad. Parish Clergy; mem. Ghent Sportsmen. Home and Office: RD 1 Box 90 Ghent NY 12075

BLAIDSELL, MACHRINA L., ecumenical agency director. Dir. Coun. Chs. of Contra Costa County, Walnut Creek, Calif. Office: Coun Chs Contra Costa County 1543 Sunnyvale Ave Walnut Creek CA 97596*

BLAINE, ALLAN, rabbi; b. N.Y.C., Mar. 4, 1930; s. Arthur M. and Frances P. Blaine; m. Suzanne Blaine, Jan. 28, 1962; children: Denna B. Seelen-Freund, Ari Michael. BA, NYU, 1953; MA, Jewish Theol. Sem., N.Y.C., 1957, DD (hon.), 1982; postgrad., Hebrew U., Jerusalem. Ordained rabbi, 1957. Assoc. rabbi East Midwood Jewish Ctr., 1960-68; rabbi Temple Beth-El, Rockaway Park, N.Y., 1969—; chmn. curriculum com. United Synagogues Am.; chmn. radio and TV commn. N.Y. Bd. Rabbis; chmn. ed. com. Solomon Schecter Day Sch.; leader study missions to Israel, Egypt and Lebanon, 1972—. Author: Idylls of the Heart, 1989; editor: Alcoholism and the Jewish Community; also articles; host (TV program) The Jewish Scene, NBC-TV, 1970-82. Advisor Munich Jewish Community. 1st. lt., chaplain U.S. Army, 1957-59. Recipient Massada award Israel Bonds Orgn., Humanitarian award United Jewish Appeal, Shalom award State of Israel. Mem. Jewish Chaplains Assn. (nat. officer), Jewish Prins. Assn., Mil. Chaplains Assn. Home: 466-B 136th St Belle Harbor NY 11694 Office: 445-B 135th St Rockaway Park NY 11694 *"Without vision a people perishes." (Proverbs).*

BLAIR, CHARLES E., minister; b. Hiawatha, Kans., Sept. 12, 1920; s. Robert O. and Elsie (Burgess) B.; m. Betty Nadine Ruppert, May 9, 1943; children: Vickie Benedict, Judith Anderson. BTh, Burton Coll. and Sem., 1955; LittD (hon.), Calif. Grad. Sch. Theology, 1970; DD (hon.), Oral Roberts U., 1973. Ordained to ministry. Pastor Calvary Temple, Denver, 1947—; bd. dirs., Network of Christian Ministries, Ch. Growth Internat. Author: The Silent Thousands Suddenly Speak, 1968, Get a Grip on Life, 1971, Americans Speak Out on This Nation's Top Ten Problems, 1972, The Man Who Could Do No Wrong, 1981, When the Journey Seems Too Great, 1988. Bd. dirs. Cath. Theol. Sem. Charles E. Blair Day proclaimed in his honor by Mayor of Denver and Denver C. of C., Denver, 1972. Mem. Assn. Internat. Mission Svcs. Home and Office: 200 S University Blvd Denver CO 80209

BLAIR, EDWARD PAYSON, theology educator; b. Woodburn, Oreg., Dec. 23, 1910; s. Oscar Newton and Bertha (Myers) B.; m. Vivian Krisel, Sept. 13, 1934; children: Phyllis, Sharon. BA, Seattle Pacific U., 1931; S.T.B., N.Y. Theol. Sem., 1934; PhD, Yale U., 1939. Ordained to ministry Free Meth. Ch., 1939; transferred to Meth. Ch., 1950. Prof. Bible Seattle Pacific U., 1939-41, dean Sch. of Religion, 1940-41; prof. Old Testament N.Y. Theol. Sem., N.Y.C., 1941-42; prof. Bibl. interpretation Garrett-Evang. Theol. Sem., Evanston, Ill., 1942-60, Harry R. Kendall prof. New Testament interpretation, 1960-71, adj. prof. New Testament interpretation, 1971-75; lectr. in field; archaeol. excavator in Israel at Anata, 1936, Herodian Jericho, 1951, Mt. Gerizim, 1966, 68. Editor Bibl. Rsch., 1964-65; co-editor, author (with others): Illustrated Family Encyclopedia of Living Bible, 1967; author: Jesus in the Gospel of Matthew, 1960, Deuteronomy and Joshua, 1964, Abingdon Bible Handbook, 1975, Illustrated Bible Handbook, 1987. Two Brothers' fellow Yale U., Jerusalem, 1935-36; recipient citation Laymen's Nat. Bible Com., 1975; named Alumnus of Yr., Seattle Pacific U., 1981. Mem. Am. Schs. of Oriental Rsch., Am. Acad. Religion, Soc. Bibl. Lit. Home and Office: 299 N Heather Dr Camano Island WA 98292 *The biblical perspectives on God, Jesus Christ, and the world and its inhabitants, while expressed in the language and thought forms of antiquity, yet offer the best insights available for meaningful living in our own difficult times.*

BLAISDELL, RUSSELL CARTER, minister, religious organization administrator; b. Chgo., Oct. 19, 1936; s. Russell Lloyd and Viola Evelyn (Hagen) B.; m. Anita Fay Cone, Jan. 4, 1964; children: David Scott, Valerie Ruth, Sarah Jane, John Milton. BA, U. Calif., Berkeley, 1959; MDiv, McCormick Theol. Sem., 1965. Ordained to ministry Presbyn. Ch. (U.S.A.), 1965. Pastor Community Presbyn Ch., Lawton, Iowa, 1965-73, 1st United Presbyn. Ch., Portage, Wis., 1973-79; assoc. gen. sec., assoc. dir. Presbyn. and Reformed Renewal Ministries Internat., Oklahoma City, 1979-91, Black Mountain, N.C., 1991—; chmn. Christian Edn., N.W. Iowa Presbytery, Storm Lake, 1969-73; commr. 191st Gen. Assembly, United Presbyn Ch. U.S.A., 1979; nat. dir. Spirit Alive for Congl. Renewal, 1990—; chmn. Congl. Devel. and Revitalization, Indian Nations Presbytery, Oklahoma City, 1985-87. Editor Renewal News, 1983—; actor, singer Portage Players, 1974; organizer, singer, bd. dirs. Portage Ecumenical Chorus, 1974-79. 1st lt. USAF, 1959-62. Calif. Alumni scholar, 1954-55; Rotary scholar, 1954-57. Mem. Presbytery Indian Nations (new ch. devel. com.), Kiwanis (bd. dirs. 1976-79). Republican. Office: Presbyn and Reformed Renewal Ministries Internat PO Box 428/115 Richardson Blvd Black Mountain NC 28711

BLAISING, CRAIG ALAN, religious educator; b. San Antonio, Sept. 28, 1949; s. Claude Lawrence and Mildred Helen (Craig) B.; m. Diane Sue Garrison, May 31, 1975; children: Emily Grace, Jonathan Craig. BS, U. Tex., 1971; ThM, Dallas Theol. Sem., 1976, ThD, 1979; PhD, U. Aberdeen, Scotland, 1988. Lic. to ministry So. Bapt. Conv., 1972. Adj. prof. dept. religion U. Tex., Arlington, 1978; asst. prof. systematic theology Dallas Theol. Sem., 1980-85, assoc. prof., 1985-89, acting dept. chmn., 1988-89, prof., 1989—. Author: (with others) Bible Knowledge Commentary, 1985, Evangelical Dictionary of Theology, 1985; contbr. articles to religious jours. Rotary Found. fellow U. Aberdeen, 1978-79. Mem. AAAS, Evang. Theol. Soc. (regional pres. 1986-87), Dispensational Study Group (pres. 1988-90), Am. Acad. Religion, Soc. Bibl. Lit., N.Am. Patristic Soc., Seminar on Devel. Early Cath. Christianity, Tau Beta Pi. Office: Dallas Theol Sem 3909 Swiss Ave Dallas TX 75204

BLAKE, BRUCE, bishop. Bishop United Meth. Ch., Dallas. Office: United Meth Ch PO Box 16069 Dallas TX 75251*

BLAKE, CHARLES, minister, bishop; b. Little Rock, Aug. 5, 1940; s. Junios Augustus and Lula (Champion) B.; m. Mae Lawrence Blake; children: Kimberly Roxanne, Charles Blake II, Lawrence Champion. BA, U.S. Internat. U., 1962; MDiv, ITC, Atlanta, 1965; DDiv, Calif. Grad Sch. Theology, 1982; ThD, Oral Roberts U., Tulsa, 1988. Ordained to ministry, Ch. of God in Christ, 1962. Interim pastor Marietta (Ga.) Ch. of God in Christ, 1963-64; co-pastor Greater Jackson Meml. Ch. of God in Christ, San Diego, 1965-69; pastor West Angeles Ch. of God in Christ, L.A., 1969—; bishop First Jurisdiction of So. Calif., L.A., 1985—; exec. bd. Bd. Regents, Oral Roberts U., Tulsa, 1986—, chmn. exec. com., 1991—; gen. bd. officer Gen. Bd. of Ch. of God in Christ Internat., 1988—; mem. Charismatic Bible Ministries, Inc., Tulsa, 1987—, Network of Christian Ministries, 1987-91. Author sermon anthology with over 500 original works. Office: West Angeles Ch of God Christ 3045 Crenshaw Los Angeles CA 90016

BLAKE, RICHARD LOUIS, minister; b. Shreveport, La., Mar. 18, 1949; s. Richard Earnest and Hilda Marie (Norris) B.; m. Stephanie Ballard, Apr. 3, 1969; children: Ryan Douglas, Cody Layne. BS, La. Tech. U., 1970; MDiv, Southwestern Bapt. Theol. Sem., 1984, D Ministry, 1992. Ordained to ministry Bapt. Ch., 1982. Assoc., adminstr. Gambrell St. Bapt. Ch., Ft. Worth, 1981-82; pastor Elkins Lake Bapt. Ch., Huntsville, Tex., 1982-85, Kingsbridge Bapt. Ch., Sugar Land, Tex., 1985-87, Immanuel Bapt. Ch., El Paso, Tex., 1987—; chmn. bd. trustees Internat. Bapt. Bible Inst., El Paso, 1988—; v.p. pastors' conf. Union Bapt. Assn., Houston, 1986-87. Mem. El Paso Bapt. Assn. (vice moderator 1989-90), Southwestern Bapt. Theol. Sem. Alumni Assn. (sec. Tex. chpt. 1989-90). Office: Immanuel Bapt Ch 1201 Hawkins Blvd El Paso TX 79925 *There is no greater poverty than to have everything in life to live with but nothing to live for.*

BLAKE, RICHARD RONALD, controller, Christian education specialist; b. Parkers Prairie, Minn., Mar. 7, 1930; s. John Paul and Marian Dorthy (Magnuson) B.; m. Thelma L. Barnes, Nov. 3, 1956; children: Richard Ronald Jr., Kenneth, James, Robert. BBA, Armstrong Coll., 1957; M of Christian Edn., Golden State Sch. Theology, Oakland, Calif., 1985, D of Ministry in Religious Edn., 1987. Regional contr. Boise Cascade Bldg., Hayward, Calif., 1968-75, Case Power and Equipment Sales and Svc. Co., San Leandro, Calif., 1974-80; owner Family Book Ctr., San Leandro, 1975—; contr. Carpet Craft, Inc., Hayward, 1989—; customer advocate Nat. Tchr. Edn. Program, Durham, 1986—; cons., bd. dirs. Christian Edn. Leadership Svc., Los Gatos, Calif., 1987-90; founder, dir. Christian Edn. Resources, San Leandro, 1980—; mem. adv. bd. Follow Up Ministries, Inc., Castro Valley, Calif., 1987—. Author: A Children's Church Curriculum; contbr. articles to The Ch. Tchr. mag., 1988. Program chmn. Bay Area Sunday Sch. Conv., Castro Valley, 1989—; active staff devel. and lay leadership Redwood Chapel Community Ch. Mem. ASCD, Profl. Assn. Christian Educators (Ariz. chpt.), Assn. Child Edn. Internat., Internat. Platform Assn., Christian Booksellers Assn., Writers Connection, Am. Legion. Avocations: church activities, writing, music. Home: 16630 Cowell St San Leandro CA 94578 *To hear the words "well done" by the Master is a goal worthy of everyone's consideration. My life is dedicated to this end.*

BLAKE, ROBERT, minister; b. Milan, Ohio, Nov. 10, 1949; s. Dean Orville and Helen Ann (Gehring) B.; m. Rebecca May Keys, June 22, 1974; children: Elizabeth, Bonnie, Brittany, Bethany. Diploma, Moody Bible Inst., 1975; BA, Trinity Coll., 1976; MDiv, Earlham Sch. Religion, 1983. Recorded friends pastor, Aug. 1983. Pastor Arba Friends Meeting, Lynn, Ind., 1976-83, Spiceland (Ind.) Friends Meeting, 1983—. Republican. Lodge: Lions. Avocation: woodworking, genealogy. Home: 437 W Main St Spiceland IN 47385 Office: Spiceland Friends Meeting 401 W Main St Spiceland IN 47385

BLANCH, STUART YARWORTH, archbishop; b. Blakeney, Gloucestershire, Eng., Feb. 2, 1918; s. William Edwin and Elizabeth Blanch; m. Brenda Gertrude Coyte, 1943; children—Susan, Hilary, Angela, Timothy, Alison. BA, Oxford U., 1948, MA, 1952; LLD, Liverpool U., 1975; DD (hon.), Hull U., 1977, Wycliffe Coll., Toronto, 1979, U. Manchester, 1984; D (hon.), U. York, 1979. Ordained priest Ch. of Eng. With Law Fire Ins. Soc. Ltd., 1936-40; curate, then vicar chs. in Oxford, 1949-57; vice prin. Wycliffe Hall, 1957-60; Oriel canon Rochester Cathedral, warden Rochester Theol. Coll., 1960-66; bishop of Liverpool, 1966-75; archbishop of York, 1975-83; prochancellor Hull U., 1975-83, York U., 1977-83; mem. House of Lords, 1972—, privy counsellor, 1975—, subprelate Order St. John, 1975—. Served as navigator RAF, 1940-46. Hon. fellow St. Catherine's Coll., Oxford, 1975, St. Peter's Coll., Oxford, 1983; decorated Baron, 1983. Mem. Royal Commonwealth Soc. Author: The World Our Orphanage, 1972; For All Mankind, 1976; The Christian Militant, 1978; The Burning Bush, 1978; The Trumpet in Morning, 1979; The Ten Commandments, 1981; Living by Faith, 1983; Way of Blessedness, 1985, Encounters with Jesus, 1988.

BLANCHARD, DONALD EDWARD, religion educator, computer scientist; b. Springfield, Ohio, Feb. 3, 1930; s. James S. and Lillian (Lyons) B.; m. Beatrice Wilkinson, May 5, 1951 (div. June 1975); children: Barbara Ann, Donald; m. Barbara Jean Cox, Sept. 6, 1975; children: Jeri Lynn, Ricardo, Mark. Grad., Air Force Inst. Tech., 1973; student bus. adminstrn. program, Capital U., 1989. Registered logistics engr., Ohio. Bible sch. tchr. Ch. of Christ, Dayton, Ohio, 1965—, edn. dir., 1969-84, youth dir., 1975-84, co-dir. edn. dept., 1984—, sec., asst. treas., 1984—; prin. engr. Computer Sci. Corp., Dayton, 1987—; mem. ch. leadership, statutory agt. Webster St. Ch. of Christ, Dayton, 1984—. Editor: Books of Bible Lessons, 1987. Sgt. USAF, 1949-52. Recipient civilian award for outstanding job performances USAF, 1965, Outstanding Tchr. award Collegiate Heights Ch. of Christ., 1972. Mem. Soc. Logistics Engrs. Home: 4750 Coulson Dr Dayton OH 45418 Office: Webster St Ch of Christ 4917 Webster St Dayton OH 45414 *I have learned that a journey toward success is more rewarding when measured by the positive influences made, rather than by percieved achievements.*

BLANCHARD, TIM, religious organization administrator. Gen. dir. Conservative Bapt. Assn. Am., Wheaton, Ill. Office: Conservative Bapt Assn Am PO Box 66 Wheaton IL 60189*

BLANCHARD, WILLIAM PAUL, minister; b. Drew, Miss., Aug. 23, 1955; s. Charles Hayward and Hettie Lee (Mitchell) B.; m. Susan Paulette Nicholass, July 30, 1977; children: Charles Wesley, Emily Lauren. AA, Miss. Delta Jr. Coll., 1975; BS in Edn., Delta State U., Cleve., Miss., 1977; MRE, Southwestern Bapt. Theol. Sem., Ft. Worth, 1981; D of Ministry, So. Bapt. Ctr. for Bibl. Study, Jacksonville, Fla., 1982. Ordained to ministry Bapt. Ch., 1972. Pastor Canaan Bapt. Ch., Crawford, Tex., 1979-81, Airport Bapt. Ch., Grenada, Miss., 1981-83, Lakeview Bapt. Ch., Leland, Miss., 1983-86, Pineview Bapt. Ch., Hattiesburg, Miss., 1986-88, Eulaton 1st Bapt. Ch., Anniston, Ala., 1988-91; dir. missions Winston Court Bapt. Assn., Louisville, Miss., 1991—; bd. dirs. So. Bapt. Ctr., Jacksonville, 1983-88, 91—; pres. Wash. County Pastor's Conf., Greenville, Miss., 1986, Lebanon Pastor's Conf., Hattiesburg, 1987. Author: Called to Minister: Commited to Serve, 1989; contbr. devotional articles to newspapers. Mem. Southwestern Bapt. Sem. Alumni. Home: 215 White Cir Louisville MS 39339 Office: Winston Bapt Assn Louisville MS 39339

BLANCHET, BERTRAND, bishop; b. Montmagny, Que., Can., Sept. 19, 1932; s. Louis and Alberta (Nicole) B. B.A., Coll. Ste-Anne-de-la Pocatiere, 1952; L.Th., Laval U., 1956, D.Sc., 1975. Ordained priest Roman Catholic Ch., 1956, consecrated bishop, 1973; tchr. biology Coll. and Coll. d'Enseignement Gen. et Profl., La Pocatiere, 1963-73; bishop of Gaspe Que., 1973—. Mem. Chevaliers de Colomb, Fonds de Recherches Forestieres. Address: 172 Rue Jacques Cartier, Gaspe, PQ Canada G0C 1R0

BLANEY, DENNIS JOSEPH, priest; b. East Chicago, Ind., Aug. 26, 1932; s. Joseph and Esther (Krieger) B. Student, Our Lady of the Lake Coll., Wawasee, Ind.; BA in Philosophy, Mt. St. Mary's of the West, Cin., 1954. Ordained priest Roman Cath. Ch., 1958. Parish priest, high sch. tchr. Hammond, Ind., 1958-64; parish priest St. Patrick's Ch., Chesterton, Ind., 1964-67, St. Thomas Ch., Munster, Ind., 1967-70; parish priest, pastor Sacred Heart Ch., Michigan City, Ind., 1970—; coord. Apostolate for Handicapped, Gary, Ind. Diocese, 1970—, Friends Club, 1978—, Respite Care, 1980—, Share Found., 1982—. Named Humanitarian of Yr. Michigan City, Ind., 1986; recipient State Gov. Profl.-in-Svc. with Handicapped award, 1986, St. Joseph the Worker award Bd. Dirs. Calumet Coll. of St. Joseph, 1987, Book of Golden Deeds award Michigan City Exch. Club. Mem. Nat. Cath. Edn. Assn., Ind. Coordinating Coun., Ind. State Assn. Cerebral Palsy, Nat. Assn. Retarded Citizens, Nat. Apostolate Mentally Retarded, Assn. Deaf in Vocat. Rehab. (state adv. bd.), Ind. Assn. Retarded Citizens (bd. dirs.). Home and Office: 1001 W 8th St Michigan City IN 46360

BLANEY, ROBERT WILLIAM, ethics educator, minister; b. L.A., Apr. 18, 1931; s. Harry French and Margaret Ethel (Clay) B.; m. Laurel Anne Hoyt, Apr. 14, 1962; children: Martha Elizabeth, Joy Marie. AB, UCLA, 1953, MPA, 1958; STB, Boston U., 1959, ThD, 1966. Ordained to ministry United Meth. Ch., 1958; elder, 1964. Pastor Brentwood United Meth. Ch., L.A., 1962-64, Los Feliz United Meth. Ch., L.A., 1964-66; assoc. prof. U. of the Pacific, Stockton, Calif., 1966-76, prof. social ethics, religious studies, 1975—, dir. Pacific Ctr. for Study of Social Issues, 1966-76, chair religious studies dept., 1975-85, 91—; assoc. dir. Wesley Found., UCLA, 1962-64; minister of residence Holy Cross United Meth. Ch., Stockton, 1969—; del. Christian Peace Conf., Prague, Czechoslovakia, 1968, 91; vis. scholar Ch. Ctr. for Study Theology and Pub. Policy, Washington, 1979, Div. Sch., Cambridge (Eng.) U., 1984; resident scholar Ecumenical Inst., St. John's U., Collegeville, Minn., 1988; chair bd. higher edn. and campus ministry Calif./Nev. Conf. United Meth. Ch., San Francisco, 1988—. Pres. San Joaquin Migrant Ministry, Stockton, 1968-70, San Joaquin Mental Health Assn., Stockton, 1974-75; chair San Joaquin County Crime Awareness/Prevention Commn., Stockton, 1980-81. Recipient Outstanding Educator award Am. Edn. Assn., 1975, Eberhardt Tchr.-Scholar award, 1990; Rockefeller Found. fellow, 1956-57, NEH fellow, 1980. Mem. Am. Acad. Religion (exec. com. western region 1973-74), Soc. Christian Ethics (chair sexuality task force 1981—), Nat. Orgn. against Sexism (men's studies task force), AAUP (exec. com. U. Pacific chpt. 1975-87), Stockton Metro Ministry (pres. 1978-79, 85-88), N.Am. Christian Peace Conf. (treas. 1990—). Democrat. Home: 2221 Dwight Way Stockton CA 95204 Office: U of Pacific Religious Studies Dept Stockton CA 95211 *Our greatest challenge today is to continue to seek for Peace and Justice in our own and others lives through nonviolent love and action.*

BLANK, KENNETH CHARLES, minister; b. Orange, N.J., Dec. 12, 1946; s. Charles Adolf and Cora (Nelson) B.; m. Audrey Barbara Davis, Jan. 7, 1978; children: Suzanne, Allison. BA cum laude, Montclair State Coll., N.J., 1976; MDiv, Gordon-Conwell Theol. Sem., So. Hamilton, Mass., 1980. Ordained to ministry Presbyn. Ch. (U.S.A.), 1980. Pastor First Presbyn. Ch., Haverhill, Mass., 1980-83; clinical pastoral edn. spvr. City Faith Med. and Rsch. Ctr., Tulsa, Okla., 1983-87; chaplain spvr. Baptist Med. Ctr., Oklahoma City, 1987-90; dir. pastoral care Presbyn. Hosp., Oklahoma City, 1990—; state rep. Coll. Chaplains, Okla., 1990—; chair standards com. S.W. Region Assn. Clinical Pastoral Edn., Houston, 1989—. Editor Wood, Hay and Stubble, 1977-80. Chair 6th congl. dist. Bread for the World, N.Y.C., 1977-80. Fellow Coll. Chaplains (state rep. 1990—); mem. Assn. for Clin. Pastoral Edn. (cert. supr.), Okla. Chaplains Assn. Presbyterian. Home: 2017 Arapaho Rd Edmond OK 73014 Office: Presbyn Hosp 700 NE 13th St Oklahoma City OK 73014

BLANTON, BETTY J., church worker; b. Jackson County, N.C., Oct. 19, 1937; d. Claude Monteith and Coral Lee (Picklesimer) Jones; m. Don A. Blanton, Dec. 23, 1955; children: Suzanne B. Shelton. Student, W. Carolina U., Cullowhee, N.C., S.W. Community Coll., Webster, N.C. Cert. profl. sec. Sec./clk. Western Carolina U., Cullowhee; sec./bookkeeper First Bapt. Ch. Proprietor, Sylva, N.C.; adminstrv. asst. First Bapt. Ch. Proprietor. Mem. NAFE, Nat. Assn. So. Bapt. Secs., N.C. Assn. So. Bapt. Secs. Home: PO Drawer 1024 Sylva NC 28779

BLASE, CHARLES DAVID, clergyman; b. Lewisville, Tex., Dec. 2, 1940; s. Charles Alvin and Nora Lou (Patterson) B.; m. Anna Katherine Taylor, Aug. 11, 1963; children: John David, Shawn Jubal. AA, Decatur Bapt. Ch., 1962; BA, Ouachita Bapt. Coll., 1964; MDiv, Southwestern Sem., 1967; DMin, Luther Rice Sem., 1978. Ordained to ministry Bapt. Ch., 1963. Pastor Tulip Bapt. Ch., Carthage, Ark., 1963-64, Bethel Bapt. Ch., Alvord, Tex., 1964-65, Bell Bapt. Ch., Decatur, Tex., 1965-67, Westview Bept. Ch., Chanute, Kans., 1967-71, Springlake Bapt. Ch., Paris, Tex., 1971-74; pastor First Bapt. Ch., Naples, Tex., 1974-78, Nashville, Ark., 1986—; pastor Highland Park Bapt. Ch., Texarkana, Tex., 1978-86; mem. state Bapt. Student Union adv. bd. Ark. Bapt. Conv., Little Rock, 1991-93. Mem. bd. Haven Home for Mentally Retarded, Texarkana, 1984-86. Mem. Ministerial Alliance (pres. Chanute 1969, Paris 1974, Naples 1976, Texarkana 1984), Rotary. Republican. Home: 901 Grove St Nashville AR 71852 Office: First Bapt Ch PO Box 339 Nashville AR 71852

BLASER, KLAUSPETER, religion educator; b. Oberthal, Switzerland, Mar. 1, 1939; s. Fritz and Ida (Schneider) S.; m. Christiane Bignens, Mar. 1, 1969; children: Jeremias, Marcos, Simeon. ThD, Univ. Mainz, 1964; BDiv, Univ. Bern, 1965. Lectr. Fed. Theol. Sem., Republic of South Africa, 1966-69; sec. Swiss Mission in South Africa, 1969-72; prof. theology U. Lausanne (Switzerland), 1972—, U. Basel (Switzerland), 1976—. Author several books; contbr. articles to profl. jours. Home: Hangweg 8, 3076 Worb Switzerland Office: U Lausanne, BFSH 2, 1015 Lausanne Switzerland

BLASZYK, CHRISTOPHER PAUL, pastor; b. Detroit, June 3, 1957; s. Virgil J. and Luella June (Harris) B.; m. Pamela Fern Gleason, Oct. 14, 1978; children: Andrea, Kimberly, Christopher. BA, Apostolic Bible Inst., 1978. Ordained to ministry United Pentecostal Ch., 1980. Evangelist United Pentecostal Ch., England, Wales, Scotland, U.S., 1979; pastor United Pentecostal Ch., Iowa City, Iowa, 1979-85, Marshfield, Wis., 1987-90; sec. youth dept. United Pentecostal Ch., Iowa, 1983-85; state dir. Harvestime Radio Ministry, United Pentecostal Ch., Wis., 1985-90; police chaplain Marshfield Police , 1987-90. *Died Sept. 3, 1990.*

BLAYLOCK, JAMES CARL, clergyman, librarian; b. Guntown, Miss., Jan. 27, 1938; s. Carl Houston and Katie Lee (Pugh) B.; m. Jo Ann Enlow, May 3, 1962; children: Jacquelyn Ann, John Thomas. AA, Southeastern Bapt. Coll., Laurel, Miss., 1962; BTh, N.Am. Theol. Sem., Jacksonville, Tex., 1964; BA, U. Tex., Tyler, 1976; MRE, Bapt. Missionary Sem., Jacksonville, 1977; MSLS, East Tex. State U., 1980. Ordained to ministry Bapt. Ch., 1962. Pastor Mt. Pleasant Ch., Bedias, Tex., 1962-64, Buena Vista Ch., Timpson, Tex., 1964-70, 1st Bapt. Ch., Maydelle, Tex., 1970-86, Corinth Ch., Jacksonville, Tex., 1986—; asst. dir. Bapt. News Svc., Jacksonville, 1969-88, dir., 1988—; asst. editor Directory and Handbook of Bapt. Missionary Assn., Jacksonville, 1969-88, editor, 1988—; libr. Bapt. Missionary Assn. Theol. Sem., Jacksonville, 1972—. Editor Mt. Olive Evangel, 1965-70; author: History of 1st Bapt. Ch. Maydelle, Tex., 1986, Buena Vista Bapt. Ch., 1986, Glimpses from the Past, 1988. Mem. Am. Theol. Libr. Assn., ALA, Tex. Libr. Assn., Evang. Theol. Soc. Home: 625 Kickapoo St Jacksonville TX 75766-4621 Office: Bapt Missionary Assn Theol Sem 1410 E Pine St Jacksonville TX 75766-5414

BLAZIER, KENNETH DEAN, minister; b. Topeka, Kans., Mar. 17, 1933; s. Edwin B. and Hazel E. (Spencer) B.; m. R. Elaine Kellogg, Aug. 25, 1956; children: Lynnette Elaine Thayer, Gregory K., Kyle W. BA, Ottawa (Kans.) U., 1955; MDiv, Am. Bapt. Sem. of West, Berkeley, Calif., 1959; DMin, N.Y. Theol. Sem., N.Y.C., 1984. Ordained to ministry Am. Bapt. Chs. USA, 1959. Pastor First Bapt. Ch., Hudson, N.Y., 1959-62, Cazenovia (N.Y.) Village Bapt. Ch., 1962-66; denominational exec. Div. Ch. Edn., Am. Bapt. Bd. Edn. and Pub., Valley Forge, Pa., 1966-86; nat. dir. Mins.-at-Large program Am. Bapt. Chs. USA, Valley Forge, Pa., 1986—; bd. dirs. Interim Ministry Network, Balt., 1990—; chmn. bd. Christian Edn., Calvary Bapt. Ch., Norristown, Pa., 1985—. Author: Building an Effective Church School, 1976, A Growing Church School, 1978, Workbook for Planning Christian Education, 1983; co-author: Planning Christian Education in Your Church, 1974; author/editor: The Teaching Church at Work, 1980. Mem and pres Norristown Chorale, 1977—. Office: ABC Ministers-At-Large Prog PO Box 851 Valley Forge PA 19482-0851

BLEDSOE, TOMMY DALTON, minister; b. Carrollton, Ga., July 23, 1942; s. Johnson Dalton and Mary Doris (Cooley) B.; m. Donna Lee Shores, June 25, 1966; children: Tommy D. Jr., Jonathan Lee, Jennifer Leigh. AB in English, Ga. State Coll., 1964; ThM, New Orleans Bapt. Theol. Sem., 1967; MEd in Counseling, Ga. State U., 1972, PhD, 1980. Ordained to ministry So. Bapt. Conv., 1966; cert marriage and family therapist, Ga. Assoc. pastor Temple Bapt. Ch., New Orleans, 1968; pastor Mt. Ararat Bapt. Ch., Gaffney, S.C., 1969-70, Arbor Heights Bapt. Ch., Douglasville, Ga., 1973-77; cons. to min. counseling 1st Bapt. Ch., Douglasville, 1977-81; interim pastor Adairsville (Ga.) Bapt. Ch., 1983-84; pastor Unity Bapt. Ch., Newnan, Ga., 1984-86; counselor The Living Ctr., Douglasville, 1986-88; pastor 1st Bapt. Ch., Soperton, Ga., 1988-90, Wrens (Ga.) Bapt. Ch., 1990—; tchr. Ctr. Hill Elem. Sch., Atlanta, 1970-74; counselor David T. Howard High Sch., Atlanta, 1974-76, Frederick Douglass High Sch., Atlanta, 1976-84; dir. Pastoral Counseling Assocs., 1982-86; asst. prof. continuing edn. Mercer U., Douglasville, 1985-86; with acad. support office Reinhardt Coll., Waleska, Ga., 1988; adj. faculty Christianity dept. Brewton-Parker Coll., Mt. Vernon, Ga., 1989—; moderator Hephzibah Bapt. Assn., 1991—; v.p. Hephzibah Bapt. Ministers' Fellowship. Contbr. articles to profl. jours. Mem. AACD, Daniell Bapt. Mins.' Assn. (v.p. 1988-89, pres. 1989-90), Treutlen County Ministerial Alliance (moderator 1988-90), Daniell Bapt. Assn. (vice-moderator 1989-90), Am. Assn. for Marriage and Family Therapy (clin.), Nat. Assn. for Career Devel., Ga. Assn. for Marriage and Family Therapy (editor newsletter 1984-86), Kiwanis. Avocations: music, fishing, drawing, cycling. Home: 408 Thompson St Wrens GA 30833 Office: Wrens Bapt Ch PO Box 217 500 N Main St Wrens GA 30833

BLEI, K., church official. Sec. gen. The Netherlands Ref. Ch., Leidschendam. Office: Nederlandse Hervormde Kerk, Overgo 11, POB 405, 2260 AK Leidschendam The Netherlands*

BLEMKER, MARGARET RUTH, educator, world mission executive; b. New Bremen, Ohio, Apr. 2, 1915; d. Rudolf William and Lillian (Kohl) B. BA, Heidelberg Coll., Tiffin, Ohio, 1936, LHD (hon.), 1958; MEd, Syracuse U., 1942. Tchr. North Canton (Ohio) High Sch., 1936-39, Timken Voc. High Sch., Canton, 1939-40, Amerikan Kiz Koleji, Izmir, Turkey, 1945-48; dir. residences Univ. Hosps., Cleve., 1942-45; Near East exec. United Ch. Bd. for World Ministries, Boston, N.Y.C., 1949-80. Mem. AAUW, LWV. Democrat. Mem. United Church of Christ.

BLEVINS, LEON WILFORD, political science educator, minister; b. Brownfield, Tex., Oct. 2, 1937; s. Bernice Wilford and Virgie Opal (Bevers) B.; m. Shannah Pharr, Aug. 28, 1960; children: Tab, Keith, Shaleah. BA, Wayland Bapt. U., 1961; postgrad., Southwestern Bapt. Theol. Sem., Ft. Worth, 1961-63; MA, U. Tex., El Paso, 1967. Ordained to ministry So. Bapt. Conv., 1963. Dir., counselor Phila. Girls Home, Ft. Worth, 1961; pastor chs. Tex., N.Mex. and Calif., 1962-65; various interim pastorates, 1967-70; chaplain Interfaith Chapel, Tex. State Tech. Inst., Amarillo, 1971-72; lectr., tchr. polit. sci. U. Tex., El Paso, 1965-67, Tex. Tech U., 1967-70, West Tex. State U., 1970-72; instr. polit. sci. El Paso Community Coll., 1972—. Author: A Topical Dictionary of American Government and Politics, 1973, Texas Government in National Perspective, 1986, also numerous text study guides and manuals; appeared as Jesus in ann. outdoor Easter Pageant, as Uncle Sam in parades and celebrations, numerous other characters. Mem. Alpha Chi, Alpha Psi Omega, Alpha Mu Gamma, Phi Alpha Theta, Pi Sigma Alpha, Pi Gamma Mu. Home: 10305 Ashwood Dr El Paso TX 79925

BLEWETT, PATRICK ALAN, clergyman; b. Lewiston, Idaho, Aug. 31, 1956; s. Pierce Nurse and Grace Johnette (Peters) B.; m. Jana Lee Tureman, July 29, 1978; children: Sheila Marie, Kraig Alan, Amanda Joy. BA in Bibl. Studies, Mont. Inst. Bible, 1978; MA in Ch. Edn., Western Conservative Bapt. Sem, 1981, MDiv, 1990, postgrad., 1990—. Ordained to ministry Community Ch., 1982. Instr. religious edn. Big Sky Bible Coll., Lewistown, Mont., 1981-82; edn. pastor First Federated Ch., Des Moines, 1982-83; edn. pastor, adminstr. First Bapt. Ch., Sheridan, Wyo., 1983-85; assoc. pastor, adminstr. Orchards Community Ch., Lewiston, Idaho, 1985-90; family ministries pastor Cole Community Ch., Boise, Idaho, 1990—; instr. Bibl. studies Cole Ctr. Bibl. Studies, Boise, 1990—; cons. Scripture Press Publs., Wheaton, Ill., 1983—; adminstrv. chaplain Lewiston (Idaho) Police Dept., 1985-90. Mem. instl. rev. bd. St. Joseph's Regional Med. Ctr., Lewiston, 1988-90; bd. mem. Lewis-Clark Coun. on Youth, Lewiston, 1988-90, Lewis-Clark Coalition on At-Risk Youth, Lewiston, 1989-90, Treasure Valley Christian Workers Conf., Boise, 1990—. Recipient Cert. of Excellence in Environ. Protection, Pres. U.S., 1973. Mem. Internat. Conf. Police Chaplains, Conservative Bapt. Assn. Am., Nat. Assn. Evangelicals, Profl. Assn. Christian Educators, Idaho Assn. Pastoral Care (bd. mem. 1988-90), Lewis-Clark Ministerial Assn. (v.p. 1988-90), Rotary (pres. 1989-90). Republican. Home: 11029 Gunsmoke Boise ID 83704 Office: Cole Community Ch 8775 Ustick Rd Boise ID 83704 *While many people desire that we demand justice in our world, I would much rather promote God's grace and care amidst an unjust society. We will never right every wrong, but we can teach peace, love, and forgiveness in the midst of wrong! I think that is what Jesus would have us do!.*

BLIEK, BEATRICE, minister; b. Surabaya, Java, Indonesia, June 5, 1925; came to U.S., 1962; d. Bastiaan and Femmy Valentine (Beemer) Onsoe; m. Frederik Claproth, May 11, 1949 (dec. Oct. 1980); children: Rosemary Ellen, Joyce Yvonne, Peter David, Lawrence James; m. Dick Anthony Bliek, July 6, 1985. Diploma in Ministry and Leadership, Shiloh Tng. Inst., 1981. Ordained to ministry Pentecostal Ch., 1982. Founder Asia for Jesus Ministries, San Bernardino, Calif., 1982—. Home and Office: 182 S Macy St San Bernardino CA 92410

BLISS, JOHN EVERETT, minister; b. Lubbock, Tex., Mar. 5, 1948; s. Tommie and Wanda May (Owen) B. BA, Rocky Mountain Coll., 1976; MDiv, Iliff Sch. Theol., 1988. Ordained to ministry United Ch. Christ, 1989. Youth dir. Northglenn (Colo.) United Ch. Christ, 1987-88, pastor, 1988—. Office: Northglenn United Ch 10500 Grant Dr Northglenn CO 80233

BLISS, MATTHEW TODD, lay worker; b. Morrisville, Vt., Oct. 2, 1964; s. L.D. Elmer and Marjorie Louise (Ruggles) B. BA, Liberty U., Lynchburg, Va., 1987; MA, Wheaton (Ill.) Coll., 1989; postgrad., U. Edinburgh, Scotland, 1990—. Itinerant preacher United Ch. of Christ, Morrisville, Vt., 1981-87; prayer leader Liberty U., 1984-85, spiritual life dir., 1985-86; layman Episc. Ch., Glen Ellyn, Ill., 1988-90; warehouseman Boise Cascade Corp., Inc., Itasca, Ill., 1987-90. Campaign worker Dem. Cen. Com., Morrisville, 1986. Mem. Soc. Bibl. Lit., Evang. Theol. Soc., Am. Soc. Ch. History. Republican. Home: Rte 2 Box 5500 Bliss Hill Rd Morrisville VT 05661 *Obedience to the gospel of Jesus Christ is the sole hope for mankind.*

BLOBAUM, GARY DUANE, minister; b. Mpls., Feb. 18, 1952; s. Duane H. and Aleta V. (Feyerherm) B.; m. Amy Joan Streit; children: Benjamin, Katie, David. BA, Concordia Tchr.'s Coll., River Forest, Ill., 1975; MDiv, Christ Sem.-Seminex, St. Louis, 1979. Ordained to ministry Luth. Ch., 1982. Pastor Millville (Pa.) Luth. Parish, 1980-84, Benscreek Luth. Ch., Thomas Mills, Pa., 1984-87, Faith Luth. Ch., Marion, Iowa, 1987—. Office: Faith Luth Ch 155 Boyson Rd Marion IA 52302

BLOCK, DANIEL ISAAC, religion educator; b. Borden, Sask., Can., May 22, 1943; came to U.S., 1983; s. Isaac Henry and Ella (Derksen) B.; m. Ellen Ruth Lepp, Aug. 6, 1966; children: Jason, Jonelle. B. Edn., U. Sask., 1968, BA, 1969; MA, Trinity Evang. Divinity Sch., 1973; PhD, U. Liverpool (Eng.), 1982. Cert. tchr., Sask. Assoc. prof. Old Testament Winnipeg Bible Coll., Otterburne, Manitoba, Can., 1973-83; prof. Old. Testament Bethel Theol. Sem., St. Paul, 1983—. Author: The Gods of the Nations, 1988; contbr. articles to religious and scholarly jours. Mem. Soc. Bibl. Lit., Evang. Theol. Soc., Inst. Bibl. Rsch., Bibl. Archaeological Soc. Baptist. Home: 4294 Brigadoon Dr Shoreview MN 55126 Office: Bethel Theol Sem Saint Paul MN 55112

BLOCK, MICHAEL DAVID, minister; b. Albuquerque, Jan. 19, 1958; s. Isaac Edward and Lucy Mac (Waide) B.; m. Rebecca Lynn Hart, June 30, 1979; 1 child, Nathanael David. BA, Wayland Bapt. U., 1980; MDiv, Southwest•n Bapt. Sem., 1983, PhD, 1990. Ordained to ministry Bapt. Ch., 1982. Min. music Finney Bapt. Ch., Plainview, Tex., 1978-79, Date St. Bapt. Ch., Plainview, Tex., 1979-80; pastor Levita Bapt. Ch., Gatesville, Tex., 1984-85, 1st Bapt. ch., Comanche, Okla., 1985—. Basketball coach Youth Sports League, Duncan, 1989-90. Mem. Comanche C. of C. (coord. Christmas food baskets 1986—), Mullins Bapt. Assn. (sec., dir. missions, search com. 1987-88, moderator 1987-89, chmn. budget com. 1990—), Ministerial Alliance. Republican. Office: 1st Bapt Ch 4th & Main Sts Comanche OK 73529 *The call of life is to walk with God. The challenge of life is to live in obedience to God. The change of life is to influence others toward God.*

BLODGET, ROBERT NEWTON, minister, religious organization administrator; b. Kansas City, Mo., June 16, 1927; s. Paul Edward and Pearl (Newton) B.; m. Dorothy Helen Randall, July 3, 1954. Student, YMCA Coll., Chgo., 1943-44, Elim Bible Inst., 1949-51; ThB, Clarksville Sch. Theol., 1954. Ordained to ministry Elim Fellowship, 1952. Pastor The Meth. Ch., Mt. Moriah, Mo., 1954-56; evangelist various locations, 1957-60; founder, pres. Mex. Border Missions, Brownsville, Tex., 1961—; pastor Ch. of the Good Shepard, Brownsville, 1975-77, Peoples Chapel, Pharr, Tex., 1982—; bd. dirs. Kingsway Missionary Inst., McAllen, Tex., 1981—. Editor Mex. Border Missions mag., 1961—. Mem. Assn. Fundamental Mins. and Chs. Home: 416 Sagittarius Mission TX 78572 Office: Mex Border Missions PO Box 789 702 W Sam Houston Pharr TX 78577

BLOEDE, LOUIS WILLIAM, seminary educator; b. Fond du Lac, Wis., Aug. 17, 1928; s. F. William and Amanda Marie (Klein) B.; m. Mary Trautmann, Nov. 12, 1955; children—Kirk, Paul. B.A., North Central Coll., 1950; B.Div., Evang. Theol. Sem., 1953; D.Th., Boston U., 1960. Ordained to ministry United Methodist Ch. 1953. Minister to students 1st United Meth. Ch., Madison, Wis., 1951-53; pastor Grace United Meth. Ch., Wautoma, Wis., 1953-57, Center United Meth. Ch., Saugus, Mass., 1958-60; founding pastor Peace United Meth. Ch., Green Bay, Wis., 1960-65; prof. worship Evang. Theol. Sem., Naperville, Ill., 1965-74; prof. parish ministry Iliff Sch. Theology, Denver, 1974—; mem. Bd. Ordained Ministry, Rocky Mountain Conf. United Meth. Ch., 1982-90; assoc. Inst. Gerontology U. Denver, 1976-84; bd. dirs. Widowed Persons Service, Denver, 1981—, Operation Nightwatch (street ministry), Denver, 1982-84. Author: Developing the New Congregation, 1965; contbr. sects. to books, articles, book revs. to publs. Bd. mgrs. Birch Homeowners Assn., Vail, Colo., 1983-89; v.p. Aspen Condominium Assn., Vail, 1989—. Hartman scholar, 1952-53; fellow Inst. for Ecumenical and Cultural Research, Collegeville, Minn., 1970-71; Assn. Theol. Schs. research fellow, 1977-78. Fellow N.Am. Acad. Liturgy; mem. Assn. Theol. Field Edn. (steering com. 1979-81, 91—), Acad. Homiletics, Assn. Practical Theology, Field Edn. United Meth. Sem. (chmn. 1975-76), Dutch N.Am. Conf. on Practical Theology. Club: YMCA Men's (pres. Green Bay 1964-65). Home: 2756 S St Paul St Denver Co 80210 Office: Iliff Sch Theology 2201 S University Blvd Denver CO 80210

BLOMGREN, DAVID KENNETH, dean, pastor; b. Rochelle, Ill., June 1, 1940; s. Darwin Wayne and Roslyn (Castle) B.; m. Susan Marie Blomgren, Nov. 3, 1961; children: Brenda Lynn, Bradley Wayne, Bryan Robert. BA, Tenn. Temple U., 1963; MA, U. Portland, 1969; MDiv, Western Cons. Bapt. Sem., 1967, ThM, 1968, DMin, 1976; ThD, Logos Grad. Sch., 1986; MACE, Luther Rice Sem., 1989. V.p. Portland (Oreg.) Bible Coll., 1967-71; pres. Logos Bible Coll. and Grad. Sch., Tampa, Fla., 1987-89; grad. dean Fla. Beacon Bible Coll., Largo, Fla., 1989—; sr. pastor Tampa Bay Christian Ctr., Brandon, Fla., 1983—; asst. mgr. Sta. KPAZ-TV Christian TV, Phoenix, 1971-73; advisor Victory Christian Univ., San Diego, 1990—. Author: The Song of the Lord, 1978, Prophetic Gatherings, 1979, Restoring God's Glory, 1985 (Bestseller 1987), Restoring Praise and Worship, 1989; exec. editor: The Trumpet Call Mag., 1989—. Chmn. Montavilla Community Assn., Portland, 1977-78. Mem. Mins. Fellowship Internat. (apostolic team Portland chpt. 1985—). Office: Tampa Bay Christian Ctr 3920 S Kings Ave Brandon FL 33511

BLOOM, HAROLD, humanities educator; b. N.Y.C., July 11, 1930; s. William and Paula (Lev) B.; m. Jeanne Gould, May 8, 1958; children: Daniel Jacob, David Moses. B.A., Cornell U., 1951; Ph.D., Yale U., 1955; L.H.D., Boston Coll., 1973, Yeshiva U., 1976. Mem. faculty Yale U., 1955—, prof. English, 1965-77, DeVane prof. humanities, 1974-77, prof. humanities, 1977—, sterling prof. humanities, 1983—; vis. prof. Hebrew U., Jerusalem, 1959, Breadloaf Summer Sch., 1965-66, Soc. for Humanities, Cornell U., 1968-69; vis. Univ. prof. New Sch. Social Research, N.Y.C., 1982-84; Charles Eliot Norton prof. of poetry Harvard U., 1987-88; Berg prof. English, NYU, 1988—. Author: Shelley's Mythmaking, 1959, The Visionary Company, 1961, Blake's Apocalypse, 1963, Commentary to Blake, 1965, Yeats, 1970, The Ringers in the Tower, 1971, The Anxiety of Influence, 1973, Wallace Stevens: The Poems of Our Climate, 1977, A Map of Misreading, 1975, Kabbalah and Criticism, 1975, Poetry and Repression, 1976, Figures of Capable Imagination, 1976, The Flight to Lucifer: A Gnostic Fantasy, 1979, Agon: Towards a Theory of Revisionism, 1981, The Breaking of the Vessels, 1981, The Strong Light of the Canonical, 1987, Freud: Transference and Authority, 1988, Poetics of Influence: New and Selected Criticism, 1988, Ruin the Sacred Truths, 1988, The Book of J, 1989, The American Religion, 1990, The Western Canon, 1991; editor, introducer Chelsea House Modern Critical Views and Interpretations, 1984—. Recipient John Addison Porter prize Yale U., 1955; Newton Arvin award, 1967; Melville Cane award Poetry Soc. Am., 1970; Zabel prize Am. Inst. Arts and Letters, 1982, Christian Gauss prize Phi Beta Kappa, 1989; Guggenheim fellow, 1962; Fulbright fellow, 1955; MacArthur prize fellowship, 1985. Mem. Am. Acad. Arts and Scis., Am. Acad. and Inst. of Arts and Letters. Home: 179 Linden St New Haven CT 06511 *Most instances of religion are mere manifestations of religiosity, which is endemic in our nation, where nine of ten say that God loves them. Spinoza observed that we should love God without expecting that God would love us in return.*

BLOOM, JAMES MARTIN, minister; b. South Akron, Ohio, May 2, 1932; s. Martin Luther and Elizabeth Gertrude (Sueper) B.; m. Carol Ann Braden, June 28, 1958 (div. Mar. 1986); children: Mark, Kathie, Ken; m. Martha Ann Gilliland Jennings, Nov. 2, 1990. BA, Otterbein Coll., 1954; MDiv, Evangel. Theol. Sem., 1957. Ordained to ministry Meth. Ch., 1957. Min. East Ohio Conf. United Meth. Ch., 1957—; also bd. dirs., 1985—; Author: A Festival of Lights, 1986, (with others) His Hands, 1977, (play) Unto Us a Child is Born, 1987. Mem. Men's Garden Club of Am., Wash. Ruritan (chaplain). Office: 3450 Beechwood Ave Alliance OH 44601

BLOOM, JOHN ANDREW, clergyman; b. Akron, Ohio, Aug. 19, 1949; s. Jesse David and Betty Monetta (Myers) B.; m. Janice Merrill Ledford, June 21, 1969; children: Paul Sterling, Deborah Michelle, Jesse David. BA in Humanities cum laude, Pensacola Christian Coll., Fla., 1981. Ordained to ministry Bapt. Ch., 1978. Pastor Cantonment (Fla.) Bapt. Ch., 1978-83; pastor, founder Community Bapt. Ch., Tucson, Ariz., 1983-84; asst. pastor Cen. Bapt. Ch., Ocala, Fla., 1984-86, sr. pastor, 1986—; pres. Cen. Bapt. Ch. Inc., Ocala, 1986—; v.p. Ocala Christian Acad., 1984—. Mem. Southwide Bapt. Fellowship, Theta Sigma Gamma. Republican. Home: 1714 SE 36th Ave Ocala FL 32671 Office: Cen Bapt Ch 1714 SE 36th Ave Ocala FL 32671 *In our quest for world peace we must realize peace works from the inside out. Nations cannot have peace until individuals have peace. Individuals cannot have peace until they have Jesus Christ as their Lord and Saviour.*

BLOOMQUIST, GEORGE ELMER, minister; b. Rockford, Ill., Mar. 9, 1939; s. Frank Elmer and Georgia Margaret (Brown) B.; m. Kay Kathryn Clark, Aug. 19, 1960; children: Phillip James, Mark David. Student, Rockford (Ill.) Coll., 1957-60, U. Minn., 1961-62; BTh, Minn. Bible Coll., 1962; ThD, Trinity Theol. Sem., Ind., 1981. Ordained to ministry Christian Ch., 1962. Assoc. pastor Christian Ch., Webster City, Iowa, 1962-65; pastor 1st Christian Ch., Green Bay, Wis., 1965-68, New Ch. Devel., State of Iowa, 1968-77, Parkwood Christian Ch., St. Louis, 1977-90, Sunset Hills Christian Ch., Kansas City, Kans., 1990—; v.p. Christian Mins. Assn., St. Louis, 1982-84, pres., 1985; pres. bd. dirs. Christian Youth Home, St. Louis, 1984-87; pres. Maryland Heights Mins. Assn., St. Louis County, 1988. Contbr. articles on edn. to profl. jours. Mem. Pattonville Sch. Dist., St. Louis County, 1988. Officey: Sunset Hills Christian Ch 6347 Leavenworth Rd Kansas City KS 66104

BLOOMQUIST, MARVIN ROBERT, music educator, singer; b. Fergus Falls, Minn., Apr. 17, 1930; s. Albin and Amy Adoline (Peterson) B.; m. Wanda Mae Nesmith; children: Brenda Kay, Craig Michael. BA in Music Theory, N.W. Nazarene Coll., 1953, B in Mus. Voice, 1954; MA in Mus. History and Lit., U. Minn., 1958; D Mus. Arts in Vocal Performance, U. Mo., Kansas City, 1970. Min. music 1st Ch. of the Nazarene, Mpls., 1956-58, Nampa, Idaho, 1960-62; prof. voice N.W. Nazarene Coll., Nampa, 1958—; prof. music Nazarene Theol. Sem., Kansas City, Mo., 1966-68; dir. choir 1st Christian Ch., Nampa, 1958-60, 1st Meth. Ch., Nampa, 1961-65, 68-72; opera singer Kansas City Lyric Opera, 1967; sec.-treas. Chambers Scale Corp., Boise, Idaho, 1969-80. Author: Songs of Ned Rorem, 1970, Thoughts of Singing, 1985; contbr. articlest to profl. jours. Mem. ch. bd. Coll. Ch. of Nazarene, Nampa, 1986-89. With USAF, 1954-56. Recipient Disting. Svc. award N.W. Nazarene Coll., 1991. Mem. Nat. Assn. Tchr. Singing (state gov. Idaho chpt. 1972-77), Am. Choral Dirs. Assn. (pres. elect 1986-89, pres. 1989-91, v.p. 1991—), Music Educators Nat. Conf. (bd. dirs. 1989—), Phi Delta Lambda, Pi Kappa Lambda. Avocations: travel, sports. Home: 215 S Rowena Nampa ID 83686 Office: NW Nazarene Coll Nampa ID 83686

BLOSSOM, TIFANIE THEYLON, minister; b. Toledo, Dec. 6, 1947; d. Jerome Harvey and Ruth Marie (Adcock) Rollins; m. Thomas Alva Downey, Jan. 28, 1967 (div. June 1975); children: Heath Thomas, Nathan Michael; m. Jon Raulph Blossom, Nov. 15, 1978. Acctg. student, Owens Tech. Sch., Toledo, 1970-73; student psychology, theology, U. Toledo, 1973-76; grad., Religious Sci. Internat. Ministerial Sch., Chgo., 1984. Lic. Religious Sci. practitioner. Mgr. Elaine Powers Figure Salon, Toledo, 1974-75; asst. comptroller, sec. Huss Enterprises, Toledo, 1975-77; cooking instr. Amana Corp., Toledo, 1977-78; med. rep. Gerber Products, Inc., Fremont, Mich., 1978-79; owner, operator Tifanie's Kitchen, Toledo, 1979-81; pres. Blossom Health Ctr., Toledo, 1981—; substitute minister North Shore Ch. Religious Sci., Evanston, Ill., First Ch. Religious Sci., Chgo.; interim minister New Beginning Ch. of Religious Sci., Toledo; lectr. various orgns., seminars on nutrition, lifestyle, self awareness, transactional analysis. Author: Breadmakers' Handbook, 1982. Bd. dirs. March of Dimes, Toledo, 1987—, mem. Gourmet Gala food com.; bd. dirs. East Toledo Community Mental Health, 1976-78; vol. St. Vincent's Hosp., Little Sisters of Poor. Mem. Internat. New Thought Alliance, Internat. Transactional Analysis Orgn. Avocations: gardening, swimming, aerobics, skiing, reading. Office: Blossom Health Ctr 5900 Southwyck Blvd Toledo OH 43614

BLOUNT, EVELYN, religious organization administrator; b. Winder, Ga., Oct. 20, 1942; d. Willie Brown and Ouida (Pool) B. BS, Woman's Coll. Ga., 1964; MRE, So. Bapt. Theol. Sem., 1969. Tchr. Blue Mountain (Miss.) Coll., 1964-66, Berkmar High Sch., Gwinnette County, Ga., 1966-67; group leader Bapt. Ctr., Louisville, Ky., 1967-69; min. edn. 1st Bapt. Ch., Auburn, Ala., 1969-70; Acteens dir. Woman's Missionary Union, Aux. Ga. Bapt. Conv., Atlanta, 1970-73; youth dept. supr., field svcs. dir., nat. enlargement plan dir., program design specialist Woman's Missionary Union Aux. So. Bapt. Conv., Birmingham, Ala., 1973-85; exec. dir. Woman's Missionary Union Aux. S.C. Bapt. Conv., Columbia, 1985—; mem. prenatal mission project adv. group S.C. Dept. Health and Environ. Control; bd. dirs. Teen Pregnancy Reduction Network, Inc. Author: Code E and Teachers Guide for Code E, 1973, (with others) Youth Ministry Missions Projects, 1978. Named hon. life mem. USAF Air Def., 1959. Mem. NAFE, Exec. Dirs. Democrat. Avocations: wood carving, camping, music. Home: 300 Friarsgate Blvd Irmo SC 29063

BLOUNT, HENRY CLAYTON, JR., minister; b. Phila., Dec. 29, 1925; s. Henry Clayton and Sally Ann (Crawford) B.; m. Marilyn A. Speede, June 12, 1949; children: Becky, Mona, Cindy, Steve, Chris. BA, Millsaps Coll., 1950; BD, Emory U., 1952, MDiv, 1972; DMin, Iliff Sch. of Theology, 1981. Ordained to ministry Meth. Ch., 1953. Pastor Grace United Meth. Ch., Ruston, La., 1953-60, Opelousas La. Meml., 1960-64, Lake Charles (La.) 1st United Meth. Ch., 1965-72, Natchitoches (La.) 1st United Meth. Ch., 1973-78, Broadmoor United Meth. Ch., Baton Rouge, 1979-84, 1st United Meth. Ch., Alexandria, La., 1989—; bd. dirs. Discipleship La. Conf. United Meth. Ch., 1984. Author: Looking for Honey, 1984, Soul Sounds, 1988. With USN, 1944-45. Mem. Assn. for Rsch. and Enlightenment, Am. Assn. Counseling Pastors, La. Assn. for Counseling Devel., La. Profl. Counselors. Home: 2550 Ave C Alexandria LA 71301 Office: 1st United Meth Ch 2727 Jackson St Alexandria LA 71301 *The purpose of life is to set us free without setting us adrift.*

BLOWERS, LAVERNE PALMER, religious educator; b. Rochester, N.Y., May 16, 1940; d. Stanley LaVerne and Willoughby (Howe) B.; m. Loretta Jayne Harmer, July 1, 1967; children: Kevin LaVerne, Kristiana Joy. BA, Seattle Pacific Coll., 1962; MDiv, Asbury Theol. Sem., Wilmore, Ky., 1967; ThM, Fuller Theol. Sem., Pasadena, Calif., 1971; D in Missiology, Trinity Evang. Div. Sch., Deerfield, Ill., 1989. Missionary-educator Free Meth. Ch. N.Am., Winona Lake, Ind., 1972-80; dean Faculdade Metodista Livre no Brasil, Sao Paulo, 1976-80; asst. prof. missions Seattle Pacific U., 1980-82; assoc prof. religion and missions Roberts Wesleyan Coll., Rochester, N.Y., 1982-86; assoc. prof. missions and theology, div. chair Bethel Coll., Mishawaka, Ind., 1986-91; dir. Ctr. Continuing Edn. for Ministry, Rochester, 1982-86; conf. del. Missionary Ch., Goshen, Ind., 1990-91. Contbr. articles to profl. jours. Key communicator Penn-Harris-Madison Sch. Dist., Osceola, Ind., 1988—. Named Alumnus with Vision, Seattle Pacific U., 1989. Mem. Am. Acad. Religion, Am. Soc. Missiology, Assn. Profs. Missiology, Wesleyan Theol. Soc., Evangelical Missiological Soc. Republican. Home: 828 Steeplechase Dr Mishawaka IN 46544 Office: Bethel Coll 1001 W McKinley Ave Mishawaka IN 46545 *The value of a person is not in possessions, real or ascribed, but in the unshakeable conviction that now she/he is seeing a dim reflection of what is yet to be fully revealed.*

BLUE, JOHN RONALD, educator; b. Milw., Sept. 4, 1935; s. Earl R. and Wretha J. (Teater) B.; m. Elizabeth Frances Wood, Sept. 7, 1962; children: Lisa, Laurie, David. BA with distinction, U. Nebr., 1957; contologist, Ohio State U., 1960; ThM with high honors, Dallas Theol. Sem., 1965; PhD, U. Tex., 1989. Missionary, field worker Cen. Am. Mission, Jalapa, Guatemala, 1965-67; internat. coord. Christian edn. Cen. Am. Mission, San Salvador, El Salvador, 1967-71; field sec. CAM, Internat., Segovia, Spain, 1971-75; world mission dept. chmn. Dallas (Tex.) Theol. Sem., 1975—; chmn. bd. Worldteam, Lilburn, Ga., 1986-90; pres. bd. Christianity Without Barriers, Inc., Dallas, 1988—; bd. mem. Outreach, Inc., Grand Rapids, Mich., 1990—. Contbr. to books, 1982-88. Lt. USN, 1957-60, PTO. Mem. Evangelical Theol. Soc., Evangelical Missiological Soc. (regional v.p. 1980-84), Epsilon Delta Pi, Theta Xi (Lincoln, Nebr. pres. 1955-57). Republican. Baptist. Home: 3504 Halifax Dr Arlington TX 76013 Office: Dallas Theological Sem 3909 Swiss Ave Dallas TX 75204

BLUESTEIN, JUDITH ANN, rabbi, educator, diversified industry executive; b. Cin., Apr. 2, 1948; d. Paul Harold and Joan Ruth (Straus) Bluestein; BA, U. Pa., 1969; postgrad. Am. Sch. Classical Studies, Athens, Greece, 1968, Vergilian Soc., 1970, 76, 77, 78, Hebrew Union Coll., Jewish Inst. Religion, Jerusalem, 1971, 1979-80, Am. Acad. in Rome, 1975; MA in Religion, Case Western Res. U., 1973, MA in Latin, 1973; MEd, Xavier U., 1984; MA in Hebrew Letters, Hebrew Union Coll.-Jewish Inst. Religion, Cin., 1983; MPhil Hebrew Union Coll., 1989. Ordained rabbi, 1984. Sec., Paul H. Bluestein & Co., Cin., 1964—; v.p. Panel Machine Co., 1966—, Blujay Corp., 1966—, Ermet Products Corp., 1966—; ptnr. Companhia Engenheiros Indsl. Bluestein do Brasil, Cin., 1971—; tchr. Latin, Cin. Public Schs., 1973-79; rabbi Temple Israel, Marion, Ohio, 1980-84, Temple Sholom, Galesburg, Ill., 1985-86, B'nai Israel Congregation, Hattiesburg, Miss., 1990—, U. So. Miss. Campus Mins., 1990—; co-chmn. Interfaith Plea for Soviet Jews, 1986; lectr. Hebrew Union Coll.-Jewish Inst. Religion, 1986-89; vis. lectr., Jewish chaplain Denison U., 1987-88; vis. lectr. Ind. U., Bloomington, 1989-90; bd. dirs. Cin. Council for Soviet Jews, 1982-84, 85-89, sec. 1985-87. Fellow Case Western Reserve U., 1970-73, Hebrew Union Coll.-Jewish Inst. Religion, 1985-90; Revson fellow Jewish Theol Sem. Am., 1984-85; Hausmon Meml. fellow Hebrew Union Coll. Jewish Inst. Religion, 1985-86; Isadore and Goldie Millstone fellow Hebrew Union Coll., 1986-87, Julia and Leo Forchheimer fellow, 1987-89., Mrs. Henry Morganthau fellow Hebrew Union Coll., 1989-90. Mem. Archeol. Inst. Am., Assn. Jewish Studies, Am. Acad. Religion, Classical Assn. Middle West and South (v.p. Ohio 1976-79), Central Conf. Am. Rabbis, Am. Classical League, Ohio Classical Conf. (council 1976-79), Vergilian Soc., Soc. Bibl. Lit., Cin. Assn. Tchrs. Classics (pres. 1976-78), Am. Philol. Assn., Hattiesburg Interfaith Alliance. Address: 2300 Lincoln Rd Apt 99 Hattiesburg MS 39401

BLUESTONE, ELLEN JANE, foundation administrator; b. St. Louis, Jan. 31, 1937; d. Albert and Fanny (Levinson) Fein; m. Daniel R. Bluestone, Jan. 12, 1958; children: Cynthia, Kenneth, Linda. Student, Washington U., 1955. Assoc. dir. women's div. Jewish Fedn., St. Louis, 1974-82, asst. campaign dir., 1982-85, assoc. campaign dir., 1985-86, campaign dir., 1986—, asst. exec. dir., campaign, 1988—; com. mem. United Jewish Appeal Nat. Campaign Planning Com., N.Y.C., 1987, 90, 91; regional membership com. Am. Jewish Community Orgn. of Personnel, N.Y.C., 1986—; vice-chmn. planning com. United Jewish Appeal Campaign Dirs. Inst., Tampa, Fla., San Francisco, Palm Beach, Fla., Phoenix, 1988-89, 90, 91; authored numerous fundraising speeches and presentations. Fundraising chmn., bd. dirs. St. Louis Friends, U. Mo. Kansas City Sch. Medicine, St. Louis, 1982-87; mem. Shaare Emeth Sisterhood, Nat. Council Jewish Women, Hadassah, Orgn. for Rehab. Through Tng., Am. Med. Ctr. Cancer Rsch. Recipient Fred A. Goldstein Meml. Svc. award Jewish Fedn. St. Louis, 1990, Vivian Rabineau Meml. award Campaign Dirs. Inst., Coun. Jewish Fedns., 1991, Pinchas Sapir award. Mem. Nat. Soc. Fund Raising Execs., Am. Jewish Community Orgn. Pers. Democrat. Avocations: reading, cooking, gardening. Office: Jewish Fedn St Louis 12 Millstone Campus Saint Louis MO 63146

BLUM, SHERI ELLEN, cantor; b. Compton, Calif., Sept. 8, 1957; d. Merwin Cordon and Janice Charlotte (Levine) B.; m. Elliott Mark Ginsburg, Nov. 20, 1983; 1 child, Rachel Gladys. B in Sacred Music, Hebrew Union Coll., 1982. Cantor Congregation Beth Am, Los Altos Hills, Calif., 1973-75, Union Reform Temple, Freeport, N.Y., 1978-82, Temple Emanuel, Worcester, Mass., 1982—. Mem. Am. Conf. of Cantors (v.p. 1983—), Justice of the Peace Assn. Republican. Jewish. Home: 2 Atwater St Worcester MA 01602 Office: Temple Emanuel 280 May St Worcester MA 01602

BLUNDELL, JAMES, ecumenical agency administrator. Pres. Associated Ministries Thurston County, Olympia, Wash. Office: Associated Ministries Thurston County Box 985 Olympia WA 98507*

BLYTHE, MARY ALGERON, lay worker; b. Portageville, Mo., July 12, 1932; d. Crit Dawson and Hettie (Ellis) Brock; m. Fagain Loranza Blythe, May 20, 1950; children: Barbara Gale (dec.), Steven Dale, Howard F. L., Sandra Dee. Grad. high sch., Gideon, Mo. Ch. clk. Lakecrest Bapt. Ch., Pontiac, Mich., 1970-75, dir. Woman's Missionary Union, 1973-76, sec., 1976; sec. Columbia Ave. Bapt. Ch., Pontiac, 1977—, ch. clk., 1982—, dir. Sunday sch., 1986-88. Mem. Oakland County Bapt. Assn. (messenger 1973-74, 78, 80, 82-88, sec. 1976-89, treas. 1977-89, sec. The Assn. Ch. Media Orgn. 1979-85, 90—). Office: Columbia Ave Bapt Ch 64 W Columbia Ave Pontiac MI 48340

BLYTHE, ROBERT RICHARD, minister, mathematics educator; b. Richmond, Ky., Nov. 5, 1949; s. Richard Mason and Vashti (Bradford) B.; m. Janice Orienda Burdette, June 6, 1981 (div. Jan. 1984). BS, Eastern Ky. U., 1971; M in Div., So. Bapt. Theol. Seminary, Louisville, 1986. Ordained to ministry Bapt. Ch., 1981; cert. secondary math. and French tchr., Ky. Math. tchr. City of Gary, Ind., 1971-72; teaching asst. French dept. Eastern Ky. U., Richmond, 1972-73; math. and French tchr. Richmond Ind. Sch. Dist., 1973-78, math. tchr., 1987—; mktg. rep. gen. systems div. IBM, Akron, Ohio, 1978-81; minister 1st Bapt. Ch., Richmond, 1981—; dean Christian edn. Bapt. Unified Christian Leadership Conf., Louisville, 1986—; pres. New Liberty Bapt. Sunday Sch. Conv., Richmond, 1986—; counselor Gov.'s Minority Student Coll. Awareness Program, Lexington, Ky., 1987—. Mem. Human Rights Commn., Richmond, 1984-86; mem., bd. dirs. ARC, Richmond, 1986-87; trustee, bd. dirs. Pattie A. Clay Hosp., Richmond, 1973-78. Mem. NEA, Ky. Edn. Assn., Richmond Edn. Assn., NAACP, Gen. Assn. Ky. Bapts. (sec. 1973—). Democrat. Avocation: piano playing. Home: 1006 Altamont St Richmond KY 40475

BOA, KENNETH DALE, minister, writer; b. Kearney, Nebr., July 22, 1945; s. Kenneth and Ruthelaine (Kelley) B.; m. Karen Rose Powelson, Dec. 29, 1967; 1 child, Heather. BS, Case Inst. Technology, 1967; ThM, Dallas Theol. Seminary, 1972; PhD, NYU, 1985; postgrad., U. Oxford, Eng., 1986—. Tchr., writer New Life, Inc., Knoxville, Tenn., 1972-75; instr., coll. chaplain The King's Coll., Briarcliff Manor, N.Y., 1976-79; tchr., writer, chief editor Walk Thru The Bible Ministries, Atlanta, 1979-82; Atlanta area dir., Ea. Div. dir. Search Ministries, Lutherville, Md., 1982—. Author numerous books including: Scripture Talks with God, 1990, Cults, World Religions, and the Occult, 1990, Night Light, 1989, Unraveling the Big Questions About God, 1988, Drawing Near: A Scripture Guide to Prayer and Renewal, 1987, Visual Survey of the Bible, 1986, The Open Bible Companion, 1986, others. Recipient C.F. Lincoln award in Bible Exposition, Dallas Theol. Seminary, 1972, Rollin Thomas Chafer award in Apologetics, 1972, W.E. Hawkins, Jr. award in Christian Svc., 1972. Mem. Evangel. Theol. Soc., Am. Scientific Affiliation, Evangel. Philos. Soc. Home: 1791 Chadds Lake Dr Marietta GA 30068 Office: Search Ministries 5038 Dorsey Hall Dr Ellicott City MD 21042 *I have came to conclude that the central theme of Biblical teaching is the qualitative transformation of relationships, and that the foundation for such a transformation on the "horizontal" dimension is entering into a growing "vertical" relationship with the infinite-personal Creator and Redeemer.*

BOADT, LAWRENCE EDWARD, priest, religion educator; b. L.A., Oct. 26, 1942; s. A. Loren and Eleanor (Power) B. MA in Religious Studies, St. Paul's Coll., Washington, 1968; STL, Cath. U. Am., 1971, MA in Semitic Langs., 1972; SSL, Pontifical Bibl. Inst., Rome, 1974, SSD, 1976. Ordained priest Roman Cath. Ch., 1969. Priest St. Andrew's Parish, Clemson, S.C., 1969-70, St. Susanna Parish, Rome, 1971-75; aux. staff St. Paul the Apostle Parish, N.Y.C., 1975-86, Good Shepherd Parish, N.Y.C., 1986—; prof. of the Bible Washington Theol. Union, Silver Spring, Md., 1976—. Editor: Toward Understanding the New Testament, 1978, Ezekiel's Oracle Against Egypt: A Literary and Philological Study, 1980, Jeremiah XXVI-LII, Zephaniah, Habakkuk and Nahum, 1983, Reading the Old Testament: An Introduction, 1985, An Introduction to Wisdom and the Book of Proverbs, 1986; editor-in-chief Theol. Inquiries; pub. editor Cath. Bibl. Quar., 1978-84; assoc. editor New Cath. World; contbr. articles to religious jours. Recipient Best Old Testament Book of Yr. Bibl. Archaeology Soc., 1986. Mem. Cath. Bibl. Assn. (regional pres. 1979-80), Am. Sch. Oriental Rsch., Soc. Bibl. Lit. (regional sec. 1984-90), Am. Acad. Religion. Office: St Paul's Coll 3015 4th St NE Washington DC 20017

BOAK, BRUCE GORDON, minister; b. Oberlin, Ohio, Aug. 10, 1947; s. Gordon E. and Vivian Marie (DuCarme) B.; m. Martha Louise Oerter, Aug. 7, 1971; Joshua, Meredith. AB, Grove City (Pa.) Coll., 1969; MDiv, Princeton Theol. Sem., 1972. Ordained to ministry Presbyn. Ch. (U.S.A.), 1972. Pastor Bessemer (Pa.) Presbyn. Ch., 1972-78, Cen. Presbyn. Ch., Downingtown, Pa., 1978-90, Christ Presbyn. Ch., Canton, Ohio, 1990—. Judge election Chester County Election Bd., West Chester, Pa., 1980-90. Recipient Honor award Chapel of Four Chaplains, Phila., 1988. Mem. Rotary. Home: 928 Southmoor Circle NE Canton OH 44721 Office: Christ Presbyn Ch 530 Tuscarawas W Canton OH 44702

BOARDMAN, DONALD PETER, minister; b. Paterson, NJ, Feb. 25, 1939; s. Harry Sr. and Adrianna (Keyzer) B.; m. Carol Paige Preston, Apr. 6, 1968. BA, Lafayette Coll., 1961; MDiv, Princeton Theol. Sem., 1964; DMin, Colgate Rochester Div. Sch., 1976. Ordained to ministry Presbyn. Ch. (USA), 1964. Exec. dir. East Trenton (N.J.) Ctr., 1967-68; pastor Union Presbyn. Ch., Sauquoit, N.Y., 1969-78, Georgetown and Cool Spring Presbyn. Chs., Georgetown, Del., 1978-84; stated clk. Presbytery West Jersey, Haddon Heights, 1987—; pastor The Presbyn. Ch., Willingboro, N.J., 1984—; missioner New Castle Presbytery, Colombia, Costa Rica, Nicaragua, 1984; commr.Gen. Assembly Presbyn. Ch. (U.S.A), Phoenix, 1984; participant Stated Clks.' Confs., Gen. Assembly and Synod, 1987—. Chairperson Mohawk Valley Coun. Chs. Social Action Com., Utica, N.Y., 1971-76, Cambodian Refugee Task Force, Georgetown, 1979-84; moderator Youth Needs Assessment Panel, Willingboro, 1985; mem. Youth Achievement Com., Willingboro, 1986-87, Alliance for Quality Edn., Willingboro, 1988-90; committeeman Dem. Party, Willingboro, 1988. Mem. Willingboro Clergy Assn. (pres. 1985), Area Presbyn. Clergy. Home: 53 Normandy Ln Willingboro NJ 08046 Office: The Presbyn Ch Beverly-Rancocas Rd Willingboro NJ 08046

BOARDMAN, KATHERINE ANNE, religion educator; b. Houston, Oct. 24, 1961; d. William Kilbourne and Katherine Baker (Blackshear) B. BA magna cum laude, Catawba Coll., 1983; MA, U. Ga., 1989, Presbyn. Sch. Christian Edn., 1989. Dir. Christian edn. Albemarle Rd. Presbyn. Ch., Charlotte, N.C., 1990—; mem. Presbytery Charlotte Youth Com., 1991; camp educator Camp Grier, Old Fort, N.C., 1991; v.p. Charlotte Fellowship of Ecumenical Religious Educators, 1991—. Mem. Assn. of Presbyn. Ch. Educators, Southeastern Theatre Conf., Kappa Delta Pi, Alpha Chi. Office: Albemarle Rd Presbyn Ch 6740 Albemarle Rd PO Box 25903 Charlotte NC 28229

BOBCOCK, FLOYD C., religious association executive. Gen. sec. Can. Bible Soc., Toronto, Ont. Office: Can Bible Soc, 10 Carnforth Rd, Toronto, ON Canada M4A 2S4*

BOCK, DARRELL LANE, religion educator; b. Calgary, Alta., Can., Dec. 8, 1953; came to U.S., 1955; s. Bertram Victor and Arlene Ann (Zuckermann) B.; m. Sarah Hallowell Painter, Dec. 23, 1975; children: Elisa, Lara, Stephen. BA, U. Tex., 1975; ThD in Old Testament, Dallas Theol. Sem., 1979; PhD in New Testament, U. Aberdeen (Scotland), 1983. Ordained to ministry Evang. Ch., 1982. From asst. prof. to prof. N.T. studies Dallas Theol. Sem., 1982—; min. of the Word Trinity Fellowship, Richardson, Tex., 1982—; chmn. steering com. CD Word Libr., Inc., Dallas, 1987—. Author: Proclamation from Prophecy and Pattern, 1987; contbr. articles to profl. jours. Rep. PTA, Dallas, 1987-88, pres., 1991—. Mem. Soc. Bibl. Lit., Evang. Theol. Soc., Tyndale Soc. (U.K.), Inst. for Bibl. Rsch. Home: 6478 Highgate Dallas TX 75214 Office: Dallas Theol Sem 3909 Swiss Ave Dallas TX 75204 *Devotion to Christ and faithfulness to others are the essence of life.*

BOCK, PAUL JOHN, religion educator; b. Beulah, N.D., Mar. 30, 1922; s. Albert F. and Lydia (Buehrer) B.; m. Eve Chybova, Jan. 28, 1949; children: Benjamin, Timothy, Jane. BA, Heidelberg Coll., 1944; BD, Yale Divinity Sch., 1950, S.T.M., 1951; PhD, Western Res. U., 1965. Ordained to ministry United Ch. Christ, 1950. Mem. publicity staff World Coun. Chs., Geneva, 1946-48; YMCA-YWCA dir. Oreg. State Coll., Corvallis, 1950-53; campus minister Bowling Green (Ohio) State U., 1953-59; prof. religion Heidelberg Coll., Tiffin, Ohio, 1959-82, Doane Coll., Crete, Nebr., 1982-89; interim pastor United Ch. of Christ, Coleridge, Nebr., 1990-91; mem. peace and justice task force Nebr. Conf., United Ch. of Christ, Lincoln, 1983—; vis. prof. Trinity Coll., Legon, Ghana, 1976-77. Author: In Search of a Responsible World Soc., 1974; editor: Signs of the Kingdom, 1984; assoc. religion editor USA Today, 1976-90. Co-dir. Jr. Yr. at Heidelberg (Fed. Republic Germany), 1980-82. Danforth Tchr. Study grantee Danforth Found., 1962, summer seminar grantee NEH, Urbana, Ill., 1973. Mem. Am. Soc. Christian Ethics, Kiwanis (pres. Tiffin club 1968), Rotary (pres. Crete, Nebr. club 1986). Home: 1600 Cherrywood Dr Crete NE 68333 *The Christian Way is no untried or uncharted road, but a road beaten hard by the footsteps of saints, apostles, prophets, and martyrs.*

BODA, REXFORD A., academic administrator. Pres. Nyack (N.Y.) Coll. Office: Nyack Coll Office of Pres Nyack NY 10960*

BODE, TIMOTHY ALAN, lay worker; b. St. Louis, May 24, 1961; s. David Allan and Evonne Carol (Stender) B.; m. Mary Ellen Cardelli, Aug. 6, 1983; children: Sarah Joy, Josiah David. BA, Concordia Coll., St. Paul, 1984. Dir. Evangelism St. John Luth. Ch., Rochester, Mich., 1984—; cir. Evangelism rep. Mich. Dist. Luth. Ch.-Mo. Synod, 1985—; mem. Networking com., 1990—. Co-editor: newsletter DE Grapevine, 1986—. Mem. Dirs. of Christian Outreach Assn. (sec. 1989—). Office: St John Luth Ch 1011 W University Dr Rochester MI 48307-1862

BODELL, ROBERT EDWAYNE, minister; b. Cadillac, Mich., Feb. 5, 1948; s. Fred Henry and Waneita Mae (Garton) B.; m. Rebecca Jane Hines, Aug. 1970 (div. April 1977); children: Tammy, Kathy, Robert E II; m. Cathy Lynn Cook, June 2, 1979; 1 child, Joshua. BA, Pacific Christian Coll., 1979, MA, 1981; MDiv, Fuller Sem., 1984; MA, Pacific Christian Coll., 1988. Ordained to ministry. Counselor Anahheim (Calif.) Viet Vet Ctr., 1982-84; pastor Larkellen Christian Ch., Fullerton, Calif., 1980-84, 1st Christian Ch., Baldwin Park, Calif., 1984—; therapist intern Curt Rounzoing Assn., Fullerton, 1989-90, Alpha Counseling, Laguna Hills, Calif., 1990—. Dir. Vietnam Leadership Program, Fullerton, Calif., 1982-85; trauma chaplain Western Med. Ctr., Santa Ana, Calif., 1982-89; v.p. Brea (Calif.) Ministerial Assn., 1983, sec., 1982; with U.S. Army, 1966-75, Vietnam. Mem. Calif. Assn. Marriage and Family Therapist, VFW, Baldwin Ministerial Assn. (sec. 1985—). Republican. Avocations: fishing, camping, walking, horseback riding, hunting. Home: 2907 E Ruby Dr Apt G Fullerton CA 92631 Office: 1st Christian Church 4161 Baldwin Park Blvd Baldwin Park CA 91706

BODENSTEIN, WALTER, theologian, educator; b. Harburg, Niedersach, Germany, Nov. 15, 1914; s. Wilhelm and Alma (Heyden) B.; m. Ilse Bartholdi; children: Michael, Christine, Wolfgang, Cornelia. 1st Theol. Exam, U. Erlangen, Fed. Republic Germany, 1937; 2nd Theol. Exam, Praktische Ausbildung, Landeskirche, Hannover, 1939; ThD, U. Erlangen, Fed. Republic Germany, 1958. Pastor Ev.luth. Landeskirche, Hannover, Fed. Republic Germany, 1945-58; pfarrer, supt. Ev.Kirche, Berlin, 1958-68; prof. Pädagogische Hochschule, Kiel, Fed. Republic Germany, 1968-80. Author: Neige des Historismus, 1959, Die Theologie Karl Holls, 1968, Glaube und Anfechtung, 1975, Christen im Röm Reich, 1981-82. Mitglied, Kiel, 1968—. Evangelical Lutheran. Avocation: music (Bach). Home: HoltenauerstraBe 194, D-2300 Kiel Federal Republic of Germany

BODEY, RICHARD ALLEN, minister, educator; b. Hazelton, Pa., Nov. 27, 1930; m. Ruth Lois Price, 1955; children: Bronnlyn Beth Spindler, Richard Allen Jr. AB, Lafayette Coll, 1952; MDiv, Princeton Theol. Sem., 1955; postgrad., U. Toronto, 1961; ThM, Westminster Theol Sem., 1972; D Ministry, Trinity Evang. Div. Sch., 1984, Seabury-Western Theol. Sem., 1985. Ordained to ministry Presbyn. Ch., 1955. Pastor Marshall Meml. Presby. Ch., Lebanon, Ill., 1955-56; instr. Bible McKendree Coll., Lebanon, Ill., 1956; pastor 3d Presbyn. Ch., North Tonawanda, N.Y., 1956-62; instr. Buffalo Bible Inst., 1961; pastor 1st Presbyn. Ch., Corry, Pa., 1962-64, Dales Meml. United Presbyn. Ch., Phila., 1964-66; prof. preaching, chmn. Practical Theol. Dept. Reformed Theol. Sem., Jackson, Miss., 1966-73; head of staff 1st Assoc. Reformed Presby. Ch., Gastonia, N.C., 1973-79; interim pastor 1st Presbyn. Ch., Hazlehurst, Miss., 1967-68; stated supply pastor Presbyn. Ch., Union Church, Miss., 1970-73; dir. Gastonia Sch. Bibl. Studies, N.C., 1979; assoc. prof. practical theol. Trinity Evang. Divinity Sch., Deerfield, Ill., 1979-87, prof., 1987—; dir. continuing edn. Trinity Evang. Divinity Sch., 1982-87, instr. preaching Moody Bible Inst., Chgo., 1982-86, vis. faculty, Westminster Theol. Sem., Phila., 1987-88, lectr., 1990, cons. in continuing edn., 1990-91; vis. faculty Columbia (S.C.) Bibl. Sem. and Grad. Sch. Missions, 1991. Author: You Can Live Without Fear of Death, 1980; editor, contbr. Good News for All Seasons: 26 Sermons for Special Days, 1987, Inside the Sermon: Thirteen Preachers Discuss Their Methods of Preparing Messages, 1990, The Voice from the Cross: Seven Sermons on the Last Words of Our Lord, 1990; editor Voices, 1980-88; contbr. to Ency. of Christianity, 1962-72, Ministers Manual, 1974, 82, Zondervan Pictorial Bible Ency., Baker Ency. of Bible, 1988; contbr. articles to profl. jours. Various exec. positions Ch. coms. Recipient Porter Bible prize Lafayette Coll., 1950, David Fowler Atkins Jr. prize, 1952. Mem. Acad. Homiletics, Evang. Theol Soc. Avocation: travel, collecting miniature cottages. *To me life's highest meaning and deepest satisfaction lie in a personal relationship with Jesus Christ as divine Saviour and Lord. My supreme aim and motive are to honor Him in everything I do. I can think of no worthier pursuit, no more challenging goal, for anyone in any age.*

BODIFORD, WILLIAM MARVIN, religion educator; b. Birmingham, Ala., Dec. 3, 1955; s. George Marvin and Helen Maria (Lablock) B.; m. Margy Sylvia Heyman, Jan. 23, 1975 (div. 1978); m. Bong Nae Lee, Sept. 2, 1984. BA, U. Kans., 1980, MA, Yale U., 1982, PhD, 1989. Asst. prof. Sch. of Religion U. Iowa, Iowa City, 1989—. Rsch. fellow Japan Found., Tokyo, 1984, edn. fellow Japanese Ministry of Edn. 1980, travel fellow Assn. for Asian Studies, 1990. Mem. Am. Acad. Religion, Assn. for Asian Studies, Kashima Shinryu (bd. dirs. North Am. chpt. 1985—). Office: U Iowa Sch of Religion 308 Gilmore Hall Iowa City IA 52242

BODINE, SISTER BERNADETTE, academic administrator; b. Velva, N.D., Oct. 9, 1935. BS, Minot (N.D.) State U., 1966; MS, N.D. State U., 1968; DA in Chemistry, U. No. Colo., 1978. Prof. chemistry U. Mary, Bismarck, N.D., 1972-76; prioress Sacred Heart Monastery, Richardton, N.D., 1981-89; pres. Presentation Coll., Aberdeen, S.D., 1990—. Pres. bd. St. Vincents Nursing Home, Bismarck, 1981-89, Marillac Retirement Ctr., Bismarck, 1981-89. Mem. Assn. Cath. Colls. and Univs., Nat. Assn. Ind. Colls. and Univs. Office: Presentation Coll 1500 N Main St Aberdeen SD 57401 *Living in a rural area keeps me aware of our home, the earth. We must keep it clean, beautify it and maintain it for future generations.*

BODINE, CARLTON WRIGHT, JR., minister; b. Neptune, N.J., Dec. 13, 1948; s. Carlton Wright Sr. and Evelyn (Mickel) B.; m. Katherine Ann Snyder, Apr. 26, 1986; 1 child, Carlton Wright III. BS in Philosophy, Asbury Coll., 1971; MDiv, Drew U., 1980. Ordained to ministry United Meth. Ch. Pastor youth Calvary Meth. Ch., Lexington, Ky., 1969-71; pastor Barnsboro (N.J.) and Mt. Zion Meth. chs., 1971-81, Waretown (N.J.) United Meth. Ch., 1981-91, 2d Meth. Ch., Millville, N.J., 1991—. Mem. Delanco Camp Meeting Assn. (bd. dirs. 1972—, camp mgr. 1980—, v.p., 1984—), King's Crusaders (founder, bd. dirs. 1971-81). Home and Office: 829 Church St Millville NJ 08332

BODINE, JOHN JERMAIN, pastor; b. Jamestown, N.Y., Jan. 21, 1941; s. Henry B. Lathrop and Josephine (Waring Bodine) Ward; Wilhelmina Thea Bijlefeld, Sept. 15, 1984; children: Melissa Heather, Courtney Joy. BA, St. John's Coll., 1963; BD, Hartford Sem. Found., 1967, PhD, 1973. Ordained to ministry United Ch. Christ, 1970. Asst. dean Hartford Sem. Found., Hartford, Conn., 1971-74; asst. dir. Macdonald Ctr. Study Islam, Hartford, 1974-77; pastor, tchr. Congl. Ch. Henniker (N.H.), 1979-83, Newent Congl. Ch., Lisbon, Conn., 1983-87, Stratham (N.H.) Community Ch., 1987—; scribe, Rockingham Assn., United Ch. Christ, N.H., 1990—; chmn., AIDS Working Group, United Ch. Christ, N.H., 1990—; mem. Task Force Homosexuality, Conn., 1985-87, Coun. Ch. Soc., United Ch. Christ., N.H., 1980-83. Contbr. articles to profl. jours. Chmn. safety programs, Conn. Red Cross, Hartford, 1972-79; mem. Child Abuse Task Force, Concord, N.H., 1981-83. Campus Ministry fellow, Danforth Found., 1974-75, Traveling fellos, Hartford Sem. Found., 1976; recipient Thompson prize Hartford Found., 1976, Tyler prize, 1976. Office: Stratham Community Ch Emery Ln Stratham NH 03885

BODMAN, WHITNEY SHEPARD, pastor; b. Princeton, N.J., Feb. 20, 1950; s. Herbert Luther and Ellen Fairbanks (Diggs) B.; m. Elizabeth Jordan, June 2, 1979; children: Noah, Elizabeth. BA, U. N.C., 1973; MDiv, Duke U., 1977. Chaplain Dana Hall Sch., Wellesley, Mass., 1979-80; assoc. pastor Evang. Ch., Westboro, Mass., 1980-85; pastor Franklin (Mass.) Federated Ch., 1985—; mem. chapel adv. com. Smith Coll., Northhhampton, Mass., 1980—; mem. planned giving com. United Ch. of Christ, Framingham, Mass., 1984-87, mem. Jewish-Christian dialogue, N.Y., 1989—; del. NCC Office for Christian and Muslim Rels., N.Y., 1989—. Mem., chair Franklin Coun. on Aging, 1986—; bd. dirs. Internat. Ctr. for Devel. Policy, Washington, 1988—. Office: Franklin Federated Ch 171 Main St Franklin MA 02038

BODO, JOHN RAINER, minister; b. Budapest, Hungary, May 10, 1920; s. Charles and Mila Maria DeBodo; m. Jeanne Pfeiffer, Oct. 12, 1950 (div. 1964); children: Erika Bodo Alarcon, Jessica Bodo Wise; m. Mary Lou Lindstrom, June 15, 1974. BD, Union Theol. Sem., 1942; ThM, Princeton Sem., 1943, PhD, 1952. Ordained to ministry Presbyn. Ch., 1942. Pastor First Nassau Presbyn. Ch., Princeton, N.J., 1951-59; prof. practical theology San Francisco Sem., San Anselmo, Calif., 1959-67; chaplain, prof. Macalester Coll., St. Paul, 1967-68; pastor Old First Presbyn. Ch., San Francisco, 1969-76; interim pastor various churches, 1977-87; retired, 1985—; broadcasting com. Presbyn. Ch., U.S.A., N.Y.C., 1954-57, ch. and soc. coun., 1960-69; com. on ministry Redwoods Presbytery, Novato, Calif., 1990—. Author: The Protestant Clergy & Public Issues, 1812-1848, 1954, Adam & Eve & You, 1977, A Gallery of New Testament Rogues, 1979; contbr. many articles to profl. jours. Democrat. Home: 730 Appleberry Dr San Rafael CA 94903

BODY, RONALD GILMOUR, minister; b. North Charleroi, Pa., Nov. 17, 1959; s. Frank and Lois Ruth (Clegg) B.; m. Candy Calvin, Aug. 12, 1978; children: Caleb, Ariel. AS, Seminole Community Coll., 1978; postgrad., Berean Sch. of the Bible, Springield, Ill., 1977, Valencia Community Coll., 1979. Ordained to ministry Assemblies of God, 1985. Christian worker Peninsular Fla. Assemblies of God, Lakeland, 1978-80; founder, adminstrv. pastor Raleigh (N.C.) Christian Community Inc., 1985—; bd. dirs. Raleigh Christian Community Inc., adminstr. bd. dirs., 1989—; bd. dirs. Airborn Single Adult Ministries, Raleigh Christian Community Sch., 1989—; exec. dir. Maranatha Springs Family Camp and Conf. Ctr., 1991—. Mem. World Changes Internat. (sec., treas., bd. dirs. 1990—), Am. Congress Christian Citizens, Raleigh People for Life, Christian Mgmt. Assn., Christian Camping Internat. Republican. Home: 1612 Colston Crossing Zebulon NC 27597 Office: Raleigh Christian Community Inc 7000 Destiny Dr Raleigh NC 27604 *Adversity can be a test of character; most can stand adversity. To really test character, give them power.*

BOECHER, OTTO HERMANN KONRAD, theology educator, art historian; b. Worms, Germany, Mar. 12, 1935; s. Otto Karl W. and Anna Katharina E. (Lumm) B.; m. Ortrud Eleonore Bauscher, Dec. 10, 1962; children: Hans Georg, Wulf Otto, Urs Peter, Dorothea. PhD in Art History, U. Mainz, 1958, Dr.theol. in N.T., 1963, D Theol. Habilitation in N.T., 1968. Curate Evangelical Ch., Wiesbaden, Fed. Republic Germany, 1960-61; parson Evangelical Ch., Selzen, Fed. Republic Germany, 1962-64; prof. Tchrs. Coll. and U. Saarbrücken, 1975-78; asst. prof. theology U. Mainz (Fed. Republic Germany), 1963-68, univ. lectr., 1968-71, prof., 1971-75, 78—, dean Theol. Faculty, 1981-83; senator Johannes Gutenberg U., Mainz, 1979-81; mem. Deutscher Hochschulverband, Bonn-Mainz, 1968—; cons., 1983—. Author: Die Alte Synagoge zu Worms, 1960, Der johanneische Dualismus, 1965, Dämonenfurcht und Dämonenabwehr, 1970, Christus Exorcista, 1972, Die Johannesapokalypse, 1975, 3d edit., 1988; editor: Ebernburg-Hefte, 1970—. Mem. Landesdenkmalrat Rheinland-Pfalz, 1968-76, Synode Evangelische Kirche in Hessen und Nassau, 1974-76. Decorated knight's cross Order of St. John; recipient Ob merita medici Germaniae medal Chamber German Physicians, 1976, Bonifatius medal German Bishops Conf., 1978. Fellow Studiorum Novi Testamenti Soc., Humboldt-Gesellschaft (corr.); mem. Kommission für die Geschichte der Juden in Hessen, Herold (corr.), Wingolf Club. Avocations: genealogy, heraldry. Home: Carl-Zuckmayer-Strasse 30, 6500 Mainz-Drais Federal Republic of Germany Office: Johannes Gutenberg U, Saarstrasse 21, D-6500 Mainz 1, Federal Republic of Germany

BOEHLKE, CRAIG ALAN, minister; b. Cleve., Aug. 25, 1947; s. Frank Carl and Polly Anna (Connelly) B.; m. Georgia Clemens Stokes, Sept. 9, 1972; children: Melissa Mae, Benjamin Andrew. BA, Capital U., 1969; MDiv, Trinity Luth. Seminary, Columbus, Ohio, 1973; postgrad., Princeton Seminary, 1985—. Ordained to ministry, Luth. Ch., 1973. Assoc. pastor Grace Luth. Ch., St. Paul, Minn., 1973-78; sr. pastor All Saints Luth. Ch., Cottage Grove, Minn., 1978—; dean Southeast Conf., St. Paul Synod, 1987—; synod coun. mem. St. Paul Area Synod, 1987—. Bd. dirs. Red Rock Manor Sr. Housing Ministry, Newport, Minn., 1983—. Leadership fellow Bush Found., St. Paul, 1985. Home: 9161 Harkness Ave S Cottage Grove MN 55016 Office: All Saints Lutheran Ch 8100 Belden Blvd Cottage Grove MN 55016

BOEHLKE, ROBERT RICHARD, theology educator, minister; b. Bismark Twp., Sibley County, Minn., Apr. 13, 1925; s. Leonard Frank and Esther Viola (Barnes) B.; m. Mary Isobel Greer, June 19, 1951; children: Lisa Greer, Eric Greg, Heidi Lori, Andrew Raden. BA, U. Dubuque, 1950, BD, 1953; PhD, Princeton Theol. Sem., 1961. Ordained minister Presbyn. Ch., 1953. Pastor 1st Presbyn. Ch., Manchester, Iowa, 1953-56, 1st Presbyn. Ch. Oxford, Belvidere, N.J., 1956-59, 2d Presbyn. Ch. Oxford (N.J.), 1956-59; prof. Jakarta Theol. Sem., Indonesia, 1963-91; cons. Indonesian Council Chs., 1963-73; resource person World Council Christian Edn., Nairobi, Kenya, 1967; acad. dean Jakarta Theol. Sem., 1972-75; adv. mem. Commn. on Ecumenical Mission, N.Y.C., 1970-71. Author: Theories of Learning in Christian Education, 1962, Who is Jesus?, 1986, A History of the Development of Christian Education Thought and Practice, 1991; various articles in Indonesian and English. Indonesian del. World Coun. Christian Edn., Huampani, Peru, 1971; adv. mem. program agy. Presbyn. Ch., 1977-78, 88—; mem. Com. Higher Edn. With U.S. Army, 1946-47. Mem. Religious Edn. Assn. Presbyterian. Avocations: swimming, snorkeling, travel, wildlife photography. Home and Office: 705 Church St Hutchinson MN 55350

BOEHNKE, JOHN HENRY, minister; b. Hooper, Nebr., Dec. 17, 1932; s. John F. and Emma Mae (Schwanamann) B.; m. Joyce Jeannine Boehnke, Apr. 11, 1954; children: Terri Lynn, Tommy Lee. BA, Phillips U., 1960, MEd, 1967; MDiv, Grad. Sem., Enid, Okla., 1977. Ordained to ministry Christian Ch., 1960. Tchr. soc. studies Hazel Green (Ky.) Acad., 1962-67; dir. counseling Cowley County Community Coll., Arkansas City, Kans., 1967-75; assoc. pastor First Christian Ch., Blackwell, Okla., 1975-80; sr. pastor First Christian Ch., Lake Jackson, Tex., 1980—; vice moderator dist. IV, Christian Chs. Okla., 1978-80; sec. coastal plains area chs., Tex., 1982-84; del. Internat. Conv. Christian Chs., Kans., Okla., and Tex., 1969-84; mem. com on the ministry CPA, 1986-90, com. of leadership devel., 1986-90; camp counselor, 1980-90. Author: Friends and Other Poems, 1988. Vice-chmn. Women's Shelter of Brazoria County, Angleton, Tex., 1982; mem. Com. to Reelect Pres., Washington, 1983-84; bd. dirs. local ARC, 1987-88, Brazosport Cares, 1988-90. With USAF, 1952-56. Recipient Master Tchr. award Cowley County Community Coll., Arkansas City, Kans., 1974-75. Mem. NEA (life), Profl. Counselors Assn., Tex. Dow Employees Credit Union, Brazosport Ministerial Alliance (pres. 1981-82), Nat. Rifle Assn., Mason. Democrat. Office: First Christian Ch 503 Oyster Creek Dr Lake Jackson TX 77566 *In all of life, tragedy occurs. Why must a tragedy occur to bring a community, a church, a family closer together?.*

BOELHOWER, GARY JOHN, theology educator, consultant; b. Appleton, Wis., June 8, 1950; s. Cornelius John and Minnie (Van Hoorn) B.; m. Patricia Lee Wahoske, May 31, 1975; children: Rebecca, Joel, Matthew. BA in Philos., Catholic U. of Am., 1973; MA in Theol., Marquette U., 1976, PhD in Religious Studies, 1986. Dir. religious edn. St. Mary Parish, Elm Grove, Wis., 1974-77, St. Mary and Joseph Parishes, Fond du Lac, Wis., 1977-81; prof. theol. Marian Coll., Fond du Lac, Wis., 1981-83, chmn. theol. dept., 1983-86, dean continuing edn., 1986-90, prof. theol., 1990-; cons. in field schs. and parishes, 1974--, cons. Wis. corps., 1989--; pres. Marian Coll. Faculty Senate, Fond du Lac, Wis., 1990-91. Author: Sacred Times, Timeless Seasons, 1986, Praying Alone, Praying Together, 1979; contbr. articles to profl. jours. Comm. mem. Milwaukee Archdiocesan Synod, 1986-87; pres., v.p. Milwaukee Archdiocesan Religious Edn. Dirs., 1981-82; chmn. Catholic Schs. Taskforce, Fond du Lac, 1990; coord. Community Meal Program, Fond du Lac, 1985--. Mem. College Theol. Soc., St. Joseph Parish Coun. (pres.), Fond du Lac Assn. of Commerce (edn. com.). Roman Catholic. Avocations: reading, computers, poetry, handball. Office: Marian College 111 E 11th St Fond du Lac WI 54935

BOENDERMAKER, JOHANNES PIETER, theology educator; b. Hilversum, The Netherlands, July 7, 1925; s. Pieter and Constance (van Hoogstraten) B.; m. Elise Anna Catharina Duyvendak, Sept. 14, 1951; children: Pieter Maarten, Constantia Maria. Student, U. Amsterdam, The Netherlands, 1945-50; ThD, 1965; student, U. Erlangen, Fed. Republic Germany, 1950-51; U. Heidelberg, 1963-64. Ordained to ministry Evangel. Luth. Ch., 1951. Pastor Evangel. Luth. Ch. Netherlands, Eindhoven, 1951-63, Naarden Bussum, 1964-68; prof. theology Evangel. Luth. Sem., U. Amsterdam, 1968—; mem. joint dialogue commn., Roman Cath. Ch.-Luth. World Fedn., 1986—; adviser, Luth. Synod, Evangel. Luth. Ch. Netherlands; cons. liturgy, Evangel. Luth. and Reformed Ch. Author: Luther's Commentary of the Epistle to the Hebrews, 1965, Luther After 500 Years, 1983, Liturgy for Pastor and Laypeople, 1975, rev. edit., 1988; contbr. articles to theol. publs. Mem. Social Democratic party. Home: van K van Veenlaan 41, 1222 LW Hilversum The Netherlands Office: U Amsterdam, Theol Inst, Herengracht 514.516.1017 CC, Amsterdam The Netherlands

BOER, JEFFREY KENT, minister; b. Sheldon, Iowa, Aug. 9, 1951; s. Frederick Allen and Geraldine Kathleen (Van Bruggen-Van Werven) B.; m. Barbara Jean Kramm, Nov. 29, 1974; children: Casey Daniel, Jordan David. BA in Psychology, Dordt Coll., 1973; postgrad., Rosemead Grad. Sch. Psychology, 1973-74; MDiv, Westminster Theol. Sem., 1979. Cert. level II counselor. Bible and sci. tchr. Naples Christian Acad., Naples, Fla., 1974-76; counselor Christian Counseling and Edn. Found., Laverock, Pa., 1978-79; dir. Sharon Christian Acad., Hialeah, Fla., 1982-86; pastor Sharon Orthodox Presby. Ch., Hialeah, Fla., 1979—; dir. Okoboji New Life Outreach, Iowa, 1973, 75, 76, staff mem. Boardwalk Chapel, Wildwood, N.J., 1974, organizing pastor, Marco Presby. Ch., Marco Island, Fla., 1978, chmn. credentials com., Presby. of South, Hialeah, 1985—. Assoc. editor: The Basis For A Christian School, 1982; contbr. articles to profl. jours. Bd. dirs. Journey Mag., Lynchburg, Va., 1986—, Caribbean Christian Ministries, Pompano Beach, Fla., 1988—, Whitefield Theol. Sem., Lakeland, Fla., 1990—. Mem. Nat. Assn. Nouthetic Counselors. Republican. Office: Sharon Presbyn Ch 17680 NW 78 Ave Hialeah FL 33015 *Some want what is rightfully theirs: equal justice, equal rights, a fair shake, just desserts...Give me grace and mercy any day!.*

BOESAK, ALLAN AUBREY, religious organization adminstrator, pastor; b. Kakamas, N.W. Cape, Republic of South Africa, Feb. 23, 1946; s. Willem Andreas and Sarah Helena (Mannel) B.; m. Dorothy Rose Martin, June 21, 1969; children: Lieneke, Belèn, Pulane, Allan Jr. Diploma in theology, Theol. Sem. U. West Cape, Bellville, 1967; ThM, Theol. Sem. Reformed Chs., Kampen, The Netherlands, 1974, ThD, 1976; DD (hon.), Victoria U., Toronto, Ont., Can., 1983, Yale U., 1984; ThD, Geneva U., 1986; LLD (hon.), U. Warwick, Coventry, England, 1989. Pastor N.G. Sendingkerk Immanuel, Paarl, Republic of South Africa, 1968-70; campus minister U. Western Cape, Bellville, Republic of South Africa, 1976-85; sr. pastor N.G. Sendingkerk Bellville, 1986—; assessor synod N.G. Sendingkerk (Dutch Reformed Mission Ch.), 1982-86, moderator synod, 1986-90; pres. World Alliance Reformed Chs., 1982-89; founder Found. for Peace and Justice, Bellville, 1986—. Author: Farewell to Innocence, 1976, The Finger of God, 1982, Black and Reformed, 1984, Comfort and Protest, 1987. Patron, co-founder United Dem. Front, Republic of South Africa, 1983—. Recipient Kaj Munk award Ch. Denmark, 1983, Humanitarian award R.F. Kennedy Found., 1985, Humanitarian award Congl. Black Caucus, 1985, M.L. King Jr. award So. Christian Leadership Conf., 1986. Mem. Assn. Christian Students in So. Africa (pres. 1984—).

BOFFO, DION LOUIS, minister; b. Akron, Ohio, Jan. 19, 1947; s. Louis Sunday and Opal Pearl (Wigner) B.; m. Irene Elizabeth Jackson, May 25, 1968; children: Todd, Kristen, Jason. Cert., Christian Counseling and Edn. Found., Laverock, Pa., 1981. Tchr. Gibbsboro (N.H.) Meth. Ch., 1978-81, lay speaker, 1981-82; founder Samaritan Ministries, Gibbsboro, 1980; pastor Saamaritan Fellowship, Gibbsboro, 1984—; coord. Del. Valley Presbytery, Gibvbsboro, 1989—. Composer: I've Got Joy, 1988, I Will Shout, 1988. Founder Christian Food Cupboard, Gibbsboro, 1980; mem. Environ. Commn., Gibbsboro, 1981; bd. dirs. Pregnancy Care Ctr., Haddon Heights, N.J.; advisor Feed My Children, Mexico City. With USN, 1968-70. Mem. Resurrection Chs. and Ministries (mem. apostolic strategy coun. 1991—), Global Apostolic Strategy Coun. (recognition 1991), Assn. Internat. Mission Svcs., Network of Christian Ministries, Team World Outreach (advisor 1990—). Office: Samaritan Ministries PO Box 51 Gibbsboro NJ 08026

BOGER, RICHARD EDWIN, JR., minister; b. Atlanta, May 13, 1952; s. Richard Edwin and Marie Yoder (Leonard) B.; m. Jill Roberta Howard, Apr. 26, 1980; 1 child, John Michael Howard. AB, Lenoir-Rhyne Coll., 1973, Hamma Sch. Theology, 1975; MDiv, Pacific Luth. Theol. Sem., 1978. Ordained to ministry Evang. Luth. Ch. Am., 1980. Vesper intern Vesper Soc., San Leandro, Calif., 1975-76; coord. vols. Care Network, San Leandro, 1978; intern Christ Our Shepherd, Peachtree City, Ga., 1979-80; pastor Luth. Ch. of Our Savior, Jacksonville, N.C., 1980-90, Nazareth Luth. Ch., Rural Hall, N.C., 1990—; counselor Neighborhood Ch. Clinic, Springfield, Ohio, 1974; pastoral counselor Eden Hayward (Calif.) Pastoral Counseling Svc., 1975-76; mem. Jacksonville Ministerial Assn., 1980-81, Onslow County Ministerial Fellowship, 1984; mem. worship com., music com. N.C. Synod Luth. Ch. in Am., 1982, 84-86; assoc. N.C. Chaplains Assn., 1984. Bd. dirs. ARC, Jacksonville, 1981-89. Mem. Alban Inst., Forsyth Luth. Area Pastors, Forsyth Luth. Coun., Rural Hall-Stanleyville Mins. Assn. Office: Nazareth Luth Ch PO Box 519 Rural Hall NC 27045 *Ours is the God who died. No other religion can make that claim. When we fully accept the fact that God became man and then died for us out of love, then and only then do we begin to live.*

BOGGS, DAVID ROBERT, minister, gerontologist; b. Haskell, Tex., Nov. 13, 1941; s. Durward and Eva Blanche (Davis) B.; m. Vearl LaVerne Turner, June 25, 1960, children: Rebecca, Jon, David. Theol. Studies, Bear Valley Sch. Bibl. Studies, Denver, 1974; BA in Edn. and Psychology, U. Auckland, New Zealand, 1981; postgrad., Utah State U., 1981-82; MS in Gerontology, Tex. Tech. U., 1990. Ordained to ministry Ch. of Christ, 1974; lic. nursing home adminstr., Tex. Asst. mgr. Wyatt Cafeterias, Inc., Irving, Tex., 1968-72; min. Ch. Christ, Auckland, 1974-81, Brigham City, Utah, 1981-83, Monahans, Tex., 1983—; lctr. civic and religious groups; leader Parkinson's disease support groups. Avocations: woodworking, car repair, music, reading. Office: Ch of Christ PO Box 167 Monahans TX 79756

BOGGS, JESSE ERNEST, minister; b. Charleston, W.Va., Dec. 27, 1954; s. James Monroe and Margaret Ruth (McPherson) B.; m. Deborah Kay Cavanaugh, May 28, 1976; children: Candice Dawn, Emily Joy, Wesley James. BA, Appalachian Bible Coll., 1977; MDiv, Grace Theol. Sem., Winona Lake, Ind., 1981. Youth pastor Tippecanoe (Ind.) Community Ch., 1978-81; sr. pastor Olathe (Kans.) Bible Ch., 1981-90, Calvary Bible Ch., Kalamazoo, 1990—; part-time prof. pastoral studies Calvary Bible Coll., Kansas City, Mo., 1989. Home: 6108 Evergreen St Portage MI 49002 Office: Calvary Bible Ch 855 S Drake Rd Kalamazoo MI 49002

BOGHAERT, ARNOLD, bishop. Bishop of Roseau Dominica. Office: Bishop's House, 20 Virgin Ln, POB 339, Roseau Dominica*

BOGHOLTZ, WILLIAM E., minister; b. L.A., Mar. 25, 1959; s. Wilhelm E. and Elizabeth F. (Caulfield) B.; m. Angela M. Apuzzo, July 12, 1981; children: Rebekah Ann, Matthew James. BA, Wagner Coll., 1981; MDiv, Luth. Theol. Sem., 1985. Ordained to ministry Luth. Ch. in Am., 1985. Intern/vicar Bethel Luth. Ch., Auburn, Mass., 1982-84; pastor Holy Trinity Luth. Ch., York Springs, Pa., 1985-88, Atonement Luth. Ch., S.I., N.Y., 1989-91, Our Saviour Luth. Ch., S.I., 1991—; mem. Christian edn. com. and parish life commn. Cen. Pa. synod Luth. Ch. in Am., 1986-87; mem. bishop's com. for ecumenical affairs Lower Susquehanna synod Evang. Luth. Ch. in Am., 1988, stewardship com. Metro N.Y. synod, 1990—; tchr. religion Trinity Luth. Sch., S.I., 1990—; convenor, mem. S.I. Luth. Ministerium, 1989—; chairperson Adams County Migrant Ministry, Gettysburg, Pa., 1986-88; chmn. adv. bd. Luth Community Svc., N.Y.C., 1989—. Editor, pub. booklet Churches of Oakwood/Richmondtown, Stated Island, 1990. Bd. dirs. United Way Adams County, 1985-87. Mem. Ecumenical Soc. Blessed Virgin Mary, Luth. Liturgical Renewal, S.I. Clergy Assn. (treas. 1990-91). Office: Our Saviour Luth Ch 549 Bard Ave Staten Island NY 10310

BOGIER, LAWRENCE, JR., minister; b. Pinewood, S.C., Mar. 23, 1941; s. Lawrence and Hattie (Davis) B.; m. Coretha Williams, Jan. 26, 1965; children: Stephanie Renee, Jeanette Danese, Lawrence III. Student, Bible Inst., Bklyn., 1971-73, Manhattan Bible Inst., N.Y.C., 1976; BTh, Am. Bible Inst., Pine Land, Fla., 1978, ThM, 1980. Ordained to ministry Original Tabernacle of Prayer for All People as elder, 1974. Min., evangelist Tabernacle of Prayer, Bklyn., 1972-74, elder, 1974-76, trustee, 1971-72; pastor Tabernacle of Prayer, Goldsboro, N.C., 1976-87; pastor, overseer nationwide chs. Tabernacle of Prayer, 1987—; bd. dirs. Inst.-Brotherhood, Tabernacle of Prayer, Bklyn., 1971-76, Inst. Bible Sch., Goldsboro, 1977—. Author: Compared the Teachings of Jesus to Judaism, 1986. Mem. Ministerial Assn. Wayne County (pres. Goldsboro chpt. 1990-91, past pres. social concern com.), United Ch. Ministries. Home: 801 S Clairborne St Goldsboro NC 27530 Office: Original Tabernacle of Prayer PO Box 1256 Goldsboro NC 27530

BOGOSIAN, PHILIP STEPHEN, missionary; b. L.A., Feb. 15, 1943; s. Abraham and Gloria Zevart) Erganian) B.; m. Juliet Elizabeth Giuntoli, Oct. 20, 1973; children: Michelle, David, Joseph, Peter, Jessica, Lydia, Naomi, Ruth, Mary. BA in Sociology, Calif. State U., Northridge, 1971. Dir. God's House, Van Nuys, Calif., 1971-73; with God's Hosp., 1973-84; dir. ch. and agy. rels. U.S. Ctr. for World Mission, Pasadena, Calif., 1984—, mem. dir.'s adv. coun., 1990—; coord. Global Network Ctrs. for World Mission, Pasadena, 1990—. Contbr. articles to religious publs. With U.S. Army, 1966-68. Mem. Internat. Soc. for Frontier Missiology, Evang. Missionary Soc. Republican. Home: 1551 Elizabeth St Pasadena CA 91104 Office: US Ctr for World Mission 1605 Elizabeth St Pasadena CA 91104

BOHANNON, DEREK SHAWN, minister; b. Torrence, Calif., June 15, 1963; s. Roger Wayne and Vivian Kaye (O'Neal) B. Grad. high sch., Cookeville, Tenn. Ordained to ministry So. Bapt. Conv. Youth dir. Eastwood Bapt. Ch., Cookeville, 1982-88; min. youth First Bapt. Ch., Sparta, Tenn., 1989—; counselor Sandy Stone Bapt. Camp, Monterey, Tenn., 1982-88. Mem. adv. bd. Bapt. Student Union, Tenn. Tech. U., 1990—. Named Outstanding Young Religious Leader Jaycees, 1987. Mem. White County Ministerial Assn., White County Bd. Chaplains, Union Bapt. Assn. Home: 1650 Iris Ave Cookeville TN 38501 Office: First Bapt Ch 308 North Spring St Sparta TN 38583

BOHLMANN, RALPH ARTHUR, clergyman, church official; b. Palisade, Nebr., Feb. 20, 1932; s. Arthur Erwin and Anne Fredericka (Weeke) B.; m. Patricia Anne McCleary, Apr. 19, 1959; children: Paul, Lynn. Student, St. Johns Coll., Winfield, Kans.; B.A., Concordia Sem., 1953; M.Div., 1956, S.T.M., 1966; Fulbright scholar, U. Heidelberg, 1956-57; Ph.D., Yale U., 1968. Ordained to ministry Lutheran Ch. (Mo. Synod), 1958; instr. history and religion Concordia Coll., 1957-58; pastor Mt. Olive Luth. Ch., Des Moines, 1958-60; prof. systematic theology Concordia Sem., St. Louis, 1960-71, acting pres., 1974-75, pres., 1975-81; pres. Luth. Ch.-Mo. Synod, 1981—; exec. sec. Commn. Theology and Ch. Relations Luth. Ch. Mo. Synod, St. Louis, 1971-74; mem. Faith and Order Commn. Nat. Council Chs., 1973-76. Author: Principles of Biblical Interpretation in the Lutheran Confessions, 1968. Office: Luth Ch Mo Synod 1333 S Kirkwood Rd Saint Louis MO 63122

BOHM, MICHAEL NEIL, religious organization administrator; b. Phila., Mar. 15, 1952; s. Herman and Ruth (Jasowitz) B.; m. Sherry Ellen Press, May 11, 1954; children: Mendel, Ariella, Joseph, Elan. BA cum laude, Temple U., 1973; MS magna cum laude, Yeshiva U., 1975; PhD, ABD, Dropsie U., Phila., 1979; MBA, Drexel U., 1989—. Prin. Greater N.E. Greenstone Hebrew High Sch., Phila., 1978-83; ednl. and youth dir. Congregation Beth El, Levittown, Pa., 1983-88; ednl. dir. Congregation Ner Zedek-Ezrath Israel, Phila., 1988—; prin. Midrasha Hebrew Jr. Coll., Cherry Hill, N.J., 1976—; pres. Educator's Coun., Trenton, N.J., 1986-88. V.p. Congregation Bnai Israel-Ohev Zedek, Phila., 1982. Mem. Prin.'s Coun., Coalition for Advancement in Jewish Edn. Avocations: reading, gardening, travel. Office: Congregation Ner Zedek Ezrath Israel Bustleton and Oakmont Sts Philadelphia PA 19152

BOHRER, RICHARD WILLIAM, religious writer, editor; b. N.Y.C., June 17, 1926; s. Jacob William and Elsie Marie (Wahlstad) B.; m. Elizabeth Anne Spencer, July 8, 1955; children: Joel Stephen, Janice Joy Bohrer Pruitt. BA, Westmont Coll., 1947; MSc, U. So. Calif., L.A., 1956; MA, Calif. State U., Long Beach, 1962. Tchr. grades 3, 4, 5 Haile Selassie I Elem. Sch., Gondar, Ethiopia, 1947-50; tchr. grades 9, 10, 11 Alhambra (Calif.) High Sch., 1954-55; tchr. grade 6 Maple Ave. Sch., Fullerton, Calif., 1955-56; tchr. grades 9, 10, 11 Orange (Calif.) High Sch., 1956-63; news editor Anaheim (Calif.) Gazette, 1961-62; prof., dir. journalism Multnomah Sch. of the Bible, Portland, Oreg., 1963-79; broker Dick Bohrer Realty Inc., Portland, 1968-81; sr. editor, mng. editor Moody Monthly mag., Chgo., 1979-83; prof. Liberty U., Lynchburg, Va., 1983-89, 91—; asst. prof., head mag. sequence Ball State U., Muncie, Ind., 1989-90; dir. Maranatha Writers Conf., Muskegon, Mich., 1980-89. Author: Easy English, 1977—, Edit, Yourself and Sell, 1980, They Called Him Shifta, 1981, 21 Ways to Write Stories for Christian Kids, 1980, 2d edit., 1982, An Everlasting Love, 1982, John Newton, 1983, Bill Borden, 1984, How to Write What You Think, 1985, How to Write Features Like a Pro, 1986, Be an Editor Yourself, 1987, Right with God, 1991, J. Edgar Beanpole: Football Detective, 1991, J. Edgar Beanpole: Volleyball Spy, 1991, J. Edgar Beanpole: Soccer Sleuth, 1991, J. Edgar Beanpole: Night Watcher, 1991; editor: The Battle for Your Faith by Willard M. Aldrich, The Schemer and the Dreamer by Luis Palau, Down to Earth by John Lawrence, Parables by the Sea by Pamela Reeve, Plague in Our Midst by Gregg Albers, MD, What Do You Say When.... by Nellie Pickard, Counseling the Terminally Ill by Gregg Albers, MD, The Self-Study of Liberty University; acting editor Moral Majority Report, 1983-85, copy editor, 1985-88. Recipient Pres.'s Svc. award Liberty U., 1985, Tchr. of Yr. award, 1987, 89. Mem. Soc. Profl. Journalists. Republican. Mem. Plymouth Brethren Ch. Avocations: oil painting, cooking, swimming. Home: 7101 Peachtree Rd Lynchburg VA 24502 Office: Liberty U PO Box 20,000 Lynchburg VA 24506-0001

BOISCLAIR, DAVID RICHARD, minister; b. Milw., Sept. 11, 1955; s. Franklin Alexander and Ruth Louise (Kettner) B. BA, Concordia Sr. Coll., Fort Wayne, Ind., 1977; MDiv, Concordia Sem., St. Louis, 1982. Ordained to ministry Luth. Ch. in Milw., 1982. Pastor St. Paul's Luth. Ch., Jonesburg, Mo., 1982—; cir. adult advisor Luth. Youth Fellowship, St. Charles, Mo., 1983-84; sec., treas. St. Charles Cir. Pastors Conf., 1988-89. Mem. Jonesburg Christian Alliance (pres. 1988-92). Home: Rte 1 Box 226 Jonesburg MO 63351-9738 Office: St Paul's Luth Ch Lion Ave & Jones St Jonesburg MO 63351-9738 *Nothing captivates me more than the image of my dear Lord Jesus on the cross. No other sight pictures pure selfless love better. My entire being is drawn into His service. I want to have taken His place on the cross, but I know I couldn't have. Even though I know that to be true, I am motivated to do His work wherever I happen to be.*

BOJARSKI, RONALD HENRY, priest, educator; b. Cleve., Nov. 15, 1934; s. Henry Edward and Frances Pauline (Ruszkowski) B. Ph.B., Borromeo Coll., 1957; postgrad. St. Mary Sem., 1957-61; M.Elem. Edn. and Adminstrn., St. John Coll., 1972; Ph.D., U. Md., 1974. Ordained priest Roman Catholic Ch., 1961. Counselor, Erieview and St. Edward High Sch., 1970-72; tchr. Cleve. Central Cath. High Sch., 1963-65; asst. supt. edn. Diocese Cleve., 1974-83, regional supt. Cuyahoga West region, 1975-83. Mem. Assn. Am. Sch. Adminstrs., Assn. Supervision and Curriculum Devel., Nat. Cath. Edn. Assn., Univ. Counseling Ednl. Adminstrs. (adv. bd. Pa., Md., Va.). Author: The Christian Code of Ethics for the Catholic Education Profession, 1976; Evaluation of Adminstrators, 1974.

BOJAXHIU, AGNES GONXHA See TERESA, MOTHER

BOL, DOUGLAS JOHN, minister, psychologist, religious broadcaster; b. Grand Haven, Mich., July 31, 1935; s. J. Edward and Jean B. (Putnam) B.; m. Marylin Seman, July 31, 1954; children: Gary Douglas, Julie Ann. LLB, LaSalle Extension U., 1960; BBA, Western Mich. U., 1963; BD cum laude, Grand Rapids Bapt. Theol. Sem., 1966, MDiv, 1970; MEd, U. Ariz., 1972, EdD, 1973. Ordained to ministry Gen. Assn. Regular Bapt. Chs., 1966. Pastor Eastview Bapt. Ch., Tucson, 1970-73; psychologist, pastoral counselor Tucson, 1970—; speaker, dir. radio broadcast Psychology in the Bible, Tucson, 1973-82; host Let's Talk radio broadcast, 1982-85, cable TV series Insight for Happiness, 1985—; clin. psychologist serving on med. staff of 9 hosps. in city of Tucson. bd. dirs., pres. Inst. Family Living, 1970—. With U.S. Army, 1966-70, Res. USANG, 1970-91. Mem. APA, Ariz. Psychological Assn., So. Ariz. Psychological Assn. Home: 9249 E 39th St Tucson AZ 85730

BOLAN, WILLIAM F., religious organization administrator. Exec. dir. N.J. Cath. Conf., Trenton. Office: NJ Cath Conf 211 N Warren St Trenton NJ 08618*

BOLAND, RAYMOND JAMES, bishop; b. Tipperary, Ireland, Feb. 8, 1932; came to U.S., 1957; Ed., Nat. U. Ireland and All Hallows Sem., Dublin. Ordained priest Roman Cath. Ch., Dublin, 1957. Vicar gen., chancellor of Washington archdiocese; ordained bishop Birmingham, Ala., 1988—. Address: PO Box 12047 Birmingham AL 35202-2047

BOLDT, FREDERICK FRANK, administrator, minister; b. Saginaw, Mich., July 7, 1946; s. Harold Pagels and Anita (Zehnder) B.; m. Barbara Louise Pergande, June 11, 1969; children: Stephen, Aaron, Nathaniel, Joshua. BA, Concordia U., River Forest, Ill., 1968, MA, 1980. Tchr., coach St. Paul Luth. Sch., Mt. Prospect, Ill., 1968-70, Our Redeemer Luth. Sch., Wauwatosa, Wis., 1970-74; prin. St. Paul's Evang. Luth. Sch., Oconomowoc, Wis., 1974—; bd. dirs. S.W. Dist. Bd. Luth. Ch. Mo. Synod, Milw.; chmn. S.W. Dist. Luth. Ch. Mo. Synod Chaplaincy Bd., Milw., 1986—. Mem. OAS task force Suicide Prevention, Oconomowoc, 1983—, Children At Risk, Oconomowoc, 1984—, Luths. for Life, Wis., YMCA, Mayor's Task Force on Cable TV, Oconomowoc, 1986; coach Little League Baseball, Oconomowoc, 1978—. Mem. Coun. of Am. Pvt. Edn., Luth. Edn. Assn., Wis. Assn. of Non-Pub. Schs., Dept. Luth. Elem. Prins., Theol. Educators in Associated Ministries, Assn. for Supervision and Curriculum Devel. Avocations: outdoor recreation, sports, hunting. Office: St Paul's Evang Luth Ch 210 E Pleasant St Oconomowoc WI 53066-3098

BOLEJACK, J. RODNEY, minister; b. Greensboro, N.C., Aug. 13, 1953; s. James William and Norma Joan (Stewart) B.; m. Tina Ann Simmons; children: Jason Neal, Christina Joyce. BArch, Va. Poly. Inst. and State U., 1977; MDiv, S.W. Bapt. Theol. Sem., Ft. Worth, 1980, D Ministry, 1988. Lic. to ministry So. Bapt. Conv., 1977, ordained, 1982. Resident chaplain Baylor U. Med. Ctr., Dallas, 1980-82; pastor Era (Tex.) Bapt. Ch., 1982-85, Meadow Oaks Bapt. Ch., Temple, Tex., 1985—; chaplain Heart of Tex. Hospice, Belton, 1990—; adj. prof. U. Mary Hardin Baylor, Belton, 1989—; mem. profl. cons. com. for chaplains dept. Scott and White Hosp., Temple, 1988—. Com. mem. Community Rev. Com. for Self-Responsibility Curriculum, Temple Ind. Sch. Dist., 1989. Mem. Temple Ministerial Assn. (sec. 1991—), Bell Bapt. Assn. (chmn. Christian Life com. 1989-90). Home: Meadow Oaks Bapt Ch 3001 Meadow Oaks Dr Temple TX 76502

BOLICH, GREGORY GORDON, religion and history educator; b. Spokane, Wash., July 7, 1953; s. Glenn Gordon and Joanne G. (Stinger) B.; m. Barbara Jo Ranson, Apr. 8, 1976; children: April Louise, Alicia Layne, Amanda Larissa, Ariell Livon; m. Marilyn M. Russell, Apr. 1, 1989. BA in Philosophy and Religion, Seattle Pacific U., 1974, M of Christian Ministries in Ednl. Psychology, 1975; MA in Religion, Western Evang. Sem., 1977, M Divinity in Christian Thought, 1978; EdD, Gonzaga U., 1983. Mem. faculty Inland Empire Sch. of the Bible, Spokane, 1975-76; adminstr. First Evang. Free Ch., Spokane, 1978-79; pres. Christian Studies Inst., Cheney, 1979-89; grad. asst. research Gonzaga U., Spokane, 1981-83, staff mem. Ctr. for Research, 1981-83; mem adj. faculty Eastern Wash. U., Cheney, 1985—; mentor Gonzaga U., 1984-86, Fuller Sem., Pasadena, Calif., 1984; elder Shadle Park Presbyn. Ch., Spokane, 1982; rep. Presbyn. Ch., 1985-86; coord. Cheney Presbyn. Fellowship, 1986-89; exec. dir. Adult Survivors of Abuse, 1991—. Author: The Christian Scholar, 1986, Authority and the Church, 1982, Karl Barth and Evangelicalism, 1980; co-author: Introduction to Religion, 1988, God in the Docket, 1991; contbr. religious articles to jours. and mags. Mem. Friends of Seven, Spokane, 1985—; active United Ministries in Higher Edn., Spokane, 1985—; assoc. mem. YWCA, Spokane, 1984-85, Cheney United Ch. Christ, 1986—. Mem. Am. Psychol. Assn., Bibl. Archaeology Soc., Internat. Thespian Soc., Soc. Bibl. Lit., N.W. Soc. Patristic and Koine Studies (v.p. 1986), Theology Forum (exec. officer 1981-84), Alpha Kappa Sigma. Democrat. Presbyterian. Avocations: basketball, theatre. Office: Ea Wash U Humanities Dept Cheney WA 99004 *I call religion that region where the ordinary and the extraordinary meet and intermingle. Within its bounds are light, life, and laughter.*

BOLIN, DANIEL STUART, religious organization administrator; b. Portland, Oreg., July 29, 1952; s. Warren H. and Margaret Jean (Read) B.; m. Catherine Pryor, Dec. 18, 1976; children: Cate (dec.), Haley. BA, Seattle Pacific U., 1975; ThM, Theol. Sem., 1981. Dir. Towers Camp Towers Camp Pine Cove Camp, Tyler, Tex., 1975-78; dir. camping ministries Pine Cove Camping, Tyler, Tex., 1980-83, exec. dir., 1983—; youth pastor Grace Bible Ch., Dallas, 1978-80; regional dir./Heartland region, Christian Camping Internat., 1985-90; speaker section., Nat. Camping Convs., 1985—; host/faculty mem. Christian Camping Internat. Devel. Inst., Buena Vista, Colo., 1991; steering com. Billy Graham Crusade '90, Tyler, 1990. Precinct del. Rep. County Caucus, Smith County, Tex., 1990. Mem. Am. Camp Assn., Camps Assn. for Mut. Progress, Rotary. Office: Pine Cove Camp PO Box 9055 Tyler TX 75711

BOLING, ROBERT GORDON, religion educator; b. Terre Haute, Ind., Nov. 24, 1930; s. Lyman Francis and Helen (Groh) B.; m. Jean Eleanor Gade, 1955; children: Gail, Ruth, Martha. BS, Ind. State U., 1952; MDiv, McCormick Theol. Sem., Chgo., 1956; PhD, Johns Hopkins U., 1959. Ordained to ministry United Presbyn. Ch., 1956. Asst. prof. religion Coll. of Wooster, Ohio; prof. Old Testament McCormick Theol. Sem., Chgo., 1964—; mem. Drew McCormick Archeol. Expdn., 1957, area supr., 1966, 68; vis. prof. Harvard U. Summer Sch., 1962-64, Pacific Theol. Coll., 1973; participant excavations, Caesarea Maritima, 1976, Tell el-Hesi, 1981, Tell el-Umeiri, Jordan, 1984; ann. prof. Am. Ctr. for Oriental Rsch., Amman, Jordan, 1984. Author: Judges: Introduction, Translation, and Commentary, 1975, Joshua: Translation, Notes, and Commentary, 1982, The Early Biblical Community in Transjordan, 1988; (with others) Crossroads, 1967; co-editor: (with Edward F. Campbell Jr.) Essays in Honor of George Ernest Wright, 1976; former mem. editorial bd. Jour. Bibl. Lit. Active presbyter's com. on preparation for ministry Presbytery of Chgo.; former trustee Am. Ctr. Oriental Rsch., Amman. Blackstone fellow McCormick Theol. Sem., 1956, Rayner fellow Johns Hopkins U., 1957, Fels fellow, 1958, Am. Sch. Oriental Rsch., 1968-69, NEH fellow, 1984. Mem. Chgo. Soc. Bibl. Rsch. (former bus. mgr., editor Bibl. Rsch. jour.), Am. Schs. Oriental Rsch., Soc. Bibl. Lit. and Exegesis. Office: McCormick Theol Sem 5555 S Woodlawn Ave Chicago IL 60637

BOLLBACK, ANTHONY GEORGE, minister; b. N.Y.C., Aug. 27, 1922; s. Anthony J. and Elizabeth Ann (Balzer) B.; m. Evelyn Watson, Aug. 14, 1943; children: James, Joy, Judith, Jonathan. Diploma, Nyack Coll., 1943. Ordained to ministry Christian and Missionary Alliance, 1945. Pastor Christian and Missionary Alliance, Coudersport, Pa., 1943-46, Chatham, N.J, 1950-52, Honolulu, 1970-77, Silver Spring, Md., 1978-85; missionary Christian and Missionary Alliance, China, 1947-49, Japan, 1952-57, Hong Kong, 1958-70; supt. western dist. Christian and Missionary Alliance, Omaha, 1985—; trustee St. Paul Bible Coll., St. Bonifacious, Minn., 1985—; pres. Evang. Missions Fellowship, Hong Kong, 1967-70, Oahu Assn. Evangelicals, Honolulu, 1974-76. Author: To China and Back, 1991. Mem. Nyack Coll. Alumni Assn. (pres. 1983-84). Republican. Office: Christian & Missionary Alliance Western Dist 1301 S 119th St Omaha NE 68144

BOLLER, JOHN HALL, JR., minister; b. N.Y.C., Sept. 4, 1949; s. John Hall Sr. and Claudia (Pinza) B.; m. Lillian Wong, June 1, 1974; children: Alisha Carole, Jenna Kaitlin. BS, Calif. State U., Long Beach, 1970; M of Christian Theology, San Francisco Theol. Sem., San Anselmo, Calif., 1972, M of Divinity, 1973; MS, Calif. State U., San Diego, 1978. Youth minister Chinese Congl. Ch., San Francisco, 1970-73; campus pastor U. Calif., Irvine, 1973-74; asst. pastor St. Mark's Presbyn. Ch., Newport Beach, Calif., 1973-74; assoc. pastor Coll. Park Presbyn. Ch., San Diego, 1974-79; pastor Northminster Presbyn. Ch., San Diego, 1979—; marriage, family and child counselor, San Diego, 1986—. Chmn. Dropout Prevention Roundtable, San Diego, 1987-89; moderator Presbytery of San Diego, 1988. Mem. Calif. Assn. Marriage and Family Therapists, Assn. Presbyn. Ch. Educators, Witherspoon Soc. Democrat. Club: San Diego Train. Avocations: reading, trains, biking, baseball cards. Office: Northminster Presbyn Ch 4324 Clairemont Mesa Blvd San Diego CA 92117-1945

BOLLIER, JOHN ALBERT, theological librarian, minister; b. North Tonawanda, N.Y., Oct. 12, 1927; s. Harold Edward and Ethel (Schurr) B.; m. Gertrude Holmes Lothian, June 21, 1952; children: Peter J., David A., John H. BA, U. Mich., 1948; BD, Princeton Theol. Sem, 1951, ThM, 1954; MLS, UCLA, 1971. Ordained to ministry Presbyn. Ch., 1952. Pastor New Harmony Presbyn. Ch., Brogue, Pa., 1952-54, 1st Presbyn. Ch., Stroudsburg, Pa., 1954-63, St. Stephen Presbyn. Ch., Chatsworth, Calif., 1963-70; reference libr. Calif. State U., Northridge, 1971-73; asst. div. libr., lectr. Yale Div. Sch., New Haven, 1973-91; dir. devel. Am. Theol. Libr. Assn., Hamden, Conn., 1991—. Author: The Literature of Theology, 1979; contbr. articles to profl. jours. Mem. Pub. Libr. Bd., Hamden, Conn., 1988—. Assn. Theol. Schs. grantee, 1976-77, 81-82, Yale Div. Sch. faculty grantee, 1989-90; Pastors fellow Presbyn. Bd. of Fgn. Missions, Ecumenical Inst., Bossey, Switzerland, 1957-58; Mutchmore fellow Presbyn. Bd. Christian Edn., 1951-52. Mem. Am. Theol. Libr. Assn. (chmn. preservation bd., 1984-90, bd. dirs. 1984-90, mem. fin. mgmt. com. 1985-90, chmn. exec. com. 1989-90), Presbytery of So. New Eng. (com. mem. 1973-78), Morys (New Haven), Beta Phi Mu. Democrat. Home and Office: 79 Heloise St Hamden CT 06517

BOLLINGER, RICHARD AMSEY, minister; b. Blacksburg, Va., Apr. 10, 1928; s. Amsey Floyd and Florence (Moyer) B.; m. Anna Mae Enrmin, June 10, 1950; children: Virginia Kaye, Rebecca Jane. BA cum laude, Manchester Coll., 1949; DivM cum laude, Union Theol. Sem., 1958; D in Ministry, Princeton Theol. Sem., 1979. Ordained to ministry Presbyn. Ch., 1958. Tchr. instrumental music Ft. Wayne (Ind.) Pub. Schs., 1949-51, Woodstock Sch., Landour, Mussourie, India, 1951-54; asst. pastor Union Congl. Ch., Richmond Hill, N.Y., 1956-58; pastor Ch. of the Brethren, Topeka, 1958-64; staff, dir. of div. Religion and Psychiatry The Menninger Found., Topeka, 1964-86; assoc. dir. The Samaritan Inst., Denver, 1986-88, v.p., 1988—; ch. cons. Menninger Found., Topeka, 1975-86; moderator Dist. of Kans., Ch. of the Brethren, 1962-63. Author: The Church in a Changing World, 1965; contbr. numerous articles to profl. jours. Concertmaster Topeka Civic Symphony, 1964-86; bd. dirs. Topeka Youth Project, 1983-86, Multiple Sclerosis Soc., Topeka, 1985-86. Fellow Fund for Theol. Edn., Princeton U., 1955-56; recipient Hope Chest award Multiple Sclerosis Soc., 1968. Fellow Am. Assn. for Marriage and Family Therapy (clin., approved supr., bd. dirs. 1984-86, Cert. of Appreciation 1982), Assn. for Clin. Pastoral Edn. (inactive supr., mem. coms. 1967-75). Democrat. Avocations: music (violinist symphony orch. and string quartet), photography, hiking. Home: 7141 S Olive Way Englewood CO 80112 Office: The Samaritan Inst 2696 S Colorado Blvd Ste 380 Denver CO 80222

BOLOIS, ROBERT WAYNE, minister; b. Sharon, Pa., Nov. 20, 1946; s. Andrew John and Mary Eugene (Davis) B.; m. Judith Ann Williams, June 17, 1966; children: Lynette, Stephen, Mark, Jay. BA in Bibl. Lit., Hobe Sound Bible Coll., 1968; MA in Psychology, Emmanuel Bapt. U., 1990; PhD in Counseling, Carolina Theol. U., 1991. Ordained to ministry Wesleyan Meth. Ch., 1977. Pastor Allegheny Wesleyan Meth. Connection, Salem, Ohio, 1966-90, Ohio Bible Meth., Barberton, Ohio, 1990—; psychologist Brink Haven Homes for Youth, North Lawrence, Ohio, 1990—; bd. dirs. Hobe Sound (Fla.) Bible Coll., 1987, Interdenominational Holiness Conv., Salem, 1986—, Allegheny Wesleyan Meth. Conv., Salem, 1979-85, Allegheny Wesleyan Meth. Connection, 1986—; dist. youth chmn.. Wesleyan Meth. Connection, Stoneboro, Pa., 1973-75, 84-85. Contbr. articles to profl. jours. Counselor Barberton Rescue Mission, 1983-90' v.p. ARC Blood-Mobile, Barberton, 1983—, Community Pregnancy Ctr., 1990—. Mem. Nat. Christian Counselors Assn. (lic. and cert. pastoral counselor and temperament therapist). Republican. Home: 3570 Eastern Rd Norton OH 44203 Office: Barberton Wesleyan Meth Ch 222 26th St Barberton OH 44203

BOLOTOWSKY, GIDEON, religious organization administrator. Pres. Jewish Community, Helsinki, Finland. Office: Jewish Community, Synagogue, Ctr, Malminkatu 26, 00100 Helsinki Finland*

BOLT, FRED FELTON, minister; b. Anderson, S.C., June 4, 1952; s. Jack Gray and Nellie (Feltman) B.; m. Tracy Rhodes, May 7, 1977; children: Kathea Jean, Kara Ellese. AA in Music, Anderson Coll., 1975; BA in Religious Edn., Central (S.C.) Wesleyan, 1977; M in Religious Edn., So. Bapt. Theol. Seminary, 1980. Minister of music Townville (S.C.) Bapt. Ch., 1974-77; minister of music and youth East Clemson (S.C.) Bapt. Ch., 1977-78; minister of music and edn. Calvary Bapt. Ch., Madison, Ind., 1978-80, Love Meml. Bapt. Ch., Gastonia N.C., 1980-87, Mon-Aetna Bapt. Ch., Union, S.C., 1987—. Home: 403 Toluca St Union SC 29379 Office: Mon-Aetna Bapt Ch PO Box 72 Union SC 29379

BOLTHOUSE, WARREN JAY, Christian broadcasting executive; b. Grand Rapids, Mich., July 13, 1927; s. Peter and Harriet (Spoelstra) B.; m. Charlotte Ann Larson, Aug. 1, 1947; children: Janice, Donna, Cheryl, Jim, Dave. Student, Grand Rapids Sch. Bible/Music, 1947-49. Youth dir. 1st Bapt., Pontiac, Mich., 1952-53; youth-music dir. Greatest Bapt., Detroit, 1953-57, Cazenonia Park Bapt., Buffalo, 1957-60; pastor Ganson St. Bapt., Jackson, Mich., 1966; pres. Family Life Radio Network, Tucson, 1966—; v.p. Youth Haven Ranches, Rives Junction, Mich., Picacho, Ariz., 1968—. Named Alumnus of Yr., Grand Rapids Sch. Bible, 1977. Republican. Home: 765 Bangor Tucson AZ 85704

BOLTON, DENNIS RUDOLPH, minister; b. High Point, N.C., Mar. 24, 1953; s. Rudolph Alexander and Gerda Sophia (Gemar) B.; m. Angela Polk, May 25, 1974; children: Jessica Kristen, Brittany Megan. BA in Religious Studies, U. S.C., 1975; MDiv, Luth. Theol. So. Sem., 1979; DMin, Union Theol. Sem., Richmond, 1984; postgrad., U. N.C., 1984-87. Ordained to ministry, Evang. Luth. Ch. in Am. Pastor Shepherd of the Sea, Morehead City, N.C., 1979-81, Christus Victor Luth. Ch., Durham, N.C., 1981-88; chaplain Duke U. Med. Ctr., Durham, 1988-89; pastor Luth. Chapel, Gastonia, N.C., 1989—; chmn. Christian Edn. Com., N.C. Synod, Salisbury, 1989-91. Coord. Crop Walk, Durham, 1984-85; bd. dirs. Mental Health Assn., Gastonia, 1989-91. Mem. Assn. Clin. Pastoral Edn., Acad. of Parish Clergy, Gastonia Ministerial Assn. (pres. 1991—). Home: 2330 Rose Garden Gastonia NC 28056 Office: Luth Chapel 702 N New Hope Rd Gastonia NC 28054 *"I beg you not to look upon (your church) as a stepping stone, but rather say: Here I shall stay as long as it pleases God; if it be His will, until I die. Look upon every child, your confirmands, every member of your congregation as if you have to give account for every soul on the day of Lord Jesus. Every day commit all of these human souls from the worst and weakest of hands - namely, your own - into the best and strongest of hands. Then you will be able to carry on your ministry not only without care, but also with joy overflowing and joyfull hope." (Friedrich von Bodelschwingh, 1821-1910).*

BOMAN, SAMUEL R., ecumenical agency executive. Pres. Interchurch Ministries Nebr., Lincoln. Office: Interchurch Ministries 215 Centenial Mall S Rm 411 Lincoln NE 68508*

BOMAN, STEN ARVID STIGSSON, minister, chaplain, counselor; b. Gävle, Sweden, Feb. 19, 1953; s. Stig Erik Boman and Grethe Lilian (Kruse) Hammershoy. BA, Nicolai, Helsingborg, Sweden, 1972; candidatus juris, U. Copenhagen, Denmark, 1979; MDiv, Yale Divinity, 1982, STM, 1985. Pastor Bethlehem Luth., Thomaston, Conn., 1986-89; chaplain St. Mary's Hosp., Waterbury, Conn., 1989—. Mem. Am. Assn. Clin. Pastoral Edn. Home: 488 Perkins Ave Waterbury CT 06704

BOMBARDIER, PAUL ALFRED, priest; b. Holyoke, Mass., Apr. 23, 1953; s. Maurice Julien Anselm and Clarisse Marie Irene (Paré) B. BS in Biology, Westfield (Mass.) State Coll., 1975; BA in Religious Studies, Cath. U. Leuven, Belgium, 1980, MA in Religious Studies, 1982. Ordained priest Roman Cath. Ch., 1982. Parochial vicar St. Thomas the Apostle Parish, West Springfield, Mass., 1982-84, St. John the Bapt. Parish, Ludlow, Mass., 1984-89; chaplain Cathedral High Sch., Springfield, 1989-90; parochial vicar Blessed Sacrament Parish, Holyoke, Mass., 1990—; mem. Diocesan Liturgical Commn., Springfield, 1987—, chmn., 1990—, editor newsletter, 1989—. Mem. Am. Recorder Soc., Early Music Am. Home: 1945 Northampton St Holyoke MA 01040-3401

BOMGARDEN, STANLEY RALPH, minister; b. Freeport, Ill., Nov. 4, 1946; s. Ralph George and Dorothy Lorraine (Heeren) B.; m. Theresa Jane McCarten, June 7, 1969 (div. 1976); children: Peter, Elizabeth; m. Sylvia Ann Stone Maurer, June 27, 1986; stepchildren: Timothy Maurer, Jane Parks, Sarah Maurer. BA, Cen. Coll., Pella, Iowa, 1969; MDiv, Western Theol. Sem., Holland, Mich., 1972; postgrad., U. Iowa, 1975-78. Ordained to ministry Ref. Ch. Am., 1975, Presbyn. Ch. (U.S.A.), 1988. Pastor 1st Ref. Ch., Rotterdam Jct., N.Y., 1973-75; assoc. pastor 1st Bapt. Ch., Iowa City, 1977-78; pastor 1st Presbyn. Ch., Beebe, Ark., 1988-91, Meml. Presbyn. Ch.,

Dayton, Ind., 1991—; counselor Highland Community Coll., Freeport, 1979-81; dir. Christian edn. 2d Presbyn. Ch., Freeport, 1983-87; guest lectr. Ark. State U., Beebe, 1989-91; program coord. Freeport Area Ch. Coop., 1984-87; moderator witness com. Presbytery of Ark., 1990-91. Illustrator: The Server's Book of the Mass, 1987; contbg. editor Festivals mag.; mem. editorial bd. newsletter Body and Soul; contbr. stories and articles to profl. jours. Mem. Lions (pres. Beebe club 1990-91). Democrat. Home: 294 Conjunction St Dayton IN 47941 Office: Meml Presbyn Ch PO Box 186 Dayton IN 47941 *When we, the heirs of western civilization, hear a story, we ask, "Is this true?" It is time that we learned from those who dwell in the East that there is a more important question: "How is this true?".*

BONACCORSO, ANTHONY, minister; b. N.Y.C., May 13, 1929; s. Concetto and Filippa Bonaccorso; m. Barbara Ruth Fogelman, Feb. 13, 1983 (div. July 1988); children: Brian David, Lisa Claire, Steven Victor. BA, San Francisco State U., 1951, MA, 1956. Ordained to ministry, 1978. Tchr. Santa Rosa (Calif.) High Sch., 1954-70; restauranteur Fiori's Italian Restaurant, Occidental, Calif., 1970-77; minister Salem Ch. of Religious Sci., Salem, Oreg., 1977-82, Miami (Fla.) Ch. of Religious Sci., 1982-88; dist. pres. Internat. New Thought Alliance, Salem, 1979-82, Miami, 1982—. Contbr. numerous articles to mags. With U.S. Army, 1952-54. Home: 1661 SW 32d Pl Miami FL 33145

BONANNO, FREDERICK RAMON, deacon, educator; b. Baton Rouge, Dec. 1, 1927; s. Joseph John and Annie (Cangelosi) B.; m. Audrey Maud Popwell, Sept. 5, 1951; children: Frederick Ramon Jr., Joel Jay, Mark Stephen. BS, U.S. Mil. Acad., 1950; MS, Iowa State U., 1957; PhD, U. Ariz., 1964; BA, St. Leo Coll., 1981. Ordained deacon Roman Cath. Ch., 1980. Commd. 2d lt. USAF, 1950, advanced through grades to lt. col., 1966, ret., 1975; dir. Office of Ecumenical and Interreligious Affairs, Pensacola, Fla., 1980-84; deacon St. Mary Parish, Ft. Walton Beach, Fla., 1984—. Contbr. articles to sci. publs. Mem. Am. Soc. for Engring. Edn. (chmn. young engring. tchrs. Rocky Mountain sect. 1958). Republican. Roman Catholic. Home: 587 L'Ombre Ct Fort Walton Beach FL 32547-1814

BONAR, CLAYTON LLOYD, minister; b. Washington County, Kans., Nov. 5, 1934; s. Earl Albert and Violet May (Doane) B.; m. Helen Ann Harmaning, Sept. 12, 1958; children: Renee, Scott. BA, N.W. Nazarene Coll., 1960; postgrad., Fuller Theol. Sem., 1974-75; MA, Point Loma Coll., 1975; postgrad., Rosemead Grad. Sch., 1975. Ordained to ministry Ch. of the Nazarene, 1963. Pastor Ch. of the Nazarene, Caldwell, Idaho, 1961-63, Pocatello, Idaho, 1963-68, Inglewood, Calif., 1968-73, Alhambra, Calif., 1973-78, Richland, Wash., 1978-89, Bremerton, Wash., 1990—; del. Gen. Nazarene World Missionary Soc., Conv. Nazarene Ch., Kansas City, 1968; regent N.W. Nazarene Coll., Nampa, Idaho, 1967-68; dist. sec. Ch. of the Nazarene, L.A., 1976-78; mem. adv. bd. N.W. Dist., 1984—; committeman Nazarene Fed. Credit Union, Whittier, Calif., 1974-78; mem. curriculum com. The Enduring World Series. Author: From Behind Closed Doors, 1981, The Spoken Law, 1985; (with others) Tough Questions: Christian Answers, 1982; contbr. articles to profl. jours. With USAF, 1953-56. Mem. Wesleyan Theol. Soc., Speakers and Writers Ink, Kiwanis. Republican. Avocation: photography. Home: 3349 Quinault Dr NE Bremerton WA 98310 Office: 1st Ch of the Nazarene 924 Sheridan Rd Bremerton WA 98310

BOND, EDWINA ELAINE, church official, lay church worker; b. Newnan, Ga., Feb. 19, 1954; d. Edward Bailey and Hazel F. (Thompson) Evans; m. Anthony Craig Bond, Mar. 22, 1974; children: Kimberly, Kyle. Student, Clayton State Coll., Morrow, Ga., 1972-74, DeKalb Jr. Coll., Clarkston, Ga., 1976-77, Cobb Tech. Inst., Smyrna, Ga., 1986. Asst. choir dir. Allgood Road United Meth. Ch., Stone Mountain, Ga., 1975-80, youth dir., 1977-80; ch. bus. adminstr. Trinity Fellowship Assembly of God Ch., Peachtree City, Ga., 1987—, dir. choirs, leader Kinship, 1990—. Recipient award of appreciation Allgood Road United Meth. Ch., 1980, Trinity Fellowship Assembly of God, 1990. Mem. Nat. Assn. Ch. Bus. Adminstrs. Home: 115 Julie Rd Tyrone GA 30290 Office: Trinity Fellowship Assembly of God Ch 8817 Hwy 54 W Sharpsburg GA 30277 *In my life I have found that every day, which is begun with prayer and meditation, is always a more successful day, than one which does not begin with prayer.*

BOND, JUNE MARILYN, principal; b. Atlanta, July 23, 1950; d. Nicholas George and Dorothy Marie (Daugherty) Mas; m. Edward Boyd Bond, Aug. 26, 1972; children: Gia Vanna, Edward Earnest. BA, Roberts Wesleyan Coll., Rochester, N.Y., 1973; MA, U. Conn., 1990. Cert. tchr., N.Y. Dir. Christian edn. Ch. of the Resurrection, Syracuse, N.Y., 1977-81, Living Waters, Harrisburg, Pa., 1981-85; dir. gifted and talented programming Mt. Morris Cen. Sch., 1986-88; tchr. Faith Temple Sch., Rochester, 1974-75, prin., dir. gifted programming, 1988—; dir. Joy Messengers-Mime-Christian Edn. Orgn., Harrisburg, 1983-85. Lab. fellow Regional Lab. for Ednl. Improvement of N.E. and Islands, 1988-89. Mem. Christian Sch. Adminstrs., Pi Lambda Theta. Republican. Home: 90 Seminole Way Rochester NY 14618 Office: Faith Temple Sch 1876 Elmwood Ave Rochester NY 14620

BOND, KERRY LAYNE, minister; b. Memphis, June 11, 1957; s. Carol Wayne and Maveline (Chrestman) B.; m. Zelanie Kay Sadler, July 9, 1976; children: Wesleigh Margaret Angelica, Alexandra Simone, Nigel Quinten. BA, Crichton Coll., Memphis, 1982; MDiv, So. Bapt. Theol. Sem., Louisville, 1985. Ordained to ministry So. Bapt. Conv., 1987. Pastor Rutledge (Tenn.) Bapt. Ch., 1987—; with J.C. Penney Co., Louisville and Memphis, 1985-87; mem. adv. bd. Appalachian Outreach/Samaritan House, Jefferson City, Tenn., 1988—. Vice chmn. Grainger County Dem. Com., Rutledge, 1989; adv. mem. Grainger County Literacy Program, 1989; alt. mem. bd. dirs. Douglas-Cherokee Econ. Authority, Morristown, Tenn., 1989. Home: Rte 4 Box 53 Rutledge TN 37861 Office: Rutledge Bapt Ch PO Box 241 Church St Rutledge TN 37861

BOND, WILLIAM CHRAMER, JR., minister; b. Atlanta, Feb. 19, 1954; s. William Chramer and Sarah June (Stephens) B.; m. Penny Rae Young, June 1, 1978; children: Daniel, John-Michael. BA, Davidson Coll., 1976; MDiv, Southeastern Sem., 1980. Ordained to ministry Bapt. Ch., 1979. Pastor Love Valley (N.C.) Presbyn. Ch., 1975-76; assoc. pastor Twinbrook Bapt. Ch., Rockville, Md., 1978-82; pastor Forest Bapt. Ch., Upperco, Md., 1982-85, Cresthill Bapt. Ch., Bowie, Md., 1985—; mem. ordination com. D.C. Bapt. Conv., 1986-87, mem. missions com., 1987-88. Mem. U.S. C. of C. Office: Cresthill Bapt Ch 6510 Laurel-Bowie Rd Bowie MD 20715

BONDI, RICHARD JOHN, religious educator; b. Cin., Nov. 26, 1951; s. August Lawrence and Catherine (Dillon) B.; m. Roberta C. Bondi, Apr. 15, 1979; stepchildren: Grace Braun, Benjamin Chesnut. BA, Oberlin Coll., Ohio, 1973; MA, U. Notre Dame, 1977, PhD, 1981. Instr. theology Marquette U., Milw., 1977, 78-79; vis. prof. Christian Ethics Emory U., Atlanta, 1979-83, asst. prof. Christian Ethics, 1983—. Author: Leading God's People: Ethics for the Practice of Ministry, 1989; contbr. articles to profl. jours. Nat. Merit fellow, 1969; U. Notre Dame fellow, 1973-77. Mem. Soc. Christian Ethics, Am. Acad. Religion, Fedn. Fly Fishers, Phi Beta Kappa. Democrat. Roman Catholic. Office: Emory Univ Atlanta GA 30322 *There are no noncombatants in the war between women and men. For men to become lovers and not enemies of women means more than renouncing our private agression. It means speaking out against what happens to our sisters and working with them to bring in the new creation.*

BONE, ALAN CLARKE, minister; b. Galesburg, Ill., Mar. 11, 1938; s. Thomas LeRoy and Sylvia Christine (Gilliland) B.; m. Mary Leta Bybee, Aug. 19, 1962 (dec. Jan. 1965); 1 child, Cynthia; m. Joan Ruth Arenberg, Aug. 7, 1968; children: Eric, Thomas. AB, Eureka Coll., 1960; MDiv., Lexington Theol. Sem., 1963; postgrad. in ministerial studies, Columbia Theol. Sem., 1983-85. Pastor Luray (S.C.) Christian Ch., 1963-66; youth, camp dir. Christian Ch. in S.C., 1965-66; assoc. pastor 1st Christian Ch., Parkersburg, W.Va., 1966-67; pastor Cen. Christian Ch., Marietta, Ohio, 1967-72, Forest Christian Ch., Jacksonville, Fla., 1972-75, Holly Ridge Christian Ch., Mechanicsville, Va., 1975-76, Prospect & Poole Christian Chs., Dinwiddie County, Va., 1977-78, 1st Christian Ch., Belvedere, S.C., 1978-85, Plymouth (Pa.) Christian Ch., 1985—; vol. chaplain Wilkes-Barre (Pa.) Gen. Hosp., 1985—, Mercy Hosp., Nanticoke, Pa., 1986—. Part-time correspondent The Times Leader, Wilkes-Barre, 1988—. Mem. Luzerne County Pub. Forum, Wilkes-Barre, 1987—. Mem. Plymouth Ministerial Assn. (convenor 1987-89), Barbershop Harmony Soc. Home: 19 W Shawnee Ave Plymouth PA 18651 Office: Plymouth Christian Ch PO Box 220 Plymouth PA 18651

BONGMBA, ELIAS KIFON, minister; b. Ntumbaw, Cameroon, Dec. 15, 1953; s. Johaness and Monica (Munkeng) B.; m. Mary Bongmba, Sept. 7, 1979; children: Donald, Dino, Douglas. BA in Mass Communications and Sociology, Sioux Falls Coll., 1987; MDiv, N.Am. Bapt. Sem., 1989; MA in Theology and Ethics, U. Iowa, 1991. Ordained to ministry Bapt. Ch., 1983. Pastor Wanti (N.W. Cameroon) Bapt. Ch., 1971-72, Ntumbaw Bapt. Ch., 1972-75; religious knowledge tchr. Gongola State, Nigeria, 1978-80; pastor Berean Bapt. Ch., Kumba, Cameroon, 1982-84, Bapt. Ch., Yaounde, Cameroon, 1982-84; interim pastor Olds (Iowa) United Ch. of Christ, 1989—; pastor Champion Hill, Franklin and Pleasant Hill (Iowa) United Meth. Chs., 1990—; radio preacher Protestant Chs. of Cameroon, 1980-84. Mem. Am. Acad. Religion, Soc. Bibl. Lit. Home: 2295 E Iliff # 311 Denver CO 80210 *The challenges that face humanity are enormous and very often disturbing. I am learning everyday that as part of my contribution to a solution the Divine requires only that I be faithful and do the very best.*

BONHAM, JOHN STEPHEN HENRY, minister; b. Calgary, Alta., Can., Jan. 7, 1936; s. Herbert Henry Bonham and Sophie Lund; m. Ruth Ellen Boyd, Aug. 23, 1958; children: Charlene, Judith, Roy, Stephen. BA, Waterloo (Ont.) Luth. U., 1963; MDiv, Cen. Baptist Sem, Toronto, 1986. Ordained to ministry Bapt. Ch., 1965. Youth pastor, asst. pastor Runnymede Bapt. Ch., Toronto, Ont., 1958-63; pastor Royal York Bapt. Ch., Toronto, 1963-72; sr. pastor Fellowship Bapt. Ch., Edmonton, Alta., 1972-89; regional sec. Fellowship of Evang. Bapt. Chs., Alta., Sask., and N.W.T., Can., 1989—. Home and Office: 42 Ironwood Dr, Saint Albert, AB Canada T8N 5J2

BONNER, WILLIAM HAVEN, bishop; b. Blytheville, Ark., Sept. 13, 1921; m. Eddie and Mattie (McBride) B.; m. Dorothy Mae Green, May 2, 1942; children: Eyness Lucinda, Willie Etta, Dorothy A., Charles Edward (dec.). DD, Trinity Hall Bible Coll., 1981. Pastor Greater Mt. Olive Ch. of God in Christ, Aurora, Ill., 1944—; bishop of 6th Ecclesiatical Jurisdiction of Ill. Chs. of God in Christ; pres. youth dept., dist. supt., asst. adminstr. to Bishop Louis Henry Ford, 1959-78, chmn. Bishop's budget com., chmn. nat. fin. com. Chs. of God in Christ. Democrat. Office: Ch of God in Christ 1039 Bonner Ave Aurora IL 60505

BONNER, WILLIAM L., religious organization administrator. Pres. bd. apostles Ch. of Our Lord Jesus Christ of Apostolic Faith, Inc., N.Y.C. Office: Ch of Our Lord Jesus Christ of Apostolic Faith Inc 2081 Adam Clayton Powell Jr New York NY 10027*

BOOHER, HAROLD HASTING, religion educator, librarian; b. Ft. Worth, July 14, 1929; s. Hugh and Bernice Beatrice (Jones) B.; m. Patricia Marie Miller, Sept. 3, 1955; children: Douglas Hugh, James Franklin. BS, Tex. Wesleyan Coll., 1951; MA, So. Meth. U., 1957; MLS, U. Tex., 1972; MPhil, Columbia U., 1975. Libr., assoc. prof. N.T. Episcopal Theol. Sem. of S.W., Austin, Tex., 1967-87, libr., prof. theol. lit. and N.T., 1987—. Mem. Am. Theol. Library Assn. Home: 7401 Chimney Corners Austin TX 78731 Office: Episcopal Theol Sem of SW PO Box 2247 Austin TX 78768

BOOHER, JOHN ARTHUR, clergyman; b. Feb. 26, 1942; s. Virgil and Lenora Booher; m. Patricia Eylene McClaflin, Aug. 1, 1964; children: Craig, Shana, Rachel. Student, N.W. Jr. Coll., 1960-62, U. Wyo., 1962, Cen. Bible Coll., Springfield, Mo., 1963-65. Ordained to ministry Assemblies of God Ch. Pastor Assemblies of God Ch., Stoneham, Colo., 1965-66, Tribune, Kans., 1966-67, Wichita, Kans., 1967-76; sr. pastor Fairlane Assembly of God, Dearborn Heights, Mich., 1976-88, Willamette Christian Ctr., Eugene, Oreg., 1988—; sectional youth leader Assemblies of God, Stoneham, 1965-66, Wichita, 1970-74, exec. presbyter Mich. dist., 1986-88; assoc. Internat. Corr. Inst., Ft. Worth, 1985—. Author: Catechism for Charismatics, 1980, I'm A New Creation, 1980, Catechism No. 2, 1989. Bd. dirs. Wichita Mental Health Assn., 1975-76, Women Aglow, Detroit, 1983-87. Mem. Studebaker Club, Lincoln Club, Chrysler 300 Club. Avocations: oil painting, fishing. Home: 1259 Courtney Pl Eugene OR 97405 Office: Willamette Christian Ctr 2500 W 18th St Eugene OR 97402

BOOKMAN, TERRY ALLEN, rabbi; b. Bklyn., May 2, 1950; s. Arthur and Lillian (Bernfeld) B.; m. Karen Sobel, Apr. 12, 1981; children: Ariel, Jonah, Micah, Jesse. BA, Richmond Coll., 1971; MAHL, Hebrew Union Coll., L.A., 1982. Ordained rabbi, 1984. Asst. rabbi Congregation Sinai, Milw., 1984-86, assoc. rabbi, 1986-89, sr. rabbi, 1989—; adj. prof. Sacred Heart Sch. Theology, Hales Corners, Wis., 1987—; lectr. Marquette U., Milw., 1991; mem. Milw. Interfaith Conf.; bd. dirs. commn. on interfaith dialogue Union Am. Hebrew Congregations, N.Y.C.; trustee Milw. Fedn. Jewish Philanthropies; co-chmn. Am. Jewish Com., Milw., 1989—; mem. rabbinic cabinet United Jewish Appeal, N.Y.C., 1990—; co-chmn. Theology group Hebrew Union Coll., N.Y.C., 1990; mem. rabbinic faculty Olin-Sang Ruby Union Camp, Chgo., 1984—, co-chmn. rabbinic adv. bd., 1988, 90. Contbr. articles to profl. jours. Marquette Acad. Achievement fellow, 1987-88; Milw. Community Found. grantee, 1990. Mem. Cen. Conf. Am. Rabbis, Wis. Coun. Rabbis (treas., v.p.), Wis. Rabbinic Fellowship, Am. Acad. Religion, Midwest Assn. Reform Rabbis. Office: Congregation Sinai 8223 N Port Washington Rd Milwaukee WI 53217

BOONE, DON MAXWELL, minister; b. Mobile, Ala., Sept. 15, 1949; s. Henry M. and Mary Sue (Douglas) B.; m. Jamie Lynn Godwin, Feb. 20, 1970; children: Chrissy L., Heather R. BS, Mobile Coll., 1974; MA, So. Bapt. Sem., 1987, D of Ministry, 1988. Ordained to ministry Bapt. Ch., 1969; lic. to preach, 1967. Pastor Magnolia Springs (Ala.) Bapt. Ch., 1980-84, Immanuel Bapt. Ch., Morgan City, La., 1984-86, Ingalls Avenue Bapt. Ch., Pascagoula, Miss., 1986-89, College Park Bapt. Ch., Mobile, 1989—; evangelist Mobile, 1975-76; music dir. Shiloh Bapt. Ch., Saraland, Ala., 1976-80, Rocky Creek Bapt. Ch., Lucedale, Miss., 1972-75. Office: College Park Bapt Ch 5860 College Pkwy Mobile AL 36613

BOONE, JOHN CLAY, minister; b. Atlanta, June 9, 1947; s. Curtis Willard Sr. and Bertha Lean (Parker) B.; m. Ella Sherrill Farmer, Jan. 20, 1968; children: Faith Simone, Christian Michael. BA, Jacksonville State U., 1970; MDiv., New Orleans Bapt. Theol Sem., 1973. Ordained to ministry Bapt. Ch., 1973. Music dir. Woodland Park Bapt. Ch., Anniston, Ala., 1967-68; minister music, youth 1st Bapt. Ch., Piedmont, Ala., 1967-68; minister youth 1st Bapt. Ch., Boaz, Ala., 1968-70; minister music, youth Elysian Fields Ave. Bapt. Ch., New Orleans, 1970-72, Buras (La.) Triumph Bapt. Ch., 1972-73; pastor Western Heights Bapt. Ch., LaGrange, Ga., 1973-80, Grace Bapt. Ch., LaGrange, Ga., 1980-85; sr. pastor Lakeview Bapt. Ch., Tallahassee, 1985-88; assoc. dir. Sunday Sch. Fla. Bapt. Conv., Jacksonville, 1988—; moderator Fla. Bapt. Assn., 1986-87; travel dir. Christian Travel Group, 1986-88. Mem. exec. bd. Leon Choral Parents Orgn., 1987-88; vol. Leon County Pub. Schs., 1987-88; officer Fla. Bapt. Religious Educators Assn., 1990. Mem. Fla. Bapt. Religious Educators Assn. (officer 1990). Avocations: golf, running, coin collecting. Office: Fla Bapt Conv 1230 Hendricks Ave Jacksonville FL 32207

BOONE, JOHN LEWIS, religious organization administrator; b. Elkton, Ky., Oct. 5, 1927; s. Benjamin Edwards and Manie (Street) B.; m. Sally Hardcastle, Dec. 30, 1952; children: Sally Boone Wieland, John L. Jr., Martha Boone Bland. BA, Vanderbilt U., 1949. CLU. Pres. Presbyns. for Democracy and Religious Freedom, 1985—; chmn. Boone, Brandon, Johnston & Evans Inc., Nashville, 1969—. Author Presbyn. Mainstream newspaper, 1986—. Recipient Faith and Freedom award Presbyns. for Democracy and Religious Freedom, Washington, 1990; named Man of the Yr., Tenn. Assn. of Life Underwriters, 1989. Mem. Nashville Chpt. CLUs (pres. 1957), Nashville Assn. of Life Underwriters (pres. 1955). Republican. Office: Boone Brandon Johnston & Evans Inc 30 Burton Hills Blvd Ste 500 Nashville TN 37215

BOONSTRA, JOHN C., ecumenical agency executive. Exec. Wash. Assn. Chs., Seattle. Office: Wash Assn Chs 4769 15th Ave NE Seattle WA 98105*

BOOTH, ALEX, religious institute administrator; b. Warfield, Ky., Oct. 24, 1924; s. Alex Lunsford and Emma (Kyle) B; m. Beatrice Thompson, Oct. 5, 1947; children: Carolyn, Daniel, Ellen Gayle, Allen, Gary. BA, King Coll., Bristol, Tenn., 1951; MDiv, Southeastern Bapt. Theol. Sem., Wake Forest, N.C., 1959; DD, Gardner-Webb, Boiling Springs, N.C., 1983. Ordained to ministry So. Baptist Ch., 1950. Pastor Cedar Fork Bapt. Ch., Yates Assn., Durham, N.C., 1957-59; pastor Spence Bapt. Ch., Md., 1959-61, Round Hill Bapt. Ch., Union Mills, N.C., 1961-64; mem. faculty Fruitland Bapt. Bible Inst., Hendersonville, N.C., 1964—, dean, 1965-74, dir., 1974—. Pres. Henderson County Mental Health Assn., 1973-74; mem. Henderson County Bd. Edn., 1973—. Mem. So. Bapt. Adult Edn. Assn. (pres.), Rotary (past dir.). Office: Fruitland Bapt Bible Inst Hendersonville NC 28739

BOOTH, CHARLES EDWARD, minister; b. Balt., Feb. 4, 1947; s. William Whiting B. and Hazel Delsenior (Willis) Sutton. BA, Howard U., 1969; MDiv, Eastern Bapt. Seminary, 1973; D Ministry, United Theol. Sem., Dayton, Ohio, 1990; DD (hon.), Va. Sem., Lynchburg, 1980. Ordained Bapt. pastor, Balt., 1970. Pastor St. Paul's Bapt. Ch., West Chester, Pa., 1970-77, Mt. Olivet Bapt. Ch., Columbus, Ohio, 1978—; instr. Trinity Luth. Sem., Columbus, Ohio, 1982-83, Meth. Theol. Sem., Delaware, Ohio, 1984-85; prof. of preaching United Theol. Sem., Dayton, 1988—. Co-author: (with others) Outstanding Black Sermons Vol. 3, 1982; writer The Worker (devotional mag.), 1985. Adv. bd. Banc Ohio Community Devel. Assn., Columbus, 1988—; bd. dirs. Columbus Urban League, 1988—. Recipient Middler scholarship Eastern Bapt. Sem., Phila., 1971, Dedicated Svc. award West Chester State Coll., 1977, Humanitarian Svc. award Alpha Kappa Alpha Sorority, Columbus, 1981. Democrat. Home: 2685 Halleck Dr Columbus OH 43209 Office: Mt Olivet Bapt Ch 428 E Main St Columbus OH 43215

BOOTH, HOWARD JOHN, religion educator; b. Detroit, June 1, 1938; s. John Edward and Helen Francis (Najjar) B.; m. Bonita Angelee Dixon, June 29, 1963; children: Gevin, Darin. BA in Religion, Graceland Coll., 1960; MA in Counseling, U. Mo., Kansas City, 1964; PhD in Religion, U. Iowa, 1972. Ordained lay min. Reorganized Ch. Jesus Christ Latter Day Saints, 1954. Exec. minister world hdqrs. Reorganized Ch. Jesus Christ Latter Day Saints, Independence, Mo., 1960-64; prof. religion, chmn. humanities div. Graceland Coll., Lamoni, Iowa, 1969—; ch. educator, speaker Reorganized Ch. Jesus Christ Latter Day Saints, 1969—. Author: Edwin Diller Starburk: Pioneer in the Psychology of Religion, 1981; contbr. to numerous religious publs. Precinct chair Dem. County Cen. Com., Lamoni and Leon, Iowa, 1980-88; profl. counselor Community Counseling Ctr., Lamoni, 1984-87. Mem. Am. Acad. Religion, John Whitmer Hist. Assn. (best lecture award 1979), Iowa Peace Studies Inst., Mormon Hist. Assn. (spl. citation as author 1981), Theol. Forum (steering com. 1987—. Democrat. Avocations: travel, writing, fishing, spectator sports. Home: 606 W Main St Lamoni IA 50140 Office: Graceland Coll Div Humanities Lamoni IA 50140 *Learning and growing is a continual process. When we see both the limitations of our understanding as well as the possibilities of learning, if we are genuinely open to new truth, we will be less critical of differing views and more open to what others can contribute to our understanding.*

BOOTH, JOHN EVANS, minister; b. Edinburg, Tex., May 30, 1956; s. Bert Evans and Lois Marie (Kennedy) B.; m. Cindy Cole, Aug. 11, 1979; children: Tyler Kennedy, Caleb Evans, Jordan Micha. BS, Howard Payne Coll., 1978; M of Religious Edn., Southwestern Bapt. Theol., Seminary, Ft. Worth, 1982. Minister of edn. and youth First Bapt. Ch., Valley Mills, Tex., 1983-85, Sealy, Tex., 1986-88; minister of edn. and youth Spring Woods Bapt., Houston, 1988—. Named to Outstanding Young Men of Am., 1988. Mem. Tex. Bapt. Ministers Edn. Assn. (registrar 1989-90). Republican. Home: 10550 Alcott Houston TX 77043 Office: Spring Woods Baptist Ch 10131 Emnora Lane Houston TX 77080

BOOTH, JOHN NICHOLLS, minister, writer, photographer; b. Meadville, Pa., Aug. 7, 1912; s. Sydney Scott and Margaret (Nicholls) B.; m. Edith Kriger, Oct. 1, 1941; 1 dau., Barbara Anne Booth Christie. BA, McMaster U., 1934; BD, Meadville Theol. Sch., 1942, MDiv, 1986; LittD, New Eng. Sch. Law, 1950. Ordained to ministry Unitarian Ch., 1942. Profl. magician, 1934-40; min. Unitarian Ch., Evanston, Ill., 1942-48, 1st Ch., Belmont, Mass., 1949-57, 2d Ch., Boston, 1958-64, Unitarian Ch., Long Beach, Calif., 1964-71; interim pastor N.Y.C., Gainesville, (Fla.), Detroit, 1971-73; celebrity platform lectr., performer on conjuring, 1942-58; ministerial adviser to liberal students MIT, 1958-63; mem. books selection com. Gen. Theol. Library, Boston, 1960-63. Author: Super Magical Miracles, 1930, Magical Mentalism, 1931, Forging Ahead in Magic, 1939, Marvels of Mystery, 1941, The Quest for Preaching Power, 1942, Fabulous Destinations, 1950, Story of the Second Church in Boston, 1959, The John Booth Classics, 1975, Booths in History, 1982, Psychic Paradoxes, 1984, Wonders of Magic, 1986, Dramatic Magic, 1988, Creative World of Conjuring, 1990; contbr. articles to mags. and newspapers; photographer full length feature travel documentary films for TV, lecture platforms made in India, Africa, S.Am., Indonesia, South Seas, Himalayas; presented first color travelogue on TV in U.S. over NBC, 1949; panel mem. radio program Churchmen Weigh The News, Boston, 1951-52; spl. corr. in Asia for Chgo. Sun-Times, 1948-49; by-line writer Boston Globe, 1952-62; producer motion picture Heart of Africa, 1954; photographer films Golden Kingdoms of the Orient, 1957, Treasures of the Amazon, Ecuador and Peru, 1960, Adventurous Britain, 1962, South Seas Saga in Tahiti, Australia and New Guinea, summer 1966, The Amazing America of Will Rogers, 1970, Spotlight on Spain, 1975. Co-founder Japan Free Religious Assn., Tokyo, 1948; co-founder Mass. Meml. Soc., 1962, dir., 1962-64; organizer Meml. Soc. Alachua County (Fla.), 1972; pres. Long Beach Mental Health Assn., 1964-66; adv. coun. Fair Housing Found. Decorated officer Ouissam Alaouite Cherifien, King of Morocco; selected for cinematographers' Wall of Fame Town Hall, N.Y.C., 1967; recipient Star of Magic award N.Y.C., 1971, H. Adrian Smith literary award, 1985, 89, John Nevil Maskelyne prize London Magic Circle, 1987; Acad. Magical Arts fellow, 1977, 90. Mem. Unitarian-Universalist Mins. Assn. (past dir.), Am. Unitarian Assn. (past com. chmn.), Unitarian Mins. Pacific S.W. Assn. (v.p.), Clergy Counseling Svc. So. Calif., Soc. Am. Magicians (inducted into Hall of Fame 1983), Magic Castle Hollywood, Internat. Motion Picture and Lectrs. Assn., L.A. Adventurers Club (pres. 1983). First regularly scheduled TV broadcasts in U.S. by clergyperson, WBKB, Chgo., mid-1940s. Home and Office: 12032 Montecito Rd Los Alamitos CA 90720 *Success often greets an imaginative, innovative approach to that which has been done in a settled way too long. An ability to time change properly and accept philosophically that which does not yield is to live maturely with one's own struggles and hopes. Bertrand Russell guides wisely in suggesting that a person living in a spirit that aims at creating rather than possessing has a certain fundamental happiness. Such a way of life is thereby freed from the tyranny of fear, since what one values most in one's existence is not at the mercy of outside power.*

BOOTH, PAUL WAYNE, minister; b. Caraway, Ark., July 30, 1929; s. Arthur Irvin and Martha Belle (Wood) B.; m. Lavanda Joan Colbert, Dec. 29, 1949; children: Dennis Paul, Donald Wayne, Karen Sue. BS in Sociology and Bus. with honors, Ark. State U., 1963; MA in Sociology, U. Louisville, 1968; postgrad., Sch. of Restoration, Independence, Mo., 1974; MDiv, St. Paul Sch. Theology, 1975. Ordained to ministry Reorganized LDS Ch., 1953. Pastor Caraway, 1953-60; dist. pres. Reorganized LDS Ch., Louisville, 1963-66, adminstr. Colo., Wyo., Kans. and Nebr. region, 1966-68, adminstr. Mo., Ill., Ind., Ky. region, 1969-70; coord. ch. relationship to Instn. Higher Edn. Reorganized LDS Ch., Independence, Mo., 1976—; chmn. Gen. Ch. Commn. on Theology, Evangelism and Zionic Community, 1970-76; min. in charge Ch. in Europe and Africa region, 1984-88; pres. Coun. of Twelf Apostles. Author: The Church and Its Mission, 1971; contbr. articles to profl. jours. Chmn. Indsl. Devel. Com., Caraway, 1958-60; pres. Outreach Internat. Found. for Third World Comprehensive Community Devel., 1980—, Restoration Trail Found.; bd. dirs. Graceland Coll., Lamoni, Iowa. Home: 12705 E 37 Terrace Ct Independence MO 64055 Office: The Auditorium Independence MO 64050 *I have found that productive living depends upon acceptance of two basic discoveries: Who I am and whose I am.*

BOOTH, STEVEN CRAIG, minister; b. Charleston, S.C., Apr. 22, 1959; s. Joseph Oscar and Grace (Mixon) B.; m. Susan Leake Maxwell, May 1, 1982; children: Robert Lee, Caleb Dow. BS, Clemson (S.C.) U., 1981; MDiv,

Southwestern Bapt. Theol. Sem., Ft. Worth, 1986, PhD, 1991. Ordained to ministry So. Bapt. Ch., 1986. Pastor Greenwood Bapt. Ch., Weatherford, Tex., 1987—. Mem. Soc. Bibl. Lit., Inst. Bibl. Rsch. Home and Office: 1504 Greenwood Cutoff Weatherford TX 76086

BOOTH, WAYNE CLAYSON, English language educator, author; b. American Fork, Utah, Feb. 22, 1921; s. Wayne Chipman and Lillian (Clayson) B.; m. Phyllis Barnes, June 19, 1946; children: Katherine, John Richard (dec.), Alison. A.B., Brigham Young U., 1944; M.A., U. Chgo., 1947, Ph.D., 1950; D. Litt. (hon.), Rockford Coll., 1965, St. Ambrose Coll., 1971, U. N.H., 1977; D.H.L. (hon.), Butler U., 1984, Lycoming Coll., 1985, SUNY, 1987. Instr. U. Chgo., 1947-50; asst. prof. Haverford Coll., 1950-53; prof. English, chmn. dept. Earlham Coll., 1953-62; George M. Pullman prof. English U. Chgo., 1962-91, dean Coll., 1964-69, disting. Service prof. dept. English and Com. on Ideas and Methods, 1970—; resident master Woodward Ct., U. Chgo., 1970-71, chmn. com. on ideas and methods, 1972-75; Beckman lectr. U. Calif., Berkeley, 1979, Sch. Criticism, Irvine, Calif., 1979; Whitney Oates vis. prof. Princeton U., 1984; vis. cons. (with wife) South African schs. and univs., 1963; cons. Lilly Endowment, NEH; examiner N. Cen. Assn. Colls. and Univs., 1959-80; nat. adv. coun. Danforth Found. Assocs. Program, 1963-69, com. on lit. Nat. Coun. on Religion in Higher Edn., 1967-70; Ryerson lectr. U. of Chgo., 1987; lectr. English Coalition Conf., 1987, seminars for high sch. English tchrs., 1987-90. Author: The Rhetoric of Fiction, 1961, Now Don't Try To Reason With Me: Essays and Ironies for a Credulous Age, 1970, A Rhetoric of Irony, 1974, Modern Dogma and the Rhetoric of Assent, 1974, Critical Understanding: The Powers and Limits of Pluralism, 1979 (Laing prize 1981); Editor: The Knowledge Most Worth Having, 1967, Harper & Row Reader, 1984, (with M. Gregory) Harper & Row Rhetoric, 1987, 90, The Company We Keep: An Ethics of Fiction, 1988, The Vocation of a Teacher: Rhetorical Occasions, 1967-88, 1988, The Art of Deliberalizing: A Handbook for True Professionals, 1990; co-editor Critical Inquiry, 1974-85, Christian Gauss Seminars in Criticism, Princeton, 1974; chmn. bd. publs., U. Chgo. Press, 1974-75, 79-80; bd. publication: Philosophy and Literature, Philosophy and Rhetoric, Novel, Critical Inquiry, 1985—. Trustee Earlham Coll., 1965-75. Served with inf. AUS, 1944-46. Recipient Christian Gauss prize Phi Beta Kappa, 1962; Disting. Alumni award Brigham Young U., 1975; Quantrell prize for undergrad. teaching U. Chgo., 1971; award for contbns. to edn. Am. Assn. for Higher Edn., 1986; Ford Faculty fellow, 1952-53; Guggenheim fellow, 1956-57, 69-70; fellow Ind. U. Sch. Letters, summer 1962; NEH fellow, 1975-76; Phi Beta Kappa vis. scholar, 1977-78; Rockefeller Found. fellow, 1981-82. Fellow Am. Acad. Arts and Scis.; mem. Acad. Lit. Studies, MLA (exec. council 1973-76, pres. 1981-82), AAUP, Nat. Council Tchrs. English (David H. Russell prize 1966, commn. on lit. 1967-70), Coll. Conf. Composition and Communication. Democrat. Mem. Ch. of Jesus Christ of Latter-day Saints. Home: 5411 Greenwood Av Chicago IL 60615

BOOTHMAN, SHERRE L., minister, religion educator; b. Houston, Nov. 28, 1953; d. Herschel Lynn and Billie Beth (Rhoads) B.; life ptnr. Marianne Van Fossen, Oct. 26, 1986. BA in History, Austin Coll., 1976, MA in Edn., 1977; postgrad., Wesley Theol. Sem., Washington, 1981-83; D Ministry, Samaritan Coll., L.A., 1988. Cert. secondary edn. tchr., Tex.; lic. to ministry Universal Fellowship Met. Community Chs., 1983, ordained, 1987. Tchr. Aldine ISD, Houston, 1977-79, Bastrop (Tex.) ISD, 1979-80; dean Samaritan Coll., L.A., 1983-87, pres., 1987-90; pastor Met. Community Ch. in the Valley, North Hollywaood, Calif., 1990—. lectr., presenter. Speaker AIDS Candlelight Vigil, L.A., 1991. Recipient Bd. of Elders' award Universal Fellowship of Met. Community Chs., Sacramento, Calif., 1985. Mem. Valley Interfaith Coun. (bd. dirs. 1990—), San Fernando Valley Lesbian/Gay Community Svc. Ctr. (bd. dirs. 1991—). Democrat. Avocations: space program, travel, horseback riding, hiking. Home: PO Box 411528 Los Angeles CA 90041 Office: Met Community Ch in the Valley 5730 Cahuenga Blvd North Hollywood CA 91601

BOOTON, RAY L., pastor; b. Spirit Lake, Iowa, Aug. 1, 1937; s. Viveon Leon Booton and Faith F. (Rieter) Kelso; m. Carolyn A. Booton, July 30, 1960; children: Russell L., Tamara C. Sedmak, Ryan C., Steven R., Lisa L., Benjamin H. Diploma, Nazarene Bible Coll., 1980; AA in Psychology, Otero Jr. Coll., 1987; BTh, Inter. Sem., 1988, MTh, 1990. Ordained to ministry Ch. of the Nazarene, 1982, as chaplain, 1991. Commd. 2d lt. USAF, 1956, advanced through grades to master sgt., 1977; pastor Tuttle (N.D.) Ch. of the Nazarene, 1980-82, Valentine (Nebr.) Ch. of the Nazarene, 1982-86, First Ch. of the Nazarene, Las Animas, Colo., 1986-89, Community Ch. of the Nazarene, Council Bluffs, Iowa, 1989-91; chaplain Bryan Meml. Hosp., Lincoln, Nebr., 1991—; supr. Recreation Ctr., Colorado Springs, Colo., 1978-80; chaplain Vets. Hosp., Omaha, 1991—. Mem. Ministers Assn., Chaplains Coup., Armed Forces Sgts. Assn., Disabled Vets. Republican. Home: 823 S 32 St Council Bluffs IA 51501 Office: Community Ch of the Nazaren 3031 7th Ave Council Bluffs IA 51501

BOOTY, JOHN EVERITT, retired religion educator; b. Detroit, May 2, 1925; s. George Thomas and Alma (Gamauf) B.; m. Catherine Louise Smith, June 10, 1950; children: Carol Holland, Geoffrey Rollen, Peter Thomas, Catherine Jane. B.A., Wayne State U., 1952; B.D., Va. Theol. Sem., 1953, DD, 1991; M.A., Princeton U., 1957, Ph.D., 1960. Ordained to ministry Episcopal Ch., 1953. Curate Christ Episcopal Ch., Dearborn, Mich., 1953-55; asst. prof. ch. history Va. Theol. Sem., 1958-64, assoc. prof., 1964-67; prof. ch. history Episcopal Theol. Sch., Cambridge, Mass., 1967-82, prof. emeritus, 1991—; acting dir. Inst. Theol. Rsch., 1974-76; dean Sch. Theology U. of South, Sewanee, Tenn., 1982-85, prof. Anglican studies, 1984-90, prof. emeritus, 1990—, historiographer Episcopal Church, 1988—; vis. prof., rsch. Yale Div. Sch., 1985-86; Disting. vis. prof. Episcopal Divinity Sch., 1990-91, prof. emeritus, 1991—. Author: John Jewel as Apologist of the Church of England, 1963, Yearning to be Free, 1974, Three Anglican Divines on Prayer: Jewel, Andrewes, and Hooker, 1978, The Church in History, 1979, The Spirit of Anglicanism, 1979, The Godly Kingdom of Tudor England, 1981, The Servant Church, 1982, What Makes Us Episcopalians, 1982, Anglican Spirituality, 1982, Anglican Moral Choice, 1983, Meditations on Four Quartets, 1983, The Christ We Know, 1987; editor: The Book of Common Prayer, 1959, John Jewel: The Apology of the Church of England, 1963, 74, The Elizabethan Prayer Book, 1976, The Works of Richard Hooker, Vol. 4, 1982, The Epicopal Church in Crisis, 1988; coeditor, contbr.: The Study of Anglicanism, 1988; editor: John Donne: Divine Poems, Sermons, Meditations and Prayers, 1990; chmn. bd. St. Luke's Jour. Theology, 1987-90; contbr. articles to profl. jours. Chmn. Nat. Youth Commn., P.E. Ch., 1948-50. Recipient Am. Philos. Soc. award, 1964; Folger Shakespeare Libr. fellow, 1964, NEH fellow, 1978-79. Mem. Soc. for Promoting Christian Knowlege (vice chmn. 1984-87). Home: RR 1 Box 167 Center Sandwich NH 03227

BOPP, LYNN A., ecumenical agency director. Adminstrv. dir. Cen. Md. Ecumenical Coun., Balt. Office: Cen Md Ecumenical Coun Cathedral House 4 E University Pkwy Baltimore MD 21218*

BORCHERT, GERALD LEO, minister, educator; b. Edmonton, Alta., Can., Mar. 20, 1932; came to U.S., 1963; s. Leo Ferdinand and Lillian Violet (Bucholz) B.; m. Doris Ann Cox, May 23, 1959; children: Mark, Timothy. Student, U. Calgary, 1951-52; BA, U. Alta., 1955, LLB, 1956; MDiv summa cum laude, Eastern Bapt. Theol. Sem., 1959; ThM, Princeton Theol. Sem., 1961, PhD in New Testament cum laude, 1967; postgrad., Princeton U., 1961-63, Am. Inst. Holy Land Studies and Albright Inst. Archeol. Rsch., 1974, Duke U., S.E. Bapt. Sem., 1981, S.W. Bapt. Sem., 1985, Theol. Sem., Hamburg, Fed. Republic Germany, 1987, Andover Newton Theol. Sch., Boston Coll., 1989. Ordained to ministry Bapt. Union of West Can., 1959. Asst. min. Christ West Hope Presbyn. Ch., Phila., 1958-60; teaching fellow, lectr. in Greek Princeton Theol. Sem., 1961-63; assoc. prof. N.T. North Am. Bapt. Sem., Sioux Falls, S.D., 1963-68, prof. N.T., 1968-77, acad. v.p., dean, 1970-77; dean, prof. N.T. No. Bapt. Sem., Lombard, Ill., 1977-80; prof. N.T. So. Bapt. Sem., Louisville, 1980-90; T. Rupert Coleman prof. N.T., 1990—; sec. commn. on cooperative Christianity Bapt. World Alliance, 1968-76, mem. Commn. doctrine, 1976-80, 85-90, chmn. 1990—; rep. Bapt. Joint Com. on Pub. Affairs for U.S.A. and Can., 1971-76, sec., 1973-75, vice chmn., 1975-76; co-tchr. Hidden Treasures of the Bible, TV studies in Gospel of John, 1977-78. Author: Great Themes From John, 1966, The Dynamics of Pauline Evangelism, 1969, Today's Model Church, 1971, Dynamics of Evangelism, 1976, Paul and His Interpreters, 1985, Discovering Thessalonians, 1986, Assurance and Warning, 1987: co-author: The Crisis of Fear, 1988; co-editor: Spiritual Dimensions of Pastoral Care, 1985; columnist The Baptist Herald, 1969-76; translator: The Revision of The Living Bible, 1990—; contbr. articles to publs. and jours. Bd. dirs. Sioux Empire Drug Edn. Com., 1970-77, treas. and chmn. speaker's bur., 1970-72; trustee Tabor Coll., Hillsboro, Kans., 1972-78, North Am. Bapt. Coll., Edmonton, 1973-77, Sioux Falls Community Coll., 1975-77, Am. Inst. Holy Land Studies, Jerusalem, 1971-74, 84-87, exec. bd., 1972-74; resource scholar Christianity Today Inst., 1985—. Office: So Bapt Theol Sem 2825 Lexington Rd Louisville KY 40280

BORDEAUX, THOMAS EUGENE, minister; b. Pensacola, Fla., July 31, 1950; s. James Wilson Bordeaux and Vernie Viola Purvis Stull; m. Ruth Anne Roberts, June 4, 1976; children: Joel Eugene, Josia Anne. Student, Centenary Coll., Shreveport, La., 1976-77, Christ for the Nations, Dallas, 1977, Miss. Gulf Coast Community Col, 1981-83, Lee Coll., Cleveland, Tenn., 1987—. Lic. to ministry Ch. of God, 1986. Pastor Tipton St. Holiness Ch., Hattiesburg, Miss., 1974-75, Prospect & Hornbeck United Meth. Ch., Florien & Hornbeck, La., 1977; music minister Gulfport (Miss.) Ch. of God, 1983-84; pastor Batesville (Miss.) Ch. of God, 1984-87, Booneville (Miss.) Ch. of God, 1987-91; Petal Ch. of God, 1991—; dist. reporter Ch. of God in Miss., 1991, dist. youth and Christian edn. dir., Clarksdale dist., 1985-87, dist. evangelism dir., N.E. dist., 1988, alt. state youth bd., Jackson, 1990—. Contbr. articles to profl. jours. Chaplain Bapt. Meml. Hosp., Booneville, 1987-91, S. Panola Hosp., Batesville, 1985. Mem. Ch. of God Instl. Chaplains Assn. (chaplain 1988-90), N.E. Miss. Writers Forum (treas. 1990-91). Office: Petal Ch of God 319 Old Richton Rd Petal MS 39465 *...Earnestly contend for the faith which was once delivered unto the saints. (Jude 3b). How can I live the New Testament example put forth in scripture? This is my lifestyle and my goal, being "all things to all men that by all means I might win some," to the glory of Jesus Christ. Amen.*

BORDEN, STANLEY PERRY, minister; b. Toronto, Ontario, Canada, Dec. 28, 1917; Arrived in U.S., Feb. 14, 1927.; s. Perry Archibald and Mary Bigelow (Whidden) B.; m. Esther Viola Knock, Oct. 10, 1942; children: Esther Mary, John Stanley, James Edward. Student, U. Toronto, Can., 1938; BA, Acadia U., Wolfville, Nova Scotia, 1939; MDiv., Union Theol. Sem., 1942; postgrad., Cornell U., 1943. Pastor Federated Ch., McLean, N.Y., 1942-46; assoc. pastor Lake Ave Baptist Ch., Rochester, N.Y., 1946-52, First Bapt. Ch., Oak Park, Ill., 1952-58; pastor First Bapt. Ch., Ames, Iowa, 1958-70, Trinity Community Ch., Mpls., 1970-74; exec. minister Cleve. Baptist Assn., 1974-84; assoc. pastor First Baptist Ch., St. Paul, 1988—; mem. adj. faculty United Theol. Sem. Twin Cities; pres. dirs. Northcrest Retirement Community, Ames, 1962-70; gen. staff coun. Am. Bapt. Chs. U.S.A., Valley Forge, Pa., 1974-84; bd. dirs. Am. Bapt. Assembly, Green Lake, Wis., 1979-84; visitor Ministers & Missionaries Benefit Bd., N.Y.C., 1984-86. Mem. Roseville (Minn.) Human Rights Commn. Mem. Rotary Club. Avocations: boating, skiing, photography. Home: 500 West County Rd B #106 Roseville MN 55113 Office: First Bapt Ch 499 Wacousta St Saint Paul MN 55101

BORDEN, STEELMAN JONATHAN, religious broadcasting executive; b. Reynoldsville, Pa., Aug. 2, 1950; s. Steelman Duane and Emma Irene (Harriger) B.; m. Jeanne Melinda Stone, May 21, 1971 (div. 1979); 1 child, Steelman Jonathan III; m. Diane Susan Dickey, Dec. 12, 1980. BS in Ministry, Atlanta Christian Coll., 1978. Ordained minister, 1976. Minister Bethal Christian Ch., Franklin, Ga., 1977-80; curriculum cons. Standard Pub. Co., Cin., 1980-83; mgr. Sta. WYNX Radio, Smyrna, Calif., 1986—. V.p. Reynoldsville C. of C., 1981-82; bd. dirs. Smyrna Bus. Assn., 1989-90; mem. Picketts Mill Christian Ch. Republican. Office: Sta WYNX Radio 2460 N Atlanta St Smyrna GA 30080

BORDERS, FRANCES ROMA B., church official; b. Deer Flat, Idhao, July 1, 1933; d. Leonard Harl and Verda Marie (Beal) Fisher; m. David Borders, Aug. 19, 1955; children: David L., Dorl A., Daniel O. Student, Eugene (Oreg.) Bible Coll., 1955. Sunday sch. tchr. Assembly of God, Lewiston, Idaho, 1969-80; bookkeeper Valley Christian Cr., Lewiston, 1980-83, dir. Christian edn., 1984—; bookkeeper Happy Day Corp., Lewiston, 1983—. Prayer leader Concerned Women Am., Lewiston. Democrat. Home and Office: Valley Christian Ctr 810 Bryden Dr Lewiston ID 83501

BORDERS, MARGARET JAMES, religious organization administrator; b. Birmingham, Ala., June 25, 1939; d. Russell William and Marian (Welsh) James; m. Raymond Alexander, June 17, 1961; children: Carolyn Ann Borders Cadman, Patricia Agnes Borders Bradley, Christine Marie Borders Signoriello, Marian Evelyn. BA in Religious Studies, Sacred Heart U., 1976, M in Religious Studies, 1982. Dir. religious edn. St. Rose Parish, Newtown, Conn., 1976-82, 86—; dir. religious edn. St. Marguerite Parish, Brookfield, Conn., 1982-83, religious edn. advisor, 1985-89; dir. religious edn. St. Francis Parish, Weston, Conn., 1983-86. Mem. Inst. for Religious Edn. and Pastoral Studies (bd. dirs. 1990—), New Eng. Dirs. Religious/Christian Edn. (cochair 1991 convocation), Bridgeport Religious Edn. Dirs. (scholarship com. 1991—), Nat. Parish Coords./Dirs. Religious Edn. (pres. 1986—, New Eng. rep. 1988—). Roman Catholic. Office: St Rose Religious Edn 40 Church Hill Rd Newtown CT 06470

BORDERS, WILLIAM DONALD, bishop; b. Washington, Ind., Oct. 9, 1913. Ed., St. Meinrad Sem., Notre Dame Sem., U. Notre Dame. Ordained priest Roman Catholic Ch., 1940; rector St. Joseph Cathedral, Baton Rouge, 1964-68; consecrated bishop, 1968, bishop of Orlando Fla., 1968-74, archbishop of Balt., 1974-89. Home: 320 Cathedral St Baltimore MD 21201

BORECKY, ISIDORE, bishop; b. Ostrowec, Ukraine, Oct. 1, 1911. Ed., Theol. Acad. Lwiw, 1932-36, Maximillian U., Munich, Germany, 1936-38. Ordained priest Ukrainian Greek Cath. Ch., 1938; missionary in Sask. and Man., Can., 1938-40; parish priest Niagara Peninsula, Ont., Can., 1940-48; titular bishop of Amathas, from 1948; 1st exarch Ukrainian Cath. Exarchate of Eastern Can., 1948-56; bishop of 1st Eparchy of Toronto, 1956. Address: 61 Glen Edyth Dr, Toronto, ON Canada M4V 2V8

BOREN, EDWARD DANIEL, priest; b. Indpls., Sept. 2, 1936; s. Edward Daniel and Mary Ann (Foreman) B. BA in Philosophy and Psychology, Quincy Coll., 1960; STB in Theology, Antonianum (Rome), Teutopolis, Ill., 1964; MA in Math. Edn., U. Tex., San Antonio, 1978. Ordained priest Roman Cath. Ch., 1964. Tchr., math. dept. head, registrar Hales Franciscan High Sch., Chgo., 1965-74; tchr., dept. head St. Francis Acad., San Antonio, 1974-85; pastor Sacred Heart Ch., Von Ormy, Tex., 1976-86; tchr. Holy Cross/St. Gerard, San Antonio, 1986-88; asst. pastor, tchr. St. Joseph's, San Antonio, 1988-89; pastor Sacred Heart Ch., Falfurrias, Tex., 1989—; advisor St. Joseph's Sch., 1988-89. Moderator Medina River Watershed Coalition, Von Ormy, 1982-85. Mem. Nat. Coun. Tchrs. of Math, Assn. for Supervision and Curriculum Devel., Math. Assn. Am. Roman Catholic. Avocation: tennis coach. Home: 1412 Twelfth St Bay City TX 77414 Office: Our Lady of Guadalupe 1412 Twelfth St Bay City TX 77414 *Life is a gift from God, meant to be shared. Its beauty is Wisdom, meant to be unveiled. Religion is the school of life. God's Word has its fulfillment when it is made flesh in this world. Our purpose here is to convey that message.*

BORER, ANTON JOSEPH, priest; b. Buesserach, Switzerland, Aug. 16, 1916; s. Arnold and Mathilda (Jeker) B. BA, Bruder Klausen Sem., 1939, BA in Theology, 1943. Ordained priest Roman Cath. Ch., 1943. Missionary China, 1946-48; asst. pastor local ch. Denver, 1949-66; founder Bethlehem Ctr., Broomfield, Colo., 1966, dir., 1966-78, spiritual dir., 1978-90; cofounder Shepherds of Bethlehem, Denver, 1991—; dist. superior Bethlehem Fathers USA, 1959-80; dir. Paepl Vols. in Denver, 1968-74; Newman chaplain Dever colls., 1969-90; personal rep. of archbishop to charismatic community in Archdiocese of Denver, 1974-81; bd. dirs. Spirit's Runway, Denver, 1970-76. Co-author: New Life: Preperation of Religious for Retirement, 1973; editor Bethlehem Call, 1974—; contbr. articles to religious jours. Office: 12550 Zuni St Broomfield CO 80020

BORG, MARCUS JOEL, theologian, educator; b. Fergus Falls, Minn., Mar. 11, 1942; s. Glenn F. and Esther (Stortroen) B.; m. Marianne Wells, Aug. 24, 1985; children: Dane, Julie. BA, Concordia Coll., Moorhead, Minn., 1964; diploma in Theology, U. Oxford, Eng., 1966; D.Phil., U. Oxford, 1972; postgrad., Union Theol. Sem., U. Tübingen, Fed. Republic Germany. Prof. religion Carleton Coll., Northfield, Minn., 1976-79; prof. religious studies Oreg. State U., Corvallis, 1979—; Disting. vis. prof. U. Puget Sound, Tacoma, Wash., 1986-87; vis. prof. N.T. Pacific Sch. Religion, Berkeley, Calif., 1989-91. Author: Year of Luke, 1976, Conflict and Social Change, 1971, Conflict, Holiness and Politics in the Teaching of Jesus, 1984, Jesus: A New Vision, 1987; contbr. articles to religious jours. Recipient Burlington-No. Teaching award Oreg. State U., 1986, Faculty Excellence award Oreg. State Legislature, 1987. Fellow The Jesus Sem.; mem. Soc. Bibl. Lit., Cath. Bibl. Assn., Am. Acad. Religion. Office: Oreg State U Dept Religious Studies Corvallis OR 97331

BORGEN, OLE EDVARD, bishop, educator; b. Lilleström, Norway, Nov. 8, 1925; s. Omar Emil and Harda (Pytte) B.; m. Martha Olava, June 4, 1949; children: May-Britt, Odd-Erik. Diploma, Tomb Agrl. Coll., Rade, Norway, 1946; AA, Brevard Coll., 1958; AB, Greensboro Coll., 1959; MDiv, Duke U., 1962; PhD, Drew U., 1968, LHD (hon.), 1986; DD (hon.), Asbury Theol. Sem., 1988. Ordained elder Meth. Ch., 1963; consecrated bishop, 1970. Jr. bus. exec. Omar E. Borgen, Lilleström, 1947-56; exec. sec. to bishop United Meth. Ch., Stockholm, 1966-69; exec. sec., leader World Meth. Coun. Office, Geneva, 1970; resident bishop No. Europe United Meth. Ch., Stockholm, 1970-89; scholar-in-residence, prof. Asbury Theol. Sem., Wilmore, Ky., 1989—; pres. Coun. of Bishops United Meth. Ch., 1985-86, European Meth. Coun. Author: John Wesley on the Sacraments, 1972, 73, 86, Taufe, Konfirmation und Mitgliedschaft im methodischen Verständnis, 1970; editor: John Wesley...The Man and His Thought, 1966. Mem. City Coun. for Christian People's Party, Lilleström, 1950-56; mem. Norwegian Underground, 1944-45. With Norwegian Army, 1946-47. Mem. World Meth. Hist. Soc. (pres. 1975-81), Wesley Hist. Soc. Eng., United Meth. Hist. Soc., Am. Soc. Ch. History, Wesleyan Theol. Soc., The Charles Wesley Soc., Rotary (sec. Sollentuna, Sweden 1984-85). Home and Office: Asbury Theol Sem Wilmore KY 40390-1199

BORGER, DAVID PAUL, minister; b. Milw., Jan. 30, 1950; s. Henry Bernard and Barbara Jean (Matz) B.; m. Roberta Nye, June 26, 1976; children: Nicole, Kimberly, Jennifer, John Michael, Shannaray, David, Shivon, Tyrone, Shawn. BA in History and Econs., U. Wis., 1972; MDiv, No. Bapt. Theol. Seminary, Lombard, Ill., 1976. Ordained to ministry Am. Bapt. Chs. in U.S.A., 1976. Pastor youth 1st Bapt. Ch., Berwyn, Ill., 1975-76; pastor 1st Bapt. Ch., Reedsburg, Wis., 1976-78, Main St. Bapt. Ch., Alton, Ill., 1978-82, 1st Bapt. Ch., El Paso, Ill., 1982-90, 1st Bapt. Richland Center and Ash Ridge (Wis.) Bapt. Ch., 1990—; mem. Am. Bapt. Ch./GRR Task Force on Criminal Justice, Springfield, Ill., 1980-82; del. Am. Bapt. Ch. USA Biennial Convs., Carbondale, Ill., 1979, Cleve., 1983, Milw., 1989. Rep. Woodford County (Ill.) Citizens Adv. Bd., Eureka, 1990, Sauk County (Wis.) Libr. Bd., Reedsburg, 1977-78. Mem. Roger Williams Fellowship, Richland County Ministerial Assn., El Paso Ministerial Assn. (pres. 1983-90), Kiwanis, Jaycees, Mason, Optimist, Rotary. Home: 392 N Church St Richland Center WI 53581 *Our conquest of earth and space, our development of new technologies and conveniences, our manipulations of the atomic and genetic structures of our world must issue forth in a new, caring policy between governments, businesses and organizations. In order for all our succeeding generations to enjoy the beauty of the earth we must heed God's call to care for one another and to replenish the earth.*

BORGFORD, NORMA JEANNE, minister; b. Seattle, July 16, 1933; d. Ulvar George and Olga Helene (Olsen) B. BSN, Pacific Luth. Coll., Tacoma, Wash., 1956; MDiv, Luther N.W. Sem., St. Paul, 1986. Ordained to ministry Luth. Ch., 1986. Commd. 2d lt. USAF, 1957, advanced through grades to maj., 1972, ret., 1979; pastor Trinity Luth. Ch., Wibaux, Mont., 1986-90; interim pastor Valier (Mont.) Luth. Ch., 1990—; bd. regents, nominating com. Pacific Luth. U., 1989-91. With. Home: care D T Oswalt 107 Yaden Ln Castle Rock WA 98611

BORGIE, JERALD RICHARD, minister; b. Thief River Falls, Minn., July 16, 1936; s. Perry Anson and Alpha (Larson) B.; m. Marcia Wilson, Aug. 17, 1968; children: Roderick, Benjamin. BA, Tex. Luth. Coll., 1960; BD, Luth. Theol. Sem., 1964; Rel.D., Calif. Grad. Sch. Theology, 1972; DD (hon.), Intrabibleskolen, Oslo, 1986. Ordained to ministry Luth. Ch. Pastor Peace Luth. Ch., Cleve., 1964-70, 1st Luth. Ch., Compton, Calif., 1970-77; sr. pastor Peñasquitos Luth. Ch., San Diego, 1977—; chmn. bd. trustees Luth. Bible Inst., Anaheim, Calif., 1990—; mem. transition team Am. Luth. Ch., L.A., 1986-88, conf. dean, San Diego, 1980-86. Author: Key to the City, 1973. Trustee Cleve. Children's Aid Soc., 1966-70; mem. Peñasquitos Town Coun., San Diego, 1978-80; mem. Poway (Calif.) Unified Sch. Dist., 1989—; mem. planning com. Cleve. Dem. Party, 1966-70. Recipient Outstanding Leadership award Luth. Bible Inst., 1986. Mem. Internat. Luth. Bible Inst. Assn. (sec. 1986-88), Kiwanis (sec. Compton club. 1974-76). Home: 11143 Socorro Ct San Diego CA 92129 Office: 14484 Peñasquitos Dr San Diego CA 92129

BORGKVIST, JOSEPH, JR., minister; b. Portsmouth, N.H., Jan. 13, 1944; s. Joseph Sr. Borgkvist and Virginia Mae (Moulton) Roy; m. Jo-Ann Marie Fenn, Aug. 19, 1967; children: Joseph Christian, Rebecca Ann. A of Div. Pastoral Ministry, New Orleans Bapt. Theol. Sem., 1978. Ordained to ministry So. Bapt. Conv., 1971. Min. of youth and edn. Northside Bapt. Ch., Valdosta, Ga., 1978-80; assoc. pastor, min. edn. White Oak Bapt. Ch., Greenville, S.C., 1980-83; pastor Hillside Bapt. Ch., Fountain Inn, S.C., 1983-85; min. edn. First Bapt. Ch., West Columbia, S.C., 1985-87; assoc. pastor, min. edn. West Side Bapt. Ch., West Columbia, 1987—; conf. leader S.C. Bapt. Conv., Columbia, 1983—, Sun. Sch. growth specialist, 1983—, youth retreat speaker, 1977—, ASSISTeam dir. Lexington (S.C.) Bapt. Assn., 1988—. Contbr. (book) 100 Great Growth Ideas, 1990; contbr. articles to profl. jours. Com. mem. Adv. com. to S.C. Dept. of Youth Svcs. Trustees, Columbia, 1987—; founder, chmn. bd. dirs. REACH Inc., West Columbia, S.C. With U.S. Army, 1964-67, Vietnam. Named Outstanding Direct Svc. Vol. of Yr. S.C. Dept. Youth Svcs., 1987. Mem. Religious Edn. & Music Assn. (pres. 1989-90), S.C. Bapt. Religious Edn. Assn. (v.p. 1987-88, pres. 1988-89), Am. Legion Post 174. Home: 1715 B Ave West Columbia SC 29169 Office: West Side Bapt Ch 2100 Platt Springs Rd West Columbia SC 29169 *The opportunity and challenge to be a servant of God and use our God-given abilities for the benefit of those whom God created and loves, is the greatest calling one can have in this life.*

BORGWARDT, ROBERT G., minister, television evangelist; b. Milw., Aug. 7, 1922; s. Erwin R. and Hilda M. (Meier) B.; m. Ruth Fossum, June 14, 1947 (dec. 1963); children: Kathryn, John, Stephen; m. Joan Renee Gullickson, Sept. 25, 1964; children: Anne, Eric. BA, St. Olaf Coll., Minn., 1944; MT, Luther Sem., St. Paul, 1947; DD (hon.), Carthage Coll., Wis., 1975. Ordained: Minister, Am. Luth. Ch. Sr. pastor Trinity Lutheran Ch., Madison, Wis., 1947-53; assoc. pastor Cen. Luth., Mpls., 1953-55; sr. pastor First Luth. Ch., Sioux Falls, S.D., 1955-63, Bethel Luth. Ch., Madison, 1963-91, cons., 1991—; pub. rels. com. Luth. Coun., U.S.A., 1964-67; pres. Madison Area Coun. Chs., 1969-70; active div. coll. and univ. services Am. Luth Ch., 1974-87; bd. regents Wartburg Coll., Waverly, Iowa, 1972-77; cscert. visit Bethel Bible Series, Japan, Korea, 1975. Author: Men Who Knew Jesus, 1958; Kind and Heavenly Father, 1967; Don't Blow Out The Candle, 1969; I am Hurting...Please Help Me. Mem. Wis. State Bd. Ethics, 1980-85, 91—. Recipient Young Man of Yr. award C. of C., Sioux Falls, 1958; Disting. Alumni award St. Olaf Coll., Minn., 1985; British Fgn. Office Conf. Participant, Wilton Park, Sussex, Eng., 1974, 84. Club: Rotary (bd. dirs. Madison 1964-66, Sr. Svc. award 1991). Avocations: cycling; golf; tennis; travel. Office: Bethel Lutheran Ch 312 Wisconsin Ave Madison WI 53703

BORNEMAN, GEORGE HOWARD, minister, social worker; b. Elkhart, Ind., Feb. 17, 1915; s. George Otto and Zella Corine (Howard) B.; m. Jean Mertens, June 25, 1957; children: Janet, Nancy, Mary, Tom, Anne McKenney. AB, BA, U. Mich., 1937; MDiv, Garrett Evang. Sem., 1961. Lic. social worker, Ill. Exec. dir. Chgo. Christian Indls. League, 1963-85; cons. The McDermott Found., Chgo., 1985-87. Interim exec. bd. dirs. Haymarket House, Chgo., 1989. With USN, 1944-46. Mem. Interfaith Coun. for Homeless (sec. 1990—), Chgo. Clergy Assn. for the Homeless (sec. 1990—), Chgo. Rotary. Presbyterian. Home: 100 W Butterfield Elmhurst IL 60126 Office: Interfaith Coun 100 S Morgan Chicago IL 60607

BOROUGHS, THADDEUS CALHOUN, III, minister; b. Greenville, S.C., Aug. 6, 1950; s. Thaddeus Calhoun Jr. and Eleanor (Armstrong) B.; m. Susan Jeanne Manning, July 14, 1975; children: Abigail, Megan. BA, Covenant Coll., 1972; MDiv, Covenant Theol. Sem., 1978. Ordained to ministry Presbyn. Ch. in Am., 1978. Co-pastor Murphy-Blair Community Ch., St. Louis, 1978-84; asst. pastor Mitchell Rd. Presbyn. Ch., Greenville, 1988-90; pastor St. Elmo Presbyn. Ch., Chattanooga, 1990—. Contbr. articles to religious publs. Bd. dirs. Human Devel. Corp., St. Louis, 1981-82, Murphy-Blair Resident Housing Bd., St. Louis, 1982-85, Confluence St. Louis, 1983-84; mem. Citizen's Adv. Com., St. Louis, 1980-84. Home: 4411 Tennessee Ave Chattanooga TN 37409 Office: St Elmo Presbyn Ch 4400 St Elmo Ave Chattanooga TN 37409

BOROW, AARON, congregational rabbi; b. Phila., Nov. 6, 1933; s. Abraham and Minnie (Janin) B.; m. Pearl Karalitzky, Dec. 12, 1955; children: Becky Borow Zimmerman, Ephraim, Yaakov, Eli, Avi. BA, Yeshiva Coll., 1955; BRE, Yeshiva U., 1955. Ordained rabbi, 1959. Rabbi Agudath Israel Congregation, Montgomery, Ala., 1959-64, Nusach Hari-B'Nai Zion Congregation, St. Louis, 1965—. Author sermons in Rabbinical Coun. Books of Sermons, 1970, 72-75, 77-79, 81, 82, 87. Active Jewish Fedn., St. Louis, 1985-90; bd. dirs. St. Louis Jewish Light, 1980-90, Cen. Agy. for Jewish Edn., St. Louis, 1980-90. Recipient life tenure Nusach Hari-B'Nai Zion Congregation, 1978. Mem. Rabbinical Coun. St. Louis (chmn. 1984-86, treas. 1991—). Office: Nusach Hari-B'Nai Zion Congregation 863 Olive Blvd Saint Louis MO 63132

BORRESON, GLENN LELAND, minister; b. LaCrosse, Wis., Apr. 29, 1944; s. Garven Lester and Cora Berdell (Sexe) B.; m. Mary Esther Jorgenson, June 17, 1967; children: Mark, Erik, Michael. BA, Luth. Coll., 1966; MDiv, Luth. Theol. Sem., 1970, ThM, 1978. Ordained to ministry Evang. Luth. Ch. Am. Pastor Jordan Luth Ch. and Our Savior's Luth. Ch., South Wayne, Wis., 1971-74, Grace Luth. Ch., Elroy, Wis., 1974-77; assoc. pastor 1st Luth. Ch., Decorah, Iowa, 1978-87; sr. pastor Bethany Luth. Ch., Mauston, Wis., 1988—; dean Decorah conf. of Iowa dist. Am. Luth. Ch., 1980-82; chair profl. candidacy com. LaCrosse Area Synod, 1988—. Author: A Taste of God's Tomorrow, 1989; contbr. articles to profl. religious publs. Bd. dirs. Winneshiek County United Way, Decorah, 1986-87, Hospice of Winneshiek County, Decorah, 1986-87, Hess Meml. Hosp., Mauston, 1989—; chmn. N.E. Iowa Refugee Agy., Decorah, 1985. Fellow Acad. Parish Clergy (bd. dirs. 1982-85, pres.-elect 1991—); mem. Internat. Bonhoeffer Soc. Home: 628 Tremont St Mauston WI 53948 Office: Bethany Luth Ch 701 Grove St Mauston WI 53948

BORSCH, FREDERICK HOUK, bishop; b. Chgo., Sept. 13, 1935; s. Reuben A. and Pearl Irene (Houk) B.; m. Barbara Edgeley Sampson, June 25, 1960; children: Benjamin, Matthew, Stuart. AB, Princeton U., 1957; MA, Oxford U., 1959; STB, Gen. Theol. Sem., 1960; PhD, U. Birmingham, 1966; DD (hon.), Seabury Western Theol. Sem., 1978, Gen. Theol. Sem., 1988; STD (hon.), Ch. Div. Sch. of Pacific, 1981, Berk Div. Sch. Yale U., 1983. Ordained priest Episcopal Ch., 1960; curate Grace Episcopal Ch., Oak Park, Ill., 1960-63; tutor Queen's Coll., Birmingham, Eng., 1963-66; asst. prof. N.T. Seabury Western Theol. Sem., Evanston, Ill., 1966-69, assoc. prof. N.T., 1969-71; prof. N.T. Gen. Theol. Sem., N.Y.C., 1971-72; pres., dean Berk Div. Sch. Yale U., Berkeley, Calif., 1972-81; dean of chapel, prof. religion Princeton U., 1981-88; bishop Episc. Diocese, L.A., 1988—; rep. Faith and Order Commn., Nat. Coun. Chs., 1975-81; mem. exec. coun. Episc. Ch., 1981-88, Anglican Cons. Coun., 1984-88; chair bd. of govs. Trinity Press Internat., 1989—. Author: The Son of May in Myth and History, 1967, The Christian and Gnostic Son of Man, 1970, God's Parable, 1976, Introducing the Lessons of the Church Year, 1978, Coming Together in the Spirit, 1980, Power in Weakness, 1983, Anglicanism and the Bible, 1984, Jesus: The Human Life of God, 1987, Many Things in Parables, 1988. Keasbey scholar, 1957-59. Fellow Soc. Arts, Religion and Contemporary Culture; mem. Am. Acad. Religion, Soc. Bibl. Lit., Studiorum Novi Testamenti Societas, Phi Beta Kappa. Home: 2930 Corda Ln Los Angeles CA 90049 Office: Episcopal Diocese of LA PO Box 2164 Los Angeles CA 90051-2145

BORSKI, CHESTER L., academic administrator. Head St. Mary's Sem., Houston. Office: St Mary's Sem 9845 Memorial Dr Houston TX 77024*

BORTHWICK, PAUL MONROE, minister; b. Arlington, Mass., Feb. 20, 1954; s. Harry M. and B. Jean (Wyse) B.; m. Christine Collazzo, May 19, 1979. BBA in Mgmt., U. Mass., 1976; MDiv, Gordon-Conwell Sem., 1980. Ordained to ministry, 1980. Youth min. Grace Chapel, Lexington, Mass., 1977-86; youth and missions min. Grace Chapel, Lexington, 1983-86, missions min., 1986—; freelance writer Lexington, 1986—; lectr. in missions Gordon-Conwell Sem., South Hamilton, Mass., 1986—, Gordon Coll., Wenham, Mass., 1986—. Author: A Mind For Missions, 1987, Youth & Missions, 1988, Feeding Forgotten Soul, 1990, But You Don't Understand, 1991, World-Class Christian, 1991. Del. Lausanne II Congress, Manila, 1989. Mem. Nat. Network Youth Ministries, Latin Am. Mission, Assn. Church Missions (coms.), Evangelistic Assn. of New Eng. (regional advisor 1990—). Home: 1 Minute Man Ln Lexington MA 02173-6726 Office: Grace Chapel 3 Militia Dr Lexington MA 02173 *We are brainwashed into thinking that life ought to be exciting. In reality, 90-95 per cent of life is average and the meaning of our character is what we do with the average times.*

BORTNER, ERNEST EDWARD, minister; b. Balt., July 3, 1930; s. Ernest Edward Sr. and Grace Lorraine (Garrett) B.; m. Martha Nicholson, June 1, 1955; children: Lorraine, E. Edward III. B.E., Johns Hopkins U., 1951; MDiv, Duke U., 1954; Th.M., Princeton Theol. Sem., 1956; DMin, Lancaster Theol. Sem., 1978. Ordained to ministry United Meth. Ch., 1952. Minister Epworth United Meth. Ch., Cockeysville, Md., 1955-61; sr. minister Corkran Meml. United Meth. Ch., Temple Hills, Md., 1961-69, Centre St. United Meth. Ch., Cumberland, Md., 1969-73, Bel Air (Md.) United Meth. Ch., 1973-79, Colesville United Meth. Ch., Silver Spring, Md., 1979-83; minister Ferndale United Meth. Ch., Glen Burnie, Md., 1983-85; assoc. dir. devel. Asbury Meth. Village, Gaithersburg, Md., 1986—. Mem. Rotary Club, Cumberland, Bel Air, Silver Spring, 1969-83. Mem. Nat. Planned Giving Assn., Nat. Soc. Fund Raising Execs., Lions (bd. dirs. Sandy Spring club 1990—). Home: 2216 Countryside Dr Silver Spring MD 20905 Office: Asbury Meth Village 201 Russell Ave Gaithersburg MD 20877

BORTZ, GARRY LYNDEN, Christian education director; b. Twin Falls, Idaho, July 25, 1953; s. Edward H. and Violet (Cox) B.; m. Virginia Verdery, Oct. 23, 1976; children: Brennon, Ryan. BS in Bibl. Lang., Lubbock Christian U., 1986. Youth minister Greenlawn Ch. of Christ, Lubbock, Tex., 1975-78; edn. minister Johnson Park Ch. of Christ, Borger, Tex., 1978-84; dir. edn. Monterey Ch. of Christ, Lubbock, 1984-91, San Jose, Calif., 1991; min. for children Campbell (Calif.) Ch. of Christ, 1991—. Co-author: A Present From Heaven, 1976,. A Present - Visual Aids, 1976. Program chmn. Am. Cancer Soc., Borger, 1982-84, bd. dirs., 1984-85; active fund raising Cystic Fibrosis Found., Borger, 1983-84. Mem. Christian Edn. Assn. (bd. dirs. 1991—, program chmn. elect 1991), Profl. Assn. Christian Educators, Kiwanis. Republican. Home: 2240 Montezuma Dr Campbell CA 95008 Office: Campbell Ch of Christ 1075 Campbell Ave Campbell CA 95008

BOS, A. DAVID, ecumenical agency administrator. Exec. dir. St. Matthews Area Ministries, Louisville. Office: St Matthews Area Ministries 4006 Shelbyville Rd Louisville KY 40207*

BOSAKOV, JOSEPH BLAGOEV (METROPOLITAN BISHOP JOSEPH), bishop; b. Slavovitza, Bulgaria, Dec. 6, 1942; came to U.S., 1983; s. Blagoy Lazarov Bosakov and Milena Ivanova Bosakova. Student, Spiritual Sem., Tcherepish, Bulgaria, 1956-61, Theol. Acad., Sofia, Bulgaria, 1966-70; Baccalaureate, Theol. Sem., Zagorsk, USSR, 1973. Joined Troiansky Monastir, Bulgarian Ea. Orthodox Ch., 1970; ordained bishop, 1980. Hierodeacon, hieromonk Lovchanska Metropolia, Lovech, Bulgaria, 1971; archimandrite Sofiiska Metropolia, 1973-80, bishop-vicar, 1980; bishop, adminstr. Am. Bulgarian Orthodox Diocese, Akron, Ohio, 1983; met. Bulgarian Ea. Orthodox Diocese of U.S., Can. and Australia, Akron, 1986, N.Y.C., 1991—; asst. met. Bulgarian Orthodox Ch. in N.Y., 1986-87. Contbr. articles to Tsarcoven Vestnik. Avocation: music.

BOSCO, ANTHONY GERARD, bishop; b. New Castle, Pa., Aug. 1, 1927; s. Joseph M. and Theresa (Pezone) B. BA, St. Vincent Sem., Latrobe, Pa.; juris canonici licentiatus, Lateran U., Rome; LLD (hon.), Duquesne U., 1971; LHD (hon.), St.Vincent Coll., 1988. Ordained priest Roman Cath. Ch., 1952. Asst. chancellor Diocese of Pitts., 1955-65, vice chancellor, 1965-67, chancellor, 1967-85, aux. bishop, 1970-87; bishop Diocese of Greensburg, Pa., 1987—; chmn. Cath. Communications Found., 1984—, U.S. Cath. Conf. Communications Com., 1990—; hon. chmn., bd. trustees Seton Hill Coll., Greensburg, 1987—; ex officio mem., bd. regents St. Vincent Sem., Latrobe, Pa., 1987—. Recipient Leonardo Da Vinci award for Religion Order of Italian Sons and Daughter, 1970; named Pitts.'s Man of Yr. in Religion Pitts. Jaycees, 1975. Mem. Nat. Conf. of Catholic Bishops (communications com. 1985-88, 90), Christian Assocs. of Southwest Pa., Christian Housing Inc. (sec.-treas.).

BOSSENBROEK, ALBERTUS GEORGE, minister; b. Brandon, Wis., Oct. 16, 1910; s. Henry and Matilda (Gysbers) B.; m. Hilda Lanting, June 10, 1936; children: Nina Kay, Margaret, Donna Louise. BA, Hope Coll., 1932; MDiv, Western Theol. Sem., Holland, Mich., 1936; DD (hon.), Hope Coll., 1977. Ordained to ministry Reformed Ch., 1936. Pastor Helderberg Reformed Ch., Guilderland Center, N.Y., 1936-41; pastor First Reformed Ch., Chatham, N.Y., 1941-47, Hastings-on-Hudson, N.Y., 1947-64; exec. sec. Synod of N.Y. Reformed Ch. Am., 1964-79; acting prof. practical theology Theol. Sem., New Brunswick, N.J., 1979-81; pres. Synod of Albany, Reformed Ch. Am., N.Y., 1946-47, N.Am. missions, 1961-63, Reformed Ch. in Am., N.Y.C., 1977-88, Warwick Conf. Ctr., N.Y., 1983-87; trustee Hope Coll., Holland, Mich., 1964-78; chaplain Fire Dept., Hastings-on-Hudson, 1947; welfare chmn. CD, Hastings-on-Hudson, 1947. Mem. Exchange Club, Chatham, N.Y. (pres. 1943-44). Home: 18 Olinda Ave Hastings-on-Hudson NY 10706

BOSSMAN, DAVID MANUEL, religious studies educator, editor; b. Buffalo, May 23, 1938; s. George L. and Margaret Rose (Owens) B. BA, St. Bonaventure U., 1961; PhD, St. Louis U., 1973; STB, Cath. U. Am., 1965; MS, SUNY, Albany, 1979. Joined Order of Friars Minor, ordained priest, Roman Cath. Ch., 1965. Assoc. prof. Siena Coll., Loudonville, 1966-82; prof., dean St. Bonaventure U., Olean, N.Y., 1982-85; provost Seton Hall U., South Orange, N.J., 1985-86, prof. Jewish-Christian studies, 1985—. Contbr. author: Authority in Judaism, 1986, Kinship in Malachi, 1989; editor: Biblical Theology Bull., 1981—; contbr. articles various publs. Trustee St. Bonaventure U., 1990—. Mem. Nat. Christian Leadership Conf. on Israel (exec. bd. 1988—), Am. Acad. Religion (regional officer 1988—), Soc. Biblical Lit., Cath. Biblical Assn. Office: Seton Hall U 400 S Orange Ave South Orange NJ 07079

BOSTON, BRUCE ORMAND, writer, editor, publications consultant; b. New Castle, Pa., Aug. 11, 1940; s. John Ormand and Williamina (Loudon) B.; m. Sandra Waymer, June 8, 1963 (div. 1973); children: Aaron Clark, Nathan Waymer, Kyle Richard; m. Jean Nelson, Dec. 23, 1989. BA, Muskingum Coll., 1962; BDiv, Princeton Theol. Sem., 1968, PhD, 1973. Instr. theology St. Joseph's Coll., Phila., 1972-73; assoc. Colloquy of Reston, Va., 1973-78; pres. Wordsmith, Inc., Reston, 1976—; publs. developer Coun. for Exceptional Children, Reston, 1973-75; asst. chief clk. com. on vets. affairs U.S. Senate, Washington, 1976; communications coun. Reston Assn., 1986-89. Author: The Sorcerer's Apprentice, 1976, (with Fortna) Testing the Gifted Child, 1976, (with Orloff) Preparing To Teach the Gifted and Talented, 2 vols., 1980, (with Cox and Daniel) Educating Able Learners, 1985, Language on a Leash, 1988, also others; editor: A Resource Manual on Educating the Gifted and Talented, 1975, Gifted and Talented: Developing Elementary and Secondary School Programs, 1975, STET! Tricks of the Trade for Writers and Editors, 1986, also numerous articles and scripts. Pres. Fairfax Farms Community Assn., 1980-81; mem. Reston Task Force on Town Governance, 1988—; lay preacher Episcopal Diocese Va., 1984—; sr. warden St. Anne's Episcopal Ch., Reston, 1990—; bd. dirs. Episcopal Awareness Ctr. on Handicaps, Washington, 1986-89. Recipient Disting. Achievement award, Edn. Press Assn., 1986, 1st place award Editor's Forum, 1986, Danforth Found. fellow, 1962-64, United Presbyn. Grad. fellow, 1968, Kent fellow in religion, 1969-73, Golden Eagle awards, Coun. for Internat. Non-Theatrical Events, 1977, 84. Mem. Assn. Editorial Bus., Washington Ind. Writers (bd. dirs. 1982-84), Rotary (bd. dirs. Reston 1988—). Democrat. Avocation: collecting books of quotations.

BOSTON, JAMES TERRELL, rector; b. Patuxent River, Md., Aug. 29, 1947; s. Leadore Glenn and Mary Jane (McCamant) B. BA, Am. U., 1968; MDiv, Ch. Div. Sch. of Pacific, 1976; cert. in theology, Ripon Coll., Oxford U., 1977. Ordained to ministry Episcopal Ch. as priest, 1978. Chaplain Good Samaritan Hosp., Portland, Oreg., 1977-78; vicar Christ the King, Stayton, Oreg., 1978-80; assoc. St. Paul's, Salem, Oreg., 1978-80; vicar St. James, Lincoln City, Oreg., 1980-86; rector St. Luke's, Grants Pass, Oreg., 1987—; pres. standing com. Diocese of Oreg., 1988-91, mem. diocesan coun., 1984-86; dep. Gen. Conv. Episcopal Ch., 1991. Pres. Lincoln County (Oreg.) Food Share, 1982-86, Lincoln Shelter and Svcs., Lincoln County, 1983-87, Symphony League, Grants Pass, 1987-89, Christian Svc. Network, Grants Pass, 1988—. Lt. comdr. USN, 1968-72, Vietnam; with USNR, 1972—. Mem. Rotary. Office: St Lukes Ch 224 NW D Grants Pass OR 97526

BOSTON, LEONA, organization executive; b. Joliet, Ill., Aug. 4, 1914; d. Dorie Philip and Margaret (Mitchell) B. Student LaSalle Extension U., 1936-37, 1946, U. Chgo., 1944-45. Tchr., Nat. Stenotype Sch., Chgo., 1937; stenotypist Rotary Internat., Evanston, Ill., 1937-44, sec. to comptroller, 1944-50, head personnel dept., 1950-65, exec. asst. to gen. sec., 1965-77; mem. exec. com. North Shore Festival of Faith, Northfield, Ill., 1978. Bd. dirs. YWCA, Evanston, 1961-63. Mem. Bus. Profl. Women's Club Evanston (chmn. fin. com. 1977-78). Evangelical (fin. sec. Bible Ch., Winnetka 1965-68, treas. 1979-80). Club: Zonta (Evanston)(v.p., chmn. program com. 1969-70, pres. 1970-71, chmn. membership com. 1976-78, historian 1979-84, mem. past pres.' com. 1972—, mem. fin. com. 1985-89, chmn. fin. com. 1987-89, chmn. club history and archives com. 1989-91, parliamentarian 1991—). Home and Office: 350 W Schaumburg Rd Schaumburg IL 60194 also: 2025 San Marcos Dr SE #34 Winter Haven FL 33880

BOSWELL, HAMILTON THEODORE, minister; b. Dallas, Aug. 11, 1914; s. Grace-Louise Majors; m. Eleanor Bernice Gragg, Dec. 10, 1939; children: Jeri Lynn, Eleanor Louise. BA, Wiley Coll., 1938, DD (hon.), 1943; MTh, U. So. Calif., L.A., 1943. Ordained to ministry United Meth. Ch. as elder, 1945. Min. Shaw Chapel, United Meth. Ch., L.A., 1939-43, Bowen United Meth. Ch., L.A., 1943-47, Jones Meml. Meth. Ch., San Francisco, 1947-76; dist. supt. Bayview Dist.-Calif., Nev. Ann. Conf., 1976-82; chaplain Calif. State Assembly, Sacramento, 1984—; bd. dirs. Jones Meth. Credit Union, San Franciso, 1954-74, Jones Meth. Homes, 1960-74; chmn. Conf. on Religion and Race, San Francisco, 1963-69; chaplain San Francisco Police Force, 1969-76. Commr. Pub. Housing, San Francisco, 1964-76; chmn. Ch. Labor Conf., San Francisco, 1962-70. Recipient Spur award San Francisco Urban Planning, 1968, Freedom award NAACP, 1973. Mem. Calif.-Nev. Ministerial Alliance, Wiley Coll. Alumni Assn., So. Calif. U. Alumni Assn., Alpha Phi Alpha. Democrat. Home: 225 Water St Point Richmond CA 94801

BOTERO, BERNARDO MERINO, bishop. Bishop of Colombia Episcopal Ch., Bogotá. Office: Bishop's Office, Carrera 6, #49-85, Apdo Aereo 52964, Bogota Colombia*

BOTHWELL, JOHN CHARLES, archbishop; b. Toronto, Ont., Can., June 29, 1926; s. William Alexander and Anne (Campbell) B.; m. Joan Cowan, Dec. 29, 1951; children—Michael, Timothy, Nancy, Douglas, Ann. BA with honors in Modern History, U. Toronto, 1948; BD, Trinity Coll., Toronto, 1950, DD (hon.), 1972; DD (hon.), Huron Coll., U. Western Ont., Wycliffe Coll. U Toronto, 1989; hon. sr. fellow, Renison Coll., U. Waterloo, 1988. Ordained priest Anglican Ch., 1952; curate St. James Cathedral, Toronto, 1951-53, Christ Ch. Cathedral, Vancouver, B.C., 1953-56; rector St. Aidan's Ch., Oakville, Ont., 1956-60, St. James' Ch., Dundas, Ont., 1960-65; canon missioner Niagara Diocese, 1965-69; nat. exec. dir. Anglican Ch. Can., 1969-71; co-adjutor bishop Niagara, 1971-73; bishop Diocese of Niagara, 1973-91, archbishop, 1985-91; met. of Ont., 1985-91, ret., 1991; chancellor Trinity Coll., U. Toronto, 1991—; mem. nat. exec. com. Anglican Ch.; hon. sr. fellow Renison Coll., U. Waterloo, 1988. Co-author: Theological Education for the 70's, 1969; author: Taking Risks and Keeping Faith, 1985, Living Faith Day By Day, 1990; contbr. articles in field to various newspapers. Active numerous nat. and ecumenical coms.; Dir., com. chmn. Hamilton (Ont.) Social Planning Council, 1965-69, 71-75, v.p., 1975-77, pres., 1977-79; v.p. United Way, 1982, 83, pres., 1984-86; bd. dirs. Hamilton Found., 1982, v.p., 1983, pres., 1985. Mem. Hamilton C. of C. Club: Dundas Golf and Country. Home: 838 Glenwood Ave, Burlington, ON Canada L7T 2J9

BOTIC, DONALD A., minister; b. Pitts., Apr. 16, 1943; s. Alexander and May Carolyn (McClatchey) B.; m. Nancy Ellen Tuft Kus, Apr. 29, 1967 (div. July 1983); children: Lisa Ann, Cheri Lee; m. Roxanne Sue Rhyan, Apr. 3, 1988. BA, Tarkio Coll., 1967; MDiv, Dubuque Theol. Sem., 1971; postgrad., McCormick Theol. Sem., 1989—. Ordained to ministry Presbyn. Ch. Pastor Buffalo Grove Presbyn. Ch., Lexington, Nebr., 1971-74; asst. pastor Crestview Presbyn. Ch., Columbus, Ohio, 1974-76; assoc. pastor 1st Presbyn. Ch., Martins Fy., Ohio, 1976-78; assoc. exec. Presbytery Western Res., Cleve., 1978-84; assoc. pastor 1st Presbyn. Ch., Gillette, Wyo., 1984-91, Community Ch. of Rockies, Estes Park, Colo., 1991—. Home: PO Box 68 Estes Park CO 80517 Office: Community Ch of Rockies 1700 Brodieve PO Box 451 Estes Park CO 80517

BOTSFORD, RONALD ARTHUR, minister; b. Buffalo, Sept. 1, 1933; s. Russell Albert and Margaret Elizabeth (Balsdon) B.; m. Patricia Joan Tuttle, Jan. 7, 1958; children: Cheryl Elaine Bostford Wilson, Michelle Kay Botsford Gavaghan. AB, Colgate U., 1955; MDiv, Columbia Theol. Sem., 1971; D of Ministry, McCormick Theol. Sem., 1977. Pastor Tallapoosa (Ga.) & Bremen Presby. Chs., 1971-74, Commerce (Ga.) Presby. Ch., 1974-81, James Island Presby. Ch., Charleston, S.C., 1981-85, 1st Presby. Ch., Highlands, N.C., 1985—; commr., P.C.U.S. 108th Gen. Assembly, Montreat, N.C., 1968, P.C. (U.S.A.) 203d Gen. Assembly, 1991; interim exec. sec. stated clerk, Athens Presbytery, Ga., 1979-80. Pres. Northeast Ga. Community Mental Health Ctr., Athens, 1979*80, pres., treas. Mental Health Assn. Trident Area, Charleston, 1982-85. Maj. USAF, 1955-75, Vietnam. Mem. Lions (Man of Yr. 1974), Rotary (internat. svc. dir. 1987-89, found. liaison 1989-91). Office: 1st Presbyn Ch PO Box 548 Highlands NC 28741

BOTT, GEORGE FREDRICK, minister, former naval officer, residential developer; b. Horseshoe Bend, Idaho, Sept. 20, 1926; s. Edward Homer and Nellie Mae (Reynolds) B.; m. Marian Nettie Housley, Feb. 2, 1948 (div. Sept. 1971); 1 dau., Kimberly Anne; m. Harriet Claire Grayson, Apr. 15, 1973; 1 child, Jonathan Edward. B.A., N.W. Nazarene Coll., Nampa, Idaho, 1952, Th.B., 1953; B.D., San Francisco Theol. Sem., 1960, Th.D. (residency), 1963. Investigator, Liberty Mut. Ins. Co., 1954-58; chaplain San Quentin Prison, 1959-60; ordained to ministry Presbyterian Ch., 1960; enlisted in U.S. Navy, 1943, commd. lt. (j.g.), 1960, advanced through grades to lt. comdr., 1966; various assignments as chaplain, 1960-81; served on USNS Barrett, USS Everglades, USS Eldorado, USS Mt. McKinley; assignments include 3d Amphibious Tractor Bn., 1st Marine Div., 1960-61, Marine Corps Recruit Depot, Parris Island, S.C., 1966-68, Naval Air Sta., Alameda, Calif., 1968-69, Naval Air Sta., Imperial Beach, Calif., 1972-75, 1st Marine Aircraft Wing, Okinawa, Japan, 1975-76, Naval Tng. Ctr., San Diego, 1977-79, U.S. Naval Hosp., Roosevelt Roads, P.R., 1979-81; ret., 1981; pres. Bott Enterprises, Inc., Pensacola, Fla., 1983—; interim and supply pastor Presbytery of Fla., 1982—. Grantee Lilly Found., 1958; scholar San Francisco Theol. Sem., 1960. Mem. Am. Legion. Republican. Author: The Robinson-McClusky Descendants, 1969, A Song at Twilight: Memoirs, 1991. *Avaricious as men and nations occasionally appear, Almighty God is Sovereign and holds exclusive title. We own nothing. At best, we are stewards. And, through His grace, or, His forbearance, we are enabled to participate with Him in this venture of living. What we do with this gift and with what sensitive ethic we exploit it, is our self-detemined judgment. Living openly with our fellows and with gratitude toward our Creator will energize a dynamic and glorious fulfillment.*

BOUCHARD, GIORGIO, minister, religious organization administrator; b. S. Germano, Torino, Italy, Aug. 1, 1929; s. Davide and Elena (Bonetto) B. Laurea in lettere, U. Torino, 1954; laurea in teologia, Waldensian Sem., Rome, 1958. Ordained to ministry Waldensian Ch. Pastor Iurea, Torino, 1958-66; leader community ctr., Cinisello, Milan, 1966-79; pastor Waldensian Ch., Naples, 1987—; pres. Protestant Fedn. Italy, 1988—. Author: I Valdesi e l'Italia, 1988, La Scritta di Pilato Spirito Protestante e Etica del Socialismo, 1991; editor Gioventu Evangelica, 1962-71. Home: Via del Cimbri 8, 80138 Naples Italy Office: Fedn Protestant Chs, Via Firenze 38, 00184 Rome Italy

BOUCHER, CHARLES VICTOR, minister, camp director; b. North Adams, Mass., Mar. 20, 1955; s. Victor Henry and Ruth Arlene (Wheeler) B.; m. Madelyn Cherryl Klose, Jan. 11, 1975; children: Elissa Joy, Joshua Charles, Kevin Paul. BA cum laude, North Adams State Coll., 1976; MDiv, Gordon-Conwell Theol. Sem., 1980. Ordained to ministry Am. Bapt. Chs. in U.S.A., 1981. Dir. Camp Advenchur, Alton Bay, N.H., 1977-79; min. of youth 1st Bapt. Ch., Belmont, Mass., 1977-80; program assoc. dir. Camp Grotonwood, Groton, Mass., 1980-81, assoc. dir., 1981-82, dir., 1985—; trustee Camp Ashmere, Hinsdale, Mass., 1975-77; pres. Am. Bapt. Students Gordon-Conwell Sem., S. Hamilton, Mass., 1978-80; deacon United Bapt. Ch., Saco, Maine, 1984-85, 1st Bapt. Ch., Littleton, Mass., 1989—. Mem. Christian Camping Internat., Conf. Bapt. Mins., Evang. Tchr. Tng. Assn. Home: Prescott St Groton MA 01450 Office: Camp Grotonwood Prescott Groton MA 01450 *There are things in our life that come and go, and we must not let our faith be one of those.*

BOUCHER, MICHAEL CHARLES, youth coordinator; b. Manchester, N.H., Apr. 11, 1968; s. Wilfrid G. and Annette I. (Labadie) B. BA in Psychology, Fairfield U., 1990. Youth coord. St. John's Parish, Bridgeport, Conn., 1989-90. Co-author: (booklet) Life on the Rocks-The Housing Crisis in N.H., 1988. Roman Catholic. Office: St Joseph's Parish 114 High St Medford MA 02155

BOUDREAUX, WARREN LOUIS, bishop; b. Berwick, La., Jan. 25, 1918; s. Alphonse Louis and Loretta Marie (Senac) B. Student, St. Joseph's Sem., Benedict, La., 1931-36, Notre Dame Sem., New Orleans, 1937, 42; LL.D., Notre Dame Sem., New Orleans, 1963; student, Grand Sem. de St. Sulpice, Paris, France, 1938-39; JCD, Catholic U. Am., 1946; hon., Pope John XXIII, 1962. Ordained priest Roman Catholic Ch., 1942; asst. pastor Crowley, La., 1942-43; vice chancellor Diocese of Lafayette, La., 1946-54; officialis Diocese of Lafayette, 1949-54; Vicar gen., 1957-61, aux. bishop., 1962-71; pastor St. Peter's Ch., New Iberia, La., 1954-71; bishop of Beaumont Tex., 1971-77; bishop of Houma-Thibodaux La., 1977—; dean New Iberia Deanery, 1954-71; Vice pres. S.W. La. Registry Newspaper, 1957-75; Mem. New Iberia Community Relations Council, 1963-71, U.S. Bishops Liturgical Commn., 1966-70, U.S. Bishop's Louvain Coll. Commn., 1970-76; imem. adv. council U.S. Cath. Conf., 1969-73; chmn. liaison com. Nat. Conf. Cath. Bishops, 1972-75, mem. liturgy commn., 1975—, mem. com. on canon law, 1975-78; state chaplain K.C. State of Tex., 1975-77; nat. moderator Marriage Encounter in U.S.A., 1975-77; mem. La. Cath. Conf., 1977—, La. Interch. Conf., 1977—. Bd. dirs. S.W. Ednl. Devel. Lab., Iberia Paris Youth Home, Consolata Home for Aged, New Iberia.; Pres. Archdiocesan Conf. Chancery Ofcls. Archdiocese New Orleans, 1950-51, bd. dirs., 1952-55. Office: Chancery Office PO Box 9077 Houma LA 70361 also: 1801 Hwy 311 Schriever LA 70395

BOULTON, EDWIN CHARLES, bishop; b. St. Joseph, Mo., Apr. 15, 1928; s. Glen Elwood and Elsa Adina Elizabeth (Person) B.; m. Betty Ann Fisher, July 17, 1949; children—Ann Lisa, Charles Mitchell, James Clay, Melanie Beth. A.B., William Jewell Coll., 1950; MDiv,Duke U., 1953; DD, Iowa Wesleyan Coll., 1974, Rust Coll., 1982, Dakota Wesleyan U., 1985, Mt. Union Coll., 1989; DHL, Simpson Coll., 1980, Westmar Coll., 1984. Ordained to ministry Meth. Ch., 1953; pastor chs., West End-Vass, N.C., 1953, Republic Community, Iowa, 1954-57, Pocahontas, Iowa, 1957-64, Bettendorf, Iowa, 1964-70; dist. supt., Dubuque, Iowa, 1970-73; adminstrv. asst. to bishop, Des Moines, 1973-80, bishop of Dakotas Area, Fargo, N.D., 1980-88; bishop of Ohio East Area, 1988—; bd. dirs. World Meth. Coun. Named Disting. Alumnus, Duke U. Div. Sch., 1980. Office: The United Meth Ch 8800 Cleveland Ave NW North Canton OH 44720

BOULWARE, JAMES L., minister; b. Duncan, Okla., Feb. 5, 1921; s. John Lafayett and Opal (Sprouse) B.; m. Virginia Lou Hanson, Feb. 5, 1943;

children: Jane Lee, Melody Ann. Grad., LIFE Bible Coll., L.A., 1944; BA in Religious Edn., Coll. of Rockies, 1960; MA in Communication, Assemblies of God Sem. Grad. Sch., 1976; PhD in N.T., Calif. Grad. Sch. Theol., 1983. Ordained to ministry Assemblies of God, 1945. Pastor Assemblies of God, Osawatomie and Hutchinson, Kans., 1944-58, Aurora, Colo., 1959-75; missionary Assemblies of God, Belgium, Fed. Republic Germany, Eng., 1976-80; prof. Am. Indian Bible Coll., Phoenix, 1981-83; pastor Assemblies of God, Montrose, Colo., 1984-86, 1st Assemblies of God Ch., Golden, Colo., 1989—; sectional youth dir. Kans. Assemblies of God, Osawatomie, 1947-51; dist presbyter Kans. Assemblies of God, Hutchinson, 1954-58; exec. presbyter, asst. supt., men's dir. and missionary Rocky Mountain Dist., 1961-91. Co-founder Ministerial Fellowship, Aurora, Colo., 1960-75; chaplain CAP, Aurora, Denver, 1965-67; founded Aurora Christian Acad., 1965—; mem. Pres.'s Coun. Trinity Bible Coll., 1973-75; bd. dirs. Am. Indian Bible Coll., 1988—; civilian chaplain U.S. Army, Augsburgh, Fed. Republic Germany, 1976-79 (numerous awards). Home: 201 Plateau Pkwy Golden CO 80403 Office: Assemblies of God 16800 W 9th Ave Golden CO 80401

BOUMAN, WALTER RICHARD, theology educator; b. Springfield, Minn., July 9, 1929; s. Walter Herman and Cordelia Ilene (Haar) B.; m. Janet Ann Gunderman, Aug. 17, 1957; children: Andrew Arthur, Lukas Lawrence, Gregory Martin. AA, Concordia Jr. Coll., 1948; BA, Concordia Sem., 1951, MDiv, 1954; DTh, Rupert-Carl U., Heidelberg, Fed. Republic of Germany, 1963. Assoc. prof. Concordia Coll., River Forest, Ill., 1963-71; vis. prof. Evang. Luth. Theol. Sem., Columbus, Ohio, 1971-74, joint prof., 1974-78; joint prof. Hamma Div. Sch., Springfield, Ohio, 1974-78; prof. systematic theology Trinity Luth. Sem., Columbus, 1978-84, Edward C. Fredt prof. systematic theology, 1984—; pres. Luth. Acad. for Schlarship, 1975-77; mem. Luth.-Episcopalian Dialogue III, 1983—, Anglican-Luth. Internat. Commn., 1985—. Author: Christianity American Style, 1970, (with others) Encyclopedia of the Lutheran Church, 1965, The Teaching of Religion, 1965, The New Church Debate, 1983. Pres. Columbus Symphony Youth Orch. Bd., 1980-82; bd. dirs. Jefferson Acad. of Music, Columbus, 1980-83, Columbus Symphony Orch. Bd. Trustees, 1981-83, Luth. Social Svcs., Columbus, 1982-85. Fulbright scholar, 1954-56; Danforth Found. fellow, 1965-71; Luth. Brotherhood Ins. grante, 1979-80, 86-87. Mem. Am. Acad. Religion, Coun. for Ethics and Econs. (bd. dirs. Columbus chpt. 1981-83). Democrat. Avocations: classical music, golf. Home: 1360 Millerdale Rd Columbus OH 43209 Office: Trinity Luth Sem 2199 E Main St Columbus OH 43209

BOUMGARDEN, DAVID LEWIS, minister; b. Sycamore, Ill., July 4, 1951; s. Lewis John and Margaret Pearl (Hyland) B.; m. D. Jane Austin, Aug. 11, 1973; children: Lindsey, Peter, John. BA with honors, Mich. State U., 1973; MDiv magna cum laude, Gordon-Conwell Theol. Sem., 1977. Ordained to ministry Presbyn. Ch., 1977. Pastor Old Stone Presbyn. Ch., Delaware, Ohio, 1977-84; organizing pastor, then first pastor River Glen Presbyn. Ch., Naperville, Ill., 1984—; chair social edn. and action com. Presbytery of Scioto Valley, Columbus, Ohio, 1978-81, mem. ecumenical rels. com., 1981-84; mem. adv. team new ch. devel. pastor/spouse retreats Presbyn. Ch. U.S.A., Louisville, 1989—; chair Delaware Ministerium, 1982-83, Naperville Ministerium, 1990-91; mem. new ch. devel. com. Chgo. Presbytery, 1985—. Chair Homemaker Home Health Aide Assn., Delaware, 1981-82; mem. Edward Hosp. Chaplaincy Found. Bd., 1985—; adj. chaplain Edward Hosp. Office: River Glen Presbyn Ch 1140 Raymond Dr Naperville IL 60563 *A worthy measuring rod for those of us called to be leaders in Christ's church is to ask how we have personally touched others and expanded their capacity to be Christ's presence to others.*

BOURBOUR, VALERIE MARIANNE, youth director, religion educator; b. Phila., Sept. 16, 1959; d. Stanley Kachnycz and Marianne (Podlaszewski) Phlanz; m. Thomas Scheetz, June 25, 1976 (div. Sept. 1986); 1 child, Jeremie Lee; m. Ahmad Bourbour, Nov. 18, 1986. AA, Bucks County Community Coll., Newtown, Pa., 1981; BA, Temple U., 1983; postgrad., U. Cen. Fla., 1986-88. Religious educator Ch. of God, Bloomington, Pa., 1981-83; tchr., second grade Our Lady of Lourdes, Ormond Beach, Fla., 1986—, sacramental instr., 1986—, youth dir., 7-12, 1990—; reviser sch. curriculum, math, English, computer; bd. dirs. Diocese of Orlando. Author: (newsletter) Youth News, 1990, church bulletin. Home: 35 Berkley Rd Ormond Beach FL 32176 Office: Our Lady of Lourdes Church 201 University Blvd Daytona Beach FL 32118

BOURDEAUX, MICHAEL ALAN, clergyman; b. Praze, Cornwall, Eng., Mar. 19, 1934; m. Gillian Davies, Aug. 27, 1960 (dec. 1978); children: Karen, Mark; m. Lorna Elizabeth Waterton, Aug. 9, 1979. BA in Russian and French with honors, St. Edmund Hall, Oxford U., 1957, MA in Theology with honors, 1959, BD, 1968. Ordained priest Anglican Ch., 1960. Parish priest, London, 1960-64; vis. fellow London Sch. Econs. and Polit. Sci., 1968-71; vis. prof. St. Bernard's Sem., Rochester, N.Y., 1969; dir. Keston Coll., 1969—; mem. staff Royal Inst. Internat. Affairs, 1971-73; Dawson lectr. Baylor U., Waco, Tex., 1972; Chavasse lectr. Oxford U., 1976; Kathryn W. Davis vis. prof. Slavic studies Wellesley Coll., Mass., 1981. Author: Opium of the People, 2nd edit., 1977; Religious Ferment in Russia, 1968; Patriarch and Prophets, 1969; Faith on Trial in Russia, 1971; Risen Indeed: Lessons in Faith from the USSR, 1983, The Gospel's Triumph over Communism, 1991; co-editor: Aida of Leningrad, 1972; Land of Crosses: the Struggle for Religious Freedom in Lithuania, 1979, Ten Growing Soviet Churches, 1987; mng. dir. quar. jour. Religion in Communist Lands (title of U.S. edit. changed to Religion, State and Society 1992), 1973—. Recipient Templeton prize for progress in religion, 1984. Brit. Council Exchange student, Moscow, 1959-60; Wyndham-Deedes traveling scholar, Israel, 1964; Centre de Recherches grantee Geneva, 1965-68. Office: Keston Rsch, 33a Canal St, Oxford OX2 6BQ, England *In the end, though even many Christians did not believe it along the way, faith in God has proved itself to be immensely more powerful and more enduring than faith in the man-made system of communism. Our work at Keston College (now moved to Oxford and called there Keston Research) has chartered this great chapter in the religious history of the Twentieth Century.*

BOURKE, GERARD JOSEPH, priest; b. Dublin, Ireland, Jan. 17, 1926; came to U.S., 1971; s. George and Katherine (Tierney) B. BA, Nat. U. Ireland, Dublin, 1948; Lic. Phil., Coll. St. Stanislaus, Tullamore, Ireland, 1951; Lic. in Sacred Theology, Miltown Pk. Inst., Dublin, 1958; MSc in Edn., Fordham U., 1972, PhD, 1976. Joined S.J., Roman Cath. Ch., 1943, ordained priest, 1957; chartered clin. psychologist, Japan. Tchr. Eiko Gakuen High Sch., Kanagawa Prefecture, Japan, 1960-71; chaplain Mt. St. Vincent Coll., N.Y.C., 1972-78; dir. Newman Ctr., U. Hawaii, Honolulu, E.W. Ctr., 1978-84; prof. dept. psychology Sophia U., Tokyo, 1985-91, dir. Counseling Inst., 1986-88; dir. Counseling Ctr., 1986-91; assoc. pastor St. Anthony's Ch., Kailua, Hawaii, 1991—; diocesan dir. Campus Ministry, Honolulu, 1978-84. Mem. Am. Counseling and Devel. Assn., Am. Psychol. Assn., Assn. Psychol. and Ednl. Counselors of Asia (exec. bd., bd. dirs. 1988—), Japan Counseling Assn., Japan Coll. Counselors Assn. Home and Office: 114 Makawao St Honolulu HI 96734 *I see life as a QUEST. But more than that, the word QUEST, as a mnemonic, expresses for me both the basic qualities of mind necessary for the QUEST, and the treasures that we seek in life. The qualities: Questioning, Understanding, Evaluating, Sharing and Trusting. The treasures: Quality of life, Understanding, Experience, Security and Truth.*

BOUTHILLETTE, RONALD JOSEPH, minister; b. Biddeford, Maine, June 1, 1950; s. Joseph Armand Bouthillette and Georgette Madaleine (Ouellette) Cofino; m. Cathy Sue Yost, July 16, 1988; children: Erich, Rachel. BA, Fla. Bible Coll., 1977; MDiv, Gordon-Conwell Theol. Sem., 1983; D Ministry (hon.), Luther Rice Sem., 1990. Ordained to ministry United Ch. of Christ, 1984. Interim pastor 1st Congl. Ch., Chelsea, Mass., 1983-85; pastor St. John's United Ch. of Christ, Fredonia, Pa., 1985-87, Brooklyn (Ohio) United Ch. of Christ, 1987-90, 1st United Ch. of Christ, Lebanon, Ind., 1990—; treas. Erie Assn. United Ch. of Christ, Pa., 1985-87. Editor (newspaper) The Messenger, 1987-90; contbr. articles to Living Faith mag. Bd. dirs. Bibl. Witness Fellowship, Knoxville, Tenn, 1985-89, cons., 1989—. Office: 1st United Ch of Christ 701 N Lebanon St Lebanon IN 46052

BOUW, LOIS MARIE SCHLAEGEL, religion educator; b. Harrison Valley, Pa., May 2, 1929; d. Waid Ernest and Esther May (Bailey) Schlaegel; m. Jacob Bouw, Jr., June 6, 1953; children: Jacob Daniel, Marlene Joy, Janet Lorene, Jonathan Henry. BS in Christian Edn., Nyack (N.Y.) Coll., 1979; postgrad., Alliance Theol. Sem., Nyack, 1983-84, 85, Columbia Bible Sem., 1983. Comm. for overseas ministries Christian and Missionary Alliance, 1955. Ch. planter Christian & Missionary, Alliance, 1956-60, 61-67, 75-79, 81-83; tchr. Mt. Apo Alliance Bible Coll., Bulatukan, The Philippines, 1963-64, 85-89; dir. Christian edn. Christian and Missionary Alliance Ch., Downsville, N.Y., 1990-91; tchr. Shekinah Alliance Bible Coll., General Santos City, The Philippines, 1991—; lectr. in field; trustee Ebenezer Bible Coll., Zamboanga City, 1985-88. Republican. Home: Campbell Brook Rd Downsville NY 13755 Office: Christian and Missionary Alliance Ch Downsville NY 13755

BOVON, FRANÇOIS, theology educator; b. Lausanne, Vaud, Switzerland, Mar. 13, 1938; s. André and Hélène (Mayor) B.; divorced; children: Pierre, Martin. BTh, U. Lausanne, 1961; ThD, U. Basel, Switzerland, 1965. Pastor Eglise Réformée, Canton de Vaud, Switzerland, 1965-67; prof. U. Geneva, 1967—; co-editor Revue de Théologie et de Philosophie, Lausanne, 1977-86, Studia Biblica, Leiden, The Netherlands, 1983-90. Author: (patristics and New Testament) De Vocatione Gentium, 1967, Luc le Théologien, 1988, 2nd edit., Lukas in Neuer Sicht, 1985, L'oeuvre de Luc, 1987, Das Evangelium nach Lukas, 1989. Mem. Studiorum Novi Testamenti Societas, Assn. pour L'étude de la Littérature Apocryphe Chrétienne (pres. 1981-87), Soc. Suisse de Théologie (pres. 1973-77), Académie Internationale des Scis. Religieuses. Avocation: sports, travel,. Home: rue François Grast, 1208 Geneva Switzerland Office: U Geneva, Faculté de Théologie, 1211 Geneva 4, Switzerland

BOWDEN, MAXINE, chef, minister; b. N.Y.C., Mar. 7, 1943; d. Philip and Frieda (Silverman) Aaron; m. Henry Earl Bowden, Aug. 22, 1983. BA, Bklyn. Coll., 1967, postgrad., 1967-69; student, Art Student's League, 1970. Tchr. Narcotic Addiction Control Commn., Staten Island, N.Y., 1967-70; writer, educator Appleton Century Crafts Pub., N.Y.C., 1970-74, Mind, Inc., N.Y.C.; chef, owner Cuisine by Maxine, N.Y.C., 1977-80; chef La Fogata Restaurant, N.Y.C., 1980-83, The Ballroom Restaurant, 1983-88, Citibank, N.Y.C.; owner Cuisine By Maxine, Queens, N.Y., 1990—; minister Hope Life, Inc.-Noah's Ark Ch., N.Y.C., 1980—. Mem. Coun. for Common Consciousness, N.Y.C., 1989—. Mem. NAFE. Republican. Avocations: painting, writing, fitness, design. Home and Office: 9740 62d Dr Rego Park NY 11374

BOWDLE, DONALD NELSON, theology educator; b. Easton, Md., Feb. 2, 1935; s. Nelson Elmer and Margaret Katherine (Kline) B.; m. Nancy Lee George, Aug. 28, 1955; children: Donald Keven, Karen Lee. BA, Lee Coll., Cleve., 1957; MA, PhD, Bob Jones U., 1959,61; ThM, Princeton Theol. Sem., 1962; ThD, Union Theol. Sem., Richmond, Va., 1970. Ordained minister, Ch. of God. Faculty, teaching adminstrn. Lee Coll., Cleve., 1962—; cons. Commn. on Religion in Appalachia, Berea, Ky., 1984—; adj. faculty Va. Commonwealth U., Richmond, 1967-69; postdoctoral fellow, visiting lectr. Yale U., New Haven, 1984-85, U. Edinburgh, Scotland, 1988-89. Author: Redemption Accomplished and Applied, 1972; editor Ellicott Bible Commentary, 1971; author/editor The Promise and the Power, 1980. Mem. Am. Soc. Ch. History, Evang. Theol. Soc. Republican. Church of God. Avocations: baseball, reading, walking, collecting selected old books, travel. Home: 3635 Edgewood Cir NW Cleveland TN 37312

BOWDON, THOMAS MICHAEL, religious school administrator; b. Memphis, Mar. 6, 1944; s. Thomas Milton and Gladys Elizabeth (Langham) B.; m. Cheryl Lynn Croley, June 5, 1966; children: Thomas Dobson, Sarah Elizabeth. BS, Cumberland Coll., 1965; MEd, Memphis State U., 1975. Secondary prin. Evang. Christian Sch., Memphis, 1972-76, headmaster, pres., 1976—; deacon 1st Evang. Ch., Memphis, 1975, elder, 1976—; chmn. ch. coun., 1983, chmn. staff search, 1985-86. Bd. dirs. Bryan Coll., Dayton, Tenn., 1988—. Mem. Assn. Christian Schs. (coun. 1986—), So. Assn. Christian Schs. (bd. dirs. 1975-85), Memphis Christian Edn. Assn. (pres. 1974-75), Memphis Christian Athletic Assn. (commr. 1973), Memphis Assn. Ind. Schs. (pres. 1986-88). Republican. Office: Evang Christian Sch 7600 Macon Rd PO Box 1030 Cordova TN 38018-1030

BOWE, BARBARA ELLEN, religion educator; b. Schenectady, N.Y., Dec. 1, 1945; d. William John and Margaret (Dinneen) B. BA, Manhattanville, 1967; MEd, Boston Coll., 1974; M.T.S., Harvard U., 1979, ThD, 1986. Asst. prof. Bibl. studies Cath. Theol. Union, Chgo., 1990—. Author: A Church in Crisis, 1988. Mem. Cath. Bibl. Assn., Soc. Bibl. Lit., Chgo. Soc. Bibl. Rsch. Roman Catholic. Office: Cath Theol Union 5401 S Cornell Ave Chicago IL 60615

BOWEN, GILBERT WILLARD, minister; b. Muskegon, Mich., Dec. 30, 1931; s. Bruce Oliver and Beatrice Lillian (Sibley) B.; m. Marlene Mary Michell, July 31, 1954; children: Kathryn Leigh, Mark Kevin, Stephen James. BA, Wheaton Coll., 1955; MDiv, McCormick Theol. Sem., 1957, PhD in Ministry, 1976; cert., Ctr. for Religion and Psychotherapy, 1976; DLL (hon.), Nat. Coll. Edn., 1987. Ordained to ministry Presbyn. Ch., 1956. Minister 1st United Presbyn. Ch., Blue Earth, Minn., 1956-63, Faith United Presbyn. Ch., Tinley Park, Ill., 1963-65, Community Presbyn. Ch., Mt. Prospect, Ill., 1965-70, Kenilworth (Ill.) Union Ch., 1970—; exchange minister Johanneskirche, Neuwied, Fed. Republic Germany, 1961-62; pres. bd. Ctr. for Religion and Psychotherapy; bd. dirs. McCormick Theol. Sem., Chgo., Anatolia Coll., Thessaloniki, Greece, Presbyn. Home, Evanston. Mem. adv. com. North Shore Sr. Ctr., Winnetka, Ill.; bd. dirs. Hospice of North Shore, Wilmette, Ill., Shelter for Battered Women, Evanston; chmn. Instl. Rev. Bd., Evanston. Mem. Am. Assn. Pastoral Counselors, Acad. Parish Clergy, Am. Waldensian Aid Soc. Republican. Club: Indian Hill. Avocations: tennis, golf, vocal music. Home: 909 Westerfield Dr Wilmette IL 60091 Office: Kenilworth Union Ch 211 Kenilworth Ave Kenilworth IL 60043

BOWEN, MICHAEL RAY, minister; b. Tyler, Tex., Apr. 4, 1954; s. Leonard Dawson and Floreice (Johnson) B.; m. Rosemarie Johnson, June 6, 1975; children: Kimberly Faith, Aaron Michael. AA, Jacksonville Coll., 1974; BS, Tex. Eastern U., 1976; MDiv, Bapt. Missionary Assn. Sem., Jacksonville, Tex., 1981. Ordained minister in Bapt. Ch. Assoc. pastor Mt. Selman Bapt. Ch., Bullard, Tex., 1980—; computer analyst Tyler (Tex.) Pipe Industries, 1974—. Home: Rte 2 Box 600 Jacksonville TX 75766

BOWENS, JOSEPH T., bishop, religious organization executive. Gen. pres. United Holy Ch. Am., Inc., Chillum, Md. Office: United Holy Ch Am 825 Fairoak Ave Chillum MD 20783*

BOWER, DOUGLAS WILLIAM, pastoral counselor, psychotherapist, clergyman; b. Niagara Falls, N.Y., Jan. 6, 1948; s. Charles Henry Bower and Phyllis June (Rank) Ayres; m. Cheryl Stewart, May 25, 1980; children: Katherine Elizabeth, Erin Colleen. AA, Manatee Jr. Coll., Bradenton, Fla., 1969; BS, Oglethorpe U., 1972; PhD, U. Ga., 1989. RN, Ga.; ordained to ministry United Meth. Ch., 1980; cert. counselor, Ga. Nurse Northside Hosp., Atlanta, 1970-80; assoc. pastor 1st United Meth. Ch., Griffin, Ga., 1980-82; pastor, pastoral counselor Oconee Street United Meth. Ch., Athens, Ga., 1982-86; dir. Asbury Woods Counseling, Athens, 1986—. Contbr. articles to profl. jours. Mem. AACD, Assn. for Religious and Value Issues in Counseling, Person-Centered Assn., N.E. Ga. Mental Health Assn., Kiwanis. Democrat. Avocations: music, weightlifting, tennis, golf, reading. Office: Asbury Woods Counseling 170 Security Circle Athens GA 30605 *While we may not make an impact on the world, we can and do make an impact on the immediate world around and within us. Persistence in maintaining faith, even in the face of adversity, makes a powerful impact on our immediate world.*

BOWER, MONTY LEE, clergyman; b. Shattuck, Okla., Sept. 2, 1954; s. Robert Albert and Leona Louise (Colten) B.; m. Jo Ann Randall, Jan. 10, 1975. BA in Religion, Bethany Nazarene Coll., 1980; MA in Religion, So. Nazarene U., 1987. Ordained to ministry Free Meth. Ch., 1981. Minister Okla. Free Meth. Ch., Oklahoma City, 1980—; supr. housekeeping ServiceMaster Deaconess Hosp., Oklahoma City, 1981-83, mgr. housekeeping, 1983-88; minister Tex. Conf. Free Meth Ch., Dallas, 1988—; adminstrv. asst. to supt. Tex. Free Meth. Ch., Dallas, 1989—. Served with U.S. Army, 1973-76. Republican. Avocations: violin, book collecting, writing, music. Home: 3931 Crepe Myrtle Ln Dallas TX 75233 Office: Kimball Free Meth Ch 3930 Boulder Dr Dallas TX 75233

BOWER, NORMA L., church secretary; b. New Philadelphia, Ohio, Aug. 9, 1939; d. Henrietta Isabelle (Fogenitz) Millisor; m. Richard J. Kuban (div. Aug. 1970); children: Barry Dean, Pamela Dawn, Brian Dale; m. Lowell Daniel Bower, Sept. 9, 1981. Grad. high sch., Brecksville, Ohio. Monitor Port Clinton (Ohio) Christian Sch., 1981-84; sec. Christian Life Community Ch., Port Clinton, 1990—; sec. Christian Action Coun., Ottawa County, Oak Harbor, Ohio, 1981-89. Republican.

BOWER, RICHARD JAMES, minister; b. Somerville, N.J., June 9, 1939; s. Oneil A. and Mildred R. (Goss) B.; m. Helen Ann Cheek, Dec. 29, 1962 (div. 1985); 1 child, Christopher Scott. Student, Sorbonne, Paris, 1959-60; B.A., Wesleyan U., 1961; M.Div., Drew U., Madison, N.J., 1965; student, Oxford U., Eng., 1983. Ordained to ministry, Congregational Christian Ch., 1965. Minister Community Congl. Ch., Kewaunee, Wis., 1965-67; sr. minister Congl. Ch., Bound Brook, N.J., 1967-78, Congl. Ch. of the Chimes, Sherman Oaks, Calif., 1978—; exec. com., dir. Nat. Assn. Congl. Christians Chs., 1973-77; chmn. Nat. Assn. Congl. Christian Chs., 1976-77, asst. moderator, 1981-82, moderator, 1982-83, exec. search com., 1990-91, nominating com., 1991—. Appeared on TV programs; contbr. poetry and articles to periodicals. Organizer, pres. Am. Field Service, Kewaunee, 1966-67; dir. Children's Bur., Los Angeles, 1981-88; bd. fellows Hollywood Congl. Ctr., 1979-82; bd. dirs. Heritage Playhouse, 1986—. Mem. Cal-West Assn. (dir., moderator 1986-87). Republican. Lodge: Bound Brook Rotary (pres. 1975-76). Home: 5737 Allott Ave Van Nuys CA 91401 Office: Congl Ch Chimes 14115 Magnolia Blvd Sherman Oaks CA 91423

BOWER, RICHARD WILLIAM, minister, medical technologist; b. Carlisle, Pa., Sept. 18, 1947; s. Richard Lutz and Dorothy Jane (Russell) B.; m. Shirley Ann Moravek, June 15, 1968; children: Christal Lynn, Amanda Mae, Abigail Joy. BS in Biology, Lebanon Valley Coll., 1972, BS in Med. Tech., 1973; MDiv, Alliance Theol. Sem., Nyack, N.Y., 1987. Ordained to ministry Christian and Missionary Alliance, 1987. Commd. 1st lt. U.S. Army, 1977; advanced through grades to maj. USNG, 1988; clin. lab. officer 825th Med. Lab. Detachment, N.Y. N.G., Bklyn., 1983—; chaplain 101 Signal Bn., Troop Command N.Y. NG, Yonkers, 1991—; sr. pastor Elim Ch., Valley Cottage, N.Y., 1987—. Vis. chaplain Nyack Manor Nursing Home, Valley Cottage, 1987—, Nyack Hosp., 1990—. Mem. Evang. Pastors Assn. Rockland County, Am. Soc. Clin. Pathology (cert.), Res. Officers Assn. (chaplain Rockland County chpt. 1990—), Alpha Phi Omega. Republican. Office: Elim Ch 82 Lake Rd Valley Cottage NY 10989

BOWER, ROY DONALD, minister, counselor; b. Pitts., June 20, 1939; s. Roy Clare and Evelyn June (Moorhead) B.; m. Sandra M. Daugherty, Mar. 16, 1963 (dec. 1976); children: Christine, Roy, Donald, Kathleen; m. Robin Jeanette Bird, Aug. 20, 1976; children: Daniel, Robin, William. Student, Indiana U. Pa., 1958, Geneva Coll., 1959-61; BS in Edn., Slippery Rock U., 1972; ThM, Am. Bible Coll., 1980; DD, Trinity Hall Sem., 1988. Ordained to ministry Ind. Christian Chs. Internat., 1970; cert. Christian counselor. Counselor La Casa Contenta, Colorado Springs, Colo., 1976-78; therapist Giles Inst., Colorado Springs, 1978-79; counselor Cheyenne Village, Manitou Springs, Colo., 1979-80, Tutoring and Counseling Svcs., Confluence, Pa., 1981—; resource counselor Family Rsch. Coun., Washington, 1985—; manuscript reviewer Nat. Coun. Social Studies, Washington, 1987; advisor Am. Pub. Welfare Assn., Chgo., 1970; rsch. theologian Ref. Faith Ctr., Confluence, Pa., 1986—, dir., 1986—; pres. Confluence Area Ministerium, 1986. Book reviewer Pastoral Counsel Newsletter, 1986—. Founder Yough Valley Symposium, Confluence, 1982—; mem. Western Pa. Conservancy, Pitts., 1980—; 1st lt. CAP, Scottdale, Pa., 1982—; state constable Somerset County Pa. Ct., 1988—. Recipient citation Dept. Social Svcs., El Paso County, Colo., 1975, Certs. of Merit ARC, Johnstown, Pa., 1987, Am. Cancer Soc., Somerset, Pa., 1990; Menninger Found. fellow, 1984—. Mem. United Assn. christian Counselors Internat., Am. Assn. Family Counselors, Nat. Christian Counselors Assn., Am. Assn. christian Counselors, Guild of Clergy Counselors (Award of Excellence 1991), Am. fedn. Police (state v.p. 1991—), Pa. State Constables Assn. Democrat. Avocations: philately, nature study, numismatics, tennis. Home: 609 Oden St Confluence PA 15424 Office: Tutoring & Counseling Svc 609 Oden St Confluence PA 15424 *Humanity's limited and created free will to think or to act pales miserably when compared to the completely free will of the sovereign Creator who foreordains all that comes to pass in the universe.*

BOWERING, GERHARD, Islamic studies educator; b. Monchen-Gladbach, Fed. Republic of Germany, Oct. 20, 1939; came to U.S., 1974; s. Franz-Josef and Anni (Leicht) B. B.A., U. Wurzburg, 1959; Ph.L., U. Munich, 1964; diploma Panjab U., Lahore, Pakistan, 1967; Th.L., U. Montreal, 1971; Ph.D., McGill U., 1975. Asst. prof. religious studies U. Pa., Phila., 1975-80, assoc. prof., 1980-84; prof. history of Islamic religion Yale U., 1984—; vis. prof. U. Innsbruck, 1982, 85; vis. assoc. prof. Princeton U., 1984. Author: the Mystical Vision of Existence in Classical Islam, 1980. Contbr. articles to profl. jours. Ford Found. grantee, 1977, Am. Rsch. Inst. grantee, 1982, 90. Office: Yale U Dept Religious Studies Yale Sta Box 2160 New Haven CT 06520

BOWERS, JOHN CARL, minister; b. L.A., Oct. 7, 1943; s. John Gordon and Georgene (Kendle) B.; m. Dorothea Adeline Geffken, July 2, 1978 (div. May 1987). BA in Philosophy, Occidental Coll., 1965; MDiv, Union Theol. Sem., N.Y.C., 1972; postgrad., Drew U., 1988—; Nat. Security Seminar, U.S. Army War Coll., 1991. Ordained to ministry Presbyn. Ch. (U.S.A.), 1973. Interim supply minister United Presbyn. Ch. of St. Andrew, Groton, Conn., 1972-73; asst. pastor Trinity Presbyn. Ch., East Brunswick, N.J., 1973-75; pastor Ft. Schuyler Presbyn. Ch., Bronx, N.Y., 1976-85, Presbyn. Ch. in Elmont (N.Y.), 1985—; co-chair regional conf. Nat. Student Christian Fedn., Berkeley, Calif., 1965; commr. Synod of N.E., 1980-82; bd. dirs. Ft. Schuyler House, Bronx, 1981-84; mem. com. on ministry Presbytery of N.Y.C., 1980-85. Mem. sch. bd. Elmont Union Free Sch. Dist., 1988—; treas. Stanforth Action Com., Elmont, 1987—; chair sub-com. Citizens Adv. Com., Elmont, 1987. Recipient Bausch and Lomb Sci. award, 1961, cert. of appreciation Greater N.Y. coun. Girl Scouts U.S., 1985, appreciation plaque Elmont Union Free Sch. Dist., 1987; Nat. Merti scholar, 1961-65. Mem. Elmont Clergy Assn. (pres. 1987-91), Presbyn. Conf. Assn. (bd. dirs. 1990—). Democrat. Home: 126 Gotham Ave Elmont NY 11003 Office: Presbyn Ch PO Box 466 Elmont NY 11003 *"Who knows? Who cares? What's the difference?"—that's what we hear, beginning the decade of the 90s. But that's wrong. We should know, because we can; we should care, because we are people of faith; and we can make a difference—the question is: will we? The truth of our faith, the depth of our love, will be judged on just that: whether our faith and love made any difference to anyone else.*

BOWERS, KEVIN LYNN, minister; b. Charleroi, Pa., Feb. 28, 1956; s. Vernon Howard and Ellamae (Owens) B. BS in Elem. Edn., Psychology, Milligan Coll., 1978; MDiv, Christian Theol. Sem., 1991. Ordained to ministry Christian Ch. (Disciples of Christ), 1991; cert. elem. tchr., Pa., Tenn. Missionary Ch. of Christ in Thailand, Bangkok, 1984-87; asst. to min. 1st Korean United Meth. Ch., Indpls., 1988; assoc. min. Linwood Christian Ch., Indpls., 1988-91; min. 1st Christian Ch., Weirton, W.Va., 1991—; tchr. Mt. Lebanon Pub. Schs., 1978-84. Mem. Emerson Elem. Community Bd., Indpls., 1991. Office: 1st Christian Ch 3252 Main St Weirton WV 26062

BOWERS, MARIANNE, clergywoman; b. Lafayette, Ind., Feb. 5, 1919; d. Gilbert Melville and Mary Frances (Montgomery) Wilson; m. Carl Eugene Bowers, June 19, 1964 (dec.); children by previous marriage—Frederic Kelly, Deborah Kelly Kivisels, Karen Kelly Wootton. B.S., Purdue U., 1940; grad. Unity Ministerial Sch., 1980. Ordained to ministry Unity Ch., 1980. Exec. sec. Tex. Lic. Vocat. Nurses Assn., Austin, Tex., 1964-66; employment counselor Tarrant Employment Agy., Austin, 1966-68; owner, mgr. Horizons Unlimited (book stores), Austin and San Antonio, 1968-72; with devel., mktg., pub. relations depts. First Nat. Bank, Harlingen, Tex., 1973-76; exec. officer Rio Grande Valley Apt. Assn., 1976-78; minister Unity Ch. of San Angelo (Tex.), 1980—. Mem. Assn. Unity Chs., Internat. New Thought Alliance, AAUW, Scriveners, Alpha Lambda Delta, Delta Rho Kappa, Chi

Omega, Nat. Assn. Female Execs., Internat. Platform Assn. Address: PO Box 1221 San Angelo TX 76902

BOWERSOX, GLEN, Episcopal priest, foundation executive; b. York, Pa., Mar. 20, 1920; s. George Edward and Anna May (Hankey) Bowersox. BA, Gettysburg Coll., 1942; MS, Northeastern U., 1942-44; postgrad., Purdue U., 1944-45, U. Chgo., 1950-54; LHD, Gettysburg Coll., 1973. Ordained priest ch. Pakistan, 1973. Civilian specialist U.S. Army, Philippines, 1945-48; instr. Muhlenburg Coll., Allentown, Pa., 1948-50; field rep. Inst. Internat. Edn., Chgo., 1951-54, asst. dir., 1954-59; asst. rep. The Asia Found., N.Y.C., 1959-60; program officer The Asia Found., San Francisco, 1960-62; asst. rep. The Asia Found., Tokyo, Japan, 1962-66; program officer The Asia Found., San Francisco, 1966-68; rep. The Asia Found., Kabul, Afghanistan, 1968-73; priest assoc. Ch. of the Advent, San Francisco, 1973—; fgn. study advisor U. Chgo., 1950-53; program officer The Asia Found., San Francisco, 1973-77; Luce Scholars coordinator The Asia Found., San Francisco, 1977-86. Home: 2484 Bush St San Francisco CA 94115 Office: Ch of the Advent of Christ the King 162 Hickory St San Francisco CA 94102

BOWES, A. WENDELL, minister, religion educator; b. San Francisco, Nov. 6, 1945; s. Alpin P. and Betty J. (Smith) B.; m. Virginia H. Miller, June 17, 1967; children: Heidi, Shelley. BA, Northwest Nazarene Coll., Nampa, Idaho, 1967; MDiv, Nazarene Theol. Seminary, Kans. City, Mo., 1970; ThM, Princeton Theol. Seminary, 1971; PhD, Dropsie Coll., Merion, Pa., 1987. Ordained, 1973. Pastor Ch. of Nazarene, Port Elizabeth, N.J., 1971-74, Bristol, Pa., 1975-78, Selinsgrove, Pa., 1979-82; prof. religion Northwest Nazarene Coll., 1982—, head dept. religion, coord. grad. studies in religion, 1986—. Named one of Outstanding Young Men Am., 1978. Mem. Soc. Bibl. Lit., Am. Schs. Oriental Rsch., Nat. Assn. Profs. Hebrew. Home: 932 W Locust Ln Nampa ID 83686 Office: Northwest Nazarene Coll Nampa ID 83686

BOWIE, DAVID BERNARD, clergyman; b. Jamaica, N.Y., Mar. 30, 1954; s. Matthew Bowie and Vanzetta Lorigné (Moore) Whittaker; m. Angela Baughman, Nov. 27, 1976; children: Courtney Alyce, Brooke Marie. BA, Talladega Coll., 1974; MDiv., Interdenominational Theological Ctr., 1983. Ordained to ministry Presbyn. Ch., 1983. Asst. Braille tchr. Erasmus Hall High Sch., Bklyn., 1975-77; employment counselor Woodward High Sch., Cin., 1978-79; student asst. pastor Westhills Presbyn. Ch., Atlanta, 1980-82; asst. pastor 1st Presbyn. Ch. East Cleveland, Ohio, 1983-84, assoc. pastor, 1984-88; stated supply pastor Heights Presbyn. Ch., Cleveland Heights, 1988-90, pastor, 1990—; mem. nominating com. Presbytery of Western Res., Cleve., 1985-87, moderator, 1987; mem. at-large mission coun., 1984-85, ex-officio mem., 1987; participant study excursion Synod of Covenant, Columbus, Ohio to Cuernavaca, Mex., 1986, alt. commr., 1987, 90; mem. Ch. Devel./Redevel., Cleve., 1984-85; sem. adv. del. Gen. Assembly, United Presbyn. Ch., Houston, 1981, observer, Hartford, Conn., 1982; mem. com. on ministry Clergy-Counselor Career Beginnings program Shaw High Sch., 1988-90, mem. Leadership Devel. com., 1991—; v.p. Heights Interfaith. Commr. 201st Gen. Assembly, Phila., 1989, tchr. Synod Sch., 1990; mem. racial ethnic recruitment adv. com. John Carroll U., 1987-90; mem. Heights Commn. on Equity and Excellence in Edn., 1990-91, Student Svcs. Adv. Bd., 1988—, student mentoring program, 1988-90. Mem. Heights Clergy, Heights Interfaith Coun. (v.p. 1991—), Kiwanis, Kappa Alpha Psi. Home: 3659 Fenley Rd Cleveland Heights OH 44121 Office: Heights Presbyn Ch 2065 Lee Rd Cleveland Heights OH 44118

BOWLES, RICHARD JOSEPH, church administrator; b. Evanston, Ill., Mar. 2, 1944; s. Richard Joseph and Virginia (Minger) B.; m. Mary Ann Singer, July 16, 1966; children—Richard S., Brian E. AB with honors, Regis Coll., 1966; MA, Cath. U. Am., 1970. Dir. religious edn. St. John's Parish, Clinton, Md., 1969-70; asst. prof. religious studies Regis Coll., Denver, 1970-75, assoc. dir. campus ministry, 1975-78; dir. liturgy Archdiocese of Denver, 1978-90, Ch. of Risen Christ, Denver, 1990—; deacon Basilica of the Immaculate Conception, Denver; archbishop's rep. Living the Good News, v.p., 1984-85. Mem. planning com. Holocaust Awareness Week, 1982-83; mem. Holocaust Inst., Bd. Judaic Studies Program, Denver U., 1985—, Jewish-Cath. Dialogue, 1982-87, Lutheran-Cath. Dialogue, 1975—; mem. planning com. Cath. Charities Run, 1982-83, Denver Symphony Marathon; mem. steering com. Denver Area Interfaith Clergy Conf., 1985-87, bishop's com. Nat. Conf. Cath. Bishops, 1985, subcom. on Book of Blessings, 1985-87. Recipient Faculty of Yr. award Regis Coll., 1974; Svc. award Denver Liturg. Commn., 1982. Mem. S.W. Liturg. Conf. Bd., Fedn. Diocesan Liturg. Commns., Alpha Sigma Nu. Office: Ch of Risen Christ 3060 S Monaco Pkwy Denver CO 80222

BOWLIN, ROBERT HENDERSON, minister, lawyer; b. Keokuk, Iowa, May 28, 1946; s. Richard Henderson and Vivian Claire (Ashline) B.; m. Ellen June Hinz, Aug. 21, 1971; childen: David, Sarah. BA, U. Iowa, 1968, JD, 1973; MDiv, Christ Sem.-Seminex, 1983. Bar: Iowa 1973, Mo. 1980. Ordained to ministry Assn. Evang. Luth. Chs., 1983. Dir., legal asst., ministry Luth. Family & Children's Svcs. of Mo., St. Louis, 1983-86; assoc. pastor Salem Luth. Ch., Moline, Ill., 1986—; cons. on constitutions No. Ill. Synod Evangelical Luth. Ch. Am. Chaplain US Army Reserve, 1984—; mem. bd. govs. Luth. Social Svc. of Ill., western region. Served with U.S. Army, 1969-70, Korea. Recipient Svc. award vol. lawyer Legal Svcs. of Ea. Mo., Inc., St. Louis, 1986. Mem. Moline Ministerial Assn. (pres. 1989-90). Democrat. Home: 2715 14th Ave Moline IL 61265 Office: Salem Luth Ch 1724 15th St Moline IL 61265

BOWLIN, S(ELDEN) CLAY, minister; b. Kansas City, Kans., May 16, 1959; s. Paul Bunyan and Joyce Luella (Wright) B.; m. Rhonda Louise Wilcox, June 20, 1987; 1 child, Rachael. BA with honors, Calvary Bible Coll., 1982, MA, 1984. Ordained to ministry Bible Ch., 1989; cert. Bible specialist. Interim pastor Bible Fellowship Ch., Olney, Ill., summers '82, 83; chaplain, tchr. Blue Ridge Christian Sch., Kansas City, Mo., 1984-90; interim pastor Hope Fellowship Ch., Kansas City, 1986; pastor Community Bible Ch., Sabetha, Kans., 1990—; dir. play Blue Ridge Christian Sch., 1984-87; sponsor class, 1984-90, student coun. 1986-90; soccer coach 1988-90, soccer official 1983—. Vol. safety hunter and instr., Independence, Mo., 1991, Kans. Dept. Wildlife and Pks., 1991—; instr. Mo. Dept. Conservation, 1988-90; official N.E. Kans. Soccer Assn., 1991—; mem. N.E. Kans. Soccer Assn.-Ofcl., 1991—; mem. sr. class pres. Calvary Bapt. Coll., 1982; missionary Gospel Mission Union, Belgium, 1981. Mem. NRA, Nat. Fed. Interscholastic Officials Assn., Assns. Christian Schs. Internat., Kiwanis. Avocations: hunting, fishing, carpentry. Home: 112 N 14th Sabetha KS 66534 Office: Community Bible Ch 623 N 6th St Sabetha KS 66534

BOWMAN, CHRISTOPHER DAVID, minister; b. Easton, Md., Jan. 9, 1962; s. Robert Cover and Martha Anne (Yoder) B.; m. Sherry Lynne Clark, May 28, 1983; children: Melissa Denae, Jacob Christopher. BS, Manchester Coll., 1984; MDiv, Bethany Theol. Sem., 1987. Chaplain Christ the King Nursing Home, West Chicago, Ill., 1985, McNeal Meml. Hosp., Berwyn, Ill., 1986; pastor First Ch. of the Brethren, Peoria, 1987—; dist. clk. Ill./Wis. Dist. of the Ch. of the Brethren, Elgin, 1988—; clk. Dist. Program and Arrangements, Elgin, 1988—, Dist. Nominating Com., 1988—. Mem. Soc. Bibl. Lit., Brethren Mins. Assn. (chmn. 1991—). Home: 1110 E Maywood Ave Peoria IL 61603 Office: First Ch of the Brethren 1225 E Corrington Ave Peoria IL 61603

BOWMAN, JOSEPH KIE, minister; b. Fairbanks, Alaska, Dec. 15, 1956; s. Van M. and Wanda Lee (Bates) B.; m. Tina L. Thornberry, Feb. 28, 1981; children: Amanda Leigh, Laura Anne, Joseph Van. BA, Cumberland Coll., 1980; MDiv, Southwestern Bapt. Theol. Sem., 1985, D Ministry, 1990. Ordained to ministry So. Bapt. Conv., 1977; cert. leader for continuing witness tng. Pastor Clarks Creek Bapt. Ch., Dry Ridge, Ky., 1979-81; min. to youth Forest Pk. Bapt. Ch., Ft. Worth, 1982-83; asst. pastor in personal evangelism Travis Ave. Bapt. Ch., Ft. Worth, 1985-87; assoc. pastor in evangelism and growth Tabernacle Bapt. Ch., Cartersville, Ga., 1987-91; pastor 1st Bapt. Ch., Canton, Ga., 1991—; mem. radio and TV com. Ga. Bapt. Conv., Savannah, 1990—; bd. dirs. Thomas Holmes House, Cartersville, 1991—. Guest speaker Kiwanis, Ret. Men's Club, Women's Club, Bartow County, Ga., 1987-91; dir. Rep. campaign Jack Kemp for U.S. Pres., Bartow County, 1988. Named one of the Outstanding Young Men of Am., U.S. Jaycees, 1983, 86. Mem. So. Bapt. Religious Educators Assn., Mid. Cherokee Assn. Baptists (dir. evangelism ch. growth asst. team 1988—, mem. evangelism com. 1988-89, chair 1989—).

BOWMAN, LEONARD JOSEPH, philosophy and religious studies educator; b. Detroit, Feb. 4, 1941; s. Joseph Leonard and Margaret Ann (Hughes) B.; m. Anne Corbi, May 29, 1971; children: Emily, Sarah, Claire. BA, Duns Scotus Coll., Southfield, Mich., 1963; MA, U. Detroit, 1967; PhD, Fordham U., Bronx, N.Y., 1973. Prof. philosophy and religious studies Teikyo Marycrest U., Davenport, Iowa, 1973—. Author: The Importance of Being Sick, 1976; author, editor: Itinerarium: The Idea of Journey, 1983; contbr. articles to profl. jours. Pres. Hospice Care of Scott County, Davenport, 1983. Home: 633 Ripley St Davenport IA 52803 Office: Teikyo Marycrest U Davenport IA 52804

BOWMAN, LOCKE E., JR., clergyman, educator, publisher; b. Henry County, Mo., Jan. 12, 1927; s. Locke E. and Naomi (McCann) B.; m. Ruth E. Halter, Aug. 11, 1952; 1 child: Locke E. III. AB, William Jewell Coll., 1948; MDiv, McCormick Theol. Sem., 1951; LHD (hon.), Schiller Coll., Fed. Republic Germany, 1972. Teaching fellow McCormick Theol. Sem., Chgo, 1951-52; pastor First Presbyn. Ch., Brookfield, Ill., 1952-55; editor Presbyn. Bd. Christian Edn., Phila., 1955-67; pres. Nat. Tchr. Edn. Program, Scottsdale, Ariz., 1967-83; prof. Va. Theol. Sem., Alexandria, 1983—; mem. Episc. Ch. task force Christian Edn., 1985-88; assoc. priest, Grace Episcopal Ch., Alexandria; dir. Project for Advancement Ch. Edn., Scottsdate, 1968-70. Author: Teaching Today: The Church's First Ministry, 1980, Teaching for Christian Hearts, Souls, & Minds, 1990; editor: This Generation mag., 1959-65; pub.: Church Teachers, 1973-85, Episcopal Teacher, 1986—; editor in chief Episcopal Children's Curriculum, 1988—. Recipient citation for achievement, William Jewell Coll., 1969, educator of the year, Presbyn. Ch., 1983. Democrat. Avocations: Needlework, gardening. Home: Seminary PO Alexandria VA 22304

BOWMAN, ROBERT WILLIAM, minister; b. San Francisco, Mar. 10, 1947; s. Harold Emmet and Jeanne Suzanne (Klinger) B. BS, U. of State of N.Y., Albany, 1970; ThB, Geneva Theol., 1972; MCEd, Reformed Theol. Sem., 1980, MEd, 1985; STD, Geneva Theol. Sem., 1990. Ordained to ministry Episcopal Ch., 1971, transferred to Presbyn. Ch. in Am., 1982; cert. tchr. elem. and secondary; cert. adminstr. Rector St. Andrew's Episcopal Ch., Savannah, Ga., 1971-78, St. Paul's Episcopal Ch., Jackson, Miss., 1978-80; supply min. Holy Trinity Episcopal, Jacksonville, Fla., 1973-78, Ch. of the Nativity, Memphis, 1981-82; asst. pastor Orangewood Presbyn., Orlando, Fla., 1983-87; adminstr. Orangewood Christian Sch., Orlando, 1983-87; asst. headmaster Northlake Christian Sch., Covington, La., 1980-82; assoc. pastor Ind. Presbyn. Ch., Savannah, Ga., 1987—; trustee Covenant Coll., Lookout Mountain, Ga., 1986-90, 91—; founder, bd. v.p. The Westminster Sch., Savannah, 1989—. Named Citizen of Day City of Savannah, 1977. Mem. Am. Assn. Tchr. French, Assn. Christian Sch. Adminstrs., Nat. Middle Sch. Assn., Nat. Assn. Secondary Sch. Prins., Cen. Ga. Presbytery PCA (chair coms., commns.). Republican. Office: Ind Presbyn Ch PO Box 9266 25 W Oglethorpe Ave Savannah GA 31412

BOWMAN, RODNEY MARTIN, minister; b. Paso Robles, Calif., Feb. 8, 1957; s. Amos Alvin and Reva Faye (Crawshaw) B.; m. Diane Louise Sagert, July 7, 1979; children: Allyson, Kathryn, Andrew. BA in Bible and Theology, San Jose Christian Coll., 1979; MDiv in Pastoral Care and Counseling, Lincoln Christian Sem., 1985. Ordained to ministry Christian Ch., 1979. Assoc. minister Willow Glen Christian Ch., Visalia, Calif., 1979-80; student supply Lincoln (Ill.) Christian Sem., 1980-82; assoc. minister Wapella (Ill.) Christian Ch., 1982-83, Cen. Ch. of Christ, Streator, Ill., 1983-86; sr. minister Petaluma (Calif.) Christian Ch., 1986—; v.p. Streator Area Ministerium, 1985-86; chmn. North Bay Christian Ch. Mins. Assn., 1987-88. Rep. Valley Vista Sch. Site Coun., Petaluma, 1989—. Mem. Petaluma Ministerial Assn. (sec. 1987-88, 89-90, pres. 1988-89). Republican. Home: 1150 Schuman Ln Petluma CA 94952 Office: Petaluma Christian Ch 1160 Schuman Ln Petaluma CA 94952

BOWMAN, WILLIAM MCKINLEY, minister; b. St. George, S.C.; s. Earline and Joseph B.; m. Annie Mae Jones (dec.); children: William McKinley Jr., Joseph Augustus, Beverly Elaine, Audrey Marie. Grad., Morris Coll. Ordained to ministry So. Bapt. Conv., 1938. Pastor So. Bapt. chs., Orangeburg, Cameron, Elloree, Fort Motte, Columbia, S.C., 1938-50, 2d Nazareth Bapt. Ch., Columbia, 1950—; former dir. pub. rels. Bapt. Ednl. and Missionary Conv.; former sec./treas. Interracial Mins. Union; past pres. Bapt. Fellowship S.C.; former v.p. Mount Hebron Progressive Assn.; former mem. Coun. for Black; former pres. Evang. Fellowship, White Bapt. Coop. Mins. S.C.; pres. Gethsemane Bapt. Sunday Sch. Congress; parliamentarian So. Region Progressive Nat. Conv.; former sales mgr. WQXL Christian Radio; former mgr. WOIC Radio. Past pres. Ward 9 Dem. Party; former chmn. OEO for Midlands; former pres. Columbia NAACP; former sec. Morris Coll. Bd. Trustees; former chmn. Emergency Assistance for Richaland Sch. Dist. One; former bd. dirs. Victory Svc. Ctr.; former chmn. adv. bd. Children's Bur. S.C.; chmn. fin. com. Richland County Sch. Dist. One Bd. Commrs., chmn. bd. Mem. Speakers Bur. Nat. Toastmaster Assn, Notary Pub. Assn. Am. Office: 2012 Hydrick St Columbia SC 29203

BOWYER, CHARLES LESTER, chaplain; b. Richwood, W.Va., June 3, 1939; s. Charles Cicero and Delores Irene (Seward) B. BA, Berea (Ky.) Coll., 1961; MDiv, Episcopal Theol. Seminary, Lexington, Ky., 1964; D of Ministry, Grad. Theol. Found. at, Notre Dame, 1991. Ordained to ministry Episcopal Ch. as deacon, 1964, as priest, 1965; lic. alcohol and drug addiction counselor. Curate St. Mary's Episcopal Ch., Big Spring, Tex., 1964-66; vicar St. John's Episcopal Ch., Snyder, Tex., 1966-75; assoc. rector St. Paul's Episcopal Ch., Lubbock, Tex., 1975-84; chaplain and addiction counselor St. Mary of the Plains Hosp., Lubbock, 1986—; sec. Episcopal Diocese of Northwest Tex., Lubbock, exec. com., mem. living and end. commn.; synod del. The Seventh Episcopal Providence. Editor/author: Alcoholism: A Spiritual Disease, 1991. Grad. Theol. Found. fellow. Mem. Tex. Assn. Alcohol and Drug Addiction Counselors, Nat. Assn. Alcohol and Drug Addiction Counselors, Soc. of St. Paul, Delta Phi Alpha. Home: PO Box 98166 Lubbock TX 79499-8166 Office: St Mary of Plains Hospital Dept Pastoral Care 4000 24th St Lubbock TX 79410-1894

BOY, MICHAEL DAVID, minister; b. Westland, Mich., Jan. 19, 1965; s. Hugh Lee Sr. and Nora Belle (Leonard) B.; m. Loida Ruth Drew, Dec. 19, 1987; children: Megan, Elaine, Michael David Jr. BA, Bob Jones U., 1988. Ordained to ministry Bapt. Ch., 1991. Child evangelist Brethern Ch., Greenville, S.C., 1982-84; teen counselor Boys Club, Greenville, 1984-85; children, youth dir. Indepent Bapt. Ch., Penscola, Fla., 1985-86; dir. youth Bapt. Ch., Clinton, S.C., 1986-88; pastor youth Bapt. Ch., Bklyn., 1988-91, Grace Bapt. Ch., Bklyn., 1991—. Leader Boy Scouts Am., Bklyn., 1990-91. Office: Grace Bapt Ch 5224 6th Ave Brooklyn NY 11220

BOYCE, (JAMES) DAVID, clergyman; b. Rancagua, Chile, Jan. 26, 1922; came to U.S., 1924; s. Clarence Robbins and Martha T. (Wilson) B.; m. Margaret Isabella Lee, May 26, 1945; children—Janet L., Martha W., Kathryn S. B.A., Western Res U., 1947; M.Div., New Brunswick Theol. Sem., 1960; S.T.M., N.Y. Theol. Sem., 1972. Ordained to ministry Reformed Ch. in America, 1960. Pastor Fourth Reformed Ch., Somerville, N.J., 1957-62; pastor Community Reformed Ch., Glenmont, N.Y., 1962-69; co-pastor, pastor Reformed Ch. of Newtown, Elmhurst, N.Y., 1969—; mem., com. chmn. Classis of Queens, Reformed Ch. Am., Synod of N.Y.; mem. commn. on evangelization Reformed Ch. in Am., 1984-85, mem. bd. edn., 1964-68; counselor Queens Fedn. Chs. Author sermons, lessons, radio broadcasts, speaker, counselor confs. Vol. clergyman Second Chance Program, Queens County, 1984-85, Jail Visitation Program, Queens, 1970-74; mem. youth com. Community Bd. 4, Queens, 1983-84; mem. bd. A-Way Out Drug Program, Queens, 1973-76. Served to lt. U.S. Army, 1950-53. Democrat. Office: Reformed Church of Newtown 85-15 Broadway Elmhurst NY 11373

BOYCE, SISTER MARY CECELIA, nun, health facility administrator, educator; b. N.Y.C., May 20, 1930; d. William Thomas Sr. and Margaret Mary (Porter) B. EdB, Mary Rogers Coll., Ossining, N.Y., 1954; MSW, Cath. U. Am., 1971. Joined Maryknoll Sisters of St. Dominic, Roman Cath. Ch., 1948. Tchr. Roman Cath. schs. N.Y.C., 1954; missioner to The Philippines and Venezuela, 1954-80; case mgr. outreach to homeless program Over Sixty Health Ctr., Berkeley, Calif., 1989—; with founderess dept. family life edn. Diocese of Tagum, Th Philippines, 1971, Stockton Family Shelter, Diocese of Stockton, Calif., 1981-83. Author: (poetry) Welcome Change With Outstretched Arms, 1990 (Gold award 1991). U.S. Govt. grantee, 1982. Democrat. Office: Over Sixty Health Ctr 1860 Alcatraz Ave Berkeley CA 94507

BOYCE, ROLAND G., minister; b. Portland, Oreg., Feb. 23, 1943; s. Francis Hays and Betty Eloise (Tyler) B.; m. Joyce Ann Saint, Aug. 15, 1969; children: Ryan M., Alana R. BA, Cascade Coll., 1965; MDiv, Western Conservative Theol Sem, 1968. Campus min. Youth for Christ, Campus Life, Portland, Oreg., 1963-70, exec. dir., 1970-75; sr. pastor Milwaukie Covenant Ch., Oreg., 1975-81, Stockton Covenant Ch., Calif., 1981-85, Loveland Covenant Ch., Colo., 1985—; Conf. Christian Edn. Bd. Covenant Ch., Stockton, 1983-84; bd. ministerial standing, Midwest Conf., Loveland, 1988—, front range ministerium pres., 1989—; nat. exec. bd., Bd. Ministerial Standing, Chgo., 1988—; spiritual life com. demon., Chgo., 1989—. Mem. Neighborhood Coun. Com., Milwaukie, 1979-81.

BOYD, GREGORY BRUCE, minister; b. Clovis, N.Mex., July 18, 1959; s. Willis Andrew and Janet Hodgkins (Maher) B.; m. Patricia Ann Gower, May 31, 1986. BA, Auburn U., 1982; MDiv., Mid-Am. Bapt. Theol. Sem., 1989. Ordained to ministry So. Bapt. Conv., 1988. Mission pastor, ch. planter Lakeview Bapt. Ch., Buffalo, 1982-84; youth intern Park Ave. Bapt. Ch., 1984-85; pastor to young adults Grace Community Ch., Memphis, 1988-89; minister of youth and recreation Circle Dr. Bapt. Ch., Colorado Springs, Colo., 1989—; associational dir. youth Pikes Peak So. Bapt. Assn., 1991—. Office: Circle Dr Bapt Ch 801 N Circle Dr Colorado Springs CO 80909

BOYD, JAMES DUNCAN, minister; b. Ft. Lauderdale, Fla., Oct. 10, 1958; s. James Duncan and Pauline Mae (Lawson) B.; m. Nancy Jean Loomis, June 18, 1983; children: Eric Andrew, James Robert, Stephanie Jean. BA, Stetson U., 1980; MDiv, Louisville Presbyn. Sem., 1983; ThD, Trinity Theol. Sem., Newburg, Ind., 1985; cert., Moody Bible Inst., 1989. Ordained to ministry Presbyn. Ch. (U.S.A.), 1983. Assoc. pastor 1st Presbyn. Ch., Royal Oak, Mich., 1983-86; pastor Erin Presbyn. Ch., Roseville, Mich., 1986-91, 1st Presbyn. Ch., Tacoma, Wash., 1991—; del. Gen. Assembly, Kansas City, Mo., 1979; moderator Detroit Presbytery Officer Devel., 1983-86; trustee div. bus. affairs Presbyn. Ch. (U.S.A.), Detroit, 1986-91; bd. dirs. Presbytery Lay Com., Detroit, 1986-90. Mem. Kiwanis (bd. dirs. Royal Oak, Mich. chpt. 1984).

BOYD, JOHN E., ecumenical agency executive. Pres. Atlantic Ecumenical Coun. Chs., Amherst, N.S., Can. Office: Atlantic Ecumenical Coun Chs, 90 Victoria St PO Box 637, Amherst, NS Canada B4H 4B4*

BOYD, JOHN MARVIN, broadcasting executive; b. Pasadena, Calif., Mar. 6, 1943; children: John Matthew, Grace Christina. BA in Oral Communications, U. Redlands, 1966; PhD in Communication, U. So. Calif., 1977. Chmn., chief exec. officer, owner Am. Sunrise Communications, Idyllwild, Calif., 1983—; media rep. Christian Rsch. Inst., San Juan Capistrano, 1977-86, Southwest Radio Ch., Oklahoma City, 1977-86, Billy Graham, Anaheim, Calif., 1985; mem. fin. com. First Bapt. Ch., Huntington Beach, Calif., 1982-89. Producer, writer video series Kingdom of the Cults, 1986 (Angel award 1987), The Gods in Paradise, 1990. Oak Knoll fellow, L.A., 1973; telecommunications scholar RCA, 1973. Mem. Nat. Religious Broadcasters, Theta Alpha Phi, Alpha Epsilon Rho. Republican. Office: Am Sunrise Communications PO Box 1976 Idyllwild CA 92349 *A smile or an occasional thank you can go a long way in generating continuing loyalty and dedication from a subordinate. It's worth the time and effort.*

BOYD, JOSEPH IAN, minister, editor, educator; b. Jan. 23, 1935, Can.; s. John Albert and Thyrza Jean (McManus) B. B.A., Sask., U., 1956; M.A., Toronto U., 1966; Ph.D., Aberdeen U., 1970. Ordained priest Roman Catholic Ch., 1963. Priest Congregation of Priests of St. Basil, Toronto, 1963—; prof. English lit. St. Thomas More Coll., U. Sask., Saskatoon, Can., 1974-86. Author: The Novels of G.K. Chesterton, 1975; editor Chesterton Rev. Home: St Thomas More Coll, 1437 College Dr, Saskatoon, SK Canada S7N 0W6

BOYD, JULIA MARGARET (MRS. SHELTON B. BOYD), lay church worker; b. Newton Grove, N.C., Mar. 7, 1921; d. Isaiah and Mary Lela (Blackman) Tart; m. Shelton Bickett Boyd, Feb. 21, 1944; children: Mary (Mrs. Edward Southerland III), Deborah (Mrs. John Wayne Pearson). BS, East Carolina U., 1942. V.p. WSCS, Lillington (N.C.) U. Meth. Ch., 1948-49; pres. WSCS, 1st United Meth. Ch., Mt. Olive, N.C., 1951-55, 59-61, sec. various coms., from 1950, mem., sec. adminstrv. bd. and coun. ministries, from 1955, mem. local work area on edn., 1960-82, chmn., 1971-75, chmn. spiritual growth, 1971-75, mem. fin. com., 1985-87, 90—; counselor United Meth. Youth Fellowship, 1960-67; adult del. Nat. Convocation Meth. Youth, 1964; pres. Goldsboro dist. United Meth. Women, 1955-59; mem. N.C. Conf. Bd. Edn., 1964-72; mem. N.C. Coun. on Youth Ministries, 1964-82, chmn., 1972-76; mem. adult staff youth, sr. high mins., 1962-81; mem. N.C. Conf. Coun. on Ministries, 1970-76; mem. Goldsboro dist. Coun. on Ministries, 1970—, sec., 1971—; also coord. youth ministries Goldsboro dist., 1964-82; del. SEJ Youth Conf., Arlington, Va., 1976, SEJ Leadership Devel. Workshop, Lake Junaluska, 1977; lay rep., Goldsboro coun. Conf. Coun. on Ministries, 1972-76, 82—, ann. conf. United Meth. Ch., 1985, 87, 90; rep. N.C. Christian, advocate N.C. Christian Advocate, 1985—. Editor Meth. Messenger, 1965-68. Pres. PTA, Mt. Olive, 1955-56, Mt. Olive High Sch. and So. Wayne High Sch. Band Patron's Club, 1964-66; leader Girl Scouts U.S.A., 1956-57; active Community Chest. Named Lay Person of Yr. N.C. Conf. United Meth. Ch., 1979, (with husband) Outstanding Sr. Citizens of Mt. Olive, 1990; recipient cert. appreciation United Meth. Youth Fellowship, 1980, 83. Mem. Women's Aux. of N.C. Pharm. Assn. (corr. sec. 1976-77, rec. sec. 1977-78, 2d v.p. 1978-79, 1st v.p. 1979-80, pres. 1980-81, mem. nominating com. 1988—, mins. com. 1988-89, hospitality com. 1989), United Meth. Women (mem. hist. com. Goldsboro dist. 1984, chairperson 1989, v.p. local chpt. 1988-89), So. Wayne Country Club. Home: 400 W Main St Mount Olive NC 28365

BOYD, KENNETH JAMES, minister; b. Ashland, Ohio, Jan. 15, 1935; s. James Donald and Doris Elverda (Casto) B.; m. Lonah Burton, Mar. 16, 1957; children: James Jerry, Mark Arthur, Shawn David. Student, Berean Bible Coll., Springfield, Mo., 1984-89. Ordained to ministry Freewill Bapt. Ch., 1987. Evangelist Assemblies of God Jail Ministry, Columbus, Ohio, 1981-87; pastor Good Shepherd Freewill Bapt. Ch., Lockbourne, Ohio, 1987—; lt. Franklin County Sheriff's Dept., Columbus, 1969—; acting chaplain Franklin County Sheriff's Dept., 1983—. Inventor posident system, 1978. With USAF, 1952-62. Recipient medal of Merit Franklin County Sheriff's Dept., 1977, Merit award, Cen. Ohio Prison Assn., 1987, 89. Mem. FOP, VFW, Moose. Home: 5370 Sherry Ct Columbus OH 43232 Office: Good Shepherd Freewill Bapt 9784 Pic-Way Rd Lockbourne OH 43137 *In this life on earth we are constantly faced with two choices, good or evil. The more you choose good, the less evil appears.*

BOYD, KEVIN ROBERT, clergyman; b. Pitts., Feb. 11, 1955; s. Robert and Valjean Delores (Stiffler) B.; m. Barbara Jane Pickens, June 11, 1977; children: Diana, Robert. BA in Religion, Westminster Coll., 1977; MDiv, Louisville Presbyn. Sem., 1982. Ordained to ministry Presbyn. Ch. (U.S.A.), 1981. Pastor First Presbyn. Ch., Hartford City, Ind., 1982-89, Trinity Presbyn. Ch., Ft. Wayne, Ind., 1989—; cantor, song leader 197th Gen. Assembly Presbyn. Ch. U.S.A., Indpls., 1985; ch. devel. chair Whitewater Valley Presbytery, P.C., Indpls., 1984-90; pres. bd. dirs. United Ministries, Ball State U., Muncie, Ind., 1987-89; del. 198th Gen. Assembly Presbyn. Ch., Mpls., 1986. Bd. dirs. Blackford United Way, Inc., Hartford City, Ind., 1982-85; dir. Hartford City Heritage Days, Inc., 1986-87. Recipient Mayor's award City Coun., Hartford City, 1988. Mem. Kiwanis (dir. 1983-86). Home: 6214 Heritage Oaks Pl Fort Wayne IN 46835 Office: Trinity Presbyn Ch 9600 St Joe Rd Fort Wayne IN 46835-9774 *The church's challenge as it moves into the twenty-first century is to assert relevance. Not adopting the dominant culture as proper, but to bring the discernment of faith to the realities of actual living. Only as we address real people and their lives will the church remain an influential part of our culture. Only as we encounter real people and their lives will we be an authentic reflection of the ministry of Jesus.*

BOYD, MALCOLM, minister, author; b. Buffalo, June 8, 1923; s. Melville and Beatrice (Lowrie) B. B.A., U. Ariz., 1944; B.D., Ch. Div. Sch. Pacific, 1954; postgrad., Oxford (Eng.) U., 1955; S.T.M., Union Theol. Sem., N.Y.C., 1956. Ordained to ministry Episcopal Ch., 1955. V.p., gen. mgr. Pickford, Rogers & Boyd, 1949-51; rector in Indpls., 1957-59; chaplain Colo. State U., 1959-61, Wayne State U., 1961-65; nat. field rep. Episcopal Soc. Cultural and Racial Unity, 1965-68; resident fellow Calhoun Coll., Yale U., 1968-71, assoc. fellow, 1971—; writer-priest in residence St. Augustine-by-the Sea Episcopal Ch., 1982—; lectr. World Council Chs., Switzerland, 1955, 64; columnist Pitts. Courier, 1962-65; resident guest Mishkenot Sha'ananim, Jerusalem, 1974; chaplain AIDS Commn. Episcopal Diocese L.A., 1989—. Host: TV spl. Sex in the Seventies, CBS-TV, Los Angeles, 1975; author: Crisis in Communication, 1957, Are You Running with Me, Jesus?, 1965, rev. 25th anniversary edit., 1990, Free to Live, Free to Die, 1967, Book of Days, 1968, As I Live and Breathe: Stages of an Autobiography, 1969, Human Like Me, Jesus, 1971, The Lover, 1972, When in the Course of Human Events, 1973, The Runner, 1974, The Alleluia Affair, 1975, Christian, 1975, Am I Running with You, God?, 1977, Take Off the Masks, 1978, Look Back in Joy, 1981, rev. edit., 1990, Half Laughing, Half Crying, 1986, Gay Priest: An Inner Journey, 1986; plays Boy, 1961, Study in Color, 1962, The Community, 1964, others; editor: On the Battle Lines, 1964, The Underground Church, 1968, Amazing Grace: Stories of Gay and Lesbian Faith, 1991; book reviewer: Los Angeles Times.; contbr. articles to numerous mags. including Newsday, Parade, Modern Maturity, also newspapers. Active voter registration, Miss., Ala., 1963, 64; mem. Los Angeles City/County AIDS Task Force. Malcolm Boyd Collection and Archives established Boston U., 1973; Recipient Integrity Internat. award, 1978; Union Am. Hebrew Congregations award, 1980. Mem. Nat. Council Chs. (film awards com. 1965), P.E.N. (pres. Los Angeles chpt. 1984-87), Am. Center, Authors Guild, Integrity, Nat. Gay Task Force, Clergy and Laity Concerned (nat. bd.), NAACP, Amnesty Internat., Episc. Peace Fellowship, Fellowship of Reconciliation (nat. com.). Address: 1227 4th St Santa Monica CA 90401 *The years have taught me the cost of getting involved in life. It is all a risk. One is on stage in an ever-new set without a script. The floor may give way without warning, the walls abruptly cave in. One may die at the hand of an assassin acting on blind impulse. Security, for which men sell their souls, is one of the few real jests in life. Yet the cost of not getting involved in life is higher; one has merely died prematurely. When one has stripped power of its mystique, its robes and artifices, it becomes vulnerable. When you stand up to power, you stand up to one or more individuals. Look an individual, then, in the eye, laugh, if you feel like it. This may be rightly received as a much-needed expression of human solidarity.*

BOYD, MILES FARRIS, minister; b. Memphis, July 19, 1953; s. Miles Farris and Ruth (Gamble) Boyd; m. Sandra Long Boyd, Dec. 17, 1977; children: Miles III, Matthew. Student, Memphis State U., 1971-74; BS, Union U., 1976; MDiv, Southwestern Bapt. Sem., 1979, D. Ministry, 1990. Ordained to ministry So. Bapt. Ch. Pastor New Prospect Bapt. Ch., Olive Branch, Miss., 1979-81, Blvd. Bapt. Ch., Memphis, 1982-88, North Trenholm Bapt. Ch., Columbia, S.C., 1988—; mem. religion adv. bd. Union U., Jackson, Tenn., 1987-88, Charleston (S.C.) So. U., 1990—; mem. jour. com. Tenn. Bapt. Convention, Nashville, 1985-88; chmn. Memphis ACTS Newtork, 1987. Author seminar Tng. in Ecclesiology, 1989. Named Chaplian of Day, Memphis City Coun., 1983, Hon. Dep. Sheriff, Shelby County (Tenn.), 1984. Mem. Columbia Metro Assn. (pres. com. 1989—, chmn. orgn. study com. 1989—). Home: 100 Silver Crest Columbia SC 29223 Office: North Trenholm Bapt Ch 6515 N Trenholm Rd Columbia SC 29206

BOYD, MURRAY MIDDLETON, pastor; b. Abilene, Tex., Nov. 29, 1934; s. Vesta Earl and Ima Oleta (Jordan) B.; m. Barbara Ann Humphreys, Aug. 2, 1953; children: Phyllis Jean, Charlotte Ann, Edmund Earl. BA, Hardin-Simmons U., 1956; MDiv, Golden Gate Bapt. Theol. Sem., Mill Valley, Calif., 1964. Ordained to ministry So. Bapt. Conv., 1957. Pastor First Bapt. Ch., Ripon, Calif., 1957-59, Clements, Calif., 1963-64; pastor Sierra Heights Bapt. Ch., Fresno, Calif., 1964-70, Immanuel Bapt. Ch., Ridgecrest, Calif., 1970-77, Cen. Bapt. Ch., Aurora, Colo., 1977-84, Grace Christian Fellowship, Aurora, 1984—; trustee Golden Gate Bapt. Sem., Mill Valley, 1977-84; bd. dirs. Fulness Mag., Ft. Worth, 1978-89. Contbr. articles to profl. jour. Mem. Kiwanis (v.p. 1972). Office: Grace Christian Fellowship 14100 E Jewell Ave #29 Aurora CO 80012

BOYD, ROBERT FRIEND, JR., evangelist; b. Jacksonville, N.C., Mar. 21, 1954; s. Robert F. and Sara (Miller) B.; m. Mallory Burkett, July 24, 1982; children: Robert F. III, Benjamin P., William L. BS, Coll. William and Mary, 1976; ThM, Dallas Theol. Sem., 1983. Pastor New Faith United Meth. Ch., Schuyler, Va., 1983-85; evangelist Bob Boyd Speaking Ministry div. Campus Crusade of Christ, Doraville, Ga., 1985—. Author: (booklet) The New Life, 1983, Bob Boyd Campus Manual, 1989. Mem. Dallas Sem. Alumni Assn. (v.p. 1990-91), Dallas 7 Group (founder 1980—). Republican. Home and Office: 617 Barefoot Dr Wilmore KY 40390 *The most exciting adventure in my life is having an intimate relationship with the living God through Jesus Christ. When I was broken, He made me whole—and gave me His love for those who are hurting.*

BOYD, ROBERT THOMPSON, minister, ministry educator; b. Charlotte, N.C., Dec. 8, 1914; s. Robert Thompson and Frances (Little) B.; m. Peggy Tuffy, Jan. 15, 1942. BA in Bibl. Edn., Washington Bible Coll., 1958; MDiv., Antietam Bible Sem., 1988, D. Ministry, 1989; DD (hon.), Indian Orthodox Ch., Madras, India, 1954. Ordained to ministry Bapt. Ch., 1942. Pastor Colerain Bapt. Ch., Kirkwood, Pa., 1941-44, Denbigh Bapt. Ch., Newport News, Va., 1944-56, Conklin (N.Y.) Ctr. Bapt. Ch., 1956-60; tchr. Bible conf. Evang. Bible Ministries, U.S., Can., 1961—; summer sch. prof. Antietam Bible Sem., Hagerstown, Md.; lectr. bibl. archaeology; spl. rep. World Radio Missionary Fellowship, Sta. HCJB, Quito, Ecuador; former program coord. Sandy Cove Bible Conf. of North East Md., former head cassette ministry. Author: A Pictorial Guide to Biblical Archaeology, 1969, Boyd's Bible Handbook, 1983, Scientific Facts in the Bible, 1983; contbg. editor Archaeology and Bibl. Rsch. Active in radio and TV ministry Sta. WNBF-TV, Binghamton, N.Y.; radio broadcaster over Sta. HCJB, Quito, Sta. KCRM, Pusan, Republic Korea, Sta. HOXO, Panama City, Panama. Named Alumnus of Yr., Washington Bible Coll., 1978; recipient Alumnus Award in Communications, Phila. Coll. Bible, 1989. Republican. Avocations: photography, Near East traveling, Bibl. archaeology. Home: 1712 Academy St Scranton PA 18504 Office: Evang Bible Ministries 1712 Academy St Scranton PA 18504

BOYD, SANDRA HUGHES, priest, librarian; b. Council Bluffs, Iowa, Dec. 29, 1938; d. Floyd Earl and Elizabeth Jane (Sturtevant) Hughes; m. J. Hayden Boyd, Dec. 28, 1963 (div. 1984); children: Jane Elizabeth, Anne Marie. BA, Colo. Coll., 1961; MALS, U. Minn., 1966; MDiv, Episcopal Divinity Sch., 1978. Ordained priest Episcopal Ch., 1979. Lay leader various Episcopal chs., Columbus, Ohio, Rochester, N.Y., Arlington, Va. and Troy, Mich., 1966-76; parish assoc. Christ Ch., Cambridge, Mass., 1978-86; interim rector St. John's Ch., Charlestown, Mass., 1983-84; parish assoc. St. Barnabas Ch., Denver, 1991—; libr. pub. svcs. Regis U., Denver, 1990—; mem. adj. faculty, libr. Episcopal Divinity Sch., Cambridge, 1978-86; bd. dirs. , v.p., editor Episcopal Women's History Project, N.Y.C., 1981—; dir. Deaconess History Project, 1983-88. Editor: Cultivating Our Roots, 1984; co-author: Women in American Religious History, 1986. Mem. Am. Acad. Religion, Am. Theol. Libr. Assn. Office: Regis U 3333 Regis Blvd Denver CO 80221-1099

BOYD, STEPHEN BLAKE, religion educator; b. Bluefield, W. Va., Feb. 10, 1954; s. Donald Early and Maxine Thompson (Dickerson) B. BA, U. Tenn., 1976; MDiv, Harvard U., 1979, ThD, 1984. Asst. to assoc. prof. Wake Forest U., Winston-Salem, N.C., 1985-90; assoc. prof. Wake Forest U., 1990—; vis. asst. prof. Colgate U., Hamilton, N.Y., 1984-85; asst. pastor Met. Bapt. Ch., Cambridge, Mass., 1979-82. Recipient Reid-Doyle prize for Excellence in Teaching, Wake Forest U., 1990, rsch. grant Deutscher Akademische Austauschdiensa, Fed. Republic of Germany, 1986; travel to collections NEH, 1986. Mem. Men's Studies Assn. (steering com. 1989—), Am. Soc. Ch. History, Am. Acad. Religion, Am. Soc. Reformation Rsch., Nat. Assn. Bapt. Profs. of Religion, Sixteenth Century Studies Conf. Democrat. Avocations: reading, bicycling, Civil War history, drawing. Home: 5084 Hutchins St Winston-Salem NC 27106 Office: Wake Forest U Dept Religion PO Box 7212 Renolds Sta Winston-Salem NC 27109

BOYD, WILLIAM ALLEN, minister; b. Birmingham, Ala., May 17, 1957; s. Allen and Maggie (Jones) B.; m. Diane Lenell McDonald, May 19, 1990. Student, Hampton (Va.) Inst., 1975-78, Chgo. Bapt. Inst., 1990—. Ordained to ministry Bapt. Ch., 1986. Dir. Clothing Care Ctr., Pacific Garden Mission, Chgo., 1985-88, Antioch Ctr. for World Mission, Chgo., 1987—; exec. dir. Mins. Conf. S. Cook County, Dixmoor, Ill., 1988-90; assoc. min. Bethlehem Temple Missionary Bapt. Ch., Harvey, Ill., 1989—; ednl. svcs. rep. Chicago Tribune, Chgo., 1990—; coord. entrepreneurial devel. Factions United to Unveil Resources thru Edn. Orgn., Harvey, 1988—; mem. speakers bur. Chicago Tribune, 1991—. Mem. United Rep. Fund Ill., Chgo., 1986—, Ill. Black Rep. Coun., Chgo., 1986—, Rep. Nat. Com., Washington, 1989—; bd. dirs. Ctr. Polit. Edn. and Rsch., Chgo., 1990—. Named to Forum of Disting. Ams., Birmingham, 1975. Mem. Internat. Ministerial Fellowship, S. Suburban Mins. Conf., Mins. Conf. S. Cook County, Alpha Phi Alpha (nat. bd. dirs. 1981-82). Home: 15430 S Loomis Harvey IL 60426 Office: Chicago Tribune 777 W Chicago Ave Chicago IL 60610 *Tenacity, always tenacity. Without it, undergirded by faith, all our greatest efforts are defeated. The pursuit of excellence can only be realized through perseverance and tenacity.*

BOYER, HARRY STARR, lay worker; b. Williamsport, Pa., Feb. 24, 1950; s. James Calvin and Helen Elisabeth (Starr) B.; m. Karen Norita Smith, July 1, 1972; children: Heather Ann, Mark Allen, Aaron Christopher. BS, Pa. State U., 1972. Cert. tchr., Pa. Youth leader, coord. Community Bapt. Ch., Montoursville, Pa., 1974-85, elder, coord., 1974-81, Christian edn. coord., 1981-84, treas., deacon, 1986—; tchr. Montoursville Area Sch. Dist., 1972—. Chmn. Upper Fairfield Twp. Zoning Hearing Bd., Montoursville, 1987—. Mem. Tech. Edn. Assn. Pa., Pa. Assn. Student Assistance Profls. Republican. Home: RD 4 Box 452 Montoursville PA 17754 Office: Community Bapt Ch 900 Loyalsock Ave Montoursville PA 17754

BOYER, RICHARD DONALD, minister; b. Pa., June 13, 1957; s. Donald Christian and Nancy Jane (Bowyer) B.; m. Rita Louise Mancha, Sept. 15, 1979; 1 child, Jared Paul. AB, Grove City Coll., 1979; MDiv, Pitts. Theol. Sem., 1982. Ordained to ministry Presbyn. Ch. U.S.A., 1982. Assoc. pastor Bethlehem Parish/Parish Outreach Program, Fredericktown, Pa., 1982-85; pastor 1st Presbyn. Ch., Finleyville, Pa., 1985—; chmn. evangelism com. Washington Presbytery, Eighty Four, Pa., 1987-88, Synod of Trinity, Camp Hill, Pa., 1989-90. Bd. dirs. Ctr. for Family Peace, Finleyville, 1988-90; bd. dirs. Hospice Care, Inc., Waynesburg, Pa., 1988—, v.p., 1991. Mem. Finleyville Area C. of C. (mem. steering com. 1990-91). Home: 5204 Lew St Finleyville PA 15332 Office: 1st Presbyn Ch 3595 Washington Ave Finleyville PA 15332 *People will give of themselves far beyond normal expectations if there is a clear sense of vision and purpose to their work.*

BOYER, WAYNE WENDELL, clergyman; b. Beloit, Wis., Mar. 15, 1941; s. James Wendell and Elizabeth Maria (Soderberg) B.; m. Lorna Kay Gohl, Aug. 3, 1963; children: Kristin Kay, Stephen Wayne, Andrew James. BA, Wheaton (Ill.) Coll., 1963; MDiv, Bethel Sem., St. Paul, 1969. Ordained to ministry Evang. Ch., 1969. Youth pastor Immanuel Community Ch., St. Paul, 1965-68; pastor Bethel Ch., Farmer City, Ill., 1969-71; sr. pastor Faircreek Ch., Dayton, Ohio, 1971—; chmn. bd. trustees United World Mission, Union Mills, N.C., 1970—; bd. dirs. WFCJ-FM, Miamisburg, Ohio, 1985—. Chaplain Dayton Fire Dept., 1985—. Mem. Nat. Assn. Evangelicals, Am. Assn. Fire Chaplains, OHio Nat. Assn. Evangelicals (bd. dirs. 1985—). Republican. Office: Faircreek Ch 51 Best St Dayton OH 45405

BOYERS, CAROL ANN, lay church worker, elementary school educator; b. Fairmont, W.Va., May 1, 1948; d. James Lester Whitecotton and Della Mary (Pyles) Sole; m. Jerry Dean Boyers, May 30, 1970; children: Melissa Ann, Christina Lynn. AB, Fairmont State Coll., 1970; MA, W.Va. U., 1977. Cert. tchr., grades 1-9, W.Va.; cert. in doctrine and catechetics, Wheeling, Charleston. Religion tchr. Fairmont (W.Va.) Cath. Sch., 1980—, religion coord., grades K-8, 1986—; lay min. Immaculate Conception Parish, Fairmont, 1986—. Mem. Internat. Reading Assn., Nat. Assn. Student Activity Advisors, Cath. Sch. Educators (Wheeling Diocese), W.Va. Univ. Alumni Assn., KC, Eagles Club, Elks, Sigma Alpha Iota. Democrat. Roman Catholic. Home: 1408 Briarwood Ln Fairmont WV 26554 Office: Fairmont Cath Grade Sch 416 Madison St Fairmont WV 26554

BOYERS, MATTHEW ERIN, program director; b. Wauseon, Ohio, Mar. 11, 1959; s. Jerry Lee and Janeth Marie (Slagle) B.; m. Lanita Jean King, May 18, 1979; children: Luke Brandon, Nicholas Michael. BS, Purdue U., 1981; M in Religious Edn., Trinity Sem. Lay youth advisor West Lafayette, Ind., 1980-81, youth dir., 1983—; lay youth advisor Wauseon, 1981-83. Contbr. articles to profl. jours. Republican. Avocations: golf, woodworking, sports, reading. Home: 408 Evergreen St West Lafayette IN 47906 Office: Covenant Presbyn Ch 211 Knox Dr West Lafayette IN 47906

BOYES, GLENN MERVIN, minister, educator; b. Owen Sound, Ont., Can., Jan. 24, 1955; s. Mervin Edwin and Dorothy Margaret (Filsinger) B.; m. Beverly Jean Francey, Sept. 3, 1977 (dec. Aug. 1991); children: Ehren, Kristen. BA in Philosophy, U. Regina, 1977; MDiv, Can. Theol. Sem., 1980. Ordained to ministry Missionary Ch., 1982. Clergyman; clergy Missionary Ch., Listowel, Ont., 1980-82; part-time prof. Emmanuel Bible Coll., Kitchener, Ont., 1981-83, prof., 1983—. Mem. Evang. Theol. Soc., Evang. Fellowship of Can. Home: 49 Betzner Ave N, Kitchener, ON Canada N2H 3B8 Office: Emmanuel Bible Coll, 100 Fergus Ave, Kitchener, ON Canada N2A 2H2

BOYKIN, GLENDA DARNELL, worship leader; b. Buffalo, Tex., Dec. 18, 1944; d. Jesse James and Lucy Marie (Gore) S.; children: Donald Allan, Victor Bradley, Brandy Layne. Youth leader, 1981-85, Sunday sch. tchr., 1981—, praise and worship leader, 1983—, prison outreach chapel svcs., 1987—; mgr., designer Buffalo (Tex.) Flower Basket, 1979—; praise leader, counselor Free Indeed Ministries, Madisonville, Tex., 1989—. V.p. Buffalo C. of C., 1986; bd. dirs. Road Home Ministries, Buffalo, 1986—; soloist, hon. mem. A.A.R.P., Buffalo, 1987—. Home: 307 S Center St Buffalo TX 75831

BOYLAN, BRIAN RICHARD, author, theologian, philosopher, director; b. Chgo., Dec. 11, 1936, s. Francis Thomas and Mary Catherine (Kane) B.; children: Rebecca, Gregory, Ingrid. Student Loyola U., 1954-58; DD, Universal Ch., 1969. Editor Jour. AMA, Med. World News, The Statesman, 1956-64; author: The New Heart, 1969; Infidelity, 1971; Benedict Arnold: The Dark Eagle, 1973; A Hack in a Hurry, 1980; Final Trace, 1983, Torquemada's The Name, Heresy 's the Game, 1989; works include 14 books, 3 plays, 2 screenplays; photographer, 1966—; theatre dir., 1970—; works include 31 plays, videotapes and films. Home: 1530 S 6th St Minneapolis MN 55454 *Perhaps the most influential words that have since guided my ministry were spoken by a failed classical scholar whom I had just helped rescue from a substance-abuse suicide attempt: "Life today resembles the Cloaca Maxima of ancient Rome. What you get out of it depends entirely on what you put in."*

BOYLE, JOHN PHILLIPS, priest; b. Iowa City, Iowa, Aug. 23, 1931; s. Clement A. and Marie Elizabeth (Phillips) B. Student, U. Iowa, 1949-50; BA, St. Ambrose Coll., Davenport, Iowa, 1953; STB, STL, Gregorian U., Rome, 1955, 57; PhD, Fordham U., N.Y.C., 1972. Ordained priest Roman Cath. Ch., 1956. Instr. Assumption High Sch., Davenport, 1957-64; mng. editor The Cath. Messenger, Davenport, 1964-67; assoc. prof. Sch. Religion, U. Iowa, Iowa City, 1972—, dir., 1979-89. Trustee Mt. St. Clare Coll., Clinton, Iowa, 1988—. Mem. Cath. Theol. Sem. Am. (pres. 1988-89), Soc. Christian Ethics (dir. 1980-84, vice chmn., sr. dir. 1991—), Am. Acad. Religion, Coun. Soc. for Study Religion. Office: Sch Religion U Iowa Iowa City IA 52242-1376

BOYLES, (CAROL) ANN, English literature educator, lay religious worker; b. Charlottetown, P.E.I., Can., May 11, 1954; d. Freeman William and Eva Frances (Ayers) B.; m. (Ivan) Stephen Gouthro, Sept. 1, 1985. BA, U. P.E.I., 1976; BEd, Dalhousie U., Can., 1977; MA, U. N.B., Can., 1983, PhD, 1987. Mem. Spiritual Assembly Bahá'ís of Charlottetown, 1973-76, 79-80; asst. to mem. aux. bd., 1980-81; exec. asst. to sec. Nat. Spiritual Assembly of Bahá'ís of Can., 1985-86; mng. editor Bahá'í Can. Publs., 1985-88; mem. Spiritual Assembly of Bahá'ís of Halifax, N.S., Can., 1989-91, asst. to mem. aux. bd., 1989-91; mem. Auxiliary Bd. of Continental Bd. of Counsellors for Protection and Propagation of Bahá '289 Faith in the Americas, 1991—; asst. prof. English Dalhousie U., Halifax, 1991—. Author: (play) the Passing of Exquisite Music: A One-Woman Play about Martha Root, 1988 (Creative Writing award Assn. for Bahá'í Studies 1989). mem. organizing com. Toronto (Can.) Interfaith Peace Festival, 1986; del. Commonwealth Conf. for Young Leaders, Ottawa, Can., 1987. Mem. Assn. for Bahá'í Studies (exec. com., editorial bd. 1987—). Home: 6253 Duncan St, Halifax, NS Canada B3L 1K4

BOYTE, ROBERT HOWARD, minister; b. Oklahoma City, Aug. 18, 1930; s. Herbert Ray and Mozelle Charlsie (French) B.; m. Barbara Ann Stout, Dec. 27, 1957; children: Kelly Boyte Peters, Edward Lee, David Mitchell. BA, Tex. Christian U., 1952, MA, 1953; MDiv, Vanderbilt U., 1956. Ordained to ministry Christian Ch. (Disciples of Christ), 1956. Assoc. min. 1st Christian Ch., Bartleville, Okla., 1956-65; sr. min. 1st Christian Ch., Pittsburg, Kans., 1965-71, Cen. Woodward Christian Ch., Troy, Mich., 1976-87, 1st Christian Ch., Decatur, Ga., 1987—; assoc. ecumenical officer Coun. on Christian Unity, Indpls., 1971-76; bd. dirs. Christian Communication Coun., Detroit, 1976-86, Bd. of Ch. Extension, Indpls., 1990—. Co-author: Spiritual Growth in the Congregation, 1988. Mem. human rights com. City of Pittsburg, 1968-71. Recipient Ch. Svc. award Christian Communication Coun., 1987. Office: 1st Christian Ch 601 W Ponce de Leon Decatur GA 30030 *One of my professors had this saying taped to the door of his office, to be seen by visitors as they left: "There is no adequate defense, except stupidity, against the impact of a new idea."*

BOZEMAN, THEODORE DWIGHT, American religious history educator; b. Gainesville, Fla.; m. Hannelore I. Wagner, June 29, 1973. BA, Eckerd Coll., 1964; BD, Union Theol. Sem., N.Y.C., 1968; ThM, Union Sem., Richmond, Va., 1970; PhD, Duke U., 1974. Instr. U. Iowa, Iowa City, 1974-75, asst. prof., 1975-79, assoc. prof., 1979-89, prof., 1989—. Author: Protestants in an Age of Science, 1978, To Live Ancient Lives, 1988; editorial bd. Am. Intellectual History Newsletter, 1987—. NEH Class A fellow, 1982. Mem. Am. Soc. Ch. History, Orgn. Am. Historians, Am. Acad. Religion (editorial bd. Jour. Am. Acad. Religion 1976-83). Office: U Iowa Sch Religion Iowa City IA 52245

BRAATEN, MARK HENDRICKS, minister; b. Virginia, Minn., Apr. 19, 1955; s. LaVerne Alvin and Lucille Carol (Hendrickson) B.; m. Karen Marie Pirner, May 23, 1987; 1 child, Amber Ashley. BA, Augsburg Coll., 1977; MDiv, Luther Northwestern Theol. Sem, 1981. Ordained to ministry Luth. Ch., 1981. Pastor St. Paul and Trinity Luth. Ch., Augusta, Ky., 1981-85, Atonement Luth. Ch., Boulder, Colo., 1985-88, Our Savior Luth. Ch., Alamogordo, N.Mex., 1988—; chaplain Meadowview Community Hosp., Maysville, Ky., 1981-84, U. Ky. Med. Ctr., Lexington, 1983-84, Boulder Community Hosp., 1985-88, Police Chaplains, Alamogorao, 1988—. Mem. Alamogordo Ministerial Alliance (sec. 1990). Office: Our Savior Luth Ch 1212 Washington Ave Alamogordo NM 88310

BRACEY, COOKIE FRANCES LEE, minister; b. Phila., Mar. 14, 1945; d. John Daniels and Evelyn (Jarvis) Bracey. B in Social Work, Temple U., 1983; MDiv, Wesley Theol. Sem., 1990. Administrv. asst. United Meth. Ch., Phila., 1963-86, parish community devel., 1984-86; local pastor United Meth. Ch., Catonsville, Ellicott City, Md., 1986-90; champlain Meth. Hosp., Phila., 1990—; pastor St. Luke Snyder Ave United Meth. Ch., Phila., 1990—; missionary Brazil, 1988, Costa Rica, 1989. Mem. Multi-Cultural Task Force, Phila. 1980, Victims & Crime Task Force. Recipient Outstanding Clergywoman award Nat. Assn. Clergywomen, 1990. Mem. Temple Univ. Soc. Adminstrn. Alumni Assn., Nat. Fellowship Local. Democrat. Avocations: music, opera, historical researcher, board games, traveling. Home: 1419 W Cayuga St PO Box 9756 Philadelphia PA 19140

BRACHLOW, STEPHEN JOHN, religion educator, minister; b. Mpls., Aug. 17, 1947; s. Calvin John and Leona Esther (Seidenkranz) B.; m. Dixie Walker, June 19, 1970; children: Andrew, Allison. BSc, Moorhead (Minn.) State Coll., 1969; MDiv, Bethel Theol. Sem., St. Paul, 1973; postgrad., Ruschlikon Bapt. Sem., Zurich, Switzerland, 1973-74; DPhil, Oxford (Eng.) U., 1978. Ordained to ministry N.Am. Bapt. Conf., 1979. Asst. prof., then assoc. prof. ch. history N.Am. Bapt. Sem., Sioux Falls, S.D., 1978-84, prof. ch. history and Christian spirituality, 1985—; assoc. prof. ch. history Ea. Bapt. Sem., Phila., 1984-85; asst. min. adult edn. 1st Presbyn. Ch., Sioux Falls, 1988—; speaker West Africa Bapt. Missionary Conf., Cameroon, 1985; lectr. seminar on Christian spirituality, Tsu, Japan, 1987; mem. European Bapt. Congress, Budapest, Hungary, 1989, gen. coun. meetings Bapt. World Alliance, Zagreb, Yugoslavia, 1989; presenter papers at profl. meetings. Author: The Communion of Saints: Radical Puritan and Separatist Ecclesiology, 1570-1625, 1988; contbr. articles and book revs. to profl. jours. Mem. steering com. for regional conf. Peace and the Arms Race, Sioux Falls, 1980, 83. Mem. Am. Soc. Ch. History, Inst. for Christian Spirituality, Conf. on Faith and History, Sixteenth Century Studies Conf., Bapt. Peace Fellowship N.Am. (bd. dirs. 1986-91). Office: NAm Bapt Sem 1321 W 22d St Sioux Falls SC 57105

BRACK, RON KEVIN, minister; b. Port Arthur, Tex., Apr. 8, 1960; s. Coy and Anabel Norene (Fillyaw) B.; m. Betsy Luanne Petrea, July 12, 1986; 1 child, Taylor Quinton. Student, Lamar U., 1978-80; B in Youth Ministry, East Tex. Bapt. U., 1988. Ordained to ministry Bapt. Ch., 1989. Min. to youth First Bapt. Ch., Kountze, Tex., summer 1984; assoc. pastor to students Waller Bapt. Ch., Bossier City, La., 1985—; asst. dean La. Super Summer Bapt. Conv., Alexandria, summer 1988; mem. planning com. La. Youth Evangelism Conf., Alexandria, 1989. Mem. N.W. La. Bapt. Assn. (pres. and youth min. 1988—, assn. youth com. 1985-88, bd. dirs. 1985—, mem. exec. bd. coun. 1988—), N.W. La. Bapt. Youth Min. Assn. (pres. 1988—), Nat. Network of Youth Mins. Home: 2601 Airline Dr # 213 Bossier City LA 71111 Office: Waller Bapt Ch 456 Waller Ave Bossier City LA 71112

BRACKEN, JAMES DONALD, minister; b. Phila., July 15, 1934; s. Guy Clark and Dolores Bertha (Fite) B.; m. Isabel Robinson Boyd, Nov. 24, 1956; children: Debra Lee, Michael James, Linda Jean. BS in Bus. Mgmt., Fla. State U., 1959. Ordained to ministry Mission Ch., 1971. Founder, exec. dir. Mission-Teens, Inc., Runnemede, N.J., 1969—, Mission Ch., Runnemede, 1974—. Trustee Come Alive Ministries, Medford, N.J., 1974—. With U.S. Army, 1955-58. Recipient Wrangler award Ranch Hope for Boys, 1976, Svc. to Humanity award Way Out, 1977, Achievement award Faith Farm, Inc., 1989. Office: Mission-Teens Inc PO Box 131 Glendora NJ 08029

BRACKEN, JOSEPH ANDREW, theology educator; b. Chgo., Mar. 22, 1930; s. Andrew Joseph and Agnes Patricia (Ryan) B. LittB, Xavier U., Cin., 1953; MA, Loyola U., Chgo., 1960; PhD, U. Freiburg, Fed. Republic Germany, 1968. Ordained priest Roman Cath. Ch., 1962. Asst. prof. St. Mary of Lake Sem., Chgo., 1968-74; assoc. prof. Marquette U., Milw., 1974-82; prof. theology Xavier U., Cin., 1982—, chmn. dept., 1982-85. Author: Freiheit und Kausalität bei Schelling, 1974; What Are They Saying About the Trinity?, 1979; The Triune Symbol—Persons, Process and Community, 1985; Society and Spirit: A Trinitarian Cosmology, 1991; contbr. articles to profl. jours. Mem. Am. Acad. Religion, Cath. Theol. Soc. Am. (bd. dirs. 1989-91), Coll. Theology Soc., Metaphys. Soc. Am. Avocations: tennis; swimming. Office: Xavier U 3800 Victory Pkwy Cincinnati OH 45207

BRACKETT, DAVID LYNN, education director; b. Chattanooga, May 5, 1961; s. Robert Lavoy and Nina Joy (Cornelison) B.; m. Debra Ann Burke, June 9, 1990. BA in Religion, Carson-Newman Coll., 1985. Ordained to ministry So. Bapt. Conv., 1983. Min. of youth East Ridge Bapt. Ch., Chattanooga, 1980-85, Silverdale Bapt. Ch., Chattanooga, 1985-86; dir. youth and spl. ministries Red Bank United Meth., Chattanooga, 1986-90; dir. Christian edn. Fairview United Meth. Ch., Maryville, Tenn., 1990—; puppet ministries dir. Hamilton County Bapt. Assn., Chattanooga, 1980-82; dist. youth coord. Chattanooga Dist. United Meth., 1988-90, Maryville Dist. United Meth., 1990—. Amb. of Goodwill State of Tenn., 1983; foster care rev. bd. mem. Blount County, Tenn., 1990; camp counselor United Cerebral Palsy, Chattanooga, 1978. Named Cert. of Appreciation, Hamilton County, Tenn., 1983. Mem. Nat. Network of Youth Ministries, Fellowship of Christian Puppeteers. Home: 2441 Old Niles Ferry Pike Maryville TN 37801

Office: Fairview United Meth Ch 2505 Old Niles Ferry Pike Maryville TN 37801

BRACKIN, JOHN LEROY, pastor; b. San Angelo, Tex., July 17, 1949; s. Alfred Coy and Doris (Sones) B.; m. Lena Anne Lloyd, Nov. 6, 1972; 1 child, Adam Lloyd. AA, Valencia Community Coll., Orlando, Fla., 1969; BA in Communications, U. Cen. Fla., 1972; MDiv, New Orleans Bapt. Theol. Sem., 1974, MRE, 1983; DMin, Trinity Theol. Sem., 1990. Ordained to ministry Bapt. Ch., 1974. Pastor First Bapt. Ch., Waverly Hall, Ga., 1974-77; fgn. missionary So. Bapt. Conv., Guatemala/Philippines, 1977-89; pastor First Bapt. Ch., Maitland, Fla., 1990—; chaplain Pine Mountain Water Soil Conservation Dist., Columbus, Ga., 1975-77. Author: Living With God, 1985; contbr. articles to profl. jours. Mem. Guatemala Bapt. Mission (v.p. 1988-89), Greater Orlando Bapt. Assn. (new work dir. 1990—). Republican. Home: 1503 Nottingham Dr Winter Park FL 32792 Office: First Bapt Ch 1950 Mohican Trail Maitland FL 32751

BRACY, ARNOLD LEE, clergyman; b. Charlotte, Mich., Jan. 13, 1938; s. Ellis Elwood and Ardis Zella (Rice) B.; m. Darlene Bracy, Sept. 20, 1957; children: Arnold, Carl, David, Diane. Diploma, Grand Rapids Sch. Bible-Music; student, Grand Rapids Bible Sem. Ordained to ministry Ind. Fundamental Chs. Am. Pastor Lake Odessa (Mich.) Bible Ch., 1959-61, Pilgrim Congl. Ch., Metamora, Mich., 1961-64, Calvary Bible Ch., Lapeer, Mich., 1964—; mgr. WMPC Radio, Lapeer, 1965—; vice moderator Mich. Conservative Cong. Christian Conf., 1962-63, moderator, 1963-64; pres. southeast sect. Mich. Ind. Fundamental Chs. Am., 1977-79. Mem. Lapeer County Bd. Social Svcs., 1968-70; county commr. Lapeer County, Mich., 1971-74. Home: 1393 Haines Rd Lapeer MI 48446 Office: Calvary Bible Ch 923 S Main St Lapeer MI 48446

BRADDOCK, NONNIE CLARKE, religious organization administrator; b. Rye, N.Y.; d. Peter Benedict and Nora Bridget (Devins) Clarke; m. Eugene Stephen Braddock, Sept. 7, 1962; children: Stephen E., Brian B., Glenn C. Adminstr. Beaver Farm Retreat and Conf. Ctr., Yorktown Heights, N.Y.; deputy city clk. City of Rye, N.Y.; founder, pres. Celebrations; dir. Security Enforcement Bur.; part-time therapist; with Marriage Encounter movement, co-founder, chmn. bd., team leader No. Westchester-Putnam (N.Y.) Interfaith Marriage Encounter, 1981-87. Vol. Boy Scouts Am., numerous polit. orgns. and community groups, 1970—; chair. "Warmth for Christmas" clothing drive, N.Y.C. shelters; facilitor mil. family support group; organizer food collections for needy; organizer, sponsor Weekly Cable TV program Featuring Peace, 1991—. Mem. Rite of Christian Initation for Adults, Right to Life. Avocations: music, travel, reading. Office: Beaver Farm Retreat Ctr Underhill Ave Yorktown NY 10598 *It seems to me that all of the problems facing humanity and its environment have at their root a lack of love. Until we learn to truly value life in all its forms we are destined to pass these problems from generation to generation. If, when I die, it can be said that "she truly loved" then my life and my work will have been a success.*

BRADENBURG, HUBERTUS, bishop. Bishop of Stockholm. Office: Office Bishop of Stockholm, Gotgt 68, POB 4098, 102 61 Stockholm Sweden*

BRADESCA, DONNA MARIE, nun, religious educator; b. Cleve., Mar. 12, 1938; d. Joseph Thomas and Ruth Mary (Kilbane) B. BS in Edn., St. John Coll., Cleve., 1961, MEd, 1969; DMinistry, United Theol. Sem., Dayton, 1988. Joined Order of Ursuline Nuns of Cleve., 1956. Tchr. elem. schs. Roman Catholic Diocese Cleve., 1961-70; dir. religious edn. St. Charles Parish, Parma, Ohio, 1970-76; tchr., adminstr. St. Mary Sem., Cleve., 1976—; tchr., Ursuline Coll., Pepper Pike, Ohio, St. John Coll., Cleve., 1969-72; coord. Ohio Field Educators Supervisory Tng. coun., Columbus, 1976-79; mem. Adult Edn. Bur., Diocese of Cleve., 1968—. Contbr. articles on edn. to theol. publs. Mem. Cath. Assn. Theol. Field Educators (coord. 1979-81), Midwest Assn. Theol. Schs. (pres. 1986-88), Assn. Nat. Field Educators. Democrat. Avocations: cooking, reading, travel. Office: Saint Mary Sem 1227 Ansel Rd Cleveland OH 44108

BRADFORD, CHARLES EDWARD, clergyman; b. Washington, July 12, 1925; s. Robert Lee and Etta Elizabeth B.; m. Ethel Lee McKenzie, May 23, 1948; children: Sharon Louise, Charles Edward, Dwight Lyman. B.A., Oakwood Coll., Huntsville, Ala., 1946; grad., Andrews U., 1958, D.D. (hon.), 1978. Ordained to ministry Seventh-day Adventist Ch.; pastor chs. in La. and Tex., 1946-51, Mo., 1953-57, N.Y., 1959-61; evangelist, dir. lay activities Central States Conf., Seventh-day Adventist Ch., Kansas City, Mo., 1952-53; dir. lay activities Northeastern Conf., St. Albans, N.Y., 1957-59; pres. Lake Region Conf., Chgo., 1961-70; assoc. sec. Gen. Conf., Washington, 1970-79; v.p. N.Am., from 1979; now pres. N.Am. div. Seventh-Day Adventist Ch.; trustee Oakwood Coll., Andrews U., Loma Linda (Calif.) U. Author: also articles. Preaching to the Times. Office: 6840 Eastern Ave NW Washington DC 20012

BRADFORD, MICHAEL LEE, religious organization administrator, clergyman; b. Johnson City, Tenn., May 4, 1942; s. Harry B. Bradford and Geneva Elizabeth (Lethco) Williams; m. Julia Ann Garrett, June 6, 1966; children: Stephen Allen, Rachel Leigh. BA, Milligan Coll., 1965; postgrad., Emmanuel Sch. of Religion, 1965-71, U. Louisville, 1985—. Ordained to ministry Christian Ch., 1965; accredited resident mgr. Inst. of Real Estate Mgmt., 1987; lic. nursing home adminstr., Ky. Minister West Walnut St. Christian Ch., Johnson City, 1963-65, Poplar Ridge Christian Ch., Piney Flats, Tenn., 1966-71, East End Christian Ch., Bristol, Va., 1971-73; supt. East Tenn. Christian Home, Elizabethton, 1973-77; sr. minister Camden Ave. Christian Ch., Louisville, 1977-84; devel. officer, dir. communications Christian Ch. Homes of Ky. Inc., Louisville, 1984-86, mgr. Friendship House, 1986-90; dir. property mgmt., 1990—; asst. adminstr. Appalachian Christian Villages, Johnson City, 1991—; chmn. emergency assistance South Louisville Community Ministry, 1979-82; bd. advisors Milligan Coll., Tenn., 1985—; mem. adv. coun. Lifespan. Bd. dirs. Neighborhood Devel. Corp. for Old Louisville. Named Hon. Col. Gov.'s Staff, State of Ky., 1981. Mem. Louisville Area Ministers Assn. (sec. 1979-80), N. Am. Christian Conv. (nat. com. 1981-84, 1987-90, chmn. local arrangements 1981, 89), Ky. Assn. Homes for Aging, Ruritan Lodge (sec. 1968-69), So. Assn. HUD Mgmt. Agts., Lions (v.p. 1977). Republican. Avocations: tropical fish, camping, salt water fishing. Home: 115 Beechnut # I-11 Johnson City TN 37601 Office: Appalachian Christian Village 2012 Sherwood Dr Johnson City TN 37601

BRADLEY, CHARLES LOWRANCE, music minister; b. Sioux City, Ia., June 14, 1938; s. Lestel and Letha (Kennedy) B.; m. Joyce Stahly, Aug. 20, 1961; children: Cheryl Lynn, Dawn Elizabeth. BA, Asbury Coll., 1961; MM, U. Ky., 1964. Organist, choir dir. St. Paul United Meth. Ch., Monroe, Mich., 1967-70; dir. youth and music 1st United Meth. Ch., Union City, Tenn., 1970-71; organist, choir master 1st United Meth. Ch., Newnan, Ga., 1971-79; min. music St. Luke United Meth. Ch., Columbus, Ga., 1979—. Author hymn lyrics. Bd. mem. Valley Rescue Mission, 1980-84, worker Contact, Columbus, Ga., 1988—. Mem. So. Ga. Bd. of Diaconal Ministry, So. Ga. Worship Comm., Am. Guild Organist (sub-dean 1979-81, dean 1981-84), Fellowship United Meth. in Music, Worship and Other Arts (pres., v.p., sec.), Kiwanis (chmn. music Columbus club 1984-89). United Methodist Church. Home: 6500 Malibu Dr Columbus GA 31909 Office: St Luke United Methodist PO Box 867 Columbus GA 31902-0867

BRADLEY, DAVID GILBERT, theology educator; b. Portland, Oreg., Sept. 1, 1916; s. Rowland Hill and Edith (Gilbert) B.; m. Gail Soules, Mar. 19, 1940 (dec. 1982); 1 dau., Katherine Ann Bradley Johnson; m. Lorene L. Greuling, Dec. 27, 1984. A.B., U. So. Calif., 1938; postgrad., Drew Theol. Sem., 1938-39; B.D., Garrett Theol. Sem., 1942; M.A., Northwestern U., 1942; Ph.D., Yale U., 1947; postgrad., Sch. Oriental and African Studies, U. London, 1955-56. Asst. prof. religion, chaplain Western Md. Coll., 1946-49; mem. faculty dept. religion Duke U., Durham, 1949—; prof. Duke U., 1970-86; retired, 1986; vis. prof. Garrett Sem., summer 1960, U. Va., summer 1969, U. N.C., Chapel Hill, 1970; mem. N.C. Conf. United Meth. Ch.; mem. Fulbright-Hays sr. screening com., religion, 1966-68. Author: A Guide to the World's Religions, 1963, Circles of Faith, 1966, The Origins of the Hortatory Materials in the Letters of Paul, 1977; contbr. articles to profl. jours. Pres. Durham Civic Choral Soc., 1959-60; mem. citizens adv. com. Durham Urban Renewal Program, 1965-67; treas. Durham Arts Council, 1968-69; pres. Durham Savoyards Ltd., 1976-77. Gt. Religions Fund fellow South and East Asia, 1969-70. Mem. Am. Acad. Religion (nat. program chmn. 1958, pres. So. sect. 1964), N.C. Tchrs. Religion (pres. 1961), Am. Soc. Study of Religion (sec. 1966-69, editor newsletter 1973—), Assn. Asian Studies, AAUP (pres. Duke U. chpt. 1971-72), Soc. Internat. Devel. (chpt. sec.-treas. 1983-85). Democrat. Office: Box 4735 D S Duke Univ Durham NC 27706

BRADLEY, FRANCIS MACLEOD, lay worker, retired lawyer, banker, educator, consultant; b. Town Creek, Ala., Apr. 29, 1921; s. Francis MacLeod and Tennie Lee (Thaxton) B.; m. Nancy Lisa Bown, Apr. 29, 1945; children: Susan Bradley Tedesco, Andrew H., Linda Bradley Morotini. BSBA, U. Fla., 11942; JD, Albany Law Sch., 1947; PhD, Union Grad. Sch., 1978. Bd. dirs. So. Am. Miss Soc., Ambridge, Pa., 1980—, Pewsaction, Asheville, N.C., 1985—, Ct. of Array, 1988—, Diocesan Coun., 1989—, Adventures in Ministry, Orlando, Fla., 1986—; bd. dirs. Episcopal Diocese of Cen. Fla., Orlando, 1988—, chmn. Diocesan Long Range Plans Commn., 1990; ret. atty., banker and educator; mem. vestry St. John's Episcopal Ch., Melbourne, Fla., 1982-85, Hope Episcopal Ch., Melbourne, 1987—; dean Greater Faith Bible Inst., 1983—; pres. Sem. Covenant Community, 1976—; bd. dirs., sec.-treas. Resurrection Ranch Ministries Inc., 1989—, Profl. Christian Assocs. Inc., 1990—. Bd. dirs., past pres. Sharing Ctr. So. Brevard, Melbourne, 1984—; pres., exec. dir. Christian Conciliation Svc., Melbourne, 1986—; mem., past sec. Habitat for Humanity, Melbourne, 1985—. 1st lt. U.S. Army, 1942-46. Mem. Rotary (past. pres. local club). Democrat. Home: 427 Timberlake Dr Melbourne FL 32940

BRADLEY, GARY MORRISON, JR., minister; b. Montgomery, Ala., May 11, 1958; s. Gary Morrison and Bobbie Jane (Strickland) B.; m. Leisa Karen Yates, Dec. 16, 1976; children: Gary III, William Edward III, Marcus Clay. BA in Speech, David Lipscomb Coll., 1980. Minister Oak Grove Ch. of Christ, Como, Miss., 1980-82, Bethel Ch. of Christ, Athens, Ala., 1982-84, Hoover Ch. of Christ, Birmingham, Ala., 1984—; mem. adv. bd. Heritage Place Retirement Home, Birmingham, 1986. Chaplain Lafayette County Rescue Squad, Miss., 1980, Limestone County Sheriff's Dept., Ala., 1982. Named one of Outstanding Young Men Am., Jaycees, 1981, 83, 85, 87; recipient B.C. Goodpsture Bible award, David Lipscomb Coll., 1980. Avocations: deer and turkey hunting, golf, softball. Office: Hoover Ch of Christ 3248 Lorna Rd Birmingham AL 35216

BRADLEY, MICHAEL LYNN, minister; b. Kansas City, Mo., Aug. 17, 1955; s. Elmer Raymond and Marjorie D. (Venable) B.; m. Toni Jean Taylor, Jan. 1, 1975; children: Michael Lynn, Christopher Allen. BA in Religion, S.W. Bapt. U., Bolivar, Mo., 1982; MDiv, Luther Rice Sem., 1990. Ordained to ministry, So. Bapt. Conv., 1980. Minister Mt. Zion Bapt. Ch., Kilbourne, Ill., 1983-87, Allen st. Bapt. Ch., Clinton, Mo., 1987-89, Sandy Bapt. Ch., Hillsboro, Mo., 1989-90, Tabernacle Bapt. Ch., Piedmont, Mo., 1991—. Home: 324 E Daniels Piedmont MO 63957

BRADLEY, PAUL JOSEPH, priest; b. McKeesport, Pa., Oct. 18, 1945; s. John Francis and V. Cecilia (Pater) B. BA, St. Meinrad Coll., 1967; MDiv, St. Meinrad Sch. Theology, 1971; MSW, U. Pitts., 1988. Ordained priest Roman Cath. Ch., 1971—. Parochial vicar local parishes Diocese of Pitts., 1971-82; dir. office of family life Pitts., 1982-88; sec. for social concerns Diocese of Pitts., 1988—; co-pastor Madonna del Castello Parish, 1991—. bd. dirs. Cath. Charities Diocese Pitts., 1988—, St. Anthony Sch. for Exceptional Children, Oakmont, Pa., 1988; chmn. rev. coms. United Way of Allegheny County,Pitts., 1989—. Home: 2021 S Braddock Ave Pittsburgh PA 15218 Office: Secretariat for Social Concerns 111 Blvd of the Allies Pittsburgh PA 15222

BRADSELL, KENNETH RAYMOND, minister; b. N.Y.C., Mar. 9, 1948; s. Robert Husted and Doris Mildred (Pennie) B.; m. Marcia Ann Van Dyke, June 25, 1971; children: Adam, Mark, Rachel. BA, Hope Coll., 1970; MDiv, New Brunswick Sem., 1974; STM, Union Theol. Sem., N.Y.C., 1983. Cert min. edn. Ref. Ch. in Am., 1982. Assoc. pastor Community Ch. Douglaston, N.Y., 1974-76; pastor Blawenburg (N.J.) Ref. Ch., 1976-81; co-pastor 1st Ch. in Albany, N.Y., 1981-84; min. for edn. Ref. Ch. in Am., Grandville, Mich., 1984—; chmn. Ministries in Christian Edn., Nat. Coun. Chs. of Christ, U.S.A., N.Y.C., 1990—, also chmn.-elect; chmn. Presbyn. and Ref. Edn. Ministry, Louisville, 1990—. Editor: Designs for Teacher and Leader Education, 1990; also articles. Mem. Christian Educators Ref. Ch. in Am. (pres. 1981-84, Educator of Yr. award 1988), Assn. Presbyn. Educators, Religious Edn. Assn. Office: Ref Ch in Am 3000 Ivanrest SW Grandville MI 49418

BRADSHAW, JAMES DANIEL, clergyman; b. Augusta, Ga., Mar. 28, 1950; s. Edwin Augustus and Annie Brinkley (Hunt) B.; m. Susan Irene Shoemaker, June 17, 1972; children: Daniel Hunt, Jared Thomas. BA in Bus., Shorter Coll., 1972; MDiv, So. Bapt. Theol. Sem., Louisville, 1975, D Ministry, 1983. Ordained to ministry Bapt. Ch., 1973. Dir. youth 1st Bapt. Ch., Rome, Ga., 1970-72; assoc. pastor 4th Ave. Bapt. Ch., Louisville, 1972-75, Cen. Bapt. Ch., Miami, Fla., 1975-79; pastor 1st Bapt. Ch., McDonough, Ga., 1979—; trustee Ga. Bapt. Homes, Inc., Atlanta, 1982-87; treas. Ga. Bapt. Pastor's Conf., Atlanta, 1985; moderator Flint River Bapt. Assn., Griffin, Ga., 1986; preaching missionary, Australia, 1983, Liberia, 1987, 88, Panama, 1990. Contbr. articles to denominational papers. Trustee Ga. Coun. on Moral and Civic Concerns, Atlanta, 1984—, Shorter Coll., Rome, Ga., 1986-91; pub. rels. chmn. United Way of Henry County, McDonough, 1985-88; treas. Habitat for Humanity, McDonough, 1986. Named Ky. Col., Commonwealth of Ky., 1975, Chaplain of the Day, Ga. Senate, 1981. Mem. Rotary (pres. Henry County chpt. 1989, Paul Harris fellow 1989). Office: First Bapt Ch 101 Macon St McDonough GA 30253

BRAGG, ELIZABETH JEAN, lay worker, computer systems analyst; b. Hagerstown, Md., Sept. 11, 1945; d. Henry E. and Sarah R. Marquiss; m. Bertrand A. Lee, Aug. 21, 1966 (div.); 1 child, John I.; m. Lincoln E. Bragg, Nov. 4, 1972 (div.); children: Willa G., Henry E., Angela R., Christopher W. BA in Math./Physics, Sacramento State Coll., 1969. Organist, dir. Suntree (Fla.) Meth. Ch., 1984-86, Ch. of Our Savior, Pal, Bay, Fla., 1986-88, St. Joseph Ch., Palm Bay, 1988—; computer system analyst System Resources, Indian Harbor Beach, Fla., 1987—. Roman Catholic. Home: 1525 Par St NE Palm Bay FL 32905 Office: St Joseph Ch 5310 Babcock St NE Palm Bay FL 32905-5040

BRAINERD, WINTHROP JOHN, priest; b. Montreal, Que., Can., Sept. 2, 1939; came to U.S., 1974, naturalized, 1987; s. Thomas Chalmers and Elizabeth Jane (Harris) B. Grad., Yale U., 1960; LittD, Haile Selassie U., Ethiopia and Cantabrigia, Eng., 1966; DD, U. London, 1967; grad., Oxford U., 1969. Ordained to ministry Anglican Ch., 1970; ordained priest Roman Cath. Ch., 1987. Chaplain Kirkland House, Harvard U., Cambridge, Mass., 1969-71; rector Parish of Battle Harbour, Labrador, Nfld., Can., 1971-73; asst. to bishop Episc. Diocese of Lexington, Ky., 1974-77; rector Episc. Christ Ch., Balt., 1977-85; pastoral asst. St. Ignatius Ch., Balt., 1985-86, St. Joseph's Ch., Washington, 1987; assoc. pastor St. Matthew's Cathedral, Washington, 1987—; adj. assoc. prof. theology Loyola Coll., Balt, 1979-81; Am. dir. Archbishop of Canterbury's Diploma in Theology, 1977-86; brigade chaplain Am. Revolution Bicentennial, 1982-84, U.S.-U.K. Diplomatic Bicentennial, 1985; chaplain Ft. McHenry Guard, Balt., 1984—; mem. N.T. com. Internat. Ecumenical Bibl. Commn., 1986—; mem. internat. adv. com. Wing Short Title Catalogue. Mem. Greater Balt. Com., 1978-85; v.p. bd. dirs. Mid-Atlantic Career Ctr., Washington, 1977-79; mem. mgmt. bd. Sta. WBJC, Balt., 1985-86; mem. Balt. Mayor's Com. on Chesapeake Bay, 1984-86; staff mem. Com. To Commemorate 125th Anniversary Battle of Gettysburg, 1986; trustee Libr. Assocs., Yale U.; mem. progress planning com. Monitor Nat. Marine Sanctuary, NOAA, 1985-87; mem. manuscripts exhbn. com. Walters Art Gallery, Balt., 1988; mem. Hist. Records Adv. Bd., D.C.; pres. Comité Jefferson-Lafayette, 1987—; also others. Decorated knight of grace Order St George, knight Order Holy Sepulchre; assoc. fellow Silliman Coll., Yale U.; recipient Silver award Balt.'s Best, 1978, also others. Mem. Most Venerable Order Hosp. St. John of Jerusalem (chaplain 1977—), Wardroom of H.M.S. Brazen (hon.), Soc. of Cincinnati in Conn., Cath. Acad. Scis., Johnsonians (chmn. 1983, 89), Co. Mil. Historians, Md. Club (Balt.), Elizabethan Club (New Haven), Harvard U. Faculty Cub, Balt. Rowing Club (bd. dirs., exec. com. 1982-86). Avocations: rowing, book collecting. Home and Office: St Matthew's Cathedral 1725 Rhode Island Ave NW Washington DC 20036

BRAISHER, MARK H., minister; b. Oklahoma City, May 3, 1963; s. William H. and Helen L. (Sears) B.; m. Michelle D. Lewis, June 1, 1984; 1 child, Jeremy M. BTh., Hillsdale Free Will Bapt. Coll, 1985; MDiv, Midwestern Bapt. Theol. Sem., 1988, postgrad., 1988—. Ordained to ministry Free Will Bapt. Ch. Pastor Victory Free Will Bapt. Ch., Kansas City, Mo., 1986—; mem. gen. bd. Mo. State Assn. Free Will Bapt., 1989—. Mem. Alban Inst. Home: 4636 N Spruce Kansas City MO 64117

BRAKEMEIER, GOTTFRIED, minister, religious organization executive; b. Cachoeira do Sul, Brazil, Jan. 4, 1937; s. Heinrich and Helma (Radünz) B.; m. Lydia Klatt, Aug. 4, 1968; children: Claus, Dietmar. BTh., U. Göttingen, Fed. Republic Germany, 1962, ThD, 1968. Ordained to ministry Luth. Ch. Pastor Luth. Ch., São Leopoldo, Brazil, 1962-66; prof. theology local univ. São Leopoldo, 1968-85; ch. pres. Evang. Ch. Luth. Confession in Brazil, Porto Alegre, 1985—; pres. Luth. World Fedn., 1990—; mem. Internat. Joint Commn. Cath.-Luth., 1986—. Author: Enfoques Bíblicos, 1980, Reino de Deus e esperança apocalíptica, 1984, O socialismo de primeira cristandade, 1985, Testemunho da fé em tempos difíceis, 1990. Office: Evang Ch Luth Confession in Brazil, Rua Senhor dos Passos, 202, 90010 Porto Alegre Brazil

BRALEY, EDNA CHRISTINE, minister, educator; b. Astoria, Oreg., Mar. 12, 1937; d. Charles Augustus and Ida Belle (Dyke) Smith; m. Don H. Braley, July 7, 1960 (div. Feb. 1976); children: Rebecca, Steven. BS with honors, Evangel Coll., 1960; MS in Edn., So. Oreg. State Coll., 1963; cert. ministerial studies, Berean Coll., 1970-81. Ordained to ministry Assemblies of God, 1986; cert. tchr., S.D., Mo., Wash. Tchr. pub. sch., Oreg. and Wash., 1960-67; missionary pastor wife Assembly of God (Makah Reservation), Neah Bay, Wash., 1968-75; edn. coord., treas. Am. Indian Youth Camp, Camp Bethel, Wash., 1969-77; tchr. Little Eagle (S.D.) Day Sch., 1978-87, curriculum cons., 1987; interim, then assoc. pastor Mobridge (S.D.) Assembly of God, 1985-88; minister, faculty Cen. Indian Bible Coll., Mobridge, 1988—; dept. chair Bible Inst. Cen. Indian Bible Coll., 1989-90; cons. various local and state schs.; presenter workshops in edn., 1985—. Author: (poems) A Ray of Light, 1955; composer; soloist sacred music, 1961—. Dir. Energy Share of S.D., 1987-90. Recipient Esther award Women's Ministries, S.D., 1981. Avocations : reading, painting, creative crafts. Home: 612 6th St W Mobridge SD 57601 Office: Cen Indian Bible Coll River Front Dr Mobridge SD 57601

BRALY, BOBBY KEY, minister; b. Bullard, Tex., Dec. 8, 1938; s. Claud Lester and Ottie B. (Key) B.; m. Carol Elizabeth Crane, Sept. 1, 1961; 1 child, Kerrie Diane. AA, Lon Morris Jr. Coll., 1959; BS, East Tex. Bapt. U., 1961; BD, MDiv, Southwestern Bapt. Theol. Sem., 1967. Ordained to ministry, 1964. Pastor Sweetwater Bapt. Ch., Commanche, Tex., 1964-67, Eastside Bapt. Ch., Henderson, Tex., 1967-70; pastor First Bapt. Ch., Tenaha, Tex., 1970-73, Pittsburg, Tex., 1973-81; pastor Horseshoe Dr. Bapt. Ch., Alexandria, La., 1981-89, Laurel Heights Bapt. Ch., Winnfield, La., 1990—; trustee East Tex. Bapt. U., Marshall, 1972-80, Lone Star Bapt. Encampment, 1977-79; mem, exec. bd. La. Bapt. Conv., Alexandria, 1982-88; moderator Winn Bapt. Assn., Winnfield, La., 1990—. V.p. Camp County C. of C., Pittsburg, 1980; pres. Family Rels. Commn., Pittsburg, 1977-80; vol. Fire Dept., Sheriff Office, Pittsburg, 1974-81; commdr. Winnfield Police Res., 1990—. Named Notable Ams. of Bicentennial, 1976. Mem. La. Moral and Civic Found., So. Bapt. Sr. Adults (leader 1989—), Kiwanis (dir. 1977-80). Office: Laurel Heights Bapt Ch 1001 San Pedro Winnfield LA 71483 *In these days of suffering, heartache and stress of all kinds, the opportunities of sharing a good work and good word allows each of us to be a better neighbor, friend, and co-laborer. I pray that our lives entwined may lead to a better world.*

BRAMBLETT, STEPHEN WALTER, lay worker; b. Arlington, Calif., May 24, 1958; s. Gerald Eugene Jr. and Evelyn Naomi (Downs) B. Student, Ga. Mil. Coll., 1978, Ga. So. U., 1979. Treas. Soldiers of God, Santa Fe, 1990-91; elder worship Mins. For Jesus Christ, Santa Fe, 1991—; organist North Facility Chapel, Santa Fe, 1988-91. Composer album Music From Within The Belly Of The Whale, rec. at Penitentiary N.Mex., 1989. Republican. Mem. Seventh-Day Adventist Ch. *Love. The ultimate gesture. God is love. It was love that created the heavens and earth. It was love that died for us while we were yet sinners. It is love which calls us to righteousness even today. When all else fails, love is there. Eternally.*

BRANCH, CHARLES EDWIN, SR., clergyman; b. Winterville, N.C., Aug. 12, 1940; s. Charles O'Hagan and Julia (Porter) B.; m. Janice Jones, May 24, 1970; children: Charles Edwin Jr., Jason D. BA, Free Will Bapt. Bible Coll., 1970. Ordained to ministry Free Will Bapt. Ch., 1969. Asst. dean men Free Will Bapt. Bible Coll., Nashville, 1969-71; pastor Saratoga (N.C.) Free Will Bapt. Ch., 1971-72, Ephesus Free Will Bapt. Ch., Blounts Creek, N.C., 1973-82, Hickory Grove Free Will Bapt. Ch., Robersonville, N.C., 1982-85, Ormondsville Free Will Bapt. Ch., Ayden, N.C., 1985—; mem. bd. ordination Conv. Original Free Will Bapt., Ayden, 1990—. Sgt. USAF, 1963-66. Home and Office: 116 Village Dr Winterville NC 28590

BRANCH, ROCKY LEE, minister; b. Spruce Pine, N.C., July 18, 1959; s. Hubert Lee Branch and Betty Jean Pitman; m. Janice Marie Thompson, Nov. 22, 1980; children: Alicia Nicole, Aaron Lee. AA, Fruitland Bible Coll., Hendersonville, N.C., 1984; BA, So. Bapt. Sem., Jacksonville, Fla., 1990, MA, 1991, D Ministry, 1991. Intern Mt. Carmel Bapt. Ch., Spruce Pine, 1983; pastor Powder Mill Bapt. Ch., Newland, N.C., 1983-84, Chestnut Grove Bapt. Ch., Little Switzerland, N.C., 1984-87, Walker Road Bapt. Ch., Morganton, N.C., 1987—; pres. Pastor's Conf., Newland, N.C., 1984; chmn. Fgn. Mission Com., Newland, 1984, Morganton, 1990; moderator Mitchell Bapt. Assn., Spruce Pine, N.C., 1986. Author, editor (newsletter) The Informer, 1991. Chmn. publicity com. campaign against Liquor-by-drink, Morganton, 1990. Home: 100 Walker Rd Morganton NC 28655

BRAND, RICHARD CLYDE, JR., pastor; b. Tuscaloosa, Ala., Feb. 28, 1943; s. Richard Clyde and Lucile (Doughty) B.; m. Elizabeth Welles Pearson, Dec. 18, 1967; children: R. Victor, Jeffery Buchanan. AB, Davidson Coll., 1965; BD, Princeton Theol. Sem., 1968. Ordained to ministry Presbyn. Ch., 1968. Assoc. minister Trinity Presbyn. Ch., Charlotte, N.C., 1968-74; pastor St. Stephen Presbyn. Ch., Houston, 1974-82; assoc. minister 1st Presbyn. Ch., Raleigh, N.C., 1982-88; pastor Bethel Presbyn. Ch., Bethel Park, Pa., 1988—; woodworker, Bethel Park; bd. dirs. South Hills Interfaith Ministries, Bethel Park, 1990—; chaplain Civitan, Raleigh, 1985-88. Contbr. articles to profl. jours. Active neighborhood ctrs. Houston Day Care-Neighborhood Ctrs., 1976-82; treas. Met. Orgn., Houston, 1979-82; precinct officer Dem. Party, Charlotte, N.C., 1972. Mem. Pitts. Presbytery, Soc. Bibl. Lit., Soc. Ch. History. Home: 5857 Horseshoe Dr Bethel Park PA 15102 Office: Bethel Presbyn Ch 2999 Bethel Church Rd Bethel Park PA 15102

BRANDENSTEIN, ROBERT LEWIS, minister; b. Phila., Dec. 16, 1923; s. Samuel Clarke and Edna A. (Bailey) B.; m. Virginia Ruth Meckel, Mar. 22, 1947 (div.); children: Sherilyn Ruth, Dawn Ellen, Norman Reed; m. Marilyn Lynn Brandenstein, Nov. 20, 1969 (div. Aug. 1983). BA, Bob Jones U., 1946; MDiv, Colgate Divinity Sch., 1985. Asst. pastor Cen. Presbyn. Ch., St. Petersburg, Fla., 1946-47; minister of edn. First Bapt. Ch., Ft. Wayne, Ind., 1961-64; pastor First Congl. Ch. of Riga United Ch. of Christ, Churchville, N.Y., 1984—; ret. banker Chase Lincoln First Bank, Rochester, N.Y., 1966-84. Mem. Am. Inst. Banking (life, hon., instr. oral communication 1976-80, pres. Rochester chpt. 1982-83), Stewardship Com. of Assn. (co-chair Rochester chpt. 1985-89), Churchville C. of C. (v.p. 1989—).

BRANDMÜLLER, WALTER, religion educator; b. Jan. 5, 1929; s. Kurt and Luise B. Dr.theol., U. Munich, 1962, Pvt. Dozent, 1967. Ordained priest, Roman Cath. Ch., 1953. Prof. ecclesiastical history U. Augsburg, Fed. Republic Germany. Author: Galilei und die Kirche-oder das Recht auf Irrtum, 1982, Papst und Konzil im Grossen Schisma-Studien und Quellen, 1991, Das Konzil von Konstanz 1414-18, 1990, Das Konzil von Pavia-Siena 1423-24, 1974; contbr. articles to profl. jours.; author books. Knight, Order of Holy Sepulchre of Jerusalem; Hon. Prelate of His Holyness the Pope;

recipient Bundesverdienstkreuz am Bande. Mem. Accademia degli Intronati Siena, Pontificia Accademia Teologica Romana, Soc. Internat. Historiae Conciliorum Investigandae (pres.), Pontificio Comitato di Scienze Storiche, Rotary. Office: U Augsburg, Universitätsstr 10, 8900 Augsburg Federal Republic of Germany

BRANDOW, WAYNE ROBERT, minister; b. Hudson, N.Y., May 4, 1952; s. Roy Herbert and Susan Jane (Miller) B.; m. Martha Stevens Leete, Apr. 17, 1976; children: Joy Lynn, Heather Beth, Lindsay Grace. BA in Biblican Edn., Fla. Bible Coll., 1975. Ordained to ministry non-denomination ch., 1975. Dir. Lauderdale South Jr. High Youth Ranch, Ft. Lauderdale, Fla., 1971-75; youth pastor Niagara Bible Conf., Olcott, N.Y., 1975-76; pastor Bible Bapt. Ch. of Galway (N.Y.), 1977—; letter carrier U.S. Postal Svc., Scotia, N.Y., 1987—; instr. Albany (N.Y.) Bible Inst., 1985-86. Mem. Internat. Fellowship Ref. Bapts. Republican. Home: PO Box 112 2076 East St Galway NY 12074-0112 Office: Bible Bapt Ch of Galway PO Box 112 2095 East St Galway NY 12074-0112 *My desire is to live for Christ, to be His ambassador. Whether it be to the multitude or the few, whether it be in good health or bad, whether it be in penury or abundance, He has appointed my lot. Therefore I will trust Him and shine for Him.*

BRANDSTRADER, FRED LUCAS, clergyman; b. Chgo., Nov. 30, 1938; s. Fred Lucas and Agnes (Golden) B.; B.A. in Sociology, Loyola U., Chgo., 1962; B.D., St. Mary-Mundelein, 1964; M.A. in Urban Studies, Loyola U., 1972. Ordained priest Roman Catholic Ch., 1968. Assoc. pastor Our Lady of Angels Ch., Chgo., 1970-76; pastor San Miguelito-Panama, Panama City, 1976-77; assoc. pastor Queen of Angels, Chgo., 1976-81; pastor Providence of God, Chgo., 1981—; mem. Chgo. Priest Senate, 1982—. Bd. dirs. Better Boys Found., Chgo., 1970—, Centro de la Causa, Chgo., 1981—, Saffer Found., Chgo., 1982; mem. Hispanic Caucus, Chgo., 1970—. Home: 717 W 18th St Chicago IL 60616 Office: Providence of God Ch 717 W 18th St Chicago IL 60616

BRANDT, KENNETH EDWARD, minister; b. Lancaster, Pa., June 14, 1959; s. Kenneth Ebersole and Jean Marie Brandt; m. Kelley Ann Rice, Aug. 18, 1979; children: Jennifer, Kristopher, Zachary. BA, U. Findlay, Ohio, 1981; MDiv, Princeton U., 1985. Ordained to ministry Presbyn. Ch. (U.S.A.), 1985. Pastor Zion Ch. of God, Hamler, Ohio, 1979-82, 1st Ch. of God, Newport, Pa., 1984-87; asst. pastor Simpson United Meth. Ch., Old Bridge, N.J., 1982-84; pastor Cedar Grove Presbyn. Ch., East Earl, Pa., 1987—; chaplain Pa. Army N.G., 1989—. Author: Passing Horizons, 1986; also articles. Mem. Lions. Republican. Office: Cedar Grove Presbyn Ch 1306 Division Hwy PO Box 96 East Earl PA 17519 *Each day is an opportunity to grow and consequently a chance to help others grow. One's value in life is determined by the number of opportunities one seizes.*

BRANDT, KONRAD, religious organization executive. Pres. World's Christian Endeavor Union, Columbus, Ohio. Office: World's Christian Endeavor Union 1221 E Broad St PO Box 1110 Columbus OH 43216*

BRANDT, ROBERT BARRY, lay worker; b. Lebanon, Pa., Nov. 13, 1948; s. Marlin Jay Brandt and Arlene Hilda (Bowman) Gable; m. Ruth Ann Peterson, June 6, 1970; 1 child, Matthew Scot. BA in Sociology, Lebanon Valley Coll., 1971; postgrad., United Theol. Sem., Dayton, Ohio, 1973. Lic. to ministry Meth. Ch., 1968. Min. Ea. Pa. United Meth. Ch., Harrisburg, Pa., 1968-72; deacon Ea. Pa. United Meth. Ch., Valley Forge, Pa., 1972-76; local ch. lay leader Ridgewood (N.J.) United Meth. Ch., 1985-87; dist. lay leader no. dist. North N.J. Conf. United Meth., Paramus, N.J., 1986-89; lay leader ann. conf. North N.J. Conf. United Meth., Madison, N.J., 1989—; chair No. N.J. Bd. of Laity, Madison, 1989—; chair coun. on ministries Ridgewood United Meth. Ch., 1988-89; mem. bishop's task force No. N.J. United Meth., Madison, 1989; mem. Walk to Emmaus Community, 1987—, Disciplined Order of Christ, Nashville, 1988—; cons., tech. mgr. Matrix Computer Cons., Inc., River Edge, N.J., 1987—. Mem. Nat. Assn. Ann. Conf. Lay Leader. Democrat. Home: 491 Dorchester Rd Ridgewood NJ 07450 Office: Matrix Computer Cons Inc 65 E Rte 4 River Edge NJ 07661 *We are each called to a life of service to others. It is in the loosing of ourselves to others that we ultimately find who and what we were meant to be when God placed us on this earth.*

BRANDT, VICTOR LEONARD, bishop; b. Wilton, N.D., July 27, 1920; s. John J. and Emma Marie (Matthias) B.; m. Irene Emma Ludwig, Aug. 20, 1950; children: James, Deborah, Ruth, John. BA, Concordia Seminary, 1941, postgrad., 1944. Pastor Trinity Luth. Ch., Bessemer, Mich., 1944-47; asst. pastor Bethlehem Luth. Ch., Balt., 1947-48; pastor Amherst Luth. Ch., Williamsville, N.Y., 1948-60, Luth. Ch. of the Good Shephard, Palos Heights, Ill., 1960-86; bishop English Synod Assn. Evang. Luth. Chs., Detroit, 1986-88; area counselor Luth. Ch.-Mo. Synod, Palos Heights, Ill., 1963-73, dist. bd. dirs. , 1973-76. Contbr. sermons to religious pubs. Adv. com. Moraine Valley Coll., Palos Hills, Ill., 1970; bd. dirs. Luth. Social Svcs. of Ill., Des Plaines, 1982-88. Mem. Assn. of Evangel. Luth. Chs. (v.p. 1976-86), Rotary (Paul Harris fellow 1986, chaplain 1976-86). Home: 701 Lake Hinsdale Dr Willowbrook IL 60514 Office: Assn Evang Luth Chs Box 19307 Detroit MI 48219

BRANHAM, MACK CARISON, JR., theological seminary president, minister; b. Columbia, S.C., Apr. 20, 1931; s. Mack Carison and Laura Pauline (Sexton) B.; m. Jennie Louise Jones, Dec. 17, 1953; children—Kenneth Gary, Charles Michael, Keith Robert, Laurie Lynn. BS, Clemson U., 1953; MDiv, Luth. Theol. So. Sem., 1958, STM, 1963; MS, George Washington U., 1968; PhD, Ariz. State U., 1974; DD (hon.), Newberry Coll., 1990; LLD (hon.), Clemson U., 1991. Ordained to ministry Luth. Ch., 1958; pastor Providence-Nazareth Luth. Parish, Lexington, S.C., 1958-59; commd. 2d lt. U.S. Air Force, 1953, advanced through grades to col., 1959; ret., 1979; adminstrv. asst., registrar Luth. Theol. So. Sem., 1979-81, v.p. adminstrn., 1981-82, pres., 1982—; instr., counselor. Decorated Bronze Star, Legion of Merit. Mem. Am. Assn. Marriage and Family Therapy. Club: Rotary. Editor Air Force Chaplain newsletter, 1974-77.

BRANNAN, CURTIS WARD, minister; b. Kansas City, Mo., Dec. 11, 1931; s. Lawrence Peter Brannan and Ruby Ina (Box) Schaefer; m. Shirley Lee McFarland, Mar. 11, 1950; children: Deborah Kay, Nancy Lynn, David Ward. AA, Southwest Bapt. Coll., 1958; BA, S.W. Mo. State U., 1961; MDiv, Midwestern Bapt. Theol. Sem., Kansas City, 1964. Pastor Bethany Bapt. Ch., Lamar, Mo., 1957-59, 1st Bapt. Ch., Forsyth, Mo., 1959-61, Fairfax Hills Bapt. Ch., Kansas City, Kans., 1961-64; chaplain, lt. comdr. USN, 1964-77; sr. pastor Grace Fellowship Ch., Camarillo, Calif., 1977-83, Ojai (Calif.) Valley Community Ch., 1983—. Republican. Home: 60 Ash Lane Ojai CA 93023 Office: Ojai Valley Community Coll 907 El Centro Ojai CA 93023

BRANNON, CLIFTON WOODROW, evangelist, lawyer; b. Fitzgerald, Ga., Apr. 14, 1912; s. George Wesley and Beulah (Green) B.; m. Ola Ruth Hall, Feb. 16, 1935; children—Beverly Mae, Madlyn Sue, Clifton Woodrow. Student, Ga. Sch. Tech., 1929-30; J.D., Woodrow Wilson Coll. Law Atlanta, 1932; LL.D., Burton Coll. and Sem., 1953. Bar: Ga. 1932, Tex. 1946, U.S. Supreme Ct. 1938. Atty. Home Owners Corp., 1933-35; trial atty. Sinclair Refining Co., 1936-40; gen. counsel, sec. R.G. LeTourneau, Inc., LeTourneau Co. Ga., LeTourneau Co. Miss., Vicksburg, Tex. Casualty Ins. Co., radio stas. KLTI, WLET, LeTourneau Tech. Inst. Tex., 1946-49; gen. counsel, dir. Winona Lake (Ind.) Christian Assembly, Inc., 1940-49; pres. Whosoever Heareth, Inc.; evangelist So. Bapt. Ch., 1949—, Word for World Pubs., Inc.; pub. Soul Winner's New American Standard New Testament, 1972; v.p., dir. All India Prayer Fellowship, Inc., 1973—; pres. Clift Brannon Evangel. Assn., 1974—; Bd. dirs. Word for World Crusade, Universal Concern Found.; Past pres. Tex. Bapt. Brotherhood Conv.; v.p. So. Baptist Conv., 1973. Editor: Soul Winner's New Testament, 1959, Soul Winner's Living Bible New Testament, 1973; notes, helps and references New Am. Standard New Testament, 1974; editor notes, helps and references The Guide to God New Testament, 1974; editor: Edicion Para Evangelismo Personal de Nuero Testamento. Bd. dirs., co-founder Longview Family Counseling Ctr., pres., 1975-85, v.p. Tex. Bapt. Men, 1985—. Mem. ABA, Tex. Bar Assn., Ga. Bar Assn. Democrat. Lodges: Masons (32 deg.), Shrine, Kiwanis. Home: 701 Coleman Dr Longview TX 75601 Office: 701 1/2 Coleman Dr Longview TX 75601 *To be fervent in spirit, diligent in business, faithful to your appointments, loyal to your friends and dedicated to God and family assures peace of mind, provisions of needs, and productivity of a life of fruitfulness.*

BRANNON, RICHARD SCOTT, minister; b. Spartanburg, S.C., Dec. 19, 1926; s. J.D. and Eunice (Whatley) B.; m. Mary Ellen Stuart, Dec. 4, 1949 (div. 1988); children: Richard Scott, Lyn Brannon Pittman, Stuart Andrew; m. Carol Ann Gushanas, Mar. 4, 1989. BA, Baylor U., 1950; BD, Southwestern Bapt. Theol. Sem., Ft. Worth, 1953, ThD, 1956; MDiv, So. Bapt. Theol. Sem., Louisville, 1954. Ordained to ministry So. Bapt. Conv., 1948. Pastor 1st Bapt. Ch., Batesville, Ark., 1956-58, Huffman Bapt. Ch., Birmingham, Ala., 1958-64, Kathwood Bapt. Ch., Columbia, S.C., 1964-70; pres., founder Good Samaritan Mission Svcs., Orlando, Fla., 1977—. Author 7 books under gen. title: Richard Brannon's Notebook; creator radio show Richard Brannon's Notebook, 1965-70; columnist newspaper, 1967-70. Spl. asst. Donald Rumsfeld-presdl. asst., Washington, 1970, Elliot Richardson-sec. HEW, Washington, 1971, George Schultz-spl. assignment, Washington, 1972-75, Pres. Gerald Ford, Washington, 1975-76. Republican. Office: Good Samaritan Mission Svcs 8323 Sand Lake Rd Orlando FL 32819 *Even though we ask for proof, I am convinced that the things most eternal can not be seen, nor touched, nor proven for certain. Confidence about spiritual matters in not necessarily a pilgrimage, but understanding is.*

BRANNON, RONALD ROY, minister; b. Aberdeen, S.D., Apr. 16, 1928; s. Walter Carlos and Mary Erma (Snyder) B.; m. Rosalee Vernela Carry, July 20, 1949; children: Rhonda Lee Storer, Rodney Vaughn, Randall Roy. BA, Bartlesville Wesleyan Coll., Okla., 1951; DD, Cen. (S.C.) Wesleyan Coll., 1987. Ordained to ministry Wesleyan Ch., 1951. Pastor Heber Wesleyan Ch., Miltonvale, Kans., 1949-52, First Wesleyan Ch., Wichita, Kans., 1952-68; dist. supt. Kans. Dist. of the Wesleyan Ch., Miltonvale, 1968-82; gen. sec. The Wesleyan Ch. Hdqtrs., Indpls., 1982—; trustee/sec. Miltonvale Wesleyan Coll. Bd., 1967-71, Bartlesville Wesleyan Coll. Bd., 1968-84, Cen. Wesleyan Coll. Bd., 1984—. Mem. Nat. Assn. Evangelicals (bd. dirs. 1970-72), Christian Holiness Assn. (treas. 1984-88). Republican. Home: 1412 Marlin Dr Marion IN 46952 Office: The Internat Ctr TWC 6060 Castleway Dr W Indianapolis IN 46250

BRANSCUM, ALFRED DEAN, minister; b. Wichita Falls, Tex., June 5, 1952; s. Donald Dean and Virginia Dea (Clanton) B.; m. Joyce Marie Wilson, June 16, 1976; children: Christopher Aaron, Jason Eric, Victor Alan. BA in Religion, Mt. Vernon (Ohio) Bible Coll., 1975. Ordained to ministry Internat. Ch. of the Foursquare Gospel, 1989. Youth leader Internat. Ch. of the Foursquare Gospel, Marion, Ohio, 1974-76; assist. pastor Internat. Ch. of the Foursquare Gospel, Wichita Falls, 1977-90, pastor, 1990—; housekeeping mgr. Wichita Falls State Hosp., 1977-90. Office: Internat Ch of Foursquare Gospel 6305 Southwest Pkwy Wichita Falls TX 76310 *It is hard to have thoughts on life without thinking of death, or at least, life after life. I pray that my earthly life is sufficient to the purpose of leading others to a life with Christ, Life after life.*

BRANSFORD, MALLORY WATKINS, music minister; b. Williamsburg, W.Va., Mar. 9, 1912; s. Wesley Henry and Martha (Fox) B.; m. Helen Elizabeth Zahn, Aug. 4, 1937; children: Marcia Ruth, Robert Wesley. MusB, Oberlin Coll., 1934; MusM, Butler U., 1936, B Music Edn., 1946; PhD in Edn., Walden U., 1976. Minister music Central Ave United Meth. Ch., 1944-46, Roberts Park United Meth. Ch., 1942-44; minister music, dir. children's music Zion Evang. United Ch. of Christ, Indpls., 1946—; chmn. organ dept. Butler U., Indpls., 1948—; music specialist Indpls. Pub. Schs., 1944-79. Author: Teaching and Learning Guide, 1976; (recordings) Choral and Organ Favorites, 1976, Sounds of Zion, 1984. Recipient Disting. Svc. award Ind. Music Educator's Assn., 1979, Caleb B. Smith medal of honor DeMolay Legion of honor, Grand Lodge Ind., 1984. Mem. Am. Guild Organists (dean 1953-55), Nat. Assn. Keyboard Artists, Columbia Club (Indpls.), Masons (organist Supreme coun. 1976—), Scottish Rite (33d degree), Phi Mu Alpha Sinfonia. Home: 4705 Melbourne Rd Indianapolis IN 46208 Office: Butler U 4600 Sunset Ave Indianapolis IN 46208

BRANSON, PHILIP B., lay worker; b. San Mateo, Calif., Nov. 7, 1941; m. Susan Smith; children: Rebecca, Teresa. BS, U. Santa Clara, 1963; MBA, Northwestern U., Chgo., 1964. Elder Presbyn. Ch., Westwood, Calif., 1982-88; lay worker United Meth. Ch., LaCrescenta, Calif., 1989—; pres. First American, Woodland Hills, Calif., 1984—. Pres. Home Warranty Assn., Calif., 1988—. Office: First American PO Box 4020 Woodland Hills CA 91365

BRANSTETTER, RUSSELL WAYNE, minister; b. Barnsdall, Okla., Dec. 28, 1946; s. Marvin Martin and Beulah Belle (Chambers) B.; m. Helen Gail Moody; children: Christopher Jon, Jennifer (Jenna) Beth. Student, Tulsa U., 1965-68; BA, So. Nazarene U., 1969, postgrad., 1969-71. Ordained to ministry Ch. of the Nazarene, 1971. Pastor Forest Home Ch. of the Nazarene, Jonesboro, Ark., 1971-74, Sun Valley Ch. of the Nazarene, Houston, 1974-80; sr. pastor First Ch. of the Nazarene, Bartlesville, Okla., 1980-84, Clovis, N.Mex., 1984-87; sr. pastor Pineville Ch. of the Nazarene, Charlotte, N.C., 1987—; Christian life chmn. Houston dist. Ch. of the Nazarene, 1979-80, mem. adv. bd. N.E. Okla. dist., 1987-88. Vol. chaplain High Plains Hosp., Clovis, 1984-87. Mem. Kiwanis (bd. dirs. Clovis chpt. 1984-87). Republican. Avocations: golf, fishing, reading, computers. Home: 202 Franklin St Pineville NC 28134 Office: Ch of the Nazarene 8614 Pineville/Matthews Rd Charlotte NC 28226

BRANTLEY, WILLIAM STANLEY, minister; b. Farmerville, La., Nov. 10, 1956; s. William Donray and Sallie Will (Smith) B.; m. Lynne Goodrum French, Feb. 28, 1986; 1 child, Eric. BA in Bible Studies, Internat. Bible Coll., 1978; BA in Psychology and Bible Studies magna cum laude, Freed-Hardeman Coll., 1986; postgrad., Murray State U., 1991—. Youth minister Hillsboro St. Ch. of Christ, El Dorado, Ark., 1976, Hamilton (Ala.) Ch. of Christ, 1976-79; minister Sulligent (Ala.) Ch. of Christ, 1979-82, Westport (Tenn.) Ch. of Christ, 1983-85, Holladay (Tenn.) Ch. of Christ, 1985—; counselor Maywood Christian Youth Camp, Hamilton, 1977-81. Mem. religious crusade Ch. of Christ, Trinidad, West Indies, 1978, 79, mem. religious campaign, Dallas, 1975, Chattanooga, 1976. Named one of top five Outstanding Young Religious Leaders Jaycees, 1977, Outstanding Young Men of Am., 1985. Mem. Alpha Chi, Psi Chi. Home: Rte 2 Box 1E Holladay TN 38341 Office: Holladay Ch of Christ Holladay TN 38341

BRASCH, RUDOLPH, rabbi, author, educator; b. Berlin, Nov. 6, 1912; s. Gustav and Hedwig (Mathias) B.; m. Liselotte Buchbinder, Feb. 16, 1952. Cert. rabbi, Jewish Theol. Sem., Berlin, 1936; PhD, U. Berlin, 1938; DD (hon.), Hebrew Union Coll., Cin., 1959. Ordained rabbi, 1936. Rabbi North London Liberal Congregation, Southgate and Enfield, Eng., 1938-48; founder, rabbi Dublin (Ireland) Progressive Synagogue, 1946-47; rabbi Springs Dist. Reform Congregation, Republic of South Africa, 1948; chief min. Temple Emanuel, Sydney, Australia, 1949-79; rabbi Temple Etz Ahayim, Montgomery, Ala., 1980; prof. in Judaica U. Hawaii, 1981; marriage celebrant Commonwealth of Australia, 1982—; vis. prof. theology various univs., Australia; guest lectr. in field; justice of peace, Australia. Author: The Midrash Shir Ha-shirim Zuta, 1936, The Prophets' Philosophy of history, 1937, The Renegade in Rabbinic Literature, 1937, The Jewish Question Mark, 1940, The Irish and the Jews, 1947, The Symbolism of King Solomon's Temple, 1954, The Star of David, 1955, The Eternal Flame, 1958, How Did It Begin?, 1965, Mexico - A Country of Contrasts, 1967, General Sir John Monash, 1968, The Unknown Sanctuary, 1969, The Judaic Heritage, 1969, How Did Sports Begin?, 1970, How Did Sex Begin?, 1973, the Supernatural and You!, 1976, Strange Customs, 1976, Australian Jews of Today and the Part They Have Played, 1977, There is a Reason for Everything, 1982, Mistakes, Misnomers and Misconceptions, 1983, Thank God I'm an Atheist, 1987, Permanent Addresses, 1987, Even More Permanent Addresses, 1989, Where Does It Come From?, 1989, The Book of the Year, 1991, A Book of Comfort, 1991; broadcaster radio and TV. Chaplain London CD, 1939-45. Decorated Order of British Empire (U.K.); Order of Australia; recipient Coronation medal Govt. of Australia, 1952, Silver Jubilee medal Govt. of Australia, 1977, Media Peace prize Assn. UN, 1979; named hon. lt. col., Ala. Militia, 1980. Mem. Australia Soc. Authors, Conf. Am. Rabbis, Rotary, Tattersalls, Vintage Club. Home: 14 Derby St, Vaucluse NSW 2030, Australia *There is a reason for everything is my philosophy of life. Though we might not recognise it right away, it will reveal itself in retrospect. And though at times we might not know where we are going, we are not going in vain.*

BRASCHLER, TODD CLIFTON, church music director; b. New Castle, Ind., July 29, 1962; s. Clifton Ray and Janice Marie (McIntire) B; m. Claudia Dean Wampler, Sept. 14, 1985; children: Nicholas Todd, Tyler Clifton. BA, Anderson U., 1984. Part-time music dir. New Hope Christian Ch., Anderson, Ind., 1982; summer intern, dir. youth and music Hercules Community Ch., Clearwater, Fla., 1982; assoc. youth and music Walnut Lawn Ch. of God, Springfield, Mo., 1985-87, 1st Ch. of God, West Palm Beach, Fla., 1987-90; assoc. youth, music and Christian edn. Eastland Ch. of God, Lexington, Ky., 1990—; planner, adviser Ch. of God Internat. Youth Conv., Anderson, 1991; mem. Ky. state music com., 1991, co-dir. State Youth Choir Ky., 1991; dir. music for Unity Forum between Christian Chs. and Chs. of God., 1991. Mem. Ch. of God (Anderson, Ind.). Office: Eastland Ch of God 2598 Liberty Rd Lexington KY 40509

BRASHEAR, ROBERT LAIRD, religious organization adminstrator; b. Huntingdon, Pa., Dec. 3, 1949; s. Robert Slagle and Hazel Irene (Laird) B.; m. Andrea Ruth Schwartz, Apr. 8, 1984; children: Micah Scott, Nathaniel Laird. BA, Coll. of Wooster, Ohio, 1971; MDiv, Yale Div. Sch., New Haven, Conn., 1975. Ordained to ministry Presbyn. Ch., 1975. Chaplain U. Bridgeport, Conn., 1973-75; assoc. pastor First Presbyn. Ch, Tulsa, 1975-85; exec. dir. Presbyn. Urban Ministry Coun., Tulsa, 1977-85; cons. Program Agy. United Presbyn. Ch., N.Y.C., 1982-85; exec. dir. S. Hills Interfaith Ministries, Bethel Park, Pa., 1985—; chair. Presbyn. Ch. (USA) Task Force on Cen. Am., N.Y.C., 1982-83, 87-88, on interfaith marriage, Louisville, 1991, adv. coun. Ch. and Society, N.Y.C., 1984-86, Natural Workshop on Christian-Jewish Rels., Pitts., 1990—; mem. Presbyn. Ch. (USA), Task Force on Christians and Jews, N.Y.C., 1983-88. Contbr. articles, photo, and poems to publs. sec. South Hills Family Hospice, Pitts., 1991, treas. Pitts. Peace Inst., 1991, mem. Holocaust Commn. Pitts., 1991, Allegheny County Bd. for Food and Shelter, Pitts., 1991, steering com. Middle East Forum, Pitts., 1991. Recipient Interfaith award, Tulsa Interfaith Coalition, 1985, Interfaith Svc. award, Tulsa Met. Ministry, 1985. Mem. N. Am. Interfaith Network, Nat. Interfaith Community Ministries, Nat. Assn. Ecumenical Staff, Presbyn. Health Edn. and Welfare Assn. (bd. dirs. 1982-84), Community Ministries and Neighborhood Orgn. (steering com. 1990—), N.Y.C. Road Runners, Washington County (Pa.) Road Runners. Democrat. Home: 346 Parkside Dr Pittsburgh PA 15228 Office: S Hills Interfaith Ministries 5171 Park Ave Bethel Park PA 15102 *I need always enough satisfaction in my work to keep going but also enough dissatisfaction to keep growing. Above all, I need some small assurance that I am where God wants me to be, doing what I am called to do.*

BRASHEAR, RUSS, communication educator, radio executive; b. Oxford, Miss., Apr. 13, 1954; s. Charles and Dorothy (Lewallen) B.; m. Alisa Louise Brashear, July 16, 1977; children: Krista, Kara. BS in Edn., Miss. Coll., Clinton, 1977; MA in Communication, Southwestern Sem., Ft. Worth, 1982. Disc jockey WWWUN, Jax, Miss., 1974-76; owner/mgr. Lawn Techniques, Ft. Worth, 1982-85; coach Trinity Valley High Sch., Ft. Worth, 1982-84; prof. communication Miss. Coll., 1982-89, gen. mgr. WHJT FM, prof. communication, 1982—; cons. WFCA FM, French Camp, 1985-87, WLVJ FM, Indianola, 1988-90. Mem. Young Reps., Clinton, 1986, Civitan, Clinton, 1990, Drug Awareness, Clinton, 1989-90. Named Sportscaster of Yr. MBA, 1987, Written Comml. of Yr., 1988. Mem. Miss. Assn. Broadcasters (bd. dirs. 1989-90)), Jaycees. Baptist. Avocations: music, sports. Home: 106 Garaway Cove Clinton MS 39058 Office: Sta WHJT FM 100 Jefferson St Clinton MS 39058

BRASHIER, JOSEPH CLARENCE, broadcasting executive, lay worker; b. Milw., Jan. 9, 1956; s. Clarence Monroe and Pearl Verna (Waymire) B.; m. Glenda Jean Gregory, June 29, 1979. Student, brown Inst., Mpls., 1977. Gospel music dir. Sta. WJKM Radio, Hartsville, Tenn., 1982-84; program dir. Sta. WNQM Radio, Nashville, 1984-87; nat. program dir. Sta. WNQM Radio/Sta. WWCR Internat. Radio, Nashville, 1987—, Sta. WITA Radio, Knoxville, Tenn., 1987—, Sta. WMQM Radio, Memphis, 1987—. Mem. Soc. Broadcast Engrs., Nat. Assn. Radio/TV Engrs. Home: 316 Hickory St Madison TN 37115 Office: Sta WNQM/WWCR World Wide Christian Radio 4647 Old Hydes Ferry Pike Nashville TN 37218

BRASWELL, CARLTON SAMUEL, pastor; b. Hawkinsville, Ga., Nov. 1, 1959; s. Carl Gene and Doris (Darsey) B.; m. Rhonda Thompson, Dec. 15, 1979; children: Heather Ann, Lori Beth, Katie Rebecca. AA, Brewton Parker Coll., 1980; BS, Ga. State U., 1983; MDiv, New Orleans Bapt. Sem., 1988. Cert. MasterLife leader, continuing witness. Interim pastor Scott (Ga.) Bapt. Ch., 1979-80; assoc./youth pastor Chapel Hill Bapt. Ch., Douglasville, Ga., 1980-83; youth minister New Ga. Bapt. Ch., Villa Rica, 1984-85; pastor High Shoals Bapt. Ch., Dallas, Ga., 1985-87, Friendship Bapt. Ch., Cartersville, Ga., 1987—. Youth baseball coach Cartersville Recreation Dept., 1988—; fund raising com. Mission Rd. Elem. PTA, Cartersville, 1990. Recipient Religious Leadership award Brewton Parker Coll., 1980; named Doctrinal Sermon speaker Mid. Cherokee Assn., 1988; nominated Parents of the Yr. Mission Rd. Elem. Tchrs., 1990. Mem. Paulding County Hosp. Chaplains, Mid. Cherokee Minister's Fellowship (sec. 1988-89), Tallapoosa Bapt. Assn. (moderator 1986-87, vice moderator 1985-86, youth com. 1984-87), Mid. Cherokee Bapt. Assn. (discipleship dir. 1987—). Home: 1116 Mission Rd SW Cartersville GA 30120 Office: Friendship Bapt Ch 606 Cassville Rd Cartersville GA 30120 *The deteriorating moral fiber of our country will only be changed when churches across America rise from an egocentric spirit to an evangelistic sphere.*

BRATCHER, DENNIS RAY, religious educator; b. Elk City, Okla., June 22, 1947; s. Earl Bud and Dona Belle (Potter) B.; m. Linda Jean Hodge; Jan. 1, 1968; children: Tamara Lynne, Todd Allan. AB, So. Nazarene Univ., 1974, MA, 1979; MDiv, Nazarene Theol. Sem., Kansas City, Mo., 1980; PhD, Union Theol. Sem., Richmond, Va., 1984. Ordained elder Ch. of the Nazarene, 1989. Assoc. pastor Hanover Ch. of the Nazarene, Mechanicsville, Va., 1980-84; adjunct prof. Va. Union U., Richmond, 1984-85; assoc. prof. So. Nazarene U., Bethany, Okla., 1985—. Author: (book) Theological Message of Habakkuk, 1984; co-author (with others) Harper's Bible Dictionary, 1985; contbr. articles to religous periodicals. Recipient teaching fellowship. Union Theol. Sem. in Va., Richmond, 1983. Mem. Wesleyan Theol. Soc., Soc. Bibl. Lit., Bibl. Archaeology Soc. Office: So Nazarene Univ 6729 NW 39 Expwy Bethany OK 73008

BRATTGARD, HELGE AXEL KRISTIAN, retired bishop; b. Gothenburg, Sweden, July 26, 1920; s. Hjalmar and Ida (Kristensson) Olsson; m. Ruth Gunhild Maria Carlson, Jan. 23, 1946; children—Kerstin Larsson, Daniel Häkan. Theology Kand., U. Lund, Sweden, 1944, Theology Lic., 1951, Theology Dr., 1956. Pastor various congregations Ch. of Sweden, 1944-51; dir. theology Nat. Com. Lutheran World Fedn., 1951-53; dean diocese of Linkoping, Ch. of Sweden, 1965-69, Bishop diocese of Skara, 1969-85, chmn. ch. commn. on confession, 1983-87; chmn. Nat. Com. Luth. World Fedn., Geneva, 1974; mem. com. for med.-ethical problems Govt. of Sweden. Author: God's Stewards, 1963. Contbr. articles to profl. jours. Lodge: Rotary. Home: Magasinsgatan 1, 44130 Alingsås Sweden

BRATTON, CONRAD CHRISTOPHER, music minister; b. Dallas, Mar. 27, 1941; s. Luther Conrad and Naomi Bernice (Clardy) B.; m. Linda Elisabeth Little, Aug. 22, 1964; 1 child, James Conrad. MusB, Hardin-Simmons U., Abilene, Tex., 1964, MusM, 1967. Choral tchr. Nolan Jr. High, Killeen, Tex., 1964-65; music tchr. Alta Vista Elem., Abilene, 1965-71; choral dir. Mann Jr. High, Abilene, 1971-79; music minister Ch. of the Heavenly Rest, Abilene, 1973—; music educator McMurry Coll., Abilene, 1974-76. Choral dir. premiere performances December Story, 1-act opera, The Easter Story, cantata, Lazarus, 1-act opera. Mem. NEA, Am. Choral Dirs. Assn., Tex. Music Educators Assn., Tex. Tchrs. Assn., Abilene Opera Assn., Brotherhood Benevolent Artists, Phi Mu Alpha Sinfonia. Episcopalian. Home: 1250 Sayles Blvd Abilene TX 79605 Office: Ch of the Heavenly Rest 602 Meander Abilene TX 79602

BRATTON, GEORGE STANFORD, minister, religious organization executive; b. Uniontown, Pa., Aug. 15, 1941; s. George A. and Mary J. (Miller) B.; m. Marietta A. Warstock; children: Barbara Brooke Bratton Tibbe, Rebecca Shellee. BA, Adrian (Mich.) Coll., 1963; BD, Andover Newton

Theol. Sem., 1967, STM, 1971, D Ministry, 1976. Ordained to ministry Am. Bapt. and Presbyn. Ch. (U.S.A.), 1967; cert. in clin. pastoral tng. Asst. min. 1st Bapt. Ch. in Am., Providence, 1966-68; urban min. Interfaith Urban Ministries, Providence, 1968-73; pastor Parsells Ave. Community Ch., Rochester, N.Y., 1973-88; exec. dir. Buffalo Area Coun. Chs., 1988—; chair pub. policy com. and futuring task force, mem. coordinating cabinet and mission coun. Synod of N.E., Presbyn. Ch. U.S.A., 1987-91; pres. Rochester/Genesee region Am. Bapt. Chs., 1987-88, mem. min.'s coun.; bd. dirs., chmn. various coms. Genesee Ecumenical Ministries, Rochester, 1976-88. Sec., bd. dirs. Action for a Better Community, Monroe County, N.Y., 1979-88; chair Western N.Y. Immigration Action Coalition, Upstate, 1986-90; mem. adv. com. N.Y. Gov.'s Inter-Agy. Task Force on Immigration Affairs, 1987-91; treas. Interfaith Coalition on Energy, Western, N.Y., 1990-91. Recipient Gabriel award Nat. Cath. Broadcasters, 1969, Testimonial of Appreciation award Haitian Community Orgn., 1975, Edward H. Rhodes award Am. Bapt. Chs., 1981. Mem. Nat. Assn. Ecumenical Staff, Presbytery Western N.Y., Greater Roch Track Club. Home: 334 Crescent Ave Buffalo NY 14214 Office: Buffalo Area Coun Chs 1272 Delaware Ave Buffalo NY 14209

BRAUCH, MANFRED T., academic administrator. Head Ea. Bapt. Theol. Sem., Phila. Office: Ea Bapt Theol Sem Lancaster and City Aves Philadelphia PA 10151-1405*

BRAUN, ALAN JAMES, pastor; b. Rolla, N.D., Aug. 14, 1942; s. Harold Carl Herman and Adele Margaret (Schwake) B.; m. Rosemary Ann Hinck, Aug. 5, 1967; children: Rebekah, Andrew, Joanna, Susanna, Deborah. AA, Concordia Coll., 1962; BA, Concordia Sr. Coll., 1964; MDiv, Concordia Sem., 1968. Ordained to Luth. ministry, 1968. Asst. pastor Pilgrim Luth. Ch., Decatur, Ill., 1968-72; pastor St. Michael Luth. Ch., Wayne, Mich., 1972-85, King of Kings Luth. Ch., Roseville, Minn., 1985—. Bd. dirs. Macon County Rehab. Facilities, Decatur, 1969-72, Community Chem. Health Coun., Roseville, 1988, 89. Home: 763 Grandview Ave W Roseville MN 55113

BRAUN, EUNICE HOCKSPEIER, author, religious order executive, lecturer; b. Alta Vista, Iowa; d. George Phillip and Lydia (Reinhart) Hockspeier; student Gates Coll., 1932-34, Coe Coll., 1937-39, Northwestern U., 1944-47; m. Leonard James Braun, May 29, 1937. Freelance writer for mags., newspapers, 1947-52; bus. mgr. Baha'i Publishing Trust, Wilmette, Ill., 1952-55, mng. dir., 1955-71; internat. news editor Baha'i News, 1952-70; tchr. Baha'i schs., Alaska, Can., Europe and U.S., 1958—; lectr. Baha'i Faith in U.S., Central Am., Europe, Africa, Asia, 1953—; cons. Baha'i Pub. Trust, New Delhi, India, 1972; mem. aux. bd. Continental Bd. Counselors, Baha'i Faith in the Ams., 1972—. Mem. Nat. League Am. Pen Women, Baha'i Faith, Iota Sigma Epsilon. Author: Know Your Baha'i Literature, 1959; The Dawn of World Peace, 1963; Baha'u'llah: His Call to the Nations, 1967; From Strength to Strength, Half Century of the Formative Age of the Baha'i Faith, 1978; A Crown of Beauty, 1982; The March of the Institutions, 1984; A Reader's Guide: The Development of Baha'i Literature in English, 1986; contbr. essays to Baha'i World, Internat. Record. Home: 1025 Forestview Ln Glenview IL 60025

BRAUNER, RONALD ALLAN, religion educator; b. Phila., Aug. 5, 1939; s. Samuel Joseph Brauner and Ann Ruth (Soloner) Levin; m. Marcia Faith Silver, Sept. 9, 1962; children: Yaakov Baruch, Miriam Aliza. Cert. in teaching, Greenberg Inst., Jerusalem, 1960; BS in Edn., Temple U., 1962; PhD, Dropsie Coll., 1974. Cert. tchr., Pa. Assoc. prof. Gratz Coll., Phila., 1967-78; acad. dean Reconstructionist Rabbinical Coll., Phila., 1972-83; dir. Brandeis-Bardin Inst., L.A., 1983-85; exec. dir. Hebrew Inst. Pitts., 1985-91; pres. Found. for Jewish Studies, Inc., Pitts., 1991—. Editor Jewish Civilization: Essays and Studies, 1979-85, Straightalk, 1991—. Mem. Coun. for Jewish Edn. (v.p. 1990—), Coalition Alternatives in Jewish Edn., Am. Oriental Soc., Soc. Biblical Lit. Democrat. Office: Found for Jewish Studies 1531 S Negley Ave Pittsburgh PA 15217

BRAUS, STEPHEN VINCENT, parish administrator; b. Bismarck, N.D., Jan. 5, 1952; s. Matthias Henry and Ruth Gertrude (Hanggi) B.; m. Elizabeth Marian Fischer, June 18, 1977; children: Stephen P., Jennifer M., Daniel M., Carolyn C. BA, BS in Secondary Edn., Math., Dickinson State Coll., 1974; MS in Edn. Adminstrn., No. State Coll., Aberdeen, S.D., 1980. Cert. asbestos inspector, mgmt. planner. Tchr. math., chemistry Killdeer (N.D.) High Sch., 1974-75; dir. religious edn. St. Anne's Parish, Bismarck, N.D., 1975-78; dir. of sacramental preparation St. Joseph's Parish, Mandan, N.D., 1978-84; cons. pastoral planning St. James Parish, Jamestown, N.D., 1988-89; parish adminstr. St. Joseph's Parish, Mandan, 1984-91, St. Mary's Parish, Bismarck, 1991—; mem. Diocesan Pastoral Planning Commn., Bismarck, 1984-90, Parish Pastoral Couns., Dickinson, Bismarck and Mandan, 1971—, Diocesan Ministry Formation Task Force, Bismarck, 1987, Diocesan Synod Adv. Com., 1990—. Contbg. author coun. manual, 1987; editor personnel manual, 1988. Named to Outstanding Young Men of Am., 1979. Fellow Nat. Assn. Ch. Bus. Adminstrs. (cert. ch. bus. adminstrn.); mem. Prairie Pastoral Ministers Assn. (pres. 1982-86, sec. 1987-90). Office: St Marys Ch 806 E Broadway Ave Bismarck ND 58501

BRAUSE, DORSEY WAYLAND, college president; b. Tiffin, Ohio, May 20, 1927; s. Earl George and Hulda Belle (Lutz) B.; m. Doris Lucile Oswalt, Aug. 30, 1953; children: Ann, Ned. BA, Otterbein Coll., 1950; MA, Ohio State U., 1953, PhD, 1963. Tchr. Republic (Ohio) Schs., 1950-52; tchr., prin. Thompson Sch., Bellevue, Ohio, 1953-55; supt. Chatfield, Alger, Newark and Dayton Schs., Ohio, 1955-64; dir. tchr. edn. Taylor U., Upland, Ind., 1964-69; dean extension svcs. Brookdale Community Coll., Lincroft, N.J., 1969-74; acad. dean Genesee Community Coll., Batavia, N.Y., 1974-76; dir. adult min. Free Meth. Ch. N.Am., Winona Lake, Ind., 1976-80; pres. Cen. Coll., McPherson, Kans., 1981-87, Spring Arbor (Mich.) Coll., 1987-91. With USN, 1945-46. Republican. Avocations: skiing, tennis, chess. Home: 25575 Budapest Mission Viejo CA 92691

BRAUZA, ELLEN LEDERER, academic administrator; b. Buffalo, N.Y., Oct. 9, 1950; d. Erwin August Lederer and Norma Lillian (Naukam) Bissell; m. Walter Kenneth Brauza, Nov. 12, 1977; children: Elisabeth Mary, Stephen Walter. BA in Theology, Valparaiso U., 1972; MA in Pastoral Ministry, Christ the King Seminary, East Aurora, N.Y., 1986. Dir. religious edn. St. Lawrence Roman Cath. Ch., Buffalo, 1986-91; dir. campus ministry Villa Maria Coll., Buffalo, 1990—; moderator Pax Christi Villa/Pax Christi USA, Buffalo, 1990—; team mem. Diocese Buffalo Campus Ministry, 1990—. Troop leader Girl Scouts U.S.A., Clarence, N.Y., 1985-88, com. mem., 1988-91. Mem. Cath. Campus Ministry Assn., Pax Christi U.S.A., Ctr. for Justice, Bread for the World. Democrat. Home: 4210 Gunnville Rd Clarence NY 14031 Office: Villa Maria Coll 240 Pine Ridge Rd Buffalo NY 14225 *The unexamined faith is like the unexamined life: not worth having. Truth matters more than we may know. But the task is not to choose between many truths; rather, it is to dance lightly on the point of their convergence.*

BRAVER, BARBARA LEIX, religious organization communications administrator; b. Pitts., Sept. 16, 1938; d. Joseph Walter and Mary (Dillon) Leix; m. Alan Braver, Sept. 7, 1963; children—Julian Ross, Margaret Elliott. B.A., Duquesne U., 1960. Tech. editor Mitre Corp., Bedford, Mass., 1961-68; copy editor The Arlingtonian, Arlington, Mass., 1970-71; dir. Communications Episcopal Diocese Mass., Boston, 1977—; free-lance writer, 1968—. Writer, editor, photographer newspaper Episcopal Times, 1984 (numeous awards). Producer videotape A Diocese Celebrates, 1985. Mem. Assoc. Ch. Press (bd. dirs. 1984—), Episcopal Communicators (bd. govs. 1982—). Democrat. Avocations: hiking; gardening; reading; films. Home: Old Salem Rd Gloucester MA 01930 Office: Episcopal Diocese of Mass 1 Joy St Boston MA 02108

BRAY, DONALD LAWRENCE, minister; b. Olwein, Iowa, Oct. 14, 1942; s. Arthur L. and Rachel C. (Archer) B.; m. Joy F. Failing, Aug. 15, 1964; children: Juli, Steven, Jeffrey. BA in Religion, Ind. Wesleyan U., 1964; MA in Religion, Olivet Nazarene U., 1965. Ordained to ministry Wesleyan Ch., 1967. Pastor Mich. Dist. Wesleyan Ch., Grand Rapids, Mich., 1965-68; missionary Wesleyan World Missions, Indpls., 1968-77, dir. personnel, 1977-84, asst. gen. sec., 1984-88; dist. supt. Delta dist. Wesleyan Ch., Jackson, Miss., 1988—; trustee Cen. Wesleyan Coll., Cen. S.C., 1989—; adj. prof. Wesley Bibl. Sem., Jackson, 1989—. Author: (tng. manual) Christian Witness, 1985; contbr. articles to profl. jours. Mem. Ind. Wesleyan U. Alumni Assn. (bd. dirs. 1984-86). Office: Delta Dist Wesleyan Ch PO Box 13100 Jackson MS 39236 *Love, self giving love, is the fullest expression of Christian faith and has the power of centrifugal force to pull others in to it. But that love becomes centrifugal in nature as it sends us out to a love starved world, in the name of Christ.*

BRAY, JAMES WALLACE, II, minister; b. Fresno, Calif., Aug. 5, 1952; s. James Wallace and Alma Jean (Higgins) B.; m. Diana Sue Rendleman, Sept. 9, 1972; 1 child, Jaime Grace. BA, Calif. Bapt. Coll., Riverside, 1974; M.Ch. Music, Golden Gate Sem., Mill Valley, Calif., 1977. Ordained to ministry, So. Bapt. Conv., 1978. Assoc pastor music and edn. Trinity Bapt. Ch., Vacaville, Calif., 1977-81; missionary So. Bapt. Fgn. Mission Bd., Costa Rica, 1981-82; assoc. pastor Canoga Park (Calif.) Bapt. Ch., 1987-89; assoc. pastor music and edn. First Bapt. Ch., Campbell, Calif., 1982-87, First So. Bapt. Ch., Apple Valley, Calif., 1989—; associational music dir. High Desert Bapt. Assn., Hesperia, Calif., 1990—; state music specialist Calif. So. Bapt. Conv., Fresno, 1980—. Mem. Calif. Singing Churchmen, Western Bapt. Religious Educators Assn. Office: First So Bapt Ch 12345 Navajo Rd Apple Valley CA 92308

BRAY, JOHN ARTHUR, minister; b. Oak Park, Ill., June 5, 1950; s. Arthur Lawrence and Rachel Charlotte (Archer) B.; m. Patricia Darlene Sexton,June 10, 1972; children: Heather Michelle, Karin Nicole. BA, Ind. Wesleyan U., 1972; postgrad., U. Iowa, 1977-78. Ordained to ministry Wesleyan Ch., 1974. Pastor Pleasantdale United Meth. Ch., Montpelier, Ind., 1972-73; sr. pastor Heritage Wesleyan Ch., Moline, Ill., 1973—; mem. steering com., dir. security Internat. Wesleyan Youth Conv., Urbana, Ill, 1981-82; pres. Christian Holiness Assn. Quad Cities, 1984-88; exec. dir. tng. Grand Rapids (Mich.) '88 Youth Conf., 1987-88. Sec. Young Republicans, Marion, Ind., 1968-69. Mem. Kiwanis. Office: Heritage Wesleyan Ch 4417 53d St Moline IL 61265 *The person who seeks to develop real faith in another must be sure to be joyful, practical and Biblical. What good is faith if these are missing?.*

BRAY, MAUREEN ELIZABETH, clergywoman; b. Medford, Oreg., Nov. 23, 1946; d. Jouett Philip and Edith Pearl (Cape) Bray. B.A., Trinity Bible Inst., Jamestown, N.D., 1970; B.A., Northwest Coll., Kirkland, Wash., 1971. Ordained to ministry Assemblies of God, 1972; assoc. pastor Lake City Tabernacle, Seattle, 1970—, youth dir., 1972—, Christian edn. dir., 1972—, asst. dir., 1970—, trustee, 1970—. Mem. Alumni Assn. Northwest Coll., Alumni Assn. Trinity Bible Inst. Democrat. Home: 529 Taylor Pl NW Renton WA 98055 Office: Lake City Tabernacle 3001 NE 127th St Seattle WA 98125

BRAY, WILLIAM DAVENPORT, minister, educator emeritus; b. Norwood, Ga., Aug. 31, 1913; s. Jouett Philip and Bernice (Anderson) B.; m. Frances Hutchison, June 13, 1944; children: James Edward, Margaret Elizabeth, Thomas Herbert. BA, So. Meth. U., 1936, ThB, 1939, ThM, 1942; PhD, U. Chgo., 1951. Pastor Turrell (Ark.) Meth. Ch., 1939-42, Tigard (Oreg.) Meth. Ch., 1942-43; prof. Multnomah Coll., Portland, Oreg., 1942-43; pastor St. Helens (Oreg.) United Meth. Ch., 1946-48; prof. New Testament Kwansei Gakuin U., Nishinomiya, Japan, 1952-80, prof. emeritus, 1980—, chaplain, 1962-66; trustee Kwansei Gakuin U., 1970-76, Seiwa Coll. for Christian Workers, Nishinomiya, 1965-80; pres. Fellowship Christian Missionaries in Japan, 1959-60. Author: The Weekday Readings in the Greek Gospel Lectionary, 1989; contbr. articles to profl. jours. Major USAF, U.S. Army, 1943-46. Recipient award for disting. svc. City of Kobe, Japan, 1978, Gov. Hyogo Prefecture, 1987. Mem. Soc. Bibl. Lit., Am. Schs. Oriental Rsch., John Wesley Soc. Japan, New Testament Soc. Japan, Inst. for Religion and Wholeness, Inst. for Preservation of Ancient Bibl. Manuscripts, Claremont U. Club, Masons. Home: 715 Plymouth Rd Claremont CA 91711

BRAY, WILLIAM HOWARD, minister; b. Shreveport, La., Feb. 8, 1952; s. Howard Maurice and Bonnie Jean (Draper) B.; m. Judy Jean Russell; children: Krista Rachelle, William Brandon. BA, Mid-Am. Nazarene Coll., 1974; MDiv., Nazarene Theol. Sem., Kansas City, Mo., 1978; D of Ministry, Phillips U., 1985. Pastor Friends Ch., Gardner, Kans., 1976-77, Fairview Nazarene Ch., Marshall, Tex., 1978-81, First Nazarene Ch., Stillwater, Okla., 1981-86; registrar/intern dir. Nazarene Bible Coll., Colorado Springs, Colo., 1986—. Author: The Church in Thy House, 1987. Republican. Office: Nazarene Bible College 1111 Chapman Dr Colorado Springs CO 80916

BRAZAUSKAS, BEVERLY MAE, religion educator; b. Manchester, Conn., June 13, 1944; d. Chester Edward and Nina Marie (Pikow) B. BA, Coll. Our Lady of the Elms, Chicopee, Mass., 1967; MEd, Wayne State U., 1974; cert., Boston Coll., 1979; MA in Theology, U. Notre Dame, 1985. Dir. religious edn. and liturgy St. Matthew Parish, Tolland, Conn., 1974-85; assoc. dir. religious edn. inst. Diocese Ft. Wayne and South Bend, Mishawaka, Ind., 1985-86; dir. religious edn. and liturgy Sacred Heart Parish, Notre Dame, Ind., 1986—; religions cons. Silver Burdett & Ginn, Dioceses Ft. Wayne and South Bend, 1987—; tchr. Workshop for U.S. Navy Chaplains, Worship and the Worshipping Community, 1989. Contbr. articles to profl. jours. Mem. Diocesan Assn. Catechetical Ministers (v.p. 1987-88, 89-90, pres. 1988-89). Office: Sacred Heart Parish Presbytery Notre Dame IN 46556

BRAZELTON, DAVID TODD, minister; b. Greenville, Pa., May 31, 1954; s. Thomas James and Mildred Elizabeth (Boot) B.; m. Cheryl Dianne Ross, May 28, 1983; children: Jessica Naomi, Nathan Thomas. BA, Thiel Coll., 1976; MA, Indiana U. Pa., 1980; MDiv, Pitts. Theol. Sem., 1984. Ordained to ministry United Meth. Ch. as deacon, 1983, as elder, 1986. Assoc. pastor Bakerstown United Meth. Ch., Gibsonia, Pa., 1981-84; pastor 4th St United Meth. Ch., Pitts., 1984-88, Muhlemon United Meth. Ch., Pitts., 1984-88, Savannah United Meth. Ch., New Castle, Pa., 1988—; dir. missions Butler dist. United Meth. Ch., 1989—, mem. global ministries, 1989—, counseling elder Western Pa. Conf., 1990—. Author: Net Results, 1991. Sec. bd. dirs. Turtle Creek Valley Mental Health/Mental Retardation, Inc., Pitts., 1984-89; coord. Lawrence County Operation Desert Storm Support Group; mem. Lawrence County chpt. Operation Desert Storm Task Force, 1990—. Mem. Greater New Castle Ministerial Fellowship. Home: 94 Savannah Gardner Rd New Castle PA 16101 Office: Savannah United Meth Ch 94 Savannah Gardner Rd New Castle PA 16101 *It is my prayer that our friendship will know not the bounds of time imposed by this pause before eternity.*

BRAZZEL, STEPHEN RAY, youth minister; b. Odessa, Tex., Aug. 18, 1964; s. Rayburn Leon and Anna Joyce (Gober) B.; m. Julie Michelle King, Sept. 15, 1989. BS in Radio-TV-Film, U. Tex., 1987; MDiv, Southwestern Bapt. Theol. Sem., 1991. Lic. to Christian Ministry, 1985. Youth min. Barton Creek Bapt. Ch., Austin, Tex., 1984-86; v.p. youth internat. World Hope Found., Austin, 1984-87; youth min. First Bapt. Ch., Seagoville, Tex., 1988—; guest speaker Various Retreats, Banquets, Baccalaureates, and Churches, 1984—; revival preacher World Hope Crusades in Japan and Korea, 1985, 86, 87. Mem. Dallas Bapt. Assn., Hillsboro Ski Team (pres. 1985-87). Home: 721 Judy Seagoville TX 75159

BRDAS, SISTER MARY ALEXINE, nun; b. Chgo., Apr. 30, 1929; d. Joseph Albert and Alexine Clare (Poirier) B. BA, St. Francis Coll., 1961; MA, DePaul U., 1975. Cert. tchr. grades 6-12, adminstrn. K-12; joined Sisters of St. Francis of Christ the King, 1948. Tchr. St. Stephen Sch., Chgo., 1949-52, St. Nicholas Sch., Pitts., 1952-53, St. Mary Nativity Sch., Joliet, Ill., 1953-55, St. Christine Sch., Euclid, OHio, 1955-60, Mt. Assisi Acad., Lemont, Ill., 1960-82; adminstr. St. George Sch., Chgo., 1982-87, St. Mary Nativity, Joliet, 1987—; CCD coord. St. Mary Nativity, Joliet, 1988-89, St. George, Chgo., 1982-87. Mem. Nat. Cath. Edn. Assn., Joliet Diocesan Prin. Assn. Roman Catholic. Office: St Mary Nativity Sch 702 N Broadway St Joliet IL 60435

BREAUX, CLIFTON LYNN, minister; b. Jennings, La., Jan. 11, 1954; s. Joseph Jules and Eltha Mae (Miller) B.; m. Denice Lynn Owens, Apr. 28, 1975; 1 child, Clifton Lynn II. BA, Mc Neese State U., 1976; MA, Southwestern Bapt. Theol. Sem., Ft. Worth, 1985. Ordained to ministry So. Bapt. Conv., 1985. Pastor 1st Bapt. Ch., Kinder, La., 1985-87, Forest Hill (La.) Bapt. Ch., 1987—; evangelist World Evangelism Found., Madrid, Southcliffe Bapt.-St. Ministry, Ft. Worth, Southwestern Bapt. Theol. Sem. Recipient Voice of Democracy award Am. Legion. Mem. Am. Radio Relay League, Masons (worshipful master), Order Ea. Star. Home: 59 9th St Forest Hill LA 71430 Office: Forest Hill Bapt Ch PO Box 158 Forest Hill LA 71430

BREAUX, HELEN ISABEL, religious organization administrator; b. Westwego, La., July 13, 1934; d. John Paul and Adelaide Isabel (Cooke) Breaux. B.S. in Edn., Loyola U. New Orleans, 1970; M.R.E., Notre Dame Sem., 1973, D.R.E., 1970. Entered Sisters of Our Lady of Mt. Carmel, Roman Catholic Ch., 1953; Sisters Christian Community, 1975; tchr. various schs., 1955-69; dir. Religious Edn., Our Lady of Prompt Succor Parish, Westwego, La., 1970-74; asso. dir. Office Religious Edn., Archdiocese of New Orleans, 1975-82; adminstr. Annunciation Inn, New Orleans, 1983—; commr.-in-charge Ward 14, Precinct 25, New Orleans, 1978—. Organist, chairperson liturgy com. St. Rita Ch., New Orleans. Recipient award for service Our Lady of Prompt Succor Parish, 1974; recipient Key to City of Westwego, 1974, 81. Mem. Nat. Cath. Educators Assn., Assn. for Supervision and Curriculum Devel., Nat. Assn. Ch. Personnel Adminstrs., Nat. Council Diocesan Dirs. Religious Edn., Religious Edn. Assn., U.S. Hist. Assn., Assn. Mgmt. Elderly Housing, New Orleans Mus. Art, St. Vincent de Paul Soc. Democrat. Club: K.C. Aux. One of several editors for religion text series, 1976-81. Home: 2719 1/2 Pine St New Orleans LA 70125 Office: 1220 Spain St New Orleans LA 70117

BRECKENRIDGE, JAMES, religion educator; b. St. Louis, June 30, 1935; s. Vance Newman and Elsa Schuarte (Breckenridge) Newman Breckenridge; m. Linda Faye Smith, June 21, 1969; children—Bonnie Lin, Rebecca Jane. B.A., Biola Coll., 1957; B.D., Calif. Bapt. Theol. Sem., 1960; M.A., U. So. Calif., 1965, Ph.D., 1968. Lectr., Am. Bapt. Sem. of West Covina (Calif.), 1967-74, Calif. Poly. Coll.-Pomona, 1969-74, U. Redlands (Calif.), spring 1972; prof. religion Baylor U., Waco, Tex., 1974—. Served to capt. USAR, 1958-66. Mem. Am. Acad. Religion, Collectors of Religion on Stamps, Japanese Assn. for Indian and Buddhist Studies, Soc. for Buddhist-Christian Studies, Phi Kappa Phi. Baptist. Contbr. religious articles to profl. publs. Home: 4612 Sanger Ave Waco TX 76710 Office: Baylor U Tidwell Bldg B 27 Waco TX 76798

BRECKENRIDGE, WILLIAM CALLOW, administrator; b. Balt., Jan. 9, 1951; s. George C. and Donna L. (Rorabaugh) B.; m. Donna Jean Anderson, Feb. 28, 1981; 1 child, Bethany Marie. BS, Liberty U., 1989; M in Bibl. Studies, Bethany Sem. Lic. to ministry Christian Ch., 1988. Ministry adminstrn. Dedication Evangelism Inc., Towaco, N.J., 1986—, The Word and The World/Newspoint, Towaco, N.J., 1986—; sr. counselor Beachmont Christian Camp, Balt., 1985. Author: (commentaries/evangelistic lit.) Newspoint radio program, 1987—. With U.S. Army, 1969-75. Republican. Office: Dedication Evangelism Inc PO Box 10 Towaco NJ 07082

BREDESON, JAMES CLEMENS, pastor; b. Forest City, Iowa, June 3, 1956; s. Clemens J. and Marilyn J. (Winkelmann) B.; m. Susan M. Waldschmidt, Aug. 27, 1981; children: John-Mark, Christopher. BA, Concordia Coll., 1978; MDiv, Concordia Sem., 1982. Ordained to ministry Luth. Ch.-Mo. Synod, 1982. Pastor St. John Luth. Ch., Chillicothe, Mo., 1982-85, Luth. Ch. of the Good Shepherd, York, Pa., 1985—; sec. York Luth. High Sch., 1986-88. Chaplain York City Police Chaplain Corps, 1986—; bd. dirs. Mental Health Assn. York County, sec. 1989—; circuit counselor Southeastern Dist. Luth. Ch. Mo. Synod, 1991—. Mem. Luth. Lay Renewal (pastoral co-advisor Mid-Atlantic Region 1990—), York County Evang. Mins. Fellowship (sec.-treas. 1987-90), First Capitol Optimist Club (bd. dirs. 1987-88). Democrat. Home: 135 S Hartley St York PA 17404 Office: Luth Ch of Good Shepherd 135 S Hartley St York PA 17404

BREED, JAMES LINCOLN, minister; b. Sept. 1, 1944; s. Stewart Harkrader and Bernice Emma (Coad) B.; m. Monika Preu, June 10, 1968; children: Thomas Stewart, Nathan Stanley, Katrina Helene. BS cum laude, U. Dubuque, 1966, MDiv summa cum laude, 1970, MST summa cum laude, 1971; PhD, Aquinas Inst. Theology, 1980. Ordained to ministry Presbyn. Ch. (U.S.A.), 1971. Pastor Garden Plain Presbyn. Ch., Fulton, Ill., 1971-79, Spring Valley Presbyn Ch., Morrison, Ill., 1971-79, Wequiock Presbyn. Ch., Green Bay, Wis., 1979-82, Robinsonville Presbyn. Ch., New Franken, Wis., 1979-82, 1st Presbyn. Ch., Kewanee, Ill., 1982—; asst. wrestling coach Kewanee High Sch., 1988—; vice moderator Blackhawk Presbytery, Presbyn. Ch. (U.S.A.), Oregon, Ill., 1985, del. Synod of Lincoln Trails, Indpls., 1989. Contbr. articles to religious publs. Mem. Am. Soc. Ch. History, Inst. Religion in Age of Sci., Kewanee Ministerial Assn. Pres. 1985-86), Kewanee Hosp. Vol. Chaplains (pres. 1985), Masons. Office: 1st Presbyn Ch 307 S Tremont St Kewanee IL 61443 *What do we have in this life that's truly valuable, if not the love of God, the love of our family and friends, the respect of our neighbors, our good name and our integrity? These things, and the ability to be of benefit to our community, have a value far beyond anything else we can possess.*

BREEN, BARTON JAMES, church business administrator; b. London, Ont., Can., Nov. 27, 1962; came to US, 1982; s. James William and Elizabeth Evelyn (Irwin) B.; m. Margaret Kay Barnes, Aug. 4, 1984; children: Ryan Paul, Evan James. Student, Oral Roberts U., 1980-81, '82-85; BS in Bus. Adminstrn., Palm Beach Atlantic Coll., 1987; postgrad., Alliance Theol. Sem., Nyack, N.Y., 1988—. Ordained to ministry Christian and Missionary Alliance Ch., Orlando, Fla., 1990. Asst. pastor Christian Missionary Alliance Ch., Lake Worth, Fla., 1988-90; fin. adminstr. Trinity United Meth. Ch., Palm Beach Gardens, Fla., 1987-90; fin. aid assoc. Palm Beach Atlantic Coll., West Palm Beach, Fla., 1986-87; pastor Community Alliance Ch., Findlay, Ohio, 1990—; treas. Trinity United Meth. Ch., Palm Beach Gardens, Fla., 1987-90. Mem. Nat. Assn. of Ch. Bus. Adminstrs., Christian Ministry Mgmt. Assn., United Meth. Computer Users Group (pres., founder 1989). Home: 1403 Washington Ave Findlay OH 45840 Office: Community Alliance Chapel 15440 US Rte 224 E Findlay OH 45840

BREEN, PAULA VIRGINIA, minister; b. Natick, Mass., Oct. 4, 1943; d. John Howard and Edna May (Davis) B. BA, Ariz. State U., 1966; MDiv, Lancaster (Pa.) Theol. Sem., 1986. Ordained to ministry United Ch. of Christ, 1987. Lay worker Faith at Work, Columbia, Md., 1968-80, Lancaster Theol. Sem., 1980-86; assoc. pastor 1st Cong. Ch., Dalton, Mass., 1987-91.

BREEN, RÍOBART ÉADBARD, youth minister; b. Cohoes, N.Y., Apr. 5, 1967; s. Robert Edward and Patricia Grace (Kilmer) B. BA, SUNY, Geneseo, 1989; postgrad., St. Bernard's Inst., Rochester, N.Y., 1990—. Religious edn. coord. St. Agnes Ch., Avon, N.Y., 1989-90; religious edn. coord. St. Augustine/St. Monica Chs., Rochester, N.Y., 1990—, youth minister, 1990—; vacation Bible sch. dir. S.W. Ecumenical Ministries, Rochester, 1990—; catechetical rep. Diocese of Rochester Cath. Sch., S.W. Quadrent Governance Bd., Rochester, 1991—. Mem. Nat. Fedn. Cath. Youth Ministry, Phi Alpha Theta. Home: 410 Chili Ave Rochester NY 14611 Office: St Augustine St Monica Chs 34 Monica St Rochester NY 14619 *The average person seeks and embraces anything that condones or justifies his or her current comfortable lifestyle. The Gospel challenges us, however, to seek truth and, despite the difficulty, modify our lives accordingly.*

BREITBARTH, STEVEN ELDOR, clergyman, marriage and family therapist; b. Truman, Minn., Sept. 28, 1949; s. Eldor and Lois Minnie (Olhoft) B.; m. Janelle Kay Young, Oct. 14, 1972; children: Jonathan, Timothy, Marcus. AA, Bethany Jr. Coll., Mankato, Minn., 1969; BS, Mankato State U., 1978; M in Div., Concordia Sem., Ft. Wayne, Ind., 1980; postgrad., U. Wis., Superior, 1981. Lic. marriage and family therapist, Minn.; Ordained to ministry, 1980. Pastor Grace Luth. Ch., Chisholm, Minn., 1977—; therapist Luth. Social Service, Hibbing, 1983; vol. therapist Family Program Cen. Mesabi Treatment Ctr., Hibbing, 1980—; adv., speaker Aid to Victims of Sexual Assault, Virginia, Minn., 1981—; advisor Luth. Youth Group, No. Minn., 1984-88; chmn. No. Minn. Dist. Youth Com., 1988—; cons., bd. dirs. Northstar Hospice, Hibbing. v.p. PTA, Chisholm, 1981; chmn. Family Life Com. No. Minn., 1985—. Mem. Am. Assn. Marriage and Family Therapy (clin.). Clubs: Chisholm Skating (bd. dirs 1981-84, pres. 1984-86), Blueline (Chisholm) (bd. dirs. 1983—, pres. 1990—). Home: 313 NW 4th St Chisholm MN 55719 Office: Grace Luth Ch 508 NW 9th St Chisholm MN 55719

BREITENBECK, JOSEPH M., retired bishop; b. Detroit, Aug. 3, 1914; s. Matthew J. and Mary A. (Quinlan) B. Student, U. Detroit, 1932-35; B.A., Sacred Heart Sem., Detroit, 1938; postgrad., Gregorian U., Rome, Italy, 1938-40; S.T.L., Catholic U., Washington; J.C.L., Lateran U., Rome, 1949. Ordained priest Roman Catholic Ch., 1942; asst. at St. Margaret Mary Parish, Detroit, 1942-44; sec. to Cardinal Mooney, 1944-58, Cardinal Dearden, 1959; pastor Assumption Grotto, 1959-67; consecrated bishop, 1965, ordained titular bishop of Tepelta and aux. bishop of Detroit, 1965-69; bishop of Grand Rapids, Mich., 1969-90; Episcopal adviser Nat. Cath. Laymens Retreat Conf. Mem. Nat. Conf. Cath. Bishops (com. chmn.). Home and Office: Chancery Office 660 Burton St SE Grand Rapids MI 49507

BREITWIESER, R., ecumenical agency administrator. Head London Inter-Ch. Coun., Ont., Can. Office: London Inter-Ch Coun, 172 High St, London, ON Canada N6C 4K6*

BRENNAN, CHRISTOPHER PATRICK, librarian; b. Rochester, N.Y., Nov. 23, 1953; s. Donald Joseph and Mildred Viola (Durnherr) B.; m. Mary Lorraine VanKeuren, Aug. 1, 1982 (div. 1990); m. Kathryn Hittle, May 18, 1991. BA, St. John Fisher Coll., 1979; MLS, SUNY, Geneseo, 1981; postgrad., Colgate Rochester Div. Sch./Bexley Hall/Crozer Theol. Sem./St. Bernard's Inst., Rochester, 1986—. Tech. svcs. libr. Colgate Rochester Divinity Sch./Bexley Hall/Crozer Theol. Sem./St. Bernard's Inst., 1985—; diocesan conv. del. Episcopal Ch., Rochester, 1990—. Contbr. articles to profl. jours. Mem. Am. Theol. Libr. Assn. (chair theol. users Group OCLC 1989-90, bd. dirs. tech. svcs. div. 1989-91), ALA, Monroe County Libr. Club (various offices), Irish Am. Cultural Inst., Comhaltas Ceoltoiri Eireann. Democrat. Office: Colgate Rochester Divinity Sch 1100 S Goodman St Rochester NY 14620

BRENNAN, JOHN JOSEPH, priest; b. Northampton, Mass., July 27, 1951; s. James Joseph and Hazel Elizabeth (Rogers) B. BA in Philosophy, St. Michael's Coll., 1973; BA in Religious Studies, U. Louvain, 1976, MA in Religious Studies, 1978. Ordained priest Roman Cath. Ch., 1978. Assoc. pastor Holy Name Ch., Springfield, Mass., 1978-80, St. Joseph's Ch., Pittsfield, Mass., 1980-86, St. Michael's Ch., East Longmeadow, Mass., 1986—; spiritual dir. Cursillo Movement, Springfield, 1988—. Mem. Amnesty Internat., Pax Christi USA, KC (4th degree knight, East Longmeadow).

BRENNER, GERALD DONALD, minister; b. Reading, Pa., Sept. 15, 1963; s. Bert Harry and Barbara Ellen (Ely) B.; m. Michelle Renee Sheffield, Aug. 10, 1985. BS, Lancaster Bible Coll., 1985; MDiv in Christian Edn., So. Bapt. Theol. Sem., 1991. Ordained to ministry Bapt. Ch., 1988. Asst. dir. Christian edn. Calvary Bible Fellowship Ch., Sinking Spring, Pa., 1981-85; youth min. Northview Bapt. Ch., Hillsboro, Ohio, 1988, Buckner Bapt. Ch., LaGrange, Ky., 1988—; chaplain Lyndon Fire Dept., Louisville, 1990—; city clk./treas. City of Plantation, Ky., 1990—; mem. exec. com. Sulphur Fork Bapt. Assn., LaGrange, 1988—. Vol. firefighter Lyndon Fire Dept., Louisville, 1988—. Mem. Fedn. Fire Chaplains, Fellowship Christian Fire Fighters. Home: 9411 Tiverton Ct Louisville KY 40242-2327 Office: Buckner Bapt Ch 3714 W Highway 146 La Grange KY 40031

BRENNER, RAYMOND ANTHONY, priest; b. Evansville, Ind., Feb. 12, 1943; s. George Frederick and Marie Catherine (Gries) B. BA, St. Meinrad (Ind.) Coll., 1965; MDiv, St. Meinrad Sch. Theology, 1969. Ordained priest Roman Cath. Ch., 1969. Deacon Nativity Ch., Indpls., 1968; assoc. pastor St. John's Ch., Loogootee, Ind., 1969-74, Sts. Peter and Paul Ch., Haubstadt, Ind., 1974-78; pastor St. Mary's Ch., Sullivan, Ind., 1978-86, St. Joan of Arc Ch., Jasonville, Ind., 1982-86, Resurrection Ch., Evansville, 1986—; mem. Cath. Charities Bd., Evansville, 1972-75; v.p. Ministerial Assn., Sullivan, 1985-86; pres. Coun. of Priests, Evansville, 1989; diocesan chaplain St. Vincent de Paul Soc., Evansville, 1990—. Mem. Wabash Valley Human Svcs., Vincennes, Ind., 1982-86, Sullivan Housing Authority, 1983-85, Fed. Emergency Mgmt. Agy., Sullivan, 1984-86, Emergency Food Bank, Sullivan, 1984-86. Mem. Optimists (chaplain Evansville club 1990—), Elks. Democrat. Home and Office: Resurrection Cath Ch 5301 New Harmony Rd Evansville IN 47720-1774 *It takes so little time to offer a smile, and the rewards are beyond imagining. Somehow they know you care and that God cares too.*

BRENNER, REEVE ROBERT, rabbi; b. N.Y.C., May 20, 1936; s. Abraham and Eva (Schwartz) B.; m. Elaine Greening, 1991; children from earlier marriage: Neeva Liat, Nurete Leor, Noga Libi. BA, CCNY, 1958; BHL, Hebrew Union Coll.-Jewish Inst. Religion, N.Y.C., 1960; MA, HUC-JIR, N.Y.C., 1964, DD, 1990. Ordained rabbi, 1964. Chaplain U.S. Army, Nuremberg, Fed. Republic Germany, 1964-66; rabbi Temple Beth Am., Monessen, Pa., 1966-67, Princeton (N.J.) Jewish Ctr., 1967-70, Genesis Ctr., Westchester, N.Y., 1972-76, Bethesda (Md.) Jewish Congregation, 1986—; mem. Cen. Conf. of Am. Rabbis, Wash. Bd. Rabbis. Author: Faith and Doubt of Holocaust Survivors, 1980 (Nat. Jewish Book award nominee 1981), American Jewry and the Rise of Nazism, 1990, Jewish Riddle Collection: A Yiddles Riddles, 1991, short stories, articles and poetry; inventor Bankshot Basketball, 1979. Recipient Yivo prize, 1967, Israel Ministry of Culture and Edn. prize, 1976-85, rsch. grant Thompson Med. Co. Home: 7911 Kentucky Ave Bethesda MD 20814 Office: Bethesda Jewish Congregation 6601 Bradley Blvd Bethesda MD 20817

BRESHEARS, JON CHANDLER, minister, educator; b. Springfield, Mo., Dec. 29, 1945; s. Edgar Ervin and Esther Lucille (Chandler) B.; m. Jan Camille BelleIsle, June 8, 1968; children: Joy, Julie. BA, U. West Fla., 1970; MA in Religious Edn., New Orleans Bapt. Sem., 1974. Ordained to ministry Bapt. Ch., 1976. Min. of music, edn. Bayou Vista Bapt. Ch., Morgan City, La., 1972-74; min. edn. 1st Bapt. Ch., Roswell, Ga., 1976-81; min. of ch. growth 1st Bapt. Ch., Lakeland, Fla., 1981-83; min. of edn. Shandon Bapt. Ch., Columbia, S.C., 1983-88; assoc. pastor, min. of edn. 2d Ponce de Leon Bapt. Ch., Atlanta, 1988—. Bd. dirs. ACTS TV, Columbia, 1980-83, S.C. Spl. Olympics, 1981-83. Recipient 4 Eagle Ch. Growth awards So. Bapt. Sunday Sch. Bd., 1979-83. Mem. Met. Atlanta Bapt. Religious Edn. Ann. (pres. 1990—), Ga. Bapt. Conv. (human resources rsch. group). Office: 2d Ponce de Leon Bapt Ch 2715 Peachtree Rd Atlanta GA 30305

BRESKY, JAN BARTON, rabbi; b. Newark, Mar. 7, 1951; s. Hebert and Gertrude (Safer) B.; divorced; children: Aaron, Ilana. BA in Religion, Temple U., Phila., 1973; MAHL, Hebrew Union Coll., Cin., 1976. Ordained rabbi 1978. Rabbi Congregation Anavat Shalom, Palm Harbor, Fla., 1978-87, Congregation Bnai Emmunah, Tarpon Springs, Fla., 1987—; leader Jewish Media Rels. Coun., Inc., Clearwater, Fla., 1986—; TV host Spiritual Light, 1986—; radio host A Time for God, 1989—. Author: Complete High Holy Day Services, 1978-81; contbr. articles to profl. jours.; author: Common Sense Religon for Americans, 1988. Mem. Cen. Conf. of Am. Rabbis, Rotary. Address: Jewish Media Rels Coun PO Box 2118 Tarpon Springs FL 34688 *Died May 15, 1991.*

BRESLAUER, SAMUEL DANIEL, religion educator, rabbi; b. San Francisco, Apr. 23, 1942; s. Daniel Joseph and Lynette Myrle (Goldstone) B.; m. Frances Pamela Gurian, June 23, 1968; children: Don Howard, Tamar Beth. BA in Near Eastern Studies, U. Calif., Berkeley, 1963; B.H.L., Hebrew Union Coll., 1965, M.H.L., 1969; PhD, Brandeis U., 1974. Ordained rabbi, 1969. Student rabbi Ealing Synagogue, London, 1965-66; asst. prof. philosophy/religion Colgate U., Hamilton, N.Y., 1971-75; vis. lectr. Judaic U. Nebr., Omaha, 1975-76; vis. lectr. religion Princeton (N.J.) U., 1977-78; asst. prof. U. Kans., Lawrence, 1978-81, prof., 1981—. Author: Martin Buber on Myth: An Introduction, 1990, A New Jewish Ethics, 1983, Meir Kahane: Idologue, Hero, Thinker, 1986, Covenant and Community in Modern Judaism, 1989. NEH grantee-in-residence Princeton U., 1976; recipient Samuel Aronowitz Prize in Jewish History, 1969, Prize for Proficiency in Modern Hebrew, 1965, 67. Mem. Midwest Jewish Studies Assn. (v.p. 1990-91), Assn. for Jewish Studies, Am. Acad. Religion. Democrat. Office: U Kans Religious Studies Dept Lawrence KS 66045

BRESLER, BORIS, consulting engineer; b. Harbin, Republic of China, Oct. 18, 1918; came to U.S., 1937, naturalized, 1943; s. Samuel and Hena (Gonopolsky) B.; m. Joy Bloom, July 5, 1946; 1 child, Deborah. BS, U. Calif., Berkeley, 1941; MS, Calif. Inst. Tech., 1946. Structural designer Kaiser Shipyards, 1941-43; stress analyst Convair Co., 1943-45; mem. faculty U. Calif., Berkeley, 1946-77, prof. civil engring., 1958-77, prof. emeritus, 1977—, asst. dean Coll. Engring., 1956-59, chmn. div. structural engring. and structural mechanics, 1963-64, dir. structural materials lab., 1963-65; prin. Wiss, Janney, Elstner Assocs., Inc. Cons. Engrs., Emeryville, Calif., 1977-87; pub. Ben-Mir Books, 1983—. Author: (with T.Y. Lin) Design of Steel Structures, 1959, 2d edit., 1968; also articles; editor: Reinforced Concrete Engineering, Vol. 1, 1974. NSF postdoctoral fellow, 1961, Guggenheim fellow, 1962; recipient State of the Art of Civil Engring. award, 1968, Engring. News Record citation, 1982. Fellow ASCE (life, chmn. structural div. exec. com. 1975), Am. Concrete Inst. (hon.; dir. 1970-73, Wason medal for research 1959, J.W. Kelly Award 1978, Raymond Davis lectr. 1982, Arthur R. Anderson award 1986); mem. NAE (hon.), Structural Engring. Assn. No. Calif., Reinforced Concrete Rsch. Coun. (Arthur J. Boase award 1989). Office: Wiss Janney Elstner & Assocs 2200 Powell Emeryville CA 94608 also: Benmir Books 1529 Cypress St Ste 105 Walnut Creek CA 94596

BRESLIN, JOHN BERNARD, university chaplain; b. N.Y.C., Aug. 19, 1943; s. Edward and Katherine (Sweeney) B. AB, Fordham U., 1967; BA, Oxford U., 1969, MA, 1973; MDiv, Woodstock Coll., N.Y.C., 1975; PhD, Yale U., 1983. Ordained Soc. of Jesus priest, 1961, Roman Catholic priest, 1973. Lit. editor Am. Mag., N.Y.C., 1971-77; sr. editor Doubleday and Co., N.Y.C., 1978-80; assoc. dir. Georgetown U. Press, Washington, 1981-82, dir., 1982-91; v.p., univ. chaplain Georgetown U., Washington, 1991—; bd. dirs. Religion Pub. Group, N.Y.C.; mem. PEN Am. Ctr., N.Y.C., 1975—; pres. Washington Book Pubs., 1988-89. Editor: The Substance of Things Hoped For, 1988; contbr. articles to profl. and popular jours. Democrat. Roman Catholic. Office: Georgetown U Office of Univ Chaplain Healy Bldg Washington DC 20057

BRESLIN, SISTER MARY, college president; b. Chgo., Sept. 27, 1936; d. William J. and Margaret D. (Hession) B. B.A., Mundelein Coll., Chgo., 1958; M.A., Marquette U., 1961; J.D., Loyola U., Chgo., 1977. Bar: Ill., Fed. Ct.; joined Sisters of Charity of Blessed Virgin Mary, Roman Cath. Ch., 1961. Internal auditor Fed. Res. Bank, Chgo., 1958-59; asst. bus. mgr. Mundelein Coll., Chgo., 1964-67, bus. mgr., treas., 1967-75, v.p. bus. affairs, treas., 1975-85, pres., 1985—; cons., evaluator North Central Accreditation Assn., Chgo., 1978—, Middle State Accreditation Assn., Phila., 1981—. Avocation: fishing. Home & Office: Mundelein Coll 6363 N Sheridan Rd Chicago IL 60660

BRETHERICK, RONALD DAVID, minister; b. Phila., Aug. 8, 1950; s. John Henry and Anna Elizabeth (Harris) B.; m. Suzanne Jean Harris, June 7, 1980; children: Rebekah Lauren, Laura Beth. BS, St. Joseph's Coll., 1975; MDiv, Reformed Episcopal Sem., Phila., 1981. Ordained to ministry Ref. Episcopal Ch. as deacon, 1981, as presbyter, 1984. Rector St. John's By the Sea Reformed Episcopal Ch., Ventnor, N.J., 1981—; trustee Synod Trustees N.Y. and Phila. Reformed Episcopal Ch., Phila., 1986-90; chaplain Atlantic City (N.J.) Med. Ctr. Hospice, 1986-90. Firefighter Glenolden (Pa.) Fire Co., 1969-79, pres. 1974. Home and Office: 6 S Sacramento Ave Ventnor NJ 08406-2754

BRETTON-GRANATOOR, GARY MARTIN, rabbi; b. Bronx, July 20, 1956; s. Jerold Mark and Sylvia Gertrude (Wollowitz) G.; m. Marianne Julia Bretton-Granatoor, May 27, 1978; children: Samantha Ariel, Jacob Daniel. BA, Sarah Lawrence Coll., Bronxville, N.Y., 1978; MAHL, Hebrew Union Coll., N.Y.C., 1982. Ordained rabbi, 1984. Assoc. dir. N.Y. Fedn. Reform Synagogues, N.Y.C., 1984-87; dir. adult studies Union of Am. Hebrew Congregations, N.Y.C., 1987-89, nat. dir. dept. interreligious affairs, 1989—; faculty Sarah Lawrence Coll., Bronxville, 1990—, NYU U. Continuing Edn., 1986-89; assoc. dir. Commn. on Social Action, 1989—, Commn. on Jewish Edn., 1986-89. Author, editor: Guidelines for Adult Jewish Study, 1989, Challenge of Tzedakah, 1991. Chmn. Interfaith Assembly on Homelessness and Housing, N.Y.C., 1984-86; adv. bd. Homes for the Homeless, 1987—. Recipient Horace J. Wolf prize Hebrew Union Coll.-Jewish Inst. Religion, 1984, Jacob Rudin prize in homiletics, 1983. Mem. Cen. Conf. Am. Rabbis, N.Y. Bd. Rabbis. Home: 351 11th St Brooklyn NY 11215 Office: Union Am Hebrew Cong 838 Fifth Ave New York NY 10021 *In Exodus, we read "Let them make for Me a sanctuary so that I may dwell among them." Notice it does not read, "...so that I may dwell in it." The spirit of God rest upon those who labor for what is good and right. We who build the world that God ordained for us work as God's partners.*

BREUER, STEPHEN ERNEST, temple executive; b. Vienna, Austria, July 14, 1936; s. John Howard and Olga Marion (Haar) B.; came to U.S., 1938, naturalized, 1945; BA cum laude, UCLA, 1959, gen. secondary credential, 1960; m. Gail Fern Breitbart, Sept. 4, 1960 (div. 1986); children: Jared Noah, Rachel Elise; m. Nadine Bendit, Sept. 25, 1988. Tchr. L.A. City Schs.; dir. Wilshire Blvd. Temple Camps, Los Angeles, 1962-88; exec. dir. Wilshire Blvd. Temple, 1980—; dir. Edgar F. Magnin Religious Sch., Los Angeles, 1970-80. Instr. Hebrew Union Coll., Los Angeles, 1965-76, U. Judaism, 1991; field instr. San Francisco State U., 1970-80, Calif. State U., San Diego, Hebrew Union Coll., 1977-81, U. of Judaism UCLA extension. Vice pres. Los Angeles Youth Programs Inc., 1967-77; youth adviser Los Angeles County Commn. Human Relations, 1969-72. Bd. dirs. Community Relations Conf. So. Calif., 1965-85; regional bd. mem. Union Am. Hebrew Congregations, 1986-88; bd. dirs. Alzheimer's Disease and Related Disorders Assn., 1984—, v.p. L.A. County chpt., 1984-86, pres., 1986-88, nat. exec. com., 1987—, Calif. state coun. pres. 1987—, chmn. of Calif. gov.'s adv. com. on Alzheimer's disease, 1988—; mem. goals program City of Beverly Hills, Calif., 1985-91; bd. dirs. Echo Found., 1986-88, Wilshire Stakeholders, exec. com., 1987—, treas. Wilshire Community Prayer Alliance, 1986-88; active United Way. Recipient Service awards Los Angeles YWCA, 1974, Los Angeles County Bd. Suprs., 1982, 87, Ventura County Bd. Suprs., 1982, 87, Weinberg Chai Achievement award Jewish Fed. Council Los Angeles, 1986, Steve Breuer Adult Ctr. named in his honor Wilshire Blvd. Temple Camps. Mem. So. Calif. Camping Assn. (dir. 1964-82), Nat. Assn. Temple Adminstrs. (nat. bd. dirs. 1987—, v.p. 1991—, Svc. to Judaism award 1989, Svc. to the Community award 1990), Nat. Assn. Temple Educators, Los Angeles Assn. Jewish Edn. (dir.), Profl. Assn. Temple Adminstrs. (pres. 1985-88), Assn. Supervision and Curriculum Devel., Am. Mgmt. Assn., So. Calif. Conf. Jewish Communal Workers, Jewish Profl. Network, Amnesty Internat., Jewish Resident Camping Assn. (pres. 1976-82), UCLA Alumni Assn., Wilderness Soc., Center for Environ. Edn., Wildlife Fedn., Living Desert, Los Angeles County Mus. Contemporary Art, People for the Am. Way, Assn. Reform Zionists Am., Union of Am. Hebrew Congregations (bd. dirs. Pacific SW region 1985-88). Office: Wilshire Blvd Temple 3663 Wilshire Blvd Los Angeles CA 90010 *You do not know at what moment you may touch the life of a child. It is rarely at the moment of our plan or choice.*

BREWER, CHARLES H., JR., bishop. Bishop Ch. of God in Christ, New Haven. Office: Ch of God in Christ 180 Osborne St New Haven CT 06515*

BREWER, H. MICHAEL, minister; b. Louisville, July 10, 1954; s. Harvey and Gail Patrick (McDonald) B.; m. Janet Faye Neff, Feb. 3, 1979; children: Bethany Megan Neff Brewer, Rachel Allyson Neff Brewer. BA in Psychology, U. Louisville, 1976; MDiv, Louisville Presbyn. Sem., 1979. Ordained to ministry Presbyn. Ch. (U.S.A.), 1979. Pastor Crescent Springs (Ky.) Presbyn. Ch., 1979—. Author sermons and articles pub. in Abingdon Ministers Manual, Clergy Jour., Preaching, Ministers Ann. Manual. Bd. dirs. Presbyn. Child Welfare Agy., Buckhorn, Ky., 1984—; chaplain Dixie Police Authority, Crescent Springs, 1990—; treas. Amnesty Internat., 1988—. Office: Crescent Springs Presbyn Ch 710 Western Res Crescent Springs KY 41017

BREWER, RONALD RAY, religious organization administrator; b. Bethany, Okla., May 9, 1951; s. Walter Ray and Bertha Lou (Stepp) B.; m. Nancy Anne Boyd, Aug. 22, 1972; children: Phillip Wayne, Allison Marie. AA, Southwestern Coll., 1972; BA, So. Nazarene U., 1974; MA, Southwestern Sem., Ft. Worth, 1978. Cert. ch. bus. adminstr. Min. youth, music Cherokee Hills Bapt. Ch., Oklahoma City, 1972-74; min. youth, family Pleasantview Bapt. Ch., Crowley, Tex., 1974-79; min. adminstrn. Trinity Bapt. Ch., Oklahoma City, 1979-85, 1st Bapt. Ch., Lawton, Okla., 1985-90, Wieuca Rd. Bapt. Ch., Atlanta, 1990—; mem. christian ethics com. Comanche-Cotton Bapt. Assn., Lawton, 1986, pers. com., 1987-88, chmn. bylaws revision com., 1989. Pres. Christian Family Counseling Ctr. Bd., Lawton, 1987-88, treas., 1988-89, chmn. fin. com., 1988-90; v.p. Bapt. edn., Music Assn. Okla., 1984-85. Named one of Outstanding Young Men Am., OYMA/Jaycees, 1981. Fellow Nat. Assn. Ch. Bus. Adminstrs.; mem. So. Bapt. Assn. for Ch. Bus. Adminstrn., Christian Ministries Mgmt. Assn., Atlanta Bapt. Assn. (bd. dirs. 1990—). Democrat. Home: 3728 Peachtree Dunwoody NE Atlanta GA 30342 Office: Wieuca Rd Bapt Ch 3626 Peachtree Atlanta GA 30326

BREWER, TINA RENE, religion educator; b. Brazil, Ind., Oct. 26, 1955; d. P. Thomas and Mary Louise (Dietz) Cox; m. Stephen Robert Brewer, Dec. 20, 1975; children: Marcy Lianne, Jed Wade. BBA, No. Ariz. U., 1976. Children's Sun. sch. tchr. Roseburg and Glendale, Oreg., 1977—; tchr. child evangelist Glendale, 1985-86, pre-sch. tchr., mission class, 1985-89, women's Bible study tchr., 1987-89; adminstr., kindergarten tchr Glendale (Oreg.) Christian Sch., 1986-89; summer camp co-dir. Bapt. Assn., Douglas County, 1989-90; tchr. Kindergarten Douglas County Christian Sch., Roseburg, Oreg., 1990—; bd. dirs. Home Mission Bd., So. Bapt. Conv., Atlanta, 1989—; asst. team children's dir. N.W. So. Bapt. Conv., Douglas County, Oreg., 1983—. Author: Big and Little in the Bible, 1987, A Sunday School Came to Life, 1988. Recipient Sun. Sch. Devel. Diploma So. Bapt. Conv. Republican. Home: 470 Amanda St Roseburg OR 97470 Office: Douglas County Sch 2079 NW Witherspoon Roseburg OR 97470

BREWSTER, DANIEL FERGERSON, minister, religious organization executive; b. Newnan, Ga., Dec. 23, 1916; s. Daniel Fergerson and Sara Josephine (Stevens) B.; m. Helen Howe Glawson, June 7, 1943. AB, Emory U., 1945; MDiv, Candler Sch. Theology, 1948; DD (hon.), LaGrange Coll., 1966. Ordained to ministry, United Meth. Ch., 1948. Pastor various chs., Ga., 1943-64; exec. dir. Ga. Meth. Commn. on Higher Edn., Atlanta, 1964-84; trustee LaGrange Coll., Ga., 1965—; mem. exec. com., sec. Southeastern Jurisdiction Commn. on Higher Edn., Atlanta, 1980-84; dean Ga. Meth. Pastors Sch., 1960-64; sec. Conf. Bd. of Edn., 1956-60. Editor: Higher Education in Southeastern Jurisdiction 1787-1984 (United Methodist Church), 1984, North Ga. Conf. Handbook, 1963-70. Chmn. history-writing com. Newnan-Coweta County Hist. Soc., 1983. Recipient Spl. Achievement award 9 Meth. Colls., 1983, Brewster Endowment in Liberal Arts, Ga. Meth. Commn. on Higher Edn.; fellow LaGrange Coll., Ga., 1981. Mem. Nat. Coun. Boy Scouts Am. (recipient Silver Beaver award 1986), Nat. Eagle Scout Assn. Democrat. Home: 20 W Broad St Newnan GA 30263

BREWSTER, GARY SCOTT, youth pastor; b. Lorain, Ohio, Jan. 16, 1965; s. Jerry Lynn and Faris Elenor (Lane) B. BA in Pastoral Ministries, Southeastern Coll. Assemblies of God, 1988; postgrad., Ashland (Ohio) Theol. Sem., 1991—. Ordained to ministry Assemblies of God. Youth pastor Ch. on the North Coast, Assemblies of God, Lorain, 1990—; speaker Kids Off Drugs, Masson Jr. High Sch., 1990, KEN Club, Adm. King. High Sch., 1991. Mem. Pumping Iron Club. Avocation: painting. Home: 545 Cleveland Ave Amherst OH 44001 Office: Ch on the N Coast 4125 Leavitt Rd Lorain OH 44052

BRICKNER, SALLY ANN, nun, educational administrator; b. Milw., May 4, 1942; d. Marcellus Victor and Evelyn Mary (DeCleene) B. BS, St. Norbert Coll., 1967; MA, Mich. State U., 1968, Tchrs. Coll. Coll., N.Y.C., 1979; PhD, Mich. State U., 1970. Joined Sisters of St. Francis of Holy Cross, 1960. Assoc. prof. St. Norbert Coll., DePere, Wis., 1970-82, dir. tchr. edn., 1982-84, chair div. social sci., 1984-89, assoc. acad. dean, 1989—. NDEA fellow, 1967-70. Mem. ASCD, Nat. Coun. Tchrs. Math., Wis. Assn. Tchr. Educators (pres. 1988), Am. Assn. Higher Edn., Common Cause. Avocations: singing, language, travel, reading. Home: 2413 S Webster Ave Green Bay WI 54301 Office: St Norbert Coll 216 Main Hall DePere WI 54115-2099

BRIDE, THOMAS ROBERT, priest; b. Middletown, Conn., Feb. 23, 1940; s. Thomas Raphael and Frances (Seraphin) B. AA, St. Thomas Sem., 1961; BA, St. Bernard Sem., 1963, ThM, 1967. Ordained priest Roman Cath. Ch., 1967. Asst. pastor St. Patrick Cathedral, Norwich, Conn., 1967-73; asst. chancellor Diocese of Norwich, 1973-76, chancellor, 1976-88, prelate of honor, 1985—, chief fin. officer, vicar gen., 1989—; dir. vocations, propagation of faith, Diocese of Norwich, 1973—; notary Diocesan Marriage Tribunal, Norwich, 1971. Mem. Diocesan Fiscal Mgmt. Conf. (pres. 1987-89, bd. dirs. 1986—), Pontifical Soc. for Holy Childhood (dir. 1979), Cath. Umbrella Pool (bd. dirs. 1991—), St. Thomas Alumni Assn. (pres. 1988-90). Home: 274 Broadway Norwich CT 06360 Office: Diocese of Norwich 210 Broadway Norwich CT 06360

BRIDGES, BOBBY LAWRENCE, minister; b. Knoxville, Tenn., Aug. 23, 1949; s. Lawrence and Mary Elizabeth (Swaggerty) B.; m. Judith Ann Freeman, June 24, 1978; 1 child, Jonathan Christian. BA, Belmont Coll., 1974; MDiv, Southwestern Bapt. Theol. Sem., 1977, MRE, 1988. Ordained to ministry Bapt. Ch., 1973. Min. of youth Belmont Heights Bapt. Ch., Nashville, 1974-76; asst. pastor Travis Ave. Bapt. Ch., Ft. Worth, 1977-79; min. youth and edn. First Bapt. Ch., Grapevine, Tex., 1979-80; sr. pastor Woods Chapel Bapt. Ch., Arlington, Tex., 1980-90, Spring Valley Bapt. Ch., Springville, Ala., 1990—; founder Arlington Pk. Bapt. Ch.; dir. Arlington Children's Camp, Glen Rose, Tex., 1982, 83, 85; pres. Arlington So. Bapt. Fellowship, 1983-84. Co-founder, bd. dirs. Children in Med. Crisis Intervention, Arlington, 1984-85. Mem. Arlington Ministerial Assn., Tarrant Bapt. Assn. (exec. bd). Avocations: skiing, golfing, book collecting. Home: 311 James St Springville AL 35146 Office: Spring Valley Bapt Ch PO Box 378 Springville AL 35146 *The lives of individual persons have the investment of all of creation in them. Therefore, we must recognize their importance over their misfortune and present conditions, and continue the investment toward their good.*

BRIDGES, CHARLIE GLENN, pastor; b. Dawson, Ga., Oct. 21, 1960; s. Don Eli and Juanita Frances (Hammond) B.; m. Lynn Marie Reams, Dec. 21, 1985; 1 child, Justin Alan. BA, Mercer U., 1982; MDiv, So. Bapt. Theol. Sem., Louisville, 1988. Ordained to ministry So. Bapt. Conv., 1982. Min. youth Faith Bapt. Ch., Cuthbert, Ga., 1981; pastor 1st Bapt. Ch., Gay, Ga., 1982-84, Summit Hills Bapt. Ch., Louisville, Ky., 1985-89, Radium Springs Bapt. Ch., Albany, Ga., 1989—. Bd. dirs. N.W. Dist. YMCA, Cartersville, Ga., 1983-84. Office: Radium Springs Bapt Ch 2402 Roxanna Rd Albany GA 31705 *Life is the experience of "Jesus loves me, this I know," within our hearts and souls. Only then have we found life.*

BRIDGES, GERALD DEAN, religious organization executive; b. Tyler, Tex., Dec. 4, 1929; s. Rufus Emmett and Lillian Ruth (Reeves) B.; m. Eleanor Louise Miller, Oct. 19, 1963 (dec. Nov. 1988); children: Kathleen Louise, Daniel Mark; m. Jane Bertha Mollet, Nov. 24, 1989. BS in Gen. Engr., U. Okla., 1951. Dept. supr. The Navigators, Colorado Springs, Colo., 1955-59, asst. to overseas dir., 1963-64, office mgr., 1965-69, sec., treas., 1969-79, v.p. for corp. affairs, 1979—; adminstrv. asst. to Europe dir. The Navigators, Hague, The Netherlands, 1960-63; bd. dirs. Evang. Coun. for Fin. Accountability, Washington, chmn. of bd., 1991—; ruling elder Grace Presbyn. Ch., Colorado Springs, 1972—. Author: (books) The Pursuit of Holiness, 1978, The Practice of Godliness, 1983, The Crisis of Caring, 1985, Trusting God, 1988, Transforming Grace, 1991. Chaplain Sertoma, Colorado Springs, 1979-80. Ensign USN, 1951-53. Republican. Office: The Navigators PO Box 6000 Colorado Springs CO 80934

BRIDSTON, KEITH RICHARD, clergyman; b. Grand Forks, N.D., Feb. 20, 1924; s. Joseph Benjamin and Anna Sofie (Pederson) B.; m. Elizabeth Onstad, Dec. 20, 1945. B.A., Yale U., 1944, B.D., 1947; Ph.D. Edinburgh U. in Div., Scotland, 1949. Ordained to ministry Lutheran Ch., 1954; grad. sec. Dwight Hall, Yale U., 1944-46; internat. sec. Student Christian Movement Gt. Brit. and Ireland, 1946-48; mem. exec. staff World's Student Christian Movement, Geneva, 1949-52; prof. theology Higher Theol. Coll., Djakarta, Indonesia and Nommensen U., P. Siantar, Sumatra, Indonesia, 1952-57; exec. sec. Commn. on Faith and Order, World Council Chs., Geneva, 1957-61; exec. dir. N.Y.C. office World Council Chs., N.Y.C., 1978-84; theol. cons. gen. secretariat Commn. on Faith and Order, World Council Chs., Geneva, 1978-84; dir. seminars Vesper Soc., San Leandro, CA, 1984-86; sr. fellow communication divinity sch. Yale U., 1984-86; mgr. China sr. service coprs program Vesper Soc., 1987-88; cons. bus. ethics project Concordia Coll., Moorehead, Minn., 1988—; dir. study on pre-seminary edn. Lilly Endowment Inc., Mpls., 1961-63; prof. systematic theology Pacific

Luth. Sem. and Grad. Theol. Union, Berkely, Calif., 1963-78; Harvard U. Corp. research fellow Div. Sch. and Grad. Sch. Bus. Adminstrn., Harvard U., Cambridge, Mass., 1971-73; dir. Case-Study Inst. (Cambridge), 1971-74; v.p. First Fed. Savs. & Loan Assn., Grand Forks, 1978-82. Author: books, latest being Pre-Seminary Education, 1966; Church Politics, 1969; editor: Orthodoxy, 1960, Old and New in the Church, 1961, One Lord-One Baptism, 1961; contbr. articles to Ency. Brit., Weltkirchenlexikon, Westminster Dictionary of Church History; mem. editorial bd.: Ecumenical Press Service, Geneva, 1949-52; mng. editor: Luth. Quar., 1973-78. Yale regional scholar, 1941; Princeton Club N.Y. scholar, 1943; Assn. Am. Theol. Schs. fellow, 1969-70. Club: Elizabethan (Yale U.). Home and Office: 1423 Calihan Ave NE Bemidji MN 56601

BRIEF, NEIL, rabbi; b. Bklyn., Oct. 10, 1934; s. Hyman and Bella (Saltzman) B.; m. Erica Greenbaum, June 16, 1957; children: Dena Brief Wald, David Chaim, Debra Pearl. BS, NYU, 1955; B of Hebrew Letters, Hebrew Union Coll. Jewish Inst. Religion, N.Y.C., 1957, M of Hebrew Letters, 1960; DD (hon.), Hebrew Union Coll. Jewish Inst. Religion, Cin., 1985; MA, Bklyn. Coll., 1958. Ordained rabbi, 1960. Post Jewish chaplain U.S. Army, Ft. Huachuca, Ariz., 1960-62; rabbi Ventura County Jewish Council, Ventura, Calif., 1962-71, Niles Twp. Jewish Congregation, Skokie, Ill., 1971—; founder, leader Jewish Marriage Encounter, 1974—; tour leader Israel, 1980, Ea. Europe, 1988, Spain and Portugal, 1990, People's Republic of China, 1991. Author: What Helped Me When My Loved One Died, 1980. Chmn. Human Relations Adv. Council, Ventura, 1963-69; mem. Skokie Human Resources Commn., 1984—; bd. dirs. Mayer Kaplan-Bernard Horwich Jewish Community Ctr. Served to capt. U.S. Army, 1960-62. Recipient Outstanding Leadership award Jewish Reconstructionist Found., N.Y.C., 1980. Mem. Cen. Conf. Am. Rabbis, Rabbinical Assembly, Chgo. Bd. Rabbis (mem. exec. com.), Clergy Forum of Niles Twp. (chmn.). Home: 4214 Suffield Ct Skokie IL 60076 Office: Niles Twp Jewish Congregation 4500 Dempster St Skokie IL 60076 *Life depends on the liver, a daily gift for which to be grateful, hopeful and productive. Life is a Becoming, a day-in, day-out challenge to become the best of one's potential, to wisely number our days and earn for ourselves a heart of wisdom.*

BRIGGS, EDWARD BURTON, JR., religion writer; b. South Attleboro, Mass., Jan. 30, 1939; s. Edward Burton and Anna Patricia (Walsh) B.; m. Janice Marie Dowdy, July 22, 1961; children: Edward Burton III, Kristal Erin. BA, U. Denver, 1965. Writer religion Richmond (Va.) Times-Dispatch, 1965—. With U.S. Army, 1959-62. Mem. Religion Newswriters Assn. (treas. 1982-86, 2d v.p. 1986-88, pres. 1988-90). Episcopalian. Office: Richmond Times-Dispatch 333 E Grace St Richmond VA 23219

BRIGHT, JOHN CALVIN, minister; b. Liao Chow, Shansi, China, Sept. 19, 1915; (parents Am. citizens); s. Jacob Homer and Minnie Minerva (Flory) B.; m. Harriett Louise Howard, May 26, 1945. BS, Berea Coll., 1943; MA, Bethany Theol. Sem., 1947. Ordained to ministry Ch. of the Brethren, 1943. Pastor Ch. of the Brethren, Peoria, Ill., 1945-47; missionary West China Union Universalists Chengtu, Szechwan, China (later People's Republic of China), 1947-51; exec. sec. univ. and mission programs West China Border Rsch. Soc., Chengtu, 1948-51; dist. exec. sec. So. Ind., pastor Ch. of the Brethren, Richmond, Ind., 1952-62; pastor Ch. of the Brethren, Decatur, Ill., 1962-66, E. Dayton (Ohio) Ch. of the Brethren, 1866—; mem. Gen. Brotherhood Bd., 1957-61, mem. standing com., 1954, 55,63-64; denom. rep. Nat. Coun. Chs., 1959-61; tchr. West China Union Theol. Sem.; also dir. West China Union U. Mus. Art, Archaeology, Ethnology and Anthropology, 1948-50. Author: Missionary Letters of Minnie Flory Bright, 1973; contbr. articles to religious jours. Bd. dirs. Boy Scouts Am., Peoria, 1945-47, Family Svc., Richmond, 1954-59; bd. dirs., life mem. Ea. Area Coun., 1967-73; mem. Parole Bd., Decatur, 1963-64; bd. dirs. Sun Rise Ctr., 1974—; mem. Human Svc. Bd., Montgomery County, 1978-84, Montgomery County Coun. on Aging, 1987—, Sch. com., Dayton, 1981-83, Belmont Sch. Adv. Bd., 1984—; bd. dirs. YMCA, 1990—; mem. United Health Bd., 1985—, Wright State U. Bd. on AIDS, 1989—, Social Health Bd., 1985-90. Mem. Brethren Chs. Assn., Dayton Mins. Assn. Home: 528 Gondert Ave Dayton OH 45403 Office: Ch of the Brethren 3520 E 3d St Dayton OH 45404-2299

BRIGHT, PAMELA MARY, religion educator; b. Brisbane, Queensland, Australia, Oct. 6, 1937; came to U.S., 1981; d. Walter John and Phyllis Mary (McCarthy) B. BA, U. Queensland, Brisbane, 1975, BD, 1978, BD Honors, 1980; MA, U. Notre Dame, 1983, PhD in Hist. Theology, 1987. Tchr. Roman Cath. schs., Queensland, 1959-79; vis. prof. Concordia U., Montreal, Que., Can., 1985-87; asst. prof. theology Loyola U., Chgo., 1987—. Author: The Book of Rules of Tyconius, 1988; co-author: A Conflict of Christian Hermeneutics in Roman Africa, 1989; also articles; translator: (from Greek and Latin) Sources of Early Christian Spirituality, 1986. Australian U. scholar Commonwealth Govt., 1970; John A. O'Brien fellow, 1984-85; summer rsch. grantee Loyola U., 1980, rsch. grantee, 1990. Mem. Am. Acad. Religion, Cath. Theol. Soc. Am., N.Am. Patristics Soc. (local convenor 1990—), Mid-West Patristics Soc. (convenor 1989-90). Roman Catholic. Office: Loyola U 6525 N Sheridan Rd Chicago IL 60626

BRIGHTON, RUTH LOUISE, lay worker, educator; b. Harrisburg, Pa., Apr. 18, 1931; d. Paul Gerhard and Ruth Genevieve (Lee) Krentz; m. Carl T. Brighton, July 27, 1954; children: David, Susan, Andrew, Joel. BA, Valparaiso U., 1953; MS in Math., U. Wis., 1955. Cert. tchr. Tchr. Sunday sch., adult Bible class Christ Meml. Luth. Ch., Malvern, Penn., 1969—; coord. adult edn., Ea. dist. Luth. Ch.-Mo. Synod, Buffalo, 1986—, bd. dirs., 1988-90; bd. dirs. Concordia Pub. House, St. Louis. Teaching fellow in math. U. Wis., 1953. Home: 14 Flintshire Rd Malvern PA 19355

BRIGHTUP, ROBERT LEROY, religion educator; b. Liberal, Kans., Nov. 9, 1936; s. Robert Everett and Mable Arlene (Perry) B.; m. Eva Marie Clark, Aug. 7, 1955; children: Robert, Lisa, Linda, Kevin. AB in Bible Study, Friends Bible Coll., Haviland, Kans., 1956; BA, Friends U., Wichita, Kans., 1958; BDiv, Nazarene Theol. Sem., Kansas City, Mo., 1961; ThD, Iliff Sch. of Theology, Denver, 1970. Recorded as minister Kans. Yearly Meeting of Friends, 1963. Pastor Plainview Community Ch., Wichita, Kans., 1957-58, First Friends Ch., Kansas City, Mo., 1960-64; adminstr. Northridge Friends Ch., Wichita, Kans., 1971-72; prof. bible & philosophy Friends U., Wichita, Kans., 1964—; chmn. Dept. of Religion, Friends U., Wichita, Kans., 1975—; coord. of Religion Grad. Studies, Friends U., Wichita, 1988—. Mem. Soc. Bibl. Lit., Bibl. Archaeology Soc., Am. Schs. of Oriental Rsch., Christian Mgmt. Assn. Office: Friends U 2100 University Wichita KS 67213 *The life of service is not only personally fufilling, but is ultimately the answer to many of the world's problems.*

BRILL, MOREDECAI LOUIS, rabbi; b. Indpls., Mar. 24, 1910; s. Henry and Esther (Schwartz) B.; m. Jeanette Kessler, Sept. 23, 1942; children: Esther Miriam, Jonathan Henry, Joel David. PhB, U. Chgo., 1936; DHL, Jewish Theol. Sem., 1948, DDiv, 1952. Ordained rabbi, 1936. Rabbi Rodef Sholom Synagogue, Johnstown, Pa., 1936-40, Brith Sholom, Bethlehem, Pa., 1940-43, Bethel Congregation, Waterbury, Conn., 1946-50; mem. staff Am. Found. Religion and Psychiatry, N.Y.C., 1962-77; chaplain Holy Cross Hosp., Ft. Lauderdale, Fla., 1989—; lectr. in field. Co-editor: Marriage, An Interfaith Guide for All Couples, 1970, Write Your Own Wedding, 1974. Capt. U.S. Army, 1943-46. Named Chaplain of the Yr., Chaplaincy Commn. of Jewish Fedn., 1988. Mem. Rabbinical Assembly N.Y.C. *We are active partners with God in eliminating the man-made evils of this world; we dare not shirk this responsibility.*

BRINDLE, BARBARA ANN, retired pastoral counselor, psychologist; b. Fort Wayne, Ind., Sept. 18, 1923; d. George W. and Florence (Burket) Myers; m. Richard L. Brindle, Apr. 24, 1942; children: David, Nancy. BA, Earlham Coll., 1958, M Ministry, 1975; MA, Miami U., 1968. Joined Secular Franciscan Order, 1980. Clin. psychologist Richmond (Ind.) State Hosp., 1960-75; pastoral family counselor Blessed Sacrament Parish, Waterloo, Iowa, 1976-84, ret., 1984.

BRINDLE, DAVID LOWELL, minister; b. Richmond, Ind., Sept. 16, 1948; s. Richard Lowell and Barbara Ann (Myers) B.; m. Linda Jean Pickard, Aug. 15, 1976; 1 child, Ruth Marie. BA, St. Meinrad (Ind.) Coll., 1972; MDiv, Earlham Sch. Religion, 1980; postgrad., United Theol. Sem., Dayton, Ohio. Ordained to ministry United Meth. Ch., 1991. Pastor Fountain City (Ind.) Friends Meeting, 1981-84; grad. asst. U. Dayton, 1984-85; dir. religious edn. St. Christopher Cath. Ch., Vandalia, Ohio, 1985-86, St. Joan of Arc Cath. Ch., Hershey, Pa., 1989-90; dir. admissions Earlham Coll. Sch. Religion, Richmond, 1986-88; interim pastor Wilmington (Ohio) Friends Meeting, 1988-89; jud. assessor Tribunal, Diocese of Harrisburg, Pa., 1990-91; pastor St. Paul United Meth. Ch., Harrisburg, 1991—; mem. Edn. Commn., Ind. Yearly Meetings of Friends, Muncie, 1981-84; chmn. Yokefellow Inst., Richmond, 1986-89. Contbr. to religious publs. Mem. Canon Law Soc. Am. (assoc.), Yokefellow Internnat., Oblates of St. Benedict. Democrat. Home: 522 Lopax Rd Harrisburg PA 17112 *Many of our creeds and personal beliefs begin as descriptions of our experience. We must guard against our tendency to turn descriptions into prescriptions which seek to regulate the experiences of others.*

BRINDLE, VAN ROGER, minister; b. Dobson, N.C., Nov. 4, 1939; s. Jasper Elmer and Stella Etta (Cave) B.; m. Faye Lee Baker, May 5, 1960; children: Van Christopher, Ginger Fae, Serena Leigh. BA in religion, Campbell U., Buies Creek, N.C., 1975. Ordained to ministry, Missionary Bapt. Ch. Interim pastor Cen. View Bapt. Ch., Dobson, N.C.; pastor Shoals (N.C.) Bapt. Ch., Salem Fork Bapt. Ch., Elkin, N.C., 1990—. With USN, 1957-60. Andy Creed scholar, 1974-75, Ministerial and Pastor Appreciation scholar, Campbell Coll., 1974-75. Democrat.

BRINK, GARY JEROME, minister; b. Memphis, Oct. 20, 1963; s. Martin Wycoff and Lenore (Peterson) B.; m. Mary Elizabeth Nelson, Oct. 4, 1986. BS, Northwestern Coll., 1986; MDiv, Golden Gate Bapt. Theol. Sem., 1991. Jr. high intern Colony Park Bapt. Ch., Edin, Minn., 1983-87; high sch. intern First Bapt. Ch., Modesto, Calif., 1987—; instr. in swimming YMCA, Modesto, 1987-88. Vol. YMCA, St. Paul, 1984. Mem. Evang. Tchrs. Tng. Assn. of Am., Nat. Network of Youth Ministries. Republican. Baptist. Avocations: running, athletics, family, marathons. Home: 1229 Brighton Ave #257 Modesto CA 95355 Office: First Bapt Ch 808 Needham St Modesto CA 95352

BRINK, WILLIAM P., clergyman; b. Chgo., Sept. 21, 1916; s. Paul W. and Cora (Wagenaar) B.; m. Alta Mae Ibershof, July 25, 1941; children: Paul William, Esther Jean Brink Leugs, John Harvey, Daniel Jay, Stephen Robert. BA, Calvin Coll., 1938; BTh, Calvin Sem., 1941. Ordained to ministry Christain Ref. Ch., 1941. Pastor Goshen (Ind.) Christian Ref. Ch., 1941-44, Archer Ave. Christian Ref. Ch., Chgo., 1944-48, Creston Christian Ref. Ch., Grand Rapids, Mich., 1948-53, Bethany Christian Ref. Ch., Holland, Mich., 1953-64, 2d Christian Ref. Ch., Fremont, Mich., 1964-70; stated clk. Christian Ref. Ch., 1970-83; Pres. Young Calvinist Fedn. N. Am., 1958-70, Gen. Synod Christian Reformed Ch., 1966, 69. Author: Learning Doctrine from the Bible, 1965; co-author: Manual of Christian Reformed Church Government, 1979, 80, 87; editor: Acts of Synod, Christian Reformed Church, 1971-82, Yearbook Christian Ref. Ch, 1971-82. Address: 5305 Queensbury Dr SE Grand Rapids MI 49508

BRINKMAN, GABRIEL, former college president; b. Indpls., Dec. 3, 1924; s. John Henry and Mary Frances (Bartsch) B. Student, Our Lady of Angels Sem., 1943-47, St. Joseph Sem., 1947-51; Ph.D. in Sociology, Cath. U. Am., 1957. Instr. ethics Our Lady of Angels Sem., Cleve., 1955-57; mem. faculty dept. sociology Quincy (Ill.) Coll., 1957-63, prof. sociology, 1970-77, 84-85, pres. coll., 1963-70, 77-83; dir. Franciscan Herald Press, Chgo., 1986—. Author: Social Thought of John de Lugo, 1957. Roman Catholic. Office: Franciscan Herald Press 1434 W 51st S Chicago IL 60609

BRISON, WILLIAM STANLEY, priest; b. West Chester, Pa., Nov. 20, 1929; s. William P. and Marion (Wilbur) B.; m. Marguerite Adelia Nettleton, June 16, 1951; children—Paul Stanley, Daniel Roy, Sarah Catherine, Martha Adelia. B.S., Alfred U., 1951; M. Div., Berkeley Div. Sch., 1957, M.S.T., 1971. Ordained to ministry Episcopal Church, 1957. Vicar to rector Christ Ch., Bethany, Conn., 1957-69, Emmanuel Ch., Stamford, Conn., 1969-72; vicar Christ Ch., Davyhulme, Manchester, Eng., 1972-81; archdeacon New Haven Archdeaconary, Conn., 1966-69; rector All Saints, Newton Heath, Manchester, 1981-85; area dean North Manchester Deanery, 1981-85; archdeacon of Bolton, Manchester, 1985-91, archdeacon emeritus, 1991—; ptnr. Ch. Missionary Soc. Mission , 1992—; gov. All Saints Primary Sch., Newton Heath, 1981-85, St. Wilfrid's Primary Sch., Newton Heath, 1981-85, Trinity Ch. of Eng. High Sch., Manchester, 1983-86; gov. Canan Slade Sch., 1987-91; chmn. Diocesan Worship Com., 1986-91, Diocesan Stewardship Com., 1987-91; mem. Diocesan Synod, Manchester, 1978—. Served to capt. USMCR, 1951-53. Home: care Mrs M Hulme, 1 College Rd, Oldham 0L8 4HU, England *I marvel still that over half a century ago, in the midst of the Depression and in suburban N.Y.C., a small boy found his own way to a church service and, in spite of contradictions, found Jesus at the center, was profoundly impressed by His radical teaching, and (against the odds because he was by nature both bellicose and agnostic) fearfully but joyfully became a disciple. This is the key for my Who's He.*

BRISTER, ARTHUR MACK, SR., clergyman; b. Vinton, La., Sept. 2, 1937; s. Rufus Arthur and Eula Belle (McNabb) B.; m. Bonnie Rae Dunn, June 13, 1958; 1 child, Arthur Mack Jr. BA, Bapt. Christian Coll., Shreveport, La., 1968. Ordained to ministry So. Bapt. Ch., 1957. Pastor Lakeview Bapt. Ch., Diboll, Tex., 1957-60, Bethel Bapt. Ch., Jefferson, Tex., 1961-62, Grand Bluff Bapt. Ch., Carthage, Tex., 1961-64, Bear Creek Bapt. Ch., Linden, Tex., 1964-65, Shiloh Bapt. Ch., Longstreet, La., 1965-66, Crims Chapel Bapt. Ch., Henderson, Tex., 1966-67, First Bapt. Ch., Oail City, La., 1967-70; edn. dir. West 14th Bapt. Ch., Houston, 1970-71; pastor 1st Bapt. Ch., Florien, La., 1971-75, 82—, Trinity Bapt. Ch., Henderson, 1975-78, 1st Bapt. Ch., Cameron, Tex., 1978-82, First Bapt. Ch., Florien, La., 1982—; police chaplain Florien City Govt., 1988—; moderator Sabine Bapt. Assn., Many, La., 1972-74, 83-84; pres. exec. bd. Dist. VIII Bapt. Conv., Pleasant Hill, La., 1974; area rep. ch. growth Campers on Missions, Alexandria, 1974; cons. La. Bapt. Conv., Alexandria, 1974; clk. Rusk-Panola Bapt. Assn., Henderson, 1976; vice-moderator Milam Bapt. Assn., Cameron, Tex., 1979, moderator, 1981; bd. mem. exec. bd. La. Bapt. Conv., Alexandria, 1989—police chaplain Sabine Parish, Many, 1989—. Pres. bd. Sabine Coun. on Aging, Many, 1986-88; trustee U. Mary Hardin Baylor, Belton, Tex., 1981-84, Sabine Med. Ctr. Hosp., Many, 1991—. Named Rural Pastor of Yr., La. Bapt. Conv., Alexandria, 1974. Mem. Nat. Christian Counselors Assn. (assoc.), Masons (master 1989). Democrat. Home: 290 E Port Arthur Ave Florien LA 71429 Office: 1st Bapt Ch 115 E Port Arthur Ave Florien LA 71429

BRISTER, C. W., religion educator; b. Pineville, La., Jan. 15, 1926; m. Gloria Nugent, Mar. 28, 1946; 1 child, Mark Allen. BA, La. Coll., 1947; postgrad., La. State U., 1948-49; BD, New Orleans Bapt. Sem., 1952, MDiv, 1973; ThD, Southwestern Bapt. Sem., 1957, PhD, 1974; postdoctoral studies, N.C. Bapt. Sch. Pastoral Care, 1960, Tex. Christian U., 1961-62, Princeton Theol. Sem., 1962-63, 67, Union Theol. Sem., N.Y.C., 1962-63, 67, Oxford (Eng.) U., 1978. Ordained to ministry Bapt. Ch.; lic. profl. counselor, Tex. Alumni sec. La. Coll., 1947-48; pastor Folsom (La.) Bapt. Ch., 1950-52, Ethel (La.) Bapt. Ch., 1952-53, Haltom Rd. Bapt. Ch., Ft. Worth, 1954-57; Disting. prof. pastoral ministry Southwestern Bapt. Theol. Sem., Ft. Worth; guest lectr. Internat. Bapt. Theol. Sem., Cali, Colombia, 1990, New Zealand Bapt. Theol. Coll., Auckland, 1990, Whitley Coll. of U. Melbourne, Australia, 1990, Kenya Bapt. Theol. Coll., 1991. Author: Pastoral Care in the Church, rev. edit., 1992, People Who Care, Dealing With Doubt, It's Tough Growing Up, Life Under Pressure: Dealing With Stress in Marriage, The Promise of Counseling, Take Care, Becoming You, Beginning Your Ministry, Caring for the Caregivers; (with others) Southwestern Sermons, Everyday, Five Minutes With God When Trouble Comes, Toward Creative Urban Strategy, Contemporary Trends in Christian Thought, Broadman Devotional Annual, An Approach to Christian Ethics; contbr. to: Holman Study Bible; contbr. articles to Pastoral Psychology, Home Life, other religious jours. With armed forces, ETO. Fellow La. State U., 1948-49, Southwestern Med. Sch., 1969-70. Mem. Soc. Pastoral Theology, Assn. Couples for Marriage Enrichment, Assn. for Clin. Pastoral Edn., Bapt. World Alliance (comm. on ch. leadership). Office: Southwestern Bapt Theol Sem PO Box 22000 Fort Worth TX 76122-0500

BRISTER, MARK ALLEN, pastor; b. New Orleans, Aug. 8, 1951; s. Commodore Webster and Gloria (Nugent) B.; m. Rhonda Rhee Evatt, June 30, 1973; children: Barrett Nugent, Austin Andrew. BA, Baylor U., 1973; MDiv., S.W. Bapt. Sem., 1976, PhD, 1980. Ordained to ministry Bapt. Ch., 1972. Pastor First Bapt. Ch., Bolivar, Mo., 1980-84, Meml. Bapt. Ch., Baytown, Tex., 1984-89, Broadmoor Bapt. Ch., Shreveport, La., 1989—; mem. resolutions com. BGCT, Dallas, 1986, long range planning com., 1988-89; parliamentarian La. Bapt. Conv., Alexandria, La., 1990, credentials com., 1990-91; mem. Baylor Univ. Devel., 1988-91. Bd. dirs. Baytown (Tex.) Welfare League, 1985-88, Baytown (Tex.) Rotary Club, 1986-89, Baytown (Tex.) C. of C., 1989, World Sickle Cell Found., 1989-91; trustee Houston (Tex.) Bapt. Univ., 1988-89. Recipient Cert. of Citation, Senate of Tex., 1989; named Outstanding Young Alumnus, Baylor Univ., Waco, Tex., 1989. Mem. Rotary Internat. (Shreveport, Paul Harris fellow 1988). Office: Broadmoor Bapt Ch 4110 Youree Dr Shreveport LA 71105

BRISTOW, WAYNE DOUGLASS, minister; b. Norfolk, Va., July 31, 1949; s. Jesse Willard and Vernelle (Grizzard) B.; m. Lynn Marie Varns, May 10, 1980; children: Meredith Renee, Stacy Marie. Diploma, Culinary Inst. Am., 1970; BBA, Campbell Coll., 1974; MRE, Southwestern Bapt. Theol. Sem., 1980. Ordained to ministry So. Bapt. Conv., 1980. Minister edn./adminstrn. West End Bapt. Ch., Petersburg, Va., 1980-85, New Bridge Bapt. Ch., Richmond, Va., 1985—. Mem. So. Bapt. Religious Edn. Assn., Va. Bapt. Religious Edn. Assn. Office: New Bridge Bapt Ch PO Box 250 Highland Springs VA 23075 *When life and death experiences occur it helps us focus on what is really important. It is not whether our church membership is a particular denomination. What truly matters is "What is our relationship with Jesus Christ and the change He has affected in our life?".*

BRITT, BRIAN MICHAEL, religious educator; b. Omaha, Aug. 28, 1964; s. Gerald Patrick and Janice Ann (Gitter) B.; m. Jessica Meltsner, Aug. 19, 1989. BA, Oberlin Coll., 1986; postgrad., U. Chgo., 1986—. Instr. basic program for adults U. Chgo., 1988—, divinity sch. fellow, 1989-90. Contbr. articles to profl. jours. Jewett prize U. Chgo., 1989. Mem. Am. Acad. Religion, Soc. Bibl. Lit. Democrat.

BRITTAIN, GARY RAY, minister; b. Gadsden, Ala., Aug. 6, 1957; s. Lee Ray and Edna Earl (Lee) R.; m. Sharon Lynn Easterwood, Aug. 7, 1982; 1 child, Ian Daniel. BA, Mobile Coll., 1979; MDiv, So. Bapt. Theol. Sem., 1987. Ordained to ministry So. Bapt. Conv., 1983. Area campus min. Ala. Bapt. State Conv., Jasper, 1981-83; pastor Mt. Moriah Bapt. Ch., Tuscumbia, Ala., 1983-86; campus min. Ala. Bapt. State Conv., Livingston, 1987-90; dir. missions Bigbee Bapt. Assn., Livingston, 1987-90; campus min. Ala. Bapt. State Conv., Jacksonville, 1990—. Mem. Asn. So. Bapt. Campus Mins., Jacksonville State Univ. Campus Mins. Assn., Jacksonville Ministerial Assn. Office: Bapt Campus Ministries PO Box 151 Jacksonville AL 36265 *The greatest challenge I find in Campus Ministry is to assist students in applying their Christian beliefs to their goals for life in a secular society.*

BRITTAIN, PAUL ALFRED ROBERT, minister; b. Montreal, Que., Can., Dec. 11, 1949; came to U.S., 1978; s. Herbert Brodie and Mary Barclay (Munro) B.; m. Edith LaFaye Smith, Dec. 27, 1975; children: Rebecca, Deborah, Adam, Bonnie. BA in History, Loyola, 1972; BA in Bibl. Edn., Fla. Bible Coll., 1975; MDiv., Bibl. Theol. Sem., 1982. Assoc. pastor People's Ch. of Montreal, 1975-78; pastor Horsham (Pa.) Bible Ch., 1982—; bass singer The Internationals, Hollywood, Fla., 1973, 73-74, 75, Bibl. Theol. Sem. Quartet, Hatfield, Pa., 1978-81; pres. North Penn. Ministerium, Horsham, 1987-89. Home: 3917 Blair Mill Rd Hatboro PA 19040 Office: Horsham Bible Ch 220 Upland Ave Box 116 Horsham PA 19044

BRITTON, CHARLES HARVEY, lay worker; b. Cin., July 24, 1941; s. Harvey B.; m. Peggy Brown; children: Rob, Chris, Amy. MusB, Campbellsville Coll., 1963; MA in Phys. Edn., Ea. Ky. U. Min. music Stithton Bapt. Ch., Radcliff, Ky., 1971-74, West Flager Pk. Bapt. Ch., Miami, Fla., 1974-76, 1st Bapt. Ch., Calhoun, Ga., 1976-79; min. youth activities 2d Bapt. Ch., Hopkinsville, Ky., 1979-82; pastor of recreation 1st Bapt. Ch., Clarksville, Tenn., 1982—. Home: 317 Irene Dr Clarksville TN 37043 Office: 1st Bapt Ch 435 Madison St Clarksville TN 37040

BRITTON, C(LARENCE) KEITH, religious organization administrator; b. Williamsfield, Ohio, July 24, 1930; s. Kline and Elsie J. (Fonner) B.; m. Lois Jean Cable, Aug. 15, 1952; 1 child, Linda J. Britton Cowden. BRE, Cleve. Bible Coll., 1954. CLU; cert. stockbroker. Dir., missionary Youth For Christ, Ashtabula, Ohio, 1954-59; bus. mgr. Word of Life, São Paulo, Brazil, 1959-69; announcer, asst. mgr., dir. devel. Sta. WEEC, Springfield, Ohio, 1969-73; field rep. devel. Narramore Christian Found., Rosemead, Calif., 1973-79; pres. Family Resources, Medway, Ohio, 1979—; exec. dir. Brazilian Evangelistic Assn., Medway and São Paulo, 1987—, also bd. dirs.; dir. music Grace Bible Ch., Springfield, 1980—. Contbr. articles to religious jours. Founder, pres. Concerned Citizens Clark County, 1981—. Recipient Outstanding Svc. award Rep. Party, 1980, 81. Mem. Nat. Fedn. Ind. Bus., Better Bus. Bur., Springfield Assn. Life Underwriters, Kiwanis (spiritual aims com. 1986-88). Office: Family Resources PO Box 100 Medway OH 45341

BRITTON, ERWIN ADELBERT, clergyman, college administrator; b. Huron, Ohio, Feb. 19, 1915; s. John Chester and Lydia Emeline (Jones) B.; m. Carolyn Anne Herron, Sept. 1, 1941 (dec. May 1, 1985); children: Margaret (Mrs. Fred C. Kolloff), Elizabeth (Mrs. Richard R. Quick), Constance; m. Alice Schriver Suffield, Sept. 27, 1986. A.B., Oberlin Coll., 1936; B.D., Grad. Sch. Theology, Oberlin, 1939; D.D., Piedmont Coll., 1961; S.T.D., Olivet Coll., 1978. Ordained to ministry Congregational Ch., 1939; pastor Community Ch., Avon Lake, Ohio, 1937-41; pastor First Congl. Ch., Wayne, Mich., 1941-64, Detroit, 1964-75; pastor Union Congl. Ch., Mackinac Island, Mich., 1982-85; exec. sec. Nat. Assn. Congl. Christian Chs., 1975-81; asst. to pres. Olivet Coll., 1982-86; Chmn. Congl. Found. for Theol. Studies, 1970-72; dir. Conf. on Crime and Religious Leadership; mem. adv. com. religious and urban studies Wayne State U. Chmn. Met. Agy. for Retarded Children, Wayne County Mental Health Soc., 1969; Trustee Olivet Coll. Named Young Man of Year Jr. C. of C., 1950, Outstanding Religious Leader of Mich. Religious Heritage Am. Mem. Detroit Pastors Union (pres. 1970), Nat. Assn. Congl. Christian Chs. (moderator 1972-73, nominating com. 1985-87), Internat. Congl. Fellowship (program com.), Phi Mu Alpha. Club: University (Winter Park, Fla.). Home: 421 Cortland Ave Winter Park FL 32789

BRIZGYS, VINCENTAS, bishop; b. Plynia, Lithuania, Nov. 10, 1903; came to U.S., 1952, naturalized, 1959; s. Mathew and Mary (Vikelis) B. Student, Priests Sem., Gizai, Lithuania, 1921-27; Dr. Philosophy and Canon Law, Gregorian U., Rome, 1935. Ordained priest Roman Catholic Ch., 1927; parish priest Lithuania, 1927-30; mem. faculty Priests' Sem., 1936-40; rector Interdiocesan Priest's Sem., Kaunas, Lithuania, 1940-41; dean, prof. Theol. Faculty, State's U., Kaunas, 1941-44; ordained bishop of Bosano and aux. bishop of Kaunsas Kaunas, 1940—; Cons. Commn. for Bishop and Adminstrs. Diocese Preparing Vatican II Ecumenic Council, 1960-61. Mem. AAAS, Pax Romana. Club: K.C. *Having everything from God I gave it back to God by serving the people, following the principles I believed. To those who are leading the society, I wish to remember that injustice, wrong and evil will never be transformed into justice, right and blessing by the erroneous opinion of the day.*

BROADAWAY, GERALD, religious organization administrator. Gen. supt. Fire Baptized Holiness Ch., Independence, Kans. Office: Fire Baptized Holiness Ch 600 College Ave Independence KS 67301*

BROADRIGHT, LARRY RAYMOND, minister; b. Pitts., July 24, 1956; s. Fred George and Shirley Anne (Knight) B.; m. Sherry Schuck, Nov. 23, 1989. BA, Westminster Coll., New Wilmington, Pa., 1978; MDiv, Pitts. Sem., 1984; ThM, Princeton Sem., 1989; postgrad., Louisville Sem., 1989—. Ordained to ministry Presbyn. Ch. (U.S.A.), 1985. Dir. Christian edn. 1st Presbyn. Ch., New Philadelphia, Ohio, 1978-81; student min. East Liberty Presbyn. Ch., Pitts., 1982-84; assoc. pastor Meml. Presbyn. Ch., Midland, Mich., 1984-87; exec. dir. ALIVE Inc., Ridgewood, N.J., 1987-89; pastor 1st Presbyn. Ch., Edgewater, N.J., 1987-89; head of staff 2d Presbyn. Ch., Portsmouth, Ohio, 1989—; adj. prof. English, religion, philosophy Shawnee State U., Portsmouth; presbyter Presbytery of Scioto Valley, 1989—. pres. Pastoral Counseling Ctr., 1990—; trustee Portsmouth Little Theatre, 1990—, bd. dirs., 1991—; mem. So. Ohio Light Opera Co., Portsmouth, 1990—; chaplain So. Ohio Med. Ctr., Portsmouth, 1991. Mem. Hanging Rock

Clergy Assn. (pres. 1990—), Scioto Christian Ministry (v.p. 1990—), Scioto County Clergy Assn., Mercy Life Ctr. Club, Rotary. Democrat. Avocations: basketball, racquetball, music, drama, gardening. Home: 1635 22d St Portsmouth OH 45662 Office: 2d Presbyn Ch 801 Waller St Portsmouth OH 45662

BROCK, FOSTER C., JR., minister; b. Springfield, Oh., Sept. 24, 1945; s. Foster C. and Virginia Katherine (Burd) B.; m. Audrey Jewell Baldridge, Oct. 10, 1964; 1 child, Deborah Jo. Student, Gulf-Coast Bible Coll., 1970-72; cert., Salem Ave. Mins. Inst., 1977, Billy Graham Sch. Evangelism, 1980. Ordained to ministry Ch. of God (Anderson, Ind.), 1975. Pastor First Ch. of God, White Pine, Tenn., 1972-73; assc. pastor First Ch. of God, E. Prairie, Mo., 1973; pastor First Ch. of God, Clarksville, Tenn., 1973-76, Mt. Carmel, Ill., 1976-84, Sullivan, Ill., 1984--. Contr. articles to local newspapers and mags. Pres./founder Wabash Christian Acad., 1981-83; mem. Indsl. Commn., 1985-87. With U.S. Army 1968-70. Mem. C. of C. of Mt. Carmel and Sullivan, Ill., Gen.. Assembly, Anderson, Ind., Sullivan Min. Assn. First Church of God. Home: 1211 E Jackson Sullivan IL 61951 Office: First Church of God 1213 E Jackson Sullivan IL 61951 *Put your trust completely in the Lord—see how far He will take you!.*

BROCK, GARY LYNN, sociology educator; b. Springfield, Mo., Oct. 4, 1942; s. Herbert Eugene and Daisy Margaret (Grizzell) B.; m. Judith Kay Sawyer, June 4, 1965; children: Kristen Kay, Tamra Lynn. BA, Harding U., 1965; MA, Harding Grad. Sch., Memphis, 1968, Syracuse U., 1977; PhD, St. Louis U., 1983. Ordained to ministry Ch. of Christ., 1967. Minister East Grand Ch. of Christ, Springfield, 1967-83; asst. prof. religious studies S.W. Mo. State U., Springfield, 1983-87, asst. prof. sociology, 1987—; Contbr. numerous revs. to profl. jours. S.W. Mo. State U. Found. grantee, 1987. Bd. visitors sociology dept. Abilene (Tex.)-Christian U., 1989—; cons. Springfield R-12 Sch. Dist., 1987-88. Mem. Am. Acad. Religion (convener 1986-89), Soc. for Sci. Study Religion, Am. Sociol. Assn., Phi Delta Kappa. Avocations: reading, travel. Home: 3652 S Nettleton Ave Springfield MO 65807 Office: SW Mo State U 901 S National Springfield MO 65804

BROCK, PATRICK LAURENCE, priest; b. Bromley, Kent, England, July 7, 1918; s. Laurence George and Ellen Margery (Williams) B.; m. Patricia Addinsell Walton, June, 1950; children: Jonathan Simon, Penelope Rachel, Jeremy Benjamin. Degree, Oxford U., 1945. Ordained to ministry Ch. Eng. as deacon, 1957, as priest 1958. With Ministry of Civil Aviation and Cabinet Office U.K. Home Civil Service, London, 1946-55; asst. curate Ch. of Eng., Malvern and London, 1957-62; vicar St. Peter, Belsize Park, London, 1962-72; rector of Finchley London, 1972-89; area dean Ctl. Barnet, London, 1980-85; staff, coun., exec. com. Coll. of Preachers, 1971-89; prebendary St. Paul's Cathedral, 1980-89. Author: Worship Beyond the Mind, 1987, Don't Preach at Me Like That!, 1991; booklet: A Theology of Church Design, 1984. Served to maj. with Brit. Army, 1939-45. Named Mem. of the Order of the British Empire His Majesty the King, 1944. Avocations: acting, theatre, photography, travel. Home and Office: 10 Albert St, Camden Town, London NW1 7NZ, England

BROCK, RALPH ELDON, camp administrator; b. Long Creek, Ill., Apr. 19, 1926; s. Lacy Edmond and Treva (Moore) B.; m. Gertrude Mae McKinney, Aug. 19, 1947; children: Eldonna Lynn Brock Long, Carolyn Christine Brock Smalligan. Pastoral diploma, Bapt. Bible Coll., Clarks Summit, Pa., 1952. Ordained to ministry Bapt. Ch., 1952. Pastor Northfield Congl. Ch., Sydny, N.Y., 1951-52, First Bapt. Ch., Castle Creek, N.Y., 1952-58, Calvary Bapt. Ch., Lockport, N.Y., 1958-67, Parr Meml. Bapt. Ch., Petoskey, Mich., 1967-71; exec. adminstr. Lake Ann (Mich.) Bapt. Camp, Inc., 1971—; coun. mem. Empire State Fellowship Regular Bapt. Chs., 1962-65, Mich. Assn. Regular Bapt. Chs., 1969-70, Fellowship Bapts. for Home Missions, Elyria, Ohio, 1961-90; chmn. Nat. Assn. Regular Bapt. Camps, 1981—; cons. trips to help missionaries improve Christian camping, S.Am., 1979, Alaska, 1982, South Africa, 1990. Recipient Outstanding Svc. award Bapt. Bible Coll., Clarks Summit, Pa., 1987. Mem. Christian Camping Internat. (bd. mem. Founds. for Excellence 1972, svc. award 1987). Republican. Home: 831 Spring St NE Grand Rapids MI 49503 Office: Lake Ann Bapt Camp Inc PO Box 109 Lake Ann MI 49650

BROCK, THOMAS LEON (TOM BROCK), religious organization administrator; b. Little Rock, Oct. 21, 1946; s. William Leon and Emma Jean (Turner) B.; m. Tommye Marie Hasley, July 25, 1970; children, Thomas Jason, Tara Marie. BA, U. Ark., 1969; postgrad., U. Cen. Ark., 1971-72. Deacon Geyer Spring 1st Bapt. Ch., Little Rock, 1978—, dir. support svcs., 1989—. Mem. Nat. Assn. Ch. Bus. Adminstrs. Office: Geyer Springs 1st Bapt Ch 5615 Geyer Springs Rd Little Rock AR 72209

BRODERICK, KILIAN J., charitable organization executive. Exec. dir. Cath. Charities, Dallas. Office: Cath Charities 3845 Oak Lawn Ave Dallas TX 75219*

BRODHEAD, CHARLES NELSON, III, lay worker; b. Phila., Nov. 1, 1963; s. Charles Lindberg Jr., and Doris Esther (Mink) B.; m. Leesa Ky Charlton, Mar. 28, 1987; children: Charles Douglas IV, Emylee Grace. BSBA, U. Redlands, 1986. Adminstrv. asst. Arlington Ave. Ch. of the Nazarene, Riverside, Calif., 1986—, youth dir., 1987—, dir. Puppeteer Express profl. puppet team, 1987—, pres. Nazarene Youth Internat., 1986-87; owner, pres. M.E. Embroidery, Riverside, 1988—. Coach, mgr. Pachappa Little League, Riverside, 1986-89; mem. Com. for Moral Concerns. Recipient Ch. Youth of Month, Kiwanis, 1986. Mem. Nazarene Multiple Staff Assn. Republican. Office: Arlington Ave Ch Nazarene 5475 Arlington Ave Riverside CA 92504

BRODRICK, ALEX, religious organization administrator; b. Phila., May 7, 1944; s. Joseph Franklin and Josephine (Kerr) B.; m. Mary Kay Allen, June 8, 1983; children: Katie Reid, Joel Alexander, Cameron Allen. AA, Warren Wilson Coll., 1966; BA, Ea. Ky. U., 1968; MSW, Fla. State U., 1971; MPA, Ky. State U., 1974. Exec. dir. Vols. of Am., Lexington, Ky., 1982-85; pres., chief exec. officer Vols. of Am. of Ky., Louisville, 1985-90; v.p. northeastern region Vols. of Am. Inc., Jeffersontown, Ky., 1990—. Pres. bd. dirs. Louisville Coalition for Homeless, 1987-90, St. John's Day Ctr., Louisville, 1989; mem. Gov.'s Adv. Coun. for Homeless, Frankfort, Ky., 1987-90; program chmn. Louisville Forum, 1990. Mem. NASW. Office: Vols of Am Inc 10518 Watterson Trail Ste 2 Jeffersontown KY 40299

BRODSKY, JEFFREY ALLAN, minister; b. Bklyn., Jan. 5, 1956; s. Seymour and Marilyn (Katz) B.; m. Sharla Fern Chapman, Sept. 22, 1980; children: Christoffer Mychal, Jason Marc, Lisa Nicole, Mandi Beth. BA in Bible summa cum laude, Living Sch. of the Bible, Upper Montclair, N.J., 1978, MA in Theology, 1979, D Ministry, 1983; MA in Bibl. Theology, Internat. Bible Inst. and Sem., Orlando, Fla., 1982. Ordained to ministry Bapt. Ch., 1980; lic. to ministry Assemblies of God, 1987. Staff evangelist Nichols Hills Bapt. Ch., Oklahoma City, 1981-86; counselor Chgo. Teen Challenge, 1986-87; pastor Cen. Assembly of God Ch., Chgo., 1987-90; admnistrv. asst. San Antonio Teen Challenge, 1990—; dir. The Jesus Ctr., N.Y.C., 1978-80. Mem. Nat. Christian Counselors Assn., Nat. Assn. Notaries, Am. Mgmt. Assn. Republican. Home: PO Box 934 Cameron TX 76520 Office: 1511 N Houston PO Box 1188 Cameron TX 76520 *The Christian Way of Living is not to demand my rights but to fufill my responsibilities.*

BROENE, G(ILBERT) RICHARD, religious organization administrator; b. Grand Rapids, Mich., May 19, 1948; s. Gilbert James and Annette (Star) B.; m. Mary Jo Katerberg, July 20, 1973; children: Richard James, Jeffrey Robert, Pamela Jo. BA, Calvin Coll., 1970. Pres. Calvinist Cadet Corps, Grand Rapids, 1977-83, exec. dir., 1983—; sec. Gideon Camp, Grand Rapids, 1982-85, v.p. 1985. Editor Crusader mag., 1983—. Republican. Avocation: youth religious activities. Home: 6962 Buchanan SW Grand Rapids MI 49548 Office: Calvinist Cadet Corps 1333 Alger SE Grand Rapids MI 49507

BROKAW, KURT JOHN, religious communication executive; b. Dubuque, Iowa, Sept. 9, 1938; s. Max Pomeroy and Harriet (Wemette) B.; children—Leslie, Christopher; m. Mona Yuter, May 25, 1980; 1 child, Kate. B.S., U. Wis., 1960, M.S., 1961. Mem. bd. dirs. Office Communication United Ch. Christ, N.Y.C., 1981-85, creative cons., 1977-86; v.p., assoc. creative dir. Al Paul Lefton Co., N.Y.C., 1979-85; lectr. New Sch., N.Y.C., 1986. Author: A Night in Transylvania; The Dracula Scrapbook, 1976. Community theatre dir. Scarsdale Congl. Ch., N.Y., 1968-82. Recipient advt. awards. Mem. Mus. Modern Art. Home: 317 W 93d St New York NY 10025

BROKERING, T. MARK, marketing director; b. Pitts., June 4, 1952; s. Herbert Frederick and Naomi Lois (Redelfs) B.; m. Amy Rood, May 5, 1990. BA in English and Psychology, St. Olaf Coll., 1974; MA in English, U. Minn., 1976. Editor Winston Press, Mpls., 1978-80, mktg. mgr., 1980-86; mktg. mgr. Harper & Row, San Francisco, 1986-90; mktg. dir. Religious Books, Harper San Francisco, 1990—. Home: 54 Loring Ave Mill Valley CA 94941 Office: Harper San Francisco 151 Union St San Francisco CA 94111

BROKHOFF, JOHN RUDOLPH, clergyman; b. Pottsville, Pa., Dec. 19, 1913; s. John Henry and Gertrude Amanda (Heiser) B.; m. Helen Leininger, June 20, 1938 (div. 1971); m. Barbara Jean Brokhoff, June 9, 1972; children: Wendy Ann, Helen Elaine, Virginia Sue, John William. AB, Muhlenberg Coll., 1935; MA, U. Pa., 1938; MDiv, Phila. Luth. Sem., 1938; DD (hon.), Muhlenberg Coll., 1951. Ordained to ministry Luth. Ch., 1938. Pastor Ebenezer Luth. Ch., Marion, Va., 1940-42, Christ Luth. Ch., Roanoke, Va., 1942-45, Luth. Ch. of Redeemer, Atlanta, 1945-55, St. Mark's Luth. Ch., Charlotte, N.C., 1955-62, Trinity Luth. Ch., Lansdale, Pa., 1962-65; prof. Candler, Emory U., Atlanta, 1965-79; pres. Christian Coun. Atlanta, 1950-52, Mecklenburg Ministers Assn., Charlotte, N.C., 1960-61; sec. Protestant Radio-TV Ctr., Atlanta, 1948-54; bd. mem. Acad. Preachrs, Phila., 1982-84. Author: Lectionary Preaching Workbook, 3 vols., Preaching the Parables, 3 vols., Preaching the Miracles, 3 vols., As One With Authority. Recipient George Washington medal Freedom Found., Valley Forge, 1966. Home: 119 Harborage Ct Clearwater FL 34630

BROKKE, CATHERINE JULIET, mission executive; b. Mpls., Dec. 25, 1926; d. Emil John and Alma (Brye) Eliason; m. Harold Joseph Brokke, Sept. 9, 1949; 1 child, Daniel. Diploma in nursing, Luth. Deaconess Hosp., Mpls., 1947; student, Concordia Coll., Moorhead, Minn., 1948-49, Bethany Coll. Missions, Mpls., 1949-51. RN, Minn. Sch. and ocupational nurse Bethany Fellowship, Mpls., 1951-75; missions sec. Bethany Fellowship Missions, Mpls., 1963-86, dir., 1986; instr. Bethany Coll. Missions, 1950-88. Mng. editor Message of Cross, 1990—; composer hymns. Organist Bethany Missionary Ch., Bloomington, Minn., 1956-89. Mem. Evang. Fellowship of Mission Agys. (trustee 1987—). Avocations: piano, organ. Office: Bethany Fellowship Missions 6820 Automobile Club Rd Bloomington MN 55438

BROM, ROBERT H., bishop; b. Arcadia, Wis., Sept. 18, 1938. Ed., St. Mary's Coll., Winona, Minn., Gregorian U., Rome. Ordained priest Roman Catholic Ch., 1963, consecrated bishop, 1983. Bishop of Duluth Minn., 1983-89; coadjutor bishop Diocese of San Diego, 1989-90, appt. bishop, 1990—. Office: Diocese of San Diego Pastoral Ctr PO Box 85728 San Diego CA 92186-5728

BROMENSCHENKEL, GIB H., church administrator; b. St. Cloud, Minn., Sept. 16, 1930; s. Alfred J. and Loretta (Feddema) B.; m. Doris Marie Miller, Apr. 18, 1955; children: Kim Marie, Jay Alan, Jill Marie. Student, St Cloud Bus. Coll., 1950-52. Sales person St. Anthony Messenger, Mpls., 1951-52; sta. agt. North Cen. Airlines, St. Cloud, 1952-54; sta. mgr. North Cen. Airlines, Land O'Lakes, Wis., 1954; sta. agt. North Cen. Airlines, Mpls. and Brainerd, 1954-57; sta. mgr. North Cen. (Republic) Airlines, Fargo, N.D., 1957-86; equip. svc. staff N.W. Airlines, Fargo, N.D., 1986-88; parish adminstr. Ch. of the Nativity, Fargo, N.D., 1988—. Pres. N.D. league of Cities, 1980-81; city commr. City of Fargo, 1970-74, vice mayor, 1974—. Mem. N.D. Jaycees (Outstanding State Vice Pres. 1964, v.p. 1963-64), U.S. Jaycees (nat. dir. 1964-66, state pres. 1966-67), Jaycees Internat. (program mgr. 1968-69), Toastmasters (Disting. Toastmaster 1961, dist. gov. 1960-61), K.C. (Grand Knight 1985-86), Elks. Republican. Roman Catholic. Avocations: clock repair and building, golf, sailing, skiing, woodworking and finishing. Home: 509 21 Ave N Fargo ND 58102

BROMLEY, ROBERT LEVAN, minister; b. Palo Alto, Calif., Nov. 10, 1931; s. LeVan Monroe and Carol Olive (Whitman) B.; m. Ruth Irene Wilson, Apr. 24, 1959 (div. May 1980); children: Delores Bromley Meyer, Jeannette Bromley Klaus, David, Timothy; m. Ann Kay Seibold, July 19, 1981. BA, Chapman Coll., 1953; BD, U. Chgo., 1957. Ordained to Christian Ch. (Disciples of Christ), 1956. Dir. admissions Eureka (Ill.) Coll., 1968-74; assoc. minister Glen Oak Christian Ch., Peoria, Ill., 1974-79; interim sr. minister Cen. Christian Ch., Jacksonville, Ill., 1979-81, Bethany Christian Ch., Lincoln, Nebr., 1981-84; sr. minister 1st Christian Ch., Cedar Rapids, Iowa, 1984—; chmn. leader devel. Christian Ch. in Mo., Jefferson City, 1967-68; chmn. com. on ministry Christian Ch. in Ill., Bloomington, 1977-81; pres. Congress of Disciples Clergy, Indpls., 1979-81, Inst. for Ministry, Christian Ch. in Upper Midwest, Des Moines, 1988-90. Author curriculum materials. Mem. Linn County Fed. Emergency Mgmt. Agy. Bd., Cedar Rapids, 1987—; vice chmn. adv. bd. Dept. Human Resources, Cedar Rapids, 1988—; mem. human svc. planning United Way, Cedar Rapids, 1989—; chmn. County Bd. Social Welfare, Cedar Rapids, 1989—; mem. Linn County Dem. Cen. Com. Mem. Conf. of Clergy. Home: 3825 Valley Pl NE Cedar Rapids IA 52402 Office: 1st Christian Ch 840 3d Ave SE Cedar Rapids IA 52403

BRONAUGH, BERT ALLEN, pastor; b. Kermit, Tex., Jan. 12, 1918; s. Frances Harold and Lela Catherine (Fox) B.; m. Joyce Ann Schmalstieg, Sept. 4, 1960; children: Bert Jr., JoBeth, Ann. BA, Austin Coll., 1959; BD, Austin Presbyn. Sem., 1962, MDiv, 1971. Pastor Boldtville Presbyn. Ch., San Antonio, 1962-65, Burnet (Tex.) Presbyn. Ch., 1965-81, St. Andrew Presbyn. Ch., Marble Falls, Tex., 1965-81, Potosi (Mo.) Presbyn. Ch., 1981-90, 1st Presbyn. Ch., Calvert City, Ky., 1990—; commr. Gen. Assembly, Presbyn. Ch. USA, Memphis, 1971; mem. leadership com. Presbytery, Hopkinsville, Ky. Mem. Zoning Commn., Burnet, 1975-80; mem. County Ministerial Alliance, Potosi, Mo., 1985; pres. Burnet Ministerial Alliance, Burnet, 1980. Named Honor Citizen of Yr., Burnet, 1975. Mem. Potosi Ministerial Alliance, Rotary (editor Marshall County, all offices Potosi chpt.), Lions (editor Calvert City chpt.), Masons (master Valley lodge Burnet 1979), Order Ea. Star. Office: First Presbyn Ch 618 Evergreen St PO Box 95 Calvert City KY 42029

BRONFMAN, EDGAR M., religious organization executive. Pres. World Jewish Congress, N.Y.C. Office: World Jewish Congress 501 Madison Ave 17th Fl New York NY 10022*

BRONKAR, CAROLYN, ecumenical agency executive. Exec. dir. Attleboro (Mass.) Area Coun. Chs., Inc. Office: Attleboro Area Coun Chs 505 N Main St Attleboro MA 02703*

BRONKEMA, FREDERICK HOLLANDER, minister, church official; b. Albany, N.Y., Feb. 1, 1934; s. Frederick and Sadie (Hollander) B.; m. Marguerite Cobble, June 5, 1959; children: Frederick David, Timothy Dunning, John Hollander, Robert Kelton. BA magna cum laude, Whitworth Coll., 1956; MDiv, Princeton Theol. Sem., 1959, ThM, 1965; postgrad., New Coll., U. Edinburgh, Scotland, 1959-60, Union Theol. Sem., 1971-72, Ctr. for Intercultural Documentation, Cuernavaca, Mex., 1972. Ordained to ministry United Presbyn. Ch. in U.S.A., 1960. Asst. min. Craigsbank Ch. of Scotland, Edinburgh, 1959-60; min. Atlantic Highlands (N.J.) Presbyn. Ch., 1960-63; assoc. min. Red Clay Creek Presbyn. Ch., Wilmington, Del., 1963-65; fraternal worker United Presbyn. Ch., Lisbon and Figueira de Foz, Portugal, 1966-71; dir. Reconciliation Ecumenical Ctr., Figueira de Foz, 1966-71; prof. Evang. Theol. Sem., Carcavelos, Portugal, 1967-70; missionary Christian Ch. (Disciples of Christ) and Commn.; assoc., fraternal worker United Presbyn. Ch., Rome, 1972-76; dir., mng. editor The Future of Missionary Enterprise, documentation/publs. project Internat. Documentation and Communication Ctr., Rome, 1972-76, assoc. gen. sec., 1974-76; U.S.A. rep. Ecumenical Devel. Coop. Soc., N.Y.C., 1977-86; fraternal worker, missionary Presbyn. Ch. (U.S.A.) and Christian Ch. (Disciples of Christ); coord. Program and Ctr. Reconciliation, Honduran Christian Commn. for Devel., Tegucigalpa, 1986-88; dir. Human Rights Office, Nat. Coun. Chs. of Christ in U.S.A., N.Y.C., 1989—; pres. Ecumenical Group of Portugal, 1967-69; cons. Commn. on World Mission and Evangelism, World Coun. Chs., 1973-75, advisor cen. com. meeting, Geneva, 1984; advisor 7th Assembly of Luth. World Fedn., Budapest, Hungary, 1984. Contbr. articles to ch. jours. Mem. Ecumenical Assn. of Acads. and Laity Ctrs. in Europe. Democrat. Home: 780 Riverside Dr Apt 6AA New York NY 10032 Office: Nat Coun Chs of Christ in USA Office Human Rights 475 Riverside Dr Rm 670 New York NY 10115 *The greatest gift we have is our common humanity. Our basic problem is our lack of humanity—our inhumanity. Life is a struggle daily to become more human.*

BRONSON, OSWALD PERRY, religious organization administrator, clergyman; b. Sanford, Fla., July 19, 1927; s. Uriah Perry and Flora (Hollingshed) B.; m. Helen Carolyn Williams, June 8, 1952; children—Josephine Suzette, Flora Helen, Oswald Perry. B.S., Bethune-Cookman Coll., 1950; B.D., Gammon Theol. Sem., 1959; Ph.D., Northwestern U., 1965. Ordained to ministry Meth. Ch., 1957; pastor in Fla., Ga. and Rock River Conf., Chgo., 1950-66; v.p. Interdenominational Theol. Center, Atlanta, 1966-68; pres. Interdenominational Theol. Center, 1968-75, Bethune-Cookman Coll., 1975—; dir. Fla. Bank and Trust Co.; Past trustee Carrie Steel Pitts Home, Atlanta; past pres. and chmn. bd. edn. Ga. Conf., Central Jurisdiction, United Meth. Ch.; now mem. bd. ministry DeLand dist., also Fla. Ann. Conf., mem., univ. senate, chmn. div. ministry, mem.-at-large bd. global ministries. Bd. dirs. United Meth. Com. on Relief; mem. Volusia County (Fla.) Sch. Bd., Fla. Gov.'s Adv. Council on Productivity; mem. exec. com. So. Regional Edn. Bd.; mem. adv. com. Fla. Sickle Cell Found., Inc.; past mem. council presidents Atlanta U. Center; past mem. Fla. Bd. Ind. Colls. and Univs.; trustee Hinton Rural Life Center; bd. dirs. Inst. of Black World, Wesley Community Center, Atlanta, Martin Luther King Center Social Change, Work Oriented Rehab. Center, Inc., Fund Theol. Edn.; mem. nat. selection com. Rockefeller Doctoral Fellowships in Religion; bd. dirs. Am. Nat. Red Cross, United Way, Nat. Assn. Equal Opportunity in Higher Edn., United Negro Coll. Fund; also mem. fund raising strategy adv. com. Ga. Pastors' Sch. Crusade scholar, 1957-64. Mem. Ga. Assn. Pastoral Care (past vice-chmn., bd. govs.), Am. Assn. Theol. Schs. (v.p. 1968-70), Ministerial Assn. of Halifax Area, Religious Edn. Assn. (past pres., past chmn. bd. dirs.), Mid-Atlantic Assn. Profs. Religious Edn., Fla. Assn. Colls. and Univs. (dir.), Atlanta Theol. Assn. (past vice chmn.), AAUP, Daytona Beach area C. of C., NAACP, Theta Phi (dir. internat. soc.), Alpha Kappa Mu, Phi Delta Kappa, Sigma Pi Phi, Alpha Phi Alpha. Clubs: Rotary, Daytona Beach area Execs, Daytona Beach Quarterback. Office: Bethune-Cookman Coll 640 2nd Ave Daytona Beach FL 32015

BRONSTED, ROGER LEWIS, educator; b. Tomahawk, Wis., Sept. 29, 1925; s. Amel Andrew and Bertha Nora Serena (Osero) B.; m. Janice Jane Nelson, May 24, 1951; children: Nathan Peter, Rebecca Kristine, Sara Serena. BA, Luth. Coll., 1947; MDiv, Concordia Sem., 1951; ThM, Luth. Theol Sem., 1965; postgrad., U. Mich., 1971. Ordained to ministry Luth. Ch. Pastor Immanuel Faith Luth. Chs., Glenburg, N.D., 1951-53, Redeemer and Centenial Ch., Deer River, Minn., 1953-59, St. John Ch., Durand, Wis., 1959-64, St. Paul Ch., Mondoville, Wis., 1959-64; tchr. Luth. High Sch. West, Detroit, 1964-66; prof. Mich. Luth. Coll., Detroit, 1966-76; pastor Getheemane Luth. Ch., Detroit, 1971-78, Unity and Bethlehem West Ch., Detroit, 1978-87; prof. part time D'Etre U., Concordia Coll., Wayne County Community Coll., Detroit, Ann Arbor, 1987—. Home and Office: 19164 Auburndale Livonia MI 48152

BRONSTEIN, HERBERT, rabbi, educator; b. Cin., Mar. 1, 1930; s. Morris and Lillian (Weisberg) B.; m. Tamar Blumenfield, June 12, 1954; children: Deborah Ruth, Miriam, Daniel Mosheh. BA in History with high honors, U. Cin., 1952; B in Hebrew Letters with honors, Hebrew Union Coll., 1954, MA in History with high honors, 1953, M in Hebrew Letters with high honors, 1956. Ordained rabbi, 1957. Rabbi B'rith Kodesh, Rochester, N.Y., 1957-72; sr. rabbi North Shore Congregation Israel, Glencoe, Ill., 1972—; lectr. religion and lit.; prof. history and philosophy of religion, U. Rochester, 1962-72; now teaching U. Ill., Chgo., 1975—. Editor Haggadah, 1972; contbr. articles to religious publs. Mem. liturgy com. Cen. Conf. Am. Rabbis, 1962—; nat. chmn. Joint Commn. on Worship, 1973—; mem. Rochester Police Adv. Bd., 1965-70; mem. Joint Met. Housing Com. of Rochester, 1966-71; bd. dirs. Rochester Jobs, Inc., 1968, also founder; chmn., founder Pastoral Counseling, 1960-70; mem. exec. com. Nat. Jewish Community Rels. Adv. Coun. Home: 595 Sheridan Rd Glencoe IL 60022 Office: North Shore Congregation Israel 1185 Sheridan Rd Glencoe IL 60022

BROOKS, ALEXANDER DOBBIN, minister, administrator; b. Dumbarton, Scotland, June 10, 1940; came to U.S., 1960; s. Thomas Gillespie and Mary (Bovil) B.; m. Joanie Carol Hegre, Oct. 11, 1963; children: David Scott, Diane Carol. Diploma, Bethany Coll. of Missions, Mpls., 1963. Ordained to Ministry Bethany Missionary Ch., 1974. Tchr. Bethany Coll. of Missions, Mpls., 1970, dean of men, 1972-80; pastor Bethany Missionary Ch., Mpls., 1974—; prin. Bethany Acad., Mpls., 1975-81; pres. Bethany Fellowship, Inc., 1980—, Bethany Corp., 1980-89; internat. dir. Bethany Fellowship Missions, Mpls., 1983-86; bd. dirs. Faith Ventures, Clarkesville, Ga. Editor-in-chief Bethany House Publs., Mpls., 1966-80; contbg. author: Message of the Cross Mag., 1975—, editor., 1982-91. Bd. dirs. Greater Mpls. Assn. Evangs., 1985. Mem. Nat. Assn. Evangs. (bd. dirs. 1986—). Home and Office: Bethany Fellowship 6820 Auto Club Rd Minneapolis MN 55438

BROOKS, BRENT THOMAS, church planter; b. Oxnard, Calif., Sept. 9, 1953; s. Otis Thomas and Clara Belle (Teague) B.; m. Vicki Jill Zelios, May 27, 1978; 1 child, Abigail Christine. BA in Polit. Sci., Southern Meth. U., 1975; JD, U. Tex., 1978; ThM, Dallas Theol. Sem., 1984. Bar: Tex. 1978; ordained to ministry Grace Fellowship Ch., 1984. Founding pastor Grace Community Ch., Columbia, Md., 1984-89; area dir. Ch. Resource Ministries, Germantown, Md., 1989—; founding pastor New Song Ch., Gaithersburg, Md., 1990—; bd. dirs. SEED Fellowship, Md., 1988—, trustee East Coast Ch. Planting Inc., Balt., 1984—, Ch. Planting Resources, Columbia, Md., 1986—, del. Leadership 88, Washington, 1988, adj. faculty Biblical Theol. Sem., Hatfield, Pa., 1989—. Contbr. articles to profl. jours. Mem. North Am. Soc. Ch. Growth. Home and Office: 11608 Summer Oak Dr Germantown MD 20874

BROOKS, DAWNE LEA, minister; b. St. Paul; d. Clinton Joseph Williamson and Beatrice (Gilbertson) Sorensen. AA in Psychology, Bellevue Community Coll., 1977; BA in Religion and Counseling, Ottawa (Kans.) U., 1982; MA in Human Rels. and Mgmt., Webster U., 1984. Ordained to ministry Unity Ch., 1982. Dir. ch. groups, counselor Unity Ch. of Practical Christianity, Seattle, 1975-79; adminstr. youth edn. Community Unity Ch., Kansas City, Kans., 1981; hostess radio programs Unity Sch. Christianity, Unity Village, Mo., 1981-82; assoc. minister, dir. edn., counselor Christ Ch. Unity, Kansas City, 1984-86, chmn. Unity Ministerial Alliance, 1984-89; sr. minister, counselor Christ Unity Ch., Chattanooga, 1989-90; chaplain intern VA Med. Ctr., St. Louis, 1991; spiritual leader U.S. Armed Forces Retreat, Ft. Jackson, S.C., 1983. Editor: Policy Manuel for a Unity Ministry, 1988. Named Vol. of Month, Assn. Unity Chs., 1988. Mem. Toastmasters (sec. 1988-89). Avocations: reading, theater, swimming, walking, symphony. *To keep our thoughts returning to the higher power of good within ourselves, in others and in life makes a difference in the quality of my life, your life and all of life. Forgiving ourselves and others at the end of each day facilitates our ability to see the best in life and people.*

BROOKS, FORREST W., SR., pastor; b. Blevins, Ark.; m. Sharon L., Nov. 3, 1972; 1 child, Forrest W., Jr. Co-pastor Assemblies of God God, 1960-75, Pentecostal Ch. of God, 1977-90. Home: 360 Elm Wenden AZ 85357

BROOKS, JAMES WRIGHT (JIM BROOKS), minister; b. Shreveport, La., Sept. 17, 1942; s. A. Q. and Ruby Estelle (Johns) B.; m. Kathy Lou Yarbrough, Apr. 8, 1966; children: Janice Brooks Kale, James Wright II. BA, La. Coll., 1972; MDiv, Southwestern Bapt. Theol. Sem., Ft. Worth, 1974. Ordained to ministry So. Bapt. Conv., 1968. Pastor Summerfield (La.) Bapt. Ch., 1966-69; min. outreach Poly. Bapt. Ch., Ft. Worth, 1971-74; pastor 1st Bapt. Ch., Hanover, Pa., 1974-75, Cen. Bapt. Ch., Ocean City, N.J., 1975-77, 1st Bapt. Ch., Grand Isle, La., 1977-78, Cherokee Pk. Bapt. Ch., Shreveport, 1978-81, Frierson (La.) Bapt. Ch., 1981-85, West Lake Bapt. Ch., Doyline, La., 1985-89; chaplain Overton Brooks VA Med. Ctr.,

Shreveport, 1990—. Chaplain CAP, N.J. and La., 1974-83; bd. dirs. Common Bond, Shreveport, 1980-84, N.W. La. Epilepsy Assn., Shreveport, 1980-87, Shreveport Met. Concert Band, 1989—. With U.S. Army, 1960s. Decorated Armed Forces Expdn. medal; Recipient Community Svc. award Grand Isle (La.) Jaycees, 1979, appreciation award Civitan Club Shreveport, 1982. Mem. Assn. for Clin. Pastoral Edn. (cert.). Office: Overton Brooks VA Med Ctr 510 E Stoner Ave Shreveport LA 71101

BROOKS, OSCAR STEPHENSON, religion educator; b. Menlo, Ga., Dec. 24, 1928; s. Charlie Alston and Jessie Alyce (Stephenson) B.; m. Sarah Ktherine Rives, Aug. 5, 1949; children: Oscar S. Jr., Philip Alston II, Amanda Katherine. BA, Carson-Newman Coll., Jefferson City, Tenn., 1949; BD, So. Bapt. Theol. Sem., Louisville, 1954, PhD, 1959; postgrad., Pacific Sch. Religion, 1965, Hebrew Union Coll., 1967, Johns Hopkins U., 1976, Ind. U., 1978, 81, Am. Sch. Classical Study, Athens, Greece, 1985, Am. Ctr. Oriental Rsch., Amman, 1989. Prof. religion Cumberland Coll., Williamsburg, Ky., 1959-63, William Jewell Coll., Liberty, Mo., 1963-82; prof. N.T. studies Golden Gate Sem., Mill Valley, Calif., 1982—; adj. prof. Midwestern Bapt. Sem., Kansas City, Mo., 1978, 82, 84, 87, So. Bapt. Sem., Louisville, 1966. Author: Drama of Decision, 1987, Sermon on Mount, 1985. NEH grantee, 1977, 79; recipient Stipend, NEH, 1981. Mem. Soc. Bibl. Lit., Am. Schs. Oriental Rsch., Cath. Bibl. Assn. Baptist. Office: Golden Gate Sem Mill Valley CA 94941

BROOKS, P. A., II, bishop. Bishop Ch. of God in Christ, Birmingham, Mich. Office: Ch of God in Christ 30945 Wendbrook Ln Birmingham MI 48010*

BROOKS, PORTER HARRISON, minister; b. Chgo., July 5, 1926; s. Hugh Moore and Lucy Elizabeth (Brooks) Woods; m. Norma Margaret Singer, Aug. 21, 1954; children: Beverly, Roland, Gloria. BA, McMurry U., 1948; MDiv, Va. Theol. Seminary, Alexandria, 1951; Diploma, U.S. Army Chaplain Sch., 1962, U.S. Army Command and Gen. Staff Coll., 1964. Commd. 2d lt. U.S. Army, 1945, advanced through ranks to col., 1971, chaplain, 1951-53, 55-81, ret.; rector St. Matthew's Ch., Pampa, Tex., 1953-55; interim rector St. Mary's, Trinity Ch., Arlington, St. Albans, Annandale, Va., 1982-86; assoc. rector St. John's Ch., McLean, Va., 1987—. Author: Cross, Crook and Candle, 1974, Chapel Windows/Ft. Myer, Va., 1973, Chapels At West Point, 1966; editor: Daily Soul Maintenance, 1970. Chmn. Am. Cancer Soc. br., Gray County, Tex., 1953-54, Cub Scouts USMA, West Point, N.Y., 1964-67. Decorated Legion of Merit, Bronze Star, others; elected to Infantry Officer Candidate Sch. Hall of Fame, Ft. Benning, Ga., 1973. Office: 6715 Georgetown Pike McLean VA 22101

BROOKS, RAY O., minister, educator; b. Emhouse, Tex., Mar. 7, 1923; s. John T. and Lalia (Ray) B.; m. Mildred Nell Evans, Sept. 8, 1945; children: Patty Dell, Jack Evans. BS, Tex. A&M U., 1946; B in Theology, Tex. Bapt. Sem., 1956, M of Theology, 1957, D of Theology, 1963. Ordained to ministry Bapt. Ch, 1952. Tchr. Blue Ridge (Tex.) Sch. System, 1946-48, Navarro County Schs., Corsicana, Tex., 1948-53; pastor Hopewell Bapt. Ch., Navarro, 1951-53, Long Branch (Tex.) Missionary Bapt. Ch., 1953—; tchr. Tex. Bapt. Inst. and Sem., Henderson, 1955—, registrar, 1957-65, dean, 1965-72, pres., 1972—. Author: Christian Doctrine, 1970; editor Bapt. Monitor, 1973—. Served to lt. (j.g.) USNR, 1942-46. Mem. Am. Bapt. Assn. (pres. 1986-87). Avocations: fishing, golf. Home: 1706 Longview Dr Henderson TX 75652 Office: 1300 Longview Dr PO Box 570 Henderson TX 75652

BROOKS, ROBERT TERRANCE, JR., minister; b. San Antonio, Sept. 8, 1963; s. Robert Terrance and Nancy Lee (MacKenney) B.; m. Lisa Marie Brown, Aug. 29, 1987; children: Ansley, Nicole. BA in Journalism, Ga. State U., 1987; postgrad., New Orleans Bapt. Theol. Sem., Atlanta, Ga., 1988—. Ordained to ministry Bapt. Ch., 1989; lic. radio broadcaster. Summer youth min. Forest Hills Bapt. Ch., College Park, Ga., 1985; youth min. Braelinn Bapt. Ch., Peachtree City, Ga., 1987-89; min. of youth and activities Clarkston (Ga.) Bapt. Ch., 1989—; officer Bapt. Student Union, Ga. State U., Atlanta, 1984-85; cons. youth ministry Fairburn (Ga.) Bapt. Assn., 1987-89; asst. dir. Light Brigade Drug and Gang Task Force, Clarkston, 1991—. Mem. Sigma Delta Chi. Office: Clarkston Bapt Ch 3895 Church St Clarkston GA 30021

BROOKS, RON ESTA, ecumenical agency executive. Head Amherst (N.S., Can.) and Area Coun. Chs. Office: Amherst and Area Coun Chs, RR 6, Amherst, NS Canada B3H 3Y4*

BROOME, RANDALL, evangelist; b. Hattiesburg, Miss., June 9, 1954; s. Eugene Wallace and Doris Vonceil (Lucas) B.; m. Barbara Ann Kelly, Dec. 18, 1976; children: Christopher Randall, Kelli Kristi Anna. BMin, Fla. Bapt. Theol. Coll., Graceville, Fla., 1981; MDiv, New Orleans Bapt. Sem., 1984. Lic. to ministry So. Bapt. Conv., 1976, ordained to ministry So. Bapt. Conv., 1979. Pastor Unity Bapt. Ch., Chipley, Fla., 1979-81, Good Hope Bapt. Ch., Franklinton, La., 1983-84, Oconee Bapt. Ch., Commerce, Ga., 1984-87, 1st Bapt. Ch. of Arabi, La., 1987-90; evangelist, pres. World Evangelism, Inc., Chalmette, La., 1990—. Contbr. articles to religion mags. With U.S. Air Force, 1973-75. Mem. Living Dividends Investment Club (founder, presiding officer 1989-90). Republican. Home and Office: 2208 Legend Dr Meraux LA 70075 *Circumstances of life are constantly changing, and we are constantly developing as persons. God has made life and living beings to function in that manner. This an absolute axiom. When a living organism ceases to change it dies, which is itself a change. Since I cannot remain the same, I have a responsibility to become everything that God intends me to be.*

BROOMFIELD, OREE, SR., bishop. Bishop 7th dist. Christian Meth. Episcopal Ch., Washington. Address: Christian Meth Episcopal Ch 6524 16th St NW Washington DC 20012*

BROOTEN, BERNADETTE JOAN, theology educator; b. Coeur d'Alene, Idaho, Jan. 29, 1951; d. Kenneth Edward and Sadie Josephine (Assad) B. BA, U. Portland, 1971; postgrad., U. Tubingen, 1971-73, 75-76, Hebrew U. Jerusalem, 1977-78; PhD, Harvard U., 1982. Instr. women's studies Leibniz Kolleg U. Tubingen, 1981; instr. Hawaii Consortium for Theol. Edn., 1982; instr. N.T. Sch. Theology at Claremont (Calif.), 1981-82; prin. investigator U. Tubingen, 1982-84; dir. rsch. women's studies, asst. prof. religion Claremont Grad. Sch., 1982-84; asst. prof. Scripture and interpretation Harvard Div. Sch., Cambridge, Mass., 1985-89, assoc. prof., 1989—; vis. asst. prof. Sch. Theology at Claremont, 1980-81; vis. instr. United Presbyn. Ch. Synod of Northeast Synod Sch., 1975; teaching fellow N.T. dept. Harvard Div. Sch., 1977, rsch. and resource assoc. in women's studies, 1978-79. Author: Women Leaders in the Ancient Synagogue: Inscriptional Evidence and Background Issues, 1982; co-editor: Frauen in der Mannerkirche?, 1982; co-editor Harvard Dissertations in Religion, 1985—; mem. editorial bd. Jour. Feminist Studies in Religion, 1984-87; contbr. articles and book revs. to profl. jours. Group facilitator Cambridge Women's Ctr., 1989—. Sinclair Kennedy traveling fellow Harvard U., 1977, NEH fellow, 1989, Buting Inst. of Radcliffe Coll. fellow, Cambridge, 1989; grantee Harvard U. Fund for Innovation, 1988, Roothbert Found., 1977, 78. Mem. NOW, Soc. Bibl. Lit. (program com. 1984-87, co-chair women in Bibl. world sect. 1982-83), Am. Acad. Religion (co-chair lesbian-feminist issues in religion group 1988-90), Cath. Bibl. Assn., Societas Novi Testamenti Studiorum, Nat. Women's Studies Assn., Assn. Jewish Studies, Am. Acad. Religion, Delta Sigma Kappa. Office: Harvard Div Sch 45 Francis Ave Cambridge MA 02138

BROSE, GREGORY LEE, minister, educator; b. Gardena, Calif., June 7, 1964; s. Lee Charles and Carmen Marie (Amos) B. Dir. Christian Edn., Christ Coll., Irvine, Calif., 1987. Youth counselor Grace Luth. Ch., Escondido, Calif., 1983-84; tchr., youth worker Christ Coll., Irvine, Calif., 1984-85; youth worker Gloria Dei Luth. Ch., Dana Point, Calif., 1985-86; fellowship coord. Christ Coll./Camp Pendleton, Irvine, Calif., 1986-87; youth min. St. Paul Luth. Ch., Ft. Worth, 1987—. Judge S.W. High Sch. Debate, Ft. Worth, 1990, 91; youth facilitator Luth. Ch. Miss. Synod, Tex. Dist., 1989—. Republican. Home: 3823 Levee Circle W #282 Fort Worth TX 76109 Office: Saint Paul Luth Ch 1800 W Freeway Fort Worth TX 76102

BROSIUS, GENE N., minister; b. Danville, Pa., Feb. 17, 1950; s. Howard Eugene and Dorothy R. (Bailey) B.; m. Roberta Louise Tucker, June 14, 1975; children: Kyle, Connolly, Kevin, Curt. AAS, Pa. Coll. Tech., 1970; BA in Bibl. Lit., Northeastern Bible Coll., 1974; MA in Religious Edn., S.W. Bapt. Sem., 1977; postgrad., Liberty U., 1990-91. Cert. emergency med. tech., Pa.; ordained minister Am. Bapt. Chs. Dir., student loans Northeastern Bible Coll., Essex Fells, N.J., 1974-75; pastor Temple Bapt. Ch., Perth Amboy, N.J., 1974-75; bus. adminstr. Shade Mt. Health Ctr., Mt. Pleasant Mills, Pa., 1978-80; pastor Montandon (Pa.) Bapt. Ch., 1980—; instr. Youth Challenge Bible Inst., Sunbury, Pa., 1979—; chaplain group home Community Svcs. Group, Montandon, 1990—. Exec. dir. Cen. Susquehanna Valley Celebration for Christ, Lewisburg, 1990; emergency med. tech. William Cameron Engine Co., Lewisburg, 1991. Mem. Profl. Ch. Leaders, Northumberland Bapt. Assn., Kiwanis. Democrat. Home: PO Box 110 Montandon PA 17850 *The secret of a fulfilling, productive life is found in the realism of the Apostle Paul, who suggested to the Philippians that while he had learned to be content with his present circumstances, he never ceased reaching for the prize ahead. Said Browning, "A man's reach should exceed his grasp, or what's a heaven for."*

BROTHERS, FLETCHER ARNOLD, minister, religious organization founder, director; b. Carthage, N.Y., Mar. 8, 1948; s. Rae L. and Hildred (Weaver) B.; m. Linda Carole Scott, Apr. 11, 1975; children: Jeremy, Jamie Lynn. Student, Houghton Coll., 1965-66, Utica Coll., 1966-67; HHD (hon.), Freedom Bible Coll., Lakemont, N.Y., 1988. Ordained to ministry Ind. Bible Chs. Am., 1975. Pastor Gates Community Chapel, Rochester and Lakemont, N.Y., 1975—; founder Freedom Village U.S.A., Lakemont, 1981—; chmn. Freedom Bible Coll., 1986—. Author several books; founder Victory Today Radio and TV Programs, 1977—. Bd. dirs. Religious Round Table, Washington, 1979—; pres. Save Am.'s Youth, Washington, 1988—; bd. govs. Coun. for Nat. Policy, Washington, 1989-90; mem. Inner Circle, Rep. Party, 1990-91. Recipient Angels award, 1989. Mem. Ind. Bible Ch. Home and Office: Freedom Village USA Rte 14 Lakemont NY 14857 *America and especially our children are in the state they are in today because we as a nation have forgotten God. We will not win the war on drugs, etc.—till we win the war declared against God!.*

BROUGH, H. O., business administrator, consultant; b. Bucklin, Mo., May 2, 1929; s. Henry Otto and Floy Alice (Williams) B.; married (div. Aug. 1979); children: Sherri Wagner, Rick, Brett; m. Penelope Raye Miller, Sept. 22, 1989. BS, Mo. State U., 1956, MA, 1959; EdS, U. Wyo., 1964. Supr. Davenport Community Schs., Iowa, 1956-59; coord. U. Wyo., Laramie, 1959-63; asst. dir. U. Iowa, Iowa City, 1963-68; asst. dean U. Colo., Boulder, 1968-89; v.p. Pacific Luth. Theol. Sem., Berkeley, Calif., 1989—; con. Mo. State U., Kirksville, 1959, U. Wyo., 1961, Nat. C. of C., Washington, 1968-79. Contbr. article to profl. jour. Fundraiser senatorial campaign, Boulder, 1979. With USN, 1949-53, Korea. Mem. Nat. Savings and Loan Assn. (edn. cons. 1977), Nat. U. Continuing Edn. Assn. (chmn. 1961-63, Key ward 1989), Colo. Assessors Assn. (edn. cons. 1979), Boulder C. of C. (bd. dirs. 1975-79). Lutheran. Avocations: fishing, restoring classic vehicles. Office: Pacific Luth Theol Seminary 2770 Marin Ave Berkeley CA 94708-1597

BROUSSARD, ALSTON DERRICK, minister; b. St. Louis, July 24, 1956; s. Alston and Dollye Moloyse (Cooksey) B. Cert., Aenon Bible Coll., Indpls., 1979, Phila. Coll. Bible, 1986; DD, Ministry Salvation Ch., Chula Vista, Calif., 1987. Ordained to ministry Pentecostal Ch., 1976. Adminstrv. asst. midwestern dist. Pentecostal Young People's Union, St. Louis, 1982-85, chief staff, 1985-88; asst. treas. MDC Sunday Sch. Assn., St. Louis, 1985-88; asst. pastor New Testament Ch. of Christ, St. Louis, 1990-91; internat. evangelist Pentecostal Power Chs., St. Louis, 1991—; pres., founder Youth Coalition for Christ, St. Louis, 1985—; Bible tchr. Ambassadors for Christ, St. Louis, 1988—, Christian Fellowship, Inc., Oklahoma City, 1989—, sec., chmn. credential com., 1991—; cert. chaplain Internat. Chaplains Assn., Rillton, Pa., 1987 . Author: The Master Touch, 1991. Telethon runner supr. Variety Club, St. Louis, 1982—, telethon runner, 1964—; active Young Dems. Am., St. Louis, 1979-81. Named one of Outstanding Young Men Am., 1988. Mem. Apostolic World Christian Fellowship, Inc., Gospel Music Workshop Am., Christian Fellowship Inc. Office: Pentecostal Power Chs Inc 4201 N Newstead Ave Saint Louis MO 63115

BROUSSEAU, SISTER NANCY MARIE, nun, school system administrator; b. Alpena, Mich., Oct. 18, 1947; d. Kenneth Thomas and Dorothy Helen (Cassan) B. BA, Aquinas Coll., 1973, MA, 1978; MDiv, St. John Sem., Plymouth, Mich., 1987. Joined Grand Rapids Dominican Sisters, Roman Cath. Ch., 1965; cert. secondary tchr., Mich. Tchr. Roman Cath. schs., Mich., 1969-79; liturgy coord. Dominican Sisters, Grand Rapids, Mich., 1979-82; liturgy coord., dir. St. John Sem., Plymouth, 1984-87; dir. total parish edn. Roscommon County Parishes, Mich., 1987-89; supt. Grand Traverse Area Cath. schs., Traverse City, Mich., 1990—. Mem. ASCD, Nat. Cath. Edn. Assn., Mich. Assn. Nonpublic Schs., Travers City C. of C. Address: St Francis Convent 120 E 10th St Traverse City MI 49684

BROUWER, ARIE RAYMOND, religious organization executive; b. Inwood, Iowa, July 14, 1935; s. Arie and Gertie (Brands) B.; m. Harriet Korver, Aug. 16, 1955; children: Milton, Charla, Steven, Patricia. A.A., Northwestern Jr. Coll., Orange City, Iowa, 1954; B.A., Hope Coll., 1956, D.D. (hon.), 1983; B.D., Western Theol. Sem., Holland, Mich., 1959; D.D., Central Coll., Pella, Iowa, 1978. Ordained to ministry Ref. Ch. in Am., 1959; pastor chs. Mich., 1959-63, N.J., 1963-68; sec. for program Ref. Ch. in Am., N.Y.C., 1968-70; exec. sec. Ref. Ch. in Am., 1970-77, gen. sec., 1977-83; dep. gen. sec. World Council Chs., Geneva, 1983-84; gen. sec. Nat. Council Chs. USA, N.Y.C., 1985-89; First chmn. Bd. Theol. Edn., Ref. Ch., 1967-68; v.p. Bd. World Missions, 1967-68; mem. Theol. Commn., 1967-68; mem. gen. bd. Nat. Council Chs., 1969-72, gov. bd., 1973-83; bd. dirs. Bread for the World, 1973-82, v.p., 1976-82; mem. central com. World Council Chs., 1979-83. Contbg. editor: Ch. Herald, 1967-68. Office: Nat Council Chs USA 475 Riverside Dr Room 880 New York NY 10115

BROWDER, MICHAEL HEATH, clergyman, educator; b. Richmond, Va., Dec. 4, 1951; s. Arville Heath and Anna Marie (Ficke) B.; m. Susan Beers, July 8, 1978; children—Michael Heath, Marjorie Elizabeth. B.A., Duke U., 1973, Th.M., 1977, Ph.D., 1982; M.Div., Harvard U., 1976. Ordained to ministry United Methodist Ch., 1977. Minister, Prospect United Meth. Ch., 1976-78, King George United Meth. Ch., 1978-80, Highland Park United Meth. Ch., 1980-82; pastor Strasburg and Mt. Zion (Va.) United Meth. Chs., 1982—; instr. religion Shenandoah Coll. and Conservatory Music, 1983—; adj. faculty Wesley Theol. Sem. Mem. Shenandoah Democratic Com., Shenandoah Bd. Human Services; active Richmond Urban Inst. Recipient grants for lang. research. Mem. Assn. Bibl. Archeologists. Lodge: Masons. Author: Al-Biruni as a Source for Mani and Manichaeism, 1982; English Translation of the Coptic Manichaen Homilies, 1983; corr. Va. Advocate. Office: 2211 Skipwith Rd Richmond VA 23229

BROWER, KENT EVERETT, religious educator; b. Calgary, Alta., Can., Sept. 4, 1946; s. Barry Howard and Jean Agnes (Dixon) B.; m. Francine Louise Taylor, Aug. 25, 1967; children: Deirdre René, Derek Leigh. B Sacred Lit., Can. Nazarene Coll., 1967; MA, Eastern Nazarene Coll., 1969; PhD, U. Manchester, Eng., 1978. Lectr., bursar Brit. Isles Nazarene Coll., Manchester, Eng., 1974-79, acad. dean, 1988—; assoc. prof. bibl. language and lit. Can. Nazarene Coll., Winnipeg, Man., 1979-88; com. mem. Ch. of the Nazarene, Kansas City, Mo., 1982—; lectr. U. Winnipeg, 1980-81, U. Man., 1983—; vis. prof. Africa Nazarene Theol. Coll., Johannesburg, Republic of South Africa, 1983, Nazarene Theol. Seminary, Kansas City, 1984. Pres. Constituency Orgn. Polit. Party, Wainwright, Alta., 1972-73. Mem. Soc. Bibl. Lit., Can. Soc. Bibl. Study, Tyndale Fellowship, Wesleyan Theol. Soc. Home: Brit Isles Nazarene Coll, The White House, Dene Rd, Didsbury M208GU, England

BROWN, ALAN MORRIS, music and youth minister; b. Walhalla, S.C., Aug. 11, 1963; s. Thomas Sloan and Betty Louise (Addis) Crumpton. B of Music Edn., Newberry Coll., 1985. Choir dir. Colony Luth. Ch., Newberry, S.C., 1984-85; lay minister Fairfax (S.C.) Luth. Parish, 1986-87; choir dir. Mill Creek United Meth. Ch., Columbia, S.C., 1987-89; choir youth dir. St. Luke United Meth. Ch., Walhalla, S.C., 1990—. Master mason Blue Ridge Masonic Lodge #92, Walhalla, 1991. Named Outstanding Young Men Am., 1987. Democrat. Home: 105 Timberline Ridge Walhalla SC 29691 Office: St Luke United Meth Ch 607 E Main St PO Box 339 Walhalla SC 29691

BROWN, AMOS CLEOPHILUS, minister; b. Jackson, Miss., Feb. 20, 1941; s. Louetta Robinson Brown; m. Jane Evangeline Smith, June 25, 1966; children: Amos Cleophilus, David Josephus, Kizzie Maria. BA, Morehouse Coll., Atlanta, 1964; MDiv, Crozer Sem., Chester, Pa., 1968; DMin, United Sem., Dayton, Ohio, 1990; DDiv, Va. Sem., Lynchburg, 1984. Ordained to ministry, Am. Bapt. Chs. ant Nat. Bapt. USA, Inc. Pastor St. Paul's Bapt. Ch., West Chester, Pa., 1966-70, Pilgrim Bapt. Ch., St. Paul, 1970-76, Third Bapt. Ch., San Francisco, 1976—; instr. philosophy Cheyney (Pa.) State Coll., 1968-70; nat. chmn. Nat. Bapt. Commn. on Civil Rights and Human Svcs., 1982—; chmn. Bay Area Ecumenical Pastors Conf., 1980—. Vice pres. governing bd. San Francisco Community Coll., 1987-89. Recipient Martin Luther King Ministerial award, Colgate Rochester Div. Sch., 1984, Man of the Yr., San Francisco Bus. and Profl. Women's Clubs, 1985. Mem. NAACP, Rotary, Masons, Alpha Phi Alpha. Democrat. Office: Third Bapt Ch 13499 McAllister St San Francisco CA 94117

BROWN, ARCHIE EARL, pastor; b. Harrisburg, Ill., Feb. 26, 1913; s. Robert Lee Brown and Rowena Maddox; div.; children: William Lee, Charles Gene. BS, Tex. Wesleyan Coll., 1945; BRE, Southwestern Bapt. Theol. Sem., 1948, DRE, 1950. Ordained to ministry So. Bapt. Conv., 1940. Pastor First Bapt. Ch., Greenwood, Tex., 1941-46, Pickneyville, Ill., 1950-54, Vandalia, Ill., 1954-79, Sandoval, Ill., 1980-86; pastor Fairman Bapt. Ch., Sandoval, 1988-90; bd. dirs. Southwestern Sem., Ft. Worth, 1952-65, Golden Gate Bapt. Sem., Mill Valley, Calif., 1966-72. Author: Million Men for Christ, 1952, Sun. Sch. lessons weekly, 1950-82. Mem. Ill. Bapt. State Assn. (pres. 1967-68, chmn. exec. com. 1967-68), Vandalia Rotary Club (pres. 1970-71). Home: 614 Randolph Vandalia IL 62471 Office: Fairman Bapt Ch RR 1 Sandoval IL

BROWN, ARTHUR CARL, JR., retired minister; b. Stockton, Calif., Dec. 16, 1915; s. Arthur Carl and Maud (Twitchings) B.; m. Inez Lundquist, May 10, 1940 (dec. Aug. 1982); 1 child, Arthur Carl III. BA, Coll. of the Pacific, 1937; MA, San Francisco Theol. Sem., 1939, BD with honors, 1940; postgrad., Stanford U.,, 1949-50. Ordained to ministry Presbyn. Ch., 1940. Pastor Presbyn. Ch., Sedro Woolley, Wash., 1940-44, Community Ch., Santa Clara, Calif., 1944-46; assoc. pastor First Presbyn. Ch., San. Jose, Calif., 1946-49; minister edn. First Presbyn. Ch., Palo Alto, Calif., 1949-51; organizing pastor Covenant Presbyn. Ch., Palo Alto, 1951-74; pastor Trinity Presbyn. Ch., Santa Cruz, Calif., 1974-78; outreach assoc. Los Gatos (Calif.) Presbyn. Ch., 1978-81; commr. to gen. assembly United Presbyn. Ch., 1947, 52, 59; moderator San Jose Presbytery, 1950, chmn. various coms., 1950-78; mem. Synod Golden Gate and Synod of Pacific coms. Synod of Calif., 1947-82; pastor emeritus Covenant Presbyn. Ch.; moderator Bellingham Prebytery-Synod of Wash., 1943. Treas., chmn. fin. com., bd. dirs. Internat. House, Davis, Calif., 1984-90, chmn. internat. house nominating com., 1990-91, mem. internat. devel. com., pers. com., 1991—. Mem. Rotary (sec. local chpt. 1941-44). Republican. Avocations: gardening, wood carving, classical music, sports, studies of Greek words in N.T., writing. Home: 4414 San Ramon Dr Davis CA 95616

BROWN, ARZA EDWARD, minister; b. Massillon, Ohio, Aug. 30, 1942; s. Edward Weldon and Olive May (Wadsworth) B.; m. Ruth Ann Inghram, July 15, 1961; children: Ruth Diane, Richard Dean, Mark Edward. ThB, Bapt. Bible Coll., Springfield, Mo., 1964; student, U. Hawaii, 1977. Ordained to ministry Ind. Bapt. Ch., 1963. Missionary World Bapt. Fellowship, Arlington, Tex., 1964—; founder, missionary Anahola (Hawaii) Bapt. Ch., 1964-73, Maranatha Bapt. Ch., Kekaha, Hawaii, 1969-75, Grace Bapt. Ch., Lahaina, Hawaii, 1974—. Contbr. articles to profl. jours. Office: World Bapt Fellowship PO Box 13459 Arlington TX 76094-0459

BROWN, ASHMUN N., priest; b. Yakima, Wash., June 9, 1930; s. Nathaniel Usher and Marie Adair (Flynn) B.; m. Suzanne Hengesch, Oct. 28, 1953 (div. 1973); children: Mara Kate Routh, Lisa Ann, Mark, Fred J.; m. Rita L. Rodda, May 23, 1981. JD cum laude, Boston U., 1958; LLM, U. Mich., 1959; D Ministry, Grad. Theol. Found., 1989. Bar: Mass., Fla., U.S. Supreme Ct. Chancellor Canterbury Retreat and Conf. Ctr., Oviedo, Fla., 1981—; vice chancellor, mem. ct. array Diocese of Cen. Fla., Orlando, 1988—; deacon Cathedral Ch. of St. Luke, Orlando, 1984-91, assoc. priest, 1991—; pres., dean Inst. for Christian Studies, Orlando, 1985—; gen. counsel Univ. Cen. Fla., Orlando, 1980—, chaplain, 1990—; diocesan bd. Diocese of Cen. Fla., Orlando, 1987-89, sexuality commn., 1990-91; bd. dirs. Inst. for Youth Ministry, Orlando. Contbr. articles to newspapers. Mem. Disabled Am. Vets., Orlando, 1989—. Lt. U.S. Signal Corps, 1951-53. Rome scholar Boston Univ. Law Sch., 1957-58, Cook fellow Univ. Mich., Ann Arbor, 1959. Mem. Fla. Bar Assn., Mass. Bar Assn. Democrat. Episcopalian. Home: 400 E Colonial Dr # 409 Orlando FL 32803 Office: Univ Cen Fla PO Box 25000 Orlando FL 32816

BROWN, AUBREY NEBLETT, JR., minister, editor; b. Hillsboro, Tex., May 6, 1908; s. Aubrey Neblett and Virginia Rose (Sims) B.; m. Sarah Dumond Hill, Oct. 4, 1932; children—Aubrey Neblett III, Zaida English Brown Field, Julia Haywood Brown Diehl, Virginia Sims Brown Ashworth, Eleanor Berkeley Brown Bigger, William Hill, Ernest Thompson, Katherine Purdie Brown Weisiger. A.B., Davidson Coll., 1929; B.D., Union Theol. Sem., Va., 1932; Litt.D., Southwestern at Memphis (now Rhodes Coll.), 1950; D.D., Maryville Coll., 1961; Litt.D., Davidson Coll., 1979. Ordained to ministry Presbyn. Ch. (U.S.A.), 1932. Pastor Presbyn. chs., Ronceverte, W.Va., 1932-38, Montgomery, W.Va., 1938-43; editor Presbyn. Outlook, Richmond, Va., 1943-78, Going-to-Coll. Handbook, 1946-78; interim pastor All Souls Presbyn. Ch., Richmond, 1963-64, 73-74; coord. Richmond Area Presbyns., 1979-90; moderator Synod of W.Va., Presbyn. Ch. U.S., 1946. Author: The Church Publicity Book, 1986. Pres. Richmond Area Council Human Relations, 1957-59, Va. Council Human Relations, 1963-65; chmn. Va. Adv. Com. to U.S. Commn. on Civil Rights, 1966-67; pres. Richmond Area chpt. UN Assn. U.S.A., 1967-69; mem. N.Am. area council World Alliance Ref. Chs., 1960-73; del. 20th Gen. Council World Alliance Ref. Chs., Nairobi, Kenya, 1970. Recipient Editorial citation Assn. Ch. Press, 1952, Torch of Liberty award Va. B'nai B'rith, 1966; co-recipient Ernest Trice Thompson award Presbyn. Outlook Found., 1989. Democrat. Home: 1600 Westwood Ave # 211-A Richmond VA 23227

BROWN, BARRON KIRKPATRICK, retired minister, organization executive; b. Jacksonville, Fla., Jan. 23, 1947; s. George Henry and Sarah Leatrice (Frazier) B.; m. Claire L. Scroggins, Sept. 19, 1970; children: William Howard, Meredith Frazier. BA, Asbury Coll., 1969; MDiv, Asbury Theol. Sem., 1973; D of Ministry, Fuller Theol. Sem., 1982. Ordained to ministry as deacon United Meth. Ch., 1970, as elder, 1975; ordained bishop, 1988. Assoc. pastor First United Meth. Ch., Melbourne, Fla., 1973-77; sr. pastor Community United Meth. Ch., Marathon, Fla., 1977-79, Cralson Meml. United Meth. Ch., La Belle, Fla., 1979-81, Calvary United Meth. Ch., Sarasota, Fla., 1981-85, The Cathedral of the Holy Spirit, Ft. Lauderdale, Fla., 1985-90; community dir March of Dimes, Miami, Fla., 1990—; adj. faculty religion Broward Community Coll., humanities and philosophy Miami-Dada Community Coll., 1990—. Editor: (one chpt.) Compendium on Ministers' Wives, 1986; contbr. articles to mags. and profl. jours; columnist: newspaper, 1988-90. Active mem. Broward County Rep. Com., 1988-90. Named Young Religious Leader of Yr., Melbourne (Fla.) Jaycees, 1976. Mem. Davie-Cooper City (Fla.) C. of C. Home: 790 Rock Hill Ave Davie FL 33325 Office: March of Dimes 900 NE 125th St Ste 200 North Miami FL 33161 *The most positive development of human progress is the ever increasing ability of the individual to gain access to objective assessments of personal abilities and motivations.*

BROWN, BETH ELAINE, religious educator; b. Rochester, N.Y., Dec. 17, 1946; d. Ernest George and Myra Aletha (Fuller) Hollenbach; m. Don Arlen Brown, Dec. 28, 1967; children: Amy, April; stepchildren: Rick, Sharon, Steve, Kayleen, David. BA, The King's Coll., Briarcliff Manor, N.Y., 1967; MA in Christian Edn., Denver Sem., 1982; EdD, U. No. Colo., 1986. Minister Christian edn. Bethel Bapt. Ch., Greeley, Colo., 1982-83; adj. prof. Christian edn. Denver Sem., 1981-84; asst. prof. Christian edn. Talbot Sch. Theology, LaMirada, Calif., 1985-87, Denver Sem., 1987—; founder, dir. Denver Sem. Sr. Sch., 1990; com. mem. Iliff Inst. for Lay and Clergy, Denver, 1989—. Author: When You're Mom #2, 1991; contbr. articles to profl. jours.; contbg. author: Dictionary of Christianity in America, 1991. Denver Sem. scholar, 1982. Mem. Nat. Assn. Profs. of Christian Edn., Christian Ministries Conv., No. Colo. Bible Inst. (bd. dirs.), Kappa Delta Pi. Office: Denver Sem PO Box 10000 Denver CO 80210

BROWN, BONNIE JEFFREYS, lay worker; b. Raleigh, N.C., Oct. 3, 1941; d. Joseph Randolph Sr. and Edna Lois (Upchurch) Jeffreys; m. Philip Michael Brown Sr., July 12, 1963; children: Philip Michael Jr., David Jeffreys, Bonnie Katherine. BA, U. N.C., Greensboro, 1964; cert., Cen. Carolina Tech. Inst., 1972, Cape Fear Tech Inst., 1980, 81. Sunday sch. tchr., pianist Inwood Bapt. Ch., Raleigh, 1958-60; chmn. Christian action and community svc. dept. First Christian Ch., Wilmington, N.C., 1977-85, deaconess, 1986-89, Sunday sch. tchr., 1987-88, chmn., youth dept., 1988-91, mem. search com. for assoc. pastor, 1990-91; counselor N.C. Soc. for Crippled Children and Adults Camp, Durham, N.C., summers 1961, 62. Bd. dirs. Children's Home Soc. of N.C., Wilmington, 1980—, United Way Info. and Referral, Wilmington, 1980-85, United Cerebral Palsy Devel. Ctr., Wilmington, 1982-85; foster parent Dept. of Social Svcs., Lee and New Hanover Counties, Sanford and Wilmington, 1973-74. Recipient Govs. Vol. award for Individual Human Svc., 1982. Mem. Am. Assn. Med. Soc. Execs. Home: 103 Green Meadows Dr Wilmington NC 28405 Office: New Hanover Pender County Med Soc PO Box 10400 Wilmington NC 28405 *Every Christian has the awesome lifelong assignment of being a positive role model. (Jesus' feelings about one's causing a believer to stumble are clear in Matthew 18:6.) Since we haven't the luxury of choosing when and upon whom our influence is felt, it follows that we should strive for behavior worthy of imitation every moment of our lives. "Example is not the most important thing in influencing others. It is the only thing." (Albert Schweitzer).*

BROWN, BRUCE RITCHIE, minister; b. Yonkers, N.Y., Apr. 27, 1936; s. Hugh Ritchie and Helen Louise (Bullock) B.; m. Shirley Ann Storie, June 9, 1962; children: Mark, Rebekah, Elisabeth, Kent. AB, Temple U., 1958; postgrad., Westminster Theol. Sem., 1957-61; BD, Gordon Div. Sch., 1962, MDiv., 1974. Ordained to ministry Congl. Ch., 1963. Asst. pastor First Congl. Ch., N. Collins, N.Y., 1962-63; pastor First Congl. Ch., N. Collins, 1963-76, San Dieguito Bible Ch., Encinitas, Calif., 1976-81, Marion (Mich.) Community Ch., 1981-84, First Congl. Ch., Middleboro, Mass., 1984—; dir. Peniel High Sch. Camp, Luzerne, N.Y., 1963-76, 79; chmn. Inter-Varsity Local Com., Buffalo, 1973-76; 2d v.p. Conservative Congl. Christian Conf., 1975-78, 1st v.p., 1978-81, pres., 1981-84; mem. teaching mission to Micronesia, Marshalls, Ponape, Kosrae, Truk, 1984-91; moderator New England Congl. Christian Fellowship. Mem. So. Erie County Community Migrant Com., N. Collins, 1960's; mem. Village Planning Commn., N. Collins, 1964-74; mem. Eden-No. Collins Rotary, 1972-80, pres. 1975-76; mem. Encinitas Rotary, 1976-80, Marion Community Men's Club, 1981-84, v.p. 1984; Protestant Fire Chaplain, Middleboro Fire Dept. Mem. Buffalo Evang. Mins. Fellowship (pres. 1969-70), San Dieguito Mins. Assn. (pres. 1977-78), Middleboro-Lakeville Clergy Assn. (pres. 1987). Republican. Home: 4 Plympton St Middleboro MA 02346 Office: First Congl Ch 6 Plympton St Middleboro MA 02346

BROWN, C. CHRISTOPHER, church business administrator; b. Blue Island, Ill., Jan. 7, 1960; s. William L. Jr. and Rosemary (Beauchamp) B.; m. Lorraine Susan Benda, Aug. 1, 1981; children: Christopher , Matthew, Andrew. Student, Oral Roberts U., 1978-80; BS, U. Mo., St. Louis, 1983. Bus. administr. First Assembly of God, St. Charles, Mo., 1989—; Christian worker papers Assembly of God North Mo., Excelsior Springs, 1991—; pres. Ch. Bus. Group, Lake Saint Louis, 1990—; treas. bd. dirs. First Assembly of God, St. Charles, Mo., 1989. Editor, contbr. (newsletter) First Edition, 1990-91. Vol. fireman Lake Saint Louis First Dept., 1985-87; mem. Young Republicans, St. Charles County, 1986-91. Mem. Nat. Assn. Ch. Bus. Adminstrs. Home: 809 Huntwood Pl Lake Saint Louis MO 63367 Office: First Assembly of God St Charles 2521 Charwood Saint Louis Charles MO 63301

BROWN, CAROL SUE, minister; b. Pitts., May 20, 1950; d. George William and Carolyn Mae (McClelland) B. BA, Slippery Rock U., 1972; MDiv, Pitts. Theol. Sem., 1975. Ordained to ministry Presbyn. Ch., 1975. Pastor Garrard and Manchester (Ky.) Presbyn. Chs., 1975-83; assoc. pastor First Presbyn. Ch., Stroudsburg, Pa., 1983—; del. Gen. Assembly, 1982; accredited visitor World Coun. Chs., Canberra, Australia, 1991. Cons. Girl Scouts U.S., Stroudsburg, 1989—. Mem. Internat. Assn. Women Mins. (treas. 1979—). Office: First Presbyn Ch 579 Main St Stroudsburg PA 18360

BROWN, CHARLES HENRY, priest, psychiatrist; b. Phila., Dec. 28, 1929; s. Charles Henry and Helen Marie (Greenan) B. BS, Villanova U., 1957; MD, Hahnemann Coll., 1961; JD, Boston U., 1974; diplomain Scientiarum Ecclesiasticarum Orientalium, Pontifical Oriental Inst., Rome, 1977. Diplomate Am. Bd. Psychiatry and Neurology; lic. N.J.; ordained to preisthood Byzantine Cath. Ch., 1987. Intern St. Luke's Hosp., San Francisco, 1961-62; surg. resident Beth Israel Hosp., Boston, 1965-65; rsch. fellow Mass. Gen. Hosp., Boston, 1965-66; resident Mass. Gen. Hosp. and VA Hosp., Boston, 1966-68; staff psychiatrist VA Outpatient Clinic, Boston, 1968-75, 79-84, Providence VA Hosp., 1976-78, VA Med. Ctrs., East Orange and Lyons, N.J., 1987-90; pastor Holy Wisdom Byzantine Cath. Ch., Flanders, N.J., 1988—. With U.S. Army, 1953-55. Recipient Dorothy Gordon Meml. award Hahnemann U., 1961. Mem. Morris County Med. Soc., N.J. Med. Soc., Mass. Med. Soc. Home and Office: 197 Emmans Rd Flanders NJ 07836

BROWN, CLARK ANTHONY, clergyman; b. Obion, Tenn., Apr. 5, 1951; s. Andrew and Sammie Nell (Reed) B.; m. Millie Jean Stephens, Apr. 17, 1970; children: Chad, Todd. BA, Mid Continent Coll., 1980; postgrad., So. Sem., 1982; M of Ministry, Luther Rice Sem., 1986. Ordained to ministry Bapt. Ch., 1977. Pastor So. Bapt. Bethel, Troy, Tenn., 1977-79, Boekerton Bapt. Ch., Portageville, Mo., 1979-81, New Bethel Bapt. Ch., Eddyville, Ky., 1981-83, Grapevine Bapt. Ch., Madisonville, Ky., 1983—; state exec. bd. Ky. Bapt. Conv., Middletown, 1987-90; trustee Midcontinent Bible Coll., Mayfield, Ky., 1987-89; moderator Little Bethel Bapt. Assn., Madisonville, 1989—; ch. adv. bd. Cumberland Coll., Williamsburg, 1988—. With U.S. Army, 1971-73. Republican. Baptist. Home: 125 Sandcut Rd Madisonville KY 42431 Office: Grapevine Bapt Ch 85 Sandcut Rd Madisonville KY 42431

BROWN, CLAY JONATHAN, religious organization administrator; b. Dallas, Dec. 11, 1958; s. Paul X. and Virginia Eloise (Smiley) B.; m. Mary Catherine Blake, Dec. 20, 1980; children: Taylor Catherine, Blake Jonathan. BA in English, Drama, East Tex. Bapt. Coll., Marshall, 1981; MA in Communication, Southwestern Bapt. Theol., Seminary, Ft. Worth, 1985; MDiv, Austin (Tex.) Presbyn. Theol., Seminary, 1988. Ordained to ministry Presbyn. Ch., 1988. Minister of edn. First Bapt. Ch., Mart, Tex., 1982-83; youth dir./asst. dir. Christian edn. Trinity Cumberland Presbyn. Ch., Ft. Worth, 1983-85; pastor St. Paul Cumberland Presbyn. Ch., Austin, 1986-88, Cumberland Presbyn. Ch., Dyer, Tenn., 1988-90; dir. of edn. for missions Cumberland Presbyn. Bd. Missions, Memphis, Tenn., 1990—; bd. dirs. Religious Interfaith Assn., Jackson, Tenn. Editor: The Missionary Messenger, 1990—. Recipient Alumni Achievement award East Tex. Bapt. Alumni Assn., Marshall, 1991. Mem. Associated Ch. Press, Evangel. Press Assn. Office: Cumberland Presbyn Bd of Missions 1978 Union Ave Memphis TN 38104

BROWN, COLON ROBERT, clergyman; b. Saginaw, Mich., Nov. 5, 1953; s. Robert Colon and Marylin Joyce (Perry) B.; m. Cynthia Jean Schellenbach, Nov. 1, 1986; children: Nicole, Troy. BA, Evangel Coll., Springfield, Mo., 1975; MDiv, Trinity Evangel. Div. Sch., Deerfield, Ill., 1980; DMin, McCormick Theol. Sem., Chgo., 1990. Ordained to ministry Assemblies of God, 1979, United Meth. Ch. as deacon, 1987, as elder, 1991. Assoc. minister Calvary Temple, Waukegan, Ill., 1976-83; minister Buffalo Grove (Ill.) Community Ch., 1983-85; assoc. minister First Meth. Ch., Michigan City, Ind., 1985-87, Mishawaka, Ind., 1987—; cons. David C. Cook, Chgo., 1977-82; retreat dir. United Meth. Ch., Michigan City, 1984-88, cons. local ch. assessment project North Ind. Conf.; cons. ch. Historicizing United Meth. Ch., Mishawaka, 1990—. Founder Blending Family Resource Ctr. of Michiana, 1989, bd. dirs., 1989—; bd. dirs. Healthy Mothers/Health Babies, 1988-90, Healthy Babies Outreach Com., 1990—, Mishawaka High Sch. Teen Pregnancy, 1990—, Family and Childrens Svcs., 1990—. Democrat. Avocations: racquetball, dining out, baseball memorabilia. Home: 52303 Carriage Hills Dr South Bend IN 46635 Office: First United Meth Ch 201 E 3d St Mishawaka IN 46544

BROWN, DALE WEAVER, clergyman, theologian, educator; b. Wichita, Kans., Jan. 12, 1926; s. Harlow J. and Cora Elisa (Weaver) B.; m. Lois D. Kauffman, Aug. 17, 1947; children: Deanna Gae, Dennis Dale, Kevin Ken. A.B., McPherson Coll., 1946; B.D., Bethany Theol. Sem., 1949; postgrad., Drake U., 1954-56, Northwestern U. and Garrett Bibl. Inst., 1956-58; Ph.D., Northwestern U., 1962. Ordained to ministry Ch. of Brethren, 1946; pastor Stover Meml. Ch. of Brethren, Des Moines, 1949-56; dir. religious life, asst. prof. philosophy and religion McPherson Coll., 1958-62; assoc. prof. Christian theology Bethany Theol. Sem., Oak Brook, Ill., 1962-70; prof. Christian theology Bethany Theol. Sem., 1970—; Del. standing com. Ch. of Brethren, 1954; moderator Middle Iowa Dist., 1952-53, mem. dist. and regional bds., gen. bd., 1960-62, moderator-elect ann. conf., 1970-71, moderator, 1971-72. Author: In Christ Jesus: The Significance of Jesus as the Christ, 1965, Four Words for World, 1968, So Send I You, 1969, Brethren and Pacifism, 1970, The Christian Revolutionary, 1971, Flamed by the Spirit, 1978, Understanding Pietism, 1978, Berea College: Spiritual and Intellectual Roots, 1982; What About the Russians, 1984; Biblical Pacifism, 1986. Mem. Am. Acad. Religion, Fellowship Reconciliation, Am. Theol. Soc. Home: 18W709 22d St Lombard IL 60148 Office: Bethany Theol Sem Oak Brook IL 60521

BROWN, DANIEL A., religion educator; b. Chgo., July 13, 1940; s. David O. and Laura A. (Burke) B.; m. Helen Jaskoski, Mar. 23, 1979; 1 child, Andrew. STB, Marianum, Rome, 1963, Licentiate in Sacred Theology, 1965; diploma in libr. sci., Vatican Libr., Vatican City, 1963; PhD, Cath. U., 1972. Chaplain Riverside (Calif.) City Coll., 1965-66; lectr. Trinity Coll., Washington, 1967-69; chaplain Claremont (Calif.) Colls., 1969-71; prof. Calif. State U., Fullerton, 1971—; chaplain U. So. Calif., L.A., 1971. Author: Options, 1980, 1233: Year of Peace, 1989; translator: Brothers and Servants, 1981, Fantasy: Old and New, 1991. Coord. funds Food for All, Redlands, Calif., 1988—; mgr. local Little League, Fullerton, 1989; bd. dirs. adult edn. dept. St. Juliana parish, Fullerton, 1989—; mem. task force bicycle com. Fullerton City Coun., 1990—. NEH fellow, 1979, 83, 87, Henry Luce Found. fellow, 1980; Fulbright grantee, 1982-83. Mem. Am. Acad. Religion, Coll. Theology Soc., Am. Soc. Ch. History, Religious Edn. Assn. Am., Nat. Edn. Assn. Democrat. Roman Catholic. Office: Calif State U Dept Religious Studies 800 N State College Fullerton CA 92634

BROWN, DARRELL HOUSTON, minister; b. Odessa, Tex., Apr. 14, 1952; s. Steve Brown and Mary Jane (Neil) B.; m. Jennifer Lynn Phillips, May 26, 1973; children: Justin, Aaron, John Clayton. BA, So. Nazarene U., 1975. Ordained to ministry Ch. of the Nazarene, 1982. Pastor Nazarene Ch., Seagraves, Tex., 1980-83, Dalhart, Tex., 1983-88, Oklahoma City, 1988—; chaplain Fire Dept., Seagraves, 1981-83, Police Dept., Dalhart, 1984-88; dist. dir. Nazarene Children's Ministries, Oklahoma City, 1989—. Contbr. articles to profl. mags. Mem. Ministerial Assn. (pres. 1983-84). Home: 6709 Johnie Oklahoma City OK 73149 Office: Southside Nazarene Ch 1537 SE 29th Oklahoma City OK 73129

BROWN, DAVID CLIFFORD, clergyman; b. Plainwell, Mich., Jan. 12, 1938; s. Maynard Fred and Geraldine Louise (Fish) B.; m. Kathleen Dianne Thomas, Aug. 25, 1979 (div. 1989); children: Lisa, Gordon, Mason, Stuart, David. BA, Kalamazoo Coll., 1960; BD, Colgate Rochester Div. Sch., 1964; D Religion, Chgo. Theol. Sem., 1970. Assoc. minister Grace United Meth. Ch., Rochester, N.Y., 1961-64; minister Wesley United Meth. Ch., Niagara Falls, N.Y., 1964-67, Geneseo (N.Y.) United Meth. Ch., 1967-69; campus minister, dir. Wesley Found. SUNY, Geneseo, 1967-69; acting clin. dir. Chgo. Inst. Pastoral Care, 1970-71; sr. minister The Community Ch., East Williston, N.Y., 1971-78; v.p. Religion in Am. Life, Inc., N.Y.C., 1978-83; sr. minister The Congl. Ch., San Mateo, Calif., 1984—. Editor: Morality: Whose Responsibility?, 1983; editor The Pastor's Jour., 1978-83; contbr. articles and book revs. to various publs. Instr. English, So. Mich. State Prison, Jackson, 1971; interim dir., Interfaith Hunger Appeal, N.Y.C., 1983-84; mem. housing task force, San Mateo County Organizing Project, 1988—. Woodrow Wilson fellow (hon.), 1960. Mem. No. Calif. Conf. United Ch. Christ (mem. ministerial standing com. 1984—), Interreligious Task Force Soviet Jews (vice-chmn. 1987—), Clergy Fellowship San Mateo (pres. 1985—), Faith and Life Com., Nat. Coun. Community Churches (bd. dirs. 1973-79), Nat. Coun. Churches of Christ in U.S.A. (governing bd. 1975-77), World Coun. Churches (stewardship coun. U.S. coun. 1976-82), Kiwanis (Clergyman of Yr. 1988), Masons. Democrat. Mem. United Church of Christ. Avocations: travel, golf, reading, music. Office: Congl Ch 225 Tilton Ave San Mateo CA 94401

BROWN, DAVID LYNN, minister; b. Pontiac, Mich., Jan. 20, 1949; s. Gordon Clifford and Donna Avis (Marshall) B.; m. Linda Lee Blount, Dec. 27, 1969; children: Steven, Karla, Sarah. Student, Cen. Mich. U., Mt. Pleasant, 1967-68; BRE, Grand Rapids (Mich.) Bapt. Coll., 1972; ThM, Clarksville Sch. Theology, Tenn., 1975. Ordained to ministry Gen. Assn. Regular Bapt. Chs., 1972. Youth pastor First Bapt Ch., Cedar Springs, Mich., 1971-74; dir. Christian edn. First Bapt Ch., Albion, Mich., 1974-75; pastor Inter-Lakes Bapt. Ch., Delton, Mich., 1975-79; sr. pastor First Bapt. Ch., Oak Creek, Wis., 1979—; pres. Christian Salvage Mission, Fowlerville, Mich., 1974-80; pres. bd. dirs. Wis. Assn. Regular Bapt. Chs., Northlake, Wis., 1981-89; chmn. Bapt. for Life of Wis., Oak Creek, 1990—; founder, pres., Logos Communication Consortium, Oak Creek, 1988—. Editor: Strength for Today, 1989—; producer video/tv spl. The Dark Side of Halloween, 1990; author booklet: The Dark Side of Halloween, 1990; contbr. articles to profl. jours. Home: 8044 S Verdev Dr Oak Creek WI 53154

BROWN, DAVID MICHAEL, minister; b. Hazleton, Pa., Nov. 18, 1953; s. David William and Lenora Lee (Rogers) B.; m. Jo Ann Campbell, May 29, 1976; children: Christy Lyn, Casey Rae; 1 foster child, Tracy. BA in Math. and Computer Sci., The Citadel, 1976; MDiv, So. Bapt. Theol. Sem., Louisville, 1983. Ordained to ministry So. Bapt. Conv., 1980. Assoc. pastor Northwood Bapt. Ch., North Charleston, S.C., 1976-80; min. evangelism Cedar Creek Bapt. Ch., Fern Creek, Ky., 1980-81; min. outreach Woodland Bapt. Ch., Middletown, Ky., 1981-83; pastor Pleasant Valley Bapt. Ch., Geneseo, N.Y., 1983—; ch. planting intern Home Mission Bd., Atlanta, 1981; exec. bd. Bapt. Conv. N.Y., Syracuse, 1989—; chaplain USNR, Buffalo, 1988—. Author: (computer book) Nastygrams in Watfive, 1976; contbr. articles to profl. jours. Treas. Geneseo Summer Festival, 1989, 91. Lt. supply corps USN, 1976-80. Recipient Outstanding Young Man of Am. award Jaycees, 1983. Mem. Greater Rochester Bapt. Assn. (exec. bd. 1980—), Groveland-Geneseo Clergy Assn. (pres. 1984—), Rotary. Home: 7514 Groveland Rd Groveland NY 14462-0021 Office: Pleasant Valley Bapt Ch 4631 Lakeville Rd Geneseo NY 14454

BROWN, DAVID VINCENT, minister; b. Nashville, Aug. 11, 1958; s. Glyn David and Helen Opal (Elam) B.; m. Charlotte Dawn Sandlin, June 5, 1981; children: Jeremiah David, Alyssa Marie. BS, Belmont Coll., Nashville, 1982. Cert. tchr., Tenn. Min. music Bordeaux Bapt. Ch., Nashville, 1976-78, Eastwood Bapt. Ch., Nashville, 1978-80; min. music 1st Bapt. Ch., Ashland City, Tenn., 1980-83, Lewisburg, Tenn., 1983-91; min. music West End Bapt. Ch., Fayetteville, Tenn., 1991—; pres. Music Educators Nat. Conf., Nashville, 1978-80; tchr. Sunday Sch. Leadership Conf., Lewisburg, 1986-90, Ridgecrest (N.C.) Bapt. Conf. Ctr., 1989-91; youth specialist ASSISTeam, Tenn., 1988-91; pres. South-Cen. Ch. Tng. Assn., Tenn., 1990. Master counselor Demolay, Nashville, 1974; founder, pres. Marshall County Softball Assn., Lewisburg, 1984-88; bd. dirs. local chpt. Am. Cancer Soc., 1985-89. Avocations: fishing, woodworking. Office: West End Bapt Ch 200 N Morgan Ave Fayetteville TN 38334

BROWN, DEAN E., social services administrator; b. Lansing, Mich.; m. Ann R. Brown, Mar. 7, 1975; 1 child, Lisa M. BA, Concordia Coll., 1975; postgrad., Concordia Theol. Sem. Cert. profl. scouter Boy Scouts Am. Minister of evangelism Luth. Ch. Miss. Synod., 1974-80; bd. missions Luth. Ch. Miss. Synod., Ann Arbor, Mich., 1977-79, instr. Gospel Communication Clinic, 1977-80; assoc. dist. exec. Lake Huron Area Coun. Boy Scouts Am., Auburn, Mich., 1980; dist. exec. Boy Scouts Am., 1981-84, fin. dir., 1985-87, field dir., 1988—; instr. Regional SBA tgn., 1987-88, Mich. Luth. Ministries Inst., 1988; active evangelism com. St. John's Luth. Ch., 1984—. Active Midland County Rep. Party, 1985. Mem. Saginaw Valley IBM-PC Users Group (treas. 1985), Rotary (youth com. chmn. 1983-84). Avocations: tennis, golf, computers. Office: Boy Scouts Am Lake Huron Council 5001 S Eleven Mile Auburn MI 48611

BROWN, DENNIS RAY, minister; b. Eldorado, Ill., Nov. 15, 1954; s. Raymond Leroy and Doris Ellen (Ludlow) B.; m. Susan Jane Foster, May 24, 1975; children: Benjamin, Christopher, Jeremy, Nathaniel. BS in Pastoral Studies, North Cen. Bible Coll., Mpls., 1981; postgrad., South Tex. Coll. Law, 1985-87. Ordained to ministry Full Gospel Ch., 1976. Min. music Salem Temple, Rock City, Ill., 1975-79, Brookdale Christian Ctr., Brooklyn Center, Minn., 1980-81; assoc. pastor Assembly of God Tabernacle, Houston, 1982-85; sr. pastor Pennelwood Ch. of God, Grand Rapids, Mich., 1987-88; founder, pastor Living Word Fellowship, Grandville, Mich., 1988—; co-founder Full Gospel Mins. Fellowship, Grand Rapids, 1990—; bd. dirs. Calvary Assembly, Caledonia, Mich., 1990; pub., editor Harvest Reign mag., Grandville, 1989—. Precinct capt. Harris County (Tex.) Rep. Com., 1986. Home and Office: Living Word Fellowship 4270 Chicago Dr Grandville MI 49418

BROWN, DONALD RAY, religious organization official; b. Crossville, Ill., May 6, 1932; s. George A. and Veda V. (Schaffer) B.; m. Shirley M. Edson, June 4, 1955; children: Rebecca L. Brown Mejdrich, Sarah A. BA, Wheaton (Ill.) Coll., 1955, MA, 1972; BD, Gordon-Conwell Theol. Sem., Hamilton, Mass., 1959. Ordained to ministry Am. Bapt. Chs. in U.S.A., 1959. Pastor 1st Bapt. Ch., Sullivan, Ill., 1959-63; editor alumni mag. Wheaton Coll., 1968-72; pres. Visualized Instrn. Prodns., Oak Brook, Ill., 1973-78; freelance writer and editor, 1978-84; editor United Evang. Action, dir. info. Nat. Assn. Evangs., Wheaton, 1984—. Author: I Was There; co-author: The Living Franklin, The Living Documents, The Real Estate Advertising Guide, How To Write A Real Estate Newsletter; writer, producer various radio and TV programs. Capt., chaplain U.S. Army, 1963-68, Vietnam; mem. Res. ret. Home: 1 N 760 Rte 59 West Chicago IL 60185 Office: Nat Assn Evangs 450 Gundersen Dr Carol Stream IL 60188

BROWN, DOROTHY LYNNE, minister; b. Pitts., Jan. 11, 1947; d. Howard Roscoe Brown and Mildred Marie (Rankin) Corwin. BS, Ind. (Pa.) U., 1968; MS, Bucknell U., 1971; MDiv, U. of the South, Sewanee, Tenn., 1986. Asst. St. James Episcopal Ch., Bozeman, Mont., 1987-89; rector Trinity Episcopal Ch., Winner, S.D., 1989—; dean Rosebud Deanery, S.D., 1990—. Bd. dirs. Home Health Care/Hospice, Winner, 1990—, Child Protection Team, Winner, 1991—. Mem. Sch. Theol. Alumni Coun., Alban Inst. Office: Trinity Episcopal Ch PO Box 468 Winner SD 57580

BROWN, DOUGLAS KENNETH, minister; b. Elmhurst, Ill., Dec. 3, 1964; s. Kenneth Truman and Janith Marylynn (Wall) B.; m. Juliana L. Carson, June 24, 1989. Diploma, Moody Bible Inst., 1986. Youth pastor First Bapt. Ch., Long Prairie, Minn., 1988—; del. to youth consultation Conservative Bapt. Assn. Am., Wheaton, Ill., 1989, Minn. point person for nat. youth task force, 1990—. Home: 520 4th Ave SE Long Prairie MN 56347 Office: Crossfire Youth Ministries care First Bapt Ch 401 4th St S Long Prairie MN 56347

BROWN, DOUGLAS LEO, priest; b. Bklyn., Mar. 29, 1937; s. Leo Francis and Sophie Margaret (Wyshnevska) B. AB, Cathedral Coll., 1959; STB, Cath. U., 1963; STM, N.Y. Theol. Sem., 1968. Ordained priest Roman Cath. Ch., 1963. Assoc. pastor Epiphany Ch., Bklyn., 1963-68; assoc. dir. St. Paul's Ctr., Bklyn., 1968-76; sec. for clergy personnel Roman Cath. Diocese, Bklyn., 1976—; dir. Diocesan Lang. Inst., Bklyn., 1976-81; chmn. Personnel Bd. Roman Cath. Ch., Bklyn., 1976—; mem. Priest's Retirement Bd., 1976—; Sem. Admissions Bd., 1977—; cons. Priest Spirituality Adv. Bd., 1978—. Mem. Nat. Assn. Ch. Personnel Adminstrs., Canon Law Soc. Am. (Prelate of Honor, 1982), Nat. Clergy Coun. on Alcholism, Holy Sepulchre Order (knight). Office: Roman Cath Diocese Pers Office P O Box C 75 Greene Ave Brooklyn NY 11202

BROWN, E. LYNN, minister; b. Jackson, Tn., Apr. 2, 1936; s. Willie T. and Ocie (Royal) B.; m. Gladys Deloris Stephens, Aug. 10, 1963; children: A. Victor, Cheronda Patrice. BD and MDiv, Interdenominational Theol. Ctr., 1963; BS, Lane Coll., 1960; DD (hon.), Tex. Coll., 1987, Miles Coll., 1979. Min. Phillips Chapel Christ Meth. Episc. Ch., Milan, Tn., 1963, Greenwood Christ Meth. Episc. Ch., Memphis, 1963-67, Mt. Pisgah Christ Meth. Episc. Ch., Memphis, 1967-78; gen. sec. Christ MEth. Episc. Nat. Hdqrs., Memphis, 1978-86; bishop 9th Episc. Dist., L.A., 1986—; bd. dirs. South Cen. Organizing Com., SCLC, Atlanta. Mem. NAACP (bd. dirs.), Nat. Coun. Chs. (bd. dirs.). Office: 9th Episc Dist 3844 E Slauson Ste 1 Los Angeles CA 90043

BROWN, EDWARD LEE, minister; b. Eads, Colo., Oct. 28, 1948; s. Kenneth R. and Margaret (Page) B.; m. Esther Corrine Lane, May 24, 1968; children: Jennifer, Jill, Justin, Jackie (dec.), Joan and Jessica (twins). Diploma, Berean Sch. of the Bible, 1985; cert., Bear Front End Alinment, Rock Island, Ill., 1971. Ordained to ministry Assemby of God Ch. Song leader Assembly of God, Stratford, Okla., 1981-83, Sun. sch. supt., 1982; song leader Assembly of God, Briscoe, Tex., 1983-85; asst. pastor Assembly of God, Wellington, Tex., 1988; pastor Assembly of God, Skellytown, Tex., 1988—; gen. maintenance Town of Skellytown, 1990—. Fireman White Deer (Tex.) Vol. Fire Dept., 1989, Skellytown Vol. Fire Dept., 1990, chaplain, 1990—. Home: 304 W 5th PO Box 335 Skellytown TX 79080 Office: Assembly of God 5th and Chamberlin Skellytown TX 79080

BROWN, EDWIN EUGENE, JR., minister; b. Edinburg, Tex., Nov. 2, 1956; s. Edwin Eugene Sr. and Angeline (Jurcak) B.; m. Carla Diann Hawkins, May 5, 1979; children: Lindsey Nicole, Jeremy Scott. BA, Southwestern U., 1979; MDiv, Tex. Christian U., 1982, postgrad., 1986. Ordained to ministry Christian Ch. (Disciples of Christ), 1982. Minister Antioch Christian Ch., Hooks, Tex., 1982-89, First Christian Ch., Monahans, Tex., 1989—. Dist. dir. dist. 11 east Tex. Am. Cancer Soc., 1984-88, state clergy com., Austin, Tex., 1984—, state golf com., Austin, 1989—. Recipient Award of Merit, Tex. Agrl. Extension Svc., 1985. Mem. Masons (deacon 1986-87). Republican. Home: 1307 S Harry Monahans TX 79756 Office: First Christian Ch 502 S Betty Monahans TX 79756

BROWN, FLAVY BUSTER, minister; b. Akron, Ohio, Sept. 12, 1928; s. Flavy Buster Brown and Elizabeth Goldie (Barnette) Miller; m. Frances Robertson, June 20, 1979; children: Mark R., Debra L., James F., Beth R., Melissa D., Kimberly A. AB, Anderson (Ind.) U., 1949; MEd, U. Pitts., 1954; MA, Western Res. U., 1957; ThD magna cum laude, Internat. Sem., Plymouth, Fla., 1988. Ordained to ministry Wesleyan Ch., 1949. Sr. pastor Ch. of God, Grove City, Pa., 1954-63, Canton, Ohio, 1954-63; sr. min. Vinton (Va.) Wesleyan Ch., 1985—; evangelist Ch. of God (Anderson), 1959-63; missionary, Australia, 1987, P.R., 1988, Haiti, 1989, 90. Speaker Gideons Internat., Anderson, 1965-70; vol. Big Bros., Anderson, 1970-71. Mem. Anderson U. Nat. Alumni Assn. (pres. 1949-52, trustee 1958-63), Lions (v.p. Roanoke, Va. 1990-91). Republican. Home: 5307 Summer Dr NW Roanoke VA 24019 Office: Vinton Wesleyan Ch Corner Jeffferson and Poplar Vinton VA 24179

BROWN, FRANK MUSTARD, chaplain, educator; b. Bland, Va., Dec. 8, 1931; s. Otis Calhoun and Lela Seagle (Mustard) B.; m. Louise Landrum, Aug. 20, 1954 (div. 1978); children: Virginia, Mark; m. Doloris Aho, Sept. 4, 1982. BA, King Coll., 1954; MDiv, Columbia Theol. Sem., 1957; STM, Dubuque Theol. Sem., 1975, D Ministry, 1978. Dir. chaplaincy services Research Med. Ctr., Kansas City, Mo., 1980. Mem. Am. Assn. Pastoral Counselors (counselor Rochester, Minn. chpt. 1973-80, counselor Kansas City chpt. 1980-86), Assn. Clin. Pastoral Edn. Presbyterian. Office: Research Med Ctr 2316 E Meyer Blvd Kansas City MO 64132

BROWN, FREEZELL, JR., minister; b. Indpls., Aug. 19, 1957; s. Freezell Brown and Alice Samuel; m. Barbara Weir, June 11, 1988. BA in Religion, Carroll Coll., Waukesha, Wis., 1979; MA in Religious Edn., Christian Theol. Sem., Indpls., 1984; MST, Garrett-Evang. Theol. Sem., 1988. Consecrated diaconal minister United Methodist Ch., 1985. Youth dir. YMCA,

Waukesha, 1980-81; minister with youth N. United Meth. Ch., Indpls., 1983, min. with youth and community, 1984-87; program coord. Crooked Creek Multi-Svc. Ctr., 1990-91; instr. PSI Inst. of Indpls., Indpls., 1991; trainer Training, Inc., 1991—; trainer Tng., Inc., Indpls., 1991—; mem. com. Religionand Race, So. Ind. Conf. United Meth. Ch., alt. com. investigation; adv. bd. Metro Adv. Ministry, Butler U. Campus Ministry, Indpls. Contbr. book revs. to The Christian Century, 1988—, The Christian Ministry, 1988—. Profl. adv. bd. Buchanan Counseling Ctr.; adv. bd. Coll. Ave. Youth Behavior Acad.; mem. Christian Educators Fellowship of United Meth. Ch.; program coord. Crooked Creek Mutli-Svc. Ctr., 1990. Democrat. Avocations: painting, music composition and performance, drama, reading. Home: 5525 N Broadway Ave Indianapolis IN 46220

BROWN, GEORGE, JR., seminary dean; b. Phila., Dec. 19, 1942; s. George and Miriam (McNeal) B.; m. Willa K. Schaver, June 4, 1965; children: Steven, Douglas, Jeffrey. BA, Cen. Coll., Pella, Iowa, 1965; BD, Western Theol. Sem., Holland, Mich., 1969; ThM, Princeton Theol. Sem., 1971; PhD, Mich. State U., 1989. Ordained to ministry Reformed Ch. in Am., 1969. Minister Pottersville (N.J.) Ref. Ch., 1969-73; minister Christian edn. Cen. Ref. Ch., Grand Rapids, Mich., 1973-88; dean faculty Western Theol. Sem., Holland, Mich., 1988—. Contbg. editor Ch. Tchrs. mag., 1986—; author: Sponsoring Faith, 1983; contbr. to Harper's Ency. of Religious Edn., 1990; copiler/writer manuals. Mem. bldg. team City High Middle Sch., Grand Rapids, Mich., 1985-87; chmn. Alger Sch. Adv. Coun., Grand Rapids, 1982-84. Recipient Humanitarian Svc. award West Mich. Assn. for Counseling & Devel., 1985. Mem. Religious Edn. Assn., Assn. for Supervision and Curriculum Devel., Christian Educators Ref. Ch. Am. (exec. com. 1989—), Phi Delta Kapp. Reformed Ch. Am. Home: 920 Reynard St SE Grand Rapids MI 49507 Office: Western Theological Sem 86 E 12th St Holland MI 49423

BROWN, GERALD EUGENE, minister; b. Garden City, Kans., July 16, 1949; s. Alva E. and Louise I. (Newcomb) B.; m. Susan L. McConnell, Nov. 14, 1970; children: Patricia, Mark Thomas, Robert. BA cum laude, S.W. Mo. State U., 1972; M Div. cum laude, Midwestern Bapt. Theol. Sem., 1975. Ordained to ministry Christian Ch., 1974. Pastor Ludlow (Mo.) Bapt. Ch., 1973-75; dir. Christian ministries Tabernacle Bapt. Ch., Kansas City, Mo., 1975-79; minister Longview Chapel Christian Ch., Lee's Summit, Mo., 1980-87, Antioch Community Ch., Kansas City, Mo., 1987—; bd. dirs. The Together Ctr., Kansas City, 1984-88, Clay-Platte Emergency Relief Assn., 1988— (pres. 1989—); asst. chaplain Lee's Summit Community Hosp., 1986-87; chaplain intern VA Med. Ctr., Kansas City, 1990-91; organizing dir. The Shepherd's Ctr. of Lee's Summit, 1985-87. Sec. Flood Relief Task Force, Kansas City, 1977-78; exec. dir. Emergency Assistance Coalition, Inc., Kansas City, 1980-84; mem. Mayor's Task Force on Energy, Kansas City, 1983-84; moderator Ch. Rels. Commn. Internat. Coun. Community Chs. Mem. Internat. Coun. Community Chs. (ch. rels. commn. 1988—, moderator 1990—), Northland Ministerial Alliance (v.p., pres.-elect 1988, pres. 1989-90). Democrat. Home: 613 NE 44th St Kansas City MO 64116 Office: Antioch Community Ch 4805 NE Antioch Rd Kansas City MO 64119 *God has given us the means to peace in our world; it falls to us to make those means effective in our world.*

BROWN, HAROLD BERGER, JR., minister; b. Augusta, Ga., Dec. 7, 1940; s. Harold Berger Sr. and Blanche Charlene Brown; m. Katherine Ward, May 18, 1967; children: Katherine Ashlyn Brown Montgomery, Courtney Ward. AB, U. Chattanooga, 1962; MDiv, Duke U., 1965. Ordained to ministry United Meth. Ch., 1963, Presbyn. Ch. (USA), 1983. Assoc. min. 1st-Centenary United Meth. Ch., Chattanooga, 1964-66; min. Max Meadows (Va.) United Meth. Cir., 1967-68; assoc. min. State St. United Meth. Ch., Bristol, Va., 1968-72, Trinity United Meth. Ch., Tallahassee, 1972-75; min. Naples (Fla.) East United Meth. Ch., 1975-83, Lely Presbyn. Ch., Naples, 1983—. Bd. dirs. Naples Family YMCA; adv. bd. Upjohn Naples, Ablecare Naples. Mem. Naples Ministerial Assn. (pres.), Rotary (chaplain Naples East club), Beta Beta Beta, Alpha Epsilon Delta, Gamma Sigma Epsilon. Office: Lely Presbyn Ch 105 St Andrews Blvd Naples FL 33962 *In response to a loving Creator, Christians who care can change things enormously in our world!.*

BROWN, HERMAN, Jewish organization executive, consultant; b. Bklyn., May 16, 1928; s. Sam and Anna (Grushkin) B.; m. Anita Lepzelter, Sept. 29, 1956; children: Lori, Kenneth, Terri. BA, Bklyn. Coll., 1953; postgrad., CCNY, 1954-55. Regional dir. Am. Jewish Congress, Queens and L.I., N.Y., 1963-68; dir. N.Y. Met. Coun., Am. Jewish Congress, 1968-72; exec. dir. Jewish Community Coun. of Met. Boston, 1972-75; dir. New Eng. area Jewish Nat. Fund, 1976; dir. New Eng. area Am. Assocs. Ben-Gurion U. of the Neyov, 1976-82; U.S. cons. Israel Coll. Optometry, 1984; dir. N.E. region Jewish Labor Com., 1985—; dir. Boston area The Workmen's Circle, 1986—. Mem. Comprehensive Health Planning Agy., N.Y.C., 1971; pres. Friends of Needham (Mass.) Pub. Libr., 1975-79; trustee Temple Israel, Boston, 1976-91. Mem. N.Y. Civil Liberties Union (bd. dirs. 1968-71), Phi Beta Kappa, Alpha Kappa Delta. Home: 33 Cynthia Rd Needham MA 02194

BROWN, HOWARD JAMES, clergyman; b. St. Louis, Aug. 6, 1907; s. John C. and Mary (O'Hara) B.; m. Helen Janney, June 18, 1931 (dec. Jan. 1983); children—Jacelyn (Mrs. Robert Dininny), Patricia (Mrs. Kenneth Kropp), H. James; m. Kathryn Tiegler, Aug. 25, 1984. B.A., Ohio Wesleyan U., 1929; D.D., 1952; B.D., Garret Theol. Sem., 1932. Ordained to ministry Methodist Ch., 1932; minister in Ft. Wayne, Ind., 1934-41, Goshen, Ind., 1941-43, Richmond, Ind., 1941-49; minister in Ch. of Savior, Cleveland Heights, Ohio, 1949-72; Dean Ind. Sch. of Prophets, 1947-48, Ohio Area Meth. Pastor's Sch., 1956-61, Coll. Preachers Ohio East Area, 1965-72; pres. Cleve. Council Chs., 1960-62; sec. gen. Commn. Pub. Relations and Meth. Information, 1964—; del. World Meth. Conf., 1951, 61. Trustee Ohio Wesleyan U., 1958—. Mem. Rotary, Masons (33 deg.), Phi Kappa Tau, Omicron Delta Kappa, Theta Alpha Phi. Home: 1801 Greencroft Dr Apt 308 Goshen IN 46526

BROWN, I. B., bishop. Bishop Ch. of God in Christ, Topeka. Office: Ch of God in Christ 1635 Hudson Blvd Topeka KS 66607*

BROWN, JAMES BARROW, bishop; b. El Dorado, Ark., Sept. 26, 1932; s. John Alexander and Ella May (Langham) B.; m. Mary Joanna Strausser, Oct. 3, 1970; 2 daus., Clare Elizabeth, Mary Laura. B.S., La. State U., 1954; B.D., Austin Presbyn. Sem., Austin, Tex., 1957; D.D., U. of South, Sewanee, Tenn., 1976. Ordained priest Episcopal Ch., 1965; teaching fellow Princeton Theol. Sem., 1962-64; curate chs. in La., 1965-70, archdeacon of, 1971-76, bishop of, 1976—. Served as chaplain AUS, 1957-59. Alumni fellow Austin Presbyn. Sem., 1957; recipient Sam Bailey Hicks prize, 1957. Mem. La. Clergy Assn., Phi Delta Theta. Club: Rotary. Address: 1623 7th St New Orleans LA 70115 also: PO Box 15719 New Orleans LA 70175

BROWN, JAMES FRANKLIN, minister; b. Cleve., Sept. 6, 1957; s. James Maurice and Marjorie Alice (Miller) B.; m. Annmarie Shoemaker, Aug. 6, 1977. Diploma in Ministerial Studies, Berean Coll., Springfield, Mo., 1985. Minister of evangelism and missions Medina (Ohio) Assembly of God, 1982-84, minister of youth, 1982-84; assoc. pastor Sunnyslope Christian Ctr., Hollister, Calif., 1984-85, sr. pastor, 1985—; coast counties youth rep. Assemblies of God, Santa Cruz, Calif., 1984-85. Office: Sunnyslope Christian Ctr 1520 Sunnyslope Rd Hollister CA 95023

BROWN, JEFFREY LAMONTE, pastor; b. Anchorage, Dec. 22, 1961; s. Jesse and Geraldine (Glover) B; m. Lesley Adair Mosley, July 13, 1985. BA, East Stroudsburg U., 1982; MEd, Ind. U. of Pa., 1984; MDiv, Andover Newton Theol., 1987. Ordained Baptist Ch., 1986. Research analyst House of Rep., Harrisburg, Pa., 1982-83; assoc. recruiter Andover Newton Theol. Sch., Newton Cen., Mass., 1985-87; pastor Union Baptist Ch., Cambridge, Mass., 1987—. Mem. bd. ministry Harvard U., 1988—; community advisor Students Against Violence and for Equality, 1990—; bd. dirs. Cambridge Children Svcs., 1991—. Recipient Outstanding Achievement award Pa. State EEO-Act 101, 1986. Mem. Jonathan Edwards Soc., Am. Baptist Chs. Mass. (gen. bd. rep. 1987—, bd. dirs. dept. ch. and soc.), United Baptist Convention, Inc. (corr. sec. 1988—), Cambridge Coun. Elders (bd. dirs. 1991—), Cambridge Black Pastors Conf. (pres. 1990—). Democrat. Office: Union Bapt Ch 874 Main St Cambridge MA 02139

BROWN, JENNAVON LEE, church organist; b. St. Louis, July 26, 1947; d. Victor Louis and Vernell L. (Lindeman) Cova; m. Robert Gerald Brown, Aug. 17, 1968; children: Jennifer Lynn and Jerolyn Lee (twins). AA, Valencia Coll., 1976. Organist, pianist various chs., 1966-78; organist North Park Bapt. Ch., Orlando, Fla., 1966-78; pianist 1st Bapt. Ch., Orlando, Fla., 1978-83; organist Coll. Pk. United Meth. Ch., 1980-83, 1st Bapt. Ch. Pine Castle, 1984-86; pianist 1st Bapt. Ch. Sanlando, 1986—; organist 1st United Meth. Ch., Cocoa Beach, Fla., 1989—; pvt. practice, 1968-76, 88—; program coord. Sacred Dance Fellowship, Orlando, 1986-88; pianist Contemporary Ensemble Group, 1st Bapt. Ch., Orlando. Mus. dir. Children's Theatre, Cocoa, Fla., 1989—. Mem. Nat. Guild, Nat. Fedn. Music Clubs, Fla. Fedn. Music Clubs. Methodist. Office: 1st United Meth Ch 3300 N Atlantic Ave Cocoa Beach FL 32931

BROWN, JERRY DUANE, minister; b. Fairport, Iowa, Jan. 30, 1934; s. Elias Henry and Gertrude Phoebe (Marlette) B.; m. Alyce Kathryn Hawkins, Aug. 26, 1956; children: Cynthia Ann, Annette Lynn. BA summa cum laude, Iowa Wesleyan Coll., 1957; M Divinity, Garrett Theol. Seminary, 1962. Pastor United Meth. Ch., Lone Tree, Iowa, 1956-64, United Ch. Christ, Lone Tree, 1962-64; pastor United Meth. Ch., New Sharon, Iowa, 1964-69, Albia, Iowa, 1969-80; sr. pastor Grace United Meth. Ch., Spencer, Iowa, 1980-88, First United Meth. Ch., Newton, Iowa, 1988—; dir., ch. action leader, Midwest Christian Ashram, 1974-76, lectr. Sch. Pastoral Care, Minn. 1979, workshop leader Holy Spirit Conf., Des Moines 1974,76,78. 1. V.p. Monroe Co Agy. on Aging, Albia 1969-80, chairperson Cross-Lines, 1969-70, dir. Monroe Co. Activity Ctr. for Retarded, 1978-80, mem. S. Cen. Iowa Mental Health bd., Oskaloosa 1970-72. Mem. Westmar Coll. Bd. Trustees, Cursillo (spiritual life dir. 1978), U.M. Organized for Renewal and Evangelism, Wesley Renewal Group, Rotary (pres. 1973-74), Jaycees (v.p. 1968-69). Republican. Avocations: swimming, water skiing, collecting old hymnals and disciplines. Office: First United Meth Ch 210 N 2d Ave E Newton IA 50208

BROWN, JIM J., campus minister, counselor; b. Milw., Apr. 24, 1941. BBA, Coll. of Santa Fe, 1966; MEd, Springfield (Mass.) Coll., 1971. Asst. provincial sec. Bros. of the Christian Schs., Lafayette, La., 1963-69; counselor St. Paul's Sch., Covington, La., 1969-72; campus min. U. Southwestern La., Lafayette, 1972-78; counselor, polit. advocate Christian Bros. Retreat House, Washington, 1978-79; counselor Cath. Social Svcs., Albuquerque, 1979-80; campus min. Regis Coll., Denver, 1980-84; counselor, social worker Big Bros./Big Sisters, Santa Fe, 1984-86; campus min. Coll. of Santa Fe, 1986—; advocate Bread for the World, Washington, 1973—; treas. Interfaith Coun., Santa Fe, 1986—; sec. Ministerial Alliance, Santa Fe, 1986-90. Roman Catholic. Office: Coll of Santa Fe St Michaels Dr Santa Fe NM 87501

BROWN, JOANNE CARLSON, religion educator; b. Pitts., Sept. 19, 1953; d. James Walker and Ruthe Eleanor (Carlson) B. AB, Mt. Holyoke Coll., 1975; M of Div., Garrett-Evang. Theol. Sem., 1978; PhD, Boston U., 1983. Lectr. Sch. Theology Boston U., 1980-82, asst. dean of chapel, 1981-82; dir. restoration program Washington Sq. Ch., N.Y.C., 1982-83; asst. prof. Pacific Luth. U., Tacoma, 1983-88; prof. ch. history, ecumenics St. Andrews Coll., Saskatoom, Sask., Can., 1988—; lectr., speaker in field. Contbr. (book): Something More Than Human, 1986, Christianity Patriarchy & Abuse: A Feminist Critique, 1989; contbr. articles to profl. jours. Elder United Meth. Ch., 1982—; v.p., bd. dirs. Pacific Peaks coun. Girl Scouts U.S., Olympia, Wash., 1984-87. United Meth. Sem. scholar, 1976-77; fellow Boston U., 1978-79. Mem. Am. Acad. Religion (regional exec. sec. 1983—), Can. Theol. Soc., Can. Soc. Ch. History, Can. Soc. for the Study of Religion, Can. Soc. Patristic Studies, Can. Women's Studies Assn. Democrat. Avocations: sports, reading. Office: St Andrews Coll, 1121 College Dr, Saskatoon, SK Canada S7N OW3

BROWN, JOHN EDWARD, bishop; b. Grimsby, Lincolnshire, Eng., July 13, 1930; arrived in Cyprus and Gulf, 1987.; s. Edward Alexander and Muriel (Burton) B.; m. Rosemary Wood, Apr. 4, 1956; 1 child, Richard Alexander. BD, London U., 1968. Ordained to ministry Anglican Ch., 1954. Tchr., chaplain St. George's Cathedral Sch., Jerusalem, 1954-56, Bishop's Sch., Amman, Jordan, 1956-57, All Saint's Cathedral, Khartoum, Sudan, 1960-64; various ecclesiastical appointments, including archdeacon Berkshire, 1977-86; Anglican bishop Cyprus and the Gulf, 1987—; Episcopal canon St. George's Anglican Cathedral, Jerusalem, k1987—; mem. Anglican Cons. Coun., 1989—. Address: Diocesan Office POB 2075, 2 Grigoris Afxentiou St, Nicosia Cyprus

BROWN, JOHN PAIRMAN, disarmament worker, church executive, writer; b. Hanover, N.H., May 16, 1923; s. Bancroft Huntington and Eleanor (Pairman) B.; m. Dorothy Emily Waymouth, June 26, 1954; children—George Waymouth, Felicity Emily Brown McCarthy, Maryam Eleanor Brown Beros, David Pairman. B.A. summa cum laude, Dartmouth Coll., 1944; jr. fellow Harvard U., 1946-49; S.T.B., Gen. Theol. Sem., N.Y.C., 1952; Th.D., Union Theol. Sem., N.Y.C., 1958. Ordained priest Episcopal Ch., 1953; joint ministerial standing Christian Ch. (Disciples of Christ). Curate, Grace Ch., Newark, 1952-54; tutor Gen. Theol. Sem., N.Y.C., 1954-56; instr. Hobart Coll., Geneva, N.Y., 1956-58; assoc. prof. classics and ancient history, Am. U., Beirut, Lebanon, 1958-65; prof. New Testament, Ch. Divinity Sch. of the Pacific, 1965-68; editorial staff U. Calif. Press, 1968-70; staff Ecumenical Peace Inst., San Francisco, 1971-76; exec. dir. No. Calif. Ecumenical Council, San Francisco, 1976-83; rep. U.S. churches and peace movement confs. Hanoi, 1967, Santiago, 1976, Belfast, 1976; non-govtl. orgn. rep. Conf. Geneva and UN Spl. Session, 1982, Uppsala Ch. World Conf. and Moscow, 1983. Active opposition to conscription during Viet Nam War, to building B-1 Bomber, to Livermore Nuclear Weapons Lab. Served with USAAF, 1944-46. Mem. Soc. Bibl. Lit., Nat. Assn. Ecumenical Staff. Editor: The Witness, 1955-58, Sequoia, 1980—; author: The Displaced Person's Almanac, 1961: The Lebanon and Phoenicia: Ancient Texts ... The Forest, 1969; The Liberated Zone, 1969; Planet on Strike, 1970; To a Sister on Laurel Drive, 1972; contbr. articles to publs. in field. Address: 1630 Arch St Berkeley CA 94709 *Reader! Please take thought and action for the suffering of the planet and of the poor.*

BROWN, JOHN ROBERT, priest, lawyer; b. Apr. 22, 1948; s. John Robert and Betty Jane (Singleterry) B. BA, Cambridge U., Eng., 1971, MA, 1972; STM, Union theol. Sem., 1973; PhD, U. Louvain, Belgium, 1981. Ordained priest Episcopal Ch., 1972. Tchr., headmaster St. John's Sch., Oklahoma City, 1973-77; novice Soc. St. John the Evangelist, Cambridge, Mass., 1979-81; minor canon Pro-Cathedral of the Holy Trinity, Brussels, 1981-83; rsch. fellow Yale U., New Haven, 1983; assoc. rector St. James' Ch., L.A., 1983-87; fellow Coll. of Preachers Cathedral of St. Peter and St. Paul, Washington, 1987; assisting priest Ch. of Ascension and St. Agnes, Washington, 1988-91; legis. aide U.S. Ho. of Reps., Washington, 1987-91; staff atty. Ga. Legal Svcs., Atlanta, 1991—; reader Ecumenical Inst., World Coun. Chs., Geneva, 1978, Huntington Libr., San Marino, Calif., 1985-86; hon. chaplain L.A. City Coun., 1986. Contbr. articles to profl. jours. Mem. Mayor's Task Force on Family Diversity, L.A., 1986; vol. NIH, 1987-88; key worker Fed. Employees Campaign of Nat. Capital Area, Washington, 1988-89; mem. Mcpl. Elections Com. of L.A., 1985-86; bd. dirs. Community Counselling Svc., 1984-86; mem. governing bd. Robert Wood Johnson Homeless Health Care Project, 1985-86. Recipient Am. Jurisprudence award, 1990; named one of Outstanding Young Men Am.,1974; Congl. fellow, 1987. Mem. ABA (vice chair fed. legis. com., gen. practice sect. 1989-90), Ga. Bar Assn., D.C. Bar Assn., Congl. Staff Club, English Speaking Union, Friends of the Kennedy Ctr., Met. Opera Guild, United Oxford and Cambridge Univ. Club (London), Harvard Club (washington). Democrat. Episcopalian. Home: 4000 Cathedral Ave NW Washington DC 20016 also: 2870 Pharr Ct S Atlanta GA 30305 Office: 1447 Peachtree St Ste 1002 Atlanta GA 30309

BROWN, KENNETH RAY, minister; b. Quincy, Mass., Sept. 14, 1946; s. Kenneth Minor and Ruth Dorothy Marie (Hedman) B.; m. Thompson O'Sullivan, Sept. 17, 1968; 1 child, Sara Beth. BA, Bethel Coll., St. Paul, 1968; postgrad., Bridgewater State Coll., 1970-71, Calif. State U., L.A., 1989—; MDiv, Andover-Newton Theol. Sem., 1974. Ordained to ministry Unitarian Universalist Assn. , 1974. Min. 1st Unitarian Soc., Exeter, N.H., 1975-78, North Shore Unitarian Universalist Soc., Plandome, N.Y., 1978-84; exec. dir. Interfaith Hunger Coalition, L.A., 1985-87, Community Rels. Conf., L.A., 1987-89; interim min. Unitarian Universalist Soc. Verdugo Hills, La Crescenta, Calif., 1990—; producer, host Cambridge Forum West Radio Sta. KPFK-FM, Pacifica Radio, L.A., 1990—; bd. dirs. Interfaith Ctr. for Corp. Responsibility, N.Y.C., 1978-84, Unitarian Universalist Peace Fellowship, 1981—; co-chmn. Unitarian Universalist Urban Ch. Coalition, 1982-85; mem. steering com. Religous Community Against the War in the Gulf, L.A., 1990—. Editor UNIPAX newsletter, 1982-85. Bd. dirs. Family Planning Assn., Exeter, 1975-78, Exeter Sch. Bd., 1976-78, ACLU, N.H., 1976-78, Clergy and Laity Conferned So. Calif., L.A., 1985-87. Mem. Unitarian Universalist Mins. Assn., Phi Alpha Theta. Democrat. Home: 421 S Sparks St Burbank CA 91506 Office: Unitarian Universalist Soc Verdugo Hills 4451 Dunsmore Ave La Crescenta CA 91214

BROWN, KETURAH, ecumenical agency executive. Exec. dir. Associated Ministries Thurston County, Olympia, Wash. Office: Associated Ministries Thurston County Box 895 Olympia WA 98507*

BROWN, KEVIN GERALD, minister; b. Oconto, Wis., Dec. 24, 1961; s. Gerald Alvin and LaVonne Ann (Woodworth) B.; m. Kathy Ann Medd, Aug. 13, 1983; children: Kristoffer Michael, Kimberly Lynn. BA, Concordia Coll., Moorhead, Minn., 1985; MDiv, Wartburg Sem., 1989. Ordained to ministry Luth. Ch., 1989. Youth dir. Bethesda Luth. Ch., Moorhead, 1983-85, St. Matthew's Luth. Ch., Dubuque, Iowa, 1985-87; intern pastor Peace Luth. Ch., Rockdale, Tex., 1987-88; interium pastor St. Matthew's Luth. Ch., Dubuque, 1988-89; pastor Minnewaukon (N.D.)-Oberon Luth. Parish, 1989-91, Wyndmere (N.D.) Luth. Parish, 1991—; young adult/youth dir. Luth. Lay Renewal, Wis., Minn., N.D., 1979-89; youth advisor Devils Lake Conf., Evang. Luth. Ch. in Am., N.D. Mem. Aid Assn. for Lutherans, N.D. Farm Bur., Eta Sigma Phi. Republican. Home: Box 99 324 3d St Wyndmere ND 58081 Office: Wyndmere Luth Parish Box 99 Wyndmere ND 58081

BROWN, L. DAVID, bishop. Bishop Evang. Luth. Ch. in Am., Waverly, Iowa. Office: Evang Luth Ch in Am 2700 5th Ave NW Waverly IA 50677*

BROWN, LAURENCE DAVID, bishop; b. Fargo, N.D., Feb. 16, 1926; s. John Nicolai and Ada Amelia (Johnson) B.; m. Virginia Ann Allen, Sept. 9, 1950; children: Patricia Ann, Julia Louise, Claudia Ruth. BS, U. Minn., 1946; BA, Concordia Coll., 1948; M of Theology, Luther Theol. Sem., 1951. Ordained to ministry Evang. Luth. Ch., 1951. Pastor Our Savior's Luth. Ch., New Ulm, Minn., 1951-55; nat. assoc. youth dir. Evang. Luth. Ch., Mpls., 1955-60; nat. youth dir. Am. Luth. Ch., Mpls., 1960-68; instn. dir. Tchr. Tng., U. Minn., Mpls., 1968-69; exec. dir. Freedom from Hunger Found., Washington, 1969-73; sr. pastor St. Paul Luth. Ch., Waverly, Iowa, 1973-79; bishop Iowa Dist. Am. Luth. Ch., Des Moines, 1979-89, N.E. Iowa Synod, Evang. Luth. Ch. in Am., Waverly, 1989—; bd. regents Luther Coll., Decorah, Iowa, 1988—, Wartburg Coll., Waverly, 1988—, Wartburg Theol. Sem., Dubuque, Iowa, 1988—, Self Help, Inc., Waverly, 1989—. Author: Take Care: A Guide for Responsible Living, 1983; contbr. articles to profl. jours. Lt. USN, 1943-46. Lutheran. Avocation: reading. Home: 501 10th Ave NW Waverly IA 50677 Office: Northeastern Iowa Synod Box 804 Waverly IA 50677

BROWN, LEE R., minister; b. Memphis, June 4, 1949; s. Mitchell Anderson and Emma (Ross) B.; m. Charles Etta Jackson, Feb. 24, 1979; children: Felicha, Le'Carl. Student, Memphis Theol. Sem., 1989—. Ordained to ministry Nat. Bapt. Conv. U.S.A., 1971. Assoc. pastor Oak Grove Bapt. Ch., Memphis, 1975-79; sr. pastor Springdale Bapt. Ch., Memphis, 1979—. Trustee Skyland Land Devel., Memphis, 1988—; alt. mem. Tenn. Selective Svc. Local Bd., Nashville, 1989—; bd. dirs. Habitat for Humanity/Mid South, Memphis, 1989—. Recipient Community Svc. award Shankman Hill Civic Club, Memphis, 1987, Outstanding Citizen award Memphis Housing Authority, 1989; named Hon. City Councilman, Memphis City Coun., 1986, one of 10 Best Dressed Men of Memphis, Tri-State Def., 1986. Mem. Memphis Distict Assn. (pres. 1990—), Memphis Bapt. Ministerial Assn. (v.p. 1989-91, pres. 1991—), Memphis African-Am. Ecumenical Assn. (bd. dirs. 1988—), Nat. Bapt. Congress (faculty 1990—). Home: 2740 Lakecrest Circle S Memphis TN 38127-8438 Office: Springdale Bapt Ch 1193 Springdale St Memphis TN 38108-2232 *God is not asking that we work for Him; He is seeking to work through us!.*

BROWN, LOUIS MILTON, pastor; b. Jackson, Miss., Nov. 26, 1939; s. Thad B. and Bonnie Bell (Jones) Davis; m. Myrna Darniece, June 21, 1969; 1 child, Chrisala Mignonne. Student, Jackson State U., 1959-60; BS, Calif. U., 1969; BA, LaVerne U., 1979; MDiv, Am. Bapt. Sem., 1981. Licentiate, min in tng. 2d Bapt. Ch., L.A., 1973-76; ministeria intern 2d Bapt. Ch., 1976-77, asst. to pastor, 1978, asst. pastor, 1978-82, assoc. pastor, 1983; pastor Community Presby. Ch., L.A., 1983-87, Faith Presby. Ch., Jackson, Miss., 1987—; chmn., racial ethnic cabinet, Synod of Living Waters, Nashville, 1987—, chmn. preparation ministry, Presby. of Miss., Hattiesburg, 1989—; v.p., Mary Magdalene Project, L.A., 1984-87. Vol. chaplain Jackson Police Dept., 1988—, Jackson City Coun., 1979—, L.A. Police Dept., 1979-87, Miss. State Senate, Jackson, 1990—; mem. Jackson City Housing Commn., 1988—; active Leadership Chaplain program Jackson C. of C., 1990—; mem., speaker So. Regional Project on Infant Mortality, 1990. Named Seminarian of Yr., Am. Bapt. Sem., 1981, Marion Bratcher Theology, 1981. Democrat. Office: Faith Presbyn Ch 3255 Bailey Ave Jackson MS 39213

BROWN, LOWELL HENRY, minister; b. Perry, Kans., Apr. 15, 1929; s. Minor Loren and Lydia Marie (Bodenhausen) B.; m. Wilma Pearl Pratt, June 24, 1951; children: Dixie Diane, Carla Renee. BA, York Coll., 1951; MDiv, United Theol. Sem., Dayton, Ohio, 1955. Pastor Council Union Ch., York, Nebr., 1949-51, Wabash Congl. Christian Ch., Celina, Ohio, 1953-56, Evang. United Brethren Ch., Alexander, Kans., 1956-62; assoc. dir. Christian Rural Overseas Prog., Topeka, Kans., 1962; dir. Christian Rural Overseas Prog., Springfield, Ill., 1963-76; asst. field dir. Ch. World Svc./CROP/Nat. Coun. Chs. of Christ in U.S.A., Elkhart, Ind., 1976-81, dir. field dept., 1981-88, acting assoc. dir. Ch. World Svc., 1989-90, dir. resource sharing Ch. World Svc., witness Nat. Coun. Chs. of Christ, 1990—. Mem. Nat. Assn. Ecumenical Staffs, Kiwanis (sec. 1956-62). Democrat. Methodist. Avocations: flying, photography, woodworking. Home: 2409 Kenilworth Dr Elkhart IN 46514 Office: Church World Svc/NCCC PO Box 968 Elkhart IN 46515

BROWN, LYN STEPHEN, minister; b. Seattle, Dec. 29, 1952; s. Lester Warren and Charlotte Macheod) B.; m. Kathryn Deanne Reiter, Dec. 16, 1975; children: Christopher Michael, Deanna Joy. BS, Western Bapt. Coll., 1975; MDiv, N.W. Bapt. Sem., 1981; PhD, Calif. Grad. Sch. of Theology, 1983; MLS, U. Wash., Seattle, 1985. Ordained to ministry. Minister Juanita Bapt. Ch., Kirkland, Wash., 1979-86; libr. Pensacola (Fla.) Christian Coll., 1986-87; dir. libr. svcs. Washington Bible Coll., Lanham, Md., 1987—. Del. Gov.'s Conf. on Librs., Balt., 1990. 1st lt. ARNG, 1990—. Mem. ALA, Am. Theol. Libr. Assn., Assn. Christian Librs., Evang. Theol. Soc. Office: Washington Bible Coll 6511 Princess Garden Pkwy Lanham MD 20706

BROWN, LYNETTE JOY, minister; b. Melbourne, Victoria, Australia, Dec. 24, 1954; d. James Lawson and Florence (Fordham) B. Religious & Bible Deg., Life Ministry Bible Coll., Yarra Glen, Victoria, 1977. Ordained to ministry Assemblies of God, 1988. Counselor, tchr. Teen Challenge, Harmony, N.C., 1982-88; singles minister First Assembly of God, Winston-Salem, 1988—; missionary Assemblies of God, Winston-Salem, 1982—; active hosp. ministry, nursing home ministry, prison and outreach ministries, First Assembly of God, Winston-Salem, 1988—. Bd. dirs. Bethesda Ctr. for Homless, Winston-Salem, 1989—, Salem Pregnancy Support Ctr., 1989—; assoc. chaplain Chaplain Assn. Forsyth Hosp., 1989—. Office: First Assembly of God 3730 University Pkwy Winston-Salem NC 27106 *In life we never know when we are making a memory. My prayer is that the memories we make will be pleasant, true and that will glorify our Lord Jesus Christ, that they will effect others in a positive way.*

BROWN, SISTER M. EDITHA, school system administrator. Supt. diocesan sch. Great Falls-Billings, Mont. Office: Office Supt Diocesan Sch 121 23rd St S PO Box 1399 Great Falls MT 59403*

BROWN, MARCUS LELAND, priest; b. Downey, Calif., Sept. 17, 1951; s. Mel E. and Janet Elaine (Morse) B.; married. AS, Sacramento (Calif.) City Coll., 1974, AA, 1979; BTh, Christian Internat. Coll., 1981; BS in Bus., U.

Cen. Calif., 1982; BSc, SUNY, Albany, 1989; DD (hon.), Coll. St. Thomas, Montreal, Que., Can., 1982. Ordained priest Assyrian Ch., 1978. Adminstr. St. Barnabas Orthodox Ch., Sacramento, Calif., 1977-78; pastor Assyrian Ch. of the East, Sacramento, Calif., 1978—; leader, tchr. Charismatic Home Groups, Sacramento, Rancho Cordova and Carmichael, Calif., 1975-77; counselor A Christian Alternative, Sacramento, 1987—; sec., adminstr. Diocese of the Western U.S., San Jose, 1985—; chaplain Los Rios Community Coll. Dist., Sacramento, 1976-78; conf. speaker numerous chs. Author: Single Again, 1990; editor: Constitution & By Laws, 1983; contbr. article to profl. jours. With U.S. Army, 1968-71, Vietnam. Decorated Purple Heart; recipient 4 other decorations. Mem. Am. Assn. Behavioral Therapists, United Assn. Christian Counselors, Fellowship Ea. Christian Clergy. Office: St Barnabas Ch 2990 Fruitridge Rd Sacramento CA 95820

BROWN, MARGARET HELEN, religion educator; b. Wis. Rapids, Wis., June 18, 1934; d. Philip Anthony and Lavina Christine (Peterson) Eron; m. Dale Brown, Nov. 18, 1961; children: Christine Therese, Lawrence Anthony. B in Music Edn., Viterbo Coll., LaCrosse, Wis., 1960; STM, St. Francis Coll., Milw., 1980; PhD in Theology, Marquette U., 1986. Cert. tchr., Wis. Youth coord. St. Charles Parish, Hartland, Wis., 1980—; instr. Marquette U., Milw., 1985—; music tchr. Milw. Pub. Schs., 1972—. Mem. Am. Guild Organists, Cath. Bibl. Assn., Soc. Bibl. Lit., Milw. Tchr. Edn. Assn., Metro Milw. Bibl. Discussion Group.

BROWN, MARGRETHE B. J., religious organization administrator. Acting sec. for N.Am., World Alliance Ref. Chs., Louisville. Office: World Alliance Ref Chs 100 Witherspoon St Louisville KY 40202*

BROWN, MARVIN LEE, minister; b. Birmingham, Ala., Nov. 11, 1933; s. Thomas Lee and Ruth (Myers) B.; m. Felisa Llanes Regner, Nov. 30, 1961 (div. 1987); 1 child, Viola Lee Brown Freeman. BA, Calif. Bapt. Coll., Riverside, 1980; M in Black Ch. Studies, Ecumenical Theology Ctr., L.A., 1983; MDiv, Am. Bapt. Sem., Berkeley, Calif., 1983; postgrad., Mt. Zion Bible Sem., Sacramento, 1990—. Ordained to ministry Bapt. Ch., 1983; Calif. (emergency) teaching credentials. Assoc. min. Temple Missionary Bapt. Ch., San Bernardino, Calif., 1976-79; asst. pastor New Hope Missionary Bapt. Ch., San Bernardino, 1980-84, pastor protem, 1984-85; sr. pastor First Bapt. Ch., Perris, Calif., 1987—; pub. rels. officer Interdenominational Mins. Alliance, Perris, 1988—; enlisted USAF, 1953, ret., 1975; pres. Interdenominational Mins. Alliance, San Bernardino, 1985-87; dist. missionary Tri County Dist. Assn., Calif., 1985-88; pres. Congress Christian Edn. Tri County, 1988—; founder, pres. Perris Valley Sch. Theology, 1988—; pres. Perris Valley Police Clergy, 1988—. Dir. edn. A. Philip Randolph Inst., San Bernardino, 1983-87; chmn. Westside Leadership Coalition, San Bernardino, 1985-87; pres. NAACP Br. #1145, Perris, 1989—. Named Pastor of Yr. Tri County Dist. Assn., So. Calif., 1990. Democrat. Home: P O Box 1381 210 E 5th St Perris CA 92370 Office: 1st Bapt Ch PO Box 1399 277 E 5th St Perris CA 92370 *In a world where such crimes as robbery, raping and killing are daily events—among the hundreds of other human problems—I believe that people who share a moment of God's love bring a ray of love, peace or joy into someone's life. Be kind to someone today.*

BROWN, MELVIN FLOYD, minister, educator; b. Chgo., Oct. 13, 1943; m. Floyd Friedrich and Mamie Leona (Boling) B.; m. Barbara Mae Carlson, June 5, 1965; children: Lori, Cheryl, Tim. BTh, Bapt. Bible Coll., 1967; BA, Evangel. Coll., 1968; MS, Western Ill. U., 1977; DD, Japan Bapt. Coll., Tokyo, 1985; EdD, No. Ill. U., 1987. Cert. marriage and family therapist, Ill.; ordained Bapt. Ch., 1963. Sr. pastor Edgewood Baptist Ch., Rock Island, Ill., 1968—; pvt. practice marriage and family therapy Rock Island, Ill., 1975—; spl. instr. Moody Bible Inst., Chgo., 1978—; cons. East Moline (Ill.) Christian Sch., 1980—; coord. Moody Bible Inst., Chgo., 1984—; pres. Marriage and Family Counseling Ctr., Rock Island, Ill.; developer marital instruction/therapy; spl. instr. Teikyo Marycrest U., U. Dubuque Theol. Sem. Named One of Outstanding Coll. Students in Am. Mem. Am. Assn. for Marriage and Family Therapy, Phi Kappa Phi, Pi Kappa Delta, Delta Psi Omega. Avocation: golf, skiing, reading. Home: 3109 29th St Moline IL 61265 Office: Edgewood Bapt Ch 2704 38th St Rock Island IL 61201

BROWN, MICHAEL BRUCE, minister; b. Asheboro, N.C., Feb. 23, 1949; s. Anderson bryant and Margaret Florence (Lowe) B.; m. Carolyn Elizabeth Davis, June 4, 1977; children: Adam Michael, Zachary David. AB, High Point (N.C.) Coll., 1971; MDiv, Duke U., 1974; DMin, Drew U. Theol. Sem., Madison, N.J., 1981. Ordained to ministry, United Meth. Ch. Minister Mt. Lebanon United Meth. Ch., Randleman, N.C., 1974-78, Center United Meth. Ch., Welcome, N.C., 1978-82, Stallings (N.C.) United Meth. Ch., 1982-87; sr. minister Boone (N.C.) United Meth. Ch., 1987—; bd. ordained ministry United Meth. Ch., Western N.C., 1980-88; bd. dirs. Meth. Counseling Ctr., Charlotte, 1982-87; chmn. Commn. on Evangelish and Ch. Growth, Westernnn N.C. Meth., 1988—; cons. Nat. Evangelistic Assn., Lubbock, 1990—; growth plus cons. Meth. Bd. Discipleship, Nashville, 1989—. Author: Ordinary Sins, 1988; contbr. articles to profl. jours. Adv. bd. dirs. Children's Home Soc. N.C., Greensboro, N.C., 1987-89, adv. bd., Charlotte, 1984-87. Recipient Cir. Rider Sermon award Meth. Pub. House, 1990, Meth. cert. of merit for contbns. to ch. growth. Mem. Order of the Lighted Lamp. Democrat. Office: Boone United Meth Ch 341 E King St Boone NC 28607 *Virtually everyone is struggling with some hardship in his/her life. Strength comes in learning the lesson of faith—that in all times or situations we are not alone. God is with us.*

BROWN, MICHAEL RICHARD, minister; b. Columbus, Ohio, Mar. 2, 1959; s. Cornelius Paul Brown and Pearl Elizabeth (Baker) Buck; m. Christine Elaine Stanley, Aug. 23, 1980; 1 child, Stephanie Nicole. BA in Bible and Religion, Huntington Coll., 1981, M in Ministry, 1983, postgrad., 1984. Ordained to ministry Christian Ch. Minister Monroe (Ind.) United Brethren Ch., 1982-89, Franklin United Brethern Ch., New Albany, Ohio, 1989—. co. dir. Adams County Soccer Clinic, Decatur, Ind., 1984-85; chmn. Adams County Child Protection Team, Decatur, 1985; v.p. Adams County Energy Assistance Inc., 1986; mem. Hoosier's For Better Schs., A-Plus Program; soccer coach New Albany Mid. Sch., 1989—. Named one of Outstanding Young Men of Am., 1985. Mem. New Albany Ministerial Assn. (pres. 1991). Republican. Avocations: soccer coach, running. Home: 6695 Albanyview Dr Westerville OH 43081 Office: Franklin United Brethren Ch 7171 Central Coll Rd New Albany OH 43054

BROWN, NEIL W., religious organization administrator; b. Columbus, Ohio, Jan. 15, 1938; s. William Dent and Grace (Wood) B.; m. Margaret Hawthorne, Aug. 20, 1960; children: Bethel Nagy, C. Todd. BA, Westminster Coll., 1959; MDiv, Pitts. Theol. Sem., 1962. Ordained to ministry Presbyn. Ch. (U.S.A.), 1962. Pastor Community Presbyn. Ch., Oakland, Oreg., 1962-66, Covenant Presbyn. Ch., Gresham, Oreg., 1966-77; assoc. exec. Synod of the Covenant, Columbus, 1977-88; exec. presbyter Presbytery San Diego, 1988—; bd. drs. San Diego Ecumenical Conf., 1988—. Precinct committeeman Douglas County, Oreg. Dem. Com., Roseburg, 1965-66, Multnomah County, Oreg. Dem. Com., Portland, 1970-74. Mem. Lions (pres. Oakland chpt. 1965-66, Portland chpt. 1966-71). Office: Presbytery San Diego 8825 Aero Dr # 220 San Diego CA 92123

BROWN, PAUL R., minister; b. Austin, Minn., Nov. 17, 1954; s. Reynold Matthew and Arlene Marie (Wise) B.; m. Brenda Sue Boyer, Aug. 1, 1975; children: Nathan Paul, Kellyn Joseph, Bethany Joy. BA, Open Bible Coll., Des Moines, 1977. Ordained to ministry Open Bible Standard Chs. Pastor Open Bible Ctr., Kankakee, Ill., 1979-87; dist. supt. Open Bible Standard Chs., Kankakee, 1984-87; pastor Lighthouse Temple, Eugene, Oreg., 1987—; seminar speaker Leadership Devel., 1987—. Contbr. articles to profl. jours. Mem. adv. bd. Trinity Christian Acad., Kankakee, 1980-81; vol. coach Kidsports, Eugene, 1987—; mem. exec. com. Eugene Bible Coll., 1988—; mem. edn. project, Eugene, 1989—. Mem. Christian Ministries Mgmt. Assn. Office: Lighthouse Temple 1790 Chenelton St Eugene OR 97401

BROWN, PAUL WILLIAM, evangelist, electronics executive; b. Niskayuna, N.Y., Aug. 29, 1948; s. Paul Walter and Esther Jean (West) B.; m. Susan Dianne Chapman, Mar. 17, 1954; children: David Paul, Charissa Joy. Grad. high sch., Schoharie, N.Y., 1966. Ordained to ministry Pentecostal Ch., 1975, 80. Prodn. specialist GE, Schenectady, N.Y., 1971-75; sr. pastor Mt. Zion Full Gospel Ch., Wellsboro, Pa., 1975-80; evangelist Oil and Wine Ministries, Canton, Pa., 1980-84; founder/pastor Bethel Family Worship Ctr., Mansfield, Pa., 1985-90; nat. sales mgr. Kingdom Tapes, Mansfield, 1985-90; gen. mgr. Nat. Cassette Svcs., Front Royal, Va., 1990—; founder/evangelist Commitment to Excellence, Front Royal, 1990—; pastor People's Ch., Manassas, Va., 1991—; conf. speaker, cons. Nat. Cassette Svcs., 1990—; conf. speaker, dir. Commitment to Excellence, 1990—. Patentee in field. With U.S. Army, 1968-80, Vietnam. Mem. The Christian Outdoorsman (pres. 1988-90). Republican. Avocations: golf, fly tying, fly fishing, hunting. Home: 9940 Portsmouth Rd Manassas VA 22110 Office: People's Ch PO Box 2427 Manassas VA 22110

BROWN, PERRY CLENDENIN, editor, marketing professional; b. Aledo, Ill., Aug. 7, 1955; m. Sarabeth Graham Brown, June 23, 1984; 1 child, Molly. BA, Sterling (Kans.) Coll., 1977; ThM, Dallas Theol. Sem., 1982. Editor, mktg. dir. Am. Tract Soc., Garland, Tex., 1984—. Mem. Evang. Press Assn., Grace Evang. Soc. Office: Am Tract Soc 1624 N First St Garland TX 75040 *Better to view one's life through a telescope than a microscope. The telescope will lead you to your dreams; the microscope will hardly let you see beyond yourself.*

BROWN, PRESTON CONDREY, pastor; b. Robinson, Ill., Dec. 21, 1926; s. Charles Dewey and Lillian (Condrey) B.; m. Billie Johns, Nov. 19, 1951; children: Rebecca Lee Ebel, Bruce Condrey. BA, DePauw U., 1948; MDiv, Garrett Evang. Theol. Sem., 1956; DD, Dakota Wesleyan, 1974. Ordained to ministry Meth. Ch., 1956. Pastor United Meth., Frankfort, S.D., 1956-60, Beresford, S.D., 1960-62, Claremont, S.D., 1962-71; dist. supt. United Meth., Rapid City, S.D., 1971-76; pastor United Meth. Ch., Williston, N.D., 1976-86, Dickinson, N.D., 1986-87; pastor United Meth., Sac City, Iowa, 1987-91; chairperson Leadership Devel. Task Force, Des Moines, 1987—. Trustee Dakota Wesleyan U., Mitchell, S.D., 1971-76, Meth. Hosp., Mitchell, 1971-75; pres. Area Alcohol Coun., Williston, N.D., 1977-86, United Way, Williston, 1981; mem. Disaster Response Team, Rapid City, 1972-75. With Med. Corps U.S. Army, 1951-53, Korea. Mem. Kiwanis (bd. dirs. Williston chpt. 1978-81, bd. dirs. Sac City chpt. 1988-91).

BROWN, RAYMOND EDWARD, educator, priest; b. N.Y.C., May 22, 1928; s. Robert H. and Loretta Brown. BA, Cath. U. Am., 1948, MA, 1949; STB, St. Mary's Sem., Balt., 1951, STD, 1955; PhD, Johns Hopkins U., 1958; SSB, Pontifical Bible Commn., Rome, 1959, SSL, 1963; DD (hon.), U. Edinburgh, Scotland, 1972, Glasgow U., Scotland, 1978; ThD (hon.), U. Uppsala, Sweden, 1974, U. Louvain, Belgium, 1976, St. Anselm's Coll., 1977; LittD, Villanova U., 1975, Boston Coll., 1977; LHD, DePaul U., 1974, Hofstra U., 1985; others. Joined Soc. St. Sulpice, 1951, ordained priest Roman Cath. Ch., 1953. Prof. sacred scriptures St. Mary's Sem., Balt., 1959-71; Auburn prof. Bibl. studies Union Theol. Sem., 1971-90; prof. emeritus, 1990; Am. mem. Roman Pontifical Bibl. Commn., 1972-78, Joint Theol. Commn. of World Coun. Chs. and Roman Cath. Ch., 1967-68, faith and order commn. World Coun. Chs., 1968—; adviser to Archbishop Hurley of St. Augustine at Vatican II Coun., 1963; lectr. Aquinas Inst. Theology, 1963, Duke U. Div. Sch., 1967, U. Sydney (Australia), 1969, Lancaster Theol. Sem., 1971, So. Bapt. Theol. Sem., 1978, U. Coll., Dublin, 1971, Vanderbilt Div. Sch. 1980; Thomas More lectr. Yale U., 1966, Shaffer lectr. 1978. Author: New Testament Essays, 1965, The Gospel According to John, (Nat. Cath. Book award, Christopher award) 1966, 70, Jesus, God and Man, 1967, The Jerome Biblical Commentary (Nat. Cath. Book award), 1968, Priest and Bishop: Biblical Reflections, 1970, The Parables of the Gospels, 1963, (with P. J. Cahill) Biblical Tendencies Today: An Introduction to the Post-Bultmanians, 1969, Peter in the New Testament, 1973, Virginal Conception and Bodily Resurrection of Jesus, 1973 (Nat. Cath. Book award), Biblical Reflections on Crises Facing the Church, 1975, The Birth of the Messiah, 1977 (Nat. Religious Book award), The Critical Meaning of the Bible, 1981, The Epistles of John (Anchor Bible), 1982, Biblical Exegesis and Church Doctrine, 1985, The New Jerome Biblical Commentary, 1990, many others; contbr. articles to religious jours.; mem. editorial bd. Cath. Bibl. Quarterly, Jour. Bibl. Lit., Theol. Studies, New Testament Studies. Mem. Soc. N.T. Studies (pres. 1986-87), Am. Schs. Oriental Rsch., Cath. Bibl. Assn. (pres. 1971-72), Soc. Bibl. Lit. (pres. 1976-77), Bibl. Theologians, Am. Theol. Soc., Phi Beta Kappa. Address: 3041 Broadway at Reinhold Niebuhr Pl New York NY 10027

BROWN, RICHARD, minister; b. McColl, S.C., Dec. 28, 1924; s. Richard and Agganora (Pipkin) B.; m. Leola Harper, Aug. 26, 1947; children: Linda Noreen, Carla Denise. BA, MEd, U. Pitts., 1955, 56; MA, Case Western Res. U., 1977; MDiv, Ashland Theol. Sem., Ohio, 1983; DMin, Trinity Theol. Sem., Evansville, Ind., 1986. Ordained to ministry Pentecostal Ch., 1956. With U.S. Steel, Clairton, Pa., 1943-56; tchr. Cleve. pub. schs., 1956-80, Clairton pub. schs., 1931-42; minister Calvary Ch., Cleve., 1961—; pres. Ministerial Alliance Greater Cleve., 1982—; bd. dirs. Calvary Bible Inst., Cleve., 1986—. Contbr. articles to profl. jours. With U.S. Army, 1944-46. Mem. Urban League, NAACP, N. Am. Christian Counselors. Democr4at. Ch. of God in Christ. Avocations: music, gardening, sports. Home: 556 E 112th St Cleveland OH 44108

BROWN, RICHARD C., minister, ecumenical agency administrator. Exec. min. R.I. State Coun. Chs., Providence. Office: RI State Coun Chs 743 Hope St Providence RI 02906*

BROWN, ROBERT EPPS, clergyman; b. Memphis, Jan. 7, 1956; s. Johnny Robert and Elsie (Benner) B.; m. Karen D. Drummond, Aug. 19, 1978; children: Robert Epps II, Richard Andrew. BS in Pastoral Studies, Wesley Coll., 1981, BS in Christian Edn., 1981; MA in Christian Edn., Wesley Bibl. Sem., 1987. Ordained to ministry Wesleyan Ch., 1977. Youth pastor Meth. Protestant Ch., Jackson, Miss., 1980-81, Ind. Meth. Ch., Jackson, 1981-86, Wesleyan Ch., Jackson, 1986-87; coll. pastor, children and sr. citizens First Wesleyan Ch., Tuscaloosa, Ala., 1987—; dist. camp dir. Delta Dist. Wesleyan Ch., Tuscaloosa, 1991-92, dist. youth pres., 1991—; mem. bd. Youth for Christ, Tuscaloosa, 1991—. Author: Breaking Through the Barriers, 1989; author video: Christian Music VS Secular, 197, Teaching Christian Education, 1990. Counselor Salvation Army - 1st Time Offenders, Jackson, 1979-81, Juvenile Ct., Tuscaloosa, 1987-90. Recipient Spl. Recognition award Youth Emergency Bd., 1988, Vol. of Yr., 1988, award of excellence Delta Dist., 1988. Mem. Christian Minister Assn. Office: The First Wesleyan Ch 1501 McFarland Blvd N Tuscaloosa AL 35405

BROWN, ROBERT LINDSAY, minister; b. Winston-Salem, N.C., Oct. 8, 1959; s. Lindsay Herbert and Jo Ann Francis (Isaacs) B.; m. Lisa Dawn Pegg, May 17, 1981; children: Jordan Lindsay, Taylor Dawn. Degree in Theology, Fruitland Bapt. Inst., 1985; BA, Mars Hill Coll., 1987; MDiv, Southwestern Bapt. Theol. Sem., 1990. Ordained to ministry So. Bapt. Conv., 1987. Min. evangelism Mud Creek Bapt. Ch., Hendersonville, N.C., 1983-87; min. media prodn. First Bapt. Ch., Euless, Tex., 1988-90; pastor Two Rivers Ch., Columbus, Ohio, 1991—; mem. home mission bd. So. Bapt. Conv., 1991—. Constance Butz Found. scholar, 1989, 90, Kesee Found. scholar, 1987-90. Mem. N.W. Apt. Chaplains Assn. (dir. 1991—), N.C. Student Fellowship (pres. 1987-90). Home: 3024 Green Arbor Ln Dublin OH 43017

BROWN, ROBERT MCAFEE, minister, religion educator; b. Carthage, Ill., May 28, 1920; s. George William and Ruth Myrtle (McAfee) B.; m. Sydney Thomson Brown, June 21, 1944; children: Peter Thomson, Mark McAfee, Alison McAfee, Thomas Seabury. B.A., Amherst Coll., 1943, D.D., 1958; M. Div., Union Theol. Sem., N.Y.C., 1945; Ph.D., Columbia, 1951; postgrad., Mansfield Coll., Oxford (Eng.) U., 1949-50, St. Mary's Coll., 1959, St. Andrews (Scotland) U., 1959-60; Litt.D., U. San Francisco, 1964; L.H.D., Lewis and Clark Coll., 1964, St. Louis U., 1966, Hebrew Union Coll., 1982; LL.D., U. Notre Dame, 1965, Loyola U., 1963, Boston Coll., 1965, St. Mary's Coll., 1968, Kenyon Coll., 1981, Lehigh U., 1988; D.D., Hamilton Coll., 1968, Pacific Sch. Religion, 1967, Kalamazoo Coll., 1980, Macalester Coll., 1985. Ordained to ministry Presbyn. Ch., 1944. Asst. chaplain Amherst Coll., 1946-48; prof. religion, chmn. dept. Macalester Coll., St. Paul, 1951-53; faculty Union Theol. Sem., N.Y.C., 1953-62, prof. systematic theology, 1962-76, prof. ecumenics and world Christianity, 1976-79; prof. religion Stanford U., 1962-76; prof. theology and ethics Pacific Sch. Religion, Berkeley, 1979-85; Hanley Disting. prof. Santa Clara (Calif.) U., 1990; Benedict Disting. vis. prof. Carleton Coll., 1987. Author: P.T. Forsyth: Prophet for Today, 1952, The Bible Speaks to You, 1955, The Significance of the Church, 1956, (with Gustave Weigel) An American Dialogue, 1960, The Spirit of Protestantism, 1961, Observer in Rome: A Protestant Report on the Vatican Council, 1964, The Collected Writings of St. Hereticus, 1964, The Ecumenical Revolution, 1967, Vietnam: Crisis of Conscience, 1967, The Pseudonyms of God, 1972, Religion and Violence, 1973, Frontiers for the Church Today, 1973, Is Faith Obsolete?, 1974, Theology in a New Key: Responding to Liberation Themes, 1978, The Hereticus Papers, 1979, Creative Dislocation—The Movement of Grace, 1980, Gustavo Gutierrez, 1980, Making Peace in the Global Village, 1981, Elie Wiesel: Messenger to all Humanity, 1983, Unexpected News: Reading the Bible with Third World Eyes, 1984, Saying Yes and Saying No: On Rendering to God and Caesar, 1986, Spirituality and Liberation, 1988, Gustavo Gutierrez: an Introduction to Liberation Theology, 1990; gen. editor: The Layman's Theological Library, 12 volumes, 1956-58; translator: (deDietrich): God's Unfolding Purpose, 1960; (Casalis), Portrait of Karl Barth, 1963; (Dumas), Dietrich Bonhoeffer: Theologian of Reality, 1971; editor: (with David Scott) The Challenge to Reunion, 1963, The Essential Reinhold Niebuhr, 1986, (with Sydney Brown) A Cry for Justice: The Churches and Synagogues Speak, 1989, Kairos: Three Prophetic Challenges to the Church, 1990; contbr. to books; mem. editorial bd. various mags. and jours. Served as chaplain USNR, 1945-46. Montgomery fellow Dartmouth Coll., 1985. Mem. Am. Theol. Soc., Soc. Theol. Discussion, Phi Beta Kappa. Home: 2090 Columbia St Palo Alto CA 94306

BROWN, RONALD TRAVIS, broadcaster; b. Bryn Mawr, Pa., Jan. 6, 1955; s. Laurence Ray and Margaret (Rushbrook) B.; m. Edythe Brodowski, July 24, 1976; children: Christian Paul, MaryAnna, Jonathan, Timothy. BS, Va. Poly. Inst. and State U., 1976. Gen. mgr. Sta. WGTH, Richlands, Va., 1979—, Sta. WKGK, Saltville, Va., 1985-90; pres. High Knob Broadcasters, Inc., Richlands, 1985—. V.p. Richlands Little League, 1990-91. Republican. Office: Sta WGTH PO Drawer 370 Richlands VA 24641

BROWN, SALLY (SARAH JANE BROWN), minister; b. Manila, Dec. 20, 1923; d. Frederick Ocean and Sarah Mathloma (Powell) England; m. David Randolph Brown, Dec. 17, 1944; children: Philip, Ellen, Polly, Ann. BA in English, U. Wash., 1945; MS in Recreation, San Jose (Calif.) State U., 1970; MDiv, Pacific Sch. of Religion, Berkeley, Calif., 1988. Cert. hosp. chaplain; cert. clin. pastor. Staff chaplain VA Med. Ctr., Palo Alto, Calif., 1988—; community chaplain Palo Alto, 1988—; co-chair United Ch. Christ com. on ministry No. Calif. Conf., 1991—. Fellow Coll. of Chaplains; mem. Assn. for Clin. Pastoral Edn. (clin.), Nat. Assn. of Vets. Affairs Chaplains, Am. Soc. Aging. Home: 1470 Sand Hill Rd #309 Palo Alto CA 94304

BROWN, SANFORD WEBSTER, minister; b. Lancaster, Calif., Nov. 20, 1957; s. Sanford Webster and Mary Martha (Nieblas) B.; m. Elizabeth Elleanor Christ, Mar. 18, 1978; children: Matthew, Luke. BA, U. Wash., 1978; MDiv, Garrett-Evang. Theol. Sem., Evanston, Ill., 1982. Ordained to ministry, United Meth. Ch., 1984. Pastor Fall City (Wash.) United Meth. Ch., 1982-86, Lake Washington United Meth. Ch., Kirkland, Wash., 1986—; mem. bd. Ordained Ministry of Pacific N.W. Conf., 1988—. Mem. sch. bd. Lake Washington Sch. Dist., Kirkland, 1989—, v.p. 1991; chmn. Eastside Human Svcs. Forum, Bellevue, Wash., 1986; v.p. E. King Coun. Social Svcs., Bellevue, 1985. Mem. Snoqualmie Valley Ministerial Assn. (pres. 1985-86), Met. United Meth. Ministers (pres. 1986-87), Kiwanis. Democrat. Home: 7506 130th Ave NE Kirkland WA 98033 Office: Lake Washington United Meth 7525 132nd Ave NE Kirkland WA 98033

BROWN, STEPHEN FRANCIS, religion educator; b. Phila., Mar. 8, 1933; s. Thomas Francis and Catherine (Fitzpatrick) B.; m. Marie La Rosa, July 14, 1974; children: Mark Stephen, Aimee Marie. BA, St. Bonaventure U., 1955; MA, Franciscan Inst., Olean, N.Y., 1959; PhL, Université de Louvain, Belgium, 1963, PhD, 1964. Prof. Boston Coll., 1979—. Author: Ockham's Philosophical Writings, 1990; editor: Opera Theologica et Philosophica Guillemi de Ockham, 5 vols., 1967-86. Mem. Am. Philos. Assn., Medieval Acad. Am., Am. Cath. Philos. Assn. (bd. dirs. 1987—), Société internationale de la philosophie médiévale (bd. dirs. 1987—). Home: 20 Riverdale Rd Wellesley MA 02181 Office: Boston Coll 410 Carney Hall Chestnut Hill MA 02167

BROWN, STEVEN KENT, minister; b. Galion, Ohio, Jan. 15, 1949; s. William Buford and Rosemary June (Geyer) B.; m. Constance Peters, June 9, 1973; children: Sarah Elizabeth, Andrew Wesley. BA, Ohio State U., 1971; ThM, Boston U., 1974, MA, 1979. Ordained to ministry United Meth. Ch. Min. Saugus Ctr. United Meth. Ch., Saugus, Mass., 1976-79; min. First United Meth. Ch., Bridgeport, Ohio, 1979-81, Ohltown United Meth. Ch., Youngstown, Ohio, 1981-85; assoc. min. Lakewood (Ohio) United Meth. Ch., 1985-88; min. Ch. of the Cross United Meth. Ch., Lexington, Ohio, 1988—. Columnist Mansfield News Jour., 1989. Jacob Sleeper fellow Boston U., 1974; Dempster grad. fellow Bd. Higher Edn. United Meth. Ch., 1975. Mem. Kiwanis. Home: 30 Mayfair Rd Lexington OH 44904 Office: Ch of the Cross United Meth 236 Otterbein Dr Lexington OH 44904

BROWN, STEVEN LEE, minister; b. Henderson, Tenn., Sept. 6, 1955; s. Charles Lee and Jane Gaither (Pierce) B.; m. Karen Sue Ulmer, June 24, 1977; children: William Brooks, Seth Walker, Margaret Negran. BA, Okla. Christian Coll., 1977; MTh, Harding Grad. Sch. Religion, Memphis, 1981. Ordained to ministry Ch. of Christ, 1981. Min. Ch. of Christ, Freehold, N.J., 1981-91, New Egypt, N.J., 1991—; chaplain Freehold Area Hosp. Chaplaincy Program, 1981-88; lectr. to orgns. Den leader Cub Scouts, Howell, N.J., 1989-90, Webelos leader, 1990-91; asst. dir. Food Bank in New Egypt. Office: Ch of Christ RR 2 Box 107 New Egypt NJ 08533-9802

BROWN, STEVEN M., pastor; b. Newman, Calif., Jan. 8, 1950; s. Elmer B. and Clarice A. (Wall) B.; m. J. LaDel Thompson, June 27, 1970; children: Scott Steven, David Timothy. BA cum laude, Bethany Coll., 1987. Lic. to preach 1987, ordained to ministry Assemblies of God 1990. Assoc. pastor Christian Life Ch., Santa Cruz, Calif., 1986—; bd. dirs. Christian Life Ch., Santa Cruz, 1970-90, Relatual Resources, Scotts Valley, Calif., 1987-90, Acess Ministries, Santa Cruz, 1988—, Word Growth Inst., Scotts Valley, 1989—. Mem. C. of C., Santa Cruz, 1971-88, adv. bd. Community Hosp., Santa Cruz, 1975-81, chmn. Downtown Derking Com., Santa Cruz, 1979-83, Dwontown Com., Santa Cruz, 1982. Mem. Christian Mgmt., Christian Forum, Delta Epsilon Chi, Elks Lodge #821. Home: 100 Seaberg Santa Cruz CA 95060 Office: Christian Life Ch 1009 Mission Santa Cruz CA 95060

BROWN, TERRENCE NEAL, library director; b. Ripley, Tenn., July 9, 1954; s. Clarence Alton and R. F. (Neal) B.; m. Millicent Ruth Brewer, Mar. 17, 1979; children: Alexander Reveley, Abigail Haston, Susanna Lancaster Brown. BA, Memphis State U., 1976; MLS, U. Tenn., 1979. Asst. dir. libr. svcs. Mid-Am. Bapt. Theol. Sem., Memphis, 1982-90, dir. libr. svcs., 1990—. Mem. Am. Theol. Libr. Assn., Tenn. Theol. Libr. Assn. (v.p. 1987-88, pres. 1988-90), Phi Alpha Theta, Phi Kappa Phi. Office: Mid Am Bapt Theol Sem 1255 Poplar Ave Memphis TN 38104

BROWN, TOD DAVID, bishop; b. San Francisco, Nov. 15, 1936; s. George Wilson and Edna Anne (Dunn) B. BA, St. John's Coll., 1958; STB, Gregorian U., Rome, 1960; MA in Theology, U. San Francisco, 1970, MAT in Edn., 1976. Dir. edn. Diocese of Monterey, Calif., 1970-80, vicar gen., clergy, 1980-82, chancellor, 1982-89, vicar gen., chancellor, 1983-89; pastor St. Francis Xavier, Seaside, Calif., 1977-82; bishop Roman Catholic Diocese of Boise, Idaho, 1989—. Named Papal Chaplain Pope Paul VI, 1975. Mem. Cath. Theological Soc. Am., Cath. Biblical Assn., Canon Law Soc. Am. Avocation: visiting health club. Office: Diocese of Boise 303 Federal Way Box 769 Boise ID 83701

BROWN, VICTOR LEE, clergyman; b. Cardston, Alta., Can., July 31, 1914; s. Gerald S. and Maggie (Lee) B.; m. Lois A. Kjar, Nov. 13, 1936; children: Victor Lee, Gerald E., Joanne K., Patricia L., Stephen M. Student, Latter-Day Saints Bus. Coll., U. Utah; spl. studies, U. Calif. at Berkeley. With United Air Lines, 1940-61; successively supr., reservations mgr. United Air Lines, Washington, Chgo.; chief payload control United Air Lines, Denver; mgr. space control United Air Lines, 1956-60; asst. to dir. reservations United Air Lines, Chgo., 1960-61; dir. Beneficial Life Ins. Co.; 2d counselor presiding bishopric Ch. of Jesus Christ of Latter-day Saints, 1961-72, presiding bishop, 1972—; pres., chmn. bd. Deseret Mut. Benefits Assn., to 1978; mem. Deseret Mgmt. Corp., Deseret News Pub. Co.; pres. Hotel

Utah Co., until 1982, chmn. bd., 1982—; vice chmn. Deseret Trust Co.; dir. Western Air Lines, O.C. Tanner Jewelry Co. Mem. Utah Bicentennial Commn., chmn. festival com., 1975-77; mem. gen. welfare services com. Ch. of Jesus Christ of Latter-day Saints, mem. bd. edn.; trustee Coll. Bus. Brigham Young U.; mem. Utah Symphony Bd. Mem. Beta Gamma Sigma. Home: 171 3rd Ave #615 Salt Lake City UT 84103-5009 Office: 50 E North Temple St Salt Lake City UT 84150

BROWN, VIRGIL JACKSON, minister; b. Argyle, Tex., May 28, 1944; s. Virgil Jackson and Essie Marie (Taylor) B.; m. Nancy Marie Hilton, Aug. 15, 1969; children: David, Stephanie, Philip. BS in Secondary Edn., U. N. Tex., 1971; MDiv, Southwestern Bapt. Sem., 1975, MA in Religious Edn., 1986. Ordained to ministry So. Bapt. Conv., 1972. Pastor Spring Creek Bapt. Ch., Weatherford, Tex., 1972-74, Center Point Bapt. Ch., Denton, Tex., 1974-76, 1st So. Bapt. Ch., Arkansas City, Kans., 1976-80, Martin Springs Bapt. Ch., Sulphur Springs, Tex., 1980-85, Garden Acres Bapt. Ch., Ft. Worth, 1985-88, 1st Bapt. Ch. Jacinto City, Houston, 1988—; chmn., Vietnamese Resettlement Com., Denton Bapt. Assn., 1975-76; mem. exec. bd. Kans./Nebr. Bapt. Conv., 1978-78; vice moderator Rehoboth Bapt. Assn., 1982-84. Chmn. bd. Helping Hands Jacinto City, 1990-91. With U.S. Army, 1965-67. Recipient Outstanding Contbn. award Progressive Farmer Mag., 1982. Office: 1st Bapt Ch Jacinto City 10701 Wiggins Houston TX 77029

BROWN, WILLIAM JOHN, clergyman; b. Pitts., Aug. 11, 1920; s. Hamilton Shepherd and Ella Lehman (Weldin) B.; m. Nancy Elizabeth Byrem, Apr. 21, 1951; children: Susan, William John Jr., Philip. BA, Grove City (Pa.) Coll., 1942; MEd, U. Pitts., 1947; MDiv, Pitts. Theol. Sem., 1950; DD (hon.), Grove City Coll., 1987. Ordained to ministry Presbyn. Ch., 1950. Assoc. pastor Dormont Presbyn. Ch., Pitts., 1950-53; pastor Ebensburg (Pa.) Presbyn. Ch., 1953-57, Clearfield (Pa.) Presbyn. Ch., 1957-63; exec. presbyter Donegal Presbytery, Lancaster, Pa., 1963-89; interim exec. dir. Lancaster County Coun. Chs., 1990—; treas., chair fin. Lancaster Career Devel. Ctr., 1965—; mem. bd. Millersville (Pa.) U. Campus Ministry, 1974-84; mem. coord. com. Asian, Hispanic, Black, Camp Hill, Pa., 1975-89; chair State Migrant Ministry, Harrisburg, Pa., 1983-86. Editor The Bull., 1963—. Pres. Recreation Commn., Lancaster, 1976-81; v.p., sch. bd. mem. Sch. Dist. Lancaster, 1975-81, 83—. Sgt. USCG, 1942-46. Mem. Homelink, Ptnrs. for Affordable Housing., Masons. Republican. Home: 453 State St Lancaster PA 17602 Office: Lancaster County Coun Chs 447 E King St Lancaster PA 17602

BROWN, WILLIS NOEL, chaplain, administrator; b. Balclutha, Otago, New Zealand, Mar. 5, 1940; s. Edward Douglas and Annie Thelma (Sinclair) B.; m. Judith Marion Miles, Feb. 16, 1963; children; Dugald Miles, Duncan Noel. BSc, U. Otago, 1961; LTh, Knox Coll., Dunedin, New Zealand, 1964; STM magna cum laude, U. Dubuque, 1967. Ordained to ministry Presbyn. Ch., 1966. Staff chaplain U. Mich. Hosps., Ann Arbor, 1970-76; dir. pastoral care Neuro-psychiat. Inst., Ann Arbor, 1976-80; pastoral cons. Presbyn. Support Svcs., Auckland, New Zealand, 1980-88, dir. human devel., 1988-90; chaplain supr. South Chgo. Community Hosp., 1990—; convenor student com. Presbytery of Auckland, 1983-90; bd. dirs. Life Line, Auckland, 1985-90; lectr. Bapt. Theol. Coll., New Zealand; mem. adj. field faculty McCormack Theol. Sem., Chgo., 1991—. Contbr. articles to profl. jours. Fellow Coll. Chaplains; mem. Suprs. Assn. for Clin. Pastoral Edn., Assn. for Clin. Pastoral Edn. (cert. supr.). Avocations: computers, collecting art. Office: South Chgo Community Hosp 2320 E 93d St Chicago IL 60617

BROWN, WINFRED JAMES, minister; b. Penokee, Kans., June 24, 1926; s. Gilbert Barton and Joann Elizabeth (McGuire) B.; m. Esther Fern Bell, Sept. 12, 1946; children: James Delbert, Charlene Ruth. ThB, Colo. Springs Bible Coll., 1950. Ordained to ministry Wesleyan Ch., 1952. Pastor Pilgrim Holiness Ch., Stratton, Nebr., 1950-55, Boulder, Colo., 1955-58; Pastor Pilgrim Holiness Ch., Colorado Springs, 1958-65, dist. supt., 1965-68; dist. supt. The Wesleyan Ch., Colorado Springs, 1968-76, pastor, 1976—; trustee Bartlesville (Okla.) Wesleyan Coll., 1960-76; del. Gen. Conf. Wesleyan Ch., 1954-76. With U.S. Army, 1944-46; EtO. Republican. Home: 2404 Providence Circle Colorado Springs CO 80909 Office: Mountain View Wesleyan Ch 1204 E Bijou Colorado Springs CO 80909

BROWNE, JAMES LOWRIE, minister; b. Princeton, N.J., Jan. 30, 1947; s. Frances William and Joan (Campbell) B.; m. Virginia Anne Kaltenborn, Sept. 5, 1967; children: Douglas David, Joan Kathleen, Andrew James. BS, Kent State U., 1974; MDiv, Pitts. Theol. Sem., 1978. Ordained to ministry Presbyn. Ch. (U.S.A.), 1978. Pastor Ft. Burd Presbyn. Ch., Brownsville, Pa., 1978-83, Shiloh Presbyn. Ch., St. Marys, Pa., 1983-86, Calvary Presbyn. Ch., Denver, 1986—. 1st lt. U.S. Army, 1970-73. Office: Calvary Presbyn Ch 1420 S Holly St Denver CO 80222

BROWNING, DON SPENCER, religion educator; b. Trenton, Mo., Jan. 13, 1934; s. Robert W. and Nelle J. (Trotter) B.; m. Carol Kohl, Sept. 27, 1958; children: Elizabeth Dell, and Christopher Robert. A.B., Central Methodist Coll., 1956; B.D., U. Chgo. Div. Sch., 1959, M.A., 1962, Ph.D., 1964. Asst. prof. Grad. Sem. Phillips U., Enid, Okla., 1963-65; instr. religion and personality U. Chgo. Div. Sch., 1965-66, asst. prof., 1967-68, assoc. prof., 1968-77, prof., 1977-80, Alexander Campbell prof., 1980—; dean Disciples Divinity House U. Chgo., 1977-83. Author: Atonement and Psychotherapy, 1966, Generative Man, 1973, The Moral Context of Pastoral Care, 1976, Pluralism and Personality, 1980, Practical Theology, 1983, Religious Ethics and Pastoral Care, 1983, Religious Thought and The Modern Psychologies, 1987, A Fundamental Practical Theology, 1991; assoc. editor: Zygon; editor Jour. of Religion; mem. editorial bd. Jour. of Pastoral Care, Pastoral Psychology, Toronto Jour. of Theology. Nat. Book award finalist, 1974; Guggenheim fellow, 1975-76. Mem. Am. Acad. Religion, Assn. Practical Theology, Internat. Acad. Practical Theology (pres. 1991—0, Soc. Sci. Study Religion., Assn. Christian Ethics. Office: Univ Chgo 1025 E 58th St Chicago IL 60637

BROWNING, EDMOND LEE, bishop; b. Corpus Christi, Tex.; s. Edmond Lucian and Cora Mae (Lee) B.; m. Patricia Sparks, Sept. 10, 1953; children: Robert Mark, Patricia Paige, Philip Myles, Peter Sparks, John Charles. B.A., U. of South, 1952, B.D., 1954, D.D., 1970; D.D., Gen. Theological Seminary, 1986, Ch. Divinity Sch. of Pacific, 1987, Seabury Western Seminary, 1987, Trinity Coll., Hartford, Conn., 1988, Va. Theol. Sch., 1989; DHL, Chaminade U., Honolulu, 1985, St. Paul's Coll., Lawrenceville, Va., 1987. Ordained priest Episcopal Ch., 1954, named bishop, 1968; curate Ch. of the Good Shepherd, Corpus Christi, 1954-56; rector Redeemer Ch., Eagle Pass, Tex., 1956-59, All Souls Ch., Okinawa, 1959-63, St. Matthews Ch., Okinawa, 1965-67; archdeacon Okinawa Episcopal Ch., 1965-67, 1st missionary bishop of Okinawa, 1968-71; bishop of convocation Episcopal Chs. in Europe, 1971-74; exec. Nat. and World Mission Exec. Council, N.Y.C., 1974-76, 82-83; bishop of Hawaii, 1976-85; Bd. dirs. Anglican Center, Rome, 1971-74, St. Stephens Sch., Rome, 1971-74; mem. Anglican Consultative Council, 1982—. Named hon. canon St. Michaels Cathedral Kobe, Japan, St. George's Cathedral, Jerusalem. Address: 815 2nd Ave New York NY 10017 also: Box 6120 Little Rock AR 72216

BROWNING, GUSTON HASSELL, minister, religious foundation administrator; b. Frankston, Tex., Dec. 21, 1926; s. Thomas Edgar and Avery Annie (Zorn) B.; m. Jacquelyn Odom, Sept. 8, 1949; children: Michael Wayne, Mark Edwin, Rebecca, Barbara Lyn. BA with high honors, U. Tex., 1949; MDiv with honors, So. Meth. U., 1953; DD (hon.), Wiley Coll., Marshall, Tex., 1975. Ordained to ministry United Meth. Ch., 1953. Rehab. counselor Tex. Commn. for Blind, Houston, 1949-51; pastor Meth. chs. in, Tatum and Henderson, Tex., 1953-58, Asbury Meth. Ch., Beaumont, Tex., 1958-61; pastor lst Meth. Ch., Livingston, Tex., 1961-66, La Porte, Tex., 1966-71; pastor Williams Meml. Meth. Ch., Texarkana, Tex., 1971-77, Gethsemane United Meth. Ch., Houston, 1977-82, St. Luke's United Meth. Ch., Kilgore, Tex., 1982-87; exec. dir. Tex. Conf. Found., Houston, 1987—; chmn. bd. ch. and sec. Tex. Meth. Conf., 1960-64, bd. health and welfare, 1972-76, bd. global ministries, 1986-87; pres. ministerial alliances, various cities, 1966-87. Trustee Meth. Home, Waco, Tex., 1972-76; chmn. bd. trustees Meth. Mission Home, San Antonio, 1980-82. Rotary Paul Harris fellow, 1984. Mem. Nat. Assn. United Meth. Found. Dirs., Houston Planned Giving, Phi Beta Kappa. Democrat. Avocations: stamps, coins, photography, tennis, mountain climbing. Home: 10309 Briar Forest Dr Houston TX 77042-2401 Office: United Meth Found 5215 Main St Houston TX 77002 *Paraphrasing William James, the great use of life (short or long) and the great use of money (be it a little or a lot) is to invest them in something worthwhile that will outlast them.*

BROWNING, ROBERT LYNN, educator, clergyman; b. Gallatin, Mo., June 19, 1924; s. Robert W. and Nelle J. (Trotter) B.; BA, Mo. Valley Coll., 1945; MDiv, Union Theol. Sem., 1948; PhD, Ohio State U., 1960; postgrad. Columbia U., 1951-53, Oxford (Eng.) U., 1978-79, 84-85; m. Jean Beatty, Dec. 27, 1947 (dec. 1977); children: Gregory, David, Peter, Lisa; m. Jackie L. Rogers, Aug. 26, 1979. Ordained to ministry Disciples of Christ Ch., 1947, transferred to United Meth. Ch., 1950; minister edn. Old Stone Ch., Meadville, Pa., 1946-51, Community Ch. at the Circle, Mt. Vernon, N.Y., 1951-53, North Broadway United Meth. Ch., Columbus, Ohio, 1953-59; prof. Christian edn. Meth. Theol. Sch., Delaware, Ohio, 1959-72, William A. Chryst prof. Christian edn., 1972-89, prof. emeritus, 1989—; sr. counselor Coun. for Ethics in Econs., 1989—; pres. Meth. Conf. on Christian edn., 1967-69; exec. dir. Commn. on Role of the Professions in Soc., fellow Acad. for Contemporary Problems, 1974-76, cons., 1976—. Bd. dirs. Southside Settlement, Columbus, 1968-74, Tray-Lee Center, Columbus, 1955-59, Ohio State U. Wesley Found., 1960-78, vice chmn. 1976-78; bd. ministry Ohio West Conf. United Meth. Ch., 1982-89. With USN, 1942-45. Recipient Paul Hinkhouse award Religious Public Relations Council Am., 1971. Mem. Assn. for Profl. Edn. for Ministry (editor proc. 1980-82), Religious Edn. Assn., Assn. of Profs. and Researchers in Religious Edn. (pres. 1989), United Meth. Profs. Christian Edn. Author: Communication with Junior Highs, 1968, Guidelines for Youth Ministry, 1970, What on Earth Are You Doing, 1966; (audiotape with Charles Foster) Communicating the Faith with Children, 1971, Ways the Bible Comes Alive, 1975, Ways Persons Become Christian, 1976, (with Charles Foster, Everett Tilson) Looking at Leadership with the Eyes of Biblical Faith, 1978, (with Roy Reed) the Sacraments in Religious Education and Liturgy: An Ecumenical Model, 1985; contbg. author: Preventing Adolescent Alienation: An Interprofessional Approach, 1983, Children, Parents and Change, 1984, Interprofessional Education, 1987; editor: Integration: Objective Studies and Practical Theology, Proc. Assn. Profl. Edn. for Ministry, 1981, The Pastor as Religious Educator, 1989; contbg. author: Congregations: Their Power to Form and Transform, 1988; contbr. articles on religious edn. to profl. jours. Home: 6613 Hawthorne St Worthington OH 43085

BROWNING, SCOTT DAVID, minister; b. Columbus, Ohio, Jan. 16, 1931; s. Dallas Lynn and Ella Mae (West) B.; m. Ruth Anna Wright, June 8, 1953; children: Donald Wayne, Douglas William. BA, Earlham Coll., 1953; BD, Garrott Theol. Sem., 1956, MDiv, 1972; DMin, Drew Theol. Sem., 1980. Ordained to ministry United Meth. Ch. Exec. sec. St. Paul Goodwill Industries, 1957-60; chaplain Goodwill Industries Pitts., 1961; pastor Mars (Pa.) United Meth. Ch., 1962-66, Homer City (Pa.) United Meth. Ch., 1966-75, Herminie (Pa.) United Meth. Ch., 1975-82, Ford Meml. United Meth. Ch., Ford City, Pa., 1982-90, Clymer (Pa.) United Meth. Ch., 1990—; dist. sec. Bd. of Missions, 1982-84; conf. sec. Global Missions, 1984-90. Bd. dirs. Keystone Tall Trees Girl Scout, 1983-89. Mem. Kiwanis (Disting. lt. gov. div. 10 1973, Disting. pres. 1979, sec.-treas. 1983-90, Internat. Found. fellow 1988), Masons. Democrat. Avocations: photography, traveling. Home: 2592 Shelley Dr Indiana PA 15701 Office: Clymer United Meth Ch Box 192 Clymer PA 15738

BROWNING, WILLIAM BLAINE, minister; b. Middletown, Ohio, Oct. 10, 1953; s. Ward Blaine and Nancy (Erwin) B.; m. Kathy Ann Hughes, Dec. 7, 1974; children: Naomi, Jesse, Seth, Zachary. Diploma in bibl. studies, Maranatha Inst., Centerville, Ohio, 1978, grad. in theology, 1979; BA in Bibl. Studies, Luther Rice Sem., Jacksonville, Fla., 1983. Lic. to ministry Bapt. Ch., 1978; ordained to ministry, 1979. Asst. pastor Wilmington (Ohio) Assembly of God, 1977-78; asst. pastor 1st Bapt. Ch. of Centerville, 1979-83, pastor, 1983—; trustee Uttermost Missions Bd., Cin., 1986—, New Life Ministries Internat. Bd., Dallas, 1989—. Home: 331 Whittington Centerville OH 45459 Office: 1st Bapt Ch Centerville 38 N Main St Centerville OH 45459 *No greater priviledge has been given to man than the invitation to come and commune with God in Christ. That each person have a private audience with God is man's greatest dignity.*

BROWNLEE, JUDITH MARILYN, Wiccan minister; b. Beaumont, Tex., May 16, 1940; d. Alvin Maurice and Juanita M. (Whittington) B.; m. Theodore Blakey Peak, Apr. 12, 1974 (div. 1981); 1 child, Daniel David Brownlee Peak. BA, Lamar U., Beaumont, Tex., 1962; postgrad., U. Denver, 1971, Avalon Inst., Boulder, Colo., 1989. Tchr. Deer Trail (Colo.) High Sch., 1963-64, Lutcher Stark High Sch., Orange, Tex., 1967-69; library technician Denver Pub. Library, 1970-73; bus. exec. Weight Watchers Rocky Mtn., Denver, 1974; mailorder div. mgr. Mile High Comics and Books, Denver, 1975-81; religious student Our Lady Perpet. Responsibility, The Silent Cir., 1975-79; religious tchr. The Silent Cir., Denver, 1979-83; gov. employee Colo. Atty. Gen. Office, Denver, 1983--; minister Fortress Temple, Denver, 1984--; pub. speaker, Denver, 1988--, workshop leader, Spring Mysteries Festival, Seattle, 1988, lectr. Isis Metaphysical Ctr., workshop leader, 1985--, organizer Front Range Pagan Festival, 1985, workshop leader Dragonfest Pagan Festival, Denver, 1987--. Author: Pagan Parenting, 1987, The Wheel of the Year, 1988. Contbr. articles to profl. jours. Interviewee KOA Radio, 1984, KUSA Channel 9, 1987, 90; community producer Mile High Cablevision, 1987; telephone counselor Lifeline of Colo., Denver, 1988. Mem. Assn. Past Life Rsch. and Therapy, Women's Spiritual Leadership Alliance, Daus. the New Moon (founder, facilitator), Soc. for Creative Anachronism (Colo. founder 1970-73, treas. 1981-83), Denver Area Sci. Fiction Assn. (editor, 1969-70, dir. 1974-75, convention chair, 1970-75), Covenant Unitarian Universalist Pagans. Avocations: reading, theatre, films, sci. fiction. Office: Fortress Temple PO Box 65 1525 Sherman C S 6 Denver CO 80203 *The two most important issues of the coming decade will be return of the Goddess (the feminine in Diety) and the re-imaging of our planet as Her Body (the Gaia Theory). We must give up our persona of "dominance over Nature" and remember again that we are part of Nature. This is true worship.*

BROWNSON, WILLIAM CLARENCE, minister, broadcast ministry company executive; b. Charlotte, N.C., June 27, 1928; s. William Clarence and Vivian Juanita (Clements) B.; m. Helen Stewart, Aug. 25, 1951; children—William C., David A., James V., Jonathan C. BA, Davidson Coll., 1949; BD, Columbia Theol. Sem., 1952; ThD, Princeton Theol. Sem., 1963; DD (hon.), Central U. Iowa, 1984, Northwestern Coll. Iowa, 1991. Pastor 2nd Reformed Ch., Lodi, N.J., 1953-59; pastor 1st Reformed Ch., Roseland, Ill., 1959-64; prof. preaching Western Theol. Sem., Holland, Mich., 1964-74; pres., broadcast minister Words of Hope, Inc., Grand Rapids, Mich., 1974—; pres. gen. synod Reformed Ch. Am., N.Y.C., 1984-85; pres. Heritage Homes, Holland, 1972-73. Author: Tried by Fire, 1972, Distinctive Lessons From Luke, 1974, Do You Believe?, 1975, Courage to Pray, 1989. Mem. Nat. Assn. Religious Broadcasters, Phi Beta Kappa. Home: 280 Sunset Bluff Ct Holland MI 49424 Office: Words of Hope 700 Ball Ave Grand Rapids MI 49503

BRUBAKER, LAUREN EDGAR, educator, minister; b. Birmingham, Ala., Oct. 8, 1914; s. Lauren Edgar and Nora (Drake) B.; m. Leonte Saye, June 6, 1944; children: Lauren Eugene, Edward Saye. A.B., Birmingham So. Coll., 1935; M.Div., Princeton Theol. Sem., 1938, postdoctoral, 1946-47; S.T.M., Union Theol. Sem., N.Y., 1943, Th.D., 1944. Ordained to ministry Presbyn. Ch., 1938. Asst. pastor in Parkersburg, W.Va., 1938-41; grad. asst. Union Theol. Sem., 1941-43; chaplain U.S. Army, 1943-46; grad. instr. Princeton Theol. Sem., 1946-47; prof. philosophy and religion, chaplain Parsons Coll., Fairfield, Iowa, 1947-49; assoc. prof. U. S.C., Columbia, 1949-58, prof., 1958-79, Disting. prof., 1979-80, Disting. prof. emeritus, 1980—, chmn. dept. religion, 1949-80, chaplain, 1949—; adj. prof. Luth. Theol. So. Sem.; moderator Univ. Forum on S.C. Ednl. TV, 1965-73. Contbr. articles to profl. jours. Dir. S.C. Council Human Relations, 1966-69; exec. committeeman Columbia and Richland County Democratic party, 1950-60. Served to maj. AUS, 1943-46. Mem. Inst. Religion (dir. 1960-63), S.C. Acad. Religion (founder 1968, pres. 1968), Am. Acad. Religion (pres. 1960), Presbyn. Edn. Assn. South, Columbia Ministers Assn. (pres. 1972), Assn. for Coll. and Univ. Religious Affairs (bd. dirs. 1985-86), AAUP (past officer), Columbia Forum on Internat. Affairs (pres. 1971), Columbia Coun. for Internats. (bd. dirs., pres. 1986, 87), Nat. Assn. Coll. and Univ. Chaplains, Soc. Bibl. Lit. (past officer), Christian Jewish Congress S.C. (sec. 1982—), Columbia CROP WALK (treas. 1983—), Common Cause of S.C. (dir. 1988—, sec. 1989—), Omicron Delta Kappa (faculty adviser 1968-71), Pi Gamma Mu, Phi Kappa Phi, Tau Kappa Alpha. Club: Executive of Columbia (pres. 1960-61). Lodge: Kiwanis (pres. 1986-87). Research teaching religion in accredited colls. and univs. Home: 9 Churchill Circle Columbia SC 29206

BRUCHARD, CHARLES E., academic administrator; b. Superior, Wis., Dec. 5, 1951; s. Charles and Catherine (Everall) B. BA, St. John's U., 1974; MA, M. Div., Aquinas Inst., 1979. Instr. Clarke Coll., 1979, Rosary Coll., 1981, The Catholic U. of Am., 1985-86;; asst. prof. Aquinas Inst. of Theology St. Louis, from 1986; now head. Mem. Cath. Theol. Soc. of Am. Office: Aquinas Inst Theol 3642 Lindell Blvd Saint Louis MO 63108*

BRUEGGEMANN, DALE ALAN., religion educator; b. Boise, Idaho, July 20, 1949; s. Homer Arthur and Mary Lou (Bundy) B.; m. Janice Colleen Steep, Aug. 19, 1968; children: Keri Lynn, Julie Ann. BA, N.W. Nazarene Coll., 1979; MA in Religion, Westminster Theol. Sem., 1983, postgrad., 1984—. Pastor Horseshoe Bend (Idaho) Assembly of God, 1972-77; asst. pastor Crossroads Assembly of God, Wilder, Idaho, 1977-79; lectr. in philosophy Valley Forge Christian Coll., Phoenixville, Pa., 1984-88; asst. prof. hermeneutics and Old Testament Cen. Bible Coll., Springfield, Mo., 1989—; lectr. in Bible studies Assemblies of God Theol. Sem., Springfield. Contbr. articles to profl. jours. With U.S. Army, 1970-71, Vietnam. Recipient Marvin Cook Bible award N.W. Nazarene Coll., 1979. Mem. Am. Acad. of Religion, Inst. Bibl. Rsch., Evang. Theol. Soc. Home: 700 S Rogers Ave Springfield MO 65804 Office: Cen Bible Coll 3000 N Grant Springfield MO 65803

BRUESKE, PATRICK JEREMY, radio announcer, radio station executive; b. Huntington, N.Y., Dec. 29, 1964; s. Robert Elroy and Mertice Adelle (Spaude) B. BS, Northwestern Coll., Roseville, Minn., 1987. On-air announcer, music dir. Sta. KBHL-FM Radio, Osakis, Minn., 1987—; asst. dir. bd. pub. rels. Zion Luth. Ch. and Sch., Alexandria, Minn., 1988-90; assoc. sound system operator Lake Community Free Ch., Alexandria, 1990—. Office: Sta KBHL-FM 515 Pike St E Osakis MN 56360

BRUESS, DAVID LINCOLN, minister; b. Springfield, Minn., July 9, 1961; s. Lincoln Frank and Freda Alvera (Schliesner) B.; m. Tracy Lynn Woodard, Aug. 21, 1982. BA in Bible/Ministry, Minn. Bible Coll., Rochester, 1983. Ordained to ministry, Christian Ch./Ch. of Christ, 1983. Minister Sunnyview Christian Ch., Oshkosh, Wis., 1984—; head chaplain Oshkosh Police Dept., 1987—. Chmn. Oshkosh YMCA Youth Com., 1986—. Mem. Wis. Christian Missionary Assn. (pres. 1989—). Office: Sunnyview Christian Ch 175 E County Y Oshkosh WI 54901

BRUINGTON, JOHN EDWARD, minister; b. Fullerton, Calif., Nov. 22, 1947; s. Gustavus Edward and Katherine Louise (Edgerton) B.; m. Sheri Sherburne, Sept. 1, 1979; children: Nathaniel, Andrew. BA, Purdue U., 1970; MDiv., Princeton Sem., 1977; DMin., McCormick Sem., 1988. Ordained to ministry United Presbyn. Ch. (U.S.A.), 1977. Asst. pastor 1st Presbyn., Great Falls, Mont., 1977-79; pastor Community Presbyn., Lingle, Wyo., 1979-84, 1st Presbyn., Huron, S.D., 1984-91; pastor, head of staff 1st Presbyn., Grand Junction, Colo., 1991—; pres. Great Falls (Mont.) Ministerial, 1977-78; sec. Huron (S.D.) Ministerial, 1986-88, pres. 1988-89. Bd. mem. Salvation Army, Huron, 1990-91. Mem. Presbyns. for Renewal (bd. dirs. 1989—). Office: 1st Presbyn 622 White Ave Grand Junction CO 81501 *It often seems to me that evil is less of a force in itself than a result of the absense of Good. As the lack of light causes darkness and the lack of order engenders chaos, so the exclusion of God from our lives and society establishes the reign of Satan.*

BRUINS, ELTON JOHN, college dean, religion educator; b. Fairwater, Wis., July 29, 1927; s. Clarence Raymond and Angeline Theodora (Kemink) B.; m. Elaine Ann Redeker, June 24, 1954; children: Mary Elaine Bruins Plasman, David Lewis. BA, Hope Coll., 1950; BD, Western Theol. Sem., 1953; S.T.M., Union Theol. Sem., 1957; PhD, NYU, 1962. Ordained to ministry Reformed Ch., 1954. Pastor, Reformed Ch., Elmsford, N.Y., 1955-61, Flushing, N.Y., 1961-66; prof. religion Hope Coll., Holland, Mich., 1966—, chmn. religion dept., 1977-84, dean arts and humanities, 1984-89, acting provost, 1989; archivist Western Theol. Sem., Holland, 1967-78, Netherlands Mus., Holland, 1968-80. Author: The Americanization of a Congregation, 1970. Contbr. articles to profl. jours. Chmn. Hist./Cultural Commn., Holland, 1978-82. Served with USNR, 1945-46. Named to Evert J. and Hattie E. Blekkink Chair of Religion, Hope Coll., 1980. Mem. Assn. for Advancement Dutch-Am. Studies (pres. 1983), Am. Soc. Ch. History, Midwest Archives Conf., State Hist. Soc. Wis. Democrat. Mem. Reformed Ch. Home: 633 Appletree Dr Holland MI 49423 Office: Hope Coll Religion Dept Holland MI 49423

BRUMM, JAMES LESLIE HART, minister; b. New Brunswick, N.J., Nov. 11, 1962; s. James Allen and Ruth Leslie (Soden) B.; m. Kathleen Louise Hart, June 1, 1985. MusB, Westminster Choir Coll., 1984; MDiv, New Brunswick Theol. Sem., 1987, MA in Theology, 1989. Ordained to ministry Reformed Ch. in Am., 1987. Choir dir. Bethel Presbyn. Ch., Plainfield, N.J., 1982-84, New Brunswick (N.J.) Theol. Sem., 1985-87; asst. clk. Classis of New Brunswick, South River, N.J., 1989—; pastor First Reformed Ch., South River, 1987—; treas. Coun. of Congregations, South River, 1987-89, trustee, 1990—, clergy co-chair, 1991. Author: Singing the Lord's Song: A History of the English Language Hymnals of the Reformed Church in America, 1990; contbr. articles to profl. jours. Trustee Nat. Ch. Residences, South River, 1989—; chair Local Assistance Bd., South River, 1990—; bd. dirs. Community Food Bank, South River, 1988-91. Recipient John W. Beardslee III Prize in Reformed Ch. History, 1989. Mem. Hymn Soc. in the U.S. and Canada, Hymn Soc. Gt. Britain and Ireland, New Brunswick Theol. Sem. Alumni/ae Assn. (v.p. 1991—). Home: 42 Thomas St South River NJ 08882-1144 Office: 1st Reformed Ch 42 Thomas St South River NJ 08882-1144

BRUMMEL, DOUGLAS JOHN, lay minister; b. Plano, Ill., Feb. 8, 1964; s. Fredrick Raymond and Lillian Regina (Kammes) B. BS, Ill. State U., 1986; MS in Counseling, Ill. Benedictine Coll., 1990. Min. youth St. Anne Parish, Oswego, Ill., 1987-91; lay youth min., dir. retreats Plano, Ill., 1991—. Roman Catholic. Address: 12480 Galena Rd Plano IL 60545

BRUMMEL, MARK JOSEPH, magazine editor; b. Chgo., Oct. 28, 1933; s. Anthony William and Mary (Helmreich) B. BA, Cath. U. Am., 1956, STL, 1961, MSLS, 1964. Joined Order of Claretians, Roman Cath. Ch., 1952; ordained priest Order of Caretians, Roman Cath. Ch., 1960; librarian, tchr. St. Jude Sem., Momence, Ill., 1961-70; asso. editor U.S. Cath. mag., Chgo., 1971-72; editor U.S. Cath. Mag., 1970—; dir. St. Jude League, Chgo., 1970—; bd. dirs. Eastern Province Claretians, 8th Day Ctr.; pres. bd. dirs. Claretian Med. Ctr., 1980—. Editor Today mag., 1970-71; contbr. article to publ. Chmn. bd. Eighth Day Ctr. For Justice, Chgo., 1988—, Claretian Med. Ctr., Chgo., 1979—; bd. dirs. United Neighborhood Orgn. South Chgo., 1981-90. Mem. Cath. Press Assn. (v.p. 1985-87), Associated Ch. Press. Avocation: photography. Home: 400 N Euclid Ave Oak Park IL 60302 Office: US Cath 205 W Monroe St Chicago IL 60606

BRUNEAU, WILLIAM JOSEPH, JR., minister; b. New Haven, Feb. 27, 1947; s. William Joseph Bruneau and Erma Luca Schipritt; m. Barbara Boynton, Mar. 28, 1970; children: Heidi Bruneau Hayes, Michael William. BA in Bibl. Studies, Breadloaf Bible Coll., Burlington, N.C., 1985; postgrad., Earlham Sch. Religion, Richmond, Ind. Ordained to ministry Elim Fellowship, 1981, The Christian and Missionary Alliance, 1987. Vice pres. World Harvest Evangelism of New Eng., Durham, Conn., 1977-80; founder, dir. The Storefront St. Ministry, Meriden, Conn., 1981—; assoc. pastor The Ch. of the Living God, Farmington, Conn., 1981-85; pastor The Community Ch. of the Cross, Richmond, Ind., 1985-91, Moreland (Ind.) Friends Meeting, 1991—; evangelist World Harvest Evangelism, Madurai, India, 1979; chmn. Christian Life and Witness, So. New Eng. Billy Graham Crusade, 1984-85; chaplain Wayne County Jail, Richmond, 1986—; founer, dir. The "Fire Escape" radio/concert ministry, Richmond, 1987—. Columnist Sr. Life Mag., 1990—. Bd. dirs. Richmond Jr. Players, 1987,

Mental Health Assn. Wayne County, Richmond, 1990—. William W. Wildman Found. scholar, 1991. Mem. Richmond Ministerial Assn. (bd. dirs., pres. 1987), Wayne County C. of C. (co-chmn. promotion and advt. devel. 1987, chmn. Quality of Life Com. 1988). Home: 305 N Broad St PO Box 180 Mooreland IN 47360 Office: Mooreland Friends Ch N Jefferson St Mooreland IN 47360 *The Church must not live in isolation from its surroundings. If we expect our communities to hear and respond to the message of Christ, then the church must hear and respond to the voice of its community. To be heard we must also hear.*

BRUNER, LAMAN HARMON, JR., priest; b. Buffalo, Aug. 14, 1917; s. Laman Harmon Sr. and Susan Kathryn (Partington) B.; m. Sarah Whitney Barnes, June 2, 1945; children: Jeffery, Laman Harmon III, Todd, Benjamin, James. BA, U. Buffalo, 1939; MA, Boston U., 1940; M of Div., Harvard U., 1942; DD (hon.), Harwick Coll., Oneonta, N.Y., 1958; LLD (hon.), U. Maine, 1959; DST (hon.), Coll. of St. Rose, Albany, N.Y., 1962. Rector St. John's Episcopal Ch., Roanoke, Va., 1942-43; asst. St. Bartholomew's Ch., N.Y.C., 1943-46; rector Trinity Ch., Indpls., 1946-52, St. Peter's Ch., Albany, 1952—, St. Ann's Ch., Kennebunkport, Maine, 1962—; chaplain N.Y. State Assembly, Albany, 1962-90. Office: St Peter's Episcopal Ch 107 State St Albany NY 12207 also: PO Box 7162 Albany NY 12224

BRUNGARDT, HELEN RUTH, minister; b. Littlefield, Tex., Sept. 2, 1931; d. Isaac Henry and Helen Irene (Hanna) Pelt; m. Guido Milton Brungardt, July 22, 1950 (div.); children: Karla Kay, Linda Gail, Mark Douglas, Celeste Dawn; m. Mark J. Pope, Jan. 1990. Student, Tex. Christian U., 1948-49, U. N.Mex., 1969, Divine Sci. Ednl. Ctr., 1976-80. Tchr. Napoleon Hill Acad., Albuquerque, 1964-66; practitioner First Ch. Religious Sci., Albuquerque, 1969-72, tchr., 1971-72; founder, minister Symphony of Life Ch., Albuquerque, 1972-81; founder, dir., pres. Inst. for the Emerging Self, Albuquerque, 1981—; cons. ministers, individuals, 1977—; lectr. various orgns., radio, tv, 1975—; instr. Profl. Leadership Tng., Albuquerque, 1965-82; bd. dirs., co-founder Grand Teton Retreat. Author: Contemplation, 1975, Mystical Meaning of Jesus, 1980, Beyond Liberation, 1985; contbr. articles to profl. jours. Mem. Divine Sci. Fedn., Internat. New Thought Alliance. Republican. Mem. Ch. Divine Sci. Avocations: fishing, pilgrimage organizer and leader. Home: PO Box 567 Columbus NM 88029 *Assuming and accepting that there is only one Presence, Power and Intelligence I practice resting in this reality reminding my ego to surrender.*

BRUNGS, ROBERT ANTHONY, theology educator, institute director; b. Cin., July 7, 1931; s. Adolph and Helen (Klosterman) B. AB, Bellarmine Coll., Plattsburgh, N.Y., 1955; Licentiate in Philosophy, Fordham U., 1956; PhD in Physics, St. Louis U., 1962; Sacred Theology Licentiae, Woodstock (Md.) Coll., 1965. Asst. prof. physics St. Louis U., 1970-75, assoc. prof. physics, 1975-83; dir. Inst. for Theol. Encounter with Sci. and Tech., St. Louis, 1968—; cons. Vatican, Rome, 1973-84, Council Cath. Bishops, Washington, 1973—; mem. adv. bd. Zygon Mag., Chgo., 1975—. Exec. producer video program DECISION, 1987, Lights Breaking, 1985; author: Building the City,1 967, A Priestly People, 1968, You See Lights Breaking Upon Us: Doctrinal Perspectives on Biological Advance, 1989; contbr. 60 articles to mags., newspapers, profl. jours. Mem. AAAS, Am. Phys. Soc., Sigma Xi, Phi Beta Kappa. Office: Inst for Theol Encounter with Sci and Tech 221 N Grand Blvd Saint Louis MO 63103

BRUNK, GEORGE E., III, academic administrator; b. Newport News, Va., May 5, 1939; s. George and Margaret (Suter) B.; m. Erma Ness; children: Douglas, Valerie. BA, Ea. Mennonite Coll., 1961; M. Div., 1964; D. Th., Union Theol. Sem., 1975. Dean & prof. Ea. Mennonite Sem., Harrisonburg, Va., from 1974; now head. Mem. Soc. Biblical Lit. Office: Ea Mennonite Sem Harrisonburg VA 22801*

BRUNKAN, WALTER LEO, priest; b. Dyersville, Iowa, Aug. 5, 1930; s. Anton C. and Mary M. (Heiring) B. BA, Loras Coll., 1952; MS in Edn., Creighton U., 1963. Assoc. pastor Immaculate Conception Ch., Charles City, Iowa, 1956-59; high sch. assoc. prin. Columbus High Sch., Waterloo, Iowa, 1959-68; high sch. prin. Columbus High Sch., Waterloo, 1968—. Youth task force mem. Met. Task Force against Gangs, 1988—. Mem. C. of C. (edn. com. 1980—), United Way Cedar Valley (bd. dirs. 1988—), Good Will Cedar Calley (bd. dirs. 1988—), ARC (blood com.), Make a Wish Found. (bd. dirs. 1985-91), Exch. Club. Home: 627 W 4th St Waterloo IA 50702 Office: Columbus High Sch 3231 W 9th St Waterloo IA 50702

BRUNNER, DAVID DERSTINE, chaplain; b. Quakertown, Pa., Oct. 12, 1938; s. Edgar Overholt and Anna Moyer (Derstine) B.; m. Fern Lois Graybill, Dec. 22, 1961 (div. July 1986); children: Wendy Marie, Marta Lane, Daryl Lynn; m. Jo Ann M. Davis, May 11, 1991. BA in Sociology, Goshen Coll., 1960; BD, Goshen Bibl. Sem., 1965; ThM, Crozer Theol. Sem., 1969. Ordained to ministry Mennonite Ch., 1967. Pastor Summit Christian Fellowship, Barberton, Ohio, 1965-70; chaplain Akron (Ohio) Gen. Med. Ctr., 1969-72; caseworker Summit County Child Welfare, Akron, 1965-68; counselor Interval Brotherhood Homes, Akron, 1971-72; dir. Letcher County Family Svcs., Whitesburg, Ky., 1972-75; pastor Nairn Mennonite Ch., Ailsa Craig, Ont., Can., 1975-83; chaplain Craigholme Nursing Home, Ailsa Craig, 1975-83; therapist Bluewater Counseling Svcs., Parkhill, Ont., 1983; chaplain Greencroft Inc., Goshen, Ind., 1984—. Bd. dirs. Goshen Area Adult Day Care, pres. 1990-91. Mem. Alzheimers Assn. North Ind. Chpt. (bd. dirs.), Mennonite Health Assn. (bd. dirs.), Goshen Ministerial Assn. Avocations: leatherwork, furniture refinishing, music. Home: 57915 CR 13 Elkhart IN 46516 Office: Greencroft Inc 1820 Greencroft Dr PO Box 819 Goshen IN 46526

BRUSH, DUANE CARTER, pastor; b. Quincy, Ill., July 18, 1950; s. Lelon Bernard and Helen Pauline (Harness) B.; m. Nora Jane Holmes, Aug. 7, 1971; 1 child, David Carter. ThB, Olivet Nazarene U., Kankakee, Ill., 1974; MDiv, Nazarene Theol. Sem., Kansas City, Mo., 1978. Ordained elder Ch. of Nazarene, 1982. Pastor lst Ch. of Nazarene, Longmont, Colo., 1978-88; assoc. pastor Longmont Ch. of Nazarene, 1988-89; pastor 1st Ch. of Nazarene, Mexico, Mo., 1989—; mem. ministerial studies bd. Colo. dist. Ch. of Nazarene, 1985-89, mem. fin. com., 1986-88, sec. ministerial studies bd. Mo. dist., 1990—. Compilor: Worship in Song: Supplementary Indexes, 1983. Founder Longmont United Hosp. Chaplaincy, 1979; regional dir. Rocky Mountain Billy Graham Crusade, Denver, 1987; coord. Longmont Pub. Safety Chaplaincy, 1988; mem. Mexico Pub. Sch. Planning and Rev. Com., 1990. Recipient cert. of merit Longmont Dept. Pub. Safety, 1989. Mem. Mex. Ministerial Alliance (v.p. 1991-91, pres. 1991-92), Kiwanis. Home and Office: 1st Ch of Nazarene 426 Teal Lake Rd Mexico MO 65265 *Inner transformation only comes when we reach outside ourselves, to God and then to others.*

BRUSHABER, GEORGE KARL, academic president, minister; b. Milw., Dec. 15, 1938; s. Ralph E. and Marie C. (Meister) B.; m. N. Darleen Dugar, Jan. 27, 1962; children: Deanna Lyn, Donald Paul. BA, Wheaton Coll., 1959, MA, 1962; MDiv, Gordon-Conwell Theol. Sem., 1963; PhD, Boston U., 1967. Ordained to ministry Bapt. Gen. Conf., 1966. Prof. philosophy, chair dept. Gordon Coll., Wenham, Mass., 1963-72; dir. admissions and registration Gordon-Conwell Theol. Sem., 1970-72; v.p., acad. dean Westmont Coll., Santa Barbara, Calif., 1972-75; v.p., dean of coll. Bethel Coll., St. Paul, 1975-82; pres. Bethel Coll. & Theol. Sem., St. Paul and San Diego, 1982—; Staley Found. lectr. Anderson U., Sioux Falls Coll.; sec. for higher edn. Bapt. Gen. Conf., Arlington Heights, Ill., 1982—; cons., evaluator Minn. Humanities Commn., St. Paul. Editor Gordon Rev., 1965-70; pub., founding editor Christian Scholar's Rev., 1970-79; exec. editor Christianity Today, 1985—; contbr. articles to religious jours. Bd. dirs. Youth Leadership, Mpls., 1982—. Mem. Christian Coll. Consortium (bd. dirs. 1982—), Nat. Assn. Evangs. (trustee 1982—), Minn. Pvt. Coll. Coun. (bd. dirs. 1982—), Coun. Ind. Colls. (bd. dirs. 1984-89), Am. Philos. Assn., Evang. Theol. Soc., Am. Assn. Higher Edn., Soc. Christian Philosophers, Fellowship Evang. Sem. Pres., Minn. Club, North Oaks Country Club. Office: Bethel Coll & Theol Sem 3900 Bethel Dr Saint Paul MN 55112

BRUSHWYLER, LAWRENCE RONALD, minister; b. E. Orange, N.J., Jan. 31, 1936; s. Vincent M. and Nan Josephine (Kjelstad) B.; m. Carol Valerie Kinney, June 24, 1961; children: Kevin Ross, Lisa Marlene Brushwyler Larson, Kurt Ronald. BA cum laude, Wheaton (Ill.) Coll., 1958; BD, Fuller Theol. Sem., Pasadena, 1963; STM, Andover Newton Theol. Sem., Newton Center, Mass., 1964; DMin, Bethany Theol. Sem., Oak Brook, Ill., 1983. Ordained to ministry, Am. Bapt. Chs. USA, 1965; lic. marriage, family counselor; nat. cert. counselor. Pastor Trinity Bapt. Ch., Poway, Calif., 1965-68; sr. pastor First Bapt. Ch., San Bruno, Calif., 1968-73; area minister Am. Bapt. Chs. of West, Oakland, Calif., 1973-77; exec. dir. Midwest Career Devel. Svc., Westchester, Ill., 1977—; chmn. strategy com. Ch. Career Devel. Coun., N.Y.C., 1985—; faculty pastoral leadership program Roman Cath. Diocese of Joliet, Ill., 1988—; adj. faculty D.Min. program No. Bapt. Theol. Sem., Lombard, Ill., 1985—. Contbr. articles to profl. jours. Mem. Am. Assn. Marriage and Family Therapists, Am. Assn. Pastoral Counselors, Ill. Psychol. Assn., Am. Assn. for Counseling and Devel. Home: 633 Brighton Dr Wheaton IL 60187 Office: Midwest Career Devel Svc 1840 Westchester Blvd #7249 Westchester IL 60154-7249

BRUSO, ROBERT ARTHUR, minister; b. Plattsburgh, N.Y., June 26, 1939; s. Truman Archie and Marion I. (Thompson) B.; m. Diane Chellis, July 25, 1959; children: Nancy Bruso Groves, Robert Alan, Mark Thomas. Grad. high sch., Plattsburgh. Ordained to ministry The Wesleyan Ch., 1969. Pastor Wesleyan Ch., Ticonderoga, N.Y., 1969-70, Long Lake, N.Y., 1970-78, Chelmsford, Mass., 1978-82; pastor Balltown Wesleyan Ch., Schenectady, 1985—; asst. dist. supt. The Wesleyan Ch., Schenectady, 1985—; mem. Dist. Bd. Adminstrn., Glens Falls, N.Y., 1972—; chmn. Dist. Bd. Ministerial Standing, 1985—; dir. Billy Graham Crusade, Albany, N.Y., 1987-90. Home: 931 Balltown Rd Schenectady NY 12309 Office: Balltown Wesleyan Ch 935 Balltown Rd Schenectady NY 12309

BRUST, LEO, bishop; b. St. Francis, Wis., Jan. 7, 1916. Student, St. Francis Sem., Wis., Canisianum, Austria, Cath. U., Washington. Ordained priest Roman Catholic Ch., 1942; ordained titular bishop of Sueli and aux. bishop Milw., 1969—. Office: 3501 S Lake Dr PO Box 2018 Milwaukee WI 53207

BRUTON, DOROTHY VIRGINIA, minister; b. Chester, Pa., June 4, 1945; d. William Edward and Alma Ellen Rea (Corbin) Minor; m. Leroy E. Bruton, Aug. 7, 1971 (dec. 1979); children: Keith Minor, Quintin Minor, Sheri Bruton. Dipl. Gen. Theology, Jameson Bible Inst., 1984; Cert., Deliverance Bible Inst., Chester, Pa., 1984, Christian Bible Ctr., Chester, Pa., 1981-83, First Pentecostal Holy Ch., Chester, Pa., 1982, 89. Ordained evangelist, Jameson Bible Inst. Bible ch. tchr. First Pentecostal Holy Ch., Chester, Pa., 1978-89, tchr. new mems., 1984-88; tchr. Pillar of Trust Ministries, Chester, 1982-83; assoc. minister First Pentecostal Holy Ch., Chester, 1981—; proprietor Dorothy V. Bruton Assocs., Chester, 1989—; bd. dirs., intercessor Women's Aglow, Chester, 1987-88; tchr. inner healing Deliverance Bible Inst., 1984-86; mem. outreach ministry Crozer Chester Extended Care, 1982-86. Author: In Search of Love/Learning the Hard Way, 1986; author booklets: The Great Summer, 1986, Inspirational Encouragement, 1986. Sec., receptionist Salvation Army, Chester, 1986, 88, 89; active mem. support group Bernardine Ctr., Chester, 1989, Chester Aids Coalition, 1990.

BRUYNZEEL, CHRIS JOHN, youth worker; b. San Jose, Calif., Nov. 2, 1966; s. John and Penelope Ann (Schneider) B. BA in Social Scis., Biola U., 1989; postgrad., Talbot Theol. Sem., La Mirada, Calif., 1991—. Summer camp Counselor Mt. Hermon Inc., Mt. Hermon, Calif., 1989; ministry asst. Peninsula Bible Ch., Cupertino, Calif., 1989-90; vol. high sch. staff Evang. Free Ch. Am., Walnut Creek, Calif., 1990, high sch. intern, 1990, jr. high sch. intern, 1990-91; coach girls and boys soccer Contra Costa Christian High Sch., Walnut Creek, 1991—; asst. coach men's varsity soccer Biola U., 1991. Republican. Home and Office: 2203 Ygnacio Valley Rd Walnut Creek CA 94598 *Life is indeed a blessing. Though we see the pain and hurt around us in the world today, there is something, or rather, someone who can bring joy, love, purpose, and hope—even through the tough times. Thank You, God, for the blessing of new life you have provided in the person of Jesus Christ!.*

BRYAN, CARDIS WILLIAM, JR., minister; b. Dallas, June 2, 1938; s. Cardis William, Sr. and Ruth Nelwyn (Brown) B.; m. Stephanie Ann Chapman, Aug. 31, 1958; children: Julia, Scott, Ruth, Heather. Diploma in theology, So. Bapt. Theol. Sem., Louisville, 1974; BTh, Hannibal LaGrange Coll., 1982; MDiv, Midwestern Bapt. Theol. Sem., Kansas City, Mo., 1983, DMin, 1986. Enlisted U.S. Army, 1958; advanced through ranks to sgt. Tea Creek Bapt. Ch.; retired U.S. Army, 1968; pastor Tea Creek Bapt. Ch., North Vernon, Ind., 1971-75, First Bapt. Ch., Mancos, Colo., 1975-77, Immanuel Bapt. Ch., Ft. Collins, Colo., 1977-80, Ramsey Creek Bapt. Ch., Clarksville, Mo., 1980-82, High Point Bapt. Ch., Raytown, Mo., 1982-88, Fifth St. Bapt. Ch., Hannibal, Mo., 1988—; started Calvary Bapt. Ch., Doloros, Colo., Calvary Bapt. Spanish Chapel, Ft. Collins, Colo.; adj. instr. Old Testament Hannibal LaGrange Coll.; pastoral field edn. supr. Midwestern Bapt. Theol. Sem. 1983-88, Kansas City, Hannibal LaGrange Coll., 1988—; teaching fellow Midwestern Bapt. Theol. Sem., Kansas City, 1985 (seminar leader). Chaplain Raytown Police Dept., bd. dirs. Raytown Community Police Chaplain Svc., mem. Concerned Citizens Com. Avocations: reading, golf. Office: Fifth St Bapt Ch 115 N 5th St Hannibal MO 63401

BRYAN, JOAN CARR, minister; b. Evanston, Ill., May 7, 1944; d. Charles William and Anne Virginia (Baisch) Carr; m. Patrick Swinney Bryan, July 23, 1966; children: David Michael, Elizabeth Anne. AA, Daytona Beach Community Coll., Fla., 1964; BA in Edn., U. Fla., 1966; MDiv, U. of South, Sewanee, Tenn., 1990. Ordained ministry Episcopal Ch. as deacon, 1990, as priest, 1990. Coord. Prayer and Study Ctr., Gainesville, Fla., 1980-82; program dir., pastoral asst. St. Joseph's Episcopal Ch., Gainesville, 1982-87; deacon Christ Episcopal Ch., Ponte Vedra Beach, Fla., 1990, priest, 1990—; mem. various diocesan coms. and commns. Diocese of Fla., Jacksonville, 1979—; mem. Acad. Affairs Com. Women Seminarians, Sewanee, 1987-89, pres. 1988-90. Editor: (book series, Episcopal edit.) Families for Prayer, 1982. Trustee Episcopal Child Care and Devel. Ctr., Inc. Mem. Beaches Ministerial Assn., Ponte Vedra Club, Pi Lambda Theta. Republican. Mailing Address: PO Box 1584 Ponte Vedra Beach FL 32004 Office: Christ Episcopal Ch 400 San Juan Dr Ponte Vedra Beach FL 32082

BRYAN, MONK, retired bishop; b. Blooming Grove, Tex., July 25, 1914; s. Gideon J. and Era (Monk) B.; m. Corneille Downer, July 22, 1941; children: Lucy (Mrs. Samuel S. Barlow, Jr.), James J., Robert M. B.A., Baylor U., 1935; M.Th., So. Meth. U., 1938; D.D., Central Meth. Coll., Fayette, Mo., 1958; L.H.D. hon., Nebr. Wesleyan U., 1977; Hum.D. hon., Westmar Coll., 1982. Ordained to ministry United Methodist Ch., 1939; consecrated bishop, 1976; minister Boyce Circuit, Waxahachie Dist. Central Tex. Conf., 1939-40, St. Luke's Meth. Ch., St. Louis, 1940-47, Centenary Meth. Ch., Bonne Terre, Mo., 1947-49, Meth. Ch., Maryville, Mo., 1949-57, Mo. United Meth. Ch., Columbia, 1957-76; bishop South Central Jurisdictional Conf. United Meth. Ch., Lincoln, Nebr., 1976-84; part-time cons. bd. discipleship Southeastern Jurisdiction United Meth. Ch., 1984—; dean Chapel Lake Junaluska Assembly, 1990—; mem. World Meth. Council, 1953—; participant confs., Lake Junaluska, N.C., 1956, Oslo, 1961, London, 1966, Denver, 1971, Dublin, Ireland, 1976, Honolulu, 1981, Nairobi, Kenya, 1986; exchange minister in Eng., 1953; pres. Mo. Conf. Bd. Edn., 1956-64, Mo. Council Chs., 1966-68; chmn. Mo. East Conf. Bd. Christian Social Concerns, 1968-72; mem. Meth. Gen. Bd., divs. ecumenical and inter-religious concerns and health and welfare Meth. Gen. Bd. Global Ministries, 1972-76; now staff cons. Gen. Bd. Discipleship; pres. World Meth. Mus., 1986-88. Bd. dirs. Wesley Found., Columbia, 1957-76, Columbia United Fund, 1964-70; trustee So. Meth. U., 1952-68, 76-84, St. Paul Sch. Theology, Kansas City, 1968-72, 76-84, Mo. Sch. Religion, Columbia, 1957-76, Philander Smith Coll., Little Rock, 1976-84, Lydia Patterson Inst., El Paso, 1976-84, Mt. Sequoyah Assembly, Fayetteville, Ark., 1976-84, Nebr. Wesleyan U., 1976-84, Omaha Meth. Hosp., 1976-84, Bryan Meml. Hosp., 1976-84, Western Nebr. Gen. Hosp., 1976-84; adv. council Gt. Rivers council Boy Scouts Am., 1960-76; pres. Friends World Meth. Mus., 1986-88. Recipient Silver Beaver award Boy Scouts Am., 1972. Lodges: Masons (33d degree), KT, Rotary. Home: 307 Crum Dr PO Box 758 Lake Junaluska NC 28745 *When ever I have found life's path to be unusually difficult, two of God's gifts have helped—the memory of solid good in days past and someone's extended hand offering to help.*

BRYAN, PHILIP R., academic administrator. Pres. Bapt. Missionary Assn. Theol. Sem., Jacksonville, Tex. Office: Bapt Missionary Assn Theol Sem 1410 E Pine St Jacksonville TX 75766*

BRYANT, DEMETRIUS EDWARD, minister, actor; b. Mobile, Ala., June 30, 1956; s. James Edward Bryant and Thelma (Kennedy) Gibbons. BA in Psychology, U. So. Calif., 1985, BA in History, 1985; DD in Religion (hon.), Ministry of Salvation Ch., Chula Vista, Calif., 1988. Ordained minister, Calif., 1986. 2nd initiate Ministry of Abundant Life, L.A., 1978-79, 1st initiate, 1979-80, pastoral clinician univ. student, 1980-85; minister, actor Ministry of Salvation Ch., Chula Vista and L.A., 1982-86, minister, actor, consultant-at-large, 1986—. Cadet Civil Air Patrol, Otis AFB, Mass., 1971-76. Fellow Internat. Biographical Assn., Am. Biographical Ctr.; mem. AFTRA, SAG, L.A. World Affairs Coun., Am. Film Inst., Smithsonian Inst., Screen Extras Guild, Assembly of the Holy Cross (initiate 1983—), Gnostic Group. Democrat. Orthodox Gnostic. Avocations: athletics, basketball, weight training, classical music, reading. Home: 2803 S Washington St Seattle WA 98144

BRYANT, GARY JONES, minister; b. Stockton, Mo., Aug. 20, 1942; s. John Franklin and Imogene Eunice (Jones) B.; m. Judy Mae Nichols, Aug. 20, 1965; children: Gary Jason Gareth Joshua. BA in Bible, Cen. Bible Coll., Springfield, Mo., 1966; BS in Religious Studies, Bethany Bible Coll., Santa Cruz, Calif., 1968; MA in Religion, Crossroad Grad. Sch. Div., Muncie, Ind., 1973, PhD in Religion, 1975. Ordained to ministry Assemblies of God, 1969. Pastor Vista (Calif.) Assembly of God Ch., 1972-75, First Assembly of God Ch., Porterville, Calif., 1976-83, Christian Life Ch., Pitts., 1982-84; dir. Heart of Am. Counseling Ctr., Kansas City, Mo., 1984-85; pastor, dir. Peoples Ch.-Peoples Counseling Ctr., Las Cruces, N.Mex., 1986—; Christian edn. advisor So. Calif. Dist. Assemblies of God, Costa Mesa, 1978-80, youth leader, San Diego, 1976-78, presbyter, Costa Mesa, 1980-83. Author: Flight of the Dove - Cedar County, 1975. Bd. dirs. So. Calif. Coll., Costa Mesa, 1980-83; adv. bd. Tulare County Mental Health Hosp. and Clinics, 1979-82; adv. com. Cen. Bus. Dist. Coun., Las Cruces, 1991. Mem. Rotary. Republican. Home: 1235 Rusty Ln Las Cruces NM 88005 Office: Peoples Ch 100 S Church St Las Cruces NM 88001

BRYANT, MARCUS DAVID, pastoral care educator, minister; b. Gilbert, Ark., July 18, 1924; s. Morton Dillard and Anna May (Boyd) B.; m. Virginia Rae Stevenson, Aug. 9, 1953; children: Barbara Lynn Bryant Martin, Steven Mark. BA, Lynchburg Coll., 1949; MA, Columbia U., 1950; MDiv, Lexington Theol Sem., 1953; PhD, U. Nebr., 1958. Ordained to ministry Christian Ch. (Disciples of Christ), 1949. Min. Newtown Christian Ch., Georgetown, Ky., 1950-54; assoc. min. First Christian Ch., Lincoln, Nebr., 1954-58; pastor First Christian Ch., Waukegan, Ill., 1958-61; assoc. prof. Div. Sch. Drake U., Des Moines, 1961-67; prof. pastoral care Brite Div. Sch. Tex. Christian U., Fort Worth, 1967-91, emeritus prof. pastoral psychology and pastoral care, 1991—; elder South Hills Christian Ch., Ft. Worth. Author: (curriculum books) Come Alive, 1971; author: (with others) The Church and Community Resources, 1977, The Art of Christian Caring, 1979; contbr. articles to religious publs. With U.S. Army, 1943-46, ETO. Rsch. grantee Tex. Christian U., 1978, 81. Mem. Am. Assn. Pastoral Counselors (diplomate, chmn. profl. relationships 1977-80), Tex. Coun. Family Relations. Democrat. Home: 3956 Wosley Dr Fort Worth TX 76133 *Caring is at the heart of the human relationship. From the first breath of life, we respond to love and to care—we learn that our lives depend upon it and it is natural to give love and care in response. We care because we have first been cared for.*

BRYANT, MICHAEL, priest, educator, counselor; b. Washington, June 21, 1940; s. Francis A. and Nelda M. (Schnopp) B. BA in Philosophy, St. Mary (Ky.) Sem., 1965; M in Div. Theology, Mt. St. Mary Sem., Emmitsburg, Md., 1969; MS in Psychology, Loyola Coll., Balt., 1983, PhD in Pastoral Counseling, 1990. Assoc. pastor Our Lady of Victory Ch., Washington, 1969-78; pastor Holy Name Ch., Washington, 1978-80; staff chaplain D.C. Detention Facility Dept. of Corrections, Washington, 1980—; part-time clin. supr. DeSales Sch. of Theology, Washington, 1985—; chairperson Nat. Convocation Jail and Prison Mins., 1989—. Author: (with others) Who Is the Prisoner, 1985. Bd. dirs. Washington Correctional Found., 1984—, Coun. on Community Corrections, 1987—, Visitors Svc. Ctr., 1989—. With USN, 1958-61. Mem. Nat. Acad. Cert. Clin. Mental Health Counselors (cert.). Democrat. Roman Catholic. Home: 1357 E Capitol St Washington DC 20003 Office: DC Detention Facility 1901 D St SE Washington DC 20003

BRYANT, ROBERT HARRY, theology educator; b. Nokesville, Va., Sept. 1, 1925; s. Harry Tucker and Frances Margaret (McAllister) B.; m. Emily Christine Rentsch (dec. Jan. 1982); children: John Robert, Miriam Joan, Mark Phillip. BA, Coll. of William & Mary, 1946; MDiv, Yale U., 1949, PhD, 1956. Asst. pastor Second Congl. Ch., Westfield, Mass., 1951-52; assoc. prof. philosophy William Jewell Coll., Liberty, Mo., 1952-53; asst. prof. religion Mt. Holyoke Coll., South Hadley, Mass., 1956-58; assoc. prof. philosophy and religion Centre Coll., Ky., 1958-61; prof. constructive theology United Theol. Sem., New Brighton, Minn., 1961-91, prof. emeritus, 1991—; vis. asst. prof. theology Vanderbilt U., Nashville, 1953-54; vis. prof. Fed. Theol. Sem., Alice, Republic of South Africa, 1973-74, St. John's U., Collegeville, Minn., 1971-72; bd. dirs. Friends Sch. of Minn., Mpls., 1988-91, Common Profits, Mpls., 1985-91. Author: Bible's Authority Today, 1968; contbr. articles to profl. jours. Mem. adv. com. Mounds View Sch. Dist. Bd., New Brighton, 1971-72; del. Dem. State Conv., Rochester, Minn., 1968, Dem. Dist. Convs., Mpls., 1968, 90. Recipient Algernon Sydney Sullivan award Coll. William and Mary, 1946, numerous others; Hooker fellow Yale Div. Sch., 1949; Fulbright Commn. scholar, 1955-56; Danforth and Lilly Found. grantee, 1960, 86, 89. Mem. Am. Acad. Religion, Am. Theol. Soc., Phi Beta Kappa. *I believe that to work for peace with social justice for all peoples is urgently important. This will be achieved to the degree a more equitable distribution of the earth's resources occurs.*

BRYANT, ROY, bishop; b. Armour, N.C., July 18, 1923; s. Augusta and Susan (Granger) B.; m. Sissieretta Burney, Oct. 11, 1942; children: Eurnetha, Roy, Larry, Ruth, Seth. DD, Fla. State Christian Coll., 1966. Ordained to ministry Bible Ch. of Christ, 1959. Elder Phila. Bible Ch., N.Y.C., 1959-61; bishop The Bible Ch. of Christ, Inc., N.Y.C., 1961—; pres. Theol. Inst., Bible Ch. of Christ, N.Y.C., 1976—, dir. Resort Community and Summer Camp, 1971—, dir. Christian Bookstore, 1978—. Exec. editor The Voice; producer, host Radio and TV Ministry. Office: The Bible Ch of Christ Inc 1358 Morris Ave New York NY 10456

BRYANT, TIMOTHY PAUL, education and youth minister; b. Opelika, Ala., Nov. 21, 1961; s. Harold and Ellen Elizabeth (Jones) B. BA in Religion, Samford U., 1984; MRE, Southwestern Bapt. Theol. Sem., 1988. Ordained to ministry So. Bapt. Conv. Min. edn. and youth Pepperell Bapt. Ch., Opelika, 1984; lay worker Wedgewood Bapt. Ch., Ft. Worth, 1984-88; min. edn. and youth Trinity Bapt. Ch., Natchitoches, La., 1988—. Home: 1651 Suzanne Ln Natchitoches LA 71457 Office: Trinity Bapt Ch 527 Howard St Natchitoches LA 71457

BRZANA, STANISLAUS JOSEPH, bishop; b. Buffalo, July 1, 1917; s. Frank and Catherine (Mikosz) B. B.A., St. Bonaventure Coll., 1938, M.A., 1946; S.T.D., Gregorian U., Rome, Italy, 1953; LL.D. (hon.), St. Bonaventure U., 1966, St. John's U., 1978, Niagara U., 1988; LHD (hon.), Christ the King Sem., 1989. Ordained priest Roman Catholic Ch., 1941; Assigned Buffalo Missionary Apostolate, 1941; asst. St. Joseph's Ch., Gowanda, N.Y., 1942, Sts. Peter and Paul, Jamestown, N.Y., 1943, 46; dir. Cath. Information Center, Buffalo; also weekend asst. Transfiguration Ch., 1949, asst., 1953; weekend asst. St. John Kanty Ch., Buffalo, 1950; vice officialis of Tribunal of Diocese of Buffalo; in charge Tribunal Office, 1954-64; weekend asst. Our Lady of Grace Parish, Woodlawn, N.Y., 1956; adminstr. Our Lady of Grace Parish, 1957; appt. officialis tribunal Diocese of Buffalo (St. Adalbert's Parish), Buffalo, 1958; adminstr. Resurrection Parish, Cheektowaga, N.Y., 1959; pastor Queen Peace Ch., Buffalo, 1959, 61-68; domestic prelate, 1959-64; apptd. titular bishop of Cufruta and aux. bishop Diocese of Buffalo, 1964-68, vicar gen., 1966-68; bishop Diocese of Ogdensburg, N.Y., 1968—; Chmn. Diocesan Commn. on Sacred Liturgy, Music and Art, 1964. Served to capt. Chaplain Corps AUS, 1944-46. Office: Chancery Office 622 Washington St PO Box 369 Ogdensburg NY 13669

BUAIA, FAM, church organization administrator; b. July 2, 1939; parents U Dosela and Daw Khuangluti; m. Laisawi Thiangi; children: Zopari, Heleni, Zomuanpuia, Laltansangi. BTh, Myanmar Inst. Theology, Insein, Yangon, 1970; BD, Trinity Theol. Coll., Singapore, 1984. Ordained to ministry Meth. Ch., 1970. Supt. Zimte Cir., Burma, 1970-72, Rihkhawdar Cir., Burma, 1973-74; chmn. Falam Dist., Hdqrs. in Falam Town, Burma, 1974-75; fin. sec. Conf. Hdqrs., Mandalay, Burma, 1977-82; lectr. Theol. Coll., Mandalay, 1985-87; pres. Conf. Hdqrs., Mandalay, 1988—. *I never see these Who's Who in Religion and Who's Who in America, therefore I am eager to have this kind of articles and books to read.*

BUBB, DAVID LESTER, minister; b. Phoenix, July 18, 1958; s. Albert Hermance and Eliza Bowling (Rowland) B. BA, Centre Coll., 1980; MDiv, Duke U., 1984. Ordained to ministry So. Bapt. Conv., 1984. Student assoc. pastor Marion (N.C.) Meth. Ch., 1982, Lewisburg (N.C.) Meth. Ch., 1983; asst. pastor Jordanhill Parish Ch., Glasgow, Scotland, 1984-86; assoc. pastor Montgomery Presbyn. Ch., Cin., 1986—; chairperson Cin. Presbyn. Youth Com., 1988—. Spl. program chair Cin. Ulster Project, 1990. Office: Montgomery Presbyn Ch 9994 Zig Zag Rd Cincinnati OH 45242 *We humans need to learn to accept and celebrate this paradox: we are each joyously unique, independent individuals full of creativity and potential, but we are also frail, finite, dependent creatures whose destiny is interwoven with the rest of the planets.*

BUCHAN, JAMES ELLIS, JR., lawyer; b. Columbus, Ohio, Jan. 30, 1951; s. James Ellis and Nan (Fraggiotti) B.; m. Mary Frances Blubaugh; children: Molly, Abigail. Student, Oral Roberts U., Tulsa, 1971; BA in History, Denison U., Granville, Ohio, 1973; JD, Capital U., Columbus, Ohio, 1976. Bar: U.S. Dist. Ct. (so. dist.) Ohio 1977. Ptnr. Buchan and Buchan, Columbus, 1976-85; pvt. practice Columbus, 1985—; pastor Christian Community Ch., Columbus, 1981—; v.p. Lawyer's Christian Fellowship, Columbus, 1981-82; mem. adv. coun. Apostolic Team Ministries, 1988—. Editor Focus Jour., 1980—; contbr. articles to profl. jours. Foudner., dir. Focus Ministries, Columbus, 1980—. Mem. Columbus Bar Assn., Capitol City Pastors Assn. Republican. Avocations: authoring Christian articles, tennis, swimming, music. Office: 972 Beechwood Rd Columbus OH 43227

BUCHANAN, RAY ALLEN, clergyman; b. Houston, Jan. 8, 1947; s. Wilbur Allen and Louise (Zwahr) B.; m. Marian Kelly, Aug. 5, 1967; children: Peter Andrew, Amy Krysteen. BA, U. N.C., Wilmington, 1972; MDiv, Southeastern Bapt. Theol. Seminary, 1976; DD, Shenandoah Coll., 1990. Ordained to ministry United Meth. Ch., 1977. Pastor North Mecklenburg United Meth. Ch., Union Level, Va., 1973-77, Oak Hall (Va.) United Meth. Ch., 1977-79, Bedford (Va.) Cir. United Meth. Ch., 1979-81; co-founder, co-dir. Soc. St. Andrew, Big Island, Va., 1979—; mem. Va. ann. conf. United Meth. Ch. Co-editor Gleanings, 1986; co-author: Prepare the Way of the Coed, 1986; author: Pass the Potatoes, 1987; contbr. articles, poems to various publs. Mem. adv. com. Va. Food Systems Study, adv. com. Lynchburg Food Bank; pvt. sector adv. bd. House Select Com. on Hunger; bd. dirs. Bedford County Red Cross; mem. nat. com. for World Food Day; co-organizer Va. Congress on Hunger; chmn. hunger com. Va. Conf. Bd. of Global Ministries; adv. bd. Rural Ministries Program U. Dubuque and Wartburg (Iowa) Coll.; bd. dirs. Va. Hunger Found. Recipient Disting. Alumnus award U. N.C.-Wilmington, 1985. Mem. Bedford County Ministerial Assn. (v.p. 1984-85, mem. exec. bd. 1985). Avocations: writing, photography, outdoor activities. Home: Rte 1 Box 867 Big Island VA 24526 *Of all the obscenity spawned by an immoral society, nothing compares to the vulgarity of hunger. Erasing this moral outrage is the greatest challenge of our age.*

BUCHANAN, ROBERT EUGENE, JR., minister; b. Valdosta, Ga., June 2, 1956; s. Robert E. Buchanan Sr. and Rose Ann (Stanford) Chmielewski; m. Mimi Francine Fogle, May 27, 1978; children: Chad Emory, Lainee Marie. BA, Stetson U., 1978; MDiv, So. Bapt. Theol. Sem., 1981, DMin, 1991. Ordained to ministry So. Bapt. Conv., 1978. Youth min. 1st Bapt. Ch., New Smyrna Beach, Fla., 1977-80, 1st So. Bapt. Ch., Floydsknobb, Ind., 1980-81; assoc. pastor, youth min. Coll. Pk. Bapt. Ch., Orlando, Fla., 1981-85; pastor 1st Bapt. Ch., Waynesboro, Ga., 1985-91, Pkwy. Bapt. Ch., Duluth, Ga., 1991—; mem. exec. com. Ga. Bapt. Conv., 1989—. Mem. spl. edn. com. Burke City (Ga.) Schs., 1988-89; mem. capital funds com. Burke City Hosp., 1988-89; chmn. blood drive com. ARC, Burk City, 1989-91. Mem. Hephzibah Bapt. Assn. (moderator 1989—), Burke City Ministerial Assn. (sec.), Rotary. Democrat. Home: 3989 Keeneland Ct Duluth GA 30136 Office: Pkwy Bapt Ch 5975 State Bridge Rd Duluth GA 30136

BUCHANAN, ROBERT RHINEHART, JR., minister; b. Poughkeepsie, N.Y., July 31, 1951; s. Robert Rhinehart, Sr., and Margaret (Wickes) B.; m. Leanita Nana Christensen, Aug. 13, 1977; children: Shaunna Joy, Abigail Lynnette. BFA in Theatre Arts, Sir George Williams U.; Lic. in Radio Broadcoasting, Brown Inst. Adminstrv. asst. Jesus People Ch., Mpls., 1979-82, assoc. pastor, 1982-85, co-pastor, 1985-87; sr. pastor Cedar Ridge Christian Ch., Eagan, Minn., 1987—. Actor, dir. The Gospel According to Scrooge, 1979. Office: Cedar Ridge Christian Ch 2024 Rahn Way Eagan MN 55122

BUCHER, OTTO NORMAN, clergyman, educator; b. Milw., June 3, 1933; s. Otto A. and Ida (Smazal) B.; B.A., Capuchin Sem. of St. Felix, Huntington, Ind., 1956; postgrad. Capuchin Sem. of St. Anthony, Marathon, Wis., 1956-60; S.T.L., Catholic U. Am., 1963; S.S.L., Pontifical Bibl. Inst., Rome, 1965. Joined Capuchin Franciscan Order, 1952; ordained priest Roman Catholic Ch., 1959; lector in scripture Capuchin Sem. of St. Anthony, Marathon, 1966-70; asso. prof. Bibl. studies St. Francis Sem., Sch. Pastoral Ministry, Milw., 1970-73; asso. prof. Bibl. studies Sacred Heart Sch. of Theology, Hales Corners, Wis., 1973—, acad. dean, 1979-85, vice rector, 1984-86, 90, dir. field edn., 1986—; mem. exec. com. Midwestern Assn. Theology Schs., 1973-74. Mem. Cath. Bibl. Assn. Am., Soc. Bibl. Lit. Democrat, Assn. Clin. Pastoral Edn., Assn. Theol. Field Edn., Cath. Assn. Theol. Field Edn. Home: St Conrad House 3138 N 2d St Milwaukee WI 53212 Office: Sacred Heart Sch Theology 7335 S Lovers Lane Rd PO Box 429 Hales Corners WI 53130

BUCHHOLZ, JAMES JOSEPH, mortuary executive; b. St. Louis, Apr. 28, 1947; s. Cletus F. and Philomena C. (Molitor) B.; m. Kathleen Mary Boman, Aug. 19, 1972; children: Julie Anne, Jennifer Marie, Christina Mary. Student, S.E. Mo. State U., 1965-68; cert. in mortuary sci., Dallas Inst. Mortuary Sci., 1969. Apprentice embalmer Buchholz Mortuaries, St. Louis, 1969-71, journeyman embalmer, 1971-76, funeral dir., 1976-81, pres., 1981—; pres. St. Angela Merili Sch. Bd., Florissant, Mo., 1987—. Bd. dirs. YMCA, North County, St. Louis, 1988—. Roman Catholic. Office: Buchholz Mortuaries 1645 Redman St PO Box 13468 Saint Louis MO 63138

BUCKEL, JOHN JOSEPH, priest, religion educator; b. Indpls., Sept. 18, 1951; s. Charles Joseph and Kathleen (Roth) B. STB, U. Louvain, Belgium, 1979, PhD in Religious Studies, 1988. Assoc. pastor Christ the King Cath. Ch., Indpls., 1980-85; asst. prof. Scripture St. Meinrad Sch. Theology, 1989—. Mem. Cath. Bibl. Assn., Soc. Bibl. Lit. Office: Saint Meinrad Sch Theology Saint Meinrad IN 47577

BUCKLEY, FRANCIS JOSEPH, priest, educator; b. Los Angeles, Aug. 31, 1928; s. Francis Joseph and Elizabeth Agnes (Haiss) B. Student, U. Notre Dame, 1944-45, U. Santa Clara, 1945-49; MST, U. Santa Clara, 1959; BA, Gonzaga U., 1951, MA in Philosophy, 1952; Licentiate in Sacred Theology, Alma Coll., 1959; STD, Gregorian U., Rome, 1964; DHL (hon.), Pacific Grad. Sch. Psychology, 1988. Joined S.J., 1945, ordained priest Roman Cath. Ch., 1958. Instr. classics, religion Bellarmine Coll. Prepatory Sch., San Jose, Calif., 1952-55; instr. theology U. San Francisco, 1960-61, asst. prof. theology, 1963-68, assoc. prof. theology, 1968-72, prof. theology, 1972—, acting chmn. dept. theology, 1971-73, chmn. dept. theology, 1978-79, 88-91, dir. grad. programs in religious edn., 1974-75, 79-82, 86-87; chaplain St. Elizabeth Infant Hosp., San Francisco, 1963—; trustee Loyola Marymount U., Los Angeles, 1974-89, Jesuit Community U. San Francisco, 1969-76, 78-82; theol. advisor to U.S. Bishops Synod of Bishops, Rome, 1977; del. to Asian Catechetical and Liturgical Conf., Manila, 1967, Latin Am. Catechetical Conf., Medellin, Colombia, 1968, Internat. Catechetical Congress, Rome, 1971; vis. scholar Ctr. for Research in Learning and Teaching U. Mich., Ann Arbor, 1973-74; bd. dirs. Paul Wattson Ecumenical Lecture Series, San Francisco; mem. Nat. Council Nat. Christian Leadership Conf. for Israel, 1979—. Author: Christ and the Church according to Gregory of Elvira, 1964, Children and God: Communion, Confession, Confirmation, 1970, I Confess: The Sacrament of Penance Today, 1972, Reconciling, 1981, Come Worship With Us, 1987, (with Johannes Hofinger) The Good News and Its Proclamation, 1968, (with Sister Maria de la Cruz Aymes) (series) With Christ to the Father, 1966, Christ's Life in Us, 1967, Jesus, 1968, Spirit, 1968, Jesus in the Gospels and the Eucharist, 1969, (with Donald Sharp) Deepening Christian Life, 1987, and various others. Trustee Pacific Grad. Sch. Psychology, Menlo Park, Calif., 1984-86, pres. bd. trustees, 1986. Mem. Coll. Theology Soc. (pres. 1972-74, bd. dirs. 1969-76, regional chmn. 1966-72), Cath. Theological Soc. Am., Cath. Bibl. Assn., Assn. Profs. and Researchers in Religious Edn., Religious Edn. Assn., Assn. Dirs. Grad. Religious Edn. Programs, Internat. Assn. Jesuit Ecumenists, Am. Soc. Ch. History, U. San Francisco Faculty Assn. (sec. 1980-88). *True wisdom is to find God in all things. This brings peace in this life and joy in the life to come.*

BUCKLEY, JOHN P., lay worker; b. La Mirada, Calif., Oct. 24, 1967; s. Philip H. Buckley and Cheri M. (Pruitt) Merrell. BA in Pastoral Studies, Maranatha Bapt. Bible Coll., 1990. Lic. ins. rep. Pres. Bereau Youth Group, Rockford, Ill., 1984-86; bus capt./songleader Berean Bapt. Ch., Rockford, 1986-87; asst. pastor Harvest Bapt. Ch., Torrington, Conn., 1988; youth pastor Emmanuel Bapt. Ch., Elkhorn, Wis., 1988—; salesman Preferred Risk Ins., Madison, 1991—. Author: The Adventures of Running Wolf, 1988, (curriculum) Why You Belive . . . What You Believe, 1989. Alderman Watertown, Wis., 1990; com. mem. Pub. Safety Com., Watertown, 1990; trustee Watertown Pub. Libr., 1990; student body pres. Maranatha Bapt. Bible Coll., Watertown, 1989-90, class officer, 1987-89. Republican. Home: 106 1/2 S Warren Watertown WI 53094 Office: Preferred Risk Ins 6400 Gisholt Dr Ste 204 Madison WI

BUCKLEY, RALPH EUGENE, minister; b. Parma, Mo., Sept. 8, 1931; s. Homer Clarence and Ruby Jewel (Oliver) B.; m. Faye Laverne Snider, July 24, 1951; 1 child, Paul Talmadge. Th.B., Th.M., Faith Baptist Coll., 1971; postgrad. Midwestern Bapt. Sem., 1971-72; D.Ministry, Crossroad Div. Sem., 1978. Owner, mgr. Standard Oil Co., Bernie, Mo., 1951-54; salesman Kirksey Pontiac Co., Malden, Mo., 1954-57; supr. Internat. Harvestor, St. Louis, 1958-60; owner, operator Buckley Farms, Bernie, 1960-66; minister So. Baptist, Malden, 1966-67, educator, minister, Jonesboro, Ill., 1967—; exec. mem. George Hutching Evang. Assn., St. Louis, 1974-78; trustee Mid-Continent Bapt. Coll., Mayfield, Ky., 1976-78; dir. Faith Christian Schs., Morgantown, Ky., 1974-79; exec. mem. Mo. Bapt., Jefferson City, 1981-82. Author: Sunday School Re-fueling Station, 1975, Commentary Matthews Gospel, 1980. Dir. Area Wide Crusade, Lawson, Mo., 1972; cert. state umpire Mo. Softball Assn., Jefferson City, 1977. Home: 2841 Bethel Blvd Zion IL 60099 Office: 1st Bapt Ch 1727 N 27th St Zion IL 60099

BUCKNELL, LARRY ALAN, religious organization administrator; b. Hastings, Nebr., Apr. 14, 1950; s. Charles Richard and Dorla Mae (Reiber) B.; m. Janet Campbell Frost, Dec. 12, 1972; 1 child, Amy Frost Bucknell. BA, Hastings Coll., 1972; M in Mgmt., Northwestern U., 1991. Cost supr. Dutton Lainson Co., Hastings, 1972; asst. to dean Hastings (Nebr.) Coll., 1972-73; asst. store mgr. F. W. Woolworth, Hastings, 1973; asst. div. mgr. Woolco Dept. Stores, Omaha, 1974-75; asst. store mgr. Allens Hastings (Nebr.), 1975-78; store mgr. B. Dalton Bookseller, Mpls., 1978-80, buyer, 1980-82; gen. mgr. Baha'i Pub. Trust, Wilmette, Ill., 1982-86; chief adminstrv. officer Baha'i Nat. Ctr., Evanston, Ill., 1986—; small bus. cons., Grayslake 1986. Mem. Am. Soc. Assn. Execs., Adminstrv. Mgmt. Soc., Mensa, Rotary, Beta Gamma Sigma. Office: Baha'i Nat Ctr 1233 Central Ave Evanston IL 60201 *The growing realization of the oneness of humanity and the inescapable interdependence we have with one another is, I believe, the key to the spiritual transformation we must all undergo if our species is to survive and flourish.*

BUDD, DONALD DEAN, minister; b. Lawrence, Kans., Feb. 15, 1944; s. John Hammond and Dolly Juanita (Dominy) B.; m. Sharlene LaLoni, Nov. 7, 1969 (div. June 1973); 1 child, Gregory Dean; m. Gloria Jean Koehler, Oct. 25, 1975; children: Renae Lynn, Jonathan Dean. BS, Bethany Nazarene Coll., 1975; MRE, Nazarene Theol. Sem., 1978; M Ch. Mgmt., Olivet Nazarene Coll., 1982; D of Ministry, United Theol. Sem., 1987. Ordained to ministry Ch. of the Nazarene, 1980. Pastor Ch. of the Nazarene, Laona, Wis., 1976-79, Eau Claire, Wis., 1979-82, Appleton, Wis., 1982-87; pastor Community Ch. of the Nazarene, Merrifield, Minn., 1987-91, Harmony (Minn.)-State Line United Meth. Ch., 1991—; mem. bd. of ministerial studies Nazarene dist. Ch. of the Nazarene, Minn., 1987—. Chairperson County Child Abuse Prevention Com., Brainerd, Minn., 1990. With U.S. Army, 1966-69, Vietnam. Republican. Home: PO Box 536 Harmony MN 55939 Office: Harmony/State Line United Meth Ch PO Box 536 Harmony MN 55939 *To me life lived in secret or in privacy is reflected and communicated in public. So live your private life as you wish for it to be known in your public life.*

BUDD, LEONARD H., minister; b. Boston, June 7, 1933; s. Henry G. and Phyllis (Leonard) B.; m. Karen Walton, July 1, 1961; children: Julia, Ellen. BA, Ohio Wesleyan U., Del., 1955; MA, Oberlin Grad. Sch. Theology, Ohio, 1959; D Ministry, Methesco, Del., 1979. Ordained to ministry United Meth. Ch. Pastor Stow United Meth. Ch., Ohio, 1961-70; sr. pastor Wadsworth Meth. Ch., Ohio, 1970-76; dist. supt. United Meth. Ch., Wooster, Ohio, 1976-80; sr. pastor Lakewood (Ohio) United Meth. Ch., 1980-88, The Ch. of the Saviour, Cleveland Heights, 1988—; trustee Meth. Theology Sch., Del. 1978, Berea Children's Home, Ohio 1982. Author: Stories of an Ancient Present, 1976, Days Multiplied, 1984, Resurrection Promises, 1986, Bethlehem's Gift, 1989. Mem. Rotary Internat. Cleve., Cleve. City Club.

BUECHLEIN, DANIEL MARK, bishop; b. Jasper, Ind., Apr. 20, 1938; s. Carl and Rose (Blessinger) B. BA, St. Meinrad Coll., 1961; student, St. Meinrad Sch. Theology, 1961-64; Licentiate Sacred Theology, Benedictine U. Sant' Anselmo, Rome, 1966. Ordained priest Roman Cath. Ch., 1964, consecrated bishop, 1987. Asst. dean students St. Meinrad Coll., 1966-68, dir. spiritual formation, 1968-71; pres., rector St. Meinrad Sch. Theology, 1971-82, St. Meinrad Sch. Theology and St. Meinrad Coll., 1982-87; bishop Diocese of Memphis, Tenn., 1987—; chmn. div. religion, St. Meinrad Coll., 1967-71, chmn. Archabbey Council, 1967—; dir. First Nat. Conf. for Sem. Spiritual Dirs., summer 1971; mem. formation com. Conf. of Major Superiors of Men of USA, 1971-78; mem. nat. steering com. for follow-up of 1983 Nat. Assembly Sem. Rectors and Ordinaries; chmn. com. on priestly formation Nat. Conf. Cath. Bishops, 1990—, mem. adminstrv. com., 1990—, com. on marriage and family life, 1987, advisor doctrine com., 1989—, mem. com. on doctrine, 1989—, adminstrv. com., 1990—, chmn. com. on priestly formation, 1990—, mem. com. on doctrine, 1989—, budget com., 1990—, bishop's emergency relief com., 1990—; peritus Internat. Synod on Priestly Formation, Rome, 1990; bd. dirs. S.E. Regional Office for Hispanics Affairs and S.E. Pastoral Inst. Co-author: (with Bleichner and Leavitt) Preparing a Diocesan Priest: The Holistic Experience, 1987; Celibacy for the Kingdom, 1990; Commentary on A Survey of Priests Ordained Five to Nie Years, 1991; contbr. articles to profl. jours. Bd. dirs. Southeast Regional Office for Hispanic Affairs and Southeast Pastoral Inst., 1987—. Hon. chaplain KC, State of Tenn., 1987. Mem. Nat. Assn. Sem. Spritual Dirs. (founding coordinator 1972), Midwest Assn. Sem. Spiritual Dirs. (founding coordinator 1971), Midwest Assn. Theol. Schs. (sec.-treas. 1972-74, ptrd. 1974-75), Theol. Edn. Assn. Mid-Am. (sec. 1972-74, 80-82, v.p. 1974-76, pres. 1976-78, 82-84), Nat. Cath. Edn. Assn. (chmn. exec. com. of sem. div. 1984-85, 85-86), Nat. Conf. Catholic Bishops (mem. com. on marriage and family life, 1987—, com. on priestly formation, 1987-89, adminstrv. com. 1988—, bd. dirs. 1988—). Office: Diocese of Memphis 1325 Jefferson Ave PO Box 41679 Memphis TN 38174-1679

BUECHNER, CARL FREDERICK, minister, author; b. N.Y.C., July 11, 1926; s. Carl Frederick and Katherine (Kuhn) B.; m. Judith Friedrike Merck, Apr. 7, 1956; children: Katherine, Dinah, Sharman. Grad., Lawrenceville Sch., 1943; AB, Princeton U., 1947; BD, Union Theol. Sem., 1958; DD, Va. Episc. Sem., Lafayette U.; LittD, Lehigh U., Cornell Coll.; DD, Yale U. Ordained minister United Presbyn. Ch. U.S.A., 1958. Tchr. English Lawrenceville Sch., 1948-53; tchr. creative writing, summer sessions N.Y.U., 1954-55; chmn. dept. religion Phillips Exeter Acad., 1958-67, sch. minister, 1960-67; William Belden Noble lectr. Harvard, 1969; Russell lectr. Tufts, 1971; Lyman Beecher lectr. Yale U., 1977; Harris lector Bangor Sem., 1979; Smyth lectr. Columbia Sem., 1981; lectr. Trinity Inst., 1990. Author: A Long Day's Dying, 1950, The Seasons' Difference, 1952, The Return of Ansel Gibbs, 1958, The Final Beast, 1965, The Magnificent Defeat, 1966, The Hungering Dark, 1969, The Entrance to Porlock, 1970, The Alphabet of Grace, 1970, Lion Country, 1971 (Nat. Book award nominee), Open Heart, 1972, Wishful Thinking, 1973, Love Feast, 1974, The Faces of Jesus, 1974, Treasure Hunt, 1977, Telling the Truth, 1977, Peculiar Treasures, 1979, The Book of Bebb, 1979, Godric, 1980 (Pulitzer Prize nominee), The Sacred Journey, 1982, Now and Then, 1983, A Room Called Remember, 1984, Brendan, 1987, Whistling in the Dark, 1988, The Wizard's Tide, 1990, Telling Secrets, 1991, The Clown in the Belfry, 1991. Trustee Barlow Sch., 1965-71. With AUS, 1944-46. Recipient Irene Glascock Meml. intercollegiate poetry award, 1947; O'Henry prize for story The Tiger, 1955; Richard and Hinda Rosenthal award for the Return of Ansel Gibbs, 1958. Mem. Nat. Council Chs. (com. on lit. 1954-57), Council for Religion in Independent Schs. (regional chmn. 1959-63), Found. for Arts, Religion and Culture, Presbytery No. New Eng., P.E.N., Author's Guild. Club: Century Assn.; University (N.Y.C.). Office: RD 1 PO Box 1145 Pawlet VT 05761

BUEHRIG, MARGA, international religious organization official. Mem. presidium World Coun. Chs., Geneva. Office: care World Coun Chs, 150 re de Ferney, PO Box 66, 1211 Geneva 20, Switzerland*

BUELOW, ALBERT HENRY, minister; b. Fresno, Calif., Nov. 24, 1934; s. Carl August and Anna Mathilda (Marty) B.; m. Karen Lou Grummer, Aug. 17, 1961; children: Paul, Philip, Timothy, Jonathan. MDiv, Concordia Seminary, St. Louis, 1960, STM, 1961; MLS, Columbia U., 1973. Prof. Concordia Coll., Bronxville, N.Y., 1961-75; pastor Trinity Luth. Ch., Odebolt, Iowa, 1976—; archivist Iowa dist. West Luth. Ch. Mo. Synod, Fort Dodge, 1978—, sec., 1982—, dist. dir., 1987-90. Mem. Soc. Bibl. Lit., Am. Acad. Religion, Beta Phi Mu. Republican. Home: 616 S Dewey St Odebolt IA 51458-0470 Office: Trinity Luth Ch Dewey and Sixth Sts Odebolt IA 51458-0470

BUETTNER, HARLAN DALE, minister; b. Grand Island, Nebr., Jan. 16, 1957; s. Leo F. and Marjorey L. (Claar) B.; m. Jennifer R. Seaney, May 24, 1980; 1 child, Ryan Lee. BA cum laude, So. Nazarene U., 1985, MS in Mgmt. summa cum laude, 1991. Ordained elder Ch. of Nazarene, 1985. Assoc. pastor El Reno (Okla.) Ch. of Nazarene, 1982-84, Choctaw (Okla.) Ch. of Nazarene, 1984-86; pastor Cozad (Nebr.) Ch. of Nazarene, 1986-88; sr. pastor Penn Ave. Ch. of Nazarene, Oklahoma City, 1988—; chmn. Sunday sch. ministries S.W. Okla. Dist. Nazarene Ch., 1990—; bd. dirs. Nebr. Dist. Nazarene Ch. Properties and Orders and Rels., 1986-88, S.W. Okla. Dist. Nazarene Ch. Sunday Sch. Bd., 1988—. Recipient Great Commn. Leader's award Nebr. Dist. Ch. of Nazarene, 1987, Honor Sunday Sch. award, 1987-88, 90-91, traveling trophy of evangelism, 1991, named to Evangelistic Honor Roll, 1987-88, 90-91, Gen. Supt.'s Great Commn. award, 1991. Office: Penn Ave Ch of Nazarene 1121 N Penn Oklahoma City OK 73107

BUFORD, ROBERT PASCHAL, foundation executive, broadcast executive; b. Okmulgee, Okla., Sept. 16, 1939; s. Paschal and Lucille (Ross) B.; m. Linda Gardner, Dec. 23, 1961; 1 child, Ross. BBA, U. Tex., 1963. Founder, chmn. Leadership Network, Tyler, Tex., 1985—, The Found. Conf., Tyler, 1987—; chmn. bd. dirs. Peter F. Drucker Found. Nonprofit Mgmt., 1990—; chief exec. officer Buford T.V., Inc., Tyler, 1970—. Mem. Young Pres. Orgn. Episcopalian. Home: 3510 Turtle Creek Dallas TX 75219 Office: Buford TV Inc PO Box 9090 Tyler TX 75711

BUGG, CHARLES BASIL, religious educator; b. Miami, Fla., Dec. 25, 1942; s. Basil Earl and Carroll (Hancock) B.; m. Diane Sue Poston, Dec. 2, 1967; children: Laura Elizabeth, Charles David. BA, Stetson U., DeLand, Fla., 1965; MDiv, So. Bapt. Sem., Louisville, 1969, PhD, 1972. Pastor First Bapt. Ch. Eau Gallie, Melbourne, Fla., 1972-74, Powers Dr. Bapt. Ch., Orlando, Fla., 1974-76, First Bapt. Ch., Deland, 1976-82; sr. minister First Bapt. Ch., Augusta, Ga., 1982-89; Carl E. Bates prof. preaching So. Bapt. Sem., Louisville, 1989—; v.p. Ga. Bapt. Conv., 1987-88, chmn. com. on nominations, 1985. Author: Things My Children Are Teaching Me, 1982, Getting on Top When Life Gets us Down, 1989; contbr. to book: Preaching and Teaching Isaiah, 1991; contbr. articles to profl. jours. Trustee Mercer U., Macon, Ga., 1983-88; chmn. trustee nominating com. Stetson U., 1978-79; bd. dirs. and chmn. personnel com. YMCA, Augusta, 1984-87; adv. bd. Shelter for Abused Children, Augusta, 1983-89; gen. chmn. Augusta Area Leighton Ford Crusade, 1986. Recipient Disting. Alumnus award, Stetson U., 1984. Mem. Acad. Homiletics, Societas Homileticas, Acad. Preachers, Rotary (bd. dirs. 1988-89). Democrat. Home: 211 Gibson Rd Louisville KY 40207 Office: So Bapt Theol Sem 2825 Lexington Rd Louisville KY 40280

BUHLER, RICHARD GERHARD, minister; b. Cottonwood, Ariz., July 18, 1946; s. Henry Richard and A. Genevieve (Woodward) B.; m. Linda M. Bates, Dec. 9, 1966; children: Karin, Kristin, Karise, Kenneth, Kevin, Kim, Keith. BA, Biola U., 1968, LLD, 1990; cert., Omega Ctr., Santa Ana, Calif., 1978. Asst. pastor Atwater (Calif.) Bapt. Ch., 1973-79, Omega Fellowship, Santa Ana, 1975-78; pastor El Dorado Ch., Long Beach, Calif., 1978-84; radio host Branches Communications, Costa Mesa, Calif., 1981—; host Tabletalk daily radio program, Costa Mesa, 1990—, Talk From the Heart radio show, 1981-90. Author: Love...No Strings Attached, 1986, Pain and Pretending, 1988, New Choices, New Boundaries, 1991. Recipient Angel award Religion in Media, L.A., 1986. Mem. Writer's Guild Am. Republican. Mem. Internat. Ch. of Foursquare Gospel. Office: Branches Communications PO Box 6688 Orange CA 92613-6688 *'"Let not the wise man boast of his wisdom or the strong boast of his strength or the rich man boast of his riches, but let him who boasts about this: that he understands and knows me, that I am the Lord who exercizes kindness, justice and righteousness on earth, for in these I delight," declares the Lord.' Jeremiah 9:23, 24.*

BUHROW, WILLIAM CARL, religious organization administrator; b. Cleve., Jan. 18, 1934; s. Philip John and Edith Rose (Leutz) B.; m. Carole Corinne Craven, Feb. 14, 1959; children: William Carl Jr., David Paul, Peter John, Carole Lynn. Diploma, Phila. Coll. Bible, 1954; B.A., Wheaton (Ill.) Coll., 1956, M.A., 1959. Ordained to ministry Gen. Assn. Regular Bapt. Chs., 1958. Asst. pastor (Hydewood Park Bapt. Ch.), N. Plainfield, N.J., 1959-63; with Continental Fed. Savs. & Loan Assn., Cleve., 1963-81; sr. v.p. Continental Fed. Savs. & Loan Assn., 1971-75, pres., chief exec. officer, dir., 1975-81; chmn. bd. Security Savs. Mortgage Corp., Citizens Service Corp., New Market Corp., CFS Service Corp., 1975-81; trustee Credit Bur. Cleve., 1975-81, Bldg. Expositions, Inc., 1974-84; registered rep. IDS/Am. Express, Cleve., 1982-83; gen. credit mgr. Forest City Enterprises, Inc., Cleve., 1983-85; pres. Forest City Ins. Agy., Inc., Cleve., 1983-85; asst. v.p. Mellon Fin. Services Corp., Cleve., 1985-87; exec. adminstr. The Gospel Ho. Ch. and Evangelistic Ctr., Walton Hills, Ohio, 1988—. Trustee Bapt. Bible Coll. and Theol. Sem., Clarks Summit, Pa., 1977-90; vice chmn. bd. deacons Cedar Hill Bapt. Ch., Cleveland Heights, Ohio, 1981-87. Mem. Internat. Consumer Credit Assn., Soc. Cert. Consumer Credit Execs., Consumer Credit Assn. Northeastern Ohio, Christian Bus. Men's Com. Internat., Nat. Assn. Ch. Bus. Adminstrn. (v.p. Northeastern Ohio chpt.), Greater Cleve. Assn. Evangelicals (treas.). Home: 1044 Linden Ln Lyndhurst OH 44124 Office: 14707 Alexander Rd Walton Hills OH 44146 *The supreme goal of my life is to please and honor the Lord Jesus Christ in all that I say and do. The standards, goals, and ideals outlined in the Bible, God's Holy Word, are the ones which I have adopted for my life. True happiness for me lies in the accomplishment of God's perfect will in my life and that of my family and in introducing others to Christ so they may know Him as their own personal Saviour, too. Herein lies the key to my success as a Christian administrator.*

BUIE, AUBREY WILLIAM, JR., clergyman; b. Alexandria, Va., June 10, 1942; s. Aubrey William and Gloria Gwendolyn (Morgan) B.; m. Sandra Kay Montague, June 2, 1961; 1 child, Michael David. BA, Apostolic Bible Coll., Esteio, Brazil, 1989. Ordained to ministry Apostolic Chs. Bd. missions Apostolic Chs. Internat., Baton Rouge, La., 1973-85, coun. elders, 1973-85, asst. gen. supt., 1985—. Home: 3411 NW 94th Ave Hollywood FL

33024 Office: Landmark Apostolic Ch 3400 NW 94th Ave Hollywood FL 33024

BUIE, BECKY RUTH LINEBERGER, religious organization executive; b. Tampa, Fla., July 27, 1941; d. Francis Marion and Margaret (Watson) Lineberger; m. Franklin Burgess Buie, June 22, 1962; children: Glenn Andrew, Thomas Franklin. BA cum laude, Columbia (S.C.) Coll., 1962. Sec. Duke U. Divinity Sch., Durham, N.C., 1962-65; sec. Anderson (S.C.) dist. The United Meth. Ch., 1970-76; bookkeeper S.C. United Meth. Conf., Columbia, 1976-84, treas., 1985—; del. United Meth. Ch. Gen. Conf., 1988—. Mem. Nat. Assn. Ann. Conf. Treas. (pres. 1991), Nat. Assn. Conf. Computer Adminstrs. (exec. com. 1991—), Nat. Assn. Ch. Bus. Adminstrn., Assn. United Meth. Ch. Bus. Adminstrn., Profl. Women in Acctg. Democrat. Lodge: Lioness (treas. Columbia Met. club 1981-90). Avocations: needlework, cats. Office: SC United Meth Conf 4908 Colonial Dr Columbia SC 29203

BUKOWIECKI, SISTER ANGELINE BERNADETTE, nun; b. Edmonton, Alta., Can., Aug. 24, 1937; came to U.S. 1960; d. Felix Peter and Stella Isabelle (Yagos) B. BA, Marillac Coll., St. Louis, 1969; MA in Dogmatic/Systematic Theology, St. Louis U., 1971. Joined Hosp. Sisters of the Third Order of St. Francis, 1962; co-foundress Franciscan Sisters of New Covenant, Roman Cath. Ch., 1979. Provincial Franciscan Sisters of New Covenant, Denver, 1979—; founder, dir. Cath. Evangelization Tng. Ctr., Denver, 1983-91; internat. dir. Assn. of Coords. of Cath. Schs. Evangelization/2000, Rome, 1991—; adminstrv. bd. Immaculate Heart of Mary Parish Coun., Northglenn, Colo., 1983-85. Author or co-author 16 books, 1983-91. Mem. Can. Soc. Radiologic Technologists, Nat. Coun. Cath. Evangelization (bd. dirs. 1983-85). Home: 10620 Livingston Dr Northglenn CO 80234 Office: Evangelization 2000, Via Boezio 21, 00192 Rome Italy *I have learned over the years to live in the present moment: the key to peace and joy. It is the only moment we have. The past cannot be changed and the future is as yet unknown. To worry about either leads to a loss of the present moment where true effectiveness is to be found. To walk in the present moment is to walk with God.*

BULA, SISTER IRMINA, nun; b. Antigo, Wis., Jan. 12, 1926; d. John Jay and Angeline Marie (Banczak) B. BA, Alverno Coll., Milw., 1955; BS, Cardinal Stritch Coll., Milw., 1956. Entered Sisters of St. Joseph, Third Order of St. Francis, 1941. Tchr. parochial schs., Milw., 1946-55, 56-59; dietitian and tchr. River Pines Santorium, Stevens Point, Wis., 1960-61, St. Joseph Home and Hosp., River Falls, Wis., 1961-63; dietitian Divine Infant Hosp., Wakefield, Mich., 1963-71, Holy Family Hosp., Manitowoc, Wis., 1971-73; treatment group home parent Manitowoc County Dept. Human Svcs., 1972—; foster parent Nat. Foster Parent Assn. Home: 3904 Martin Ln Two Rivers WI 54241-1399

BULKOWSKI, DAVID ALLEN, youth minister; b. Grand Rapids, Mich., Sept. 5, 1963; s. James Walter and Linda Frances (O'Hearn) B. BA, U. Waterloo, Ont., 1985, Cath. U. Louvain, Belgium, 1987; MA, Cath. U. Louvain, Belgium, 1988, BST, 1988. Pastoral intern Holy Family Ch., Caledonia, Mich., 1985, St. Thomas Ch., Muskegon, Mich., 1987, S.H.A.P.E. Cath. Community, Mons, Belgium, 1986, 88; pastoral assoc. St. Thomas Ch., Grand Rapids, Mich., 1989-90; pastoral assoc. for youth St. Thomas Ch., Grand Rapids, 1990-91; youth min. St. James Ch., Novi, Mich., 1991—; bd. dirs. Dymo Camp, Inc., Grand Rapids, 1989—; rep. Diocesan Rsch. Task Force, Grand Rapids, 1990—. Editor, author Literary Mag., 1990. Chairperson Liz's House Task Force, Grand Rapids, 1988—; vol. God's Kitchen, Capitol Lunch, Grand Rapids, 1981—. Mem. KC, Mins. United for Youth, Bread for the World, Pax Christi, USA. Office: St James Ch 24491 Riverview Ln Novi MI 48374

BULLARD, GEORGE WOODROW, JR., minister, religious organization administrator; b. Raleigh, N.C., July 22, 1950; s. George Woodrow and Anna Mozelle (Bridgers) B.; m. Betty Boyd, June 17, 1972; children: Jonathan, Allison. BA, Mars Hill (N.C.) Coll., 1971; MDiv, So. Bapt. Theol. Sem., Louisville, 1974, ThM, 1976, D Ministry, 1980. Ordained to ministry Bapt. Ch., 1973. Community minister West Side Bapt. Ch., Louisville, 1972-74, pastor, 1974-76; chs. in transition cons. Bapt. Conv. Md.-Del., Lutherville, Md., 1977-78; dir. missions ministries Mecklenburg Bapt. Assn., Charlotte, N.C., 1979-81; assoc. dir. met. missions Home Missions Bd., So. Bapt. Conv., Atlanta, 1981-85; dir. missions div. S.C. Bapt. Conv., Coluumbia, 1985—; vis. prof. ch. and community So. Bapt. Theol. Sem., 1987; vis. prof. ministry Golden Gate Bapt. Theol. Sem., Mill Valley, Calif., 1988, 92—; bd. dirs. S.C. Christian Action Coun., Columbia, 1987—; pres. So. Bapt. New Work Fellowship, 1990—, Master Design Assocs., 1990—. Co-author: Shaping a Future for the Church in the Changing Community, 1981. Recipient Outstanding PACT Cons. Leadership award home mission bd. So. Bapt. Conv., 1979. Democrat. Office: SC Bapt Conv 907 Richland St Columbia SC 29201 *A sense of dynamic spiritual vision is essential for the world God created to become more loving and just. A life dedicated to such a vision will bear much fruit.*

BULLARD, JOHN MOORE, religion educator, church musician; b. Winston-Salem, N.C., May 6, 1932; s. Hoke Vogler and May Evangeline (Moore) B. AB, U. N.C., 1953, AM, 1955; MDiv, Yale U., 1957, PhD, 1962. Ordained to ministry United Meth. Ch., 1955. Asst. in instrn. Yale U., New Haven, 1957-61; asst. prof. religion Wofford Coll., Spartanburg, S.C., 1961-65, assoc. prof., 1965-70, Albert C. Outler prof. religion, 1970—, chmn. dept., 1962—; minister music (organist-choirmaster) Cen. United Meth. Ch., Spartanburg, 1961-72, Bethel United Meth. Ch., Spartanburg, 1972-88; vis. prof. Biblical Lit. U. N.C., Chapel Hill, 1966, 67, U. N.C. at Charlotte, summer 1974; vis. prof. comparative religion Converse Coll., Spartanburg, S.C., 1984. Contbr. articles to Interpreter's Dictionary of Bibl. Interpretation and profl. jours. With Naval ROTC, 1950-52. Grantee NEH summer seminar Harvard U., 1982, U. Pa., 1986, Yale U., 1987; Fulbright-Hays grantee, Pakistan 1973, Fund for the Study of Gt. Religions in Asia, 1970-71; named to Ky. Cols.; Dana Fellow Emory Univ's. Grad. Inst. Liberal Arts, 1989-90. Mem. Soc. Bibl. Lit. (pres. so. sect. 1968-69), Am. Acad. Religion, Am. Guild Organists (dean chpt. 1965-67), S.C. Acad. Religion (pres. 1974-75), Southeastern Hist. Keyboard Soc., New Bach Soc. (Leipzig), Phi Mu Alpha Sinfonia. Avocation: early keyboard music. Home: 104 Hickman Ct Hillbrook Forest Spartanburg SC 29302 Office: Wofford Coll Dept Religion 429 N Church St Spartanburg SC 29303-3663

BULLARD, KEVIN LEE, minister; b. Ft. Worth, Aug. 15, 1956; s. Raymond Edward and Letris Laverne (Elkins) B.; m. Tammy Darlene Tibbles, Apr. 22, 1978; children: Matthew Raymond, Tiffany Nicole, April Breann. BA in Bible, Okla. Christian Coll., 1978; MA in Christian Ministry, Friends Univ., 1990. Youth minister Pryor (Okla.) Ch. of Christ, 1978-79, Coll. Terrace Ch. of Christ, Ft. Smith, Ark., 1979-80; minister Okemah (Okla.) Ch. of Christ, 1980-83, East Main Ch. of Christ, Holdenville, Okla., 1983-84, Derby (Kans.) Ch. of Christ, 1984—; tour host trips to Holy Land, 1984, 87; marriage and family dir. Equipping to Serve Workshop com., Wichita, Kans., 1987—. Named to Outstanding Young Men of Am., 1989; recipient Nat. Leadership award Soc. of Disting. Am. High Sch. Students, 1988, Hugo McCord Bible award Okla. Christian Coll., 1978. Home: 1719 Evergreen Ct Derby KS 67037 Office: Derby Church of Christ 225 N Derby Derby KS 67037

BULLARD, LAWRENCE EDWARD, minister; b. Conway, S.C., Oct. 15, 1943; s. John G. and Willie M. (Burney) B.; m. Mary C. Brown, Aug. 4, 1968; children: Eddie, Andy. AA, North Greenville Coll., 1965; BA, Carson-Newman Coll., 1967; MRE, Southeastern Bapt. Theol. Sem., Wake Forest, N.C., 1970; D Ministry, Drew U., 1989. Ordained to ministry So. Bapt. Conv., 1968. Min. Braggtown Bapt. Ch., Durham, N.C., 1968-70, Beecher Hills Bapt. Ch., Atlanta, 1970-71, Riverland Hills Bapt. Ch., Columbia, S.C., 1971-83, 1st Bapt. Ch., Easley, S.C., 1983—; mem. nominating com. S.C. Conv., 1990—; mem. Interracial Mins. Conf., 1983. Author: Church Committees, 1989. Coord. United Way, Columbia, 1977-82; leader Boy Scouts Am., Columbia, 1982-83; trustee S.C. Bapt. Ministries for Aging, 1983-88; participant The White House Conf. for Aging, Columbia, 1987; chairperson centennial com. North Greenville Coll., 1990; treas. United Christian Ministries, Easley, S.C., 1990-91. Mem. Nat. Assn. Ch. Bus. Adminstrn., So. Bapt. Alliance, Ea. Religious Edn. Assn. Office: 1st Bapt Ch 300 E 1st Ave Easley SC 29640 *No amount of religious rhetoric can equal the value of that gift of something needed from one who has to one who needs.*

BULLARD, MARY ELLEN, religious study center administrator; b. Elkin, N.C., Jan. 12, 1926; d. Roy Brannoch and Mattie Reid (Doughton) H.; m. John Carson Bullard Sr., Apr. 27, 1957; children: John Carson Jr., Roy Harrell. BS, U. N.C., Greensboro, 1947; postgrad., Union Theol. Sem., N.Y.C., 1956; MA, Troy State U., Montgomery, Ala., 1979. Dir. women's and girls' work Gilvin Roth YMCA, Elkin, 1947-49; dir. Christian edn. 1st United Meth. Ch., Salisbury, N.C., 1949-51, Charlotte, N.C., 1951-55; dir. youth ministry United Meth. Ch., Western N.C. Conf., 1956-57; dir. ednl. ministries, div. continuing edn. Huntingdon Coll., 1979-88; dir. U.S. office Bibl. Resources Study Ctr., Inc., Jerusalem, 1988—; mem. World Meth. Coun., 15th World Meth. Conf., Nairobi, Kenya, 1986; del. Gen. Conf. United Meth. Ch., St. Louis. Bd. dirs. LWV, Montgomery, 1966-70, Am. Cancer Soc., Montgomery, 1975-81, Ala. Dept. Youth Svcs., Mt. Meigs Campus, 1984-85; mem. Montgomery Symphony League, 1984-90, Ala. World Affairs Coun., Montgomery, 1989-90. Recipient award of recognition Christian Higher Edn., Ala.-West Fla. Conf. United Meth. Ch., 1975, Conf. Coun. on Ministries, Ala. West Fla. Conf., 1987. Mem. Christian Educators Fellowship (sec. Ala.-West Fla. Conf. 1989-90), Kappa Delta Pi. Home: 3359 Warrenton Rd Montgomery AL 36111 Office: Bibl Resources Study Ctr care Huntington Coll 1500 Fairview Ave Montgomery AL 36111

BULLARD, ROGER AUBREY, religion educator; b. Memphis, Aug. 1, 1937; s. Roger Maurice and Ladye Mable (Bennett) B.; m. Carol Louise Hawthorne, May 21, 1961; children: Kenneth, Floyd. BA, Union U., Jackson, Tenn., 1958; MA, U. Ky., 1959; BD, Southeastern Sem., 1962; PhD, Vanderbilt U., 1965. Prof. Barton Coll., Wilson, N.C., 1965—. Author: Hypostasis of the Archons, 1970; co-translator: Today's English Version, 1976; assoc. editor: Abingdon Dictionary of Living Religions, 1981, Mercer Dictionary of the Bible, 1990. Mem. AAUP, Nat. Assn. Bapt. Profs. of Religion, Soc. Bibl. Lit. Democrat. Baptist. Home: 4002 Little John Dr Wilson NC 27893 Office: Barton Coll Wilson NC 27893

BULLOCK, CLIFTON VERNICE, minister; b. Lincoln County, Miss., Feb. 12, 1928; s. Obie and Gertrude (Hughes) B.; m. Voncile C. Bowman, Sept. 28, 1951; children: Vidette K., Kim V. Bullock Joseph, Ivan A. BS, Nebr. Wesleyan U., 1967; MTh, So. Meth. U., 1971. Ordained to ministry United Meth. Ch., 1971. Min. Newman United Meth. Ch., Lincoln, Nebr., 1962-67; pastor, dir. Eastwood Ministry, Ft. Worth, 1968-71; chaplain Nebr. Wesylan U., Lincoln, 1971-76; min. Washington Heights United Meth. Ch., Battle Creek, Mich., 1976—; mem. Coun. of Ministries, North Cen. Jurisdiction, United Meth. Ch., 1976—; chmn. Commn. on Religion and Race, West Mich. Ann. Conf., United Meth. Ch., 1978-84;mem. New Black Ch. Task Force, Black Meths. for Church Rrenewal, 1978-82; founder, pres. United Community Ministerial Alliance, Battle Creek, 1979—; del. to gen. and jurisdictional confs. United Meth. Ch., 1980, 84, 88, World Meth. Coun., 1981, 86, 91; chaplain Racial-Ethnic Local Ch. Com., United Meth. Ch., mem. Gen. Bd. of Discipleship, 1988—. Mem. Battle Creek City Commn., 1982-88. Recipient George award Battle Creek Enquirer & News, 1980; named Religious Leader Mich. Religious Heritage Am., Inc., 1982. Mem. NAACP, Forward in Faith Clergy Fellowship, Urban League. Home: 26 W Roosevelt Battle Creek MI 49017 Office: Washington Heights United Meth Ch 153 N Wood St Battle Creek MI 49017

BULLOCK, DONALD MELVIN, minister; b. Reading, Ohio, Feb. 15, 1933; s. Coy and Leta Pearl (Herrin) B.; m. Jewel Willene Beal, May 10, 1952; children: Pamela Kay, Denise Diane, Lynnette Lynne, Rebecca Joy, Timothy Coy. AB, Ky. Christian Coll., 1955, M Ministry, 1984; BA, St. Francis Coll., 1969. Ordained to ministry Chs. of Christ, 1953. Min. Stinson, Ky., 1952, Higginsport, Ohio, 1952-53, Waco, Ky., 1953-55, Tollesboro, Ky., 1955-56, Butler, Ind., 1956-57, Edgerton, Ohio, 1957-67, St. Joe, Ind., 1967-69; min. Parkview Ch. of Christ, Findlay, Ohio, 1969-74, Kenwood Ch. of Christ, Livonia, Mich., 1974-75, West Village Christian Ch., Oak Ridge, Tenn., 1975—. Contbr. articles to profl. jours. Home: 639 Robertsville Rd Oak Ridge TN 37830 Office: West Village Christian Ch 637 Robertsville Rd Oak Ridge TN 37830

BULLOCK, ROBERT HAYDON, JR., religious publication editor; b. Houston, July 17, 1945; s. Robert Haydon and Sarah Adelia (Perry) B.; m. Gretchen Weicker, Aug. 24, 1968; 1 child, Richard Austin. BA, Austin Coll., 1967; MA, U. Mich., 1969; MDiv, Austin Presbyn. Sem., 1971; MA, Princeton U., 1973, PhD, 1975. Ordained to ministry Presbyn. Ch. (U.S.A.), 1971. Dir. Ecumenical Ministries Callaway County, Fulton, Mo., 1975-77; assoc. pastor Covenant Presbyn. Ch., Austin, Tex., 1978-81, 1st Presbyn. Ch., Lynchburg, Va., 1981-83; organizing pastor 1st Presbyn. Ch., Allen, Tex., 1983-88; editor The Presbyn. Outlook, Richmond, Va., 1988—. Contbg. author: The Diversity of Discipleship, 1991. Mem. Am. Acad. Religion, Am. Soc. Ch. History, Presbyn. Hist. Soc. SW. Democrat. Office: Presbyn Outlook Found 3711 Saunders Ave Richmond VA 23227

BULLOCK, WILLIAM H., bishop; b. Maple Lakes, Minn., Apr. 13, 1927; s. Loren W. and Anne C. (Raiche) B. B.A., Notre Dame U., 1948, M.A., 1962; Ed.S., St. Thomas Coll., St. Paul, 1969. Ordained priest Roman Catholic Ch., ordained bishop Roman Catholic Ch. Assoc. pastor Ch. of St. Stephens, Mpls., 1952-55, Ch. of Our Lady of Grace, Edina, Minn., 1955-56, Ch. of Incarnation, Mpls., 1956-57; instr. St. Thomas Acad., Mendota Heights, Minn., 1957-61, headmaster, 1968-71; pastor Ch. of St. John the Baptist, Excelsior, Minn., 1971-80, Ch. of Our Lady of Perpetual Help, Mpls., 1980—; aux. bishop Archdiocese of St. Paul and Mpls., 1980-87; bishop Diocese of Des Moines, 1987; chmn. agenda com. U.S. Catholic Conf., mem. communications com.; mem. Iowa Catholic Conf., Catholic Relief Svcs. Bd., Tri-Conf. Commn. Religious Life and Ministry. Mem. U.S. Bishops-Region II. Lodges: KC; Knights of Holy Sepulchre. Office: Diocese of Des Moines 818 5th Ave PO Box 1816 Des Moines IA 50306

BULTEMA, HARRY J. R., minister; b. Grand Rapids, Mich., Feb. 29, 1936; s. Harry and Magdalena (Potter) B.; m. Janice Bernice Ebels, Aug. 7, 1959; children: Deborah Faith, Timothy James, Stephen John. BA, Grace Bible Coll., Grand Rapids, 1961; M of Div., Covenant Theol. Sem., St. Louis, 1974. Ordained to ministry Bible Ch., 1963, Grace Gospel Fellowship. Pastor Berean Bible Ch., Cadillac, Mich., 1962-66, Alton, Ill., 1966-74; pastor Highland Hills Bible Ch., Lombard, Ill., 1974-76, Community Bible Ch., Grandville, Mich., 1977—; bd. dirs. Grace Ministries, Internat., Grand Rapids, 1968—, Grace Youth Camp, Mears, Mich., 1985—. Served with USN, 1955-57. Republican. Home: 7552 Astronaut St Jenison MI 49428 Office: Community Bible Ch PO Box 52 Grandville MI 49418

BUMSTEAD, DAWN D., radio executive; b. Flint, Mich., July 15, 1965; d. Charles Stanley and Wanda June (Atchley) B. BA in Communications, Olivet Nazarene U., Kankakee, Ill., 1986. Lic. FCC radio telephone operator. Ops. mgr. Sta. WKOC-FM, Kankakee, 1986-88; news and community rels. dir. Sta. WUFL, Detroit, 1988—; pres. dawn bumstead communications, Mt. Clemens, Mich., 1989—; program dir. CV-one, Rochester Hills, Mich., 1989-91. Producer Information Plus, 1984-86, Single Walk, 1990-91, Kidminute, 1990-91. Instr. Brandon Community Edn., Ortonville, Mich., 1982; min. youth, dir. choir Lake Louise Ch. of Nazarene, Ortonville, 1990—. Mem. Nat. Religious Broadcasters, Concerned Women for Am., Nat. Right to Life, Rotary (hon.). Republican. Avocations: softball, music, biblical studies. Home: 4400 Grange Hall Rd Holly MI 48442 Office: WUFL 42669 Garfield Rd Ste 328 Mount Clemens MI 48044

BUNCH, ALBERT WILLIAM, minister; b. Eldon, Mo., Feb. 3, 1933; s. Tade W. and Leta Beatrice (Hees) B. AB, William Jewell Coll., 1954; BD, Cen. Bapt. Theol. Sem., Kansas City, Kans., 1958; MDiv, Cen. Bapt. Theol. Sem., Kansas City, Mo., 1972; postgrad., Mo. Valley Coll., 1970-75, U. Mo., 1971. Ordained to ministry So. Bapt. Conv., 1954. Pastor Bethlehem Bapt. Ch., Carrollton, Mo., 1957-61, New Salem Bapt. Ch., Marshall, Mo., 1961—; clk. Saline Bapt. Assn., 1965-67, 75-91, mem. exec. bd., 1961-91, strategy planning com., 1988-90, historian, 1976—; mem. Carroll-Saline Bapt. Assn. Joint Mission Bd., 1966-69, 71-76; Bible tchr. Happy Adult Singles, 1978-90. Author: History of the SBA, 1976. Chmn. student work com. Mo. Valley Coll., Marshall, 1975-80; pres. Friends Libr. Svcs., Marshall, 1984-90. Recipient cert. So. Bapt. Conv., 1976, Alumnus of Yr. award Cen. Bapt. Theol. Sem., 1983. Mem. ACLU, People for the Am. Way, Nat. Cathedral Assn., So. Bapt. Alliance, State Hist. Soc. Mo., S.C. Hist. Soc., Friends of Arrow Rock, Mo. Religion Coalition for Abortion Rights, Saline County Assn. for Mental Health (exec. bd.), Planned Parenthood, Marshall Philharm. Orch., Lyceum Theatre of Arrow Rock. Home: Rte 1 Marshall MO 66340 Office: New Salem Bapt Ch Interstate Hwy at US Hwy 65 Marshall MO 65340

BUNCH, RICHARD ADDISON, clergyman; b. Springfield, Mo., Oct. 28, 1940; s. Clyde A. and Elsie Fern (Bird) B.; m. Kay Ann Burtch, Sept. 12, 1962; children: Kerby, Amy. AB, Graceland Coll., 1962; MS, Ind. U., 1965, D of Recreation and Park Adminstrn., 1971; postgrad., St. Paul's Sem., 1979-80. Ordained priest Reorganized Ch. of Jesus Christ of Latter-day Sts., 1956, ordained high priest, 1980. Dist. youth leader Reorganized Ch. Jesus Christ Latter Day Sts., Chgo., 1966-69, Nauvoo, Ill., 1969-71; tech. advisor Reorganized Ch. Jesus Christ Latter Day Sts., Papeete, French Polynesia, 1971-73; regional youth commr. Reorganized Ch. Jesus Christ Latter Day Sts., Macomb, Ill., 1974-79; chaplain Graceland Coll., Lamoni, Iowa, 1980—; bd. dirs. Midwest Coll. Retreat, Stewartsville, Mo., 1981—; mem. camping task force Reorganized Ch. Jesus Christ of Latter Day Sts., Independence, Mo., 1982—. Contbr. articles to profl. jours. Mem. Lamoni Park Bd., 1981—; mem. bd. Community Counseling Service, Lamoni, 1982—. Mem. Nat. Assn. Coll. and Univ. Chaplains, Nat. Recreation and Park Assn. (chmn. Recreation and Religion Com. 1974-79), Soc. Park and Recreation Educators (bd. dirs. 1977). Lodge: Lions. Avocations: tennis, golf, adventure programming, camping, canoeing. Office: Graceland Coll PO Box 1493 Lamoni IA 50140

BUNDY, DAVID DALE, librarian, educator; b. Longview, Wash., Sept. 27, 1948; s. Cedric Dale and Florence (Prichard) B.; m. Consuelo Ann Briones, Dec. 19, 1969 (div. 1982); children: Keith Dale, Cheryl Ann; m. Melody Lynn Garlock, June 14, 1985; children: Rachel Lynn, Lydia Marie. BA, Seattle Pacific U., 1969; MDiv, ThM, Asbury Theol. Sem., Wilmore, Ky., 1973; Licentiate, Cath. U. Louvain, Louvain-la-Neuve, Belgium, 1978. Dean Inst. Univ. Ministry Louvain, 1977-81; rsch. asst. Cath. U. Louvain, 1978-85; assoc. prof. Christian Origins, collection devel. libr. Asbury Theol. Sem., Wilmore, 1985-91; libr., assoc. prof. ch. history Christian Theol. Sem., Indpls., 1991—; dir. Wesleyan Holiness Studies Ctr., Wilmore, 1990-91. Author: Keswick, 1985; contbr. articles to profl. jours. Pew Charitable Trusts grantee, 1988. Mem. N.Am. Patristic Soc., Symposium Syriacum (internat. dir. 1988—), Am. Acad. Religion, Assn. Christian Arabic Studies (editor Mid. Ea. Christian Studies), Wesleyan Theol. Soc. Democrat. Mem. United Meth. Ch. Office: Christian Theol Sem 1000 W 42d St Indianapolis IN 46208

BUNGE, MARCIA JOANN, educator; b. Dubuque, Iowa, Apr. 14, 1954; d. Richard and Myrene (Larson) B.; m. Gary Stephen Dulin, June 2, 1990. BA magna cum laude, St. Olaf Coll., 1976; MA, U. Chgo., 1979, PhD, 1986. Asst. prof. Luther Northwestern Theol. Sem., St. Paul, 1985-90, Luther Coll., Decorah, Iowa, 1990—; vis. asst. prof. Knox Coll., Galesburg, Ill., 1985, Theologisches Seminar, Leipzig, German Democratic Republic, 1989. Mem. exec. bd. Word and World, 1987-88, 89-90; contbr. articles to profl. jours. World Coun. of Chs. fellow, 1979-81, U. Chgo. fellow, 1984, Charlotte Newcombe Found. fellow, 1984-85, Assn. Theol. Schs. fellow, 1986, Evang. Ch. in Am. fellow, 1989. Mem. Internat. Herder Soc. (exec. bd. 1985-90), Am. Acad. Religion, Soc. for Values in Higher Edn., Gesellschaft für die Erforschung des 18. Jahrhunderts, Phi Beta Kappa. Office: Luther Coll Dept Religion and Philosophy 700 College Dr Decorah IA 52101

BUNGE, WILFRED FRANKLIN, religion educator; b. Caledonia, Minn., Nov. 21, 1931; s. Franklin Henry George and Hilda Mathilda Emma (Fruechte) B.; m. Ruth Ann Jensen, Nov. 29, 1963; children: Paul Dieter, Maren Kjersti. BA summa cum laude, Luther Coll., Decorah, Iowa, 1953; MA, U. Iowa, 1955; BTh. with honors, Luther Theol. Sem., St. Paul, 1958; ThD, Harvard U., 1966. Instr. Luther Coll., Decorah, 1956-57, asst. prof., 1962-69, assoc. prof., 1969-74, prof., 1974—, head dept. classical langs., 1976-80, head dept. religion, 1979-87, dir. PAIDEIA program, 1979—; instr. Greek lang. Luther Theol. Sem., St. Paul, 1957-58; teaching fellow Harvard Div. Sch., Cambridge, Mass., 1961-62; mem. program evaluation panel NEH, 1985, 87. Author: (with others) Theological Perspectives, 1964; editor book rev. sect. Dialog, 1965, 66-70; contbr. articles to profl. jours. Recipient Faculty Growth award Am. Luth. Ch., 1971, 84; essay recipient prize Div. Coll. Univ. Svcs., 1986; Univ. fellow U. Iowa, 1954-55, George Chase Christian Meml. fellow Harvard U., 1958-59, 60-61, fellow Luth. World Fedn., 1959-60, fellow Luth. Brotherhood, 1964-65. Mem. AAUP, Soc. Bibl. Lit., Assn. Luth. Coll. Faculties (v.p. 1985-86, pres. 1986-87, past pres., mem. exec. com. 1987-88). Lutheran. Home: 902 W Pearl Decorah IA 52101 Office: Luther Coll Decorah IA 52101

BUNN, JOHN D., music minister; b. Madrid, Sept. 25, 1959; s. Lionell Dwight and Ruth (Pate) B.; m. Lisa Jane Phillips, May 28, 1982. BA in Music, Mars Hill (N.C.) Coll., 1981. Assoc. min. Naples (N.C.) Bapt. Ch., 1982-83; pianist Parkview Bapt. Ch., 1985-86; min. music, promotional dir. 1st Bapt. Ch., Elizabethton, Ten.., 1986—; dir. Upper East Tenn. Mins. Music, 1988-89. Mem. Watauga Assn. Bapts. (associational music dir. 1990-92). Office: 1st Bapt Ch 212 E F St Elizabethton TN 37643

BUNNELL, DON CARLOS, minister; b. Horse Cave, Ky., Jan. 21, 1930; s. Carlos and Elizabeth Myrrell (Davis) B.; m. Annelle Petty, May 21, 1955; children: Leesa Ann, Laura Kay, Carla Beth, Donna Lea. AA, Fla. Christian Coll., 1952; BA, Abilene Christian U., 1954; MA in Teaching, Southeastern State U., Durant, Okla., 1965. Min., dir. Bible chair Ch. of Christ, Madill, Okla., 1959-66; min., Bible camp bd. Strafford (Mo.) Ch. of Christ, 1966-68; minister, Bible chair dir. Ch. of Christ, Brigham City, Utah, 1969-71; minister Ch. of Christ, Casa Grande, Ariz., 1971-80, Caddo, Okla., 1980-87; minister Audubon Dr. Ch. of Christ, Laurel, Miss., 1987—; Bible camp tchr., mem. bd. Strafford, Mo., 1966-68; Bible camp counselor and dir. Pine Ridge, Utah, 1970, 71; Bible camp tchr., counselor Pettijohn Springs Bible Camp, Madill, Okla., 1981-85. Host TV evangelism program, Madill, Okla., 1963. Bd. dirs. ARC, Laurel, Miss., 1988—. With Civil Air Patrol, 1987— (Chaplain of the Yr. 1989). Recipient Thomas C. Casaday award, Civil Air Patrol, 1980, Miss. Wing Chaplain of Yr., 1989, Gil Robb Wilson award, 1989. Mem. AARP (bd. dirs Pinebelt chpt. 1991),Lions (pres. 1986-87), Kiwanis (bd. dirs. 1968-71). *Of all the things expected of one who is called a minister, there is the one thing to forever occupy his life if he is a true servant of the Lord. That one thing is to live and proclaim the message of the Lord Jesus Christ without fear or favor to anyone.*

BURCHETT, DARYL WAYNE, minister, emergency medical technician; b. Hiawatha, Kans., May 28, 1959; s. Lowell Alan and Lois Merlene (Link) B.; m. Kelly Dawn Crawford, Mar. 3, 1979; children: Jennifer, Matthew, Nathan, Isaac, Hannah, Emily. BA, Manhattan Christian Coll., 1982. Minister Christian Ch., Clyde, Kans., 1980-82, Norwich, Kans., 1982-88, LaCrosse, Kans., 1988—; emergency med. technician Rush County Cen. Ambulance, LaCrosse, 1988—. Councilman City of Norwich, 1983-87. Home: 521 Poplar La Crosse KS 67548 Office: Christian Ch 619 Oak La Crosse KS 67548

BURCHETT, JAMES CLARK, minister; b. New Boston, Ohio, Apr. 25, 1932; s. James Harvey and Goldie Blanch (May) B.; m. Carolyn Jeanette Carmichael; children: Cynthia, Michael, Darla, Scott. BA, Anderson (Ind.) Coll., 1955; M of Div., Internat. Sem., 1983, DD, 1985. Ordained to ministry, 1955. Assoc. pastor Second Ch. of God, Springfield, Ohio, 1955-56; pastor First Ch. of God, Concord, N.C., 1956-63, Trinity Ch. of God, Huntington, W.Va., 1963-71, Dayspring Ch. of God, Cin., 1971—; mem. bus. com., exec. council Nat. Office of Ch. of God, 1981—; pres. Regal Investments Inc., 1989. Author: A Biblical Trace of God's People, 1983, Lessons From a Bird, 1985; bd. pub. Warner Press, 1970-80. Active Cabell County (W.Va.) Bd. Edn., 1968-71; chmn. Conv. Program, Ind., 1965-66; trustee Mid Am. Bible Coll., Okla., 1978-83; vice-chmn. Citizens Concerned for Community Values, Cin., 1986—. Lodge: Kiwanis. Avocations: flying, reading. Office: Dayspring Ch of God 12010 Winston Rd Cincinnati OH 45240

BURDAN, DANNY REID, religion educator; b. Ft. Worth, May 6, 1952; s. Homer and Pauline (Taylor) B.; m. Linda Kay Marion, Nov. 5, 1971; children: Evan, Nathan. BA in Bible, OCUSA City U., Edmond, Okla., 1974; postgrad., Bethany Sem., 1990—. Min. Kopperl (Tex.) Ch. Christ, 1971-72; youth min. Cen. Ch. Christ, Shawnee, Okla., 1974-77; min. edn. Preston Rd. Ch. Christ, Dallas, 1977-85, Airline Ch. Christ, Bossier City, La., 1986—. Bd. dirs. Ark., La., Tex., Camp, Shrevesport, La., 1986-90, N.W. La. Tchrs. Workshop, Bossier City, 1988—, N.W. La. Bible Bowl, 1986—. Office: Airline Ch Christ 2125 Airline Dr Bossier City LA 71111

BURDASHAW, JOHN TIMOTHY, pastor; b. Washington, Jan. 17, 1958; s. John E. and Shirley Dee (Johnson) B.; m. Debora Sue Barker, June 17, 1978; children: John-Paul Timothy, Becky Sue. BA, Lee Coll., Cleveland, Tenn., 1980; master diploma, Christian Tng. Course, 1986. Ordained to ministry Ch. of God, 1984. Sr. pastor Marion (Ala.) Ch. of God, 1981-83, Lineville (Ala.) Ch. of God, 1983-84; youth pastor Parkview Ch. of God, Natchez, Miss., 1984-86; chaplain Cook County Corrections Dept., Chgo., 1986-88; sr. pastor NW Ch. of God, Wichita, Kans., 1988—; del. Wichita Pentecostal Fellowship, 1988—; speaker Kans. Mins. Tng. Conf., Wichita, 1990, 91. Contbr. articles to religious publs. Organizer Wichita Homeless Feeding Program, 1989—; mem. adv. bd. Wichita/Sedgwick County Regional Prevention Ctr. for Drug/Alcohol Abuse, 1991—. Mem. Wichita Evang. Assn. (del. 1988—), Ch. of God Instnl. Chaplains Assn. Home: 5914 Franklin Wichita KS 67212 Office: NW Ch of God 4600 W Central PO Box 9563 Wichita KS 67227-9563 *In my opinion, there is only one way for social concerns to be addressed: when men and women quit talking about the problems and become involved with the solutions. As long as one talks, one remains in the relative 'safe-zone' of friends and family. Even through public demonstrations and picketing, there is a certain 'safe-zone.' However, when one becomes involved, one-on-one, with an alcoholic or addict or a pregnant teen or whatever, then and only then does one leave the 'safe-zone' and risks—risks success or failure, intimacy or estrangement, relationship or non-involvement. It is past time for safe-zoners to become risk-takers.*

BURDEN, JERRY DON, religious organization administrator; b. Granite, Okla., July 20, 1944; s. Thomas George and Vivian Julianne (Savage) B.; m. Virginia Carol McCune, Dec. 28, 1966; children: Christina, Julia. BS, Okla. State U., 1967; MS, Ariz. State U., 1971. Cert. secondary sch. tchr. U.S.A. field rep. Gideons Internat., Nashville, 1976-81, adminstr. internat. dept., 1981-87, promotion mgr., 1987—; trustee Bapt. Sunday Sch. Bd., Nashville, 1984—. Mem. Religious Conf., Mgmt. Assn. Republican. Home: 139 Medearis Dr Old Hickory TN 37138 Office: Gideons Internat 2900 Lebanon Rd Nashville TN 37214

BURDICK, GARY LEE, minister; b. Pasadena, Calif., Apr. 19, 1952; s. James Alfred and Roberta (Jones) B.; m. Jacqueline Ruth Massaro, Oct. 8, 1978; children: James Vincent, Caralyn Ruth, Matthew John. BA, Point Loma Coll., 1974; MDiv, Princeton Theol. Sem., 1977. Ordained to ministry United Ch. of Christ, 1977. Chaplain Meth. Hosp., Bklyn., 1977-78; assoc. minister Wilson Meml. Union Ch., Watchung, N.J., 1978-82, East Congregational Ch., United Ch. of Christ, Grand Rapids, Mich., 1982-86; pastor 1st Congl. Ch. of Ada (Mich.) United Ch. of Christ, 1986—; chmn. ch. and ministry com. Grand Rapids Area Assn. United Ch. of Christ, 1988-90; mem. Commn. for Ch. & Pastoral Ministries, Mich. Conf. United Ch. of Christ, 1988-90. Trustee Pilgrim Manor Retirement Home, Grand Rapids, 1987-90; bd. dirs. All County Chs. Emergency Support System, Ada, 1986—; chmn. clergy adv. com. Community Counseling Ctr., Grand Rapids, 1984-87. Mem. Grand Rapids Clergy Assn., Forrest Hills Clergy Assn. Republican. Office: 1st Congl Ch of Ada United Ch of Christ PO Box 135 Ada MI 49301 *Happiness and growth come to us as we faithfully seek to love our God and our neighbor. Go and Grow!.*

BURG, GERALD WILLIAM, religious organization administrator; b. Pitts., Oct. 16, 1923; s. Julius Samuel and Anna (Shapiro) B.; student Walsh Inst., 1940-43; m. Flavia Kafton, Aug. 12, 1945; children—Cindy, Melinda, Andrew. Engring. rep. U.S. Rubber Co., 1943-45; adminstr. Beverly Hills (Calif.) B'nai B'rith, 1945-52, Univ. Synagogue, Brentwood, 1952-55; exec. dir. Wilshire Blvd. Temple, Los Angeles, 1956-80; mgmt. and fin. cons., 1980-85; adminstr. Sinai Temple, 1985—. Mem. Jewish relations com. Los Angeles council Boy Scouts Am., 1959-85; mem. Mayor's Adv. Com. on Community Activities, Los Angeles, 1963-73; chmn. Crime Prevention Fifth Councilmanic Dist., Los Angeles, 1968-73. Bd. dirs. McCobb Home for Boys, Los Angeles Psychiat. Service, Maple Ctr. for Crises Intervention, Save a Heart Found., Didi Hirsch Community Mental Health Services, pres., 1975-77; bd. dirs., chmn. finances, chmn. adminstrv. com. Community Care and Devel. Services, 1975—. Mem. Nat. (bd. dir., pres. 1975-77), Western (pres. 1969-71, bd. dirs.), So. Calif. (pres. 1958-60) assns. temple adminstrs., NCCJ (bd. dirs. brotherhood anytown 1966-82), Los Angeles Jewish Communal Execs. (dir.). Mem. B'nai B'rith (youth dir. 1945-82, Akiba award 1950, Beverly Hills pres. 1953-54). Club: Sertoma (v.p. 1973-82). Home: 5115 Kester Ave #202 Sherman Oaks CA 91403 Office: Sinai Temple 10400 Wilshire Blvd Los Angeles CA 90024

BURGE, GARY MITCHELL, religion educator; b. Covina, Calif., Apr. 28, 1952; s. John Theodore and Shirlee Ellen (Horn) B.; m. Carol Elizabeth Wright, June 19, 1976; 1 child, Ashley Elizabeth. BA, U. Calif., Riverside, 1974; MDiv, Fuller Theol. Seminary, Pasadena, Calif., 1978; PhD, U. Aberdeen, Scotland, 1983. Ordained to ministry Presbyn. Ch., 1982. Asst. prof. New Testament King Coll., Bristol, Tenn., 1981-87; assoc. prof. New Testament, Karl A. Olsson prof. religion, chair dept. Bibl. theol. studies North Park Coll., Chgo., 1987—. Author: The Anointed Community, The Holy Spirit in the Johannine Tradition, 1987, Interpreting the Gospel of John, 1992; contbr. articles to profl. jours. Lt. USNR, 1987—. Recipient Everett Harrison award in New Testament Fuller Seminary, 1978. Mem. Soc. Bibl. Lit., Bibl. Archaeology Soc., Tyndale Fellowship, Inst. for Bibl. Rsch. Office: North Park Coll 3225 W Foster Ave Chicago IL 60625-4895

BURGER, JOHN EDWARD, religion educator; b. Phila., Nov. 28, 1946; s. John Jacob and Frances Mary (Marley) B. BA, St. Columban's Coll., 1969; BD, St. John's Seminary, Brighton, Mass., 1972; MS, Loyola Coll., Balt., 1986. Ordained priest Roman Cath. Ch., 1973. Asst. pastor St. Patrick's Ch., Tokyo, 1975-77; pastor Queen of Peace Ch., Wakayama, Japan, 1979-83; dist. superior Columban Fathers, Wakayama, 1981-85; rector St. Columban's Theologate, Chgo., 1986—; trustee Cath. Theol. Union, Chgo., 1989—. Contbr. articles to profl. jours. Mem. Religious Formation Conf. (vice-chmn. region 1982-90), U.S. Cath. Mission Assn. Roman Catholic. Home: 5722 South Drexel Ave Chicago IL 60637 Office: Columban Fathers Saint Columbans NE 68056

BURGER, KENNETH EUGENE, minister; b. Washington, Feb. 13, 1950; s. Clarence Melvin and Eva (Smith) B.; m. Suzanne Thompson, Aug. 1971; children: Melinda Anne, Stephenie Leigh. BS in Secondary Edn., U. Ala., 1971; MDiv, Lexington Theol. Sem., 1975. Ordained to ministry Christian Ch., 1974. Student min. Laurence Creek Christian Ch., Maysville, Ky., 1972-74; min. First Christian Ch., Girard, Ill., 1974-77, 79-86; assoc. min. Cen. Christian Ch., Jacksonville, Ill., 1977-79; min. Bedford (Va.) Christian Ch., 1986—; chmn. N.B.A. Task Force, Christian Ch. in Va., 1989—; dir. Canoe Camp, Christian Ch. in Va., 1988-90, in Ill., 1983-85; chair Outdoor Ministries Fin. Com., Christian Ch. in Va., 1989—. Mem. Bedford Curbside Recycling Com., 1990—; chair Spl. Edn. Citizens Adv. Com., 1987—; pres. Liberty High Sch. Band Boosters, 1988-90. Mem. Bedford County Ministerial Assn. (pres. 1988-90). Office: Bedford Christian Ch 305 N Bridge St Bedford VA 24523 *From its very foundations, life is basically, inherently good...and can continue to be good if we so choose.*

BURGESS, D. GENE, minister; b. Memphis, Oct. 24, 1939; m. Heather A. Burgess; children: Deborah Michelle, Doyle Som. PharmD, U. Tenn., 1963; MA, Assembly of God Theol. Sem., Springfield, Mo., 1980. Ordained to ministry Assembly of God Ch. Overseas evangelist Assemblies of God, 1968-71; missionary Assemblies of God, Thailand, 1971-73, 82-84, Philippines, 1975-82; pastor First Assembly of God, Jackson, Miss., 1988—. Contbr. articles to profl. jours. Office: First Assembly of God 1201 Cooper Rd Jackson MS 39212

BURGESS, DAVID STEWART, former religious organization director, former trade union, diplomatic and international organization official; b. N.Y.C., June 15, 1917; s. John Stewart and Stella (Fisher) B.; m. Alice Stevens, Nov. 20, 1941; children: Laurel, Lyman, John, Emagene Burgess Castro, Stevens. BA, Oberlin Coll.; MDiv, Union Theol. Sem., N.Y.C., 1944. Ordained to ministry Congl. and Christian Ch., 1944. Migrant min. Home Mission Coun., Fed. Coun. Chs., 1942-43, Bd. Homeland Ministries, United Ch. of Christ, 1944-47; labor organizer CIO, N.C., S.C., Ga., 1947-55; with U.S. Fgn. Svc., New Delhi, Djakarta (Indonesia), Washington, 1955-66; dep. regional dir. for East Asia UNICEF, 1966-72; sr. officer Office of Exec. Dir. UNICEF, N.Y.C., 1972-77; dir. Latin Am. scholarship program Am. Univs., Cambridge, Mass., 1977-78; pastor Zion United Ch. of Christ, Newark, 1979-86, St. Stephen's United Ch. of Christ, Newark, 1979-89; exec. dir. Met. Ecumenical Ministry, Newark, 1981, 84-90. Author: (with others) Half Century of Religious Dialogue: 1939-1989; also articles in Christian Century, Progressive mag., New Republic, other jours. Recipient Social Action award Congl. and Christian Chs., 1946, Meritorious Svc. award U.S. Dept. State, 1957. Democrat. Home: 128 Ardmore Way Benicia CA 94510-2023

BURGESS, JOHN PAUL, minister, religion educator; b. Denver, Dec. 18, 1954; s. Charles Samuel and Elizabeth Ann (Bulger) B.; m. Deborah Lynn Shoemaker, July 9, 1988; 1 child, Hannah Ruth. BA, Colo. Coll., 1976; MA, U. Chgo., 1980; MDiv, McCormick Sem., 1983; PhD, U. Chgo., 1986. Ordained to ministry Presbyn. Ch. (U.S.A.), 1984. Asst. prof. religion, campus minister Doane Coll., Crete, Nebr., 1986-91; parish assoc. Westminster Presbyn. Ch., Lincoln, Nebr., 1989-91; assoc. for theol. studies Presbyn. Ch. (U.S.A.), Louisville, 1991—. Contbr. articles to profl. publs. NEH grantee, 1990-91. Mem. Am. Acad. Religion, Soc. Christian Ethics. Office: 100 Witherspoon St Louisville KY 40206

BURGESS, ROGER, church official; b. Sioux City, Iowa, 1927; s. Frederick Earl and Mabel (Irwin) B.; m. Donah Jean Salyer, 1953; 4 children. BA, Morningside Coll., 1950, LLD (hon.), 1965; postgrad., Am. U. Grad. Sch. Journalism, 1966. Dir. Morningside Coll. Press Bur., Sioux City, 1948-50; projects sec., editor youth publs. Nat. Conf. Meth. Youth, Nashville, 1950-53; editor publs., dir. communications Meth. Gen. Bd. Temperance, 1953-56, assoc. gen. sec., 1956-60; dir. communications, editor news mag. Meth. Gen. Bd. Christian Social Concerns, 1960-61, assoc. gen. sec., responsible div. alcohol problems and gen. welfare, 1961-65; exec. v.p. charge creative planning in advt., graphic arts and audio visuals Design Ctr., Inc., 1965-67; nat. exec. dir. Joint Action in Community Service, 1967-68, sec. bd. dirs.; gen. sec. Bd. Health and Welfare Ministries United Meth. Ch., 1968-72, assoc. gen. sec. Bd. Global Ministries, 1972-73; editorial dir. United Meth. Pub. House, 1974-76, v.p. pub. relations, 1976-84; gen. sec. United Meth. Communications, 1984—; treas. Communications Commn.; Communication Chmn., bd. dirs. Religion in Am. Life. Contbr. articles to profl. jours. Former bd. dirs. Scarritt Coll.; former v.p., bd. dirs. United Way Nashville. With USN, 1945-46, USNR, 1946-48. Office: PO Box 320 Nashville TN 37202

BURGESS, STANLEY MILTON, religious studies educator; b. Nagercoil, India, Nov. 27, 1937; s. John H. and Bernice F. (Andrews) B.; m. Ruth Lenora Vassar, Feb. 26, 1960; children: John Bradley, Stanley Matthew, Scott Vassar, Justin David, Heidi Amanda. AB, U. Mich., 1957, MA, 1959; PhD, U. Mo., 1971. Prof. religious studies S.W. Mo. State U., Springfield, 1976—. Author: The Spirit and the Church: Antiquity, 1984, The Holy Spirit: Eastern Christian Traditions, 1989; editor: Reaching Beyond: Chapters in the History of Perfectionism, 1986, Dictionary of Pentecostal and Charismatic Movements, 1988 (on of top 15 books of yr. Internat. Bull. Missionary Rsch., Critics' Choice award Christianity Today 1990). Mem. Am. Acad. Religion, Rotary. Home: Rte 2 Box 307A Strafford MO 65757 Office: SW Mo State U 901 S National Springfield MO 65804

BURGHARDT, WALTER JOHN, priest, theologian, author; b. N.Y.C., July 10, 1914; s. John Albert and Mary (Krupp) B. MA, Woodstock Coll., 1937, Licentiate in Philosophy, 1938; STD, Cath. U. Am., 1957. Joined S.J., 1931; ordained priest Roman Cath. Ch., 1941. Prof. hist. theology Woodstock (Md.) Coll., 1946-74; prof. patristic theology Cath. U. Am., Washington, 1974-78; theologian in residence Georgetown U., 1978-90; sr. fellow Woodstock Theol. Ctr., 1990—; mem. U.S. dialogue group Luth.-Roman Cath. Theol. Conversations, 1965-76; mem. Faith Order Commn., World Coun. Chs., 1968-75, Nat. Coun. Chs., 1971-75; mem. Internat. Papal Theol. Commn., 1969-80. Author: The Image of God in Man According to Cyril of Alexandria, 1957, The Testimony of the Patristic Age Concerning Mary's Death, 1957, (with William F. Lynch) The Idea of Catholicism, 1960; All Lost in Wonder: Sermons on Theology and Life, 1960, Saints and Sanctity, 1965, Towards Reconciliation, 1974, Seven Hungers of the Human Family, 1976, Tell the Next Generation, 1980, Sir, We Would Like To See Jesus, 1982, Still Proclaiming Your Wonders, 1984, Grace on Crutches, 1986, Preaching: The Art and the Craft, 1987, Lovely in Eyes Not His, 1988, To Christ I Look, 1989, Dare To Be Christ, 1991; mng. editor Theol. Studies, 1946-67, editor in chief, 1967-90. Recipient Mariological award, 1958, Outstanding Contbn. Sacred Theology award Cardinal Spellman, 1962, Andrew White medal Loyola Coll., 1968, Cath. Press award, 1979, Pres.'s medal Cath. U. Am., 1982; recipient 18 hon. degrees. Office: Manresa-on Severn PO Box 9 Annapolis MD 21404

BURGIN, MAX EDWARD, minister, military officer; b. Forest City, N.C., Feb. 26, 1934; s. Robert Cheek and Nannie Bell (Harris) B.; m. Mickie Jean Kelly, June 30, 1962; children: Kelli Lynn, Edward Lee. BA, Wake Forest U., 1959; BD, Southwestern Bapt. Theol. Sem., 1962; MA, L.I. U., 1974; D Ministry, N.Y. Theol. Sem., 1976. Ordained to ministry Bapt. Ch., 1962. Pastor Union Bapt. Ch., Shelby, N.C., 1963-65; commd. 1st lt. U.S. Army, 1963, advanced through grades to col., 1985; dir. dept. ministry and pastoral care Walter Reed Army Med. Ctr., Washington, 1986-91; ret., 1991. Contbr. articles to profl. jours. Chmn. personnel com. Sch. Bd., Fort Benning, Ga., 1978-81. Decorated Bronze Star, Nat. Def. Ribbon, others. Fellow Coll. of Chaplains. Home: Rte 2 Box 73E Ellenboro NC 28040 *If one person calls you a jackass you can ignore it, if two you should consider buying the saddle.*

BURGUIERE, JULIUS EDWARD, broadcasting executive, radio announcer; b. Tarrytown, N.Y., June 17, 1958; s. Julius Edward and Eleanor Ruth (Carlson) B.; m. Cheryl Dawn Pilcher, Aug. 11, 1979; children: Joseph Arthur, Jenava Diane. BS, Evangel Coll., 1981. Radio announcer Sta. KLFJ Radio, Springfield, Mo., 1980-82; music dir./announcer Sta. WIBI Radio, Carlinville, Ill., 1987—. Mem. Assemblies of God. Office: Sta WIBI Radio Box 140 Carlinville IL 62626

BURHOE, RALPH WENDELL, religion and science educator; b. Somerville, Mass., June 21, 1911; s. Winslow Page and Mary Trenaman (Stumbles) B.; m. Frances Bickford, Aug. 4, 1931 (dec. Aug. 1967); children: Winslow Newton, Laura Jean Burhoe Maier, Thomas Allen, Diana May Burhoe Chase; m. Calla Crawford Butler, Apr. 6, 1969. Student, Harvard, 1928-32, Andover Newton Theol. Sch., 1934-36; Sc.D., Meadville Lombard Theol. Sch., Chgo., 1975; L.H.D., Rollins Coll., 1979. Observer, research asst., librarian, asst. to dir. Blue Hill Meteorol. Obs., Harvard U., 1936-47; asst. sec. Am. Meteorol. Soc., Milton, Mass., 1936-47; treas. Am. Meteorol. Soc., 1942-47; exec. officer Am. Acad. Arts and Sciences, Boston, 1947-64; research prof. theology and scis. Meadville Theol. Sch., Chgo., 1964-74, dir. Ctr. for Advanced Studies in Theology and the Scis., 1965-66, prof. emeritus, 1974—; founder Ctr. for Advanced Studies in Religion and Sci., 1973, treas., bd. dirs., 1974-89; co-founder, operator Chgo. Ctr. for Religion, 1988—. Author: Toward a Scientific Theology, 1981; editor: (with Hudson Hoagland) Evolution and Man's Progress, 1962; author, editor: Science and Human Values in the Twenty-first Century, 1971; editor Zygon: Jour. Religion and Sci., 1966-79, founding editor, 1979—; contbr. to profl. jours. and books. 1st Am. recipient Templeton prize for progress in religion, London, 1980. Fellow AAAS, World Acad. Art and Sci., Am. Acad. Arts and Scis., Inst. on Religion in an Age of Sci. (founder 1954, hon. pres. 1959—), Soc. Sci. Study of Religion (treas. 1965-70, Disting. Career Achievement award 1984); mem. Am. Acad. Religion, Am. Theol. Assn., Inst. Theol. Encounter with Sci. and Tech. Home and Office: Montgomery Place 5550 South Shore Dr #715 Chicago IL 60637 *The religions of the world are fast losing their effectiveness for transmitting human values and moral behavior, primarily because religions have lost their credibility in the context of the science-believing world. If the religions of the world were more adequately understood in the light of some newer scientific interpretations of religion published in Zygon and elsewhere, then essential religious truths would thereby increasingly be revitalized and harmonized to bring wider altruism, peace, and meaning to humanity. One illustration of why our group can be confident of this outcome stems from what B.F. Skinner told us: that positive is more effective than negative behavioral reinforcement. Hence a religion which establishes belief in an all-knowing and -powerful God of love, will be selected in the long run of cultural evolution as more fit or necessary for good behavior than a state's legal or military compulsion.*

BURKACKI, GARRY SHAWN, minister; b. Mt. Clemens, Mich., Mar. 8, 1961; s. Eugene Anthony and Beverly Jean (Higgins) B. Cert. Pastoral Ministry, So. Sem., 1983; Cert. Seminar Study, Calvary Fellowships, 1983; Cert., Billy Graham Sch. Evangelism, 1985. Ordained to ministry So. Bapt. Conv., 1982. Pastor Elkton (Mich.) Bapt. Chapel, 1977-79, Grosse Pointe Park (Mich.) Bapt. Ch., 1979-80, Faith Bapt. Chapel, Sandusky, Mich., 1980-81, Laneview Bapt. Ch., Kenton, Tenn., 1981-85, 2d Bapt. Ch., Indianola, Miss., 1990—; moderator Gibson Bapt. Assn., Trenton, 1982-89; pres. Gibson Bapt. Pastors Conf., Trenton, 1987-88; bd. dirs. Gibson Bapt. Evangelism Coun., 1983-87, Delta U. Bapt. Student Union, 1990—. Mem. planning com. Good Old Days Festival, Richmond, Mich., 1979-80, adv. com. Macomb County CETA Program, 1979-80; pool dir. ACTION Club, Rutherford, Tenn., 1985, planning com. Kenton Homecoming Festival, 1986-87. Recipient Appreciation award Gibson Bapt. Pastors, 1988, Gibson Bapt. chs., 1989. Bethpage Bapt. Ch., 1990. Mem. Sunflower Bapt. Assn. Office: 2d Bapt Ch PO Box 207 Indianola MS 38751

BURKE, ANNE M., ecumenical agency director. Exec. dir. Urban Ministry Ctr., Raleigh, N.C. Office: Urban Ministry Ctr 310 W Edenton St Raleigh NC 27603*

BURKE, AUGUSTIN EMILE, bishop; b. Sluice Point, N.S., Can., Jan. 22, 1922. Ordained priest Roman Cath. Ch., 1950. Consecrated bishop of Yarmouth, N.S., 1968—. Office: PO Box 278, 53 Rue Park St, Yarmouth, NS Canada B5A 4B2

BURKE, JOHN, priest; b. Washington, Sept. 15, 1928; s. William Francis and Grace Allison (Logan) B. AB, Cath. U. Am., 1950, MA, 1965, STD, 1969. Joined Order Preachers, ordained priest Roman Cath. Ch., 1960. Prof. homiletics St. Stephen's Coll., Dover, Mass., 1961-64, Immaculate Conception faculty, 1964-67, 90, asst. prof., summers 1964-69, asst. prof. drama, 1968-72, dir. Preaching Workshop, 1965-67, dir. Preachers Inst., 1967-72; mem. faculty Washington Theol. Coalition, 1968-69; coord. Nat. Congress for the Word of God, 1972; founder, exec. dir. Nat. Inst. for the Word of God, Washington, 1972—. Author: Bible Sharing Youth Retreat Manual, 1983, Beginners' Guide to Bible Sharing, Vol. I, II, 1984, The Homilist's Guide to Scripture, Theology and Canon Law, 1987; editor: Gospel Power: Toward the Revitalization of Preaching, 1978, Bible Sharing: How to Grow in the Mystery of Christ, 1979, A New Look at Preaching, 1983; contbr. articles to profl. jours.; producer TV film Chimbote, 1964. Mem. Radio-TV Dirs. Guild of AFTRA, Phi Beta Kappa. Address: 487 Michigan Ave NE Washington DC 20017 *For lasting happiness in life, one needs to experience the active presence of God.*

BURKE, KENNETH EDISON, minister; b. Norfolk, Va., Apr. 15, 1936; s. Kenneth Edison and Ida Pearle (Nunnally) B.; m. Ruby Jane Brown, Dec. 23, 1960 (div. 1989); children: Kenneth H., Robert E. BA, U. Richmond, 1958; MDiv, So. Bapt. Theol. Sem., 1962. Ordained to ministry So. Bapt. Conv., 1962. Pastor 1st Bapt. Ch., Jamestown, Ky., 1962-66; career missionary Home Mission Bd., So. Bapt. Conv., Washington, 1966-68; pastor Westminster Bapt. Ch., Norfolk, 1968-69; min. Christian edn. Shiloh Bapt. Ch., Washington, 1969-81; pastor East Washington Heights Bapt. Ch., Washington, 1981—; v.p. D.C. Bapt. Conv., 1990-91, pres., 1991-92; bd. dirs. Coun. Chs. Greater Washington, 1990—, Pastoral Care Counseling Ctr., Mt. Airy Bapt. Ch., Washington, 1990—. Sec., bd. dirs. Oxon Hill (Md.) Vol. Fire and Rescue Assn. Inc., 1983—. Mem. Missionary Bapt. Mins. Conf., Am. Bapt. Mins. Coun. Greater Washington Met. Area, Mins.' Fellowship of D.C. Bapt. Conv., Kiwanis (chmn. Ea. br. 1988-90, spiritual aims com.). Democrat. Office: East Washington Heights Bapt Ch 2220 Branch Ave SE Washington DC 20020-3340

BURKE, LAWRENCE A., bishop. Bishop of Nassau, Roman Cath. Ch., The Bahamas. Office: The Hermitage, Eastern Rd, PO Box N-8187, Nassau The Bahamas*

BURKE, LESLIE CARLTON, minister; b. Memphis, Nov. 30, 1941; s. William Leslie and Corinne (Whitten) B.; m. Dee Vonne Clark, Dec. 29, 1960; children: Carlton, Stephen, Deborah, Sarah. BA, Harding Coll., 1964. Min. Ch. of Christ, Chehalis, Wash., 1970-76, Sandy, Oreg., 1976-80, Manteca, Calif., 1980-84, Hanford, Calif., 1984—; mem. corp. King's Stewards, Inc., Hanford, 1984—, Western Christian Sch., Hanford, 1984—. Mem. Kiwanis (sec. 1986-89). Republican. Office: Ch of Christ 1596 W Grangeville Rd Hanford CA 93230

BURKE, MARNIE SPARRE, church business administrator; b. Toledo, June 7, 1937; d. Fin Dallas Sparre and Geraldine (Downs) Purdy; m. William Alvord Burke, Jr., Aug. 10, 1957; 1 child, Maren Louise. Student, Middlebury (Vt.) Coll., 1955-57; cert. in ch. bus. adminstrn., Emory U., 1986. Sec. St. Stephen's Ch., Plainfield, N.J., 1972-75; editor First United Meth. Ch., Westfield, N.J., 1975-87; adminstr. sec., property mgr. First United Meth. Ch., Westfield, 1981-87; bus. mgr. The Presbyn. Ch., Westfield, 1988—. Mem. Bicycle Bd. Westfield, N.J.; active in Sanctuary Choir, Oratorio Singers, Wesley Singers, 1st United Meth. Ch., Westfield, Scherzo Bell Ringers, The Presbyn. Ch., Westfield. Fellow Nat. Assn. of Ch. Bus. Adminstrs., United Meth. Assn. Ch. Bus. Adminstrs. (bd. dirs. 1986-89), Presbyn. Ch. Bus. Adminstrs. Assn., Community Players Westfield (v.p. bus. 1965-67). Home: 728 Hanford Pl Westfield NJ 07090 Office: The Presbyn Ch 140 Mountain Ave Westfield NJ 07090

BURKE, THOMAS JOHN, JR., minister, educator; b. Dalhart, Tex., Dec. 25, 1943; s. Thomas John and Dorothy Ann (Mileti) B.; m. Maria Elizabeth Aguilar, June 13, 1970. Student, Nyack (N.Y.) Missionary Coll., 1961-63; BA in History, Baylor U., 1965; MDiv, Trinity Evang. Div. Sch., Deerfield, Ill., 1969; PhD in Religion, Garrett-Evang. Theol. Sem.-Northwestern U., 1978; MA in Philosophy, Mich. State U., 1983, PhD, 1989. Ordained to ministry Am. Bapt. Conv., 1969. Asst. pastor Bapt. Ch., Milw., 1967-69; pastor Bapt. Ch., Pewaukee, wis., 1970-72, Coll. Bapt. Ch., Hillsdale, Mich., 1974-82; asst. prof. Hillsdale Coll., 1982-88, assoc. prof., 1988—, chmn. dept. philosophy and religion, 1984—, chmn. humanities div., 1990—; mem. social concerns com. Am. Bapt. Assn., 1972-75. Editor: The Christian Vision: Man and Morality, 1986, Man and Mind: A Christian Theory of Personality, 1987, Man and State: Religion, Society and the Constitution, 1988; contbr. articles to profl. jours. Mem. Am. Philos. Assn., Soc. Christian Philosophers, Am. Sci. Affiliation (assoc.), Soc. for Philosophy and Psychology, Rotary. Office: Hillsdale Coll Hillsdale MI 49242

BURKE-SULLIVAN, EILEEN CATHERINE, liturgist; b. Laramie, Wyo., Apr. 5, 1949; d. M. Joseph and Mary Josephine (Sirridge) Burke; m. Michael Joseph Sullivan, July 16, 1982. BA, St. Mary Coll., Leavenworth, Kans., 1971; MusM, U. Colo., 1975; M in Spiritual Theology, Creighton U., Omaha, 1984. Dir. music, liturgy Cathedral Parish, Cheyenne, Wyo., 1976-77; dir. music, coord. worship Archdiocese of Omaha, 1977-80; nat. exec. dir. Christian Life Communities of U.S., St. Louis, 1980-83; dir. worship All Saints Cath. Ch., Dallas, 1984—; adj. prof. Creighton U., Omaha, summers 1984—, U. Dallas, Irving, 1989—; v.p. for ecumenical rels. Greater Dallas Community of Chs., Dallas, 1988-90; diocesan rep. Tex. Conf. Chs., Austin, 1986—; mem. rep. Inter-Faith Dialogues, Dallas, 1987—; mem. Diocesan Strategic Planning Commn., Dallas, 1991—, Worship Commn., Dallas Diocese, 1990—. Script writer tv documentary: Built of Living Stones, 1988; contbr. articles to profl. jours., chpts. to books. Chmn. by-laws Grapevine Neighborhood Assn., 1989-90, pres., 1991—. Mem. Fedn. Diocesan Lit. Commns., Nat. Pastoral Musicians. Democrat. Home: 533 Post Oak Rd Grapeview TX 76051 Office: All Saints Cath Ch 5231 Meadow Creek Dallas TX 75248

BURKETT, EDWARD EUGENE, minister, educational consultant; b. Greencastle, Pa., Jan. 15, 1955; s. George Lester and Kathryn Marie (Keim)

B.; m. Vanessa Kay Howell, Mar. 5, 1977; children: Jennifer Rebekah, Timothy Andrew, Ethan Edward. BS in Secondary Edn. Earth and Space Sci., Bloomsburg U., 1975; M in Ministry in Pastoral Theology, Antietam Bibl. Sem., 1983; postgrad., Liberty U., 1990—. Cert. profl. tchr., Pa.; ordained minister, 1986. Jr. high sch. instr. Upper Adams Sch. Dist., Biglerville, Pa., 1976-78; jr. and sr. high sch. instr. Broadfording Christian Acad., Hagerstown, Md., 1980-82; instr. Antietam Biblical Coll., Hagerstown, 1983; minister Highland Brethren Ch., Marianna, Pa., 1983-85; minister, founder Cornerstone Bible Ch., Washington, Pa., 1985—; adminstr., prin. Washington Christian Sch., 1987-88; ednl. cons. Self-Contract, Washington, 1984—. Author: (study series) Discipleship in Action, 1984; Biblical Foundations for Local Church Government, 1983. Activist pro-life orgns., Hagerstown and Washington, 1975—. Mem. Alpha Phi Omega. Republican. Avocations: hunting, camping, golfing, reading, computer technology. Home: 368 Burton Ave Washington PA 15301 Office: 995 Addison St Washington PA 15301 *Jesus Christ is my life, there is absolutely no substitute for a vital relationship with Jesus, who is both Savior and Lord.*

BURKETT, RANDALL KEITH, educator; b. Union City, Ind., Oct. 23, 1943; s. Forrest and Frances Louise (Ullery) B.; m. Nancy Hall, Aug. 21, 1965. BA, Am. U., 1965; M of Theol. Studies, Harvard U., 1969; PhD, U. So. Calif., 1975. From assoc. dir. spl. studies to coord. grants and rsch. Holy Cross Coll., 1973-85; assoc. dir., W.E.B. DuBois Inst. Harvard U., Cambridge, 1985—. Author: Garveyism as a Religious Movement, 1978, Black Redemption, 1978; co-editor: Black Apostles, 1978), (with Nancy Hall Burkett and Henry Louis Gates, Jr.) Black Biography 1790-1950: A Cumulative Index, 3 vols., 1991; editor Afro-Am. Religions newsletter, 1976—. Oakley fellow U. So. Calif., 1969-72, rsch. fellow NEH, 1979-80; Ford Found. grantee, 1971. Mem. Am. Acad. Religion, Am. Soc. Ch. History, Assn. for the Study of Afro-Am. Life and History, Orgn. of Am. Historians, Worcester Com. on Fgn. Rels. Office: Harvard U W E B DuBois Inst 44 Brattle St Cambridge MA 02138

BURKHAMMER, EUGENE RONALD, clinical counselor, evangelist; b. Clarksburg, W.Va., Feb. 24, 1944; s. Eugene Dawson and Lucille Iowa (Murphy) B.; m. Cynthia Jean Gaver, May 7, 1964; children: Eugene Ronald Jr., Sean Richard, James Robert, Joshua Heath. AA, Nazarene Bible Coll., 1974, Kent State U., 1984; BS, Friends U., 1985; MA, Internat. U., 1987; PhD, Internat. Assn. Christian Clin. Counselors, 1989. Ordained to ministry Ch. of the Nazarene, 1977. Assoc. pastor Ch. of the Nazarene, Colorado Springs, Colo., 1970-74; pastor Ch. of the Nazarene, Amarillo, Tex., 1974-77; evangelist Ch. of the Nazarene, Monaca, Pa., 1977; pres. E.R. Burkhammer Evang. Assn., Inc., Rochester, Pa., 1979—; bd. dirs. Agape Outreach Ctr., Rochester, 1988—; clin. counselor, Rochester, 1989—. Mem. Internat. Assn. Christian Clin. Counselors. Home: 416 Vermont Ave Rochester PA 15074

BURKHART, JOHN ERNEST, minister, religion educator; b. Riverside, Calif., Oct. 25, 1927; s. Joseph Ernest and Lockie Louisa (Dryden) B.; m. Virginia Bell French, Sept. 16, 1951; children: David Aaron, Audrey Elizabeth, Deborah Ann. BA, Occidental Coll., 1949; BD, Union Theol. Sem., 1952; PhD, U. So. Calif., 1959; DD, Occidental Coll., 1964. Ordained to ministry United Presby. Ch., 1952. Pastor Presbyn. U. U. So. Calif., L.A., 1953-59, from instr. to prof. of Theology, 1959-1990; prof. Systematic Theology McCormick Theol. Sem., Chgo., 1990—; vis. prof. Garrett Theol. Sem. Evanston, Ill., 1966, DePaul U., Chgo., 1970. Author: Kingdom, Church, and Baptism, 1959, Understanding the Word of God, 1964, Worship, 1982; contbr. articles to profl. jours. Fellow Royal Anthrop. Inst., Soc. for Values in Higher Edn.; mem. Am. Acad. Religion, Cath. Theol. Soc. of Am., N.Am. Acad. Liturgy, Am. Theol. Soc. (pres. 1969-70), Midwest Alumni Club (v.p. 1985—), Quadrangle Club, Blue Key, Phi Beta Kappa. 1st lt., chaplain USAF, 1952-53. Home: Four Elm Creek Dr # 117 Elmhurst IL 60126 Office: McCormick Theol Sem 5555 S Woodlawn Ave Chicago IL 60637

BURKHART, ROBIN LEE, minister; b. Adrian, Mich., Apr. 28, 1952; s. Paul Leon and Madelyn Lela (Still) B.; m. Linda Luigina D'Achille, July 27, 1974; children: Erika Lynn, Paul D'Achille, Mark David. BA, Cen. Bible Coll., 1974; Mdiv, Fuller Theol. Sem., 1977; PhD, Mich. State U., 1987. Ordained to ministry Assemblies of God, 1979. Min. christian edn. Christian Life Ch., LaCresenta, Calif., 1974-77, Bethany Assembly of God, Adrian, Mich., 1977-88; dir. extension edn. Assemblies of God Theol. Sem., Springfield, Mo., 1988-89; dir. christian edn. Assemblies of God Mich. Dist., Dearborn, 1989—; pres. bd. dirs., The Christian Mission, Adrian, 1978-80, Lenawee Christian Sch., Adrian, 1987-88; pres., Lenawee County Ministrial Assn., Adrian, 1985-86; founding dir., Bethany Day Care, Adrian, 1987-88. author: To Be Like Jesus, 1990; contbr. articles to profl. jours. Mem. Profl. Assn. Christian Educators. Office: Assemblies of God Mich 6053 Chase Rd Dearborn MI 48239 *No one is born a winner or a loser. Life is about what we choose and create, not about what we have or inherit.*

BURKS, ROBERT EDWARD, minister, educator; b. Washington, Aug. 20, 1930; s. Jesse Audie and Elizabeth (Morton) B.; m. Norma Jean Banner, Sept. 5, 1953 (div. Oct. 1984); children: Jennifer Burks Dawson, Kari Beth Burks Parchment, Robert Tucker; m. Elizabeth Steadman, Oct. 23, 1987. BA, Mercer U., 1951; BD, So. Bapt. Theol. Sem., 1954, ThM, 1955, PhD, 1961. Ordained to ministry So. Bapt. Conv., 1953. Pastor Bethel Bapt. Ch., Scottsburg, Ind., 1955-60; assoc. pastor 1st Bapt. Ch., Anderson, S.C., 1961-65; prof., chmn. dept. religion Anderson Coll., 1965—. Former chmn. bd. dirs. ARC; bd. dirs. Anderson Scholastic Loan Fund, 1963—, past pres.; bd. dirs. Anderson Sch. Theology for Laymen, 1962—, also past pres. Recipient Svc. to Community award Kiwanis, 1965. Mem. Soc. Bibl. Lit., Nat. Assn. Bapt. Profs. Religion (mem. editorial bd. 1980-85, sec. S.E. region 1984-89), Rotary. Democrat. Home: 504 Squire Circle Clemson SC 29631 Office: Anderson Coll Anderson SC 29621

BURLEIGH, DOUGLAS GLEN, religious organization executive; b. Norman, Okla., Mar. 31, 1945; s. Gilbert Emmett and Grace Lorene (Cochran) B.; m. Deborah Jan Coe, Nov. 30, 1974; children: John Douglas, James David, Katherine Elizabeth, Peter Gilbert. BA in Polit. Sci., Willamette U., 1966; MA in Polit. Sci., U. Wash., 1967; M of Divinity, Fuller Theol. Sem., 1979. Ordained to ministry Presbyn. Ch. Area dir. Young Life Internat., Bellevue, Wash., 1967-72, Tacoma, 1972-74; regional dir., Seattle, 1974-78, Western states field dir., 1978-84; Ea. states field dir., Washington, 1984-87; pres., Colorado Springs, Colo., 1987—; cons. Nat. Student Movement, Washington, 1985—. Contbr. articles to ministry jours. Eagle scout Boy Scouts Am., Seattle, 1958; student body officer Willamette U., Salem, 1965-66. Recipient God and Country award Boy Scouts Am., 1957; Nat. Defense fellow U.S. Dept Health, Edn. and Welfare, 1965; Guy F. Atkinson scholar Willamette U., 1965-66. Mem. Phi Eta Sigma, Phi Delta Theta (pledge trainer 1965). Republican. Lodge: Rotary (boys work chmn. Tacoma club 1973-74). Home: 1630 Pinnacle Ridge Ln Colorado Springs CO 80919 Office: Youth Life Internat 720 W Monument St Colorado Springs CO 80919

BURLESON, DANIEL EVAN, minister; b. San Pedro, Calif., June 28, 1967; s. Roy Evan Burleson and Alice Susan (Mahler) Starr. BA, The Master's Coll., 1990. Youth pastor Bethany Bapt. Ch., Thousand Oaks, Calif., 1990—. Office: Bethany Bapt Ch 200 W Bethany Ct Thousand Oaks CA 91360

BURLESON, TIMOTHY WARREN, minister; b. Asheville, N.C., Aug. 22, 1954; s. Harley Warren and Ruby Mae (Mc Craw) B.; children: Timothy Gabriel, Elizabeth Erin. BA, Appalachian State U., Boone, N.C., 1977; MRE, S.E. Bapt. Theol. Sem., 1979. Ordained to min. So. Bapt. Ch., 1978. Assoc. pastor Mt. Vernon Bapt. Ch., Raleigh, N.C., 1977-78; pastor Boissevain (Va.) Bapt. Ch., 1979-80, Mt. Moriah-Calvert Bapt. Ch., Brevard, N.C., 1980-82, Greens Creek Bapt. Ch., Sylva, N.C., 1982—, Fort Barnwell Missionary Bapt. Ch., Dover, N.C., 1987—. Coach Jackson County Little League, Sylva, 1985—; chaplain assoc. C.J. Harris Community Hosp., Sylva, 1986—. Mem. Jackson County Ministerial Assn. (pres. 1986—); Tuckaseigee Bapt. Assn. (evangelism chmn. 1983-85). Avocations: reading, sports. Home and Office: 109 Campbell St Swannanoa NC 28778 :

BURMAN, MARY MORTENSEN, religious education director, former educator; b. Chgo., Apr. 8, 1930; d. Axel Christian and Mabel Geneva (Ide) Mortensen; m. Robert Duane Burman, Nov. 17, 1951; children: James, John, William, Mary Evelyn, Thomas, Edward. BA in Enlish and Edn., U. Wyo., 1952. Dir. Christian edn. 1st Bapt. Ch., Laramie, Wyo., 1985—; tchr. pub. schs. Laramie; del. Am. Bap. Chs. Rocky Mountain, Denver, 1985—, mem. dept. edn., 1988—; dir. Jr. High Camp, Wyo. Bapt. Assn., Casper, 1985-90, mem. camp bd., 1986—. Trustee Albany County Sch. Bd., Laramie, 1985—, also chmn. bd.; bd. dirs. Cathedral Home for Children, Laramie, 1988—. Mem. Laramie Ministerial Assn. (sec. 1985-87). Republican. Home: 1214 Downey St Laramie WY 82070 Office: 1st Bapt Ch 1517 Canby St Laramie WY 82070

BURNEKO, GUY CHRISTIAN, interdisciplinary studies educator; b. Oneida, N.Y., Nov. 14, 1946; s. Julian Jerome and Mary Elizabeth (LoFaro) B.; m. Grace Manning Bailey, May 10, 1980 (div. 1987); 1 child, Eva Eugenia. BA, Fordham U., 1968; MA, U. Alaska, 1971; PhD, Emory U., 1981. Asst. prof. Alaska Pacific U., Anchorage, 1988—; social worker Jesuit Vol. Corps., Bethel, Alaska, 1972-74. Contbr. articles to profl. publs. NEH fellow, 1974, 85. Mem. Am. Acad. Religion, Internat. Jean Gebser Assn., Assn. for Integrative Studies, C. G. Jung Assn. (pres. 1990—), Asheville Noetics Group. Home and Office: Alaska Pacific U 4101 University Dr 536 Anchorage AK 99508

BURNES, DONALD EDWARD, minister; b. Forsyth, Mont., Sept. 18, 1926; s. Ira Calvin Burnes and Mary Ann (Bell) Rask; m. Hilda Jean Koch, June 5, 1952; children: Christel Jean, Donald Edward Jr., Linda Annalesa, Deborah Lynn. AS, Altus Jr. Coll., 1973; BS, U. Md., 1984; postgrad., Nazarene Theol. Sem., Kansas City, Mo., 1984, So. Nazarene U., 1985. Ordained to ministry Ch. of the Nazarene, 1973. Pastor Ch. of the Nazarene, various U.S. cities, 1959-81; missionary Ch. of the Nazarene, Japan, 1981-85; pastor Ch. of the Nazarene, Eldorado, Okla., 1985-86, Kaiserslautern, Fed. Republic Germany, 1986-90; evangelist Ch. of the Nazarene, Altus, Okla., 1990—, min. outreach, 1991—; asst. missionary Ch. of the Nazarene, The Philippines, 1966-68; tchr. religion, Topeka, 1971-72; CLT dir. La. Dist. Ch. of the Nazarene, 1962-63. With USAF, 1945-74; Vietnam. Democrat. Home and Office: 1105 Darla Ave Altus OK 73521

BURNETT, BOBBY J., minister; b. Alexander City, Ala., Jan. 28, 1932; s. Rueben J. and Mollie (Newman) B.; m. Nobie Ruth O'Neal, Sept. 8, 1963; children: Tracy Ann Burnett Taylor, Bobby J. Jr. MusB, La. State U., 1956; DD (hon.), Bapt. Christian U., 1982. Ordained to ministry Bapt. Ch. Pastor Temple Bapt. Ch., Baton Rouge, La., 1956—; evangelist; tchr. music Stamps Quartet Sch. Music, Dallas, 1954-58, Gospel Singers of Am. Sch. Gospel Music, Pass Christian, Miss., 1956—; song writer Stamps Quartet Music Co., Dallas; bd. dirs. Gospel Singers Am., Inc., Pass Christian, 1956—; prin. Temple Christian Ch., Baton Rouge, 1973—. Composer various gospel songs. Mem. La. Bapt. Bible Fellowship (chmn. 1980-81). Home: 9398 W Darryl Pkwy Baton Rouge LA 70815 Office: Temple Bapt Ch 7513 Prescott Rd Baton Rouge LA 70812-4312

BURNETT, FREDRICK WAYNE, religious studies educator; b. Birmingham, Ala., Dec. 18, 1944; s. Arthur Fredrick and Pauline Nellie (Gunn) B.; m. Carol Jean Struthers, June 23, 1967; children: Brian, Kelli. BA, Anderson Coll., 1967; MDiv, Anderson Theol. Sem., 1970; D of Ministry, Vanderbilt Div. Sch., 1973; MA, Vanderbilt U., 1976, PhD, 1979. Minister Post Oak Presbyn. Ch., Cookeville, Tenn., 1971-74; teaching asst. religion Vanderbilt U., Nashville, 1975-76; instr. Greek Am. Bapt. Sem., Nashville, 1975-76; prof. religion and classics Anderson (Ind.) Coll., 1976—. Author: The Testament of Jesus-Sophia, 1981; contbr. articles and revs. to religious jours. Asst. youth dir. Anderson YMCA, 1967-70. NEH grantee, 1980, 83; Andrew Mellon Found. grantee, 1981, 86, 87, 88, Eli Lilly Found. grantee, 1985, 90, Anderson U. Faculty grantee, 1987, 90, 91, 92, U. Chgo. Midwest Faculty fellow, 1985, 89, 91. Mem. Soc. Bibl. Lit., Am. Acad. Religion, Cath. Bible. Assn. Office: Anderson U Dept Bible & Religion Anderson IN 46012

BURNETT, KENNETH C., church business administrator; b. Chardon, Ohio, Sept. 15, 1950; s. Richard F. and Jeanette M. (Matthews) B.; m. Ruth Marie Yoder, July 10, 1971; children: Rachel E., Joseph M. BS in Fin. & Banking, Bowling Green State U., Ohio, 1972. Bus. adminstr. Faith Fellowship Ch., Bedford Heights, Ohio, 1984—; counselor Christian Fin. Concepts, Ga., 1987—. Mem. Geauga County Bd. Edn., Chardon, Ohio, 1990. Mem. Nat. Assn. Ch. Bus. Adminstrs. (pres. N.E. Ohio chpt. 1989—). Office: Faith Fellowship Ch 23600 Columbus Rd Bedford Heights OH 44021

BURNETT, ST. CLAIRE Y., bishop. Bishop, fin. sec. Ch. of God in Christ, Altamonte Springs, Fla. Office: Ch of God in Christ PO Box 245 Altamonte Springs FL 32715*

BURNETTE, JOE EDWARD, clergyman; b. Denison, Tex., Dec. 27, 1918; s. Joe Stevenson and Lula Viola (Sisk) B.; m. Betty Ann Huguley, Oct. 8, 1954; 1 child, Joann. BA, Carson-Newman Coll., 1942; MRE, Southwestern Sem., 1946. Ordained to ministry, Bapt. Ch. Minister of edn. Immanuel Bapt. Ch., Tulsa, 1946-50; minister of edn. First Bapt. Ch., Baton Rouge, 1950-52, Columbia, S.C., 1952-61; adminstr. Bapt. Home for Aging, Florence, S.C., 1961-63; assoc. pastor First Bapt. Ch., Charlotte, N.C., 1963—. Mem. Nat. Alumni Assn. Southwestern Sem. (pres. 1977), So. Bapt. Religious Edn. Assn. (pres. 1972), Gator Bowl Assn., Rotary (pres. Charlotte chpt. 1985-86; Paul Harris fellow). Democrat. Avocations: sports, travel, history, reading. Home: 4244 Wright Ave Charlotte NC 28211 Office: First Bapt Ch PO Box 31046 Charlotte NC 28231

BURNS, ALFRED WARREN, rector, minister; b. Boston, Apr. 5, 1921; s. Alfred Aretus and Frances Agnes (Stone) B.; m. Elisabeth Treat Simonds, May 30, 1944; children: Rosalind Ayrault, Alison Gaylord, Christopher Deming. BA, Bowdoin Coll., 1942; BDiv, Episcopal Theol. Sch., 1945. Curate Grace Episcopal Ch., Lawrence, Mass., 1945-47; priest-in-charge, rector Calvary Episcopal Ch., Bridgeport, Conn., 1947-51; rector St. Matthew's Parish, Hyattsville, Md., 1951-64; rector St. Luke's Parish, East Greenwich, R.I., 1964-86, ret., 1986. Contbr. articles to profl. jours. Commr. East Greenwich Housing Authority, 1987—. Coll. of Preachers fellow, 1951. Mem. Rotary. Democrat. Episcopalian. Avocations: mountain climbing, skiing, golf. Home: 74 London St East Greenwich RI 02818

BURNS, CATHY JEAN, lay worker, writer; b. Pottsville, Pa., Dec. 22, 1955; d. Malcolm William and Jean Delores (Cappel) B. BTh, ThM, Internat. Sem., 1984, D in Bible Philosophy, 1985. Deaconess Mt. Zion Interdenominational Ch., Stroudsburg, Pa., 1988-89. Author: Hidden Secrets of Masonry, 1990, Alcoholics Anonymous Unmasked, 1991; contbr. articles to profl. jours. Home: 212 E Seventh St Mount Carmel PA 17851-2211 *Trust in the Lord with all thine heart; and lean not unto thine own understanding. In all thy ways acknowledge Him, and He shall direct thy paths. (Proverbs 3:5-6).*

BURNS, SISTER JACQUELINE, college president; b. Kearny, N.J., Sept. 1, 1927; d. John Francis and Elizabeth Louise (Calmar) B. BA, Coll. St. Elizabeth, Convent, N.J., 1957; MA, Cath. U. Am., Washington, 1964; PhD in History, Cath. U. Am., 1968; LHD (hon.), Seton Hall U., 1987. Secondary sch. tchr. St. John Cathedral High Sch., Paterson, N.J, 1957-64; instr., asst. prof. Coll. of St. Elizabeth, Convent, N.J., 1967-71, asst. dean of studies, 1971-76, dean of studies, 1976-81, pres., 1981—; bd. dirs. Chestnut Hill Coll., Phila., 1990—. Trustee N.J. Ind. Coll. Fund (treas. 1985-87); mem. N.J. Com. for Humanities, New Brunswick, 1982-86; bd. dirs. N.J. Coun. on Econ. Education, Trenton, 1984-88, Morris County Consumer Credit Union, Morristown, 1984-88; mem. N.J. Bd. Higher Edn., Trenton, 1988—, exec. com., 1990—, chair acad. affairs com., 1990—; trustee St. Joseph Hosp. and Med. Ctr., Paterson, 1984-88; bd. dirs. Nat. Assn. Ind. Colls. & Univs., 1985-88. Recipient Pres.'s award for ednl. leadership Northeast Coalition of Ednl. Leaders, 1987, Woman of Achievement award Bus. and Profl. Women's Clubs N.J., Morris County, 1984, Fulbright scholarship, France, 1964. Mem. Am. Hist. Assn., Am. Cath. Hist. Assn., Am. Coun. on Edn., Am. Cath. Colls. and Univs., Nat. Assn. Ind. Colls. and Univs., Assn. Ind. Colls. and Univs. of N.J. (bd. dirs. 1978—, chmn. 1985-87), Morris County C. of C. (bd. dirs. 1988—). Office: Coll St Elizabeth Office of Pres 2 Convent Rd Morristown NJ 07960-6989

BURNS, JAMES MICHAEL, minister; b. Orange, Calif., Oct. 21, 1953; s. Robert W. and Donna M. (Hadsell) B.; m. Catherine Lynn, May 11, 1974; children: Christy, Rebecca, Heidi. BA in Psychology and Religion, Azusa Pacific U., 1975; MA in Pastoral Theology, Princeton Theol. Sem., 1977. Ordained to ministry Evang. Ch. Alliance, 1977. Min. to students 1st Presbyn. Ch., Orange, Calif., 1977-80; mem. staff Youth Spltys. Assn., El Cajon, Calif., 1980—; min. to students South Coast Community Ch., Costa Mesa, Calif., 1980-85; pres. Nat. Inst. Youth Ministry, San Clemente, Calif., 1985—. Author: Putting God First, 1983, Handling Your Hormones, 1986, Surviving Adolescence, 1990 (all Gold Medallion winners ECAP); also 20 other books. Office: Nat Inst Youth Ministry 940 Calle Amanecer #G San Clemente CA 92672 *The decisions we make today will affect us for the rest of our lives.*

BURNS, JOHN LANIER, religion educator, minister; b. Knoxville, Tenn., Nov. 8, 1943; s. David Brantley and Lollie Ellis (Newton) B.; m. Katherine Gaines Oates, July 8, 1966; children: John, Laura, Katherine, Mary. BA, Davidson Coll., 1965; ThM, Dallas Theol. Sem., 1972, ThD, 1979; postgrad. in humanities, U. Tex., Dallas, 1981—. Ordained to ministry Plano Bible Ch., 1973. Youth dir. Davidson (N.C.) Presbyn. Ch., 1962-65; youth min. Grace Bible Ch., San Antonio, 1966-67; evangelistic ministry The Navigators, 1966-68; youth min. Believer's Chapel, Dallas, 1968-72; min. Plano (Tex.) Bible Ch., 1972-82; asst. prof. systematic theology Dallas Theol. Sem., 1982-83, assoc. prof., 1983-84, prof., dept. chair., 1984—; co-founder Asian Christian Acad., India, 1973, tchr. summer 1980; pres. Am. Coun. Asian Christian Acad., Bangalore, India, 1973-82; tchr. home Bible studies in San Antonio, Irving, Dallas, and Plano, Tex.; elder Plano Bible Chapel, 1974-82, counselor and visitation worker, 1974-77; conf. speaker, tchr. Hesed Class, Northwest Bible Ch., Dallas, 1986—; editorial cons. Academic Books Div., Zondervan Pub. Corp., 1986—. Contbr. articles to religious jours. Bd. Advisors, Providence Sch., 1988—; com. on Acad. Excellence, Highland Park Independent Sch. Dist., 1989-90. Served to capt. M.P., U.S. Army, 1965-68. W. H. Griffith Thomas scholar. Mem. Am. Philol. Soc., Evang. Theol. Soc., Soc. Bible Lit., Soc. Christian Philosophers, Truth Internat., Internat. Platform Assn. Home: 3505 Wentwood Dallas TX 75225 Office: Dallas Theol Sem 3909 Swiss Dallas TX 75204

BURNS, JONATHAN GILBERT, administrator, theological librarian; b. New Haven, June 12, 1946; s. William Jackson and Evelyn Rose (Stapleton) B.; divorced. BA, Haverford Coll., 1970; MS in Libr. Svc., Columbia U., 1981; MDiv, Earlham Coll., 1986; postgrad., Boston U., 1986—. Mem. ministry team West Richmond Friends Mtg., Richmond, Ind., 1984-86; teaching fellow Boston U., 1987-89; dir. Gen. Theol. Ctr. of Maine, Portland, 1988-91, Beacon Hill Friends House, Boston, 1991—; mem. Maine Ann. Conf., United Meth. Ch., 1989-91, Commn. on Archives and History, Maine Conf., United Meth. Ch., 1990-91. Editor Bull of Gen. Theol. Ctr. of Maine, 1989-90. Conservation chmn. Appalachian Mountain Club, Maine chpt., Portland, 1990-91, chpt. chmn., 1979-81. Univ. Presdl. fellow Boston U., 1986-87, Univ. Presdl. Teaching fellow, 1988-89; Univ. Teaching fellow, Boston U., 1987-88. Mem. Soc. Bibl. Lit., Am. Acad. Religion, Am. Theol. Libr. Assn. Democrat. Mem. Soc. of Friends. Office: Beacon Hill Friends House 6 Chestnut St Boston MA 02108

BURNS, MARY CLAUDE, nun, secondary educator; b. Roxbury, Mass.; d. John J. and Annie (Sheehan) B. BSEd, Notre Dame U., Balt., 1945; MA, Villanova U., 1962, Providence Coll., 1969. Joined SSND. Tchr. English, religion Acad. of Holy Angels, Demarest, N.J. Grantee Tufts U., U. Ill. Mem. N.J. Edn. Assn., Nat. Coun. Tchrs. English.

BURNS, MELISSA EMERSON, lay worker, college administrator; b. Austin, Minn., July 8, 1957; d. Edgar Allen and JoAnn L. (Smart) Emerson; m. Marlyn Earl Burns Jr., Sept. 16, 1989. BA, Pepperdine U., 1980, MA, 1986; postgrad., U. Minn., 1990—. Organizer, tchr. Athletes in Christ, Malibu, Calif., 1986-88; study group leader campus ministry Pepperdine U., Malibu, 1986-88, U. Minn., Mpls., 1988—; tchr. Culver Palms Ch. of Christ, L.A., 1985-88, Ch. of Christ, Brooklyn Center, Minn., 1990—; sr. acad. adviser U. Minn., 1988—. Speaker talk show KUOM Radio, 1990-91. Tutor, vol. Plus Literacy Program, Pasadena, Calif., 1986-88, Literacy Plus Program, St. Paul, 1988—; student tutor Highland High Sch., St. Paul, 1989—; student-athlete tutor Pepperdine U., U. Minn., 1984—; campaign vol. Paul Wellstone for Senator, St. Paul, 1990. Mem. Nat. Assn. Coll. Acad. Advisors, Am. Acad. Relgion, Soc. Bibl. Lit. Democrat. Home: 692 Macalester St Saint Paul MN 55116

BURNS, (JAMES) PATOUT, JR., religion educator; b. New Orleans, Oct. 14, 1939; s. James Patout and Mary Theodosia (Weber) B.; m. Patricia Colling Egan, 1986. B.A., Spring Hill Coll., Mobile, Ala., 1963; M.A., Spring Hill Coll., 1964; M.Div., Regis Coll., Toronto, 1970; M.Th., Univ. St. Michael's Coll., Toronto, 1971; Ph.D., Yale U., 1974. Ordained priest Roman Catholic Ch., 1970, laicized, 1987. Tchr. math. Jesuit High Sch., Shreveport, La., 1964-66; instr. philosophy Spring Hill Coll., Mobile, Ala., 1966-67; acting instr. religious studies Yale U., 1973; asst. prof. hist. theology Jesuit Sch. Theology, Chgo., 1974-79; assoc. prof. Jesuit Sch. Theology, 1979-80; assoc. prof. theology Loyola U., Chgo., 1980-86; chmn. dept. Loyola U., 1980-85; prof. religion U. Fla., Gainesville, 1986—; lectr. ch. history Catholic Theol. Union, Chgo., 1974-81; adj. prof. ch. history Lutheran Sch. Theology, Chgo., 1976-80; trustee Loyola U. of the South, 1982-85; Am. Council Edn. adminstrv. fellow, 1985-86; bd. dirs. M.A. Patout & Son Ltd., 1987—. Author: The Development of Augustine's Doctrine of Operative Grace, 1980; Theological Anthropology, 1981; (with others) The Holy Spirit, 1984, Christians and the Military: The Early Experience, 1985. Editor: Grace and Freedom: Operative Grace in the Thought of St. Thomas Aquinas (by Bernard Lonergan), 1971. Contbr. articles to theol. publs. Editorial bd. Theol. Studies, 1977-80. Chaplain Misericordia Home, Chgo., 1980-85; group home resident staff Heart of Mercy Village, Chgo., 1984-85. Grantee Assn. Theol. Schs., 1978; Am. Council on Edn. Leadership Devel. fellow, Ga. State U., 1985-86. Mem. Am. Acad. Religion, Cath. Theol. Soc. Am., Coll. Theol. Soc., N.Am. Patristics Soc. Democrat.

BURNS, PATRICIA HENRIETTA, religious association founder and administrator; b. L.I., N.Y., Dec. 9, 1934; d. Henri Jacob and Rolanda Katherine (Berger) Verwayen; m. John Christopher Burns, Sept. 10, 1933 (dec. Jan. 1977); children: Stephanie, David, John Henri. Student, Warren Harding, 1952, Maricopa Tech. Coll., 1978-86, Rio Salado Community Coll., 1980-88, Lamson Bus., 1981. Advt. mgr. W. T. Grant Phoenix Area Stores, 1970-74; with securities sales dept. Waddell & Reed Securities, Phoenix, 1975-76; commr.'s aide Maricopa County Superior Ct., Phoenix, 1976-82; sec. to dept. mgrs. Motorola, Inc., Chandler, Ariz., 1984—; pres. Non-Denominational Bible Prophecy Study Assn., Tempe, 1983—. Author: The Book of Revelation Explained, 1982. Avocations: travel, entertaining, golf, crafts, studying.

BURNS, ROBERT WALLACE, minister; b. Omaha, July 21, 1950; s. George Robert and Eleanore Maude (Wallace) B.; m. Janet Sue Alcorn, July 15, 1977; children: Robert Wallace II, Christopher W. BA, U. Md., 1972; MDiv, Covenant Theol. Sem., St. Louis, 1977; D Ministry, Westminster Theol. Sem., Phila., 1985. Ordained to ministry Presbyn. Ch. in Am., 1979. Pastor Evang. Presbyn. Ch., Cape Coral, Fla., 1979-80; pastor of single adults Ch. of the Saviour, Wayne, Pa., 1980-85; pastor Perimeter Ch., East Congregation, Stone Mountain, Ga., 1985-89; pastor of single adults and family devel. Perimeter Ch., Norcross, Ga., 1989—; founder, pres. bd. dirs. Fresh Start Seminars Inc., Wayne, 1981—); bd. dirs. Gwinett Ctr. for Christian Counseling, Lilburn, Ga., 1985—. Author: Through the Whirlwind, 1989; co-author: The Adult Child of Divorce, 1991, The Fresh start Divorce Recovery Workbook, 1992; ; contbg. author: Singles Ministry Handbook, 1988. Bd. dirs., founder Amnion Crisis Pregnancy Ctr., Wayne, 1983-85. Office: Perimeter Ch 5701 Spalding Dr Norcross GA 30092 *In the midst of a contantly changing and volatile world, I have found the only consistant hope is in the God who has revealed Himself through Jesus Christ.*

BURNSIDE, BURNIE R., minister; b. Madison, W.Va., July 23, 1953; s. Arthur U. and Fay A. (Calvin) B.; m. Peggy L. Hallam, Aug. 10, 1974; children: Benjamin, Tiffany. BA, Olivet Nazarene U., Kankakee, Ill., 1975, MA, 1980; postgrad., U. N. Tex., Denton, 1988—. Ordained to ministry, Ch. of the Nazarene, 1980. Assoc. pastor Northside Ch. of the Nazarene,

Chgo., 1973-77; pastor First Ch. of the Nazarene, Dubuque, Iowa, 1978-84; sr. pastor First Ch. of the Nazarene, Denton, Tex., 1984—; adult dir. W. Tex. Dist. Ch. of the Nazarene, Lubbock, Tex., 1989—, mem. bd. credentials, 1989—, evangelism dir., Iowa Dist., Des Moines, 1984, IMPACT dir., 1980. Bd. dirs Crisis Pregnancy Ctr., Denton, Tex., 1987-90. Recipient Grand Commn. award, W. Tex. Dist. Ch. of the Nazarene, 1990, Blue Ribbon Ch. award, 1990. Mem. Fitness Club of Denton. Office: First Ch of the Nazarene 2321 E Sherman Dr Denton TX 76201 *"Commit to the Lord whatever you do, and your plans will succeed." (Prov. 16:3).*

BURRELL, CALVIN ARCHIE, minister; b. Fairview, Okla., June 22, 1943; s. Lawrence Lester and Lottie Eona (Davison) B.; m. Barbara Ann Mann, May 29, 1966; children: Debra, Darla, Donna. BS, Northwestern State U., 1965; M.A., So. Nazarene Coll., Bethany, Okla., 1978. Ordained to ministry Ch. of God. tchr., prin., dean of boys, Spring Vale Acad., Owosso, Mich., 1964-76; Pastor Ch. of God (Seventh Day), Ft. Smith, Ark., 1970-73, Shawnee, Okla., 1976-78, Denver, 1978-88; pres. Gen. Conf. of Ch. of God (Seventh Day), Denver, 1987-91; instr. Summit Sch. Theology, Denver, 1978-91. Office: Ch of God 330 W 152nd Ave PO Box 33677 Denver CO 80233

BURRELL, DAVID BAKEWELL, philosophy educator; b. Akron, Ohio, Mar. 1, 1933; s. Roger Allen and Nancy deLauriel (Bakewell) B. BA, U. Notre Dame, 1954; STL, Gregorian U., Rome, 1960; PhD, Yale U., 1965. Ordained priest Roman Catholic Ch., 1959. Asst. prof. philosophy U. Notre Dame, Ind., 1965-70, assoc. prof., 1970-77, prof., 1977—, T. M. Hesburgh prof. arts and letters, 1988—, chmn. dept. theology, 1971-80; rector Ecumenical Inst. for Theol. Rsch., Jerusalem, 1980-81. Author: Analogy and Philosophical Language, 1973, Exercises in Religious Understanding, 1975, Aquinas: God and Action, 1979, Knowing the Unknowable God, 1986, Al-Ghazali on the Naming God, 1991. Woodrow Wilson fellow, 1954, Fulbright fellow, 1954, Kent fellow, 1963. Mem. Am. Philos. Assn., Soc. for Values in Higher Edn. Home: Box 402 Notre Dame IN 46556

BURRILL, RUSSELL CLAYTON, clergyman; b. Haverhill, Mass., June 19, 1941; s. Arnold Franklin and Norma Ruth (Ward) B.; m. Cynthia Lynn Hartmann, Aug. 25, 1963; children: James David, Ruth Anne. BA, Atlantic Union Coll., 1963; MA, Andrews U., 1964, MDiv Equivalency, 1988. Ordained to ministry Seventh-day Adventists, 1968. Pastor So. New Eng. Conf. Seventh-day Adventists, Willimantic, Conn., 1964-68, Mountain View Conf. Seventh-day Adventists, Cumberland, Md., 1968-70; evangelist Parkersburg, W.Va., 1970-72, Chesapeake Conf. Seventh-day Adventists, Columbia, Md., 1972-75; evangelist Upper Columbia Conf. Seventh-day Adventists, Spokane, Wash., 1975-77, pastor, 1977-83; pastor Kans.-Nebr. Conf. Seventh-day Adventists, Wichita, 1983-85; dir. evangelism N. Am. Div. of Seventh-day Adventists Evangelism Inst., La Grange, Ill., 1985—; mem. com Mountain View Conf. Seventh-day Adventists, 1968-72, Kans.-Nebr. Conf. Seventh-day Adventists, Topeka, 1983-85. Home: 117 Ainslie Ct Westmont IL 60559 Office: N Am Div Evangelism Inst 1120 64th St La Grange IL 60525

BURRIS, STEPHEN EUGENE, religion educator; b. Mpls., Mar. 10, 1950; s. Daniel Lee and Esther Beth (Bartow) B.; m. Cynthia Ann Burris; children: Andrea, Matthew, Jennifer. BS, Puget Sound Christian Coll., 1976; MA, Lincoln Christian Sem., 1980. Cert. ednl. adminstr. Prof. Lincoln (Ill.) Christian Coll., 1977-80, St. Louis Christian Coll., Florissant, Mo., 1980-81; min. First Christian Ch., Granite City, Ill., 1981-83, Marysville (Wash.) Christian Ch., 1984-87; adminstr. Cornerstone Christian Sch., Camarillo, Calif., 1987—. Editor, author: Critical Issues Facing Christian Schools, 1990, Christian Schools Guide to the Christian Mind, 1991; contbr. author: Ency. for Christian Living, 1991. Republican. Office: Cornerstone Christian Sch 1777 Arneill Rd Camarillo CA 93010

BURROUGHS, ROBERT HOWARD, minister; b. Houston, Nov. 9, 1937; s. Charlie Howard Roys and Lillie Adeline (Schultz) B.; m. Rebecca Faye Allen, Feb. 7, 1959; children: Rebecca Ann, Robert H. Jr., Ray Warren. BS, Sam Houston U., 1960; postgrad. in acctg., U. Houston, 1964-67; MDiv, Southwestern Bapt. Theol. Sem., 1983, MA in Religious Edn., 1984. Ordained to ministry So. Bapt. Conv., 1984; cert. secondary sch. tchr., Tex. Assoc. pastor N.E. Bapt. Ch., San Antonio, 1979-80; assoc. pastor, adminstr. 1st Bapt. Ch., Springfield, Mo., 1984—. Sec. Exch. Club, Houston, 1971-72, sponsor, 1971. Mem. Nat. Assn. Ch. Bus. Adminstrs., NSS & LC & F.O. (pres. 1966, dist. gov. 1967 Houston chpt.), Houston Livestock Show and Rodeo (life). Office: 1st Bapt Ch 525 South Ave Springfield MO 65806

BURROUGHS, SHANE EDWARD, minister; b. Columbus, Ohio, Sept. 29, 1956; s. Flavis Leland and Doris June (Lovelle) B.; m. Barbara Alice High, Oct. 27, 1978; children: Amber Cherié, Dustin Shane. BS, Lee Coll., 1984. Ordained to ministry Ch. of the Rock, 1990. State evangelist Ch. of God., Ala., 1980-82; sr. pastor Kings' Forest Ch. of God, Leeds, Ala., 1982-84; evangelist Assemblies of God, Ala., 1984-87; founder, pastor Cathedral of Praise, Ch. of the Rock, Coker, Ala., 1987-90, sr. pastor, 1987—. Home: 130 Wickstead Rd Hueytown AL 35023 Office: Cathedral of Praise PO Box 158 Coker AL 35452

BURROWS, ELIZABETH MACDONALD, religious organization executive; b. Portland, Oreg., Jan. 30, 1930; d. Leland R. and Ruth M. (Frew) MacDonald. Certificate, Chinmaya Trust Sandeepany, Bombay; PhD (hon.), Internat. U. Philosophy and Sci., 1975. Ordained to ministry First Christian Ch., 1976. Mgr. credit Home Utilities, Seattle, 1958, Montgomery Ward, Crescent City, Calif., 1963; supr. Oreg. Dist. Tng. West Coast Telephone, Beaverton, 1965; pres. Christian Ch. Universal Peace, Seattle, 1971—, Archives Internat., Seattle, 1971—; v.p. James Tyler Kent Inst. Homeopathy, 1984—, Internat. Coll. Universal Psychology, 1986—. Author: Crystal Planet, 1979, Pathway of the Immortal, 1980, Odyssey of The Apocalypse, 1981, Maya Sangh, 1981, Harp of Destiny, 1984, Commentary for Gospel of Peace of Jesus Christ according to John, 1986, American Poetry Anthology, 1989. Mem. Internat. Speakers Platform, Internat. New Thought Alliance, Cousteau Soc., Internat. Order of Chivalry. Home: 10529 Ashworth Ave N Seattle WA 98133 Office: Christian Ch Universal Peace 10529 Ashworth Ave N Seattle WA 98133 *Oneness with God is mankind's ultimate vision. This results in a profound journey which covers strange and wonderful worlds beyond mortal boundaries, for to reach oneness is to reach more than anyone can imagine, or more than anyone has ever dreamed.*

BURROWS, EVA EVELYN, religious organization administrator; b. Newcastle, Australia, Sept. 15, 1929; d. Robert John and Ella Maria (Watson) B. BA, Queensland U., 1950; postgrad. cert. in edn., U. London, 1952; MEd, Sydney U., Australia, 1959; PhD (hon.), EWHA Woman's U., Seoul, Korea, 1988; LLD (hon.), Asbury Coll., U.S.A., 1988. Missionary educator Howard Inst., Zimbabwe, 1952-67; prin. Usher Inst., Zimbabwe, 1967-69; vice prin. Internat. Coll. for Officers, London, 1970-73, prin., 1974-75; leader Women's Social Services of Great Britain and Ireland, 1975-77; territorial comdr. Salvation Army, Sri Lanka, 1977-79, Scotland, 1979-82, Australia, 1982-86; gen. (internat. leader) The Salvation Army, London, 1986—. Named Officer Order of Australia, 1986. Office: Salvation Army Internat Hdqrs, 101 Queen Victoria St, Box 249, London EC4P 4EP, England

BURT, JOHN HARRIS, bishop; b. Marquette, Mich., Apr. 11, 1918; s. Bates G. and Emily May (Bailey) B.; m. Martha M. Miller, Feb. 16, 1946; children—Susan, Emily, Sarah, Mary. B.A., Amherst Coll., 1940, D.D. (hon.), 1960; B.A., Va. Theol. Sem., 1943, D.D., 1967; D.D., Youngstown U., 1958, Kenyon Coll., 1967. Boys worker Christodora House, N.Y.C., 1940-41; ordained to ministry Episcopal Ch., 1943; canon (Christ Ch. Cathedral); rector (St. Paul's Ch.), St. Louis, 1943-44; chaplain to Episc. students U. Mich., 1946-50; rector St. John's Ch., Youngstown, Ohio, 1950-57, All Saints Ch., Pasadena, Calif., 1957-67; bishop coadjutor Ohio, 1967-68, Episc. bishop of, 1968-84; pres. So. Calif. Council Chs., 1962-65; mem. bd. Ch. Soc. Coll. Work, 1964-71; chmn. clergy deployment bd. Episc. Ch., 1971-73. Co-author: World Religions and World Peace, 1969; author: Economic Justice and the Christian Conscience, 1987. Pres. Youngstown Coordinating Council, 1954-56, Pasadena Community Council, 1964-66; trustee Pomona Coll., 1963-66, Va. Theol. Sem., 1967-72, Colgate-Rochester Div. Sch., 1968-84, Kenyon Coll., 1967-84; bd. dirs. United Way Los Angeles, 1964-67, Cleve. Urban Coalition, 1968-70, Ams. for Energy Independence, 1975-85; bd. dirs. Nat. Com. Against Censorship, 1974—; chmn. bd. dirs. St. John's Home for Girls, Painesville, Ohio, 1968-84; governing bd. Nat. Council Chs., 1970-81; mem. Com. on Ch. Order, Consultation on Ch. Union, 1980-88; chmn. com. on theology Episc. Ch. House Bishops, 1973-80; chmn. Urban Bishops Coalition, 1977—, Faith and Order Commn. Ohio Council Chs., 1970-74; bd. dirs. Episcopal Ch. Pub. Co., 1985—, pres., 1990—; chmn. commn. ecumenical relations Episc. Ch., 1973-79, also chmn. commn. middle judicatories, cons. on ch. union, 1975-79; chmn. com. human affairs and health Epis. Ch., 1982-85; chmn. Bishops Com. Nat. and Internat. Affairs, 1982-85; chmn. Ecumenical Gt. Lakes Project on Econ. Crisis, 1983-87; chmn. Presiding Bishop's Com. Christian-Jewish Relations, 1986—; pres. Nat. Christian Leadership Conf. on Israel, 1988—; mem. ch. rels. com. U.S. Holocaust Meml. Coun., 1989—; mem. Ecumenical Consultation on New Religions Movements, 1985-87; bd. dirs. religious task force Mobilization for Survival, 1987—. Served as chaplain USNR, 1943-46. Recipient Arvona Lynch Human Relations award Youngstown, 1956; Rissica Human Relations award Jewish War Vets., 1966; Pasadena Community Relations award, 1967; Cleve.'s Simon Bolivar award, 1972; Pitts.'s Thomas Merton award, 1978; Human Rights award Ohio br. ACLU, 1980; Ecumenical Leadership award Christian Ch. (Disciples of Christ), 1986, Am. Jewish Com., 1991. Mem. Phi Gamma Delta. Home: Middle Island Point 25 Marquette MI 49855

BURTCHAELL, JAMES TUNSTEAD, priest; b. Portland, Oreg., Mar. 31, 1934; s. James Tunstead Jr. and Marion Margaret (Murphy) B. BA, U. Notre Dame, 1956; Sacrae Theologiae Baccalaureatus, Pontifical U. Gregoriana, Rome, 1958; Sacrae Theologiae Licentiatus, Cath. U. Am., 1960; postgrad., Ecole Biblique Francaise, Jerusalem, 1961-63; SSL, Pontifical Bibl. Commn., 1964; PhD, Cambridge U., 1966; LHD (hon.), St. Mary's Coll., Moraga, Calif., 1974, Rose Hulman Inst. Tech., 1976, Coll. Mt. St. Joseph, Cin., 1987. Ordained priest Roman Cath. Ch., 1960. Prof. theol. U. Notre Dame, Ind., 1966—, provost, 1970-77. Author: Catholic Theories of Biblical Inspiration, 1969, Philemon's Problem, 1973, Rachel Weeping, 1982, (Christopher award 1982), For Better, For Worse, 1985, A Just War No Longer Exists, 1988, The Giving and Taking of Life, 1989, From Synagogue to Church, 1992. Bd. dirs., v.p. Protective Svcs. Bd., South Bend, Ind., 1982-90, bd. dirs. Inst. Religion and Pub. Life, N.Y.C., 1986—, Justlife, Phila., 1989—; chmn. Ctr, Constl. Studies, Notre Dame, 1977-79. Sr.Fulbright scholar, 1985-86, S.A. Cook Bye fellow, 1965-66, Assn. Theol. Schs. Rsch. fellow, 1985-86, 90-91. Mem. Am. Acad. Religion (pres. 1970-71), Cath. Commn. Intellectual and Cultural Affairs. Office: Our Lady of Princeton Great Rd at Drakes Corner Princeton NJ 08540

BURTON, BETTY JUNE, minister, pastor; b. Muskegon, Mich., June 11, 1923; d. Bernard J. and Louise Ella (Weaver) Mulder; mem. Harold Ver Berkmoes, June 4, 1943 (div. 1966); children: Suzanne, James, Michael, William, Judith, David (dec.); m. Eldon Franklin Burton, June 27, 1971. Student of music and psychology, Hope Coll., 1941-45; student, Garrett Evang. Theol. Sem., 1984-85. Ordained to ministry United Meth. Ch., 1986. Librarian Vassar Hosp. Sch. Nursing, Poughkeepsie, N.Y., 1958-60, Hackley Pub. Library, Muskegon, 1960-64, Boyne City (Mich.) Pub. Library, 1972-74; reporter Ludington (Mich.) Daily News, 1975-81; caseworker Aid to Dependent Children Mich. Dept. Social Services, Hart, 1974-78; pastor various Meth. Chs., Norwood, Barnard and Charlevoix, Mich., 1981-83, Mears (Mich.) United Meth. Ch., 1985, 86; assoc. pastor United Meth. Centenary, Pentwater, Mich., 1986—; assoc. realtor Shaw Real Estate, Pentwater, 1975-81, Real Estate One, Traverse City, Mich., 1981-82, Century 21 Williams Real Estate, Pentwater, 1986—. Sec. Pentwater Planning Commn., 1985. Mem. International Platform Assn., Am. Assn. Christian Counselors, Nat. Assn. Female Execs., Nat. Christian Counselors Assn., Nat. Trust Hist. Preservation, Am. Museum Natural History, Nat. Audubon Soc., Hist. Soc. Mich., Oceana County Hist. Soc., Kappa Beta Phi (pres. 1943), Xi Gamma Beta (sec. 1970). Republican. Clubs: Women's of Pentwater (v.p. 1986—), Garden of Pentwater (pres. 1986—), Sierra. Avocations: writing, fishing, gardening, birding, travel. Home and Office: 610 Maple Ln PO Box 860 Pentwater MI 49449

BURTON, DEWITT A., bishop. Bishop Ch. of God in Christ, Wyncote, Pa. Office: Ch of God in Christ 1400 Wistar Dr Wyncote PA 19095*

BURTON, KEITH AUGUSTUS, minister, theological researcher; b. London, Aug. 1, 1963; came to U.S., 1984; s. Nehemiah Augustus and Cynthia Yvonne (Morgan) B.; m. Hyacinth Louise Henry, June 19, 1989. BA, Oakwood Coll., 1987; MTS, Garrett-Evang. Theol. Sem., 1989. Ordained to ministry Seventh-day Adventist Ch., 1987. Asst. pastor Seventh-day Adventist Ch., Evanston, Ill., 1987—; theol. researcher Garrett-Evang. Sem., Evanston, 1989—; presl. advisor Nat. Conf. Black Seminarians, Evanston, 1988; del. First Seventh-day Adventist Ch., Evanston, 1989; v.p. Seventh-day Adventist Youth Fedn., Chgo., 1989—. Dir. personal ministries, Evanston, 1990—. Recipient Greek award Am. Bible Soc., 1986. Mem. Soc. Bibl. Lit. (compiler Pauline bibliography), Police Clergy Assn. Home: 2207 Maple Ave #B3 Evanston IL 60201 Office: Garrett-Evang Theol Sem 2121 Sheridan Rd Evanston IL 60201

BURTON, ROBERT DALE, minister; b. Mt. Vernon, Ill., Sept. 16, 1960; s. Charles M. and Glenda (Wilson) B.; m. Dana Lou Larimore, May 20, 1990; 1 child, Andrew Charles. AA, Rend Lake Coll., 1980; B in Religion, S.W. Bapt. U., 1982; MRE, Midwestern Bapt. Theol. Sem., Kansas City, Mo., 1985. Ordained to ministry So. Bapt. Conv., 1986. Assoc. pastor Armour Heights Bapt. Ch., Kansas City, 1983-84, Belle Rive (Ill.) Bapt. Ch., 1984-85; pastor Havana (Ill.) So. Bapt. Ch., 1985-87; assoc. pastor youth and edn. Pleasant Hill Bapt. Ch., Mt. Vernon, 1988—; dir. youth, asst. team-youth specialist Salem South Bapt. Assn., Mt. Vernon, 1984-91; mem. Havana Ministerial Alliance, 1985-87. Mem. Drug Free Adv. Bd., Mt. Vernon, 1988-91. Mem. Jefferson County Ministerial Alliance (bd. dirs. Mt. Vernon City wide rally 1989-90). Home: Rte 1 Box 264 Woodlawn IL 62898 Office: Pleasant Hill Bapt Ch Rte 5 Box 318 Mount Vernon IL 62864

BURTON, ROSS BLAND, education and administration clergyman; b. Kansas City, Mo., June 13, 1956; s. Ernest Bland and Thelma Nadine (Stevens) B.; m. Elizabeth Jane Straight, July 17, 1982; children: Lisa Michaelle, Anna Beth. AA, Longview Community Coll., Lee's Summit, Mo., 1975; BA, S.W. Bapt. Coll., Bolivar, Mo., 1978; MRE, Southwestern Bapt. Sem., Ft. Worth, 1980. Minister edn. 1st Bapt. Ch., Bolivar, 1980-84; minister edn. and adminstrn. Calvary Bapt. Ch., Little Rock, 1984—. Mem. Nat. Assn. Ch. Bus. Adminstrs., So. Bapt. Religious Edn. Assn. Avocations: hunting, jogging. Office: Calvary Bapt Ch 1901 N Pierce St Little Rock AR 72207

BURY, DAVID ALFRED, minister; b. Mpls., June 19, 1933; s. Alfred Frank and Annie Viola (Howard) B.; m. Joyce Annette Steen, Aug. 6, 1955; children: Michael David, Diane Joyce, Steven George, Cheryl Jean. ThB, North Cen. Bible Coll., 1956; postgrad., Seattle Pacific U., 1968-70. Ordained to ministry, 1959. Youth pastor Peoples Ch., Mpls., 1955-57; youth pastor, music dir. Fremont Tabernacle, Seattle, 1958-60; club dir. Seattle Youth for Christ, 1960-63, exec. dir., 1963-71; exec. dir. Portland (Oreg.) Youth for Christ, 1975-84, San Gabriel-Pomona Valley Youth for Christ, Calif., 1984—; v.p. Pacific N.W. area Youth for Christ Internat., 1964-68; instr. music North Cen. Bible Coll., Mpls., 1955-56. Mem. adv. bd. Campus Life mag., 1966-69; producer religious radio and multi media presentations. Mem. C. of C., Rotary. Office: 440 S Cataract Ave Ste J San Dimas CA 91773

BUSCH, EBERHARD, theology educator; b. Witten, Germany, Aug. 22, 1937; s. Johannes and Margarete (Johann) B.; m. Beate Blum; children: Emanuel, Christian, Sara, Nathanael. ThD, U. Basel, Switzerland, 1977. Asst. to prof. K. Barth, Basel, 1965-68; pastor Uerkheim, Switzerland, 1968-86; guest lectr. U. Tübingen, Fed. Republic Germany, 1982-83; prof. theology U. Göttingen, Fed. Republic Germany, 1986—. Author: Karl Barths Lebenslauf, 1975, 4th edit. 1986; contbr. to various publs. Home: Lindenstrasse 13, 3403 Friedland 4, Federal Republic of Germany Office: U Göttingen, Platz der Göttinger Sieben 2, 3400 Göttingen Federal Republic of Germany

BUSELT, CLARA IRENE, religious organization administrator; b. Detroit, Jan. 30, 1921; d. Andrew and Bernice (Marcian) Kochanowski; m. Michael Leo Buselt, Apr. 18, 1940; children: Edwin, Nancy, Robert, John, Jane. Student, MacGregor Beauty Coll., Kansas City, 1939. Cosmetician various beauty shops, Leavenworth, 1940-45; surp. dir. Sch. Lunch Program Sacred Heart Cafeteria, Immaculata High, Leavenworth, 1957-68; dietetic worker VA Med. Ctr., Leavenworth, 1968-81; office clk. Storage Box Inc., Leavenworth, 1987—; sr. Times corr. Leavenworth Times, 1990—. Photographer (contest) Congress Americas, 1986. Mem. Sr. Coun. Park and Recreation, Leavenworth 1988. Mem. Women's Div. C. of C., Parish Council Sacred Heart Ch., Sacred Heart Alter Soc. (pres. 1977-87), Am. War Mothers (state pres. 1983-85, nat. color bearer 1985-87, nat. chaplain 1987-89), Cath. Literary Club (pres. 1983-85), Sch. Food Svc. Assn. (charter pres. 1958), St. John Hosp. Guild (pres. 1975-76), Loyal Christian Benefit Assn. (br. pres. 1977-88, nat. trustee 1981—), Daughters Isabella, Arch Diocese Coun. (pres. 1981-83), Nat. Assn. Ret. Fed. Employees, Loyal Christian Benefit Assn. (br. pres. 1977—), Ret. Eagle Activity Club (v.p. 1991—). Avocations: vol. work, sewing, photography. Home: 1413 S 16th St Leavenworth KS 66048 *In my lifetime I have found that you must place your trust in God, and have a positive attitude; there is good in every person, but sometimes someone has to bring it out.*

BUSH, BERNARD JOSEPH, JR., clergyman, religious organization administrator; b. Garberville, Calif., Sept. 13, 1934; s. Bernard Joseph and Anne Josephine (Kelly). MA in Philosophy, Gonzaga U., 1957; MA in Theology, St. Mary's U., Halifax, N.S., Can., 1967; STL in Theology, St. Mary's U., 1967; PhD in Human Sci., Saybrook Inst., 1985. Joined S.J., 1951; ordained priest Roman Catholic Ch., 1965. With campus ministry U. San Francisco, 1967-69; spiritual dir. Grad. Theol. Union, Berkeley, Calif., 1969-71; chaplain, psychology intern Boston State Hosp., 1971-74; dir. House of Affirmation, Boston, 1974-77, Montara, Calif., 1977—; cons. Saybrook Inst., 1985-86. Author: Living in His Love; contbr. articles to profl. mags. Mem. Internat. Fedn. for Systems Research. Democrat. Avocations: sculpting, private piloting. Office: House of Affirmation 1185 Acacia St Montara CA 94037

BUSH, CHARLES JAY, minister; b. Victoria, Tex., June 3, 1935; s. Henry Jay and Hattie Beatrice (Bush) B.; m. Patricia Adele Myers, June 12, 1953; children: Deborah Elaine Bush Beadle, Sharon Faye Bush Mullens. BA, East Tex. Bapt. U., 1964; MDiv, Southwestern Bapt. Theol. Sem., Ft. Worth, 1969. Ordained to ministry So. Bapt. Conv., 1961. Pastor Pope City Bapt. Ch., Woodlawn, Tex., 1961-63, 1st Bapt. Ch., Redwater, Tex., 1963-66, 2d Bapt. Ch., Ranger, Tex., 1966-69; pastor 1st Bapt. Ch., Roscoe, Tex., 1969-77, Devine, Tex., 1977—; vice chmn. area bd. Mitchell-Scurry-Sweetwater (Tex.) Area, 1970-71, chmn., 1971-72; mem. exec. bd. Bapt. Gen. Conv. Tex., Dallas, 1982-88; moderator Frio River Bapt. Assn., Pearsall, Tex., 1986-88. With U.S. Army, 1957-60. Recipient outstanding svc. plaque Bapt. Gen. Conv. Tex. Exec. Bd., 1988. Mem. Devine Ministerial Fellowship (sec.-treas. 1990—), Lions. Democrat. Home: 703 Atkins Devine TX 78016 Office: 1st Bapt Ch 308 W Hondo Box 468 Devine TX 78016

BUSH, JUDY LYNN, church program administrator; b. Madison, Wis., Aug. 6, 1938; d. Marvin Leonard and Alberta Ruth Martha (Wagner) Anderson; m. James Paul Rasmussen (div.); children: Linda Bradley, Nancy Carlisle, Dan Rasmussen; m. George L. Bush. BS, U. Wis., 1960, MS, 1979; Cert. vol. mgmt. program, U. Colo., 1987. Tchr. Neenah Pub. Schs., Neenah, Wis., 1960-61; tchr. Menasha Pub. Schs., Menasha, Wis., 1961; med. sec. U. Wis. Hosp., Madison, 1974-77, 79-81; adminstrv. sec. Luth. Campus Ministry, Madison, 1981-83; coord. vol. ministries Luther Meml. Ch., Madison, 1984-91. Founding mem. Capitol City Opera Co., Madison, 1983; adv. to bd. Madison Opera Guild, 1987-88; bd. dirs., edn. chair Friends of Univ. Hosp., Madison, 1987-88; pres. Madison-Freiburg Sister City Com., Madison, 1988-89, v.p., 1989-90). Mem. Vol. Adminstrs. Dane County (bd. dirs., chair edn. com. 1988-89). Lutheran. Avocations: reading, music, walking, knitting, traveling. Home: 3420 Valley Creek Circle Middleton WI 53562

BUSH, L. RUSS, dean, theology educator; b. Alexandria, La., Dec. 25, 1944; s. Luther Russell and Sara Frances (Warnock) B.; m. Cynthia E. McGraw, June 2, 1968; children: Joshua Russell, Bethany Charis. BA, Miss. Coll., 1967; MDiv, Southwestern Sem., 1970, PhD, 1975. From instr. to assoc. prof. Southwestern Bapt. Theol. Sem., Ft. Worth, 1972-89; prof. philosophy of religion, dean of faculty Southeastern Bapt. Theol. Sem., Wake Forest, N.C., 1989—. Author: Baptists and the Bible, 1980, Handbook for Christian Philosophy, 1991; editor; Classical Readings in Christian Apologetics, 1985. Mem. Evang. Philos. Soc. (pres. 1989-90), Am. Acad. Religion, Soc. Biblical Lit., Evang. Theol. Soc., Am. Sci. Affiliation, Soc. Christian Philosophers. Avocations: computing, amateur radio, travel. Office: Southeastern Sem Box 1889 Wake Forest NC 27588 *The urgent will always crowd out the important. I keep things in stacks and I consistently find that last year's stacks can be disposed of quite easily. It is today's stack that gives me trouble.*

BUSH, MARK STUART, minister, publisher; b. Washington, Aug. 21, 1960; s. James Richard and Joan Denson (Colquitt) B.; m. Cheryl Celeste Hyatt, Dec. 14, 1985. BA in History, Ga. Southwestern Coll., 1982; MDiv, Southeastern Bapt. Theol. Sem., 1985. Ordained to ministry So. Bapt. Conv., 1985. Min. music and youth Carey Bapt. Ch., Henderson, N.C., 1984; campus min. intern Shorter Coll., Rome, Ga., 1984-85; asst. dir. admissions Truett-McConnell Coll., Cleveland, Ga., 1985-87; min. edn. and Youth Pearisburg (Va.) Bapt. Ch, 1987-89, Rivermont Ave. Bapt. Ch., Lynchburg, Va., 1989—; owner Text FX Desktop Pub. Co., Lynchburg, 1989—; vol. campus min. Randolph-Macon Woman's Coll. Bapt. Student Union, 1990—. Mem. com. Georgetown Forest Homeowners Assn., Lynchburg, 1991. Mem. Lynchburg Bapt. Assn. (student ministries chair, 1991—), Va. Bapt. Religious Educators Assn., So. Bapt. Religious Educators Assn. Democrat. Home: 121 Kettering Ln Lynchburg VA 24501 Office: Rivermont Ave Bapt Ch 1301 Rivermont Ave Lynchburg VA 24504

BUSH, RANDALL BRUCE, religion educator; b. Houston, July 23, 1953; s. Dudley M. B. and Iris Elaine (Myers) Morris; m. Cynthia Gail Walker, Jan. 22, 1952; children: Christopher Alan, Laura Elaine. BA, Howard Payne U., Brownwood, Tex., 1975; MDiv, Southwestern Bapt. Seminary, Fort Worth, 1978, PhD, 1981; DPhil, U. Oxford, 1990. Asst. prof. Bible Howard Payne U., 1981-86, v.p. for student affairs, 1985-86; Rockwell vis. theologian U. Houston, 1989-90; asst. prof. philosophy and religion Union U., Jackson, Tenn., 1991—; coord. grad. seminar Regent's Park Coll., Oxford, England, 1987-89. Author: Recent Ideas of Divine Conflict, 1991. Fellow Bapt. Gen. Conv. Tex., 1985; Asheville scholar Regent's Park Coll., 1987-89. Mem. Am. Acad. Religion, Soc. Bibl. Lit. Home: 4852 Highway 412 Bells TN 38006

BUSH, WILLIAM EDWARD, minister; b. Birmingham, Ala., Oct. 7, 1959; s. Raymond Howard and Zelma Frances (Pepper) B.; m. Deborah Lynn Stewart, June 9, 1979; children: Matthew Stephen, Thomas Edward. BA, Harding U., 1981. Ordained to ministry Ch. of Christ, 1990. Admissions counselor Faulkner U., Montgomery, Ala., 1981-83; min. Marcella (Ark.) Ch. of Christ, 1980-81, Alpharetta (Ga.) Ch. of Christ, 1990—. Named One of Outstanding Young Men in Am., Jaycees, 1981. Republican. Home: 400 Milton Ave Alpharetta GA 30201 Office: Alpharetta Ch Christ 54 Duluth St Alpharetta GA 30201 *Possessions--some good, others burdensome. Our most cherished possession is that one moment in time when we face death. For it is at that moment that we shall be with the Father in all His glory. And that, my friends, is what life is all about.*

BUSSE, RICHARD PAUL, religion educator; b. Valparaiso, Ind., June 4, 1950; s. Edward E. and Virginia M. (Paul) B.; m. Barbara J. Schmidt, Jan. 24, 1974; children: Matthew, Kristin. BA, Valparaiso U., 1972; MTS, Luth. Sch. of Theology, 1975, ThM, 1979, ThD, 1984. Asst. prof. religion Valparaiso U., 1984-85, part-time asst. prof. religion, 1985-88; lectr. in theology Luth. Sch. of Theology, Chgo., 1986—; instr. in philosophy St. Francis Coll., Joliet, Ill., 1987; mem. assoc. faculty Ind. U. N.W., Gary, 1989—; mem. coms. Editor Bull. on the Coun. of Socs. for the Study of Religion, 1988—. Mem. Am. Acad. Religion, Chgo. Ctr. for Religion and Sci. (assoc., founder, editor 1989—), Inst. on Religion in an Age of Sci., Ctr. for Process Studies, Ind. Civil Liberties Union (pres. Gary chpt. 1986—, bd. dirs. Indpls. chpt. 1986—). Home: 1706 Calumet Ave Valparaiso IN 46383-3129

BUSWELL, ROBERT EVANS, JR., religion educator; b. Cocoa Beach, Fla., Mar. 25, 1953; s. Robert Evans and Miriam Josephine (Dunn) B.; m.

Kyoko Tokuno, Feb. 17, 1985. AB, U. Calif., Berkeley, 1981, MA, 1983, PhD, 1985. Bhikkhu Thammayut Order of Theravada Buddhism, Thailand, 1972-73; Bhiksu Ch'an Sch. Chinese Buddhism, Hong Kong, 1973-74, Chogye Order Korean Buddhism, Songgwang-sa, Republic of Korea, 1974-79; prof. UCLA, 1986—; bd. dirs. Kuroda Inst. for the Study of Buddhism, L.A., 1989—. Author: Korean Approach to Zen, 1983, Formation of Ch'an, 1989, Chinese Buddhist Apocrypha, 1990; editorial bd. Studies in East Asian Buddhism series, U. Hawaii Press, 1989—; editor-in-chief Korean Culture, 1989—; contbr. articles to profl. jours. Cultural advisor Korean Cultural Svc., L.A., 1986-89. Rsch. grantee NEH, 1989-90, conf. grantee Am. Coun. Learned Socs./Social Sci. Rsch. Coun., 1988; recipient award of merit Ctr. for the Study of Chinul's Thought, Seoul, Republic of Korea, 1988. Mem. Internat. Assn. Buddhist Studies, Am. Acad. Religion, Assn. Asian Studies (exec. com. 1990-93, com. on Korean studies), Am. Oriental Soc. Buddhist. Office: UCLA Dept East Asian Langs 405 Hilgard Ave Los Angeles CA 90024-1540

BUTCHART, WAYNE M., minister; b. Riverton, Wash., Mar. 21, 1915; s. John Marshall and Maude Mae (Harm) B.; m. Alice M. Roberts, June 3, 1940 (wid. Feb. 1990); children: Dennis (dec.), Joanna, Marcia; m. Arlene A. Berry, Oct. 13, 1990. AB, N.N. Coll., Nampa, Idaho, 1940. Pastor various Nazarene Chs., Northwest region, 1940-62; traveling tchr./ch. renewal movement/interdenominational, 1962-89; minister Open Gates Ch., Stanwood, 1989—. Capt. (chaplain) U.S. Army, 1944-46. Office: Open Gates Church Stanwood WA 98292

BUTEYN, DONALD PETER, minister, educator; b. Fond du Lac, Wis., Nov. 10, 1924; s. Cornelius and Jessie Louise (Felsman) B.; m. Marian Schroeder, June 24, 1949; children: Richard, Joyce, Jean, Carol, Douglas, Steven. BA, Hope Coll., 1948; MDiv, Western Theol. Sem., 1951; DD, Whitworth Coll., 1974. Pastor Jamestown (Mich.) Reformed Ch., 1951-53, Midland (Mich.) Reformed Ch., 1953-58; sr. pastor 1st Reformed Ch., Kalamazoo, Mich., 1958-64; assoc. pastor 1st Presbyn. Ch., Berkeley, Calif., 1964-69; exec. pastor 1st Presbyn. Ch., Hollywood, Calif., 1973-79; sr. pastor 1st Presbyn. Ch., Bakersfield, Calif., 1986—; exec. Seattle Presbery, 1969-73; chaplain L.A. Police Dept., 1975-79; Flora Lampson Hewlett prof. evangelism and mission San Francisco Theol. Sem., San Anselma, Calif., 1979-86, dean, 1983-86, prof. emeritus, 1989—; adj. prof. Fuller Theol. Sem. Contbr. articles to profl. jours. Mem. Kern County Human Rels. Commn.; chmn. Hollywood Devel. Commn., L.A., 1976-79; bd. dirs. Bethany Svc. Ctr., Bakersfield, Kern County Food Banks, Inc., Bakersfield, Friends Outside Agy., Bakersfield, Frontier Fellowship Presbyn. Ch.; mem. governing bd. Nat. Coun. Chs. of Christ, 1988—. Named Presbyn. Preacher of Yr., Gen. Assembly Presbyn. Ch., 1983. Mem. Nat. Assn. Profs. of Mission, Rotary. Democrat. Avocations: miniature railroads, gardening. Home: 9600 Lea Oak Rd Bakersfield CA 93311 Office: First Presbyn Ch 1705 17th St Bakersfield CA 93301 *Fill each day to the full knowing that you may not have another; plan your life knowing that you are destined to live forever. And in the midst of living be less concerned about doing things right and more concerned about doing the right thing.*

BUTHOD, MARY CLARE (SISTER), school administrator; b. Tulsa, Aug. 20, 1945; d. Arthur Paul and Mary Rudelle (Dougherty) B. MA in Teaching, Tulsa U., 1969; M Christian Spirituality, Creighton U., 1981. Joined Order of St. Benedict. Asst. tchr. HeadStart, Tulsa, 1966; tchr. Madalene Parish Sch., Tulsa, 1968-69, Monte Cassino Pvt. Sch., Tulsa, 1969-79; prin. Monte Cassino Elem. Sch., Tulsa, 1979-86; dir. Monte Cassino Sch., Tulsa, 1986—; mem. convent coun. Benedictine Sisters, Tulsa, 1975-88, dir. formation programa, 1983—. Mem. State Congl. Ednl. Com., Tulsa, 1989-90; co-chair for edn. and human devel. Tulsa Coalition Against Illegal Use of Drugs, 1990-91. Mem. Tulsa Reading Coun. (sec. 1975-77), Nat. Cath. Edn. Assn., Delta Kappa Gamma. Home: 220 S Lewis Tulsa OK 74114 Office: Monte Cassino Sch 2206 S Lewis Tulsa OK 74414

BUTLER, CHARLES WILLIAM, clergyman; b. Dermott, Ark., May 4, 1922; s. George Jackson and Effie (Russell) B.; m. Helen Odean Scoggins, Aug. 26, 1946; children: Charles, Jr., Beverly, Keith, Kevin. B.A., Philander Smith Coll., 1943; B.D., Union Theol. Sem., 1949, M.Div., 1971; D.D., Interdenominational Theol. Ctr., Morehouse Sch. Religion, 1980, Birmingham Bapt. Bible Sch., 1980. Ordained to ministry Bapt. Ch. Asst. pastor St. James Presbyn. Ch., N.Y.C., 1947-50; released time tchr. N.Y.C. Mission Soc., 1950-51; tchr. Bapt. Center, N.Y.C., 1950-51; tchr. bibl. lit. and religion Morehouse Coll., Atlanta, 1951-54; pastor Met. Bapt. Ch., Detroit, 1954-63, New Calvary Bapt. Ch., Detroit, 1963—; pres. Mich. Progressive Bapt. Conv., Detroit, 1962-64; bd. dirs. Interdenominational Theol. Ctr., Detroit, 1978—, Morehouse Sch. Religion, Atlanta; 1st v.p. Bapt. Pastor's Coun., Detroit, 1983—, pres., 1987-89; pres. Progressive Nat. Bapt. Conv., Washington, 1982-84. Dir., organizer 1st Ind. Nat. Bank, Detroit, 1970-80; chmn. bd. Police Commn., City Detroit, 1976; mem. adv. bd. Mich. Consol. Gas Co., Detroit, 1980-86. Served with U.S. Army, 1943-46, ETO. Named Man of Year Mich. Chronicle, 1962. Mem. Congress Nat. Black Chs. (chmn. Washington chpt. 1989—), Alpha Phi Alpha. Office: New Calvary Baptist Ch 3975 Concord St Detroit MI 48207

BUTLER, DOLORES J., nun, education educator; b. Canton, Mass., Aug. 23, 1930; d. Joseph E. and Helen M. B. BS in Elem. Edn., Villanova U., 1960; EdM in Spl. Edn., St. Louis U., 1968, PhD in Edn., 1973. Prin. St. Michael (Ariz.) Ind. Sch., 1970-73; teaching asst. St. Louis U., 1970-73; rsch. asst. U. Solothurn, Switzerland, 1973-74; prin. Holy Ghost Sch., New Orleans, 1975-80; asst. prof. Xavier U. La., New Orleans, 1981-87, assoc. prof. Grad. Sch. Edn., 1988—; early childhood cons. Archdiocese of New Orleans. Mem. NEA, ASCD, Assn. Early Childhood Internat., Nat. Assn. Edn. Young Children, Coun. Exceptional Children, Nat. Cath. Edn. Assn., Phi Delta Kappa. Avocations: cooking, gardening, reading. Office: Xavier Univ La 7325 Pine and Palmetto St New Orleans LA 70125

BUTLER, DONALD EDWARD, minister; b. Donaldsonville, Ga., Dec. 21, 1946; s. Howard Edward and Leila Mae (Johnson) B.; m. Wanda Jean Smith, June 10, 1966; children: Don Jr., Christy. B in Div., Luther Rice Coll., 1974; MDiv, Luther Rice Seminary, 1975, D in Ministry, 1976; post-grad., U. Fla., 1981-82, Liberty U. Rep. Ind. Life, Donaldsonville, Ga., 1967-71; minister West St. Baptist Ch., Bainbridge, Ga., 1971-73; minister First Baptist Ch., New Hope, Ala., 1973-76, Cherokee, Ala., 1976-77; minister Don Butler Evangelist Assn., Donaldsonville, 1977-79, FIrst Baptist Ch. of Colbert Heights, Tuscumbia, Ala., 1979-81; sr. minister Hilton Terr. Baptist Ch., Columbus, Ga., 1981—. Author: The Second Coming, 1975. Co-chair City Wide Crusade, Columbus, 1984. Mem. Southern Baptist Convention (messenger), Columbus Baptist Assn. (moderator 1986-87), Colbert-Lauderdale Baptist Assn. (moderator 1980-81). Republican. Avocations: weightlifting, fishing, golf. Office: Hilton Terr Baptist Ch 2236 Warm Springs Rd Columbus GA 31904

BUTLER, EDWARD LEE, pastor, consultant; b. Frostproof, Fla., June 29, 1945; s. Willie and Lucinda (Hays) B.; m. Thelma Ruth Moore; children: Adina Zaneta, Edward Lee II. BA, Pacific States U., 1972; MDiv, Payne Theol. Sem., 1982. Ordained to ministry Episcopalian Ch., 1973. Pastor Bethel A.M.E. Ch., Mt. Union, Pa., 1973-74, St. Paul A.M.E. Ch., Uniontown, Pa., 1974-79, Quinn Chapel A.M.E. Ch., Wilmington, Ohio, 1979-82, Trinity A.M.E. Ch., Pitts., 1982-90, Ebenezer A.M.E. Ch., Aliquippa, Pa., 1990—; mem. edn. com., cons. Interdenominational Social Action Alliance, Pitts., 1984—; part-time chaplain Pa. Coun. Chs., 1990—, Western Ctr. Mental Health Facility, Canonsburg, Pa., 1990—. Mem. council Am. Cancer Soc., Pitts., 1985-86; mem. adv. bd. Black Adoption Services, Pitts., 1987—; mem. publicity com. Black Polit. Enpowerment Project, Pitts., 1987—. Fellow Black Child Devel. Inst., Met. Crusade for Voters, Urban League; mem. NAACP. Democrat. Lodge: Kiwanis (bd. dirs. Uptown Hill club 1986—). Avocations: table tennis, chess, gourmet cooking. Home: 1015 Davis St Aliquippa PA 15001

BUTLER, JAMES PATRICK, minister; b. Phoenix, Mar. 17, 1957; s. Howard Manuel and Mabel (Jennings) B.; m. Cynthia Lynn Carpenter, May 31, 1980; children: Stephen James, William Scott. BA, Grand Canyon U., 1980; MDiv, Southwestern Bapt. Theol. Sem., 1984, DMin, 1990. Ordained minister Laveen (Ariz.) Bapt. Ch., 1984. Chaplain extern Baylor Univ. Med. Ctr., Dallas, 1982; pastor Laveen (Ariz.) Bapt. Ch., 1984-89; chaplain New Life Treatment Ctr., Phoenix, 1989-90; pastor Community Meth. Ch., Buckeye, Ariz., 1991—; co-spiritual dir. Walk to Emmaus Retreat, 1988, spiritual dir., 1989. Mem. Estrella Baptist Assn. (ch. tng. dir. 1985-86, exec. bd. mem. 1988-89, moderator 1989). Avocations: bicycling, reading, poetry, computers, home do-it-yourself projects. Home: 808 Eason Ave Buckeye AZ 85326

BUTLER, JIM GLEN, minister; b. Shawnee, Okla., Nov. 29, 1950; s. Glen Eldon and Reba Jean (Hamon) B.; m. Lawanda Shrene Pinkston, Aug. 3, 1973; children: Meredith Ann, Ashley Shrene, Lauren Leigh. BA, Okla. Bapt. U., 1973; MDiv, Southwestern Bapt. Sem., 1976; PhD, Luther Rice Sem., 1990. Ordained to ministry So. Bapt. Conv., 1974; cert. continuing witness tng. equipper. Sr. pastor Cache Rd. Bapt. Ch., Lawton, Okla., 1977-83, 1st Bapt. Ch., Midwest City, Okla., 1983-86, 1st Bapt. Ch. Lakewood, Tacoma, 1986-88, Calvary Bapt. Ch., McAllen, Tex., 1988-90, Trinity Bapt. Ch., Memphis, 1990—; messenger Okla. Bapt. Conv., Oklahoma City, 1976-86, N.W. Bapt. Conv., Portland, Oreg., 1986-88, Tex. Bapt. Conv., Dallas, 1988-90, Tenn. Bapt. Conv., Nashville, 1990—. Author: What Every Southern Baptist Should Know, 1988, Revelation: The Keys to Unlocking Its Mystery, 1990. Recipient Evangelism Equipper award Fgn. Mission Bd., 1978, Eagle Ch. Growth award Sunday Sch. Bd., 1980, 86, 87. Mem. Shelby Bapt. Assn. (bd. dirs. 1990—), Rotary. Republican. Office: Trinity Bapt Ch 4225 Airways Blvd Memphis TN 38116

BUTLER, ROBERT JOHN, priest, social worker; b. Boston, May 8, 1936; s. Matthew Patrick and Katherine (Morrison) B. Student, St. John's Sem., Boston, 1958, MDiv, 1962; MSW, Boston Coll., 1971. Clin. social worker Family Counseling & Guidance Inc., Danvers, Mass., 1971-86; pastor St. Mary's Parish, Hull, Mass., 1986—. Home and Office: 58 Nantasket Ave Hull MA 02045

BUTLER, ROBERT MILLER, minister; b. Scranton, Pa., Jan. 7, 1946; s. Robert M. and Ida (Smith) B.; m. Elaine D. Weber, Aug. 10, 1968; children: Amy Elizabeth, Brandon Robert, Corey Nathan. BS in Econs., Albright Coll., 1967; MDiv, Gordon Conwell Theol. Sem., 1970; D Ministry, Fuller Theol. Sem., 1985. Ordained to ministry Am. Bapt. Chs. in U.S.A, 1970. Pastor Parsons Bapt. Ch., Wilkes-Barre, Pa., 1970-73, Evang. Bapt. Ch., Sharon, Mass., 1973-80; missionary Bapt. Gen. Conf., Mexico City, 1980-89; pastor Richmond Pla. Bapt. Ch., Bellaire, Tex., 1990—; mem. Com. on Ministerial Guidance, Worcester, Mass., 1975-78; chmn. Mex. Field Coun., 1983-84. Office: Richmond Pla Bapt Ch 7115 Mapleridge Bellaire TX 77401

BUTMAN, HARRY RAYMOND, minister; b. Beverly, Mass., Mar. 20, 1904; s. John Choate and Elsie Louise (Raymond) B.; m. Jennette Alice Stott, Jan. 5, 1929; children: Beverly, Raymond, Jack, Jennette. BD, Bangor Sem., 1928; postgrad., U. Vt., 1933; DD (hon.), Piedmont Coll., 1955. Ordained to ministry Congregational Ch., 1932. Minister Federated Ch., Edgartown, Mass., 1932-37, Congl. Ch., Randolph, Mass., 1937-49, Allin Congl. Ch., Dedham, Mass., 1949-53, Ch. of the Messiah, L.A., 1953-78; interim minister First Congl. Ch., L.A., 1978-81, cons., 1982—; moderator Nat. Assn. Congregational Christian Chs., 1963-64; chmn. Internat. Congregational Fellowship, London, 1977-81. Author: History of Randolph, 1942, Far Islands, 1954, Serve with Gladness, 1971, The Lord's Free People, 1968, The Argent Year, 1980, The Desert Face of God, 1985, Brown Boy, 1987, The Good Beasts, 1991; contbr. articles to profl. jours. Named for Best Patriotic Sermon, Freedom Found., 1972. Republican. Avocations: boating, desert driving. Home: 2451 Soledad Cyn Rd Acton CA 93510

BUTTERFIELD, JAMES D., minister; b. Nevada, Mo., June 18, 1960; s. James Dale and Lorene Maxine (Scott) B.; m. Margaret Joan Blair, May 23, 1981; children: Joshua David, Justice Daniel. BA in Religious Studies, S.W. Bapt. U., 1983; grad., Southwestern Bapt. Theol. Sem., Midwestern Bapt. Theol. Sem., 1989-90; postgrad., Trinity Theol. Sem., 1990—. Ordained to ministry So. Bapt. Conv., 1983. Pastor Harmony Bapt. Ch., Lowry City, Mo., 1982-83; min. youth and edn. Murphy (Tex.) Bapt. Ch., 1983-84; min. youth and music 1st Bapt. Ch., Junction, Tex., 1987-89; pastor 1st Bapt. Ch., Syracuse, Mo., 1989—. Contbr. articles to profl. jours. Ch. music. dir. Medina River Bapt. Assn., Junction, 1988-89; children's camp dir., chmn. coun., asst. moderator Harmony Bapt. Assn., Sedalia, Mo., 1990-91; grad. speaker at several high schs.; participant numerous revival meetings as preacher and music dir. Named one of Outstanding Young Men of Am., 1989. Mem. Rotary (sgt. at arms Junction club 1987-89). Republican. Home and Office: 1st Bapt Ch Hwy 59 and Washington PO Box 96 Syracuse MO 65354 *Life's greatest fulfillment comes not from one's service to God but rather from one's relationship to and fellowship with God. Then, that service to Him and others begins to become truly satisfying.*

BUTTERWORTH, DARRELL DAVID, minister; b. Montebello, Calif., May 3, 1950; s. Ralph Joe and Betty Katherine (Johnson) B.; m. Jean Ellen Melton, Dec. 12, 1970; children: Nelson Alexander, Nicholas Adam. AS, West Valley Jr. Coll., Saratoga, Calif., 1970; BA summa cum laude, San Jose Bible Coll., 1973; MDiv, Lincoln (Ill.) Christian Sem., 1982. Ordained to ministry Ch. of Christ, 1974. Min. Prophetstown (Ill.) Ch. of Christ, 1976-79, Yorktown (Ill.) Ch. of Christ, 1977-79, Putnam (Ill.) Christian Ch., 1979-85; assoc. min. Canby (Oreg.) Christian Ch., 1985-88; min. 1st Christian Ch., Bell, Calif., 1988-91, The Christian Ch., Los Alamos, N.Mex., 1991—; pres. Prophetstown Ministerial Assn., 1977-79; dean of faculty Rock River Christian Camp, Polo, Ill., 1983-85; covenant group leader Nat. Missionary Conv., Anaheim, Calif., 1989. Speaker Community Meml. Day Svcs., Putnam, 1979-85; coord. Community Health Fair, Canby, 1987; judge S.E. L.A. Pilot Club, Bell, 1989. Mem. Tri-City Ministerial Assn. (pres. 1990-91), Delta Epsilon Chi. Republican. Office: The Christian Ch 93 East Rd Los Alamos NM 87544 *Living a moral life is easy: just don't do anything that shouldn't be done with your mother's blessing.*

BUTTERWORTH, EDWARD JOSEPH, systematic theology educator; b. Pittsfield, Mass., Sept. 21, 1951; s. Clarence Joseph and Mary Concetta (Maffuccio) B.; m. LindaSue F. Schlee, Sept. 26, 1981. BA in Math., U. Mass., 1973; MA in Religion, Fordham U., 1977, PhD in Theology, 1985. Asst. prof. Niagara U., Lewiston, N.Y., 1986-89, Sacred Heart Major Sem., Detroit, 1989-90; adj. prof. religion U. Detroit, 1990-91; asst. prof., chair theology St. Mary's Coll., Orchard Lake, Mich., 1991—. Author: Anselm-Aquinas: Existence of God, 1990; contbr. articles to profl. jours. Mem. Am. Cusanus Soc. Roman Catholic. Home: 3221 Christopher Ln # 221 Keego Harbor MI 48320 Office: St Mary's Coll Dept Theology Orchard Lake MI 48324

BUTTGEN, JOSEPH CHRIS, minister; b. Davenport, Iowa, Dec. 31, 1955; s. Kenneth Eugene and Nari (Chirpas) B.; m. Darlene Francis Beasley, June 27, 1980; 1 child, Christopher James. BA, Free Will Bapt. Bible Coll., 1982. Ordained to ministry Free Will Bapts., 1985. Tchr. Shenandoah Christian Acad., Baton Rouge, 1982-85; pastor Christ's Free Will Bapt. Ch., Corpus Christi, Tex., 1985-88, Fellowship Free Will Bapt. Ch., Richton, Miss., 1988—. Home and Office: Rte 1 Box 96 Richton MS 39476-9663 *Our life and actions are an outpouring from the reservoir of our mind where we receive, store and disperse knowledge.*

BUTTINGER, RICHARD WALTER, army officer, retail professional; b. Boston, June 2, 1932; s. Walter Byron and Helen Gertrude (Graves) B.; m.k Sally Patricia Scanlon, Apr. 19, 1986. BBA, Norwich U., 1956. Commd. U.S. Army, 1958, advanced through grades to maj., 1969, ret., 1976; dist. mgr., distbr. Christian lit. and products, 1976—; distbr. Successful Living, Inc., Norwood, Mass., 1979—. Mem. Ch. of the Nazarene. Home and Office: 256 Railroad Ave Norwood MA 02062-2230

BUTTRAM, JAMES DAVID, publishing company executive; b. Springfield, Mo., May 7, 1941; s. Lester Leo and Ethel Bernice (Thiemer) B. BS, Cen. Mo. State U., Warrensburg, 1971. Contr. Gospel Tract Soc. Inc., Independence, 1965-70, sec./treas., 1970-90, pres., 1991—; pres. Bethel Bible Sch., Port au Prince, Haiti, 1976—; supt. Ebenezer Christian Schs., Haiti, 1983—. Author numerous religious tracts. Editor: Gospel Tract Harvester, 1978—. Active Rep. Nat. Com., 1976—; bd. dirs. Teen Challenge Kansas City, Mo., 1980-82, Bethesda Missionary Fellowship, Bungoma, Kenya, 1988—. Staff sgt. USAFR, 1964-70. Named hon. fellow, Harry S. Truman Libr. Inst., 1978. Mem. Independence C. of C. Mem. Assembly of God Ch. Club: Kiwanis (pres. Independence chpt. 1982-83). Office: Gospel Tract Soc Inc 1105 S Fuller St Independence MO 64050 *Life is moving so quickly that without a permanent foundation there is no stability—no basis from which to reach forth a helping hand or uplifting word.*

BUTTRICK, DAVID GARDNER, religion educator; b. N.Y.C., May 21, 1927; s. George Arthur and Agnes (Gardner) B.; m. Betty More Allaben, Dec. 21, 1950; 1 child, Anne Jackson Buttrick Crumpler. BA, Haverford (Pa.) Coll., 1948; BD, Union Theol. Sem., 1951; postgrad., Garrett Inst., Evanston, Ill., 1963-64, Northwestern U., 1963-64. Ordained minister Presbyn. Ch. U.S.A., 1951. Pastor 1st Presbyn. Ch., Fredonia, N.Y., 1951-60; editor Presbyn. Ch. Bd. Edn., Phila., 1960-61; prof. Pitts. Theol. Sem., 1961-75, William Oliver Campbell prof., 1972-75; Marten prof. St. Meinrad (Ind.) Sch. Theology, 1975-82; prof. Homiletics and Liturgics Divinity Sch. Vanderbilt U., Nashville, 1982—; vis. prof. St. Francis Sem., Loretto, Pa., 1972, Sts. Cyril and Methodius Sem., Pitts., 1974, So. Bapt. Sem., Louisville, 1972, Lexington (Ky.) Theol. Sem., 1979, Iliff Sch. Theology, Denver, 1987, others. Writer, editor: The Worshipbook, 1970; author: Homiletic, 1987 (Book of Yr. Preaching mag. Acad. Parish Clergy), Preaching Jesus Christ, 1988, The Mystery and the Passion, 1991; editor: Jesus and Man's Hope, 1970. Mem. Acad. Homiletics, Sociatas Homileticas, N.Am. Acad. Liturgy, Religious Speech Assn., Am. Acad. Religion, ACad. Parish Clergy. Democrat. Office: Vanderbilt U Div Sch Nashville TN 37240

BUTTS, DAVID LESTER, minister; b. Terre Haute, Ind., June 11, 1953; s. Lester L. and Margaret L. (Crumrin) B.; 1 adopted child, Ronald L. BA, Lincoln Christian Coll., 1975, Ind. State U., 1979; MS, Ind. State U., 1982. Min. Christian edn. Maplewood Christian Ch., Terre Haute, 1975-78; youth min. Agape Christian Ch., Terre Haute, 1979-80; min. Five Points Christian Ch., Marshall, Ill., 1980-82, Kansas (Ill.) Christian Ch., 1982—; Christian Ch. del. Denomination Prayer Leaders Conf., Atlanta, 1990—; assoc. bd. mem. Pioneer Bible Translators, 1990—; prayer chmn. Task Force on Missions, 1990—; nat. prayer chmn. Nat. Missionary Conv., Springfield, Ill., 1991. Contbr. articles to Christian jour. State legislator Ind. Ho. of Reps., Indpls., 1980-81. Home and Office: Kansas Christian Ch Box 301 Kansas IL 61933

BUTTS, S. L., bishop. Bishop Ch. of God in Christ, Upper Marlboro, Md. Office: Ch of God in Christ PO Box 4504 Upper Marlboro MD 20775*

BUTZ, GENEVA MAE, pastor; b. Emmaus, Pa., May 11, 1944; d. Edwin F. and Arlene E. (Engler) B. BA, Hood Coll., 1966; MRE, Union Theol. Sem., 1968. Ordained clergywoman United Ch. of Christ, 1972. Dir. Christian edn. United Ch. of Christ, Palos Verdes, Calif., 1968-72; mng. editor Youth mag., United Ch. Bd. for Homeland Ministries, Phila., 1972-75; affiliate rep. Ecumenical Community of Taizé, France, New Zealand, Australia, Indonesia, India and others, 1975-77; parish worker Temple Presbyn. Ch., Phila., 1978-83; pastor Old First Reformed Ch., United Ch. of Christ, Phila., 1984—; bd dirs. exec. com. Met. Christian Coun. of Phila., 1985—; chair Ch. and Ministry Com., Phila. Assn. United Ch. Christ, 1983-86; cons. Auburn Theol. Sem., N.Y., 1988-89; coord. 5-Day urban seminar for incoming students Lancaster Theol. Sem., 1986—, The Small Ch. and Cultural Change, Bangor Theol. Sem., 1988; mem. adv. com. on evangelism and membeship growth priority, United Ch. Christ, 1989—; team chair Toward the 21st Century, A Church-wide Planning Process for the United Ch. Christ, 1990-91; speaker Faith Journey, consultation XVI on Parish Ministry for United Ch. Christ Clergy, Orlando, Fla., 1991. Author: Color Me Well, 1986, Christmas Comes Alive, 1988; contbr. Women Pray, Karen Roller, Ed, 1986. Mem. Old City Civic Assn., Phila., 1984—; bd. dirs. Bethesda Project, Inc., Phila., 1986; del. Gen. Synod-United Ch. of Christ, Cleve., Ft. Worth, 1987-89; ecumenical del. Gen. Assembly Presbyn. Ch. (U.S.A.), 1989; bd. dirs. Phila. Religious Leadership Devel. Fund, 1988—, Protestant adv. bd. Temple U., Phila., 1987; mem. dialogue group Reformed Ch. in Am./United Ch. of Christ. Recipient Human Rels. award Nt. Conf. of Christians and Jews, Phila., 1985; named One of 85 People to Watch Phila. mag., 1985, One of 7 Clergy Leading U.S. Constl. BIcentennial Parade, 1987. Mem. Nat. Orgn. of Women, Ch. Women United of Greater Phila. (bd. mgrs. 1985-87), Old Phila. Clergy (v.p. 1986-87), Assn. Uniting Arts and Religion (steering com.), Phila. Assn. (ministrial standing). Democrat. Office: Old First Reformed Ch 4th & Race St Philadelphia PA 19106 *Being religious is so simple that we find it hard to achieve. Children do it easily. We need to work with children so we don't destroy their natural religious inclination. The future of the faith lies in our ability to evoke the innate religious sensitivity in all people.*

BUTZIGER, ROBERT ANTON, minister; b. Pawtucket, R.I., Jan. 17, 1937; s. Edwin Lewis and Edna (Myers) B.; m. Marianne Stahowski, Sept. 1, 1962; children: Caryl M., Peter, Laura. BA, U. R.I., 1958; postgrad., U. Conn., 1962; MDiv, Princeton Theol. Sem., 1969; D Ministry, San Francisco Theol. Sem., 1988. Ordained to ministry Presbyn. Ch., 1969. Pastor W.Va. Mountain Project, Dry Creek, 1969-71; supr. clin. pastoral edn. Appalachian Reg. Hosp., Middlesboro, Ky., 1971-72; dir. Morgan-Scott Project, Deer Lodge, Tenn., 1972-80; pastor Farragut (Tenn.) Presbyn. Ch., 1980-86, St. Andrew Presbyn. Ch., Albuquerque, 1986—; sec. com. on ministry Presbytery of Santa Fe.; marriage and family therapist, 1980—. Author: Family Commitments, 1988. Bd. dirs. Contact Teleministry, Knox, Tenn. & Albuquerque, 1982-88; v.p. Assn. for Couples in Marriage Enrichment, Winston-Salem, N.C., 1979-84. Lt. USN, 1960-64. Mem. N.Mex. Conf. of Churches (marriage and family chmn. 1988—). Home: 2200 Marie Park NE Albuquerque NM 87112 Office: Saint Andrew Presbyn Ch 5301 Ponderosa NE Albuquerque NM 87110 *One of the greatest tasks facing families today is the recognition that for the first time in recorded human history, we are in the process of change from an authoritarian, one-vote system to a more egalitarian, two-vote system which demands tremendous communication skills in decision making, negotiation, and conflict resolution.*

BUXTON, ZANE KELLY, pastor; b. Austin, Minn., Apr. 4, 1946; s.Harry Lee Buxton and Kathryn Martha (Miller) LaDue; m. Karol Kay Kelly, June 3, 1967; 1 child Kristin Kelly. BA in History, Bethel Coll., 1968; BD, Fuller Theological Seminary, 1971; ThM, Princeton Theol. Sem., 1989. Pastor E Friesland Presbyn. Ch., Rushmore, Minn., 1971-75; assoc. pastor North Shore Presbyn. Ch., Shorewood, Wis., 1975-81, Westminster Presbyn. Ch., Des Moines, 1981-85; pastor Community Presbyn. Ch., Clarendon Hills, Ill., 1985—. Pres. North Shore Neighbors, Shorewood, 1983-84. Mem. Milw. Mental Health Cons., Milw. Broadcast Ministry, Chgo. Presbytery (moderator 1991). Democratic. Avocations: reading, cabinet-making, bicycling, canoeing. Home: 2 Woodstock Clarendon Hills IL 60514 Office: Community Presbyn Ch 39 N Prospect Ave Clarendon Hills IL 60514

BUZITIS, BETTY JEAN, gifted and talented educator, daycare provider; b. Englewood, Ohio, Nov. 5, 1933; d. Wilbur B. and Neva Mae (Lochner) Sando; m. Leon William Buzitis, Aug. 1, 1953; children: Dale Edward, Janice Marie Jacobson, Cynthia Kay Wick, Jon Lynn, Kevin Leon. BA, Bethel Coll., 1955; postgrad., Cen. Wash. U., 1966; MEd, U. Wash., 1976. Cert. elementary, secondary tchr., Wash. Tchr. gifted, talented Mishawaka (Ind.) Sch. Dist., 1955-57, Moxee Sch. Dist, Yakima, Wash., 1962-66, Edmonds (Wash.) Sch. Dist., 1966-67, 69-90, 91—; dir. Lynnwood (Wash.) Day Care, 1990-91; cons. Newspaper in Classrm., 1970-76; seminar leader Ednl. Svc. Dist., 1976-80; workshop leader Northwest Gifted and Talented, Wash., 1982, 86, 88. Author: Bloom's Recipes, 1986; (curriculum book) Alpha Omega, 1979, Math Nuggets, 1975. Dir. Christian Edn. Free Meth. Ch., Lynnwood, 1974—; v.p. missions Free Meth. Ch. Am., Seattle, 1990—. Named Tchr. of Yr. Bethel Coll., Mishawaka, 1974; recipient Math. and Gifted Girls award Dept. Edn. State of Wash., 1978, Visual Arts and Gifted award State of Wash., 1979, Inventions and Inventors award Pub. Edn. Fund Edmonds, 1989. Mem. NEA, Wash. Edn. Assn., Edmonds Edn. Assn., Wash. Gifted and Talented. Methodist. Avocations: camping, travel, reading, sewing, handwork.

BUZZARD, SIR ANTHONY FARQUHAR, religion educator; b. Godalming, Surrey, Eng., June 28, 1935; came to U.S., 1981; s. Anthony W. and Margaret E. (Knapp) B.; m. Barbara Jean Arnold, July 21, 1970; children: Sarah J., Claire J., Heather E. MA in Modern Langs., Oxford U., 1960; ThM, Bethany Theol. Coll., 1990. Tchr. fgn. langs. Am. Sch., London, 1974-81; lectr. in Bible Oregon (Ill.) Bible Coll. (now Atlanta Bible Coll.), Morrow, Ga., 1982—; coord. Restoration Fellowship, Oregon, 1981—. Author: The Coming Kingdom of the Messiah: A Solution to the

Riddle of the New Testament, 1988. Home: 1194 Mud Creek Rd Oregon IL 61061 *The most remarkable fact of church history is that the churches bearing the name 'Christian' have never clearly announced Jesus' Gospel about the Kingdom of God.*

BYAM-BALDWIN, CARMEN SYLVIA, minister; b. Trinidad, W.I.; came to U.S., 1966; d. James Teopholus Baldwin and Virginia D. Smith; m. George E. Byam, Apr. 18, 1954. BA, Mary Mount Manhattan Coll., 1975; M in Community Health Edn., NYU, 1979. Ordained to ministry Unity Temple of Christ, 1984; RN and midwife, Eng., Wales; RN, N.Y. Founder, min. Unity Temple of Christ, Laurelton, N.Y., 1984—. Mem. Ea. Region Assn. of Unity Chs. (alt. regional rep. 1990-93, sec., v.p. 1987-90). Home: 139-11 222nd St Laurelton NY 11413 Office: 228-20 137th Ave Laurelton NY 11413

BYARS, RONALD PRESTON, minister; b. Beatrice, Nebr., July 5, 1937; s. Preston Randolph Florence Ione (Penny) B.; m. Susan Eleanor Rhodes, Sept. 5, 1959; children: Stephen Rhodes, Matthew Mason. BA, U. Nebr., 1959; BD, Yale U., 1962; MA, Mich. State U., 1972, PhD, 1979. Ordained to ministry Christian Ch. (Disciples of Christ), 1962. Pastor First Christian Ch. (Disciples), Fremont, Mich., 1962-66; asst. pastor Allen Park (Mich.) United Presbyn. Ch., 1966-68; pastor United Presbyn. Ch. of Okemos, Mich., 1968-80, Second Presbyn. Ch., Lexington, Ky., 1980—; chmn. Ky. Commn. on Christian Unity, Lexington, 1985; trustee Presbytery of Transylvania, Lexington, 1985—; bd. dirs. Ky. Coun. Ch. Editor: Eucharist and Ecumenical Life, 1985. Bd. dirs. Appalachian Regional Healthcare, Lexington, 1986—, Lexington Coun. on Child Abuse, 1985-88; chmn., bd. dirs. Samaritan Counseling Ctr., Lexington, 1982-85; chmn. ch. campaign United Way of the Bluegrass, Lexington, 1990-91. Mem. Orgn. Am. Historians, Rotary, Phi Kappa Phi. Home: 1220 Tishoff Dr Lexington KY 40502 Office: Second Presbyn Ch 460 E Main St Lexington KY 40507-1572

BYERS, GARY WILLIAM, religious organization administrator; b. Pitts., May 30, 1948; s. William and Wilma (Gaal) B.; m. Kathy M. Byers, June 27, 1970; children: Erika, Jill, Nathan, Christina, Holly. AA, Concordia Coll., 1969; BA, Concordia Theol. Sem., Ft. Wayne, 1970; MDiv, Concordia Theol. Sem., 1974. Pastor St. Andrew Luth. Ch., Flint, Mich., 1975-79, St. Paul's Luth. Ch., Decatur, Ill., 1979-89; dist. exec. Cen. Ill. Dist. Luth. Ch. Mo. Synod, Springfield, Ill., 1989—; speaker in field. Chaplain USAR. Maj. USAR, 1983—. Home: 29 Meander Pike Chatham IL 62629 Office: Cen Ill Dist Luth Ch Mo Synod 1850 N Grand W Springfield IL 62702

BYERS, HAROLD HILL, religious organization executive; b. Bellwood, Pa., Nov. 26, 1928; s. Harold Hill and Ruth (Conley) B.; m. Phyllis E. Stahl, June 11, 1949 (div. Feb. 1975); children—Anne L., Stephen P., Cynthia R.; m. Jeanne McBeath Byers, Nov. 5, 1977. B.A., Ashland Coll. (Ohio), 1951; M.Div., Pitts. Theol. Sem., 1954; D.D. (hon.), Tusculum Coll., Greenville, Tenn., 1983. Ordained to ministry Presbyn. Ch. (U.S.A.), 1954; pastor Upper Buffalo Presbyn. Ch., Buffalo, Pa., 1951-55; assoc. pastor 1st Presbyn. Ch., Lansdowne, Pa., 1955-57; pastor 1st Presbyn. Ch., DuBois, Pa., 1957-64, Presbyn. Ch. of Apostles, Burnsville, Minn., 1964-73; program dir. Program Agy. Upcusa, N.Y.C., 1973-81; exec. Synod of South, Atlanta, 1981-87; adminstrv. assoc. exec. Presbytery of Grand Canyon, Phoenix, 1988; interim assoc. synod exec. Presbytery of Cascades, Portland, Oreg., 1992.

BYERS, J DONALD, JR., minister; b. Lynwood, Calif., Sept. 1, 1947; s. J. Donald Sr. and Ruthanna (Wilson) B.; m. Cynthia Joyce Wamhoff, Sept. 7, 1968; children: Tracy Lynn, Kerry Elizabeth, David Christopher. AA, Rio Hondo Jr. Coll., Whittier, Calif., 1968; BA in Sociology, Calif. State U., Long Beach, 1973; MA in Bibl. Studies, Grace Grad. Sch., Long Beach, 1977, D of Ministry, 1987. Pastoral staff Grace Brethren Ch., Long Beach, 1976-77; sr. pastor Grace Ch. of Orange, Calif., 1977-88; dir. ch. rels. Grace Coll. and Sem., Winona Lake, Ind., 1988-89, dir. constituent rels., 1989—, dir. D Ministry program, 1990—; chaplain Orange Police Dept., 1986-88, cons. 1984-86; v.p. So. Calif.-Ariz. Dist. Ministerium, 1978, pres. 1979; asst. conf. coord. Nat. Conf. Fellowship of Grace Brethren Ch., So. Calif., 1982, 88, v.p., bd. dirs. C.E. Nat., Winona Lake, 1982-90. Sgt. U.S. Army, 1969-71. Mem. Christian Mgmt. Assn., Assn. of Ch. Missions Commns. Republican. Home: 207 Sandpoint Dr Warsaw IN 46580 Office: Grace Coll and Sem 200 Seminary Dr Winona Lake IN 46590 *None of us know ourselves completely, but if we listen objectively to the observations of others and determine what we enjoy doing most, we can begin to identify what areas may bring the greatest reward in our occupational pursuit.*

BYERS, JOHN A., bishop. Bishop Brethren in Christ Ch., Elizabethtown, Pa. Office: Brethren in Christ Ch Elizabethtown PA 17022*

BYERS, JOHN BRUCE, minister; b. Pitts., Oct. 7, 1952; s. John Agnew and Dolores Mary (Morrissey) B.; m. Shelley Jane Long, Apr. 16, 1974; children: Sarah Rebekah, Shannon Elisabeth. BA, Millikin U., 1974; MDiv, Princeton Theol. Sem., 1977; PhD, U. St. Andrews, Fife, Scotland, 1984. Ordained to ministry Presbyn. Ch., 1977. Asst. min. Southminster Presbyn. Ch., Pitts., 1977-80; sr. min. St. Andrews Presbyn. Ch., Butler, Pa., 1984—; chmn. evangelism com. Beaver-Butler Presbytery, 1986—. Howard C. Scharfe Meml. fellow Shadyside Presbyn. Ch., St. Andrews, Scotland, 1981-84. Mem. Alban Inst., Butler Fellowship of Chs. (exec. bd., youth com. chmn. 1984-86), Butler Lodge 272. Republican. Office: St Andrews United Presbyn Ch 201 E Jefferson St Butler PA 16001

BYERS, LAURENCE PRIMM, minister; b. Kachek, Island of Hainan, China, Feb. 8, 1921; s. George Douglas and Clara Laura (Primm) B.; m. Muriel May Anderson, May 27, 1947; children—Helen Elizabeth, George Douglas II, Laureen Claire. A.A., Marin Jr. Coll., 1941; B.A., Occidental Coll., 1943; M.Div., San Francisco Theol. Sem., 1947; D.Div. (hon.) Pacific Sch. of Religion, 1966. Mem. ednl. mission, Presbyterian Ch., Brazil, 1947-52; pastor Presbyn. Ch., Red Bluff, Calif., 1952-55, Community Presbyn. Ch., Vallejo, Calif., 1955-59, Union Ch. Monterrey, Mex., 1959-61, Calvary Presbyn. Ch., Berkeley, Calif., 1961-66, Westminster Presbyn. Ch., Portland, Oreg., 1967-75; minister adult edn. Village Ch., Prairie Village, Kans., 1975-77; pastor Trinity United Presbyn. Ch., Burlington, Sedro Woolley, Wash., 1977-85. Author: Christians in Crossfire, 1967, Beyond the Abyss, 1977, The Forbidden Zone, 1991; contbr. articles to newspapers and profl. jours. Pres. Vallejo Ministerial Assn., 1957-59; chmn. pastors for Fair Housing Legislation, Berkeley, 1963, Clergyman for Sch. Bonds and Integrated Pub. Schs., Berkeley, 1962-63; bd. dirs. Bd. of Edn., Berkeley, 1964-66, Mental Health Assn., Mem. No. Coastal Area Council (bd. dirs., moderator 1957-58), Presbyn. Interracial Council (bd. dirs., chmn. 1963-64), Ch. and Soc. Com. (bd. dirs., chmn. 1969-73), Mission Strategy, Presbytery of North Puget Sound (dept. head, Wash. chmn. 1978-83). Democrat. Club: Portland City (Oreg.). Lodges: Rotary, Kiwanis. *The greatest threats to the world are nationalism as idolatry, ecological devastation resulting from technological weaponry and political provincialism on an over-populated planet.*

BYLES, SISTER MARY JOSEPHINE, retired religion educator; b. N.Y.C., Nov. 29, 1913; d. William Esdaile and I. Katherine (Russell) B. BA, Manhattanville Coll., 1934; MA, Fordham U., 1947, PhD, 1951. Joined Soc. Sacred Heart. From faculty instr. to asst. prof. Manhattanville Coll., Purchase, N.Y., 1945-53; acad. dean U. Sacred Heart, P.R., 1953-69; faculty full prof. Maryville Coll., St. Louis, 1972-90, prof. emeritus, 1990—; religion educator several chs., St. Louis, 1990—; dir. retreats Cenacle, St. Louis, St. Louis U. Princeton Theol. Sem. fellow, 1969-70. Home: 13648 Conway Rd Saint Louis MO 63141

BYRD, CHARLES EVERETT, clergyman; b. Brinkerhoff, N.Y., Mar. 19, 1909; s. James Edward and Mamie (Lovelle) B.; m. Violetta Eleanor Price. AB, Howard U., 1932; MDiv, Union Theol. Sem., 1935; MA, Columbia U., 1947; D in Ministry, Drew U., 1978. Pastor Cen. Bapt. Ch., Salt Point, N.Y., 1939-47, Mt. Zion Bapt. Ch., Green Haven, N.Y., 1936-52, Ebenezer Bapt. Ch., Poughkeepsie, N.Y., 1947-52; program rep. Am. Bapt. Svc. Corp., Valley Forge, Pa., 1969-74; chaplain Dutchess County Jail, Poughkeepsie, 1974-89. Author: Review of the Policies of the Baptist Home in Light of the Theology of Service, 1978. Bd. dirs. Bapt. Home, Rhinebeck, N.Y., 1972—, Dutchess County Office Aging, Poughkeepsie, 1976—, The Rural and Migrant Ministry, New Paltz, N.Y., 1980—, Dutchess County Mental Health Assn., Poughkeepsie, 1981—. With USAAF, 1943-46; lt. col. USAF, 1952-68. Decorated Commendation medal with oak leaf cluster. Mem. Dutchess Interfaith Coun. (Disting svc. medal 1987), Rotary. Home: 123 Carpenter Rd Hopwell Junction NY 12533 *During the time of my prayers prior to very high risk cancer surgery, the third with 2 in 1987, my courage and faith grew as I reached the point that nothing could change or diminish the goodness of God to me over the past 78 years.*

BYRD, GLENN NELSON, minister; b. Hartford, Ala., May 21, 1922; s. William Arthur and Jimmie Gertrude (Stewart) B.; m. Melba Kyser, June 27, 1948; children: Joel Glenn, Jeanene Karen. Cert. Christian tng., Samford U., 1954; AB, Mercer U., 1959. Ordained to ministry So. Bapt. Conv., 1951. Pastor various chs., Ga., 1952-70, Richmond Hill (Ga.) Bapt. Ch., 1969-70; dir. missions Grady County Bapt. Assn., Cairo, Ga., 1970-88; retired, 1988; pres. Ga. Bapt. Tng. Union Cov., 1964-65; cons. Discipleship Tng. for Bapt. Sunday Sch. Bd., So. Bapt. Conv. Active Boy Scouts Am. (Scouter's Key), 1970—. Recipient Wilburn S. Smith award Grady County Bapt. Youth Assn.. Mem. Grady County Ministerial Assn. (past pres., sec.), So. Bapt. Conv. Dirs. Missions Assn. Home: 340 Horseshoe Bend SE Cairo GA 31728 *If a door of opportunity closes for us, we must remember that God never closes a door without opening another.*

BYRD, GRANT TRAVIS, minister, educator; b. Baytown, Tex., Aug. 27, 1962; s. Zack and Melba Ruth (Bumstead) B. B, East Tex. Bapt. U., 1984; M, Southwestern Bapt. Theol. Sem., 1986. Ordained to ministry Bapt. Ch. 1987. Min. youth 1st Bapt. Ch., Greenwood, La., 1981-82, Mount Pleasant, Tex., 1983-84; assoc. min. Sagemont, Houston, 1985-86; min. of students 2d Bapt. Ch., Baytown, Tex., 1987-91, 1st Bapt. Ch., Mc Kinney, Tex., 1991—; chmn. Youth Baytown Christian Crusade, 1987-91; exec. dir. Super Summer Recreation, 1989-90; mem. Nat. Network Youth Mins., 1988—. Contbr. articles to profl. jours. Mem. San Jacinto Associational Youth Com., Baytown, 1987-91; mem. Big Brothers and Sisters, Ft. Worth, 1984-86; mem. Young Reps., Arlington, Tex., 1984. Avocations: snow skiing, rock climbing, rappeling, backpacking, golf. Office: 1st Bapt Ch 1615 W Louisiana St Mc Kinney TX 75069 *The greatest opportunity that people have to impact the world (starting with their city) for God, is most often overlooked...Prayer! Use the power!.*

BYRD, GWENDOLYN PAULINE, school system superintendent; b. Mobile, Ala., July 21, 1943; d. Marley and Frances (Ramsay) B. BS in History, Marillac Coll., St. Louis, 1966; MA in Sch. Adminstrn., DePaul U., 1975. Tchr. St. Matthias Sch., St. Louis, 1966-70; prin., tchr. Cathedral Elem. Sch., Natchez, Miss., 1970-74; prin. St. Francis De Sales Sch., Lake Zurich, Ill., 1974-77; curriculum coord. for sch. system Archdiocese of Mobile, 1977-83, sch. supt., 1983—. Chairperson Little Flower Liturgy Com., Mobile, 1980—; pvt. sch. rep. to adv. com. on tchr. edn. State of Ala., 1983—; active Mobile Bay Area Partnership for Youth, 1987—; mem. adv. bd. Cath. Svc. Ctr., Mobile, 1989—; bd. dirs. Mobile Mental Health Assn., 1990—. Named Outstanding Career Woman, Cayfer's Career Club, 1985, Outstanding Supt., Ala. Assn. Learning Disabilities, 1988. Mem. Nat. Cath. Edn. Assn., Chief Adminstrs. Cath. Edn., Phi Delta Kappa. Office: Office Cath Schs 308 S Dearborn St Mobile AL 36603

BYRD, MARY ELAINE, music director; b. West Point, Miss., Aug. 5, 1953; d. Oliver Carroll and Mary Ellen (May) B. AA, East Miss. Jr. Coll., 1972; B of Music Edn., Miss. U. for Women, 1975; M of Music Edn., Miss. State U., 1988. Youth choir dir. 1st United Meth. Ch., West Point, Miss., 1974-75, organist, 1982-88; dir. music LeMoyne Blvd. Bapt. Chapel, Biloxi, Miss., 1976-77; organist 1st Presbyn. Ch., West Point, 1977-80; dir. music and activities 1st United Meth. Ch., Waynesboro, Miss., 1988-91; dir. music ministries 1st United Meth. Ch., West Point, Miss., 1991—; pvt. music instr., Waynesboro, 1979-91, West Point, 1991—. Mem. Kiwanis (editor bull. 1990-91, key club advisor 1989-91), West Point Music Coterie, Pilot Club, Phi Delta Kappa. Home: PO Box 61 West Point MS 39773-0061 Office: 1st United Meth Ch PO Box 293 West Point MS 39773

BYRD, VERNON R., bishop. Bishop A.M.E. Ch., Nashville. Address: AME Ch 500 8th Ave Nashville TN 33204*

BYRNE, ALLAN DEAN, minister; b. Pontiac, Ill., Oct. 3, 1930; s. Ira Council and Vera Ruth (Rittenhouse) B.; m. Louise Marie Wichmann, Aug. 12, 1951 (div. Mar. 1983); children: Allan Mark, Wesley Charles, Rae Marie; m. Mary Elizabeth Gottula, Apr. 27, 1985. B. Philosophy, Ill. Wesleyan U., 1952; MDiv, Garrett Theol. Sem., Evanston, Ill., 1955; DMin, Christian Theol. Sem., Indpls., 1980. Ordained minister in Meth. Ch., 1955. Pastor Dyer (Ind.) Meth. Ch., 1954-59; assoc. pastor City Meth. Ch., Gary, Ind., 1959-64; pastor Grace Meth. Ch., Rochester, Ind., 1964-68; sr. pastor First United Meth. Ch., Hobart, Ind., 1968-73, Waynedale United Meth. Ch., Ft. Wayne, Ind., 1973-77, College Ave. United Meth. Ch., Muncie, Ind., 1977-83, Woodmar United Meth. Ch., Hammond, Ind., 1983-86, First United Meth. Ch., South Bend, Ind., 1986—; commn. mem. Commn. on Christian Unity and Interreligious Concerns, Ind., 1987-91; chairperson South Bend Cluster of United Meth. Ministers, 1987-91; mem. exec. com. South Bend Dist. Coun. on Ministries, 1987-91. Bd. dirs. Madison Ctr., South Bend 1989-91, Bashor Children's Home, Goshen, Ind., 1989-91. Mem. Rotary. Home: 1701 E Wayne St South Bend IN 46615 Office: First United Meth Ch 333 N Main St South Bend IN 46601 *"It is in giving that we receive." The happiest moments in life are those times of greatest service.*

BYRNE, HARRY J., priest; b. N.Y.C., Feb. 7, 1921; s. Harry T. and Mary E. (Whelen) B. BA, Cathedral Coll., 1942; JDC, Cath. U. Am., 1948. Ordained priest Roman Cath. Ch., 1945. Sec. to marriage tribunal Archdiocese of N.Y., N.Y.C., 1950-63, asst. chancellor, 1963-68; pastor St. Joseph's Ch., N.Y.C., 1971-82, Epiphany Ch., N.Y.C., 1982—. Pub. mem. Rent Guidelines Bd., N.Y.C., 1978-81; bd. dirs. Doctor's Hosp., N.Y.C., 1978—, Boys Brotherhood Republic, N.Y.C., 1960—, Burden Ctr. for Aging, N.Y.C., 1972—. Democrat. Address: Ch of Epiphany 239 E 21st St New York NY 10010

BYRNE, JAMES JOSEPH, retired archbishop; b. St. Paul, July 28, 1908; s. Philip Joseph and Mary Agnes (McMonigal) B. STB, Cath. U., Washington, 1933; STD, U. Louvain, Belgium, 1937; PhD (hon.), St. Mary's Coll., Winona, Minn., 1955, U. Portland, Oreg., 1958. Prof. St. Thomas Coll., St. Paul, 1937-45, St. Paul Sem., 1945-47; pastor and bishop Nativity Parish, St. Paul, 1948-56; pastor and aux. bishop Archdiocese of St. Paul, 1947-56; bishop Diocese of Boise, Idaho, 1956-62; archbishop Archdiocese of Dubuque, Iowa, 1962-83; ret. Archdiocese of Dubuque, 1983—. Home: PO Box 479 Dubuque IA 52004-0479

BYRNES, THOMAS ANTHONY, religion educator; b. Waterbury, Conn., Nov. 2, 1943; s. Thomas Joseph and Ann (Shanahan) B.; m. Carol Joan Rigmark, May 17, 1980. AB, Holy Cross Coll., 1965; MA, Boston Coll., 1969; MDiv, Weston Coll., 1973; PhD, U. Chgo., 1982. From asst. prof. to assoc. prof. Ill. Benedictine Coll., Lisle, 1982-89, prof. Religious Studies, 1990—. Contbr. articles to profl. jours. Mem. Am. Acad. Religion, Soc. of Christian Ethics. Democrat. Roman Catholic. Office: Ill Benedictine Coll 5700 College Rd Lisle IL 60532

BYRON, THOMAS E., minister; b. Norristown, Pa., May 22, 1949; s. LeRoy Thomas and Mae Jean (Madtes) B.; m. Nancy MacQueen, July 19, 1975; children: Allison, Rebecca. BA, Eastern Bapt. Coll., 1971; MA in Religion, E.B. Theol. Sem., 1973. Ordained to ministry Am. Baspt. Ch., 1975. Minister of youth North Wales (Pa.) Bapt. Ch., 1972-75; coord. Peoples Emergency Ctr., Phila., 1973-75; asst. minister Cen. Schwenkfelder Ch., Worcester, Pa., 1975-81, assoc. minister, 1982—; pres. Schwenkfelder Bd. Publ., Pennsburg, Pa., 1979—; v.p. Pa. Christian Endeavor, 1976-77; del. Pa. Interfaith Disaster Response Com., 1980—. Author: From One Place to Another, 1984. Chaplain Worcester Vol. Fire Dept., 1976—, asst. fire chief, 1991; dir. North Penn Vol. Fire Co., North Wales, 1974; chaplain 5th Dist. Firemen's Assn., 1976—. Named Firefighter of Yr., North Penn C. of C., 1989; recipient Earl Mayers award 5th Dist. Firemen's Assn., 1984; Alban Inst. rsch. fellow.

BYRUM, REGINALD DALE, evangelist; b. Indian Trail, N.C., Aug. 30, 1961; s. Walter Mason and Lorraine Janie (Helms) B.; m. Susan Leona Gregory, May 15, 1985; 1 child, Christopher Dale. Student, Cen. Piedmont Comm. Coll., Charlotte, N.C., 1990—. Dir. evangelism Calvary Ch., Midland, N.C., 1980-82; dir. evangelism, Sunday sch. tchr. Revival Cen. Ch., Matthews, N.C., 1982-84; founder, pres. Street Priests Evangelistic Assn., Indian Trail, 1984-86; youth pastor Word of Faith Family Ch., Charlotte, 1986-89; evangelist Reggie Byrum Ministries, Indian Trail, 1989—; graphics specialist CEM Corp., Matthews, 1981—. Mem. Concerned Charlotteans, Charlotte, 1989. With USNR, 1985—. Home: 849 Fairview Rd Indian Trail NC 28079

BYRUM, RONALD LANE, JR., youth minister; b. Decatur, Ga., Mar. 20, 1968; s. Ronald L. and Laura Suzanne (Bonner) B. Student, Cin. Bible Coll., 1987-90, Lincoln Christian Coll., 1990—. Youth min. Roachdale (Ind.) Christian Ch., 1988—; camp dean of sr. high wk. Hanging Rock Christian Assembly, West Lebanon, Ind., 1990—. Republican. Office: Roachdale Christian Ch Box 287 Forest Home/Walnut Roachdale IN 46172 *As Christians, we are called to be responsible. We are also called to be free. We are responsible to be free. In Christ, there is a freedom that surpasses all others. To live life free in Christ is a joy, yet also a command.*

BZOSKIE, JAMES STEVEN, minister; b. Owatonna, Minn., Sept. 18, 1949; s. Lawrence Justin and Margret Lucille (James) B.; m. Charlotte Anne Carroll, Mar. 2, 1971; children: James Steven Jr., Sarah Anne, Isaiah John. BA, Kingsway Bible Coll., 1986; ThM, Kingsway Sem., 1987, ThD, 1987. Ordained to ministry Pentecostal Ch., 1978. Pastor Jesus Believers Ch., Hastings, Minn., 1978-79; co-pastor Assemblies of God, Hastings, 1979-83; pastor Cornerstone Bible Ch., Hastings, 1983—; pres. Cornerstone Bible Coll.; chaplain Dakota County Sheriff Dept. (Jail), Hastings, 1983—. Author: The Book of Revelation, 1983. Community advisor Edn. Adv. Coun., Hastings, 1989—. Home: 311 State St Hastings MN 55033 *A successful person is one who puts his faith in Jesus Christ and recognize his need of God in every area of his life.*

CABABE, SISTER LOUISE DIANA, nun, educational administrator; b. Paterson, N.J., Sept. 12, 1944; d. Charles and Mary (Hayek) C. BA, Mt. St. Mary Coll., Newburgh, N.Y., 1967; MA, Jersey City State Coll., 1975; postgrad., Fordham U., 1989—. Joined Dominican Sisters, Roman Cath. Ch., 1962; cert. sch. adminstr. and supr., N.Y.; cert. sch. adminstr., N.J. Tchr. St. Paul's Sch., Jersey City, 1972-75, Pope Pius XII High Sch., Passaic, N.Y., 1980-81; adminstr. Holy Rosary Sch., Hawthorne, N.Y., 1975-80; tutor Mt. St. Mary Coll., 1982-83; adminstr. St. Mary's Sch., New Monmouth, N.J., 1983—; rep. 4th Synod Diocese of Trenton, 1991—. Chmn. Parent Setting Standards, New Monmouth, 1986-88. Grantee U.S. Dept. Edn., Cath. U. Am., 1987. Mem. Nat. Cath. Edn. Assn. Office: St Mary's Sch 538 Church St New Monmouth NJ 07748 *Every day is a wonderful gift from God to be celebrated and enjoyed. To live this precious gift is to use our talents for the service of others and to help build the kingdom of God here and now. Humanity and a peacefull world will develop if each person contributes willingly to this endeavor.*

CABANILLA, RAQUEL BLANCAFLOR, lay worker, charitable organization executive; b. Bangued, Abra, The Philippines, June 30, 1916; came to U.S., 1952; d. Isabelo Villareal and Fredesvinda (Panlasigui) Blancaflor; m. Cari Sanidad Cabanilla; children: Nathaniel, Israel, Johanna. BS, Far Ea. U., Manila, 1939; MS, Simmons Coll., Boston, 1962. Libr. Union Theol. Sem., Manila, 1948-65; libr. city schs. Balt., 1966-83; nat. sec. Spiritual Life, Women's Soc. of Christian Svc., The Philippines, 1952-56; mem. Bread for the World, Balt., 1974—; mem. hunger com. United Meth. Ch. Balt. Conf., 1978-82; chmn. commn. on missions Mt. Vernon United Meth. Ch., Balt., 1982-84; founder, pres. HEART, Inc., Balt., 1986—. Recipient award Com. on Relief, United Meth. Ch., N.Y.C., 1986, The Philippine Govt., 1991, Humanitarian Svc. award Filipino Am. Women's Network, 1991. Mem. Ch. Women United (award N.Y.C. chpt. 1987), Balt. Clergy and Laity Concerned. Republican. Home: 5507 York Rd Baltimore MD 21212

CABLE, KENNETH, academic administrator. Head Manhattan (Kans.) Christian Coll. Office: Manhattan Christian Coll 1415 Anderson Manhattan KS 66502*

CABLE, KENNETH A., ecumenical agency director. Exec. dir. Broom County Coun. Chs., Inc., Binghamton, N.Y. Office: Broome County Coun Chs Inc 81 Main St Binghamton NY 13905*

CACCIAVILLAN, AGOSTINO, archbishop; b. Vicenza, Italy, Aug. 14, 1926. JCD, Pontifical Lateran U.; JD, State U., Rome. Ordained priest Roman Cath. Ch., 1949, archbishop, 1976. Joined diplomatic svc. Holy See, Rome, 1959; served The Philippines, Spain, Portugal in Vatican Secretariat of State, until 1976; apostolic pro-nuncio Kenya, 1976-81, India, 1981-90; joint appointment to Nepal, 1985-90, apptd. apostolic pro-nuncio to U.S., 1990—; permament observer of the Holy See to OAS, 1990—. Home and Office: 3339 Massachusetts Ave NW Washington DC 20008

CACERES, ADRIAN, bishop. Bishop Episcopal Ch., Quito, Ecuador. Office: Episcopal Ch, Apdo 353-A, Quito Ecuador*

CADIEUX, DENNIS BARRY, religious organization administrator, minister; b. Chicago Heights, Ill., Jan. 2, 1936; s. Lawrence C. and Leone E. (Parks) C.; m. Louise E. Mehlhorn, Oct. 26, 1955; children: Catherine, Jennifer, Michael, Joshua. Grad. high sch., Aurora, Ill. Ordained to ministry Evangelistic Messengers Assn., 1977; ministerial lic. for pastoral office Evang. Covenant Ch., 1989—. Regional dir. Christian Action Coun., Chgo., 1984—; min. Jesus People USA Covenant Ch., Chgo., 1975—, also bd. dirs. Editor newsletters Action/Alert, 1984, View From the Towers, 1990. Sec. Cornerstone Community Outreach, Chgo., 1990—; tchr., adminstr. Cornerstone Festival, Chgo., 1985—; mem. adv. bd. Harry S. Truman Coll., Chgo., 1985-91; em. Task Force Against Displacement of Poor, Chgo., 1987—; active Aldermn's Community Svc., Chgo.; activities dir. Sr. Citizens at Friendly Towers. Mem. Northside Evang. Fellowship (exec. bd. 1980—), Kiwanis (chair spiritual aims Lake View club, bd. dirs. 1985-91). Home and Office: 920 W Wilson Ave Ste 436 Chicago IL 60640

CADWALLADER, DOUGLAS STEPHEN, clergyman; b. Orlando, Fla., Feb. 1, 1944; s. Harold Lee and Lenora Vada (Still) C. BA in History, La. State U., 1966, BS in Psychology, 1972, postgrad., 1990; MDiv, Va. Theol. Sem., 1977. Ordained priest, Episcopal Ch., 1977. GS 9 analyst The Def. Intelligence Agy., Washington, 1966-70; priest Episcopal Diocese of Tex., Houston, 1977-89. Mem. Rotary, Masons. Republican. Avocations: reading, firearms (shooting and collecting). Home: 9585 Donna Dr Baton Rouge LA 70815

CADWALLADER, EVA HAUEL, philosopher, educator; b. Cologne, Fed. Republic Germany, Jan. 11, 1933; came to U.S., 1939, naturalized, 1951; d. Karl August and Anna Paula Hauel; BS cum laude, Bucknell U., 1954; MS, U. Louisville, 1964; PhD, Ind. U., 1972; m. Thomas Christy Cadwallader, Aug. 3, 1954 (div. 1970); children: Mark Elliot, Lorraine Diane. Vis. instr. Cornell Coll., Mt. Vernon, Iowa, 1965-66; teaching assoc. Ind. U., 1966-69; adj. prof. Rose-Hulman Poly. Inst., Terre Haute, Ind., 1972; asst. prof. Western Ill. U., 1972-73; asst. prof. Westminster Coll., New Wilmington, Pa., 1973-77, assoc. prof., 1977-85, prof., 1985—; cons. Macmillan Pub. Co., Wadsworth Pub. Co., Fla. State U. Press. Author: Searchlight on Values: Nicolai Hartmann's Twentieth-Century Value Platonism, 1985, Balancing, 1987; guest editor spl. issue Depression and Religion, Counseling and Value, 1991; contbr. articles to profl. jours. Commonwealth speaker Pa. Humanities Coun., 1989. NSF grantee, 1962, Coun. of Learned Societies grantee, 1982; editorial bd. Counseling and Values, 1987—. Mem. Am. Soc. Value Inquiry (pres. 1978-79, v.p. 1976-77), Am. Philos. Assn., Tri-State Philos. Assn. (exec. com.), Am. Assn. Counseling and Devel., Metaphys. Soc. Am., Phi Beta Kappa, Phi Sigma Tau (exec. coun., pres.), Omicrom Delta Kappa. Episcopalian. Home: RD 1 Box 37 New Wilmington PA 16142 Office: Westminster Coll Dept Philosophy New Wilmington PA 16172

CAFFEY, WILLIAM BALLARD, JR., minister; b. Washington, Nov. 4, 1941; s. William Ballard Sr. and Margaret Louise (Stephens) C.; m. Jimmie Jo Stack, Aug. 23, 1963; children: Marvilyn Lee, James Ballard. B of Music Edn., East Tex. Bapt. Coll., Marshall, 1964; DD (hon.), Grace Bible Coll.,

New Delhi, 1987. Ordained to ministry Bapt. Ch., 1969. Asst. pastor, tchr. Liberty Ministries, Pensacola, Fla., 1966-78; tchr. Fountain Gate Ministries, Plano, Tex., 1978-79; pastor Cen. Park Ch., Richardson, Tex., 1980—. Office: Cen Park Ch 1001 E Arapaho Rd Richardson TX 75081

CAGLE, TERRY DEE, clergyman; b. Charlotte, N.C., June 7, 1955; s. James Clarence and Jean (Belk) C.; m. Julia Ann Conner, June 30, 1979; children: Julia Lynn, Christopher Terry. BA, Gardner-Webb Coll., 1979; postgrad., Southeastern Bapt. Theol. Sem., 1982, 87. Ordained to ministry So. Bapt. Conv., 1982. Pastor Mountain Creek Bapt. Ch., Oxford, N.C., 1982-85, Southside Bapt. Ch., Gaffney, S.C., 1985-88, Pleasant Ridge Bapt. Ch., Boiling Springs, N.C., 1988—; adj. prof. O.T. Gardner-Webb Coll., Boiling Springs, 1989—; mem. Christian Life com. King Mountain Bapt. Assn., Shelby, N.C.; v.p. Greater Gaffney Ministerial Fellowship, 1987-88. Mem. Boiling Springs Area Rotary Club (v.p. elect, club svc. chmn. 1989—), Shelby Amateur Radio Club. Home: 203 Gordon Ave PO Box 1084 Boiling Springs NC 28017 Office: Pleasant Ridge Bapt Ch 198 Pleasant Ridge Ch Rd Shelby NC 28150 *Adam and Eve dismissed the consequences of their decision. We are reminded that every deed is followed by its own consequence. Today should be lived in full, knowing full well that tomorrow's consequences are the results of today's decisions.*

CAHILL, LISA SOWLE, educator, author, lecturer; b. Phila., Mar. 27, 1948; d. Donald Edgar and Gretchen Elizabeth (MacRae) Sowle; m. Lawrence R. Cahill, Mar. 25, 1972; children: Charlotte Mary, James Donald, Donald Robert, William MacRae. B.A., U. Santa Clara, 1970; M.A., U. Chgo., 1973, Ph.D., 1976. Instr., Concordia Coll., Moorhead, Minn., 1976; asst. prof. theology Boston Coll., Chestnut Hill, 1976-82, assoc. prof. theology, 1982-89, prof. theology, 1989—; vis. scholar Kennedy Inst. Ethics Georgetown U., fall 1986. Author: Between the Sexes: Toward a Christian Ethics of Sexuality, 1985, (with Thomas A. Shannon) Religion and Artificial Reproduction: An Inquiry into the Vatican Instruction, 1988; contbr. articles to profl. jours.; assoc. editor Religious Studies Rev., 1981—, Jour. Religious Ethics, 1981—, Jour. Medicine and Philosophy, 1989—, Concilium, 1989—; adv. bd. Logos: Philos. Issues in Christian Perspective, Jour. of Law and Religion, 1983—, Interpretation, 1989—; assoc. editor Horizons: A Publ. of the Coll. Theology Soc., 1983—; mem. editorial bd., bd. dirs. Jour. Religion and Philosophy. Active Instnl. Rev. Bd. Harvard Community Health Plan, 1979-85; mem. bioethics com. March of Dimes, 1985—; mem. theology and ethics com. Cath. Hosp. Assn., 1985—. Boston Coll. Summer Rsch. grantee, 1977; Faculty fellow, 1986. Mem. Am. Acad. Religion (program com. 1979-82), Soc. Christian Ethics (dir. 1983-86). Cath. Theol. Soc. Am. (moral theology steering com. 1984-87, v.p. 1990-91, pres.-elect 1991—), Coll. Theology Soc. Democrat. Office: Boston Coll Dept Theology Chestnut Hill MA 02167

CAHILL, ROSALIE MARIE, writer, publisher; b. N.Y.C., Oct. 11, 1923; d. Peter A. and Grace (Callahan) Saitta; m. James Q. Cahill, May 31, 1957; children: Joseph, Stephen, Christopher. BA, St. Joseph's Coll., Bklyn., 1940; MLS, Columbia U., 1941; postgrad., U. Dubuque, 1969-70. Asst. librarian Pace Coll., NYC, 1941-42, Equitable Life Assn. Soc., NYC, 1942-45; librarian Lenox Hill Hosp., NYC, 1945-52; chemistry, physics librarian Columbia U., NYC, 1952-58; freelance research writer NYC, 1959-67, Iowa, 1967-71; librarian Dubuque (Iowa) Pub. Sch. System, 1971-72, Clear Creek Dist. Sch. System, Iowa City, 1972-79; freelance research writer publisher, 1980-. Co.-mgr. West Br. Food Pantry, 1981—; mem. Citizens Adv. Bd. Iowa Dept. Human Svcs., 1981-84, Cedar (Iowa) Task Force on Needs of Mentally Retarded, 1983-85, Iowa Bd. of Examiner Nursing Home Adminstrs., 1985-88. Mem. AAUW (pres. Tipon chpt. 1989—), Iowa Farm Bur. Women (chmn. Cedar County div. 1986-88). Democrat. Roman Catholic. Home and Office: Rt 2 Box 92 West Branch IA 52358

CAIN, CLIFFORD CHALMERS, chaplain, educator; b. Zanesville, Ohio, Feb. 15, 1950; s. Clifford Chalmers Sr. and Ethel Virginia (Bokelman) C.; m. Louise E. Lueckel, June 7, 1975; children: Rachel Mariël, Zachary Matheüs. BA, Muskingum Coll., 1972; M Div., Princeton Theol. Seminary, 1975; postgrad., Rijksuniversiteit te Leiden, The Netherlands, 1975-78; D in Ministry, Vanderbilt U., 1981. Ordained to ministry Am. Bapt. Ch., 1975. Assoc. pastor The Am. Protestant Ch., The Netherlands, 1975-78; chaplain Muskingum Coll., New Concord, Ohio, 1978-81; chaplain, assoc. prof. Franklin (Ind.) Coll., 1981—; pres. Met. Indpls. Campus Ministry, 1984-85, Ind. Office for Campus Ministries, 1985-88. Author: Faith Faces the World, 1989; contbr. articles to profl. jours. and book revs.; contbg. editor: The Intersection of Mind and Spirit, 1985. V.p. The Am. Community Council, The Hague, The Netherlands, 1977-78; bd. dirs. Evergreen Village, New Concord, Ohio, 1980-81. Mem. Am. Acad. Religion, Soc. Bibl. Lit., Bapt. Peace Fellowship N.Am., Ind. Bapt. Peace and Justice Fellowship (pres.), Nat. Assn. Coll. and U. Chaplains (bd. dirs., v.p., pres.). Avocations: photography, music, traveling, sports, archaeology. Home: 300 W Jefferson St Franklin IN 46131 Office: Franklin Coll East Monroe St Franklin IN 46131

CAIN, SISTER GLORIA, school system administrator; b. New Orleans, Oct. 8, 1941; d. Albert Sidney and Grace Dorothy (Connolly) C. BA, Notre Dame Coll., 1963; MEd, Our Lady of the Lake, 1974. Tchr. elem. Our Lady of Fatima Sch., Galena Park, Tex., 1963-66, San Jose Cath. Sch., Albuquerque, 1966-68, St. Paul Cath. Sch., Ft. Worth, 1968-69, St. Gerard Cath. Sch., Baton Rouge, 1969-72; Tchr. elem. Our Lady Queen of Heaven Sch., Lake Charles, La., 1972-73, elem. prin., dir. day care ctr., 1973-83; deputy supt. Diocese of Lake Charles, 1983-85, supt. cath. schs., 1985—; coord. primary sch. San Jose Cath. Sch., Albuquerque, 1966-68; coord. intemediate sch. St. Gerard Sch. Baton Rouge, 1969-72; dir. day care ctr. Our Lady Queen of Heaven Sch., Lake Charles, 1973-83; dir. renewal of lay orgns. Diocese of Lake Charles, 1983-85, communications adv. com., 1983—; mem. La. Cath. Conf., Chief Adminstrs. of Cath. Edn. Bd. dirs. Citizens for Edn. Freedom, Baton Rouge, 1985—; mem. Calcasieu Ministerial Alliance Lake Charles, 1983-84. Named to Order of St. Charles Bishop of the Diocese of Lake Charles, 1990. Mem. Nat. Cath. Edn. Assn., Assn. of Supervision and Curriculum Devel. Roman Catholic. Office: Diocese of Lake Charles 4029 Avenue G Lake Charles LA 70601

CAIN, RICHARD WILSON, minister; b. Marlow, Okla., Feb. 26, 1926; s. Lloyd D. and Zelma (Leddy) C. AB, U. Southern Calif., 1949; STB, Boston U., 1952, MST, 1954; DD, U. Pacific, 1964. Ordained to ministry, 1952. Min. Silverado United Meth. Ch., Long Beach, Calif., 1954-58, Mont Park (Calif.) United Meth. Ch., 1958-62; dist. supt. L.A. Dist., 1962-68; min. Phoenix United Meth Ch., 1968-77; pres. Claremont (Calif.) Sch. Theology, 1977-90. Office: Claremont Sch Theology 1325 N College Ave Claremont CA 91711

CAIN, SISTER THECLA, religious schools superintendent. BA in Elem. Edn., U. Portland, MA in Adminstrn. and Supervision; postgrad., Loyola U., Internat. Grad. Sch. Edn., St. Norbert Coll., St. Cloud State U., Aquinas Inst., Devel. Inst., U. San Diego. Tchr. All St's. Sch., Portland, Oreg., 1950-65, St. Mary Sch., Dubuque, Iowa, 1950-65; prin. St. Mary Sch., Manchester, Iowa, 1965-69; instr. summer sessions Sch. curriculum I and II Briar Cliff Coll., Sioux City, Iowa, 1967-69; edn. cons. Archdiocesan Office Edn., Dubuque, Iowa, 1969-80; dir., counselor Personal Growth Ctr., St. Cloud, Minn., 1980-84; cons. edn. Archdiocesan Office Edn., Omaha, 1984-87, Diocese of Austin, Tex., 1988-89; supt. schs. Diocese Austin and San Angelo, Tex., 1989—. Mem. ad hoc govt. com. gen. chpt. Dubuque Franciscan, 1971-72, chairperson steering com. gen. chpt. election and affairs, 1975-76l; chairperson safety com. Franciscan Community Fleet, 1977-80; assembly rep. Franciscan Area Group 20, 1989-91; co-presenter and condr. in field. Mem. Nat. Cath. Edn. Assn. Home: 13005 Heinemann Dr #606 Austin TX 78727 Office: Diocese of Austin Office of Edn 8000 Centre Park Dr Ste 160 Austin TX 78754

CAIRD, DONALD ARTHUR RICHARD, archbishop; b. Dublin, Ireland, Dec. 11, 1925; s. George Robert and Emily Florence (Dreaper) C.; m. Nancy Ballatyne Sharp, Jan. 12, 1963; children: Ann, John, Helen. BA, Dublin U., 1949, MA, BD, 1955, H.Dip Edn., 1959, DD (hon.), 1988. Ordained priest Ch. of Ireland. Curate-asst. St. Mark's Dundela, 1950-53; master Portora Royal Sch., Enniskillen, Ireland, 1953-57; lectr. in philosophy St. David's Coll., U. Wales, 1957-58; rector Rathmichael Parish, Dublin, 1960-69; dean of Kilkenny Ireland, 1969-70, bishop of Limerick, Ardfelt and Aghadoe, 1970-76, bishop of Meath and Kildare, 1976-85; archbishop of Dublin, 1985—; chmn. Ch. of Ireland Coll. Edn., 1985. Author: Directions, 1970. Mem. Radio/TV Rev. Commn., Ireland, 1971-74; bd. govs. St. Patrick's Hosp., Dublin, 1985, High Sch. Dublin, 1985; chmn. bd. govs. Alexandra Coll., Dublin. St. Columba's Coll. fellow, 1971. Mem. Bord Na Gaeilge, Kildare St. and Univ. Club. Home: The See House, 17 Temple Rd, Milltown, Dublin 6, Ireland

CAKEBREAD, STEVEN ROBERT, minister; b. Pitts., Calif., June 19, 1946; s. Robert Harold Cakebread and Mildred Irene (McQeen) Cowing; m. Margaret Anne Spandau, July 16, 1967; children: Robert, Scott, Andrew. ABS, Nazarene Bible Coll., Colorado Springs, Colo., 1977; BA, Mid. Am. Nazarene Coll., 1979; MDiv, Am. Bapt. Sem. of the West, Berkeley, Calif., 1983. Ordained to ministry Ch. of the Nazarene, 1980, Am. Bapt. Ch.,1984. Pastor Ch. of the Nazarene, Brookfield, Md., 1978-80; hosp. chaplain VA Hosp., San Francisco, 1988—, Oakland (Calif.) Naval Hosp./ Operation Desert Storm, 1990-91, Naval Reserves/Naval Base, San Francisco, 1985—; pastor 21st Ave Bapt. Ch., San Francisco, 1984—; Coun. mem. Coun. of Chs., San Francisco, 1988. E-5 USN, 1966-70, Vietnam. Decorated Humanitarian Svc. medal USN, Navy Achievement medal (Desert Storm). Mem. Naval Res. Assn., ABA/USA Chaplains Coun. Avocations: profl. chef, caterer, movies, walking a foggy beach. Home: 316 Burbank Rd Antioch CA 94509 Office: Am Baptist Personnel Svc PO Box 851 Valley Forge PA 19482-0851

CALABRESE, ALPHONSE FRANCIS XAVIER, psychotherapist; b. Bklyn., Apr. 27, 1923; s. Charles Angelo and Josephine Maria (Ambrosino) C.; m. Florence E. Schumacher, Aug. 15, 1950 (div. Oct. 1979); children: Charles, Theresa, Thomas, Catherine, John, Bernardette, Eileen, James; m. Eleanor A. Wallace, July 13, 1980; children: William, Paul. BA, St. John's U., 1948; MSW, Cath. U. of Am., 1950; PhD, Fla. State Christian U., 1976. Bd. cert. diplomate in social work; cert. psychoanalyst. Psychiat. social worker Cath. Charities Psychiat. Clinic, Bklyn., 1950-53; psychiat. social worker Postgrad. Inst. for Psychotherapy, N.Y.C., 1953-55, fellow, psychoanalysis, 1955-58, fellow analytic group psychotherapy, 1958-60; pvt. practice psychotherapy N.Y.C., 1960—; exec. dir. Christian Inst. for Psycho-Therapeutic Studies, Hicksville, N.Y., 1975—. Author: The Christian Love Treatment, 1977; contbr. articles to profl. jours. Dir. edn. Vt. Right to Life, Montpelier, 1986. Recipient grant Postgrad. Inst. for Psychotherapy, N.Y.C., 1953, scholarship St. Vincent DePaul Soc., Bklyn., 1948. Fellow Nat. Assn. for Psychoanalysis; mem. AAAS, NASW, Assn. of Christian Therapists (pres. 1976-77), Christian Assn. for Psychol. Studies, KC, 3d Order St. Francis. Republican. Roman Catholic. Avocations: theol. studies, lecturing. Home: RR 1 PO Box 1107 Ludlow VT 05149 Office: Christian Inst for Psychotherapeutic Studies 183 S Broadway Hicksville NY

CALAGNA, STEPHEN LEE, pastor; b. South Gate, Calif., Apr. 25, 1952; s. Anthony and Josephine (Samples) C.; m. Cathleen Chapman, July 2, 1970; children: Melinda, Joshua, Christopher, Laura, Joseph. Cert. in christian leadership, Melodyland Sch. of Theology, 1976. Ordained to Christian ministry, 1978. Youth pastor First Christian Ch., Paso Robles, Calif., 1976-78; pastor North County Christian Fellowship, Paso Robles, 1978—; pres. bd. dirs. Leaves & Fishes Crisis Ministry to the Poor, Paso Robles, 1988—. Bd. dirs. Tree of Life Crisis Pregnancy Ctr., Atascadero, Calif., 1987-88. Mem. Paso Robles Ministerial Assn. (pres. 1988—). Office: North County Christian Fellowship 1745 Riverside Paso Robles CA 93446

CALBERT, WILLIAM EDWARD, minister; b. Lemoore, Calif., June 11, 1918; s. William Riley and Sadie Emma (Hackett) C.; m. Katie Rose Baker, Sept. 4, 1942 (div. 1961); children: William E. (dec.), Rose M. Calbert Findley, Muriel L., Katherine E. Calbert-Jackson, Yvonne A.; m. Madlyn Gwendolyn Williams, June 15, 1963; 1 child, William Eugene. AB, San Francisco State U., 1949; MDiv, Berkeley Bapt. Div. Sch., 1952; MA, Columbia U., 1963; postgrad., The Am. U., 1969-70. Ordained to ministry Am. Bapt. Chs. U.S.A., 1952. Enlisted U.S. Army, 1942, commd. 1st lt., 1952, advanced through grades to lt. col., 1966; orgn. chaplain U.S. Army, Korea, Fed. Republic Germany, 1952-62; instr. U.S. Army Chaplain Sch., Bklyn., 1963-67; supr. chaplain Army Commands, Vietnam, 1967-68; assst. chaplain ops. tng. hdqrs. 1st U.S. Army, Ft. Meade, Md., 1968-69; ret. U.S. Army, 1969; dir. religious edn. Concord Bapt. Ch., Bklyn., 1964-67; chaplain St. Elizabeth Hosp., Washington, 1973-81; min. edn. Shiloh (D.C.) Bapt. Ch., 1981-85, pulpit asst., 1987—; interim dir. chaplaincy and pastoral counseling svcs. Am. Bapt. Chs., Valley Forge, Pa., 1986-87; del. Coun. Chs., Washington, 1981-85; mem. missions and evangelism com. D.C. Bapt. Conv., 1987-91. Contbr. articles to profl. jours. Asst. dir., exec. dir. Far East Community Svcs., Washington, 1970-73; bd. dirs. Housing Devel. Corp., Washington, 1972-76; mem. Mayor's Health Planning Adv. Com., Washington, 1972-77; mem. D.C. State Adv. Coun. on Adult Edn., 1990—. Decorated Bronze Star, Meritorious Svc. medal; recipient cert. appreciation Chief of Chaplains, U.S. Army, 1969, D.C. Govt., 1973, Spl. Fraternal Leadership award Sigma Gamma Rho, 1983. Mem. NAACP, Far East Ministerial Assn. (pres. Washington chpt. 1973-74), Nat. Mil. Chaplains Assn. (trustee 1984-87), Assn. Mental Health Chaplains, Bapt. Mins. Conf. D.C., Urban League, Am. Bapt. Sem. of West Alumni Assn. (pres. ea. region 1989—, internat. pres., trustee 1990—), Alpha Phi Alpha (chaplain Washinton chpt. 1980-81, pres. 1982-83). Democrat. Home: 1261 Kearney St NE Washington DC 20017

CALCOTE, ALAN DEAN, priest, headmaster; b. Shreveport, La., July 25, 1933; s. Aucei Daniel and Patty Lewis (Redditt) C.; m. Maree Elizabeth Minturn, Aug. 12, 1961; children: Alan, Sarah. BA, Tulane U., 1955; MDiv, Gen. Theol. Sem., 1958, STM, 1963. Ordained to ministry Episcopal Ch. as priest, 1959. Curate St. Paul's Episcopal Ch., New Orleans, 1958-61; lect. Gen. Theol. Sem., N.Y.C., 1962-63; chaplain, asst. headmaster All Saints Episcopal Sch., Vicksburg, Miss., 1963-69; asst. headmaster Episcopal High Sch., Baton Rouge, 1969-74; headmaster All Saints Episcopal Sch., Beaumont, Tex., 1974—; assoc. rector St. Mark's Episcopal Ch., Beaumont, 1974—; chmn. Bishop's Commn. on Schs., Diocese of Tex., 1978—. Mem. S.W. Assn. Episcopal Schs. (pres.), Nat. Assn. Episcopal Schs. (governing bd.), Rotary. Home: 5615 Duff Beaumont TX 77706 Office: All Saints Episcopal Sch PO Box 7188 Beaumont TX 77706

CALDERONE, JOSEPH DANIEL, campus ministry director, educator; b. Bryn Mawr, Pa., Feb. 26, 1948; s. Joseph Albert and Sara Jane (Giangiulio) C. B.A. in Social Scis. Villanova U., 1970, M.A. in Counseling, 1973. M.A. in Theology, Washington Theol. Union, 1975; Cert. Advanced Grad. Study in Higher Edn. Adminstrn., Northeastern U., 1976, Ed.D. in Higher Edn. Adminstrn., 1982. Ordained priest Roman Catholic Ch., 1973. Campus minister Villanova U., Pa., 1973-74; assoc. dir. campus ministry Merrimack Coll., North Andover, Mass., 1974-76, dir. campus ministry, 1976-78; diocesan dir. campus ministry, Orlando and Winter Park, Fla., 1978—; prof. mgmt. and counseling theory St. Leo Coll., St. Leo, Fla., 1984—; prof. bus. ethics Rollins Coll., Winter Park, Fla., 1983—. Mem. Nat. Assn. Diocesan Dirs. Campus Ministry (sec., treas. 1984—), Nat. Assn. Coll. and Univ. Chaplains (mem. at large 1985—). Democrat. Home and Office: 430 E Lyman Ave Winter Park FL 32789

CALDERWOOD, DONALD HUGH, minister, educator; b. Sterling, Kans., Mar. 5, 1931; s. Robert Orr and Nelle Mae (Lindsay) C.; m. Evelyn Campbell, June 22, 1956; children: Douglas Hugh, Brian Campbell, Timothy Donald. BS, Sterling Coll., 1953; MDiv, Pitts.-Xenia Sem., 1956; MS inEdn., Emporia (Kans.) State Coll., 1963. Ordained to ministry, Presbyn. Ch. (U.S.A.), 1956. Prin. Presbyn. Ch. (USA), Murree, Pakistan, 1956-61, counselor, tchr., 1963-87; pastor Presbyn. Ch. (USA), Lahore, Pakistan, 1987-89, Gardner, Kans., 1990, Wichita, Kans., 1991—. Mem. Presbytery of So. Kans. Home: 2244 Marigold Wichita KS 67204-5513

CALDERWOOD, ROBERT CHARLES, minister; b. Waldoboro, Maine, Apr. 22, 1901; s. Ephraim Benson and Edla Matilda (Hallgren) C.; m. Doreas Evelyn Gaylord, June 17, 1927; 1 child, Mary Helen Calderwood Reeve. BA, U. Maine, 1923; BD, Garrett Theol. Sem., 1926; MA, U. Chgo., 1927. Ordained to ministry United Meth. Ch., 1926. Pastor United Meth. Ch., Neoga, Ill., 1927-30, Catlin, Ill., 1930-35, Pittsfield, Ill., 1935-40, Abingdon, Ill., 1940-44, Dwight, Ill., 1944-49, Macomb, Ill., 1949-54; exec. sec. Conf. Bd. Edn. United Meth. Ch., 1954-60, supt. Decatur Dist., 1960-1966; ednl. asst. Wesley United Meth. Ch., Bloomington, Ill., 1966-74, min. membership, 1974-86, min. visitation, 1986-89. Vol. preacher, nursing homes, ; mem. Agy. on Aging, 1991; police chaplain, jail visitor. Democrat. Home: 304 Riley Dr Bloomington IL 61701

CALDWELL, EDWARD SABISTON, minister, editor; b. Seattle, Sept. 18, 1928; s. Henry Parker and Rose Hilda (Money) C.; m. Clara La Belle Neeley, Mar. 29, 1948; children; Robert, Mark, James, Scott. Diploma, N.W. Coll. Assemblies of God, Seattle, 1949; student, N.W. Nazarene Coll., Nampa, Idaho, 1964, 66. Ordained to ministry Assemblies of God, 1952. Clergyman Assembly of God Chs., 1949-83; assoc. editor Ministries Today mag. Strang Communications Co., Lake Mary, Fla., 1984-89, assoc. editor Charisma mag., 1990; mng. editor Charismalife Sunday sch. curriculum Strang Communications Co., Altamonte Springs, Fla., 1991—; publicity dir. Assemblies of God Radio Dept., Springfield, Mo., 1966-76, Assemblies of God Home Missions, Springfield, 1982-83. Author: Only One Life, 1975, She's Gone, 1977, God's Promises for Spirit-Filled Living, Words of Faith for Daily Living, 1988, Words of Victory for Defeating the Enemy, 1989.

CALDWELL, FRANKLIN D., minister; b. Havana, Fla., Sept. 18, 1934; s. Denver C. and Catherine (Nelson) C.; m. Katie B. Williams, Mar. 21, 1960 (div. Mar. 1969); children: Frankie and Frederick (twins); m. Bunnie Williams, Feb. 23, 1972; children: Deborah and Amelia (twins). BA, Va. Wesleyan Coll., 1980; MDiv, Howard U. Div. Sch., 1983; postgrad., Boston U., 1985-88; HHD, Richmond (Va.) Sem., 1991. Assoc. min. Mt. Olive Bapt. Ch., Lebanon, Ill., 1976-77; pastor United Meth. Ch. Va. Conf., Virginia Beach, Va., 1978-81, Portsmouth, Va., 1981-83, Hampton, Va., 1983-85; assoc. pastor King St. First Bapt. Ch., Hampton, 1985-86; sr. pastor Aloyssinia Bapt. Ch., Newport News, Va., 1986—; instr. St. Leo Coll., Ft. Eustis, Va., 1985—, Richmond Sem., 1987—; dean Christian edn. Tidewater/ Peninsula Assn., Hampton, 1991; chmn.-elect trustees Children's Home Va. Bapt., Petersburg, 1990. Bd. dirs. Big Bros./Big Sisters, Hampton, 1990. With USAF, 1953-77. Mem. Hampton Rds. Mins. Alliance (pres. 1989—), Masons (D.D. at large 1970-76). Democrat. Home: 806 Homestead Ave Hampton VA 23661 Office: Aloyssinia Bapt Ch 3001 Wickham Ave Newport News VA 23607

CALDWELL, JOHN WILLIAM, pastor; b. Springfield, Mo., Aug. 26, 1943; s. Manville Olen and Ella Francis (Larimore) C.; m. Janis Thelma Stenzinger, Aug. 15, 1965; children: John Shannon, Jennifer Noel. BTh, Ozark Christian Coll., Joplin, Mo., 1967, M of Ministry, 1974; MDiv, Cin. Christian Sem., 1985; D of Ministry, Trinity Evang. Div. Sch., Deerfield, Ill., 1989. Ordained to ministry Ind. Christian Ch., 1967. Student min. Louisburg (Mo.) Christian Ch., 1964-68; evangelist, 1968-74; pastor Kingsway Christian Ch., Indpls., 1974—; adj. prof. Cin. Bible Sem., 1986—; mem. continuation com. N.Am. Christian Conv., nat. prayer chmn., 1991-92. Author: Growing Up in Christ, 1974, Reaching the Lost, 1975; contbr. articles to profl. jours. Recipient Seth Wilson Disting. Alumnus award Ozark Christian Coll., 1991. Mem. Ind. Christian Men's Fellowship (pres. 1981). Republican. Office: Kingsway Christian Ch 12313 W 10th Indianapolis IN 46112

CALDWELL, WAYNE EUGENE, editor; b. Culver, Kans., Nov. 2, 1923; s. Robert Vernon and Cora Helena (Fischer) C.; m. Joan Marie Wiese, June 6, 1946; children: Joy A., Eunice L., Philip W. BRE, Miltonvale Wesleyan Coll., 1949; BD, Nazarene Theol. Sem., 1953; ThB, Cen. Bapt. Theol. Sem., 1957; ThD, Iliff Sch. Theology, 1969. Ordained elder Wesleyan Ch., 1950. Pres. Wesleyan youth Wesleyan Meth. Ch., Miltonvale, Kans., 1948-60; v.p. Kans. conf. Wesleyan Meth. Ch., Miltonvale, 1959-68; pastor, gen. pres. Wesleyan youth Wesleyan Meth. Ch., Denver, 1960-68; pastor Kans. conf. Wesleyan Meth. Ch., 1948-68; gen. editor The Wesleyan Ch., Indpls., 1984—; bd. adminstrn. Coll. Wesleyan Ch., Marion, Ind., 1978-84, Trinity Wesleyan Ch., Indpls., 1989—; asst. prof. religion Ind. Wesleyan U., Marion, Ind., 1972-74, assoc. prof. religion, 1974-79, prof. religion, 1979-84, adj. prof. relgiion 1984-87, faculty rep., bd. trustees 1978-81, faculty advisor, 1978-83 and others; bd. trustees ednl. ministry Bethany Bible Coll., Sussex, New Brunswick, Can., 1984—. Author: (with others) And They Shall Prophesy-In Quest of Glory, 1978, The Fruit and Gifts of the Holy Spirit, 1979, Beacon Dictionary of Theology, 1983, Contemporary Wesleyan Theology, 1983; co-author: Marriage, The Biblical Perspective, 1984; contbr. articles to profl. jours. Trustee Miltonvale Wesleyan Coll., 1955-68, chmn. 1965-68; mem. Nat. Arbor Day Found., 1987—. Mem. Wesleyan Theol. Soc. (sec.-treas. 1978-84), Ind. and Am. Coun. for the Blind, Christian Holiness Assn., Plains States Philos. Soc., Ind. Assn. of Workers for the Blind, Lions Internat., Christian Bus. Men's Assn., VFW, Am. Legion of Ind., Evang. Press. Assn., AARP. Home: 117 Rush Ct Fishers IN 46038-1374 Office: Wesleyan Ch Internat Ctr PO Box 50434 Indianapolis IN 46250-0434

CALDWELL, WENDY JEAN, secretary; b. Newport Beach, Calif., July 13, 1966; d. Garfield James and Jeanne Ann (Wise) Bova; m. Rick Allan Caldwell, May 20, 1989. Youth leader Little Country Ch., Palo Cedro, Calif., 1987—; jr. minister Little Country Ch. Office: Little Country Ch 21945 Old 44 Dr Palo Cedro CA 96073

CALDWELL, WILLIAM GERALD, educator, minister; b. Atlanta, Jan. 21, 1934; s. George Wesley and Evelyn (Albright) C.; m. Emily Dianne Clemm, May 29, 1954; children: William Gerald, Janis Marie. BA, Howard Coll. (now Samford U.), 1954; MRE, Southwestern Bapt. Theol. Sem., Ft. Worth, 1956, DRE, 1963, EdD, 1972. Ordained to ministry So. Bapt. Conv., 1971. Min. edn. 1st Bapt. Ch., Ferguson, Mo., 1959-63, Hunter Street Bapt. Ch., Birmingham, Ala., 1963-66, Cliff Temple Bapt. Ch., Dallas, 1966-69; prof. religious edn. Bapt. Bible Inst., Graceville, Fla., 1969-73; cons. adult work Bapt. Sunday Sch. Bd., Nashville, 1973-75; prof. adminstrn. Southwestern Bapt. Theol. Sem., 1976—. Contbr. articles and curriculum materials to So. Bapt. periodicals. Mem. So. Bapt. Religious Edn. Assn., Southwestern Bapt. Religious Edn. Assn., Ea. Bapt. Religious Edn. Assn. (pres. 1974-75), Nat. Assn. Ch. Bus. Adminstrn., So. Bapt. Ch. Bus. Adminstrn. Assn., Church Mgmt. Hall of Fame, 1991. Home: 3905 Wosley Dr Fort Worth TX 76133 Office: Box 22000 Fort Worth TX 76122

CALHOUN, DAVID VAN, minister; b. Colorado Springs, Colo., Sept. 18, 1956; s. Richard Guy and Elizabeth Jane (Swearingen) C.; m. Lynne Werner (div. Apr. 1991); children: Rachel Marie and Sarah Elizabeth (twins). BA, Met. State Coll., Denver, 1979; MDiv, Iliff Sch. Theology, 1989. Ordained to ministry United Meth. Ch. as deacon, 1989, as elder, 1991. Assoc. min. St. Luke United Meth. Ch., Omaha, 1989—; mem. clergy adv. bd. to Mayor of Omaha, 1990—. Illustrator: Gail Bird Vestments, 1985. Senatorial intern for Senator Gary Hart, Denver, 1979; organizer food and clothing for homeless Iliff Sch. Theology, Denver, 1989. 2d lt. USAF, 1988—. Mem. Rotary (svc. project com. Omaha club), Masons (32 degree), Phi Alpha Theta. Home: 424 N 118th Pla #11 Omaha NE 68154 Office: St Luke United Meth Ch 11810 Burke Omaha NE 68154 *Life can be a wonderful journey if we can learn to accept the world as it is, and change our inward attitudes.*

CALHOUN, DOUGLAS ALAN, minister; b. Ashland, Ohio, June 30, 1951; s. Charles Eugene and Donna (Glenn) C.; m. Adele Ahlberg, Aug. 13, 1977; children: Nathaniel, Annaliese. MDiv, Gordon Conwell Theol. Sem., 1986. Ordained to ministry Conservative Congl. Christian Conf., 1987. Staff and team leader Intervarsity Christian Fellowship, N.Y., Maine, 1974-81; staff and trainer Internat. Fellowship Evangelical Students, Trinidad, W.I., 1981-83; asst. pastor Park St. Ch., Boston, 1986—. Author: (with others) Single Adult Ministries, 1989. Recipient Whittemore's award, Gordon Conwell Theol Sem., 1986; Byington fellow Gordon Conwell Theol. Sem., 1984-86. Mem. Nat. Assn. Single Adult Leaders (bd. dirs. 1990—). Office: One Park St Boston MA 02108

CALHOUN, PAUL, III, physician, international medical missions executive, lay church worker; b. Burlington, Iowa, Aug. 5, 1938; s. Paul Bailey and Ruth Calhoun; m. Brenda Lynn, June 24, 1978; children: Sean, Shane, Shelly. BA, Occidental Coll., Pasadena, Calif., 1960; BTh, San Francisco Theol. Sem., 1963; MD, U. N.Mex., 1971. Intern Pacific-Presbyn. Hosp., San Francisco, 1971-72; resident dermatology Stanford U., 1973-75; exec. dir. Med. Ambs. Internat., Modesto, Calif., 1987—; elder Big Valley Grace Community Ch., Modesto, 1981-89; bd. dirs. Issachar Frontier Missions, Seattle, 1986-89. Fellow Am. Acad. Dermatology. Republican. Home: 1533 River Rd Modesto CA 95351 Office: Med Ambs Internat 4048 Tully Rd PO Box 576645 Modesto CA 95356

CALHOUN, WILLIAM MICHAEL, religious organization administrator; b. Birmingham, Ala., June 13, 1952; s. William Marion and Ann Christine (Booth) C.; m. Elizabeth Ann Phillips, June 1, 1973; children: Misty, Joshua, Caleb. BA in Bible, Tenn. Temple U., 1975. Area missionary Word of Life Clubs, Schroon Lake, N.Y., 1973-78, regional dir., 1978-85, dir. nat. field, 1985-87, dir., 1987—. Republican. Baptist. Home: Pine Ln Box 529 Schroon Lake NY 12870 Office: Word of Life Fellowship Rte 9 Schroon Lake NY 12870

CALIAN, CARNEGIE SAMUEL, academic administrator, theology educator; b. N.Y.C., July 1, 1933; s. Frank and Zekieh (Halajian) C.; m. Doris Zobian, Sept. 12, 1959; children: Lois, Philip, Sara. BA, Occidental Coll., L.A., 1955; BD, Princeton Theol. Sem., 1958; ThD, U. Basel, Switzerland, 1963; LLD, Westminster Coll., 1983. Ordained to ministry Presbyn. Ch., 1958. Asst. min. Calvary Presbyn. Ch., Hawthorne, Calif., 1958-60; prof. theology U. Dubuque (Iowa) Theol. Sem., 1963-81; pres., prof. theology Pitts. Theol. Sem., 1981—; cons. Acad. for Contemporary Problems, Columbus, Ohio, 1977-79; vis. disting. prof. Juniata Coll., Huntingdon, Pa., 1975-77;. Author: The Significance of Eschatology in the Thoughts of Nicolas Berdyaev, 1965, Berdyaev's Philosophy of Hope, 1968, Icon and Pulpit, 1968, Grace Guts and Goods, 1971, The Gospel According to the Wall Street Journal, 1975, Today's Pastor in Tomorrow's World, 1977, 2d edit., 1982, For All Your Seasons: Biblical Direction Through Life's Passages, 1979, Where's the Passion for Excellence in the Church, 1989, Theology without Boundaries, 1992; contbr. to Ency. Britannica, 1974, Ency. of Religion, 1987, Dictionary of Ecumenical Movement, 1991; contbr. over 200 articles and revs. to profl. jours. Mem. Pitts. Presbytery, 1981—, mem. jud. com., 1984; mem. adv. com. Spina Bifida, Pitts., 1986; bd. dirs. Foxwall, Fox Chapel, Pa., 1987-89; mem. Allegheny Conf. Citizens' Com., 1985—, Pitts. Chamber Music Soc., 1991—. Recipient Patriarchal Medal of Honor, Patriarch Justinian of Romania, 1971. Fellow Soc. for Human Values in Higher Edn.; mem. Am. Theol. Soc. (pres. M.W. 1979-80), Am. Acad. of Religion, Soc. of Christian Ethics, Cath. Theol. Soc. Avocations: tennis, racquetball, reading. Office: Pitts Theol Sem 616 N Highland Ave Pittsburgh PA 15206 *Understanding that life is a gift from God is the drawing force for me. Each day I seek to be a good steward of the time and talents I have.*

CALIVAS, ALKIVIADIS, academic administrator. Head Holy Cross Greek Orthodox Sch. Theology, Brookline, Mass. Office: Holy Cross Greek Orthodox Sch Theol 50 Goddard Ave Brookline MA 02146*

CALKINS, HAROLD LEROY, minister; b. Ruthren, Iowa, Mar. 8, 1920; s. Ernest Alva and Daisy (Zielstra) C.; m. Fern Louise Wagner, Sept. 17, 1944; children: Kent LeRoy, Ross Calvin. BA, Andrews U., 1943, MA, 1958, MDiv, 1966. Ordained to ministry Seventh-day Adventist, 1947. Pastor Seventh-day Adventist, Temple City, Calif., 1956-66; pres. So. Calif. Seventh-day Adventist Conf., Glendale, Calif., 1972-81, British Union Seventh-day Adventist, Watford, Herts, Eng., 1981-86; ret. British Union Seventh-day Adventist, Watford, Eng., 1986; pres. So. Calif. Assn. Seventh-day Adventists, Glendale, 1972-81. Author: Master Preachers, 1960; contbr. articles to mags. Vice-chmn. bd. White Meml. Med. Ctr., L.A., 1972-81, Glendale Adventist Med. CTr., 1972-81; bd. dirs. Loma Linda (Calif.) U., 1972-81.

CALKINS, MARILYN RUTH, minister; b. Albuquerque, Oct. 15, 1939; d. Llewelyn Ira and Margaret Lee (Owen) C. Pre-med. student, U. N.Mex., 1957-60; MD, Universidad Nacional Autonoma, Mexico City, 1966. Ordained to ministry Christ Gospel Chs. Internat., Inc., 1973. Tchr. phys. edn. Harwood Girls Sch., Albuquerque, 1958-60; intern Gen. Hosp., Mexico City, Mex., 1966-67; with Govt. Social Svc., Mexico City, 1967-68; child welfare coord. Christian Children's Fund, Mex., 1969-71; med. missionary Christ Gospel Ch., Mex., 1971-82; prin. Christian sch. Christ Gospel Ch., Jeffersonville, Ind., 1982-83, dir. spiritual edn., 1983-90; dir. Calif. chs. Christ Gospel Ch., L.A. area, 1990—; bd. dirs. River Falls Christian Assn. Home Educators, Jeffersonville, 1986-90. Author various study manuals; editor Sunday sch. curriculum. Home and Office: 309 N San Dimas Cyn Rd San Dimas CA 91773

CALL, ROBERT E., minister; b. Claremont, N.H., Apr. 28, 1934; s. Maurice S. and Marion (Walker) C.; m. LeeAnne Bockoven, Sept. 1, 1977; children: Shannon Harner, Shaun Harner, Erik Harner, Cynthia Call. BA, W. Va. Wesleyan Coll., 1956; MDiv, Garrett Evang. Theol. Sem., 1961. Ordained to ministry United Meth. Ch., 1961. Pastor Pierce-Osmond (Nebr.) United Meth. Ch., 1961-66, Grand Island Trinity Ch., 1966-70, Louisville Meth. Ch., 1970-75, Lincoln St. Marks Ch., 1975-78, Imperial Lamar Ch., 1978-86, York First United Meth. Ch., 1986—; del. World Meth. Conf., Honolulu, 1981; dean Conf. Schs. of Christian Mission, 1988-90; conf. chmn. Vocations Com., United Meth. Ch., 1966-70; chairperson bd. Global Ministries World Div., 1980-88. Recipient Sheridan Watson Bell award, W. Va. Wesleyan Coll., 1956, Wesleyan Key award, 1956, Harry Denman award, Nebr. Ann. Conf. United Meth. Ch., 1983. Mem. Lions (pres.), Rotary (chaplain), Order Eastern Star (worthy patron), Mason (32 degree). Home: 722 Nebraska Ave York NE 68467 Office: First United Meth Ch 309 E 7th St York NE 68467-3007

CALLAHAN, NELSON JAMES, priest, theology educator; b. Cleve., Aug. 20, 1927; s. Nelson James and Mary Katherine (Mulholland) C. Student, St. Mary Sem., 1947-53, Lumen Vitae Ctr., Belgium, 1962. Ordained priest Roman Cath. Ch., 1953. Asst. pastor 2 parishes Cleve., 1953-65; dir. guidance St. Peter High Sch., Cleve., 1965-67; resident chaplain, asst. prof. theology St. John Coll., Cleve., 1967-74; pastor St. Raphael Ch., Bay Village, Ohio, 1974—; historian and archivist Diocese of Cleve., 1967-78; moderator First Friday Club of Cleve., 1968—; prof. synodal judge Cleve. Diocese Matrimonial Tribunal, 1969—; bd. dirs. nat. ethnic studies assembly Cleve. State U., 1974—; co-dir. Area Clergy Dialog, Cleve., 1978—. Author: A Case For Due Process In the Church, 1971; (with others) Irish Communities of Cleveland, 1978; editor: Diary of Richard Burtsell 1865-68, 1978, Catholic Journey Through Ohio, 1976, The History of St. Ignatius High School: 100 years, 1986, St. Malachi Church: 125 years, 1990. Mem. Canon Law Soc. Am., Cath. Hist. Soc., Coll. Theol. Soc., Gt. Lakes Hist. Soc. Home and Office: St Raphael Ch 525 Dover Rd Bay Village OH 44140

CALLAM, DANIEL, priest, educator, editor; b. Windsor, Ont., Can., June 12, 1935; s. Walter William and Mary Eileen (Kelly) C. BA, U. Toronto, Ont., 1959; STB, U. St. Michael's Coll., Ont., 1964, MA, 1966; MA, Wayne State U., 1969; PhD, Oxford (Eng.) U., 1978. Ordained priest Roman Cath. Ch., 1964, joined Congregation St. Basil, 1964. Prof. St. Thomas More Coll., Saskatoon, Sask., Can., 1977—. Mng. editor Chelsea Jour., 1978-80; editor Can. Cath. Rev., 1983—. Mem. Can. Theol. Soc., Can. Patristics Soc. Home and Office: 1437 College Dr, Saskatoon, SK Canada S7N 0W6

CALLIER, M. ALICE, gifted and talented education coordinator; d. Frank and Mary (Underwood) Dowe; m. M. Ernest Callier, Aug. 4, 1962; 1 child, Myron Ernest. BS, Cen. State Univ., Wilberforce, Ohio, 1962; MEd, Wright State U., 1970; ABD, Ohio State U., 1977. Cert. tchr. gifted edn., elem. prin., curriculum, supervision, Ohio. Tchr. Dayton (Ohio) Pub. Schs., 1962-68, reading supr., 1971-83, asst. prin., 1983-84, supr. gifted edn., 1984-88; lang. arts coord. Longfellow Sch., Dayton, 1968-71; supr. gifted edn. West Muskingum Schs., Zanesville, Ohio, 1988—; workshop presenter Internat. Reading Assn., Ohio and Pa., 1975—; pvt. cons. in field, 1985—; lectr. Univ. Cin., 1986-87, Sinclair Community Coll., Dayton, 1987—. Author: (film) The Gift: Ohio Rule For Gifted Units, 1984, (books) Excell/K-12 Plan for Gifted Education, 1987, Gifted Education: Honors/Advanced Placement Criteria, 1986. Recipient award Writing Prog.: COLAWP Jennings Found., Cleve., 1981-82; grantee Ohio Dept. Edn., Columbus, 1983. Mem. Ohio Assn. Gifted Children, Toastmasters, Ohio Coords. of the Gifted (regional rep. 1988-90), Phi Delta Kappa (com. chmn. 1984-87, Pi Lambda Theta. Lutheran. Avocations: reading, gardening, tennis, travel. Home: 4000 Colemere Circle Dayton OH 45415

CALVERT, JODY LEE, minister; b. Montgomery, Ala., Sept. 20, 1961; s. Hearl Dee and Geneva Mae (Tillery) C.; m. Angela Christine Newsome, Apr. 5, 1990. AA in History, Fla. Coll., 1981; ASEE, R.E.T.S. Electronics, Birmingham, Ala., 1983. Ordained to ministry Ch. of Christ, 1979. Evangelist Dawson (Tex.) Ch. of Christ, 1985, Stanley Ave. Ch. of Christ, Andalusia, Ala., 1985-86; min. Hillsboro Hts. Ch. of Christ, Moulton, Ala., 1986-89, S.E. Ch. of Christ, Montgomery, Ala., 1989—; missionary to Jamaica, 1991. Author: Hunter and the Peacock, 1986, The Deadly Game, 1984; editor: Lawrence County Reminiscences, 1989; contbr. to sermon book: Outlines for Young Preachers, 1991. Pres. Lawrence County Hist. Commn., Moulton, 1988-89. With USAR, 1985-86. Recipient Achievement award Lawrence County Hist. Commn., 1989. Mem. Sons. of Confederate Vets., Cen. Ala. Artifacts Soc., Kiwanis. Republican. Home: 2704 Locust St Montgomery AL 36107-2910 Office: SE Ch of Christ 2401 Plum St Montgomery AL 36107-2910 *Not all the angels of heaven, nor all the saved of earth, can protect me from wrath at Judgement if I've failed to declare the whole counsel of God, and done so understandably.*

CALVIN, LARRY NELSON, clergyman, educator; b. Ft. Worth, Sept. 5, 1946; s. Nelson W. and Vera N. Calvin; m. Joan L. Turner, June 4, 1966; children: James David, Laura Lynette, Lisa Loette. BA, Abilene Christian U., 1967, MA, 1973, DMin, 1990. Ordained to ministry Ch. of Christ, 1965. Minister Smithfield Ch. of Christ, Ft. Worth, 1982—; instr. marriage and family Ft. Worth Christian Sch., 1982—; cons. on marriage and family LJC Assocs., Ft. Worth, 1978—. Family life editor Christian Jour. Mem. Ch. of Christ.

CALVO, DAVID JAIME, clergyman, consultant; b. Montevideo, Uruguay, Dec. 14, 1934; came to Argentina, 1935; s. Jaime and Amaydela (dos Santos) C.; m. Ljubica Cobrda, July 8, 1961; children—Martin, Miguel, Andres David. B. in Theology, Facultad Luterana de Teologí a, J.C. Paz, Argentina, 1960. Ordained to ministry Luth. Ch., 1960; pastor United Evangel Luth. Ch., La Falda, José C. Paz, Rosario, Argentina, 1960-68, San Miguel, Argentina, 1976-79; editor Publicaciones El Escudo, Buenos Aires, 1969-75; cons. Lutherans United in Communication, Buenos Aires, 1980—; v.p. United Evang. Luth. Ch., Buenos Aires, 1983—. Author: The Congregation, 1982; Martin Luther, 1983; contbr. articles in field to profl. jours. Mem. Assn. Photographers Internat., Profl. Photographers Assn. Argentina, The Alban Inst. Office: Lutherans United in Communication, Simbron 4661, 1417 Buenos Aires Argentina

CAMACHO, TOMAS AGUON, bishop; b. Chalon Kanoa, Saipon, Sept. 18, 1933. Ed., St. Patrick's Sem., Menlo Park, Calif. Ordained priest Roman Cath. Ch., 1961, ordained first bishop of Chalon Kanoa, 1985. Bishop Roman Cath. Ch., Chalon Kanoa, Northern Marianas, U.S. trust territory, 1985—. Address: PO Box 745 Saipan MP 96950

CAMANDARI, MANUEL TALAMAS, bishop; b. Chihuahua, Mexico, June 16, 1917; s. Felix Talamas and Isabel (Camandari) Sapah. Ed., Gregorian U., Rome, Italy. Ordained priest Roman Catholic Ch., 1943, consecrated bishop, 1957. Bishop Ciudad Juarez, Chihuahua, Mexico, 1957—. Author books; contbr. articles to newspapers and religious publs. Home: Zaragoza 1119, Ciudad Juarez Chihuahua, Mexico 32000 Office: Mejia y Peru, Ciudad Juarez Chihuahua, Mexico 32030

CAMBERS, PHILIP WILLIAM, music minister, music educator; b. Kansas City, Mo., May 5, 1957; s. William Hammond Cambers and Mary Elizabeth (Sharp) Kehrer; m. Sharon Kay Thompson, Apr. 28, 1984; children: Ashley Carmen, Jeffrey Philip, Scott William. B of Music Edn., Cen. Mo. State U., 1979, BA of Sci. Edn., 1979. Lic. to ministry Assemblies of God, 1987; cert. tchr. music and French. Youth min. First Assembly of God, St. Joseph, Mo., 1982; min. of music Calvary Assembly of God, Toledo, 1982-85, First Assembly of God, Mobile, Ala., 1985, N. Highland Assembly of God, Columbus, Ga., 1985-86, Southside Assembly of God, Jackson, Miss., 1986—; tchr. music Calvary Christian Sch., Toledo, 1982-85, Briarcrest Christian Sch., Columbus, Ga., 1985-86, Southside Christian Sch., Jackson, Miss., 1986—; dist. music dir. Miss. Dist. Coun. Assembly of God, Jackson, 1986—; host Miss. Dist. Coun. Choral Workshop, Jackson, 1987; adjudicator Nat. Fine Arts Festival Assembly of God, Springfield, Mo., 1988; choral clinician Evangel Assembly of God, Columbus, Miss., 1988-90. Contbr. articles to profl. jours. Choir dir. Children's Choir & Handbell Choir (for nursing homes), Jackson, 1989-90; handbell choir dir. TV comml. Sta. WAPT-TV, Jackson, 1990. Recipient First Place Nat. Assn. Tchrs. Singing, 1979. Mem. Am. Guild English Handbell. Home: 323 Barfield Dr Jackson MS 39212 Office: Southside Assembly of God 665 Raymond Rd Jackson MS 39204-3699 *Through all my life's toils, the only things that really matter are the ones that glorify God.*

CAMBLIN, RON E., youth and education minister; b. Lawrence, Kans., May 24, 1954; s. Glenn E. Camblin and Betty N. (Jordan) Shepherd; m. Barbara Sue Thompson, May 31, 1975; children: Justin Ryan and Ashley Brooke. Student, Ozark State Coll., 1972-75; BS, Fla. Christian Coll., 1982. Youth min. Villa Heights Christian Ch., Joplin, Mo., 1973-75; min. Dadeville (Mo.) Christian Ch., 1975-78; youth min. 1st Christian Ch., Wauchula, Fla., 1978-80, Pine Hills Christian Ch., Orlando, Fla., 1980-92, 1st Christian Ch., Largo, Fla., 1982-88, Westwood-Cheviot Ch. of Christ, Cin., 1988-89; min. of youth and edn. Harborside Christian Ch., Safety Harbor, Fla., 1989—; pres. Fla. Christian Youth Conv., 1973-74; cons. Standard Pub. Co., Cin., 1987—. Recipient Ch. Growth award Nat. Ch. Growth Rsch. Ctr., 1981. Mem. Fla. Christian Coll. Alumni Assn. (pres. k1982-83), Nat. Network Youth Mins. Republican. Office: Harborside Christian Ch 3380 SR 580 Safety Harbor FL 34695

CAMERON, LAWRENCE MICHAEL, minister, social worker; b. Muskegon, Mich., Jan. 15, 1959; s. Roger William and Paula Marie (McNally) C.; m. Cindy Lou Remboski, Mar. 17, 1990; 1 child, Joseph Thomas. BA in Religious Studies, Albion Coll., 1981; MDiv, Methesco Sem., Delaware, Ohio, 1985; D Ministry, Ashland (Ohio) Sem., 1991. Ordained to ministry United Ch. of Christ, 1991; registered social worker, Mich. Min. East Liberty (Ohio) United Meth. Ch., 1982-85; therapist Monroe County, Monroe, Mich., 1988—; min. Immanuel United Ch. Christ, Detroit, 1989—; pvt. practice Pastoral Therapy Ctr., Detroit, 1991. Dir. religious affairs Monroe County Youth Ctr., 1988—. With U.S. Army, 1985-88. North Greenfield Trustees grantee, Europe and Middle East, 1983. Mem. NAACP (dir. religious affairs local chpt., exec. bd. 1989—), Am. Assn. Christian Counselors, Am. Assn. Mental Health Counselors, Am. Assn. for Counseling and Devel., Order of St. Luke, Order of Ecumenical Franciscans, Alpha Tau Omega. Home: 2390 Hollywood Dr Monroe MI 48161 Office: Immanuel United Ch 4600 Livernois Detroit MI 48210

CAMERON, MARVIN GLEN, minister; b. Knoxville, Aug. 7, 1953; s. Glen Allen Cameron and Mary Jean (Whitt) Phillips; m. Penny Rae Greer, June 14, 1980; 1 child, Christopher Glen. BA, Union U., 1975; MDiv, So. Bapt. Theol. Sem., 1978. Ordained to ministry Bapt. Ch., 1980. Assoc. minister First Bapt. Ch., Gatlinburg, Tenn., 1980-83, minister, 1984—; mem. exec. com. So. Bapt. Alliance, 1987—, bd. dirs. Active Sevier County bicentennial com. Sevierville, Tenn., 1985, Gatlinburg Strategic Task Force, 1987. Recipient Broadman award for Outstanding Achievement in Biblical Studies So. Bapt. Conv., 1978. Mem. Tenn. Bapt. Conv. (constitution by-laws com. 1984-87, speaker 1985), Gatlinburg Ministerial Assn. (pres. 1985—). Lodge: Rotary (bd. dirs. Gatlinburg club 1983—, pres. 1985-86). Avocations: golf, tennis, snow skiing. Home: Rt 3 Box 274 Gatlinburg TN 37738 Office: First Bapt Ch 600 S Parkway Gatlinburg TN 37738

CAMIN, BALDWIN ALBERT, minister; b. Helmstedt, Germany, Nov. 8, 1940; came to U.S., 1953, naturalized, 1963; s. Albert and Emmi Loni (Meyer) C.; m. Janet Mina Nahodyl, June 12, 1965; children: Timothy, Jonathan, Marc. BA, Montclair State U., 1963; BD, Concordia Theol. Sem., 1967, MDiv, 1972. Ordained to ministry Luth. Ch.-Mo. Synod, 1967. Pastor Duncan-Trinity (B.C., Can.) Luth. Ch., 1967-69, Youbou (B.C.) Luth. Ch., 1967-69; pastor local chs. Alta., Can.; founder mission Grande Cache, Alta., 1969-72; pastor Zion Luth. Ch., Decatur, Ind., 1972-76, Messiah Luth. Ch., Marysville, Wash., 1976-90, St. Paul's Luth. Ch., Jerome, Idaho, 1990—; instr. Bible Stony Plain and Decatur cirs. Luth. Ch.-Mo. Synod, 1967; sec. Edson Ministerial Assn. and Pastoral Group, 1970-71, chmn., 1971-72. Vice chmn. Ind. Dist. Youth Commn., 1974-76; vice-chair Jerome Devel. Com. Mem. Jerome Ministerial Assn. (chair), South Idaho Pastoral Conf. (sec.). Home: 39 W, 600 S Jerome ID 83338 Office: 1301 N Davis Jerome ID 83338

CAMP, JIMMY D. (HAMBONE CAMP), minister; b. Tryon, N.C., Oct. 26, 1954; s. Ella Mae Camp Childers; m. Debra B. Camp, Aug. 13, 1977; children: Heather Nicole, Marci DeeAnn, Cassie Jo. AS in Bus., Spartanburg Tech. Coll., 1974; BA in Religion, Carson-Newman Coll., 1984; MDiv, MRE, Southeastern Bapt. Theol. Sem., Wake Forest, N.C., 1988. Ordained to ministry Soc. Bapt. Conv. Min. youth Lebanon Bapt. Ch., Talbott, Tenn., 1983-84; min. youth, edn. and activities Hope Valley Bapt. Ch., Durham, N.C., 1984-88, Virginia Heights Bapt. Ch., Roanoke, Va., 1988-90, Riverside Bapt. Ch., Greer, S.C., 1990-91; family min. Southside Bapt. Ch., Spartanburg, S.C., 1991—. Mem. S.C. Bapt. Youth Recreation Mins. Assn. Office: Southside Bapt Ch 316 S Church St Spartanburg SC 29301

CAMP, THOMAS EDWARD, librarian; b. Haynesville, La., July 12, 1929; s. Charles Walter and Annie Laura (Brazzel) C.; m. Elizabeth Anne Sowar, Sept. 4, 1952; children: Anne Winifred, Thomas David. BA, Centenary Coll. Shreveport, 1950; M.L.S., La. State U., 1953. Binding asst. La. State U. Library, Baton Rouge, 1951-53; circulation librarian Perkins Sch. Theology Bridwell Library, So. Meth. U., Dallas, 1955-57; librarian Sch. Theology, U. of South, Sewanee, Tenn., 1957—, assoc. univ. librarian, 1976—, acting univ. librarian, 1981-82. Co-author: Using Theological Libraries and Books, 1963; contbr. articles to profl. jours. Pres. Franklin County Assn. for Retarded, 1971-72. Served with AUS, 1953-55. Mem. Am. Theol. Library Assn. (exec. sec. 1965-67), ALA, Tenn. Library Assn. Democrat. Episcopalian. Home: Carruthers Rd PO Box 820 Sewanee TN 37375 Office: U of South Library Sewanee TN 37375

CAMPBELL, ALAN RICHARD WILLIAM, minister; b. Ft. Wayne, Ind., Feb. 7, 1937; s. Joe Richard and Neva Alice (Lintz) C.; m. Janet Lee Updike, Sept. 28, 1957; children: Bruce Alexander, Brian Alan. AB, Baldwin-Wallace Coll., 1958; STB, MDiv, Boston U. Sch. Theology, 1961; MST, Oberlin Grad. Sch. Theology, Vanderbilt Div. Sch., 1967, D Ministry, 1974. Ordained to ministry Congl. Christian Ch. (now United Ch. of Christ), 1961. Student pastor Union Congl. Ch., Medford, Mass., 1958-61; pastor East Oberlin (Ohio) Community Ch., United Ch. of Christ, 1961-65; assoc. min. Mariemont Community Ch., Cin., 1965-68, Bushnell Congl. Ch., Detroit, 1968-71; sr. min. Washington Park United Ch. of Christ, Denver, 1971-77, 1st Congl. Ch., United Ch. of Christ, Freemont, Nebr., 1977-81, St. Lucas United Ch. of Christ, St. Louis, 1981—; field supr. Eden Theol. Sem., Webster Groves, Mo., 1981—; chmn. Chgo.-United-Eden com. Mo. Conf. United Ch. of Christ, St. Louis, 1982—; participant large ch. growth com. Evangelism Div., United Ch. of Christ, N.Y.C., 1983—. Author: (booklet) A Festival of Banners, 1975. Trustee Elmhurst (Ill.) Coll. Bertha Walker fellow Boston U. Sch. Theology, 1958, Frank D. Howard fellow Boston U. Sch. Theology, 1961,. Mem. St. Louis Ministerium (pres. 1983—), Assn. United Ch. Educators, Assn. for Psychol. Type. Democrat. Office: St Lucas United Ch Christ 11735 Denny Rd Saint Louis MO 63126 *Too frequently, our faith is limited by our expectations, which are limited by our experience, which is limited by our perceptions, which are limited by where we are willing to look. Faith, to be fruitful, must look beyond our expectations in the direction of our hope.*

CAMPBELL, ANTOINE LAMONT, minister; b. Indpls., Dec. 24, 1954; s. John Robert and Earline (Salters) C.; m. Julie Glen Barker, Aug. 23, 1980; children: Benjamin Lloyd, Sarah Allison, Paul Robert. BS in Econs., U.S. Naval Acad., Annapolis, Md., 1977; MDiv, Yale U., 1985. Ordained to ministry Episcopal Ch. as deacon, 1985, as priest, 1986. Rector Baskervill Ministries, Pawleys Island, S.C., 1985—; canon missioner Diocese of S.C., Charleston, 1991; mem. Nat. Ch. Congl. Devel., N.Y.C., 1987—; trustee Kanuga Conf., Hendersonville, N.C., mem. standing com., 1988—. Trustee Voorhees Coll., Denmark, S.C., 1988—, Palmetto Project, Charleston, 1990—, Trident Community Found., Charleston, 1991. Recipient Citizen of Yr. award Georgetown County club Omega Psi Phi, 1988-89, S.C. Religious Leader award S.C. Jaycees, 1990-91, Peace award Louis Gregory Bahai Inst., 1991; Benjamin Mays fellow, 1984; Heptagonal Games High Hurdler champion, 1977. Office: Diocese of SC PO Box 20127 Charleston SC 29413-0127

CAMPBELL, BARBARA ELLEN, deaconess, religious organization administrator; b. Olney, Ill., Sept. 6, 1926; d. Ernest Melancthon and Sibyl Elizabeth (Johnston) C. BA, Scarritt Coll., 1953, MA, 1954; DD, McKendree Coll., 1977. Dir. Christian edn. Niedringhaus Meth. Ch., Granite City, Ill., 1954-58; asst. sec. visual edn., Woman's Div. Bd. Missions, N.Y.C., 1958-64; exec sec. leadership devel. Bd. Missions(now Gen. Bd. Global Ministries), N.Y.C., 1964-74, asst. gen. sec. in adminstrn., 1974—; clk. F.W. Woolworth Co., Olney, 1942-50. Author: United Methodist Women: In the Middle of Tomorrow, 1975, book supplement, 1983. Trustee Sibley Hosp., Washington, 1987—; bd. dirs. Scarritt Bennett Ctr., Nashville, 1988—. Home: 235 E 22nd St New York NY 10010 Office: Gen Bd Global Ministries Women's Div 475 Riverside Dr Rm 1504 New York NY 10115

CAMPBELL, BRENDA C., lay worker; b. Fort Hood, Tex., Mar. 16, 1957; d. Virgil Wayne and Ida Mae (Combs) Mowrey; divorced Feb., 1982; 1 child, Michael Logan Taylor; m. Alan L. Campblee, Jan. 21, 1983; 1 child, Lara Lee. Student, Cameron U., 1975-77, Okla. State U., 1981-82. Sec. 1st Bapt. Ch. West, Lawton, Okla., 1989-91, mem. evangelism com., 1989—, mem. nominating com., 1990—, children's ch. dir., 1990—, tchr. sr. high girls, 1990—; sec. Workshop Track 1, Southwestern Bapt. Theol. Seminar, Ft. Worth, 1989; trainer Evangelism Explosion, 1990, tchr. pre-sch. discipleship tng., 1991. Mem. Southwestern Oklahomans for Life. Home: 7304 Compass Lawton OK 73000 Office: 1st Bapt Ch West 7302 Cache Rd Lawton OK 73505

CAMPBELL, CHALEN J., minister, educator; b. Alton, Ill., Feb. 17, 1937; s. Chalen and Dorothy (Dossett) C.; m. Ellen Stickels, Dec. 13, 1958; children: Annette Ellen, Jayne Renee. Diploma, Moody Bible Inst., 1968; BS, Calvary Bible Coll., 1969; MA, Trinity Theol. Seminary, 1974; DEd, Trinity Bible Coll. Seminary, 1980; DD (hon.), Wesley Coll., 1979. Pastor First Assembly of God, Pocahontas, Ill., 1962-65, Dolton Assembly of God, Dolton, Ill., 1965-68, Bethel Assembly of God, Elmhurst, Ill., 1969-74, First Assembly of God, Merrillville, Ind., 1974—; prof. Christian Life Coll., Mt. Prospect, Ill., 1970—, Berean Coll. of the Bible, Merrillville, 1982—; pres. Living Hope Ministries, Merrillville, Ind., 1983—; founder Good Shepherd Day Care Ctr., 1976, Merrillville Christian Sch., 1978. Bd. dirs. Chgo. Teen Challenge, 1970-74. Served with USN, 1954-57. Mem. Assemblies of God Ministerial Assn., Ross Township Clergy Assn. Avocations: golf, swimming, softball. Office: 7525 Taft St Merrillville IN 46410

CAMPBELL, CYNTHIA ANN, lay worker; b. Somerville, N.J., Oct. 23, 1960; d. Gerald Francis and Carole Jane (Ahrensfield) C. Student, Cath. U. Am., 1978-79, Fairleigh Dickinson U., 1989—. Organist, choir dir. jr. and sr. choirs Reformed Ch. of Round Brook, South Round Brook, N.J., 1975—; treas. Reformed Ch. of Round Brook, South Round Brook, 1988—, deacon, 1989—; asst. staff mgr. AT&T Bus. Communications Systems, Bridgewater, N.J., 1980—. Mem. Am. Mgmt. Assn.

CAMPBELL, DAVID LLOYD, minister; b. Ft. Worth, Oct. 8, 1941; s. Hilton Coleman and Ida Cozette (Jones) C.; m. Ann Orlene Shirley, July 27, 1963; children: Christopher David, Kimberly Ann, Coleman Edward. BS in Music Edn., East Tex. State U., Commerce, 1965. Lic. to ministry So. Bapt. Conv., ordained. Min. music and youth 1st Bapt. Ch., Cooper, Tex., 1964-65; min. music, youth and edn. 1st Bapt. Ch., Friona, Tex., 1965-67; min. music and youth Casa View Bapt. Ch., Dallas, 1967-69, 1st Bapt. Ch., Pampa, Tex., 1969-71; min. music Westbury Bapt. Ch., Houston, 1971-73, 1st Bapt. Ch., Midland, Tex., 1974-80; dir. awareness World Hunger Relief, Inc., Waco, Tex., 1980-83; assoc. pastor Elkins Lake Bapt. Ch., Huntsville, Tex., 1985-89; min. music 1st Bapt. Ch., Nacogdoches, Tex., 1989—; dir. Singing Men West Tex., Midland, 1976-80, Singing Men SE Tex., Houston, 1987—. Contbr. articles to Ch. Musician. Pilot Senator Phil Gramm, Waco, 1983-84. Mem. Am. Choral Dirs. Assn., Centurymen (charter). Avocations: piloting, basketball, skiing. Office: 1st Bapt Ch 411 North St Nacogdoches TX 75961

CAMPBELL, DENNIS MARION, theology educator, university dean; b. Dalhart, Tex., Aug. 23, 1945; s. Francis Marion and Margaret (Osterberg) C.; m. Leesa Heydenreich, June 13, 1970; children: Margaret Heyden, Robert

Trevor. AB, Duke U., 1970, PhD, 1973; BD, Yale U., 1970; DD (hon.), Fla. So. U., 1986. Ordained to ministry United Meth. Ch., 1974. Min. Trinity United Meth. Ch., Durham, N.C., 1973-74; chmn. dept. religion Converse Coll., Spartanburg, S.C., 1974-79; dir. continuing edn. Div. Sch. Duke U., Durham, 1979-82, prof. theology, 1982—, dean. Div. Sch., 1982—; mem. Oxford (Eng.) Inst. Theol. Studies, 1982, 87; gen. conf. United Meth. Ch., Balt., 1984, St. Louis, 1988; del. World Meth. Coun., Nairobi, Kenya, 1987, World Coun. Chs. 7th Assembly, Canberra, Australia, 1991. Author: Authority and the Renewal of American Theology, 1976, Doctors, Lawyers, Ministers: Christian Ethics in Professional Practice, 1982, The Yoke of Obedience: the Meaning of Ordination in Methodism, 1988. Chmn. Protection of Human Subjects Com.; bd. dirs. Family Health Internat., Rsch. Triangle Park, 1986—; bd. visitors Perkins Sch. Theology So. Meth. U., Dallas, 1987. Mem. Am. Theol. Soc., Am. Acad. Religion, Soc. Christian Ethics, Assn. Theol. Schs. (accrediting com. 1986—), Phi Beta Kappa, Omicron Delta Kappa. Home: 3 Pilling Pl Durham NC 27707 Office: Duke U Div Sch Durham NC 27706

CAMPBELL, DONALD FISHER, retired minister; b. Cranbury, N.J., July 1, 1909; s. William John and Jennie Frances (Bowers) C.; m. Charlotte Morris, Aug. 31, 1934; children: William, David, Bruce. BSc, U. Mo., 1934; MEd, U. Pitts., 1936; MDiv, Pitts. Theol. Sem., 1937; postgrad., Cambridge (Eng.) U., 1937-38; DD (hon.), Bloomfield Coll., 1962. Ordained to ministry Presbyn. Ch. (U.S.A.), 1937. Asst. pastor Presbyn. Ch., Sewickley, Pa., 1935-37, interim pastor, 1938-40; pastor Presbyn. Ch., Brentwood, Pa., 1940-43; assoc. pastor Shadyside Presbyn. Ch., Pitts., 1943-45; pastor 1st Presbyn. Ch., Stamford, Conn., 1945-75; mem. com. on worship and music Presbyn. Ch. (U.S.A.), 1960-72; moderator Presbytery of Conn. Valley and Synod, New Eng., del. Nat. Coun. Chs., 1950, mem. ch. ecumenical life com., 1952-56. Active in past various charitable orgns. Named Citizen of the Yr., Jewish War Vets, 1959, Am. Heritage award, 1965. Mem. Stanford Yacht Club (chaplain), Burning Tree Country Club. Republican. Home: RD 1 Middlebury VT 05753

CAMPBELL, DONALD K., theological seminary administrator, educator; b. Ft. Wayne, Ind., July 6, 1926; s. Dwight V. and Evelyn G. (Pfeiffer) C.; m. Beatta Ruth Carlson, Mar. 10, 1926 (dec. 1991); children: Stephen, John Timothy, Mary Joy, Jonathan. AB in History with highest honors, Wheaton Coll., 1947; ThM with high honors, Dallas Theol. Sem., 1951, ThD in Bible Exposition, 1953; DD, Liberty U., 1989. Tchr. Dallas Bible Inst., 1951-53; chmn. dept., asst. prof. Bryan Coll., Dayton, Tenn., 1953-54; registrar Dallas Theol. Sem., 1954-67, asst. prof. Bible exposition, 1954-61, acting chmn. Bible exposition, 1960-61, acad. dean, 1961-84, exec. v.p., 1985-86, vice chmn. faculty, 1961-86, pres., chmn. faculty, 1986—; bd. dirs. Covenant Life Ins. Co.; mem. adv. com. Mt. Hermon (Calif.) Assn. Inc. Author: Nehemiah: Man in Charge, 1979, Joshua: Leader Under Fire, 1981, Daniel: God's Man in a Secular Society, 1988, Judges: Leaders in Crisis Times, 1989; editor: Walvoord: A Tribute, 1982; contbr. to Bible Knowledge Commentary, Old Testament edit.: Book of Joshua, 1985, N.T. edit.: Book of Galatians, 1985, Essays in Honor of J. Dwight Pentecost: The Church in God's Prophetic Program; cons. editor: Chafer's Systematic Theology, abridged edit., vols. 1 and 2; contbg. writer: Baker Encyclopedia of the Bible; also articles and revs. Bd. advisers Dallas Assn. for Decency; mem. steering com. Citizens for Dallas; mem. bd. of reference Christian Counseling Ctr., McPherson, Kans., Found. for Thoughts and Ethics, Richardson, Tex., Family Ministry, Little Rock, Ark., Outreach Inc., Grand Rapids, Mich., Patkai (India) Christian Coll., Uppsala (Sweden) Theol. Sem., Capturing Poland for Christ, Nashville Bible Coll.; bd. advisers Dallas Christian Leadership, Barnabas Internat., Rockford, Ill., Fair Park Friendship Ctr. Mem. Wheaton Coll. Scholastic Honor Soc., Pi Gamma Mu. Office: Dallas Theol Sem Office of Pres 3909 Swiss Ave Dallas TX 75204

CAMPBELL, DONALD PERRY, music minister; b. Birmingham, Ala., June 30, 1951; s. David Henry and Lena Loraine (Shaver) C.; m. Debra Rockenbaugh, Dec. 18, 1976; children: Clifton Reed, Kathryn Loraine. BS in Music Edn., Samford U., 1974; M. Ch. Music, Southwestern Bapt. Theol. Sem., 1976, postgrad. in musical arts, 1986—. Minister of music and youth Westwood Bapt. Ch., Birmingham, Ala., 1972-74, minister of music, 1977-86; minister of music Carroll Bapt. Ch., Southlake, Tex., 1974-77, East Meadows Bapt. Ch., Ft. Worth, 1986—; asst. dir. Ala. Singing Men, Birmingham, 1984-86; associational music dir. Birmingham Bapt. Assn., 1982-83. Named Youth Minister of Yr., Birmingham Bapt. Assn., 1971. Mem. Phi Mu Alpha (pres. Pi Sigma chpt. 1971-72). Home: 2901 Yates St Fort Worth TX 76133 Office: East Meadows Bapt Ch 2000 Morrison Dr Fort Worth TX 76112

CAMPBELL, DWAYNE LOUIS, minister; b. Washburn, Maine, Feb. 16, 1944; s. Vaughn Weldon and Margaret Sarah (McDuff) C.; m. Jeanette Patricia Mitchell, June 30, 1966. Student, Aroostook State Tchrs. Coll., 1962-63, Faith Sch. Theology, 1963-66. Ordained to ministry Assembly of God, 1969. Assoc./youth pastor First Assembly of God, Anchorage, 1966-69; sr. pastor Kodiak (Alaska) Assembly of God, 1969-73; sr. pastor First Assembly of God, Indiana, Pa., 1973-77, York, Pa., 1977—; presbyter Pa./Del. Dist. Coun. of the Assemblies of God, Camp Hill, 1990-91; internat. bd. dirs. New Life for Girls, Dover, Pa., 1985-91; area bd. advisor Women's Aglow, 1990-92. Office: First Assembly of God 2270 Susquehanna Trail N York PA 17404

CAMPBELL, EDWARD FAY, JR., religion educator; b. New Haven, Jan. 5, 1932; s. Edward Fay and Edith (May) C.; m. Phyllis Kletzien, Sept. 4, 1954; children: Thomas Edward, Sarah Ives. B.A., Yale U., 1953; B.D., McCormick Theol. Sem., 1956; Ph.D., Johns Hopkins U., 1959. Ordained to ministry Presbyn. Ch., 1956. Asst. pastor 1st Presbyn. Ch., Balt., 1956-58; from instr. to prof. McCormick Theol. Sem., Chgo., 1958—; mem.-at-large ch. and soc. com. Chgo. Presbytery, 1987—. Author: The Chronology of the Amarna Letters, 1964, Anchor Bible: Ruth, 1975, Shechem II: Profile of a Hill Country Vale, 1991; (with others) Harper Bible Dictionary; co-editor (with David Freedman) Biblical Archaeologist Reader 2, 3, 4; contbr. articles and revs. to profl. jours. Assoc. trustee Rush-Presbyn.-St. Luke's Hosp., Chgo., 1976—. Am. Coun. Learned Socs. fellow, 1972-73. Mem. Cath. Bibl. Assn., Soc. Bibl. Lit. (sr. editor monograph series), Am. Schs. Oriental Rsch. (trustee 1972-82, v.p. 1973-81, Ann. Prof. award 1964-65), Archaeol. Inst. Am., Israel Exploration Soc. Democrat. Home: 2535 Bennett Ave # 2W Evanston IL 60201-1383 Office: McCormick Theol Sem 5555 S Woodlawn Ave Chicago IL 60637 *Life finds its ultimate value in relationship to a sovereign, loving, suffering deity and to one's companions in the entire human family—including especially those who are oppressed and victimized.*

CAMPBELL, FRANK ROSS, academic administrator, educator; b. Roanoke, Va., Jan. 4, 1936; s. Clarence Robert and Frances Louise (Slayden) C.; m. Janet Faye Hale, July 5, 1957; children: Cathy Burgess, Donna Burki. BA cum laude, Carson-Newman Coll., 1958; BD, Southeastern Bapt. Theol. Sem., 1961, ThM, 1965, MDiv, 1973, D. Ministry, 1975; DD, Wake Forest U., 1980. Supr. of students Southeastern Theol. Sem., 1975-85; prof. religion Averett Coll., 1986—; pres. Averett Coll., Danville, Va., 1985—; pastor English Creek Bapt. Ch., Newport, Tenn., 1957-58, Corinth Bapt. Ch., Oxford, N.C., 1958-61, Peace's Chapel Bapt. Ch., Oxford, 1958-61, New Hope Bapt. Ch., Raleigh, N.C., 1961-66, First Bapt. Ch., Statesville, N.C., 1966-85; adj. instr. Gardner-Webb Coll., spring 1981, fall 1981, 82; bd. dirs. Signet Bank. Mem. Danville Concert Assn., Danville Arts and Humanities, Danville Friends of the Libr.; mem. adv. bd. Danville Hospice, 1985-88; mem. steering com. Dan Daniel Meml. Pk., 1990—; chmn. Delius com. Danville Internat. Centennial Celebration, 1985-86, Danville United Way, 1991—; trustee Davis Hosp., Statesville, N.C.; chmn. Mayor's Citizen Adv. Com., 1967-72; bd. dirs. Iredell Day Care Ctr. for Handicapped Children, 1967-80, Statesville United Fund, 1968-72, David Found., Inc., 1982-89, Danville Mus. Fine Arts and History. Mem. Coun. Ind. Colls. of Va. (chmn.), Bapt. State Conv. of N.C. (1st v.p. 1979-81, pres. 1981-83, chmn. spl. com. Coun. on Christian Higher Edn. 1979, com. on bds. 1977, com. on tellers 1983), Danville Area C. of C. (bd. dirs. 1986—, 1st v.p. 1987, pres. 1988), Va. C. of C. (bd. dirs.), Danville Rotary, Phi Delta Kappa, Phi Eta Sigma. Baptist. Avocations: jogging, tennis, travel, reading. Home: 500 Hawthorne Dr Danville VA 24541 Office: Averett Coll 420 W Main St Danville VA 24541

CAMPBELL, JOAN BROWN, religious organization executive. Gen. sec. Nat. Coun. Chs. of Christ in U.S.A., N.Y.C. Office: Nat Coun Chs of Christ in USA 475 Riverside Dr Rm 1062 New York NY 10115*

CAMPBELL, JOHN DOUGLAS, minister; b. Westfield, Ont., Can., Jan. 8, 1943; s. A. Douglas and Gladys Laura (Good) C.; m. Betty Lou Walker, Aug. 17, 1963; children: Laura Lee, Douglas Bruce. Ministerial diploma, Gardner Bible Coll., Camrose, Alta., Can., 1967. Ordained to ministry Ch. of God (Anderson, Ind.), 1967. Min. Ch. of God, Schuler, Alta., 1967-72, Swift Current, Sask., 1972-75, Grand Bend, Ont., 1975-85, London, Ont., 1985-88; min. North Haven Ch. of God, Welland, Ont., 1988—; Mem. Missionary Bd., Ch. of God, Anderson, 1980—, chmn. Gen. Assembly, 1988—, bd. dirs., chmn. Missionary Bd., 1989—. Home: 48 Leaside Dr, Welland, ON Canada L3C 6B2

CAMPBELL, JOHN HOWARD, minister; b. Balt., Sept. 17, 1949; s. Robert Chalmers and Ethel May (Canfield) C.; m. Donna Sue Caulk, Jan. 3, 1969 (div. Oct. 1978); m. Bonnie Bell MacCallum, Dec. 23, 1978; children: John, Joy, Jill, Katherine. BA, W.Va. Wesleyan Coll., 1971; Mdiv, Meth. Theol. Sem., Delaware, Ohio, 1974, MA in Christian Edn., 1978. Ordained to ministry United Meth. Ch., 1972. Pastor Cheltenham (Md.) United Meth. Ch., 1974-75; min. of nurture and mission Foundry United Meth. Ch., Washington, 1975-78; pastor St. John's of Hamilton United Meth. Ch., Balt., 1978-83, Calvary United Meth. Ch., Mt. Airy, Md., 1983-86; missionary Alaska Missionary Confs., Juneau, 1986—; mem. Bd. of Ordained Ministry, Anchorage, 1986—; chair Western Jurisdiction Cong. Devel. Com., Portland, Oreg., 1989—, Regional Program Coun. S.E., Anchorage, 1988-90; bd. dirs. Glory Hole Soup Kitchen/Shelter, Juneau, 1987—. Recipient Denman award Found. for Evangelism, 1990. Office: Aldersgate United Meth Ch PO Box 33491 Juneau AK 99803

CAMPBELL, JOYCE, church official. Coord. youth dept. Glyndon (Md.) United Meth. Ch. Office: Glyndon United Meth Ch 4713 Butler Rd Glyndon MD 21071

CAMPBELL, SISTER MAURA, religious studies educator; b. Bayonne, N.J.; d. Patrick John and Helena Marie (Collins) C. BS, Seton Hall U., 1940, MA, 1945; MA, Providence Coll., 1953; PhD, St. Mary's Sch. Theology, Notre Dame, Ind., 1955; hon. doctorate in religious edn., Providence Coll., 1985; postgrad. Marquette U, Ottawa U., 1969, Cath. U. Am., 1970-71. Joined Dominican Order, Roman Cath. Ch., 1927. Tchr. elem. and secondary schs., 1930-53; dir. postulants Mt. St. Dominic, Caldwell, N.J., 1955-59, dir. scholastics, 1959-69; mem. faculty Caldwell Coll., 1955—, prof. religious studies, 1957-86, prof. emerita, 1986—, chmn. dept., 1969-86; permanent rep. internat. Cath. edn. office UN Non-Govtl. Orgns., 1969—; v.p. internat. Cath. orgns. N.Y. Info. Ctr., 1978, pres., 1982-87; permanent rep. World Assembly Internat. Cath. Edn. Office, Bangkok, 1982. Recipient Recognition award for outstanding achievement in higher edn. State of N.J., 1989, Award for Svc. Caldwell Coll., 1989. Mem. editorial bd. The Cath.c Adv. Mem. Ecumenical/Interfaith Commn. Archdiocese of Newark, 1986—; elected mem. exec. bd. NGO/DPI at UN, 1988. Recipient 40th Anniversary Faculty award Caldwell Coll., 1979. Mem. Dominican Edn. Assn. (past pres.), Coll. Theology Soc. (past v.p., sec.), Am. Acad. Religion, Religious Edn. Assn., Cath. Theology Soc., Council Religion and World Affairs, Theta Alpha Kappa (hon., Veritas award 1989, Outstanding Professor of Religion 1989). Address: Caldwell Coll 9 Ryerson Ave Caldwell NJ 07006

CAMPBELL, PHILLIP CRAIG, music minister; b. Wadesboro, N.C., Sept. 29, 1952; s. Joseph Amberth and Mary Lilly (Brigman) C.; m. Melissa Ann Gold, May 31, 1975; children: Laura Ann, Lee Phillip. BA, Gardner-Webb Coll., 1975; M. Ch. Music, So. Bapt. Theol. Sem., 1977. Minister of music/youth 2d Bapt. Ch., Mt. Holly, N.C., 1971-74, Pleasant Grove Bapt. Ch., Anchorage, Ky., 1975-77; minister of music/youth 1st Bapt. Ch., Lincolnton, N.C., 1978-88, music minister, 1978—; state children's worker N.C. Bapt. State Convention, Mais Hill, N.C., 1988-91; vol. missionary, Alexandria, Va., 1989, Sao Paulo, 1991. Recipient Assoc. Music Standard of Excellence award Bapt. Sunday Sch. Bd., 1990. Mem. South Fork Bapt. Assn. (assoc. youth dir. 1979-85, assoc. mudic dir. 1985—, assoc. program chmn. 1987-88, assoc. chmn. nominating com. 1991—). Republican. Office: 1st Bapt Ch 201 Robin Rd Lincolnton NC 28092

CAMPBELL, ROBERT CHARLES, clergyman, religious organization administrator; b. Chandler, Ariz., Mar. 9, 1924; s. Alexander Joshua and Florence (Betzner) C.; m. Lotus Idamae Graham, July 12, 1945; children: Robin Carl, Cherry Colleen. AB, Westmont Coll., 1944; BD, Eastern Baptist Theol. Sem., 1947, ThM, 1949, ThD, 1951, DD (hon.), 1974; MA, U. So. Calif., 1959; postgrad., Dropsie U., 1949-51, U. Pa., 1951-52, NYU, 1960-62, U. Cambridge, Eng., 1969; DLitt (hon.), Am. Bapt. Sem. of West, 1972; HHD (hon.), Alderson-Broaddus Coll., 1979; LHD (hon.), Linfield Coll., 1982; LLD (hon.), Franklin Coll., 1986. Ordained to ministry Am. Bapt. Ch., 1947; pastor 34th St. Bapt. Ch., Phila., 1945-49; instr. Eastern Bapt. Theol. Sem., Phila., 1949-51; asst. prof. Eastern Coll., St. Davids, Pa., 1951-53; assoc. prof. N.T. Am. Bapt. Sem. of West, Covina, Cal., 1953-54, dean, prof., 1954-72; gen. sec. Am. Bapt. Chs. in U.S.A., Valley Forge, Pa., 1972-87; pres. Eastern Bapt. Theol. Sem., Phila., 1987-89, ret.; Vis. lectr. Sch. Theology at Claremont, Calif., 1961-63, U. Redlands, Calif., 1959-60, 66-67; Bd. mgrs. Am. Bapt. Bd. of Edn. and Publ., 1956-59, 65-69; v.p. So. Calif. Bapt. Conv., 1967-68; pres. Am. Bapt. Chs. of Pacific S.W., 1970-71; Pres. N.Am. Bapt. Fellowship, 1974-76; mem. exec. com. Bapt. World Alliance, 1972-90, v.p., 1975-80; mem. exec. com., gov. bd. Nat. Council Chs. of Christ in U.S.A., 1972-87; del. to World Council of Chs., 1975, 83, mem. central com., 1975-90. Author: Great Words of the Faith, 1965, The Gospel of Paul, 1973, Evangelistic Emphases in Ephesians, Jesus Still Has Something To Say, 1987. Home: 125 Via Alicia Santa Barbara CA 93108

CAMPBELL, RONALD MICHAEL, minister; b. Elgin, Ill., Jan. 22, 1957; s. Wallace Michael and Ruth Isabel (MacKenzie) C.; m. Catherine Marie Deuber, June 27, 1981. BA, Wheaton Coll., 1978, MA, 1981; MDiv, No. Bapt. Theol. Sem., 1983; ThM, Calvin Theol. Sem., 1987. Youth pastor First United Presbyn. Ch., Barberton, Ohio, 1979-81, Bethel Presbyn. Ch., Wheaton, Ill., 1981-83; asst. pastor Calvary Presbyn. Ch., Flint, Mich., 1983-84, First Presbyn. Ch., River Forest, Ill., 1985-88; pastor Elmwood Park (Ill.) Presbyn. Ch., 1988—; teaching asst. Northwestern U., Evanston, Ill., 1988—. Mem. Am. Acad. Religion, Soc. Bibl. Lit.

CAMPION, OWEN FRANCIS, priest, publisher; b. Nashville, Apr. 24, 1940; s. Owen F. and Frances (Bass) C. AB, St. Bernard Coll., Cullman, Ala., 1962; postgrad., St. Mary's Sem., Balt., 1964-66, Cath. U., 1968, 69. Ordained priest Roman Cath. Ch., 1966. Various pastoral positions in Nashville, Chattanooga and Knoxville, 1966-71; editor in chief Tenn. Register, Nashville, 1971-88; assoc. pub. Our Sunday Visitor, Huntington, Ind., 1988—. Mem. Cath. Press Assn. (bd. dirs. 1980-89, treas. 1981-84, pres. 1984-86, St. Francis de Sales award 1989), Internat. Cath. Union of Press (ecclesiastical asst. 1989—), Religious Pub. Relations Coun. (Hinkhouse-de Rose award 1975), Assoc. Ch. Press, Internat. Fedn. Cath. Press Assn. (v.p. 1986-89), Nat. Press Club, Overseas Press Club. Home: 3389 E County Rd 722 N Huntington IN 46750 Office: Our Sunday Visitor 200 Noll Plaza Huntington IN 46750

CANADAY, MARVIN CLEVELAND, religion educator; b. Walterboro, S.C., May 3, 1954; s. Marvin Edward and Mary Lea (Langdale) C.; m. Connie Elizabeth Steedly, Dec. 18, 1976; children: Kristin Elizabeth, Lauren Steedly. BS in Polit. Sci., Charleston So. U., 1976; MDiv, S.E. Bapt. Theol. Sem., Wake Forest, N.C., 1980. Ordained to ministry So. Bapt. Conv., 1982. Min. edn. First Bapt. Ch., Waynesboro, Ga., 1982-84, Ridge Bapt. Ch., Richmond, Va., 1984-87; min. edn. and youth Walnut Grove Bapt. Ch., Mechanicsville, Va., 1987—; missionary intern So. Bapt. Conv. Home Mission Bd., Ithaca, N.Y., 1978; campus ministry intern, Old Dominion U., Norfolk, Va., 1979-80; dir. women's shelter, Salvation Army, Raleigh, N.C., 1981; outreach dir. Dover Bapt. Assn. Assisteam, Richmond, 1989—, v.p. Pastors' Conf., Dover Bapt. Assn., 1989—, dir. student ministries, Norfolk, Va., 1987-90; vol. chaplain Henrico Doctor's Hosp., Richmond, 1991—. mem. (assoc.) NEA, Va. Edn. Assn.; mem. Va. Bapt. Religious Edn. Assn., Richmond Area Religious Edn. Assn., Coop. Bapt. Fellowship. Home: 1019 Dunwoody Rd Mechanicsville VA 23111 Office: Walnut Grove Bapt Ch P O Box 428 Mechanicsville VA 23111

CANESTRI, GIOVANNI CARDINAL, archbishop; b. Castelspina, Alessandria, Italy, Sept. 30, 1918; s. Paolo Antonio and Giuseppina Canestri. Diploma in Arts, State U. Rome, 1950. ordained priest, 1941. Parish priest Rome, 1951-59; spiritual dir. Higher Roman Seminary, Rome, 1959-61; aux. bishop to Cardinal Vicario Rome, 1961-71; bishop Tortona, 1971, Rome, 1975-84; archbishop Cagliari, 1984-87; archbishop Genoa, 1987-88, cardinal, 1988—. Address: Piazza Matteotti 4, Genoa Genoa-Liguria, Italy

CANFIELD, FRANCIS XAVIER, clergyman, English language educator; b. Detroit, Dec. 3, 1920; s. Edward and Adelle (Berg) C. B.A., Sacred Heart Sem., Detroit, 1941; M.A., Catholic U., 1945; A.M. in L.S, U. Mich., 1950; Ph.D. U. Ottawa, 1951; spl. courses, Notre Dame U., Wayne U., U. Detroit. Ordained priest Roman Cath. Ch., 1945. Named domestic prelate Roman Cath. Ch., 1963; with English dept. Sacred Heart Sem., Detroit, 1946-70; librarian Sacred Heart Sem., 1948-63, rector-president, 1963-70; pastor St. Paul's Parish, Grosse Pointe Farms, Mich., 1971-91; instr. library sci. Immaculate Heart Coll., Los Angeles, summers 1955-61; chaplain Detroit Police Dept., 1965-72. Author: Condensed History of the Catholic Church in the Archdiocese of Detroit, 1984, With Eyes of Faith, 1984; editor: Philosophy and the Modern Mind, 1961, Literature and the Modern Mind, 1963, Political Science and the Modern Mind, 1963; Author articles, book revs. Bd. dirs. Bon Secours Hosp., Grosse Pointe, Mich., 1982—. Recipient Alumni Recognition award U. Mich. Sch. Info. and Libr. Studies, 1990. Mem. Cath. Library Assn. (chmn. Mich. unit 1950-52, 54-56, exec. council 1957-63, pres. 1961-63), Grosse Pointe Ministerial Assn. (pres. 1972-73), Council Nat. Library Assns. (vice chmn. 1962-63), Am. Friends of Vatican Library (pres. 1981—). Home: 157 Lake Shore Grosse Pointe Farms MI 48236 *In whatever circumstances of life I find mysejf, I feel called somehow to bring God to man and man to God.*

CANFIELD, TERRY LEE, minister; b. Dover, Ohio, Oct. 8, 1955; s. Edward L. and Thelma Elizabeth (Everett) C.; m. Ruth A. Abel, Mar. 30, 1985; children: Joshua, Nathan. BS in Christian Edn. & Bible, Mid-Am. Bible Coll., Oklahoma City, 1980; student, Anderson Sch. Theology, Ind., 1987-88, Ind. Wesleyan U., Marion, 1990—. Ordained to ministry, Ch. of God, 1983. Assoc. pastor Sioux City (Iowa) Ch. of God, summer 1979; minister of youth and outreach Fourth Ave. Ch. of God, Lake Charles, La., 1980-83; assoc. pastor Akron (Ind.) Ch. of God, 1983-88, Eaton (Ind.) First Ch. of God, 1988—; active in youth camps Ohio, La., Ind.; resource/conf. leader for youth convs., Christian edn. workshops, youth retreats. Chmn. Boy Scouts Am., Akron, 1984-85; mem. camp com. No. Ind. Youth, 1984-86, dir., 1983-85; ministerial advisor La. State Youth; chaplain Civil Air Patrol of Lake Charles. Mem. Fellowship of Christian Athletes in Lake Charles, Ind. Assn. Bd. Dirs., Lions. Home: 714 E Harris Box 31 Eaton IN 47338 Office: Eaton First Ch of God 700 E Harris Eaton IN 47338

CANNON, ALBERRY CHARLES, priest; b. Greenville, S.C., May 12, 1936; s. Alberry Charles and Mary (Cogswell) Cannon; m. Nancy Sterling, June 15, 1957; children: A. Charles, J.M. Sterling, Caroline, Michael D.W. BA, The Citadel, Charleston, S.C., 1957; MDiv, U. of the South, Sewanee, 1963. Priest Episcopal Ch., S.C., Fla., 1963-85; vicar Calvary Episcopal Ch., Glenn Springs, S.C., 1986-91, St. Andrew's Episcopal Ch., Greenville, S.C., 1991—; employment counselor United Ministries, Greenville, S.C., 1986-89; mgr. Place of Home, Unit Ministries, Greenville, 1989—. Author: History of the Cotillion Club of Greenville, S.C., 1988, The Maxwells of Greenville, 1989. Mem. Greenville Homeless Coalition, 1989—; chaplain Greenville Soup Kitchen, 1986—; pres. Greenville Meml. Hosp. Adv. Bd., 1989; mem. homeless task force S.C. Gen. Assembly, 1990—, chmn. sub-com. on urban issues. Mem. NASW, Greenville County Hist. Soc. (v.p. 1988—), Cotillion Club (bd. dirs. 1989—). Democrat. Episcopalian. Avocations: duplicate bridge, pug dogs, England and its history. Home: 105 W Prentiss Ave Greenville SC 29605 Office: United Ministries 600 Pendleton St Greenville SC 29601

CANNON, CHRISTOPHER JOHN, minister; b. Santa Monica, Calif., Feb. 25, 1961; s. George William and Vicky (Adamson) C.; m. Anne Elizabeth, Sept. 10, 1986. BA in Psychology, Westmont Coll., 1983; MA in Counseling, Loyola Marymount U., 1988. Assoc. pastor Hope Chapel Foursquare Ch., Hermosa Beach, Calif., 1987—. Mem. Nat. Network Youth Ministry (coord. 1989). Office: Internat Ch Foursquare Gospel Hope Chapel 2420 Pacific Coast Hwy Hermosa Beach CA 90254

CANNON, ROBERT LESTER, minister, former educational administrator, theological educator; b. Dallas, Mar. 7, 1942; s. Charles W. and Lois Marie (Peal) C.; m. Corene Kelly, June 1, 1968; children—Chris, Keith, Laurie. B.S., North Tex. State U., 1964; M.Div., Southwestern Bapt. Theol. Sem., 1968; D.Ministry, Golden Gate Baptist Theol. Sem., 1981. Dir. Bapt. Student Union, So. Meth. U., Dallas, 1965-69, Stephen F. Austin State U., Nacogdoches, Tex., 1969-72, Tex. Tech, Lubbock, 1972-75; dir. church services N.W. Bapt. Conv., Can., 1977-80; v.p. Golden Gate Sem., Mill Valley, Calif., 1980-85; pastor University Heights Bapt. Ch., Stillwater, Okla., 1985—. Mem. adv. council Keesee Found., Martinsville, Va., 1982—. Recipient Canadian Merit award, 1978. Democrat. Home: 323 S Knoblock St Stillwater OK 74074

CANNON, WILLIAM RAGSDALE, bishop; b. Chattanooga, Apr. 5, 1916; s. William Ragsdale and Emma (McAfee) C. A.B., U. Ga., 1937; B.D. summa cum laude, Yale U., 1940, Ph.D., 1942; D.D., Asbury Coll., 1950; LL.D., Temple U., 1955; L.H.D., Emory U., 1962; S.T.D. (hon.), Wesleyan Coll., 1980; Litt.D. (hon.), La Grange Coll., 1980, Duke U., 1983; D.C.L. (hon.), N.C. Wesleyan Coll., 1982; D.H., Meth. Coll., 1984. Ordained to ministry Methodist Ch., 1940; pastor Allen Meml. Methodist Ch., Oxford, Ga., 1942-43; prof. ch. history and hist. theology Candler Sch. Theology, Emory U., 1943-68, dean sch. theology, 1953-68; bishop Raleigh area United Meth. Ch., 1968-72, 80-84, Richmond area, 1970-72, Atlanta area, 1972-80; lectr. Fondren Found. So. Meth. U., 1948; vis. prof. Garrett Bibl. Inst., summer 1949, Richmond Coll., U. London, 1950; Mem. commn. on ritual and worship Meth. Ch., 1948-64; chmn. bd. ministerial tng. North Ga. Conf., Meth. Ch., 1948-64; del. to gen. and jurisdictional confs. Meth. Ch., 1948, 52, 56, 60, 64, 68; also mem. commn. on worship, commn. ecumenical affairs; del. Ecumenical Conf. Methodism, Oxford, Eng., 1951, World Meth. Conf., Lake Junalaska, N.C., 1956; fraternal del. from World Meth. Council to World Conf. on Faith and Order, Lund, Sweden, 1952, Nairobi, Kenya, 1975; chmn. exec. com. World Meth. Council; pres. World Meth. Conf., 1980—; hon. pres. World Meth. Council, 1986—; accredited visitor World Council Chs., Evanston, Ill., 1954; Meth. ch. del. 3d assembly World Council of Chs., New Delhi, 1961, Lund, Sweden, 1968, Nairobi, Kenya, 1976; del. World Meth. Conf., Oslo, Norway, 1961; Meth. Ch. del. Conf. on Faith and Order, Montreal, Can., 1963; pres. N. Am. sect., chmn. exec. com. World Methodist Council; mem. presidium; pres. World Meth. Conf.; ofcl. protestant observer from council to II Vatican Council of Roman Catholic Church; co-chmn. Conversations of Methodists and Roman Catholics at Internat. Level; deliverer Episcopal address Bicentennial Gen. Conf. United Meth. Ch., 1984; one of ten observers to Extraordinary Synod of Roman Cath. Ch., 1985; gave prayer at Inauguration of Jimmy Carter as Pres., 1977 and opening of Carter Presdl. Ctr., 1986. Author: A Faith for These Times, 1944, The Christian Church, 1945, The Theology of John Wesley, 1946, Accomplishments to Wesley's Death in Methodism (edited by W.K. Anderson), 1947, Our Protestant Faith, 1949, The Redeemer, 1951, History of Christianity in the Middle Ages, 1960, journeys after St. Paul, 1963, Evangelism in a Contemporary Context, 1973, A Disciple's Profile of Jesus: On the Gospel of Luke, 1975, Jesus the Servant: On the Gospel of Mark, 1978, The Gospel of Matthew, 1983, The Gospel of John, 1985, The Book of Acts, 1989; editor: Selections from Augustine, Table Talk (Martin Luther), 1950. Trustee La Grange (Ga.) Coll., Asbury Coll.; trustee, vice chmn. bd. Emory U.; chmn. trustees Protestant Radio and TV Center, 1953-63. Mem. Oxford Inst. Wesleyan Studies, Phi Beta Kappa, Phi Beta Kappa Assos. (exec. com.), Theta Phi, Phi Kappa Phi. Gave bicentennial Episc. address Gen. Conf. United Meth. Ch., 1984; one of ten non-Roman Caths. to be invited to Extraordinary Synod of Bishops, Vatican, 1985. Address: The Plaza Towers 12F 2575 Peachtree Rd NE Atlanta GA 30305 *The principles by which I have tried to live are: complete devotion to Jesus Christ; loyalty to His Church as represented by the United Methodist Church; daily Bible reading and prayer; service to others; and concern for the betterment of humanity. I have pursued scholarship, organized my time and energy, and enjoyed the simple things of life.*

CANTERBURY, HUGH FRANKLIN, SR., minister, music minister; b. Camden, Ark., Apr. 22, 1930; s. James Franklin and Myrl (Scoggin) C.; m. Mary Jean Holloway, Jan. 24, 1952; children: Hugh Franklin Jr., Danna Floyd, Michael Joe. BME, U. So. Ark., 1953; student, New Orleans Bapt. Theol. Sem., 1954-55. Min. music & edn. Weller Ave. Bapt. Ch., Baton Rouge, La., 1954-61; min. music & edn. First Bapt. Ch., Sulphur, La., 1961-63, Buna, Tex., 1963-66; min. music & admin. Second Bapt. Ch., Griffin, Ga., 1966-70; min. edn. West Rome Bapt. Ch., Rome, Ga., 1970-72; min. music First Bapt. Ch., Summerville, Ga., 1972-76, Second Bapt. Ch., Griffin, Ga., 1976-85; assoc. pastor/min. music First Bapt. Ch., Eastman, Ga., 1985-91; rep. La. Bapt. Music Dept. Baton Rouge, 1956-59, v.p. Baton Rouge Religious Ed. Assn. 195759, pres. La. Training Union Conv. 1960-61, soloist La. Bapt. Conv. 1959, songleader Ga. Bapt. Conv. 1974. Seaman 1st, USN, 1948-49. Mem. Ga. Bapt. Music Assn., Dodge County Bapt. Assn. (music dir.), Hosp. Chaplains Assn., Ministerial Assn., Bapt. Pastor's Assn. Southern Baptist. Home: 203 Pine St Eastman GA 31023 Office: First Baptist Ch 201 Oak St Eastman GA 31023

CANTRELL, ALMOS CALVIN, minister; b. Haynesville, La., June 27, 1932; s. David DeVan and Clara Bell (Bruer) C.; m. Dorothy Mae Adcock, Dec. 28, 1952; children: Beth Cantrell Lord, Calvin, Paul E. DD, United Bapt. Theol. Sem., 1980. Ordained to ministry So. Bapt. Conv., 1952. Pastor Gilliam (La.) Bapt. Ch., 1952-58, Bethany (La.) Bapt.Ch., 1958-65, Chapel Hill Bapt. ch., West Monroe, La., 1965-73; assoc. dir. evangelism La. Bapt. Conv., Alexandria, 1973—; led 12 evang. crusades overseas. Named Outstanding Pastor of Yr., La. Bapt. Conv., 1973. Home: 67 Western Heights Dr Boyce LA 71409 Office: PO Box 311 Alexandria LA 71309 *The greatest contribution to life here and hereafter is to share a good Witness to Jesus Christ and to encourage others to do the same.*

CANTWELL, RICHARD E., minister, music educator; b. Omaha, Sept. 10, 1943; s. Virgil R. and Alma L. (Parrish) C.; m. Linda Sue DeVore, Aug. 4, 1967; children: Richard II, Julie, Daniel. BFA, U. Nebr., Omaha, 1967; MusM, U. Nebr., Lincoln, 1969; D of Mus. Arts, U. Mo., Kansas City, 1990. Min. music, organist 1st Nazarene Ch., Omaha, 1961-65; min. children's music Coll. Ch., Wollaston, Mass., 1967-69; min. music 1st Ch. of the Nazarene, Lawrence, Kans., 1970-72; min. music and drama Cen. Ch. of the Nazarene, Lenexa, Kans., 1972—; prof. music Mid-Am. Nazarene Coll., Olathe, Kans., 1969-85, Ea. Nazarene Coll., Quincy, Mass., 1991—. Contbr. articles to profl. jours.; arranger chorals. Mem. Coll. Band Dirs. Nat. Assn., Multiple Staff Ministries Assn. Office: Cen Ch of the Nazarene 12600 W 87th St Pkwy Lenexa KS 66215

CANTY, CARRIE REBECCA, clergywoman, educator; b. Sumter, S.C., Aug. 2, 1927; d. Frank Clifford and Marie (Willis) C. B.S., Morris Brown Coll., Atlanta, 1950; M.Ed., Temple U., 1970; Th.M. summa cum laude, Trinity Theol. Sem., Newburgh, Ind., 1982; Th.D. summa cum laude, Trinity U., Newburgh, 1983, Ph.D. summa cum laude, 1984. Ordained to ministry Fire Baptized Holiness Ch. of God of the Ams., 1965; cert. tchr., Pa., N.J.; cert. counselor, Pa., Ind. Tchr. Fuller Normal Indsl. Inst., Greenville, S.C., 1950-51, S.E. Delco Sch. Dist., Folcroft, Pa., 1955-74; instr. Youth Leadership, Greenville, 1971—; pastor Mt. Pleasant Ch., Phila., 1973-78, Mt. Finai Fire Baptized Holiness Ch., Mount Vernon, N.Y., 1979-82, Gethsemane Fire Baptized Holiness Ch., Phila., 1982—; instr. religious edn. dept. Pa. Dist., Phila., 1986—. Chairperson Be Ye Kind to One Another, Phila., 1974-78. Recipient Ambassador of Yr. award Young People Inst., 1972; Preservance award Religious Edn. Dept. of Pa. Dist., 1975; Bishop F.C. Canty award Religious Edn. Dept. of Pa. Dist., 1978; Leadership award Young People Inst., Pa. Dist., 1984. Mem. Ministerial Alliance (Pastor of Yr. 1983), Young People Inst. (coordinator 3 dists. fellowship 1982—), Nat. Assn. Female Execs. Democrat. Avocations: reading; basketball. Home: 5832 Webster St Philadelphia PA 19143 Office: Gethsemane Fire Baptized Holiness Ch 2629 W York St Philadelphia PA 19132

CAPENER, REGNER ALVIN, minister, electronics engineer; b. Astoria, Oreg., Apr. 18, 1942; s. Alvin Earnest and Lillian Lorraine (Lehtosaari) C.; divorced; children: Deborah, Christian, Melodie, Ariella; m. Della Denise Melson, May 17, 1983; children: Shelley, Danielle, Rebekah, Joshua. Student, U. Nebr., 1957-58, 59-60, Southwestern Coll., Waxahachie, Tex., 1958-59, Bethany Bible Coll., 1963-64. Ordained minister Full Gospel Assembly Ch., 1971. Engr., talk show host Sta. KHOF-FM, Glendale, Calif., 1966-67; youth min. Bethel Union Ch., Duarte, Calif., 1966-67; pres. Intermountain Electronics, Salt Lake City, 1967-72; assoc. pastor Full Gospel Assembly, Salt Lake City, 1968-72, Long Beach (Calif.) Christian Ctr., 1972-76; v.p. Refuge Ministries, Inc., Long Beach, 1972-76; pres. Christian Broadcasting Network-Alaska, Inc., Fairbanks, 1977-83; gen.mgr. Action Sch. of Broadcasting, Anchorage, 1983-85; pres., pastor House of Praise, Anchorage, 1984—; chief engr. KTBY-TV, Inc., Anchorage, 1988—; area dir. Christian Broadcasting Network, Virginia Beach, 1977-83; cons., dir. Union Bond and Trust Co., Anchorage, 1985-86; author, editor univ. courses, 1984-85; dep. gov. Am. Biog. Inst. Rsch. Assn., 1990—. Author: Spiritual Maturity, 1975, Spiritual Warfare, 1976, The Doctrine of Submission, 1988, A Vision for Praise, 1988; author, composer numerous gospel songs; creator numerous broadcasting and electronic instrument inventions. Sec., Christian Businessmen's Com., Salt Lake City, 1968-72; area advisor Women's Aglow Internat., Fairbanks, 1981-83; local co-chmn. campaign Boucher for Gov. Com., Fairbanks, 1982; campaigner for Boucher, Anchorage, 1984, Clark Gruening for Senate Com., Barrow, Alaska, 1980; TV producer Stevens for U.S. Senate, Barrow, 1978; fundraiser City of Refuge, Mex., 1973-75; statewide rep. Sudden Infant Death Syndrome, Barrow, 1978-82; founder Operation Blessing/Alaska, 1981; mem. resch. bd. advisors Am. Biog. Inst., 1990—; advisor Anchorage chpt. Women's Aglow Internat., 1990—. Mem. Soc. Broadcast Engrs., Internat. Soc. Classical Guitarists (sec. 1967-69), Alaska Broadcaster's Assn., Nat. Assn. Broadcasters, Anchorage C. of C. Republican. Avocations: musician, ancient history, ancient langs. Office: Sta KTBY Inc 1840 S Bragaw Ste 101 Anchorage AK 99508 *The word "impossible" need never be a part of the vocabulary of one whose life is intertwined with the Lord Jesus Christ. I have learned that there are no problems in life which do not have clear and definitive solutions when approached from the standpoint of a personal relationship with Jesus Christ.*

CAPLAN, MARSHA, ecumenical agency administrator. Exec. dir. Interfaith Coun. of Boulder, Colo. Office: Interfaith Coun 2650 Table Mesa Dr Boulder CO 80303*

CAPPELLO, FATHER RICHARD, priest, librarian; b. Providence, 1949; s. Anthony and Teresa Cappello. BSLS, St. Bonaventure U., 1970; ThM, St. John's U., 1975, MLS, 1976. Joined Josephite Fathers, Roman Cath. Ch., 1967, ordained priest, 1972. Priest various parishes Roman Cath. Ch., N.Y.C., 1971-76; tchr. various schs. Archdiocese of N.Y.C., 1976-79; libr. Loyola Marymount U., 1979-85, Werik Found. for Christian Studies, Boston, 1986—; adj. instr. information scis. Boston Coll., Chestnut Hill, Mass., 1987-88. Office: Werik Found for Christian Studies 80 Boylston St Rm 618 Boston MA 02116-4961

CAPPO, LOUIS CESARE, priest; b. Baltic, Mich., Dec. 16, 1919; s. Caesar and Jennie (Marie) C. BA in Theology, St. Francis Sem., Milw., 1943. Ordained priest Roman Cath. Ch., 1946. Min. Diocese of Marquette, Mich., 1946-52; adminstr. Christ the King Parish, Ramsay, Mich., 1952-58, pastor, 1956-65; pastor St. Cecilia Parish, Hubbell, Mich., 1965-68, Sacred Heart Parish, L'Anse, 1969, St. Ann's Parish, Escanaba, 1969-72; rector St. Peter's Cathedral, Marquette, 1975—; exec. dir. Dept. Community Svcs. and Family Life, Marquette, 1972-85; chaplain Mich. State Police, 1966—; diocesan rep. to Social Action Bd., Mich. Cath. Conf., 1963; past pres. Bishop Baraga Assn.; bd. dirs. Bishop Noa Home; health coord. Diocese of Marquette, diocesan dir. of cemeteries, exec. dir. Tower of History.; v.p. bd. dirs. Cath. Social Svcs. Bd. dirs. Marquette Gen. Hosp., 1973—, United Way; mem. bd. of control Lake Superior State Coll.; co-founder, chairperson Lake Superior Jobs Coalition; chairperson Mich. Tourist Coun.; mem. Internat. Trade Commn., adv. coun. SBA, Planning Commn. Houghton County, Water Commn. of Adams Township and Village of South Range, Ancillary Manpower Planning Bd., Vol. Commn.; vice chmn. Tri-State Interfaith Devel. Enterprise; adv. com. Inst. Wood Rsch., Mich. Tech. U., Houghton; chmn. Action Non-Profit Housing Corp. Recipient Pres.'s award No. Mich. U., 1974. Address: St Peter Cathedral 311 W Baraga Ave Marquette MI 49855

CAPPS, ROBERT VANBUREN, minister; b. Atlanta, Aug. 19, 1938; s. Homer Buren and Grace Ione (Ward) C.; m. Nancy Patricia Radford, Feb. 14, 1964; 1 child, Joy Lynn. BA, Furman U., 1960; BD, Southwestern Bapt. Theol. Sem., 1963, MDiv, 1973. Ordained to ministry So. Bapt. Conv., 1961. Pastor Poynor (Tex.) Bapt. Ch., 1961-62; assoc. pastor 1st Bapt. Ch., Enterprise, Ala., 1963-65; pastor Pine Crest Bapt. Ch., Tampa, Fla., 1965-67; evangelist, founder Van Capps Evangelistic Assn., Lake Hamilton, Fla., 1967—. Mem. Conf. So. Bapt. Evangelists, Alpha Phi Gamma. Home: 3 E Lake Dr Paradise Island Haines City FL 33844 Office: PO Box 337 Lake Hamilton FL 33851 *The greatest thought ever penned by a Christian writer is the statement of the Apostle Paul, found in Philippians 4:13: "I can do all things through Christ who strengthens me."*

CAPPS, WALTER HOLDEN, religion educator; b. Omaha, May 5, 1934; s. Holden Frances and Mildred Linnea (Bildt) C.; m. Lois Ragnhild Grimsrud, Aug. 21, 1960; children: Lisa Margarit, Todd Holden, Laura Karolina. BS, Portland (Oreg.) State U., 1957; BD, Augustana Theol. Sem., Rock Island, Ill., 1960; STM, Yale U., 1961, MA, 1963, PhD, 1965. Prof. religious studies U. Calif., Santa Barbara, 1964—. Author: The Unfinished War, 1982, The Monastic Impulse, 1983, New Religious Right, 1990, Thomas Merton, 1990. Bd. dirs. Pacific Luth. Sem., Berkeley, Calif., 1965-73, La Casa de Maria Retreat Ctr., Santa Barbara, 1966-84; chair Calif. Coun. for Humanities, San Francisco, 1984-87; pres. Fedn. State Humanities Couns., Washington, 1985-87. Lutheran. Home: 1724 Santa Barbara St Santa Barbara CA 93101 Office: U Calif Santa Barbara Dept Religious Studies Santa Barbara CA 93106

CAPRIO, JOSEPH GIUSEPPE CARDINAL, clergyman; b. Lapio, Italy, Nov. 15, 1914. Ordained priest Roman Catholic Ch., 1938. Served in diplomatic missions, China, 1947-51, Belgium, 1951-54, South Vietnam, 1954-56; internuncio in China with residence at Taiwan, 1959-67; ordained titular archbishop of Apollonia, 1961; pro-nuncio in India, 1967-69; sec. Adminstrn. of Patrimony of Holy See, 1969-77, pres., 1979-81; substitute sec. of state, 1977-79; elevated to Sacred Coll. of Cardinals, 1979; deacon St. Mary Auxiliatrix in Via Tuscolana; pres. Prefecture of Econ. Affairs of Holy See, 1981—; mem. Congregation Evangelization of Peoples; mem. commn. Revision Code of Canon Law. Office: Econ Affairs, The Holy See, Vatican City Vatican City

CARABALLO, JOSE, minister, educator; b. Fajardo, P.R., Mar. 24, 1932; came to U.S., 1944; s. Ines and Angelina (Rios) C.; m. Elba A., Oct. 25, 1952; children—Mildred, Elba Ruth, Elizabeth, Joe, Robert. B.A., Adelphi U., 1974; M.Div., N.Y. Theol. Sem., 1976; M.S.T., Union Theol. Sem., 1978; Dr. Ministry, Drew U., 1983; Dr. h.c., Latin Am. Bible Coll., 1980; diploma (hon.), Spanish Am. Bible Inst., 1958. Ordained to ministry Assemblies of God, 1955. Pastor, Macedonia Ch., Assemblies of God, 1955-65, Pentecostal Ch. The Light of the World, 1965-69; dir. Spanish dept. N.Y. Bible Soc. Internat., 1971-76; prison chaplain City Correctional Instn., 1971-76; cons. on Hispanic ministry United Ministry in Higher Edn., 1978, to N.Y.C. Missions Soc., 1978; adj. prof. urban community coll. of New Rochelle (N.Y.), 1977-81, Empire State Coll., 1976; dir. coll. program for minority clergy N.Y. Theol. Sem., 1976-81, dean Hispanic concerns, asst. prof. urban theology, dean pastoral ministries program and Sing Sing Program, 1976—; pastor Trinity United Presbyn. Ch., Bklyn., 1979—; mem. statewide com. N.Y. State Council Chs., adv. com. on Hispanic affairs Union Theol. Sem., N.Y.C. Author: A Certificate Program for Hispanic Clergy and Lay Leaders in an Accredited Theological Seminary, 1982. Mem. majors com. of Religious Leaders, N.Y.C.; past mem. adv. com. Green Point Hosp.; past bd. dirs., chmn. Bethesda Day Care Ctr.; past v.p. com. Denominational Execs., N.Y.C.; bd. dirs. Auburn Theol. Sem. program com., 1982; bd. dirs. Inter-Religious Bail Fund Inc.; active various orgns. in Hispanic Community. Served with U.S. Army, 1952-54. Mem. Assn. Profl. Edn. for Ministry. Democrat. Office: New York Theol Seminary 5 W 29 St New York NY 10001

CARBALLOSA, EVIS L., minister. Grad., Detroit Bible Inst., 1960; PhD in History. Exec. dir. Spanish World Gospel Mission, Inc., Winona Lake, Ind., 1990—; with Spanish Evang. Ent., Inc., Miami, Fla. Office: Spanish World Gospel Mission PO Box 542 Winona Lake IN 46590

CARDEN, ALLEN, college president; b. St. Charles, Ill., June 18, 1949. Registrar Biola U., La Mirada, Calif., 1974-77, prof. history, 1977-87, assoc. provost, 1986-87; v.p. acad. affairs Spring Arbor (Mich.) Coll., 1987-91, pres., 1991—. Home: 218 W Arbor Heights Dr Spring Arbor MI 49283 Office: Spring Arbor Coll 106 E Main St Spring Arbor MI 49283

CARDILLO, CLEMENT JOHN, priest, psychologist; b. Port Chester, N.Y., June 20, 1925; s. Anthony and Beatrice (Pitera) C.; BA, Don Bosco Coll., Newton, N.J., 1950; MEd in Counseling Psychology, Boston Coll., 1965, PhD in Counseling Psychology, 1972. Ordained priest Roman Catholic Ch., 1954; prin., superior Sacred Heart Jr. Sem., Ipswich, Mass., 1960-65; pastor St. Anthony's Ch., Paterson, N.J., 1965-80; dir. Consultation Services Center, Clifton, N.J., 1968—; chmn. N.J. Bd. Psychol. Examiners, 1981-83; lectr. on psychol. topics. Pres. Harbor House. Recipient citation Congressional Record, 1980. Mem. Am. Psychol. Assn., N.J. Psychol. Assn. Club: Paterson Rotary. Author: Empathy and Personality Traits, 1972. Home: 501 W Broadway Paterson NJ 07522 Office: 737 Valley Rd Clifton NJ 07013

CARDIN, SHOSHANA SHOUBIN, religious organization administrator, consultant; b. Tel Aviv, Oct. 10, 1926; came to U.S., 1927; d. Sraiah and Chana (Barbalot) Shoubin; m. Jerome Stanley Cardin, Aug. 17, 1948; children: Steven Harris, Ilene Marcia, Nina Beth, Sanford Ronald. Student, Johns Hopkins U., 1942-45; BA, UCLA, 1946; MA, Antioch U., 1979; LHD (hon.), Western Md. Coll., 1985, Jewish Theol. Seminary, 1989. Tchr. elem. schs. Balt., 1946-50; pres. Fedn. of Jewish Women's Org., Md., 1965-67; sec. Voluntary Action Ctr. Cen. Md., 1973-75; pres. Associated Jewish Charities and Welfare Fund, 1975-77; chmn. bd. The Associated, 1983-85; pres. Coun. Jewish Fedns., 1984-87; vice chmn. Gov.'s Vol. Coun., 1985—; chmn. Nat. Conf. on Soviet Jewry, 1988—, Conf. of Pres. of Major Am. Jewish Orgns., 1991—; gov. Jewish Agy. for Israel, 1985—. Co-Editor: Leadership Logic, 1974, Volunteerism: Moving into the 1980's, 1979, Strategies for Success-Surviving the New Federalism, 1982; contbr. editor, author of numerous pubs. Bd. dirs. Am. Jewish Joint Distbn. Com., United Israel Appeal, United Way Cen. Md., 1983-85, Health Welfare Council Cen. Md., 1980-85, Jewish Community Ctr. Balt., 1970-76, Balt. County Gen. Hosp. Aux., 1972-74, Park Sch. Parent's Assn., 1966-71, Md. Assn. Mental Health, 1965-66, March of Dimes Balt. Chpt., 1966-68, Levindale Ladies Aux., 1961-65, Chizuk Amuno Sch. Bd., 1963-65; Balt. Jewish Council, 1963-70, 1980-82 (sec. 1967-70); chmn. bd. Assn. Jewish Charities and Welfare Fund, 1983-85; pres. Chizuk Amuno PTA, 1964-65, Jewish Community Ctr. Assocs. 1969-71 (exec. com. 1969—); chmn. Md. State Employment and Trng. Council, 1979-83, Md. Vol.Network, 1980-82, Md. Comm. Women, 1974-79 (commr. 1968-79), Maryland Women's Conf., 1977; trustee United Jewish Appeal, Nat. Retinitis Pigmentosa Found., Loyola-Notre Dame Library, 1980-84, Balt. Hebrew Coll., 1979-82, Antioch U., 1977-78, Nat. Assn. Comms. for Women, Edn. and Research Fund, 1976-77; sec. Voluntary Action Ctr. Cen. Md., 1973-76 (exec. com. 1971-76); commr. Md. Comm. Human Relations, 1979-82; coordinator Women's Fair Balt., 1975; co-founder Women Together, 1973 (exec. com. 1973-76); co-chmn. Md. Interfaith Conf. Peace, 1966; del. Md. Constln. Conv., 1967; mem. Md. Jr. League (hon. life). Recipient Louise Waterman Wise award Am. Jewish Congress, 1970, Citizen Civics Affairs award B'nai B'rith, 1968, Jimmie Swartz medallion, 1983, Governor's Citation State of Md., 1982, Cert. of Merit U.S. Congress, 1979, Cert. of Distinguished Citizenship State of Md., 1969, Na'Amat Golda Meir award, 1989; named Outstanding Citizen of Md. Jewish War Vets., 1978, Woman of Yr. B'nai B'rith Women Md., 1967, one of Women of Distinction Fashion Group Balt. Inc., 1975, Honored and Outstanding Citizen City of Balt., 1969; inductee Md. Jewish Hall of Fame Jewish Hist. Soc. Md., 1979; Organizational and Community Devel. Fellow Johns Hopkins, 1976-77. Mem. Md. Assn. Parliamentarians (bd. dirs. 1976-77), Nat. Coun. Jewish Women (bd. dirs. 1963-65, 68-72, 73-74, Hannah G. Solomon award 1975), Assn. Voluntary Action Scholars. Democrat. Avocation: gardening. Office: Nat Conf on Soviet Jewry 10 E 40th St New York NY 10016

CARDONE, JAMES JOSEPH, JR., priest; b. Montclair, N.J., Aug. 21, 1948; s. James Joseph and Lucy Ann (Maffei) C.; m. Sheryl Helen Larson, Jan. 17, 1970; children: Thomas, Benjamin. BA in Psychology, Thiel Coll., 1970; MA in Psychology, John Carroll U., 1974; MDiv, Bexley Hall, 1979. Cert. rehab. counselor, 1974-78. Rector Trinity Ch., Houghton, Mich., 1979-82, Emmanuel Ch., Rockford, Ill., 1982-88, Grace Ch., Utica, N.Y., 1988—; professed mem. Tertiary Soc. St. Francis, Mt. Sinai, N.Y., 1984—, bd. dirs., chaplain St. Luke's Meml. Hosp., Utica, 1988—, bd. dirs. Mohawk Valley Coun. Chs., Uitca, N.Y., standing com. mem. on constitution, canons, rules of order, Ciocesn Coun., 1991—, Diocese Cen. N.Y., Syracuse, 1989—. Contbr. articles to profl. jours. bd. dirs. Utica Area C. of C., 1989—; founder, pres. Shelter Care Ministries for Homeless, Rockford, 1984-88, founder, supr. Community Soup Kitchen, Rockford, 1982-88. Recipient Elizabeth A. Connelly Svc. award, Rome, N.Y., 1990. Mem. Rotary Club Utica N.Y. Home: 110 Paris Rd New Hartford NY 13413 Office: Grace Ch 6 Elizabeth St Utica NY 13501 *True knowledge of our limitations is a greater virtue than the realization of our gifts.*

CAREY, GEORGE LEONARD, archbishop of Canterbury; b. Nov. 13, 1935; s. George and Ruby Carey; m. Eileen Harmsworth Hood, 1960; 4 children. BD with honors, London Coll. Div., ThM; PhD, King's Coll., London. Ordained priest Ch. of Eng. Curate St. Mary's, Islington, Eng., 1962-66; lectr. Oak Hill Coll., Southgate, Eng., 1966-70, St. John's Coll., Nottingham, Eng., 1970-75; vicar St. Nicholas' Ch., Durham, Eng., 1975-82; prin. Trinity Coll., Stoke Hill, Bristol, Eng., 1982-87; hon. canon Bristol Cathedral, 1983-87; bishop of Bath and Wells Eng., 1987-91, archbishop of Canterbury, 1991—. Author: I Believe in Man, 1975, God Incarnate, 1976; co-author: (with others) The Great Acquittal, 1980, the Meeting of the Waters, 1985, The Gate of Glory, 1986, The Message of the Bible, 1988, The Great God Robbery, 1989; also numerous articles. With RAF, 1954-56. Avocations: reading, writing, walking. Address: Old Palace, Canterbury Cathedral, Canterbury England*

CAREY, LINDA MARIE, lay worker; b. Greenfield, Ohio, June 10, 1962; d. Allen Dean CArey and Elaine Bridget Duffy Miller. BS in Elem. Edn., Ohio Dominican Coll., 1985, BA in Theology, 1986; postgrad., Athenaeum of Ohio, Cin. Dir. youth ministry St. Susanna Ch., Mason, Ohio, 1986-88, St. Antoninus, Cin., 1988—; chmn. Westside Youth Nights, Cin., 1990—, World Youth Day, Cin., 1989. Mem. Cin. Youth Ministers Assn. Office: St Antoninus Cath Ch 1500 Linneman Rd Cincinnati OH 45238

CARGO, WILLIAM ABRAM, minister; b. Petoskey, Mich., June 20, 1947; s. Paul Morris and Martha (Hatcher) C.; m. Alice Jo Younggren, Jan. 2, 1976; children: John Abram, James Oliver. BA, MusB, Ohio Wesleyan U., 1970; MDiv, Union Theol. Sem., N.Y.C., 1973; D Ministry, Vanderbilt U., 1978. Ordained deacon United Meth. Ch., 1971; elder, 1975. Pastor Waukau-Elo-Eureka of Wis. Conf. United Meth. Ch., 1973-74, Nennelly-Bethel Ch. of Mid. Tenn. Conf., 1975-76, Jefferson Ave. United Meth. Ch., Detroit, 1976-81, Riverview (Mich.) United Meth. Ch., 1981-88, Oscoda (Mich.) United Meth. Ch., Oscoda Indian Mission of Detroit Conf., 1988—; adminstrv. asst. to acting pres. Union Theol. Sem., N.Y.C., 1974-75; sec. evangelism Detroit East dist. of Detroit Conf., 1977-81, dir. communication Detroit West dist., Riverview, 1982-87, also mem. music worship and arts. Condr. music Community Messiah Performance, Oscoda, 1989—, singer Miss Iosco Scholarship Pageant, 1989—. Mem. Lions. Home: 108 W Dwight Oscoda MI 48750 Office: Oscoda United Meth Ch 120 W Dwight Oscoda MI 48750

CARIGNAN, SHANDA MULFORD HEISER, priest; b. Jersey City, N.J., May 22, 1950; d. Joseph Herman and Victoria (White) Heiser; m. Donald Richard Carignan, Dec. 19, 1970; children: Jeremy Joseph, Shantih Stephanie, Benjamin Richard. BA, Goucher Coll., Towson, Md., 1972; MDiv, Princeton Theol. Sem., 1976. Ordained priest Episcopal Ch., 1986. Counselor, cons. Retreat/Conf. Cons., Holly, Mich., 1981-83; counselor Ednl. Opportunity Ctr., Dayton, Ohio, 1983-85; asst. rector St. Andrew's Episcopal Ch., Dayton, 1985-87; assoc. rector St. Paul's Episcopal Ch., Richmond, Va., 1987—. Mem. Downtown Coop. Ministries. Democrat. Avocation: swimming. Office: St Paul's Episcopal Ch 815 E Grace St Richmond VA 23219 *In my life I have found that most people are good, but many bad things are done by these good people! The problem is largely in our systems—family, political, economic, religious. The church needs to challenge bad systems and confront systemic evil.*

CARL, EDWARD LEE, minister; b. Akron, Ohio, Sept. 6, 1945; s. John P. and Dorothy (Knowles) C.; m. Phyllis K. Wise, Aug. 12, 1967; 1 child, Jason Matthew. BA, Malone Coll., 1968; MDiv, Bethany Theol. Sem., 1971. Ordained to ministry Ch. of the Brethren, 1971. Assoc. pastor First United Meth. Ch., Westmont, Ill., 1969-71; pastor Salamonie Ch. of the Brethren, Warren, Ind., 1971-77, Scalp Level Ch. of the Brethren, Windber, Pa., 1978-86, Ch. of the Brethren, Uniontown, Pa., 1986—; del. standing com. Ch. of the Brethren, Elgin, Ill., 1983-84; mem. Dist. Bd. Adminstrn., Davidsville, Pa., 1985-91; chmn. Dist. Ministry Commn., Davidsville, 1988, 89, 91. Mem. Lions (Windber, Pa.). Home: 45 Belmeade Ln Uniontown PA 15401 Office: Ch of the Brethren 20 Robinson St Uniontown PA 15401

CARLILE, KEITH SMITH, minister; b. Boswell, Ind., Mar. 8, 1928; s. Jasper Leslie and Mearl Jane (Smith) C.; m. Joyce Evelyn Gottschall, June 16, 1949; children: Donald, John, Roger, Paul. AB, Ind. State U., 1949; MDiv, Garrett-Evang. Theol. Sem., 1953; MA, Northwestern U., 1954. Min. North Liberty (In.d) United Meth. Ch., 1950-54; missionary Honolulu, 1954-59; min. Portage Chapel-Asbury United Meth. Ch., South Bend, Ind., 1959-64, Trinity United Meth. Ch., Crawfordsville, Ind., 1964-70, Wesley United Meth. Ch., Indpls., 1970-74, Christ United Meth. Ch., Indpls., 1974-76, Maple Ave. United Meth. Ch., Terre Haute, Ind., 1976-81, Old North United Meth. Ch., Evansville, Ind., 1981-85; dist. supt. South Ind. Conf. United Meth. Ch., Bloomington, 1985-91; ret., 1991; chmn. Bd. Ordained Ministry, 1975-80, Coun. Fin. and Adminstrn., 1984-85; del. World Meth. Coun., 1991. Contbr. articles to profl. jours.

CARLIN, CHARLES STEPHEN, religious organization administrator, quality assurance executive; b. Lexington, Mass., Oct. 8, 1943; s. Donald Stewart and Winifred (Gilligan) C.; m. Susan Edith Keene, Apr. 11, 1971; children: Rebecca Sue, Stephen Charles. BSEE, Northeastern U., 1967, MS in Engring. Mgmt., 1970. Configuration mgmt. mgr. Raytheon Co., Andover, Mass., 1969—; treas. New Colony Bapt. Ch., Billerica, Mass., 1973-79, deacon, 1975-79; treas. Nashua (N.H.) Bapt. Ch., 1983—, deacon, 1986—; messenger Bapt. Conv. New Eng., Northborough, Mass., 1984-86, 90; photographer Centrifuge-N.E. Bapt., 1985-91; coord. Centrifuge-Nashua Bapt. Ch., Rumney, N.H., 1986-89, Wenham, Mass., 1990, 91. Chmn. Raytheon Co. United Way, Andover, 1989. Mem. Nat. Assn. Ch. Treas. (charter), Am. Soc. for Quality Control (cert.). Republican. Mem. So. Bapt. Conv. Home: 27 Seminole Dr Nashua NH 03063 Office: Nashua Bapt Ch 555 Broad St Nashua NH 03063

CARLISLE, JAMES PATTON, clergyman; b. Miami Beach, Fla., May 7, 1946; s. William Olin and Evelyn Obie (Ogden) C.; m. Laima Kristina. BA, Auburn U., 1969; MDiv, Emory U., 1976. Ordained to ministry Methodist Ch., 1975. Adminstrv. asst. Radney for Lt. Gov. Ala. campaign, 1969-70; asst. adminstr. Lee County Head Start, Auburn, Ala., 1970-72; assoc. pastor 10th St. United Meth. Ch., Atlanta, 1974-76; dir. continuing edn. N. Ga. Ann. Conf., United Meth. Ch., Atlanta, 1975-78; program dir. Ctr. for Profl. Devel. in Ministry, Lancaster, Pa., 1978-80; pres. Carlisle Leadership Group, 1984—; dir. Ctr. for Profl. Devel. in Ministry, Lancaster Theol. Sem., 1980-90, Ctr. for Creative Ch. Leadership, 1990—, also dir. programs and continuing edn. events for clergy and religious leaders; leader career planning events for clergy Uniting Ch. of Australia, Australia and N.Z., 1983; cons. mem. task force Pastoral Counseling Center, Lancaster, 1980-81; mem. nat. consultation on ch. ministry systems and racism, edn. and tng. for ethnic minorities Nat. Council Chs., 1983; elder N.Y. Ann. Conf. United Meth. Ch. Mem. Nat. Vocat. Guidance Assn., Assn. Clin. Pastoral Edn., Soc. Advancement Continuing Edn. for Ministry, Assn. for Creative Change (profl. mem.), Omicron Delta Kappa. Contbr. articles to profl. jours. Home and Office: 1722 Niblick Ave Lancaster PA 17603 *As leaders we must engage ourselves and others in the mysterious adventure of life; whether through prayer and contemplation, social action or the adventure of living, engage life.*

CARLISLE, THOMAS JOHN, minister emeritus; b. Plattsburgh, N.Y., Oct. 11, 1913; s. Thomas Houston and Ruby Grace (Mann) C.; m. Dorothy Mae Davis, Aug. 20, 1936; children: Thomas, Christopher, David, Jonathan. BA, Williams Coll., 1934; MDiv, Union Theol. Sem., 1937. Ordained to ministry Presbyn. Ch. (U.S.A.), 1937. Pastor Tupper Lake (N.Y.) Presbyn. Ch., 1937-42, 2d Presbyn. Ch., Delhi, N.Y., 1942-49; pastor Stone St. Presbyn. Ch., Watertown, N.Y., 1949-78, pastor emeritus, 1978—. Author: (poetry) You! Jonahs, 1968, Celebration!, 1970, Mistaken Identity, 1973, Journey with Job, 1976, Eve and After, 1984, Tales of Hopkins Forest, 1984, Beginning with Mary, 1986, Invisible Harvest, 1987; contbr. articles to mags. in field. Recipient Philips-Rice award Jefferson County Assn. for Mental Health, 1960. Mem. Poetry Soc. Ga., Poetry Soc. Va., Watertown Rotary (pres. 1960-61, Paul Harris fellow). Home: 437 Lachenauer Dr Watertown NY 13601

CARLISLE, WAYLON ARNOLD, minister; b. Opp, Ala., Feb. 13, 1937; s. Dozier and Grace Inez (Eiland) C.; m. Jean I. Rogers, Aug. 29, 1955; children: Pam, Kim, Lisa, Lorrie. BA, Carson Newman Coll., 1972; MS, Emmanuel Bapt. U., 1990. Lic. to ministry So. Bapt. Conv., 1964, ordained, 1965; lic. pastoral counselor, 1988. Pastor Warrensburg Bapt. Ch., Mohawk, Tenn., 1965-67, Magna View Bapt. Ch., Talbott, Tenn., 1967-72, Westside Bapt. Ch., Lake Wales, Fla., 1972-79, Eastside Bapt. Ch., Plant City, Fla., 1979—; bd. dirs. Eastside Bapt. Daycare, Plant City, 1979—; moderator Ridge Bapt. Assn., Winter Haven, Fla., 1975-76, Shiloh Bapt. Assn., Plant City, 1981-82, 89-90; loans com. mem. State Bd. Missions, Fla. Bapt. Conv., Jacksonville, 1990—. Mem. Nat. Christian Counselors Assn., Civitans (chaplain), East Hillsborough C. of C. (legis. com. 1988—). Democrat. Home: 1207 W Sandalwood Dr S Plant City FL 33566 Office: Eastside Bapt Ch 1318 E Calhoun St Plant City FL 33566

CARLOCK, JON THOMPSON, minister; b. Birmingham, Ala., Sept. 14, 1964; s. Herbert William and Betty Jane (Thompson) C. BA, Bethel Coll., 1985; MDiv, Vanderbilt U., 1988, D Ministry, 1989; postgrad., U. St. Andrews, Scotland, 1990—. Ordained minister Cumberland Presbyn. Ch. Supply min. Mt. Zion Cumberland Presbyn. Ch., McKenzie, Tenn., 1983-85, Bethel Cumberland Presbyn. Ch., McLemoresville, Tenn., 1984-85; youth min. Loudon (Tenn.) Cumberland Presbyn. Ch., 1985; supply min. Bank's Cumberland Presbyn. Ch., Smithville, 1986-87; min. Mt. Tabor Cumberland Presbyn. Ch., Murfreesboro, 1986-89, Beech Grove (Tenn.) Cumberland Presbyn. Ch., 1987-89; assoc. minister, family counselor Cookeville 1st Cumberland Presbyn. Ch., 1989—. Vice pres. Bethel Coll. Young Reps., McKenzie, 1984-85. Named one of Outstanding Young Men in Am., 1986, 89. Mem. Sigma Phi Omega (chaplain 1983-85), Gamma Beta Phi. Avocations: skeet shooting, martial arts, collecting antiques.

CARLSON, BRUCE LYMAN, minister; b. Youngstown, Ohio, Oct. 25, 1938; s. Harold Lawrence and Edith Christine (Johnson) C.; m. Jean Elise Ditzler, Dec. 22, 1962; children: Douglas Bruce, Eric Lee. BA, Elmhurst (Ill.) Coll., 1961; MDiv, Garrett Theol. Sem., Evanston, Ill., 1964; DMin, Drew U., Madison, N.J., 1977. Ordained to ministry United Meth. Ch., 1965. Pastor Rondout Valley United Meth. Ch., Stone Ridge, N.Y., 1964-68, United Meth. Ch., New Milford, Conn., 1968-74; sr. pastor Shrub Oak (N.Y.) United Meth. Ch., 1974-80, Community United Meth. Ch., Poughkeepsie, N.Y., 1980—; pres. Coun. on Fin. and Adminstrn., N.Y. Ann. Conf. United Meth. Ch., 1987—, registrar Bd. of Ordained Ministry, 1972-80; trustee Vassar Warner Home, Poughkeepsie, 1990—; dir. Garrett Evang. Sem., Evanston, 1989—; bd. advisors Boston U. Sch. Theology, 1976-80. Contbr. articles to profl. jours. Dutchess County Clergy Assn. (pres. 1986-87), Rotary (pres. 1980). Home: 16 Meadow View Dr Poughkeepsie NY 12603 Office: Community United Meth Ch 112 New Hackensack Rd Poughkeepsie NY 12603

CARLSON, DENNIS NOBEL, minister, religious organization executive; b. Lincoln, Nebr., Mar. 26, 1946; s. Nobel August and Hildur Eulila (Bengtson) C.; m. Annalee Whieldon, Aug. 10, 1968; children: Jonathan Dennis, Julie Ann. Ordained to ministry Seventh-day Adventist, 1974. Pastor Seventh-day Adventist Ch., East Dayton, Ohio, 1970-72, Willoughby and Brooklyn, Ohio, 1972-74, Mansfield, Ohio, 1974-80, Puyallup, Wash., 1980-84; dir. stewardship edn. and communication Wash. Conf. Seventh-day Adventists, Bothell, 1984-86, exec. sec., 1986—, mem. exec. com., 1981-83; mem. exec. com. Ohio Conf., Mt. Vernon, 1978-80, mem. K-16 Bd. Edn., 1978-80. Contbr. articles to profl. jours. Office: Wash Conf Seventh-day Adventists 20015 Bothell Way SE Bothell WA 98012

CARLSON, GUY RAYMOND, minister, religious organization administrator; b. Crosby, N.D., Feb. 17, 1918; s. George and Ragna Louise (Rassum) C.; m. Mae Adeline Steffler, Oct. 7, 1938; children: Gary Allen, Sharon Carlson Bontrager, Paul Raymond. Student, Western Bible Coll., Winnipeg, Man., Can., 1934-35; D. of Div. (hon.), N. Cen. Bible Coll., Mpls., 1968. Ordained to ministry Assemblies of God Ch., 1941. Pastor Assembly of God Tabernacle, Thief River Falls, Minn., 1940-48; Minn. dist. Sunday sch. dir. Assemblies of God Council, Mpls., 1944-48, Minn. dist. supr., 1948-61; pres. N. Cen. Bible Coll., Mpls., 1961-69; asst. gen. supt. Assemblies of God Council, Springfield, Mo., 1970-85, gen. supt., 1986—. Contbr. articles to profl. jours. Bd. dirs. Cen. Bible Coll., Evangel Coll., Assemblies of God Theol. Sem., Springfield. Named to Order of Golden Shield, Evangel Coll., 1977. Mem. Nat. Assn. Evangelicals (exec. com. 1983—), Pentecostal Fellowship N.Am. (exec. com.). Office: Assemblies of God 1445 Boonville Ave Springfield MO 65802

CARLSON, JAMES LESLIE, minister; b. Canton, Ill., May 26, 1932; s. Leslie A.F. and Helen Marie (Teed) C.; m. Greta Adair Nelson, June 24, 1954; children: Kristen, Gretchen, Marcus, Steffen. BA, Bethany Coll., 1954; BD, Augustana Sem., Rock Island, Ill., 1958; MDiv., Luth. Sch. Theology, Chgo., 1964; DMin., Luth. Sch. Theology, 1983. Ordained to ministry Luth. Ch., 1958. Pastor Luth. Ch. of the Good Shepherd, Largo, Fla., 1958-61, Gloria Dei Luth. Ch., Durant, Iowa, 1961-63; chaplain resident Austin (Tex.) State Hosp., 1963-64; sr. pastor Trinity Luth. Ch., Victoria, Tex., 1964—; mem. planning coun. Tex.-La. Synod Luth. Ch. Am., 1973-75, synodical dean, 1975-82, mem. synod coun., 1975-78, 87-91; chairperson Luth. Inst. for Religious Studies, Continuing Edn. Agy. for Tex.; del. Nat. ELCA Assembly, 1991—. Bd. dirs., mem. founders group Gulf Bend Ctr., Victoria, 1964; pres. Victoria (Tex.) County Sr. Citizens Assn., 1979; pres. City PTA, Victoria, 1975, DeLeon Villa-HUD 302 Housing, Victoria, 1983. Fellow Assn. Large Luth. Chs.; mem. Ministerial Alliance Victoria. Home: 2403 Terrace St Victoria TX 77901 Office: Trinity Evangelical Luth Ch 106 N DeLeon St Victoria TX 77901

CARLSON, RICHARD PAUL, minister; b. Hazard, Ky., Apr. 7, 1945; s. Harold Nathaniel and Verma Elnora (Granlund) C.; m. Virginia Ann Piatt, June 16, 1967; children: Amy Marie, Heather Adele, Gretchen Ann, Audrey Joy, Aaron Richard, Nathaniel August, Amanda Beth. BA cum laude, Trinity Coll., Ill., 1967; MDiv magna cum laude, Trinity Evang. Div. Sch., 1970. Ordained to ministry Evang. Free Ch. Am., 1973. Pastor Evang. Free Ch., Bloomington-Normal, Ill., 1970-76, Rock Springs, Wyo., 1976—; v.p. McLean County Ministerial Assn., 1970-73; chmn., co-chmn. Evang. Ministerial Fellowship, 1974-76; Christian edn. Coord. So. Ill. Area 7, Great Lakes Dist. Evang. Free Ch. Am., 1970-76; pres. Sweetwater County Ministerial Alliance, 1979-81. Author: Hope for the Home, 1981; contbr. articles to Evang. Beacon. Mem. Youth Svcs. Agy., Bloomington, 1973-74, assoc. mem. 1975-76; v.p., sec., treas. Right to Read, Inc., 1977-82. Mem. Key '73, Evang. Free Ch. Am. Ministerial Assn. (chmn. Rock Springs-Green River 1979-81, 88-90), Sweetwater County Right to Life (bd. dirs. 1983—). Home and Office: 523 Q St Rock Springs WY 82901 *There are two dimensions to the reconciliation available at the cross of Christ. Until first the vertical and then the horizontal dimensions are experienced, reconciliation is incomplete and man is at war with his Creator and with himself.*

CARLSON, ROBERT JAMES, bishop; b. Mpls., June 30, 1944; s. Robert James and Jeanne Catherine (Dorgan) C. B.A., St. Paul Sem., 1964, M.Div., 1976; J.C.L., Catholic U. Am., 1979. Ordained priest Roman Catholic Ch. 1970. Asst. St. Raphael Ch., Crystal, 1970-72; assoc. St. Margaret Mary Ch., Golden Valley, 1972-73, adminstr., 1973-76; vice chancellor Vocation Office, 1976-79, dir., 1977; temp. adminstr. St. Peter Ch., Mendota, 1977, chancellor, 1979—; temp. adminstr. St. Peter Claver, St. Paul, 1982; pastor St. Leonard of Port Maurice, Mpls., 1982-84; aux. bishop St. Paul and Mpls., Mpls., 1983—; vicar Eastern Vicariate Archdiocese of St. Paul and Mpls., Mpls., 1984—; pres., bd. dirs. Nat. Evangelization Teams, 1991; mem. com. on the laity Nat. Conf. Cath. Bishops, 1990. Author: Going All Out: An Invitation to Belong, 1985. Pres. Nat. Found. Cath. Youth Ministry, Washington, 1989—. Recipient Friendship award Knights and Ladies of St. Peter Claver, 1990, St. De LaSalle Meml. award Cretin High Sch. Alumni Assn., 1990. Mem. Canon Law Soc. Am. Avocations: canoeing, downhill and cross country skiing. Office: The Chancery 226 Summit Ave Saint Paul MN 55102

CARLSON, WAYNE HAROLD, priest; b. Fremont, Nebr., May 16, 1944; s. Harold G. and Verla Elaine (Rasmussen) C.; m. Diane Marie Krull, June 10, 1967; children: Sarah, David. BS in Edn., U. Nebr., 1965; MDiv, Seabury-Western Theol. Sem., 1971. Vicar St. John's Episcopal Ch., Albion, Nebr., 1971-77; rector Christ Episcopal Ch., Central City, Nebr., 1971-77; editor Nebr. Churchman Diocese of Nebr., 1975-77; vicar St. Luke's Episcopal Ch., Manchester, Mo., 1977-80, rector, 1980—; mem. Commn. on Ministry, Mo., 1978-83; mem., chmn. Music/Liturgical Commn., Diocese of Mo., 1978-89; trustee St. Monica's Home, Lincoln, 1972-77. Mem. citizens adv. coun. Parkway Sch. Bd., Chesterfield, Mo., 1978—, pres., 1978—, chmn. study group on character edn., 1987-88. Republican. Home: 806 Catania Dr Manchester MO 63021 Office: St Lukes Episcopal Ch 1101 Sulphur Springs Rd Manchester MO 63021

CARLTON, JOHN WAYNE, minister; b. Tuscaloosa, Ala., Sept. 7, 1946; s. Myers Cecil and Dorothy (Morgan) C.; m. Mary Jean Johnson, July 6, 1968; children: Joel Wayne, Joy Alicia. Student, U. South Fla., 1963-66, Mercer U., 1973-74. Ordained to ministry So. Bapt. Conv., 1977. Min. music and youth Shurlington Bapt. Ch., Macon, Ga., 1971-73, Glover Bapt. Ch., Norcross, Ga., 1973-74; min. music and youth Calvary Bapt. Ch., Jesup, Ga., 1974-85, min. music, 1985—. Mem. Altamaha Bapt. Pastor's Conf. (sec. 1975-78), Altamaha Bapt. Assn. (music dir. 1974-84, 91—), Ga. Bapt. Ch. Music Conf. (area rep. 1976-78), Wayne County Ministerial Assn. Home: 212 Charlton St Jesup GA 31545 Office: 411 E Cherry St Jesup GA 31545

CARMAN, ED BRADLEY, minister; b. Doniphan, Mo., Feb. 22, 1955; s. Warren T. and Valla Jo (Stevenson) C.; m. L. Gail Carman, Aug. 25, 1974; children: Amy Dawn, Carrie Jo, Allan Bradley, Dani Gail. BA, Freed-Hardeman Coll., 1979. Ordained to ministry Ch. of Christ, 1979. Min. youth Ch. of Christ, Camden, Tenn., 1976-79; min. edn. Ch. of Christ, East Peoria, Ill., 1979-82; min. preaching Ch. of Christ, 1982-90, CH. of Christ, Maryland Hts., Mo., 1990—; treas., bd. dirs., Peoria Area Christian Sch., East Peoria, 1981-85; instr., listening lab., Lead Cons., 1988—, conflict mediator, 1990—. Mem. Peoria Area Civic Chorale, 1986-89. Mem. Assn. Couples Marriage Enrichment (facilitator), Theta Alpha Gamma (coun. del. 1974-75). Home: 11352 Dorsett Rd Maryland Heights MO 63043 Office: Ch of Christ 107 Midland Ave Maryland Heights MO 63043

CARMICHAEL, CLIFFORD LEE, minister; b. Linton, Ind., Sept. 3, 1914; s. Lee and Grace (Beem) C.; m. Jeanette Ridgway, May 1, 1941; children: Morris, Morton, Mark. BA, Ind. U., 1943; BD, Garret Sem., 1946. Ordained to ministry, United Meth. Ch., 1946. Asst. supt. Chgo. United Mission, 1936-37; pastor various chs., Ind., 1937-80, Brownsburg United Meth. Ch., Ind., 1976-80; ret.; chmn. Town and Country Commn., United Meth. Ch., Ind. Conf., chmn. camping com., mem. Conf. Corp. Trustees. Mem. Kiwanis (pres. 1981, 88). Republican. Methodist. Avocations: lapidary, golf, fishing, travel. Home: 207 W 4th St Bicknell IN 47512

CARMICHAEL, MARGARET SUSAN, retired theology educator; b. Laurel, Miss., Dec. 25, 1923; d. William Merritt and Mary Annie (Williams) C. AA, Jones County Jr. Coll., 1943; BA, Scarritt Coll., 1948, MA, 1959. Ordained deaconess United Meth. Ch., deaconess, 1960, diaconal min., 1977. Dir. Christian edn. St. Luke's United Meth. Ch., Jackson, Miss., 1948-61; assoc. prof. Christian edn. Pfeiffer Coll., Misenheimer, N.C., 1961-88, prof. emerita, 1989—; mem. bd. diaconal ministries N.C. Conf., United Meth. Ch., 1983—, dist. dir. childrens ministries Albemarle dist. Western N.C. Conf., 1978-87. Sec. Stanly County Coun. Status of Women, 1984-85. Mem. Nat. Christian Educators Fellowship, Western N.C. Christian Educators Fellowship, Southeastern Jurisdiction Deaconess and Home Missionary Assn., United Meth. Assn. Profs. Christian Edn., Albemarle Bus. and Profl. Womens Club (pres. 1987-88). Home: Box 561 Misenheimer NC 28109 Office: Pfeiffer Coll Misenheimer NC 28109

CARMICHEL, ALEXANDER CAMPBELL, IV, minister, religious organization administrator; b. Syracuse, N.Y., Sept. 5, 1949; s. Alexander Campbell III and Elizabeth (Tracy) C.; m. Karen Stitham, June 6, 1970; children: Erin Elizabeth, Megan Katherine. BA, W.Va. Wesleyan Coll., Backhannon, 1971; MDiv, Colgate Rochester Div. Sch., N.Y., 1977. Assoc. pastor 1st United Meth. Ch., Clearwater, Fla., 1977-78; pastor 1st United Meth. Ch., Safety Harbor, Fla., 1978-83, Friendship United Meth. Ch., Punta Gorda, Fla., 1983-86; chaplain Fla. United Meth. Children's Home, Deltona, Fla., 1986-90, assoc. dir., 1990=91, dir. fin. devel., 1991—; mem. World Meth. Coun., Lake Junaluska, 1986-91; chair Dist. Coun. on Ministries, DeLand, Fla., 1988—; mem. Fla. Conf. Coun. on Ministries, Lakeland, Fla., 1988—; treas. Fla. Coun. of Chs., Orlando, Fla., 1988-90; speaker workshops, 1986—. Contbr. articles to newspaper. Recipient Ecumenical Leadership award Fla. Ann. Conf., 1987. Mem. Nat. Assn. Fund Raising Execs., Nat. Child Care Devel. Assn. and Conf., Rotary (bd. dmem. 1988-90). Office: Fla United Meth Childrens Home 51 Main St Enterprise FL 32725

CARMINES, ALVIN ALLISON, JR., minister, educator, composer, playwright; b. Hampton, Va., July 25, 1936; s. Alvin Allison Sr. and Katherine Elizabeth (Graham) C. BA, Swartmore Coll., 1958; BD, Union Theol. Sem., 1961, STM, 1963. Ordained to ministry Meth. Ch., 1960. Pastor Judson Meml. Ch., N.Y.C., 1961-81; sr. pastor Rauschenbusch Meml. Ch., N.Y.C., 1982—; prof. Columbia U., N.Y.C., 1988—. Composer hymns; plays include In Circles, What Happened, Joan, Peace, Promenade. Mem. campaign com. Lindsay for Mayor, Robert Kennedy for Pres., Michael Dukakis for Pres., Ronnie Elderidge for Coun. Mem.; bd. dirs. Metro-Suffolk United Ch. Christ, 1986—. Mem. Arts, Religion and Culture (bd. dirs. 1976-83), N.Y. Coun. NCCCJ (bd. dirs. 1973-74). Democrat. Home: 24N 400 W 43d St New York NY 10036

CARNEY, SISTER MARGARET, religious order superior; b. Pitts., July 8, 1941; d. Edmund Earl and Margaret (Mawe) C. BS in Edn., Duquesne U., 1966, MA in Theology, 1984; MA in Franciscan Studies, St. Bonaventure U., 1985; STD in Theology, U. Antonianum, Rome, 1988. Joined Sisters of St. Francis of Providence of God, Roman Cath. Ch., 1959; cert. tchr., Pa. Assoc. vicar for religious Diocese of Pitts., 1972-79; mem. gen. coun. Sisters of St. Francis of Providence of God, Pitts., 1976-84, gen. superior, 1988—; mem. faculty Franciscan Inst., Olean, N.Y., 1985-86; mem. internat. work group Internat. Franciscan Conf., Rome, 1979-82. Co-author: Tor Rule, 1981. Mem. bd. regents St. Fidelis Sem., Herman, Pa., 1975-78, St. Vincent Sem., Latrobe, Pa., 1979-86; bd. dirs. Pennsylvanians for Human Life, Pitts., 1975-77, exec. dir., 1978-79. Recipient Franciscan Portiuncula Celebration award U. Steubenville, 1982. Mem. Leadership Conf. Women Religious (role mem.), Franciscan Fedn. USA (chair rule and life com. 1981-86), Internat. Franciscan Conf. Home and Office: Grove & McRoberts Rds Pittsburgh PA 15234

CARNINE, ALBERT J., music educator, minister of music; b. Bloomington, Ill., Aug. 3, 1943; s. Albert G. Carnine and Ruth (Bierbaum) Sayre; m. Nancy Lee Isaacson, Aug. 2, 1969; children: Michelle Lee, Holly Ann, David Christopher. B in Music Edn., Ill. Wesleyan U., 1965; MusM, M in Music Edn., So. Meth. U., 1966; D Mus. Arts, U. Tex., 1977. Min. music numerous Bapt. chs., 1962-90; min. music Calvary Bapt. Ch., Joplin, Mo., 1991—; faculty music Mo. So. State Coll., Joplin; local, state and nat. adjudicator for ch. and high sch. choral festivals; mem. North Cen. Evaluation Team Assessing Carl Junction, Mo. Sch. System, 1991. Book reviewer. Parliamentarian citizens adv. coun. Carl Junction Sch. Dist., 1988. Recipient Friend of Edn. award Joplin Pub. Sch. Dist., 1982. Mem. Am. Choral Dirs. Assn. (life), Music Educators Nat. Conf. (life), Am. Choral Found. (life). Republican. Avocations: Bible study, travel. Home: Rte 3 Box 740 Joplin MO 64801 Office: Calvary Bapt Ch 50th and Brookwood Dr Joplin MO 64801

CAROTHERS, CHUCK, minister; b. Jackson, Tenn., Oct. 23, 1957; s. James Lowell Carothers and Janie Nowell Hickman; m. Leni Suzanne Lumbley, July 19, 1986; 1 child, Tyler Christopher. BA, Union U., 1982; MDiv, Southwestern Bapt. Theol. Sem., 1986. Ordained to ministry So. Bapt. Conv., 1988. Assoc. pastor/youth Walnut Hill Bapt. Ch., Bells, Tenn., 1979-81; assoc. pastor First Bapt. Ch., Huntingdon, Tenn., 1987-89, Millington, Tenn., 1989-91; assoc. pastor Sherwood Bapt. Ch., Albany, Ga., 1991—. Mem. REIMA, SBERA. Home: 3222 Saddleleaf Ave Albany GA 31707 Office: Sherwood Bapt Ch 2011 Whispering Pines Albany GA 31707-1855

CAROZZA, DAVY ANGELO, Italian educator; b. Montenerodomo, Italy, Oct. 10, 1926; came to U.S., 1947, naturalized, 1952; s. Nicola and Maria A. (Mariotti) C.; m. Anna G. Carozza, Feb. 3, 1952; children—Daniel, Walter, Janet, Paolo. B.A. summa cum laude, Cath. U. Am., 1956, M.A. (Woodrow Wilson fellow), 1957, Ph.D. (Woodrow Wilson fellow), 1964. Tchr. Italian, 1943-47; lectr. summer sessions Cath. U. Am., 1957-65, lectr. in French, 1960-61; instr. Italian and French U. Md., College Park, 1961-64; asst. prof. Italian U. Md., 1964-65; lectr. Sch. Advanced Internat. Studies, Johns Hopkins U., 1964-65; asso. prof. comparative lit. U. Wis., Milw., 1965-68; prof. U. Wis., 1968—, chmn. dept., 1967-69, 73-76, coordinator M.A. program in Fgn. Lang. and Lit., 1976-86; vis. asso. prof. comparative lit. Northwestern U., Evanston, Ill., 1966; mem. panel discussion on Dante Georgetown U. Forum radio program, 1965; adviser, coordinator Italian program for adults and children Cardinal Stritch Coll., 1971-73; mem. symposia on Baroque U. Ky., 1965, Cath. U. Am., 1975. Author: European Baroque, 1976, Petrarch's Secretum, 1989; contbr. book revs. and articles to lit. jours. Served with AUS, 1948-52. U. Wis. grantee, (8 awards) 1966-87. Mem. Midwest MLA (pres. 1969-70, exec. com. 1970-71), MLA (exec. council 1969-70), Internat., Am. Comparative lit. assns., Renaissance Soc. Am., Dante Soc. Am., Internat., Am. assns. tchrs. Italian, Am. Assn. Tchrs. French, Am. Assn. Tchrs. Spanish and Portuguese, Phi Beta Kappa, Delta Epsilon Sigma, Phi Kappa Phi. Home: 5549 N Berkeley Blvd Milwaukee WI 53217 Office: U Wis Dept English & Comparative Lit Milwaukee WI 53201

CAROZZOLO, SHIRLEY JEAN, minister; b. Buffalo, Nov. 21, 1935; d. Albert A. and Jean Louise (Hanna) La Chiusa; m. Vito A. Carozzolo, Sept. 17, 1966; children: Michael John Kurban, David Charles Kurban. Various secretarial positions, 1953-55, 68-74; office mgr. Haney Erection Services Inc., Tonawanda, N.Y., 1975-76, corp. sec., 1976-84, EEO officer, 1980-84; ordained to ministry Full Gospel Assemblies Internat.; corp. sec.-treas. New Covenant Evang. Ministries Inc., 1984-87; fin. adminstr. World Outreach Conf., 1985; treas. New Covenant Tabernacle, 1985—. Mem. Niagara Frontier Subcontractors Assn. (membership chmn. 1978), Leadership Council Western N.Y., Prison Fellowship Local Council of Western N.Y., Am. Mgmt. Assn., Am. Soc. Profl. and Exec. Women, Christian Ministries Mgmt. Assn. (1st v.p. 1985-87), Nat. Assn. Ch. Bus. Adminstrs., Christian Found. for the Performing Arts (treas. 1986-87, v.p. 1989), Zonta (1st v.p. 1979-81, pres. 1981-82, treas. 1990—, local area bd. dirs. 1991—). Republican. Home: 426 Ashford Ave Tonawanda NY 14150 Office: 1 World Ministries Ctr Buffalo NY 14223 *To live is to serve God. To exist is to go through life searching but never finding who you are in Christ.*

CARP, RICHARD MERCHANT, educational administrator; b. Madison, Wis., June 10, 1949; s. Abraham and Frances (Merchant) C.; m. Jana Elizabeth Carp, Nov. 6, 1985; 1 child, Jamie. BA, Stanford U., 1971; MA, Pacific Sch. Religion, 1977; PhD, Grad. Theol. Union, 1981. Youth dir. St. Mark Episcopal Ch., Berkeley, Calif., 1984-86; program dir. United Meth. Jr. High Ch. Camp, No. Calif., 1985-87; dir., editor Image Bank for Teaching Religious Studies U. Hawaii, Manoa, 1988—; v.p. acad. affairs Kansas City Art Inst., 1989—; bd. advisors TV course WGBH, Boston, 1989—. Author: (play) Maiden, Mother, Crone: Women and Spirituality in the West, 1987; contbr. chpts. to books. Bd. dirs. Coun. for Arts in Palo Alto (Calif.) and Mid-Peninsula Area, 1976-77, Theatre Community Ctr. of Bay Area, San Francisco, 1979-84; artistic dir. Bur. Western Mythology, San Francisco Bay area, 1977-88; pres., art dir. Arts in Process, Berkeley, 1986-88. NEH grantee, 1987, 89; named to Outstanding Young Men Am., Jaycees, 1984. Mem. Am. Acad. Religion, Am. Studies Assn., Assn. for Integrative Studies, Coll. Art Assn., Phi Beta Kappa. Office: Kansas City Art Inst 4415 Warwick Blvd Kansas City MO 64111

CARPENTER, CHARLES, religious organization administrator. Dir. overseas ministries Missionary Ch., Ft. Wayne, Ind. Office: Missionary Ch 3901 S Wayne Ave Fort Wayne IN 46807*

CARPENTER, DENNIS D., minister; b. Hillsboro, Wis., Jan. 16, 1954; s. Darrel Orvis and Avis Jean (Moore) C.; m. Selena Fox, June 7, 1986. BS, U. Wis., Madison, 1976; MS in Edn., U. Wis., Stout, 1978; postgrad., Saybrook Inst., San Francisco, 1988—. Cert. sch. psychologist, Wis. Min./adminstr. Circle Sanctuary, Mt. Horeb/Madison, Wis., 1984—. Editor/pub.: Circle Network News jour. 1984—, The Wisconsin Sch. Psychologist Jour., 1981-85; author: (cassette tape) Magick Mirror Past Life Journey, 1988. Bd. dirs. Counseling and Personal Devel. Ctr., Price County, Wis., 1982-84; profl. adv. Parents Without Ptnrs., Inc., Phillips, Wis., 1982-84; adv. bd. mem. Women's Devel. Ctr., Wausaw, Wis., 1982-84. Mem. Assn. Humanistic Psychology, Assn. Transpersonal Psychology, Assn. Past Life Rsch. and Therapy, Am. Assn. Counseling and Devel., Wis. Sch. Psychologists Assn. Mem. Circle Sanctuary/Nature Spiritualist. Office: Circle Sanctuary PO Box 219 Mount Horeb WI 53572 *The most significant theological issues of our time center around humans' relationship with nature. Continued exploitation of the Earth's resources and uncontrolled human population growth threaten the ecological well-being of the planet as well as human survival.*

CARPENTER, FRANK ROBERT, minister; b. Southampton, England, Apr. 13, 1946; came to U.S., 1946; s. Frank Ralph and Margaret Joan (Trezise) C.; m. Merrilee Yvonne Quiring, Mar. 16, 1974; children: Karen Johanna, Lisa Marie, Brittany Brooke. BS in Sociology/Polit. Sci., U. Oreg., 1968; MDiv, Western Conservative Bapt. Sem., 1977. Ordained to ministry Bapt. Ch., 1982. Assoc. pastor Palo Verde Bapt. Ch., Tucson, 1977-79, Hillsboro (Oreg.) First Bapt. Ch., 1980—. Chaplain Oreg. Legislature, Salem, 1985—; del. Rep. Nat. Conv., New Orleans, 1988; chmn. Hillsboro Mayors Prayer Breakfast Com., 1986-88; vol. police chaplain City of Hillsboro, 1982—; long range planning com. mem. Hillsboro C. of C., 1990—. Recipient Sr. Achievement award Western Conservative Bapt. Sem., 1977, Am. Legion Citizenship award, 1964. Mem. Oreg. Assn. Evangs. (v.p. 1991—, exec. com. 1987—), Lower Columbia Assn. (chmn. camping com. 1982-87). Republican. Home: 2754 SE Brent Hillsboro OR 97123 Office: First Bapt Ch 177 NE Lincoln PO Box 186 Hillsboro OR 97123 *The great adventure of life is to discover the plans that the Creator has set before us, and this is only realized by knowing the Creator Himself through His son, Jesus the Christ.*

CARPENTER, JAMES ALLEN, minister; b. Houston, Sept. 24, 1936; s. Allen Lawrence and Ninnah Leona (Thurmond) C.; m. Dolly Syletta Still, June 7, 1958; children: Lydia, Ninnah. BA, Johnson Bible Coll., 1958; MDiv, Christian Theol. Seminary, 1966; D Ministry, Phillips U., 1982. Ordained to ministry Christian Ch., 1957. Pastor Blvd. Christian Ch., Balt., 1958-62, Christian Ch., Edwardsport, Ind., 1962-66, Bethany Christian Ch., Detroit, 1966-73, Community Christian Ch., Manchester, Mo., 1973-76; sr. pastor Midwest Blvd. Christian Ch., Midwest City, Okla., 1976-86, First Christian Ch., Noblesville, Ind., 1986—. Author: Faith in Action, 1975. Pres. Mid-Del Group Homes, Inc., Midwest City, 1982-84; dir. Hamilton County Emergency Shelter, Noblesville, 1987. Named Outstanding Vol., Okla. Dept Human Services, 1985. Democrat. Lodge: Kiwanis. Home: 7695 Creekside Ct Noblesville IN 46060 Office: First Christian Church PO Box 189 Noblesville IN 46060

CARPENTER, JOHN LORING, minister; b. Providence, Oct. 27, 1948; s. Cheslie N. and Delight (Swanson) C.; m. MaryAnne Gorman, June 6, 1970; children: John, Christine, Rebekah. BSBA, Babson Coll., 1969; MDiv, Colgate-Rochester Div. Sch., 1973. Ordained to ministry Am. Bapt. Chs. in the U.S.A., 1972. Pastor, Hague Bapt. Ch., N.Y., 1972-74, Voluntown Bapt. Ch., Conn., 1974-80, 1st Bapt. Ch., Middletown, N.Y., 1980-81; adminstr. Camp Koinonia, Geneva, Ohio, 1982-84; sr. pastor 1st Bapt. Ch., Bridgeport, Conn., 1985-89; pastor The Congl. Ch., West Newbury, Mass., 1989—; mem. dept. camps and confs. Ohio Bapt. Conv., 1982-84; treas. Coun. Chs. Greater Bridgeport, 1986-89; pres. Bd. Campus Ministry, U.

Bridgeport, 1986-89; sec. Greater Bridgeport Evang. Fellowship; ch. growth assoc. Inst. for Am. Ch. Growth; founder Alpha Home, Inc., 1988-89, also bd. dirs.; founding bd. dirs., treas. Habitat for Humanity, Lower Merrimac Valley, 1990—. Mem. adv. bd. Parents Anonymous Lake County, Ohio, 1983-84; basketball coach, 1983-89. Recipient Ecumenical Ministry award Coun. Chs. Greater Bridgeport, 1988. Mem. Ministers Council Am. Bapt. Ch., Am. Camping Assn., Christian Camping Internat. Home: 7 Chestnut Hill St West Newbury MA 01985

CARPENTER, M. RICK, minister; b. Dothan, Ala., May 23, 1950; s. Marion Coolidge and Linnie (Godfrey) C.; m. Deborah Kay Meredith, Jan. 1976; children: Landon Godfrey, Logan Meredith. AA, Wallace Jr. Coll., Dothan, 1970; BA, Samford U., 1972; MRE, So. Bapt. Theol. Sem., 1974. Ordained to ministry So. Bapt. Conv., 1979. Min. youth Milltown (Ind.) Bapt. Ch., 1972-73; min. edn. and youth Eastwood Bapt. Ch., Bowling Green, Ky., 1974-78; min. youth and recreation Judson Bapt. Ch., Nashville, 1978-82, min. adminstrn. pastoral care, 1982—; summer missionary Jonah Missions, Birmingham, Ala., 1971-73. Author: (musical drama) A Special Place, 1986; contbr. articles to Ch. Adminstrn. Mag. Bd. dirs. Maplewood Homeowners Assn., Franklin, Tenn., 1985-88. Mem. Nat. Assn. Ch. Bus. Adminstrn. (pres. Music City chpt. 1989-90), So. Bapt. Assn. Ch. Bus. Adminstrn. Home: 202 Julia Ct Franklin TN 37064 Office: Judson Bapt Ch 4900 Franklin Rd Nashville TN 37220 *Our sons often respond to seeming injustice with, "That's not fair." My latest response is, "Whoever told you life is fair?" Beautiful, yes. Fulfilling, yes. But, fair? The challenge of life is not in finding "A fair shake," but in dealing fairly with others.*

CARPENTER, MICHAEL JAMES, minister; b. Hamilton, Ohio, Dec. 9, 1943; s. Glenn and Anita Elsie (Thompson) C.; m. Kitty Lynn Noland, June 15, 1963; children: Michael Christopher, Matthew Glenn. AA, Ea. Bapt. Sem., Milford, Ohio, 1967, BA, 1968, MA, 1969; PhD, Covington Theol. Sem., Rossville Ga., 1981. Ordained to ministry Ind. Bapt. Ch. Pastor asst. Fairmont Bapt. Ch., Kettering, Ohio, 1964-65; pastor Calvary Bapt. Temple, Burnside, Ky., 1965-67; pastor asst. Fairmont Bapt. Ch., Kettering, 1967-69; pastor First Bapt. Ch., Frankton, Ind., 1969-76, Loveland Park Bapt. Ch., Loveland, Ohio, 1977—; bus. dir. Gospel Bapt. Ch., Montgomery, Ohio, 1975-76; jail pastor Warren County Jail, lebanon, Ohio, 1981—. Ky. Col., 1988—. Mem. Southwide Bapt. Fellowship, CCCV. Home: 2200 Rose Dr Loveland OH 45140 Office: Loveland Park Bapt Ch 2288 Lilac Dr Loveland OH 45140

CARPENTER, THOMAS ROBERTS, JR., minister; b. Washington, June 14, 1955; s. Thomas Roberts and Shirley Ann (Shriver) C.; m. Patricia Lynn Hartley, Oct. 27, 1973; children: Angela Dawn, Thomas Roberts III. BA, Trinity Bapt. Coll., 1983; MDiv, Luther Rice Sem., 1991. Ordained to ministry Bapt. Ch., 1983. Deacon Victory Bapt. Ch., Mechanicsville, Md., 1979, interim pastor, 1980; tchr. Trinity Bapt. Ch., Jacksonville, Fla., 1980-81, bus capt., 1981-83; founding pastor Ind. Bapt. Ch., Silver Spring, Md., 1983—; tchr. Ind. Bapt. Inst., Clinton, Md., 1989—; owner Ind. Reprographic Svcs., Camp Springs, Md., 1990—; missionary Bapt. Internat. Missions Inc., Chattanooga, 1988-90. Campaign asst. Montgomery County Rep. Party, 1988. With USN, 1973-80. Mem. Trinitarian Bible Soc., Trinity Coll. Alumni Assn. (pres. 1985-86).

CARPENTER, WALTER J(ULIAND) G(RANT), minister; b. Elmira, N.Y., Apr. 16, 1939; s. Juliand Grant and Augusta (Shaul) C. BS, Cornell U., 1961; MS, U. R.I., 1963; postgrad., Wesley Theol. Sem., Washington, 1986. Lic. preacher United Meth. Ch., 1981; ordained to ministry as deacon, 1990. Min. visitation Drew United Meth. Ch., Carmel, N.Y., 1981-86; pastor Germantown & Elizaville (N.Y.) United Meth. Chs., 1986-88; pastor chs. Germantown, Elizaville, West Taghkanic, Glenco Mills, N.Y., 1988—; chair dist. stewardship work area Hudson East Dist. of N.Y. Ann. Conf. United Meth. Ch., 1990-91, vice chair dist. coun. on ministries, 1989-90, chair, 1990-91, mem. com. on superintendency, 1986-91, nominations com., 1987-90, conf. suicide task force, 1989-91, spl. conf. stewardship task force, 1990-91; co-vice chair Bishop's Convocation, 1989-90, co-chair, 1990-91; mem. Columbia Coun. Chs., 1989-91, Germantown Clergy Group, 1987-91; bus. mgr. N.Y. Coop. Sch. Christian Missions, 1975-77. Editor Parish News, 1987-91; contbr. articles to profl. jours. Past charter mem. Putnam Symphony Orch. Com.; Putnam County Mediation Com.; past trustee Putnam Arts Coun.; mem. Germantown's Substance Abuse Program, 1989-91, Germantown's Emergency Program, 1990-91. Recipient Disting. Svc. award Nat. Assn. County Agrl. Agts., 1986, others. Mem. Nat. Fellowship Assoc. and Local Pastors, Order of St. Luke, Order of St. Luke the Physician, Sigma Xi, Phi Kappa Phi, Phi Sigma, Alpha Zeta. Republican. Home and Office: 26 Camp Creek Rd Germantown NY 12526-5313 *Life without Christ as the core is meaningless. Fullness of life comes when one becomes empty. Strength comes through faith and trust in the Living Christ. One's independence depends on dependence on God through Christ. Life is more than just possessing things: it's giving and receiving.*

CARPINO, FRANCESCO CARDINAL, former archbishop of Palermo; b. Palazzolo Acreide, Italy, May 18, 1905; Ordained priest Roman Catholic Ch., 1927; ordained titular archbishop of Nicomedia and coadjutor archbishop of Monreale, 1951, archbishop of Monreale, 1951-61; titular archbishop of Sardica, 1961; assessor Sacred Consistorial Congregation, 1961; pro-prefect of Sacred Congregation of the Council, 1967; elevated to Sacred Coll. of Cardinals, 1967; archbishop of Palermo, 1967-70; entered order of cardinal bishops as titular bishop of Albano, 1978. Referendary of the Congregation of Bishops, 1970. Mem. Council for Public Affairs of the Ch., Congregation, Tribunal, Causes of Saints, Apostolic Signatura. Office: Piazza St Calisto 16, I-00153 Rome Italy

CARR, ANNE ELIZABETH, theology educator; b. Chgo., Nov. 11, 1934; d. Frank James and Dorothy Margaret (Graber) C. AB, Mundelein Coll., 1956; AM, Marquette U., 1963, U. Chgo., 1968; PhD, U. Chgo., 1971. Instr. Mundelein Coll., Chgo., 1963-66, asst. prof., 1971-73; asst. prof. Ind. U., Bloomington, 1971-73; asst. prof., asst. dean U. Chgo. Divinity Sch., 1975-78, assoc. prof., assoc. dean, 1978-88, prof., 1988—; Donnelian vis. prof. Trinity Coll., Dublin, Ireland, 1983. Author: Theological Method of K. Rahner, 1977, Transforming Grace, 1988, Search for Wisdom and Spirit, 1988; editor: (with E.S. Fiorenza), Women, Work, and Poverty, 1987, Motherhood: Experience, Institution, Theology, 1989, Women's Special Nature? 1991; bd. cons. Jour. of Religion, 1975-86, co-editor, 1987—; assoc. editor Horizons, 1974—; editorial bd. Concilium, 1985-91. Trustee Mundelein Coll., Chgo., 1977-91. Postdoctoral fellow Harvard Divinity Sch., 1983-84. Mem. Am. Acad. Religion (program com. 1978-80), Cath. Theol. Soc. Am., Coll. Theology Soc. Roman Catholic. Office: U Chgo Divinity Sch 1025 E 58th St Chicago IL 60637

CARR, CALVIN JOHNSON, youth minister; b. Jacksonville, Fla., July 13, 1960; s. C.J. Carr and Christine (Warren) Boote; m. Kelly Brannen Carr, May 1, 1982; children: Paul Johnson, Katherine Leigh, Rachel Christine. BA, U. Fla., 1982; MDiv, Southwestern Bapt. Theol. Sem., 1985. Ordained to ministry Bapt. Ch., 1985. Asst. youth minister North Cen. Bapt. Ch., Gainesville, Fla., 1982; summer missionary Santa Fe River Bapt. Assn., Gainesville, 1982; youth pastor Oak Park Bapt. Ch., Gainesville, 1982; summer youth activities dir. Prestonwood Bapt. Ch., Dallas, 1984; assoc. pastor to youth North Cen. Bapt. Ch., Gainesville, 1985-89; sr. high youth ednl. dir. First Bapt. Ch., Jacksonville, 1989—; speaker various chs. and groups, 1985—. Avocations: running, racquet sports. Office: First Bapt Ch 124 W Ashley St Jacksonville FL 32202

CARR, CAROLYN SUE DEAN, religious organization meeting planner; b. Tonapah, Nev., May 31, 1943; d. John Thomas Dean and Laura Frank (Lofland) Rhoads; m. Harold Lawrence Carr, 1963; children: Jason Anthony, Dena Gale. BS magna cum laude, U. No. Tex., 1977. Cert. meeting profl. Adminstrv. asst. Annuity Bd. So. Bapt. Conv., Dallas, 1977-82, meeting coord., 1982—; seminar instr. Religious Mgmt. Conf. Assn., 1988-90; grad. MPI Inst. I and II; pub. speaker to various profl. groups. V.p. Girls Softball League, Carrollton, Farmers Br., Tex., 1983-85; leadership tng. Boy Scouts Am., Carrollton, Farmers Br., 1983-85; CPR instr. ARC, Dallas, 1983-90; counselor N.W. Dallas County Crises Ctr., Carrollton. Recipient Tuition grant, Meeting Planners Internat., Dallas, 1989. Mem. Meeting Planners Internat. (bd. dirs. 1988-89, nominee Meeting Planner of Yr. 1988), Religious Cong. Mgmt. Assn. (bd. dirs. 1988-91), Diversity (pres. 1981-82, program dir. 1979-81). Republican. Avocation: gardening. Home: Rt 2 Box 109 A-3 Point TX 75472 Office: Annuity Bd So Bapt Conv 2401 Cedar Springs Dallas TX 75201 *Forgiveness is a vital key to finding joy.*

CARR, CHARLES LOUIS, religious organization administrator; b. Rockport, Ind., Sept. 9, 1930; s. Louis E. and Loris B. (Lindsey) C.; m. Shirley R. Cron, Nov. 15, 1950; children: Kathleen Carr Wright, Charles Stephen, Jeffrey Louis, David Wayne. Student, Ind. State U., 1949-50, Oakland City Coll., 1958-59, So. Bapt. Theol. Sem., 1965-67. Ordained to ministry Gen. Assn. Gen. Bapts., 1957. Pastor East Oolitic Gen. Bapt. Ch., Bedford, Ind., 1959-63, Mt. Zion Gen. Bapt. Ch., Indpls., 1963-65, Hunsinger Lane Gen. Bapt. Ch., Louisville, 1965-67; missionary to Saipan Mariana Islands, 1967-73; exec. dir. Gen. Bapt. Fgn. Mission Soc., Poplar Bluff, Mo., 1973—. Editor: Capsule; contbr. articles to various publs. Mem. Am. Soc. Missiology, Evang. Fgn. Missions Assn. Home: 706 S 9th St Poplar Bluff MO 63901 Office: 100 Stinson Dr Poplar Bluff MO 63901

CARR, GARY, priest, elementary educator; b. St. Louis, Apr. 11, 1954; s. Russell Michael and Jeanne Teresa (King) C. BS in Elem. Edn., Southeast Mo. State U., 1978; MSDiv, Josephinum Theology Sem., 1982; postgrad., DePaul U., St. Mary's Coll. Sem., Perryville, Mo. Ordained priest Roman Cath. Ch.; cert. tchr., Mo. Tchr. Immaculate Conception Sch., Springfield, Mo.; tchr., vice-prin. St. Peter's Cath. Middle Sch., Joplin, Mo.; priest Diocese of Springfield, Cape Girardeau, Mo.; pastor, tchr., vice-prin. St. Teresa Cath. Sch., Glennonville, Mo.

CARR, HARRY ELWOOD, minister; b. Elizabethtown, Ill., May 29, 1932; s. James Roy and Ollen Remona (Page) C.; m. Opal Alberta Brandt, July 16, 1951; children: Salinda Ann LaTurneau, David Michael, Lisa Janna Montgomery. Grad., Evang. Tchrs. Tng. Assn., 1949; student, Oakland Community Coll., 1969-71; BRE, Midwestern Bapt. Coll., 1980, DD, 1983; MA, Bapt. Christian U., 1989. Ordained to ministry Bapt. Ch., 1954. Pastor New Home Social Brethren Ch., Eddyville, Ill., 1953-57, Cedar Grove Social Brethren Ch., Glendale, Ill., 1955-56, Bethesda Social Brethren Ch., Herod, Ill., 1955-57, Union Social Brethren Ch., Golconda, Ill., 1957-59, Palestine Social Brethren Ch., Stonefort, Ill., 1957-60, Spring Valley Social Brethren Ch., Harrisburg, Ill., 1960-67, First Social Brethren Ch., Pontiac, Mich., 1967-76; founder, pastor Shalom Bapt. Ch., Pontiac, 1976—; dir., founder Shalom Bapt. Bible Classes, Orion, Mich., 1986—; instr. Bible dept. Midwestern Bapt. Coll., Pontiac, 1980—, chmn. dept. Christian ministries, 1989, trustee to bd., 1987—; moderator Union Assn. Chs., 1956, 57, 62, 63, 64, Gen. Assembly Social Brethren, 1971-73, Midwestern Assn. Chs., 1973-75, Presbytery; sec.-treas. Bd. Christian Edn., Midwestern Assn. Social Brethren, 1968-76; mem. Union and Midwestern Assn. Missionary Bd., 1967-76; sec. Greater Pontiac Area Minister's Fellowship, 1971-72, pres., 1973-75. Author workbooks for Midwestern Bapt. Coll. Office: Shalom Bapt Ch 3400 Morgan Rd Orion MI 48359

CARR, JAY D., minister; b. Joliet, Ill., Mar. 6; s. Jewell Dean and Mary Janet (Lawrence) C.; m. Brenda Lynn Cook, Dec. 12, 1981; children: Jason David, Joshua Daniel. AA, Joliet Coll., 1979; BMus, No. Ill. U., 1981; MDiv, Garrett-Evang., Evanston, Ill., 1984; D of Ministry, McCormick Theol. Sem., 1990. Ordained to ministry United Meth. Ch., 1984. Asst. pastor Tinley Park (Ill.) United Meth. Ch., 1982-84; pastor Malden (Ill.) United Meth. Ch., 1984-86; assoc. pastor First United Meth. Ch., Dixon, Ill., 1986-89; pastor Prairie United Meth. Ch., Oswego, Ill., 1989—; tchr. Sch. Relgion, Oswego, Ill., 1990—; asst. sec. No. Ill. Conf., Chgo., 1989—; mem. rsch. and planning, Chgo., 1988—. Bd. dirs. Ct. Appointed Spl. Advocates, Dixon, 1989; steering com. Farm Crisis Support, Princeton, 1985; chair Food for Sharing, DeKalb, Ill., 1987-88. Hunt scholar McCormick Theol. Sem., 1990. Mem. Oswego Coun. Chs. (treas. 1990—), Phi Kappa Phi. Home: 75 Wolf Rd Oswego IL 60543 *The real challenge facing the church today is whether or not it will assert its moral and ethical authority as we continue to struggle with societal dilemmas.*

CARR, JOHN F., minister; b. Donalsonville, Ga., Sept. 27, 1932; s. Frank Samuel and Lillie Mae (Ward) C.; m. Nancy Jean Kinnett, Sept. 1, 1956; children: John Franklin Jr., Richard Dabney. AA, Norman Coll., 1951; BA, Mercer U., 1953; B of Div., So. Bapt. Theol. Seminary, 1956. Ordained to ministry Bapt. Ch., 1956. Pastor Bethany and Mountain Hill Bapt. Chs., Pine Mountain, Ga., 1956-59, Bethsaida Bapt. Ch., Dublin, Ga., 1959-63, Ellaville (Ga.) Bapt. Ch., 1963-75; area missionary Altamaha, Consolation, Southeast Assns., Brunswick, Ga., 1975—. Avocation: philately. Office: SE Area Mission Program 2410 Ellis St Brunswick GA 31520

CARR, JOHN MARK, minister, customs brokerage firm representative; b. Danville, Ill., Mar. 20, 1953; s. John Paul and Betty Lee (Brattain) C.; m. Kathy Jean Iman, Aug. 8, 1981; children: John Michael, James Matthew, Kara Jean, Jared Mark. BA in Christian Ministries, Cin. Bible Coll., 1975; student, Cin. Christian Sem., 1980-81, Ball State U., 1981; BS, Ind. U.-Purdue U., Indpls., 1984; postgrad. in edn., Liberty U., 1989-90. Ordained to ministry Chs. of Christ, 1975. Assoc. minister Southglen Christian Ch., Anchorage, 1984, Homer (Alaska) Christian Ch., 1984-85; elementary tchr. Indpls. Pub. Schs., 1985-89; elem. tchr. Anchorage Sch. Dist., 1989-90; tech. svcs. rep. Fritz Co., Inc., 1990—. Ofcl. observer CAP, Homer, 1984-85; mem. South Peninsula Amateur Radio Club, Homer, 1984-85; insp. Rep. Party, Indpls., 1985-88; mem. Parkside Christian Ch., Anchorage, 1989-90, Palmer (Alaska) Christian Ch., 1990—. Avocations: amateur radio, outdoor sports, spectator sports. Home: PO Box 3205 Palmer AK 99645

CARR, MARY ELIZABETH, lay worker; b. Anniston, Ala., Jan. 21, 1925; d. Robert Bryan and Chollie Mae (House) C. Student, U. Ala., 1948, Huntingdon Coll., 1957. Youth dir. St. Mark's Meth. Ch., Montgomery, Ala., 1956; youth, recreation dir. 1st United Meth. Ch., Montgomery, Ala.; youth dir. Grace Episcopal Ch., Anniston, Ala., 1975-85, chalice bearer, 1990-; personnel, camp dir. Presbyn. Home for Children, Talladega, Fla., 1988-91. Recipient Betty Carr Service to Youth, Anniston YMCA, 1986, Paul Grist Service to youth Southeast YMCA, Blue Ridge Assembly, 1985. Democrat. Home: 619 Goodwin St Anniston AL 36201

CARR, NORINE JOYCE, minister; b. St. Louis, Oct. 29, 1937; d. Eugene Stuart and Lillian Bush (Hedrick) Ansley; m. James Ray, Oct. 12, 1962 (div. Jan. 1971); 1 child, Curtis Ray; m. Donald E. Carr, July 6, 1991. Cert., Candler Sch. Theology, 1978. Ordained to ministry United Meth. Ch., 1979. Ch. sec. St. Matthew United Meth. Ch., Belleville, Ill., 1968-75, adminstrv. asst., 1975-78, ch. bus. adminstr., 1978-79, diaconal minister ch. bus. adminstrn., 1979-91; dir. Christian edn. 1st Presbyn. Ch., Lexington, Ky., 1991—. Fellow Nat. Assn. Ch. Bus. Adminstrs.; mem. UMACBA (exec. bd., mem. at large 1985-89), Christian Ministry Mgmt. Assn. Home: 1424 Blanche Dr Belleville IL 62223 Office: 1st Presbyn Ch 171 Market St Lexington KY 40510

CARRAL, ANSELMO, ecumenical agency administrator. Pres. Austin (Tex.) Met. Ministries. Office: Austin Met Ministries 44 East Ave Ste 302 Austin TX 78701*

CARRANZA, ANDRES, lay worker; b. Mexico City, Mexico, Oct. 20, 1951; came to U.S., 1989.; s. Alberto and Domitila (Mayen) C.; m. Gail Ellen Hobson, Dec. 1, 1984. DVM, Nat. U. Mexico, 1988; MA in Theology Studies, No. Bapt. Theol. Sem., 1991; MDiv, McCormick Theol. Sem., Chgo., 1991. Mem. campus staff Campus Crusade for Christ, Mexico City, 1971-74, 77-78, Villahermosa, Tabaso, 1975-76; S.E. area dir. Campus Crusade for Christ, Villahermosa, Tabasco, 1978-79; No. area dir. Campus Crusade for Christ, Chihuahua, 1983-84; campus staff Nat. U. Campus Crusade for Christ, Mexico City, 1984-86; coord. Jesus Film Ministry Campus Crusade for Christ, Morelos State, 1986-88; del., tchr. Nat. Evang. Youth Congress, Campus Crusade for Christ, Cuernavaca, Morelos, 1975; del. Alternative '82 Evangelism Congress, Mexico City, 1982; del. Nat. Congress for Pastors and Christian Leaders, Oaxtepec, Mexico, 1984; del., tchr., organizer Explo '85 Nat. Congress in Evangelism Discipleship and Missions, Mexico City, 1985; coord. med. and social svc. brigades Campus Crusade for Christ, Morelos, Guerrero, 1986-87; coord. outreach Emmanuel Presbyn. Ch., Chgo., 1990-91. Sec. appointment com. Tchrs. Union, Superior Inst. Agr. Guerrero, Iguala, 1981, high sch. tchr., Agrl. Tng. Ctr., Huitzuco; coll. tchr. Superior Inst. of Agr., Iguala, 1980-82, coord. social svcs. Agrl. Tng. Ctr., Huitzuco, 1980-82, tchr. and community devel. bee farming, Huitzuco and Iguala. Home: 322 N Princeton Apt B Villa Park IL 60181 *During my generation I have seen men and women who don't profess any faith do great things, and I have seen men and women who claim to have much faith, yet achieve very little. I believe we should be men and women of both faith and action.*

CARRAS, GEORGE PETER, educator; b. Turlock, Calif., Jan. 27, 1950; s. Peter George and Vivian (Mageras) C.; m. Elizabeth Carol Chaffee, Dec. 20, 1974; children: Jonathan, Joel, Megan. BA with honors, U. Calif., Berkeley, 1974; diploma theology, Regent Coll., Vancouver, B.C., 1979; MA in Bibl. Criticism, Manchester U., Eng., 1982; postgrad., U. Oxford, Eng., 1984-90, PhD, 1989. Tutor N.T. Lady Margaret Hall, Queens Coll., U. Oxford, 1984-88; lectr. in theology London U., 1987-89; vis. prof. new testament Gonzaga U., Spokane, Wash., 1989-90; lectr. in N.T. Mansfield Coll., Oxford U., 1983-90; postdoctoral fellow U. Calif., Berkeley, 1991-92; coll. dean Mansfield Coll., U. Oxford, 1985-88; mem. faculty theology U. Oxford, 1983-90; vis. rsch. scholar Grad. Theol. Union, Berkeley, 1988-89, Ctr. for Jewish Studies, Berkeley, 1991-92. Contbr. articles to profl. jours. Rsch. stipend Christ Ch. Coll., U. Oxford, 1980-82; Denyer and Johnson student U. Oxford, 1981-83; Hall-Houghton student in Bibl. Studies, U. Oxford, 1981-83. Mem. Brit. Assn. for Jewish Studies, European Assn. of Jewish Studies, Am. Acad. Religion, Soc. Bibl. Lit. Democrat. Home: N 10708 Nelson Rd Spokane WA 99218 Office: U Calif Dept Nr Ea Studies Berkeley CA 94720

CARRASCO BRICENO, BARTOLOME, archbishop; b. Tlaxco, Mex., Aug. 18, 1918. Ordained priest Roman Cath. Ch., 1945. named bishop of Huejutla, Mex., 1963, titular bishop of Claterna, 1967, bishop of Tapachula, 1971; named archbishop of Antequera, Oaxaca, Mex., 1976. Address: Diocese of Oaxaca, Apartado Postal 31, Oaxaca City Oaxaca, Mexico

CARR-HAMILTON, JACQUELINE DIANE, minister, educator; b. Washington, Aug. 24, 1951; d. James David and Willie Marion (Durham) Carr; divorced; 1 child, Felicia Milaya Hamilton. BA in Philosphy and Religion, Monmouth Coll., 1976; M Div, cert. tchr. English, Princeton Theol. Sem. and Princeton U., 1979; postgrad., Drew U., 1985—. Ordained to ministry Bapt. Ch., 1985. Assoc. minister Second Bapt. Ch., Asbury Pk., N.J., 1975—; chaplain Phila. House of Corrections, Holmsberg Prison, Phila., 1978-79; tchr. St. Benedict's Prep. Sch., Newark, 1979-81; sec., library asst. Ft. Monmouth, Drew U., U. Va., NYU, 1981—. Author plays The Prophets, Moses and Me, 1978-79, How I Got Over, 1983, Gonna Move a Mountain, 1983. Chairperson Dr. Martin Luther King, Jr. Com., Asbury and Neptune, N.J., 1981-87. Named one of Outstanding Young Women Am., 1982; Benjamin Mays fellow Princeton Theol. Sem., 1978-79. Mem. NAACP. Avocations: piano, tennis, swimming, skating, reading. Home: 203 Belmar Ave Neptune NJ 07753 Office: Second Bapt Ch Asbury Park NJ

CARRICK-SCHREIBER, CHARLES RAPHAEL, minister; b. Clinton, Md., Apr. 3, 1961; s. Charles Raphael and Violet Ella (Fonner) Carrick; m. Linda Maries Schreiber, Sept. 8, 1984; 1 child, Jordan Charles. BS in Computer Sci., Drexel U., 1984; MDiv, Yale Divinity Sch., 1987. Ordained to ministry United Meth. Ch., 1989. Asst. chaplain United Meth. Home for Children, Phila., 1984-85; asst. pastor Diamond Hill United Meth. Ch., Cos Cob, Conn., 1985-87; assoc. pastor St. John's United Meth. Ch., Ivyland, Pa., 1987-89; exec. dir. Hazleton (Pa.) Enlarged Ministry, 1989—; commn. mem. United Ministries in Higher Edn. in Pa., 1987—. Pres. Big Bros./Big Sisters Hazleton, 1990-91; chairperson child advocacy com. Child Adv. Com., Hazleton, 1990—; bd. dirs. Serento Gardens Drug & Alcohol Svcs., Hazleton, 1990—. Democrat. Office: Hazleton Enlarged Ministry 314 W Broad St Hazleton PA 18201

CARRIER, HERVE, priest, sociology educator; b. Grand-Mere, Que., Can., Aug. 26, 1921; s. Fortunat and Cora (Gelinas) C. B.A., U. Montreal, Que., 1944; M.A. in Sociology, Cath. U. Am., 1953; Dr. Sociology, Sorbonne, Paris, 1959; Hum.D. (hon.), Sogang U., Seoul, 1970, Fu Jan Cath. U., Taipei, Republic of China, 1975. Joined S.J., 1944; ordained priest Roman Catholic Ch., 1955, licentiate in Theology, Montreal. Prof. sociology Gregorian U., Rome, 1959—, rector, 1966-78; sec. Pontificial Council for Culture, Vatican City, 1982—. Author: Sociology of Religious Belonging, 1965; Higher Education facing New Cultures, 1982; Cultures: Notre Avenir, 1985, Gospel Message and Human Cultures, 1989, The Social Doctrine of the Church Revisited, 1990, Evangélisation et Développment des Cultures, 1990. Decorated officer Legion of Honor (France). Mem. Royal Soc. Can., Internat. Fedn. Cath. Univs. (pres. 1970-80). Home: Piazza della Pilotta 4, 00187 Rome Italy Office: Pontifical Council for Culture, Vatican City Vatican City

CARRINGTON, JAMES DONALD, minister; b. Pitts., Sept. 25, 1933; s. Edward and Susie Mae (Jones) C.; m. Doris Jones, Apr. 9, 1960; children: Darlene Denise Carrington Haynes, Roderick. BTh, Reed Coll. of Religion, 1964; DD, Reed Christian Coll. and Sem., 1981. Ordained to ministry Bapt. Ch., 1958. Pastor Friendship Bapt. Ch., Yorba Linda, Calif., 1964—; v.p. Am. Bapt. Chs. of Pacific S.W., 1984, pres., 1985, bd. mgrs., 1991—; bd. dirs. Am. Bapt. Chs. U.S.A., 1986—, Am. Bapt. Credit Union, 1991—, Bapt. World Alliance, 1991—, Mins. and Missionaries Bd., 1991—. V.p. Orange County Br. NAACP; advisor Calif. State U., Fullerton Martin Luther King, Jr. Com.; mem. Fullerton Police Community Coun., North Orange County Fair Housing Adv. Bd., Youth Devel. Coun., Minority Adv. Bd.; pres. Am. Bapt. Black Caucus of Pacific S.W., 1984. Named Man of Yr. Ford Motor Co. of Orange County, 1971. Office: Friendship Bapt Ch 17145 Bastanchury Rd Yorba Linda CA 92686

CARRINGTON, SHIRLEY STANCIL RICE, minister, educator; b. Balt., June 27, 1934; d. Ocar and Blanche (Cornick) Stancil; m. Edward W. Rice, Sept. 11, 1954 (div. June 1962); children: Edwin, Pamela; m. William Arthur Carrington,July 23, 1962; 1 child, Prayera. BS, Morgan State U., 1969; MA, St. Mary Sem., 1983; MDiv, Howard U., 1990. Ordained to ministry United Meth. Ch. Religious educator Calvary Bapt. Ch., Balt., 1978-90; organist, educator Lewin United Meth. Ch., Balt., 1978-91. Recipient Ford Found. grant Howard U., 1989-90. Mem. NAACP, Black Seminarians Inc. Home: 3708 Campfield Rd Baltimore MD 21207

CARROLL, MONSIGNOR AIDAN M., academic administrator. Supt. Dept. Cath. Schs., L.A. Office: Cath Schs Dept Office of Supt 1520 W 9th St Los Angeles CA 90015*

CARROLL, BENJAMIN FRANKLIN, JR., minister; b. Buckner, Ark., Sept. 11, 1932; s. Benjamin Franklin Sr. and Era Letha (Mayfield) C.; m. Sadie Namoi McKamie, May 22, 1955. BSE, U. Cen. Ark., 1962; MDiv, Southwest Bapt. Theol. Sem., Ft. Worth, Tex., 1972. Cert. secondary sci. tchr. Minister First Bapt. Ch., Pocola, Okla., 1966-69, Foreman, Ark., 1972-79, Oil City, La., 1979—; chmn. Camp Bethany Com., 1983-87; mem., exec. bd. Ark. Bapt. Conv., 1976-78; stewardship and budget com. mem. Northwest La. Bapt. Assn., 1989—. Pres. Ministerial Alliance, Foreman, 1972-79. Recipient Pub. Sch. Vol. award Dist. Sch. Bd., Oil City, 1981. Mem. Kiwanis, Masons. Republican. Home: PO Box 398 Oil City LA 71061 Office: First Baptist Ch PO Box 298 Oil City LA 71061

CARROLL, CECIL EARL, retired minister; b. Corinth, Miss., Mar. 11, 1925; s. Walter and Ruby (Strickland) C.; married; children: Judith, Marcell, Duane. AB, South Western Bapt. Theol. Sem, Ft. Worth, 1961. Minister edn. and youth Ellison Bapt., Memphis, 1961-62; with First Bapt. Ch., North Little Rock, Ark., 1963-65; minister edn. and youth Ellison Bapt., Memphis, 1968-90. Probation officer Juvenile Ct., Memphis, 1968-76. Home: 3643 Wilshire Memphis TN 38111 Office: VIP Tours Sr Citizens Christian Tours 3643 Wilshire Memphis TN 38111

CARROLL, CLIFFORD ANDREW, priest, educator; b. Duluth, Minn., Apr. 23, 1906; s. Andrew P. and Nellie (Beladeau) C. AB, Santa Clara U., 1932, Gonzaga U., 1933; AM, Gonzaga U., 1934; S.T.L., Alma Coll., Calif., 1942; PhD, St. Louis U., 1946. Joined S.J., Roman Cath. Ch., 1928; ordained priest, 1941. Instr. Seattle Coll., 1935-38, vis. prof., 1942; dean Gonzaga U. Sch. Econs. and Bus., Spokane, Wash., 1945-53, regent, 1953-63, dir. librs., prof., 1963-73, archivist, adj. prof., 1973—; chmn. Pacific N.W. Cath. Regional Libr. Conf., 1961-63; mem. Adv. Coun. on Librs., Office of

Gov. of Wash., 1971—. Mem. Am. Arbitration Assn. (nat. panel), Am. Econ. Assn., Cath. Econ. Assn., Royal Econ. Soc., Indsl. Rels. Inst. Address: Gonzaga U Spokane WA 99258

CARROLL, DANIEL THOMAS, priest, counselor; b. Chgo., Apr. 6, 1934; s. Daniel Thomas and Lillian Ruth (Hogle) C. BA in Philosophy, St. Bonaventure U., 1958; MS in Edn., Chgo. State U., 1974. Ordained priest Roman Cath. Ch. 1960. Tchr., counselor Mt. Carmel High Sch., Chgo., 1961-68, counselor, 1974-78; tchr., counselor De Sales High Sch., Louisville, 1969-79. Avocations: athletics, listening to jazz music. Home and Office: 6428 S Dante Ave Chicago IL 60637

CARROLL, FRANCIS P., archbishop. Archbishop of Canberra and Goulburn, Roman Cath. Ch., Australia. Office: Archbishop Canberra and Goulburn, PO Box 89, Canberra ACT 2601, Australia*

CARROLL, HOWARD W., school system administrator. Supt. schs. Office of Edn., Diocese of Sioux Falls, Iowa. Office: Diocesan Edn Supt 3000 W 41st St Ste 126 Sioux Falls IA 57105*

CARROLL, JACKSON WALKER, theology educator; b. Chester, S.C., Jan. 29, 1932; s. Jackson Walker and Eileen (Little) C.; m. Jo Anne Ewing, Aug. 25, 1954; children: Susan Ewing, Frances Carroll Strumph. AB magna cum laude, Wofford Coll., Spartansburg, S.C., 1953; BD, Duke U., 1956; PhD, Princeton Theol. Sem., 1970. Asst. min. St. Michael's Ch., Dumfries, Scotland, 1956-57; min. Mt. Holly Meth. Ch., Rock Hill, S.C., 1957-61; chaplain Duke U., Durham, 1961-65; lectr. Princeton U., 1968; from asst. to assoc. prof. Emory U., Atlanta, 1968-74; prof. religion and soc., dir. research Hartford (Conn.) Sem., 1974-88, v.p., 1988-89, interim pres., 1989—; mem. adv. com. research United Meth. Ch., 1972—; cons. in field. Author: Ministry as Reflective Practice, 1986; co-author: Religion in America, 1950 to the Present, 1977, Too Many Pastors?, 1980, Women of the Cloth, 1982, Handbook for Congregational Studies, 1986, also editor; editor: Small Churches Are Beautiful, 1977, Patterns of Parish Leadership, 1989. Bd. dirs. Capital Region Conf. Chs., Hartford, 1975-82; mem. Bloomfield (Conn.) Human Relations Com., 1976-82, Leadership Greater Hartford. Recipient Danforth Campus Ministry, Danforth Found., 1965-67; named one of Outstanding Young Men in Am. U.S. Jaycees, 1966; Rockefeller Found. Doctoral fellow,1967-68. Mem. Am. Sociol. Assn., So. Sociol. Soc., Assn. for the Sociol. Religion, Religious Research Assn. (pres. 1983-84), Soc. for the Sci. Study Religion (council mem. 1981-84). Democrat. Avocations: growing roses, tennis, photography, fishing. Home: 7 Bear Ridge Dr Bloomfield CT 06002 Office: Hartford Sem 77 Sherman St Hartford CT 06105

CARROLL, JOHN TIMOTHY, religion educator; b. Buffalo, Apr. 22, 1954; s. James Rose and Mildred E. (Lester) C.; m. Cynthia Ann Walker, June 2, 1977; children: Andrew Walker Carroll, Anna Lynn Walker Carroll. BA, Tulsa U., 1976; diploma in theology, Oxford (Eng.) U., 1978; MDiv, Princeton Theol. Sem., 1979, PhD, 1986. Ordained to ministry Presbyn. Ch.,1979. Assoc. pastor First Presbyn. Ch., Dearborn, Mich., 1979-82; vis. instr. Luth. Theol. Sem., Phila., 1984-86; interim pastor 1st Presbyn. Ch., Denham Springs, La., 1988-89; asst. prof. La. State U., Baton Rouge, 1986-91, assoc. prof., 1991—. Author: Response to the End of History, 1988; editor: Faith and History, 1990; contbr. articles to profl. jours. Rsch. grant La. State U. Rsch. Coun., 1987; recipient Henry Snyder Gehman Prize, Princeton Theol. Sem., 1978. Mem. Soc. Bibl. Lit. (chair group on passion narrative 1988—), Cath. Bibl. Assn., Omicron Delta Kappa. Democrat. Home: 6775 Menlo Dr Baton Rouge LA 70808 Office: La State U Program Religious Studies Baton Rouge LA 70803-3901

CARROLL, MARY ANN, philosophy educator; b. Baton Rouge, May 31, 1947; d. Frank Theodore Jr. and Patricia Ann (Farr) C.; m. Bruce Nicholas Richter, Sept. 1, 1967 (div. Dec. 1980). B.A., U. New Orleans, 1969; M.A., U. N.C., 1971, Ph.D., 1973. Lectr. U. N.C., Chapel Hill, summer 1973; asst. prof. Appalachian State U., Boone, N.C., 1973-77, assoc. prof., 1977-83, prof. philosophy, 1983—; applied ethics cons.; vis. prof. U. Richmond, 1986-87. Mem. Am. Philos. Assn., So. Soc. for Philosophy and Psychology, N.C. Philos. Soc., Am. Assn. Philosophy Tchrs. Co-author: Moral Problems in Nursing: Case Studies, 1979; Ethics in the Practice of Psychology, 1984; also book revs. Office: Appalachian State U Philosophy & Religion Dept Boone NC 28608

CARROLL, SISTER MARY TERESA, nun, religion education director; b. Canton, Mass.; d. John Francis and Helen (Guild) C. BA, Manhattan Coll., 1948; MA, Seton Hall U., 1958, postgrad. Joined Sch. Sisters of Notre Dame, Roman Cath. Ch., 1944; cert. tchr., Mass., N.H., Conn., N.Y.; cert. administr. Tchr. various schs., 1958-74, secondary sch. adminstr., 1974-82, religious edn. coord., 1982-87, pastoral asst., 1987—; adj. prof. English Bryant Coll., Smithfield, R.I., 1986—; dir. of religious edn. Diocese of Providence, Johnston, R.I., 1987—. Editor: (newsletter) Renew, 1985-88; contbr. children's stories to mags. Vol. CASA, Providence, 1985—. Recipient scholarship Wall St. Jour., N.Y., 1963, 66, award Am. Assn. Tchrs. of French, N.Y., 1966, 68, Vol. award Juv. Ct, 1970.

CARROLL, RICHARD ELLIS (DICK CARROLL), minister, educator, workshop leader, writer, actor, media consultant; b. Tampa, Fla., Dec. 22, 1955; s. James Carlton Sr. and Shirley Mae (Bailey) C.; m. Sherry Lynn McGee, July 9, 1988. BA, Palm Beach Atlantic Coll., 1981; MDiv, Southwestern Bapt. Theological Seminary, 1984, MA in Communications, 1986. Asst. dir. continuity Sta. WFUZ-FM, Ocala, Fla., 1981-82; internship in master control Sammons Cable of Ft. Worth, 1985; media cons. Rehab., Edn., Advocacy for Citizens with Handicaps, Ft. Worth, 1987-88; personal and profl. workshop leader Carroll & Carroll Enterprises, Ft. Worth, 1989—; pub. access cable producer Sammons Cable, Ft. Worth, 1986-88. Author, dir., actor Memoirs of the Fisherman; author: Three One Man Shows, 1986, (TV movie) Fire and Rain, 1989, (movies) Problem Child, 1990, Ruby, 1991. Served with U.S. Army, 1974-80. Recipient Albert G. Wade Acting Award Palm Beach Atlantic Coll., 1981, Girl Scout Svc. award, 1990; named one of Outstanding Young Men in Am. Mem. Alpha Psi Omega, Fellowship of Christian Communicators. Democrat. Avocations: writing, martial arts, swimming, scuba diving, line art. Home: 7520 Parkwood Ln Fort Worth TX 76133 Office: Carroll & Carroll Enterprises PO Box 330261 Fort Worth TX 76163-0261 *Learning to see the world through Jesus's eyes, to feel with Jesus' heart and to act with Jesus' tender touch is the only thing that will change our world.*

CARRUTH, THEODORE RAYMOND, religious educator; b. Pampa, Tex., May 20, 1941; s. Glenn Raymond and Lela Silverene (Grant) C.; m. Georgia Carolyn Ridgeway, Oct. 7, 1966; children; Amy, Ellen, Karen. BA, Harding U., 1964, ThM, 1966; PhD, BAylor U., 1973. Ordained to minstry Chs. of Christ, 1963. Instr. Lubbock (Tex.) Christian Coll., 1971-73, asst. prof., 1973-76; assoc. prof. religion David Lipscomb Coll., Nashville, 1976-83, prof., 1983—; mem. editorial bd. Restoration Quarterly, 1977—. Contbr. articles to profl. jours. Bd. dirs. Coronado Children's Home, Lubbock, 1971-76. David Lipscomb Coll. grantee, 1982; Named Outstanding Tchr., David Lipscomb Coll., 1983. Home: 755 Elysian Fields Rd Nashville TN 37204 Office: David Lipscomb Coll 3901 Granny White Pike Nashville TN 37203

CARSON, ANTHONY BRUCE, minister; b. Huntsville, Tenn., Apr. 4, 1940; s. Robert Lee Carson and Katherine Jualynn (Wright) Johnson; m. Peggy Jayne Rector, Sept. 25, 1959; children: Bruce, Lynnette, Pam, Rob. BS magna cum laude, Cumberland Coll., 1970; ThM, Internat. Sem., Orlando, Fla., 1982, ThD, 1983. Ordained to ministry Bapt. Ch., 1968. Sr. pastor Mill Creek Bapt. Ch., Radcliff, Ky., 1976-79, Southside Bapt. Ch., Ft. Pierce, Fla., 1979-81, 1st Bapt. Ch., Jenkins, Ky., 1982-85, Emmanuel Bapt. Ch., Jenkins, Ky., 1985-87, 1st So. Bapt. Ch. of Greater Louisville, 1988—; bd. dirs. home mission bd. So. Bapt. Conv., Atlanta, 1987-91; mem. ch. rels. coun. Campbellsville (Ky.) Coll., 1982-91; bd. overseers The Criswell Coll., Dallas, 1991. Dir. Right to Life, Elizabethtown, Ky., 1978-79; pres. Citizens Against Pornography, Ft. Pierce, 1981; mem. Sewer Planning Commn., Jenkins, 1987; chaplain Shively (Ky.) Police Force, 1990-91. With USAF, 1957-59. Office: 1st So Bapt Ch Louisville 2627 Crums Ln Louisville KY 40216

CARSON, (JOHN) EBEN, minister, educator; b. Brunswick, Ga., Apr. 23, 1951; s. William T. Thomas and Ollie Pauline (Morgan) C.; m. Bonnie Marie Bridges, Oct. 12, 1974; children: Kathryn Delane, Morgan Bridges. AA, Brunswick Jr. Coll., 1971; BA, Ga. So. Coll., 1973; MDiv, Southwestern Bapt. Sem., Ft. Worth, Tex., 1978. Ordained to ministry, 1974. Minister of youth Byne Meml. Bapt. Ch., Albany, Ga., 1972-75, South Hills Bapt. Ch., Ft. Worth, 1976-78; pastor Poulan (Ga.) Bapt. Ch., 1978-83, First Bapt. Ch., Jesup, Ga., 1983—; instr. ext. course Brewton Parker Coll., Mt. Vernon, Ga., 1986—, Ga. Bapt. Ext. Sch., Sylvester, 1979-83; trustee Bapt. Village, Waycross, Ga., 1983-87; missionary So. Bapt. Fgn. Mission Bd., Zimbabwe, 1984, 88, 89. Active Dist. 1 Adv. Coun. for Drug Free Schs. Named one of Outstanding Young Me Am. Nat. Jaycees, 1981, 85, 88. Mem. Wayne County Ministerial Assn. (pres. 1985-86), Atlanta Bapt. Assn. (sch. dir. 1984-89, moderator 1989—), Wayne County C. of C.. Kiwanis, Rotary. Lodges: Kiwanis, Rotary. Avocations: guitar, gardening. Home: 211 Harrington St Jesup GA 31545 Office: First Bapt Ch PO Box 1115 Jesup GA 31545

CARSON, JAMES DONALD, clergyman; b. Sparta, Ill., July 4, 1929; s. Melville Kennedy and Margaret Faith (Coleman) C.; m. Dorothy Jane Mersereau, May 16, 1952; children: Douglas, Kenneth, Thomas, Rebecca. B.A., Geneva Coll., 1950, D.D., 1970; diploma, Reformed Presbyn. Theol. Sem., 1953; D.Min., Calif. Grad. Sch. Theology, 1980. Ordained to ministry Ref. Presbyn. Ch., 1953; pastor Ref. Presbyn. Ch., Portland, Oreg., 1953-57, Ref. Presbyn. Ch. of North Hills, Pitts., 1957-73, Ref. Presbyn. Ch. of Los Angeles, 1973—; Pres. bd. Ref. Presbyn. Theol. Sem., 1964-72, guest lectr., 1972-73; pres. bd. corporators Geneva Coll., 1964-72, trustee, 1976-91; moderator Synod, Ref. Presbyn. Ch., 1973; trustee Westminster Theol. Sem. Calif., 1981-87, 88—. Contbr. articles to ch. jours. Mem. Nat. Reform Assn. (sec. 1962-72), Calif. Council on Alcohol Problems (dir. 1973—, pres. 1982-86). Home: 230 Cherry Dr Pasadena CA 91105 Office: 3557 Fletcher Dr Los Angeles CA 90065

CARSON, JOHN LITTLE, historical theology educator; b. Wilmington, N.C., Jan. 31, 1945; s. Everette Crawford and Emmaline Mayme (Little) C.; m. Sarah Ellen Patrick, June 3, 1967; children: Marana Tha, Emily Ruth, Rebekah Jean, James Everette. BA, Erskine Coll., 1967; MDiv, Ref. Theol. Sem., 1973; PhD, Aberdeen U., 1988. Ordained to ministry Assoc. Ref. Presbyn. Ch., 1973. Pastor Ebenezer Assoc. Ref. Presbyn. Ch., Charlotte, N.C., 1973-83; prof. hist. theology Erskine Sem., Due West, S.C., 1985—; moderator Gen. Synod, Assoc. Ref. Presbyn. Ch., 1989-90; chmn. N.Am. Presbyn. and Ref. Coun., 1990-91. Mem. Evang. Theol. Soc. Home: PO Box 576 Due West SC 29639 Office: Erskine Sem Main St Due West SC 29639

CARSTENSEN, ROGER NORWOOD, educational institute executive, educator; b. Tilden, Nebr., Apr. 1, 1920; s. Lorenz Thomas and Birdie Alwilda (Norwood) C.; m. Maretta Marie Murphy, June 7, 1942; children: Karel, Karen, Roger L., Connie, Phillip, Deborah. BTh, Northwest Christian Coll., 1940; AB, U. Oreg., 1943, MA cum laude, 1946; MDiv, Phillips U., 1952; PhD, Vanderbilt U., 1960. Ordained Minister, Christian Ch. Minister Christian Ch., Scotts Mills, Oreg., 1938-40, Junction City, Oreg., 1940-46, Sisters, Oreg., 1946-49, Ceres, Okla., 1949-52; assoc. prof. N.W. Christian Coll., Eugene, 1941-48, Phillips U., Enid, Okla., 1952-59; prof. Phillips U., Enid, 1960-66; dean, pres. Christian Coll. Ga., Athens, 1966-78; pres. Inst. for Bibl. Literacy, Athens, 1978—. Author: Job: Defense of Honor, 1963, Jonah, 1970, Help Stamp Out Biblical Illiteracy, 1984, Life Through the Lens of Scripture, 1986; editor Biblical Literacy Today, 1986. Chmn. task force on aging Christian Coun. Met. Atlanta, Inc., 1974-75; dir. of secretariat Nat. Interfaith Coalition on Aging, 1972-76. Mem. Soc. Biblical Lit., Am. Acad. Religion, Am. Inst. Oriental Rsch. Republican. Christian Church. Avocations: piano compositions, poetry. Home: 67 Gail Dr Athens GA 30606 Office: Inst For Bibl Literacy 337 S Milledge Ste 109 Athens GA 30605

CART, PAULINE HARMON, minister, educator; b. Jamestown, Ky., Nov. 3, 1914; d. Preston L. and Frances L. (Sullivan) Harmon; m. William C. Cart, July 3, 1936; children—Charles W., David N. BS Berea Coll., 1955; MA U. Mich.-Ann Arbor, 1957, postgrad., 1957; postgrad. Ea. Mich. U., 1957, Nanjing Coll. Traditional Medicine, 1987, PhD in Homeopathic Philosophy. Cert. Tuina instr. Mgr., owner Gen. Store, Beattyville, Ky., 1936-41; def. worker GM, Dayton, Ohio, 1941-46; tchr. Ann Arbor Pub. Schs., 1955-83, Leads Sch., Eng., 1963-64 myomassologist Coll. Naturopathic Physicians, St. Louis, 1959-84; minister, counselor Ch. of Universology, Ann Arbor, 1972—; full prof. nutrition and body balancing Inst. Natural Health Scis., Wis. Contbr. poems and short stories to mags. Instr. Touch for Health Found., Pasadena, Calif., 1972—, Ir. dology, Escondido, Calif., 1972—; bd. dir. Music in Trauma Release Touch for Health in Profl. Health Practitioner; mem. Conservative Caucus, Washington, 1973—. Mem. NEA (del. 1959, cons. 1987—), Am. Nutrition Counselors Am., Internat. Myomathetics Fedn. (sec. edn. 1985—), Assn. Mich. Myomassologists Inc. (v.p. 1987—), Federated Organic Garden & Farming of Mich. (v.p. 1985-86), Alumni Assn. U. Mich. (life), Berea Alumni Assn., Delta Kappa Pi. Republican. Avocations: painting, quilting, crafts, writing, traveling. Home: 2564 Hawks Ave Ann Arbor MI 48108 Office: 2450 Hawks Ave Ann Arbor MI 48108

CARTER, AMBROSE WAYNE, minister; b. Benton, Ark., June 19, 1948; s. Ambrose Marion and Mildred Janice (Dees) C.; m. Enita Joy Heflin, Aug. 8, 1970; children: Christopher, Terri, Melissa. MusB, Henderson State U., 1972; M in Ch. Music, New Orleans Bapt. Sem., 1983. Cert. behavioral analyst. Min. music and youth Stevendale Bapt. Ch., Baton Rouge, 1974-78; min. ednl. music 1st Bapt. Ch., Cen., Baton Rouge, 1978-80; min. ednl. music 1st Bapt. Ch., Russellville, Ala., 1980-82, Charleston, Miss., 1982-84, Saltillo, Miss., 1984—; asst. team dir. Tallahatchie Bapt. Assn., Charleston, 1982-84; ch. growth specialist Miss. Bapt. Conv., Jackson, 1988—, area music coord., 1990—; associational music dir. Lee County Bapt. Assn., 1987—. Composer: In This Hour, 1987 (Anthem of Yr. award 1987), Rise Up!, 1988. Chmn. St. Jude Children's Hosp. Bike-A-Thon, Saltillo, 1989. Name one of Outstanding Young Religious Leaders, Ala. Jaycees, Huntsville, 1981, Outstanding Young Men Am., 1981. Mem. Miss. Bapt. Religious Edn. Assn., So. Bapt. Ch. Bus. Adminstrs., Miss. Singing Churchmen. Home: Rte 2 Box 3W Saltillo MS 38866 Office: 1st Bapt Ch Mobile St Saltillo MS 38866 *I believe that of all the things men work so furiously to possess none has been more passively ignored than that "free gift of eternal life."*

CARTER, CAMERON AUGUSTUS, minister; b. Balt., Oct. 23, 1961; s. Clifton Andrew Norman and Helen Beatrice (Carter) Simms. Cert., Balt. Sch. of the Bible, 1981; BA, Coppin State Coll., 1985; DD (hon.), Millis Inst. Religion, Easton, Md., 1985; DLitt (hon.), Walter Sch. Religion, Unionville, Md., 1986. Lic. to ministry Bapt. Ch., 1979. Interim pastor Nazare Bapt., Balt., 1980-81, Prince of Peace Bapt., Unionville, 1986-87; assoc. minister New Shiloh Bapt., Balt., 1979—; chaplain Vet. Med. Ctr., Balt., 1990—; tchr. Balt. City Pub. Sch., 1988—; chmn. Student Com. Philos. Theology, Balt., 1983-84. Contbr. articles to profl. jours. Youth dir. South Clifton Park Com., Balt., 1977-81; mem. NAACP, Balt., 1980, Operation PUSH, Chgo., 1984, Afro-Am. History Group, Cambridge, Mass., 1985; vol. chaplain Balt. Vets. Med. Ctr. Recipient Gov.'s Citation, State of Md., 1986, Mayoral Citation, City of Balt., 1988, Congl. Citation, U.S. Congress, 1981. Democrat. *It is by the grace of God Almighty I have arrived at the level of success that I have and knowing this I give thanks to Him.*

CARTER, DIAN JEAN, lay worker; b. Erie, Pa., Sept. 22, 1952; d. Robert Lawrence and Jean Marie (Jensen) Carter; m. James Joseph Jensen Carter Albert, Oct. 13, 1979. RN, Villa Maria Hosp., Erie, 1977; BA, Mercyhurst Coll., Erie, 1975. Asst. choir dir. St. Matthew's Ch., Erie, 1979-80, St. Paul's Ch., Erie, 1980-88; Sun. sch. tchr. St. John's Ch., Erie, 1982-86, choir dir., 1986—; dir. Luth. Chs. of Erie, 1987-90, asst. dir., 1980-86. Poll worker Rep. Party, Erie, 1988, 91, transporter, 1990. Lt. USNR, 1975-77. Named Citizen of the Yr., Summit Twp., Pa., 1981. Mem. Erie Mus., Pa. Pet Club (sec. 1984), DAR (sec. 1980-85). Home: 3907 Lewis Ave Erie PA 16504

CARTER, DOUGLAS BRIAN, church administrator; b. DeLand, Fla., July 1, 1958; s. Howard Ernest and Diana Kay (Batchelder) C.; m. Lynta Clarice Johnston, July 26, 1980; children: Preston James, Glen Brian, Andrew David. MusB, Stetson U., 1980; M. Ch. Music, Southwestern Bapt. Theol. Sem., Ft. Worth, 1983. Ordained to ministry Bapt. Ch., 1991. Organist Faith Luth. Ch., DeLand, 1978-79; minister music Harbor Oaks Bapt. Ch., Daytona Beach, Fla., 1979-80, First Bapt. Ch., Ellenton, Fla., 1984-85; minister music and youth First Bapt. Ch., Parrish, Fla., 1985-87; dir. music and youth United Bapt. Ch., Caribou, Maine, 1987—; dir./producer The Living Christmas Tree, Caribou, Maine, 1987-90. Asst. dean Labor Day Retreat Sr. High Camp, Mapleton, Maine, 1987-88, dean, 1989-90. Home: 153 Main St Caribou ME 04736 Office: United Bapt Ch 74 High St Caribou ME 04736

CARTER, GENE STRATTON, minister; b. Dawson, Ill., Aug. 4, 1926; s. George William and Edna Belle (Stroub) C.; m. Mary Margaret Kent, May 15, 1947; children: Edward K., Mary Gene Little, Rebecca Ahlberg, Carol Gingrich, Wendy Sandy, Peggy Riesco. BA, Cin. Christian Coll., 1950; MA, Mich. State U., 1971, Pacific Christian Coll., Fullerton, Calif., 1979; DD (hon.), Pacific Christian Coll., Fullerton, Calif., 1989. Ordained to ministry Ch. of Christ, 1950. Min. Franklin St. Christian Ch. (renamed Woodview Christian), Grand Rapids, Mich., 1950-52, 56-64, Kentwood Christian Ch., Grand Rapids, 1964-68; asst. to the pres. Pacific Christian Coll., 1972-73, vice chmn., bd. dirs., 1978-92; min. U. Christian Ch., L.A., 1973-89, First Christian Ch., Long Beach, Calif., 1989—; chmn. North Burma Christian Mission, Chiang Mai, Thailand, 1972-91; pres. Westwood Christian Found., L.A., 1976-91111; treas. N.Am. Christian Conv., Cin., 1990-92. With USN, 1944-46. Named Disting. Alumni of Yr. Pacific Christian Coll., 1988. Mem. Long Beach C. of C., Downtown Lions (dist. gov. Mich. chpt. 1971-72, internat. bd. dirs. 1978-79, 91-92, Amb. of Goodwill 1979). Office: 1st Christian Ch 440 Elm Ave Long Beach CA 90802

CARTER, GEORGE DENNIS, minister; b. Laurens, S.C., Feb. 22, 1947; s. James Louis and Mary Viola (Fuller) C.; m. Linda Gail Waters, July 2, 1967; children: Melody, Marla, Dennis Jr., Patrick, John, Joy. Student, Tenn. Temple Coll., 1967-72, Bethany Coll., 1983-84; BTh., Bethany Coll., 1987. Ordained to ministry Bapt. Ch., 1974. Visitation min. Faith Bapt. Ch., Laurens, 1975-78; high sch. supr. Faith Christian Sch., Laurens, 1975-78; pastor Trinity Bapt. Ch., Spartanburg, S.C., 1978—; bd. dirs. Ark Youth Shelter, Spartanburg, S.C., Sauliner-Roberson Haven, Chattanooga. Author: Fear Not's in the Bible, 1988, Teen-Ager's Have a Friend, 1989. Bd. dirs. Save-Our-Babies, Spartanburg, 1987. Home: 390 Wingo Heights Rd Spartanburg SC 29301

CARTER, GEORGIAN L., minister; b. St. Mary's, Ga., July 3, 1939; d. Leroy Sr. and Abbie (Myers) Logan; m. Calvin L. Carter, Mar. 26, 1956; children: Janice Carter Slocumb, Arlette Carter Fletcher, Eric. AA, Prince Georges Community Coll., Largo, Md., 1973; cert., Dale Carnegie Sch., 1980. Ordained to ministry Deliverance Ch. of Christ. Clk., trustee Deliverance Ch. of Christ, Seat Pleasant, Md., 1968-87, Bible class tchr., 1983-89; sec., sick and shut-in ministry Full Gospel A.M.E. Zion Ch., Temple Hills, Md., 1989—; with HUD, Washington, 1967-89; tchr. noon-time Bible study U.S. State Dept. Fellowship, 1989-91. Asst. dir. Glenarden (Md.) Housing Authority, 1973-75. Democrat. Home: 909 Byrum Dr Hinesville GA 31313 *Many of my desires for life conflicted with God's requirements. However, insight gained from the word of God has changed my way of thinking and has produced great rewards for my life.*

CARTER, GERALD EMMETT, retired archbishop; b. Montreal, Que., Can., Mar. 1, 1912; s. Thomas Joseph and Mary (Kelty) C. BTh, Grand Sem. Montreal, 1936; BA, U. Montreal, 1933, MA, 1940, PhD, 1947, LTh, 1950; DHL, Duquesne U., 1963; LLD (hon.), U. Western Ont., 1966, Concordia U., 1976, U. Windsor, 1977, McGill U., Montreal, 1980, Notre Dame (Ind.) U., 1981; LittD, St. Mary's U., Halifax, 1980. Ordained priest Roman Cath. Ch., 1937. Founder, prin., prof. St. Joseph Tchrs. Coll., Montreal, 1939-61; chaplain Newan Club McGill U., 1941-56; charter mem., 1st pres. Thomas More Inst. Adult Edn., Montreal, 1945-61; mem. Montreal Cath. Sch. Commn., 1948-61; hon. canon Cathedral Basilica Montreal, 1952-61; aux. bishop London and titular bishop Altiburo, 1961; bishop of London, Ont., 1964-78; archbishop of Toronto, 1978-90, ret., 1990; elevated to cardinal, 1979; Chmn. Episcopal Commn. Liturgy Can., 1966-73; mem. Consilium of Liturgy, Rome, 1965, Sacred Congregation for Divine Worship, 1970; chmn. Internat. Com. for English in the Liturgy, 1971; appointee Econ. Affairs Coun. of Holy See, 1981; vice pres. Can. Cath. Conf., 1973, Cath. Conf. of Ont., 1971-73; pres. Can. Conf. Cath. Bishops, 1975; mem. coun. Synod of Bishops, 1977. Author: The Catholic Public Schools of Quebec, 1957, Psychology and the Cross, 1959, The Modern Challenge to Religious Education, 1961. Decorated companion Order of Can. Office: Chancery Office, 355 Church St, Toronto, ON Canada M5B 1Z8

CARTER, HERBERT RANDAL, minister; b. Clinton, N.C., July 29, 1960; s. Herbert Franklin and Mary Elizabeth (Key) C.; m. Gwendolyn Gail Collum, May 9, 1982; children: Jonathan Randal, Jena Rebecca, Kristen Ashleigh. B of Religious Edn., Heritage Bible Coll., Dunn, N.C., 1983; postgrad., Columbia (S.C.) Grad. Sch., 1984. Pastor Johnson Chapel Ch., Benson, N.C., 1982-83; missionary Pentecostal Free Will Bapt. Ch., Guadalajara, Jalieco, 1984-88; pastor Restoration Assembly Ch., Cary, N.C., 1990—. Office: Restoration Assembly 1600 Piney Plains Rd Cary NC 27511

CARTER, HOWARD JULIAN, minister; b. Auckland, New Zealand, Sept. 10, 1936; arrived in Australia, 1969; s. Claude and Enid (Abel) C.; m. Jean Eleanor Muir; children: Morrison, Craig, Amanda, Vickie. Diploma in Teaching, Auckland Tchrs. Coll., 1956; LTh, Coll. Div., Melbourne, Australia, 1962; diploma in Ministry, Bapt. Theol. Coll., Auckland, 1965; MA, Pacific Coll. Theol., Melbourne, 1987. Ordained min. Tchr. Dist. High Sch., Reporoa, New Zealand, 1960-61; min. Manurewa (New Zealand) Bapt. Ch., 1962-68; min. Covenant Evangel. Ch., Blackheath, Australia, 1969-80, 85-87, Surrey, Can., 1980-85, Toowoomba, Australia, 1987—; dir. Logos Found., Blackheath, 1969-80, 85-87, Surrey, Can., 1980-85, Toowoomba, Australia, 1987—. Editor: Logos Jour., 1986-89, (mag.) Restore, 1977-86; author: Bill of Rights or Bill of Violations, 1986, Education: The Parent, The Church and the State, 1987, 1988: The Bi-Centenary Celebration or Constitutional Crisis, 1987, AIDS: The Plague to End all Plagues, 1987, Go Through the Gates, 1981, The Wolf in Sheep's Clothing, 1987, Introducing the Kingdom, 1985, Voter's Veto: The Voice of the People, 1988 Confronting Babylon, 1979, Local Assembly, 1975. Founding chmn. Australians Speaking Up, 1986—, Voters Veto-Voice of the People, Australia, 1987—. Office: Logos Found, 2 Burnage St, Toowoomba Queensland 4350, Australia

CARTER, JAMES EDWARD, minister, religious organization administrator; b. New Edinburg, Ark., Jan. 19, 1935; s. Edward Floyd and Sue (Reaves) C.; m. Carole Ann Hunter, Sept. 4, 1955; children: James Craig, Edward Keith, Chyrisse Ann Carter. BA, La. Coll., 1957; MDiv, Southwestern Bapt. Theol. Sem., Ft. Worth, 1960, PhD, 1964. Ordained to ministry Bapt. Ch., 1955. Pastor Wise Meml. Bapt. Ch., Lena, La., 1955-57, John T. White Bapt. Ch., Ft. Worth, 1958-61, Temple Bapt. Ch., Gainesville, Tex., 1961-64, 1st Bapt. Ch., Natchitoches, La., 1964-77, Univ. Bapt. Ch., Ft. Worth, 1978-88; exec. asst. to exec. dir. La. Bapt. Conv., Alexandria, 1977-78, dir. ch. min. rels. div., 1988—. Author: A Source Book for Stewardship Sermons, 1972, People Parables, 1973, The Mission of the Church, 1974, What is to Come?, 1975, Following Jesus: The Nature of Christian Discipleship, 1977, Christ and the Crowds, 1981, Layman's Bible Book Commentary, 1984, Help for the Evangelistic Preacher, 1985, Facing the Final Foe, 1986, Cowboys, Cowtown and Crosses: A Centennial History of Tarrant Baptist Association, 1986; contbg. author: The Bible Teacher's Commentary, Encyclopedia of Southern Baptist, vol. III, Zondervan's Pastor's Annual, 1973-86, The Lord's Free People in a Free Land, Award Winning Sermons, vol. I-II, Doran's Minister's Manual, 1978, Salvation in Our Time, Illustrating the Gospel of Matthew, Illustrating the Book of Romans, Who Am I. Recipient Freedoms Found. award, 1971, 79; named Alumnus of the Yr., La. Coll., 1979. Mem. La. Bapt. Hist. Assn., So. Bapt. Hist. Assn., Am. Mgmt. Assn., Am. Soc. Ch. History, Rotary. Democrat. Home: 1105 W Pointe Alexandria LA 71303 Office: La Bapt Conv 1250 Mac Arthur Dr Alexandria LA 71309

CARTER, JAMES PAUL, clergyman; b. Kirbyville, Tex., Apr. 30, 1940; s. James D. and Bonnie (Beard) C.; m. Nancy K. VanPelt, Nov. 24, 1960;l children: James Paul, Mark S. AA, Lon Morris Coll., 1960; BS, Stephen F. Austin State U., 1962; MTh, So. Meth. U., 1966; DMin, San Francisco

Theol. Sem., 1987. Lic. profl. counselor, Tex.; ordained deacon United Meth. Ch., 1963, elder, 1967. Student pastor United Meth. Ch., various cities, Tex., 1958-62; pastor United Meth. Ch., various cities, 1962-67; chaplain VA Med. Ctr., San Antonio, 1973-79, Olin E. Teague VA Med. Ctr., Temple, Tex., 1979—. Chmn. Temple Mayor's Com. for Employment of Handicapped, 1987; chaplain various profl. orgns. Capt. (chaplain) U.S. Army, 1967-70. Named Outstanding Handicapped Employee, VA Hosp., 1974, 81-86. Mem. Mil. Chaplains Assn., Nat. Assn. VA Chaplains, Am. Assn. Protestant Chaplains, Assn. protestant Chaplains of Tex. Home: 16 Admiral Circle Belton TX 76513 Office: Olin E Teague Vets Center 1901 South First St Temple TX 76501

CARTER, JOANN BELL, lay worker; b. Nashville, Mar. 5, 1943; d. Mary (Callie) Bell; m. Hosea E. Carter Jr., Apr. 12, 1963; children: Clifton, Maurice, Leslie, Stacy, Preston. Student, Tenn. State U., 1967-68, 70. Clk. Sunday Sch. & Ch., Riddleton, Tenn., 1968—; sec. Lilly Hill Ch., Riddleton, 1969—, fin. clk., 1978—, treas., 1978—, advisor, social missionary, 1980—; co-svc. dir. Cordell Hull Community Action Agy., Carthage, Tenn., 1967—. Lili inner guard Golden Circle, Carthage. Mem. Hearn of Jericho, Home Soc., Order Ea. Star (assoc. matron Carthage chpt.), Beta Sigma Phi (Woman of Yr. 1989). Home: PO Box 40 Hwy 25 Riddleton TN 37151 Office: Cordell Hull CAA 207 W 3d Ave Carthage TN 37030 *I do not feel you can be successful at any task without help from God. I feel through prayer all things are possible. If you truly believe, go on His strength and fear not.*

CARTER, JOHN CROWLEY, minister; b. Nashville, May 14, 1932; s. John Franklin C. and Birdie Elizabeth (Crowley) Rainey; m. Shirley Mae Yoes, Dec. 1, 1952 (div. Feb. 1975); children: John, Steven, Eric, Jeffrey, Brent; m. Judith Anne Riddell, July 19, 1975; 1 stepchild, Patricia. BA, Belmont Coll., 1960; MDiv, So. Bapt. Theol. Sem., 1966. Ordained to ministry Am. Bapt. Ch. Pastor First Bapt. Ch., Red Boiling Springs, Tenn., 1959-62; pastor Oak Park Bapt. Ch., Jeffersonville, Ind., 1962-66; pastor First Bapt. Ch., Tell City, Ind., 1966-70, Crawfordsville, Ind., 1970-74; chaplain, Dept. Corrections State of Ind., 1974-90; pastor Am. Bapt. Ch., Munster, Ind., 1990—; bd. dirs. Mennonite Prison Ministry, 1991; group leader Transactional Analysis, 1990—. Author: (booklet) To The Morning: a Tool for Grief Ministry. With U.S. Navy, 1949-52. Mem. Westville (Ind.) C. of C. (pres. 1989-90); Lions (dist. sec. 1986-88). Home: 137 Tulip Dr Westville IN 46391 Office: Munster Am Bapt Ch 8635 Calumet Munster IN 46391

CARTER, JOHN ROSS, philosophy and religion educator; b. Baytown, Tex., June 22, 1938; s. Robert Louis and Virginia Annette (Cook) C.; m. Sandra McNeill, June 24, 1960; children: Christopher John, Mary Elizabeth. BA, Baylor U., 1960; BD, So. Bapt. Theol. Sem., 1963; ThM, U. London, 1965; PhD, Harvard U., 1972. Prof. Colgate U., Hamilton, N.Y., 1972—, dir. Chapel House, 1976—. Author: Dhamma: Western...; editor: Religiousness in Sri..., 1979, Religiousness in Yoga, 1980; translator: Dhammapada, a New English, 1987. Frank Knox Meml. fellow, Rockefeller fellow; Spalding Trust Gt. Britain grantee; Fulbright-Hays scholar. Mem. Am. Acad. Religion, Am. Oriental Soc., Assn. for Asian Studies, Japan Soc., Asia Soc., Rotary. Baptist. Office: Colgate U Chapel House 13 Oak Dr Hamilton NY 13346

CARTER, KENNETH HARPER, JR., minister; b. Greensboro, N.C., Aug. 23, 1957; s. Kenneth Harper Carter and Frieda (Ensminger) Moye; m. Pamela B., Jan. 3, 1981; children: Elizabeth, Abigail. BS, Columbus Coll., Ga., 1980; MDiv magna cum laude, Duke U., 1983; MA, U. Va., 1986. Ordained to ministry Meth. Ch. as elder, 1983. Assoc. pastor Trinity United Meth. Ch., Kannapolis, N.C., 1983-84; pastor Smithtown United Meth. Ch., East Bend, N.C., 1985-88; minister of prog. Christ United Meth. Ch., Greensboro, N.C., 1988—; chmn. Hispanic Ministry, West N.C., 1987—. Author: The Pastor As Steward, 1991. Speaker's bur. N.C. Humanities Coun., 1990—; bd. dirs. Hospice of Yadkin County, Yadkinville, N.C., 1986-88. Home: 1513 Alderman Dr Greensboro NC 27408 Office: Christ Church United Meth 410 N Holden Greensboro NC 27410

CARTER, PAUL DENNIS, pastor; b. St. Joseph, Mo., May 9, 1950; s. Frank Clem and Nancy (Operman) C.; m. Linda Lee Wennihan, Sept. 12, 1971; children: Erica Nancy, Alan Lowell. Degree in law enforcement, Colby Community Coll., 1974; BA cum laude, Criswell Coll., 1985; MA in Counseling, Liberty U., 1988. Ordained minister So. Bapt. Ch. Emergency med. technician Thomas County Ambulence Svc., Colby, Kans., 1972-74; police officer Colby Police Dept., 1972-74, Olathe (Kans.) Police Dept., 1974-76, Green River (Wyo.) Police Dept., 1976-79; pastor Wamsutter (Wyo.) Bapt. Ch., 1979-81; adminstrv. asst. Criswell Coll., Dallas, 1981-86; sr. pastor Del Ray Bapt. Ch., Alexandria, Va., 1986-89; pastor Hillcrest Bapt. Ch., Riverton, Wyo., 1989—. Contbr. articles to profl. publs. Bd. dirs. Good News Jail and Prison Ministry, Arlington, Va., 1988-89; chaplain Alexandria Hosp., 1986-89, Fremont County Sheriff's Office, 1989—, Riverton Police Dept., 1989—. Mem. Am. Assn. Counseling Devel., Energy Basin Bapt. Assn. (chmn. evangelism 1978-79), Mt. Vernon Bapt. Assn. (bd. dirs., ethnic commn. 1987-88, evangelism commn. 1988—), Kiwanis. Republican. Avocations: computers, telecommunications. *"For other foundation can no man lay than that is laid, which is Christ Jesus." (Romans 3:11). My task is this...to point men and women, boys and girls, to faith in Jesus Christ.*

CARTER, RICHARD BERT, church and retired government official; b. Spokane, Wash., Dec. 2, 1916; s. Richard B. and Lula Selena (Jones) C.; BA in Polit. Sci., Wash. State U., 1939; postgrad. Georgetown U. Law Sch., 1941, Brown U., 1944, Brigham Young U. Extension, 1975-76; m. Mildred Brown, Sept. 6, 1952; children: Paul, Mark, Janis, David. Advt. credit mgr. Elec. Products Consol., Omaha, 1939-40; pub. communications ofcl., investigator FBI, Washington, 1940-41, Huntington, W.Va., 1941, Houston, 1942, Boston, 1943, S. Am., 1943, Providence, 1944-45, N.Y.C., 1945, Salt Lake City, 1945, P.R., 1946-48, Phoenix, 1948-50, Washington, 1950-51, Cleve., 1952-55, Seattle, 1955-75, ret., 1975; assoc. dir. stake and mission pub. communications dept. Ch. Hdqrs., Ch. of Jesus Christ of Latter-day Saints, Salt Lake City, 1975-77. Dist. chmn. Chief Seattle coun. Boy Scouts Am., 1967-68, coun. v.p., 1971-72, coun. commr., 1973-74, nat. coun. rep., 1962-64, 72-74, area II, Eagle Scout Assn., 1984—. Mem. Freedoms Found. Valley Forge, Utah chpt., 1988—; bd. dirs. Salvation Army, 1963, United Way, 1962-63, mem. allocations com., 1962, 1987-88. Served to 1st lt., Intelligence Corps, U.S. Army, 1954. Recipient Silver Beaver award Boy Scouts Am., 1964, Vigil Honor, 1971; named Nat. Media Man-of-Month Morality in Media, Inc., N.Y.C., 1976. Mem. Profl. Photographers Am., Internat. Assn. Bus. Communicators, Am. Security Council (nat. adv. bd.), Internat. Platform Assn., Sons Utah Pioneers (pres. 1982, Disting. Svc. award 1985), SAR (pres. Salt Lake City chpt. 1987-88, Law Enforcement Commendation medal 1987, Meritorious Svc. medal 1989, Pres.-Gen.'s Program Excellence award, Oliver R. Smith medal 1990, Grahame T. Smallwood award 1990, Liberty medal 1991), Utah State Soc. (pres. 1989-90), Amicus Club (chmn. membership com. Deseret Found. 1988—, world sr. games adv. com. 1987—), William Carter Family Orgn. (nat. pres.), Nat. Assn. Chiefs of Police (Am. Police Hall of Fame, John Edgar Hoover Distin. Pub. Svc. medal 1991), Scabbard and Blade, Am. Media Network (nat. adv. bd.), Assn. Former Intelligence Officers, Alpha Phi Omega, Pi Sigma Alpha, Sigma Delta Chi, Phi Delta Theta. Mem. LDS Ch. (coord. pub. communications council Seattle area 1973-75, br. pres. 1944-45, dist. pres. 1954-55, high priest 1958—, stake pres. counselor 1959-64, stake Sunday Sch. pres. 1980-81, temple staff 1987—). Clubs: Bonneville Knife and Fork (bd. dirs. 1982-85), Rotary (dir., editor The Rotary Bee, 1982-83, Paul Harris fellow 1982, Richard L. Evans fellow 1987, Best Club History in Utah award 1988, Best Dist. Newsletter award 1983, Rotarian of Month 1988). Author: The Sunbeam Years-An Autobiography, 1986; assoc. editor FBI Investigator, 1965-75; contbg. author, editor: Biographies of Sons of Utah Pioneers, 1982; contbr. articles to mags. Home: 2180 S Elaine Dr Bountiful UT 84010 *Live each day so as to have no regrets. Do not defile the temple which houses the spirit given you by God. With a positive and commendatory attitude, love and serve your fellow beings.*

CARTER, ROBERT FELTON, minister; b. Eden, N.C., Mar. 8, 1935; s. Robert Lee and Carrie Minnie (Grey) C.; m. Martha J. Smith, June 29, 1956; children: Celia Carter Bryant, Cynthia Carter Davis, Christopher Robert II, Catherine Lori Carter Eakin. SLB, Atlanta Christian Coll., East Point, Ga., 1957; DMin, Drew U., Madison, N.J., 1987. Ordained to ministry Fellowship of Christian Chs., 1954. Pastor Gosport (Ind.) Christian Ch., 1959-65, Bethany Christian Ch., Indpls., 1965-75, Hickory Valley Christian Ch., Chattanooga, 1975-79, Valley Mills Christian Ch., Indpls., 1979—; pres. Alexander Christian Found., Indpls., 1965—; arrangements chmn. N. Am. Christian Conv., Indpls., 1973; trustee Atlanta Christian Coll., E. Point, Ga., 1976-88. Author: Preparing for the Preaching Event, 1987; contbr. articles to profl. jours. Recipient citation Govt. of Israel. Mem. Christian Ch. Evangelizing Assn., Decatur Ministers Fellowship (pres. 1981-87), Pilot Club, Lions (pres. 1964), Masons. Home: 4440 Tincher Rd Indianapolis IN 46241 Office: Valley Mills Christian Ch 5555 Kentucky Ave Indianapolis IN 46241 *The glory of underachievement is pervasive and is potentially more insidious than heresy. Jesus' concept of 'take up your cross daily' is believed by fewer than we like to suppose. What are we to become without high purpose? Move over Bart Simpson.*

CARTER, RONNIE EUGENE, minister; b. Columbus, Ga., Sept. 28, 1937; s. Raymond P. and Ruth Viola (Landon) C.; m. Nora Elizabeth Martin, Aug. 24, 1956; children: Ronnie Eugene Jr., Rhonda Elizabeth, Robin Angela. Student, Auburn U., 1955-56; diploma in ch. music, New Orleans Bapt. Theol. Sem., 1973. Ordained to ministry Bapt. Ch., 1974. Min. music and youth Port Sulphur (La.) Bapt. Ch., 1972-73, 1st Bapt. Ch., Ashburn, Ga., 1974-77; min. music and outreach Ardsley Pk. Bapt. Ch., Savannah, Ga., 1977-89; min. music and edn. King St. Bapt. Ch., Cocoa, Fla., 1989—; sec., treas. Turner County Ministerial Conf., Ashburn, Ga., 1977; pres. Savannah Bapt. Min.'s Conf., 1983-84. Home: 905 Prosperity Pl Rockledge FL 32955 Office: King St Bapt Ch 1040 W King St Cocoa FL 32922 *Passion: knowing your destiny and loving others enough to take them with you!.*

CARTER, RUFUS EARL, college president, minister; b. Greenwood, Miss., Nov. 3, 1938; s. Eddie Earl and Rosie Lee (Holmes) C.; m. Maxine Mae Bess, Mar. 10, 1974; children: Jaquetta, Jacquline, Natasha, Sonja, Kenneth, Rufus Earl Jr. B Ministry, Family Bible Coll., Balt., 1980, ThM, 1982; ThD, Covington Theol. Sem., Rossville, Ga., 1983, PhD, 1987. Ordained to ministry Bapt. Ch., 1981. Youth coord. Wildwood Bapt. Ch., Greenwood, 1948-50; deacon New Abisenia Ch. of Christ, Balt., 1962-73; pres. Assoc. Mins. Conf., Balt., 1973-75; pastor Phila. Bapt. Ch., 1974—; pres. Phila. Bible Coll., 1974—, chmn. bd. trustees, 1984—; trustee Family Bible Coll., 1977-82; mem. Evening Mins. Conf., 1984—, Nat. Bapt. Conf., 1984—. Author: Telescope of Prophecy, 1987. Voter registrar NE Dem. Club, Balt., 1985—. Staff sgt. U.S. Army, 1956-66. Recipient honor plaque Assoc. Mins. Conf., 1975. Mem. Nat. Evangelistic Assn., Masons. Home: 2800 Ashland Ave Baltimore MD 21205 *One must realize that everything has a purpose. And each purpose has yet another purpose, one above the other. For example, the purpose of building a house is so that a person should have a place to rest. But the purpose of his resting is so that he should have enough strength to serve God.*

CARTER, SAMUEL EMMANUEL, archbishop; b. St. Andrew, Jamaica, W.I., July 31, 1919; s. Wilfred George and Eugenie Marie (Williams) C. BA, MA in Theology, Weston (Mass.) Coll., 1950, STL in Theology, 1951; postgrad. in Ascetical Theology, St. Beuno's Coll., North Wales, 1955-56; MSW, Boston Coll., 1958, STD, 1988; DD (hon.), 1966; LLD (hon.), Coll. of Holy Cross, Worcester, Mass., 1970, LeMoyne Coll., Syracuse, N.Y., 1976, Loyola U., Chgo., 1979, U. W.I., 1988. Ordained as priest Roman Cath. Ch., 1954, as bishop, 1966, appointed archbishop, 1970. Instr. Latin S. Simon's Coll., 1939-41; ivil servant Treas. Dept., 1941-44; instr. sociology Holy Cross Coll., Worcester, 1950-51; asst. parish priest, master ceremonies Holy Trinity Cathedral Partish, Jamaica, 1958-59; founder, headmaster Campion Coll., 1960-64; rector St. George's Coll., 1964—; aux. bishop Kingston, Jamaica, 1966; vicar gen. Archdiocese of Kingston, pastor Holy Cross Ch. Kingston, 1966-70; archbishop of Kingston, 1970—; dir. Pre-Cana Conf., 1959-65; vice chmn. Ecumenical Com. on Religious Edn., 1966-68; chmn. Archdiocesan Edn. Bd., 1968—; marriage counsellor Boston Children's Svc. and Family Svc. Greater Boston; del. 4th and final session of 2d Vatican Coun., Rome, as adviser to Bishop McEleney, 1965; chmn. Archdiocesan Commn. on Ecumenism,1966-70; chmn. Liturgical Commn. Antilles Episcopal Conf., 1966, pres., 1968, 70, 72, 74, 77, 79, 83, 86, 88; rep. 2d Synod of Bishops, Rome, 1969, rep. 3d Synod of Bishops, Rome, 1970; chmn. Caribbeaan Conf. Chs., 1973; mem. Commn. of Enquiry into adminstrn. justice, police brutality in State of Grenada, W.I., 1973; moderator Internat. Co-operation for Socio-Econ. Devel., mem. Bur., European Ch. Devel. Agy., 1975; chmn. Antilles Episcopal Commn. on Missions, 1975; chmn. Commn. for Missionary Activities, Communications Commn., Antilles Episcopal Conf., 1982; del. World Synod of Bishops, Rome, 1983; leader Caribbean Conf. Chs. Fact Finding Mission to Haiti, 1987. Editor in chief Mental Health Conf. Report, 1962. Chaplain Cath. Women's League, 1958-66; hon. sec. Jamaica Save the Children Fund, 1958-66, Fort Augusta Prison vis. com., 1960-74; mem. exec. com. Jamaica Mental Health Assn., 1961-63; moderator St. George's Coll. Old Boys' Assn., 1964-66; chmn. Archdiocesan Edn. Bd., 1968—, Holy Childhood High Sch. Bd., 1968-70, Holy Trinity Jr. Secondary Sch. Bd., 1968—; hon. v.p. Girl Guides Assn., Jamaica Scout Coun.; chmn. Dupont Primary Sch., Cockburn Pen.; mem. Coun. U. W.I., 1976—. Decorated Comdr. Order of Distinction Govt. Jamaica; recipient Rale medallion, Bicentennial award Boston Coll. Sch. Social Work, 1976. Mem. Jamaica Coun. Chs. (pres. 1979, 80), Edn. Adv. Coun., Ministry Edn. Com. on Orgn. and Structure of Ednl. System (chmn.), Schs. and Colls. Labour Rels. Coun. (chm. 1965-66). Address: Archbishop's Residence, 21 Hopefield Ave POB 43, Kingston 6, Jamaica

CARTER, STEPHEN JAMES, religious publishing company executive, minister; b. Indpls., Mar. 23, 1941; s. Homer J. and Irene Laura (Olsen) C.; m. Gail Roane Dobberstein, June 27, 1964; children: Mark Stanton, Amy Elizabeth, Rebecca Dawn. BA with high distinction, Concordia Sr. Coll., Ft. Wayne, Ind., 1962; MDiv, Concordia Sem., St. Louis, 1966, STM, 1967; D Ministry, United Theol. Sem., Dayton, Ohio, 1984. Ordained to ministry Luth. Ch.-Mo. Synod, 1967. Asst. pastor St. Paul Luth. Ch., Decatur, Ill., 1967-71; pastor Trinity Luth Ch., Utica, Mich., 1971-74, St. John Luth. Ch., Peru, Ind., 1974-82; mem. faculty, dir. continuing edn. and D Ministry program Concordia Sem., Ft. Wayne, 1982-87; v.p. editorial div. Concordia Pub. House, St. Louis, 1987—; chmn. adult and family com. Ind. dist. Luth. Ch.-Mo. Synod, 1979-82, chmn. ministerial health com., 1985-87, chmn. continuing edn. com., 1986-89. Author: Questions about Marriage, 1979, Learning Plan Workshop, 1984, Pastors on the Grow, 1986, Preaching for Pastors, 1986, My Daily Devotion, 1988; co-author: Keeping a Good Thing Going, 1979, More of a Good Thing, 1982, How to Develop a Team Ministry and Make It Work, 1985. Scholar Luth. Brotherhood, 1966-67; grantee Aid Assn. for Luths., 1982-84. Mem. Concordia Hist. Inst., Soc. for Advancement Continuing Edn. in Ministry, Luth. Edn. Assn., Protestant Ch.-Owned Pubs. Assn. Home: 12142 Theiss Meadows Dr Saint Louis MO 63128 Office: Concordia Pub House 3558 S Jefferson Ave Saint Louis MO 63118 *In my relationships with others I have learned to lead with my weakness. We meet on the common ground of our humanity and dependence on God.*

CARTER, WILLIAM GLENN, minister; b. Angola, Ind., Feb. 21, 1960; s. Glenn W. and Elizabeth Ann Carter; m. Colleen Lane, Aug. 18, 1984. BA, SUNY, Binghamton, 1982; MDiv, Princeton Sem., 1985. Ordained to ministry Presbyn. Ch. (U.S.A.), 1985. Pastor Presbyn. Ch., Catasauqua, Pa., 1985-90, 1st Presbyn. Ch, Clarks Summit, Pa., 1990—; jazz pianist 200th Gen. Assembly, Phila., 1989; chmn. Pastor as Educator Task Force, Camp Hill, Pa., 1987-90, Lehigh Presbyn. Christian Edn. Com., Allentown, Pa., 1989-90; educator adminstr. Homiletical Feast, Princeton, N.J., 1990—. Contbr. articles to religious jours. Mem. Abington Ecumenical Ministerium, Alban Inst., Rotary (bd. dirs. Catasauqua 1986-90). Office: 1st Presbyn Ch 300 School St Clarks Summit PA 18411-1536

CARUSILLO, SISTER JOAN GLORIA, nun; b. Washington, June 10, 1931; d. Louis J. and Anna (Thomas) C. BA, Dunbarton Coll., 1953; MA, Cath. U., Washington, 1965, STB, 1967. Tchr. high sch. English, Latin and theology various high schs., 1957-75; asst. prin. St. Mary's Acad., Alexandria, Va., 1975-77, prin., 1977-81; eastern regional superior Sisters of the Holy Cross, 1981-87; v.p. philosophy and mission Mount Carmel Health, Columbus, Ohio, 1988-91; mem. leadership group Sisters of the Holy Cross, Notre Dame, Ind., 1981-87; bd. dirs. Holy Cross Health System, South Bend, Ind., 1981-87; bd. trustees Mount Carmel Health, Columbus, 1981-87; vice-chmn. Leadership Conf. Women Religious, region 4, Pitts., 1983-86. Mem. diocesan sch. bd. Cath. Diocese Arlington, 1979-81; mem. hunger seminar adv. coun. Bread for World, Washington, 1983-86; vice chair bd. trustees Holy Cross Hosp., Silver Spring, Md., 1989—. Avocations: walking, painting. *The center of my life is Jesus Christ. In my opinion, the most important message He gave us was, "Love one another as I have loved you." Happiness for me lies in striving to live these words.*

CARVALHO, EMILIO JÚLIO MIGUEL DE, bishop; b. Cazengo, Angola, Aug. 3, 1933; s. Júlio João and Eva Pedro (de Andrade) Miguel; m. Marilina Stella de Jesus F., Aug. 6, 1966; children: Ari César, Eunice Paula, David Mauro Figueiredo. BD, Methodist Sch. Theology, São Paulo, Brazil, 1958; MA, Northwestern U., 1960. Prof., prin. Emmanuel Theol. Sem., Dondi, Angola, 1965-72; chmn. Angolan Coun. of Chs., Luanda, Angola, 1977-80, Ecumenical Assn. 3d World Theologians, 1981-86; v.p. Oxford Inst. Meth. Theol. Studies, Luanda, 1987—; pres.-designate Coun. of Bishops, United Meth. Ch., Luanda; mem. exec. com. World Meth. Coun., 1986-91; del Wordl Coun. of Chs. VI Assembly, Vancouver, Can., 1983. Contbr. articles to profl. jours. Chmn. bd. dirs. Africa U., Old Mutari, Zimbabwe, 1988—; gov. Bd. Higher Edn. and Ministry, Nashville, 1984-92. Home: Rua NS Muxima 18, Luanda Angola Office: United Meth Church, Rua NS da Muxima 12, Luanda Angola

CARVER, DAVID BRUCE, minister; b. St. Albans, W.Va., June 22, 1960; s. Frank William and Lorraine Helen (Shutt) C.; m. Sharon Lee McCoy, May 30, 1982; 1 child, Ariel Rose. BA in English magna cum laude, Geneva Coll., 1982; MDiv, Colgate-Rochester Div. Sch., 1990. Ordained to ministry Presbyn. Ch. (U.S.A.), 1990. Youth and campus min. Coalition for Christian Outreach, Pitts., 1982-85, staff specialist for youth ministry, 1985-88; asst. Christian edn. Summerville Presbyn. Ch., Rochester, N.Y., 1989-90; assoc. pastor 12 Corners Presbyn. Ch., Rochester, 1990—. Author: Opening the Door--A Youth Ministry Primer, 1987, Building Relationships with Teens, 1990; also articles. Founder The Open Door Youth and Community Ctr., Pitts., 1987. Dave Carver Day proclaimed in his honor, Pa. Ho. of Reps. and Pitts. City Coun., 1988. Democrat. Office: 12 Corners Presbyn Ch 1200 S Winton Rd Rochester NY 14618

CARVER, FRANK GOULD, theology educator; b. Crookston, Nebr., May 27, 1928; s. Frank Alonzo and Greeta G. (Gould) C.; m. Betty Joan Ireland, Mar. 31, 1949; children: Mark Erwin, Carol Denise. BA, Taylor U., 1950; BD, Nazarene Theol. Sem., 1954; MTh, Princeton Theol. Sem., 1958; PhD, New Coll., U. Edinburgh, Scotland, 1964. Pastor Ch. of Nazarene, Kimball, Nebr., 1954-56, Edison, N.J., 1956-58, Edinburgh, Scotland, 1959; from asst. to full prof. Pasadena/Point Loma (Calif.) Nazarene Coll., 1961—, chmn. dept. philosophy and religion, 1967-82, 1991—, dir. grad. programs in religion, 1981—, dir. summer ministries, faculty officer, 1986-89; Mem. numerous coms. including curricular exceptions, academic policy, coun. on ednl. policy and program, graduate studies, profl. devel., rank and tenure and many others Point Loma Nazarene Coll., San Diego, Calif.; guest prof. Olivet Nazarene Coll., fall 1972, Nazarene Theol. Sem., 1976, 79, 81, 85, Nazarene Theol. Coll., S. Africa, 1979, Inst. Biblico Nazareno Ensenada, Mex., 1987; mem. Ch. Growth Symposium, 1978-79; mem. curriculum com. Enduring Word Series, 1976-80; many lecturing positions. Author: Peter the Rock Man, 1973, Matthew Part One: To Be a Disciple, 1984, Matthew Part Two: Come...and Learn From Me, 1986, The Cross and the Spirit: Peter and the Way of the Holy, 1987; contbr. articles to profl. jours.; editorial bd. Lockman Found., 1961—. Tchr. adult Sunday Sch. Pasadena First Ch. Nazarene, San Diego First Ch. Nazarene, 1961-89. Mem. Inst. Biblical Rsch. (West Coast chmn. 2 terms, nat. exec. com. 2 terms), Soc. Biblical Lang., Wesleyan Theol. Soc. (1st v.p. 1985-86, pres. 1986-87), Evangel. Theol. Soc. Home: 4037-95 Porte De Palmas San Diego CA 92122 Office: Point Loma Nazarene Coll 3900 Lomaland Dr San Diego CA 92106

CARVER, LOYCE CLEO, clergyman; b. Decaturville, Tenn., Dec. 13, 1918; s. Oscar Price and Mae Joanne (Chumney) C.; m. Mary Rebecca Frymire, Dec. 14, 1940; children—Judith Ann Carver Tyson, Linda Carver Sheals, Rebecca Carver Bishop. Ordained to ministry Apostolic Faith, 1947; real estate appraiser, dep. county tax assessor Klamath County, Oreg., 1943-44; bookkeeper Pacific Fruit Co., Los Angeles, Klamath Falls, Oreg., 1945-47; pastor Apostolic Faith Ch., Dallas, Oreg., 1948-49, San Francisco, 1949-52, Los Angeles, 1952-56, Medford, Oreg., 1956-65; gen. overseer Apostolic Faith, Portland, Oreg., 1965—; chmn. bd. dirs. World-Wide Movement, 1965—, trustee, 1959-65, pres., 1965—. Editor: Light of Hope, 1965—. Served with USNR, 1944. Home: 3322 SE Raymond St Portland OR 97202 Office: 6615 SE 52d Ave Portland OR 97206

CARVER, W. EDMUND, minister; b. Evanston, Ill., May 3, 1928; s. Wallace Harper and Bertha (Edmond) C.; m. Norean Byrons, Nov. 22, 1969; children: David John, Kevin Edmund, Janine C. Carver Reister, Brian Wallace, Kimberly Ann. AB, Lafayette Coll., Easton, Pa., 1950; MA, Princeton Theol. Sem., 1953; DDiv (hon.), Bloomfield (N.J.) Coll., 1976, Tuculum Coll., Greeneville, Tenn., 1987. Ordained minister Presbyn. Ch. Pastor Tremont Presbyn. Ch., N.Y.C., 1953-58, Trinity Presbyn. Ch., Cherry Hill, N.J., 1958-68, 2d Presbyn. Ch., Knoxville, Tenn., 1976—; exec. v.p. Nat. Coun. Crime and Deliquency, N.Y.C., 1968-76; co-owner Moxham, Carver, Inc., Knoxville, 1989—. Author: A New Beginning, 1968, The Book of Acts, 1968, Role of Business in Combatting Organized Crime, 1970. Chmn. devel. Bloomfield Coll., 1959-60; bd. dirs. Maryville (Tenn.) Coll., 1978—; bd. dirs. Shannondale retirement homes and healthcare ctr., 1983—; bd. dirs. Presbyn. Ctr., U. Tenn., 1976-84; mem. speakers' bur. com. Knoxville-Knox County Constitution bicentennial Commn., 1985—; mem. Bd. Control of Corrections, State of Tenn., 1977-86; bd. dirs. Knoxville Miltiple Sclerosis Soc., 1978-82, Mixtec Project in Mex., 1978-82, Knoxville Young Adult Redevel. Inst., 1980-84. Mem. Presbyn. Ministers' Assn. (pres. 1984-85), Presbytery of East Tenn. (chmn. com. 1987—, moderator 1984-85), Union Presbytery (chmn. com. 1981-84, mem. gen. coun. 1976-84), Knoxville United Ministries (bd. dirs. 1977-82), Assn. Religious Ministries (bd. dirs. 1978-81), Knoxville Ministerial Assn., Rotary. Home: 209 Suburban Rd Knoxville TN 37923 Office: 2d Presbyn Ch 2829 Kingston Pike Knoxville TN 37923

CARVER, WILLIAM LOUIE, minister; b. Marshall, N.C., Mar. 23, 1939; s. Clarence T. and Ollie A. (Hensley) C.; m. Mary C. Gaines, Aug. 26, 1961; children: Pamela, Timothy, Charity, Rebecca. BA, Lexington Bapt. Coll., 1966; ThM, Teays Valley Bapt. Coll., 1978; ThD, Bapt. Christian U., 1981, PhD, 1983. Ordained to ministry Bapt. Ch., 1958. Missionary Mt. Missions, Irvine, Ky., 1963-68; pastor Bentley Meml. Bapt. Ch., Lexington, Ky., 1968-71; missionary Bapt. Faith Missions, Seoul, Korea, Manila, 1971-81; missions field rep. Bapt. Faith Missions, Lexington, 1981-87; pastor Harmony Bapt. Ch., Pine Bluff, Ark., 1987—; dir. Bluegrass Bapt. Schs., Lexington, 1969-71, Korean Ind. Bapt. Coll., Seoul, 1979—; regular dir. Nat. Christian Coun. Assn., Kitting, Pa., 1989—. Author: A Bird's Eye View of the Book, 1978, The Apocalypse, 1980, Marks of a N.T. Church, 1981, Missions: The Missionary and His Work, 1983. With USAF, 1959-63. Mem. Nat. Christian Counselor Assn. (counselor, nat. dir. to Korea 1989—). Home: 1911 Edmar Pine Bluff AR 71603 Office: Harmony Bapt Ch 2101 E 6th Pine Bluff AR 71601 *It has been my experience that God uses the individual who makes himself available to Him.*

CARY, LOWELL, religious organization director. Dir. world missions Ch. of God, Cleveland, Tenn. Office: Ch of God PO Box 2430 Cleveland TN 37320*

CARY, WILLIAM STERLING, church executive; b. Plainfield, N.J., Aug. 10, 1927; s. Andrew and Sadie C.; m. Marie B. Phillips; children: Yvonne, Denise, Sterling, Patricia. Ed., Morehouse Coll., also D.D.; student, Union Theol. Sem.; LL.D., Bishop Coll.; D.D., Elmhurst Coll.; L.H.D., Allen U., Ill. Coll. Ordained to ministry Baptist Ch., 1948; pastor Butler Meml. Presbyn. Ch., Youngstown, Ohio, 1953-55, Interdenominational Ch. of Open Door, Bklyn., 1955-58, Grace Congl. Ch., N.Y.C., 1958-68; area minister Met. and Suffolk assns. N.Y. Conf. United Ch. Christ, 1968-75; pres. Nat. Council Chs., N.Y.C., 1972-75; conf. minister Ill. conf. United Ch. Christ, 1975—; chmn. United Ch. Christ Council Conf. Execs., Council Religious Leaders Met. Chgo., 1986-92; mem. governing bd. Nat. Council Chs.; mem.

rep. consultation on ch. union United Ch. of Christ; mem. exec. council United Ch. of Christ; mem. Council on Ecumenism, Ch. World Service, Pres.'s Adv. Com. Vietnam Refugees; lectr. in field. Named One of 100 Most Influential Blacks in Am. for 1974-75 Ebony mag. Address: 1840 Westchester Blvd Westchester IL 60154

CASALE, ALFRED PAUL, eucharistic minister; b. N.Y.C., Aug. 1, 1955; s. Alfred Victor Dante and Clara (Lembo) C.; m. Sandra Leonor Sanchez, June 23, 1990. BA, Fordham U., 1990; postgrad., Union Theol. Sem., 1991—. Charismatic group seminar leader Children of Light Prayer Group, Bronx, 1982-84; young adult group core mem. Our Lady of the Assumption Parish, Bronx, 1984-85, eucharistic min., 1985—. Fordham U. scholar, 1987, 88, 89. Mem. Pax Christi, Contemplative Outreach, Alpha Sigma Nu, Alpha Sigma Lambda.

CASALE, FRANCIS JOSEPH, minister to the deaf; b. Hartford, Conn., Jan. 14, 1947; s. Joseph Lawrence and Elizabeth Frances (Torza) C.; m. Kimie Hiasa, Apr. 25, 1982; children: Naomi Ruth, Grace Megumi. BA, Gallaudet U., 1970; MA, Calif. State U., Northridge, 1974, BA, 1988; AA in Practical Theology, Christ for all Nations Inst., Dallas, 1984; ThD, Internat. Sem., 1989, PhD, 1990. Ordained to ministry Internat. Ministerial Assn., 1989. Evangelist, tchr. Christ for Nations Inst., Dallas, 1983-84; ind. missionary-tchr. various orgns., world-wide, 1984-87; evangelist, tchr. Christian Deaf Fellowship Mission, Downey, Calif., 1987-90; spiritual counselor Immanuel Deaf Bible Coll. and Immanuel Ch. Deaf, Downey, 1987-90; tchr. Bible, spiritual counselor Ind.-Internat. Ministerial Assn., Downey, 1990—; tchr. Calif. State U., Northridge, 1976-79; jr. bd. dirs. Immanuel Church of the Deaf., Downey, 1985—; asst. dir. Immanuel Deaf Bible Coll., Downey, 1986-89; adv. coun. bd. Christian Deaf Fellowship (Mission Orgn.), Downey, 1986—; counselor various locations, Calif. and Conn., 1980—. Illustrator: (sign lang.) L. A. Pierce Coll., Woodland Hills, Calif., 1975-78; editor: (mag.) Silent Evangel, 1988—, (newsletter) The Casales' Times/Teaching the Gospel, 1989—. Active in deaf ministry. Mem. Nat. Christian Counselors Assn. (assoc.), Internat. Ministerial Assn., Deaf Evang. Assn. N.Am. (treas. 1988—). Home and Office: 504 E Covina Blvd Covina CA 91722-2953 *In my life there are many wonderful and successful leaders to look up to and follow. It is confusing to decide which one to follow. I have found the One who is an infallible leader. I have chosen this infallible leader which is the Lord Jesus Christ.*

CASAROLI, CARDINAL AGOSTINO, Vatican secretary of state; b. Castel San Giovanni, Nov. 24, 1914. Ordained priest Roman Cath. Ch., 1938, titular archbishop, Cartagina, 1967; elevated to Sacred Coll. of Cardinals, 1979. Entered service of Vatican secretariat, 1940, undersec., 1961-67; sec. Congregation for Extraordinary Ecclesiastical Affairs, 1967-79; sec. of state and prefect of Council for Pub. Affairs of the Ch., 1979-90. Address: Vatican City Vatican City

CASE, CINDEE, youth minister; b. Akron, Ohio, Aug. 15, 1967; d. Charles Case and Barbara Putman. BA, Kent State U., 1990. Tchr. religion Holy Family Parish, Kent, Ohio, 1987-89; min. youth St. Patrick Parish, Stow, Ohio, 1989—; vol. retreat worker SEARCH program Cath. Youth Orgn., Akron, 1983-91; day camp dir., young adult coord., youth ministry parish facilitator, staff mem. Cath. Youth Orgn. of Summit County, Akron, 1991—. Mem. Nat. Orientation Dirs. Assn., Am. Camping Assn., Women's Network, Ladies Ancient Order of Hibernians (historian 1989, chair program com. 1990-92). Office: Holy Family Parish 3450 Sycamore Dr Stow OH 44224

CASE, JANE MCFARLING, religious educator; b. Owensboro, Ky., Apr. 13, 1955; d. Norman Henry and Beverly Jean (Ogle) McFarling. BME, Ky. Wesleyan Coll., Owensboro, Ky., 1979; MA in Communication, Western Ky. U., 1989; EdD, U. Ky., 1990—. Minister music and youth Panther Creek Bapt. Ch., Owensboro, Ky., 1978-83; pianist Eaton Meml. Bapt. Ch., Owensboro, Ky., 1987-89; dir. Christian edn. and music Cumberland Presbyn. Ch., Owensboro, Ky., 1989—; instr. Owensboro Community Coll., 1990—; presbyterial cons. for leadership devel. Cumberland Presbyn. Denomination, 1990—. Corres. sec. exec. com. Daviess County Rep. Party, 1989—. Mem. So. State Communication Assn., Ky. Assn. Communication Arts, Delta Omicron. Republican. Home: 1401 W 12th St Owensboro KY 42301 Office: Cumberland Presbyn Ch 910 Booth AVe Owensboro KY 42301

CASE, STEVE WAYNE, clergyman; b. San Francisco, Sept. 13, 1957; s. Marvin E. and Billie Ann (Wright) C.; m. Deborah Pontynen, Aug. 20, 1978; 1 child, Katharine Pontynen. BS in Phys. Edn., Pacific Union Coll., 1979, BA in Theology, MA in Phys. Edn., 1980; MDiv, Andrews U., 1985, PhD in Religious Edn., 1987. Ordained to ministry Seventh-day Adventist Ch., 1986. Youth pastor English Oaks Ch., Lodi, Calif., 1980-82; youth ministry asst. Pioneer Meml. Ch., Berrien Springs, Mich., 1982-85; asst. prof. youth ministry Andrews U. (Sem.), Berrien Springs, 1985-89; youth pastor Carmichael Seventh Day Adventist Ch., Sacramento, Calif., 1989—; dir. Youth Resource Ctr., Berrien Springs, Mich., 1985-89; founder Seventh Day Adventist Youth Ministry Profls., Berrien Springs, 1987; co-investigator valuegenesis Seventh-day Adventist Ch., Silver Spring, Md., 1989—. Author: Growing Kids: Making Your Youth Ministry Count, 1989; editor UTH MIN, 1988—. Mem. Soc. Sci. Study Religion, Religious Rsch. Assn. Office: Carmichael Seventh Day Adventist Ch 4600 Winding Way Sacramento CA 95841 *Life is full of non-neutral enrichments—opportunities to see what a person is made of and a motivation for positive character development.*

CASE, STEVEN CHARLES, minister; b. Mariemont, Ohio, Sept. 4, 1951; s. Charles Robert and Estelle Margaret (Bryan) C.; m. Gayle Louise Milay, June 23, 1973. BA, Judson Coll., 1973; MDiv, Ea. Bapt. Sem., 1978. Ordained to ministry Am. Bapt. Chs. in the U.S.A., 1978. Min. Norwayne Bapt. Ch., Westland, Mich., 1970-73, 1st Bapt. Ch., Somerdale, N.J., 1974-79, Bergen Point Community Ch., Bayonne, N.J., 1979-80, Grace Bapt. Ch., Westmont, N.J., 1981—; mem., chmn. ann. session Am. Bapt. Chs. in N.J., 1979, chmn. com. pub. mission, 1982-85, pres., 1989. Trustee, v.p. bd. trustees Bapt. Home South Jersey, Riverton, N.J., 1982-87, chmn. pers. com., 1982-87; organizer community food pantry Grace Bapt. Ch., Haddon Twp., N.J., 1983—; chmn. commn. on impact of pub. witness N.J. Coun. Chs., 1991—; mem. community ethics and values com. Haddon Township Pub. Schs., 1990—. Mem. Bapt. Peace Fellowship. Home: 23 Reeve Ave Westmont NJ 08108 Office: Grace Bapt Ch 25-27 Reeve Ave Westmont NJ 08108

CASE, SYLVESTER QUEZADA, minister; b. La Vega, Dominican Republic, June 25, 1941; s. Sylvester and Digna Quezada; m. Juanita Rodriguez, Aug. 29, 1961; children: Larry, Alvin, Edward. BA in Theology, Andrews U., Berrien Springs, Mich., 1982, MDiv, 1985; MA in New Testament, Denver Bapt. Seminary, 1987. Ordained to ministry Seventh-day Adventists, 1987. Min. Rocky Mountain Conf. Seventh-day Adventists, Denver, 1984—; dist. dir. Seventh Day Adventists Chs. Farmington, Waterflow, La Vida, N.Mex., 1988—; del. Rocky Mountain Conf. Seventh Day Adventists, Denver, 1984—, Mid Am. Union Seventh Day Adventists, Lincoln, Nebr., 1987—. Named Outstanding Student of Yr. Am. Bible Soc. Mem. Soc. Bibl. Lit., Phi Kappa Phi, Alpha Mu Gamma. Republican. Home: 712 N Dustin Farmington NM 87401 Office: Rocky Mountain Conf Seventh Day Adventists 2520 S Downing Denver CO 80210 *There is no crime in being inquisitive. On the contrary, one of the great joys of life radicates in finding things out for ourselves.*

CASE-WINTERS, ANNA, theology educator; d. Henry Burton and Emma Lucile (Barksdale) Case; m. R. Michael Winters III, June 7, 1975; 1 child, R. Michael Winters IV; 1 stepdaughter, Jennifer Gwyn. BA in Bible and Religion, Psychology, Agnes Scott Coll., 1975; MDiv summa cum laude, Columbia Theol. Sem., 1978; PhD in Theology, Vanderbilt U., 1988. Assoc. pastor Cen. Presbyn. Ch., Oklahoma City, 1978-80; assoc. dir. field edn. Vanderbilt Divinity SCh., 1981-86; instr. theology McCormick Theol. Sem., Chgo., 1986-88, asst. prof. theology, 1988-90, assoc. prof. theolgoy, 1990—; Presbyn. Ch. USA rep. World Alliance of Reformed Chs.; mem. Reformed Theology Work Group, Presbyn. Ch. USA, com. on preparation for ministry Chgo. Presbytery; theologian in residence for synod sch. Synod of Mid-Americas, 1990; lectr. for ch. retreats. Author: Divine Power: Traditional Understandings and Conteporary Challenges; contbr. articles to profl. jours.; book reviewer Religious Studies Rev., 1986—. John H. Smith fellow Vanderbilt U., grad. fellow Columbia Theol. Sem. Mem. Am. Acad. Religion, Am. Theol. Soc., Phi Beta Kappa, Eta Sigma Phi. Office: McCormick Sem 5555 S Woodlawn Chicago IL 60637

CASEY, BROTHER DANIEL F., school system administrator. Supt. of Schs. Dept. of edn., Diocese of Providence, R.I. Office: Edn Dept Supt 1 Cathedral Sq Providence RI 02903*

CASEY, DANIEL JOSEPH, priest; b. County Kerry, Ireland, Jan. 25, 1935; came to U.S., 1958; s. Daniel D. and Julia Ann (Collins) C. Student, All Hallows Coll., Dublin, 1952-58; MSW, Sacramento State U., 1972. Ordained priest Roman Cath. Ch., 1958. Assoc. pastor Holy Rosary Ch., Woodland, Calif., 1958-65, St. Isidore's Ch., Yuba City, Calif., 1965-66, Cathedral of Blessed Sacrament, Sacramento, 1966-69; founding dir. Dept. Mex.-Am. Affairs, Diocese of Sacramento, 1969-71, coord. for Spanish speaking Apostolate, 1971-76, mem. commn. for Spanish speaking West Coast Bishops, 1973-76, dir. community devel., 1976-77; producer Mex.-Am. Forum and Chicano Press Conf. TV, 1973-76; pastor St. Mary's Ch., Vacaville, Calif., 1977-90, Presentation Ch., Sacramento, 1990—. Mem. Sacramento Redevel. Commn., 1973-75; mem. Calif. State Office Econ. Opportunity Bd., 1973-76. Mem. Calif. State Marriage Counselors Assn., Nat. Assn. Social Workers, Sacramento Bd. Realtors, Acad. Cert. Social Workers, Nat. Conf. Cath. Charities.

CASEY, DEBORA DE VORE, youth director; b. Denver, May 2, 1964; d. Gerald Edmond and Dorothy (Ramsdale) De V.; m. Paul Lambert Casey, Jan. 2, 1988. BS in Animal Sci., Tex. A&M U., 1986; MS in Animal Sci., La. State U., 1989. Youth dir. 1st United Meth. Ch., Sylacauga, Ala., 1989-91. Member Fayetteville (Ala.) Vol. Fire Dept., 1990-91; co-organizer Fayetteville Country Fair, 1991. Mem. Ala. Cattlewoman Assn. Home: 386 Talladega Springs Rd Sylacauga AL 35150 Office: 1st United Meth Ch 105 E Spring St Sylacauga AL 35150

CASEY, EDWARD JOHN, minister; b. Dover, N.J., Aug. 7, 1953; s. Edward Gerard and Eva (Reule) C. B.Engring., Stevens Inst. Tech., Hoboken, N.J., 1975, M.Engring., 1980; MDiv, Drew Theol. Sem., 1988. Ordained to ministry United Meth. Ch., 1990; registered profl. engr., N.J. Pastor Barryville (N.Y.) United Meth. Ch., 1985-86, Eldred (N.Y.) United Meth. Ch., 1985-86, 1st United Meth. Ch., Stony Point, N.Y., 1986-91, Stockholm (N.J.) United Meth. Ch., 1991—; chaplain Nyack (N.Y.) Hosp., 1990-91; pres. United Meth. Parish of Rockland County, 1990-91. Mem. IEEE. Office: Stockholm United Meth Ch RD # 1 27 Vernon Rd Stockholm NJ 07460

CASEY, STEPHEN JOSEPH, religious studies educator; b. N.Y.C., Oct. 24, 1941; s. Michael Joseph and Marion (LeBrun) C.; m. Ellen Miller, Aug. 1965; children—Roberta Katherine, Amy Clare, Paul Joseph. B.A., Iona Coll., 1963; postgrad., U. Wis., 1963-65; M.A., Marquette U., 1969; postgrad., 1974-75. Assoc. prof. theology/religious studies U. Scranton, Penn. since 1969—. Mem. Soc. Christian Ethics, Soc. Sci. Studies Religion, Coll. Theology Soc. (regional officer 1984—). Roman Catholic. Office: U Scranton Dept Theology Scranton PA 18510

CASEY, TIMOTHY FRANK, lay worker; b. Beaver Falls, Pa., Mar. 31, 1947; s. Frank and Carmella (Dinello) C.; m. Judith Servello, Aug. 7, 1976 (div. Apr. 1980). BS in Edn., Clarion Univ. of Pa., 1969, MS in Libr. Sci., 1972. Sec. Fellowship of Christian Athletes, Kane, Pa., 1985—; libr. Kane Pub. and Sch. Libr., 1983—. Republican. Home: 20 Greeves St Kane PA 16735

CASH, RICK GORDON, minister; b. Winston-Salem, Dec. 15, 1947; s. Marvin Edgar and Audrey (Gwaltney) C.; m. Janet Louise Ernest, Mar. 17, 1984; 1 child, Lauren Suzanne. BA, U. N.C., 1971; MDiv, Southeastern Sem., Wake Forest, N.C., 1974; PhD, So. Sem., Louisville, 1991. Ordained to ministry, So. Bapt. Conv., 1974. Assoc. pastor Mineral Springs Bapt. Ch., Winston-Salem, 1973-79; pastor Hiddenite (N.C.) Bapt. Ch., 1980-86; interim pastor Calvary Bapt. Ch., Madison, 1988; supply pastor So. Bapt. Ch. in Ind. and Ky., 1988—; temp. staff Billy Graham Evangelistic Assn., Amsterdam, 1986; summer missionary Home Mission Bd., So. Bapt. Conv., 1971, 72, 73. Bd. dirs. United Way, Alexander County, N.C., 1982-86, Heart Fund, Alexander County, 1982-86. Named Outstanding Young Religious Leader, Jaycees, Taylorsville, 1984; All Union Coun. of Evang. Christians vis. scholar, 1990, Spl. Studies scholar, Harvard U., 1988; Garret fellow, So. Bapt. Theol. Sem., 1987-90. Mem. Acad. of Homiletics. Office: So Bapt Theol Sem Box 8-1202 Louisville KY 40280

CASHMAN, CHARLES WILLIAM, III, minister; b. Norfolk, Va., June 22, 1951; s. Charles William Jr. and Lucy Ellen (Bourdon) C.; m. Barbara Jo Perkins, June 23, 1973; children: Barbara Christine, Katie Nicole, Charles Stephen. AA, Lees-McRae Jr. Coll., 1971; BA, Wake Forest U., 1973; MDiv, Southwestern Bapt. Theol. Sem., 1976; postgrad., Luther Rice Sem. Ordained to ministry So. Bapt. Conv., 1975. Min. youth and music Providence Bapt. Ch., Roxboro, N.C., 1972, 1st Bapt. Ch., Lucas, Tex., 1973-74; pastor Dunn's Mountain Bapt. Ch., Salisbury, N.C., 1976-79, Brookwood Bapt. Ch., Burlington, N.C., 1979-83, York River Bapt. Ch., Williamsburg, Va., 1983—; chmn. Missions Growth Com., 1990—; pres. Peninsula Bapt. Pastor's Conf., Newport News, Va., 1990—, Bapt. Gen. Assn. Va. Pastor's Conf., 1990—; chmn. evangelism com. Peninsula Assn., 1989—. Mem. Sch. Reorgn. Com., Williamsburg, 1987-89. Mem. Williamsburg Clergy Assn., Civitan (Granite Quarry, N.C. chaplain 1977-79), Grove Kennel Club (chaplain 1984—). Republican. Home: 118 Plains View Rd Williamsburg VA 23188 Office: York River Bapt Ch 8201 Croaker Rd Williamsburg VA 23188 *The buzzards flying across a meadow won't be impressed with the beauty of the wild flowers but in the midst of the flowers they will light upon the carcass of a dead rabbit, because buzzards major on dead things. What you are determines what you see. I've discovered this is true for you and me as well.*

CASHMAN, DONALD P., rabbi; b. Newburgh, N.Y., May 3, 1955; s. Allan B. and Elaine (Siegfried) C.; m. Sharona R. Wachs, Mar. 25, 1984; children: Avraham Dov Wachs, Eliana Leah Wachs, Ayelet Na'arah Wachs. MA, Hebrew Union Coll., N.Y.C., 1982. Ordained rabbi, 1983. Rabbi Temple Israel of Greater Miami (Fla.), 1983-85; rabbi B'nai Sholom Reform Congregation, Albany, N.Y., 1985—; sec. Interfaith Social Action Coalition, Albany, 1990—; treas. Capital Dist. Religious Coalition for Abortion Rights, 1986-90. Editor Albany JGS Newsletter, 1988-91. Mem. Albany Jewish Genealog. Soc. (pres. 1990—), Cen. Conf. Am. Rabbis, Kutz Camp Alumni and Friends Assn. (pres. 1985-87). Office: B'nai Sholom 420 Whitehall Rd Albany NY 12208-1792

CASIANO VARGAS, ULISES, bishop; b. Lajas, P.R., Sept. 25, 1933. Ordained priest Roman Cath. Ch., 1967. Elected to bishop, 1976 bishop of Mayaquez, P.R., 1976—. Address: Diocese of Mayaquez Apartado 2272 PO Box 2272 Mayaquez PR 00708

CASON, DEE MARIE, religious organization administrator; b. Washington, Oct. 7; d. Warren Lee and Jessie Marie (Schulz) O.; m. Ron K. Cason, May 24, 1969; children: Adam Gerard, Matthew Todd. Student, Lee Coll., 1967-70. Sec. sales dept. Chris Craft Corp., Ft. Lauderdale, Fla., 1965-67; sr. sec. student aid office Lee Coll., Cleveland, Tenn., 1967-68, exec. sec., bus. mgr., 1968-71; sec. temporary svcs. various corps., Warner Robins, Ga., 1971-75; word processing sec. Armco Steel Corp., Middletown, Ohio, 1975; exec. sec., dir. mfg. Johnson Wax, Racine, Wis., 1975-80; account analyst Property Tax Svcs., Denver, 1982-83; sec. GM and Dow Corning, Saginaw, Mich., 1983-85; trademark analyst legal dept. Dow Corning, Midland, Mich., 1985; adminstrv. coord. pub. rels. internat. offices Ch. of God, Cleveland, Tenn., 1985-91, coord. convs. and spl. events Internat. Offices, 1991—; Active ladies ministries, 1971—; speaker for denominational local, dist. and state meetings, confs. and seminars, 1974—; Sunday sch. tchrs., 1975; coord. state girls club Ch. of God, Wis., 1978-80. Mem. NAFE, Religious Conf. Mgmt. Assn., Nat. Assn. Bus. and Profl. Women. Republican. Home: 106 Vermont Circle NW Cleveland TN 37312 Office: Ch of God 2490 Keith St NW Cleveland TN 37311

CASORIA, GIUSEPPE CARDINAL, Italian ecclesiastic; b. Acerra, Italy, Oct. 1, 1908. Ordained priest Roman Catholic Ch., 1930; jurist, ofcl. Roman Curia, 1937—; under-sec. Congregation for Sacraments, 1959-69, sec., 1969-73, pro-prefect, 1981-83, prefect, 1983; consecrated titular archbishop of Vescovia, 1972; elevated to Sacred Coll. of Cardinals, 1983; deacon St. Joseph of Via Trionfale. Mem. Congregation for Doctrine of Faith, Congregation for Causes of Saints, Commn. for Interpretation of Canonical Directives. Correggere e confrontare con l'annesso foglio aggiornato. Address: Via Pancrazio Pfeiffer 10, 00193 Rome Italy

CASSEL, HERBERT WILLIAM, religion educator; b. Cressona, Pa., July 13, 1931; s. William K. and Mabel O. (Heimbach) C.; m. Elva Jean Segerlund, June 27, 1954 (div. Jan. 1978); children: Eric William, Scott David; m. Nancy Jo Kivett, Nov. 23, 1978. BA, Huntington (Ind.) Coll., 1953; STB, Temple U. Sch. Theology, 1956; ThM, Princeton (N.J.) Theol. Sem., 1963; PhD, Temple U., 1973. Pastor Trinity Evang. Congl. Ch., Harrisburg, Pa., 1956-60, Evang. Congl. Ch., Pine Beach, N.J., 1960-63; asst. prof. religion U. Indpls., 1966-68, assoc. prof. religion, 1968-78, prof., 1978—, chair philosophy and religion dept., 1971-79, 83—, Raines Mueller prof. philosophy and religion, 1979—. Bd. dirs. Southside Youth Coun., Indpls., 1976-78, Metro Ministries, Indpls., 1976-80. Mem. Am. Acad. Religion, Am. Philos. Assn., Soc. Christian Philosophers, South Ind. Conf. United Meth. Ch. (bd. ordained ministry 1983—), AAUP (pres. Ind. conf. 1989-90), Alpha Chi (faculty sponsor 1984—, pres. region V 1986-88). Office: U Indpls 1400 E Hanna Ave Indianapolis IN 46227-3697

CASSIDY, EDWARD IDRIS CARDINAL, archbishop; b. Sydney, NSW, Australia, July 5, 1924; s. Harold George and Dorothy May (Philipps) C. Grad., St. Columba Sem., Springwood, Australia, 1943, St. Patrick's Coll., Manly, Australia, 1949; JCD, Lateran U., Rome, 1955; Diploma in Ecclesiastical Diplomacy, Pontifical Ecclesiastical Acad., Rome, 1955. Ordained priest Roman Cath. Ch., 1949, archbishop, 1970, created cardinal, 1991. Asst. priest Parish Yenda, Wagga Wagga, NSW, 1950-52; with Vatican Diplomatic Svc., India, Ireland, El Salvador, Argentina, 1955-70; titular archbishop of Amantia, 1970; Pontifical rep. Republic of China, Bangladesh, So. Africa and Lesotho, The Netherlands, 1970-88; substitute Vatican Secretariat of State, 1988-89; pres. Pontifical Coun. for Promoting Christian Unity, Vatican City, 1989—. Decorated comendador en la Orden Nacional José Matias Delgado (El Salvador); officer Order of Brilliant Star with Grand Cordon (Republic of China); grootkruis in de Orde van Oranje-Nassau (The Netherlands); cavaliere de Gran Croce dell'Ordine Al Merito della Repubblica Italiana; companion in Gen. Div. of Order of Australia; commandeur de la Légion d'Honneur (France). Office: Pontifical Coun for Promoting, Christian Unity, 00120 Vatican City Vatican City

CASSIDY, JAMES PATRICK, priest, university chancellor, health care administrator; b. Mt. Vernon, N.Y., May 10, 1925; s. Patrick J. and Helen (Curran) C. BA, St. Joseph's Sem. & Coll., Yonkers, N.Y., 1950; PhD, Fordham U., 1963. Ordained priest Roman Cath. Ch., 1951; lic. psychologist, N.Y., Conn., N.J. Parish priest Archdiocese N.Y., N.Y.C., 1951-64, marriage counselor family life bur.,, 1957-65, dir. Cana Confs., 1960-64, dir. family cons. svcs., 1965-72, exec. dir. dept. health and hosps., 1972—; guidance counselor St. Barnabas High Sch., Bronx, 1954-57; intern clin. psychology St. Vincent's Hosp., N.Y.C., 1964-65, sr. clin. psychologist, 1965-72; chancellor N.Y. Med. Coll., Valhalla, N.Y., 1987—; adj. prof. Fordham U., Bronx, 1965-66; assoc. prof. St. John's U., Jamaica, N.Y., 1965-75, dir. pastoral counseling, 1969-75. Mem. task force N.Y.C. Planning Commn., 1973; mem. adv. coun. on youth drug and alcohol problems N.Y.C. Dept. Mental Health, 1974; mem. steering com.on alcoholism Gov. of N.Y., N.Y.C., 1976; mem. Assn. for a Better N.Y., 1985, Cath. Charities, U.S.A.; mem. adv. coun. health com. N.Y. State Senate, 1985. Recipient Terence Cardinal Cooke award N.Y. Med. Coll., 1985, Gran Ofcl. award Orden Heraldica Cristobal Colon, 1988; inducted into Knights of Malta, 1988. Fellow N.Y. Acad. Medicine; mem. Am. Hosp. Assn., Am. Pub. Health Assn., N.Y. State Psychol. Assn., N.Y. Athletic Club, Larchmont Shore Club. Avocations: photography, reading, boating. Home: 1249 Fifth Ave New York NY 10029 Office: NY Med Coll Sunshine Cottage Valhalla NY 10595

CASTELEIN, JOHN DONALD, theology educator; b. Linselles, France, Dec. 30, 1948; s. Donald and Julienne (Geiregat) C.; m. R. Marie Cornett, Dec. 21, 1968. AB, Lincoln Christian Coll., 1970; MA, MDiv, Lincoln Christian Sem., 1977; PhD in Theology, U. Chgo., 1988. Prof. theology Lincoln (Ill.) Christian Coll. and Sem., 1977—. Mem. Am. Acad. Religion. Mem. Christian Ch. Home: 210 Campus View Dr Lincoln IL 62656

CASTELLAW, EARLENE JOHNSON, clergywoman; b. Carroll County, Ga., Jan. 11, 1928; d. Earl Clifton and Beulah (Walker) Johnson; m. Chet Lee Castellaw, Mar. 20, 1947 (dec. 1977); children: Gary Lee, Jeffrey, Debra Susan. D Religious Sci., Religious Sci. Inst., Fillmore, Calif., 1975; DD, Religious Sci. Inst., San Diego, 1984. Ordained to ministry, 1964. Asst. minister Ch. of Religious Sci., San Diego, 1961-77, pastor, 1977—; mem. bd. edn. Religious Sci. Inst., Spokane, Wash., 1961—, bd. dirs., 1978—, mem. exec. com., 1980—, chair sponsor program, 1987—; pres. Religious Sci. Inst., San Diego, 1980-84. Avocations: gardening, reading. Home: 3509 Carleton St San Diego CA 92106 Office: Ch Religious Sci Ste 310 1260 Morena Blvd San Diego CA 92110

CASTELLOE, RALEIGH ROOSEVELT, JR., minister; b. Windsor, N.C., Jan. 3, 1939; s. Raleigh Roosevelt and Mary Elizabeth (Pearce) C.; m. Phyllis Coleman, Dec. 19, 1961; children: Raleigh Roosevelt III, Karen Sue, Andrew Coleman. AA, Campbell U., Buies Creek, N.C., 1959; BA, Carson-Newman Coll., Jefferson City, Tenn., 1961; BDiv, Southeastern Bapt. Theol. Sem., Wake Forest, N.C., 1964. Ordained to ministry, So. Bapt. Ch., 1962. Minister Horton's and Oak Grove Bapt. Chs., Aulander, N.C., 1961-65, Macedonia Bapt. Ch., Liberty, N.C., 1965-72; assoc. minister First Bapt. Ch., Newton, N.C., 1972-78; minister Flint Groves Bapt. Ch., Gastonia, N.C., 1978-84, First Bapt. Ch., Troy, N.C., 1985—; mem. gen. bd. Bapt. State Conv. of N.C., Cary, 1990—. Bd. dirs. N.C. div. Am. Cancer Soc., Raleigh, 1990; advisor bd. advisors Montgomery Meml. Hosp., Troy, N.C., 1991. Democrat. Home: 219 E Chestnut St Troy NC 27371 Office: First Bapt Ch 401 E Main St Troy NC 27371

CASTILLO, DENNIS ANGELO, theology and history educator; b. Detroit, Oct. 21, 1958; s. Pasquale Anthony and Josephine (Zammit) C.; m. Kathleen Murphy, July 7, 1984; children: Paul Joseph, John Louis. BA in History and Religion, Mich. State U., 1981; MDiv, U. Chgo., 1982, PhD in History of Christianity, 1990. Dir. religious edn. St. Alphonsus Ch., Chgo., 1983-86; asst. prof. history and theology, chair theology dept. St. Mary's Coll., Orchard Lake, Mich., 1986-91; adj. prof. religious studies U. Detroit Mercy, 1988—. Bd. dirs. Caritas Found., Detroit, 1984—. Mem. Am. Acad. Religion, Am. Hist. Assn., Am. Cath. Hist. Assn., Am. Soc. Ch. Historians, Phi Kappa Phi. Democrat. Office: 306 E Michigan Ave Albion MI 45224

CASTILLO LARA, ROSALIO JOSE CARDINAL, archbishop; b. Sept. 4, 1922, San Casimiro, Venezuela; s. Rosalio Castillo Hernandez and Guillermina Lara Pena. J.C.D., Ateneo Salesiano, Torino, Italy, 1953. Ordained priest Roman Catholic Ch., 1949. Asst. for studies Liceo San Jose, Los Teques, Venezuela, 1949-50; pres. Assn. Venezuelana degli Educatori Cattolici, 1953; prof. Ateneo Salesiano, Torino, 1954-57, Rome, 1957-65; provincial superior Venezuela, Salesians, 1966-67, regional superior Latin Am., 1967-71, gen. councillor for pastoral care to youth, 1971-73; consecrated bishop Titular Ch. of Precausa, 1973, archbishop, 1982; co-adjutor bishop, Trujillo, Venezuela, 1973-74; del. Episcopal Conf. Venezuela, Synod of Bishops, Rome, 1974-75; sec. Pontifical Commn. for Revision of Code of Canon Law, Rome, 1975, pro-pres., 1982-84; pres. Disciplinary Commn. of Roman Curia, 1981, Pontifical Commn. for Authentic Interpretation of Code of Canon Law, 1984—; elevated to cardinal, 1985; pres. Pontifical coun. Interpretation of Legis. Texts, 1989—, Adminstrn. of Patrimony of Apostolic See, 1989—, Pontifical Commn. Vatican City State, 1990. Contbr. articles to scholarly jours. Mem. Academia Ciencias Sociales y Politicas del Venezuela, Academia Nacional de la Historia di Venezuela (corr.). Address: Vatican City Vatican City

CASTLE, CARLYLE FAIRFAX, clergyman; b. Honolulu, Aug. 4, 1955; s. William Donald and Jacqueline (Meredith) C. B Christian Edn., Simpson

Coll., 1978, MA in Bible and Theology, 1979. Ordained to minsitry Assembly of God Ch. Dean men First Assembly of God, Honolulu, 1982-83; counselor Teen Challenge Hawaii, Honolulu, 1983-84; assoc. pastor Pahoa (Hawaii) Assembly of God Ch., 1984-86, New Life Ch., Haleiwa, Hawaii, 1987-90, GateWay Tabernacle, St. Louis, 1990—. Republican. Home and Office: GateWay Tabernacle 3225 A Nebraska Ave Saint Louis MO 63118

CASTLE, HOWARD BLAINE, religious organization administrator; b. Toledo, July 15, 1935; s. Russell Wesley and Letha Belle (Hobbs) C.; m. Patricia Ann Haverty, Aug. 12, 1957; 1 child Kevin Blaine. AB, Marion Coll., 1958; postgrad., Valparaiso U., 1960. Pastor The Wesleyan Ch., Valparaiso, Ind., 1958-60, Toronto, Ohio, 1963-69; assoc. pastor Northridge Wesleyan Ch., Dayton, Ohio, 1960-63; exec. dir. gen. dept. youth Wesleyan Ch. Hdqrs., Marion, Ind., 1968-72, dir. field ministries gen. dept. Sunday schs., 1972-74, exec. dir. curriculum, 1980-81; mng. editor WIN Mag., Marion, Ind., 1969-72; asst. gen. sec. Gen. Dept. of Local Ch. Edn., Marion, Ind., 1974-80; gen. dir. estate planning Wesleyan Ch. Internat Ctr., Indpls., 1982—; Editor Ohio dist. The Wesleyan Ch., Columbus, 1961-69; gen. conf. del. The Wesleyan Ch., Anderson, Ind., 1968. Writer: Curriculum-Religious Adult Student/Teacher, 1982—, Light from the Word, 1982—. Mem. Christian Holiness Assn., Christian Stewardship Assn., Christian Mgmt. Assn. Avocations: music, reading. Office: The Wesleyan Ch Internat 6060 Castleway Dr W Indianapolis IN 46250 *Life's choices impact more than any other factor the measure of our success and achievements. Circumstances cannot defeat one who chooses to rise above them by acting in accord with his choice.*

CASTRILLON, URIEL, minister; b. Guatemala, Guatemala, Mar. 5, 1961; came to U.S., 1982; s. Uriel and Blanca Argentina (Flores) C.; m. Rebecca Ruth Beaty, June 28, 1986; children: Rebecca Rachelle, Miriam Elizabeth. Student, Mariano G. U., 1979-81; BBA, U. Balt., 1983. Ordained to ministry Ch. of God, 1991. Min. of youth Ch. of Nazarene, Huntington Park, Calif., 1982-83; pastor for Hispanics Ch. of Nazarene, Dundalk, Md., 1983-85; ethnic ministries dir. Ch. of God, Middle River, Md., 1985-88; sr. pastor Ch. of God, Halethorpe, Md., 1988-91; outreach dir. House of Prayer, Cleve., 1991—; evangelistic work of preaching and teaching in fgn. nations Ch. of God, 1980-91. Author: This Great Salvation, 1990. Home: 24202 Elm Rd North Olmsted OH 44070 Office: House of Prayer 3106 Woodbridge Ave Cleveland OH 44109 *True life begins with faith in Jesus...knowing that God is always for you, with you, and in you.*

CASTRO, JOHN GONZALES, clergyman, educator; b. San Antonio, Nov. 18, 1935; s. John Riojas and Elvira (Medrano) Gonzales C. B.A. in Philosophy, Oblate Coll. S.W., 1959, M.Div. (equivalent), 1963; Ph.D. in Counseling Psychology, Mich. State U., 1975. Ordained priest Roman Catholic Ch., 1962; cert. counselor Nat. Bd. Cert. Counselors. Joined Missionary Oblates of Mary Immaculate, 1956; tchr. Spanish, St. Anthony High Sch. Sem., San Antonio, 1972; grad. asst. Mich. State U., East Lansing, 1973-75, coordinator Chicano program com. Coll. Edn., 1972-73; assoc. pastor Our Lady of Guadalupe, Austin, Tex., 1975-78; prof. Mexican Am. psychodynamics, counseling psychology and homiletics, dir. dept. cultural awareness and devel. Oblate Coll. S.W., San Antonio, 1978-81; prof. Hispanic psychodynamics, social, emotional, interpersonal devel., pastoral psychology, homiletics, Spanish, dir. dept. Hispanic ministries Mt. Angel Sem., St. Benedict, Oreg., 1981-83; prof., dean Hispanic Intercultural Ministry Program, St. Thomas Theol. Sem., Denver, 1983—; mem. diaconate program teaching staff Archdiocese of San Antonio, 1978-81; trustee El Visitante Dominical, nat. weekly newspaper, 1978—; co-dir. undergrad. coll. program Missionary Oblates of Mary Immaculate, Austin, 1975-76; coordinator master's program Antioch Juarez Lincoln U., Austin, 1976-77; program dir. Mexican Am. Ctr. for Econ. Devel., Austin, 1978-79; psychologist Diocese of Austin, 1975-78; mem. San Salvador Vicariate for Hispanic Affairs, Archdiocese of Portland (Oreg.), 1981—. Charter mem. Juvenile Rev. Bd. Brownsville (Tex.), 1971-72; mem. central council Mental Health and Mental Retardation Adv. Bd., Austin, 1976-77; chmn. adv. bd. Drug Abuse Mental Health and Mental Retardation, Austin, 1976-78; chmn. adv. bd. VISTA, Austin, 1976-77. Mem. Am. Assn. Counseling and Devel., Nat. Council Cath. Bishops (trustee N.W. region for Hispanic affairs Region XII, 1981-83), Priests Organized for Religious, Econ. and Social Rights, Assn. Religious and Value Issues in Counseling (editorial bd. quar. Counseling and Values, trustee 1982—), Assn. Humanistic Edn. and Devel., Mich. State U. Alumni Assn. Democrat. Club: K.C. Home: 2695 So Ames Way #6 Denver CO 80227 Office: 1300 S Steele St Denver CO 80210

CASTRONIS, JOHN MICHAEL, minister; b. Athens, Ga., Dec. 20, 1948; s. Michael John C.; m. Danielle Baudouin, July 18, 1990. BA, U. Ga., 1967, MEd, 1973; MDiv, Columbia Sem., 1988, D of Ministry, 1991. Ordained to ministry Presbyn. Ch., 1988. Staff asst. Cen. Presbyn. Ch., Atlanta, 1986; pastor asst. New Hope Presbyn. Ch., Comer, Ga., 1987-88; assoc. pastor 1st Presbyn. Ch., Delray Beach, Fla., 1989—; pres. Certgy Assn., Delray Beach, 1991; mem. Food Pantry Coord. Coun., Delray Beach, 1990-91; ethics com., Hospice By the Sea, Boca Raton, Fla., 1989-91; chaplain CROS Camp for Underprovileged, West Palm Beach, Fla., 1989-90. Mem. Delran Beach Community Drug Abuse Task Force, 1991—. Grad. Studies grantee, Columbia Sem., 1988; recipient Ch. History award, Columbia Sem., 1986, Theology award, 1988; named Top Grad., Columbia Sem., 1988. Office: 1st Presbyn Ch 33 Gleason St Delray Beach FL 33483

CASTRO RUIZ, MANUEL, archbishop; b. Morelia, Michoacan, Mex., Nov. 9, 1918; s. Castro Tinoco and Mercedes (Ruiz de) C. Student, Morelia Sem., 1930-37, Pontifical Pius, Latin Am. Coll., 1940, Gregorian U., Rome, 1940, Puebla Sem., 1943. Ordained priest Roman Cath. Ch., 1943. Pvt. sec. to archbishop of Morelia, 1943; prefect of Valladolid Inst.; spiritual dir. Minor Sem., 1947-50; spiritual dir. major Sem. of Morelia, prof. math. and philosophy, 1950-65; aux. bishop of Yucatan, 1965-69, archbishop of Yucatan, 1969—; asst. to Episcopal Synod, 1974. Office: State of Yucatan, Numero 501 Calle 58, City of Merida CP 97000, Mexico

CASURELLA, ANTHONY, religion educator; b. Chgo., May 11, 1946; s. Anthony and Anna Mildred (Hibbett) C.; m. Sharon Marie Yardy, June 15, 1968; children: Stephan A., Joy M., Jonathan P., Alison K. BA, Greenville (Ill.) Coll., 1968; MDiv, Asbury Theol. Sem., 1971; PhD, U. Durham, Eng., 1981. Ordained to ministry Free Meth. Ch., 1971. Chaplain St. Marys Coll., U. Durham, 1975-76; minister Claypath United Reformed Ch., Durham, 1975-76; lectr. in new testament Emmanuel Bible Coll., Birkenhead, Eng., 1976-77, prin., 1977-87; prof. of new testament Western Evang. Sem., Portland, Oreg., 1987—; mem. Emmanuel Denomination Exec. Coun., Birkenhead, 1977-87, chmn. 1983-84. Author: The Johannine Paraclete in The Church Fathers, 1983. Fellow Inst. Bibl. Rsch.; mem. Studiorum Novi Testamenti Societas, Soc. Bibl. Lit., Tyndale Fellowship for Bibl. Rsch. Office: Western Evang Sem 4200 SE Jennings Ave Portland OR 97267-6498 *We Americans have a firm commitment to our rights and freedoms. Now we need an equally lively appreciation of our responsibilities.*

CATALDO, CHET WILLIAM, minister; b. Omaha, July 6, 1955; s. Robert Gene and Lloydine Marie (Grimes) C.; m. Jodi Lynn Carpenter, Nov. 1, 1975; children: Jeremiah William, Tobin Mathias. BA summa cum laude, Friends Bible Coll., 1982; MA in Religious Studies, Cen. Bapt. Theol. Sem., 1983; ThD, Internat. Sem., 1988. Ordained to ministry Gen. Bapt. Ch., 1982. Pastoral intern 1st Bapt. Ch., Pratt, Kans., 1978-79; pastor 1st Bapt. Ch., Belpre, Kans., 1979-81, Olathe (Kans.) Gen. Bapt. Ch., 1982-85; missionary, tchr. Gen. Bapt. Mission, Davao City, Philippines, 1985-88; home mission pastor New Horizons Bapt. Ch., Marion, Ill., 1989-90; pastor Zion United Meth. Chs., Wishek and Lehr, N.D., 1990—; del. N.D. Annual Confs. of United Meth. Chs., 1991—; mem. Ministerial Alliance, Wishek, 1990—. Contbr. articles to profl. jours. With USN, 1973-77.

CATE, CHARLES THOMAS, educator, administrator; b. Tuepelo, Miss., Jan. 23, 1945; s. James Lee and Mada Marie (Lummus) C.; m. Lillie Katherine Morris, June 13, 1969; children: Charles Thomas II, Christy Marie. BS, Murray State U., 1967, MA, 1972, postgrad., 1983. Cert. educator in art, adminstr. Minister Ch. of Christ, Springville, Tenn., 1982-88; prin. Henry County Bd. Edn., Paris, Tenn., 1979—. Mem. NAESP. Home: 1618 Patriot Ave Paris TN 38242 Office: Springville Elem Sch Rte 2 Box 45 Springville TN 38256

CATE, PATRICK O'HAIR, mission executive; b. San Antonio, Oct. 19, 1940; s. Julian O'Hair and Jesse Mary (Ramsey) C.; m. Mary Ann Seume, Aug. 31, 1968; children: Jennifer Ann, Amy Sherene, Julie Esther. BA in History, Wheaton Coll., 1963; ThM in Missions, Dallas Theol. Sem., 1968; PhD in Islamics, Hartford Sem., 1974. Ordained to ministry, Congl. Ch., 1974. Pastor Nepaug Congl. Ch., New Hartford, Conn., 1969-74; missionary Internat. Missions, Inc., Kermanshah, Iran, 1974-79; v.p., candidate sec. Internat. Missions Inc., 1980-84; missionary Internat. Missions, Inc., Cairo, 1984-89; pres. Internat. Missions, Inc., Reading, Pa., 1989—; instr. Dallas Theol. Sem., 1980; vis. instr. in missions and Islamics Wheaton (Ill.) Coll., Dallas Theol. Sem., Columbia (S.C.) Bible Coll. Author: Each Other's Scripture, 1974, Muslim World Pulse, 1978. Mem. Interdenominational Fgn. Missions Assn. (Islamics com. 1990). Home: 108 Rose Ct Shillington PA 19607 Office: Internat Missions Inc 621 Centre Ave Reading PA 19601 *Only three things are eternal: God, The Word of God and the souls of men. Let us give our lives to that which has eternal significance—especially the Asian majority of this world who have yet to hear of God's love in Christ.*

CATE, ROBERT LOUIS, religion educator; b. Nashville, Aug. 11, 1932; s. George Harrison and Lucile (Cowherd) C.; m. Dorothy Wright, Aug. 17, 1951; children: Ruth Cate Ackermann, Robert L. Jr., Fred Harrison. B in Engring., Vanderbilt U., 1953; BD, So. Bapt. Sem., 1956, PhD, 1960; postgrad., Oxford (Eng.) U., 1980-81. Ordained to ministry Bapt. Ch., 1952. Pastor Walnut Hill Bapt. Ch., Campbellsville, Ky., 1955-57, McRae (Ga.) Bapt. Ch., 1959-64, First Bapt. Ch., Aiken, S.C., 1964-74; prof. O.T. Golden Gate Sem., Mill Valley, Calif., 1975-90, dean acad. affairs, 1984-90; Phoebe Schertz Young prof. religion Okla. State U., Stillwater, 1991—; gen. bd. S.C. Bapt. conv., Columbia, 1966-68. Author: Study Guide on Exodus, 1977, Exodus, Layman's Bible Commentary, 1979, Introducing the Old Testament, Parts I, II, and III, 1980, Old Testament Roots for New Testament Faith, 1982, Teologia del Antiquo Testamento, 1989, How to Interpret the Bible, 1983, These Sought a Country, 1985, An Introduction to the Old Testament and Its Study, 1987, Discovering Judges, Ruth, and 1 and 2 Samuel, 1988, A History of the Bible Lands in the Interbiblical Period, 1989, A History of New Testament Times, 1991; contbr. articles to profl. jours. Trustee Tift Coll., Forsythe, Ga., 1961-63, Furman U., Greenville, S.C., 1970-74, So. Bapt. Theol. Sem., Louisville, 1974; bd. dir. Aiken-Barnwell Mental Ctr., 1966-70, chmn., 1970-74; pres.-elect Aiken Rotary Club, 1974. Edn. Commn. of So. Bapt. Conv. grantee Oxford U. Mem. Soc. Bibl. Lit., Nat. Assn. Profs. Hebrew, Soc. Old Testament Studies (Brit.), Nat. Assn. Bapt. Profs. Religion. Home: 1410 E Connell Ave Stillwater OK 74057

CATE, WILLIAM BURKE, religious organization administrator; b. Itasca, Tex., Mar. 25, 1924; s. Emmet Cate and Irene N. (Kincaid) Moberly; m. Janice McLeod Patterson, Aug. 20, 1946; children: Lucy, Nancy, Michael, Sara, Rebecca, Mary. BA, Willamette U., 1945; STB, Boston U., 1948, PhD, 1953; DD (hon.), Lewis and Clark U., 1965. Ordained minister United Meth. Ch., 1952. Exec. dir. Interchurch Council of Greater New Bedford, Mass., 1953-58, Greater Portland (Oreg.) Council of Chs., 1958-70; pres., dir. Ch. Council of Greater Seattle, 1970-90; ret., 1990; v.p. Nat. Council of Chs., N.Y.C., 1970-73; pres. Nat. Assn. of Ecumenical Staff, 1972-73. Served with USN, 1943-46. Recipient Disting. Alumni award Boston U. Sch. Theology, 1968. Lodge: Rotary. Home: 12642 NE 5th Bellevue WA 98005

CATES, PHILLIP KEITH, minister; b. High Point, N.C., Oct. 11, 1958; s. Eural Fletcher and Dorothy Frances (Gardner) C.; m. Toni Marie Hemphill, Sept. 21, 1985. BA in Religion and Philosophy, Greensboro Coll., 1986; MDiv, Candler Sch. of Theology, Atlanta, 1988, MTh, 1989. Ordained to ministry United Meth. Ch. as deacon, 1987, as elder, 1991. Evangelism min. Grace United Meth. Ch., Greensboro, N.C., 1985; assoc. pastor Cherokee Heights United Meth. Ch., Macon, Ga., 1986-89; congl. devel. cons. Covenant United Meth. Ch., High Point, N.C., 1989; pastor Mt. Lebanon United Meth. Ch., Randleman, N.C., 1989—; chaplain Greensboro (N.C.) Coll., 1990—; ch. growth cons., 1989—; herald, missioner Gen. Bd. Discipleship, Nashville, 1989—; dist. dir. of children, youth and youth adult ministries, High Point Dist., United Meth. Ch., 1990—; mem. WNCC Commn. on Children, Youth, Youth Adults, Charlotte, 1990—. Editor: (study book) Choose Christ: Faith-Sharing Workbook, 1991. Mem. NCCJ, Atlanta, 1988; mem. Randolph County AIDS Resorce Group; chaplain Greensboro Coll. Alumni Bd., 1990—. Recipient Hardee Christian Svc. award Greensboro Coll., 1986. Mem. Assn. for Clin. Pastoral Edn., Western N.C. Conf./United Meth. Ch., Phi Kappa Phi Alumni Assn. (pres. 1986, Alumni of Yr. award Gamma Epsilon chpt., Cullowhee, N.C. 1986), Randolph County Grief Coun., Greensboro Walk to Emmaus (spiritual dir. 1990—). Republican. Home: 149 West River Dr Randleman NC 27317 Office: Mt Lebanon United Meth Ch 119 West River Dr Randleman NC 27317 *When life is seen as a gift from God, it can be seen as a journey of potential. Being made in God's image human potential is limitless; therefore, life should be seen as a quest...a quest for the best!.*

CATOE, SAMUEL GEORGE, minister; b. Camden, S.C., Dec. 25, 1946; s. Audrey Columbus and Grace (Adams) C.; m. Joyce Marie Huckaby, Jan. 27, 1968. BA, Furman U., Greenville, S.C., 1976; MDiv, Midwestern Bapt. Theol. Sem., Kansas City, Mo., 1979; DMin, Southeastern Bapt. Theol. Sem., Wake Forest, N.C., 1986. Ordained to ministry So. Bapt. Ch., 1976. Assoc. pastor Jackson Creek Bapt. Ch., Columbia, S.C., 1976; assoc. pastor Leavenworth (Kans.) Bapt. Ch., 1976-77; pastor First Bapt. Ch., Marceline, Mo., 1978-81; gen. evangelist Fgn. Mission Bd., So. Bapt. Conv., West Africa, 1981-83; pastor Emmanuel Bapt. Ch., Huntingtown, Md., 1983-89, Victor Bapt. Ch., Greer, S.C., 1989—; gen. mission bd. Bapt. Conv. of Md./Del., 1984-89. Mem. spiritual resources com. Widowed Persons Svc. of Calvert County, Prince Frederick, Md., 1987-89. Mem. Greer C. of C. (community devel. com. 1991), Greer Bapt. Assn. (stewardship dir. 1990—), Potomac Bapt. Assn. (stewqardship dir. 1986-89, moderator 1983-85), Clergy Coun. of So. Md. (vice chmn. 1984-86). Home: PO Box 2023 Greer SC 29652-2023 Office: Victor Bapt Ch 105 S Line St Greer SC 29651

CATON, KENNETH LLOYD, minister; b. Portland, Oreg., Nov. 5, 1943; s. Earnest Edward and Lula May (Barnes) C.; m. Erika Ruth Phillips, Nov. 25, 1967 (div. Nov. 1979). MusB, Lewis and Clark Coll., 1965, PhD (hon.), 1975; MusM, San Diego State U., 1967. Ordained to ministry Universal Fellowhip Met. Community Chs., 1991. Minister music Apostolic Faith Ch., L.A., 1966-72, Denver, 1972-76; minister music St. Paul's United Meth. Ch., Albuquerque, 1978-79; assoc. pastor, minister music Met. Community Ch., San Diego, 1987-89; assoc. pastor All God's Children Met. Community Ch., Mpls., 1989-91; sr. pastor Met. Community Ch., Las Vegas, Nev., 1991—; prof. Samaritan Coll., L.A., 1991—, faculty, 1991—; music coord. Universal Fellowship Met. Community Chs., L.A., 1986-87. Composer (sacred music album) Free To Be, 1988 (nominee Gospel Album of Yr. Billboard Mag. 1989). Mem. Am. Choral Dirs. Assn., Nat. Assn. Tchrs. Singing. Home: 4365 Terrace Hill Rd # 202 Las Vegas NV 89103 Office: Met Community Ch Las Vegas 1110 S Main St Las Vegas NV 89104 *We must learn to treat each other with dignity, and respect and until we have truly learned to love ourselves, we can only then begin to "love one another!".*

CATRETT, JOHN THOMAS, III, minister; b. Pascegoula, Miss., June 20, 1947; s. John T. Catrett II and Dorothy M. (Demouey) Morgan. BA in Ministry, Midwest Christian Coll., 1971, BA in Christian Edn., 1972; postgrad., Ky. Christian Coll., 1987—. Student minister Cere Christian Ch., Red Rock, Okla., 1969-71; student youth minister Forest Hills Christian Ch., Oklahoma City, 1971-72; youth minister Davis Park Christian Ch., Enid, Okla., 1972-74, Sandusky Area Christian Ch., Tulsa, 1974-85; minister Cen. Christian Ch., Carlsbad, N.Mex., 1986—; chmn. trustees Midwest Christian Coll., Oklahoma City, 1984-85; regional bd. dirs. Dallas Christian Coll. Donor ARC, 1974—; asst. coach T-Ball Team, 1980-82; coach Basketball Jr. High Teams, 1979-81; mem. N.Mex. for Life, 1987—, Camp Fire Bd., 1987—, Little League Umpires, 1987—; pres. N.Mex. Christian Conv., 1990, treas., 1991—. Avocations: jogging, travel, reading, writing. Home: 1114 W Ash St Carlsbad NM 88220

CATT, MICHAEL CAMERON, pastor; b. Pascagoula, Miss., Dec. 25, 1952; s. Grover Hickman and Winnie Virginia (Bethea) C.; m. Terri Payne, Aug. 10, 1974; children: Erin Bethea, Hayley Amanda. BA in Bible, Miss. Coll., 1975; ThM, Luther Rice Seminary, 1988. Student min. Ruskin Heights Bapt. Ch., Kansas City, Mo., 1975-76, First Bapt. Ch., Yukon, Okla., 1976-78, First Bapt. North Spartanburg, Spartanburg, S.C., 1978-81, Roswell St. Bapt. Ch., Marietta, Ga., 1981-85; assoc. pastor Sagamore Hill Bapt. Ch., Fort Worth, 1985-87; pastor First Bapt. Ch., Ada, Okla., 1987—; featured speaker The Baptist Light, Radio/TV, Ada, 1987—; youth ministry cons. various locations, 1976-87; masterlife cons. Bapt. Sunday Sch. Bd., Nashville, 1984—. Contbr. articles to mag.; author (with others) Ch. training materials. Mem. adv. bd. Lassiter High Sch., Marietta, 1982. Mem. Network, Ada C. of C., Okla. Fellowship Christian Athletes (bd. dirs.). Republican. Southern Baptist. Avocations: golf, tennis, basketball. Office: First Baptist Church 521 South Broadway Ada OK 74820

CATTERMOLE, RICHARD A., bishop. Chmn. adminstrv. coun. Evang. Congl. Ch., Myerstown, Pa. Office: Evang Congl Ch 100 W Park Ave PO Box 186 Myerstown PA 17067*

CATUCCI, PAUL FRANK, priest; b. New Britain, Conn., July 22, 1956; s. Vito Paul and Lucy (Mazzarella) C. BA, Cen. Conn. State U., 1979, St. Mary's Sem., 1982; MDiv, St. Mary's Sem., 1982; D of Ministry, Hartford Sem., 1989. Parochial vicar St. Lucy Ch., Waterbury, Conn., 1983-86, Holy Spirit Ch., Newington, Conn., 1986-90; temporary adminstr. Sts. Peter and Paul, Waterbury, 1990-91; co-pastor St. Francis Ch., Naugatuck, Conn., 1991—; staff rep. Civil Svc. Employees Affiliated, Hartford, Conn., 1983—; presbyteral coun. Archdioces of Hartford, 1983-86. Author: The Role of Clergy in Labor and Management Relations, 1989. Mem. KC. Democrat.

CAUCAU, ISIRELI M., religious organization administrator. Pres. Meth. Ch., Suva, Fiji. Office: Meth Ch, GPO Box 357, Suva Fiji*

CAULLEY, THOMAS SCOTT, religion educator; b. Eugene, Oreg., Apr. 16, 1952; s. James M. and Zena F. (Vail) C.; m. Cherie L. Zook, June 23, 1972; children: Alisha Nicole, Justin Lee Mark. BA, Puget Sound Coll. Bible, 1974; MA, Fuller Theol. Sem., 1976; Dr Theol, U. Tuebingen, 1983. Ordained to ministry Christian Ch., 1974. Instr. Puget Sound Coll. Bible, Seattle, 1974-76, Seattle Pacific U., 1974-76, 82-83; asst. prof. religion Eastern N. Mex. U., Portales, 1983-88; assoc. dir. Christian Campus House, 1983-88; assoc. prof. New Testament Manhattan (Kans.) Christian Coll., 1988—. Fellow Inst. Bibl. Rsch.; mem. Soc. Bibl. Lit. (sect. advisor 1984-88), Assn. for Case Teaching. Democrat. Office: Manhattan Christian Coll 1415 Anderson Ave Manhattan KS 66502

CAUSEY, C. HARRY, music director, music minister; b. Rockingham, N.C., Oct. 19, 1942; s. Clyde Harold and Edna Ann (Bruton) C.; m. Elizabeth Ann Reinoehl, Aug. 27, 1966; children: David Andrew, Debbie Elaine. BA, Davidson (N.C.) Coll., 1965; MusM, Fla. State U., 1967. Min. music Coll. Hill Presbyn. Ch., Cin., 1969-80, 4th Presbyn. Ch., Bethesda, Md., 1980-81; pres. Music Revelation, Rockville, Md., 1983-91; music dir., chm. bd. The Nat. Christian Choir, WAshington, 1984-91. Author: Open the Doors to Creativity in Worship, 1983, Things They Didn't Tell Me About Being a Minister of Music, 1988, If Only I Could Read Music, 1991. Republican. Mem. Christian Missionary Alliance. Avocations: computers, movies, tropical fish. Home and Office: 7 Elmwood Ct Rockville MD 20850-2935

CAUSEY, CALVIN GERALD, minister, chaplain; b. Columbus, Ga., Apr. 18, 1930; s. Moss Schelly and Norma May (Clark) C.; m. Patricia J. Norgrove, Sept. 1, 1952; children: Calvin G. Jr., Carol P., Nathanael P., Charles M. BA, Emory U., 1952; MDiv, Nazarene Theol. Sem., 1955; STM, N.Y. Theol. Sem., 1979. Ordained to ministry Ch. of the Nazarene, 1955. Pastor Ch. of the Nazarene, Salisbury, N.C., 1955-56; chaplain U.S. Army, 1956-76, VA Med. Ctr., Leavenworth, Kans., 1977—; mem. Chaplains' Adv. Coun., 1977—, VA Patient Treatment Team, 1979—, VA Equal Employment Com., 1984—. Editor Reserve Chaplains' Training, 1969-71. Col. U.S. Army, 1956-76, Fed. Republic Germany, Korea, Vietnam. Decorated Legion of Merit, Bronze Star, Air medal. Mem. Leavenworth Clergy Assn., Mil. Chaplains Assn., Ret. Officers Assn. Republican.

CAUSEY, GERALD DAVID, lay church worker; b. Hendersonville, N.C., July 9, 1934; s. Herman Columbus and Tempie Faye (Bagwell) C.; m. Beverly Jean Hicks, Nov. 2, 1956; children: Mark David, Steven Craig, Tara Renee, Amber Jean. BA, Wayland Coll., 1962; MA, Appalachian State U., 1963. Min. music 1st Bapt. Ch., Alamogordo, N.Mex., 1957-59, Edmundson, Tex., 1959-62, Hendersonville, N.C., 1963-70, Tucker, Ga., 1970-76; pres. Master Media, Tucker, 1976—. Ind. photographer, multimedia producer. Mem. nat. evangelism support team So. Bapt. Conv.; bivocat. min. music Bapt. Tabernacle, Atlanta, 1979-85, Yellow River Bapt. Ch., 1985-86, Valley Brook Bapt. Ch., 1986—. Recipient cert. of merit Southeastern U.S. Fair, 1975, cert. of appreciation DeKalb County Juvenile Ct., 1976, Exceptional Achievement award Nat. Coun. Advancement and Support of Edn., 1983, Award of Merit Ala. Hosp. Pub. Rels. and Mktg. Soc. Mem. Am. Guild English Handbell Ringers, Am. Choral Dirs. Assn., Nat. Assn. Tchrs. Singing, Nat. Audio-Visual Assn., Phi Mu Alpha Sinfonia. Home: 1441 Camelot Ln Tucker GA 30084 *The Christian life is usually experienced on the fringe by a vast majority of church members. The positive message of Christ Jesus is for us to be sure we are born again, then, let Him live out the life of victory over circumstances for us. Are we too self-centered?.*

CAUSEY, JOHN NORMAN, minister; b. Greensboro, N.C., Dec. 1, 1952; s. William Mitchell and Helen Marie (Clapp) C.; m. Margaret McClintock, Dec. 25, 1976; 1 child, Gregg Patrick. BSBA, U. N.C., Chapel Hill, 1977; MDiv, Union Theol. Sem. Va., 1981. Ordained to ministry Presbyn. Ch. (U.S.A.), 1981. Pastor Covenant Presbyn. Ch., Wendell, N.C., 1981-88; assoc. for planned giving Union Theol. Sem., Richmond, Va., 1988—. With U.S. Army, 1972-74. Mem. Coun. for Advancement and Support of Edn., Wendell Coun. Chs. (pres. 1986-88), Lions (pres. Wendell chpt. 1986-87, v.p. Richmond-Lakeside chpt. 1990-91). Democrat. Office: Union Theol Sem 3401 Brook Rd Richmond VA 23227

CAUSEY, MARION EDWARD, II, clergyman, counselor; b. Centreville, Miss., Dec. 21, 1947; s. Marion Edward and Mary Lucrecia (Strait) C.; m. Janice Lee Parfitt, Aug. 7, 1971; children: Emilee Kaye, Jessica Erin. AA, Southwest Miss. Jr. Coll., 1968; BA, Miss. Coll., 1971; MDiv, So. Bapt. Theol. Sem., Louisville, 1976. Ordained Bapt. min., 1974. Asst. dir. Bapt. Student Union Miss. Coll., Clinton, 1971-73; pastor Mt. Hermon Bapt. Ch., Carrollton, Ky., 1974-76; tng. chaplain Jewish Hosp., Louisville, 1976-77; chaplain intern Bapt. Hosp. East, Louisville, 1977-78; assoc. paster Buechel Park Bapt. Ch., Louisville, 1978-79; pastoral counselor Louisville Bapt. Hosps., 1979-82; dir. Pastoral Counseling and Consultation Ctr., Inc., Louisville, 1982—; cons., St. Anthony Med. Ctr., Louisville, 1979—, Bapt. Hosp. East, Louisville, 1979—, Jewish Hosp. Cardiac Rehab., Louisville, 1988—. Bd. dirs. Louisville unit Am. Diabetes Assn., 1989, greater Louisville div. Am. Heart Assn., 1989. Mem. Am. Assn. Pastoral Counselors (chmn. nominating com. Midwest region 1982-87, mem. nat. nominating com. 1982-87). Democrat. Avocations: tennis, sailing. Office: Pastoral Counseling Ctr 4007 Kresge Way Louisville KY 40207

CAUSEY, RICHARD WAYNE (JACK CAUSEY), minister; b. Meridian, Miss., May 26, 1935; s. Harry and Genevieve Cecilia (Davis) C.; m. Mary Elizabeth May, July 18, 1959; children: Kimberly Ann Causey Summers, Richard Wayne Jr. BA, Miss. Coll., 1957; BDiv, So. Bapt. Theol. Sem., 1960, MDiv, 1967, DMin, 1983. Ordained to ministry So. Bapt. Conv. Assoc. pastor First Bapt. Ch., Greensboro, N.C., 1960-66; pastor First Bapt. Ch., Gaffney, S.C., 1966-74, Statesville, N.C., 1986—; pastor Pendleton St. Bapt. Ch., Greenville, S.C., 1974-86; mem. ministerial bd. assocs. Gardner-Webb Coll., Boiling Springs, N.C. Bd. dirs. Hospice Iredell County, Inc., Statesville; mem. health adv. coun. Iredell-Statesville Sch., 1987—. Home: 240 Glen Eagle Rd E Statesville NC 28677 Office: First Bapt Ch 815 Davie Ave Statesville NC 28677

CAVALLO, JOSEPH CHARLES, JR., clergyman; b. Riverside, Calif., Jan. 12, 1944; s. Joseph Charles and Ruth Caroline (Elfner) C. AA, St. Thomas Seminary, 1964; BA in Philosophy, St. Mary's U., 1966; MDiv, St. Meinard Seminary, 1970. Ordained priest Roman Catholic Ch., 1970. Asst. pastor Immaculate Heart of Mary, Atlanta, 1970-71, Sacred Heart Ch., Atlanta, 1971-74, St. Jude Ch., Sandy Springs, Ga., 1974-75, St. Thomas Ch.,

Smyrna, Ga., 1975-77; chaplain Emory U., Atlanta, 1977-81, Atlanta U. Ctr., 1981-86; pastor Our Lady of Lourdes Ch., Atlanta, 1986—; chaplain Civil Air Patrol, DeKalb County, Ga., 1971-81; pres. Atlanta Senate of Priests, 1979-81; chaplain Dignity, Atlanta, 1979—. Chmn. bd. dirs. So. Center for Mil. and Vet. Rights, Atlanta, 1978; co-pres. Ecumenical Coalition of Ch. and Labor, Atlanta, 1979-83; mem. bd. Urban Tng. Orgn., Atlanta, 1981-83. Served to maj., Air Force CAP, 1971-81. Mem. Atlanta Bus. and Profl. Guild. Lodge: Rotary. Office: Our Lady of Lourdes Cath Ch 25 Boulevard NE Atlanta GA 30312

CAVANAGH, KAREN MARIE, pastoral associate; b. Bklyn., Apr. 10, 1941; d. Joseph James and Agnes Rita (Fagan) C. BS in Edn., Brentwood (N.Y.) Coll., 1966; MS in Edn., CCNY, 1972; MA in Religious Edn., Fordham U., Bronx, 1982. Tchr. O.L.M.C., Bklyn., 1962-63, St. Rita Sch., L.I., 1963-71; tchr. Immaculate Conception Sch., Jamaica, N.Y., 1971-77; adminstr. Blessed Sacrament Sch., Bklyn., 1977-85; pastoral assoc. Immaculate Conception Ch., Jamaica, 1985—; retreat preacher various parishes, religious cong. Author children's religious paperbacks, prayerbooks including: We Go to Mass, The Rosary, The Saints, vol. I, The Saints, vol. II, The Bible, The Life of Jesus, The Life of Mary, The Way of the Cross, The Christmas Story, The New Testament, others. Democrat. Home: 111-20 115th St Jamaica NY 11420 Office: Immaculate Conception Ch 86-45 178 St Jamaica NY 11432

CAVANAGH, MARY JO, church music director, educator; b. Vallejo, Calif., Feb. 13, 1956; d. Paul Leo and Elizabeth Irene (Caprini) C. B.A. in English, U. Calif.-Davis, 1976; M.A. in Music Lit., Dominican Coll., San Rafael, Calif., 1983. Cert. community coll. educator, Calif. Tchr. music English Big Valley Sch. Dist., Bieber, Calif., 1977-79; tchr. guitar Lassen Coll. Extension, Bieber, 1978-79; tchr. English John Swett High Sch., Crockett, Calif., 1979-80; choir dir. St. Catherine Ch., Vallejo, 1979-82; tchr. English and math. St. Patrick's Sch., Vallejo, 1979-82; dir. music St. Rita's Cath. Ch., Fairfax, Calif., 1982—; pvt. music tchr.; flutist Dominican Chamber Orch., San Rafael, Calif., 1982-84. Community producer Marin Video Channel 31, San Rafael, 1984; mem. exec. bd. Mill Valley Chamber Music Soc. (Calif.), 1983-84. Mem. Coll. Music Soc., Am. Musicol. Soc., Nat. Assn. Pastoral Musicians, Phi Beta Kappa. Democrat. Roman Catholic.

CAVANAUGH, VONTROS EUGENE, minister, director; b. Mason City, Ill., May 25, 1928; s. Thomas Harold and Eva Evelyn (Forbis) C.; m. Gloria Jean Ford, June 25, 1955; children: Cynthia Jean, Bonnie Lou, Thomas William, Robert William Robson. Student, Ft. Wayne (Ind.) Bible Coll., 1951-56. Pastor Free Meth. Ch., Harbor Beach, Mich., 1959-61, Cheboygan, Mich., 1961-63, Saginaw, Mich., 1963-65; pastor W. Grout F. M. Ch., Gladwin, Mich., 1965-68, Roosevelt Ave F.M. Ch., Flint, Mich., 1968-70; founder, dir. Inner-City Youth Ministries, Flint, 1970—; counselor Probate Ct., Flint, 1969—; advisor D.O.T. Caring Progam, Flint, 1988—. Master Cub Scouts Am., Mason City, 1950-51; asst. scoutmaster Boy Scouts Am., Mason City, 1948-50; asst. dir. Youth for Christ, Manito, Ill., 1949-51, bd. dirs., Harbor Beach, 1960-61. With U.S. Army, 1946-47. Mem. East Mich. Conf. Free Meth. Ch. Home: 5215 S Genesee Rd RR # 4 Grand Blanc MI 48439

CAVINS, WILLIAM ROBERT, evangelization director, educator; b. Homestead, Pa., May 15, 1953; s. Samuel James and Joan ELizabeth (Witkowski) C.; m. Karen René Steele, Oct. 19, 1985; children: Zachary A., Suzannah E. AA, BA, U. Cen. Fla., Orlando, 1974; student, St. Meinrad Sem., Ind., 1975-76; MS, Nova U., Ft. Lauderdale, Fla., 1980. Cert. tchr., Fla. Dir. religious edn. Mary Help of Christians Ch., Mariah Hill, Ind., 1975-76; youth dir. Blessed Sacrament Ch., Clermont, Fla., 1976-77; dir. of family life St. Clare Cath. Community, Deltona, Fla., 1990-91; dir. rcia/evangelization St. Clarke Cath. Community, Deltona, Fla., 1991—; tchr. Sch. Bd. of Seminole County, Sanford, Fla., 1982—; pastoral ministry canidate Diocese of Orlando, Fla., 1990— (ministry of acolyte, 1976—). Precinct leader Dem. Exec. Com., Lake County, Fla., 1981-82 (chmn. 1982); pres. Groveland/Mascotte C. of C., Fla., 1981-82. Recipient Tchr. Merit award Walt Disney World Co., Lake Buena Vista, Fla., 1990, 91, Louie Camp award for creative teaching Fla. Coun. Elem. Edn., 1990. Mem. Nat. Assn. Lay Ministry, Seminole Reading Coun., Seminole Edn. Assn., K.C. (founding grand knight Assisi coun.), Phi Delta Kappa (found. rep. 1989-90). Democrat. Roman Catholic. Office: St Clare Cath Community 1330-B Howland Blvd Deltona FL 32738

CAYCE, W. H., elder, religious organization leader. Elder Primitive Bapts., Thornton, Ark. Office: Primitive Bapts S 2nd St PO Box 38 Thornton AR 71766*

CAYLOR, CHESTER A., minister; b. Jasper, Tex., Nov. 30, 1933; s. Chester A. and Lottie P. (Seale) C.; m. Glenrose Lee Caylor, Feb. 25, 1956; children: Glenda Sue, Randy Michael. Student, S.W. Tex. U., 1952-53, S.W. Assembly of God Coll., Waxahachie, Tex., 1958-59. Cert. property mgr. Min. Assembly of God, Springfield, Mo., 1957-75, Austin (Tex.) Revival Ctr., 1975-79, Pentecostal Ch. of God, Joplin, Mo., 1979—; missionary Laredo, Tex., 1975—; gen. bd. Pentecostal Ch. of God, San Marcos, Tex., 1979-80; world mission dir. Pentecostal Ch. of God, Joplin, Mo., 1987—; exec. bd. Latin Am. Bible Ch., Laredo; v.p. Broadway Asset Mgmt., San Antonio, 1990—. Sec. Helping Our Bros. Out, Austin, 1987. Named Pastor of Yr. Austin Revival Ctr., 1976. Fellow Austin Apt. Assn. (faculty 1983-88), Inst. of Real Estate Mgmt. (treas. 1984-85, sec. 1986-89, Cert. Property Mgr. of Yr. award 1986, 88), Christ's Mission, Inc. (pres. 1989—); mem. Exchange Club (com. 1980-85), C. of C. Home: Rte 1 Box 53 Red Rock TX 78662 Office: Christs Mission Community 4115 Ave D Austin TX 78751

CAYTON, MARY EVELYN, minister; b. Morgantown, W. Va., July 7, 1926; d. Adam Johnson and Dorothy Ena (Bigler) C. Student, Internat. Bible Coll., San Antonio, Tex., 1955. Founder, pastor Morgantown (W.Va.) Revival Ctr., 1956—; staff, controller's office W. Va. Univ., Morgantown, 1951-55, '58-84; chmn. Morgantown Revival Ctr. Assn., 1956—. Home and Office: Morgantown Revival Ctr Rt 3 Box 542-A Morgantown WV 26505 *I have found through life that "With Man some things are possible but "With God nothing is impossible".*

CAYWOOD, DAVID MIKEL, minister; b. Cleve., July 22, 1962; s. Jimmy Lester and Faye Arlene (Geren) C.; m. Dana Louise Bennett, Dec. 29, 1984; children: David Andrew, James Mikel. AA, Cleve. State Community Coll., 1982; MusB, Carson-Newman Coll., 1984; MA in Religious Edn., Southwestern Bapt. Theol. Sem., Ft. Worth, 1988. Ordained to ministry So. Bapt. Conv., 1984. Min. music Covenant Bapt. Ch., Cleveland, Tenn., 1980-82, Trinity Bapt. Ch., Knoxville, Tenn., 1982-84; min. music and youth 1st Bapt. Ch., Celeste, Tex., 1985-86, Live Oak Bapt. Ch., Jacksboro, Tex., 1986-89; min. youth East Side Bapt. Ch., Paragould, Ark., 1989-90; min. music and youth 1st Bapt. Ch. Gravel Ridge, Jacksonville, Ark., 1990—; associational min. youth Jack County Bapt. Assn., Jacksboro, 1986-89; mem. steering com. jr. high jamboree Ark. Bapt. State Conv., 1989—, guest tchr., 1990-91; guest tchr. Ark. State Bapt. Youth Assembly, 1991. Chmn. edn. com. Crop Walk of Jacksboro, 1988-89. Republican. Home: 66 Creekwood Jacksonville AR 72076 Office: 1st Bapt Ch Gravel Ridge 14322 Hwy 107 Jacksonville AR 72076-9310 *There are few things in life that really make a difference on "the big picture"; however, choosing to be a servant of others is one of them!.*

CÉ, MARCO CARDINAL, patriarch of Venice, former bishop of Bologna; b. Izano, Italy, July 8, 1925. Ordained priest Roman Catholic Ch., 1948; tchr. sacred scripture and dogmatic theology at sem. in Diocese of Crema (Italy); rector seminary, 1957; presided over diocesan liturgical commn., preached youth retreats; ordained titular bishop of Vulturia, 1970; aux. bishop of Bologna (Italy), 1970-76; gen. eccles. asst. of Italian Cath. Action, 1976-78; patriarch of Venice, 1978—, elevated to Sacred Coll. of Cardinals, 1979; titular ch., St. Mark. Mem. congregations Clergy, Cath. Edn. Office: Curia Patriarcale, S Marco 320-A, 30124 Venice Italy

CECIL, EARL IVAN, minister; b. Ft. Wayne, Ind., Mar. 31, 1946; s. Kenneth Everett and Amy Ilene (Leonard) C.; m. Cheryl Ann Roth, July 8, 1967; children: Angela Beth, Aric Nathan, Andrew Jon, April Joy. BA in Pastoral Ministries, Ft. Wayne Bible Coll., 1968; postgrad., Trinity Evang. Div., 1972-74, Grace Theol. Sem., 1976-79; M of Christian Ministries, Huntington Grad. Sch. Christian Ministries, 1983. Ordained to ministry Mennonite Ch., 1971. Min., pastor 1st Evang. Mennonite Ch., Lafayette, Ind., 1968-72; houseparent, counselor Saelm Children's Home, Flanagan, Ill., 1972-73; asst. pastor, chaplain Salem Children's Home, Flanagan, Ill., 1973-76; pastor Thorncreek Ch. of God, Columbia City, Ind., 1976-77, Woodburn (Ind.) Evang. Mennonite Ch., 1977-86; assoc. pastor missions and pastoral care Grace Evang. Mennonite Ch., Morton, Ill., 1986—; chmn. Evang. Mennonite Conf. Commn. on Christian Edn., Ft. Wayne, 1980-84; program chmn. Miracle Camp, Lawton, Mich., 1980-85; bd. dirs. Gen. Bd., Evang. Mennonite Ch., Ft. Wayne, 1980-84. V.p. PTA, Woodburn, 1983. Home: 201 E Madison Morton IL 61550 Office: Grace Evang Mennonite Ch 1050 S 4th St Morton IL 61550 *Two things are eternal - God's word, the Bible, and people - invest in both generously.*

CECIL, STEPHEN DON, minister; b. Sikeston, Mo., Nov. 26, 1958; s. Leeman Donald and Naomi Ruth (Ball) C.; m. Peggy Lee Denny, Aug. 15, 1981; children: Leigh-Ann, Stephanie Michelle, Emily Rebecca, Stephen Palmer. BA, Mid-Am. Nazarene Coll., 1981. Assoc. pastor Community Ch. of Nazarene, San Antonio, Tex., 1981-83; pastor Ch. of Nazarene, Kempton, Ill., 1983-86, Grace Ch. of Nazarene, Inver Grove Heights, Mnn., 1986—; zone youth coord. San Antonio, 1982, Kankakee, Ill., 1985, Minn. Nazarene Youth Internat., Inver Grove Hts., 1986-90; chmn. ch. planting com. Minn. Dist. Ch. of Nazarene, 1988—, home missions and ministerial studies bds., 1988—. Named One of Outstanding Young Men Am., 1982, 85. Avocation: various athletics. Home: 7268 Clay Ave E Inver Grove Heights MN 55076 Office: Grace Ch of Nazarene 7950 Blaine Ave E Inver Grove Heights MN 55076 *Wherever the enemy is operating, there is a victory to be won.*

CECIRE, ROBERT CLYDE, minister; b. Norwalk, Conn., Nov. 3, 1940; s. Bernard Francis and Elva L. (Buchanan) C.; m. Sarah Marie Hull, June 19, 1971. BA, Wheaton Coll., 1962; BD, Gordon Divinity Sch., Wenham, Mass., 1965; MA, U. Kans, 1976, PhD, 1985. Ordained to ministry Bapt. Ch., 1967. Min. United Bapt. Ch., Biddeford, Maine, 1967-70, Southwest Bapt. Ch., Topeka, Kans., 1970-80; min. (interim) Gage Park Bapt. Ch., Topeka, 1980, Terra Heights Bapt. Ch., Topeka, 1980-81; min. First Bapt. Ch., Silver Lake, Kans., 1981-86, Wamego, Kans., 1987-90; sec. Wamego (Kans.) Coun. of Chs., 1987-90; adj. faculty Bethel Coll., 1991, Anoka-Ramsey Community Coll., 1991. Contbr. articles to profl. jours. Fellow (rsch.) Dept. of Hist., U. Kans.; mem. Soc. of Bibl. Lit., Conference on Faith and Hist., Nat. Hist. Honor Soc., White Lakes Optimist Club (sec. 1972). Home: 11440 Jonquil St NW Coon Rapids MN 55453 *Inherent in the idea of Christian love is a sense of responsibility to God and the world in which He has placed us. We need to absorb the truth contained in Jesus' parable of the Good Samaritan.*

CEDAR, PAUL ARNOLD, minister; b. Mpls., Nov. 4, 1938; s. Carl Benjamin and Bernice M. (Peterson) C.; m. Jean Helen Lier, Aug. 25, 1959; children: Daniel Paul, Mark John, Deborah Jean. BS, No. State Coll., Aberdeen, S.D., 1960; postgrad., U. Iowa Grad. Sch. of Religion, 1965; MDiv, No. Bap. Theol. Sem., 1968; postgrad., Calif. State U., Fullerton, 1971; D Ministry, Am. Baptist Sem. of the West, 1973. Ordained to ministry Evang. Free Ch., 1966. Youth for Christ, crusade dir. Billy Graham Evang. Assn., Leighton Ford Team, 1960-65; pastor Evang. Free Ch., Naperville, Ill., 1965-67, Yorba Linda, Calif., 1969-73; exec. pastor 1st Presbyn. Ch. Hollywood, Calif., 1975-81; sr. pastor Lake Ave. Congl. Ch., Pasadena, Calif., 1981-90; pres. Evang. Free Ch. Am., Mpls., 1990—; pres. Dynamic Communications, Pasadena, Calif., 1973-90; mem. adv. bd. World Wide Pictures, Mpls., 1982-86; dean Billy Graham Sch. Evangelism, Mpls., 1983—; vis. prof. Fuller Theol. Sem., Pasadena, Talbot Theol. Sem., LaHabra, Calif., Trinity Div. Sch., Deerfield, Ill. Author: How to Make Love Your Motive, 1977, Becoming a Lover, 1978, Seven Keys to Maximum Communication, 1980, Sharing the Good Life, 1980, Communicators Commentary, 1983, Strength in Servant Leadership, 1987, There is Hope!, 1991, Mastering the Pastoral Role, 1991. Vice chmn. Billy Graham So. Calif. Crusade, 1984-85; vice chmn. U.S. Lausanne Com. for World Evangelization; mem. John M. Perkins Found. Mem. Leighton Ford Ministries (bd. of reference), Caleb Ministries, Calif. Fellowship Christian Athletes, Leadership Renewal Ctr., Nat. Prayer Com., Providence Mission Homes, Revival Prayer Fellowship, Barnabas Internat., Russia for Christ, World Opportunities Internat., Phi Kappa Delta, Univ. Club. Avocations: athletics, music, writing, carpentry. Office: Evang Free Ch Am 901 E 78th St Minneapolis MN 55420-1300 *I am convinced that when all of life is over, only one thing will matter ultimately-fufilling the will of God.*

CEDARLEAF, JOHN LENNART, minister; b. Rockford, Ill., Aug. 5, 1915; s. Bror Samuel and Ellen Josephine (Johnson) C.; m. Agnes Swanson, Sept. 14, 1943. BA, U. N.D., 1941; cert., North Pk. Sem., 1944, Chgo. Psychoanalytic Inst., 1949. Ordained to ministry Presbyn. Ch. (U.S.A.), 1946. Chaplain Ill. State Tng. Sch. for Boys, St. Charles, 1948-54, clin. dir., 1953-54; chaplain No. Reception Ctr., Sacramento, 1954-78; adj. prof. Dominican Sch. Theology, Berkeley, Calif., 1979-82; supr. clin. pastoral edn., 1948-78. Author: (with Paul Maves): Older People and Church, 1948; contbr. articles to religious jours. Vol. Sierra Club, Sacramento, 1991. Mem. Assn. for Clin. Pastoral Edn. (pres. 1978-79, dir. Pacific region 1980-88, Disting. Svc. award 1986). *To live a full life today demands that we be in touch with yesterday's history.*

CEDARLEAF, JOHN NEVINS, minister; b. Chgo., Apr. 20, 1943; s. Nevins N. and Viola (Hedstrom) C.; m. Jean Berg, Sept. 19, 1970; children: Karl, David. BA, North Park Coll., 1965; BD, Andover Newton Theol. Sch., 1969, D Ministry, 1981. Ordained to ministry United Ch. of Christ, 1969. Pastor 1st Congl. Ch., Turners Falls, Mass., 1969-75, Evang. Congl. Ch., Grafton, Mass., 1975-84, 1st Congl. United Ch. of Christ, Fairport, N.Y., 1984—; chair worship com. N.Y. Conf. United Ch. of Christ, 1987; adj. faculty Andover Newton Theol. Sch., 1979-81, Colgate Rochester Div. Sch. Contbr. articles to profl. jours. Mem. Genesee Valley Assn. United Ch. of Christ (sec. ch. and ministry com. 1990—), Mercersburg Soc. Democrat. Home: 1 Clifford St Fairport NY 14450 Office: First Congl Ch 26 E Church St Fairport NY 14450

CENKNER, WILLIAM, religion educator, academic administrator; b. Cleve., Oct. 25, 1930; s. Joseph Paul and Sophia (Gladis) C. BA, Providence Coll., 1954; STB, Dominican Faculty, Washington, 1956, STL, 1959; PhD, Fordham U., 1969. Ordained priest Roman Cath. Ch., 1958. Lectr. Aquinas Coll. High Sch., Columbus, Ohio, 1959-64, St. Charles Coll., Columbus, 1962-64; asst. prof. religion Marist Coll., Poughkeepsie, N.Y., 1964-65; asst. prof. religion Cath. U. Am., Washington, 1969-73, assoc. prof., 1973-83, prof., 1983—, dean Sch. Religious Studies, 1985—; mem. exec. com. Am. Conf. on Religious Movements, Washington, 1988—. Author: The Hindu Personality in Education, 1976, A Tradition of Teachers: Sankara and Jagadgurus Today, 1983. Chmn. Faiths in the World Com., Washington, 1985—. Rsch. grantee Chauncy Stillman Found., India, 1969, C. Vander-Linde Found., India, 1979, Nanzan Inst. Religion and Culture, Japan, 1983. Mem. Am. Acad. Religion, Cath. Acad. Scis. in U.S., Assn. Asian Studies, Am. Oriental Soc., Coll. Theology Soc. (pres. 1978-80), Internat. Assn. History of Religions. Roman Catholic. Office: Cath Univ of Am Sch of Religious Studies Washington DC 20064

CERCE, TIMOTHY PAUL, minister; b. Paterson, N.J., Feb. 4, 1958; s. Franklin Richard and Elizabeth Jane (Rowan) C.; m. Sharon Lee Fox, Oct. 4, 1980; children: Lauren Elizabeth, Stephanie Erin. BS in Bible, Valley Forge Christian Coll., 1980. Ordained to ministry Gen. Council of the Assemblies of God. Asst. pastor Fairfax Assembly of God, Fairfax, Va., 1980-81; asst. pastor First Assembly of God, Alexandria, Va., 1981—, minister of music, 1987—; pastoral counselor Op. Blessing-CBN, Fairfax, 1984—; prof. First Assembly Christian Acad., Alexandria, 1982-84. Named one of Outstanding Young Men of Am., 1985. Mem. Ch. Assemblies of God. Office: First Assembly of God 700 W Braddock Rd Alexandria VA 22302

CERNERA, ANTHONY JOSEPH, academic administrator; b. Bronx, N.Y., Mar. 21, 1950; children: Anthony, Philip, Thomas, Anne Marie. BA in History and Theol., Fordham U., 1972, MA in Religious Edn., 1974, PhD in Theology, 1987. Tchr./chmn. Aquinas High Sch., Bronx, N.Y., 1972-77; asst. exec. dir. Bread for the World Ednl. Fund, 1977-80; exec. dir. Bread for the World Ednl. Fund, N.Y.C., 1980-81; exec. asst. to pres. Marist Coll., Poughkeepsie, N.Y., 1981-84, asst. v.p. acad. affairs, dean acad. programs & svcs., 1984-85, v.p. coll. advancement, 1985-88; pres. Sacred Heart U., Fairfield, Conn., 1988—; mem. com. on edn. U.S. Cath. Conf., 1989—; bd. dirs. U.S.T. Bank Conn. Bd. dirs. Pax Romana, Stamford, Conn., 1989—, United Way Ea. Fairfield County. Office: Sacred Heart U Office of Pres 5151 Park Ave Fairfield CT 06432-1000

CERNIGLIA, MARK ANDREW, minister; b. Miami, Fla., Feb. 8, 1954; s. Alfred Mario and Eloise Gertrude (Nelson) C.; m. Constance Susan Flanery, Nov. 5, 1977; children: Benjamin, Joseph, Adam. AA, Broward Community Coll., 1975; BA in Clin. Psychology, Fla. State U., 1977; MDiv, Luth. Theol. So. Sem., 1982. Ordained to ministry Evang. Luth. Ch. in Am., 1982. Asst. pastor Faith Luth. Ch., 1982-84; pastor Prince of Peace Luth. Ch., Indpls., 1984—; dean Indpls. Conf., Evang. Luth. Ch. Am., 1987-91, del. Churchwide Assembly, 1991; bd. dirs. Indpls. Ch. Fedn., 1987-89, Luth. Campus Ministry of Ind.-Ky., 1984-90; mem. steering com. Luth./Episc. Dialog for Ind., 1984-87. Mem. Vasa Lodge, Phi Beta Kappa. Office: Prince of Peace Luth Ch 3650 Guion Rd Indianapolis IN 46222

CERRETTO, MICHAEL PATRICK, religion educator, principal; b. Long Beach, Calif., Aug. 3, 1940; s. Michael James and Margaret (Lioi) C. BS, St. John Fisher Coll., Rochester, N.Y., 1963; STB, U. St. Michael, Toronto, Ont., Can., 1969; MA, U. Detroit, 1971. Ordained priest Roman Cath. Ch., 1969; cert. profl. in adminstrn. and supervision, Ind.; lic. social studies specialist, Ind. Tchr., treas. Aquinas Inst., Rochester, 1969-82; religious superior Basilian Fathers-Andrean High Sch., Merrillville, Ind., 1982-86; prin. Andrean High Sch., Merrillville, 1986—, dean dept. theology, 1989-91. Mem. Nat. Cath. Ednl. Assn., Nat. Assn. Secondary Sch. Prins. (div. student activities), Nat. Arbor Day Found. Republican. Home and Office: Andrean High Sch 5959 Broadway Merrillville IN 46410

CERULLO, MORRIS, evangelist, educator; b. Passaic, N.J., Oct. 2, 1931; s. Joseph and Bertha (Rosenblatt) C.; m. Vivian Theresa LePari, July 27, 1951; children: Charles David, Susan Darlene Gilhuis, Mark Stephen. Graduate, New England Bible Coll., 1951; HHD (hon.), Fla. Beacon Coll., 1974; DD (hon.), Oral Roberts U., 1987. Ordained Assembly of God, 1952, Evang. Ch. Alliance, 1984. Pastor Clairmont (N.H.) Assembly of God Ch., 1951-52; internat., domestic evangelistic crusade speaker various locations, 1952-59; pres. Morris Cerullo World Evangelism, Inc., San Diego, 1960—, Morris Cerullo Sch. of Ministry, San Diego, 1960—; owner New Inspirational Network & Heritage USA; instr. in field. Author more than 50 books including Two Men from Eden, You Can Know How to Defeat Satan, Proof Producers; monthly pub. Footprints, Frontlines, Victory Miracle Library; producer TV spls. Masada, 1976, Advent II, 1980, Advent III, 1981. Named one of Community Leaders and Noteworthy Americans, 1973-76. Mem. Can. Acad. Cultural Exchange (hon. dir.), Nat. Assn. Evangs., Evang. Press Assn., San Diego C. of C., San Diego Visitors and Conv. Bur., World Affairs Council. Office: Morris Cerullo World Evangelism PO Box 85277 San Diego CA 92186

CERVELLA, ALBERT THOMAS, priest; b. Phila., Feb. 27, 1935; s. Alberto Francesco and Concetta Mary (Petrone) C.; m. Mary Anne Connors, Sept. 28, 1963 (dec. Aug. 1973). BS in Bus. and Pub. Adminstrn., Temple U., 1957; MDiv., Pope John XXIII Nat. Sem., 1979; voice student, Hilda Rainer-Settlement Sch., 1952-62, Martial Singher-Curtis Inst., 1964-66. Ordained priest Roman Cath. Ch., 1979. Assoc. pastor Holy Rosary Ch., Reading, Pa., 1979-82, St. Anthony of Padua Ch., Easton, Pa., 1982-87, Holy Guardian Angels Ch., Reading, 1987-90, St. Columbkill Ch., Boyertown, Pa., 1990—. Writer, producer, dir. Benefit Opera Concert, Reading, 1982, The Padua Follies, Easton, 1984, The Shower of Stars, Easton, 1986, The Shower of Stars, Boyertown, 1991. Bd. dirs. State Theater, Easton, 1985-86; founding mem. Rittenhouse Opera Soc., Phila., 1960. With U.S. Army, 1958-60. Recipient Outstanding Svc. award Dept. Army, Ft. Sill, Okla., 1959. Mem. KC (4th degree, Phila., Knight of Yr. award, Phila., 1972). Democrat. Home and Office: 200 Indian Spring Rd Boyertown PA 19512

CERVENY, CAROLINE JEANNE, religious education and instructional design consultant; b. Cleve., May 9, 1943; d. Robert Theodore and Ethel Margaret (Bailey) C. BA, Ursuline Coll., Pepper Pike, Ohio, 1967; MA, St. Mary's Coll., Winona, Minn., 1977; D in Ministry, McCormick Sem., Chgo., 1985. Tchr. Regina High Sch., Warren, Mich., 1965-66; dept. chmn. Cleve. Central High Sch., 1967-69; pastoral assoc. Holy Trinity Parish, Bedford Heights, Ohio, 1969-69, St. Dorothy Parish, Warren, 1969-72, Sacred Heart Parish, Chgo., 1976-78; cons. Office Religious Edn. Archdiocese Chgo., 1978-89; ind. cons., 1989—; mem. evaluation team Loyola U., New Orleans, 1986-88, McCormick Sem., 1987. Producer videos in field. Mem. Assn. Psychol. Type, Chgo. Assn. Religious Educators, Chgo. Nat. Soc. for Performance and Instrn., Nat. Fedn. Local Cable Programmers, Religious Edn. Assn. of U.S. and Can., Instrl. Interactive Communications Soc. Office: Sisters of St Joseph 6804 Joliet Rd Indian Head Park IL 60525-4471

CERVENY, FRANK STANLEY, bishop; b. Springfield, Mass., June 4, 1933; s. Frank Charles and Julia Victoria (Kulig) C.; m. Emmy Pettway, Nov. 1, 1961; children: Frank Stanley, Emmy Pettway, William DeMoville. BA, Trinity Coll., Hartford, Conn., 1955, M in Divinity (hon.), 1977; M in Divinity, Gen. Theol. Sem., N.Y.C., 1958; M in Divinity (hon.), U. of South, 1977. Asst. rector Ch. of Resurrection, Miami, Fla., 1958-60; assoc. priest, dir. Christian edn. Trinity Ch., N.Y.C., 1960-63; rector St. Lukes Ch., Jackson, Tenn., 1963-68, St. Johns Ch., Knoxville, Tenn., 1968-72, St. John's Cathedral, Jacksonville, 1972-74; bishop Episc. Diocese of Fla., Jacksonville, 1974—. trustee Gen. Theol. Sem., N.Y.C., U. of South, Sewanee, Tenn. Club: Rotary. Office: Episcopal Ch 325 Market St Jacksonville FL 32202

CEYNAR, MARVIN EMIL, minister; b. Fairfax, Iowa, Sept. 30, 1934; s. Emil Vincent and Mary Marie (Roshek) C.; m. Barbara Jeanette Shepard, Dec. 18, 1957; children: Susanna Barbara Ceynar Karagoez, John Marvin. BA, U. Iowa, 1957; MDiv, Garrett Sem., 1962; MA, U. Iowa, 1965. Ordained minister United Meth. Ch. Minister various congregations United Meth. Ch. and United Ch. Christ, Iowa and Ill., 1957-90, St. Mark's United Meth. Ch., Cedar Rapids, Iowa, 1990—; prof. oral communications No. Ill. U., DeKalb, 1965-74; dir. numerous writers workshops, 1982—; mem. Iowa Annual Conf. United Meth. Ch., 1962—. Author: Writing for the Religious Market, 1986, Healing the Heartland, 1989, rev., 1991; author, editor: Creativity in the Communicative Arts, 1975; contbr. articles to profl. publs. Active Dem. Party, Iowa and Ill., 1962—; chair Chgo. CORE, 1960-62. Mem. Interstate Religious Writers Assn. (founder, pres. 1981—, editor newsletter 1981—). Avocations: fishing, walking, reading, swimming. Home: 300 Cherry Hill Rd NW Cedar Rapids IA 52405 Office: St Mark's United Meth Ch 4700 Johnson Ave NW Cedar Rapids IA 52405

CHACKO, MATHEW CHETHIPURACKAL, minister; b. Thalavady, Kerala, India, Dec. 19, 1932; came to U.S., 1968; s. Varkey C. and Sosamma (Mathew) C.; m. Ruthamma Thomas, May 25, 1969; children: Jacob, Susan. BSc, C.M.S. Coll., Kottayam, India, 1954; BD, Bishops Coll., Calcutta, India, 1957; MA, Univ. Coll., Trivandrum, India, 1964; MST, Union Theol. Sem., N.Y.C., 1969; PhD, Hartford Sem., 1973. Ordained to ministry Ea. Orthodox Christian Ch., 1957. Pastor Orthodox Chs. in India, 1957-68; assoc. pastor various chs. in U.S., 1968-73; assoc. pastor, coord. Orthodox Chs. in U.S.A., 1974-77; chaplain Sea View Hosp. and Home, S.I., N.Y., 1977—; pastor St. Basilios-Gregorian Orthodox Ch., S.I., 1989—; pres. Coun. Chs., N.Y.C., 1986-88. Mem. S.I. Clergy Assn. (pres. 1984-86), Bhargt Aid Assn. N.Y. (chmn. 1974-75), Kerala Samajans of S.I. (pres. 1988-90). Home: 29 Bache St Staten Island NY 10302 Office: Sea View Hosp and Home 660 Brielle Ave Staten Island NY 10314

CHADWICK, RONALD PAUL, academic administrator, religion educator; b. Buffalo, July 16, 1935; s. George Maurice and Edna Eleanor (Schmidt) C.; m. Sarah Alice Dolson, Aug. 24, 1956; children: Randall Scott, Stephen Michael, Robert Paul, Scott Michael. AB, Bryan Coll., 1958; ThM, Dallas Theol. Sem., 1962; PhD, U. Mo., Kansas City, 1974; PhD (hon.), Oxford Grad. Sch., Dayton, Tenn., 1989. Min. Christian edn. Bible Chapel and Christian Sch., Phoenix, 1963-64; assoc. prof. Ariz. Bible Coll., Phoenix, 1964-68, Calvary Bible Coll., Kansas City, 1968-73; prof. religious edn. Grand Rapids (Mich.) Bapt. Sem., 1973-86; dir. ednl. ministry Radio Bible

Class, Grand Rapids, 1986-91; pres. Grand Rapids Sch. Bible and Music, Comstock Park, Mich., 1991—. Author: Teaching and Learning: An Integrated Approach to Education, 1982, Christian School Curriculum: An Integrated Approach; (with others) An Introduction to Biblical Christian Education. Trustee Springhill Camp, Evart, Mich., 1989—; elder Calvary Ch., Grand Rapids, 1991—. Mem. Nat. Assn. Profs. Christian Edn. (pres. 1973-76), Christian Camping Internat., Am. Assn. Bible Colls. Republican. Home: 1715 Rodney Cir Grand Rapids MI 49505 Office: Grand Rapids Sch Bible and Music 109 School St NE Comstock Park MI 49321

CHAE, YOON KWON, minister, educator; b. Seoul, Korea, Feb. 13, 1932; came to U.S., 1973; s. Sang H. and Bong Soo (Cho) Chae (Choi); m. Geon Min, Mar. 3, 1981 (dec.); m. Kook Ja Park, Dec. 4, 1982; 1 child, John Wooshik. BA, San Jose Bible Coll., 1960; MA, Lincoln Christian Sem., 1961; DD, Am. Bible Inst., 1968; ThD, Immanuel Bapt. Sem., 1976. Ordained to ministry Christian Ch., 1960. Pastor numerous Christian Chs., Korea and U.S., 1962—; pres., chancellor Korea Christian Sem., Seoul, 1965—; prof. San Jose Christian Coll., 1985—; bd. dirs. Geon Christian Children's Home, Seoul, 1966—, Korea Gospel Mission, San Jose, 1974—. Author: My Dear American Friends I, 1973, II, 1982, III, 1989, The Shattered Cross I, 1972, II, 1978, III, 1985, Yoon Kwon Chae Column, 1988, Sermons for 52 Weeks, 1987. 1st lt. Korean Army, 1953-56. Mem. Kiwanis (pres. Seoul 1983-84, gov. 1987-88). Republican. Home: 1043 Forest Knoll Dr San Jose CA 95129 Office: San Jose Christian Coll 12th and Virginia San Jose CA 95112

CHAFFEE, ESTHER RIDENOUR (MRS. THOMAS K. CHAFFEE), church organist; b. Lima, Ohio; d. Joshua Mechling and Jennie (Hitchcock) Ridenour; m. David R. Meily, May 23, 1934 (dec. 1972); children: Helen Adelia Bayer, Martha Frances Senechal, Sara Elizabeth Hayden; m. Thomas K. Chafee Jr., Aug. 1975. Student, Wittenberg U., 1929-30, Ball State U., 1956-57, Bluffton Coll., 1932-33, U. Mich., 1950-51; BA in Music Edn. Lawrence U., 1963. Elem. vocal music tchr., Lima, 1932-34, Morgan Sch., Appleton, Wis., 1963-75; substitute tchr., Washington, 1934-36, Pontiac and Birmingham, Mich., 1945-55; high sch. music tchr., Marion, Ind., 1955-58. Asst. organist Nat. City Christian Ch., Washington, 1934-36; organist, choir dir. First Bapt. Ch., Birmingham, 1950-53, All Sts. Episcopal Ch., Appleton, 1958-64, St. Thomas Episcopal Ch., Menasha, Wis., 1964-75; organist, choirmaster St. Albans Episcopal Ch., Olney, Ill., and St. Mary's Episcopal Ch., Robinson, Ill., 1975-77, St. Anne's Ch., De Pere, Wis., 1977—. Vol. tchr., programmer Children's Hosp., Detroit, 1950-54; dir. Civic Music Series, Marion, 1952; music tchr. Retarded Children's Sch., Marion, 1954-55; asst. music therapist Winnebago State Hosp., Oshkosh, Wis., 1967-71; music coordinator Opportunity Centers, S.E. Ill. Daycare Center. Mem. Organ Guild, Wis. Acad. Arts, Nat. Music Educators Guild, Wis. Music Educators Guild, Am. Contract Bridge League (life master). Composer: St. Thomas and St. Anne Mass, other sacred works.

CHAFFIN, JOHN CRAIG, minister; b. Ft. Wayne, Ind., Apr. 28, 1955; s. Frank Stanley and Maxine Margret (Miller) C.; m. Laura June Mummery, June 4, 1977; children: Brice, Daniel, Jesse, Elizabeth. BA in English, Okla. State U., 1977; MDiv, Western Bapt. Sem., 1985. Ordained to ministry Christian and Missionary Alliance, 1987. Pastor Alliance Bible Ch., Oklahoma City, 1985—. Pres. Metro-South Crisis Pregnancy Ctr., Moore, Okla., 1989—. Mem. Moore Area Ministerial Allinace (sec.-treas. 1987-89, v.p. 1990). Republican. Home: 117 S Woods Moore OK 73160 Office: Alliance Bible Ch 204 SW 104th Oklahoma City OK 73139

CHAKAIPA, PATRICK FANI, archbishop; b. Mhondoro, June 25, 1932. Ordained priest Roman Cath. Ch., 1965. Asst. priest Makumbi Mission, 1967-69; priest-in-charge All Souls Mission, 1969; episcopal vicar Mutoko and Murewa, 1970; aux. bishop of Harare, 1972; archbishop of Harare Zimbabwe, 1976—. Author: Karikoga Gumiremiseve, 1958, Rudo and Pfumo Reropa, 1961, Garandichauya, 1963, Dzasukwa Mwana Asina Hembe, 1967. Office: Archdiocese of Harare, PO Box 8060, Causeway, Harare Zimbabwe

CHALFANT, EDWARD COLE, bishop; b. Pitts., Aug. 14, 1937; s. Edward Trimble and Helen Louise (Cole) C.; m. Marydee Wimbish, Aug. 29, 1959; children—Edward Cole, Margaret Louise. B.A., Wesleyan U., Middletown, Conn., 1960; cert. St. Augustines, Canterbury, Eng., 1962; M.Div., Va. Theol. Sem., 1963, D.D. (hon.), 1985. Ordained to ministry Episcopal Ch., 1963. Assoc. rector Ch. of Ascension, Clearwater, Fla., 1963-67; vicar St. John's Episcopal Ch., Clearwater, 1967-72; rector St. Mark's Ch., Columbus, Ohio, 1972-84; bishop coadjutor Diocese of Maine, Portland, 1984-86, bishop, 1986—; cons. in field. Contbr. articles to profl. publs. Bd. dirs. Clearwater YMCA, 1966-72, Mantal Health Assn. and Clinic, Clearwater, 1969-72, United Way, 1988—; incorporator Maine Med. Ctr., 1989—. Clubs: Bucks Harbor Yacht (So. Brooksville, Maine); Athletic (Columbus). Avocations: sailing; skiing. Home: PO Box 215 Orrs Island ME 04066-0215 Office: Diocese Maine 143 State St Portland ME 04101

CHALKER, KENNETH WAYNE, minister; b. Alliance, Ohio, Jan. 22, 1949; s. Wayne Calvin Chalker and Vernita Colletta (Chaffee) Nail; m. Grace Elaine Bird, Aug. 14, 1971; children: Laura Elaine, Wayne Charles. BA, Mt. Union Coll., 1971; MDiv, Duke U., 1974; D in Ministry, Northwestern U., Evanston, Ill., 1982. Ordained to ministry Meth. Ch., 1975. Pastor Lexington (Ohio) Ch. of the Cross, 1974-82, Union Ave. United Meth. Ch., Alliance, 1982-86, First United Meth. Ch., Cleve., 1986—; registrar Bd. Ordained Ministry East Ohio Conf., 1976-84, chmn. conf. nominating com., 1984-88; del. Jurisdictional Conf., Duluth, Minn. and DeKalb, Ill., 1984, 88; sec. East Ohio Ann. Conf., Canton, 1988—; weekly news commentator Sta. WEWS-TV, Cleve. Author: Dare to Defy, 1980; contbr. articles to profl. jours. Trustee Midtown Corridor Assn., Cleve., 1988—; pres., trustee Berea Children's Home; trustee United Theol. Sem., 1987—, Cleve. Alcoholism Services, 1987—; mem. adv. bd. Playhouse Sq., 1987—, St. Luke's Hosp. Assn.; councilman Lexington Village Council, 1978-82; del. Nat. Security Forum Air War Coll., Maxwell AFB, Montgomery, Ala., 1978. Recipient Communication Achievement of Yr. award Cleve. Advt. Club, 1988. Mem. Univ. City Club, Kiwanis. Avocations: boating, woodworking. Office: First United Meth Ch 3000 Euclid Ave Cleveland OH 44115

CHAMBERLAIN, CAROL MOORE, priest; b. Princeton, N.J., Nov. 17, 1946; d. Frank L. Jr. and Lucille M. (Kipp) Moore; m. Barry D. Chamberlain, June 12, 1976; children: Matthew, John. BS, Syracuse U., 1968; MDiv, Episcopal Div. Sch., 1975. Ordained deacon Episcopal Ch., 1975, priest, 1977. Deacon Fairmount Team Ministry, Phila., 1975-76, coord., 1976-78; interim St. John the Evangelist, Phila., 1981; rector St. Aidan's Ch., Cheltenham, Pa., 1982—; coord. Deacon Intern Program, Phila., 1990—; chmn. Commn. on Ministry, Phila., 1984-88. Bd. dirs. Phila. Protestant Home, 1991—. Mem. Rotary. Office: St Aidans Church 1 Central Ave Cheltenham PA 19012

CHAMBERLAIN, DAVID MORROW, priest; b. Chattanooga, Oct. 10, 1946; s. Augustus Wright and Myrle Delano (Hancock) C.; m. Patricia Ann Magill, Jan. 8, 1972; children: Michael, Carolyn. BA, U. Chattanooga, 1968; MDiv, Va. Theol. Sem., 1971. Ordained to ministry Episcopal Ch. in the U.S.A. as deacon, 1971, as priest, 1972. Deacon, priest in tng. St. John's Episcopal Ch., Johnson City, Tenn., 1971-72; asst. to rector Calvary Episc. Ch., Memphis, 1972-73, St. Andrew's Episcopal Ch., Arlington, Va., 1973-76; rector St. John's Episcopal Ch., Glencarlyn, Arlington, 1976-80; dean Region III Episcopal Diocese of Va., 1978-80; canon educator Episcopal Cathedral St. Philip, Atlanta, 1980-87; rector St. John's Episcopal Ch., Fayetteville, N.C., 1987—; field edn. supr. Va. Theol. Sem., Alexandria, 1973-80; exec. com. Region III, Diocese of Va., 1978-80; com. of ann. coun., Diocese of Atlanta, 1980-87, com. overseeing bishop election, 1983. Author: The Bible in Capsule Form,1987; film critic in the Tenn. Churchman, 1971-73. 1st lt. U.S. Army, 1968-73. Mem. Kiwanis. Avocations: banjo, coins, film, piano. Home: 274 Westwood Ct Fayetteville NC 28303 Office: St John's Episcopal Ch 302 Green St PO Box # 722 Fayetteville NC 28302 *In my life I have yet to run into an issue that was more important than a relationship.*

CHAMBERLAIN, ERNEST HENRY, minister, educator; b. Corbett, Oreg., Aug., 1915; s. George Henry and Virginia Pearl (Owen) C.; m. Zella Lucile Webb, Jan. 2, 1937; children—Gloria Ann, Martha Ann. B.Theology, N.W. Christian Coll., 1938, B.Oratory, 1939; B.Div., Butler U., 1946. Ordained to ministry, Christian Ch., 1936. Minister, various pastorates, 1936-76; dir. devel. Boise Bible Coll., Idaho, 1976-85; minister Peninsula Christian Ch., Gig Harbor, Wash., 1985—. Contbr. articles to profl. jours. Editor news bull. Boise Bible Coll., 1976-85. Mem. N.Am. Christian Conv. (pres. 1962-63). Republican. Club: Kiwanis. Home: 6601 40th Street Ct NW Gig Harbor WA 98335

CHAMBERLAIN, GARY LEE, theology educator; b. Denver, Aug. 21, 1938; s. John L. and Marie M. (Thomson) C.; m. Sharon Anne Demong, June 15, 1968; children: Michael and Benjamin (twins). BA in Philosophy, St. Louis U., 1962, PhL in Philosophy, 1963; MA in Polit. Sci., U. Chgo., 1967; PhD, Grad. Theol. Union, Berkeley, Calif., 1973. Prof. theology and religious studies Seattle U., 1979—; lectr. parishes and group, Seattle. Author: Fostering Faith, 1989, Empowering Authority, 1990. Mem Am. Acad. Religion, Assn. Profs. and Researchers in Religious Edn. (task force coord. 1985-88), Pax Christi U.S.A. Democrat. Home: 1012 W Bothwell Seattle WA 98122 Office: Seattle U Broadway and Madison Seattle WA 98119

CHAMBERLAIN, MARK STEVEN, pastor; b. Culver City, Calif., Mar. 25, 1954; s. Melvin Eugene and Ruth Ann (Connell) C.; m. Teresa Marie Roberts, Dec. 16, 1978; children: Sarah Diane, Noel Steven, Laura Marie. BA in Communication, Biola Coll., 1980; MDiv in Christian Formation, Fuller Sem., 1983. Ordained minister in Presbyn. Ch. Co-asst. pastor La Canada (Calif.) Presbyn. Ch., 1983-88; co-assoc. pastor First Presbyn. Ch., Aurora, Colo., 1988-90; pastor Crosby-Ironton Presbyn. Ch., Crosby, Minn., 1990—; mem. polity and records com. San Fernando, Calif., 1987-88, com. on preparation, Denver, 1989-91; chair com. on representation, Minnesota Valleys, Minn., 1991—. Mem. Nat. Presbyn. Educators. Office: Crosby Ironton Presbyn Ch Hallett Ave at First SE Crosby MN 56441

CHAMBERLIN, HERBERT CHARLES, minister; b. Yonkers, N.Y., Mar. 7, 1932; s. Robert Mason and Muriel Lucille (Whipple) C.; m. Deena Hunter, Aug. 21, 1958; children: Lisa Lynne Whitby, Douglas Arthur. BA, Adelphi U., Garden City, N.Y., 1953; MRE, Southwestern Sem., Ft. Worth, Tex., 1959; MDiv, Andover Newton Theol. Sch., 1965; D Ministry, Drew U., 1976. Ordained to ministry United Ch. of Christ, 1963. Minister of edn. Grandin Ct. Bapt. Ch., Roanoke, Va., 1959-63; pastor First Bapt. Ch., Scituate, Mass., 1964-69, Wantagh Meml. Congl. Ch., 1970-79, Pleasantville United Ch. of Christ, Chalfont, Pa., 1979-90; sr. pastor Hillcrest Congl. Ch., La Habra Heigths, Calif., 1990—; chmn. Div. Evangelism, Pa. S.E. Conf., United Ch. of Christ, Collegeville, Pa., 1987-90, others in past. Author sermons in Master Sermon series. With U.S. Army, 1953-55. Democrat. Office: Hillcrest Congl Ch 2000 West Rd La Habra Heights CA 90631

CHAMBERS, CRAIG VAN, minister; b. Torrance, Calif., May 26, 1953; s. Donald Elsworth and Elizabeth Jo Ann C.; m. Katrina Whittington, Aug. 27, 1977 (div. June 1983); 1 child, Anika Nicole; m. Denise Marie Krainik, June 14, 1985; children: Matthew James, Paul Timothy, Luke Nathanael, Thaddaeus John. M of Ministry, Talbot Sem., 1988. Ordained to ministry, 1988. Pastor Silver Lakes Community Ch., Helendale, Calif., 1988-90; pastor Grace Bible Ch., Helendale, 1990—. Author: (booklets) Believer's Baptism, Communion, 1990. Mem. Helendale Sch. Dist. Com., 1990-92. Sgt. U.S. Army, 1976-83. Republican. Home: PO Box 1203 26837 Water Rd Helendale CA 92342 Office: Grace Bible Ch PO Box 498 Helendale CA 92342

CHAMBERS, CURTIS ALLEN, clergyman, church communications executive; b. Damascus, Ohio, Sept. 24, 1924; s. Binford Vincent and Margaret Esther (Patterson) C.; m. Anna June Winn, Aug. 26, 1946; children: David Lloyd, Curtis Allen II, Deborah Ann, Charles Cloyde. Th.B., Malone Coll., 1946; A.B., Ind. Wesleyan U., 1947; B.D., Asbury Theol. Sem., 1950; postgrad., Oberlin Grad. Sch. Theology, 1951-53; S.T.M., Temple U., 1955, S.T.D., 1960; D.D. (hon.), Lebanon Valley Coll., 1967. Ordained to ministry Evang. United Brethren Ch., 1954. Pastor 1st Ch., Cleve., 1951-53, Rockville Ch., Harrisburg, Pa., 1953-59; editor adult publs. Evang. United Brethren Ch., 1959-65; assoc. editor Ch. and Home mag., Dayton, Ohio, 1963-66; editor Ch. and Home mag., 1967-69; asst. editorial dir. Together and Christian Advocate, Meth. Pub. House, Park Ridge, Ill., 1969; editor Together mag., 1969-73; acting editorial dir. gen. periodicals United Meth. Ch., 1971-72, editorial dir., 1972-73; gen. sec. United Meth. Communications, 1973-84; gen. mgr. Alternate View Network, 1984-85; minister edn. and communication First United Meth. Ch., Shreveport, La., 1985-87, minister pastoral care and communication, 1987-88; minister program and communication St. Paul's United Meth. Ch., Monroe, La., 1988-90; religious communication cons. Nashville, 1990—; assoc. pastor Andrew Price United Meth. Ch., Nashville, 1991—; book editor Evang. United Brethren Ch., 1965-68; co-editor Plan of Union, United Meth. Ch., 1965-68, Plan of Union, United Meth. Ch. (Book of Discipline), 1968, chmn. staff com. long range planning, 1969-72, mem. commn. on ch. union, 1965-68; dir. radio-TV relations gen. confs. Evang. United Brethren Ch., 1958, 62, 66, United Meth. Ch., 1966, 68; Chmn. commn. on ednl. media Nat. Council Chs., 1965-66, chmn. com. on audio visual and broadcast edn., 1962-65, exec. com. broadcasting and film commn., chmn. communications commn., 1975-78, v.p., 1975-78; chmn. Religious Communications Congress, 1980; named 1 of 12 editors sent to Middle East on fact-finding trip, 1969. Contbr. articles to religious lit. Served as capt. (chaplain) CAP, 1960-65. Recipient Distinguished Alumni award Malone Coll., 1967, Alumni of Year, 1978. Mem. Aircraft Owners and Pilots Assn., United Meth. Assn. Communicators (v.p. 1968-72), World Assn. Christian Communications (central com., chmn. Jour. editorial bd. 1975-82, chmn. periodical devel. com., exec. com., sec. 1978-82), Asso. Ch. Press (hon. life), Religious Pub. Relations Council. Clubs: Chgo. Press (Dayton), Torch (Dayton). Home: 120 Saddle Tree Ct Hermitage TN 37076 *When I was young I thought that anything was possible for me and that I had a long, long time to achieve it. With maturity I have come to a recognition of mortality, finitude, a limitation of time and opportunity. Thus my life has taught me three things: 1) Choose the best. Life is too precious to squander it on the second rate. 2) Live for others. The quality of one's life is enhanced rather than diminished as one shares himself/herself with others. 3) Fulfill your dreams. Tomorrow may never come; act now so that life's opportunities may not be lost forever.*

CHAMBERS, ELIZABETH, missionary, librarian; b. New Cumberland, Va., July 24, 1916; d. Boyd Blaine and Edith (Marshall) C. BA, U. Cin., 1938; BS in Libr. Sci., MS, U. Ill., 1941, 61; MA, Berkeley Bapt. Div. Sch., 1954; cert. in edn., Peabody Coll., 1972. Missionary, libr. Am. Bapt. Chs., Iloilo City, Philippines, 1954-72, 81-83; libr. Am. Bapt. Sem., Covina, Calif., 1984-88; dir. librs. Cen. Philippine U., Iloilo City, 1954-72, mission correspondent Am. Bapt. Chs., Valley Forge, Pa. Pres., treas. Iloilo City YWCA, 1954-71. Mem. ALA, Am. Theol. Libr. Assn. Home: 727 Plymouth Rd Claremont CA 91711

CHAMBERS, JIMMIE JOE, minister, educational consultant; b. Pawhuska, Okla., Feb. 2, 1951; s. Jimmie J. Chambers and Frances F. (Adolph) Rivera; m. Diana Lynette Burrus, Feb. 10, 1971; children: Joe, Amanda Christine. BA in Bibl. Studies, NW Bible Coll., Minot, N.D., 1986; MA in Bibl. Lit., Assemblies of God Theol. Sem., Springfield, Mo., 1988. Ordained to ministry Ch. of God, 1985. Pastor Union (Mo.) Ch. of God, 1975-80; sr. pastor Joplin (Mo.) Ch. of God, 1980-85; instr. NW Bible Coll., 1985-87; tchr. Mt. Paran Christian High Sch., Marietta, Ga., 1987-89; program specialist Mt. Paran Ch. of God, Atlanta, 1988-89, dir. small group ministries, 1990—; program dir. Sch. for Ministry Devel., Atlanta, 1988-89; clin. coord. Clin. Ministerial Internship Program, Minot, 1986-87; dist. overseer Ch. of God, Minot, 1986-87. Author: Life and Times of John, 1988, The Holy Spirit and Ministry, 1989, Handbook for Small Group Leaders, 1991, Vine Life Ministry: A Strategy for Small Group Evangelism, Nurture and Discipleship, 1991; also tng. courses. Recipient Academia-Scholarship award Minot C. of C., 1987. Avocations: golf, fishing. Office: Mt Paran Ch of God 2055 Mt Paran Rd NW Atlanta GA 30327

CHAMBERS, ROBERT BEN, music minister; b. Houston, Mar. 12, 1949; s. Ben William and Vira L. (Marshall) C.; m. Cheryl Ann Sharbutt, Nov. 21, 1973; children: Micah, Emily. BMusEdn, Tex. Christian U., 1971, MMusEdn, 1973; DMA, Southwestern Bapt. Theol. Sem., Ft. Worth, 1984. Ordained to ministry So. Bapt. Conv., 1978. Minister of music and youth Main St. Bapt. Ch., Williamsburg, Ky., 1978-80, Calvary Bapt. Ch., Newport News, 1980-82; minister of music Trinity Bapt. Ch., Amarillo, Tex., 1982-91, First Bapt. Ch., Maryville, Tenn., 1991—. Mem. So. Bapt. Ch. Music Conf., Am. Choral Dirs. Assn., The Hymn Soc. Am., Choristers Guild, Am. Guild of English Handbell Ringers. Office: First Bapt Ch 202 W Lamar Alexander Pkwy Maryville TN 37801-4985 *The quest of my life has always been consistency—consistency in thought, action, and relationship to God and others.*

CHAMBLIN, STEVEN KYLE, minister; b. Oklahoma City, Apr. 4, 1959; s. Kenneth Wayne and Beverly T. (Byrum) C.; m. Jaqueline Marie DuBois, June 9, 1979; children: Steven Kyle II, Jaqueline Crystal. BS in Indsl. Supervision, U. Houston, 1987; MusM, Southwestern Bapt. Theol. Sem., Ft. Worth, 1991. Lic. and ordained to ministry So. Bapt. Conv., 1987. Min. music 1st Bapt. Ch. West Houston, 1979-87, dir. outreach and youth, 1985-87; min. music 1st. Bapt. Ch., Everman, Tex., 1987-91; min. music and edn. 1st. Bapt. Ch., Sachse, Tex., 1991—; treas. Everman Ch. Alliance, 1990-91. Recipient 1st pl. award Nat. Assn. for Tchrs. Singing, 1977. Office: 1st Bapt Ch 2412 Third Sachse TX 75048 *The highest ideal in life is to live in absolute devotion to God and under the complete Lordship of Jesus Christ. It is the bedrock upon which all of our service, both to God and to mankind, is built.*

CHAMPION, RICHARD GORDON, editor, journalism educator; b. Elkhart, Ind., Mar. 25, 1931; s. Gordon Champion and Ruby Estelle (Jenkin) C.; m. Norma Jean Black, Oct. 3, 1953; children: Jeffrey Bruce, Ashley Brooke. BA, Central Bible Coll., Springfield, Mo., 1953; student, Drury Coll., 1957-59. Ordained minister Assemblies of God, 1953. Assoc. pastor 1st Assembly of God, Macomb, Ill., 1953-55; circulation mgr. Pentecostal Evangel, Springfield, Mo., 1955-57; editor CA Herald; CA Guide, Springfield, 1958-64; instr. journalism Central Bible Coll., Springfield, 1961—; mng. editor Pentecostal Evangel, Springfield, 1964-84; editor Pentecostal Evangel, 1984—. Author: Above and Beyond, 1961, What's Mine..., 1964, Go On Singing, 1976, The Assemblies of God at 75, 1989; chmn. adv. com. Advance Mag., 1971—. Sec., bd. dirs. Gen. Coun. Credit Union, Springfield, 1974-91; bd. dirs. Springfield chpt. Am. Cancer Soc., 1990—. Mem. Evang. Press Assn. (pres. 1976-77, bd. dirs. 1971-77), Internat. Pentecostal Press Assn. (bd. dirs. 1982—, 1st v.p. 1988—). Avocations: gardening, stamp collecting. Home: 3609 S Broadway Springfield MO 65807 Office: Pentecostal Evang 1445 Boonville Springfield MO 65802

CHAN, SILAS CHENG-YI, religious educator; b. Taiwan, China, Nov. 11, 1940; came to U.S., 1976; m. Rachel R. Liao, Feb. 11, 1971; 1 child, Evan. MDiv, Denver Seminary, 1978; PhD in Theology, Fuller Seminary, Pasadena, Calif., 1986. Lectr. Taiwan Coll., Hsilo, 1969-71, asst. prof., dean, 1971-80; dir. 1st Evang. Ch., Glendale, Calif., 1980-85; gen. dir. China Evang. Seminary, L.A., 1986-90; prof. Old Testament Logos Theol. Sem., Pasadena, 1991—. Editor: Living Spring Publs., 1981—; author: The Prophetic Concept of Kingship, 1987, Barclay of Taiwan, 1975. Recipient Spiritual Leadership awards Denver Seminary, 1978, Most Outstanding Achievement award for handicapped person Govt. of Taiwan, 1976. Mem. Soc. Bibl. Lit., Evang. Theol. Soc. Home: 153 Alta St Arcadia CA 91006 Office: Logos Theol Sem Pasadena CA 91101

CHANCE, HUGH E., religious organization official; b. Winfield, Kans., Dec. 28, 1911; s. Hugh Chester and Edna Mary (Johnson) C.; m. Margaret Chamberlin, May 29, 1934; 1 child, Mary Ann. BA, Cornell Coll., Mt. Vernon, Iowa, 1933; JD, State U. Iowa, 1935. Mem. Nat. Spiritual Assembly Bahá'í Faith, Wilmette, Ill., 1961-63; mem. Universal House of Justice Bahá'í Faith, Haifa, Israel, 1963—. Author: A Crown of Beauty. Lt. (j.g.) USN, 1944-46, PTO. Mem. Rotary (pres. Haifa club 1971-72). Home: 37 Harofe, Haifa Israel Office: Bahá'í World Ctr, PO Box 155, Haifa 31 001, Israel

CHANCE, JAMES BRADLEY, religion educator; b. Topeka, Kans., May 17, 1954; s. James Melvin and Annette Myrtle (Huke) C.; m. Mary Venters Jenkins, Aug. 16, 1975; children: Marianne, Jay Bradley. AB, U. N.C., 1975; MDiv, Southeastern Bapt. Seminary, Wake Forest, N.C., 1978; PhD, Duke U., 1984. Vis. instr. of New Testament Southeastern Bapt. Seminary, 1978-82; assoc. prof. of religion William Jewell Coll., Liberty, Mo., 1982—; editorial bd. Perspectives in Religious Studies, 1990—. Author: Jerusalem, the Temple, and the New Age in Luke-Acts, 1988; contbr. articles and book revs. to profl. jours. Mem. Soc. Bibl. Lit., Nat. Assn. Bapt. Profs. of Religion (pres. Midwest region 1989-90). Democrat. Office: William Jewell Coll Liberty MO 64068

CHANCEY, DUDLEY H., minister; m. Vicki E. DuPriest, Apr. 12, 1974; children: Andrew Paul, Matthew Kyle. AA in Bus. Adminstrn., Albany Jr. Coll., 1981; BS in Indsl. Tech., Tenn. Technol. U., 1985, postgrad., 1986—; postgrad., U. Tenn., 1990—. Ordained to ministry Ch. of Christ. Prodn. supe. MacGregor Golf Co., 1973-81; youth min. Collegeside Ch. of Christ, Cookeville, Tenn., 1981—; bd. dirs. UPLIFT, Harding U. Named one of Outstanding Young Men of Am., 1984. Mem. Engrs.' Joint Count., Am. Foundrymen's Soc., Am. Welding Soc., Soc. Advancement Mgmt., Univ. Christian Student Ctr., Alpha Beta Gamma, Phi Theta Kappa. Avocations: golf, backpacking, skiing, building cherry furniture, computers. Home: 3426 Buck Mt Rd Cookeville TN 38501 Office: Collegeside Ch Christ 252 E 9th St Cookeville TN 38501

CHANDLER, BRIAN KEITH, minister; b. Wyndotte, Mich., Nov. 4, 1960; s. Richard and Doris Nadean (Mahaffey) C. BRE, William Tyndale Coll., 1984; MA in Christian Edn., Talbot Sch. Theology, 1987. Ordained to ministry Ref. Ch., 1988. Couselor, staff Camp Hiawatha, Piatt Lake, Mich., 1980-83; youth pastor Grosse Ile (Mich.) Bapt. Ch., 1983-85; program dir. Laurel Pines Camp, Barton Flats, Calif., 1987; youth minister Bethany Reformed Ch., Redlands, Calif., 1987—; co-founder Nat. Youth Speakers Assn., Redlands, Calif., 1989—; camp dir. Laurel Pines Camp, Barton Flats, Calif., 1991—. Chmn. Redlands Youth Com., 1989—; mem. Laurel Pines Bd. Mem. Nat. Youth Speakers Assn. (bd. dirs.), Calif Classis Youth Com. Home: 1498 Brookside Apt I-231 Redlands CA 92373

CHANDLER, CHARLES HOWARD, minister; b. Cedartown, Ga., July 26, 1935; s. Gordon Russell and Kathleen Maude (Green) C.; m. Betty Lou Horton, Mar. 22, 1957; children: Charles Howard, Sheri Lynn, Clayton Anthony, Cynthia Dawn. AB, Samford U., 1957; MDiv, So. Bapt. Theol. Sem., 1961, MRE, 1964, D Ministry, 1974. Ordained to ministry So. Bapt. Conv., 1957. Pastor Fellowship Bapt. Ch., Harrodsburg, Ky., 1960-62; assoc. pastor Deer Pk. Bapt. Ch., Louisville, 1962-65; pastor Bapt. Tabernacle Ch., Paducah, Ky., 1965-71, 1st Bapt. Ch., Metropolis, Ill., 1971-76, Pennsylvania Ave. Bapt. Ch., Urbana, Ill., 1976-89, Huguenot Rd. Bapt. Ch., Richmond, Va., 1989—; bd. dirs. Bapt. Bd. Child Care, Ky., 1968-71; bd. dirs. Ill. Bapt. State Assn., 1973-82, chmn. spl. ministries com., 1976-78, assn. pres., 1984-86; mem. exec. stewardship adv. coun., 1973-89; host pastor, speaker convs., retreats, confs.; condr. revivals, numerous states; pres. Paducah Area Ministerial Assn., 1967, Massac County Ministerial Alliance, Metropolis, 1975-76, Champaign-Urbana Ministerial Assn., 1981-83; participant devotional Sta. WPSD-TV, Paducah, Sta. WCIA-TV, Champaign; mem. com. on coms. So. Bapt. Conv., 1981; field supr. D Ministry program So. Bapt. Theol. Sem., Louisville, 1975—; tchr. Ctr. of Boyce Bible Sch., Springfield, Ill., 1979-87. Author: The Deacon Family Ministry Plan Really Works, 1982, Preaching from Prairie Pulpits, 1985, Minister's Support Group: Alternative to Burnout, 1987; contbr. chpts. to books, articles to profl. jours. Chmn. Metropolis Little League Football Program, 1972-75; mem. Mayor's Adv. Com. for City Improvement through HUD, Metropolis, 1975-76; bd. dirs. Devel. Svcs. Ctr., Champaign, 1982-87. Recipient Duke of Paducah award, 1967, Superman of Metropolis award, 1972; named to Ky. Cols., 1976. Mem. So. Bapt. Theol. Sem. Alumni Assn. (pres. Ill. chpt. 1980-81), Rotary. Home: 2641 Cromwell Rd Richmond VA 23235 Office: Huguenot Rd Bapt Ch 10525 W Huguenot Rd Richmond VA 23235 *Though I cannot always determine my lot in life, I can determine the attitude by which I respond to life. Believing that God can work for good through all experiences enables me to grow through that experience. Each stage of life has helped prepare me for the next stage. A positive attitude is an essential ingredient in reaching our God given potential.*

CHANDLER, E(DWIN) RUSSELL, journalist; b. Los Angeles, Calif., Sept. 9, 1932; s. Edwin Russell Sr. and Mary Elizabeth (Smith) C.; m. Sandra Lynn Swisher, Aug. 24, 1957 (div. 1977); children—Heather, Holly, Timothy John; m. Marjorie Lee Moore, Dec. 21, 1978; 3 stepchildren. Student, Stanford U., 1950-52; B.S. in Bus. Adminstrn., UCLA, 1952-55; postgrad., U. So. Calif. Grad. Sch. Religion, 1955, New Coll., Edinburgh, Scotland, 1955-56; M.Div.,, Princeton Theol. Sem., 1958; grad., Washington Journalism Ctr., 1967. Ordained to ministry Presbyterian Ch., 1958. Asst. pastor 1st Presbyn. Ch., Concord, Calif., 1958-61; pastor Escalon Presbyn. Ch., Calif., 1961-66; reporter Modesto Bee, Calif., 1966-67; religion editor Washington Star, 1968-69; news editor Christianity Today, Washington, 1969-72; reporter Sonora Daily Union Dem., Calif., 1972-73; religion writer L.A. Times, 1974—. Author: The Kennedy Explosion, 1972, Budgets, Bedrooms and Boredom, 1976; co-author: Your Family—Frenzy or Fun?, 1977, The Overcomers, 1978, Understanding the New Age, 1988 (Silver Angel award 1989), Wilbur award 1989; contbr. articles to profl. jours. Recipient Arthur West award United Methodist Communications Council, 1978; co-recipient Silver Angel award, Religion in Media, 1985. Mem. Religion Newswriters Assn. (pres. 1982-84, James O. Supple Meml. award, 1976, 1984, 86, John M. Templeton Reporter of Yr. award 1984, 87, 89), Phi Delta Theta. Republican. Avocations: tennis; beekeeping. Home: 930 Figueroa Terr # 414 Los Angeles CA 90012 Office: Los Angeles Times Times Mirror Sq Los Angeles CA 90053

CHANDLER, JOHN EDWARD, minister; b. Peterman, Ala., July 13, 1927; s. John T. and Ida Cornelia (Downs) C.; m. Sylvia Christine Craft, July 14, 1949; children: Wanda, Sharon, John Edward Jr. BA, Asbury Coll., 1960; MDiv, Asbury Theol. Sem., 1962. Ordained to ministry United Meth. Ch. Min. 1st United Meth. Ch., Graefenburg, Ky., 1958-62, Louisville, 1962-63, Pine Grove, 1964-67, St. John, 1967-71, Butler, Ala., 1972-76, Myrtle Grove, 1977-82, Niceville, Fla., 1983—; chmn. minimum salary commn. Ala.—West Fla. conf. United Meth. Ch., 1966-72, chmn. bd. evangelism, 1972-80, mem. bd. ordained ministry, 1980-88, mem. com. on superintendency, 1986—, mem. coun. on fin. and adminstrn., 1988—, del. jurisdictional conf., 1991. Contbr. articles to religious jours. With USAAF, 1943-44. Recipient Denman award for evangelism, 1991; named Min. of Yr., Ala.—West Fla. conf. United Meth. Ch., 1967. Office: Firt United Meth Ch PO Box 278 Niceville FL 32588

CHANDLER, JOHN PRESTON, minister; b. Chapel Hill, N.C., Apr. 30, 1961; s. John Edward III and Martha Ethel (Sprinkle) C.; m. Mary Celeste Maddrey, May 26, 1984; children: J. Preston Jr., James Roland. BA, U. N.C., 1983; MDiv, Princeton Theol. Sem., 1986, ThM, 1987. Ordained to ministry So. Bapt. Ch., 1985. Youth min. Friendly Ave. Bapt. Ch., Greensboro, N.C., 1980; survey missionary South Jersey/Pa. Bapt. Assn., 1984-85; pastor Twin County Bapt. Ch., Kendall Pk., N.J., 1985-87, Effort Bapt. Ch., Palmyra, Va., 1987—; chaplain Lake Monticello Rescue Squad, Palmyra, 1987—. Home: 63 Wildwood Dr Palmyra VA 22963 Office: Effort Bapt Church Rte 2 Box 353 Palmyra VA 22963

CHANES, JEROME ALAN, religious organization administrator; b. N.Y.C., Mar. 29, 1943; s. Manuel S. and Berta (Gottlieb) C.; m. Eva Fogelman, June 19, 1988. BA, Yeshiva U., 1964, MSW, 1974; postgrad., Columbia U., 1966-68, Brandeis U., 1974-76. Dir. interreligious affairs, nat. affairs dir. Nat. Jewish Community Rels. Adv. Coun., N.Y.C., 1983—; adj. prof. of Jewish communal issues Wurzweiler Sch. Social Work, Yeshiva U., N.Y.C., 1990—. Contbr. articles to profl. publs., chpts. to books. Benjamin Hornstein fellow, 1974. Mem. Labor Zionist Alliance (nat. sec. 1988—). Home: 60 Riverside Dr Apt 11G New York NY 10024 Office: Nat Jewish Community Rels Adv Coun 443 Park Ave S 11th Floor New York NY 10016

CHANEY, ALBERT ANDREW, pastor; b. Chgo., Sept. 4, 1954; s. Fredrick Raymond and Freda Virginia (Wood) C.; m. Marjorie Elaine Calhoun, Apr. 19, 1975; children: Marie Elaine, Mindy Elaine, Martha Elaine. Rhema Bible Tng. Ctr., 1980-82. Ordained to ministry Faith Christian Fellowship, 1981. Ministry of helps Faith Christian Fellowship, Tulsa, 1980-82; pastor Faith Christian Fellowship, Litchfield, Ill., 1989—; ministry of helps New Life Christian Fellowship, Urbana, Ill., 1979, 82; interim pastor Victory Flame Fellowship, Fisher, Ill., 1983; assoc. pastor Full Gospel Christian Fellowship, 1983-87; evangelist, tchr. Fountain of Life Family Fellowship, Tolono, Ill., 1987-89. Sgt. USMC, 1973-77. Mem. Women's Aglow Fellowship (local advisor 1989-90, area advisor 1990-91), Charismatic Bible Ministries, Rhema Alumni Assn. Home: 1010 N Van Buren Litchfield IL 62056 Office: Faith Christian Fellowship 1004 N Van Buren Litchfield IL 62056

CHANEY, ALBION HENRY, pastor; b. King City, Calif., Nov. 12, 1921; s. Leonardo Eldridge and Marie Bertha (Menke) D.; m. Mary Jacqueline Mooney, Apr. 1, 1945; children: Kathleen, James, Steven, Terri Eileen, David, Colleen. Student, U. Calif., Davis, 1941; naval officer, USN U. of Air, Corpus Christi, Tex., 1943; student, Moody Bible Inst., Chgo., 1950, Missionary Training Inst., Seattle, 1961. Lic. C.B.A. Ch., 1954; ordained to ministry Am. Evang. Christ Chs., 1956. Pastor various chs., Calif. and Iowa, 1954-1985, First Bapt., Healdsburg, Calif., 1986; pres. San Joaquin Conservative Bapt. Assn., Mariposa, Calif., 1966-67. Lt. USNR, 1942-45. Recipient Presdl. Citation USN, 1944. Republican. Home: 725A Heron Dr Healdsburg CA 95448

CHANEY, ROBERT GALEN, religious organization executive; b. LaPorte, Ind., Oct. 27, 1913; s. Clyde Galen and Maree (Francis) C.; student Miami U., Ohio, 1931-33; D.D., Coll. Universal Truth, 1954; m. Earlyne Cantrell, Oct. 4, 1947; 1 dau., Sita. Ordained to non-denominational ministry, 1939; pastor various parishes, Eaton Rapids and Lansing Mich., 1938-50; founder, pres. Astara, Los Angeles, 1956-76, Upland, Calif., 1976—. Republican. Lodges: Mason, Kiwanis. Author: The Inner Way, 1962; Adventures in ESP, 1975; Mysticism: The Journey Within, 1979. Office: Astara 800 W Arrow Hwy Upland CA 91786

CHANG, KWAI SING, retired educator; b. Honolulu, Aug. 22, 1921; s. Jan and Agnes (Lee) C.; m. Miyoko Hokama, July 10, 1951; children: Forsythia, Jasmine. BA, U. Hawaii, 1944; BD, Princeton Theol. Sem., 1947, ThM, 1948; PhD, U. Edinburgh, Scotland, 1952. Ordained to ministry, United Ch. of Christ, 1948. Min. Lanai Union Ch., Lanai City, Hawaii, 1948-50, Kalahikiola Congl. Ch., Kohala, Hawaii, 1952-56; prof. Bible and religion Agnes Scott Coll., Decatur, Ga., 1956-86. Mem. Am. Acad. Religion. Home: 351 S McDonough St Decatur GA 30030

CHANG, SHENG-YEN, Buddhist monk, educator; b. Nan T'ung, People's Republic China, Dec. 4, 1930; came to U.S., 1975; s. Hsuan Ts'ai and Chin Chang. MA, Rissho U., Tokyo, 1971, LittD, 1975. Prof., dir. Chinese Culture U., Taipei, Republic of China, 1978-87; pres. Chung-Hwa Inst. Buddhist Culture, Taipei and Elmhurst, N.Y., 1980—; dir. Chung-Hwa Inst. Buddhist Studies, Taipei, 1985—; pub. Tungchu Pub. Co., Taipei, 1980—, Dharma Drum Publs., N.Y.C., 1982—, Humanity Monthly, Taipei, 1982—; prof. Tung-Wu U., Taipei, 1986—, Fu-Jen U., Taipei, 1989—. Author: Getting the Buddha Mind, 1982, Poetry of Enlightenment, 1987, Faith in Mind, 1988, Zen: Tradition and Transition, 1988, Ox Herding at Morgan's Bay, 1989; The Life and Practice of Ou-Yi Chih-Hsu, 1975 (in Japanese), The Infinite Mirror, 1990, the Sword of Wisdom, 1990; also numerous books in Chinese. Mem. Japanese Assn. Indian Buddhist Studies, Internat. Assn. Buddhist Studies (founding). Office: Ch'an Meditation Ctr 90-56 Corona Ave Elmhurst NY 11373

CHANG-HIM, FRENCH KITCHENER, bishop. Bishop of Seychelles, archbishop of Province of Indian Ocean Anglican Communion. Office: Anglican Communion, POB 44, Victoria Seychelles*

CHAPIN, SHELLEY, religious organization administrator; b. Dallas, Dec. 30, 1953; d. Charles Hall and Melita Louise (Johnson) C. BS, Dallas Theol. Sem., 1979, M.Bibl. Studies, 1989, postgrad., 1990—; postgrad., U. N. Tex., 1990—. Asst. to dir. Pine Cove Conf. Ctr., Tyler, Tex., 1981-85; dir. Pine Cove Outreach, Tyler, Tex., 1985-86; psychology prof. Taylor U., Upland, Ind., 1990—; gen. mgr. KVNE/KGLY Radio, Tyler, 1984—; exec. dir. CSC Ministries, Dallas, 1983—; marriage and family counselor French Jones & Assocs., Dallas, 1990—; trustee St. Marcus Compassion House, Tyler, 1990—; del. Christian Counselors Assn., Dallas, 1989—; bd. dirs., dir. CSC Ministries, 1984—. Author: Within the Shadow, 1991; contbr. articles to profl. jours.; author, songwriter tape cassettes: For the Times We've Cried, Through the Eye of a Needle, Windows, The Hidden Gifts of Pain, Peacemaker, In Remembrance: An Attitude to Live Wity, others; author, host radio programs. Bd. dirs. Hospice of E. Tex., 1988-90, CSC Ministries, 1984—; com. mem. Com. for Celebration of Bicentennial, Tyler, 1986-88; bd. dirs. All Saints Sch., 1989-90, others. Recipient Mary T. Seume award, Dallas Theol. Sem., 1989, Local Screenwriters award, Screenwriters Guild, Dallas, 1989. Mem. Am. Psychol. Assn., Am. Assn. for Counseling and Devel., Assn. for Multi-cultural Counseling and Devel. Office: CSC Ministries PO Box 130338 Tyler TX 75713-0338

CHAPMAN, CHARLES TAYLOR, JR., rector; b. Memphis, Dec. 23, 1955; s. Charles Taylor Sr. and Betty Jane (Shelton) C. BA, Union U., 1976; MDiv, So. Bapt. Theol. Sem., 1979; cert. ind. theol. studies, Episcopal Theol. Sem. S.W., 1986. Asst. to rector Grace-St. Luke's Episcopal Ch., Memphis, 1980-90, chaplain sch., 1981-90; rector Grace Episcopal Ch., Winfield, Kans., 1990-91; with St. Andrew's Episcopal Sch. of Amarillo, Tex., 1991—; chmn. Diocesan Youth Adv. Com., 1991; mem. diocesan coun. Diocese of Kans., Topeka, 1990-91. Lyricist Holy Gifts, 1983, Easter Hymn, 1983. Mem. adv. bd. Family Link Runaway House, Memphis, 1983-85, Good Samaritan Village, Winfield, 1990-91. Office: St Andrew's Episcopal Sch Amarillo 1515 S Georgia Amarillo TX 79102

CHAPMAN, CRAIG BRUCE, clergyman; b. Trenton, Mich., Sept. 10, 1958; s. Bruce Everett and Carole Ann (Remilard) C.; m. Lori Kay McConnell, Sept. 12, 1981; children: Andrea Robin, Andrew Craig. AA, Washtenaw Community Coll., Ann Arbor, Mich., 1980; BA, U. Mich., 1983; MDiv, Bexley Hall Sem., Rochester, N.Y., 1987. Draftsperson Livingston Home Planners, Howell, Mich., 1977-78; with UPS, Ypsilanti, Mich., 1978-84; asst. to bishop Diocese of Rochester (N.Y.), 1984-87; safety inspector U. Rochester, 1984-87; youth worker St. Thomas Episc. Ch., 1984-87; priest Christ Episc. Ch., Warren, Ohio, 1987-89, St. Martin In The Fields Episc. Ch., Atlanta, 1989—; youth minister Diocese of Ohio, 1987-89, Nat. Episc. Ch. youth projects, 1988—, Diocesan Youth Commn., Atlanta. Board dirs. Rebecca William Community Ctr., Warren, Ohio, 1987, Scope of Trumbul County, Warren, 1989; chmn. Warren/Trumbul Country, Warren, 1989; chmn. Warren/Trumbul C.R.O.P. Walk, 1989; mem. Mikel Camp and Conf. Ctr., Toccoa, Ga., Diocese Atlanta Youth Ministries Program, conf. leader; dean Inter Summer Camp, 1991,. Mem. Warren Area Clergy Assn., Howland Area Clergy Assn., Ea. Valley Regional Council, Ea. Valley Clergy Assn. Republican. Avocations: photograhy, swimming, music, reading.

CHAPMAN, DAN G., minister; b. Brownwood, Tex., Jan. 29, 1939; s. Bert A. and Mary Louise (Pelton) C.; m. Delores Sue Thomas,June 20, 1964; 1 child, Jason Carter. BTh, Internat. Sem., 1985, MTh, 1988, DM, 1989; DTh, Sch. Bible Theology, 1989. Ordained to ministry Pentecostal Ch. God. Dist. youth dir. S.W. Tex. Dist. Pentecostal Ch. God, San Marcos, 1971-79, sectional presbyter S.W. Tex. Dist., 1986—, dir. Christian Edn. S.W. Tex. Dist., 1988-90; internat. evangelist Pentecostal Ch. God, Joplin, Mo., 1979-83; adminstr. Trinity Day Care, Early, Tex., 1983—; prin. Trinity Christian Acad., Early, 1983—; sr. pastor Trinity Chapel Ch., Early, 1983—; area advisor Heart of tex. Area Aglow, Killeen, 1987—; chaplain Police and Fire Depts., Brownwood, 1987—. Author: Youth Leadership and Development, 1978. Mem. Tex. Youth Coun. Adv. Bd., Brownwood, 1991—, Noah Project Bd., Brownwood, 1991—. With U.S. Army, 1961-63. Mem. Internat. Conf. Police Chaplains, Early C. of C., Lions Club (pres. 1969-70). Home: 207 Crescent Dr Early TX 76801 Office: Trinity Chapel Ch 1040 Early Blvd PO Box 3246 Early TX 76803

CHAPMAN, ELIZABETH NINA, counselor; b. Canton, N.Y., July 5, 1947; d. Kenneth Wallace and Kathryne Mary (Moulton) Loucks; m. Edwin Tracy Chapman, Jr., Aug. 31, 1968; children: Scott, Brian, Lori, Katie. Nursing Diploma, Hepburn Sch. of Nursing, Ogdensburg, N.Y., 1968; BS in Profl. Arts, St. Joseph's Coll., North Windham, Maine, 1981; M in Counseling, Internat. Sem., Plymouth, Fla., 1991. RN, N.Y. Counselor, speaker, writer Restoration Women's Ministries, DeKalb Jct., N.Y.; past mem. social concerns com. Koinonia, Potsdam, N.Y.; mem. bd. deacons 1st Bapt. Ch., Gouverneur, N.Y., 1980, treas. 1988-90, v.p. 1990. Author: Patchwork, 1987; Christian songwriter. Mem. Nat. Right to Life. *Biblical counsel is the best avenue of human counsel and restoration. (See 2 Tim 3:16, 17, and 1 Peter 5:10).*

CHAPMAN, GARY LEVI, minister; b. Champaign, Ill., Aug. 13, 1946; s. Harold H. and Vena M. (Warfel) C.; m. Janet R. Chapman, Aug. 31, 1968; children: Alicia Kathrin, Nathan Paul. BA, Ill. Wesleyan U., 1968; DMin, Chgo. Theol. Seminary, 1973. Ordained to ministry United Ch. of Christ, 1974. Min. United Ch. Tilton, Danville, Ill., 1973-80; pastor St. Paul's United Ch. of Christ, Minonk, Ill., 1980-88, Zion United Ch. of Christ, Burlington, Iowa, 1988—; del. gen. synod United Ch. of Christ, Ames, Iowa, 1985; del., dir. Ill. Conf. Coun., Westchester, 1984-88. Dir. YMCA, Burlington, 1990—; scoutmaster troop 878 Boy Scouts Am., Minonk, 1983-88; bd. dirs. Ill. Farm Worker Ministry, Downers Grove, 1986—. Named Outstanding Young Religious Leader Danville Jaycees, 1978; recipient recognition Chgo. Theol. Sem. Alumni Coun., 1979. Mem. Soc. Bibl. Lit., Jewish-Christian Dialogue Project, Amnesty Internat., Nat. Impact, Ill. Impact, Iowa Impact, Burlington Area Coun. Chs. (pres. 1990—), Southeastern Iowa Assn. (v.p., pres. 1990—). Democrat. Office: Zion United Ch of Christ 412 N Fifth St Burlington IA 52601

CHAPMAN, IAN M., school system administrator. Head No. Bapt. Theol. Sem., Lombard, Ill. Office: No Bapt Theol Sem Office of Pres 660 E Butterfield Rd Lombard IL 60148*

CHAPMAN, JANET WARNER, minister; b. Kalispell, Mont., Apr. 20, 1962; d. Harvey Glenn and Phyllis (Thrasher) Warner; m. John E. Chapman, Sept. 10, 1988. BS, Northwest Christian Coll., Eugene, Oreg., 1984; MDiv, Tex. Christian U., 1988. Ordained to ministry Christian Ch. (Disciples of Christ), 1989. Youth min. Springfield (Oreg.) First Christian Ch., 1984-85, Grapevine (Tex.) Presbyn. Ch., 1985-86; chaplain Edna Gladney Maternity Home, Ft. Worth, 1986-87; assoc. min. Benbrook (Tex.) United Meth. Ch., 1987-90, Hurst (Tex.) Christian Ch., 1990—; mem. youth adv. com. Trinity Brazos area Christian Ch. in SW, Ft. Worth, 1990—; co-dir. Christian Ch. Youth Camp, Ft. Worth, summer 1991. Grantee Christian Bd. Publ., 1988. Mem. Mid Cities Mins. Assn., Disciples Mins. Assn., Theta Phi (honor soc. 1987—). Office: Hurst Christian Ch 745 Brown Trail Hurst TX 76053 *I'm on a daily journey to discover the divine Spirit present in all God's children and cherish such an opportunity.*

CHAPMAN, MICHAEL RAY, minister; b. Laurens, S.C., Aug. 22, 1951; s. Ray Calhoun and Sara Elizabeth (Davis) C.; m. Trudy Elaine Leverette, Dec. 19, 1970; children: Shannon, Michael. BA, Lee Coll., 1973; Th.M., Luther Rice Sem., 1977; postgrad., Faith Evang. Luth. Sem., 1978-84; DMin, North Am. Bibl. Sem., 1988. Lic. to ministry Ch. of God (Cleveland, Tenn.), 1973, ordained, 1978. Minister of youth South Cleveland Ch. of God, Cleveland, Tenn., 1972-73; pastor Fremont (Calif.) Ch. of God, 1973-74; state youth dir. Ch. of God in Hawaii, Honolulu, 1974-76; pastor Hawaii Kai Ch. of God, Honolulu, 1974-76; sr. pastor Lee Hwy. Ch. of God, Chattanooga, 1976—; mem. state coun. Ch. of God in Tenn., Chattanooga, 1987-90, state evangelism bd., 1984-87, state edn. bd., 1982-84; guest lectr. Lee Coll., Cleveland, 1990. Contbg. editor: Discipleship 90: Discovering the Christlife, 1990, Welcome to the Family, 1991; contbr. articles to profl. jours. Bd. dirs. Chattanooga Team Challenge, 1978-81; advisor Women's Aglow Fellowship, Chattanooga, 1980-84; clergy coun. Moccasin Bend Mental Health Inst., Chattanooga, 1980-82. Recipient Outstanding Young Pastor award Lee Coll., 1986. Home: 2017 Hickory Valley Rd Chattanooga TN 37421 Office: Lee Hwy Ch of God 7120 Lee Hwy Chattanooga TN 37421 *Prayer is not something we do, but it is someone we are with. To see this discipline in this light has greatly enhanced my enjoyment of prayer.*

CHAPMAN, ROBERT L., bishop. Bishop Ch. of God in Christ, Cleve. Office: Ch of God in Christ 3194 E 18th St Cleveland OH 44120*

CHAPMAN, ROBERT LEE, minister; b. Tiffin, Ohio, Mar. 12, 1926; s. Harry and Ruth Elizabeth (Bailey) C.; m. Cora Ann Briggs, June 2, 1946; children: Robert Lewis, Paula Jean, Thomas Lynn. Diploma, Libert Bapt. U., 1978; postgrad., Cascade Bible Coll., 1983; AMDiv, Southwestern Bapt. Sem., 1982; D of Divinity, Kent Coll., 1990; postgrad., Bethany Theol Sem., Chgo., 1990—. Ordained to ministry Ch. of the Brethren, 1984. Minister Ch. of the Brethren, Seattle, 1973-85, Arcadia, Fla., 1985—. With USN, 1943-46. Home: Rte 7 Box 910 Arcadia FL 33821 Office: Ch of the Brethren 25 N Mills Ave Arcadia FL 33821

CHAPPELL, BONNIE DELL, religion educator; b. Silverton, Tex., Feb. 1, 1927; d. Andrew Houston and Glen Josephine (Graham) C. AA, Wayland Coll., 1946; BS, Howard Payne Coll., 1948; MRE, Southwestern Bapt Theol. Sem., 1950. Edn. sec. First Bapt. Ch., Brownfield, Tex., 1950-51, Greenville, Tex., 1951-54; edn. sec. Beech St. Bapt. Ch., Texarkana, Ark., 1954-55, First So. Bapt. Ch., Costa Mesa, Calif., 1955-60; assoc. chmn. tng., dept. field worker So. Bapt. Conv., Fresno, Calif., 1960-64; asst. to bus. mgr. Calif. Bapt. Coll., Riverside, Calif., 1964-70; instr. Golden Gate Bapt. Sem., Mill Valley, Calif., 1970—. Mem. So. Bapt. Religious Edn. Assn., Western Bapt. Religious Edn. Assn. Home: 201 Isle Royale San Rafael CA 94903 Office: Golden Gate Bapt Sem Strawberry Point Mill Valley CA 94941 *Rewarding experiences have been mine in these years in Christian education as I've encountered those who are in training to become more effective leaders in helping persons to live meaningful and purposeful lives for the betterment of all humankind.*

CHAPPELL, DAVID WELLINGTON, religion educator; b. Saint John, N.B., Can., Feb. 3, 1940; came to U.S., 1966; s. Hayward Lynsin and Mary Elvira (Mosher) C.; m. Bertha Vera Bidulock, Aug. 23, 1960 (div. Jan. 1976); children: Cynthia Joan, Mark Lynsin David; m. Stella Quemada, July 11, 1981. BA, Mt. Allison U., Sackville, N.B., 1961; BD, McGill U., Montreal, Can., 1965; PhD, Yale U., 1976. Min. United Ch. Can., Elma, Ont., Can., 1964-66; prof. U. Hawaii, Honolulu, 1971—; asst. prof. U. Toronto, Can., 1977-78; vis. prof. U. Pitts., 1982; vis. lectr. Taisho U., Tokyo, 1986-88; dir. East West Religions Project, Honolulu, 1980—, Buddhist Studies Program, U. Hawaii, 1987—. Editor: T'ien-t'ai Buddhism, 1983, Buddhist and Taoist Practice, 1987; editor Buddhist-Christian Studies jour., 1980—. Mem. Am. Acad. Religion, Assn. Asian Studies, Internat. Assn. Buddhist Studies, Soc. Buddhist-Christian Studies. Democrat. Avocations: interreligious dialogue, tennis. Home: 47 696 1 Hui Kelu St Kaneohe HI 96744

CHAPPELL, ROY M., clergyman; b. Pollard, Ark., May 1, 1932; s. Frank and Velma (Garrett) C.; m. Wille Mae Haggard, Nov. 6, 1954; children—Steven Roy, Janiece Marie. B.A., Pentecostal Bible Coll., Livermore, Calif., 1954, D.Div. (hon.), 1976. Ordained to ministry Pentecostal Ch. of God. Pastor chs. Calif. and Mo., 1954-66; field rep. Pentecostal Ch. of God, 1963-67; exec. missions Pentecostal Ch. of God, Joplin, Mo., 1967-74; dist. supt. No. Calif. Pentecostal Ch. of God, 1974-75; gen. supt., pres. Pentecostal Ch. of God, Joplin, Mo., 1975—; editor in chief Messenger Pub. House, Joplin, Mo., 1975—. Mem. U.S. Adv. Bd., Washington, 1984-85, Presdl. Task Force, 1984-85. Served with USNG, 1950-52. Republican. Home: 1830 Delaware St Joplin MO 64804

CHAPPELL, WADE MILLARD, minister; b. Jackson, Miss., June 7, 1946; s. Arthur Chester and Milda Estelle (Wooten) C.; m. Glenda Jo Talbert, June 14, 1968; children: Sharon, Amy, Christopher. AA, East Cen. Jr. Coll., Decatur, Miss., 1968; BS, Miss. Coll., 1970; MDiv, New Orleans Bapt. Theol. Sem., 1978. Ordained to ministry So. Bapt. Conv., 1968. Pastor New Harmony Bapt. Ch., Philadelphia, Miss., 1968-71, Old Pearl Valley Bapt. Ch., Philadelphia, 1971-77, Freeny Bapt. Ch., Carthage, 1977-80, Grandview Bapt. Ch., Pearl, 1980—; moderator Rankin County Bapt. Assn., Pearl, 1986-88; bd. dirs. Miss. Bapt. Conv., Jackson, 1989—; vol. chaplain Rankin Med. Ctr., Brandon, Miss., 1988—, River Oaks Hosp., Flowood, Miss., 1988—. Mem. Pearl High Sch. Band Boosters Club, 1987-90. Home: 546 Monica Ln Pearl MS 39208 Office: Grandview Bapt Ch 900 S Pearson Rd Pearl MS 39208

CHAPPLE, CHRISTOPHER, theology educator; b. Medina, N.Y., Sept. 4, 1954; s. Hugh Edward I and Julia Dolores (Peton) C.; m. Maureen Shannon, Aug. 10, 1974; children: Dylan Edward, Emma Catherine. BA, SUNY, Stony Brook, 1976; MA, Fordham U., 1978, PhD, 1980. Assoc. prof. dept. theology Loyla Marymount U., L.A., 1985—, chair dept. theology, 1990—. Author: Karma and Creativity, 1986; co-author, translator: Yoga Sutras of the Patanjali, 1990; editor: Bhagavad Gita, 1984; compiler: (book) Religious Experience and Scientific Paradigms, 1985. Mem. Coll. Theology Soc., Soc. for Buddhist-Christian Studies, Am. Acad. of Religion, Soc. for Asian & Comparative Philosophy, So. Calif. Seminar on South Asia (chair 1986—). Home: 5839 W 78th Pl Los Angeles CA 90045 Office: Loyola Marymount U Dept of Theology Los Angeles CA 90045

CHAPPLE, JOHN HUNT, minister; b. Worcester, Mass., May 2, 1928; s. Robert and Mabel (Ingham) C.; m. Josephine Haynes, Aug. 2, 1951 (div. 1979); children—Kevin Peter, Karen Elizabeth, John Lawrence; m. Joylyn Marie Winters Brammer, Apr. 11, 1982; children—Debra, Diane, Donna. A.B. in Sociology, Tufts U., 1951, B.Div., 1952; postgrad., St. Andrews U., Scotland, 1971, Christ Coll., Canteberry, Eng., 1978. Ordained to ministry United Ch. of Christ, 1952. Pastor United Ch., Bethel, Vt., 1952-56, Armour, S.D., 1956-68, Hampton, Iowa, 1968-81, United Ch. First Congl., Belchertown, Mass., 1982—; sr. pastor United Ch. of Christ, Mitchell, S.D.; moderator Missouri Valley Assn., United Ch. of Christ; cons., leader Vol. Service United Ch. Christ, Pottstown, Pa. and N.Y.C.; mem. bd. of rev. Mental Health Davison, 1986. Chief hearing officer, chmn. rent control Belchertown, 1984; trustee, chairperson Mitchell Pub. Libr. Recipient Community Service award Armour, 1968, Svc. award Town of Belchertown, 1984, Boy Scout award Belchertown Council, 1985. Mem. United Ch. of Christ Clergy, Hampshire Assn. (bd. dirs. 1982-80), City Club (Armour), Masons, Rotary, Shriners. Avocations: fishing; raising prize roses; photography; travel. Home: 1200 E University Blvd Mitchell SD 57301 Office: 301 E 4th St Mitchell SD 57301

CHAPUT, CHARLES J., bishop; b. Concordia, Kans., Sept. 26, 1944. Student, St. Fidelis Coll., Capuchin Coll., Cath. U., U. San Francisco. Ordained priest Roman Cath. Ch., 1970; consecrated bishop Diocese Rapid City, S.D., 1988. Office: Chancery Office 606 Cathedral Dr PO Box 678 Rapid City SD 57709

CHARLES, E. OTIS, bishop; b. Norristown, Pa., Apr. 24, 1926; s. Jacob Otis and Elizabeth Francis (Abraham) C.; m. Elvira Latta, May 26, 1951; children: Christopher, Nicholas, Emilie, Timothy, Elvira. B.A., Trinity Coll., Hartford, Conn., 1948; S.T.B., Gen. Theol. Sem., N.Y.C., 1959, D.D., 1983. Ordained deacon Episcopal Ch., 1951, priest, 1951, bishop, 1971; curate St. Johns Ch., Elizabeth, N.J., 1951-53; priest-in-charge St. Andrews Ch., Beacon, N.Y., 1953-59; rector St. Johns Ch., Washington, Conn., 1959-68; assoc. dir. Montford House Ecumenical Center, 1968-69; exec. sec. Asso. Parishes, Inc., 1968-71; bishop Episcopal Diocese Utah, Salt Lake City, 1971—; bishop in charge Navajo Episc. Ch., 1976-79; mem. Episcopal Standing Liturgical Commn., 1970-79; dir. Epis. Ch. Pub. Co. Trustee Episcopal Radio TV Found., 1972-78; pres. bd. trustees St. Marks Hosp., Rowland Hall St. Marks Sch.; trustee Hospice of Salt Lake, 1978-80; adviser U. Utah Coll. Nursing, 1980-83; mem. Utah State Health Coordinating Council, 1981—; adviser Utah Camp Fire Council, 1980-82; bd. dirs. Episcopal Urban Caucus, 1981, Planned Parenthood of Utah, 1980-83; Mem. Utah Arts Festival Council, 1981—, Utah Assn. Autism, 1980—; mem. Health Systems Agy. Governing Body, 1981—, State Health Coordinating Council, 1981—; exec. com. Utahns United Against the Arms Race, 1982—. Served with USNR, 1943-46, PTO. Recipient Washington Community Fund grants, 1962, 68. Club: Alta (Salt Lake City). Office: 231 E 1st S Salt Lake City UT 84111 *My personal and professional life may be described in words attributed to Prince William, Founder of the House of Orange: " Even without hope to undertake; even without success to persevere." The motivating desire of my life is to make a difference in the continuing evolution of this planet earth. Ecumenism provides the principal focus of this desire—the harmony of diverse spiritual and political experience lending toward unity and peace.*

CHARLES, REX STEPHEN, minister; b. Lakeville, Ind., Aug. 28, 1953; s. Joseph Harding and Peggy Mae (Judd) C.; m. Kathryn Anne Losicki, July 6, 1985; 1 child, Christine Michelle. BA in Bible Lit., Bethel Coll., 1977; MDiv, Asbury Sem., 1980. Youth pastor People's Ch., South Bend, Ind., 1976; chmn. edn. work area Sumption Prairie United Meth. Ch., South Bend, 1977; assoc. pastor Yorktown (Ind.) United Meth. Ch., 1980-83; pastor Star City (Ind.) United Meth. Ch., 1983-88, Pleasant Chapel/Zion United Meth. Ch., Roanoke, Ind., 1988—. Contbr. articles to newspapers.

CHARLES, SYDNEY ANICETUS, bishop. Bishop Roman cath. ch., St. George's, Grenada. Office: Bishop House, Morne Jaloux, POB 375, Saint George's Grenada*

CHARLESWORTH, JAMES HAMILTON, religion educator, minister; b. St. Petersburg, Fla., May 30, 1940; s. Arthur Riggs and Martha Jean (Hamilton) C.; m. Jerrie Lynn Pittard, Apr. 10, 1965; children: Rachel Michelle, Eve Marie, James Hamilton. AB, Ohio Wesleyan U., 1962; BD, Duke U., 1965, PhD, 1967; ET, Ecole Biblique de Jerusalem, 1969. Ordained to ministry United Meth. Ch., 1963. Fulbright fellow U. Edinburgh, Scotland, 1967-68; Thayer fellow Am. Sch. Oriental Rsch., Jerusalem, 1968-69; prof. dept. religion Duke U., Durham, N.C., 1969-84, dir. Internat. Ctr. on Christian Origins, 1975-84; George L. Collord prof. N.T. lang. and lit. Princeton (N.J.) Theol. Sem., 1984—; dir. Princeton Theol. Sem. Dead Sea Scrolls Project, 1985—. Author: The Pseudepigrapha and Modern Research, 1976, 2d edit., 1981, The Pseudepigrapha and the New Testament, 1985, The New Testament Apocrypha and Pseudepigrapha, 1987, The Old Testament Pseudepigrapha and The New Testament, 1985, 87, Jesus Within Judaism, 1988; editor, translator: The Odes of Solomon, 1973, The History of the Rechabites, 1982; editor: The Old Testament Pseudepigrapha, 1983, 85, Eleve Titulaire de l'Ecole Biblique avec la Mention Tres Honorable, Jerusalem, 1968, Paul and the Dead Sea Scrolls, 1990, John and the Dead Sea Scrolls, 1990, Jews and Christians, 1990; editor Jour. for Study of Pseudepigrapha and Explorations, Mysteries and Revelations, 1991, Graphic Concordance to the Dead Sea Scrolls, 1991. Fellow Am. Coun. Learned Socs., 1973-74, Alexander von Humboldt fellow, 1983-84, Lady Davis prof. Hebrew U., Jerusalem. Mem. Soc. Bibl. Lit. (sec. pseudepigrapha group 1969-84), Soc. N.T. Studies (editorial bd. 1979-83), Am. Acad. Religion, Found. Christian Origins (pres.), Bibl. Archaeology Soc. (editorial bd.). Democrat. Home: 51 Ross Stevenson Circle Princeton NJ 08540 Office: Princeton Theol Sem CN 821 Princeton NJ 08542

CHARLOP, ZEVULUN, rabbi, seminary administrator; b. N.Y.C., Dec. 14, 1929; s. Jechiel Michael and Ida (Schocher) C.; m. Judith Rosner, Dec. 27, 1954; children: Betty, Rochelle, Anna Riva, Shoshana, Zev, Alexander Z., Fay Gila, Miriam. BA, Yeshiva Coll., 1951; MA, Columbia U., 1959; student, Rabbi Isaac Elchananan Theol. Sem. Ordained rabbi, 1954. Rabbi Young Israel Mosholu Pkwy., Bronx, N.Y., 1954—; dean Rabbi Isaac Elchanan Theol. Sem., N.Y.C., 1986—; instr. Talmud Yeshiva U., 1967-71, lectr. Am. history, 1967—, dir. Rabbi Isaac Elchanan Theol. Sem., 1971-86, Internat. chmn. The Rabbi Abraham Isaac HaCohen Kook 50th Anniversary of His Death com., 1985-86; pres. Yeshiva Beth Zvul, Jerusalem; Am. pres. Eitz Chaim Yeshiva, Jerusalem, Meah Shearim Yeshiva, Jerusalem, Gen. Israel Orphan Home for Girls, Jerusalem. Editor: Chavrusa, 1967. Mem. exec. com. Bronx chpt. Am. Cancer Soc. Grand Chaplain Free Sons of Israel, 1956-58. Mem. Nat. Coun. Young Israel (pres. coun. rabbis 1968-71), Rabbinical Coun. Am. (co-chmn. coll. campus com. 1966-68). Home: 100 E Mosholu Pkwy S New York NY 10458 Office: Rabbi Isaaac Elchanan Theol Sem 2540 Amsterdam Ave New York NY 10033

CHARLTON, GORDON TALIAFERRO, JR., retired bishop; b. San Antonio, Sept. 29, 1923; s. Gordon Taliaferro and Enid Lynn (Jones) C.; m. Landon Cutler Crump, Dec. 23, 1948; children—Virginia, David, Duncan. B.A., U. Tex-Austin, 1944; M.Div., Va. Sem., 1949, D.D. (hon.), 1974. Ordained priest Episcopal Ch. Asst. rector St. James Ch., Houston, 1949-51; rector St. Mathews Ch., Fairbanks, Alaska, 1951-54; personnel sec. Overseas dept. Nat. Council Episcopal Ch., N.Y.C., 1954-58; rector Christ Ch., Mexico City, 1958-63, St. Andrews Ch., Wilmington, Del., 1963-67; asst. dean Va. Sem., Alexandria, 1967-73; dean Sem. of Southwest, Austin, Tex., 1973-82; Suffragan bishop Episcopal Diocese of Tex., Houston, 1982-89, ret., 1989. Served to lt. (j.g.) USNR, 1943-46; PTO. Episcopalian.

CHARLTON, JOHN FREDERICK, III, minister; b. Elgin, Ill., July 24, 1944; s. John F. Jr. and Ivagene E. (Householder) C.; m. Barbara Jean Ring, Oct. 10, 1987; 8 children. BA, Judson Coll., 1966; MDiv, Ea. Bapt. Theol. Sem., 1970; D Ministry, McCormick Theol. Sem., 1978; cert. in Teaching, Cen. Mich. U., 1987. Ordained to ministry Bapt. Ch., 1970. Pastor First Bapt. Ch. of Harbor Beach, Mich., 1970-73; pastor First Bapt. Ch. of Alma, Mich., 1973-90, Harvard Park Bapt. Ch., Springfield, Ill., 1990—. Mem. Masons (sr. deacon 1989-90). Home: 26 Lake Knolls Dr Chatham IL 62629 Office: Harvard Park Bapt Ch 2401 S 9th St Springfield IL 62703

CHARMÉ, STUART ZANE, religion educator; b. Elizabeth, N.J., Apr. 16, 1951; s. Samuel Louis and Miriam (Aronson) C.; m. Nancie Zane, May 29, 1988; 1 child, Sara. BA, Columbia U., 1973; MA, U. Chgo., 1975, PhD, 1980. Prof. religion Rutgers U., Camden, N.J., 1978—. Author: Meaning and Myth in the Study of Lives, 1984, Vulgarity and Authenticity, 1991; also articles. NEH fellow, 1981, Am. Coun. Learned Socs. fellow, 1983, Coolidge Rsch. Colloquium fellow Assocs. for Religion and Intellectural Life, 1985. Mem. Am. Acad. Religion, Soc. for Sci. Study of Religion, Assn. for Jewish Studies, Religious Rsch. Assn. Home: 763 S 10th St Philadelphia PA 19147

CHARRON, SISTER ESTELLE IRMA, religious association executive; b. Duluth, Minn., Nov. 17, 1928; d. Harold Frederick and Amy Estelle (Hill) C. B.S. in Med. Tech., Marquette U., 1958; M.S. in Adminstrn., U. Notre Dame, 1984. Joined Benedictine Sisters, Roman Cath. Ch. Med. technologist Oconomowoc Meml. Hosp., Wis., 1962-69; mgr. printshop Coll. St. Scholastica, Duluth, Minn., 1973-74, mgr. bookstore, 1974-81; treas. Benedictine Sisters Benevolent Assn., Duluth, 1981—, bd. dirs., 1985—. Trustee St. Mary's Hosp., Duluth, 1981-87; bd. dirs. St. Francis Regional Med. Ctr., Shakopee, Minn., 1987—, Benedictine Health System, Duluth, 1985—. Mem. Nat. Assn. Treasurers Religious Insts., Conf. Religious Treasurers. Avocations: canoeing, hiking, camping, painting. Home: St Scholastica Priory 1200 Kenwood Ave Duluth MN 55811

CHARTIER, MYRON RAYMOND, minister; b. Ft. Morgan, Colo., Jan. 13, 1938; s. Raymond Earl and Margaret Carol (Winegar) C.; m. Janet A., Dec. 18, 1959; children: Melody Song, Timothy Paul. BA, U. Colo., 1960; BD, Am. Bapt. Sem. of the West, 1963; MA, Ft. Hays State U., 1969; PhD, U. Denver, 1971. Ordained to ministry Bapt. Ch., 1963. Campus minister Ft. Hays State Coll. Bapt. Student Found., Hays, Kans., 1963-68; grad. teaching asst. U. Denver, 1968-71; asst. prof. speech communication Am. Bapt. Sem. of West, Covina, Calif., 1971-74; dir. doctoral programs Ea. Bapt. Theol. Sem., Phila., 1974-87; co-minister Christian edn. and family life Am. Bapt. Chs. Mich., Kalamazoo, 1987—. Author: Preaching as Communication, 1981 (award 1981); co-author: Trusting Together in God, 1984, Caring Together: Faith, Hope and Love in Your Family, 1986; co-editor: Judson Family Life Series, 9 vols., 1984-86; contbg. editor Jour. Psychology and Theology, 1987—, Marriage and Family, 1987-91; corr. The Am. Bapt., 1989—; asst. editor Minister, 1989—. Pres. Kansans Concerned About Vietnam, Hays, 1967-68. Fellow Case Study Inst., 1973. Mem. Ministers Coun., Assn. Couples in Marriage Enrichment. Democrat. Avocations: music appreciation, walking, writing, reading. Home: 1606 Suffolk Portage MI 49002-2542 Office: Am Bapt Chs Mich 315 W Michigan Ave Kalamazoo MI 49007-3742

CHASE, ALAN LEWIS, minister; b. Newburyport, Mass., Apr. 22, 1947; s. Lewis Furlong and Frances Louise (Champoux) C.; m. Susan Harriet Bangs, Aug. 27, 1972; children: Alan L. Jr., Scott David, Timothy Michael, Christopher Daniel. BA in Sociology, Wheaton Coll., 1970; MDiv, Gordon-Conwell Theol. Sem., 1978; D of Ministry, Fuller Theol. Sem., 1989. Ordained to ministry Am. Bapt. Chs. U.S.A., 1979. Missionary Haiti Bapt. Mission; pastor First Bapt. Ch., Lynn, Mass., 1979-82; nat. dir. Prison Fellowship Ministries, Reston, Va., 1982-87; assoc. pastor Bethany Congl. Christian Ch., Rye, N.H., 1988—; central dir. Operational Blessing, Inc., Portsmouth, N.H., 1988—; founding pres., dir. Greater Lynn Com. for Racial Harmony, 1980-82, Greater Lynn Vols. in Probation, 1980-84; dir. North Shore Christian Sch., Lynn., 1980-83. Author: Surviving and Thriving: Steps to Christian Growth, 1987. Dir. Portsmouth Acad. of Performing Arts, 1989-91; founder, dir. The Bethany Players, Rye, 1989—; dir. We Are Incarcerated Too, Exeter, N.H., 1989—. Mem. The Evangelistic Assn. New Eng. Home: 8 Gill St Exeter NH 03833 Office: Bethany Congl Christian Ch Washington Rd Rye NH 03870 *For Christ's followers to make an impact in this world in the 1990s, two things must happen: we must reaffirm our commitment to preach an unchanged and uncompromised Gospel; we must constantly be vigilant to discover new ways and creative means to deliver the changeless message of hope to a changing world.*

CHASE, KEITH WILLIAM, religious educator, clergyman; b. St. Louis, July 25, 1953; s. Max William and Ara May (Jones) C.; m. Joanne Elise Reynolds; 1 child, William Christopher. BS in Am. History, USCG Acad., 1975; M Div. in Bibl. Studies, New Orleans Bapt. Theol. Sem., 1982, ThD in N.T., Greek, 1987. Ordained to ministry Bapt. Ch. Prof. N.T., Greek Union Bapt. Theol. Sem., New Orleans, 1983—. Served to lt. (j.g.) USCG, 1975-80. Mem. Soc. Bibl. Lit. Avocations: acoustic guitar, sports. Home: 8021 Wave Dr New Orleans LA 70128

CHASTEEN, JOHN RAY, minister; b. Quantico, Va., Jan. 6, 1955; m. Betky K. Griffin, Sept. 8, 1973; children: Amy, Andrew, Jonathan. Student, Cen. Bible Coll., Springfield, Mo., 1989—. Ordained to ministry Pentecostal Holiness Ch. Internat., 1983. Youth pastor Calvary Temple Ch., Mountain Grove, Mo., 1978-80, assoc. pastor, 1980-83, sr. pastor, 1983—; asst. dir. Christian edn. Ozarks Conf., Oklahoma City, 1987—, bd. dirs., Westville, Okla., 1990—. Mem. Mountain Grove Drug and Alcohol Com., 1987—. Named Profl. of Yr., Mountain Grove C. of C., 1987. Mem. Mountain Grove Ministrial Alliance (pres. 1985-87). Home: Rte 2 Box 161R Mountain Grove MO 65711 Office: Calvary Temple Ch PO Box 547 Mountain Grove MO 65711

CHASTINE, RONALD FREEMAN, pastor; b. Atlanta, Ga., Oct. 13, 1940; s. John Freeman and Carolyn (Crumbley) C.; m. Helen McDuffie, Apr. 22, 1961; children: Greg, Alan, Rhonda. AA, Brewton-Parker Coll., 1968; BS, Ga. So. U., 1970; MDiv., Trinity Theol. Sem., 1982, ThD, 1983. Pastor North Tucson (Ariz.) Bapt. Ch., 1977-81, First Bapt. Ch., Deming, N.Mex., 1981-84, Bapt. Temple, Oklahoma City, Okla., 1984-88, First Bapt. Ch., Clinton, Mo., 1988—; adj. prof. Okla. Bapt. Univ., Shawnee, 1986-88; moderator Capitol Bapt. Assn., Oklahoma City, 1987-88, conf. pres. 1987; chmn. Christian Life Commn., 1987-88. Author: (book) Counseling Confortations of Jesus, 1983, (weekly column) Chastine's Comments. Chaplain Clinton (Mo.) Police Dept., 1988—; pres. Henry County Cancer Bd., Clinton, 1991; mem. Charles Haddon Spurgeon Soc. of William Jewell Coll. With USN, 1958-62. Mem. Internat. Conf. Police Chaplins, Rotary. Republican. Home: 1041 Hogan Pl Clinton MO 64735 Office: First Bapt Ch 2nd & Jefferson Clinton MO 64735 *After surviving for a half-century, it is crystal clear to me that the "impact" one makes upon people in this short life comes not through theology or politics alone but blossoms forth via the personal touch in life.*

CHATFIELD, DONALD F(RANKLIN), theologian, educator; b. Boston, Jan. 29, 1935; s. George Irving and Marie Margaret (Walters) C.; m. Martha Jane Daily, 1959 (div. 1967); 1 child, Nicholas Walters; m. Kathleen Hurley, Aug. 12, 1967 (div. Nov. 1983); children: Amy Ruth, Gregory Van Cleve; m. Judith Lane, June 20, 1987. AB, Yale U., 1956; BD, Princeton Theol. Seminary, N.J., 1959; PhD, U. Edinburgh, Scotland, 1964. Ordained to ministry Presbyn. Ch., 1959. Intern/asst. minister Erie Chapel and Neighborhood House, Chgo., 1959-60; instr. in homiletics Princeton Theol. Sem., 1964-67; prof. of preaching Garrett-Evang. Theol. Sem., Evanston, Ill., 1967—; interim preacher various congregations in Scotland, N.J., Ill., 1963—. Author: (book) Dinner With Jesus, 1988, (chancel drama) The Big Trade, 1975; founder/dir. three religious drama groups. Office: Garrett-Evang Theol Seminary 2121 Sheridan Rd Evanston IL 60201

CHATFIELD, JOAN, church administrator; b. Elizabeth, N.J., Oct. 7, 1932; d. Henry Summers and Angela Dorothea (McCahill) Chatfield. BA, Manhattanville Coll., 1956; MA, U. San Francisco, 1968; PhD, Grad. Theol. Union, Berkeley, Calif., 1983. Secondary sch. tchr. Cath. Sch. Dept., Hawaii, 1956-72; dir. Maryknoll (N.Y.) Mission Inst., 1974-78; exec. dir. Inst. for Religion and Social Change, Honolulu, 1980—; ecumenical officer Roman Cath. Diocese of Honolulu, 1983-90, chair ecumenical commn., 1983—; dean Sch. Humanities and Fine Arts Chaminade U. Honolulu, 1990—; pres. Hawaii Inst. for Theol. Studies, Honolulu, 1988—; v.p. Western Fellowship for the Profs. of Mission, Calif., 1989—; sec. Interfaith Ministries of Hawaii, Honolulu, 1985—. Contbr. articles to profl. jours. Vice chair City & County Status of Women, Honolulu, 1981-86; pres. Project Realize Effective Support Programs for the Elderly through Chs. and Temples, Honolulu, 1983—. Named Tchr. of Yr., Finance Factors, Honolulu, 1964, one of Women of Note, Honolulu Status of Women Commn., 1982; recipient Pres.'s award Internat. Assn. Mission Studies, 1988. Mem. AAUW (chair ednl. found. program, pres. 1986-88), Am. Soc. Missiology (pres. 1984-86), Rotary. Democrat. Home: 2880 Oahu Ave Honolulu HI 96822 Office: Inst for Religion & Social Change 3146 Waialae Ave Honolulu HI 96816

CHATMAN-ROYCE, EDGAR TRUITT, deacon; b. Gloucester, N.J., Sept. 3, 1924; s. Edgar Truitt and Gertrude Frances (Hewitt) Chatman; m. Monique Charlotte Timmermans, Sept. 20, 1945 (div. 1955); children: Edgar Truitt III, Vivian Mary; m. Barbara Joan Royce, Dec. 24, 1955; children: Robert Charles, Mark Edgar. Ordained deacon Episc. Ch., 1987. Deacon Diocese of Pa., Coatesville, 1987—; architect Gibbons & Hatt, Inc., Exton, Pa., 1970—; chmn. subcom. on Diaconate, Phila., 1989—; asst. rector Trinity Ch., Coatesville, 1987—; assoc. chaplain Episcopal Community Svcs., Chester County, Pa., 1987—. Panel mem. United Way Allocation Panel, Chester County, 1984-91. 1st lt. U.S. Army, 1942-47, 51-53, ETO. Republican. Home: PO Box 333 Highspire Rd Lyndell PA 19354

CHAVEZ, GILBERT ESPINOZA, bishop; b. Ontario, Calif., Mar. 19, 1932; ed. St. Francis Sem., El Cajon, Calif., Immaculate Heart Sem., San Diego, U. Calif., San Diego. Ordained priest Roman Cath. Ch., 1960; titular bishop of Magarmel and aux. bishop Diocese of San Diego, 1974—. Office: 1535 3rd Ave San Diego CA 92101

CHAVEZ, JOSEPH PHILIP, minister, evangelist, counselor; b. Santa Fe, Nov. 2, 1946; s. Luther Philip Chavez and Maria Louise (Trujillo) Valdez; m. Mary Dorothy Vigil, Dec. 23, 1967; children: Maurice Chandler, Simona Anissa. Ministerial diploma, Latin Am. Bible Inst., El Paso, Tex., 1967; student, AIMS Community Coll., Greeley, Colo., 1971-72; BTh, Internat. Bible Sem., Plymouth, Fla., 1983, M Ministry, 1986; DD, Am. Bible Inst., 1978; paralegal studies, Profl. Career Inst., 1990—. Ordained to ministry Assemblies of God, 1973. Dir. dist. youth ministries Cen. Latin Am. dist. coun. Assemblies of Gods, 1979-82; dir. Hispanic dept. Christian Anti-Communism Crusade, Long Beach, Calif., 1982-83; missionary evangelist Riverside Chapel, Laramie, Wyo., 1983-84; sr. pastor, counselor New Life Assembly, Rupert, Idaho, 1984-86; sr. pastor Emmanuel Christian Assembly, Fruita, Colo., 1988-91; founder, dir. Living Room Coffee House Ministry, Sterling, Colo., 1973-79; founder, pres. Trinity Christian Acad., Roswell, N.Mex., 1976-79; founder, counselor Magic Valley Christian Counseling, Rupert, 1984-86; behavioral analyst Lower Valley Christian Counseling, Fruita, 1988—. Mem., chmn. Chaves County Community Action Agy., 1977-79; rep. Logan County Coun. on Youth Placement, Sterling, Colo., 1973-76, Logan County Coun. on Aging, 1973-76, Regional Coun. on Aging, Twin Falls, Idaho, 1985-86; mem. Minidoka County Coun. on Aging, Rupert, 1984-85, Minidoka County Comm. on Devel. Disabled Adults, 1984-86. Recipient spl. recognition Nat. Assn. Disting. Am. High Sch. Students, 1978, 79, 88, award of recognition Chaves County Community Action Agy., 1979. Republican. Home and Office: 1055 E Cleveland Ave Fruita CO 81521

CHAVEZ, RICHARD RALPH, pastor; b. Tampa, Fla., Apr. 6, 1943; s. Ralph and Josephine Chavez; m. Carolyn Jean Shaughnessy, June 16, 1963; children: Richard Ralph Jr., Sean Michael. Ordained to ministry So. Bapt. Conv., 1980; cert. lay evangelism sch. instr., Taylor-Johnson temperament analysis; interfaith witness assoc. Pastor Garrison Forest Bapt. Ch., Owings Mills, Md., 1979-82; sr. pastor Burtonsville (Md.) Bapt. Ch., 1982—; brotherhood pres. Bapt. Conv. Md. and Del., Columbia, Md., 1974-79, coord. disaster relief, 1976-80, v.p. state mission bd., 1987-88. Home: 14579 Dowling Dr Burtonsville MD 20866 Office: Burtonsville Bapt Ch 3400 Spencerville Rd Burtonsville MD 20866

CHEATHAM, GARY LYNN, educator; b. Wichita, Kans., Aug. 9, 1953; s. Clifford Eugene and Dolores Mae (Burt) C.; m. Rebecca Jo Wheeler, Apr. 16, 1977 (div. Mar. 1989); 1 child, Erin Whitney; m. Linda Marie York, June 29, 1991. BS, N.W. Christian Coll., 1976; MDiv, Tex. Christian U., 1980; MLS, U. Tenn., 1984. Ordained to ministry Christian Ch. (Disciples of Christ), 1981. Ministerial intern Peachtree Christian Ch., Atlanta, 1974; asst. prof. Northeastern Okla. State U., Tahlequah, 1986—. Contbr. articles to history jours. Mem. ALA, Am. Theol. Libr. Assn., Okla. Libr. Assn., Okla. chpt. Assn. Coll. and Rsch. Librs., Amnesty Internat. Office: Northeastern Okla State U John Vaughan Libr Tahlequah OK 74464

CHEDID, JOHN G., bishop; b. Eddid, Lebanon, July 4, 1923. Educated, Sems. in Lebanon and Pontifical Urban Coll., Rome. Ordained priest Roman Cath. Ch., 1951. Titular bishop of Callinico and aux bishop St. Maron of Bklyn., 1981. Office: 333 S San Vicente Blvd Los Angeles CA 90048

CHEEK, DENNIS WILLIAM, educator, minister, consultant; b. Harrisburg, Pa., Apr. 13, 1955; s. Clarence William Jr. and Laura Priscilla (Rockey) C.; m. Kim Anita Douglas, Mar. 9, 1980; children: Carol Annette, Michael William. BA, Towson State U., 1979; MA, U. Md., 1984; BS, U. State N.Y. Regents Coll., 1988; PhD, Pa. State U., 1989; postgrad., Grad. Theol. Found., 1992—. Cert. sci. and social studies tchr., N.Y.; ordained to ministry Assemblies of God Ch., 1979. Assoc. evangelist Don Summers Evangelistic Assn., Bristol, Eng., 1976-78; asst. pastor Gospel Tabernacle Balt., Inc., 1978-83; pastor Rhaunen (Fed. Republic Germany) Tabernacle, 1983-84; chmn. high sch. sci. dept. Def. Dependents Sch., Bitburg, Fed. Republic Germany, 1984-87; rsch. asst. sci., tech. and society program Pa. State U., University Park, 1987-88; project coord. Nat. Sci., Tech. and Soc. Network, University Park, 1988-89; coord. curriculum devel. N.Y. Sci., Tech. Soc. Edn. Project State Edn. Dept., Albany, 1989—; tchr. Tabernacle Christian Sch., Balt., 1978-80; lectr. history European div. U. Md., Heidelberg, Fed. Republic Germany, 1985-87; aux. protestant chaplain USAF, Buechel, Fed. Republic Germany, 1984-87; field tester, reviewer nat. security in nuclear age series Mershon Ctr., Ohio State U., Columbus, 1986-87; advisor Discovering Sci. and Tech. through Am. History Project of the Soc for the History of Tech., 1990—, advisor task force on environ. edn. and pollution prevention EPA, Fed. Interagy. Task Force on Environ. Cancer, Heart and Lung Disease, Tech. Media Project AIME, 1990—; cons. on sci., tech. and society edn. to numerous sch. dists. and nat. orgns.; cons. on ch. growth and Chrstian edn. to numerous chs.; mem. task force on sci. and tech. Evang. Luth Ch. in Am., 1989—. Editor STS Reporter, 1988-89; co-editor Proc. 5th Ann. Tech. Lit. Conf., 1989; editor Proc. 4th Ann. Tech. Lit. Conf., 1990, Proc. 6th Ann. Tech. Lit. Conf., 1991; editoral bd., book rev. editor Jour. Tech. Edn., 1989—; cons. editor Odyssey; contbr. numerous articles, essays and curriculum materials. Troop coord. Dulaney dist. Boy Scouts Am., Balt., 1979-83. U. Md. gen. univ. fellow, 1983. Mem. AAAS, NSTA (task force on scope, sequence and coordination secondary sch. sci. 1989, chmn. task force on NSTA-Sponsored presentations at non-NSTA convs. and meetings), ASCD (facilitator network for sci., math. and tech. edn. 1990—, nat. adv. panel U.S. maths. and sci. achievement 1991), Soc. for History Tech. (advisor Discovering Sci. and Tech. through Am. History project), Nat. Assn. Sci., Tech. and Soc. (chmn. site and confs. liaison com., chmn. subcom. on STS assessment position paper, com. on STS evaluation), Acad. Parish Clergy, Alban Inst. (book reviewer), Religious Rsch. Assn., Am. Ednl. Rsch. Assn. (liaison spl. interest group in sci. and tech. to ASCD and Coun. State Sci. Suprs.), Nat. Coun. Social Studies (manuscript reviewer, book reviewer 1991—, mem. sci. and soc. com. 1991-94), Nat. Mid. Sch. Assn. (publs. rev. bd. 1991—), Internat. Network for Info. in Sci. and Tech. Edn., UNESCO, Nat. Mid. Level Sci. Tchrs. Assn., Coun. of State Sci. Suprs., Sci. Tchrs. Assn. of N.Y., Kappa Delta Pi (assoc. counselor Sigma Mu chpt.), Phi Alpha Theta, Epsilon Pi Tau. Republican. Office: NY Sci Tech Soc Edn Project State Edn Bldg Rm 232-M EB Albany NY 12234 *A person must willingly give up what cannot be kept to gain that which cannot be lost.*

CHEEK, NICHOLAS BYRON, minister; b. Statesville, N.C., Dec. 28, 1952; s. Jones Culver and Ruth Marie (Caudill) C.; m. Janice Bell Mathis, Mar. 12, 1977; children: Candace, John Wesley, Nathan. AA, Wilkes Community Coll., 1973; Assoc. Divinity, Mid-Am. Bapt. Theol. Sem., 1986. Ordained to ministry So. Bapt. Ch. Pastor, tchr. Mineral Springs Bapt. Ch., Jonesville, N.C., 1986-91, Antioch Bapt. Ch., Lincolton, N.C., 1991—. Author: Effective Witnessing: Bringing Men to Christ, 1987. Mem. Elkin Bapt. Assn. (MasterLife instr. 1989-90, SonShine Bible tchr. 1990-91), Tandem Club Am. Home: Rte 3 Box 755 Lincolnton NC 28092

CHEEK, RANDY MICHAEL, minister; b. Atlanta, Aug. 14, 1952; s. James Lee and Frances Odene (Richards) C.; m. Connie Lois Brantley, Nov. 17, 1972; children: Michael James, Bethany Leigh. BA in Theology, Mercer U., 1974; Mdiv, So. Bapt. Sem., 1978. Minister to youth First Bapt. Ch., Shepherdsville, Ky., 1975-78; pastor First Bapt. Ch., Grantville, Ga., 1978-79; minister to youth Mt. Zion Bapt. Ch., Snellville, Ga., 1979-82, First Bapt. Ch., Smyrna, Ga., 1982-88, Brainerd Bapt. Ch., CHattanooga, Tenn., 1988—; chmn. Noonday Bapt. Youth Com. Noonday Assn., Marietta, Ga., 1987, Hamilton County Youth Mins.'s Fellowship, 1989; clown ministry seminar leader Ga. Bapt. Conv., Atlanta, 1983—; disc jockey WYNX-Radio, Smyrna, 1983-86. Named one of Outstanding Young Men of Am., 1985. Mem. Ga. Bapt. Youth Minister's Fellowship, Clowns of Am. Internat., World Clown Assn. Avocations: reading, electric trains, yard work, woodworking, writing. Home: 8212 Fallen Maple Dr Chattanooga TN 37421 Office: Brainerd Bapt Ch k300 Brookfield Ave Chattanooga TN 37411

CHEESMAN, JOHN MICHAEL, aeronautics company administrator, lay church worker; b. Wichita, Kans., Feb. 4, 1943; s. Norman Carlyle and Anne Lucille (Norris) C.; m. Sharon Lindsey, Feb. 8, 1964; children: Mary Kathleen, Deborah Kristine. AA in Math., Social Scis., Wichita (Kans.) State U., BBA, 1986, AA in Social Scis., 1987; postgrad., Calif. State U., Carson. Cert. quality engr., Kans. Mgr. Guardian Industries, Wichita, 1966-72; supr. Cessna Aircraft Corp., Wichita, 1972-78; stats. analyst Boeing Airplane Co., Wichita, 1978-85; lead engr. Boeing Mil. Airplanes, Wichita, 1985-89; coord. prodn. conformance Boeing Comml. A/P Group, Wichita, 1989—. Contbr. articles to religious jours. Vol. United Meth. Urban Ministries Wichita, 1984—; numerous positions local and regional chpts. Boy Scouts Am., including commr. of scouting Quivira coun., Wichita; leader United Meth. Men and Boys Retreat Youth Ministries, 1984—; chmn. United Meth. Neighborhood Outreach, 1988—; chmn. communication com. Grace United Meth. Ch., Wichita, 1988—; vice chmn. endowment com., United Meth. Ch., Wichita; institutional rep. United Meth. Coun. on Ministries, Wichita; active Wichita-Sedgwick County Hist. Mus. Assn., 1985—, Rep. Nat. Com., 1981—, Nat. Rep. Congl. Com., 1986—, Wichita Children's Home, 1989—, Big Bros./Big Sisters, Wichita/Sedgwick County, 1989—; vol. leader Wichita Spl. Olympics, 1985—; bd. dirs. Dept. Human Svcs., City of Wichita, 1991—. Recipient Campaign Victory cert., 1983, Presdl. Achievement award Rep. Nat. Com., 1986, Cert. of merit, 1990, George Meany award Nat. Fedn. Unions, 1986, God and Svc. award United Meth. Ch., 1986, Torch award Kans. West conf. United Meth. Ch., 1986, 88, Community Vol. of Yr. awards Boeing Co., 1987-89, Cross and Flame award United Meth. Ch., 1988, 91, Award of Merit Boy Scouts Am., 1988, Arrowhead Honor award Boy Scouts Am., 1988, God and Svc. award Presbyn. Ch. U.S.A., 1991, William M. Allen award Boeing Corp., 1989, Cert. of Appreciation Nat. Rep. congl. Com., 1990, 91, Whitney M. Young award Salvation Army, 1991. Mem. Am. Mgmt. Assn., Adminstrv. Mgmt. Soc., Boeing Mgmt. Club, Am. Soc. for Quality Control, Wichita State U. Alumni Assn. (life), Wichita State U. Soc. of 1985 (life), Wichita State U. Endowment Assn. (life), Wichita Aero. Hist. Assn./Kans. Aviation Mus., United meth. Men (past pres.), Nat. Assn. United Meth. Scouters (life, coord./chartered organizational rep.), Nat. Assn. Presbyn. Scouters (life), Nat. United Ch. of Christ Assn. Scouters (life mem. Nat. Adv. Coun. 1984—), Orders and Medals Soc. Am., Medal of Honor Hist. Soc., Token and Medal Soc. Am., Masons (32 degree), Shriners, Order of the Arrow. Avocations:

collecting, travel, reading. Home: 1470 Hornecker Dr Wichita KS 67235 Office: United Meth Ch 944 S Topeka Wichita KS 67211

CHELETTE, RICKY PAUL, clergyman; b. New Orleans, May 10, 1962; s. Leonard Paul Jr. and Anna Anita (Attardo) C.; m. Merlinda Lee Allen, Dec. 10, 1988. BA, La. Coll., 1985; MRE, New Orleans Bapt. Theol. Sem., 1988. Lic. to ministry So. Bapt. Conv., 1980. Min. youth 1st Bapt. Ch., Alpine, La., 1983-84, music evangelist, 1984-85; min. student edn. 1st Bapt. Ch., Pineville, La., 1988—; assoc. pastor of edn. and youth 1st Bapt. Ch., Ponchatoula, La., 1985-88; associational youth dir. Chappapeela (La.) Bapt. Assn., 1986-88; adj. instr. La. Coll., Pineville, 1990—. Mem. Pearl River Planning Commn., 1981-82; chaplain Ponchatoula High Sch. Football, 1985-88; bd. dirs. Fellowship Christian Athletes, Ponchatoula, 1985-88; v.p. exec. com. Celebration of Life, Pineville, 1989, vice chair, 1989—, also bd. dirs. Recipient Nat. Collegiate Student Govt. award, 1988; named Teenager of Yr. Elks Clubs Am., 1980. Mem. So. Bapt. Religious Edn. Assn., La. Bapt. Religious Edn. Assn., Omicron Delta Kappa. Home: 324 Pearce Rd Pineville LA 71360 Office: 1st Bapt Ch 901 Main St Pineville LA 71360

CHEN, TAR TIMOTHY, biostatistician; b. Fuching, China, June 23, 1945; came to U.S., 1967, naturalized, 1979; s. Lin-Tsang and Ai-Ging (Chang) C.; m. Meei-Ming Li, Aug. 9, 1969; children: Stephen, Daniel. BS, Nat. Taiwan U., 1966; MS, U. Chgo., 1969, PhD, 1972; MDiv, Southwestern Bapt. Theol. Sem., 1989. Statistician Ill. Bell Tel., Chgo., 1971-73; asst. prof. Calif. State U., Hayward, 1973-74; vis. assoc. prof. Chung-Hsing U., Taichung, Taiwan, 1974-75; biostatistician The Upjohn Co., Kalamazoo, 1975-79; asst. prof. biometrics M.D. Anderson Cancer Ctr. U. Tex., Houston, 1979-84; sr. biostatistician Alcon Labs., Fort Worth, 1984-89; math. statistician Nat. Cancer Inst., Bethesda, Md., 1989—. Contbr. articles to profl. jours. Treas. Chinese for Christ Chgo. Fellowship Ch., 1972-73; deacon, Houston Chinese Ch., 1981-83, McKinney Meml. Bible Ch., Ft. Worth, 1988-89. 2d lt. Republic of China Army, 1966-67. Mem. Am. Statis. Assn., Biometric Soc., Soc. Clin. Trials, Sigma Xi. Office: Biometric Rsch Br Nat Cancer Inst EPN-738 Bethesda MD 20892

CHENG-CHUNG, JOHN BAPTIST, bishop. Bishop Roman Cath. Ch., Hong Kong. Office: Cath Diocese Ctr, 16 Caine Rd, Hong Kong Hong Kong*

CHENOWITH, LONNIE LYNN, pastor; b. Covina, Calif., Jan. 12, 1959; s. Billy Kay and Madeline (Baker) Cooper; m. Katherine Jean Shelley, Aug. 1, 1981; children: Jonathan Malachi, Nathanael Paul, Karis Elizabeth. BA, Okla. Bapt. U., 1980; MDiv, Southwestern, 1983; doctoral studies, Luther Rice, 1991—. Lic. min., 1976; ordained to ministry So. Bapt. Conv., 1984. Pastor First Bapt., West Pembroke Pines, Fla., 1984-88, Mineral Wells (W.Va.) Bapt. Fellowship, 1988—; mem. com. on coms. So. Bapt. Conv., New Orleans, 1990; chmn. Order Bus. Com., W.Va. Conv., 1991; pres. Southwestern Sem. Alumni, Parkersburg, W.Va., 1990; coord. Conservative Fellowship, 1990—. Republican. Home: Rte 2 Box 148 Mineral Wells WV 26150 Office: Mineral Wells Fellowship Rte 14 Mineral Wells WV 26150 *Life is to be enthusiastically lived for the glory of God and benefit to man. Both merge at Calvary. Thus life should be lived in the shadow and light of the cross, waiting for the promised morning.*

CHERAMIE, SISTER MILDRED, hospital pastoral care director; b. Gretna, La., Nov. 8, 1928; d. Leopold Jules and Edwina Cleona (Borné) C. B., Marillac Coll., 1959; MA in Theology, Marquette U., 1976; postgrad., St. Louis U., 1970-74. RN. Clin. instr. pediatrics Hotel Dieu Hosp., New Orleans, 1951-53; supr. pediatric nursing St. Mary's Hosp., Evansville, Ind., 1955-57; supr. pediatrics DePaul Health Ctr., St. Louis, 1959-64; supr. child psychiatry Child Ctr. Our Lady of Grace, St. Louis, 1965; supr. nursing obstetrics St. Mary's Hosp., Milw., 1966-68; instr. sacred scripture Marillac Coll.-Notre Dame Coll., Normandy, Mo., 1972-77; dir. pastoral care DePaul Health Ctr., Bridgeton, Mo., 1984—; chmn. bd. trustees Hotel Dieu Hosp., New Orleans, 1987—; bd. dirs. Hotel Dieu Hosp., New Orleans; mem. ethics com. DePaul Health Ctr., Bridgeton, 1985—. Named hon. leutenant-forest ranger Shawnee Nat. Forest, Ozark, Ill., 1965-66. Mem. Gateway Catholic Ethics Network, Daughters Charity St. Vincent de Paul (local supr. 1971-84). Avocations: oil painting, watercolor painting, langs., translator, traveling, crossword puzzles. Home: 7800 Natural Bridge Rd Normandy MO 63121 Office: De Paul Health Ctr 12303 DePaul Dr Bridgeton MO 63044

CHERNOFF, ROBERT, rabbi; b. Bklyn., Sept. 4, 1922; s. Louis and Sarah Dorothy (Grotsky) C.; m. Lea Rosen, Nov. 23, 1943; children—Howard, Shira, Frances. Student Yeshivah D'Bklyn., 1939; BA Elysion Coll., 1978, PhD, 1979. Rabbi, Rabbinical Acad. Am., 1972. Ordained rabbi, 1972. Rabbi Congregation Sons of Israel, Chambersburg, Pa., 1974-90, ret., 1990; Pa. state chaplain South Mountain Restoration Ctr., Pa., 1974—. Author: Shechitah, The Jewish Method of Slaughtering and Attendant Dietary Laws, 1973; Aspects of Judaism, 1975, Some Other Aspects of Judaism, 1987. Recipient Meritorious Service award Dept. Air Force, 1956, Commendation award Dept. Def., 1972. Mem. Am. Assn. Rabbis (nat. sec. 1981, hon. pres.), Greater Carolinas Assn. Rabbis, Chambersburg Area Ministerium, Jewish Chaplains Orgn. Pa. Lodge: Kiwanis (past pres.).

CHERRY, CHARLES CONRAD, religion educator; b. Kerens, Tex., Mar. 31, 1937; s. Charles and Laura (Vaughn) C.; m. Mary Ella Bigony, Aug. 22, 1959; children: Charles Kevin, Cynthia Diane. BA, McMurry U., 1958; MDiv, Drew U., 1961, PhD, 1965. Prof. Pa. State U., University Park, 1964-81; Disting. prof. Ind. U., Indpls., 1988—; dir. Scholars Press, Atlanta, 1981-88. Author: Theology of Jonathan Edwards, 1966, God's New Israel, 1971, Nature and Religious Imagination, 1980; editor jour. Religion and Am. Culture, 1990—. Recipient Best Article award Am. Quar., 1969; Soc. for Religion in Higher Edn. fellow, 1970, Pa. State U. fellow, 1978. Fellow Soc. for Values in Higher Edn.; mem. Am. Acad. Religion, Am. Soc. Ch. History. Presbyterian. Office: Ind U 425 University Blvd Indianapolis IN 46202

CHESHIER, JOFFRE PAUL, youth clergyman; b. Camden, Ark., Dec. 2, 1961; s. Joe Toney and Billie Margaret (Edwards) C.; m. Barbara Hope Brantley, Oct. 6, 1984; 1 child, Ashley Victoria. BA in Bible, Columbia Bible Coll., 1984; postgrad., Moody Bible Inst., 1988—. Ordained to ministry, 1988. Youth pastor Dunn's Chapel Ch., Columbia, S.C., 1984-87, Faith Bible Ch., Robins, Iowa, 1987—; chmn. Youth Ministry Coalition, Cedar Rapids, Iowa, 1990. Avocations: hunting, fishing, hanging wallpaper, woodworking, gardening. Home: 40 Timber Ln Robins IA 52328 Office: Faith Bible Ch 95 S Mentzer Robins IA 52328

CHESNUT, FRANKLIN GILMORE, clergyman; b. Bowling Green, Ky., Mar. 2, 1919; s. Walter Franklin and Fannie (Meador) C.; m. Laurelyn Travillian, Aug. 19, 1950; children: Franklin Gilmore, Kathryn Lynne. Student, W. Ky. State Tchrs. Coll., Bowling Green, 1937-39; B.A., Bethel Coll., 1941; B.D., Cumberland Presbyn. Theol. Sem., 1943. Ordained to ministry Cumberland Presbyn. Ch., 1940. Pastor in Brunswick, Tenn., 1943-44; denominational youth dir., 1944-53; mgr. Cumberland Presbyn. Book Store, Memphis, 1953-54; pastor Callco Rock, Ark., 1954-58, Russellville, Ark., 1958-75, Booneville, Ark., 1975-90; moderator Logan Presbytery, Ky. Synod, 1941, W. Tenn. Synod, 1945, Cumberland Presbyn. Gen. Assembly, 1963, White River Presbytery, 1956, Ewing Presbytery, 1959, 61, 64, Porter Presbytery, 1975; stated clk., Ark. Synod, 1956-86; stated clk. Porter Presbytery, 1977-88; moderator Ark. Synod, 1988, 89; mem. Denominational Commn. on the Ministry, 1975-84, Gen. Bd. Ark. Presbytery, 1988—; trustee Cumberland Presbyn. Children's Home, 1962-71. Co-author: Arkansas Cumberland Presbyterians, 1812-1984. Address: 908 N Erie Russellville AR 72801

CHESSER, JOE MAX, minister; b. Paragould, Ark., May 14, 1948; s. Joe Memory and Tomazine (Wood) C.; m. Areva Ovaughn Ward, Aug. 3, 1968; children: Joe MAx Jr., Andrew Ward, Jennifer Casey. AA, Crowley's Ridge Coll., 1968; BA, Harding U., 1970, postgrad. Ordained to Ch. Christ, 1970. Min. Ch. of Christ, Edgar Springs, Mo., 1970-71, Marshfield, Mo., 1971-73; missionary, evangelist Ch. of Christ, Brainard, Minn., 1973-82, Mankato, Minn., 1982-85; min. Ch. of Christ, Brookland, Ark., 1985-91, Crowder Blvd. Ch. of Christ, New Orleans, 1991—; charter mem., bd. dirs., Flaming Pines Youth Camp, Togo, Minn., 1975-85; bd. dirs., Campaign for Christ, Brainard, 1976, NEARK Youth Meetings, Brookland, 1989-90; missionary campaign dir. Guyana, S.A.; other missionary trips to Guyana and Kenya. Editor: The Challange of Mission Work in the Upper Mid-West, 1980. Mem. adv. coun. Crowley's Rdige Acad., Paragould, Ark., 1989-91. Office: Crowder Blvd Ch Christ 7301 Crowder Blvd New Orleans LA 70127

CHEVEALLIER, J. CLINT, religious organization executive; b. Dec. 16, 1943; s. J. C. and Eula Mae Cheveallier; m. Sue Steel, 1965; children: Jervey Clint Jr., Jean DeWayne. Student, La. State U.; B in Sociology and Psychology, Bethany Nazarene Coll., 1966; postgrad., Tulane U. Ordained to ministry Vols. of Am., 1980. Various positions Vols. of Am., Baton Rouge, New Orleans, Indpls.; exec. dir. Vols. of Am., Baton Rouge, 1968-82; sec. nat. correctional svcs. Vols. of Am., regional dir. So. region, 1979, with tech. and support svcs. nat. staff, 1987, pres., chief exec. officer, 1990—. Mem. U.S. Power Squadron (various offices Baton Rouge chpt., sec., chaplain, adminstrv. officer dist. 15), Kiwanis (past v.p., pres.). Office: Vols Am Nat Hdqrs 3813 N Causeway Blvd Metairie LA 70002

CHEYNEY, THOMAS EDWARD, JR., minister; b. Cecilton, Md., May 30, 1957; s. Thomas Edward and Joan Pauline (Drumheller) C.; m. Cheryl Lynn Weigand, Sept. 5, 1982; 1 child, Thomas Andrew. Lic. to preach So. Bapt. Conv., 1979, ordained to ministry, 1981; cert. ch. growth specialist. Min. youth 1st Bapt. Ch., Delray Beach, Fla., 1980-82; youth pastor Calvary Bapt. Ch., Aberdeen, N.J., 1982-84; pastor intern Metairie (La.) Bapt. Ch., 1985-87; pastor Haven Bapt. Ch., New Bedford, Mass., 1987-89; sr. pastor Calvary Bapt. Ch., Morgantown, W.Va., 1989—; messenger So. Bapt. Conv., Nashville, 1990—; mem. nominating com. W.Va. Conv. of So. Bapt., Scott Depot, 1990—. Author: The Total Church Communication Planbook, 1991; co-author: Evanglism Tools for the 90's, 1990; contbr. articles to Ch. Adminstrn. Mag. Recipient John Dansforth Citizenship award 4-H Club, 1976, John Leesberg award SAR, 1978. Mem. Monongahela Bapt. Assn. (assoc. evang. dir. 1990—), W.Va. Fellowship Christian Athletes (bd. dirs. 1990—), Rotary (chmn. pub. rels. Morgantown club 1991). Republican. Home: 24 Cedarwood Dr Morgantown WV 26505 Office: Calvary Bapt Ch 519 Burroughs St Morgantown WV 26505

CHIANG, SAMUEL EDWARD, theological educator; b. Taipei, Taiwan, Republic of China, Oct. 20, 1959; s. William L. and Gladys (Chao) C.; m. Roberta Jean Bush, Dec. 31, 1987; children: Zachariah Asa, Micah Kaleem. B. Commerce, U. Toronto (Can.), 1982; MA in Bibl. Studies, Dallas Theol. Sem., 1989. Ordained minister Peoples' Ch., 1990. Writer, researcher Can. Broadcasting Co., Toronto, Ont., Can., 1980-81; audit automation coord. Can. nat. office Ernest & Young, Toronto, 1982-86; asst. to the pres. Dallas Sem. Found., 1988—; East Asia regional coord. Ptnrs. Internat., San Jose, Calif., 1991—; tchr. Applied Principle of Learning-Walk Thru the Bible, 1990—. Contbr. articles to profl. jours.; editor, contbr. World Christian Perspective, 1988—. Youth dir. jr. high The Peoples' Ch., Toronto, 1980-82; youth pastor Korean Philadelphia Presbyn. Ch., Toronto, 1983-85; youth dir. Dallas Chinese Fellowship Ch., 1987-90; bd. dirs. Dallas Chinese Ch. Youth Camps, 1987—; adv. bd. dirs. I Too Have A Dream, Harare, Zimbabwe, 1989—, Foyer Fraternal, Ndjamena, Chad, 1990—, Student Christian Outreach for China, U.S., 1991. Mem. Evang. Missiological Soc. Avocations: reading, music, hiking, writing, tennis. *Matters in this world are seldom urgent. Accept that which lasts for eternity—the souls of individuals.*

CHIAPPERINO, FRANK ANTHONY, lay worker; b. Astoria, N.Y., Mar. 5, 1952; s. Anthony and Mary (Bonise) C.; m. Jeanette Suzanne Calhoun, Sept. 24, 1972; children: Frank Jr., David, Peter. AAS, N.Y.C. Community Coll., Bklyn., 1972; BS in Criminal Justice, Mercy Coll., Dobbs Ferry, N.Y., 1981; postgrad., L. I. U., 1990—. Trustee Italian Christian Ch. of Astoria, N.Y., 1975-77; youth leader, children's ch. dir. Trinity Assembly of God, Middletown, N.Y., 1977-79, sec., 1980—, trustee, 1984—; correction counselor N.Y. State Dept. of Correctional Svc., 1977—; Sunday sch. tchr. adults Trinity Assembly of God, Middletown, 1982—; staff advisor Alcholics Anonymous, Fishkill, N.Y., 1982-85, Narcotics Anonymous, Photo Club Camp Beacon, N.Y., 1985-90, Alternatives to Violence, Wallkill, N.Y., 1990—. V.p. Village on Green Homeowners Assn., Middletown, 1979-80; chmn. scheduling com. Quality of Worklife Bldg., Beacon, 1985-90; community advisor N.Y. State Div. of Youth, Middletown, 1986-90. Recipient vol. svc. awards, Fishkill Correctional Facility, 1980, 81, gold medal and silver medal N.Y. Dept. of State Olympic Com., Albany, 1988, numerous certs. N.Y. State Dept. Correctional Svc. Home: 4 Commonwealth Ave Middletown NY 10940-4711 Office: Trinity Assembly of God Ch Blumel Rd P O Box 277 Middletown NY 10940

CHIARA, JOHN CARMEN, pastor; b. New Brunswick, N.J., Oct. 21, 1949; s. John Joseph and Mary Catherine (DeSantis) C.; m. Carolyn Jean Pittman, Aug. 24, 1975; children: J.J. and James. BS, Lee Coll., Cleveland, Tenn., 1977; MDiv, Melodyland Sch. of Theol., Anaheim, Calif., 1981. Youth pastor Ch. of God, Salinas, Calif., 1982-84; pastor Ch. of God, Dinuba, Calif., 1986-89, San Bruno, Calif., 1989—. Republican. Home: 949 Huntington Ave San Bruno CA 94066 Office: Church of God 953 Huntington Ave San Bruno CA 94066

CHIASSON, DONAT, archbishop; b. Paquetville, N.B., Can., Jan. 2, 1930. Ordained priest Roman Catholic Ch., 1956; archbishop of Moncton N.B., 1972—. Office: Chancery Office, 452 rue Amirault, PO Box 248, Moncton, NB Canada E1C 8K9

CHICHESTER, DONALD WALLACE, minister; b. Amityville, N.Y., Aug. 23, 1933; s. Jesse Ketcham and Ingar Elizabeth (Schaller) C.; m. Jane A. Reid, Apr. 26, 1958; children: Deborah Louise, Elizabeth Mae, Stephen Wallace. BS in Applied Physics, Hofstra U., 1955; MDiv, Pitts. Theol. Sem., 1964. Ordained to ministry Presbyn. Ch. (U.S.A.), 1964. Asst. and interim pastor 6th Presbyn. Ch., Pitts., 1964-67; assoc. pastor lst Presbyn. Ch., Monongahela, Pa., 1967-68, Southampton, N.Y., 1968-72; pastor Eastminster United Presbyn. Ch., Erie, Pa., 1972-90, Gilbert (W.Va.) Presbyn. Ch., 1990—; commr. to Synod of Trinity, United Presbyn. Ch. (U.S.A.), 1976, mem. resource staff synod sch. Wilson Coll., 1976; former mem. L.I. Coun. Chs., Lake Erie Presbytery; mem. W.Va. Presbytery. Contbg. author: Contemporary Worship Services (James L. Christensen), 1971. Pres. bd. dirs. Erie Family and Child Svc., 1976-83. Recipient award for religious broadcasting L.I. Coun. Chs., 1972. Home: Wharncliffe Ave Box 1031 Gilbert WV 25621 Office: Box 496 Gilbert WV 25621 *In our tense and fast-paced world, I have found that humor is an effective means of releasing pressure, and giving a new perspective to our life's goals. Humor is a great healer.*

CHIKOSI, DAVIDSON, Bible Tng. Coll., 1989-90airport administrator, clergyman; b. Mutare, Manialand, Zimbabwe, Jan. 15, 1961; s. Davidson and Lois (Kanogoiwa) C. Student Inst. of Langs. and Acad. Studies, Zimbabwe, 1980. Aerodeommes' officer Civil Aviation Dept., Harare, Zimbabwe, 1982-83, airport mgr., Bulawayo, 1983-87; pastor Bulawayo Christian Centre Ch., 1987-88, dean of Christian Tng. coll., 1989-90; sales and buying mgr. Polywire Pvt. Ltd., 1991—; founder, sr. pastor Grace Christian Fellowship, 1991—; mng. dir. Pinnacle Supplies Pvt. Ltd., 1991—. Mem. Chartered Inst. Secs. Mem. Christian Ch. Avocations: lawn tennis, basketball, baseball. Home: 34 Park Rd, Darlington, Mutare Manicaland, Zimbabwe Office: 16 Munn Rd, Fortune's Gate Rd, Bulawayo Zimbabwe

CHILD, CHARLES JUDSON, JR., bishop; b. North Bergen, N.J., Apr. 25, 1923; s. Charles Judson and Alice Sylvia (Sparling) C. B.A., U. of the South, 1944, M.Div., 1947, D.D. (hon.), 1978; Lic. in Theology, St. Augustine Coll.-Eng., 1961. Ordained priest Episcopal Ch., 1948, bishop, 1978. Asst., St. Paul's Episc. Ch., Paterson, N.J., 1947-51; rector St. Bartholomew's Episc. Ch., Ho-Ho-Kus, N.J., 1951-67; canon pastor Cathedral of St. Philip, Atlanta, 1967-78; bishop suffragan Diocese of Atlanta, 1978-83, bishop, 1983-89. Home: 3138 Peachtree Dr NE Atlanta GA 30305 Office: Episcopal Diocese 2744 Peachtree Rd NE Atlanta GA 30363

CHILD, JOSEPH ALAN, minister; b. Gary, Ind., Jan. 6, 1959; s. Larry Gene and Dorothy Marcella (Walton) C.; m. Teri Lynn Geil, Nov. 10, 1979; children: Michael, Madison, Mackenzie. Diploma, Rhema Bible Tng. Ctr., 1982; BA summa cum laude, Bethel Christian Ctr., 1988, MRE magna cum laude, 1990. Ordained to ministry Rhema Ministerial Assn. Internat., 1989. Assoc. pastor Victory Christian Ctr., Palm Springs, Calif., 1986—; prof. grad. sch. theology, Bethel Christian Coll., Riverside, Calif., 1989—. Mem. Western States Ministerial Assn., Rhema Alumni Assn., Rhema Ministerial Assn. Internat. Republican. Home: PO Box 1595 Cathedral City CA 92235 Office: Victory Christian Ctr PO Box 5060 Palm Springs CA 92263 *A lifetime of success, riches, glory and honor cannot even remotely compare to the satisfaction and fulfillment of ten minutes in the true presence of God.*

CHILDRESS, CAROL SUE, research consultant; b. Springfield, Mo., July 10, 1948; d. Paul C. and Iva M. (Dampier) C. BA in Govt., Tex. Tech U., 1970; MA in Urban Studies, U. Tex., 1971; MDiv., S.W. Bapt. Theol. Sem., 1982. Ch. extension intern Bapt. Gen. Conv. Tex., Dallas, 1980-82, ch. planter apprentice, 1982-84, rsch. cons., 1984—; mem. world evangelism strategy work group Bapt. World Alliance, Fairfax, Va., 1990—. Mem. Am. Sociol. Assn., Soc. Religious Researchers, Am. Soc. Missionary, N.Am. Ch. Growth Soc., So. Demographic Assn. Office: Bapt Gen Conv Tex 333 N Washington Dallas TX 75246

CHILDRESS, JAMES FRANKLIN, theology and medical educator; b. Mt. Airy, N.C., Oct. 4, 1940; s. Roscoe Franklin and Zella Bessie (Wagoner) C.; m. Georgia Monroe Harrell, Dec. 21, 1958; children—(twins) Albert Franklin, James Frederic. B.A., Guilford Coll., N.C., 1962; B.D. cum laude, Yale Div. Sch, New Haven, 1965; M.A., Yale U., New Haven, 1967, Ph.D., 1968. Asst. prof. dept. religious studies U. Va.-Charlottesville, 1968-71; assoc. prof. dept. religious studies U. Va.-Charlottesville, 1971-75, chmn. dept. religious studies, 1972-75, 86—, prof. religious studies and med. edn., 1979—; prof. Christian ethics Kennedy Inst. Ethics, Georgetown U., Washington, 1975-79.; vis. prof. U. Chgo. Divinity Sch., 1977, Princeton U., 1978, Coll. Physicians and Surgeons, Columbia U., 1978; cons. and lectr. in field. Author: Priorities in Biomedical Ethics, 1981; Moral Responsibility in Conflicts, 1982; Who Should Decide?, Paternalism in Health Care, 1982; co-author: Principles of Biomedical Ethics, 1979, 1983, 1989; co-editor: Westminster Dictionary of Christian Ethics, 1986; contbr. chpts. to books, articles to profl. jours. Trustee Guilford Coll., Greensboro, N.C., 1983-85; mem. subcom. on human gene therapy NIH, Bethesda, Md., 1984—, mem. NIH recombinant DNA adv. com., 1988-90; mem. Biomed. Ethics Adv. Com., 1988-89; vice-chmn. Task Force on Organ Transplantation, HHS, 1985-86; bd. dirs. United Network for Organ Sharing, 1987-89. Recipient numerous awards and grants in field including Disting. Prof. award U. Va., 1984, Va. Prof. of Yr. award Coun. for Advancement and Support Edn., 1990; Am. Coun. Learned Socs. fellow, 1972-73, Wilson Ctr. fellow, 1984-85, Guggenheim fellow, 1984-85. Fellow Inst. Soc. Ethics and Life Scis., Am. Acad. Arts and Scis.; mem. Soc. Christian Ethics (bd. dirs. 1973-76), Am. Theol. Soc., Am. Philos. Assn. Democrat. Quaker. Avocations: tennis; reading; music. Office: U Va Dept Religious Studies Charlottesville VA 22903

CHILDS, BREVARD SPRINGS, religious educator; b. Columbia, S.C., Sept. 2, 1923; s. Richard A. and Reaux (Jones) C.; m. Ann Taylor, Aug. 7, 1954; children—John, Catherine. BA, U. Mich., 1946, MA, 1948; BD, Princeton, 1950; ThD, U. Basel, Switzerland, 1955; DD, U. Aberdeen, Scotland, 1984. Ordained to ministry Presbyn. Ch., 1958. Prof. O.T., Mission House Sem., Plymouth, Wis., 1954-58; prof. religion Yale U., New Haven, 1958—. Author: Myth and Reality in the Old Testament, 1960, Memory and Tradition in Israel, 1962, Isaiah and the Assyrian Crisis, 1967, Biblical Theology in Crisis, 1970, The Book of Exodus, 1974, Old Testament Books for Pastor and Teacher, 1977, Introduction to the Old Testament as Scripture, 1979, the New Testament as Canon: An Introduction, 1985, Old Testament Theology in a Canonical Context, 1986. Served with AUS, 1943-45. Guggenheim fellow, 1963-64; Nat. Endowment for Humanities fellow, 1977-78; Fulbright-Hays fellow, 1981; Deutscher Akademischer Austauschdienst fellow, 1987. Home: 508 Amity Rd Bethany CT 06525 Office: 409 Prospect St New Haven CT 06511

CHILDS, GARY LEE, minister; b. Indpls., July 11, 1959; s. Robert George and Virginia Joyce (Byrd) C.; m. Anita Ruth Strohschein, July 25, 1981; children: Aaron, Eric, Kathleen. BSW, Valparaiso (Ind.) U., 1981; MDiv, Concordia Sem., 1987. Dir. youth guidance Youth for Christ, Valparaiso, 1980-83; pastor Zion Luth. Ch., Bogalusa, La., 1987-89; assoc. pastor St. Matthew Luth. Ch., Bel Air, Md., 1989—; asst. chaplain Luth. Mission Soc., Balt., 1990—; chaplain CAP, Bogalusa, 1987-89. Bd. dirs. Sunshine Town Boys Home, Bogalusa, 1988, 89; active Bogalusa Diamond Jubilee, 1989. Republican. Office: St Matthew Luth Ch 1200 Churchville Rd Bel Air MD 21014

CHILSTROM, HERBERT WALFRED, bishop; b. Litchfield, Minn., Oct. 18, 1931; s. Walfred Emanuel and Ruth (Lindell) C.; m. Ella Corinne Hansen, June 12, 1954; children: Mary, Christopher. BA, Augsburg Coll., Mpls., 1954; BD, Augustana Theol. Sem., Rock Island, Ill., 1958; ThM, Princeton Theol. Sem., 1966; EdD, NYU, 1976; DD (hon.), Northwestern Luth. Theol. Sem., Mpls., 1979, Gustavus Adolphus Coll., 1987, Capital U., Columbus, Ohio, 1988, Wittenberg U., 1988, Gettysburg (Pa.) Coll., 1988, Midland (Nebr.) Coll., 1988, Newberry (S.C.) Coll., 1989; LHD (hon.), Capitol U., 1988. Ordained to ministry Luth. Ch., 1958. Pastor Faith Luth. Ch., Pelican Rapids, Minn., 1958-62; prof., acad. dean Luther Coll., Teaneck, N.J., 1962-70; sr. pastor First Luth. Ch., St. Peter, Minn, 1970-76; pres., bishop Minn. Synod, Luth. Ch. Am., Mpls., 1976-87, mem. exec. council, 1978-82; pres., bishop Evang. Luth. Ch. in Am., Chgo., 1987—; mem. Faith and Order Commn. Nat. Council Chs., N.Y.C., 1982; mem. Commn. for a New Lutheran Ch., 1982-86; v.p. Luth. World Fedn., 1990—. Author: Hebrews, A New and Better Way, 1984, When We Reach for the Sun, 1986, Foundation in the Future, 1987. Decorated Royal Order of North Star (Sweden); recipient Pub. Service award Suomi Coll., Hancock, Mich, 1979, Disting. Alumnus citation Augsburg Coll., Mpls., 1979. Avocations: photography; golf; travel; picture framing; fishing. Office: Evang Luth Ch Am 8765 W Higgins Rd Chicago IL 60631

CHILTON, BRUCE DAVID, theologian, religion educator, minister; b. Roslyn, N.Y., Sept. 27, 1949; s. Bruce David and Virginia Marie (Bové) C.; m. Odile Juilette Micheline Sevault, July 3, 1982; 1 child, Samuel Georges Norbert. AB, Bard Coll., 1971; MDiv, Gen. Theol. Sem., 1974; PhD, Cambridge (Eng.) U., 1976. Ordained to ministry Episcopal Ch., 1974. Lectr. Sheffield U., Eng., 1976-85; assoc. prof. Yale Divinity Sch., New Haven, 1985-86, Lillian Claus assoc. prof., 1986-87; prof. religion Bard Coll., Annandale, N.Y., 1987-89, Bernard Iddings Bell prof. religion, 1990—; rector Ch. of St. John the Evangelist, Barrytown, N.Y., 1987—. Author: A Galilean Rabbi, 1984, Targumic Approaches to the Gospels, 1986, The Isaiah Targum, 1987, Jesus and the Ethics, 1988, Profiles of a Rabbi, 1989; editor Studiorum Novi Testamenti Societas, 1990—, Inst. for Bibl. Rsch., 1989—. Episc. Ch. Found. rsch. fellow, 1974, Edelman fellow, 1981; Aidan scholar St. John's Coll., Cambridge U., 1974, Heinrich Hertz scholar, Fed. Republic Germany, 1981. Mem. Soc. Bibl. Lit. Office: Bard Coll Annandale NY 12504 *God is not as much defined by the angle of our perspective as by the direction of our movement.*

CHILTON, CLAUDE LYSIAS, minister, former career officer; b. N.Y.C., Feb. 19, 1917; s. Claude Lysias and Clara Caroline (Weidman) C.; m. Juanita Christine Eastis, Aug. 17, 1939; children: Robert Hamilton, Claudia Jeanne Britt, Linda Christine Morgan. BTh, Bethany Nazarene Coll. (now So. Nazarene U.), 1939, BA, 1940; MA, Calif. Grad. Sch. Theology, Glendale, 1974, PhD, 1975. Ordained to ministry Ch. of the Nazarene, 1939. Pastor Ch. of the Nazarene, Ala., Okla, Ohio, 1936-43, Calif., Ala., 1946-51, Phoenix, 1971-79; ret. Ch. of the Nazarene, 1982; commd. 1st lt. U.S. Army, 1943-46; recalled to active duty as capt. USAF, 1951, advanced through grades to lt. col., 1962, chaplain various Air Force bases, 1951-71, ret., 1971. Author: The Nazarene Serviceman, 1953, Chaplains in Mission: Fifty Years of Ministry, 1992; co-author: Chaplains See World Missions, 1946; contbr. articles to profl. jours. Trustee Trevecca Nazarene Coll., Nashville, 1949-52; pres. Mobile Ministerial Assn., Ala., 1950-51; active ministerial assns., Phoenix, 1976—. Recipient various mil. decorations and awards. Mem. Air Force Assn., Ret. Officers Assn., Christian Holiness Assn., Nat. Assn. Evangels., Wesleyan Theol. Soc., Mil. Chaplains Assn. Republican. Avocation: collecting more than 14,000 different religious periodicals. Home: 13215 N 56th Ave Glendale AZ 85304 *Time and experience have convinced* *me that the two most indispensable components of human personality required to be socially responsible, emotionally stable and spiritually sound are INTEGRITY and ACCOUNTABILITY.*

CHILTON, DAVID LEE, lay worker; b. Newport News, Dec. 21, 1954; s. Robert Gregg and Ruth Lee (Martin) C.; m. Carol Cotton, Dec. 13, 1980. BS, USCG Acad., 1979; MA in History, Rice U., Houston, 1990. Lay worker St. Paul's United Meth. Ch., Houston, 1985-89; lay worker First United Meth. Ch., Charlotte, N.C., 1989-90, sec. coun. on ministries, 1990—; history tchr. N.W. Cabarrus High Sch., Concord, N.C., 1990—. With USCG, 1974-85. Mem. Nat. Coun. on Religion and Pub. Edn., World History Assn. Home: 1538 Clayton Dr Charlotte NC 28203

CHIMY, JEROME ISIDORE, bishop; b. Radway, Alta., Can., Mar. 12, 1919; s. Stanley and Anna (Yahnij) C. J.C.D., Lateran U., Rome, 1966. Ordained priest Ukrainian Cath. Ch., 1944; consecrated bishop, 1974; consultor to Provincial Superior, 1958-61; sec. to Superior Gen. of Basilian Order, Rome, 1961-63; consultor Superior Gen. of Basilian Order, 1963-74; rector St. Josaphat Ukrainian Pontifical Coll., Rome, 1966-74; former consultor to Sacred Congregation for Eastern Chs.; former commissario for matrimonial cases at Sacred Congregation for Doctrine of Faith; bishop of New Westminster B.C., Can., 1974—; consultor to Pontifical Comm. for Revision Oriental Canon Law. Author: De Figura Luridica Archiepiscopi Maioris in Iure Canonico Orientali Vigenti, 1968. Home and Office: 502 5th Ave, New Westminster, BC Canada V3L 1S2

CHING, ANDY KWOK-YEE, minister; b. Shanghai, People's Republic of China, Apr. 12, 1956; arrived in Hong Kong, 1961; arrived in Can., 1973; came to U.S., 1989.; s. Jan Wai and Hon Wah (Kwan) C.; m. Rosita Wai-Mui Tsoi, June 4, 1989. B of Applied Sci., U. Toronto, 1981; M of Theol. Studies, Ontario Theol. Sem., 1982; DD, Internat. Sem., 1988. Ordained to ministry Chinese Christian Alliance Chs., 1989. Asst. pastor North York Chinese Bapt. Ch., Willowdale, Ont., Can., 1982-83; interim pastor Montreal Chinese Bapt. Ch., Quebec, Can., 1984; lit. coord. Christian Reformed Ch., Toronto, Ont., 1988; gen. sec. Harvester Evangelical Press, Willowdale, 1985-89; pastor Chinese Christian Alliance Ch., Northridge, Calif., 1989—; bd. dirs., Harvester Evangelical Press, 1985—; guest lectr., Christ Internat. Theol. Sem., Alhambra, Calif., 1990—; reporter, mem., Evangelical Press. Assn., Canoga Park, 1990—; tchr. trainer, Evangelical Tchr. Tng. Assn., Wheaton, Ill., 1989—; interpreter, Toronto Bd. Edn., 1986-88, instr,m 1986-87. Editor: Onward Christian Soldiers, Toronto, 1982, Three Episodes of Life, 1982; translator (books) Reasons to Believe, 1988, Called to Ministry, 1989; contbr. articles to profl. jours. Vol. Scott Missions to Native People, Toronto, 1983-84. Mem. Internat. Missions Inc. Office: Chinese Christian Alliance Ch 18827 Roscoe Northridge CA 91325 *The two Josephs in the Old and New Testament teach us one thing: there is a price to pay if we want to actualize the dreams given by God.*

CHING, JULIA, religion educator; b. Shanghai, China, Oct. 15, 1934; came to Can., 1951; d. William Ching and Christina Ching Tsao; m. Willard G. Oxtoby, 1981. PhD, Australian Nat. U., Canberra, 1972. Prof. U. Toronto (Ont., Can.), 1978—. Author: Confucianism and Christianity, 1977 (Outstanding Acad. Book of Yr., Choice), Probing China's Soul, 1990; co-author: Christianity and Chinese Religions, 1989. Trustee United Bd. for Christian Higher Edn. in Asia, N.Y., 1977-86; co-organizer Spirit of Asia Pacific Gala, Toronto, 1990; co-pres. 33d Internat. Congress for Asian and N.African Studies, Toronto, 1990. Fellow Royal Soc. Can.; mem. Am. Soc. for Study of Religion. Office: U Toronto, Victoria Coll, Toronto, ON Canada M5S 1K7

CHINNICI, JOSEPH PATRICK, priest; b. Altadena, Calif., Mar. 16, 1945; s. Gregory Francis and Lucile Elizabeth (Rogers) C. BA, San Luis Rey Coll., 1968; MA, Grad. Theol. Union, Berkeley, Calif., 1971; MDiv, Franciscan Sch. Theology, Berkeley, Calif., 1972; PhD, Oxford U., Eng., 1976. Joined Franciscan Friars, 1966; ordained priest Roman Cath. Ch., 1972. Prof. ch. history Franciscan Sch. Theology, Berkeley, 1980—; vicar provincial St. Barbara province Franciscan Friars, Oakland, Calif., 1984-88, provincial, 1988—; Cath. Daus. of the Ams. vis. prof. Cath. U. Am., 1987. Author: The English Catholic Enlightenment, 1980, Living Stones: The History and Structure of Catholic Spiritual Life in the United States, 1989; author, editor: Devotion to the Holy Spirit in American Catholicism, 1985. Grantee NEH, 1977, U. Notre Dame, 1979. Mem. Am. Hist. Assn., Am. Cath. Hist. Assn. Home and Office: 1712 Euclid Ave Berkeley CA 94709

CHIN-TSUNG-CHIEN, JOHN, bishop. Bishop Anglican Communion, Taipei, Taiwan. Office: Bishop Taiwan, 7 Lane 105, Hangchow South Rd, Sec 3, Taipei 10763, Taiwan*

CHIONA, JAMES, archbishop. Archbishop of Blantyre Malawi; pres. Episcopal Conf. Malawi. Office: Episcopal Conf Cath Sec, Capital City/ POB 30384, Lilongwe 3, Malawi*

CHIPHANGWI, S. D., religious organization administrator. Chmn. Christian Coun. of Malawi, Lilongwe. Office: Christian Coun Malawi, Capital City, POB 30068, Lilongwe 3, Malawi*

CHIPLEY, BENJAMIN NED, minister; b. Carthage, Miss., Apr. 24, 1935; s. William Everett and Lilla Gertrude (Ivey) C.; m. Martha Ann Veal, Aug. 29, 1954; children: Benjamin Evered, Debra Sue McDowell, Brent Dwaine. BS, East Tex. State U., 1960. Ordained to ministry Meth. Ch., 1954. Dir. dept. home missions Congl. Meth. Ch., Florence, Miss., 1961-72; sec. Gen. Conf. of Congl. Meth. Chs., Florence, 1964-72; founder, pastor Wesleyan Bible Ch., Dallas, 1973—; editor The Messenger Congl. Meth. Ch., Dallas, 1985-86. Mem. S.E. Dallas C. of C. (life). Home: 318 Crenshaw Dr Dallas TX 75217 Office: Wesleyan Bible Ch 10747 Bruton Rd Dallas TX 75217

CHIPMAN, CHARLES JOSEPH, minister; b. Sycamore, Kans., Feb. 2, 1931; s. Charles Claude and Mary Alice (Potts) C.; m. Alicia Lopez, June 13, 1954 (div. 1958); m. Margaret Elaine Keiser, June 7, 1959; children: Gary (dec.), Ulrich, Karen, Tony, Michael, Dennis. BA, York Coll. (now Westmar Coll.), 1953; MDiv, United Theol. Sem., 1957; postgrad., U. Dayton, 1957-58. Ordained to ministry United Meth. Ch., 1961. Pastor Detroit and Bethany United Meth. Ch., Detroit, Kans., 1962-68, 1st United Meth. Ch., Syracuse, Kans., 1968-75, St. Paul's United Meth. Ch., Wichita, Kans., 1975—; del. World Meth. Coun., Dublin, Ireland, 1976, Honolulu, 1981, coun. mem., Nairobi, Kenya, 1986, Singapore, 1991. Active AIDS Community Edn. Ctr., Wichita, 1985—; chair Sedgwick-Wichita Drug Adv. Bd., 1990; mem. Wichita Housing Adv. Bd., 1990, Outside Connection Prison Ministry, Wichita, 1990; exec. com. Inter-Faith Ministries, Wichita, 1990. Recipient award for effective ministry United Theol. Sem., 1983, Good Neighbor award Mid Town Assn., Wichita, 1988. Home: 1433 Park Pl Wichita KS 67203 Office: St Paul's United Meth Ch 1356 N Broadway Wichita KS 67214 *It is by God's Grace, not our attempts at being holy, that each of us is locked in God's Heart. It is also God's continuing gift that persons will come into our lives, and through them we may more fully experience God's grace.*

CHIRICO, PETER FRANCIS, priest, theologian; b. Bklyn., May 4, 1927; s. Peter Francis and Anna Marian (Marotta) C. BA, St. John's U., 1952; STL, St. Mary's Sem., 1956; STD, Gregorianum, Rome, 1960. Ordained priest Roman Cath. Ch., 1956. Assoc. to prof. of systematic theology St. Thomas Sem., Kenmore, Wash., 1960-69, prof. systematics, 1976-77; prof. systematics St. Patrick's Sem., Menlo Park, Calif., 1969-76, 86-89; theologian in residence Archdiocese of Seattle, 1977-86, 89—; mem. theol. commn. Wash. State Cath. Conf., 1989—. Author: Infallibillity: The Crossroads of Doctrine, 1977; contbr. articles to profl. jours. With U.S. Army, 1945-46. Mem. Cath. Theol. Soc. Am. (bd. dirs. 1987-89).

CHIRISA, FARAI JONAH, minister; b. Chivhu, Zimbabwe, May 29, 1940; m. Gladys Pazuichaenda, Aug. 19, 1972; children: Shingirai, Tapiwa, Chipo, Ngoni. Student, Mutare Tchrs. Coll., 1961-62; diploma in theology, United Theol. Coll., Harare, Zimbabwe, 1967; BA in Theol., Hartley Victoria U., Manchester, Eng., 1977. Ordained to ministry Meth. Ch., 1971. Cir. min. Meth. Ch., Norton, Eng., 1968-70, Bulawayo, Zimbabwe, 1971-74, Harare, Zimbabwe, 1974—; bishop Meth. Ch., 1986—; sec. conf. Meth. Ch., Harare, 1983-86; vice prin. United Theol. Coll., Harare, 1985-86; mem. exec. com. Zimbabwe Christian Coun., 1986—. Mem. World Meth. Coun., World Coun. Chs. (exec. com.). Home: #6 Clare Rd Avondale, Harare Zimbabwe Office: Meth Ch Connexional Office, 7 Central Ave PO Box 8298, Causeway Harare Zimbabwe

CHISHOLM, WALTER SAMUEL, minister; b. East Cleveland, Ohio, Oct. 16, 1926; s. Walter J. and Anna Mae (Wagoner) C.; m. Patricia Joan West, Dec. 27, 1950; children: Shirli Ann, Walter Steven, Patti Liane. BS in Edn., Kent State U., 1950; MDiv, Northwestern U., 1964; D in Ministry, Drew U., 1984. Ordained to ministry United Meth. Ch. Pastor Culver (Ind.) Emmanuel, 1961-64, Montrose-Zion United Meth. Ch., Akron, Ohio, 1964-75; supt. Painsville (Ohio) dist. East Ohio Conf. United Meth. Ch., 1975-81; pastor Epworth Euclid United Meth. Ch., Cleve., 1981-83, Norwalk (Ohio) First United Meth. Ch., 1983—; chmn. Akron Dist. Coun. on Ministry, 1974-75; conf. sec. EOC Bd. Global Ministry, North Canton, Ohio, 1972-75; pres. bd. trustees Elyria (Ohio) Meth. Home, 1988—.0. Pres. Univ. Circle Housing, Cleve., 1982-83; v.p. Norwalk Area United Way, 1990—. Petty officer 3d class USN, 1944-46, PTO. Named Citizen of Yr. City of Fairlawn, Ohio, 1971; recipient Pioneer Svc. award Elyria United Meth. Home, 1989. Mem. Am. Assn. Homes Aging, Nat. Assn. United Meth. Men, Fairlawn C. of C. (pres. 1974-75), Kiwanis (pres. Portage lakes club 1960-61). Home: 117 W Main St Norwalk OH 44857 Office: First United Meth Ch 60 W Main St Norwalk OH 44857

CHISHOLM, WILLIAM DEWAYNE, retired contract manager; b. Everett, Wash., Mar. 1, 1924; s. James Adam and Evelyn May (Iles) C.; m. Esther Troehler, Mar. 10, 1956; children: James Scott, Larry Alan, Brian Duane. BS in ChemE, U. Wash., 1949, BS in Indsl. Engring., 1949; MBA, Harvard U., 1955. Chemist, unit leader, tech. rep. The Coca-Cola Co., Atlanta and Los Angeles, 1949-59; contract adminstr. Honeywell Inc., Los Angeles, 1959-61, mktg. adminstr., 1961-64, contracts work dir., 1964-66, contracts mgr., Clearwater, Fla., 1966-73, contracts supr., 1973-75, sr. contract mgmt. rep., 1975-80, prin. contract mgmt. rep., work dir., 1980-82, contracts mgr., 1982-89; ret.; chmn. bd. Creative Attitudes, Inc., 1987—; adj. faculty Fla. Inst. Tech., 1976—. Contbr. articles to profl. jours. Trustee, John Calvin Found., 1974-82; mem. budget adv. com. City of Clearwater, 1983-85; commr. to 196th gen. assembly Presbyn. Ch. (USA), 1984; sec. bd. trustees, treas. Presbytery of Tampa Bay, 1990—, City of Clearwater rep. on the Long Ctr. Bd. Dirs., 1991—. With USN, 1944-46. Cert. profl. contracts mgr. Recipient Award of Distinction Fla. Inst. Tech. Grad. Ctr., 1987. Fellow Nat. Contract Mgmt. Assn. (chmn. S.E. region fellows 1985-87, past nat. dir., pres., v.p. Suncoast chpt.). Republican. Presbyterian (elder session mem. 1964-65, 73-76, 77-80, 81-84, 86-90). Club: Breakfast Optimist of Clearwater (dir. 1982—, disting. sec.-treas. 1983-84, disting. pres. 1984-85). Home: 1364 Hercules Ave S Clearwater FL 34624 *We can't be too generous in sharing understanding and words of comfort, encouragement, and support to those facing adversity and challenge at various times in their lives.*

CHISNELL, JOHN GILBERT, SR., clergyman; b. Atlanta, Jan. 19, 1938; s. John Patrick and Ada Inez (Key) C.; m. Harriet Blanche Popham, Mar. 10, 1958; children: Lisa Renae, John Gilbert, Kellie Jean, Julia Lynnette. BA in Bible, Beulah Heights Bible Coll., Atlanta, 1973; student, Evang. Theol. Sem., Goldsboro, N.C., 1978-79. Ordained to ministry Assemblies of God Ch., 1975. Missionary tchr. Am. Indian Bible Inst., Phoenix, 1973-78; missionary, dir. NW Indian Bible Inst, Port Angeles, Wash., 1978-84; pastor Forest Park (Ga.) Assy. of God, 1984-86, Glad Tidings Assy. of God, Dexter, Ga., 1986—; petitioner Teen Challenge Ctr., Atlanta, 1970-71; mem. bd. adminstrn. Am. Indian Bible Inst., 1977-78, mem. curriculum com., 1975-78; founder continuing edn. Advanced Ministers Inst., 1980. Presbyter Dublin sect. Ga. Dist. Council Assys. of God, 1986—; chaplain Clayton Gen. Hosp., 1984—. Served with USAF, 1955-64. Club: Greenacres Golf (Dexter). Avocation: golf. Office: Glad Tidings Assembly of God S Nam St PO Box 26 Dexter GA 91019

CHITTENDEN-BASCOM, CATHLEEN, priest; b. Denver, Jan. 27, 1962; d. Bruce Eugene and Marilyn (Ward) Chittenden; m. Timothy Paul Bascom, Nov. 27, 1987. BA in English Lit. with distinction, U. Kans., 1984; MDiv, Seabury-Western U., 1990; MA in English Lit., Exeter (Eng.) U., 1991. Ordained priest Episcopal Ch., 1991. Coord. Logan Sq. Arts and Scis., Chgo., 1987-89; asst. priest St. Gregory's Episcopal Ch., Deerfield, Ill., 1990—. Editor mag. Crossroads, 1988-89. Mem. S.E. Lake County Clergy Assn. Democrat. Office: St Gregory's Episcopal Ch Deerfield and Wilmot Rds Deerfield IL 60015 *The "American Dream" is both crude and beautiful. Yet I see through its cracks a more lasting Mystery: a word spoken through prophets, a love made flesh which waits to save America too.*

CHITTY, MONTE L., minister; b. Alice, Tex., Sept. 26, 1961; s. Alfred L. and Sherry Louise (Martin) C.; m. Sylvia Ann Bohrn, Nov. 16, 1983; children: Jessica, Roger, Rachael. BA in Bible Studies, Hannibal (Mo.)-Lagrange Coll., 1991. Pastor 1st Bapt. Ch., Plainville, Ill., 1989—. Home: 208 North Ave Plainville IL 62356

CHIU, PETER CHING-TAI, religious organization administrator; b. China, July 23, 1944; came to U.S., 1968; s. Ping-Kee and Chun-Yuk (Yim) Yau; m. Josephine C. Chiu, May 27, 1970; children: Nia, Joshua, Caleb. BA in Fgn. Languages and Literatures, Nat. Taiwan U., 1965; MEd in Counseling, No. Tex. State U., 1970; EdD, Columbia U., 1975. Lic. marriage, family and child counselor, Calif. Chmn. dept. psychology Chung Yuan U., Chung-Li, Taiwan, 1975-79; dir. dept. counseling Chinese Christian Mission, Petaluma, Calif., 1979-86, asst. to gen. sec., 1988-90; dir. San Francisco counseling ctr. Chinese Christian Mission, 1981-86; marriage and family counselor Family Wellness Ctr. Tunghai U., Taichung, Taiwan, 1986-88; pres. Chinese Family for Christ, Hayward, Calif., 1990—; visiting prof. China Evang. Sem., Taipei, Taiwan, 1986-88. Mem. Am., Calif. assns. Marriage and Family Therapists. Home: 744 E Charleston Rd Palo Alto CA 94303 Office: Chinese Family for Christ 22416 Meekland Ave Hayward CA 94541

CHLAPEK, MARVIN, religious organization administrator. Pres. Unity of the Brethren, Pasadena, Tex. Office: Unity of Brethren 2513 Revere Dr Pasadena TX 77502*

CHO, DAVID DONG-JIN, missiologist; b. Pyung Buk, Republic of Korea, Dec. 19, 1924; s. Sang Hang Cho; married; children: Eung Chun, Eung Soon, Eung Oak, Eung Sun, Eun Hea. BD, Presbyn. Sem., Seoul, Republic of Korea, 1949; ThM, Asbury Sem., Wilmore, Ky., 1960; DD (hon.), Belhaven Coll., 1979, Asbury Sem., 1981. Chief editor Christian Weekly News, Seoul, Republic of Korea, 1951-54; gen. sec. Korean Evang. Fellowship, Seoul, Republic of Korea, 1953-57; pres. Korea Internat. Mission, Seoul, Republic of Korea, 1968—; gen. dir. East-West Ctr. Missions, Seoul, Republic of Korea, 1973—; gen. sec. Asia Missions Assn., Seoul, Republic of Korea, 1973-86; coordinating dir. Billy Graham Seoul Crusade, Seoul, Republic of Korea, 1973; pres. Cen. Coll. Social Industries, Dae-Jeoun, Republic of Korea, 1984—; chmn. Joint Council Third World Missions Advance, Pasadena, Calif., 1986—. Author: Church Administrations, 1963, New Forces in Mission, 1976, The Third Forces, 1986; editor jour. Asia Missions Advance, 1977—. Home: CPO Box 2732, Seoul 100, Republic of Korea Office: Korea Internat Mission, CPO Box 3476, Seoul 100, Republic of Korea also: PO Box 40288 Pasadena CA 91104

CHOATE, MITCHELL KENT, minister; b. Tulsa, Mar. 10, 1960; s. Doyle and Jo Ann (Dunn) C.; m. Carmen Lyn Cunningham, Oct. 9, 1982; children: Kendall Thomas, Kyle Evan. BA, Okla. Bapt. U., 1982; MA, Southwestern Bapt. Theol. Sem., 1985. Min. youth Connell Bapt. Ch., Ft. Worth, 1983-85, Field St. Bapt. Ch., Cleburne, Tex., 1985-88, Pioneer Dr. Bapt. Ch., Abilene, Tex., 1988—; conf. leader Bapt. Gen. Conv. Tex., Dallas, 1987-91, Women's Missionary Union Tex., Dallas, 1989-91, Sunday Sch. Bd., So. Bapt. Conv., Nashville, 1990. Mem. Nat. Network Youth Ministries, Johnson Bapt. Assn. (dir. youth 1986-88), Abilene Bapt. Assn. (dir. youth 1991—). Avocations: racquetball, golf, collecting baseball cards. Office: Pioneer Dr Bapt Ch 701 S Pioneer St Abilene TX 79605

CHOCK, STEPHEN K(AN) L(EONG), minister; b. Honolulu, Nov. 10, 1955; s. Leon L.O. and Gertrude Y. C. BS in Human Devel., U. Hawaii, 1980; MA in Psychology, Ohio State U., 1984, PhD in Psychology, 1988. Lic. psychologist, Tex. Internat. student Bible study leader Great Commn. Ch., Mpls., 1985; discussion group leader Great Commn. Ch., Columbus, Ohio, 1985-87; home group leader Grace Community Ch., Dallas, 1988; youth minister Grace Community Ch., Plano, Tex., 1989—; psychologist Minirth-Meier Clinic, Richardson, Tex., 1990—; bd. advisors Grace Community Ch., Plano, 1989—; pastor intern Great Commn. Assn. of Chs., Dallas, 1990—; lectr. in field. Contbr. articles to profl. jours. Ohio State U. Minority fellow, 1982. Mem. Am. Psychol. Assn., Dallas Psychol. Assn. Republican. Office: Minirth-Meier Clinic 2100 N Collins Blvd Richardson TX 75080 *Daily experiencing of God's unconditional acceptance and unlimited love and grace in Jesus Christ frees me to live my life to the fullest and help others experience the same. This is the abundant life.*

CHODOS, ROBERT IRWIN, editor, writer; b. Montreal, Que., Can., Mar. 16, 1947; s. Louis and Constance (Routtenberg) C.; m. Andrea Ceil Leis, Dec. 26, 1977; children: Sarah, David. BSc in Math. with honors, McGill U., Montreal, 1967; postgrad., Johns Hopkins U., 1967-68; MA in Liberal Arts, Clark U., 1990. Freelance book editor, 1976—, translator Que. social sci. books, 1980—; prin., tchr. Temple Shalom Religious Sch., Kitchener, Ont., Can., 1986—; editor briefings This Magazine, Toronto, Ont., 1986—; editor Compass: A Jesuit Jour., Toronto, 1987—; adj. instr. English Fisher Jr. Coll., Clinton, Mass., 1983-84; instr. journalism Conestoga Coll., Kitchener, 1985. Author: Right-of-Way: Passenger Trains for Canada's Future, 1971, The CPR: A Century of Corporate Welfare, 1973, The Caribbean Connection, 1977; co-author: Winners, Losers: The 1976 Tory Convention, 1976, Your Place or Mine?, 1978, Brian Mulroney: The Boy from Baie-Comeau, 1984, Write All About It, 1986, Selling Out: Four Years of the Mulroney Government, 1988, The Unmaking of Canada, 1991, Quebec and the American Dream, 1991; co-editor: Quebec: A Chronicle 1968-72, 1972, Let Us Prey, 1974; mem. editorial bd. Last Post mag., 1969-80, parliamentary corr., 1971-72, 76-77, news editor, 1972-74; rsch. cons. CBC radio and TV, 1974-79; contbr. numerous articles to profl. jours. Recipient 1st pl. awards Can. Ch. Press, 1990, 91, Cath. Press Assn., 1990, 91. Jewish. Avocations: travel, folk music. Home: PO Box 1311, New Hamburg, ON Canada N0B 2G0 Office: Compass: A Jesuit Jour, 10 St Mary St Ste 300, Toronto, ON Canada M4Y 1P9

CHOE, VICTOR HEE SEUNG, lay church worker, architectural company executive; b. Seoul, Republic of Korea, Mar. 2, 1963; came to U.S., 1974; s. Myung S. and Chang Soon (Son) C. BArch, Calif. State Poly. U., Pomona, 1987. Dir. youth Agape United Presbyn. Ch., Los Alamitos, Calif., 1982-86, Monterey Park (Calif.) United Meth. Ch., 1987—; gen. mgr. Advance Architects & Devel., L.A., 1987—. Home: 3933 Marathon St #202B Los Angeles CA 90029 Office: Advance Architects & Devel 4643 W Beverly Blvd #201 Los Angeles CA 90004

CHOI, CHAN-YOUNG, minister, religious organization administrator; b. Pyong Yang, Korea, Sept. 16, 1926; came to U.S., 1971; m. Kwang Kim, Nov. 24, 1954; children: Samuel, Helen, Mizar, Daniel. BTh, Presbyn. Theol. Sem., Seoul, Republic of Korea, 1951; BA, Hong Ik U., Seoul, 1954; EdM, U. Pitts., 1962; MDiv, Pitts. Theol. Sem., 1962; DD (hon.), Calif. Grad. Sch. Theology, 1991. Ordained to ministry Presbyn. Ch. Korea, 1952. Missionary to Thailand Presbyn. Ch. Korea, 1955-70; gen. sec. Bible Socs. in Thailand, Bangkok, 1962-70; distbn. sec. Am. Bible Soc., 1971-74; cons. mktg. Asia Pacific region United Bible Socs., Manila, 1974-77, coord. mktg., 1977-78; regional sec. United Bible Socs., Hong Kong, 1978—; chmn. Printing Co., Ltd. of United Bible Socs., Hong Kong, 1987—; vice chmn. Amity Printing Co., Ltd., Nanping, Republic of China, 1987—; fraternal del. Christian Ch. of Asia., Hong Kong, 1991, others; speaker, lectr. various profl. meetings; prin. Korean sch. for Korean children, Bangkok, 1962-66. Subject of film This High Calling, 1954, Better Than Fine Gold, 1970. Chaplain Republic of Korea Army, 1952-55. Office: United Bible Socs, 1001-2 S Seas Centre Tower 1, Hong Kong Hong Kong

CHOI, THOMAS SUNGSOO, minister; b. Los Angeles, Jan. 24, 1958; s. Young Yong and In Soon (Shin) C. BA, Pomona Coll., Claremont, Calif., 1979; M Div., Yale U., 1986. Ordained deacon United Meth. Ch., 1985. Assoc. minister Westwood United Meth. Ch., Los Angeles, 1986—; mem. communications com. Calif. Pacific Annual Conf., United Meth. Ch., Pasadena, Calif., 1988—. Mem. Korean Am. Coalition, Los Angeles, 1986, del. Supporters Fingerprint Refusers for Japan, 1988. Democrat. Office: Westwood United Meth Ch 10497 Wilshire Blvd Los Angeles CA 90024

CHOLODOWSKI, SISTER ANTONIA MARIE, religious organization administrator; b. Norwich, Conn., Aug. 8, 1932; d. Dominic Francis and Joanna Mary (Przekop) C. BA, Holy Family Coll., 1962; MS Counselor of Edn., Marywood Coll., 1973. Joined Sisters of the Holy Family of Nazareth, Roman Cath. Ch., 1950; cert. elem. tchr. Tchr. St. John Cantius Sch., Phila., 1953-60, St. Mary Sch., Ambler, Pa., 1960-67; child care worker St. Mary Villa for Children, Ambler, 1960-67; prin. Queen of Peace Sch., Ardsley, Pa., 1967-73, Our Lady Calvary Sch., Phila., 1973-79; dir. ministry Sisters of the Holy Family of Nazareth, Phila., 1979-90; asst. adminstr. St. Mary Villa for Children, Ambler, Pa., 1990—, trustee, 1979-90. Trustee Nazareth Hosp., Phila., 1979-90, Holy Family Coll., Phila., 1979-90, Nazareth Acad., Phila., 1979-90. Home and Office: St Mary Villa for Children Bethlehem Pike Ambler PA 19002

CHOMSKY, JACK (STEVEN), cantor; b. N.Y.C., May 9, 1955; s. William Alexander Chomsky and Doris Mae (Bobker) C.; m. Susan Gellman, July 4, 1982; children: Benjamin Gellman-Chomsky, Addie Gellman-Chomsky. AB, Brown U., 1977; BSM, Hazzan, Jewish Theol. Sem., 1982. Cantor Congregation Tifereth Israel, Columbus, Ohio, 1982—. Editor Jour. of Synagogue Music, 1989—. Mem. mus. adv. panel Ohio Arts Coun., Columbus, 1989-91, chair, 1991—. Recipient Community award of excellence Columbus Jewish Fedn., 1985. Mem. Cantors Assembly (chair Tri-State Region Pa., Mich., Ohio 1989-91, exec. coun., 1990—), Am. Soc. Jewish Music, Coalition for Advancement Jewish Edn. (co-chair Evening Entertainment Nat. Conv. 1990). Democrat. Office: Congregation Tifereth Israel 1354 E Broad St Columbus OH 43205

CHOO, SAMUEL KAM-CHEE, retired clergyman; b. Malaysia, Mar. 16, 1916; arrived in Can., 1960, naturalized, 1968; s. Seng and Foon (Wong) C.; m. King Cheung Man, Feb. 4, 1950. BSc, Lingnan U., Canton, China, 1941; MRE, Golden Gate Bapt. Theol. Sem., Berkeley, Calif., 1958; postgrad. U. Calif., Berkeley, 1958-59. Ordained to ministry United Ch. Can., 1962. Min. Ottawa (Ont., Can.) Chinese United Ch., 1960-68; min., sec. bldg. com. Chinese United Ch., Winnipeg, Man., Can., 1968-77; ret., 1977; pres. Chinese United Ch. Conf. Can., 1963-67. Bd. dirs. Chinatown Redevel. Non-Profit Housing Corp., Winnipeg, 1982—, sec., 1984; sec. Sr. Citizen's Home Bldg Com., Winnipeg, 1975-82; sec. bldg. com. Sek On Toi Chinese Sr. Citizens Home, Winnipeg, 1978; sec. fund raising com. Harmony Mansion, Winnipeg, 1986. Recipient City of Winnipeg Community Svc. award Mayor of Winnipeg, 1984. Home: 120 Donald St Apt 204, Winnipeg, MB Canada R3C 4G2 Office: 281 Pacific Ave, Winnipeg, MB Canada R3B 0M7

CHOPKO, MARK E., lawyer; b. Kingston, Pa., Nov. 4, 1953; s. Michael E. and Rose Ann C. (Gavlick) C.; m. Mary Ann C. Suhocki, June 17, 1978; children: Michael, Jessica, Laura. BS summa cum laude, U. Scranton, 1974; JD cum laude, Cornell U., 1977. Bar: Pa. 1977, U.S. Supreme Ct. 1984, D.C. 1987. Gen. counsel Nat. Conf. Cath. Bishops, U.S. Cath. Conf., Washington, 1987—; mem. religious liberty com. Nat. Coun. Chs., N.Y.C., 1987—. Mem. bd. editors Religious Freedom Reporter, N.C., 1987—; contbr. articles to profl. jours. Mem. bd. Blessed Sacrament Sch., Alexandria, Va., 1986-88; legal advisor Ams. United for Life, Chgo., 1987—; mem. legal scholars bd. DePaul Inst. for ch.-State Studies, Chgo., 1988—; asst. coach basketball Cath. Youth Orgn., Alexandria, 1989—. Recipient High Quality award U.S. Nuclear Regulatory Commn., 1982. Mem. ABA (vice chair religious, charitable and non-profit orgns. tort sect. 1990—), Cath. Health Assn. (legal affairs com. 1988—). Office: US Cath Conf 3211 4th St NE Washington DC 20017

CHORNY, AMMOS, rabbi; b. Bogota, Colombia, July 2, 1961; came to U.S., 1978; s. Jorge and Nima (Hony) C.; m. Aviva Rosenbaum, Dec. 11, 1982; children: Joel, Daniel, Michal. BA, Jewish Theol. Sem., N.Y.C., 1982, Columbia U., N.Y.C., 1982; MHL, Jewish Theol. Sem., N.Y.C., 1986.

Ordained rabbi, 1987. Rabbi Pelham Jewish Ctr., Pelham Manor, N.Y., 1985-87, B'nai Israel Congregation, Rockville, Md., 1987-89, Beth David Synagogue, Greensboro, N.C., 1989—; chaplain USAR, 1983—; adj. chaplain Moses H. Cone Hosp., Greensboro, 1989—. Recipient Army Achievement medal USAR, 1989. Mem. Rabbinical Assembly, N.Y. Bd. Rabbis. Home: 806 Winview Dr Greensboro NC 27410 Office: Beth David Synagogue 804 Winview Dr Greensboro NC 27410

CHORZEMPA, SISTER MARIE ANDREE, nun, religious order administrator; b. Mpls., Dec. 26, 1926; d. Andrew and Louise (Galant) C. BS, St. Teresa Coll., Winona, Minn., 1958; MST, St. Louis U., 1963; PhD, Oreg. State U., 1970; cert. in theol. studies, Regis Coll., Toronto, Can., 1981. Joined Sisters St. Francis of Sylvania, Roman Cath. Ch., 1945. Mem. gen. coun. Sisters St. Francis of Sylvania, Ohio, 1972-76, asst. superior gen., 1976-80, chpt. del., 1976, 80, 84, 88, superior gen., 1984-88, min. gen., 1988—. Editor: Our Covenant with the Lord Jesus, 1977. Mem. Franciscan Fedn., Leadership Conf. Women Religious, Internat. Union Superiors Gen., Internat. Franciscan Conf. (bd. dirs. 1989—). Office: Sisters St Francis Sylvania 6832 Convent Blvd Sylvania OH 43560

CHOTTINER, LAWRENCE R., minister; b. McKeesport, Pa., July 11, 1949; s. Lawrence and Caroline (Stright) C.; m. Nancy T. Johnson, Aug. 30, 1975; children: Brett L., Meghan T. BA, Waynesburg (Pa.) Coll., 1971; MDiv, Pitts. Theol. Sem., 1974; DMin, McCormick Theol. Sem., Chgo., 1982. Pastor Mt. Pisgah Presbyn. Ch., Pitts., 1974-79, Lewistown (Pa.) Presbyn. Ch., 1979-85, Westmont Presbyn. Ch., Johnstown, Pa., 1985—. Sch. dir. Westmont Hilltop Sch. Dist., 1990—. Office: Westmont Presbyn Ch 601 Luzerne St Johnstown PA 15905

CHOUN, ROBERT JOSEPH, JR., Christian education educator; b. Bridgeport, Conn., Aug. 17, 1948; s. Robert Joseph and Mildred Fitz C.; AA, Luther Coll., 1969; BA, Gustavus Adolphus Coll., 1971; MRE, Trinity Evang. Div. Sch., 1974; MA, Wheaton Coll., 1975; DMin, Faith Sem., 1980; postgrad. N. Tex. State U., 1978; postgrad. Dallas Theol. Sem., 1989; m. Jane Willson, July 12, 1975. Media rels. asst. Am. Bible Soc., N.Y.C., 1969-74; prof. Christian edn. Dallas Theol. Sem.; sem. leader early childhood Internat. Center Learning, Ventura, Calif., 1977—; minister edn. Pantego Bible Ch., Arlington, Tex., 1975-85; prof. edn. Dallas Theol. Sem., 1984—. Mem. bd. evaluation Pioneer Ministries, Wheaton, Ill. Mem. Nat. Assn. Dirs. Christian Edn., Christian Camping Internat., Booth Meml. Astron. Soc., Kappa Delta Phi, Phi Delta Kappa. Co-author: What the Bible Is All About, Young Explorers edit., 1987-88, Quick Reference edit., 1987-88, Directing Christian Education, 1992, The Complete Book of Children's Ministry, 1993; contbr. articles to profl. jours. and mags.; denominational rep., editorial cons., denom. cons., Gospel Light Publs., Ventura, Calif. Home: 818 Clover Park Dr Arlington TX 76013 Office: 3909 Swiss Ave Dallas TX 75204

CHOW, MARTIN MEI-TA, evangelist; b. Taipei, Taiwan, Republic of China, Sept. 11, 1956; s. Allan I-Lin and Shirley Shin-Yu (Chou) C.; m. Sharmaye Chou, Sept. 9, 1989. BA, Yale U., 1979; MDiv, Fuller Theol. Sem., 1984, postgrad., 1990—. Ordained to ministry So. Bapt. Conv., 1985. Info. coord. United Evangelism to the Chinese, Inter-Aid Inc., Camarillo, Calif., 1981-83; student chaplain Hollywood Presbyn. Med. Ctr., L.A., 1983; pastoral intern Mandarin Bapt. Ch. L.A., Alhambra, Calif., 1983; English min. Mandarin Bapt. Ch. Pasadena, Arcadia, Calif., 1985-90; evangelist Martin Chow Evangelistic Assn., Arcadia, 1990—; chaplain, music evangelist Joyful Melody, Monterey Park, Calif., 1984—; ch. coord. Billy Graham Crusade in L.A., Anaheim, Calif., 1985; participant Leadership '88, Lausanne Com. on World Evangelization, Washington, 1988. Vocalist L.A. Master Chorale, 1980; cassettes include Joyful Melody I, 1985, Joyful Melody II, 1987. Mem. Greater L.A. Chinese Ministers Assn. Republican. Home: 611 1/2 W Longden Ave Arcadia CA 91007

CHOY, WILBUR WONG YAN, bishop; b. Stockton, Calif., May 28, 1918; s. Lie Yen and Ida (Lee) C.; m. Grace Ying Hom, Sept. 26, 1940 (dec. Dec. 1977); children: Randolph W., Jonathan W., Phyllis W. (Mrs. Lawrence Uno), Donnell W.; m. Nancy S. Yamasaki, Dec. 1981. A.A., Stockton Jr. Coll., 1944; B.A., Coll. of Pacific, Stockton, 1946; M.Div., Pacific Sch. Religion, Berkeley, Calif., 1949, D.D., 1969; L.H.D., U. Puget Sound, Tacoma, 1973. Ordained deacon Methodist Ch., 1947, elder, 1949; asso. pastor Chinese Meth. Ch., Stockton, 1943-49; pastor Chinese Meth. Ch., 1949-54, St. Marks Meth. Ch., Stockton, 1954-59; asso. pastor Woodland (Calif.) Meth. Ch., 1959-60; pastor Oak Park Meth. Ch., Sacramento, 1960-69; also Chinese Meth. Ch., Sacramento, 1968-69; dist. supt. Bay View Dist., Calif.-Nev. Conf., United Meth. Ch., 1969-72; resident bishop United Meth. Ch., Seattle Area, 1972-80, San Francisco Area, 1980—; mem. exec. com. World Meth. Council; mem. Gen. Bd. of Ch. and Soc., United Meth. Ch., 1972-80, Gen. Bd. of Global Ministry, 1980—; v.p., chmn. div. gen. welfare, 1972-76; chaplain Calif. Senate, 1967; del. United Meth. Western Jurisdictional Conf., 1952, 56, 60, 64, 72, alt., 1968; del. United Meth. Gen. Conf., 1972; mem. Meth. Gen. Bd. of Temperance, 1952-56; mem. adv. com. Asian-Am. Ministries, 1968-72; mem. exec. com. Nat. Conf. Chinese Chs., 1971-74; Rep. Chinese Assn. of Stockton to Nat. Conf. Chinese Communities in U.S.A., 1954; cons. Pacific and Asian Center Theology and Strategies, Berkeley, Calif., 1972—. Bd. dirs. Goodwill Industries, Stockton, 1958-59; Bd. dirs. Family Service Agy., Stockton, 1958-59, Woodland, 1959-60; Bd. dirs. Center for Asian-Am. Ministries, Sch. Theology at Claremont (Calif.), 1977—; trustee Pacific Sch. Religion, Berkeley, U. Puget Sound, Tacoma, 1972-80; mem. exec. com. Oak Park Neighborhood Council, Sacramento, 1964-67. Club: Press (San Francisco). Office: 330 Ellis St PO Box 467 San Francisco CA 94101

CHRISTELL, ROY ERNEST, minister; b. Oak Park, Ill., Sept. 21, 1952; s. Jack Vally and Shirley Eleanor (Quenzer) C.; m. Theresa Lynn Jensen, Aug. 18, 1973; 1 child, Kelly Jean. BA, Augustana Coll., 1974; MDiv, Luth. Theol. Sem., 1978. Ordained to ministry Luth. Ch. in Am., 1978. Asst. pastor Bethany Luth. Ch., Crystal Lake, Ill., 1978-80; pastor, developer Living Lord Luth. Ch., Lake St. Louis, Mo., 1980-81, pastor, 1981—; mem. youth ministry task force Ill. Synod, Luth. Ch. in Am./Evang. Luth. Ch. in Am., 1978-81, youth ministry dist. resource, 1979-80, witness dist. resource, St. Louis, 1982-84, witness com., 1984-87, group leader youth leadership lab., 1985-87, 90, retreat chaplain, rep. Mo. Coun. Chs., 1983, music coord. youth events, 1984, 86-87, 90, mem. plannin com. Mo. Christian Leadership Forum, 1984-89; mem. audication team Mo.-Kans. synod Evang. Luth. Ch. in Am., 1989—, chairperson synod assembly resolutions com., 1990, pastor-mentor, 1990-91; chaplain Lake St. Louis Police Dept., 1981—. Editor (newsletter) The Wood Works, 1978-81. Blood drive chmn., chaplain Crystal Lake Jaycees, 1979-80; mem. adv. bd. coun. St. Charles County dist. ARC, 1981—, chairperson, 1985—, bd. dirs. Bi-State chpt., 1982-89, exec. bd., 1985-89, mem. long range planning com., 1989—, vol. svcs., 1989—; state bd. dirs., chaplain Mo. Jr. Miss Scholarship Program, 1983-84. Recipient Honor award Bi-State chpt. ARC, 1988, Clara Barton award, 1989; Ill. State scholar, 1970. Mem. Lake St. Louis Ambs. (charter, bd. dirs. 1981-86, sec. 1982-84, pres. 1985). Home: 204 Rue Grand Lake Saint Louis MO 63367 Office: Living Lord Luth Ch 1799 Lake Saint Louis Blvd Lake Saint Louis MO 63367

CHRISTENSEN, ARTHUR ROY, minister; b. N.Y.C., Apr. 17, 1937; s Jacob and Gudrun Amanda (Hansen) C.; m. Joan Beverly Elms, July 25, 1959; children: Stephen, Thomas, Timothy. Diploma in Bible and Theology, Barrington Coll., 1959, BA, 1960; ThB summa cum laude, 1961. Ordained to ministry Conservative Bapt. Assn. Am., 1959. Pastor chs., Mass., 1959-61, 65-70, N.H., 1962-65, 81-86, Maine, 1979-81; pastor Leffingwell Bapt. Ch., Norwich, Conn., 1970-79, 1st Bapt. Ch., Port Jervis, N.Y., 1986-91; sec.-treas. Evang. Ministers Strafford County, N.H., 1963-65; pres. Everett, Mass. Ministerial Assn., 1968, 69, Evang. Ministers Ea. Conn., 1971-73; pres. Conservative Bapt. Assn., Conn., 1972-74, State rep., 1975-79; dir., 1st v.p. Merrmac Mission, Boston, 1966-69. Law enforcement chaplain police dept. Hollis, N.H., 1982-86. Mem. Conservative Bapt. Assn. New Eng. (coun. mem. 1982-85) Conservative Bapt. Assn. Am. (bd. dirs. 1982-88), Conservative Bapt. Assn. N.Y. (corr. sec. 1989—).

CHRISTENSEN, DUANE LEE, seminary educator; b. Park Rapids, Minn., May 27, 1938; s. John William and Elsie Annabelle (DeFoer) C.; m. Carol Russell Christensen, June 10, 1960; children: Beth, Sharon, Julie. BS, MIT, 1960; MDiv, Am. Bapt. Sem., 1963; ThD, Harvard U., 1972. Ordained to ministry Bapt. Ch., 1963. Min. of edn. First Bapt. Ch., Melrose, Mass., 1965-68; instr. Bridgewater (Mass.) State Coll., 1969-71, asst. prof., 1971-74, assoc. prof., 1974-78; pastor Winter Hill Bapt. Ch., Somerville, Mass., 1972-78; prof. O.T. Am. Bapt. Sem., Berkeley, Calif., 1978—; acting dean Christian Witness Theol. Sem., Berkeley, 1991—; vis. prof. U. Calif., Berkeley, 1984; pres. Berkeley Inst. of Bible, Archaeology & Law Bibal Corp., 1987--; bd. trustees Am. Schs. Oriental Rsch., Balt., 1986-89. Author: Transformations of War Oracle, 1975; editor: Experiencing the Exodus, 1988, Deuteronomy (Word Biblical Commentary), 1991; contbr. articles to profl. jours. Grantee Hebrew U., Inst. for Adv. Studies, 1983, Assn. Theol. Schs., Vienna, Austria, 1980; Nat. Def. Fgn. Lang. fellow Harvard U., 1963-64, 68-70; Zion Rsch. Found. fellow, 1976. Mem. Cath. Bibl. Assn. (task force com. 1984-89), Soc. Bibl. Lit., Am. Oriental Soc., Internat. Orgn. for Study of O.T. Democrat. Baptist. Avocations: carpentry, gardening. Home: 845 Bodega Way Rodeo CA 94572 Office: Christian Witness Theol Sem 1525 Solano Ave Berkeley CA 94707

CHRISTENSEN, GWEN JOYNER, media director, diaconal minister; b. Mpls., Feb. 21, 1930; d. Albert and Victoria (Krienke) J.; children: Grant, Vicki, Emily, Bert. BA, Hamline U., 1951; MA, Sch. Theology, Claremont, Calif., 1989. Cert. tchr.; ordained to ministry United Meth. Ch. as diaconal min. Tchr. English local jr. high sch. Mpls., 1951-52; dir. jr. high sch. sect. United Meth. Ch., Mpls., 1952-54; dir. media ctr. United Meth. Ch., L.A., 1975—; diaconal min. United Meth. Ch., Pasadena, Calif., 1980—; cons. media for ch. workshops and seminars; vice-chair Bd. Diaconal Ministry, 1988-89. Contbg. writer Ch. Tchrs. mag., 1986—; writer Ch. Educator mag., 1991—. Supt. Sunday sch. local ch. United Meth. Ch., Tujunga, Calif., 1960-63, tchr. Sunday sch. local ch., Glendale, Calif., 1977—, chair ministries coun., Glendale, 1985-86. Recipient Bishop's award Calif.-Pacific conf. United Meth. Ch., 1991. Mem. United Meth. Communicators, Religious Pub. Rels. Coun., Christian Edn. Fellowship. Avocations: reading, travel, cooking, media, gardening.

CHRISTENSEN, HOMER COBB, religious organization administrator; b. St. Paul, Apr. 15, 1940; s. Wayne Edgar and Ruth Louise (Cobb) C.; B.S.B.A., Sioux Falls Coll., 1963; m. Charlene Kaye Foerster, June 8, 1968; children—Michele Lynn, Kevin Wayne. Store mgr. Judson Book Store, Valley Forge, Pa. and Green Lake, Wis., 1963-68; hosp. adminstr. Cordova (Alaska) Community Hosp., 1968-72; ch. bus. adminstr. Calvary Baptist Ch., Washington, 1972—. Baptist. Home: 6353 Parramore Dr Alexandria VA 22312 Office: 755 8th St NW Washington DC 20001

CHRISTENSEN, PAUL, ecumenical agency administrator. Pres. Evanston (Ill.) Ecumenical Action Coun. Office: Evanston Ecumenical Action Coun PO Box 1414 Evanston IL 60204*

CHRISTENSON, ALFRED MANDT, minister; b. Hartford, Wis., Mar. 16, 1943; s. Robert Irving and Esther Synneva (Lunde) C.; m. Sylvia Febus, July 26, 1980; children: Selene, Sylvia Esther, Mark, Amber, Rebecca. Student, Capital U., 1961-64; BA, U. Wis., Milw., 1970; MDiv. cum laude, Luth. Theol. Sem., 1974. Ordained to ministry Am. Luth. Ch., 1975. Pastor Kingsbridge Luth. Ch., Bronx, N.Y., 1975-81; campus pastor Lehman Coll., Bronx, 1975-81; pastor Community Luth. Ch., Butler, Pa., 1981, Bethlehem Luth. Ch., Baldwin, N.Y., 1982-87, Community of St. Dysmas Luth. Ch., Jessup, Md., 1987—; mem. Riverdale Clergy Conf., 1976—, chmn., 1980; mem. synod coun. Metro N.Y. Synod-Evang. Luth. Ch. Am., N.Y.C., 1987. Sgt. USAF, 1964-68. Republican. Home: 6357 Barefoot Boy Columbia MD 21045-4501 Office: Community St Dysmas Luth Ch 6004 Waterloo Rd Columbia MD 21045-2631 *The challenge is there—in the prisons of our land—to embody Christ's Love for persons whose overhelming experience of life is a negation of this. It has to be the Gospel, the Gospel over and over again, that predominates our message. For me, St. Dysmas has been that challenge—and hope.*

CHRISTIAN, FRANCIS JOSEPH, priest; b. Peterborough, N.H., Oct. 12, 1942; s. Joseph Lucien and Dorothy Mary (Parent) C. BA, PhB, U. Ottawa, Can., 1964; MA in Theology, U. Louvain, Belgium, 1968, PhD in Religious Studies, 1975. Ordained priest Roman Cath. Ch., 1968. Asst. pastor Our Lady of Mercy Parish Roman Cath. Ch., Merrimack, N.H., 1968-71; asst. pastor St. Joseph Cathedral Parish Roman Cath. Ch., Manchester, N.H., 1971-72; asst. chancellor Diocese Manchester Roman Cath. Ch., 1975-77, chancellor, sec. for administrn. canonical affairs Diocese Manchester, 1978—. Named Monsignor (Prelate of Honor), Pope John Paul II, 1986. Home: 2345 Candia Rd Auburn NH 03032 Office: Diocese of Manchester 153 Ash St Manchester NH 03105

CHRISTIAN, J. C., JR., minister; b. San Angelo, Tex., Mar. 9, 1957; s. J.C. and Jeanette (Johnson) C.; m. Patty Sue Kilgore, Jan. 17, 1976; 1 child, Leslie Brook. AS in Sacred Lit., Covington Theol. Sem., Rossville, Ga., 1988; student, Chattanooga State Tech. Community Coll., 1989—. Lic. to ministry So. Bapt. Conv., 1981, ordained, 1984; cert. pastor-leader in continual witness tng. Interim pastor 1st Bapt. Ch., Sequatchie, Tenn., 1982-83; assoc. pastor, min. youth Cartwright 1st Bapt. Ch., Whitwell, Tenn., 1983-84; pastor Harmony Bapt. Ch., Whitwell, 1984-85, Richard City 1st Bapt. Ch., South Pittsburg, Tenn., 1986-91, Rover Bapt. Ch., Eagleville, Tenn., 1991—; v.p. Marion County Ministerial Assn., 1987-88; dir. evangelism Sequatchie Valley Bapt. Assn., Whitwell, 1990—. Mem. South Pittsburg High Sch. Band Boosters, 1990—, South Pittsburg Parks and Recreation Planning Com., 1990. Mem. South Pittsburg Ministerial Assn. (pres. 1987-90), Phi Theta Kappa. Republican. Home and Office: Rover Baptist Ch 204 Baptist Church Rd Eagleville TN 37060 *In this world most of the news a person receives is bad. I enjoy telling people the "Good News" of Jesus Christ. In Christ people can find the cure for all their hurts and disappointments.*

CHRISTIAN, MARK ROBERT, clergyman; b. South Bend, Ind., Feb. 6, 1965; s. Harold Dale and Marilyn Ann (Bailey) C.; m. Heather Rae Christian, Aug. 15, 1987. B Religious Edn., Great Lakes Bible Coll., 1987; postgrad., Cen. Mich. U., 1988—. Ordained to ministry Ch. of Christ, 1987. Assoc. minister First Ch. of Christ, Mt. Pleasant, Mich., 1986-90, sr. minister, 1990—. Office: First Ch of Christ 1610 E Broadway Mount Pleasant MI 48858

CHRISTIAN, PATRICIA LANE HOLMES, education director; b. Richlands, Va., Apr. 22, 1953; d. Alvin Lane and Betty Jean (Burress) Holmes; m. Farley A. Christian Jr., Apr. 1, 1983; 1 child, Hannah Beth. Student, S.W. Va. Community Coll., 1971-72; BA in Christian Edn., Gateway Coll. Evangelism, 1979; MA in Edn. Adminstrn., Twin Cities U., 1983. Dir. Christian edn. 1st Apostolic Christian Sch., Richlands, Va., 1979—. Author poetry, short stories. Recipient Outstanding Alumnus award Gateway Coll. Evangelism, 1987. Home: PO Box 704 Sixth St Richlands VA 24641-0974 Office: 1st Apostolic Christian PO Drawer P Sixth St Richlands VA 24641-0974

CHRISTIANSON, CONRAD JOHAN, JR., minister, church official; b. Stoughton, Wis., Oct. 13, 1935; s. Conrad Johan and Edith Lysle (Thomas) C.; m. Eva Elisabeth Strasser, June 24, 1965; 1 child, Katrin. BA, U. Ill., 1957; BDiv, Luth. Theol. Sem., Gettysburg, Pa., 1966, STM, 1973, DMin, 1984. Ordained to ministry Luth. Ch. in Am., 1966. Min. Bethel Luth. Ch., Winchester, Va., 1966—; dean No. Valley area Luth. Ch. in Am., 1983-87; ecumenical rep. Va. Synod Evang. Luth. Ch. Am., 1988—, mem. steering com. Luth. Ecumenical Rep. Network, 1988—; mem. Va. Synod Coun., 1990—. Bd. dirs. Cath. Charities, Winchester, 1978-81, Big Bros. Am., Winchester, 1982-89; pres. Social Svcs. Coun., Winchester, 1975, 76, Ministerial Assn./Frederick County, Va., 1982-83; chaplain W.Va. State Soc. SAR, 1983. With U.S. Army, 1958-59. Home: 1040 Devland Dr Winchester VA 22601 Office: Bethel Luth Ch HC-36 Box 117A Winchester VA 22601

CHRISTIE, LES JOHN, youth minister; b. Liverpool, Eng., June 6, 1947; s. Les Arthur and Margaret May (Blain) C.; m. Gretchen Martha Hintz, June 19, 1976; children: Brent Paul, David Andrew. BS, Pacific Christian Coll., 1971; M, Fuller Theol. Sem., 1974. Youth min. Cardiff Ave. Ch., L.A., 1966-67, Compton (Calif.) 1st Christian, 1967-69, 1st Christian, Garden Grove, Calif., 1969-71, Eastside Christian Ch., Fullerton, Calif., 1971—; lectr. Pacific Christian Coll., 1971—, others. Author: Dating and Waiting, 1983, Unsung Heroes, 1987, Positive Discipline, 1988; contbr. numerous articles to profl. jours. Recipient Pilgrimage 1984 award Israeli Govt.; named Alumni of Yr. Pacific Christian Coll., Fullerton, 1981, 86. Mem. Network. Home: 1212 Puerto Natales Placenta CA 92670 Office: Eastside Christian Ch 2505 E Yorba Linda Blvd Fullerton CA 92634-4178

CHRISTIE, PAUL C., ecumenical agency administrator. Exec. dir. Ctr. City Chs., Hartford, Conn. Office: Ctr City Chs 170 Main St Hartford CT 06106*

CHRISTIE, ROBERT LUSK, priest; b. Olympia, Wash., Aug. 13, 1936; s. Elmer Burton and Margaret (Lusk) C.; m. Marjorie Reinhardt, Sept. 28, 1957; children: Carol Louise, Margaret Rose, Robert Lincoln. BA, Seattle Pacific U., 1967; MDiv, Ch. Div. Sch. of Pacific, Berkeley, Calif., 1970. Ordained to ministry Episcopal Ch., 1970. Curate St. James Episcopal Ch., Kent, Wash., 1970-72; vicar Ea. Grays Harbor Mission, Montesano, Wash., 1972-79; reg. archdeacon Diocese of Olympia, Seattle, 1976-90; vicar All Saints Episcopal Ch., Vancouver, Wash., 1979-90, St. Georges Episcopal Ch., Seattle, 1990—; trainer Tng. and Cons. Svcs., Diocese of Olympia, Seattle, 1974—; spiritual dir. Cursillo secretariat, Seattle, 1975-77; diocesan coun. diocese of Olympia, Seattle, 1977-81, standing com., 1983-86, dep. gen. conv., 1988-91. Editor: Mission Manual, 1974-90. Bd. dirs. Grays Harbor County Alcoholism Adminstrv. Bd., Aberdeen, 1976-79. With USAF, 1955-59. Mem. Clergy Assn. Diocese of Olympia, Kiwanis. Office: St Georges Episcopal Ch 2212 NE 125th St Box 25535 Seattle WA 98125

CHRISTOPHER, GREGORY THEODORE, minister; b. Colo. City, Mar. 15, 1958; m. Deborah Christopher, June 11, 1977; children: James, Sharon. ThM in New Testament, Grace Seminary, Winona Lake, Ind., 1985; postgrad., U. Tex., Arlington. Min. Faith Bapt. Ch., Columbia City, Ind., 1984-86, Bapt. Temple, Grand Prairie, Tex., 1986-91, Bethel Bapt. Ch., Arlington, 1991—; vis. prof. Bapt. Bible Grad. Sch., Springfield, Mo., 1987-91. Mem. Soc. Bibl. Lit., Evang. Theol. Soc. Home: 607 Town North Dr Arlington TX 76011

CHRISTOPHER, HUW, minister; b. Mountain Ash, Wales, U.K., Nov. 11, 1945; came to U.S. 1970; s. Edwin Jones and Gladys Mary (Castree) C.; m. Rachel Jeanette Micol, June 11, 1972; 1 child, Micol Huw. BA with honors, U. Coll., Cardiff, Wales, 1967, BD, 1970; ThM, Union Theol. Sem., Richmond, Va., 1971; DMin, Columbia Theol. Sem., Decatur, Ga., 1991. Ordained to ministry Presbyn. Ch. (U.S.A.), 1972. Pastor First Presbyn. Ch., Washington, N.C., 1972-77, Kinston, N.C., 1977-86; pastor Little Chapel on the Boardwalk, Wrightsville Beach, N.C., 1986—; moderator Presbytery of Albemarle, 1981; commr. Gen. Assy., Presbyn. Ch. (U.S.A.), Houston, 1981. World Coun. of Chs. Ecumenical scholar, Geneva, Switzerland, 1970. Mem. Rotary. Home: 25 W Oxford St # 4906 Wrightsville Beach NC 28480-1885 Office: Little Chapel on Boardwalk N Lumina & W Fayetteville Wrightsville NC 28480 *I find hope and encouragement from Paul's word that nothing in life or in death can separate us from the love of God which is in Christ Jesus our Lord.*

CHRISTOPHER, JAMES ALEXANDER, minister; b. Pulaski, Tenn., June 28, 1938; s. James Hayden and Helen (Moore) C.; m. Nancy Ada Trites, Apr. 2, 1960 (div. 1982); m. Carole Ann Synder, May 7, 1983; children: Cynthia, Karen, Jonathan. BA, Colgate U., 1961; BD, Iliff Sch. Theology, 1963; D of Ministry, Andover Newton Sch. Theology, 1973. Ordained to ministry United Ch. of Christ, 1964. Pastor Ashburnham Community Ch., Mass., 1965-69, Ridgeview Ch., White Plains, N.Y., 1969-76; sr. pastor Faith United Protestant Ch., Park Forest, Ill., 1976-82; sr. pastor 1st Congl. Ch., Elgin, Ill., 1982-87, Bloomfield, Conn., 1987—; bd. dirs. Ill. conf. United Ch. of Christ, Westchester, 1984-85. Author: Gifts Believers Seek, 1988. Bd. dirs. C.G. Jung Ctr., Evanston, Ill., 1983, Dumcaster Life Care Ctr., Bloomfield, Conn.; mem. adv. bd. C.G. Jung Inst., 1984; v.p. Econ. Devel. Commn., Park Forest, 1981-82. Mem. Profl. Assn. Clergy, Assn. Clin. Pastoral Edn., Bloomfield Clergy Assn. (pres. 1991—), Current History Club. Democrat. Address: 10 Wintonbury Ave Bloomfield CT 06002

CHRISTOPHER, SHARON A. BROWN, bishop; b. Corpus Christi, Tex., July 24, 1944; d. Fred L. and Mavis Lorraine (Krueger) Brown; m. Charles Edmond Logsdon Christopher, June 17, 1973. BA, Southwestern U., Georgetown, Tex., 1966; MDiv, Perkins Sch. Theology, 1969; DD, Southwestern U., 1990. Ordained to ministry United Meth. Ch., 1970; elected bishop 1988. Dir. Christian Edn. First United Meth. Ch., Appleton, Wis., 1969-70, assoc. pastor, 1970-72; pastor Butler United Meth. Ch., Butler, Wis., 1972-76, Calvary United Meth. Ch., Germantown, Wis., 1972-76, Aldersgate United Meth. Ch., Milw., 1976-80; dist. supt. Ea. Dist. Wis. Conf. United Meth. Ch., 1980-85; asst. to bishop Wis. Conf. Wis. Confs. United Meth. Ch., Sun Prairie, Wis., 1986-88; bishop North Cen. jurisdiction United Meth. Ch., Minn., 1988—. Contbr. articles and papers to religious publs. Bd. dirs. Nat. Coun. Churches of Christ, U.S.A., 1988—, United Meth. Ch. Bd. of Ch. & Soc., 1988—, Walker Meth. Health Ctr., Mpls., 1988—, Meth. Hosp., Mpls., 1988—; trustee Hamline U., St. Paul, 1988—; gen. and jurisdictional conf. del., 1976, 80, 84, 88; mem. North Cen. Jurisdiction Com. on Episcopacy, 1984-88, Gen. Bd. Global Ministries, 1980-88, chmn. Mission Pers. Resources Program Dept., 1984-88; mem. North Cen. Jurisdiction Com. on Investigation, 1980-88, Nat. United Meth. clergywomen's. Named one of Eighty for the Eighties, Milw. Jour., 1980. Office: United Meth Ch 122 W Franklin Ave Rm 400 Minneapolis MN 55404

CHRISTOPHER, STEVEN LEE, religion educator; b. Long Beach, Calif., May 29, 1956; s. Lehland James and Harriet Ann (Werner) C.; m. Doris Dianne Deterding, Aug. 19, 1978; children: LeAnna Helen, Brett Steven. BS in Edn., Concordia Coll., Seward, Nebr., 1979; MA, U. San Diego, 1989. Ordained to ministry Luth. Ch.-Mo. Synod, 1979; tchr.'s diploma, cert. dir. Christian edn. Min. youth and edn. Bethany Luth. Ch., Long Beach, 1979-85; coord. youth ministries Christ Luth. Ch., La Mesa, Calif., 1985-88; prof., dir. Christian edn. program Christ Coll. Irvine, Calif., 1988—; chmn. youth com. Pacific SW dist. Luth. Ch.-Mo. Synod, Irvine, 1983-88, mem. extended staff bd. for youth svcs., St. Louis, 1988-91, com. mem. nat. youth gathering, 1986, 89; chmn. 1991 Nat. Dirs. Christian Edn. Conf., River Forest, Ill., 1989-91; mem. youth bd. Abiding Savior Luth. Ch., El Toro, Calif., 1989—. Author young adult Bible study and youth Bible study, 1985, 3 devotions for children, 1988, chapel talks for children, 1989. Mem. Theol. Educators in Assoc. Ministries (pres.-elect 1988-90, pres. 1990-92), Profl. Assn. Christian Educators, Religious Edn. Assn. Democrat. Office: Christ Coll Irvine 1530 Concordia Dr Irvine CA 92715 *It is becoming increasingly important in this tech age, that we be involved in high touch ministry. Life in the world is becoming less personal. A relationship with a personal Jesus gives spiritual meaning and direction and personal meaning and direction. This is our challenge!.*

CHRISTOPHERSON, VIOLET MARGARET, minister; b. Gooding, Idaho, Oct. 23, 1922; d. William J. Rice and Amanda Elizabeth (Wilkens) Hughes; m. Leander William Christopherson, June 30, 1940 (dec.); 1 child, Sandra Lee Hodge. Student, Berean Sch. Bible, Springfield, Mo. Ordained to ministry Assemblies of God, 1979. Pastor Gustavus (Ark.) Chapel Assemblies of God, 1976-85, pastor Haines (Ark.) Christian Ctr., 1987—. Home: Box 730 Haines AK 99827 Office: Haines Christian Ctr 2nd and Union Haines AK 99827

CHRISTY, JAMES T., minister, writer; b. Leavenworth, Kan., Dec. 3, 1936; s. Peter Frederick Christiansen and Frances Grace (Somers) Christy; m. Velma June Snodgrass, July 17, 1962; children: Jamey, Greg. BA, Southern Nazarene U., 1959, Nazarene Theological Seminary, Kansas City, Mo., 1962; MA, Nazarene Theological Seminary, Kansas City, Mo., 1972, DM, 1978. Pastor Ch. of the Nazarene, Drexel, Mo., 1960-62; pastor Ch. of the Nazarene, Kimball, Nebr., 1962-65, Rochester, Minn., 1965-72, Greeley, Colo., 1972—; chaplain Ch. of the Nazarene to The Mayo Clinic, Rochester 1965-72; counselor Northeast Health Assn., Greeley 1975-85; regent Northwest Nazarene Coll. Nampa, Idaho 1982—; bd. dirs. several orgns. with Ch. of the Nazarene 1962—. Author: book, The Puppet Ministry 1978, dozens of articles and writing contests. Chmn. Centennial-Bi-Centennial Religious Heritage, Greeley, Colo. 1976; dir. Budget Counseling, Greeley, 1980, Food/Aid, Greeley, 1986. Mem. Greeley Area Ministeral Assn. (pres.

1978), Long's Peak Council. Avocations: writing. Office: SunnyView Nazarene 4100 W 20th St Greeley CO 80634

CHRISTY, JOHN WICK, minister; b. Winding Gulf, W.Va., Jan. 3, 1927; s. Harry Pierce and B. Ethel (Maloney) C.; m. Marilyn E. Mitchell, Nov. 30, 1951; children: Janet, Mark, Philip, Colette, Sharon, Caroline. BA, Tarkio Coll., 1951, DD (hon.), 1973; postgrad., U. Dubuque, 1958-59; MDiv, Drake U., 1965. Ordained to ministry United Ch. of Christ, 1965. Dir. Christian edn. United Ch. of Christ, Reinbeck, Iowa, 1959-63; pastor Community Ch., Union, Iowa, 1964-66, United Ch. of Christ, Manson, Moorland, Iowa, 1966-78, Little Brown Ch. in Vale, Nashua, Iowa, 1978-86, United Ch. of Christ/Chapel United Meth. Ch., Green Mountain, Iowa, 1986—; farmer, 1952-63. Mem., pres. sch. bd. Manson Sch. Dist., 1972-74; parliamentarian Calhoun County Dem. Party, Rockwell City, Iowa, 1976; mem. sch. bd. Nashua Sch. Dist., 1982-86. With USN, 1945-46; PTO. Recipient Svc. to Community award City of Manson, 1976, 25-yrs. ministry award Cen. Assn. Iowa Conf., 1990; Ea. Star scholar, grantee, 1964. Mem. Nat. Assn. Parliamentarians, Iowa State Assn. Parliamentarians, Lions (pres. Nashua and Green Mountain clubs), Kiwanis (pres. Manson and Union clubs). Home and Office: PO Box 506 503 Woolston St Green Mountain IA 50637 *Love God and people; trust each other; have hope in humanity and the eternal God. Doing this wisdom of life will be yours.*

CHRYSOSTOMOS, ARCHBISHOP (CHRYSTOFOROS ARISTODOMOU), archbishop of Cyprus; b. Statos, Cyprus, Sept. 28, 1927. Ordained deacon Greek Orthodox Ch., 1951, priest, 1961. Suffragan bishop, 1968-73, met. of Paphos, 1973; archbishop of Nova Justiniana and all Cyprus, Nicosia, 1977—. Office: Orthodox Ch of Cyprus, PO Box 1130, Nicosia Cyprus

CHRYSOSTOMOS OF OREOI, BISHOP (GONZÁLEZ-ALEXOPOULOS), bishop, psychologist, educator; b. Apr. 6, 1945; s. A.E. and J. (Rothmann) González-Alexopoulos. BA, U. Calif.-Riverside, 1964, Calif. State U., San Bernardino, 1971; MA, U. Calif., Davis, 1970, Princeton U., 1974; PhD, Princeton U., 1975. Bishop True Orthodox Ch. of Greece. Preceptor in psychology Princeton U., 1972-75; asst. prof. psychology U. Calif., Riverside, 1975; adj. asst. prof. Christian thought Ashland (Ohio) Theol. Sem., 1981-83; asst., assoc. prof. psychology Ashland U., 1980-83; dir. Ctr. for Traditional Orthodox Studies, Etna, Calif., 1981-85, scholar-in-residence, 1986, acad. dir., 1986—; vis. scholar Harvard Divinity Sch., 1981; vis. assoc. prof. Uppsala U., Sweden, 1987—. Marsden research fellow Oxford U., 1985. Greek Orthodox. Address: Ctr for Traditionalist Orthodox Studies PO Box 398 Etna CA 96027

CHRYSOULAKIS, GENNADIOS See GENNADIOS, BISHOP

CHU, C. F., bishop. Bishop Myanmar Meth. Ch., Yangon. Office: Meth Hdqrs, 22 Signal Pagoda Rd, Yangon Myanmar*

CHURCH, FRANK FORRESTER, minister, author, columnist; b. Boise, Idaho, Sept. 23, 1948; s. Frank Forrester and Bethine (Clark) C.; m. Amy Furth, May 30, 1970 (div. 1991); children: Frank Forrester, Nina Wynne. AB, Stanford U., 1970; MDiv, Harvard U., 1974, PhD, 1978. Sr. min. All Souls Unitarian Ch., N.Y.C., 1978—; columnist The Chicago Tribune, 1987-88, The New York Post, 1989; vis. prof. Dartmouth Coll., Hanover, N.H., 1989. Author: Father and Son: A Personal Biography of Senator Frank Church of Idaho, 1985, The Devil and Dr. Church, 1985, Entertaining Angels, 1987, The Seven Deadly Virtues, 1988, Everyday Miracles, 1988, Our Chosen Faith: An Introduction to Unitarian Universalism, 1989; translator: Greek Word-Building (Matthias Stehle), 1976; editor: Continuity and Discontinuity in Church History, 1978, The Essential Tillich, 1987, The Macmillan Book of Earliest Christian Prayers, 1988, The Macmillan Book of Earliest Christian Hymns, 1988, The Macmillan Book of Earliest Christian Meditations, 1989, One Prayer at a Time: A 12 Step Anthology, 1989, The Jefferson Bible, 1989, God and other Famous Liberals, 1991; contbr. articles to Harvard Theol. Rev., Church and State Quar., Vigiliae Christianae, others. Bd. dirs. Union Theol. Sem., N.Y.C., 1989—, Coun. on Econ. Priorities, N.Y.C., 1984-91, Religion in Am. Life, 1990—, Christianity in Crisis, 1991—, Franklin and Eleanor Roosevelt Found., N.Y.C, 1987—; mem. Unitarian Universalist Svc. Com., 1978—. Montgomery fellow Dartmouth Coll., 1989. Mem. Am. Acad. Religion, Unitarian Universalist Mins. Assn., Soc. Bibl. Lit., Citizens United for Separation of Church and State. Democrat. Home: 108 E 82d St New York NY 10028 Office: All Souls Unitarian Church 1157 Lexington Ave New York NY 10021

CHURCH, STEVEN MORGAN, minister; b. Mason City, Iowa, Nov. 27, 1947; s. Kenneth Ray and Marilyn Jean (Greenlee) C.; m. Heather Roseberry (div. Mar. 1977); 1 child, Heather; m. Karen Faye Johnson, June 30, 1979; children: Ryan, Morgan, Lauren. BA, Culver-Stockton Coll., 1970; MDiv, Tex. Christian U., 1974. Ordained to ministry Disciples of Christ. Min. First Christian Ch., Havana, Ill., 1968-69, Eastland, Tex., 1972-75; assoc. min. First Christian Ch., Midland, Tex., 1978-84; sr. min. First Christian Ch., Ft. Worth, 1984-91; min. Greentop Christian Ch. and Gifford Christian Ch., Mo., 1970, Hagerstown, 1991—; youth min. East Dallas Christian Ch., Dallas, 1970-71; min. ch. edn. Hemphill Presbyn. Ch., Ft. Worth, 1972; interim min. Kingwood (Tex.) Christian Ch., 1977-78; dean Sch. Christian Living, Midland, 1981-82; supr. Brite Divinity Field Edn., Ft. Worth, 1987-89; pres. Ft. Worth Area Disciple Mins., Ft. Worth, 1988-91; adj. prof. Southwestern Bapt. Theol. Sem., Ft. Worth, 1988-91. Dir. Am. Cancer Soc., Midland, Tex., 1979-84; reporter Mayor's Commn. on the Homeless, Ft. Worth, 1985-87; chair Italian Com. Sister Cities, Ft. Worth, 1986-90. Home: 6412 Canyon Circle Fort Worth TX 76133 Office: First Christian Ch 612 Throckmorton Fort Worth TX 76102

CHURCHILL, DAVID CHARLES, minister; b. Syracuse, N.Y., Mar. 17, 1958; s. Donald W. and Shirley A. (Barrett) C.; m. Linda Sarah Rogers, Oct. 5, 1985; children: Sarah, Matthew, Timothy. BA, Northeastern Bible Coll., Essex Fells, N.J., 1980; MA, Bibl. Theol. Sem., Hatfield, Pa., 1984.

CIANCIOLO, SISTER ROSEMARY, school system administrator. Supt. schs. Roman Cath. Diocese of Pensacola, Fla. Office: Office Supt Schs PO Box 17329 Pensacola FL 32522*

CIANGIO, SISTER DONNA LENORE, religious organization administrator; b. Newark, Feb. 2, 1949; d. Nicholas Gabriel and Elizabeth Helen (Cwikla) C. BA, Caldwell (N.J.) Coll., 1971, 82; MA, NYU, 1980. Joined Sisters of St. Dominic of Caldwell, N.J., Roman Catholic Ch., 1967. Tchr. Blessed Sacrament Sch., Bridgeport, Conn., 1971-73, St. Ann Sch., Newark, 1973; chairperson art dept. St. Dominic Acad., Jersey City, 1974-78; art instr., gallery dir. Caldwell Coll., 1978-80; art dept. chairperson St. Cecilia High Sch., Englewood, N.J., 1979-81; assoc. dir. internat. office RENEW, Plainfield, N.J., 1981—; cons. in art for secondary schs. Archdiocese of Newark, 1976-79. Recipient awards for paintings and drawings. Office: RENEW Internat Office 1232 George St Plainfield NJ 07062

CIAPPI, MARIO LUIGI CARDINAL, ecclesiastic; b. Florence, Italy, Oct. 6, 1909. Ordained Roman Catholic priest, 1932, bishop, 1977. Papal theologian, 1955—; bishop of Misenum, 1977, elected Sacred Coll. Cardinals, 1977; deacon Our Lady of Sacred Heart. Mem. Causes of Saint Congregation, Apostolic Signatura Tribunal. Address: Città del Vaticano, 11120 Rome Italy

CIARROCCHI, JEROME WILLIAM, deacon; b. Centerville, Pa., Aug. 3, 1921; s. Emilio and Catherine (Capozzoli) C.; m. Maura Barry, Dec. 23, 1963; children: Catherine, Regina, David. BA, Our Lady of the Lake U., 1966, MEd, 1968; M Theol. Studies, Oblate Sch. Theology, 1980. Ordained deacon Roman Cath. Ch., 1972; lic. profl. counselor, Tex. Permanent deacon St. Thomas More Cath. Ch., San Antonio, 1972—, pastoral counselor, 1972—; marriage counselor St. Helena's Cath. Ch., San Antonio, 1985—, St. Mark the Evangelist Cath. Ch., San Antonio, 1989—; ednl. diagnostician N.E. Ind. Schs., San Antonio, 1972-91; instr. pastoral counseling Permanent Diaconate Program, Archdiocese San Antonio, 1983—; mem. St. Thomas More Pastoral Coun., 1983-91. Mem. Community Cath. Counselors (treas. 1987-91), Assn. Tex. Profl. Educators, Third Order St. Francis, St. Vincent de Paul Soc., 3d Order St. Francis, KC. Home: 201 Windcrest Dr San Antonio TX 78239 Office: St Thomas More Ch 4411 Moana Dr San Antonio TX 78218

CIBIK, ROSEMARIE E., school system administrator. Supt. Dept. for Cath. Schs., Pitts. Office: Dept Cath Schs Office of Supt 111 Blvd of Allies Pittsburgh PA 15222*

CIESLEWSKI, PETER HENRY, pastor; b. Waterbury, Conn., May 24, 1955; s. Henry Stanley and Sophie Margaret (Kocsowicz) C.; m. Michelle Dawne Huffman, June 6, 1987; children: Jeremy Oglesby, Joseph. AS in Bus. Mgmt., Post Coll., 1981; BS in History, So. Conn. State U., 1984; MDiv, Luther Rice Sem., 1988. Ordained to ministry Bapt. Ch., 1990. Ministerial asst. Calvary Bapt. Ch., Las Cruces, N.Mex., 1988-89; assoc. pastor S.E. Bapt. Ch., Salt Lake City, 1989—; pastoral ministry dir. Salt Lake Bapt. Assn., 1990—. With U.S. Army, 1973-75. Mem. DAV (life), Am. Assn. Christian Counselors, Paralyzed Vets. Am. Republican. Home: 8261 S Viscounti Dr Sandy UT 84093 Office: 1700 E 7000 South PO Box 21399 Salt Lake City UT 84121

CILKE, ROBERT HENRY, minister; b. Petoskey, Mich., June 27, 1941; s. Robert Emil and Eleanor (Baines) C.; m. Barbara Eleene Hatch, Dec. 28, 1963; children: Debra, Brenda, Robert F. Diploma in music, North Cen. Bible Coll., 1962; B in Music Edn., MacPhail Coll. Music, 1963; MA, Cen. Mich. U., 1969. Ordained to ministry Assemblies of God, 1966. Min. music and youth Bethel Assembly of God, Rapid City, S.D., 1963-64; pastor 1st Assembly of God, Cheboygan, Mich., 1964-65, Faith Assembly of God, Rogers City, Mich., 1965-72; assoc. pastor, min. music Brookdale Assembly of God, Brooklyn Center, Minn., 1972-74, assoc. pastor, 1976—; assoc. pastor Brookdale Christian Ctr. Assembly of God, 1976—; chmn. music dept. North Cen. Bible Coll., 1972-76; music dir. State of Minn. Assemblies of God, 1972-76; Christ amb., rep. N.E. sect. Mich. for Assemblies of God Ch., 1966-68. Condr. Ohio Teen Tempos, 1975-76; bd. dirs. King's Acad., 1976—, North Hennepin Mediation Project, 1986-87, Peacemakers Ctr., 1987-88, Brooklyn Center Charitable Found., 1988—; mem. Brooklyn Center Housing Commn., 1977-83; mem., chair Brooklyn Center Prayer Breakfast Com., 1981—; pres., bd. dirs. N.W. Suburbs Community TV, 1982—; mem. Drug Awareness Task Force, 1987-88. Mem. North Twin Cities Mins. Assn. (sec.-treas. 1982), Brooklyn Center C. of C. (chmn. legis com. 1979-81), Rotary (v.p. 1981-82, pres. 1982-83, Paul Harris fellow 1983). Home: 11718 River View Rd NE Hanover MN 55341 Office: Brookdale Christian Ctr Assembly of God 6030 Xerxes Ave N Brooklyn Center MN 55430

CIMINO, RALPH LIEBERT, religion educator; b. Rocca, Isernia, Italy, June 27, 1918; came to U.S., 1924; s. Anthony and Sarah (DiFrancesco) C.; m. Esther Rose Calvanico, June 10, 1944; children: Faith E., Ralph P., Jacqueline J. BA, Cen. Bible Coll., 1962; MA, Assemblies of God Theol. Sem., 1979. Ordained to ministry Assembly of God, 1946. Pastor Assemblies of God, Augusta, Ill., 1944-54, Ewing, Mo., 1944-54; missionary, bible coll. tchr. West Africa, 1954-86; pres. Cen. Bible Coll. of Nigeria, West Africa, 1955-83; missionary in residence Zion Bible Inst., Barrington, R.I., 1987-89, Cen. Bible Coll., Springfield, Mo., 1990—; chmn. Missionary Field Fellowship, Nigeria, 1963-65; gen. sec. Nigeria Assemblies of God, 1975-85. Author: (booklet) Book of Acts, 1960, History of the Old Testament, 1964. Office: Assemblies of God 1445 Boonville Springfield MO 65802

CINTRON, CARMEN DELIA, religious organization administrator; b. Las Piedres, P.R., Feb. 6, 1939; d. Bernardo and Juanita (Fernandez) C.; divorced; children: Mario Ramirez, Humberto Jose Ramirez. AA, Boricua Coll., 1983; postgrad. Baruch Coll., 1984. Sec. labor dept.-unemployment div. Office of Gov. P.R., Santurce, 1958-60; posting-machine operator Corona Brewer Corp., Santurce, 1960-62; consumer service rep. II Aqueduct and Sewer Authority, Rio Piedras, P.R., 1962-71; exec. sec. First Spanish Presbyn. Ch., Bklyn., 1975—; colloquim rep. Boricua Coll., Bklyn., 1983-84. Helper Presbyn. Sr. Citizens, Bklyn., 1975—; mem. Puerto Rican Traveling Theatre, 1983—, N.Y. Mus. Natural History, 1985. Mem. Am. Hort. Soc., Nature Conservancy, Citizens for Decency through Law, Am. Film Inst., NOW, Smithsonian Inst., Postal Commemorative Soc., Nat. Trust for Historic Preservation, People's Med. Soc., Nat. Health Fedn. Republican. Avocations: reading, bicycling, walking. Home: 84-25 Elmhurst Ave Apt 1-I Queens NY 11373

CIONCA, JOHN RICHARD, dean, religion educator, minister; b. Chgo., Aug. 25, 1946; s. Aaron and Anne C.; m. Barbara Kay Lowden, Sept. 6, 1969; children: Benjamin John, Elizabeth Anne. BA in Psychology, Elmhurst Coll., 1968; MRE, Denver Sem., 1971; MA in Adult Edn., Ariz. State U., 1975, PhD in Adult Edn., 1977. Ordained to ministry Conservative Bapt. Assn. Am., 1971. Campus min. Bethany Bapt. Ch., Boulder, Colo., 1968-70; youth min. Trinity Bapt. Ch., Wheatridge, Colo., 1970-71; assoc. pastor Trinity Ch., Mesa, Ariz., 1971-79; sr. pastor Southwood Bapt. Ch., Woodbury, N.J., 1979-85; assoc. dean for student affairs Bethel Sem., St. Paul, 1985—; pres. Phoenix Area Christian Educators, 1978-79; bd. dirs. Denver Sem., 1983-85, Romanian Missionary Soc., Wheaton, Ill., 1986—; interim pastor Minnetonka (Minn.) Bapt. Ch., 1990—. Author: The Trouble Shooting Guide to Christian Education, 1986, The Victors, 1987, Solving Church Education's Ten Toughest Problems, 1990; co-author: What Every Pastor Should Know About Music, Youth and Education, 1986. Mem. Nat. Assn. Profs. Christian Edn. Office: Bethel Sem Saint Paul MN 55112-6998

CIROU, JOSEPH PHILIP, priest, organist, educator; b. Chgo., Nov. 3, 1943; s. Ernest Henry and Virginia (Milord) C. BA, St. Mary of the Lake Sem., Mundelein, Ill., 1965, STB, 1967, Sacred Theology Licentiate, 1969; MA, Govs. State U., 1985. Ordained to ministry Byzantine-Bielarusian Cath. Ch. as deacon, 1968, as priest, 1969. Deacon St. John Berchmans' Ch., Chgo., 1968-69; asst. pastor St. Mary of the Assumption Ch., Chgo., 1969-76, St. Gerald Majella Ch., Markham, Ill., 1976-81, St. Irenaeus Ch., Park Forest, Ill., 1981-87, St. Florian Ch., Chgo., 1987—; adminstr. Christ the Redeemer Ch., Chgo., 1987—; tchr. music Cath. Sch. System, Chgo., 1980-82, 89—; mem. Cons. on Ecumenical Hymnody, 1970-80. Editor Johannine Hymnal, 1970; contbr. articles to profl. jours. Mem. Ea. Cath. Clergy Assn. (sec. Chgo. chpt. 1972-76, 88-90, treas. 1976-80, pres. 1990—), Am. Cath. Press (bd. dirs. 1989—). Democrat. Home: 13145 S Houston Chicago IL 60633 Office: Christ the Redeemer Ch 3107 W Fullerton Ave Chicago IL 60647-2809

CIVARDI, ERNESTO CARDINAL, titular archbishop of Sardica; b. Fossarmato, Italy, Oct. 21, 1906. Ordained priest Roman Catholic Ch., 1930; asst. rector Pontifical Lombard Sem., Rome; held various curial offices; undersec., 1953-67, sec. Congregation for Bishops (known as the Consistorial Congregation until 1967), 1967-79; consecrated titular archbishop of Sardica, 1967, elevated to Sacred Coll. of Cardinals, 1979; deacon St. Theodore; sec. Coll. of Cardinals, 1967-79; filled office of sec. at 1978 conclaves which elected Popes John Paul I and John Paul II. Mem. Congregations: Causes of Saints, Evangelization of Peoples. Office: Piazza del S Uffizio 11, 00193 Rome Italy

CLAIR, JOHN JOSEPH, priest; b. Chgo., Nov. 26, 1956; s. William Patrick and Geraldine Marie (Creighton) C. BA in Communications, Loyola U., Chgo., 1978; MDiv, St. Mary of Lake Sem., Mundelein, Ill., 1982. Ordained priest Roman Cath. Ch., 1982. Deacon St. Michael's Ch., Orland Park, Ill., 1981-82; assoc. pastor St. Hubert's Ch., Hoffman Estates, Ill., 1982-90; dir. recruitment dept. Niles Coll. Sem., 1990—; dir. Cath. and Proud, 1988—. Dir. 10 mus. plays. Lord mayor St. Patrick's Day Parade, Hoffman Estates, 1988, 89. Democrat. Home and Office: 7135 N Harlem Ave Chicago IL 60631

CLANCY, EDWARD BEDE CARDINAL, archbishop; b. Lithgow, NSW, Australia, Dec. 13, 1923; s. John Bede and Ellen Lucy (Edwards) C. Grad., St. Columba's Coll., Springwood, NSW, St. Patrick's Coll., Manly, NSW; LSS, Pontifical Bibl. Inst., Rome; DD, Propaganda Fide U., Rome. Ordained priest Roman Cath. Ch., 1949, ordained bishop, 1974. Parish min. Belmore, NSW, 1950-51, Liverpool, NSW, 1955; sem. staff Springwood, NSW, 1958, Manly, 1966-73; aux. bishop Archdiocese of Sydney, Australia, 1974-78; apptd. and installed archbishop of Canberra and Goulburn Australia, 1979; archbishop of Sydney, 1983—, created cardinal,, 1988. Author: The Bible-The Church's Book, 1974; contbr. to Australian Cath. Record. Avocations: reading, golf. Office: St Mary's Cathedral, Archbishop of Sydney, Sydney NSW 2000, Australia

CLANCY, SISTER MADELINE, school system administrator. Supt. schs. Roman Cath. Diocese of Stockton, Calif. Office: Office Supt Schs PO Box 4237 Stockton CA 95204*

CLANCY, THOMAS HANLEY, seminary administrator; b. Helena, Ark., Aug. 8, 1923; s. Thomas Hornor and Ruth (Lewis) C. AB, Spring Hill Coll., 1948; MA, Fordham U., 1950; STL, Facultes S.J., Louvain, Belgium, 1956; PhD, U. London, 1960. Joined S.J., Roman Cath. Ch., 1942, ordained priest, 1955. Instr. Spring Hill Coll., Mobile, Ala., 1950-52; assoc. editor America mag., N.Y.C., 1970-71; provincial supr. New Orleans Province S.J., 1971-77, archivist, 1977—; asst. prof. history and polit. sci. Loyola U., New Orleans, 1960-68, chmn. dept., 1966-69, v.p. acad. affairs, 1968-70, v.p. communications, 1978-89, trustee, 1968-72, 78-89; dir. Jesuit Sem. and Mission Bur., New Orleans, 1989—; lectr. on constns. and history of S.J., 1970—. Author: English Catholic Books 1641-1700: A Bibliography, 1974, An Introduction to Jesuit Life, 1976, Our Friends, 1978, 2d edit., 1989, The Conversational Word of God, 1978 (Japanese edit. 1986); contbr. articles and book revs. to profl. jours. Vol. chaplain Orleans Parish Prison; trustee Spring Hill Coll., 1980-89, Loyola Marymount U., L.A., 1989—; chmn. Inst. Politics, New Orleans, 1968—. Folger Shakespeare Libr. fellow, 1961. Mem. Cath. Record Soc. Democrat. Avocation: golf. Home and Office: 150 Baronne St # 211 New Orleans LA 70112

CLAPP, KENNETH WAYNE, campus minister; b. Greensboro, N.C., Mar. 16, 1948; s. James Ernest and Lillian (Hutchens) C. AB in Sociology, Catawba Coll., 1970; M of Divinity, Yale U., 1973; PhD, Lancaster (Pa.) Theol. Sem., 1989. Ordained to ministry Christian Ch., 1973. Minister edn. North Haven (Conn.) Congl. Ch., 1971-73; pastor Emanuel United Ch. of Christ, Lincolnton, N.C., 1973-79; exec. dir. Blowing Rock (N.C.) Assembly Grounds, 1979-89; campus minister, asst. prof. religion Catawba Coll., Salisbury, N.C., 1989—; del. Gen. Synod-United Ch. of Christ, Washington, 1977-79; v.p. Market Art, Inc., Greensboro, 1972—; bd. dirs. nat. adv. com. Outdoor Ministries, chmn., 1989—. Author: (book) Tried and Tested Retreats, 1976, Making Retreats Work, 1981, Two Approaches To Confirmation Education, 1989; editor (curriculum) Confirmation Studies, 1975; composer Shalom For You and Me, 1975; creator (board game) Wilderness, 1973. Advancement chmn. Lincoln dist. Boy Scouts Am., 1976-78; bd. dirs. Mental Health, Lincolnton, 1978-79; mem. adv. com. Dunn Fund, Blowing Rock, 1981—. Mem. Assn. United Ch. Educators (regional rep. 1974-79). Republican. Lodge: Rotary (pres. Blowing Rock club 1985). Avocations: restoring automobiles, woodworking, handball, sailing. Home: Summit Ave Salisbury NC 28144 Office: Omwake-Dearborn Chapel Catawba Coll PO Box 1039 Salisbury NC 28144-2488

CLAPP, MARGARET ANN, religious education director; b. Ravenna, Ohio, July 26, 1954; d. Earl J.R. and Mary Ann (Hissem) Clark; m. George William Clapp, Oct. 26, 1974; children: Sarah Elizabeth, AnnMarie Ellen, Kathleen Mary. BA in Edn., Kent (Ohio) State U., 1977; MRE, Loyola U., New Orleans, 1991; postgrad., Ursuline U., Pepperpike, Ohio, 1983. CCD catechist St. Joseph Parish, Mantua, Ohio, 1978-85, prin., 1985-87, catechist rite of Christian initiation adults, 1985—, parish dir. religious edn., 1987—, dir. rite of Christian initiation adults, 1991—; mem. Diocesan Bd. Religious Edn., Youngstown, Ohio, 1987—; chmn. Diocesan Ad Hoc Com. on Children's Catechumenate, 1988—. Author children's book: Jason's New Tennis Shoes, 1975. Mem. nat. Cath. Edn. Assn., St. Joseph Garden Club (treas. 1982-85). Home: 9645 Diagonal Rd Mantua OH 44225 Office: Blessed Sacrament Parish 3020 Reeves St NE Warren OH 44483 *People think that you need to find ways to get more out of life. I think that if we are to make the world a better place we need to find ways to put more into life.*

CLAPP, WAYNE GEORGE, minister, educator; b. Detroit, Feb. 11, 1950; s. Dwayne Paul Sr. and Bernadette Gertrude Clapp; m. Ferne Elise O'Malley, Feb. 26, 1973; children: Kellie, Marlene, Ted, Jason, Christine, Sara Beth. BA in Social Rels., Harvard U., 1972; MA in Edn., U. Tex., San Antonio, 1976. Ordained to ministry Christian Ch., 1981. State coord. The Way of Iowa, Des Moines, 1979-81; campus coord. The Way Coll. Bible Rsch., Rome City, Ind., 1982—. With U.S. Army, 1973-76. Home and Office: 2730 E Northport Rome City IN 46784

CLAPPER, GREGORY SCOTT, religion and philosophy educator; b. Chgo., Oct. 3, 1951; s. Allen Bernard and Martha (Garrett) C.; m. Jody Rigg, Oct. 30, 1973; children: Laura, Jenya. AB, Carthage Coll., 1974; MA, U. Wis., Milw., 1977; MDiv, Garrett-Evang. Theol. Sem., 1979; PhD, Emory U., 1985. Ordained to ministry United Meth. Ch., 1978. Asst. prof. Westmar Coll., Le Mars, Iowa, 1985-89; assoc. prof. Teikyo Westmar U., Le Mars, 1989-91; sr. min. Trinity United Meth. Ch., Waverly, Iowa, 1991—. Author: John Wesley on Religious Affections, 1989. Mem. United Meth. Acad. for Spiritual Formation, 1988-90; chaplain Iowa Air N.G., Sioux City, 1989—. Recipient Westmar Trustees Svc. award of excellence Westmar Coll., 1987, Iowa Meritorious Svc. award State of Iowa, 1990. Fellow Soc. John Wesley Fellows; mem. Am. Acad. Religion. Home: 1210 Park Ave Waverly IA 50677 Office: Trinity United Meth Ch 1400 W Bremer Waverly IA 50677

CLARK, BETH, minister; b. Bradford, N.H., Apr. 15, 1914; d. John Scott and Bessie (Murdock) Pendleton; m. John Guill Clark, June 20, 1940 (dec. 1955); children: John Guill Jr., Beverly Estelle Clark Daggett. BA, Colby Coll., 1935; BD, Andover Newton Theol. Sch., 1938; MDiv, Ea. Bapt. Theol. Sem., 1967; D Ministry, Lancaster Theol. Sem., 1981; postgrad., U. Athens, 1970, Jungian Inst., Zurich, 1980, Mansfield Coll., Oxford, Eng., 1982, 85, Caribbean Inst., 1989. Ordained to ministry United Ch. of Christ, 1967. Interim min. various chs. Penn Cen. Conf., United Ch. of Christ, Harrisburg, 1968—. Author: Grief in the Loss of a Pastor, 1981; editor: Meditations on the Lord's Supper (John G. Clark), 1958. Bd. mgr. Bethany Children's Home, Womelsdorf, Pa., 1982-88; mem. adv. com. Sun Home Nursing Svcs., Northumberland, Pa., 1982—, sec., bd. dirs., 1989—. Mem. Interim Network (steering com. 1978-80), Assn. Ret. State Employees, Alban Inst., Interagency Club (pres. 1966-68), Triangle Club (v.p. 1970-74). Democrat. Home: 709 N 9th St Selinsgrove PA 17870 *Our world is crying out for honesty, for absolute truth. Communication is impossible without belief and trust in the sincerity of the other person. Better the bitter truth than favor catering deception.*

CLARK, DANIEL COOPER, priest; b. Winshester, Ind., May 1, 1948; s. Kenneth Raymond and Henrietta Finnerty (Sayers) C. BA, St. Meinrad (Ind.) Coll., 1967; MDiv, Athenaeum of Ohio, Cin., 1980; postgrad., Highland Baptist Hosp., Louisville, 1987-89, Cen. State Hosp., Louisville, 1980. Ordained priest Roman Cath. Ch., 1980. Priest Roman Cath. Ch., Louisville, 1980-89; Chaplain, Highland Baptist Hosp., Louisville, 1986-88. Author: Hope in Cross Addiction 1989, Walking with a Modern Day Christ 1989. Sponsor, Al Anon, Louisville, 1986—, Adult Children of Alcoholics, 1986—. Mem. Amnesty Internat.: Urgent Action, 1981—, Peace & Justice Commn., Archdiocese of Louisville, 1982-83, Nat. Assn. of Cath. Chaplains, Milwaukee, Wis., 1988, Springfield Ministerial Assn. (sec. 1983), KC, Bass Anglers Spsortsman Soc. Roman Catholic. Avocations: fishing, bluegrass banjo, photography. Home and Office: 1924 Newburg Rd Louisville KY 40205-1498

CLARK, DENNIS LEE, clergyman; b. Chgo., Sept. 22, 1947; s. Lloyd Harding and Lorraine C. (Heintz) C.; m. Sharon Lee Pisegna, June 19, 1971; children: Jason Joseph, Jesse Dennis. Student, Youngstown (Ohio) State U., 1966-67, Inst. Motivational Living, New Castle, Pa., 1985, Inst. Basic Youth Conflicts, Wheaton, Ill., 1982. Founder Christian Couples Fellowship, Sharon, Pa., 1978-81, Community Ministries, Sharon, 1981-84; founder, sr. pastor New Life Community Ch., Hermitage, Pa., 1984-86, New Life Covenant Ch., Sharpsville, Pa., 1986—; advisor Womens Anglo Fellowship, Hermitage, 1988-90; bd. govs. Internat. Congress Local Chs., St. Louis, 1990; active Charismatic Bible Ministries, Tulsa, 1989—. Author: Sunshine through Raindrops, 1980; contbr. articles to religious publs. With U.S. Army. Republican. Home: 3878 Holly Ln Hermitage PA 16148 Office: New Life Covenant Ch 3050 Saranac Rd Sharpsville PA 16150

CLARK, DONALD JAMES, minister; b. New Castle, Ind., Dec. 1, 1957; s. Jearldine M. (Wilhelm) C. BTh, Ind. Bible Coll., 1986; postgrad., Earlham Sch. Religion, Richmond, 1991—; ThM, ThD (hon.), Crossroads Grad. Sch., 1988. Ordained to ministry Evang. Christian Chs., 1987. Tchr. youth ministry Loomis (Calif.) Christian Sch., 1978-79; youth min. Emmanuel Ch., Morgantown, Ind., 1979; min. youth and Christian edn. United Pentecostal Ch., New Castle, Ind., 1985; pastoral staff New Creations Christian Ctr., Richmond, 1986; pastor Milton (Ind.), Pershing (Ind.) United Meth. Ch., 1988-90, Peaceful Valley Friends Ch., Lynn, Ind., 1990—. With USAF, 1979-82. Hoosier scholar, 1976. Mem. Western Wayne Ministerial Assn. (v.p. 1990). Home and Office: RR 2 Box 147 Lynn IN 47355

CLARK, DONALD LEWIS, minister, psychology educator; b. Lynchburg, Va., Aug. 31, 1926; s. Myron L. and Edis (Webb) C.; m. M. Sue Stocks, Jan. 9, 1966; children: Rebecca A., Donna J., Michael William. BA, George Washington U., 1950; BD, Southeastern Bapt. Theol. Sem., 1956; MA, Appalachian State Tchrs. Coll., 1958; EdD, U. Fla., 1962. Ordained to ministry Episcopal Ch. as priest, 1986; diplomate Am. Bd. Profl. Psychology. Pastor Middleburg (N.C.) Bapt. Ch., 1953-56; counselor Coop. Christian Counseling Ctr., Hickory, N.C., 1979-85; priest Ch. of Our Saviour (Episcopal-Luth.), Newland, N.C., 1988-89, St. Stephens Episcopal Ch., Morganton, N.C., 1989-90; interim chaplain Patterson (N.C.) Sch., 1990—; prof. psychology Appalachian State U., Boone, N.C., 1969—. Contbr. articles to profl. jours. Commr. N.C. Commn. on Mental Health, Substance Abuse and Devel. Disabilities, Raleigh, 1989—. Mem. Am. Psychol. Assn., N.C. Psychol. Assn., Soc. for the Sci. Study of Religion. Republican. Home: PO Box 502 Boone NC 28608 Office: Appalachian State U Boone NC 28608

CLARK, GARY KENNETH, religious ministries executive; b. New Castle, Pa., June 17, 1936; s. Stanley Kenneth and Melba Sunshine (Brickner) C.; m. Dorothy Agnes MacGregor, Aug. 23, 1958; children: Bethany Jane, Nathan Douglas, David Stanley, Kathryn Joy. BA, Barrington (R.I.) Coll., 1958; MDiv, Gordon Sem., Wenham, Mass., 1965, M of Christian Edn., 1969; DDiv (hon.), Trinity Coll., Nigeria, 1990. Asst. pastor Woodlawn Bapt Ch., Pawtucket, R.I., 1958-61; pastor Calvary Covenant Ch., Cranston, R.I., 1961-63, 1st Bapt. Ch., Salem, N.H., 1963-85; pres. Holy Spirit Renewal Ministries, Pasadena, Calif., 1984—; internat. field coord. Assn. of Internat. Mission Svcs., Pasadena, 1989—; assoc. dir. of program Lausanne Congress of World Evangelism, Monrovia, Calif., 1988-89; pres. Gordon-Cornwell Sem. Alumni, Wenham, 1978-84. Editor: (newletter) Lausanne Internat., 1988-89, Refreshing Times, 1985-91, AD2000, 1987-89. Mem. ABC Ministers Coun., Rotary Internat. Republican. Baptist. Avocations: running, tennis, photography, international travel. Home: 1386 Sierra Bonita Ave Pasadena CA 91104

CLARK, JAMES ERNEST, minister; b. Blue Earth, Minn., Dec. 22, 1942; s. DeVere Elwood and Lorene (Kark) C.; m. Pamela Ann Long, Sept. 10, 1966; children: Christopher Wade, Deborah Lynn. BA, Buena Vista Coll., 1965; MDiv., Princeton Theol. Sem., 1968. Pastor 1st Presbyn. Ch., Elbow Lake, Ashby, Minn., 1968-70; assoc. pastor 1st Presbyn. Ch., Burlington, Iowa, 1970-73; pastor St. Andrew Ch., Davenport, Iowa, 1973—; bd. dirs. Quad City Interfaith, Davenport. Mem. Albin Inst. Office: St Andrew Presbyn Ch 2501 E Pleasant St Davenport IA 52803

CLARK, JERRY DALE, minister; b. Athens, Tenn., July 28, 1955; s. Columbus Eugene and Mary Christine (Ledford) C.; m. Rebecca Darlene Manning, Aug. 24, 1979; children: Donald Scott, Hope Maria. BS, Tenn. Tech. U., Cookeville, 1981; MDiv, Southeastern Bapt. Sem., Wake Forest, N.C., 1988. Ordained to ministry So. Bapt. Conv., 1989. Singles minister Apex Bapt. Ch., Apex, N.C., 1987-88; sr. minister Abbottsburg Bapt. Ch., Bladenboro, N.C., 1988—. Fundraiser Am. Cancer Soc., Elizabethtown, N.C., 1989. With USAF, 1974-77. Named Outstanding Vet. award, Roane State Community Coll., 1979. Mem. Bladen Bapt. Assn. (missions devel. dir.), Phi Alpha Theta (sec. 1979-81). Republican. Home and Office: RR 3 Box 500 Bladenboro NC 28320 *The secret of one's success is not what they have accomplished as much as how they have handled their failures.*

CLARK, MALCOLM GRAY, minister; b. Lumberton, N.C., Oct. 1, 1947; s. George Ellis and Martha Cromartie (Campbell) C.; divorced; m. Janet Phillips, Jan. 27, 1991; children: Josh, Will, Kelly, Aaron, Jacob. BA, St. Andrews Presbyn. Coll., 1969; postgrad., Union Theol. Seminary, Richmond, Va., 1969-70; MDiv, Eden Theol. Seminary, St. Louis, 1973; D of Ministry, McCormick Theol. Seminary, Chgo., 1979. Ordained to ministry Presbyn. Ch. (USA), 1974. Minister Little River Presbyn. Ch., Hurdle Mills, N.C., 1974-77; assoc. minister First Presbyn. Ch., Asheboro, N.C., 1977-79; minister Fellowship Presbyn. Ch., Greensboro, N.C., 1979—; del. to gen. assembly Presbyn. Ch., Biloxi, Miss., 1985; chmn. budget com. Salem Presbytery, Clemmons, N.C., 1988-90, spl. ministries com. Orange Presbytery, Durham, N.C., 1981. Chmn. Britt for Congress Campaign, Greensboro, 1985-86. Democrat. Home: 2602 Beaconwood Dr Greensboro NC 27405 Office: Fellowship Presbyterian Church 3713 Richfield Rd Greensboro NC 27410

CLARK, MARGARET, clergywoman; b. Miami, Fla., Feb. 15, 1949; d. George Earle and Margaret (Richards) Owen; m. Gerald Daniel Clark, Sept. 1, 1973. BA with honors, Ind. U., 1970; MA, Columbia U., 1973, Union Theol. Sem., 1973; D in Min., N.Y. Theol. Sem., 1982; DHL (hon.), Chapman Coll. Ordained to ministry Christian Ch. Asst. minister Park Ave. Christian Ch., N.Y.C., 1971-74; asst. to pres. Nikko Ceramics, N.Y.C., 1974-77; assoc. minister Union Meml. Ch., Stamford, Conn., 1977-80; assoc. regional minister Northeast region Christian Ch., N.Y.C., 1980-89, regional minister Pacific S.W. region, 1989—; chmn. Ecumenical Ministries Higher Edn., N.Y.C., 1982-83, Com. Denominational Execs., N.Y.C., 1981-82; pres. So. Calif. Ecumenical Coun.; bd. dirs. Disciples Seminary Found., Church Fin. Coun., Chapman Coll. Author: Voices, 1982; contbr. to book: Go Quickly and Tell, 1966. Recipient Community Leadership Devel. award Stamford Coun. Chs., 1978. Mem. Coun. of Chs. City of N.Y. (bd. dirs.), Religion in Am. Life (bd. dirs.), Tri-State Media Ministry (pres., bd. dirs.), Coun. on Christian Unity (bd. dirs.). Home: 11322 Lull St Sun Valley CA 91352 Office: 3126 Los Feliz Blvd Los Angeles CA 90039

CLARK, MATTHEW HARVEY, bishop; b. Troy, N.Y., July 15, 1937; s. M. Harvey and Grace (Bills) C. Student, Coll. Holy Cross, Worcester, Mass.; BA, St. Bernard's Sem., Rochester, N.Y.; STL, N. Am. Coll., Rome; JCL, Gregorian U., Rome. Ordained priest Roman Catholic Ch., 1962—; vice chancellor Diocese of Albany, N.Y.; Cath. chaplain Albany Law Sch.; mem. faculty Vincentian Inst.; chmn. personnel bd. Diocese of Albany; spiritual dir. N. Am. Coll.; bishop Diocese of Rochester, 1979—. Office: Chancery Office 1150 Buffalo Rd Rochester NY 14624

CLARK, MAURICE COATES, hospital chaplain, retired educator; b. Stamford, Conn., Feb. 4, 1921; s. Loyal Brown and Ada Agnes (Coates) C.; m. Cynthia Ann Reed, Aug. 25, 1945 (div. 1965); children: Steven, Judith, Daniel, Peter; m. Harriett Anne Stovall, Oct. 17, 1965. BA, Wesleyan U., 1942; M Div., Yale U., 1945. Ordained to ministry United Ch. of Christ, 1945. Chaplain Columbus (Ohio) State Hosp., 1950-68; pastoral counselor Bay County Guidance Clinic, Panama City, Fla., 1968-70; dir. pastoral services Brevard County Mental Health Ctr., Rockledge, Fla., 1970-77; teaching chaplain Toronto (Can.) Inst. Pastoral Tng., 1977-79; chaplain supr. Hosp. Chaplaincy Council, Troy, Ohio, 1979-80, Cen. Ohio Psychiat. Hosp., Columbus, 1980-90; mental health cons. Roman Cath. Diocese of Columbus, 1981-87, Trinity Luth. Sem., Columbus, 1984—; mem. dept. ministry United Ch. Christ; exec. dir. Council Clin. Tng., N.Y.C., 1962-67; cons. Samaritan Counseling Ctr., Cleve., 1991—. Contbr. articles to profl. jours. Mem. Am. Acad. Psychotherapists, Am. Assn. Pastoral Counselors (diplomate), Am. Group Therapy Assn., Am. Protestant Hosp. Assn. (coll. of chaplains), Assn. Clin. Pastoral Edn. (chaplain supr. 1948—), Assn. Mental Health Chaplains (profl. mem.). Home: 7200 Riverside Dr Dublin OH 43017

CLARK, ODIS MORRISON, minister; b. Frankfort, Ky., Jan. 23, 1944; s. Leonard Raymond and Waldien (Hammond) C.; m. Sharon Louise Patrick, Aug. 3, 1968; children: Brian Patrick, Jonathan Raymond, Amy Katherine. AB, Louisville Bible Coll., 1967, M. Sacred Lit., 1988; M. Ministry, Ky. Christian Coll., 1988. Minister Mt. Eden (Ky.) Christian Ch., 1966-72, River Drive Christian Ch., Irvine, Ky., 1972-76, Indian Hills Christian Ch., Danville, Ky., 1976—. Mem. continuation com. So. Christian Youth Conf., Lexington, Ky., 1980, 1966—, pres., 1986; pres. Temperance League of Ky., Louisville, 1983-89, v.p., 1989—; v.p. Child Devel. Ctr., Danville, 1987-88; active D.A.R.E. Com., Danville, 1988. Recipient Outstanding Leadership award Salt River Men's Fellowship, Shelbyville, Ky., 1972, Estill/Madison County Men's Fellowship, Richmond, Ky., 1976; named one of Outstanding Young Men of Am. Mem. Danville/Boyle Ministers Assn. (pres. 1984), Rotary (sec. Danville chpt. 1983—). Avocations: fishing, basketball, softball. Home: 409 Streamland Danville KY 40422 Office: Indian Hills Christian Ch 516 Grabruck Danville KY 40422

CLARK, RICHARD STANLEY, minister; b. Portsmouth, Va., Mar. 3, 1955; s. Albert Bernhard and Margaret Ann (Barnes) C.; m. Deborah Joanne McKinney, Mar. 29, 1975; children: Joshua Albert, Haley. BS, Roanoke Bible Coll., 1978. Ordained to ministry Ch. of Christ, 1978. Youth minister Zion's Chapel Ch. of Christ, Roper, N.C., 1976-79; minister youth and music North Scales Ch. of Christ, Reidsville, N.C., 1979-86; youth minister Central Christian Ch., Carmel, Ind., 1986—; pres. Ind. Jr. High Christian Conv., Indpls., 1990-91, Carolina Christian Youth Conf., Chapel Hill, N.C., 1981-82, N.C. Bible Bowl League, 1982-83; instr. youth ministers Roanoke Bible Coll., Elizabeth City, N.C., 1986—. Mem. Delta Epsilon Chi. Republican. Home: 719 Winter Way Carmel IN 46032 Office: Central Christian Ch 1242 W 136th St Carmel IN 46032 *When I remember what God has done, I cannot doubt what God can do.*

CLARK, RICHARD W., minister; b. Pitts., Feb. 11, 1954; s. Norman N. and Betty Jane (Fast) C.; m. Patricia Ruth Richards, Aug. 21, 1976; children: Charissa Lynn, Sarah Elizabeth. BA in Religion magna cum laude, Westminster Coll., 1976; MDiv magna cum laude, Gordon-Conwell Theol. Sem., 1979; postgrad., Fuller Theol. Sem. Ordained to ministry Presbyn. Ch. (U.S.A.), 1979. Pastor Paris Presbyn. Ch., Burgettstown, Pa., 1979-83, Dormont Presbyn. Ch., Pitts., 1983-86, Forest Park Presbyn. Ch., Hutchinson, Kans., 1986—; mem. com. on ministry So. Kans. Presbytery, Wichita, 1991—. Home: 603 E 25th Ave Hutchinson KS 67502 Office: Forest Park Presbyn Ch 700 E 25th Ave Hutchinson KS 67502

CLARK, ROBERT EUGENE, religion educator; b. Cheyenne, Wyo., Aug. 19, 1931; s. Glen E. and Anna W. (Shaw) C.; m. Marian A. Anderson, June 13, 1954; children: Kathleen, Kevin, Kristine, Karen, Ken, Kraig. BA, Wheaton Coll., 1961; MS, U. Nebr., Omaha, 1965; EdD, U. Denver, 1968. Dir. Christian edn. Bethel Bible Ch., Hammond, Ind., 1954-58; instr. Faith Bapt. Bible Coll., Ankeny, Iowa, 1958-59, chmn. Christian edn. dept., 1961-69; prof. Christian edn. faculty Moody Bible Inst., Chgo., 1969-91, ret., 1991. Author: (with others) Understanding People, 2d edit., 1981; editor: Childhood Education in the Church, 1975, rev. edit., 1986, Teaching Preschoolers, 1983, Study Guide, Keys to Happy Family Living, 1990, Christian Education: Foundations for the Future, 1991; contbr. to publs. in field. Recipient Faculty Citation award Moody Bible Inst., 1983. Baptist. Home: 10360 E Jewell Ave # 90 Denver CO 80231

CLARK, ROSS ALAN, minister; b. Austin, Tex., Oct. 14, 1960; s. James Lamar and Clara Cathrine (Pickett) C. BA, Baylor U., 1984; MRE, Midwestern Bapt. Sem., Kansas City, Mo., 1989. Ordained to ministry Bapt. Ch., 1989. Min. youth and music Calvary Bapt. Ch., Santa Fe, N.Mex., 1983-85, Bethel Bapt. Ch., Independence, Mo., 1987-91; tchr. People's Republic of China, 1991—. Pledge pres. APO Fraternity, Baylor U., 1983. Mem. Pub. Rels. Soc. (v.p. Baylor Univ. chpt. 1983-84).

CLARK, STEPHEN MORRIESON, minister; b. Mandeville, Jamaica, July 26, 1950; came to U.S., 1977; s. Ernest Morrieson and Elizabeth Jane (Jesperson) C.; m. Olivia Faith Arscott, Aug. 20, 1972; children: Stephen Matthew, Jean-Paul Morrieson, Alisha Katherine. Diploma in theology, U. London, 1972; MDiv, Gordon-Conwell Sem., 1980; ThM, Princeton U., 1980; MPhil, Drew U., 1983, PhD, 1986. Ordained to ministry Presbyn. Ch. in Am., 1973. Pastor Grace Ch., Kingston, Jamaica, 1973-77, Knowlton Presby. Ch., Columbia, 1981—; lectr. Jamaica Theol. Sem., Kingston, 1977, Westminster Theol. Sem., Phila., 19890—; chmn. theol. exams. Presbytery of N.J., 1984-90; chaplain Knowlton Twp., Columbia, N.J., 1990—. Mem. Am. Acad. Religion. Office: Knowlton Presbyn Ch Rd 1 Box 1432 Columbia NJ 07832

CLARK, VICTOR JOSEPH, abbot; b. Cullman, Ala., Jan. 7, 1930; s. Marcus Rene and Anna Marie (Schwann) C. AA, St. Bernard Jr. Coll., Cullman, 1948; BS, St. Benedict Coll., 1951; MS, Auburn U., 1957; postgrad., St. Bernard Abbey, 1951. Joined Order of St. Benedict, 1949, ordained priest Roman Cath. Ch., 1954. Biology tchr. St. Bernard Coll., Cullman, 1952-79, dean of men, 1965-69; bus. officer St. Bernard Abbey, Cullman, 1976-82, 86-87; pastor St. Bartholemew Ch., Elberta, Ala., 1983-86; abbot St. Bernard Abbey, Cullman, 1987—; chmn. bd. dirs. St. Bernard Prep. Sch., Cullman, 1987—. Mem. (abbey) Am. Cassinese Congregation of the Order of St. Benedict, KC (chaplain 1975). Home and Office: 1600 St Bernard Dr SE Cullman AL 35055 *"Ut in Omnibus glorificetur Deus" is the Benedictine motto which translated means "That in all things may God be glorified."*

CLARK, WESLEY GLENN, minister; b. Three Sands, Okla., Sept. 1, 1929; s. Willis A. C. and Roberta A. (Hayes) C.; m. Gladys E. Carrithers, Sept. 5, 1969. Student, Grand Canyon Coll., Phoenix, 1973, Cen. Ariz. Coll., 1974; diploma, So. Sem., Louisville, 1976; BTh, Internat. Sem., Plymouth, Fla., 1982, MDiv, 1983. Ordained to ministry So. Bapt. Conv., 1972. Enlisted man U.S. Army, 1948; ret., 1968; pastor 1st So. Mammoth Ch., Mammoth, Ariz., 1972-74, Ashby Lane Bapt. Ch., Valley Station, Ky., 1974—. Democrat. Home: 6623 Ashby Ln Louisville KY 40272 Office: Ashby Ln Bapt Ch 6617 Ashby Ln Louisville KY 40272 *We are citizens of two worlds and the energizing power of these worlds is Jesus Christ. However, to perpetuate this power we are obligated to have more confidence and more faith in our young. To lose confidence in our youth is to admit defeat.*

CLARKE, CAROLYN CARPENTER, minister; b. Attleboro, Mass., Apr. 9, 1937; d. Lloyd Wesley and Elsie Marvis (Hager) Carpenter; m. James Davis Clarke, July 13, 1963; children: Sabra, Benjamin, Heather. BS, Ursinus Coll., 1959; cert. in occupational therapy, U. Pa., 1961; MDiv, Andover Newton Theol. Sch., 1987. Ordained to ministry Am. Bapt. Chs. in USA, 1985. Asst. pastor Am. Bapt. Chs. Strafford, N.H., 1981-83; pastor 2d Bapt. Ch., Strafford, 1983-86, New Boston (N.H.) Fellowship, 1987-89; vol. bd. internat. mis. Am. Bapt. Chs., Zaire, 1989-90; pastor Georga Plain (Vt.) Bapt. Ch., 1990—; sec. Am. Bapt. Charismatic Fellowship, 1984-88; sec., pres. bd. dirs. United Campus Ministry U. N.H., 1984-87. Mem. Am. Bapt. Chs. in USA (mins. coun.). Home and Office: RD 3 Box 4637 Milton VT 05468

CLARKE, EDWIN KENT, archbishop; b. Rankin, Ont., Can., Jan. 21, 1932; s. J. Roy and Margaret G. (Brown) C.; m. Norma L. Griffith, July 25, 1964; children—John, Susan, Myles. B.A., Bishop's U., Lennoxville, Que., Can., 1954; L.S.T., Bishop's U., 1956; M.R.E., Union Theol. Sem., N.Y.C., 1960; D.D. (hon.), Huron Coll., London, Ont., Can., 1977. Ordained to ministry Anglican Ch., 1957; consecrated bishop, 1976. Curate All Saint's Westboro Ch., Ottawa, Ont., 1956-59; diocesan dir. Christian edn. Anglicn Diocese of Ottawa, 1960-66; rector St. Barnabas Anglican Ch., St. Lambert, Que., 1966-73; archdeacon of Niagara Anglican Ch. of Can., Hamilton, Ont., 1973-76; suffragan bishop of Niagara Anglican Ch. of Can., 1976-79, bishop of Edmonton, 1979—; elected met. Rupert's Land, 1986, resigned, 1987; mem. Immigration and Refugee Bd., Can., 1988. Home: RR 3, Pembroke, ON Canada K8A 6W4

CLARKE, GORDON, clergyman; b. Charleston, W.Va., Mar. 3, 1931; s. Leonard Gordon and Marguerite (Lyons) C.; m. Martha Thompson, Nov. 3, 1950; children: Daniel Gordon, David Allen. AB in Religion, Marion (Ind.) Coll., ThM; DD (hon.), C.T.S. Ordained to ministry Friends Ch. Dir. Creative Ministries, Indpls., 1959-69; regional exec. sec. Am. Bible Soc., Chgo., 1959-77; pastor Forsyth Friends Ch. Winston-Salem, N.C., 1977-79; sr. pastor Garden Grove (Calif.) Friends Ch., 1979—; chaplain Garden Grove Police Dept.; chmn. Bd. Spiritual Life Friends United Meeting, chmn. program meeting 1987, mem. meeting ministries commn.; mem. exec. com. bd. adminstrn. S.W. Yearly Meeting, chmn. spiritual life com.; pres. bd. trustees Calif. Friends Homes; founder Chaplain-on-Call. Mem. Spl. Task Force of Religious Well Being for White House Conf. on Aging; mem. Gov.'s Commn. on Aging, Gov.'s Commn. on Tourism, Gov.'s Com. on Migrant Labor. Sgt. USAF. Mem. Coll. Chaplains Am. Protestant Hosp. Assn., Correctional Chaplains Assn., Internat. Platform Assn., Nat. Assn. Religious Broadcasters, Leisure Fellowship Ministry. Home: 11571 Varna St Garden Grove CA 92640 Office: Garden Grove Friends Ch 12211 Magnolia St Garden Grove CA 92641

CLARKE, RITA-LOU, minister; b. Riverside, Calif., Apr. 7, 1934; d. Cleopas John and Mary Rebecca (Rolfe) Messer; m. Russell Charles Reid, July 23, 1955 (div. 1980); children: Mark Allan, Anne Reid Opperman, Paul James, Janis Lynn; m. George James Clarke, July 19, 1980. BSc in Home Econs., U. Wash., 1956; MDiv, Sch. of Theology at Claremont, 1982, D of Ministry, 1985. Ordained to ministry United Presbyn. Ch. in the U.S.A., 1985. Elde Arcadia (Calif.) Presbyn. Ch., 1975-80; intern Calvary Presbyn. ch., South Pasadena, Calif., 1982, 1st Presbyn. Ch., Baldwin Park, Calif., 1983-84; assoc. pastor 1st Presbyn. Ch., Garden Grove, Calif., 1985-88; pastor 1st Presbyn. Ch., Williamsburg, Ohio, 1989—; pres., bd. dirs. Evangelical Women's Caucus, So. Calif., 1980-81; del. Gen. Assembly, Presbyn. Ch. in U.S.A., St. Louis, 1988. Author: Pastoral Care of Battered Women, 1986; (with others) Voices of Experience: Lifestories of Clergywomen in the Presbyterian Church (U.S.A.), 1991; contbr. articles to jours. in field. Chaplain Clermont (Ohio) Mercy Hosp., 1989—; mem. YWCA Protection from Abuse Bd., Cin., 1990—. Recipient Vol. of Yr. award YWCA, Cin., 1990. Mem. Nat. Assn. Presbyn. Clergywomen, Williamsburg Garden Club. Democrat. Home: 3222 Williamsburg-Batavia Pike Batavia OH 45103 Office: 1st Presbyn Ch 2d and Gay Sts Williamsburg OH 45176

CLARY, BRUCE MAXFIELD, minister; b. Berwyn, Ill., July 30, 1939; s. Bruce Homer and Jane (Maxfield) C.; m. Myra Lee Hughes, Dec. 27, 1969 (div. 1974); 1 child, David Hughes Clary; m. Dorothy Newton Moore, Apr. 16, 1978. BA, U. Tulsa, 1961; BD, Meadville Theol., Chgo., 1965. Ordained to ministry Unitarian Universalist Ch., 1965. Min. various chs. Mass., Okla. and Vt., 1965-78; min. 1st Parish Universalist Ch., Stoughton, Mass., 1978-91, East Shore Unitarian Universalist Ch., Mentor, Ohio, 1991—. Author: Views From the Iceberg, 1987. Active Stoughton Arts Coun., 1988—, ACLU, Mass., 1988—, NOW, Mass., 1988—. Recipient govs. OKIE award Okla., 1978. Mem. Ballou Channing Dist. of UUA (pres. 1983-84), Ballou Channing Ministers Assn. (pres. 1983-84), Unitarian Universalists Ministers Assn. (sec. 1969-70), Liberal Religious Edn. Dir. Assn., Unitarian Sunday Sch. Soc. (pres. 1990—), Masons, Shriners, Sigma Chi (historian 1960-61). Democrat. Avocations: painting, photography, writing, antiques, model railroading. Home: 98 Bassick Circle Stoughton MA 02072 Office: East Shore Unitarian Universalist Ch 8181 S Center St Mentor OH 44060

CLARY, WILLIAM VICTOR, minister; b. Baraboo, Wis., May 27, 1946; s. Harry Theone and Ruth Margaret (Harris) C.; m. F. Marie Bush, Aug. 12, 1966; children: Donna, Vicki, William. AA, Mich. Christian Coll., 1966; BA, Okla. Christian Coll., 1968; postgrad., Abilene Christian U., 1972, No. Ill. U., 1973. Ordained to ministry Ch. of Christ, 1966. Min. Clinton, Ill., 1974-78, Lincoln, Ill., 1978-84, Anchorage, 1984—. v.p. Ill. Christian Camp, Decatur, 1978-84, dir. 1976-84; dir. Ill. Ch. of Christ Exhibit, Springfield, Ill., 1977-84; chaplain Abraham Lincoln Hosp., Licoln, 1978-84, Logan County Jail, Lincoln, 1983-84; host-parent Am. Field Svcs., 1988, 89, 90 (chpt. pres. 1988-91). Republican. Avocations: reading, athletics, fishing, photography, traveling. Home: 1031 W 73d Ave Anchorage AK 99518 Office: PO Box 91735 Anchorage AK 99509 *No matter at what stage one is in life, the best is yet to come. Live each day joyfully knowing that a victory is certain for those in Christ!.*

CLAUSEL, NANCY KAREN, minister; b. Jackson, Tenn., Jan. 1, 1948; s. Clinton Prentice and Martha Juanita (Felker) C.; children: Richard D. Harwood Jr., Kara Denise Harwood. Student Lambuth Coll., 1966-67, George Peabody Coll. for Tchrs.; BEd, Memphis State U., 1971; MDiv summa cum laude, Memphis Theol. Sem., 1980. Ordained to ministry United Meth.; lic. counselor Tenn. Ch. Dir. Christian edn. Grimes United Meth. Ch., Memphis, 1977-79, Wesleyan Hills United Meth. Ch., Memphis, 1979-80; assoc. minister St. James United Meth. Ch., Memphis, 1981-82; dir. Wesley Pastoral Counseling Ctr., Memphis, 1982-85; co-dir. Connection: Holistic Counseling Ctr., Memphis, 1985-87; co-founder, co-minister The Connection Ch., 1986—; bd. dirs. Wesley Found.-Memphis State, 1979-80, 82-84; vice chmn. commn. on status and role of women Memphis Ann. Conf., 1980-86; mem. work area on worship McKendree Dist. Memphis Ann. Conf., 1980-84; mem. Bd. Pensions Memphis Ann. Conf., 1983-84; supervising pastor Candidacy for Minister program Memphis Ann. Conf., 1984-86. Vol. Johnson Aux. City of Memphis Hosp., 1975; sec. Peacemakers Memphis, 1979; clergy rep. adv. bd. Memphis chpt. Parents Without Ptnrs., 1984-85; mem. Network, Memphis, 1984-87. Mem. Internat. Transactional Analysis Assn. (clin. mem. 1981—, provisional teaching mem. 1982—), Assn. for Specialists in Group Work, Memphis Ministers Assn. (treas. 1985-86), Altrusa Internat., Phi Kappa Phi. Columnist: The Light (newspaper). Avocations: aerobics, music. Home: 4114 Henderson Blvd SE Olympia WA 98501 *The development of trust is at the heart of the spirit's journey. Our lives provide constant and unerring reflections of our consciousness.*

CLAUSING, JOHN MAURICE, minister; b. Clay City, Iowa, July 21, 1934; s. Mortiz Gustav and Bertha Alvina (Korspeter) C.; m. Ruth Lea Storm, Dec. 13, 1958; children: James, Debra, Judith, Mary Jo. BA, Lakeland Coll., Plymouth, Wis., 1956; BD, Mission House, Plymouth, Wis., 1959; ThM, Princeton Theol. Sem., 1963. Ordained to ministry United Ch. of Christ, 1959. Pastor Bowmansville-Center (Pa.) Charge, 1959-64, Lake Ave. United Ch. of Christ, Elyria, Ohio, 1964-74; sr. pastor Trinity United Ch. of Christ, Miamisburg, Ohio, 1974-81; interim pastor S.W. Ohio Assn., Dayton, 1981—; chmn. Ohio Conf. Intentional Ministers, Columbus, 1988-91; staff S.W. Ohio Assn. Tng. and Support Group, Dayton, 1987-91. Editor, pubr. Jour. for Interim Ministers, Moving On, 1988-91; radio and TV preacher: One for All, 1986-89, 90-91. Pres. Burg. Ctr., Miamisburg, Ohio, 1979-81; founder Ecumenical Resettlement Com., Miamisburg, 1978-81; pres. Firelands Retirement Ctr., Elyria, Ohio, 1972-74; co-founder United Ch. of Christ Homes, Annville, 1960-64. Mem. Interim Ministry Network. Home: 3316 Ultimate Way Dayton OH 45449 *True freedom is not to pursue whatever passing thought happens to flit through our minds at the moment, but to follow with commitment those deep interests and gifts which God has placed in our soul.*

CLAUSSEN, RUSSELL GEORGE, minister, church organization administrator; b. Chgo., Aug. 10, 1934; s. Herman William and Eleanor Martha (Seiferth) C. BA, DePauw U., 1955; MDiv, Yale U., 1959. Ordained to ministry United Ch. of Christ, 1959. Chaplain U. Mass., Amherst, 1959-61; pastor North Congl. Ch., Amherst, 1961-66; editor curriculum United Ch. Bd. for Homeland Ministries, N.Y.C., 1973-82; dir. youth work United Ch. of Christ, N.Y.C., 1966-73, editor publs. Office for Ch. in Soc., 1982-90; editor United Ch. Press, N.Y.C., 1990—; dir. Cen. Com. for Conscientious Objectors, Phila., 1970-79; mem. staff Met. Assn. United Ch. of Christ, 1991—. Mem. editorial bd. Voices: Jour. for Psychotherapists, 1981—. Chmn. Prisoner Visitation and Support, Phila., 1972-81; vol. mgr. AIDS Bailey House, N.Y.C.; mem. N.Y.C. Dem. Com. Recipient Disting. Svc. award Prisoner Visitation and Support, 1988. Home: 171 Court St Brooklyn NY 11201

CLAWSON, ARTHUR EMORY, minister, missionary; b. Erie, Pa., Dec. 23, 1953; s. Arthur Ellsworth Clawson and LaVerne Magdalene (Allen) Kochanowski; m. Suetta Ruth Batchelor, Apr. 26, 1973. BA, Warner So. Coll., 1978; MS, Fla. State U., 1980, postgrad., 1991—. Ordained to ministry Ch. of God (Anderson, Ind.), 1985. Pastor First Ch. of God, Richmond, Va., 1978-79; coord. student devel. Warner So. Coll., Lake Wales, Fla., 1979-85; coord. community devel. missionary bd. Ch. of God (Anderson, Ind.), 1986-91; mem. faculty Warner So. Coll., Lake Wales, 1981-85. Contbr. articles to religious jours. Sgt. USAF, 1971-74. Mem. Rotary. Home: PO Box 2615 Tallahassee FL 32316-2615 *In this day and age we have lost the realization that God can use us beyond our wildest imagination.*

CLAY, DONALD OWEN, JR., minister; b. Cin., Nov. 7, 1959; s. Donald Owen and Ada Mae (Freeman) C.; m. Sharon Anita Hooper, Oct. 9, 1982.

B.A. in Religious Studies, U. Ariz., 1981. Ordained to ministry Baptist Ch., 1979. Assoc. minister Mt. Sinai Bapt. Ch., Cin., 1976-77; dir. evangelism Youth for Christ, Dallas, 1979, bd. dirs., 1979; asst. pastor Grace Temple Missionary Bapt. Ch., Tucson, 1980-81; pastor United Missionary Bapt. Ch., Middletown, Ohio, 1981-85, Mt. Ararat Bapt. Ch., Pitts., 1985—. Chief editor The Voice, 1984. Mem. ad hoc com. Miami U., Middletown, 1984; 8th Congl. Dist. coordinator Jesse Jackson Presdl. campaign, 1984; cons. Middletown Pub. Schs., 1981-85; founder "Just Us" Drug Abuse Program, Middletown, 1982—. Mem. NAACP, Progressive Nat. Bapt. Conv. (del. 1981—), Lott Carey Fgn. Missions Conv. (del. 1985—), NAACP (Middletown chpt.; pres. 1984-85), Kappa Alpha Psi. Avocation: golf. Office: Mt Ararat Bapt Ch 271 Paulson Ave Pittsburgh PA 15206

CLAYBOURN, COLLEEN TALMADGE, lay worker; b. Gary, Ind., Oct. 11, 1934; d. Paul Preston and Leonora May (Hill) Talmadge; m. James Leo Penland, Mar. 27, 1952 (div. Jan. 1971); children: Sharon Melita Cress, Sarah Leonora Binder, Rhoda Allene Garrett, Aaron Altha II (dec.); m. Guy Raymond Claybourn Jr., Nov. 19, 1972; stepchildren: Clayton Alan, Carolyn Guilaine Goforth. Student, Savannah (Ga.) Jr. Coll., 1952. Deacon First Presbyn. Ch., Palacios, Tex., 1976, elder, 1980—; mission and svc. com. Mission Presbytery, San Antonio, 1978-84, chmn. Presbyn. devel. corp., 1980-85, moderator, 1988-89, mem. spiritual task force com., 1988-91; exec. dir., trustee The Trull Found., Palacios, 1981—; commr. Mission Presbytery to Gen. Assembly Presbyn. Ch. (U.S.A.), 1989; bd. dirs. Presbyn. Hist. Soc. S.W., Dallas. Author: A History of the First Presbyterian Church, 1982 (Tex. Hist. Commn. award 1983), Palacios—Past & Present, 1985; editor: Historic Matagorda County, 1986 (Tex. Genealogy Soc. award 1987). Chmn. Palacios Bay Fest, Inc., 1979, bd. dirs. 1979-90; chmn. Palacios Area Hist. Assn., 1984—; bd. dirs. Rainbow Land Day Care Ctr., Palacios, 1967-68; active Matagorda County Hist. Commn., Bay City, Tex., 1984—, Matagorda County Hist. Soc., 1984—. Named Woman of Yr. Palacios C. of C., 1986, Historian of Yr. Palacios Area Hist. Assn., 1987. Mem. Conf. S.W. Found. (sec. 1978-80, bd. dirs. 1980-81, archivist 1987—), Sigma Tau Nu. Democrat. Home: 1511 Bayshore Dr Palacios TX 77465 Office: The Trull Foundation 404 Fourth St Palacios TX 77465 *I am, like E.B. White, always torn between savoring (enjoying) the world or saving (improve) it, which makes it hard to plan the day.*

CLAYMAN, DAVID, rabbi, academic administrator; b. Cambridge, Mass., Sept. 8, 1933; s. Benjamin and Sophie (Kushner) C.; m. Rachel Kestenbaum, June 17, 1956; children: Tamar, Daniel, Jonathan. BA, Harvard Coll., 1954; B.H.L., Hebrew Coll., Brookline, Mass., 1955; M.H.L., Jewish Theol. Sem., N.Y.C., 1959, DD (hon.), 1986. Chaplain U.S. Navy, 1959-61; assoc. rabbi Temple Har Zion, Phila., 1961-64; rabbi Congregation Ramat El, Phila., 1964-70; Israel dir. Am. Jewish Congress., Jerusalem, 1980—. Author: (jour.) The Congress Monthly, (newsletter) The Jerusalem Letter. Dir. Louise Waterman Wise Youth Hostel, Jerusalem, 1980—. Lt. USN, 1959-61. Fellow Jerusalem Ctr. for Pub. Affairs, 1976—. Mem. Rabbinical Assembly. Home: 19 Hachish St, Jerusalem Israel Office: Am Jewish Congress, 3 Mapu St, Jerusalem Israel

CLAYPOOL, JOHN ROWAN, IV, priest; b. Franklin, Ky., Dec. 15, 1930; s. John Rowan III and Mary Etta (Buchanan) C.; (div. Oct. 1981); children: John R. V, Laura Lue (dec.); m. Ann Wilkinson Scheyd, June 25, 1982; children: Charles T. Williams III, Laura C. Williams. AA, Mars Hill Coll., 1950; BA, Baylor U., 1952; BD, So. Bapt. Theol. Sem., 1955, ThD, 1959. Ordained to ministry Episcopal Ch. as priest, 1986. Sr. pastor Broadway Bapt. Ch., Ft. Worth, 1971-76, Northminster Bapt. Ch., Jackson, Miss., 1976-81; co-pastor Second Bapt. Ch., Lubbock, Tex., 1982-85; theologian-in-resident Christ Episcopal, San Antonio, 1985-87; rector St. Luke's Episcopal Ch., Birmingham, Ala., 1987—; bd. dirs. St. Martin's-in-the-Pines Retirement Home, Birmingham; adv. bd. dept. Pastoral Care, U. Ala., Birmingham, 1988—, Bapt. Montclair Hosp., Birmingham, 1988. Author: Tracks of a Fellow Struggler, 1974, Stages, 1977, The Preaching Event, 1980, The Light Within You, 1982, Opening Blind Eyes, 1983, Glad Reunion, 1984. Named Young Man of Yr. Jr. C. of C., Louisville, 1965. Mem. Birmingham C. of C., Birmingham County Club. Home: 4313 Fair Oaks Dr Birmingham AL 35213 Office: St Lukes Episcopal Ch 3736 Montrose Rd Birmingham AL 35213

CLAYTON, ALLEN LEE, librarian; b. Santa Monica, Calif., Sept. 1, 1951; s. Harold Amos and Ada Mae (Lloyd) C.; m. Mary Rachel Gutel, Jan. 5, 1973; 1 child, Monica Mary. BA, So. Calif. Coll., 1973; MDiv, Yale U., 1976; PhD, So. Meth. U., 1988. Asst. govt. documents libr. U. Tex.-Dallas, Richardson, 1987—; grad. fellow So. Meth. U., Dallas, 1976-85; vis. adj. prof. St. Paul Sch. Theology, Kansas City, Mo., 1989; speaker in field. Contbr. articles to profl. publs. Alt. del. Dallas County Dem. Party, 1980. Layne Found. scholar, 1973. Mem. N.Am. Patristic Soc., Soc. Biblical Lit., Am. Soc. Ch. History, S.W. Sem. on Catholic Christianity. Home: 2113 Spanish Trail Irving TX 75060-7342 Office: U Tex-Dallas PO Box 830643 Sta MC33 Richardson TX 75083-0643

CLEARY, EDWARD LOUIS, university administrator; b. Chgo., Aug. 4, 1929; s. Emmet Vincent and Mary Veronica C.; student Marquette U., 1947-50; B.A., Aquinas Inst., 1953, M.A., 1954; Ph.D., U. Chgo., 1975. Entered Dominican Order, 1950, ordained priest Roman Catholic Church, 1957; instr., dean of students Nat. Sem., Bolivia, 1958-62; asst. prof. St. Xavier Coll., Chgo., 1963-66; asst. prof., asst. dir. U. Pitts., 1971-76; prof., dean Aquinas Inst., Dubuque, Iowa, 1976-79; research assoc. Columbia U. and Research Inst. for Study of Man, N.Y.C., 1979-81; coordinator social research, adj. prof. MaryKnoll Sch. Theology, 1982-83; research assoc. Columbia U., N.Y.C., 1983—. Ford Found. fellow, 1970-72; Comparative Edn. fellow, 1971-72. Mem. Am. Acad. Religion, Soc. Sci. Study of Religion, Am. Cath. Theol. Soc., Am. Anthropol. Assn., Am. Sociol. Assn. Editor, co-founder Estudios Andinos, 1969-76, contbg. editor, 1976—; editor: Shaping a New World, 1971; contbr. articles to scholarly jours. Home: 431 Bedford Rd Pleasantville NY 10570

CLEARY, MICHAEL J., religious organization administrator. Pres. Gambia Christian Coun., Banjul. Office: Gambia Christian Coun, POB 27, Banjul The Gambia*

CLEAVER, LUCY TEMPLETON, religion educator; b. Calvert, Tex., Apr. 11, 1929; d. Monroe and Eunice Alma (Derrick) Templeton; m. Houston L. Tidwell Jr., Dec. 31, 1947 (dec. Dec. 1964); 1 child, Terry Tidwell Cleaver Eaton; m. Kenneth Ray Cleaver, July 29, 1967 (dec.). BS, Tex. Wesleyan, 1978; MRE, Tex. Christian U., 1980. Cert. Christian educator, Tex. Dir. Christian edn. First Presbyn. Ch., Tyler, Tex., 1983-87, Ridglea Presbyn. Ch., Ft. Worth, 1987—. Pres. womens div. C. of C., Arlington, Tex., 1972, Soroptimist Club of Arlington, 1971. Mem. Assn. Presbyn. Ch. Educator (pres. 1990-91, south cen. region rep. 1986-90, rep. educator certification coun., 1987—), Quadrangle Club. Home: 1703 Larkspur Arlington TX 76013

CLEETON, ROGER EARL, minister; b. Lancaster, Mo., July 3, 1949; s. Theodore Earl and Beulah Ivalee (Crump) C.; m. Janice Marie Thomas, July 31, 1971; children: Tracy, Terry, Tamela. Student, Bethany Coll. Missions, 1971, Robert Schuller Inst., Garden Grove, Calif., 1975, Emmaus Bible Coll., Dubuque, Iowa, 1986, Liberty U., Lynchburg, Va., 1990. Ordained elder Free Meth. Ch. N.Am., 1978. Min. Irving Park Free Meth. Ch., Chgo., 1974-77, Beaver Dam (Wis.) Free Meth. Ch., 1977-84, Livingston (Wis.) Free Meth. Ch., 1984-86, Leslie (Mich.) Free Meth. Ch., 1986-89, Faith Free Meth. Ch., Snover, Mich., 1989—; dir. children's ministry Ill.-Wis. Conf., Woodstock, Ill., 1976-86; bd. dirs. Olive Branch Mission, Chgo., 1975-78; chaplain McKenzie Meml. Hosp., Sandusky, Mich., 1989—. Editor Childrens Ministries Memo newsletter, 1978-86. Mem. Snover Ministerial Assn. Home: 2390 Deckerville Rd Snover MI 48472 Office: Faith Free Meth Ch 2380 Deckerville Rd Snover MI 48472

CLEGG, ALBERT LAWRENCE, minister, religious organization administrator; b. Crystal Springs, Miss., Feb. 16, 1931; s. Cecil Grey and Winnie (Gardner) C.; m. Dorothy Ann Beckman, Feb. 11, 1956; children: Lauranne, Lawrence, Ronald, David. AA, Jones County Jr. Coll., 1951; BA, Miss. Coll., 1953; BD, New Orleans Bapt. Theol. Sem., 1956, ThD, 1958. Ordained to ministry So. Bapt. Conv., 1953. Pastor Coyt Bapt. Ch., Waynesboro, Miss., 1955-57, Silver Creek Bapt. Ch., McComb, Miss., 1957-59; pastor 1st Bapt. Ch., Greensburg, La., 1959-61, Ponchatoula, La., 1961-80; dir. Associational Missions for S.E. La., La. Bapt. Conv., Hammond, 1980—; sec. So. Bapt. Conv. Dirs. of Associational Missions Conf., 1987-91; v.p. La. Bapt. Conv., 1974-75, chmn. missions com., 1968-72, mem. exec. bd., 1966-72; pres. Dist. 11 Bapt. Conv., 1963-65; pres. Dist. Bapt. Pastor's Conf., 1961-63, 66-68. Mem. Ponchatoula C. of C. Home: 221 S 2d St Ponchatoula LA 70454 Office: PO Box 1249 Ponchatoula LA 70454 *Years ago I determined that I would look for the best in everything that happened. This meant that I would look for the best part of the good things and for something good in the bad. This has made a tremendous difference in my outlook on life and on my ability to accomplish in life.*

CLEMENS, DAVID ALLEN, minister; b. Camden, N.J., Aug. 8, 1941; s. Arleigh Allen and Mae Elizabeth (Browne) C.; m. Janice Ruth Bonino, Feb. 13, 1965; children: Stephen David, Daniel Lee. BA magna cum laude, Houghton Coll., 1963; MA, Nat. Christian U., 1972; ThD, Clarksville Sch. Theology, 1980; PhD, Christian Bible Coll., 1990. Ordained to ministry Ind. Bapt. Ch., 1963. Missionary Pocket Testament League, Argentina, Paraguay, Brazil, S.Am., 1963-66; min. Richfield (Pa.) Mennonite Ch., 1966-67; itinerant Bible tchr. Bible Club Movement Inc., Upper Darby, Pa., 1968-71, nat. rep., 1971-77, dir. family adult ministries dept., 1977-80, min. at large, 1980—; preaching and teaching tours Eng., The Netherlands, Belgium, Sweden, Spain, Ireland, Can., Middle East, The Philippines, Zimbabwe. Author: Steps to Maturity, Vols. I-III, 1973-79. Mem. Nat. Home Missions Fellowship. Home: 72 Knox Blvd Marlton NJ 08053 Office: 237 Fairfield Ave Upper Derby PA 19082 *To know, love, and serve God (as revealed in Jesus Christ) is the highest privilege of life.*

CLEMENT, JOHN EDWARD SIMPSON, minister, religious organization administrator; b. Enid, Okla., Jan. 9, 1934; s. Joseph Alvis and Sarah Evelyn (Brown) C.; m. Elenore Jan Simpson-Clement. MDiv, Union Theol. Sem., 1960. Ordained to ministry, 1960. Pastor Williamsport, Pa., 1960-65, Wilmington, Del., 1965-69; project leader S. Cen. Ministry, Minn., 1969-74; mission enabler Los Ranchos Presbytery, Long Beach, Calif., 1974-91; exec. presbyter Cayuca-Syracuse Presbytery, Syracuse, N.Y., 1974-91, Pitts. Presbytery, 1991—. Office: Pitts Presbytery 801 Union Ave Pittsburgh PA 15212 *I believe God loves our world and has become one of us to redeem us and guide us toward a new humanity. I see our ministry standing on the side of the poor and oppressed as well as loving the oppressor.*

CLEMENT, PATRICIA ELLEN, director of religious education; b. New Orleans, La., May 30, 1955; d. Gregory Vance and Sharon (Ferguson) C. BA, La. Tech. U., 1977; MRE, U. St. Thomas, 1982. Cert. tchr., La. Tchr. St. Francis Cabrini Sch., Alexandria, La., 1977-78; campus ministry team McNeese State U., Lake Charles, La., 1978-82; edn. cons. Jesuit Mission Soc., Juarez, Mex., 1980; dir. religious edn. Immaculate Conception Cathedral, Lake Charles, 1982-88, St. Martha's Parish, Sarasota, Fla., 1988—; edn. cons. Jesuit Missionary Soc., Juarez, 1980, Diocese of Lake Charles, 1982-88, Pelican Man's Bird Sanctuary, Sarasota, 1990—; supporting mem. Maryknoll Missionary Soc., 1982—; dir. of arts and letters festival Diocese of Venice, Sarasota, 1988-91. Author: Sadlier Resource & Review Book, 1988. Mem. Bread for the World, 1978—. Recipient Commendation New Orleans Art Assn., 1973. Mem. Nat. Cath. Educators Assn., Soc. Creative Anachronism (hospitaler 1989—, Award of Arms 1990). Democrat. Office: St Marthas Parish PO Box 1706 Sarasota FL 34230 *It is not important to find out who you are—but "whose" you are. Once you realize that we are simply creatures, and not the creator, then it is easy to see who is really in charge.*

CLEMENT, THE MOST REVERENT BISHOP OF SERPUKHOV See **KAPALIN, JERMAN**

CLEMENTS, BRANT ALISTARI BRUCE, minister; b. Detroit, May 3, 1957; s. Hugh Huston and Gloria Diane (Crall) C.; m. Melanie K. Little, June 28, 1980. BA, Augustana Coll., Rock Island, Ill., 1979; MDiv, Luth. Sch. Theology Chgo., 1984. Ordained to ministry Luth. Ch., 1984. Pastor Trinity Luth. Ch., Utica, Ill., 1984-87, Immanuel Luth. Ch., Amboy, Ill., 1987—; chaplain Nachusa (Ill.) Luth. Home. Office: Immanuel Luth Ch Box 201 Amboy IL 61310

CLEMENTS, ERIC LEE, youth minister; b. Tulsa, Sept. 7, 1963; s. Fred Lynn and Bettye Ruth (Phillips) C.; m. Marchel Word, June 9, 1990. B in Christian Edn., Ozark Bible Coll., 1985. Youth ministry intern Paramount Terr. Christian Ch., Amarillo, Tex., 1984; youth min. 1st Christian Ch., Drumright, Okla., 1984-86, East Bartlesville (Okla.) Christian Ch., 1986—; camp dean Hidden Haven Christian Camp, Thayer, Kans., 1989—. Republican. Office: East Bartlesville Christian Ch 321 SE Tuxedo Blvd Bartlesville OK 74006

CLEMENTS, WILLIAM LEWIS, JR. (BILL), minister; b. Sacramento, Nov. 5, 1952; s. William L. C. Sr. AA, Am. River, 1973; BA, Southern Calif., 1976; MS, Calif. State U., Fresno, 1980; MBA, Nat. U., 1986. Assoc. Assembly of God, Orange, Calif., 1975-79, Cerritos, Calif., 1979-80; pastor Assembly of God, Folsom, Calif., 1980-83; bus. adminstr. Trinity Ch., Sacramento, 1983—. Mem. Nat. Assn. Ch. Bus. Adminstrn. (pres. 1989-90), Christian Mgmt. Assn. (pres. 1990-91), CMMA. Office: Trinity Ch 5225 Hillsdale Blvd Sacramento CA 95842

CLEMMONS, ITHIEL, bishop. Bishop Ch. of God in Christ, Hollis, N.Y. Office: Ch of God in Christ 190-08 104th Ave Hollis NY 11412*

CLEMMONS, JANE GOODRICH, religious organization administrator; b. Casper, Wyo., Apr. 10, 1934; d. Leon Chauncey and Grace (Austin) Goodrich; m. Thomas Powell Clemmons; 1 child, Bradley Powell. AA, Casper Coll., 1954; BA, U. Wash., 1976. Tchr. Stitchin' Time Sewing Sch., Bellevue, Wash., 1966-73, dir. sch., 1970-73; chmn. Bishops Commn. Edn., Seattle, 1981-84, 86-89; mem. N.W. Episc. educators Diocese of Olympia, Episc. Ch., Seattle, 1983—, pres. overlake convocation, 1983-85, mem. bishop's adv. com. on admission to the ministry, 1985—, mem. sch. of theology bd., 1983-84, 86—, mem. diocesan coun., 1987-90; v.p. diocesan coun. Diocese of Olympia, Episc. Ch., 1988-90; pres. Clemmons Cons. Group, 1990—; mem. Tng. and Cons. Svcs., Seattle, 1984—. cons. Girl Scouts USA, Totem Coun., 1989; publicity chmn. League of Women Voters, Colo., 1961-62. Recipient Bishops Cross award for vol. svcs., 1989. Mem. Omicron Nu, Phi Theta Kappa (nat. historian 1953-54). Episcopalian. Avocations: sewing, running, knitting, music, gardening. Home: 15650 Main Bellevue WA 98008

CLEVELAND, CROMWELL COOK, JR., priest, counselor; b. Newport News, Va., Dec. 6, 1948; s. Cromwell Cook Sr. and Gene Ruth (Rickey) C. BA, Centre Coll., 1971; MDiv, Gen. Theol. Sem., 1975. Ordained priest Episcopal Ch., 1975. Asst. rector Ch. of St. Michael & St. George, Clayton, Mo., 1975-77; parish assoc. Holy Communion Episcopal Ch., University City, Mo., 1977-78; chaplain adminstr. Bishop Anderson Found., Chgo., 1979-87; interim rector St. Andrews Episcopal Ch., New Orleans, 1987-88; vicar St. Andrews Episcopal Ch., Paradis, La., 1989—; outreach facilitator Christ Ch. Cathedral, New Orleans, 1988-90; coord. social ministry Greater New Orleans Fedn. Chs., 1988—; dir. community svcs. Community Youth Activity Project, La. State Med. Sch., 1990—; priest assoc. St. James Cathedral, Chgo., 1979-87; pres. Assembly Episcopal Hosps. and Chs., 1985-87. Chaplain coord. New Orleans Fire Dept., 1989—; bd. dirs. New Orleans Coalition for the Homeless, 1989—, Uptown Shepherd Ctr., New Orleans, 1989—; chmn. bd. feed program Friends of the New Orleans Revival Ctr., 1989—. Recipient Horace B. Donnegan prize Gen. Theol. Sem., 1975. Fellow Am. Protestant Health Assn.; mem. Assn. Mental Health Clergy, Caledonian Club (pres. 1983-85), Reiki Internat. Office: St Andrew's Episcopal Ch PO Box 621 Luling LA 70070

CLEVELAND, JOHN PAUL, youth worker; b. Tampa, Fla., Feb. 21, 1970; s. Charles Louis Cleveland and Marilee (Ragsdale) McAnespie. Student, Fla. So. Coll., 1988—. Youth worker, Brandan (Fla.) Youth Group Brandon (Fla.) Youth Group/1st United Meth., 1989—; tram driver Busch Entertainment Corp., Tampa, Fla., 1989—; pres. All Campus Fellowship, Lakeland, 1990-91; mission trip worker to Haiti and Costa Rica, 1990-91. Mem. Wesley Fellowship, Young Life, Sigma Rho Epsilon, Theta Chi Beta, Omicron Delta Kappa. Democrat. Home: 2416 Stonehill Ave Valrico FL 33594 *The world, as well as the Christian Church, is constantly undergoing change. In order to meet the needs and challenges of all of humanity, we need to be in continual dialogue.*

CLEVELAND, ROGER PECKE, minister; b. Plymouth, Conn., Apr. 16, 1901; s. George A. and Clare Truesdell (Fenn) C.; A.B., Middlebury Coll. of Vt., 1928; M.Div., Bangor Theol. Sem., 1929; A.B. (hon.), Hesser Coll.; 1 adopted child, William Fenn; foster children: Henri J.P. Therrien, Robert E. Rowe, Henry Therrien, Richard Williams. Ordained to ministry Congl. Ch., 1929; asst. minister Community Ch., Miami Beach, Fla., 1928-29; minister Evang. Congl. Ch., Grafton, Mass., 1929-49; permanent rector Chapel of St. John of Mountains, Ellsworth, N.H., 1940—, minister Grace Ch. Orient Heights, East Boston, Mass., 1949-69, pastor emeritus, 1969—; minister St. Mary's United Ref. Ch., Devizes, Wiltshire, Eng., 1969-73; exchange minister to Eng. and No. Ireland, 1949. Mem. Kennet & Avon Canal Trust, Ltd. (Eng.). Former mem. East Boston Area Planning Action Council; former mem. Boston Unity Com. Former trustee North Suffolk Mental Health, Clinic, Family Service Assn. Greater Boston; former bd. dirs. Boston Seaman's Friend Soc., Mass. Dept. Mental Health, Govt. Center Area Bd.; former Protestant chaplain East Boston Dist. Ct. Fellow Royal Hort. Soc. (Eng.); mem. Worcester County Mechanics Assn. (life), Nat. Trust Eng., Nat. Trust Hist. Preservation (U.S.), Soc. Preservation New Eng. Antiquities, Eastern Amateur Ski Assn., Boston Council Internat. Visitors, N.H. Hist. Soc., New Hampton Hist. Soc. (pres.), N.H. and Mass. Psychic Research Soc. (hon., life mem.), Theta Chi. Kiwanian (pres.). Clubs: Appalachian Mountain, Eastern Slopes Ski. Mason. Author: Up The Trail, 1936; Look Upon The Rainbow, 1962; The Heritage of Friends, 1974; Garment of Holiness, 1977. Home: Fenn Gate Townhouse Rd New Hampton NH 03256 *I go on dialysis 3 times a week, but I am so lucky to have friends supporting me.*

CLIBORN, DENNIS ELVIN, SR., minister; b. San Benito, Tex., Feb. 28, 1950; s. Roy Lee and Lillian Corrine (Swallow) C.; m. Sue Carol Sindle, July 10, 1970; children: Dennis Jr., Christopher. Student, East Tex. Bapt. Coll., 1969-72; B in Bible Theology, Internat. Bible Sem., 1989, ThM magna cum laude, 1990; D in Ministry, Andersonville Bapt. Sem., 1991. Ordained to ministry Bapt. Ch., 1972; lic. Christian counselor. Pastor Alamance Bapt. Ch., Atlanta, Tex., 1972-74, 1979-82, Bethel Cass Bapt. Ch., Linden, Tex., 1974-79, Zion Hill Bapt. Ch., Linden, 1982-86, Park Heights Bapt. Ch., Tyler, Tex., 1987—; min. Goodwill Industries, Tyler, 1987—; chaplain Queen City (Tex.) Police and Fire Depts., 1987—. Camp sponsor Chapel Hill Ind. Sch., New Chapel Hill, Tex., 1988-91, vocat. adv. coun., 1989. Mem. Nat. Christian Counselor Assn. (area rep. 1989—), Bapt. Gen. Conv. (cert. Masterlife group leader 1990), Cass County Peace Officers Club. Republican. Home: 3108 Shady Tr Tyler TX 75702 Office: Park Heights Bapt Ch 2726 Van Hwy Tyler TX 75702 *It has been a lesson throughout my ministry that the word Love has to be more than a word you use from the pulpit. The minister has to sincerely LOVE the people in order to minister unto them effectively, no matter who they may be.*

CLIFF, JUDITH ANITA, author, biblical studies lecturer; b. Chgo., July 13, 1941; d. Howard Allen and Anita Caroline (Bell) Cliff. Student, Whittier Coll., 1962-64. Lectr. Bibl. studies Santa Rosa, Calif., 1971-74; author, lectr. Bibl. studies Jerusalem, Israel, 1974-78, Santa Rosa, St. Helena, Napa and San Francisco, 1978-89; author Bibl. studies La Jolla, Calif., 1989—. Author: Jesus: A Gospel Guide to His Life, 1976; Land of the Bible, 1978; The Christmas Journey, 1984; The Leaves of the Tree, 1984; The Healing Teachings of Jesus, 1985; author, pub. newsletter The Bibl. Rev., 1978, 89; author/narrator numerous lecture cassettes. Home: PO Box 5375 Clearlake CA 95422

CLIFFORD, GEORGE, ecumenical agency administrator. Head Brockville (Ont., Can.) and Dist. Inter-Ch. Coun. Office: Brockville and Dist Inter-Ch, Coun/5 Wall St, Brockville, ON Canada K6V 4R8*

CLIFFORD, BROTHER PETER, academic administrator, religious educator; b. N.Y.C., Feb. 17, 1925; s. Peter and Mary (Lynch) C. AB, Manhattan Coll., 1950; MA, Fordham U., 1957; EdD, Harvard U., 1970; EdD (hon.), St. Mary's Coll., Winona, Minn., 1987. Cert. sch. supt., N.Y. Tchr., prin. Cath. schs., N.Y.C., 1947-57; dean De La Salle Coll., Manila, 1957-61; asst. prin. Bishop Loughlin High Sch., Bklyn., 1962-64; assoc. supt. schs. Diocese Bklyn., 1968-71; exec. sec. Nat. Cath. Edn. Assn., Washington, 1971-74; assoc. dean edn. St. John U., N.Y.C., 1974-76; pres. St. Mary's Coll., Winona, Minn., 1976-84; provincial Bros. Christian Schs., Narragansett, R.I., 1984-87; staff asst. higher edn. U.S. Cath. Conf., Washington, 1987-89; pres. St. Mary Coll., Leavenworth, Kans., 1989—. Mem. Leavenworth Area Devel., 1989—. Recipient Avila award Coll. St. Teresa, Winona. Mem. Kans. Ind. Coll. Assn., Kans. Ind. Coll. Fund, Bros. of the Christian Schs (Christian Bro. 1943—). Home and Office: St Mary Coll Office of the President 4100 S 4th Trafficway Leavenworth KS 66048

CLIFT, CHARLES KENNETH, minister; b. Dearborn, Mich., Aug. 7, 1938; s. Charles Anderson and Irene (Storey) C.; m. D. Denise Moore, Sept. 29, 1978; children: Tricia, Janelle, Amanda, Kimberly. AA in Div., Southwestern Bapt. Theol. Sem., 1981; BA, Trinity Div. Coll., Deerfield, Ill., 1983, MDiv, 1984; STD (hon.), Am. Bible Inst., Falls Church, Va., 1991. Ordained to ministry So. Bapt. Conv., 1982. Asst. pastor Tate Springs Bapt. Ch., Arlington, Tex., 1980-83; pastor Rush Creek Bapt. Ch., Arlington, 1984-89, South Arlington Community Ch., 1989—; chaplain Arlington Police Dept., 1988—; pres. Arlington Bapt. Fellowship, 1984-85, Tarrant Bapt. Assn., Ft. Worth, 1985-86. Author: Command and Staffing, 1959. Lt. USN, 1959-64. Mem. Am. Assn. Christian Counselors, North Tex. Assn. Small Group Ministries, Internat. Conf. Police Chaplains, Rotary (pres. Arlington, 1988, bd. dirs. 1990, gov.'s rep. dist. 579, 1989, Rotarian of Yr. award 1989, Dist. Outstanding Rotarian award 1989). Republican. Home: 2616 Charolais Way Arlington TX 76017 Office: South Arlington Community Ch 2311 Roosevelt Dr Ste C Arlington TX 76016

CLIFT, DAVID BRIAN, minister; b. Concord, Calif., May 10, 1962; s. Everett Ray and Joyce Lorraine (Attenborough) C.; m. Cindy Sue Lockwood; 1 child, Jenelle Sue. BA in Bible, Bob Jones U., 1985, BA in Speech, 1985; MA, San Francisco Bapt. Theol. Sem, 1986; MDiv, Bapt. Coll. & Grad. Sch. West, 1989. Lic. to ministry Gen. Assn. Regular Bapt. Chs. Assoc. pastor Bethany Bapt. Ch., Martinez, Calif., 1986-88; interim pastor 1st Bapt. Ch. of Clayton Valley, Concord, Calif., 1989; sr. pastor Hillside Bapt. Ch., Antioch, Calif., 1989—; song leader Bapt. Alive Youth Ministries, Concord, 1990—. Republican. Office: Hillside Bapt Ch 108 Hillside Rd Antioch CA 94509

CLIFT, WALLACE BRUCE, educator, priest, lawyer; b. Robert Lee, Tex., Mar. 27, 1926; s. Wallace Bruce Sr. and Ruth (Simpson) C.; m. Jean Dalby, Jan. 23, 1954; children: Anne Boris, Lucy Clifthorne, Bruce. BA, U. Tex., 1949; JD, Harvard U., 1952; MDiv, Ch. Div. Sch. of Pacific, 1960; MA, U. Chgo., 1968, PhD, 1970. Bar: D.C., Tex. Adminstrv. officer U.S. Civil Svc., Seoul, Republic of Korea, 1946-48; assoc. Baker & Botts, Houston, 1953-57; Episcopal vicar Diocese of Tex., Houston, 1960-64; prof. U. Denver, 1969—. Author: Jung and Christianity, 1982, Journey Into Love, 1990; (with Jean Dalby) Symbols of Transformation in Dreams, 1985, Hero Journey in Dreams, 1988. Assoc. priest St. John's Episcopal Cathedral, Denver, 1987—. Lt. (j.g.) USNR, 1944-46. Farish Found. fellow, 1964-69; NEH grantee Fordham U., 1988. Mem. Am. Assn. Pastorial Counselors (affiliate), Am. Acad. Religion, Soc. for Pastoral Theology, Jung Soc. Colo. (pres. Denver chpt. 1975-89). Office: U Denver Religious Studies Dept Denver CO 80208

CLIFTON, MICHAEL CRAWFORD, minister; b. Eugene, Oreg., May 23, 1948; s. Garnett Crawford and Lola Darlene (Richey) C.; m. Christine Ann Sims, Aug. 2, 1975; children: Jeremy Crawford, James Michael. BA, Northwest Christian, 1970; BS, U. Oreg., Eugene, 1970; MDiv, Phillips Sem., 1975. Ordained to ministry Christian Ch. (Disciples of Christ). Youth minister Parkwood Christian Ch., Portland, Oreg., 1969-70; minister Burton (Kans.) Christian Ch., 1970-71, South Haven (Kans.) Christian Ch., 1972-74; shared minister Davis St. and Bladenburg Chs., Ottumwa, Iowa, 1975-77; sr. minister 1st Christian Ch., Newkirk, Okla., 1986—; brigade chaplain 3d Bde., 95th Div. (Tng.) USAR, Stillwater, Okla., 1986—; Army chaplain 9th Div. and 3d Armored Div., Ft. Lewis, Wash., Fed. Republic Germany, 1977-86; chmn. Okla. Ch. in Soc. Com., Oklahoma City, 1986—, Kay Disaster

Relief Com., Newkirk, Okla., 1986—; pres. Newkirk Ministerial Alliance, 1987—. Chmn. Newkirk Community Chest, 1989-90; 2d and 3d v.p. Newkirk Lions Club, 1989-90; cubmaster pack 28, 101 dist. Boy Scouts Am., Newkirk, 1988. Major USAR, 1973—. Mem. Mil. Chaplain Assn., Disciples Chaplain Assn., Ruritan Club (Ottumwa), Lions. Democrat. Home: 313 S Walnut Newkirk OK 74647-6019 Office: 1st Christian Ch 9th & Walnut Newkirk OK 74647-0462

CLIMACO, VICENTE MARIANO, clergyman; b. Zamboanga City, Zamboanga, Philippines, Apr. 5, 1950; s. Nicomedes de Leon and Teresa (Labanacruz Mariano) C. A.A., Trinity Coll., Quezon City, 1972; B.Th., St. Andrew's Theol. Sem., Quezon City, 1976; B.A., U. of the East, Manila, 1978. Ordained priest Philippine Episcopal Ch., 1978. Fellow in residence St. Andrew's Theol. Sem., Quezon City, 1976-78; chaplain St. Francis High Sch., Maguindanao, 1978-82; priest in charge St. Andrew's Mission, Maguindanao, 1979-80; cathedral canon Sts. Peter and Paul, Cotabato City, Philippines, 1980-82; theol. tutor Patteson Theol. Centre, Ch. of Melanesia, Solomon Islands, 1982-85. Mem. Philippine Episcopal Ch. Commn. on Christian Living, 1980-82, 85—, Bd. Examing Chaplains, 1982, del nat. conv., 1980, 86; trustee Brent Hosp., Zamboanga, 1979; sec. Episcopal Diocese of So. Philippine Standing Com., 1986—, Diocesan Personnel Com., 1986—; mem. Diocesan Com. on Social Concern, 1986—, conv. registrar, 1986—. Home: Sinsuat Ave, PO Box 113, Cotabato City Philippines Office: Bishop Patteson Theol Ctr, Honiara GPO Box 19, Guadalcanal Solomon Islands

CLINE, BILLY H., minister; b. Valdese, N.C., Dec. 19, 1927; s. Sterling Lenoir and Marie (Burns) C.; m. Ruth Geneva Jamison, Jan. 12, 1947; children: Gail Lynae Cline Lawrence, Joel David. AA, Gardner-Webb Coll., 1956; BA, Lenoir-Rhyne Coll., 1958; D Ministry, Luther Rice Sem., 1977. Ordained to ministry So. Bapt. Conv. Pastor Pisgah Bapt., Casar, N.C., 1954-57, High Peak Bapt., Valdese, N.C., 1957-65, Merrimon Ave. Bapt., Asheville, N.C., 1965—. Trustee Southeastern Bapt. Sem., Wake Forest, N.C., 1980—. Sgt. U.S. Army, 1946-49. Billy Cline Day established in his honor City of Asheville, 1985, 89. Mem. Optimist (sgt. of arms Asheville club, Community Svc. award 1988). Home: 149 S Wildflower Rd Asheville NC 28804 Office: Merrimon Ave Bapt 283 Merrimon Ave Asheville NC 28801

CLINE, HAROLD EDWIN, minister; b. Canton, Ohio, May 10, 1930; s. Lloyd DeWitt Talmadge and Hilda Margaret (Welty) C.; m. Ruby Ann Dawson, May 31, 1952; children: Sally Jane Cline Beerman, Chad Erwin, Carol Ann Cline Saenz. BA magna cum laude, Butler U., 1953, MA, 1959; MDiv in Hebrew cum laude, Christian Theol. Sem., 1959; DST, Emory U., 1971. Ordained to ministry Christian Ch. (Disciples of Christ), 1953. Minister Arcadia (Ind.) Christian Ch., 1955-59; sr. minister South Side Christian Ch., Kokomo., Ind., 1959-71; sr. minister 1st Christian Ch., Ft. Wayne, Ind., 1971-81, South Bend, Ind., 1981-85; area minister Hi-Plains area Christian Ch. (Disciples of Christ) in S.W., Amarillo, Tex., 1985—; mem. adminstrv. com., gen. bd. Christian Ch. (Disciples of Christ), 1973-76; mem. regional coun. Christian Ch. in Ind., Indpls., 1964-68, 72-80, mem. com. on ministry, 1960-68, chmn., 1966-68, mem. com. on evangelism and renewal, 1972-80, chmn., 1973-80. Contbr. articles to mag. The Disciple. Mem. adv. coun. Dept. Human Svcs., 1987—; bd. dirs., fundraiser YMCA, Kokomo, 1964-68; chmn. dept. youth work Ind. Coun. Chs., Indpls., 1960-63. Recipient Disting. Svc. award Kokomo Jaycees, 1963, Disting. Alumni award Christian Theol. Sem., 1979, Outstanding Svc. and Leadership award Coun. Christian Unity, 1979. Mem. Nat. Evang. Assn. Christian Ch. (Disciples of Christ) (pres. 1977-83, exec. com. 1983-91), Pioneer Promenaders, Yellow Rock Plus Dancers, Theta Phi. Democrat. Home: 2221 S Fannin St Amarillo TX 79109-2132 Office: Christian Ch SW Hi-Plains 2201 Civic Circle Ste 902 Amarillo TX 79109 *Right relationships with self, others and God are the keys to fulfillment and growth in the life pilgrimage.*

CLINE, JAMES RALPH, JR., minister; b. Birmingham, Ala., May 18, 1928; s. James Ralph Sr. and Minnie Pauline (Graves) C.;m . Bobbie Jean Walker, May 21, 1951; children: James Ralph III, Paula Jeanne Cline Clements, David Thomas. BA, Samford U., 1952; BTh, Southeastern Bible Coll., 1954; MD, So. Bapt. Theol. Sem., 1958. Pastor Mt. Signal Bapt. Ch., Sterrett, Ala., 1952-55, Mill Creek Bapt. Ch., Salem, Ind., 1955-56, Rock Haven Bapt. Ch., Brandenburg, Ky., 1956-57, Immanuel Bapt. Ch., Elizabethtown, Ky., 1957-59, Oak Grove Bapt. Ch., Bessemer, Ala., 1959-62, Smith's (Ala.) Sta. Bapt. Ch., 1962-65, Hopewell Bapt. Ch., Pinson, Ala., 1965-75; assoc. pastor 1st Bapt. Ch., Sylacauga, Ala., 1975-87; pastor Calvary Heights Bapt. Ch., Alexander City, Ala., 1987—; pres. Tallapoosa Christian Crisis Ctr., Alexander City, 1988—. Served with USN, 1946-49. Mem. Civitans (chaplain Alexander City chpt. 1988—). Avocations: music, collecting old books and fountain pens. Home: 206 Clubview Dr Alexander City AL 35010 Office: Calvary Heights Bapt Ch Elkahatchee & US 280 Alexander City AL 35010

CLINE, RICHARD LEE, clergyman; b. Kansas City, Mo., Dec. 26, 1950; s. Robert Paul and Mary Elizabeth (Hall) C.; m. Lou Ann Manley, June 21, 1975; children: Melissa, Shannon. BSBA, Emporia State U., 1972; MA in Counseling and Guidance, U. Mo., Kansas City, 1978. Assoc. minister Ch. of Christ, Chillicothe, Mo., 1972-73, Overland Park (Kans.) Ch. of Christ, 1973-79; pulpit minister Cen. Ch. of Christ, Wichita, Kans., 1979—. Contbr. articles religious publs. Mem. adv. bd. Widowed Persons Svc.-YMCA, Wichita, 1988—, Sedgwick County Regional Drug/Alcohol Abuse Prevention Ctr., 1991—; coach and vol. Am. Youth Soccer Orgn., Wichita, 1984—. Named one of Outstanding Young Men of Am., 1978, 83, 85, 86, 87, 88. Mem. Christian Edn. Assn. Office: Cen Ch of Christ 225 N Waco Wichita KS 67202

CLINGAN, WANDA JACQUELINE, minister; b. Hunnewell, Kans., Oct. 29, 1928; d. Claude Charles Stephenson and Leta Nette (Davison) Phillips; m. Donald F. Clingan, Aug. 26, 1952; children: Stephen F., Jane Ellen Clingan Reynolds. BA, Phillips U., 1950. Lic. minister, 1973. State youth and children's worker Christian Ch. in Kans., Topeka, 1950-52; asst. to registrar Tex. Christian U., Fort Worth, 1952-55; dir. children's ministries and family life Downey Ave. Christian Ch., Indpls., 1967-73; mgr. Bethany Bookstore, Indpls., 1973-79; ministry dir. Ministry on Ch. Response to Family Violence Ill. Conf. Chs., Springfield, 1986—. Contbr. articles to profl. jours. Registered lobbyist Christian InnerCity Assn., Indpls., 1966; sec. to bd. dirs. Broadway Christian Ctr., Indpls., 1967; precinct committeewoman Dem. Cen. Com., Indpls., 1973-75. Mem. AAUW (chair cultural arts 1987-88, chair study group 1986-87), Nat. Assn. Ecumenical Staff. Home: 41 Westwood Terr Springfield IL 62702 Office: Ill Conf Chs 615 S 5th St Springfield IL 62703

CLINTON, STEPHEN MICHAEL, academic administrator; b. Wichita, Kans., Aug. 21, 1944; s. Thomas Francis and Bettie Lee (Harrison) C.; m. Virginia Ann Schoonover, Aug. 30, 1964; children: Matthew, Michael, Shanna. MA in Philosophy, Trinity Evang. Div. Sch., Deerfield, Ill., 1969, MDiv, 1970; PhD in Theology, Calif. Grad. Sch. Theology, 1979; MA in Counseling, Internat. Sch. Theology, San Bernardino, Calif., 1987; MA in Edn., Calif. State U., San Bernardino, 1988; postgrad., U. Calif., Riverside, 1991—. Ordained to ministry Evang. Free Ch. Am., 1973; cert. gifted edn. tchr., Calif. Dir. extension degree programs Internat. Sch. Theology, 1974-86, assoc. prof., 1978-86; dir. Internat. Leadership Coun., San Bernardino, 1986-91; pres. New Life Inst., Orlando, Fla., 1991—; pres. Ministry Devel., Inc., San Bernardino, 1978-86; elder Community Bible Ch., San Bernardino, 1981-91. Author: The Doctrine of the Christian Life, 1981, Cultural Apologetics, 1983, Calvinism and Arminianism, 1985, The Everlasting God, 1989; also 40 articles. Pres. Advs. for Gifted and Talented Edn., San Bernardino, 1979-85; chmn. state parent coun. Calif. Assn. for Gifted, 1978-83; mem. adv. bd. for gifted and talented edn. San Bernardino Unified Sch. Dist., 1984-87; chmn. bd. dirs. Ctr. for Individuals with Disabilities, San Bernardino, 1984-88. Mem. Evang. Philos. Soc. (editor 1979-81, 84-92, pres. 1983), Evang. Free Ch. Ministerial Assn., Evang. Theol. Soc. (chmn. 1982), John Dewey Soc. Office: 100 Sunport Ln Orlando FL 32809

CLOHERTY, THOMAS PATRICK, priest; b. Dublin, Ireland, July 3, 1948; s. Joseph Francis and Catherine (Griffin) C. BA in History, U. Dallas, 1970, MDiv, 1974, postgrad., 1977-79. Ordained priest Roman Cath. Ch., 1974; joined Equestrian Order of Holy Sepulchre, 1986. Parochial vicar Diocese of Dallas, 1974-76, vocation dir., 1977-85; spiritual dir. Holy Trinity Sem., Irving, Tex., 1976-79, dean, 1979-83, trustee, 1990; adminstr. St. Francis Ch., Frisco, Tex., 1977-80; pastor St. Jude's Ch., Allen, Tex., 1983-89, Holy Spirit Ch., Duncanville, Tex., 1989—; bd. dirs. Duncanville Outreach Ministry, 1990. Contbr. articles to profl. jours. Home and Office: Holy Spirit Cath Ch 1111 W Danieldale Duncanville TX 75137

CLOPINE, SANDRA LOU, religious organization administrator; b. Ft. Wayne, Ind., May 12, 1936; d. Clarence Melvin and Gwendola Louise (Copp) Burry; m. Sidney Ray Goodwin, July 12, 1957 (dec. 1963); 1 child, Gwenda Lynn Goodwin Stewart; m. Myron Stanley Clopine, Aug 7, 1982; stepchildren: Charles, Dan, Linda Clopine Palser, Lynnette Clopine Blackstone. BA, Southwestern Assemblies of God, Waxahachie, Tex., 1958; BS, West Tex. State U., 1968; MA, Assemblies of God Theol. Sem., Springfield, Mo., 1979. Ordained to ministry West Tex. Assemblies of God, 1971. Fgn. missionary Assemblies of God Ch., Ghana, West Africa, 1961-65; social worker Tex. Ctr. Human Devel., Amarillo, 1968-69, dir. vol. svcs., 1969-70; instr. Arusha Bible Sch., Tanzania, East Africa, 1970-80; instr. sociology Evang. Coll. Assemblies of God, Springfield, 1979-80; office of info. coord. Internat. Corr. Inst., Brussels, 1980-82; state dir. Women's Ministries, Nebr., 1984-85; nat. sec., dept. head for denomination Assemblies of God Women's Ministries, Springfield, Mo., 1986—; speaker women's convs., leadership seminars, other orgns. Recipient Outstanding Contbn. award Internat. Corr. Inst., 1983, Leadership Friend of Yr. award Highland Child Placement Ctr., Kansas City, Mo., 1989; named Disting. Alumnus Southwestern Assemblies of God Coll., 1989. Mem. Nat. Assn. Evangs. Women's Commn. (exec. bd., 1st vice-chmn. 1989—), Evang. Press Assn., Nat. Women's Leadership Task Force (steering com. 1990—), Internat. Pentecostal Press Assn., Delta Epsilon Chi. Republican. Avocations: swimming, reading, basketball, ice skating, horseback riding. Office: Assemblies of God 1445 Boonville Ave Springfield MO 65802

CLORE, FRANK CALDIN, pastor, chaplain; b. Bremerton, Wash., Feb. 3, 1942; s. Frank H. Clore and Audrey F. (Garinger) Wrestling; m. Teresa Mae Scofield, May 19, 1984; 1 child, Frank Anthony. Student, Oreg. Coll. Edn., 1960-64, Warner Pacific Coll., Portland, Oreg., 1984-87. Ordained to ministry Ch. of God (Anderson, Ind.), 1990. Pastor Milwaukie (Oreg.) Congl. Ch., 1984-85; interim pastor Olney (Oreg.) Community Ch., 1985; sr. pastor 1st Ch. of God, Grants Pass, Oreg., 1986-91, Oregon City, Oreg., 1991—; sr. chaplain Josephine County Sheriff's Office, Grants Pass, 1987-91; chaplain Hull & Hull Funeral Home, Grants Pass, 1987-91; state dir. primary camp Chs. of God, Oreg., 1987-91; mem. Social Concerns Commn., Oreg. Ch. of God, 1988—. State dir. Josephine County Juvenile Svcs. Commn., 1989; mem. Josephine County Mental Health Adv. Bd., 1988-91, Josephine County Juvenile Adv. Coun., 1991—; mem. nat. steering com. Nat. Sheriff's Chaplaincy Program; past bd. dirs. Lovejoy Hospice; mem. Josephine County Dist. Atty.'s Adv. Coun., 1989. Mem. Grants Pass Ministerial Assn. (v.p. 1987, pres. 1988-90), Internat. Conf. Police Chaplains. Address: 1st Ch of God Oregon City OR 97045

CLOSSER, PATRICK DENTON, artist, radio evangelist; b. San Diego, Apr. 27, 1945; s. Edward and Helen Thompson. Diploma, Am. Schs. of Cinema, 1970; hon. doctorate cinema arts, World U., Tucson, 1985. Artist Sta. KBFI-TV, Dallas, 1972-73; with Stas. KVTT and KDTX, Dallas, 1976-81, Stas. KTER and KTXO, Dallas, 1980-83; broadcaster Radio Newspaper, Panama, 1990-91. Worked on TV commls. for Dr. Pepper, Am. Chiropractic Assn., feature movies, show Comment on Our Times, Bible's Forecast; evangelist Stas. KDTX-FM, KVTT-FM; worked on theatre trailers, network TV shows, Nelson Golf Classic, Operation Entertainment; radio evangelist Sta. Radio Africa, KXVI, WINB-shortwave, Radio Caroline; contbr. articles on evangelism and learning disabilities to various mags. Mem. coalition for Better Television CBTV, Tupelo, Miss. Named to Life History Ctr., Conroe, Tex., Internat. Hall of Leaders, 1988, to Nobility and Peerage, Country of Tasmania, 1989; recipient grant of arms Grand Duke of Avram, 1989. Fellow Internat. Platform Assn., Internat. Biog. Assn. (life). Mem. Anglo-Am. Acad., Internat. Christian Broadcasters Assn., Am. Biog. Assn. Religious Broadcasters, Soc. Motion Picture and TV Engrs., Nat. Fedn. Decency. Home: PO Box 540881 Dallas TX 75220 *The Grand Duke of Avram gave me an ecclesiastical coat of arms, and made me an ecclesiastical nobleman, of the United Kingdom. I am proud to have served God and Jesus, as machinery fabricator, control-room engineer, and religious broadcaster, for almost 20 years. If it weren't for God and Jesus, I wouldn't be here.*

CLOTFELTER, VIRGIL JACKSON, JR., minister; b. Atlanta, Mar. 18, 1954; s. Virgil Jackson and Thelma Gladys (Sayles) C.; m. Dorri Susan Puckett, Jun. 29, 1975;; children: Andrew McClain, Alexander Wade. BA, Atlanta Christian Coll., 1976, BTh., 1977; MA, Cinn. Chr. Sem., 1989. Youth min. Peachtree City Christian Ch., Peachtree City, Ga., 1975-77; assc. min. Garden City Church of Christ, Columbus, Ind., 1977--; Sec.-treas. Ind. Christian Youth Conv., 1981-82, 1989--; dean Hilltop Christian Assembly, 1979--. Poll sheriff Barth. Co. Rep. Party, Columbus, Ind., 1990. Republican. Independent Christian Churches/Churches of Christ. Home: 264 Lincoln St Columbus IN 47201-7986 Office: Garden City Church Christ 3245 Jonesville Rd Columbus IN 47201-7932

CLOTHEY, FREDERICK WILSON, religious studies educator, researcher; b. Madras, Tamil Nadu, India, Feb. 29, 1936 (parents Am. citizens); s. Frederick and Vesta Averill (Wilson) C.; m. Ann Irene Forbes, June 20, 1962; children—Phillip W., Rebecca A., Frederick M., Sharmali J., Fathima. B.A., B.Th., Aurora Coll., 1957; B.D., Evang. Theol. Sem., 1959; M.A., U. Chgo., 1965, Ph.D., 1968. Dir. youth work Gen. Conf., Adventist Ch., Aurora, Ill., 1959-62; asst. prof. religion Boston U., 1967-74; from asst. prof. to prof. religious studies U. Pitts., 1975—, chmn. dept., 1978-88, acting dir. Asian studies, 1979-80; resident coordinator Gt. Lakes Colls. Assoc. Yr. in India Program, Madurai, 1971-72. Author: The Many Faces of Murukan, 1978; Rhythm and Intent: Ritual Studies from South India, 1983, Quiescence and Passion: The Vision of Arunakiri, Tamil Mystic, 1984; editor: Images of Man: Religion and Historical Process in South Asia, 1982; co-editor: Experiencing Śiva: Encounters with a Hindu Deity, 1983; co-founder, assoc. editor Jour. Ritual Studies; dir., producer of 5 films: Yakam: A Fire Ritual of South India, 1973, Skanda-Sasti: A Festival of Conquest, 1973, Pankuni Uttiram: Festival of Fertility, 1974, Consecration of a Temple, 1979, Pilgrimage to Pittsburgh, 1990. Fulbright-Hays fellow, 1978, 82, 91; grantee Pa. Pub. Com. for Humanities, 1978, 87. Fellow Am. Inst. Indian Studies (trustee 1966-67, 81, 90); mem. Am. Acad. Religion, Assn. for Asian Studies, Soc. for South Indian Studies, Conf. on Religion in South India. Democrat. Avocations: hiking; gardening. Home: 939 Heberton St Pittsburgh PA 15206 Office: U Pittsburgh Dept Religious Studies 2604 Cathedral Learning Pittsburgh PA 15260

CLOUSE, BONNIDELL, psychology educator; b. San Jose, Costa Rica, July 5, 1928; came to U.S., 1930; d. Ranselaer and Lela (Freeland) Barrows; m. Robert Gordon Clouse, June 17, 1955; children: Gary, Kenneth. BA, Wheaton Coll., 1950; MA, Boston U., 1953; PhD, Ind. U., 1968. Psychiat. aide Inst. of Living, Hartford, Conn., 1950-52; asst. prof. edn. and psychology Bryan Coll., Dayton, Tenn., 1953-55; elem. tchr. Marion Twp. Schs., Marion, Iowa, 1958-63; teaching assoc. Ind. U., Bloomington, 1965-67; prof. ednl. and sch. psychology Ind. State U., Terre Haute, 1967—. Author: Moral Development: Perspectives in Psychology and Christian Belief, 1985; editor: Women in Ministry: Four Views, 1989; contbg. editor jours. Psychology and Theology, 1976—, Christian Parenting Today, 1988—; contbr. articles to profl. jours. Tchr. Sunday sch. 1st Brethren Ch., Clay City, Ind., 1964—; bd. dirs. YWCA, Terre Haute, Ind., 1976-79. Mem. Am. Psychol. Assn., Christian Assn. Psychol. Studies, Phi Kappa Phi. Democrat. Brethren. Avocation: needlework. Home: 2122 S 21st St Terre Haute IN 47802 Office: Ind State U Sch Edn Terre Haute IN 47809 *I believe that prayer serves not so much to establish cognitive and affective equilibrium on the part of the intercessor as to provide a means of communication with the Creator and Redeemer. God hears our prayers and answers them in the way that in the long run is best for us and meets the divine purpose for the universe.*

CLOUSE, ROBERT GORDON, history educator, minister; b. Mansfield, Ohio, Aug. 26, 1931; s. Garry A. and Marion Katherine (Ost) C.; m. Bonnidell Amelia Barrows, June 17, 1955; children: Gary R., Kenneth D. BA, Bryan Coll., 1954; BD, Grace Theol. Sem., 1957; MA, U. Iowa, 1957, PhD, 1963. Ordained to ministry Brethren Ch., 1958. Min. Grace Brethren Ch., Cedar Rapids, Iowa, 1957-60; prof. history Ind. State U., Terre Haute, 1963—; min. First Brethren Ch., Clay City, Ind., 1964—; J. Omar Good vis. disting. prof. evang. Christianity Juniata Coll., 1982-83. Author: The Church in an Age of Orthodoxy and Enlightenment, 1980; author, editor: The Meaning of the Millennium, Four Views, 1977, Women in Ministry, Four Views, 1989, War, Four Christian Views, 1991. Dir. Conf. on Faith and History, Terre Haute, 1965—, Eugene V. Debs Found., Terre Haute, 1968—, Cen. Renaissance Conf., 1986—; active Sixteenth Studies Conf. Postdoctoral grantee Folger Shakespeare Libr., 1964; postdoctoral fellow Inst. for Advanced Christian Studies, 1970, Lilly Libr., 1976. Mem. Am. Soc. Ch. History, Calvin Studies Soc., Am. Hist. Assn., Nat. Fellowship Grace Brethren Mins. Avocations: travel, walking, reading. Home: 2122 S 21st St Terre Haute IN 47802 Office: Ind State U History Dept Terre Haute IN 47809

CLOUTIER, WILLIAM JOSEPH, priest; b. Chgo., Aug. 25, 1949; s. William Vladimar and Dolores Ellen (Wisner) C. BA with honors, Loyola U., Chgo., 1971; MDiv, St. Mary of Lake, Mundelein, Ill., 1975, STL, 1976, DMin, 1979. Ordained priest Roman Cath. Ch., 1975. Assoc. pastor Archdiocese of Chgo., 1975-79; adj. prof. edn. U. Ill., Chgo., 1979-85, ednl. cons., 1985—; chaplain Providence-St. Mel High Sch., Chgo., 1975-79. Mem. Niles Twp. Clergy Forum, Skokie, Ill., 1985—. Meme. Assn. Chgo. Priests, K.C. Democrat. Avocations: computer programming, race walking, Chicago Symphony. Home and Office: St Peter Ch 8116 Niles Center Rd Skokie IL 60077-2520

CLUNE, JOSEPH HENRY, insurance consultant; b. N.Y.C., June 15, 1914; s. Henry Patrick and Nora Mary (O'Dea) C.; m. Ann Marie Smith, Nov. 21, 1940; 1 son, Christopher Gerard. Student, St. Francis Coll, CCNY, Duke U., U. Oxford, Eng. With Met. Life Ins. Co., N.Y.C., 1936-82, mgr. group nat. accounts, to 1982; ins. cons., 1982—. Ordained permanent deacon Roman Cath. Ch., 1974. Pres. Diaconate Assembly, Diocese of Paterson; asst. chaplain Passaic (N.J.) Gen. Hosp.; bd. dirs. Med. 21 Corp., Med. Care Internat., Inc., 1983-85. With U.S. Army Criminal Investigation Div., 1942-45. Mem. Federated Ambulatory Surgery Assn. (dir. 1973), Cath. Chaplains Assn., Cath. War Vets., K.C. Contbr. articles to profl. jours. Home and Office: 191 Beechwood Dr Wayne NJ 07470

CLUNE, ROBERT BELL, bishop; b. Toronto, Ont., Can., Sept. 18, 1920; s. William Robert and Agnes Anne (Higgins) C. B.A., U. Toronto, 1941; Dr. Canon Law, Cath. U. Am., 1948. Ordained priest Roman Catholic Ch., 1945. Vice-chancellor Archdiocese of Toronto, 1948-53, vice ofcl. Marriage Tribunal, 1953-65, aux. bishop, 1979—, now regional bishop Northeast Pastoral Region; pastor St. Wilfrid's Parish, Toronto, 1965-71; pres. Cath. Ch. Extension Soc., Toronto, 1971-79. Avocations: golf; hiking; reading. Home and Office: 903 Gifford Ave, Whitby, ON Canada L1N 2S3

CLUNEY, J(OHN) C(HARLES) (JACK CLUNEY), minister; b. Buffalo, Aug. 16, 1948; s. Edward Cecil and Edna Mary (Kinley) C.; m. Evelyn Mae Chapman, July 11, 1970; children: John C. Jr., Carrie Lynn. Ordained to ministry So. Bapt. Conv., 1983. Assoc. pastor Starlight Park Bapt. Ch., Phoenix, 1982-83; pastor Rainbow Valley Bapt. Ch., Buckeye, Ariz., 1983-85, Hopewell Bapt. Ch., Pana, Ill., 1985-89, Forsyth (Ill.) Bapt. Ch., 1989—; area rep. fulness fellowship of leaders, Ft. Worth, 1989—; state dir. Nat. Christian Counselors Assn., Pitts., 1987—; exec. dir. The Light House Project, Inc., Forsyth, Ill., 1989—; mem. Evang. Ministers Alliance, 1990. Author: Satanism and the Occult A Rational Look, 1989. Mem. Nat. Christian Counselors Assn. (state dir. 1987—), Evang. Ministers Alliance, Optimist Club (Decatur chpt., past pres. Pana, Ill. chpt.). Home: 144 E Cox St Box 285 Forsyth IL 62535 Office: Forsyth Bapt Ch 144 E Cox Box 139 Forsyth IL 62535 *Every man has lodged in his Being, the very purpose of God for his life. It remains his mission to discover it and use it to serve mankind. Know God, and enjoy the peace that only the manifest will of God can bring.*

CLUTE, DONNA LEE, lay youth worker; b. St. Petersburg, Fla., July 24, 1964; d. Donald A. and Wanda E. (Denhart) Logan; m. Robert M. Clute, Apr. 18, 1986; children: Shannon Leigh, Alexander Daniel. Student, Milligan Coll., 1983, Fla. Christian Coll., 1984. Youth vol. 1st Christian Ch., Largo, Fla., 1980-90, personnel asst. to youth, 1989; sr. high Sunday sch. tchr. Harborside Christian Ch., Largo, Fla., 1990—. Home: 12781-102 Way N Largo FL 34643 Office: Harborside Christian Ch 3380 SR 580 Safety Harbor FL 34695

CLYDE, ELMORE LOUIS, religious foundation administrator; b. Page, Nebr., Oct. 5, 1929; s. Henry E. and Edna E. (Van Kleeck) C.; m. Arlene A. Tice, Aug. 23, 1953; children: Steven M., Sheryl K. BA, Seattle Pacific U., 1951, DD, 1987; MDiv, Asbury Theol. Sem., 1954. Ordained to ministry Free Meth. Ch., 1954. Pastor Free Meth. Ch., Tonasket, Wash., 1954-56; missionary Free Meth. Ch., South Africa, 1957-74; exec. asst. World Missions-Free Meth. Ch., Winona Lake, Ind., 1975-84, gen. dir., 1984-89; exec. asst. Free Meth. Found., Spring Arbor, Mich., 1990—; del. gen. conf. Free Meth. Ch., Winona Lake, 1964, 69, 79, 85, 89; trustee Union Bible Sch., Pietermaritzburg, South Africa, 1958-74, Deaconess Hosp., Oklahoma City, 1985-90. Contbr. articles to Missions Mag., 1958—. Home: 159 Burr Oak Spring Arbor MI 49283 Office: Free Meth Found PO Box 580 Spring Arbor MI 49283 *Life's most pleasant moments can not always be planned but often come unexpectedly from the hand of God.*

CLYMER, WAYNE KENTON, bishop; b. Napoleon, Ohio, Sept. 24, 1917; s. George Arnold and Sallie Grace (Hulvey) C.; m. Helen Eloise Graves, Sept. 3, 1939; children: Kenton James, Richard George. A.B., Asbury Coll., 1939; M.A., Columbia, 1942; B.D., Union Theol. Sem., 1944; Ph.D., N.Y. U., 1950; LL.D., Westmar Coll., 1969; D.Litt., Hamline U., 1975; D.D., Iowa Wesleyan Coll., Rust Coll., Garrett-Evang. Theol. Sem. Ordained to ministry Evang. Ch., 1942; pastor Emanuel Ch., Ozone Park, N.Y.C., 1939-41, St. Paul's Ch., Forest Hills, N.Y.C., 1941-46; prof. Evang. Theol. Sem., Naperville, Ill., 1946-57; dean Evang. Theol. Sem., 1957-67, pres., 1967-72; bishop United Meth. Ch., Mpls., 1972-80, Des Moines, 1980-84; lectr. St. Andrews Theol. Coll., Manila, 1966, Trinity Coll., Singapore, 1967, U. Dubuque, 1985, Ill. Coll., 1990, United Theol. Sem. in Twin Cities, 1990; pres. United Meth. Com. on Relief, 1976-84; mem. del. UN Conf. Refugee, 1979; liaison to theol. sems. Coun. of Bishops, 1984-87; chair Grannis-Martin Found., 1984—. Author: Affirmation, 1971, Membership Means Discipleship, 1976; Contbr. to: Ency. Religious Edn. Pres. Naperville Sch. Bd., 1959-63; Mem. bd. Naperville Community Fund, 1966; pres. Chgo. Pastoral Counseling Center. Mem. Soc. Sci. Study Religion, Kappa Delta Pi. Club: Kiwanian.

COAKER, GEORGE MACK, minister; b. McLain, Miss., Jan. 9, 1927; s. George Mack and Kate Dean (Leeke) C.; m. Catherine Sabina Pennington, Mar. 19, 1948; children: Carol Dean Coaker Brewer, JoaAnn Coaker Littlejohn, Cathy Kay Coaker Vickers. BA, Howard Coll., Birmingham, Ala., 1948; BD, New Orleans Bapt. Theol. Sem., 1951; MA, U. Miss., 1955; PhD, Vanderbilt U., 1962. Ordained to ministry, So. Bapt. Conv., 1948. Pastor Chunchula (Ala.) Bapt. Ch., 1948-51, Ecru (Miss.) Bapt. Ch., 1951-53; chaplain USAF and VA, various locations, 1957-83; pastor Milton (Tenn.) Bapt. Ch., 1983-91, Greenvale (Tenn.) Bapt. Ch., 1991—; exec. bd. Tenn. Bapt. Conv., Nashville, 1983-90. Lt. col. chaplain corps USAF, 1953-57. Mem. Res. Officers Assn., Ret. Officers Assn., Am. Legion, DAV. Home and Office: 2535 Oregon Rd Milton TN 37118 *Life is Hard: Life is Harder without God. "With God all things are possible." Genesis 18:14.*

COALTER, MILTON J, JR., library director, educator; b. Memphis, July 5, 1949; s. Milton J. and Jewel (Mitchel) C.; m. Linda M. Block, May 20, 1973; children: Martha Claire, Siram Jacob. BA, Davidson Coll., 1971; MDiv, Princeton Theol. Sem., 1975, ThM, 1976, PhD in Religion, 1982. Asst. prof. Am. Religion N.C. State U., Raleigh, 1981-82; pub. svcs. libr. The Iliff Sch. Theology, Denver, 1982-84, acting libr. dir., 1984-85; libr. dir., prof. bibliography and rsch. Louisville Presbyn. Theol. Sem., 1985—; bd. dirs. Inst. for Study of Protestantism and Am. Culture, Louisville; mem. Gen. Assembly Coun. Task Force on Ch. Membership Growth, Presbyn. Ch. (U.S.A.), Louisville, 1989-91. Author: (with John M. Mulder) The Letters of David Avery, 1979, Gilbert Tennent, Son of Thunder, 1986, (with John M.

Mulder and Louis B. Weeks) The Presbyterian Presence in the Twentieth Century, 7 vols., 1989-92; contbr. articles to profl. jours. Recipient Jonathan Edwards award Princeton U., 1977-80, teaching award Assn. Princeton Grad Alumni, 1979-80; Lilly Endowment grantee Presbyn. Ch., 1987-90, N.J. Hist. Commn. grantee, 1979-80, Pew Charitable Trust grantee, 1990—; Princeton U. Whiting fellow, 1980-81. Mem. Am. Theol. Libr. Assn. (chmn. collection evaluation and devel. com., 1988-89), Am. Soc. Ch. History, Am. Acad. Religion, Orgn. Am. Historians. Presbyterian. Office: Louisville Presbyn Theol Sem 1044 Alta Vista Rd Louisville KY 40205

COATES, CECIL GRAY, pastor; b. Nathalie, Va., Sept. 16, 1931; s. Callie William and Nellie (Mason) C.; m. Margaret Carver, Dec. 28, 1951; children: Delores, Phyllis Kay, Elaine, Bettyy Jean, Steve. Student, Elon Coll., Holmes Bible Coll., Greenville, S.C. Ordained to ministry Pentecostal Holiness Ch. Pastor West Durham (N.C.) Pentecostal Holiness Ch.; pres. Mins.' Fellowship of Evangs., Danville, Va., 1976-79. With U.S. Army, 1951-53, Korea. Home and Office: West Durham Pentecostal Holiness Ch 322 N Lasalle St Durham NC 27705

COATS, ARTHUR WILLIAM, clergyman; b. Froid, Mont., Jan. 18, 1930; s. Arthur Henry and Severine Austrid (Scott) C.; m. Virginia Irene Morgan, June 5, 1952; children: Vicki Irene, David Arthur. Diploma Bible, Multnomah Sch. of Bible, 1953; BS in Edn., Lewis and Clark Coll., 1955; MS in Edn., Western Mont. Coll., 1966. Cert. guidance counselor and tchr.; ordained to ministry Bapt. Ch., 1955. Pastor Bethel Bapt. Ch., Lewistown, Mont., 1955-60, First Bapt. Ch., Dillon, Mont., 1960-67, Nyssa (Oreg.) Conservative Bapt. Ch., 1969-73, Prior Lake (Minn.) Bapt. Ch., 1974-80, Lakeview Bapt. Ch., Orr, Minn., 1980-85, First Bapt. Ch., Milltown, Wis., 1985—; adminstr. Heritage Christian Sch., Ft. Collins, Colo., 1973-74; founder Prior lake (Minn.) Christian Sch., 1977-80, Lakeview Bapt. Sch., Orr, Minn., 1984-85; trustee N.T. Assn. Ind. Bapt. Chs., Lakewood, Colo., 1986—. Author: Sunday School Commentary of Gospel of John, 1978, Sunday School Commentary on Book of Isaiah, 1979, Sunday School Commentary on Book of Judges, 1983. Precinct coord. Rep. party, Prior Lake and Orr, 1979, 83; pres. Milltown Manor, Inc., 1991. Home: 208 Milltown Ave N Box 125 Milltown WI 54858 Office: First Bapt Ch 216 Milltown Ave N Milltown WI 54858 *Serving the Supreme Being is supreme service. Serving the Savior (Jesus Christ) He sent to die for our sins is no sacrifice. Serving the people the Savior came to save is a privilege.*

COBB, SISTER ELIZABETH, school system administrator. Supt. schs. Roman Cath. Diocese of Portland, Maine. Office: Office Supt Cath Schs 510 Ocean Ave PO Box 6750 Portland ME 04101*

COBB, J., bishop. Bishop Ch. of God in Christ, Cairo, Ill. Office: Ch of God in Christ 323-30th St Cairo IL 62914*

COBB, JAMES GURLEY, minister; b. Hickory, N.C., Sept. 29, 1947; s. James Kevitt and Sara Ellen (Wingard) C.; m. Judith Ann Dawson, May 19, 1973; children: Christopher, Stephen. BA, William and Mary Coll., 1969; MDiv, Luth. Theol. Seminary, Gettysburg, Pa., 1973, D of Ministry, 1980. Ordained to ministry Evang. Ch. in Am., 1973. Asst. pastor St. Martin Luth. Ch., Annapolis, Md., 1973-74; pastor Christ Luth. Ch., Fredericksburg, Va., 1974-81; sr. pastor Trinity Luth. Ch., Grand Rapids, Mich., 1981-88, First Luth. Ch., Norfolk, Va., 1988—; active Nat. Ch. Coun./ Evangel. Luth. Ch. in Am., Chgo., 1987—; del. Va. Coun. Churches, 1976-81. Contbg. author: Augsburg Sermons II, 1984, In Sure and Certain Hope, 1985; contbg. author/editor: Rooted in Remembering, 1989. Mayor's adv. com. Fredericksburg, 1980-81; pres. Fredericksburg Ministerial Assn., Grand Rapids Area Ctr. for Ecumenism, 1986-87. Recipient Honor award Freedom's Found., Valley Forge, Pa., 1966. Office: First Lutheran Church 1301 Coiley Ave Norfolk VA 23517

COBB, JOHN BOSWELL, JR., clergyman, educator; b. Kobe, Japan, Feb. 9, 1925; s. John Boswell and Theodora Cook (Atkinson) C.; m. Jean Olmstead Loftin, June 18, 1947; children: Theodore, Cliford, Andrew, Richard. M.A., U. Chgo. Div. Sch., 1949, Ph. D., 1952. Ordained to ministry United Meth. Ch., 1950. Pastor Towns County Circuit, N.Ga. Conf., 1950-51; faculty Young Harris Coll., Ga., 1950-53, Candler Sch. Theology and Emory U., 1953-58, Sch. Theology, Claremont, Calif., 1958-90; Avery prof. Claremont Grad. Sch., 1973-90; ret., 1990; mem. commn. on doctrine and doctrinal standard United Meth. Ch., 1968-72; mem. commn. on mission, 1984-88. Author: A Christian Natural Theology, 1965, The Structure of Christian Existence, 1967, Christ in a Pluralistic Age, 1975, (with Herman Daly) For the Common Good, 1989. Dir. Center for Process Studies. Fulbright prof. U. Mainz, 1965-66; fellow Woodrow Wilson Internat. Ctr. for Scholars, 1976. Mem. Am. Acad. Religion, Am. Metaphys. Soc.

COBURN, JOHN BOWEN, retired bishop; b. Danbury, Conn., Sept. 27, 1914; s. Rev. Aaron Cutler and Eugenia Bowen (Woolfolk) C.; m. Ruth Alvord Barnum, May 26, 1941; children: Thomas, Judith, Michael, Sarah. AB with high honors, Princeton U., 1936, DD, 1960; BD cum laude, Union Theol. Sem., 1942; DD, Amherst Coll., 1955, Harvard U., 1964, Huron Coll., 1964, Middlebury Coll., 1970, Bucknell U., 1971, Trinity Coll., 1980, Hamilton Coll., 1982, Williams Coll., 1982; STD, Berkeley Div. Sch., 1958; DD, Hobart Coll., William Smith Colls., 1967; D of Canon Law, Kenyon Coll., 1968; DST, Gen. Theol. Sem., 1968; DCL, U. Kent, Canterbury, Eng., 1978. Ordained to ministry Protestant Episcopal Ch., as deacon, 1943, as priest, 1943. Tchr. English and biology Robert Coll., Istanbul, Turkey, 1936-39; asst. minister Grace Ch., N.Y.C., 1942-44; rector Grace Ch., Amherst, Mass.; chaplain Amherst Coll., 1946-53; dean Trinity Cathedral, Newark, 1953-57, Episcopal Theol. Sch., Cambridge, Mass., 1957-68; tchr. St. Acad., Urban League, Harlem, N.Y.C., 1968-69; rector St. James' Ch., N.Y.C., 1969-75; Episcopal bishop of Mass., 1976-86; Dir. Corning Glass Works.; del. Episcopal Gen. Conv., 1955, 61, 64, 67, 69, 70, 73, pres. house deps., 1967-76. Author: Prayer and Personal Religion, 1957, One Family in Christ, 1958, Minister, Man in the Middle, 1963, Anne and the Sand Dobbies, 1964, Twentieth Century Spiritual Letters, 1967, A Life to Live: A Way to Pray, 1973, A Diary of Prayers: Personal and Private, 1975, The Hope of Glory, 1976, Christ's Life: Our Life, 1978, Feeding Fire, 1980; editor: (with Norman Pittenger) Viewpoints, 1959. Trustee Princeton, Wooster Sch., Union Theol. Sem. Lt. (s.g.), Chaplains Corps USNR, 1944-46. Address: 17 Scallop Way Sears Point Brewster MA 02631

COBURN, THOMAS BOWEN, religious studies educator, college administrator; b. N.Y.C., Feb. 8, 1944; s. John Bowen and Ruth Alvord (Barnum) C.; m. Cynthia Diane Mueller, Sept. 3, 1967 (div. 1987); children: Brooke Bowen, Jesse Cutler. AB magna cum laude, Princeton U., 1965; M of Theol. Studies, Harvard U., 1969, PhD, 1977. Teaching fellow religion Phillips Acad., Andover, Mass., 1965-66; instr. math and physics Am. Community Sch., Beirut, 1966-67; house dir. Dana Hall Sch., Wellesley, Mass., 1971-74; teaching fellow, rsch. asst. Harvard U., 1971-74; instr. religious studies and classical langs. St. Lawrence U., Canton, N.Y., 1974-77, asst. prof., 1977-81, assoc. prof., 1981-88, prof., 1988-90, Charles A. Dana prof., 1990—, assoc. dean acad. affairs, 1983-85, dean acad. affairs, v.p. univ., 1985-86; vis. scholar Harvard Div. Sch., 1986-87; vis. lectr. U. Pitts., 1987; dir. N.Y. State Ind. Coll. Consortium for Study in India, 1990. Author: Devi-Mahatmya: Crystallization of the Goddess Tradition, 1984, Encountering the Goddess, 1991; contbr. articles to scholarly jours. Fund for Theol. Edn. fellow, 1967-68, Am. Inst. Indian Studies fellow, 1981-82; NEH grantee, 1982. Mem. Am. Oriental Soc., Assn. for Asian Studies, Am. Acad. Religion (co-chmn. sect. com. 1986—). Democrat. Episcopalian. Home: 16 Crescent St Canton NY 13617 Office: St Lawrence U Dept Religious Studies & Classical Langs Canton NY 13617

COCANOUGHER, G(EORGE) TRUETT, minister; b. Danville, Ky., Apr. 16, 1941; s. George Wesley and Zelma (Hundley) C.; m. Jeanene Nichols, June 23, 1963; children: Sara, Lela. BA, Georgetown (Ky.) Coll., 1962; MDiv, So. Bapt. Theol. Sem., 1968. Ordained to ministry So. Bapt. Conv., 1966. Assoc. pastor Valley Station Bapt. Ch., Louisville, 1966-68; pastor Mt. Pleasant Bapt. Ch., Nicholasville, Ky., 1968-70; Pastor Cecilia (Ky.) Bapt. Ch., 1970-72; pastor Kento-Boo Bapt. Ch., Florence, Ky., 1972-78, Reid Village Bapt. Ch., Mt. Sterling, Ky., 1978-81, Cen. Bapt. Ch., Maysville, Ky., 1981-91; dir. missions Bracken Assn. Bapts., Maysville, 1991—; mem. exec. bd. Ky. Bapt. Conv., 1976-78, 84-87, mem. nominating com., 1984-86, mem. Hist. Commn., 1989—; mem. pastoral care bd. St. Elizabeth Hosp., Covington, Ky., 1973-78. Mem. Greater Mason County Amateur Radio Assn. (pres. 1989-91). Home: 1234 Lewis St Maysville KY 41056 Office: Bracken Assn Bapts 315 Market St Maysville KY 41056

COCHRAN, KENT HAYS, minister; b. Clarksdale, Miss., Oct. 26, 1949; s. Frank Ralph and Josephine (Hays) C.; m. Millie Linda Boyd, June 14, 1974; children: Kelli Jo, Ryan Kent. AA, Meridian (Miss.) Jr. Coll., 1970; BS in Health, Phys. Edn. and Recreation, Delta State U., Cleveland, Miss., 1972; MDiv, New Orleans Bapt. Theol. Sem., 1981. Ordained to ministry So. Bapt. Conv., 1986. Dir. activities and youth Midway Bapt. Ch., Jackson, Miss., 1975-79; min. edn. and youth Midway Bapt. Ch., Meridian, 1982-86; pastor Calvary Bapt. Ch., Louisville, Miss., 1986—; conf. leader Miss. Bapt. Conv., Jackson, 1983—, growth specialist, 1989—; moderator Winston Bapt. Assn., Louisville, 1989—. Contbr. to religious publs. Home and Office: Calvary Bapt Ch Rte 2 Box 301 Louisville MS 39339 *It takes fewer muscles in the face to form a smile than it does to form a frown. So, smile!.*

COCHRANE, RICHARD JAMES CHRISTOPHER, priest, educator; b. Lawrence, Mass., Feb. 12, 1945; s. David Ernest and Ada Elizabeth (Haynes) C. BA, Merrimack Coll., 1966; MA, Washington Theol. Union, 1972; postgrad., Oxford U., 1987. Ordained priest Roman Cath. Ch., 1972. Dir. religious edn. Holy Rosary Sch., Lawrence, Mass., 1972-73; theol. dept. chmn. Malvern (Pa.) Prep. Sch., 1974-82, chaplain, dir. religious edn., 1974-80, admissions dir., 1982-89, adminstr. classical music program, 1976—, prof. biblical studies, 1976—. Contbr. articles to newspapers. Study grantee Hebrew U., Jerusalem, Order of St. Augustine, 1978; Brit. Art grantee Worcester Coll., Oxford U., Eng., 1987. Mem. Nat. Assn. Pvt. Schs. (Phila. area admissions dir.), Ednl. Records Bur. Republican. Avocations: skiing, hiking, sailing, tennis, scuba diving. Home and Office: Malvern Prep Sch Warren Ave Malvern PA 19355

COCHRANE, ROBERT H., bishop; s. William Arthur H. and Raven (Hume) C.; m. Theresa M. Tripi; two children. BA, CUNY, 1948; STB, Gen. Theol. Sem., N.Y., 1951, DD, 1976. Ordained to ministry, Episcopal Ch., 1951; consecrated bishop coadjutor, Diocese of Olympia, Wash., 1976. Vicar Redeemer Ch., Delano, Calif., 1951-52; curate Trinity Ch., Reno, 1952-54; vicar St. Timothy Ch., Henderson, Nev., 1954-60; rector All Saints Ch., Salt Lake City, 1960-69, Christ Ch., Tacoma, Wash., 1969-76; bishop, Olympia, 1976—. Office: Diocese of Olympia PO Box 12126 1551 Tenth Ave Seattle WA 98102

COCKBURN, CLIFF J., minister; b. Sioux City, Iowa, Feb. 21, 1963; s. Dean James and Charlotte (Henderson) C. BS in Ministry, Neb. Christian Coll., 1985, BTh, 1986. Ordained to ministry Christian Ch., 1986. Sr. min. First Ch. of Christ, Modale, Iowa, 1983-88, First Christian Ch., Central City, Nebr., 1988—; regional pub. rels. North Am. Christian Conv., Cin.; bd. dirs. Cult Awareness Project, Norfolk, Nebr.; adv. bd. Coll. Career Christian Fellowship, Lincoln, Nebr., pub. rels. chmn. Nebr. State Christian Conv., Kearney, Nebr. Mem. Central City C. of C., Lions Club (pres. 1990—). Office: First Christian Church 407 Ave A Central City NE 68826-1315

COCKMAN, RICHARD LEE, minister; b. Greensboro, N.C., Sept. 13, 1949; s. Herbert Eugene and Mary Matilda (Hussey) C.; m. Malissa Eve Moore, Aug. 2, 1975; children: Malissa, Rebekah, Keturah. AA, Broward Community Coll., Ft. Lauderdale, Fla., 1969; BS, Nyack Coll., 1972; MDiv, Asbury Theol. Sem., Wilmore, Ky., 1975; D Ministry, Luther Rice Sem., 1989. Ordained to ministry Christian and Missionary Alliance, 1975. Student minister Old Springfield Presbyterian Ch., Ky., 1974-75; asst. minister East Lake Alliance Ch., Birmingham, Ala., 1975-76; minister Arlington (Tex.) Alliance Ch., 1976-81; sr. min. Christian and Missionary Alliance Ch., Lake Worth, Fla., 1981-87; sr. minister Faith Missionary Alliance, Winston-Salem, N.C., 1987—; family and marital therapist Caroline Christian Counseling Ctr., High Point, N.C., 1989-91; mem. designation com. Billy Graham Crusade, Ft. Lauderdale, Fla., 1985; agenda chmn. Christian and Missionary Alliance, Nyack, N.Y., 1985—, mem. exec. com. southwestern dist., Dallas, 1979-81, southeastern dist., Orlando, Fla., 1985-87; v.p. North Davidson Ministerium, Davidson County, N.C., 1988-89; v.p. Palm Coast Ministerium, West Palm Beach, Fla., 1982-83, pres., 1983-84. Parsell scholar Nyack Coll., 1972. Republican. Home: Rte 16 Box 9 4D Winston-Salem NC 27107 Office: Faith Missionary Alliance Route 16 Box 3 Winston-Salem NC 27107

COCORIS, GEORGE MICHAEL, minister; b. Pensacola, Fla., Sept. 22, 1939; s. George Theodore and Laura Belle (Rutherford) C.; m. Judith Iola Eaves, June 2, 1962; children: James Michael, Careth Ruth, Christine Hope. BA, Tenn. Temple U., 1962; ThM, Dallas Theol. Sem., 1966; DD (hon.), Biola U., 1984. Ordained to ministry So. Bapt. Conv., 1963. Pastor 1st Bapt. Ch., Pattonville, Tex., 1963-66; evangelist, Chattanooga, 1966-74; staff evangelist, v.p. Evantel, Dallas, 1974-79, bd. dirs., 1974—; sr. pastor Ch. of Open Door, Glendora, Calif., 1979—; adj. prof. Dallas Sem., 1974-79; speaker The Open Door radio, L.A., 1979-91, the Biola Hour, 1991—; founder, tchr. Torrey Bible Inst., L.A., 1982—. Author: Evangelism: A Biblical Approach, 1984, (booklet) Lordship Salvation, Is It Biblical?, 1983; contbr. articles to profl. jours. Bd. dirs. S.O.S., Irvine, Calif., 1979-89, Biola U., 1987-91; arbitrator Better Bus. Bur., 1984. Home: 767 Kilnaleck Ln Glendora CA 91740 Office: Ch of Open Door 701 W Sierra Madre Ave Glendora CA 91740 *The greatest need of mankind is to know Jesus Christ personally through faith and be obedient to the Word of God. Everyone in the ministry should be dedicated to the task of getting that job done.*

CODER, SAMUEL MAXWELL, clergyman, dean emeritus; b. Straight, Pa., Mar. 25, 1902; s. Emmanuel Miller and Abbie Mary (Bailey) C.; m. Elizabeth Maria Dieterle, Feb. 20, 1932; children—Margaret Elizabeth (dec.), Maxine Joyce, Donald Maxwell. Student, Evang. Theol. Coll., Dallas, 1932-35; B.S., Temple U., 1938; Th.B., Dallas Theol. Sem., 1938; Th.M., 1940; D.D., Bible Theol. Sem. of Los Angeles, 1949. Ordained to ministry Presbyn. Ch., 1938. Bus. exec., 1928-32; pastor Grace Ch., Camden, N.J., 1935-38, Chelsea Ch., Atlantic City, N.J., 1938-43, Evangel Ch., Phila., 1944-45; mem. faculty Moody Bible Inst., Chgo., from 1945, v.p. and dean edn., 1947-69, now dean emeritus. Editor in chief, Moody Press, 1946; gen. editor: The Wycliffe Series of Christian Classics, 1950—; Author: Youth Triumphant, 3 vols., Moody Corr. Course, 1946, Dobbie, Defender of Malta, 1946, God's Will for Your Life, 1950, Jude: the Acts of the Apostates, 1955, Israel's Destiny, 1978, The Moody Christian Worker's New Testament, 1980, The Final Chapter, 1984; editor: Memoirs of McCheyne, 1947, Our Lord Prays for His Own, 1950, The World to Come, 1954, Nave's Topical Bible, 1976; Contbr. articles to religious jours. Republican. Home: 1860 Sherman Ave Evanston IL 60201 *The greatest discovery of my life was that the Bible is the Word of God. All who honor its precepts experience peace of mind and a joyful abundant life. It contains the answer to every problem of the human heart and to the problems of our nation.*

COELHO, JOSEPH RICHARD, educator; b. Evanston, Ill., Apr. 27, 1946; s. Richard Joseph and Helene Christine (Lindquist) C.; m. Pauline Gloria Bailey, May 21, 1971 (div.). BS, Mich. State U., 1968; BA, U. Minn., 1975; MDiv, Yale U., 1978; postgrad., Columbia U., 1980-82. Research asst. U. Minn., Mpls., 1972-75; mgr. Meridian Mall, Okemos, Mich., 1978-79; cons. Gen. Motors, Detroit, 1979-80; mgr. Am. Mgmt. Assn., N.Y.C., 1981-82; cons. Pitney Bowes Inc., Stamford, Conn., 1982-85; exec. Bridgeport (Conn.) Deanery, 1985-88; adj. prof. philosophy Sacred Heart U., Fairfield, Conn., 1985-86; pres. Isaiah 61:1 Inc., Bridgeport, Conn., 1985—; lectr. applied ethics Fairfield (Conn.) U., 1986-90. Author and editor various works in art history, strategy and military history. Served to comdr. USNR, 1965—. Mem. Yale Club (N.Y.C.), Coasters Harbor Navy Yacht Club (Newport, R.I.), Phi Kappa Phi.. Republican. Episcopalian. Home: 11 Main St Newtown CT 06470 Office: Isaiah 61:1 Inc Bridgeport CT 06604

COFFEN, RICHARD WAYNE, minister, editor; b. Stoneham, Mass., Nov. 19, 1941; s. George Albert and Dorothy Cowan (Hayward) C.; m. Rosalia Jane Clausen, June 9, 1963; children: Robert W., Ronald D. BA, Atlantic Union Coll., 1963; MA, Andrews U., 1964. Ordained to ministry Seventh-day Adventists, 1968. Pastor So. New Eng. conf., Seventh-day Adventists, Mass., 1964-70; editor So. Pub. Assn., Nashville, 1970-81; editor, assoc. editor books div. Rev. & Herald Pub. Assn., Hagerstown, Md., 1981—. Author: Time of the Sign, 1975, Ten Steps to Successful Bible Study, 1976. Mem. Soc. Bibl. Lit., Andrews Soc. for Religious Studies. Home: 25 Bittersweet Dr Hagerstown MD 21740 Office: Rev & Herald Pub Assn 55 W Oak Ridge Dr Hagerstown MD 21740

COFFEY, JACK FRANKLIN, minister; b. Granite Falls, N.C., Nov. 18, 1928; s. Frank Bynum Coffey and Lottie (Lefevers) Hill; m. Sarah Elizabeth Buie, May 9, 1959; children: Jack Franklin Jr., Sarah Catherine. Student, Mars Hill Coll., 1950; BA, Wake Forest U., 1954; student, Duke Div. Sch., Durham, N.C., 1955; BD, Southeastern Sem., Wake Forest, N.C., 1958; MDiv, Southeastern Sem., 1970. Ordained to ministry Bapt. Ch., 1954. Pastor Island Creek Bapt. Ch., Henderson, N.C., 1954-58; assoc. pastor Petworth-Montgomery Hills Bapt. Ch., Washington, 1958-62; sr. pastor Downtown Bapt. Ch., Alexandria, Va., 1962-67, New Hope Bapt. Ch., Raleigh, N.C., 1967—; mem. bd. mins. Campbell U., Buies Creek, N.C., 1976—, trustee, 1984—; trustee Annuity Bd. So. Bapt. Conv., Dallas, 1988—; bd. dirs. Life Enrichment Ctr., Raleigh, 1975-85. Mem. Raleigh Bapt. Assn. (moderator 1983-85), Kiwanis. Democrat. Home: 3801 Valley Stream Dr Raleigh NC 27604 Office: New Hope Bapt Ch 4301 Louisburg Rd Raleigh NC 27604 *Selfless love is a dynamic force that works toward good in all relationships, an example of which can be found in Jesus, whose life should well be our pattern.*

COFFIN, ROY RIDDELL, priest; b. Bryn Mawr, Pa., Mar. 9, 1932; s. Roy Riddell and Catharine Marie (Pfingst) C.; m. Caroline Compton Clarkson, Mar. 9, 1963; children: Cynthia Parker, Deborah Osborne, John Tristram. BA, Dartmouth Coll., 1954; MBA, U. Mich., 1959; MDiv, Va. Theol. Sem., 1977; DMin, Wesley Sem., 1987. Ordained priest Episcopal Ch., 1978. Interim rector Diocese of Washington, 1978—; asst. St. Columba's Ch., Washington, 1977-78; chaplain St. Patrick's Elem. Day Sch., Washington, 1977-79. Founding bd. dirs. Interim Ministry Network, Balt., 1981—. Address: 124 Hesketh St Chevy Chase MD 20815

COFFMAN, JAMES RAYMOND, pastoral counselor; b. Brownsville, Tenn., Mar. 29, 1946; s. Robin Ernest and Helen Elizabeth (Thornley) C.; m. Mary Kathryn Stinson, June1, 1968; children: Kathryn Alice, Raymond Lincoln. BA, Union U., 1968; MDiv, So. Bapt. Theol. Sem., 1971, ThM, 1972; D of Ministry, Vanderbilt U., 1980. Ordained to ministry Bapt. Ch., 1968. cert. profl. counselor, cert. marriage and family therapist. Pastor Mt. Zion Bapt. Ch., Beaver Dam, Ky., 1969-72; counselor Berea (Ky.) Coll., 1972; assoc. pastor 1st Bapt. Ch., Kirksville, Mo., 1972-75, interim pastor, 1974; pastor Arran Lake Bapt. Ch., Fayetteville, N.C., 1975-78; chaplain Jesse Holman Hosp., Springfield, Tenn., 1978-80; resident chaplin Bapt. Med. Ctrs., Birmingham, Ala., 1980-82, assoc. dir., 1982-85; exec. dir. Pastoral Counseling & Consultation Ctrs. Tenn., Nashville, 1985—; cons., VA Med. Ctr., Nashville, 1986—; lectr., Vanderbilt U., 1985—. Fellow Am. Assn. Pastoral Counselors (com. ctr. and tng. 1985-91), Coll. Chaplains; mem. Assn. Clin. Pastoral Edn. (cert. supr., com. accreditation 1985-91), Nat. Coun. Family Rels., Am. Assn. for Marital and Family Therapy (clin.). Avocations: tennis, jogging, travel, photography. Office: Pastoral Counseling and Consultation Ctrs 100 Vine Ct Nashville TN 37205

COFFMAN, MARK ANTHONY, clergyman; b. Atlanta, Dec. 23, 1966; s. Gerald Thomas and Sheryl Elaine (Dickerson) Cantrell; m. Cindy Joyce Perry, Mar. 12, 1988; children: HIllary, Noel. BS, Atlanta Christian Coll., 1991. Ordained to ministry Christian Ch., 1989. Youth/singles minister First Christian Ch., Cumming, Ga., 1987—. Office: First Christian Ch 1270 Sawnee Dr Cumming GA 30130

COFFY, ROBERT CARDINAL, archev252que; b. Le Biot, Haute Savoie, France, Oct. 24, 1920; s. Jean and Henriette (Morand) C. Student, Petit Séminaire de Thonon Les Bains, Haute Savoie, Grand Séminaire d'Annecy, Haute Savoie; grad., Faculté de Théologie de Lyon, Rhone; Licentiate in Theology. Ordained priest Roman Cath. Ch., 1944, bishop, 1967, created cardinal, 1991. Vicar à Bernex Roman Cath. Ch., 1946-48, prof. au Petit Séminaire de Thonon les Bains, 1948-49, prof. de dogme au Grand Séminaire d'Annecy, 1949-52, supérieur du Grand Séminaire d'Annecy, 1952-67, vicaire général du diocèse d'Annecy, 1956, eveque de Gap, 1967-74, archbishop d'Albi, 1974-85, archbishop de Marseille, 1985—, cardinal, 1991—; mem. Conseil Permanent Episcopat Français, Paris. Author: Dieu des Athées: Theilhard de Chardin et le Socialisme, Eglise, signe de salut, Une Eglise qui célèbre et qui prie. Home: 4, place Colonel Edon, 13007 Marseilles France

COGAN, MORDECHAI, biblical studies educator; b. Phila., Dec. 24, 1939; s. Jack and Elizabeth C. BA in Semitics, U. Pa., 1961, PhD in Biblical Studies, 1971. Assoc. prof. biblical studies Ben-Gurion U., Beer Sheba, Israel, 1972—, Hebrew U., Jerusalem. Author: Imperialism and Religion, 1974, Second Kings, 1988, Obadiah, 1992. Grantee Meml. Found. for Jewish Culture, 1968-69. Mem. Am. Oriental Soc., Assn. Jewish Studies, Am. Schools of Oriental Research, Israel Exploration Soc., World Union Jewish Studies. Home: 19 Shaked, Omer Israel 89465

COGGAN, FREDERICK DONALD, former archbishop of Canterbury; b. London, Eng., Oct. 9, 1909; s. Cornish Arthur and Fanny Sarah (Chubb) C.; m. Jean Braithwaite Strain, Oct. 17, 1935; children—Dorothy Ann, Ruth Evelyn. B.A., St. John's Coll., Cambridge U., 1931, M.A., 1935; student, Wycliffe Hall, Oxford, 1934; B.D., U. Toronto, 1941; D.D. (hon.), Wycliffe Coll., Toronto, Can., 1944; Lambeth D.D., U. Leeds, 1958, Cambridge (Eng.) U., 1962, U. Aberdeen, Saskatoon, Huron, Tokyo, Hull, 1963, U. Manchester, 1972, Moravian Theol. Sem., 1976; H.H.D., Westminster Choir Coll., Princeton, 1966; D.Litt., Westminster Choir Coll., Lancaster, 1967; S.T.D., Gen. Theol. Sem., 1967; LL.D., Liverpool U., 1972; D.C.L., Kent U., 1975; D.Univ., U. York, 1975, King's Coll., London, 1975. Ordained to ministry Ch. of Eng., 1934; asst. lectr. Semitic langs. and lit. Manchester U., 1931-34; curate St. Mary, Islington, London, 1934-37; prof. N.T. Wycliffe Coll., Toronto, 1937-44; prin. London Coll. Div., 1944-56, bishop of Bradford, 1956-61, archbishop of York, 1961-74, archbishop of Canterbury, 1974-80; chmn. Coll. of Preachers.; Prelate Order St. John Jerusalem, 1967-89. Created baron of Canterbury and Sissinghurst, 1980. Author: A People's Heritage, 1944, The Ministry of the Word, 1945, The Glory of God, 1950, Stewards of Grace, 1958, Five Makers of the New Testament, 1962, Christian Priorities, 1963, The Prayers of the New Testament, 1967, Sinews of Faith, 1969, Word and World, 1971, Convictions, 1975, On Preaching, 1978, Great Words of the Christian Faith, 1978, Sure Foundation, 1981, Paul: Portrait of a Revolutionary, 1984, The Sacrament of the Word, 1987, Cuthbert Bardsley: Bishop, Evangelist, Pastor, 1989, God of Hope, 1991. Home: 28 Lions Hall, St Swithun St, Winchester England SO23 9HW

COGGIN, WALTER ARTHUR, clergyman; b. Richmond, Va., Feb. 10, 1916; s. Walter Arthur and Mary Veronica (Moshy) C. Student, Belmont (N.C.) Abbey Jr. Coll., 1934-36, Belmont Abbey Sem., 1939-43; A.B., St. Benedict's Coll., Atchison, Kan., 1939; postgrad, U. N.C., 1942; M.A., Cath. U., 1948, Ph.D., 1954. Became Benedictine monk, 1937; ordained priest Roman Catholic Ch., 1943; vicar Belmont Abbey Monastery, 1956-59; abbot-ordinary of Belmont Abbey Nullius, 1960-70; tchr. philosophy Belmont Abbey Coll., 1954—; Mem. 2d Vatican Council, 1962-65. Mem. N.C. Philos. Soc. (pres. 1955-56), Am. Cath. Philos. Assn. Address: Belmont Abbey Belmont NC 28012

COGSWELL, ROBERT ELZY, librarian; b. Houston, Aug. 9, 1939; s. Ray Boyd Cogswell and Reba Pauline (Pendergrass) Mullen; m. Betty Jo Dornberger, Feb. 2, 1967. BA in Govt., U. Tex., 1972, MLS, 1978; MA in Religion, Luth. Sem. Program S.W., Austin, Tex., 1990. Cataloger, reference libr. Episcopal Theol. Sem. S.W., Austin, 1979—. Editor, pub. Abba, a Jour. of Prayer, 1976-77; contbr. book revs. and articles to profl. jours. Founder, bd. dirs. Casa Marianella, Austin, 1985-88. Mem. Am. Theol. Libr. Assn., Amnesty Internat., Fellowship of Reconciliation. Democrat. Lutheran. Home: 3913 Wilbert Rd Austin TX 78751

COHEN, ARMOND E., rabbi; b. Canton, Ohio, June 5, 1909; s. Samuel and Rebecca (Lipowitz) C.; m. Anne Lederman; children: Rebecca Long, Deborah (dec.), Samuel. BA, NYU, 1931; rabbi, Jewish Theol Sem. Am., 1934, M Hebrew Lit., 1945, DD, 1966; LLD, Cleve. State U., 1969; LHD, Baldwin-Wallace Coll., 1989. Ordained rabbi, 1934. Rabbi Pk. Synagogue, Cleve., 1934—; adj. prof. psychiatry Jewish Theol. Sem. Am., N.Y.C., 1970-

75; bd. dirs. Inst. Religion and Health, N.Y.C. Author: All God's Children, Selected Readings on Zionism, Outline of Jewish History, Readings in Medieval Jewish Literature; mem. editorial bd. Jour. Religion and Health, 1943-67; contbr. articles to profl. jours. Bd. govs. Hebrew U., Jerusalem; trustee Am. Friends of Hebrew U.; bd. dirs. consumers League Ohio, Cleve., Jewish Community Fedn., Cleve., Coun. World Affairs, Cleve.; hon. v.p. Zionist Orgn. Am. Recipient Nat. Humanitarian award NCCJ, 1983; hon. fellow Hebrew U., 1979. Mem. Rabbinical Assembly Am., Cleve. Bd. Rabbis (founder), Lotos Club (N.Y.C.), Oakwood Club (Cleve.). Home: 8 Sherwood Ct Beachwood OH 44122 Office: The Park Synagogue 3300 Mayfield Rd Cleveland Heights OH 44118 *Anyone can struggle through life without faith but everyone needs faith if he would confront life's inevitable challenges and sorrows and stand erect. It is easier to go through this life with faith than without it.*

COHEN, EUGENE JOSEPH, rabbi; b. N.Y.C., Aug. 22, 1918; s. Philip J. and Rose (Cohen) C.; Rabbi, Yeshiva U., 1942; Ph.D., Boston U., 1954; m. Ada Twersky, Dec. 1, 1948; children: Burton, Bethsheva, Leeber. Rabbi, Congregation Derech Emunoh, Arverne, N.Y., 1948-66, Internat. Synagogue, Queens, N.Y., 1967-85, Brith Milah Bd. Am., N.Y.C., 1960—; chief chaplains VA Hosp., Bklyn., 1969—. Active Bricha underground rescue movement, World War II. Served to capt. AUS, 1945-47. Recipient award Fedn. Jewish Philanthropists, 1964. Mem. Religious Zionists Am. (v.p.), Jewish Chaplains U.S. (past pres.), Rabbinical Council (sec. 1984), Rabbinical Alumni, N.Y. Bd. Rabbis, Brith Milah Am., Fedn. Jewish Philanthropies (mem. med. ethics com.). Lodge: B'nai Brith (pres. Milah bd. of world). Author: Jewish Concepts of the Servant, 1954; Ritual Circumcision and Redemption of the First-Born Son, Presentation and Analysis of Routine Rescue Circumcision (40 vols. in print), Hope for Humanity; also articles; editor: Pediatrics and Urology and Their Relationship to Brith Milah; Medical Dilemmas and the Practise of Milah; Brith Milah and Medicine; speaker radio and tv. Home: 258 Riverside Dr New York NY 10025 Office: 800 Poly Pl Brooklyn NY 11209

COHEN, JACOB, bishop. Bishop Ch. of God in Christ, Miami, Fla. Office: Ch of God in Christ 3120 NW 48th Terr Miami FL 33142*

COHEN, JEFFREY, hospital chaplain; b. Sydney, Australia, Jan. 4, 1950; s. Leonard and Gwen (Abbott) C.; m. Edith Feldman, June 27, 1982; children: Moshe-Lieb, Miriam. B in Commerce, U. New South Wales, Australia, 1973; Dr. Ministries, Eden Theol. Sem., 1986. Ordained rabbi, 1979. Exec. dir. Assn. Internat. des Etudiants Sciences Economiques et Commerciales, South Pacific, 1972-74, Europe World Coun. Synagogues, London, 1979-80; assoc. rabbi Congregation B'Nai Amoona, St. Louis, 1980-82; chaplain Jewish Fedn., St. Louis, 1983-84; coord. pastoral svcs. St. Louis State Hosp., 1984-88; dir. div. pastoral resources Dept. Mental Health, Mo., 1988—; dir. Inst. for Pastoral Edn., 1989—; cons. Pathways to Promise: Interfaith Ministry and Prolonged Mental Illness, 1988—. Active Holocaust Commn., St. Louis; bd. dirs. Solomon Schechter Day Sch. St. Louis, Sr. Svc. Bd., University City, Mo.; Jewish Community Rels. Coun., St. Louis. Coun. Jewish Fedn. rabbinical fellow, 1981, 86. Fellow Assn. Jewish Chaplains in Spl. Settings (pres. 1986—), Coll. Chaplains; mem. Assn. Mental Health Clergy (pres. 1990—), Assn. for Clin. Pastoral Edn., Rabbinical Assembly St. Louis (pres. 1985-86), St. Louis Rabbinical Assn. (pres. 1989-90), U. New South Wales Alumni Assn. (award 1974), Leo Baeck Coll. Alumni Assn. (bd. dirs.), Jewish Family and Childrens' Svc. (bd. dirs.), Congress on Ministry in Specialized Settings (v.p. 1990—). Home: 7822 Stanford Saint Louis MO 63130 Office: Dept Mental Health 5400 Arsenal Saint Louis MO 63139

COHEN, KENNETH LOUIS, rabbi; b. Rahway, N.J., June 19, 1952; s. Joseph and Sylvia (Daniels) C.; m. Gillian Papilsky, Mar. 1, 1987 (dec. Oct. 1991); 1 child, Zachary Natan; stepchildren: Tal, Daniel. BSFS, Georgetown U., 1974; MA, Balt. Hebrew U., 1976; postgrad., Leo Baeck Coll., 1980; PhD (hon.), Found. for Amateur Radio, 1990. Ordained rabbi, 1980. Rabbi Cardiff (Wales) New Synagogue, 1980-84; assoc. rabbi Shaarey Zedek, Southfield, Mich., 1984-86; rabbi Beth Shalom, Columbia, Md., 1986—; dep. Bd. Deps. of Brit. Jews, London, 1981-83; chair Balt. Washington Union of Jewish Studies, 1972-74; mem. exec. com. Jewish Community Coun. Greater Washington, 1972-74; religious broadcaster BBC, 1980-83; chair pastoral care com. Howard County Hosp., Columbia, 1990. Contbr. articles, book revs. to various newspapers and profl. publs. Mem. Howard County Pub. Ethics Commn., Ellicott City, Md., 1988—, chairperson, 1991. Chaplain USNR, 1983-91. Recipient cert. of merit U.S. Senator Barbara Mikulski, 1988. Mem. Rabinnical Assembly, Cen. Conf. Am. Rabbis, Wash. Bd. Rabbis, Balt. Bd. Rabbis, N.Y. Bd. Rabbis, Am. Radio Relay League (sect. mgr. Md.-D.C. sect. 1989—). Home: 7308 Silent Bird Ctrcle Columbia MD 21046 Office: Beth Shalom of Howard Co Box 2878 Columbia MD 21045 *Beware the person who preaches much but reads little.*

COHEN, SAMUEL ISRAEL, clergyman, organization executive; b. Asbury Park, N.J., Apr. 17, 1933; s. Meyer and Henrietta (Gershman) C.; m. Mira Hager, Sept. 5, 1960; children: Baruch Chaim, Michael Nachum, Miriam Rachel. BA, Bklyn. Coll., 1955; MRE, Yeshiva U., 1959, EdD, 1967. Ordained rabbi, 1956. Exec. dir. L.I. Zionist Youth Commn., Queens, N.Y., 1957-61; regional dir. Supreme Lodge B'nai B'rith, Queens, 1961-66; dir. membership dept. dist. 1 Supreme Lodge B'nai B'rith, N.Y.C., 1966-72; nat. dir. orgn. Am. Jewish Congress, N.Y.C., 1972-74; exec. dir. Am. Zionist Fedn., N.Y.C., 1974-77; exec. v.p. Jewish Nat. Fund, N.Y.C., 1977—; adj. asst. prof. sociology L.I. U., 1967; lectr. sociology Queensborough Community Coll., 1968, adj. asst. prof., 1971-74; lectr. Borough of Manhattan Community Coll., 1968, adj. asst. prof., 1970-72; adj. asst. prof. John Jay Coll. Criminal Justice, 1973—; lectr. Herzl Inst., N.Y.C., 1974-78. Contbr. articles to nat. publs. Chmn. edn. adv. bd. Yeshiva Toras Chaim, Woodmere, N.Y., 1971-74; mem. Religious Zionists Am., 1960—, Zionist Orgn. Am., 1960—, Nat. Coun. Jewish Edn., 1970—; mem. Conf. Jewish Communal Svc., 1970—; mem. Congregation Shaarei Tephila, Lawrence, N.Y., 1983-87, Congregation Kneseth Israel, 1983—; sec Olam Chadash, 1980—; bd. dirs. Union Orthodox Jewish Congregations Am., 1973—, United Israel Appeal, 1984—. Co-recipient Boneh Israel award, Mercaz Horav Kook. Mem. Adult Edn. Assn. (nat. com. on goals and objectives religious edn. sect. 1967-68), Educators Council Am., Young Israel of Wavecrest and Bayswater (v.p. 1973-75), Assn. Jewish Community Orgn. Profls., Nat. Council for Adult Jewish Edn., Nat. Soc. Fund Raising Execs, B'nai B'rith (v.p. Briarwood Lodge, 1964). Home: 112 Rand Pl Lawrence NY 11559 Office: 42 E 69th St New York NY 10029

COHEN, SEYMOUR JAY, rabbi; b. N.Y.C., Jan. 30, 1922; s. Philip J. and Rose (Cohen) C.; m. Naomi Greenberg, June 11, 1946; children: Grace, Marc, Leeber. BSS, CCNY, 1942; postgrad., Jewish Theol. Sem., 1942-46, Hebrew U., Jerusalem, 1946-47; MA, Columbia U., 1949; PhD, U. Pitts., 1953. Ordained rabbi, 1946. Rabbi Patchogue (N.Y.) Jewish Ctr., 1947-51, B'nai Israel Synagogue, Pitts., 1951-60, Anshe Emet Synagogue, Chgo., 1961—; instr. industry and econs. U. Pitts., 1954-57; vis. prof. St. Mary of Lake, Mundelein, pres. Synagogue Coun. Am., 1965-67; chmn. Am. Jewish Conf. on Soviet Jewry, 1965; sec. Rabbinical Assembly, 1962-64, v.p., 1978-80, pres., 1980-82; co-chmn. Interreligious Com. Against Poverty, 1966-68; pres. Chgo. Bd. Rabbis, 1968-70; mem. com. medicine and religion AMA, 1961-66; bd. dirs. Jewish Theol. Sem. Author: Judaism and the Worlds of Business and Labor, 1961, Negro-Jewish Dialogue, 1963, Religious Freedom and the Constitution, 1963, A Time to Speak, 1968, Form, Fire and Ashes, 1978; translator: Ways of the Righteous, 1969, rev. edit., 1982, Book of the Righteous, 1978, The Holy Letter, 1976, Affirming Life, 1986. Am. Travelling fellow Zionist Orgn. Am., 1946-47. Mem. Phi Beta Kappa. Home: 3800 Lake Shore Dr Chicago IL 60613 Office: 3760 N Pine Grove St Chicago IL 60613

COHEN, STEVEN MARTIN, religion educator; b. Bklyn., Apr. 3, 1950; s. Max and Toby (Fassman) C.; m. Susan segal, July 31, 1983; 1 child, Edeet. BA, Columbia U., 1970, PhD, 1974. Prof. Queens Coll., Flushing, N.Y., 1974—. Author: American Modernity and..., 1983, American Assimilation or..., 1988, Cosmopolitans and Parochials, 1989, Two Worlds of Judaism, 1990. Democrat. Home: 162 Cleveland Rd New Haven CT 06515 Office: Queens Coll Dept Sociology Flushing NY 11367

COHN, EDWARD PAUL, rabbi; b. Balt., Sept. 24, 1948; s. Rudolph J. and Rebecca (Weiner) C.; m. Andrea Levy, June 18, 1972; children: Jennifer, Debra. BA, U. Cin., 1970; BHL, Hebrew Union Coll., 1974, MAHL, 1974; DMin, St. Paul Sch. Theology, Kansas City, Mo., 1983. Ordained rabbi. Asst. rabbi The Temple, Atlanta, 1974-76; rabbi Temple Beth Israel, Macon, Ga., 1976-79, The New Reform Temple, Kansas City, Mo., 1979-84, Temple Sinai, Pitts., 1984-87; sr. rabbi Cong. Temple Sinai, New Orleans, 1987—; nat. chmn. interreligious activities Cen. Conf. Am. Rabbis, 1990—, bd. dirs., Jewish Reg. Ctr., New Orleans, 1989—; pres. New Orleans Rabbinical Coun., 1991—; adj. prof. dept. religion Dillard U., 1991—. Contbg. editor Pulpet Digest, 1987-90; producer, moderator: Talking Faith to Faith, Channel 47, 1987—, Shalom New Orleans, 1990—; author: Suicide and the Elderly, 1988. Mayor's rep. Human Rels. Com., new Orleans, 1989—; bd. dirs. United Way, New Orleans, 1991—, Trinity Sch. Bd. Visitors, New Orleans, 1990—, Ethics Com., Touro Infirmary, New Orlenas, 1989—. Mem. Cen. Conf. Am. Rabbis. Office: Temple Sinai 6227 St Charles Ave New Orleans LA 70118

COHN, HILLEL, rabbi; b. Berlin, Germany, Sept. 4, 1938; came to U.S., 1939; s. Franklin and Miriam (Finkelstein) C.; m. Rita Jarson, Dec. 25, 1960; children: Elana Cohn-Rozansky, Marc S. BA, UCLA, 1959; B Hebrew Letters, Hebrew Union Coll., L.A., 1959, DD (hon.), 1988; MA, Hebrew Union Coll., Cin., 1963; D Min, Sch. of Theology, Claremont, Calif., 1984. Ordained rabbi, 1963. Rabbi Congregation Emanu El, San Bernardino, Calif., 1963—; mem. Nat. Commn. on Rabbinic-Congregation Rels., Union Am. Hebrew Congregations, Cen. Conf. Am. Rabbis, 1989—; mem. rabbinic cabinet United Jewish Appeal, N.Y., 1984—. Author: Haggadah for Passover, 1990 (Best Sermons award); contbr. articles, sermons to religious publs. Trustee St. Bernardine Med. Ctr. Found., San Bernardino, 1987—, San Bernardino Community Hosp., 1986—; bd. dirs. Operation Home Run, San Bernardino, 1988—, Frazee Community Ctr., San Bernardino, 1990—. Recipient Emanuel Gamoran Meml. award Nat. Assn. Temple Educators, 1964, 73, citizen of achievement award LWV, 1989, Citizen of Yr. award Inland Empire coun. Boy Scouts Am., 1988. Mem. San Bernardino Clergy Assn. (pres. 1980-81), Pacific Assn. Reform Rabbis (pres. 1977-78), Cen. Conf. Am. Rabbis (exec. com. 1976-78), Bd. Rabbis Southern Calif., Priest-Rabbi Consultation of Bd. of Rabbis and Cath. Archdiocese, B'nai Brith (pres. Paradise lodge 1968-69), Arrowhead Country Club, Kiwanis. Home: 3947 Ironwood St San Bernardino CA 92404 Office: Congregation Emanu El 3512 E St San Bernardino CA 92405 *From the prophets I am mandated to work for a more just human society. From my tradition I am encouraged to prize the intellect and nurture the soul. The goal of life should be to pursue justice for all.*

COKER, DAVID, academic administrator. Head Wesley Coll., Florence, Miss. Office: Wesley Coll Florence MS 39073-0070*

COLANER, ROBERT LEE, principal; b. Canton, Ohio, July 10, 1953; s. Robert Paul Colaner and Esther Clara (Swyter) Houk; m. Barbara Anne Johnson, Jue 27, 1976; children: Nathan, Seth, Anna. B music edn., Mount Union Coll., 1975; MEd, Ashland (Ohio) U., 1987. Ordained min. Tchr. vocal and gen. music Jackson Schs., Massillon, Ohio, 1975-77; youth pastor Calvary Chapel, Massillon, 1977-78, asst. pastor, 1978-82; pastor Calvary Bible Fellowship, Massillon, 1982—; tchr. Calvary Christian Acad., Massillon, 1978-79, prin., head tchr., 1979—. Musical dir. Soc. for Preservation of Barbershop Singing in Am., Sebring, Ohio, 1973-77. Named one of Outstanding Young Men Am., 1985. Mem. Conservative Congl. Christian Conf. Republican. Mem. Ind. Bible Ch. Avocations: fishing, guitar, piano, singing, homesteading. Office: Calvary Bible Fellowship 708 Federal Ave NE Massillon OH 44646 *Only two things will last forever: the word of God and people. Happy is he who spends his time fostering a bond between them.*

COLAW, EMERSON S., clergyman. Bishop N. Central jurisdiction United Methodist Ch., Mpls. Office: 4469 Sentry Hill Ct Dayton OH 45440

COLAW, NATHAN RENÉ, minister; b. Fredonia, Kans., Jan. 12, 1941; s. C. B. and Mabel E. (Kauth) C.; m. Betty A. Friend, Dec. 31, 1961; children: Shari, Darrel, Sheila. BA, So. Nazarene U., 1964; postgrad., Nazarene Theol. Sem., Kansas City, Mo., 1965-70, 90-91. Ordained to ministry Ch. of Nazarene, 1973. Pastor 1st Ch. of Nazarene, Miami, Okla., 1970-71; assoc. youth pastor 1st Ch. of Nazarene, Bartlesville, Okla., 1971-73; pastor 1st Ch. of Nazarene, Lake Charles, La., 1973-76, Salina, Kans., 1976—; chmn. Pastoral Care Adv. Com., Salina, 1980-91; mem. adv. bd. Kans. Dist. Ch. of Nazarene, Wichita, 1990-91. Com. mem. Goals for Salina; mem. task force Salina All-Am. Prevention Partnership, Salina, 1990-91. Mem. Lions. Office: 1st Ch of Nazarene 1425 S Ohio Salina KS 67401

COLBERT, RICHARD A., clergyman; b. Cleve., May 1, 1942; s. Richard I. and Nora (Lavelle) C. BA, U. Dayton, 1965; MDiv, St. Charles Sem., 1969; M.P.S., St. Paul U., 1980, MA, 1981. Cert. counselor, Nebr. Assoc. pastor chs. N.D., Mo., Nebr., 1969-75; with formation program ch. Mo., Minn., 1976-79; chaplain hosp. Nebr., 1984-87; pastor ch. Pilot Grove, Mo., 1988—; marriage and family therapist ch., Pilot Grove, 1988—; supr. tng. St. Joseph Hosp., Omaha, 1984-86. Mem. Am. Assn. Marriage and Family Therapy (clin.), Lions Internat., K.C. Home and Office: 407 Harris Pilot Grove MO 65276

COLBETH, RICHARD STANLEY, religious organization administrator, minister; b. Brattleboro, Vt., July 21, 1938; s. Ralph Stanley and Martha C.; m. Julianna Unger, Aug. 23, 1957 (div. Mar. 1970); children: James Richard, Jonathan Andrew, Debbra A.; m. Margaret Ann Kissling, Dec. 23, 1976 (div. Jan. 1986); m. Sandra May Harrison, Nov. 7, 1987; 1 child, John James. BA, Ariz. Bible Coll., 1982; MA, San Antonio Theol. Inst., 1988. Ordained to ministry Charismatic/Pentecostal Ch., 1990. Chaplain's asst. VA Hosp., Phoenix, 1978-81; co-pastor Willcox (Ariz.) Bapt. Ch., 1985; also co-pastor chs. Klondyke and Bonita, Ariz.; sr. adult pastor True Life Fellowship Ch., Portland, Oreg.; pres. Concerned Christians II, Phoenix, 1979-85, Portland Am. Family Assn. Pres. George Mid. Sch. PTA, Portland; dist. capt. Oreg. Citizens Alliance, Portland, 1990; Rep. precinct com. person, Portland, 1990. With USAF, 1956-76, Vietnam. Mem. Mensa, U.S. Chess Fedn. Home: 8870 N Columbia Blvd # 9 Portland OR 97203 Office: Portland Am Family Assn PO Box 83203 Portland OR 97283

COLBURN, RALPH JONATHAN, minister; b. Wheatland, N.D., Oct. 22, 1916; s. Franklin and Alvina (Ritter) C.; m. Julia Elizabeth Rowland, Apr. 10, 1954; children: Mark Jonathan, Timothy Joel. AA, Long Beach (Calif.) City Coll., 1936; BTh, Bible Inst. of L.A., 1940; BA, Westmont Coll., Santa Barbara, Calif., 1941. Ordained minister, 1941. Founding pastor Grace Community Ch., Seal Beach, Calif., 1939-42; pastor First Brethren Ch., Compton, Calif., 1942-48; nat. youth dir. Fellowship of Brethren Chs., Winona Lake, Ind., 1948-54; founding pastor Grace Brethren Ch., Ft. Lauderdale, Fla., 1955-68; pastor Community Grace Brethren Ch., Long Beach, Calif., 1968-78; assoc. pastor Grace Ch., Los Alamitos, Calif., 1978—; exec. sec. Nat. Fellowship of Grace Brethren Ministers, Winona Lake, 1975—; officer Brethren Missionary Herald Bd., Winona Lake, 1961—. Mem. Biola Alumni Assn., Westmont Coll. Alumni Assn. Republican. Avocation: music. Home: 3490 La Jara St Long Beach CA 90805 Office: Grace Ch 3021 Blume Dr Los Alamitos CA 90720

COLBY, NEAL D., JR., charitable organization executive. Exec. dir. Cath. Charities, Kansas City, Mo. Office: Cath Charities 1112 Broadway Kansas City MO 64105*

COLBY, VIRGINIA LITTLE, lay worker; b. Saugus, Mass., May 1, 1917; d. Guy L. and Alberta M. (Chadwick) Little; m. Robert G. Colby, Dec. 25, 1951. AB, U. Mass., 1940. Svc. rep. N.E.T. and T. Co. Bus. Office, Concord, N.H., 1940-67; tchr. Shaker Regional Sch. Dist., Belmont, N.H., 1967-77. Contbr. articles to profl. publs. Mem. AAUW (past pres. Concord br.), Lakes Region Retired Tchrs. Assn. (past pres.), No. N.H. Telephone Pioneers Am. (past pres.), Boscawen Hist. Soc., Inc. (sec., libr.), Concord Ch. Women United (past pres., v.p.), N.H. State Ch. Women United (v.p.), Delta Kappa Gamma (hon. mem. Beta chpt.). Home: 134 Mountain Rd Concord NH 03301

COLCORD, ELMER DANFORTH, minister; b. Canton, Mass., Nov. 4, 1895; s. Frederick Elmer and Sadie Holway (Hill) C.; m. Evelyn Ruth Huntsinger, May 6, 1930; children: Robin Hill, Carol Ann. AB, Tufts U., 1917, STB, 1919; HM, Springfield Coll., 1923, EdM, 1928. Minister 2d Universalist Ch., Springfield, Mass., 1919-26, Unitarian Ch., Trenton, N.J., 1926-30, Mt. Vernon (N.Y.) Unitarian-Universalist Ch., 1930-39; minister Universalist Ch., Provincetown, Mass., 1939-42, Gardiner, Maine, 1942-50; minister Unitarian Universalist Ch., Somerville, Mass., 1950-87; minister Universalist Ch., Greene, Maine, summers 1943-90; prof. psychology Springfield Coll., 1925-26; tchr. Boston Ctr. for Adult Edn., 1966-72; lectr. on poet Edwin Arlington Robinson. Author: Cultural History of a Small Town, (poetry) The Smiling of the Mind, The Progressive Vertical, others. Sec., dir. Nat. Universalist Summer Meetings, Ferry Beach, Maine, 1922-44; pres. City Somerville Council Chs., 1972-79. Named Poet of Yr., World Poetry Assn., 1987. Mem. Odd Fellows, Lions, KP, Rotary, Phi Delta Kappa. Avocations: philately, numismatics, collecting old books. Home: 11 Morrison Ave West Somerville MA 02144 also: 14 William St Boothbay Harbor ME 04538

COLE, BRUCE KASNER, rabbi, organization executive; b. Cleve., Feb. 28, 1939; s. Morris and Pauline (Kasner) C.; m. Marianne Presner, June 20, 1965; children: Michael Edward, Jennifer Karen. BA, U. Mich., 1961; BHL, Hebrew Union Coll., 1964, MA, 1966, DD (hon.), 1991. Ordained rabbi Reform Jewish Congregations, 1966. Community cons. Columbus (Ohio) Regional Office, Anti-Defamation League, B'nai B'rith, 1966-68; dir. interreligious affairs Anti-Defamation League, B'nai Brith, N.Y.C., 1968-80, assoc. dir. N.Y., 1980-90; dir. L.I. Anti-Defamation League, B'nai Brith, Jericho, N.Y., 1990—; rabbi Temple Emanu El Queens, 1988—; exec. co-sec. Cath.-Jewish rels. com. Diocese of Bklyn. and Anti-Defamation League, 1970—; mem. exec. com. Commn. on Inter-religious Affairs, Am. Zionist Fedn., 1976-80; co-chmn. adv. com. on Jewish rels. Episcopal Diocese of N.Y., 1975; mem. religious adv. com. N.Y. State Div. Human Rights, 1975-81; mem. exec. com. Ctr. for Jewish-Christian Studies and Rels., Gen. Theol. Sem. N.Y.; mem. Cath.-Jewish rels. com. Archdiocese of N.Y., 1982—. Co-editor: The Future of Jewish-Christian Relations, 1982; also articles. Bd. dirs. Ralph W. Alvis Halfway Houe for Prisoner Rehab., Columbus, 1967-68; mem. exec. com. Civil Rights Coun., Columbus, 1966-68; vice chmn. Raoul Wallenberg Com. U.S., 1980—. Mem. Cen. Conf. Am. Rabbis, N.Y. Assn. Reform Rabbis. Home: 166 E 63d St New York NY 10021 Office: 100 Jericho Quadrangle Jericho NY 11753

COLE, CARLOS LANE, minister; b. Pasadena, Tex., June 28, 1958; s. Gerald F. and Charlotte (Williams) C.; m. Kathy Smith, June 30, 1979; children: Justin Lane, Karla Denae. BA in Religion, Ouachita Bapt. U., Arkadelphia, Ark., 1980; MDiv, Southwestern Bapt. Theol. Sem., 1983, DMin, 1988. Ordained to ministry, So. Bapt. Conv., 1983. Dir. activities Al-Church Home for Children, Ft. Worth, Tex., 1980-81; assoc. pastor Park Temple Bapt. Ch., Ft. Worth, 1981-83; pastor Sharon Bapt. Ch., Dubach, La., 1983-89, First Bapt. Ch., Monterey, La., 1989—; moderator Ouachita Bapt. Assn., Jonesville, 1990—; founder, pres. Black River Christians United Monterey, 1989—; cons. La. Drug Edn. Taskforce, Baton Rouge, 1990—; chaplain Lincoln Parish Detention Ctr., Ruston, 1984-87. Author: A Program for Senior Adults, 1989, Drug Education in the Church, 1990, The Church and Aging, 1988. Bd. dirs. Concordia Coun. on Aging, Vidalia, La., 1990—; VIP vol. Monterey Pub. Schs., 1989—; vol. coach Boys Baseball Program, 1989—; pres./v.p. PTO, Monterey, Hico, 1988-90. Named Outstanding Young Pastor, La. Bapt., 1985, Vol. of the Yr., Claiborne Parish, Homer, La., 1986, La. Vol. of the Yr., La. Civic Soc., New Orleans, 1987. Mem. Southwestern Alumni Assn., La. Assn. Ministers, Ministerial Alliance, Sandy Hills Golf Club. Home: HC73 Box 7A Monterey LA 71354 Office: First Bapt Ch PO Drawer 310 Monterey LA 71354

COLE, CLIFFORD ADAIR, clergyman; b. Lamoni, Iowa, Nov. 16, 1915; s. Fayette V. and Mable F. (Adair) C.; m. Harriett Lucile Hartshorn, June 28, 1936; children—Alethea Rae (Mrs. Justus S. Allen), Beverly Sue (Mrs. Lloyd G. Hilburn, Jr.), Lawrence Dean. Student, Graceland Coll., Lamoni, 1934-35, 41-42, U. Wyo., 1938; B.S. in Edn, Central Mo. State Coll., 1943; postgrad., U. Iowa, 1946, U. Chgo., 1952; M.A. in Edn, U. Mo. at Kansas City, 1957. Ordained to ministry Reorganized Ch. of Jesus Christ of Latter Day Saints, 1939. High sch. tchr. Lamoni, 1943-46, Bellevue, Ia., 1946- 47; min. Iowa, 1947-51; dean students Graceland Coll., 1951-53; dir. dept. religious edn. Reorganized Ch. of Jesus Christ of Latter Day Saints, 1955-58, apostle in council twelve, 1958-80, pres. council, 1964-80, cons. to 1st presidency, 1980-82; ret., 1982. Author: The Prophets Speak, 1954, Working Together in our Families, 1955, Celebrating Together in our Families, 1955, Faith for New Frontier, 1956, The Revelation in Christ, 1963, Modern Women in a Modern World, 1965, The Mighty Act of God, 1984. Mem. Phi Sigma Pi, Zeta Kappa Epsilon, Kappa Delta Pi. *Everyone who thinks deeply must answer the question: "What is the Ultimate Reality undergirding our universe?" The answer is not found in proof but rather in faith. The struggle has led me to a profound and abiding faith in God.*

COLE, DAVID CHRISTOPHER, minister; b. L.A., Sept. 2, 1962; s. Leon and Susan (Porter) C.; m. Christie Gordon, Mar. 14, 1989. AB in Theology, Liberty Bible Inst., Lynchburg, Va., 1986, cert. Christian counselor, 1987; cert. youth counselor, Youth Ministry U., L.A., 1989. Ordained to ministry Northwestern Bapt. Assn., 1987. Youth pastor Maranatha Ch., L.A., 1980-83; asst. pastor Faith Bapt. Ch., L.A., 1983-87, pastor, 1987-90, sr. pastor, 1991—; dir. Youth Evangelism Caucus, L.A., 1990—; pres. media div. Ch. Growth Book and Media, Burbank, Calif., 1989—; dir. Cole, Inc., ch. growth inst., L.A., 1988—. Author: Evangelizing Today's Youth, 1987; also articles. Calif. chmn. Nat. Traditionalist Caucus, 1988—; Calif. del. United Conservatives Am., Leesburg Pike, Pa., 1989—; Calif. rep. Heritage Found., 1990; v.p. West Los Angeles Parents for Life, 1989—; mem. Rep. Nat. Comn., 1987—, Rep. Presdl. Task Force, 1988—. Recipient medal of merit Rep. Nat. Com., 1989, medal of honor Rep. Presdl. Task Force, 1989, Youth and Excellence award Nat. Traditionalist Caucus, 1990, Youth Educator of Yr. award L.A. Youth Ministry Assn., 1990. Mem. Nat. Assn. Evangelicals, Christian Educators Am. (chpt. head L.A. 1988—), Christian Coalition, L.A. Am. Family Assn. (pres. 1989—), United Taxpayers Am. (state rep. 1991—). Office: 2508 Castle Heights Ave Los Angeles CA 90034 *Religion, that is to say, a person's spiritual life, must consist of more than one day a week of worship. It should be called upon, used and reflected i your daily life. That is what makes Christianity more than a simple set of rules. The living word of God lives daily in the lives of all Christians.*

COLE, DONALD WILLARD, clergyman, consulting psychologist; b. San Diego, Jan. 12, 1920; s. Rolland Ames and Genevieve (Bender) C.; m. Ann Bradford, Sept. 18, 1942; 1 son, Timothy Bradford. Student, U. Redlands; A.B., Stanford, 1942; B.D., Eastern Bapt. Theol. Sem., 1945; Ed.D., Southwestern Bapt. Theol. Sem., 1952; Ph.D., U. London, 1962. Ordained to ministry Bapt. Ch., 1945; pastor Linden Bapt. Ch., Camden, N.J., 1944-46; asso. pastor First Bapt. Ch., San Diego, 1946-48; univ. pastor, dir. Bapt. student work So. Calif., 1948-52, dean, dir. Bapt. confs., camps, coll. and univ. students, 1948-52; pres. Calif. Bapt. Theol. Sem. and Coll., 1952-59; Brit. Nat. Health Service fellow, 1959-61; dean students, prof. psychology Fuller Theol. Sem., Pasadena, Calif., 1962-70; pvt. practice cons. clin. psychology, psychotherapy, religion Monrovia, Calif., 1970-74; pastor S. Shores Bapt. Ch., Laguna Niguel, Calif., 1974-90, ret., 1990. Author: The Role of Religion In The Development of Personality; Contbr. articles to religious publs. Fellow Royal Geog. Soc. London; mem. NEA, Religious Edn. Assn., Am. Group Psychotherapy Assn., Nat. Assn. Mental Health, Acad. Religion and Mental Health, Am. Psychol. Assn., Am. Assn. Schs. Religious Edn., Western, Cal. State, Los Angeles County psychol. assns., Nat. Council Family Relations, Am. Soc. Psychical Research, Am. Acad. Polit. and Social Sci., U.S. Air Force Assn., Alpha Gamma Nu, Alpha Phi Omega. Republican. Home: 245 Via Ballena San Clemente CA 92672 Office: 32712 Crown Valley Pkwy Laguna Niguel CA 92677

COLE, FRANCIS BERNARD, JR., deacon; b. Hartford, Conn., July 10, 1933; s. Francis B. and Cecil (Farley) C.; m. Gladys Pelletier, Aug. 10, 1957; children: Francis B. III, Christopher B., Victoria Ann Galo, Anthony B. BBA, St. Anselm Coll., 1957; MA in Counseling, St. Joseph Coll., 1981. Deacon St. Peter Claver, West Hartford, Conn., 1978-82, Trinity Coll., U. Hartford, 1982-86, St. Patrick, Farmington, Conn., 1986—; claim acct. exec. Travelers Inc. Co., Hartford, 1972—. Mem. KC. Home: 1155 Farmington

Ave W Hartford CT 06107 Office: Saint Patrick Ch 116 Main St Farmington CT 06034 *His servant.*

COLE, GLEN DAVID, minister; b. Tacoma, Dec. 21, 1933; s. Ray Milton and Ruth Evelyn (Ranton) C.; m. Mary Ann Von Moos, June 6, 1953; children: Randall Ray, Ricky Jay. BA in Theology, Cen. Bible Coll., 1956; DD, Pacific Coast Bible Coll., 1983. Pastor Assembly of God, Marion, Ohio, 1957-60, Maple Valley, Wash., 1960-65; assoc. pastor Calvary Temple, Seattle, 1965-67; sr. pastor Evergreen Christian Ctr., Olympia, Wash., 1967-78, Capital Christian Ctr., Sacramento, 1978—; exec. presbyter Assemblies of God, Springfield, 1985—; trustee Bethany Bible Coll., Santa Cruz, Calif., 1979—; bd. dirs. Cen. Bible Coll., Springfield, Mo., 1988—; bd. dirs. Calif. Theol. Sem., Fresno, 1985-90. Mem. Rotary (pres. Olympia chpt. 1977-78). Republican. Office: Capital Christian Ctr 9470 Micron Ave Sacramento CA 95827 *It seems that the people God uses most are not those with greater ability, or more education, or superior talent but those who become totally dependent on him.*

COLE, LAWRENCE FREDERICK, minister, counselor; b. Takoma Park, Md., Apr. 27, 1947; s. Kenneth Edward and Grace Mae (Myer) C.; m. Marjorie Suzzanne Fellers, June 28, 1969; children: Traci Lynn, Johnathan Lawrence. BA in Theology, So. Coll., 1983; MA in Counseling Psychology, Bowie State U., 1983—. Technician Xerox Corp., Washington, 1969-70; sr. svc. specialist Saxon Bus. Products, Orlando, Fla., 1970-77; minister Chesapeake Conf. Seventh-day Adventists, Columbia, Md., 1980-84, Potomac Conf. of Seventhúday Adventists, Staunton, Va., 1984—. With USMC, 1965-69, Vietnam. Mem. Am. Assn. for Counseling and Devel., Jaycees (bd. dirs. Jr. Miss Pageant 1975). Democrat. Avocations: woodworking, golf. Home and Office: 18 Nichols Rd Luray VA 22835

COLE, WALLACE BARTZ, minister; b. Lake Crystal, Minn., May 30, 1928; s. Garner Henry and Laura Dorothy (Bartz) C.; m. Fern Darlene Olson, May 29, 1955; children: David, Steven. BA, St. Olaf Coll., 1954; BTh, Luther Theol. Sem., 1958. Ordained to ministry Luth. Ch., 1958. Pastor Medo Luth. Ch., Mapleton, Minn., 1958-65; mission dir. Navajo Evang. Luth. Mission, Rock Point, Ariz., 1965-90, dir. devel., 1990—. Trustee Christian Hope Indian Eskimo Fellowship., Phoenix, 1982-90, Navajo Hymnal Conf., Farmington, N.Mex., 1970-90. Recipient Exemplar award Calif. Luth. U., 1990. Home and Office: 333 W Leroux E7 Prescott AZ 86303

COLE, WILLIAM OWEN, religion educator, consultant, writer; b. Sheffield, Yorkshire, Eng., Sept. 22, 1931; s. William Owen Cole and Clara Coupland; m. Gwynneth Bowen; children: Eluned, Siân Rhiannon. BA in History, Durham U., 1954, Diploma in Edn., 1955; BD, London U., 1966; MPhil with distinction, Leeds U., 1975, PhD, 1979. Tchr. primary schs., Wiltshire, Eng., 1957-60, comprehensive schs., Essex, Eng., 1960-63; lectr. No. Counties Coll., Northumberland, Eng., 1963-68, James Graham Coll. and Leeds Poly., Yorkshire, Eng., 1968-80; part-time lectr. religious studies Leeds U. and Open U.; cons. in religious edn. Open U., 1981-84; interfaith cons. to archbishops of Canterbury and York, 1981-91; vis. prof. religious studies Punjab U., Patiala, India, 1983; moderator com. for rels. with people of other faiths Religious Edn. Panel Brit. Coun. Chs., 1982—, also editor workshop in edn., 1990. Author: The Sikhs, 1978, Guru in Sikhism, 1982, Sikhism in its Indian Context 1469-1708, 1984, Six Religions in the Twentieth Century, 1984, Christianity, 1989; editor: World Faiths in Education, 1978, Religion in the Multifaith School, 1983, Popular Dictioary of Sikhism, 1990, Moral Issues in Six Religions (Heinemann), 1991, Religious Education in the Primary Curriculum (Chansitor and Wheeler), 1991; contbr. articles to various publications. Served with Friends Ambulance Unit Internat. Service, 1955-57. Founding mem. Shap Working Party on World Religions in Education (chmn. 1978-81, publicity officer 1988—). Anglican. Office: West Sussex Inst of Higher Edn, Bishop Otter Coll Coll Ln, PO19 4PE Chichester England *Religions can be instruments for the oppression or liberation of individual spirituality and for the creation of tolerant or intolerant societies. I would like to think that my work and my life have contributed to a wholeness of humanity.*

COLEMAN, CLINTON R., bishop. Bishop A.M.E. Zion Ch., Balt. Office: AME Zion Ch 8605 Caswell Ct Raleigh NC 27612*

COLEMAN, DAVID MICHAEL, religious organization executive; b. Cedar Hill, Tenn., Oct. 24, 1942; s. Julian Turner and Dorothy (Cobb) C.; m. Linda Ruth Gholdston, Dec. 21, 1963; children: Melissa Jeanette, Michael Carl. BS, Belmont Coll., 1965; postgrad., Midwestern Bapt. Theol. Sem., 1965-67, So. Bapt. Theol. Sem., 1979. Pastor Maple Grove Bapt. Ch., Dickson, Tenn., 1963-65, Kingsville (Mo.) Bapt. Ch., 1965-67; office mgr. Bapt. Sunday Sch. Bd., Nashville, 1967-69; missionary Zimbabwe So. Bapt. Fgn. Mission Bd., Richmond, Va., 1969-86, assoc. dir. vols. in missions dept, 1986-87, assoc. to v.p. for devel., 1987-89, dir. for devel., 1989—; chmn. Bapt. Internat. Mission Services Bd., Johannesburg, South Africa, 1982-83, 84-85. Co-author: (book) Baptist Beliefs, 1972. Pres. Frank Johnson Sch. PTA, Harare, Zimbabwe, 1975-77; chmn. Planning and Devel. Coun., Harare, 1983-85; chmn. bd. trustees Bapt. Theol. Sem., Gweru, Zimbabwe. Mem. Nat. Soc. Fund Raising Execs., Va. Assn. Fund Raising Execs. Republican. Lodge: Kiwanis (pres. local chpt. 1963-64, treas. 1965). Avocations: golf, tennis. Home: 8730 Sheldeb Dr Richmond VA 23235 Office: Fgn Mission Bd So Baptist Conv PO Box 6767 3806 Monument Ave Richmond VA 23230

COLEMAN, MICHAEL ANDREW, minister; b. Kansas City, Mo., July 9, 1950; s. Andrew Franklin and Helen E. Coleman; m. Nancy Gayle Beach, Dec. 19, 1970; 1 child, Abigail Michal. B.E.S. with honors, U. Mo., 1981, MEd in Health Edn., 1982; MDiv, MRE, St. Paul Sch. Theology, Kansas City, 1987. Ordained to ministry Meth. Ch.; cert. minister Christian edn. Dir. Christian edn. Centenary Meth. Ch., Cape Girardeau, Mo., 1982-84; student pastor Concordia (Mo.) Charge, 1984-87; assoc. pastor edn. St. Mark's United Meth. Ch., Florissant, Mo., 1987-89; sr. pastor Moscow Mills (Mo.) Charge, 1989-91; assoc. pastor United Meth. Ch. of the Shepherd, Saint Charles, Mo., 1991—; vice-chmn. Mo. East Conf. Bd. Edn., United Meth. Ch., St. Louis, 1990-91, Hosp. Chaplains Bd., Troy, Mo., 1991—; chmn. Dist. Edn. Com. St. Louis North, 1990-91; cons. in field. Author: The Academy of Christian Growth, 1987. Designer-implementer Sch. Respiratory Therapy, Cape Area Vo-Tech Sch., Cape Girardeau, 1979; mem. adv. bd. Foster Grandparents (Bi-County) Higginsville, Mo., 1986. Mem. Nat. Reg. Outstanding Coll. Grads., Order of St. Luke United Meth. Ch. (pres. 1985-86, Conf. Pres. 1990), Ministerial Alliance, Kappa Delta Pi (pres. 1980-81), Phi Delta Kappa. Democrat.

COLEMAN, SHALOM, rabbi; b. Liverpool, Eng., Dec. 5, 1918; s. Samuel and Fruma (Levin) C.; B.A., U. Liverpool, 1939, Litt.B., 1939; diploma, Jewish Coll., London, 1955; M.A., U. S.Africa, 1956; Ph.D., U. Orange Free State, 1960; m. Anna Daviat, Mar. 29, 1942 (dec. 1982); children: Romaine, Hilary, Marilyn, Martin Howard; m. Elena Doktorovich, 1985. Ordained rabbi, 1955. Minister Potchefstroom Hebrew Congregation, S. Africa, 1946-47, Bloemfontein Hebrew Congregation, S. Africa, 1947-60, S. Head Synagogue, Sydney, Australia, Dayan of Sydney, Beth Din (Jewish Ecclesiastical Ct.), 1961-66; chief rabbi Perth Hebrew Congregation, 1966-85, chmn. Perth Beth Din, Western Australia, 1966-85; hon. prof. bibl. studies, Maimonides Coll., Toronto; lectr. dept. adult edn. U. Western Australia; V.p. Save the Children Fund, 1967—; vice patron St. Johns Ambulance Brigade; padre to spl. unit Fleet Air Arm Assn. Western Australia, 1970—, patron, 1975—; mem. senate Murdoch U., West Australia, 1978-87; chmn. Com. on Nat. Pride in Schs., 1981-91, Com. on Religious Studies in Schs., 1983-85. Justice of Peace, Western Australia, 1967. Trustee Karrakatta Cemetery Bd., 1973-88; state exec. Returned Services League, 1985-87; trustee Pinaroo Valley Meml. Park, 1973-88; chmn. Perth Dental Hosp. Bd., 1984-89. Served with R.A.F., World War II. Decorated comdr. Order Brit. Empire, Queen's Honours (U.K.); officer Order of Australia; recipient Queen's Silver Jubilee medal; Sir Robert Waley Cohen Internat. Meml. scholar, 1964. Mem. Assn. Jewish Ministers Australia and New Zealand (pres. 1984), Rotary (pres. Perth 1985-86, Kyle orator 1986). Author: Hosea in Midrash and Talmud, 1960; Habakkuk in Rabbinic Doctrine, 1966; What Every Jew Should Know, 1974; What is a Jewish Home, 1978; A Short History of the Karrakatta Cemetery, 1979; What Is A Synagogue, 1982. Contbr. articles to profl. jours. Home: 38 Bradford St, Mt Lawley, Western Australia Australia *Life is a corridor in which we prepare to enter the kingdom of heaven and give an account of it to our Maker. It passes like a dream and every minute must be used to praise Him in our relations with all mankind.*

COLEMAN, STEVEN EUGENE, minister; b. North Little Rock, Ark., Feb. 12, 1955; s. Joseph Benson and Gertrude (Oxford) C.; m. Rita Kay Henson, Aug. 15, 1987; 1 child, Karissa Ann. BA in Religion, So. Nazarene U., 1977, MA in Religion, 1979; MDiv, Nazarene Theol. Sem., 1982; doctoral studies, Calif. Grad. Sch. Theology, 1982-83, Rice U., 1984—. Ordained minister Ch. of Nazarene, 1984. Resident dir. Bethany Nazarene Coll., 1977-79; pub. relations asst. Nazarene Theol. Sem., 1980-82; v.p. Houston Dist. Nazarene Youth Internat., 1983-87, pres., 1987-89; faculty Houston Nazarene Bible Inst., 1988-90, Nazarene Bible Coll., Dallas Extension, 1991—; chmn. Christian Action Com., Houston Dist. Ch. of Nazarene, 1985-86, bd. dirs. Boys and Girls Camp, 1987. Vol. chaplain Katy Community Hosp., 1983-85, Renaissance Place Nursing Home, Katy, 1986-88. Recipient Citation Okla. Ho. of Reps., 1976, Ch. Planter award Houston Dist. Ch. of Nazarene, 1983, Great Commn. Fellowship award Houston Dist. Ch. of Nazarene, 1984-85, Evangelistic Honor Roll award Houston Dist. Ch. of Nazarene, 1983-86; named one of Outstanding Young Men Am., 1981, 83-85. Republican. Avocations: basketball, softball, tennis, racquetball. Home: 3012 Kathleen Longview TX 75604 Office: 1801 S Moberly PO Box 7007 PO Box 7007 Longview TX 75607

COLEMAN, T. RUPERT, retired minister; b. Granville County, N.C., May 10, 1908; s. Henry Gordon and Ina Jenette (Wilkerson) C.; m. Lucille Knight, June 27, 1934; 1 child, Larry Knight. BA, Duke U., 1928, MA, 1930, BD, 1931; PhD, So. Bapt. Theol. Sem., Louisville, 1939. Ordained to ministry So. Bapt. Conv., 1929. Min. Ginter Park Bapt. Ch., Richmond, Va., 1934-56, Univ. Bapt. Ch., Coral Gables, Fla., 1956-64, Southside Bapt. Ch., Lakeland, Fla., 1964-73; ret., 1973; vol. missionary Fgn. Mission Bd., So. Bapt. Conv., Taipei, Republic China, 1974, Athens, Greece, 1976, Ankara, Turkey, 1977, also former trustee; numerous offices Va. Bapt. Gen. Assn., Fla. Bapt. Conv., So. Bapt. Conv.; former dir. Christianity Commn., So. Bapt. Conv. Author: Paul's Prison Life, 1939; contbr. numerous articles to profl. jours. Former trustee Stetson U., DeLand, Fla.; founder Christian Freedom Found. T. Rupert and Lucille K. Coleman chair of N.T. established in their honor So. Bapt. Theol. Sem. Mem. Richmond Jaycees (life chaplain), Kiwanis. Home: 21 Claridge House 1600 Lake Parker Dr W Lakeland FL 33805

COLEMAN, TERRY LEE, minister; b. Memphis, Apr. 13, 1959; s. Neb and Alma Dean (Hicks) C.; m. Lea Ann Clausel, Mar. 16, 1979; children: Nathan Scott, Emily Rachel, Joel Christopher. BA, Trinity Bapt. Coll., Jacksonville, Fla., 1983. Ordained to ministry Ind. Bapt. Ch., 1983. Asst. pastor Grace Bapt. Temple, Memphis, 1976-79; pastor Bethany Bible Ch., St. Augustine, Fla., 1985-89, Trinity Bapt. Ch., Lake Butler, Fla., 1989—. Mem. Trinity Bapt. Coll. Alumni Assn. (pres. 1987-91, editor The Specialist newsletter 1987-91). Republican. Home and Office: Trinity Bapt Ch 325 SW 6th St Lake Butler FL 32054 *Life is a paradox. The trials, features and sorrows of life seem overwhelming at times. However, The opportunities, sucesses and joys of life work to offset difficulties. What is the balance and glue of life? It is found in the grace, mercy and forbearance of Almighty God.*

COLERIDGE, CLARENCE NICHOLAS, bishop; b. Georgetown, Guyana, Nov. 27, 1930; came to U.S., 1950; s. Charles and Ina (DeWeever) C.; m. Euna Jervis, Sept. 8, 1962; children—Cheryl Lisa, Carolyn Bridgett. B.S., Howard U., 1954; M.Div., Drew U., 1960; M.S.W., U. Conn., 1973; D.Min., Andover-Newton Theol. Sch., 1977. Ordained deacon Episcopal Ch., 1961, priest, 1962, consecrated bishop, 1981. Asst. minister St. Philip's Episc. Ch., N.Y.C., 1961; curate, dir. youth St. George's Episc. Ch., Bklyn., 1962-66; chaplain Sea View Hosp., Staten Island, N.Y., 1964-66; rector St. Mark's Episc. Ch., Bridgeport, Conn., 1966-81; counselor, dir. counseling Episc. Social Service, Diocese of Conn., 1974-81; suffragan bishop Diocese of Conn., Hartford, 1981—; dir. Pastoral Devel. of Episc. Ch., 1981—. Dir. Gov.'s Task Force on Racial Justice, 1981—, United Fund Fairfield County, 1967-71; v.p. Bridgeport Day Car, Inc., 1978-81. Recipient cert. of appreciation Afro-Am. Educators Assn., 1978, Outstanding Service award Eldorado Club Inc., 1981; named Citizen of Yr. Omega Psi Phi, 1968, Man of Yr. Nat. Council Negro Women, 1980. Democrat. Home: 29 Indian Rd Trumbull CT 06611 Office: Episcopal Diocese 1335 Asylum Ave Hartford CT 06105

COLESON, JOSEPH EDWARD, religion educator; b. Hart, Mich., Feb. 5, 1947; s. Albert Herman and Maxine Matilda (Rickard) C.; m. Charlotte DeLee West, June 20, 1970; children: Jeremy, Sarah. BA, Marion Coll., 1968; MA, Brandeis U., 1976, PhD, 1982. Ordained to ministry Wesleyan Ch., 1979. Curriculum editor Wesleyan Ch., Marion, Ind., 1970-72; prof. Western Evang. Sem., Portland, Oreg., 1977—. Contbr. articles to profl. publs., chpts. to books; mem. editorial bd. Shalom Oreg., 1978-80. Mem. Wesleyan Theol. Soc., Soc. Biblical Lit., Am. Acad. Religion, Oreg. Classical Assn., Theta Alpha Kappa. Republican. Home: 18609 SE River Rd Milwaukie OR 97267 Office: Western Evang Sem 4200 SE Jennings Ave Milwaukie OR 97267

COLFLESH, TRUDY PATTERSON, religion counselor; b. Steubenville, Ohio, June 6, 1939; d. Robert Meade and Gertrude (Lippencott) Patterson; m. George William Colflesh, Aug. 5, 1961; children: Michael, Christopher, Karen. BA in Religious Studies, Coll. Wooster, 1961; postgrad., Oberlin Sch. Theology, 1962; MA in Counseling and Human Devel., Montclair State Coll., 1990. Dir. Christian Edn. Calvary Presbyn. Ch., Canton, Ohio, 1961-63; counselor Christian Counseling Ctr., Clifton, N.J., 1990—; founder women's support groups St. Andrew's Presbyn. Ch., Berea, Ohio, 1966-72, elder, 1972; founding v.p. Women's Aglow Fellowship Internat., Miami, Fla., 1973-75, area v.p. Outreach and Retreats, No. N.J., 1980-86. Author: Too Precious to Die, 1984. Mem. Am. Assn. Christian Counselors, Am. Assn. for Counseling and Devel., Phi Kappa Phi. Home: 33 Northwood Dr West Milford NJ 07480 Office: Christian Counseling Ctr 352 Clifton Ave Clifton NJ 07011 *While the accomplishments of my years of service and achievements are presented in this book with pride and delight, my greatest joy is in the accomplishment of Jesus Christ who saved and redeemed me and entered my name in His Book of Life.*

COLLARD, EUGENE ALBERT, clergyman, publisher; b. Liège, Belgium, July 1, 1915; s. Jules Marie and Eugenie Marie (Deronchêne) C. Student philosophy and theology Diocesan Sem., Tournai, Belgium, 1933-40; D.C.L., Université Catholique de Louvain (Belgium), 1942, diploma in Social and Polit. Scis., 1943. Ordained priest Roman Catholic Ch., 1940. Curator, Our Lady Parish, Farciennes, Belgium, 1942-44; dir. media orgn. Diocese of Tournai, Mons, Belgium, 1945-88; pub. weekley Dimanche, Mons, 1946-90; lectr. sociology of religion Université Catholique de Louvain, 1951-80; dir. Instituto Pastoral Conf. dos Bispos do Northeast Brazil, Natal, 1964-65. Mem. M.N.B. (resistance orgn.), occupied Belgium, 1943-44. Served with Belgian Health Service, 1937, 39-40. Decorated chevalier de l'Ordre de Leopold, Belgium, 1956; hon. canon Diocese of Tournai, 1965. Mem. Union des Editeurs de la Presse Périodique Belge (adminstr. 1955-88, pres. 1974-75). Roman Catholic. Home: Place de Vannes 19, B 7000 Mons Hainaut, Belgium *"Go into all the world, and preach the Gospel to the whole creation". Mark 16:15.*

COLLETT, D. WALTER, minister; b. St. Louis, Aug. 20, 1954; s. Walter and Mildred Collett; m. Karen Marie Willey, Aug. 10, 1974; children: Erin Kay, Kellie Rene, Katie Marie. BA in Religion, Carson-Newman Coll., 1976; MDiv, New Orleans Bapt. Theol. Sem., 1978; ThD, Trinity Theol. Sem., 1984. Ordained to ministry So. Bapt. Ch., 1975. Pastor Old Silver Creek (Miss.) Bapt. Ch., 1976-78, 1st Bapt. Ch., Savage, Md., 1978-82; sr. pastor Covenant Bapt. Ch., Columbia, Md., 1982—; bd. dirs. Home Mission Bd., So. Bapt. Conv., Atlanta; trustee Gen. Mission Bd, Bapt. Conv. of Md., Del., 1987—; mem. Columbia Evang. Pastors' Assn., 1985-89. Author: Philippians, 1981. Bd. dirs. Columbia Inst. Bibl. Studies, Columbia, 1988-89; bd. overseers Criswell Coll., 1990—. Capt. USAR, 1983-89. Republican. Home: 6312 Early Red Ct Columbia MD 21045 Office: Covenant Bapt Ch 5901 Cedar Fern Ct Columbia MD 21044

COLLETT, DAVID MARK, minister; b. Salem, Oreg., July 14, 1952; s. W. Gene Collett and Donna L. Kempthorne; m. Roberta (Bobbi) Constans, June 20, 1971; children: Micah J., Sarah C. BA in Religion, Warner Pacific Coll., 1984; MDiv, Anderson U., 1987. Ordained to ministry Ch. of God (Anderson, Ind.), 1989. Min. music and edn. Community Ch. of God, Washougal, Wash., 1983-84; min. music Meadowbrook Bapt. Ch., Anderson, 1984-86; pastor Olive Bethel Ch. of God, Akron, Ind., 1986-89, First Ch. of God, Marion, S.D., 1989—; mem. corp. Tieszen Meml. Nursing Home, Marion, 1990—. Mem. Ministerial Assn. Ch. of God in S.D. (chmn. 1989-91), North Cen. Ministerial Assembly Ch. of God (vice chair 1991—), Lions. Home: 5 E Center PO Box 477 Marion SD 57043 Office: First Ch of God 455 N Broadway Marion SD 57043

COLLETTI, DANIEL ALON, music and education minister; b. New Orleans, Apr. 1, 1954; s. Alon Joseph and Edna Lucille (Dasinger) C.; m. Jenny Lee Swindle, Nov. 28, 1975; children: Molly Susan, Brennis Lyn, Jesse Alon (dec.). Student, Chiploa Jr. Coll., Marianna, Fla., 1972-74, Southwestern Bapt. Theol. Sem., Ft. Worth, 1976-79; MusB, William Carey Coll., Hattiesburg, Miss., 1976. Min. music and youth Goodwater Bapt. Ch., Magee, Miss., 1974-76, Riverside Bapt. Ch., Ft. Worth, 1976-80; min. music and youth 1st Bapt. Ch., Chipley, Fla., 1980-84, Brewton, Ala., 1984-86; min. music and edn. 1st Bapt. Ch., Chipley, Fla., 1986—; pres. DJ Cons., Chipley, 1990—. Mem. West Fla. Assn. (pres. pastor's conf. 1990, associational music dir. 1987—), Chipley Ministerial Assn. (pres. 1990), Optimists (pres. 1987-88). Office: 1st Bapt Ch 200 S Boulevard W Chipley FL 32428

COLLIER, CURTIS NEWTON, minister; b. Rosedale, Ind., July 14, 1933; s. Charles LeRoy and Mildred (Mae) C.; m. Joan Rosabelle Hicks, June 25, 1955; children: Catharine Marie, Paul Stephen, Philip Wayne, John Thomas. BS in Religion, Bethel Coll., 1955; BA in Psychology, Counseling, John Wesley Coll., 1974; MA in Psychology, Small Coll. Adminstrn., U. Mich., 1976; PhD in Ethics, Religion Edn., Columbia Pacific U., 1991. Diplomate Internat. Assn. Christian Clin. Counselors. Sr. min. United Missionary Ch., South Bend, Ind., 1955-70; evangelist United Missionary Ch. Inc., Owosso, Mich., 1970-79; exec. dir. Life-Line Youth Home, Kansas City, Kans., 1979-81; sr. min. First Missionary Ch., St. Petersburg, Fla., 1981-84; evangelist, tchr. Missionary Ch. Assn., St. Petersburg, Fla., 1984-89; assoc. min. Sylvan Abbey United Meth. Ch., Clearwater, Fla., 1984—; profl. counselor Assn. Christian Marriage Counselors, Chgo., 1984—; counselor United Assn. Christian Counselors, Chattanooga, 1983—. Author: Laying a New Life Foundation, 1991. Publicity chmn. Sertoma Club, Johnson City/Kansas City, Kans., 1979-81; pub. rels. vol. Am. Cancer Soc., Kansas City, 1980-81; v.p. Rotary, Sturgis, Mich., 1967-69; tenor soloist Symphony Orchestra & Chorus, Wichita, Kans., 1978-79, Flint, Mich., 1963-67. Avocations: walking, golfing, tennis, choral performing and directing. Home: 5209 Robin Lane N Saint Petersburg FL 33714 Office: Sylvan Abbey United Meth 2817 Sunset Point Rd Clearwater FL 34619

COLLIER, ELIZABETH JANE, minister; b. Ft. Benning, Ga., Sept. 21, 1954; d. Thomas Bardin and Katherine Ann (Guest) C. BA, Winthrop Coll., 1975; MDiv, Southeastern Bapt. Theol. Sem., 1978. Cert. mental health clergy; lic. profl. counselor; ordained to ministry United Meth. Ch., 1981. Chaplain Spartanburg (S.C.) Gen. Hosp., 1978-79; assoc. pastor Bethel United Meth. Ch., Charleston, S.C., 1979-80; pastor Tranquil Ctr. Charge United Meth. Ch., Mullins, S.C., 1980-82; clin. counselor, chaplain Pee Dee Mental Health Ctr., Florence, S.C., 1982-84; chaplain assoc. McLeod Regional Med. Ctr., Florence, 1983-85; assoc. pastor Highland Park United Meth. Ch., Florence, 1983-85; chaplain resident S.C. Dept. Mental Health, Columbia, 1985-86; exec. dir. Family Shelter, Inc., Columbia, 1986—; mem. task force role of religious systems S.C. Dept. Mental Health, 1987; cons., tchr. Highland park united Meth. Ch., 1984-85. Rep. poll watcher, Rock Hill, S.C. 1972; presenter Councl on Homelessness, Columbia, 1987. Mem. Assn. Clin. Pastoral Edn., Assn. mental Health Clergy (cert.), Sierra Club. Democrat. Avocations: whitewater canoeing and kayaking, camping, cooking, reading, calligraphy. Office: Family Shelter Inc 2411 Two Notch Rd Columbia SC 29204

COLLIER, ROGER MALCOLM, minister; b. Richmond, Va., Nov. 10, 1950; s. Edward Malcolm and Vallie Pauline (Cuthbertson) C.; m. Sarah Catherine Carter, Apr. 5, 1980; children: Leigh Anne, Paula Kay, Edward Malcolm II. BA, U. Richmond, 1972; postgrad., Yale U. Div. Sch., 1972-73; MDiv, Southeastern Bapt. Theol. Sem., 1976; D of Ministry, Union Theol. Sem., Richmond, 1984. Ordained to ministry So. Bapt. Conv., 1975. Min. Hunton Bapt. Ch., Glen Allen, Va., 1975-85, West End Bapt. Ch., Suffolk, Va., 1985-86, Glen Allen Bapt. Ch., 1986—. Trustee Community Rels. Referral Bd. of Henrico County, Richmond,1989—; pres. Glen Allen Elem. PTA, 1990-91; bd. dirs. Virginians for Integrity in Govt., 1991—. Named Outstanding Young Religious Leader, Glen Allen Jaycees. 1981. Mem. Bapt. Gen. Assn. Va. (chmn. Christian Life Com. 1982-85), Laurel Glen Allen Mins.' Conf. (pres. 1976, 84), Phi Beta Kappa. Home: 2909 Susan Sheppard Ct Glen Allen VA 23060 Office: Glen Allen Bapt Ch PO Box 1245 Glen Allen VA 23060

COLLINGSWORTH, JOE B., minister; b. Monroe, La., Aug. 17, 1952; s. Joseph B. and M. Justine (Roberts) C.; m. Anne Leavell Mann, Feb. 12, 1983; children: Mary Margaret, Robert Leavell, Wesley Joseph. BA in Communication Arts, La. Coll., 1974; MRE, Southwestern Bapt. Theol. Sem., Ft. Worth, 1977. Lic. to ministry So. Bapt. Conv., 1967, ordained to ministry, 1971. Pastor Lake Lilly Bapt. Ch., Jonesville, La., 1970-72; min. youth Glenmora (La.) Bapt. Ch., 1972-74; assoc. pastor, youth and coll. min. Oakland Heights Bapt. Ch., Longview, Tex., 1977-80, 82-84; assoc. pastor, min. youth Putnam City Bapt. Ch., Oklahoma City, 1980-82, Grand Avenue Bapt. Ch., Ft. Smith, Ark., 1984-87; state youth and cons. La. Bapt. Conv., Alexandria, 1987-89; asst. pastor 1st Bapt. Ch., Orlando, Fla., 1989—; mem. exec. bd. Lone Star (Tex.) Bapt. Camp, 1982-84; leader growth confs. for ch., assn. and state Sunday schs.; preacher state youth camp, Siloam Springs, Ark., 1984; mem. super summer Ark. bd. Ark. Bapt. Conv., 1986-87; spl. Sunday sch. worker Ark. and and Okla. Bapt. Convs.; contract worker Bapt. Gen. Conv. Tex.; adj. prof. youth ministry La. Coll., Pineville, 1987-89. Co-author: The Work of the Ministry of Youth, 1989; author: 10 Minute Devotions for Youth Groups, 1989; contbr. to denominational publs. Mem. Community Day Care Bd., Longview, 1977-80; fund raiser LeTourneau Coll., Longview, 1979-81, Am. Heart Assn., 1979. Home: 5340 Keswick Ct Orlando FL 32812 Office: 1st Bapt Ch 3701 LB McLeod Rd Orlando FL 32812

COLLINS, BARBARA ANNE, minister, business educator; b. Dallas, May 8, 1935; d. Paul Norton and Pauline (Coats) Henderson; m. Philip Linn Collins, June 16, 1956; children: Stephen-Andrew-Paul, Jeffrey Linn, Byron Keith. BBA, So. Meth. U., 1955; BTh, Fountain Gate Bible Coll., 1980; ThM, Fla. Beacon Bible Coll., 1991. Ordained to ministry, 1980. Legal sec. Scurry, Scurry & Pace, Dallas, 1955-56; tchr. bus. Pflugerville (Tex.) High Sch., Dallas, 1956-57; legal sec. Hutchison, Shipp & Guinn, Dallas, 1959-60; sec., bd. elders Fountain Gate Ministries, Dallas and Plano, 1976-91, dir. Alms Ministry, 1980-91, co-pastor, 1988-91; tchr. bible Fountain Gate Bible Coll., Dallas and Plano, 1974-91, dean of student affairs, 1983-86. Del. State Rep. Conv., Dallas, 1986, numerous county and state Rep. convs. Mem. Sigma Kappa (pres. SK Corp. Bd. of Tex. 1960-63, Nat. Pledge Trainer, 1963-70). Home and Office: 912 Tanglewood Plano TX 75075 *My greatest honor has come from Him who counted me faithful, appointing me to the stewardship of the ministry to be a co-laborer with Him. My effectiveness in this high calling is related to assisting, equipping and training others in the Body of Christ to do the work of the ministry toward building up the church.*

COLLINS, DAVID BROWNING, religious institution administrator; b. Hot Springs, Ark., Dec. 18, 1922; s. Charles Frederick and Agnes Elizabeth (George) C.; m. Maryon Virginia Moise, Oct. 14, 1945; children: Melissa, Christopher, Matthew, Geoffrey. BA, U. of the South, 1943, BD, 1948, STM, 1962, DD, 1974. Rector St. Andrew's Episc. Ch., Marianna, Ark., 1948-53; priest-in-charge Holy Cross Episc. Ch., West Memphis, Ark., 1949-53; chaplain and assoc. prof. of religion U. of the South, Sewanee, Tenn., 1953-66; dean Cathedral of St. Philip, Atlanta, 1966-84; exec. dir. Windsong Ministries, Inc., 1984—; pres. House of Deps. Episcopal Ch., 1985-91; trustee Ch. Pension Fund, N.Y.C., 1976-88; mem. Bd. of Clergy Deployment, N.Y.C., 1971-76. Contbr. articles to profl. jours. Pres. Christian

Council of Met. Atlanta, 1977-78; chaplain Atlanta Braves Booster Club, 1966-84. Served to lt. (j.g.) USNR, 1943-46. Avocation: baseball. Home and Office: Rte 2 Box 2511 Townsend GA 31331

COLLINS, DAVID HARVEY, pastor; b. Marlboro, Mass., Aug. 7, 1951; s. Harvey Herman and Annalee (Harwood) C.; m. Meryl Ann Hopkins, Aug. 19, 1978; children: Jeremy David, Zachary Lucas. BS in Naval Architecture-Marine Engring., Webb Inst. Naval Architecture, 1973; MDiv, Trinity Evang. Div. Sch., Deerfield, Ill., 1978. Ordained to ministry Plymouth Brethren, 1978. Pastor Sea Cliff (N.Y.) Gospel Chapel, 1978—; cachet artist dhc Cachet, Sea Cliff, 1983—. Pres. PTA, Sea Cliff, 1990-92. Mem. L.I. Cover Soc. (v.p. 1986-91). Home and Office: Sea Cliff Gospel Chapel 40 Ransom Ave Sea Cliff NY 11579 *The only thing worthwhile in life is seeking to please Jesus Christ.*

COLLINS, F. DONALD, religious organization executive. Gen. sec. Bapt. Missionary Assn. Am., Little Rock. Office: Bapt Missionary Assn Am 721 Main St Little Rock AR 72201*

COLLINS, MICHAEL EDWARD, religious newspaper editor; b. Columbus, Ohio, Nov. 17, 1938; s. Martin Patrick and Monica Louise (Metzger) C. Student, MIT, 1956-57, Ohio State U., 1957-61. Staff writer Cath. Times, Columbus, 1962-66, news editor, 1966-70, editor, 1970—; pres. Cath. Men's Luncheon Club, 1972-73, Holy Name Parish Coun., 1972-73; chmn. communications Diocesan Coun. Cath. Men, 1964-67; chmn. communications sect. Cath. Conf. Ohio, 1978-80; instr. Gabriel Richard Inst., 1963-69. Contbr. articles to religious jours. Mem. Cath. Press Assn. (various coms.), Soc. Profl. Journalists (pres. Cen. Ohio chpt. 1980-82), Mensa, Press Club Ohio, KC. Home: 82 Georgetown Dr Columbus OH 43214 Office: PO Box 636 Columbus OH 43216 *I think it is impossible to be a Christian by yourself. If a person is to follow Matthew 25, he or she has to be involved in a real church—one with old people, young people, poor people, sick people, people who need each other.*

COLLINS, MICHAEL EUGENE, pastor; b. Pensacola, Fla., Aug. 28, 1955; s. Benjamin Franklin and Vergie (House) C.; m. Pamela Diane Jacobs, June 7, 1975; children: Jeffrey, Benjamin, Matthew. AA, Pensacola Jr. Coll., 1975; BA in Communication Arts, U. West Fla., 1977; M in Religious Edn., New Orleans Bapt. Sem., 1979. Youth, music Westwood Christian Ch., Pensacola, Fla., 1974-75, Olivet Bapt. Ch., Milton, Fla., 1975-78, Empire Bapt. Ch., La., 1978-79; sr. pastor Charity Chapel, Pensacola, Fla., 1979—; bd. dirs. Alpha Ctr., Pensacola, 1987—, Loaves and Fishes Soup Kitchen, Pensacola, 1988— (v.p.), Inner City Ministries, Pensacola, 1989—; adj. tchr. Liberty Christian Coll., Pensacola, 1982—. Bd. dirs. United Cerebral Palsy, Pensacola, 1989—; mem. Handicapped Awareness Com., Pensacola, 1989—; instr. Parent Ednl. Network, Pensacola, 1987—, Supportive Employement Project, Pensacola, 1987—. Mem. Pentecostal Fellowship North Am. (Pensacola chpt. pres. 1990-91), Pensacola Area Mins. Assn., Liberty Fellowship of Mins. and Chs. Republican. Office: Charity Chapel 5820 Montgomery Ave Pensacola FL 32526

COLLINS, MICHAEL LEE, SR., minister; b. Hickory, N.C., Mar. 14, 1952; s. Hume Self Sr. and Naoma (Cline) C.; m. Sheila Harris, Nov. 7, 1981; children: Courtney, Michael Jr., Candace. BS, Appalachian State U., 1974; MDiv, Luth. Theol. So. Sem., 1978; DMin, Grad. Theol. Found., Notre Dame, Ind., 1989. Ordained to ministry Luth. Ch., 1978. Pastor Christ Luth. Ch., Winston-Salem, N.C., 1978-81, A Mighty Fortress Luth. Ch., Charlotte, N.C., 1981-84, Calvary Luth. Ch., Morganton, N.C., 1984-89; sr. pastor Emmanuel Luth. Ch., Naples, Fla., 1989—; bd. trustees Lutheridge Conf. & Camping Ctr., Arden, N.C., 1986-90; chmn. worship planning com. 1991 Fla. Assembly, Tampa, 1990-91; sec., bd. dirs. Hospice of Burke County, Morganton, 1985-88. Editor, contbr. Soli Deo Gloria worship newsletter, 1987-89; contbr. articles to publs. Mem. Mayor's Task Force on Drug Abuse, Morganton, 1986-87, Naples Task Force on Homeless, 1991—; mem. exec. com. United Way, Morganton, 1986-89; v.p. Burke United Christian Ministries, Morganton, 1986-89; county coord. CROP Hunger Walk, Burke County, N.C., 1988-89; mem. coordinating com. Spl. Olympics, Burke County, 1986-89, Collier County, 1991. Recipient Human Rights award Baha'is, Morgantown, 1988. Fellow Grad. Theol. Found.; mem. Am. Assn. Christian Counselors, Acad. of Evangelists, Acad. Parish Clergy, Naples Ministerial Assn. (pres. elect 1991), Jaycees, Rotary (pres. Morganton chpt. 1988-89). Office: Emmanuel Luth Ch 777 Mooring Line Dr Naples FL 33940 *The longer I am alive, the more I yearn to know, experience and celebrate the depths of "the joy of God's salvation" in my heart, spirit and soul!.*

COLLINS, PATRICK WINCHESTER, priest, educator; b. Peoria, Ill., Dec. 1, 1936; s. Eugene Stowell and Juanita (Winchester) C. MusB, U. Ill., 1959; PhB, St. Paul Sem., 1960, MA in History, 1963; PhD in Hist. Theology, Fordham U., 1972; M in Music Edn., Bradley U., 1982. Ordained priest Roman Cath. Ch., 1964. Asst. pastor, dir. music St. Mary's Cathedral, Peoria, 1964-67; pastor, rector St. Mary's Cathedral and St. Peter's Ch., Peoria, 1987-90; asst. chancellor Diocese of Peoria, 1967-69, chair preparatory commn., synod 6, 1972-74, chair continuing edn. of clergy com., 1974-76, dir. diocesan office of worship and music, 1979-87; dir. campus ministry, adj. prof. Cath. U. Am., Washington, 1976-79; founder, dir. St. Peter's House of Prayer, Peoria, 1987-90; instr. liturgical music St. Joseph Sem., Yonkers, N.Y., 1970-71, U. Notre Dame, Ind., 1972, St. Joseph's Coll., Renssaeler, Ind., 1974; instr. hist. theology Maryknoll (N.Y.) Sem., 1971-72; instr. theology Cath. U. Am., 1976-79; instr. liturgy Duquesne U., Pitts., 1983-84, St. Meinrad (Ind.) Sem., 1984, Loyola U., Chgo., 1987-89, St. Louis U., 1989-90; vis. scholar U. Notre Dame, 1990-91; chair continuing edn. com. Canon Law Soc. Am., 1975-77; v.p., bd. dirs. Cath. Campus Ministry Assn., 1977-79; vis. scholar Grad. Theol. Union, Berkeley, Calif., spring 1992. Author: More Than Meets the Eye, 1983, Bodying Forth: Liturgy Is an Art, 1992, Gustave Weigel, S.J., A Pioneer of Reform, 1992; mem. editorial bd. Modern Liturgy, 1981-84, contbr. articles to profl. jours.; condr. Peoria Schola Cantorum; creator, writer, producer, host over 40 TV programs Peoria NBC/Cath. Telecommunications Network Am.; writer, producer, host Paulist Press video Understanding the Mass. Bd. dirs. Peoria Symphony Orch., 1965-69, 82-88, Royal Sch. Ch. Music in Am., 1982-84; condr. Carmel (Ind.) Symphony Chorus, 1990-91. Avocations: sports, gardening, cooking, writing, music. Home: 1983 S Oldfields Circle Indianapolis IN 46208 *Two phrases of Jesus enlighten my life's journey: "Seek first the Reign of God", and "I have come so that you may have life more abundantly."*

COLLINS, THOMAS ASA, minister; b. Rome, Ga., Aug. 31, 1921; s. Earle Strathmore and Hazel (Alverson) C.; m. Anna E. Galloway, Aug. 17, 1944; children—Faye Anne (Mrs. Cullen B. Rivers), Thomas Asa, Robert Earle, William Ray. B.A., Asbury Coll., Wilmore, Ky., 1941, B.D., 1944; M.Div., Emory U., 1944; D.D. (hon.), High Point (N.C.) Coll. Ordained to ministry Methodist Ch., 1944; pastor in Atlanta, 1942-43; pastor Talbot, Ga., 1943-44, Gatesville, N.C., 1944-49, Raleigh, N.C., 1949-53; exec. dir. Meth. Conf. Bd. Missions, 1953-59; 1st pres. N.C. Wesleyan Coll., Rocky Mount, 1959-75; sr. pastor 1st Meth. Ch., Roanoke Rapids, 1976-80; sr. pastor St. Mark's United Meth. Ch., Raleigh, 1980-86, asst. to bishop for ch. extension, 1986-88; dist. supt. Raleigh dist., 1988-90, asst. to bishop for ch. extension, 1990—; prin., tchr. high sch., Gates County, 1944-46; dir. People's Bank & Trust Co., Rocky Mount, 1966-69; del. gen. conf. and jurisdictional confs. Meth. Ch., 1960-64, 68, 70, 84, World Meth. Conf., 1971, 76, 81, 86, 91; pres. Bd. Global Ministries N.C. United Meth. Conf., 1972-76, N.C. Council Chs., 1967-70; mem. bd. Commn. Christian Edn., Nat. Council Chs., 1959-68; pres. Raleigh Ministerial Assn., 1982-83. Sermon editor: Carolina Cooperator, 1949-85; Contbr. articles to religious jours. Pres. Roanoke Rapids United Way, 1976-78, Roanoke Rapids chpt. N.C. Symphony Soc.; chmn. bd. dirs. Life Enrichment Center, 1982-83. Named N.C. Tar Heel of Week, 1959; recipient Disting. Service award N.C. Council Chs., 1971. Mem. Am. Acad. Religion, Am. Assn. Colls. and Univs., N.C. Assn. Coll. and Univ. (pres. 1972-74), Omicron Delta Kappa. Democrat. Clubs: Kiwanis (lt. gov. 1972-73), Ruritan (pres. 1947-49). Home: 1200 Manchester Dr Raleigh NC 27609 *The one principle which has clearly dominated all others in my life has been a conviction of the inherent rightness of the life and teachings of Jesus Christ. I have been committed to His service since my early youth and I have tried my best to serve my fellow man, with a particular concern for the youth of my world, as I have believed He would have wanted me to do.*

COLLINS, THOMAS HENRY, minister; b. New Bedford, Mass., Nov. 7, 1961; s. Charles Henry and Alice Louise (Jones) C.; m. Marianne Louise Somers, Aug. 15, 1981; children: Jacquelyn, Stephanie, Joshua. BA, Barrington Coll., 1983; MDiv, Southeastern Sem., 1986. Ordained to ministry So. Bapt. Ch., 1986. Min. music Wake Union Bapt. Ch., Wake Forest, N.C., 1985-86; pastor Union Chapel Bapt. Ch., Lynch Station, Va., 1986-89, Blackstone (Va.) Bapt. Ch., 1989—. Pres., founder Altavista (Va.) Housing Assn., 1988-89, Helping Every Life Prosper, Blackstone, 1990-91; dir. Southside Va. Food Distbn. Ctr., Dolphin, 1990-91; bd. dirs. Fed. Emergency Mgmt. Assn., Nottoway County, Va., 1990-91; chaplain P TA, Blackstone, 1990-91. Recipient Excellence in Bibl. Greek award Am. Bible Soc., 1983. Mem. Va. Bapt. Hist. Soc., South Side Assn. Pastors Conf. (treas. 1990-91), Blackstone Ministerial Assn. (treas. 1990-91), Staunton River Assn. Pastors Conf. (pres. 1987-88, chmn. ordination com. 1987-89). Office: Blackstone Bapt Ch 407 S Main St PO Box 53 Blackstone VA 23824

COLLINS, TRAVIS MURRAY, missionary, educator; b. Anniston, Ala., May 27, 1959; s. J.D. and Maude Murray (Copeland) C.; m. Keri Ellen Williams, July 23, 1983; children: Landan, Brennan, Grant. BA, Samford U., Birmingham, Ala., 1981; MDiv, So. Bapt. Theol. Sem., Louisville, 1987, PhD, 1990. Ordained to ministry, So. Bapt. Conv. Missionary journeyman Fgn. Mission Bd., So. Bapt. Conv., Venezuela, 1981-83; pastor Lucas Grove Bapt. Ch., Upton, Ky., 1984-87, Valley Creek Bapt. Ch., Elizabethtown, Ky., 1987-90; missionary Fgn. Mission Bd., So. Bapt. Conv., Nigeria, 1991—; prof.'s asst. So. Bapt. Theol. Sem., Louisville, 1988-90; prof. missions and ch. history Nigerian Bapt. Theol. Sem., Ogbomosho, 1991—. Home and Office: Nigerian Bapt Theol Sem, Bay 30, Ogbomosho Nigeria

COLLINS, TRUMAN EDWARD, clergyman; b. Advance, Mo., Aug. 22, 1919; s. Edward and Pearl (Shell) C.; m. Dorothy Virginia Eaker, Dec. 23, 1939; 1 child, Edward Alan. Diploma, Calvary Bible Coll., Kansas City, Mo., 1952. Ordained to ministry Bapt. Ch., 1949. Pastor Mt. Zion Gen. Bapt. Ch., Granite City, Ill., 1950-64, First Gen. Bapt. Ch., Princeton, Ind., 1964-67, Dover Chapel Gen. Bapt. Ch., Louisville, 1967-69, Southland Gen. Bapt. Ch., Louisville, 1969-85, Lutesville (Mo.) Gen. Bapt. Ch., 1986-88; Pres. Nat. Sunday Sch. Bd. Gen. Bapt., 1956-63, moderator nat. conv., 1961-62; pres. Gen. Bapt. Publs. and Edn. Bd., Inc., 1964-66; mem. Liberty Presbyter Gen. Bapt. Assn., Ind., 1965-67, Christian Edn. and Publs. Bd., Inc. of Gen. Baptist Denomination, 1963-66, pres., 1964-65; pres. Illmo Assn. Endowment Corp., 1959-64; dir. Illmo Assn. Youth Camp of Gen. Bapt., 1954-64; mem. Hahn Chapel Gen. Bapt. Ch., 1987—; mem. Tri-City Ministerial Alliance, 1988. Author: Sun Rays In the Sickroom. Pres. Emerson Sch. PTA, 1962-63. Mem. Nat. Congress PTA, Quad City Ministerial Assn. (treas.), Kentuckana Assn. Gen. Bapts., S.E. Mo. Assn. Gen. Bapts., Greater Louisville Evang. Fellowship (v.p.), Old Liberty Assn. Gen. Bapts. Address: Box 371 Marble Hill MO 63764

COLOMBO, GIOVANNI CARDINAL, former archbishop; b. Milan, Dec. 6, 1902. Ordained to priesthood, 1926. Consecrated Titular Bishop of Philippopolis in Arabia, 1960, Archbishop of Milan, 1963-79, created Cardinal, 1965; mem. Com. of the Ecumenical Council on Cath. Sems. and Edn. Address: Corso Venezia 11, 20121 Milan Italy

COLON, JAC AGUSTIN, minister; b. New Orleans, Aug. 19, 1942; s. Jose Agustin and Grace Elsie (D'Ingianni) C.; m. Eldena Kay Walter, Sept. 4, 1975; children: Paul Elden, Jason Jac. BA, Union Coll., Lincoln, Nebr., 1964. Ordained to ministry Adventist Ch., 1980. Pastor Seventh-day Adventist Ch., Claremore and Sand Spring, Okla., 1974-79; evangelist Seventh-day Adventist Ch., various locations, 1979-87; v.p. Tex. Conv. Seventh-day Adventist, Harlingen, Tex., 1987-89; dir. N.W. Evang. Inst., Federal Way, Wash., 1989—; condr. evangelistic crusade and tng. for pastors in USSR, 1991; lectr. in field. Author: Standing in the Shaking, 1982, Persuasive Influence, 1984. Capt. USAF, 1966-71. Mem. Adventist Theol. Soc. Office: NW Evangelism Inst 810 S 312th St Federal Way WA 98003 *I am amazed to see the extent to which the entire world is frantically searching for peace through politics, diplomacy and technology while peace can only come by planting the banner of God's kingdom in the hearts of men and women on planet Earth.*

COLON, JAMES ANTHONY, religious organization administrator; b. San Juan, P.R., Feb. 14, 1943; s. Raymond and Dolly C.; m. Eileen Joy Dennison, Feb. 6, 1968; children: Holly, Ramon, Joel, Micah. BA, Citadel Bible Coll., 1976; MDiv, Talbot Theol. Sem., 1980; postgrad., Biola U., 1987—. Missionary Overseas Crusades Ministries (now Overseas Ministries), Milpitas, Calif., 1980-87; pastor Bell Bapt. Ch., Conservative Bapt. Denom., Cudahy, Calif., 1987-89; v.p. Overseas Ministries United World Mission, Union Mills, N.C., 1989—. With U.S. Navy, 1960-64. Republican. Office: United World Mission PO Box 250 Union Mills NC 28167-0250 *"When all else fails, read the directions." This adage is as true of life as it is of mechanical contraptions. The book of life is the Bible. If one is interested in living right, the Bible is the handbook.*

COLSON, CHARLES WENDELL, lay minister, writer; b. Boston, Oct. 16, 1931; s. Wendell Ball and Inez (Ducrow) C.; m. Nancy Billings, June 3, 1953; children: Wendell Ball II, Christian B., Emily Ann; m. Patricia Ann Hughes, Apr. 4, 1964. AB, Brown U., 1953; JD, George Washington U., 1959; LLD (hon.), Wheaton Coll., 1982, Houghton Coll., 1983, Eastern Coll., 1983, Anderson Coll., 1984, Taylor U., 1985, Geneva Coll., 1987, John Brown U., 1988, Asbury Coll., 1989, LeTourneau U., 1990. Pvt. practice Washington, 1961-69; asst. to asst. sec. Navy, 1955-56; adminstrv. asst. Senator Leverett Saltonstall U.S. Senate, 1956-61; sr. ptnr. Gadsby & Hannah, 1961-69; spl. counsel to pres. of U.S., 1969-72; ptnr. Colson & Shapiro, Washington, 1973-74; assoc. Fellowship House, Washington, 1975-76, Prison Fellowship, 1976—. Author: Born Again, 1975, Life Sentence, 1979, Crime and The Responsible Community, 1980, Loving God, 1983, Who Speaks for God?, 1985, Kingdoms in Conflict, 1987, Against the Night, 1989, The God of Stones and Spiders, 1990, (with Jack Eckerd) Why America Doesn't Work, 1991. Campaign mgr. Saltonstall campaign, 1960. Capt. USMCR, Korea. Recipient Religious Heritage award Freedom Found., 1977, Abe Lincoln award So. Bapt. Conv., 1984, Poverello award U. Steubenville, 1986, Disting. Svc. award Salvation Army, 1990, Humanitarian award So. Bapt. Conv., 1991, Domino's Pizza award; named Layman of Yr., Nat. Assn. Evangelists, 1983. Mem. Order of Coif, Beta Theta Pi. Baptist. Office: Prison Fellowship PO Box 17500 Washington DC 20041

COLVERT, KENNETH RONALD, minister, educator; b. Little Rock, June 9, 1942; s. Joe Bumpass and Virginia (Hicks) C.; m. Carolyn Norman, Aug. 16, 1963. BA in Bible, Cen. Bapt. Coll., Conway, Ark., 1965; BS in Elem. Edn., U. Cen. Ark., 1969; MS in Elem. Adminstrn., Ark. State U., 1974, EdS in Elem. Adminstrn., 1981. Ordained to ministry Bapt. Missionary Assn. Am., 1963; cert. tchr., elem. prin., Ark. Pastor Park Grove Bapt. Ch., Clarendon, Ark., 1963-75; dir. children's ch. Trenton Bapt. Ch., Marvell, Ark., 1975-87; dir. youth Bethel Bapt. Ch., Forrest City, Ark., 1987-91; elem. tchr. Moro (Ark.) Elem. Sch., Lee County Schs., 1965-74, 1981—; prin. Aubrey (Ark.) Lee County Schs., 1974-81; dir. Mt. Vernon Dist. Galileans, 1985—, Ark. Galileans, Bapt. Missionary Assn. Am., 1989—, asst. dir. Am. Galileans, Writer's Family-Bapt. Pub. House, 1989—. Contbr. worship devotions to religious publs. Scoutmaster Boy Scoutss Am., Moro, 1966-77, fund raising chmn., Lee County, Ark., 1978-85. Mem. NEA, ASCD, Nat. Coun. Tchrs. Social Studies, Internat. Reading Assn., Ark. Edn. Assn., Lee County Edn. Assn. (pres. 1970-73). Home: PO Box 5 Hwy 238 S Moro AR 72368 *The greatest pay for a teacher/preacher is the reward of beholding the success and accomplishments of those individuals he has taught.*

COLVIN, GARY LEE, religion educator; b. Las Animas, Colo., Apr. 20, 1940; s. Arthur L. Colvin and Mary Cecil McCasland; married; children: Joanne, Donna, Rhonda, Randy. BA, Abilene Christian U., 1962, MA, 1969; D. Ministry, Pacific Sch. Religion, 1985. Assoc. prof. Abilene (Tex.) Christian U., 1985—, dir. off-campus grad. studies, 1985-87, assoc. chmn. undergrad. Bible, 1987-88. Mem. A. Acad. Religion, Soc. Bibl. Lit., Evang. Theol. Soc., Inst. Nautical Archaeology. Home and Office: 833 Washington Blvd Abilene TX 79601

COLVIN, JOHN ALEXANDER, campus minister; b. N.Y.C., Sept. 14, 1950; s. Donald Roy Colvin and Alice Justine (Berry) Stone; m. Linda Lorraine Duxbury, July 1, 1982; children: Hana Lyn, Dena Bari. BA, U. Balt., 1983; MDiv, Unification Theol. Sem., 1986; MA, U. Balt., 1990. Ordained to ministry Unification Ch., 1986. Lay missionary Unification Ch., Balt., 1976-83; dir. outreach Unification Theol. Sem., Barrytown, N.Y., 1984-86; state dir. Unification Ch., Ohio, 1986; dir. campus ministry Unification Campus Mins. Assn., Balt., 1989—; state dir. Am. Constitution Com., Md., 1987—; staff Orgn. Interfaith Activity in N.Y.C., Assembly of World Religions, McAttra, N.J., 1985; participant Youth Seminar on World Religions, various countries, 1985; dir. United Christian Citizens, Md., 1987—. Contbr. articles to jours. bd. dirs. Am. Freedom Coalition of Md., 1987—, sec.-treas. 1990—; co-founder, dir. pub. rels. Univ. Balt., Fgn. Affairs Coun., 1989—; co-founder, sec. Coalition for Harmony, Balt., 1990—; treas. Ann Arundel Sch. Bd. Nominating Conv., Anne Arundel County, Md., 1990—. Named Outstanding Young Men of Am., 1987. Mem. Internat. Religious Fedn., Federalist Soc., Prince George County Rep. Club, Anne Arundel County Elephant Club. Home: 205 Marie Ave Glen Burnie MD 21060 Office: Am Constitution Com 205 Marie Ave Glen Burnie MD 21060 *The challenge of life is to be a good person. When I succeed in maintaining my own personal integrity and directing my actions in the service of God and mankind, problems are transformed into exciting growth experiences and the blessings of love, success, and joy are assured.*

COLWELL, STEVEN MICHAEL, minister; b. Aurora, Mo., Sept. 16, 1954; s. James William and Doris Loretta (Hough) C.; m. Karen Sue Blakely, Feb. 14, 1976. BA, Ouachita Bapt. U., 1977; MDiv, Midwestern Bapt. Sem., Kansas City, Mo., 1984; MA in Religion, Cen. Bapt. Sem., Kansas City, Kans., 1985. Ordained to ministry Bapt. Ch., 1976. Pastor Perla (Ark.) Bapt. Ch., 1976-77, Trinity So. Bapt. Ch., Waterloo, Iowa, 1986-87; chaplain candidate U.S. Army Res., Kansas City, 1982-86; chaplain intern VA Med. Ctr., Kansas City, 1984-86; chaplain 588th combat engr. bn. U.S. Army, Ft. Polk, La., 1987—. Capt. U.S. Army, 1977-81. Mem. Assn. U.S. Army. Office: 588th Engr Bn Chaplain Bldg 1072 Fort Polk LA 71459

COMBITSIS, CONSTANTINE, clergyman; b. Salonica, Greece, Oct. 15, 1932; came to U.S., 1946; s. Apostolos and Arhondia (Psomiades) C.; m. Argeroula Loutraris, May 13, 1962; children—Paul, Maria. Th.M., Internat. Theol. Sem., 1980, Th.D., 1981, D.D. (hon.), 1981. Ordained priest Greek Orthodox Ch., 1962. Priest, St. Spyridon Greek Orthodox Ch., Clarksburg, W.Va., 1962-66, Annunciation Greek Orthodox Ch., Endicott, N.Y., 1966-73, St. Catherine Greek Orthodox Ch., West Palm Beach, Fla., 1973-75, Holy Trinity Greek Orthodox Ch., Harrisburg, Pa., 1975-80, St. Nicholas Greek Orthodox Ch., Atlantic City, 1980—. Contbr. articles to religious jours. Served with USAF, 1952-60. Elevated to title of Sakelarios, 1974, Economos, 1977, Stavroforos, 1979. Mem. Harrisburg Council Chs. (bd. dirs., dir. inter-ch. relations 1976-78), Greek Orthodox Ministerial Assn., Greek Orthodox Presbyters Council. Home: 3 Saddle Ridge Ln Pleasantville NJ 08232 Office: 13 S Mt Vernon Ave Atlantic City NJ 08401

COMBS, CURTIS FLOYD, music minister; b. Ft. Thomas, Ky., Sept. 24, 1959; s. E. Mitchell and Eileen Marie (Turner) C.; m. Judith Dean Yelton, May 15, 1982; 1 child, Caitlin DeAnna. BFA in Theatre Performance, No. Ky. U., 1982; M Ch. Music, So. Bapt. Theol. Sem., 1989. Ordained to ministry So. Bapt. Conv., 1989. Min. music Calvary Bapt. Ch., Newport, Ky., 1975-77, Trinity Bapt. Ch., Newport, Ky., 1977-79, Rosedale Bapt. Ch., Latonia, Ky., 1980-83; min. music/youth Willoughby (Ohio) Bapt. Ch., 1989—; mission team leader Frenchburg (Ky.) Bapt. Ch., 1986; associational music dir. Cleve. Bapt. Assn., 1989—. Recipient 1st place vocalist award NATS, Lexington, Ky. Mem. So. Bapt. Ch. Music Conf., Ohio Bapt. Music Specialists. Office: Willoughby Bapt Ch 37927 Euclid Ave Willoughby OH 44094

COMBS, IRA, JR., pastor, social services administrator; b. Inkster, Mich., Apr. 21, 1958; s. Ira Sr. and Hazel M. (Cosper) C.; m. Kimberly Loretta Marshall, Jan. 12, 1980; children: Sarah Michelle, Ira III. Student, Mich. State U., 1976-79; AS in Theology, Ind. Bible Coll., 1989, BTh, 1991. Owner Combs Landscaping & Gardening, Detroit, summer 1975; quality control insp. Ford Motor Co., Dearborn, Mich., summer 1977; installment loan adjuster Am. Bank & Trust, Lansing, Mich., 1978-79; pastor, founder The Greater Bible Way Temple, Inc., Jackson, Mich., 1980—; mem. customer svc. support team Xerox Corp., Lansing, 1979-84; dist. mgr., sales leader A. L. Williams Mktg./Ins., Lansing and Jackson, 1985-86; exec. dir. Christ Centered Homes, Inc., Jackson. Contbr. articles to profl. jours. Pres. Mich. Housing Coalition, Community Reinvestment Action Network, 1990-91; mem. com. to integrate county cert. mental health contracts Mich. Dept. Mental Health, Lansing and Jackson, 1990—; chmn., founder Ad-Hoc Coalition on Fair Banking Practice, Jackson County, 1988—; bd. dirs. state resolution com. NAACP, Mich.; bd. dirs. adv. coun. Jackson Fair Housing Ctr., 1989—. Named one of Outstanding Young Men of Am., Nat. Jaycees, 1982; recipient Community Svcs. award Jackson Negro Bus. and Profl. Women's Club, Inc., 1989, Community Svcs. award Human Rels. Commn., 1990. Mem. Police Officer's Assn. Am., Mich. Sheriff's Assn., Omega Psi Phi. Pentecostal. Avocations: body building, basketball, baseball, running. Home: 1704 Plymouth St Jackson MI 49201 Office: Christ Centered Homes Inc 327 W Monroe St Jackson MI 49202

COMBS, K(ERMIT) STEPHEN, JR., minister; b. Richmond, Va., Apr. 19, 1941; s. Kermit Stephen Sr. and Geraldine Mary (Ellis) C.; m. J. Sue Moore, Nov. 27, 1982; children: Paul B., Mary Ellen, Joshua S., James N. BA in Edn., U. Fla., 1964; M. Religious Edn., So. Bapt. Theol. Sem., 1968, EdD, 1978; postgrad., U. Louisville, 1975, 76. Cert. deacon trainer. Jr. high sch. tchr. Maitland Jr. High Sch., Orlando, Fla., 1964-65; state dir. boys missions State Conv. Baptists in Ind., Indpls., 1966-67; minister edn./activities Bethlehem Bapt. Ch., Louisville, 1967-68; assoc. pastor Murray Hill Bapt. Ch., Jacksonville, Fla., 1968-70; assoc. minister edn./adminstrn. 1st Bapt. Ch., Hendersonville, N.C., 1970-72; minister edn./youth 1st Bapt. Ch., Shelbyville, Ky., 1972-74; high sch. tchr. Ky. Country Day Sch., Louisville, 1975-76; growth cons. Bapt. Sunday Sch. Bd., Nashville, 1976-82; assoc. pastor 1st Bapt. Ch., Carrollton, Ga., 1982-87; min. edn. and evangelism 3rd Bapt. Ch., St. Louis, 1987-91; exec. dir. Shepherd's Ctr. St. Louis, 1991—; Garrett teaching fellow So. Bapt. Theol. Sem., Louisville, 1974-76; adminstrv. intern Boyce Bible Sch., Louisville, 1975; vis. prof. So. Bapt. Theol. Sem., Louisville, 1978; adj. prof. Midwestern Bapt. Theol. Sem., Kansas City, Mo., 1979. Co-author: Equipping Disciples Through Church Training, 1980; contbr. articles to profl. jours. Pres. bd. dirs. Family Devel. Ctr., Hendersonville, 1971-72, So. Sem. Alumni Assn., Mo.-Ill., ABC, 1989-91; bd. dirs. Head Start Coun., Shelbyville, 1974; mem. exec. bd. St. Louis Metro Bapt. Assn., 1989-90; mem. Kiwanis Club, Carrollton, 1983-84. Fla. State Tchr.'s scholar State Dept. Edn., Tallahassee, Fla., 1959. Mem. ASCD, Religious Edn. Assn., So. Bapt. Religious Edn. Assn. (bd. dirs. 1991—), Mo. Bapt. Religious Edn. Assn. Avocations: photography, tennis, woodworking, gardening, bicycling. Office: Shepherd's Ctr St Louis PO Box 30550 Saint Louis MO 63116-0550

COMBS, PHILIP DEE, minister; b. Aurora, Mo., Sept. 4, 1947; s. Joe B. and Ada (Lockard) C.; m. Marydell Austin; children: La Betha, Naara, Erin. Student, Cen. Bible Coll., Springfield, Mo., 1965-66, 73-74, Assy. of God Theol. Sem., Springfield, Mo., 1974, 80; Dipl., Taipei Lang. Inst., Taiwan, 1976-78. Ordained to ministry Assemblies of God, 1971. Pastor Assemblies of God, Mo., 1967-73; missionary Assemblies of God, 1974-91, Taiwan, 1974-88; exec. dir. Taiwan TV Ministry, 1984-88; supt. Taiwan Mt. Dist. Coun., 1978-84; coord. Internat. Outreach Ctr., Palisades Park, N.J., 1990—; exec. com. Taiwan Field Fellowship, 1978-88; del. Assemblies of God Asian Mission Assn., 1978-84; mem. Asia Project 2000, 1985-88; lectr. in field. Contbr. articles to profl. jours.; producer TV and radio programs. Participant Found. for Free Ent., N.J., 1991; English tchr. N.Y. Performing Artists Gospel Fellowship, 1989-90. NSF scholar, 1964; recipient Community Svc. Commendaion, Mayor City of Taipei, 1987. Mem Gen. Coun. of Assemblies of God, Nat. Coun. of Light for the Lost, So. Mo. Dist. Coun. Assemblies of God (hon. mem.), N.J. Dist. Coun. Assemblies of God. Office: Internat Outreach Ctr PO Box 95 Palisades Park NJ 07650 *What is important is not that I am able to serenely accept life's passing; neither is it that I can aggressively, with success, move through life; it is, rather, that my life count for eternity.*

COMER, JOHN FLETCHER, JR., minister; b. Memphis, Dec. 7, 1946; s. John Fletcher and Bettie Blair (Thomson) C.; m. Judith Lynn Walton, Mar. 15, 1969; children: John Fletcher, Patrick Brittan, James Lamar Walton, Sun Mee. BS, Auburn U., 1968, MBA, 1969; MDiv, U. South, Sewanee, Tenn., 1975. Ordained priest Episcopal Ch., 1975. Youth dir. All Sts. Episcopal Ch., Birmingham, Ala., 1971-72; chaplain Advent Episcopal Day Sch., Birmingham, 1970-72, 79-85; rector St. Andrew's Episcopal Ch., Sylacauga, Ala., 1975-79, St. Mary's Episcopal Ch., Childersburg, 1975-79; canon adminstr. Cathedral Ch. of the Advent, Birmingham, 1979-85; rector St. Mark's Episcopal Ch., Prattville, Ala., 1985—; mem. dept. parish devel. Diocese of Ala., 1986—, dept. world mission, 1987—, dept. Christian edn., 1972-76; stewardship cons. Diocese of Iowa, 1985—, trainer, 1988, Diocese of West Tex., 1990. Co-founder Sml. Parish Assn. Ala., 1976, Downtown Coop. Ministry, Birmingham, 1982, North of the Ala. River Orgn. of Anglican Helpers, 1987; core mem. Karanta Community, 1982—; chmn. adv. coun. Ret. Sr. Vol. Program, Autauga County, 1989-90; mem. drug awareness com. Autauga County Bd. of Edn., and others; chmn. advancement and tng. Frontier Dist. Boy Scouts am., 1989-90, chmn. membership com., 1990—; mem. Libr. Bd., 1990—; treas. Autauga County Libr. Bd., Prattville, 1990—. 1st lt. U.S. Army, 1969-71. Recipient Algeron Sidney Sullivan award, Auburn U., 1968; Cubmaster award, Boy Scouts Am., 1985, Weblos Leader award, 1987. Mem. Nat. Assn. Ch. Bus. Adminstrs., Prattville Ministerial Assn. (v.p. 1987-90, pres. 1991), Rotary (pres. Prattville club 1991—), Omicron Delta Kappa. Episcopalian. Avocations: bridge, golf, tennis, fishing, racquetball. Office: Saint Marks Episcopal Ch 178 E 4th St Prattville AL 36067

COMFORT, WILLIAM MICHAEL, minister; b. Bklyn., Sept. 5, 1934; s. William Henry Comfort and Beatrice (Cannizzaro) Hurlbert; m. E. Shirley Evans, Feb. 5, 1960; children: Derrick Mark, Paul William. BA, Bob Jones U., 1958; MA, Capital Bible Sem., Lanham, Md., 1975; MLitt, Oxford Grad. Sch., Dayton, Tenn., 1985, PhD, 1986; postgrad., Oxford U., Eng., 1986. Ordained to ministry Bapt. Ch., 1962. Counselor Christian Servicemen's Ctr., San Antonio, 1957-58; co-founder Christian Servicemen's Ctr., Norfolk, Va., 1958-62; pastor Victory Bapt. Ch., Chesapeake, Va., 1963-68; assoc. pastor Alexander Bapt. Ch., Portsmouth, Va., 1969-71; founder Kettering Bapt. Ch., Largo, Md., 1971-73; pastor 1st Bapt. Ch. of Eastport, Annapolis, Md., 1973-76, New Covenant Ch., Queenstown, Md., 1976—; prof. Va. Bible Coll., Norfolk, 1960; vice moderator Prince Georges Bapt. Assn., Largo, Mdd., 1973; pres. New Covenant Christian Acad., Queenstown, 1981—, New Covenant Christian Coll., Queenstown, 1990. Columnist Queen Anne Record Observer, 1976-78, New Life Jour., 1977-79, Christian Growth Report, 1978, Koinonia mag., 1978-79. Chaplain Acad. Park Elem. Sch. PTA, Portsmouth, 1970; mem. Queen Anne's Econ. Devel. Commn., Centreville, Md., 1984; chmn. Queen Anne's County Commn. on Aging, 1985-87; sec. Queenstown Planning and Zoning Commn., 1990. With USAF, 1951-53; mem. Rep. Nat. Com. Recipient mayor's citation City of Portsmouth, 1968. Mem. Evang. Philos. Soc., Evang. Theol. Soc., Evang. Tchr. Tng. Assn., Anglo-Am. Acad., Oxford Soc. Scholars, Internat. Biog. Assn. Republican. Home: PO Box 419 Queenstown MD 21658 Office: New Covenant Ch Main St and Bowlingly Ln Queenstown MD 21658 *My daily creed: (1) Don't worry about anything. (2) Don't compare yourself with anyone else. (3) Do what you are supposed to do today. Our only security in this world is doing and being right!.*

COMISKEY, ANNE TERESE (TERRY COMISKEY), lay church worker; b. Bklyn., Aug. 3, 1941; d. John Dominick and Anne Rebecca (McCaffrey) Abbate Marco; m. Michael Richard Comiskey, May 13, 1967; children: Michael Kevin, John Kenneth, Ryan Andrew, Gregory Martin. BA, St. Mary's Coll., Notre Dame, Ind., 1963. Jr. High Sch. coord. St. Stephen's Ch., Walnut Creek, Calif., 1985—; religion coord. St. Jarlath Sch., Oakland, Calif., 1988-91, St. Anthony Sch., Oakland, 1989-90. Vice chair Walnut Creek Community Against Substance Abuse, 1987-90; chmn. bd. dirs. Las Lomas Music Found., Walnut Creek, 1990-91; coord. Youth Ministries, 1991—. Home: 1309 Ramsay Circle Walnut Creek CA 94596 Office: St Stephen's Ch 525 Madonna Ln Walnut Creek CA 94596 *The joys in my life have come from experiencing the moment and cherishing its memory forever.*

COMPAGNONE, NICK PETER, educational administrator; b. Bklyn., Sept. 3, 1952; s. Edward Peter and Cathrine Ann (LoMonaco) C.; m. Cindy Ann Hoffman, Aug. 21, 1973; children—Craig Joseph, Chris Edward, Catrina Ann, Curt Nicholas. B.A., St. Mary of the Plains Coll., 1974; M.S., Wichita State U., 1978. Acting prin. Sacred Heart, Larned, Kans., 1974-75; asst. prin., coach Blessed Sacrament Sch., Wichita, Kans., 1975-78; sch. adminstr. St. Joseph Sch., Oakley, Kans., 1978-82, St. Mary's Sch., Salina, Kans., 1982—; chmn. Colby Commn. Edn., Bd. Edn., Salina Diocese, 1978-82. Mem. United Sch. Adminstrs., Nat. Assn. Elem. Sch. Prins., Assn. Supervision and Curriculum Devel. Democrat. Roman Catholic. Lodge: K.C. Office: 2810 Bret Ave Salina KS 67401 also: United Bldg 7th & Iron 9th Fl PO Box 825 Salina KS 67402

COMPAORE, JEAN-MARIE, bishop. Pres. Bishops' Conf., Ougadougou. Office: Conf Episcopale du Burkina Faso, BP 1195, Ouagadougou Burkina Faso*

COMPTON, LINDA, ecumenical agency administrator. Exec. dir. Marin Interfaith Coun., San Rafael, Calif. Office: Marin Interfaith Coun 35 Mitchell Blvd Ste 13 San Rafael CA 94903*

COMPTON, ROBERT BRUCE, religion educator, chaplain; b. Long Beach, Calif., Feb. 27, 1944; s. Robert Hayes Compton and Shirley Ines (Doll) Dayton; m. Mari Huffaker, May 15, 1971; children: Joel David, Jared Michael. BA, UCLA, 1966; MDiv, Denver Bapt. Sem., 1977, ThM, 1979; ThD, Grace Theol. Sem., 1986. Ordained to ministry Bapt. Ch., 1987. Asst. prof. religion Denver Bapt. Theol. Sem., 1977-84; assoc. prof. religion Detroit Bapt. Theol. Sem., 1984-86, prof. religion, 1986—. Contbr. articles, book revs. to religious jours. Chaplain (maj.) Ohio Air N.G., 1987—. Capt. USAF, 1968-74. Mem. Soc. of Bibl. Lit., Evang. Theol. Soc. Republican. Office: Detroit Bapt Theol Sem 4801 Allen Rd Allen Park MI 48101

COMPTON, ROGER ELLSWORTH, clergyman; b. Dayton, Ohio, Dec. 10, 1932; s. Earl Eli and Marie (Stegman) C.; m. Sara Jo Young, Aug. 11, 1956; children: Beth Compton Neel, Lisa Compton Zimmerman, Lori, Eric. AB, Wheaton Coll., 1955; MDiv, No. Bapt. Theol. Sem., Oakbrook, Ill., 1958; MA, Northwestern U., Evanston, Ill., 1960; DD (hon.), Judson Coll., 1978. Ordained to ministry Bapt. Ch., 1958. Assoc. pastor Mannheim Bapt. Ch., Franklin Park, Ill., 1957-60; pastor First Bapt. Ch., Nokomis, Ill., 1960-64, Rantoul, Ill., 1964-70; sr. pastor First Bapt. Ch., Mattoon, Ill., 1970-79, Cen. Bapt. Ch., Springfield, Ill., 1979—; mem. gen. bd. Am. Bapt. Chs., U.S.A., Valley Forge, Pa., 1974-79, bd. mgrs. Great Rivers region, Springfield, 1968-78, pres. Great Rivers region, 1980. Trustee Vis. Nurse Assn., Mattoon, 1970-79, Wesley Towers Retirement Ctr., Mattoon, 1974-80, Judson Coll., Elgin, Ill., 1979—, No. Bapt. Theol. Sem., 1979—; bd. dirs. Vols. in Literacy, Springfield, 1986—; commentator Sta. WCIA-TV, Champaign, Ill., 1964—, Sta. WMAY AM-FM, Springfield, 1984—; dir. Sangamon County Sr. Citizens Commn., Springfield, 1987-89. Fellow Acad. of Parish Clergy; mem. Internat. Platform Assn., Springfield C. of C., Rotary (bd. dirs. 1990). Republican. Avocations: golf, tennis, photography. Office: Cen Bapt Ch 501 S 4th St Springfield IL 62701-1793

COMSTOCK, GARY LYNN, philosophy educator; b. Oak Park, Ill., Feb. 23, 1954; s. Roy L. and Marie (Pippert) C.; m. Karen Werner, Aug. 28, 1976; children: Krista Marie, Benjamin Dhruva Werner. BA, Wheaton Coll., 1976; AM, U. Chgo., 1977, PhD, 1983. Assoc. prof. Iowa State U., Ames, 1982—; mem. Ctr. Theol. Inquiry, Princeton, N.J., 1990; ctr. assoc. Nat. Rural Studies Com., Oreg. State U., 1988-89. Editor: Is There a Moral Obligation to Save the Family Farm?, 1987, Is There a Conspiracy Against Family Farmers?, 1990; contbr. articles to profl. jours. Mem. Am. Acad. Religion, Am. Philos. Assn., Soc. Christian Philosophers, Soc. Christian Ethics. Office: Iowa State U Dept Philosophy Ames IA 50011

CONARD, ARLYN MARK, minister, historian; b. Ashland, Kans., June 22, 1948; s. Arlyn Elmer and Mary Lockie (Mast) C.; m. Joyce Marie Fieser, Aug. 21, 1971; children: Jonathan, Andrew, Kristin. BA, Southwestern Coll., Winfield, Kans., 1970; MDiv, St. Paul Sch. Theology, Kansas City, Mo., 1974; ThM, Union Theol. Sem. in Va., 1975, ThD, 1979. Ordained to ministry United Methodist Ch., Deacon, 1971, elder, 1979. Pastor United Meth. Ch., Geneseo, Kans., 1978-81, Maize, Kans., 1981-87; pastor Pleasant Valley Ch., Wichita, 1987—; chmn. conf. commn. on archives and history, United Meth. Ch., 1980-88, vice chmn. jurisdictional com. on archives and history, 1984-88, vice chmn., 1988—, mem. gen. commn. on archives and history, 1984-91, v.p., 1988-91. Contbr. articles and book revs. to profl. jours. Grad. fellow Union Theol. Sem. in Va. 1975-78. Mem. Am. Soc. Ch. History, Am. Assn. for State and Local History, Conf. on Faith and History, Alban Inst., Acad. Parish Clergy, Kans. State Hist. Soc. Avocation: philately. Home: 3160 Carlock Wichita KS 67204 Office: Pleasant Valley Ch 2801 Coolidge Wichita KS 67204

CONDITT, MARION WITHERSPOON, minister; b. Dallas, Nov. 19, 1928; s. Marion Uri and Helen (Clough) C.; m. Bonnie Warren, June 12, 1954; children: Calvin, Karla, Craig. BA, Trinity U., San Antonio, 1951; BD, Princeton Theol. Sem., 1954; ThD, Basel (Switzerland) U., 1961. Ordained to ministry Presbyn. Ch. (U.S.A.), 1954. Pastor First Presbyn. Ch., Winters, Tex., 1954-56, Temple, Tex., 1962-72; pastor Ferguson Presbyn. Ch., St. Louis, 1972-83; pastor First Presbyn. Ch., Arlington, Tex., 1983-88, Woodward, Okla., 1988—; stated clk. Cimarron presbytery Presbyn. Ch. (USA), 1990—. Author: More Acceptable Than Sacrifice, 1973. With AUS, 1946-48. Named Outstanding Newcomer Arts Theater, 1990. Mem. Ministerial Alliance (pres. Arlington, Tex. 1987, sec. Woodward, Okla., 1990), Rotary (Paul Harris fellow 1987). Home: 1030 Ridgecrest Woodward OK 73801 Office: First Presbyn Ch 721 Oklahoma Ave Woodward OK 73801

CONDON, DEAN FRANCIS, religious organization official; b. Liverpool, Eng., Feb. 1, 1962; came to U.S., 1962; s. James David Condon and Anita (Dorrian) Nicoletta; m. Janet Rose Hesenius, Aug. 27, 1988. BA, Boston Coll., Chestnut Hill, Mass., 1984; MDiv, Harvard U., 1988. Dir., dir. newsletter Charismatic Renewal Svcs., Waltham, Mass., 1988—; liaison to cardinal for charismatic renewal, Boston, 1990—. Office: Charismatic Renewal Svcs 20 Pond St Waltham MA 02154

CONE, JAMES HAL, theologian, educator, author; b. Fordyce, Ark., Aug. 5, 1938; s. Charlie M. and Lucy (Frost) C. BA, Philander Smith Coll., 1958; BD, Garrett Theol. Sem., 1961; MA, Northwestern U., 1963, PhD, 1965. Asst. prof. religion and philosophy Philander Smith Coll., Little Rock, 1964-66; asst. prof. religion Adrian (Mich.) Coll., 1966-69; asst. prof. theology Union Theol. Sem., N.Y.C., 1969-70; asso. prof. Union Theol. Sem., 1970-73, prof., 1973-77, Charles A. Briggs prof. systematic theology, 1977-87, Briggs disting. prof., 1987—; vis. prof. Afro-Am. history U. of Pacific, Stockton, Calif., summer, 1969; vis. asso. prof. religion Barnard Coll., N.Y.C., 1969-71, 74; vis. prof. theology Drew U., Madison, N.J., 1973; lectr. systematic theology Woodstock Coll., N.Y.C., 1971-73; vis. prof. theology Princeton (N.J.) Theol. Sem., 1976, Notre Dame Sch. Theology, New Orleans, summer, 1977, Howard U. Sch. Religion, Washington, 1980. Author: Black Theology and Black Power, 1969 (transl. into Dutch, 1970, German, 1971, Japanese, 1971, Korean, 1979), A Black Theology of Liberation, 1970 (transl. into Spanish, 1973, Italian, 1973, Japanese, 1974), The Spirituals and the Blues: An Interpretation, 1972 (transl. into German, 1973, Japanese, 1975, Korean, 1987), God of the Oppressed, 1975 (transl. into Japanese, 1976, Italian, 1978, Korean, 1978, German, 1982, French, 1989), My Soul Looks Back, 1982 (transl. into Japanese, 1987), For My People, 1984 (transl. into German, 1987), Speaking the Truth, 1986, Martin and Malcom and America: A Dream or a Nightmare, 1991; contbr. articles to profl. publs.; mem. editorial bd.: Jour. Religious Thought, 1975—, Jour. Interdenominational Theological Ctr.; co-editor: Black Theology: A Documentary History, 1966-79, 1979. Rockefeller Found. grantee, 1973-74. Mem. Black Theology Project Theology in Ams., Am. Acad. Religion, Soc. Study Black Religion, Ecumenical Assn. Third World Theologians. Mem. African Methodist Episcopal Ch. Office: Union Theol Sem 3041 Broadway New York NY 10027

CONGDON, GAYLA COOPER, minister; b. Inglewood, Calif., June 30, 1954; d. Herbert Schooler Jr. and Virginia Lea (Lindley) Cooper; m. Scott Newton Congdon, Oct. 17, 1981; children: San Juana, Jordan. BA in Communications, Pacific Christian Coll., 1977, MA in Urban Missions, 1989. Forwarding agt. Tijuana Christian Mission, Mexico, 1978-88; youth minister Lemon Grove (Calif.) Christian Ch., 1978-79; exec. dir., co-founder Amor Ministries, San Diego and Fullerton, Calif., 1980—; past of evangelism, missions Community Christian Ch., San Diego, 1989—; adj. prof. Pacific Christian Coll., Fullerton, 1984—; coord. World Inst., Cin., 1988—; bd. dirs. Tijuana Christian Mission, 1977—. Contg. author: Creative Urban Youth Ministry, 1990; producer: (curriculum series) Casa de Amor, 1988; creator: (manual) Project Lovetide, 1985 (Disneyland Community Svc. award 1988, 89). Vice-pres. Crawford High Sch. sch. site coun., San Diego, 1989—. Recipient Christian Svc. award Pacific Christian Coll., 1985. Democrat. Home: 4002 Olympic San Diego CA 92115 Office: Amor Ministries 7850 Golden Ave Lemon Grove CA 92045

CONGDON, ROGER DOUGLASS, theology educator, minister; b. Ft. Collins, Colo., Apr. 6, 1918; s. John Solon and Ellen Avery (Kellogg) C.; m. Rhoda Gwendolyn Britt, Jan. 2, 1948; children: Rachel Congdon Lidbeck, James R., R. Steven, Jon B., Philip F., Robert N., Bradford B., Ruth A. Mahner, Rebecca Congdon Skones, Rhoda J. Miller, Marianne C., Mark Alexander. BA, Wheaton Coll., 1940; postgrad, Eastern Bapt. Sem., 1940-41; ThM, Dallas Theol. Sem., 1945; ThD, Dallas Theology Sem., 1949. Ordained to ministry Bapt. Ch., 1945. Exec. sec., dean Altanta Bible Inst., 1945-49; prof. theology Carver Bible Inst., Atlanta, 1945-49; prof. Multnomah Sch. of the Bible, Portland, Oreg., 1950-87; pastor Emmanuel Bapt. Ch., Vancouver, Wash., 1985—; served as past dean of faculty, dean of edn., v.p., chmn. library com., chmn. achievement-award com., chmn. lectureship com., advisor grad. div. and mem. pres.'s cabinet all at Multnomah Sch. of the Bible; chmn. Chil Evang. Fellowship of Greater Portland, 1978—; founder, pres. Preaching Print Inc., Portland, 1953—. Founder, speaker semi-weekly radio broadcast Bible Truth Forum, KPDQ, Portland, Oreg., 1989—; author: The Doctrine of Conscience, 1945. Chmn. Citizen's Com. Info. on Communism, Portland, 1968-75. Recipient Outstanding Educators of Am. award, 1972, Loraine Chafer award in Systematic Theology, Dallas Theol. Sem. Mem. Am. Assn. Bible Colls. (chmn. testing com. 1953-78), N.Am. Assn. Bible Colls. (N.W. rep. 1960-63), Near East Archaeol. Soc., Evang. Theol. Soc. Republican. Home: 16539 NE Halsey St Portland OR 97230 Office: Emmanuel Bapt Ch 14810 NE 28th St Vancouver WA 98682 *A base person's problems usually consist in selecting between overt evils. The average person chooses between the shady and the good. But the truly noble person, who follows Jesus Christ, never bothers with evils or shady acts; he ever seeks to discern the transcendent, to choose the best of all good choices.*

CONGRAM, JOHN DOUGLAS, minister, editor; b. Toronto, Ont., Can., Mar. 18, 1937; s. Wilfrid Douglas and Elsie Irene (Blackhall) C.; m. Elizabeth Anne McKinney, May 13, 1961; children: Mark, Robbin, Timothy, Blair. BA, U. Western Ont., London, 1962; BD, Knox Coll., Toronto, 1965. Ordained to ministry Presbyn. Ch., 1962. Pastor St. Andrew's Ch., Biggar, Sask., Can., 1962-65, Knox/Calvin Ch., Hamilton, Ont., 1965-68; min. outreach St. Paul's Ch., Hamilton, 1968-71; pastor St. Gile's Ch., Sarnia, Ont., 1971-77, St. Mark's Ch., Don Mills, Ont., 1977-88; editor Presbyn. Record, Toronto, 1988—; mem. various coms. in East Toronto Presbytery, Synod and Gen. Assembly; mem. numerous workshops on Death and Dying, and Stories and Storytelling; active in ministerial assns. Editor The Knoxonian mag., in 1960s; contbr. articles, poems, book revs. to religious jours. Chmn. Adv. Com. on Community TV, Sarnia, 1973-76. Burgess scholar Knox Coll., 1962. Mem. Associated Ch. Press, Can. Ch. Press (exec. com.). Office: Presbyn Record, 50 Wynford Dr, Don Mills, ON Canada M3C 1J7

CONKLIN, DANIEL GEORGE, clergyman; b. Phoenixville, Pa., Sept. 27, 1943; s. Henry Clayton and Evelyn Ruth (Potts) C. B.A., Pa. State U., 1965; M. Div. with honors, Phila. Div. Sch., 1968; postgrad., Kart-Eberhards U., Fed. Republic Germany, 1970-72. Ordained to ministry Episcopal Ch. 1968. Curate St. Paul's Chestnut Hill, Phila., 1968-70; religion educator St. Moriz Roman Cath. Ch., Rottenburg, Fed. Republic Germany, 1973-77, scholarships sec. Diakonisches Werk, Stuttgart, Fed. Republic Germany, 1977-83; pastor Old Cath. Ch., Blumberg, Fed. Republic Germany, 1983—; del. Anglican Old Cath. Theol. Commn., 1982—; mem. Ecumenical Soc. Blessed Virgin Mary, Surrey, Eng., 1980—. English Speaking Union grantee, 1969. World Council Chs. scholar 1971-73. Democrat. Home and Office: Haupt Strasse 95, D-7712 Blumberg Federal Republic of Germany

CONKLIN, DEBORAH LYNN, project director; b. Toledo, June 30, 1950; d. Herbert Edward and Delores F. (Abbajay) O'Leary; m. James Norman Conklin, Aug. 25, 1973; children: Rebecca Marie, Andrew James. BA in Religious Studies, Lourdes Coll., 1991. Jobs project dir. Toledo Met. Mission, 1989—. Member adult basic edn. adv. bd. Toledo Pub. Schs., 1990—. Mem. Luth. Coalition and Conf. (dean, pres. Toledo chpt. 1989-91, sec. 1991—), Kappa Gamma Pi, Theta Alpha Kappa. Republican. Home: 9719 Schadel Waterville OH 43566 Office: Toledo Met Mission 444 Floyd Toledo OH 43620

CONLEY, CARL EDWARD, minister; b. Terre Haute, Ind., Sept. 30, 1938; s. Howard Pierce and Winifred Virginia (Roberts) C.; m. Ellene Rhoda Migliore, July 31, 1959; 1 child, Virginia Rose. BTh, Internat. Sem., 1974, MTh, 1976. Ordained to ministry Christian Covenant Ch., 1963. Missionary Assemblies of God, Springfield, Mo., 1962-74; v.p. World Changers, Tulsa, 1975-77, Don Stewart Assn., Phoenix, 1977-79; pastor Christian Life Assembly of God, Santa Fe, N.Mex., 1979-84; v.p. Don Stewart Assn., Phoenix, 1985-89; pres. The Life Link, Santa Fe, 1989—, Joy Junction, Albuquerque, 1990—, Assn. Vida, Mex., 1990—, Life Link Philippines, 1990—; Contbr. articles to various mags. Mem. Christian Law Assn., Christian Press Assn. Home: 7 Apache Ridge Rd Santa Fe NM 87505 Office: The Life Link 2325 Cerrillos Rd Santa Fe NM 87502

CONLEY, THOMAS ANTHONY, clergyman, counselor; b. Oak Hill, Ohio, Aug. 7, 1954; m. Susan B. Kemp, June 21, 1981; children: Gabriel S., Zachary D. Student, Ohio U., 1972-74; BA, Circleville (Ohio) Bible Coll., 1981; postgrad., Olivet Nazarene U., Kankakee, Ill., 1989-91. Ordained to ministry Ch. of the Nazarene, 1983. Min. Ch. of the Nazarene, Mt. Sterling, Ill., 1984-86, Crothersville, Ind., 1986-90, Salem, Ohio, 1990—; dir., pastoral counselor Nazarene Counseling Svcs., Salem, 1990—. Home: 2310 Kennedy Dr Salem OH 44460 Office: Ch Nazarene 1431 N Ellsworth Salem OH 44460

CONN, JAMES STEPHEN, clergyman; b. Leadwood, Mo., Jan. 26, 1945; s. Charles W. and Edna Louise (Minor) C.; m. Patricia Elizabeth Miller, Oct. 24, 1965; children: Gregory, Christopher, Jeremy. Grad. Lee Coll., Cleveland, Tenn., 1966; postgrad Jerusalem Cen. for Bibl. Studies, 1985. Ordained to ministry Church of God, 1966; transferred ordination to Assemblies of God, 1988. Pastor Ch. of God, Casper, Wyo., 1966-67, state youth dir., Albuquerque, 1967-68, pastor, Cleveland, Tenn., 1968-72, new field evangelist, Pineville, W.Va., 1972-73, dist. overseer, Harrisburg, Pa., 1973-77; pastor, founder Maranatha Christian Ctr., Augusta, Ga., 1977—. Mem. nat. bd. govs. Am. Coalition for Traditional Values, Washington, 1984—. Author: Damascus Appointment, 1976, Run With the Vision, 1977, Miracles Don't Just Happen, 1979, Jesus Never Called Anyone a Sinner, 1989. Contbr. articles to profl. jours. Editorial columnist Augusta Chronicle Herald, 1982—, syndicated in others. Republican. Avocations: mountain climbing, farming. Home: 1036 Conn Rd Evans GA 30809 Office: Maranatha Christian Ctr 400 Warren Rd Augusta GA 30907

CONN, WALTER EUGENE, religion educator, counselor; b. Providence, July 11, 1940; s. Earl Furness and Ethel Helen (Keough) C.; m. Joann Wolski, Oct. 14, 1972. BA, Providence Coll., 1962; MA, Boston Coll., 1966; PhL, Weston Coll., 1966; PhD, Columbia U., 1973; MS, Villanova U., 1988. Assoc. prof. Christian ethics St. Patrick's Sem., Menlo Park, Calif., 1973-78; prof. religious studies Villanova (Pa.) U., 1978—; counselor Cath. Social Svcs., West Chester, Pa., 1988—. Author: Conscience, 1981 (named Best Book Coll. Theology Soc. 1982), Conversion, 1986 (Best Book award Cath. Press Assn. 1987); also articles; editor: Christian Conversion, 1978, Mainstreaming, 1985; mem. editorial adv. bd. Religious Studies Rev., 1980—. Mem. Am. Acad. Religion, Cath. Theol. Soc. Am., Coll. Theology Soc. (bd. dirs., editor in chief Horizons jour. 1980—), Soc. for Christian Ethics, Amnesty Internat. USA, Bread for the World. Roman Catholic. Home: 25 Aldwyn Ln Villanova PA 19085 Office: Villanova U Religious Studies Dept Villanova PA 19085

CONNARE, WILLIAM GRAHAM, bishop; b. Pitts., Dec. 11, 1911; s. James J. and Nellie T. (O'Connor) C. BA, Duquesne U., 1932, LittD, 1961; MA, St. Vincent Coll., Latrobe, Pa., 1934, LHD, 1962; LLD, Seton Hill Coll., 1960. Ordained priest Roman Cath. Ch., 1936. Named domestic prelate, 1955; asst. pastor St. Canice, Pitts., 1936-37, St. Paul's Cathedral, 1937-49; adminstr. St. Richard's Ch., Pitts., 1949-55; pastor St. Richard's Ch., 1955-60; chaplain Univ. Cath. Club, Pitts., 1947-60, Cath. Interracial Council Pitts., 1953-60; dir. Soc. Propagation of Faith, 1950-59; vicar for religious as rep. Bishop of Pitts., 1959-60; consecrated bishop of Greensburg Pa., 1960—. Bd. dirs., chmn. community services com. Urban League Pitts., 1950-60; mem. Pitts. Commn. Human Relations, 1953-60; mem. Allegheny County Council Civil Rights, 1953-60, bd. dirs., 1958-60; bd. dirs. Pitts. br. NAACP, 1959-60; Episcopal chmn. Nat. Cath. Com. on Scouting, Boy Scouts Am., 1962-70; Episcopal moderator div. youth activities U.S. Cath. Conf., 1968-70; mem. Bishop's Commn. for Liturgical Apostolate, 1967-72; chmn. commn. on missions Nat. Conf. Cath. Bishops, 1967-71, mem. adminstrv. bd., 1967, chmn. com. for inter-rite affairs, 1975—; mem. Bishop's Com. on Missions, 1971; mem. council Christian Assos. Southwest Pa., 1972; chmn. Am. Bd. Cath. Missions, 1972; mem. Episcopal adv. bd. Word of God Inst., 1974; Episcopal adviser Nat. Cath. Stewardship Council, 1974; exec. bd. Cath. Relief Services, 1979-84. Address: 723 E Pittsburgh St Greensburg PA 15601 also: Neumann House 2900 Seminary Dr Greensburg PA 15601

CONNELL, DESMOND, archbishop. Archbishop of Dublin, primate of Ireland. Office: Archbishop House, Drumcondra, Dublin 9, Ireland*

CONNELL, FOSTER GLADWIN, minister, church administrator; b. Prescott, Ark., Oct. 9, 1938; s. Lewis Leonard and Clara Lou (Foster) C. BA, Hendrix, 1960; MTh, So. Meth. U., 1963; DMin, United Theol. Sem., 1991. Ordained to ministry Meth. Ch., 1961. Assoc. pastor 1st United Meth. Ch., Hope, Ark., 1963; asosc. dir. Coun. on Ministry, Little Rock, 1964; pastor St. Paul United Meth. Ch., El Dorado, 1969, 1st United Meth. Ch., Malvern, Ark., 1976; dist. supt. Camden (Ark.) Dist. United Meth. Ch., 1989—; del. gen. conf. United Meth. Ch., St. Louis, 1988, del. jurisdictional conf., New Orleans, 1988; del. World Meth. Conf., Singapore, 1992. Author: History of Malvern 1st UMC, 1986; contbr. articles to religious publs. Trustee Hendrix Coll., Conway, 1984—, Children's Home, Little Rock, 1986-89, Camp Tanako, Hot Springs, Ark., 1974-82, Camp Aldersgate, Little Rock, 1982-89; chair West Cen. Ark. Agy. Bd., Hot Springs, 1982-86, Hot Springs unit Am. Cancer Soc., Malvern, 1985-86, vice-chair Ouachita unit, Camden, 1990—. Democrat. Office: United Meth Ch 484 Elaine Ave NW Camden AR 71701

CONNELL, JACK, minister; b. Rochester, N.Y., Oct. 26, 1961; s. Melvyn Samuel and Rachel (Bence) C.; m. Wendy Kipp, May 28, 1988. BS, Houghton Coll., 1983; MDiv, Asbury Theol. Sem., 1987. Ordained to ministry Wesleyan Ch., 1988. Asst. pastor Houghton (N.Y.) Wesleyan Ch.; pastor Lyncourt Wesleyan Ch., Syracuse, N.Y., 1989—; v.p. Greater Syracuse Assn. Evangelicals, 1990—; Sun. sch. sec. Cen. N.Y. Dist. Wesleyan Ch., Syracuse, 1990—. Mem. Theta Phi. Office: Lyncourt Wesleyan Ch 2626 Court St Syracuse NY 13208

CONNELLY, BETTY FEES, lay ministries consultant; b. L.A., Apr. 13, 1924; d. Ferdinand R. and Margaret (Lewis) Fees; m. Daniel Snyder Connelly, Apr. 20, 1946; children: Richard, Kathleen, Patrick. BA, Pomona Coll., Claremont, Calif., 1945; BS in Edn., U. Minn., 1947; postgrad., Claremont Grad. Sch., 1962-63. Presiding officer Women of Ch. Triennial, Denver, 1977-80; lay min., cons. St. James Episcopal Ch., Newport Beach, Calif., 1981-83, dir. lay ministries and evang. svc. and outreach, 1988—; trustee Pension Fund Episcopal Ch., 1988—; mem. Coun. for Devel. Ministry, Anglican Fellowship of Prayer; dep. gen. conv. Episcopal Ch., 1982, 85, 88, 91. With USN, 1944-46. Republican. Home: 3706 Sea Breeze Santa Ana CA 92704 Office: St James Episcopal Ch 3209 Via Lido Newport Beach CA 92663

CONNER, DAVID EMORY, clergyman; b. Jackson, Miss., Jan. 24, 1950; s. James Sydney Jr. and Betty Jane (Langdon) C.; m. Nancy Blair Fulgham, Aug. 28, 1971; children: Rebecca Carol, James Henry Langdon, Rachel Catherine. BS, Millsaps Coll., 1972; MDiv with distinction, Iliff Sch. Theology, 1975; postgrad., Claremont Grad. Sch., 1975-76; ThD, Iliff Sch. Theology, 1981. Pastor St. James United Meth. Ch., Central City, Colo., 1974-75; assoc. pastor 1st United Meth. Ch., Golden, Colo., 1975-79; pastor Sandy Hook (Miss.) Charge United Meth. Ch., 1979-80, Americus Charge United Meth. Ch., George County, Miss., 1980-81, Cedaredge (Colo.) United Meth. Ch., 1981-86, Estes Park (Colo.) United Meth. Ch., 1986—; alternate del. western jurisdiction United Meth. Ch., San Diego, 1988-91; chair conf. rels. Cong. Bd. of Ordained Ministry, Rocky Mountain Conf., United Meth. Ch., 1988—. Author: Our 1988 Doctrinal Statement, 1988; author: (with others) Functional Philosophy of W.H. Bernhardt, 1988. Pres. Estes Park Interfaith Assn., 1989—; trustee Frasier Meadows Manor, Boulder, 1989—. Elizabeth Iliff Warren fellow Iliff Sch. Theology, 1975-76, Claremont Grad. Sch. fellow, 1975-76. Mem. Am. Acad. Religion. Democrat. Home: PO Box 1906 Estes Park CO 80517

CONNER, RONALD PARKS, priest; b. Washington, June 15, 1945; s. Francis Willard and Vivian (Parks) C. BA magna cum laude, U. of South, 1967; STB cumm laude, Gen. Theol. Sem., N.Y.C., 1970, STM, 1971; ThM, Princeton U., 1980; DMin, Drew U., 1982. Ordained priest Episcopal Ch., 1970. Curate Holy Trinity Ch., Hicksville, N.Y., 1970-71; teaching fellow Gen. Theol. Sem., 1971-72, Princeton (N.J.) U. Theol. Sem., 1972-74; assoc. All Sts. Ch., Princeton, 1974-75, curate, 1975-78; mem. staff Trinity Ch., 1976-78, St. Columba's Ch., Washington, 1978; vicar St. Martin's Ch., Martinsville, N.J., 1978-81; dean Province Deanery, 1982-88; chmn. Diocesan Continuing Edn. Com., 1982—, Diocesan Commn. on Higher Edn. Editor: Prayers for Eastertide, 1970. Mem. Phi Beta Kappa. Office: St Stephen's Ch 114 George St Providence RI 02906

CONNER, VICTOR RANDAL, camp administrator; b. Gibson City, Ill., July 16, 1953; s. Victor Kalman and Jean (Minor) C.; m. Kathryn Ann Canfield, Aug. 30, 1990; children: Joshua David, Jeremy Ryan. BA, Rockmont Coll., 1980; MA, Denver Sem., 1982. Dir. pub. rels. Rockmont Coll., Denver, 1981-85; regional rep. World Concern, Seattle, 1985-87; dir. info. svcs. Forest Home Christian Conf. Ctr., Forest Falls, Calif., 1987-89; spl. asst. to pres. Mission Aviation Fellowship, Redlands, Calif., 1989-90; mng. dir. Tonto Rim Bapt Camp, Payson, Ariz., 1990—. Author, editor mag. Rockmont Rev., 1981-85, Forest Home Life, 1987-89.

CONNERY, GLORIA JEAN, minister; b. Hartford, Conn., May 20, 1951; d. Henry Francis and Helen Alice (Lingner) C. BA, U. Conn., 1973; MDiv, Trinity Luth. Sem., Columbus, Ohio, 1989. Ordained to ministry, Evang. Luth. Ch. Am. 1990. Pastor Evang. Luth. Ch. of Redeemer, Lawrence, Mass., 1990—. Author articles, book reviews. Campaign chmn. Conn. Rep. Com., 1980; mem. Glastonbury (Conn.) Bd. Youth and Family Svcs., 1983. Mem. New Eng. Luth. Clergy Assn. (steering com.), Alban Inst., Liturgical Conf. Office: Redeemer Luth Ch 163 E Haverhill St Lawrence MA 01841

CONNICK, CHARLES MILO, retired religion educator, clergyman; b. Conneaut Lake Park, Pa., Mar. 23, 1917; s. Walter and Iola Belle (Wintermute) C.; m. Genevieve Shaul, June 7, 1941; children: Joy (Mrs. J. Bruce Parker), Christopher Milo, Nancy (Mrs. David F. Jankowski). Student, Edinboro State U., 1935-36; AB, Allegheny Coll., 1939, DD, 1960; STB, Boston U., 1942, PhD, 1944; Roswell R. Robinson fellow, Harvard U., 1942-43; postgrad., Episcopal Div. Sch., 1942-44. Ordained deacon United Meth. Ch., 1941, elder, 1942; assoc. minister St. Paul's Methodist Ch., Lowell, Mass., 1940-41, Copley Meth. Ch., Boston, 1941-42; dir. Wesley Found., Harvard U.; also minister to students Harvard Epworth Meth. Ch., Cambridge, Mass., summers 1943-44; sr. instr. pub. speaking Curry Coll., Boston, 1942-44; head Bible dept. Northfield Sch., East Northfield, Mass., 1944-46; prof. religion, chmn. dept. philosophy, religion Whittier (Calif.) Coll., 1946-82, prof. religion emeritus, 1982—; chmn. social sci. div., 1950, 60, pres. faculty senate, 1970-71, dir. coll. study tour to Europe, Middle East, around the world, summers 1955-69; pres. I-TAC, 1976-87; Danforth assoc., 1959—, Danforth sr. assoc., 1964-82; spl. lectr. Bibl. lit. Sch. Religion, First Congl. Ch., Los Angeles, 1948-61; mem. Western Pa. Conf., United Meth. Ch., 1942—; exec. sec. Presdl. Selection Com., 1969-70; cons. for colls. and univs. seeking new presidents, 1971-82; adv. council Calif. Christian Com. for Israel, 1974-82. Author: Build on The Rock, You and the Sermon on the Mount, 1960, Jesus, the Man, the Mission, and the Message, 1963, 2d edit., 1974, The Message and Meaning of the Bible, 1965, The New Testament: An Introduction to its History, Literature and Thought, 1972, 2d edit., 1978; editorial adviser to maj. pubs., 1964-88; contbr. articles to religious jours. and mags. Trustee Whittier Coll., 1982—. Recipient Distinguished Alumnus award Boston U., 1971, Gold award Allegheny Coll., 1989; C. Milo Connick chair in religion established Whittier Coll., 1982. Mem. Consumers Coop. Whittier Inc. (pres. 1949-53), AAUP (Whittier pres. 1970-72), Pacific Coast Assn. for Religious Studies (exec. com. 1947-60), Am. Acad. Religion (pres. Western Region 1953-54), Soc. Bibl. Lit., Am. Oriental Soc., Am. Christian Assn. for Israel (mem. nat. adv. com. 1964-69), Phi Sigma Tau, Kappa Phi Kappa, Chi Delta Sigma, Omicron Delta Kappa. Home: 6249 Roundhill Dr Whittier CA 90601 Office: Whittier Coll 13421 E Philadelphia St Whittier CA 90608 *Perhaps the greatest misunderstanding about courtship and marriage is the nature of love. A person does not "fall in love." Love is not an accident; it is an achievement. One falls into passion and climbs into love.*

CONNOLLY, KENNETH SCOTT, lay worker; b. Wurzberg, Fed. Republic Germany, Apr. 20, 1965; s. Marilyn Agnes Connolly-Overbey. BA, U. Notre Dame, 1987. Pastoral asst. to youth min. St. John Bosco, Tacoma, Wash., 1987—. Mem. Archdiocesan Assn. Youth Mins., Pierce County Parish Ministry Assn. (chair 1987-90), Kiwanis (bd. dirs. Clover Pk. chpt. 1988-91). Democrat. Home and Office: St John Bosco 10508 112th St SW Tacoma WA 98498

CONNOLLY, MICHAELA, nun, religious organization administrator; b. N.Y.C., Apr. 12, 1945; d. Michael James and Mary Bridget (Kiernan) C. B.S. in Edn., Dominican Coll., 1968; M.S. in Edn., Fordham U., 1973. Cert. elem. edn., N.Y.; joined Sisters of St. Dominic, Roman Catholic Ch., 1963. Tchr. Holy Spirit Sch., N.Y.C., 1967-68, St. Luke Sch., N.Y.C., 1968-72; dir. pub. relations Dominican Coll., Orangeburg, N.Y., 1972-73, dir. devel., 1973-87; pastoral assoc. St. Margaret's Ch., Pearl River, N.Y., 1987—. Mem. adv. bd. Rockland County Vicariate, 1979-86; bd. dirs. Tappan Zee Playhouse Preservation Com., 1985-87; mem. Town of Orangetown Affordable Housing Com., 1987-89. Named to Outstanding Young Women Am., U.S. Jaycees, 1977. Mem. Rockland County Assn. Home: 33 N Magnolia St Pearl River NY 10965 Office: St Margaret's Ch 115 W Central Ave Pearl River NY 10965

CONNOLLY, THOMAS JOSEPH, bishop; b. Tonopah, Nev., July 18, 1922; s. John and Katherine (Hammel) C. Student, St. Joseph Coll. and St. Patrick Sem., Menlo Park, Calif., 1936-47, Catholic U. Am., 1949-51; JCD, Lateran Pontifical U., Rome, 1952; DHL (hon.), U. Portland, 1972. Ordained priest Roman Cath. Ch., 1947. Asst. St. Thomas Cathedral, Reno, 1947, asst., rector, 1953-55; asst. Little Flower Parish, Reno, 1947-48; sec. to bishop, 1949; asst. St. Albert the Gt., Reno, 1952-53; pastor St. Albert the Gt., 1960-68, St. Joseph Ch., Elko, 1955-60, St. Theresa's Ch., Carson City, Nev., 1968-71; bishop Baker, Oreg., 1971—; Tchr. Manogue High Sch., Reno, 1948-49; chaplain Serra Club, 1948-49; officialis Diocese of Reno; chmn. bldg. com., dir. Cursillo Movement; moderator Italian Cath. Fedn.; dean, mem. personnel bd. Senate of Priests; mem. Nat. Bishops Liturgy Com., 1973-76; region XII rep. to adminstrv. bd. Nat. Conf. Cath. Bishops, 1973-76, 86-89, mem. adv. com., 1974-76; bd. dirs. Cath. Communications Northwest, 1977-82. Club: K.C. (state chaplain Nev. 1970-71). Home: 63255 Overtree Rd Bend OR 97701 Office: 911 SE Armour PO Box 5999 Bend OR 97708

CONNOR, BRIAN NICHOLS, clergyman; b. Charleston, S.C., May 23, 1946; s. George Nichols and Mary Jane (Crooks) C.; m. Vivian Faye Vickery, Sept. 6, 1969; children: Amy Beth, Carey Lynn. BA, Carson-Newman Coll., 1968; MDiv, So. Bapt. Theol. Sem., 1971, DMin, 1977. Ordained to ministry, So. Bapt. Ch., 1971. Houseparent Ky. Dept. Child Welfare, Louisville, 1968-69; lectr., asst. debate coach Bellarmine Coll., Louisville, 1969-70; staff minister Portland Bridge Mission, Crescent Hill Bapt. Ch., Louisville, 1970-71; pastor Marion St. Bapt. Ch., Aiken, S.C., 1971-75, Portside Bapt. Ch., North Charleston, S.C., 1975-83, Redland Bapt. Ch., Derwood, Md., 1983—; supr. ministry program So. Bapt. Theol. Sem., 1986; adj. faculty, Bapt. Coll. Charleston, 1981-82; moderator, Montgomery Bapt. Assn., Rockville, Md., 1985-87. Contbr. articles to various publs. Bd. dirs., Aiken County Mental Health Assn., 1975; chmn. bd. dirs., Hope Ctr. for Retarded, Charleston, 1983. Mem. Assn. Couples in Marriage Enrichment, Potomac Appalachian Trail Club. Democrat. Avocations: hunting, fishing, amateur radio. Home: 16913 Briardale Rd Derwood MD 20855 Office: Redland Bapt Ch 6922 Muncaster Mill Rd Derwood MD 20855

CONRAD, ARNOLD SPENCER, minister; b. Jersey City, Aug. 9, 1942; s. Christian and Carrie (Johnsen) C.; m. Sharon Lee Leff, June 12, 1965; children: Cynthia, Nathan. BA, Trinity Coll., Deerfield, Ill., 1965; MDiv, Trinity Evan. Div. Sch., 1969. Ordained to ministry Evang. Free Ch., 1972. Pastor Maple Ridge Evang. Free Ch., Braham, Minn., 1969-72, Marshall (Minn.) Evang. Free Ch., 1972-80, Manassas (Va.) Evang. Free Ch., 1980-83; sr. pastor Moorhead (Minn.) Evang. Free Ch., 1983-87, Grace Evang. Free Ch., Davenport, Iowa, 1987—; tchr. Moody Bible Inst., Chgo., 1991; sec. North Cen. Dist. Assn., Mpls., 1977-80, 84-86, chmn., treas., 1986-87. Contbr. articles to religious publs. Mem. Nat. Assn. Evangelicals (treas. 1988—), Evang. Fee Ch. Ministerial Assn. (sec. 1982-85), Lions (chaplain local chpt. 1977-80), Optimists. Republican. Office: Grace Evang Free Ch 5520 Eastern Ave Davenport IA 52806

CONRAD, DIETHELM, theology educator; b. Ludwigshafen, Germany, Sept. 26, 1933; s. Johannes and Elisabeth (Fraedrich) C.; m. Katharina Fett, Aug. 28, 1959; children: Till, Wiebke, Jan. Student, U. Marburg, 1953-55, U. Basel, Switzerland, 1955-56, U. Utrecht, Netherlands, 1956-58; ThD, U. Marburg, 1966. Lektor U. Marburg, 1963-75, prof. Old Testament, 1975—, dean dept. protestant theology, 1978-80. Author: Studien zum Altargesetz Ex 20:24-26, 1968. Mem. Deutscher Palestina Verein, Deutsche Orient Gesellschaft, Am. Schs. Oriental Research, Israel Exploration Soc., Wissensch. Gesellschaft für Theologie. Social Democratic Party of Ger. Home: Friedrichstrasse 5, D-3550 Marburg Federal Republic of Germany Officed: Dept Protestant Theology, Lahntor 3, D-3550 Marburg Federal Republic of Germany

CONRAD, FLAVIUS LESLIE, JR., minister; b. Hickory, N.C., May 5, 1920; s. Flavius Leslie and Mary Wilhelmina (Huffman) C.; m. Mary Elizabeth Isenhour, Nov. 4, 1944; children: Ann (Mrs. Bruce E. Meisner), Susan (Mrs. James A. Amis). AB, Lenoir Rhyne Coll., 1941; MDiv, Luth. Theol. So. Sem., 1944; MST, Temple U., 1955, STD, 1959. Ordained to ministry Evang. Luth. Ch. Am., 1944. Pastor St. Timothy Luth. Ch., Hickory, 1944-49, Holy Comforter Luth. Ch., Belmont, N.C., 1949-50; youth dir. United Luth. Ch. Am., Phila., 1950-60; pastor St. Luke's Luth. Ch., Richardson, Tex., 1960-86, pastor emeritus, 1986—; dean Dallas and East Tex. dist. Luth. Ch. Am., 1973-77, mem. publ. bd., 1974-82; del. convs. Luth. Ch. Am., 1968, 74, 76; exec. sec. Luther League Am., 1950-60; mem. exec. bd. and gen. assembly Nat. Coun. Chs. of Christ in U.S.A., 1954-60. Author: A Study of Four Non-Denominational Youth Movements, 1955, Poetic Potshots at People and Preachers, 1977; contbg. editor Ch. Mgmt. mag., 1966-74; corr. The Lutheran from S.W., 1962-87; contbr. sermons, articles and poems to various mags. V.p. Piedmont (N.C.) coun. Boy Scouts Am., 1948-49. Winner Nat. Poetry Contest, 1960. Home: 1108 Pueblo Dr Richardson TX 75080

CONRAD, HAROLD AUGUST, pension board executive; b. Cleve., Dec. 18, 1928; s. August and Olga (Heise) C.; m. Anne (Chernosky) Conrad, July 10, 1948 (widowed Mar. 1956); children: Deborah Anne Hamer, Loren Harold Conrad, Rebecca Faith Towle; m. Naomi Ruth (Sweeny) Conrad, Dec. 31, 1960; 1 child, Paul Alan Conrad. BA, Anderson U., Ind., 1952; MDiv, Christian Theo. Sem., Indpls., 1970; DD, Mid-Am. Bible Coll., Oklahoma City, 1975. Pastor Akron Ch. of God, Akron, Ind., 1952-63, First Ch. of God, Winchester, Ky., 1963-66, Glendale Ch. of God, Indpls., 1966-74; exec. sec. treas. Bd. of Pensions of Ch. of God, Anderson, Ind., 1974—; state chmn. Ind. Ministerial Assembly, Indpls., 1961-62; vice chmn. Ky. Ministerial Assembly, Winchester, Ky., 1965-66; bd. mem. Bd. of Pensions of Ch. of God, Anderson, Ind., 1964-74; bd. dirs. Exec. Coun. of Ch. of God, Anderson, Ind., 1976-84, 87-90. Mem. Nat. Ch. Pensions Conf. (pres. 1985), Kiwanis. Republican. Mem. Ch. of God. Avocations: stamp collecting, gardening, walking, reading, traveling. Home: 810 Northwood Dr Anderson IN 46011

CONRAD, JUANA CAROL, court administrator; b. Callaway, Nebr., July 4, 1939; d. Norris Elwood and Madeline Gwendolyn (Stapelman) Whaley; m. James Edward Williams, Feb. 7, 1959 (div. July 1963); m. Samuel Charles Conrad, Sept. 2, 1966; children: Scott James, Jason Charles. Asst. supr. Los Angeles Mcpl. Ct., 1964-65, supr., 1965-66, ct. clk., 1966-79, dep. chief, 1979-82; ct. adminstr. East Los Angeles Mcpl. Ct., 1982—. Pres. Women for Internat. Peace and Arbitration, Glendale, Calif., 1985, founder; appointed to nat. com. on women Baha'is of U.S. Fellow Inst. Ct. Mgmt.; mem. Mcpl. Cts. Los Angeles, Assn. of Los Angeles County Mcpl. Ct. Adminstrs. (mem. jury auto. com. 1982—), Nat. Assn. Trial Ct. Adminstrs. Avocation: skiing. Office: East Los Angeles Mcpl Ct 4837 E Third St Los Angeles CA 90022

CONRAD, LARRY WAYNE, pastor; b. E. St. Louis, Ill., July 11, 1961; s. Wayne Melvin and Phyllis Ann (Schroll) C.; m. Mary Beth Baker, June 29, 1985; children: Benjamin Michael, David Wayne. BA, Graceland Coll., 1983; postgrad., Vanderbilt U., 1983-84; MDiv, Emory U., 1988. Ordained to ministry Meth. Ch., 1987. Pastor Aragon (Ga.) United Meth. Ch., 1986-88, Polk City (Iowa) United Meth. Ch., 1988—, Hopkins Grove United Meth. Ch., Madrid, Iowa, 1988—. Merit badge counselor Polk City Boy Scouts Am., 1988—. Emory U. scholar, 1986-87, Charles S. Wright scholar Emory U., 1987-88. Mem. Iowa Ann. Con. United Meth. Ch., Kiwanis (program chair Polk City chpt. 1988-89, bd. dirs. 1989-91 local chpt.), Madrid Ministerial Assn. (sec., treas. 1989-91, pres. 1991—). Home: 503 Broadway PO Box 185 Polk City IA 50226 Office: United Meth Ch 11905 NW Madrid Dr Box 185 Polk City IA 50226

CONRAD, LOLA IRENE, religious association administrator; b. Dayton, Ohio, May 14, 1943; d. Basil Henry and Jeanette Mae (Goins) Fourman; m. Gary F. Arnett, Feb. 17, 1962 (div. Aug. 1973); children: Rick G., Janie Lynn; m. Duane E. Conrad, June 28, 1978. Student, Sinclair Coll., 1973—. Owner Verona (Ohio) Cafe, 1970-73; adminstrn. sec. Gen. Council on Ministries United Meth. Ch., Dayton, 1973-86, dir. council ops., 1987—. Mem. Nat. Assn. Cert. Profl. Secs., Profl. Assn. United Meth. Ch. Secs., Cert. Profl. Sec. Acad. (cert.), Religious Conf. Mgmt. Assn., Nat. Assn. Female Execs. Republican. Avocations: travel, reading. Office: United Meth Ch Gen Council on Ministries 601 W Riverview Ave Dayton OH 45406

CONRAD, TRUDE LOIS, religious organization administrator; b. Gregory, S.D., June 13, 1923; d. Clifford and Licy (Horton) Ketchum; m. Ray Conrad, July 6, 1947 (dec. Oct. 1990); 1 child, Kent. Student, Kletzing Coll., University Park, Iowa, 1942-43, Bethany Nazarene Coll., 1946-47. Missionary pres. Ch. of the Nazarene, Denver, 1972-79; sec. dist. missions Colo. Dist. Nazarene, Denver, 1979-82, pres. dist. missions, 1982—; adminstrv. asst. Ch. of the Nazarene, Denver, 1969—; gen. coun. Internat. Ch. of the Nazarene, Kansas City, Mo., 1989—; bd. regents N.W. Nazarene Coll., Nampa, Idaho, 1984—. Office: Lakewood Ch of the Nazarene 1755 Dover Denver CO 80217

CONREY, THERON ALBERT, minister; b. Oskaloosa, Iowa, Mar. 4, 1948; s. Duane Moore and Madeline Jeanne (Grate) C.; m. M. Susan Anderson, Apr. 14, 1972; 1 child, Theron A. Jr. AS, Cuyahoga Community Coll., 1974; BGS, Drake U., 1980; MDiv, Dubuque Theol. Sem., 1986. Ordained to ministry Presbyn. Ch., 1987. Physician asst. Davis Clinic, Marion, Ind., 1974-75; physician asst. V.A. Hosp., Marion, 1975-77, Des Moines, 1977-83; chaplain Iowa Meth. Med. Ctr., Des Moines, 1986-87; pastor Community United Presbyn. Ch., Hartford, Iowa, 1987—; counselor Dubuque Counseling Ctr., 1984-86. Vol. Hartford Fire and Rescue Dept., 1987—; scoutmaster boy Scouts Am., 1988—; chaplain Iowa Air Guard, Des Moines, 1988—. With USN, 1967-71, Res. Mem. Nat. Assn. Clergy Hypnotists, Assn. Advancement Ethical Hypnosis. Hartford Lodge. Avocations: blacksmithing, rifles, hunting, fishing, camping. Home: PO Box 48 235 N Washington St Hartford IA 50118 Office: Community United Presbyn Ch PO Box C Hartford IA 50118

CONSTANT, CHRISTOPHER ANDREW, lay worker; b. Dixon, Calif., Feb. 11, 1966; s. Barbara Ann (Duncan) C. Diploma, Nat. Bus. Coll., Sioux Falls, S.D., 1986; student, Moody Bible Inst., Chgo., 1990—. Sunday Sch. tchr. Trinity Ch., Greensboro, N.C., 1987—, youth leader, 1987-89, youth dir., 1989—; sales rep. Hilti Fastening Systems, Inc., Greensboro, 1987—; softball coach Trinity Ch., 1990—. Author poetry (awards 1984). Republican. Avocations: wildlife, judo, softball. Home: 3546 B Lynnhaven Dr Greensboro NC 27409 Office: Trinity Church 5200 W Friendly Ave Greensboro NC 27410

CONSTANTELOS, DEMETRIOS JOHN, priest, educator; b. Spilia, Greece, July 27, 1927; came to U.S., 1955; naturalized, 1958; s. John and Christine (Psilopoulos) C.; m. Stella Croussouloudis, Aug. 15, 1954; children: Christine, John, Eleni, Maria. BTh, Holy Cross Sch. Theology, 1958; ThM, Princeton Theol. Sem., 1959; MA, Rutgers U., 1963, PhD, 1965. Ordained priest Greek Orthodox Ch., 1955. Pastor St. Demetrios, Perth Amboy, N.J., 1955-64, St. Nicholas Ch., Lexington, Mass., 1965-67; interim pastor St. Barbara Ch., Toms River, N.J., 1972-74, St. Anthony Ch., Vineland, N.J., 1975-82, Holy Trinity Ch., Northfield, N.J., 1982-89; prof. Holy Cross Sem., Brookline, Mass., 1965-71; prof. history Stockton State Coll., Pomona, N.J., 1971-86, Charles Cooper Townsend Disting. prof. history and religious studies, 1986—; mem. Orthodox-Cath. Theol. Consultation, 1965-84, New Rev. Standard Version Bible Com., 1974—, Anglican-Orthodox Theol. Consultation. Author: Byzantine Philanthropy, 1968, 2d edit. 1991, Understanding the Greek Orthodox Church, 1982, 2d edit., 1990, Poverty, Society and Philanthropy in the Late Mediaeval Greek World, 1991; editor: Encyclicals, 1976, Orthodox Theology, 1981; assoc. editor Greek Theol. Rev., 1971—, Jour. Ecumenical Studies, 1976—. Lane Cooper fellow Rutgers U., 1962, Jr. fellow Dumbarton Oaks, 1964. Mem. Orthodox Theol. Soc. (pres. 1968-71), Soc. for Ch. History, Am. Hist. Assn., Medieval Acad. Am., Modern Greek Studies Assn., U.S. Nat. Com. for Byzantine Studies. Home: 304 Forest Dr Linwood NJ 08221 Office: Stockton State Coll Pomona NJ 08240

CONSTANTINE, CLEMENT, charitable organization administrator. Dir. Cath. Charities, Ft. Worth. Office: Cath Charities 1404 Hemphill Fort Worth TX 76104*

CONTOIS, JOY FAITH, religion educator, biblical archaeologist; b. Haverhill, Mass., July 1, 1943; d. Harding Lawton and Florence Nora (Riley) Porter; m. John Sewell Contois, Mar. 17, 1962; children: Kimberly, William, Pamela, Deborah. Student, Fitchburg State Coll., 1978-87; BA, Logos Bible Coll., San Diego, 1988; MA in Theol. Studies, Gordon-Conwell Theol. Sem., South Hamilton, Mass., 1991. Lic. lay speaker Meth. Ch. Educator, sec. Assembly of God Ch., Fitchburg, Mass., 1974-81; educator, interim pastor Fitchburg Meth. Ch., 1986; educator Pilgrim Covenant Ch., Lunenburg, Mass., 1986—; substitute tchr. Oakmont Regional High Sch., Ashburnham, Mass., 1988—; lectr. in field, various groups, retreats, confs. and chs. throughout New Eng., 1976—; v.p. leadership tng. Southeastern New Eng. area Bd. Women's Aglow Fellowship, 1980-81; art dir., tchr. Trinity Christian Academy, Fitchburg, Mass., 1980; tour guide to Israel, Jordon, and Egypt, 1984—. Designed (teaching tool) scaled model of Mosaic Tabernacle, 1979; contbr. articles to newspapers. Mem. Women's Rep. Club Mass., 1978—. Mem. Biblical Archaeol. Soc., Found. Bibl. Rsch. Home: 106 Phillips St Fitchburg MA 01420-3710

CONWAY, EDWIN MICHAEL, priest, church administrator; b. Chgo., Mar. 6, 1934; s. Edwin Michael and Nellie Veronica (Rooney) C. ThM, St. Mary of the Lake Sem., Mundelein, Ill., 1960; MSW, Loyola U., Chgo., 1970. Ordained priest Roman Cath. Ch.; lic. social worker, Ill. Assoc. pastor St. Bonaventure Parish, Chgo., 1960-65; assoc. pastor St. Mary of the Lake Parish, Chgo., 1965-67, priest-in-residence, 1967—; dir. dept. human svcs. Archdiocese of Chgo., 1991—; assoc. adminstr. Cath. Charities, Archdiocese of Chgo., 1967-83, dept. dir., 1970-78, div. mgr., 1978-83, adminstr., 1983—, nat. treas., 1985-91. Editor manuals. Bd. dirs. citizens com. Juvenile Ct., Chgo., 1985-90; bd. dirs. planning com. United Way Chgo., 1985-88; mem. planning com. Crusade of Mercy, met. Chgo., 1988—; mem. Mayor's Com. for a Clean Chgo., 1990. Decorated knight comdr. Order of Holy Sepulcher (Italy); award South Chgo. Legal Clinic, 1988, Outstanding Svc. award United Way Chgo., 1988, Alumni Citation award Loyola U. Alumni Assn., 1989. Mem. Cath. Conf. Ill. (social svc. com. 1971—), Coun. Community Svcs. (adv. vol. com. 1971-75), Nat. Conf. Cath. Charities (bd. dirs. 1973-78). Office: Cath Charities 126 N Desplaines Chicago IL 60661

CONWAY, LYNDA DIANE, minister; b. Longview, Tex., Dec. 26, 1951; d. Denis Austin and Betty Jean (Gilbert) Sheeran. BS, Stephen F. Austin State U., 1973; MA, Southwestern Bapt. Theol. Sem., Ft. Worth, 1975. Dir. childhood edn. Allandale Bapt. Ch., Austin, Tex., 1975-77; dir. edn. Manchaca (Tex.) Bapt. Ch., 1983-85; ch. adminstr. Cen. Christian Ch., Austin, 1985-88; min. 1st Christian Ch., Lexington, Tex., 1988—; treas. Camp and Conf. Dept. Bluebonnet Area, San Antonio, 1986-90; Bluebonnet Area rep. Tex. Conf. Chrs., Austin, 1989—; 1st vice moderator Bluebonnet Area Christian Ch., San Antonio, 1990—. Mem. Lee County Coun. on Drug/Alcohol Abuse, Giddings, Tex., 1989—; founding mem. Lexington Inreach, 1990—. Mem. Austin Bus. and Profl. Women (Woman of Yr. 1989, parlimentarian 1989—), Lexington Ministerial Alliance, Lions (sec. Lexington chpt. 1990—). Office: 1st Christian Ch PO Box 406 Lexington TX 78947-0406

COOK, BOBBY RAY, minister; b. Searcy, Ark., Apr. 5, 1946; s. Billy Bob and Dura Winefred (Tidwell) C.; m. Helen Hoyle, Apr. 18, 1969; children: Connie Renae, Bobby Rex. BA, Quachita Bapt. U., 1979; postgrad., Midwestern Bapt. Theol. Sem., 1990—. Pastor Raynor Grove Bapt. Ch., McCrory, Ark., 1974-75, Mt. Bethel Bapt. Ch., Arkadelphia, Ark., 1975, DeGray Bapt. Ch., Arkadelphia, 1976-80, First Bapt. Higginson, Ark., 1980-84, First Bapt. Ch. Curtis, Ark., 1984-87, Park Hill Bapt., Arkadelphia, 1987—. Alderman City Coun., McRae, Ark., 1975. With U.S. Army, 1965-67. Named to Outstanding Young Man of Am., 1976. Mem. Arkadelphia Ministerial Alliance, Red River Bapt. Assn. (chmn. nominating com. 1985-86, assn. moderator 1986-88, pastoral ministries dir. 1989-90). Republican. Home: 2600 Sylvia St Arkadelphia AR 71923 Office: Park Hill Bapt Ch 2410 Pine St Arkadelphia AR 71923

COOK, CARL EDWARD, religious association administrator; b. Paintsville, Ky., Aug. 19, 1952; s. David and Ruby (Castle) C.; m. Carol Ann Hix, Mar. 17, 1973 (div. Mar. 1990); children: Stephanie Dawn, Mark Douglas. AA, Southwestern Assemblies of God, 1980, BS, 1981. Ordained to ministry Assemblies of God, 1976. Rep. Christian edn. Denton sect., North Tex. dist. Assemblies of God, 1981-84; pastor 1st Assembly of God, Princeton, Tex., 1981-83; children's pastor San Jacinto Assembly of God, Amarillo, Tex., 1989-90; adminstrv. asst. Forest Hill Assembly of God, Amarillo, 1990—; telephone operator Southwestern Bell Telephone Co., Amarillo, 1991—. Home: 2703 S Seminole Amarillo TX 79103 *In my life I have learned to place my faith and trust in God and not in man. Man, even your closest friend, will fail you, but God will never fail you.*

COOK, CHARLES LOWELL, business administrator; b. Shelbyville, Ky., Apr. 23, 1927. Student, Georgetown Coll., 1946-48; BA, Transylvania U., 1950. Bus mgr. Immanuel Bapt. Ch., Lexington, Ky., 1980-89, bus. adminstr., 1989—. Mem. Nat. Assn. Ch. Bus. Adminstrn. (fellow, pres. Ky. chpt. 1982-83, 89-90), So. Bapt. Ch. Bus. Adminstrn. (cert. ch. bus. adminstrn.). Office: Immanuel Bapt Ch 3100 Tates Creek Rd Lexington KY 40515

COOK, CLAUDE, minister; b. Eastman, Ga., Feb. 20, 1936; s. Robert Lee and Celestia (Rogers) C.; m. Bertha L. Taylor, Sept. 2, 1966. Diploma in Christian ministry, Ga. Bapt. Conv., 1979, cert., 1983. Ordained to ministry So. Bapt. Conv. Min. gospel film Cook's Visual Aids, Eastman, 1976-83; pastor Bethel Bapt. Ch, Eastman, 1984-86; interim pastor Sweet Home and

Browndale Chs., Eastman, 1986-87; pastor Dubois Bapt. Ch., Eastman, 1987—. With U.S. Army, 1954-57; with USN, 1959-61. Home: Rte 4 Box 369 Eastman GA 31023-9236

COOK, DONALD RAY, pastor; b. L.A., May 24, 1943; s. Burnie and Ardie Mae (Dewitt) C.; m. Debra Rue Cotton, Nov. 1981; children: Chisha Christine, Donald R. II, Barrington Jason. BA, Pepperdine U., 1976; MA, Eula Wesley U., 1984; DD (hon.), L.A. Bible Coll. and Sem., 1986; PhD, Eula Wesley U., 1990. Lic. to ministry Chs. of God in Christ, 1966; ordained, 1972; cert. mental health counselor. Chaplain L.A. County Jail Sheriffs Dept., 1973-76; sr. pastor, organizer Calif. Harvest Tabernacle Ch., L.A., 1976—; police clergy coun. L.A. Police Dept., 1970—; exec. bd. Southwest Ecclesiastic Jurisdiction of Calif., 1988—, supt. of 4th dist., 1988—; commr. edn. Chs. of God in Christ, Santa Monica, Calif., 1988—; reserve L.A. Police Dept., 1990—; bd. dirs. Pentecostal Heritage Found., L.A., 1989—; rsch. cons. in field; acad. tutor, Dublin Magnet Sch., L.A., 1991; lectr., West Coast Coll. Assn., Calif., 1974-79; pub. rels., L.A. Police Dept., 1991. With U.S. Army, 1966-68. Mem. Martinist Soc., Ancient Mystic Order Rosicrucian, Internat. Soc. Athletes (life). Office: Calif Harvest Tabernacle Ch 1744 E 55th St Los Angeles CA 90058 *I have found that there is an external spirit which, when followed, leads one to fulfillment and contentment.*

COOK, DOUGLAS JOHN, deacon, manufacturing executive; b. South Bend, Ind., Oct. 4, 1944; s. Everett Clarence and Lillian Irene (Weinkauf) C.; m. Sheila Frances Welch, June 12, 1965; children: Troy, Todd. BS in Indsl. Engring., Purdue U., 1967. Ordained to ministry Roman Cath. Ch. as deacon, 1979. Deacon San Antonio Cath. Ch., Anaheim, Calif., 1979—; mgr. mfg. Hughes Aircraft Co., Fullerton, Calif., 1983—; bd. dirs. San Antonio Homeless Ministry, Anaheim, 1986-91.

COOK, FREDERICK WILLIAM, minister; b. Watertown, N.Y.; s. Floyd Albert and Mary Rosina (Stephenson) C.; m. Aletha Beverley Brown, June 29, 1952; children: Alan, Frederick. BA, St. Lawrence U., 1953, BDiv, 1955; MA, Syracuse U., 1961. Ordained to ministry United Meth. Ch., 1953. Pastor Colton (N.Y.) United Meth. Ch., 1951-55, St. Johnsville (N.Y.) United Meth. Ch., 1955-57; asoc. pastor Rome (N.Y.) United Meth. Ch., 1960-64, Hollywood (Calif.) First United Meth. Ch., 1964-70; pastor Community Ch., Blythe, Calif., 1970-73, S. Pasadena (Calif.) Ch., 1973-89, Westchester United Meth. Ch., L.A., 1989—; dir. Wesley Found., Calif. State U., L.A., 1972—, Baker Home for Retired Religious Workers, Rowland Hts., Calif., 1986—; pres. Westchester-Ladera Hts. Clergy Assn., 1990—. Mem. S. Pasadena Unified Sch. Bd. Trustees, 1981-85. Office: Westchester United Meth Ch 8065 Emerson Ave Los Angeles CA 90045

COOK, GARRY DAVID, pastoral counselor; b. Louisville, Jan. 3, 1953; s. Ben J. and Irene (Taylor) C. BA, Campbellsville (Ky.) Coll., 1977; M Div., So. Bapt. Theol. Seminary, 1980. Pastor White Oak Bapt. Ch., Columbia, Ky., 1974-75, Grace Union Bapt. Ch., Edmonton, Ky., 1975-77; assoc. pastor River View Bapt. Ch., Cox's Creek, Ky., 1977-79; pastor Pleasant Mount Bapt. Ch., Remlap, Ala., 1981-84; Pastor Mt. Olive Bapt. Ch., Trussville, Ala., 1984-87; pastoral care/counseling resident Bapt. Med. Ctrs., Birmingham, Ala., 1984—. Recipient Joe Boone Abbott Research award Bapt. Med. Ctrs. 1985. Mem. Assn. Clin. Pastoral Edn., Am. Assn. Pastoral Counselors. Democrat. Club: Bookbinders Fellowship (pres. 1979-80). Avocations: guitar, backpacking, electronics, radio. Office: Pastoral Counseling & Edn 750 Montclair Birmingham AL 35213

COOK, JAMES IVAN, clergyman, religion educator; b. Grand Rapids, Mich., Mar. 8, 1925; s. Cornelius Peter and Cornelia (Dornbos) C.; m. Jean Rivenburgh, July 8, 1950; children: Mark James, Carol Jean, Timothy Scott, Paul Brian (dec.). B.A., Hope Coll., 1948; M.A., Mich. State U., 1949; B.D., Western Theol. Sem., 1952; Th.D., Princeton Theol. Sem., 1964. Ordained to ministry Reformed Ch. America, 1953. Pastor Blawenburg Reformed Ch., N.J., 1953-63; instr. bibl. langs. Western Theol. Sem., Holland, Mich., 1963-65, asst. prof. bibl. langs., 1965-67, prof. bibl. langs. and lit., 1967-77, Anton Biemont prof. N.T., 1977—; chmn. Theol. Commn., Reformed Ch. Am. N.Y.C., 1980-85; pres. Gen. Synod-Reformed Ch. Am., N.Y.C., 1982-83. Author: Edgar Johnson Goodspeed, 1981, Shared Pain and Sorrow: Reflections of a Secondary Sufferer, 1991, One Lord/One Body, 1991; editor Reformed Rev.; contbg. editor: Grace Upon Grace, 1975; book rev. editor: Perspectives, A Journal of Reformed Thought, 1986—; contbg.: Saved by Hope, 1978, The Church Speaks, 1985. Served with U.S. Army, 1943-45, ETO. Mem. Soc. Bibl. Lit. Home: 1004 S Shore Dr Holland MI 49423 Office: Western Theol Sem 86 E 12th St Holland MI 49423

COOK, JOHN KEITH, minister; b. Madrid, Nebr., Feb. 21, 1935; s. John Edward and Angie Elizabeth (Carlsen) C.; m. Ruth L. Ollis, Aug. 17, 1956; children: Andrew J., J. Paul, C. Todd. BA, Hastings Coll., 1957; Master of Divinity, San Francisco Theol. Sem., 1960, Doctor of Ministry, 1979. Ordained to ministry Presbyn. Ch. (U.S.A.), 1960. Pastor Union Presbyn. Ch., Belden, Nebr., 1960-70, United Presbyn. Ch., Laurel, Nebr., 1960-70; sr. pastor Presbyn. Ch. of the Master, Omaha, 1970-90; ch. cons., seminar dir., 1990—; pastor Underwood Hills Presbyn. Ch., Omaha, 1990—; adj. prof. continuing edn. Dubuque (Iowa) Theol. Sem., 1989—; bd. dirs. the Omaha Sem. Found., The U. of Dubuque; officer, Support Agy. of Gen. Assembly, N.Y.C., 1975-87. Author: The First Parish, 1983, Six Stages of a Pastor's Life, 1990. Bd. dirs. N.E. Nebr. Community Coll., Norfolk, 1967-70; chmn. The Nat. Found. March of Dimes, Nebr., 1963-72. Republican. Avocations: writing, seminar leadership, geneaology. Home and Office: 9816 Sprague St Omaha NE 68134-3713 *To me, the key words are 'Be kind and do good!'—not to garner salvation but as an expression of salvation.*

COOK, MARSHA EICHENBERG, religious organization administrator; b. Jefferson City, Mo., Dec. 3, 1943; d. Barnett Samuel and Iona Katherine (Hudson) E.; m. Duane Wilbert Cook, Nov. 29, 1980; 1 child, Joshua Barnett. BS in Edn., U. Mo., 1965; M in Religious Edn., So. Bapt. Theol. Sem., Louisville, 1969. Tchr. speech, drama and debate, pub. high sch. Buchannan County Schs., St. Joseph, Mo., 1965-67; dir. weekday activities 4th Ave. Bapt. Ch., Louisville, 1968-69; dir. Christian Social Ministries Etowah Bapt. Assn./So. Bapt. Home Mission Bd., Gadsden, Ala., 1969-76, Wilmington (N.C.) Bapt. Assn./So. Bapt. Home Mission Bd., 1977-89, Bapt. State Conv. N.C., Wilmington, 1977—; dir. ch. and coummunity ministries Raleigh (N.C.) Bapt. Assn., 1989—; sr. adult cons. So. Baptist Sunday Sch. Bd., 1978—; adv. conversational English/literacy New Hanover and Pender Cos., N.C., 1977—, Christian life and pub. affairs New Hanover and Pender Cos., 1985—. Contbr. articles to Ch. Tng. and Recreation mags.; contbr. to several books on recreation. Chmn. adv. coun. Ret. Sr. Vol. program, New Hanover County, 1980—; co-chmn., then chmn. Fetal Alcohol Task Force, New Hanover County, 1985-87; chmn. Nursing Home Community Adv. Bd., New Hanover County, 1980-87; active Community Council Women's Correctional Facility, New Hanover County, 1977—, chmn., 1978-81; dir. Summer Recreation Programs for Inner City, Wilmington, 1977—; mem. adult Sunday sch. benevolence com. Wrightsboro Bapt. Ch., Wilmington, also adult Sunday sch. mission leader; bd. dirs. N.C. Literacy Coun., 1990; mem. task force for Healthy Mother, Healthy Baby, Wake County Health Dept., 1990, N.C. Farmworker Coun., 1990; chmn. arrangements Raleigh Cropwalk for World Hunger, 1989-91; chmn. bd. trustees N.C. Literacy Assn., 1991; mem. community resources coun. Raleigh Correctional Ctr. for Women. Home: 901 Buckhorn Rd Garner NE 27529 Office: Raleigh Bapt Assn 2600 New Bern Ave Raleigh NC 27610

COOK, ROBERT BRUCE, JR., minister; b. Attleboro, Mass., Dec. 21, 1943; s. Robert Bruce and Elizabeth Ann (Plattner) C.; m. Sandy Elizabeth Mastin, Nov. 1, 1987; children: Robert III, Jonathan Aldan, David Christopher. BS, BA, No. Mich. U., 1967; postgrad., Wayne State U., 1967-69; MDiv, Episcopal Theol. Sch., Cambridge, Mass., 1973; D Ministry, U. of the South, 1979. Ordained to ministry Episcopal Ch. as deacon, 1973, as priest, 1974. Asst. St. John's Ch., Plymouth, Mich., 1973-75, St. Mary's Ch., Tampa, Fla., 1975-77; asst. to bishop Diocese of S.E. Fla., Miami, 1977-80; rector St. David's Ch., Lakeland, Fla., 1980-86; assoc. priest St. Francis Ch., Greensboro, N.C., 1986—; chaplain St. Peter's Home for Boys, Detroit, 1973-75, St. Francis Day Sch., 1986—; adj. chaplain Moses Cone Hosp., Greensboro, 1988—. Co-author: Managament Theory and Practice, 1969. Bd. dirs. YMCA, Lakeland, 1983-86, United Cerebral Palsey, Greensboro, 1987—; support mem. Greensboro Human Rels. Commn., 1987-89. Office: St Francis Ch 3506 Lawndale Dr Greensboro NC 27408-2804

COOK, RONALD J., school system administrator. Supt. Cath. edn. Buffalo. Office: Office Supt Cath Edn 795 Main St Buffalo NY 14222*

COOK, RUSSELL LYNN, minister; b. Harrisburg, Ill., Feb. 15, 1954; s. Lynn O. and Ann (Lemon) C.; m. Rhonda L. Warpula, June 17, 1977; children: Allison M. and Michael L. BS, Freed-Hardeman Coll., 1976; MS, Abilene Christian U., 1988, MDiv, 1986-89. Min. Ch. of Christ, Miami, Fla., 1976-79, Memphis, 1979-81, West Point, Miss., 1981-82, Albany, Ga., 1982-91, Jackson, Tenn., 1991—; pres. South Ga. Christian Acad., 1983-85. Named one of Outstanding Young Men of Am., 1983, 85. Republican. Avocations: hunting, fishing. Home: 36 Valleyview Cir Jackson TN 38305 Office: North Jackson Ch of Christ 2780 Hwy 45 Bypass Jackson TN 38305

COOK, WILLIAM ROBERT, theology educator; b. Portland, Oreg., Nov. 18, 1928; s. Floyd Newton and Alice (Schmidt) C.; m. Elaine Lucille Johnson, June 8, 1951; children: David, Kimberly. BA, Westmont Coll., 1951; ThM, Dallas Theol. Sem., 1955, ThD, 1960; postgrad., Hebrew U., Jerusalem, Israel, 1975. Pastor Galvin (Wash.) Bible Chapel, 1955-58; assoc. prof. theology Northwestern Coll., Mpls., 1960-65; dean of students Western Conservative Bapt. Sem., Portland, 1966-69, acad. v.p., 1969-86, prof. bibl. theology, 1965—. Author: Theology of John, 1979; author chpt. in book: God What is He Like?, 1977; contbr. numerous articles to profl. jours. Mem. Evang. Theol. Soc. Avocation: rose gardening. Office: Western Conservative Bapt Sem 5511 SE Hawthorne Blvd Portland OR 97215

COOKE, E(LBERT) RONALD, III, pastor; b. Balt., July 14, 1963; s. Elbert Ronald Jr. and Dorothy Ann (Wildner) C.; m. Barbara Lynn Hoegger, June 30, 1985. BDiv, Concordia Coll., 1985; MDiv, Concordia Theol. Sem., 1988. Pastor Divine Shepherd Luth. Ch., Bolinbrook, Ill., 1988—. Chaplain Bolingbrook Fire Dept., 1989—, Bolingbrook Police Dept., 1990—. Mem. No. Ill. Confessional Luths. (sec. 1988—, 90, Evangelism rep. 1989—), Concordia Theol. Sem. Alumni Assn. Office: Divine Shepherd Luth Ch 985 Lily Cache Ln Bolingbrook IL 60440

COOKE, HARLAN WALTER, minister; b. Elkhart, Kans., Aug. 19, 1936; s. Walter Abbot and Pearl Ethel (Hanna) C.; m. Barbara June Dixon, Dec. 7, 1957; children: Monica Joan Cooke Barringer, Laura June Cooke Hunter, Stephen Harlan, Eric Walter. Grad. in theology, Bapt. Bible Coll., Springfield, Mo., 1964; DD, Covington Theol. Inst., Rossville, Ga., 1982; DD (hon.), Internat. Bible Inst., Orlando, Fla., 1983. Ordained to ministry Ind. Bible Bapt. Ch., 1964. Pastor Bible Bapt. Ch., Talhequah, Okla., 1965-66, 1st Bapt. Ch., Walsh, Colo., 1966-68, Fellowship Bapt. Ch., Lincoln, Nebr., 1968-79, Grace Bapt. Ch., Madison Heights, Va., 1979—; dir. Bapt. Bible Fellowship Internat., Springfield, 1977—, mission field rep., 1980-83; dir. Atlantic Bapt. Bible Coll., Chester, Va., 1991—; chmn. Va. Bapt. Bible Fellowship, Gainesville, Va., 1982-84, Nebr. Bapt. Bible Fellowship, 1970-75. Presenter messages weekly radio program Hour of Victory, 1979-89; contbr. articles to newspapers and mags. Area chmn. Am. Coalition for Traditional Values, Washington, 1984-86; trustee Temple Deaf Coll., Kansas City, Mo., 1978. Recipient Plaque award Taiwan Bapt. Bible Fellowship, 1982, award Australian Bapt. Bible Fellowship, 1988, Asia for Christ, 1991. Republican. Home: 117 Hilltop Dr Madison Heights VA 24572 Office: Grace Bapt Ch 1312 Lakeview Dr Madison Heights VA 24572 *As I look back upon my years of Christian experience, two very important things stand out as being imperative. First is to know Jesus Christ as a personal savior, and secondly is to find and get into God's perfect will.*

COOKE, MARK GRISHAM, pastor; b. Abilene, Tex., May 24, 1954; s. Paul Raymond and Bette Jo (Grisham) C.; m. Roseann Beha, Aug. 11, 1979; children: Matthew Shawn, Nathan Paul. Student, Baylor U., 1975-77; MusB with honors, U. Louisville, 1979; M in Ch. Music, So. Bapt. Theol. Sem., Louisville, 1981. Ordained to ministry Bapt. Ch., 1982. Min. music 1st Bapt. Ch., Kenova, W.Va., 1982-86; assoc. pastor music and singles Manassas (Va.) Bapt. Ch., 1986—; mem. State Music Task Force, W.Va., 1985-86, Va. Bapt. Male Chorale, 1987—. Bd. mem. SERVE, Inc., Manassas, 1987—. With U.S. Army, 1972-75. Mem. Fellowship Am. Bapt. Musicians (workshop leader 1984). Office: Manassas Bapt Ch 8800 Sudley Rd Manassas VA 22110

COOKE, MARVIN LEE, religious organization administrator, consultant, minister; b. Tulsa, Dec. 9, 1947; s. Marvin Joel and Mary Lee (Sleeper) C.; m. Sandra Pauline Creason, Dec. 23, 1967 (div. Mar. 1979); 1 child, Francis Wesley; m. Mary Lou Albitz, Nov. 25, 1981. BA summa cum laude, Cen. State U., Edmond, Okla., 1970; M in Divinity summa cum laude, Phillips U., Enid, Okla., 1975. Ordained to ministry United Meth. Ch., 1972, withdrew, 1985. Pastor Carmen (Okla.) United Meth. Ch., 1973-75, Turley United Meth. Ch., Tulsa, 1975-78; assoc. dir. Tulsa Met. Ministry, 1978-82, exec. dir., 1982—; mem. staff planning group Met. Human Services Commn., Tulsa, 1982—; human resources cons. Meals on Wheels program, Tulsa, 1987—; fund-raising cons. Hospice of Green County, Tulsa, 1987—; adj. prof. Phillips Grad. Sem., 1991—. Cons. in program devel. grad. sem. Phillips U., 1987—; exec. com. Citizens' Action for Safe Energy, Tulsa, 1975-78; co-chmn. Fair Law Enforcement in North Tulsa, 1987—; founder Western Neighbors, Tulsa, 1980, Job Support Ctr., Tulsa, 1982; mem. Giv.'s Task Force on the Homeless, Okla., 1988. Mem. Nat. Assn. Ecumenical Staff, Am. Sociol. Assn. Democrat. Episcopalian. Avocations: running, biking, hiking. Home: 302 N Santa Fe Tulsa OK 74127

COOKE, ROBERT WAYNE, minister; b. Farrockaway, N.Y., Nov. 2, 1927; s. Edward Minor and Jessie Elizabeth (Bailey) C.; m. Marion Edna Childs, June 24, 1950; children: Wayne Allen, Cheryl Ann, Ruth Yvonne, Robert Timothy. Diploma missions/bible, Barrington (R.I.) Coll., 1950; BS, Cornell U., 1952, MS, 1962; postgrad., CUNY, 1973-74. Cert. tchr.; cert. adminstr. in edn.; ordained to ministry Bapt. Ch., 1985. Missionary SIM Internat., 1953-65; camp dir. Christian Svc. Brigade, Wheaton, Ill., 1966-69; pastor First Bapt. Ch., Dix Hills, N.Y., 1985—; moderator Conservative Bapt. Assn. of N.Y., N.Y.C., 1990—, outreach com., 1988—, exec. com., 1990—; substitute tchr. Lawrence (N.Y.) Pub. Schs., 1987—; steering com. Urban Acad., Bklyn., 1986—. Mem. Am. Scientific Affiliation, Greater N.Y. Sunday Sch. Assn. Home: 195 W 3rd St Deer Park NY 11729 Office: First Bapt Ch 377 Deer Park Ave Dix Hills NY 11746

COOKSEY, BOBBY JOE, minister, educator; b. Pueblo, Colo., Aug. 4, 1942; s. Forrest Glynn and Willie Ovada (Griffing) C.; m. Jackie LaVern Threadgill, July 17, 1965; children: Jennifer Lea, Sarah Elizabeth, Glynn Edward. AA, Kilgore Coll., 1962; BS, E. Tex. Bapt. U., 1965; M Combined Scis., U. Miss., 1969; MRE, Southwestern Bapt. Theol. Sem., 1987. Ordained to ministry So. Bapt. Conv., 1978. Min. music and youth 1st Bapt. Ch., Queen City, Tex., 1975-77; min. edn. 1st Bapt. Ch., Alvin, Tex., 1977-84, Lamar Bapt. Ch., Wichita Falls, Tex., 1984-87, 1st Bapt. Ch., Miami, Okla., 1987-90; assoc. pastor edn. and adminstrn. Skelly Dr. Bapt. Ch., Tulsa, 1990—. Mem. So. Bapt. Religious Edn. Assn., Southwestern Bapt. Religious Edn. Assn., Nat. Assn. Ch. Bus. Adminstrs., Okla. Bapt. Edn./Music Assn. Republican. Home: 10010 E 24th St Tulsa OK 74129 Office: Skelly Dr Bapt Ch 8504 E Skelly Dr Tulsa OK 74129

COOLEY, JAMES FRANKLIN, minister; b. Rowland, N.C., Jan. 11, 1926; s. James F. and Martha (Buie) C.; m. Carolyn A. Butler, Mar. 23, 1976; children: Virginia M. Cooley Lewis, James Francis, Gladys M. Cooley Taylor, Franklin Donell, Stephen Lamar, Stetson Laron. BA in Social Sci., Johnson C. Smith U., Charlotte, N.C., 1953, BTh, 1956; MA in Sociology, St. John U., Valley, Nebr., 1971; M of Divinity, Interdenom. Theol. Sem., Atlanta, 1973, D of Civil Law, 1977; DD, Shorter Coll., 1971, Life Sci. Coll., Rolling Meadows, Ill., 1972; D of Social Sci., World U., 1982. Cert. law enforcement officer, instr. Pastor Grant Chapel Presbyn. Ch., Darien, Ga., 1956-57, St. Andrews Presbyn. Ch., Forrest City, Ark., 1957-69; tchr. social studies Forrest City Spl. Sch. Dist. #7, 1957-69; juvenile probation officer St. Francis County, Forrest City, 1959-68, assoc. juvenile judge, 1963-64; polit. sci. dir. Minister of Services, North Little Rock, 1969-73; dean of men, acad. dean Shorter Coll., North Little Rock, 1969-73; chaplin Ark. Dept. of Corrections, 1971; exec. dir. County Contact Com., North Little Rock, 1976—; constable elect Pulaski County Dist. 3A, Little Rock, 1978-80; developer inmate coll. ednl. program Ark. Dept. Corrections, 1969. Host TV program On the Educational Scene, 1989—; featured in Ebony Mag., 1969, HEP Mag., 1972, HIP Mag., 1979. Active Ref. to Challenge to Juvenile or Youths; radio program host Sta. KITA Radio, Little Rock, 1984—; committeman, del. Dem. Party of Ark., 1985—; bd. dirs. AWARE Alcohol and Drug Prevention, Little Rock, 1986—, YMCA Young Br., North Little Rock, 1986-87; legis. liaison on community affairs, 1985—; mem. Ark. Commn. on Juvenile Justice, 1988—; probation officer 5th, 6th and 7th Divs. Cir. Ct.; mem. adv. bd. Am. Security Coun.; cert. McAlmont fireman; agt. Consumer Protection, Atty. Gen.'s Office; com. mem. Boy Scouts Am., 1987; elected sch. bd. mem. Pulaski County Spl. Sch. Dist. 7, 1988. Decorated 6 Bronze Stars, 3 Campaign medals; recipient Order of Long Leaf Pine Gov. James G. Martin, Raleigh, N.C., 1986, Cert. of Appreciation Nat. Chaplain's Assn., 1987, Big Heart award Nat. Bank of Ark., 1987, Sesquicentennial Medallion Gov. Bill Clinton, 1986, Community Svc. award NAACP, 1989, Key to the City Mayor Mitchell Walker, Key to the City of Jacksonville, 1991, Key to the City of North Little Rock, 1991, Letter of commendation Pres. of U.S., 1991, Capitol citation Dept. State, 1991, cert. of appreciation City of Little Rock, 1991, Ark. cert. of merit, 1991, Gov.'s Vol. Excellence award, Ark., 1991, award of merit Muslim Soc., 1991; named Citizen of Day Sta. KLRG-AM, 1990; numerous other awards and honors; James Franklin Cooley Day proclaimed by Gov. David Pryor, 1977, proclaimed by Gov. Bill Clinton, 1988, 91, James Franklin Cooley Day proclaimed by City of Rowland, 1986, City of Little Rock, 1982, 87, City of Jacksonville, Ark., 1986, City of Wrightville, Ark., 1986, 91, City North Little Rock, 1987, City of Sherwood, Ark., 1991; Dr. J.F. Cooley Rd. named in honor, North Little Rock, Ark., 1986; Cooley Rd. named in his honor Rowland, 1990; Dr. J.F. Cooley Dr. named in his honor County Judge Buddy Villines, 1991. Mem. Am. Biog. Inst., Nat. Bd. Advisors, Internat. Platform Assn., Internat. Chiefs of Police, Am. Legion, Nat. Chaplains Assn. (life, maj. gen.), DAV (life), Am. Legion (life), VFW (life), Omega Psi Phi (Citizen of the Yr. 1974). Democrat. Presbyterian. Avocations: reading, writing, debating, playing music, sports. Home: PO Box 17225 North Little Rock AR 72117

COOLEY, JAMES HOWARD, minister; b. Birmingham, Ala., Mar. 18, 1955; s. Bobby Gene and Betty Jean (Chastain) C.; m. Judith Lee Sanders, June 14, 1984; 1 child, James Sanders. BA, Samford U., 1977; MDiv, Southeastern Bapt Theol. Sem., Wake Forest, N.C., 1982; D Ministry, New Orleans Bapt. Theol. Sem., 1991. Ordained to ministry So. Bapt. Conv., 1981. Minister to youth First Bapt. Ch., South Hill, Va., 1978-82; assoc. pastor First Bapt. Ch., Clanton, Ala., 1983-88; pastor First Bapt. Ch., Aliceville, Ala., 1988—; credentials com. Ala. Bapt. State Conv., 1990-91, youth evangelism specialist, 1988-91. Ala. alumni pres. Southeastern Sem., Wake Forest, 1986-87. Named Outstanding Young Religious Leader, South Hill Jaycees, 1981, Outstanding Religious Leader, Clanton Jaycees, 1985. Mem. Aliceville C. of C. (vitalization com. 1989-91), Rotary, Kiwanis, Sigma Tau Delta. Home: 202 3d St SE Aliceville AL 35442 Office: Aliceville First Bapt Ch Broad St at 4th Ave Aliceville AL 35442

COOLEY, JOHN DIBRELL, minister; b. Springfield, Ill., Feb. 17, 1963; s. J.D. and Janice Katherine (Ande) C.; m. Lisa René Hughes, Nov. 4, 1989; 1 child, Joshua Dibrell. BS, SE Mo. State U., 1989. Lay campus min. Cath. Newman Ctr., Cape Girardeau, Mo., 1988—; state advisor Mo. Assn. Cath. Coll. Students, Columbia, 1989—, conv. speaker, 1990, 91; lectr. Teens Encounter Christ, 1989. Author Crossroads newsletter, 1989. Religious edn. tchr. St. Mary Parish, Cape Girardeau, 1989-90; instr. Riverside Gymnastics Acad., Cape Girardeau, 1989-90. Avocations: lecturing, workshops, golf, play music (guitar, drums). Office: Cath Newman Ctr 512 N Pacific Cape Girardeau MO 63701

COOLEY, ROBERT EARL, religion and archaeology educator; b. Kalamazoo, Sept. 12, 1930; m. Eileen H. Carlson; children: Robert Carl, Gerald Earl. BA in Bibl. Studies and Archaeology, Wheaton Coll., 1955, MA in Religious Edn., 1957; PhD in Hebrew Studies and Near Ea. Archaeology, NYU, 1968. Grad. asst. in archaeology Wheaton (Ill.) Coll., 1955-57, dir. archaeol. studies, asst. prof. archaeology, 1965-68; dean of men Cen. Bible Coll., Springfield, Mo., 1957-59, dean of students, 1959-64, acad. dean, 1964-65; asst. prof. Bilbe and archaeology Wheaton (Ill.) Coll., 1965-68; dir. religious activities NYU, 1962-63; asst. to pres. Dropsie U., Phila., 1967-68; assoc. prof. Evangel Coll., Springfield, 1968-70, dean of coll., 1970-73; vis. prof. Drury Grad. Sch., Springfield, 1971-73; prof. anthropology and religious studies, dir. Ctr. for Archaeol. Rsch. S.W. Mo. State U., Springfield, 1973-81; pres., prof. Bibl. studies and archaeology Gordon-Conwell Theol. Sem., South Hamilton, Mass., 1981—; area supr., architect Dothan Archaeol. Expdn., Israel, 1959, 60, 64; mem. staff Oyster Bay Site 7, N.Y., 1963; site supr. joint expdn. to Ai, Khirbet Haiyan and Khirbet Raddana, Israel, 1969; field dir. expdn., Raddana, Israel, 1970, 72, 74; dir. field schs. various sites, Mo., 1971-81; with Phase I surveys, 1974-81; field archaeologist Tell Retaba Expdn., Arab Republic of Egypt, 1977-78; dir. publs. project Dothan II, 1978—; field dir., prin. investigator Smith Cabin site, Mo., 1979; lectr. various profl. confs., Brazil, Belgium, Israel, Portugal, Korea, 1972-88. Asst. issue editor spl. edit. Jour. Ednl. Sociology, 1963; creator concept film, 1968; contbr. articles to profl. jours. Bd. dirs. Hist. Site Bd., City of Springfield, 1970-78, chmn., 1974-78; bd. dirs. Mo. Heritage Trust, 1977-81, Appalachian Ministries Edn. Resource Ctr., 1985—, World Relief, Wheaton, Ill., 1985—; mem. Gov.'s Adv. Coun. on Hist. Preservation, State of Mo., 1977-81, interfaith adv. coun. Harvard Semitic Mus., Harvard U., 1985—; mem. planning bd. Bicentennial Commn.; corporator Beverly (Mass.) Hosp., 1985—. Founder's Day award NYU, 1969. Mem. Am. Schs. Oriental Rsch. (trustee 1978-80), Archaeol. Inst. Am., Evang. Theol. Soc. (pres. 1970), Near East Archaeol. Soc. (v.p. 1972-78), Soc. Bibl. Lit., Nat. Assn. Profs. Hebrew (treas. 1968-73), Am. Anthrop. Assn., Soc. Am. Archaeology, Soc. Profl. Archaeologists, Assn. Field Archaeology, Israel Exploration Soc., Mo. Archaeol. Soc. (site preservation bd. 1975-81, pres. Ozarks chpt. 1969-75), Mo. Assn. Profl. Archaeologists (v.p. 1978-79, pres. 1980-81), Assn. Theol. Schs. (sec. 1986-88, pres. 1991—), Nat. Assn. Evangs. (bd. adminstrn. 1982—), World Relief (pres. 1990—), Rotary (program com. Springfield 1970-81). Avocations: fishing, golf, photography, outdoor activities. Home: 31 Hilltop Dr Wenham MA 01984

COOLIDGE, ROBERT TYTUS, deacon, historian, educator; b. Boston, Mar. 30, 1933; s. Lawrence and Victoria Stuart (Tytus) C.; m. Ellen Osborne, Sept. 10, 1960; children: Christopher, Miles, Matthew. Grad., Groton (Mass.) Sch., 1951; AB, Harvard U., 1955; MA, U. Calif. at Berkeley, 1957; BLitt, U. Oxford, Eng., 1966. Ordained deacon Episcopal Ch., 1967. Non-stipendiary min. Christ Ch. Cathedral, Montreal, Que., Can., 1967-69, 71—, dir. Montreal Fund for the Diaconate, 1984—; non-stipendiary min. St. Marylebone Ch., London Clin., 1969-71; mem. faculty Loyola Coll. (now Concordia U.), Montreal, 1963—, assoc. prof. history, 1968-88, adj. assoc. prof., 1988—. Contbr. to hist. vol. Fellow Royal Hist. Soc.; mem. Am. Soc. Ch. History, Ecclesiastical History Soc., Medieval Acad. Am., Am. Hist. Assn., Soc. d'Histoire de l'Eglise de France, Oxford and Cambridge Club (London). Home: POB 4070, Westmount, PQ Canada H3Z 2X3 *If you really want to help your fellow humans, don't think it is their fault if they refuse or reject your help. Look instead at how you react to help offered to you.*

COOMER, KENNETH H., minister; b. Louisville, Apr. 20, 1953; s. Kenneth H. Coomer and Mary Rita (Robert) Naiden; m. Joyce Ann Davis, Nov. 17, 1973; children: Chris, K.C., Clayton. BS, N.W. Bible, Minot, N.D., 1979. Pastor Ch. of God, Millry, Ala., 1980—. Served with USMC, 1971-73. Named one Outstanding Young Men Am. Jaycees, 1979, 81, 83, 85, Pacesetter Paster Ch. of God, 1983-85. Mem. Ministers Assn. Georgetown, Ky. (pres. 1985-86). Republican. Home and Office: Ch of God Rt 2 Box 131 Millry AL 36558

COON, MARION GENE, minister; b. Hooks, Tex., Aug. 6, 1950; s. Thomas Noil and Francis Isabell (Rose) C.; m. Nancy Sue Roberts, Oct. 5, 1969; 1 child, Thomas Wayne. BA, East Tex. Bapt. U., 1979; MDiv, New Orleans Bapt. Theol., Seminary, 1990. Interim pastor Everett Bapt. Ch., Hoos, 1976; minister Athey Bapt. Ch., Harleton, Tex., 1977-80, Calvary Bapt. Ch., Talco, Tex., 1980-84, Little Flock Bapt. Ch., Longview, Tex., 1984—; trustee Lakeview Bapt. Encampment, Lone Star, Tex., 1990—; spiritual affairs advisor East Tex. Bapt. Univ., Marshall, 1987—; evangelism chmn. Gregg Bapt. Assn., Longview, 1989—. With USMC, 1969-72.

Democrat. Home: Rte 1 PO Box 398 Longview TX 75602 Office: Little Flock Bapt Church Rte 1 PO Box 398 Longview TX 75602

COONEY, PATRICK RONALD, bishop; b. Detroit, Mar. 10, 1934; s. Michael and Elizabeth (Dowdall) C. B.A., Sacred Heart Sem., 1956; S.T.B., Gregorian U., Rome, 1958, S.T.L., 1960; M.A., Notre Dame U., 1973. Ordained priest Roman Cath. Ch., 1959 ordained bishop, 1983. Assoc. pastor St. Catherine Ch., Detroit, 1960-62; asst. chancellor Archdiocese of Detroit, 1962-69, dir. dept. worship, 1969-83; rector Blessed Sacrament Cathedral, 1977-83; regional bishop Roman Cath. Ch., Detroit, 1983-89; apptd. bishop Diocese of Gaylord, Mich., 1989—. Office: Diocese of Gaylord Pastoral Ctr 1665 M 32 W Gaylord MI 49735

COOPER, CHARLES WILLIAM, JR., minister; b. Feb. 7, 1931; s. Charles William Sr. and Edris Marguerite (Burgess) C.; m. JoAnn Marie Weinert, June 30, 1952; children: James Burgess, Lawrence Charles, Janette Lynn Ridley. BA in History, Whittier Coll., 1952; MDiv, Yale U., 1955; M in Communications, Temple U., 1971. Pastor Brea (Calif.) Congregational Ch., 1955-58, La Mesa Community Ch., Santa Barbara, Calif., 1958-62; editor Stewardship Council, United Ch. Christ, Phila., 1962-79; assoc. mission info. position Stewardship Council, United Ch. Christ, N.Y.C., 1979-85; asst. to pres. United Ch. Christ, N.Y.C., 1985-89; cons. for spl. projects stewardship coun. United Ch. of Christ, Cleve., 1990—. Mem. Park Commn. and Recreation Commn., Santa Barbara, 1960-62. Fellow Danforth Found., 1952-54. Mem. Kiwanis, Lions. Republican. Avocations: travel, reading.

COOPER, DIANE, minister, religious organization administrator. Elder, pres. fgn. mission Bible Ch. of Christ, Inc., Bronx, N.Y. Office: Bible Ch Christ Inc 1358 Morris Ave Bronx NY 10456*

COOPER, EDGAR MAUNEY, minister; b. Kings Mountain, N.C., Oct. 17, 1922; s. Edgar Claudius and Vera Lavine (Mauney) C.; m. Jacqueline Eloise Golden, Apr. 16, 1977. A.B., Lenoir Rhyne Coll., 1943; B.D., Mt. Airy Lutheran Sem., 1945, S.T.M., 1950. Ordained to ministry Luth. Ch., 1945. Pastor New Hanover Luth. Ch., Gilbertsville, Pa., 1945—; Luther League advisor Norristown Conf., 1953; bd. dirs. Artman Luth. Home, Ambler, Pa., 1962-69; sec. Trappe dist. Southeast Pa. Luth. Synod, 1964-69. Chmn., contbr.: New Hanover Township History 1741-1991, 1991; also hist. articles, play. Mem. adv. bd. Nat. Bank Boyertown, Pa., 1961—. Chaplain Am. Automobile Assn., Pottstown, Pa., 1947-68; mem. Selective Service Bd., Pottstown, 1966-73; chmn. hist. com. New Hanover 250th Ann. Observance. Mem. Boyertown Ministerial Assn. (pres. 1961), Eastern Pa. Luth. Hist. Soc. (pres. 1974-80). Democrat. Avocation: gardening. Home: 2971 Lutheran Rd Gilbertsville PA 19525 Office: New Hanover Luth Ch 2941 Lutheran Rd Gilbertsville PA 19525

COOPER, ELLIS, minister; b. Dixon, June 30, 1921; s. Robert Adam and Vaida (Livingston) C.; m. Mildred Ann Queen, Aug. 10, 1946 (dec. 1984); children: Rebecca Elaine, Keith Ellis, Kenneth Robert, Benjamine Eugene; m. Doris Evelyn Dawson, Dec. 28, 1984. BS, S.W. Mo. State U., 1952; MEd, U. Mo., 1972; DMin, Luther Rice Sem., Jacksonville, Fla., 1980. Ordained to ministry So. Bapt. Conv., 1948. Pastor Galloway Bapt. Ch., Springfield, Mo., 1949-52; mission pastor First Bapt. Ch., Clinton, Mo., 1955-56; pastor Reedville Bapt. Ch., Sullivan, Mo., 1964-66, 74-81, Crest Bapt. Ch., Creston, Iowa, 1981-83, Lancaster (Mo.) Bapt. Ch., 1984-91; exec. bd. Franklin County Bapt. Assn., Sullivan, 1974-81; pastoral dir. N. Mo. Bapt. Assn., Lancaster, 1986-90, exec. bd., 1984-91. With U.S. Army, 1942-45. Decorated Bronze Star medal. Mem. Luther Rice Sem. Alumni Assn., Charles Haddon Spurgeon Soc. Democrat. Home: Route 3 Box 38B Lancaster MO 63548 *All humanity has some good; therefore, one great ambition should be to find the good and use it to overcome the evil that we may have peace one with another.*

COOPER, HUGH ADAIR, minister; b. Greenville, S.C., June 19, 1937; s. Carlos Alton and Sara Elizabeth (Adair) C.; m. Alice Carol Gwinn, Feb. 6, 1960; children: Steven, Susan. AB, N. Greenville Coll.; BA, U. Ga.; BD, Luther Rice Sem., ThM. Ordained to ministry Bapt. Ch., 1962. Pastor Nicholson (Ga.) Bapt. Ch., 1961-62, Mt. Carmel Bapt. Ch., CLarkesville, Ga., 1962-64, Lee Rd. Bapt. Ch., Taylors, S.C., 1964-73, First Bapt. Ch., Liberty, S.C., 1973-76, Calvary Bapt. Ch., Williamston, S.C., 1976—; trustee Anderson (S.C.) Coll., 1985-90. Mem. Masons. Republican. Home: 15 Springdale Dr Williamston SC 29697 Office: Calvary Bapt Ch 10 Academy St Williamston SC 29697

COOPER, JEANETTE IRENE, religious educator; b. Houston, June 2, 1939; d. Vernon Roy and Mildred Irene (Mars) Hanser; m. Dwaine Eugene Cooper, May 15, 1959; children: Trent Eugene, Neal Forrest, Michele Renee, Amy Denise. Grad., Galena Park High Sch., Tex. Sun. sch. tchr. Houston, 1956-59; children's ch. tchr., 1956-59, children's ch. dir., 1969-74, Sun. sch. supt., 1974-82, 84-86; Sun. sch. supt. Pasadena, Tex., 1987-88; ret. Leader local chpt. Girl Scouts U.S., 1972-76; pres. PTA, Houston, 1978-80. Mem. Ladies of Oriental Shrine, Daus. of Nile, Order Eastern Star (matron 1987-88), Social Order Beauceant (neighborhood chmn. 1977, pres. 1990). Republican. Home: 1062 Eastlake Houston TX 77034

COOPER, JEFFERY BERNARD, minister, university administrator; b. Savannah, Ga.; s. James and Idella (Goodwin) C.; m. Joanne Elizabeth Williams, Nov. 25, 1983; children: Ako, Ethan, Charity, Jeffery B. II. BA, U. Ga., 1980, MPA, 1983. Ordained to ministry A.M.E. Ch., 1980. Pastor St. Paul A.M.E. Ch., Siloam, Ga., 1977-79, St. Luke and Nimnoe A.M.E. Ch., Athens, Ga., 1979-80; sr. pastor Greater Bethel A.M.E. Ch., Athens, 1980-88, Trinity A.M.E. Ch., Atlanta, 1988—; chmn. Bethel Ch. Homes, Athens, 1980-88; sec. Augusta (Ga.) Ann. Conf., 1983-88; dir. minority admissions U. Ga., Athens, 1984—; mem. gen. bd. A.M.E. Ch., Washington, 1984-88. Trustee Turner Theol. Sem., Atlanta, 1984-91; active Athens/Clarke County Ethics Bd., 1985-89; hon. dep. sheriff Fulton County, Ga., 1991. Mem. A.M.E. Mins. Union, Optimists. Office: Trinity AME Ch 604 Lynhurst Dr Atlanta GA 30311

COOPER, JERRY RONALD, minister; b. Rolla, Mo., Apr. 21, 1941; s. Lester Cooper and Juanita Anna (Skidgle) Wilmoth; m. Carole Ann Sollberger, Oct. 12, 1962. BDiv, Internat. Bible Sch. & Sem., 1985; MDiv, Midwestern Bapt. Theol. Sem., 1983. Ordained to ministry Bapt. Ch. Pastor New Liberty Bapt. Ch., Oak Grove, Mo., 1980-84, Ozark Bapt. Ch., Houston, Mo., 1984-86, Internat. Ch. Ougadougou, Burkina Faso, West Africa, 1986, Four Way Bapt. Ch., Fort Lupton, Colo., 1987—; bd. dirs. Colo. Bapt. Conv., Denver, 1988—; missionary Burkina Faso, West Africa, 1986. Mem. Rotary Club Internat., Springfield, Mo., 1981. With USN, 1958-62. Recipient Pres.'s award Pastor's Conf. of Colo., 1990, Moderator award Long's Peak Assn., 1989-90; named to Exec. Bd. of Colo., 1989-90. Mem. Pastor's Conf. Bapt. of Colo. (pres. 1989-90), Long's Peak Assn. (moderator 1988-90, vice-moderator 1990—). Republican. Home: 9966 W C R #41 Fort Lupton CO 80621

COOPER, JOHN DANIEL, rabbi; b. Mpls., Jan. 1, 1949; s. Melvin S. and Frayda F. (Myers) C. Student, MIT, 1969-70; BA in Psychology, Brandeis U., 1969; postgrad., Columbia U., 1975-77; MA in Hebrew Lit., Hebrew Union Coll.-Jewish Inst. Religion, N.Y.C., 1976; cert. in gerontology, CCNY Hunter Coll., 1977-78. Ordained rabbi, 1978; CLU. Rabbi Victorian Union for Progressive Judaism, 1978-81; rabbinic chaplain Century Village, Robina, Queensland, Australia, 1991—; vis. rabbi Jewish Homes for Elderly, Culver City, Calif. and Bronx, N.Y., 1974-76, Temple Beth Israel, Charlottesville, Va., 1976-78, Australian Union for Progressive Judaism, 1986—; dir. Jewish Communal Centre of Old, Burbank, Queensland, 1987-91. Mem. Brandeis U. Alumni Admissions Coun., 1974—; vice chmn., hon. sec. Jewish Social Svc. Coun., Melbourne, 1979-86; chmn. pub. rels. com., bd. dirs. Australian Jewish Welfare Soc., Melbourne, 1980-86; co-initiator, bd. dirs. Univ. of 3d Age, Sunshine Coast and Queensland, 1986-91; bd. dirs. found. of Sunshine Coast Univ. Assn., 1990-91. Mem. Cen. Conf. Am. Rabbis, Australian Jewish Dem. Soc. (founding), Victorian Union for Progressive Judaism (hon. life), Am. Soc. CLUs, Australian Assn. Gerontology, Am. Soc. on Aging (forum on religion and aging 1989—), Queensland Orgn. for Adult and Community Edn. (exec. com. 1988—), Queensland Recreation Coun. (area com. 1987-91), Queensland Croquet Assn. (sr. v.p., state coaching dir. 1991—, croquet mgr. nat. masters games 1991), Caloundra Club (life), Nambour Croquet Club (coach 1989-91), B'nai Brith. Home: PO Box 335, Buderim QLD 4556, Australia Office: Century Village, PO Box 100, Robina QLD 4226, Australia

COOPER, JOHN PAUL, priest; b. N.Y.C.; s. Charles Tracy and Ruth Mary (Menesee) C. Student, SUNY, New Paltz; cert. in Edn., Duarte Costa Sch., Altoona, Pa., 1988. Missionary priest Servants Jerusalem Covenant, Poughkeepsie, N.Y.; home health care Hudson Valley Home Care, Poughkeepsie, N.Y. Head usher Bardevon Theatre, Poughkeepsie. Liberal. Independent Cath. Avocations: religion, poetry, hiking, bicycling. Home: 77 Academy St Poughkeepsie NY 12601

COOPER, KENNETH ROBERT, minister; b. Ridley Park, Pa., Nov. 21, 1942; s. Earl Kenneth and Catherine (Owens) C.; m. Marilyn J. Clore, Aug. 4, 1963; children: Kevin, Corey. BD, Bible Bapt. Seminary, Arlington, Tex., 1963; BA, U. Tex., Arlington, 1970, MA, 1974. Field rep. Inst. Judaic-Christian Rsch., Arlington, 1974-85, pres., 1985—; human svcs. specialist Tex. Dept. Human Svcs., Arlington, 1974—; edn. dir. Temple Bapt. Ch., Fort Worth, 1963-65. Contbr. articles to profl. jours. Active program com. YMCA, Fort Worth, 1975-79; chaplain troop 83 Boy Scouts Am., Fort Worth, 1980—. Recipient Good Shepherd award Assn. Bapts. for Scouting, 1984. Mem. Soc. Bibl. Lit. Republican. Home: 7533 Castillo Rd Fort Worth TX 76112 Office: Inst Judaic Christian Rsch PO Box 120366 Arlington TX 76012

COOPER, LEE E., JR., minister; b. Oklahoma City, June 24, 1960; s. Lee E. Sr. and Dorothy R. (Ponder) C.; m. Shelia D. Wiley, Dec. 9, 1989. BA, Bishop Coll., 1983; MDiv, Va. Union U., 1986. Ordained to ministry Progressive Nat. Bapt. Ch., 1983. Asst. min. St. John Bapt. Ch., Oklahoma City, 1979-83; assoc. min. Concord Bapt. Ch., Dallas, 1981-83; youth dir. Quioccasin Bapt. Ch., Richmond, Va., 1985-86; interim pastor Mt. Olive Bapt. Ch., Glen Allen, Va., 1985-86; pastor Prospect Bapt. Ch., Oklahoma City, 1986—; bd. dirs. exec., edn. and publ. Progressive Okla. Bapt. Conv., Oklahoma City; pres. Progressive Okla. Bapt. Conv., 1989—. Bd. dirs. Urban League Greater Oklahoma City, 1988—, One Ch. One Child Black Adoption, 1989—; chaplain Oklahoma State Senate, 1990; chmn. Alliance for Better Community, 1988-89. Mem. Interdenominational Ministerial Alliance (v.p. 1990—), Alpha Phi Alpha, Masons. Democrat. Home: 2200 Sandy Creek Trail Edmond OK 73013 Office: Prospect Bapt Ch 2809 N Missouri Oklahoma City OK 73111

COOPER, LESLIE FRANCIS, deacon, film producer; b. Paterson, N.J., Feb. 15, 1949; s. Leslie Van Wagner and Virginia Rose (Marron) C.; m. Evelyn Ann Popp, Sept. 7, 1970; children: Jennel, Christine, Jason, Michael. Student, Mary Knoll Sem., Glen Ellyn, Ill., 1967-69; BA in Psychology, Franklin Pierce Coll., 1971. Ordained deacon Roman Cath. Ch., 1984. Deacon Christ the Good Shepherd Ch., Spring, Tex., 1984—, chair peace and justice com., 1982-85; v.p. Reel Spirit Prodns., Inc., Houston, 1989—; mem. peace and justice commn. Diocese of Galveston-Houston, 1985-87, 89. Mem. Bread for the World, Washington, 1983—. Mem. Pax Christi. Home: 6607 Oak Masters Dr Spring TX 77379

COOPER, LYNN DALE, minister, retired navy chaplain; b. Aberdeen, Wash., Aug. 11, 1932; s. Lindsey Monroe and Mattie Ann (Cattron) C.; m. Doris Marlene Aydelott, June 2, 1956; children: Kevin Dale, Kathy Lois, Karen Doris Cooper Henthorn. Student, Gray's Harbor Coll., 1950-51; BTh, Northwest Christian Coll., 1955; MDiv, Phillips U., 1961, D Ministry, 1977. Ordained to ministry Christian Ch., 1955. Commd lt. (j.g.) USN, 1965, advanced through grades to comdr., 1988, ret., 1988; assoc. pastor First Christian Ch., Olympia, Wash., 1955-57; minister First Christian Ch., Aline, Okla., 1957-61, Sumner, Wash., 1961-66; chaplain U.S. Navy, 1966-88; minister Cen. Christian Ch., Prosser, Wash., 1988—; bd. dirs. Jubilee Ministries, Prosser, Wash., 1988—, Annie Tran Ctr. for Grief and Loss. Recipient many Navy and Marine Corps awards and medals; decorated Bronze Star medal. Mem. Mil. Chaplains Assn. U.S.A. (life), Disciples of Christ Hist. Soc. (life), Navy League of U.S., Kiwanis (sec., treas. Prosser, Wash. chpt.), De Molay (past master, councillor 1950—). Avocations: hiking, snowshoeing, backpacking. Home: 1818 Benson Ave Prosser WA 99350 Office: Cen Christian Ch 1000 Sixth St Prosser WA 99350

COOPER, MARY ANDERSON, religious organization executive; b. Honolulu, June 4, 1938; d. William Lovett and Frances Emily (Lux) Anderson; m. Bert H. Cooper, Mar. 26, 1960. BS, U. S.C., 1959; MA, George Washington U., 1978. Parish sec. St. Marks Episcopal Ch., Washington, 1962-65; adminstrv. asst. Nat. Coun. Chs., Washington, 1965-75, program specialist, 1975-77, asst. dir., 1977-89, acting dir., 1989-91, assoc. dir., 1991—; del. U.S. Com. on the Ecumenical Decade, N.Y.C., 1988—. Contbr. articles to profl. jours. Nat. bd. dirs. Emergency Food and Shelter Nat. Bd. Program, Washington, 1983—. Home: 3313 Porter St NW Washington DC 20008 Office: Nat Coun Churches 110 Maryland Ave NE Washington DC 20002

COOPER, PEGGY LOU, minister; b. Washburn, N.D., May 6, 1933; d. Weldon Wayne and Pearl Lamoine (Massey) C. BA, U. Minn., Duluth, 1962; MDiv, United Theol. Sem., New Brighton, Minn., 1976. Ordained to ministry United Meth. Ch., 1976, Presbyn. Ch. (U.S.A.), 1985. Community min. Simpson United Meth. Ch., Mpls., 1973-78; pastor Minn. Ann. Conf. United Meth. Ch., 1973-89, Gethsemane Presbyn. Ch., Council Bluff, Iowa, 1986-88; interim pastor Missouri River Valley Presbytery, Iowa, Nebr., 1988-90, John Calvin Presbytery, Mt. Vernon, Mo., 1991—; parish assoc. St. Simsons Episcopal Ch., Conyers, Ga., 1985-86; cons. Inst. Cultural Affairs, Atlanta, 1984-86. Author: The Witch and Me, 1967. Co-founder Counsel for Religious Involment Mentally Handicapped Persons, Twin City Area, 1975, The Mission Store Project, Osakis-Villard, Minn., 1979, Counseling, Referral, Ednl. Svc. Team, Conyers, 1984, The Good Samaritan Project, Conyers, 1985; co-worker, co-organizer Project for the Homeless, Council Bluffs, 1987. Mem. Rotary. Home: Rte 1 Isle MN 56342 *If we align ourselves with Jesus, we will know that we have the Holy Spirit of Truth within us as our sustainer, teacher and guide, being able to stand strong in all circumstances. If we align ourselves with persons of strong will and stubborn pride, we will remain empty vessels and be useless as friends and advocates of the people of God.*

COOPER, VIRGIL DAVID, minister, chaplain; b. Kennett, Mo., Sept. 18, 1949; s. Millage Franklin and Helen (Glessnor) C.; m. Sherry Malyn Martin, May 15, 1971; children: Amy Beth, Jared David, Ryan Martin. BA, Sch. of Ozarks, 1971; MDiv, Lexington Theol. Sem., 1978, D Ministry, 1985. Ordained to ministry Christian Ch. (Disciples of Christ, 1978. Assoc. min. Victory Christian Ch., Lexington, Ky., 1975-76; min. Newtown Christian Ch., Georgetown, Ky., 1976-78, Cen. Christian Ch., Beaufort, S.C., 1978-83, lst Christian Ch., Covington, Ky., 1984—; mem. S.C. Regional Evangelism Com., Charleston, 1979-80, N.C.-S.C. Alighment Com., Charleston, 1979-81; del. S.C. Regional Bd., Charleston, 1979-83; chmn. S.C. Regional Com. on Ministry, Charleston, 1980-83, Beaufort Ministerial Assn., 1980; mem. Ky. Regional Bd., 1986-90, Ky. Regional Coun., 1986-90; rep. Ky. Coun. for United Ministries in Higher Edn., 1987-88; chmn. Ky. Higher Edn. Commn., 1988-90; pres. dist. 7, Disciples of Christ in Ky., 1987-88; mem. bd. for children's and family svcs. Christian Ch. Homes Ky. Adviser HELP Orgn., Beaufort, 1980; chmn. Wheels for Life, St. Jude Hosp., Beaufort, 1982-83; mem. Cin. Symphony and Chorus, 1984—. Chaplain USAFR, 1981—. Recipient Key to City, City of Hollister, Mo., 1974; scholar Lexington Theol. Sem., 1976. Mem. Mil. Chaplains Assn., Disciples Chaplains Assn., Res. Officers Assn., Kiwanis (funding chmn. 1983). Avocations: music, camping, canoeing, racquetball, hunting and fishing. Office: lst Christian Ch 14 W 5th St Covington KY 41011 *In Ecclesiastes 3:1, it is written, "To everything there is a season, and a time to every purpose under heaven." My life is occupied with trying to attune myself to the right time and season.*

COOPER, WALLACE LEGRAND, church administrator; b. Sumter, S.C., Jan. 30, 1951; s. Wallace LeGrand and Blanche Connice (Lawson) C.; m. Beverly Loving Myers, Mar. 2, 1974. BS, U. S.C., 1973. Chmn. bd. Covenant Day Sch., Cola, S.C., 1979-82; rep., co-mgr. Kroger Co., 1982-87; adminstr. First Presbyn. Ch., Columbia, S.C., 1987—. Mem. Sons Am. Revolution. Office: First Presbyn Ch 1324 Marion St Cola SC 29201

COOTS, BILLY EDWARD, minister; b. Cindy, Ky., Apr. 28, 1939; s. Charlie and Edna (Vernon) C.; m. Shirley Lynn Baker, June 11, 1960; children: Donna Lynn, Danetta Louise. Student, Ohio U., 1974-76, Ohio State U., 1987-88. Ordained to ministry Ch. of Nazarene, 1970. Pastor Galena (Ohio) Ch. of Nazarene, 1968-72, The Plains (Ohio) Ch. of Nazarene, 1972-77, Columbus (Ohio) Cooke Rd. Ch. of Nazarene, 1977—; chmn., Evangelism Ch. Growth Continuing Edn., Cen. Ohio Dist., Columbus, 1984-90; mem., examiner, Bd. Ministrial Studies, Columbus, 1984-91; stat. sec., Cen. Ohio Dist., Columbus, 1986-89; mem., Dist. Fin. Com., Columbus, 1983-91. With U.S. Army, 1956-59. Home: 1375 E Cooke Rd Columbus OH 43224-2061 Office: Columbus Ch of Nazarene 1389 E Cooke Rd Columbus OH 43224-2061 *In building the Kingdom of God we must be willing to pay the price, no matter what the costs are! Our forefathers did! Do I think I need not be as dedicated as they to hear the Master say "Well done, thou good and faithful servant." I need to walk and talk His way!.*

COPE, O. LAMAR, religion educator; b. Somers, Iowa, July 13, 1938; s. A. Baker and Ruth M. (Moeller) C.; m. Sandra Dyne Patrick, June 11, 1960; children: Stephen, Rebecca. AB, Morningside Coll., 1961; MTh, Wesley Theol. Sem., 1964; ThD, Union Theol. Sem., 1971. Prof. religion Carroll Coll., Waukesha, Wis., 1969—. Author: Mt. A Scribe, 1976, Faith for a New Day, 1986; contbr. articles to profl. jours. Mem. Soc. Bibl. Lit., Cath. Bibl. Assn., Soc. for New Testament Studies, Chgo. Soc. Bibl. Rsch. (pres. 1989-90). Home: 217 N Racine Ave Waukesha WI 53186 Office: Carroll Coll 100 N East Ave Waukesha WI 53186

COPELAND, KENNETH EDWARD, lawyer, minister; b. Kansas City, Mo., Aug. 7, 1962; s. William Henry and Leola (Coley) C.; m. Starla Lynne Starks, Aug. 5, 1989; 1 child, William Jibri. BA in English-Rhetoric, U. Ill., 1984; JD, U. Calif., Berkeley, 1987; postgrad., Golden Gate Bapt. Theol. Sem., 1989—. Bar: Ill. Intern Alameda County Legal Aid Soc., Oakland, Calif., 1987; pub. defender Kankakee (Ill.) County, 1987-88; jr. ptnr. Sacks, Albrecht & Copeland, Kankakee, 1987-88; min. of music, youth dir. Cornerstone Bapt. Ch., Oakland, 1989—; assoc. Julius Echeles, Chgo., summer 1985; intern Kankakee County State Atty.'s Office, summer 1986; instr. choir workshop Nat. Black Gospel Coll., Atlanta, 1988—, Nat. Evangelism Movement Workshop, L.A., 1988—; clinician/guest artist 1st Ann. Black Sacred Music Symposium, U. Ill., Champaign. Site coord. after sch. tutor program project SPIRIT Cornerstone Gapt. Ch., Oakland, 1989—. Mem. ABA, Ill. Bar Assn. Avocations: poetry, key board playing, reading. Office: Cornerstone Bapt Ch 3535 38th Ave Oakland CA 94619

COPPICK, GLENDON CLEON, priest; b. Stigler, Okla., Mar. 18, 1926; s. Cleo Clarence and Gertie (Speer) C.; m. Shirley Jane Pederson, Nov. 21, 1954; children: Stephen Cleon, John Christen, Mary Katherine. BA, Tex. Christian U., 1952; MDiv, Ch. Divinity Sch., Berkeley, Calif., 1955; STD, San Francisco Theol. Seminary, 1987. Rector Ch. of the Good Shepherd, Dallas, 1955-59; lectr. Brescia Coll., Owensboro, Ky., 1970-80; rector Trinity Ch., Owensboro, 1959—; trustee Univ. of the South, Sewanee, Tenn., 1967-87, Diocese of Ky., Louisville, 1982-85; mem. Diocese of Ky. Standing Com., Louisville, 1979-82, 85-88; dep. Episcopal Ch. Gen. Conv., Houston, 1970. Pres. Hospice Assn., Owensboro, 1980-84, Owensboro Churches for Better Homes, 1990—; mem. profl. adv. com. Green River Comprehensive Care Ctr., Owensboro, 1981-82. With USN, 1944-46, ATO. Mem. Am. Acad. Reigion, Soc. Bibl. Lit. Democrat. Home: 1517 Dean Ave Owensboro KY 42301 *As long as theological and ethical debates remain vigorous I have great hope for the future.*

COPPINGER, JOHN F., religious society administrator. Pres. Soc. of St. Vincent de Paul, St. Louis. Office: Soc of St Vincent de Paul 4140 Lindell Blvd Saint Louis MO 63108*

CORA, GEORGE F., ecumenical agency administrator. Exec. dir. Christian Coun. of Del. and Md. Ea. Shore, Wilmington, Del. Office: Christian Coun Del and Md Ea Shore 1626 N Union St Wilmington DE 19806*

CORBETT, GORDON LEROY, minister; b. Melrose, Mass., Dec. 11, 1920; s. Winfield Leroy and Lalia Estey (Fiske) C.; m. Winifred Pickett, Sept. 7, 1946; children: Douglas Leroy, Christine, Patricia, Carolyn. AB, Bates Coll., 1943; MDiv, Yale U., 1948. Ordained to ministry Bapt. Ch., 1948. Pastor Montowese Bapt. Ch., North Haven, Conn., 1948-52; assoc. pastor First Presbyn. Ch., Glen Falls, N.Y., 1952-59; synod exec. Synod of Ky., Lexington, 1959-71; assoc. synod exec. for Alaska, 1971-84; interim synod exec. Synod of Lincoln Trails, Indpls., 1987-88; interim Presbyn. exec. Santa Barbara (Calif.) Presbytery, 1991—; trustee Appalachian Regional Hosps., Lexington, 1969-72, Sheldon Jackson Coll., Sitka, Alaska, 1972-84; chmn. chaplaincy com. Alaska Christian Conf., 1975-78, Alaska Pipeline Chaplaincy. Dist. chmn. Rep. Party, Anchorage, 1974-78. 1st lt. USAAF, 1944-45, China. Recipient Christian Citizenship award Sheldon Jackson Coll., 1984. Mem. Whitewater Valley Presbytery. *"Since we are surrounded by so great a cloud of witnesses... let us run with perserverance and the race that is set before us". (Hebrews 12:1).*

CORBETT, STEVEN BRADLEY, SR., minister; b. Berkeley Springs, W.Va., May 1, 1959; s. Donald Franklin and Wilma Jean (Divel) C.; m. Lisa Lynne' Heidler, Aug. 21, 1982; children: Steven Jr., Elisabeth, Rebekah, Daniel. Student, Union Bible Sch., Westfield, Ind., 1983-85; BS summa cum laude, Liberty U., 1989; postgrad., Liberty Bapt. Theol. Sem., 1990. Ordained to ministry Free Will Bapts., 1990. Pastor Shiloh Meth. Ch., Lynchburg, Va., 1986-90, Shady Grove Free Will Bapt. Ch., Whitesburg, Tenn., 1990—; evangelist Camp Joshua, Greeneville, Tenn., 1991. Republican. Home: Rte 2 Box 495-1 Whitesburg TN 37891

CORBETT, WILLIAM LYNNWOOD, clergyman; b. Springfield, S.C., Sept. 27, 1927; s. Albert S. and Margaret (Tarrant) C.; m. Hazel Clark Crosby, Feb. 12, 1949; children—Patricia Lynn, Robert Stokes. Cert. in Bible, Columbia Bible Coll., S.C., 1947. Ordained to ministry So. Methodist Ch., 1946. Pres. So. Meth. Ch., Orangeburg, S.C., 1955-66, minister, 1962-82, pres., 1982—. Recipient Christian Service award So. Meth. Coll., Orangeburg, 1966, 69, 70. Mem. Evangel. Tchrs. Tng. Assn., Am. Council Christian Chs. (officer 1956-66). Lodge: Lions (bd. dirs. Orangeburg 1985). Office: So Meth Ch 872 Broughton St PO Box 132 Orangeburg SC 29116

CORBIN, RONALD EUGENE, pastor; b. Springfield, Mo., Sept. 3, 1942; s. Carl Eugene and Norma Francis (Mathenia) C.; m. Joyce Marie Gould, July 11, 1964; children: Dena Marie Kastner, Ronald Jr., Brenda Kay. BA, Pasadena Coll., 1964; PhD, New World Bible Inst., 1989. Ordained to ministry Ch. of Nazarene, 1967. Pastor Ch. of the Nazarene, Yucalpa, Calif., 1972-79, Livermore, Calif., 1979-82, El Paso, Tex., 1982-84, Oiai, Calif., 1984-88, Westchester, 1988—; dist. young people's pres. So. Calif. dist. Ch. of the Nazarene, Orange, Calif., 1978-82; chmn. L.A. Dist. Camp Bd., Pasadena, Calif., 1986-90, L.A. Dist. Sunday Sch. Ministry Bd., Pasadena, 1990—. Contbr. articles to profl. jours. Del. Gen. Assembly, Indpls., 1989. Mem. Rotary (chaplain 1984-88). Republican. Home: 7330 W 89th St Los Angeles CA 90045 Office: Ch of the Nazarene 7299 W Manchester Los Angeles CA 90045

CORDEIRO, JOSEPH CARDINAL, archbishop of Karachi; b. Bombay, India, Jan. 19, 1918. BA, U. Bombay, 1939; MA, Oxford (Eng.) U., 1950. Ordained priest Roman Catholic Ch., 1946. Archbishop of Karachi Pakistan, 1958—, created cardinal, 1973. Mem. congregation Religious and Secular Insts.; mem. Secretariate Non-Christian Religions. Address: Archbishop's House, St Patrick's Cathedral, Karachi 3, Pakistan

CORDIS, MARIA, nun, English educator; b. Princeton, N.J., Mar. 16, 1929; d. Joseph Leonard and Florence Louise (Berset) Richey. AB, Georgian Court Coll., Lakewood, N.J., 1950; MA, Fordham U., 1959, PhD., 1964. Joined Sisters of Mercy, Roman Cath. Ch., 1951. Tchr. English St. Mary High Sch., Perth Amboy, N.J., 1952-57; prof. English Georgian Court Coll., 1957—, pres., 1974-80. Contbr. poetry to Sewanee Rev., Continuum Quar., Sign mag., Cath. World, Sisters Today, others. Mem. Kappa Gamma Pi. Home and Office: Georgian Court Coll Lakewood NJ 08701

CORDLE, KENNETH EDWIN, JR., clergyman; b. Monroe, Mich., Apr. 13, 1964; s. Kenneth Edwin and Shirley Lucille (Gazaway) C. BA,

Anderson (Ind.) U., 1988; postgrad., Ball State U., Muncie, Ind., 1988-89, Anderson Sch. Theology, 1990—. Student sec. Anderson U. Alumni Office, 1985-87; music/youth dir. Ch. of the Brethren, Anderson, 1986-88, dir. supporting ministries, 1988—; minister of youth, asst. organist, music dir. Anderson Ch. of the Brethren, 1986—. Mem. Anderson Symphonic Choir, 1989-90. Mem. Madison County Ministerial Assn., Madison County, Ind., 1988—. Avocations: world peace, world hunger, mus. events, sports.

CORDLE, WILLIAM LANCE, minister; b. Florence, Ala., Dec. 7, 1959; s. William Raymon and Nellie Jollie (Revod) C.; m. Laura Gail Gulley, June 26, 1982; 1 child, Drew. BA in Bible, Freed-Hardeman Coll., 1982; MA in Religion, David Lipscomb U., 1989. Min. Atwood (Tenn.) Ch. of Christ, 1982-89, Calvert City (Ky.) Ch. of Christ, 1989—. Contbr. articles to Freed-Hardeman College Lectures, 1985, 87. Office: Calvert City Ch of Christ Hwy 62 PO Box 466 Calvert City KY 42029

COREY, ESTHER MARIE, church administrator; b. Providence, Jan. 26, 1927; d. Anders Ludvig and Emily Lenore (Jacobsen) Schroder; m. Hugh MacLeod Corey, May 17, 1958; children: Bonnie Jeane, Barry Hugh. Student, New England Bible Coll., 1954. Licensed to ministry, Assemblies of God, 1954. Dir. Christian edn. Assemblies of God Ch., New Eng. Dist., 1954-59; co-pastor Assemblies of God Ch., Quincy, Mass., 1960-68; dir. Missionette Girls Club Assemblies of God Ch., So. New England, 1968-78, dir. women's ministries, 1978-87, dir. ministry wives, 1987—; organizer retreats, convs., seminars Assemblies of God. Office: Assemblies of God So New England Dist Hdqr Ctr PO Box 535 Sturbridge MA 01566

COREY, STUART MERTON, minister; b. Tacoma, Wash., Apr. 20, 1933; s. Harold Marvin and Vera Lydia (Wonderly) C.; m. Laraine Kathryn Ober, May 1, 1956; children: Nathan, Rebecca, MaryBeth. BS, U.S. Naval Postgrad. Sch., 1961, MS, 1965. Ordained to ministry, 1984. Commd. USN, 1955, advanced through ranks to capt., 1977; served in Korea, Vietnam, ret., 1978, Bible tchr., conf. speaker, 1961—; pres., founder Island Ministries, Oak Harbor, Wash., 1979—; owner Corey Oil Co., Oak Harbor, Wash., 1978—. Adv. coun. Coupeville (Wash.) Pub. Sch., 1982-83; mem. Econ. Devel. Coun., Island County, Wash., 1984-85. With USNR, 1950-53. Mem. North Whibey Ministerial Assn., Petroleum Marketers Assn., Aircraft Pilots & Owners Assn. Home: 431 S Race Rd Coupeville WA 98234 Office: Island Ministries 3124 300th Ave E Oak Harbor WA 98277

CORIATY, GEORGE MICHAEL, clergyman, vicar general, chancellor, cultural center executive; b. Sao Paulo, Brazil, Jan. 1, 1933; came to Can., 1960, naturalized, 1967; s. Michael A. and Marie (Nassif) C.; B.A., St. Savior's Sem., Saida, Lebanon, 1950; Ph.D. in Social Psychology and Polit. Sci., 1977; postgrad. in canon law Strasbourg U., France, 1986—; Ph.D. in Byzantine Studies (hon.), Internat. U. Found. Ordained priest Roman Catholic Ch., 1956; prof. St. Savior's Sem., Lebanon, 1952-56; asst. pastor Our Lady Annunciation Ch., Boston, 1957-60; pastor St. Savior's Ch., Montreal, Que., Can., 1960—; apostolic visitor, patriarchal vicar for Melkites in Can., 1972—; nominated judge for Ecclesiastical Maronite Tribunal in Can., 1987; chaplain Golden Age Assn., 1985; organizer, administrator Community Youth Club, 1986; superior Basilian Order in Can.; founder Our Lady Assumption Parish, Toronto, Ont., Can., Our Lady of Lebanon Parish, Quebec City, Que., St. George's Parish, Vancouver, B.C., Can., 1976; founder Middle-East Immigrant Aid Soc. Can., 1963; mem. multiculturalism Council Can., Que. Region; founder, pres. Centre Multicultural Bois de Boulogne, 1973—; mem. ecumenical movement. Decorated mem. Order of Can.; Highest Medal of Merit (Egypt); named First Citizen of Montreal, 1973; recipient Bronze medal for peace Albert Einstein Internat. Acad. Found., 1986. Mem. Can. Canon Law Soc., House of Trade of Montreal, Can. and Am. Hist. and Geog. Assn., U.S. Tennis Assn. (hon. life), Assn. Quebeçoise de la Solidarité Internationale (exec. mem.), Council of the Internat. Scholarship Found.-Que. Founder, pub., editor Trait D'Union Rev., 1964; founder Byzantine Mus., 1975. Office: 329 Viger St, Montreal, PQ Canada H2X 1R6 *I lived for others. I welcomed over 200,000 persons: new immigrants or refugees, with a smile and a great patience, from all religions and races. I am happy today, after 30 years, to have done such charitable and humanitarian works.*

CORK, HOWARD DEAN, church lay worker; b. Hundred, W.Va., Sept. 18, 1942; s. Warner Paul and Dorothy Jean (Henderson) C.; m. Carolyn Jean Fetty, Jan. 31, 1963; 1 child, Shana Jean. Cert., Rhema Bible Tng. Ctr., Tulsa, 1978. Tchr. Mt. Olivet Ch., Porters Falls, W.Va., 1982-85; tchr., assoc. pastor Chapel of Victory, Pine Grove, W.Va., 1986—; aluminum worker Conalco, Hannibal, Ohio, 1965—; trustee Proclaim Word Ministries, New Martinsville, W.Va., 1980-90. With USAF, 1960-64. Mem. Photographers W.Va. (bd. dirs.), Full Gospel Fellowship Internat. (past bd. dirs.), Profl. Photographers Am., Triangle Inst. Photography. Home: Box 302 Pine Grove WV 26419 Office: Chapel of Victory Box 82 Pine Grove WV 26419 *You can do and be anything you set your mind to, with God's help. (Phil. 4:13) Through Christ Jesus, though I grew up stuttering very badly, I basicly overcame and became a successful photographer and Christian Bookstore owner, all to the glory of God.*

CORLEY, ROBERT KEITH, minister; b. Thomaston, Ga., June 22, 1955; s. Robert Leon and Barbara (Stewart) C.; m. Harriet Walker, Aug. 15, 1975; children: Jason Zack, Robert Walker. AA, Gordon Jr. Coll., Barnsville, Ga., 1979; BS, Tift Coll., 1984; MDiv, So. Bapt. Theol. Sem., 1988. Ordained to ministry Bapt. Ch., 1982. Pastor The Rock Bapt. Ch., The Rock, Ga., 1982-85; adult tchr. Farmdale Bapt. Ch., Louisville, 1985-86; interim pastor Union Bapt. Ch., Cynthiana, Ky., 1986-87; student intern Long Run Bapt. Assn., Louisville, 1987; min. of youth First Bapt. Ch., Fort Valley, Ga., from 1988. Home: 117 Forsyth St Fort Valley GA 31030 *In life we are called upon to make many choices. From observation and experience it is very evident to me that those who choose the life style of a servant, as Christ did, are the most happy and content in this world.*

CORNELL, JAMES MARK, minister, music educator; b. Blue Ridge, Ga., Oct. 23, 1953; s. Charles George and Dorothy (Cheatham) C.; m. Patricia Stewart Payton; children: James Mark Jr., Nathan Stewart, Elizabeth Anne. BMus, West Ga. Coll., 1976; MA in Ch. Music, New Orleans Bapt. Theol. Sem., 1979. Min. music and youth St. Philip United Meth. Ch., Marietta, Ga., 1975-77, Galilee Bapt. Ch., Zachary, La., 1977-79, Ingalls Ave. Bapt. Ch., Pascagoula, Miss., 1979-80; assoc. pastor music and youth First Bapt. Ch., Clermont, Fla., 1980-83, assoc. pastor music and sr. adults, 1983-85, assoc. pastor music and edn., 1985-90; min. music First Bapt. Ch., Sanford, Fla., 1990—; co-leader trainee MasterLife, facilitator on state convention level Bapt. Sunday Sch. Bd., 1982-86, 91. Vol. haplain South Lake Meml. Hosp., Clermont, 1980-90; mem. Exec. Com. Vol. Chaplains, 1987-90; mem. adv. com. Lake Sumter Community Coll., 1984-89. Mem. Fla. Ch. Music Conf., So. Bapt. Ch. Music Conf., Am. Guild English Handbell Ringers, South Lake Ministerial Assn. (sec.-treas. 1981-83, pres. 1983-84), Lake County Bapt. Assn. (mem. exec. com. 1980-90, chmn. youth com. 1982-83, pres. pastor staff fellowship 1984-86, dir. music 1989-90, chmn. nominating com. 1989-90), Seminole Bapt. Assn. (mem. exec. bd. 1981-86), Kiwanis. Avocations: music, sports, fishing, reading, piano. Home: 733 Lakeview Dr Winter Springs FL 32708 Office: First Bapt Ch 519 Park Ave Sanford FL 32771

CORNELL, VINCENT JOSEPH, religious educator; b. Detroit, Sept. 25, 1951; s. Marvin Joseph and Eleanor Mary (Toth) C.; m. Rkia Elaroui, Aug. 15, 1976; 1 child, Sakina al-Moujahid. BA with highest honors, U. Calif., Berkeley, 1974; PhD in Islamic Studies, UCLA, 1989. V.p. Islamic Ctr. South Bay, Lomita, Calif., 1987-88; adviser on Islam State's Atty. of Cook County, Ill., 1989-90; asst. prof. religion U. Ga., Athens, 1990-91; asst. prof. Islamic studies Duke U., Durham, N.C., 1991—; vis. prof. religion Northwestern U., Evanston, Ill., 1989-90. Author: The Way of Abu Madyan, 1991; translator: The Glory of the Black Race, 1981; contbr. articles to profl. jours. Recipient Rsch. award Del Amo Found., 1988, Malcolm H. Kerr Dissertation award Mid. East Studies Assn. N.Am., 1990. Mem. Middle East Studies Assn., Am. Acad. Religion, Soc. for Bibl. Lit., Maghrib Studies Assn., Am. Oriental Soc. Democrat. Muslim. Office: Duke U Dept Religion 118 Gray Bldg Durham NC 27706

CORNELSEN, LINDA SUE, children's ministries director; b. East St. Louis, Ill., May 1, 1951; d. George Ule and Alfreda (Thacker) Frizzell; m. Edmer Gordon Cornelsen, Aug. 7, 1976; children: Amanda Suzanne, Sarah Noelle. BA in Music and Religious Edn., Mid-Am. Nazarene Coll., 1976. Asst. min. music Linwood Ch. of Nazarene, Wichita, Kans., 1976-84, Oscaloosa (Iowa) Ch. of Nazarene, 1984-87; min. music Dallas First Ch. of Nazarene, 1987-88, children's Sun. sch. dir., 1988-89; children's ministries dir. Lubbock (Tex.) First Ch. of Nazarene, 1990—. Contbr. articles to profl. jours. mem. Civic Chorale, Wichita, 1979-80; bd. dirs. PTA, Duncanville, Tex. Republican. Home: 5714 67th St Lubbock TX 79424 Office: Lubbock First Ch Nazarene 4510 Ave Q Lubbock TX 79412 *In order for our children to survive in this somtimes hostile world, parents must make a top priority of training and nurturing their children in the areas of the mental, physical and spiritual rather than leaving this job to the educational system or federal government.*

CORNELSEN, RUFUS, clergyman; b. Colony, Okla., Jan. 29, 1914; s. Isaac and Anna (Boese) C.; m. Frances Louise Deen, Aug. 4, 1946; children: Susan Kathleen Cornelsen France, David Alan, Sara Ann Cornelsen Kaminski. A.B., Southwestern State Tchrs. Coll., Weatherford, Okla., 1935; Th.B., So. Bapt. Theol. Sem., 1937; B.D., Union Theol. sem., 1939; postgrad., Columbia U., 1939-40, Lutheran Theol. Sem., 1941-42, Princeton Theol. Sem., 1948-49; Litt.D., Gettysburg Coll., 1964. Ordained to ministry United Lutheran Ch., 1942; pastor Emanuel Luth. Ch., New Brunswick, N.J., 1942-57, Luth. Student Assn., Rutgers U., 1942-57; assoc. dir. social action United Luth. Ch. Am., 1957-58, dir. social action, 1958-62; sec. for civil and econ. life Luth. Ch. in Am., 1962-65; rep. to UN, 1964-65; assoc. gen. sec. for planning and program Nat. Council Chs. of Christ in U.S., 1965-68; exec. dir. Met. Christian Council Phila., 1968-79; dir. Office of Christian-Jewish Relations, Nat. Council Chs., 1980-82; chmn. Nat. Inst. on the Holocaust, 1982—; exec. sec. New Brunswick Council Chs., 1945-46; mem. social missions com. Luth. Synod N.Y., 1947-50; exec. bd. Luth. Synod N.J., 1950-52, mem. bd. social missions, 1950-56, pres., 1955-56; mem. commn. social responsibility United Luth. Ch., 1952-57; Luth. World Fedn. fellow study laymen's insts., Europe, 1958; mem. bd. social ministry Luth. Ch. Am., 1966-72, cons. div. mission to, N.Am., 1973-76; bd. dirs. Union Theol. Sem., 1958-76, Phila. Fellowship Commn., 1968—; past trustee Protestant Found. Students, Rutgers U.; bd. dirs. NCCJ, 1982—. Contbr. articles, chpts. to religious publs. Mem. nat. council, nat. bd. YMCA, 1967-72, mem. armed services com., 1967-72; bd. govs. USO. Mem. Urban League New Brunswick (dir. 1944-68, pres. 1946- 48), Nat. Council Chs. (rep. Latin Am. Conf. Ch. and Soc. 1962), World Council Chs. Home: 415 S Chester Rd Swarthmore PA 19081

CORNER, MARK ADRIAN, religious studies educator; b. London, Feb. 10, 1953; s. Eric Dennis Sennett and Renee Eleanor (Eyers) C. B.A. with honors in History and Theology, 1975; M.A., Cambridge U., 1978; Ph.D., U. Durham, 1983. Lectr. religious studies U. Newcastle-on-Tyne, Eng., 1978-89; mem. theol. and religious studies bd. Council for Nat. Acad. Awards, U.K., 1984—. Contbr. articles to profl. jours. and newspapers. Mem. Campaign for Nuclear Disarmament, U.K., 1980—; mem. com. Newcastle U. Nuclear Disarmament Group, 1983—; mem. City Conv., Newcastle, 1988—; chair Newcastle City Coun. Edn. Com., 1991—. Found. scholar Corpus Christi Coll., Cambridge, 1974. Mem. Soc. for Study of Theology, Fabian Soc. Anglican. Avocations: films; reading; writing fiction. Home: 47 Claremont Rd, Spital Tongue, Newcastle-upon-Tyne Tyne and Wear, England Office: Civic Centre, Newcastle-on-Tyne Tyne and Wear NE1 7RU, England

CORNO, CHARLES JOSEPH, JR., minister, educator; b. Bklyn., Apr. 13, 1946; s. Charles Joseph and Connie Anne (Moratorio) C.; m. Lucinda K. Vieux, Aug. 2, 1965; children: Darlene Danette, Richard Joseph, Charles Joseph III. BA, Walla Walla Coll., 1975. Lic. to ministry Seventh-day Adventist Ch., 1975, ordained, 1985. Pastor Seventh-day Adventist Ch., Manhassett, N.Y., 1975-77, pastor, chmn. Bible dept. Greater N.Y. Acad. of Seventh-day Adventists, Woodside, N.Y., 1978-86, history and Bible instr., 1977-78, sponsor Adventist youth for better living team, 1980-86, Babylon Seventh-day Adventist Ch., 1985-89; pastor Co-op City Seventh-day Adventist Ch., Hartsdale Seventh-day Adventist Ch.; chairperson Cong. Hebrew Adventists. Served with USN, 1963-69. Mem. Bibl. Archaeol. Soc., Am. Philatelic Soc. Adaptor: Walking with Hashem, 1991. *It has been my experience that it is in His tough love that I really experience what it means to be a child of God.*

CORR, SISTER MARY ANN, school system administrator. Supt. Cath. schs. Steubenville, Ohio. Office: Office of Supt Schs PO Box 1196 Steubenville OH 43952*

CORRADADEL RIO, ALVARO, bishop; b. Santurce, P.R., May 13, 1942. ordained priest Roman Cath. Ch., 1974. Titular bishop of Rusticana and aux. bishop Washington, 1985; pastoral coordinator Northeast Cath. Hispanic Ctr., N.Y., 1982-85. Office: Chancery Office 5001 Eastern Ave PO Box 29260 NW Washington DC 20017*

CORREA, YAMIL, clergyman; b. San Juan, P.R., Sept. 30, 1943; parents Correa Americo and Negron Carmen M.; m. Rivera Mercedes, Jan. 20, 1968; children: Enid M., Zaira N. B, P.R. U., Rio Piedras, 1964; M, Evangelical Sem., Rio Piedras, 1967. Ordained to ministry Meth. Ch. Social technician Social Svcs. P.R., Comerio, 1970-75; pastor United Meth. CH., Comerio, 1976-87; chairperson P.R. Bd. Pensions, Rio Piedras, 1977-89; treas., adminstr. United Meth. Ch., Rio Piedras, 1987—; chairperson Day Care Ctr., Comerio, 1984-87, Children Abuse Shelter, Comerio, 1985-87. Editor: (song books) Coleccion de Coritos, 1979; author: El Artista Eterno, 1985, Iglesia de 70 Revolut., 1987, Recurse Dev. Funerals, 1988, Special Ceremonies, 1988. Mem. Social Problem Cokm., Comerio, 1982. Mem. Hogares Crea. Mem. Popular Party. Home: 2G-34 Elodea St Lomas Verdes Bayamon PR 00619

CORREIA-AFONSO, JOHN, priest, history institute executive; b. Goa, India, July 15, 1924; s. Francis and Luzia (de Heredia) C.-A. BA, U. Bombay, 1943, MA, 1945, PhD, 1953; Licentiate in Sacred Theology (STL), Weston (Mass.) Coll., 1958. Ordained priest Roman Cath. Ch., 1957. Prof. history St. Xavier's Coll., Bombay, 1960-65, 75-84, prin., 1963-65, 80-84; dir. Heras Inst. Indian History and Culture, Bombay, 1960-67, 76-90; sec.-gen. S.J., Rome, 1967-70, asst. to superior-gen., 1970-75. Author: Jesuit Letters and Indian History, 1955, The Soul of Modern India, 1960; editor: Letters from the Mughal Court, 1980, Tntrepid Itinerant, 1990. Fellow Royal Asiatic Soc., Portuguese Acad. History; mem. Assn. for Asian Studies. Avocations: reading, music, travel. Home and Office: 5 Mahapalika Marg, Bombay 400 001, India

CORRELL, PATRICK GERALD, minister; b. Ft. Worth, July 16, 1955; s. Gerald Lester and Mary Alice C.; m. Lynda Ann Smith, Aug. 21, 1976; children: Christina, Shannon, Kelli. BA, Baylor U., 1977; MDiv, Southwestern Bapt. Theol., Seminary, Ft. Worth, 1980; D of Ministry, Fuller Theol. Seminary, Pasadena, Calif., 1987. Ordained to ministry Bapt. Ch., 1974. Sr. pastor Ochre Hill Bapt. Ch., Sylva, N.C., 1980-82, First Bapt. Ch., Garrison, Tex., 1982-85, Calvary Bapt. Ch., Abilene, Tex., 1985-87, Meml. Bapt. Ch., Pasadena, Tex., 1987—. Mem. N. Am. Soc. Ch. Growth, Baylor Alumni Assn. (v.p. 1981-82). Home: 4618 Merion Circle Pasadena TX 77505 Office: Memorial Baptist Church 6715 Fairmont Pasadena TX 77505

CORRIGAN, CHARLES LAWRENCE, minister, counselor; b. Gary, Ind., Jan. 22, 1936; s. Charles Edward and Anne Belle (Horne) C.; m. Gay Nell Boykin, Jan. 25, 1957; children: Charles Lawrence II, William Edward, David Wayne. BS, Bapt. Coll., 1976; MS in Edn., So. Ill. U., 1978; MDiv, So. Bapt. Theol. Sem., 1984. Ordained to ministry Bapt. Ch.; lic. ind. social worker, lic. profl. counselor, S.C. Hosp. corpsman USN, 1954-74; vet. counselor Bapt. Coll., Charleston, S.C., 1974-77; counselor S.C. Dept. of Mental Health, Charleston, 1978-81; pastor Mt. Zion Bapt. Ch., Cromwell, Ky., 1982-83, New Albany (Ind.) Bapt. Mission, 1983-84; dir. Bapt. Children's Home, Middletown, Ky., 1984-86; mental health counselor S.C. Dept. of Mental Health, Beaufort, S.C., 1986-89; owner, counselor Agape Family Counseling Svc., Beaufort, 1989—; pastor Oaktee Bapt. Ch., Bluffton, S.C.; mem. Gray's Hill Bapt. Chapel, Burton, S.C., 1986—. Mem. Am. Assn. of Counseling and Devel., Am. Mental Health Counselor's Assn., Psychiat. Patient and Family Educators. Republican. Avocations: bowling, jogging, camping. Home: 1632 Hampton Dr Beaufort SC 29902

CORRIGAN, JUDITH ANN, religious charities organization administrator; b. Springfield, Ill., Aug. 26, 1937; d. John James and Leonarda Bernadine (Gorey) C. AB, Notre Dame Coll., St. Louis, 1960; MA, St. Louis U., 1972. Primary tchr. St. Philomena Parish, Our Lady Queen of Peace Parish, House Springs, Mo., 1959-62; secondary tchr. St. Paul High Sch., Downey, Calif., 1963-64, St. Pius X High Sch., Santa Fe Springs, 1964-66, Duchesne High Sch., St. Charles, Mo., 1966-70; tchr./dir. Acad. of Notre Dame, Belleville, Ill., 1970-71; tchr./chmn./dir. Notre Dame High Sch., St. Louis, 1971-83; acad. dean, devel. dir. Our Lady of Angels Franciscan Sem., Quincy, Ill., 1983-87; grants dir. Franciscan Charities, St. Louis, 1987-91; dir. devel. Sch. Sisters of Notre Dame of the Dallas Province, 1991—. Mem. Cath. Interscholastic Speech League (pres. 1974-76), Sch. Sisters of Notre Dame (wellness com., spiritual dirs. com.). Roman Catholic. Home: 4431 Highview Dallas TX 75211 Office: Sch Sisters of Notre Dame of the Dallas Province PO Box 229295 Dallas TX 75222-7275

CORRIPIO AHUMADA, ERNESTO CARDINAL, archbishop; b. Tampico, Mex., June 29, 1919. Ordained priest Roman Catholic Ch., 1942. Aux. bishop, Zapara, Mex. 1953; named bishop of Tampico, 1956, of Artequera, 1967, of Puebla de los Angeles, 1976; archibishop of Mexico City, primate of Mex., 1977—, created cardinal, 1979; tchr. sem., Tampico, 1945-50. Address: Apartado Postal 22-796, Mexico City 14000, Mexico

CORSELLO, LILY JOANN, minister, counselor, educator; b. Newark, Mar. 30, 1953; d. Joseph DiFalco and Antonietta (Gandolfo) C.; BA, Fla. State U., 1974; MEd, Fla. Atlantic U., 1977; MA, Southwestern Bapt. Theol. Seminary, 1987. Media coordinator, sec. Church-by-the-Sea, Ft. Lauderdale, Fla., 1968-71; student asst. Fla. State U., 1972-73; lang. arts tchr. Plantation (Fla.) High Sch., 1974-80; guidance counselor Boyd Anderson High Sch., Lauderdale Lakes, Fla., 1980-81, Lauderhill (Fla.) Middle Sch., 1981-83; guidance dir. B.F. James Adult Ctr., Hallandale, Fla., 1983-84; minister single adults Park Place Bapt. Ch., Houston, 1985-87; pres. SinglePlus, Inc., 1989—; drama and communications tchr., coordinator John Robert Powers Sch. Modeling, 1978-80; mem. ops. com. Sta. WAFG, 1974-75. Writer, lectr. singles ministry and Christian Single mag. So. Baptist Conv., Nashville, 1979-89. Mem. NEA, AACD, Nat. Council Tchrs. English, Nat. Educators Fellowship, Fla. Council Tchrs. English (lobbyist 1978), Fla. Adult Edn. Assn., Fla. Teaching Profession and Classroom Tchrs. Assn. (rep. 1975), Internat. Platform Assn., Pilot Club of Ft. Lauderdale (chaplain 1982-83), Lambda Iota Tau. Republican. Club: Women of Flower Mound (pres. 1989-90). Home and Office: 3300 Heather Glen Dr Flower Mound TX 75028

CORSON, DAVID ALLAN, church administrator; b. Miami, Fla., Jan. 15, 1951; s. William Milton and Florence Julia (Yentsch) C.; m. Sherry Ann Icard, July 29, 1972; children: Leah, John. BS in Social Work, Fla. State U., 1973; MDiv, Southwestern Bapt. Theol. Sem., Ft. Worth, 1976. Ordained to ministry So. Bapt. Conv. Min. music Crawfordville (Fla.) Bapt. Ch., 1969-71; min. music and youth 1st Bapt. Ch., Monticello, Fla., 1971-73; adminstr., youth min. Tate Springs Bapt. Ch., Arlington, Tex., 1974-84; adminstr. 1st Bapt. Ch., Winter Park, Fla., 1985—; Pres. Arlington Youth Mins. Fellowship, 1977; treas. Arlington So. Bapt. Mins. Fellowship, 1980. Treas. Jim Norwood City Coun. Campaign, Arlington, 1984; sec. Sleepy Hollow Homeowners Assn., Longwood, Fla., 1989. Mem. Nat. Assn. Ch. Bus. Adminstrs. (pres. Cen. Fla. chpt. 1989-91). Republican. Office: 1st Bapt Ch PO Drawer P Winter Park FL 32790

CORSON, MAURICE S., rabbi, foundation administrator; b. Phila., Dec. 4, 1933; s. David and Pearl Dorothy (Lipshitz) C.; m. Ruth Ann Cohen, Dec. 26, 1955; children: Rishona Yael, Aliza Rachel. BA, U. Cin., 1955; M. Hebrew Letters, Jewish Theol. Sem., 1960, DD (hon.), 1986. Ordained rabbi, 1960. Dir. interreligious and internat. programs Jewish Community Rels. Coun., Phila., 1971-76; sr. rabbi Chizuk Amuna Congregation, Balt., 1976-79; nat. exec. dir. United Israel Appeal Can., Toronto, Ont., 1979-80; dir. devel. B'nai Brith Internat., N.Y.C., 1980-85; pres. Wexner Found., Columbus, Ohio, 1985—; mem. exec. com. B'nai Brith Hillel Commn., Washington, 1987—; pres. Religious Edn. Assn., Seattle, 1964-6, Zionist Orgn. Am., Atlantic City, 1973-75; adj. prof. religion Trinity Luth. Sem., Columbus, Ohio, 1988-89, Meth. Theol. Sch. Ohio, Delaware, 1991—. Contbr. articles to religious publs. Bd. dirs. Pub. Sch. Fund, Columbus, 1985-90; mem. exec. com. Nat. Assn. Jewish Community Rels. Workers, N.Y.C., 1972-75. Chaplain U.S. Army, 1960-62. Mem. Rabbinical Assembly, Assn. for Jewish Studies. Office: Wexner Found 41 S High St Ste 3390 Columbus OH 43215

CORUM, RAYMOND KEITH, minister; b. Webb City, Mo., Dec. 20, 1947; s. Raymond Cleo and Esther Virginia (Schleppy) C.; m. Judy Marlene Frazier, June 20, 1972; children: Jenee Annette, Ryan Keith. Student, Ozark Christian Coll., 1966-69; BA, San Jose (Calif.) Christian Coll., 1972; postgrad., Pacific Christian Coll., Fullerton, Calif., 1991—. Ordained to ministry Christian Chs. and Chs. of Christ, 1982. Min. Willows (Calif.) Christian Ch., 1973-76, 80—, Northridge (Calif.) Christian Ch., 1976-78. Mem. Willows City Coun., 1982-86; mayor City of Willows, 1984-85, planning commr., 1987—, chmn. planning commn., 1990-91. Home: PO Box 327 Willows CA 95988 Office: Willows Christian Ch 200 S Plumas St Willows CA 95988 *The titles to two books written by Robert H. Schuller have helped me when I have been discouraged. The books were also very inspirational. The titles are: "Success is never ending, failure is never final," and "Believe in the God who believes in you."*

CORYELL, DANIEL CARL, minister; b. Oakland, Calif., Dec. 25, 1951; s. Carroll Clifford and Carmel Juanita (Loggins) C.; m. Martha Benavidez; children: Raul, Mario, Regina, Daniel, Aimee. BA, Patten Coll., 1976; teaching credential, U. Calif., Berkeley, 1979; postgrad. Liberty U., 1989—. Ordained min. Evang. Ch. Alliance, 1989. Disk jockey Sta. KFMR-FM, 1972-73; chief engr. TV prodn. services Patten Coll., 1973-90, instr. broadcast arts, 1979-90; corp. dir. CWE Systems, Inc., Oakland, 1979-90, pres., chief fin. officer corp. ops., 1980-90; owner, pres. Dan Coryell Assocs., cons. firm; guest lectr., instr. martial arts YMCA; vol. Protestant chaplain San Quentin State Prison, 1988-90; chaplain Alameda County Sheriff's Dept., 1990—. Recipient Heart award Patten Coll., 1978; holder 1st class radio-telephone lic. FCC; holder Black Belt in Am. Judo and Ju Jitsu Fedn., 1981, Tae Kwon Do, 1981. Mem. Nat. Acad. Arts and Scis., Am. Entrepreneurs Assn., Soc. Motion Picture and TV Engrs., Soc. Broadcast Engrs., Am. Correctional Assn., Am. Protestant Correctional Chaplain's Assn., Nat. Assn. Evangs., Nat. Sheriff's Assn., Soc. Profl. Journalists. Office: PO Box 2114 Oakland CA 94621

CORZINE, VERNON DALE, minister; b. Cypress, Ill., Nov. 17, 1933; s. Herman Cecil and Nellie Pauline (Meadows) C.; m. Gladys Martin, Dec. 13, 1952; children: Terry, Richard, Donald. BA, Olivet Nazarene Coll., 1971. Min. Ch. of the Nazarene, 1970-91, West Side Ch. of the Nazarene, Decatur, Ill., 1991—; chief acct. Tut Hill Spring Co., Momence, Ill., 1958-62; pvt. practice accountancy Bradley, Ill., 1960-75. Contbr. articles to profl. jours. Home and Office: West Side Ch of the Nazarene 2260 Longwood Dr Decatur IL 62526

COSBY, JANE WHYKOFF ROYSTER, lay worker; b. Phila., Aug. 11, 1929; d. Charles Alexander Royster and Vivian Highgate (Carter) Gardner; m. Thornhill Olie Cosby, Feb. 11, 1951; children: Thornhill O. Jr., Jane Anne, Paul Stuart. Student, Cheney U., 1948, Temple U., 1948; MEd in Counselling, Antioch U., Phila., 1981. Mem. program staff Episcopal Diocese, Phila., 1986—. Home: 124 W Washington Ln Philadelphia PA 19144 Office: Episcopal Diocese Pa 240 S 4th St Philadelphia PA 19106

COSBY, MICHAEL RAY, religion educator; b. Douglas, Ariz, Jan. 31, 1950; s. Cecil M. and Gretchen L. (Gildehous) C.; m. E. Lynne Nave, Dec. 22, 1978; children: Allen M., Evan P. BS, U. Mont., 1972; MA, Western Ky. U., 1980; PhD, Emory U., 1985. Campus staff worker InterVarsity Christian Fellowship, Moscow, Idaho, 1973-78; from asst. to assoc. prof. Warner Pacific Coll., Portland, Oreg., 1985—; instr. Emory U., Atlanta, 1980-85. Author: The Rhetorical Composition and Function of Hebrews II, 1988, Sex in the Bible, 1984; contbr. articles to profl. jours. Mem. Soc. Bibl. Lit. (convener N.W. Oreg. chpt. 1987-89, chair N.T. and Hellenistic religion sect. of N.W. region 1991—). Mem. Ch. of God. Office: Warner Pacific Coll 2219 SE 68th Portland OR 97215

COSSEY, JAMES EDWIN, pastor; b. Hot Springs, Ark., Dec. 25, 1947; s. George Othel and Toye A. (Moore) C.; M. Myrlene Cain; children: Ca Sondra, Dawn. BTh., Clarksville Sch. Theol., 1976, MTh., 1977, ThD, 1978. Ordained to ministry Ch. of God. Pastor Ch. of Cog, Heber Springs, Ark., 1966, Caraway, Ark., 1967-68, Caraway, McCrory, Ark., 1970-71, Russellville, Ark., 1971-72, Knoxville, Iowa, 1972-74, Pontiac, Mich., 1980-86, La Follette, Tenn., 1986-87, Warren, Mich., 1987-90, Lakeland, Fla., 1990—; state youth dir. Ch. of God, Iowa, 1972-76, Okla., 1976-78; editor missions, Ch. of God., Tenn., 1978-80; mem. radio and TV bd., Ch. of God, Tenn., 1988—. Author: Sunday School and Missions, 1980, R.M. Evans: First of His Kind, 1982, Friendship Evangelism, 1983; contbr. articles to jours. in field. Mem. Assn. Christian Counselors. Republican. Avocations: radio broadcasting, yard work, hunting, camping. Home: 4804 Musket Dr Lakeland FL 33809 Office: West Lakeland Ch of God 1900 W Memorial Blvd Lakeland FL 33801

COSSITT, JAN, religion educator, consultant; b. New Albany, Miss., May 20, 1950. AA, N.E. Miss. Jr. Coll., 1970; BS, Miss. U. for Women, 1972; MEd, Miss. Coll., 1979. Min. youth and activities Morrison Heights Bapt. Ch., Clinton, Miss., 1975-85; youth cons. Miss. Bapt. Conv. Bd., Jackson, 1985—. Contbr. articles to profl. jours. Chmn. Recreation Coun., Clinton, 1988; vice chmn. Clinton Christmas Parade, 1988-89. Named one of Outstanding Young Women in Am., Miss. Coll. 1986, 87, 88, Outstanding Religious Leader in Clinton, 1979. Mem. Clinton C. of C. (chmn. lit. com. 1988-90). So. Baptist. Office: Miss Bapt Conv Bd PO Box 530 Jackson MS 39205 *Keep on keeping on is my motto for life. It is one thing to have a relationship with The Lord and spend some time with Him, but a whole different thing to make it a lifetime experience!.*

COSTANZO, MARIE ALLEN, religion educator; b. Bklyn., Mar. 25, 1957; d. Robert James and Rita Dorothy (Hugel) Allen; m. Gabriel William Costanzo, Nov. 9, 1980; children: Jason William, Meghan Dorothy. AAS, Fashion Inst. Tech., N.Y.C., 1984. Religion educator St. James Sch. of Religion, Hopewell, Va., 1984—; chairperson CCD com. St. James Sch. of Religion, Hopewell, 1986-88, sec. CCD com., 1988-90, mem. CCD com., 1991—; tchr. 1st Bapt. WEE Sch., Hopewell, 1991—; sr. bank teller Signet Bank, Petersburg, Va., 1989—. Office: 1st Bapt Ch 2d and Randolph Rd Hopewell VA 23860

COSTELLO, ANDREW JACKSON, theologian; b. Bklyn., Nov. 10, 1939; s. Michael and Mary (Connelly) C. BA, Mt. St. Alphonsus, Esopus, N.Y., 1962, MDiv, 1966, M of Religious Edn., 1978; ThM, Princeton Theol. Seminary, 1973. Ordained priest Roman Cath. Ch., 1965. Parish priest Most Holy Redeemer Parish, N.Y.C., 1967-69; retreat master San Alfonso Retreat House, West End, N.J., 1969-75; cons. Redemptorists, Washington, 1975-76; retreat master St. Alphonsus Retreat House, Tobyhanna, Pa., 1976-84; novice dir. Immaculate Conception Novitiate, Oconomowoc, Wis., 1984-85, Mt. St. Alphonsus Novitiate, Esopus, 1985—. Author: How To Deal with Difficult People, 1980, Listenings, 1980, Cries But Silent, 1981, Thank God It's Friday, 1987. Democrat. Home: Mt St Alphonsus Esopus NY 12429 Office: Redemptorist Novitiate Mt St Alphonsus Espous NY 12429

COSTELLO, THOMAS JOSEPH, clergyman; b. Camden, N.Y., Feb. 23, 1929; s. James G. and Ethel A. (Dupont) C. S.T.L., Cath. U. Am., 1954, J.C.B., 1960. Ordained priest Roman Cath. Ch., 1954; sec. Diocesan Tribunal, Diocese of Syracuse, 1958; supt. schs. Cath. Diocese of Syracuse, 1960-75; pastor Our Lady Lourdes Ch., Syracuse, N.Y., 1975-78; aux. bishop Syracuse, 1978—. Home: 1515 Midland Ave Syracuse NY 13205 Office: 240 E Onondaga St Syracuse NY 13202

COTHRAN, TERRELL EUGENE, church administrator; b. Nov. 13, 1946; s. Howard William and Mai Frances (Jewell) C.; m. Judy Ann Barrett, Aug. 14, 1971; children: Timothy Blake, Wendi Leigh. BS, Vanderbilt U., 1968, MA, 1973; postgrad., So. Bapt. Theol. Sem., 1981; cert. in ch. bus. adminstrn., Southwestern Bapt. Theol. Sem., 1990. Min. music Whitsitt Chapel Bapt. Ch., Nashville, 1971-73; min. music Dalewood Bapt. Ch., Nashville, 1973-75, min. music, ednl. assoc., 1975-80, min. music and youth, 1980-86; min. edn. and adminstrn. First Bapt. Ch., Norcross, Ga., 1986—. Mem. Metro Atlanta/Ga. Bapt./So. Bapt. Religious Edn. Assn., So. Bapt. Bus. Officers Conf., So. Bapt. Ch. Bus. Adminstrn. Assn., Nat. Assn. Ch. Bus. Adminstrn., Choristers Guild, Am. Guild English Handbell Ringers. Office: First Bapt Ch 706 N Peachtree St Norcross GA 30071

COTNER, ROBERT EUGENE, minister; b. Broken Arrow, Okla., Mar. 19, 1946; s. Eddie James and Ruth (Weldon) C.; m. Betty J. Butler, Mar. 19, 1991. Student, U. Calif., Berkeley, 1979; certs., CIA, Langley, Va., 1969, 72; D in Religion (hon.), U. P.R., 1976; D in Common Law (hon.), Freedom U., 1989. Ordained to ministry Ch. of the Remnant Inc., 1975. Min. Ch. of the Remnant, Bixby, Okla., 1975-89, min., tchr. instr., 1989—; researcher CIA Mkultra Project, 1964-72; instr. Freedom U., Mounds, Okla., 1991—. Mem. Am. Correctional Assn. (cons., counselor 1983—), Okla. Correctional Assn. (tchr., cons. 1983—). Home: Box 557 Mounds OK 74047 Office: Ch of the Remnant Inc Box 728 Bixby OK 74008 *A Manipulative religion stresses the inability of man, and an Actulized religion stresses that the 'God' kingdom is within. The experience convinces only the experiencer because we normally only see a dim part of reality, from a limited point of view.*

COTOV, PAULA ROBIN, youth leader, computer programmer; b. Perth Amboy, N.J., Dec. 31, 1961; d. Paul and Rose Elizabeth (Gall) Sarik; m. Thomas Joseph Cotov, Sept. 8, 1990. BBA, Rutger's U., 1983. Leader jr. high sch. youth 1st Presbyn. Ch., Carteret, N.J., 1981—, women's Bible study leader, 1988-90, Sunday sch. tchr., 1988-90; computer programmer Buck Cons., Inc., Secaucus, N.J., 1987—; God Squad mem. evang. outreach 1st Reformed Ch. of Palisades, Ft. Lee, N.J., 1988-90. Big sister S.P.A.N. with Middlesex County Coll., Edison, N.J., (outstanding vol. awards 1988, 89, 90), 1987—. Home: 2 Camelot Dr East Brunswick NJ 08816 Office: Buck Cons Inc 500 Plaza Dr Secaucus NJ 07096-1533

COTTER, JEFFREY LEE, pastor; b. Los Angeles, May 14, 1946; s. Lawrence L. and Frankie Marie (Marlow) C.; m. Patricia Allen Hodges, May 19, 1973; children: Meghan, Marlo. BA, UCLA, 1969; M of Divinity, Fuller Theol. Sem., 1973. Ordained to ministry Presbyn. Ch., 1973. Dir. drug rehab. Hollywood (Calif.) First Presbyn. Ch., 1968-71; dir. student ministries Bel Air Presbyn. Ch., Los Angeles, 1971-73; univ. pastor Fremont Presbyn. Ch., Sacramento, Calif., 1973-76, pastor and founder, dir. Logos Study Ctr.,, 1976-79; pastor Santa Ynez Valley Presbyn. Ch., Solvang, Calif., 1979—; speaker Calvin Crest Confs., Fresno, Calif., 1973-78, Young Life Campaign Sacramento Young Life, 1974-78; cons. in Youth Outreach Sacramento Area Youth Ministries, 1974-76; cons. New Ch. Devel. Presbyn. Ch., Santa Barbara; lectr. Japan Ch. Growth Inst., Tokyo, 1986; cons., speaker Nepali Pastors Conf., Nepal. Contbr. articles to profl. jours. Mem. adv. bd. Drug Rehab., Hollywood, Calif., 1968; mem. steering com. Extension Edn. Grad. Theol. Union, Berkeley, Calif., 1981, Fuller Theol. Sem. for Santa Barbara County, 1982-84; preaching pastor for President and Mrs. Ronald Reagan, Santa Ynez Valley, Calif., 1982, 86; mem. gen. council Santa Barbara Presbytery; co-founder Cross Roads Counseling Ctr., Santa Ynez, Valley Friendship Ctr., Santa Ynez; cons., charter founder Great Commn. Tng. Ctr., Bangalore, India. Named one of Outstanding Young Men of Am., 1975. Mem. Presbyn. Panel (research and mktg. 1982, 84), Serving God Found. (adv. com. bd. dirs. 1984—). Republican. Avocations: piano, competition road bicycle racing, writing. Office: Santa Ynez Presbyn Ch 1825 Alamo Pintado Rd Solvang CA 93463

COTTO, IRVING, minister; b. N.Y.C., Aug. 4, 1954; s. Efrain and Lydia (Perez) C.; m. Lilian Lucrecia de Paz, Oct. 4, 1979; children: Julio, Andrés, Alejandro. BA in Psychology, Bayamon Cen. U., 1977; MDiv, Union Theol. Sem., N.Y.C., 1979; D of Ministry in Pastoral and Mission Studies, Ea. Bapt. Theol. Sem., Phila., 1986. Ordained to ministry United Meth. Ch. Pastor for Hispanic ministries United Meth. Ch., Reading, Pa., 1979-82; pastor Emanuel United Meth. Ch., Lancaster, Pa., 1982-83, El Redentor United Meth. Ch., Lancaster, 1983—; 1st alt. 13th jurisdictional conf. United Meth. Ch., Buckhannon, W.Va., 1988. Mem. adv. bd. local chpt. Salvation Army, Lancaster; active S.E. Area Comml. and Indsl. Revitalization Program, Lancaster, 1991—. Recipient Community Svc. award Spanish-Am. Civic Assn., 1991. Mem. Acad. Parish Clergy, Lancaster Peace and Justice Coalition, Order of St. Luke (ea. Pa. chpt.). Democrat. Home: 1804 Wilderness Rd Lancaster PA 17603 Office: El Redentor United Meth Ch 548 S Ann St Lancaster PA 17602

COTTON, JERRY LEE, church administrator; b. Ardmore, Okla., Mar. 29, 1939; s. Victor Glenn and Marian Madeline (Haines) C.; m. Rhonda Lou Collins, Jan. 11, 1961; children: David, Deborah. BBA, S.W. Tex. State U., 1976. Cert. fellow in ch. bus. adminstrn. Instr., adminstr. San Marcos Bapt. Acad. (Tex.), 1967-76; asst. bus. mgr. E. Tex. Bapt. Coll., Marshall, 1977-81; ch. bus. adminstr. North Richland Hills Bapt. Ch. (Tex.), 1981—. Served with U.S. Army, 1959-67. Mem. Nat. Assn. Ch. Bus. Adminstrs., Tex. Bapt. Pub. Rels. Assn., Lions. Baptist. Home: 6708 Karen Dr North Richland Hills TX 76118 Office: 4001 Vance Rd North Richland Hills TX 76118

COUCH, CHARLES EDWARD, minister; b. Hazard, Ky., Aug. 13, 1944; s. Alfred and Alice (Stedham) C.; m. J. Eileen Adomson, Oct. 23, 1964; children: Michael, Pamela, Aaron. BS, Cin. Bible Coll., 1976. Ordained to ministry Christian Chs., 1974. Youth minister Bethel (Ohio) Ch. of Christ, 1970-74; sr. minister Monterey Ch. of Christ, Batavia, Ohio, 1974-76, Worland (Wyo.) Christian Ch., 1976-83, Libby (Mont.) Christian Ch., 1983—; bd. dirs. Boise (Idaho) Bible Coll., 1989—. Named Ky. Col., Commonwealth of Ky., 1990, Ky. Admiral, 1990. Mem. Mont. Evangelizing Assn. (chmn. 1990—). Home: 1028 Mineral Libby MT 59923

COUCOUZIS, DEMETRIOS A. See IAKOVOS, ARCHBISHOP

COUEY, DUANE EMERSON, church administrator; b. Milw., Sept. 13, 1924; s. Ralph Emerson and Hazel Viola (Lindsey) C.; m. Edith Rosalyn Griswold, Sept. 6, 1947 (dec. Sept. 1982); children: Patricia Louise, Ralph Floyd; m. Margaret Paschall Rushing, Feb. 18, 1989. Student, U. Wis., 1946-47; B.A. in Religious Studies, Park Coll., 1978. Lithographer, Moebious Printing Co., Milw., 1942; fabricator Product Miniature Co., Inc., Milw., 1946-54, supt. mfg., 1947-54; ch. adminstr. Memphis dist. Reorganized Ch. Jesus Christ of Latter Day Saints, 1954-57; asst. to first presidency Reorganized Ch. Jesus Christ of Latter-day Saints, 1958, pres. Los Angeles Stake, 1959-60, mem. council Twelve Apostles, 1960, mem. first presidency, 1966-82, presiding patriarch, 1982—. Contbr. articles to religious jours. Mem. Citizens' Adv. Com. Selection Chief of Police, Independence, Mo., 1968; bd. corporators Independence Regional Health Ctr., trustee, 1966-72. Served with USNR, 1943-51. Mem. U.S. Naval Inst. Office: The Auditorium PO Box 1059 Independence MO 64051

COUGHENOUR, ROBERT ALLEN, religion educator; b. Youngwood, Pa., Nov. 28, 1931; m. Betty Zane Reed, 1953; children: Reed Allen, Mary Jo, John Mark, Amy Elizabeth. BS in Music Edn., Indiana U. Pa., 1953; MDiv cum laude, Pitts. Theol. Sem., 1960; MA, Western Res. U., 1967; PhD, Case Western Res. U., 1972. Ordained to ministry United Presbyn. Ch. in USA, 1960; transferred credentials to Reformed Ch. in Am., 1978. Music instr. Pa. high schs., 1953, 55-57; min. Christian edn. Wallace Meml. United Presbyn. Ch., Greentree, Pa., 1959-62; instr., asst. prof. Bible Westminster Coll., New Wilmington, Pa., 1962-69; from assoc. prof. to prof. bibl. studies Hope Coll., Holland, Mich., 1969-75; Cornelius Van Der Meulen prof. of Old Testament Western Theol. Sem., Holland, 1975—, acad. dean, 1982-86; prof. theology Reformed Ch. in Am., 1981—; del. 1st Internat. Conf. on History and Archaeology of Jordan, Christ Ch. Coll., Oxford, Eng., 1980; lectr. Brit. Mus., London, 1982; Ann. prof. Am. Ctr. for Oriental Rsch., Amman, Jordan, 1986; vis. rsch. prof. Regent's Park Coll., U. Oxford, 1987. Author: For Me To Live: Essays in Honor of James Leon Kelso, 1972, In Search of a City: Biblical Mahanaim, 1979, What's New in Biblical Archaeology, 1984, Essays in Jewish Literature, 1990; also numerous articles on religion and archaeology to profl. jours., book revs. Bd. dirs., sec.-treas. Kyle-Kelso Found., Inc., Holland, 1969—; trustee Am. Ctr. Oriental Rsch., Amman, Jordan, 1981-91; pres. bd. trustees, 1988-91. With U.S. Army, 1953-55. Recipient Outstanding Prof.-Educator award Hope Coll., 1974; James Purdy scholar Pitts.-Xenia Sem., 1957, resident scholar Inst. Ecumenical and Cultural Rsch., Minn., 1979; Univ. fellow Western Res. U., 1966-67, Rosenstiel fellow Notre Dame U., 1973, Den Uyl fellow Hope Coll., 1973. Mem. Soc. Bibl. Lit., Am. Acad. Religion, Am. Schs. Oriental Rsch., Calvin Studies Soc. Home: 13935 Ridgewood Dr Holland MI 49424

COUGHLIN, MAUREEN ELIZABETH, minister; b. Cleve., Oct. 28, 1956; d. Frank Walter and Mildred Rose (Grob) C. BA in Communications, John Carroll U., 1978, postgrad., 1981, 83-85; postgrad., Ursuline Coll., 1986, Notre Dame Coll., Cleve., 1986. Cert. lay pastoral min. Tchr. theology St. Augustine Acad., Lakewood, Ohio, 1980-83, Lumen Cordium High Sch., Bedford, Ohio, 1984-85; dir. religious edn. Annunciation Ch., Cleve., 1985-88; tchr. theology Padua High Sch., Parma, Ohio, 1988-90; lay pastoral min. St. Matthias Ch., Parma, 1990—; bd. dirs. Urban Region CYO, Cleve., 1985-88; advisor Youth Bd. Urban Region, 1985-88; mem. Bishop's Urban Planning Commn., Cleve., 1985-88; coord. Urban Region Cluster, Cleve. Orgn. Religious Educators, 1991—; rep. Ohio Dirs. Religious Edn., 1991—. Recipient 9 yr. svc. cert., Diocese Cleve. Religious Edn. Dept., 1986. Mem. Ohio Dirs. Religious Edn., Cleve. Diocese Lay Pastoral Mins. Home: 1480 Warren Rd #411 Lakewood OH 44107 Office: St Matthias Ch 1200 W Sprague Rd Parma OH 44134

COULSON, JESSE EDWARD, counselor, minister; b. Davis, Okla., July 11, 1940; s. Ola and Eula Willie (Etherton) C.; m. Gunilla Birgitta Louise Jonsson, Sept. 3, 1960; children: Karen Louise Coulson Kobe, Nancy Sue, Linda Kay. Ministerial diploma Life Bible Coll., L.A., 1963; B.A. in Psychology and Religion, Pacific Coll. Fresno, Calif., 1971; M.S. in Clin. Psychology, N. Tex. State U., 1974, EdD, U. North Tex., 1987. Lic. profl. counselor, Tex. Minister, Internat. Ch. of the Foursquare Gospel, Calif. and Oreg., 1963-71; clin. supr., staff psychologist Texoma Mental Health Ctr., Denison, Tex., 1974-82; pvt. practice counseling, Dallas and Denison, 1982-87; clin. psychologist Wichita Falls (Tex.) State Hosp., 1987—; pastor Mission United Meth. Ch., Gainesville, Tex., 1985-86; assoc. pastor St. Marks United Meth. Ch., Wichita, 1987—. Mem. citizens road and subdiv. com. Grayson County Tex., Sherman, 1983. Mem. Am. Assn. Marriage and Family Therapy (clin.), Am. Assn. Counseling and Devel., Tex. Assn. Counseling and Devel. (bd. dirs. 1983-86), Tex. Assn. for Measurement and Evaluation in Counseling and Devel. (bd. dirs. 1985-86), Am. Acad. Behavioral Medicine, Texoma Counselors Assn. (pres. 1984-85), North Cen. Tex. Assn. Counseling & Devel. (bd. dirs. 1985-87), Greenbelt Assn. Counseling & Devel. (pres.-elect 1989), Sherman Area C. of C. (leadership com. 1983, youth devel. com. 1982-84). Democrat. Methodist. Avocations: raising small animals, oil painting; writing poetry, public speaking, sailing. Home: 4117 Seymour Rd Wichita Falls TX 76309-2807

COULTER, WILLIAM ROBERT, clergyman, religious organization administrator; b. Parkersburg, W.Va., July 21, 1930; s. Jesse Henderson and Mary Jamison (Hensworth) C.; m. Flora Emogene Fletcher, June 9, 1951; children: William Robert, James Eric, Jill Marie, Alan Lee. Student, Salem Coll., 1950-51, U. Colo., 1953-54. Ordained to ministry Ch. of God (Seventh Day), 1957. Pastor Ch. of God (Seventh Day), New Auburn, Wis., 1956-61; overseer Gt. Lakes dist. Ch. of God (Seventh Day), Detroit, 1961-63; chmn. Gen. Conf. Ch. of God (Seventh Day), Denver, 1963. Mem. Nat. Assn. Parliamentarians. Address: 6104 Bay Hill Arlington TX 76018

COUNCIL AUSTIN, MARY H., minister; b. Stantonsburg, N.C., Jan. 4, 1953; d. Charles E. and Martha Ann (McMillian) Council; m. Clarence Austin, June 20, 1981. BS, N.C. A&T State U., 1975; MDiv, Howard U., 1978. Assoc. pastor United Meth. Ch., Washington, 1975-77; pastor St. Matthias United Meth. Ch., Beloit, Wis., 1978-79; assoc. program dir. Wis. Conf. United Meth. Ch., Sun Prairie, 1979-81; min. Kenwood young adult U. Wis., Milw., 1981-82; staff assoc. South Madison Community Ctr., 1982; pastor Community United Meth. Ch., Brooklyn, Wis., 1983-85; asst. exec. sec. Gen. Bd. Ch. and Soc. United Meth. Ch., Washington, 1985-90; chaplain Howard U., Washington, 1990—; del. World Meth. Coun., Gen. Conf. United Meth. Ch. Contbr. articles to religious publs. Mem. NOW, NAACP, Link Inc., Nat. Assn. Univ. Chaplains, United Meth. Clergywomen, United Meth. Clergy, Campus Ministry Women, Home Econ. Assn. Home: 9085 Blarney Stone Dr Springfield VA 22152 Office: Howard Univ Wesley Found 2405 First St MW Washington DC 20001

COUNTRYMAN, LOUIS WILLIAM, religion educator; b. Oklahoma City, Okla., Oct. 21, 1941; s. Louis and Bera Sue Frances (Gray) C. AB, U. Chgo., 1962, MA, 1974, PhD, 1977; STB, Gen. Theol. Sem., 1965. Curate St. Philip's Episcopal Ch., Ardmore, Okla., 1965-67; rector St. Paul's Episcopal Ch., Logan, Ohio, 1968-72; prof. S.W. Mo. State U., Springfield, 1976-79; prof. Brite Divinity Sch. Tex. Christian U., Ft. Worth, 1979-83; prof. Ch. Divinty Sch. of the Pacific, Berkeley, Calif., 1983—. Author: The Rich Christian in the Church of the Early Empire, 1980, Biblical Authority or Biblical Tyranny?, 1982, The Mystical Way in the Fourth Gospel, 1985, Dirt, Greed, and Sex, 1988. Mem. N.Am. Patristics Soc., Soc. Bibl. Lit. Office: Ch Divinity Sch of Pacific 2451 Ridge Rd Berkeley CA 94709

COURSON, DAVID MERLE, religious organization administrator, minister; b. Glendale, Calif., July 10, 1947; s. Merle D. and Mary E. (Stine) C.; m. Terri Feess. AA, West Valley Coll., 1970-73; BA, Calif. State U., 1971; postgrad., Western Theol. Sem., 1971-73. Ordained to ministry Christian Ch., 1976. Sr. min. South Valley Chapel, San Jose, Calif., 1974-78; pres. Christian Emergency Relief Teams, Internat., Carlsbad, Calif., 1979—; pres. Nat. Christian Fellowship, Carlsbad, 1979—, Victory Christian High Sch., Carlsbad, 1983-85; dir. Internat. Health Svs., Lancaster, Pa., 1989—. Dir. Fed. Sch. Site Coun., Carlsbad, 1987-88; mem. Conservative Polit. Action Com., 1989-91. Sgt. USMC, 1966-68, Vietnam. Named Man of Yr. Pro-Am., 1989. Mem. Evang. Coun. for Fin. Accountability, San Diego C. of C., San Diego Evang. Assn., Kiwanis. Office: Christian Emergency Relief Teams Internat 2075 Corte del Nogal #S Carlsbad CA 92009

COURTNEY, ESAU, bishop. Bishop Ch. of God in Christ, Trenton, N.J. Office: Ch of God in Christ 12 Clover Hill Cir Trenton NJ 08538*

COURTNEY, HOWARD PERRY, clergyman; b. Frederick, Okla., Dec. 20, 1911; s. Columbus C. and Dotty Lee (Whelchel) C.; m. Vaneda Harper, Mar. 21, 1932; 1 child, Howard Perry. Grad., L.I.F.E. Bible Coll., 1932, D.D., 1944. Ordained to ministry Internat. Ch. of the Foursquare Gospel, 1933; pastor chs. Racine, Wis., 1932-34, Terre Haute, Ind., 1934, Portland, Ore., 1935-36, Riverside, Calif., 1936-39, Urbana, Ill., 1939; dist. supr. Great Lakes dist., Internat. Ch. of the Foursquare Gospel, 1940-44, gen. supr., v.p., 1950; gen. supr., dir. fgn. missions, 1944-50, v.p., 1953-80, gen. supr., 1953-74; pastor Angelus Temple, Los Angeles, 1950-53, 77-81; mem. faculty L.I.F.E. Bible Coll., 1937-39, 44-74; Chmn. adv. com. Pentecostal World Conf., 1958-61. Mem. Pentecostal Fellowship North Am. (chmn. 1953, 54, 65-66), Nat. Assn. Evangelicals (bd. mem. 1953-54, 59-60, 66-67, 69-77). Office: 1130 Sonora Ave Glendale CA 91201

COURTRIGHT, PAUL BARBER, religion educator; b. Nashville, Aug. 12, 1942; s. Harold Franklin and Norma Gibbs Courtright; m. Ruth Ann Unruh, June 11, 1966 (div. 1973); 1 child, Benjamin; m. Margaret Crosby, Feb. 16, 1975; children: Jonathan, Rachel, David. BA, Grinnell Coll., 1964; MDiv, Yale U., 1968; MA, Princeton U., 1970, PhD, 1974. Prof., chmn. dept. religion Emory U., Atlanta, 1989—. Author: Ganesa, 1985 (named Best Book Am. Coun. Learned Socs. 1986). Recipient Excellence in Teaching award U. N.C., Greensboro Alumni Soc., 1981; Am. Coun. Learned Socs. grantee, 1977, 87; NEH fellow, 1979, 87. Mem. Am. Acad. Religion, Assn. for Asian Studies. Office: Emory U Dept Religion 312 Physics Bldg Atlanta GA 30322

COURY, MICHAEL, school system administrator. Supt. schs. Diocese of Columbus, Ohio. Office: Sch Office 197 E Gay St Columbus OH 43215*

COUSER, THOMAS DONALD, religion educator; b. Detroit, Mar. 6, 1946; s. Thomas William and Dolores Helen (Ulbrich) C.; m. Barbara Ruth Brown, June 14, 1969; children: Peter, Mark, Katie. BA, Concordia Coll., 1969, MA in Edn., 1980; postgrad., S.E. Mo. State, 1970-72. Youth dir. Trinity Luth. Ch., Cape Girardeau, Mo., 1969-72; dir. Christian Edn. Immanuel Luth. Ch., Downers Grove, Ill., 1972-80, Bethlehem Luth. Ch., West Dundee, Ill., 1980-88; youth dir. Holy Cross Luth. Ch., Dallas, 1988—; pres. Parish Ministries Resources, Inc., Maywood, Ill., 1982—; chaplain Dundee C. of C., 1982-88. Co-author: (text) Come Follow, 1979, Alive In Our Lord, 1980, Pathlight, 1990; editor jour. Insights Into Christian Edn., 1984—. Trustee Luth. High Sch., Dallas, 1990—; mem. Mayor's Commn. on Youth, Downers Grove, 1977-78. Recipient Cal P. Rogers award Dirs. Christian Edn., 1978. Mem. Luth. Edn. Assn. (chair editorial com. 1988—, pres. TEAM 1978-80). Home: 2921 Meadow Green Dr Dallas TX 75234 Office: Holy Cross Luth Ch 11425 Marsh Ln Dallas TX 75229 *Ministry happens when people care enough to share their Faith and give others the Freedom to do the same.*

COUSIN, PHILIP R., clergyman; b. Pittston, Pa., Mar. 26, 1933; m. Joan Cousin; children—Philip Jr., Steven, David, Michael, Joseph. Ed., Central State U., Boston U.; Th.M., Colgate Rochester Div. Sch., Ph.D. Ministry. Pastor various chs., N.C., Va., Fla.; bishop A.M.E. Ch., Ala.; bishop 11th Episc. Dist. A.M.E. Ch.; chmn. bd. trustees Edward Waters Coll.; pres. Kittrell Coll., 1960-65, Nat. Council Chs. of Christ in U.S.A., N.Y.C., 1983-87. Chmn. Durham Human Relations Commn., N.C., 1968-69; trustee Lincoln Hosp., Durham, 1966-72, Fayetteville State U. from 1972; mem. Durham County Bd. Edn. from 1972, Durham County Bd. Social Service from 1970; del. Dem. Nat. Conv., 1968. Served to 2d lt. AUS, 1952. Kellogg Found. fellow, 1965; Martin Luther King fellow in Black Ch. Studies, 1972. Office: 11th Dist PO Box 2140 Jacksonville FL 32203

COUSINEAU, R. DAVID, charitable organization executive. Exec. dir. Cath. Charities, L.A. Office: Cath Charities 1400 W 9th St PO Box 15095 Los Angeles CA 90015*

COUTU, CHARLES ARTHUR, deacon; b. Central Falls, R.I., Oct. 3, 1927; s. Charles Arthur and Aldea Alma (Laliberte) C.; m. Yvette Rhea Dery, Nov. 26, 1953. AA, Our Lady of Providence Sem., 1949; Etudes Speciales de Philosophies, Sem. Philosophy, Montreal, Que., Can., 1951; A in Casualty Claims Law, Am. Ednl. Inst. N.J., 1966. Ordained deacon Roman Cath. Ch., 1978. Master of ceremonies Bishop Tracy, Lafayette, La., 1958-59; tchr. St. Teresa's High Sch., Decatur, Ill., 1964-65, Pitts., 1964-68; tchr. Holy Family Ch., Dale City, Va., 1971—, permanent diaconate commn. mem., 1986-89; procurator, adv. Tribunal, Arlington, Va., 1990—; subrogation mgr. United Svcs. Automobile Assn., Reston, Va., 1976—; advocate Tribunal, Arlington, 1976—; chmn. Arbitration Com., Washington, 1975-88; mem. Diaconal Coun. Exec. Com., 1987-90; vice-chmn. Evangelization Commn., Diocese of Arlington, 1979-80. Religious emblem counselor Cath. Com. on Scouting and Campfire, 1990. Sgt. 1st class U.S. Army, 1952-55. Mem. KC. Home: 13401 Keating Dr Dale City VA 22193 Office: US Automobile Assn 1902 Campus Commons Dr Reston VA 22091 *I want to try to develop and nurture a deeper love and respect for God through His Mother, the Blessed Virgin Mary.*

COUTURE, JEAN GUY, bishop; b. Quebec, Que., Can., May 6, 1929; s. Odilon and Eva (Drolet) C. B.A., Laval U., Quebec, 1949, B.Ph., 1949, L.Theol., 1953, L.Sc.Phys., 1959. Ordained priest Roman Cath. Ch., 1953; prof. math. and scis. St. Georges High Sch. and Coll., Beauce, Que., 1953-65; adminstr. coll. St. Georges High Sch. and Coll., 1961-68; mem. adminstrn. Roman Cath. Diocese Quebec, 1968-75; bishop of Hauterive Que., 1975-79, of Chicoutimi, 1979—. Home and Office: 602 E Racine, Chicoutimi, PQ Canada G7H 6J6

COUTURE, MAURICE, archbishop; b. Saint-Pierre-de-Broughton, Que., Can., Nov. 3, 1926. Ordained priest Roman Cath. Ch., 1951; ordained titular bishop of Talaptula and aux. bishop of Quebec, 1982; bishop of Baie Comeau, Que., 1988-90; archbishop of Que., primate Ch. of Can., 1990—. Home: 2 Port Dauphin CP 45 HV, Quebec, PQ Canada G1R 4R6 Office: Archidiocese de Quebec, 1073 Saint-Cyrille Ouest, Sillery, PQ Canada G1S 4R5

COUTURIER, GUY, priest, educator; b. St. Joseph, N.B., Can., Apr. 22, 1929; s. Treffle and Leona (Cyr) C. Licentiate in theology, Angelicum, Rome, 1956; MA, Johns Hopkins U., 1957; licentiate in Bible, Vatican, 1959; PhD, Ecole Biblique, Jerusalem, 1961. Ordained priest Roman Cath. Ch., 1955. Mem. faculty U. Montreal, Que., Can., 1963—; prof. theology U. Montreal, 1962—; trustee Stonehill Coll., North Easton, Mass., 1976—,

Kings Coll., Wilkes-Barre, Pa., 1987—; mem. Bibl. Commn., Vatican, 1977-84. Mem. Am. Schs. Oriental Rsch., Archaeol. Inst. Am. (pres. 1979-91), Soc. Bibl. Lit., Brit. Sch. Archeology, Israel Exploration Soc. Office: U Montreal, Montreal, PQ Canada

COVENEY, MAURICE JOHN, minister; b. London, July 2, 1933; arrived in Can., 1957; s. John Herbert and Mary Ann (Roden) C.; m. Eileen Lois Ryba, Aug. 16, 1958; children: Graham Brent, Caren Lynn. Grad., Western Pentecostal Bible Coll., Vancouver, B.C., Can., 1963. Ordained to ministry Pentecostal Ch., 1968. Pastor Salmo (B.C.) Pentecostal Ch., 1965-67, Cache Creek (B.C.) Pentecostal Ch., 1967-70; asst. pastor Williams Lake Pentecostal Tabernacle, 1970-74; tchr. ministry St. Catharines, Ont., Can., 1974—. Author: (tape) How to Witness to the Jehovah's Witnesses, 1976. Home: 7 Vollette St, Saint Catharines, ON Canada L2R 6L4 Office: PO Box 2272, Saint Catharines, ON Canada L2M 6P6

COVINGTON, JOHN EWBANK, priest; b. Charlotte, N.C., Sept. 10, 1946; s. William Thomas Jr. and Winona Hill (Ewbank) C. BA, Trinity Coll., Hartford, Conn., 1968; MDiv, Gen. Sem., N.Y.C., 1973, STM, 1986. Ordained to ministry Episcopal Ch. as deacon, 1973, as priest, 1973. Asst. min. Christ Episcopal Ch., Easton, Md., 1973-75; asst. min. St. John's Episcopal Ch., Larchmont, N.Y., 1975-76, priest-in-charge, 1977; rector St. Alban's Episcopal Ch., S.I., N.Y., 1977—; pres. S.I. Interparish Coun., 1986-88, Interfaith Counseling Ctr., S.I., 1986-90. Bd. dirs. South Shore Ctr., YMCA, S.I., 1991—. Mem. S.I. Coun. of Chs. (pres. 1989—). Home and Office: 76 St Alban's Pl Staten Island NY 10312

COVINO, PAUL FRANCIS XAVIER, religious executive, consultant; b. Methuen, Mass., Aug. 3, 1958; s. Benjamin Gene and Lorraine Mary (Gallagher) C.; m. Anne Elizabeth Hallisey, Apr. 23, 1983. BA, Georgetown U., 1980; MA, U. Notre Dame, 1981. Mem. staff Diocesan Office for Worship, Worcester, Mass., 1980; assoc. dir. Georgetown Ctr. for Liturgy, Spirituality and Arts, Washington, 1981-89; pvt. practice liturgical resource cons. Upton, Mass., 1989—; dormitory min. in residence Georgetown U., Washington, 1981-83; mem. pastoral planning steering com. Diocese of Worcester. Editor: Celebrating Marriage: Preparing the Wedding Liturgy, 1987; contbr. articles to profl. jours. Mem. Nat. Assn. for Lay Ministry, N.Am. Acad. Liturgy (assoc.), Religious Conf. Mgmt. Assn., Nat. Conf. on Environment and Art for Cath. Worship (nat. com.). Roman Catholic. Address: 28 Elm St Upton MA 01568-1321

COWDEN, CLARK DOUGLAS, minister; b. Cleve., May 24, 1961; s. Robert Laughlin and Corinne Lucille (Leister) C.; m. Linda Joyce Britton, June 4, 1984; children: Ryan, Justin. BS, Taylor U., 1984; MDiv, Fuller Sem., 1988. Ordained to ministry Presbyn. Ch., 1988. Club dir. Youth for Christ, Marion, Ind., 1980-84; dir. youth Southminster Presbyn. Ch., Indpls., 1984-86; pastoral intern First Presbyn. Ch. of Newhall, Calif., 1986-87; evangelism intern LaCanada (Calif.) Presbyn. Ch., 1987-88; assoc. pastor First Presbyn. Ch. of Anderson, Ind., 1988—; chmn. Presbyn. Evangelism Com., Indpls., 1991—; mem. Presbytery Com. on Congl. Mission, Indpls., 1989-90. Author worship leaflets, 1990. Elections vote verifier Rep. Party, Anderson, 1990. Mem. Presbyns. for Renewal, Evang. Tchr. Tng. Assn., Kiwanis. Home: 1315 W 9th St Anderson IN 46016 Office: First Presbyn Ch 230 W 9th St Anderson IN 46016

COWELL, RONALD JAMES, radio engineer; b. Grosse Pointe Farms, Mich., May 17, 1941; s. Lambert Bowman and Vivian Beatrice (Soggs) C.; m. Sally Elizabeth Erickson, Dec. 16, 1967; children: Amy Joy, Wendy Ann, Melody Sue. BS in Elec. Engring., Wayne State U., Detroit, 1963; student, Moody Bible Inst., Chgo., 1965-66. Cert. sr. broadcast engr. Chief engr. WRVM, Suring, Wis., 1970-76, KOQT/Help Ministries, Bellingham, Wash., 1976-86, KNTR/Help Ministries, Ferndale, Wash., 1987—. Mem. Soc. Broadcast Engrs. Mem. Assembly of God Ch. Office: Sta KNTR PO Box 308 5538 Imhof Rd Ferndale WA 98248

COWELL, WILBURN JAMES, minister; b. Memphis, Jan. 11, 1940; s. Wilburn Jackson and Hazel Eugenia (Babb) C.; m. Norma Jean Bratton, Dec. 30, 1961; children: James Andrew, Norma Lynn, Janet Raye. BA, Emory U., 1962, M in Divinity, 1965. Ordained to ministry United Meth. Ch. as elder. Assoc. pastor Madison Heights United Meth. Ch., Memphis, 1965-68; pastor Trinity United Meth. Ch., Paris, Tenn., 1968-70; assoc. pastor Mullins United Meth. Ch., Memphis, 1970-74; pastor First United Meth. Ch., Clinton, Ky., 1974-76; minister of evangelism First United Meth. Ch., Colorado Springs, Colo., 1976-80; pastor Sunrise United Meth. Ch., Colorado Springs, 1980-83; dir. congl. devel. Gen. Bd. Discipleship United Meth. Ch., Nashville, 1983-91; pastor Hilltop United Meth. Ch., Sandy, Utah, 1991—. Author: Sponsoring New Congregations, 1985, Extending Your Congregation's Welcome, 1989; editor: Organizing New Congregations, 1986; editor newsletter New Congl. Devel., 1984-91. Mem. Memphis United Meth. Conf. (dist. chairperson evangelism), Rocky Mountain United Meth. Conf. (past dist. chairperson evangelism, conf. chairperson). Democrat. Office: Hilltop United Meth Ch 985 E 10600 South Sandy UT 84094

COWLES, JAMES ARTHUR, school administrator; b. Wellsville, N.Y., May 9, 1952; s. Mary Elizabeth Laven; m. Marva Jane Mapes, July 31, 1976; children: Chris, Cory. BS in Edn., Bowling Green (Ohio) U., 1973; MEd, Ohio U., 1976, PhD, 1991. Tchr. Lancaster (Ohio) City Schs., 1974-85, supr. math./sci./computers, 1984—, asst. prin., 1989—; instr. Ohio U., Athens, 1980—; cons. in field. Author 12 Pascal text books, 1984—. Mem. Nat. Assn. Sec. Sch. Prins., Ohio Assn. Sch. Adminstrs., Lancaster Assn. Sch. Adminstrs. (pres. 1987-89), Mensa, Kiwanis (v.p. 1990—). Avocations: computers, sports. Office: Lancaster City Schs 345 E Mulberry St Lancaster OH 43130

COWLEY, WILLIAM AUSTIN, religion educator; b. Meade County, Ky., Feb. 20, 1931; s. William H. and Elva (Brown) C.; m. Audrey C. Evans, Sept. 3, 1954; children: Carol E., Karen C. Bergquist. BA, Georgetown Coll., 1951; MA, U. Fla., 1954; PhD, Mich. State U., 1972. Sec. Bapt. student union Georgetown (Ky.) Coll., 1951-53, asst. prof., 1954-55; fgn. missionary Fgn. Mission Bd. So. Bapt. Conv.-Nigeria, 1955-77; prof. religion Samford U., Birmingham, Ala., 1977—; interim and supply pastor various chs. Contbr. study materials to mags. Mem. So. Bapt. Profs. Religion Edn., Nat. Assn. Profs. Christian Edn., Phi Kappa Phi. Home: 433 Glenwood Rd Birmingham AL 35216

COWLING, RANDAL KEITH, minister; b. Killeen, Tex., Nov. 13, 1957; s. Marion F. and Ollie L. (Hosey) C.; m. Doris Jean Lorenz, May 28, 1978; children: Jennifer Ann, Emily Megan. BA, SW Bapt. Coll., 1979; MDiv, Midwestern Bapt. Sem., 1983. Ordained to ministry So. Bapt. Conv., 1987. Interim minister edn., ch. extension intern Park Hill Bapt. Ch., Kansas City, Mo., 1986-87; dir. ch. and community ministries Clay-Platte Bapt. Assn., Kansas City, 1987-89, dir. ch. programs, 1988-89; founder, pastor Boardwalk Chapel, Atlantic City, 1989—; dir. Atlantic City Ministries, 1989—; founder, co-pastor Iglesia Bautista Hispana, Atlantic City, 1990, Hope Fellowship Ch., Galloway Township, N.J., 1991. Compiler (community ministries manual) Northland Directory, 1987. Co-founder-pres., v.p. Northland Homes Partnership, Kansas City, 1988. Named Outstanding Young Man of Am., Jaycees, Kansas City, 1987, 89. Mem. South Jersey Bapt. Assn. (sec.-treas. ministers fellowship 1989—), So. Bapt. Social Svcs. Assn. (charter, v.p. publs.), Assn. Resort and Leisure Mins. Office: Atlantic City Ministries 3123 Atlantic Ave Atlantic City NJ 08401

COX, ALBERT EDWARD, pastor; b. Turtle Creek, Pa., Oct. 30, 1935; s. Albert Earl and Naomi (Page) C.; m. Ruth Lynne Gray, July 5, 1958; children: Lynne Ellen Cox Chenot, Lisa Diane Cox Shutt. BS, Houghton, 1957; BS in Mission, St. Paul Bible, 1958. Ordained to ministry Christian and Missionary Alliance, 1966 and in United Meth. Ch., as deacon, 1971, as elder, 1983. Pastor C&MA, Pa., 1963-68, Cen. Pa. Conf. United Meth. Ch., 1968—. Republican. Home and Office: Saginaw-Starview Parish 765 Market St Mount Wolf PA 17347-9774

COX, DANIEL G., bishop. Bishop Ref. Episcopal Ch., Catonsville, Md. Office: Reformed Episcopal Ch 9 Hiltop Pl Catonsville MD 21228*

COX, ELDON WESTON, minister; b. Chandler, Okla., Nov. 26, 1939; s. Weston Francis Cox and Winifred Irene (Jones) Lyon; m. Anita Gayle Key, Aug. 1, 1958; children: Kevin, Kim, Kris, Karmen. Diploma, Friends Bible Coll., Haviland, Kans., 1962; BA, Friends U., 1974. Ordained to ministry Soc. Friends Ch. Pastor North Houston Friends Ch., 1962-66, Lawrence (Kans.) Friends Ch., 1966-72, Homestead Friends Ch., Cedar Point, Kans., 1973-80, Paonia (Colo.) Friends ch., 1980—; chmn. com. Spiritual Life Dist. Bd., Rocky Mountain area, 1990—, Recording (Ordination) of Pastors, 1982-90. Vol. van driver for sr. citizens' dinners, 1988—. Mem. Nat. Pastors Conf. (mem. com. 1990—). Republican. Home: 409 3d St PO Box 278 Paonia CO 81428 Office: Evang Friends Ch 3d and Poplar Sts Paonia CO 81428

COX, GEORGE SHERWOOD, minister; b. McAllen, Tex., Jan. 12, 1963; s. Jerry Alton and Eldora (Chrismier) C. BA in Communication, U. Tex. Pan Am., Edinburg, U.K., 1985; MA in Religious Edn., Southwestern Bapt. Theol. Sem., Ft. Worth, 1988. Lic. to ministry So. Bapt. Conv., 1985, ordained, 1990. Assoc. min. edn. South Hills Bapt. Ch., Ft. Worth, 1987-88; min. youth, assoc. pastor Trinity Bapt. Ch., McAllen, 1989-91; account exec. Christian radio Sta. KVTY, McAllen, 1991—; dir. Bapt. Student Union, U. Tex., Brownsville, Bapt. Gen. Conv. Tex., Dallas, 1988—. Mem. So. Bapt. Religious Educators Assn., Network for Youth Ministry. Republican. Home: 320 S Peking McAllen TX 78501

COX, HARVEY GALLAGHER, theologian; b. Phoenixville, Pa., May 19, 1929; s. Harvey Gallagher and Dorothea (Dunwoody) C.; m. Nancy Nieburger, May 10, 1957; children—Rachel Lianelly, Martin Stephen, Sarah Irene. A.B. with honors in history, U. Pa., 1951; B.D. cum laude, Yale, 1955; Ph.D., Harvard, 1963. Dir. religious activities Oberlin Coll., 1955-58; program asso. Am. Baptist Home Mission Soc., 1958-62; fraternal worker Gossner Mission, East Berlin, 1962-63; asst. prof. Andover Newton Theol. Sch., 1963-65; asso. prof. church and soc. Harvard, 1965-70, Victor Thomas prof. divinity, 1970—; cons. Third Assembly World Council Chs., New Delhi, India, 1961. Author: The Secular City, 1965, God's Revolution and Man's Responsibility, 1965, The Feast of Fools, 1969, The Seduction of the Spirit: The Use and Misuse of People's Religion, 1973, Turning East: The Promise and Peril of the New Orientalism, 1977, Just As I Am, 1983, The Silencing of Leonardo Boff: The Vatican and the Future of World Christianity, 1988, Many Mansions: A Christian's Encounter With Other Faiths, 1988; editorial bd.: Christianity and Crisis. Chmn. bd. Blue Hill Christian Center, 1963-66; chmn. Boston Indsl. Mission. Office: Harvard Univ Divinity Sch Cambridge MA 02140

COX, HUGH RONALD, music minister; b. Trumann, Ark., July 5, 1939; s. Marvin and Virgie Ouella (Thorne) C.; m. Elizabeth Joy, Feb. 26, 1960; children: Gregory Lynn (dec.), Ernest Randall (dec.). MusB, Ark. State Coll., 1961; MS, Ark. State U., 1969. Music dir. Pocahontas (Ark.) First Bapt., 1961-63, Morrilton (Ark.) First Bapt., 1963-65, Carruthersville (Mo.) First Bapt. Ch., 1965-67, Bay (Ark.) First Bapt. Ch., 1968-70, 3 chs., Tulsa, 1970-76, First Bapt. Ch., Brinkley, Ark., 1976-78, First So. Bapt. Ch., Del City, Okla., 1978-81; min. of music Olivet Bapt. Ch., Wichita, Kans., 1981—; mus. dir. Sedgewich Assn., Wichita, Kans., 1984-86; music coord. Jay Strack Evangelistic Crusade, Wichita, 1983—; city chaplain Coun. of City of Brinkley, 1977. Mem. Kans./Neb. Conv. So. Bapt. Music Dirs. (past pres.). Office: Olivet So Bapt Ch 3440 W 13th St Wichita KS 67203

COX, IVAN WILLIAM ROBERT, clergyman, social worker; b. Dallas, Aug. 25, 1950; s. Bob J. and M. Bernice (Slaughter) C.; m. Beverly K. Porter Pike, Aug. 15, 1987. AB, Dallas Christian Coll., 1972; MS, Am. Tech. U., 1981, M in Criminal Justice, 1982. Lic. profl. counselor; lic. childcare adminstr.; cert. social worker; ordained to ministry Christian Ch., 1972. Minister Woodland Christian Ch., Timpson, Tex., 1972-77, First Christian Ch., Florence, Colo., 1977-80; exec. dir. Cen. Tex. Youth Services Bur., Killeen, 1981-85; pres., gen. mgr. Cen. Tex. Exposition, Killeen, 1982-87; minister Northview Christian Ch., Taylor, Tex., 1983—; dir. Williamson County Mental Health Ctr., Taylor, 1987—; planner ann. workshop Regional Network for Children, Austin, Tex., 1982-84; cons. Tex. Evangelism, Dallas, 1972—. Co-author (course guide) Successful Living, 1982; contbr. articles to profl. jours. Mem. exec. bd. Ret. Sr. Vol. Program, Nacogdoches, Tex., 1973-77; founding chmn. Florence Council on Aging, 1978-80. Recipient Appreciation award Florence Council on Aging, 1982, Citation of Merit, Ladies Aux. to VFW, 1979, Outstanding State Chaplain, U.S. Jaycees, 1984. Mem. Tex. Assn. Alcohol and Drug Abuse Counselors, Tex. Network Youth Services (bd. dirs. 1982-83), Tex. Assn. Christian Counselors, Regional Network Children (bd. dirs. 1983, Service Appreciation award 1982), Tex. Jaycees (i.d. trainer 1983—, Outstanding Appointed Officer, 1984), Jaycees Internat. (senator), Killeen Jaycees (pres., pub. relations dir., v.p. 1982—), Am. Tech. U. Alumni Assn. (pres. 1983-84), Alpha Kappa Delta. Republican. Lodge: Lions. Avocations: hunting, fishing, horseback riding, travel. Home: 4416 County Rd 123 PO Box 304 Hutto TX 78634 Office: Northview Christian Ch Hwy 94 N PO Box 1031 Taylor TX 76574

COX, J. ARTHUR, minister; b. Utica, N.Y., Aug. 5, 1940; s. James F. and Margaret (Craig) C.; m. Mahailie Tillson, Dec. 29, 1962; children: Deborah Jean, James Andrew. AAS, Mohawk Valley Community Coll., 1961; BTh, Concordia Sem., 1975; D Ministry, Faith Sem., Tacoma, 1991. Ordained to ministry Luth. Ch.-Mo. Synod, 1975. Pastor Grace Luth. Ch., Bradford, Pa., 1975—; del. Synodical Conv., Dallas, 1977; counselor Cattaraugus Cir., Bradford, 1978-82; chmn. Dist. Open House, Bradford, 1982, Dist. Extension Fund, Buffalo, 1982-85; chmn. ea. dist. Alive in Christ, bd. dirs. Mission Svcs. Bd. dirs. Evergreen Hylands, 1979, Am. Cancer Soc., 1980, Vis. Nurse Assn., 1980-86, Bradford Hosp., 1985—. Mem. Rotary (bd. dirs. 1978-82, pres. 1982-83). Republican. Home: 465 Interstate Pkwy Bradford PA 16701 Office: Grace Luth Ch 79 Mechanic St Bradford PA 16701 *Life is a sequence of God-given opportunities to serve Him and His people. The excitement is derived from accepting His call to service and experiencing His magnificent power working through you to accomplish His purpose.*

COX, JAMES WILLIAM, religious educator; b. Kingston, Tenn., Jan. 18, 1923; s. Isham Monroe and Carrie Eva (Driskill) C.; m. Patricia Parrent, Aug. 4, 1951; children: David Allan, Kenneth Mitchell. BA, Carson-Newman Coll., Jefferson City, Tenn., 1944; MDiv, So. Bapt. Theol. Sem., Louisville, 1947, PhD, 1953. Ordained to ministry So. Bapt. Conv., 1943. Pastor Nance's Grove Bapt. Ch., New Market, Tenn., 1943-44, Meml. Bapt. Ch., Frankfort, Ky., 1945-54, Cen. Bapt. Ch., Johnson City, Tenn., 1954-59; Lester prof. preaching So. Bapt. Theol. Sem., Louisville, 1959—; vis. lectr. Protestant Episcopal Sem., Alexandria, Va., 1977, Princeton Theol. Sem., 1964-65, 86, Golden GAte Bapt. Sem., Mill Valley, Calif., 1985, 86. Editor Pulpit Digest, Jackson, Miss., 1983-85; author: A Guide to Biblical Preaching, 1976, Preaching, 1985; editor book (ann.): The Ministers Manual, 1984—, Best Sermons, 1988—. Named Disting. Alumnus, Carson-Newman Coll., Jefferson City, Tenn., 1979. Fellow Assn. Theol. Schs.; mem. Acad. of Homiletics (pres. 1976-77). Home: 516 Dover Rd Louisville KY 40206 Office: So Bapt Theol Sem 2825 Lexington Rd Louisville KY 40280

COX, JOHN B., minister; b. Rochester, Tex., July 20, 1932; s. Arthur B. and Leora (Bradley) C.; m. Mozelle D. Cox, May 20, 1949 (dec. June 1989); children: Roy L., Tim B., Robin Cox Ankrom, Michelle Cox Mirelez; m. Karen D. Scott, Dec. 12, 1989; children: LaTisha Renae, Brandon Joel. BTh, Southwestern Bapt. Theol. Sem., Ft. Worth, 1965; postgrad., U. Nebr., 1970-71; BA, Ebert Inst., Colombia, Mo., 1979, D of Ministry, 1980; postgrad. law sch., Meridian U., 1989—. Ordained to ministry So. Bapt. Conv., 1968. V.p., sec., treas. Kans.-Nebr. Bapt. Found., Topeka, 1983-86; sr. pastor Univ. Bapt. Ch., Lubbock, Tex., 1987—; del. So. Bapt. Conv., Atlanta, 1972-91; mem. Com. on Bds., Nashville, 1982; missionary Home Mission Bd., Atlanta, 1965-87; adj. faculty Meridian U., Lafayette, La. Author: Prayer in The First Degree, 1982. Vol. Dem. Party to Elect James Exon for Gov., Lincoln, Nebr., 1967-68; bd. dirs. Nebr. Coun. on Alcohol Edn., Lincoln, 1969-74; pres., bd. dirs. United Cerebral Palsy, Lincoln, N.Y.C., 1967-75. Mem. Lubbock Bapt. Assn. (bd. dirs. 1987—), Christian Counseling Assoc. (pres. 1980—), Inst. for Adolescent Studies (cert. tchr.). Democrat. Home: 4905 11th St Lubbock TX 79416 Office: Univ Bapt Ch 2420 10th St Lubbock TX 79401 *Commitment is the most important trail we may possess. With commitment one may "stay on course" to reach our life goals. The most important commitment one may make is to follow Jesus Christ as Savior.*

COX, JOHN HENRY, religious organization administrator, aeronautical engineer; b. Dorking, Surrey, Eng., May 17, 1941; s. William Edward and Ethel May (Bailey) C.; m. Elizabeth Mary Iris O'Brien, June 26, 1965; children: Jared Selvoy, Rachel Sonia. Diploma, Southall Coll. Technology, Eng., 1965. Lic. airline engr.; chartered engr. Asst. chief engr. British Airways, Eng., 1965-72, chief engr., 1972-77; national dir. Latter-day Saints Ch., Eng., 1977-83; internat. dir. Latter-day Saints Ch., Salt Lake City, 1983-85, welfare dir., 1985—. Mem. Inst. Mech. Engrs., Royal Aero. Soc., Brit. Inst. Mgmt. Avocation: photography.

COX, JOHN HORACE, minister; b. Greenville, S.C., Dec. 7, 1944; s. Horace Nelson and Nell (O'Neal) C.; m. Mary Ann Bryant, Dec. 23, 1967; children: Mary Angelique, Rhonda Michelle. Student, Fruitland Bapt. Bible Coll., 1973-75; AA, N. Greenville Coll., 1978; BA in Bibl. Studies, Luther Rice U., 1987; postgrad., Covington Theol. Sem. Ordained to ministry Bapt. Ch., 1975. Pastor Faith Bapt. Ch., Norris, S.C., 1975-78, Jupiter Bapt. Ch., Weaverville, N.C., 1978-79; assoc. pastor outreach and evangelism City View First Bapt. Ch., Greenville, S.C., 1979-80; pastor Beaumont Bapt. Ch., Spartanburg, S.C., 1980—; Mem. Gen. Bd. S.C. Bapt. Conv., 1990—. With USN, 1964-67. Home: 412 Jasmine St Spartanburg SC 29303 Office: Beaumont Bapt Ch 717 N Liberty St Spartanburg SC 29303

COX, JOHN SAMUEL, evangelist; b. Lincoln, Ill., Aug. 13, 1959; s. John David Cox and Roseann (Leith) Jackson; m. Deanna Lea Brant, June 19, 1982; children: Jonathan David, Jennifer Leanne. B in Christian Edn., Lincoln Christian Coll., 1981, MDiv in New Testament, 1989; postgrad., Trinity Evang. Div. Sch., 1989—. Ordained to ministry Christian Ch., 1980. Youth min. Atlanta Christian Ch., 1978-81, sr. min., 1981-86; preaching min. South Fork Ch. of Christ, Rochester, Ill., 1986-89; state evangelist for Ga. New Ch. Evangelism, Dallas, 1989—; founding pastor Pickett's Mill Christian Ch., Dallas, 1990—; Pres. Little Galilee Christian Assembly Camp, Clinton, Ill., 1986, Rochester (Ill.) Ministerial Alliance, 1988, Imago Dei-Right to Life, Lincoln, 1989. Contbr. articles to profl. publs. Co-chmn. Leadership Paulding, Dallas, 1991; mem. Rochester Cert. City Program, 1987; co-founder Area Drug and Alcohol Prevention Team, Atlanta, Ill., 1984. Named Outstanding Young Min., N.Am. Christian Conv., 1989. Mem. Paulding County C. of C. (bd. dirs. 1991—), Rotary (bd. dirs. Atlanta, Ill. club 1985). Home: 2383 Park Ave E Dallas GA 30132 Office: Picketts Mill Christian Ch 3323 Hiram Acworth Rd Dallas GA 30132 *Success belongs to those who, having taken God's hand, have acknowledged great risks, have overcome incredible odds, and have accepted the challenge to seize the future by the hand. This is visionary leadership at its best.*

COX, K. K., JR. (KEN COX), minister; b. Ft. Worth, Mar. 6, 1951; s. K.K. and Clara Lorene (Ellison) C.; m. Martha Lynne McFarland, Oct. 2, 1976; children: Amanda Kay, Brooks Kennedy, Rachel Lynne, Clara Louise. BBA, Tex. A&M U., 1973; MDiv, Southwestern Bapt. Theol. Sem., Ft. Worth, 1982, DMin, 1988. Ordained to ministry So. Bapt. Conv., 1981; CPA, Tex. Pastor Pike Bapt. Ch., Blue Ridge, Tex., 1980-83, Pine Burr Bapt. Ch., Beaumont, Tex., 1983-87, Woodland Pl. Bapt. Ch., Magnolia, Tex., 1987-91, 1st Bapt. Ch., New Boston, Tex., 1991—; moderator Tryon-Evergreen Bapt. Assn., Conroe, 1989-90, chmn. fin. com., 1987-89; trustee E. Tex. Bapt. Encampment, Newton, 1984-87; cons. ACTS TV Network, Beaumont, 1983-87. Home and Office: 506 McCoy Blvd S New Boston TX 75570 *A very simple motto that I like to repeat in times of trial and triumph is: Prayer will be answered, patience will be rewarded, and perserverance will be blessed.*

COX, KATHRYN HONAKER, clergywoman; b. Beckley, W.Va., Mar. 22, 1924; d. William Wesley and Daisy Elizabeth (Lilly) Honaker; m. Lewis Kimber Cox, June 4, 1944; children—Mary Kathrine Cox Southwood, Lewis Kimber. Student Salvation Army Officers Tng., Atlanta, 1943-44; A.A. in Journalism and Psychology, Richland Coll., Dallas, 1974; B.S. in Criminal Justice, U. Tex.-Arlington, 1976, M.A. in Urban Affairs, 1977. Ordained minister, Salvation Army, 1944. Officer, Salvation Army, N.C., Ky., Tenn., Md., Ga., Fla., Va., Tex., 1944-84, assoc. dir. correctional services, Tex., 1972-81, ret., 1984, adminstrv. asst. property dept., Dallas, 1984—. Contbr. articles to Nat. War Cry. Kiest Found. scholar, Dallas, 1973; U. Tex.-Arlington scholar, 1975-76; Am. Bus Women scholar, 1977, recipient merit award, 1977. Vol., VA hosps. and mental instns. Mem. Ch. Women United (pres. Kingsport, Tenn. 1950's, sec.-treas. Waco 1970), Social Workers Assn. (sec. 1970), Bus. and Profl. Women (scholar, named Woman of Yr. 1970). Republican. Home: 6354 Velasco Ave Dallas TX 75214 Office: State Hdqrs The Salvation Army 500 N Ervay St Dallas TX 75214

COX, RANDY CARTER, minister; b. El Paso, Tex., Jan. 5, 1960; s. A.O. and Edith (Mueller) C.; m. Shari Renee Treybig, June 20, 1987. BA in Bus. Adminstrn., Tex. Tech. U., 1984; MA in Religious Edn., Southwestern Bapt. Theol., Seminary, Ft. Worth, 1988. Lic. to ministry So Bapt. Conv., 1984. Youth minister First Bapt. Ch., Wilson, Tex., 1982-85; assoc. pastor First Bapt. Ch., Willow Park, Tex., 1987—; camp dir. Youth Camp '89, '90, Ouachita, Ark., 1988-89; assn. youth dir. Parker County Bapt. Assn., Weatherford, Tex., 1991. Home: 134 North Chase Willow Park TX 76087 Office: First Baptist Church 601 Ranch House Rd Willow Park TX 76087 *In life, it is not so much "what" you go through but "how" you go through it that counts. Christianity is not another area of our lives but something that should permeate and affect every area of our lives.*

COX, TIMOTHY M., religion educator; b. Cadillac, Mich., Nov. 20, 1957; s. Richard Solomon and Phyliss (Davidson) C.; m. Diane Daggy, June 20, 1980; children: Philip, Stephen, Melissa, Christina. BA, William Jennings Bryan Coll., 1980; M of Religious Edn., Southwestern Bapt. Theol. Sem., 1982. Christian edn. pastor Bible Bapt. Ch., Traverse City, Mich., 1982-88, Pulpit Rock Ch., Colorado Springs, Colo., 1988—; Christian edn. cons. Scripture Press Publs., Wheaton, Ill., 1985—. Mem. Profl. Assn. Christian Educators. Baptist. Office: Pulpit Rock Church 301 Austin Bluffs Pkwy Colorado Springs CO 80918 *To God be any glory or praise I receive. It is a joy to be a participant in His ministry on this earth.*

COX, WILLIAM ALBERT, JR., minister, musician; b. Jefferson, Tex., May 2, 1927; s. William Albert and Dollye (Spradley) C.; m. Catherine Ward, Dec. 5, 1948; children: Catherine Rose Cox Jones, Carole Nan Cox Hammock. BS, East Tex. Bapt. Coll., 1949; MRE, Southwestern Bapt. Theol. Sem., 1954. Ordained to ministry So. Bapt. Conv., 1952. Minister edn. First Bapt. Ch., Dallas, 1960-63; supr. sales Bapt. Sunday Sch. Bd., Nashville, 1967-74, music specialist, 1974-75, trade sales supr., 1975-80, supr. programs, 1980-90, ret., 1990; music dir., soloist Gideons Internat., Indpls., 1983, soloist, Kansas City, Mo., 1990; music dir., soloist Pastor's Conf., Dallas, 1965, revivals and confs. over U.S. Soloist So. Bapt. Conv., L.A., 1982; featured soloist Gov.'s Prayer Breakfast, Nashville, 1982, Oil Industry Pres.'s Prayer Breakfast, Nashville, 1984; soloist (record) God Gave Me Love, 1973, From Glory to Heaven, 1983; compiler: (music book) Time of Salvation, 1973. Nat. coord. Vols. in Evangelism, Home Mission Bd., So. Bapt. Conv., 1990—. Republican. Avocations: fishing, travel. Home and Office: 104 Blue Hills Ct Nashville TN 37214

COX, WILLIAM ARGUS, music and youth minister; b. Tulsa, July 3, 1959; s. Luther M. and Florence S. (Wasson) C.; m. Cathrine Diane Bush, Feb. 16, 1980; children: Michelle Dawn, James Luther. B in Music Edn., Cen. State U., 1981; M in Ch. Music, Southwestern Bapt. Theol Sem., 1983. Min. music and youth Millwood Bapt. Ch., Oklahoma City, Okla., 1977-78, Noble Ave. Bapt. Ch., Guthrie, Okla., 1978-79; min. music and youth 1st Bapt. Ch., Cashion, Okla., 1979-81, Heritage Bapt. Ch., 1981-84; assoc. pastor music and youth Vista Grande Bapt. Ch., Colorado Springs, Colo., 1984—; v.p. Pikes Peak Bapt. Pastor's Conf., Colorado Springs, 1984-85, music. dir. Pikes Peak Bapt. Assn., Colorado Springs, 1985-86, 2d v.p. Colo. Bapt. Pastor's Conf., 1987-88, mem. CENTURYMEN, Southern Bapt. Conv., 1988—. Conductor Vista Grande Area Choral Groups Christmas Program, Colorado Springs, 1987. Mem. Am. Choral Dirs. Assn., Am. Guild English Handbell Ringers, Colorado Singing Churchmen, Phi Mu Alpha Sinfonia (historian 1980-81). Republican. Home: 3960 Topsail Dr Colorado Springs CO 80918 Office: Vista Grande Bapt Ch 5075 Flintridge Dr Colorado Springs CO 80918

COX, WILLIAM JACKSON, bishop; b. Valeria, Ky., Jan. 24, 1921; s. Robert Lee and Ora Ethel (Lawson) C.; m. Betty Drake, Dec. 20, 1941;

children—Sharon Lee, William Richard, Michael Colin. Student, U. Cin., 1939-40, George Washington U., Washington, 1945-46, U. Md. overseas extension, London, 1951-53, Va. Theol. Sem., Alexandria, 1957; D.Div. (hon.), Va. Theol. Sem., Alexandria, 1974, Episcopal Theol. Sem. Ky., Lexington, 1980. Ordained priest Episcopal Ch., 1957. Pres., gen. mgr. McCook Broadcasting Co., McCook, Nebr., 1947-49; rector Church of the Holy Cross, Cumberland, Md., 1957-72; suffragan bishop of Md. Episcopal Ch., Frederick, Md., 1972-80; asst. bishop Okla. Episcopal Ch., Tulsa, 1980—; pres. Appalachian Peoples Service Orgn., Blacksburg, Va., 1974-80; chmn. Standing Com. on the Church in Small Communities, N.Y.C., 1976-82. Pres., Nursing Home Bd. of Allegany County, Cumberland, Md., 1965-72; pres. Episcopal Ministries to the Aging, Balt., 1973-80. Served to lt. col. U.S. Army, 1942-46, 1949-54; ETO. Avocation: private pilot. Home: 6130 S Hudson Pl Tulsa OK 74136 Office: Diocese of Okla 501 S Cincinnati Ave Tulsa OK 74103

COY, WILLARD JENE, church school administrator; b. Indpls., Dec. 22, 1955; s. Charlie George and Katrina Janet (Kaufman) C.; m. Jean Raynal Easterday, July 5, 1980; children: Timothy Mark, Jennifer Raynal, Summer Marie. AA in Acctg., Ind. Bus. Coll., 1976; T.H.G. in Missions, Bapt. Bible Coll., Springfield, Mo., 1980, BS in Theology, 1981; MRE in Ch. Ministry, Bapt. Theol. Sem., Chattanooga, 1984. Cert. ETTA. Bible clubs organizer Springfield Bapt. Ch., 1977-81; visitation officer Highland Park Bapt., Chattanooga, 1981-84; Awana club leader, Sunday sch. tchr. Grace Bapt. Ch., Chattanooga, 1985-87, tchr. single adults, 1987-90, pre-primary div. Sunday sch. supt., 1990—; machine operator McKee Baking Co., Collegdale, Tenn., 1981-91. Recipient Master Degree in Free Enterprise, Jr. Achievement Indpls., 1974. Mem. Evang. Tchr. Tng. Assn. (life, Standard Tchr. Diploma 1984). Home: 4909 Scenic View Dr Chattanooga TN 37409

COYLE, GRADY ELLIS, organist, music director; b. Oklahoma City, Okla., Oct. 3, 1946; s. Volley Tine and Julia Madge (Ellis) C. BA, U. N. Tex., 1968; MusM, So. Meth. U., 1973; D of Mus. Arts, U. Ill., 1988. Organist, choirmaster St. Stephen United Presbyn. Ch., Irving, Tex., 1977-79; dir. music, organist Northridge Presbyn. Ch., Dallas, 1979—; mem. Worship Com. Grace Presbytery, Tex., 1984-88. Staff sgt. USAF, 1968-72. Mem. Am. Guild Organists (cert., dean 1989-91), Choristers Guild (Dallas chpt. pres. 1987-88), Presby. Assn. Musicians (Grace Presbytery chpt. pres. 1989-91). Home: 3237 Carlisle 139 Dallas TX 75204 Office: Northridge Presbyn Ch 6920 Bob-o-link Dr Dallas TX 75214

COYLE, PATRICK OTIS, music minister; b. Gaffney, S.C., July 14, 1960; s. George Wallace and Lorene Helen (Patterson) C. MusB, Furman U., 1982; MusM, Converse Coll., 1987. Ordained to ministry So. Bapt. Conv., 1985. Min. of music and activities Park Hills Bapt. Ch., Spartanburg, S.C., 1983-87; organist, min. of music First Bapt. Ch., Conway, S.C., 1987—; ch. music specialist S.C. Bapt. Conv., Columbia, S.C., 1983—; assoc. conductor S.C. Bapt. Singing Churchmen, Columbia, 1987—. Composer religious music, 1985, 87. Mem. Myrtle Beach (S.C.) Community Chorus, 1990. Mem. Am. Choral Dirs. Assn., So. Bapt. Ch. Music Conf. Home: 240 Myrtle Greens Dr Conway SC 29526 Office: First Bapt Ch 603 Elm St Conway SC 29526 *So much of modern religion is based on fear—fear of freedom and the unknown. We must let go of legalistic "dos and don'ts." True faith should serve as an example of love, acceptance and inclusiveness.*

COZZI, SISTER JOANNE, school system administrator. Supt. Cath. schs. Diocese Biloxi, Miss. Home: 3900 16th St Gulfport MS 39501*

CRABB, GERALD ALLEN, minister; b. Detroit, Sept. 16, 1949; s. Cecil Arthur and Grace (Simpson) C.; m. Eunice Anne Wright, May 14, 1971; children: Gerald II, Geoffrey Cecil. AA, Macomb Community Coll., 1969; MRE, Midwestern Bapt. Coll., 1972; MEd, Faith Evangelistic Coll., 1976, PhD, 1978. Ordained to ministry Bapt. Ch., 1973; cert. sch. adminstr., Fla. Assoc. pastor First Bapt. Ch., Ruskin, Fla., 1972-81; sr. pastor Bible Bapt. Ch., Callahan, Fla., 1981-87, Grace Bapt. Ch., Miami, Fla., 1988—; v.p., bd. dirs. Beebe Evangelistic Assn., Stockbridge, Ga., 1978—; pres. Grace Bapt. Acad., Miami, 1988—; trustee Midwestern Bapt. Coll., Pontiac, Mich., 1990—; regional v.p. Trinity Bapt. Coll., Jacksonville, Fla., 1991—. Co-editor articles in religious jours., 1982—. Mem. A Women's Pregnancy Ctr., Homestead, Fla., 1991. Recipient Soc. Disting. High Sch. Students, 1981; named Hon. Lt. Col. Govs. Office, 1974. Mem. Nat. Assn. Christian Athletes (chaplain 1984—), Accelerated Christian Edn. (cons., officer 1985—, chmn. Fla. state student conv. 1985—), Fla. Christian Activities Assn. (sec., treas. 1986—), U.S. Golf Assn., Southwide Bapt. Fellowship. Republican. Office: Grace Bapt Ch & Acad 19301 SW 127 Ave Miami FL 33177 *In life you will find that you have many acquaintances, but very few Real Friends. The key to a successful friendship is forgiveness. I believe the gift of forgiveness is a lost gift in today's society. To have a friend you must be a friend.*

CRABTREE, ARTHUR BAMFORD, retired religion educator; b. Stalybridge, Cheshire, Eng., May 5, 1910; came to U.S., 1957; s. George and Harriet (Bamford) C.; m. Hanna Utzinger; 1 child, Martin. BA, Manchester (Eng.) U., 1933, BD, 1935; Dr. Theology, Zürich U., Switzerland, 1946; postgrad., Tübingen U., Fed. Republic Germany, 1965-66. Ordained to ministry Bapt. Ch., 1937. Min. Bapt. Ch., Fleetwood, Eng., 1937-39, Harehills Bapt. Ch., Leeds, Eng., 1939-45; youth sec. Bapt. Union Gr. Britain, London, 1945-39; prof. systematic theology Bapt.Theol. Sem., Rüschlikon, 1949-57, Ea. Bapt. Theol. Sem., Phila., 1957-68; prof. ecumenism Villanova (Pa.) U., 1968-87. Home: Normandy Farms Estates Box 1108 C212 Blue Bell PA 19422 *I am deeply concerned about the future of life on earth—human life and plant and animal life. To ensure the survival of life we humans will need to make drastic and speedy changes in the way we think and act.*

CRABTREE, DAVIDA FOY, minister; b. Waterbury, Conn., June 7, 1944; d. Alfred and Davida (Blakeslee) Foy; m. David T. Hindinger Jr., Aug. 28, 1982; stepchildren: Elizabeth Anne, D. Todd. BS, Marietta Coll., 1967; MDiv, Andover Newton Theol. Sch., 1972; D of Ministry, Hartford Sem., 1989. Ordained to ministry United Ch. of Christ, 1972. Founder, exec. dir. Prudence Crandall Ctr. for Women, New Britain, Conn., 1973-76; min., dir. Greater Hartford (Conn.) Campus Ministry, 1976-80; sr. min. Colchester (Conn.) Federated Ch., 1980-91; bd. dirs. Conn. Conf. United Ch. of Christ, Hartford, 1982-90; conf. min. So. Calif. Conf., United Ch. of Christ, Pasadena, 1991—; rsch. assoc. Harvard Div. Sch., Cambridge, Mass., 1975-76. Author: The Empowering Church, 1989 (named one of Top Ten Books of Yr. 1990); editorial advisor Alban Inst., 1990—. Bd. dirs. Hartford region YWCA, 1979-82; trustee Cragin Meml. Libr., Colchester, 1980-91, Hartford Sem., 1983-91; founder Youth Svcs. Bur., Colchester, 1984-89; pres. Creative Devel. for Colchester Inc., 1989-91. Recipient Antoinette Brown award Gen. Synod, United Ch. of Christ, 1977, Conf. Preacher award Conn. Conf., United Ch. of Christ, 1982, Woman in Leadership award Hartford region YWCA, 1987; named one of Outstanding Conn. Women, UN Assn., 1987. Mem. Nat. Coun. Chs. (bd. dirs. 1969-81), Christians for Justice Action (exec. com. 1981-91).

CRABTREE, ROBERT DEE, minister; b. Mt. Vernon, Mo., Nov. 11, 1935; s. Cecil Sherman and Wanda Marie (Bennett) C.; m. Roberta Mae Davidson, June 8, 1957; children: Douglas Todd, Daniel Howard, Deona Marie. Student, Cen. Bible Coll., Springfield, Mo., 1959; BA, Ind. U. Extention, Ft. Wayne, 1962; MA, John Carroll U., 1967. Ordained to ministry Assemblies of God, 1961. Student, pastor Assembly of God, Flint Hollow, Mo., 1957-58; pastor Assembly of God, Hicksville, Ohio, 1959-62, Decatur, Ind., 1962-63; pastor Calvary Assembly of God, Willoughby Hills, Ohio, 1963-66; missionary Assemblies of God, Germany, Austria, Yugoslavia, 1966-77; coll. pres. Continental Bible Coll., Brussels, 1974-77; pastor Falls Assembly Of God, Cuyahoga Falls, Ohio, 1977-79, Bethel Temple Assembly of God, Parma, Ohio, 1979-83; Ohio dist. supr. Assemblies of God, Columbus, 1983—; bd. dirs. Emerge Counseling Ctr., Akron, Ohio, 1986—, Cen. Bible Coll., Springfield, Nat. Bd. Edn. Assemblies of God 1990—. Author: New Wave Theology, 1987. Pres. Ministerial Assn., S.W. Cleve., 1981-83, Ministerial Assn., Cuyahoga Falls, Ohio, 1978-79, Ministerial Assn., Euclid., Ohio, 1965-66. Home: 4107 Broadview Court Columbus OH 43230 Office: Ohio Dist Coun Inc Assemblies of God 3107 E Dublin-Granville Rd Columbus OH 43229

CRABTREE, SAMUEL WILLIAM, pastor, counselor; b. Dixon, Ill., Oct. 25, 1950; s. Samuel William Crabtree Sr. and Adele Rose (Joop) Cross; m. Vicki Gail Anderstrom, Aug. 4, 1973; children: Dawn, Mandi. BA, St. Cloud (Minn.) State U., 1974; MEd, S.D. State U., Brookings, 1979. Asst. mgr. Riverside Resort, Richmond, Minn., 1966-73; custodian ServiceMaster, St. Cloud, 1967-73; tchr. Watertown (S.D.) Pub. Schs., 1974-81; asst. to pastor Brookings Wesleyan Ch., 1981—; found. Inst. for Scholastic Pursuit, Brookings, 1984-90; mem. exec. coun. S.D. State Sunday Sch. Assn., 1985-89; dist. bd. adminstr. Dakota Dist. Wesleyan Ch., Rapid City, S.D., 1989-90. Author: Feeling Good About Feeling Bad, 1979, Imitating Jesus, 1988, 16 Irrelevant & Boring Exercises, 1990. Keynote speaker Dakota Leadership Conf., Brookings, 1985, 88; dir. rallies Denver "88", 1986-89; mem. Gov. Janklow's Blue Ribbon Panel for Reading is Fundamental Week, 1990; mem. respite care adv. bd. Easter Seals Soc., 1985-86; asst. area dir. Western Area Wesleyan Youth, 1986-90; co-chair Watertown for Jesus campaign, 1980-81. Mem. NEA (del. 1975), Coun. on Emergency Svcs. (bd. dirs. 1985-90), Watertown Edn. Assn. (pres. 1976-77). Avocations: drawing, basketball.

CRADDOCK, JAMES RICHARD, minister; b. Chatham, Va., Oct. 7, 1921; s. Richard Irvin and Elna May (Cox) C.; m. Frances Smith, Aug. 20, 1943; 1 child, Lynn Josephine. BSME, Va. Poly. Inst., 1942; BD in Theology, Lexington (Ky.) Theol. Sem., 1951; D of Ministry, Eden Theol. Sem., Webster Groves, Mo., 1973. Ordained to ministry Christian Ch., 1951. Aero. engr. G.L. Martin Co., Balt., 1945-48; mech. engr. Aberdeen (Md.) Proving Grounds, 1948; minister Christian Ch., Willisburg, Ky., 1948-51, First Christian Ch., Richmond, Mo., 1951-57, Cen. Christian Ch., Granite City, Ill., 1957-70, First Christian Ch., Centralia, Ill., 1970-74, Augusta Christian Ch., Indpls., 1975-86; pres. Greater Indpls. Disciples Housing, Inc., 1985-86; mktg. counselor Robin Run Village, Indpls., 1987—; bd. dirs. Christian Ch., Indpls., 1980-84. Bd. dirs. Lenoir Home, Columbia, Mo., 1969-73, Greater Indpls. Disc. Housing Bd., 1980-84, Nat. Benefit Assn., St. Louis, 1986. Served to capt. USAF, 1942-45. Mem. Am. Assn. Pastoral Counselors, Assn. Clin. Pastoral Edn. Democrat. Lodges: Kiwanis, Optimists, Masons, Shriners. Home: 6439 Chapelwood Ct Indianapolis IN 46268-4020 Office: Robin Run Village 5354 W 62d St Indianapolis IN 46268

CRADY, SHANNON LOUISE, lay church worker, athletic coach; b. Jacksonville, Fla., July 12, 1962; d. George Abraham and Virginia Lee (Roerig) C. BS in Recreation, Mars Hill (N.C.) Coll., 1985. Music dir. Mars Hill Coll., 1983-85; youth dir. Christ United Meth. Ch., Weaverville, N.C., 1984-85; gymnastics coach All Am. Gymnastics, Jacksonville, 1986—; youth worker Christ Community Ch., Jacksonville, 1988-90. Worker Spl. Olympics, Fernandina, Fla. and Jacksonville, 1981-83. Mem. U.S. Gymnastics Fedn. (fl. coach mem. 1986—), Lioness Club. Democrat. Home: Rte 3 Box 779 Yulee FL 32097 Office: All Am Gymnastics 730 St John's Bluff Rd N Jacksonville FL 32225

CRAFT, RICHARD HOWARD, minister, small business owner; b. L.A., Feb. 25, 1944; s. Claude Howard and Dorothy (Thomas) C.; m. Sharon Anne Giddings, Apr. 6, 1968; children: Jonathan Winslow, Emily Suzanne, Stephen Paul. Student, Occidental Coll., 1961-63; BA, Whittier Coll., 1965; D in Religion, Claremont Sch. Theology, 1972. Ordained to ministry Presbyn. Ch. (U.S.A.),1970. Asst. pastor Whittier (Calif.) Presbyn. Ch., 1970-72; assoc. pastor Presbyn. Ch., Barrington, Ill., 1972-76; pastor Elmwood Park (Ill.) Presbyn. Ch., 1976-80; adminstrv. pastor St. Peter's By the Sea Presbyn. Ch., Rancho Palos Verdes, Calif., 1980-88; interim pastor First Presbyn. Ch., Ouray, Colo., 1988-90; stated clk. Presbytery Western Colo., Ouray, 1990—; owner Just Us Missionary Shop, Ouray, Tin Lizzie Tours, Ouray, 1988—. Councilman City of Ouray, 1990—. Mem. Elks. Home and Office: PO Box 526 Ouray CO 81427

CRAGG, DONALD GEORGE LYNN, minister; b. Bloemfontein, Orange Free State, Republic South Africa, July 5, 1933; s. Ernest Lynn and Doris Jenny (Mitchell) C.; m. Doreen May Kidson, June 29, 1957; children: Carol Diane, Geoffrey Lynn, Brian Lynn. BA, Rhodes U., Grahamstown, South Africa, 1952, Oxford U., Eng., 1955; MA, DPhil, Oxford U., Eng., 1959. Ordained to ministry Meth. Ch., 1956. Min. Orange Grove Meth. Ch., Johannesburg, Republic of South Africa, 1961-63; lectr. Fed. Theol. Sem., Alice, Republic of South Africa, 1964-72; prin. tutor Meth. Theol. Coll., Grahamstown, 1973-82; supt. min. Meth. Ch. So. Africa, Grahamstown, 1982-89, sec. ch. unity commn., 1990—; exec. com. World Meth. Coun., 1986—, South African Coun. Chs., Johannesburg, 1990—; sec. dept. ecumenical affairs Meth. Ch. So. Africa, 1982—; min. St. Paul's United Ch., Johannesburg, 1990—. Author: (pamphlet) Christian Liberation, 1977; contbr. articles to Dictionary of South African Biography, Ency. of World Methodism, Internat. Dictionary of the Christian Ch. Exec. mem. Kingswood Coll. Coun., Grahamstown, 1978-89; chmn. trustees Masibambane Community Devel. Ctr., Peddie, Republic of South Africa, 1986-89. Rhodes scholar Oxford U., 1953. Home: 31 Koedoe St Mayfield Park, Johannesburg 2053, Republic of South Africa Office: Ch Unity Commn, PO Box 990508 Kibler Park, Johannesburg 2053, Republic of South Africa

CRAIG, DANIEL ROBERT, broadcasting executive; b. San Diego, Oct. 1, 1957; s. R. E. and Doris T. (Trew) C.; m. Vickie Lynn Jacob, Feb. 25, 1984; children: Erin Elizabeth, Leah Christine. Cert., KCBQ Broadcast Workshops, San Diego, 1977. Announcer Family Stations Inc., El Cajon, Calif., 1977-81; youth dir. 1st So. Bapt. Ch., San Diego, 1981-83; program dir. Sta. KWBI, Denver, 1983-86; ops. mgr. Sta. KPRZ, San Diego, 1988—; announcer, producer Considerations, Inc., Lakewood, Colo., 1989—, Denver Sem., 1984-89; owner Custom Audio Communication, 1990—. Author, creator games: Denarii, The Ultimate Bible Game, 1984, Trivia Express, 1986. Mem. AFTRA. Republican. Office: Sta KPRZ 1635 S Rancho Santa Fe Rd San Marcos CA 92069

CRAIG, DAVID HOWARD, minister; b. Nashville, Dec. 29, 1951; s. Mack Wayne and Dorothy Ann Craig; m. Yvonne Blackwell, Aug. 16, 1974; 1 child, James. BA, David Lipscomb Coll., 1973; MA, Harding Grad. Sch. Religion, Memphis, 1975; PhD, U. Miss., 1987. Lic. psychol. examiner. Minister 3d Ave. Ch. Christ, Nashville, 1971-72; assoc. minister Centerville (Tenn.) Ch. Christ, 1972-83, Graymere Ch. Christ, Columbia, Tenn., 1983—; guidance counselor Columbia Acad., 1983—; outpatient therapist Columbia Mental Health Ctr., 1983—; social worker Agape, Nashville, 1976-79; frequent speaker, presenter workshops. Contbr. religious articles to mags. Bd. dirs. Maury County Christian Camp, Columbia, 1983—, Maury County Cancer Soc., 1986; chaplain, pilot Civil Air Patrol, Centerville, 1977-83; county fund drive chmn. Am. Heart Assn., Centerville, 1974-75. Mem. Am. Assn. for Counseling and Devel., Phi Kappa Phi. Lodge: Civitan. Avocations: canoeing, reading, family activities. Home: 202 Sunnymeade Dr Columbia TN 38401 Office: Graymere Ch Christ 1320 Mount Pleasant Pike Columbia TN 38401 *I believe that life should be lived with intensity. The world is an open door of possibility to the person who greets each day with enthusiasm.*

CRAIG, JOHN JAMES, minister; b. Scranton, Pa., Aug. 14, 1950; s. John and Grace Marie C.; m. Debra Elizabeth Miller, Nov. 18, 1972; children: Kimberly, Scott, Kristen. AA, Keystone Jr. Coll., 1970; BS, Mansfield U., 1972; MS, U. Scranton, 1978; postgrad., Wesley Sem., 1982-90. Min. Bidwell United Meth. Ch., Hamlin, Pa., 1982—, Grace United Meth. Ch., Maplewood, Pa., 1986—; tchr. North Pocono Sch. Dist., Moscow, Pa., 1972—. Mem. Pa. State Edn. Assn. Republican.

CRAIG, JUDITH, clergywoman; b. Lexington, Mo., June 5, 1937; d. Raymond Luther and Edna Amelia (Forsha) C. BA, William Jewell Coll., 1959; MA in Christian Edn., Eden Theol. Sem., 1961; MDiv, Union Theol. Sem., 1968; DD, Baldwin Wallace Coll., 1981; DHL, Adrian Coll., 1985. Youth dir. Bellefontaine United Meth. Ch., St. Louis, 1959-61; intern children's work Nat. Coun. of Chs. of Christ, N.Y.C., 1961-62; dir. Christian edn. 1st United Meth. Ch., Stamford, Ct., 1962-66; inst. adult basic edn. N.Y.C. Schs., 1967; dir. Christian edn. Epworth Euclid United Meth. Ch., Cleve., 1969-72, assoc. pastor, 1972-76; pastor Pleasant Hills United Meth. Ch., Middleburg Heights, Ohio, 1976-80; conf. council dir. East Ohio Conf. United Meth. Ch., Canton, 1980-84; bishop United Meth. Ch., Detroit, 1984—; mem. Nat. Task Force on Itineracy, 1977-80; responder to World Coun. of Chs. (document on Baptism, Eucharist and Ministry 1975); gen. conf. del., 1980, 84. Contbr. articles to ministry mags. Bd. dirs. YWCA, Middleburg Heights, 1976-80. Recipient Citation of Achievement William Jewell Coll., 1985. Mem. Internat. Women Minister's Assn. Office: The United Meth Ch 155 W Congress Ste 200 Detroit MI 48226

CRAIG, STANLEY FRANCIS, minister; b. Oakland, Calif., Mar. 22, 1952; s. Donald Francis and Lois Ann (O'Connell) C.; m. Pattye LeAnn; children: Ryan, Kyle, Brandon, Erin. BA with honors, U. Colo., Colorado Springs, 1983; MDiv, Western Theol. Sem., Holland, Mich., 1987. Ordained to ministry Reformed Ch. in Am., 1987. Founding pastor Gun Lake Community Ch., Wayland, Mich., 1986-90; pastor Peace Reformed Ch., Mt. Prospect, Ill., 1990—; ch. planter Reformed Ch. in Am., Wayland, 1986-90. Recipient recognition award Synod of Mich., 1990.

CRAIN, JAMES ARNOLD, clergyman; b. Longview, Tex., Feb. 5, 1952; s. Arnold Abijah and Billie Jean (Matthews) C.; m. Bevery Denise Goodson, June 8, 1973; children: Anthony Lee, Rebecca Arlene. BTh, La. Missionary Bapt. Sem., 1987, MTh, 1988. Ordained to ministry Bapt. Ch. Pastor Cen. Missionary Bapt. Ch., Jonesboro, La., 1974-78, Greenwood Hills Missionary Bapt. Ch., Greenwood, La., 1978-82, Stamps (Ark.) Missionary Bapt. Ch., 1982-83, Park Missionary Bapt. Ch., Prescott, Ark., 1983-88, Cen. Missionary Bapt. Ch., Bastrop, La., 1988—; moderator 1st Colombia Missionary Bapt. Assn, Magnolia, Ark., 1982-83, 1st Union Missionary Bapt. Assn., Nevada County, Ark., 1984-86, N.E. La. Missionary Bapt. Assn., Bastrop, 1989—, La. State Missionary Bapt. Assn., Bastrop, 1991—. Author: Two Natures, 1987; contbr. articles to Missionary Bapt. newsletter, 1989—. Chmn. Nevada County Rep. party, Prescott, Ark., 1986-87; election commr. Nevada County, Prescott, 1986, 87; zoning commr. City of Greenwood, La., 1981, 82. With USAF, 1971-74. Mem. Kiwanis. Republican. Office: Cen Missionary Bapt Ch 1231 Leavell Bastrop LA 71220

CRAIN, JAMES HARRY, minister; b. Fayetteville, Ark., Nov. 30, 1951; s. Hubert Arthur and Lillian Frances (Mitchell) C.; m. Karen Jo Keeler, Mar. 26, 1977; children: Benjamin James, Kristin Joelle. BS, Abilene Christian U., 1974, MS, 1976. Assoc. minister Ch. of Christ, Cen., Topeka, Kans., 1977-79, Ch. of Christ, White Rock, Dallas, 1979-83; minister Ch. of Christ, Haskell, Tex., 1983-87, Rogers, Ark., 1987—. Mem. bd. dirs. Haskell Meml. Civic Ctr., 1987. Named one of Outstanding Young Men of Am., 1985; recipient Outstanding Citizenship award Springfield (Mo.) C. of C., 1970. Mem. Rotary (Rogers), Lions (pres. 1986-87, dep. dist. gov. 1986-87). Avocations: golf, travel. Home: 912 Oak Hill Dr Rogers AR 72756 Office: PO Box 66 Dogwood and S Dixieland Rogers AR 72757

CRAKER, WENDEL DEAN, minister; b. Baraboo, Wis., July 19, 1929; s. Harold Vivian and Orlow (Emery) C.; m. Norma Jean Kramer, Aug. 3, 1949; children: Sharon Joy, Timothy Dean. AB, Ind. Wesleyan U., 1949; MDiv, Columbia Theol. Sem., Decatur, Ga., 1972; MA, U. Ga., 1977, PhD, 1990. Ordained to ministry Wesleyan Ch., 1954, Presbyn. Ch. (U.S.A.), 1984. Min. Ill. dist. Wesleyan Ch., Chgo., 1952-64; min. Va. dist. Wesleyan Ch., Rockville, Md., 1964-69; min. Ga. dist. Wesleyan Ch., Winder, 1969-78; min. Clayton (Ga.) Presbyn. Ch., Chapel Sky Valley, Ga., 1986—; dir. Sch. Communication, Toccoa Falls (Ga.) Coll., 1978-86; adj. prof. Central (S.C.) Wesleyan Coll., 1990—; chair com. on constn. N.E. Ga. Presbytery, Athens, 1988—; del. Synod of South Atlantic, Jacksonville, Fla., 1991. Mem. selection com. Habitat for Humanity, Clayton, 1991—. Mem. Am. Sociol. Assn., Am. Acad. Religion, Alban Inst., Rotary. Home: Rte 1 Box 134 Rabun Gap GA 30568 Office: Clayton Presbyn Ch PO Box 734 Clayton GA 30525 *To know one's self to be loved and accepted in the present moment, and yet to be open to change and new vision, are essential ingredients to a happy and productive life.*

CRANCH, HAROLD COVERT, minister; b. Bryn Athyn, Pa., Oct. 10, 1911; s. Walter Appleton and Clara (Covert) C.; m. Jean Seville Smith, June 20, 1936; children—Virginia, Walter, Jonathan, Suzanne, Nora, Claudia, Margaret, Gabrielle. AA, Coll. Acad. of the New Ch., 1933, BTh, 1941, MDiv, 1990. Ordained to ministry Swedenborgian Ch., 1941. Pastor Sharon Ch., Chgo., 1941-52, Gabriel Ch., Glendale, Calif., 1952-66, Olivet Ch., Toronto, Ont., Can., 1966-76; assoc. pastor Immanuel Ch., Glenview, Ill., 1976-80; pastor Boston Soc., 1980-82; assoc. pastor Gabriel Ch., LaCrescenta, Calif., 1982—; dir. religion lesson, 1941-45, evangelization, 1952-66, religious programming Sta. WMWA-FM, Glenview, Ill, 1978-80; mem. Bishop's Consistory, 1955-70; exec. v.p. Gen. Ch. of New Jerusalem in Can., 1972-74; lectr. Edn. Coun. Archaeology, Acad. of New Ch., 1990. Recipient Glencairn Found. award, 1986. Author: Building Succesful Sunday Schools, 1954, Leader of His People, 1957, Principles of Evangelization, 1958, Ten Commandments, 1968, Teach Us to Pray, 1977, Monotheism and the Gods, 1989; contbr. articles to profl. jours. Mem. Coun. Clergy, Swedenborg Sci. Assn., Swedenborg Found. (life), Swedenborg Soc. (London, life), Bibl. Archaeology Soc. Republican. Home: 501 Porter St Glendale CA 91205 *Today many shun evils only because of fear of punishment or loss of reputation. Evil should be rejected from conscience because it is against God's will and would harm our neighbor. Even if we could "get away with it" we must not do it. It would harm our relationship with God, with our neighbor, and our happy acceptance of ourselves.*

CRANE, CHARLES EDWARD, educational administrator, minister; b. Pitts., Apr. 7, 1950; s. Don C. and Kathryn (Cyphers) C.; m. Sarah Grant, Sept. 9, 1972; children: Aaron, Chara, Jonathan, Benjamin. BS, U. Pitts., 1972; MA, Fuller Theol. Sem., Pasadena, Calif., 1980. Ordained to ministry Evang. Luth. Ch. in Am., 1981. Assoc. pastor Eagle Rock Bapt. Ch., L.A., 1980-84; prin. Westminster Acad., L.A., 1981-86; adminstr. Plumas Christian Sch., Quincy, Calif., 1986-88; headmaster Penn Christian Acad., Norristown, Pa., 1988—. Coach YMCA, Am. Youth Soccer Orgn., Little League, Pasadena, Quincy, 1982-86; block leader Neighborhood Watch, Altadena, Calif., 1984. With USNR, 1968-74. Mem. ASCD, Internat. Fellowship Christian Sch. Adminstrs. Home: PO Box 166 Obelisk PA 19492 Office: Penn Christian Acad 50 W Germantown Pike Norristown PA 19401

CRANE, GREGORY SCOTT, minister; b. Lafayette, Ga., Oct. 11, 1955; s. Kenneth Lamar and Betty Sue (Glass) C.; m. Melanie Kay Brock; children: Nicholas John Oliver, Lee Robinson. B in Music Edn., Samford U., 1978, MusM, 1983. Lic. to ministry Bapt. Ch., 1974, ordained, 1978. Min. music and youth Moundville (Ala.) Bapt. Ch., 1974-75, South Highland Bapt. Ch., Bessemer, Ala., 1976-78, South Roebuck Bapt. Ch., Birmingham, Ala., 1979-83, 1st Bapt. Ch., Brevard, N.C., 1983-85; min. music 1st Bapt. Ch., Columbia, Tenn., 1985—; tchr. music Shades Mountain Elem. Sch., Jefferson County, Ala., 1978-79. Bd. dirs. Brevard (N.C.) Men's Glee Club, 1984-85. Home: Rte 7 Box 118A-1 Columbia TN 38401 Office: 1st Bapt Ch 812 S High St Columbia TN 38401

CRANK, CHARLES EDWARD, JR., retired clergyman; b. Richmond, Va., July 20, 1923; s. Charles Edward and Mary Frances (Cochran) C.; m. Melba Louise Cornett, June 7, 1947; children—Charles Edward III, Stephen Lee, Brian Cornett, Melba Kathryn. Student Hampden-Sydney Coll., 1940-42; B.A., Lynchburg Coll., 1947; B.D., Lexington Theol. Sem., 1950; D.D. (hon.), Bethany Coll., 1970. Ordained to ministry Christian Ch., 1947. Pastor, Ky. and Va., 1945-58; dist. minister N.E. Mo., 1958-65; assoc. prof. religion Culver-Stockton Coll., Canton, Mo., 1958-65; regional minister Christian Ch., Parkersburg, W.Va., 1965-88; dir. Div. Homeland Ministries, 1971-80, W.Va. Council Chs., 1965-88; chaplain Lions Club, 1952-55, Am. Legion, 1944-45. Dir. Hazel Green Acad., 1972-83; chmn. Shenandoah County (Va.) ARC, 1954; mem. PTA, 1955-73; worker Community Little League, 1959-65, Tb, Assn., 1956-58. Served with U.S. Army, 1943-44. Recipient Outstanding Alumni award Lexington Theol. Sem., 1971; Assoc. award Bethany Coll., 1969; Ch. Exec. Devel. Bd. scholar, 1968. Mem. Disciples Peace Fellowship, Council Christian Unity, Disciples of Christ Hist. Soc., Am. Philatelic Soc., Congress Disciples Clergy, Blennerhasset Hist. Found., Blennerhasset Stamp Soc. Democrat. Lodge: Masons. Editor W.Va. Christian Ch. News, 1965-88.

CRANK, ROBERT NEIL, minister; b. Buckner, Ark., Apr. 20, 1938; s. E. Day and Hazel G. (Eddy) C.; m. Linda Lee Magee, Sept. 5, 1964; children: Mikel Shane, Amy La Shay. BBA, So. Ark. U., 1960; MRE, Bapt. Missionary Assn. Sem., Jacksonville, Tex., 1966. Ordained to ministry Bapt. Missionary Assn. Am., 1966. Dir. Assn. Bapt. Students So. Ark. U., Magnolia, 1967-75, 1986—; pres. Columbia Bapt. Bible Sch., Magnolia, 1968-75; dir. Assn. Bapt. Students Stephen F. Austin State U., Nacogdoches, Tex., 1975-77, Assn. Bapt. Students La. Tech. U., Ruston, 1977-80; pastor various chs.,

Ark., Tex.; mem. Nat. Youth Com. Bapt. Missionary Assn. Am., 1969-72, 76-79; staff writer Bapt. Pub. House, Texarkana, Tex., 1973-75; mem. Ark. State Youth Com. Bapt. Missionary Assn. Ark., Magnolia, 1985-87, 91—. Author: Journies in Galatians, 1967. With U.S. Army, 1961-63. Recipient achievement award U.S. Engr. Ctr., Ft. Belvoir, Va., 1963. Mem. Ministerial Alliance (various coms. 1967-75), Alpha Chi. Home: 524 E McNeil Magnolia AR 71753 Office: Assn Bapt Students 2223 N Washington St Magnolia AR 71753

CRANSTON, JEFFREY SCOTT, minister; b. Balt., Nov. 15, 1961; s. Edward William and Joan Ellen (Stutzka) C.; m. Linda Darlene Baughman, Aug. 13, 1983; children: Tiffany Lynn, Lauren Joy . BS, Columbia Bible Coll., 1983; postgrad., Moody Bible Inst., 1990—. Ordained to ministry So. Bapt. Conv., 1983, Christian and Missionary Alliance, 1989. Min. music and youth 1st Bapt Ch., Oakwood, Ga., 1983-84, Hampstead (Md.) Bapt. Ch., 1984-86; pastor youth ministries Lilburn (Ga.) Alliance Ch., 1986-91; assoc. pub. ministries Ravi Zacharias Internat. Ministries, Norcross, Ga., 1991—; del., seminar leader Amsterdam, The Netherlands, 1986. Mem. Nat. Right to Life Com., Washington, 1990—. Mem. Nat. Network Youth Ministries. Office: Ravi Zacharias Internat Ministries Norcross GA 30092

CRAVEN, PAUL JOHN, JR., minister, academic director; b. Charleston, S.C., Dec. 15, 1934; s. Paul John Sr. and Thaye (Burk) C.; m. Joye Meares, July 27, 1957; children: Elizabeth Craven Simmons, Melanie Craven Ross, Paula Craven Henderson, Lexie. BA, Furman U., 1957; BD, Southeastern Bapt. Theol. Sem., Wake Forest, N.C., 1960, ThM, 1962, D of Ministry, 1975; DD (hon.), Charleston Southern U., 1974. Pastor Spring Hill Bapt. Ch., Cottageville, S.C., 1953-59, Jackson Hill Bapt. Ch., Atlanta, 1960-66; sr. min. 1st Bapt. Ch., Charleston, 1966-81, Winston-Salem, N.C., 1981-90; dir. Coll. of Charleston, 1990—; mem. exec. com. So. Bapt. Conv., Nashville, 1972-80. Co-author: Adventures in Faith-The First Baptist Church-300 years, 1982. Trustee Beathea Home for Aging, Darlington, S.C., 1970-74, Furman U., Greenville, S.C., 1974-78, Gardner-Webb Coll., N.C., 1984-88; charter mem. Leadership Winston-Salem, 1985. Mem. CASE. Office: Coll Charleston 66 George St Charleston SC 29401

CRAVER, BENNIE DALE, minister; b. McKinney, Tex., Aug. 18, 1950; s. John Davis and Ruby Alice (Carman) C.; m. Elizabeth Ann Gattis, June 30, 1973; 1 child, Emily Suzanne. BBA, East Tex. State U., 1972; MDiv, Southwestern Bapt. Sem., Ft. Worth, 1986. Ordained to ministry Southern Bapt. Conv., 1979. Pastor Friendship Bapt. Ch., McKinney, 1981-82, Nevada (Tex.) Bapt. Ch., 1982-88, 1st Bapt. Ch., Justin, Tex., 1988—. Contbr. articles to profl. jours. Recipient H.C. Brown Jr. Meml. award in preaching Southwestern Bapt. Theol. Sem., 1986, teaching fellow, 1988. Mem. Soc. Bibl. Lit., Nat. Assn. Bapt. Profs. Religion. Home: 217 S Snyder PO Box 463 Justin TX 76247 Office: 1st Bapt Ch 116 N Jackson PO Box 309 Justin TX 76247

CRAVEY, CHARLES EDWARD, minister, publisher, poet; b. Eastman, Ga., June 17, 1951; s. Carise Lee and Irene (Cooper) C.; m. Charlotte Renee Dennis, July 12, 1972; children: Angela Marie, Jonathan Edward. BS in Sociology, Ga. So. U., 1979; student, Candler Sch. Theology, 1983; M of Sacred Literature, Trinity Theol. Sem., 1989, PhD in Theology, 1991. Ordained to ministry Meth. Ch. as elder, 1987. Assoc. pastor Cochran (Ga.) Meth. Ch., 1972-73, St. Peter's United Meth. Ch., Fitzgerald, Ga., 1973-77; Newington charge pastor, 1977-79, Bartow charge pastor, 1979-82; pastor Alamo (Ga.) United Meth. Ch., 1982-86, Northview United Meth. Ch., Warner Robins, Ga., 1986-90; sr. min. 1st United Meth. Ch., Reidsville, Ga., 1991—; pres., founder In His Steps Pub. Co., Warner Robins, 1979—, The Soc. Am. Poets, Warner Robins, 1988—; chaplain Houston County Hosp., Warner Robins, 1987—. Author: 15 books on poetry and religious themes; (weekly newspaper column) Fruits From The Vineyard, Daily Prayers, 1986—; editor, pub.: (quar. poetry newspaper) The Poet's Pen, also 53 books of poetry by various authors, 1988—; recorded 18 personal song albums. Bd. dirs. Warner Robins Teen Ctr., 1987—; pres. Vol. Houston County, Warner Robins, 1991. Mem. Gospel Music Assn. (nominated for 10 Dove awards 1989, 90, 91), Ga. State Poetry Soc., The Soc. of Am. Poets (pres., founder), So. Poetry Assn., Warner Robins Ministerial Assn., Reidsville Ministerial Assn. (v.p. 1991—). Home and Office: Reidsville United Meth Ch PO Box 147 Reidsville GA 30453 *One day, as you stand in an emergency room holding the hand of a dying individual, you suddenly realize that every word you utter has far-reaching consequences for time and eternity!.*

CRAWFORD, BARRY STEELE, religion educator; b. Phila., Apr. 24, 1946; s. Walter Mallach Crawford and Doris Mae (Dodds) Wright; m. Janet Elaine Myers, Sept. 28, 1970 (div. 1976); 1 child, Granville Scott; m. Christena Lee, Sept. 20, 1982; children: Todd M., Spencer E. BA, Catawba Coll., 1969; MA, Wake Forest U., 1971; PhD, Vanderbilt U., 1978. From asst. prof. to prof. religion Washburn U., Topeka, 1978—; vis. instr. religion U. of the South, Sewanee, Tenn., 1976-77; vis. asst. prof. New Testament, U. Iowa, Iowa City, 1977-78. Contbr. articles and book revs. to profl. jours. Fellow NEH, 1982, 88, NCCJ, 1986. Mem. Soc. Bibl. Lit. Office: Washburn U 1700 College Ave Topeka KS 66621

CRAWFORD, DAN REAVIS, minister, educator; b. Temple, Tex., Dec. 30, 1941; s. William Edwin and Inez (Gilliam) C.; m. Joanne C. Crawford, Aug. 8, 1964; children: Danna, James Edwin. BA, Howard Payne U., 1964; BD, Southwestern Bapt. Theol. Sem., Ft. Worth, 1967, MDiv, 1976, D of Ministry, 1981. Campus min. Pan Am. U., Edinburg, Tex., 1967-73, East Tex. State U., Commerce, Tex., 1973-76, U. Tex., Austin, 1976-82; nat. evangelism cons. home mission bd. Southern Bapt. Conf., Atlanta, 1982-85; assoc. prof. evangelism and missions Southwestern Bapt. Theol. Sem., Ft. Worth, 1985—; Author: Evangelife: A Guide to Lifestyle Evangelism, First Things First: Daily Guide for Summer Missionaries, Where One is Gathered in His Name, Church Growth Words From the Risen Lord, Families Reaching Families; author: (with others) Opening Doors to Multifamily Housing; editor: Single Adults: Resource and Recipient for Revival; contbr. articles to mags. Mem. Acad. for Evangelism in Theol. Edn., N.Am. Soc. for Ch. Growth, Am. Soc. Missiology, Assn. Profs. of Mission. Office: Southwestern Theol Bapt Sem PO Box 22298 Fort Worth TX 76122 *Spend little time with God and you will grow weary in well-doing; spend much time with God and you will find seasons of refreshing for your soul.*

CRAWFORD, ISAAC BENJAMIN, pastor; b. Bklyn., Apr. 23, 1948; s. Isaac Benjamin Sr. and Rubie (May) C.; m. Betty Anderson, Nov. 20, 1967; children: Anthony, Curtis, Towanda. AS, N.Y.C. Community Coll., Bklyn., 1968; MST, Va. Sem. and Coll., Lynchburg, 1974, postgrad., 1991—. Ordained to ministry Bapt. Ch., 1975; lic. min., 1964. Assoc. min. Zion Bapt. Ch., Bklyn., 1964-75; asst. pastor Greater Jerusalem Bapt. Ch., Bklyn., 1975-76, Brown Meml. Bapt. Ch., Bklyn., 1976-81; interim pastor Union Reformed Ch., Bronx, N.Y., 1981-82; assoc. min. Ft. Washington Collegiate Ch., N.Y.C., 1982-84; exec. asst. Friendly Bapt. Ch., Bronx, 1984-86; pastor Mt. Cella Bapt. Ch., Bronx, 1986—; co-chmn. Black Caucus of South Bronx Chs. Inc., 1985—; Bronx rep. to Coun. Chs. of Greater N.Y., 1990—; v.p. Bronx Coun. Chs., 1991—. Active Bedford-Stuyvesant Early Childhood Devel. Ctr., Bklyn.; mem. city-wide coun. Agy. for Child Devel., N.Y.C.; mem. 44th Precinct Community Coun. Com., Bronx; mem. community bd. #4 apptd. by Borough Pres. Ferrer, Bronx; bd. dirs. Embassy Day Care. 1st lt. USAF N.G., 1965—. Mem. NAACP, Operation P.U.S.H., Nat. Bapt. Conv. USA, Bapt. Pastors Ch. Union, Bapt. Mins. Conf. N.Y., United Missionary Bapt. Assn., Empire State Missionary Assn. (mem. reconstrn. com.), 265 Decatur St. Parent Assn. (chmn., co-chmn. del. agy.), Dems. Club (v.p. 1982-85), Masons. Home: 129 W 170th St Bronx NY 10452 Office: Mt Cella Bapt Ch Inc 1480 Jesup Ave Bronx NY 10452

CRAWFORD, JAMES WINFIELD, minister; b. Rochester, N.Y., July 17, 1936; s. Henry Baker and Elizabeth (Keenholts) C.; m. Linda Lovett, June 8, 1961; children: Hanry, Elizabeth, Robert, Benjamin. BA, Dartmouth Coll., 1958; BD, MDiv, Union Theol. Sem., 1962; D of Ministry, Andover-Newton Theol. Sch., 1990. 1st Federated Ch., Bayonne, N.J., 1962-65, East Harlem Prosestant Parrish, N.Y.C., 1965-68, Cen. Presby. Ch., N.Y.C., 1968-74; Sr. min. The Old South Ch., Boston, 1974—. Home: 40 Taylor Crossway Brookline MA 02146 Office: The Old South Ch Boston Boston MA 02116

CRAWFORD, MICHAEL DAVID, youth ministry director; b. Titusville, Fla., Oct. 2, 1964; s. David Clark and Blondell (Sewell) C.; m. Blondell Crawford, Oct. 1, 1960; children: Michael, Clark Anthony. BS, Fla. So. Coll., 1986. Youth dir. First United Meth. Ch., St. Cloud, Fla., 1982-84, Ft. Myers, Fla., 1984-85; dir. youth ministry First United Meth. Ch., Lakeland, Fla., 1985-87, Killearn United Meth. Ch., Tallahassee, Fla., 1987—; cons. in field; instr. in field. Pres. Alumni Adv. Bd., Lambda Chi Alpha Frat. Mem. Christian Educators Fellowship, Youth Workers Network, Meth. Youth Worker Assn. Democrat. Home: 4046 Delvin Dr Tallahassee FL 32308 Office: Killearn United Meth Ch 2800 Shamrock St Tallahassee FL 32308 *Let God lead!.*

CRAWFORD, PAUL DOUGLAS, friar; b. Boston, Feb. 9, 1952; s. Paul Douglas and Mary Elizabeth (Manning) C. AA, St. Anthony's Coll., Hudson, N.H., 1974. Joined Franciscan Order, Roman Cath. Ch., 1969. Formation team Capuchin Franciscans, Boston, 1975-76; pastoral staff Capuchin Franciscans, Yonkers, N.Y., 1976-81, N.Y.C., 1981-88; youth worker Diocese of Manchester (N.H.) Capuchin Franciscans, 1988—; archdiocesan liaison Charismatic Renewal Svcs., N.Y.C., 1986-88; founder Bread of Life Food Prog., N.Y.C., 1984-87; deanry dir. Manchester CYO, 1990—; mem. youth evangelism com. Nat. Svc. Com., Diocesan Liaisons, 1986-87; pres. Charismetro Broadcasting Co., 1978-81; bd. dirs. N.H. Conf. Religious Educators. Recipient Founders award, Manchester Summer Basketball, 1990, Youth Leadership award, CYO, 1989. Home: 14 Elm St Manchester NH 03103

CRAWFORD, ROBERT FRANKLIN, minister; b. Detroit, Nov. 6, 1951; s. Willie Allmon and Sara Nell (Jones) C.; m. Teresa Dianne Bishop, Dec. 31, 1972. BA, Samford U., 1974; MDiv, New Orleans Bapt. Theol. Sem., 1979; DMin, So. Bapt. Theol. Sem., 1991. Ordained to ministry So. Bapt. Conv., 1972. Pastor Cedar Grove Bapt. Ch., West Blocton, Ala., 1972-75; staff assoc. 1st Bapt. Ch., Birmingham, Ala., 1975-76; pastor 3d St Bapt. Ch., New Orleans, 1976-78, Simcoe Bapt. Ch., Cullman, Ala., 1979-85, Fairview Bapt. Ch., Valley, Ala., 1985—; mem. edn. commn. Ala. Bapt. State Conv., Montgomery, 1991—. Chaplain Sr. Adult Ctr., Valley, 1985—, Self Discovery Drug Rehab. Unit, Valley, 1990—. Home: 112 Leta Ln Valley AL 36854-4340 Office: Fairview Bapt Ch 600 River Rd Valley AL 36854-4943 *To help one's self requires helping someone other than self.*

CRAWLEY, BEVERLY ANN, minister; b. Balt., Aug. 11, 1940; d. Jerome and Madeline (Butler) Thomas; m. Earl Crawley Jr., Jan. 30, 1965; children: Tanya, Thomas, Timothy. Student, Morgan State U., 1958-61; diploma, Cortez Peters Bus. Sch., 1961-63; student, Coppin State Coll., 1977-81; cert., Bethel Bible Inst., 1987. Missionary, sr. New Psalmist Bapt. Ch., Balt., 1984-86, lay speaker, 1986-90; evangelist Ind. Zoe Ministries, Balt., 1986—; student chaplain Liberty Med. Ctr., Balt., 1990-91; announcer Sta. WJRO-AM Radio, Glen Burnie, Md., 1986-87, 91—; substitute tchr. Mark of Excellence, Balt., 1989-91; mem. Mount Bethel Bapt. Assn., Washington, 1989-91; prayer, counselor 700 Club, Balt., 1976-81; mem. United Prayer Warriors, Balt., 1991—, Interdenom. Ministerial Women's Alliance, 1986, Power of Faith Evangelistic Ch.; facilitator decision making seminar, 1991. Contbr. to From My Heart to Yours mag. Voting mem. Dem. Orgn. of Md., Balt., 1961-91; mem. Ednor Gardens and Lakeside Orgn., Balt., 1975-76. Recipient Helping Students in Pub. Schs. award Mercentile Bank, Balt., 1978. Democrat. Home and Office: Zoe Ministries 3602 Rexmere Rd Baltimore MD 21218 *As we trod through life, down the road least traveled by many, we must contemplate on "what must I do for God each and every day?" Above all, pray first.*

CRAWSHAW, CRAIG FREDERICK, music and worship minister; b. Berkeley, Calif., May 30, 1947; s. Frederick Story Crawshaw and Shirley (Frolich) Crawshaw-Wiggins; m. Joanne Lois Gardner, Aug. 30, 1970; children: Shelley Lyn, Curtis Frederick. BA in Math. and Music, U. Calif. Santa Barbara, 1970, MA in Music Composition, 1972. Ordained to ministry Bapt. Gen. Conf., 1977. Min. music and worship Trinity Bapt. Ch., Santa Barbara, 1972—; tour dir. Forerunners Youth Choir, Santa Barbara, 1972—, Cornerstone Coll. Career Choir, Santa Barbara, 1972—; chaplain Santa Barbara County Jail, 1976—. Arranger handbell music, 1984-86; composer (anthem) Come Unto Me, 1986, (choral works) May the Fruit of My Lips, 1987, I Can do All Things, 1988, Woman of God, 1988, Wise and Worthy, 1990, Living Water, 1990, Teach Me to Be Kind, 1991, Something You Give, 1991. Mem. Am. Guild English Handbell Ringers, Am. Soc. Composers and Pubs. Republican. Avocations: record collecing, Disney collecting. Office: Trinity Bapt Ch 1002 Cieneguitas Rd Santa Barbara CA 93110

CREAMER, JAMES LARRY, minister; b. Belton, S.C., Feb. 5, 1954; s. James Washington and Lula Mae (Bell) C; m. Pamela Teresa Lollis, July 7, 1973; children: Marshall Kent, Aaron Joseph. BTh, Fla. Bapt. Theol. Coll., 1981; MDiv, Southwestern Bapt. Theol. Sem., 1986. Ordained to ministry So. Bapt. Conv., 1978. Pastor 1st Bapt. Ch., Baker, Fla., 1978-83, Loveview Bapt. Ch., Itasca, Tex., 1983-85, Friendship Bapt. Ch., Fort Atkinson, Wis., 1987—, Milton (Wis.) Bapt. Ch., 1987—; evangelism chmn., moderator Oakaloosa Bapt. Assn., Crestview, Fla., 1981-83; stewardship chmn. Cen. Bapt. Assn., Madison, Wis., 1987-90; pres. Minn.-Wis. So. Bapt. Conv., Rochester, Minn., 1990—. Home: 508 Maple St Fort Atkinson WI 53538 Office: Friendship Bapt Ch 116 N Main St Fort Atkinson WI 53538

CREASMAN, JAMES CRAIG, clergyman; b. L.A., Apr. 3, 1957; s. Walter Cecil and Marilyn Sue (Dougherty) C.; m. Kimberly Eileen Coventon, June 22, 1985. BA in Econs., UCLA, 1979; MDiv with high honors, Talbot Theol. Sem., La Mirada, Calif., 1984. Ordained to ministry Evang. Covenant Ch., 1991. Staff mem. Campus Crusade for Christ, Guam, 1979-81; instr. L.A. Bible Tng. Sch., 1984-88; pastoral intern 1st Evang. Free Ch., Fullerton, Calif., 1984-85; pastor missions and evangelism Rolling Hills Covenant Ch., Rolling Hills Estates, Calif., 1985—; v.p. Theol. Students for Frontier Missions, Phila., 1982-84; mem. Bd. of World Mission, Evang. Covenant Ch., Chgo., 1987—. Named one of Oustanding Youn Men in Am., 1983; Rotary scholar, 1982. Mem. Kappa Tau Epsilon. Home: 1418 Brett Pl #124 San Pedro CA 90732 Office: Rolling Hills Covenant Ch 2222 Palos Verdes Dr N Rolling Hills Estates CA 90274

CREECY, RACHEL ALICE, missionary, librarian; b. Honolulu, Aug. 24, 1950; d. Carson Henry and Dorothy Lee (Roberts) C. BA cum laude, U. N.Mex., 1972; MLS, U. Calif., Berkeley, 1973; postgrad., Golden Gate Bapt. Theol. Sem., 1976. Career missionary fgn. mission bd. So. Bapt. Conv., Richmond, Va., 1976—; sem. libr. Hong Kong Bapt. Theol. Sem., Kowloon, 1977—; del. Hong Kong Bapt. Conv., Kowloon, 1983-86, 89-90, mem. religious edn. bd., 1984-86; Hong Kong rep. Bapt. World Alliance, 16th Congress, Seoul, Republic of Korea, 1990. N.Mex. Libr. Assn. scholar, 1972. Mem. ALA, Am. Theol. Libr. Assn., Hong Kong Libr. Assn. Home: 169 Boundary St, Kowloon Hong Kong Office: Hong Kong Bapt Theol Sem, 1 Homantin Hill Rd, Kowloon Hong Kong *God honors us in no greater way than by allowing us to serve His people in His world.*

CREED, JOHN BRADLEY, minister; b. Jacksonville, Tex., Apr. 20, 1957; s. Charles H. and Jeanette (Walden) C.; m. Kathy Harton, Aug. 9, 1980; children: Caitlin E., Charles V. BA, Baylor U., 1979; MDiv, Southwestern Sem., 1982, PhD, 1986. Ordained to ministry Bapt. Ch., 1986. Pastor Easterly (Tex.) Bapt. Ch., 1980-82, Wheatland Bapt. Ch., Ft. Worth, 1983-86, McCart Meadows Bapt. Ch., Ft. Worth, 1986-88, First Bapt. Ch., Natchitoches, La., 1988—; advisor Bapt. Student Union, La., 1989-90. Contbr. Holman Bible Dictionary, 1991. Bd. mem. Crisis Pregnancy Ctr., Natchidoches, 1990—. Pres. merit scholar Southwestern Sem., Ft. Worth, 1982. Mem. Audubon Soc., Kiwanis Club. Office: First Bapt Ch 508 2d St Natchitoches LA 71457

CREEL, AUSTIN BOWMAN, religion educator; b. Alexandria, Va., Nov. 8, 1929; s. Benjamin Kemper and Bertha A. (Naff) C.; m. Patricia Ann Harrison, June 26, 1954 (dec. Aug. 1985); children: Stephen, Kathryn. BS, Northwestern U., 1950; BD, Colgate Rochester Div. Sch., 1954; MA, Yale U., 1957, PhD, 1959. Ordained to ministry Am. Bapt. Convs., 1952. Asst. chaplain U. Rochester Coll. for Men, 1950-52; del. ecumenical confs. in India, travel in Asia, 1952-53; student minister Calvary Presbyn. Ch., Rochester, N.Y., 1953-54; asst. prof. religion U. Fla., Gainesville, 1957-64, assoc. prof., 1964-77, prof., 1977—, dir. Asian studies, 1973-75, chmn. dept. religion, 1977-90, interim dir. Ctr. for Jewish Studies, 1983-85; chmn. Humanities Council, 1987-89. Author: Dharma in Hindu Ethics, 1977; editor: A Larger View: Delton L. Scudder's Prayers and Addresses, 1973; co-editor: (with Vasudha Narayanan) Monasticism in the Christian and Hindu Traditions, 1990. Trustee Alachua Gen. Hosp., Gainesville, 1969-72, vice chmn., 1970-71. Recipient Sigmund Livington Interfaith prize Northwestern U., 1949, Agnes Crabtree Internat. Rels. award Fla. Coun. for the Social Studies, 1988; postdoctoral fellow in Asian religions Poona, India, 1965. Mem. Am. Acad. Religion (bd. dirs. 1988—, chair com. on edn. and study of religion 1988—), Am. Inst. Indian Studies (trustee 1974—, v.p. 1990-91, mem. exec. com. 1980-82, 89-91), Assn. Asian Studies (pres. S.E. conf. 1978-79), Soc. Asian and Comparative Philosophy, Nat. Coun. Religion and Pub. Edn. (exec. com. 1990—). Home: 1228 NW 36th Dr Gainesville FL 32605 Office: U Fla Dept Religion Gainesville FL 32611

CREMEANS, JAMES L., minister; b. Rayland, Ohio, Dec. 22, 1939; s. Leroy and Waneda (Montgomery) C.; m. Mary McCormick, Oct. 4, 1956; children: James, David, Jeffery, Diane, Janet. DD (hon.), Internat. Bible Sem., 1985. Ordained to ministry 1st Tabernacle Ch., Ironton, Ohio, 1967. Pastor City Mission Ch., Ironton, 1967—; exec. dir. City Welfare Mission, Ironton, 1967—; dir. corr. sch. Evangelistic Outreach, Pedro, Ohio, 1982—, v.p., 1975—, also bd. dirs. Mem. Lawrence County (Ohio) Welfare Adv. Bd., 1980-82, Home Health Care Bd., Ironton, 1980—, Lawrence County Youth Coun., 1988—. Named Citizen of Yr., Community Betterment Club, Lawrence County, 1979. Mem. Lawrence County Ministerial Assn. (chmn. radio and TV 1975-80). Home: Rte 1 Box 18 Pedro OH 45659 Office: City Mission Ch 710 N 5th St Ironton OH 45638

CRENSHAW, H(ENRY) C(ARLTON), minister; b. Quitman, Miss., Apr. 1, 1929; s. Henry Grady and Eunice (Hudson) C.; m. Bertha Elzine Mangum, Aug. 16, 1949; children: Kareen Crenshaw Brantley, David B., Terry C. Student, Meridian (Miss.) Jr. Coll., 1952-53, U. Tenn. ext., 1974-75; diploma, So. Sem., Nashville, 1979. Ordained to ministry So. Bapt. Conv., 1969; cert. in pastoral ministries, counseling to deaf. Min. to deaf 1st Bapt. Ch., Meridian, 1969-83; pastor Emmanual Bapt. Ch., Meridian, 1973-83, Grandview Bapt. Mission, Meridian, 1983-85, Cen. Grove Bapt. Ch., Meridian, 1985-90; missionary to deaf, pastor Corinth Bapt. Ch., Kemper County, Miss., 1990—; vol. missionary to deaf So. Bapt. Conv., Neshoba County, 1968—; tchr. sign lang. Choctaw Indian High Sch., Neshoba, Choctaw Cen. High Sch., 1968, 82. Mem. Ind. Gov.'s Com. on Rehab. of Handicapped, Meridian, 1982-86. Sgt. USMC, 1950-52. Recipient Talking Hand award 1st Bapt. Ch., Meridian, 1973. Mem. Lauderdale Mins. Assn., Kemper County Min. Assn. Home: Rte 7 Box 214-A Meridian MS 39301 *It is indeed heartening to see the people of the silent world excel in every area of life and in so doing glorify God with their talents and abilities.*

CRENSHAW, JAMES L(EE), theology educator; b. Sunset, S.C., Dec. 19, 1934; s. B. D. and Bessie (Aiken) C.; m. Juanita Rhodes, June 10, 1956; children: James Timothy, David Lee. AA, North Greenville Coll., 1954; BA, Furman U., 1956; BD, So. Bapt. Theol. Sem., 1960; PhD, Vanderbilt U., 1964. Asst. prof. religion Atlantic Christian Coll., Wilson, N.C., 1964-65; assoc. prof. Mercer U., Macon, Ga., 1965-69; prof. Old Testament Vanderbilt Div. Sch., Nashville, 1970-87, Duke U., Durham, N.C., 1987—. Author: 10 books; editor, contbg. author: 5 books; series editor: 12 books; contbr. articles to profl. jours. Grantee NEH, 1974, Am. Coun. Learned Socs., 1981; fellow Soc. Values in Higher Edn., 1972-73, Assn. Theol. Schs., 1978-79, 90-91, Guggenheim Found. 1984-85, NEH, 1990-91. Mem. Soc. Bibl. Lit. (editor 1978-84), Cath. Bibl. Assn. (editor 1991—), Soc. Values in Higher Edn., Colloquium Bibl. Rsch., Internat. Orgn. Study of Old Testament, The Soc. for Old Testament Study, Phi Beta Kappa. Democrat. Home: 8 Beckford Pl Durham NC 27705 Office: Duke U The Div Sch PO Box 4735 Durham NC 27706 *Accepting the accuracy of the Egyptian proverb, "Without love there can be no learning," I cultivate a love for my discipline and for those whom I seek to instruct.*

CRESWELL, NORMAN BRUCE, minister; b. Balt., Aug. 16, 1954; s. Norman Bruce and Ruth Lorraine (Hardin) C.; m. Carolyn Dale Main, June 9, 1979; children: Mary Elisabeth, Norman Bruce III, David Jeremiah, Gregory Frederick. Student, Balt. Sch. Bible, 1971; BA, Bob Jones U., Greenville, S.C., 1977. Ordained to ministry Ind. Bapt. Ch., 1980. Non-com leader Christian Svc. Brigade, Balt., 1969-72; asst. pastor Temple Bapt. Ch., Athens, Ga., 1974-78; tchr. Bible and U.S. history Cross Lanes Christian Sch., Charleston, W.Va., 1980-82; pastor Bellepoint Bapt. Ch., Hinton, W.Va., 1982—; chaplain Summers County Hosp., Hinton, W.Va., 1983—; chaplain, min. Hinton House, 1982—; min. (local radio) Morning Light Program, 1984-89; missionary Scotland, 1985, 87, 91. Recipient Herald of Christ award, Christian Svc. Brigade, Balt., 1972, Voice of Democracy award, VFW, 1972. Mem. W. Va. Right to Life, Bapt. Std. Bearer Soc. Republican. Home: 213 Miller Ave Hinton WV 25951 Office: Bellepoint Bapt Ch 211 Miller Ave Hinton WV 25951 *The greatest purpose of life is to glorify God in walking in His Word and this is not done with sounding brass or clanging cymbals but by the heart of man who has been redeemed and cleansed by the shed blood of Jesus Christ.*

CREWS, CLARENCE LEO, minister; b. Newark, N.J., Aug. 10, 1929; s. Lundy and Cynthia (Hester) C.; m. Felecia Martin (widowed); 1 child, Clarenece Leo; m. Varee Rhodes, May 27, 1983; children: Anthony Brent, Angela Dawn. BA, Bloomfield Coll., 1954; MDiv, Va. Union U., 1957; DD, Urban Bible Inst., Detroit, 1983. Asst. pastor Union Bapt. Ch., Montclair, N.Y., 195-54; pastor Union Grove Bapt. Ch., Petersburg, Va., 1957; asst. pastor Tabernacle Bapt. Ch., Detroit, 1957-61; dir., assoc. prof. Tex. Coll., Tyler, 1961-65; pastor Hopewell Bapt. Ch., Detroit, 1966—; probation officer Mich. Dept. of Corrections, Detroit, 1968—. Mem. Detroit Econ. Club. Home: 1967 Pembridge Place Detroit MI 48207 Office: Mich Dept Corrections 4242 Cass Ave Detroit MI 48201

CREWS, SANDRA JOANNE, minister, librarian; b. Reno, May 28, 1961; d. Robert Hewitt and Emma Doris (Cote) C. BA, U. Nev., 1985. Chmn. Search of Nev., Reno, 1982-85; youth min. Community Bapt. Ch., Reno, 1986—; libr. U.S. Bur. Mines, Reno, 1984—; 4-day chmn. Cusillo, Reno, 1985-86; mem., team leader Wittenberg Hall, Reno, 1989—; mem. Kairos Prison Ministry, Reno, 1990—. Democrat. Home: 4870 Ellis St Reno NV 89502 Office: Community Bapt Ch 246 Crampton St Reno NV 89502

CREWS, WILLIAM ODELL, JR., seminary administrator; b. Houston, Feb. 8, 1936; s. William O. Sr. and Juanita (Pearson) C.; m. Wanda Jo Ann Cunningham; children: Ronald Wayne, Rhonda Ann Crews Patterson. BA, Hardin Simmons U., 1957, HHD, 1987; BDiv, Southwestern Bapt. Theol. Sem., 1964; DD, Calif. Bapt. Coll., 1987. Ordained to ministry Bapt. Ch., 1953. Pastor Grape Creek Bapt. Ch., San Angelo, Tex., 1952-54, Plainview Bapt. Ch., Stamford, Tex., 1955-57, 1st Bapt. Ch., Sterling City, Tex., 1957-60, 7th St. Bapt. Ch., Ballinger, Tex., 1960-65, Woodland Heights Bapt. Ch., Brownwood, Tex., 1965-67, Victory Bapt. Ch., Seattle, 1967-72, Met. Bapt. Ch., Portland, Oreg., 1972-77; dir. communications Northwest Bapt. Conv., Portland, 1977-78; pastor Magnolia Ave Bapt. Ch., Riverside, Calif., 1978-86; pres. Golden Gate Bapt. Theol. Sem., Mill Valley, Calif., 1986—; pres. NW Bapt. Conv., Portland, 1974-76, So. Bapt. Gen. Conv. Calif., Fresno, 1982-84. Trustee Fgn. Mission Bd., Richmond, Va., 1973-78, Golden Gate Bapt. Theol. Sem., 1980-85; bd. dirs. Midway-Seatac Boys Club, Des Moines, 1969-72. Mem. Marin County C. of C. (bd. dirs. 1987—), Midway C. of C. (bd. dirs. 1968-72). Lodge: Rotary (pres. Portland club 1975-76, pres-elect Riverside club 1984-85). Home: 10 Chapel Dr Mill Valley CA 94941 Office: Golden Gate Bapt Theol Sem Strawberry Point Mill Valley CA 94941

CREWSE, DOYLE GENE, minister; b. Boise, Idaho, Nov. 28, 1930; s. Eldridge A. and Alma Faye (Crawford) C.; m. Helen Le Anna Myers, Aug. 27, 1955; children: Gregory H., Gretchen Elizabeth Crewse Smith. BS in Edn., Southwest Mo. State U., 1954; MRE, Cen. Bapt. Theol. Sem., 1956; MDiv, So. Bapt. Theol. Sem., 1958. Ordained to ministry So. Bapt. Conv. Tchr., acting prin. Bloodland C-7 Dist., Palace, Mo.; student pastor New Hope Bapt. ch., Butler, Mo.; student asst. 1st Bapt. Ch., St. Joseph, Mo.; asst. pastor Dauphin Way Bapt. Ch., Mobile, Ala.; pastor 1st Bapt. Ch., Demopolis, Ala., Ballwin (Mo.) Bapt. Ch., Mountain View Bapt. Ch., Boise. Contbr. to Bapt. jours. V.p., chmn. edn. Boise Mayor's Com. for Hiring the Handicapped and Older Worker; mem. steering com. Boise Mayor's Inaugural Prayer Breakfast, 1986; steering com. alt. The Idaho Citizens Health Parliament, 1986; chaplain Pacific Northwest Water Works of Am.

Conv.; acting chaplain Idaho Ho. of Reps.; cons. Family Ministry sect. Bapt. Sunday Sch. Bd., Nashville, Family Ministry of Utah-Idaho So. Bapt. Conv., Sandy, Utah, 1985-91. Mem. Am. Assn. Pastoral Counselors, Idaho Assn. Pastoral Care. Republican. Avocations: jogging, golf. Home: 11299 W Cartridge St Boise ID 83704

CRIDER, MELODY ANN, religious organization administrator; b. Spokane, Wash., Nov. 4, 1955; d. Roy Cook and Martha Jane (Jackson) Morey; m. Ronald Claud Crider, Mar. 22, 1975; children: Joni, Shane. Cert., Yakima Valley Coll., 1982. Tchr. St. Paul's Cathedral, Yakima, Wash., 1979-80; asst. dir. St. Paul's Cathedral, Yakima, 1980-81, tchr., 1985-88, dir., 1988-91; substitute tchr. and asst. St. Joseph Cathedral, Wenatchee, Wash., 1981-82; sec. House of Real Estate, Yakima, 1987-91; mem. Ready, Yakima (attendant 1988-88, treas. 1989-90, sec. 1990-91). Office: St Paul's Cathedral 1208 W Chestnut Yakima WA 98902-3169

CRIM, KEITH RENN, editor, writer, translator; b. Winchester, Va., Sept. 30, 1924; s. Abram Harry Marshall and Mable Grace (Renn) C.; m. Evelyn Ritchie, Aug. 26, 1947 (div.); children: Deborah Ann, Gregory Marshall (dec.), Edward McDonald, Julia Ruth, Martin Ritchie; m. 2d, Julia Firr Hickson, June 29, 1979; 1 dau., Laura Renn. B.A., Bridgewater Coll., 1947; B.D., Union Theol. Sem. in Va., 1950, Th.M., 1951, Th.D., 1959. Ordained to ministry Presbyterian Ch. U.S., 1950; missionary to Korea, Taejon, 1952-66; prof. Taejon Coll., 1956-65, acting pres., 1958-59, 64-65; book editor John Knox Press, Richmond, Va., 1967-69; spl. sec. for translations Am. Bible Soc., N.Y.C., 1969-73; prof. religious studies, Va. Commonwealth U., Richmond, 1973-83; pastor New Concord (Va.) Presbyn. Ch., 1991—; editorial dir. Westminster Press, Phila., 1983-89; mem. editorial bd. Jour. Bibl. Lit., 1975-78, Quarterly Review, Nashville, 1980-84; mem. translation team Old Testament, Good News Bible, 1978; gen. editor supplementary vol. Interpreters' Dictionary of the Bible, 1978; gen. editor Abingdon Dictionary of Living Religions, 1981; pub. editor Perennial Dictionary of World Religions, 1989. Author: The Royal Psalms, 1962; Limericks—Lay and Clerical, 1979. Staff sgt. U.S. Army, 1943-46; ETO. Mem. Am. Acad. Religion, Soc. Bibl. Lit., Catholic Bibl. Assn., Va. Writers' Club (pres. 1977-78).

CRIMMINS, JOHN BLAINE, minister; b. Chattanooga, Dec. 6, 1951; s. John Blaine Jr. and Marie Ward (Bryson) C.; m. Debra Kay Bailey, July 21, 1974; 1 child, John IV. BA, U. Tenn., 1974; MDiv, Trinity Divinity Sch., Deerfield, Ill., 1984. Asst. minister pastoral care Ward Presbyn. Ch., Livonia, Mich., 1984-85, minister of evangelism, 1985-87, adminstrv. pastor, 1986—; chmn. Ch. Devel. Com./Presbytery of Midwest, Evangelical Presbyn. Ch., Detroit, 1987-89. Mem. Christian Ministries Mgmt. Assn. Office: Ward Presbyn Ch 17000 Farmington Rd Livonia MI 48154

CRISCOE, ARTHUR HUGH, educator; b. Union Grove, Ala., Feb. 21, 1939. BA, Samford U., 1964; MDiv, Southwestern Seminary, Ft. Worth, 1968, M in Religious Edn., 1969, EdD, 1975. Min. New Hope Bapt. Ch., Mansfield, Tex., 1965-71; prof. Columbia (S.C.) Bible Coll., 1972-76; mgmt. support dir. Sunday Sch. Bd., Nashville, 1976—; adj. prof. Cumberland U., Lebanon, Tenn., 1988—. Author: Original, Youth Becoming Leaders, 1984, The Doctrine of the Laity Teaching Workbook, 1985, The Doctrine of Prayer Teaching Workbook, 1986, The Doctrine of the Believers Teaching Woorkbook, 1987, (with others) A Biblical Model for Training Leaders, 1985. Mem. World Future Soc., Assn. for Ednl. Communications, Nat. Soc. for Performance and Instrn., Nat. Assn. Profs. Christian Edn., Internat. Brotherhood Magicians, Am. Soc. Magicians. Baptist. Avocation: magic. Office: Sunday Sch Bd 127 9th Ave N Nashville TN 37234

CRISS, DIANE RAMSEY, community and church worker; b. Brunswick, Ga., Jan. 21, 1941; d. Leroy and Beatrice (Powell) R.; m. Gary Wayne Criss, Nov. 5, 1977. BA in Religion, Scarritt Coll., 1966. Staff Lake-of-the-Ozark (Mo.) Parish, 1966; church and community worker Global Ministries of United Meth. Ch., N.Y.C., 1967-81; deaconess United Meth. Ch. Contbr. articles to various newspapers. Bd. dirs. Barrow County Benevolence Com., Winder, Ga., 1988-89; vol. Barrow County Sr. Citizens, Winder, 1989. Recipient Outstanding Young Women of Am award, 1970-74, 80, Community Svc. award Seneca Mental Health, 1980, Vol. award Family and Children Svcs., 1978-80; grantee in field. Mem. Barrow County Benevolence Com., Ga. Poetry Soc. Democrat. Methodist. Avocations: reading, writing, photography, people. Home: 108 Evergreen Ln Winder GA 30680

CRISTELLI, JOSE GOTTARDI, archbishop. Archbishop of Montevideo Uruguay. Office: Arzobispado, Calle Trenta, y Tres 1368, Casilla 356, 11100 Montevideo Uruguay*

CRISWELL, E. G., church administrator; b. Tulsa, Aug. 11, 1940; s. Victor Earl and Doris (Messenger) C.; m. Beverly Jo Criswell, Dec. 12, 1960; children: Diana Jo Neff, Jeffrey Dean. BSBA, Phillips U., Enid, Okla., 1978; postgrad., Emory Sch., Atlanta, Ga., 1978—. Bus. adminstr. 1st Christian Ch., Tulsa, 1976-81, Asbury United Meth. Ch., Tulsa, 1981-88, 1st Presbyn. Ch., Arlington, Tex., 1988-89, Polk St. United Meth. Ch., Amarillo, Tex., 1989—. Fellow Nat. Assn. Ch. Bus. Adminstrn. (treas. 1984-85), United Meth. Assn. of Bd. Ch. Bus. Adminstrn. (cert.). Office: Polk St United Meth Ch 1401 S Polk St Amarillo TX 79101

CRITES, STEPHEN DECATUR, religion educator; b. Elida, Ohio, July 27, 1931; s. Beryl Anderson and Martha Crites; m. Gertrud Elizabeth Bremer, Sept. 11, 1955 (div. June 1990); children—Dorothea, Stephanie, Lilian, Hannah; m. Ann Lindberg, Dec. 26, 1990. B.A., Ohio Wesleyan U., 1953; B.D., Yale U., 1956, M.A., 1959, Ph.D., 1961; student U. Heidelberg (Ger.), 1959-60. Ordained to ministry United Meth. Ch., 1956. Minister Grace Meth. Ch., Southington, Conn., 1956-58; instr. philosophy and religion College U., 1960-61; asst. prof. religion Wesleyan U., Middletown, Conn., 1961-66, assoc. prof., 1966-69, prof., 1969—, prof. philosophy, 1991—. Author: In the Twilight of Christendom: Hegel vs. Kierkegaard on Faith and History, 1972. Translator: Kierkegaard, Crisis in the Life of an Actress and Other Essays on Drama, 1967. Editor: Studies in Religion, Am. Acad. Religion monograph series, 1971-79. Mem. Am. Acad. Religion, Soc. for Religion in Higher Edn. Home: 281 Beaver Brook Rd Lyme CT 06371 Office: Wesleyan U Middletown CT 06457

CRITTENDEN, WILLIAM, retired bishop; b. New Boston, Pa., June 28, 1908; s. Ernest H. and Susan B. (Cook) C.; m. Eleanor Setchell, Dec. 36, 1931 (dec.); 1 child, William; m. Helen Cotton, May 11, 1976 (dec.); 1 child, Joan Merritt; m. Mary Bedell Alexander, Aug. 6, 1985. BS, Lafayette Coll., 1929, DD (hon.), 1954; BD, MDiv, Episcopal Div. Sch., Cambridge, Mass., 1936; LLD (hon.), Gannon U., 1963. Ordained to ministry Episcopal Ch. as deacon, 1934, as priest, 1935; ordained bishop, 1952. Curate St. Paul's Episcopal Ch., Brookline, Mass., 1934-35; vicar Grace Ch. Episcopal Ch., Dalton, Mass., 1936-39, St. Luke's Episcopal Ch., Lanesboro, Mass., 1936-39; rector St. John's Episcopal Ch., Adams, Mass., 1939-42; prof. Lafayette Coll., Easton, Pa., 1942-45; exec. sec. youth div. Nat. Episcopal Ch., 1945-49; archdeacon Episcopal Diocese of So. Ohio, 1949-52; bishop Episcopal Diocese of NW Pa., 1952-74; ret., 1974; leader Bible study World Conf. Youth, Oslo, 1947; leader U.S. youth sect. World Coun. Chs., Amsterdam, The Netherlands, 1949; bd. dirs., v.p. Nat. Coun. Chs., 1960-66; adj. prof. Garza Law Sch., Edinboro, Tex., 1982-84. Trustee Western Coll. for Women, Oxford, Ohio, 1964-72. Recipient Currick award Jewish Community, 1966.

CROCKER, J. A. FRAZER, JR., minister, social worker; b. Detroit, Oct. 4, 1935; s. J. A. Frazer, Sr. and Marjorie Olievia (May) C.; m. Jaqueline Fairchild Arnold, Apr. 15, 1961 (div. Aug. 1972); children: John A. F. III, Matthew M.; m. Diana Worden, June 4, 1977; 1 stepchild, Colin E. Brayton. AB, Kenyon Coll., Gambier, Ohio, 1957; MDiv, Ch. Div. Sch. of the Pacific, Berkeley, Calif., 1960; MSW, U. Utah, 1974. Lic. clin. social worker; ordained to ministry Episcopal Ch. as deacon then priest, 1960. Asst. min. Trinity Cathedral, Davenport, Iowa, 1960-61; priest in charge St. Paul's Ch., Sioux City, Iowa, 1961-64; assoc. rector Grace Ch., Jamaica, N.Y., 1964-67; rector St. Mary's Ch., Provo, Utah, 1967-72; program dir. Utah State Prison Alcohol Treatment Program, Draper, 1974-81; pvt. practice Salt Lake City, 1981-83; dir. mental health Family Health Plan, Salt Lake City, 1983-88; bishop's canon Episcopal Diocese Utah, Salt Lake City, 1988—; protestant chaplain Utah State Prison, 1968-74; asst. chaplain St. Mark's Hosp., Salt Lake City, 1983; exec. dir. Episcopal Social and Pastoral Ministries, 1990—. Pres. Utah Mental Health Assn., Salt Lake City, 1970-72; flotilla comdr. USCG Aux., Salt Lake City, 1980; bd. dirs. Family Support Ctr., Salt Lake City, 1989—, pres., 1991—. Mem. Great Salt Lake Yacht Club (bd. dirs. 1980-82). Avocations: sailing, reading, back-packing, fishing. Office: Episcopal Diocese Utah PO Box 3090 Salt Lake City UT 84110-3090

CROCKETT, CHRISTINE HOLMES, music director; b. Princeton, Ind.; d. Hilary Herbert and Christine (Warnock) Holmes; m. William Mabon Crockett; 1 child, Geoffrey. BA, U. Chgo., MA. Choir dir., organist Temple Israel, Duluth, Minn., 1961—; music dir., organist St. Paul's Episcopal Ch., Duluth, Minn., 1961—. Contbr. articles to profl. jours. Mem. Am. Guild Organists (former dean), Guild of Temple Musicians (bd. dirs.), Assn. Anglican Musicians. Democrat. Home: 2724 E Second St Duluth MN 55812 Office: Temple Israel 1602 E Second St Duluth MN 55812 *In 30 years of working with two congregations, Episcopal and Jewish, I have observed that things go better when you believe in something or someone rather than in nothing or no one; and that you should endeavor "to do justly, to love mercy, and to walk humbly with your God." (Micah).*

CROCKETT-DICKERMAN, MARGARET WILLIAMS, minister, pastoral counselor; b. Dallas, Aug. 26, 1918; d. George Burgoyne and Margaret Ellen (Schultz) Williams; m. James Underwood Crockett, July 28, 1943 (dec. July 1979); children: Carol Ellen, Robert Bryan, Jean Crockett Ritchie, Mary Crockett Richardson; m. Frederick Emery Dickerman, Nov. 5, 1988; stepchildren: David L., Ruth Ann Dickerman Randall. BA, Rice U., 1939; MDiv, Harvard U., 1978; D Ministry, Andover Newton Theol. Sch., 1979. Ordained to ministry United Ch. of Christ, 1979. Interim min. Edwards Ch., Framingham, Mass., 1979-80, min., 1980—; interim min. 2d Ch., West Newton, Mass., 1980; staff counselor Middleton (Mass.) Pastoral Counseling Ctr., 1979-87, North Shore Pastoral Counseling Ctr., Lynnfield, Mass., 1987-89; clergy rep. Metro West Hospice, Framingham, 1982-87. Author (with others): Spinning a Sacred Thread; contbr. articles to profl. jours. Mem. Am. Assn. Pastoral Counselors (cert.), Assn. Clin. Pastoral Edn. (advanced cert.), PEO Sisterhood Club (Lexington chpt.). Home: 315 Musketaguid Rd Concord MA 01742 Office: Edwards Ch 39 Edwards St Framingham MA 01701

CROMPTON, ARNOLD, minister, educator; b. Leeds, Yorkshire, Eng., Dec. 19, 1914; came to U.S., 1923; s. Harold and May Almyeria (Milward) C. BA, Case Western Res. U., 1936; MA, U. Chgo., 1939; BD, Meadville Theol. Sch., Chgo., 1939; ThD, Pacific Sch. of Religion, 1956; DD (hon.), Meadville-Lombard Theol. Sch., 1972. Ordained to ministry Unitarian Ch., 1939. Minister 1st Unitarian Ch. of Erie, Pa., 1939-45; minister 1st Unitarian Ch. of Erie, Oakland, Calif., 1945-82, minister emeritus, 1982—; lectr. ch. history Starr King Sch. for the Ministry, Berkeley, Calif., 1953-67; dir. Earl Morse Wilbur Library, Berkeley, 1961-67, tutor, 1990—; anniversary lectr. Taegu (Republic of Korea) U., 1986; Wilbur Meml. lectr. on religion on Pacific Rim, Berkeley, 1990; bd. dirs., past pres. Oakland-Fukuoka Soc., Oakland, 1975—; pres. Rossmoor Religious Coun., Walnut Creek, Calif., 1989—. Author: Apostle of Liberty, 1950, Unitarianism on Pacific Coast, 1954, Aurelia H. Reinhardt, 1981; contbr. articles to profl. jours. Lectr. Ebell Soc., Oakland, 1982—; pres. Internat. Inst. of the East Bay, Oakland, 1981-82, Rossmoor Activities Coun., Walnut Creek, 1989—; chmn. Alameda County Crime Prevention Commn., Calif., 1978-80; bd. dirs. English summer sch. Bir Zeit Coll., Jordan, 1963-64, English Lang. Program-Komagane, Japan, 1967. Recipient Silver Beaver award Boy Scouts Am., 1966, citation Calif. State Assembly, 1970, Calif. State Senate, 1975, Ho. of Reps., 1990, Ohio Ho. of Reps., 1989, Disting. Alumnus award Case Western Res. U., 1989; named one of Outstanding Immigrants, Internat. Inst., 1976. Mem. Unitarian Universalist Ministers Assn. (pres. Pacific Coast chpt. 1970, spl. envoy to chs. of Japan 1989), Rotary (pres. Rossmoor chpt. 1986-87), Masons (grand chaplain 1979-80), Phi Alpha Theta (hon.), Phi Kappa Tau. Avocations: hiking, mountain climbing, traveling, music, rare books. Home: 1449 Skycrest Dr #1 Walnut Creek CA 94595 Office: 1st Unitarian Ch 685-14th St Oakland CA 94612

CROMWELL, ROBERT JOSEPH, minister; b. Charlotte, N.C., June 23, 1956; s. Robert Varney C. and Mildred Elizabeth (Cesky) Crissman; m. Susan Diane Zylstra, May 26, 1979; 1 child, Joseph Edwin. Student, Cen. Bible Coll., 1974-75; BA, Dordt Coll., 1978; student, U. Mo., 1978-80; MDiv, Princeton Theol. Sem., 1983. Ordained to ministry Presbyn. Ch., 1983. Pastor Fayette City and Little Redstone Presbyn. Chs., Fayette City, Pa., 1983—. Area coord. Fayette County CROP Walk, 1988. Mem. World Federalist Assn. (Pitts. chpt.), Alban Inst., Fayette City Area Clergy Assn. (pres. 1985—), Evangelicals for Social Action, Fellowship of Reconciliation. Democrat. Home and Office: RD #1 Box 198 B Fayette City PA 15438

CRONIC, DAVID WILLIAM, minister; b. Winder, Ga., Mar. 12, 1960; s. Henry Virgil Jr. and Marjorie (Boyd) C.; m. Jane Ellen Fanslow (div. Nov. 1990). BA, Emory U., 1982; MDiv, Lexington (Ky.) Theol. Sem., 1986. Ordained to ministry Christian Ch. (Disciples of Christ). Pastor First Christian Ch., Morgantown, W.Va., 1986—. Mem. Monongalia County Ministerial Assn. (pres. 1990—). Home: 701 Park St Morgantown WV 26505 Office: First Christian Ch Cobun Ave at Grand St Morgantown WV 26505

CRONIN, DANIEL ANTHONY, bishop; b. Newton, Mass., Nov. 14, 1927; s. Daniel George and Emily Frances (Joyce) C. S.T.L., Gregorian U., 1953, S.T.D. summa cum laude, 1956; LL.D., Suffolk U., Boston, 1969, Stonehill Coll., North Easton, 1971. Ordained priest Roman Cath. Ch., 1952; attache Apostolic Internunicature, Addis Ababa, Ethiopia, 1957-61, Secretariat of State, Vatican City, 1961-68; named Monsignor by His Holiness Pope John XXIII, 1962; named titular bishop of Egnatia and aux. bishop of Boston, 1968-70; Episcopal ordination from Richard Cardinal Cushing (archbishop of Boston), 1968; pastor St. Raphael Ch., Medford, Mass., 1968-70; bishop Fall River, Mass., 1970—. Club: K.C. (4). Office: 47 Underwood St PO Box 2577 Fall River MA 02722

CRONIN, THOMAS JOSEPH, priest; b. Kansas City, Mo., July 20, 1943; s. Thomas Joseph and Mary Katherine (Farley) C. BA, Immaculate Conception Sem., 1964, postgrad., 1964-68; MA, U. Mo., Kansas City, 1988. Ordained priest Roman Cath. Ch.,. Assoc, pastor Cath. Diocese of Kansas City-St. Joseph, Mo., 1968-79; pastor Sacred Heart Ch., Hamilton, Mo., 1979-85; chaplain Truman Med. Ctr., Kansas City, 1985—, Children's Mercy Hosp., Kansas City, 1985—, Western Mo. Mental Health Ctr., Kansas City, 1985—, Kansas City (Mo.) Police Dept., 1991—. Com. chairperson Nat. Cath. Com. on Scouting, Irving, Tex., 1989-90. Mem. APA, AACD, Nat. Assn. Cath. Chaplains, Assn. for Vol. Adminstrn., Am. Critical Incident Stress Found., Christian Assn. for Psychol. Studies. Home: 2552 Gillham Rd Kansas City MO 64108 Office: Truman Med Ctr 2301 Holmes Kansas City MO 64108

CRONK, SISTER ANN S., librarian; b. Waterbury, Conn., Jan. 3, 1928; d. Abram Sylvester and Anna C. (Overton) C. BS in Edn., St. Bonaventure, 1966; MLS, U. R.I., 1969. Joined Franciscan Sisters of Allegany; lic. edn. media specialist, Fla. Tchr. various schs., 1948-64; adminstrv. asst. vocation dept. Diocese of Providence, 1968-72; libr. high sch., 1973-82, 84-89; ins. contact for gen. treas. FSA, Allegany, N.Y., 1982-84; dir. diocesan libr. Diocese of St. Petersburg (Fla.), 1989—; spiritual asst. Secular Franciscan, Melbourne, Fla., 1984-89, Hudson, Fla., 1990—. Mem. Cath. Libr. Assn. Home: 1822 12th St N Saint Petersburg FL 33704-4042 Office: Diocesan Libr 6533 9th Ave N Saint Petersburg FL 33704

CROOK, NORRIS CLINTON, minister, psychology educator; b. Speaker, Mich., June 24, 1923; s. Herbert James and Hazel Mildred (Kipp) C.; m. Bernice Gertrude Gabram, June 21, 1947. B.Theology, Concordia Theol. Sem., 1947; B.Sc. in Edn., U. Omaha, 1953; M.A., Western Res. U., 1959; Ph.D., U. Wis.-Madison, 1968. Ordained to ministry Lutheran Ch.-Mo. Synod, 1947. Pastor, tchr. Faith Lutheran Ch., Council Bluffs, Iowa, 1947-51; pastor Trinity Lutheran Ch., Mallard, Iowa, 1951-56; pastor, tchr. St. John Lutheran Ch., Elyria, Ohio, 1956-59; founding pastor All Sts. Luth. Ch., Slippery Rock, Pa., 1977-83; interim pastor in Key West, Fla., 1986, Cape Coral, Fla., 1988; asst. prof. Concordia Coll., Milw., 1959-62; headmaster Secondary Schs., Kitui and Narok, Kenya, 1962-64; assoc. prof. psychology Slippery Rock U., Pa., 1968—. Recipient Fulbright, Smith & Mundt award Dept. State, Kenya, 1962-64. Mem. Assn. Overseas Educators Inc. (pres. 1981-83), Greater Pitts. Psychol. Assn., NEA. Republican. Club: Wally Byam Caravan (pres. 1982-83). Lodge: Rotary (pres. Slippery Rock chpt., 1984-86). Office: 615 Greenwood Ave Lehigh Acres FL 33936 *God's declaration in the Bible of His great love for mankind through Jesus Christ gives comfort and direction to our lives as nothing else can do. The more we read the Bible the better we will be—the greater our reliance upon God will be.*

CROOM, HERMAN LEE, lay worker, retired federal official; b. Wilmington, N.C., Nov. 21, 1909; s. Walter Judson and Carrie Murray Croom; m. Mildred Mamie Cain; 1 child, Ellen Lee Croom Barker. BS, NYU, 1950; MA, Am. U., 1955. Deacon 1st Bapt. Ch., Alexandria, Va., 1966-70, Stuart, Fla., 1972-73; deacon North Stuart Bapt. Ch., 1975-84; ruling elder Grace Presbyn. Ch. Am., Stuart, 1986-91; mem. bd. trustees Midestern Bapt. Theol. Sem., Kansas City, Mo., 1970-72. Home: 1996 NW Fork Road Stuart FL 34994 *The greatest things we can do in life are to trust in our savior and Lord, Jesus Christ, and to love our fellow men.*

CROSBY, DANIEL EARL, minister; b. Indiana, Pa., Mar. 21, 1956; s. Russell Bryan and Donna Mae (Riethmiller) C.; m. Deborah Diane Tatum, Jan. 27, 1978; children: Andrew Wade, Danielle Elizabeth. BA, Baylor U., 1978; M of Div., Southwestern Bapt. Sem., 1984, PhD, 1990. Ordained to ministry Bapt. Ch., 1983. Minister music and youth Live Oak Bapt. Ch., Gatesville, Tex., 1975-79, staff missionary, 1979; pastor Levita Bapt. Ch., Gatesville, 1980-84, First Bapt. Ch., Oglesby, Tex., 1984-87, Taylor's Valley Bapt. Ch., Temple, Tex., 1987—; Ordained to ministry Bapt. Ch. Mme. Bell Bapt. Assn. (bd. dirs. pastoral ministries, missions com. 1988—, student ministries 1988—, clk. 1990-91, vice moderator 1991-92). Avocations: hunting, carpentry, mechanics. Home and Office: 36 Taylor's Valley Rd Temple TX 76502

CROSBY, DONALD ALLEN, philosophy educator; b. Mansfield, Ohio, Apr. 7, 1932; s. Edmund Bevington Crosby and Mary Lou (Bogan) Foster; m. Charlotte Mae Robinson, Sept. 15, 1956; children: Colleen Judith Davis, Kathleen Bridgett Carnahan. BA, Davidson Coll., 1953; BD, Princeton Sem., 1956, ThM, 1959, PhD, Columbia U., 1963. Minister Christiana (Del.) Presbyn. Ch., 1956-59; asst. minister First Congregational Ch., Norwalk, Conn., 1959-62; asst. prof. philosophy and religion Centre Coll., Danville, Ky., 1962-65; prof. philosophy Colo. State U., Ft. Collins, 1965—. Author: Horace Bushnell's Theory of Language, 1975, Interpretive Theories of Religion, 1981, The Specter of the Absurd, 1988; mem. editorial bd. and exec. com. Am. Jour. Theology and Philosophy. Dist. capt. Larimer County (Colo.) Dem. Party, 1969-70. Recipient Excellence in Grad. Rsch. and Teaching award, 1989; named Honors Prof., 1981; Presbyn. Grad. fellow Presbyn. Ch. USA, 1961-62. Mem. Am. Philos. Assn., Am. Acad. Religion (bd. dirs.), Highlands Inst. for Am. Religious Thought, Soc. Philosophy of Religion, N.Am. Soc. for Social Philosophy. Home: 3517 Canadian Pkwy Fort Collins CO 80524 Office: Colo State U Dept Philosophy Fort Collins CO 80523

CROSBY, MICHAEL HUGH, priest; b. Fond du Lac, Wis., Feb. 16, 1940; s. Hugh John and Blanche Hannah (Bouser) C. BA, St. Mary's Capuchin Coll., 1963; ThM, St. Anthony Coll., 1967; M in Econs., New Sch. Social Research, 1985; PhD in Theology, Grad. Theol. Union, 1989. Ordained priest Roman Cath. Ch., 1966. Assoc. pastor St. Elizabeth Ch., Milw., 1968-73; mem. staff Justice & Peace Ctr., Milw., 1973-83, coord. beatitudes program, corp. responsibilities, 1983—; mem. governing bd. Interfaith Ctr. on Corp. Responsibility, N.Y., 1973—; mem. Justice and Peace Com. Conf. of Maj. Superiors of Men, Washington, 1982—. Author six books on scriptures, spirituality and theology; contbr. articles on spirituality, theology and corp. responsibility to profl. jours. Avocations: racquetball, swimming. Home: 1534 Arch Berkeley CA 94708 Office: 1001 E Keefe Milwaukee WI 53212

CROSE, LESTER ALTON, minister; b. Santa Cruz, Calif., July 28, 1912; s. John Davis and Pearl Parthenia (Conrad) C.; m. Ruthe Marie Hamon, Sept. 26, 1934; children: Alta Ruthe (Mrs. Ronald Jack), John Lester. BA, Anderson (Ind.) Coll., 1945, DD, 1959. Ordained to ministry Ch. of God, 1937. Overseas missionary Ch. of God, 1933-54; sec.-treas. Ch. of God, Barbados and Trinidad, 1941-44, Lebanon, 1945-50, Egypt, 1950-52; exec. sec.-treas. missionary bd. Ch. of God, 1954-75, sec. for rsch. and devel., 1975-76, prof. missions Sch. of Theology, 1976-78, mem. gen. assembly; cons. Mediterranean Bible Coll., Beirut, Lebanon. Author: Passport for a Reformation, 1981. Mem. Am. Soc. Missiology, Middle East Inst. Home: 303 Central Ave Anderson IN 46012 Office: Ch of God Exec Offices Anderson IN 46012

CROSS, HAMAN, II, minister; b. Detroit, Jan. 28, 1949; s. Haman Sr. and Malettor (Gause) C.; m. Roberta Aneette Alexander, June 26, 1971; children: Haman III, Gilvonna, Sharryl. BA, William Tyndale Coll., 1971; postgrad., Nyack Missionary Coll., 1967-68. Ordained to ministry Bapt. Ch. Dir. Detroit's Afro Am. Mission, 1971-82; sr. pastor Rosedale Park Bapt. Ch., Detroit, 1982—; instr. Bible Rsch. Inst., Detroit, 1971-82; assoc. satff Campus Crusade for Christ, 1975—; instr., cons. Christian Rsch. and Devel., Phila., 1980—, also bd. dirs.; assoc. staff trainer Leadership Dynamics, Inc., Atlanta, 1984—; coach William Tyndale Coll., Farmington, Mich., 1973-79. Author: Dating and Courtship, God's Honor Roll of Faith, The Life of Moses. Bd. dirs. Carver Fgn. Missions, Joy of Jesus, Jubilee Found., Here's Life Am., also city dir. Home: 14017 Robson Detroit MI 48227 Office: Rosedale Park Bapt Ch 14161 Vaughan Detroit MI 48223

CROSS, IRVIE KEIL, religious organization executive; b. Huntington, Ark., Mar. 21, 1917; s. William Earl and Bertha Frances (Harris) C.; m. Johnnie Maxine Sharpe, June 9, 1939; children: Johnnie Keilene Cross Barnes, Maxine Irviene Cross Perkins. Th.M., Missionary Baptist Sem., 1938, Th.D., 1944; D.D., Orthdox Bapt. Inst., 1946, Eastern Bapt. Inst., 1959, Internat. Free Protestant Episcopal U. of London, Eng., 1964. Ordained to ministry Am. Baptist Assn., 1936. Pastor Pauline Bapt. Ch., Monticello, Ark., 1939-41, County Ave Bapt. Ch., Texarkana, Ark., 1941-50, Langdon St. Bapt. Ch., Somerset, Ky., 1950-59; founder, pres. Eastern Bapt. Inst., 1953-67; pres. Eastern Bapt. Assn., 1958-62; founder, dir. office of publicity Am. Bapt. Assn., Texarkana, Ark.-Tex., 1952-67; dir. office of promotion and pub. rels. Am. Bapt. Assn., Texarkana, 1967-74, 86-91, v.p., 1975-78, pres., 1978-79, mem. history and archives com., 1974—, chmn. history and archives com., 1988-91, mem. chaplains commn., 1964—; adminstrv. v.p. Calif. Missionary Bapt. Inst. and Sem., Bellflower, Calif., 1974-86; condr. study tours to, Europe and Middle East. Author: Truth About Conventionism, 1955, The Church Covenant, 1955, Paul's Lectures, 1956, Non-Denominational Denomination, 1956, I Believe God, 1966, Tongues, 1973, Baptism Holy Spirit, 1973, Great Commission, 1974, Divine Healing, 1974, Lectures on Israel in Prophecy, 1974, Baptist Heritage Abandoned, 1981, The Universal Church, 1983, Landmarkism: An Update, 1984, The Work of a Deacon, 1984, The Work of a Pastor, 1984, Paul's Lectures, 1986, Studies in Practicalities for Young Ministers, 1987, Protestant Reformation and Baptist Compromise, 1989, Austin T. Powers As I Knew Him, 1989, According to Matthew, 1990, The Battle for Baptist History, 1990; editor Sword, 1944-49, Am. Bapt. Digest, 1949-50, Missionary, 1953-67, Bapt. Sentinel, 1974-86, Christian Education Bulletin, 1986—. Mem. adv. bd. Salvation Army, 1947-50; pres. Kidco, Inc., 1962-74, Lake Cumberland-Dale Hollow Tourist and Travel, 1965; mem. Ky. Devel. Council, 1962. Mem. Four States Aviation Assn. (pres. 1946-47), Somerset-Pulaski County (Ky.) C. of C. (pres. 1962), Somerset Ministerial Assn. (pres. 1954), Ky. Guild Artists and Craftsmen (pres. 1963-67). Club: Masons. Home: 8 Park Ln Texarkana TX 75503 *I have lived by the concept that honesty, truthfulness and moral cleanliness form the foundation of character. I prefer to pursue my own ideas, and am not satisfied short of the top in any endeavor undertaken.*

CROSS, MARY HARRINGTON, theology educator, organizational consultant; b. Norwich, Conn., Mar. 9, 1943; d. Charles Ellsworth and Albina Marie (Richard) Harrington. B.A., U. Conn., 1967; M.L.S., U. Calif.-Berkeley, 1974; postgrad. Wright Inst., Berkeley, 1983. Dir. disabled services Wilbur Cross Library, Storrs, Conn., 1968-72; dir. ministry-in-action Sch. Applied Theology, Berkeley, Calif., 1975—; dir. Ctr. for Women and Religion, Berkeley, 1977—. Bd. dirs. Chrysalis, Oakland, Calif. Mem. Assn.

Theol. Field Educators (steering com. 1981-85), Ctr. for Orgnl. Studies, Calif. Library Assn. Democrat. Roman Catholic. Office: Ctr for Women and Religion 2465 LeConte St Berkeley CA 94709

CROSS, MIKE W., minister; b. Spokane, Wash., Jan. 19, 1960; s. Wayne H. Cross and Bernice (Jones) Haas; m. Michele Renee Angevine, Oct. 24, 1984; children: Hannah, Rachel. BA in History, U. Wash., 1982; postgrad., Western Evang. Sem., 1989—. Ordained to ministry Evang. Ch. N.Am. Jr. high sch. dir., intern Edgewood Bapt. Ch., Edmonds, Wash., 1979-82; youth pastor Cedarhome Bapt. Ch., Stanwood, Wash., 1982-85, Renton Park Chapel-Evang. Ch., Renton, Wash., 1985-88, Oregon City (Oreg.) Evang. Ch., 1988—; camp. dir. Conf. High Sch., Evang. Ch., Portland, Oreg., 1986—, high sch. camp tchr., 1988—. Office: Oregon City Evang Ch 1024 Linn Ave Oregon City OR 97045

CROSSIN, JOHN WILLIAM, academic administrator; b. Phila., May 17, 1947; s. John William and Marie (Astley) C. BS in Math., Allentown Coll., 1972; MA in Psychology, Cath. U., 1978, PhD in Theology, 1982. Asst., assoc prof., moral theology DeSales Sch. Theology, Washington, 1980-90, pres., 1987—; ethics com. Providence Hosp., Washington, 1988—; bd. trustees Allentown Coll., Pa., 1987—. Author: What are They Saying About Virtue?, 1985; contbr. articles to profl. jours. Mem. Cath. Theol. Soc. Am., Soc. Christian Ethics, Nat. Cath. Ednl. Assn. Roman Catholic. Office: De Sales Sch Theology 721 Lawrence St NE Washington DC 20017

CROSSMAN, KENNETH CHARLES, clergyman; b. Toledo, Apr. 4, 1933; s. Elliott Andrew and Mabel Irene (Miller) C.; m. Cecily Riley, July 2, 1960; children—Catherine Ann, Scott Elliott, Sarah Elizabeth, John Mark. B.A., Wabash Coll., 1955; postgrad. Harvard Bus. Sch., 1955; M.Div., Candler Sch. Theology, Emory U., 1968. Regional sales mgr. Yardley or London, Inc., Ft. Lauderdale, Fla., 1958-65; student pastor United Methodist Ch., Atlanta, 1965-68, minister, Ft. Lauderdale, 1968-77, Orlando, Fla., 1977-81, Melbourne, Fla., 1981—, sr. minister St. Paul's United Meth. Ch., 1981—; host weekly local TV program; producer nat. TV commls. for United Meth. Ch.; chmn. TV and Radio Task Force, United Meth. Ch., Fla., 1980—; pres. Rebuild Found., Ft. Lauderdale, 1970-77; founder Specialized Urban Ministries, Ft. Lauderdale, 1970-77; v.p. Religion and Race Com. United Meth. Ch., Lakeland, Fla., 1977-80. Author: Questions Jesus Asked, 1981; producer various TV programs, 1983. Minister Orange County Commn., 1981, Orlando City Council, 1981; co-chmn. Broward County Community Relations Com., 1972-74; mem. Areawide Council on Aging, 1971-75; dir. Broward County Legal Aid Bd., pres., 1974-77; del. state Democratic Conv., 1981. Served with U.S. Army, 1956-58. Recipient Community Service award Broward Times, 1970; Outstanding Contbns. award Broward County Community Relations Commn., 1974; cert. of appreciation Broward County Commn., 1974-77; Human Relations award Fla. Edn. Assn., 1974; Community Service award Broward County Areawide Council on Aging, 1975; commendation Ft. Lauderdale City Commn., 1977; Human Relations award Broward County Classroom Tchrs. Assn., 1977; commendation Orlando City Council, 1981, Orange County Commn., 1981; named Outstanding Religious Leader, Melbourne Jaycees, 1981-82. Mem. United Meth. Assn. Ch. Bus. Adminstrs. (cert. ch. bus. adminstr.), Greater Ft. Lauderdale Ministerial Assn. (pres. 1974-75), Assn. Regional Religious Communicators. Office: United Meth Palm Beaches 612 Florida Ave PO Box 1156 West Palm Beach FL 33402-1156

CROTTS, STEPHEN MICHAEL, minister; b. Burlington, N.C., Apr. 14, 1950; s. George Byron and Elizabeth (Aiken) C.; m. Kathryn Cook, June 16, 1973; children: Claire Elizabeth, Bryan Patrick, David Stephen. BA in Philosophy, Furman U., 1972; MDiv, Emory U., 1975. Ordained to ministry Presbyn. Ch., 1975. With missions New Directions Ministries SE USA, Jamaica, Haiti, 1968-71; youth pastor One Way Bapt. Ch., Augusta, Ga., 1975-78; with Village Presbyn. Ch., Drakes Branch Ch., Charlotte Court House, Va., 1975-78, Westview Presbyn. Ch., Elon College, N.C., 1978-81; sr. min. Christ Ch., Burlington, 1981—. Contbr. articles to numerous mags.; guest columnist The Fellowship of Christian Athletes. Republican. Home: 728 W Davis St Burlington NC 27215 Office: Christ Ch PO Box 2665 Burlington NC 27216 *Early Christians did not stand around complaining, "Look what the world has come to!" Rather, they joyfully proclaimed, "Look who has come to the world!".*

CROUCH, ANTHONY LEE, minister; b. Indpls., Aug. 21, 1957; s. Edgar Ira and Ruth Louise (Wirey) C.; m. Marla Jill Collins, Aug. 20, 1978; children: Caleb Anthony, Cameron Philip. BA, Lincoln Christian Coll., 1984; postgrad., Lincoln Christian Sem., 1990, Ky. Christian Coll., 1991—. Ordained to ministry Ind. Christian Ch., 1983. Assoc. min. Antioch Christian Ch., Decatur, Ill., 1981-84; min. Ellery (Ill.) Christian Ch., 1984-86, Ch. of Christ (Christian), Rushville, Ill., 1986-87, Lockport (Ill.) Christian Ch., 1987—. Office: Lockport Christian Ch 315 E Eleventh St Lockport IL 60441-3432 *In my life I have tried to follow the golden rule set forth by Jesus in Mathew 7:12 as a guide to my own life. It answers a hundred differnet questions or situations.*

CROUCH, LEON, clergyman, educator; b. Trenton, Tex., Nov. 28, 1928; s. Jimmy W. and Annie E. (Goodman) C.; m. Peggy J. Crouch, Feb. 8, 1953; children: Cathy Crouch Akin, Jimmy, Edward, Charles. BS, West. Tex. State U., 1956; MA, Harding Grad. Sch., Memphis, 1961; DMinistry, Luther Rice Sem., Jacksonville, Fla., 1977; ThD, Trinity Sem., Tennyson, Ind., 1980. Ordained minister Ch. of Christ, 1956. Minister Ch. of Christ, Minot, N.D., 1956-59, Leachville, Ark., 1959-61, Liverpool, Eng., 1965-68, London, 1968-72; tchr., Bible chair Tex. Tech U., Lubbock, 1961-65; tchr., dir. Wembley (Eng.) Bible Sch., 1968-72; tchr. Lubbock Christian U., 1972—. Author: The Deity of Christ, 1977, Commentary on 1 a 2 Thessalonians, Beginning Greek Textbook; contbr. articles to profl. jours. Cpl. USMC, 1948-53, Korea. Mem. Evang. Theol. Soc. Republican. Home: 5433 31st St Lubbock TX 79407 Office: Lubbock Christian U 5601 W 19th St Lubbock TX 79407

CROUCH, PAUL FRANKLIN, minister, church official; b. St. Joseph, Mo., Mar. 30, 1934; s. Andrew Franklin and Sarah Matilda (Swingle) C.; m. Janice Wendell Bethany, Aug. 25, 1957; children—Paul F., Matthew W. B.Th., Central Bible Coll. and Sem., Springfield, Mo., 1955. Ordained to ministry, 1955; dir. fgn. missions film and audio visual dept. Assemblies of God, 1955-58; assoc. pastor 1st Assembly of God, Rapid City, S.D., 1958-60, Central Assembly of God, Muskegon, Mich., 1960-62; gen. mgr. TV and film prodn. center Assemblies of God, Burbank, Calif., 1962-65; gen. mgr. Sta. KREL, Cornona, Calif., 1965-71, Sta. KHOF, KHOF-TV, Glendale, Calif., 1971-73; founder, pres. Sta. KTBN-TV, Trinity Broadcasting Network, Los Angeles, 1973—. Recipient Best Religious film award Winona Lake Film Festival, 1956. Mem. Nat. Assn. Religious Broadcasters, Western Religious Broadcasters Assn., Assn. Christian TV Stas. (founder). Office: Trinity Broadcasting Network 2442 Michelle Dr Tustin CA 92680

CROUCH, ROBERT ANDREW, minister; b. San Rafael, Calif., May 25, 1959; s. Arthur E. and Alice Augusta (Lindquist) C.; m. Suzanne Marie Pederson, Dec. 1, 1990. BA in Sociology, UCLA, 1982; MDiv, San Francisco Theol. Seminary, 1986. Ordained to ministry Presbyn. Ch., 1989. Asst. minister First Presbyn. Ch., Encino, Calif., 1986-87; prog. asst./prog. agy. The Presbyn. Ch. USN, N.Y.C., 1987-89; assoc. minister First Presbyn. Ch., Santa Monica, Calif., 1989—; chmn. Presbytery of the Pacific, L.A.; del. Gen. Assembly 1983, Atlanta, 1983. Producer/editor: (video) Voices of the Future, 1988; contbr. articles to profl. jours. Bd. dirs. Coalition of Santa Monica Homeless, Laubach Literacy; hosp. chaplain UCLA Med. Ctr. Democrat. Home: 3321 Keystone # 4 Los Angeles CA 90034 Office: First Presbyterian Church 1220 2 St Santa Monica CA 90401-1109

CROUCH, RONALD GENE, SR., minister; b. Ceres, Calif., Dec. 23, 1952; s. George and Donna Mae (Aifs) C.; m. Rose Marie Chipponeri, July 12, 1976; children: Ron Jr., Adam D., Samantha M., Serena L. Youth dir. Orchard Ave. Bapt. Ch., Vacaville, Calif., 1987—; trustee chmn. Orchard Ave. Bapt., 1990—. Home: 445 Wilmington Way Vacaville CA 95688 Office: Orchard Ave Baptist Church 301 N Orchard Ave Vacaville CA 95688

CROUCH, W. EUGENE, minister; b. Sioux City, Iowa, Nov. 27, 1945; s. Leland Eugene and Bessie E. (Tillis) C.; m. Janice Ilene Davis, Aug. 13, 1977; children: Karis E., Abigail Hannah, Nathan Eugene. BA, Biola U., La Mirada, Calif., 1967; MDiv, Talbot Theol. Sem., La Mirada, 1978; ThM, Grace Theol. Sem., Winona Lake, Ind., 1990. Ordained to ministry Evang. Ind. Chs. Am., 1978. Tchr. various pub. sch. dists., Anaheim and Buena Park, Calif., 1967-70, Norwalk (Calif.) Brethren Christian Sch., 1969-70; prof. L.A. Bible Tng. Sch., 1972-77, Grace Bible Inst. and Grad. Sch., Long Beach, Calif., 1981-83; pastor Berea Bapt. Ch., Long Beach, 1981-83; missionary UFM Internat., Brazil, 1976-81; misssionary, prof. Word of Life Bible Inst., Portugal, 1986-88; pastor Evang. Free Ch., Plum City, Wis., 1988—. Home: W2524 County Rd S Maiden Rock WI 54750-8415 Office: Evang Free Ch 501 1st Ave E Plum City WI 54761

CROUCH, WILLIAM HENRY, minister; b. Hickory, N.C., June 14, 1928; s. W. Perry and Floy (Hornaer) C.; m. Janice Y. Crouch, July 10, 1929; children: Bill, Thomas, Debbie, Sarah. AA, Mars Hill Coll.; BA, Wake Forest U., 1949; MDiv, So. Bapt. Sem., 1953, MTh, 1954. Ordained to ministry Bapt. Ch., 1948. Minister Taylorsville (Ky.) Bapt. Ch., 1952-54, Northside Bapt. Ch., Jackson, Mich., 1954-59, Ardmore Bapt. Ch., Winston-Salem, N.C., 1959-68, Providence Bapt. Ch., Charlotte, N.C., 1968—; dir. devel. Bapt. Sem., Richmond, Va., 1991—; chaplain Meklenburg Police, 1970-92, Charlotte Police Dept., 1971-84, Hornets, NBA, Charlotte, 1989-91; pres. So. Bapt. Alliance, Washington, 1988-89. Mem. Kiwanis (pres.). Home: 318 Burleigh St Charlotte NC 28211 Office: Providence Bapt Ch 4921 Randolph Rd Charlotte NC 28211

CROUSE, STEPHEN GARY, minister; b. Burlington, N.C., Mar. 12, 1955; s. Clair Hurley and Laura Louise (Rhodes) C.; m. Martha Jean Drum, Feb. 4, 1989. BS, Gardner-Webb Coll., 1977. Min. youth and activities Glen Hope Baptist Ch., Burlington, N.C., 1977-78; min. music and youth Enoree Baptist Ch., Travelers Rest, S.C., 1979-87; dir. joyful sound No. Greenville Coll., Tigerville, S.C., 1984-87; min. music and youth Mt. Zion Baptist Ch., Hudson, N.C., 1987—; chmn. bd. dirs. Regal Venture, Inc., Kings Mountain, N.C., 1985--. Co-author: Disciples Under Construction, 1990, author: Kingdom Studies, 1989. Mem. Natl. Network Youth Mins. Republican. Southern Baptist. Office: Mt Zion Baptist Ch Rte 3 Box 481 Hudson NC 28638 *We have but two lasting gifts to pass on to those who follow us, roots and freedom. Roots come through faithfulness and commitment to eternal truth. Freedom give individuals the opportunity to be creative and inventive.*

CROUSE, TERRY EDWIN, minister; b. Lenoir, N.C., May 11, 1954; s. J. B. and Mary Joan (Prestwood) C.; m. Sherry Brown, July 22, 1953; children: Joseph Matthew, Andrew David. Student, Gardner Webb Coll., 1972-75. Ordained to ministry So. Bapt. Conv., 1988. Min. music and youth Mountain Grove Bapt. Ch., Granite Falls, N.C., 1975-78, Trinity Bapt. Ch., Whiteville, N.C., 1978-81, Concord Bapt. Ch., Granite Falls, 1981—; instrumental dir. Caldwell (N.C.) Music Coun., 1990-91; dir. Associational Youth Music Coun., Lenoir, 1990-91; mem. New Life Singers Am., Marion, N.C., 1972. Bd. dirs. Caldwell Youth for Christ, Caldwell County, 1977. Recipient Nat. Leadership award Soc. Disting. High Sch. Students, 1990. Mem. ASCD. Republican. Office: Concord Bapt Ch 74 Falls Ave Granite Falls NC 28630

CROUSE, WILLIAM ARNOLD, JR., music minister; b. Columbus, Ohio, Oct. 3, 1939; s. William Arnold Sr. and Thelma Ida (Soulsby) C.; m. Devonnia Gerene Lewallen, July 6, 1963; children: Jeffrey Alan, Joy Alane. BA, Belmont Coll., 1971. Min. of music First Bapt. Ch., Mt. Juliet, Tenn., 1971-73, Magnolia Springs Bapt. Ch., Theodore, Ala., 1973—; dir. of music Am. Bapt. Assn., 1987-90, asst. dir. music, 1991. With U.S. Army, 1958-60. Home: 6070 Old Spanish Trail Theodore AL 36582 Office: Magnolia Springs Bapt Ch 6058 Theodore-Dawes Rd Theodore AL 36582

CROUSE, WILLIAM CHARLES, religious educator; b. Lewisburg, Pa., July 20, 1944; s. Charles Albert and Mary Good (Zechman) C.; m. Susan Lynn Brown, June 1, 1974; children: Jamie Sue, Heidi, Tammi, Mary, Robert. AB, Goshen Coll., 1966; ThM, Dallas Sem., 1970; postgrad., U. Tex. at Dallas, Richardson, 1983-85. Asst. pastor Calvary Bapt. Ch., Vestal, N.Y., 1970-71; tchr. Trinity Christian Acad., Addison, Tex., 1972-75; sr. scholar Probe Ministries Internat., Richardson, 1975-85; founder, pres. Christian Info. Ministries Internat., Richardson, 1985—. Editor Ararat Report newsletter, 1986—. Mem. Evang. Theol. Soc., Evang. Philos. Soc. Office: Christian Info Ministries 2050 N Collins Blvd Ste 100 Richardson TX 75080

CROUTER, RICHARD EARL, religion educator; b. Washington, Nov. 2, 1937; s. Earl Clinton and Neva J. (Crain) C.; m. Barbara Jean Williams, Jan. 30, 1960; children—Edward, Frances. A.B., Occidental Coll., 1960; B.D., Union Theol. U., N.Y.C., 1963, Th.D., 1968. Asst. prof. religion Carleton Coll., Northfield, Minn., 1967-73; assoc. prof. Carleton Coll., 1973-79, prof., 1979—; Translator, editor: On Religion (F. Schleiermacher), 1988. Chmn. parents adv. council Greenvale Sch. Northfield, 1977-78; resident dir. A Better Chance Program, Northfield, 1968-70. Fulbright scholar, 1976-77, 87, 91—; Am. Council Learned Socs. fellow, 1976-77. Mem. Am. Acad. Religion (steering com. 19th century theol. group 1982—, chmn. 1987—), Hegel Soc. Am. Democrat. Avocations: hiking, tennis, travel, biking. Home: 808 E 2d St Northfield MN 55057 Office: Carleton Coll Northfield MN 55057

CROW, PAUL ABERNATHY, JR., clergyman, religious council executive, educator; b. Birmingham, Ala., Nov. 17, 1931; s. Paul Abernathy and Beulah Elizabeth (Parker) C.; m. Mary Evelyn Matthews, Sept. 11, 1955; children: Carol Ann, Stephen Paul, Susan Margaret. BS, U. Ala., 1954; BD, Lexington Theol. Sem., 1957; MST, Hartford Sem. Found., 1958, PhD, 1962; postdoctoral studies, Oxford U., 1967-68, U. Geneva, 1981, Phillips U., 1983; DD, Bethany Coll., 1983; postdoctoral studies, Yale U., 1986, Va. Theological Sem., 1987, Ecumenical Inst., Bossey, 1987. Ordained to ministry Disciples of Christ, 1957. Minister various Disciples congregations various Disciples congregations, Ala., Ky., 1955-57; min. First Congl. Ch., Hadley, Mass., 1957-61; assoc. prof. ch. history Lexington Theol. Sem., 1961-66, prof., 1966-68; Am. Assn. Theol. Schs. vis. fellow Oxford U., 1967-68; gen. sec. Consultation on Ch. Union, Princeton, N.J., 1968-74; pres. Coun. on Christian Unity, Indpls., 1974—; Mem. cen. com. World Coun. Chs., exec. com., plenary faith and order commn., 1975—; del. faith and order confs., St. Andrews, Scotland, 1960, Montreal, Que., Can., 1963, Bristol, Eng., 1967, Louvain, Belgium, 1971, Accra, Ghana, 1974, Bangalore, India, 1978, Lima, Peru, 1982, Stavanger, Norway, 1985, Budapest, Hungary, 1989; del. World Coun. Chs. assembly Uppsala, Sweden, 1968, Nairobi, Kenya, 1975, Vancouver, Can., 1983, Canberra, Australia, 1991; del. ch. union confs., Limuru, Kenya, 1970, Toronto, Ont., Can., 1975, Colombo, Sri Lanka, 1981, Potsdam, German Democratic Republic, 1987; mem. exec. com. Consultation on Ch. Union; chmn. Disciples of Christ del., mem. exec. com., mem. gen. bd. Nat. Coun. Chs.; co-chmn. Disciples of Christ-Roman Cath. Internat. Bilateral; co-chmn. Disciples-Russian Orthodox Internat. Bilateral; vis. prof. Princeton Theol. Sem., 1968-78; affiliate prof. Christian Theol. Sem., 1974—; gen. sec. Disciples Ecumenical Consultative Coun., 1975—. Author: Where We Are in Church Union, 1965, The Ecumenical Movement in Bibliographical Outline, 1965, No Greater Love: The Gospel and Its Imperatives, 1967, Church Union at Mid-Point, 1972, Christian Unity: Matrix for Mission, 1982, The Anatomy of a Nineteenth Century United Church, 1983; editor: Mid-Stream: An Ecumenical Jour., 1974—. Bd. govs. Ecumenical Inst., Bossey; trustee Disciples of Christ Hist. Soc. Recipient Disting. Alumni award Hartford Sem. Found., 1986; Jacobus fellow Hartford Sem. Found., 1958. Mem. Am. Soc. Ch. History, North Am. Acad. Ecumenists, Societas Oikoumenicus, Nassau Club (Princeton, N.J.), Indianapolis Athletic Club, Omicron Delta Kappa, Theta Phi. Democrat. Home: 7215 Vauxhall Rd Indianapolis IN 46250 Office: 222 S Downey Ave PO Box 1986 Indianapolis IN 46206

CROWELL, GILBERT EARL, minister, accountant; b. Macon, Miss., Nov. 20, 1952; s. Billy and Era Jean (McGaugh) C.; m. Teresa Lyn Hoxworth, May 26, 1984; children: Katie, John, Jim. BBA with honors, U. Tex., 1974; ThM, Dallas Sem., 1984. Ordained to ministry Northwest Bible Ch., 1984; CPA, Md. Missionary pastor Internat. Students, Cascais, Portugal, 1985-88; assoc. pastor single adults Eastside Bapt. Ch., Marietta, Ga., 1988—, assoc. pastor missions, 1991—. Mem. Nat. Assn. Single Adult Leaders. Office: Eastside Bapt Ch 2450 Lower Roswell Rd Marietta GA 30068 *"I do not consider my life of any account as dear to myself in order that I may finish my course and the ministry which I received from the Lord Jesus, to testify solemnly of the Gospel of the grace of God." Acts 20:24.*

CROWETIPTON, VAUGHN ERIC, minister; b. Columbus, Ohio, Oct. 13, 1962; s. Clyde Vernon and Shirley Faye (Saucer) T.; m. Beverly Cheryl CroweTipton, Oct. 21, 1989. BA, Miss. Coll., Jackson, 1985; MDiv, So. Bapt. Theol. Seminary, Louisville, 1988; PhD, Baylor U., 1991. Min. youth Forrest Hill Bapt., Jackson, 1983-86; assoc. pastor 1st Bapt. Ch., Sellersburg, Ind., 1987-89; chaplain Meth. Children's Home, Waco, Tex., 1989-91; minister to coll. students Seventh and James Bapt. Ch., Waco, Tex., 1991—. Vol. Caratas, Waco, 1989-90, Habitat for Humanity, Waco, 1989-90; active Fellowship of Reconciliation, N.Y.C., 1987—. Named one of Outstanding Young Men Am., 1985, 87, 89, 90. Mem. Soc. Bibl. Lit., Religious Edn. Assn. Democrat. Baptist. Home: 1918 Mountainview Dr Waco TX 76710

CROWLEY, JOSEPH R., bishop; b. Ft. Wayne, Ind., Jan. 12, 1915. Student, St. Mary's Coll., St. Mary, Ky., St. Meinrad (Ind.) Sem. Ordained priest Roman Cath. Ch., 1953. Ordained titular bishop of Maraguis and aux. bishop of Ft. Wayne-South Bend, Ind., 1971. Editor: Our Sunday Visitor, 1958-67. Office: 1701 Miami St South Bend IN 46613

CROWLEY, LEONARD JAMES, auxiliary bishop; b. Montreal, Que., Can., Dec. 28, 1921; s. James and Agnes (Wheeler) C. B.A., U. Montreal, 1941, Licentiate in Theology, 1947; Licentiate in Canon Law, U. Ottawa, Ont., Can., 1950. Ordained priest Roman Catholic Ch., 1947, bishop, 1971. Aux. bishop Diocese Montreal, 1971—, dir. Office for English Lang. Affairs. Home: 1071 rue de la Cathédrale, Montreal, PQ Canada H3B 2V4 Office: Archeveche de Montreal, 2000 Sherbrooke St W, Montreal, PQ Canada H3H 1G4

CROWNFIELD, DAVID RING, religion and philosophy educator; b. Quincy, Mass., June 24, 1930; s. Frederic Rudolph and Margaret Elizabeth (Robbins) C.; m. Eleanor L. Bostwick, Aug. 29, 1953 (div. 1979); children: Elizabeth E., Nonie B. Quinlan, Eleanor C. Ray. BA, Harvard U., 1951; BD, Yale U., 1954; ThM, Harvard U., 1958, ThD, 1964. Ordained to ministry Congl. Ch., 1955. Pastor Hatfield (Mass.) Congregational Ch., 1955-56, Cen. Congregational Ch. Dorchester, Boston, 1957-58; prof. U. No. Iowa, Cedar Falls, 1964—. Co-editor, author (with others): (anthology) Lacan and Theological Discourse, 1989; contbr. articles to profl. jours. Mem. Am. Acad. Religion (unit chair 1981-86), Am. Theol. Soc. (pres. Midwest chpt. 1987-88), Person, Culture and Religion (chair 1980-81), Soc. for Phenominology and Existential Philosophy, Am. Philos. Assn., Heidegger Conf. Office: U No Iowa Dept Philosophy and Religion Cedar Falls IA 50614-0501

CROWTHER, CLARENCE EDWARD, bishop; b. Bradford, Eng., Mar. 4, 1929; came to U.S., 1959, naturalized, 1964; s. Joseph Austin and Margaret Edith Ellen (Simm) C.; m. Margaret Hird, Apr. 1, 1955; children: Paul, Alison, Deborah; m. Ingrid Schunemann, Dec. 5, 1982. B.A., U. Leeds, Eng., 1950, LL.B., 1952, LL.M., 1953; Ph.D, U. Calif., 1975. Ordained to ministry, Episcopal Ch., 1956. Tutor law Exeter Coll., Oxford U., 1952-54; curate Sts. Philip and James Ch. Oxford, Eng., 1956-58; sr. chaplain UCLA, 1958-64; dean St. Cyprian's Cathedral, Kimberly, South Africa, 1964-65; bishop of Kimberly South Africa, 1965-67; asst. bishop Calif. San Francisco, 1971-85; asst. bishop Diocese of L.A., 1991—; hon. canon Grace Cathedral, San Francisco; lectr. black studies U. Calif.- Santa Barbara, 1970-75; exec. dir. Operation Connection (N.Y.C. and Santa Barbara), 1970-72. Author: Where Religion Gets Lost in the Church, 1969, The Face of Apartheid, 1971, Intimacy: Strategies for Successful Relationship, 1986. Vis. fellow Ctr. for Study Democratic Instns., Santa Barbara, Calif., 1968-70. Mem. Calif. Assn. Marriage and Family Therapists (clin. life). Home: 210 San Ysidro Rd Montecito CA 93108

CROY, DANIEL ALBERT, religious organization administrator, consultant; b. Kansas City, Kans., July 10, 1951; s. Arthur Albert and Esther Naomi (Hieronymus) C.; m. Carolyn Kay Hawkins, Dec. 16, 1972; children: Kasey Dawn, Nathan Daniel. BS, Mid-Am. Nazarene Coll., 1973; MA, U. No. Colo., 1978; EdD, Vanderbilt U., 1988. Assoc. prof. Nazarene Bible Coll., Colorado Springs, Colo., 1978-81; assoc. minister First Ch. of the Nazarene, Denver, 1981-83; counselor Carolina Christian Counseling Ctr., High Point, N.C., 1983-84, Christian Counseling Svcs., Nashville, 1984-87; coord. exec. devel. Hosp. Corp. Am., Nashville, 1988-89; dir. counseling and learning ministries First Wesleyan Ch., High Point, 1989—. Mem. ASTD, Am. Assn. for Counseling and Devel., Am. Mental Health Counselors Assn. Home: 3905 Waldorf Ct High Point NC 27265 Office: First Wesleyan Ch 1915 North Centennial High Point NC 27262

CRUDUP, W., bishop. Bishop Ch . of God in Christ, Oxon Hill, Md. Office: Ch of God in Christ 5101 Martin Dr Oxon Hill MD 20745*

CRUDUP, WARREN GEORGE, SR., bishop; b. Norfolk, Va., Aug. 1, 1923; s. George Albert and Mary Lue (Person) C.; m. Parthenia Betty Anne Turner, Apr. 28, 1944; children: Warren G. Jr., Carolyn Yvonne, Carlton Lovelis. BTh, Northwestern Coll., 1965, DD (hon.), 1968. Ordained to ministry Ch. of God in Christ as elder, 1956, bishop, 1989. Pastor Ch. of God in Christ, Washington, 1955—, supt., 1973-89, adminstrv. asst., 1982-89, bishop, 1989—; area dir. C.H. Mason System Bible Coll., Washington and Md., 1975-78, regional dir., 1978—; mem. Coun. of Chs., Washington, 1960—; advisor to seminarians Howard U., Am. U., Washington, 1990—. Booster Census Bur., Washington, 1990. With U.S. Army, 1943-46, ETO. Democrat. Office: St Paul Temple Ch of God in Christ 3420-16th St NE Washington DC 20018

CRUEL, RONNIE, minister; b. Moultrie, Ga., Sept. 15, 1957; s. James H. and Earlene L. C.; m. Sonya Tracy Riley, July 4, 1989. BS, Liberty U., 1990. Ordained to ministry Nat. Bapt. Conv. U.S.A., 1979. Pastor Flak Gospel Fellowship, Augsburg, Fed. Republic Germany, 1976-77; interim pastor Mt. Calvary Bapt. Ch., Cairo, Ga., 1979-80; pastor Cornerstone Ministry Ctr., Augusta, Ga., 1983-89; min. Living Word Christian Ctr., Augusta, 1989—; mem. clergy staff Univ. Hosp., Augusta, 1989—. Author: Now That You're in the Kingdom, 1986, The Knowledge of God, 1987; editor Living World Trumpet newsletter, 1989. Sgt. U.S. Army, 1975-86. Home: 3918 Bowen Dr Hephzibah GA 30815 Office: Living Word Christian Ctr PO Box 6285 Augusta GA 30916

CRUM, ALFREDA FOSTER, church choir director; b. Columbia, S.C., Feb. 16, 1953; d. John Wesley and Maria (Green) Foster; m. Albert Lee Crum, Sept. 1, 1990; children: Scheri Charmaine, Eboni Nichole Eichelberger, Chariti Faith. Student, Benedict Coll., Columbia, 1971-72, 78; cert., Midlands Tech. Coll., Columbia, 1978. Dir. choir Mt. Zion Bapt. Ch., Cayce, S.C., 1970-73, 78-81, Cornerstone Bapt. Young Gospel Choir, Columbia, 1987-91; organizer, dir. choir Cornerstone Bapt. Friends and Family Day Choir, Cornerstone Bapt. Mass Choir, Columbia, 1988—; receptionist S.C. Lt. Gov.'s Office, Columbia, 1991—; mem. The Caravan Gospel Singers, Columbia, 1970-77, 83-86, All in Family Gospel Singers, Columbia, 1977-80. Mem. Singing Angels Gospel Singers. Home: 105 Dove Dr Lexington SC 29072

CRUMBLY, DOUGLAS GARNER, clergyman; b. Rome, Ga., Sept. 25, 1962; s. Billy Charles Crumbly and Gloria Yvonne (Hubbard) Judd; m. Debbie Francis Manning, Jan. 16, 1982; children: Amanda Leigh, Anne, Lauren Danielle. BS in Sacred Lit., Covington Theol. Sem., 1991. Youth pastor Assembly of God Ch. - East Gate, Rome, Ga., 1989—; self-employed heating, ventilation and air conditioning svc., Rome, 1990—. deacon First So. Bapt. of Apple Valley, Calif., 1983-85; membership chmn. Full Gospel Businessmen, Rome, 1990—. With USAF, 1982-87. Home: 9 Monroe Dr Rome GA 30161 Office: East Gate Assembly of God Hwy 411 S Rome GA 30161

CRUMBLY, JOHN QUANTOCK, priest; b. Union Point, Ga., Nov. 2, 1916; s. Frank and Anna (Walden) C.; m. Meda Lamb Crouch, May 31, 1936. BD, U. of the South, 1952; MDiv, 1972; MEd, The Citadel, 1985. Ordained priest Episcopal Ch., 1949; lic. profl. counselor, 1986. Rector various parishes S.C., 1948-51, Fla., 1951-58, Washington, 1958-63, Upper S.C., 1963-79; chaplain VA Med. Ctr., Charleston, S.C., 1969-79, Crafts

Farrows Hosp., 1970-79, Diocese of S.C., 1979-89; treas. bd. camps and confs. Episcopal. Ch., 1952-54; mem. bd. missions, 1953-57; sec. Diocese of South Fla., 1953-57. Trustee Porter Mil. Acad. Home: 4304 Exum Dr West Columbia SC 29169

CRUMES, WILLIAM EDWARD, bishop; b. Louisville, Mar. 8, 1914; s. William E. Sr. and Della (McDowell) C.; m. Dorothy E. Marshall, May 21, 1934; 1 child, Vernita E. Crumes Mays. BTh cum laude, God's Bible Sch. and Coll., Cin., 1951. Ordained to ministry Ch. of Living God, 1948. Gen. sec. Ch. of Living God, Cin., 1950-62, overseeing elder, 1955-58, bishop, 1958-62, vice chief bishop, 1962-79, chief exec. officer, 1979—. Bd. mem. Charter Party, Cin., 1965—. Mem. NAACP (life). Office: Ch of the Living God 434 Forest Ave Cincinnati OH 45229

CRUMLEY, JAMES ROBERT, JR., clergyman; b. Bluff City, Tenn., Mar. 30, 1925; s. James Robert and Ida Frances (Fine) C.; m. Sara Annette Bodie, May 26, 1950; children: Frances Crumley Holman, James Robert, Jeanne Crumley Lindemann. BA, Roanoke Coll., 1948, DD (hon.), 1973; MDiv, Luth. Theol. So. Sem., Columbia, S.C., 1951; DD (hon.), Newberry (S.C.) Coll., 1971, Augustana Coll., 1982, Muhlenberg Coll., Allentown, Pa., 1983; LLD (hon.), Susquehanna U., Selinsgrove, Pa., 1977; LHD (hon.), Lenoir-Rhyne Coll., Hickory, N.C., 1979; LittD (hon.), Bethany Coll., 1981; LHD (hon.), Manhattan Coll., 1984, U. S.C., 1987. Ordained to ministry Luth. Ch. in Am., 1951; pastor chs. in Greenville and Oak Ridge, Tenn., Savannah, Ga., 1951-74; sec. Luth. Ch. in Am., N.Y.C., 1974-78; bishop Luth. Ch. in Am., 1978-88; vis. prof. ecumenism Luth. Theol. So. Sem., Columbia, S.C., 1988. Home: 362 Little Creek Dr Leesville SC 29070 Office: 4201 N Main St Columbia SC 29203

CRUMM, DAVID MARK, writer; b. LaGrange, Ind., Aug. 20, 1955; s. Donald Otis and Barbara Ruth (Yunker) C.; m. Amy Jo Weil, May 20, 1978; children: Megan, Benjamin. BA, U. Mich., 1977. Reporter, editor Oakland Press, Pontiac, Mich., 1978-81; feature writer Lexington (Ky.) Herald-Leader, 1981-83; reporter, editor Detroit Free Press, 1983-86, religion writer, 1986—. Recipient Wilbur award Religious Pub. Rels. Coun., 1988, 90, 91. Mem. Religion Newswriters Assn. Home: 41646 Ravenwood Canton MI 48187 Office: Detroit Free Press 321 W Lafayette Detroit MI 48226 *The two toughest challenges in life are to love and to share, but it is in pursuing these challenges that our lives are fulfilled.*

CRUSOE, JAMES MICHAEL, minister; b. Dayton, Ohio, Feb. 27, 1956; s. Willie Bernard and Geraldine (Carter) C.; m. Debra Denise Dilworth, July 19, 1980; children: Cory, Rebekah, Brittney. BA, Wittenberg U., Springfield, Ohio, 1978; MS, Abilene Christian U., 1983. Ordained to ministry Ch. of Christ, 1977. Min. Ch. of Christ, Tucson, 1983-85, Kansas City, Kans., 1985-87, Hopewell, Va., 1987—; bd. dirs. Camp Idlewild Christian Camp, Hopewell, 1989—; adminstr. Arlington Rd. Daycare Ctr., Hopewell, 1989—. Abilene Grad. Bible scholar, 1981-83; recipient cert. Kans. Children's League, 1986. Office: Ch of Christ 2106 Arlington Rd Hopewell VA 23860

CRUTCHER, GABRIEL, bishop. Bishop Apostolic Oercoming Holy Ch. of God Inc., Detroit. Office: Apostolic Overcoming Holy Ch of God Inc 526 E Bethune St Detroit MI 48202*

CRUTE, BEVERLY JEAN, minister; b. Kansas City, Mo.; d. Robert Scott and Rossie Nell (Locke) C. BA, Baker U., Baldwin City, Kans., 1961; MA, U. Mo., Kansas City, 1969; PhD, Boston Coll., 1981; MDiv, Princeton Theol. Sem., 1984. Ordained to ministry Presbyn. Ch., 1985. Summer intern Berkeley (Mo.) Presbyn. Ch., 1981-83; sem. asst. Faith Presbyn. Ch., Medford, N.J., 1981-82, First Presbyn. Ch., Morrisville, Pa., 1982-83; asst. pastor First Presbyn. Ch., Willmar, Minn., 1984-85, assoc. pastor, 1986—; vis. lectr. Washington U., St. Louis, 1980; lectr. Boston Coll., Chestnut Hill, Mass., 1974-79; instr. N. Shore Community Coll., Beverly, Mass., 1972-79; dean women Baker U., Baldwin City, Kans., 1967-71, instr. sociology, 1967-71; tchr. Shawnee Mission High Sch. Dist., Kans., 1961-67; chmn. Presbytery Social Justice Com., Willmar, 1985-90; mem. Synod Work Group in Social Justice, 1989—, moderator, 1991—. Author: (instr.'s guide) Introduction to Sociology, 1979; contbr. numerous book revs. in Theology Today, 1982-85. Mem. City of Willmar Heartland Express Bd., 1990—. Recipient Disting. Svc. award, Kiwanis, 1990, Spiritual Aims award, Minn.-Dakotas Dist., 1989-90. Mem. AAUW, Am. Sociol. Assn., Soc. for Sci. Study of Religion, Kiwanis (bd. dirs. 1991—). Home: 1128 Par Ln Willmar MN 56201 Office: First Presbyn Ch 605 W Litchfield Ave Willmar MN 56201 *In my desire for growth as well as wholeness, I have found a need for the "four-fold" balance of the physical, mental, social, and religious aspects of life.*

CRUZ, DAVID RAMIREZ, priest; b. Lubbock, Tex., Feb. 6, 1961; s. Florentino and Margarita (Ramirez) C. Student, Immaculate Heart Sem., Santa Fe, 1979-82; BA in History, Coll. Santa Fe, 1982; M in Religious Studies, U. Louvain, Leuven, Belgium, 1986; Major in Sem., Am. Coll., Leuven, Belgium, 1986. Ordained priest Roman Cath. Ch., 1986. Assoc. pastor Christ the King Cathedral, Lubbock, 1986-87, Sacred Heart Ch., Lubbock, 1987-88; adminstr. St. Theresa's Ch., Lubbock, 1988—; assoc. dir. Office of Renew, Lubbock, 1987-89; exec. dir. Christian Renewal Ctr., Lubbock, 1989—; dir. Cursillo Movement, Lubbock, 1989—. Exec. dir. West Tex. Community Orgn., Lubbock, 1988—. Mem. KC (hon.).

CRUZ, MARIA, church lay worker; b. Havana, Cuba, June 13, 1961; came to U.S., 1967; d. Arnaido and Emma Rosa (Prado) C. AA in Bus., Miami-Dade Community Coll., 1983. Dir. Sunday sch., substitute Sunday sch. tchr. Nazaret (Spanish) Bapt. Ch., Miami, Fla., 1984-85; dir. 7th grade Sunday sch. Univ. Bapt. Ch., Coral Gables, Fla., 1988—; sec. Dade County Sch. Bd., Miami, 1990—. Republican.

CRUZAN, EARL, minister; b. North Loup, Nebr., Sept. 12, 1913; s. Roy and Stella E. (Clement) C.; m. Mabel Elizabeth Davis, June 30, 1936; children: Barbara J., Earl Wayne, Nancy E., Jonathan D. BA, Salem Coll., 1938; BD, Alfred U., 1941. Ordained to ministry Seventh-day Bapt. Ch., 1941. Pastor Seventh Day Bapt. Ch. of Waterford, Conn., 1940-42; pastor Seventh Day Bapt. Ch. of Boulder, Colo., 1942-46, Seventh Day Bapt. Ch. of Dodge Ctr., Minn., 1946-51, Seventh Day Bapt. Ch. of Adams Ctr., N.Y., 1951-59, Pawcatuck Seventh Day Bapt. Ch., R.I., 1959-66; pastor Seventh Day Bapt. Ch. of Milton, Wis., 1966-81, extension pastor, 1981—; chmn. Evangelism, Home Field com. Seventh Day Bapt. Missionary Bd., Westerly, R.I., 1960-66, 79—; exec. v.p. Seventh Day Bapt. North Cen. Assn., 1981—; pres. Seventh Day Bapt. Gen. Conf., 1957-58; mem. Seventh Day Bapt. Commn., 1953-59. Mem. Boy Scouts Am. com., Adams Ctr., N.Y., Westerly, R.I., Milton, Wis. Home: 106 Rogers St Milton WI 53563-1447 *Life is a gift from God. It is to be lived and enjoyed in responsible loving relationships with others.*

CRYANS, ANDREW WILLIAM, priest; b. Littleton, N.H., Dec. 23, 1947; s. Andrew William and Evelyn (Howard) C. AB, Rockhurst Coll., 1971; MA, Fordham U., 1972; MDiv, Woodstock Coll., 1975; STM, Union Theol. Sem., 1976. Assoc. pastor Our Lady of Guadaleupe Ch., Topeka, 1975-78; vice-supr. Tagaste Monastery, Suffern, N.Y., 1978-81; assoc. pastor St. Joseph Cathedral, Manchester, N.H., 1981-86, St. Johns, Concord, N.H., 1986-87; assoc. dir. Our Lady of Perpetual Help, Manchester, 1987-89; vocation dir. Diocese of Manchester, 1987—; pastor Sacred Heart, Wilton, N.H., 1989—; mem. Diocesan Ecumenical Commn., Manchester, 1987—. Democrat. Home: 27 Maple St Wilton NH 03086 Office: Diocese of Manchester 153 Ash St Manchester NH 03105

CRYSTAL, ELEANOR, ecumenical agency director. Coord. Christian Community Action, South Norwalk, Conn. Office: Christian Community Action 98 S Main St South Norwalk CT 06854*

CUBILLOS, ROBERT HERNAN, church administrator, philosophy educator; b. Long Beach, Calif., Sept. 16, 1957; s. Roberto Hernan and Jacqueline Lee (Smith) C.; m. Deborah Sue Forbes, June 21, 1986; children: Robby, Kelli. BS, Calif. State U., Carson, 1983; cert. in human rights, Internat. Inst. Human Rights, Strasbourg, France, 1984; MA in Apologetics, Simon Greenleaf Sch. of Law, Orange, Calif., 1985; MA in Theology, Fuller Theol. Sem., Pasadena, Calif., 1986; postgrad. studies, Claremont (Calif.) Grad. Sch., 1987., U. So. Calif., 1990—. Ch. bus. adminstr. The Harbor Ch., Lomita, Calif., 1983-87, Rolling Hills Covenant Ch., Rolling Hills Estates, Calif., 1987—; asst. prof., co-editor Law Review Simon Greenleaf Sch. of Law, Orange, Calif., 1987—; thesis sec., dean of students Simon Greenleaf Sch. of Law, Orange, 1988—. Contbr. articles to religious and philos. jours. Mem. Am. Acad. Religion, Christian Mgmt. Assn., Evangel. Theol. Soc., Soc. Bibl. Lit., Pi Delta Phi. Office: Rolling Hills Covenant Ch 2222 Palos Verdes Dr N Rolling Hills Estates CA 90274

CUBINE, MARGARET VIRGINIA, retired educator; b. Flinstone, Ga., Mar. 28, 1919; d. Ralph Darrell and Anna Lou-Genia (Morgan) C. AB, LaGrange Coll., 1939; MA in English, U. N.C., 1944; MA in Religion, Northwestern U., 1947; BD, Garrett Theol. Sem., 1949; PhD, Northwestern U., 1955. Tchr. English Chattanooga Valley High Sch., 1939-42; tchr. English Bethany High Sch., Reidsville, N.C., 1942-43; instr. English Reinhardt Coll., Waleska, Ga., 1943-45; instr. English, religion Ward-Belmont, Nashville, 1947-50; instr. English Martin Coll., Pulaski, Tenn., 1947; asst. prof. religion Aurora (Ill.) Coll., 1952-53, Huntingdon Coll., Montgomery, Ala., 1953-55; prof. English, religion LaGrange (Ga.) Coll., 1955-61; prof. religion Erskine Coll., Due West, S.C., 1961-89. Mem. Amnesty Internat. Mem. AAUW (various local offices 1965—), Am. Acad. Religion (regional pres. 1976), Assn. for Clin. Pastoral Edn. (clin.), Mental Health Assn. (pres. 1984). Democrat. Presbyterian. Avocations: reading, yoga. Home: 18 Depot St PO417 Due West SC 29639

CUDDY, WILLIAM FRANCIS, JR., military chaplain; b. Boston, Mar. 16, 1949; s. William Francis and Mary Elizabeth (Connelly) C. BS in Edn., Fitchburg State U., 1974; MDiv., St. John's Sem., 1979. Deacon St. Ann's Parish, Somerville, Mass., 1978-79; asst. pastor Holy Family Parish, Rockland, Mass., 1979-84; chaplain Cathedral High Sch., Boston, 1984-90, USN, Cherry Point, N.C., 1990—. Lt. commdr. USN, 1986—. Mem. Mass. Indsl. Arts Assn., Internat. Tech. and Edn. Assn., CTTA, Harelock (N.C.) Ministerial Assn., Am. Legion, KC.

CUDNEY, GERALD EDWARD, minister, real estate professional; b. Tacoma, Wash., Feb. 28, 1941; s. Henry Edward and Lucille Ellen (Ward) C.; m. Donna Jo Stowell, Dec. 17, 1961; children: Carin, Jerilynn, Amy, Jill. BA, Western Bapt. Coll., 1963. Ordained to ministry Gen. Assn. Regular Bapt. Chs., 1965. Min. edn. Cedar Ave. Bapt. Ch., Fresno, Calif., 1963-66, Northland Bapt. Ch., Grand Rapids, Mich., 1966-72; sr. pastor Eastgate Bapt. Ch., Bellevue, Wash., 1972-82, First Bapt. Ch., Woodland, Calif., 1982-84, Maranatha Bapt. Ch., Issaquah, Wash., 1986—; sales assoc. Heritage West Properties, Bellevue, Wash., 1986—. Author: Administering The Ministry, 1980. Trustee Western Bapt. Coll., Salem, Oreg., 1978—; chmn. bd. dirs. Bapt. Family Agy., Seattle, 1978—; mem. adv. bd. Assn. Baptists for World Evangelism, Cherry Hill, N.J., 1978—. Home: 21904 SE 35th St Issaquah WA 98027 Office: Maranatha Bapt Ch PO Box 952 Issaquah WA 98027

CUESTAS, FELIX VINCENT, minister; b. Bklyn., July 11, 1934; s. Felix Vincent and Ruth (King) C. Student, Northeastern Bible Coll. N.J., 1971-74, Empire State Coll., 1971-74; BDiv, Nat. Theol. Coll. Sem., 1981; MDiv, Nat. theol. Coll. Sem., 1985. Ordained to ministry Ethiopian Orthodox Ch., 1980. Supply pastor Bethel Community Ch., Staten Island, N.Y., 1979-90, pastor, 1980-86; assoc. min. Mt. Sinai Bapt. Ch., Bklyn., 1986-89; chaplain Harlem Hosp., N.Y.C., 1989—; Contbr. articles to Staten Island Advance. With U.S. Army, 1954-56. Mem. Omega Psi Phi (chaplain 1986-91). Home: 1247 President St Brooklyn NY 11225

CUFFEY, KENNETH HUGH, minister; b. Bloomington, Ind., Apr. 21, 1956; s. James and Rita (Paraboshi) C.; m. Lori Lee Baird, June 28, 1980; children: Stephen, Joel, Abigail, Daniel. BA, Ind. U., 1978; MDiv, Trinity Evang. Div. Sch., Deerfield, Ill., 1982; MPhil, Drew U., Madison, N.J., 1985, PhD, 1987. Teaching fellow in Greek Trinity Evang. Div. Sch., 1980; coll. pastor Evang. Community Ch., Bloomington, Ind., 1981-83; adj. faculty Trinity Evang. Div. Sch., Deerfield, 1987; sr. pastor Wyckoff (N.J.) Bapt. Ch., 1988—; adj. faculty Alliance Theol. Sem., Nyack, N.Y., 1991. Contbr. Ancher Bible Dictionary; also articles. Hopper fellow, 1983-86; Trinity Faculty scholar, 1981. Mem. Soc. Bibl. Lit., Bibl. Archaeol. Soc., Evang. Theol. Soc., Phi Beta Kappa, Phi Eta Sigma. Home: 709 Timberline Dr Wyckoff NJ 07481 Office: Wyckoff Bapt Ch Wyckoff & Russell Aves Wyckoff NJ 07481

CUKURAS, VALDEMAR MICHAEL, priest; b. Latvia, Apr. 11, 1915; s. William and Maria (Grumslyte) C. MA, U. Kaunas, Lithuania, 1938; PhD, Gregorian U., Rome, 1948; ThD, Angelicum U., Rome, 1950. Ordained priest Roman Cath. Ch., 1938. Tchr. Theology and Philosophy Lithuania, 1938-50; lectr. in Philosophy Wesleyan U., Middletown, Conn., 1958-64; prof. Theology and Philosphy Annhurst Coll., Woodstock, Conn., 1955-80; prof. Psychology Holy Apostles Sem., Cromwell, Conn., 1959-65; nat. chaplain Lithuanian Holy Youth Fedn., 1983—; nat. sec. Lithuanian Roman Cath. Priests' League of Am., 1979—; nat. chaplain Lithuanian Boy Scouts, Girl Scouts in Exile, 1956-65; nat. chaplain Lithuanian Cath. Fedn., 1983—; lectr. at Am. Philosopy and Theol. convs., 1958-80; retreat master at various Lithuanian communities in U.S. and Can., 1970—. Author: (theol. study) Dark Night of the Soul, 1958, Theology of Concrete Realities, 1969, Dialectic of Christianity with Individualism and Communism, 1976, Situation Ethics and Its Debilitating Influence on Religious Life Today, 1984, The Story Telling and Theology, 1988, Liberation Theology and Religion in Lithuania, 1990. Mem. Cath. Acad. Arts and Scis., Lithuanian Cultural Inst. Am. Home: ICC 600 Liberty Hwy Putnam CT 06260

CULBERSON, DAVID CHRISTOPHER, church music educator, minister; b. Charlotte, N.C., July 25, 1961; s. Robert Edward and Lillian Ruth (Richardson); m. Laura Ann Morton, Jun. 4, 1983; children: Christopher David, Courtney Elyse. BS, East Coast Bible Coll., 1983; MusM, Winthrop Coll., 1988. Min. music West Asheville Church of God, Asheville, N.C., 1983-84, East Belmont Church of God, Belmont, N.C., 1984-86, Eastway Church of God, Charlotte, N.C., 1986-87, Oakdale Church of God, Charlotte, N.C., 1987--; asst. prof. church music East Coast Bible Coll., Charlotte, N.C., 1986--. Composer: religious songs, various arrangements and recording sessions. Named one of Outstanding Young Men of America, 1982/83. Mem. East Coast Bible Coll. Alumni Assc. (pres.) 1986-, Church of God N.C. State Music Com. 1990--. Home: 7408 Pawtuckett Rd Charlotte NC 28214 Office: East Coast Bible College 6900 Wilkinson Blvd Charlotte NC 28214

CULBERSON, GUY, JR., pastor; b. Branchill, Ohio, Apr. 18, 1930; s. Guy and Dorothy (Maines) C.; m. Janice Jo Fugett, Apr. 18, 1947; children: Cynthia, June, Daniel, Warren. Grad. in theology, Tenn. Temple U., 1957; DD (hon.), New World Bible Inst., Hayti, Mo., 1987. Ordained to ministry Bapt. Ch., 1957. Youth leader Kings Mills (Ohio) Bapt. Ch., 1957-68; founder, pastor, now sr. pastor Maranatha Bapt. Ch., Mason, Ohio, 1970—. Bd. dirs. Tri-County Preegnancy Crisis Ctr., Mason, 1988—. Office: Maranatha Bapt Ch 4505 US 42 N Mason OH 45040-9998

CULBERTSON, MARVIN CRIDDLE, JR., general assembly representative; b. Vernon, Tex., Aug. 30, 1927; s. Marvin Criddle and Henrietta May (Beal) C.; m. Elizabeth Abshier, Dec. 9, 1950; children: Marvin C. III, Kathryn Lynn, Donald G., Diane Seward. MD, U. Tex., 1950. Diplomate Am. Bd. Pediatrics, Am. Bd. Otolargyn. Ruling elder, 1948—; moderator North Tex. Presbyn. Ch. in Am., 1986-87, mission to world com., 1989—; gen. assembly rep. Presbyn. Ch. Am., Dallas, 1991—; pvt. practice, Dallas, 1956—; clin. prof. U. Tex. S.W. Med. Ctr., 1956—; med. tchr. India, Korea and others. Lt. USN, 1950-53. Mem. ACS, Am. Acad. Otolargyn. Home: 3405 Colgate Dallas TX 75225 Office: 8617 NW Plaza Dr Dallas TX 75225

CULBERTSON, MATTHEW, minister; b. Marion, Ohio, Jan. 12, 1967; s. Bobby Gene and Wilma Jean (Stepp) C. BA, Cedarville (Ohio) Coll., 1989. Ordained to ministry So. Bapt. Conv., 1989. Minister of youth Hillcrest Bapt. Ch., Carlisle, Ohio, 1989—; camp co-dir. Seneca Lake Bapt. Camp, 1989—; chaplain Carlisle Basketball, 1989. Mem. Phi Mu Alpha. Home and Office: Hillcrest Bapt Ch 820 Central Ave Carlisle OH 45005

CULBERTSON, PHILIP LEROY, theology educator; b. Bartlesville, Okla., Oct. 10, 1944; s. Walter LeRoy and Wanda Miriam (Atkins) C. MusB, Washington U., St. Louis, 1966; MDiv, Gen. Theol. Sem., N.Y.C., 1970; doctoral research, The Hebrew U., Jerusalem, 1974-76; PhD, NYU, 1977. Assoc. rector Ch. of the Holy Trinity, N.Y.C., 1970-74; rector Christ Episcopal Ch., Oberlin, Ohio, 1976-85; prof. pastoral theology U. of the South, Sewanee, Tenn., 1985—; cons. presiding Episcopal Bishop's Adv. Com. on Christian-Jewish Relations, 1986; interim rector Christ Episcopal Ch., Tracy City, Tenn., 1986-87. Author: The Pastor: Readings from the Patristic Period, 1990, New Adam: The Future of Male Spirituality, 1991; contbr. articles to profl. jours. Assoc. dir. Ctr. for Ethics and Religious Pluralism, Shalom Hartman Inst., Jerusalem, 1988—. Mem. Conf. of Anglican Theologians, Guild of Clergy Counselors, Christian Study Group on Judaism and the Jewish People. Office: U of South Sch of Theology Sewanee TN 37375

CULLEN, HARRY PATRICK, II, administrative coordinator; b. Oklahoma City, July 14, 1949; s. Harold L. and Glennora T. (Thompson) C.; m. Carol Sue Kerr, Aug. 3, 1968 (div. 1977); m. Pamela Sue Allen, Apr. 30, 1983; children: Amanda M., James A. BA in Bus., So. Nazarene U., 1989. Pvt. practice homebuilder Oklahoma City, 1971-73, 80-85; coord. Okla. CAth. Charismatic Renewal, Oklahoma City, 1973-75; dir. social ministry St. Charles Borromeo, Oklahoma City, 1976-78; pvt. practice entertainer Oklahoma City, 1978—; adminstrv. coord. Christ the King Ch., Oklahoma City, 1985—; cons. St. Eugene Cath. Ch., Oklahoma City, 1989—; advanced cathechist Archdiocese of Oklahoma City, 1990—. Democrat. Avocation: golf. Home: 8113 NW 114th Oklahoma City OK 73162 Office: Christ the King Ch 8005 Dorset Dr Oklahoma City OK 73120

CULLEN, RANDOLPH FENTON, minister; b. Balt., Nov. 12, 1955; s. James Kimmy and Britt Marie (Thornander) C.; m. Christine Dee Johnson, Apr. 16, 1983; 1 child, Emily Meredith. BA, Furman U., 1978; MDiv, Princeton Theol. Sem., 1981; postgrad., Lancaster Theol. Sem. Ordained to Presbyn. Ch. Assoc. pastor First Presbyn. Ch., Marshfield, Wis., 1981-84; pastor The Presbyn. Ch. Columbia, Pa., 1984-89, Highland Presbyn. Ch., Street, Md., 1989—; v.p. bd. campus ministries Millersville (Pa.) U., 1986-88. Bd. dirs. Columbia Area Improvement, 1985-89, Children's Ctr. N. Hartford, Street, 1989—. Home: 704 Highland Rd Street MD 21154 Office: Highland Presbyn Ch 701 Highland Rd Street MD 21154

CULLEN, WILLIAM, school system administrator. Supt. schs Roman Cath. Diocese of Jackson, Miss. Office: Schs Supt 237 E Amite St PO Box 2248 Jackson MS 39225-2248*

CULLINAN, ALICE RAE, religion educator; b. Richmond, Va., May 21, 1939; d. James Michaux and Sarah Elizabeth (Burger) C. BA, Carson-Newman Coll., 1963; MRE, Southwester Bapt. Theol. Sem., 1965, EdD, 1974. Min. music and edn. Triangle (Va.) Bapt. Ch., 1966-70; counselor Southwestern Sem. Counseling Clinic, 1971-73; cons., tchr. tng. dept. Va. Bapt. Gen. Assn., 1973-74; prof. religion and religious edn. Gardner-Webb Coll., Boiling Springs, N.C., 1974—; instr. psychology Tarrant County Jr. Coll., 1972; interim music dir. Stanley (N.C.) Bapt. Ch., 1974-75, Upper Fair Forest Bapt. Ch., Union, S.C., 1975-76; min. of music and edn. Mt. Sinai Bapt. Ch., Shelby, N.C., 1979-83; min. edn. Zoar Bapt. Ch., Shelby, 1983—. Mem. So. Bapt. Religious Edn. Assn., Religious Edn. Assn. Am., N.C. Bapt. Profs. Religion. Home and Office: PO Box 833 Boiling Springs NC 28017 *I believe that faith and education are compatible, and that intelligence should never be an obstacle to one's trust in God.*

CULLUM, ROBERT FRANCIS, chaplain; b. St. Louis, Aug. 9, 1932; s. Ralph Francis Cullum and Mildred McMekin; m. Shirley Rose Harvengt, Dec. 22, 1957; children: Pamela Kay, Barbara Lynn, Christi Coleen. BA, So. Ill. U., 1960; MDiv, So. Western Bapt. Sem., Ft. Worth, 1965, M of Religious Edn., 1988; ThD, Luther Rice Sem., Jacksonville, Tenn., 1973. Chaplain Masonic Home and Sch., Ft. Worth, 1963-65, Bapt. Meml. Hosp., San Antonio, 1965-66, San Antonio State Hosp., 1966—; coord. chaplains Tex. Dept. Mental Health and Retardation, 1980—. Contbr. articles to jours. Pres. Mental Health Assn. of Bexar County, San Antonio, 1972, Half Way House, Inc., San Antonio, 1990, Pres.'s Club SA, San Antonio, 1988; treas. Mental Health Clergy, 1986-90. Sgt. USAF 1951-59, Morroco. Recipient Vol. award Am. Bible Soc., N.Y.C., 1990. Fellow Coll. Chaplains (state rep.); mem. Assn. Clin. Pastoral Educators, Lions (pres. 1984-85). Republican. Baptist. Avocations: freelance writing, woodcarving, golf. Home: 446 Saipan San Antonio TX 78221 Office: San Antonio State Hosp PO Box 23991 San Antonio TX 78223

CULLY, IRIS VIRGINIA, religion educator emerita; b. N.Y.C., Sept. 12, 1914; d. James Aikman and Myrtle Marie (Michael) Arnold; m. Kendig Brubaker Cully, Sept. 9, 1939 (dec. Mar. 1987); children: Melissa Iris Mueller, Patience Allegra Ecklund. BA, Adelphi U., 1936; MA, Hartford Sem. Found., 1937; BD, Garrett-Evang. Theol. Sem., 1954; PhD, Northwestern U., 1955. Assoc. prof. Yale U. Divinity Sch., New Haven, 1965-72; prof. Lexington (Ky.) Theol. Sem., 1976-85, prof. emerita, 1985—; vis. prof. Garrett Theol. Sem., 1958-61, Union Theol. Sem., 1964-66, Northwestern U., 1960, 63, Drew U. Sch. Theology, 1964, NYU, 1964-65, Fordham U., 1970, SCh. of Theol. Claremont, Calif., 1987, 89, Pacific Sch. of Religion, 1961. Author: Education for Spirtual Growth, 1984, Christian Child Development, 1979, Planning and Selecting Curriculum for Christian Education, 1983, New Life for Your Sunday School, 1976, Change, Conflict and Self-Determination, 1972, Christian Worship and Church Education, 1967, Ways to Teach Children, 1966, Imparting the Word, 1962, Children in the Church, 1960, The Dynamics of Christian Education, 1958; co-author: (with Kendig Brubaker Cully) Two Seasons: Advent and Lent, 1954, Introductory Theological Wordbook, 1963, From Aaron to Zerubbabel, 1977, Process and Relationship, 1978, Guide to Biblical Resources, 1981, Harper's Encyclopedia of Religious Education, 1990. Mem. Assn. Profs. and Researchers in Religious Edn. (v.p. 1972-73, pres. 1973-74), Religious Edn. Assn. (bd. trustees 1975-79), Am. Acad. Religion, Soc. Bibl. Lit. Democrat. Episcopalian. Home: 627 Alden Rd Claremont CA 91711

CULP, DONNA LEA, lay worker; b. Joplin, Mo., May 28, 1959; d. Richard Lee and Betty Jo (Eutsler) Evans; m. Gary Gene Culp, Mar. 20, 1978; children: Adrienne, Aaron, Seth. Diploma, Inst. Children's Lit., Redding Ridge, Conn., 1989. Lay worker, pastor's wife Hart Bapt. Ch., Seneca, Mo., 1983-87, Pineville (Mo.) Bapt. Ch., 1987—; youth dir., Hart Bapt. Ch., 1985-87, tchr. Sunday sch., 1983-87; youth coord. 1st Bapt. Ch., Pineville, 1989—, tchr. Sunday sch., 1987—; assn. leader Vaction Bible Sch. Shoal Creek Bapt. Assn., Neosho, Mo., 1987-89. Author: (short stories) Gus and Us, 1990, Bird on Board, 1990. Pres. Pineville Schs. PTO, 1989-90, v.p., 1990. Mem. Woman's Missionary Union (mission action dir. Seneca 1985-86). Republican. Home: PO Box 506 Pineville MO 64856 *No matter who we are, what we are, or what we achieve in life, the only thing that will make any difference is how we answer the question, "What will I do with Jesus Christ."*

CULP, L(YLE) D(ELANE), minister; b. Palestine, Ill., Mar. 19, 1951; s. Lyle Delane Sr. and Rosealee (Smith) C.; m. Eileen Pearl, June 8, 1973; children: Lyle D. III, Janella E. BA, NW Bible Coll.-Lee Coll., 1977. Ordained to ministry Ch. of God, 1986. Fellowship leader Ch. of God, Mannheim, Fed. Republic Germany, 1971-72; pastor Indian missions Ch. of God, New Town, N.D., Parshall, N.D., 1972-75; pastor Ch. of God, Greenville, Ohio, 1977-79; sch. tchr. Paw Creek Christian Acad., Charlotte, N.C., 1979-81; evangelist Ch. of God, Porterville, Ill., 1982-85; pastor Ch. of God, Rantoul, Ill., 1985-87, Chenoa, Ill., 1987-89, Anna, Ill., 1989-91, Norris City, Ill., 1991—; dir. transient food voucher program Chenoa Ministerial Alliance Assn., 1987-89. Counselor Mannheim Drug Abuse Coun., 1971-72. With U.S. Army, 1970-72. Republican. Home: PO Box 5 211 Conger St Norris City IL 62896 *While not able to save the whole world, nor change the world in my life time, I have chosen to serve Jesus Christ, and fulfill His high calling to His satisfaction.*

CULP, TIMOTHY A., lay worker, interior designer; b. Chester, Ill., Oct. 7, 1958; s. Andrew George and Margie Lee (Word) C. AA, Belleville Area Coll., 1978. Salesman, interior designer Lynn Furniture Co., Inc., Sparta, Ill., 1978—; dir. chancel choir, handbell choir Trinity United Presbyn. Ch., Sparta, 1985—, dir jr. choir, 1991. Accompanist Sparta Community Chorus, 1978—; former dir. Gateway Men's Chorus, St. Louis, 1989-90. Mem. Am.

Soc. Interior Designers (allied mem.), Am. Guild of Organists. Home: 200 W Main St Sparta IL 62286

CULVER, JOHN BLAINE, minister; b. Urbana, Ill., Nov. 3, 1938; s. Lawson Blaine and Sunray Lillian (Cooper) C.; m. Rosa Bertha Diaz-Mori, Feb. 28, 1970; children: Janice Lillian, John Manuel, Edward Blaine. BA, U. Ill., 1962, MA, 1964; MDiv cum laude, Chgo. Theol. Sem., 1972; postgrad., Escuela de Idiomas, Sociedad de Santiago Apostol, Pontifical U., Lima, Peru, 1969-70. Ordained to ministry United Ch. of Christ, 1973. Pastor, adminstr. Winnebago Indian Mission, United Ch. of Christ, Black River Falls, Wis., 1972-75; pastor Bethany United Ch. of Christ, San Antonio, 1975-78, Bethany Congl. Ch., San Antonio, 1978—; interim pastor Pilgrim Congl. Ch., San Antonio, 1978, Iglesia Unida de Cristo Betania, San Antonio, 1982-83; part-time instr. San Antonio Coll., 1978—; bd. dirs. South Cen. conf. United Ch. of Christ, Austin, Tex., 1982, 84-87, 90—; mem. exec. com., sec.-registrar South Tex. Assn. United Ch. of Christ, 1982-90, moderator, 1982, 90—. Bd. dirs., program chmn. Illini Young Reps., Urbana, Ill., 1963; bd. dirs. Greater San Antonio Community of Chs., 1976-80, San Antonio Urban Coun., 1984-86, 88; sec. Tobin Hill Neighborhood Assn., San Antonio, 1978-79. Mem. Masons (chaplain 1981-82, 90-92, tiler 1980-81, 84-85). Home: 102 Shadywood Ln San Antonio TX 78216 Office: Bethany Congl Ch 500 Pilgrim Dr San Antonio TX 78213-2800 *For the Christ Disciple the most important thing about life is to become a vehicle of God's love and peace in the world and to minister to others in their need as an instrument of Christ's presence and compassion.*

CULVER, MAURICE EDWIN, minister, theology educator; b. Max, N.D., Dec. 21, 1915; s. Charles P. and Nina V. (Wilkinson) C.; m. Verna Murphree (div.); children: Shirley E., Tara E., Garth E., Melody, Vickie, Clay; m. Mary Byrene Taylor, Dec. 19, 1989. BA, Asbury Coll., 1939; BD, Asbury Theol. Sem., 1941; MA, Hartford (Conn.) Sem., 1944; PhD, Drew U., 1952. Ordained to ministry United Meth. Ch., 1943. Pastor U. Meth. Ch., Commercial Point, Ohio, 1943-44, Jersey City, 1944-45; dist. supt. U. Meth. Ch., Zimbabwe, Africa, 1945-49; prof. Drew Theol. Sem., Madison, N.J., 1951-52, Claremont (Calif.) Sch. Theology, 1962-63; dean Asbury Theol. Sem., Wilmore, Ky., 1963-66, United Theol Coll., Harare, Zimbabwe, Africa, 1966-80; prof. ethics Oral Roberts U., Tulsa, 1980—. Editor Africa Discipline of United Meth. Ch. Home: 8418 S Florence Ave Tulsa OK 74137 Office: Oral Roberts U 7777 S Lewis Tulsa OK 74137

CUMMINGS, DARRELL WILLIAM, pastor; b. San Antonio, Jan. 8, 1960; s. Claude William and Faith Joyce (France) C.; m. Valerie Bernice Vaugh, June 23, 1979; children: Melanie Faith, Claude Vaughn. AA, Cuyahoga Community Coll., Cleve., 1980, AS in Applied Bus., 1981; student, Baldwin Wallace Coll., 1983, Cleve. State Coll., 1984. Youth pastor Ebenezer Assembly of Christ, Cleve., 1976-82; treas. North Ohio Dist. Sunday Sch., Youngstown, 1979-82, Northern Ohio Dist. Young People Union, Akron, Ohio, 1976-80, North Ohio Dist. Sunday Sch., Youngstown, Ohio, 1980-82; founder, pastor Greater Love Ch., Ashtabula, Ohio, 1982—; auditor Fed. Res. Bank, Cleve., 1980-82; trustee D.W. Cumming Evang. Assocs., Ashtabula; dir. Shary Flaring Ministry, Ashtabula. Author: The Power of Dreams, 1983, I Am A Winner, 1984; editor The Lamplighter mag., 1982—. Secretary Apostolic Ministerial Alliance, Cleve., 1982-84; v.p. Community Action Agy., Ashtabula, 1988—. Home: 3233 Station Ave Ashtabula OH 44004 Office: Greater Love Ch 906 Joseph Ave Ashtabula OH 44004

CUMMINGS, FRANK C., bishop; b. Minter, Ala., Apr. 4, 1929; s. Edmond and Annie (Moultrie) C.; m. Martha Coleen Colly, Mar. 5, 1954; 1 dau., Paschell Coleen. B.A., Seattle Pacific Coll., 1949, 1952; B.D., D.D., Shorter Coll., 1970. Ordained to ministry A.M.E. Ch., 1948; pastor A.M.E. Ch., Alridge, Ala., 1948-49, Bremerton, Wash., 1952-53, Santa Barbara, Calif., 1954-60; pastor A.M.E. Ch., St. Louis, 1960-68, sec.-treas. dept. ch. extension, 1968-76; elected bishop A.M.E. Ch., 1976; assigned 8th Episc. Dist. (La.-Miss.) A.M.E. Ch., New Orleans, 1976-85; bishop 1st Episc. Dist. A.M.E. Ch., Phila., 1985—; pres. A.M.E. Mgmt. Agy., Inc., 1969-76; founder Frontier Ins. Agy., Allen Travel Service. Vice chmn. St. Louis Civil Service Commn., 1965-71; pres. bd. dirs. West End Hosp. Assn. Mem. Alpha Phi Alpha. Office: A M E Ch 1st Dist 5070 Parkside Ste 1410 Philadelphia PA 19131

CUMMINGS, JAMES ALEXANDER, religious organization administrator; b. Des Moines, Oct. 27, 1952; s. Ray Cummings and Shirley (Boyt) Booth; m. Bonnie Lou Cashler, Oct. 11, 1975; children: Jennifer, Ryan, Andrew, Sarah. BS in Elec. Engring., U. Wis., 1974; MBA, U. Houston, 1981. Ordained to ministry Bible Ch., 1987. Adminstr. Westlake Bible Ch., Austin, Tex., 1986—, also bd. dirs., sec., elder, 1986—. Coach Little League baseball, Lake Travis Youth Assn., Austin, 1989-90, soccer coach, 1989-90. Mem. Nat. Assn. Ch. Bus. Adminstrs. Office: Westlake Bible Ch 3423 Bee Cave Rd Austin TX 78746

CUMMINGS, KEVIN BRYAN, minister; b. Lake Charles, La., Dec. 8, 1967; s. Kenneth Richard and Sharon Elaine (Kinchen) C.; m. Terri Lynn Pickering, June 11, 1988. BS cum laude, Liberty U., 1989. Ordained to ministry Bapt. Ch., 1989. Camp counselor Milldale Bapt. Teen Retreat, Zachary, La., 1985-86; pastor Tamuning (Guam) Bapt. Ch., 1986-87; dir. campus club Thomas Rd. Bapt. Ch., Lynchburg, Va., 1987-88; youth worker Temple Bapt. Ch., Madison Heights, Va., 1988-89; pastor youth and Christian edn. Ch. of the Open Door, Ft. Washington, Pa., 1989—. Republican. Office: Ch of the Open Door 1260 Ft Washington Ave Fort Washington PA 19034 *When all you can do is pray, you have done all you can do!.*

CUMMINS, JOHN STEPHEN, bishop; b. Oakland, Calif., Mar. 3, 1928; s. Michael and Mary (Connolly) C. A.B., St. Patrick's Coll., 1949. Ordained priest Roman Catholic Ch., 1953; asst. pastor Mission Dolores Ch., San Francisco, 1953-57; mem. faculty Bishop O'Dowd High Sch., Oakland, 1957-62; chancellor Diocese of Oakland, 1962-71; rev. monsignor, 1962, domestic prelate, 1967; exec. dir. Calif. Cath. Conf., Sacramento, 1971-77; consecrated bishop, 1974; aux. bishop of Sacramento, 1974-77; bishop of Oakland, 1977—; Campus minister San Francisco State Coll., 1953-57, Mills Coll., Oakland, 1957-71; Trustee St. Mary's Coll., 1968-79. Home: 634 21st St Oakland CA 94612 Office: Oakland Diocese 2900 Lake Shore Ave Oakland CA 94610

CUMMINS, WILLIAM LEE, minister; b. Detroit, Aug. 20, 1947; s. Edgar Lee and Viola Mae (Ewing) C.; m. Dorothy Marie Cummins, June 19, 1971; children: Joshua, Daniel, Matthew. BE, Taylor U., 1969; MA, Trinity Div. Sch., Deerfield, Ill., 1971; PhD (hon.), Columbia Pacific U., 1977. Ordained to ministry Am. Bapt. Chs. U.S.A. Assoc. pastor Calvary Ch., Grand Rapids, Mich., 1971-77; pastor Ebenezer Bapt. Ch., Detroit, 1977-85; area dir. Bibles for India, Lodi, Calif., 1986-89; founding pastor Bear Creek Community Ch., Stockton, Calif., 1989—. Author: India Journal, 1987. Mem. Am. Bapt. Mins. Coun. (v.p. 1989—), Rotary. Home: 401 Applewood Dr Lodi CA 95242 Office: Bear Creek Community Ch 678 Crider Way Stockton CA 95209

CUNHA, IRENEU DA SILVA, minister; b. Porto, Portugal, Nov. 11, 1930; s. José Ferraz da Cunha and Irene da Silva Cunha; m. Maria Teresa Guedes Coelho, Sept. 19, 1956; children: Iolanda Maria, Jorge Emanuel. Student theol. course, Ecumenical Sem. Lisbon, Portugal, 1949-56; grad. in theology, Didsbury Coll., Bristol, Eng., 1955. Ordained to ministry Portuguese Meth. Ch. Pastor Meth. Ch., Porto, Aveiro, Coimbra, Porto, 1956-90; gen. sec. Portugal Coun. Chs., Coimbra, 1970-84; gen. supt. Meth. Ch., Porto, 1984—; bd. dirs. Ecumenical Reconcilitation Ctr., Figueira Foz, Portugal, 1970-82; newspaper dir. Portugal Evangelico, Porto, 1957-90. Contbr. numerous articles to profl. jours. Mem. Rotary (pres. Coimbra club 1977-78, Porto club. Home: Rua Direita das Campinas 91-20, 4100 Porto Portugal Office: Portuguese Meth Ch, Praca Coronel Pacheco, 4000 Porto Portugal

CUNNINGHAM, SISTER AGNES, patristic theology educator, author; b. Middlesborough, Yorkshire, Eng., May 26, 1923; came to U.S., 1926; d. Michael Steven and Monica Gertrude (Burns) C. BS, St. Louis U., 1954; MA, Marquette U., 1963; STL, Facultés Catholiques, Lyon, France, 1964, STD, 1968. Tchr. Holy Family Acad., Beaverville, Ill., 1943-52; prin., tchr. St. Mary Magdalene Elem. Sch., Joliet, Ill., 1954-57; prin. St. Gall Elem. Sch., Chgo., 1957-60; instr. Mundelein Coll. for Women, Chgo., 1960-63; dir., asst. prof. Newman Found. at the U. Ill., Champaign, 1967-69; prof. patristic theology and early Christianity Mundelein (Ill.) Sem., U. of St. Mary of the Lake, 1967-90; mem. com. on Role of Women in Soc. and Ch., Washington, 1971-89; exec. sec. Chgo. Theol. Inst., 1981-90; Disting. vis. prof. Barry U., Miami, Fla., 1991—. Author: Prayer: Personal & Liturgical, 1985, The Significance of Mary, 1988; translator, editor: The Early Church and the State, 1982; assoc. editor: Chicago Studies, 1985—; cons. editor Communio, 1991—; contbr. articles to profl. jours. ATS grantee, 1980. Mem. Am. Theol. Soc., Cath. Theol. Soc. Am. (pres. 1977-78), Internat. Assn. Patristic Scholars. Roman Catholic. Avocations: reading mystery stories, zoos, music, travel. Home: 717 N Batavia Batavia IL 60510 Office: Mundelein Sem U St Mary of the Lake Mundelein IL 60060

CUNNINGHAM, DAVID SCOTT, religion educator; b. Wichita, Kans., June 2, 1961; s. Donald M. and Patsy Elaine (Barrett) C.; m. Teresa Anne Hittner, Aug. 13, 1983. BS, Northwestern U., 1983; BA, MA, U. Cambridge, England, 1985; PhD, Duke U., 1990. Vis. instr. Austin Coll., Sherman, Tex., 1989-90; asst. prof. theology U. St. Thomas, St. Paul, 1990—. Author: Faithful Persuasion: In Aid of a Rhetoric of Christian Theology (Bross prize 1990), 1991; contbr. articles and book revs. to profl. jours. Newton Minow scholar, 1982-83; Jacob Javits fellow 1986-90. Mem. Am. Acad. Religion, Soc. Bibl. Lit., Soc. Christian Ethics, Speech Communication Assn. Democrat. Episcopalian. Office: U Saint Thomas Mail #4195 Saint Paul MN 55105

CUNNINGHAM, SISTER FRANCES PATRICIA, nun, religious order administrator; b. Chgo., Mar. 7, 1937; d. Theodore and Margaret Veronica (Owens) C. BA, Alverno Coll., 1965; MEd, DePaul U., 1970. Joined Sch. Sisters of St. Francis, Roman Cath. Ch., 1955. Adminstr. Immaculate Conception Sch., Chgo., 1967-71; exec. dir., dir. pub. rels. Holy Name province, Sch. Sisters St. Francis, Chgo., 1971-80; with internat. elections generalate Sch. Sisters St. Francis, Milw., 1980-92; chair Nat. Sisters Communication Svc., L.A., 1977-79; mem. task force and commn. on women Archdiocese of Milw., 1981-88. Editor: Images of Women in Mission, 1981. Chmn. bd. 8th Day Ctr. for Justice and Peace, Chgo., 1976-78, Ill. Women's Agenda, Chgo., 1977-78, Sojourner Truth House, Inc., Milw., 1990—. Mem. Leadership Conf. Women Religious (chair region VIII 1976-78, nat. sec. 1978-81), Internat. Union Superiors Gen., Nat. Assn. Religious Women. Office: Sch Sisters St Francis 1501 S Layton Blvd Milwaukee WI 53215

CUNNINGHAM, HUBERT D., minister; b. Nashville, June 6, 1956; s. Lillard Thomas and Hazel (Felts) C.; m. Karen Williams, July 8, 1978; children: Rachel Leah, Megan Victoria. BA, Trevecca Coll., 1978; MDiv, Vanderbilt U., 1988. Ordained to ministry United Meth. Ch., 1990. Minister Kingston Springs (Tenn.)/Craggie Hope United Meth. Ch., 1985-88, Mt. Carmel United Meth. Ch., Clarksville, Tenn., 1988-90, Glencliff United Meth. Ch., Nashville, 1990—; mem. Tenn. Ann. Conf., United Meth. Ch. Named Outstanding Young Man in Am., Internat. Jr. C. of C., 1982, Colonel, Gov. State of Tenn., 1988. Mem. Nashville Assn. Rabbis, Priests, and Ministers, Emmaus Community, Masons (32 Degree). Home: 760 Winthorne Dr Nashville TN 37217 Office: Glencliff United Meth Ch 2901 Glencliff Rd Nashville TN 37211

CUNNINGHAM, JAMES R., religious organization director. Exec. dir. Nebr. Cath. Conf., Lincoln. Office: Nebr Cath Conf 521 S 14th St Lincoln NE 68508*

CUNNINGHAM, JOSEPH LEONARD, priest, seminary president; b. Bklyn., Mar. 4, 1937. Student, Cathedral Coll., Bklyn., 1955-57; BA, St. Mary's Sem. and U., Balt., 1959, Lic. Sacred Theology, 1963; MA, U. Notre Dame, 1969. Ordained priest Roman Cath. Ch., 1963. Assoc. pastor Our Lady of Mercy Ch., Forest Hills, N.Y., 1963-66; asst. chancellor Diocese of Bklyn., 1966-67, exec. sec. liturgical commn., 1968-79; prin. Cathedral Preparatory Sem. Diocese of Bklyn., Elmhurst, 1979-84; rector, pres. St. Vincent de Paul Regional Sem., Boynton Beach, Fla., 1986—. Author (Tapes) Needs of Parish Liturgy-Presidential Style, 1976; contbg. editor: Prayer of Christians, 1971, Confirmation: Pastoral Concerns, 1973; contbr. articles to profl. jours. Adv. bd. Pastoral Inst., 1967-78, Bioethics Inst. St. Francis Hosp., 1986—; bd. dirs. Fedn. Diocesan Liturgical Commn., 1969-70, chmn., 1972-75; bd. dirs. Liturgical Conf., 1975-79; trustee St. John Vianney Coll. Sem., 1987—; vocation bd. Archdiocese of Miami, 1986—. Mem. Catholic Theol. Soc. Am., N.Am. Acad. Liturgy. Home and Office: St Vincent de Paul Reg Sem 10701 S Military Tr Boynton Beach FL 33436

CUNNINGHAM, LAWRENCE DAVID, religious organization specialist; b. Little Rock, Nov. 5, 1936; s. Lawrence Edward and Mable Eunice (Woods) C.; children: David Edward, Shannah Delise. BA, Ouachita Bapt. U., 1959; MRE, Southwestern Bapt. Theol. Sem., 1965. Ordained minister Bapt. Ch. Minister of music Towson Ave. Bapt., Ft. Smith, Ark., 1955-57, First Bapt. Cullendale, Camden, Ark., 1957-59; dir. youth music Field City Bapt. Ch., Dallas, 1961-62; music educator First Bapt. Ch., Seagoville, Tex., 1962-63; dir. youth music First Bapt. Ch., Durant, Okla., 1963-65; minister of edn. First Bapt. Ch., Orlando, Fla., 1973-84; music youth minister Pleasant Valley Bapt. Ch., Amarillo, Tex., 1965-68; minister edn. Plymouth Park Bapt. Ch., Irving, Tex., 1968-73; Sunday sch. dir. Fla. Bapt. Conv., Jacksonville, 1984—; founder Ch. Resource Cons., Orlando, 1978—; assoc. cons. Performax Learning Co., Mpls., 1981—; cons. Sunday Sch. Work, Jacksonville, 1984—. Author: Dual Sunday School; contbrg. author Ideas For V.B.S. Promotion. Capt. USAR, 1959-68. Mem. So. Bapt. R.E.A. Assn., Fla. R.E.A. Assn., Rotary. Avocations: photography, travel, music. Home: 3636 Sarah Brooke Ct Jacksonville FL 32211 Office: Fla Bapt Conv 1230 Hendricks Ave Jacksonville FL 32207

CUNNINGHAM, LAWRENCE SPRINGER, theology educator; b. Pitts., Sept. 23, 1935; s. Lawrence S. and Helen Anne (Shimkus) C.; m. Cecilia Davis, Oct. 13, 1972; children: Sarah Mary, Julia Clare. AB, St. Bernard's Coll., 1961; STL, Gregorian U., Rome, 1961; MA, Fla. State U., 1963, PhD, 1968. Asst. prof. religion Fla. State U., Tallahassee, 1969-74, assoc. prof. religion, 1975-79, prof. religion, 1980-87; prof. theology U. Notre Dame, Ind., 1988—; chair dept. theology U. Notre Dame, Ind., 1991—; NEH vis. prof. U. Scranton, Pa., 1980-81. Author: Catholic Faith, 1988, Catholic Prayer, 1989. Mem. Am. Acad. Religion, Coll. Theology Soc., Cath. Theol. Assn. Am., Medieval Acad. Am. Democrat. Roman Catholic. Home: 909 Riverside Dr South Bend IN 46616 Office: U Notre Dame Dept of Theology Notre Dame IN 46556

CUNNINGHAM, LOREN DUANE, religious organization executive; b. Taft, Calif., June 30, 1935; s. Thomas Cecil and Jewell Etta (Nicholson) C.; m. Darlene Joy Scratch; children: Karen Joy, David Loren. BA in Bible Studies, BA in Religious Edn., Cen. Bible Inst. and Sem., 1957; BA in Religion, MA in Adminstrn. of Edn., U. So. Calif., 1958; DD (hon.), Latin Am. Bible Coll., 1982. Founder, pres. Youth With A Mission, Kailua-Kona, Hawaii, 1960—; chmn. nat. exec. bd. Yr. of the Bible, Hawaii, 1983—; mem. exec. bd. Freedom Council Nat. Am. for Jesus, Virginia Beach, Va.; mem. internat. council Second Internat. Conf. on World Evangelization; pres. U. of the Nations, Kailua-Kona; mem. exec. com. Wash. for Jesus, 1988—; mem. adv. com. Open Doors with Bro. Andrew, Assn. Internat. Missions Services. Author: Is That Really You God?, 1984, Winning, God's Way. Mem. Women's Aglow (internat. adv. bd.), Christian Broadcasting Assn. (exec. bd.), Active Am. Coalition (exec. bd.), Full Gospel Chaplains Assn. (exec. bd.). Home: Kuakini Hwy Kailua Kona HI 96740 Office: Youth With A Mission 75-5851 Kaukini Hwy Kailua Kona HI 96740

CUNNINGHAM, SISTER MADONNA MARIE, nun, congregation president; b. Trenton, N.J., Aug. 31, 1933. AB, Villanova U., 1961; MA, Fordham U., 1964, PhD, 1968. Joined Sisters of St. Francis, Roman Cath. Ch., 1953. Intern in psychology St. Elizabeth's Hosp., Washington, 1965-66; elem. tchr. Spokane, Wash., 1956-60, Elsmere, Del., 1956-60; dir. counseling, asst. prof. psychology Our Lady of Angels Coll., Aston, Pa., 1967-71, pres., assoc. prof., 1971-83; lectr. Dept. Edn., St. Joseph's Coll., Phila., 1968-70; staff psychologist Phila. Archdiocesan Counseling Svc. for Religions, 1969-76. Trustee St. Joseph Hosp., Towson, Md., Archmere Acad., Claymont, Del., Franciscan Health System, Neumann Coll. Mem. Am. Psychol. Assn., Pa. Psychol. Assn., Psychologists Interested in Religious Issues, Sigma Xi. Office: Our Lady of Angels Convent Aston PA 19014

CUNNINGHAM, MURRELL THOMAS, minister; b. Knoxville, Tenn., July 14, 1933; s. Millard Arthur and Josie Mae (Gosnell) C.; m. Rebecca Hale, Aug. 20, 1955; 1 child, Stephanie Ann. BS, Washington U., St. Louis, 1966; MDiv, Eden Theol. Sem., St. Louis, 1969; DD, Cen. Meth. Coll., Fayette, Mo., 1979. Ordained to ministry Meth. Ch. as deacon, 1964, in United Meth. Ch. as elder, 1969. Assoc. min. United Meth. Ch., Farmington, Mo., 1963-66; min. Mellow Meml. United Meth. Ch., Farmington, Mo., 1966-69, St. Andrew United Meth. Ch., Florissant, Mo., 1969-74, St. John's United Meth. Ch., St. Louis, 1974-82; dist. supt. St. Louis South Dist., 1982-87; sr. min. Webster Hills United Meth. Ch., St. Louis, 1987—; del. World Meth. Coun., Dublin, Ireland, 1976; mem. Inter-Faith Clergy Coun., St. Louis, 1981. Bd. curators Cen. Meth. Coll., 1980-85; dir. Eden Theol. Sem Bd., 1977-84. Mem. Mo. Athletic Club, Tuscan (chaplain 1975-76). Office: Webster Hills Meth Ch 698 W Lockwood Saint Louis MO 63119

CUNNINGHAM, PAUL GEORGE, minister; b. Chgo., Aug. 27, 1937; s. Paul George Sr. and Naomi Pearl (Anderson) C.; m. Constance Ruth Seaman, May 27, 1960; children: Lori, Paul, Connie Jo. BA, Olivet Nazarene U., 1960; BDiv., Nazarene Theol. Sem., 1964; DD, Mid Am. Nazarene Coll., 1975. Sr. pastor Coll. Ch. of the Nazarene, Olathe, Kans., 1964—; adv. bd. Kansas City Dist. Ch. of the Nazarene, Overland Park, Kans., 1971—; trustee Mid Am. Nazarene Coll., Olathe, 1971—; chmn. book com. Nazarene Pub. House, Kansas City, Mo., 1974-90; pres. gen. bd. Internat. Ch. of the Nazarene, Kansas City, 1985—. Police chaplain Olathe (Kans.) Police Dept., 1975—; adv. bd. Good Samaritan Ctr., Olathe, 1990—. Recipient Disting. Svc. award Jaycees, Olathe, 1967, Paul Harris fellow Rotary Internat., Olathe, 1989. Mem. Nat. Assn. Evangelicals, Rotary. Home: 1109 Clairborne Olathe KS 66062 Office: Coll Ch of the Nazarene 2020 E Sheridan Olathe KS 66062

CUNNINGHAM, ROBERT CYRIL, clergyman, editor; b. Peterborough, Ont., Can., Dec. 23, 1914; came to U.S., 1935, naturalized, 1942; s. John James and Cecelia (Simpson) C.; m. Helen Marian Platte, May 14, 1941; children—Robert Stephen, Philip Joseph, Andrew Platte, Bethel Marian. B.A., Central Bible Coll., 1962; M.A., Assemblies of God Theol. Sem., 1980. Ordained to ministry Assemblies of God, 1945; pastor Assembly of God, Ozark, Mo., 1943-47; mem. editorial staff Gospel Pub. House, Springfield, Mo., 1937-84; editor Christ's Ambassadors Herald, 1940-45; asso. editor The Pentecostal Evangel, 1943-49, editor, 1949-84; missionary Assemblies of God Ch., Lome, Togo, 1985-86. Author: Filled With The Spirit, 1972, Getting Together With Luke and Acts, 1973, Senior Adults Ministries Manual, 1985; contbr. articles to mags. Mem. Evang. Press Assn. (pres. 1961-63), Internat. Pentecostal Press Assn. (pres. 1973-76, 80-84), Central Bible Coll. Alumni Assn. (pres. 1946-48). Club: Univ. Home: 2338 E Bancroft St Springfield MO 65804 *On life's turbulent sea I am constantly buoyed by a blessed hope. I have Christ's threefold promise (1) that He will return, (2) that He will take me to a better world, and (3) that I shall live with Him forever in a beautiful place He has prepared for all who love Him.*

CUNNINGHAM, RONALD M., religious education director. Gen. sec. Christian edn. Christian Meth. Episcopal Ch., Memphis. Office: Christian Meth Episcopal Ch 2805 Shoreland Dr Atlanta GA 30331*

CUNNINGHAM, THOMAS WILLIAM, clergyman, retired English educator; b. Jersey City, June 7, 1911; s. Joseph A. and Mary A. (Snell) C. Student, St. Peter's Prep. Sch., 1923-27; A.B., Seton Hall U., 1931; student, Immaculate Conception Theol. Sem., 1931-35; M.A., Fordham U., 1943, Ph.D., 1950. Ordained priest Roman Cath. Ch., 1935; asst. pastor St. John's Ch., Orange, N.J., 1935-40; instr., later asst. prof. English lit. Seton Hall U., 1940-46, prof. English lit., head dept. English, 1946-53, dean coll. arts and scis., co-ordinating dean all schs., 1951-53, v.p. charge instrn., 1953-63; pastor Immaculate Conception Ch., Montclair, N.J., 1963-77; apptd. domestic prelate, 1964; lectr. Cath. Forum Newark Critic's Circle N.Y.; Chmn. Newark Archdiocese Ecumenical Commn.; mem. Priest's Senate, Newark, 1971-77; synodal judge Archdiocesan Tribune, 1964-80. Author: Saints Off Pedestals, 1953; also articles, book revs. Appointed Papal Chamberlain, 1958. Recipient James Roosevelt Bayley award Seton Hall U., 1964; Coronat award St. Edward's U., 1964; For God and Country award Cath. War Vets., 1968. Mem. Modern Lang. Assn., Mediaeval Acad. Am., Am. Cath. Hist. Assn., Nat. Cath. Ednl. Assn., St. Paul's Guild N.Y. Clubs: K.C, Serra Vocation, Mercier. Home: 3436 Stirling Rd Palm Harbor FL 34684 *The realization that God underlies our beginnings, our culture, our laws and our ideals gives me reason to participate in all phases of society's activities and bolsters my hopes in times of crisis. My love for my American roots urges me to greater efforts in creating a noble society around me so as to keep aglow the magnificent spirit of our founding fathers.*

CUPP, JOYCE ANN, religion educator; b. Douglas, Ariz., Feb. 20, 1950; d. Eldon Joseph and Esther Lavern (Sparks) Coons; m. Kent Phillip Cupp, Sept. 19, 1987; stepchildren: Benjamin Abner, Joseph Lee. BS, Ariz. Coll. of the Bible, 1972. Youth dir., christian edn. Westlane Christian Ch., Indpls., 1989—; kindergarten tchr. Indpls. Christian Sch., 1972-73, Clermont (Ind.) Christian Acad., 1973-74, Bethesda Christian Sch., Brownsburg, Ind., 1974-80; children's coord. FOCUS, Indpls., 1989; co-chmn. program com. Ind. Christian Youth Conv., Indpls., 1991. Mem. Big Sisters, Indpls., 1986-90. Republican. Office: Westlane Christian Ch 7220 Grandview Dr Indianapolis IN 46260

CURIS, CARLO, bishop; b. La Maddalena, Sardinia, Italy, Nov. 2, 1923. D of Canon Law, Pontifical Lateran U., Rome. Ordained priest Roman Cath. Ch., 1947. Mem. Diplomatic Corps of Holy See, Uruguay, Chile, India, U.S., Italy, 1956—; apptd. apostolic del. Sri Lanka; raised to archepiscopal titular see of Medeli, 1971, consecrated bishop, 1971, apostolic pro-nuncio to Sri Lanka, 1976, apostolic pro-nuncio in Nigeria, 1978-84; apptd. apostolic del. for Israel and Jordan, apostolic pro-nuncio in Cyprus Jerusalem, 1984-90; apostolic pro-nuncio in Can., 1990—. Address: 724 Manor Ave, Ottawa, ON Canada K1M 0E3

CURLEE, ROBERT C., JR., minister; b. Ellaville, Ga., Apr. 2, 1935; s. Robert C. and Grace (Willis) C.; m. Sue Lenox, July 11, 1959; children: Robert, Lisa, Cathy, Jamey. BA, Samford U., 1957; BD, So. Sem., 1962; D Ministry, New Orleans Sem., 1977; DD (hon.), Judson Coll., 1988. Ordained to ministry Bapt. Ch., 1956. Pastor Ashland (Ala.) Bapt. Ch., 1963-67, Ensley Bapt. Ch., Birmingham, Ala., 1967-72, Centercrest Bapt. Ch., Birmingham, 1972—; exec. dir. Jonah Missions, 1969—; trustee Birmingham Bapt. Camp, B.M.C. Author: Jonah and the Whale, 1969, From Haystacks to Skylabs, 1974, Cross Roads, 1990. Recipient Brother Bryan award, Birmingham, 1973. Mem. Ministers' Assn. Greater Birmingham (pres. 1976). Home: 2533 5th St N E Birmingham AL 35215 Office: Centercrest Bapt Ch 3025 Wood Dr N E Birmingham AL 35215

CURLESS, ROBERT BRUCE, minister; b. Elwood, Ind., June 25, 1945; s. Wilbur Carl and Violet Alice (Watson) C.; m. Betty Jo Summitt, Apr. 11, 1969; children: Robert Andrew, Jennifer Dawn. MusB, U. Miami, 1967; postgrad., Salvation Army Sch. for Officers, Atlanta, 1967-68, 70-71, So. Bapt. Seminary, Louisville, 1969-70, Emory U., 1970-71. Band dir., tchr. Bishop David High Sch., Louisville, 1969-70; asst. officer Salvation Army, Clearwater, Fla., 1968-69, Pensacola, Fla., 1969; commanding officer Salvation Army, Melbourne, Fla., 1971-77, Ocala, Fla., 1977-78; home officer, bandmaster, coordinator music dept., tchr. Sch. for Officers Salvation Army, Atlanta, 1978-83; commanding officer Salvation Army, Ponca City, Okla., 1983-85, Enid, Okla., 1985—; tuba player Okla.-Ark. Divisional Brass Sextet, 1985-87, tuba sect. leader, 1986-87, dep. bandmaster, 1987—; tuba player So. U.S. Territorial Band, 1972-87; adj. faculty So. Territorial Music Inst. Mem. Enid Council of Chs., 1986-87. Recipient Spl. Merit award Melbourne C. of C., 1973-74, Norm Keller Disting. Service award Melbourne Jaycees, 1973-74, Service to Mankind award Sertoma Internat., 1974, Outstanding Service award Ocala Adv. Bd., 1978. Mem. Ministerial Assn., Okla. Welfare and Health Orgn., Enid C. of C., Okla.-Ark. Music Com. Club: Exchange (West Palm Beach). Lodges: Rotary, Kiwanis. Avocations: fishing, hunting, swimming, skindiving, camping. Office: Salvation Army 516 N Independence PO Box 708 Enid OK 73702

CURLEY, JOHN E., JR., religious health association director. Pres. Cath. Health Assn., St. Louis. Office: Cath Health Assn 4455 Woodson Rd Saint Louis MO 63134*

CURNUTT, BRIAN JOE, religion educator; b. Montebello, Calif., Jan. 26, 1962; s. Gerald Ray and Barbara Jean (Cichirillo) C.; m. Heidi Elizabeth Notter, June 28, 1986. AA in Bibl. Lit., Cascade Bible Coll., 1986, M Ministry, 1990; BA in Bibl. Lit., Northwest Coll., 1988. Cert. cons. Youth pastor Kirkland (Wash.) 1st Bapt. Ch., 1984-86; assoc. pastor Calvary Chapel, Seattle, 1988; prof. Cascade Bible Coll., Bellevue, Wash., 1988—; spl. rep. of pres. Cascade Bible Coll., 1989—. Author/programmer: (software database) Kyrios Church Manager and Accounting, 1990-91, Counseling Reference Database, 1991. Office: PC Answers Inc 18700 33d Ave W Ste B245 Lynnwood WA 98037 *As we rise to the challenge of living in a rapidly changing world, let us not forget the greatest challenge of all—to bear each other's burdens, to love unconditionally and to lay down our lives for the sake of our brother.*

CURRAN, CHARLES E., theologian, educator, priest; b. Rochester, N.Y., Mar. 30, 1934; s. John F. and Gertrude (Beisner) C. BA, St. Bernard's Coll., 1955; Licentiate in Sacred Theology, Pontifical Gregorian U., Rome, 1959, STD, 1961; STD, Acad. Alfonsiana, Rome, 1961; PhD (hon.), U. Charleston, 1987. Ordained priest Roman Cath. Ch. Prof. moral theology St. Bernard's Sem., Rochester, 1961-65; from asst. prof. to prof. Cath. U. Am., Washington, 1965-87; vis. Kaneb prof. Cath. studies Cornell U., Ithaca, N.Y., 1987-88; vis. Brooks prof. Religion U. So. Calif., L.A., 1988-89, vis. Firestone prof. Religion, 1989-90; vis. Goodwin-Philpott eminent scholar in Religion Auburn (Ala.) U., 1990-91; Elizabeth Scurlock prof. of Human Values So. Meth. U., Dallas, 1991—; external examiner in Christian ethics U. W.I., 1982-86; lectr. in field. Author: Christian Morality Today, 1966, A New Look at Christian Morality, 1968, Contemporary Problems in Moral Theology, 1970, Catholic Moral Theology in Dialogue, 1972, The Crisis in Pirestly Ministry, 1972, Politics, Medicine and Christian Ethics: A Dialogue with Paul Ramsey, 1973, New Perspectives in Moral Theology, 1974, Ongoing Revision: Studies in Moral Theology, 1976, Themes in Fundamental Moral Theology, 1977, Issues in Sexual and Medical Ethics, 1978, Transition and Tradition in Moral Theology, 1979, Moral Theology: A Continuing Journey, 1982, American Catholic Social Ethics: Twentieth Century Approaches, 1982, Critical Concerns in Moral Theology, 1984, Directions in Catholic Social Ethics, 1985, Directions in Fundamental Moral Theology, 1985, Faithful Dissent, 1986, Toward an American Catholic Moral Theology, 1988, Sexualitat and Ethik, 1988, Tensions in Moral Theology, 1988, Catholic Higher Education, Theology, and Academic Freedom, 1990; also articles; (with others) Dissent In and For the Church: Theologians and Humanae Vitae, 1969, The Responsibility of Dissent: The Church and Academic Freedom, 1969; editor: Absolutes in Moral Theology?, 1968, Contraception: Authority and Dissent, 1969, Moral Theology: Challenges for the Future, 1990; co-editor book series: (with Richard A. McCormick) Readings in Moral Theology: No. 1: Moral Norms and Catholic Tradition, 1979, No. 2: The Distinctiveness of Christian Ethics, 1980, No. 3: The Magisterium and Morality, 1982, No. 4: The Use of Scripture in Moral Theology, 1984, No. 5: Official Catholic Social Teaching, 1986, No. 6: Dissent in the Church, 1988, No. 7: Natural Law and Theology, 1990; mem. editorial bd. Eglise et Theologie, Horizons, Internat. Christian Digest, 1986-90. Am. Assn. Theol. Schs. fellow, 1971; Georgetown U. Kennedy Ctr. for Bioethics scholar, 1972. Mem. Cath. Theol. Soc. Am. (pres. 1969-70, John Courtney Murray award 1972), Soc. Christian Ethics (pres. 1971-72, mem. editorial bd. Ann. 1991—), Am. Theol. Soc. (pres. 1989-90), Coll. Theology Soc. Avocations: golf, swimming, reading. Home: 4125 Woodcreek Dr Dallas TX 75220 Office: So Meth U 317 Dallas Hall Dallas TX 75275-0235

CURRIE, SISTER EILEEN, college president; BA in Psychology, Cabrini Coll., 1966; MA in Religious Edn., LaSalle Coll., 1976; postgrad. Bryn Mawr Coll./HERS Summer Inst., 1982, Inst. for Ednl. Mgmt./Harvard U., 1983. Tchr. religion/English, coordinator Confraternity Christian Doctrine programs, mem. vicariate religious edn. bd. Sacred Hearts of Jesus and Mary Sch., Bklyn., 1970-73, mem. parish council, 1971-77, prin., 1973-77, chairperson area cluster schs. for consol., 1975-77; tchr. Mother Cabrini High Sch., N.Y.C., 1977-81, acting prin., 1978-79, coll. advisor, 1979-80, moderator student body assn., 1979-81; dean student affairs Cabrini Coll., Radnor, Pa., 1981-82, pres., 1982—, past trustee; chairperson Apostolic Evaluation Team U.S. Provinces, Missionary Sisters of Sacred Heart, 1975-76, mem. provincial council ea. province, 1978-81; trustee St. Clare's Health Ctr., N.Y., 1981-82; mem. bd. adminstrn. Santa Cabrini Hosp., Montreal, Can., 1983—. Office: Cabrini Coll 610 King Of Prussia Rd Radnor PA 19087

CURRIN, KIMBERLI JOYCE, church secretary; b. Corsicana, Tex., Nov. 4, 1958; d. Joe Miller and Marjorie Marie (Gilliam) Tidwell; m. William Douglas Currin, Jan. 6, 1978; children: Jennifer Marie, Justin Douglas, Nathan Scott. AS, Eastfield Coll., Mesquite, Tex. Vacation Bible sch. dir. First Bapt. Ch., Sunnyvale, Tex., 1985-89; ch. sec. Edgemont Pk. Bapt. Ch., Mesquite, Tex., 1988—, Sun. sch. dir., 1982—. Pres. Rutherford Elem. PTA, 1988-90. Home: 1326 Caladium Mesquite TX 75149 Office: Edgemont Pk Bapt Ch 1804 Hickory Tree Rd Mesquite TX 75149-6339

CURRY, EVERETT WILLIAM, JR., minister; b. Glendale, Calif., Mar. 7, 1942; s. Everett William and Sylvia Pauline (Burkholder) C.; m. Barbara Kay Orman, June 13, 1964; children: Kimberly Suzanne Curry McSwain, Kevin Everett. BA, Calif. State U., Northridge, 1964; MDiv, Am. Bapt. Sem., Berkeley, Calif., 1967; Doctor of Ministry, San Francisco Theol. Sem., San Anselmo, Calif., 1977. Cert. fin. planner. Minister to youth First Bapt. Ch., San Fernando, Calif., 1960-62; assoc. pastor Valley Park Bapt. Ch., Sepulveda, Calif., 1962-66; dir., media ministries Coachella Valley Bapt. Found., Thermal, Calif., 1966-68; pastor Lakeview Terrace Bapt. Ch., Lakeview Terrace, Calif., 1968-71; dir., media ministries L.A. Bapt. City Mission Soc., 1971-74; pastor Community Bapt. Ch., Pearl Harbor, Hawaii, 1974-78, First Bapt. Ch., Coos Bay, Oreg., 1978-86; planned giving counselor Am. Bapt. Found., Valley Forge, Pa., 1986—. Chmn., bd. dirs. Coos Bay Sch. Dist., Coos Bay, 1988-89; chief, chaplain corps, Coos Bay Police Dept., 1979-85; pres. Hawaiian Islands Pub. Radio, Honolulu, 1977-78. Mem. Am. Bapt. Ministers Coun. (sen. 1983-87), Western Commn. on Ministry (sec. 1988—), Coos-Bay North Bend Rotary (Outstanding Citizen award 1985). Republican. Baptist. Avocations: amateur radio, backpacking, photography, travel. Home: 1546 NE Greensword Dr Hillsboro OR 97124 *The test of my generation is found in whether we pass along values in faith and democracy for adoption by the new generation—then adapted by them for their world.*

CURRY, JOEL BRUCE, public relations executive; b. Fairmont, W.Va., Mar. 28, 1948; s. Carroll Hugh and Opal Corrine (Gates) C.; m. Shara Jean Belknap, Aug. 1, 1970; children: Andrea Christine, Alicia Gail. BA, Fairmont State Coll., 1970; postgrad., Grace Theol. Seminary, Winona Lake, Ind. Accredited pub. rels. specialist. Staff assoc. C&P Telephone, Charleston, W.Va., 1970-74; pub. rels. staff supr. C&P Telephone, Washington, 1974-76; pub. rels. staff mgr. C&P Telephone, Charleston, 1976-82; pub. rels. mgr. Appalachian Power Co., Roanoke, Va., 1982-86; pub. rels. dirs. Grace Coll. and Seminary, Winona Lake, 1986—. Author: Public Relations for the Local Church, 1991, Tell the Good News About Your Christian School, 1991. Founder Oakland VA/Jaycees, 1976; mem. South Charleston Jaycees, 1970-80; bd. dirs. Crisis Pregnancy Ctr., Roanoke, 1985-86. Mem. Pub. Rels. Soc. Am. Avocation: photography. Home: 1121 East Market St Warsaw IN 46580 Office: Grace Coll and Seminary 200 Seminary Dr Winona Lake IN 46590

CURRY, JOSEPH C., minister; b. DeKalb, Miss., Apr. 3, 1918; s. William and Suzanne (Jack) C.; m. Martha Ann Grace, Jan. 4, 1947; children: Paticia Ann Moore, Lou E., Josiah, Ondria Jackson. Pastor Macedonia Bapt. Ch., Flint, Mich., 1961—; vice moderator Great Lakes Dist. Assn. Bapt. Ch., Flint, 1980-90. With U.S. Army, 1940-45, NATOUSA. Named Humanitarian, Human Relations Com., Flint, Mich., 1977; cited for Loyalty, Faithfulness and Dedication, Wolverine State Cong. of Ch. Educators, Flint, Mich., 1984; honored in resolution by City of Flint, 1985. Mem. NAACP (lifetime), Masons. Home: G-5444 Summit Flint MI 48505

CURRY, MITCHELL LEE, minister, psychotherapist; b. Augusta, Ga., Feb. 5, 1935; s. Walter Lee and Ernestine (Battle) C.; m. Carolyn Davenport, Sept. 11, 1974; children: Rachael, Michele; children by previous marriage, Sonja, Reuben. BA, Morris Brown Coll., 1960; MDiv, Andover Newton Theol. Sem., 1964; MS in Social Work, U. Louisville, 1972; PhD, D Ministry, Sch. Theology, Claremont, 1979; LHD (hon.), Reed Christian Coll., 1976. Ordained to ministry A.M.E. Ch. as elder, 1951; lic. clin. social worker, Calif. Exec. dir. Harlem div. Protestant Coun. N.Y.C., 1963-65; pastor Richard Allen African Meth. Episcopal Ch., St. George's, Bermuda, 1965-69; interim pastor Florence Ave. Presbyn. Ch., L.A., d1976-79, Imperial Heights Ch., L.A., 1980-84; pvt. practice psychotherapy L.A., 1980—; psychotherapist L.A. County Mental Health Dept., 1976-85; bd. govs. Nat. Coun. Chs., N.Y.C., 1981—; mem. So. Calif. Coun. Chs., L.A., 1982—, L.A. Coun. Chs., 1973-76.—. Bd. dirs. Crenshaw Counseling Svcs., L.A., 1980—. Am. Missionary Assn. scholar, N.Y.C., 1960-64, NIMH scholar, Md., 1970-72. Fellow Am. Assn. Pastoral Counselors; mem. NAACP, Acad. Cert. Social Workers (cert. diplomate), Alpha Phi Alpha. Home: 1809 Virginia Rd Los Angeles CA 90019 Office: 3875 Wilshire Blvd Ste 408 Los Angeles CA 90010

CURTIS, CHARLES EDWARD, minister; b. Cooperstown, N.Y., Feb. 2, 1943; s. Edward Romine and Lucy May (Matthews) C.; m. Jayne Lamont Newcomb, Jan. 17, 1981; 1 child, Katherine. BA, Mich. State U., 1964; MDiv, Episcopal Theol. Sch., Cambridge, Mass., 1967. Ordained to ministry Episcopal Ch., 1967. Curate St. Thomas Episcopal Ch., Trenton, Mich., 1967-69; vicar Christ the King Episcopal Ch., Taylor, Mich., 1969-77; asst. rector St. John's Episcopal Ch., Royal Oak, Mich., 1977-88; rector All Saints Episcopal Ch., Nevado, Mo., 1980-86, St. Alban's Episcopal Ch., Bay City, Mich., 1986—; mem. standing com. Diocese of West Mo., Kansas City, 1984-86; convocation dean Saginaw (Mich.) Valley Convocation, 1990—, Downriver Convocation, Detroit, 1971-73. Bd. dirs. Boy County Emergency Food Pantry Network, Bay City, 1989—, pres., 1990—; pres. Meals on Wheels, Nevada, 1984-86; mem. Taylor Mayor's Community Block Grant Adv. Com., 1975-77, Bay City Sch. Supt.'s Adv. Com., 1990. Mem. Episcopal Clergy Assn. of Mich. (treas. 1990—), Associated Parishes for Liturgy and Mission, The Alcuin Club, The Anglican Soc., Nat. Geographic Soc. Office: St Albans Episcopal Church 105 S Erie Bay City MI 48706

CURTIS, JOHN BARRY, bishop; b. June 19, 1933; s. Harold Boyd and Eva B. (Saunders) C.; m. Patricia Emily Simpson, 1959; four children. BA, U. Toronto, 1955, LTh, 1958; student, Theol. Coll., Chichester, Sussex, Eng.; DD (hon.), Trinity Coll., 1985, U. Toronto, 1985. Ordained to deacon The Anglican Ch. of Can., 1958, priest, 1959. Asst. curate Holy Trinity, Pembroke, Ont., 1958-61; rector Parish of March, Kanota, Ont., 1961-65, St. Stephen's Ch., Buckingham, Que., 1965-69, All Saints (Westboro), Ottawa, Ont., 1969-78; program dir. Diocese of Ottawa, 1978-80; rector Christ Ch., Elbow Park, Calgary, Alta., 1980-83; bishop Diocese of Calgary, 1983—. Mem. Ranchmen's Club (Calgary). Office: Diocese Calgary, 3015 Glencoe Rd SW, Calgary, AB Canada T2S 2L9

CURTIS, JOSEPH ROBERT, music minister; b. Espanola, N.Mex., Mar. 20, 1962; s. Theodore Grant and Carol Elaine (Miller) C.; m. Michelle Tina Cook, Dec. 27, 1986. BS, Grand Canyon U., Phoenix, 1989. Dir. sound and lighting Agape Players, Lake Wales, Fla., 1980-85; youth dir. Historic First Presbyn. Ch., Phoenix, 1987-88, dir. music and media, 1988—; voice tchr. Phoenix, 1989—; mem. nominating com. Historic First Presbyn. Ch., 1989-91. Author, composer musical drama, Liberty, 1989, Something Different About Him, 1991. Vol. Interfaith Coop. Ministries, Phoenix, 1990—, Care Ctr., Lake Wales, 1985. Ray Meben scholar, 1989; Paul Douglas grantee, 1988. Mem. Am. Guild Organists, Am. Choral Dirs. Assn., Presbyn. Assn. Musicians. Republican. Home: 349 E Thomas E205 Phoenix AZ 85012 Office: Historic First Presbyn Ch 402 W Monroe Phoenix AZ 85003

CURTIS, RICHARD LEWIS, pastor; b. Indpls.; s. Lewis Richard and Patricia Ellen (Scribner) C.; m. Mayetta Eloise Wirth, Dec. 30, 1983; children: Nathaniel, Rebekah, Phillip. BA, Cen. Bible Coll., 1985; MDiv, Assemblies of God Theol. Sem., 1988. Ordained to ministry Assemblies of God, 1988; lic. pastoral counselor. Pastor March (Mo.) Assembly of God, 1986, Renault (Ill.) Assembly of God, 1987-89; pastor First Assembly of God, Clay Center, Kans., 1989, Watonga, Okla., 1990—; founder, counselor Christ in Counseling Ministries, Watonga, 1990—; Christian edn. profl. Ill. Dist. Coun. Assemblies of God, Carlinville, Ill., 1988-89; area rep. Nat. Christian Counselors Assn., Pitts., 1989—. With U.S. Army, 1975-78; with USN, 1978-80. Decorated Meritorious Achievement. Mem. Nat. Christian Counselors Assn. Republican. Home: 702 N Burford St Watonga OK 73772-2218 Office: First Assembly of God 400 N Harmon St Watonga OK 73772-2842 *A personal relationship with God cannot insure you against the crisis of poverty, illness, or disaster. It can, however, help you to overcome your trials, rather than succumb to them.*

CURTIS, STEPHEN DOUGLAS, minister; b. Morganton, N.C., July 17, 1954; s. Henry Earnest and Bessie (Bean) C.; m. Suzanne Bess Mull, July 1, 1972; children: Chandler, Danielle. Diploma, Fruitland Bible Bapt. Inst., 1982; student, Wingate Coll., 1983-84; B in Ministry, So. Bapt. Ctr., 1985, M in Ministry, 1986. Ordained to ministry So. Bapt. Conv., 1982. Pastor Bethel Bapt. Ch., Morganton, 1982-88, Mt. Anderson Bapt. Ch., Maiden, N.C., 1988—; bd. dirs. Tar Hill Prison Ministries Inc., Maiden, 1989—; v.p. external studies Ala. Bible U., Notasulga, 1989—; mentor So. Bapt. Ctr., Jacksonville, Fla., 1991—. Editor: Exciting Adventures Through the Scriptures, 1988. Mem. adv. bd. Citizens United Burke County, Morganton, 1987. Recipient Missions Outreach award Bethel Bapt. Ch., Morganton, 1987. Fellow Compassion Internat. Evang. Assn. (bd. dirs. 1985—, award 1990), South Fork Bapt. Assn. (mem. nominations com. 1990-91). Home and Office: Rte 1 Box 301 Maiden NC 28650 *I have learned that with God, dreams can become reality, goals can be achieved, for where God guides, He provides.*

CURTIS, WALTER W., retired bishop; b. Jersey City, May 3, 1913. Student, Fordham U., Seton Hall U., Immaculate Conception Sem., N.Am. and Gregorian U., Rome; S.T.D., Cath. U. Am. Ordained priest Roman Catholic Ch., 1937; appointed bishop of Bisica in Tunis and aux. bishop of Newark, 1957-61; bishop of Bridgeport, Conn., 1961-88. Office: The Catholic Ctr 238 Jewett Ave Bridgeport CT 06606

CURTISS, ELDEN F., bishop; b. Baker, Oreg., June 16, 1932; s. Elden F. and Mary (Neiger) C. B.A., St. Edward Sem., Seattle, M.Div., 1958; M.A. in Ednl. Adminstrn, U. Portland, 1965; postgrad., Fordham U., U. Notre Dame. Ordained priest Roman Catholic Ch., 1958; campus chaplain, 1959-64, 65-68; supt. schs. Diocese of Baker (Oreg.), 1962-70; pastor, 1968-70; pres./rector Mt. Angel Sem., Benedict, Oreg., 1972-76; mem. bd. regents Mt. Angel Sem., Benedict, 1990—; bishop of Helena (Mont.), 1976—; mem. priests senate Archdiocese of Portland, 1974-76; mem. ecumenical ministries State of Oreg., 1972; mem. pastoral services com. Oreg. State Hosp., Salem, 1975-76; mem. adminstrv. bd. Nat. Conf. Cath. Bishops, 1976-80, 89—; mem. pro-life com., 1977-89, chmn. com. on vocations, 1989—, mem. com. on priestly formation, also mem. com.. Nat. Cath. News Svc., bd. dirs. Cath. Mut. Relief Soc., 1977—, Mont. Cath. Conf., 1976—, Mont. Cath. Social Svcs., Inc.; mem. N.W. Assn. Bishops and Major Religious Superiors, 1976—, Mont. Assn. Chs., 1976—, bd. regents U Portland, bishops and pres's com ednl. dept. U.S. Cath. Conf.; chancellor Carroll Coll., Helena. Mem. Nat. Cath. Ednl. Assn. (Outstanding Educator 1972, bishops and pres's com. coll. dept.). Office: 515 N Ewing PO Box 1729 Helena MT 59624

CURTS, MARK STEPHEN, pastor; b. Waco, Tex., Dec. 29, 1957; s. Allen Andrew and Jean (Crowley) C. BA, Calif. Bapt. Coll., Riverside, 1981; student, Fuller Theol. Sem., Pasadena, Calif., 1981, William Carey Internat. U., 1983-84; MA in Religious Edn., Southwestern Bapt. Theol. Sem., Ft. Worth, 1988. Ordained to ministry Bapt. Ch. 1989. Min. youth Calif. So. Bapt. Gen. Conv., Fresno, 1979; min. music Calvary Bapt. Ch., Riverside, 1979-80; children's intern The Ch. on Brady, L.A., 1981-82; staff chaplain Tex. Dept. Mental Health, Ft. Worth, 1985-87; assoc. pastor First So. Bapt. Ch., Oxnard, Calif., 1989-91; pastor First So. Bapt. Ch., Riverbank, Calif., 1991—; youth rally coord. Gold Coast Bapt. Assn., Oxnard, 1991—. Named Outstanding Young Man in Am., 1988. Mem. Southwestern Bapt. Religious Educators Assn. Home: 1721 Harvard Ave Clovis CA 93612 Office: First So Bapt Ch Po Box 181 Riverbank CA 95367 *Travel light in life. Take only what you need: a loving family, good friends, simple pleasures, someone to love and someone to love you, enought to eat and a little more than enough to drink, for thirst is a dangerous thing.*

CUSHING, VINCENT DEPAUL, theology educator, college president, priest; b. N.Y.C., Apr. 6, 1934; s. Joseph Patrick and Anna Veronica (O'Connell) C. BA, St. Bonaventure U., 1960; STL, Cath. U. Am., 1964, STD, 1972; DLitt (hon.), Villanova U., 1984. Joined Order of St. Francis, 1953, ordained priest Roman Cath. Ch., 1964. Instr. theology Christ the King Sem., Olean, N.Y., 1964-66, Holy Name Coll., Washington, 1966-69; asst. prof. Washington Theol. Union, Silver Spring, Md., 1970—, pres., 1975—; trustee St. Bonaventure U., Olean, 1969-78, Siena Coll., Loudanville, N.Y., 1969-75, Christ the King Sem., 1972-74. Mem. Cath. Theol. Soc. Am., Assn. Theol. Schs. in U.S. and Can. (pres. 1982-84). Office: Washington Theol Union 9001 New Hampshire Ave Silver Spring MD 20903

CUSHMAN, EARLE LYNWOOD, minister; b. Thomaston, Maine, Aug. 24, 1940; s. Lynwood George and Virginia Marie (Taylor) C.; children: Rebecca Jean Hance, Debra Jayne. ThB, Emmanuel Bible Coll., 1974; ThM, Clarksville Sch. Theology, 1975, ThD, 1978; D of Ministry, Southeastern Sem., 1988. Ordained to ministry Ch. of God, 1972. Pastor Ch. of God, Pittsfield, Maine, 1962-65, Portland, Maine, 1965-66, Boston, 1966-67, Groton, Conn., 1968-79, Akron, Ohio, 1982-84; state youth dir. New Eng., 1965-66, So. New Eng., 1968-74, Mo., 1974-76, Pa., 1976-78; state evangelism dir. No. Ohio, 1978-82; state youth dir. No. Ohio, 1982-84; crosscultural dir. L.A., 1984-86, Fla., 1986-89; internat. evangelist, 1989—; planter over 100 chs. Bd. dirs. Groton Resource Organized, 1970-74. Republican. Home and Office: PO Box 70802 Fort Lauderdale FL 33307

CUSHMAN, ROBERT EARL, minister, retired theology educator; b. Fall River, Mass., Dec. 26, 1913; s. Ralph Spaulding and Maud (Hammond) C.; m. Barbara Priscilla Edgecomb, Sept. 12, 1936; children—Robert Earl, Thomas Spaulding, Elizabeth Jane. Student, Denver U., 1932-34; A.B., Wesleyan U., Middletown, Conn., 1936; B.D., Yale, 1940, Ph.D., 1942; L.H.D., Belmont (N.C.) Abbey, 1966. Ordained elder Methodist Ch., 1940; asst. pastor Meth. Ch., South Meriden, Conn., 1936-40, Park Meth. Ch., Hamilton, N.Y., 1941; instr. theology Yale Div. Sch., 1942-43; prof. religion U. Oreg., 1943-45; assoc. prof. theology Duke Div. Sch., 1945-48, prof., 1948-58, dean, 1958-71, rsch. prof., 1971-79, lectr. in residence, 1980-84, ret., 1979; ofcl. Meth. del. World Conf. Faith and Order, Lund, Sweden, 1952; founding mem. commn. ecumenical consultation Meth. Ch., 1958-64; mem. commn. ecumenical affairs United Meth. Ch., 1964-72, v.p., 1971-72; mem. N.A. commn. worship World Council Chs., 1954-63; ofcl. Meth. del. 4th World Conf. Faith and Order, Montreal, 1963; Meth. ofcl. observer 2d Vatican Council, Rome, 1963-65; mem. N.C. conf. Wesley Soc., 1955-62; mem. commn. ecumenical affairs Nat. Council Chs., 1965-70; mem. World Meth. Council, 1968-72; chmn. bd. dirs. Oxford Edit. Wesley Works Project, Inc., 1959-71, gen. editor, 1971-88, v.p., 1976-88; fellow Ecumenical Inst. Advanced Theol. Studies, Jerusalem, 1971-72; del. Gen. Conf., Meth. Church, 1964, 66, 68, 70, 72; mem. univ. senate United Meth. Ch., 1966-71; Meth. del. N.C. Council Chs., 1970-74. Author: (with Ralph S. Cushman) More Hilltop Verses and Prayers, 1947, Therapeia; Plato's Conception of Philosophy, 1958, The Heritage of Christian Thought, 1966, Faith Seeking Understanding, 1981; Wesley's Experimental Divinity: Studies in Methodist Doctrinal Standards, 1989, Socrates, Encyclopedia of Religion, 1987; contbr. articles to profl. jours. including Religion in Life, Church History, Contemporary Theology, et al. Recipient Tchr.-Scholar award Wesleyan U., 1967; Robert E. Cushman Chair of Christian Theol. Duke U. named in his honor, 1981. Mem. Assn. United Meth. Theol. Schs. (pres. 1964-66, mem. exec. com.), Duodecim Theol. Group, Am. Theol. Soc., Soc. Mayflower Descendents, Delta Kappa Epsilon, Phi Beta Kappa. Home: RR 1 PO Box 225 Newcastle ME 04553 *Other things being more or less equal, I find achievement to be perseverance in worthy causes and, in the face of obstacles, a determination to give the job what it takes. In my observation, resiliency and attainment are closely paired. Yet resiliency without verve may become doggedness, so that loyalty that is sparked by vision is that quality in greater men that objectifies motivation. The latter sires the rarity of self-transcendence and perhaps is, in turn, the signature of something we call faith. It is this, I believe, that keeps endeavor from going stale, that outruns misgivings and weighty evidence to the contrary, and alone has survival value for imperfect fulfillments of which life is composed.*

CUSTER, QUESSNAL STEWART, JR., minister, educator; b. Chgo., Apr. 1, 1931; s. Quessnal Stewart and Bessie M. (Akerstrom) C.; m. Carol Kistner, June 10, 1959; 1 child, Charles Steven. BA, Bob Jones U., 1955, MA, 1957, PhD, 1966. Ordained to ministry Bible Ch., 1983. Asst. prof. Bob Jones U., Greenville, S.C., 1955-60, prof. Bible, 1960—, chmn. div. Bible, 1967—, dir. Planetarium, 1960—; pastor Trinity Bible Ch., Greer, S.C., 1982—. Author: Does Inspiration Demand Inerrancy?, 1968, Treasury of New Testament Synonyms, 1975, The Stars Speak, 1977, Tools for Preaching and Teaching the Bible, 1979; founder, editor Biblical Viewpoint, 1967—. Mem. Western S.C. Gem and Mineral Soc. (life). Republican. Avocations: photography, mineral collecting, chess, travel.

CUTLER, LEROY RESPESS, clergyman; b. Washington County, N.C., Mar. 1, 1934; s. Leonard Leroy and Rosa Marie (Respess) C.; m. Eleanor Wilson Keech, July 20, 1952; children: Cynthia Elaine Cutler Biddle, Joseph Leroy, Gary LaVerne. BD, Free Will Bapt. Bible Coll., 1958; MDiv, Luther Rice Sem., 1977, DMin, 1979; postgrad. Tex. A. and M. U., 1965-66. Ordained to ministry Baptist Ch., 1955; comml. pilot CFII. Pastor First Free Will Bapt. Ch., Jacksonville, N.C., 1958-64, First Free Will Bapt. Ch., Bryan, Tex., 1964-74, Immanuel Free Will Bapt. Ch., Jacksonville, Fla., 1974—; moderator Greater St. Johns River Assn.; mem. Fla. State Mission Bd., Nat. Home Missions Bd., 1984-85, Hymn Book Revision Com., 1985-86; pres. Wing Air, Inc., 1986-89; cert. flight instr., 1969-89. Chaplain maj. CAP, 1986. Mem. Nat. Assn. Free Will Bapts. (chmn. steering com. 1989), Fla. State Assn. (moderator 1987—), Free Will Bapts. (moderator 1987-89), Aircraft Owners and Pilots Assn. Democrat. Baptist. Contbr. articles to Contact mag. Home: 10561 Villanova Rd Jacksonville FL 32218 Office: 6225 Norwood Ave Jacksonville FL 32208

CUTRONE, EMMANUEL JOSEPH, theology educator; b. Morgan City, La., Sept. 16, 1938; s. Lawrence Paul and Genevieve (Dimiceli) C.; m. Marcella Hrdina; children: Julie, Mary, Thomas, Joseph. BA in History, Notre Dame Sch. Theology, New Orleans, 1960, MA in History, 1963; MA in Liturgy, U. Notre Dame, 1964, PhD in Theology, 1975. Prof. theology Quincy (Ill.) Coll., 1970-86; prof. Spring Hill Coll., Mobile, Ala., 1986—; prof. liturgy U. Notre Dame, Ind., 1982—, St. John U., Collegeville, Minn., 1984-88; dir. Spring Hill Venice (Italy) Ctr., 1989-91. Ctr. for Ecumenical and Cultural Rsch. fellow, 1983. Mem. N.Am. Acad. Liturgy, Societas Liturgica. Roman Catholic. Office: Spring Hill Coll 4000 Dauphin St Mobile AL 36608

CUTTER, WILLIAM, educator; b. St. Louis, Feb. 9, 1937; s. Jack Robert and Gladys (Frank) C.; m. Georgianne Fischer, Oct. 25, 1970; 1 child, Benjamin Joseph. AB, Yale U., 1959; MA, Hebrew Union Coll., 1965; PhD, UCLA, 1971. Ordained rabbi, 1965. Asst. dean Hebrew Union Coll., L.A., 1965-70, dir., sch. edn., 1970-82, prof., 1982—; cons. Behrman House Pubs., West Orange, N.J., 1985—. Contbg. editor Jewish Spectator; contbr. articles on lit. and edn. to profl. publs. Bd. dirs. L.A. Jewish Feminist Ctr., Am. Jewish Congress; active numerous civic orgns. Recipient Cultural Arts award Jewish Fedn. of L.A., 1986. Mem. Yale Club, Cen. Conf. Am. Rabbis (bd. dirs.), Jewish TV Network (bd. dirs.), others. Avocations: tennis, reading, health activities. Office: Hebrew Union Coll 3077 University Los Angeles CA 90007

DACIUK, MYRON MICHAEL, bishop; b. Mundare, Alta., Can., Nov. 16, 1919; s. Lucas and Ksenia (Bruchkowsky) D. Student in philosophy and theology, Basilian Sem. Mundare, Grimsby, Ont., 1943-45. Ordained priest Ukrainian Catholic Ch., 1945, aux. bishop, 1982. Priest Ukrainian Cath. Ch., Can., 1945-82; bishop Ukrainian Cath. Ch., Winnipeg, Man., Can., 1982-90; superior Basilian Fathers, Mundare, 1959-64; superior Basilian Fathers, Edmonton, Alta., 1976-79, provincial superior, 1964-70. Home: 235

Scotia St, Winnipeg, MB Canada R2V 1V7 Office: Winnipeg Archeparchy, 235 Scotia St, Winnipeg, MB Canada R2V 1V7

DAECKE, SIGURD MARTIN, systematic theology educator; b. Hamburg, Germany, Nov. 22, 1932; s. Herbert and Maria (Rueth) D.; m. Rosemarie Seeger, Dec. 4, 1964; children: Dirk Martin, Nils Christian. ThD, Hamburg U., 1967. Asst. pastor Luth. Ch., Hamburg, 1957-59; asst. prof. Hamburg U., 1959-61; ch. editor Deutsches Allgemeines Sonntagsblatt, Hamburg, 1961-63; pastor Luth. Ch., Hamburg, 1963-64; pastor, editor Evangelical Ch. in Germany, Stuttgart, 1964-70, chief editor Evangelische Kommentare, 1970-72; prof. Aachen (Fed. Republic Germany) U. Edn., 1972-80; prof. systematic theology Aachen U. Tech., 1980—. Author: Teilhard de Chardin, 1967, The Death-of-God Myth, 1969, also editor: Basis of Theology, 1974, Kann man Gott aus der Natur erkennen?, 1990; editor, author introduction: Albert Einstein, Worte in Zeit und Raum, 1991; contbr. articles to profl. jours. Mem. Sci. Soc. for Theology, Acad. Assn. Theology. Avocations: sailing, skiing. Home: Flandrische Str 36, W-5100 Aachen Federal Republic of Germany Office: Univ Tech, Templergraben 55, W-5100 Aachen Federal Republic of Germany *Matter of our faith is not only the relation between God and man but also between God and nature, God and environment. The peace of God is peace with nature too.*

DAGNEL, BOBBY CHARLES, minister; b. Tyler, Tex., Aug. 2, 1958; s. Charles Moran and Barby Nell (Fowler) D.; m. Patti Ann Calley, May 21, 1983; 1 child, Courtney Brooke. BBA, U. Tex., Tyler, 1984; MDiv, Southwestern Bapt. Theol. Sem., Ft. Worth, 1987. Ordained to ministry Bapt. Ch. Asst. min. recreation Green Acres Bapt. Ch., Tyler, 1983-84; min. bus. adminstrn. First Bapt. CH., Tuscaloosa, Ala., 1985-88; pastor First Bapt. Ch., Hemphill, Tex., 1989—. Sustaining mem. Rep. Nat. Com. Fellow Nat. Assn. Ch. Bus. Adminstrs. Home: P O Drawer R Hemphill TX 75948 Office: First Bapt Ch P O Drawer Hemphill TX 75948

DAHDAH, PAUL, archbishop. Archbishop of Baghdad Roman Cath. Ch., Iraq. Office: Archeveche Latin, POB 2090, Wahdah 904/8/44, Baghdad Iraq*

DAHLBERG, GILBERT EDWARD, priest; b. Chgo., Oct. 11, 1933; s. Gilbert Edward and Helen Miriam (Watkiss) D.; m. Mary Garrett Price, Feb. 2, 1985. AB, U. Chgo., 1954; MDiv., Seabury Western Theol. Sem., Evanston, Ill., 1962. Ordained priest Episcopal Ch., 1962. Chgo. area dir. U. Chgo. Alumni Found., 1956-57; curate St. Gregory's Episcopal Ch., Deerfield, Ill., 1962-65; rector St. Barnabas Episcopal Ch., Denver, 1965-83; v.p. Extensive Care Inc., Dayton, Ohio, 1984-88; rector Episcopal Ch. of Epiphany, Urbana, Ill., 1989—; Treas. Capitol Hill Community Ctr., Denver, 1977-82; bd. dirs., treas. ch. community svc. Colo. Coun. Chs., Denver, 1979-81. Founding dir., bd. dirs. Family Svc. Agy. of Champaign and Clark Counties; bd. dirs. Rocky Mountain Kidney Found., Denver, 1968-72; mem. Huffman Hist. Area Soc., Dayton. With U.S. Army, 1957-58. Named one of Outstanding Young Men of Am., U.S. Jaycees, 1965. Fellow Coll. of Preachers of Washington Nat. Cathedral; mem. Phi Delta Theta (treas. 1952-54). Republican. Home: 119 Lafayette Ave Urbana OH 43078 Office: Episcopal Ch of Epiphany 230 Scioto St at Kenton Urbana OH 43078

DAHLBURG, ANDREW DICKENS, lay worker; b. Upper Montclair, N.J., Sept. 24, 1956; s. Donald Russell and Madeline (Blackadore) D. BA, Geneva Coll., Beaver Falls, Pa., 1979; PhM, St. Andrews (Scotland) U., 1985; MDiv, Edinburgh U., Scotland, 1988; postgrad., Rutgers U., 1990—. Health technician VA, Lyons, N.J., 1989—; youth dir. St. Bernard's Ch., Bernardsville, N.J., 1989-90; singles dir. Good Samaritan Ch., Paoli, Pa., 1988-89; pres. New Coll. Missionary Soc., U. Edinburgh, 1985-88. Mem. Toastmasters. Home: 40 S Fifth Ave Highland Park NJ 08904 Office: VA Med Center Lyons NJ 07939

DAHLING, DANIEL FRED, clergyman; b. Milw., Jan. 4, 1957; s. Fred W. and Suzanne E. (Foelber) D.; m. Tamara S. Buhr, July 11, 1981; children: Henry, Lydia. BA, Ind. U., 1979; MDiv, Concordia Theol. Sem., Ft. Wayne, Ind., 1983. Ordained to ministry Luth. Ch., Mo. Synod., 1983. Pastor Trinity Luth. Sch., Lansing, Ill., 1983-87, Zion Friedheim Luth. Ch. and Sch., Decatur, Ind., 1987—; advisor Decatur Zone Luth. Layman's League, 1988—. Author: O Come Let Us Worship The Lord, 1989. Mem. Lutherans for Life. Republican. Avocations: gardening, sports. Home and Office: Rte 8 Box 289A Decatur IN 46733

DAHLSTEIN, DAVID KEITH, minister; b. Indepedance, Mo., Dec. 24, 1959; s. Richard Oscar and Hilda Darlene (Richardson) D.; m. Vanessa Faye Lowe, June 5, 1982; children: Mary Elizabeth, Sarah Dianne, Leann Renee, David Keith Jr. B in Biblical Literature, Ozark Bible Coll., Joplin, Mo., 1982; M of Ministry, Cin. Christian Sem., 1986. Ordained to ministry Grain Valley Christian Ch., 1981. Asst. basketball coach Cin. Bible Coll., 1982-83; min. Ch. of Christ, St. Mary's, Ohio, 1983-90, Park St. Christian Ch., El Dorado Springs, Mo., 1990—; instr. Christian Tng. Ctr., St. Mary's, 1985—. Mgr. St. Mary's Little League, 1986. Named one of Outstanding Young Men Am., 1985. Mem. St. Mary's Ministerial Assn. Republican. Avocations: golf, baseball card collecting. Home: 212 W Fields El Dorado Springs MO 64744 Office: Park St Christian Ch PO Box 32 El Dorado MO 64744

DAHM, DONALD JAMES, lay worker, chemical company executive; b. Mahaska County, Iowa, Oct. 26, 1941; s. Leonard and Gertrude (Bandstra) D.; m. Arlene Faye Tysseling, June 5, 1964; children: Jeffrey Michael, Kevin Douglas, Melissa Lee. BA, Cen. Coll., Pella, Iowa, 1963; PhD, Iowa State U., 1968. Dir. R&D Monsanto Chem. Co., Springfield, Mass., 1968—; moderator, bd. deacons St. Mark United Presbyn. Ch., Ballwin, Mo., 1974-77; moderator, bd. deacons Southminster United Presbyn. Ch., Centerville, Ohio, 1979-81, chmn. bd. govs., 1989-90; lectr. sci. and religion; ch. sch. instr. various chs., 1973—. Contbr. articles to various periodicals. Organizer, 1st pres. Lafayette Work Ctr., Manchester, Mo., 1975; v.p. Pioneer Valley Child and Family Svcs. Bd., Springfield, 1985-90. Mem. United Ch. of Christ. Home: 90 Chapin Green Ludlow MA 01056 Office: Monsanto Chem Co 730 Worcester St Springfield MA 01151 *Many people assume the "faith" is being intellectually convinced that something is true. Actually, faith is deciding to live as if something were true, frequently in the absence of evidence and somtimes in the face of evidence to the contrary.*

DAILY, JAMES MILFORD, minister; b. Fairmount, Ind., Apr. 9, 1926; s. James Arthur and Olive Elizabeth (Johnson) D.; m. Twila Jean Parker, June 30, 1962; children: Thomas R., Shelly L., Michael F. BS, Ball State U., 1952; MDiv, Lexington Theol. Sem., 1982, DMin, 1986. Ordained to ministry Christian Ch. (Disciples of Christ). Commd. 2d lt. USAF, 1952, advanced through grades to maj., ret., 1973; assoc. pastor First Christian Ch., Fayetteville, N.C., 1978-79; pastor Morgan (Ky.) Christian Ch., 1979-83; sr. pastor Ayden (N.C.) Christian Ch., 1983—; chair pers. com. N.C. region Disciples of Christ, Wilson, N.C., 1989—, rep. to United Ch. of Christ, 1987-89; chair ecumenical com. Gov.'s Coun. on Substance Abuse Among Children and Youth, 1987—. Contbr. articles to religious jours. Active Ayden Mental Health Assn. Mem. Acad. Parish Clergy, Nat. Christian Counselors Assn., Rotary (pres. Ayden club 1985-86). Office: Ayden Christian Ch 115 W 2d St PO Box 488 Ayden NC 28513

DAILY, SANDRA, minister; b. Davenport, Iowa. BA, U. Nebr., Omaha, 1972; MTh, Boston U., 1976; D Ministry, Andover Newton Theol. Sch., 1980. Ordained to ministry Luth. Ch., 1976. Co-pastor Our Saviour Luth. Ch., East Boston, Mass., 1976-79, St. Olaf Evang. Luth. Ch., Detroit, 1979-82; pastor Good Hope Luth. Ch., Detroit, 1987—; chaplain Mich. Dept. Corrections, Plymouth, Mich., 1985—; sec. banking and legal cos., 1959-62; adminstrv. asst. U.S. Ho. of Reps., Washington, 1962-68; com. chmn. specialized ministry SE Mich. Synod Evang. Luth. Ch. in Am., 1991, mem. specialized ministry com., 1990, mem. profl. leadership, 1989. Contbr. articles to profl. jours. Mem. Am. Correctional Assn., Coll. of Chaplains, Am. Correctional Chaplain's Assn. Office: Western Wayne Correctional Facility 48401 Five Mile Plymouth MI 48170 *We need to relook at our concept of the separation of church and state, invest more in pastoral psychotherapy expertise and establish a source to license chaplains for state correctional facilities.*

DAILY, THOMAS V., bishop; b. Belmont, Mass., Sept. 23, 1927. Student, Boston Coll., St. John's Sem., Brighton, Mass. Ordained priest Roman Cath. Ch., 1952; missionary Peru as mem. Soc. St. James the Apostle; ordained titular bishop of Bladia and aux. bishop Boston, 1975-84; first bishop Palm Beach, Fla., 1984-90; bishop Diocese of Bklyn., 1990—. Address: Chancery Office 75 Greene Ave Box C Brooklyn NY 11202

DAILY, TODD EUGENE, missionary; b. Grand Island, Nebr., Oct. 17, 1963; s. Delbert Dean Daily and Virginia Rae (Pearson) Gwinner; m. Dawn Arlana Carlblom, June 4, 1988. BA with honors, Faith Bapt. Bible Coll., 1987; MTh summa cum laude, Faith Bapt. Theol. Sem., 1989, MDiv summa cum laude, 1990. Ordained to ministry Bapt. Ch., Iowa. Missionary Bapt. Mid-Missions, Cleve., 1989—. Mem. Delta Epsilon Chi. Republican.

DAKE, CHARLES SAFELY, JR., minister; b. St. Paul, Minn., Nov. 11, 1952; s. Charles Safely and Margaret Lorraine (Zakariasen) D.; m. Sharon Gail Houston, June 24, 1978. BA in History and Philosophy summa cum laude, Trinity Coll., Deerfield, Ill., 1975; MDiv summa cum laude, Trinity Evang. Div. Sch., 1979. Ordained to ministry Evang. Free Ch. Am., 1984. Intern pastor Elim Mission Ch., Cokato, Minn., 1976; pastor Saguaro Evang. Free Ch., Tucson, 1979-85, sr. pastor, 1983-85; dean students, internat. student advisor Trinity Evang. Div. Sch., 1985-90; sr. pastor Glenview (Ill.) Evang. Free Ch., 1990—; bd. dirs. S.W. Border dist. Evang. Free Ch. Am., Phoenix, 1980-83, vice chmn., 1981-82. Recipient Lincoln Medallion State of Ill., 1975. Mem. Evang. Free Ch. Ministerial Assn., Trinity Evang. Div. Sch. Alumni Assn. (bd. dirs., sec. 1981-85). Democrat. Home: 135 Montgomery Ln Glenview IL 60025-4924 Office: Glenview Evang Free Ch 2 Shermer Rd Glenview IL 60025 *Faith in Jesus Christ as one's Savior and Lord brings ultimate meaning to life. Our sojourn on earth becomes an important, but brief, preface co-authored by God and ourselves. The best remains to be written.*

DAKE, JAMES EMMIT, minister; b. Mountain Grove, Mo., Sept. 6, 1925; s. Jacob Huston and Lillie Ellen (Long) D.; m. Dolores Rosalie Cross, Sept. 20, 1956; children: Rosalie Dake Alcoser, Emily Dake Inman. BD, Clarksville Theol. Sem., 1955; PhD, Pioneer Theol. Sem., 1959; ThD, Burton Theol. Sem., 1965; DD (hon.), Burton Coll. and Sem., 1956. Ordained to ministry So. Bapt. Conv., 1949. Pastor Galloway Bapt. Ch., Springfield, Mo., 1956-57, Howlandville Bapt. Ch., Warrensville, S.C., 1957-59, DeSoto Park Bapt. Ch., Rome, Ga., 1959-67, 1st Bapt. Ch., Graniteville, S.C., 1967-75, Providence Bapt. Ch., New Bloomfield, Mo., 1975-86, Solid Rock Bapt. Ch., Linn, Mo., 1986—; moderator Aiken (S.C.) Bapt. Assn., 1974-75, Callaway Bapt. Assn., Auxvasse, Mo., 1984-85. Mem. Dixon Bapt. Assn. (moderator-elect 1991), Charles Haddon Spurgeon Soc. Home: Rte 2 Box 214 Linn MO 65051 Office: Solid Rock Bapt Ch Rte 2 Box 214 Linn MO 65051 *Life is full of decisions. For the right choices we must read the Bible to find God's principles and apply them to our decision making for successful living.*

DAKIN, PAUL EDWARD, minister; b. Key West, Fla., July 5, 1956; s. John Castle and Mary Ellen (Friemuth) D.; m. Miriam Marie Goodwin, June 13, 1987. B in Music Edn., U. Montevallo, 1979; postgrad., So. Bapt. Theol Sem., Louisville, 1986—. Lic. to ministry Bapt. Ch., 1986. Min. music and youth Zama Bapt. Ch., Tokyo, 1980-82, 4th Ave. Bapt. Ch., Birmingham, Ala., 1983-86; min. music Lynn Acres Bapt. Ch., Louisville, 1986-89, Audubon Bapt. Ch., Louisville, 1989—; chair spiritual life So. Bapt. Theol. Sem., 1991—. Mem. Hymn Soc. in the U.S. and Can. (pres. Louisville chpt. 1990-91), Am. Guild English Handbell Ringers. Home: 2825 Lexington Rd Box 1477 Louisville KY 40280 Office: Audubon Bapt Ch 1046 Hess Ln Louisville KY 40217

DALAGER, LLOYD, religious organization head. Chmn. Israelite House of David, Benton Harbor, Mich. Office: Israelite House of David PO Box 1067 Benton Harbor MI 49022*

DALAI LAMA (TENZIN GYATSO), supreme temporal and religious head of Tibet; b. Taktser, Amdo province, Tibet, July 6, 1935; s. Chokyong and Diki Tsering. LittD (hon.), Banaras Hindu U., Varanasi, India, 1957; D in Buddhist Philosophy, Monasteries of Sera, Drepung and Gaden, Lhasa, 1959; DD, The Carroll Coll., Waukesha, Wis., 1979, Cen. Inst. for Higher Tibetan Studies, 1990; D of Buddhist Philosophy, U. of Oriental Studies, L.A., 1979; HHD, Seattle U., 1979; D (hon.), U. de Paris X Naterre Cedex, 1984. Enthroned Dalai Lama XIV Lhasa, 1940; was requested to assume full polit. power, 1950, fled to Chumbi in South Tibet on Chinese invasion, 1950, negotiated with China, 1951, fled to India after abortive revolt of Tibetan people against Communist Chinese, 1959; established govt.-in-exile Dharamsala, India; mem. nat. com. Chinese People's Polit. Consultative Conf., 1951-59; hon. chmn. China Buddhist Assn., 1953-59; del. Nat. Productivity Council, 1954-59, vice chmn. standing com.; chmn. preparatory com. Autonomous Region Tibet, 1955-59; announced Five-Point Peace Plan on future of Tibet in speech to U.S. Congl. Human Rights Caucus, 1987; speaker at European Parliament, Strasbourg, France, 1988. Author: My Land and My People, 1962, The Opening of the Wisdom Eye, 1963, An Introduction to Buddhism, 1965, Key to the Middle Way, 1971, Universal Responsibility and Good Heart, 1977, Four Essential Buddhist Commentaries, 1982, Kindness, Clarity and Insight, 1984, 87, A Human Approach to World Peace, 1984, Freedom in Exile, 1990, others. Recipient Magsaysay award, 1959, Admiral Richard E. Byrd Meml. award Internat. Rescue com., 1959, Lincoln award Rsch. Inst. Am., 1960, Plakett award Norwegian Refugee Council, Alber Schweitzer Humanitarian award, 1987, Special medal Asian Buddhist Council for Peace, 1979, Nobel Peace prize, 1989, Raoul Wallenberg Congl. Human Rights award Congl. Human Rights Found., 1989, Le Prix De La Memoire, Found. Danielle Mitterrand, 1989. Address: Thekchen Choeling, McLeod Ganj, 176219 Dharamsala Himachal Pradesh, India

DALBERG, LEONARD EDWIN, retired minister; b. Stratton, Ont., Can., Oct. 9, 1925; came to U.S., 1946; s. Carl and Signe (Carlson) D.; m. Anabelle Shirley Hanson, Sept. 9, 1950; children: Denise, Lana, Ben, Janelle. BA, Augsburg Coll., 1952; BD, Luth. Sch. Theology Chgo., 1955. Ordained to ministry Luth. Ch., 1956. Minister Faith Luth. Ch., Caldwell, Idaho, 1955-61, Elim Luth. Ch., Ogden, Utah, 1961-67, Good Shepherd Luth. Ch., Concord, Calif., 1967-76, Our Saviour's Luth. Ch., Orange, Calif., 1976-84, Bethania Luth. Ch., Solvang, Calif., 1984-89; retired, 1989; dean Utah dist. Am. Luth. Ch., 1962-67, Sem. dist., No. Calif., 1969-70, So. dist., So. Calif., 1982-84, Intermountain dist., Idaho and Utah, 1957-61. Mem. Rotary (sec. Santa Ynez Valley club 1987-89). Democrat. Home: 330 W Hwy 246 # 39 Buellton CA 93427

DALE, ALFRED STUART, missionary, minister; b. Bismarck, N.D., Mar. 18, 1926; s. Alfred S. and Jenny (Lusk) D.; m. Dorothy Anna Pikas, Sept. 5, 1948; children: Eric S., Daniel T., Ana K. Gobledale. BS, George Williams Coll., 1949; BD, U. Chgo., 1952; MA, U. So. Calif., L.A., 1959; postgrad., San Francisco State U., 1961-68; MTh, D Religion, Chgo. Theol. Sem., 1969. Ordained to ministry United Meth. Ch., 1950. Campus pastor U. So. Calif. Wesley Found., L.A., 1952-54, Western Wash. U., Bellingham, 1955-58, San Francisco State U., 1961-68; exec. v.p., provost Cen. YMCA Coll., Chgo., 1969-75; pres. Soc. Edn. Rsch. Devel. Inc., Santa Cruz, Calif., 1978-82; missionary Gen. Bd. Global Ministries United Meth. Ch., Fiji, Poland, 1982-88; missionary Peace with Justice Educators, 1988-91; participant confs. Student Christian Movement, 1946-78. Author: Christ and Culture in Fiji, 1983, Plant for Tomorrow, 1984, To Be a Pilgrim, 1991. Chair Ocean View, Merced Heights, Ingleside Community Orgn., San Francisco, 1962-68. 1st lt. U.S. Army, 1943-48, 59-65. Home and Office: 741 Chuckanut Dr Bellingham WA 98226

DALE, DARYL D., religious organization administrator; b. Dallas, Oreg., June 11, 1943; s. Charles H. and Elizabeth (Grandia) D.; m. Janet L. Johnson, Sept. 14, 1978; children: Julie Ann, Timothy Chip, Heidi Jo. BA in Psychology, San Diego State U., 1976; MA in Christian Edn., Wheaton (Ill.) Grad. Sch., 1978. Pastor Wilmot Alliance Ch., Tucson, 1978-84; dist. dir. Christian edn. The Christian and Missionary Alliance, Canby, Oreg., 1984-88; nat. dir. Christian edn. The Christian and Missionary Alliance, Colorado Springs, Colo., 1988—. Author: Teaching Basics for Primaries, 1985, Teaching Basics for Juniors, 1985, Teaching Basics for Youth, 1985, Teaching Basics for Adults, 1985, Christian Education Basics for Smaller Churches, 1990. Office: The Christian and Missionary Alliance 8595 Explorer Dr Colorado Springs CO 80920

DALE, JUDY RIES, religious organization administrator, educational consultant; b. Memphis, Dec. 13, 1944; d. James Lorigan and Julia Marie (Schwinn) Ries; m. Eddie Melvin Ashmore, July 12, 1969 (div. Dec. 1983). BA, Rhodes Coll., 1966; M in Religious Edn., So. Bapt. Theol. Sem., 1969, Grad. Specialist in Religious Edn., 1969. Cert. tchr. educable mentally handicapped, secondary English adminstrn. and supervision in spl. edn. EMH tchr., curriculum writer, tchr. trainer Jefferson County Bd. Edn., Louisville, 1969-88, ednl. cons., 1988-90; dist. coord. Great Lakes Dist. Universal Fellowship Met. Community Chs., Louisville, 1990—; lectr. Jefferson Community Coll., Louisville, 1987—, U. Louisville, 1976-77, 1987—; mem. program advisory com. Internat. Conf. Spl. Edn., Bejing, 1987-88; gen. coun. Universal Fellowship Met. Community Chs., mem. steering com. Women's Secretariat; mem. Elder's Ministry on Evangelism, Samaritan Coll. Task Force. Editor, writer: (handbook) Handbook for Beginning Teachers, 1989, A Manual of Instructional Strategies, 1985; author: (kit) Math Activities Cards, 1978. Bd. sec. Comm. Ten, Inc., Louisville, 1987—; active Greater Louisville Human Rights Commn., 1985—, Ky. Civil Liberties Union, 1986—; v.p. GLUE, 1988—. Recipient Honorable Order of Ky. Cols., 1976; named Outstanding Elem. Tchr. Am., 1975. Mem. NOW, Coun. Exceptional Children (keynote speaker 1984-88, internat. pres. 1986-87, exec. com. 1984-88, bd. govs. 1981-88), Ky. Coun. Exceptional Children (bd. 1976—, Mem of Yr. 1987), Internat. Platform Assn., Women's Alliance, Phi Delta Kappa. Democrat. Universal Fellowship of Metro. Community Chs. Avocations: people, church work, reading, handwork. Home and Office: 1300 Ambridge Dr Louisville KY 40207-2410

DALE, LEONARD ALVIN, missionary; b. Hiawatha, Kans., Jan. 7, 1921; s. Charles Fred Dale and Melda Diller; m. Meta Dargatz, Apr. 7, 1945; children—Sharon, Leonard, Roxane, E'Lona, Yvonne. M.S.T., Concordia U., 1945. Ordained to ministry Lutheran Church Missouri Synod, 1945. Pastor, Chambers, Nebr., 1945-50, Wichita, Kans., 1950-69; missionary, Seoul, Korea, 1969-76, Luth. Ctr., Philippines, 1976—. Named Man of Yr., Kans. Jaycees. Lodges: Lions, Rotary. Home: 1648 Rizal Ave, Olongapo City 2201, The Philippines

DALE, LEONARD ALVIN, JR., pastor; b. Norfolk, Nebr., May 11, 1949; s. Leonard Alvin and Meta (Dargatz) D.; m. Anne Catherine Taylor, June 26, 1971; children: Emily, Aaron, Ryan. AA, St. John's Jr. Coll., Winfield, Kans., 1969; BA, Concordia Sr. Coll., 1971; MDiv, Christ Sem., 1975. Assoc. pastor Calvary Luth. Ch., Ferguson, Mo., 1975-77; pastor Hope Luth. Ch., Fergus Falls, Minn., 1977-88; chaplain Fergus Falls Treatment Ctr., 1977-88; pastor Trinity Luth. Ch., Great Bend, Kans., 1988—; instr. in polit. sci. Fergus Falls Community Coll., 1986-88; guest lectr. Larned (Kans.) St. Hosp., bd. dirs. Barton County Youth Care, Great Bend, 1989—, Barton County Young Men's Orgn., Great Bend, 1988—; synod rep. Task Force on Youth and Sexuality, 1989—. Coord. Mo./Kans. Jr. Youth Event, 1991; mem., pres. New Life for Teen Parents, Great Bend, 1991—. Mem. Great Bend Ministerial Alliance (pres. 1990-91), Ambucs, Rotary (treas. Fergus Falls 1986-87). Home: 3108 28th St Great Bend KS 56537 Office: Trinity Luth Ch 2701 24th Great Bend KS 56537

DALE, ROBERT DENNIS, minister, church official; b. Neosho, Mo., Aug. 23, 1940; s. Ivan A. and Jewel (Kingry) D.; m. Carrie Kondy, Aug. 25, 1962; children: Cass, Amy. BA, Okla. Bapt. U., 1962; BD, Southwestern Bapt. Theol. Sem., 1966, PhD, 1970. Ordained to ministry Bapt. Ch., 1960. Min. local chs. Kans., Tex., Okla. and Mo., 1959-73; cons. Bapt. Sunday Sch. Bd., Nashville, 1973-77; prof. Southeastern Bapt. Theo. Sem., Wake Forest, N.C., 1977-88; dir. ch. and min. support Va. Bapt. Gen. Bd., Richmond, 1989—; bd. dirs. Life Enrichment Ctr., Raleigh, N.C., 1985-88, Va. Inst. for Pastoral Care, Richmond, 1989—, Richmond Hill, Richmond, 1991—; cons. Master Design, Inc., 1990—. Author: To Dream Again, 1981, Keeping the Dream Alive, 1988, Pastoral Leadership, 1988, also 12 other profl. books. Office: Va Bapt Gen Bd PO Box 8568 Richmond VA 23226

DALEY, ALEXANDER SPOTSWOOD, priest; b. Boston, Apr. 4, 1935; s. Robert Francis and Louisa (Watson) D. AB, Harvard Coll., 1957; STB, Episcopal Theol. Sch., 1971; D of Ministry, Pitts. Theol. Sem., 1984. Ordained to ministry Episcopal Ch. as deacon, 1971, as priest, 1972. Asst. rector St. George's Ch., Dayton, Ohio, 1971-73; chaplain Bishop of Fulham and Gibraltar, London, 1973-75; priest-in-charge St. Augustine's Anglican Ch., Stephenville, Newfoundland, 1975-76; rector St. Paul's Episcopal Ch., North Andover, Mass., 1976—; chaplain First Corps of Cadets, Boston, 1989—; dep. chaplain Soc. of Colonial Wars in Mass., Boston, 1990—; exec. com. Lawrence (Mass.) Coun. of Chs., 1983—; treas. Phillips Brooks Clericus, Cambridge, 1990—; Episcopal commisary to archbishop Diocese of Western Newfoundland, 1991—; chmn. Order of St. Luke. Gov. Groton (Mass.) Sch., 1984—; dir. C.L.A.S.S., Inc., Lawrence, 1983. Lt. comdr. USNR, ret. Republican. Office: St Pauls Episcopal Ch 390 Main St North Andover MA 01845

DALLEN, (RICHARD) JAMES, priest, religious educator; b. Concordia, Kans., Apr. 16, 1943; s. Vern L. and Clementine (Breault) D. BA, St. Mary's Coll., 1965; STB, Cath. U., 1968, MA, 1969, STD, 1976. Assoc. pastor St. Andrews Parish, Abilene, Kans., 1969-73; assoc. prof. Rosemont (Pa.) Coll., 1975-82; assoc. prof. Gonzaga U., Spokane, Wash., 1982—, chair religious studies dept., 1990—; chair Diocesan Liturgical Commn., Spokane, 1986-90. Author: Reconciling Community, 1986, Gathering for Eucharist, 1983; contbr. articles to profl. jours. Mem. Cath. Theol. Soc., Coll. Theology Soc. (Best book 1987), N.Am. Acad. Liturgy, Socs. Liturgica, Am. Acad. Religion. Office: Gonzaga U Spokane WA 99258

DALLENBACH, ROBERT BARNEY, bishop, educator; b. Brunswick, N.J., Aug. 6, 1927; s. Jacob William and Bertha Cornelia (Christenson) D.; m. Pauline Alma White; children: Alma Beth, Joel William. Cert., Zarephath Bible Sem., 1947; AB, Alma White Coll., 1949; MA in Physics, Columbia U., 1956; PhD, U. Colo., 1973. Cert. tchr., Colo. Deacon Pillar of Fire Ch., Zarephath, N.J., 1948-52, elder, 1952-67, presiding elder, 1967-84, bishop, 1984—; pres. Friends of Alma White Coll. (Alumni Assn.), Zarephath, 1956-60; acting dean Alma White Coll., Zarephath, 1962-63, Belleview Coll., Westminster, Colo., 1966-67; pres. Belleview Coll., Westminster, 1974—; teaching assoc. engrng. dept. U. Colo., Boulder, 1968 summer; dean Belleview Bible Sem., Westminster, 1971-74; gen. mgr. Radio Sta. KPOF, Denver, 1965—; pres. Belleview Schs., Westminster, 1984—. Photographer: (book) Dear Friends, 1952. Pres. Brico Symphony Orch., Denver, 1980, Centennial Philharmonic, Denver, 1985—; mem. com. People for Progress, Westminster, 1973; mem. exec. com., mem. at large Northwest Metro Denver Crusade for Christ; mem. com. Colo. Prayer Network. Recipient Disting. Svc. to Community award Westminster and Dist. 50, Colo., 1969; U. Colo. grantee Ednl. Media Inst., 1967-68. Mem. Nat. Religious Broadcasters Assn. (with press credentials), Colo. Working Press, Columbia U. Grad./Faculty Alumni Assn., Alumni Assn. U. Colo., Phi Delta Kappa (Colo. U. chpt.). Republican. Avocations: photography, cycling, mountain climbing, skiing, vocal and instrumental music. Home: 8201 King St Westminster CO 80030 Office: Sta KPOF 910 AM 3455 W 83rd Ave Westminster CO 80030

DALRYMPLE, INA LYNN, deaconess, retired hospital administrator; b. Portalnd, Jamaica, Jan. 7, 1926; d. Lorenzo Joachiam and Eva Retinella (Fuller) Clachar; m. Lawrence A. Dalrymple, Oct. 15, 1955; children: Lawrence A. Jr., Denise. BA, CUNY, 1952. Ordained deacon So. Bapt. Ch., 1987. Tchr. Christian edn. Assembly of God, N.Y.C., 1958-65, pres. women's ministries, 1965-73; dir. children and youth ministries various chs., N.Y., 1975-82; sec.-treas. Fla. Bapt. Mins. Wives Assn., Ft. Lauderdale, 1985-86; deaconess, pres. Women's Missionary Union, Bethel Bapt. Ch., Ft. Lauderdale, 1987—, pres. corp., 1985—, del., 1986-90; religious counselor Calvary and Cathedral chs., L.I., N.Y., 1975-82; Editor monthly children's newsletter Spotlight, 1975-82. Commr. deeds City of N.Y., 1956-83; mem. policy com. Baldwin (N.Y.) Schs., 1974-75. Mem. Christian Bus. Women's Fellowship, Notary Pub. Assn. Davie-Ft. Lauderdale. Democrat. Home: 2390 NW 34th Terr Fort Lauderdale FL 33311 Office: 150 NW 46th Ave Plantation FL 33317 *Life has a way of molding us into creatures who are either spiritually mellow or else hardened and bitter. To fear God and to think positive will ultimately mold us into vessels for adequate service.*

DALTON, RONNIE THOMAS, minister; b. Dayton, Ohio, Apr. 25, 1953; s. Merl Thomas and Luttie (Scrimager) D.; m. Martha Gomer, Oct. 15, 1977; children: John Thomas, James Douglas, Stephen Wade. AA, Mt. Vernon Nazarene Coll., 1973; BA, Trevecca Nazarene Coll., 1975; MDiv, Nazarene Theol. Sem., 1979; D Ministry, Vanderbilt U., 1984. Ordained to ministry Ch. of Nazarene, 1983. Pastor Ch. of Brethren, St. Joseph, Mo., 1977-78; assoc. pastor Grace Nazarene Ch., Chattanooga, 1979-80; v.p. Nazarene Youth Internat., Dist. E. Tenn., 1982-84; teaching asst. Vanderbilt Div. Sch., Nashville, 1983-84; pastor West View Nazarene Ch., Lebanon, Tenn., 1980-85, Montana Ave Nazarene Ch., Cin., 1985—; adj. prof. religion Mt. Vernon Nazarene Coll.; dir. mins. tng. seminars Antioch U. Mem. Soc. Bibl. Lit., Religious Rsch. Assn., Wesleyan Theol. Soc. Avocations: computer programming and design, golf, antique auto rebuilding. Home and Office: 2559 Montana Ave Cincinnati OH 45211 *The challenge of holiness is to reconcile our experiences of Being in the World and those of Being in Christ. It is an ethic which is both personal and social, attained by both personal struggle and Divine gift.*

DALUZ, SISTER LUCIA, school system administrator. Supt. schs. Roman Cath. Diocese of El Paso, Tex. Office: Office Supt Schs 499 St Matthews El Paso TX 79907*

DALY, ALEXANDER JOSEPH, minister; b. Jersey City, May 23, 1930; s. Alexander Joseph and Viola (Fell) D.; m. Mary Kay Baughman, Aug. 20, 1960. BA, Lenoir-Rhyne Coll., 1958; MDiv, Luth. Sch. Theol., 1962. Ordained to ministry Luth. Ch. in Am., 1962. Pastor St. James Luth. Ch., Folsom, N.J., 1962-64; assoc. pastor Trinity Luth. Ch., Lemoyne, Pa., 1964-71, Redeemer Luth. Ch., Atlanta, 1971-80; campus pastor Ga. Inst. Tech., Atlanta, 1980—; chaplain Luth. Towers, Atlanta, 1980—; cons. Downtown Atlanta Sr. Svcs., 1983-84. Coord. Community Head Start Program, Lemoyne, 1977-78; chmn. County-Wide Meals on Wheels, Lemoyne, 1978-79. Office: Luth Towers 727 Juniper St NE Atlanta GA 30308

DALY, CAHAL BRENDAN CARDINAL, cardinal, archbishop; b. Loughguile, Northern Ireland, Oct. 1, 1917. Student, St. Malachy's Coll., Belfast, Northern Ireland; M.A., Queen's U., Belfast, hon. doctorate; D.D., St. Patrick's Coll., Maynooth, Ireland, 1944; L.Ph., Institut Catholique, Paris, 1953. Ordained priest Roman Cath. Ch. Lectr., reader in scholastic philosophy Queen's U., 1946-67; bishop of Ardagh and Clonmacnois Roman Cath. Ch., Longford, Ireland, 1967-82; bishop of Down and Connor Belfast, 1982-90; archbishop of Armagh, primate of all Ireland, 1990—; cardinal archbishop Roman Cath. Ch., 1991—. Author: Morals, Law and Life, 1962, Natural Law, Morality Today, 1965, Violence in Ireland and Christian Conscience, 1973, Peace, the Work of Justice, 1980, The Price of Peace, 1991. Office: Archdiocese Roman Cath Ch, Armagh Northern Ireland

DALY, SISTER CATHERINE MARY, nun, religious community administrator; b. Jersey City, May 25, 1938; d. Michael and Mary J. (Fynn) D. BA, Caldwell Coll., 1965; MS, Marquette U., 1970. Joined Dominican Sisters, Roman Catholic Ch., 1955. Tchr. chemistry Lacordaire Sch., Upper Montclair, N.J., 1962-68; assoc. prof. Caldwell (N.J.) Coll., 1971-79, CUNY, 1979-81; dir. Campaign Human Devel. Cath. Community Services, Newark, 1983-86; dir. social ministry Cath. Community Services, Newark, 1987—; cons. N. Hudson Chs., W. New York, N.J., 1984—. Mem. adv. bd. women's ctr. Essex Community Coll., 1982—, cons., 1983—; mem. selectors com. Regional Health Planning Commn., Newark, 1984—; trustee Calwell Coll., 1983—. Research grantee Boston Coll., 1966, U. Dayton, 1971-72; research fellow U. Medicine and Dentistry N.J., 1976-77. Mem. AAUP. Home: 158 Nesbit St Weehawken NJ 07087 Office: Cath Community Services 1 Summer Ave Newark NJ 07087

DALY, JAMES JOSEPH, bishop; b. Bronx, N.Y., Aug. 14, 1921; s. Thomas and Catherine (Cass) D. Grad., Immaculate Conception Sem., Huntington, 1948; LL.D., Molloy Coll., Rockville Centre, N.Y., St. John's U., Jamaica, N.Y., 1979. Ordained priest Roman Catholic Ch., 1948; priest Our Lady of Snow, Blue Point, N.Y., 1948-51, Holy Child Jesus, Richmond Hill, 1951, St. William the Abbot, Seaford, 1951-58; procurator Immaculate Conception Sem., Huntington, 1958; dir. Priests' Personnel Bd., 1968-72; pastor St. Boniface, Elmont; aux. bishop of Rockville Centre, 1977—; vicar gen. Diocese of Rockville Centre, 1989—; now aux. bishop Suffolk County.

DALY, MARY F., feminist philosopher; A.B., Coll. of St. Rose, Albany, N.Y.; A.M., Cath. U.; S.T.L., S.T.D., Ph.D., U. Fribourg; Ph.D. in Religion, U. Notre Dame. Assoc. prof. dept. theology Boston Coll. Author: The Church and the Second Sex, 1968, 3d rev. ed., 1985; Beyond God the Father, 1973, 2nd edit. rev. 1985; Gyn/Ecology, 1979, Pure Lust, 1984; Websters' New Intergalactic Wickedary of the English Language, 1987. Address: Boston Coll Dept Theology Chestnut Hill MA 02167

DALY, BROTHER RICHARD, religious organization administrator. Exec. dir. Tex. Cath. Conf., Austin. Office: Tex Cath Conf 3001 S Congress Ave Austin TX 78704*

DALY, ROBERT J., theology educator; b. Quincy, Mass., Apr. 22, 1933; s. Timothy Patrick and Stella M. (Deschenes) D., A.B., Boston Coll., 1956, M.A. in Philosophy, 1957; M.A. in English, Catholic U., 1961; Dr.Theol., Julius Maximilians U., Wurzburg, Fed. Republic Germany, 1972. Instr., dept. theology Boston Coll., Chestnut Hill, Mass., 1971-72, asst. prof., 1972-75, assoc. prof., 1975-84, prof., 1984—, dept. theology chairperson, 1973-88; acting dir. Boston Coll. inst. religious edn. and pastoral ministry, 1980-82; bd. trustees Boston Theol. Inst., 1973-88, chairperson, 1981-82; dir. Jesuit Inst. at Boston Coll., 1987—. Author Christian Sacrifice, 1978; The Origins of the Christian Doctrine of Sacrifice, 1978. Author, editor Christian Biblical Ethics, 1984, Christians and the Military, 1985; editor Rising From History, 1987, In All Things, 1990; editor in chief Theol. Studies, 1991—; co-translator The von Balthasar Reader, 1982; editor, translator: Spirit and Fire (Anthology of Writings of Origen), 1984; contbr. articles to profl. jours. Mem. AAUP, Am. Acad. Religions, Am. Schs. Oriental Research, Assn. Internat. d'Etudes Patristiques, Boston Theol. Soc., Cath. Biblical Assn. Am., Cath. Theol. Soc. Am., Coll. Theology Soc., Boston Patristic Soc. (co-founder 1979), Soc. Bibl. Lit., N.Am. Acad. Liturgy, N.Am. Patristic Soc., Societas Liturgica. Democrat. Office: Boston Coll Dept Theology Chestnut Hill MA 02167 *We can accept and enjoy life only by handing on what we have received, and by accepting the fact that what we are handing on is God's, not ours.*

DALY, SIMEON PHILIP JOHN, librarian; b. Detroit, May 9, 1922; s. Philip T. and Marguerite I. (Ginzel) D. BA, St. Meinrad Coll., 1945; Licentiate in Sacred Theol., Cath. U., 1949, MLS, 1951; MDiv, St. Meinrad Sch. Theol., 1985. Joined Benedictines, 1943, ordained priest Roman Cath. Ch., 1948. Libr. dir. St. Meinrad (Ind.) Coll. and St. Meinrad Sch. Theol., 1951—; pres. Four Rivers Area Libr. Svcs. Authority, Ind., 1974-75, Am. Theol. Libr. Assn., St. Meinrad, 1979-81; exec. sec. Am. Theol. Library Assn., St. Meinrad, 1985-90. Mem. ALA, Ind. Library Assn., Am. Theol. Library Assn. (bd. dirs., pres., exec. sec.), Am. Benedictine Acad. Home: St Meinrad Archabbey Saint Meinrad IN 47577 Office: St Meinrad Coll Archabbey Libr Saint Meinrad IN 47577

DALY, THOMAS J., academic administrator. Head St. John's Sem., Brighton, Mass. Office: St John's Sem Brighton MA 02135*

DAMGAARD, NEIL CHRISTIAN, minister; b. Washington, Dec. 10, 1952; s. Martin Jens and Joe Evelyn (Porch) D.; m. Renée Ann English, Oct. 4, 1975; children: Jocelyn Charis, Susanna Jo. BS, Va. Poly. Inst. and State U., 1975; ThM, Dallas Sem., 1983. Ordained to ministry Grace Ch., 1982; Cert. mgmt. engring. Cons. Cons. mgmt. engring. Mc Lean, Va., 1975-77; ministerial intern to campus min. Grace Ch., Roanoke, Va., 1982; youth pastor Grace Ch., Dallas, 1978-79, Trinity Fellowship, Dallas, 1982-83; sr. pastor Dartmouth Bible Ch., N. Dartmouth, Mass., 1983—; past pres. S.E. Mass. Evang. Mins. Fellowship, 1987-90 (sec. 1990—); active mem. Evang. Theol. Soc., 1988—. Editor newsletters Lifeline Action Com, 1985—. Vol. Hospice of St. Luke's Hosp, New Bedford, Mass., 1987; bd. dirs. Christian Day Sch., Fall River, Mass.; mem., newletter editor Lifeline Action Com., New Bedford, Mass. Mem. Evang. Theol. Soc., Nat. Assn. Evang. (officer), Dallas Sem. Nat Evap. Alumni Assn. (sec.)

DAMM, JOHN SILBER, minister; b. Union City, N.J., June 21, 1926; s. John William and Lillian (Meisse) D. BA, BD, MDiv, Concordia Sem., St. Louis, 1945-51; MA, Columbia U., 1952; EdD, Tchrs. Coll. N.Y., 1959; DD (hon.), Susquehanna U., 1982. Ordained to ministry Luth. in Am. (now Evang. Luth. Ch. in Am.), 1951. Prof. Concordia Sem. in exile, St. Louis, 1974-81, acting pres., 1974-75, acad. dean, 1974-81; sr. pastor St. Peter's Ch., N.Y.C., 1981-91; asst. pastor Grace Ch., Teaneck, N.J., 1991—; chmn. bd. trustees Hosp. Chaplaincy, Inc., N.Y.C., 1983-87; synod rep. Luth. Ch. Dialogue with Archdiocese of N.Y., 1984. Mng. editor Am. Luth., 1962-66; mem. editorial staff Concordia Theol. Monthly, 1966-74; contbr. articles to profl. jours. Asst. chmn. Community Scholarship Fund, Teaneck, N.J., 1964; chmn. Cerebral Palsy Lily campaign, 1965; mem. nat. adv. com. Forum for Corp. Responsibility, N.Y.C., 1982. Fulbright scholar, 1959, Amerika-Kreis-Muenster Auslands scholar, 1960, Luth. Brotherhood ann. faculty scholar, 1981; Case Study Inst. fellow, 1972. Home: 1200 River Rd Teaneck NJ 07666

DANCY, PAUL BARTLETT, minister; b. Detroit, June 23, 1954; s. Robert Bartlett and Joan Arda (LeMond) D.; m. Heidi Lynn Scherfling, Aug. 28, 1976; children: Rachel, Adam, Rebecca. BA in Edn., Concordia Coll., 1976; MDiv, Concordia Theol. Sem., Ft. Wayne, Ind., 1980; postgrad., Grad. Theol. Found., Donaldson, Ind., 1990—. Ordained to ministry Luth. Ch.-Mo. Synod, 1980. Pastor Trinity Luth. Ch., Pontiac, Ill., 1980-88; assoc. pastor St. Paul's Evang. Luth. Ch., Chicago Heights, Ill., 1988—; clergy counselor mentally retarded Martin Luther Homes, Pontiac, 1983-88; v.p. Pontiac Area Ministerial Assn., 1984-88; vacancy pastor Emmanuel Luth. Ch., Dwight, Ill., 1984; spiritual counselor Deaconess Program, Luth. Ch.-Mo. Synod, 1991—. Bd. dirs. Christian Action Coun. of Pontiac, 1984-88; chaplain Pontiac Correctional Ctr., 1987-88. Republican. Home: 136 Indiana St Park Forest IL 60466 Office: St Paul's Evang Luth Ch 330 Highland Dr Chicago Heights IL 60411

DANDRIDGE, DOUGLAS BATES, minister; b. Connersville, Ind., Aug. 9, 1939; s. Charles Lorn Stoup and Anne (Douglas) Bates; m. Deborah D.R., Feb. 29, 1976; children: Douglas II, Adam B.C., Brian C., Anne D., D. Airen. BA, Ohio State U., 1968; MDiv, Lancaster (Pa.) Theol., Seminary, 1977; PhD, So. Calif. Grad. Sch. Theology, Fresno, 1990; grad., Tri State Inst. Traditional Chinese Acupuncture, 1991. Ordained to ministry United Ch. Christ, 1976, Am. Bapt. Ch. in U.S., 1988. Pastor Market Street Bapt. Ch., Harrisburg, Pa., 1988—; dir. Lancaster Analgesia Assocs., Ltd., 1991—. With U.S. Army, 1961-63, Vietnam. Home: 245 Millersville Rd Lancaster PA 17603

DANEKER, ROBERT MILTON, minister; b. Palmerton, Pa., Nov. 25, 1938; s. Matthew M. and Mildred E. (Dunbar) D.; m. Barbara A. Wehr, June 18, 1960; children: Robert M. Jr., Laurie Ann Kuhns, James Matthew. BA, Moravian Coll., Bethlehem, Pa., 1960; MDiv, Evang. Sch. Theology, Myerstown, Pa., 1964. Ordained to ministry Evang. Congl. Ch. 1961. Pastor Grace Evang. Congl. Ch., Cetronia, Pa., 1958-60, Reedsville Bethesda Evang. Congl. Ch., Schuykill Haven, Pa., 1960-67, Blvd. Evang. Congl. Ch., Allentown, Pa., 1967-75; assoc. pastor Grace Evang. Congl. Ch., Lancaster, Pa., 1975-86; ea. dist. supt. Evang. Congl. Ch., Allentown, 1986—; gen. conf. del. Evang. Congl. Ch., Myerstown, Pa., 1974—; trustee Evang. Sch. Theology, Myerstown, 1986—; chmn. social action commn. Nat. Assn. Evangs., 1990—; vice chmn. gen. and ann. confs. Evang. Congl. Ch., 1986—. Home: 122 S Emerson St Allentown PA 18104 Office: Dist Office Evang Ch Ctr 100 W Park Ave Box 186 Myerstown PA 17067 *Among the greatest challenges of the twenty-first century Church will be developing awareness of the principles that govern growth through service by a spiritual body in a material world.*

DANES, C. W., minister. Chaplain The Anglican Communion, Monte Carlo, Monaco. Office: St Paul's Ch House, ave de Grande Bretagne, Monte Carlo Monaco*

DANESH, HOSSAIN B., psychiatrist, religious organization official; b. Yazd, Iran, Jan. 15, 1938; arrived in Can., 1968; s. Jaafar and Khadijeh (Malek-Afsali) D.; m. Michele Lyn Bernstein, Dec. 2, 1967; children: Arman Eric, Roshan Philip. MD, Isfahan U., Iran, 1961; diploma in psychiatry, Ill. State Psychiat. Inst., Chgo. 1966. Mem. Nat. Spiritual Assembly of Bahá'ís of Can., Thornhill, Ont., Can., 1972—, chmn., 1980-85, sec. gen., 1985-90; dir. Marriage Therapy Ctr., Toronto, Ont.; cons. Bahá'í Faith, N.Y.C., 1970—; founding mem., chmn. Bahá'í Internat. Health Agy., Montreal, Que., Can., 1979-85. Author: The Violence-Free Society: A Gift For Our Children, 1976, Unity: The Creative Foundation of Peace, 1986; also articles; editor: To The Peoples of the World: A Bahá'í Statement on Peace. Fellow Royal Coll. Physicians and Surgeons Can.; mem. Assn. for Bahá'í Studies (founding mem. 1973, chmn 1973—). Office: Marriage Therapy Ctr, 500-615 Yonge St, Toronto, ON Canada M4Y 1Z5

DANG, MINH NGOC, minister; b. Quang-Nam, DaNang, Socialist Republic of Vietnam, May 3, 1958; came to U.S., 1975; s. Cang Ngoc Dang and Duyen Thi Nguyen. BS, U. Akron, 1980; M Divinity, Grace Theol. Sem., 1983; D Ministry, Ashland Theol. Sem., 1987. Ordained minister. Dir. Vietnamese Evangelistic Outreach, Akron, 1984—; vis. prof. theology Vietnamese Theol. Sem., Weztlar, Fed. Republic Germany, 1990—. Author: The Evacuation Route 1975, 2d edit., 1978. Mem. Vietnamese Pastor Assn. Am., Vietnamese Christian Youth Assn. Am. (bd. leadership Des Moines chpt. 1986—). Mem. Ind. Ch. Avocations: writing, reading, ping pong. Home: 105 Mayfield Ave Akron OH 44313

DANHELKA, ANTHONY GEORGE, minister, religious organization administrator; b. Chgo., June 15, 1945; s. Tony Lewis and Emily Rosemary Danhelka; m. Donna Jean Russell, Jan. 25, 1969; 1 child, Anthony David. BA, Trinity Coll., 1972; MDiv, Garrett Evang. Sem., 1975. Ordained to ministry Bapt. Ch., 1974. Instr. Christian Identity Seminars, Deerfield, Ill., 1969-72; children's ch. pastor Western Springs (Ill.) Bapt. Ch., 1968-72, assoc. pastor, 1972-76; exec. dir. Riverwoods Christian Ctr., St. Charles, Ill., 1976—; itinerate preacher Chgo., 1977—; 1st Bapt. Ch., Geneva, Ill, 1976—, Aawana leader, 1989—. Sgt. E-5 Arty., U.S. Army, 1966-68. Recipient Disting. Anglers' award Sports Afield mag., 1970. Mem. Christian Camping Internat. (bd. dirs. 1985—), Am. Camping Assn., Christian Laity Chgo. (chairperson forum team). Office: Riverwoods Christian Ctr 35 W 701 Riverwoods Ln Saint Charles IL 60174

DANIEL, ELEANOR A., academic administrator; b. Milton, Ill., Feb. 28, 1940; d. Donald W. Daniel and Bernice Hillig. BA summa cum laude, Lincoln Christian Coll., 1962; MA, Lincoln Christian Seminary, Ill., 1965; EdM, U. Ill., 1969, PhD, 1975. Youth min. 1st Christian Ch., Tuscola, Ill., 1961-65; dir. Christian edn. Ch. of Christ, Buchanan, Mich., 1965-67; instr. Christian edn. Lincoln (Ill.) Christian Coll., 1964-65, 72, 74-78; prof. Christian edn. Midwest Christian Coll., Oklahoma City, 1967-71; min. Christian edn Christian Ch., Lincoln, 1973-78; prof. Christian edn. Cin. Bible Sem., 1978—; cons. Standard Pub. Co., Cin., 1982—; dean grad. studies Cin. Bible Coll. and Seminary. Author: Introduction to Christian Education , 1980, rev., 1987, What the Bible Says About Sexual Identity, 1982, The ABC's of VBS, 1983; contbr. articles to profl. jours. Active several bds. and coms. of religious orgns. and ednl. task forces. Recipient Restoration Award for Outstanding Svc. in Edn., Lincoln Christian Col. and Seminary Alumni Assn., 1974; named Runnerup for Educator of the Yr., Logan City, Ill., 1974. Mem. AAUW, Am. Edn. Rsch. Assn., Nat. Assn. Profs. of Christian Edn., Nat. Assn. Dirs. of Christian Edn., Assn. Tchr. Educators, Assn. Profs. and Researchers in Religious Edn., Delta Kappa Gamma Soc., Delta Alpha Tau, Delta Epsilon Chi, Gamma Alpha Chi. Mem. Christian Ch. Office: Cin Bible Sem 2700 Glenway Ave Cincinnati OH 45204

DANIEL, ELINOR PERKINS (PERKY DANIEL), clergywoman; b. Louisville, Dec. 9, 1952; d. James Gordon and Lenora (Lisle) Perkins; m. James Wallace Daniel III, Sept. 21, 1974. BA in Music, Agnes Scott Coll., 1974; MDiv, Columbia Sem., 1986; postgrad., Ga. State U., 1991—. Ordained to ministry Presbyn. Ch., 1986. Co-founder, assoc. music dir. Young Singers of Callanwolde, Atlanta, 1975-82; dir., developer youth, chil-

dren, handbell choirs Peachtree Presbyn. Ch., Atlanta, 1976-78; dir., developer youth, handbell choirs Decatur (Ga.) Presbyn. Ch., 1978-84; sr. pastor Morningside Presbyn. Ch., Atlanta, 1984—; mem. Task Force on Urban Ministry/Atlanta Presbytery, 1989—; trustee Westminster Homes, Ga. Presbyn. Homes, Atlanta, 1991—; vice-chmn. Columbia Sem. Alumni Coun. Decatur, Ga., 1992—; co-author mus. Piedmont Hosp., Atlanta, 1989—; mem. Atlanta Presbytery's Com. on Urban Ministry, 1987-89; baccalaureate preacher Columbia Sem., 1990; preacher in Eng., Scotland, Switzerland. Co-creator, author mus.: Petros/Life of Peter, 1980; co-creator, composer mus.: Innkeeper and The Room, 1982-83; contbr. articles and book revs. to profl. jours. Mem. Leadership Ga., 1990. Mem. Assn. Clin. Pastoral Edn. (individual mem., steering coun. to organize Ga.'s Interfaith Intercultural Coalition, 1991). Office: Morningside Presbyn Ch 1411 N Morningside Dr NE Atlanta GA 30306

DANIEL, GEORGE FRANCIS, archbishop; b. Pretoria, Transvaal, Republic of South Africa, Apr. 23, 1933; s. Robert Francis and Catherine Mary (Pattison) D. Licentiate in Theology, St. Paul's Coll., Republic of South Africa, 1956; postgrad., St. John Vianney Sem., Republic of South Africa, 1961; BD, Urbanianum, Rome, 1965. Ordained priest Roman Cath. Ch., 1964. Curate Archdiocese of Pretoria, 1965-67, parish priest, 1968-69; parish priest Tembisa, 1969-75; archbishop of Pretoria, 1975—; with Mil. Ordinariate, Republic of South Africa, 1976—; coun. mem. Internat. Com. Mil. Ordinariates, Rome, 1985-87; v.p. II So. African Cath. Bishops' Conf., 1990—. Mem. Coun. for Promoting Christian Unity. Home: Archbishop's House, 125 Main St, Waterkloof Pretoria Transvaal 0181, Republic of South Africa Office: Archdiocese of Pretoria, PO Box 17245, Groenkloof, Pretoria Transvaal 0027, Republic of South Africa

DANIEL, JILL RANKIN, lay worker; b. Shreveport, La., Mar. 23, 1959; d. Lennis Morgan and Audrey Wynona (Cook) Rankin; m. Kenneth Ray Daniel, Mar. 26, 1977; children: Stephanie Leann, Kathryn Rene'. B.Elem. Edn., Texarkana (Tex.) Coll., 1980. Dir. children's ministries First United Meth. Ch., Atlanta, Tex.; adminstrv. bd. First United Meth. Ch., Atlanta, 1989—; family life coord., coun. on ministries and edn. coun., 1989—. Vol. coord. PTA, Atlanta, 1989; leader Girl Scouts of the U.S.A., Atlanta, 1989-91; vol. coord. Early Childhood Intervention, Mt. Pleasant, Tex., 1990—. Mem. Curriculum Devel. Coun., Nat. Pre-Sch. Religious Tchrs. Home: Rt 4 Box 60 Atlanta TX 75551 Office: First United Meth Ch 103 N Louise Atlanta TX 75551

DANIEL, ROBERT EDWIN, retired investment banker; b. Joplin, Mo., Aug. 19, 1906; s. Robert Brown and Lilian (Boswell) D.; m. Margaret Moir, July 16, 1932; children: Robert William, Phillip Merrill, Linda Jane. A.B. magna cum laude, Ottawa U., 1927; LL.D., Whitworth Coll., 1971. With Blyth & Co., 1928-31, Pacific Northwest Co., Seattle, 1931-41, 46-66; pres. Pacific Northwest Co., 1959-66; v.p. United Pacific Corp.; ret., 1961; Chmn. regional bus. conduct com. Nat. Assn. Securities Dealers, 1959-60; gov. Midwest Stock Exchange, 1959-60. Trustee, treas. Wash.-Alaska Synod United Presbyn. Ch., dir. finance, 1966-72; trustee United Presbyn. Found., 1973-82. Served to maj. AUS, 1941-45. Republican. Presbyn. (elder). Home: 3214 8th St W Seattle WA 98119

DANIELS, GEORGE MORRIS, former religious publishing company editor, writer; b. St. Louis, July 9, 1927; s. Stafford Cecil and Hattie W. (Nichols) D.; m. Cecilia Adams, 1959 (div. 1960); 1 child, Margaret Ann; m. June Aline Smith, July 20, 1961 (div. 1973); 1 child, Lisa Marguerite. BA in Journalism, Drake U., 1951; MA in Journalism, Columbia U., 1970. Assoc. news dir. United Meth. Bd. Missions, 1961-67; dir. interpretive svcs. United Meth. Bd. Global Ministries, 1967-81, exec. editor New World Outlook, 1981-89; editor Renewal mag., N.Y.C., 1974-76; free-lance writer N.Y.C., 1989—; specialist in African and Caribbean affairs. Author: The Church in New Nations, 1964; editor: Southern Africa: A Time for Change, 1969, Drums of War: The Continuing Crisis in Rhodesia, 1974. Recipient Page One award Chgo. Newspaper Guild, 1955; named to Hall of Fame, United Meth. Assn. Communicators, 1990; Ralph Stoody fellow, 1969; mag. grantee Columbia U., S.Am., 1970. Mem. UN Assn. N.Y. (bd. dirs. 1990—), Columbia U. Grad. Sch. Journalism Nat. Alumni Assn. (pres. 1983-85), Soc. Profl. Journalists, NAACP, Alpha Phi Alpha. Home and Office: 392 Central Park West #1-N New York NY 10025

DANIELS, JIMMIE LEROY, minister; b. Saginaw, Mich., Jan. 29, 1941; s. Olin Lee and Elvira Cordelia (Millering) D.; m. Hazel Edna Holbrook, Nov. 11, 1972; children: Daren Kerry, Braden Wade, Steven Todd, Janie Rae, Spencer Gene, Teri Lin, David Allen. BTh., Citadel Bapt. Theol. Sem., 1985; M of Ministry, Bethany Theol. Sem., 1989. Ordained to ministry Bapt. Ch., 1986. Vice pastor First Bapt. Ch., E. Tawas, Mich., 1977-81; sr. pastor Trinity Bapt. Ch., Saginaw, 1981-83, Liberty Bapt. Ch. (formerly Trinity Bapt. Ch.), Carrollton, Mich., 1986—; janitor Saginaw div. Gen. Motors Corp., 1962—; pres. Total Evangelism Inc., Saginaw, 1984-89. Author: The Gift Shoppe. With USMC, 1958-61. Home: 1021 Congress Ave Saginaw MI 48602 Office: Liberty Bapt Ch PO Box 278 Carrollton MI 48724 *Life, that incredible journey of trial and error, leading to the ultimate confrontation of choice, either to continue on alone to destruction or to accept God's gracious gift and eternal companion, Jesus Christ, the author and joy of life.*

DANIELS, VIVIAN CECILLE, lay worker; b. Alleene, Ark., July 18, 1939; d. Esco Cecil and Nelle Agnes (Seastrunk) Thompson; m. Leon Windsor Daniels, Oct 24, 1958; children: Mark, David, Lori Daniels Froidl. Student, Draughons Bus. Coll., Dallas, 1957-58. Southwestern Bapt. Theol. Sem., Nashville. Preschool dir. sunday sch. Oakland Heights Bapt. Ch., Longview, Tex., 1975-86, choir, 1975—, mem. coms., 1975—, libr., 1980—, presch. dir., 1987—. Mem. Gregg Assn. So. Bapt. Secs. (v.p. 1991, pres. 1988), Tex. Assn. So. Bapt. Secs. (nominating coun. 1986), Nat. Assn. So. Bapt. Secs. (charter), So. Bapt. Conv. (basic cert. 1976, advanced cert. 1984, advanced Christian devel. 1986-89, ch. office adminstrn. 1990). Democrat. Office: Oakland Heights Bapt Ch 108 Eden Dr Longview TX 75601

DANIELSON, MICHAEL JON, minister; b. Moscow, Idaho, May 30, 1960; s. Jon Jay and Marilyn Ann (Stewart) D. BS in Archtl. Studies, Wash. State U., 1982, BArch cum laude, 1983; M in Ministry, Seattle U., 1987. Youth minister St. John Vianney Ch., Spokane, Wash., 1983-84, St. Mary's Ch., Spokane, 1983-88; mem. dir. Cath. Youth Ministries of Spokane, 1983-85; mem. Channel Lay Ministers Program, Spokane, 1983-85; founder, dir. Christian Rock Music workshops and seminars, 1983—. Roman Catholic. Avocations: tennis, snow and water skiing, juggling, drama, dancing. Office: St Mary's Religious Edn S 304 Adams Spokane WA 99216

DANKER, FREDERICK WILLIAM, retired religion educator; b. Frankenmuth, Mich., July 12, 1920; s. Wilhelm Friedrich Julius and Wilhelmina (Classen) D.; m. Lois Roberta Dreyer, June 2, 1948; children: Kathleen, James. BD, Concordia Sem., St. Louis, 1950; PhD, U. Chgo. 1963. Ordained to ministry Luth. Ch., 1945. Parish minister Trinity Luth. Ch., Bay City, Mich., 1948-54; prof. Concordia Sem., St. Louis, 1954-74, Christ Sem.-Seminex, St. Louis, 1974-83, Luth. Sch. Theology, Chgo., 1983-88. Author: No Room in the Brotherhood, 1977, Benefactor: Epigraphic Study, 1982, A Century of Greco-Roman Philology, Jesus and the New Age: Luke, 1988; co-editor: A Greek-English Lexicon of the New Testament, 1979. Named for Disting. Svc., Aid Assn. for Lutherans, St. Louis, 1982. Mem. Soc. Bibl. Lit., Studiorum Novi Testamenti Societas, Cath. Bibl. Assn. Am. Philological Assn., Am. Soc. Papyrologists. Home: 3438 Russell Blvd 203 Saint Louis MO 63104

DANKER, WILLIAM JOHN, religion educator; b. Willow Creek, Minn., June 19, 1914; s. William Frederick Julius and Wilhelmine Agnes (Classen) D.; m. Elizabeth Marie Miller, June 16, 1942; children: Elizabeth, William, Deborah. Diploma summo cum honore, Concordia Coll., 1948; MA, Wheaton Coll., 1948; ThD magna cum laude, Ruprecht-Karl U., Heidelberg, Fed. Republic of Germany, 1967; LittD (hon.), Valparaiso U., 1991. Ordained to ministry Luth. Ch., 1945. Pastor Luth. Chs., Harvard, West Chicago, Ill., 1937-48; missionary 2560 Luth. Ch., Mo. Synod, Japan, 1948-56; prof of mission Concordia Sem., St. Louis, 1956-74; prof. of mission Christ Sem.-Seminex, St. Louis 1974-83; prof. of mission emeritus Luth. Sch. Theology, Chgo., 1983—; vis. prof. of mission, U. Heidelberg, Fed. Republic of Germany, 1966; founder, pres. Ctr. for World Christian Interaction, Chgo., 1974—; organizer, chair Conf. on Econ. Activities in Christian World Mission, St. Louis, 1971; coord. World Hunger Appeal (2650) St. Louis. 1974-77. Composer: (song) The Sending Lord, 1969; author: Two Worlds or None, 1964, Profit for the Lord, 1971; co-author: More Than Healing 1973; contbr. articles to profl. jours.; editor more than 20 books. Exec. dir. Heifer Project Internat., Little Rock, 1977-78; mem., chair Mo. State Bd. of Christian Rural Overseas Project of Ch. World Svc., 1977-83, Community World Hunger Appeal, 1977-83. Recipient Festschrift, Christian Presence in Japan: essays in his honor, Luth. Lit. Soc., Tokyo, 1981. Mem. Assn. Profs. of Mission (pres. 1979-80), Am. Soc. Missiology (editor book 12 vol. book series), Internat. Assn. Mission Studies, Am. Acad. Religion, Assn. for Asian Studies. Home: 5842 Stony Island Ste 10G Chicago IL 60637 Office: Luth Sch Theology Chicago 1100 E 55th St Chicago IL 60615 *As you walk, step by step, I will open your way before you. (Transl. from Syriac version of Prov. 4:12).*

DANNA, C. S., SR., pastor; b. New Iberia, La., July 15, 1927; s. Sebastian B. and Sarah C. (Curcio) D.; m. Joyce B. Danna, Sept. 9, 1953; children: Theresa, C.S. Jr., Maria. Diploma, Austin (Tex.) Tech. Sch., 1947; D of Biblical Studies (hon), Universal Christian Coll., 1989. Pastor Living Word Fellowship, Erath, La., 1987—; trustee Full Gospel Bus. Men's Fellowship, Abbeville, La., 1989-90. Capt. USN, 1948-50, PTO. Office: Living Word Fellowship PO Box 89 Erath LA 70533

DANNEELS, GODFRIED CARDINAL, archbishop of Mechelen-Brussel; b. Kanegem, Belgium, June 4, 1933. Ordained priest Roman Cath. Ch., 1957; prof. liturgy and sacramental theology Cath. U. Louvain (Belgium), 1969-77; consecrated bishop of Antwerp, 1977; apptd. archbishop of Mechelen-Brussel (Belgium), 1979; elected mem. gen. secretariat Synod of Bishops, 1981; elevated to Sacred Coll. of Cardinals, 1983. Mil. bishop, Belgium; pres. Belgian Episcopal Conf. Mem. Congregation of Cath. Edn., Congregation of Doctrine of Faith, Congregation of Bishops, Congregation of Evangelisation, Congregation of Divine Worship, Coun. for pub. affairs of ch. Secretariate for non-believers. Address: Aartsbisdom, Wollemarkt 15, B-2800 Mechelen Belgium

DANNER, DAN GORDON, theology educator; b. Salt Lake City, July 5, 1939; s. Glen Curtis and Katherine (Kyker) D.; m. Dorothy Marie Holland, June 1, 1961; children: J. Darin, Kirt Holland. BA, Abilene (Tex.) Christian Coll., 1961, MA, 1963; PhD, U. Iowa, 1969. Ordained to ministry Ch. of Christ, 1961. Campus minister Ch. of Christ Bible Chair, Tyler, Tex., 1961-65; asst. prof. theology U. Portland (Oreg.), 1969-72, assoc. prof. theology, 1972-80, prof. theology, 1980—. Author books, articles and revs. to profl. jours. Folger-Shakespeare fellow, Washington, 1969, 71. Mem. Am. Acad. Religion, Am. Soc. Ch. History, Am. Soc. Reformation Rsch., Historians Modern Europe, Riverside Golf and Country Club (bd. dirs. 1987-90). Office: U Portland Theology Dept Portland OR 97203

DANNER, JAMES SEAGER, minister; b. Mobile, Ala., Mar. 14, 1957; s. Robert Marshall and Jean (Seager) D.; m. Susan Berry, Sept. 25, 1979; 1 child, Jillian Ruth. BA, U. Fla., 1980; MDiv, Reformed Theol. Sem., Jackson, Miss., 1985. Ordained to ministry Presbyn. Ch. Am. Pastor Old Madison Presbyn. Ch., Canton, Miss., 1985-87, Grace Fellowship Presbyn. Ch., Albertville, Ala., 1987—. Home: 201 Graceson St Albertville AL 35950 Office: Grace Fellowship Presbyn Ch PO Box 1214 Albertville AL 35950

DANNER, ROBERT LEA, SR., minister; b. Seattle, Dec. 12, 1929; s. Albert Lea and Stella (Bright) D.; m. Marilyn M. Davis, June 10, 1951; children: Deborah, Robert Lea, Mary, Steven. AB, Chapman U., 1952; BD, Lexinton Theol. Sem., 1955; postgrad., Calif. State U., Northridge, 1961; PhD, Pacific Western U., 1979; postgrad., Boston U., 1987—, Lexington Theol. Sem., 1987—. Ordained to ministry Christian Ch., 1955; cert. tchr., Calif.; cert. coll. tchr., Va. Pastor Christian Ch., Smithfield, Ky., 1952-55; assoc. minister Cen. Christian Ch., Van Nuys, Calif., 1955-57; minister edn. Hollywood (Calif.)-Beverly Christian Ch., 1957-59; pastor 1st Christian Ch., Reseda, Calif., 1959-62; tchr. Porter Jr. High Sch., Los Angeles City Schs., 1962-80; pastor Diamond Springs Christian Ch., Virginia Beach, Va., 1980-85; co-pastor Park View Christian Ch., Chesapeake, Va., 1985—; prof. St. Leo Coll., 1982—, Golden Gate U., 1986, Atlantic U., 1986—; marriage and family cons., 1981—. Bd. dirs. Bayside Jr. High Sch., Virginia Beach, Va., 1982-83; pres. Dist. 8 Christian Chs., Va., 1982-83; chmn. Ministers Assn., 1983-84; mem. Capital Campaign for Christian Chs. Va., 1982-84, mem. clergy com., 1984-86, mem. goals and promotion com., 1983-85. Radio host Deliberately Different, WCMS-AM, 1982-83. Mem. Hemlock Soc., Peta Soc., Concern for Dying, Nat. Victim Ctr., Internat. Assn. Near Death Studies, Mensa.

DANTER, ALBERT FRANCIS, priest; b. Redbud, Ill., Mar. 9, 1918; s. Albert Alois and Rose (Mudd) D. BA, Kenrick Seminary, St. Louis, 1943, MA, 1978; PhD, St. Louis U., 1989. Pastor St. Joseph Ch., Tiff, Mo., 1960-66, St. Alphonsus Ch., Millwood, Mo., 1966-74, St. Catherine of Siena Ch., Pagedale, Mo., 1974-78; chaplain St. Joseph Home, St. Charles, Mo., 1986—. Mem. Cath. Bibl. Assn., Soc. Bibl. Lit., K.C., Theta Alpha Kappa. Republican. Home and Office: 723 First Capitol Dr Saint Charles MO 63301

D'ANTONIO, NICHOLAS, bishop; b. Rochester, N.Y., July 10, 1916; s. Pasquale and Josephine (Salza) D'A. Student, St. Francis Seraphic Sem., Andover, Mass., 1931, St. Anthony Friary, Catskill, N.Y., 1939. Joined Order of Friars Minor; ordained priest Roman Catholic Ch., 1942; pastor Trail, B.C., Can., 1943-45; provincial del. of U.S.A. Friars working in Guatemala, Honduras and El Salvador, 1953-63; named prelate of Olancho, Honduras, 1966; bishop Diocese Olancho, 1966-76; vicar gen. Archdiocese of New Orleans, 1977-91, also vicar of Hispanics; pastor Annunciation Ch., New Orleans, 1979-91, pastor emeritus, 1991—; Liaison Family Life in La.; observer Nat. Conf. of Cath. Bishops. Mem. KC (2d and 3d degree), Equestrian Order of the Holy Sepulchre. Home: 1221 Mandeville St New Orleans LA 70117

DANTZLER, WILLIAM A., minister, educator; b. Winona, Miss., Sept. 15, 1933; s. John Aldridge and Maggie (Watson) D.; m. Kelly Wren, July 10, 1959; children: Carolyn Wren, John Andrew. BA, Presbyn. Coll., Clinton, S.C., 1956; MDiv, Columbia Theol. Sem., 1959, D Ministry, 1990. Ordained to ministry Presbyn. Ch. (U.S.A.); cert. supr. clin. pastoral edn. Asst. pastor Meml. Presbyn. Ch., West Palm Beach, Fla., 1959-61; pastor 1st Presbyn. Ch., Dadeville, Ala., 1961-63, Glencliff Presbyn. Ch., Nashville, 1963-67, Kelley Presbyn. Ch., McDonough, Ga., 1967-71; corp. dir. clin. pastoral edn. Bapt. Med. Ctrs., Birrmingham, Ala., 1971—; moderator Birmingham Presbytery Presbyn. Ch. (U.S.A.), 1975, Midsouth Synod, Nashville, 1983, 85. Recipient Devoted Svc. award Louisville Presbyn. Theol. Sem, 1984. Fellow Coll. of Chaplains; mem. Assn. for Clin. Pastoral Edn. (chmn. certification com. S.E. region 1986-89, chmn. S.E. region 1991—, rsch. award 1991), Blue Key. Democrat. Avocations: classical music, reading, writing, yard work, photography. Home: 313 Lucerne Blvd Birmingham AL 35209 Office: Bapt Med Ctrs Corp Pastoral Care 750 Montclair Rd Birmingham AL 35213

DAOUST, JOSEPH PATRICK, priest, educator, lawyer; b. Mpls., Aug. 24, 1939; s. Joseph Henry and Bernadette Nan (Gannon) D. A.B., St. Louis U., 1963, Ph.L., 1964, M.A., 1964; M.Div., Woodstock Coll., 1969; M.A., U. Pa., 1966, Ph.D. candidate, 1968; J.D., U. Mich., 1982. Joined S.J., Roman Cath. Ch., ordained priest, 1969; bar: Mich. 1982, U.S. Dist. Ct. (ea. dist.) Mich. 1982. Social devel. worker Indian Social Inst., Pune, India, and Kandy, Sri Lanka, 1972-73; prof. econs. U. Detroit, 1973—, assoc. prof. law and econs., 1982—, v.p. adminstrn. and student affairs, 1975-77, dean humanities and philosophy, 1977-80; dir. social ministry Detroit Province Jesuits, 1980-88, provincial superior, 1989—; mem. nat. bd. Jesuity Social Ministry, Washington, 1982-88. Vol. atty. Wayne County Neighborhood Service, Detroit, 1981-83. NSF fellow, 1964-67. Mem. Am. Econ. Assn., Order of Coif. Contbr. articles to profl. jours. Address: Jesuit Provincial Offices 7303 W 7 Mile Rd Detroit MI 48221

DARBY, WESLEY ANDREW, minister, educator; b. Glendale, Ariz., Sept. 19, 1928; s. Albert Leslie and Beulah E. (Lamb) D.; student Bible Inst. L.A., 1946, No. Ariz. U., 1946-47, Rockmont Coll., Denver, 1948-50, Ariz. State U., 1965, St. Anne's Coll., Oxford (Eng.) U., 1978; m. Donna Maye Bice, May 29, 1947; children: Carolyn Darby Eymann, Lorna Dale, Elizabeth Darby Bass, Andrea Darby Perdue. Ordained to ministry Bapt. Ch., 1950; pastor Sunnyside Bapt. Ch., Flagstaff, Ariz., 1947-48, First Bapt. Ch. of Clifton, Ariz., 1950-55, West High Bapt. Ch., Phoenix, 1955-90; pastor emeritus, 1990—; dep. assessor Greenlee County, 1951-55; instr. English lit. and pastoral subjects Southwestern Conservative Bapt. Bible Coll., Phoenix, 1961-87. Chmn. bd. Conservative Bapt. Found. Ariz., 1974-83, Gospel Wings, 1960-88; v.p. Ariz. Bapt. Conf., 1976-83; pres. Ariz. Alcohol-Narcotic Edn. Assn., 1968—. Recipient God, Family and Country award Freeman Inst., 1981. Mem. Evang. Philos. Soc., Greater Phoenix Assn. Evangelicals (pres. 1960-63), Ariz. Breakfast Club, (chaplain 1969—). Contbr. articles to profl. jours. Republican. Home: 5628 N 11th Dr Phoenix AZ 85013 Office: 3301 N 19th Ave Phoenix AZ 85015

DARCY, HAROLD P., chaplain; b. Newark, July 10, 1929; s. Michael and Annie (Keaney) D. BA magna cum laude, Seton Hall U., 1951; Licentiate in Sacred Theology magna cum laude, Gregorian U., 1955, JCD summa cum laude, 1960. Assoc. pastor St. Joseph of Palisades Ch., West New York, N.J., 1955-56; asst. chancellor, actuary of tribunal Archdiocese of Newark, N.J., 1956-57; sec. Apostolic Delegate, Washington, 1961-71; pastor St. Vincent de Paul Ch., Bayonne, N.J., 1971-72; rector Immaculate Conception Sem., Mahwah, N.J., 1972-74, North Am. Coll., Rome, Italy, 1974-79; pastor Notre Dame Ch., North Caldwell, N.J., 1979-87; chaplain, adj. faculty mem. sch. law Seton Hall U., Newark, 1988—; bd. trustees Seton Hall U., South Orange, N.J., 1972-74; vicar del. Military Ordinariate, Rome, 1974-79; mem. commn. ecumenical and interreligious affairs Archdiocese of Newark, 1984—, dir. med. moral commn., 1988—. Contbr. articles to profl. jours.; mem. editorial bd. The Cath. Advocate, Archdiocese of Newark, 1972-74, bd. trustees, 1980—. Mem. Supreme Ct. N.J. Dist. Ethics Com. for Essex County, Newark, 1984-87. Named Hon. Prelate, Pope Paul VI, 1971, Chaplain of His Holiness, Pope John XXIII, 1962. Mem. Canon Law Soc. Am., Cath. Theol. Soc. Am. Office: Seton Hall U Sch Law 1111 Raymond Blvd Newark NJ 07102

D'ARCY, JOHN MICHAEL, bishop; b. Brighton, Mass., Aug. 18, 1932. Student, St. John's Sem., Brighton, 1949-57; ThD, Angelicum U., Rome, 1968. Ordained priest Roman Cath. Ch., 1957. Spiritual dir., prof. theology St. John's Sem., 1968-85; ordained titular bishop of Mediana and aux. bishop of Boston Archdiocese of Boston, 1975-85; bishop Archdiocese of Ft. Wayne-South Bend, Ind., 1985—. Office: Diocese of Ft Wayne-South Bend PO Box 390 Fort Wayne IN 46801

DARCY, KEITH THOMAS, educator, finance company executive; b. N.Y.C., June 18, 1948; s. Donald and Geraldine (Kindermann) D.; m. Lynne Alison Cumming, June 17, 1972; children: Erin Lyn, Timothy James. BS in Econs., Fordham U., 1970; MBA, Iona Coll., New Rochelle, N.Y., 1974; postgrad., N.Y. Theol. Sem. With Bankers Trust Co., N.Y.C., 1970-77; v.p. Marine Midland Bank N.A., N.Y.C., 1977-82; chief exec. officer IGM div. of Frank B. Hall & Co., Inc., Briarcliff Manor, N.Y., 1982-83; dir. human resource div. Marine Midland Bank, N.Y.C., 1984-89; pres., chief exec. officer Found. For Leadership, Quality and Ethics Practice, N.Y.C., 1989—; adj. faculty mem. Marymount Coll., 1978—, Mercy Coll., 1975-82; mem. faculty consumer bankers Assoc. Grad. Sch. of Bank Mgmt., U. Va. Author: I Quit My Job Today. Treas. Westchester County Rep. Com., White Plains, N.Y., 1979-89; asst. treas. N.Y. State Friends for Jim Buckley, 1976; dir NCCJ, 1977-85; trustee Bedford Presbyn. Ch., N.Y., 1982-87; mem. Westchester Blue Ribbon Commn. to Formulate County Housing Policy, 1979; trustee March of Dimes, Westchester, 1978-84, chmn. Exec. Walkathon, 1978-81. Mem. Delta Mu Delta. Club: Soc. Friendly Sons of St. Patrick (pres. 1985). Home: Horseshoe Hill W Pound Ridge NY 10576

DARETY, PAUL RAYMOND, minister; b. Humboldt, Tenn., May 4, 1962; s. Raymond Reams and Bettye Jean (Luckey) D.; m. Trena Suzanne DePriest, July 6, 1984; 1 child, Ethan Paul. BA, Freed-Hardeman Coll., 1984; student, David-Lipscomb Coll., 1984-87. Student intern Ch. of Christ, Milan, Tenn., 1981-83; min. Ch. of Christ, Trezevant, Tenn., 1984-86, Bradford, Tenn., 1986—; speaker Bradford Sr. Citizens Ctr., 1986—. Participant Gov.'s Alliance Drug Free Tenn., Bradford, 1988. Mem. Alpha Chi. Home: 127 Bradford Acres Bradford TN 38316 Office: Ch of Christ 138 W Front St Bradford TN 38316

DARK, DANIEL HERBERT, minister; b. Beaumont, Tex., Dec. 18, 1954; s. Jack and Edra L. (Jenkins) D.; m. Priscilla Jo James, Aug. 12, 1978; children: Jonathan, James, Miriam, Rachel, Joseph. BA, William Jennings Bryan Coll., 1977; ThM, Dallas Theol. Sem., 1982; postgrad., La. Christian U., 1990—. Cert. Christian counselor, Tex. Youth min. Richland BIble Fellowship, Richardson, Tex., 1979-81; assoc. min. Westwood Bible Ch., Beaumont, Tex., 1982-84, sr. pastor, 1985—; prof. Bible La. Christian U., Lake Charles, 1990—; part-time counselor, Beaumont. Invocation City Coun. Meetings, Beaumont, 1982-90; mem. Young Men's Bus. League, Beaumont, 1989-90. Home: 996 W Lucas Beaumont TX 77706 Office: Westwood Bible Ch 2394 W Lucas Beaumont TX 77706

DARKES, ANNA SUE, religious organization administrator, writer; b. Lebanon, Pa., Feb. 5, 1927; d. John W. and Anna S. (Flinchbaugh) Darkes; diploma Lebanon Bus. Coll., 1945, Phila. Coll. Bible, 1949. Bookkeeper, E. H. Gerhart & Co., Jonestown, Pa., 1945-47; missionary Scripture Memory Mt. Mission, 1950-73; mem. Corp. Calvary Fellowship Homes, 1979—; co-founder, exec. dir. Faith Venture Visuals, Inc., Lititz, Pa., 1972—; co-founder Mayking Bapt. Ch., 1958; overseas seminar lectr., Australia, Japan, New Zealand, Ireland, Ecuador, Brazil, Holland. Recipient Alumna of Yr. award Phila. Coll. Bible, 1977. Author: Sailing on Life's Sea, 1973; Pioneering of Life's Trail, How To Be Saved and Know It, 1974; Exploring God's Word, 1975; God of Space, 1976; Campsites of Victory, 1977; Christ Our Shepherd, 1978; How to Make and Use Overhead Transparencies, 1977; 80 Cool Ideas for Your Summer Outreach, 1984; author, filmer video tng. tapes 30 Whys and Ways of Overhead Use, The Basics for Making Transparencies, Teaching Your Overhead Good Manners and New Tricks, 1983, The Innovative Teaching Team: You and Your Overhead Projector, 1987; Faith Venture Visual In-Depth Communication Enrichment Seminar, 1991, designer Faith Venture Visual's Instaframe. Office: 510 E Main St Lititz PA 17543

DARLING, FRANK CLAYTON, former political science educator, educational institute administrator; b. Chgo., May 8, 1925; s. Frank D. and Nora (Pomeroy) D.; m. Ann Bardwell, June 10, 1952; children: Diane Christine, Heather Ann, Elizabeth Carolyn. B.A., Principia Coll., Elsah, Ill., 1951; M.A., U. Chgo., 1957; Ph.D., Am. U., 1960. Lectr. Chulalongkorn U., Thailand, 1953-56; prof. U. Colo., 1960-67; prof. polit. sci., head dept. DePauw U., 1967-79; prof. polit. sci. Principia Coll., 1981-87; adminstr. Inst. Study of Christian Healing, 1987-88; pres., editor Vista Publs., Boulder, Colo., 1989—; writer on religion and politics, 1988—. Author: Thailand and the United States, 1965, Thailand: The Modern Kingdom, 1971, The Westernization of Asia: A Comparative Political Analysis, 1979, Biblical Healing: Hebrew and Christian Roots, 1989, Christian Healing in the Middle Ages, 1990. Served with USNR, 1943-46. Address: 36 Benthaven Pl Boulder CO 80303

DARLING, GEORGE CURTIS, minister, administrator; b. Xenia, Ohio, Nov. 23, 1928; s. Russell M. and Mary Elizabeth (Young) D.; m. Edna Pearlen Phillips, May 1, 1960; (div. Apr. 1973) 1 child, Curtis; m. Mary Elizabeth Miller, Oct. 24, 1952 (div. Aug. 1956), 1 child, Kirk; m. Evelyn Cornelia Woodfork, Apr. 10, 1976. Diploma in Theology, Am. Bapt. Theol. Sem., Dayton, Ohio, 1970. Ordained to ministry Bapt. Ch., 1963. Pastor 2nd Bapt. Ch., Del., Ohio, 1966-71; supply pastor Tabernacle Bapt. Ch., Columbus, Ohio, 1974; pastor Flintridge Bapt. Ch., Columbus, 1980-91; v.p. Springfield (Ohio) Dist. Sunday Sch. and Bapt. Tng. Union. Author: (booklet) How to Find God, 1969. Bd. dirs., pres. Liberty Ctr., Delaware, Ohio, 1968-70; mem. Delaware County Community Action Orgn., 1967. With U.S. Army, 1950-52, Korea.; ret. USAF, 1988. Recipient Hon. Sci. award, Bausch & Lomb, 1946. Mem. Eastern Union Missionary Bapt. Assn. (statistical clk Ohio 1981-85, 3rd vice moderator 1985-87, 2nd vice moderator, 1987-91), Columbus Bapt. Ministers and Laity Bible League (instr. 1987—). Home: 3546 Eisenhower Rd Columbus OH 43224 *On cloudy days when the sun is hidden from view, flying above the clouds enables one to see the brightness of the sun. When things go wrong in my life, I take a spiritual trip beyond the darkness of the moment into the sunlight of hope.*

DARLING, PAMELA ANN WOOD, religious consultant, educator; b. Lake Forest, Ill., Aug. 31, 1943; d. Charles Edwards Jr. and Ann (Rayner) Wood. BA, Northwestern U., 1965; MS, Columbia U., 1971; MA, Gen. Theol. Sem., 1987, ThD, 1991. Cons. Episcopal Ch. Women's Program, 1985—; adminstr. Episcopal Women's History Project, N.Y.C., 1985-91; fellow Gen. Theol. Sem., N.Y.C., 1987-91; adj. prof. ch. history Gen. Theol. Sem., 1991—; mem. steering com. Nat. Network of Lay Profls., Episcopal Ch., 1987-90; mem. Gen. Bd. Examining Chaplains, Episcopal Ch., 1991—; bd. dirs. Episcopal Ch. Pub. Co., 1991—. Author: Preservation Planning Program, 1982; editor: Reaching Toward Wholeness: Women in Episcopal Church, 1988; contbr. numerous articles to profl. jours. Recipient Esther J. Piercy award ALA, 1979. Mem. Am. Acad. of Religion, Coll. Theology Soc., Episcopal Women's History Project (asst. treas. 1987-91), Episcopal Women's Caucus, Episcopal Communicators. Democrat. Home and Office: 11 Brookshire Ln Philadelphia PA 19116

DARLING, RICHARD, ecumenical agency director. Head Thunder Bay Coun. Chs., Ont., Can. Office: Thunder Bay Coun Chs, 1800 Moodie St E, Thunder Bay, ON Canada P7E 4Z2*

DARMOJUWONO, JUSTIN CARDINAL, retired archbishop; b. Godean, Yogyakarta, Indonesia, Nov. 2, 1914; s. Yoseph Surodikoro and Mary Ngatinah. Diploma, Tchr. Sch., Muntilan, Indonesia, 1935, Minor Sem., Yogyakarta, 1942, Major Sem., Yogyakarta, 1947, Gregorian U., Rome, 1955. Ordained Roman Cath. priest, 1947. Tchr. Minor Sem., 1947-48; priest local parish Yogyakarta, 1948-50, Klaten, Indonesia, 1950-54, Surakarta, Indonesia, 1956-62; priest, vicar gen. Semarang, Indonesia, 1962-63; archbishop Semarang, 1963-81; ret., 1981; bishop Indonesian Army, 1964-81; cardinal 1967—. Home: Kamfer Raya 49, Semarang 50237, Indonesia

DART, JOHN SEWARD, religion news writer; b. Peekskill, N.Y., Aug. 1, 1936; s. Seward Homer and Vella Marion (Haverstock) D.; m. Gloria Joan Walker, Aug. 31, 1957; children—Kim, John W., Randall, Christopher. B.A., U. Colo., 1958. Staff writer UPI, Indpls. and Los Angeles, 1961-65; sci. writer Calif. Inst. Tech., Pasadena, 1966-67; religion writer Los Angeles Times, 1967—. Author: The Laughing Savior, 1976, The Jesus of Heresy and History, revised, expanded edit., 1988. Served with U.S. Army, 1958-61. Recipient Supple Meml. award Religion Newswriters Assn., 1980; Merrell Meml. award Jim Merrell Religion Liberty Found., 1980, William E. Leidt award Episcopal Ch., 1980, Angel award Religion in Media, 1985; NEH fellow Stanford U., 1973-74. Mem. Soc. Prof. Journalists (chpt. pres. 1976), Religion Newswriters Assn. (pres. 1990—), Soc. Bibl. Lit. (mem.-at-large exec. com. Pacific Coast region 1990—). Democrat. Office: Los Angeles Times Times Mirror Sq Los Angeles CA 90053

DASCOLI, MICHAEL ANTHONY, youth pastor; b. Tucson, Feb. 4, 1959; s. Ralph Albert and Jean Marie (Beni) D.; m. Valerie Ann Jones, Aug. 3, 1985; 1 child, Carlyn Rianna. Student, No. Ariz. U., 1977-78; cert., Tucson Skill Ctr., 1979; BA in Theology, Bartlesville (Okla.) Wesleyan Coll., 1985. Electrician Gates Learjet Corp., Tucson, 1979-82, Bartlesville Wesleyan Coll., 1982-85; youth minister Bartlesville First Wesleyan Ch., 1985-87, Greeley (Colo.) Wesleyan Ch., 1987—; dist. youth pres. Colo. Wesleyan Youth, Denver, 1984—; mem. Youth for Christ, Greeley, 1987—; chaplain football team Greeley West High sch., 1989—; mem. steering com. Wesleyan Ch., Marion, Ind., 1989—. Mem. steering com. Greeley Dream Team, 1989; chaplain CAP, Bartlesville, 1986; min. Wesleyan Ch., 1985—. Mem. Youth Network, Bartlesville Wesleyan Coll. Alumni Assn. (pres. 1987—). Republican. Avocations: music, rocketry, outdoors, family. Home: 903 24th Ave Greeley CO 80631 Office: Greeley Wesleyan Ch 3600 W 22d Greeley CO 80634

DATTILO, NICHOLAS C., bishop. Ordained priest Roman Cath. Ch., 1958, apptd. Eighth Bishop of Harrisburg, 1989, ordained Bishop of Harrisburg, 1990. Home and Office: 4800 Union Deposit Road Harrisburg PA 17111

DAUSEY, GARY RALPH, minister; b. Chgo., Jan. 8, 1940; s. Ralph S. and Theresa (Campbell) D.; m. Julie, Greg. Student, Moody Bible Inst., 1958-59; BA, Taylor U., 1962; MA, Wheaton Grad. Sch. Theol., 1965. Ordained to ministry Christian Ch., 1963. Pastor Noble Congl. Christian Ch., Noble, Ind., 1959-62; asst. dir. Moody Bible Inst., Audio-visual Dept., Chgo., 1962-63; v.p. Youth for Christ Internat., Wheaton, Ill., 1964-81; exec. v.p. Youth for Christ USA, Wheaton, Ill., 1982-87; assoc. pastor Wheaton Bible Ch., Ill., 1987—; bd. dirs. Metro-Chgo. Youth for Christ, Chgo. Author, editor: Youth Leader's Source Book, 1984 (recipient Gold Medalion); (with others) Parents and Teenagers, 1985, Parents and Children, 1986, Practical Christianity, 1987; translator: Life Application Bible, 1987. Recipient Editorial award, Evang. Press Assn., 1967, Pres. award, Youth for Christ USA, 1985. Mem. Christian Ministry Mgmt. Assn. Home: 309 Brookside Circle Wheaton IL 60187 Office: Wheaton Bible Ch Main at Franklin Wheaton IL 60187

DAVENPORT, DAVID, university president, lawyer; b. Sheboygan, Wis., Oct. 24, 1950; s. E. Guy and Beverly J. (Snoddy) D.; m. Sally Nelson, Aug. 13, 1977; children—Katherine, Charles, Scott. B.A., Stanford U., 1972; J.D., U. Kans., Lawrence, 1977. Bar: Calif. 1977, U.S. Dist. Ct. (so. dist.) Calif., 1977. Assoc. Gray, Cary, Ames & Frye, San Diego, 1977-78; min. Ch. of Christ, San Diego, 1979; law prof. Pepperdine U., Malibu, Calif., 1980—, gen. counsel, 1981-83, exec. v.p., 1983-85, pres., 1985—. Contbr. articles to profl. jours.; contbr. to Fed. Antitrust Law, 1985. Mem. Adminstrv. Conf. of U.S., Washington, 1984-86; bd. overseers Hoover Inst., Stanford U.; bd. dirs. L.A. World Affairs Coun., Nat. Legal Ctr. for Pub. Interest, Washington. Mem. Mchts. and Mfrs. Assn. Calif. (bd. dirs. 1985—), Am. Assn. Pres. of Ind. Colls. and Univs. (bd. dirs. 1985—, pres.), Young Pres. Orgn., L.A. Area C. of C. (bd. dirs.), Order of Coif. Republican. Home: 24255 Pacific Coast Hwy Malibu CA 90265 Office: Pepperdine U Office of Pres 24255 Pacific Coast Hwy Malibu CA 90265

DAVENPORT, HAROLD ALLEN, minister; b. Daisy, Tenn., Dec. 22, 1926; s. James W. and Martha Elizabeth (Swafford) D.; m. Jean Deloris Usher, Aug. 31, 1952; 1 child, Dixie Ann. BA, U. Tenn., 1949; MDiv, Vanderbilt Sch. of Divinity, 1952; DD (hon.), Piedmost Coll., 1978. Ordained to ministry United Ch. of Christ. Pastor First Congregational United Ch. of Christ, Ankeny, Iowa, 1952-57, Council Bluffs, Iowa, 1957-68; pastor Miami Shores (Fla.) Community United Ch. of Christ, 1968—. Mem. Human Rights Com., North Shore Med. Ctr., Miami, Fla., 1982—. With USN, 1944-46, Atlantic. Paul Harris Fellow, Rotary Internat., Miami Shores, 1987. Mem. Dade Monroe Mission Coun., Fla. Conf. United Ch. of Chrsit (bd. dirs. 1978-80), Rotary, Clams. Office: Miami Shores Community United Church of Christ 9823 NE 4th Ave Miami Shores FL 33138

DAVENPORT, J. LEE, clergyman, social work consultant; b. Mayo, Fla., Oct. 2, 1935; s. Jesse David and Fronie Bell (Hadley) D.; m. Bernice M. Webb, Dec. 22, 1958; children: Valarie, Velina, Otis, David. BA in History, Cameron U., Lawton, Okla., 1970; MS in Psychiat. Social Work, U. Okla., 1975; student, Am. Bapt. Theol. Seminary, Nashville, 1962-65; postgrad., U. Tex., Arlington, 1981-87. Lic. clin. social worker, Okla.; diplomate Am. Bd. Examiners in Clin. Social Work; ordained to ministry Bapt. Ch. Social worker Okla. Dept. Mental Health, Lawton, 1970-85; individual and family therapist Christian Family Counseling Ctr., Lawton, 1985-87; sr. pastor St. John's Bapt. Ch., Lawton, 1965—; v.p. Okla. Bapt. State Conv.; discussion leader Nat. Bapt. Congress Christian Edn.; instr. Okla. Bapt. Congress Christian Edn.; dir. Lawton br. Okla. Sch. Religion; dir. leadership edn. Western Dist. Assn. Pres. Okla. One Church One Child Corp., Coalition for Minority Affairs Okla.; bd. dirs. Cameron U. Found., Lawton-Ft. Sill United Way. With USAF, 1953-58. Recipient Internat. Awareness and Involvement award Delta Sigma Theta, 1985, Richard Allen award Davis Chapel African-Meth.-Episcopal Ch., 1987, Humanitarian award Alpha Kappa Alpha, 1988, speaker's award III U.S. Corp. Arty., 1990, NW Kiwanis, 1990, Human Svc. and Human Rights award Lawton Pub. Schs., 1990. Mem. NASW, Christian Assn. for Psychol. Studies, NAACP (life, Outstanding Leadership award 1986, Humanitarian award 1987), Omega Psi Phi

(Omega Citizen of Yr. award 1986). Office: St John's Bapt Ch 1501 Roosevelt St Lawton OK 73501

DAVENPORT, JAMES GUYTHON, minister; b. Columbia, N.C., Sept. 15, 1932; s. Llewellyn Harrison and Lillian Mae (Brickhouse) D.; m. Bethany Lavinia Sawyer, Nov. 23, 1956 (div. July 1983); 1 child, Kathleen Nina Davenport Ingram; m. Jacqueline Ann Wilson, Aug. 5, 1983; children: Daniel, Jeffrey, Jack, Jerry. AA, Chowan Coll., 1963; BA, Miss. Coll., 1965; MDiv, Southeastern Bapt. Theol. Sem., 1968; Clin. Pastoral Edn. Cert., Cen. State Hosp., Milledgeville, Ga., 1971; DD, Bethany Theol. Sem., 1991. Ordained to ministry So. Bapt. Conv., 1963; cert. hosp., instnl., mil. chaplain. Pastor Holy Grove Bapt. Ch., Powellsville, N.C., 1963, Siloam Bapt. Ch., Windsor, NC., 1965-68, Fellowship Bapt. Ch., Ettrick, Va., 1968-70, 71-83, Dinwiddie (Va.) Bapt. Ch., 1983-85, McKenney (Va.) Bapt. Ch., 1983—; substitute tch. Dinwiddie County Sch. Bd., 1985—; chaplain CAP, Hopewell, Va., 1969-83, Ellrick-Matoaca Rescue Squad, 1973-74, Petersburg (Va.) Correctional Ctr., 1974-83; staff counselor Southside Area Counseling Svc., Petersburg, 1968—. Vol. fireman Saint Brides Fire Dept., Chesapeake, Va., 1959-61; mem. Ettrick-Matoaca Rescue Squad, 1968-74, Planning Commn., McKenney, 1989—, electorial bd. Dinwiddie County, 1985—; chaplain Petersburg Fraternal Order Police, 1975-80 (Outsanding Svc. plaque 1977). Mem. Petersburg Bapt. Assn. (sec. 1974). Home: Box 14 McKenney VA 23872 Office: McKenney Bapt Ch Zehmer Ave McKenney VA 23872 *I have found that all too often when people want to change their life for the better they depend only on their own will power and never realize that God has given us the power of the Holy Spirit to work with ours in our transformation.*

DAVENPORT, L. B., bishop. Bishop Ch. of God in Christ, Plymouth, N.C. Office: Ch of God in Christ PO Box 156 Plymouth NC 28803*

DAVENPORT, MITCHELL FRANCIS, pastor; b. Clinton, Iowa, July 17, 1960; s. Adrian Mitchell and Frances Arlynn (Eckel) D.; m. Judy Kay Simmons, June 18, 1983; children: Keith Mitchell, Kent Michael, Kayla Michele. BA in Religion, Olivet Nazarene U., 1987, postgrad., 1988. Ordained to ministry, 1989. Pastor Princeton (Ill.) Ch. of the Nazarene, 1987—; ch. plantin com. Northwestern Ill. Dist. Ch. of the Nazarene, 1989-90. Contbr. articles to profl. jours. Treas. Princeton Ministerial Assn., 1988—; mem. Dist. Bd. Ministerial Studies, 1991. Recipient Am. Bible Soc. Award for Biblical Scholarship Am. Bible Soc., 1987. Mem. Wesleyan Theol. Soc., Christians for Biblical Equality. Church of the Nazarene. Avocations: reading, outdoor activities, computers. Office: Princeton Ch of Nazarene 30 N Dallas St Princeton IL 61356

DAVES, DON MICHAEL, minister; b. Wichita Falls, Tex., Mar. 4, 1938; s. Floyd Lee and Johnnie Majorie (Dunn) D.; m. Patricia N. McLean, Aug. 29, 1958; children: Paul Lee, Donna Michelle. BA, Midwestern U., 1959; ThM, So. Meth. U., 1963; D. Humanities (hon.), Southwestern Coll., 1971. Ordained to ministry Meth. Ch., 1963. Pastor 1st United Meth. Ch., Holliday, Tex., 1963-66, Prarie Heights United Meth. Ch., Grand Prairie, Tex., 1966-72; minister to soc. North Tex. Conf. United Meth. Ch., 1972-77; pastor Meml. United Meth. Ch., Dallas, 1977-78; assoc. pastor Preston Hollow United Meth. Ch., Dallas, 1978-81, 1st United Meth. Ch., Duncanville, Tex., 1981-85; pastor 1st United Meth. Ch., Cedar Hill, Tex., 1985—; mem. North Tex. Conf., United Meth. Ch.; trustee Charlton Meth. Hosp., Dallas. Author: Devotional Talks for Children, 1961, Famous Hymns & Their Writers, 1962, Sermon Outlines on Romans, 1962, Meditations on Early Christian Symbols, 1963, Come with Faith, 1964, Young Readers Book of Christian Symbolism, 1967, Advent: A Calendar of Devotions, 1971, Joy is Now, 1988. Named for Best Children's Book by a Tex. Author, Tex. Inst. Letters, 1968. Mem. Am. Assn. Pastoral Counselors, Ministerial Alliance Cedar Hill (pres. 1987—), Lions. Home: 1101 Balfour Cedar Hill TX 75104 Office: 1st United Meth Ch 127 Roberts PO Box 187 Cedar Hill TX 75104

DAVID, AUSTIN, brother, educator; b. N.Y.C., Nov. 22, 1935; s. Hugh Felix and Gertrude (Jordan) Carroll. BA in Physics, Cath. U., 1958; MAT in Physics, Brown U., 1963; PhD in Sci. Edn., NYU, 1978. Cert. secondary math. and sci. tchr., N.Y.; joined Bros. of Christian Schs., 1953. Instr. De La Salle Acad., Newport, R.I., 1958-62, vice prin., 1961-62; instr. Hillside Hall, Troy, N.Y., 1962-63, Mater Christi High Sch., Astoria, N.Y., 1963-64; data processing cons. Diocese of Bklyn., 1964-68; asst. to chancellor for info svcs. Archdiocese of N.Y., N.Y.C., 1968-82; dir. rsch. Pope John Paul II Ctr. of Prayer for Study of Peace, N.Y.C., 1982-85; dir. info. svc. Cath. Near East Welfare Assn., N.Y.C., 1985—; advisor on Middle East affairs Holy See Mission to UN, N.Y.C., 1985—; adj. prof. NYU, N.Y.C., 1978—; assoc. provincial for fin. L.I.-New Eng. Province, 1978-82. Editor-in-chief mag. Catholic Near East, 1990—; contbr. numerous articles to profl. jours. Treas. FSC Found., Oak Brook, Ill., 1985—; chmn. bd. dirs. Christian Bros. Investment Svc., Oak Brook, 1982-87; bd. dirs., pres. Martin De Porres Community Ctr., Astoria, N.Y., 1977-81; trustee La Salle Mil. Acad., Oakdale, N.Y. Named knight Equestrian Order Holy Sepulchre, Jerusalem, 1987. Mem. Cath. Acad. Scis. (sec. 1986—), World Future Soc., Am. Teilhard Assn., Nat. Sci. Tchrs. Assn. (Star award 1971). Earth Soc. Found. (bd. dirs. 1982—). Home: 367 Clermont Ave Brooklyn NY 11238 Office: Cath Near East Welfare Assn 1011 1st Ave New York NY 10022

DAVIDSON, ELIZABETH BECK, minister; b. Pitts., July 22, 1908; d. William Porter and Ethel Mae (Higgins) Beck; m. James A. Davidson, June 9, 1933 (dec.); children: David B., John, W. Lee, J. Porter. BA, Denison U., 1930; postgrad., Andover Newton Theol. Sem., 1933-34. Ordained to ministry Bapt. Ch., 1980. Min. various chs. Active in various YWCA's. Mem. AAUW, Chi Omega. Republican. Avocations: travel, music, continuous education, reading. Home: 4676 Park Mirasol Calabasas Park CA 91302

DAVIDSON, ERIC NATHAN, minister, credit manager; b. Asheboro, N.C., Apr. 28, 1959; s. James Wilson and Virginia Lucille (Brown) D.; m. Deborah Louise Pell, June 12, 1982; 1 child, Jonathan Wilson. Student, John Wesley Coll., 1981-82, Cen. Carolina Community Coll., 1991, Southeastern Bapt. Theol. Sem., 1991. Treas. N.C. east dist. Wesleyan Ch., 1980-83; youth pastor Reynolds Meml. Wesleyan Ch., Troy, N.C., 1981, Sawyersville Wesleyan Ch., Asheboro, 1981-86; min. youth/children Jonesboro Heights Bapt. Ch., Sanford, N.C., 1986—; office, credit mgr. Lowe's of Sanford, 1983—. Bd. dirs. Lee County Am. Heart Assn., Sanford, 1990—. Mem. Fellowship Christian Athletes (adult chpt. 1990—), Sandy Creek Bapt. Assn. (exec. bd., youth dir. 1989—). Republican. Home: 5109 Briarwood Dr Sanford NC 27330 Office: Jonesboro Heights Bapt Ch 316 W Main St Sanford NC 27330-5922 *Life is too short to let one precious moment be wasted in anger. Live each day as if it were your last opportunity to ever be in contact with that person. Let God control your life, and live life to its fullest, because that's the way God intended for us to live.*

DAVIDSON, GEORGE THOMAS, JR., minister, educator; b. Winchester, Mass., Dec. 4, 1916; s. George Thomas and Allie Elizabeth (Patterson) D.; B.S., Bowdoin Coll., 1938; D.Ed. (hon.), 1976; postgrad. Columbia U., 1938-39; M.A., Boston U., 1954, postgrad., 1959-61; m. Frances Ray, Sept. 30, 1944; children—Richard G., Raylene Alice Newbury. Tchr., coach Kennett High Sch., Conway, N.H., 1939-42, vice-prin., 1946-47, prin., 1947-57, tchr.-coach, 1957-59, sch. counselor, 1959-61, dir. guidance services, 1961-76; cons. admissions testing program Regional Office of Coll. Bd., 1976-80; interim lay preacher Congl. Chs., Bartlett, Jackson, Fryeburg, Chocorua, Tamworth, Conway, Ossipee, N.H., 1951-53; lay minister First Christian Ch., Freedom, N.H., 1953-70; ordained to ministry Christian Ch., 1970; minister First Christian Ch., Freedom, N.H., 1970-89, 2d Congl. Ch., Ossipee, N.H., 1969-89; Protestant chaplain N.H. State Police, 1973—; vis. instr. U. N.H., 1964-67, 71-72, Gorham State Coll., 1967-70, N.H. Dept. Edn., 1970-72. Mem. Carroll County YMCA Com., State YMCA Youth Com.; mem. Gov's. Adv. Bd. Tech. Services in Health Field; mem. N.H. Interscholastic Athletic Assn.; pres. N.H. Assn. Secondary Sch. Prins., 1953-54; owner, dir. Camp Wakuta for Boys, 1951-67; mem. county com. Gov's. Com. on Crime and Juvenile Delinquency; bd. dirs. Carroll County Mental Health Services; co-founder, exec. sec. Mount Washington Citizens Scholarship Found.; dir. Conway Adult Basic Edn. Program; moderator 2d Congl. Ch., Conway, N.H.; coach North Conway Am. Legion Baseball; vice-chmn. N.H. State Adv. Council Vocat.-Tech. Edn.; tour guide N.H. Coll. and Univ. Council; sports announcer Sta. WBNC, Conway, N.H.; test center supr. Coll. Bd., Fryeburg, Maine; trustee Fryeburg Acad., 1985-89; chaplain Carroll County Sheriff's Dept., 1985—, Conway Fire Dept., 1985—. Served to capt. USAAF, 1942-46. Named Carroll County Educator of Year, 1954; recipient First Achievement award N.H. Personnel and Guidance Assn., 1966, Disting. Bowdoin Educator award Bowdoin Coll. Alumni Assn., 1967, Carl Lundholm award State N.H., 1972, Granite State award U. N.H., 1976, Disting. Service award New Eng. Assn. Coll. Admissions Counselors, 1976, Gov's. Commendation for Service to Youth, 1976, Community Service award Freedom Old Home Week Sunday Service, 1979, Service to Community award Conway Grange, 1979; Disting. Service award Mt. Washington Valley Kiwanis Club, 1983. Mem. Nat. Assn. Coll. Admissions Counselors (assembly del. 1967-69), New Eng. Assn. Coll. Admissions Counselors (dir. 1970-74), N.H. Vocat. Assn. (pres.), N.H. Sch. Counselors Assn. (pres. 1969-70), Rotary (Paul Harris Fellow North Conway chpt. 1988). Home: RD 1 Box 214 Freedom NH 03836

DAVIDSON, GERALD RAY, minister; b. Moberly, Mo., Jan. 14, 1936; s. Robert Andrew and Geneva Gay (Farris) D.; m. Verlena Stone, July 10, 1955; children: Douglas, Debra, Darla. AA, Hannibal LaGrange Coll., 1958, DDiv (hon.), 1986; BA, N.E. Mo. State U., 1960; MDiv, S.W. Bapt. Sem., 1968. Ordained to ministry So. Bapt. Conv., 1958. Pastor Ten Mile and Arbela Bapt. Chs., Mo., 1957-58; pastor First Bapt. Ch., Wyaconda, Mo., 1958-61, Kahoka, Mo., 1961-66, Venus, Tex., 1966-68, Mansfield, Tex., 1968-70, Memphis, 1970-76, Arnold, Mo., 1976—; pres. Mo. Bapt. Pastor's Conf., 1989-90, Mo. Bapt. Conv., 1991-92; 1st v.p. Mo. Bapt. Conv., 1990-91, So. Bapt. Conv. Pastor's Conf., 1988. Office: First Bapt Ch 2012 Missouri State Rd Arnold MO 63010

DAVIDSON, GLEN WILLIAM, medical humanities educator, researcher, author; b. Wendell, Idaho, July 26, 1936; s. W. Dean and Grace (Barnum) D.; m. Shirlee Proctor, Nov. 26, 1971; children—Heather, Kristin. B.A., U. Pacific, 1958; M.Div., Drew U., 1961; Ph.D., Claremont Grad. Sch., 1964. Ordained to ministry United Meth. Ch. as elder, 1962. Asst. prof., chaplain Colgate U., Hamilton, N.Y., 1964-67; asst. prof. history of religions U. Chgo., 1968-70; fellow U. Iowa Coll. Medicine, Iowa City, 1970-72; assoc. prof. culture and medicine So. Ill. U., Springfield, 1972—, prof., chmn. dept. med. humanities Sch. Medicine, 1974—; founding chmn., bd. advisors SHARE, a mutual help group for parents of prenatal loss, 1980; chmn. bd. Park Ridge Ctr. for the Study of Health, Faith and Ethics, Chgo., 1980-89. Author: Understanding Mourning, 1984; (also editor) Hospice: Development and Administration, 1985; (with Lila Hill) They Came to Build A Community, 1986, Living with Dying, revised and expanded, 1990, Human Remains: Contemporary Controversies, 1990; editor Caduceus A Mus. Jour. for the Health Scis., 1985—; So. Ill. U. Med. Humanities Series. Author 10 patient counseling films, 1985, assoc. editor Death Studies, 1976-89. Dir. Pearson Mus., Springfield, 1972—; pres. Med. Mus. Assn. Recipient Spl. Merit award Am. Hosp. Assn., 1980, Disting. Alumnus award Claremont Grad. Sch., 1982, Spl. Recognition award Am. Assn. for State and Local History, 1986; named Louis Forman Disting. Lectr., St. Lukes's Hosp., Kansas City, Mo., 1984; grantee So. Ill. U. Found., 1978—, Ill. Med. Soc. Found., 1981, Luth. Gen. Hosp., Park Ridge, 1983-85, Inst. for Mus. Svcs., 1990. Mem. Dirs. of Human Values Programs (convenor 1980-83), Am. Assn. Marriage and Family Therapists (cert. 1974), Am. Acad. Religion, Soc. for Values in Higher Edn. Methodist. Avocations: gardening, philately, music. Home: 13 Pinehurst Dr Springfield IL 62704 Office: So Ill U Sch Medicine PO Box 19230 Springfield IL 62794-9230

DAVIDSON, JAMES WILSON, clinical psychologist; b. Muncie, Ind., Apr. 22, 1950; s. James Wayne and Mary Marguerite (Sanford) D.; m. Nancy Lee Hendershot, Aug. 30, 1969; children: Melissa Ann, Amanda Corynne, Kevin Patrick. BS, Mich. State U., 1972; PhD, Kent State U., 1975; postgrad., Ashland (Ohio) Theol. Sem., 1980-82. Ordained to ministry Assemblies of God, 1988. Coord. Ctr. on Rsch. and Evaluation, Ashtabula, Ohio, 1974-77; pres. The Children's Ctr., Ashtabula, 1978-80, Computech Data Systems, Ashtabula, 1978-82; v.p. Davidson Assocs., Ashtabula, 1977-86; assoc. pastor First Assembly of God, Ashtabula, 1986-88; sr. pastor Metro Ch., Cleve., 1988—; chief exec. officer Heart and Hand Found., Cleve., 1988—; dir. Ohio Dist. Coun. Urban Missions Ministries, Columbus, 1990—. Recipient 414th Point of Light award White House, 1991; Kent State U. fellow, 1973-74. Mem. Christian Ministries Mgmt. Assn., Christian Camping Internat., Am. Camping Assn., Kiwanis. Republican. Avocations: flying, writing, travel, snorkeling. Home: Box 604266 Cleveland OH 44104 Office: Heart and Hand Found 2570 Woodhill Box 604209 Cleveland OH 44104

DAVIDSON, NEAL R., minister, educator; b. Milw., Nov. 25, 1934; s. Russell Norman and Eleanor Clara (Geller) D.; m. Jean Colette Okstel, Feb. 14, 1981; children: Craig, Roger. BS, Iowa State U., 1956; MDiv, Cen. Luth. Theol. Sem., Fremont, Nebr., 1963; ThM, Princeton U., 1974; EdM, Columbia U., 1980, EdD, 1983. Ordained to ministry Evang. Luth. Ch. in Am., 1963. Pastor St. Stephen Luth. Ch., Portland, Tex., 1963-70; commd. 2d lt. U.S. Army, 1970, advanced through grades to lt. col., 1985, chaplain, 1970-87; ret., 1987; pastor Our Redeemer Luth Ch., Kalamazoo, 1987—; chmn. youth com. Tex.-La. Synod, Luth. Ch. in Am., 1965-70; chmn. communication com. Mich. Synod, Evang. Luth. Ch. in Am., 1987—. Editor NW Lower Mich. mag. supplement The Luth., 1988—. Bd. dirs. Kalamazoo Consultation Ctr. Mem. Religious Speech Communication Assn., Acad. Preachers, Liturgical Arts, Rotary. Republican. Office: Our Redeemer Luth Ch 2508 Gull Rd Kalamazoo MI 49001

DAVIDSON, THOMAS JAMES, minister; b. Sewickley, Pa., Jan. 22, 1952; s. Thomas James Jr. and Clara Arvella (Near) D.; m. Coleen Marie Kalamasz, July 14, 1978; children: Lori Ann, Caroline Marie, Jessica Brooks. Grad., Hosanna Bible Coll., Bedford Heights, Ohio, 1985; BTh, MTh, Christian Bible Coll., Rocky Mount, N.C., 1988, PhD in Religion, 1989. Ordained to ministry Assn. Evang. Gospel Assemblies, Inc., 1988; cert. behavioral analysis cons. Inst. Motivational Living; cert. Assn. Christian Counselors. Min. of helps Word Alive Ch., Ellwood City, Pa., 1984-86; pastor Homecoming Christian Fellowship, Frankfort Springs, Pa., 1986-87; mem. staff Christian Assembly Ch., New Brighton, Pa., 1987-89, Ellwood City, Pa., 1989-90; pastor, pres., bd. dirs. Homecoming Christian Fellowship, Aliquippa, Pa., 1990—; bd. dirs. Mike Hovonec Ministries, New Brighton, Pa., 1991—. Home and Office: Homecoming Christian Fellowship 103 Mengle Ave Aliquippa PA 15001 *The most important thing in my life is the concept of salvation that Jesus spoke to Nicodemus about in John 3:1-3..."I say unto thee, except a man be born again, he cannot see the kingdom of God." I pray it will mean as much to you.*

DAVIES, HORTON MARLAIS, clergyman, religion educator; b. Cwmavon, South Wales, Mar. 10, 1916; s. D. Marlais and Martha Reid (Davies) D.; m. Brenda Mary Deakin, Sept. 8, 1942; children: Christine Mary, Hugh Marlais, Philip Marlais; m. Marie-Hélène Baudy, Apr. 14, 1973. MA with high honors, U. Edinburgh, 1937, BD with highest honors, 1940; DPhil, Oxford U., 1943, DLitt, 1970; DD, U. South Africa, 1950; DLitt (hon.), LaSalle Coll., 1966. Ordained to ministry Congl. Ch., 1942. Minister Wallington Ch., South London, Eng., 1942-45; religious adviser, dir. edn. YMCA; operating with Brit. Army, 1945-46; prof., head dept. div. Rhodes U., Grahamstown, S. Africa, 1946-53; dean faculty Rhodes U., 1951-53; travelling fellow U.S., Carnegie Corp. of N.Y., also; Old St. Andrew's Meml.; lectr. Emmanuel Coll., U. Toronto, 1952; head joint dept. ch. history Mansfield and Regent's Park colls.; Oxford U., 1953-56; prof. religion Princeton U., 1956-59, Henry W. Putman prof., 1959-84, chmn. dept., 1983-84, emeritus prof., dept. religion, 1984—; Guggenheim Found. fellow, 1959-60, 64-65; vis. prof. ch. history Union Theol. Seminary, N.Y.C., 1959, 1966; cons. on missionary research com. Joint Internat. Missionary Council and World Council Chs., 1954-60; Select preacher, vis. lectr. Cambridge U., Eng., 1960; Mullins lectr So. Bapt. Theol. Sem., Louisville, 1961; sr. F. Council Humanities Princeton U., 1961-62; vis. lectr. Princeton Theol. Sem., numerous occasions 1962—, Pacific Sch. Religion, Berkeley, 1962, Eden Theol. Seminary, Webster Groves, Mo., 1965; vis. lectr. Christian Theol. Sem., Indpls., 1977, Presbyn. Theol. Sem., Austin, Tex., 1977, 84, St. John's U., Collegeville, Minn., 1967, 79; Zabriskie lectr. P.E. Sem., Alexandria, Va., 1963; vis. lectr. ecclesiastical art Union Theol. Sem., Richmond, Va.; vis. lectr. Mansfield Coll., Oxford, 1969; vis. prof. Drew U., 1969, adj. prof., 1978—; vis. prof. New Brunswick Theol. Sem., 1980; research grantee Huntington Library, San Marino, 1967-68, vis. fellow, 1981-82; fellow Ctr. Theol. Inquiry, Princeton, 1987—. Author: Christian Worship: Its Making and Meaning, 1946, The Worship of the English Puritans, 1948, The English Free Churches, 1952, Christian Deviations, 1954, A Mirror of the Ministry in Modern Novels, 1959, Worship and Theology in England, vols. 1-5, 1961-75, Varieties of English Preaching, 1900-1960, 1963, (with Hugh Davies) Sacred Art in a Secular Century, 1978, (with Marie-Hélène Davies) Holy Days and Holidays, 1982; Like Angels on a Cloud: The English Metaphysical Preachers 1588-1645, 1986, The Worship of the American Puritans, 1990, The Communion of Saints: The Prayers of the Famous, 1990, The Vigilant God: The Doctrine of Providence in Augustine, Aquinas, Calvin and Barth, 1991; editor: (with R.H.W. Shepherd) An Anthology of South African Missions, 1953; assoc. editor Worship, 1967-72; contbg. editor: Studia Liturgica (Rotterdam); contbr. to periodicals. Founding trustee Inst. Ecumenical and Cultural Research, St. John's Abbey and U., Collegeville, Minn., 1967-72. Decorated Queen's Coronation medal U.K.; recipient Berakah prize N.Am. Acad. Liturgy, 1979. Mem. Am. Soc. Ch. History, Am. Theol. Soc., Am. Acad. Religion. Home: 120 McCosh Circle Princeton NJ 08540 Home (summer): 155a Cream St Thetford Center VT 05075

DAVIES, JACQUELINE MARIE, school system strategist; b. Opelousas, La., Mar. 10, 1950; d. John W. and Elna (Dupre) Bertrand; m. Robert Jeffrey Davies; 1 child, Jacqueline Nicole. BA, U. So. La., 1983, MEd, 1987. Cert. elem. tchr., supr., assessment prof., La. Spl. edn. tchr. Vermilion Parish Schs., Abbeville, La., 1983-84, Maurice, La., 1984-85; spl. edn. tchr. Lafayette (La.) Parish Schs., 1985-90, ednl. assessment strategist, 1990—. Judge young authors' contest La. Reading Assn., 1987; vol. regional and internat. games Spl. Olympics; block chair March of Dimes; vol. La. Assn. Retarded Citizens; fundraiser Broadmoor Elem. Sch., Episc. Sch. of Acadiana, St. Thomas More High Sch. Mem. Coun. for Exceptional Children (editor newsletter 1988-89, treas. 1989-90), Assoc. Profl. Educators of La., Phi Kappa Delta, Phi Kappa Phi. Avocations: tennis, needlework. Home: 808 Canaan Dr Lafayette LA 70508 Office: Lafayette Parish Sch Bd Chaplin Dr Lafayette LA 70501

DAVIES, KENNETH JOHN, religious writer; b. Oceanside, Calif., Sept. 9, 1958; s. Lloyd A. and Rae A. D.; m. K. L. Hopkins, Nov. 2, 1979; children: September, Nakota, Michael. BS in History and Bible, Christian Heritage Coll., 1990. Ordained to ministry Christian Ch., 1989. Staff writer Kingdom Counsel, Bradford, Pa., 1990—; owner, operator K & K Enterprises, El Cajon, Calif., 1990-91. Contbr. book revs. and articles to profl. jours. Republican. Home and Office: 13320 Camino Canada #6 El Cajon CA 92021 *As Philip James Bailey said, "It matters not how long we live, but how."*

DAVIES, TREVOR, religious organization and social services administrator; b. Liverpool, Merseyside, Eng., Jan. 10, 1940; s. Arthur Stanley and Alice (Hughes) D.; m. Dorothy Irene Blair, July 31, 1965; children: Rosalind Jane, Alistair James. BS with honors, U. Birmingham, 1962; Diploma in Social Work, Home Office, London, 1963. Probation officer Manchester (Eng.) City Cts., 1963-65; lectr. social administrn. Lancaster Poly., Coventry, Eng., 1965-68, sr. lectr. social policy, 1968-72; dep. head social affairs sect. personnel div. European Orgn. Nuclear Research, Geneva, 1972-78; dir. personnel office World Council Chs., Geneva, 1978—; cons. Joint Inspection Unit UN, Geneva, 1977-78, World Intellectual Property Orgn., Geneva, 1977, Joint Working Group on Social Security U. Geneva, 1986—; pres. social commn., mem. exec. com. Fedn. Internat. Non-Govtl. Orgns. in Geneva, 1978—. Mem. vestry com. Holy Trinity Ch., Geneva, 1973-80; Ferney Voltaire elder Crossroads Community Ch., 1981—. Mem. Soc. Suisse Gestion Personnel. Anglican. Avocation: skiing, wind surfing. Office: World Council Chs, DCI PO Box 88, 1211 Geneva Switzerland Office: 1 rue Varembe, 1211 Geneva Switzerland

DAVIGNON, CHARLES PHILIAS, priest; b. Albany, Vt., Nov. 5, 1930; s. Nellie Mae (Pudvah) D. STL, U. Montreal, Que., Can., 1956; MA, Cath. U. Am., 1960, PhD, 1973. Ordained priest Roman Cath. Ch., 1956. Assoc. pastor St. Augustine's Parish, Montpelier, Vt., 1960-66; prin. St. Michael's High Sch., Montpelier, 1960-66; assoc. mem. Maryknoll Fathers, dir. lang. dept. Sch. Spl. Studies, San Marcos Nat. U., Lima, Peru, 1967-69; dir. Communication Ctr., Puno, Peru, 1969-72, Diocesan Office Communications, Burlington, Vt., 1972-74, 88—; v.p. devel., dir. Ctr. for Mission Studies Maryknoll (N.Y.) Sch. Theology, 1974-79; pastor St. Mary Star of Sea Ch., Newport, Vt., 1980-88, St. John Vianney Ch., South Burlington, Vt., 1988—; coord. Office of Justice and Peace, Maryknoll, N.Y./Latin Am. Desk-Office of Internat. Justice and Peace, U.S. Cath. Conf., Washington. Home: 160 Hinesburg Rd South Burlington VT 05403 Office: Office Communications 351 North Ave Burlington VT 05401 *Once a person is called, gifted and graced, one mission remains—to seek ways and means of sharing who and what you are with others.*

DÁVILA, DANIEL, religion educator; b. Montemorelos, Mexico, Feb. 28, 1946; came to U.S., 1947; naturalized, 1968; s. Eliseo and María (Díaz) D.; m. Holly Annette Rinne, June 14, 1970; children: Daniel II, Erin María. AA in Bibl. Found., Midwest Bible Coll., Stanberry, Mo., 1970; BA, Evang. Coll., 1973; MDiv, Phillips U., 1979; MA in Religion, Iliff Sch. Theology, 1990. Pastor Ch. God, Buffalo, Mo., 1970-73, Saginaw, Mich., 1973-76, Oklahoma City, 1976-77, Claremore, Okla., 1977-79; tchr. Spring Vale Acad., Owosso, Mich., 1973-76; dir., instr. Summit Sch. Theol., Denver, 1979—; constrn. laborer, Denver, summer, 1971-72; cotton picker Fields in Nuecess County, Corpus Christi, Tex., summer, 1956-64. Editor: (journal) North American Minister Forum, 1979-82, International Minister Forum, 1982-90; contbr. articles to profl. jours. Reporter Hispanic Dem. for Adams County, 1990. With U.S. Army, 1965-67. Recipient Ministerial Recognition award Consejo Ejecutivo Ministerial, Mexico City, 1981, Pastoral Recognition award Shebet Ministerial Dept., Mexico City, 1983. Mem. No. Am. Ministerial Coun. (v.p. 1985-87, chmn. ministerial lic. and credentials com.), Internat. Ministerial Congress (1st v.p. 1982-86). Democrat. Home: 1001 E 105th Pl Northglenn CO 80233-1203 Office: Summit Sch Theology PO Box 33677 Denver CO 80233

DAVILA, JAMES R., classics educator; b. San Diego, Aug. 8, 1960. BA, UCLA, 1982, MA, 1983; PhD, Harvard U., 1988. Vis. asst. prof. Tulane U., New Orleans, 1988—. Office: Tulane U Dept Classics New Orleans LA 70118

DAVIS, ARTHUR WILLIAM, clergyman; b. Scranton, Pa., Apr. 10, 1933; s. Hosie and Mildred Henrietta (Evans) D.; m. Carol Ann Bambach, Juiy 16, 1955; children: Arthur Kevin, Nancy Carol Davis Guzzi, Scott William Davis (dec.). BA, U. Scranton, 1982. Ordained to ministry Meth. Ch., 1972. Pastor First United Meth. Ch., Jermyn, Pa., 1968-79, Maplewood/Cortez (Pa.) Ch., 1979-81, Embury United Meth. Ch., Scranton, Pa., 1981-85, First United Meth. Ch., Carbondale, Pa., 1985—; chmn. dist. supt. com. Wyo. Conf. United Meth. Ch., 1990—; chmn. Salvation Army Upper Valley Svc.; sec.-treas. Carbondale Ministerium. Republican. Office: First United Meth Ch 76 Terrace St Carbondale PA 18407-2338

DAVIS, BENJAMIN GEORGE, clergyman, theologian, educator; b. Honesdale, Pa., July 6, 1941; s. Benjamin George and Laura Teneyck (Swingle) D.; m. Janet Marie Gorden, June 21, 1980; children: Leslie Anne, John Nathan. AB, U. Mich., 1967, AM, 1969; M.Th., U. Nottingham, England, 1982; D. Min., St. Mary's Sem. & Univ., Balt., 1985. Draftsman, designer Munson Mill Machinery Co., Utica, N.Y., 1961-62; design engr. Gen. Motors Corp., Warren, Mich., 1963-66; devel. coord. City of Ann Arbor, Mich., 1967; research economist Exec. Office of the Pres., Washington, 1970; sr. assoc. RMC Research Corp., Bethesda, Md., 1971-75; dir. Research Svcs., Inc., Clinton, Md., 1975-80; regional dir. World Relief, Landover, Md., 1981-86; dir. Evangelicals for Social Action, Washington, 1987-89; pastor St. John United Ch., Columbia, Md., 1989—; bd. dirs. Columbia Inst. for Psychotherapy, 1986—; adj. prof. St. Mary's Sem. & Univ., Balt., 1986—, Balt. Internat. Culinary Coll., 1988—; cons. Md. Office Refugee Affairs, Balt., 1986. Author: A Modern Interpretation of Revelation, 1982, Group Building Designs for Adults, 1989, Understanding World Cultures: The United States and Canada, 1990, A Commentary on the Gospel of Mark, 1991; editor: The Dictionary of Essential English, 1987. Pres. Fgn.-born Info. and Referral Network, Columbia, 1986—; chmn. Coalition fo r Refugee Resettlement, Washington, 1985-86; chairperson Md.

Refugee Adv. Coun., Balt., 1985-86. Recipient Gov.'s Citation State of Md., 1985, 86; NDEA fellow in economics U. Md., 1969-71, Rickard's fellow in theology U. Nottingham, 1980-81. Mem. Assn. for Psychol. Type, Assn. Overseas Educators, Mensa, Omicron Delta Epsilon. Avocations: jazz, photography, motorcycling. Home: 6580 Madrigal Terr Columbia MD 21045 Office: St Marys Sem and U 5400 Roland Ave Baltimore MD 21210 *The search for certainty in life leads only up blind alleys. Accepting the ambiguity and moving forward in faith is all.*

DAVIS, BENJAMIN LLOYD, religion educator, musician; b. Seattle, Mar. 20, 1961; s. Nathaniel J. and Addie Bell (Beleer) D. AA in Music, Shoreline Community Coll., 1982; BA, Seattle Pacific U., 1989. Prin. percussionist Seattle Philharmonic Orch., 1987-91, Thalia Symphony Orch., Seattle, 1988-91, Rainier Symphony Orch., Kent, Wash., 1989-91; Sunday sch. supt. Bethel Christian Ch., Seattle, 1989-91, music adminstr., 1990-91, pvt. tchr., 1990-91, Bible Coll. coord., 1990-91, music condr., 1989-90. Recipient Outstanding Svc. award Bethel Christian Ch., 1089. Mem. Pacific Northwest Dist. Conm. Music Instructors. Mem. Pentecostal Assemblies of the World. Home: 11614 54th St Seattle WA 98178 Office: Bethel Christian Ch Seattle WA 98178

DAVIS, BRIAN NEWTON, primate, archbishop; b. Stratford, Taranaki, New Zealand, Oct. 28, 1934; s. Leonard Lancelot and Ethel May (Newland) D.; m. Marie Lynette Waters, Jan. 21, 1969; children: Megan Elizabeth, Susan-Mary, Jane Louise, Fiona Catherine. MA, Victoria U., Wellington, New Zealand, 1959; Licentiate in Theology, 1965. Ordained priest Anglican Ch., 1961. Asst. curate St. Mark's Wellington, 1960-62, Karori West and Makara, 1962-64; vicar of Dannevirke, 1967-73; vicar Cathedral Parish St. John the Evangelist; Napier and dean of Waiapu, 1973-80, vicar gen. of Waiapu, 1979-80, 1979-80, bishop of Waikato, 1980-86, primate, archbishop of New Zealand, bishop of Wellington, 1986—. Author: (with others) An Encyclopaedia of New Zealand, 1966; also articles; columnist Ch. Scene newspaper. Office: Anglican Diocese Wellington, PO Box 12-046, Wellington New Zealand

DAVIS, CALVIN GRIER, clergyman, college president; b. Wilmar, Ark., Sept. 15, 1906; s. Coleman Robert and Ollie Pearson (Hilliard) D.; m. Rebecca Spencer McDowell, July 6, 1935; children—Calvin Grier, James McDowell. B.A., Davidson Coll., 1927; B.Div., Union Theol. Sem., 1931, M.Th., 1933, Th.D., 1943; D.D. (hon.), Davidson Coll., 1943, Tusculum Coll., 1943. Ordained to ministry Presbyn. Ch., 1931. Asst. minister Grace Covenant Ch., Richmond, Va., 1931-33; minister Second Presbyn. Ch., Norfolk, Va., 1933-38, First Presbyn. Ch., Asheville, N.C., 1938-59; pres. Mt. Retreat Assn., 1959-72, Montreat-Anderson Coll., N.C., 1959-72; ret. 1972; trustee Davidson Coll., 1940-59, King Coll., Bristol, Tenn., 1950-59, Mt. Retreat Assn., Montreat, 1945-59, Montreat-Anderson Coll., 1945-59; bd. mgrs. Lords Day Alliance, U.S., Atlanta, 1940—; bd. dirs. Annuities and Relief of Presbyn. Ch. in U.S., Atlanta, 1948-58. Contbg. editor Presbyn. Outlook, 1938-60. Author: A Mountain Retreat, 1986; radio preacher The Protestant Hour, 1950. Mem. Ministers Assn. Asheville (pres. 1952). Club: Biltmore Forest Country. Lodge: Kiwanis. Avocations: golf, physical fitness. Home: 306 Sales Health Care Sweeter Creek Rd Asheville NC 28803

DAVIS, CARL LYNN, minister; b. Ganado, Tex., Mar. 2, 1941; s. Forest Rivers and Mary Margaret (Martin) D.; m. Geraldine Louise Jones, July 3, 1971; children: Jana Suzanne, Justin Bryan. BA, East Cen. Okla. State U., 1975; M Behavior Studies, Southeastern Okla. State U., 1976; D Christian Counseling, Bethany Theol. Seminary, Dothan, Ala., 1985. Pastor Brock (Okla.) Bapt. Ch., 1972-74, Roady Bapt. Ch., Wynnewood, Okla., 1974-76; instr. of Bible Southeastern Okla. State U., Durant, 1977-79; pastor Calvary Bapt. Ch., Ardmore, Okla., 1986-88; dir. spl. ministries for the blind Enon Bapt. Assn., 1980-91; pastor Grantham Bapt. Ch., Madill, Okla., 1990—; vol. chaplin for Okla. prisons, Enon Bapt. Assn., 1986-91. Hon. bd. dirs. Sheltered Workshop, Durant, 1979-81; vol. counselor Carter County Group Home, Ardmore, 1986-88; active Gov.'s Com. for the Handicapped, State Capitol, Okla., 1977. Recipient scholastic award Bethany Theol. Seminary, 1985. Home: 716 Davis NW Ardmore OK 73401

DAVIS, CAROLYN LEIGH, priest, psychotherapist; b. Houston, Mar. 18, 1936; d. William Harvey Speight and Veral Audra (Nunn) Speight Poole; m. John C. Rogers, June 22, 1957 (div. Nov. 1970); children: Elizabeth Leigh Porterfield, Rena Kathleen Stephan, John; m. L.B. Davis Sept. 14, 1972. Diploma in nursing, U. Houston, 1956; MSW, U. Denver, 1981; MDiv, Iliff Sch. Theology, 1990; cert. individual theol. studies, Episcopal Theol. Sem. of S.W., 1990. RN, Tex., Colo.; lic. clin. social worker, Colo.; cert. alcohol, drug counselor, Colo.; ordained to ministry Episcopal Ch. as deacon, 1990, as priest, 1990. Therapist Bethesda Mental Health Ctr., Denver, 1972-73; supr. emergency alcoholism services Denver Gen. Hosp., 1973-74; dir. alcoholism services Jefferson County Health Dept., Lakewood, Colo., 1974-78; pvt. practice psychotherapy Lakewood and Englewood, Colo., 1981—, Curate St. Joseph's Episc. Ch., Lakewood, 1991. Author: The Most Important Nine Months of Your Child's Life: Fetal Alcohol Syndrome, 1976. Mem. Nat. Assn. Social Workers. Democrat. Avocations: bridge, music. Office: 720 Kipling Ste 119 Lakewood CO 80215 also: 6909 S Holly Cir Ste 260 Englewood CO 80112 also: St Joseph Episcopal Ch 11202 W Jewell Ave Lakewood CO 80232

DAVIS, CHARLES ROBERT, minister; b. Indpls., Feb. 11, 1943; s. Robert Roudebush and Dorothy Frances (Hanna) D.; m. Mary Ann Pitchford, Aug. 22, 1970; children: Melia Sang, Marikim Hyun. BSBA, U. Indpls., 1967; MA, Lincoln Christian Sem., 1970, MDiv, 1972. Ordained to ministry Christian Chs. Min. Darlington (Ind.) Christian Ch., 1973-76, Bedford (Tex.) Christian Ch., 1980-81, 1st Christian Ch., Green Bay, Wis., 1988-91, South Side Ch. of Christ, Danville, Ill., 1991—; prof. religion and Bible, Minn. Bible Coll., Rochester, 1976-80; instr. theology Dallas Christian Coll., 1980-85; pres. Christian Harbor Youth Camp, Holcombe, Wis., 1989-91; vis. prof. Chiangmai (Thailand) Bible Inst., 1990. Mem. Wis. Christian Missionary Assn. (2d v.p. 1990-91, chmn. outreach 1990-91). Home: 622 Bensyl Danville IL 61832 Office: 611 Forrest Danville IL 61832

DAVIS, CHARLES THOMAS, III, religion educator; b. Marion, Ala., July 25, 1939; s. Charles Thomas Jr. and Ruby C. (Coplin) D.; m. Mary Holland King, June 17, 1962; 1 child, Eric R. AS, Marion Mil. Inst., 1958; BS in Edn., U. Ala., 1960; BD, Emory U., 1963, PhD, 1967. Ordained to ministry United Meth. Ch. as deacon, 1961, as elder, 1963. Min. Lower Peachtree (Ala.) Cir., United Meth. Ch., 1958, Maplesville (Ala.) Cir., 1958-60, Thorsby (Ala.)-Jemison Cir., 1960-63; prof. Appalachian State U., Boone, N.C., 1967—. Author: Speaking of Jesus, 1978; also articles. Mem. Soc. Bibl. Lit., Am. Acad. Religion, N.C. Tchrs. Religion (v.p. 1982, pres. 1983). Office: Appalachian State U Dept Philosophy and Religion Boone NC 28608

DAVIS, CLARENCE EPHRAIM, minister, seminary president; b. Tampa, Fla., Sept. 5, 1941; s. John Henry and Alice (Forbes) D.; m. Ada Belle Jones, Sept. 8, 1962; children: Clarence Ephraim Jr., Bryon K., Cherry E., Eric A. AA, Allan Hancock Coll., Santa Maria, Calif., 1972; BA, U. La Verne, 1975; MRE, St. Stephen's Sem., L.A., 1976, PhD, 1977; MA, Webster U., 1979. Ordained to ministry Nat. Bapt. Conv. U.S.A., 1972; cert. tchr., counselor, Calif. Asst. pastor Mt. Sinai Bapt. Ch., Okinawa, Japan, 1971-72, Grace Temple Bapt. Ch., Lompoc, Calif., 1972-73; pastor Vandenberg Bapt. Ch., Lompoc, 1973-77, Kelivak (Iceland) Bapt. Ch., 1977-79, Tabernacle Bapt. Ch., Oklahoma City, 1980-85; sr. pastor Jesus' Ch. Ministries, Oklahoma City, 1985—; pres. Cornerstone Theol. Sem., Jerusalem, 1990—; dean Dist. Congress Ch. Edn., Oklahoma City, 1982-84; bd. dirs. Nat. Bapt. Conv., USA, Inc., 1981-83, trustee, 1983-84. Author: Blood of Jesus, 1990, Husband Love Your Wife, 1990, How To Study the Bible, 1991. Mem. exec. bd. NAACP, Oklahoma City, 1981-83; chmn. Oklahoma City Human Rights Commn., 1981-84; vice chmn. Alternative for Incarceration, Okla., 1982-85; bd. dirs. A Chance for Youth, Oklahoma City, 1991—. With USAFR, 1960-80, ret. Named Outstanding Citizen, Oklahoma City Citizens Coun., 1980; scholar Martin Luther King Found., 1974. Mem. Bapt. Mins. Assn., Omega Psi Phi (chaplain Oklahoma City 1981-83). Home: 9433 NE 13th St Midwest City OK 73110 Office: Jesus' Ch Ministries Inc 2201 NE 15th St Oklahoma City OK 73117 *Living each day to its fullest. Completely forgetting about yesterday's failures and never thinking on tomorrows's problems. Because the only thing that I can do anything about is today.*

DAVIS, CLAUD EDWIN, III, clergyman; b. Danville, Va., Nov. 4, 1958; s. Claud Edwin and Dorothy Wingfield (Asbury) D.; m. Lu Ann Harris, July 1, 1977; children: Michael Andrew, Emily Anne. BA, Southeastern La. U., 1979; MDiv, New Orleans Bapt. Theol. Sem., 1983; D Ministry, Southwestern Bapt. Theol. Sem., 1988. Ordained to ministry Bapt. Ch., 1981. Minister youth/children Hebron Bapt. Ch., Denham Springs, La., 1977-83; pastor Pine Hill Bapt. Ch., Sicily Island, La., 1983-85; assoc. pastor evangelism First Bapt. Ch., Zachary, La., 1985-88; pastor Scotts Hill Bapt. Ch., Wilmington, N.C., 1988—; youth dir. Ea. La. Bapt. Assn., Hammond, 1978-83; pastor's conf. pres. Ouachita Bapt. Assn., Jonesville, La., 1984; budget com. William Wallace Bapt. Assn., Zachary, 1987-88; discipleship tng. dir. Wilmington (N.C.) Bapt. Assn., 1989—. Author: The Utilization of Spiritual Gifts in the Local Church, 1988, Welcome to Our Church, 1990; illustrator Proclaim mag., 1990. Mem. Zachary Kiwanis (chaplain 1987). Democrat. Office: Scotts Hill Bapt Ch 15 Scotts Hill Loop Rd Wilmington NC 28405

DAVIS, DANIEL OSCAR, JR., minister; b. Orlando, Fla., May 20, 1932; s. Daniel Oscar and Lavon Marie (Ruemmele) D.; m. Virginia Dare McDaniel, Apr. 25, 1948; children: Pamela Rose Dukes, Cynthia Diane Johns, Elva Yvonne Smith. AB, John B. Stetson U., 1959; BD, MDiv, Southwestern Bapt. Theol. Sem., 1963; STM, N.Y. Theol. Sem., 1977; D of Ministry, Columbia Theol. Sem., 1987; grad., Army War Coll., 1988. Ordained to ministry So. Bapt. Conv. Enlisted USAF, 1948; commd. 2d lt. U.S. Army, 1962, commd. 1st lt. in Chaplain Corps, 1964, advanced through grades to lt. col., 1987; chaplain USAR, 1964-67, Ala. N.G., 1967-70; with 7th Spl. Forces Group U.S. Army, Fort Bragg, N.C., 1970-71; with Spl. Forces U.S. Army, Vietnam, 1971-72; with 20th Engr. Bn. and 3/187th Inf., 101st Airborned Div. U.S. Army, Ft. Campbell, Ky., 1972-74; with Army Security Agy. U.S. Army, Udorn, Thailand, 1974-76; asst. div. chaplain 82nd Airborne Div., dep. corps chaplain 18th Airborne Corps U.S. Army, 1980-83; div. chaplain 2d Inf. Div. U.S. Army, Rep. Korea, 1983-84; chaplain staff officer Office of FORSCOM Chaplain U.S. Army, Atlanta, 1984-87; corps chaplain VII U.S. Corps U.S. Army, Stuttgart, Fed. Republic Germany, Persian Gulf, 1990-91; installation chaplain U.S. Army, Ft. Stewart, Ga., 1991—; pastor S. Side Estates Bapt. Ch., Jacksonville, Fla., 1963-70; student U.S. Army Chaplain Ctr. and Sch. U.S. Army, 1976-77. Democrat. Home: 12657 Aladdin Rd Jacksonville FL 32223 Office: US Army Box 839 HQ VII Corps APO NY 09107

DAVIS, DANNY ANDREW, minister; b. Richlands, Va., Nov. 22, 1947; s. Britt Andrew and Doris (Sumpter) D.; m. Katherine Louise Penniston, June 8, 1971; children: Robert Andrew, Krystal Jeannette. BA in Bible, Mt. Vernon Bible Coll., 1978. Ordained to ministry Internat. Ch. of the Foursquare Gospel, 1979. Pastor's asst. Internat. Ch. of the Foursquare Gospel, Vincennes, Ind., 1978-79; pastor Internat. Ch. of the Foursquare Gospel, Burlington, Iowa, 1979-86, Calvary Foursquare Ch., Keokuk, Iowa, 1986—; dir. regional men's ministry Internat. Ch. of the Foursquare Gospel, Keokuk, 1990—. With U.S. Army 1967-70. Home: 1503 Timea Keokuk IA 52632 Office: Calvary Foursquare Ch S 7th and Ave G Keokuk IA 52632

DAVIS, DAVID COLEMAN, minister, chaplain supervisor; b. Portsmouth, Ohio, Sept. 9, 1932; s. Edward Thomas and Julia Alveretta (Fox) D.; m. Barbara Kathryn Redinger, Dec. 19, 1952; children: Kathryn Sue, Kimberle Anne, Karyn Dawn. BA, Otterbein Coll., 1955; MDiv, United Theol. Sem., 1958; M of Sacred Theology, Trinity Sem., 1973. Pastor of chs. Evangel. United Brethern Ch., Ohio and Pa., 1952-68; staff chaplain St. Elizabeths Hosp., Washington, 1968-75; dir. human relations Bronson Meth. Hosp., Kalamazoo, 1975-83; staff chaplain Meth. Hosp., Jacksonville, Ill., 1983-84; dir. pastoral care Carle Found. Hosp., Urbana, Ill., 1984—. Bd. dirs. Mich. Hospice Orgn., 1978-83; bd. dirs., founder Hospice Greater Kalamazoo, 1978-83; me. clergy com. Am. Cancer Soc., Mich., 1980-82. Named Chaplain of Yr., United Meth. Health and Welfare, 1981. Fellow Coll. Chaplains (com. mem. 1981-83); mem. Assn. Clin. Pastoral Edn. (cert. supr.), Assn. Mental Health Clergy (mag. editor 1977-82). Club: Toastmasters (local officer 1979-91). Avocations: golf, photography, horseshoe nail art, camping, speaking. Home: 2508 Valkar Ln Champaign IL 61821 Office: Carle Found Hosp 611 W Park St Urbana IL 61801

DAVIS, DONALD JAMES, bishop; b. New Castle, Pa., Mar. 12, 1929; s. LeRoy Francis and Rya Anne (Stewart) D.; B.A., Westminster Coll., 1949, D.D. (hon.), 1975; M.A., Bowling Green State U., 1971; M.Div., Princeton U., 1952; postgrad. Ind. U.; m. Gray Schofield, Sept. 6, 1952; children—Stewart, Kristin, Addison. Ordained priest Episc. Ch.; curate Ch. of the Epiphany and Christ Ch., Washington, 1955-57; rector St. Christopher's Ch., Indpls., 1957-63, Trinity Ch., Toledo, 1963-71, Trinity Ch., Bloomington, Ind., 1971-73; chaplain Ind. U., 1971-73; bishop co-adjutor Diocese of Erie (Pa.), 1973, bishop, 1974—; press officer Ho. of Bishops, 1976—; mem. exec. council Episcopal Ch., 1982—; chmn. Bd. of Hood Conf., 1976-77; mem. Standing Commn. on Ch. Music; mem. Gen. Bd. of Examining Chaplains. Bd. assocs. St. Paul's Coll., Richmond, Va. bd. mem. Coalition of Human Needs, Nat. Ch.; mem. standing commn. on ch. in small communities; bd. mem. Gannon U., Erie Met. Coll., Seabury-Western Theol. Sem. Ill., Erie Philharm., OIC; pres. St. Barnabas House N.E. Pa.; pres. St. Patricks Found. Episcopal Edn. Fund., 1983—. Mem. Erie Area Bus. and Labor Council, 1983—. Named Hon. Alumnus, Bexley Hall Sem. Named Hon. Alumnus, Bexley Hall Sem. Office: 145 W 6th St Erie PA 16501

DAVIS, DONNIE BRUCE, minister; b. Danville, Va., June 27, 1965; s. Jackie Bruce and Shirley (Dawson) D.; m. Debra McCann, Oct. 28, 1989. BS, Liberty U., 1988. Interim min. music North Main Bapt. Ch., Danville, 1987-88; min. music Woodland Bapt. Ch., Danville, 1989—; tchr. piano Leed's Music Ctr., Danville, 1986—; pianist, dir. choir Bapt. Tabernacle, Danville, 1988. Home: 174 Mimosa St Danville VA 24541 Office: Woodlawn Bapt Ch 2500 Westover Dr Danville VA 24541

DAVIS, F. BENJAMIN, academic administrator. Head Cen. Bapt. Theol. Sem., Indpls. Office: Cen Bapt Theol Sem 1535 Dr A J Brown Ave N Indianapolis IN 46202*

DAVIS, FRANCIS RAYMOND, priest; b. Washington, Feb. 10, 1920; s. Frank Raymond and Ruth Madeline (Donovan) D.; B.A., St. Bernard's Sem., Rochester, N.Y., 1941; M.L.S., Cath. U. Am., 1953. Ordained priest Roman Cath. Ch., 1945; asst. pastor St. Ambrose Ch., Rochester, 1945-50; prof. lit. St. Bernard's Sem., 1950-51, librarian, 1950-69, prof. speech., 1958-67; pastor Our Lady Lourdes Ch., Elmira, N.Y., 1969-78; pastor St. Mary's Ch., Dansville, N.Y., 1978-80, St. Patrick's Ch., Corning, N.Y., 1980-90. Mem. Chemung county gen. edn. bd. Diocese of Rochester, 1971-78; mem. exec. com. Chemung County (N.Y.) Council Aging, 1972-76; mem. adv. com. Chemung County Office for Aging, 1973-78; mem. exec. com. Ecumenical Preaching Mission, 1977-78; bd. dirs. All Saints' Acad., Corning, 1986-90, founder. Fellow Internat. Biog. Assn.; mem. ALA, Cath. Library Assn. (officer sem. sect. 1958-61), Ch. and Synagogue Library Assn. (nominating com. 1979), Elmira Vicinity Ministerial Assn. (officer 1972-73). Author articles and book revs. Address: St Vincent's Ch 222 Dodge Ave Corning NY 14830

DAVIS, GLADYS, evangelist, educator; b. N.Y.C., July 25, 1937; d. Robert and Pearl Gertrude (Vaughan) D.; divorced; m. Lesly Lezeau, Sept. 10, 1976; 1 son, Leonel. BS, SUNY, 1960; MS, Pace U., 1977. Ordained to ministry Ind. Holiness Assembly Ch., Inc., 1990. Tchr. adult edn. Yonkers (N.Y.) Bd. Edn., 1960—; nat. evangelist Ch. of God in Christ, 1961-77; founder Women for Christ-Worldwide, 1970; founder Prayer and Praise, 1978, exec. dir., 1978-80; radio evangelist St. Paul's Ch., Westchester, 1968-80; founder, dir. Sun's of God, Inc., 1980—. Recipient award for dedicated service Women for Christ-Worldwide, 1968; Am. Studies fellow Eastern Bapt. Coll., summer 1970. Mem. N.Y. State Home Econs. Assn., Yonkers Fedn. Tchrs., 700 Club. Home: 105 Bruce Ave Yonkers NY 10705 Office: 145 Palmer Rd Yonkers NY 10701

DAVIS, GLENN EARNEST, minister; b. East St. Louis, Ill., Jan. 23, 1944; s. John Howard and Adele (Koch) D.; m. Ann Marie Mosbacher, Feb. 14, 1970; children: Phyllis, Heather. BA in Sociology, Southern Ill. U., 1970; MDiv, Eden Sem., 1972. Pastor St. Paul United Ch. Christ, Edwardsville, Ill., 1969-77, Mounds (Ill.) and Tamms United Ch. Christ, 1977-78, Spencer County Parish West United Ch. Christ, Chrisney, Ind., 1977-84, Zion United Ch. Christ, Calumet, Iowa, 1984—; county chmn. Crop Walk, Spencer County, 1979-83; pres. Ministrial Alliance, Spencer County, 1981-83; organizer United Ch. Christ Pastor Support Group, Hartley, Iowa, 1988-90. Editor The Northwestern, 1987-89, The New Creation, 1989-91. Pres. Spencer County Coun. on Aging, 1981-83; county rep. Southwestern Ind. Coun. on Aging Adv., 1979-81; vol. fireman Calumet Fire Dept., 1985-91; sec. 4H Youth Bd., Spencer County, 1979-83. Mem. Northwestern Assn. Adv. Coun., Northwestern Assn. Ch. and Ministry, Lincolnland Assn. Evangelism Commn. (chmn. 1981-84), Lions Club (Ind. pres. 1980-83), Cubmaster Mason, Mason Lodge (chaplain 1988-91). Democrat. *Any organization that loses members consistently desperately needs reformation, to allow the cries of its members to be heard and responded to in a timely fashion! Excuses for membership loses are too easy!!!.*

DAVIS, HAROLD, religious organization administrator. Bd. chmn. YMCA of U.S.A., Chgo. Office: YMCA of the USA 101 N Wacker Chicago IL 60606*

DAVIS, HARRELL DUANE, minister; b. Carson City, Nev., Mar. 5, 1950; s. Neil Sexton and Ethel Pearl (Ocobo) D.; m. Carol Louise West, Mar. 21, 1970; children: Allison Kay, Sarah Jane. BS, Cen. State U., 1976; MDiv, Louisville Presbyn. Theol. Sem, 1981. Ordained to ministry, 1981. Prof., dir. native Am. studies United Theol. Sem. of Twin Cities, New Brighton, Minn., 1981-83; instl. rep. Native Am. Theol. Assn., Mpls., 1981-83, also bd. dirs., exec. dir., 1983—. Gen. editor: Jour. Native American Theology. Vol. Stilwater (Minn.) State Prison, 1982-83. Mem. Nat. Fellowship Indian Workers, Nat. Council Chs. (ethnic minority ministries). Address: 17 Waverly San Anselmo CA 94960

DAVIS, JAMES HAROLD, minister; b. Bowling Green, Fla., May 29, 1937; s. Alvie Alto and Dolly Jane (Thomas) D.; m. Myrtie Sue Smith, June 29, 1958 (widowed May 2, 1987); children: Deborah Jane Magann, Stephanie Ann Herriman; m. Marilyn M. Duden Zippay-Davis, July 19, 1988. Bachelor Ministry, Bethany Bible Coll., Dothan, Ala., 1983; Master Ministry, Bethany Theol. Sem., 1984. Pastor Lake Ruth Bapt. Ch., Bartow, Fla., 1963-69; assoc. pastor Lake Ruth Bapt. Ch., 1969-71; pastor Wauchula Hills Bapt. Ch., Wauchula, Fla., 1971, Good News Bapt. Ch., Wauchula, Fla., 1971-73, First Bapt. Ch., Lake Mary, Fla., 1973-76, Oneco First Bapt. Ch., Oneco, Fla., 1977-78, 1st Bapt. Ch., Terra Ceia, Fla., 1978-90; min. to sr. adults, dir. Golden Agers West Bradenton Bapt. Ch., Bradenton, Fla., 1990—; bd. dirs. United Christian Action, Jacksonville, Fla., 1974-90. With U.S. Army, 1956-59. Mem. Rotary (Paul Harris fellow South Manatee 1987). Democrat. Baptist.

DAVIS, JAN DEBORAH, lay worker; b. Norfolk, Va., Jan. 31, 1950; d. Joseph Douglas and Lydia Virginia (Gimbert) Zimmerman; m. Wilbur Earl Davis Jr., Dec. 2, 1968; 1 child, Lisa Letitia. Pastoral ministries diploma, So. Bapt. Sem. Extension. Ordained deacon Bapt. Ch., 1984. Dir. Woman's Missionary Union, Moyock (N.C.) Bapt. Ch., 1982-83, libr. chmn., 1982-85, deacon, 1984-87, Sunday sch. tchr., 1987-88; dir. Associational Mission Friends, Norfolk Bapt. Assn., Virginia Beach, Va., 1989-90. Contbg. author: (books/anthology) American Poetry Anthology, 1989, Sparrowgrass Poetry Forum, 1990, Argus Literary Digest, 1990. Second soprano Albemarle Community Chorus, Elizabeth City, N.C., 1990-91. Recipient Cert. of Recognition, Assn. Woman's Missionary Union, Norfolk Bapt. Assn., 1988, Spl. Citation-Christian Devel., The Sunday Sch. Bd. of So. Bapt. Conv., 1989. Home: Rt 3 Box 358 Moyock NC 27958 *Change comes from within, and my responsibility and control rests with my own choices; I can not choose for another. By my life I am to witness for Christ, testifying to the Holy Spirit's inner work of conviction.*

DAVIS, JEFFERY LEE, pastor; b. Bluefield, W.Va., July 16, 1956; s. Ellis Vaden Jr. and Mildred Marie (Billips) D.; m. Donna Kay Culbreath, July 9, 1982; children: Nathan Ryan, Ashley Renae. BA, Southeastern Coll. Assembly of God, 1981; MA, Assembly of God Theol. Sem., Springfield, Mo., 1989. Ordained to ministry Assemblies of God, 1984; lic. preacher, W.Va.; cert. Evang. Tchrs. Tng. Assns. Youth pastor Assembly of God, Tazewell, Va., 1979-81, assoc. pastor, 1982-84; missionary evangelist Assembly of God, Mex., Africa and U.S.A., 1981-82; assoc. pastor Assembly of God, Raven, Va., 1984-88; pastor Assembly of God, Archdale, N.C., 1988—, sectional youth rep., 1989—. Mem. planning/transportation com. Concerned Citizens Against Alcohol, Randolf County, N.C., 1989-90. Recipient Outstanding Svc. award Applachian Dist./Sectional Youth, 1987. Mem. Christian Action League. Home: 123 Brookhollow Ln Archdale NC 27263 *I have found it is better to do what God is blessing, rather than ask God to bless what I am doing.*

DAVIS, JEFFREY G., youth minister; b. Wichita, Kans., July 26, 1961; s. Donald Ray Davis and Freda Ellois George Sanborn; m. Laurie Kathleen Gower, June 4, 1983; children: Glenn Huston, Donald James. AB in Bible, Ministries, Manhattan Christian Coll., Kans., 1984. Youth pastor Anthony (Kans.) Christian Ch., 1984-87, First Christian Ch., Yuma, Ariz., 1987—. Republican. Office: First Christian Ch 221 E 26th Pl Yuma AZ 85364

DAVIS, JOHN JAMES, religion educator; b. Phila., Oct. 13, 1936; s. John James and Cathryn Ann (Nichols) D.; m. Carolyn Ann. BA, Trinity Coll., Dunedin, Fla., 1959, DD (hon.), 1968; MDiv, Grace Coll. & Grace Theol. Sem., Winona Lake, Ind., 1962, ThM, 1964, ThD, 1967. Instr. Grace Coll. & Grace Theol. Sem., 1963-65, prof. of Old Testament, 1965—, exec. v.p., 1976-82, pres., 1986—; exec. dean Near East Sch. Archaeology, Jerusalem, 1970-71; area supr. Tekoa Archeol. Expdn., Jordan, 1968, 70, Raddana Expdn., Jordan, 1974, Heshbon Expdn., Jordan, 1976, Abila Archeol. Expdn., Jordan, 1982, 84. Author: Paradise to Prison, 1975 (Book of Yr.), The Perfect Shepherd, 1979 (Book of Yr.), 10 other books. Recipient Gold award United Way, 1980, Conservation award Barbee Property Owners Assn., 1983; named Outdoor Writer of Yr., Ind. Dept. Natural Resources, 1986. Mem. Am. Schs. of Oriental Research, Near East Archeol. Soc., Outdoor Writers Assn., Hoosier Outdoor Writers Assn. (pres. 1984-86). Avocations: fishing, hunting, stamp collecting, photography. Home: PO Box 635 Winona Lake IN 46590 Office: Grace Theol Sem 200 Seminary Dr Winona Lake IN 46590

DAVIS, JOHN LOUIS, II, pastor; b. Hampton, Va., June 6, 1934; s. John Louis and Thelma (Rogers) D.; m. Jeanne Claytor, June 8, 1957; children: Elizabeth Anne, Leila Katherine, John Mark. BA, King Coll., Bristol, Tenn., 1956; MDiv, Union Theol. Seminary, Richmond, Va., 1959, ThM, 1960, DMin, 1974. Lic. marriage and family therapist, profl. counselor; ordained min. Pastor Vandalia Presbyt. Ch., Greensboro, S.C., 1960-69; assoc. pastor 1st Presbyt. Ch., Knoxville, Tenn., 1969-78; pastor Fountain City Presbyt. Ch., Knoxville, 1978—. Active Leadership Knoxville, 1989—; bd. dirs. Downtown YMCA, Knoxville, 1989—, Knoxville Mental Health Assn., Knoxville Youth Connection. Chaplain USNG, 1967-69. Mem. Am. Assn. Marriage and Family Therapists. Avocations: jogging, cinema. Home: 3410 Kesterwood Rd Knoxville TN 37918 Office: Fountain City Presbyn Ch 500 Hotel Rd Knoxville TN 37918 *I am convinced of the reality of the psyche and that through joy and despair, light and darkness and creativity and chaos we are led to the wholeness that God has for us.*

DAVIS, JUDITH ANNE, lay worker; b. Troy, N.C., June 17, 1969; d. John Leon and Aletha Maxine (Story) Sheets; m. Kenneth Wade Davis, Sept. 12, 1987; children: Kenneth Wade Jr., Nathan Paul. Student, United Wesleyan Coll., Allentown, Pa., 1986-87, John Wesley Coll., High Point, N.C., 1990—. Youth leader Calvary Wesleyan Ch., Greensboro, N.C., 1989—; dealer Tupperware Home Parties, Greensboro, 1990—. Republican. Home: 2418 N Centennial St #1F High Point NC 27265

DAVIS, KATHERINE ADAMS MARTIN, broadcast consultant; b. Seattle, Jan. 22, 1944; d. Edward Trueblood and Anne (Northrop) Martin; m. Edward Eli Davis, July 19, 1969. BA in French and Religion, Fla. So. Coll., 1966; postgrad., No. Va. Community Coll., Sterling, 1980-81; cert., Omega Recording Studios, 1981. Singer, composer KAD Prodn., Alexandria, Va., 1973-76, Slidell, La., 1976-79; singer, mem. New Testament Gospel Group, Silver Spring, Md., 1974—; audio engr. Studio House North Gospel, Washington, 1981-83; TV prodn., cons. A New You, Chantilly, Va., 1986—; video, editor Fairfax Cable Gospel Spl., Annandale, Va., 1986; cons. in field. Producer: (TV spl.) Fairfax Cable TV Spl., Annandale, 1985-86; producer:

(tape) Brand New Child, 1982; author: (poetry) Slidell Daily Times, 1977; composer various gospel and folk music; audio prodn. various video and TV shows. Active Nat. Trust for Hist. Preservation, Washington, 1991, Voice of Retarded, Rolling Meadows, Ill., 1991, Nat. Alliance for Mentally Ill, Arlington, Va., 1990. Recipient Telly award for All That Jazz and Christmas Spl., Fairfax Cable, Annandale, 1985. Mem. Fairfax Cable Access Corp., Friends Christain Performing Artists Fellowship, Delta Zeta. Home and Office: KAD Prodns 8807 Trafalgar Ct Springfield VA 22151 *One can obtain comfort and peace in this troubled world through Biblical Scripture memory.*

DAVIS, KENNETH WESLEY, pastor, educator; b. Woodbury, N.J., Sept. 11, 1946; s. Warren Russell and Dorothy (Elliott) D. BA in Theology, Andrews U., 1983, MAT in Elem. Edn., 1988. Ordained to ministry Seventh-day Adventists, 1988. Pastor, tchr. Texico Conf. of Seventh-day Adventists, Raton, N.Mex., 1983-84, Hobbs, N.Mex., 1984—. With USN, 1967-71. Home: 6620 Knowles Rd Hobbs MN 88240 Office: Seventh-Day Adventist Ch and Sch 6620 Knowles Rd Hobbs MN 88240

DAVIS, KEVIN WYNSTON, educator; b. Boston, Nov. 11, 1955; s. Robert Lewis and Helen Adeline (Kemp) D.; B.A., Pacific Union Coll., 1977; M.A., Loma Linda (Calif.) U., 1982. Cert. tchr., Calif. Head resident asst. Pacific Union Coll., Angwin, Calif., 1977; ordained to ministry Seventh-day Adventist Ch.; assoc. minister Seventh-day Adventist Ch., Los Angeles, 1977-80, elem. tchr., 1980—. Hon. mem. Spl. Olympics Com. Seventh-day Adventist Ch. grantee, 1980. Mem. Calif. Reading Assn., Assn. Supervision and Curriculum Devel. Democrat. Club: Brookinairs. Office: 15548 Santa Ana Ave Bellflower CA 90706

DAVIS, MARK BRYAN, minister; b. Enterprise, Ala., Oct. 8, 1960; s. Vernon Ray and Sara Nell (Adams) D.; m. Lorna Nanette Bruso, June 6, 1981; 1 child, Andrew. BA, U. Ala., 1982. Lic. to ministry Assemblies of God, 1987, ordained, 1990. Youth/music min. Temple Assembly, Clanton, Ala., 1987-91; missionary, evangelist Assemblies of God, Springfield, Mo., 1991—; youth rep. Ala. Assemblies of God, Clanton, 1987-91. Media co-chair Concerned Citizens of Clanton, 1990; ch. coord. Ala. Pro-Life Coalition, Clanton, 1990. Mem. Kappa Tau Alpha. Home and Office: Rt 1 Box 191 Enterprise AL 36330

DAVIS, MARK HERMAN, minister; b. Louisville, Ky., Dec. 25, 1962; s. Thomas Jefferson and Joyce Reece (Roach) D.; m. Catherine Ann Cline, Nov. 30, 1985; child: Christopher Mark. BS, Tenn. Temple U., 1985. Assc. pastor Hawthorne Bapt. Ch., Lilburn, Ga., 1985-90; pastor Sunny Hill Bapt. Ch., Lawrenceville, Ga., 1990--. Independent Baptist. Home: 91 Caldwell Rd Lawrenceville GA 30245 Office: Sunny Hill Bapt Ch 2209 Sunny Hill Rd Lawrenceville GA 30243-2212

DAVIS, MARVIN ROBERT, minister; b. Lexington, Va., Oct. 15, 1956; s. William Avery and Ernestine (Armentrout) D.; m. Debra Ann Driver, May 27, 1977; children: Andrew Robert, Christopher Avery, Daniel Lee. BS, Cen. Meth. Coll., 1979; MDiv, St. Paul Sch. Theology, 1983. Ordained to ministry United Meth. Ch., 1984. Min.'s asst. Meyer Blvd. Ch., Kansas City, Mo., 1979-82; pastor Holt (Mo.) United Meth. Ch., 1982-85; assoc. pastor Platte Woods United Meth. Ch., Kansas City, 1985-88; pastor 1st United Meth. Ch. Platte City (Mo.), 1988-90, Hood United Meth. Ch., Republic, Mo., 1990—; dir. edn., Springfield (Mo.) Dist., Coun. on Ministries, 1990—; sec., Mo. Area Commn. Higher Edn., 1988—; bd. dirs. Diaconal Ministry, 1988—; page Gen. Conf., St. Louis, 1988. Mem. Boy Scouts Am., 1983—, God & Svc. award, 1989. Recipient The Torch award, Mo. West Annual Conf., 1989, Harry Denman Evangelism award, 1988. Mem. Disciplined Order Christ (life), Kiwanis, York Rite, Ararat Shrine, Order of St. Luke, Scottish Rite, Alpha Phi Omega. Republican. Office: Hood United Meth Ch PO Box 304 Republic MO 65738 *By remembering our collective history, we may be able to "Re-Member" our destiny.*

DAVIS, MARY DUESTERBERG (MIMI), lay worker; b. Houston, June 27, 1934; d. Leonard A. Duesterberg and Lillian Palmire (Walter) Van Pelt; m. James Watson Davis, June 3, 1953 (div. May 1982); children: James Watson Jr., John Van Pelt (dec.), Mary Lynn, Kenneth Walter (dec.). BS in Psychology, U. Houston, 1980; postgrad., Rice U., 1981-82; M in Theol. Studies, So. Meth. U., 1986; MS, U. North Tex., 1990. Lay adv. bd. mem. Southern Meth. U., Dallas, 1985-86; reference libr. Southern Meth. U., Bridwell Theol. Libr., Dallas, 1986-89, Plano Pub. Libr. System, Tex., 1989—; Sunday sch. tchr. 1st Meth. Ch., Houston, 1980-83, retreat leader, 1980—, summer faculty Perkins Sch. Theology, So. Meth. U., Dallas, 1987—. Mem. Am. Theol. Libr. Assn., ALA, Tex. Libr. Assn., Spl. Librs. Assn. Home: 3101 Townbluff Dr #412 Plano TX 75075 *My religious beliefs are my rules and guide for living—sometimes that means keeping things and pondering them in my heart and sometimes it means speaking openly to the world, at great risk—such is the paradox.*

DAVIS, MAURICE, retired rabbi; b. Providence, Dec. 15, 1920; s. Jack and Sadie (Marks) D.; m. Marion Cronbach, Dec. 10, 1944; children: Jay R., Michael A. BA, U. Cin., 1945; B in Hebrew Letters, Hebrew Union Coll., 1949, M in Hebrew Letters, 1949, DD (hon.), 1974; LHD (hon.), Marion Coll., 1969. Ordained rabbi, 1949. Rabbi Euclid Ave. Temple, Cleve., 1949-51; sr. rabbi Temple Adath Israel, Lexington, Ky., 1951-56, Indpls. Hebrew Congregation, 1956-67, Jewish Community Ctr., White Plains, N.Y., 1967-87; faculty Acad. for Jewish Religion, N.Y.C., 1977—, Manhattan Coll., Riverdale, N.Y., 1973-87; pres. Westchester Bd. Rabbis, 1978-80. Columnist Nat. Jewish Post & Opinion, 1958—. Hon. chmn. NAACP, 1964-65. Recipient Medal of Honor, U. Evansville, Ind., 1970, testimonial Purdue U., 1967, Community Svc. award B'nai B'rith, Anti-Defamation League, White Plains, N.Y., 1977, Congressman Lou Ryan award Citizens Freedom Found., N.Y.C., 1982. Mem. Flagler Ared Ministerial Assn., Cen. Conf. Am. Rabbis. Democrat. Home: 2 Classic Ct S Palm Coast FL 32137 *The worship of God is out there in the street where we life. Out there in the world we inhabit. Not with our lips, but with our lives we worship God.*

DAVIS, MICHAEL JOSEPH, pastor, educator, psychologist; b. Quantico, Va., May 1, 1956; s. Harold Glenn and Dorothy Jeanne (Bundy) D.; m. Patricia Frances Delmar, Oct. 28, 1978; children: Diana, Christopher, Miriam, Stephen. BS, Carolina Christian Coll., 1988; MS, Emmanuel Bapt. U., Charlotte, N.C., 1990, PhD, 1991. Lic. pastoral counselor, temperment therapist, cert. behavior cons. Supr. data systems Assn. Am. R.R.s, Washington, 1983-86; counselor, treatment therapist Doulos Counseling Svcs., Charles Town, W.Va., 1983—; prin. Doulos Christian Acad., Charles Town, 1987—; pastor Liberty Christian Fellowship, Charles Town, 1989—; cons. safety tng. Doulos Svcs., Charles Town, 1986—. Co-author: Financial Freedom Seminar, 1990; author: Ammunition/Explosives Handling Safety, 1989. Bd. me. Comunity Minsitries, Charles Town, 1989—. Recipient Merit award Assn. Am. R.R.s, 1986; named Competent Toastmaster, Toastmasters Internat., 1988. Mem. ASCD, Nat. Safety Mgmt. Soc., Nat. Christian Counselors Assn., Network Kingdom Chs., Internat. Fellowship Christian Sch. Adminstrs. Avocations: skiing, gardening, reading. Office: Liberty Christian Fellowship Ch 210 N Church St Charles Town WV 25414

DAVIS, MOSHE, historian; b. Bklyn., June 12, 1916; s. William and Ida (Schenker) D.; m. Lottie Keiser, June 11, 1939; children: Zev, Tamar. B.S., Columbia U., 1937; Pd.B., Jewish Theol. Sem. Am., 1937, M.H.L., 1942; Ph.D., Hebrew U. Jerusalem, 1946; L.H.D. (hon.), Hebrew Union Coll.-Jewish Inst. Religion, 1974; D.H.L. (hon.), Jewish Theol. Sem. Am., 1986. Rabbi, 1942; registrar Jewish Theol. Sem. Am., N.Y.C., 1942-46, dean Tchrs. Inst., 1946-51, provost, 1950-63, dir. Am. Jewish History Center, 1953-65, editor Regional History Series, 1963-78, asso. prof. Am. Jewish history, 1956-63, research prof., 1963—; founding head Inst. Contempory Jewry, Hebrew U. Jerusalem, Israel, 1959—, vis. prof., 1959-63, assoc. prof. Am. Jewish history, 1963-70, Stephen S. Wise prof. Am. Jewish history and instns., 1970—; chmn. Internat. Ctr. for Univ. Teaching Jewish Civilization, 1980—; vis. scholar univs. in Latin Am., U.S., Can., Europe; mem. adv. com. Centre National des Hautes Etudes Juive, Brussels, 1962-75; chmn. Israel Pres.'s Study Circle on World Jewry, 1966-83, Pres.'s Continuing Seminar on World Jewry and State of Israel, 1973-83; committeeman Irving Neuman Hebrew Lit. award Bar Ilan U., Israel; chmn. J. Machover Trust for Contemporary Jewish History, London. Program editor: Eternal Light, NBC-Radio, 1942-52, Frontiers of Faith, NBC-TV, 1951-53; author: (with L. Davis) Land of Our Fathers: Biblical Place-names in America, Guide and Map, 1950, Shaping of American Judaism, 1951, Jewish Religious Life and Institutions, 1953, rev. edit., 1971, (with V. Ratner) Birthday of the World, 1959, Emergence of Conservative Judaism, 1963, From Dependence to Mutuality: The American Jewish Community and World Jewry, 1970; editor: M.M. Kaplan Jubilee Volumes, 1951, Israel: Its Role in Civilization, 1956, Publications of Study Circle in Home of President of Israel, series I, 1967—, series XIII, 1983, Contemporary Jewish Civilization Series, Vol. I, 1970, Vols. II and III, 1971—, (with A.J. Karp) Texts and Studies in American Jewish History in Hebrew, Vol. I, 1970, Vols. II, III, 1971, Vol. IV, 1977, Vol. V, 1980, Vol. VI, 1984, The Yom Kippur War—Israel and the Jewish People, 1974, Hebrew vol., 1975, (with Y. Bauer and I. Kolatt) Studies in the History of Zionism, 1976, World Jewry and the State of Israel, 1977, With Eyes Toward Zion, 1977, Zionism in Transition, 1980, Sir Moses Montefiore: American Jewry's Ideal, 1985, Jewish Distinctiveness Within The American Tradition: The Eretz-Yisrael Dimension as Case Illustration, 1986, With Eyes Toward Zion II, 1986, American Christian Devotees in the Holy Land, 1987, (with Y. Ben-Arieh) With Eyes Toward Zion-III, 1991; advisory editor: America and the Holy Land Collection, 1977; mem. adv. bd. Jewish Jour. Sociology, 1966—; project dir. Am. Holy Land Studies. Recipient Louis LaMed award for Hebrew Lit., 1951, citation B'nai Brith, 1973, Lee M. Friedman Scholar's award, 1977, Israel Knesset Speaker's award, 1987, Samuel Rothberg prize for World Jewish Edn., 1989, medal Jewish Theol. Sem., 1991; Lena Sokolow fellow, 1937-38; Guggenheim fellow, 1956, 59. Mem. Am. Jewish Hist. Soc. (hon. v.p. 1956—), World Union of Jewish Studies (hon. exec. coun.). Office: Hebrew U Jerusalem, Inst Contemporary Jewry, Jerusalem Israel *"Success" is a complex word. How can it be gauged? Position? Public respect? Private welfare? Or is it creativity, dedication and search for truth. If the former, then others determine. If the latter, then I suggest success is continuing tension in the direction of one's goals. Above all, success is inviolate dedication. In my life—to the extent I know myself—my tension derives from my need to comprehend and interpret the meaning of the historic Jewish experience in our conflicted world, and to try to raise myself each day to live by Judaism's teachings.*

DAVIS, OTIS JAY, chaplain; b. Chgo., Sept. 7, 1937; s. Wendell D. and Phyllis Mae (Rockefeller) D.; children: Cindy Davis Houghton, Buffy Davis Bruskas. BA, Hardin-Simmons U., 1964; M in Religious Edn., SWBTS, 1973; D. Min with honors, Internat. Sem., 1981, DD (hon.), 1982, PhD in Thanatology summa cum laude, 1991. Ordained min., 1964. Child placement specialist Dept. Human Svcs., Dallas, child protective svc. specialist, adult protective svc. specialist; chaplain Lovelace Med. Ctr., Albuquerque. With U.S. Army, 1955-58. Mem. Nat. Coun. Social Welfare, Albuquerque Com. for Social Action, Child Abuse Rsch. Ctr. (Father of Yr. 1982). Home: 4510 Joe Dan Pl NE Albuquerque NM 87110

DAVIS, PAUL MILTON, religion educator; b. Winslow, Ind., Jan. 30, 1934; s. Norval Milton and Margaret (Fine) D.; m. Shirley Jean Noland, Aug. 24, 1957; children: Tresa Marie Davis Heath, Lisa Beth. BS, Oakland City Coll., 1957; MS, Ind. State U., 1963; ThM, Trinity Sem., 1991. Cert. tchr., Ind. Pastor First Bapt. Ch., New Harmony, Ind., 1970-71; tchr. Evansville(Ind.)-Vanderburgh Schs., 1957—. Mem. NEA (life), Ind. State Tchrs. Assn., Evansville Tchrs. Assn. Republican. Home: 3515 N Red Bank Rd Evansville IN 47720

DAVIS, PAUL WESLEY, music minister; b. Springfield, Ill., Aug. 14, 1945; s. D. Walter and Lucy Belle (Swords) D.; m. Faith Pearl Edmonds Davis, July 14, 1973; children: Matthew, Theresa, Christina. MusB, Biola U., 1971; MA in Music, Calif. State U. at Fullerton, 1979. Ordained to ministry Bapt. Ch. Minister music Ch. of the Open Door, Los Angeles, 1972-78; Assn. pastor and music dir. Whittier Area Bapt. Fellowship, Calif., 1978—; guest lectr. and speaker for music confs. and retreats Glass Conv., Musicalifornia, 1971—. Pres. REJOICE, Inc., Walnut, Calif., 1971-87. Mem. Choral Conductors Guild (v.p. 1971-72), Am. Choral Dirs. Assn. Republican. Baptist. Avocations: photography, raquetball. Home: 20038 E Wild Blossom Circle Walnut CA 91789 Office: Whittier Area Bapt Fellowship 8175 Villa Verde Dr Whittier CA 90605

DAVIS, PETER (PETER PATHFINDER DAVIS), priest; b. Jersey City, Mar. 22, 1937; s. Joseph Anthony and Adele Elizabeth (Claveloux) D.; m. Catharine Buenz, 1958 (div. 1979); children: Richard, Robert; m. Cynthia Anne Tibbetts, Apr. 30, 1987. Student, Rutgers U., 1973, U. Okla., 1979, Pacific Luth. U., 1980. Founder, archpriest Aquarian Tabernacle Ch. (Wicca), Seattle, 1979—; pub. info. officer Covenant of the Goddess, Berkeley, Calif., 1985-86; founding bd. dirs. Wiccan Info. Network, Vancouver, Can.; advisor to mgr. religious program Wash. Dept. Corrections; organizer Pagan Ch. Conf., 1990, other ann. confs. Contbg. author: Witchcraft Today, 1991; editor Panegyria, 1984—. Councilman, then mayor Andover Twp., N.J., 1960-76; mem. Selective Svc. Bd., Newton, 1971-76; commr. Sussex County Election Commn., 1973-74; trustee Ctr. for Non-Traditional Religion, Seattle, 1980—. With N.J.A.R.N.G., 1956-62. Mem. Interfaith Coun. Wash. (sr. del. 1990—), Am. Soc. for Indsl. Security (cert. protection profl.), Fellowship of Isis. Democrat. Office: Aquarian Tabernacle Ch PO Box 85507 Seattle WA 98145 *Our whole society is in disarray and our children, in confusion. What is desperately needed is the re-establishment of clear limits of societally acceptable behavior, for both ourselves and our youngsters. Ecology should be considered a sacramental duty. Only by abandonment of today's "maybe" limits in favor of clear, firm, unequivocal yet equitable behavioral limits can we hope to restore moral stability. Personal responsibility starts at home with each of us, where "no" once again needs to mean, simply, "no", and not "maybe."*

DAVIS, (CLONNIE) PHILIP, minister, architect; b. Oklahoma City, Jan. 4, 1952; s. Clonnie Levon and Thelma Lorene (Harris) D.; m. Rebecca Irene Taylor. BS in Environ. Design with honors, Okla. U., 1974, BArch, 1975, MArch, 1976; MA, Tenn. Bible Coll., 1982. Registered architect, Tex.; ordained to ministry Ch. of Christ, 1982. Archtl. draftsman Harwood K. Smith & Assocs., Dallas, 1976-77, EDI-Cape Clement, Hopkins, Dallas, 1977-78; architect The Architects Partnership, Dallas, 1978-79, William Charles Maffett & Assocs., Architects & Engrs., Cookeville, Tenn., 1980-82; minister Athens Ch. of Christ, Sparta, Tenn., 1981-82, South Woodward St. Ch. of Christ, Oklahoma City, 1982-86, Seminole (Okla.) Ch. of Christ, 1986—; speaker various religious lecture programs, Tex., Tenn., Okla., Miss., Mo., Ind., 1984—. Contbr. articles to profl. jours., various religious anthologies. Former mem., past pres. Rotary. Named one of Outstanding Young Men of Am., 1984, 85, 86, 87, 88. Avocations: horticulture, music. Home: 1505 Kellye Ln Seminole OK 74868 *Humanity will make a marvelous stride toward unity when finally people reject subjectivistic pluralism and acknowledge the transcendency, objectivity and unanimity of the God—ordained trinity of ethics, religion and truth.*

DAVIS, R. KEITH, minister; b. Kearney, Nebr., Oct. 4, 1953; s. Robert Keith and Marcia Rose (Reger) D.; m. Kathryn Joyce Anderson, July 20, 1974; children: Kody, Keilah, Kelton. BS in Sacred Music, Open Bible Coll., Des Moines, 1975. Ordained to ministry Open Bible Standard Ch., 1976. Min. youth and music First Free Meth. Ch., Des Moines, 1973-75, Ch. of the Open Bible, Aberdeen, Wash., 1975-76; assoc. pastor Ch. of the Open Bible, Tujunga, Calif., 1976-86; founding pastor Desert Streams Ch., Canyon Country, Calif., 1986—; dist. youth dir. Open Bible Standard Chs., So. Calif., 1976-86, dist. supr., 1987-90; bd. dirs. Pacific div. Open Bible Standard Chs., 1987-90, Eugene (Oreg.) Bible Coll., 1987-90, Santa Clarita Valley Women's Aglow, Canyon Country, Calif., 1986—. Composer: (sacred music) Anoint My Head With Fresh Oil, 1990, Holiness, Majesty, 1990; contbr. articles to Message and Overcomers (mags.). bd. dirs. Calif. Coun. on Alcohol Problems, Sacramento, 1987—. Mem. So. Calif. Dist. Min's. Assn. Home: 20131 Gilbert Dr Canyon Country CA 91351 Office: Desert Streams Ch 26873 Ruether Ave Canyon Country CA 91351

DAVIS, RANDOLPH DEAN, minister; b. Decatur, Ill., May 30, 1952; s. Paul and Beverly Jean (Bailey) D.; m. Rebecca Fae Madden, Aug. 16, 1974; children: Steven Dean, Erin Fae. BA, Mo. Bapt. Coll., St. Louis, 1974; M Religious Edn., Southwestern Bapt. Seminary, Ft. Worth, Tex., 1976. Ordained to ministry So. Bapt. Conv., 1973. Assoc. min. Westview Bapt. Ch., Belleville, Ill., 1977-80; min. of edn. Southwest Bapt. Ch., St. Louis, 1980-82; min. Charity Bapt. Ch., Carlinville, Ill., 1982-87, Sterling Bapt. Ch., Fairview Heights, Ill., 1987-91, Chandler Acres Bapt. Ch., Omaha, 1991—. Office: Chandler Acres Bapt Ch 7505 Chandler Acres Dr Omaha NE 68147 *I have found that the greatest joy in life is to be in the center of God's Will.*

DAVIS, RANDY LYNN, youth minister; b. Oklahoma City, June 2, 1960; s. Rosby Levon and Sue Ella (Brown) D.; m. Amy Lynn Cantrell, May 27, 1989. AS, Anderson Coll., 1982; BA in Youth Ministry, Okla. Bapt. U., 1989. Minister of youth Pope Dr. Bapt. Ch., Anderson, S.C., 1981-82, Trinity Bapt. Ch., Yukon, Okla., 1983-86; mid. sch. minister Sagamore Hill Bapt. Ch., Ft. Worth, 1986-87; assoc. pastor youth edn. First Bapt. Ch., Piedmont, Okla., 1987-89; minister youth edn. First Bapt. Ch., Kingfisher, Okla., 1989—. Named to Soc. Disting. Americans. Democrat. Home: 836 Clark Dr Kingfisher OK 73750

DAVIS, RONALD GLENN, minister; b. Bloomfield, Ky., Apr. 14, 1959; s. Tracy Davis and Betty (Beasley) Martin; m. Valencia Renee Smith, June 9, 1990. BS in Bus. Edn., U. Minn., 1982; MDiv, Fuller Theol. Sem., Pasadena, Calif., 1986. Lic. to ministry Bapt. Gen. Conf., 1987. Missions pastor Elim Bapt. Ch., Detroit, 1986-88; assoc. pastor Bethel Bapt. Ch., Cleveland Heights, Ohio, 1989—; prison chaplain NE Pre-Release Ctr., Cleve., 1990—; rep. Christian edn. com. Mich. Bapt. Conf., Grand Rapids, 1987-88; chmn., rep. adult com. Mid. East Bapt. Conf., Canfield, Ohio, 1989—. Office: Bethel Bapt Ch 2706 Noble Rd Cleveland Heights OH 44121

DAVIS, RONALD MERLE, minister; b. Hamilton, Ohio, Nov. 18, 1948; s. James Allen and Margaret (Ross) D.; m. Joan Carol Flaherty, Oct. 21 1972; 1 child, Christopher Ronald. BA in Bibl. Studies, Cen. Bible Coll., Springfield, Mo., 1976. Assoc. pastor Eagle Heights Assembly of God, Springfield, Mo., 1974-75; evangelist Assemblies of God, 1976-80; sr. pastor New Life Tabernacle Assembly of God, West Carrolton, Ohio, 1980-85, First Assembly of God, Greenville, Ohio, 1985—; counseling tng. Emerge Ministries, Akron, Ohio, 1985—. Chmn. bd. dirs. Senior Citizens Orgn. SCOPE, Greenville, Ohio, 1988—; pres. bd. dirs. Beacon House Maternity Home, Greenville, 1988—; Repub. Presidential Task Force, 1988—. Sgt. U.S. Army, 1969-71. Home: 1393 Chippewa St Greenville OH 45331 Office: First Assembly of God Ch Rt 118 N 7219 St Greenville OH 45331 *I have found it is easier to get along with people when you accept them where they are rather than where you expect them to be.*

DAVIS, ROY WILLIAM, minister; b. Canton, Ohio, Mar. 30, 1950; s. Roy Beasley and Elizabeth Mathilda (Marquart) D.; m. Cynthia Ann Huggins, Apr. 22, 1972. AA, Pensacola Jr. Coll., 1970; BA, U. West Fla., 1972; MRE, New Orleans Bapt. Theol. Sem., 1974. Ordained to ministry So. Bapt. Conv., 1975. Min. edn. and youth Smithwood Bapt. Ch., Knoxville, Tenn., 1974-76; min. edn. 1st Bapt. Ch., Burlington, N.C., 1976-78; min. edn. and youth Rock Bapt. Ch., Rex, Ga., 1978-79; tchr. jr. high schs. Escambia and Hillsborough counties, Fla., 1979-81; min. edn. and youth Keene Terr. Bapt. Ch., Largo, Fla., 1981-83; tchr. Taylor Meml. Bapt. Ch. and Sch., Tampa, Fla., 1983-84; min. edn. and youth Temple Bapt. Ch., Norfolk, Va., 1984-85, Kempsville Bapt. Ch., Virginia Beach, Va., 1985-87; elem. tchr. Norfolk Pub. Schs., 1987-89; tchr. Clayton County Schs., Jonesboro, Ga., 1989-90, Landmark Christian High Sch., Fayetteville and Fairburn, Ga., 1990-91; coord. vol. resources Ga. Regional Hosp. at Atlanta, Decatur, 1991—. Exec. vol. coord. Atlanta Clothing Bank Network. Mem. Ea. Bapt. Religious Edn. Assn., Vols. for People. Office: PATH 1141 Spring St Atlanta GA 30309

DAVIS, RUDOLPH JEFFERY, minister, educator; b. Vallejo, Calif., July 30, 1964; s. James Oscar and Charlestine (Williams) D.; 1 child, Christine M.L. AA, Solano Community Coll., 1985; BA, Sonoma State U., 1987, postgrad., 1991—; DD, Universal Bible Coll., 1991. Ordained to ministry Pentecostal Ch., 1984. Assoc. min. True Pentecostal Ch. of Calif., Vallejo, 1979—, youth pastor, 1985-86; pastor Ch. of Jesus Christ, Rohnert Park, Calif., 1988-89; lectr. Sonoma State U., Rohnert Park, Calif., 1987-90; pres. Young Min.'s Coun., Vallejo, 1990—. Office: True Pentecostal Ch Calif 131 Mendocino St Vallejo CA 94590

DAVIS, RUSSELL RAY, minister; b. Eagle Lake, Tex., July 12, 1954; s. Clarence Luther (stepfather) and Irene (Hartman) Jenkins; m. Marie Elizabeth Baxter, June 7, 1975; children: Jana Danielle, Lauren Michelle. Student, Wharton (Tex.) Jr. Coll., 1972-73; BA, Houston Bapt. U., 1976; M of Div., Southwestern Bapt. Theol. Sem., 1981, MRE, 1983; postgrad., North Tex. State U., 1984-85, United Inst. Bibl. Counseling, 1985—. Ordained to ministry Bapt. Ch., 1973. Pastor Rock Island (Tex.) Bapt. Ch., 1973-76; assoc. pastor First Bapt. Sugar Land, Tex., 1976-79; asst. mgr. La-Z-Boy Showcase, Ft. Worth, 1981-84; teaching asst. North Tex. State U., Denton, 1984-85; pastor East Dallas Bapt. Ch., 1986-89, Urban Pk. Bapt. Ch., Dallas, 1989—; pulpit supply Coastal Plains Bapt. Assn., Wharton, Tex., 1969-72; youth evangelist Southwest Tex. Area, 1969-75; tchr. youth bible camp Peach Creek Encampment, Humble, Tex., 1975; evangelist revivals Tex. and Okla. Compiler: Study Outlines of the Bible, 1977. Grantee Tex. Edn. Agy., 1985; named one of Outstanding Young Mem of Am., 1987. Mem. Dallas Bapt. Assn. (exec. bd. dirs. 1986—, inner city ministries com. 1986-89, chmn. pub. rels. & media com., com. on coms. 1990). Home: 7119 Dillon Dr Dallas TX 75227 *I have discovered that Nothing comes into your life without God's permission and, with His permission, grace to deal with it.*

DAVIS, S. KENNETH, minister; b. Plainfield, N.J., Apr. 7, 1927; s. Courtland VanHorn and Frankie Alice (Lowther) D.; m. C. Jean Bailey, Jan. 4, 1947; children: Susan Bond, Deborah Giles, Kenneth H., Paul D., Janice Noel. AB in Elem. Edn., Salem (W.Va.) Coll., 1949; BDiv, Alfred U., 1961. Ordained to ministry Seventh Day Bapt. Gen. Conf., 1961; cert. tchr., W.Va., N.J., Ohio, N.Y. Pastor Daytona Beach (Fla.) Seventh Day Bapt. Ch., 1961-66, Pawcatuck Seventh Day Bapt. Ch., Westerly, R.I., 1966-70, Seventh Day Bapt. Ch., Battle Creek, Mich., 1970-85, Battle Creek Ch. of Brethren, 1977-85, Salem Seventh Day Bapt. Ch., 1985—; mem. commn. Seventh Day Bapt. Gen. Conf., 1965-68, 73-76, pres., 1974-75. Pres. Salem and Greenbrier Cemetery Assn., 1986—; chmn. Salem Apple Butter Festival Com., 1987—; co-chmn. Salem Bicentennial Com., 1989—; mem. Salem City Coun., 1989—. With USMC, 1945-46. Mem. Seventh Day Bapt. Hist. Soc. (pres. 1990—), Salem Area Ministerial Assn. (pres. 1987-90), Harrison County Ministerial Assn., Vol. Chaplains at Hosp., Kiwanis (pres. Salem 1988-89). Home and Office: 171 E Main St Salem WV 26426

DAVIS, STEVEN BRAD, minister; b. Newark, June 7, 1953; s. Roosevelt and Ozzie Florence (Windom) D.; m. Denise Arlene Quarles, July 17, 1976; children: Teriq Crosby, Constance Victoria, Jonathan Steven. BA, ThB, Internat. Sem., Plymouth, Fla., 1986, DDiv, 1988. Ordained to ministry, Nat. Bapt. Conv. Am., 1984. Minister to youth Calvary Gospel Ch., Newark, 1977-81; assoc. minister Mt. Olive Bapt. Ch., Norfolk, Va., 1981-85; campus minister Norfolk State U., 1981—; pastor Westminster Bapt. Ch., Norfolk, 1985—; trustee Peniel Bible Conf., Lake Lurcerne, N.Y., 1985—; bd. dirs. Young Adult and New Adult Conf., 1978—; del. Va. Fellowship, Hampton, 1982—. Bd. dirs. Va. Task Force Justice Fellowship, 1983—. Home: 5641 Darby Close Portsmouth VA 23703 Office: Westminster Bapt Ch 3412 Westminster Ave Norfolk VA 23504

DAVIS, TERRI M., pastoral counselor; b. Binghampton, N.Y., Dec. 2, 1947; d. Michael Sr. and Patricia Ann (Bentz) Maslak; m. Thomas Leon Davis, Dec. 20, 1969; children: Eric, Annette. BS in Dietetics, Okla. State U., 1970; MA in Pastoral Care and Counseling, Phillips Grad. Sem., 1988; postgrad., Coll. for Fin. Planning, 1984-86. Pub. relations cons. TMD Enterprises, Tulsa, 1984-85, proprietor, cons., 1985-86; systems analyst Arrow Specialty Co. div. Masco Corp., Tulsa, 1986; dir. communication services Arrow Specialty Co. div. Masco Industries, Tulsa, 1986-87, inventory control mgr., 1987-89; cons. computer systems Resonance for Women, Tulsa, 1983-86, pastoral counselor, 1989—; cons. Cascia Hall Prep Sch., Tulsa, 1986-87. Editor (newsletters) Arrow Update, Arrow News. Cabinet advisor Camp Fire, Tulsa, 1986-87, advisor, 1984—, discovery treas., 1987-89; active Mothers Against Drunk Driving. Elks Found. scholar, Endicott, 1965. Mem. NAFE, Nat. Math Scholarship Assn., Holland Hall Parents Assn. (treas. 1982-83). Republican. Episcopalian. Home: 1810 E 43d St Tulsa OK 74105 Office: Resonance for Women 2524 E 41st St Tulsa OK 74105

DAVIS, THEODORE ROOSEVELT, bishop, contractor; b. Hazelhurst, Miss., Mar. 28, 1903; s. Moses and Narcissus D.; m. Freddie Wilhemett, Aug. 30, 1923 (dec. 1984); children—Myrtle, Wilma, Dorothy, Connie, Frankie, Theo, Roosevelt; m. Emma Hawthrone, Jan. 12, 1985. Hon. degree Saints Acad., Lexington, Miss., 1969, Anthony Les Ctr., Hattiesburg, Miss., 1972. Ordained minister Pentecostal Ch., 1930. Contractor Wise Constrn., 1930-50; pastor Ch. of God in Christ, Bolton, Miss., 1930-45, Rankin, Miss., 1931-42, Vicksburg, Miss., 1937-47; sec. Jurisdiction So. Miss., 1940-55; dist. supt. 7th Dist., 1947-62; jurisdiction bishop So. Miss., 1962—; gen. contractor hdqrs. 1st jurisdiction Ch. of God in Christ, Jackson, Miss., 1972—, nat. treas., Memphis, 1980-85, also mem. bd. bishops; chaplain Westside Housing, Jackson, 1983—, Hinds County Republican Com., Jackson, 1977-85; cons. for housing Chisca Hotel, Memphis, 1978-85, chmn. bldg. commn., 1979-85; Bd. dirs. Saints Jr. Coll., Lexington, 1974-79; mem. Jackson Pub. Service Commn., 1984-85. Named Man of Yr., Religious Workers Guild, 1972; recipient Leadership award Ch. of God in Christ, 1984. Mem. Miss. Ministerial Allowance. Club: Millionaires (Memphis). Avocation: fishing.

DAVIS, THOMAS CRAWLEY, III, minister; b. Annapolis, Md., Feb. 21, 1945; s. Thomas Crawley Jr. and Emily Ruth (Myers) D.; m. Alice Goodfellow David, Mar.22, 1969; children: Matthew Myers, Adam Goodfellow. BA, Wash. & Lee U., 1967; MA, Northwestern U., Evanston, Ill., 1969; PhD., U. Pitts., 1981; postdoctoral, St. Thomas U., Miami, Fla., 1989. Adminstrv. asst. U. and city ministries U. and city ministires, Pitts., 1973-75; campus minister Duke U., Durham, N.C., 1976-81, U. Miami, 1981-84; chaplain Krome Ave I.N.S. Processing Ctr., Miami, 1985-87; pastor North Miami Beach Presbyn. Ch., 1985—; assoc. prof. christian ethics and theology South Fla. Ctr. for Theol. Studies, Miami, 1985—; urban ministry cons. Tropical Fla. Presbytery, Miami, 1985-87. Founder, mem. Amnesty Internat. (chpt. 248), Miami, 1982. Lt. USNR, 1969-71. Decorated Bronze Star; Woodrow Wilson fellowship Northwestern U., 1968. Mem. Am. Assn. of Counseling and Devel., League of Am. Wheelmen, Phi Beta Kappa, Omicron Delta Kappa. Democrat. Avocations: bicycling, water sports. Office: N Miami Beach Presbyn Ch 16951 NE 4 Ave North Miami Beach FL 33162

DAVIS, WALLACE TERRY, minister, association executive; b. Andalusia, Ala., July 15, 1949; s. Marion Elmer Davis and Helen Myrtice Hall Davis; m. Carol McCall, June 2, 1974; children: Joshua, Amanda. BS, Samford U., 1971; ThM, New Orleans Bapt. Theol. Sem., 1974, DEd, 1977. Ordained to ministry So. Bapt. Conv., 1969; lic. profl. counselor. Chaplain Vols. Am., New Orleans, 1975-77, pres., chief exec. officer, 1981—; assoc. pastor Oakdale Bapt. Ch., Mobile, Ala., 1977-81, interim pastor, 1981-85; interim pastor Westlawn Bapt. Ch., Mobile, 1986. Author: How Churches in Transition Can Grow, 1988. Home: 3110 Riviere du Chien Loop E Mobile AL 36693 Office: Vols of Am 600 Azalea Rd Mobile AL 36609 *When it's over, all that is left are the seeds that we have sown. Good seeds will produce good for eternity. I want to broadcast His seeds of love, joy, goodwill, and preach to all.*

DAVIS, WALTER BOND, minister; b. Balt., Jan. 16, 1930; s. Everett Fogg and Fanny-Fern (Smith) D.; m. Catherine Fixx, Sept. 18, 1934 (div. 1981); m. Barbara Buschmeyer, Nov. 24, 1928; children: Ward, Peter, Eric, Craig, Jean, Martha, Neil, Tom. BA with honors, Cornell U., 1951; MDiv, Yale U., 1954; postgrad., Harvard U., 1957-60. Ordained to ministry United Ch. of Christ, 1954. Assoc. pastor First Ch., Oberlin, Ohio, 1954-57, Cen. Congl. Ch., Newtonville, Mass., 1957-60; sr. pastor First Congl. Ch., United Ch. Christ, Verona, N.J., 1960-65, Santa Barbara, Calif., 1965-71, Winchester, Mass., 1971-89, Attleboro, Mass., 1989—; vis. scholar Claremont (Calif.) Sch. Theology, 1975, 86, Vienna, 1986; dean youth confs., United Ch. of Christ, Ohio, N.J., 1950-70; exec. com., bd. dirs. Mass. Conf., 1980; recording sec. United Ch. Bd. for World Ministries, 1982-86, steering com. FOCUS, 1988—; community rep. protocol com. Winchester Hosp., 1985-89. Contbr. articles to profl. jours. and newspapers; composer hymns. Chmn. Community Rels. Commn., Santa Barbara, Calif., 1966-70, Dept. Coll. and Univ. Ministries, N.J. Coun. Chs., 1962-65; founding pres. Winchester Interagy. Coun.; founder Family to Family Fellowship, Santa Barbara, 1967; bd. dirs. United Way, 1990—, Habitat for Humanity, 1990—, Attleboro Area Literacy Coun., 1990—. Recipient Outstanding Program award Exch. Club, Outstanding Svc. award ABI. Mem. Congl. Christian Hist. Soc. (clk. 1981—, exec. bd.), Winchester Interfaith Coun. (pres. 1988-89), Theol. Study Mass. Coun. Chs., Winthrop Club Boston (pres. 1982-84), Rotary Club. Avocations: sailing, writing, walking, music, traveling. Office: Second Congl Ch 50 Park St Attleboro MA 02703

DAVIS, WAYNE RODERICK, minister; b. Cin., May 16, 1951; s. Wilfred and Anna Mae (Wilhite) D.; m. Norma Jeanette Holt, June 14, 1975; 1 child, Kalila Ain. BA, Morehouse Coll., 1977; MDiv, Colgate-Rochester Div. Sch., 1979; MSW, Ohio State U., 1988; postgrad., So. Bapt. Sem., 1990—. Ordained to ministry Nat. Bapt. Conv. U.S.A., 1972; lic. social worker, Ohio. Asst. min. Zion Bapt. Ch., Walton, Ky., 1968-75, 1st Genesis Bapt. Ch., Rochester, N.Y., 1976-79; pastor Bethel Bapt. Ch., Cin., 1980—. Bd. dirs. SUMA, 1980-85, HIP, Cin., 1982-86, Walnut Hills/Evanston Med. Ctr., 1984; chmn. Cin. Task Force for Affirmative Action, 1988, Community Chest/United Way, 1990—. Mem. Ohio State Social Workers. Office: Bethel Bapt Ch 2712 Alms Pl Cincinnati OH 45206 *One of mankind's greatest gifts is relationships, with another, oneself and with God.*

DAVIS, WILLIAM ALBERT, minister, educator; b. Portland, Oreg., Feb. 26, 1934; s. Earl A. and Mary Ruth (Pratt) D.; B.A. in History, Wash. State U., 1961, B.A. in Philosophy, 1962, M.A. in History, 1962; Th.M., So. Meth. U., 1967; postgrad. U. Denver, 1967-73, 79-80, U. No. Colo., 1982-83, Colo. State U., 1983-84, 87, U. Colo., Denver, 1988-89; m. Vineta Alice Rensink, July 2, 1960; children—David Albert, Daniel Alyn, Derek Andrew. Tchr. social sci. Wenat High Sch., Wenatchee, Wash., 1962-63; chmn. social scis., asst. to pres. Wenatchee Valley Coll., 1963-64; ordained to ministry United Meth. Ch., 1965, elder, 1967; pastor United Meth. Ch., Celeste, Tex., 1964-67; pastor Burns Meml. United Meth. Ch., Aurora, Colo., 1967-70, 74-75; youth and edn. minister Montclair United Meth. Ch., Denver, 1970-71; polit. scientist, philosophy faculty Community Coll. Denver (now Front Range Community Coll.), 1969-81, dir. div. arts and humanities, 1981-87, exec. dir. spl. projects, 1987; asst. dir. vocal edn. Aurora (Colo.) Pub. Schs., 1987-88; pvt. practice cons., 1988-91; supt. McCurdy Sch., Espanola, N.Mex., 1991—; cons. Denver Urban Observatory, 1970-71; faculty rep. Colo. Bd. Community Colls. and Occupational Edn., 1972-74; treas. Bd. Edn. Adams-Arapahoe Dist. 28J, 1973-75, sec., 1975-77, pres., 1977-79, sec., 1979-81, v.p., 1981-83, bd. dirs., 1983-85, pres., 1985-87; precinct committeeman Arapahoe County Democratic Party, 1969-71, 1980-82, dist. capt., 1972-73; bd. dirs. Aurora Community Mental Health Center, 1976-85, 89-91, pres., 1981-83; trustee Aurora Community Mental Health Found., 1976-78, Aurora Community Living Resources, Inc., 1981—, pres., 1987—; trustee Aurora Mental Health Research Inst., Inc., 1981—, pres., 1985, sec., 1988—; trustee Aurora Community Hosp., 1977-80, moderator, 1978-80; mem. Aurora Citizens Adv. Utilities Budget Com., 1983-91, vice chair, 1988-91. Served with AUS, 1954-57, USAR, 1957-62, USNR, 1968-75. Mem. United Ministries in Higher Edn. (chmn. Colo. commn. 1974-75, treas. 1982-88), Colo. Assn. Community Jr. Colls. (pres. faculty unit 1972-74, parliamentarian 1974-75), Am. Legion. Clubs: K.T., Masons (32 deg., hon. past master 1991), Kiwanis (pres. 1990-91), Shriners, Lions (pres. 1965), Optimists (pres. 1980-81). Home: PO Box 700 Santa Cruz NM 87567-0700 Office: McCurdy Sch No NMex PO Box 127 Espanola NM 87532-0127

DAVIS, WILLIAM EMRYS, religious organization official; b. Lexington, Ky., Oct. 13, 1942; s. Evans Jefferies and Martha Louise (Crain) D.; m. Constance Ann Shrawder, Aug. 25, 1968; children: Marya Elizabeth, Hillary Louise. AB, Transylvania U., 1964; JD, U. Ky., 1972. Bar: Calif. 1974, U.S. Ct. Appeals (9th cir.) 1974. Regional rep. Peace Corps, Chile, 1968-71; dir. adminstrv. office of cts. State of Ky., 1975-79; dist. exec. for fed. cts. U.S. Ct. Appeals (9th cir.), 1981-86; dir. adminstrv. office of cts. State of Calif., 1987-91; pers. officer Baha'i World Ctr., Hafia, Israel, 1979-81; with com. for teaching Nat. Spiritual Assembly, Wilmette, Ill., 1982-83, with com. for social and ednl. devel., 1984-85, mem., 1985—, treas., 1988—; chair fed. cts. com. State Bar Calif., 1985-86; sr. advisor for jud. adminstrn. in Latin Am. Nat. Ctr. for State Cts., Williamsburg, Va., 1991—. Bd. dirs. Pre-trial Resource Ctr., 1990—. Recipient Outstanding Leadership award Ky. Bar Assn., 1979, Outstanding Contbn. award Ky. Lawyers Assn., 1979, Outstanding Contbn. award Calif. Judges Assn., 1991. Mem. Am. Judicature Soc. (bd. dirs. 1991—). Home: 414 Bay Rd Menlo Park CA 94025

DAVIS, WILLIAM MARK, minister; b. Lexington, Ky., June 28, 1963; s. Robert Edward Davis and Helen (Youngman) Lucky; m. Dawna Elaine Davis, July 21, 1990. BA in Psychology, Georgetown Coll., 1986; MDiv, Lexington Theol. Sem., 1989. Ordained to ministry Disciples of Christ Ch., 1989. Assoc. min. Twin Pines Christian Ch., Lexington, 1988-90, South Side Christian Ch., Lima, Ohio, 1990—. Mem. Assn. Christian Ch. Educators, Lima Area Clergy Acad. Office: South Side Christian Ch 540 S Central Ave Lima OH 45804

DAVISSON, SISTER MARY FRANCES, nun, elementary school educator; b. Lima, Ohio, Dec. 27, 1948; d. Robert George and Catherine Elizabeth (Moriarity) D. BA in Elem. Edn., Coll. Mt. St. Joseph, 1972, MA in Edn., 1988. Cert. tchr. Ohio; joined Sisters of Charity, Roman Cath. Ch. Tchr. grades 1-3 St. Saviour Sch., Cin., 1972-74, Mount Campus Sch., Cin., 1975-78; tchr. grades 1, 4-6 St. Boniface Sch., Cin., 1978-82; 2nd grade tchr. St. William Sch., Cin., 1982-85, Our Lady of Lourdes Sch., Cin., 1985-89; math. insvc. specialist K-6 Cin. Archdiocesan Schs., 1989—; active curriculum revision com. Archdiocese of Cin., 1984, 89; workshop presenter various meetings, convs.; tutor Diamond Oaks Joint Vocat. Sch., Cin., 1988; coop. tchr. Coll. Mt. St. Joseph, 1988, 89. Chairperson United Appeal Campaign, Our Lady of Lourdes Sch., 1987, 88; music min. Sisters of Charity, Cin., 1984—; vol. (Mrs. Claus) Cin. Zoo, 1988—. Mem. Nat. Cath. Edn. Assn., Nat. Coun. Tchrs. Math., Ohio Coun. Tchrs. Math., Greater Cin. Coun. Tchrs. Math. Roman Catholic. Avocations: bicycling, knitting, needlepoint, tennis, walking. Office: Office for Cath Schs 100 E Eighth St Cincinnati OH 45202

DAWE, JERRY LYLE, pastor; b. Marion, Ill., Sept. 14, 1942; s. Raymond Eugene and Mary Isabelle (Hunter) D.; m. Charolette Ann Moore, Dec. 15, 1973; children: Jeremy Eugene, Jonathon Bartholomew, Pilar Elizabeth, Simon Timothy. MusB, So. Ill. U., 1968; degree in pastoral theology, ECA Inst., 1979. Ordained to ministry Christian Ch., 1979. Minister of music 1st Christian Ch., Poplar Bluff, Mo., 1978-80; tchr. 1st Assembly of God, Poplar Bluff, 1980-81; pastor Christian Ch., Mill Spring, Mo., 1983-89, Bethany Bible, LeRoy, Minn., 1989—; chaplain Full Gospel Businessmen Internat., Poplar Bluff, 1987-89. With USAF, 1960-63. Recipient Fellowship Presser Found., 1966. Mem. Evang. Pastor's Assn., Rotary. Home: 146 E Main Le Roy MN 55951 Office: Bethany Bible Ch 142 E Main LeRoy MN 55951

DAWES, DENNIS RICHARD, minister; b. Greenfield, Ohio, July 31, 1950; s. Delbert Wayne and Omalee (Comer) D.; m. Teresa Joan Kamer, Aug. 6, 1971; children: Andrew, Daryn, Steve. BA, Ky. Christian Coll., 1972. Min. Pond Creek Ch. of Christ, Portsmouth, Ohio, 1969-71, Pricetown Ch. of Christ, Hillsboro, Ohio, 1971-76, 5th Ave. Ch. of Christ, Williamson, W.Va., 1976-84, Cen. Ch. of Christ, Portsmouth, 1984—; speaker radio program Look to Jesus, Portsmouth, 1990—. Mem. Ky. Christian Coll. Alumni Assn. (pres. 1990-92), Tri-State Min.'s Assn. (pers. 1986-88). Office: Cen Ch Christ 1211 Grandview Ave Portsmouth OH 45662

DAWKINS, ROSE MARIE, religious educator; b. Mack, Colo., Sept. 19, 1936; d. Milo Roy and Flora Ella (Bennet) Douglas; m. Robert Clyde Dawkins, Mar. 2, 1957; children: Debra Wynice, Ella Marie, Robert Clyde Jr. AA, Lee Coll., 1956; BA, Berean Coll., 1972. Missionary Ch. of God, Okinawa, Japan, 1964-68; tchr. Berean Fellowship, Dallas, 1968-72; tchr., prin. Internat. Life Corps, Atlanta, 1972-91; music dir., publs. editor Internat. Life Corps, Atlanta, 1972-91; sec. Atlanta Deaf Action Ctr., 1985-91. Editor: Sweetwater Digest, 1972-91. Home: 1774 Bolton Rd NW Atlanta GA 30318 *My only desire is to let Christ so live through me that others will desire to know more of Him from God's Word.*

DAWN, MARVA JENINE, theologian; b. Napoleon, Ohio, Aug. 20, 1948; d. Herold C. and Louise A. (Bayer) Gersmehl; m. Myron L. Sandberg, June 10, 1989. MDiv, Western Evang. Seminary, Portland, Oreg., 1978; STM, Pacific Luth. Seminary, Berkeley, Calif., 1983; MA in Ethics, U. Notre Dame, 1986, postgrad. Dir. youth and edn. Concordia Luth Ch., 1972-75; dir. spl. ministries Good Shepherd Luth. Ch., Olympia, Wash., 1976-79; founder, author, educator Christians Equipped for Ministry, Tumwater, Wash., 1979—; vis. prof. Western Evang. Seminary, 1981, 83, 84; chmn. Inter-Luth. Commn. on Campus Ministry, 1979-82, vice chmn., 1978; organizer Inter-Luth. Task Force on Ministry to Single Adults, 1980; bd. dirs. state and dist. youth bds. Luth Ch. Mo. Synod, 1973-79. Author: Keeping the Sabbath Wholly, 1989, I'm Lonely, LORD—How Long? The Psalms for Today, 1983, To Walk in the Kingdom: God's Call to Discipleship, 1982, To Walk and Not Faint: God's Comfort from Isaiah 40, 1980 (Bibl. Writer of Yr. 1981); translator, editor: Holy War in Ancient Israel (Gerhard von Rad), 1990; contbr. articles to profl. jours. Active Bread for the World, 1982—, Fellowship of Reconciliation, 1982—, Luth. Peace Fellowship, 1985—, Evangelicals for Social Action, 1986—. Mem. Am. Acad. Religion, Soc. Bibl. Lit. Home: 304 Fredricksburg Way Vancouver WA 98664 Office: Christians Equipped for Ministry 524 S 4th Ave Tumwater WA 98502 *Through numerous struggles with physical and visual handicaps, I have learned this essential truth: God is faithful. One of the greatest gifts that God's people can offer to the world is the gift of hope founded on God's unchanging grace.*

DAWSON, JOHN DAVID, religious organization administrator; b. Auckland, New Lealand, Nov. 19, 1951; came to U.S., 1971; s. James Cummings and Adaline Joy (Manins) D.; m. Julie Alaine Schmaltz, May 19, 1973; children: David James, Paul Steven, Matthew John. Evangelist Youth with a Mission, various countries, 1971-75; founder, dir. Youth with a Mission, L.A., 1975-83; dir. 1986 Olympic Outreach, L.A., 1983-84, Youth with a Mission, Southwestern, U.S., 1984-88; dist. dir. Youth with a Mission North Am. Coun., 1988—; Author: Taking our Cities for God, 1984 (Best Seller), Strategy for Cities, 1988, LEaders Guide, 1990, The Father Heart of God (booklet), 1983; contbr. articles to profl. jours. Mem. bd. regents U. of the Nations, Kona, Hawaii. Office: Youth with a Mission PO Box 296 Sunland CA 91041-0296 *Success in spiritual leadership is not measured by how many people I control. Rather, it is demonstrated by the number of people whom I have helped release into their full potential who now surpass me.*

DAWSON, LEWIS EDWARD, minister, retired military officer; b. Louisville, Oct. 26, 1933; s. Lewis Harper and Zelma Ruth (Hocutt) D.; m. Margaret Ellen Poor, July 29, 1956; children: Edward Rhodes, David Harper, Deborah Louise, Virginia Ruth. BA, Baylor U., 1954; MDiv, So. Bapt. Sem., 1960; postgrad., Presbyn. Sch. Christian Edn., 1977—. Ordained to ministry So. Bapt. Conv., 1960. Pastor Finecastle (Va.) Bapt. Ch. and Zion Hill Bapt. Ch., 1960-63, First So. Bapt. Ch., Great Falls, Mont., 1963-67; commd. capt. USAF, 1967, advanced through grades to col., 1983; chaplain McCoy AFB, 1967-69, Vietnam, 1969-70, Sheppard AFB, 1971-73, RAF, Chicksands, Eng., 1973-76, Keesler AFB, 1977-79; sr. chaplain Ankara (Turkey) Air Sta., 1979-81; mem. USAF Chaplain Res. Bd. Maxwell AFB, 1981-84; sr. chaplain Wright-Patterson AFB, 1984-87; sr. chaplain Elmendorf AFB, Alaska, 1987-89, ret., 1989; assoc. dir. mil. chaplaincy Home Mission Bd., Atlanta, Ga., 1989—; clk. Triangle Bapt. Assn., 1965-66; chmn. Mont. Indian mission com. Mont. So. Bapt. Fellowship, 1965-66, treas., 1965-66. Mem. exec. coun. Save the Children Fund, Shefford, Eng., 1973-76. Decorated Bronze Star, Meritorious Svc. medal with 4 oak leaf cluster, Legion of Merit, Air Force Commendation medal. Home: 1926 Coventry Way Jonesboro GA 30236 Office: Home Mission Bd 1350 Spring St Atlanta GA 30367 *When the weapons of war are exploding all around you as well as when you are secure at home with family, God is with you. God is in the logistics business, supplying all that people need as we make ourselves available to God.*

DAWSON, MARTHA MORGAN, minister; b. Anderson, Ind., Aug. 30, 1908; d. Earl R. and Elena (Hill) Morgan. Student, Colo. U.; D. in Div. Sci. (hon.), Brooks Divinity Coll., 1986. Ordained to ministry, 1982. Sales profl., owner Denver, 1959-68; copywriter Maginot Advt. Co., Denver, 1968-71; travel host Middle East, 1971-84; instr. Brooks Divine Sci. Coll., 1979-91. Columnist: Aspire, 1978-81; contbr. articles, stories, poems to religious and gen. publs. Mem. Colo. Poetry Soc. (pres. 1977-79), Altrusa, Denver Woman's Press Club (pres. 1973-74).

DAWSON, WAYNE LOWELL, minister; b. Independence, Mo., Mar. 29, 1961; s. Lowell Allison Dawson and Marian (Rosbrugh) Walker; m. Robin Kay Jensen, June 5, 1982; children: Roxanne L., Michelle L. BA in Ch. Music and Religious Edn., Mid-Am. Nazarene Coll., 1988. Music minister Ch. of the Nazarene, Omaha, 1977-79; with pub. relations Mid-Am. Nazarene Coll., Olathe, Kans., 1979-81; music minister Ch. of the Nazarene, Overland Park, Kans., 1982; assoc. pastor music and youth First Ch. of the Nazarene, Independence, Kans., 1982-88; assoc. pastor music First Ch. of the Nazarene, Independence, 1988—. Sr. Youth Dir. Nazarene Ch. Joplin dist., 1984-87; pres. Nazarene Youth Internat., Joplin Dist., 1987—. Fellow Independence Ministerial Alliance. Republican. Avocations: automobiles, photography, outdoor activities, woodworking. Home: 316 S 12th Independence KS 67301 Office: 3200 S 10th St Box 595 Independence KS 67301

DAY, DONALD SHELDON, lawyer; b. Boston, Nov. 3, 1924; s. Israel and Frances (Goldberg) D.; m. Edythe Greenberg, July 8, 1945; children—Clifford L., Richard J., Halee Beth. BA, Bates Coll., 1946; LLB, Cornell U., 1948. Bar: N.Y. 1948. Chmn. bd. Saperston and Day P.C., Buffalo, 1979—; pres. World Union for Progressive Judaism; bd. dirs. various corps. Gen. chmn. United Jewish Fund campaign, Buffalo, 1971-73, 75; past co-chmn. Western N.Y. chpt. NCCJ; past pres. United Jewish Fedn. Buffalo; chmn. bd. Children's Hosp. of Buffalo; trustee Forest Lawn Cemetery and Crematory, Hebrew-Union Coll.; past chmn. bd. Union Am. Hebrew Congregations; bd. dirs. Coun. Jewish Fedns. With AUS, 1942-45. Mem. Am., N.Y. State, Erie County bar assns., Order of Coif, Phi Kappa Phi. Jewish (past pres. temple). Office: Saperston & Day PC 1 Fountain Pla Buffalo NY 14203

DAY, DOUGLAS DEE, religious organization administrator; b. Memphis, Aug. 21, 1949; s. Douglas F. and Anna L. (Tate) D.; m. Deborah Jean East, Aug. 18, 1973; children: Michael Douglas, Laura Ashlyn. BS, U. Tenn., 1971; postgrad., Southwestern Bapt. Theol. Sem., 1973. Cert. fin. planner, recording agt. property and casualty. Minister of students 1st Bapt. Ch., Houston, 1972-75; mninster edn. 1st Bapt. Ch., Sharkville, Miss., 1975-80; dir. video tape svcs. So. Bapt. Conv., Ft. Worth, 1980-86; dir. spl. gifts div. Bapt. Gen. Conv. Tex., Dallas, 1984-86; v.p. annuity bd. So. Bapt. Conv., Dallas, 1986—; adj. prof. Sch. Religious Edn. Southwestern Bapt. Theol. Sem., Ft. Worth, 1990-91; mem. leadership com. 1st Bapt. Ch., Arlington, Tex. Contbr. articles to profl. jours. Mem. Tex. Bapt. Men (v.p. 1988-91), So. Bapt. Religious Educators, Nat. Ch. Bus. Administrs., Internat. Bd. Cert. Fin. Planner. Republican. Home: 521 Whistler Arlington TX 76006 Office: Southern Bapt Conv Annuity Bd 2401 Cedar Springs Dallas TX 75221-2190 *In my work I have often reflected on a saying Henry Ford used, "Never complain, never explain!".*

DAY, JACKSON HARVEY, minister, health care administrator; b. Oakland, Calif., Mar. 18, 1942; s. Jackson Wesley and Ruthlydia (Slayton) D.; m. Martha Ann Taylor, May 30, 1964 (div. 1970); 1 child, James Wesley; m. Emily Ann Roberts, Nov. 13, 1971 (div. 1978); 1 child, Catherin; m. Frances Kathleen Irvin, Apr. 8, 1989. AB, Western Md. Coll., 1963; MDiv, Wesley Theology Sem., 1967; MPH, U. N.C., 1987. Ordained to ministry United Meth. Ch. as deacon, 1964, as elder 1967. Pastor Piney Plains Meth. Charge, Little Orleans, Md., 1964-67, Epworth United Meth. Ch., Washington, 1970-71; clergy mem. Capitol Hill United Meth. Ch., Washington, 1971-75, Christ United Meth. Ch., Columbia, Md., 1975—; v.p. program devel. JSA Healthcare Corp., Columbia, 1986—; treas. Nat. Conf. Vietnam Vet. Min., Washington, 1990—; bd. dirs. Owen Brown Interfaith Ctr., Columbia, 1988-89; coord. Interagency Coun. on Family Planning, Washington, 1971-72; program mgr. Westinghouse Health Systems, 1973-82; deputy dir. mgmt. svcs. King Fahad Hosp. Riyadh, Saudi Arabia, 1982-84. Author: James Day of Browningsville, 1977; author: (poetry) Reclaiming the Pieces, 1988. Sec., chaplain Vietnam Vets. of Am., Balt., 1989—. Capt. U.S. Army, 1967-70, Vietnam. Decorated Bronze Star, Air medal. Mem. The Liturgical Conf., Am. Pub. Health Assn., Nat. Coun. for Internat. Health. Democrat. Home: 11892 Blue February Way Columbia MD 21044

DAY, JERRY KEITH, minister; b. South Bend, Ind., May 15, 1938; s. Bruce E. and Grace L. (Buck) D.; m. Shirley Joseph, Nov. 3, 1956; children: Debbie Marvin, Jerry Jr. BA, Bryan Coll., 1960; MDiv, Grace Theol. Sem., 1963. Sr pastor Berean Bible Ch., Columbus, Ind., 1963--. Mem. Y-Med (bd. dirs. 1968-69), ARC (bd. dirs. 1973-82), Evang. Pastors' Fellowship, 1987--. Home: 31 N Brooks St Columbus IN 47201 Office: Berean Bible Church 51 N Brooks St Columbus IN 47201

DAY, WAYNE ALLAN, religious educator; b. Paducah, Ky., Dec. 6, 1955; s. Howard Len and Joan (Hileman) D.; m. Patricia Hannaford, Oct. 3, 1981; 1 child, Bryan. BA in Music Edn., Union U., Jackson, Tenn., 1977; MS in Human Svc., Murray (Ky.) State U., 1979; MA in Religious Edn., Southwestern Bapt. Theol. Sem., Ft. Worth, 1981, EdD of Youth Edn., 1990. Ordained to ministry Bapt. Ch., 1990. Min. music and edn. Lovelaceville (Ky.) Bapt. Ch., 1980-81; tchr., therapist Ft. Worth State Sch., 1982-85, Willow Creek Adolescent Ctr., Arlington, Tex., 1984-87; asst. prof. Union U., 1988—; min. music Poplar Corner Bapt. Ch., Bells, Tenn., 1989—; sponsor Youth Edn. Assn., Jackson, 1989—; sponsor, dir. Youth Leadership Conf., Jackson, 1988—; intern First Bapt. Ch., Arlington, 1986-88. Named one of Outstanding Young Men Am., 1989. Mem. Assn. Profs. Researchers Religious Edn., Religious Educators Am. Avocations: model building, woodworking, refinishing. Home: 17 LaPlace Jackson TN 38305 Office: Union U 2447 Hwy 45 Bypass Box 1824 Jackson TN 38305-9901

DAYA MATA, SRI (FAYE WRIGHT), clergywoman; b. Salt Lake City, Jan. 31, 1914; d. Clarence Aaron and Rachel (Terry) Wright. Grad. high sch., 1931. Ordained to ministry Self-Realization Fellowship, 1935. Min. Self-Realization Fellowship, L.A., 1935—, bd. dirs., 1941—, sec., 1944-45, treas., 1945-71, lectr., 1952—, pres. brs. U.S., Can., Mex., S.Am., Europe, Africa, Asia, Australia and New Zealand, 1955—; pres. Yogoda Satsanga Soc. of India/Self-Realization Fellowship Found., India, Pakistan, Nepal, and Sri Lanka, 1955—, Gemeinschaft der Selbst-Verwirklichung, 1974—, Self Realization Inst. of Va., Inc., 1981—. Author: (books) Only Love, 1976, Finding the Joy Within You, 1990; (videocassette) Security in a World of Change, 1989; contbr. articles to mags. Pres. Homeopathic Mahavidyalaya, Yogoda Satsanga Mahavidyalaya, Yogoda Satsanga Vidyalaya, Yogoda Satsanga Kanya Vidyalaya, Yogoda Satsanga Sangeet Kala Bharati, Yogoda Satsanga Shilpa Kala Bharati, Yogoda Satsanga Balkrishnalaya, Yogoda Satsanga Sevashram Hosp., others. Home and Office: Self-Realization Fellowship 3880 San Rafael Ave Los Angeles CA 90065

DAYLONG, STEVEN GEORGE, minister; b. Mt. Clemens, Mich., Nov. 19, 1961; s. George Gale and Sharon Marie (Hill) D.; m. Carla Marie Sattler, June 21, 1986. BA in Bibl. Rsch., Puget Sound Christian Coll., 1989; postgrad., Emmanuel Sch. Religion, Johnson City, Tenn., 1989—. Ordained to ministry Christian Ch/Ch. of Christ, 1989. Youth min. Mountlake Terrace (Wash.) Christian Ch., 1988-89; broadcaster, host Upward Vision program Sta. WZAP Christian Radio, Bristol, Va., 1990—. Weight room instr. YMCA, Seattle, 1987-88; youth sponsor Downtown Christian Ch., Johnson City, 1990—. Mem. Christian Chs. and Chs. of Christ. Home: 1610 Cherokee Rd Johnson City TN 37604 *I design to take my religion from the scriptures, and then, whether it suits or suits not any other denomination, I am not much concerned; for I think, at the last day it will not be inquired whether I was of (any particular denomination), but whether I sought or embraced truth in the love of it.*

DAYRINGER, RICHARD LEE, medical educator, minister; b. Carthage, Mo., Feb. 3, 1934; s. Joseph Allen and Sarah Marlin (Ruppert) D.; m. Evelyn Janet Hymer, Jan. 26, 1952; children: Stephen Lee, David Carter, Deborah Evelyn, Daniel Hymer, James Ray. AA, Southwest Bapt. Coll., Bolivar, Mo., 1953; AB, William Jewell Coll., 1955; MDiv, Midwestern Bapt. Theol. Sem., 1961; ThD, New Orleans Bapt. Theol. Sem., 1968. Ordained to ministry Bapt. Ch., 1952. Pastor various Bapt. Chs. Mo., Kans., La., 1951-65; interim pastor Santa Fe Hills Bapt. Ch., Kansas City, Mo., 1968-69; intern So. Bapt. Hosp., New Orleans, 1961-63; resident in psychiatry East La. State Hosp., Jackson, 1963-64; instr. pastoral care Immaculate Conception (Mo.) Sem., 1967-72; clin. instr. in pastoral care, then adj. prof. Midwestern Bapt. Theol. Sem., Kansas City, 1968-74, guest prof., 1967, 69; instr. religion and pastoral counseling sch. medicine U. Mo., Kansas City,

1971-74; dir. dept. pastoral care and counseling Bapt. Meml. Hosp., Kansas City, 1965-74; adj. prof. human devel. counseling Sangamon State U., Springfield, Ill., 1979—; dir. clin. edn. in psychosocial care sch. medicine So. Ill. U., Springfield, 1974—, assoc. prof., 1974-82, prof. depts. family practice and med. humanities, 1982—, chief behavioral sci., dept. family practice, 1990—; assoc. dir. Alcohol Edn. Project, Nat. Inst. Alcoholics Anonymous Assn., 1977-79; mem. adv. com. on tenure grievance, 1976; mem. promotion and tenure com. 1977-79, 84—; mem. student progress com., 1979-84; chmn. med. edn. dept. rev. com., 1982; mem. med. student faculty advisory program, 1983—; mem. med. service and research plan, 1984-87; med. staff affiliate and clin. counselor St. John's Hosp., Springfield, 1975—; founder and supr. Interfaith Counseling, Inc., Springfield, 1979—; tchr. Boyce Bible Sch., Springfield, 1980-82. Author: God Cares for You, 1983, The Heart of Pastoral Counseling, 1989; editor: Pastor and Patient, 1982; mem. editorial bd. Jour. Pastoral Care, 1989, Jour. Sex Edn. and Therapy, 1990—; contbr. numerous chpts. to books, articles to profl. jours. Served as asst. scoutmaster, then scoutmaster, Troop 11 Boy Scouts Am., Springfield, 1978-84; also v.p. Abraham Lincoln council, 1985, council chaplain, 1986—. Recipient Cen. Rsch. award So. Ill. U. Sch. Medicine, 1979-81, Rsch. award Joint Council for Rsch. in Pastoral Care and Counseling, 1981, Humanitarian Svc. award Greater Springfield Interfaith Assn., 1985, Comiss Rsch. award, 1991; grantee Midwestern Bapt. Theol. Sem., 1959-61, New Orleans Bapt. Theol. Sem., 1961-62, East La. State Hosp., 1963-64, Eastern Star Lodge, 1961-62, NEH, 1977. Fellow Coll. Chaplains Am. Protestant Hosp. Assn. (chair nat. research com. 1968, nat. editorial com. 1973-74); mem. Am. Assn. Marriage and Family Therapy (supr. 1983—, chair Ill. div. devel. com. 1983-84, 87), Am. Assn. Pastoral Counselors (diplomate 1969—, chair membership com. cen. region 1970-82), Am. Assn. Sex Educators, Counselors and Therapists (cert. sex therapist 1979—), Am. Soc. Clin. Hypnosis, Assn. Clin. Pastoral Edn., Inc. (chaplain supr. 1964—, various coms., 1968—, Researcher of Yr. award 1984), Assn. Bapt. Chaplains (pres. 1970), Assn. Mo. Chaplains (pres. 1967-68), Jackson County Med. Soc. (mem. mediation com. 1974), Kaw Valley Bapt. Assn. (moderator 1960), Ministers in Med. Edn. (newsletter editor 1978-81), Nat. Found. Sudden Infant Death (bd. dirs. Kansas City chpt. 1973-74), Soc. Health and Human Values (publs. com. 1979-80), Soc. Tchrs. Family Medicine (mem. task force on humanities, 1981—), So. Bapt. Conv. Democrat. Lodge: Optimist (program chmn. Kansas City chpt. 1970-73). Home: 56 Maple Grove Springfield IL 62707 Office: So Ill U Sch Medicine Box 3926 Springfield IL 62708

DEAHL, SALLIEJEAN, elementary educator; b. Muncie, Ind., Oct. 27, 1937; d. Oren Albin and Cornelia May (McMaken) Skinner; m. Richard Thomas Deahl, Aug. 25, 1956 (dec.); children: John, Eric, Steven, Joseph. BS in Edn., Bowling Green State U., 1967; MS in Edn., St. Francis Coll., Fort Wayne, Ind., 1971. Cert. elem. tchr., Ind. Dir. Sunday and vacation Bible sch., deaconess Antioch Luth. Ch., Hoagland, Ind.; tchr. Sunday sch., dir. vacation Bible sch., youth dir. St. John Luth. Ch., Monroeville, Ind.; day sch. tchr. St. John Luth. Sch., Monroeville, 1976-84, teaching prin., 1984-87; prin., day sch. tchr. Ascension Luth. Sch., Charlotte, N.C., 1987—, outreach coord., 1990—. Active Fort Wayne Children's Zoo. Mem. Hoagland Area Advancement Assn., Luth. Edn. Assn. Office: Ascension Luth Ch and Sch 1225 E Morehead St Charlotte NC 28204

DEAHL, WILLIAM EVANS, JR., minister; b. Twin Falls, Idaho, Apr. 21, 1945; s. William Evans Deahl Sr. and Cora Elizabeth Hardberger; m. Diane Elizabeth Davis, June 4, 1967. BS, Nebr. Wesleyan U., Lincoln, 1966; MA, No. Ill. U., DeKalb, 1968; MDiv., MST, Iliff Sch. Theology, Denver, 1970, 81; PhD, So. Ill. U., Carbondale, 1974. Ordained to ministry United Meth. Ch., 1969. Tchr. speech and theatre Nebr. Wesleyan U., Lincoln, 1970-71, 82-84; chair speech and theatre Va. Intermont Coll., Bristol, 1972-74; tchr. speech and theatre Eastern Mont. Coll., Billings, 1974-76; chair speech and theatre Midland Luth. Coll., Fremont, Nebr., 1976-82; minister Nebr. Wesleyan U., Lincoln, 1984—; minister United Meth. Ch., Ryegate, Mont., 1975-76, Rising City, Nebr., 1976-82, First United Meth. Ch., Springfield, Nebr., 1982-83, Grace United Meth. Ch., Lincoln, 1983—. Co-author: Speech Liberal Arts Context, 1981; contbr. articles to profl. jours. Recipient Bishop Baker Grad. award United Meth. Ch., 1989. Mem. Am. Acad. Religion, Assn. for Religion and Intelligent Life, Assn. Coll. and Univ. Chaplains, Schuyler Inst. Worship/Arts, Order of St. Luke. Office: Nebr Wesleyan U 5000 St Paul Ave Lincoln NE 68504 *The unceasing quest for excellence and beauty in life, especially in relationship to the divine, community, and friendship, is necessary to escape the constant lure of conformity and mediocrity so rampant in our culture.*

DEAL, MICHAEL LEE, minister; b. Cortland, N.Y., May 6, 1961; s. Thomas Lowel and Anna Belle (Graves) D.; m. Christine Kay Spickler, Aug. 13, 1983; children: Jonathan Michael, Joshua Caleb, Rachel Elizabeth. BS in Sociology, Bridgewater Coll., 1983; MDiv, Gordon-Cornwall Theol., Seminary, South Hamilton, Mass., 1987. Pastor Hughesville (Pa.) Bapt. Ch., 1987—; minister/advisor Muncy Valley Bapt. Men, Hughesville, 1989-90; exec. officer Northumberland Bapt. Assn., Hughesville, 1990—. Mem. East Lycoming Ministorium (pres. 1989—). Home: 128 North Fourth St Hughesville PA 17737 Office: Hughesville Bapt Church 37 North Third St Hughesville PA 17757

DE ALMEIDA, LUCIANO P. MENDES, religious organization administrator. Pres. Bishops' Conf. Roman Cath. Ch., Brasilia, Brazil. Office: SES, Quadra 801, Conj B, CP 13-2067, Brasilia 70.401, Brazil*

DEAN, DAVID ARNOLD, minister, educator; b. Brockton, Mass., June 1, 1929; s. Ellery Cushing and Phoebe Estelle (Chase) D.; m. Dorothy Mae Pierce, June 2, 1951; children: Dwight S., David E., Paul M., Nathan E., Bethany E. BA, Berkshire Christian Coll., 1951; MDiv, Hartford (Conn.) Theol. Sem., 1963; MTh, Westminster Theol. Sem., 1965, ThD, 1976. Ordained to ministry Christian Ch., 1951. Pastor Advent Christian Ch., Danville, Can., 1951-57, Blessed Hope Ch., Springfield, Mass., 1957-64; prof. theology Berkshire Christian Coll., Lenox, Mass., 1959-87, acad. dean, 1969-84; pastor United Ch. of New Marlborough, Southfield, Mass., 1983-91; prof. theology, dir. Ctr. for Advent Christian Studies, Gordon-Conwell Theol. Sem., South Hamilton, Mass., 1991—. Author: Resurrection: His and Ours, 1977, The Gift from Above, 1989; contbr. articles to profl. jours.; editor: Resurrection mag., 1986—. Mem. adv. bd. Salvation Army, New Marlborough, 1985-91; bd. dirs. Right to Life of Berkshire County, Pittsfield, Mass., 1964-84, Am. Cancer Soc. Mass. chpt., Boston, 1981-83, Vernon (Vt.) Retirement Homes, 1958-65. Montgomery fellow Westminster Theol. Sem., 1964, 65. Mem. Evang. Theol. Soc. (chmn. New Eng. chpt. 1968-70), Evang. Philos. Soc., Acad. Advent Mission Soc. (recording sec. Boston chpt. 1959-76), Ea. Assn. Bible Coll. Deans (chmn. 1974-76), West Mass. Advent Christian Conf. (pres. 1980-84). Republican. Home: 140 Essex St Apt 103 South Hamilton MA 01982-2304 Office: Gordon-Conwell Theol Sem 130 Essex St G-C TS Box 209 South Hamilton MA 01982-2304

DEAN, JAMES ROBERT, minister; b. Nashville, Nov. 21, 1961; s. Joe B. and Ruth (James) D. Student, Belmont Coll., Nashville, 1987, So. Bapt. Theol. Sem., Louisville, 1990. Youth intern Park Ave. Bapt. Ch., Nashville, 1981-85, 88, dir. family life ctr., 1982-83, interim minister of youth, 1988-89; minister of youth and edn. First Bapt. Ch., Joelton, Tenn., 1989—. Mem. So. Bapt. Religious Educators Assn. Office: First Bapt Ch of Joelton PO Box 86 7140 White Creek Joelton TN 37080

DEAN, JOHNNY LYDELL, lay minister; b. Cleveland, Miss., Oct. 20, 1946; s. John Robert and Gertrude Louise (Skelton) D.; m. Cheryl Anne Martin, Feb. 14, 1969 (div. 1976); children: Devin Michael, John Martin; m. Joann Elizabeth Daugherty, Jan. 18, 1980; 1 child, Theresa Joann. Student, Syracuse U., 1965, Memphis State U., 1988-89, Memphis Theol. Sem., 1989—. Interim minister St. Luke's Christian Ch., Newbern, Tenn., 1988; interim minister Univ. Christian Ch., Memphis, 1990-91, sr. minister, 1991—; computer ops. specialist Seabrook Wallcoverings, Memphis, 1987—. With USAF, 1964-68. Mem. Memphis Area Disciples Ministers Assn., Disciples Men of Memphis. Home: 1221 Wells Station Rd Memphis TN 38122 Office: Univ Christian Ch 685 S Highland St Memphis TN 38111

DEAN, JOSEPH ANTHONY, minister; b. Jamaica, West Indies, May 29, 1941; came to U.S., 1975; s. Francis and Doris (Ross) D.; m. Lucy Rebecca Dennis, Aug. 10, 1966; children—Mark, Daniel, Paul, Reba, Lydia, Wendy, Tracy. Ordained to ministry United Pentecostal Ch., 1966. Pastor Venetian Acres Apostolic Temple; pres. Native Constrn., Kingston, Jamaica, 1968-75, Allstate Bldg. Contractors, Miami, Fla., 1975-83, Gospelight Evang. Assn., Kingston, 1965-75, Apostolic Temple, Inc., Miami, 1975—, Carpenters of Fla., Inc., 1983—, Dean Investment Inc., Miami; dir., dean Miami Campus of Internat. U. Bible. Studies.

DEAN, RANDOLL ERIC, pastor; b. Breese, Ill., Mar. 25, 1953; s. Earl Hendricks and Helen Mae (Meredith) D.; m. Ginger Ann Warrick, Aug. 9, 1974; children: Elizabeth Rochelle, Jonathan Randall. BS, S.W. Assembly God Coll., 1975. Youth pastor 1st Assembly of God, Athens, Tex., 1973-75; asst. pastor Calvary Temple, Plainview, Tex., 1975-78; pastor Trinity Community Ch., Clyde, Tex., 1978-84, Branch Harvest Ch., Austin, Tex., 1984-88, Living Word Chapel, Emerald, Wis., 1988—. Home and Office: Living Word Chapel 2694 200th Ave Emerald WI 54012

DEAN, RUSSELL SCOTT, minister; b. Greenville, S.C., Apr. 1, 1964; s. Donald Emory and Betty (Mauldin) D.; m. Scottie Lynn McCaffery, May 18, 1984; children: Marsha Lynn, Sarah Janette, Donald Jacob. BS in Religion, Liberty U., Lynchburg, Va., 1986. Asst. pastor Choice Hills Bapt. Ch., Greenville, S.C., 1976-82, Jordan Bapt. Ch., Lynchburg, Va., 1982-84; pastor Calvary Bapt. Ch., Appotomax, Va., 1984-85, Liberty Bapt. Ch., Altavista, Va., 1985-90; founder Gospel Light Bapt. Ch., Altavista, 1990—; founder WSBV Gospel Radio Station, South Boston, Va., 1989. Speaker (Radio Ministry) Gleanings from Calvary, 1980—. Home: 2360 Cobbs St Lynchburg VA 24501 Office: PO Box 625 Altavista VA 24517

DEAN, TREVIE CRILE, minister, educator; b. Albuquerque, Apr. 1, 1947; s. Crile Rupert and Avanelle (Timmons) D.; m. Linda Colleen England, Sept. 30, 1967; children: Glynda Sue, David Trevett. BA, Calif. Bapt. Coll., 1971, BS, 1989; MDiv, Golden Gate Bapt. Sem., 1974, MRE, 1979; EdD, Southwestern Bapt. Theol. Sem., 1985. Minister music and youth Immanuel Bapt. Ch., La Puente, Calif., 1968-71; pastor Montalvin Bapt. Ch., Pinole, Calif., 1971-74, Trinity S. Bapt. Ch., Tracy, Calif., 1978-79; adj. prof. Pacific Christian Coll., Fullerton, 1978-79; pastor Quartz Hill (Calif.) S. Bapt. Ch., 1976-79, 1st So. Bapt. Ch., Roseville, Calif., 1979-83; ch. bus. adminstr. Woods Chapel Bapt. Ch., Arlington, Tex., 1983-85; adj. prof. Southwestern Bapt. Theol. Sem., Ft. Worth, 1985; prof. religious edn. Calif. Bapt. Coll., Riverside, 1985-88; growth cons. So. Bapt. Gen. Conv., Fresno, Calif., 1974-82; pres. Calif. Bapt. Coll. Devel. Found., Riverside, 1988—. Umpire March/Moreno Valley Little League. Named Tchr. Yr. Associated Students Calif. Bapt. Coll., 1987. Fellow Nat. Assn. Ch. Bus. Adminstrs.; mem. Assn. Ministers and Coordinators Discipleship (pres. Garland, Tex. chpt. 1987—). Republican. Avocations: swimming, baseball, water skiing, reading, movies. Home: 10471 Agave St Moreno Valley CA 92387 Office: Calif Bapt Coll Devel Found 8432 Magnolia Ave Riverside CA 92504

DEAN, WILLIAM DENARD, religion educator, author; b. South Bend, Ind., July 12, 1937; s. William Stover and Eleanor (Hatcher) D.; m. Patricia Ann Fletcher; children—Jennifer, Colin. B.A., Carleton Coll., 1959; M.A., U. Chgo., 1964, Ph.D., 1967. Asst. prof. philosophy, religion Northland Coll., Ashland, Wis., 1966-68; asst. prof. religion Gustavus Adolphus Coll., St. Peter, Minn., 1968-73, assoc. prof. religion, 1973-80, prof. religion, 1980—, chmn. dept. religion, 1979-83; rsch. fellow Inst. for Advanced Study of Religion, U. Chgo., Ill., 1984-85; vis. scholar Luth. Sch. Theology, Chgo., 1984-85; vis. rsch. scholar Ctr. on Philanthropy, Ind. U., 1991—. Author: Coming To: A Theology of Beauty, 1972, Love Before the Fall, 1976, American Religious Empiricism, 1986, History Making History, 1988; co-editor: The Size of God, 1987; mem. editorial bd. Am. Jour. Theology and Philosophy, 1983—, Religion and Am. Culture: A Jour. of Interpretation, 1990—; also articles. Del. Wis. Dem. Nat. Conv. committed to McCarthy, Chgo., 1968. Mem. Am. Acad. Religion. Methodist. Home: 2718 Stone Circle Minnetonka MN 55343 Office: Gustavus Adolphus Coll Saint Peter MN 56082 *If, as postmodernists tell us, there are no longer any acceptable universal answers, then our task may be to develop a distinctly American style of religious thought.*

DEANER, JEFFREY LEE, lay worker; b. Big Rapids, Mich., May 4, 1963; s. Gary Lee Deaner and Donna Lee (Gracey) Bryce; m. Wendi Sue Ellerd, July 21, 1989; 1 child, Dane; stepchild, Brittany Brumett. Student in Econs., Mktg., U. Minn., 1986. Mktg. mgr. Edge Tele-Serve Ctr., L.A., 1986-91. Mem. Young Christians for a Better Life, Charhasser, Minn., 1984. Mem. Valencia Young Christians Soc. (founder, dir. 1986-91). Republican. Home: 29682 Alicarte Dr Valencia CA 91355 Office: Edge Tele-Serve Ctr 3057 Roswell St Los Angeles CA 90065

DEANS, WILLIAM ANDERSON, III, minister; b. Lumberton, N.C., Feb. 3, 1941; s. George Thomas Jr. and Emma Marjalene (Tolar) D.; m. Mary Elizabeth Morgan, June 23, 1962; children: Donna Elizabeth, Sarah Louise, Rachel Marie, Michael William. BA in History, Mars Hill Coll., 1965; MRE, So. Bapt. Theol. Sem., Louisville, 1974; MDiv, So. Bapt. Theol. Sem., 1978, MA in Christian Edn., 1974. Ordained to ministry So. Bapt. Conv., 1966, transferred credentials to Am. Bapt. Chs. in U.S.A., 1979. Community min. West Side Bapt. Ch., Louisville, 1974-78; pastor Lake Dreamland Bapt. Ch., Louisville, 1978-79, Meml. Bapt. Ch., Ft. Wayne, Ind., 1979—; asst. dir. ministry studies So. Bapt. Theol. Sem. Louisville, 1977-79; pres. Fedn. Ch. Soc. Agys., Louisville, 1977-78; bd. dirs. Assoc. Chs., Ft. Wayne, 1980-83, Samaritan Pastoral Counseling Ctr., Ft. Wayne, 1980-83, Ind. Office for Campus Ministry, Indpls., 1982—; state rep. Met. Ministry Conf., Phila., 1982; bd. mgrs. ABC-Ind., 1986-89; mem. gen. bd. ABC-U.S.A., 1989—, bd. Internat. Ministries ABC-U.S.A., 1989—; exec. comm. bd. Internat. Ministry, 1991, others commns. in field. Author: An Evaluation and Redesign of the Supervised Ministry Studies Staff Development Program for Campus Ministries at Southern Baptist Theological Seminary, 1979, Psalms of a Reluctant Shepherd, 1990, A Hound, a Bay Horse and a Turtle Dove, 1991. Bd. dirs. Coalition on Housing, Louisville, 1978; panelist, bd. dirs. LaLeche League Internat. Conv., Atlanta, 1979; senator Ministries Coun. Am. Bapt. Chs. in U.S.A., 1983-87; v.p. Brentwood Elem. Sch. PTA, Ft. Wayne, 1983. Mem. Am. Bapt. Peace Fellowship, So. Bapt. Theol. Sem. Alumni Assn. (pres. Ind. chpt. 1982, nat. chpt. 1983-85). Home: 2410 Santa Rosa Dr Fort Wayne IN 46805 Office: Meml Bapt Ch 2900 N Anthony Blvd Fort Wayne IN 46805 *The search for God's shalom takes us into the fray with the assurance that we are sent even as the one whom we follow.*

DE ARAUHO SALES, EUGENIO CARDINAL, archbishop of Rio de Janeiro; b. Acari, Brazil, Nov. 8, 1920. Ordained priest Roman Catholic Ch., 1943. Titular bishop of Tibica and aux. bishop of Natal, 1954; archbishop of Sao Salvador, 1968-71; elevated to sacred Coll. of Cardinals, 1969; archbishop of Rio de Janeiro, 1971—; also ordinary for Eastern Rite Catholics, Brazil.

DEARMIN, DENNIS DALE, minister; b. Stockton, Calif., Oct. 5, 1950; s. Mark Twain and Virginia Rose (Heinrichs) D.; m. Kathleen Joy Severin, Sept. 23, 1972; children—Michelle Renee, Lisa Marie, Melissa Ann. B.A., Calif. State U.-Sacramento, 1975; MA in Ministry, Trinity Theol. Sem., 1986, postgrad., 1986—; cert. FBI Nat. Acad., 1983; ordained to ministry Bapt. Ch., 1987. Cadet, San Joaquin Sheriffs Office, Stockton, Calif., 1970-71, dep. sheriff, 1971-77, sgt., 1977-81, lt., 1981-84, comdr., 1984-87; sr. Pastor Valley Community Bapt. Ch., Tracy Calif., 1987— cons. Modesto and Delta Coll., Stockton and Modesto, Calif., 1978-83; 911 coordinator San Joaquin County, 1978—. Author manuals, articles to profl. jours. Mem. Assn. Pub. Safety Commn. (bd. dirs. 1983—, pres. no. Calif. chpt.), Nat. Acad. Grads., Assn. Police Planners and Researchers. Republican. Home: 25787 S Corral Hollow Rd Tracy CA 95376 Office: 932 B St Tracy CA 95376

DEAS, ALBERTA D., educator, educational administrator; b. Charleston, S.C., Mar. 15, 1934; d. Michael and Carrie Lee (Waring) D.; m. Joe Major Williford, Dec. 19, 1957 (div. Oct. 1964); children—Joel Major, Jon Michael. B.S., S.C. State Coll., 1956; M.Ed., U. Mass., 1975, Ed.D., 1978. Gen. mgr. Sta. WMOZ, Mobile, Ala., 1959-62; chmn. bus. edn. dept. Carver Tech., Mobile, 1962-68; project dir. Westfield State Coll., Mass., 1975-77; asst. prof. S.C. State Coll., Orangeburg, 1977-82; gen. mgr. Sta. WLGI-FM, Hemingway, S.C., 1982-84; sch. adminstr. Louis Gregary Inst., Hemingway, 1980-85; owner, dir. Tiny Tot Presch., Mobile, 1961-65; adminstr. Ind. State U., Terre Haute, 1968-69; owner Garden of Eden, Orangeburg, S.C.; program analyst Office of Econ. Opportunities, Charleston, 1969-71; adminstr. Baha'i Regional Office, Goose Creek, S.C., 1971-74; del UN Internat. Women's Conf., Nairobi, Kenya. Author: (filmstrip) Parenting: Early Childhood, 1980; (manual) Exchange Student/Australia, 1976. Mem. Children Defense Fund, Washington, 1985—. Mem. Nat. Council of Women, Nat. Spiritual Assembly of Baha'is of U.S., Phi Delta Kappa (Coll. Tchr. Yr. 1979). Avocations: health and fitness; dancing; travel; reading. Home: PO Box 2152 Orangeburg SC 29115 Office: Garden of Eden 389 Russell St Orangeburg SC 29115

DEATON, JULIE FRANCES, church lay worker; b. Lexington, Ky., Aug. 31, 1961; d. Larry Alonzo and Sharon Lee (Kizer) Freshwater; m. Donald Alan Deaton, July 11, 1981; children: Laura Ann, Kevin Alan. AAS, Clark State Coll., Springgfield, Ohio, 1981. Youth leader Lena Bapt. Ch., Conover, Ohio, 1981-86, Piqua (Ohio) Bapt. Ch., 1986—; youth advisor Western Assn. Am. Bapt. Chs. Ohio, 1987—; trustee, 1989—. Mem. Am. Soc. Clin. Pathologists (cert. med. lab. technician). Home: 140 W Snodgrass Rd Piqua OH 45356 Office: Piqua Bapt Ch 1402 W High St Piqua OH 45356

DEATON, PAUL REAGAN, navy chaplain; b. Houston, Nov. 18, 1957; s. Frank Norman and Norma Dean (Tautenhahn) D.; m. Cynthia Kay Brewer, Apr. 28, 1979; children: Nathan, Michelle, Eric. BA, E. Tex. Bapt. Coll., Marshall, Tex., 1980; MDiv, New Orleans Bapt. Theol. Sem., 1985. Ordained to ministry, So. Bapt. Conv., 1985. Pastor Oakville (Tex.) Bapt. Ch., 1986-88; chaplain 2nd Marine Div., Camp Lejeune, N.C., 1988-90, Marine Barracks 8th & I, Washington, 1990—. Mem. Realm of the Arctic Cir. Home: 1519E Carswell Cir Washington DC 20336

DEATS, PAUL KINDRED, JR., religion educator emeritus, clergyman; b. Graham, Tex., Oct. 1, 1918; s. Paul Kindred and Agnes (Craig) D.; m. Ruth Miller Zumbrunnen, Sept. 10, 1941; children: Patricia Zee (Mrs. Alain Jehlen), Carolyn Kay, Frances Ann Deats, Randall Kin. AA, Tarleton (Tex.) State Coll., 1937; BA, So. Meth. U., 1939; BD, Union Theol. Sem., N.Y.C., 1943; PhD (Gen. Edn. Bd. Rockefeller fellow, Kent fellow), Boston U., 1954. Ordained to ministry Meth. Ch., 1944. Assoc. minister Highland Park Meth. Ch., Dallas; Met. Duane Meth. Ch., N.Y.C., 1939-41, 41-42; dir. Wesley Found., U. Tex., 1942-51; dir. United Ministry, Boston U., 1953-55, asst. prof. religion in higher edn., 1954-58, assoc. prof. religion in higher edn. and social ethics, 1958-63, prof. social ethics, 1963-86, Walter G. Muelder prof., 1979-86, Walter G. Muelder prof. emeritus, 1986—; chmn. div. theol. and religious studies Boston U. (Grad. Sch.), 1969-81; Mem. Gen. Commn. on Ch.-Govt. Relations, 1965-68. Author: (with others) The Responsible Student, 1957, (with H.E. Stotts) Methodism and Society: Guidelines for Strategy, 1962; editor: Toward a Discipline of Social Ethics, 1972; (with Carol Robb) The Boston Personalist Tradition in Philosophy, Theology and Social Ethics, 1986. Trustee CarEth Found. Am. Assn. Theol. Schs. fellow, 1961-62. Mem. Soc. Christian Ethics, Soc. for Sci. Study Religion, Fellowship of Reconciliation. Democrat. Home: 69 Ruane Rd West Newton MA 02165

DEATS, RICHARD LOUIS, religious agency executive; b. Big Spring, Tex., Feb. 8, 1932; s. Charles Wesley Deats Sr. and Helen Marie (Mueller) Horton; m. Janice Baggett, June 2, 1956; children: Mark, Stephen, Elizabeth, Katherine. BA magna cum laude, McMurry Coll., 1953; BD with honors, So. Meth. U., 1956; PhD, Boston U., 1964. Ordained to ministry United Meth. Ch., 1954. Assoc. pastor 1st Meth. Ch., Big Spring, 1956-57; prof. social ethics Union Theol. Sem., Manila, 1959-72; dir. interfaith activities Fellowship of Reconciliation, Nyack, N.Y., 1972-79, 84—, exec. sec., 1979-84; chmn. bd. dirs. Meth. Social Ctr., Manila, 1969-71; sec., treas. Philippine Theol. Soc., Manila, 1964-66; exec. com. Internat. Fellowship Reconciliation, Alkmaar, Holland, 1976-84. Author: The Story of Methodism in The Philippines, 1964, Nationalism and Christianity in The Philippines, 1967; (with others) Studies in Philippine Church History, 1968, Responsible Parenthood in The Philippines, 1970; editor: Ambassador of Reconciliation, 1991; co-editor: The Filipino in the Seventies, 1973. Trustee Philippine Wesleyan Coll., Cabanatuan, 1964-70; chmn. Fred. Johnson Congl. Campaign, Spring Valley, 1978; mem. steering com. 20th Anniversary King March on Washington, 1983; treas. Nyack Coop. Market, 1982-83; vice-chmn. June 12th Com., N.Y.C., 1982; active in Martin Luther King Singers, Spring Valley, 1982—; commr. King Fed. Holiday Commn., 1990—. Mem. Soc. Christian Ethics. Democrat. Home: 117 N Broadway Nyack NY 10960 Office: Fellowship of Reconciliation Box 271 Nyack NY 10960 *Just as violence expresses the destructive side of human nature, nonviolence expresses humanity's constructive side, our potential for truth, goodness and beauty.*

DE BARY, WILLIAM THEODORE, Asian studies educator; b. N.Y.C., Aug. 9, 1919; s. William Emil and Mildred (Marquette) de B.; m. Fanny Brett, June 16, 1942; children: Mary Brett, Paul Ambrose, Catherine Anne, Mary Beatrice. BA, Columbia U., 1941, MA, 1948, PhD, 1953; DLitt (hon.), St. Lawrence U., 1960; LHD (hon.), Loyola U., Chgo., 1970. Mem. faculty Columbia U., N.Y.C., 1949—, prof. Chinese and Japanese, 1959-66, chmn. dept. East Asian langs. and cultures, 1960-66, chmn. univ. com. Oriental studies, 1953-61, dir. East Asian Lang. and Area Ctr., 1960-72, Horace Carpentier prof. Oriental studies, 1966-78, exec. v.p. for acad. affairs, provost, 1971-78, John Mitchell Mason prof., 1979-89, John Mitchell Mason prof., provost emeritus, 1990—, dir. Heyman Ctr. for Humanities, 1990—; Ch'ien Mu lectr. Chinese U. Hong Kong, 1982; inaugural lectr. Edwin O. Reischauer lectureship in East Asian affairs, Harvard U., 1986; guest lectr. Coll. de France, 1986; Tanner lectr. U. Calif., Berkeley, 1988. Author, co-author: Approaches to the Oriental Classics, 1958, Sources of Japanese Tradition, 1958, Sources of Chinese Tradition, 1960, Sources of Indian Tradition, 1960, rev. edit., 1988, A Guide to Oriental Classics, 1964, Approaches to Asian Civilizations, 1964, The Buddhist Tradition, 1969, Self and Society in Ming Thought, 1970, Letters from War Wasted Asia, 1975, The Unfolding of Neo-Confucianism, 1975, Principle and Practicality: Neo-Confucianism and Practical Learning, 1979, Neo-Confucian Orthodoxy and the Learning of the Mind and Heart, 1981, Yuan Thought: Essays on Chinese Thought and Religion under the Mongols, 1982, The Liberal Tradition in China, 1983, The Rise of Neo-Confucianism in Korea, 1985, East Asian Civilizations: A Dialogue in Five Stages, 1987, The Message of the Mind in Neo-Confucianism, 1988, Neo-Confucian Education, 1989, Approaches to Asian Classics, 1990, Learning for One's Self, 1991, The Trouble with Confucianism, 1991; (transl.) Five Women Who Loved Love (Ihara Saikaku), 1956; mem. editorial bd. The Am. Scholar. Lt. comdr. USNR, 1942-46, PTO. Recipient Watumull prize Am. Hist. Assn., 1958, Fishburn prize Ednl. Press Assn., 1964, award Grad. Faculties Alumni, 1983, Lionel Trilling Book award, 1983, Mark Van Doren Gt. Tchr. award, 1987; Fulbright scholar, 1948-49; Henry Evans traveling fellow, 1941-42, William Bayard Cutting traveling fellow, 1948-49, Guggenheim fellow, 1981-82. Mem. Assn. Asian Studies (bd. dirs. 1961-64, pres. 1969-70), China Soc., Japan soc. N.Y. (bd. dirs. 1964-66), Am. Coun. Learned Socs. (chmn. subcom. Chinese thought, bd. dirs. 1978-86, fellow 1947-48), Am. Acad. Arts and Scis. (coun.), Phi Beta Kappa. Home: 98 Hickory Hill Rd Tappan NY 10983 Office: Columbia U 502 Kent Hall New York NY 10027

DEBERG, BETTY ANN, theology educator; b. Watertown, S.D., Sept. 25, 1953; d. John Richard and Dorothy Carey (Berg) DeB. BA, Concordia Coll., Moorhead, Minn., 1975; MDiv, Vanderbilt U., 1980, MA, 1987, PhD, 1988. Dir. admissions and fin. aid Vanderbilt Divinity Sch., Nashville, 1980-87; asst. prof. theology Valparaiso (Ind.) U., 1988—. Author: Ungodly Women: Gender and the First Wave of American Fundamentalism, 1990. Mem. Am. Acad. Religion, Am. Soc. Church History, Luth. Hist. Soc.

DEBOER, JAMES RONALD, religious organization administrator; b. Oak Park, Ill., Aug. 27, 1956; s. John and Edith Agatha (Boerema) DeB.; m. Nancy R. Bushhouse, July 7, 1978; children: Eric, Maria, Jordan. BA, Calvin Coll., 1978; MA, Western Mich. U., 1982. Cert. tchr., Mich. Ch. adminstr., min. music Providence Christian Reformed Ch., Holland, Mich., 1988—. Mem. Nat. Assn. Ch. Bus. Adminstrs., Christian Ministries Mgmt. Assn. Republican. Home: 157 W 40th St Holland MI 49423 Office: Providence Christian Reformed Ch 821 Ottawa Ave Holland MI 49423

DEBUSMAN, PAUL M(ARSHALL), librarian, minister; b. Wichita, Kans., Dec. 6, 1932; s. Paul Louis and Lillian Gertrude (Larson) D.; m. Amelia Orr, Aug. 29, 1958; children: Melanie Lynn, Amelia Ann. BA, Baylor U., 1954; MDiv, So. Bapt. Theol. Sem., 1957, PhD, 1962; MSLS, Spalding U., 1970.

Ordained to ministry So. Bapt. Conv., 1957. Acquisitions libr. So. Bapt. Theol. Sem., Louisville, 1963-74, reference and serials libr., 1974-84, reference libr., 1984—; chmn. bd. dirs. Paradigms jour., Louisville, 1986—. Mem. Crescent Hill Community Coun., Louisville, 1974—, Nature Conservancy, 1990—. Mem. Am. Theol. Libr. Assn. (chmn. periodical exch. com. 1973-74), Ky. Bapt. Hist. Soc. Home: 2934 Grinstead Dr Louisville KY 40206 Office: So Bapt Sem 2825 Lexington Rd PO Box 80294 Louisville KY 40280

DECAMP, HAROLD LEWIS, evangelist, computer draftsman; b. Corning, N.Y., Nov. 10, 1952; s. Ivan Albert and Beulah Winefred (Davis) DeC.; m. Marie Elaine Whitman, Aug. 16, 1985. Cert., Corning Community Coll., 1978, AAS, 1980; lic., Valley Forge Coll., 1987. Assoc. pastor Williamsport (Pa.) Christian Worship, 1987-89; evangelist FGFCMI, 1989—; CAD operator Anchor/Darling Valve Co., Williamsport, 1988—. Composer Christian songs. With U.S. Army, 1970-73. Democrat. Home: 760 Brandon Ave Williamsport PA 17701

DE CELLES, CHARLES EDOUARD, theologian, educator; b. Holyoke, Mass., May 17, 1942; s. Fernand Pierre and Stella Marie (Shooner) De C.; B.A., U. Windsor (Ont., Can.), 1964; MA in Theology, Marquette U., Milw., 1966; PhD, Fordham U., 1970, MA in Religion, Temple U., Phila., 1979; m. Mildred Manzano Valdez, July 17, 1978; children—Christopher Emanuel, Mark Joshua, Salvador Isaiah. Mem. faculty Marywood Coll., Scranton, Pa., 1970—, prof. religious studies, 1980—; mem. bd. examiners U. Calicut, Kerala, India, 1985-86; moderator Students Organized to Uphold Life, Marywood Coll., 1982—; bd. dirs. Scranton UN Assn., 1974-75, chmn. UN Day, 1974; mem. ProLife Prep. Commn. Scranton Diocesan Synod, 1984-85; bd. dirs. Scranton chpt. Pennsylvanians for Human Life, 1983—; leader Cath. Charismatic Prayer Group, Scranton, 1970-76; mem. com. local pack Cub Scouts, Scranton, 1990—. Recipient cert. of appreciation U.S. Cath. Conf., 1976, Disting. Svc. award UN Assn. U.S., 1974, cert. appreciation Boy Scouts Am., 1991, numerous athletic awards for rd. running, 1987-91, several awards for speed walking, 1990-91; admitted to the Order Cor Mariae, Marywood Coll., 1987-90. Mem. Cath. Acad. Sci. in U.S.A. (pub. com. 1991—), Filipino-Am. Assn. N.E. Pa. (pub. rels. officer 1985-91, award 1990, editor newsletter, 1988-91), Coll. Theology Soc. Am., Theta Alpha Kappa (chpt. moderator). Roman Catholic. Author: Paths of Belief, Vol. 2, 1977, prin. co-author rev. edit., 1987; The Unbound Spirit: God's Universal Sanctifying Work, 1985; also pamphlets, articles, book revs., letters; occasional columnist Nat. Cath. Register, 1983-87; contbr. articles to profl. jours., mags. and newspapers. Home: 923 E Drinker St Dunmore PA 18512 Office: Marywood Coll Dept Religious Studies Scranton PA 18509 *What the world needs is compassion. It needs me to climb out of the confines of my own little ego and embrace humankind: humanity created not in my image but God's—the senile man, the pathetic drunk, the starving Ethiopian, the abused woman, the child in the womb.*

DECHANT, VIRGIL C., fraternal organization administrator; b. Antonino, Kans., Sept. 24, 1930; s. Cornel J. and Ursula (Legleiter) D.; m. Ann Schafer, Aug. 20, 1951; children—Thomas, Daniel, Karen, Robert. Hon. degree, Pontifical Coll. Josephinum, Columbus, Ohio, St. Anselm's Coll., Manchester, N.H., St. Leo's Coll., Fla., Mt. St. Mary's Coll., Emmitsburg, Md., St. John's U., S.I., N.Y., Providence Coll., Sacred Heart U., Bridgeport, Conn., Pontifical U. Santo Tomas, Manila, Assumption Coll., Worcester, Mass., Albertus Magnus Coll., New Haven. With K.C., 1948—, dir., Asst. Supreme Sec., Supreme Master 4th degree, 1963, Supreme Sec., 1967-77; Supreme Knight, chief exec. officer K.C., New Haven, 1977—; mem. Pontifical Coun. for the Family, 1982—; consultor Pontifical Coun. for Social Communications, 1990—; hon. consultor of Vatican City State, 1988. Bd. dirs. Nat. Shrine Immaculate Conception, Washington, Pontifical Coll. Josephinum, Columbus; appointee Pontifical Council for Family, 1982—, commr. Christopher Columbus Quincentenary Commn. for 1992 celebration Christopher Columbus founding of Americas. Decorated Knight St. Gregory the Great promoted to comdr. with Star elevated to Knight Grand Cross, Knight Grand Cross Equestrian Order Holy Sepulchre, Holy Land Pilgrim Shell, Knight Grand Cross Order Pius IX, Knight Sovereign Mil. Order of Malta; named one of Gentleman of His Holiness, Pope John Paul II, 1987; appointed to Extraordinary Synod of Bishops in Vatican, 1985, Synod of Bishops on Laity, 1987; recipient Cross of Merit with Golden Star of Holy Sepulchre of Jerusalem, 1990. Office: KC 1 Columbus Pla New Haven CT 06507

DE CHEVIGNY, ROBERT, bishop. Bishop Roman Cath. Ch., Nouakchott, Mauritania. Office: Eveche, BP 353, Nouakchott Mauritania*

DECKARD, LOREN DEAN, minister; b. Athens, Ill., July 27, 1939; s. John Hobart and Ruth Ellen (Clemens) D.; m. Mary Jane Diveley, June 12, 1960; children: Lori Jo, Karen Beth, Kirby Dwayne, Jill Colleen. BA, Lincoln (Ill.) Christian Coll., 1962; MA, Lincoln Christian Sem., 1967. Ordained to ministry Christian Ch., 1963. Minister Bartonville (Ill.) Christian Ch., 1959-67, Joppatowne (Md.) Christian Ch., 1967—; officer Greater Peoria (Ill.) Evangelizing Assn., 1962-66; pres. Mid-Atlantic Christian Ch. Evang., Balt., 1969-86; vis. lectr. Ea. Christian Coll., Bel Air, Md., 1979-84; coord. Ea. Christian Conv., Joppa, Md., 1984—; vis. lectr. Springdale Coll., Selly Oak Coll., Birmingham, Eng., 1991. Leader Boy Scouts Am., Joppa, 1976-77; com. mem. Com. to Recommend Sch. Bd. Mems. to Gov., Harford County, Md., 1977. Recipient Restoration award, Lincoln Christian Coll., 1990. Office: Joppatowne Christian Ch 725 Trimble Rd Box 216 Joppatowne MD 21085

DECKER, DALLAS BURR, rector; b. Elmira, N.Y., Aug. 10, 1939; s. George Bentley and T. Gertrude (Hager) D.; m. Cynthia Prichard, Aug. 21, 1960; children: Denise, David, Katie, Richard. AAS, SUNY, Albany, 1972, BS in Biology, 1975; MDiv, St. Augustine's Sch., Bradenton, Fla., 1984. Ordained to ministry Episcopal Ch. as deacon, 1976, as priest, 1976. Priest-in-charge various chs., N.Y., 1976-77; vicar Laurel/Hardin/Bridger Mission Field, Laurel, Mont., 1977-82; rector Ch. of the Holy Spirit, Gallup, N.Mex., 1982-87, Zion Episcopal Ch., Douglaston, N.Y., 1987-90; assoc. rector St. Ann's Ch., Sayville, N.Y., 1990—; cytology supr. Enzolabs Inc., Farmingdale, N.Y., 1990-91; cytotechnologist Metpath, Massapequa, N.Y., 1991—; founding dir. Gallup Area Ecumenical Coun., Gallup, 1984-87, Gallup Area Transient Relief Inc., 1984-87; bd. dirs. N.Mex. Conf. Chs., Albuquerque, 1985-87. Mem. Am. Soc. Cytology, Am. Soc. Clin. Pathologists, Order of the Holy Family (clergy oblate), Order of the Ascension (clergy oblate), Order of St. Luke, Kiwanis, Rotary (bd. dirs. 1982-87), Masons. Home: 3 Fernwood Dr Commack NY 11725-4701 Office: St Ann's Episcopal Ch 257 S Main St Sayville NY 11782

DECKER, DAVID LEE, minister; b. Spokane, Wash., Jan. 29, 1946; s. Walter Lee and Mabel Abigail (Turner) D.; m. Barbara Jean Hart, June 17, 1967; children: Christine Renee, Mark Allen. BTh, NW Christian Coll., Spokane, 1968; MDiv, Phillips U., 1971; postgrad., Iliff Sem., Denver, 1979. Ordained to ministry Christian Ch. (Disciples of Christ), 1964. Min. 1st Christian Ch., Humboldt, Nebr., 1971-75, Cen. Christian Ch., Billings, Mont., 1979-82; sr. min. Univ. Christian Ch., Boise, Idaho, 1975-79, 1st Christian Ch., Springfield, Oreg., 1982-86, Country Homes Christian Ch., Spokane, 1986—. Contbr. numerous articles to religious publs. Office: Country Homes Christian Ch N 8415 Wall St Spokane WA 99208

DECKER, GEORGE DAVID, minister; b. Birmingham, Ala., Oct. 14, 1955; s. Hazel Leigh (Trice) Decker; m. Debbie Louise Moultrie, June 1, 1979; children: Sarah Beth, Ashley Marie. BA, Freed-Hardeman Coll., 1981; MA, Harding U., 1983. Program dir. Sta. WFHC, Henderson, Tenn., 1978-81; minister Mt. Zion Ch. of Christ, Hornbeak, Tenn., 1980-83, Fairview Ch. of Christ, Stockbridge, Ga., 1983—; family bible week dir. Fairview Ch. Christ, Stockbridge, Ga., 1985—. Invocation officiant Henry County Bd Commrs., McDonough, Ga., 1983—. Named One of Outstanding Young Men of Am. Jaycees, 1983, 84, 85. Mem. Iota Beta Sigma (past pres.). Republican. Mem. Ch. Christ. Avocations: golf, guitar playing, songwriting, body building. Office: Fairview Ch of Christ 1048 Swan Lake Rd Stockbridge GA 30281

DECOURTRAY, ALBERT CARDINAL, cardinal; b. Wattignies, France, Apr. 9, 1923; s. Paul and Marie Louise (Pouille) D. D in Theology. Ordained priest Roman Cath. Ch. 1947. Consecrated bishop Titular Ch. of Ippona Zárito, 1971; with Titular Ch. of Dijon, 1974; archbishop of Lyons, 1981—, created cardinal, 1985. Chmn. French Episcopal Conf., 1987-90. Office: Archevêché, 1 place de Fourvière, 69321 Lyon Cedex 5, France

DEDMON, GEORGE LEROY, minister; b. Ringgold, Ga., June 27, 1939; s. Grodon Lee and Ruby Viola (Dickson) D.; m. Jane C., Apr. 5, 1959; children: Gary, Gwen. BA, Nat. Christian U., 1971; MA, Ala. Christian Sch. Religion, 1976. Min. Ch. Christ, Gurley, Ala., 1960-64; house parent Childhaven Children's Home, Cullman, Ala., 1964; min. New Union Ch. Christ, Manchester, Tenn., 1964-68, Morrison Ch. Christ, Tenn., 1968-72; house parent Sunny Acres Home for Children, Morrison, Tenn., 1970-72; min. Ch. Christ, Springfield, Tenn., 1972-85, Bremen, Ga., 1985—; bd. dirs. Camp Inagehi, Douglasville, Ga.; chaplian Robinson County Sheriff's Dept., Springfield, 1975-76. Bd. dirs. Home Health Care, Springfield, 1980-85; mem. Job Opportunity Com., Springfield, 1975. Home and Office: 650 Ala Ave Bremen GA 30110-0672

DEEDS, MOSES EARNSHAW, minister; b. Oilton, Okla., Oct. 31, 1932; s. Franklin Pierce and Gracie Fanny (Johnson) D.; m. Willie Jean Barker, June 18,1957; children: Lyndon, LaDonna, Jeffrey, James, Daniel. BA, Free Will Bapt. Bible Coll., 1958. Ordained to ministry Free Will Bapt. Ch., 1958. Pastor 1st Free Will Bapt. Ch., Warren, Ark., 1958-60, Conway, Ark., 1960-62; missionary to Brazil Free Will Bapts., Nashville, 1962—; prof. Free Will Bapt. Bible Inst., Jaboticabal, Sao Paulo, 1968-70; radio broadcaster Free Will Bapt. Mission, Brazil, 1969-72, 74-88, field chmn., 1975-87, sec.-treas., 1989-90. Contbr. articles to profl. jours. With U.S. Army, 1951-54. Office: Free Will Bapt Fgn Missions PO Box 5002 Antioch TN 37011-5002 *To know the Eternal God through faith in Jesus Christ enables one to discover the design and purpose for which He gave life. Success is the result of knowing and fulfilling that purpose or will in life.*

DEEGAN, JOHN EDWARD, college president; b. Newburgh, N.Y., Mar. 31, 1935; s. John Francis and Kathleen Marguerite (McGrath) D. BA, Villanova U., 1957, MA in Modern European History, 1960, MA in Secondard Sch. Adminstrn, 1965; PhD in Student Pers. Adminstrn. in Higher Edn, Am. U., 1971. Joined Order St. Augustine, 1954; ordained priest Roman Cath. Ch., 1961. Dir. studies Msgr. Bonner high Sch., Drexel Hill, Pa., 1961-69; asso. dean student activities Villanova U., 1972-73, asst. prof. edn., 1972-81, chmn. dept. edn., 1975-76, v.p. student life, 1976-81; pres. Merrimack Coll., North Andover, Mass., 1981—. Mem. Order St. Augustine. Mem. Am. Assn. for Higher Edn., Am. Assn. Colls., Assn. Cath. Colls. and Univs., Phi Delta Kappa, Kappa Delta Pi. Roman Catholic. Club: K. of C. Office: Merrimack Coll Office of Pres North Andover MA 01845

DEEKENS, ELIZABETH TUPMAN, lay worker; b. Washington, Aug. 25, 1926; d. William Spencer Tupman and Isabelle McNeil Roberts; m. William Carter Deekens, July 30, 1955 (dec. 1988); children: Arthur Carter, Christine Isabelle, Catherine Deekens Ward. Student, George Washington U., 1945-49. parish sec. All Souls Episcopal Ch., Washington, 1951-52; Washington corres. The Living Ch., Mpls., 1951-52; woman's editor Episcopal Churchnews, Richmond, Va., 1952-57; mem. Episcopal Churchwomen Bd., Diocese of Va., Richmond, 1968; mem. Bishop's Liturgical Commn., Diocese of Va., 1975; newsletter editor Vestry, Ch. of Epiphany, Richmond, 1974-82; editor, layreader St. Martin's Ch., Richmond, 1983—. Contbr. articles to mags. including Seventeen, Good Housekeeping, features to various newspapers. Publicity staff First Mills Godwin Gubernatorial Campaign, 1965. Fellow Am. Soc. Hosp. Mktg. and Pub. Rels.; mem. Va. Soc. Hosp. Mktg. and Pub. Rels. (bd. dirs. 1969-88, treas. 1975-85), Richmond Pub. Rels. Assn. (pres. 1983-84), Va. Press Women, Order of St. Luke (sec.-treas. 1989—). Republican. Home: 9711 Royerton Dr Richmond VA 23228

DEEL, BRUCE LYNN, minister; b. Richlands, Va., Aug. 10, 1960; s. Cecil B. and F. Dawn (Landreth) D.; m. Rhonda Lynn Ramsey, Feb. 14, 1987; 1 child, Kassandra Brooke. BS in Bibl. Edn., Lee Coll., 1990. Ordained to ministry Ch. of God, 1990. Youth min. Riverhills Ch. of God, Tampa, Fla., 1983-85, Snellville (Ga.) Ch. of God, 1985-87, Fleming Ch. of God, Augusta, Ga., 1987-89, Pulaski (Va.) Ch. of God, 1989—. Mem. Nat. Youth Leaders Assn. (del. Cleve., Tenn. 1986—), Va. Lee Alumni Assn. (pres. 1990—), Delta Zeta Tau. Republican. Office: PO Box 2109 Pulaski VA 24301

DEELEY, MARY KATHARINE, religion educator; b. Elmhurst, Ill., Sept. 16, 1951; d. William Francis Deeley and Katharine Isabel (Anderson) Goes; m. Daniel Tuck Wai Lum, May 16, 1981; children: Katharine, Annie. B in Mus. Edn., Rosary Coll., River Forest, Ill., 1974; MDiv, Yale U., 1978; PhD in Bibl. Studies, Northwestern U., Evanston, Ill., 1989. Lectr. Inst. Pastoral Studies Loyola U., Chgo., 1987—. Contbr. articles to religious publs. Mem. Soc. Bibl. Lit., Chgo. Soc. Bibl. Rsch., Cath. Bibl. Soc. Roman Catholic. Home: 913 Cherry Winnetka IL 60093 Office: Loyola U 6363 N Sheridan Chicago IL 60660

DEEM, HARLAN LEE, minister; b. Sasakwa, Okla., June 1, 1930; s. Marvin E. Deem and Jessie (Redick) Griffith; m. Dorothy Mae Andrus, Sept. 4, 1948; children: Linda Kay Deem Goodman, Harlan Ray, Richard Lee, Ronald Dee. Student, Lamar U., 1954-71. Founder, dir. In Jesus Name Ministries, Beaumont, Tex., 1980—; founder, pastor Christ Ctr., Beaumont, 1988—; owner Deem Welding Svc., Beaumont. Precinct chmn. Rep. Party of Tex., Beaumont, 1988—, state conv. del., Houston, 1988, Ft. Worth, 1990. Home: 980 Sunnyside Dr Beaumont TX 77707

DEERING, RONALD FRANKLIN, librarian, minister; b. Paxton, Ill., Oct. 6, 1929; s. Minor Franklin and Grace Gilmour (Perkins) D.; m. Geraldine Gibbons, June 27, 1953 (dec. Jan. 1965); m. Edith Ann Proctor, June 12, 1966; children: Mark David, Daniel Timothy. BA summa cum laude, Georgetown (Ky.) Coll., 1951; MDiv, So. Bapt. Theol. Sem., 1955, PhD, 1962; MLS, Columbia U., 1967. Ordained to ministry So. Bapt. Conv., 1950. Pastor 1st Hilltop Bapt. Ch., North College Hill, Ohio, 1949-50; instr. in Bible Georgeton (Ky.) Coll., 1950-51; pastor Blue River Bapt. Ch., Salem, Ind., 1954-59; instr. Greek, N.T. So. Bapt. Theol. Sem., Louisville, 1958-61, theol. libr., 1962—; chmn. So. Bapt. Hist. Commn., Nashville, 1987-90; interim pastor 31 chs. in Ind., Ky., 1961-90; del. Bapt. World Alliance, Miami, Fla., Toronto, Ont., Can., L.A., 1965, 80, 85. Contbr. articles to profl. jours. Eli Lilly Theol. Librarianship grantee, 1967. Mem. AAUP, ALA, Southeastern Libr. Assn., Am. Theol. Libr. Assn. (nat. pres. 1984-85), Ky. Libr. Assn., Phi Alpha Theta, Beta Phi Mu, Sigma Tau Delta. Democrat. Home: 3111 Dunleith Ct Louisville KY 40241 Office: So Bapt Theol Sem 2825 Lexington Rd Louisville KY 40280

DEES, JAMES PARKER, bishop; b. Greenville, N.C., Dec. 30, 1915; s. James Earl and Margaret Burgwyn (Parker) D.; m. Margaret Lucinda Brown, Aug. 10, 1940; children—Margaret Lucinda Dees Lane, Eugenia Johnston Dees Osteen. B.A., U. N.C., 1938, postgrad., 1938-39; M.Div., Va. Theol. Sem., 1949; D.Div. (hon.) Bob Jones U., 1965. Ordained deacon Episcopal Ch., 1949, priest, 1950, resigned, 1963; ordained bishop Anglican Orthodox Ch., 1964. Shipping clk. Atlantic Coast Line R.R., Greenville, N.C., 1939-42; priest Protestant Episcopal Ch., Aurora and Beaufort, N.C., 1949-55, Episcopal Ch., Statesville, N.C., 1955-63; founder, presiding bishop Anglican Orthodox Ch., Statesville, 1963—; founder Cranmer Sem., Statesville, 1971; mem. Diocesan Exec. Council Episcopal Ch., 1951-60, sec., 1952-54, sec. conv., 1953-54, chmn. dept. youth, 1952-55, mem. dept. Christian edn., 1954-60, mem. dept. camps and confs., 1951-52. Author: Reformation Anglicanism, 1971, Runnymede, 1983. Founder, pres. N.C. Defenders of States' Rights; bd. dirs. Fedn. Constl. Govt., New Orleans, Independence Found., Portland, Ind.; mem. bd. policy Liberty Lobby, Washington; bd. dirs. Nat. Conservative Council, Richmond, Va.; mem. Com. to Restore the Constitution, 1976; pres. PTA, Statesville; baritone soloist N.Y. Opera Co., 1945-46. Served with U.S. Army, 1943-45. Recipient Liberty award Congress of Freedom, 1968-74; Solidarity Freedom award Polish Freedom Fighters, Salem, Mass., 1983. Avocation: Historical reading. Office: Anglican Orthodox Ch PO Box 128 Statesville NC 28677 *Life is the gift of God. It is meant to be sacred, holy. The wages of sin is death, the obliteration of that life. Death is not the end, eternal existence in hell is the end. Life is given to us to live for God and to praise His holy Name.*

DEFELICE, JONATHAN PETER, college president, priest; b. Bristol, R.I., Nov. 7, 1947; s. Ralph Thomas and Eleanor Ida (Balzano) DeF. AB, St. Anselm Coll., 1970; JCL, Pontifical Gregorian U., Rome, 1983. Joined Order of St. Benedict, Roman Cath. Ch., 1968, ordained priest, 1974. Lectr. theology St. Anselm Coll., Manchester, N.H., 1974—, campus min., 1974-75, dean freshmen, 1975-76, dean students, 1976-81; dir. St. Anselm Abbey Sem., Manchester, 1985—; prior, dir. formation St. Anselm Abbey, Manchester, 1986-89, acting pres., 1989-90; pres. St. Anselm Coll., Manchester, 1989—; del. gen. chpt. Am.-Cassinese Congregation, Order of St. Benedict, 1989, 1992. Mem. Postsecondary Edn. Commn., State of N.H., Concord, 1990—; mem. bd. incorporators Fidelity Health Alliance, Manchester, 1990—; bd. dirs. Federated Arts of Manchester, 1991—. Mem. Canon Law Soc. Am., Nat. Assn. Ind. Colls. and Univs., Assn. Cath. Colls. and Univs., Assn. Benedictine Colls. and Univs. (founding). Home: St Anselm Abbey Manchester NH 03102-1310 Office: St Anselm Coll 87 St Anselm Dr Manchester NH 03102-1310

DEFFENBACHER, MARK EDWIN, minister; b. Eugene, Oreg., Sept. 25, 1945; s. Fred and Esther (Stolsig) D.; m. Judith Ann Peelman, Aug. 12, 1967; children: Brent, Kristin. BA, Warner Pacific Coll., 1967; M of Religion, Anderson U., 1969. Ordained to ministry Ch. of God, 1986. Youth min. Park Place Ch., Anderson, Ind., 1967-69; dean Warner Pacific Coll., Portland, Oreg., 1969-81; dir. advancement Warner Pacific Coll., 1981-86; exec. pastor Cen. Community Ch., Wichita, 1986—; exec. dir. 1st Ch. of God Found., Wichita, 1986—; bd. advisors, Warner Pacific Coll., 1986—; trustee, Ch. of God Ch. Svc., Anderson, 1977-78; advisor, Chs. of God in Kans., Topeka, 1989—; rec. sec. Internat. Gen. Assembly of the Ch. of God, 1991—. Annual fund solicitation Chisholm Trail Boy Scouts Am., Wichita, 1987; eme. C. of C., Wichita, 1991. Named Outstanding Educators Am., 1973. Mem. Nat. Fund Raising Execs. Home: 3033 Benjamin Ct Wichita KS 67204 Office: Cen Community Ch 6100 W Maple Wichita KS 67209 *"Where there is no vision, the people perish!" (Proverbs 29:18).*

DEFIORE, LEONARD F., academic administrator. Supt. of schs. Roman Cath. Diocese of Metuchen, N.J. Office: Schs Supt PO Box 191 Metuchen NJ 08840*

DEFOOR, DAVID MARTIN, religion educator; b. Toccoa, Ga., Dec. 11, 1959; s. Maurice Fred Sr. and Sarah Eleanor (Haulbrook) DeF.; m. Cynthia Moorhead, June 19, 1982; 1 child, Walter Martin. BA, Furman U., 1981; MDiv, So. Bapt. Theol. Seminary, 1985. Ordained to ministry So. Bapt. Conv., 1983. Student missionary S.C. Bapt. Conv., Columbia, 1978; minister of music/youth Roper Mountain Bapt. Ch., Greenville, S.C., 1979; pastor Underwood (Ind.) Bapt. Ch., 1983-86, Olive Chapel Bapt. Ch., Apex, N.C., 1986-90; teaching asst. U. N.C., Chapel Hill, 1990—; chair So. Bapt. Women in Ministry N.C., 1989-90; pres. Apex Ministerial Assn., 1988-90. Editor Excursus jour., 1992—. Mem. Am. Soc. Church History, Am. Acad. of Religion, Nat. Assn. Bapt. Profs. of Religion, Raleigh Area Theol. Soc. Home: 109 Perdue St Garner NC 27529

DEFOOR, W. ROBERT, minister; b. Atlanta, Dec. 2, 1941; s. Joseph T. and Mary Louise (Sheriff) DeF.; m. Sandra Bailey, June 22, 1962; children: Jennifer Louise, W. Robert, Stephanie Ruth. BA, Baylor U., 1964; MDiv, So. Bapt. Theol. Sem., Louisville, 1968, D in Ministry, 1975. Ordained to ministry So. Bapt. Conv., 1965. Pastor Mt. Moriah Bapt. Ch, Boston, Ky., 1965-68, Gilead Bapt. Ch., Glendale, Ky., 1969-73; assoc. pastor Druid Hills Bapt. Ch., Atlanta, 1973-75, pastor, 1976-79; pastor Harrodsburg (Ky.) Bapt. Ch., 1979—; evangelist So. Bapt. Home Mission Bd, Atlanta, 1977-83, 85, 88; pres. Ga. Bapt. Pastor's Conf., 1978-79; dir. Western Recorder, Middletown, Ky, 1983—; mem. exec. bd, Ky. Bapt. Conv., 1985-1988; field supr. So. Bapt. Theol. Sem. 1987—. Author: Sunday sch. lessons for religious publs. Coach Harrodsburg Little League, 1980-83; mem. Harrodsburg Bd. Edn., 1982-87; bd. dirs. Harrodsburg YMCA, 1983-86, United Way, 1988. Mem. Mercer Ministerial Assn. (pres. 1981-83), Rotary (bd. dirs. 1984, v.p. 1990, Rotarian of Yr. 1983). Democrat. Home: 815 Southgate Harrodsburg KY 40330 Office: Harrodsburg Bapt Ch Main at Office St Harrodsburg KY 40330

DEGA, SISTER MARY BENEDICTA, religious education administrator; b. Milw., June 8, 1934; d. Frank Arthur and Rose Frances (Piszczek) D. BA in History, Rosary Hill Coll., 1964; MA in History, Marquette U., 1968; MA in Theology, Christ the King Seminary, East Aurora, N.Y., 1975; MA in Franciscan Studies, St. Bonaventure U., 1983. Entered Franciscan Sisters of St. Joseph, 1948, professed final vows 1956; cert. tchr. Mich., N.Y., Wis., Ala.; cert. religious edn. tchr. Archdiocese of Detroit and Lansing, Mich. Various to vocation dir. Franciscan Sisters of St. Joseph, 1988; prin. elem. sch. St. Francis of Assissi, Bessemer, Ala., 1989—; vicar of religious/Diocese of Birmingham, 1990—; pastoral minister of St. Francis of Assisi Parish, 1989—, fin. dir. St. Francis of Assisi Sch., 1989—; others. Named Religious Educator of Yr., St. Joseph Parish, Albion, N.Y., 1977; recipient Nat. Valley Forge Tchrs. medal Freedoms Found. at Valley Forge, 1971. Avocations: travel, handwork, reading, nature walking, working with people. Home and Office: St Francis of Assisi 2410 7 Ave N Bessemer AL 35020-4006

DEGGES, RONALD JOSEPH, minister; b. Washington, Aug. 14, 1954; s. Randall Clark and Kathleen (Krahling) D.; m. Jami Lynn Biles (div. 1984); 1 child, Joshua Martin; m. Deniese Ruth Sullivan, Nov. 22, 1986; children: Randall Clark II, Ronald Joseph Jr., Deniese Hope. BA, Carsen-Newman Coll., 1975; MA in Religion, Yale Div. Sch., 1977. Ordained to ministry So. Bapt. Conv., 1973. Chaplain intern St. Elizabeths Hosp., Washington, 1977; assoc. min. North Chevy Chase (Md.) Christian Ch., 1977-78; min. Mitchellville (Iowa) Christian Ch., 1979-80, 1st Christian Ch., Wilmington, Del., 1980-87; sr. min. 1st Christian Ch., Alexandria, Va., 1987—; del. at large Christian Ch. Capital Area, Chevy Chase, 1984-88. Bd. dirs. Alexandria YMCA, 1987-88, Woodbine Adv. Coun., 1989—; mem. adv. bd. Salvation Army, 1988—; vol. chaplain Alexandria Hosp., 1989—. Democrat. Office: 1st Christian Ch 2723 King St Alexandria VA 22302 *We live each day of our lives under an illusion. The illusion simply stated is that death is the "grim reaper" from which no one can escape. Let not yourselves be deceived, what seems illusory is the truth, and what parades as the truth is the illusion. God has swallowed up death. Christ is risen! Christ is risen indeed!.*

DEGNER, GERHARD WALDEMAR, theology educator; b. Hampton, Nebr., Aug. 9, 1935; s. Hugo William and Louise Clara (Bloomenkamp) D.; m. Anita Duescher; children: Daniel, David, Mary, Evangeline, Joel. BA, Concordia Sem., St. Louis, 1948, MDiv, 1950; MA, Washington U., St. Louis, 1951; PhD, U. Chgo., 1972. Ordained to ministry Luth. Ch., 1950. Pastor St. John's Luth. Ch., Tyndal, S.D., 1951-53, Grace Luth. Ch., Breckenridge, Minn., 1953-57; assoc. prof. theology Concordia Coll., Milw., 1957-67; pastor Trinity Luth. Ch., Ithaca, N.Y., 1967-76; prof. Concordia Theol. Sem., Fort Wayne, Ind., 1976—, chmn. dept. exegetical theology, 1980-87; ednl. cons. Mission Services Staff China Evang. Luth. Ch., Taiwan, Republic of China, 1987-88; mem. St. Louis Commn. on Theology and Ch. Relations, 1986—. Contbr. articles to profl. jours. Bd. dirs. Park Ctr., Fort Wayne, 1986—. Fulbright scholar, 1960. Mem. Soc. Bibl. Lit., Am. Inst. Parliamentarians (bd. dirs.), 356 Registry Club. Home: 7934 Garman Rd Auburn IN 46706 Office: Concordia Theol Sem 6600 N Clinton Fort Wayne IN 46825

DEGRAFFENREIDT, KERMIT J., minister, religious organization official. Sec.-treas. dept. overseas missions A.M.E. Zion Ch., N.Y.C. Office: AME Zion Ch 475 Riverside Dr Ste 1910 New York NY 10115*

DEHEYMAN, WILLIAM MARQUAND, minister; b. Sept. 3, 1933; s. Frank Grover and Luella (Marquand) deH.; m. Martha Ann Diana, June 4, 1960; children: Elizabeth, Deborah. BA, Wagner Coll., 1955; MDiv, Luth. Theol. Sem., 1960. Ordained to ministry Evang. Luth. Ch. in Am., 1960. Pastor, mission developer King of Kings Luth. Ch., New Windsor, N.Y., 1960-63; assoc. pastor St. Paul's Luth. Ch., Allentown, Pa., 1963-69; pastor St. John's Luth. Ch., Phoenixville, Pa., 1969-70, Good Shepherd Luth. Ch., King of Prussia, Pa., 1971-82, Christ's Luth. Ch., Oreland, Pa., 1984-85, Redeemer Luth. Ch., Phila., 1986—; trustee Luth. Home at Germantown, Phila., 1981—; dir. pub. rels. Southeastern Pa. Synod, Evang. Luth. Ch. in Am., 1986—. Recipient Youth award Sta. KYW-TV, 1966. Republican. Home: 3300 W Queen Ln East Falls Philadelphia PA 19129 Office: Redeemer Luth Ch 3462 Midvale Ave East Falls Philadelphia PA 19129

DEIBLER, SAMUEL ELWOOD, JR., religious organization director; b. Pottsville, Pa., Aug. 17, 1945; s. Samuel Elwood and Miriam Elizabeth (Houser) D.; m. Nancy Carroll Wesselman, Sept. 8, 1973; children: Peter Brandt, Jill Kathryn. BA in Psychology, Pa. State U., 1967; BD, Colgate Rochester Div. Sch., 1970. Staff chaplain East Midtown Protestant Chaplaincy, N.Y.C., 1971-75; dir. outreach ministries Assn. Religious Communities, Danbury, Conn., 1975-82, exec. dir., 1982—; mem. Bd. Edn. and Publ., Am. Bapt. Chs. in U.S.A., Valley Forge, Pa., 1967-71, mem. Gen. Bd., 1972. Mem. Danbury Commn. on Equal Rights and Opportunities, 1981-87; bd. dirs. Danbury Hosp. Corp.; chmn. Danbury Housing Authority, Danbury Housing Partnership. Recipient Liberty Bell award Danbury Bar Assn., 1989. Office: Assn Religious Communities 213 Main St Danbury CT 06810

DEIDA, JOSE FERNANDO, lay worker; b. Buffalo, Nov. 6, 1957; s. Fernando and Carmen (Colon) D.; m. Dora Garcia, July 8, 1979; children: Michael, Andrew E. AA, Antillian Coll., Mayaguez, P.R., 1978, Southern Coll., Collegedale, Tenn., 1981. Pres. religion club Seventh-day Adventist Ch., P.R., 1978-87; asst. youth leader Seventh-day Adventist Ch., Miami Springs, Fla., 1988—, tchr. Sabbath sch., 1987-90. Editor Changes mag., 1988; patentee in field. Mem. Unum et Idem, P.R. (pres. 1977). Republican. Home: 381 W 14th St Hialeah FL 33010

DEINHARDT, CAROL LUCY, psychologist, minister; b. Huntington, N.Y., Nov. 8, 1946; d. John and Florence (Hoag) D.; m. Roger Tishleu. Student, Douglass Coll., Rutgers U., 1964-66; BA in Anthropology with honors, Stanford U., 1969; MA, Harvard U., 1973; PhD in Psychology, Calif. Western U., 1982; BTh L.I.F.E. Bible Coll., 1987. Vol. VISTA, 1966; rsch. asst. Johns Hopkins U., Balt., 1967; teaching fellow Harvard U., Cambridge, Mass., 1970-73; psychologist Salem Hosp., Mass., 1972-73; dir., psychologist Child Devel. Ctr., S.E. La. Hosp., Mandeville, 1973-75; asst. prof. City Coll., Loyola U., New Orleans, 1975-80; dir. Women's Ctr. for Greater New Orleans, 1975-80; research assoc., psychology bd. U. Calif., Santa Cruz, 1982-84; counselor Alpha Counseling Ctr., L.A., 1985-89, psychologist, 1989—; minister Grace Chapel, Westlake Village, Calif., 1988—; asst. pastor Thousand Oaks (Calif.) Foursquare Ch., 1987; cons. in field. Author: Personality Assessment and Psychological Interpretation, 1983; contbr. articles to profl. jours. Recipient YWCA Bicentennial Achievement award, 1976; Ford Found. Research grantee, 1968; NSF fellow, 1969-71; NIMH fellow, 1972. Mem. Am. Assn. Counseling and Devel., Am. Psychol. Assn., Am. Mental Health Counselors Assn., Nat. Vocat. Guidance Assn. Club: Harvard (N.Y.C.). Address: 1412 Oldbury Westlake Village CA 91361

DEITZ, JAMES GILBERT, minister; b. Phila., Dec. 10, 1928; s. Purd Eugene and Thisbe Elizabeth (Shultz) D.; m. Elizabeth May Cummings, June 16, 1951; children: Dorothy Jane, Daniel Purd, Charles David, Ruth Ellen Thisbe. AB, Haverford Coll., 1950; BD, Eden Theol. Sem., 1955; STM, Yale U., 1960. Ordained to ministry United Ch. of Christ. Pastor Beaver United Ch. of Christ, Xenia, Ohio, 1955-59, St. John United Ch. of Christ, Strasburg, Ohio, 1960-64; sr. pastor Trinity United Ch. of Christ, Miamisburg, Ohio, 1964-73; pastor North Congl. United Ch. of Christ, Columbus, Ohio, 1973-88, The Congl. United Ch. of Christ, Amherst, Ohio, 1988—; moderator Ohio Conf. United Ch. of Christ, Columbus, 1980-81; del. Gen. Synod United Ch. of Christ, Boston and Grand Rapids, Mich., 1969, 71; bd. dirs. United Ch. Bd. for Homeland Ministries, N.Y.C., 1969-75. Trustee Crossroad, Ft. Wayne, Ind., 1989—, Heidelberg Coll., Tiffin, Ohio, 1976-84. Fellow Acad. Parish Clergy (pres. 1991—); mem. Kiwanis. Democrat. Home: 109 Hickory Hollow Ct Amherst OH 44001 Office: The Congl United Ch Christ 379 S Main St Amherst OH 44001

DE JESUS, BENJAMIN, religious organization administrator. Pres. Alliance World Fedn., Colorado Springs, Colo. Office: Alliance World Fellowship PO Box 35000 Colorado Springs CO 80935*

DE JONG, JAMES A., seminary president, historical theology educator; b. Patterson, N.J., July 10, 1941; s. Peter Ymen and Joanne Henriette (Heyns) De J.; m. Lois Jean De Kock, June 14, 1963; children: Kurtis, Kristin, Kyle. AB, Calvin Coll., 1963; BD, Calvin Sem., 1966; ThD, Free U., Amsterdam, The Netherlands, 1970. Ordained minister Christian Reformed Ch. in N.Am., 1970. Asst. prof. theology Trinity Christian Coll., Palos Heights, Ill., 1970-74; asst. prof. theology Dordt Coll., Sioux Ctr., Iowa, 1974-76, pastoral counselor, 1974-80, assoc. prof., 1976-80, prof., 1980-82; pres. Calvin Theol. Sem., Grand Rapids, Mich., 1983—, prof., 1983—; bd. dirs. Synodical Com. on Race Rels., 1986. Author: As the Waters Cover the Sea, 1970, Into His Presence, 1985; (with others) A Lion Handbook: The History of Christianity, 1977, rev. edit., 1990; contbr. to: The New International Dictionary of the Christian Church, 1974, The World Book Encyclopedia, 1988, The New 20th-Century Encyclopedia of Religious Knowledge, 1991, Encyclopedia of the Reformed Faith, 1991; co-editor: Building the House, 1981; assoc. editor The Banner, 1979-82; editor Renewal jour., 1979-82; founder, editor Calvin Theol. Sem. in Focus quar., 1983—; cons. editor Reformed Worship, 1984—; contbr. articles to religious jours. Vol. chaplain St. Mary's Hosp., Grand Rapids, 1989-91; assoc. pastor Plymouth Heights Christian Reformed Ch., Grand Rapids, 1981, elder, 1991—, various ch. positions, 1973—. Centennial Mission scholar Bd. World Missions Christian Reformed Ch. in N.Am., 1966; ZWO-Govt. of The Netherlands grantee, London, 1968, The Hague, 1970, NEH grantee, Princeton U., 1977; recipient Hometown Hero award Grand Rapids Conv. and Bus. Bur., 1990. Mem. Internat. Congress Calvin Rsch. (exec. com. 1986-90), Assn. Theol. Schs. (exec. com. 1988—), Am. Soc. Ch. History, Am. Soc. Missiology, Calvin Studies Soc., Evang. Theol. Soc., Assn. Advancement Dutch-Am. Studies. Avocations: gardening, travel. Office: Calvin Theol Sem 3233 Burton St SE Grand Rapids MI 49506

DEJONG, LLOYD GERALD, chaplain; b. Orange City, Iowa, Aug. 11, 1917; s. John G. and Hattie (Van Rooyen) DeJ.; m. Bernice E. Hammond, May 1, 1940; children: Joann, Judy, Jane, James, Jerry. BA, Coe Coll., 1939; BD, McCormick Theol. Sem., 1942; DD, Carroll Coll., 1963. Ordained to ministry Presbyterian Ch., 1942. Pastor 1st Presbyn. Ch., Chippewa Falls, Wis., 1942-44, Portage, Wis., 1947-63, Fond du Lac, Wis., 1963-85; chaplain Buena Vista Coll., Storm Lake, Iowa, 1985—; moderator Presbyn. Synod of Wis., 1965. Trustee Carroll Coll., Waukesha, 1962-66, McCormick Theol. Sem., Chgo., 1979-83, Buena Vista Coll., Storm Lake, 1982—; bd. dirs. Town and Gown, Fond du Lac, 1972-84, YMCA, Fond du Lac, 1975-80; apptd. mem. housing com. City of Fond du Lac, 1971-76. Lt. USNR, 1944-46. Mem. Kiwanis (bd. dirs. Fond du Lac chpt. 1976-80, Storm Lake chpt. 1987-90). Republican. Home: 1300 W 6th St Storm Lake IA 50588 Office: Buena Vista Coll Storm Lake IA 50588

DEJONG, PETER, minister; b. Grand Rapids, Mich., July 10, 1915; s. John and Jennie (Elenbaas) DeJ.; m. Thelma Marie Klooster, Oct. 19, 1939; children: Jeanne Louise, Arthur Allen, Douglas Jay, Dennis Ray, David Lee, Daniel Warren, Mark William, Kenneth John. Student, Modesto (Calif.) Jr. Coll., 1932-33; AB, Calvin Coll., Grand Rapids, 1936; ThB, Calvin Theol. Sem., Grand Rapids, 1939; AM, U. Wash., 1963. Ordained to ministry, Christian Reformed Ch. Pastor Christian Reformed Ch., Hamshire, Tex., 1939-42, Oak Harbor, Wash., 1942-44, East Saugatuck, Mich., 1949-52, Seattle, 1952-62, Smithers, B.C., Can., 1962-66; Telkwa, B.C., Can., 1962-64; pastor Christian Reformed Ch., Sarnia, Ont., Can., 1966-70, Dutton, Mich., 1970-80; editor The Outlook, Grand Rapids, 1977-89. Contbr. articles to profl. publs. Lt. (j.g.) USNR, 1944-46. Home: 4985 Sequoia Dr SE Grand Rapids MI 49512

DE JONG, WILBUR LEON, minister; b. Oskaloosa, Iowa, Sept. 21, 1929; s. Martin P. and Marie (Van Wyngarden) De J.; m. Marilyn Joyce Groenendyk, Aug. 6, 1953; children: Judith, Carl, Mary, Cheryl, Karen, Wesley. BA, Calvin Coll., 1954; BD, Calvin Sem., 1957, MDiv, 1975. Pastor Houston (Can.) Christian Reformed Ch., 1957-61, Oak Harbor (Wash.) Christian Reformed Ch., 1962-66, Prairie Lane Christrian Reformed Ch., Omaha, 1966-72, Sherman St. Christian Reformed Ch., Grand Rapids, Mich., 1972-79, Ann Arbor (Mich.) Christian Reformed Ch., 1979—; synodical del. Christian Reformed Ch., Grand Rapids, Mich., 1964, 71, 76, 84, bd. world missions, 1969-72, 89—. Bd. trustees Calvin Coll. and Sem., Grand Rapids, 1972-78. Avocations: fishing, golf, woodworking. Home: 3334 Yellowstone Ann Arbor MI 48105

DE JONGE, MARINUS, religious literature educator; b. Vlissingen, The Netherlands, Dec. 9, 1925; s. Jacobus and P. Dorothea (Kloosterman) de J.; m. Vera Abrahams, Feb. 10, 1951; children: Christiaan, Henriëtte, Anne D. Student, U. Leiden, The Netherlands, 1945-50, U. Manchester, Eng., 1951-52; ThD, U. Leiden, The Netherlands, 1953. Ordained to ministry Netherlands Reformed Ch., 1952. Minister Netherlands Reformed Ch., Wedde, The Netherlands, 1952-56, Blija, The Netherlands, 1956-61, Barchem, The Netherlands, 1961-62; lectr. N.T., faculty theology U. Groningen, The Netherlands, 1962-65, reader early Christian and intertestamentary lit., 1965-66; prof. N.T. and early Christian lit. U. Leiden, 1966-90; Manson Meml. lectr. U. Manchester, 1970, Shaffer lectr. Yale Div. Sch., 1989, Ethel M. Wood lectr. U. London, 1991; vis. prof. N.T., Yale U., New Haven, Conn., 1981; Ida Beam Disting. prof. U. Iowa, 1989. Author: The Testaments of the Twelve Patriarchs: A Study of their Text, Composition and Origin, 1953, The Letters of John, 1968, Jezus: Inspirator en Spelbreker, 1971, Jesus: Inspiring and Disturbing Presence, 1974, Jezus: Stranger from Heaven and Son of God, 1977, Christology in Context: The Earliest Christian Response to Jesus, 1988, Eschatology, Early Christian Christology and the Testaments of the Twelve Patriarchs: Collected Essays, 1991, Jesus: The Servant-Messiah, 1991, Dutch transl., 1990; (with C. Haas and J.L. Swellengrebel) A Translator's Handbook on the Letters of John, 1972, (with H.M.J. van Duyne) Words and Signs: Encounters with Jesus in the Gospel of John, 1978, (with H.W. Hollander, H.J. de Jonge and Th. Korteweg) The Testaments of the Twelve Patriarchs: A Critical Edition of the Greek Text, 1978, (with H.M.J. van Duyne) From Text to Interpretation: Exercises in Listening to the New Testament, 1982, (with H.W. Hollander) The Testaments of the Twelve Patriarchs: A Commentary, 1985; editor, co-author (book) Studies on the Testaments of the Twelve Patriarchs Text and Interpretation, 1975; editor Outside the Old Testament, 1985; contbr. articles to profl. jours. Mem. Soc. Bibl. Lit., Studiorum Novi Testamenti Soc. (pres. 1985-86), Colloquium Biblicum Lovaniense (pres. 1975). Home: Libellenveld 19, 2318 VE Leiden The Netherlands

DEKKER, LOIS ANN, ministry representative; b. Sheboygan, Wis., Apr. 1, 1929; d. Theodore R. Stuedeman and Gladys R. (Eichenberger) Kaufmann; m. Russell E. Rydberg, June 4, 1949 (dec. 1973); children: Marcia A. Rydberg Soerens, Sandra R. Rydberg Miller, Virginia L. Rydberg; m. John Dekker, June 29, 1977; stepchildren: Ruth Even, Gary J., Debra L. Dekker Leftwich. Student, U. Wis., Sheboygan, 1974-75; EdD in Christian Edn. (hon.), Carthage Coll., 1984. Cert. lay profl. leader Luth. Ch. in Am., 1982. Christian edn. coord. First United Luth. Ch., Sheboygan, 1963-83; assoc. dir. dept. leadership support, div. profl. leadership Luth. Ch. in Am., Phila., 1983-88; congl. resource svc. rep. Augsburg Fortress Pubs., Phila., 1988—; synod rep. Wis. Broadcast Ministry, Wis. Coun. Chs., Madison, 1970-74; del. convs. Luth. Ch. in Am., Boston, 1976, Chgo., 1978, mem., v.p. bd. publs., Phila., 1976-83; communicator Luth. Brotherhood, Mpls, 1983. Editor: Life Within newsletter, 1975-76; contbr. articles to publs. Trainer Sheboygan County coun. Girl Scouts U.S.A., 1957-62; trustee Mead Pub. Libr., Sheybogan, 1975-83, Sheybogan County Federated Libr., 1978-83; mem. Women for Greater Phila., 1983-84, budget com. United Way, Sheboygan, 1978-79; dist. chair. Heart Fund, Sheboygan, Community Fund, Sheboygan, Mother's March, Sheboygan. Recipient Citation award Sheboygan Jaycettes, 1963. Office: Augsburg Fortress Publishers 4700 Wissahickon Ave Philadelphia PA 19144

DEKLAVON, ROBERT ALLEN, minister; b. Pitts., Feb. 12, 1954; s. William F. and Rachel (Hunker) DeK.; m. Janice E. Wiebe, Aug. 15, 1981; children: Evangeline, Elizabeth. BA, Miami Christian Coll., 1976; MDiv, Trinity Evang. Div. Sch., Deerfield, Ill., 1983. Ordained to ministry Cavalry Bapt. Ch., 1986; lic. to ministry Evang. Free Ch. Am., 1989, ordained, 1991. Youth worker Maranatha Community Ch., Miami, Fla., 1972-75; dir. Youth for Christ, Miami, 1976-78; Christian edn. intern Calvary Bapt. Ch., Mundelein, Ill., 1980-82; min. youth and Christian edn. Calvary Bapt. Ch., Bradenton, Fla., 1982-86; min. Ft. Myers (Fla.) Evang. Free Ch., 1986—; advisor ch. planting Miami Team, Evang. Free Ch. Am., 1990—, bd. dirs. SE dist., Orlando. Office: Ft Myers Evang Free Ch 1198 Hemingway Dr Fort Myers FL 33912

DE KLERK, ABEL JACOBUS, minister; b. Kakamas, Cape Province, Republic of South Africa, Nov. 12, 1935; arrived in Namibia, 1967; s. Christiaan Jacobus and Margaretha (Burger) de K.; m. Wilhelmina Alida du Toit, Aug. 9, 1956; children: Riaan, Dawie, Jacques. BA, U. Stellenbosch, Republic of South Africa, 1962, BTh, 1965, Licentiate in Theology, 1966. Ordained to ministry Dutch Reformed Ch. Min. Dutch Reformed Ch., Jobabis-Suid, Namibia, 1967-76, scribe of synod, 1975-76; min. Dutch Reformed Ch., Villiersdorp, Republic of South Africa, 1976-82; min. Dutch Reformed Ch., Pionierspark, Namibia, 1982—, moderator of synod, 1987—. Trustee Windhoek Theol. Sem., Namibia, 1986-91; bd. dirs. Namibia Evang. Theol. Sem., 1991—. Home and Office: 32 Albert St, PO Box 30068, Windhoek 9000, Namibia

DE LA CHAPELLE, FRANCES PASSERAT, religion educator; b. Englewood, N.J., Feb. 3, 1940; d. Richard and Frances (Barr Malone) de la C. BA, Maryville Coll., 1961; MA, Cath. U. Am., 1969; MSA, U. Notre Dame, 1977; CE, Jesuit Sch. Theology, 1981. Joined Soc. of Sacred Heart, Roman Cath. Ch. Tchr. Kenwood High Sch., 1964; tchr., adminstr. Stone Ridge Country Day Sch., Bethesda, Md., 1965-67, Stuart Country Day Sch., Princeton, N.J., 1967-69; dean students Newton (Mass.) Coll., 1969-75; head high sch. Stuart Country Day Sch., Princeton, N.J., 1975-80; tchr., dir. admissions and coll. guidance Newton Country Day Sch., 1981-83; headmistress, prin. Woodlands Acad. Sacred Heart, Lake Forest, Ill., 1983-91; dir. ongoing formation for ministry Soc. of Sacred Heart, U.S. Province, St. Louis, 1991—; trustee Carollton, Miami, Fla., 1971-78, Newton Acad., Stone Ridge Country Day, Stuart Country Day, 91st St., N.Y., 1976-77, Woodlands Acad., 1980-83, Sacred Heart Schs., Chgo., 1983-89, Duchesne Acad., Omaha, 1989—; speaker in field. Mem. planning commn. Washington Province, 1968-69. Mem. Religious of Sacred Heart, Nat. Assn. Women Deans, Nat. Assn. Ind. Schs., Ind. High Sch. Assn. Greater Chgo. Home and Office: Soc of the Sacred Heart 4389 W Pine Blvd Saint Louis MO 63108

DELAMARIAN, MICHAEL, III, minister; b. Oak Park, Ill., Nov. 22, 1953; s. Michael and Eleanor (Milan) D.; m. Joan Ellen Snead, Aug. 4, 1979; children: Adrienne, Amber, Michael IV. AA, Palomar Coll., San Marcos, Calif., 1973; BA, U.S. Internat. U., San Diego, 1975; MDiv, Talbot Theol. Sem., La Mirada, Calif., 1980. Ordained to ministry, Evang. Free Ch. Am. Assoc. pastor Evang. Free Ch. of Laguna Hills (Calif.), 1980-83; sr. pastor Hydesville (Calif.) Community Ch., 1983—. Home: 3053 Johnson Rd Hydesville CA 95547 Office: Hydesville Community Ch 3296 Hwy 36 Hydesville CA 95547

DELANCEY, ROBERT HOUSTON, JR., minister; b. Union City, Tenn., Aug. 24, 1936; s. Robert Houston and Mary J. (Burlison) DeL.; m. Donna Jean Goble, Dec. 18, 1953; children: Robert Houston III, Diana K., Sherri L. BA, Oklahoma City U., 1958. Ordained to ministry Assembly of God Ch., 1967. Acct. Kerr-McGee Oil Co., Oklahoma City, 1957-63; sr. pastor University Assembly of God Ch., Denton, Tex., 1963-67; sr. pastor 1st Assembly of God Ch., Seagraves, Tex., 1967-70, Pauls Valley, Okla., 1970-75; sr. pastor Bethel Assembly of God, Hobbs, N.Mex., 1975-81, The Rock Inc., Oklahoma City, 1981—. Republican. Home: 7308 S Western Oklahoma City OK 73139 Office: The Rock Inc 7308 S Western Oklahoma City OK 73139

DELANCY, MICHAEL ROBINSON, minister; b. Abilene, Tex., Nov. 1, 1948; s. Leslie Jack Delancy and Gloria Eileen (Baker) Barnes; m. Fairy Marguerite Johnston, Nov. 23, 1966 (div. Aug. 1974); children: Lisa Marie, Michael Gary, Joseph Lamont; m. Patricia Robinson, Dec. 17, 1976; children: Patrick Sean, Mary Elizabeth. AA, St. John's Jr. Coll., 1975; BA, Concordia Sr. Coll., Ft. Wayne, Ind., 1977; MDiv, Concordia Theol. Sem., Ft. Wayne, Ind., 1981. Ordained to ministry Luth. Ch., 1981. Vicar Mt. Olive Luth. Ch., Billings, Mont., 1979-80; head min. Zion Evangelical Luth. Ch., Vassar, Kans., 1981-90; min. Outreach Calvary Luth. Ch., Topeka, 1990—; workshop leader Dist. Evangelism, Wichita, Kans., 1981, Dist. Singles, Wichita, 1983, Luth. Women's Missionary League Wksp., Vassar, 1983, Cir. 14 Sunday Sch., Salina, Kans., 1984; constitution ad hoc Kans. dist. Luth. Ch., Topeka, 1982-83, mgr. dist. conv., 1991, mgr. continuing edn. seminar, 1991; cir. youth rep. Cir. 4, Vassar, 1983—, youth pastoral advisor, 1983—, singles pastoral advisor, 1991—. Scoutmaster Boy Scouts Am., Oklahoma City, 1970-73, chaplain local troop, 1991—; organizer, chmn. Cub Pack, Ft. Wayne, 1977-79, treas., 1991—; organizer Young Reps. Fundraiser, Ft. Wayne, 1978; mem. Vet. Counseling Ctr., Ft. Wayne, 1979; bereavement coord. Osage County Hospice, 1987-88. Named Vol. of Yr., Boy Scouts Am., Ft. Wayne, 1979, Best New Poet, Am. Poetry Soc., 1988. Avocations: poetry, mechanics, woodworking, water skiing, nature. Home: 4106 SW West Dr Topeka KS 66606 Office: Calvary Luth Ch 4211 NW Topeka Ave Topeka KS 66617

DELANEY, JOSEPH P., bishop; b. Fall River, Mass., Aug. 29, 1934. Student, Cardinal O'Connell Sem., Mass., Theol. Coll., Washington, N.Am. Coll., Rome, R.I. Coll. Ordained priest Roman Catholic Ch., 1960; ordained bishop of Fort Worth, 1981—. Office: 800 W Loop 820 S Fort Worth TX 76108

DE LANGE, NICHOLAS ROBERT MICHAEL, rabbinical scholar; b. Nottingham, Eng., Aug. 7, 1944; s. George David and Elaine (Jacobus) de L. M.A., Oxford U., Eng., 1969, D.Phil., 1970. Ordained rabbi, 1973. Lectr. in rabbinics U. Cambridge, Eng., 1971—, fellow Wolfson Coll., 1984—. Author: Origen and the Jews, 1976; Apocrypha, 1978; Atlas of the Jewish World, 1984; Judaism, 1986; also various translations, articles. Mem. Jewish Hist. Soc. Eng. (mem. council). Home: 18 Bateman St, Cambridge CB2 1NB, England Office: The Divinity Sch, Saint John's St, Cambridge CB2 1TW, England

DELAQUIS, NOEL, bishop; b. Notre-Dame de Lourdes, Man., Can., Dec. 25, 1934; s. Louis and Therese (Hebert) D. B.A., U. Man., 1954; B.Th., U. Laval, 1958; J.C.L., Latran, Rome, 1962. Ordained priest Roman Catholic Ch., 1958; asst. priest Christ the King Parish, St. Vital, Man., 1958-60; prof. canon law St. Boniface Sem., Man., 1962-68; chancellor Archdiocese of St. Boniface, Man., 1965-73; bishop of Gravelbourg, Sask., Can., 1974—. Address: CP 690, Gravelbourg, SK Canada S0H 1X0

DELARUE, LOUIS C(HARLES), priest; b. Orange, Tex., Mar. 24, 1939; s. Garrett Louis and Ethel Marie (Walker) D. Student, St. Joseph Sem., Washington; BS in Secondary Edn., Lamar U.; postgrad., U. St. Thomas; MDiv, St. Mary's Sem., 1978. Ordained priest Roman Cath. Ch., 1976. Assoc. pastor St. Mary's Ch., Port Arthur, Tex., 1976-77, pastor, 1978-83; pastor Our Lady of Lourdes, Chireno, 1983-85; assoc. pastor St. Anne's Ch., Beaumont, Tex., 1985-86; deacon Diocese of Beaumont, Port Arthur, 1978-79; assoc. pastor St. Mary's Cath. Ch., Port Arthur, 1979-80; pastoral adminstr. St. Mary Ch., Port Arthur, 1980-81; campus minister Stephen F. Austin U., Nacogdoches, Tex., 1983-86; pastor St. Therese, Orange and St. Maurice Mission, Mauriceville, Tex., 1986—; del. Nat. Fedn. Presbyn. Couns., Hosp. Ministry; spiritual asst. Secular Franciscan and other assns.; chaplain Cath. Student Ctr., Stephen F. Austin U., Nacogdoches, Lamar U., Beaumont, 1985; ecumenical dir. Diocese Beaumont, Tex. Cath. Conf.; spiritual dir. Parish Afro-Am. Ecumenical Dance Group Henderson Sch. Dance; cons. Afro-Am. Diocesan Cath. Commn., Diocese Beaumont, 1987-91; pres. Diocesan Presbyteral Coun., Diocese of Beaumont, 1991-92; adminstr. St. Maurice Cath. Ch. Mission, Mauriceville. Recipient Outstanding Preacher award Black Preachers Assn., 1980. Mem. NAACP, Canon Law Soc., Nat. Black Seminarian Assn., Nat. Black Clergy Caucus, Assn. Pastoral Counseling, Interfaith Groups, Nat. Assn. Cath. Ecumenical Dirs., Nat. Black Cath. Clergy Caucus, Tex. Cath. Campus Ministry Assn., Nat. Cath. Campus Ministry Assn., Assn. Spiritual Dirs., Toastmasters, Kiwanis, KC. Home and Office: St Therese Ch 1409 N 6th St Orange TX 77630-3927

DELAY, LARRY G., minister; b. McAlester, Okla., July 13, 1955; s. Truman Eugene and Mae Foy (Smith) D.; m. Cynthia Diane Woodard, Jan. 7, 1978; children: Justin Ryan, Jeremy Ross. BA, Okla. Bapt. U., 1978, Northeastern State U., 1985; MDiv, Trinity Theol. Sem., 1990, DMin, 1991. Ordained to ministry So. Bapt. Conv., 1976. Author: How to Move Your Church Off Dean Center, 1991; composer In His Name, 1988, In Harmony, 1989-90, I Can, 1991. Mem. com. Nowata (Okla.) Cablecom, 1989—; bd. dirs. Birthright Crisis Pregnancy Ctr., Nowata, 1991; trustee Bapt. Retirement Ctr., Owasso, Okla., 1990-91. Named Outstanding Young Man in Am. Jaycees, 1983. Republican. Office: First Bapt Ch 433 N Mississippi Nowata OK 74048

DE LEON, DANIEL BENITZ, minister; b. Uvalde, Tex., Mar. 15, 1941; s. Gilbert de Leon and Rosa Benitez; m. Ruth Ibarra, Aug. 6, 1966; children: Daniel B. Jr., Joseph Lee, Stephen Peter. BA, So. Calif. Coll., Costa Mesa, 1967; MA, Chapman Coll., Orange, Calif., 1969; MDiv, Melodyland Sch. Theology, Anaheim, Calif., 1977; DD (hon.), Gran Convencion, L.A., 1984. Ordained to ministry Assembly of God Ch., 1969. Youth coord. Western region Pacific Dist. Assembly of God, various locations, 1967-73; nat. youth coord. Latin Am. Assembly of God, 1969-71; chaplain Race Track Chaplain of Am., So. Calif., 1973-76; sr. pastor Templo Calvario, Santa Ana, Calif., 1976—; gen. presbyter Assembly of God, Springfield, Mo., 1982—, nat. coord. lang. groups, 1989—; v.p. L.A. '88, Santa Ana, Calif., 1985—; bd. dirs. Open Doors Internat., Santa Ana, 1989—. Mem. bd. Mayor's Prayer Breakfast, Santa Ana, 1983-87, Mayor's Study Com., Santa Ana, 1987-88, Orange County coun. Boy Scouts Am., 1989—. Named Fastest Growing Ch. in Calif., Nat. Assn. Sunday Schs., 1983, Largest Hispanic Ch. Am., 500 Largest Chs. in Am., 1983—. Mem. Nat. Assn. Evangelicals, Nat. Religious Broadcasters, Pacific Latin Am. Dist. (exec. presbyter 1980—), Hispanic Assn. for Bilingual Bicultural Ministries (founder, pres. 1985—). Republican. Office: Templo Calvario 2617 W Fifth St Santa Ana CA 92703

DELL, J. HOWARD, bishop. Bishop, Ch. of God in Christ, No. Ga., Atlanta. Address: Ch of God in Christ PO Box 6118 Knoxville TN 37914

DELLINGER, CHARLES WADE, minister; b. Lincolnton, N.C., Feb. 25, 1949; s. Coy Hillard Dellinger and Lorene (Russ) Harbinson; m. Sarah Lynn Baxter, July 20, 1969; children: Sarah Beth, Charles Matthew. AA, Gardner-Webb Coll., 1969, BA cum laude, 1971; MDiv, S.E. Bapt. Sem., 1975, D of Ministry, 1983. Ordained to ministry Bapt. Ch., 1969. Pastor Roseland Bapt. Ch., Lincolnton, N.C., 1969-71; assoc. pastor, pastor Temple Bapt. Ch., Gastoma, N.C., 1971-74; pastor Mulls Meml. Bapt. Ch., Shelby, N.C., 1975-87; sr. pastor Old Town Bapt. Ch., Winston-Salem, N.C., 1987—; bd. dirs. Gardner-Webb Coll., Bolling Springs, N.C., 1980-84, 86-90; assoc. chaplain Cleveland Meml. Hosp., Shelby, 1985-87. Author: Personal Moments, 1990. Bd. dirs. Boy Scouts Am., Winston-Salem, 1989—, dist. advancement chmn., 1990—; moderator Kings Mountain Bapt. Assn., Shelby, 1985-87; chmn. ministry coun., Bapt. State Conv., Raleigh, 1987-88. Recipient Disting. Citizen award State of N.C., 1973. Mem. Am. Family Counselors. Democrat. Baptist. Avocations: golf, fishing, hunting, reading. Home: 1625 Turfwood Dr Pfafftown NC 27040 *A precious gift called "life" has been given to us. How we use that gift will bring blessing or curse. The length of life matters little. The honor to the giver comes if the gift is used for blessing.*

DEL MESTRI, GUIDO CARDINAL, cardinal; b. Banja Luka, Yugoslavia, Jan. 13, 1911. Cardinal titular ch. St. Eustachio; elevated to the Sacred Coll. Cardinals, 1991. Office: Mommenstrasse 24, Nurnberg 20, Federal Republic of Germany*

DEL MONTE, CARLOS, minister. Pastor Waldensian Evang. Ch., Montevideo, Uruguay. Office: Waldensian Evang Ch, Avda 8 de Octobre 3037, 11600 Montevideo Uruguay*

DELOACH, MICHAEL ALLEN, minister; b. Wilmington, Del., May 21, 1962; s. William Edward and Ann Murl (Hall) D.; m. Jamie Moree Patterson, June 6, 1986; 1 child, Micahia Moree. BRE, Fla. Bapt. Coll., 1987, MRE, 1989. Ordained to ministry Am. Bapt. Assn., 1990. Youth dir. 1st Missionary Bapt. Ch., Pace, Fla., 1981-85; ch. planter 1st Thonotosassa (Fla.) Missionary Bapt., 1989—; pastor, ch. planter 1st Missionary Bapt. Mission, Odessa, Del., 1990—. Mem. Nat. Christian Counselor Assn. (lic., cert. Christian counselor, area rep. 1990—). Office: 1st Missionary Bapt Mission 506 High St PO Box 65 Odessa DE 19730

DELONG, ANDREW, minister; b. Fed. Republic Germany, Aug. 8, 1961; s. Lambert Vincent and Mary Kathryn (L'auster) DeL.; m. Reneé Adele Wendel, Aug. 27, 1982; children: Jillian Reneé, Justin Andrew, Ashley Marie, Andrew Phillip. Ministerial internship program, minor in Bible, Lee Coll., 1980-82. Lic. to ministry Ch. of God, 1989. Assoc. pastor of youth and evangelism Pompano Beach (Fla.) Ch. of God, 1986-88; asst. pastor of youth and ch. edn. Naples (Fla.) Ch. of God, 1988—; Pres. Fla. Youth Leader Assn., Ch. of God, 1987-89, bd. dirs., 1989—; bd. dirs. Morality Media, Naples, 1988-90, pres., 1990-91; travel with Evang. Outreach Program to Yugoslavia, Romania, Bulgaria, 1989, 91. Contbr. articles to religious publs. Home: 1086 11th St N Naples FL 33940 Office: Naples Ch of God 1086 11th St N Naples FL 33940

DELONG, MICHAEL BEN, clergyman, college president; b. Bellefonte, Pa., Sept. 24, 1956; s. Bernard Lincoln and Priscilla (Hobson) DeL.; m. Terry Arlene Stone, Dec. 3, 1978; children—Benjamin, Jonathan, Matthew, Samuel. Student Centerville Bible Coll., 1975-78; B.A., Temple Baptist Coll., 1981, M.A., 1985. Ordained to ministry Baptist Ch. 1979. Minister of music First Bapt. Ch. Centerville, 1978—; instr., registrar Centerville Bible Coll., 1978—, pres., 1985—; asst. pastor First Bapt. Ch. Centerville, 1983—. Editor The Light, 1981-83. Republican. Avocations: tennis, flying, racquetball. Home: 2886 Washington Mill Rd Bellbrook OH 45305 Office: First Baptist Ch Centerville 38 N Main St Centerville OH 45459 *Each day I try to learn more about God, creation, myself and others.*

DELONG, TERRY LEE, clergyman; b. Chgo., Mar. 2, 1950; s. Bernnard Authur and Jacqueline (Fish) DeL.; m. Michelle Suzanne, Travis Lee. AA in Practical Ministries, Olivet Nazarene U., 1985. Ordained to ministry The Salvation Army, 1985. Corps asst. The Salvation Army, Anderson, Ind., 1981, Lafayette, Ind., 1981-82, Evanston, Ill., 1982; corps officer The Salvation Army, Madison, Ind., 1985-88, Marion, Ind., 1988—; mem. Mayor's Prayer Breakfast Com., Marion, 1990—; mem. divisional men's fellowship com. The Salvation Army, Indpls., 1987-89, mem. divisional music com., Indpls., 1988—. Pres. Grant County Ministerial Assn., Marion, 1990, Grant County Farmworkers Task Force, 1991—; mem. Prins. Citizens Com., Marion, 1990; bd. dirs. Meals on Wheels, Marion, 1991. Sgt. U.S. Army, 1968-77. Decorated Army Commendation medal. Mem. Rotary. Office: The Salvation Army 2001 S Gallatin St Marion IN 46953

DELP, DOUGLAS A., minister; b. Lincoln, Nebr., Apr. 21, 1955; s. Jimmie LeRoy and Marjory (Stover) D.; m. Cindy Sue Bates, Nov. 12, 1983. BS, U. Nebr., 1976; ThM, Perkins Sch. Theology, Dallas, 1980; D Ministry, United Theol. Sem., 1989. Ordained to ministry United Meth. Ch., 1983. Pastor Hemingford (Nebr.) United Meth. Ch., 1981-85; sr. pastor Tecumseh and Sterling (Nebr.) United Meth. Chs., 1985-91, Meml. United Meth. Ch., McCook, Nebr., 1991—; coord. sem. scholarships Bd. Ordained Ministry, Nebr. Conf., 1986-91; chairperson S.E. Dist. Com. on Ministry, Beatrice, Nebr., 1989-91. Coord. Adult Basic Edn., Tecumseh, 1989-91; group leader START (Econ. and Strategic Planning), Johnson County, Nebr., 1990. Recipient Denman Evangelism award Found. for Evangelism, Lake Junaluska, N.C.,1991. Office: Meml United Meth Ch 105 East E St McCook NE 69001 *We live in a world in which people, who have little or no awareness of the cost to self or others, are both starving and striving for power, but who have yet to discover that the joy of true power comes through the Spirit of Christ rather than a pursuit of self.*

DELP, RANDY LEE, religion educator; b. Josephine, W.Va., Jan. 11, 1950; s. Raymond Cromwell and Chloe Roverta (Hornsby) D.; m. Terry Renee Workman, July 11, 1969; 1 child, Kevin. BS in Bibl. History, Lee Coll., 1985; postgrad., Southern Meth. U., 1986—, Liberty U., 1989—. Ordained to ministry Ch. of God, 1971. Pastor Ch. of God, Weirton, W.Va., 1976-80, Solid Rock/Vineyard Ch., Weirton, 1981-82; instr. Christ for the Nations, Dallas, 1983—, adminstr., 1988—; v.p., founding dir. Caribbean Christ for the Nations, Montego Bay, Jamaica, 1988—; bd. dirs. Christ for Asia, Soporro, Japan, 1987. State del. Rep. Party, Houston, 1988, Ft. Worth, 1990. Named Most Outstanding Religious Leader, Ohio River Valley Jaycees, 1979. Mem. Soc. for Pentecostal Studies (on site coord. annual meeting 1990), Upsilon Xi (chaplain 1971). Home: 545 Fawn Ridge Dr # 121 Dallas TX 75224

DEL RICCI, JOHN ANTHONY, clergyman; b. Providence, May 2, 1951; s. John and Mary (Matano) Del R.; m. Janis Phyllis D'orazio, June 17, 1972. Assoc., R.I. Jr. Coll., 1971; BA, Roger Williams Coll., 1973. Ordained to ministry Bapt. Ch. Minister music Ocean State Bapt. Ch., Smithfield, R.I., 1975—. Republican. Office: Ocean State Bapt Ch Douglas Pike Smithfield RI 02917

DEL TURCO, JOHN, minister, religious organization administrator. Dir. dept. fgn. and home missions Christian Ch. N.Am. Gen. Coun., Transfer, Pa. Office: Christian Ch NAm Gen Coun RD 1 Box 141-A Transfer PA 16154*

DE LUKIE, DONALD ADRIAN, religion educator; b. Minden, La., June 25, 1944; s. A.F. and Edith Sue (Thompson) De L.; m. Jean Davidson, July 30, 1965; children: Donna, Marla, Tina, Don Jr. AA, White Ferry Rd Sch., 1972; BA, Ala. Christian Sch. Religion, 1974, MA, 1975; postgrad., Troy State U., 1978. Ordained to ministry Ch. of Christ, 1972. Min. Palo Alto Ch. of Christ, Panama City, Fla., 1972-78; instr. Sch. Bibl. Studies White's Ferry Rd. Ch. of Christ, West Monroe, La., 1978-90; minister Jackson St. Ch. of Christ, Monroe, La., 1989-90; pres. Am. Christian Sch. of Religion, West Monroe, La., 1980—; com. mem. African Evangelism Com., West Monroe, 1988—; dir. African Leadership Seminars, West Monroe, 1984—. Author syllabuses; editor Far & Near Sch. Paper, 1983-85. Pres. Mental Health Assn., Bay County, Fla., 1976, 77, Toastmasters, Bay County, 1978, Positive Attitude Yields Success, Monroe, La., 1982. Recipient medal Fla. Future Scientists, 1976; named Outstanding Young Man of Am. Jaycees, 1980. Avocations: rock collecting, hunting, canoe. Home: 1120 Flanagan Rd West Monroe LA 71291 Office: Church of Christ 3201 N 7th St West Monroe LA 71291

DELUMEAU, JEAN, religion educator; b. Nantes, France, June 18, 1923; s. Leon and Claire (Seguinaud) D.; m. Jeanny Le Goff, Sept. 2, 1947; children: Jean-Pierre, Marie-Christine, Jean-Christophe. Student, Agrege d'Histoire, 1947, Ecole Francaise, Rome, 1948-50; DLitt, U. Paris, 1955. Prof. faculty of letters U. Rennes, France, 1955-70; prof. U. Pantheon-Sorbonne, Paris, 1970-74, Coll. de France, Paris, 1974—. Author: Le Christianisme va-t-il Mourir?, 1977, La Peur en Occident, 1978, La Peche et la Peur, 1983, La Cas Luther, 1983, Ce Que Je Crois, 1985, Rassurer autrefois. Le sentiment de sécurité en l'Occident (XIVe-XVIIIe siécles), 1989, L'Aveu et le Pardon, 1990. Mem. Acad. Inscriptions et Belles Lettres. Home: 29 Rue des Lauriers, 35510 Cesson-Sevigne France Office: Coll de France, 11 Place Marcelin Berthelot, Cedex5, 75231 Paris France

DE LUNA, SISTER ANITA, religious organization administrator; b. Robstown, Tex., Aug. 15, 1947; d. Anastacio Herrera and Carmen (Mata) de L. BA, Our Lady of the Lake Coll., San Antonio, 1972; MRE, Seattle U., 1976; MAS, U. San Francisco, 1987. Entered Missionary Catechists of Divine Province. Dir. religious edn. Cath. parishes, Gonzales and Brownsville, Tex., 1969-84; major superior Missionary Catechists of Divine Province, San Antonio, 1984—; pres. Leadership Conf. of Women Religious, Region XII, 1989—, nat. bd. dirs., Washington, 1989—, exec. com., 1990—. Editor: Divine Delicacies, 1987; musician: For You Our People, 1980; composer/musician: Holy is the People, 1990; co-author prayer booklet: Holy is the People, 1991. Bd. dirs. Mexican Am. Cultural Ctr., San Antonio, 1988—. Home: 4650 Eldridge San Antonio TX 78237 Office: Missionary Catechists 4650 Eldridge San Antonio TX 78237

DELVAUX, WILLIAM PRESTON, minister; b. Durham, N.C., Mar. 23, 1957; s. Thomas Childs and Martha Jean (McConnell) D.; m. Heidi Ann Coulter, Mar. 15, 1986; 1 child, Abigail. BA, Duke U., 1979; MDiv, Trinity Evangelical Div. Sch., Deerfield, Ill., 1985. Ordained to ministry Presbyn. Ch. in Am., 1989. Youth minister Cen. Pres. Ch., Balt., 1984-88; assoc. pastor Christ Community Ch., Franklin, Tenn., 1988-90; pastor Christ Fellowship Ch., Nashville, 1990—; bd. dirs. World Harvest Mission, Jenkintown, Pa. Home: 5025 Hillsboro Pike #17D Nashville TN 37215 Office: Christ Fellowship Church 136 3rd Ave S Franklin TN 37064

DEMAREST, GERALD GREGORY, minister; b. Greeley, Colo., July 16, 1959; s. Walter Lewis and Dorothea Evangeline (Miller) D.; m. Cynthia Diane Harkins, July 18, 1987. BA in Communications, Oral Roberts U., Tulsa, 1981, BA in English Bible, 1981, MDiv, 1985. Ordained to ministry Christian Ch. (Disciples of Christ), 1985. Evangelist Oral Roberts U. World Outreach Club, Tulsa, 1978-79, Pentecostal Assemblies of Can., Waxeham Bay, Que., 1980; minister First Christian Ch., Holdenville, Okla., 1985-90, Sherman, Tex., 1990—; mem. ch. in soc. com. Christian Ch. in Okla., Oklahoma City, 1987-89, sml. membership congregation com., 1985-88. Leader Cub Scouts Troop #60, Holdenville, Okla., 1988, exec. coun. Boy Scouts Am., Holdenville, 1988-90, asst. scoutmaster, Sherman, Tex., 1990—. Mem. Sherman Assistance Ministries, Sherman Ministerial Alliance, Kiwanis, Odd Fellows. Republican. Office: First Christian Ch 1515 N Travis Sherman TX 75090

DE MARGERIE, BERNARD, minister, ecumenical agency administrator. Head Ctr. for Ecumenism, Saskatoon, Sask., Can. Office: Ctr Ecumenism, 1006 Broadway Ave, Saskatoon, SK Canada S7N 1B9*

DEMARINIS, JOHN HENRY, priest; b. Youngstown, OH, Oct. 2, 1937; s. John and Lucille Elizabeth (Pavone) DeM. BA, Athenaium of Ohio, Cin., 1959, MDiv, 1963; MA, Xavier U., 1962. Ordained priest Roman Cath. Ch., 1962. Assoc. pastor St. Paul's Ch., Canton, Ohio, 1963-66; instr. theology Ursuline High Sch., Youngstown, Ohio, 1966-73; pastor St. Anthony Ch., Youngstown, 1973—; pro-synodal judge Diocesan Priests Senate, Youngstown, 1976-83; treas. Diocese of Youngstown, 1981—, dir. adult edn., 1963, 65, mem. ins. bd., 1981—, priorities study steering com., 1983—, chmn. fin. adv. bd., 1981—; mem. adv. bd. Oblate Sisters, 1966—; mem. com. Synod 76, Youngstown, 1976; tchr. rep. Diocesan Tchr. Confedn., Youngstown, 1968-70; chaplain Mahoning Valley coun. Boy Scouts Am., 1963-66; moderator Home and Sch. Assn. Ursuline High Sch., 1969-73. Democrat. Home: 1125 Turin Ave Youngstown OH 44510 Office: Diocese of Youngstown 144 W Wood St Youngstown OH 44503

DEMBOWSKI, HERMANN, systematic theology educator; b. Carlshof, East Prussia, Nov. 20, 1928; s. Heinz and Christel (Besch) D.; m. Hiltrud Brock, June 3, 1955; 1 child, Ulrike. Theol. exam., U. Goettingen, Goettingen, Fed. Republic Germany, 1952; ThD, U. Goettingen, 1953; Habilitation, U. Bon, Bonn, Fed. Republic Germany, 1967. Parson Evang. Kirche Kurhessen-Waldeck, Solz, Fed. Republic Germany, 1955-60; Lectr. theology Technische Hochschule, Aachen, Fed. Republic Germany, 1960-69; prof. systematic theology U. Bonn, 1970—. Author: Grundfragen der Christologie, 1969, Karl Barth-Rudolf Bultmann-Dietrich Bonhoeffer, 1976, Menschliches Leiden und der Dreieinige Gott, 1979, Gott im Wort, 1982, Das unsere Augen aufgetan werden..., 1989. Evang. Avocations: lit., arts, music. Home: Luisenstrasse 31, D 5300 Bonn 1, Federal Republic of Germany Office: Evangelisch Theologisches, Seminar, Am Hof 2, D 5300 Bonn 1, Federal Republic of Germany

DE MENDENG, GREGOIRE AMBADIANG, minister, administrator. Gen. sec. Eglise Presbyterienne Camerounaise, Yaounde, Cameroon. Office: Eglise Presbyterienne, Camerounaise, BP 519, Yaounde Cameroon*

DEMES, DENNIS THOMAS, religious educator; b. Jersey City, N.J., Apr. 10, 1949; s. Thomas Joseph and Lillian (Harabedian) D. BA, St. John's Coll., Brighton, Mass., 1974; MS in Edn., Princeton U., 1979, ThM, 1979. Cert. advanced religious educator; ordained to ministry as religious educator Roman Cath. Ch., 1984. Religious Educator Archdiocese of Boston, 1974-79; dir. religious edn. St. John's the Evangelist Parish, Winthrop, Mass., 1976-81, Holy Rosary Parish, Lawrence, Mass., 1981-83; Prior Soc. St. Benedict of Nursia, Boston, 1984—; moderator: young adults, youth group, berievement group, div. and separated Caths., Boca Raton, Fla., 1990—. Mem. Nat. Cath. Educators Assn., Soc. St. Benedict. Office: Ascension Cath Ch 699 N E 70 St Boca Raton FL 33487-2427 *As the first stage of life in the womb prepares and nourishes us for the stage after birth, so too does earthly life nourish and prepare us for ultimate life with God.*

DEMONTE, SISTER MARIA, nun, pastoral associate; b. Martins Creek, Pa., Sept. 28, 1930; d. Antonio and Giovina (Coccia) DeM. BA cum laude, St. Rose Coll., 1972; M.T.A. Cert., Cath. U., 1971; MA in Pastoral Ministry, St. Joseph Coll., 1980; MDiv, Immaculate Conception Sem., 1992. Cert. adolescent depression and suicide counseling, spiritual direction. Religion tchr. Walton, Altamont, Deposit, Delhi and Bainbridge, N.Y., 1960-75; sec., program dir. Consultation Ctr.-Diocese, Albany, N.Y., 1984-90; bd. dirs. Adminstrv. Rev. Bd., Albany, 1991—; del. Congregation St. Catherine de'Ricci, Media, Pa., 1978—; instr. Our Lady of Angels Sem., Glemont, N.Y., 1988; dir. religious edn., pastoral assoc. Latham, N.Y., 1987—; religion tchr. Loudonville, N.Y., 1979-81; catechetical cons. Wm. Sadlier Co., Latham, 1989—; coord. Formation for Laity, Latham, 1987—; candidate dir. Congregation of St. Catherine de'Ricci, Media, 1980-86, gen. coun., 1986-90; v.p. Still Point house of Prayer, 1988-89; chairperson Congregation Centennial Celebration, Elkins Park, Pa., 1980. Author: (text) Look At Life, 1980. Counselor Billy Graham Crusade, Capital Dist., N.Y., 1990; dir. Inner City Food Pantry, Latham, Albany, 1987; coord. World Hunger, Latham, 1986, 88, Drug Program, North Colonie, N.Y., 1985. Recipient Maria de LaCruz award Diocesan Religious Edn., 1989, Mary Reed Newland award, 1988, Alumni award Easton Cath. High Sch., 1991; the Sister Maria DeMonte Religious Edn. Ctr. was dedicated in her honor, Aug. 15, 1991. Mem. Diocesan Coun. Sisters, Diocesan Religious Edn. Office (spl. asst. 1976-80), North Colonie Ambulance, Formation for Ministry (instr. 1981—), Religious Edn. Diocese (instr. 1976—). Home: 500 Watervliet Shaker Rd Latham NY 12110 Office: Our Lady Assumption Ch 498 Watervliet Shaker Rd Latham NY 12110

DEMOS, ALBERT LINCOLN ARIES, priest, counselor; b. Chgo., May 1, 1939; s. Lincoln Albert and Margaret (Mason) D.; m. Carol Thessalia Psaros, Oct. 13, 1968; children: Constantine, Mark. BA, Holy Cross Sch. Theology, 1965; MDiv, Hellenic Coll., 1968; D in Ministry, Andover-Newton Theol. Sch., 1988. Ordained minister Greek Orthodox Ch., 1968. Assoc. pastor St. Vsilios Ch., Peabody, Mass., 1968-70; pastor St. John Children's Ch., Charleston, W.Va., 1970-73; pastor Annunciation Ch., Binghamton, N.Y., 1973-76, Rochester, N.Y., 1976-78; assoc. dean students and admissions Hellenci Coll/Holy Cross, Brookline, Mass., 1978-80; dean cathedral Cathedral of New Eng., Boston, 1980-82; priest Greek Orthodox Archdiocese, Boston, 1982—; tour guide, leader, counselor London Village, Bartholomew, Greece, summer 1976-80. Bd. trustees Bay State Coll., Boston, 1988—. Mem. New Eng. Clergy Brotherhood (pres. 1990-91). Avocations: travel, reading, sports, family. Home: 44A Lincoln St Extension Natick MA 01760 Office: Annunciation Greek Orthodox Cathedral of New Eng Parker & Ruggles Sts Boston MA

DEMOSS, LYNN ALLYN, minister; b. Wabash, Ind., Dec. 25, 1934; d. Lowell H. and Helen (McCarty) DeM.; m. Lois Likes, July 23, 1960; children: Jeffrey, Jennifer. AB, U. Mich., 1956; MDiv, Garrett Evang., 1963; DD (hon.), Adrian Coll., 1982. Ordained to ministry Meth. Ch., 1961. Missionary The Meth. Ch., Belgian Congo, Africa, 1957-60; pastor chs. Wis. and Mich., 1960—; sr. pastor 1st United Meth. Ch., Grand Rapids, Mich., 1988—; sec., treas. Blodgett Press, Grand Rapids, 1978—; pres. Meth. Found. of Mich.; trustee Adrian (Mich.) Coll., 1981—; chairperson New Ch. Commn., West Mich. Conf., 1982—; vis. instr. Kimbulu-Kayeke Sem., Mulungwishi, Zaire, 1982. Contbr. articles to profl. jours. Chairperson Sch. Dist. Excellence Com., Muskegon, 1985-86, County Youth Ctr. Study Com., 1986-87. Recipient Disting. Svc. award Jaycees, 1976, Mich. Minute Man award, 1979; named Friend of Edn. Mona Shores Sch. Dist., 1985. Mem. Rotary. Home: 1245 Woodshire SE Grand Rapids MI 49506 Office: First United Meth Ch 227 E Fulton Grand Rapids MI 49503 *I have received from God life and meaning; from family, a legacy of love; and from the world, joy and inspiration. I serve all, out of gratitude.*

DEMPSEY, JOHN KNOWLES, priest; b. San Bernardino, Calif., Sept. 18, 1936; s. John K. and Mary Virginia (Hartshorn) D.; m. Rosemeri Ann Fairchild, July 8, 1972. B.B.A., Golden Gate Coll., 1967; M.Div., Ch. Div. Sch. of Pacific, Berkeley, Calif., 1967. Ordained priest Anglican Ch., 1967. Vicar, St. Mark's Ch., Ritzville, Wash., 1967-69, Holy Trinity Ch., Wallace, Idaho, 1969-72; chaplain U.S. Air Force, 1972-82; rector All Souls' Ch., Okinawa, Japan, 1982—; radio-TV coordinator Episcopal Diocese Spokane, Wash., 1968-71; instr. N.C. Wesleyan Coll., Rocky Mount, 1977-78; pres. Okinawa Missionary Fellowship, 1983-84; chaplain Missions to Seamen, Naha, Japan, 1983—; sec. Anglican Clergy in Central Europe, Germany, 1980-81. Editor: Okinawa, Where Is It? Contbr. articles to Anglican Digest. Served with USN, 1954-64, Far East; served to maj. USAF, 1972-82, Thailand, Fed. Republic Germany. Decorated various mil. medals. Mem. Am. C. of C., Ret. Officers Assn. (sec. Okinawa 1985). Episcopalian. Avocation: music. Home: All Souls' Church, 935 Makiminato, Urasoe City, Okinawa 901-21, Japan

DEMPSEY, RAYMOND LEO, JR., radio and television producer, moderator, writer; b. Providence, June 18, 1949; s. Raymond Leo Sr. and Louise Veronica (Gambuto) D.; m. Patricia Batchelder (div. 1984); children: Joab, Jahdeam, Deezsha, Nathaniel, Talitha. BA in Liberal Arts, R.I. Coll., 1973; Cert. in Bus., U. R.I., 1979; cert., Blake Computer Programming Inst., 1977, Billy Graham Sch. Evangelism, 1989. Lic. real estate agt., R.I.; cert. secondary sch. teacher, R.I., cert. videographer, R.I., cert. contractor, R.I.; Notary Pub. Writer local and nat. publs., 1980—; producer, moderator Chapter & Verse TV, RICA-TV, Providence, 1983—; tchr. R.I. Pub. High Schs., Providence and Cranston, 1988—; producer, moderator radio programs Ch. Focus and Page Seven, WRIB AM Radio, East Providence, R.I., 1989—; bd. dirs. Blessing, Inc., Providence; spl. reporter for U.S.A. Radio network, 1991; host Striaght Talk, WKRI AM Radio, 1989; producer, co-host The Bible Answer Program, WARV AM Radio, 1986. Producer, co-host (radio program) The Bible Answer Program, 1986. Bd. dirs. R.I. Right to Life, Cranston, 1973—; witness R.I. Gen. Assembly, 1973—,R.I. Bd. Health, 1973—; vol. ARC, R.I. Hosp.; registrar voters, State of R.I., 1980, 91; sponsor World Vision, Pasadena, Calif., 1981—, Compassion Internat., Colorado Springs, Colo., 1989—; chief boys instr. Mattson Acad. Karate, Providence, 1969-71; del. Gov.'s Conf. on Libr. and Info. Svcs., 1991; elector White House Conf. on Libr. and Info. Svcs.; Justice of the Peace, 1991. Named one of Top 4 Local Cable TV Producers in Nation, Nat. Assn. Local Cable Programming, 1987; recipient Internat. Angel award for excellence in cable TV presentations, 1991, and others. Mem. ASCD, R.I. Assn. for Edn. Young Children, Am. Math. Soc., Smithsonian Air and Space, Am. Soc. Oriental Rsch., Mental Health Assn. R.I., Nat. Geog. Soc., Bread for the World, Evangs. for Social Action, Musical Heritage Soc., Archaeol. Inst. Am., Internat. Platform Assn., Phi Theta Kappa. Avocations: scuba diving, marksmanship, bibl. archeology. Home and Office: 75 Marion Ave Providence RI 02905 *Orthodoxy presumes orthopraxy, and correct knowledge must precede correct action.*

DEMPSTER, MURRAY WAYNE, religion educator, minister; b. Melville, Sask., Can., June 27, 1942; came to U.S., 1965; s. Raymond Daniel Rudolph and June (Bellamy) Rynbend; m. Coralie Faith Erickson, Sept. 26, 1964; 1 child, Marlon Murray. Ministerial diploma, N.W. Bible Coll., Can., 1963; BA in Bibl. Studies summa cum laude, So. Calif. Coll., 1968; MA in Social Ethics, U. So. Calif., 1969, PhD in Social Ethics, 1980. Ordained to ministry Assemblies of God, 1965. Asst. min. Cen. Pentecostal Ch., Edmonton, Alta., Can., 1963-65; assoc. min. 1st Assembly of God, Long Beach, Calif., 1965-68; dean of men So. Calif. Coll., Costa Mesa, 1969-70, campus pastor, 1970-71, asst. prof. religion, 1971-78, assoc. prof., 1980-87, prof. social ethics, 1987—; vis. prof. Fuller Theol. Sem., Pasadena, Calif., 1980—; Pentecostal lectr. Regent Coll., Vancouver, B.C., Can., 1988; Staley lectr. Southeastern Coll., Lakeland, Fla., 1991. Co-author: Salt and Light: Evangelical Political Thought in Modern America, 1989; author: (with others) Pastoral Problems in the Pentecostal-Charismatic Movement, 1983; co-editor: Called and Empowered: Global Mission in Pentecostal Perspective, 1991, Agora mag., 1977-81; mem. editorial adv. bd.: The Study of Philosophy, 3d edit., contbr. articles to religious jours. Mem. instl. rev. team Calif. State Dept. Edn., 1984, 86. Recipient Outstanding Faculty award Associated Student Body, So. Calif. Coll., 1981-82; scholar So. Calif. Coll., 1967-68, U. So. Calif., 1968-69; Layne Found. fellow U. So. Calif., 1971-74. Mem. Soc. for Pentecostal Studies (2d v.p. 1989, 1st v.p., program chair ann. meeting 1990, pres. 1990-91), Am. Acad. Religion, Soc. for Sci. Study of Religion, Soc. Christian Ethics, Soc. Christian Philosophers. Democrat. Home: 2 Toulon Laguna Niguel CA 92677 Office: So Calif Coll Div Religion 55 Fair Dr Costa Mesa CA 92626

DENDE, CORNELIAN EDMUND, priest, radio program director; b. Scranton, Pa., Aug. 15, 1915; s. John and Mary (Borowski) D. Student, Seminaire de Philosophie, Montreal, Que., Can., 1935, U. Lwow, Poland, 1937, Gregorian U., Rome, 1939, St. Hyacinth Coll., Sem., Granby, Mass., 1940; LHD (hon.), Alliance Coll., 1985. Ordained priest Roman Cath. Ch., 1941. Dir. Cath. Press Agy., N.Y.C., 1943; master novices Order Friars Minor Conventual, 1948-58; rector St. Hyacinth Coll., Sem., Granby, 1959; dir. Father Justin Rosary Hour, Athol Springs, N.Y., 1959—. Author radio speeches in Polish, 31 vols., 1959-90. Recipient medal of merit Cath. U. Lublin, Poland, 1984, Pro Ecclesia et Pontifice medal Pope John Paul II, 1991, Primate's medal of merit, Poland, 1991. Office: Father Justin Rosary Hour Sta F Box 217 Buffalo NY 14212

DENEUI, JOEL ARTHUR, minister; b. Spencer, Iowa, Nov. 7, 1941; s. Arthur Joe and Doris Austrid (Lindberg) DeN.; m. Jackie Jean Gaston, Sept. 24, 1965; children: Jodi Ann, Jeffrey Paul. MA in Ministry, Talbot Theol. Sem., 1986. Ordained minister Bapt. Ch., 1989. Choir dir. Berean Bapt. Ch., Orange, Calif., 1971-73; choir dir., jr. ch. pastor Calvary Bapt. Ch., Albert Lea, Minn., 1973-74; camp adminstr., dir. Whispering Pines Camp, Miraposa, Calif., 1979-80; assoc. pastor Grace Bapt. Ch., Anaheim, Calif., 1981-84; sr. pastor Calvary Bapt. Ch., Monrovia, Calif., 1985—; chmn. bd. 3-1 Camp Big Bear-Conservative Bapt. of Am. Camp, Calif., 1986, registrar, 1986, 89,; corr. sec. Conservative Bapt. of Am. of So. Calif., Anaheim, 1989, 90, rec. sec., 1990. Rep. to city coun. Ministerial Coun., Monrovia, 1985. With USN, 1961-65. Recipient Presdl. accommodation USN, 1964. Republican. Home: 615 Terrado Dr Monrovia CA 91016

DEN EXTER BLOKLAND, A. FRANÇOIS, religious educator; b. Hilversum, Holland, July 28, 1949; s. Adriaan Willem and Dingena de Cock (Sofras) den Exter B.; m. Vicki Lynn Bawsel, Aug. 19, 1972; children: Rebecca Ann, Elizabeth Adriana. MDiv, Trinity Evang. Divinity Sch., Deerfield, Ill., 1985, ThM, 1988; Drs., Free U., Amsterdam, 1990. Dir. tng. Campus Crusade for Christ, Netherlands, 1973-82; interpreter Berlitz Translation Svcs., Chgo., 1989—. Mem. Evang. Theol. Soc., Soc. Bibl. Lit. Home: 310 Channel Dr Island Lake IL 60042

DENHAM, MICHAEL THOMAS, minister; b. Tulsa, June 29, 1955; s. Leonard Patrick and Jean (Dowdy) D.; m. Elizabeth Callender, June 6, 1981. MusB, Wheaton (Ill.) Coll., 1978; MusM, U. Ill., 1980; ThM, Dallas Theol. Sem., 1986; postgrad., U. North Tex., Denton, 1990—. Ordained to ministry Northwest Bible Ch., 1986. Dir. music Town North Presbyn. Ch., Richardson, Tex., 1987-90; doctoral teaching fellow U. North Tex., Denton, 1987-90; opera singer Ft. Worth Opera, 1987-91; asst. prof. music Lamar U., Beaumont, Tex., 1991—, Walles Chair artist in residence, 1991; dir. music Trinity United Meth. Ch., Beaumont; lectr. music U. Tex., Arlington, 1989—, Walles Chair artist in residence, 1991. Named Outstanding Univ. Teaching fellow U. North Tex., Denton, 1990. Mem. Nat. Assn. Teachers Singing, Evangelical Theol. Soc. Republican. Avocations: golf, tennis, biking, gardening, sports events. Office: Lamar U PO Box 10044 Beaumont TX 77710

DENHAM, WILLIAM ERNEST, JR., minister, counselor; b. Louisville, Oct. 8, 1911; s. William E. and Myrtle (Lane) D.; m. Priscilla Kelley, June 27, 1941 (dec.); children: William Ernest III, James Kelley, Priscilla, Elizabeth Denham Thompson; m. 2d, Louise D. Yelvington, Nov. 23, 1974. AB, Washington U., 1933; ThM, So. Bapt. Theol. Sem., 1940, PhD, 1944; postgrad. U. Tex., Austin, 1971-73. Lic. profl. counselor, Tex. Sec. Bapt. Student Union, Mo. Baptist Conv., 1933-35, Atlanta, 1935-37; pastor 1st. Bapt. Ch., Newport, Tenn., 1944-47, Macon, Ga., 1947-52, River Oaks Bapt. Ch., Houston, 1952-64, 1st. Bapt. Ch., Austin, 1964-75; founder, dir. Counseling and Pastoral Care Ctr., Austin, 1975-90, dir. spiritual growth, 1987—; mem. bd. Bapt. Radio Commn., So. Bapt. Conv.; exec. com. mem. Bapt. Gen. Conv., Tex.; 1st bd. chmn. Houston Bapt. U.; founding sponsor Amigos de las Americas; Protestant chaplain gen. Boy Scouts Am., 1969. Mem. Family Meditation Assn. (cert.), Am. Assn. Marriage and Family Therapists, Am. Assn. Sex Educators, Counselors and Therapists, Am. Assn. Pastoral Counselors (diplomate), Omicron Delta Kappa. Democrat. Lodges:

Rotary, Kiwanis. Contbr. articles to profl. jours. Address: Counseling and Pastoral Care Ctr 5425A Burnet Rd Austin TX 78756

DENISON, JAMES C., minister; b. Houston, May 29, 1958; s. Lester Irvin and Ruth (Payne) D.; m. Janet Lynn Croswhite, June 7, 1980; children: Ryan, Craig. BA, Houston Bapt. U., 1980; MDiv, Southwestern Bapt. Theol. Sem., 1983, PhD, 1989. Ordained to ministry So. Bapt. Conv. Youth min. Temple Oaks Bapt. Ch., Houston, 1977-78, Coll. Pk. Bapt. Ch., Houston, 1978-79; pastor New Hope Bapt. Ch., Mansfield, Tex., 1984-88; instr. religion philosophy Southwestern Bapt. Theol. Sem., Ft. Worth, 1987-89; pastor First Bapt. Ch., Midland, 1989—. Contbr. articles to dictionary, Youth Alive mag. Teaching fellow Southwestern Bapt. Theol. Sem., 1984-87. Home: 1302 Brighton Ct Midland TX 79705 Office: First Bapt Ch 2104 W Louisiana Midland TX 79702

DENISON, MARK EDWIN, minister; b. Houston, Jan. 16, 1960; s. Lester I. and Ruth (Payne) D.; m. Elizabeth Ann Solomon, Feb. 26, 1983; 1 child, David James. BA, Houston Bapt. U., 1982; MDiv, Southwestern Bapt. Theol. Sem., Ft. Worth, 1989. Ordained to ministry So. Bapt. Conv., 1983. Minister of youth First Bapt. Ch. of Genoa, Houston, 1979-81, First Bapt. Ch., Tomball, Tex., 1981-82; interim pastor First Bapt. Ch. of Genoa, Houston, 1982-84; pastor Baybrook Bapt. Ch., Friendswood, Tex., 1984—; chmn. lang. missions com. Union Bapt. Assn., Houston, 1986-89, chmn. ministerial tng., 1989—; youth evangelist Bapt. Gen. Conv. of Tex., Dallas, 1977-82. Home: 2211 Leading Edge Friendswood TX 77546 Office: Baybrook Bapt Ch 15775 Hope Village Rd Friendswood TX 77546

DENLINGER, JOHN ARTHUR, pastor; b. Lancaster, Pa., Dec. 29, 1941; s. Arthur Abram and Violet (Lamparter) D.; m. Mary Hazel Fahringer, Sept. 1, 1962; children: Mark Allen, Pamela Sue, Todd Andrew, Bethany Ann. BA in Religion and Philosophy Magna Cum Laude, Catawba Coll., 1965; MDiv cum laude, Lancaster Theol. Sem., 1970. Ordained to ministry, 1970. Assoc. pastor St. John's United Ch. of Christ, Lansdale, Pa., 1970-73; pastor St. Luke's United Ch. of Christ, Lititz, Pa., 1973-80, McClure (Pa.) Parish United Ch. of Christ, 1980-82, Mt. Bethel United Ch. of Christ, McClure, 1983-86, Emmanuel United Ch. of Christ, McClure, 1986—; with maintenance and cleaning dept. U.S. Post Office, Wrightsville, Pa., 1989—; chairperson Middle Creek Valley Food Bank, Beaver Springs, Pa., 1982-86. Organizer Western Snyder County Polit. Recognition Dinner, McClure, 1985; graduation speaker West Snyder High Sch., Beaver Springs, 1981, 83; mem. McClure Vol. Fire Co., 1984-86; chaplain Goodwill Fire Co. 5, York, Pa., 1989—. Mem. Cen. Assn. Ministerium (chairperson McClure chpt. 1984-86), York Assn. Ministerium (chairperson 1988-89), Pa. Cen. Conf. (chairperson outdoor ministries com. 19766), Lancaster County Ministerial Fellowship (sec., treas. 1974-77, chairperson 1977-80, chairperson parish life com. 1976-78), Lansdale Ministerium (sec., treas. 1972-73), Rotary (sec. West York, Pa. chpt. 1989-90, pres. elect 1990, pres. 1991—). Home: 1639 Fourth Ave York PA 17403-2624 Office: Emmanuel United Ch Christ 813 E Market St York PA 17403-1101

DENMAN, KATHLEEN ANNE, hospital chaplain; b. Stockton, Calif., Aug. 23, 1955; d. Attilio Dominic and Cora Ellen (Trotter) Bregante; m. Marshall L. Denman, Oct. 30, 1976 (dec. Oct. 1980); 1 child, Paul Michael. BMus, U. of the Pacific, 1977; MDiv cum laude, North Park Theol. Sem., 1988. Youth minister Community Covenant Ch., Rocklin, Calif., 1981-83; faculty asst. North Park Theol. Sem., Chgo., 1983-88; assoc. pastor First Covenant Ch., Red Wing, Minn., 1986-87; chaplain resident Luth. Gen. Hosp., Chgo., 1988-89, Hermann Hosp., Houston, 1989-90; chaplain supr. Meth. Hosp., Houston, 1990, Meth. Med. Ctr. Ill., Peoria, 1991—. Mem. Evang. Covenant Ministerium, Assn. for Clin. Pastoral Edn., Coll. Chaplains, Soc. Bibl. Lit. Democrat. Home: 5250 N Knoxville # 604 Peoria IL 61614 Office: Meth Med Ctr Dept Pastoral Care Peoria IL 61614 *I have learned that pain does not have to render us victims in life. If we allow ourselves to feel our pain and to befriend it, pain can bless us and render us victors in life.*

DENNEY, JAMES TYRE, pastor; b. Atlanta, Aug. 25, 1930; s. Homer Uclet and Leone (Little) D.; m. Betty Ann Nash, Aug. 14, 1948; children: Jennifer, Jim, Jeff, Joel, Jody, Jana. BS in Human Rels., Samford U., 1966; MDiv, So. Bapt. Theol. Sem., 1970. Min. of youth 4th Ave Bapt. Ch., Birmingham, Ala., 1959-61, Calvary Bapt. Ch., Marion, Ala., 1961-62, Happy Home Bapt. Ch., Leeds, Ala., 1962-64, Westside Bapt. Ch., Pell City, Ala., 1965-67; minister of youth Alton Bapt. Ch., Lawrenceburg, Ky., 1967—. Author: (newspaper column) The Anderson News, 1983—. Mem. Rotary, Ruritan. Republican. Home: 1481 Alton Rd Lawrenceburg KY 40342 Office: Alton Bapt Ch 1321 Bypass N Lawrenceburg KY 40342 *There is a vast difference between those who are merely church members and those who have had a life changing experience with Christ and thus are the Church.*

DENNIE, DEBORAH THOMAS, minister; b. Memphis, Sept. 20, 1939; d. Willie Timothy and Beatrice (Bell) Thomas; m. Thurman Paul Dennie, Sept. 30, 1965; children: Deirdre Beatrice, Thurman Phillip. BA, Cen. State U., Wilberforce, Ohio, 1961; MA, Memphis State U., 1967; postgrad., Vanderbilt U., 1969-70. Lic. marriage and family therapist, profl. counselor, Tenn. Tchr. Memphis City Schs., 1962-65; instr. S.A. Owen Jr. Coll., Memphis, 1965-68, Lemoyne-Owen Coll., Memphis, 1968-69; assoc. editor Tri-State Defender Newspaper, Memphis, 1970-76; radio host WLOK Radio, Memphis, 1976-78; counselor Shelby County Sheriff's Dept., Memphis, 1978-87; chief hearing officer Shelby County Sheriff's Dept., 1987-89, asst. to chief jailer, 1989-90, dir. programs, 1990—; dir. Crisis & Stress Mgmt. Inst., Memphis, 1982-86; psychotherapist in pvt. practice Memphis, 1982—; pastor African Meth. Episcopal Ch., Memphis, 1983—. Author: Sing Sweet Orpheus, Sing, 1976; editor-in-chief newspaper, Ministers' Alliance of W. Tennessee, 1990. Bd. dirs. N. Memphis Health Clinic, 1978-83. Named Outstanding Citizen Seventh Day Adventists, 1985; Rev. Deborah Thomas Dennie Day named in honor by Sheriff of Shelby County, 1990. Mem. AAUW, Tenn. Corrections Assn. Shelby County (treas. 1989), AME Ministers Alliance of W. Tenn. (pres. 1990), Phi Delta Kappa. Republican. Avocations: writing, sculptoring. Home: 3294 Harris Ave Memphis TN 38111

DENNIS, BOBBY GENE, pastor; b. Albemarle, N.C., May 29, 1938; s. Henry Fay and Jettie Mae (Chandler) D.; m. Barbara Ann Thomas, Sept. 10, 1960; 1 child, Melanie Lane. Intermediate cert. in Bible, Washington Bible Coll., 1972; cert. in pastoral counseling, Southeastern Sem., Nashville, 1972; ThB, Internat. Sem., Orlando, Fla., 1985, ThM, 1986, DD (hon.), 1986. Ordained to ministry Bapt. Ch., 1967; lic. gospel min., 1964. Interim pastor Cedar Grove Bapt. Ch., Charlotte, N.C., 1969-70, Gloryland Bapt. Ch., Charlotte, 1971, Pine Grove Bapt. Ch., Concord, N.C., 1971, 73-74, Albemarle Rd. Bapt. Ch., Charlotte, 1971-72, Tabernacle Bapt. Ch., Mt. Holly, N.C., 1973, Trinity Bapt. Ch., Statesville, N.C., 1974-75, Grace Bapt. Ch., Hagerstown, Md., 1976-78, 80-82, Wayside Bapt. Ch., Leitersburg, Md., 1978, Faith Bapt. Ch., Altoona, Pa., 1984-85; assoc. pastor Harvest Bapt. Ch., Hagerstown, 1985-86; pastor Marantha Bapt. Ch., Statesville, 1986—; hon. assoc. pastor Coll. Pk. Bapt. Ch., Charlotte; evangelist and counselor. Bd. dirs. Iredell Developmental Ctrs., Statesville, 1989-92. With U.S. Army, 1956-62. Recipient Pride award Ryder Truck Lines, 1974. Republican. Home: 254 Ethel Ln Statesville NC 28677 Office: Maranatha Bapt Ch Rte 13 Box 35-A Statesville NC 28677

DENNIS, GARY OWEN, minister; b. Waynesville, N.C., Feb. 17, 1946; s. Daniel Shaefer and Shirley Carlene (Owen) D.; m. Sara Bright, June 14, 1969. BA, Taylor U., 1968; MDiv, Princeton Theol. Seminary, 1972, D.Min., Union Theol. Seminary, 1986. Ordained to ministry Presbyn. Ch., 1972; assoc. pastor Second Presbyn. Ch., Memphis, 1972-73, Hollywood Presbyn. Ch., Los Angeles, 1973-76; pastor Westlake Hills Presbyn. Ch., Austin, Tex., 1976-90; pastor La Canada Presbyn. Ch., L.A., 1990—; adj. prof. Fuller Theol. Sem., Pasadena, Calif., 1973-76; mem. stewardship com. Mission Presbytery, San Antonio, 1980-85, mem. edn. com., 1976-80; founder, dir. Youth Leadership Devel. Am., Los Angeles, 1973-76; cons. Lilly Endowment, Indpls., 1974-76. Contbr. articles to various publs. Bd. dirs. Central City Counseling Svc., Austin, 1982-83, Ronald McDonald House, Austin, 1984, 85, 86, Austin Children's Cancer Clinic, 1987. Mem. Kiwanis. Democrat.

DENNIS, JAN PHILIP, publishing executive; b. Evanston, Ill., Nov. 21, 1945; s. Clyde Harold and Muriel Lucile (Benson) D.; m. Jeanne Archer Schaap, June 12, 1968; children: Graham, Mary, Leslie, Christopher, Cory, Robyn. BA, Westmont Coll., 1967; MA, Ind. U., 1972. Contbg. editor Am. Bible Soc., N.Y.C., 1971-72; assoc. editor Cultural Info. Svcs., N.Y.C., 1972-73; rep. sales Lithocolor Press, Westchester, Ill., 1973-75; exec. v.p. editorial dept. Good News Pubs./Crossway Books, Wheaton, Ill., 1976—. Author: The How-To Book, 1976. Mem. adv. bd. Ams. United for Life, Ill. With U.S. Army, 1968-71. Mem. Evang. Christian Pubs. Assn. Republican. Office: Good News Pubs/Crossway Books 1300 Crescent St Wheaton IL 60187

DENNIS, JOHN DAVISON, minister; b. Pitts., Sept. 18, 1937; s. John Wellington and Helen Isabella (Davison) D.; m. Nancy Schumacher, Jan. 7, 1967; children: Michael, Andrew. AB, Wesleyan U., 1959; BD, Princeton Theol. Sem., 1962, ThM, 1965. Ordained to ministry United Presbyn. Ch. (USA), 1962. Asst. pastor First Presbyn. Ch., Germantown, Pa., 1962-69; sr. pastor First Presbyn. Ch., Corvallis, Oreg., 1969—; exch. min. St. Columbia's Presbyn. Ch., Johannesburg, Republic of South Africa, 1978. Chaplain Germantown Hosp., 1965-69; west coast dean Presbyn. Young Pastors Seminars, 1983-85; vice chmn. Westminster Found. Oreg., 1974-76; pres. Madison Ave. Task Force, 1975-77, Corvallis Community Improvement, Inc., USSR Sister City Assn., 1989-90; founder Corvallis Summer Music Festival, 1979, v.p., 1979-83; trustee, charter mem. Good Samaritan Hosp. Found.; mem. Benton County Mental Health Bd., 1972-76, chmn. 1975-76; founder, mem. exec. com. Corvallis Fish Emergency Aid Svc., 1969-76; trustee Ecumenical Ministries of Oreg., 1989—; bd. dirs. United Way of Benton County, 1986—; candidate U.S. Congress from Oreg. 5th dist., 1988. Fellow Aspen Inst., 1987. Mem. Rotary (charter mem., dir. local club). Home: 2760 NW Skyline Dr Corvallis OR 97330 Office: 114 SW 8th St Corvallis OR 97330

DENNIS, PATSY ANN, lay worker; b. Versailles, Ky., Sept. 20, 1948; d. William Railey and Florence Mildred (Edwards) Richards; m. Larry Edwin Dennis, June 4, 1966; children: Kimberly Dawn Dennis Seyberth, Larry Kevin, Kelly Shawn. Grad. high sch., Versailles. Children's dir. Ch. of God of Prophecy, Versailles, 1967-76; children's pastor King's Way Assembly of God, Versailles, 1976—, bus. ministry dir., 1976-80, youth staff, 1980-85, tchr. Sunday sch., 1980-86, bd. dirs., 1982—, activities dir., 1985—; cartographer Rand McNally Co., Versailles, 1966-80, sec., 1980-91; seminar leader. Recipient Excellence in Ministry award Children's Pastors' Conf., 1989. Home: 106 Dan Dr Versailles KY 40383 Office: Kings Way Assembly of God 4175 Versailles Rd PO Box 425 Versailles KY 40383

DENNIS, WALTER DECOSTER, suffragan bishop; b. Washington, Aug. 23, 1932. B.A., Va. State Coll., 1952; M.A., NYU, 1953; M.Div., Gen. Theol. Sem., 1958; D.D. (honoris causa) Interdenominational Theol. Ctr.-Absalom Jones Theol. Inst., 1977, Gen. Theol. Sem., 1980; L.H.D. (hon.), Va. State U., 1983, Episcopal Sem. of S.W., 1983. Ordained deacon Protestant Episcopal Ch., 1956, ordained priest, 1958, ordained suffragan bishop, 1979. Curate St. Phillip's Ch., Bklyn., 1956; asst. minister Cathedral Ch. of St. John the Divine, N.Y.C., 1956-60, canon residentiary, 1965—; vicar St. Cyprian's Ch., Hampton, Va., 1960-65; suffragan bishop of N.Y., 1979—; adj. asst. prof. Am. history and constl. law Hampton Inst., 1961-65; adj. prof. Christian ethics Gen. Theol. Sem., 1975—; lectr. U. of South Div. Sch., Sewanee, Tenn., 1974-75; mem. Nat. Task Force on Hunger, Episc. Ch., 1975—; mem. adv. bd. Episc. Ch.'s Teaching Series: Ethics, 1975—; convenor Black Caucus Diocese of N.Y., 1976—; served as Diocese examining chaplain; mem. religious liberty com. Nat. Council Chs.; research fellow Episc. Theol. Sem. of SW, 1978; N.Y. dep. Gen. Conv., 1979; mem. numerous coms. Diocese of N.Y.; adminstr. numerous programs for Cathedral Ch. of St. John the Divine; chmn. standing commn. Constn. and Canons; mem. Joint nominating com. for election of presiding bishop. Author: (booklets) Puerto Rican Neighbors, 1958, Mexican American Neighbors, 1960. Contbg. author: (chpt.) On the Battle Lines, 1962. Bd. dirs. Manhattanville Community Ctr., Inc., Abortion Repeal Assn., Assn. For Study of Abortion, Inst. for Study of Human Resources, Homosexual Community Counselling Ctr., Nat. Orgn. for Reform of Marijuana Laws, N.Y. Tng. Sch. for Deaconesses, Soc. Juvenile Justice and Sex Info. and Edn. Counsel of U.S., Planned Parenthood Fedn. of Am., Lenox Hill Hosp. Mem. Union Black Episcopalians, Guild of St. Ives (founder, sec.). Address: 1047 Amsterdam Ave New York NY 10025

DENNIS, WILBURN DWAYNE, minister; b. Abilene, Tex., July 26, 1937; s. Wilburn Parker and Beulah Isabella (Dearing) D.; m. Marcia Ann Todd, June 23, 1959; children—Wilburn Todd, Sherrie Ann, Marcia Leigh. B.A., Abilene Christian U., 1958, M.A., 1959; M.Ed., West Tex. State U., 1975. Ordained to ministry Ch. of Christ. Minister, Crescent Park Ch. of Christ, Littlefield, Tex., 1959-62, Univ. Ch. of Christ, Canyon, Tex., 1967-75, Broadway Ch. of Christ, Paducah, Ky., 1975-78, Oakcrest Ch. of Christ, Oklahoma City, 1962-67, 78-84, Missouri St. Ch. of Christ, Baytown, Tex., 1984-86, Cen. Ch. Christ. Shawnee, Okla., 1986—; mem. adv. bd. Lubbock Christian Coll., Tex., 1959-62, Okla. Christian Coll., Oklahoma City, 1963-70, Freed-Hardeman Coll., Henderson, Tenn., 1975-80. Contbr. articles to religious jours. Republican. Lodge: Rotary. Avocations: jogging; travel; reading; music. Home: 27 Pam Dr Shawnee OK 74801 Office: Cen Ch Christ PO Box 1228 Shawnee OK 74801

DENNISON, SISTER MARY ELIZABETH, religion educator, nun; b. Alton, Ill., Apr. 24, 1928; d. John Thomas and Emelie Ann (Gschwend) D. BS, St. Louis U., 1949; MRE, Loyola U., Chgo., 1969; EdD, U. Houston, 1984. Joined Religious Order of Cenacle, Roman Cath. Ch. Mem. staff Cenacle Retreat House, Ill., Mo., Calif., Tex., 1951-59; mem. staff Office Religious Edn., Sacramento Diocese, 1957-63, Houston Diocese, 1964-69; dir. religious edn. St. John Vianney, Houston, 1968-80; assoc. prof. religion U. St. Thomas, Houston, 1968-92, dir. MRE program, 1983—, dir. Spiritual Direction Inst., 1985—; chmn. Diocesan Social Concerns Commn., 1990-92. Co-author: (high sch. text) Church, 1982, God with Us, Guides 1 and 2, 1983; also articles. Recipient Constantin award for faculty devel. U. St. Thomas, 1982. Mem. Nat. Cath. Edn. Assn., Assn. Profs. and Researchers in Religious Edn., Religious Edn. Assn., Assn. Dir. Grad. Religious Edn. Programs (treas. 1972-74). Home: Cenacle Retreat House 420 N Kirkwood St Houston TX 77079 Office: U St Thomas 3812 Montrose St Houston TX 77006

DENNY, FREDERICK MATHEWSON, religious studies educator; b. Burlington, Vt., Mar. 2, 1939; s. Franklin Eulah and Ella Mabel (Mathewson) D.; m. Alexandra Ivanoff, Aug. 25, 1962; children: Joshua Mathewson, Sydney Eldridge. AB, Coll. of William and Mary, 1961; BDiv, Andover-Newton (Mass.) Theol. Sch., 1965; MA, U. Chgo., 1969, PhD, 1974. Instr. in religious studies Colby-Sawyer Coll., New London, N.H., 1964-67; lectr. in religious studies Yale U., New Haven, 1971-72; asst. prof. religious studies U. Va., Charlottesville, 1972-78; assoc. prof. religious studies U. Colo., Boulder, 1978-88, prof., 1988—. Author: (textbook) An Introduction to Islam, 1985, Islam and the Muslim Community, 1985; co-editor: (scholarly book) The Holy Book in Comparative Perspective, 1985; series editor: (scholarly book) Studies in Comparative Religion, 1985—; contbr. articles to profl. jours. NEH fellow, 1976-77, U. Colo. fellow, 1984-85, 91-92; Fulbright Commn. and U.S. Info. Agy. grantee, 1984-85. Mem. Am. Acad. Religion (regional pres. 1987-88, chair Islam sect. 1986-88), Am. Oriental Soc., Am. Rsch. Ctr. in Egypt, Soc. for the Sci. Study of Religion, Omicron Delta Kappa, Phi Beta Kappa. Democrat. Office: U Colo Dept Religious Studies Campus Box 292 Boulder CO 80309 *The most significant development in the religious life of the coming century will be the domestication of Islam in North America.*

DENNY, RANDAL EARL, pastor; b. L.A., Jan. 27, 1937; s. Earl Winburne and Thelma Ruth (Willis) D.; m. Ruth Beatrice Gladden, May 30, 1958; children: Shannon Ruth, Shelley Kathleen. BA, Pasadena Coll., 1958; BD, Nazarene Theol. Sem., Kansas City, Mo., 1961; grad. studies, Denver Sem., 1965. Pastor Thornton Ch. of the Nazarene, Denver, 1961-63, Golden Ch. of the Nazarene, Denver, 1963-68; pastor First Ch. of the Nazarene, Modesto, Calif., 1968-75, L.A., 1975-79, San Luis Obispo, Calif., 1979-82; pastor Spokane (Wash.) Valley Ch., 1982—; editor The Preacher's Mag., Kansas City, Mo., 1989—; dist. ch. schs. chmn. Central Calif. Dist., Fresno, 1969-73; chmn. ministerial credintials Colo., Calif., Wash., 1966-91; dist. adv. bd. L.A. Dist., Pasadena, 1975-82; trustee Point Loma Nazarene Coll., San Diego, 1976-82. Bass violin player Golden Symphony Orch., Colo., 1966-68, Modesto Symphony Orch., Calif., 1968-75 (bd. mem. 1973-75); singer Gold Coast Chorus, San Luis Obispo, Calif., 1979-82. Republican. Office: Spokane Valley Church 10814 E. Broadway Spokane WA 99206

DENO, LAWRENCE M., academic administrator. Supt. of schs. Roman Cath. Diocese of Ogdensburg, N.Y. Office: Schs Supt 622 Washington St PO Box 369 Ogdensburg NY 13669*

DENTON, BILLY RAY, minister; b. Oxford, Miss., Mar. 19, 1949; s. Clo Ray and Vivian Christine (Reaves) D.; m. Linda Jean Leist, Dec. 17, 1972; children: Melody Joy, Olivia Christine. AA in Sacred Lit., Whites Ferr Rd. Sch. Bible, 1979; BA in Bibl. Studies, Am. Christian Bible Coll., 1979; ThM, Internat. Bible Inst., 1980. Ordained to ministry Ch. Christ, 1979; lic. pastoral counselor. Min. Vicksburg (Miss.) Ch. Christ, 1979-80, Rodenburg Ave. Ch. Christ, Biloxi, Miss., 1980-82, 43d St. Ch. Christ, Bradenton, Fla., 1982-85, Pineville (La.) Ch. Christ, 1985-88, Forest Park (Ga.) Ch. Christ, 1988—; dir. Atlanta World Missions Forum, Forest Park, 1989—; campaign coord. South Met. Atlanta Campaign Christ, 1990—. Editor: (Newsletter) Living the Word, 1990—. Mem. Clayton County C. of C., Jonesboro, Ga., 1991. Staff sgt. USAF, 1969-76. Named Outstanding Young Men Am., 1980, 82. Mem. Nat. Christian Counselors Assn., Optimist Club (pres. 1988). Office: Ch of Christ PO Box 1401 Forest Park GA 30051-1401 *The world is in need of more good people. We need kind, gentle, generous people. Those qualities ought to appeal to us, but is is easier to follow the opposite trail. The positive qualities we need are in short supply because they are hard to develop. Praise God for people who are good before they try to become anything else.*

DENTON, DOUGLAS GUY, minister; b. Tallahassee, Fla., Sept. 1, 1945; s. Guy Otha and Jacquelyn (Melton) D.; m. Linda Kay Daniel, Aug. 21, 1971; children: April Dawn, Bonnie Heather, Amber Eve. BA, U. Tex., Arlington, 1971; MDiv, Southwestern Bapt. Theol. Sem., 1974, MRE, 1979. Ordained to ministry So. Bapt. Conv., 1973. Pastor Hibbit Bapt. Ch., Whitesboro, Tex., 1973-74; pastor Trinity Bapt. Mission, LaGrande, Oreg., 1974-75, Parkhurst Bapt. Ch., Shreveport, La., 1975-76; dir. Bapt. Student Union Tex. A&I U., Kingsville, 1976-78; pastor Ranchland Heights Bapt. Ch., Midland, Tex., 1986-89, Skyline Bapt. Ch., El Paso, Tex., 1989—; trustee Internat. Bapt. Bible Inst., 1991—, adj. instr., 1989—. Author: Outlines on the Sermon on the Mount, 1990, Sermons on the Savior, 1990, Challenging Sermon Outlines, 1991, Sermons for the Last Days, 1991; contbr. articles to religious periodicals. With USAF, 1966-70. Republican. Home: 5449 Ketchikan El Paso TX 79924 Office: Skyline Bapt Ch 10061 Rushing Rd El Paso TX 79924 *The humanistic dream of moral progress apart from divine aid has become a personal and social nightmare from which religious truth alone can awaken us. Man has lost his way and is too proud to ask God for directions.*

DENTON, JOHN G., religious organization administrator. Gen. sec. Nat. Office of Anglican Ch., Sydney, Australia. Office: Nat Office Anglican Ch, Box Q190, Queen Victoria PO, Sydney NSW 2000, Australia*

DENTON, RENA WILSON, religion educator; b. Atlanta, Jan. 20, 1943; d. Warren Russell and Mildred (Carr) Wilson; children: Anna Holland Denton, Kimball Clark Denton, Robyn Carr Denton. BA in History, Emory U., 1965; postgrad., U. Ga., 1967; MA in Theology, Fuller Theol. Sem., 1989, postgrad., 1990—. Cert. tchr., Calif. Tchr. adult edn. La Jolla (Calif.) Presbyn. Ch., 1978—; tchr. Bible Village Ch., Rancho Santa Fe, Calif., 1988—; speaker in field; elder La Jolla Presbyn. Ch., 1978—, mem. long range planning and adult edn. coms., 1978—, chmn. Circle, 1976-77. Member Community Concert Bd., Rancho Santa Fe, 1981; v.p. Rancho Santa Fe Elem. Sch. PTO, 1982, 83; advisor Nat. Charity League, San Diego, 1987—. Mem. DAR, Alpha Alpha Tau, Omicron Alpha Upsilon. Home: PO Box 1748 Rancho Santa Fe CA 92067

DENTON, THOMAS MILLARD, minister; b. Clinton, N.C., May 26, 1947; s. Wayland Millard and Marion Ruth (Riverbark) D.; m. Connie Bass, June 6, 1971; children: Josh, Whitney. AA, Mars Hill Coll., 1967; BA, Wake Forest U., 1969; MDiv, Southeastern Bapt. Sem., Wake Forest, N.C., 1972, D Ministry, 1974. Ordained to ministry So. Bapt. Conf., 1973. Youth dir. 1st Bapt. Ch., Fayetteville, N.C., 1970-71; assoc. pastor Lakeside Bapt. Ch., Rocky Mount, N.C., 1971-74; pastor 1st Bapt. Ch., Hillsborough, N.C., 1974-87, New Bern, N.C., 1987—; mem. exec. com. Bapt. State Conv., N.Y., Cary, 1987-89, mem. gen. bd., 1990—; pres. Coun. on Christian Life, Cary, 1987-89; co-founder Orange Congregations in Missions, 1981; trustee Religious Community Svcs., 1991. Pres. United Way Orange County, Hillsborough, 1979; chmn. bd. N.C. Dept. Social Svcs., Hillsborough, 1986, vice chmn. bd., New Bern, 1991; trustee Chowan Coll., Murphreesboro, N.C., 1990; founder, pres. Samaritan Relief Fund, 1977. Recipient Gov.'s Vol. award State of N.C., 1987. Mem. Civitans (chaplain New Bern), Exch. Club (Hillsborough). Home: PO Box 1463 New Bern NC 28563 *As we openly share our sense of weakness and vulnerability with others we find new friends and strength to face our fears courageously.*

DENYER, DAVID ALEXANDER, minister, religion educator; b. Colville, Wash., Oct. 27, 1933; s. Charles Frederick and Hannah Lois (Blackwood) D.; m. Dorothy Jeanne SWeem, Aug. 31, 1957; children: Debra Ann Denyer Hammond, Donna Lee Denyer Opperman, Douglas Jay. BA, Simpson Coll., 1955, Wheaton Coll., 1958; MDiv, Golden Gate Sem., 1968; PhD, So. Bapt. Sem., Louisville, 1976. Ordained to ministry Christian and Missionary Alliance, 1959. Pastor Alliance Ch., Wenatchee, Wash., 1958-62; dean students, prof. Simpson Coll., Redding, Calif., 1962-72; prof. Old Testament Columbia (S.C.) Bible Coll., 1976-77; prof. Old Testament and Archaeology Alliance Theol. Sem., Nyack, N.Y., 1977—; mem. ordaining coun. Met. Dist. Christian and Missionary Alliance, North Plainfield, N.Y., 1981-90; mem. bd. mgrs. Christian and Missionary Alliance, Colorado Springs, Colo., 1990—. Named Citizen of the Day, City of San Franciso, 1971. Mem. Soc. Bibl. Lit., Am. Schs. Oriental Rsch., Near East Archaeology Soc., Bibl. Archaeology Soc., Israel Exploration Soc., Delta Epsilon Chi. Republican. Home: 25 Short Hill Rd New City NY 10956 Office: Alliance Theol Sem Nyack NY 10960

DE PAUW, GOMMAR ALBERT, priest, educator; b. Stekene, Belgium, Oct. 11, 1918; came to U.S., 1949, naturalized, 1955; s. Desiré and Anna (Van Overloop) De P. Diplomate Classical Humanities, Coll. St. Nicholas, Belgium, 1936; JCB, U. Louvain, 1943, JCL, 1945; Juris Canonici Dr., Catholic U. Am., 1953. Ordained priest Roman Cath. Ch., 1942. Parish priest, chaplain Cath. Social Action, Ghent, Belgium, 1945-49, N.Y.C., 1949-52; successively prof. moral and fundamental dogmatic theology and canon law sem. div., assoc. prof. philosophy coll. div. Mt. St. Mary's Coll., Emmitsburg, Md., 1952-65, dean studies maj. sem. div., 1954-64, mem. council adminstrn., 1957-65; Theol. adviser II Vatican Ecumenical Council, 1962-65; founder-pres. Cath. Traditionalist Movement, Inc., 1964—. Author: The Educational Rights of the Church, 1953, The Rebel Priest, 1965, The Traditional Roman Catholic Mass, 1977, Bishops on War and Peace, 1983, The Traditional Requiem Mass, 1989, The Challenge of Peace Through Strength, 1989; co-author: New Catholic Ency.; Dictionary of the Bible, Ephemerides Theologicae Lovanienses; editor: Sounds of Truth and Tradition, Quote... Unquote; producer Latin radio mass, various religious phonograph records, audio and video cassettes. With Belgian Army inf. M.C., 1939-45, World War II Resistance and Free Polish Forces. Decorated Honor Cross (Free Polish Forces); recipient Achievement Citation, U.S. Army. Mem. AAUP, Internat. Platform Assn., Cath. Theol. Soc., Am. Canon Law Soc. Am., Am. Security Coun., Am. Cath. Philos. Assn., Nat. Cath. Ednl. Assn., Univ. Prof. for Acad. Order. Home: Cath Traditionalist Movement 210 Maple Ave Westbury NY 11590 Office: Pan Am Bldg Ste 303E New York NY 10166 *Especially since my founding of the Catholic Traditionalist Movement in 1964 has made me somewhat "controversial," I draw great inspiration from two sayings adorning the walls of my office. One, attributed to Davy Crockett: "Be sure you're right. Then go ahead!" The other, quoting Saint Athanasius: "If the whole world goes against the truth, then Athanasius must go against the whole world!" And when living by those axioms becomes heavy at times, I just brace myself and coin another one of my own: "It's better to be right alone, than to be wrong with a thousand others!".*

DEPEW, THOMAS ANDREW, mission administrator; b. Pittsfield, Mass., Nov. 30, 1927; s. George Edward and Rose Delma (Major) D. BA, U. N.Y., 1950; M in Religious Edn., Maryknoll, N.Y., 1955. Ordained priest Roman Cath. Ch., 1955. Pastor, educator Maryknoll Mission, Huehuetenango, Guatemala, 1955-60; diocesan consultor Prelature Huehuetenango, Guatemala, 1960-65, dir. edn., 1958-65; asst. superior Maryknoll Mission, Cen. Am., 1960-65; new missionary Maryknoll Mission, Caracas, Venezuela, 1965-66, asst. superior, 1966-74, superior, 1974-77, coordinator, adminstr., 1977-85, adminstr. formation ctr., 1985—; pres. Ecumenical Assn., Caracas, 1970-72. Avocations: planning and managing social workshops. Home: Apartado Postal 30319, Correos de Pro-Patria, 1030-A Caracas Venezuela Office: Catia Formation Ctr, Casa # 4 Vereda # 2 Urdaneta, 1030 Caracas Venezuela

DEPRATER, WILLIAM ARTHUR, III, minister; b. Fayetteville, N.C., Apr. 12, 1947; s. William Arthur Jr. and Mary Blue (Monroe) DeP.; m. Margaret Lee Rogers, Nov. 25, 1972; children: Elizabeth Monroe, Mary Margaret, Katherine Lee. BA, Meth. Coll., 1969; cert. in clin. pastoral edn., N.C. Bapt. Hosp., Winston-Salem, 1971; MDiv, Erskine Sem., 1973; D Ministry, McCormick Sem., 1977; cert. in clin. pastoral education residency, Wm. S. Hall Psychiat. Inst., Columbia, S.C., 1978. Ordained to ministry Presbyn. Ch., 1973. Pastor Blenheim, Dunbar & Reedy Creek Presbyn. Chs., Clio, S.C., 1972-75, Barnwell (S.C.) Presbyn. Ch., 1975-77; dir. chaplaincy Pee Dee Mental Retardation Ctr., Florence, S.C., 1978-83; pastor Sunnyside Presbyn. Ch., Fayetteville, N.C., 1983—; vice moderator Synod Bicentennial Com., Richmond, Va., 1990—; moderator Presbytery Stewardship Mission Com., Fayetteville, 1988—; mem. Presbytery Camp Com., Fayetteville, 1984-88, Presbytery Coordinating Coun., Fayetteville, 1989—; pres. Fayetteville Ministerial Assn., 1986-87, v.p., 1985-86. Recipient E.T. George Preaching award Union Theol. Sem., 1970. Mem. Kiwanis (Fayetteville). Democrat. *Life's excitement is the pregnant possibilities it offers for creative personal growth and contribution to humanity.*

DERBY, WILLIAM, ecumenical agency administrator. Head Montreal Ecumenical Assn., Que., Can. Office: Montreal Ecumenical Assn, 158 Sta B, Montreal, PQ Canada H3H 3J5*

DEREA, PHILIP, priest, religious organization executive; b. Roseto, Pa., Mar. 26, 1942; s. Philip and Irene Elizabeth (Bajan) DeR. BS in Philosophy, Sacred Heart Sem., Shelby, Ohio, 1965, MDiv, 1969. Ordained priest Roman Cath. Ch., 1968. Devel. dir. Missionaries of Sacred Heart, Aurora, Ill., 1969-76; dir. vocation and communications, Missionaries of Sacred Heart, Center Valley, Pa., 1976-79; assoc. pastor Our Lady of Guadalupe, Cali, Colombia, 1979-80; chaplain Sacred Heart Hosp., Allentown, Pa., 1980-81; nat. dir. Missionary Vehicle Assn., Washington, 1981—; canon Cathedral of La Paz, Bolivia, 1985—; mem. Nat. Cath. Devel. Conv., Hempstead, N.Y., 1969—. Mem. Wings of Hope, KC (3 and 4 degree). Democrat. Address: 1241 Monroe St NE Washington DC 20017

DERESIENSKI, STANLEY MITCHELL, priest; b. Hartford, Conn., Sept. 28, 1950; s. Stanley John and Sophie Jane (Zenesky) D. BA in Sociology, St. Michael's Coll., 1974, MS in Counseling, 1975; MDiv in Theology, U. St. Michael's Coll., 1978. Dir. vol. programs St. Michael's Coll., Winooski, Vt., 1975; dir. black ministry rsch. Soc. St. Edmund, Selma, Ala., 1980-81; instr. Xavier U., New Orleans, 1982-84, dir. housing edn., 1981-84; superior, dir. Edmundite Apostolate Ctr., Mystic, Conn., 1989—; trustee St. Michael's Coll., Winooski, 1986—, Bethsaida Community, Norwich, Conn., 1988-90; del. ecumenical coun. Ecumenical Coun. of New Orleans, 1983, Ecumenical Coun. Vt., 1979. Author: Black Perspectives, 1981. Del. New Eng. Conf. Bishops, Holyoke, Mass., 1979. REcipient Pres.'s award St. Michael's Coll., 1989. Mem. Spiritual Dirs. Internat., Assn. Humanistic Psychology, Retreats Internat., Internat. Assn. Conf. Ctrs. Adminstrs., KC. Home: Enders Island Mystic CT 06355 Office: Edmundite Apostolate Ctr Enders Island Mystic CT 06355

DERFELT, JERRY LEROY, music minister, funeral director; b. Joplin, Mo., Aug. 16, 1953; s. Roy L. and H. Virginia (Tyler) D.; m. Lucy Carver, Apr. 16, 1971 (div. July 1981); children: J. Matt, Angel D.; m. Peggy S. Daniels, Nov. 28, 1981; children: Jenny Lynn, Emily Jo, Stephen T. Student, Mo. So. State Coll., 1971-72, Kans. State Coll. Pittsburg, 1972-73; AS, Cen. State U., Edmond, Okla., 1974. Lic. funeral dir. Kans., Mo., Okla. Asst. min. music First Bapt. Ch., Galena, Kans., 1974-83, min. music, 1983—; asst. sec./treas. Bapt. Missionary Assn. of Kans., 1984-88; asst. editor Bapt. Herald, 1984-88, editor, 1988—; sec., treas. Bapt. Missionary Assn. of Kans. and West Mo., 1988—; Sunday sch. tchr. First Bapt. Ch., Galena, 1976-77, 80, trustee, 1983-89; singer Gospelaires Quartet, Galena, 1973-88; pres. Derfelt Funeral Homes Inc., Galena, 1982—. Fireman Galena Vol. Fire Dept., 1972—; pres. Galena Mining and Hist. Mus. Assn., 1983-88, treas., 1988—; com. mem. Vocat. Tng. Commn. USD #499, Galena, 1978-86. Named Jaycee of Quar. Galena Jaycees, 1980. Mem. Nat. Funeral Dirs. Assn., Kans. Funeral Dirs. Assn. (dist. pres. 1984), Lions, C. of C. Democrat. Home: 1119 Short St Galena KS 66739 Office: Derfelt Funeral Home PO Box 367 Galena KS 66739

DE ROO, REMI JOSEPH, bishop; b. Swan Lake, Man., Can., Feb. 24, 1924; s. Raymond and Josephine (De Pape) De R. Student, St. Boniface (Man.) Coll.; STD, Angelicum U., Rome, Italy.; LLD (hon.), U. Antigonish, N.S., 1983, U. Brandon, Man., 1987, U. Victoria, B.C., Can., 1991; DD (hon.), U. Winnipeg, Man., 1990; LLD (hon.), U. Victoria, B.C., 1991. Ordained priest Roman Catholic Ch., 1950; curate Holy Cross Parish, St. Boniface, 1952-53; sec. to archbishop of St. Boniface, 1954-56; diocesan dir. Cath. action Archdiocese St. Boniface, 1953-54; exec. sec. Man. Cath. Con., 1958; pastor Holy Cross Parish, 1960-62; bishop of Victoria, B.C., Can., 1962—; Canadian Episcopal rep. Internat. Secretariat Apostleship See, 1964-78, Pontifical Commn. Culture, 1984-87; chairperson Human Rights Commn. B.C., 1974-77; mem. social affairs commn. Can. Conf. Cath. Bishops, 1973-87; pres. Western Cath. Conf. Bishops, 1984-88; mem. theology commn. Can. Conf. Cath. Bishops, 1987—. Hon. fellow Ryerson Poly. Inst., 1987. Address: 4044 Nelthorpe St # 1, Victoria, BC Canada V8X 2A1

DEROULHAC, JOSEPH HAROLD, JR., minister; b. Albuquerque, Jan. 5, 1953; s. Joseph Harold and Bettie Leah (Wilson) DeR.; m. Lucinda Paglinawan Custodio, Mar. 29, 1980; 1 child, Christina. BA in Sociology, U. Ark., 1975; MDiv., So. Bapt. Theol. Sem., 1979; PhD in Religion and Social Ethics, U. So. Calif., L.A., 1983. Ordained to ministry Am. Bapt. Ch., 1983. Field staff Young Life in Ark., Little Rock, 1975-76; assoc. pastor Fourth Ave. Bapt. Ch., Louisville, 1978-79; coord. young adult ministries First Bapt. Ch., L.A., 1982-83; pastor North Hills Community Bapt. Ch., Pitts., 1984-89; sr. min. The First Bapt. Ch. of Redlands, Calif., 1989—; pres. Am. Bapt. Mins. Coun. of Pitts., 1986-88; bd. dirs. Am. Bapt. Theol. Ctr., Pasadena, Calif.; trustee Am. Bapt. Homes of the West, Oakland, Calif., 1990—. Bd. dirs. Pitts. Bapt. Assn., 1986-88, North Hills Youth Ministry, Pitts., 1985-88; mem. bio-ethics com. Redlands (Calif.) Community Hosp., 1990—; bd. mgrs. Plymouth Village, Redlands, 1990—; environ. scan com. United Way, Redlands, 1991. Oakley fellow Univ. So. Calif., L.A., 1979-82; recipient Eagle award Boy Scouts Am., North Little Rock, 1968. Mem. Mins. Coun. of the Am. Bapt. Chs. USA (senator 1986-88, nat. sec.-treas. 1990—), Bapt. Peace Fellowship N.Am., Phi Kappa Phi. Office: The First Bapt Ch Redlands 51 W Olive Ave Redlands CA 92373

DERR, AMANDUS JOHN, clergyman; b. Wilkes-Barre, Pa., Apr. 11, 1949; s. Amandus Ambrose and Elizabeth Sue (Balla) D.; m. Bonnie Laura Genser, June 29, 1975 (dec. Aug. 1981); 1 child, Amandus John; m. Carole Evelyn Faller, Nov. 28, 1982; 1 child, Jonathan Peter. AA in Theology, Concordia Coll., Bronxville, N.Y., 1969; BA in Theology, Concordia Sr. Coll., Ft. Wayne, Ind., 1971; MDiv, Christ Sem., St. Louis; 1975. Ordained to ministry Luth. Ch., 1975. Pastor Grace Luth. Ch., Teaneck, N.J., 1975—; chmn. transition team N.J. Synod, Evang. Luth. Ch. Am., 1986-87, mem. synod coun., 1988—. Rev. editor Luth. Ptnrs. mag., 1986—; contbr. articles, sermons and book revs. to religious pubs. Sec.-treas. Teaneck Clergy Coun., 1976—; pres. Teaneck Community Chest, 1980—; co-chmn. One Roof Inc., Carlstadt, N.J., 1989—. Mem. Teaneck City Club (pres. 1978), Rotary (pres. Teaneck 1988, Walter D. Head award 1988). Democrat. Avocations: fishing, swimming, reading, coaching little league. Home: 362 Madison Ct New Milford NJ 07646 Office: Grace Luth Ch and Sch 1200 River Rd Teaneck NJ 07666

DERR, TERESA MARIE, chaplain; b. Jamaica, N.Y., Nov. 26, 1953; d. Emmanuel Henry and Catherine Elizabeth (Junker) D. BA magna cum laude, Georgian Ct. Coll., Lakewood, N.J., 1975; MDiv, Princeton Theol. Sem., 1980; therapist in tngs. Dynamics of Psycho., Washington Sch. Psychiatry, 1989-91; postgrad., Nat. Cath. Sch. Social Svc., Cath. U. Am., 1991—. Tchr. religion Notre Dame High Sch., Lawrenceville, N.J., 1975-76; tchr. religion, campus minister Stuart Country Day Sch., Princeton, N.J., 1977-78; chaplain AMI Presbyn.-St. Luke's Med. Ctr., Denver, 1978, 84-85, supr., 1984-85; chaplain Bethesda PsycHealth System, Denver, 1978-79; alcohol counselor Rescue Mission Trenton (N.J.), Inc., 1979-80; chaplain St. Peter's Med. ctr., New Brunswick, N.J., 1980-83, Children's Hosp., Denver, 1983-84; assoc. dir. pastoral care Luth. Med. Ctr., Bklyn., 1985-88; assoc. dir. pastoral care, dir. clin. pastoral edn. Washington Hosp. Ctr., 1988-90; dep. dir. devel. Women in Mil. Svc. for Am., Meml. Found., Washington, 1990-91; therapist Eugene Meyer II Treatment Ctr., 1990-91; chaplain, bereavement coord. Children's Hospice Svcs., Washington, 1991—; lay minister St. Francis Ch., Brant Beach, N.J., summer 1977; dir. children's summer prog. St. Michael's Episcopal Ch., Trenton, summer 1979; workshop leader Ctr. for Humanizing Healthcare, Washington, 1988-90; mem. employee and physician devel. com. Ctr. for Humanizing Healthcare. Choral singer various groups incl. Oratorio Soc. of N.Y. Mem. Bread for World; co-leader, organizer support group for people with cancer, Bklyn., 1985-86; rep. Trenton Diocesan Pastoral Coun., 1976. Mem. AAUW, Nat. Assn. Social Workers, Nat. Hospice Orgn., Assn. Clin. Pastoral Edn. (assoc. supr., com. mem. 1986—), Am. Orthopsychiat. Assn., Pastoral Care Network for Social Responsibility, Washington Psychologists for Study of Psychoanalysis, Women's Ordination Conf., Cath. Alumni Club, Sigma Phi Sigma, Phi Delta Phi. Democrat. Episcopalian. Avocations: exercise and sports, reading, art, music, dance. Office: Children's Hospice Svcs 111 Michigan Ave NW Washington DC 20010-2975 *Besides being curious teachers, children are prophets, for they point us beyond what we can see and remind us what is most important and precious in our lives—relationships. With love and concern for all peoples we are then called forth to act for the good of the larger community.*

DERR, THOMAS SIEGER, religion educator; b. Boston, June 18, 1931; s. Thomas Sieger and Mary Ferguson (Sebring) D.; m. Virginia Anne Bush, June 9, 1956, (div. 1977); children—Peter Bulkeley, Laura Seely, Mary Williams; m. Janet Hackman, Apr. 12, 1980 (div. 1985); 1 child, Philip Henry; m. Linda Vincent, Feb. 14, 1986. AB, Harvard U., 1953; MDiv, Union Theol. Sem., 1956; PhD, Columbia U., 1972. Ordained to ministry, United Ch. of Christ, 1956. Researcher World Council Chs., Geneva, 1961-62; asst. chaplain Stanford U., Calif., 1956-59; asst. chaplain Smith Coll., Northampton, Mass., 1963-65, asst. prof. religion, 1965-71, assoc. prof., 1972-77, prof., 1977—; cons. World Coun. Chs., 1965—; dir. Inst. on Religion in Pub. Life, N.Y.C.; mem. complemental faculty Rush Med. Coll., Chgo., 1979-84. Author: The Political Thought of the Ecumenical Movement, 1972; Ecology and Human Need, 1975; Church State, and Politics, 1981; Barriers to Ecumenism: The Holy See and the World Council of Churches on Social Questions, 1983; Believable Futures of American Protesantism, 1988; contbr. articles to profl. jours. Danforth Found. grantee, 1959-60, 65-66; Inst. for Advanced Study of Religion, U. Chgo. fellow, 1981. Soc. for Christian Ethics. Home: 60 Harrison Ave Northampton MA 01060 Office: Smith Coll Dept Religion Northampton MA 01063

DERRICK, IRVIN HENDRIX, lay worker, government contracting consultant; b. Ballentine, S.C., Nov. 18, 1921; s. Ollie Jessie and Anna Viola (Lowman) D.; m. Betty Ruby Koon, July 10, 1948; children: Karen Susan, Robin Anna, David Michael, Stephen Hendrix. BS in Engring. Mgmt., Air Force Inst. Tech., 1953; BS in Indsl. Engring., U. Mich., 1959, MS in Indsl. Engring., 1960; BA in Bibl. Studies, Southwestern Coll., Oklahoma City, 1971. Registered profl. engr., Fla.; cert. profl. contracts mgr. Enlisted USAF, 1942, advanced through grades to lt. col., 1962; tchr. adult Sunday sch. Base Chapel, Wright Patterson AFB, Ohio, 1963-65; supt. Sunday sch. Base Chapel, Elmendorf AFB, Alaska, 1966-68; chmn. Protestant Fund Coun., Elmendorf AFB, Alaska, 1966-68; asst. adult Sunday sch. tchr. Christian Tabernacle, Dayton, Ohio, 1969-77; pres. Govt. Contracting Cons. Inc., Melbourne, FL, 1988—. Author: Contract Asministration, 1970, Government Property Administration, 1972, Government Procurement for Labor Department, 1973. Chmn. bd. Dayton Christian Schs., 1969-71. Mem. Nat. Contract Mgmt. Assn. Home and Office: 2255 Pine Meadow Ave Melbourne FL 32904 *Experience has verified that "one cannot outgive God." As we contribute to His work in advancing the Christian message, we have found that He always meets all our needs.*

DERRICK, ROBERT WAYNE, pastor; b. Texas City, Tex., Sept. 13, 1947; s. Xenophen Lucian and Flomar (Cushing) D.; m. Valla Ellen Brewington, Sept. 3, 1967; children: Rebekah Elizabeth, Stephen Daniel. BA, U. Tex., 1969; MDiv, Talbot Theol. Sem., La Mirada, Calif., 1981. Ordained minister in Bapt. Ch., 1977. Assoc. pastor Mid-Cities Bapt. Ch., Westminster, Calif., 1977-81; sr. pastor Orangewood Ave. Bapt. Ch., Garden Grove, Calif., 1981—; adj. faculty, instr. Greek Talbot Theol. Sem., La Mirada, 1982-87, Golden Gate Bapt. Theol. Sem., Garden Grove, Calif., 1986-88. Mem. Phi Beta Kappa. Home: 6402 Freeborn Dr Huntington Beach CA 92647 Office: Orangewood Ave Bapt Ch 8421 Orangewood Ave Garden Grove CA 92641

DERSHOWITZ, A. MENASHE, retired rabbi; b. Bklyn., Oct. 31, 1910; s. Louis Alexander and Ida (Maultasch) D.; m. Anne Deresiewicz, June 11, 1939; children: Alan N., Isaac M., Zachary B. (dec.). BS, CCNY, 1933, MS in Edn., 1934. Ordained rabbi, 1937. Rabbi Talmud Torah, North Bergen, N.J., 1937-38, Congregation Adath Jeshuran, Newport News, 1940-42, Congregation Sons of Abraham, LaCrosse, Wis., 1942-44; chaplain Middletown (N.Y.) Psychiat. Ctr., 1954-75, Lakewood, N.J., 1975-91; ret.; pvt. pastoral counselor, Lakewood. Democrat. Home: 518 Forest Ave Lakewood NJ 08701

DESCOTEAUX, CAROL J., academic administrator; b. Nashua, N.H., Apr. 5, 1948; d. Henry Louis and Therese (Arel) D. BA, Notre Dame Coll., 1970; MEd, Boston Coll., 1975; MA, U. Notre Dame, 1984, PhD, 1985. Jr. high sch. instr., dir. religious studies St. Joseph's Sch., North Grosvenordale, Conn., 1970-73; jr. high sch. tchr., dir. religious edn. Notre Dame Sch., North Adams, Mass., 1973-77; jr. high sch. instr. Sacred Heart Sch., Groton, Conn., 1977-78; chairperson religious studies discipline U. Notre Dame, Grad. Theol. Union, Notre Dame, Ind., 1982-83, 84-85; pres. Notre Dame Coll., Manchester, N.H., 1985—; trustee King's Coll., Wilkes-Barre, Pa., 1987—; pres. Fedn. of Holy Cross Colls., 1985—; mem. adv. bd. Manchester Christian Life Ctr., 1978-80; treas. N.H. Coll. and Univ. Council, Manchester, 1985—; trustee N.H. Higher Edn. Assistance Found., 1986—. Mem. Manchester United Way campaign, 1985—; bd. incorporators, mem. ethics com., instl. research com. Cath. Med. Ctr., Manchester, 1986—. Named Disting. Woman Leader of Yr., So. N.H. region YWCA, 1985. Mem. Am. Acad. Religion, Coll. Theology Soc. Am., N.H. Women's Forum, Soc. Christian Ethics, AAUW, N.H. Women in Higher Edn. Democrat. Roman Catholic. Avocations: art, music, theater, fishing, bowling. Office: Notre Dame Coll Office of the Pres 2321 Elm St Manchester NH 03104

DE SHAY, WILLIAM LESLIE, minister; b. Columbus, Ohio, Sept. 23, 1930; s. William Henry Dewey and Aleatha Delilah (Brantley) De S.; m. Corinne Fauntleroy, Oct. 25, 1959; children: William Leslie, Mark Antoine. BA in Theology, Oakwood Coll., 1952; MS in Counseling Psychology, A&M U., Normal, Ala., 1971; PhD in Counseling, Ohio State U., 1975. Ordained to ministry Seventh-day Adventist Ch., 1959. Pastor Allegheny Conf. Seventh-day Adventists, 1954-64, Dupont Park Ch., Washington, 1965-69; chaplain, counselor adminstr. Oakwood Coll., Huntsville, Ala., 1969-72; adminstr., dir. black affairs, mem. exec. com. So. Calif. conf. Seventh-day Adventists, Glendale, 1976-87; pastor Altadena (Calif.) Seventh-day Adventists Ch., 1987-88, Del. Ave. Seventh-day Adventists Ch., Santa Monica, Calif., 1989—; trustee So. Calif. Conf. Assn., Glendale, 1976-91; mem. minority groups com. Pacific Union Conf., 1976—; del. youth congress Columbia Union Conf., Paris, 1951. Named Hon. Citizen State of Tenn., 1977; recipient Century Soul award South Cen. Conf., 1972. Democrat. Home: 18951 Milmore Ave Carson CA 90746 Office: So Calif Conf Seventh-day Adventists 1535 E Chevy Chase Dr Glendale CA 91206 *There is no limit to the good one can be used to accomplish if he does not care who gets the credit.*

DE SIMONE, LOUIS A., bishop; b. Phila., Feb. 21, 1922. Student, Villanova U., St. Charles Borromeo Sem., Pa. Ordained priest Roman Catholic Ch., 1952; ordained titular bishop of Cillium and aux. bishop of Phila., 1981—. Office: Chancery Office 222 N 17th St Philadelphia PA 19103

DESKUR, ANDRZEJ MARIA CARDINAL, cardinal; b. Sancygniow, Kielce, Poland, Feb. 29, 1924. Ordained priest Roman Cath. Ch., 1950. Consecrated bishop Titular See of Gnenae, 1974, archbishop, 1980; created cardinal, 1985; pres.-emeritus Pontifical Commn. for Social Communications; pres. Pontifical Acad. Immaculate Conception. Office: 00120 Vatican City Vatican City

DESMARAIS, NORMAN PAUL, librarian, editor; b. Lowell, Mass., Dec. 15, 1946; s. Ernest M. and Cecile Helen (Bouvier) D.; m. Barbara Rose Hughes, June 18, 1977; children: Jeanne, Denise. PhB, Gregorian U., Rome, 1969, STB, 1972; MLS, Simmons Coll., 1977; MBA, Providence Coll., 1990. Acquisitions libr. Providence Coll., R.I., 1984—; libr. St. Mary's Sem. and U., Balt., 1977-82; head order and cataloging Cath. U. Am., Washington, 1982-84. Author: Automated Acquisitions Systems, 1988, Librarian's CD-ROM Handbook, 1989, CD-ROMs in Print, 1990—; editor in chief CD-ROM Libr. jour., 1989—. Mem. Am. Theol. Libr. Assn. (head readers svcs. com. 1979-82), R.I. Libr. Assn. (feature editor 1984—), Spl. Librs. Assn. Roman Catholic. Office: Providence Coll Phillips Meml Libr Providence RI 02918

DESMET, KATHLEEN MARIE (KATE DESMET), journalist; b. Detroit; d. Andrew and Helen D. B.A. in Journalism, Wayne State U., 1980. Staff writer Marine and Recreation News, 1973-75; mng. editor The South End, 1975-77; feature writer The Advisor, Utica, Mich., 1977-78; summer intern The Boston Globe, 1979; religion writer The Detroit News, 1978—; sec. The Newspaper Guild, Local 22, 1980—. Recipient Wilbur award Religious Pub. Relations Assn., 1986. Mem. Religion Newswriters Assn. (one of 10 finalists Templeton Religion Writer of Yr. award, 1986). Office: Detroit News 615 Lafayette Blvd Detroit MI 48231

DE SOUSA RIBAS, ABILIO RODAS, bishop. Bishop Roman Cath. Ch., Sao Tome and Principe. Office: Centro Diocesano, CP 104, Sao Tome Sao Tome And Principe*

DE SOUZA, ERNEST HENRIQUES, religious organization administrator, photographer, accountant; b. Kingston, Jamaica, Sept. 28, 1933; s. Ernest de Souza and Nora Rebecca (Henriques) de S.; m. Judy Mary Bate, July 11, 1971; children: David Richard, Robert Charles. Grad., Wolmer's Boys Sch., Kingston. Lay reader, tchr. religion sch. United Congregation of Israelites, Kingston, from 1946, now hon. lay leader, dir. of synagogue, 1960-75, v.p., 1963-66, pres., 1966-67, treas., 1969-75, sec., 1975—; acting spiritual leader Jewish Community, 1978—; profl. photograher, 1954—. Author: Prayers, Meditations and Order of Services for the Synagogue, 1984, Pictorial History of the Jewish Community in Jamaica, 1986. Mem. Island coun. and exec. com. Girl Guides Assn., 1961—, hon. treas. and acct., 1967—; mem. Island coun., exec. com. Scout Assn. of Jamaica, 1967—, hon. v.p., 1980—; mem. bd. govs. Hillel Acad., 1972—, trustee, 1978-82, sec., 1984—, vice chmn., 1989—. Recipient Gevaert Gold medal and Blue Ribbon award Scenic Photographic Competition for Jamaica's Tercentenary's Yr., 1955; Thanks Badge award Girl Guides Assn., 1962, Torch award, 1967, Silver Bee award, 1975, 75th Anniversary plague and citation, 1990; certs. of merit Jaycees of Jamaica, 1963, 65, 67; Silver Salver for 25-yr. svc. United Congregation of Israelites, 1971, for 35-yr. svc., 1981, for 40-yr. svc., 1986; Pro Mundi, Beneficio medal Brazilian Acad. Humanities, 1975, medal of appreciation Prime Min. of Jamaica, 1983, Layman's award Kiwanis, 1983, 86, Silver Pine Apple award Scout Assn. of Jamaica, 1986, Silver Tray award Jewish Community, 1986. Mem. Jr. Chamber Internat. (life senator), Profl. Photographers Assn. (founder), Jamaica Camera Club (founder), B'nai Brith (founder Jewish svc. club, Ben Brit of Yr. award 1969, award of merit 1972, treas.' plague 1980), Masons (master Sussex Mark club 1976, comdr. Royal Ark Marines of Jamaica club 1980, founder, 1st master Friendly Mark club 1981, Friendly Royal Ark Marines 1981, hon. mem. Sussex club, hon. Bible bearer of grand lodge of Scotland, mark master lodge of Engl, others). Avocations: collecting coins, stamps and souvenirs, preserving historical records. Home: 2A King's Dr, Kingston 6, Jamaica Office: United Congregation Israelites, 92 Duke St, Kingston Jamaica

DE SOUZA, NEVILLE WARDSWORTH, bishop. Bishop of Jamaica The Anglican Communion, Kingston. Office: Ch House, 2 Caledonian Ave, Kingston 2, Jamaica*

DES ROSIERS, CAMILLE, head of religious order. Superior Father Roman Cath. Ch., Funafuti, Tuvalu. Office: Roman Cath Ch, Cath Mission, Funafuti Tuvalu*

DESSLER, NAHUM W., rabbi; b. Kelme, Lithuania, Feb. 27, 1921; came to U.S., 1940; s. Eliase and Bluma (Ziv) D.; married, June 5, 1945; children: Reuven, Sarika, Peshy, Elloyhu, Malka, Simcha Z. Telshe Coll., Lithuania, 1936-40. Ordained rabbi Jewish Ch. Ednl. dir. Hebrew Acad. Cleve., 1944-87, dean, 1987—. Home: 3664 Shannon Rd Cleveland Heights OH 44118 Office: 1860 S Taylor Rd Cleveland Heights OH 44118

DETAMORE, GEORGE EDWARD, lay worker; b. Warren, Ind., Feb. 25, 1924; s. Milford and Hazel (James) D.; married, June 15, 1944; children: William, George Jr., Patsy. Student, God's Bible Sch., 1945, Marion Coll., 1950. Missionary Haiti, 1950; Sunday shc. tchr. Mt. Etna Wesleyan Ch., Warren, 1950-75, treas., 1975—, supt., 1986—; missionary India, 1986; nurse VA Hosp., Marion, 1954-78. Scout master Boy Scouts Am., Mt. Etna, 1950. Office: Mt Etna Wesleyan 10478 S 500th W Warren IN 46792-9715

DETERDING, CURTIS LYNN, minister; b. Kansas City, Mo., Aug. 31, 1958; s. Darold Willard and Willa Jean (Morales) D.; m. Jo Ann Katherine Hermann, Apr. 3, 1982; children: Eva Marie, Katherine Elizabeth, Rebecca Lynn. BA in Elem. Edn., Concordia Coll., St. Paul, 1981; MDiv, Concordia Sem., St. Louis, 1987. Ordained to ministry Luth. Ch.-Mo. Synod. Athletic dir., tchr. 9th grade Holy Cross Luth. Sch., North Miami, Fla., 1981-83; pastor youth and edn. Bethel Luth. Ch., Claremont, N.C., 1987-91; asst. pastor Prince of Peace Luth. Ch., Spring Lake Park, Minn., 1991—; coord. Project Samuel Concordia Coll., St. Paul, 1991—; mem. adv. bd. recruitment and student aid com. Minn. South dist. Luth. Ch.-Mo. Synod, 1991; membership rep. Luth. Layman's League, Salina, Kans., 1975-76; youth del. Internat. Luth. Layman's League, Kans., 1976-79; sec. cir. 16 Luth. Ch.-Mo. Synod, Clarmont, 1987-91, cir. youth advisor, Catawba Valley, 1988-91, adv. del., Wichita, Kans., 1989, project coord. Servant Event, Linnville, 1991; organizer, chmn. Catawba Valley Servant Events, 1988-90; worship coord. Southeastern Dist. Youth Gathering, Raleigh, N.C., 1990. Asst. coach Lenior-Rhyne Coll., Hickory, N.C., 1988-89; head coach Catawba Valley Luth. High Sch., Hickory, 1990; adj. chaplain Catawba Meml. Hosp., Hickory, 1988-91; chmn. Crisis Pregnancy Ctr., Hickory, 1988-90. St. John's Coll. scholar, 1976-77, Aid Assn. for Luths. scholar, 1976-82, 83-87. Home: 1467 Blair Ave Saint Paul MN 55104 Office: Concordia Coll 275 N Syndicate St Saint Paul MN 55104

DETHOMASIS, BROTHER LOUIS, college president; b. Bklyn., Oct. 6, 1940; s. Costantino and Anna (Maggio) DeT. B.S. in Fgn. Service,, Georgetown U., 1963; Ph.D., Union Grad. Sch., 1982. Tchr. LaSalle Acad., Providence, 1969-71; assoc. headmaster LaSalle Mil. Acad., Oakdale, N.Y., 1971-73, pres., 1976-84; v.p. for fin. The Christian Brothers, Narragansett, R.I., 1973-76; pres. St. Mary's Coll., Winona, Minn., 1984—. Author: The Finance of Education, 1978; Investing With Options, 1981; Social Justice, 1982; My Father's Business, 1984. Recipient Pres.'s medal for Christian edn., St. John's Coll. High Sch., 1985, Christian Edn. award Franz W. Sichel Found., 1974. Roman Catholic. Home and Office: Box 30 Winona MN 55987

DETRICK, DONALD HOWARD, minister; b. Newberg, Oreg., Dec. 13, 1954; s. Howard Raymond and Madeline F. (Roth) D.; m. Jodi Lanette

Dunlap, June 8, 1974; children: Kristina Lynne, Mark Andrew, Jana Kathleen. Student, Eugene Bible Coll., 1974-77; BA, Bapt. Christian Coll., 1985; MA in Counseling, Luther Rice Sem., 1990. Ordained to ministry Assemblies of God, 1980. Sr. pastor Dayton (Oreg.) Assembly of God, 1977-78; assoc. pastor First Assembly of God, Newberg, 1979-83; sr. pastor Abundant Life Ctr., Toledo, Oreg., 1983-91, Bethel Ch., Chehalis, Wash., 1991—; presbyter Oreg. Coun. Assemblies of God, Salem, 1986-91, exec. prebyter, 1987-91. Contbr. articles to religious publs. Republican. Office: Bethel Ch 132 Kirkland Rd Chehalis WA 98532

DEUEL, DOUGLAS JAMES, minister; b. California, Mo., Oct. 12, 1956; s. James Roy and Janet Rae (Cunningham) D.; m. Mellony Kay Gutshall, Apr. 4, 1985; children: Christopher James, Jeffrey Alan. Student, U. Oxford, Eng., 1977-78; BA, William Jewell Coll., 1979; MDiv, Midwestern Bapt. Sem., 1982; ThD, New Orleans Bapt. Sem., 1989. Ordained to ministry Disciples of Christ. Pastor Cego (Tex.) Bapt. Ch., 1983-84; founding pastor North Woods Christian Ch., Kansas City, Mo., 1984-87; assoc. min. Country Club Christian Ch., Kansas City, 1987—; assoc. min. Holmeswood Bapt. Ch., Kansas City, summers 1977-83; mem. com. Regional New Congregational Establishment Co., Kansas City, 1989—, Regional Mission Interpretation Co., Kansas City, 1989—, William Jewell Alumni Spiritual Life Co., Liberty, Mo., 1989—, Regional Mission to Haiti Co., Kansas City, 1990—. Work project leader Habitat for Humanity Global Village, El Rosario, Guatemala, 1990, Enriquilla, Dominican Republic, 1991, Esparza, Costa Rica, 1991; house organizer Habitat for Humanity, Kansas City, 1990-91. Mem. Disciples Mins. Assn. Home: 15231 Dearborn Overland Park KS 66223 Office: Country Club Christian Ch 6101 Ward Pkwy Kansas City MO 66113

DEUTSCH, LAWRENCE IRA, minister; b. Bklyn., June 17, 1939; s. Meyer Irving and Lillian (Ilkovitz) D.; m. Carolyn Ann Beaton, June 2, 1960 (div. Oct. 1986); children: Michael Keith, Eric Scott; m. Karol White, Dec. 31, 1987. AAS, Bklyn. Coll., 1961; BTh, Calvary Bible Coll., Lake Charles, La., 1990; MA, Cornerstone U., 1991. Ordained to ministry Am. Bapt. Assn., 1982. Pastor Congregation Beth Ha'Shem, Houston, 1988—; chaplain T.D.C. & Houston Downtown Med. Ctr., 1981—; nat. assessment and referral counselor, Rapha, Houston, 1988—; bd. dirs. Jesus the Messiah , 1990—, Beth Ha'Shem Christian Counseling Ctr. Author: (poetry) various publs. (silver award 1986, golden award 1987-89), 1986-89. Pub. rels. officer to mayor, Gulfport, Miss., 1986. With USMC, 1958-64. Mem. Southern Bapt. Messianic Alliance, Internat. Writers Alive (v.p. 1990—). Republican. Mem. Messianic Ch. Home: 3510 Greenwood Pl Deer Park TX 77536 Office: 8990 Kirby Dr Ste 250 Houston TX 77054 *LaChaim (To Life!). Life is very precious and very exciting. We need to make each day count to bring honor and glory to Yeshua Ha'Mashiach (Jesus the Messiah).*

DEVANTIER, PAUL W., communications executive, broadcaster; b. Wausau, Wis., Mar. 25, 1946; s. Walter Herman and Ella Marie (Mundt) D.; m. Ellen Stapel, Aug. 2, 1970; children: Richard, John, Andrew, Katie. BA, Concordia Coll., 1968; M in Divinity, Concordia Seminary, 1972; postgrad., So. Ill. U., Edwardsville. Radio announcer Sta. WXCO, Wausau, 1965-68, Sta. KRCH, St. Louis, 1968-72; dir. devel. Sta. KFUO-AM-FM, St. Louis, 1972-74, gen. mgr., 1974-82; exec. dir. communications Luth. Ch.—Mo. Synod, St. Louis, 1982—; speaker By the Way (internat. syndicated radio program) 1974—. Exec. producer religious documentary film hymn A Celebration of Change, 1984 (Angel award), variety of network religious pub. service programs, announcements; mag. Luth. Witness. Trustee, pres. Luth. Film Assocs., N.Y.C., 1982—. Mem. Religious Pub. Rels. Coun., World Assn. Christian Communicators, Nat. Assn. Broadcasters, Phi Kappa Phi. Office: The Luth Ch—Mo Synod Communication Svc 1333 S Kirkwood Rd Saint Louis MO 63122

DEVER, DANIEL, academic administrator. Supt. of schs. Roman Cath. Diocese of Honolulu. Office: Cath Schs Dept 6301 Pali Hwy Kaneohe HI 96744*

DEVER, HOMER HOBART, elementary school educator; b. Portsmouth, Ohio, July 29, 1928; s. Hobart Samuel and Hazel Corine (Allen) D.; m. Arlene Lynore Detamore, July 21, 1955; children: Lorna, Beth, Ronda. BS in Elem. Edn., So. Missionary Coll., 1957; MA in Elem. Edn., Andrews U., 1964. Cert. elem. tchr., Tenn. Elem. tchr. Ohio Conf. 7th-day Adventists, Mt. Vernon, Ohio, 1957-60, Ga.-Cumberland Conf. 7th-day Adventists, Calhoun, Ga., 1960-88, Mountain View Conf. 7th-day Adventists, Parkersburg, W.Va., 1988—. Author: Log Cabin Poems, 1953. Youth leader McMinnville (Tenn.) Adventists, 1960-67. With U.S. Army, 1950-52. Republican. Avocations: gardening, carpentry, antiques, walking, writing poetry. Home: PO Box 357 Dunlap TN 37327 Office: Willowbrook Sch Rte 9 Box 300A Cumberland MD 21502

DEVITO, ALBERICO, religious organization administrator, minister. Gen. supt. Italian Pentecostal Ch. Can., Boussard, Que., Can. Office: Italian Pentecostal Ch Can, 7685 Treblay St, Boussard, PQ Canada J4W 2W2*

DEVNICH, D. D., religious organization administrator. Pres. Seventh-day Adventist Ch. in Can., Oshawa, Ont. Office: Seventh-day Adventist Ch, 1149 King St E, Oshawa, ON Canada L1H 1H8*

DE VRIES, CALVIN THOMAS, minister; b. Sibley, Tex., June 6, 1921; s. John Martin and Elsa Amelia (Reineking) De V.; m. Janet Clark, May 19, 1945; children: Janet Margaret De Vries Myer, Nancy Ann De Vries. Student, N.W. Jr. Coll., Orange City, Iowa, 1939-41; BA, Hope Coll., 1943; MDiv, New Brunswick Theol. Sem., 1947. Ordained to ministry Presbyn. Ch. Assoc. pastor 4th Presbyn. Ch., Chgo., 1947-57; pastor Sherwood Presbyn. Ch., Washington, 1957-62, 1st Presbyn. Ch., Danville, Ill., 1962-70, Larchmont (N.Y.) Ave Ch., 1970-77; pastor 1st Presbyn. Ch., Cedar Rapids, Iowa, 1977-89, pastor emeritus, 1989—; instr. Mt. Mercy Coll., Cedar Rapids, Iowa, 1983-89; mem. Consortium for Internat. Peace and Reconciliation State of Iowa, 1978-81; trustee Coe Coll., Cedar Rapids, Ill. Coll., Jacksonville; speaker McCormick Theol. Sem., Chgo., Hope Coll., Holland, Mich. Mem. Christian Dialogue Group, Cedar Rapids. Recipient Citation for Interfaith Work Anti-defammation League of B'nai Brith, 1966, Jewish-Christian Dialogue Group, 1989. Home: 301 Red Fox Rd SE Cedar Rapids IA 52403

DE VRIES, DAWN ANN, religion educator; b. Hammond, Ind., June 11, 1961; d. Martin Richard and Janet Ruth (Van Ramshorst) De Vries; m. Brian Albert Gerrish, Aug. 3, 1990. BA, U. Chgo., 1983, MA, 1984, PhD, 1991. Asst. prof. ch. history San Francisco Theol. Sem., San Anselmo, Calif., 1988-90, McCormick Theol. Sem., Chgo., 1990—. Editor, translator: Servant of the Word, 1987. Newcombe fellow, 1987; recipient Deutsche Akademische Austauschdienst Govt. of Fed. Republic Germany, 1987. Presbyterian. Office: McCormick Theol Sem 5555 S Woodlawn Chicago IL 60637

DE VRIES, EGBERT, lay minister, agriculture science educator emeritus; b. Grijpskerke, Zeeland, The Netherlands, Jan. 29, 1901; came to U.S., 1966; s. Jan de Vries and J. Willemina Luuring; m. Tine Berg, Feb. 18, 1924 (dec. May 1945); m. A. Duvekot, July 14, 1947. Degree in agrl. engring., Agrl. U., The Netherlands, 1923, DAgr, 1931; MA, Duvekot, 1947. Horticulture officer Jakarta, Malang, Indonesia, 1924-29; sr. agrl. officer Bogor, Jakarta, Indonesia, 1929-34; chief devel. officer Jakarta, Indonesia, 1935-41; chmn. agrl. faculty U. Indonesia, Jakarta, 1941-46; prof. tropical agr. U. Wageningen, The Netherlands, 1947-50; chief agrl. dept. IBRD, Washington, 1950-56; rector Internat. Inst. Social Studies, The Hague, The Netherlands, 1956-66; prof. internat. devel. U. Pitts., 1966-82; Mem. nat. bd. United Protestant Chs. Indonesia, 1937-47; chmn. dept. on ch. and soc., World Coun. Chs., 1953-66. Mem. UN Assn., World Federalists, Internat. Devel. Svcs. (chmn. bd. 1987—), Rotary. Home: 3955 Bigelow Blvd #601 Pittsburgh PA 15213-1235 *Having lived in three continents (in Asia in a predominantly Moslem country) brought me and my family dear friends everywhere.*

DE VRIES, JANET MARGARET, clergywoman; b. Chgo., Feb. 24, 1950; d. Calvin Thomas and Janet May (Clark) DeV.; B.A., Hope Coll., Holland, Mich., 1972; M.Div., Union Theol. Sem., N.Y.C., 1978; m. William J. Cowfer, Sept. 6, 1980; stepchildren—David E., Jonathan C., Stephanie L. Ordained to ministry United Presbyterian Ch., U.S.A., 1977; coordinator tng. Support Agy., United Presbyn. Ch., N.Y.C., 1980-83, mng. dir. div. stewardship/tng. support agy., program specialist vols. in mission, Program Agy., N.Y.C., 1973-78, coordinator communication and ch. support Synod S. Calif., Los Angeles, 1973-80; instr. Claremont (Calif.) Sch. Theology, 1979. Gannett Newspaper scholar, 1967. Mem. UN Assn., Religious Public Relations Council. Author: Learning the Pacific Way: A Guide for All Ages, 1982; also articles. Office: Room 921 475 Riverside Dr New York NY 10115

DE VRIES, PHILIP JOHN, worship and music minister; b. Sutton, Mass., Sept. 19, 1947; s. Nicholas and Jennie (Haringa) De V.; m. Elizabeth Daniels; children: Sharyn Lee, Thomas Michael Philip. BA, Barrington Coll., 1963; MusB, Westminster Choir Coll., 1968; cert. in opera theater, Temple U., 1977. Cert. tchr., Mass. Min. music 1st Ref. Ch., Xenia, Ohio, 1968-70; developer dept. music Delaware County Christian Sch., Newtown Square, Pa., 1970-77; min. music 1st Bapt. Ch., Newtown Square, 1981-83, Evang. Covenant Ch., Buffalo, Minn., 1984-88; min. music and worship Chelten Bapt. Ch., Dresher, Pa., 1988—; exec. dir. Accent Ministries, Ambler, Pa., 1989—; concert tour dir. Delaware County Christian Sch., 1971-77; freelance oratorio tenor Greater Phila. Ch. and Colls. Assn., 1974-88; owner, performer Ind. Sacred Concert Ministry, West Chester, Pa., 1977-84; adjudicator Mid-Atlantic Christian Sch. Assn., 1976-82, Phila. Coll. Bible Scholarships, Langhorn, Pa., 1988-89; chorus mgr. Sandi Patti Tours, 1990-91. Author: (musicals) Ragman, 1988, Come Celebrate Jesus, 1989, Bethlehem, 1990. Founder, dir. Phil de Vries & Children of Truth Singers, West Chester, 1973-79, Accent Mus. Drama Ministries, Dresler, Pa., 1988—; soloist, asst. dir. Am. Youth Chamber Orch. and Singers, Eng. and Scotland, 1976; leading tenor Berks Grand Opera, Reading, Pa., 1976-83; mus. dir. Chester County Christian Chorale, 1980-84. Mem. Christian Instrumental Dirs. Assn., Am. Choral Dirs. Assn., Am. Guild English Handbell Ringers. Republican. Presbyterian. Avocations: furniture building, bicycling, hiking. Home: 1004 Welsh Rd W Ambler PA 19002

DEVRIES, ROBERT K., religious book publisher; b. Sully, Iowa, July 6, 1932; s. Fred G. and Selena Irene (Willetts) DeV.; m. Carolyn Jo Schroeder, June 2, 1962 (div. 1978); children—Stephen Robert, Suzanne Mishael; m. Carolyn Gail Bergmans, May 26, 1979; children—Staci Ann, Keri Gail. A.B., Wheaton Coll., 1954; Th.M., Dallas Theol. Sem., 1958, Th.D., 1969. Asst. registrar Dallas Theol. Sem., 1959-63; editor-in-chief Moody Press, Chgo., 1963-68; dir., v.p. pubs. Zondervan Pub. House, Grand Rapids, Mich., 1968-76, exec. v.p. book div., 1976-85; exec. v.p., publisher Zondervan Book Group, Zondervan Corp., Grand Rapids, Mich., 1985-86; pub. cons. Evang. Christian Pubs., 1987; pub., bd. dirs. Discovery House Pubs., Grand Rapids, 1987—; bd. dirs. Media Assocs. Internat., Bloomingdale, Ill., Oswald Chambers Pub. Assn. Ltd., South Croydon, Eng., Serendipity House, Littleton, Colo., Christian Counseling Ctr., Grand Rapids, Mich. Bd. dirs. Ligonier Valley Study Ctr., Stahlstown, Pa., 1979-83, Bd. Publ. Evang. Covenant Ch. Am., Chgo., 1989—; advisor Internat. Coun. Bibl. Inerrancy, Walnut Creek, Calif., 1978-87. Recipient Outstanding Young Man in Am. award Jaycees, 1965. Mem. Evang. Christian Pubs. Assn. Republican. Mem. Evangelical Covenant Ch. Avocation: model railroading. Home: 7554 Lime Hollow SE Grand Rapids MI 49546 Office: Box 3566 Grand Rapids MI 49501

DEW, WILLIAM WALDO, JR., bishop; b. Newport, Ky., Dec. 14, 1935; s. William Waldo and Thelma (Dittus) D.; m. Mae Marie Eggers, Jan. 5, 1958; children: Linda Dew-Hiersoux, William, Marilyn. BA, Union Coll., Barbourville, Ky., 1957; MDiv, Drew Theol. Sch., 1961. Ordained to ministry United Meth. Ch. as deacon, 1958, as elder, 1963. Pastor Springville (Calif.) United Meth. Ch., 1961-64, Lindsay (Calif.) United Meth. Ch., 1964-67, Meml. United Meth. Ch., Clovis, Calif., 1967-72, Epworth United Meth. Ch., Berkeley, Calif., 1972-79; dist. supt. Cen. Dist. Calif.-Nev. Annual Conf., Modesto, Calif., 1979-84; pastor San Ramon Valley United Meth. Ch., Alamo, Calif., 1984-88; bishop United Meth. Ch., Portland, Oreg., 1988—; lectr. Pacific Sch. Religion, Berkeley, 1976-79. Trustee Willamette U., Salem, Oreg., 1988—, Alaska Pacific U., Anchorage, 1988—. Paul Harris fellow Rotary Internat., 1988. Democrat. Avocations: fishing, golf, reading, travel. Office: United Meth Conf Ctr 1505 SW 18th Ave Portland OR 97201

DEWEY, S. DAYTON, priest; b. Hampton, Va., Nov. 29, 1944; arrived in Eng., 1986; s. Sanford Dayton and Betty (Clark) D. AB, Syracuse U., 1967, MA, 1972; MDiv, Gen. Theol. Sem., N.Y.C., 1979. Ordained deacon Episcopal Ch., 1979, priest, 1980. Tchr. Syracuse (N.Y.) City Schs., 1968-76; assoc. dir. religious svcs. St. Luke's Roosevelt Hosp. Ctr., N.Y.C., 1979-86 asst. priest St. Mary Le Bow Ch., London, 1986—, dir. counseling ctr. 1989—; cons. AIDS Ministry, Ch. of Eng., 1987—; lectr., presenter work shops for AIDS Ministry. Mem. Brit. Assn. Counseling, Assn. Pastoral Car and Counseling U.K.

DEWING, CHARLES BENJAMIN, clergyman, missionary; b. Cambridge, Mass., Oct. 5, 1942; s. Norman F. and Ethel M. (Stoylis) D.; m. Joan F. O'Connell, July 17, 1971; children: Francis, Nathan, Andrew. Ministerial diploma, Zion Bible Inst., East Providence, R.I., 1971; BTh, Internat. Bible Coll., San Antonio, 1972; MRE, Internat. Sem., Plymouth, Fla., 1985, PhD in Missions, 1990. Ordained to ministry United Evang. Chs., 1971. Tchr. Bible, Trinity Episcopal Ch., Bridgewater, Mass., 1967-71; asst. pastor Trinity Chapel, San Antonio, 1971-74; dir. Christian edn. Wyncote (Pa.) Assembly of God Ch., 1975-76; internat. rep., missionary in SE Asia, United Evang. Chs., Thomasville, Ga., 1976—; internat. rep. Christian United in Action, Thomasville, 1976, Evang. Bible Inst., Thomasville, 1976—; fgn. missionary Internat. Ministrial Assn., Bloomington, 1976—. Named Missionary of Yr., Zion Bible Inst., 1982. Mem. Full Gospel Businessmens Fellowship Internat. (life). Office: United Evang Chs PO Box 1175 Thomasville GA 31799

DEWIRE, NORMAN EDWARD (NED DEWIRE), minister; b. Cin., Mar. 5, 1936; s. Ormsby and Lucille (Binder) D.; m. Shirley W. Dewire, June 16, 1957; children: Cathy Dewire Blum, Deborah Dewire Bolmida. BS in Edn., Ohio U., 1958; MDiv, Boston U., 1962; D Ministry, McCormick Sem., Chgo., 1979; DD (hon.), Adrian Coll., 1976. Ordained deacon United Meth. Ch., 1959. Pastor Jacksonville United Meth. Cir., Athens County, Ohio, 1957-58, Charlton City (Mass.) United Meth. Ch., 1958-62; mem. pastoral team Cen. United Meth. Ch., Detroit, 1962-67; exec. dir. Detroit Conf. Bd. Missions, 1967-69, Joint Strategy and Action Com., N.Y.C., 1969-75; gen. sec. Gen. Coun. on Ministries, United Meth. Ch., 1975-86; pres. Meth. Theol. Sem., Delaware, Ohio, 1986—; dir. United Meth. Commn. on Unity, 1988—; vice chair West Ohio United Meth. Conf. Coun.; del., staff 5th, 6th, 7th World Coun. of Chs. Assemblies; chmn. social concerns com. World Meth. Coun., 1981-91. Bd. dirs. The Otterbein Homes, Lebanon, Ohio; exec. com., bd. dirs. Riverside Meth. Hosps., Columbus, Ohio; treas., mem. Ohio Commn. Dispute Resolution, Columbus. Recipient award U.S. Atty. Gen., 1975. Mem. World Meth. Coun. (chmn. social concerns com. 1981-91), Newcomen Soc. N.Am., Capital Club (Columbus), Ohio State U. Faculty Club, Torch Club, Kappa Delta Pi. Office: Meth Theol Sch 3081 Columbus Pike PO Box 1204 Delaware OH 43015-0931

DEWITT, EDWARD ELBERT, clergyman; b. Galesburg, Ill., Oct. 22, 1946; s. Elbert Eugene and Thelma (Oatman) DeW.; m. Linda Arlene Guenther, Sept. 22, 1968; children: Amy Lynn, Ethan Edward. AA, Carl Sandburg Coll., 1979; BA, Western Ill. U., Macomb, 1982; ThB, Am. Bible Coll., 1978, ThM, 1982. Ordained to ministry Am. Evang. Christian Ch. Pastor Glade Br. Bapt. Ch., Pitkin, La., 1970-71, Christian Faith Chapel, Galesburg, Ill., 1972—; dir. Bible Questions Ministries, Galesburg, 1983—; speaker Bible Questions Ministries Presents, Galesburg, 1986—. Author: Evangelism: The Order of the Day of the Army of the Redeemed, 1978, Public Education Vs. Religion - Problem or Paranoia, 1980; (study outlines) Inspiration, Return of the Savior, Bible From Outlines, 1987-91. With U.S. Army, 1968-71, Vietnam. Office: Bible Questions Ministries PO Box 1413 Galesburg IL 61402 *All else must be secondary when compared with the eternal destiny of the immortal soul.*

DE WITT, JESSE R., bishop; b. Detroit, Dec. 5, 1918; s. Jesse A. and Bessie G. (Mainzinger) DeW.; m. Annamary Horner, Apr. 19, 1941; children: Donna Lee (Mrs. William Wegryn), Darla Jean (Mrs. William Inman). B.A., Wayne State U., 1948; B.D., Garrett Theol. Sem., 1948; D.D., Adrian Coll., 1965, Northland Coll., 1976, Wiley Coll., 1981; H.H.D. (hon.), North Central Coll., 1977. Ordained deacon, received in full membership Methodist Ch. (Detroit conf.), 1945, ordained elder, 1948; student pastor, 1944-46; minister Aldersgate Ch., Detroit, 1946, Faith Ch., Oak Park, Mich., 1952-58; exec. sec. Detroit Conf. Bd. Missions, 1958-67; dist. supt. Detroit Conf. Bd. Missions (West dist.), 1967-70; asst. gen. sec. sect. ch. extension Nat. Bd. Missions, 1970-72; bishop United Meth. Ch.; resident bishop United Meth. Ch. (Wis. area), 1972-80; bishop United Meth. Ch. (Chgo. area), 1980-89; del. gen. conf. Meth. Ch., 1964, 66, 68, 70, 72, 76; past epis. rep. Commn. on Status and Role Women; epis. rep. Consultation on Ch. Union, Bd. Ch. and Society (other coms. and task forces); pres. nat. div. Bd. Global Ministries, 1976-80, pres., 1980—; past pres. North Central jurisdiction Coll. Bishops; chmn. pastoral concerns com. Council Bishops, United Meth. Ch. Trustee North Central Coll., Naperville, Ill., Garrett Evang. Sem.; bd. dirs. No. Ill. Conf., Meth. Youth Services, Marcy-Newberry Assn., United Meth. Homes and Services, Lake Bluff-Chgo. Homes for Children. Office: No Ill Conf United Meth Ch 77 W Washington St Suite 1806 Chicago IL 60602

DEWITT, LARRY DALE, minister; b. Royal Oak, Mich., Mar. 23, 1937; s. Austin and Helen Alice (Dickinson) DeW.; m. Rebecca Joan Shufelt, Aug. 17, 1962; children: Kirk Stratton, Laurel Joan, Cynthia Lynn Bausman. BS, Wheaton Coll., 1959; MDiv, Fuller Theol. Sem., 1964. Assoc. pastor Royal Oak (Mich.) Missionary Ch., 1959-61, Pasadena (Calif.) Alliance Ch., 1962-64; sr. pastor Orangevale (Calif.) Community Ch., 1964-67; sr. pastor 1st Missionary Ch., Flint, Mich., 1967-71, Ft. Wayne, Ind., 1972-76; sr. pastor Calvary Community Ch., Westlake Village, Calif., 1976—. Avocations: travel, boating. Home: 2378 McCrea Rd Thousand Oaks CA 91362 Office: Calvary Community Ch 31293 Via Colinas Westlake Village CA 91362

DEWOLFE, WILLIAM ARTHUR, religious organization administrator, clergyman; b. Boston, Aug. 21, 1927; s. John Campbell Gordon and Miriam Elbridge (Ford) DeW.; m. Barbara Louise Mosher, Sept. 10, 1949; children: Mark Mosher, Richard Scott, Paul Howard. AB, Tufts U., 1950; BS in Theology, Harvard U., 1953; EdM, Springfield Coll., 1964. Ordained to ministry Unitarian Universalist Ch., 1952. Student minister 1st Universalist Ch., Norwell, Mass., 1950-52; minister 1st Universlaist Soc., Wakefield, Mass., 1953-55, 1st Parish Universalist Ch., Stoughton, Mass., 1956-60, Sixteen Acres Universalist Ch., Springfield, Mass., 1960-64; minister 1st Unitarian Ch., San Antonio, 1964-70, St. Louis, 1970-73; interdist. rep. Unitarian Universalist Assn., Berea, Ohio, 1973-85, Hopedale, Mass., 1985-86; dist. exec. Springfield, 1986—; pres. Mass. Universalist Conv., Boston, 1960-62. Pres. Universalist Hist. Soc., Medford, Mass., 1958-63; founder, pres. San Antonio Civil Liberties Union, 1965-68; bd. dirs. ACLU, N.Y.C., 1968-70; pres. Tex. Civil Liberties Union, Austin, 1968-70; treas. East Mo. Civil Liberties Union, St. Louis, 1970-73; trustee Doolittle Home for the Aged, Foxboro, Mass., 1985—. Served as pfc. U.S. Army, 1945-47. Named Advisor of Yr. Liberal Religious Youth, 1965. Mem. Unitarian Universalist Ministers (trustee 1981-83), Liberal Religious Edn. Dirs. Democrat. Lodge: Rotary (pres. Stoughton chpt. 1960, v.p. University City, Mo. chpt. 1972-73). Avocations: furniture refinishing, collecting antiques. Home: 75 Tioga St Springfield MA 01128-1343 Office: Unitarian Universalist Assn Conn Valley Dist Office 245 Porter Lake Dr Longmeadow MA 01106

DEXTRAS, MARY LOU, religious organization coordinator; b. Youngstown, Ohio, Sept. 20, 1922; d. Guido and Catherine (Spagnola) Bernard; m. Albert Raymond Dextras, Feb. 9, 1946; children—Suzanne, Paul A., Cathie, Mary Alice, Dee Anne. Student Youngstown Bus. Sch., Wichita State U., 1984—. Exec. sec. U.S. Air Force, Kadena, Okinawa, 1957-62; youth dir. McConnell AFB, Wichita, Kans., 1963-64; real estate agt. Egan Realtors, Derby, Kans., 1965-80; coordinator Congregation Sisters of St. Joseph Coordinated Services, Wichita, 1980-88; tchr. religion and edn. St. Mary's Ch., 1991—. Mem. Derby Bd. Edn., pres. 1978-79, 84-85; moderator Sr. Citizens of Derby, 1991—; mem. Community Edn., Students at Risk; lectr. St. Mary's Ch. Sr. Citizen program. Served to sgt. USMCWR, 1942-45. Mem. Derby Arts Council, Kans. Named Mother of Yr., Bergstrom AFB, Austin, 1956; recipient Koza Shi Fujenkai award Women's Fedn., Okinawa, 1960; People-to-People award Pres. Eisenhower, 1961. Democrat. Roman Catholic. Lodges: Soroptimists, K.C. Aux. (Derby, Kans.). Avocations: Tap dancing; piano. Office: Congregation of Sisters of St Joseph Coordinated Services 3720 E Bayley Wichita KS 67218

DEYE, ARMIN ULFERT, retired minister; b. Arst, Sask., Can., July 10, 1913; came to U.S., 1916; s. John Herman and Meta Sophia (Iben) D.; m. Gladys Myrtle Hahs, June 29, 1941; children: Harold, Dorothy, Kathryn, Donald, Carol. Student, St. Paul's Coll., Concordia, Mo., 1932-34; grad., Concordia Sem., St. Louis, 1938. Pastor 1st Eng. Luth. Ch., Spring Valley, Minn., 1940-44, Grace Luth. Ch., Rochester, Minn., 1944-49, St. Peter's Luth. Ch., St. Paul, 1949-61, St. Martin's Luth. Ch., Winona, Minn., 1961-81; pastor St. Mark's Luth. Ch., Rushford, Minn., 1981-86, ret., 1986—; circuit counselor Luth. Ch. Mo. Synod, del. to Synod conv., San Francisco, chmn. pub. rels., Minn. dist. Author Luth. Prayer Book; editor The Luth. Jour., 1950— (Conn. Hist. Soc. award). Bd. dirs. Ramsey County Hosp., St. Paul, 1959-61. Mem. Winona Luths. for Life (pastoral advisor 1987—), Lions. Home: 80 Whitewater Ct Winona MN 55987

DEYNEKA, PETER, JR., religious organization executive; b. Chgo., Sept. 13, 1931; s. Peter and Vera (Demidovich) D.; m. Anita Marson, June 14, 1968. BA in Bibl. Lit., Wheaton Coll., 1953; MDiv, No. Bapt. Sem., 1957. Missionary Slavic Gospel Assn., Ecuador, Argentina, 1961-63; asst. dir. Slavic Gospel Assn., Chgo., 1966-74; gen. dir. Slavic Gospel Assn., Wheaton, Ill., 1975—; dir. Russian Bible Inst., Buenos Aires, 1962-63; missionary, chaplain U.S. Army Seoul, Republic of Korea, 1963-65; elder Coll. Ch., Wheaton, 1983-85; guest lectr. Fuller Theol. Sem., 1984, Grad. Sch., Wheaton Coll., 1984; guest speaker TV and radio programs; cons. on religion in USSR and Eastern Europe, Billy Graham Assn., Trans World Radio, others. Co-author: Christians in the Shadow of the Kremlin, 1974, Peter Dynamite, 1975, A Song in Siberia, 1977. Mem. Interdenominational Fgn. Mission Assn. (bd. dirs.), S.Am. Crusades (bd. dirs.), Soc. for Study Religion and Communism (bd. dirs. 1979-81), Romanian Missionary Soc. (bd. dirs.), Soc. for Cen. Asian Nationalities (coun. advisors). Home: 1263 Casa Solana Wheaton IL 60187 Office: Slavic Gospel Assn 139 N Washington Box 1122 Wheaton IL 60189

DE ZWAGER, H., ecumenical agency administrator. Pres. Greater Victoria Coun. Chs., B.C., Can. Office: Greater Victoria Coun Chs, 1457 Clifford St, Victoria, BC Canada V8S 1M1*

DEZZA, PAOLO CARDINAL, cardinal, theologian; b. Parma, Italy, Dec. 13, 1901; s. Giovanni and Carla (Riccadonna) D. Doctorate in Philosophy, Colegio de San Ignacio, Barcelona, Spain, 1924; Doctorate in Theology, Facoltà di San Luigi, Naples, Italy, 1929; Doctorate in Philosophy (hon.), Universidad Catholica, Santiago de Chile, 1953. Ordained priest Roman Cath. Ch., 1928, created cardinal, 1991. Prof. philosophy Gregorian U., Rome, 1929-62; provincial superior Jesuit Province, Milan, Italy, 1935-39; rector Gregorian U., Rome, 1941-51; gen. asst. Soc. Jesus, Rome, 1965-75, papal del., 1981-83; peritus Vatican Coun. II, Rome, 1962-65; cons. various congregations of Holy See, 1929-91. Author: Alle origini del Neotomismo, 1940, Metaphysica Generalis, 1962, Filosofia, sintesi scholastica, 1988. Decorated comendador de la Orden de Alfonso X el Sabio (Spain). Fellow Pontificia Accademia di San Tommaso d'Aquino. Home and Office: Borgo Santo Spirito 4, CP 6139, Rome Italy

DIAL, DONNA KAY, economics educator; b. Smithers, W.Va., Aug. 7, 1940; d. James L. and Helen Rosamond (Curry) D.; m. David Lee Morgan, May 29, 1982. BA, Fla. State U., 1962, MS, 1964, PhD, 1969. Rsch. asst. Fed. Res. Bank, Richmond, Va., 1964; instr. U. N.C., Wilmington, 1965; cost analyst Hayes Internat. Corp., Eau Gallie, Fla., 1965-66; instr. Fla. State U., Tallahassee, 1966-69; asst. prof. Ind. U.-Purdue U., Indpls., 1969-75, assoc. prof., 1975—, dir. hons. program, 1978-81, asst. dir. continuing studies, 1986-91; pres. Econ. Edn. for Clergy, Indpls., 1987—; bd. dirs. European Evagelistic Soc., Ctr. for Minority Entrepreneurs; cons. small bus., Fla. and Ind., 1980—. Author: (handbook) Church Resource Planning, 1978, Program Development for Clergy Workshops, 1989; editor: (book) Readings in Economics of North Atlantic Community, 1976. Mem. Nat. Contract Mgmt. Assn., Assn. of Christian Economists, Soc. for the

Advancement of Continuing Edn. for Clergy, Assn. of Theol. Schs., History of Econ. Soc., Econ. Club. Avocations: music, reading, hiking, cooking. Office: Econ Edn for Clergy 620 Union Dr Indianapolis IN 46202

DIAMOND, MALCOLM LURIA, religion educator; b. Bklyn., Nov. 6, 1924; s. Walter Joseph and Jeannette Civia (Luria) D.; m. Barbara Reingold, June 1953 (div. 1974); children: Michael, Jonathan; m. Denise J. Landry, July 1976. B.Engring., Yale U., 1945; postgrad., Trinity Coll., Cambridge (Eng.) U., 1947-48; Ph.D., Columbia U., 1956; EdS in Marriage and Family Counselling, Seton Hall U., 1985. Mem. faculty Sarah Lawrence Coll., Bronxville, N.Y., 1950-51, N.Y. U., 1951-53; mem. faculty Princeton U., 1953—, prof. religion, 1968—, William H. Danforth prof., 1978—; therapist Corner House, Princeton, 1983-88; pvt. practice therapy, 1987—. Author: Martin Buber: Jewish Existentialist, 1960, Contemporary Philosophy and Religious Thought, 1974; co-editor: The Logic of God, 1975. Served with USNR, 1942-45. Recipient Harbison Teaching award Danforth Found., 1970; Kent fellow, 1951; Guggenheim fellow, 1976. Mem. Am. Acad. Religion (exec. com. 1975-77), Soc. Values in Higher Edn., Princeton Assn. Human Rights. Jewish. Home: 24 Wheatsheaf Ln Princeton NJ 08540 Office: Dept Religion 613 Seventy Nine Hall Princeton NJ 08544

DIANALAN, JAMIL, religious organization administrator. Nat. chmn. Confedn. Muslim Orgns. of The Philippines, Manila. Office: Conf Muslim Orgn, Manila Metro Manila, The Philippines*

DIBBLE, RUSSELL KURT, minister, educator; b. Clintwood, Va., May 3, 1945; s. Russell Spencer and Elsa Teresa (Osberg) D.; m. Marsha Lou Ramsey, Dec. 16, 1967; children: Laura Reneé Dibble Mayo, Klinton Spencer. BS in Music Edn., Bryan Coll., Dayton, Tenn., 1971. Ordained to ministry, 1966. Pastor Mill Creek Bapt. Ch., Liverpool, W.Va., 1969-70; dir. juvenile rehab. City Mission, Niagara Falls, N.Y., 1970-71; assoc. pastor Holston Bapt. Ch., Bluff City, Tenn., 1971-72; dir. Child Evangelism Fellowship, Kingsport, Tenn., 1972-75; state dir. Child Evangelism Fellowship, Nashville, 1975-78; city dir. Child Evangelism Fellowship, Charlotte, N.C., 1986—; asst. to pastor Cedarview Ind. Meth., Kingsport, 1978-80; mgr. Greenwood Hills Bible Conf., Fayetteville, Pa., 1980-81; mgr. ops. Alethia Springs Christian Edn. Ctr., Ferrum, Va., 1982-86. Active Charlotte chpt. ARC, Salvation Army, Boys Club., 1986—. Mem. United Assn. Christian Counselors, Metrolina Fellowship of Evang. Pastors, Fellowship Christian Magicians, Mid-Atlantic Sunday Sch. Assn. (workshop leader 1987—), Columbia Sch. Bibl. Edn. (ext. com. 1989—). Republican. Avocations: music, fine arts, camping. Home and Office: 3700 Western Blvd Raleigh NC 27606

DICICCO, MARIO MICHAEL, priest, religious organization administrator; b. Memphis, Jan. 15, 1933; s. Michael Angelo and Pasqualina (Saluppo) DiC. MA in English, U. Chgo., 1964; PhD in English, Case Western Res. U., 1970; MA in Psychology, Loyola U., Chgo., 1974; MA in New Testament, Cath. Theol. U., Chgo., 1980. English tchr. Padua Franciscan High Sch., Cleve., 1961-70; prof. English Quincy (Ill.) Coll., 1970-72; marriage and family counselor Archdiocese of Chgo., 1973-77; assoc. pastor St. Jude Ch., New Lenox, Ill., 1980-82; prin. Hales Franciscan High Sch., Chgo., 1982-89, pres., 1990—. Home: 4930 Cottage Grove Chicago IL 60615

DICK, HENRY HENRY, minister; b. Russia, June 1, 1922; s. Henry Henry and Mary (Unger) D.; m. Erica Penner, May 25, 1946; children—Janet (Mrs. Arthur Enns), Judith (Mrs. Ron Brown), James, Henry. Th.B., Mennonite Brethren Bible Coll., 1950. Ordained to ministry Mennonite Brethren Ch., 1950; pastor in Orillia, Ont., Can., 1950-54, Lodi, Calif., 1954-57, Shafter, Calif., 1958-69; faculty Tabor Coll., 1954-55; gen. sec. Mennonite Brethren Conf. of U.S.A., 1969-72; pres. Mennonite Brethren Bibl. Sem., Fresno, Calif., 1972-76; vice moderator Gen Conf. Mennonite Brethren Ch., 1975-78, moderator, 1979-84; pastor Reedley Mennonite Brethren Ch., 1976-88; ret., 1989; dir. ch. and constituency relations Mennonite Brethren Biblical Sem., 1987-89; moderator Pacific Dist. Conf., 1959-60, 61-63, 75-77; mem. exec. com. Mennonite Central Com. Internat., 1967-75, mem. bd. reference and counsel, 1966-69, 72-75, mem. bd. missions and services, 1969-72; exec. sec. Bd. Edn. Mennonite Brethren, 1969-72; chmn. Bd. Missions and Services, 1985-91; pastor emeritus Reedley Mennonite Brethren Ch., 1987. Columnist bi-weekly publ. Christian Leader, 1969-75. Bd. dirs. Bob Wilson Meml. Hosp., Ulysses, Kans., 1969-72; dist. minister Pacific Dist. Conf. Mennonite Brethren, 1989—. Recipient Humanitarian award Shafter C. of C., 1969, Citation bd. dirs. Bibl. Sem. Clubs: Kiwanis, Reedley Rotary. Home: 783 W Carpenter St Reedley CA 93654 Office: 1632 L St Reedley CA 93654

DICKENS, DEBORAH E., music and youth director, customer service specialist; b. Louisville, Miss., June 16, 1951; d. Delbert D. and Patricia (Lashley) Estes; m. James Earl Dickens, Aug. 22, 1970; children: Deedra, Darren. Student, Miss. Coll., 1969-71. Music/youth dir. Bethany Bapt. Ch., Prentiss, Miss., 1983-87, Whitesand Bapt. Ch., Prentiss, Miss., 1987—; cust. svc. specialist Miss. Power & Light, Prentiss, Miss., 1986—; youth-ASSIST Team Jeff Davis Assc., Prentiss, Miss. 1987—. Mem. GFWC-MFWC Jr. Civic League (pres.), GJWC-MFWC Twentieth Century Club (v.p 1990, pres. 1991). Baptist. Home: 1471 Third St Prentiss MS 39474-0331

DICKENS, GEORGE MECOM, minister; b. Washington, June 27, 1947; s. George Willis and Margaret Winifred (Lee) D.; m. Patricia Ellen Galt, Aug. 26, 1969; children: Polly Ann, Heather Michelle, Joel Edward, George Wilson. AA, Prince George Community Coll., Largo, Md., 1977; BS, U. Md., 1978; B of Christian Theology, Atlantic Bapt. Bible Coll., 1990. Ordained to ministry Ind. Bapt. Ch., 1990. Dir. Awana Clubs 1st Bapt. Ch., Calvert County, Md., 1983-86; pastor North Woods Bapt. Ch., Cumberland, Va., 1989-90, Cen. Bapt. Ch., Charleston, W.Va., 1990—. With USN, 1967-71. Mem. Atlantic Bapt. Bible Fellowship, W.Va. Bapt. Bible Fellowship (exec. sec. 1991). Office: Cen Bapt Ch 3845 Chesterfield Ave Charleston WV 25304-2617

DICKENSON, DANIEL DAVID, minister, retirement home administrator; b. Richmond, Va., Nov. 5, 1932; s. Daniel David Dickenson and Ellen Armistead (Guerrant) Barnes; m. Margaret Lois Boyer, June 11, 1954; children: Daniel David III, Thomas Boyer, Elizabeth Guerrant. BA, Washington & Lee U., 1954; BD, Union Theol. Sem., Richmond, 1957, ThM, 1963, D in Ministry, 1973. Ordained to ministry Presbyn. Ch., 1957; lic. nursing home adminstr., Va., Fla. Pastor Ben Salem and Poplar Hill Presbyn. Chs., Lexington, Va., 1957-60; asst. to ednl. sec. Bd. of World Missions U.S. Presbyn. Ch., Nashville, 1960-62; pastor Berryville (Va.) and Stone's Chapel Presbyn. Chs., 1963-70, Lafayette Presbyn. Ch., Norfolk, Va., 1970-77; pres. Westminster-Canterbury in Hampton Rds., Inc., Va. Beach, Va., 1977-85; exec. dir. Fla. Presbyn. Homes, Inc., Lakeland, 1986-87, Vicar's Landing, Ponte Vedra Beach, Fla., 1987-89, Meadowood, Worcester, Pa., 1990—. Commr. Ea. Va. Med. Authority, Norfolk, 1985. Am. Coll. Health Care Adminstrs., Pa. Assn. Homes for the Aging, Am. Assn. Homes for the Aging. Republican. Lodge: Rotary (pres. Northside Norfolk club 1977, founding pres. Cape Henry club, Virginia Beach, 1983, Paul Harris fellow 1982). Home: 2035 Ryans Run Lansdale PA 19446 Office: PO Box 670 Worcester PA 19490

DICKERMAN, DAVID LESLIE, pastor; b. Lynn, Mass., Jan. 27, 1943; s. Frederick Emery and Bessie Ruth (Butler) D.; m. Susan Helen Pavlovich, Aug. 13, 1967 (div. 1990); children: Peter Frederick, Andrew John. BA, Springfield Coll., 1965; MDiv, Yale U., 1969; D in Ministry, Hartford Sem., 1980. Ordained to ministry United Ch. of Christ, 1969. Parish assoc. United Ch. on the Green, New Haven, Conn., 1967-69; asst. min. 1st Congl. Ch., Dalton, Mass., 1969-70; assoc. min. Immanuel Congl. Ch., Hartford, Conn., 1970-77; sr. min. Mittineague Congl. Ch., West Springfield, Mass., 1977-85; sr. pastor Grace Ch., United Ch. of Christ, Framingham, Mass., 1985—; corporator United Ch. Bd. for Homeland Ministries, Cleve., 1987—; pres. Star Island United Ch. of Christ, Boston, 1976-87; chairperson Family Life Task Force, Mass. Conf., United Ch. of Christ, Framingham, 1981-87; bd. dirs. Star Island Corp., Rye, N.H. Author: On First Looking Into Chapman's Piloting, 1976; editor: Of Things Not Seen, 1969, Karl Barth and the Future of Theology, 1969, Dear Folks: The War Letters of Frederick E. Dickerman, 1983; author numerous hymns; contbr. articles to profl. publs. Chmn. Community Devel. Adv. Group, Framingham, 1987—; mem. South Middlesex Homelessness Task Force, Framingham, 1988—; corporator Framingham Union Hosp., 1987—; dir. Metrowest Leadership Acad., Framingham, 1988—. Mem. Am. Guild Organists, Rotary (pres. Framingham chpt. 1985—). Democrat. Office: Grace Ch United Ch Christ 73 Union Ave Framingham MA 01701

DICKEY, GARY ALAN, minister; b. Santa Monica, Calif., Jan. 25, 1946; s. Charles Harry and Audrey W. (White) D.; m. Tamara Jean Kimble, Jan. 11, 1976. BA, UCLA, 1968; MDiv, Fuller Theol. Sem., Pasadena, 1972; DMin, Sch. Theology, Claremont, Calif., 1974. Assoc. pastor Magnolia Pk. United Meth. Ch., Burbank, Calif., 1974-78; sr. pastor St. James United Meth. Ch., Pasadena, 1978-90, First United Meth. Ch. of Canoga Park, 1990—; exec. com. mem. Calif.-Pacific Ann. Conf. Bd. of Ordained Ministry, 1980-88; chmn. Pasadena Dist. Com. on Ordained Ministry, 1978-90; supervising pastor Bd. Higher Edn., Nashville, 1978—. Recipient Polonia Restituta, Polish Peoples Republic, 1990. Mem. Soc. Colonial Wars, Soc. War of 1812 (chaplian 1989—), Soc. of Sons of Am. Revolution (chaplain 1988—, Outstanding Citizenship award 1990), Soc. of Sons of the Revolution, Descendants of Soldiers of Valley Forge, Rotary (pres. 1989-90, Paul Harris fellow 1986). Republican. Methodist. Avocations: photography, travel, genealogical research. Home: 22167 Bryant St West Hills CA 91304 Office: First United Meth Ch 22700 Sherman Way West Hills CA 91307

DICKIE, ARTHUR WILLIAM, minister, engineer; b. Dunedin, New Zealand, Jan. 6, 1927; came to U.S., 1985; s. Matthew Alexander and Jane (Scarlet) D.; m. Catherine Elizabeth Burton, Jan. 8, 1955; children: Mark, Andrew, Elizabeth, Anne, Alice. Grad., Trinity Meth. Theol. Coll., Aukland, New Zealand, 1953; degree in art, Auckland U., 1953. Ordained to ministry United Ch. Christ.; chartered engr., Eng. Pastor Meth. Ch. New Zealand, Ohura and Whakatane, New Zealand, 1954-60, Waihi-Paeroa, 1977-85; engr., worker priest Tasman Pulp & Paper Co., Kawerau, New Zealand, 1960-74; engr., interim pastor Standards Assn. New Zealand, Wellington, 1974-77; pastor Bethel Congl. Ch. United Ch. Christ, White Salmon, Wash., 1985—. Mem. Inst. Energy (com. 1975-77), Inst. Profl. Engrs. New Zealand, Rotary (editor newsletter White Salmon club 1978-88). Home: 522 Grandview PO Box 219 White Salmon WA 98672 Office: Bethel Congl Ch 480 E Jewett Blvd PO Box 219 White Salmon WA 98672

DICKINSON, CHARLES CAMERON, III, theologian, educator; b. Charleston, W.Va., May 13, 1936; s. Charles Cameron and Frances Ann (Saunders) D., Jr.; m. JoAnne Walton. BA cum laude, Dartmouth Coll., 1958; BD, Pitts. Theol. Sem., 1965; PhD, U. Pitts., 1973. Prof. English, Greek and N.T. Ecole de Theologie Kimbanguiste, Zaire, 1972; asst. prof. systematic theology and philosophy Union Theol. Sem., Richmond, Va., 1974-75; asst. prof. religion and philosophy Morris Harvey Coll., Charleston, 1975-79; prof. Am. Coll. of Rome, 1979; research prof. U. Charleston, 1980-81; curatorial assoc. manuscript collections Andover-Harvard Theol. Library, 1981-86; vis. scholar Christ Ch., Oxford (Eng.) U., 1979, Harvard U. Div. Sch., 1980; prof. linguistics and lit. Hebei Tchrs U., Shijiazhuang, Hebei Province, China, 1983-84; dir. Univ. Press Edits./Mountain State Press, Charleston, 1980-83; lectr. Harvard Med. Sch., 1985-88. Author: One Thing Necessary: The Word of God in Preaching, 1988; contbr. articles, revs. to profl. jours. Bd. dirs., mem. ednl. coun. River Sch., Charleston, 1978-81; bd. dirs. Charleston Chamber Music Soc., Kanawha Valley Youth Orch., Charleston Ballet, W.Va. Opera Theater, Kanawha Pastoral Counseling Ctr., Boston Conservatory. With USMC, 1958-61. Entrance fellow Chgo. Theol. Sem., 1962; Chgo. U. Div. Sch. scholar, 1962. Fellow Royal Soc. Arts; mem. AAAS, Karl Barth Soc. N.Am. (dir.), Am. Acad. Religion, Soc. Bibl. Lit., Am. Theol. Soc., Am. Philos. Assn., Am. Assn. Advancement Humanities, W.Va. Philos. Soc., W.Va. Assn. Humanities, Internat. Bonhoeffer Soc., Edgewood Country Club (Charleston), Wichita Club, Univ. Club (Wichita Falls, Pitts.), Yale Club (N.Y.), Harvard Club (Boston, Dallas, France), Boston Athenaeum, Am. Club of Paris, Cercle de l'Union Interalliée, Rotary (chmn. Charleston Club student exchange com. 1978-79). Democrat. Office: 1111 City National Bldg Wichita Falls TX 76301-3309 *On proud days, I swell with the Protestant spirit which brought the "rise of the West." On black days, I am glad I shall not live to see us kill all the animals, cut down all the trees, and crowd the earth with 20,000,000,000 people. Which shall it be? Earth's fate lies in our hands.*

DICKINSON, MARYANNA, ecumenical agency administrator. Pres. Chs. United, Inc., Cedar Rapids, Iowa. Office: Chs United Inc 222 29th St SE Cedar Rapids IA 52403*

DICKINSON, RICHARD DONALD NYE, clergyman, educator, theological seminary administrator; b. Monson, Mass., Aug. 1, 1929; s. Richard Donald Nye and Phoebe Abigail (Naylor) D.; m. Nancy Leland Stone, Nov. 26, 1955; children: Elizabeth Stone, Richard Donald Nye III, Edward David McCrea. B.A., Am. Internat. Coll., 1950, M.A., 1951; S.T.B., Boston U., 1954, Ph.D., 1959; Certificate, Institut Oecumenique, Geneva, 1955. Ordained to ministry United Ch. of Christ; chaplain, instr. Wheaton Coll., Norton, Mass., 1957-62; assoc. dir. Quaker Confs. in So. Asia, 1962-64; sr. research officer Inst. for Social Studies, The Hague, Netherlands, 1964-67; sec. for specialized assistance World Council Chs., 1967-68; now cons.; prof. Christian social ethics Christian Theol. Sem., Indpls., 1968-74, v.p., dean, 1974-86, acting pres., 1986-87, pres., 1987—; chmn. devel. commn. World Coun. Chs.; mem. edn. commn. Nat. Coun. Chs., 1972-74; mem. ch. world service com.; incorporating mem. Center for Exploration Values and Meaning.; bd. dirs. internat. affairs div. Am. Friends Service Com., div. overseas ministries of Christian Ch. Author: The Christian College and National Development, 1967, Line and Plummet, 1968, The Christian College in Developing India, 1969, To Set at Liberty the Oppressed, 1975, Poor, Yet Making Many Rich, 1983. Bd. dirs. The Gemmer Found., Ind. Com. Econ. Edn.; mem. Greater Indpls. Progress Com. Mem. Am. Soc. for Christian Ethics, Soc. for Sci. Study Religion, Rotary. Home: 445 Blue Ridge Indianapolis IN 46208 Office: 1000 W 42d St Indianapolis IN 46208

DICKSON, ALEX DOCKERY, bishop; b. Alligator, Miss., Sept. 9, 1926. B.B.A., U. Miss., 1949; M.Div., U. of the South, 1958; M.E., Miss. Coll., 1972; m. Charlotte Perkins. Ordained to ministry Episcopal Ch., 1958. Rector, Chapel of the Cross, Rolling Fork, Miss.; vicar St. Paul's Ch., Hollandale, Miss., 1958-62; rector St. Columb's Ch., Jackson, Miss., 1962-68; rector, headmaster All Saints' Episcopal Sch., Vicksburg, Miss., 1968-83; first bishop Diocese of West Tenn., Memphis, 1983—. Office: Episcopal Ch 692 Poplar Ave Memphis TN 38105

DICKSON, JOHN B., minister; b. Gettysburg, Pa., Sept. 5, 1909; s. James Allen and Mary Edna D.; m. Alice McCollum, Feb. 1, 1938; children: Martha Dickson Hiller, Mary Dickson Card. AB, Gettysburg Coll., Pa., 1931; MD, Columbia Sem., Decatur, Ga., 1934; postgrad., Princeton Sem.; DD, Rhodes Coll., Memphis, 1947. Ordained to ministry, Presbyn. Ch. (USA), 1934. Minister Morningside Ch., Atlanta, 1934-43; minister First Presbyn. Ch., Greenwood, Miss., 1943-48, Tampa, Fla., 1948-72; minister emeritus First Presbyn. Ch., Tampa, 1972—; parish assoc. Peace Meml. Presbyn. Ch., Clearwater, Fla., 1979—; pres. Fla. Coun. Chs., 1958-60; trustee Eckerd Coll., St. Petersburg, 1958—. Author: Living Echoes, 1957. Active in past ARC, Travelers Aid Soc., Family Svcs., all Tampa. Mem. Sigma Chi, Masons. Home: 221 N Osceola Ave Clearwater FL 34615

DICKSON, RICHARD SCOTT, youth and music minister; b. Sparta, Ga., Aug. 1, 1957; s. George Lee and Earline (Frazier) D.; m. Donna Christine Finger, Jan. 21, 1983. BS, Ga. Coll., 1978; M of Ch. Music., Southwestern Bapt. Theol. Sem., 1982. Ordained to ministry Bapt. Ch. 1982. Min. music and youth Southside Bapt. Ch., Ft. Pierce, Fla., 1982-84, min. music and edn., 1984-86; min. youth and music 1st Bapt. Ch., Trion, Ga., 1987—; associational dir. music. Indian River Bapt. Assn., Ft. Pierce, 1985-86, Chattooga Bapt. Assn., Trion, 1987-89, 90—, Vacation Bible Sch. team, 1988-89; state music specialist, Ga. Bapt. Conv., Atlanta, 1990—. Mem. System Media Com. Trion City Schs., 1989-90. Mem. Ga. Bapt. Youth Mins. Fellowship (regional v.p. 1990), Ga. Bapt. Ch. Music Conf. Home: 321 Church St Trion GA 30753 Office: 1st Bapt Ch 336 Church St Trion GA 30753 *It seems that much of what we do in our hectic lives is relatively unimportant. Viewed from a thousand years in the future it surely pales in significance. Maybe we should heed the writer of Ecclesiastes who said, "Fear God, and keep his commandments: for this is the whole duty of man."*

DICKSON, WILLIAM HAROLD, JR., church program administrator; b. Andrade, Calif., Oct. 18, 1937; s. William Harold and Lola Virginia (Swinson) D.; m. Barbara Jean Claudette Beebe, Mar. 29, 1956 (div. Dec. 1975); children: Laurie, Rachel, Nicci, Andrew; m. Jacqueline Scott Lesure, Jan. 13, 1976; children: Bryan, Dean Langenfeld. BA, Calif. State U., Hayward, 1978, MPA, 1982. Adminstrv. officer St. Michael's Epsicopal Ch., Issaquah, Wash., 1984-85; exec. asst. to bishop Episcopal Diocese of Spokane, 1989—; sec. Diocesen Corp., Spokane, 1989—; dir. Cen. Terr. Diocesan Housing, Spokane, 1989—; mgr. FAA, Seattle, 1959-84, ret. 1984. Comdr. Spokane Squadron CAP, Spokane, 1987-90. With USAF, 1955-59. Mem. Brotherhood of St. Andrew, MPA Alumni Assn. Calif. State U., Exchange Club, (pres. 1989—), St. Andrews Soc. (v.p. 1989-90), Elks. Republican. Home: E 15319 8th Ave Veradale WA 99037 Office: E 245 13th Ave Spokane WA 99202

DIEDERICH, SISTER ANNE MARIE, college president; b. Cleve., Apr. 8, 1943. BA in English, Ursuline Coll. for Women, 1966; MA in Ednl. Adminstrn., John Carroll U., 1975; PhD in Edn. Policy and Leadership, Ohio State U., 1988. Joined Order St. Ursula, Roman Cath. Ch., 1961. Tchr. Villa Angela Acad., Cleve., 1966-70, asst. prin., 1971-76, prin., 1976-82; tchr. Beaumont Sch. for Girls, 1982-84; pres. Ursuline Coll., Pepper Pike, Ohio, 1986—. Mem. Leadership Cleve. '89. Dan H. Eikenberry scholar Ohio State U., 1985; William R. and Marie A. Flesher fellow Ohio State U., 1986. Mem. Ohio Tchr. Edn. and Adv. Commn., Phi Kappa Phi. Office: Ursuline Coll 2550 Lander Rd Cleveland OH 44124

DIEMER, CARL JOHN, JR., minister; b. Mobile, Ala., July 2, 1938; s. Carl John Diemer and Nellie Mary Robine; m. Gayle Carolyn Sparks, July 6, 1963; children: Curtis, Christy. BSME, Va. Inst. Tech., 1960; MDiv, Southwestern Bapt. Theol. Sem., 1965, ThD, 1972. Ordained to ministry Bapt. Ch., 1966. Pastor Forestburg (Tex.) Bapt. Ch., 1966-69, Villebrook Bapt. Ch., Hazelwood, Mo., 1969-73; prof. Liberty Bapt. Theol. Sem., Lynchburg, Va., 1973—. Contbr. articles to profl. jours. Mem. Evang. Theol. Soc., Am. Hist. Soc., Va. Bapt. Hist. Soc., Profl. Tennis Registry, Profl. Tennis Assn. Home: 105 Pacos St Lynchburg VA 24502 Office: Liberty Bapt Theol Sem 3765 Candlers Mountain Rd Lynchburg VA 24506 *Living a life that is pleasing to God is not easier than the alternative, but is better.*

DIETER, SISTER MARY, religious organization executive, accountant; b. Pitts., Feb. 14, 1949; d. Jacob I. and Rita R. (Haffner) D. BA in Math., La Roche Coll., Allison Park, Pa., 1971; MBA, Duquesne U., 1975. CPA, Pa.; joined Sisters of Divine Providence, Roman Cath. Ch., 1967—. Tchr. Sacred Heart Elem. Sch., New Philadelphia, Ohio, 1971=72, Divine Providence Acad., Cheswick, Pa., 1972-73; asst. to treas. La Roche Coll., 1976-77, treas., 1977-8l, trustee, 1982-88; treas. Sisters of Divine Providence, Allison Park, 1982-88; fin. analyst Entek, Inc., 1988-89; computer cons. Sisters Divine Providence, Allison Park, Pa., 1989—; assoc. dir. parish reorgn. and revitalization project Diocese of Pitts., 1990-91. Trustee Divine Providence Hops., Pitts., 1980-88. Mem. AICPA, Pa. Inst. CPA's. Democrat. Home and Office: 9000 Babcock Blvd Allison Park PA 15101

DIETRICH, RICHARD SMITH, minister, educator; b. Dover, N.J., Oct. 25, 1947; s. Richard Vincent and Frances Elizabeth (Smith) D.; m. Robin Lee Smail, Aug. 28, 1969; children: Christopher Roy William, Nathanael Richard Smail. BA, Carleton Coll., 1969; MA, Tulane U., 1971; D Ministry, Union Theol. Sem., Richmond, Va., 1981. Ordained to ministry Presbyn. Ch. (U.S.A.), 1981. Assoc. minister 1st Presbyn. Ch., Gainesville, Fla., 1981-85; min. Huffman Presbyn. Ch., Birmingham, Ala., 1985—; adj. instr. Jefferson State Community Coll., Birmingham, 1988—; v.p. bd. Disciples-Presbyn. Student Ctr., Gainesville, 1982-83, St. Francis House, Gainesville, 1983-85; del. Synod of Living Waters, Nashville, 1990; vol. chaplain hospice Med. Ctr. East, Birmingham, 1990—. Editor: The Hebrew Scriptures, 1984, Estraightaway newsletter, 1990—; contbr. articles and book revs. to jours. Democrat. Office: Huffman Presbyn Ch 9312 Parkway E Birmingham AL 35215

DIETZ, FRANK HERBERT, minister; b. New Orleans, Sept. 28, 1940; s. Harold F. and Ione (Canty) D.; m. Karen E. Pantermuehl, Aug. 14, 1941; children: Kevin P., Mark D. AB magna cum laude, Elmhurst Coll., 1962; MDiv with honors, Eden Theol. Sem., 1965; MS in Edn., Tex. A&M U., 1970; DDiv, Huston-Tillotson Coll., 1983. Ordained to ministry United Ch. of Christ, 1965. Pastor Irving Park Emmanuel United Ch. of Christ, Chgo., 1965-66; assoc. pastor Congl. United Ch. of Christ, Lockport, Ill., 1966-68; pastor Faith United Ch., Bryan and College Station, Tex., 1968-75, St. Peter United Ch. of Christ, Houston, 1975-82; exec. dir. Tex. Conf. of Chs., Austin, 1982—; mem. Coun. for Lay Life and Work, United Ch. of Christ, 1972-82, Coun. on Ecumenism, N.Y.C., 1986—; cons. Town and Country Ch. Conf. Tex. A&M U., 1982—, Ch. Rels. Adv. Group Tex. Dept. Human Svcs., 1983—; bd. dirs. Corp. Child Devel. Fund, Tex., 1987—; liaison for region World Council Chs., 1989, World Mission and Evangelism Conf. Contbr. articles to various religious jours. Bd. dirs. Tex. IMPACT, 1982—; bd. dirs. Huston-Tillotson Coll., Austin, 1983—, chmn. bd. dirs., 1989—; pres. Tex. Valley Disaster Relief, Austin, 1983; mem. Gov.'s Vol. Conf., State of Tex., Austin, 1983-89; coord. internat. travel seminar Nat. Assn. Ecumenical Staff, 1990; mem. exec. com. Texans Who Care, 1987—; bd. dirs. Projecto LIbertad Tex., 1982—, Rural Social Sci. by Extension Dept. Rural Sociology and Agrl. Extension Service, 1986—, Corp. Child Devel. Fund, Tex., 1987—, Coalition for Justice in the Maquiladoras, 1989—; mem. adv. bd. Tex. Ch. World Svc./CROP, 1982—, mem. nat. edn. and fund raising com., 1986—; panel mem. Beneficial Fin. Scholarships for Tex., Collaborative Elder Abuse Prevention Progam, 1986—; mem. Council Regional and Local Ecumenism of Nat. Council of the Chs. of Christ, U.S.A., 1988—, mem. ch. world svc. and witness unit, 1991—; mem. adv. coun. Tex. Adolescenty Pregnancy Prevention, 1988—, chair, 1991-92. Recipient Ecumenical Leadership award Eden Theol. Sem., 1991. Avocations: reading, drama, art. Home: 7613 Barcelona Cove Austin TX 78752

DIETZ, JOHN FREDERICK, minister; b. Canonsburg, Pa., Mar. 4, 1944; s. Herman Frederick and Martha Lucille (McCrory) D.; m. Frances Virginia Cockrell, Aug. 20, 1966; children: Allyson, Jeremy. BA, Muskingum Coll., 1966; MA, Tufts U., 1968; MDiv, Pitts. Theol. Sem., 1971; PhD, Duke U., 1976. Ordained to ministry Presbyn. Ch., 1974. Min. Calvary United Presbyn. Ch., Wilson, N.C., 1974-82, North Buffalo United Presbyn. Ch., Washington, Pa., 1982—; dir. Washington Presbytery Acad., Eighty Four, Pa., 1982—; moderator Synod of the Piedmont, United Presbyn. Ch. USA, 1981-82; adj. prof. religion Waynesburg (Pa.) Coll., 1990—. Trustee Barber-Scotia Coll., Concord, N.C., 1982-88. Mem. Soc. Christian Ethics, Assn. Profl. Ch. Educators. Home: 447 2d St Washington PA 15301 Office: Washington Presbytery Acad PO Box 146 Eighty Four PA 15330

DIETZE, CHARLES EDGAR, minister; b. Savannah, Ga., Jan. 21, 1919; s. Ernest and Mary Edith (Fetzer) D.; m. Mary Nettie Peavyhouse, Dec. 28, 1940 (dec. 1980); children: Mary Katherine Dietze Ballance, Charles William; m. Irma Spencer, Nov. 30, 1980. BA, Transylvania U., 1940; BD, Lexington Theol. Sem., 1944; DD (hon.), Atlantic Christian Coll., 1965. Ordained to ministry Disciples of Christ Ch., 1941. Min. 1st Christian Ch., Morehead, Ky., 1943-47; min. 1st Christian Ch., Henderson, Ky., 1948-52, min. emeritus, 1983—; min. Christian Ch., North Middletown, Ky., 1952-55; v.p. Lexington (Ky.) Theol. Sem., 1955-65; regional min. Christian Ch. N.C., Wilson, 1965-81; nat. pres. Disciples Peace Fellowship, 1956-57; nat. v.p. Bd. Higher Edn., 1968-69; pres. N.C. Coun. Chs., Durham, 1970-71; nat. pres. Conf. Regional Mins., 1974-76. Author: God's Trustees, 1976, The Henderson Crusade, 1983, (novel) The Place, 1991. Pres. St. Anthony's Hospice, Henderson, 1983. Recipient Spl. Centennial citation Lexington Theol. Sem., 1965. Mem. Lions (chmn. sight conservation com. Henderson club 1983-84). Democrat. Home: 322 Hancock St Henderson KY 42420 *I believe that life is a gift from God; that I am a trustee of that gift, to be used responsibly for the benefit of all humankind.*

DIGNAZIO, EILEEN KAZOKAS, religious education administrator; b. New Britain, Conn., June 7, 1946; d. Alexander Richard and Mary Catherine (Piatek) Kazokas; m. Thomas Dignazio, July 13, 1968 (div. Dec. 1986); children: Jennifer, Joyanne, Kristen. BS, Cen. Conn. State Coll., New Britain, 1968; MS, Cen. Conn. State Coll., 1974; MA, St. Joseph Coll., West Hartford, Conn., 1989. Dir. religious edn. Our Lady of Mercy Ch.,

Plainville, Conn., 1981-88, Sacred Heart Ch., Southbury, Conn., 1989—; dir./founder Sacred Heart Parish Libr., 1990; chmn. Children's Liturgy Commn., Southbury, 1989-91, Plainville, 1983-88. Participant March for Life, Washington, 1990, Hartford, 1990, 91. Democrat. Roman Catholic. Home: 58 Washburn Dr Plainville CT 06062 Office: Sacred Heart Parish 910 Main Street S Southbury CT 06062

DILDAY, RUSSELL HOOPER, seminary president; b. Amarillo, Tex., Sept. 30, 1930; s. R. Hooper and Opal Dilday; m. Betty Doyen, Aug. 15, 1952; children: Robert, Nancy Dilday Duck, Ellen Dilday Garrett. B.A., Baylor U., 1952, LL.D., 1978; B.Div., Southwestern Baptist Theol. Sem., 1955, Ph.D. in Philosophy of Religions, 1959; D.D. (hon.), Mercer U., 1975; L.H.D. (hon.), William Jewell Coll., 1979. Ordained to ministry Baptist Ch. Pastor 1st Bapt. Ch., Antelope, Tex., 1952-56; pastor 1st Bapt. Ch., Clifton, Tex., 1956-59; instr. religion Baylor U., Waco, Tex., 1957-58; pastor Tallowood Bapt. Ch., Houston, 1959-69, 2d-Ponce de Leon Bapt. Ch., Atlanta, 1969-77; pres. Southwestern Bapt. Theol. Sem., Fort Worth, 1978—; pres. Assn. Theol. Schs. in U.S. and Can., 1988-90. Author: The Teacher's Bible Commentary, 1972, You Can Overcome Discouragement, 1977, Prayer Meeting Resources, Vol. I, 1977, The Doctrine of Biblical Authority, 1982, Personal Computer: A New Tool for Ministers, 1985, I & II Kings, Word Communicator's Commentary, 1987. Recipient Valley Forge Honor Cert. award, 1976, Outstanding Alumnus award Baylor U., 1977, Disting. Alumnus award Southwestern Bapt. Theol. Sem., 1979, Baylor U., 1983. Mem. AAUP, Am. Acad. Religion, Fort Worth C. of C., Kiwanis, Rotary. Lodges: Kiwanis, Rotary. Office: Southwestern Bapt Theol Sem PO Box 22000-0040 Fort Worth TX 76122

DI LELLA, ALEXANDER ANTHONY, biblical studies educator; b. Paterson, N.J., Aug. 14, 1929; s. Alessandro and Adelaide (Grimaldi) Di L. B.A., St. Bonaventure U., 1952; S.T.L., Cath. U. Am., 1959, Ph.D., 1962; S.S.L., Pontifical Bibl. Inst., Rome, 1964. Entered Franciscan Order, Roman Catholic Ch., 1949; ordained priest, 1955. Lectr. O.T. and bibl. Greek Holy Name Coll., Washington, 1964-67; asst. prof. Semitic lang. Cath. U. Am., 1966-68, assoc. prof., 1968-76, assoc. prof. Bibl. studies, 1976-77, prof., 1977—; adj. prof. O.T., Washington Theol. Union, 1969-72; mem. Rev. Standard Version Bible Com., 1982—; chmn. bd. of control New Am. Bible, 1988—. Assoc. editor, translator New American Bible, 1965-87; author: The Hebrew Text of Sirach: A Text-Critical and Historical Study, 1966, The Book of Daniel, 1978, Proverbs in the Old Testament in Syriac According to the Peshitta Version, 1979, The Wisdom of Ben Sira, 1987; contbr. articles and revs. to scholarly and popular publs. Mem. instnl. rev. bd. Dubroff Eye Ctr., Silver Spring, Md., 1982—; mem. adv. com. oncology unit George Washington U. Hosp., Washington, 1983—. Am. Sch. Oriental Research fellow, 1962-63; Guggenheim fellow, 1972-73; Assn. Theol. Schs. in U.S. and Can. fellow, 1979-80. Mem. Soc. Bibl. Lit. (pres. Chesapeake Bay region 1972-73), Cath. Bibl. Assn. (pres. 1975-76, del. to Council on Study of Religion 1971-72). Home: Curley Hall Cath U Am Washington DC 20064 Office: Cath U Am Rm 420 Caldwell Washington DC 20064 *Most of my adult life I have been a student of Biblical languages and literatures, interpretation and theology. Teaching, research and publications enable me to convey to others the value of the Bible as a primary document of Judaism and Christianity and as a significant factor in Western culture and civilization.*

DILL, ELLEN RENÉE, minister; b. Detroit, Jan. 2, 1949; d. Clarence Lorenzo and Melvin Elizabeth (Knowles) D.; m. Norval Ignatius Brown, May 24, 1980; children: Christopher Edward Brown, Crystal Elizabeth Brown. BA, Nazareth Coll. Mich., 1972; MDiv, Garrett Evang. Sem., Evanston, Ill., 1979; postgrad., Northwestern U., Evanston, Ill., 1979-82, Chgo. Theol. Sem., 1988—. Lic. to ministry United Meth. Ch., 1974. Teaching asst. Head Start St. Agnes Ch., Detroit, 1966-68; tchr. Eastside Vicariate Sch., Detroit, 1972-77; pastor St. Luke United Meth. Ch., Chgo., 1980-82; assoc. pastor First United Meth. Ch., Chgo., 1982-84; pastor Clair-Christian United Meth. Ch., Chgo., 1984-88, Community United Meth. Ch., Markham, Ill., 1988-90, Woodlawn United Meth. Ch., Chgo., 1990—; condr. seminar on women in ministry Garrett Evang. Sem., 1981, condr. seminar on ch. and soc., 1980, instr. continuing edn. seminar for clergy in adminstrn., 1987; bd. dirs. So. Dist. Bd. Ordained Ministry, Bd. Ch. Bldg. Location; mem. So. Dist. Coun. on Ministries, So. Dist. Strategy Com.; former chmn. No. Ill. Conf. Bd. Edn., So. Dist. Bd. Edn.; former asst. chmn. bd. edn. United Meth. Ch.; mem. Detroit Conf. Elders Orders, 1985; spiritual dir. Walk to Emmaus, 1991; mem. No. Ill. Conf. Commn. on Status and Role of Women, 1991—, United Meth. Found., U. Chgo., 1990—; mem. monotoring com. on implementation recommendations of Task Force on Configuration, No. Ill. Conf.; mem. planning com. Western Dist. Lab. Sch Innovation, Chgo. City Coun. meeting, 1991. Co-author: Teachers Guide: Two Hundred Years of American Methodism, 1981; editorial advisor The Christian Ministry jour., 1987—; contbr. articles to profl. jours. Bd. dirs. Austin Christian Law Ctr., 1983—, Child Serve Community Coun., Chgo., 1984-88, Garrett-Evang. Sem., 1978; area chairperson Mayor's Com. to Keep Detroit Beautiful. Recipient citation Mayor's Com. To Keep Detroit Beautiful, 1966, citation for excellence in journalism Mich. Press Assn., 1978; Hartman scholar, 1979; Dempster Grad. fellow, 1980, Hartman fellow, 1981. Mem. NAFE, Nat. Assn. Bus. and Profl. Women, Nat. Platform Soc., Black United Methodists for Ch. Renewal (citation for svc. 1982), Clergy Cluster, So. Suburban Clergy Cluster, Ecumenical Ministrial Assn., Lay Acad. No. Ill. Conf. Avocations: sewing, reading, teaching, writing, studying. Home: 8600 S Cregier Chicago IL 60617 Office: Woodlawn United Meth Ch 1208 E 64th St Chicago IL 60637 *In my life I have found that the power of evil is impotent when confronted by that which is good.*

DILL, GREGORY ALLAN, evangelist; b. Nassawadox, Va., May 22, 1949; s. George Thomas Jr. and Augustine (Kelley) D.; m. Barbara Brown, May 26, 1969; children: Rebecca Dianne, Sarah Elizabeth. B of Sacred Lit., Roanoke Bible Coll., 1971. Ordained to ministry Ch. of Christ, 1969. New ch. evangelist Dagsboro (Del.) Ch. of Christ, 1971-73; evangelist Rosedale (Va.) Ch. of Christ, 1973-77; assoc. min. Grundy (Va.) Ch. of Christ, 1977-80; evangelist worldwide, 1980-84; sr. min. Macedonia Ch. of Christ, Abingdon, Va., 1984—. Home: 5620 Lee Hwy Abingdon VA 24210 Office: PO Box 1385 Abingdon VA 24210

DILLAMAN, ROCKWELL LANE, minister; b. Butler, Pa., Apr. 8, 1949; s. Howard Cecil and Ethel Louise (Brandon) D.; m. Karen Jacalyn Staley, Aug. 5, 1972; children: Jason Rockwell, Shannon Rochelle, Autumn Marie. Student, Duquesne U., 1967-69; BA, Nyack Coll., 1973; MDiv, Asbury Theol. Sem., Wilmore, Ky., 1976. Ordained to ministry Christian and Missionary Alliance, 1977. Asst. pastor 1st Alliance Ch., Lexington, Ky., 1975-76, New Castle, Pa., 1976-77; sr. pastor North East (Pa.) Alliance Ch., 1977-84, Allegheny Ctr. Alliance Ch., Pitts., 1984—; pres. Edinboro (Pa.) Conf. Grounds, 1979-83; mem. numerous coms. Christian and Missionary Alliance, 1976—, conf. speaker in U.S. and overseas, 1986—; guest Christian TV program Project 90, 1989—. Contbr. articles to mags. Trustee Nyack (N.Y.) Coll., Alliance Theol. Sem., 1983—. Republican. Home: 128 Rene Dr Glenshaw PA 15116 Office: Allegheny Ctr Alliance Ch 250 E Ohio St Pittsburgh PA 15212 *God is looking for men with whom He can trust His message and His glory. If we will preach the unchanging Christ in a compassionate yet uncompromising manner, and humbly give the honor for any success to God, we will know His power in our work and His peace in our hearts.*

DILLARD, GEORGE STEWART, III, minister; b. Jacksonville, Fla., Dec. 17, 1958; s. George Stewart II and Carolyn Faye (Brown) D.; m. Reneé Cheryl Barnes, Mar. 26, 1988; 1 child, Tiffany Reneé. BS, Atlanta Christian Coll., 1983; postgrad., Emmanuel Sch. Religion, 1983-85. Ordained to ministry Christian Ch., 1980. Min. Countyline Christian Ch., Brooks, Ga., 1980-82, New Hope Christian Ch., Rogersville, Tenn., 1983-85; sr. min. 1st Christian Ch., Rincon, Ga., 1985—; pres. Min. Asst., Christian Ch., Savannah, Ga., 1986-88; v.p., treas., bd. dirs. Bd. Coastal Empire Christian Camp, Sylvania, Ga., 1986—; com. mem. Ga. Christian Youth Conv., Atlanta, 1987, Ga. Christian Missionary Rally, Atlanta, 1989—; chaplain Effingham County (Ga.) Sheriffs Dept., 1986—, Effingham County High Sch. Football, 1986—. Author column Mins. Thoughts, 1985—. Chmn. com. George Bush for Pres., 1988; chmn. Victims/Witness Asistance Program, Effingham County, 1989—; mem. Tidelands Coun. Prevention of Drug Abuse, Effingham County, 1989—; pres. Effingham County Athletic Booster Club, 1990—. Recipient Outstanding Young Mins. award N.Am. Christian Conv., Louisville, Ky., 1990. Mem. Rotary (bd. dirs. 1989-91). Home: 530 John Glenn Dr Rincon GA 31326 Office: 1st Christian Ch Hwy 21 Rincon GA 31326 *Have this attitude in yourselves which was in Christ Jesus. (Phil. 2:5). The world needs a Church which understands and lives this truth, that there is no price to great to pay in order to be obedient to the Father.*

DILLENBECK, HADLEY HERMAN, JR., religion educator; b. Ft. Plain, N.Y., June 5, 1964; s. Hadley H. Sr. and Marlene (Bailey) White; m. Diance C. Marshall, Dec. 12, 1984. Tchr. Body of Christ, Winchendon, Mass., 1989—; herd mgr. Otter River Farm, Winchendon, 1989—. Home: 188 Old Baldwinville Rd Winchendon MA 01475

DILLENBERGER, JANE, theology and visual arts educator. BA in Art History, U. Chgo., 1940; MA in Art History, Radcliffe Coll., 1944; postgrad., Drew U., 1958-59, LHD (hon.), 1991. Lectr. in Christianity and art Drew Theol. Sem., 1950-62, extension div. U. Calif., 1963-65; lectr. in Christianity and arts San Francisco Theol. Sem., 1963-65, assoc. prof., 1965-71; assoc. prof. visual arts and theology Grad. Theol. Union, Berkeley, Calif., 1967-76, prof. visual arts and theology, 1976-78, prof. emerita, 1978—; adj. prof. Jesuit Sch. Theology, 1976-78, Lone Mountain Coll., 1974-78, Trinity Coll., 1980-83, Pacific Sch. Religion, 1978—; guest curator various mus.; spl. researcher San Francisco Mus. Art, 1963-66; docent, mem. staff Newark Mus., 1945-55; head art dept. Boston Atheneum, 1944-45. Author: Style and Content in Christian Art, 1966, repub. under title Crossroad, 1986, Secular Art with Sacred Themes, 1969, Image and Spirit in Sacred and Secular Act, 1990; co-author: The Hand and the Spirit: Religious Art in America, 1700-1900, 1972, Perceptions of the Spirit in 20th-Century American Art, 1977, Perceptions of the Spirit: The Art of Elihu Vedder, 1969; editor: Paul Tillich: On Art and Architecture, 1987; Studies in Humanities series; mem. editorial bd. Isaac Hecker Studies in Religion and American Culture; contbr. articles to profl. publs. Fellow Lilly Endowment Fund, Inc., 1971-72, NEH, 1973-74, NEA, 1975-76; Rockefeller Found. grantee, 1961, 70-71. Mem. Am. Acad. Religion, Coll. Art Assn., Soc. for Art, Religion and Contemporary Culture (pres. 1987-90). Home: 1536 Le Roy Ave Berkeley CA 94708

DILLENBERGER, JOHN, emeritus educator, minister; b. St. Louis, July 11, 1918; s. Charles and Bertha (Hoffmann) D.; children: Eric John, Paul Gregor. B.A., Elmhurst Coll., 1940, D.D. (hon.), 1959; B.D., Union Theol. Sem., 1943; Ph.D., Columbia, 1948; D.D. (hon.), U. Vt., 1957; S.T.D. (hon.), Ch. Divinity Sch. Pacific, 1965, Ripon Coll., 1966; L.H.D. (hon.), U. San Francisco, 1966. Ordained to ministry United Ch. of Christ, 1943. Tutor asst. theology Union Theol. Sem., N.Y.C., 1947-48; instr. religion Princeton U., 1948-49; asst. prof. religion Columbia U., 1949-52, assoc. prof., 1952-54; assoc. prof. theology Harvard U. Div. Sch., 1954-57, Parkman prof. theology, 1957-58; Ellen S. James prof. systematic and hist. theology, grad. sch. and sem. Drew U., Madison, N.J., 1958-62; prof. hist. theology, dean grad. studies San Francisco Theol. Sem., San Anselmo, Calif., 1962-64; dean, pres., prof. hist. theology Grad. Theol. Union, Berkeley, Calif., 1962-72; prof. hist. theology Grad. Theol. Union, 1962-78, prof. emeritus, 1983—; pres. Hartford Sem., 1978-83. Author: God Hidden and Revealed, 1953, (with Claude Welch) Protestant Christianity: Interpreted Through Its Development, 1954, rev. and enlarged edit., 1987, Protestant Thought and Natural Science, 1960, Contours of Faith, 1969, Benjamin West: The Context of His Life's Work, 1971, (with Jane Dillenberger) Perceptions of the Spirit in 20th Century American Art, 1977, The Visual Arts and Christianity in America, 1984, rev. and enlarded edit., 1988, A Theology of Artistic Sensibilities, 1986.; editor: Martin Luther: Selections from His Writings, 1961, John Calvin: Selections from His Writings, 1971, Paul Tillich: On the Visual Arts and Architecture, 1987; chmn. editorial bd. Libr. of Protestant Thought, 1958-72. Mem. exec. com. Assn. Theol. Schs. U.S. and Can., 1970-74. Chaplain USN, 1943-46. Rsch. scholar Nat. Collection Fine Arts, Smithsonian Instn., 1973-74; grantee Nat. Endowment for Arts, 1973-77, NEH, 1977. Fellow Soc. for Values in Higher Edn., Soc. Arts, Religion and Contemporary Culture; mem. Am. Acad. Religion (chmn. rsch. and publs. com. 1977-79, v.p. 1985, pres.-elect 1986, pres. 1987). Home: 322 Hanover Ave # 201 Oakland CA 94606

DILLEY, TIMOTHY EUGENE, minister; b. Auburn, Ind., Nov. 25, 1958; s. David Eugene and Judy Ann (Duncan) D.; m. Deborah Ann Feher, July 11, 1981. BA cum laude, United Wesleyan Coll., Allentown, Pa., 1981; postgrad., Ashland (Ohio) Theol. Sem., 1983-86; MDiv, Meth. Theol. Sch., Delaware, Ohio, 1989. Minister visitation Zion Wesleyan Ch., Bath, Pa., 1979-81; minister Deland Wesleyan Ch., Temperance, Mich., 1981-85; sr. minister Epworth United Meth. Ch., Bluffton, Ind., 1986—. Named one of Outstanding Young Men of Am., 1985. Mem. Wesleyan Theol. Soc., Wells County Ministerial Assn. Republican. Methodist. Lodge: Masons. Avocations: piano, boating, fishing, reading. Home: 1211 W Cherry St Bluffton IN 46714 Office: Epworth United Meth Ch 1204 W Cherry St Bluffton IN 46714

DILLINGHAM, GRACE VOORHIS, lay worker; b. N.Y.C., Oct. 16, 1927; d. Frederic William and Mary Steeles (Voorhis) D. BA, Bryn Mawr Coll., 1949. Assoc. actuary Am. Coun. Life Ins., Washington, 1952-90; treas. St. Dunstan's Ch., Bethesda, Md., 1976—; del. Diocesan convs.; chmn. Commn. on Health and Life Ins., Episcopal Diocese Washington; alt. lay dep. to Gen. Conv., Episcopal Diocese Washington, 1988; lay dep. to Provincial Synod, Episcopal Diocese Washington, 1990. Fellow Soc. Actuaries. Home: 4601 N Park Ave #701 Chevy Chase MD 20815

DILLMAN, CHARLES NORMAN, religion educator; b. North Robinson, Ohio, Mar. 31, 1938; s. Robert Herman Dillman and Mildred (Baker) Fitzgerald; m. Alice Marie Bear; children: James Robert, Angie Beth. BA, Otterbein (Ohio) Coll., 1960; BDiv, Evang. Luth. Sem., 1964; ThM, Columbia Theol. Sem., 1968; PhD, U. Edinburgh, Scotland, 1978. Pastor Evang. United Brethren Ch., Ohio, 1958-67; min. West Ohio Conf., United Meth. Ch., 1968—; prof. Greenville (Ill.) Coll., 1970-74, Spring Arbor (Mich.) Coll., 1974—; chmn. profl. standards com. Spring Arbor Coll., 1989—; observer in attendance East German Ann. Conf., Evang. Meth. Ch., 1990-91; tchr. ch. youth; substitute preacher local chs. Contbr. articles to profl. jours. With Ohio N.G. NEH grantee U. Chgo., 1978. Mem. Soc. Bibl. Lit., Wesleyan Theol. Soc. (editorial com. 1976-84), Spring Arbor Coll. Alumni Assn. Home: 153 Burr Oak Spring Arbor MI 49283 Office: Spring Arbor Coll Spring Arbor MI 49283

DILLON, JOSEPH NEIL, pastor; b. Fresno, Calif., July 31, 1945; s. Howard Arthur and Blanch Marie (Nichols) D.; m. Paula Ann Gunovich, June 17, 1973; children: Chandra M., Ryan A. 0BA, Pacific Luth. U., 1970; MDiv, Northwestern Luth. Theol. Sem., 1976. Ordained to ministry, Luth. Ch., 1976. Pastor 1st Luth. Ch., Anconda, Mont., 1976-82, Messiah Luth. Ch., Billings, Mont., 1982-85; assoc. pastor Messiah Luth. Ch., Auburn, Wash., 1985-88; sr. pastor Messiah Luth. Ch., 1988—; dean, Evergreen Conf., South King Coun., Wash., 1990—; regional coun. Region I ELCA Southwest Wash., 1987-90, pres., 1988-90; pres., Auburn Ministrial Assn., 1988-90. Mem. Gov. Coun. Employment Planning, Anaconda, 1980-83; pres., bd. dirs., Anaconda Devel. Disabled, 1978-82; bd. dirs., Auburn Youth Resources, 1987—; mem. Human Resources Commn., City Auburn, 1987—. Sgt. U.S. Army, 1963-66. Mem. Lions. Home: 6307 37th Pl SE Auburn WA 98002 Office: Messiah Luth Ch 805 4th St NE Auburn WA 98002

DILLON, ROBERT CHAPMAN, church organization administrator; b. Proctorville, Ohio, June 5, 1926; s. Robert Evvan and Harriet Irene (Marks) D.; m. Shirley Ann Winget, Dec. 10, 1950; children: Kathryn, Mark, Douglas. Student, Ohio State U., 1946, 47; BA, Northwestern Coll., Mpls., 1954; postgrad., Trinity Coll. and Sem., Chgo., 1954-55, Belgium Colonial Sch., Brussels, 1955-56. Ordained to ministry Evang. Free Ch. Am., 1955. Missionary Evang. Free Ch. Am., Zaire, 1956-62; min. Evang. Free Ch. Am., Greeley, Colo., 1962-64; exec. dir. Evang. Free Ch. Am., Mpls., 1964—; dir. world missions Internat. Fedn. Evang. Free Ch. Am., Oslo, 1986—. Editor Evang. Beacon, 1972; contbr. numerous articles to religious publs. With AUS, 1945-46. Mem. Evang. Fgn. Missions Assn. (pres. 1987-89). Office: Evang Free Ch Am 901 E 78th St Minneapolis MN 55420

DILLON, RONALD GAY, minister; b. Matoaka, W.Va., June 29, 1948; s. Tresler Gay and Norma Lorraine (Belcher) D.; m. Elizabeth Ann Thompson, June 7, 1968; children: Daniel, Jonathan, Peter. AA, Bluefield (Va.) Coll., 1968; BA, Bluefield (W.Va.) State Coll., 1970; MDiv, New Orleans Bapt. Theol. Sem., 1973, D Ministry, 1975. Ordained to ministry So. Bapt. Conv., 1968. Pastor Fellowship Bapt. Ch., Princeton, W.Va., 1968-71, New Sharon Bapt. Ch., Husser, La., 1971-74, Grace Bapt. Ch., Parkersburg, W.Va., 1974-86, Highland Park Bapt. Ch., Charleston, S.C., 1986—; pres. W.Va. Conv. of So. Bapt. Conv., 1977, 78, 83-84; mem. gen. bd. S.C. Bapt. Conv., 1988—. Republican. Home: 1230 Woodside Dr Hanahan SC 29406 Office: Highland Park Bapt Ch 6211 Murray Dr Hanahan SC 29406 *God does not work in us or through us because we are worthy or ever will be. He chooses to use us because of who He is. It is a matter of grace.*

DILLON, VALERIE VANCE, church executive, author, magazine columnist; b. Chgo., Oct. 19, 1930; d. James Robert and Rose Matilda (Beauchamp) Vance; m. Raydon Thomas Dillon, Sept. 26, 1953; children: Karen, Patricia, Valerie, Donna. BS in Journalism, U. Ill., 1952; MA in Religion, Butler U., 1979; MA in Family Studies, Regis Coll., Denver, 1990. Radio newswriter UPI, Chgo., 1952-53; reporter Austin News and Garfieldian, Chgo., 1953-54; researcher, writer N.J. Cath. Conf., Trenton, 1966-73; family life educator Cath. Diocese of Trenton, 1968-73; dir. communications Ind. Cath. Conf., Indpls., 1973-79; news editor Criterion newspaper, Indpls., 1979-82; dir. family life Archdiocese of Indpls., 1982-91; advisor U.S. Bishops' Com. on Family, Washington, 1987—. Author: Your Child's Sex Life, 1966, Life in Our Hands, 1973, Becoming a Woman, 1990, (sch. curriculum) Choose Life, 1976; monthly columnist Columbia mag., 1981—. Trustee St. Meinrad (Ind.) Sem. and Coll., 1987—. Recipient various writing awards Cath. Press Assn., 1981, 83, Women's Press Club, Indpls., 1984, 86, Nat. Leadership award Nat. Family Life Drs. Assn., 1991, Respect Life award Assn. Indpls., 1991. Mem. Nat. Assn. Cath. Family Life Ministers (pres. 1987-89). Avocations: oil painting, golf, grandparenting. Home: 2740 Pomona Ct Indianapolis IN 46268

DIMINO, JOSEPH T., archbishop; b. N.Y.C., Jan. 7, 1923; s. Joseph Thomas and Mary (Helbig) D. B.A., Cathedral Coll., N.Y.C., 1945; M.A., Cath. U., 1962. Ordained priest, Roman Catholic Ch., 1949, bishop, 1983. Assoc. pastor Archdiocese of N.Y., N.Y.C., 1949-53; commd. lt. Chaplain Corps, U.S. Navy, 1952, advanced through grades to capt.; dir. Chaplains Sch. Chaplain Corps, U.S. Navy, Newport, R.I., 1971-74; with 11th Naval Dist. Chaplain Corps, U.S. Navy, San Diego, 1974-76; with Office of Chief of Chaplains Chaplain Corps, U.S. Navy, Washington, 1976-77; ret. Chaplain Corps, U.S. Navy, 1977; chancellor Mil. Vicariate, N.Y.C., 1977-83, vicar gen., 1983-91; mem. exec. bd. Nat. Conf. on Ministry of the Armed Forces, 1980-83; chmn. N.Y. State Cath. Com. on Chaplaincy, 1983-85. Author: Religious Education Curriculum for Navy, 1970. Decorated Meritorious Service medal, Legion of Merit. Mem. Ret. Officers Assn., Nat. Conf. Cath. Bishops, N.Y. State Conf. Bishops. Avocations: collecting anecdotes-human interest stories relating to military personnel. Home: 832 Varnum St NE Washington DC 20017 Office: Mil Archdiocese 962 Wayne Silver Spring MD 20910

DING GUANGXUN, bishop. Chmn. Three-Self Patriotic Movement Com. of Protestant Chs. of China; pres. China Christian Coun., Shanghai. Office: China Christian Coun, 168 Yuan Ming Yuan Lu, Shanghai People's Republic of China*

DINGMAN, MAURICE J., bishop; b. St. Paul, Iowa, Jan. 20, 1914; s. Theodore and Angela (Witte) D. Ed., St. Ambrose Coll., Davenport, Iowa, 1936, N.Am. Coll. and Gregorian U., Rome, Catholic U. Am. Ordained priest Roman Cath. Ch., 1939; instr. St. Ambrose Acad., 1940-43; vice chancellor Diocese of Davenport, Iowa, 1942-45; prin. Hayes High Sch., Muscatine, Iowa, 1950-53; domestic prelate, 1956; appointed bishop Diocese of Des Moines, 1968-87.

DINKEL, JAMES RICHARDSON, minister; b. Springfield, Ohio, Sept. 30, 1952; s. J. Edward and Betty (Richardson) D.; m. Martha Gaw, June 21, 1980; children: Jesse Carley (dec. 1990), Stephen James. BS, Defiance Coll., 1975; MDiv, Trinity Luth. Sem., 1979. Ordained to ministry Evang. Luth Ch. Am., 1979. Pastor Galilee Luth. ch., Russells Point, Ohio, 1979—, All Saints Luth. Ch., Cin., 1991—; chaplain USNR, 1987—; mem. Outreach Com. So. Ohio Synod, Columbus, 1988—; del. Nat. Conv. Evang. Luth. Ch. Am., 1991. Bd. dirs. Am. Cancer Soc., Bellefontaine, Ohio, 1982-88; v.p. Logan County Concert Assn., Bellefontaine, 1985—; mem. Emergency Food and Shelter Bd., Bellefontaine, 1986—, Mental Health Svcs. Bd., Bellefontaine, 1991. Recipient Outstanding Svc. award United Way, 1982, 88. Mem. Indian Lake (Ohio) Pastor Fellowship (pres. 1984-90, Dedicated Svc. award 1988), Internat. Cultural Edn. Program, Naval Res. Assn., Mil. Chaplains Assn. U.S.A., Retired Officers Assn., Indian Lake Svc.Club, Logan County Hist. Soc. Home: 4790 Powderhorn Dr Cincinnati OH 45244 Office: All Saints Luth Ch 445 Craig Cincinnati OH 45244 *Soli Deo Gloria.*

DINKINS, GORDON SCOTT, religion educator; b. Porterville, Calif., Dec. 20, 1956; s. Donald Eugene and Arletta (Nadine) D.; m. Jill Christine White, Dec. 7, 1979. BA, Fresno Pacific Coll., 1982; DPhil, U. London, 1988. Ordained to ministry Calvary Chapel, 1988. Instr. Pacific Coll., Fresno, Calif., 1986-88, Calvary Chapel of Costa Mesa, Calif., 1989—; pastor Calvary Chapel of Visalia (Calif.), 1988-89. Author: In the Balance, 1989, Psalm 119, 1990, poems; contbr. articles to profl. publs. Mem. Am. Acad. Religion, Soc. Biblical Lit., Royal Inst. Philosophy, Sci. and Religion Forum. Republican. Home: 1601 W MacArthur Blvd #11N Santa Ana CA 92704 Office: Calvary Chapel Costa Mesa 3800 S Fairview Santa Ana CA 92704

DINNER, LUCY H. FRIED, rabbi; b. New Orleans, July 7, 1960. BA, U. N.C., 1982; MA in Hebrew Letters, Hebrew Union Coll.-Jewish Inst. Religion, Cin., 1988. Ordained rabbi Union Am. Hebrew Congregations (Ref.), 1988. Assoc. rabbi Congregation Shaare Emeth, St. Louis, 1988—; chmn. congregation rels. Jewish Fund for Human Needs, St. Louis, 1989—; mem. com. on family Union Am. Hebrew Congregations. Bd. dirs. Older Adult Community Action Program, St. Louis, 1989—, Religious Coalition for Abortion Rights, St. Louis, 1989—, Vis. Nurses Assn., St. Louis, 1989—. Mem. Cen. Conf. Am. Rabbis, St. Louis Rabbinical Assn. (chmn. Adult Inst.), St. Louis Assn. Reform Rabbis (pres. 1991—). Office: Congregation Shaare Emeth 11645 Ladue Rd Saint Louis MO 63141

DINNINGER, DONALD HARRY, minister, retired law enforcement professional; b. Saginaw, Mich., Apr. 13, 1946; s. Donald Joseph and Peggy Lou (Pharis) D.; m. Bonnie Lou McLeod, Nov. 23, 1967; children: Andrea, Donald Joseph II. AA, Delta Coll., Bay City, Mich., 1974; BA in Criminal Justice summa cum laude, Saginaw Valley State U., 1977; MA, U. Detroit, 1979; cert. in pastoral studies, Berean Coll., Springfield, Mo., 1983. Grad. FBI Nat. Acad., 1979. Police sgt. City of Saginaw, Mich., 1967-85; bd. dirs. Valley Bible Inst., Saginaw, Mich., 1985—; chaplain Saginaw Police Dept., 1985-90. Author: (books) The Shield of Faith, 1985, The Christian Warrior, 1988. Pres. Mid-Mich. Teen Challenge, Saginaw, 1985—; dir. Christ's Constrn. Crew, worked in Chile, 1987, Ecuador, 1988, Jamaica, 1989, Bonaire, 1990, Clothed with Love Ministries, Saginaw, 1990. With USMC, 1964-67, Vietnam. Named Policeman of the Yr., Saginaw Police Dept., 1984. Office: First Assembly of God 4570 Mackinaw Rd Saginaw MI 48603

DI NOIA, JOSEPH AUGUSTINE, educator, priest; b. N.Y.C., July 10, 1943; s. Giacomo and Matilda (Carucci) Di N. Student, Proficence Coll., 1961-63; BA, St. Stephen's Coll., 1966, MA, 1970; STB, Pontifical Faculty Immaculate Conception Sem., 1969, STL, 1971; PhD, Yale U., 1980. Ordained Dominican priest Roman Cath. Ch., 1970. Instr. dept. religious studies Providence Coll., 1971—, asst. chaplain, 1971-74; prof. systematic theology Dominican House of Studies, 1980—; subprior Dominican Community. Editor-in-chief: The Thomist. Mem. Cath. Theol. Soc. Am., Am. Acad. Religion. Home and Office: 487 Michigan Ave Washington DC 20017

DIODOROS I (DAMIANOS GEORGE KARIVALIS), patriarch of Jerusalem; b. Chios, Greece, Aug. 14, 1923; arrived in Israel, 1938; Degree in theology, U. Athens, Greece, 1957; PhD (hon.), Theol. Acad., Leningrad, USSR, 1981. Ordained priest Patriarchate of Jerusalem, 1947. Deacon Ch. of the Nativity, Bethlehem, 1944; superior Ch. of the Praetorium, Jerusalem, 1947-52; tchr., libr., archivist High Sch. of Patriarchate; pres. Eccles. Ct. Patriarchate Patriarchate of Jerusalem, 1958, draguman, 1959-62; consecrated titular archbishop of Hierapolis, 1962; apptd. patriarchal vicar Ammam, Jordan, 1962; elected patriarch of Jerusalem, 1981. Office: Patriarch of Jerusalem, PO Box 19, Jerusalem Israel

DIONNE, JOSEPH GERARD, bishop; b. St. Basile, N.B., Can., June 19, 1919; s. Aurele and Octavie (Pelletier) D. B.A., Laval U., 1944; Ph.D. in Canon Law, Angelicum U., 1963. Ordained priest Roman Cath. Ch., 1948. Asst. pastor Parish Our Lady of Sorrows, Edmundston, N.B., Can., 1948-56, pastor, 1971-75; chaplain orphanage Edmundston, 1956-60. Hotel-Dieu, St. Basile, 1963-67; dir. Nat. Missions Office Cath. Bishops, Ottawa, Ont., 1967-71; aux. bishop Diocese Sault Ste.-Marie, Ont., 1975-83; bishop Roman Catholic Diocese, Edmundston, 1984—. Lodge: K.C. (4 degree). Home and Office: Centre Diocesain, Edmundston, NB Canada E3V 3K1

DIPBOYE, LARRY KEITH, minister; b. Poteau, Okla., Aug. 6, 1939; s. Walter Faye and Dessa Mable (Babb) D.; m. Nelrose Martin, Sept. 3, 1961 (wid. Apr. 1968); children: Michelle Sames, L. Keith Jr.; m. Carolyn Sue Cook, July 20, 1970. BA, Baylor U., 1961; BD, Southwestern Bapt. Theol. Seminary, Ft. Worth, 1965; MTh, So. Bapt. Theol. Seminary, Louisville, 1967, PhD, 1970. Ordained to ministry Bapt. Ch., 1962. Pastor Chisholm Bapt. Ch., Terrell, Tex., 1962-65, West Point (Ky.) Bapt. Ch., 1965-70, Green Trails Bapt. Ch., Chesterfield, Mo., 1971-74, Buechel Park Bapt. Ch., Louisville, 1974-88, First Bapt. Ch., Oak Ridge, Tenn., 1988—. Contbg. author: Ministers Manual, 1985-89. Mem. TV panel WHAS-TV/radio, The Moral Side of the News, Louisville, 1982-88. Mem. Oak Ridge Ministerial Assn. (pres. 1991), Rotary. Home: 108 Wimberly Lane Oak Ridge TN 37830 Office: First Baptist Church 1101 Oak Ridge Tpk Oak Ridge TN 37830

D'IPPOLITO, NANCY E. S., minister; b. Lynwood, Calif., May 28, 1950; d. Carl Henry and Mary Agnes (Ready) Schiermeyer; m. Daniel A.S. D'Ippolito, Sept. 29, 1984; children: Corinne, Laura, Michelle. BA, Calif. State U., L.A., 1972; MDiv, McCormick Seminary, Chgo., 1982. Pastor Community Ch., Pinewood Springs, Colo., 1984-85; pastor at large Boulder (Colo.) Presbytery, 1986—. Democrat. Home and Office: 795 Gilpin Dr Boulder CO 80303

DIRIR, MOGUE HASSAN, religious court minister; b. Djibouti, 1937; s. Hassen Dirir; m. Amina Dirir (separated); 1 child; m. Asha Dirir; 3 children. Diploma in religion, Sudan U. Religion educator Muslim Community of Djibouti, 1970—, pres., 1977—; min. Muslim Ct. of Djibouti, 1977—. Pub.: Law of Issa, 1991. Mem. RPP Party. Office: Qadi of Djibouti, PO Box 168, Djibouti Republic of Djibouti

DIROKPA, BALUFUGA, bishop. Bishop of Bukavu The Anglican Communion, Zaire. Office: BP 2987, Bukavu Zaire*

DISCHER, GERALD ROGER, clergyman; b. Wausau, Wis., July 20, 1929; ss. William Frederick annd Lillie (Bloedel) D.; m. Betty Jane Halbardier, Jan. 17, 1951; children: Claryllie, Cynthia, Stephen. BTh, Concordia Sem., Springfield, Ill., 1961; MDiv, Concordia Sem., Ft. Wayne, Ind., 1980; postgrad., Tex. A&M U., 1965-75. Ordained to ministry Luth. Ch.-Mo. Synod. Pastor Ascension Luth. Ch., Apple Valley, Calif., 1961-65, Trinity Luth. Ch., Navasota, Tex., 1965-82; chaplain Tex. Dept. Corrections, Navasota, 1982—; cir. counsellor Tex. dist. Luth. Ch.-Mo. Synod, also mem. town and country com., 1965-71. Chmn. Grimes Substance Abuse Coun., Navasota, 1965-82; scoutmaster Sam Houston coun. Boy Scouts Am.; chaplain Tex. Wing, CAP, 1981—. With USAF, 1947-55, chief master sgt. Res. ret. Recipient honor cert. Freedoms Found., 1977, Outstanding Svc. award Brazos Valley Devel. Coun., 1980-82. Mem. Am. Assn. Protestant Correctional Chaplains, Air Force Assn., Kiwanis (Kiwanian of Yr. award 1970), Alpha Kappa Delta. Home: RR 3 Box 311 Navasota TX 77868 Office: Tex Dept Corrections Pack I Rte 3 Box 300 Navasota TX 77868

DISTANT EAGLE See AUDLIN, JAMES DAVID

DISTLER, CHARLES, minister, administrator; b. N.Y.C., June 21, 1915; s. William and Anna Elizabeth (Weiscuff) D.; m. Daisy Laura Smith, March 21, 1936; children: Charles Jr., Daisy-Anna Powell, Ruth Naomi Gabel. D Bible Philosophy, Lighthouse Bible Coll., Rockford, Ill., 1945; BA, Shelton Coll., Cape May, N.Y., 1948; postgrad., East Bapt. Theol. Sem., Overbrook, Pa., 1949-54. Ordained to the ministry Conference of Fundamental Chs., 1945, Am. Bapt. Conv., 1949. Pastor various chs., N.Y. Ohio, 1948-70, Ill. Mich., 1970-87; adminstr. dir. Victory Mission, Salinas, Calif., 1988—; pres. Ohio Regional IFCA, Akron, 1965-68; bd. mem. Akron Christian Schs., 1965-68; chaplain Carthage Mem. Hosp., Ill., 1972-75; radio preacher WCAZ, Carthage, Ill., 1971-76. Chaplain N.Y.C. Post Office Dept., 1950-55; tank comdr. World War II, China-Burma, India, 1944-45; with U.S. Army 1944-46. Mem. Am. Numismatic Assn., Am. Legion. Home: 926 Padre Dr 5 Salinas CA 93901 Office: Victory Mission 43 Soledad St Salinas CA 93901

DITTERICH, ERIC KEITH VON, clergyman; b. East Melbourne, Victoria, Australia, Feb. 8, 1913; s. Richard and Christiana (Shand) D.; B.A., B.D., Dip.Ed., Queen's Coll., Melbourne U.; m. Nancy Moyle Russell, Aug. 6, 1940; children—Anne (Mrs. Roger T. McLeod), Helen (Mrs. Kenneth I. Williams), Elizabeth (Mrs. Ross S. Fraser), Robert J.R., Julianne B. Pardee. Ordained to ministry Methodist Ch., 1940; minister in East Malvern, 1946-50, Benalla, 1950-55, Horsham, 1955-58; chmn. Wimmera Dist., 1955-58; mng. treas. Meth. Gen. Conf. Supernumerary Fund, 1958-77; mng. treas. Uniting Ch. in Australia Beneficiary Fund, 1977-79, chmn., 1980; dir. Meth. Publishing House, Melbourne, 1945-77; convener Uniting Ch. Pub. Agy., 1977-79. Pres., Victoria and Tasmania Conf., Meth. Ch., 1969-70; mem. Joint Commn. for Uniting Ch. in Australia, 1966-72; chmn. Meth. World Council Com. Pub. Interests 1971-76. Pres. council Queen's Coll., U. Melbourne, 1965-68; pres. council Wesley Coll., Melbourne, 1966-81, hon. fellow, 1983; trustee F.J. Cato Charitable Fund, 1977-90, chmn., 1982. Served as chaplain Royal Australian Air Force, 1940-46; chaplain Citizen Air Force, 1948-70, Nepean Presbytery, 1981-84. Decorated mem. Order Brit. Empire. Mem. Royal Philatelic Soc. London, Royal Automobile Club. Lodge: Rotary (past pres.). Club: Port Philip Probus. Author: Food Available to Air Crew shot down in Tropical Areas, 1942, The Church on Active Service, 1945, Some Distortions of the Christian Faith, 1953, A Methodist Member's Manual, 1956, Three Curious Creeds, 1961, Our Faith and Its Fruits, 1965, Inflation, The Church and The Ministry, 1973, others. Home: 1574 High St, Glen Iris, Victoria 3146, Australia

DITTES, JAMES EDWARD, psychology of religion educator; b. Cleve., Dec. 26, 1926; s. Mercein Edward and Mary (Freeman) D.; children: Lawrence William (dec.), Nancy Eleanor, Carolyn Ann, Joanne Frances; m. Anne Hebert Smith, Nov. 27, 1987. A.B., Oberlin Coll., 1949; B.D., Yale U., 1954, M.S., 1955, Ph.D., 1958. Instr. Am. Sch., Talas, Turkey, 1950-52; ordained to ministry United Ch. Christ, 1954; mem. faculty Yale U., 1955—, prof. psychology of religion, 1967-84, prof. pastoral theology and psychology, 1984—, chmn. dept. religious studies, 1975-82; chmn. Council on Grad. Studies in Religion in U.S. and Can., 1970-71. Author: The Church in the Way, 1967, Minister on the Spot, 1970, Bias and the Pious, 1973, When the People Say No, 1979, The Male Predicament, 1985, When Work goes Sour, 1987, (with Robert Menges) Psychological Studies of Clergymen, 1965, (with Donald Capps) The Hunger of the Heart, 1990. Served with USNR, 1945-46. Guggenheim fellow, 1965-66; Fulbright Research fellow Rome, 1965-66; sr. fellow NEH, 1972-73. Mem. Soc. Sci. Study of Religion (exec. sec. 1959-63, editor jour. 1966-71, pres. 1971-73). Home: 85 Viscount Blvd #A24 Milford CT 06460 Office: 409 Prospect St New Haven CT 06511

DITTMER, JOHN MARK, minister; b. Central City, Nebr., Aug. 16, 1959; s. Ivan Eldon and Lois Jane (Cherry) D.; m. Kristin Sue Livgren, Aug. 17, 1985; children: Philip Scot, Matthew Clayton. AA in Criminal Justice, N.E. Tech. Community Coll., 1979; BA in Pastoral Ministries cum laude, Nebr. Christian Coll., 1981, BTh. in Pastoral Ministries cum laude, 1982; postgrad., Cin. Bible Sem. Minister Christian Ch./Chs. of Christ. Vocat. coord., case mgr. Liberty Centre br. No. Nebr. Comprehensive Mental Health Ctr, Norfolk, 1983-86; minister Ch. of Christ, Indianola, Nebr., 1986-90, 1st Christian Ch., Concordia, Kans., 1990—; pres. youth program coun. for Pibel Bible Camp, 1990; mem. com. Nebr. State Christian Conv., 1989-90. Named Outstanding Young Minister, N.Am. Christian Convention, 1989, Outstanding Young Man of Am. for 1987. Mem. Rotary (pres. Indianola chpt. 1990). Republican. Office: 1st Christian Ch 6th and Cedar Sts Concordia KS 66901

DIULIO, ALBERT JOSEPH, university president, priest; b. Laona, Wis., Feb. 14, 1943; s. Albert Joseph and Louise Frances (Bradle) D. BS, Marquette U., 1965, AM, 1969; MDiv, Weston Sch. Theology, Cambridge, Mass., 1974; MA, Stanford U., 1976, PhD, 1979, MBA, 1983. Joined S.J., Roman Cath. Ch., ordained priest, 1974. Mem. faculty Campion High Sch., Prairie Du Chien, Wis., 1969-70, 73-74, headmaster, 1970-71, 74-75; prin. Campion Jesuit High Sch., 1975; asst. to dean Coll. Arts & Scis., Marquette U., Milw., 1978-80, mem. bus. faculty, 1983-84, assoc. dean Sch. of Bus., 1984-86, pres., 1990—; asst. to pres. Loyola Marymount U., Los Angeles, 1980-81; pres. Xavier U., Cin., 1986-90, Marquette U., Milw., 1990—; trustee Marquette High Sch., Milw., 1985—; bd. dirs. Wis. Assn. Ind. Colls. and Univs., Baird Capital Devel. Fund, Inc., Baird Blue Chip Fund, Inc. Chmn. Greater Milw. Com. Task Force to review governance Milw. County Med. Complex; mem. Pres.'s Commn. Nat. Collegiate Athletic Assn.; chmn. mayor's com. Police and Community Rels., Milw. Decorated Equestrian Order of the Holy Sepulchre of Jerusalem; recipient Outstanding Bus. Leadership award Marquette U.; Lockheed fellow Stanford Bus. Sch. Mem. AAUP, Am. Assn. Ednl. Rsch., Am. Fin. Assn., Am. Mgmt. Assn., Acad. Mgmt., Am. Assn. Higher Edn., Assn. Jesuit Colls. & Univs. (bd. dirs. 1986—), Greater Milw. Com., Wis. Found. Ind. Coll., Internat. Fedn. Cath. Colls. and Univs., Newcomen Soc. of U.S., Phi Delta Kappa, Alpha Sigma Nu, Beta Gamma Sigma, Beta Alpha Psi., Milw. Club, Univ. Club Milw., Milw. Athletic Club. Avocations: California wines, gardening, reading. Home and Office: Marquette U Milwaukee WI 53233

DIVELY, EMORY KEVIN, missionary, religious education administrator; b. Flint, Mich., Aug. 21, 1956; s. Emory M. and Elaine R. (Wong) D.; m. Cynthia Anne Garwood, June 7, 1980; children: Erica Anne, Emory David. BSW, Rochester Inst. Tech., 1980; MA in Cross Cultural Communications, Assemblies of God Theol. Sem., 1982. Ordained to ministry Assemblies of God, 1982. Deaf pastor Rochester (N.Y.) Deaf Assemblies of God, 1977-80; chaplain Nat. Tech. Inst. for the Deaf, Rochester, 1977-80, 82-88; missionary Assemblies of God, Springfield, Mo., 1982—; faculty Deaf Internat. Bible Coll., Mpls., 1986-88, missionary, dir., 1989—; bd. dirs. Christian Coalitation for Person with Disability, Wis., 1989-91. Co-founder, chair Coun. for Mental Health for Deaf, Rochester, 1979-81. Mem. Minn. Assn. Deaf Citizens, Nat. Assn. Deaf. Republican. Home: 3668 Cardinal Way Eagan MN 55123 Office: Deaf Internat Bible Coll 800 S 10th St Ste 5 Minneapolis MN 55404 *Greatest of all beside salvation is the Pentecostal experience among the Deaf Culture Community demonstrating the ability to use sign language as the physical evidence rather than the vocal language to prove Him omnipotent!.*

DIXON, BARRY PERCY, religion educator; b. Bklyn., June 3, 1950; m. Maria Theresa Ambos, June 14, 1974; children: Rahim, Yasmeen. BA, Calif. Bapt. Coll., 1972. Instr. Noohra Found., Irvine, Calif., 1983—; bus. devel. officer Govt. Funding Corp., Riverside, Calif., 1989—, Pacific Inland Bank, Ontario, Calif., 1991—. Contbr. articles to profl. publs. Mem. Soc. Biblical Lit., Am. Acad. Religion, Ancient and Mystical Order Rosae Crucis (master 1983-84). Home: 3191 Kilkenny Dr Riverside CA 92503 Office: Pacific Inland Bank 337 N Vineyard Ave Ontario CA 91764 *We must be cognizant that there is no religion higher than truth, and that all truth lies outside any kind of fixed pattern. Truth grows from within, and is sensed in a spiritual way without the limitation of words. For truth is the fruit of the tree of knowledge and is not the tree itself.*

DIXON, DONALD KEITH, minister; b. Ashland, Ky., Sept. 18, 1940; s. Ralph Heiller and Carrie (Adams) D.; m. Victoria Elaine Gough, Aug. 10, 1968; 1 child, Keith Nathaniel. BA, Georgetown (Ky.) Coll., 1963; BDiv, So. Bapt. Theol. Sem., 1966; postgrad., Bapt. Sem., Ruschlikon, Switzerland, 1972. Ordained to ministry So. Bapt. Conv., 1966. Pastor Dawson Bapt. Ch., Philpot, Ky., 1966-70, Hahn Bapt. Ch., Hahn Air Base, Fed. Republic Germany, 1970-73, Mt. Moriah Bapt. Ch., Brevard, N.C., 1974-78, Mt. Pleasant Bapt. Ch., Bogalusa, La., 1979-84, Highland Bapt. Ch., Tullahoma, Tenn., 1984—. chmn. Sr. Citizen Coun., Transylvania County, N.C., 1975-78; bd. dirs. Contact Life Line, Tullahoma, 1989—; trustee Belmont Coll., 1990—; organizer Pub. Forum of Persian Gulf, Tullahoma, 1991; co-founder Friends of Families of 251st, 1991. Mem. Police Chaplains (sec. 1988—), Duck River Bapt. Assn. (moderator), Tullahoma Ministerial Assn. (pres. 1988-89). Office: Highland Bapt Ch 808 W Hickory St Tullahoma TN 37388 *My experience has been that the more I am open to others the more I find that I have in common with them. No matter what tags we wear or have put on us by society, there is more that we share than what divides us.*

DIXON, ERNEST THOMAS, JR., bishop; b. San Antonio, Oct. 13, 1922; s. Ernest Thomas and Ethel Louise (Reese) D.; m. Lois F. Brown, July 20, 1943 (dec. 1977); children—Freddie Brown, Ernest Reese, Muriel Jean, Leona Louise; m. Ernestine Gray Clark, May 18, 1979; 1 child, Sherryl D. Clark. B.A. magna cum laude, Samuel Huston Coll., 1943; B.D., Drew Theol. Sem., 1945; D.D. (hon.), Huston-Tillotson Coll., 1962; L.H.D. (hon.), Southwestern Coll., Winfield, Kans., 1973; LL.D. (hon.), Baker U., 1973; Litt.D. (hon.), Westmar Coll., 1978; H.H.D. (hon.), Kans. Wesleyan Coll., 1980. Ordained to ministry Methodist Ch., 1946, consecrated bishop, 1972. Pastor Methodist Ch., Brackettville, Tex., 1943; asst. pastor East Calvary Meth. Ch., Harlem, N.Y., 1943-44, Wallace Chapel, A.M.E. Zion Ch., Summit, N.J., 1944-45; dir. religious extension service Tuskegee Inst., Ala., 1945-51; exec. sec. West Tex. Conf. Bd. Edn., 1951-52; staff mem. Div. Local Ch. Bd. Edn., Meth. Ch., 1952-64; pres. Philander Smith Coll., Little Rock, 1965-69; asst. gen. sec. div. coordination, research and planning Program Council United Meth. Ch., 1969-72, bishop Kans. area, 1972-80; bishop San Antonio area United Meth. Ch., Tex., 1980—; pres. Council of Bishops, 1988-89; pres. bd. dirs. Bethlehem Ctr., Nashville, 1953-64; del. gen. conf. Meth. and United Meth. Chs., 1964-72; pres. Gen. Bd. Higher Edn. and Ministry, United Meth. Ch., 1972-76; Ala. del. Midcentury White House Conf. Children and Youth, 1950. Citizens adv. com. Gov. Ark., 1967-69; bd. dirs. Little Rock C. of C., 1967-69; pres. Tex. Conf. Chs., 1984-86; trustee Gammon Theol. Sem., Atlanta, Gulfside Assembly, Waveland, Miss., 1978—, Huston-Tillotson Coll., Austin, Tex., Lydia Patterson Inst., Mission Home, San Antonio, Meth. Home, Waco, Morningside Manor, Mt. Sequoyah Assembly, Southwestern U., Georgetown, Tex., S.W. Meth. Hosp., others. Mem. Alpha Phi Alpha, Sigma Pi Phi. Office: United Meth Ch PO Box 28509 San Antonio TX 78228

DIXON, FREDDIE BROWN, SR., minister; b. San Antonio, June 6, 1944; s. Ernest T. and Lois Freddie (Brown) D.; m. Barbara Watson, June 1, 1968; children: Freddie Brown, Douglass L. BA, Philander Smith Coll., 1967; MDiv., Gammon Sem., 1970. Ordained to ministry, United Meth. Ch., 1970. Assoc. pastor First United Meth. Ch., Beeville, Tex., 1970-73; pastor Wesley United Meth. Ch., Austin, 1973—. Mem. Alpha Phi Alpha. Home: 1602 Astor Pl Austin TX 78721 Office: 1164 San Bernard St Austin TX 78702

DIXON, JAMES GEORGE, JR., minister, headmaster; b. Wichita, Kans., Feb. 3, 1922; s. James George and Lena Mae (Wertz) D.; m. Dorothy Beatrice Hoidale, Aug. 14, 1941 (dec. June 1991); children: Richard, Paul, Paula, James III, Peter, Deborah. Grad. cum laude, Biola Coll., 1944; BD cum laude, Grace Theol Sem., 1947, MDiv, 1949; BA, Wooster Coll., 1949. Ordained to ministry Grace Brethren Ch., 1947. Pastor Sunnymede Brethren Ch., South Bend, Ind., 1944-47, W. 10th St. Brethren Ch., Ashland, Ohio, 1947-51, 1st Brethren Ch., Washington, 1951-61, Grace Brethren Ch. Greater Washington, Temple Hills, Md. and Washington, 1961—; Pres. Christian Edn. and Sunday Sch. Bd., 1951-81; dir. Grace Theol. Sem., Winona Lake, Ind., 1951-68; cons. Gospel Light Publs., Calif., 1961-65. Named Pastor of Yr., Fellowship Grace Brethren Chs. Mins., 1988. Republican. Home: 5920 John Adams Dr Camp Springs MD 20748 Office: Grace Brethren Ch 5000 St Barnabas Temple Hills MD 20748

DIXON, JOHN WESLEY, JR., retired religion and art educator; b. Richmond, Va., Aug. 18, 1919; s. John Wesley and Margaret (Denny) D.; m. Vivian Ardelia Slagle, Jan. 9, 1943; children: Susan Raglan, Judith Ann, Miriam Elizabeth. B.A., Emory & Henry Coll., 1941; Ph.D., U. Chgo., 1953. Instr. Mich. State U., East Lansing, 1950-52; asst. prof. Emory U., Atlanta, 1952-57; exec. dir. Faculty Christian Fellowship, N.Y.C., 1955-57; assoc. prof. Dickinson Coll., Carlisle, Pa., 1957-60; prof. Fla. Presbyn. Coll., St. Petersburg, 1960-63; prof. religion and art U. N.C., Chapel Hill, 1963-87, prof. emeritus, 1987—. Author: Nature and Grace in Art, 1964, Art and the Theological Imagination, 1978, The Physiology of Faith, 1979. Served to 1st lt. U.S. Army, 1941-45. Recipient Tanner Teaching award, 1967. Democrat. Episcopalian. Home: 216 Glenhill Ln Chapel Hill NC 27514 Office: U NC Dept Religion Chapel Hill NC 27514

DIXON, SAMUEL ROZZELL EBENEZER, deacon; b. Clayashland, Liberia, Mar. 20, 1921; s. Rozzell Emmons and Rosina Rebecca (Freeman) D.; B.S., U. Liberia, 1961, D.D., 1969; B.D., Interdenominational Theol. Center, 1965, M.Div., 1973; m. Mary Deborah Carter, Dec. 19, 1955; 1 son, Rozzell L. Clerk, Liberia Co., Monrovia, 1952-55, personnel mgr., liaison officer, 1955-62; ordained deacon United Methodist Ch., 1960, elder, 1962; pastor First United Meth. Ch., Monrovia, 1965-73; dir. religious affairs, community relations Firestone Plantations Co., Harbel, Liberia, 1973—, pastor Harbel Chapel, Harbel Community Ch., Harbel Duside Chapel, 1973—. Trustee Coll. W. Africa; bd. dirs. Family Planning Assn. Decorated knight grand comdr. Humane Order of African Redemption, Govt. of Liberia, 1969. Mem. Christian Ministers Assn. Liberia, Inc. (nat. pres. 1971—). Clubs: Rotary of Monrovia, Masons (33 deg.), Order Eastern Star (patron). Contbr. articles to religious jours. Office: Firestone Plantations Co, Harbel Liberia

DIYANNI, DAVID, minister; b. Hackensack, N.J., Apr. 28, 1954; s. Henry and Irene (Caminini) DiY.; m. Roxanna Rae Beals, Dec. 19, 1976; children: Michael, Hannah, Stephany, Jason, Christopher. AA in Bus., Lane Community Coll., Eugene, Oreg., 1977; student, Capital U., Columbus, Ohio, 1981-82. Ordained to ministry Shiloh Youth Revival Ctrs., 1976l cert. tax preparer. Youth min. Shiloh Youth Revival Ctr., Dexter, Oreg., 1973-77; sr. min. Faith Chapel, Reynoldsburg, Ohio, 1978—; ministerial tax cons. pvt. practice, Reynoldsburg, 1980—; chmn. bd. dirs. Lighthouse Christian Counseling Ctr., Reynoldsburg, 1985—; pres. Reynoldsburg Ministerial Assn., 1986-88. Contbr. articles to publs. Recipient Good Citizenship Award, Am. Legion, Dover, N.J., 1970, commendation, President Ronald Reagan, 1987. Home: 15131 Palmer Rd Reynoldsburg OH 43069 Office: Faith Chapel 15187 Palmer Rd Reynoldsburg OH 43068

DJOKIC, GEORGIJE, bishop; b. Bijeljina, Bosna, Yugoslavia, May 6, 1949; arrived in Can., 1984; s. Krsto and Krunija (Arsenovic) D. BA in Theology, Faculty of Theology, Yugoslavia, 1981. Ordained priest Serbian Orthodox Ch., 1971. Parish priest, spiritual advisor Monastery Tauna, Bosna, 1971-82; parish priest St. Peter and Paul Serbian Orthodox Ch., Darby, Eng., 1982-84; bishop, pres. Serbian Orthodox Diocese Can., Toronto, 1984—; pres. Diocesan Eccles. Ct. Can., 1984—, Diocesan Exec. Bd. Can., 1984—; v.p. Cen. Ch. Coun., Serbian Orthodox Ch. in U.S.A. and Can., 1984—; mem. Holy Assembly Bishops, Belgrade, Yugoslavia, 1984—. Author Istocnik jour., 1987—. Mem. Can. Coun. Chs. Home: 5A Stockbridge Ave, Toronto, ON Canada M8Z 4M6 Office: Serbian Orthodox Diocese Can, 2520 Dixie Rd, Mississauga, ON Canada L4Y 2A5

DMITRI OF DALLAS, BISHOP See ROYSTER, ROBERT

DOAN, GILBERT EVERETT, JR., minister; b. Phila., Sept. 14, 1930; s. Gilbert Everett and Alice Curtis (Olney) D.; m. Janice Yelland (div. 1976); children: Gilbert Everett III, Robert Bruce, Stephen Olney, James Sibbald; m. Roberta McKaig. AB, Harvard U., 1952; MDiv, Luth. Theol. Sem., Phila., 1955; MA, U. Pa., 1962; DD (hon.), Wagner Coll., 1984. Ordained to ministry United Luth. Ch. in Am. Campus pastor Luth. Found., Phila., 1955-61; regional dir. Luth. Coun. U.S.A., Phila., 1961-84; pastor Luth. Ch. of Holy Communion, Phila., 1984—; chmn. com. on hymn texts Inter-Luth. Commn. on Worship, 1972-78, sec. 1972-78; mem. coun. Acad. of Preachers, Phila., 1982-86. Editor: (with others) Oremus, 1962; editor: Preaching of F. W. Robertson, 1964. Recipient Campus Ministry award Danforth Found., 1964. Republican. Home: 142 Drexel Rd Ardmore PA 19003 Office: Ch of Holy Communion 2111 Sansom St Philadelphia PA 19103

DOANE, ANTHONY WAYNE, music director; b. Covington, Ky., Dec. 4, 1956; s. Norman Dirille and Frances Elaine (Livingood) D.; m. Gail Sue Owens, May 29, 1982; children: Jamie Nicole, Jill Catherine, Jordan Dirille. MusB in Ch. Music, Eastern Ky. U., 1979. Music dir. Crittenden (Ky.) Bapt. Ch., 1975-76, Red House Bapt. Ch., Richmond, Ky., 1976-79, Hebron (Ky.) Bapt. Ch., 1980—; maintenance electrician GE Aircraft Engines, Evendale, Ohio, 1985—; organizer, leader Community Choir Messiah, Hebron, 1988, Community Nativity Scene, 1990. Composer spl. event songs including Fathers Day, 1988, Mothers Day, 1989, Sanctity of Human Life, 1989. Republican. Home: 6783 Hillock Ct Florence KY 41042 Office: Hebron Bapt Ch Box 92 Hebron KY 41048

DOBBINS, C(LAUDE) RAY, minister, editor, journalist; b. Denton, Tex., Jan. 25, 1919; s. James Dewitt and Sallie Pearl (Wilkinson) D.; m. Mary Alice Smith, June 4, 1943; children: Mary Catherine, Dorothy, James, Alice, Cynthia, William, John. BA, Bethel Coll., McKenzie, Tenn., 1941, DD (hon.), 1960; MDiv, Memphis Theol. Sem., 1943; ThM, U. Chgo., 1951. Ordained to ministry Cumberland Presbyn. Ch. Min. Cumberland Presbyn. Ch., Bowling Green, Ky., 1945-48; editor The Cumberland Presbyn., Memphis, 1948-84; moderator Gen. Assembly, Cumberland Presbyn. Ch., Chattanooga, 1984-85; exec. dir. Tenn. Assn. Chs., Nashville, 1986—. Mem. editorial bd. A People Called Cumberland Presbyn., 1968-75. C. Ray Dobbins lectureship established in his honor Bethel Coll., McKenzie, 1984. Mem. Civitans (chaplain Memphis chpt., dist. chaplain). Home: 413 Moss Creek Ct Nashville TN 37221

DOBRANSKI, ROBERT EDWARD, clergyman, church administrator; b. Kingston, Pa., Mar. 11, 1944; s. Peter Paul and Stella (Januszewski) D.; m. Kathleen Yvonne Stringfellow, Dec. 28, 1985. BSBA, King's Coll., Wilkes-Barre, Pa., 1970; MDiv, Biola U., 1984. Ordained to ministry Conservative Bapt. Assn. Am. Adminstrv. pastor Community Bapt. Ch., Manhattan Beach, Calif., 1987—. Sgt. USAF, 1962-66. Office: Community Bapt Ch 1243 Artesia Blvd Manhattan Beach CA 90266

DOBSON, EDWARD G., minister; b. Ireland, Dec. 30, 1949; s. Calvin C. and Eileen (McKnight) D.; m. Lorna Dobson, June 2, 1972; children: Kent Edward, Heather Elizabeth, Daniel Calvin. BA, Bob Jones U., 1970, MA, 1972; DD, Calif. Grad. Sch. Theology, 1981; EdD, U. Va., 1986. V.p. student affairs Liberty U., Lynchburg, Va., asst. prof. religion; sr. minister Calvary Ch., Grand Rapids, Mich. Mem. Am. Personnel and Guidance Assn., College State Personnel Assn., Nat. Assn. of Student Personnel Adminstrn. Home: 6875 Blue Ridge NE Belmont MI 49306

DOBSON, KAREN, religious studies educator; b. Boston, Mar. 24, 1932; d. Chester A. and Katherine (Smith) D.; m. Alcide J. Lessard, June 23, 1984. BA, Regis Coll., 1957; MA, Emmanuel Coll., 1972; PhD, Walden U., 1984. Cons. religious edn. Archdiocese of Boston, 1969-75; vicar for religious edn. Diocese Grand Island, Nebr., 1976-79; dean campus ministry Salve Regina Coll., Newport, R.I., 1980-85, seminar dir. religious edn., 1987-88; dir. religious edn. Diocese of Bridgeport, Conn., 1989—, Diocese of Providence, 1989—; religious edn. cons. Boys Town, Omaha, 1982; mem. adv. bd. MA program Emmanuel Coll., Boston, 1990. Author: The Gift of Life, 1976; editor: newsletter Boston Arch Diocese Office of Religious Edn., 1971-76; published Vatican II and Social Change, 1990, Consciousness of God Witnessed by Thomas Merton, 1990; contbr. to Register, West Nebr., 1988, 89, also articles to profl. jours. Mem. Faculty Senate (v.p. Newport chpt. 1989, 90, 91, appointed chair dept. religious studies 1990), Theta Alpha Kappa. Roman Catholic. Home: 15 Ruby Ct Box 9186 North Dartmouth MA 02747 Office: Salve Regina U Ochre Point Ave Newport RI 02840

DOCHERTY, ROBERT KELLIEHAN, II, minister; b. Newton, Mass., May 27, 1935; s. Alexander Harper and Mary (Campbell) D; m. Eileen Joyce Rockefeller, June 14, 1958; children: Robert K. III, Scott Rockefeller, Stacy Jean. BA, Sterling Coll., 1961, Moody Bible Inst., 1970; MS, Pittsburg (Kans.) State U., 1972; PhD, Kans. State U., 1981. Ordained to ministry

Presbyn. Ch. (U.S.A.), 1977. Min. 1st Bapt. Ch., Frederick, Kans., 1959-63, Russell, Kans., 1964-67; campus min. Pittsburg State U., 1967-72; mem. State Staff Kans. Bapt. Conv., Topeka, 1972-77; min. United Presbyn. Ch., Pittsburg, 1977-85; co-pastor The Presbyn. Ch., Pittsburg, 1985-87; organizing pastor John Knox Presbyn. Ch., Wichita, Kans., 1988, pastor, 1988—; moderator Synod Ministries Div., Overland Park, Kans., 1990—, Church Related Colls., Overland Park. Author: Community Education with School Superintendents, 1980. Founder Help NOW Inc., Pittsburg, 1972; bd. dirs. Elm Acres Youth Home, Girard, Kans., 1973-79; chmn. United Way, Pittsburg, 1974, co-chmn., 1983; treas. Mt. Carmel Hosp. Found., Pittsburg, 1984-87; chaplain CAP, Wichita, 1988—. Nat. Coun. Chs. Christ fellow, 1976; C.S. Mott Found. fellow Kans. State U., 1978. Mem. Presbytery So. Kans., Com. on Ministry, Kiwanis (Gov. Kans. 1972-73). Office: John Knox Presbyn Ch 7202 E 9th St Wichita KS 67206 *Life is a quest, made up of many relationships, the most important one is to the giver of Life, God.*

DOCKER, JOHN THORNLEY, religious organization administrator, minister; b. Reading, Pa., June 2, 1937; s. John Thornley and Evelyn Clara (Deam) D.; m. Georgie Elizabeth Dawson, Dec. 31, 1968; children: Sean Thornley, Robert Kenneth. BA, Lehigh U., 1960; MDiv, Gen. Theol. Sem., 1963; D. Ministry, Bexley Hall, 1987. Ordained to ministry Episcopal Ch. as deacon, 1963, as priest, 1964. Vicar St. Mary's Ch., Wind Gap, Pa., 1963-68, St. Joseph's Ch., West Bangor, Pa., 1963-68; program asst., rector native Diocese of Cen. Pa., Newport, Pa., 1968-74; canon missioner Christ Ch. Cathedral, Rochester, N.Y., 1974-76; program dir. Canon to Bishop of Bethlehem, 1976-82; coord. for ministry devel., mem. presiding bishop's staff Episcopal Ch. Ctr., N.Y.C., 1982—, program dep., edn. for mission and ministry unit, 1988—; priest assoc. St. Paul's Ch., Ossining, N.Y., 1987—; field officer Coun. for Devel. of Ministry, N.Y., 1983—; coord. Nat. Task Force for Total Ministry, 1982—. Author: Toward A Totally Ministering Church, 1987, Fluffing the Tangled Skein, 1990; editor: From Survival to Renewal, 1989; producer videos; Day By Day, 1984 (Golden Eagle award 1986), Snapshots, 1985, Callings, 1987, Faith on a Tightrope, Part 1, 1988 (Assoc. Ch. Press award 1990), Faith on a Tightrope, Part 2, 1989, Signs of Service, 1990.

DOCKERY, DAVID SAMUEL, theology educator, editor; b. Tuscaloosa, Ala., Oct. 28, 1952; s. Samuel Wesley and Pansye (Pierson) D.; m. Lanese Huckeba, June 14, 1975; children: Jonathan Samuel, Benjamin Paul, Timothy David. BS, U. Ala., 1975; MDiv magna cum laude, Grace Theol. Sem., Winona Lake, Ind., 1979; MDiv, Southwestern Bapt. Theol. Sem., Ft. Worth, 1981; MA, Tex. Christian U., 1986; PhD, U. Tex., Arlington, 1988. Ordained to ministry So. Bapt. Conv., 1982. Pastor Met. Bapt. Ch., Bklyn., 1981-84; prof. theology Criswell Coll., Dallas, 1984-88; asst. prof. N.T., So. Bapt. Sem., Louisville, 1988—; gen. editor Broadman Press, Nashville, 1990—; bd. dirs. Billy Graham Ctr., Louisville, 1989-91. Author: Doctrine of the Bible, 1991; editor: Baptist Theologians, 1990, People of God, 1991, New Testament Criticism and Interpretation, 1991; gen. editor The New American Cmmentary, 1991—. Bd. advisors Alternative Pregnancy Ctr., Louisville, 1990. Fellow Inst. Bibl. Rsch.; mem. Evang. Theol. Soc., Soc. Bible Lit., Am. Acad. Religion, Nat. Assn. Bapt. Profs. Religion. Home: 139 Woodvale Hendersonville TN 37075 Office: Broadman Press 127 9th Ave N Nashville TN 37234 *While change is constant—I have found the unchanging Christ to be the supreme source of security to which life can be anchored.*

DOCKERY, ROBERT GERALD, minister; b. Fayetteville, Ark., Nov. 2, 1948; s. Geroge Lawson and Zelen (Bradley) D.; m. Meredy Jane Roberts, July 15, 1971; children: Jared Nathan, Rachael Marie, Robert Luke. BA, Harding U., 1971. Ordained to ministry Ch. of Christ, 1970. Min. Habberton Ch. of Christ, Fayetteville, 1968-69, Baldwin Ch. of Christ, Fayetteville, 1971—; dir. Ozark Christian Leadership Program, Fayetteville, Gospel Tracts Internat., Fayetteville. Author: Sermons For Special Occassions, 1977, The Holy Spirit: Unraveling the Mystery, 1990; contbr. articles to profl. jours. Co-founder Pro-Life Edn. Alliance, 1983; speaker Ark. Right To Life Rally, Little Rock, 1983. Home and Office: 4377 E Huntsville Fayetteville AR 72701

DODD, CHARLIE HERRING, minister; b. San Angelo, Tex., Nov. 27, 1950; s. William H. and Dorothy V. (Hall) D.; m. Mary Jan Welch, May 21, 1972; children: Ryan, Kristen, Jordan. BA, Baylor U., 1973; M Religious Edn., Southwestern Bapt. Theol., Seminary, Ft. Worth, 1975. Minister of youth and recreation First Bapt. Ch., Georgetown, Tex., 1971-72, Temple, Tex., 1972-76; minister of youth and recreation Northwest Bapt. Ch., Oklahoma City, 1976-79; minister of youth First Bapt. Ch., Midland, Tex., 1979—; conf. leader Bapt. Sunday Sch. Bd., Nashville, Glorieta, N.Mex., 1979—, Bapt. Gen. Conv. of Tex., 1979—, Bat. Gen. Conv. Okla.; assn. youth minister Midland Bapt. Assn., 1989—; del. State Missions Task Force, Dallas, 1990—. Contbg. author: (manuals) Budgeting, 1988, Radical Evangelism, 1989; contbr. articles to profl. jours. Bd. dirs. Palmer Drug Abuse Prog., Midland, 1985—, Hearthstone Foster Group Home, Midland, 1983—; task force Midland Introspective/Adolescent Issues Task Force, 1990—, United Way, Midland, 1987-89. Recipient Disting. Svc. award Focus on Family, L.A., 1982-83, Clergyman of Yr. award Midland Downtown Kiwanis, 1986, God and Svc. Recognition award Boy Scouts Am. # 1106. Mem. Metro Youth Ministers Assn., Baylor Univ. C. of C. (parlimentarian 1972). Home: 409 N Bentwood Midland TX 79703 Office: First Baptist Church 2104 W Louisiana Midland TX 79701 *I really believe that God gives everyone help and a chance to change. So we should never give up.*

DODD, GARY WAYNE, minister; b. Huntington, W.Va., May 21, 1958; s. Harold Frank and Virginia Marie (Boland) D.; m. Faith Rankin; children: Andrew Wayne, Rebekah Marie. AA, Ohio Valley Coll., 1978; BA, David Lipscomb Coll., 1980; MA in Edn., Tenn. State U., 1983, postgrad.; MS in Bible and Related Studies, Abilene Christian U., 1990. Asst. minster Ch. Christ, Reynoldsburg, Ohio, 1980-81; youth minister Hermitage (Tenn.) Ch. Christ, 1981-84; assoc. minister Hillsboro Ch. Christ, Nashville, 1985-88, Southside Ch., Shelbyville, Tenn., 1988, Wingate Ch. Christ, Nashville, 1989-90; Brownsville Rd. Ch. of Christ, Memphis, 1990—; lectr., speaker throughout South and Midwest. Fundraiser Fannie Battle Day Care, Nashville, 1986, Am. Heart Assn. Republican. Office: Brownsville Rd Ch of Christ 3333 Old Brownsville Rd Memphis TN 38134

DODD, TRAVIS CURTIS, pastor; b. Wharton, Tex., Oct. 19, 1951; s. Travis Curtis Jr. and Cleo (Blake) D.; m. Melody Ann Bisagno, June 1, 1975; children: Jonathan, Zachary, Britni. BA, Houston Bapt. U., 1974; MDiv, Southwestern Sem., 1977, D Ministry, 1981. Ordained to ministry So. Bapt. Conv., 1974. Assoc. pastor Urban Park Bapt. Ch., Dallas, 1974-76; pastor First Bapt. Ch., Eden, Tex., 1977-80, Gonzales, Tex., 1980-82; pastor Met. Bapt. Ch., Houston, 1982—. Author: And One to Grow On, 1989, Hearts On Fire, 1989, Running On Empty, 1990. Steering com. Houston Campaign for Homeless, Houston, 1989-90; bd. dirs. KSBJ Ednl. Found., Houston, 1984-87. Named Pastor of the Day State of Tex. Ho. of Reps., Austin, 1988, 89. Mem. Bapt. Gen. Conv. (exec. bd. 1989—, E. European Task Force, 1990—), Conf. Tex. Bapt. Evangelists (pastor, advisor 1989-90), Houston Bapt. U. Alumni (bd. dirs. 1989-90). Republican. Office: Met Bapt Ch 13000 Jones Rd Houston TX 77070

DODD, WENDELL RAY, minister; b. Winfield, Ala., Nov. 4, 1958; s. Bud and Edith (Evans) D.; m. Lorie Jane Ernst, Jan. 3, 1987. BS in Religious Edn., Miss. Coll., 1985; MA in Religious Edn., Southwestern Bapt. Theol. Sem., Ft. Worth, 1988. Ordained to ministry So. Bapt. Conv., 1989. Min. youth and activities Southside Bapt. Ch., Jackson, Miss., 1982-83; recreational asst. 1st Bapt. Ch., Jackson, 1983-85; min. activities Emmanuel Bapt. Ch., Alexandria, La., 1988-80; min. edn. 1st Bapt. Ch., Pontotoc, Miss., 1990—. With USAF, 1977-82. Mem. Lions. Home: 83 S Liberty St Pontotoc MS 38863 Office: 1st Bapt Ch 31 Washington St Pontotoc MS 38863

DODD, WILLIAM FERRALL, educator; b. Louisville, Miss., Mar. 31, 1942; s. William S. and Elsie Rae (Chappell) D.; m. Kaysie Dawn Deaton, Aug. 24, 1968; children: Kaysie, Patton. BA, Colo. Christian U., 1989; MA, U. No. Colo., 1991. Pastor So. Bapt. Ch., Medina, Tenn., 1969-70; v.p., bus. adminstr. Ea. European Bible Mission, Colorado Springs, Colo., 1985-89; educator Colo. Christian Univ., Colorado Springs, 1989—; prof. Pikes Peak Community Coll., Colorado Springs, 1991—; deacon First So. Bapt. Ch., Colorado Springs, 1989—. Sec. Exchange Club, Jackson, Tenn., 1974, Christian Ministries Assn., Colorado Springs, 1989. With USNG, 1959-68. Mem. Colo. Speech Communication Assn. (chair interest group 1991—). Home: 5030 Montebello Pl Colorado Springs CO 80918 *Generally what we least like or admire in others becomes a mirror of ourselves.*

DODDS, ALAN ROBERT, chemist, church organist; b. Beaver Falls, Pa., Oct. 20, 1951; s. Robert Warren Jr. and Virginia May (Martsolf); m. Ruth Elizabeth Stiening, Apr. 27, 1973; children: Evan Thomas, Martha Lynn, Catherine Elisabeth. BS, Geneva Coll., 1973; PhD, U. Utah, 1980. Rsch. chem. UOP Inc., Des Plaines, Ill., 1977-79; plant chemist Syntex Labs., Inc., Elgin, Ill., 1979-81; new product chemist Aldrich Chem. Co., Sheboygan Falls, Wis., 1981-83; chemist Kohler (Wis.) Co., 1984—. Co-contbr. articles to profl. jours; patentee in field. Organist 1st United Meth. Ch., Dundee, Ill., 1980-81, Wesley United Meth. Ch., Sheboygan, Wis., 1981-82, Ebenezer United Ch. of Christ, Sheboygan, 1982—. Faculty fellow U. Utah, 1974-76. Mem. Am. Chem. Soc., Organ Hist. Soc., Soc. Applied Spectroscopy, Sheboygan Music Club, Sigma Xi. Mem. United Ch. of Christ. Avocations: music, travel, history, literature. Home: 1323 N 7th St Sheboygan WI 53081 Office: Kohler Co 444 Highland Dr Kohler WI 53044

DODDS, JAPHETH EVANS, minister; b. Wesley, Dominica, W.I., Jan. 24, 1942; came to U.S. 1985; s. Jonathan Adam and Dulcina (Lawrence) D.; m. Carlotta Rosalind Dodds, Aug. 4, 1971; children: Eldon Sigmund, Curtis Lysander, Japheth Evans Jr. MA, Princeton Theol. Sem., 1977; MDiv, Trinity Theol. Sem., Newburgh, Ind., 1988, DMin, 1988; EdD, Calif. Coast U., Santa Ana, Calif., 1982. Ordained to ministry, United Meth. Ch., 1974. Pastor Meth. Ch. Caribbean, Belize, 1971-76, various locations, 1977-85; pastor So. N.J. Ann. Conf.-Hamilton Meml. Ch., Atlantic City, N.J., 1985—; mem. Commn. of Religion and Race, 1988—; bd. ordained ministry, chmn. recruitment com. United Meth. Ch., 1990—. Author: Meditation for Youth Through the Year with God, 1984. Home: 745 Sewell Ave Atlantic City NJ 08401 Office: Hamilton Meml Meth Ch 605-611 Arctic Ave Atlantic City NJ 08401 *We are living at a critical time in our history. Christians are faced with the challenge to help make the gospel of Jesus Christ become a redemptive power in the midst of drug and alcohol addiction, racism, world hunger and the AIDS epidemic.*

DODDS, MICHAEL JOHN, priest, theology educator, academic dean; b. Des Moines, Nov. 14, 1950; s. John Joseph and Margaret Evelyn (Farrell) D. BA, St. Albert's Coll., Oakland, Calif., 1973; MA in Philosophy, Dominican Sch. Philosophy & Theology, Berkeley, Calif., 1975; MA with distinction in Theology, Grad. Theol. Union, Berkeley, 1978; PhD summa cum laude, U. Fribourg, Switzerland, 1986. Joined Western Dominican Province Order Preachers, 1970, ordained priest Roman Cath. Ch., 1977. Tchr. St. Mary's Coll., Moraga, Calif., 1978-81; asst. prof. dept. philosophy and theology Dominican Sch. Philosophy and Theology, 1985—, acad. dean, 1988—. Author: The Unchanging God of Love, 1986. Mem. Cath. Theol. Soc. Am., Soc. Christian Philosophers.

DODGE, DAVID FREDERICK, minister; b. Salem, Mass., Mar. 25, 1949; s. Frederick Henry and Elaine Joyce (Marden) D.; divorced; children: David Sr., Christopher, Heather, Robyn; m. Susan Lesli Rideout, July 25, 1986. BA in Communications, U. Southern Maine, 1982; MDiv, Bangor Theol. Sem., 1989. Ordained to ministry United Ch. of Christ, 1989. Minister with youth Swampscott (Mass.) Congl. Ch., 1982-83, Falmouth (Maine) Congl. Ch., 1986-87; minister Forest Ave. Congl. Ch., Bangor, Maine, 1987-89, Union Ch. of Stow (Mass.), 1989—; mem. commn. for ch. life and leadership United Ch. of Christ, Framingham, 1990—, student del. bd. homeland ministries, N.Y.C., 1987-89; trustee Maine Theol. Ctr., Portland, 1984-89; mem. Cen. Assn. Mass. Conf. United Ch. of Christ, 1988—. Chaplain Stow Police Dept., 1991; bd. dirs. Stow Food Pantry, 1991; vol. Stow Fire Dept., 1990. Mem. Acton, Boxboro Stow Clergy Assn., Golden Fleece, Bangor Consistory, Masons. Home and Office: Box 246 Stow MA 01775

DODRILL, DENVER KEITH, minister; b. Columbus, Ohio, Apr. 11, 1953; s. Donald Everett and Dorcas Orlena (Hash) D.; m. Marilyn Diane Dean, Jan. 5, 1974; children: Michelle Renée, Jonathan Denver. B in Sacred Lit., Circleville Bible Coll., Ohio, 1975; BA, Ind. Wesleyan U., Marion, 1977. Asst. pastor South High St. United Meth. Ch., Columbus, Ohio, 1974-75; pastor Jonesboro (Ind.) 1st United Meth. Ch., 1975-77, Coshocton (Ohio) Burt Ave. Wesleyan Ch., 1977-85; sr. pastor Kenney Mem. Wesleyan Ch., Athens, Ohio, 1985—; trustee Dist. Bd. of Adminstrn., Columbus, Ohio, 1980-91, Dist. Bd. Ministerial Standing, 1980-90, Wellspring Retreat & Resource Ctr., Albany, Ohio, 1987—, Ind. Wesleyan U., Marion, 1990—; active mem. Host Com. of Christian Holiness Assn., Columbus, 1991. Active Kiwanis, Athens, Ohio, 1987. Mem. Athens Ministerial Assn. (pres. 1987-88). Office: Kenney Memorial Wesleyan Ch 88 East State St Athens OH 45701

DOERMANN, RALPH WALTER, religion educator, archaeologist; b. Kodaikanal, South India, June 25, 1930; came to U.S., 1948; s. Carl Martin and Cora Charlotte (Knupke) D.; m. Laurel Diane Ackermann, June 13, 1953; children: Roger James, Gail Marie, Richard Carl, William Frederick. BA, Capital U., 1952; BDiv, Luth. Theol. Sem., 1958; PhD, Duke U., 1961. Pastor Trinity Luth. Ch., Albert Lea, Minn., 1961-63; asst. prof. O.T. Trinity Luth. Sem., Columbus, Ohio, 1963-64; assoc. prof. Luth. Theol. Sem., Columbus, 1964-72, prof., 1972-78; prof. O.T. and Archaeology Trinity Luth. Sem., Columbus, Ohio, 1978—; ann. prof. Albright Inst. Archaeol. Rsch., Jerusalem, 1977, 84; mem. excavation staff Expedition to Tell el-Hesi, Israel, 1970-83; field supr. Idalion (Cyprus) Excavations, 1972, 74. Author: Biblical Concern for the Poor, 1972, God's Hand Stretched Out: Isaiah, 1976, (chpt. in book) Archaeology and Biblical Interpretation, 1987. Mem. Columbus Open Housing Assn., 1966-70, Ohio Civil Rights Edn. Commn., Columbus, 1968-71; bd. dirs. Tell el-Hesi, 1975—. Lt. USNR, 1952-54. James B. Duke fellow Duke U., 1960-61, J.A. Montgomery fellow Am. Schs. of Oriental Rsch., 1969, NEH fellow, 1985; recipient Schiotz award Aid Assn. for Luths., 1984. Mem. Soc. Bibl. Lit., Ea. Great Lakes Bibl. Soc. (pres. 1986-87). Democrat. Lutheran. Avocations: travel, photography, gardening. Home: 2485 Brookwood Rd Columbus OH 43209 Office: Trinity Luth Sem 2199 E Main St Columbus OH 43209

DOERR, EDD, religious liberty organization administrator; b. Indpls., Dec. 21, 1930; s. Eugene Henry and Mary Catherine (Burk) D.; m. Herenia Isabel Osma, Apr. 21, 1956; children: Eric E., Helena T. BS, Ind. U., 1956. Cert. secondary educator, Ind.; counselor Am. Humanist Assn. Exec. dir. Americans for Religious Liberty, Silver Spring, Md., 1982—; v.p. Am. Humanist Assn., Amherst, N.Y., 1985-91, also bd. dirs.; bd. dirs. Internat. Humanist and Ethical Union, Utrecht, The Netherlands, 1985—, N.Am. Com. for Humanism, Farmington Hills, Mich., 1985—. Author: Religious Liberty in Crisis, 1988, A Hitch in Time, 1988, (poems) Images, 1991; co-author: Religion and Public Education: Common Sense and the Law, 1991, Church Schools and Public Money: The Politics of Parochiaid, 1991; co-editor: Abortion Rights and Fetal "Personhood", 1989, The Great Quotations on Religious Freedom, 1991. Campaign leader Md. Coalition for Pub. Edn. and Religious Liberty, Sliver Spring, 1972, 1974; bd. dirs. Religious Coalition for Abortion Rights, Washington, 1973—, Nat. Coalition Pub. Edn. and Religious Liberty, 1970—. Mem. Fellowship Religious Humanists (bd. dirs. 1989—), Phi Delta Kappa. Democrat. Office: Americans for Religious Liberty PO Box 6656 Silver Spring MD 20916 *If full religious liberty for every American is to survive and grow, it is imperative that we halt every effort to erode our constitutional principle of separation of church and state.*

DOEUNG, SOK T., minister; b. Siemreap, Cambodia, Feb. 23, 1936; came to U.S., 1975; d. Mey and Touch (Keo) Pich; m. Banan San Doeung, July 22, 1964; children: Yuttevong, Panhavong, Seilavong, Chansorya, Chanleakhena. Diploma, Nat. Sch. Agr., Phnom Penh, Cambodia, 1957; BS, U. Fla., 1961, MS, 1963; postgrad., Southwestern Bapt. Theol. Sem., 1980-81. Chief crop protection div. Ministry of Agr., Phnom Penh, 1963-64; dir. Vocat. Sch. Agr., Prek Leap, Cambodia, 1964-66; head studies and rsch. dept. People U., Phnom Penh, 1967-69; dean Coll. Arts & Trade Tech. U., Phnom Penh, 1970-74; ops. mgr. Khmer Devel. Co., Kompong Som, Cambodia, 1974-75; nurseryman City of Ft. Worth Pk. and Recreation, 1975-76; pest control technician, 1976; salesperson Ency. Britannica Co., Ft. Worth, 1977-79; mission pastor Bapt. Gen. Conv. Tex., Dallas, 1979-82; home missionary Home Mission Bd., SBC, Dallas, 1981—; bus. mgr., editor Cambodian Bapt. Standards, Ft. Worth, 1985—; gen. coord. Cambodian Bapt. Fellowship, So. Bapt. Conv., Ft. Worth, 1985—; catalytic missionary Bapt. Gen. Conv. Tex. and Home Mission Bd., Dallas, 1988—; cons. in field. Editor: Cambodian Bapt. Standard mag., 1985—; contbr. articles to profl. jours. Mem. adv. coun. Ft. Worth Ind. Sch. Dist., 1977-78; mem. Rep. Party, Ft. Worth, 1981—; bd. dirs. Tex. Bapt. Sch. Theology, 1987—, Mayfield Christian TV, San Antonio, 1988—. Mem. New Work Fellowship, Assn. Agrl. Technicians (gen. sec. 1963-65), Optimists. Avocations: photography, history, writing, newspaper clipping, reading. Home: 1813 Barron Ln Fort Worth TX 76112 Office: Bapt Gen Conv Tex 333 N Washington St Dallas TX 75246-1798

DOGGETT, JOHN NELSON, JR., clergyman; b. Phila., Apr. 3, 1918; s. John Nelson and Winola (Ballard) D.; BA, Lincoln U., 1942; MDiv, Union Theol. Sem., N.Y.C., 1945; MEd, St. Louis U., 1969, PhD, 1971; m. Juanita Toley, Aug. 2, 1973; children by previous marriage: Lorraine, John, William, Kenneth Riddick. Ordained to ministry United Methodist Ch., 1943; civilian chaplain South Gate Community Ch., San Francisco, 1945-47; organizing pastor Downs Meml. Meth. Ch., Oakland, Calif., 1947-49; pastor Scott Meml. Meth. Ch., Pasadena, Calif., 1950-53, Hamilton Meml. Meth. Ch., L.A., 1953-64, Union Meml. United Meth. Ch., St. Louis, 1964-76; dist. supt. United Meth. Ch., St. Louis, 1976-82; sr. pastor Grace United Meth. Ch., St. Louis, 1982-85; ret. pastor Cabanne United Meth. Ch., 1986-89; staff Pastoral Counseling Inst., St. Louis, 1968-89 ; pres. Midwest Cons., 1989—. instr. founds. edn. Harris Tchrs. Coll., St. Louis, 1971-75; assoc. prof. practical theology Met. Coll., St. Louis, 1976-77; commr. Nat. Coun. Chs. of Christ, 1981-84. Pres. bd. dirs. St. Louis C.M.C. Retirement Village Ctr., Cen. Med. Ctr. Hosps., St. Louis, 1973-86 ; pres. St. Louis NAACP, 1973-81, Limelight Mag. Health Issues Chronicle, Clergy Coalition Ch. Ea. Mo. AIDS Summit, 1990; bd. dirs. United Way St. Louis, 1974-81; mem. Commn. on Alternatives to Prison, 1981, Citizens Com. Mo. Dept. Corrections, 1974-80, Mayor's Task Force on Hunger, 1981, Mo. Minority Health Task Force; trustee Mo. Hist. Soc., 1980-85; adv. com. St. Louis U. Sch. Social Work; advisor John N. Doggett Scholarship Found.; mem. Interfaith Clergy Coun., World Meth. Coun., St. Louis U. Pres. Coun.; mem. mayor's ambassadors World Affairs Coun., ACLU, Pub. Schs. Drug Free Commn. Named Minister of Year, St. Louis Argus Newspaper, 1971; recipient Outstanding Alumni award St. Louis U., 1981, Human Rights award E.P. Lovejoy Soc., Martin Luther King Alpha/Anheuser-Busch Spl. Plaque, M.L. King Day Plague award Job Corp., 1990. Mem. Am. Assn. Pastoral Counselors, Metro Ministers Coalition, 1981-91, UN Assn. (clergy-pub. edn. com.), Masons, Shriners, Chi Alpha Lit. Forum, Phi Delta Kappa, Alpha Phi Alpha (nat. chaplain, D. Bowles/R. Anderson Svc. award, regional hall fame 1987). Democrat. Home: 4466 W Pine Blvd # 2C Saint Louis MO 63108

DOGGETTE, JACKSON MICHAEL, JR., minister; b. Ardmore, Okla., Mar. 24, 1957; s. Jackson Michael Sr. and Edythe Marie (Young) D.; m. Emily Kaye Dunn, Dec. 23, 1984; children: Jacquelyn Michelle, Jackson Michael III. Student, Calif. State U., L.A., 1982; BTh, Oakwood Coll., 1982; postgrad., Loma Linda (Calif.) U., 1983, Indian U., 1985; MA in Religion, Andrews U., 1986; JD, Thomas M. Cooley Law Sch., 1990. Ordained to ministry Adventist Ch., 1986. Pastor, evangelist, mem. sch. bd. Seventh-Day Adventist Ch., Los Angeles, 1979-83, pastor, evangelist, 1979-85; pastor, evangelist Seventh-Day Adventist Ch., Ft. Wayne, Ind., 1985-86; pastor, evangelist, mem. sch. bd. Seventh-Day Adventist Ch., Detroit, 1986—; cons. So. Calif. Conf. of Seventh-Day Adventists, Glendale, Calif., 1979. Contbr. articles to profl. jours. Co-founder Children's Ednl. Watch, Ft. Wayne, 1986; bd. dirs. Met. Open Housing Commn., Ft. Wayne, 1985, Gingerbread House, Inc., Ft. Wayne, 1985, Learning Acad., Ft. Wayne, 1986; chief legal officer Fla. Hosp., Orlando. Named one of Outstanding Young Men of Am., U.S. Jaycees, 1980. Mem. NAACP, Lake Region Ministerial Alliance (Excellence award 1985-87), Inkster Ministerial Alliance. Avocations: flying airplanes, musician, athlete, author. Office: PO Box 80244 Lansing MI 48908 *My philosophy of life is simple: I daily strive to reach my fullest potential in order to bring glory to God through service to my fellow man.*

DOHERTY, SISTER BARBARA (ANN DOHERTY), academic administrator; b. Chgo., Dec. 2, 1931; d. Martin James and Margaret Eleanor (Noe) D. Student, Rosary Coll., 1949-51; BA in Latin, English and History, St. Mary-of-the-Woods Coll., 1953; MA in Theology, St. Mary's Coll., 1963; PhD in Theology, Fordham U., 1979; LittD (hon.), Ind. State U., 1990. Tchr. Jr. and Sr. High Schs., Ind. and Ill., 1953-63; asst. prof. religion St. Mary-of-the-Woods Coll., Ind., 1963-67, 71-75, pres., 1984—; provincial supr. Chgo. Province of Sisters of Providence, 1975-83; summer faculty NCAIS-KCRCHE, Delhi, India, 1970. Author: I Am What I Do, 1981, Make Yourself an Ark, 1984; editor: Providence: God's Face Towards the World, 1984; contbr. articles to New Cath. Ency. Vol. XVII, 1982, Dictionary of Spirituality, 1990. Pres. Leadership Terre Haute, Ind., 1985-86; bd. regents Ind. Acad., 1987—; bd. dirs. 8th Day Cen. for Justice, Chgo., 1978-83, Family Svcs., Swope Art Mus., Terre Haute, Ind., 1988—. Arthur J. Schmidt Found. grantee, 1967-71. Mem. Women's Coll. Coalition (nat. bd. dirs. 1984—), Assn. Colls. Ind., Ind. Colls. and Univs. of Ind. (exec. bd.), Assn. Am. Colls., Leadership Conf. of Women Religious of USA (program chairperson nat. assembly 1982-83). Democrat. Roman Catholic. Avocation: walking, reading, traveling. Home and Office: Office of the Pres Saint Mary-of-the-Woods IN 47876

DOHERTY, EDWARD J., academic administrator. Supt. of schs. Roman Cath. Diocese of Ft. Worth. Office: Edn Dept 800 W Loop 820 S Fort Worth TX 76108*

DOHSE, CRAIG CLAYTON, minister; b. Carroll, Iowa, Nov. 22, 1948; s. Clayton Henry and Maxine Ruth (Bauer) D.; m. Eileen F. Henn, June 28, 1975 (div. 1983); m. Roberta L. Shellum, May 25, 1984; children: Gretchen, Kari, Shea, Seth, Christian. AA, Concordia Coll., Ann Arbor, Mich., 1969; BA, Concordia Coll., Ft. Wayne, Ind., 1971; MDiv., Concordia Sem., St. Louis, 1975; postgrad., U. Houston, 1987—. Ordained to ministry Luth. Ch., 1975. Pastor Trinity Luth. Ch., Borger, Tex., 1975-80; chaplain M.D. Anderson Hosp. U. Tex., Houston, 1980-81; pastor Mt. Calvary Luth. Ch., Houston, 1981-82; sr. pastor Beautiful Savior Luth. Ch., Houston, 1982-83; regional v.p. A.L. Williams Corp., Atlanta, 1980—; sr. pastor North Land Ch., Houston, 1985-88; sr. ptnr. Holy Trinity Luth. Ch., Houston, 1988—; regional pastoral counselor Luth. Ch., No. Tex., 1978-80, youth counselor, 1975-78; counselor Luth. Women's Missionary League, Tex., 1978-80; mem. exec. bd. regents Christian Coll. Am., Houston, 1984-86; adj. prof. North Harris County Coll., Houston, 1985—; asst. prof. Christian Coll. Am., 1985-86; task force for Evangelism S.E. Tex. Synod of Evang. Luth. Ch. in Am., bishop's com. Instr. Evangelism Explosion, 1977—, Effectiveness Tng. Inc., 1977—; chmn. bd. Cornerstone House (daycare for families with AIDS); founder Joy Ctr. Social Svc. Agy. Lutheran. Avocations: singing. Home: 727 Redleaf Houston TX 77090 Office: 7822 Northline Dr Houston TX 77037

DOLINAY, THOMAS V., bishop; b. Uniontown, Pa., July 24, 1923. Student, St. Procopius Coll., Ill. Ordained priest Roman Catholic Ch., 1948. Ordained titular bishop Tiatira and aux. bishop Byzantine rite Diocese of Passaic, 1976-81; aux. bishop Byzantine rite Diocese of Van Nuys Calif., 1981; installed, 1982—. Editor: Eastern Cath. Life, 1966-82. Office: Diocese of Van Nuys 18024 Parthenia St Northridge CA 91325

DOLL, ALICE MARY, religion educator; b. Perham, Minn., Mar. 29, 1921; d. Peter Henry and Ann (Delaney) D. Student, Coll. St. Benedict, 1945-46; BA in Art and Chemistry, Mt. Mary Coll., 1949; postgrad., Marquette U., 1955; MRE, Notre Dame U., 1965. Cert. secondary tchr., Minn. Tchr. St. Francis High Sch., Little Falls, Minn., 1949-64; dir. jr. sisters Franciscan House of Studies, St. Paul, 1964-69; dir. religious edn. Assumption Parish, Morris, Minn., 1969-72; diocesan dir. Office of Religious Edn., St. Cloud, Minn., 1972—; chmn. Franciscan Edn. Com., Little Falls, 1970-72; sec. Diocesan Pastoral Coun., St. Cloud, 1972-80; instr. St. John's U., Collegeville, Minn., 1980-85; mem. ecumenical commn. Diocese. Columnist: St. Cloud Visitor, 1980—; contbr. articles to profl. jours. Recipient Excellence in Art award St. Otto's Home, Little Falls, 1970. Mem. Nat. Conf. Diocesan Dir. (bd. dirs. 1980-82), Nat. Cath. Edn. Assn., Diocesan Centennial (com. mem.), Franciscan Sisters Centennial (com. mem.). Home: 1600 11th Ave S Saint Cloud MN 56301 *I hope that my life will help many others value beauty, truth and goodness.*

DOLL, MARY ASWELL, English educator; b. N.Y.C., June 4, 1940; d. Edward Campbell and Mary Louise (White) Aswell; m. William Elder Doll, June 25, 1966; 1 child, William Campbell. BA, Conn. Coll., 1962; M in Liberal Arts, Johns Hopkins U., 1972; PhD, Syracuse U., 1980. Instr. Garrison (Md.) Forest Sch., 1962-65, Sidwell Friends Sch., Washington, 1965-66, Park Sch., Brooklandville, Md., 1966-70; instr. SUNY-Oswego State Coll., 1978-84, asst. prof., 1982-84; instr. U. Redlands (Calif.), 1985-88; vis. asst. prof. Tulane U., New Orleans, 1988-89; assoc. prof. Our Lady of Holy Cross Coll., New Orleans, 1989—. Author: Beckett and Myth, 1989; co-editor: In the Shadow of the Giant, 1989; contbr. articles to profl. publs. Chmn. Beckett's Archetypal Imagination, Columbus, 1981; bd. dirs. Friends of Library, New Orleans, 1989—; pres. Dem. Com., Fulton, N.Y., 1983-85; sec. bd. dirs. United Way, Fulton, 1983-85; pres. bd. dirs. Fulton Libr., 1983-85. Mem. Am. Acad. Religion, Nat. Coun. Tchrs. of English, Samuel Beckett Soc., Thomas Wolfe Soc. (bd. dirs. 1989—), MLA (chmn. Jung session NE chpt. 1986). Roman Catholic. Avocation: tennis. Home: 69 Belle Grove Destrehan LA 70047 Office: Our Lady of Holy Cross Coll 4123 Woodland Dr New Orleans LA 70131-7399

DOLLAHITE, DAMIAN GENE, priest; b. Yukon, Okla., Nov. 2, 1939; s. LC and Mabel Lucille (Jackson) D.; m. Loni Jeanne Dill, June 19, 1976; 1 child, Michael Saint-Damian. AA in Behavioral Sci., Coll. of Marin, Kentfield, Calif., 1971; BA in Counseling, Antioch Coll. West, San Francisco, Calif., 1976; MDiv, Ch. Divinity Sch. of Pacific, Berkeley, Calif., 1981. Ordained to ministry Episcopal Ch. as deacon, 1973, as priest, 1981. Founder, pres. Bread of Life Ministries, 1974—; assoc. priest Holy Innocents Episcopal Ch., Corte Madera, Calif., 1981-82; vicar The Episcopal Ch. in the Bridger Wilderness, Pinedale, Wyo., 1982-85; priest-in-charge St. George's Episcopal Ch., Lusk, Wyo., 1986-87; rector St. Philip's Epsicopal Ch. of Benzie County, Beulah, Mich., 1987—; mem. diocesan evangelism devel. team Diocese of Western Mich., 1989—; chair evangelism and mission commn., 1990—; chaplain Internat. Order of St. Luke the Physician, 1979—. Author: (passion play) Amen: So Be It, 1970. Bd. dirs. Commn. on Aging, Benzie County, Mich., 1987—, chmn., 1991—; bd. dirs. Sr. Companions, Grand Traverse Area, Mich., 1990—; cubmaster pack 141 Cub Scouts Am., Beulah, 1990-91, asst. scoutmaster troup 41, 1990—. With U.S. Navy, 1957-60. Mem. Benzie County Ministerial Assn. (pres. 1990—), Western Mich. Episcopal Cursillo (spiritual advisor), Confraternity of the Blessed Sacrament (life), Anglican Priest Eucharistic League, Nat. Order of Episcopalians for Life, Order of Holy Cross (clergy assoc.). Republican. Home: 5627 River Rd Benzonia MI 49616 Office: St Philip's Ch 785 Beulah Hwy Beulah MI 49617

DOLOREY, SISTER MARY, nun, college administrator. BS in Biology, Coll. Misericordia, Dallas, Pa.; MA in Ednl. Adminstrn., Fairfield U.; postgrad., Syracuse U. Prin. Our Lady of Pilar High Sch., Rio Piedras, P.R.; registrar Alvernia Coll., Reading, Pa., 1978-79, pres., 1982—. Office: Alvernia Coll Office of the Pres Reading PA 19607

DOMBALIS, CONSTANTINE NICHOLAS, minister; b. Norfolk, Va., July 29, 1925; s. Nicholas John and Helen Constantine (Matinos) D.; m. Mary Christine Fourgis, June 6, 1954; children: Nicholas, Christopher. BTh, Hellenic Coll., 1947; BD, Holy Cross Sem., 1949; STB, Gen. Theol. Sch., 1951; DD (hon.), U. Richmond, 1988. Ordained to ministry Greek Orthodox Ch., 1954. Pastor Greek Orthodox Ch., Richmond, Va., 1954-71; dean Greek Orthodox Cathedral, Richmond, Va., 1971—; vicar Archdiocese of Va., Richmond, Va., 1976—; exec. com. Va. Coun. of Chs., Richmond, 1978—; U.S. del. to UN 38th Gen. Assembly, 1983; mem. coun. religious leaders U.S. Holocaust Meml., Washington, 1989—; exec. bd. dirs. Sts. Cosma and Damianos Sr. Residence, Richmond, 1988—. Contbr. articles to profl. jours. Chmn. Va. Dept. of Rehab., 1979-83; chmn. religious com. Va. Statute for Religious Freedom, 1989—; mem. bd. visitors Va. Commonwealth U., 1991—. Recipient DAR award, 1968, NCCJ award 1974, B'nai Brith Torch of Liberty award 1976; named one of 100 Most Influential Richmonders 1986. Mem. UNESCO (bd. dirs. 1980-82), Holy Cross Theol. Sch. Alumni Assn. (pres. 1978-82). Home: 304 Sandalwood Dr Richmond VA 23229 Office: Greek Orthodox Cathedral 30 Malvern Ave Richmond VA 23221

DOMKE, MICHAEL JOHN, pastor; b. Flint, Mich., Sept. 21, 1963; s. Earl Joseph and Mary Francis (Miller) D.; m. Juli An Swartz, June 3, 1989. BS, Liberty U., Lynchburg, Va., 1990. Ordained to ministry Bapt. Ch., 1990. Min. youth 1st Bapt. Ch., Flushing, Mich., 1987; min. youth, coll. lay staff Old Forest Rd. Bapt. Ch., Lynchburg, 1988-89; assoc. pastor, min. youth and edn. 1st Bapt. Ch. Oceanway, Jacksonville, Fla., 1990—; youth chmn. City Wide Bailey Smith Crusade, Jacksonville, 1990-91. With USN, 1981-87. Mem. Jacksonville Bapt. Assn. (youth coun. 1990—, discipleship com. 1990—), David Burton-Fla. Bapt. Assn. (state bd. regents for evangelism 1991—). Republican. Home: 357 Shamrock Ave S Jacksonville FL 32218

DOMOKOS, ROBERT LEWIS, college administrator; b. Windsor, Ohio, July 2, 1938; s. Martin and Helen (Molnar) D.; m. Shirley Ann Harrington, June 30, 1962; children: Michael Lewis, Brenda Louise. BA, Cedarville (Ohio) Coll., 1962; MDiv, Grace Sem., Winona Lake, Ind., 1965, ThM, 1972; D Ministry, Trinity Div. Sch., Deerfield, Ill., 1980. Itinerant minister Winona Lake, 1965; pastor Bible Bapt. Ch., Huntington, Ind., 1965-69, Village Bapt. Ch., Poland, Ohio, 1969-72; faculty mem. Faith Bapt. Bible Coll., Ankeny, Iowa, 1972-87; pres. Faith Bapt. Bible Coll. and Sem., Ankeny, Iowa, 1988—; interim pastor 15 different chs., Iowa, 1972-88; ch. cons., Iowa, 1972-88. Named Alumnus of Yr., Cedarville Coll., 1988, Hon. Alumnus, Faith Bapt. Bible Coll. and Sem., Ankeny, 1990. Mem. Evang. Theol. Soc. Office: Faith Bapt Bible Coll & Sem 1900 NW 4th St Ankeny IA 50021

DOMSCH, JOHN FRANCIS, minister; b. Council Bluffs, Iowa, Dec. 13, 1941; s. John Traugott and Constance Concordia (Mencke) D.; m. Linda Ellen Patzer, June 8, 1968; children: Lara Lyn, Jeremy John, Jeffrey James. BA, Concordia Sr. Coll., 1964; MDiv, Concordia Theol. Sem., St. Louis, 1968. Ordained to ministry Luth. Ch.-Mo. Synod, 1968. Pastor 1st Luth. Ch., Sabetha, Kans., 1968-76, Redeemer Luth. Ch., Marshalltown, Iowa, 1976—; del. Luth. Ch.-Mo. Synod Nat. Conv., Milw., 1971, del., mem. floor com., Dallas, 1977, St. Louis, 1983, cir. counselor Iowa dist. East, Luth. Ch.-Mo. Synod, 1981—, chmn. continuing edn. com., 1985—, dist. rep. to nat. continuing edn. com., 1988—; pastoral advisor Kans. dist. Luth. Women's Missionary League, 1974-76. Bd. dirs. Svc. to Mil. Families, Nemaha County chpt. ARC, Sebetha, 1973, county chmn., 1975; active N.E. Kans. Alcoholism Coun., 1975-76. Home: 1603 S 2d Ave Marshalltown IA 50158 Office: Redeemer Luth Ch 1600 S Center St Marshalltown IA 50158

DOMSKE, RENNY, minister; b. Washington, Pa., Sept. 10, 1950; s. R. William and Martha Alice (Weaver) D.; m. Ronee Christy, Oct. 14, 1972; children: Tobyn, Tyler, Kirby, Addison. BA in Psychology, Duke U., 1974; MDiv, D Ministry, Union Theol. Sem., 1978. Ordained to ministry Presbyn. Ch. (U.S.A.), 1978. Club asst. Young Life, Durham, N.C., 1968-69; club dir., Bible quiz dir. Washington County Youth for Christ, 1969-73; minister of youth and edn. Beulah Presbyn. Ch., Pitts., 1978-82; minister of youth Abington Presbyn. Ch., Phila., 1982-86; minister to youth and families United Presbyn. Ch., Washington, Iowa, 1986—; mem. candidates and credentials com. Pitts. Presbytery, 1981-82; mem. ch. oversight com. Phila. Presbytery, 1985-86, trustee presbytery, 1985-86; mem. Christian edn. com. East Iowa Presbytery, 1987—, chair youth com., 1989—, mem. com. on preparation for ministry, 1989—. Bd. dirs. Washington YMCA; coach Little League Baseball, Washington, 1989—; high sch. basketball referee, 1976—; state chmn. alumni admissions coun. Duke U., 1991—. Mem. Soc. Biblical Lit., Am. Acad. Religion, World Bible Quiz Assn. (quizmaster world finals 1987, 90), Washington County Bible Quiz League (founder, bd. dirs. 1987—, coach 1st place team 1987, 89, 91). Home: RR 3 Box 33 Washington IA 52353 Office: United Presbyn Ch 209 E Main St Washington IA 52353 *How can I live the life God has created for me to live? How can I hear God's voice most clearly instead of substituting my own or another religious leader's? How can I have ears to hear? This I pursue...*

DONADIEU, JOSEPH MARTIN, religious editor, lay church worker; b. Phila., Jan. 13, 1943; s. Joseph G. and Teresa A. (McElhatton) D.; m. Phyllis A. Jaeger, Aug. 6, 1966; children: Marc V., John J. BA, La Salle Coll., 1964; MA, Duquesne U., 1967; postgrad., U. Notre Dame, 1967-69. Ordained deacon Roman Cath. Ch., 1984. Editor in chief Monitor Communications, Trenton, N.J., 1978—; deacon St. Joseph's Parish, Beverly, N.J., 1984—. Office: Monitor Communications 315 Lowell Ave PO Box 3095 Trenton NJ 08619

DONAHUE, WILLIAM PATRICK, priest; b. Belvidere, Ill., June 2, 1958; s. Robert Michael and Marlene Louise (Brehmer) D. BA in Classics, U. Calif., Santa Barbara, 1980; MA in Classics, Boston Coll., 1982; MDiv, St. Patrick's Sem., Menlo Park, Calif., 1986. Ordained priest Roman Cath. Ch., 1986. Sec. to bishop Cath. Diocese of Santa Rosa, Calif., 1986-87; assoc. pastor St. John the Bapt. Ch., Napa, Calif., 1987-89; chaplain St. Vincent High Sch., Petaluma, Calif., 1989—; dir. Propagation of Faith, Santa Rosa, 1990—; mem. Diocesan Priests' Coun., Santa Rosa, 1989—, Priests' Health and Retirement Bd., Santa Rosa, 1989—. Editor (diocesan newspaper) The Redwood Cruzier, 1990—. Recipient 2d pl. poetry award Jessamyn West Contest, 1989. Home: 125 Ely Blvd N Petaluma CA 94954 Office: Diocese of Santa Rosa 547 B St Santa Rosa CA 95401

DONALD, MICHAEL J(OSEPH), pastor; b. Van Wert, Ohio, Dec. 25, 1960; s. Ronald Joseph Donald and Shirley (Bailey) Tyson; m. Drusilla Adams, June 7, 1980; children: Matthew Joseph, Brittany Nichole. Grad. in theology, Bapt. Bible Coll., Springfield, Mo., 1981, BA, 1982. Ordained to ministry Bapt. Bible Fellowship, 1986. Pastor youth Braeburn Bapt. Ch., Houston, 1982-86; sr. pastor Liberty Bapt. Ch., Van Wert, 1986—; traveling speaker as youth counselor, East Coast, Midwest, Brazil, 1986—; pres. Gulf Coast Youth Fellowship, Houston, 1984-86; leader Youth for Christ, Van Wert, 1986-89. Speaker to numerous local orgns., 1986—. Home: 618 W Main St Van Wert OH 45891 Office: Liberty Bapt Ch 101 S Harrison St Van Wert OH 45891

DONALDSON, GENE MICHAEL, minister; b. Washington, Nov. 26, 1953; s. Charles Joseph and Rose Elaine (Patterson) D.; m. Barbara Naomi Carter, May 1, 1976; children: Dawn, Trevor. BA, Hampton U., 1975; MDiv, Andrews U., 1984. Ordained to ministry Seventh-day Adventist Ch., 1988. Min. Allegheny East Conf., Seventh-day Adventist Ch., Pine Forge, Pa., 1984—. Recipient Outstanding Svc. award Allegheny East Conf., 1985-86, 87-88; named Pastor of Yr. Allegheny East Conf. Prison Ministry, 1987. Home: 30 Marquis Rd Ewing NJ 08638 Office: Mt Sinai Seventh-day Adventist Ch 35 Arlington Ave Trenton NJ 08618

DONALDSON, MARCIA JEAN, lay worker; b. Wilmington, Del., June 20, 1925; C. Aubrey Smith and Marcia Allen (Hall) Whitman; m. Robert Donald Donaldson, Jan. 8, 1944; children: Robert Gary, Pamela Lynn, David Keith. Student pub. schs., Wilmington. Sunday Sch. tchr. Del., N.J., 1943-70; tchr. Child Evangelism Fellowship, Wilmington, 1943-55; tchr., bd. dirs. Child Evangelism Fellowship, N.J., 1955-64; dir. Child Evangelism Fellowship, Ocean County, N.J., 1964-73; pres., exec. dir. Christian Children's Assocs., Toms River, N.J., 1973—. Writer radio and TV syndicated programs for children; producer, hostess radio and TV program Adventure Pals. Mem. Nat. Religious Broadcasters Assn. (bd. dirs), Gideons Aux. Office: 511 Dover Rd Toms River NJ 08754 *Of all the important achievements one can accomplish in this life I believe the most rewarding is to be able to introduce another person to the one true and living God, who alone can give us real joy and hope and peace.*

DO NASCIMENTO, ALEXANDER CARDINAL, archbishop; b. Malanje, Angola, Mar. 1, 1925. Ordained priest Roman Catholic Ch., 1952; prof. dogmatic theology in maj. sem. of Luanda (Angola); editor Cath. newspaper O Apostolada; in exile, Lisbon, Portugal, 1961-71, returned to Angola, 1971; then prof. Pius XII Inst. Social Scis.; consecrated bishop of Malanje, 1975; nominated archbishop of Lubango and apostolic adminstr. of Onjiva, 1977, archbishop of Luanda, 1986—; held hostage by Angolan guerrillas in 1982; elevated to Sacred Coll. of Cardinals, 1983; titular see, St. Mark in Agro Laurentino. Mem. Congregation for Evangelization of Peoples, Caritas Internationalis (pres. 1983-91). Address: Arcebispado CP 87, Luanda Angola

DONAT, REX, bishop. Bishop of Mauritius The Anglican Communion, Phoenix. Office: Bishop of Mauritius, Bishop's House, Phoenix Mauritius*

DONEHOO, PARIS NOLAN, minister; b. Atlanta, Aug. 14, 1952; s. John Timothy and Peggy Joyce (Paris) D.; m. Iris Anne Mills, Aug. 3, 1974; children: Margaret Elizabeth, Kathryn Peggy. BA, Ga. So. Coll., 1974; MDiv, Southwestern Sem., 1977; D of Ministry, Columbia Sem., 1988. Ordained to ministry Bapt. Ch., 1973. Pastor Little Ogeechee Bapt. Ch., Oliver, Ga., 1973-74, Sardis Bapt. Ch., Palmetto, Ga., 1977-80, Lost Mountain Bapt. Ch., Powder Springs, Ga., 1981-90; sr. min. Park Ridge (Ill.) Community Ch., 1991—; instr. New Orleans Bapt. Seminary, North Ga. Ctr; clk. Noonday Bapt. Assn., Marietta, Ga., 1984-90; chaplain Kennestone Hosp., Marietta, 1981-88. Author: Prayer in the Life of Jesus, 1984; contbr. articles to profl. jours. Adv. com. Pine Mountain Mid. Sch., Kennesaw, Ga., 1989-90; speaker Cobb/Douglas Symposium on Infant Mortality, Marietta, 1987, State BSU Conf., Rock Eagle, Ga., 1986. Named to Outstanding Young Men of Am., 1981; recipient Grant Knights Templar of Ga., 1976. Mem. Chgo. Metro Assn. United Ch. of Christ, Internat. Coun. Community Chs. Home: 607 S Knight Park Ridge IL 60068 Office: Park Ridge Community Ch 100 S Courtland Park Ridge IL 60068 *I never cease to be amazed and suprised by a God who accepts me for who I am, and who calls me to a journey for which there is always one more step.*

DONER, COLONEL VAUGHN, religious organization administrator, religious writer; b. Pomona, Calif., Sept. 23, 1948; s. Joseph Byron and Grace (Chapman) D.; m. Miriam Norman, Oct. 12, 1985; 1 child, Brant Eric Vaughn. BA, Calif. State U., Fullerton, 1971. Dir. World Emergency Relief Fund, Pasadena, Calif., 1972-74; chief exec. officer Christian Voice Inc., Washington, 1979-85; chmn., chief exec. officer Christian Action Network Found., Santa Rosa, Calif., 1984-90, Internat. Ch. Relief Fund, Santa Rosa, 1986—. Author: The Samaritan Strategy, 1988, Parents Guide to TV, 1988; editor Recipes for Successful Living, 1980, Christian Voice Strategy Guide, 1984. Chmn. Orange County, Calif. Young Reps., 1970, United Student Assn. Inc., Orange County, 1971; dir. Calif. Young Reps., Sacramento, 1970; chmn. Christians for Reagan Campaign, Washington, 1980, 84; mem. exec. com. Am. Coalition for Traditional Values, Washington, 1984-88; mem. adv. bd. World Emergency Relief Fund, San Diego, 1989—, Nat. Citizens Network, Costa Mesa, Calif., 1989—. Recipient Outstanding Achievement award Orange County Press Club, 1969, Outstanding Achievement award Freedoms Found., Valley Forge, Pa., 1971, Disting. Svc. award Nat. Child Protection Program, Dallas, 1990. Mem. Assn. Reformed and Charismatic Chs. (bd. dirs. 1991—), Evang. Fgn. Missions Assn., Network Christian Ministries. Office: Internat Ch Relief Fund 131 Stony Circle Ste 1000 Santa Rosa CA 95401

DONEY, JUDITH KAREN, minister, educator, consultant; b. Winston-Salem, N.C., Aug. 24, 1942; d. Parks Harvey and Dorothy (Hanna) Vanderlip; m. Arnold Bokhoven, May 26, 1961 (div. Mar. 1968); m. Marion Van Wyk, Mar. 16, 1968 (div. June 1975); m. Malcolm Edwards Doney, Sept. 30, 1981. Student, U. N.C., 1965-66, Vennard Coll., 1970-71, U. So. Miss., 1976, Phillips Coll., 1981-82. Audit clk. Consol. Credit Corp., Charlotte, N.C., 1963-64; operating rm. technician Mercy Hosp., Charlotte, 1965-66; operating and emergency rms. technician St. Dominics Hosp., Jackson, Miss., 1975-76; acute care technician U. Miss. Med. Ctr., Jackson, 1981; co-founder, sec.-treas., bd. dirs, dir. rehab. svcs. New Beginnings Ministries, Inc., Jackson, 1983—. Campaign mgr. U.S. senatorial candidate, Mahaska County, Iowa, 1968; mem. disaster team, instr. ARC, Jackson, 1980-81. Mem. NAFE, Nat. Chronic Pain Outreach Assn., Nat. Head Injury Found. Republican. Mailing Address: PO Box 776 Dallas TX 75221-0776

DONFRIED, KARL PAUL, minister, theology educator; b. N.Y.C., Apr. 6, 1940; s. Paul and Else (Schmuck) D.; m. Katharine E. Krayer, Sept. 10, 1960; children: Paul Andrew, Karen Erika, Mark Christopher. AB, Columbia U., 1960; BD, Harvard U., 1963; STM, Union Theol. Sem., 1965; ThD, U. Heidelberg, Fed. Republic Germany, 1968. Ordained to ministry Lutheran Ch. in Am., 1963; named ecumenical canon Christ Ch. Cathedral, Springfield, Mass., 1977. Assoc. pastor ch. N.Y.C., 1963-64; acting Luth. chaplain (Columbia U.), 1963-64; mem. faculty Smith Coll., Northampton, Mass., 1968—, prof. N.T. and early Christianity, 1968—, chmn. dept. religion and mem. N.T. panel Nat. Luth.-Roman Cath. Dialogue, 1971-73, 75-78; chmn. Columbia Seminar for Study of N.T., 1976-77; vis. prof. Assumption Coll., Worcester, Mass., 1975, Amherst Coll., 1976, 78, 85, St. Hyacinth Coll. and Sem., Granby, Mass., 1976, Brown U., 1979, Mt. Holyoke Coll., 1983, U. Hamburg, 1985. Author: (with R.E. Brown, J. Reumann) Peter in the New Testament, 1973, The Setting of Second Clement in Early Christianity, 1974, (with others) Mary in the New Testament, 1978, The Dynamic Word, 1981; editor: The Romans Debate, 1977, The Romans Debate: New and Expanded Edition, 1991; mem. editorial bd.: Jour. Bibl. Lit., 1975-81. Mem. Am. Acad. Religion (dir. 1972-73, pres. New Eng. region 1971-72), Studiorum Novi Testamenti Societas (chmn. Paul seminar 1975-78, exec. com. 1979-83, chmn. New Testament Texts in their Cultural Environment seminar 1990—), Soc. Bibl. Lit. (pres. New Eng. region 1975-76), Cath. Bibl. Assn. (participant internat. congresses of scholars in following cities, Aberdeen, Basel, Bern, Bielefeld, Cambridge, Canterbury, Eindhoven, Göttingen, Heidelberg, Frankfurt, Louvain, Milan, Newcastle, Oxford, Rome, Sigtuna, Toronto, Tübingen). Office: Smith Coll Dept Religion Northampton MA 01063 *As the son of immigrant parents, I learned early the value of hard and honest work, the necessity for integrity in all human relations and the blessings of generosity to those less fortunate. These values, together with my commitment to Christianity, have shaped, and continue to shape, my life.*

DONGALEN, GEOFFREY OMBIAN, priest; b. Besao, Mountain Province, Philippines; Aug. 30, 1937; s. Anacleto Dalison and Constancia Lingayo (Ombian) D.; m. Christiana Tabeban Aglit, June 2, 1965; children: Geoffrey Dalison, Jason Nineu. BA, U. Philippines, 1964, MPA, 1972; BTh cum laude, St. Andrew's Theol. Sem., 1964, MDiv, 1989. Ordained to ministry Anglican Ch., as deacon, 1964, as priest, 1965. Chaplain coll. students Philippines Episc. Ch., Manila, 1964-67; priest St. Gabriel's Mission, Mountain Province, 1968-70; chaplain Trinity Coll., Quezon City, 1970-73; worker-Priest Fund Assistance Pvt. Edn., Philippines, 1973-76; chaplain Tng. Ctr., Sunbury, Melbourne, 1977-83, Mental Health Div., Victoria, Australia, 1983—; sec. Australian Health and Welfare Chaplains Assn., 1979-80; Australian del. Asian Conf. Pastoral Care and Counselling, Manila, 1982, Tokyo, 1984. Author: Mental Health Chaplaincy in the 1980's, 1982; A Sojourn, 1982; Methodology and Philosophy, C.P.E. Supervision, 1983; Journey into Freedom, 1983. Mem. Filipino-Australian Soc., Victorian Assn. Mental Health, Assn. Supervised Pastoral Edn. Australia (exec. sec. 1981—). Lodge: Rotary. Home and Office: Psychiatric Hosp Royal Park, 3052 Parkville Victoria, Australia

DONIGER, WENDY, history of religions educator; b. N.Y.C., Nov. 20, 1940; d. Lester L. and Rita (Roth) Doniger; m. Dennis M. O'Flaherty, Mar. 31, 1964; 1 child, Michael Lester. BA summa cum laude, Radcliffe Coll., 1962; PhD, Harvard U., 1968. Lectr. Sch. Oriental and African Studies U. London, 1968-75; vis. lectr. U. Calif., Berkeley, 1975-77; prof. history of religions Div. Sch., dept. South Asian langs., com. on social thought U. Chgo., 1978-85, Mircea Eliade prof., 1986—. Author: (under name of Wendy Doniger O'Flaherty) Asceticism and Eroticism in the Mythology of Siva, 1973, Hindu Myths, 1975, The Origins of Evil in Hindu Mythology, 1976, Women, Androgynes and Other Mythical Beasts, 1980, The Rig Veda: An Anthology, 1981, Karma and Rebirth in Classical Indian Traditions, 1980, Dreams, Illusion and Other Realities, 1984, Other Peoples' Myths, 1988, (under name of Wendy Doniger), Mythologies, 1991, The Laws of Manu, 1991, Mythologies, 1991; editor Jour. Am. Acad. Religion, 1977-80, History of Religions, 1979—; mem. bd. editors Ency. Britannica, 1987—, Daedalus, 1990—. Recipient Lucy Allen Paton prize, 1961, Phi Beta Kappa prize, 1962; Jonathan Fay Fund scholar, 1962, Am. Inst. Indian Studies fellow, 1963-64, NEH summer stipend, 1980, Guggenheim fellow, 1980-81. Fellow Soc. for the Arts, Religion and Culture, Am. Acad. Arts and Scis.; mem. Am. Acad. Religion (pres. 1984), Am. Soc. for Study Religion, Am. Oriental Soc., Assn. Asian Studies, Phi Beta Kappa. Home: 1319 E 55th St Chicago IL 60615 Office: U Chgo Div Sch 1025 E 58th St Chicago IL 60637

DONKERSLOOT, WILLIAM MARTIN, minister; b. Passaic, N.J., Dec. 28, 1947; s. Martin Jr. and June M. (Walsh) D.; m. Marcia Kay Bleeker, June 12, 1971; children: Scott, Michelle, Jason. AA, Iowa Lakes Community Coll., Esterville, Iowa, 1970; BA, Northwestern Coll., Orange City, Iowa, 1972; MDiv, New Brunswick Theol. Sem., 1988. Ordained to ministry Ref. Ch. in Am., 1988. Dir. edn. 1st Ref. Ch., Tampa, Fla., 1972-75; assoc. pastor Morningside Ref. Ch., Sioux City, Iowa, 1975-81, Ch. on Hill, Norco, Calif., 1981-84, Pompton Ref. Ch., Pompton Lakes, N.J., 1985—. Fireman, chaplain Pompton Lakes Vol. Fire Dept., 1989—. Mem. Christian Educators Ref. Ch. in Am., Assn. Presbyn. Ch. Educators. Office: Pompton Ref Ch 59 Hamburg Tpke Pompton Lakes NJ 07442

DONLEY, BRIAN C., academic administrator. Head John Wesley Coll., High Point, N.C. Office: John Wesley Coll 2314 N Centennial St High Point NC 27265*

DONNELL, JAMES KNOX, minister; b. Waterloo, Iowa, Dec. 27, 1931; s. Allan Douglas and Anita Louise (Rath) D.; m. Barbara Doan Pendleton, June 18, 1955; children: Bridget Stevens, Jane Knox, Calvin Rath. BA, Princeton U., 1953; BD, Yale U., 1958. Ordained to ministry Presbyn. Ch. (U.S.A.), 1958. Pastor 1st Presbyn. Ch., West Carrollton, Ohio, 1958-72, College Hill Presbyn. Ch., Beaver Falls, Pa., 1972-85; assoc. exec. presbyter for ministry and candidates Pitts. Presbytery, 1985—; pres. West Carrollton Coun. Religious Edn., 1958-66; dir. summer youth camps, 1963-68; commr. to Synod, Ohio, 1961, 66, Trinity, 1973, 80; commr. to Gen. Assembly, 1965, 78; del. Ohio Coun. Chs., 1960-64, 70-72; chmn. Presbytery's Com. on Ministerial Rels., Miami Presbytery, 1969-72, Beaver-Butler Presbytery, 1972-79, 80-85; mem. Beaver Falls Ministerium, 1972-85. Bd. dirs. Big Bros. Assn. Greater Dayton, 1965-72, FISH, 1972-75; pres. West Carrollton Bd. Edn., 1966-72; chmn. steering com. Meals on Wheels, Beaver Falls, 1972-85; mem. adv. group profl. pers. Home Health Agy., Med. Ctr. Beaver County, 1973-81. Mem. College Hill Ministerial Assn. Home: 9468 N Florence Rd Pittsburgh PA 15237 Office: 801 Union Ave Pittsburgh PA 15212

DONNELLY, ANDREA (MARY KATHRYM), nun, educator, counselor; b. Muskegon, Mich., July 7, 1937; d. Andrew John and Valeria Janet (Gregory) D. BA, Marquette U., 1960; MEd, Duquesne U., 1972. Joined Pallottine Missionary Sisters, Roman Catholic Ch. Tchr. St. Mary's Sch., Laurel, Md., 1964-66, Holy Family Sch., Richwood, W.Va., 1966-68, St. Mary's Sch., Spring Lake, Mich., 1968-71; guidance dir., counselor Pallotti High Sch., Laurel, 1971-75, Cath. Cen., Muskegon, 1975-76; pastoral care asst. St. Mary's Hosp., Huntington, W.Va., 1977-84; tchr. St. Joseph Cen. High Sch., Huntington, 1984—. Mem. Am. Assn. Counseling and Devel., Assn. Religious Value in Issues s in Counseling, W.Va. Counseling Assn. Roman Catholic. Avocations: stamp collecting, reading, water skiing. Home: 2900 1st Ave Huntington WV 25701

DONNELLY, JOHN, philosophy educator; b. Worcester, Mass., Mar. 30, 1941; s. Donald Smith and Viola Frances (Norton) D.; m. Joyce Marie Mattress, June 10, 1967; children: Colin, Maria. BS, Holy Cross Coll., 1963; MA, Boston Coll., 1965; AM, Brown U., 1967, PhD, 1969. Prof. U. San Diego, 1976—. Editor: Suicide: Right or Wrong, 1990, Reflective Wisdom, 1989, Language, Metaphysics and Death, 1978, Logical Analysis and Contemporary Theism, 1972, Conscience, 1973; editorial bd. Internat. Philos. Quar., N.Y.C., 1972-76. Recipient award NEH, 1980. Mem. Am. Philos. Assn., Soc. Christian Philosophers, Am. Acad. Religion, Soren Kierkegaard Soc. (v.p. 1988, pres. 1989). Democrat. Roman Catholic. Home: 1773 Glidden Ct San Diego CA 92111 Office: U San Diego Alcala Park San Diego CA 92110 *Despite the opposing current tide, I continue to believe that the amelioration of the human condition requires the personal appropriation of the "seamless garment" ethic.*

DONNELLY, JOHN PATRICK, priest; b. Milw., Sept. 23, 1934; s. John Patrick and Margaret Mary Donnelly. BA, St. Louis U., 1958, MA, 1963,

S.T.L., 1967; PhD, U. Wis., 1972. Joined S.J., ordained priest Roman Cath. Ch., 1965. From asst. prof. to prof. history Marquette U., Milw., 1971—. Author: Calvinism and Scholasticism in Vermigli's Doctrine of Man and Grace, 1976, Reform and Reneval, 1977; co-editor, co-translator: Robert Bellarmine: Spiritual Writings, 1989. Mem. Soc. for Reformation Rsch. (pres. 1990-91), 16th Century Studies Conf. (pres. 1977), Am. Hist. Assn., Renaissance Soc. Am., Am. Cath. Hist. Assn. Home and Office: Marquette U 1404 W Wisconsin Ave Milwaukee WI 53233

DONNELLY, SISTER KATHLEEN, nun, educational administrator; b. West Palm Beach, Fla., Oct. 7, 1921; d. Charles Henry and Kathleen Marie (O'Hare) D. B.A., Barry Coll., 1949, M.A., 1957; postgrad. U. Fla.; Mich. State U., Fla. Atlantic U., Cath. U. Am. Joined Adrian Dominican Sisters, 1937. Tchr. St. Matthew Sch., Chgo., 1939-43, St. Dominic Sch., Detroit, 1943-44, St. Patrick Sch., Miami Beach, Fla., 1944-52; prin. Sacred Heart Sch., Pensacola, Fla., 1952-58; asst. prin., tchr. St. Matthew Sch., Jacksonville, Fla., 1958-61, Little Flower Sch., Hollywood, Fla., 1961-66, Holy Family Sch., St. Petersburg, Fla., 1966-67; prin. Our Lady Queen of Martyrs Sch., Fort Lauderdale, Fla., 1967-74, St. Hugh Sch., Coconut Grove, Fla., 1974—; superior Sacred Heart Convent, Pensacola, 1952-58. Leader Girl Scouts U.S.A., Detroit, 1943. Mem. Nat. Catholic Edn. Assn., Nat. Assn. Elem. Sch. Prins., Internat. Platform Assn., Fla. Assn. for Supervision and Curriculum Devel., Fla. Cath. Conf. (chmn.), Kappa Delta Pi. Office: St Hugh Sch 3460 Royal Rd Coconut Grove FL 33134

DONNELLY, MARY LOUISE, religion education director; b. San Antonio, Tex., Nov. 26, 1926; d. Leo H. and Martha Almyra (Tollett) D. BS, St. Mary Coll., Leavenworth, Tex., 1961, MS, 1966; postgrad., New Sch. of Religion, Pontiac, Mich., 1970-74, Cath. U., 1976. Dir. religious edn. Blessed Sacrament Ch., Midland, Mich., 1971-74, Nativity Ch., Burke, Va., 1974-84, St. Luke's Ch., McLean, Va., 1984-87, St. John's Ch., Ennis, Tex., 1987—. Author: (genealogy books) Maryland Elder and Kin, 1976 (Parker award Md. Hist. Soc. 1977), Arnold Livers Family in American, 1977 (Parker award 1978), William Boarman Descendants, 1990, Hayden/Rapier & Allied Families, 1991. Mem. Nat. Cath. Edn. Assn. (dir. religious edn. of the month, 1990-91). Home: PO Box 97 Ennis TX 75120 Office: St Johns Ch 401 E Lampasas Ennis TX 75119 *Life's journey in the sunshine of God's loving presence brings meaning and happiness to my life as I share God's love and my story with others. My journey helped me discover my ancestral roots in Colonial Maryland and Catholic Church history, and the marvelous avocation of genealogy.*

DONNELLY, ROBERT WILLIAM, bishop. Attended, St. Meinard (Ind.) Sem. Coll., Mt. St. Mary's West Sem., Norwood, Ohio. Ordained priest Roman Cath. Ch., 1957. Ordained titular; bishop Garba; aux. bishop Toledo, 1984—. Home: 2544 Parkwood Ave Toledo OH 43610

DONOGHUE, JOHN F., bishop; b. Washington, Aug. 9, 1928. Student, St. Mary's Sem., Cath. U. Ordained priest Cath. Ch., 1955. Chancellor and vicar gen. Washington Archdiocese, 1973-84; bishop Charlotte, N.C., 1984—. Home: 1521 Dilworth Rd Charlotte NC 28203 Office: Diocese of Charlotte PO Box 36776 Charlotte NC 28236

DONOHUE, EDWARD LEON, deacon; b. Glassboro, N.J., Dec. 19, 1929; s. John Frank Sr. and Estella (White) D.; m. Nancy Lee Middleton, May 24, 1952; children: Robin Ann, Rosemary, Edward Leon Jr., Patrice, Christopher, Janet Lee,Kathleen (dec.). AA, St. Charles' Coll., Catonsville, Md., 1945; BA, St. Mary's Sem., Balt., 1946; MA, Villanova U., 1950. Ordained deacon Roman Cath. Ch., 1976; cert. elem. tchr., N.J. Asst. pastor St. Aloysius' Ch., Oaklyn, N.J., 1976-80, Transfiguration Ch., West Collingswood, N.J., 1980—; Pres. St. Aloysius' Parish Coun., 1968-70. Councilman Oaklyn Borough Coun., 1956-58; chmn. Oaklyn Planning Bd., 1961-68; undersheriff County of Camden, 1964-68; gerontol. cons. Diocese of Camden, N.J., 1968—; exec. dir. Camden County Office on Aging, 1968—; asst. chaplain Our Lady of Lourdes Med. Ctr., Camden, 1977-80. Recipient Disting. Svc. award Gov. N.J., 1987, Others award Salvation Army, 1989. Mem. N.J. Assn. Area Agys. on Agine (Disting. Svc. award 1986), Gerontol. Soc. Am., KC (grand knight 1954-56, chmn. Gloucester County chpt. 1956-58). Home: 21 E Haddon Ave Oaklyn NJ 08107 Office: Camden County Office Aging 120 White Horse Pike Haddon Heights NJ 08059

DONOVAN, DENNIS DALE, priest; b. Nyack, N.Y., Feb. 26, 1954; s. Thomas A. and Helen I. (Rudolph) D. BA in Philosophy, Don Bosco Coll., 1977; MA in Theology, Pontifical Coll. Josephinum, 1983, MDiv in Theology, 1983. Joined Soc. St. Francis de Sales, Roman Cath. ch., 1973, ordained priest, 1983; cert. tchr. N.Y., N.J. Asst. adminstr. Salesian Sch., Goshen, N.Y., 1983-85; adminstr. Salesian Ctr., Columbus, Ohio, 1985—; assoc., youth min. St. Andrew Parish, Upper Arlington, Ohio, 1985—. Chaplain Ohio Senate, Columbus, 1987—; mem. Juvenile Delinquency Task Force, Franklin County, 1988-90. Recipient Senate Resolution award Ohio Senate, 1988. Mem. Am. Guild Organists (bd. dirs., chaplain, 1986—), KC (chaplain 1987—). Address: Salesian Ctr 80 S Sixth St Columbus OH 43215

DONOVAN, EGBERT HERBERT, clergyman, consultant; b. Buffalo, Jan. 15, 1913; s. James D. and Laura-Mary (Thompson) D. A.B., St. Vincent Coll., Latrobe, Pa., 1936; M.A., 1940; M.Ed., Cath. U. Am., 1945; Ed.D. (hon.), St. Francis Coll., 1968; LL.D. (hon.), Seton Hill Coll., 1969. Headmaster St. Vincent Prep. Sch., Latrobe, Pa., 1945-54; dean of men St. Vincent Coll., 1957-62; chaplain Pa. State U., 1962-67; archabbot, chancellor St. Vincent Archabbey and Coll., Latrobe, 1967-79; now cons. Bd. dirs. St. Vincent Coll., 1947-62, 67-79. Mem. Nat. Newman Chaplains Assn., Am. Benedictine Acad. Club: K.C. Address: St Vincent Archabbey Latrobe PA 15650

DONOVAN, HERBERT ALCORN, JR., bishop; b. Washington, July 14, 1931; s. Herbert Alcorn and Marion Mitchell (Kirk) D.; m. Mary Gertrude Sudman, July 7, 1959; children—Mary Ellen, Herbert Alcorn III, Jane. B.A., U. Va., 1954; M.Div., Va. Theol. Sem., 1957, D.D. (hon.), 1981; D.D. (hon.), U. South, 1985. Ordained to ministry Episcopal Ch., 1957. Rector St. John's Ch., Green River, Wyo., 1957-59; vicar, rector St. Andrew's Ch., Basin-Greybull, Wyo., 1959-64; exec. officer Diocese of Ky., Louisville, 1964-70; rector St. Luke's Ch., Montclair, N.J., 1970-80; bishop Diocese of Ark., Little Rock, 1980—; sec. House of Bishops, 1986—; chmn. adv. council Ark. Conf. Chs. and Synagogues, Little Rock, 1983-84; chmn. bd. Heifer Project Internat., Little Rock, 1985-87; vis. fellow Harvard Divinity Sch., 1987. Author: (with others) (study guide) God Willing: Decision in the Church, 1973; Forward Day-by-Day, 1983. Trustee U. South, Sewanee, Tenn., 1980—; bd. dirs. All Saints Sch., Vicksburg, Miss., 1980—. Named hon. canon Christ Ch. Cathedral, Louisville, 1966. Fellow Coll. of Preachers. Democrat. Office: Diocese of Ark 300 W 17th St PO Box 164668 Little Rock AR 72216

DONOVAN, JAMES C., academic administrator. Head Atlanta Christian Coll., East Point, Ga. Office: Atlanta Christian Coll 2605 Ben Hill Rd East Point GA 30344*

DONOVAN, JOHN CARL, priest; b. Muncie, Ind., July 20, 1930; s. Carl Edwin and Eleanor Law (Pickerill) D.; m. Joal Harris, Feb. 5, 1962; children: Mark, Harris, Thomas. BA, Univ. Tex, 1952, LLB, 1954; BD, Epis. Sem. of S.W., 1957. Ordained to ministry Episcopal Ch., as priest, 1958. Vicar and chaplain Christ Ch. & Baylor Univ., Mexia & Waco, Tex., 1957-63; assoc. rector Trinity Epis. Ch., Galveston, Tex., 1963-65, rector, 1976—; rector St. Stephens's Epis. Ch., Beaumont, Tex., 1965-71, St. Paul's Epis. Ch., San Miguel de Allende, Mex., 1971-76; Chmn. Diocese of Tex. examining chaplains 1982—, com. on Constitution and Canons 1978—; fellow Coll. of Preachers, Washington Cathedral; dep., gen. conv. Epis. Ch. 1979, 82, 85. Former pres. bd. St. Vincent's House, Seaman's Ctr. Galveston; exec. com. United Way Galveston 1983. Mem. Rotary, Phi Beta Kappa. Democrat. Episcopalian. Avocations: walking, bicycling, reading. Home: 15 Cedar Lawn N Galveston TX 77551 Office: Trinity Episc Church 2216 Ball St Galveston TX 77550 *The coming of God's Kingdom depends not on us, but on Him. We are promised that it will come. Our task is to learn to watch, to work, and to hope in the light of that promise.*

DONOVAN, PAUL V., bishop; b. Bernard, Iowa, Sept. 1, 1924; s. John J. and Loretta (Carew) D. Student, St. Joseph Sem., Grand Rapids, Mich.; BA, St. Gregory Sem., Cin., 1946; postgrad., Mt. St. Mary Sem. of West, Cin.; JCL, Pontifical Lateran U., Rome, 1957. Ordained priest Roman Catholic Ch., 1950; asst. pastor St. Mary Ch., Jackson, Mich., 1950-51; sec. to bishop of Lansing Mich.; adminstr. St. Peter Ch., Eaton Rapids, Mich., 1951-55; sec. to bishop, 1957-59; pastor Our Lady of Fatima Ch., Michigan Center, Mich.; and St. Rita Mission, Clark Lake, Mich., 1959-68; pastor St. Agnes Ch., Flint, Mich., 1968-71; bishop of Kalamazoo, 1971—; mem. liturgical commn. Diocese of Lansing, chmn., 1963; mem. Cath. Bd. Edn., Jackson and Hillsdale counties; mem. bishop's personnel com., priests' senate. Bd. dirs. Family Services and, Mich. Children's Aid. Office: 2131 Aberdeen Kalamazoo MI 49008 Address: 215 N Westnedge Ave PO Box 949 Kalamazoo MI 49005

DOODY, LORETTA IRENE, clergywoman; b. Caribou, Maine, Oct. 24, 1937; d. Morris Henry and Annie Mae (Drost) St. Peter; m. Richard Louis Doody, Apr. 30, 1955; children: Michael, Charmaine, Marty, Scott. Student, U. South Fla., Tampa, 1980-81; BA, U. Maine, Presque Isle, 1983, BS, 1983. Ordained to ministry Pentecostal Ch. Sunday sch. tchr. Ch. of God, Caribou, 1978-84, Christian edn. dir., 1981-82; Bible sch. dir., tchr. Ch. of God, 1982; pastor Abundant Life Mission, Caribou, 1985—; social worker State of Maine, Caribou, 1989—; founder Abundant Life Mission, Caribou, 1985, pres., 1987—. Home: Rt 1 Box 230 Caribou ME 04736

DOOLEY, DAVID GRANT, minister; b. Louisville, Nov. 17, 1943; s. Raymon Richard Emmett and Mary Catheringe (Compton) D.; m. Esther Marie Hoot; children: Trisha, David Richard-Wilson. AB, Olivet Nazarene U., 1967, MA, 1969; Ad. cert., U. Va., 1971. Ordained to ministry Nazarene Ch. Tchr. Peotone (Ill.) Elem. Sch., 1967-69; tchr. Shenandoah Sch. System, Woodstock, Va., 1969-71, prin., 1971-75; pastor Woodstock Ch. of Nazarene, 1960-75, Williamsburg (Va.) Ch. of Nazarene, 1975-76, Edison (N.J.) Ch. of Nazarene, 1976-80, Paulding (Ohio) Ch. of Nazarene, 1980—; mem. credentials bd. N.Y. Dist. Ch. of Nazarene, 1976-80, mem. dist. adv. bd., 1977-80; mem. credentials bd. N.W. Ohio Dist. Ch. of Nazarene, St. Marys, Ohio, 1982—. Contbr. articles to local news publs. Vice chairperson Bd. Mental Retardation, Paulding County, Ohio, 1983—; chaplain Paulding County Hosp. Bd., 1984—; treas. Paulding County Ministerial Assn., 1987—; mem. Paulding County Vis. Nurses, 1989—. Named Pastor of Yr., Va. Dist. Ch. of Nazarene, 1971; named Pastor of Yr. N.W. Ohio Dist. Ch. of Nazarene, 1987. Home and Office: Ch of Nazarene Rte 3 Box 1859 Paulding OH 45879

DOOLEY, SISTER MARY AGNES, college president; b. Sommerville, Mass., Mar. 5, 1923; d. Richard and Mary A. (O'Neill) D. BA, Elms Coll., 1944; MA, Assumption Coll., 1960, LHD (hon.), 1982; Doctorat d'Université, U. Paris, 1968; LLD (hon.) Am. Internat. Coll., 1981; DMinistry, St. Louis U. Aquinas Inst., 1983; LittD (hon.), Fitchburg State Coll., 1985. Joined Congregation of the Sisters of St. Joseph, Roman Cath. Ch., 1944; tchr. St. Joseph's High Sch., North Adams, Mass., 1946-65; chmn. lang. dept. Elms Coll., Chicopee, Mass., 1968-70, pres., 1979—; pres. Leadership Conf. Women Religious U.S., Washington, 1978-79; pres. Congregation Sisters of St. Joseph, Springfield, Mass., 1971-79. Contbr. articles to profl. jours. Recipient Disting. Alumna award Elms Coll., 1979, Human Rels. award NCCJ, 1988; decorated chevalier dans l'Ordre des Palmes Academiques (France), 1981; named Woman of Yr., Chicopee Bus. and Profl. Women's Club, Woman of Yr., Greater Springfield C. of C., 1987, Woman of Yr. Quota Club of Holyoke, 1991. Mem. Assn. Cath. Colls. and Univs. (bd. dir. 1980-85), Leadership Conf. Women Religious, Delta Epsilon Sigma.

DOOLIN, JOSEPH, social services administrator; b. Boston, June 16, 1937; s. Joseph Patrick and Zita M. (Pelose) D.; m. Mary E. Daigle, Sept. 1, 1962; children: Joel A., Seth A., Matthew J. AB, Boston U., 1960; MPA, U. Mass., 1980, PhD, 1988. Lic. social worker, Mass. Promotion dir. United Ch., Boston, 1963-69; dir. program devel. Federated Dorchester Neighborhood Houses, Inc., Boston, 1970-78; exec. dir. Kit Clark Sr. House, Dorchester, Mass., 1979-89; dir. Office on Aging Archdiocese of Boston, 1989, dir. Cath. Charities, 1989—; prof. Boston U., 1973-89, U. Mass., Boston, 1984-88. Contbr. articles to profl. jours. Pres. Boston Elder Emergency Fund, 1978—. With USN, 1960-62. Roman Catholic. Office: Archdiocese of Boston Cath Charities 49 Franklin St Boston MA 02110

DOOLIN, SYLVA ALPHA, minister; b. Selvin, Ind., Nov. 3, 1913; d. James Oliver and Emma Cordillia (Thiry) Bolin; m. Marvin Lawson Doolin, July 15, 1939 (dec. 1972); children: Marvin, Roy Edward, Daniel Lee. G-rad., Glad Tidings Bible Inst., 1937; cert., Bethany Bible Coll., 1937; master diploma worker's tng., Assemblies of God, Springfield, Ill., 1958; diploma, Christian Writers Inst., 1963. Ordained to ministry, 1947. Pastor Assemblies of God Chs., Carrollton, Ill., 1939-40, Jerseyville, Ill., 1940-45, Renault, Ill., 1945-53, Olney, Ill., 1953-63, Browning, Ill., 1963-70; Bible tchr., music tchr., evangelist, christian writer Browning, 1970—; mem. adv. coun. for ch. sch. lit. Assemblies of God, 1958. Contbr. short stories and articles to numerous religious mags. and jours. Treas. Salvation Army; Olney WCTU worker; mem. Schuyler County Sr. Citizns Coun.; active Ret. Sr. Vols. Program. Recipient Manuscript award Harvest Publs., 1966, Fifty Yrs. Continuous and Dedicated Svc. award Gen. Coun. Assemblies of God, Springfield, 1987. Home and Office: Rte 1 Browning IL 62624 *Becoming a Christian is like an election. God sent His Son to redeem you. Satan is determined to destroy you. You cast the deciding vote.*

DOPKINS, SISTER ARITA LEYELE, religion educator; b. Beldenville, Wis., Sept. 21, 1920; d. Mearl Lynn and Ellen Marie (Hurley) D. BS in Edn., Viterbo Coll., 1953; MA, St. Mary's Coll., Notre Dame, Ind., 1967. Joined Franciscan Sisters of Perpetual Adoration, Roman Cath. Ch. Tchr. Cath. schs. Iowa, Wis., 1939-68; prin. Cath. elem. schs. Wis., 1961-69; mem. faculty Viterbo Coll., La Crosse, Wis., 1968-90, chair dept. religious studies, 1972-90; mem. faculty La Ministry Program, La Crosse, 1975-92; mem. faculty, consultation com. Clin. Pastoral Edn. program St. Francis Med. Ctr., La Crosse, 1983—. Contbr. articles to profl. jours. Mem. Franciscan Sisters of Perpetual Adoration. Recipient J. Thomas Finucan award, 1983, Tchr. of the Yr. award, 1985. Mem. Coll. Theology Soc. Home: 805 Mississippi St Apt E La Crosse WI 54601 Office: Viterbo Coll 815 S 9th St La Crosse WI 54601

DORAN, DONALD LEO, minister; b. National City, Calif., Jan. 22, 1957; s. David Leo and Lula Faye (Causey) D.; m. Melinda Gean Power, Mar. 4, 1978; children: Justin Wayne, Abigail Joy, Jared Craig. Ordained to ministry United Pentecostal Ch., 1976. Youth pastor United Pentecostal Ch., Rio Dell, Calif., 1973-78; asst. pastor United Pentecostal Ch., Roseburg, Oreg., 1978-79; pastor United Pentecostal Ch., Ukiah, Calif., 1984-85; prin. Northwoods Christian Sch., Eureka, Calif., 1989-90; assoc. pastor Triumphant Life Tabernacle, Rio Dell, 1989-90, pastor, 1990—; apt. mgr. Hank Fisher Properties, Rio Dell, 1989—; sunday sch. regional dir. United Pentecostal Ch., Rio Dell, 1990—; youth dir. regional, Roseburg, 1978-79. Republican. Home: 753 Rigby Ave Rio Dell CA 95562 Office: Triumphant Life Tabernacle PO Box 374 Rio Dell CA 95562

DORMAN, JAMES LOWELL, minister; b. McKees Rocks, Pa., June 29, 1951; s. Lowell Dean and Nedra Aileen (Crawford) D.; m. Phyllis Marie Herman, Mar. 16, 1973; children: Jeffrey William, Bradley James, Carrie Lynn. AB in Bible Study, Ministries, Manhattan Christian Coll., 1983. Ordained to ministry Christian Ch., 1983. Recruiter Manhattan (Kans.) Christian Coll., 1980-83; min. of evangelism Christ's Ch. of Valley, Phoenix, 1983-84; founding min., sr. pastor Christ's Ch. of Flagstaff (Ariz.), 1984—; chaplain Flagstaff Fire Dept., 1990-91; pres. elect. Ariz. Christian Conv., Phoenix, 1991; pres. Evang. Mins. Fellowship, Flagstaff, 1985. Pres. Flagstaff 25, 1986; del. Flagstaff Town Hall, 1985, 1991. Mem. Rotary (Flagstaff chpt., dir. 1988-89, v.p. 1991). Republican. Office: Christ's Ch Flagstaff 306 W Cedar Ave Flagstaff AZ 86001

DORN, LOUIS OTTO, minister, editor; b. Detroit, July 1, 1928; s. Theodore Herman and Thekla Maria (Frederking) D.; m. Erna Ruth Koessel, June 14, 1953; children: Margaret Ligaya Dorn White, Peter Bayani, Martin Louis, Judith Anne Dorn Depuydt. BA, Concordia Theol. Sem., St. Louis, 1951, BD, 1962; MA in Linguistics, Ateneo de Manila U., Quezon City, The Philippines, 1974; ThD, Luth. Sch. Theology, Chgo., 1980. Ordained to ministry Luth. Ch.-Mo. Synod, 1953. Missionary Luth. Ch. in The Philippines, Manila, 1953-74; candidate Ohio dist. Luth. Ch. -Mo. Synod, 1975-80; candidate N.J. dist. Luth. Ch.-Mo. Synod, 1980—; transls. rsch. assoc. Am. Bible Soc., N.Y.C., 1979-90; transl. cons. United Bible Socs., N.Y.C., 1990—; chmn. Luth. Philippine Mission, Manila, 1962-63, 71-72; sec. Luth. Ch. in The Philippines, Manila, 1962-63, commn. for ecumenical affairs. 1964-74, dir. transls. dept., 1966-74; hon. transls. advisor Philippine Bible Soc., Manila, 1968-74; bd. dirs. Interchurch Lang. Sch., Quezon City, 1964-74, chmn. bd., 1967-74. Contbr. articles and revs. to religious publs. Grantee Cen. dist. Luth. Ch.-Mo. Synod, 1944-53; scholarship grantee Luth. Sch. Theology, Chgo., 1974-78. Mem. Soc. Bibl. Lit. Democrat. Office: Am Bible Soc 1865 Broadway New York NY 10023 *People often don't know how to live under God's grace because they can't forgive themselves and know only God's law. To accept God's grace, to be willing to be forgiven, results in an amazing life of freedom that honors the Savior.*

DORNBUSH, VONN KEVIN, religion educator; b. Fargo, N.D., May 6, 1959; s. Merlin and Alfrieda Dornbush; m. Martha Elizabeth Anderson, Sept. 10, 1983; children: Luke Gerrit, Andrew Michael. BA in Social Studies Secondary Edn., U. Minn., 1981; MDiv in Christian Edn., Trinity Evang. Divinity Sch., 1985; postgrad., Tenn. Temple U., 1988—. Lic. secondary edn. social studies tchr., Minn.; lic. min. Evang. Free Ch. Intern Hope Evang. Free Ch., Oakdale, Minn., 1983-84; pastor Christian edn. Beacon Community Evang. Free Ch., New Port Richey, Fla., 1985-91, Trinity Evang. Free Ch., Lakeville, Minn., 1991—; mem. Student Ministry Coun., Evang. Free Ch., Mpls., 1989-90, S.E. dist. bd. dirs., Orlando, Fla., 1987-90, chmn. Challenge 90 conf., Orlando, 1989-90; mem. Nat. Right to Life Com., Washington, 1987—. Mem. Nat. Assn. Dir. Christian Edn., Edn. Honor Soc. Republican.

DORNETTE, RALPH MEREDITH, church organization executive, educator, minister; b. Cin., Aug. 31, 1927; s. Paul A. and Lillian (Bauer) D.; m. Betty Jean Pierce, May 11, 1948; 1 child, Cynthia Anne Dornette Orndorff. AB, Cin. Bible Coll., 1948. Ordained to ministry Christian Ch., 1947. Min. Indian Creek Christian Ch., Cynthiana, Ky., 1946-51; assoc. prof. Cin. Bible Coll., 1948-51; sr. min. First Christian Ch., Muskogee, Okla., 1951-57; founding min. Bellaire Christian Ch., Tulsa, 1957-59; exec. dir. So. Calif. Evangelistic Assn., Torrance, Calif., 1959-62, 68-77; sr. min. Eastside Christian Ch., Fullerton, Calif., 1962-68; dir. devel., prof. ministries Cin. Bible Coll. & Sem., 1977-79; chief exec. officer Ch. Devel. Fund, Inc., Fullerton, 1968-79; sr. preaching minister 1st Christian Ch., Downey, Calif., 1971, 91; pres. So. Calif. Christian Mins. Assn., Fullerton, 1975. Author: Bible Answers to Popular Questions, 1954, Walking With Our Wonderful Lord, 1955, Bible Answers to Popular Questions II, 1964. Pres. Homeowners Assn., Anaheim, Calif., 1980-81. Named Churchman of Yr. Pacific Christian Coll., Fullerton, 1973. Mem. N.Am. Christian Conv. (conv. com. Cin. chpt. 1963, chair nat. registration com. 1963-68, v.p. 1972, exec. com. 1963, 70-72, 80-82). Office: Ch Devel Fund Inc 905 S Euclid St Fullerton CA 92632

DORNHEIM, JOHN FREDRICK CHRISTIAN, XIX, minister; b. Rockville Centre, N.Y., Nov. 5, 1951; s. John Fredrick Christian XVIII and Maritza George (Baltas) D.; m. Meredith Anne Mayer, Sept. 6, 1987. BA, Concordia Sr. Coll., 1973; MDiv., Concordia Sem. in Exile, 1977. Ordained minister Evangelical Luth. Ch., 1990. Pastor St. James Luth. Ch., Huntingdon, Pa., 1990—; bd. dirs. Sch. for Social Work-Refugee Assistance Program Adelphi Univ., Long Island, N.Y., Allegheny Luth. Homes, Holidaysburg, Pa. Co-chmn. McGovern Presdl. Campaign, Fort Wayne, Ind., 1972; election inspector Bd. Elections, Suffolk County, N.Y., 1984-90. Democrat. Home: 271 Standing Stone Ave Huntingdon PA 16652 Office: St James Luth Ch 525 Mifflin St Huntingdon PA 16652

DORNISCH, LORETTA, religious studies educator. BA, Edgewood Coll., Madison, Wis., 1962; ME, Marquette U., Milw., 1969, PhD, 1973. Prof. Edgewood Coll., Madison, Wis., 1969—. Author: Faith and Philosophy in the Writings of Paul Ricoeur, 1990; contbr. articles to profl. jours. Mem. Am. Acad. Religion (chairperson study group on the interpretation theory of Paul Ricoeur 1976-82), Soc. Bibl. Lit., Chgo. Soc. Bibl. Researchers, Madison Bibl. Archeol. Soc. Office: Edgewood Coll 855 Woodrow St Madison WI 53711

DORNISH, MARGARET HAMMOND, religion educator; b. St. Marys, Pa., July 25, 1934; d. Karl and Helen (Hammond) D. AB, Smith Coll., 1956; MA, Claremont Grad. Sch., 1967, PhD, 1969. Assoc. prof. Asian religions, religion in Am. Pomona Coll., Claremont, Calif., 1969—. Editor Jour. of the Blaisdell Inst.; contbr. articles on D.T. Suzuki as interpretor of Buddhism to profl. jours. Mem. Am. Acad. Religion. Office: Pomona Coll Dept Religion Claremont CA 91711

DOROSHUK, JOHN, bishop. Pres., nat. overseer Ch. of God of Prophecy in Can., Strathmore, Alta. Office: Ch God Prophecy Can, PO Box 952, Strathmore, AB Canada T0J 3H0*

DORRIEN, GARY JOHN, religion educator, chapel dean; b. Midland, Mich., Mar. 21, 1952; s. John Ellis and Virginia Catherine (Hank) D.; m. Brenda Louise Biggs, Aug. 4, 1979; 1 child, Sara Biggs Dorrien. BA, Alma Coll., 1974; MDiv, Union Theol. Sem., 1978; MA, ThM, Princeton Theol. Sem., 1979; PhD, Union Grad.. Sch., 1989. Ordained priest Episcopal Ch., 1982. Chaplain Doane Stuart Sch., Albany, N.Y., 1982-87; asst. pastor St. Andrew's Episc. Ch., Albany, 1982-87; asst. prof. religion, dean of chapel Kalamazoo (Mich.) Coll., 1987—. Author: Logic and Consciousness, 1985, The Democratic Socialist Vision, 1986, Reconstructing the Common Good, 1990; contbr. articles to profl. jours. Mem. Episc. Peace Fellowship, Washington, Amnesty Internat., N.Y., Rainbow Organizing Com. of Kalamazoo. Mem. Am. Acad. Religion, Soc. Christian Ethics. Democrat. Office: Kalamazoo Coll 1200 Academy St Kalamazoo MI 49007

DORSCH, LOUIS H., clergyman; b. Cin., Dec. 25, 1947; s. Louis Herbert and Evelyn (Chitwood) D.; m. Donna Semler, June 10, 1972; children: Aaron M., Nathan A. BA, Heidelberg Coll., 1970; MDiv, Eden Theol. Sem., 1973, D in Ministry, 1979. Ordained minister in United Ch. of Christ, 1973. Minister Trinity United Ch. of Christ, McCutchenville, Ohio, 1973-79, Immanuel United Ch. of Christ, Zanesville, Ohio, 1979—; del. gen. synod United Ch. of Christ, 1991; pres. Muskingum County Ministerial Assn., Zanesville, 1986-87. Mem. Ohio Conf. United Ch. of Christ (moderator 1990-91). Home: 2175 Newark Rd Zanesville OH 43701 Office: Immanuel United Ch of Christ 105 S 7th St Zanesville OH 43701 *In a complex world such as ours, we need to be reminded of those simple, basic values for living; such as honesty, love, sharing with others, and doing unto others as you would have them do unto you. It is such qualities as these that give our lives meaning and help us live life with integrity.*

DORSEY, NORBERT M., auxiliary bishop; b. Springfield, Mass., Dec. 14, 1929; s. Leonard Edward and Mary Ann (Dowd) D. ThM, St. Michael's Passionist Monastery, 1956; Maestro Sacred Music, Pontifical Inst. Sacred Music, Rome, 1960; DST, Gregorian U., Rome, 1986. Ordained priest, 1956. Dir. formation Eastern U.S. Province, West Hartford, Conn., 1960-65; monastery rector Eastern U.S. Province, West Springfield, Mass., 1965-68; provincial consultor, exec. asst. to provincial Eastern U.S. Province, Union City, N.J., 1968-76; asst. Generas, Passionist Congregation, Rome, 1976-86; aux. bishop Archdiocese of Miami, Fla., 1986-90; titular bishop of Mactaris, 1986—; bishop of Orlando Fla., 1990—. Office: Chancery Office 421 Robinson PO Box 1800 Orlando FL 32802

DOSKOCIL, WILLIAM ROBERT, lay preacher; b. Chgo., Jan. 8, 1950; s. Robert William and Delores Eunice (Mertes) D.; children: Jason Allen, Jenny Lynne. BS in Secondary Edn. and Sociology, U. Wis., Superior, 1971. Salesman Physicians Mut., Wisconsin Physicians, N.Y. Life ins. cos., 1977—; elder, lay preacher Christian Fellowship, Hayward, Wis., 1980—; prin. Health Ins. Specialties, Stone Lake, Wis., 1991—; sec., treas. Christian Fellowship, Hayward, 1984—; dir. Rock and Cornerstone Ministries, Stone Lake, Wis., 1989—; trade sales rep. Gospel Light Publs., Ventura, Calif., 1989-91; self employed ins. agt. Author: (book) Cannons and Sails: Meeting the Challenges to Marriage, 1989. Recipient Nat. Sales Achievement award

Nat. Assn. Life Underwriters, 1984. Republican. Charismatic. Home: Rt 1 Box 30 Stone Lake WI 54876 *There are two steps in accurately determining what is right. First, it must originate in the God of Creation, the Triune God, the Father of Jesus Christ. Second, it must be motivated and brought to life by His Holy Spirit living in us. If its origin and motivation are not these, then, in spite of how noble or fitting or proper it may seem, it has nonetheless, failed the test of true righteousness and will eventually perish.*

DOSS, THOMAS WAYNE, youth and music minister; b. Lynchburg, Va., Oct. 12, 1963; s. Ferrelle Wayne and Lorene Frances (Miles) D.; m. Elizabeth Joyce Goodwin, Jan. 13, 1990. BS, Liberty U., 1986. Ordained to ministry Ind. Bapt. ch., 1989. Assoc. children's pastor Thomas Rd. Bapt. Ch., Lynchburg, 1987-89; min. of music, youth Guess Rd. Bapt. Ch., Durham, N.C., 1989—; mem. pub. rels. staff 1992 World Missions Conf. Yates Bapt. Assn., Durham, 1991. Composer (children's music) Who Is A God Like Thee, 1988, Love Is Not A Word, 1989, Opportunity, 1990, The Heart Is Deceitful, 1990. Republican. Home: 2636 Kirk Rd Durham NC 27705 Office: Guess Rd Bapt Ch 3102 Guess Rd Durham NC 27705

DOS SANTOS, ALEXANDRE JOSE MARIA CARDINAL, cardinal; b. Inhambane, Mozambique, Mar. 18, 1924. Ordained bishop Roman Cath. Ch., 1953. Elected to Ch. in Lourenço Marques (now Maputo), 1974; consecrated bishop, 1975, created cardinal, 1988. Office: Paco Arquiepiscopal CP 258, Avda Eduardo Mandlane 1448, Maputo Mozambique

DOSSEH-ANYRON, MONSIGNOR ROBERT-CASIMIR TONYUI MESSAN, archbishop. Archbishop of Lome Roman Casth. Ch., Togo. Office: Archeveche, BP 348, Lome Togo*

DOSTER, GEORGE ELLIOTT, JR., clergyman; b. Ft. Benning, Ga., Mar. 27, 1962; s. George Eliott and Bonnie Estell (Baker) D.; m. Michelle Renee Brown, May 29, 1987. Student, Denver Inst. Tech., 1980; B Bibl. Lit., Ozark Christian Coll., 1987, BTh, 1987. Ordained to ministry Christian Ch., 1987. Minister Weableau (Mo.) Christian Ch., 1984-85; youth minister intern Littleton (Colo.) Christian Ch., 1986; music dir., disc jockey KOBC-Radio, Joplin, Mo., 1982-87; campus minister Colo. Christian Campus Ministries, Greeley, Colo., 1987—; camp rep. Colo. Christian Svc. Camp, Colorado Springs, 1988-90; planning com. Colo. Christian Youth Conv., Denver, 1988-90; local coord. College, Career and Singles Prog., N. Am. Christian Conv. Com. mem. Nat. Parents Rights Conf., Greeley, Colo. Mem. Computer Users Group, Delta Upsilon Alumni. Republican. Office: Christian Student Fellowship 924 20th St Greeley CO 80631

DOSTER, JUNE MARKEN, minister; b. Des Moines, June 10, 1930; d. DeLoss Irving and Helen (Roberts) Marken; m. Harold Charles Doster, June 19, 1955; children: Deborah, Diana, Donald, Denise. BA magna cum laude, Iowa State U., 1952; MRE, Yale U., 1957. Ordained to ministry Christian Ch. (Disciples of Christ), 1982. Instr. sociology Bethany Coll., W.Va., 1961-62; dir. religious edn. Meml. Christian Ch., Ann Arbor, Mich., 1966-68; min. ch. edn. First Christian Ch., Wilson, N.C.; assoc. regional min. Christian Ch., Macon, Ga., 1984—; mem. cabinet Ch. Women Fellowship, Canton, Mo., 1975-77, Wilson, 1979-83, mem. exec. com., Indpls., 1985-90. Author retreat, jr. camp curriculum Christian Ch. in N.C. Leader Girl Scouts U.S., Ky., W.Va., 1968-73, treas. neighborhood coun. Wilson, N.C., 1978-83; bd. dirs. Wilson Concerts, 1981-83, Parents Anonymous, Wilson, 1982-83; mem. adv. bd. Villa Internat., 1985-90, Christmount Christian Assembly, 1985—. Sr. woman scholar Iowa State U., 1951. Mem. PEO, Gen. Fedn. Women (Keyser, W.Va. and Canton chpts.), Wilson Women's Club, Phi Beta Kappa, Alpha Xi Delta. Republican. Avocations: cello, piano, organ, swimming, water skiing. Home: 1974 Ellwyn Dr Chamblee GA 30341 Office: Christian Ch in Ga 2370 Vineville Ave Macon GA 31204

DOTTERER, DONALD WILLIAM, minister; b. Oil City, Pa., Mar. 26, 1953; s. Clarence Donald and Sarah Icel (Gilmore) D.; m. Pamela Yvonne Zimmer, June 18, 1983; 1 child, Steven Matthew. BA, Grove City Coll., 1975; MA, Drew U., 1977; MDiv, Boston U., 1979, PhD, 1983. Ordained to ministry Meth. Ch., 1985. Assoc. min. Greenburg (Pa.) First United Meth. Ch., 1983-86; min. Christy Park United Meth. Ch., McKeesport, Pa., 1986-91, Wesley United Meth. ch., New Castle, Pa., 1991—, Western Pa. Conf., 1983—; chair Bd. of Higher Edn. & Campus Ministry, 1988-92; mem. United Ministries in Higher Edn., 1988-92. Author: Up & Down the Mountain, 1991; contbr. sermons and articles to profl. jours. Jacob Sleeper fellow Boston U., 1979, 80, Lowstuter fellow Boston U., 1981, 82. Democrat. Home: 14 Cecil Ave New Castle PA 16101

DOTTS, M. FRANKLIN, retired religious publications editor; b. Williamsport, Pa., May 26, 1929; s. Merrill M. and Helen (Holt) D.; 1 child, Ruthann Catherine. BA, U. Pitts., 1951, MEd, 1954; MDiv, Garrett Evang. Theol. Sem., 1961; EdD, Columbia U., 1969. Ordained to ministry, Meth. Ch., 1961. Tchr. high schs. Pa., 1951-57; youth min. 1st United Meth. Ch., Arlington Heights, Ill., 1958-61; min. Christian edn. St. Paul United Meth. Ch., Omaha, 1961-65; editor children's publs. United Meth. Ch. Gen. Bd. of Discipleship, Nashville, 1967-73, dir. curriculum planning, 1973-86, exec. editor children's publs., 1986-90; ret., 1990. Co-author: Clues to Creativity, vols. 1, 2, 3, 1976. Mem. Rel. Edn. Assn., World Future Soc., Christian Educators Fellowship, Assn. for Supervision and Curriculum Devel., Phi Delta Kappa.

DOTTS, MARYANN J., lay worker, educator; b. Pitts., Nov. 11, 1933; d. Charles A. and Mary J. (Dryer) Dreese; m. M. Franklin Dotts, Aug. 8, 1958 (div. Oct. 1982); 1 child, Ruthann Catherine Dotts Martin. BA in Religious Edn., Nat. Coll. Christian Workers, 1956; MA in Christian Edn., Scarritt Coll., 1974; MLS, Vanderbilt U., 1975. Cert. lab. leader tchr. tng. With transit dept. People's First Nat. Bank, Pitts., 1951-52; dir. Christian edn. First United Meth. Ch., Erie, Pa., 1956-58, Arlington Heights, Ill., 1958-61; tchr., supr. children's sect. edn. staff Riverside Ch., N.Y.C., 1965-67; libr., cataloger Upper Rm. Libr. and Mus. United Meth. Bd. Discipleship, Nashville, 1975; dir. children's ministries and adult ministries and presch. Belle Meade United Meth. Ch., Nashville, 1976-79; dir. Christian edn. Andrew Price United Meth. Ch., Nashville, 1980-84, Mulberry St. United Meth. Ch., Macon, Ga., 1984-85, First United Meth. Ch., Cape Coral, Fla., 1985-89; dir. Christian edn. and program Gulf Breeze (Fla.) United Meth. Ch., 1989—; pres. Ch. and Synagogue Libr. Assn., Portland, Org., 1978-79; lab. leader tng. events Ch. Librs. and Elem. Grades, 1962—; free lance writer curriculum United Meth. Ch., 1963—. Author: I Am Happy, 1971, Clues to Creativity: Providing Learning Experiences for Children, 3 vols., 1974, The Church Resource Library, 1975, When Jesus Was Born, 1979, You Can Have a Church Library, 1988. Mem. Ch. and Synagogue Libr. Assn. (bd. mem. 1976—, chpts. coord. 1987—), Christian Educator's Fellowship (mem. design team 1980), Ala.-West Fla. Christian Educator's Fellowship, West Fla. Writers Guild, United Meth. Women. Republican. Office: Gulf Breeze United Meth Ch 75 Fairpoint Dr Box 338 Gulf Breeze FL 32562-0338

DOTY, JAMES EDWARD, pastoral psychologist; b. Lakewood, Ohio, May 8, 1922; s. Ordello Luce and Margaret (McCurdy) D.; m. Mary Merciel Smith, Sept. 8, 1943; children: Mark Allen, David Wesley, Martha Suzanne. AB, Mt. Union Coll., Alliance, Ohio, 1944, DD (hon.), 1965; MDiv cum laude, Boston U., 1947, PhD, 1959; postgrad., Harvard U., Oxford U.; DD (hon.), DePauw U., 1966. Ordained to ministry Meth. Ch., 1945. Pastor in Salem, Mass., 1947-51, Lynn, Mass., 1951-57; founder, dir. Greater Lynn Pastoral Care and Counselling Ctr., 1954-57; dir. pastoral care and counselling Ind. Area Meth. Ch., 1957-66; pres. Baker U., 1966-73; pvt. practice pastoral psychology Corpus Christi, Tex., 1973—; exec. dir. Corpus Christi Pastoral Counselling Ctr., 1973-84; mem. staff Boston Ctr. Adult Edn., 1949-53; spl. lectr. Union Theol. Sem., Buenos Aires, 1962, Meth. Theol. Sem., Sao Paulo, Brazil, 1962, Epworth Theol. Sem., Salisbury, Rhodesia, 1963, Meth. Theol. Sem., Mulungwishi, Congo, 1964, Trinity Theol. Coll., Singapore, 1967; mem. First Student Christian Movement Conf. in postwar Germany, Heidelberg U., summer 1947; del. World Family Life Consultation, Birmingham, Eng., 1966; chmn. World Family Life, 1981-86; mem. World Meth. Coun., London, 1966, Denver, 1971, Dublin, 1976, Honolulu, 1981; del. World Meth. Coun., Nairobi, Kenya, 1986, Singapore, 1991—. Author: The Pastor as Agape Counselor, 1964, Postmark Lambarene: A Visit with Albert Schweitzer, 1965; editor: Authentic Man Encounters God's World, 1967, Students Search for Meaning, 1971; producer, moderator weekly program Focus, Sta. KEDT-TV, 1984—. V.p. Pike Twp. Sch. Bd., Marion County, Ind., 1960-66. Recipient Alumni of Year award Mt. Union Coll., 1963, Alumni award of merit, Boston U., 1969. Mem. APA, S.W. Conf. United Meth. Ch., Tex. Bd. Profl. Counselors, Am. Bd. Sexology (diplomate), Am. Assn. Pastoral Counselors (diplomate, bd. dirs.), Am. Assn. Marriage and Family Therapy, Am. Assn. Sex Educators, Counselors and Therapists, Rockport Country Club, Neuces Club, Rotary, Sigma Alpha Epsilon, Zeta Chi. Home and Office: 502 Peerman Pl Corpus Christi TX 78411

DOTY, WILLIAM GUY, religion educator; b. Ratón, N.Mex., Aug. 7, 1939; s. William Henry and Marcia Constance (Freeman) D.; m. Joan T. Mallonée, Sept. 7, 1965. BA, U. N.Mex., 1961; MDiv, San Francisco Theol. Sem., 1963; PhD, Drew U., 1966. Instr. religion Rutgers U., 1965-66; instr. Garrett Theol. Sem., 1966-67; lectr. Vassar Coll., Poughkeepsie, N.Y., 1967-68; asst. prof. Douglass Coll., Rutgers U., New Brunswick, N.J., 1968-75; vis. lectr. in classics U. Mass., Amherst, 1976-77; mem. faculty Goddard Coll., Plainfield, Vt., 1978-80; assoc. prof. dept. religious studies U. Ala., Tuscaloosa, 1981-82, prof., 1982—, dept. chair, 1983-88, rsch. prof., 1991—; vis. assoc. prof. Hampshire Coll., Amherst, 1978; mem. faculty, program advisor Beacon Coll., Boston, 1978-82; vis. scholar Emory U., 1988, adj. faculty, 1989-90, 1992-93; judge Carlie Meml. Prize. Author: Contemporary New Testament Interpretation, 1972, Letters in Primitive Christianity, 1973, Mythography: The Study of Myths and Rituals, 1986 (named Outstanding Acad. Book, Choice mag. 1987); also articles; editor: The Daemonic Imagination: Biblical Text and Secular Story, 1990; (with Wendell C. Beane) Myths, Rites, Symbols: A Mircea Eliade Reader, 1976; translator: Candid Questions Concerning Gospel Form Criticism: A Methodological Sketch of the Fundamental Problematics of Form and Redaction Criticism (Erhardt Güttgemanns), 1979; editor (with Norman R. Petersen) Semeia jour., 1976; guest editor Arché jour., 1981; co-editor Issues in Integrative Studies, 1991; exhbns. include Festival for the Arts, Somerset County Coll., Bicentennial History Exhbn., 1976; contbr. photography and photog. reproductions to: Portrait of a Village: A History Of Millstone. Pres. exec. com. Friends of Arboretum, Tuscaloosa; bd. dirs. com. on traditional arts of Ams., Africa, and Oceania Birmingham Mus. Art, 1987-88. Recipient Alumni Achievement award Alumni Soc. of Grad. Sch./Drew U., 1991; San Francisco Theol. Sem., Drew U., Alumni fellow San Francisco Theiol. Sem., Presbyn. Grad. fellow, B'nai B'rith fellow, 1970, Soc. for Religion in Higher Edn fellow, 1971-72, Woodrow Wilson Inst. fellow, 1986, 90; Mellow grantee, 1984, NEH grantee, 1984, 91. Fellow Soc. for Values in Higher Edn. (editorial bd. Soundings: An Interdisciplinary Jour. 1980—, bd. dirs. cen. com. 1987-90, guest editor 1988), mem. Am. Acad. Religion (coord. juries awards for excellence in study of religion com. 1987-93), So. Humanities Coun. (del.-at-large exec. com. 1988-91). Home: 4343 Springhill Dr Tuscaloosa AL 35405-4746 Office: U Ala Dept Religious Studies 212 Manly Tuscaloosa AL 35487-0264

DOUBLEDAY, WILLIAM ALAN, religious administrator, educator; b. Northampton, Mass., Feb. 9, 1951; s. Elwyn John and Margaret Ann (Webster) D. BA magna cum laude, Amherst Coll., 1972; M of Div. with distinction, Episcopal Div. Sch., 1976. Ordained to ministry Episcopal Ch. as deacon and priest, 1980. Research staff Com. on the Study of History, Amherst, Mass., 1967-71; edn. staff Hist. Deerfield (Mass.), Inc., 1972-73; asst. to dir. of field edn. Episcopal Div. Sch., Cambridge, Mass., 1976-77; cons. edn. N.Y.C., 1978-79; curate St. James Episcopal Ch., Great Barrington, Mass., 1979-80; chaplain Morningside House Nursing Home, Bronx, N.Y., 1980-82; hospice chaplain St. Luke's-Roosevelt Hosp. Ctr., N.Y.C., 1983-85, AIDS chaplain, 1985-86; assoc. prof. pastoral theology, dir. of field edn. The Gen. Theol. Sem., N.Y.C., 1986—; priest assoc. Christ and St. Stephen's Ch., N.Y.C., 1984—; dep. gen. conv., 1988, 91. Author: (with others) AIDS: Facts and Issues, 1986; contbr. articles to profl. jours. Founder Hospice of South Berkshire, Inc., Great Barrington, Mass., 1980. Mem. Assn. for Theol. Field Edn., Assn. for Clin. Pastoral Edn. (sem. rep.). Democrat. Home and Office: 175 9th Ave New York NY 10011

DOUD, JOHN FOSTER, minister; b. Milw., Feb. 7, 1953; s. Donald Budlong and Jane Ellen (Foster) D.; m. Catherine Ellen Roberts, Aug. 21, 1976. BA, Albion Coll., 1975; MDiv, Duke U., 1978; D in Ministry, Drew U., 1989. Ordained to ministry Nat. Assn. Congl. Christian Chs., 1978. Chaplain U. N.C. Hosp., Chapel Hill, 1978; min. First Congl., Lake Odessa, Mich., 1978-80; sr. min. Arbor Grove Congl. Ch., Jackson, Mich., 1981—; chmn. Christian Edn. Nat. Assn. Congl. Chs., 1983-85; moderator Cen. Mich. Assn. Congl. Chs., 1983-84, Mich. Conf. Congl. Christian Chs., 1986-87, chmn. ch. and pastoral counselling, 1983-84; pres. Jackson Area Ministerial Assn., 1983-84; mem. Found. for Econ. Edn., Inc. Author pamphlets for ch. devotions; contbr. articles to religious publs. V.p. Big Bros./Big Sisters Am., Jackson County, 1983-84; mem. Voice of Reason, Jackson, 1982-84. Fellow Internat. Congl. Fellowship; mem. Ecumenical Inst. Jewish/Christian Studies, Fellowship of Religious Educators, Fellowship of Religious Humanists. Home: 2510 Spring Arbor Rd Jackson MI 49203 Office: Arbor Grove Congl Ch 2621 McCain Rd Jackson MI 49203 *The opposite of love is not hate; nor is it fear or anger. Rather, the opposite of love is apathy. Love, hate, joy, sadness, courage, fear: these are emotions and feelings which give substance to our life together. But apathy is the enemy of life-it is feeling nothing at all.*

DOUD, ROBERT EUGENE, philosophy and religion educator; b. Bklyn., Apr. 15, 1942; s. Robert Eugene and Cecilia Mary (McGuinness) D.; m. Jacqueline Powers, Feb. 12, 1977. BA, Cathedral Coll., 1963; MA, De Paul U., Chgo., 1971; PhD, Claremont Grad. Sch., 1977. Ordained priest in Roman Cath. Ch., 1968. Asst. pastor Missionary Servants of the Most Holy Trinity, Silver Spring, Md., 1968-73; asst. prof. Washington Theol. Union, Silver Spring, 1974-76, Pasadena (Calif.) City Coll., 1985—; lector, choir mem. Incarnation Cath. Ch., Glendale, Calif., 1986—. Contbr. articles and rev. to profl. jours. Mem. Cath. Theol. Soc. Am., Coll. Theol. Soc., Am. Acad. Religion, Am. Philos. Assn., Corpus. Democrat. Office: Pasadena City Coll 1570 E Colorado Blvd Pasadena CA 91106-2003

DOUDNA, JOHN CHARLES, retired religion educator; b. St. Clairsville, Ohio, July 7, 1907; s. Joseph Elmer and Alice Cary (McMillen) D.; m. Evelyn Gertrude Blaisdell, Dec. 26, 1939; children: Roger Blaisdell Doudha, Christine Evelyn Doudna Grand Jean. AB, Washington & Jefferson Coll., 1928; S.T.B., Western Theol. Sem., 1931; PhD, Yale U., 1939. Ordained to ministry Meth. Ch., 1933. Pastor Pitts. Conf., 1931-53; prof. Baker U., Baldwin City, Kans., 1953-75. Author: The Greek of the Gospel of Mark, 1939. Chmn. bd. trustees Santa Fe Trail Hist. Soc., 1957-79. Capt., Chaplain Corps, USAF, 1942-45, ETO. Sem. fellow Western Theol. Sem., 1931. Democrat. Home: 1314 8th St Baldwin City KS 66006

DOUEK, HAIM, rabbi. Chief rabbi Jewish community, Cairo. Office: Jewish Community, 13 Sharia, Sebil alKhazindar, Abbassia, Cairo Arab Republic of Egypt*

DOUGAN, PHILIP JEROME, minister; b. Butler, Pa., May 3, 1932; s. Richard Francis and Margaret Evelyn (Scowden) D.; m. Helen Norene Chavers, Aug. 16, 1952; children: Philip David, Barbara Jean, William Franklin. BA in Bible, Columbia (S.C.) Bible Coll., 1956. Ordained to ministry Bapt. Ch., 1967. Pastor 1st Bapt. Ch., Alexandria, Tenn., 1967-71, Franklin St. Bapt. Ch., Centerville, Ohio, 1971-76, 1st Bapt. Ch., Enon, Ohio, 1976-80, Gath Bapt. Ch., McMinnville, Tenn., 1981-86, Madison Creek Bapt., Goodlettsville, Tenn., 1986-90; mission pastor First Bapt. Ch., Portland, Tenn., 1990—; moderator Bledsoe Bapt. Assn., Gallatin, Tenn., 1988-90; pres. Bapt. Pastor's Conf., McMinnville, 1982-85, Dayton, Ohio, 1977-79; chmn. Wilson County Evangelistic Crusade, Lebanon, Tenn., 1970-71. Author: (Sunday Sch. lessons) Baptist and Reflector, 1985, (devotionals), 1971. Steering com. Mayor's Prayer Breakfast, Springfield, Ohio, 1977-79; chmn. DeKalb County Adv. Com., Smithville, Tenn., 1969-71. Home: 130 Chippendale Dr Hendersonville TN 37075 Office: Oak Street Baptist Church 300 Oak St Portland TN 37148 *In the final analysis, all that really counts in life is what I have done to help others find God and to make this a better world.*

DOUGHERTY, BERNARD GLENN, minister; b. Cleve., Jan. 30, 1949; s. Hugh and Lillian (Thomas) D.; m. LaDonna Harriet Bella, July 26, 1969; children: Michael Patrick, Dawnya Christina. BA, Kent (Ohio) State U., 1971, MA, 1973; MDiv, Candler Sch. Theology, Atlanta, 1976. Ordained to ministry United Meth. Ch. as deacon, 1974, as elder, 1979; cert. min. Christian edn. and youth ministry. Pastor Sawyerwood United Meth. Ch., Akron, Ohio, 1970-73, Holly Springs Cir., Canton, Ga., 1973-77; assoc. pastor First United Meth. Ch., Cambridge, Ohio, 197778; minister edn. Rocky River (Ohio) United Meth. Ch., 1978-90; pastor Newton Falls (Ohio) United Meth. Ch., 1990—; sec. communications Cleve. Dist. United Meth. Ch., 1982-84, youth coord., 1978-83; mem. Coun. of Chs., Greater Cleve. Internch. Coun., 1982-89. Contbr. articles to profl. jours.; author plays: Isn't This What Christmas is About?, 1984, The Meaning of a Gift, 1986. Recipient Legion of Honor, Order DeMolay, 1980. Mem. Newton Falls Ministerial Assn., E. Ohio Christian Educators Fellowship (sec. 1983-87), Nat. Christian Educators Fellowship, Masons, Kiwanis (spiritual aims chmn. 1990—). Office: Newton Falls United Meth Ch 336 Ridge Rd Newton Falls OH 44444

DOUGHERTY, JOHN JOSEPH, bishop; b. Jersey City, Sept. 16, 1907; s. John J. and Christina (Farrell) D.; A.B., Seton Hall U., 1930; student U. Propaganda, Rome, 1930-32; S.T.L., Gregorian U., Rome, 1934; student Pontifical Bibl. Inst., Rome, 1934-37, D.S.S., 1948; L.H.D. (hon.), U. Detroit, 1960; LL.D., Rutgers U., 1962, St. Peter's Coll., 1964, St. Ambrose Coll., 1964; L.H.D., Seton Hall U., 1969. Ordained priest Roman Cath. Ch., 1933, papal chamberlain, 1954, domestic prelate, 1958, titular bishop of Cotenna and auxiliary to archbishop of Newark, 1963—; pastor St. Rose of Lima Ch., Short Hills, N.J., 1969-77; prof. sacred scriptures Immaculate Conception Sem., Darlington, N.J., 1937-59; radio broadcasting CBS, NBC, ABC, 1946—, TV broadcasting CBS, NBC, 1951—; regent Inst. Judaeo Christian Studies, Seton Hall U., 1954-59, pres. univ., 1959-69, scholar in residence, 1977—; mem. Vatican Commn. on Radio and TV, 1956-60; mem. Vatican Com. on Peace Studies, 1972-76; chmn. World Conf. Religion and Peace, 1974—. Bd. dirs. Cath. Bibl. Assn., 1957-59, UNDA (Internat. Assn. Cath. Radio and TV), 1956-59; mem. nat. council UNA-USA, 1977—; mem. Nat. Citizens Commn. Internat. Coop., 1965; mem. Adv. Com. Edn. of the Deaf, 1966; vice chmn. com. of dept. internat. affairs U.S.C.C., 1969-74; trustee Council Religion and Internat. Affairs, 1971—, chmn., 1973-77. Decorated Star of Solidarity (Italy); recipient Freedoms Found. medal, 1953; award Cath. TV Arts, 1959; Ann. Americanism award B'nai B'rith, 1965; citation NCCJ, 1965. Author: Searching the Scriptures, 1959. Address: Seton Hall U South Orange NJ 07079

DOUGHERTY, MARK ALLEN, minister; b. Wichita, Kans., Sept. 30, 1960; s. Raymond Joseph and Claudeen V. (Martin) D.; m. Melony Joan Williams, May 28, 1983; children: Kyle Allen, Trevor Ray. Diploma in emergency medicine, Wichita State U., 1979; student, Mo. So. State Coll., 1985; BTh in Preaching Ministry, B in Biblical Lit., Ozark Christian Coll., 1986. Ordained to ministry Christian Ch., 1985. Firefighter Sedgwick County Fire Dept., Wichita, 1979-81; youth min. Salina (Okla.) Christian Ch., 1982-83; min. McCune (Kans.) Christian Ch., 1984-86, First Christian Ch., Muskogee, Okla., 1988—; Youth worker 1st Christian Ch., Derby, Kans., 1980-81; acctg. clk. Tamko Asphalt Products, Joplin, Mo., 1983-86. Program dir. Joplin Family YMCA, 1986-88. Mem. Muskogrr C. of C. (contact com., pub. rels. com.). Avocations: religious study, philosophy, exercise. Home: 2926 W Broadway Muskogee OK 74403 Office: First Christian Ch 400 Court St Muskogee OK 74401

DOUGHTIE, BONNIE LYNN, clergywoman; b. Portsmouth, Va., Sept. 1, 1950; d. Claxton McCray and Dorothy (Copeland) D. BS, Mars Hill Coll., 1972; MDiv, Southeastern Bapt. Theol. Sem., 1979; postgrad., Spartanburg Regional Med. Ctr., 1989. Ordained to ministry So. Bapt. Conv., 1985. Min. edn. and youth Durham (N.C.) Meml. Bapt. Ch., 1978-80; min. edn. and outreach Indian River Bapt. Ch., Chesapeake, Va., 1980-83; min. edn. Boiling Springs (N.C.) Bapt. Ch., 1983—. Mem. So. Bapt. Religious Edn. Assn., N.C. Bapt. Religious Edn. Assn. (sec.-treas. 1989—), Southeastern Bapt. Theol. Sem. Alumni Assn. (pres. N.C. 1987-88). Home: 233 N Main St Box 337 Boiling Springs NC 28017 Office: Boiling Springs Bapt Ch 307 S Main St Box 917 Boiling Springs NC 28017

DOUGHTY, A. GLENN, minister; b. Somers Point, N.J., Aug. 30, 1942; s. Alfred and Irene Dorothy (Colhouer) D.; m. Carole True, June 17, 1967; children: Matthew Glenn, Lynn Carole. BS in Bible Studies, Phila. Coll. of Bible, 1965; MDiv, Faith Theol. Sem., 1968. Ordained to ministry Fellowship Fundamental Bible Chs., 1970. Pastor Community Bible Ch., Barrington, N.J., 1968-70, The Bible Ch. of Westville, N.J., 1970—; chmn. Bible Protestant Ch. Extension, 1970-73; sec. Ministerial Qualifications Com., 1980—; sec. Fellowship of Fundamental Bible Chs., 1976—; pres. Bible Protestant Conf. Trustees, 1985-91. Chmn. Community Dispute Resolution Com., Westville, 1976—. Home and Office: 134 Delsea Dr Westville NJ 08093

DOUGLAS, GARY KENT, minister; b. Excelsior Springs, Mo., May 14, 1953; s. Kenneth Harold and Elizabeth Frances (Craven) D.; m. Deborah Kay Ireland, Mar. 16, 1974; children: Sandra Kristine, Joel Kent, Benjamin Kurtis, Matthew Kirby. BA, William Jewell Coll., 1975; MDiv, Midwestern Bapt. Theol., 1980. Ordained to ministry So. Bapt. Conv., 1976. Assoc. pastor youth 1st Bapt. Ch., Grain Valley, Mo., 1978-80; chaplain Bethany Hosp., Kansas City, Kans., 1980; pastor Lewis & Clark Bapt. Ch., Rushville, Mo., 1983-85, 1st Bapt. Ch., Paris, Mo., 1985—. Contbr. articles and book revs. to profl. jours. Mem. Monroe Bapt. Assn. (moderator 1987-89, camp dir. 1985—, dir. evangelism 1985—), Associational Tri-Bd. (moderator 1989), Ministerial Alliance (pres. 1986-89), Mark Twain Lake Ministries (v.p. 1986-89), Rotary (bd. dirs. 1986—, sec. 1987, pres. elect 1988, pres. 1989). Office: 1st Bapt Ch 100 N Main Paris MO 65275

DOUGLASS, HERBERT EDGAR, academic administrator; b. Springfield, Mass., May 16, 1927; s. Herbert Edgar Sr. and Mildred (Munson) D.; m. Norma Campbell, Nov. 16, 1974; children: Janelle, Herbert III, Reatha, Vivienne, Donna, Clifford. AB, Atlantic Union Coll., 1947; MA, Andrews U., 1953, BDiv, 1957; ThD, Pacific Sch. of Religion, 1964. Min. Ill. Conf. of Seventh Day Adventists, Peoria and Aurora, Ill., 1947-53; tchr. Pacific Union Coll., Angwin, Calif., 1953-60; dean, pres. Atlantic Union Coll., 1960-70; editor Review & Herald, Washington, 1970-76; v.p. Pacific Press Pub. Assn., Mountain View, Calif., 1978-85; pres. Weimar (Calif.) Inst., 1985—. Author: If I Had One Sermon to Preach, 1971, Why Jesus Waits, 1976, Jesus, The Model Man, 1977, Faith-Saying Yes to God, 1978, The End, 1980. Named Disting. Alumnus, Andrews U., 1976. Mem. Rotary Internat. Home: PO Box 933 Weimar CA 95736 Office: Weimar Inst PO Box 486 Weimar CA 95736

DOUGLASS, JANE DEMPSEY, theology educator; b. Wilmington, Del., Mar. 22, 1933; d. Hazell Brownlie and Ethel Katherine (Smith) Dempsey; m. Gordon Klene Douglass, Aug. 23, 1964; children: Alan Bruce, Anne Lorine, John Gordon. AB, Syracuse U., 1954; postgrad., U. Geneva, 1954-55; AM, Radcliffe Coll., 1961; PhD, Harvard U., 1963. Assoc. dir. Presbyn. Student Ctr., Columbia, Mo., 1955-58; teaching fellow Harvard Divinity Sch., Cambridge, Mass., 1959-62; from instr. to prof. Sch. of Theology and Claremont Grad. Sch., Claremont, Ca., 1963-85; Hazel Thompson McCord prof. hist. theology Princeton (N.J.) Theol. Sem., 1985—; pres. Am. Soc. Ch. History, 1983; v.p. World Alliance of Reformed Chs., 1989-90, pres. 1990—. Author: Justification in Late Medieval Preaching: A Study of John Geiler of Keisersberg, 1966, 2d edit., 1989, Women, Freedom and Calvin, 1985; editor: (with Jack L. Stotts) To Confess the Faith Today, 1990; contbr. articles to profl. jours. Presbyterian. Office: Princeton Theol Seminary CN 821 Princeton NJ 08542

DOUKHAN, JACQUES BENJAMIN, religion educator; b. Constantine, Algeria, Nov. 17, 1940; s. Kalfa Albert and Fortunee Honorine (Attal) D.; m. Lilianne Ubersax, May 17, 1966; 1 child, Myrte Abigail. Lic. Theology, Saleve Adventist Inst., Collonges, France, 1967; Lic. Hebrew, Maitrise Hebrew, U. Strasbourg (France), 1970, 71, DHL, 1973; ThD, Andrews U., Berrien Springs, Mich., 1978. Prof. O.T. Saleve Adventist Inst., Collonges, 1965-66, prof. Hebrew and Bibl. studies, 1970-73; pastor Seventh-day Adventist Franco-Belgian Union, Strasbourg, 1974-76; pres. Seventh-day Adventist Union Sem., Phoenix, 1980-84; prof. O.T. Andrews U., Berrien Springs, 1984—. Author: Drinking at the Sources: Essay on the Jewish-Christian Problem, French ed., 1977, English ed., 1981; The Genesis Creation Story, Its Literary Structure, 1978, Aux Portes de l'Espérance, 1983, E.G. White and the Jews, 1985, Daniel, The Vision of the End, 1987, 2d edit., 1989, German edit., 1989; editor-in-chief L'Olivier, 1989—, Hebrew for

Theologians. With French Army, 1961-63. Mem. Soc. Bibl. Lit., Nat. Assn. Profs. Hebrew, Midwest Jewish Studies Assn. Home: 4797 Kimber Ln Berrien Springs MI 49103 Office: Andrews U OT Dept Berrien Springs MI 49104 *To live is to be ready for surprises--the new which disturbs me and changes me into a new being--but one who also remembers and remains faithful to my roots and to what I have received.*

DOUTY, HORACE DALE, clergyman; b. Rockbridge, Va., June 18, 1932; s. Reuben Franklin and Mary Flotelle (Coffey) D.; m. Madeline Carole Gillespie, Aug. 31, 1956 (div. Sept. 1989); children: Dale Christopher, Ellen Hope; m. Ellen Baker Harris, June 15, 1991; stepsons: Gillette Harris, Michael Harris. BA, Washington & Lee U., 1954; BD, Union Thel. Sem., 1957, D in Ministry, 1985. Minister, pastor Collierstown Presbyn. Ch., Lexington, Va., 1957-61, Ch. of the Covenant, Greensboro, N.C., 1961-63, Culpeper (Va.) Presbyn. Ch., 1963-88. Mem. City Coun. of Culpepper, 1972-84; mem. planning commn. Dist. 9 State of Va., 1973-80. Avocations: gunsmithing, choral music, farming, machinery, hunting. Home: 1703 Rolling Hills Dr Culpeper VA 22701 Office: Milford Presbyn Ch 10 Church St PO Box 96 Milford VA 22514

DOUTY, ROBERT WATSON, minister; b. Phila., June 20, 1943; m. Marshalee Wood, Apr. 22, 1972. BA in Psychology, Calif. State U., Long Beach, 1969; MS in Edn., U. Bridgeport, 1974; postgrad., Alliance Theol. Sem., Nyack, N.Y., 1984—. Ordained to ministry Bapt. Ch., 1990; teaching cert., N.Y. Tchr. Garrison (N.Y.) Sch., 1980—; chmn. bd. deacons 1st Bapt. Ch., Ossining, N.Y., 1980-82, dir. Christian edn., 1985-91; assoc. pastor 1st Bapt. Ch., Ossining, 1991—; deacon 1st Bapt. Ch., 1973-82, chmn. missions, 1990—; chaplain Phelps Hosp., Tarrytown, N.Y., 1988—. Author: Star City: A Classroom Management System, 1989; author: (with others) In the Footsteps of Birdy Edwards, 1980; contbr. articles to mags. With U.S. Navy, 1962-65. Mem. N.Y. State English Coun., Baker St. Irregulars (The Priory Sch.). Republican.

DOVICH, LAUREL MAY, lay worker, structural engineer; b. Rosthern, Sask., Can., Dec. 9, 1962; came to U.S., 1967; d. John and Luvamay (Epp) D. BS in Engring., Walla Walla Coll., 1986; MS in Civil Engring., U. Mich., 1990, postgrad., 1990—. Cert. engr. in tng. Student missionary SDA Lang. Schs., Seoul, Republic of Korea, 1981-82; sec. campus ministry Andrews U., Berrien Springs, Mich., 1982-83, Walla Walla Coll., College Place, Wash., 1984-86; youth leader Holly (Mich.) Seventh-day Adventist Ch., 1986-87; missionary, faculty, advisor West Indies Coll., Mandeville, Jamaica, 1987-89; dir. campus ministries Ann Arbor (Mich.) Seventh-day Adventist Ch., 1990—; founder, dir. newsletter editor Collegiate Adventists for Re-Creation, Ann Arbor, 1991—. Leadership scholar Campus Ministries, Walla Walla Coll., 1985, CEW scholar, U. Mich., 1990. Mem. ASCE (v.p. 1985-86), Am. Concrete Inst. Home: Box 133 Holly MI 48442

DOW, IRVING APGAR, JR., minister, consultant; b. Elizabeth, N.J., Sept. 8, 1920; s. Irving Apgar Sr. and Freda Anna (Schenk) D.; m. Barbara Alice Davidson, Oct. 16, 1943; children: Mark I., Matthew A. BA, Columbia Union Coll., 1950; M In Religious Edn., Tenn. Christian U., 1974, PhD in Sacred Theology and Philosophy, 1975; MDiv, Shaw U., 1977. Ordained minister Seventh Day Adventist Ch. 1950, ordained minister Bapt. Ch., 1973. Pastor N.J. Conf. Seventh Day Adventists, Trenton, 1950-54; pres. Dow Home Builders, Inc., Alexandria, Va., 1956-60; cons., lectr. pastoral, clin. counseling in psycho-theology Elizabeth, 1975—. Patentee oil saving device used in oil burning boilers. With USAAC, 1943-45; lt. col. USAR, 1975-90. Republican. Avocations: church restoring, wood carving. Home and Office: 20 Vista Ave Elizabeth NJ 07208 *Living in a frightening and unprecedented period in human history, we are faced with new, overwhelming, destructive perplexities and anxieties. The, heretofore, stabilizing influence of love is now, itself, misunderstood and faith seems futile. With hope crushed beneath the load, I have verified to scientists and countless others, there is an answer to human despair. "Peace is what I leave with you...I do not give as the world does. Do not be worried and upset: Do not be afraid" (Good News Bible, Jn. 14:27). God, the spokesman, is there and does care!.*

DOW, THOMAS EDWARD, college president; b. Royal Oak, Mich., Feb. 5, 1940; arrived in Can., 1942; s. Harold Walter Dow and Herbena May (Buckner) LeNeve; m. Carolyn Ruth Spice, Sept. 23, 1961; children: Stephen Thomas, Beverly Susan, Marianne Elizabeth. BTh, Emmanuel Bible Coll., 1961; BA, Wilfrid Laurier U., 1963, MA, 1972; BD, Waterloo Luth. Sem., Ont., Can., 1966; PhD, U. Waterloo, Ont., Can., 1981. Ordained to ministry Missionary Ch., 1963. Pastor Missionary Ch., Stratford, Ont., Can., 1962-66; prof. Emmanuel Bible Coll., Kitchener, Ont., Can., 1966-72, 74-79, acad. dean, 1979-88, pres., 1988—; pastor Lincoln Heights Missionary Ch., Waterloo, 1967-72, Beechwood Missionary Ch., Waterloo, 1980-86; missionary Missionary Ch., Nigeria, 1972-74; mem., bd. dirs. Missionary Ch. Can., 1979—. Recipient scholarship U. Waterloo, 1979-80. Mem. Can. Assn. Bible Colls. (exec. com. 1980—). Home: 30 Simpson Ave, Kitchener, ON Canada N2A 1L3 Office: Emmanuel Bible Coll, 100 Fergus Ave, Kitchener, ON Canada N2A 2H2

DOWD, KARL EDMUND, priest; b. Nashua, N.H., May 3, 1934; s. Karl Edmund Sr. and Edna Louise (Burque) D. BS, Coll. of Holy Cross, 1956; BTh, U. Ottawa, Ont., Can., 1958, Licentiate in Sacred Theology, 1960; MEd, Rivier Coll., 1964. Ordained priest Roman Cath. Ch., 1960. Tchr. Bishop Bradley High Sch., Manchester, N.H., 1960-62; tchr., athletic dir. St. Thomas Aquinas High Sch., Dover, N.H., 1960-62; adminstr. St. Mary's, Rollinsford, N.H., 1967; assoc. pastor St. Bernard's Parish, Keene, N.H., 1968-69, St. Joseph's Parish, Nashua, 1969-71, Immaculate Heart of Mary, Concord, N.H., 1971-75; pastor St. Joseph's Ch., Salem, N.H., 1975-86; dean Salem Deanery, 1980-86; pastor St. Christopher Ch., Nashua, 1986—; asst. dir. diocesan camps, Fatima and Bernadette, N.H., 1960-62, diocesan dir., 1971-90; mem. New Eng. regional com. Nat. Liturgical Conf., 1961—; adv. diocesan marriage tribunal Diocese of Manchester, 1975—, diocesan consultor, 1980-86. Chaplain Nashua coun. KC, 1970-76, State Prior Columbian Squires, 1973-76; Salem div. chaplain Ct. Holy Name, Cath. Daus. Ams., 1977-80, state chaplain, 1989—; bd. dirs., exec. com. Concord Mental Health Clinic; chmn. interfaith svc. com. N.H. Hosp., Concord, 1974-75; past. pres., bd. dirs. Salemhaven, Inc.; bd. dirs., pres. Silverthorne, Inc.; treas., bd. dirs. Marklin Candle Design. Named knight of the Holy Sepulchre, 1986; recipient Noyes medal, 1952. Mem. Am. Camping Assn. (nat. bd. dirs., past. pres. and bd. dirs. New Eng. sect., regional chair 1986-90, chair ethics com. 1990—), N.H. Camp Dirs. Assn. ((bd. dirs. 1971—, pres. 1974-78), U.S. Cath. Conf. (com. on camping 1972-76). Home: 15 Denise St PO Box 3810 Nashua NH 03061-3810 Office: St Christopher Ch 62 Manchester St Nashua NH 03060-6296

DOWDY, HELEN MARIE, educational administrator; b. Macon, Ga., Mar. 10, 1930; d. Manly Calvin and Eriel Marie (Merriman) Britt; m. Lemuel Stroud Dowdy, Sept. 5, 1953 (dec.); children: Lemuel David, Donald Manly. A.A., Mars Hill Coll., 1950. Cert., N.C. Pub. Mgr. Program. Sec. First Citizens Bank, Raleigh, N.C., 1950-53, N.C. State U., Raleigh, 1953-55; adminstrv. asst. N.C. Dept. Curriculum Study, Raleigh, 1959-63; adminstrv. asst. N.C. Dept. Community Colls., Raleigh, 1963-77, spl. asst. to pres., 1977—; cons. N.C. Employees Tng. Ctr., Raleigh, 1974-76; mem. adv. com. N.C. Employee Suggestion System, 1978—. Pres. Congl. Coun. Christ the King Luth. Ch., 1989—. Named Tar Heel of Week Raleigh News and Observer, 1988; recipient Pres.' award Community Coll. System, 1990, Gov.'s award State of N.C., 1991. V.p. Cary Jr. Woman's Club (N.C.), 1964. Mem. N.C. Assn. Ednl. Office Personnel (pres. dist. 10, 1977-78, scholarship fund named in her honor 1979), Am. Bus. Womens Assn. (chmn. edn. com. Cary chpt. 1979-80), Women in Mgmt., Am. Acad. Cert. Pub. Mgrs., N.C. Soc. Cert. Pub. Mgrs. (chmn. bd. dirs.), Soroptomists. Democrat. Lutheran. Office: NC Dept Community Colls 200 W Jones St Raleigh NC 27603

DOWDY, JOHN WESLEY, minister, theology educator, mayor; b. Albertville, Ala., Jan. 7, 1912; s. Sherman and Beulah Bee (Strange) D.; m. Floy Weaver Thurston, Apr. 2, 1930; children—John Wesley, David Sherman, Floyd William, Paul Philip. A.B., Okla. Baptist U., 1934, D.D., 1960; Th.B., So. Bapt. Theol. Sem., Louisville, 1939, Th.M., 1940; Th.D., Central Baptist Theol. Sem., Kansas City, 1945; M.R.E., 1948. Ordained to ministry Bapt. Ch. as elder, 1933. Served pastorates in Baptist Church, Shawnee, Okla., 1933-34, Haskell, Okla., 1934-36, English, Ky., 1936-39, Wheatley, Ky., 1939-4O; asst. exec. sec. Ky. Baptist Gen. Assn., Louisville, 1940-43; asst. gen. supt. Mo. Baptist Gen. Assn., Kansas City, 1943-45; prof. systematic theology Central Baptist Theol. Sem., 1945-48; pres. S.W. Baptist Coll., Bolivar, Mo., 1948-61; pastor 1st Bapt. Ch., Guthrie, Okla., 1961—; mayor City of Guthrie, 1977—; Moderator Central Bapt. Assn.; bd. dirs. Bapt. Gen. Conv. of Okla. Mem. Logan County Hosp., Assn.; chmn lay adv. bd. Alverno Heights Hosp.; chmn. Guthrie Human Relations Com.; Bd. dirs. United Community Chest Fund; trustee Okla. Bapt. U. Decorated Order Red Cross of Constantine. Mem. Order of Eastern Star, DeMolay Legion Honor (hon. life), Rotary. Democrat. Lodges: Mason (33 deg.) (past master Guthrie, past grand chaplain Most Worshipful lodge, past venerable master), KT (past prelate), Shriners. Home: 410 E Mansur St Guthrie OK 73044

DOWDY, JOHN WESLEY, JR., minister; b. Muskogee, Okla., Nov. 15, 1935; s. John Wesley and Floy Weaver (Thurston) D.; m. Joycelyn Adele Pinnell, June 9, 1956; children: Barbara Annette, Gina Marie (dec.). AA, Southwest Baptist Coll., 1954; BA, Southwest Mo. State U., 1956; M in Div., Midwestern Baptsit Theol. Sem., 1962, D in Ministries, 1974. Pastor Cedar City (Mo.) Bapt. Ch., 1956-59, First Bapt. Ch., Maysville, Mo., 1959-64, Tabernacle Bapt. Ch., Kansas City, Mo., 1964-75; dir. Christian social ministries Metro Mission Bd., Kansas City, 1975-78; dir. Christian social ministries Mo. Bapt. Conv., Jefferson City, Mo., 1978-80, dir. missions dept., 1980-88, dir. missions evangelism div., 1988—; field supr., adj. prof. D of Ministries program Midwestern Bapt. Theol. Sem., Kansas City, Mo., 1976-88; cons. SBC Home Mission Bd., Atlanta, 1976—. Pres. Inter Faith Chaplain's Commn. of Mo., Jefferson City, 1983-88; bd. dirs. Am. Field Svc., Jefferson City, 1985-88. Mem. So. Baptist Convention Research Soc., So. Baptist Social Service Soc., Futurist Soc. Am. Avocation: avid reader. Home: 1004 Winston Dr Jefferson City MO 65101 Office: Mo Bapt Conv 400 E High Jefferson City MO 65101

DOWNEY, CHARLES HART, minister, speaker; b. Beaumont, Tex., June 8, 1930; s. Marvin LeRoy and Edna Mae (Hardy) D.; m. Joan Alleen Sanders; children: Charles Jr., David Roy, Catherine Downey Chambers. BS, Hardin Simmons U., 1951; MEd., Sam Houston State U., 1953. Cert. real estate profl. Minister of music Second Baptist Ch., Houston, 1956-58, Parkplace Baptist Ch., Houston, 1958-60, Queensborough Baptist Ch., Shreveport, La., 1960-65; minister of music, assoc. pastor First Baptist Ch., Springfield, Mo., 1965-69; cons. Southern Baptist Conv. Sunday Sch. Bd., Nashville, 1969-72; minister of music, assoc. pastor Woodmont Baptist Ch., Nashville, 1972-74; self-employed Quitman, Tex., 1974-84; assoc. pastor First Baptist Ch., Conroe, Tex., 1984-90; founder Conroe Chaplaincy Assn., 1990—; seminar dir. Southern Baptist Conv., Nashville, 1969; speaker/humorist Charles Downey Enterprises, 1965—. Recording artist (two albums), 1965, 70; co-author: Church Music Administration, 1974; composer sheet music, 1970-84; contbr. articles to various publs.; soloist Houston Grand Opera Assn., Houston Symphony Orchestra. Bd. dirs. Springfield (Mo.) Symphony, 1965-69. With U.S. Army, 1953-56. Republican. Avocations: speed biking, mountain biking, SCUBA diving. Home: 1704 N Thompson Conroe TX 77301

DOWNEY, JAMES LEROY, minister; b. Tuscola, Ill., Apr. 14, 1950; s. Robert Francis and Dorthy Louese (Price) D.; m. DeAnna Ruth Hughes, Dec. 12, 1970; children: John Eric, Bradley Dee. BA, Carson-Newman Coll., 1981; MDiv, So. Sem., Louisville, 1987. Ordained to ministry Bapt. Ch., 1975. Pastor First Bapt. Ch., Loogootee, Ind., 1975-77, Little Flat Creek Bapt. Ch., Corryton, Tenn., 1980-83, Mt. Tabor Bapt. Ch., Paint Lick, Ky., 1984-87, First Bapt. Ch., Waterville, Ohio, 1987—; state exec. bd. dirs. State Conv. Bapt. in Ohio, Columbus. Active Right to Life Group, Loogootee, 1975. Recipient Cert. Appreciation award So. Bapt. Foreign Mission Bd., Richmond, Va., 1982. Mem. Maumee Valley Assn. Bapt. (asst. moderator 1989—, dir. misson coun. 1988—), Waterville Ministerial Assn. (pres. 1991). Home: 8814 Waterville/Neapolis Rd Waterville OH 43566 Office: First Bapt Church 8239 St Rte 64 Waterville OH 43566

DOWNEY, JOHN KENNETH, religion educator; b. L.A., Jan. 16, 1948; s. B.K. and Doris Downey; m. Alexis Anne Nelson, Aug. 19, 1972; children: Benjamin, Meara. AB in Latin, Marquette U., 1971, MA in Theology, 1975, PhD in Religious Studies, 1983. Dir. edn. Newman Found., U. Ill., Champaign, 1981-82; assoc. prof. Gonzaga U., Spokane, 1982—. Author: Beginning at the Beginning, 1986. Grantee Wash. Ctr. for Undergrad. Edn., 1989, Coolidge Rsch. Colloquium, 1990. Mem. Am. Acad. Religion, Cath. Theol. Soc. Am., Coll. Theology Soc. (convener philos. sect. 1989—, regional chair 1984—), Danforth Assocs N.W., Phi Beta Kappa, Alpha Sigma Nu. Office: Gonzaga U Dept Religious Studies Spokane WA 99258

DOWNEY, RONALD DEAN, minister; b. Santa Paula, Calif., Jan. 24, 1950; s. Donald Dean and Ruth Ann (Johnston) D.; m. Shirley Ann Brown, Feb. 5, 1972; children: John, Rebecca, Jenna, Nick. AA, Yuba Coll., 1970; cert., Sunset Sch. Preaching, Lubbock, Tex., 1972, Sunset Sch. Missions, Lubbock, Tex., 1977. Ordained to ministry Ch. of Christ, 1972. Min. Ch. of Christ, Livermore, Calif., 1973-75; min. Ch. of Christ, Fairfield, Calif., 1975-76; missionary Ch. of Christ, Sask., Can., 1977-79, Melbourne, Australia, 1980-85; min. Ch. of Christ, Martinez, Calif., 1986—; official Costa Christian Edn. Fund, 1989—. Pub. Sancho Panza newsletter, 1988—. Chaplain Rotary Internat., Livermore, 1975. Named one of Outstanding Young Men of Am. U.S. Jaycees, 1979. Republican. Home: 1281 Maywood Ln Martinez CA 94553 Office: Martinez Ch of Christ 1865 Arnold Dr Martinez CA 94553

DOWNING, BARRY HOWARD, minister; b. Syracuse, N.Y., Oct. 14, 1938; s. Franklin Vivian and Beatrice Anna (Barry) D.; m. Kathleen Esther Schrader, June 10, 1960; children: Scott, Ross, Todd. BA in Physics, Hartwick Coll., 1960; BD, Princeton Sem., 1963; PhD, U. Edinburgh, Scotland, 1966. Ordained to ministry Presbyn. Ch., 1967. Asst. pastor Northminster Presbyn. Ch., Endwell, N.Y., 1967-68, assoc. pastor, 1968-71, sr. pastor, 1971—; moderator Presbytery of Susquehanna Valley, Bainbridge, N.Y., 1979; pres. SEPP Housing Inc., Binghamton, 1986-87; lectr. MUFON MIT Conf., 1981; theol. cons. Mut. UFO Network, Seguin, Tex., 1971—; bd. dirs. fund for UFO Research, Washington. Author: The Bible and Flying Saucers, 1968. Pres. Union Soccer Assn., Endwell, 1975-76, Broome County Soccer Assn., N.Y., 1980-81; chmn. Broome County Jail Ministry, 1981, Broome County Hunger Walk, 1985-86. Lodge: Rotary (pres. Endwell club 1977-78). Avocations: soccer coaching, raising beef cattle, collecting and restoring 19th century oil landscapes. Home: 3663 Rath Ave Endwell NY 13760 Office: Northminster Presbyn Ch Box 8655 Endwell NY 13760

DOWNING, CHRISTINE ROSENBLATT, religious studies educator; b. Leipzig, Germany, Mar. 21, 1931; came to U.S., 1935; d. Edgar Fritz and Herta (Fischer) Rosenblatt; m. George Downing, June 9, 1951, (div. Jan. 1978); children: Peter, Eric, Scott, Christopher, Sandra; m. River Malcolm, Sept. 2, 1984. BA, Swarthmore Coll., 1948; PhD, Drew U., 1966; MA, U.S. Internat. U., 1982. From instr. to assoc. prof. religion Rutgers U., New Brunswick, N.J., 1963-75; prof., chmn. dept. religious studies San Diego State U., 1974—; mem. core faculty Calif. Sch. Profl. Psychology, San Diego, 1974-90. Author: The Goddess, 1981, Journey Through Menopause, 1987, Psyche's Sisters, 1988, Myths and Mysteries fo Same Sex Love Continuum, 1989; co-author: Face to Face to Face, 1975; editor: Mirrors of the Self (Tarcher), 1991; contbr. articles to profl. jours. Fellow NEH, 1982-83. Fellow Soc. Values in Higher Edn. (bd. dirs. 1966-81); mem. AAUP, Am. Acad. Religion (pres. 1973-74). Office: San Diego State U Dept Religious Studies San Diego CA 92182

DOWNING, DANIEL REX, minister; b. Louisville, Dec. 12, 1963; s. David Michael and Carole Joyce (Spears) D.; m. Merry Linda Alexander, Aug. 3, 1985; children: Carole Ann, Merry Emily. BA, Mercer U., 1985; MA in Religious Edn., Southwestern Bapt. Theo. Sem., 1988. Ordained to ministry Bapt. Ch., 1989. Recreation asst. Dawson Meml. Bapt. Ch., Birmingham, Ala., 1983-85; minister edn. and recreation First Bapt. Ch., Marietta, Okla., 1985-88; minister to youth First Bapt. Ch., Gainesville, Ga., 1988—; mem. Bapt. Student Union, Macon, Ga., 1981-85. Mem. Drug-Free Schs. Adv. Coun., Gainesville, 1989—; mem. Hall County Commn. on Children and Youth, Gainesville, 1990—. Mem. Chattahoochee Bapt. Assn. (youth com. Gainesville chpt. 1989—), So. Bapt. Religious Edn. Assn., Sigma Nu (pledge trainer 1984-85). Home: 3935 Summit Chase Gainesville GA 30506 Office: First Bapt Ch 751 Green St Gainesville GA 30501

DOWNS, DAVID RUTHERFORD, minister; b. Birmingham, Ala., Nov. 5, 1957; s. Glen and Beatrice (Roy) D.; m. Laurie Ann Smith, June 20, 1980; 1 child, David. BA cum laude, William Jennings Bryan Coll.; ThM magna cum laude, Dallas Theol. Sem., 1989, postgrad., 1991—. Lic. to ministry So. Bapt. Conv., 1975; ordained to ministry Bible Ch., 1990. Min. youth/music Grace Community Ch., Largo, Fl., 1975-83; assoc. pastor Redeemer Bible Ch., Ft. Worth, 1986-89; pastor Westminster Bible Ch., Henderson, Tex., 1989—. Author: Power Evangelism Exposed, 1988; co-author: God's View of Sex, 1991. Office: Westminster Bible Ch 1018 S Main St Henderson TX 75652 *Like the story of the Good Samaritan there are three ways to treat people: Beat 'em up, pass 'em up, or help 'em up. I like the last one.*

DOWNS, DAVID WILLIAM, minister, educator; b. Birmingham, Ala., Jan. 31, 1954; s. Orville Clinton and Eula Elizabeth (Reno) D.; m. Dorothy Susan Sanford, Dec. 18, 1976; children: Deidre Michelle, Drew Sanford. BA, Samford U., 1976; MDiv., So. Bapt. Theol. Sem., 1979, ThM, 1980, PhD, 1984; postgrad, Oxford U., 1981. Ordained to ministry, Bapt. Ch., 1978. Youth minister Wilsonville (Ala.) Bapt. Ch., 1976, First Bapt. Ch., Marietta, Ga., 1977, St. Matthew's United Meth. Ch., Louisville, 1977-78; pastor Macedonia Bapt. Ch., Madison, Ind., 1978-85, Edison (Ga.) Bapt. Ch., 1985—; adj. prof. theology Bellarmine Coll., Louisville, 1985. Contbr. Ency. So. Bapts., 1982, articles to profl. and religious jours. Active centennial pageant City of Edison, 1986; bd. dirs. nat. bd. So. Bapt. Alliance, 1988—. Named One of Outstanding Young Men of Am. Mem. Am. Soc. Ch. History, So. Bapt. Hist. Soc., Ga. Bapt. Hist. Soc. Democrat. Lodge: Lions. Office: Edison Bapt Ch Box 296 Edison GA 31746

DOWNS, STURDIE W., bishop. Bishop of Nicaragua Episcopal Ch., Managua. Office: Bishop Nicaragua, Apdo 1207, Managua JR, Nicaragua*

DOYAL, KERRY SHAWN, pastor; b. Jonesboro, Ga., Aug. 6, 1961; s. Ronald Mailon and Joan (Bartlett) D.; m. Robin Cornelius, Dec. 1, 1984; children: Karissa Annette, Kimsey William. AA, Clayton State Coll., Morrow, Ga., 1982; BA in Bible and Missions, Columbia (S.C.) Bible Coll., 1985; MDiv cum laude, Trinity Evang. Divinity Sch., Deerfield, Ill., 1990. Lic. to ministry Evang. Free Ch. Am., 1991. Asst. pastor 1st Evang. Free Ch., Bkyln., 1985-88; pastor, ch. planter Waukegan (Ill.) Evang. Free Ch., 1990—; dir. Christian edn. Lake Region Bible Ch., Round Lake, Ill., 1988-90. Publicity chmn. Coll. Polit. Union Clayton State Coll., 1981; prayer group leader Columbia Bible Coll., 1984. Mem. Greater Waukegan Ministerial Assn. Home and Office: 1022 Pacific Ave Waukegan IL 60085 *Objective truth exists. Its ultimate expression is in Scripture and personifed by Jesus Christ. If this were not so, all else would be vain and up for debate.*

DOYLE, FRANCIS XAVIER, religious organization administrator; b. Bklyn., July 13, 1933; s. Francis Xavier Sr. and Marie Louise (Farley) D.; m. Carole Helen Saunders, Aug. 15, 1959; children: Kevin, Brian, Nancy, Claire. AB, Holy Cross, 1955; JD, St. John's Law Sch., 1961; MS in Edn., Hofstra U., 1963. Bar: N.Y., 1963. Exec. dir. Nat. Cath. Devel. Conf., N.Y.C., 1968-71; asst. dir. govt. liaison Nat. Conf. Cath. Bishops/U.S. Cath. Conf., Washington, 1971-77, deputy dir. fin., 1977-78, dir. fin., 1978-84, assoc. gen. sec., 1984—; special agent FBI, Washington, 1961-62; spl. deputy atty. gen. N.Y. State, 1963-64. pres. parish coun. St. Francis Ch., Greenlawn, N.Y., 1969-70, St. Mark Ch., Vienna, Va., 1976-77; v.p. Kilmer Jr. High Sch. PTA, Vienna, 1974-75. Capt. USMC, 1955-63, Japan. Mem. State of N.Y. Bar, Am. Soc. Assn. Execs. Office: US Catholic Conf 3211 4th St NE Washington DC 20017

DOYLE, JAMES JOSEPH, priest, theology educator; b. Lynn, Mass., Mar. 29, 1923; s. James and Nellie (Cronin) D. AB, Boston Coll., 1943; STL, Cath. U. Am., 1951, MA, 1972. Ordained priest Roman Cath. Ch., 1950. Inst., asst. prof. Stonehill Coll., North Easton, Mass., 1951-60, acad. dean, 1955-60; assoc. prof. theology King's Coll., Wilkes-Barre, Pa., 1960, prof., 1968—, disting. svc. prof., 1983-85; rsch. assoc. Kennedy Inst., Georgetown U., Washington, 1974-76. Asst. editor Ency. Bioethics, 1978. Vice pres. Community Counseling Svcs., Wilkes-Barre, 1968—, M.L. King Com., Wilkes-Barre, 1970—; coord. Wyoming Valley Peace Com., Wilkes-Barre, 1980—. With AUS, 1943-45. Recipient Silverblatt award Wilkes-Barre chpt. Am. Jewish Com., 1978, 15-Yr. Svc. plaque Luzerne-Wyoming Mental Health-Mental Retardation Program, 1984. Mem. Coll. Theology Soc., Cath. Theol. Soc., Assn. for Religion and Intellectual Life, Torch Club, Theta Alpha Kappa (nat. sec. 1976—), Delta Epsilon Sigma. Home and Office: 133 N Franklin St Wilkes-Barre PA 18711

DOYLE, JAMES LEONARD, bishop; b. Chatham, Ont., Can., June 20, 1929; s. Herbert Lawrence and Mary Josephine (Ennett) D. B.A., U. Western Ont., 1950; D.D., St. Peters Sem., London, 1954. Ordained priest Roman Catholic Ch., 1954. Then consecrated bishop; asso. rector St. Peter's Cathedral, London, Ont., 1954-60; rector St. Peter's Cathedral, 1974-76; pastor Sacred Heart Ch., Windsor, Ont., 1960-66; prin. Brennan High Sch., Windsor, 1966-68; pastor Holy Name Ch., Windsor, 1968-74; bishop of Peterborough Ont., 1976—. Address: 350 Hunter St W, Box 175, Peterborough, ON Canada K9J 6Y8

DOYLE, LLOYD ALLEN, III, minister; b. Atlanta, Apr. 13, 1962; s. Lloyd Allen Jr. and Betty Glen (Barksdale) D.; m. Mary Clare Golson, May 21, 1988. BBA, Lambuth Coll., 1984; MDiv, Vanderbilt U., 1988. Ordained deacon United Meth. Ch., 1987; elder, 1990. Intern, asst. pastor Tulip St. United Meth. Ch., Nashville, 1986-87; intern chaplain VA Med. Ctr., Nashville, 1987-88; min. Evangelism First United Meth. Ch., Murray, Ky., 1988-90; pastor Cowell's Chapel and Shiloh Ch., Camden, Tenn., 1990—; cons. on baby boomers Memphis Annual Conf. United Meth. Ch., Jackson, Tenn., 1990—; bd. dirs. Benton County Ministerial Alliance, Camden. Vol. Habitat for Humanity, Murray, 1989; active Nat. Trust for Hist. Preservation, Washington, 1980—, Greenpeace, Washington, 1990—. Blakemore Trust fellow, 1987-88; Magee Christian Found. grantee, Lake Junaluska, N.C., 1987-88; named one of Outstanding Young Men of Am., Montgomery, Ala., 1990. Mem. Conf. Issues Group, Omicron Phi Tau, Kappa Sigma (treas. 1982-84). Office: Cowells Chapel Church 371 Natchez Trace Rd Camden TN 38320

DOYLE, SISTER MARY ANNE, religious organization administrator; b. Boston, Mar. 17, 1943; d. Walter Andrew and Loretta Mary (Burgoyne) D. AB in Math. cum laude, Regis Coll., 1967; MS in Nuclear Physics, Ohio State U., 1973, PhD in Nuclear Physics, 1976. Joined Congregation of Sisters of St. Joseph, Roman Cath. Ch., 1960. Lectr., asst. prof. physics Regis Coll., Weston, Mass., 1975-82, dir. research ctr., 1978-80, rsch. physicist rsch. ctr., 1980-85; asst. prof. Wellesley (Mass.) Coll., 1980-81; adminstrv. resident Carney Hosp., Boston, 1985-86; assoc. dir. Office of Synod Archdiocese Boston, 1986-89, dir. office of planning and rsch., 1989—; vis. scientist accelerator lab. U. Lowell, Mass., 1977-78; facilitator, cons. congregations of religious women, 1979—. Contbr. articles to profl. jours. Mem. Am. Geophys. Union, Am. Phys. Soc., Stoneham Citizens for Peace. Roman Catholic.

DOYLE, SISTER MARY DOLORES, academic administrator. Supt. of Cath. schs. Diocese of Brownsville, Tex. Office: Cath Schs Supt Box 2279 Brownsville TX 78522*

DOYLE, WILFRED EMMETT, retired bishop; b. Calgary, Alta., Can., Feb. 18, 1913; s. John Joseph and Mary (O'Neill) D. B.A., U. Alta, 1935; D.C.L., U. Ottawa, Ont., Can., 1949. Ordained priest Roman Cath. Ch., 1938; chancellor Archdiocese Edmonton, Alta., Can., 1949-58; bishop Nelson, B.C., Can., 1958-89, bishop emeritus, 1989—; Chmn. bd. govs. Notre Dame U., Nelson, 1963-74. Address: 10661-82 Ave, Edmonton, AB Canada T6E 2A6

DRABISKA, FRANK JOHN, priest, educator; b. Ellwood, Pa., Oct. 7, 1950; s. Martin and Eugenia (Galat) D. BA in Philosophy, Duquesne U., 1972, postgrad., 1991—; MDiv, St. Francis Coll., 1976. Ordained priest Roman Cath. Ch., 1976. Parochial vicar Diocese of Pitts., 1976—, deanery dir. religious edn., master catechist, 1982—. Roman Catholic. Home and Office: 7446 McClure Ave Pittsburgh PA 15218

DRAHMANN, BROTHER THEODORE, academic administrator; b. Perham, Minn., June 7, 1926; s. Vincent Henry Drahmann and Louise Cecile Speiser. BS in History, St. Mary's Coll., Winona, Wis., 1949, DEd (hon.), 1981; M in Social and Indsl. Relations, Loyola U., Chgo., 1956; degree in edn. adminstrn., Coll. St. Thomas, St. Paul, 1974. Joined Cath. order Bros. of the Christian Schs. Tchr. De La Salle High Sch., Chgo., 1949-56, prin., 1956-62; counselor St. Mary's Coll., 1963-66; prin. Cretin High Sch., St. Paul, 1966-70; supr. schs. Christian Bros., St. Paul, 1970-72; supt. schs. Archdiocese of St. Paul/Mpls., 1972-76; dir. grad. studies Coll. St. Thomas, 1978-80; pres. Christian Bros. U., Memphis, 1980—. Author: (manual) Catholic School Principal-Outline for Action, 1980, (brochure) Governance & Administration in Catholic Schools, 1985. Trustee St. Mary's Coll., 1972-81, Lewis U., Romeoville, Ill, 1982—. Named Disting. Grad. Coll. St. Thomas, 1984, Oustanding Tennessean Gov. of Tenn., Nashville, 1988. Mem. Nat. Cath. Ednl. Assn. (Outstanding Educator of Yr. award 1985, bd. dirs. 1986—), Assn. Cath. Colls. and Univs. (bd. dirs. 1985—), NCCJ (chmn. bd. Memphis chpt. 1980—, Humanitarian award 1990), Econ. Club Memphis (bd. dirs. 1988—), Rotary (bd. dirs. Memphis club 1984-89, pres. 1987-88), KC, Mil. and Hospitaller Order St. Lazarus Jerusalem (knight comdr. 1991—), Pi Gamma Mu, Alpha Kappa Delta, Delta Epsilon Sigma. Avocations: reading, jogging, cycling. Home and Office: Christian Bros U 650 E Parkway S Memphis TN 38104

DRAKE, CHESTER LEE, minister; b. New Brunswick, N.J., Dec. 2, 1946; s. Chester LeRoy and Elizabeth (Reed) D.; m. Deborah Jane Smith, July 9, 1977; children: Timothy, Rebekah. BA, Covington Sem., 1982, MA, 1984, DD, 1986, DST, 1988, PhD, 1988; BA, Miami Christian Coll., 1990. Founder, pastor Broward Community Chapel, Ft. Lauderdale, Fla., 1971—; S.E. Regional coord. Moody Bible Inst., Chgo., 1983-88; aftercare counselor T.M. Ralph Plantation funeral Home, Plantation, Fla., 1990—; chaplain Fla. Funeral Dirs., Tallahasse, 1982—, Christian Funeral Dirs., Pahokee, Fla., 1982—. Author: Helping the Hurting, 1987, Grief Counseling: Lost Art of the Clergy, 1988. Mem. Kiwanis (bd. dirs. 1981-85, treas. 1983-85 Plantation/Jacaranda chpt.). Home and Office: 11501 Rexmere Blvd Fort Lauderdale FL 33325

DRANE, JOHN WILLIAM, minister, religion educator; b. Hartlepool, Eng., Oct. 17, 1946; s. John Wallace and Marjorie (Ireland) D.; m. Olive Mary Fleming, Sept. 16, 1967; children: Andrew James Jonathan, Mark Samuel Paul, Alethea Joy Frances. MA with 1st class honors, U. Aberdeen, Scotland, 1969; PhD, U. Manchester, Eng., 1972. Ordained to ministry Bapt. Ch., 1970. Minister Bapt. Ch., Eng., 1971-73; prof. religious studies U. Stirling, Scotland, 1973—; mission convener Scottish Chs. Coun., 1984-90; mem. joint ministerial bd. Bapt. Union Scotland, 1985—; mem. evangelism com. Brit. Coun. Chs., 1985-90; cons. evangelism World Coun. Chs., 1990—. Author: Introducing the New Testament, 1986, Introducing the Old Testament, 1987, What Is the New Age Saying to the Church?, 1991; contbr. articles to profl. and religious jours. Mem. Studiorium Novi Testamenti Societas, Soc. Authors. Avocations: snow skiing, beekeeping, hill walking, boating, travel. Home: 39 Fountain Rd, Bridge of Allan FK9 4AU, Scotland Office: U Stirling, Dept Religious Studies, Stirling FK9 4LA, Scotland *Too many Christian evangelists today are like Rambo—shoot down the "opposition" at any price. Jesus always affirmed people and lifted them up. We need more Christians like that—we can do without Rambo.*

DRAPER, ALBERT LEE, minister; b. Beaumont, Tex., July 20, 1938; s. Chester Oren and Mary Elizabeth (Cash) D.; m. Linda Lou Burgess, Jan. 30, 1960; children: Lori Rae, Derek Jackson. BS, U. Houston, 1964; MRE, Southwestern Bapt. Theol. Sem., 1968. Ordained to ministry So. Bapt. Conv., 1959. Pastor Joy Bapt. Ch., Gladewater, Tex., 1959-62, Lakeview Park Bapt. Ch., Houston, 1962-65, Justin (Tex.) Bapt. Ch., 1966-69, First Bapt. Ch., Wylie, Tex., 1969—; mem. exec. bd. Bapt. Gen. Conv. Tex., 1973—, cons. lifestyle evangelism, 1975—; pres. Wylie Ministerial Alliance, 1973-75; chaplain Wylie Vol. Fire Dept., 1969-79; moderator exec. bd. Collin Bapt. Assn., McKinney, Tex., 1975—, chmn. missions com., 1983-84, mem. steering com., 1984. Field rep. Salvation Army, Wylie, 1970—; v.p. Wylie Community Edn. Adv. Coun., 1976—; bd. dirs. Tex. Alcohol Narcotics Edn., Dallas; mem. citizens adv. com. Wylie Pub. Sch., 1873-74; key communicator Wylie Independent Sch. Dist., 1989-91; pres. Wylie Christian Community Care Ctr., 1990-91; sec. Project Care Adult Adv. Bd. Named Wylie Area Citzen of Yr., 1980. Home: 100 Tanglewood Ct Wylie TX 75098 Office: First Bapt Ch 100 N 1st St Wylie TX 75098

DRAPER, DAVID EUGENE, seminary president; b. Hagerstown, Md., Feb. 6, 1949; s. James Thomas and Irene Virginia (Seylar) D.; m. Linda Marie Mills, June 26, 1971; 1 child, Andrew Thomas. BS, Frostburg (Md.) State Coll., 1971; MDiv, Winebrenner Sem., Findlay, Ohio, 1979; MEd, Bowling Green (Ohio) U., 1985, PhD, 1988. Ordained to ministry Chs. of God, Gen. Conf., 1978. Pastor Mt. Pleasant Ch. of God, Mt. Victory, Ohio, 1976-79; assoc. in ministry Chs. of God, Findlay, 1979-82; dir. devel. Winebrenner Sem., Findlay, 1982-85, v.p., 1985-88, pres., 1988—; trustee U. Findlay, 1989—; mem. Fellowship of Evang. Sem. Pres. Co-author: Bound but Free, 1978. Adv. bd. Trust Corps Bank, Findlay, 1987-89. Lilly grantee, 1987. Democrat. Home: 3218 St Andrews Dr Findlay OH 45840 Office: Winebrenner Sem 701 E Melrose Ave Findlay OH 45840 *Life is a matter of priorities. I believe these should include in order of importance: God, family, others, self. I am surrounded by people who have chosen these priorities and because of them I am a better person.*

DRAPER, JAMES THOMAS (JIMMY DRAPER), clergyman; b. Hartford, Ark., Oct. 10, 1935; s. James T. D.; m. Carol Ann Floyd, 1956; children—Randy, Bailey, Terri. B.A., Baylor U., 1957; B.D., Southwestern Bapt. Theol. Sem., M.Div.; hon. degree, Howard Payne U., Brownwood, Tex., Dallas Bapt. Coll.; D.D. hon., Campbell U., Buies Creek, N.C. Ordained to ministry Baptist Ch.; pastor Steel Hollow Bapt. Ch., Bryan, Tex., Iredell Bapt. Ch., Tex., Temple Bapt. Ch., Tyler, Tex., Univ. Park Bapt. Ch., San Antonio, Tex., Red Bridge Bapt. Ch., Kansas City, Mo., First So. Bapt. Ch., Del City, Okla.; assoc. pastor First Bapt. Ch., Dallas, pastor, Euless, Tex., 1975—; mem. adminstrv. com. Bapt. Gen. Conv., Tex., mem. exec. bd., mem. missions funding com., mem. exec. dir. search com.; pres. So. Bapt. Conv., 1982-84, So. Baptist Conv. Pastors Conf., 1979—; trustee So. Bapt. Conv. Annuity Bd.; preacher numerous convs., confs. Author 16 books. Contbr. articles to religious jours. Office: First Baptist Ch PO Box 400 Euless TX 76039

DREIBELBIS, JOHN L., priest; b. Miles City, Mont., Dec. 1, 1934; s. John Calvin and Regina Theresa (Pestka) D.; m. Patricia Ann Wagner, June 11, 1960; children: Anne, Catherine, David, Rachel. Student, U. Chgo., 1952-56, PhD, 1990; MDiv, Seabury-Western Sem., 1959. Ordained priest Episcopal Ch., 1959. Curate St. Matthew's Episcopal Ch., Evanston, 1959-60; pastor Good Samaritan Ch., Oak Park, Ill., 1960-63, Christ Episcopal Ch., Chgo., 1964-71; rector Grace Episcopal Ch., Huron, S.D., 1971-75; asst. St. Christopher's Ch., Oak Park, 1981-84, Grace Ch., Oak Park, 1986—; dir. profl. programs, continuing edn. U. Chgo., 1983-86, dir. mgmt. devel. seminars U. Chgo., 1989—, mem. faculty, mgmt. devel. seminars, 1977—; mem. coun. Episcopal Diocese of Chgo., 1963-66, chmn. Commn. on Met. Affairs, 1968-71; mem. bishop and coun. Episcopal Diocese of S.D., 1971-75; prin. investigator Lilly Endowment Diocese Chgo. Rsch. Project, 1988-90; cons. educator Borg-Warner Fin. Svcs., Chgo., 1977-88; dir. White Farm Equip. Co., Oak Brook, 1983-85. Del. Woodlawn Orgn., Chgo., 1964-68. Mem. Episcopal Clergy Assn. Chgo. (nat. del. 1971, pres. 1970-71). Office: U Chgo 5835 Kimbark Ave Chicago IL 60637 *Forty odd years ago, George Kennan and others taught us that peace is the hardest thing for dictators to endure, provided aggression is contained, and the Russian empire crumbled. Have we learned anything from this?.*

DREISBACH, ALBERT RUSSEL, JR., priest; b. Watertown, N.Y., Apr. 27, 1934; s. Albert Russel and Florence Agnew (Young) D.; m. Jane Adelaide Corey, June 1, 1957; children: Diane Corey Dreisbach Weber, Daniel Agnew. AB, Wesleyan U., Middletown, Conn., 1956; MDiv, Union Theol. Sem., N.Y.C., 1962. Ordained to ministry Episcopalian Ch. as deacon, 1962, as priest 1963. Asst. to dean Cathedral of St. John, Wilmington, Del., 1962-65; assoc. dir. Episcopal Soc. for Cultural and Racial Unity, Atlanta, 1965-67, exec. dir., 1967-70; rector Ch. of Incarnation, Atlanta, 1973-85; reader Nat. Bd. Exam. Chaplains, 1974-78; dean, editor Lay Readers Acad. Lay Reader's Manual, 1980; exec. dir. Atlanta Internat. Ctr. for Continuing Study Shroud of Tourin, 1985—; liaison to bd. Shroud of Turin Rsch. Project, Amston, Conn., 1981—. Contbr. articles to religious publs. 1st Lt. USMC, 1956-59. Mem. Internat. Platform Assn. Democrat. Avocations: photography, international travel. Home and Office: 2657 Vance Dr East Point GA 30344

DRENNAN, HARRY JOSEPH, minister; b. Dallas, Jan. 29, 1933; s. Harry Brown and Ora (Ware) D.; m. Elva Phyllis Rice, Dec. 13, 1952; children: Brian Joseph, Kathryn Phyllis, Paul David. BS, U. Houston, 1957; ThM, ThD, Internat. Sem., 1986; DRE, Northgate Grad. Sch., 1987; EdD, Cornerstone U. and Sem., Jerusalem, 1990; PhD in Psychology, Emmanual Bapt. U., 1991. Lic. profl. counselor, temperment therapist. Assoc. pastor Evangelistic Temple, Houston, 1971-87; dir. Teen Challenge Ministry, Houston, 1972-79, 700 Club Ministry, Houston, 1973-79, Today's World Ministry Counseling Ctr., Houston, 1976-80; pres. Cornerstone Sem. and Univ., Jerusalem, Israel, 1986—, Hawaii, 1988—. Author: (books) Man's Relationship to Spirit, 1987, Pheumatology, 1988, Hermenutics, 1989, A Study of the Pentateuch, 1990; (O.T. survey) Plus, 1991. With USN, 1952-56, Korea. Recipient Man-of-the-Yr. award, Ford Motor Co., Phila., 1965. Mem. Nat. Christian Counselor Assn. (dir. 1989—), World Ministry Fellowship Counseling (dir. 1990—), Cornerstone Ministrial Assn. (pres. 1988—). Home: 14619 Moss Creek Ln Cypress TX 77429 Office: Living Stones Ch 26605 Peden Rd Magnolia TX 77355

DRENNAN, MERRILL WILLIAM, clergyman; b. Washington, Oct. 17, 1915; s. Milton William and Balbena (Altman) D.; m. Frances Emily Dunn, Apr. 26, 1937; children—Marilyn Drennan Brus, Kathleen; m. Arianne Hadley Lowell, Oct. 3, 1987. B.C.S., Southeastern U., 1939; A.B., U. Md., 1950; M.Div., Westminster (now Wesley) Theol. Sem., 1953; D.D., Western Md. Coll., 1970. Ordained to ministry Meth. Ch., 1953. With banking dept. Am. Security and Trust Co., Washington, 1933-37; office mgr. Brewood Engravers and Printers, Washington, 1937-42; spl. agt. FBI, 1942-48; minister in Ashton, Md., 1950-54; minister Millian Meml. Ch., Rockville, Md., 1954-65; supt. Balt. Southeast Dist., 1965-67; sr. minister Met. Meml. United Meth. Ch., Washington, 1967-74; supt. Washington W. Dist., Balt. Conf., 1974-79, assoc. council dir., 1979-83;; del. Northeastern Jurisdictional Conf. Meth. Ch., 1964, 68, 72, 76, 80, Gen. Conf. United Meth. Ch., Dallas, 1968, Atlanta, 1972, Portland, Oreg., 1976, Indpls., 1980. Pres. Deering Woods Condominiums, 1984-85, Park Ave. Residence Lodge, Balt., 1985-87. Home: 3505 Woodbine St Chevy Chase MD 20815

DRESCHER, JOHN MUMMAU, bishop, author; b. Manheim, Pa., Sept. 15, 1928; s. John L. and Anna (Mummau) D.; m. Betty Keener, Aug. 30, 1952; children: John Ronald, Sandra Kay, Rose Marie, Joseph Dean, David Carl. Student, Elizabethtown Coll., 1947-49; A.B., Eastern Mennonite Coll., 1951, Th.B., 1953; B.D., Goshen Bibl. Sem., 1954. Ordained to ministry Mennonite Ch., 1954. Pastor Crown Hill Mennonite Ch., Rittman, Ohio, 1954-62, Scottdale Mennonite Ch., Pa., 1973-78; editor Gospel Herald weekly mag., 1962-73; bishop Ohio, Eastern Mennonite Conf., 1959-64; asst. moderator Mennonite Ch., 1967-69, bishop, 1959-64, moderator, 1969-71; pastor Zion Mennonite Ch., Broadway, Va., 1989—; writer, lectr., 1979—; mem. faculty Eastern Mennonite Sem., Harrisonburg, Va., 1979—; pres. Ohio Memmonite Mission Bd., 1956-62; overseer Va. Mennonite Conf., 1985—. Author: Meditations for the Newly Married, 1969, Blessings By Your Bedside, 1969, Heartbeats, 1970, Now is the Time to Love, 1970, Follow Me, 1971, In Grief's Lone Hour, 1971, May Your Marriage be a Happy One, 1971, Spirit Fruit, 1974, Talking It Over, 1975, I Lift My Eyes, 1976, Seven Things Children Need, 1976, The Way of the Cross and Resurrection, 1978, If I Were Starting My Family Again, 1979, For Better-For Worse, 1979, When Opposites Attract, 1980, What Should Parents Expect, 1980, Testimony of Triumph, 1980, When You Think You Are in Love, 1981, You Can Plan a Good Marriage, 1982, Why I am a Conscientious Objector, 1982, If We Were Starting Our Marriage Again, 1985, When Your Child, 1986, God's Presence in Time of Trouble, 1989, The Lord is Near, 1989; contbr. articles to mags. and jours. Office: Zion Mennonite Ch Broadway VA 22815

DREYFUS, ALFRED STANLEY, rabbi; b. Youngstown, Ohio, Jan. 31, 1921; s. Marcel and Isabella (Mervis) D.; m. Marianne Cecilia Berlak, July 25, 1950; children—James Nathaniel, Richard Baeck. B.A., U. Cin., 1942; B. Hebrew Letters, Hebrew Union Coll., Cin., 1942, M. Hebrew Letters, 1946, Ph.D., 1951, D.D., 1971. Rabbi Terre Haute, Ind., 1951-56, Galveston, Tex., 1956-65; rabbi Union Temple, Bklyn., 1965-79; lectr. liturgy and commentaries N.Y. Sch., Hebrew Union Coll.-Jewish Inst. Religion, 1966—; dir. placement Rabbinical Placement Commn., 1979-91; pres. Assembly Tex. Rabbis, 1962-63, Bklyn. Assn. Reform Rabbis, 1967-68, Bklyn. Bd. Rabbis, 1970-72; mem. governing body World Union Progressive Judaism, 1967—; bd. govs. N.Y. Bd. Rabbis, 1967-83; co-chmn. Cath. Jewish Relations Com., Bklyn.-Queens Diocese, 1974-79; bd. dirs. Synagogue Council Am., 1968-72. Pres. Friends of Rosenberg Library, Galveston, 1961-62, bd. dirs., 1962-65; chmn. home service of Galveston chpt. ARC, 1956-65; vice chmn. Bklyn. chpt., 1973-79; hon. chmn. Bklyn. div. United Hosp. campaign, 1965-79. Served as chaplain AUS, 1953-55; lt. col. Res. ret. Mem. Central Conf. Am. Rabbis, Assn. Jewish Chaplains (pres. 1973-75), N.Y. Assn. Reform Rabbis (pres. 1975-77). Clubs: Masons (32 deg.), Shriners, Elks, B'nai B'rith. Home: 9 Prospect Park W Brooklyn NY 11215 Office: 192 Lexington Ave New York NY 10016

DRIEDGER, FLORENCE GAY, social agency executive, social work educator, consultant; b. Plum Coulee, Man., Can., Feb. 21, 1933; d. Jake and Gertrude (Harms) Hooge; m. Otto Driedger, Oct. 10, 1954; children: Joan, Karen. BA, Bethel Coll., Newton, Kans., 1954; MSW, McGill U., Montreal, Que., Can., 1958. Social worker Dept. Social Svcs., Govt. of Sask., Saskatoon, Can., 1955-56, Prince Albert, 1958-59; social worker, supr. dept. social svcs. Dept. Social Svcs., Govt. of Sask., Moose Jaw, 1959-62; social worker Dept. Social Svcs., Govt. of Sask., Swift Current, 1964-65; coord. edn. Dept. Social Svcs., Govt. of Sask., Regina, 1967-80; co-coord. Conf. Mennonites Can., Nat. Ministries, Winnipeg, Man., 1980-83; exec. dir. Family Svc. Bur. of Regina, 1983—; social worker Family Svcs., Montreal, 1956; mem., chairperson Family Life Sask., 1971-81; mem. membership bd. confs. Mennonites in Sask. and Mennonites in Can., 1961-80; moderator Gen. Conf. Mennonite Ch., Newton, 1986—. Recipient Women's award YWCA, 1985. Mem. Can. Coun. Children and Youth, Can. Assn. Social Workers (exec. com. Ottawa div. 1983-85), Sask. Assn. Social Workers (pres. 1980-83), Family Svc. Sask. (exec. dir., chairperson subcom. 1987—). Home: 3833 Montague St, Regina, SK Canada S4S 3J6 Office: Family Svc Bur, 2020 Halifax St, Regina, SK Canada S4P 1T7

DRIGGERS, RAYMOND ROLAND, minister; b. Coleman, Fla., May 2, 1923; s. John Jonas and Mable L. D.; m. Mary Pearl Golden, Jan. 25, 1946; children: Sharon Mary Driggers Blanton, Larry Raymond. BA, Southeastern Bible Coll., 1966; postgrad. in edn., U. Miss., 1969-76. Ordained to ministry, 1955. Pastor 1st Assembly, Coleman, Fla., 1952, Polk City, Fla., 1953-55; asst. pastor Auburndale (Fla.) 1st Assembly, 1955-62; pastor 1st Assembly, Arcadia, Fla., 1964-65; asst. pastor 1st Assembly, Winter Haven, Fla., 1973—; chaplain, dist chartering officer, Royal Rangers, Winter Haven. Contbr. articles to various publs. Srs. coord., Cypress Cathedral, Winter Haven. Home: 110 Rose St Auburndale FL 33823

DRISCOLL, SISTER BRIGID, college president; b. N.Y.C.; d. Daniel Driscoll and Delia Duffy. B in Math., Edn., Marymount Manhattan Coll., 1954; M in Math., Cath. U., 1957; PhD in Math., CUNY, 1967; EdD (hon.), Siena Coll. Joined Religious of Sacred Heart of Mary, Roman Cath. Ch., 1954. Prof. math., assoc. acad. dean, dir. continuing edn. Marymount Coll., Tarrytown, N.Y., founder Weekend Coll., 1975, pres., 1979—; mem. Commr. of Edn.'s Adv. Council on Post-Secondary Edn. in N.Y. State; trustee Commn. on Ind. Colls. and Univs. Bd. dirs. Girl Scouts U.S., Phelps Meml. Hosp. Ctr., North Tarrytown, N.Y., Axe-Houghton Funds; bd. dirs. Westchester/Putnam chpt. United Way, mem. nat. vol. involvement com. 2d Century Initiative; mem. Statue of Liberty/Ellis Island Commn.; trustee Marymount Sch., N.Y.C. Named Woman of Yr. Sleepy Hollow C. of C., 1982; honored for disting. service Westchester (N.Y.) chpt. NCCJ; NASA fellow, 1967. Mem. Assn. Cath. Colls. and Univs. (bd. dirs., chairwoman Neylan Commn.), Commn. on Ind. Colls. and Univs. (trustee). Office: Marymount Coll Office of Pres Tarrytown NY 10591-3796

DRISCOLL, CECIL LILLIAN, retired religion educator; b. Apr. 23, 1915; d. Andrew Melville and Linnie (DeWeese) D. AB, Cascade Coll., 1948. Ordained to ministry Ky. Mt. Holiness Assn., 1941, transferred to Faith Missionary Assn., 1953. Co-pastor Ky. Mt. Holiness Assn., Vancleve, 1940-41; missionary World Gospel Mission, Honduras, 1943-48, Cuba, 1950-60; refugee worker Miami, Fla., 1961-63; mem. faculty Hobe Sound (Fla.) Bible Coll., 1963-72, 73-88, ret., 1988; with Pilgrim Pub. House, Indpls., summers 1960-61. Author: Cloud By Day; Fire By Night, 1983; (play) The Message of Christmas, 1947; asst. editor religious periodical The Torch, 1970-87; contbr. articles, lessons to religious publs. Republican. Home: PO Box 1065 Hobe Sound FL 33475 *By allowing the Holy Spirit to work in our hearts as He desires to do, we are made free indeed. Our wills are brought into harmony with the Divine will. Thus, the inner struggle is ended, relieving life of much of its pressure. We enjoy a peace hitherto unknown. This experience God has for each of His children.*

DRISCOLL, DONALD THOMAS, priest; b. Bronx, N.Y., Nov. 17, 1931; s. John Francis and Helen Kathleen (McArdle) D.; student St. Jerome's Coll., Kitchener, Ont., Can., 1950-52; A.B. in Philosophy, St. Joseph's Sem. Coll., 1960; M.S. Ed. in Counseling and Personnel, Fordham U., 1977. Ordained priest Roman Catholic Ch., 1964; expediter Ruben H. Donnelly Corp., Mt. Vernon, N.Y., 1953-56; parish minister, S.I., N.Y., 1964-65, Larchmont, N.Y., 1965-68; dir. guidance and counseling Bishop Dubois High Sch. in Harlem, N.Y.C., 1968-76; counselor jr. year students Cardinal Hayes High Sch., Bronx, N.Y., 1976-77; dir. evangelization project Iona Coll., New Rochelle, N.Y., 1977-80; dir. guidance and counseling Moore Cath. High Sch., 1980-82; counselor Cathedral High Sch., N.Y.C., 1982-86; appointed R.C. Chaplain Rockland Psychiatric Ctr., Orangeburg, N.Y., 1986— ; adj. instr. Marymount Coll., 1980—; cons. unwed mothers shelter, N.Y.C.; Rockland County Human Rights Commn., 1988—. Served with U.S. Army, 1956-58. Cert. neuropsychiat. technician; lic. cert. sch. counselor, N.Y. State. Mem. N.Y.C. Personnel and Guidance Assn. (chmn. ethics com, bd. dirs.), Nat. Cath. Guidance Conf. (bd. dirs., awards com., program chmn. N.Y.C. nat. conv. 1975, pres. 1977), Am. Coll. Personnel Assn., Am. Sch. Counselor Assn., Assn. for Measurement and Evaluation in Guidance, Nat. Assn. for Religious and Value Issues in Counseling (pres. 1978), Am., N.Y. State, Fordham personnel and guidance assns., Assn. for Counselor Edn. and Supervision, Nat. Vocat. Guidance Assn., Assn. for Humanistic Edn. and Devel., Am. Rehab. Counseling Assn., Nat. Employment Counselors Assn., Assn. for Non-White Concerns in Personnel and Guidance, Assn. for Specialist in Group Work. Office: Our Lady Queen Peace Chapel Rockland Psychiat Ctr Orangeburg NY 10962

DRISCOLL, JOHN GERARD, college president; b. N.Y.C., Apr. 17, 1933; s. John P. and Mary T. (Kennedy) D. B.S., Iona Coll., 1954; M.S., St. John's U., 1957; Ph.D., Columbia U., 1969; D.Sc., Coll. New Rochelle, 1971. Tchr. elem. schs. Rice High Sch., 1956-57, St. Joseph Sch., Antigua, 1957-61, Power Meml. Sch., 1961-65; prof. math. Iona Coll., New Rochelle, N.Y., 1965—; asst. to pres. Iona Coll., 1969-71, pres., 1971—; bd. dirs. Chase N.B.W. Bank, City Harvest, Inc., N.Y. Trustee St. Joseph's Sem. and Sch. Theology, Yonkers, N.Y.; bd. dirs. Drexel Burnham Scholarship Fund, New Rochelle Hosp. Med. Ctr., Nat. Com. Bishops and Pres., Assn. Colls. and Univs. State N.Y.; bd. dirs. Irish Am. Sports Found. Mem. World Trade Inst. Office: Iona Coll 715 North Ave New Rochelle NY 10801

DRISCOLL, THOMAS JOHN, deacon; b. Rochester, N.Y., July 14, 1949; s. John Joseph and Dorothy (Doscher) D.; m. Michele B. Szembrot, June 7, 1974; children: Brendan, Kevin, Padraic, Aisling. BA in Sociology, St. John Fisher Coll., 1971; MA in Theology, St. John's U., 1977; D Ministry, Colgate Rochester Div. Sch., 1987. Cert. religious edn.; ordained deacon Roman Cath. Ch., 1984. Dir. religious edn. St. James Ch., Rochester, N.Y., 1973-74; tchr. Our Lady of Mercy High Sch., Rochester, 1973-74; dir. religious edn. St. Jerome Ch., East Rochester, N.Y., 1974-80; minister Christian formation St. Louis Ch., Pittsford, N.Y., 1980—; chairperson Diocesan Liturgical Commn., Diocese of Rochester, 1978-81, instr. permanent deacon program, 1990—; vis. lectr. ministry studies St. Bernard's Inst., Rochester, 1990—; founder, dir. adult edn. program Spirituality Faire, 1989—. Mem. Religious Edn. Assn., Friends of Creation Spirituality, Pittsford Clergy Assn., Comaltas Ceoltiori Eireann. Home: 105 School St Victor NY 14564 Office: St Louis Ch 46 S Main St Pittsford NY 14534

DRISKILL, JAMES LAWRENCE, minister; b. Rustburg, Va., Aug. 18, 1920; s. Elijah Hudnall and Annie Farr (Carwile) D.; m. Ethel Lillian Cassel, May 29, 1949; children: Edward Lawrence, Mary Lillian. BA, Pa. State U., 1946, BD, San Francisco Theol. Sem., 1949; ThM, Princeton Sem., 1957; S.T.D., San Francisco Theol. Sem., 1969. Ordained minister in Presbyn. Ch., 1949. Missionary Presbyn. Ch. USA, Japan, 1949-72; stated supply pastor Madison Square Presbyn. Ch., San Antonio, 1973; minister Highland Presbyn. Ch., Maryville, Tenn., 1973-82; supply pastor of Japanese-Am. chs. Presbyn. Ch. USA, Long Beach, Calif., Hollywood, Calif., Altadena, Calif., 1984—; vis. prof. religion dept. Trinity U., 1972-73. Contbr. articles to profl. jours. Mem. Sierra Club, Calif., 1988—, Nat. Parks and Conservation Assn., 1989—, Am. Farmland Trust, 1989—; trustee Osaka (Japan) Girls Sch., 1952-65, Seikyo Gakuen Christian Sch., Japan, 1953—. With USN, 1943-46. Mem. Am. Acad. Religion, Presbyn. Writers Guild. Democrat. Home and Office: 1420 Santo Domingo Ave Duarte CA 91010 *Experience has taught me that, ultimately, the meaning and value of a person's life is determined by the quality of one's personal relationships, especially by the quality of one's relationship to God.*

DRISKILL, JOSEPH DENVER, minister; b. Peoria, Ill., Jan. 7, 1946; s. Joseph Abraham and Evelyn Jane (Skinner) D.; m. Anne Louise Cummings, June 2, 1971 (div. 1979); m. Leslie Jane Bryant, July 27, 1985. BA, Culver-Stockton Coll., 1968; MDiv, Vanderbilt U. Div. Sch., 1971; MA, U. Regina, Can., 1976; postgrad., Grad. Theol. Union, 1988—. Ordained to ministry Christian Ch. (Disciples of Christ), 1971. Min. Mt. Zion Christian Ch., Hannibal, Mo., 1965-68, Union Chapel Christian Ch., Center, Mo., 1965-68, Marion (Ky.) Christian Ch., 1969-71, Regina (Sask., Can.) Ave. Christian Ch., 1971-75; chaplain U. Western Ont., London, Can., 1976-88; lectr. Huron Coll., London, 1983-88; asst. to dean Disciples Sem. Found., 1990—; exec. Regina Gen. Ministerial Assn., 1974-76; mem. com. on union and joint mission Anglican United and Disciples Chs. Can., 1972-75; mem. cons. com. Sask. Coun. for Internat. Coop. Govt. and Agy., 1974-76. Exec. Regina Housing Assn., 1973-75. Mem. Can. Assn. Pastoral Edn., Am. Acad. Religion. Home: 817 Pomona Ave El Cerrito CA 94530 Office: Pacific Sch Religion Disciples Sem Found Rm 40, 1798 Scenic Berkeley CA 94709

DRIVER, TOM FAW, theology educator, writer; b. Johnson City, Tenn., May 31, 1925; s. Leslie Rowles and Sarah (Broyles) D.; m. Anne L. Barstow, June 7, 1952; children: Katharine Anne, Paul Barstow, Susannah Ambrose. A.B., Duke U., 1950; M.Div., Union Theol. Sem., 1953; Ph.D., Columbia U., 1957; D.Litt., Denison U., 1970. Ordained to ministry United Meth. Ch., 1951. Dir. youth work Riverside Ch., N.Y.C., 1955-56; faculty Union Theol. Sem., N.Y.C., 1956—; Paul J. Tillich prof. theology and culture Union Theol. Sem., 1973—; drama critic Christian Century, 1956-62, Sta. WBAI-FM, 1960-61, The Reporter, 1963-64; vis. assoc. prof. English Columbia U., 1964-65; vis. assoc. prof. religion Barnard Coll., 1965-66, Fordham U., 1967; cons. humanities and arts Coll. Old Westbury (N.Y.), 1970; William Evans vis. prof. religion U. Otago, N.Z., 1976; vis. prof. religion Vassar Coll., 1978, Montclair State Coll., 1981; vis. prof. English lit. Doshisha U., Kyoto, Japan, 1983. Author: libretto for oratorio The Invisible Fire, 1957; The Sense of History in Greek and Shakespearean Drama, 1960, Jean Genet, 1966, Romantic Quest and Modern Query: A History of The Modern Theater, 1970, Patterns of Grace: Human Experience as Word of God, 1977, Christ in a Changing World: Toward an Ethical Christology, 1981, The Magic of Ritual: Our Need for Liberating Rites that Transform Our Lives and Our Communities, 1991; editor: (with Robert Pack) Poems of Doubt and Belief, 1964; also articles. Bd. dirs. dept. worship and arts Nat. Council Chs., 1958- 63, Found. for Arts, Religion and Culture, 1963-67. Served with AUS, 1943-46. Kent fellow, 1953; Guggenheim fellow, 1962-63. Mem. Am. Acad. Religion, New Haven Theol. Group, Soc. Values in Higher Edn., AAUP, ACLU, Pen, Clergy and Laity Concerned, Dem. Socialists of Am., Phi Beta Kappa, Omicron Delta Kappa. Home: 90 LaSalle St New York NY 10027

DROBENA, THOMAS JOHN, minister, educator; b. Chgo., Aug. 23, 1934; s. Thomas and Suzanne (Durec) D.; m. Wilma S. Kucharek, Dec. 27, 1980; 1 child, Thomas Samuel. BA, Valparaiso U., 1964; ThB, Concordia Theol. Sem., 1961, MDiv, 1974; MA, Hebrew U., Jerusalem, 1968; PhD, Calif. Grad. Sch. Theology, 1975; MST, Luth. Theol. Sem., 1986. Ordained to ministry Evang. Luth. Ch. in Am. English pastor Redeemer Luth. Ch., Jerusalem, 1967-68; prin. St. Mark's Luth. Ch., Bklyn., 1968-69; pastor Ascension Luth. Ch., Binghamton, N.Y., 1969-78, Holy Emmanuel, Mahoney City, Pa., 1981-86; pastor St. Johns, St. Clair, Pa., 1981-86, Nanticoke, Pa., 1981-86; co-pastor Holy Trinity Luth. Ch., Torrington, Conn., 1986—; adj. prof. SUNY, Binghamton, 1975-77; chairperson Global Missions, Evang. Luth. Ch. in Am., Chgo., 1985—; v.p., treas. Slavic Heritage Inst., Torrington, 1965—. Co-author: Heritage of the Slavs, 1976; contbr. articles to profl. jours. Chaplain Civil Air Patrol USAFA, Conn., 1964—; bd. dirs. ARC, 1986—; v.p. Crimestoppers, 1988—, New Eng. Hist. Soc., 1990—. Grantee U.S. State Dept., Jerusalem, 1967-68, U. Ill. Russian and East European Ctr., Urbana, 1980—. Fellow Istituto Slovacco; mem. Am. Assn. for the Advancement of Slavic Studies, Am. Assn. of Tchrs. of Slavic and East European Langs., Czechoslovak Soc. for the Arts and Scis., New Eng. Hist. Soc. (v.p.). Office: Slavic Heritage Inst PO Box 1882 Torrington CT 06790

DROEGE, THOMAS ARTHUR, theology educator; b. Seymour, Ind., Apr. 10, 1931; s. Walter Henry and Minna Lydia (Strasen) D.; m. Esther K. Kuehn, Jan. 29, 1956; children: Donna, Paula, Karla. BA, Concordia Sem., St. Louis, 1953, MST in Theology, 1956; MA in Theology, U. Chgo., 1963, PhD in Theology, 1965. Ordained to ministry Luth. Ch.-Mo. Synod, 1956. Pastor Redeemer Luth. Ch., Oneida, N.Y., 1956-60; instr. in theology Valparaiso (Ind.) U., 1964-65, asst. prof., 1966-67, assoc. prof., 1968-77, prof., 1978—, chairperson dept. theology, 1978-91, Univ. rsch. prof., 1988-89; study dir. Med. Mission Conf., India, 1966-67. Author: That Thy Saving Health May Be Known, 1968, Self-Realization and Faith: Beginning and Becoming in Relation to God, 1978, Theological Roots of Wholistic Health Care, 1979, Ministry to the Whole Person: Eight Models of Healing Ministry in Lutheran Congregations, 1982, Faith Passages and Patterns, 1983, Guided Grief Imagery: Exercises in Guided Imagery for Death Education and Grief Ministry, 1987, The Faith Factor in Healing, 1991; also articles; (with others) The Church and Pastoral Care, 1988, Death Imagery, 1991. Recipient O. P. Kretzmann Rsch. award Valparaiso U., 1978, 81, 84, 88, Disting. Teaching award, 1986-87; Lilly faculty fellow, 1981-82. Mem. Am. Assn. Pastoral Counselors. Office: Valparaiso U Valparaiso IN 46383

DROEL, WILLIAM LOUIS, educator; b. Rochester, N.Y., July 28, 1948; s. Louis W. and Alice (Melvin) D.; m. Mary Ann Gallagher, Oct. 19, 1985; children: Elizabeth, Robert. BA, St. John Fisher Coll., 1970; MA, Mundelein Coll., 1982. Assoc. dir. Orgn. for Better St. Paul, 1972-74; dir. Office Urban-Ethnic Affairs, Buffalo, 1975-77; tchr. Notre Dame High Sch., Niles, Ill., 1978-80; campus min., instr. Moraine Valley Community Coll., Palos Hills, Ill., 1981—; cons. Fund for Intercultural Edn., Chgo., 1988—; officer Nat. Ctr. for the Laity, 1980—. Author: Confident and Competent, 1987; editor Initiatives, 1981—; host TV series Conversation on Faith, 1985—. Pres. Zone 32 Pantry, Chgo., 1982—; bd. dirs. S.W. YMCA, Alsip, Ill., 1986-90, S.W. Cath. Cluster Project, Chgo., 1989—. Mem. Cath. Campus Ministry Assn. Democrat. Office: Newman Ctr PO Box 311 Worth IL 60482

DROGIN, EVE ROSHEVSKY, editor, writer; b. N.Y.C., Apr. 17, 1946; d. Philip M. and Sarah (Fuhrer) Roshevsky; m. Barry J. Drogin, May 26, 1986. Student, Oberlin Coll., 1964-66. Editor Doubleday & Co., Inc., N.Y.C., 1973-85, Orbis Books, Ossining, N.Y., 1986-90; staff exec. Nat. Fedn. Temple Sisterhoods, N.Y.C., 1990—; free-lance author, journalist Pubs. Weekly, N.Y.C., 1976—, UAHC Press, N.Y.C., 1991—. Mem. Religion Pub. Group (pres. 1981-82, 89-90), Jewish Book Coun. (v.p. 1980-89). Jewish. Home: 118 E 92d St # 2B New York NY 10128 Office: Nat Fedn Temple Sisterhoods 838 5th Ave New York NY 10021

DROPKO, WILLIAM G., religious organization administrator; b. Drumheller, Alta., Can., Apr. 2, 1938; s. William Alexander and Ruth (Henderson) D.; m. Judy JoAnn Brookshine, June 8, 1963. Th.B., No. Calif. Bible Coll., 1975; MRE, Christian Internat. U., 1979. Assoc. pastor Fellowship Tabernacle, Phoenix, 1965-69; dean No. Calif. Bible Coll., San Jose, 1970-75, v.p., 1975-79; dir. Christian Outreach Ministry, Spokane, Wash., 1979—; bd. dirs. Love Ch. Svcs. Network, Spokane, 1989—; presenter seminars on emergency-crisis intervention; police chaplain Spokane Police Dept., 1982. Mem. Police adv. bd. Spokane Police Dept. Home and Office: Christian Outreach Ministry PO Box 18083 Spokane WA 99208

DRUMMOND, LEWIS A., seminary president, minister; b. Dixon, Ill.; s. Wendall Addison and Elsie Lottie (Newbury) D.; m. Betty Rae Love. AB in English, Samford U., 1950; BD in N.T., Southwestern Bapt. Theol. Sem., Ft. Worth, 1955; ThM in Philosophy, Southwestern Bapt. Theol. Sem., 1958; PhD, U. London, 1963; postdoctoral studies, Oxford (Eng.) U. Ordained to ministry Bapt. Ch. Pastor New Bethel Bapt. Ch., Columbiana, Ala., 1949-50, 8th Ave. Bapt. Ch., Ft. Worth, 1951-53, 1st Bapt. Ch., Granbury, Tex., 1953-56, Glen Iris Bapt. Ch., Birmingham, Ala., 1956-61, 9th and O Bapt. Ch., Louisville, 1964-68; chair evangelism and practical theology Spurgeon's Theol. Coll., Oxford U., London, 1968-73; Billy Graham prof. evangelism, dir. Billy Graham Ctr. So. Bapt. Theol. Sem., Louisville, 1973-88; pres. Southeastern Bapt. Theol. Sem., Wake Forest, N.C., 1988—; prof.-at-large U. Zagreb, Yugoslavia; assoc. evangelist Billy Graham Evangelistic Team, Poland, Australia; mem. faculty Billy Graham Sch. Evangelism; lectr. Southwestern Bapt. Theol. Sem., Ft. Worth, Golden Gate Bapt. Theol. Sem., San Francisco, New Orleans Bapt. Theol. Sem., Luther Rice Theol. Sem., St. Petersburg, Fla., Hong Kong Bapt. Theol. Sem., Philippine Bapt. Theol. Sem., Baguio, East Germany Bapt. Theol. Sem., Boukow, German Dem. Republic, Yugoslavia Bapt. Theol. Sem., Novi Sad, Poland Bapt. Theol. Sem., Warsaw, West Australia Bapt. Theol. Sem., Perth, Sydney (Australia) Bapt. Theol. Sem., Guatemala Bapt. Theol. Sem., Carfif (Wales) Bapt. Theol. Sem., Scottish Bapt. Theol. Sem., Glasgow, Trinity Evang. Div. Sch., Deerfield, Ill., Asbury Theol. Sem., Wilmore, Ky., Samford U., Birmingham, Mobile (Ala.) Coll., Carson-Newman Coll., Jefferson City, Tenn., U. Sydney, Union U., Jackson, Tenn., Miss. Coll., Clinton, Okla. Bapt. U., Shawnee, Campbellsville (Ky.) Bapt. Coll., Wheaton (Ill.) Coll., S.W. Bapt. U., Bolivar, Mo., Wingate (N.C.) Bapt. Coll., Campbell Coll., Buies Creek, N.C., Fla. Bapt. Theol. Coll., Graceville. Author: Evangelism: The Counter-Revolution, 1972, Life Can Be Real, 1974, Leading Your Church in Evangelism, 1976, The Awakening That Must Come, 1979, Witnessing for God to Men, 1980, The Revived Life, 1981, Charles G. Finney: The Birth of Modern Evangelism, 1982, The Life and Ministry of Charles G. Finney, 1984, If My People Will...I Will, 1985, The People of God in Ministry, 1985, How to Answer a Skeptic, 1986; also articles in Christianity Today, Bapt. Theol. Quar.; editor: What the Bible Says, 1974, Here They Stand: Sermons from Eastern Europe, 1976. With U.S. Army Air Corps, World War II. Mem. Bapt. World Alliance (com. on evangelism and edn. 1975—), Royal Inst. Philos., Evang. Philos. Soc., Acad. Profs. Evangelism (pres. 1978-80). Office: Southeastern Bapt Theol Sem PO Box 1887 Wake Forest NC 27588-1887

DRUMMOND, RICHARD HENRY, religion educator; b. San Francisco, Dec. 14, 1916; s. John Albert and Clara (Jacobson) D.; m. Pearl Estella Oppegaard, June 5, 1943; children: Donald Craig, Angela Claire, Lowell Henry. BA, UCLA, 1938, MA, 1939; PhD, U. Wis., 1941; BD, Gettysburg Theol. Sem., 1944. Ordained to ministry, 1947. Fraternal worker United Presbyn. Ch. (USA) in Japan, 1949-62; prof. Christian studies and classical langs. Meiji Gakuin U., Tokyo, 1958-62; Florence Livergood Warren prof. comparative religions U. Dubuque (Iowa) Theol. Sem., 1962-87, prof. emeritus, 1987—. Author: A History of Christianity in Japan, 1971, Gautama the Buddha, 1974, Unto the Churches, 1978, Toward a New Age in Christian Theology, 1985, A Life of Jesus the Christ, 1989. With U.S. Army, 1945-46. U. Wis. fellow, 1940-41, Sealntic Fund fellow, 1968-69. Mem. Fellowship Christian Missionaries in Japan (pres. 1960-61), Internat. Assn. Mission Studies, N. Am. Acad. Ecumenists, Am. Acad. Religion, Am. Soc. Missiology, Midwest Fellowship of Profs. Mission (pres. 1966-67), Rotary. Democrat. Home: 135 Croydon Crest Dubuque IA 52001 Office: U Dubuque Theol Sem 2000 University Ave Dubuque IA 52001 *Peace in our world seems intimately related to peace among the religions of the world. There can be no such peace, I believe, apart from sincere efforts to appreciate and respect one another.*

DRUMMOND, TERENCE MICHAEL, church official; b. Scarborough, Yorkshire, Eng., Mar. 30, 1950; s. Harold and Mary Hannah Charlotte (Shepherd) D.; m. Linda Roe, Dec. 28, 1974; 1 child, Matthew. Interdiocesan cert. Ch. Army Tng. Coll., London, 1972; cert. in Religious Studies, U. Manchester, 1984. Sr. counselor Ch. of Eng., City of London, 1975-79; fieldwork services officer Ch. Army, London, 1980—. Contbr. articles on social issues to profl. jours. Mem. British Assn. Social Workers. Social Democrat. Anglican. Avocations: classical music; theatre. Home: 27 Chevening Rd, Greenwich,, London, England Office: Ch Army Hdqrs Independents Rd, Blackheath, 9LG, London SE3, England

DRURY, STEPHEN MAX, minister, religious organization administrator; b. Frankfort, Ind., Feb. 28, 1948; s. Robert Lee and Audra Browning (DeFord) D.; m. Evelyn Louise Ratcliff, Dec. 17, 1972; children: James Kent, Stephanie Louise, Mendy Christine. ThB, Apostolic Bible Inst., 1969. Ordained to ministry United Pentecostal Ch., 1976. Pastor United Pentecostal Ch., Hennepin, Okla., 1974-76; supt. Tupelo (Miss.) Children's Mansion, 1976—; pastor, founder Abundant Life Tabernacle, Tupelo, 1983—; supt., founder Tupelo Christian Acad., 1979—; chmn., founder New Beginnings Adoption Agy., Tupelo, 1989—. Home: 123 Windsor Circle Tupelo MS 38801 Office: Tupelo Children's Mansion PO Box 167 Tupelo MS 38802 *The greatest thrill in life is a servant's heart, especially for those who have been hurt by the volatile sins of this generation. It is more than a worthwhile ministry for life.*

DRURY, THOMAS T., pastor; b. Jacksonville, Fla., Dec. 25, 1943; s. John David and Thelma Jenny (Moore) D.; m. Carolyn Deloris Cox, June 3, 1961; children: Thomas Ethan, Mark Anthony, Timothy Tyrone, William Arthur. AS, Jones Coll., Jacksonville, 1969, BS, 1976; ThM, North Fla. Bapt. Theol. Sem., 1989, ThD, 1990. Ordained to ministry So. Bapt. Conv. Pastor Pleasant Park Bapt. Ch., Jacksonville, 1986—. With U.S. Army, 1961-64. Mem. North Fla. Bapt. Theol. Sem. Alumni Assn. (v.p. 1990—). Home: 11335 Avery Dr Jacksonville FL 32218

DRUSEDUM, JOHN WILLIAM, JR., minister; b. Sellersville, Pa., Sept. 11, 1952; s. John William and Mary Anna (Flickinger) D.; m. Sharon Ann Bennett, May 23, 1981; children: Julia Ann, Kelley Rene. BA, So. Nazarene U., Bethany, Okla., 1987, MA in Religion, 1991. Ordained to ministry Ch. of the Nazarene, 1987. Asst. pastor El Reno (Okla.) Ch. of the Nazarene, 1983-87, Mustang (Okla.) Ch. of the Nazarene, 1987; pastor Crown Hts. Ch. of the Nazarene, Oklahoma City, 1987—; dist. pres. Nazarene Youth Internat., 1990—, v.p., 1988-90. Chmn. bd. I CARE, Oklahoma City, 1990—; bd. dirs. Edn. and Employment Ministry, Oklahoma City, 1987—, Reg. AIDS Interfaith Network, 1990—. With USN, 1974-80. Mem. Soc. Bibl. Lit., Am. Acad. Religion, Wesleyan Theol. Soc. Office: 1st Ch of the Nazarene 1044 Don Diego Santa Fe NM 87501 *I am constantly amazed at the increasing number of choices we are forced to make and when we assume responsibility for those choices, that is when we will make a drastic difference in this world.*

DRYE, SAMUEL T., minister; m. Rheba Ballard; children: Jennifer, Jeffrey. BTh, Internat. Sem., Orlando, Fla., 1988. Pastor Holy Spirit Harvest Ch., Macon, Ga., 1988—. With U.S. Navy, 1964-66. Mem. Evangelical Fellowship of Chs., Macon Ministerial Assn. (sec. 1987-88). Office: Holy Spirit Harvest Ch 2254 Rocky Creek Rd Macon GA 31206

DRYER, RICHARD EDWARD, rabbi; b. N.Y.C., Nov. 29, 1930; s. Oscar Albert and Anna (Frankl) D.; m. Arlene Terry Gottlieb, Dec. 25, 1955; 1 child, Deborah. BA, CCNY, 1951; BHL, Hebrew Union Coll., 1954, MAHL, 1957, DD (hon.), 1982. Ordained rabbi, 1957. Commd. 2d lt. U.S. Army, 1957, advanced through grades to col., 1979, chaplain various locations, 1957-87, ret., 1987; rabbi Temple Mizpah, Abilene, Tex., 1987-90, Temple Beth Emeth, Sherman, Tex., 1990—; faculty Tex. Luth. Coll., Seguin, 1992—; chmn. armed svcs. com. San Antonio Jewish Community Ctr., 1988—, chmn. Judaic practices com., 1989—. Mem. allocations panel United Way, San Antonio, 1987—. Recipient Four Chaplains award B'nai B'rith, N.Y.C., 1965, Medal of Merit, Jewish War Vets. USA, Atlantic City, N.J., 1966; named Chaplain of Yr., Assn. Jewish Chaplains of Armed Forces, 1986; decorated Legion of Merit, Bronze Star. Mem. Cen. Conf. Am. Rabbis (bd. dirs. 1979-80), Kallah of Tex. Rabbis (pres. 1989-90), Am. Acad. Religion. Home: 2411 Shadow Cliff San Antonio TX 78232

DUARTE, HAROLD JORGE, minister; b. San Juan, Argentina, Sept. 21, 1950; came to U.S., 1972; s. A. and Laura (Bernhardt) D.; m. Johanna Ruth Nikkels, Sept. 23, 1979; children: Halcyon Johanna, Harold Johannes, Heidi Joy. BA, River Plate Coll., Argentina, 1972; postgrad., Sch. Theology at Claremont, Calif., 1990—. Ordained to ministry Seventh-day Adventists, 1979. Youth pastor Seventh-day Adventist Ch., Bakersfield, Calif., 1973-76, L.A., 1976-77; pastor Seventh-day Adventist Ch., La Crescenta, Calif., 1977-81, East Los Angeles, Calif., 1981-85; exec. dir. Listen, Seventh-day Adventist Ch., Glendale, Calif., 1985-87; assoc. pastor Downey (Calif.) Seventh-day Adventist Ch., 1987—; chmn. youth ministries com. Seventh-day Adventist Ch. in Cen. Calif. Conf., San Jose, 1974-75, Glendale, 1976-78, mem. communication steering com., 1979—. Contbr. articles to religious mags. Mem. AACD, Nat. Assn. Ch. Bus. Adminstrn., Assn. for Religious Values and Issues in Counseling. Home: 1159 W Nicholas St Upland CA 91786-7311 Office: Seventh-day Adventist Ch 9820 S Lakewood Blvd Downey CA 90240 *The most humbling dilemma I face as a pastor is the realization that religion and morality in all its cultural expressions are perhaps the single most dehumanizing forces of society. Whoever said life and God were supposed to be this complicated? Why do we as the church attack the social maladies born out of our own insensitivity to existing needs? For the child it is either engaging and absorbing or tedious. Relevant or irrelevant. Connected to the whole of life or expected behavior for the preservation of "adult cultural traditions." I am convinced that people naturally search for God the Creator. It is the dysfunctional expressions of a God that does not exist that they resent. The Gospel of Christ is life at its best and it is liberating. It is wholistic and basic. Let's stop using religion and cultural values in order to control and feel better about ourselves. Let God be at last!.*

DUBA, ARLO DEAN, academic administrator, theology educator; b. Brule County, S.D., Nov. 12, 1929; s. Frank Joseph and Alvera Mae (Forman) D.; m. Doreen Elizabeth Eckles, June 18, 1954; children: Paul Douglas, Bruce Franklin, John David, Anne Elizabeth. B.A., U. Dubuque, 1952; B.D., Princeton Theol. Sem., 1955, Ph.D., 1960; postgrad., l'Institut Superieur de Liturgie, Paris, 1968-69. Chaplain, assoc. prof. religion Westminster Choir Coll., 1957-68; dir. chapel, dir. admissions Princeton Theol. Sem., 1969-82; dean, prof. worship U. Dubuque Theol. Sem., 1982-85, univ. v.p., 1985—; mem. adminstrn. com. Presbyn. Office of Worship, 1979-84. Author: (with Mary F. Carson) Praise God—Worship Through the Year, 1979, Principles of Protestant Worship (in Indonesian), 1980; composer musical settings for psalms, 1980-82. Mem. Liturg. Conf. (bd. dirs. 1978-82, exec. com. 1979-82), N. Am. Acad. Liturgy (charter mem., exec. bd. 1981-83), Societas Liturgica, Acad. Homiletics. Office: U Dubuque Theol Sem 2000 University Ave Dubuque IA 52001

DUBINA, SISTER MARY REGINA, head of religious order; b. Chgo., Dec. 5, 1922; d. John Joseph and Anna (Sirovatka) D. BA, DePaul U., 1967, MEd, 1972. Elem. sch. tchr. various schs., Chgo., Tex. and Wis., 1946-62; elem. sch. prin. various schs., Wis., Tex., 1962-64; high sch. tchr. Benet Acad., Lisle, Ill., 1965-85; sixth prioress Benedictine Sisters, Lisle, 1984—; community treas. Benedictine Sisters, Lisle, 1966-84; mem. Benet Acad. Bd., Lisle, 1967—, Benedictine Sisters council, Lisle, 1967—; treas. Conf. Religious Treas. Region 8, 1980-84. Mem. Leadership Conf. of Women Religious, Am. Benedictine Acad., Conf. Am. Benedictine Prioresses. Avocations: swimming, crafts, visiting sick and shut-ins. Home: 1910 Maple Ave Lisle IL 60532 *I believe this is the age of Benedictinism because Benedictine spirituality has what the world needs: prayer, stability, humility, community, balance, obedient listening, stewardship of the earth, etc.*

DUBOSE, FRANCIS MARQUIS, clergyman; b. Elba, Ala., Feb. 27, 1922; s. Hansford Arthur and Mayde Frances (Owen) DuB.; BA cum laude, Baylor U., 1947; MA, U. Houston, 1958; BD, Southwestern Bapt. Sem., 1957, ThD, 1961; postgrad. Oxford (Eng.) U., 1972; m. Dorothy Anne Sessums, Aug. 28, 1940; children: Elizabeth Anne Parnell, Frances Jeannine Stevens, Jonathan Michael, Celia Danielle. Pastor Bapt. chs., Tex., Ark., 1939-61; supt. missions. So. Bapt. Conv., Detroit, 1961-66; prof. missions Golden Gate Bapt. Sem., 1966—, dir. World Mission Ctr., 1979—; lectr., cons. in 115 cities outside U.S., 1969-82; v.p. Conf. City Mission Supts., So. Bapt. Conv., 1964-66; trustee Mich. Bapt. Inst., 1963-66; mem. Mayor's Inter-Faith Task Force on Homelessness. Mem. Internat. Assn. Mission Study, Am. Soc. Missiology, Assn. Mission Profs. Co-editor: The Mission of the Church in the Racially Changing Community, 1969; author: How Churches Grow in an Urban World, 1978, Classics of Christian Missions, 1979, God Who Sends: A Fresh Quest for Biblical Mission, 1983, Home Cell Groups and House Churches, 1987; contbr. to Toward Creative Urban Strategy; Vol. III Ency. of So. Baptists, also articles to profl. jours. Home: 2 Carpenter Ct San Francisco CA 94124 Office: Golden Gate Bapt Sem Mill Valley CA 94941

DUBOSE, PIERRE WILDS, JR., minister; b. Miami, Fla., Aug. 26, 1928; s. Pierre Wilds Sr. and Gwynn (Ewell) DuB.; m. Lois Harris, Oct. 17, 1950 (Div. 1978); children: Pierre III, Lois E., Rebekah H., George H.; m. Roselis DaCunha Pacheco, May 8, 1981. BA, U. Fla., 1950; MDiv, Columbia Theol. Sem., Decatur, Ga., 1954. Ordained to ministry Presbyn. Ch., 1954. Pastor Tallapoosa-Bremen (Ga.) Presbyn. Chs., 1951-57; missionary Presbyn. Ch., Brazil, 1957-80; pastor Westminster Presbyn. Ch., Miami, Fla., 1983—; bus. exec. Brazil and U.S., 1971—; profl. engraver pvt. practice, North Miami, Fla., 1982—; area dir. Presbyn. Mission, Paraiba-Rio Grande, Brazil, 1957-65; pres., organizer ABC Crusade Literacy, Recife, Brazil, 1966-70. Named Honored Citizen of Guanapara State, Rio de Janeiro, Brazil, 1968. Office: Westminster Presbyn Ch 4201 N 2nd Ave Miami FL 33137-3521

DUCE, S. ALAN, minister; b. Bryan, Tex., Aug. 9, 1961; s. P. Hubert and Phyllis A. (Turner) D.; m. Janice Sharpes, Aug. 22, 1987. BA in Religion, Bethany (Okla.) Nazarene Coll., 1983, BS in Music, 1984, MA in Religion, 1985; MDiv., Nazarene Theol. Sem., 1987. Ordained to ministry Ch. of the Nazarene, 1989. Asst. funeral dir. Carson Funeral Home, Kansas City, Mo., 1985-87; pastor Ch. Nazarene, Bowling Green, Ohio, 1987—; pub. relations dir. N.T.S. Women's Support Group, Kansas City, Mo., 1985-86; shut in ministry coordinator Nazarene Ch., Kansas City, 1986-87. Mem. Wesleyan Theol. Soc. Republican. Avocations: golf, reading. Home: 219 Evergreen # 45 Bowling Green OH 43402 Office: 1291 Conneaut Bowling Green OH 43402 *At no time in history has humanity's dependence upon God and responsibility for one another been more important.*

DUCK, RUTH CAROLYN, minister, religion educator, writer; b. Washington, Nov. 21, 1947; d. Jesse Thomas and Louise (Farmer) Duck; m. John Webb Stoppels, Sept. 26, 1987. MDiv, Chgo. Theol. Seminary, 1973; MA in Theology, U. Notre Dame, 1987; ThD, Boston U., 1989; DD, Chgo. Theol. Seminary, 1983. Ordained to ministry United Ch. Christ, 1974. Assoc. min. Pilgrim Congregation UCC, Oak Park, Ill., 1974-75; pastor St. John's UCC, Hartford, Wis., 1975-79, Bethel-Bethany UCC, Milw., 1979-84; asst. prof. worship Garrett Evang. Theol. Seminary, Evanston, Ill., 1989—. Author: Gender and the Name of God, 1991; editor: Bread For the Journey, 1981, Everflowing Streams, 1981, Touch Holiness, 1990; contbr. articles to profl. jours. Mem. North Am. Acad. Liturgy (assoc.), Hymn Soc. Am., Soc. Bibl. Lit. Home: 2207 Maple Ave B1 Evanston IL 60201 Office: Garrett Evang Theol Sem 2121 Sheridan Rd Evanston IL 60201

DUCKWORTH, JOHN HOWARD, clergyman; b. Parkersburg, W.Va., Mar. 27, 1949; s. James Wellington and Fern Mildred (Larsen) D.; m. Patricia Gaye Nichols, Aug. 14, 1976; children: Jonathan Douglas, James David. BA, Sioux Falls Coll., 1977; MDiv, Cen. Bapt. Sem., 1980. Ordained to ministry Am. Bapt. Chs. in U.S.A., 1980. Interim and student pastor Burke (S.D.)-Lucas Parish, 1976-77; student pastor Wyandotte Bapt. Ch., Kansas City, Mo., 1979-80; pastor lst Bapt. Ch., Greybull, Wyo., 1980-84, Ridgecrest, Calif., 1984-91; sr. pastor lst Bapt. Ch., Great Falls, Mont., 1991—; bd. dirs. New Ch. Devel., Denver, 1980-84; sec.-treas. min.'s coun. Am. Bapt. Chs. of the Rocky Mountains, 1983-84. With USN, 1967-71. Mem. South Big Horn County Ministerial Assn. (pres. 1981-83), Indian Wells Valley Ministerial Assn. (pres. 1985), Rotary (sec.-treas. Greybull 1981-83). Office: 1st Bapt Ch 1350 South Downs Ridgecrest CA 93555 *Never has there been a greater need for high moral standards in our world. In a time when everything competes for our attention, we must learn to focus on Godliness.*

DUDDLEY, JOB, head of religious order. Leader, Holymama Christian Fellowship ch., Solomon Islands. Office: Christian Fellowship Ch, Paradide, Munda, Western Province Solomon Islands*

DUDICK, MICHAEL JOSEPH, bishop; b. St. Clair, Pa., Feb. 24, 1917; s. John and Mary (Jurick) D. BA, Ill. Benedictine Coll., Lisle, 1943; postgrad., St. Procopius Sem., Lisle, 1943-45; HHD (hon.), Kings Coll., 1987; DD (hon.), Scranton U., 1989. Ordained priest Roman Cath. Ch., 1945. Vice chancellor Exarchate of Pitts., 1946-55; chancellor Diocese of Passaic, N.J., 1963-68; bishop Diocese of Passaic, 1968—; mem. N.J. Coalition of Religious Leaders; cons. ecumenical and interreligious com. Nat. Conf. Cath. Bishops. Bd. regents Seton Hall U., 1968—.

DUDLEY, CARL SAFFORD, religion educator; b. Balt., Oct. 27, 1932; s. Harold Jenkins and Margaret (Safford) D.; m. Shirley Sanford, June 18, 1955; children: Nathan, Rebecca, Andrew, Deborah, Steven. BA, Cornell U., 1954; postgrad., N.Y. Sch. Social Work, 1954-56; MDiv, Union Theol. Sem., 1959; D of Ministry, McCormick Theol. Sem., 1974. Social worker Manhattanville Community Ctr., N.Y.C., 1954-56; asst. pastor 1st Presbyn. Ch., Buffalo, 1959-62; pastor Berea Presbyn. Ch., St. Louis, 1962-73; prof. McCormick Theol. Sem., Chgo., 1973—; exec. dir. Ctr. for Ch. and Community Ministries. Author: Making the Small Church Effective, 1978, Where Have All Our People Gown, 1979, Orientations to Faith, 1982; co-editor, co-author: Building Effective Ministry, 1983, Handbook for Congregational Studies, 1986, New Testament Tensions in the Contemporary Church, 1987, Developing Your Small Church's Potential, 1988, Carriers of Faith, 1991, Basic Steps toward Community Ministry, 1991. Commr. St. Louis Housing Authority, 1970-73; bd. dirs. Sch. Bd. 200, Oak Park, Ill., 1981-87. Mem. Religious Rsch. Assn. (exec. com. 1979-82, assoc. editor Religious Rsch. Rev. 1980-82), Soc. Sci. Study of Religion, Assn. Sociology of Religion. Home: 210 S Elmwood Ave Oak Park IL 60302 Office: McCormick Theol Sem 5555 S Woodlawn Ave Chicago IL 60637

DUDLEY, HARRY JOSEPH, religion educator; b. Yonkers, N.Y., July 18, 1949; s. Harry Neil and Theresa Marie (Fisher) D.; m. Patricia Ann Goodman, Mar. 18, 1978; children: Martin, Neil, Kathleen. BA cum laude, SUNY, Stony Brook, 1971; STB, Cath. Univ. of Am., 1975. Tchr. St. Anselm's Abbey Sch., Washington, 1975-78; coord. Anchor Social Ctr. and Communications, Anchor Mental Health Assn./Archdiocese Washington, 1978-80; tchr., campus minister Bishop McNamara High Sch., Forestville, Md., 1981-84; area coord. Dept. of Cath. Edn. Ministries, Ctr. of Cen. Md., Archdiocese of Balt., Frederick, 1990—. Mem. Nat. Assn. Parish Coords. and Dirs. of Religious Edn. of Nat. Cath. Ednl. Assn., Balt. Assn. Catechetical Ministers, Balt. Assn. Profl. Youth Ministers. Home: 2068 C Virts Lane Jefferson MD 21755 Office: Cath Edn Ministries Ctr Cen Md Chapel Alley and Church St PO Box 645 Frederick MD 21701

DUDLEY, JOHN CLEVELAND, minister; b. Dixiana, Ala., Mar. 18, 1928; s. John Brightly and Clevie Mae (Collins) D.; m. Ella Louise Peoples, Oct. 5, 1953; children: Cathy Dianne Dudley Bedenbender, John Cleveland Jr. Student pub. schs., Ala. Ordained to ministry Ch. of God. Dist. youth dir. Ch. of God, Ala., 1957-59; dist. overseer Ch. of God, Ky., 1960-65, Monroe, La., 1967-78; mem. state coun. Ch. of God, Hazard, Ky., 1960-65, Baton Rouge, 1966—. Mem. Ouaxhita Parish Ministerial Assn. (officer 1980-85. Office: Ch of God 205 Alpha St West Monroe LA 71291

DUDLEY, MERLE BLAND, minister; b. Norfolk, Va., Feb. 19, 1929; s. Harry Roy and Merle (Garrett) D.; m. Lillie M. Pennington, Oct. 12, 1950; children: Carter Bland, Jane Merle. BA, Lynchburg Coll., 1950; MDiv, Union Theol. Sem., 1954; MA, Presbyn. Sch. Christian Edn., 1969; PhD,

Glasgow (Scotland) U., 1973. Ordained to ministry Presbyterian Ch., 1954; pastor McQuay Meml. Presbyn. Ch., Charlotte, N.C., 1954-56, Holmes Presbyn. Ch., Cheriton, Va., 1956-59; asst. pastor First Presbyn. Ch., Roanoke, Va., 1959-60; pastor Christ Presbyn. Ch., Virginia Beach, Va., 1960-67; asso. pastor First Presbyn. Ch., Winston-Salem, N.C., 1967-70; pastor Westminster Presbyn. Ch., Waynesboro, Va., 1971-89, ret. 1989; mem. adj. faculty dept. philosophy and religion Blue Ridge Community Coll., Weyers Cave, Va., 1977-89. Mem. Am. Acad. Religion, Soc. Bibl. Lit., Ch. Service Soc., Am. Schs. Oriental Research, Waynesboro Ministers' Assn. (pres. 1978-79), Va. Hist. Soc., Va. Soc. Sons of Am. Revolution, Jamestowne Soc. Republican. Lodge: Rotary (pres. 1974-75) (Waynesboro, Va.). Author: New Testament Preaching and Twentieth Century Communication, 1973. Home: PO Box 1639 Tappahannock VA 22560-1639

DUDLEY, PAUL V., bishop; b. Northfield, Minn., Nov. 27, 1926; s. Edward Austin and Margaret Ann (Nolan) D. Student, Nazareth Coll., St. Paul Sem. Ordained priest Roman Cath. Ch., 1951. Titular bishop of Ursona, aux. bishop of St. Paul-Mpls, 1977-78; bishop of Sioux Falls S.D., 1978—. Office: Chancery Office 423 N Duluth Ave PO Box 5033 Sioux Falls SD 57117

DUDUIT, J(AMES) MICHAEL, clergyman, public relations executive, university official; b. Sandwich, Ill., Aug. 18, 1954; s. James Loren and Sarah Lee (baker) D.; m. Laura Ann Niemann, Jan. 11, 1986. BA, Stetson U., 1975; MDiv, So. Bapt. Sem., 1979; PhD in Humanities, Fla. State U., 1983. Ordained minister Bapt. Ch.; cert. fund raising exec. accreditation. Pastor Union Flatrock Bapt. Ch., Osgood, Ind., 1976-78; news dir. So. Bapt. Sem., Louisville, 1975-78, dir. communications, 1984-87; dir. pub. affairs Palm Beach Atlantic Coll., West Palm Beach, Fla., 1978-80; asst. to pres. Cuneo Advt., Inc., Tallahassee, 1980-81; assoc. campus minister Bapt. Campus Ministry, Tallahassee, 1981-83; assoc. pastor Immanuel Bapt. Ch., Tallahassee, 1982-84; pres. Preaching Resources, Inc., Jacksonville, Fla., 1985—; dir. devel. Samford U., Birmingham, 1987—. Author: Joy in Ministry: Messages from Second Corinthians, 1989; editor: Great Preaching 1990, 1990; editor, pub. Preaching jour.; contbr. articles to profl. jours. Mem. Nat. Soc. Fund-Raising Execs., Bapt. Pub. Relations Soc. (newsletter editor 1977-78), Homewood C. of C. (v.p. 1988-89), Religious Conf. Mgmt. Assn., Religious Speech Communication Assn., Nat. Conf. on Preaching (bd. dirs.), Acad. of Homiletics. Democrat. Avocations: reading, creative writing, travel. Home: 2448 Regent Ln Birmingham AL 35226

DUECKER, ROBERT SHELDON, bishop; b. Medina County, Ohio, Sept. 4, 1926; s. Howard LaVerne and Sarah Faye (Simpson) D., m. Marjorie Louise Clouse, June 13, 1948; children: Philip Lee, Cristine Cay Duecker Haney. B in Religion, AB, Indiana Wesleyan U., 1948; BD, MS, Christian Theol. Sem., Indpls., 1952, DD (hon.), 1969. Ordained to ministry United Meth. Ch., 1952. Pastor Dyer (Ind.) United Meth. Ch., 1952-54; sr. pastor Gethsemane United Meth. Ch., Muncie, Ind., 1954-62, Grace United Meth. Ch., Hartford City, Ind., 1962-65, 1st United Meth. Ch., Warsaw, Ind., 1965-70, Simpson United Meth. Ch., Ft. Wayne, Ind., 1970-72; dir. No. Ind. Conf. Coun. Ministries United Meth. Ch., Marion, 1973-77; dist. supt. No. Ind. Conf. United Meth. Ch., Ft. Wayne, 1977-82; sr. pastor High St. United Meth. Ch., Muncie, 1982-88; bishop Chgo. area United Meth. Ch., 1988—; trustee United Theol. Sem., Dayton, Ohio, 1985—, Kendall Coll., Evanston, Ill., 1988—, North Cen. Coll., Naperville, Ill., 1988—, Garrett Theol. Sem., Evanston, 1988—; mem. gen. bd. publ. United Meth. Ch. Author: Tensions in the Connection, 1982; also monographs. Mem. Kosciusko County Health Planning Coun., Warsaw, Ind., 1968-70; bd. dirs. Goodwill Industries, Ft. Wayne, Muncie, 1977-88; former pres. Del. County Mental Health Assn., Muncie. Named Sagamore of the Wabash Gov. of Ind., 1988. Mem. Coun. Bishops United Meth. Ch., North Cen. Jurisdiction Coll. Bishops, Kiwanis, Rotary, Theta Phi. Avocations: stamp collecting, golf. Office: United Meth Ch 1661 N Northwest Hwy Park Ridge IL 60068

DUEITT, GEORGE MALCOLM, minister; b. Mobile, Ala., Jan. 13, 1955; s. Malcolm Deloss and Ruby Doreen (Moore) D.; m. Sandra Veleria Dennis, Dec. 30, 1975; children: Elizabeth Michelle, Phillip Malcolm. BS, Mobile Coll., 1978. Lic. to ministry So. Bapt. Conv., 1986, ordained, 1991. Min. music Smithtown Bapt. Ch., Eight Mile, Ala., 1974-76; min. music and youth 1st Bapt. Ch., Leroy, Ala., 1976-79, Sardis Bapt. Ch., Wawbeek, Ala., 1979-82, Park Ave. Bapt. Ch., Enterprise, Ala., 1982-84, Smiths Sta. Bapt. Ch., Smiths, Ala., 1984-91, Oates Ave. Bapt. Ch., Columbus, Ga., 1991—. Mem. Smiths Ruritan, 1986-87. Mem. Russell Bapt.Assn. (music dir. 1988-90, chmn. youth com., 1990, Ala. Bapt. Youth (evangelism com. 1988-89). Home: PO Box 461 2093 Lee Rd 430 Smiths AL 36877

DUERBECK, JULIAN JOSEPH FRANCIS, priest, educator; b. Chgo., May 3, 1949; s. Joseph and Frances (Dankowski) D. BA in English Lit., St. Procopius Coll., 1971; MA Theology in Liturgy, St. John's U., Collegeville, Minn., 1975; postgrad., U. Toronto, 1981, 82, 84, U. Calif., Berkeley, 1989, Harvard Div. Sch., 1990. Professed Benedictine monk, 1970; ordained priest Roman Cath. Ch., 1976. Instr. religious studies Ill. Benedictine Coll., Lisle, 1975-78; instr. monastic novices St. Procopius Abbey, Lisle, 1976, liturgist, 1976-88, coord. interreligious dialogue, 1990—; Sunday asst. Joliet Diocese Parishes, DuPage County, Ill., 1976-84; councillor for parliament World Religions, Lisle, 1990—; tchr. world religion Benet Acad., Lisle, 1986—; active East-West Monastic Dialogue, 1989—. Author: Alternate Psalm Prayers, 1989; editor: Liturgy of the Hourse, 3 vols., 1979. Mem. Field Mus. (Chgo.), Oriental Inst. (Chgo.). Home: St Procopius Abbey 5601 College Rd Lisle IL 60532 Office: Benet Acad Lisle IL 60532

DUEY, CHARLES JOHN, SR., minister; b. Miami, Fla., Aug. 1, 1928; s. William John and Florence Isabel (Isgren) D.; m. Alice E. Lindquist, May 16, 1951 (dec. June 1977); children: Cheryl Alice, Charles John Jr., Craig William; m. Eleanor Marie Johnson, Feb. 11, 1978; children: Jeanne Elizabeth Peterson, Karen Louise Peterson. BEd, U. Miami, Coral Gables, Fla., 1954; MDiv, Fuller Theol. Sem., 1957; ThM, Princeton Theol. Sem., 1964; D. Ministry, Andover Newton Theol. Sem., 1977. Ordained to ministry Evang. Covenant Ch., transferred to United Ch. of Christ; cert. Spanish tchr., Conn. Missionary tchr. Evang. Covenant Ch., Chgo., 1958-67; pastor Covenant Congl. Ch., West Hartford, Conn., 1967-87; interim pastor Congl. Ch., Newington, Conn., 1987—, Stratford, Conn., 1990—; chmn. east coast conf. Evang. Covenant Ch., Cromwell, Conn., 1972-73, mem. commn. on inter-ch. rels., 1983-88; moderator Conn. conf. United Ch. of Christ, Hartford, 1978-81; co-founder Cooperative Ministries, 1972. Author: Covenant Missions in Ecuador, 1965, Ensayos Evangélicos, 1965. Bd. dirs. Children's home of Cromwell, 1982-85; co-founder West Hartford Pastoral Counseling Ctr., 1979. With USN, 1946-51. Mem. Cen. Assn. Conn. Clergy United Ch. of Christ, Ministerium Evang. Covenant Ch. Am. (life), Masons. Home: 125 Goodale Dr Newington CT 06111

DUFAULT, WILFRID JOSEPH, religious organization administrator; b. Spencer, Mass., Dec. 11, 1907; s. Stephen and Alma (Kasky) D. AB, Assumption Coll., 1929, DD (hon.), 1970; lic. in theology, Angelicum, Rome, 1933; lic. in philosophy, Laval U., Que., 1938; LHD (hon.), Rivier Coll., 1980; EdD (hon.), Anna Maria Coll., Paxton, Mass., 1980. Joined Augustinians of Assumption Soc., 1930, ordained priest Roman Cath. Ch., 1934. Prof. philosophy Assumption Coll., Worcester, Mass., 1934-37, 40-46, pres., 1946-47, acting pres., 1971-72, 77-78, v.p., 1972-82, chancellor, 1982—; provincial superior Augustinians of Assumption, N.Y.C., 1944-52, superior gen., Rome, 1952-69, postulator, 1983—. Office: Assumption Coll Office of Chancellor 500 Salisbury St Worcester MA 01609-1296

DUFFEY, PAUL ANDREWS, bishop; b. Brownsville, Tenn., Dec. 13, 1920; s. George Henderson and Julia Griffin (McKissack) D.; m. Anna Louise Calhoun, June 20, 1944; children: Melanie Duffey Hutto, Paul Andrews Jr. Student, U. Ala., 1938-40; A.B., Birmingham-So. Coll., 1942; M.Div., Vanderbilt U., 1945; DD, Birmingham-So. Coll., 1966; DHL, Union Coll., 1987; LLD, Ky. Wesleyan Coll., 1987. Ordained to ministry as deacon United Meth. Ch., 1944, elder, 1946; pastor Chapel Hill Ch., Tenn., 1944-46; pastor Abbeville, Ala., 1946-50, Marion, Ala., 1950-54; pastor Dexter Ave United Meth. Ch., Montgomery, Ala., 1954-61; pastor First Ch., Pensacola, Fla., 1961-66, Dothan, Ala., 1966-70, Montgomery, Ala., 1970-76; supt. Montgomery dist. United Meth. Ch., from 1976, mem. jud. council, 1976-80; bishop United Meth. Ch., Louisville, 1980-91; ret., 1991. Chmn. community council United Appeal, 1974; trustee Birmingham-So. Coll., 1956—, chmn. bd., 1956-73. Recipient Leadership award Lindsay Wilson Coll., 1987, Trustees award Sue Bennett Coll., 1987. Address: 3643 Fernway Montgomery AL 36111

DUFFEY, PERRY L., clergyman; b. Fairfax, Ala., Oct. 26, 1934; s. Clyde B. and Dorothy (Kilgore) D.; m. Sara Meadows, Dec. 19, 1954; children: Perry L. Jr., Amanda Duffey Proctor. BA, Huntingdon Coll., 1985; postgrad., Candler Sch. Theology, 1987. Ordained elder Meth. Ch., 1989. Pastor Riverview United Meth. Ch., Valley, Ala., 1980-81, Riverview-Plant City United Meth. Ch., Valley, 1981-85, Bethany United Meth. Ch., Sylacauga, Ala., 1985-88, Morgan United Meth. Ch., Bessemer, Ala., 1988—. With U.S. Army Nat. Guard, 1954-82. Home: 3981 Methodist Circle SE Bessemer AL 35023 Office: Morgan United Meth Ch 2701 Morgan Rd SE Bessemer AL 35023

DUGAN, HERSCHEL CEDRIC, minister; b. Mankato, Minn., Apr. 13, 1931; s. Charles E. and Harriet (Van Buren) D.; m. Shirley Joan Tietsort, July 28, 1960; children: Denise Louise, Mark Van Buren. BA, Phillips U., 1953; MDiv, Div. Sch. Drake U., 1956; D of Ministry, Phillips U., 1981. Ordained to ministry Christian Ch., 1956. Assoc. min. First Christian Ch., Omaha, 1956-60; min. First Christian Ch., Aurora, Nebr., 1963-68, Olathe, Kans., 1968-86; min. No. Heights Christian Ch., Tulsa, 1960-63, Grant Park Christian Ch., Des Moines, 1986—; intersem. rep. div. sch. Drake U., Des Moines, 1953-56; state bd. dirs. Christian Ch. in Kans., 1982-85, chmn. com. on min., 1980-82; moderator Christian Ch. Kansas City, Mo., 1984-85. Active Nebr. Adv. Commn./U.S. Civil Rights Commn., Omaha, 1962-63. Mem. Des. Moines Ministerial Assn., Des Moines Area Religious Coun. (adminstrn. com. 1988—), Rotary, Ancient Form (chaplain 1971-72), Masons. Democrat. Home: 2958 Tiffin Des Moines IA 50317 Office: Grant Park Christian Ch 2440 Capitol Des Moines IA 50317

DUGAN, ROBERT PERRY, JR., minister, religious organization administrator; b. Morristown, N.J., Jan. 19, 1932; s. Robert P. and Marion Frances (Sahrbeck) D.; m. Marilyn I. Wertz, Aug. 8, 1953; children: Robert Perry III, Cheryl. AB, Wheaton Coll., 1953; MDiv, Fuller Theol. Sem., 1956, postgrad. (teaching fellow in Hebrew), 1956-57; DD, Denver Conservative Bapt. Sem., 1985; LHD, Geneva Coll., 1985; LLD, Roberts Wesleyan Coll., 1990. Ordained to ministry Conservative Baptist Assn. Am., 1957; minister of youth ch. Bloomfield, N.J., 1957-58; pastor Rochester, N.H., 1959-63, Elmhurst, Ill., 1963-69; pastor Trinity Baptist Ch., Wheat Ridge, Colo., 1970-75; chaplain Senate of State of Colo., 1974-75; pres. Conservative Baptist Assn. Am., 1973-76; v.p. Rockmont Coll., Lakewood, Colo., 1976-78; dir. Office of Pub. Affairs, Nat. Assn. Evangelicals, Washington, 1978—; bd. dirs. Denver Conservative Baptist Sem., Denver; Staley disting. Christian scholar lectr., 1973, 82, 84, 86, 88; participant Internat. Congress on World Evangelism, Lausanne, Switzerland, 1974. Author: Winning the New Civil War: Recapturing America's Values, 1991; editor monthly newsletter NAE Washington Insight. Candidate for U.S. Congress, 1976; mem. ethics adv. bd. USIA, 1982-84; bd. dirs. Justice Fellowship, 1983—, Transformation Internat., 1987—; bd. trustees Williamsburg Charter Found., 1988-89. Home: 1712 Paisley Blue Ct Vienna VA 22182 Office: Nat Assn Evangs Office Pub Affairs 1023 15th St NW Suite 500 Washington DC 20005

DUKE, DAVID NELSON, religion educator; b. Gadsden, Ala., Jan. 4, 1950; s. G. Nelson and Wilma (Awbrey) D.; m. Marcia Sowell; children: Wesley Sowell, Hillary Kathryn. BA, Samford U., 1972; MDiv, So. Bapt. Theol. Sem., Louisville, 1975; PhD, Emory U., 1980. Instr., chaplain North Greenville Coll., Tigerville, S.C., 1978-80; successively asst. prof., assoc. prof., prof. William Jewell Coll., Liberty, Mo., 1980—, chair dept. Co-author: Anguish and the Word: Preaching That Touches Pain, 1991; contbr.: Remembering For the Future, Vol. II, 1989; (dictionary) Mercer Bible Dictionary, 1990; mem. editorial bd. Perspectives in Religious Studies, 1991—; contbr. articles to Christian Century, Encounter, other jours. With speakers bur. Mo. Humanities Coun., 1989—, mem. adv. bd. scholars, St. Louis, 1990—. Recipient Excellence in Teaching Northland C. of C., 1988. Mem. Am. Acad. Religion, Internat. Bonhoeffer Soc., Nat. Assn. for Bapt. Profs. Religion (pres. Midwest region 1985-86). Baptist. Home: 116 N Jewell Liberty MO 64068 Office: William Jewell Coll 500 College Hill Liberty MO 64068-1896

DUKE, JAMES OLIVER, religion educator; b. Balt., Nov. 8, 1946; s. James Roy and Florence Gertrude (Hanes) D.; m. Jeanne Scott, May 15, 1991. BA, U. Md., 1968; MDiv, Vanderbilt U., 1971, MA, 1973, PhD, 1975. Ordained to ministry Christian Ch. (Disciples of Christ), 1971. Vis. prof. U. Mont., Missoula, 1975-76; asst. prof. Brite Div. Sch., Tex. Christian U., Ft. Worth, 1976-80, assoc. prof., 1980-85, prof., 1991—; prof. Pacific Sch. Religion, Berkeley, Calif., 1985-91; mem. theology commn. Coun. on Christian Unity, Christian Ch. (Disciples of Christ), 1976—, cons. Ch. Union, Princeton, N.J., 1978-84; guest prof. Evangelische Theologische Fakultat, U. Munich, Fed. Republic Germany, 1984. Author: Horace Bushnell, 1984; co-editor, translator: Schleiermacher, Practical Theology, 1988; co-translator: Schleiermacher's Hermeneutics, 1977, Schleiermacher's Lücke Letters, 1981. Recipient Jr. Scholars award Deutscher Akademischer Austauschdienst, 1973-74, Younger Scholars award Assn. Theol. Schs., 1984. Mem. Am. Acad. Religion, Am. Soc. Ch. History, N.Am. Assn. Ecumenists. Office: Tex Christian U Brite Div Sch Fort Worth TX 76109

DUKE, LAURA J., religious organization administrator; b. San Rafael, Calif.; m. David William Duke; children: Christian David, Kov Sum, Pann Sum. BS, U. Mich., 1978; MSW, Washington U., St. Louis, 1981. Lic. social worker. Social worker County Adoptions, San Bernardino, Calif.; dir. Bethany Christian Svcs., Bellflower, Calif., Adoption Agy.; pvt. practice social work; exec. dir., founder, chief exec. officer Internat. Christian Adoptions, Temecula, Calif., 1990—; cons. in field. Vol., founder various crisis ctrs., Calif. Mem. Acad. Cert. Social Work. Office: Internat Christian Adoptions 41745 Rider Way Ste 2 Temecula CA 92390

DUKE, THOMAS ALLEN, clergyman, religious organization executive; b. Eaton, Ohio, May 6, 1941; s. Leonard L. and Edith (Larsh) D.; m. Joan Mayer, Aug. 24, 1963; children: Karen E., Laura J. BA, Capital U., Columbus, Ohio, 1963; BD, Luther Theol. Sem., St. Paul, 1967; STM, Andover-Newton Theol. Sem., 1968; PhD, U. Minn., 1979. Ordained to ministry Evang. Luth. Ch. in Am., 1969. Asst. pastor Bethlehem Luth. Ch., St. Paul, 1969-72; instr. pastoral theology Luther Theol. Sem., 1968-76; program dir. community care unit Amherst-Wilder Found., St. Paul, 1976-88; exec. dir. St. Paul Area Coun. Chs., 1988—. Mem. Am. Assn. Pastoral Counselors (diplomate). Office: St Paul Area Coun Chs 1671 Summit Ave Saint Paul MN 55113

DUKES, DOROTHY, lay church worker; b. Birmingham, Ala., Jan. 24, 1926; d. Charlie and Elizabeth (Smiler) Dixon; m. Leonard Dukes, Mar. 11, 1957; children: Charlie Mae Dukes Johnson, Lauretta. Grad., Detroit Bible Coll., 1976; DH (hon.), Trinity Hall Coll. and Sem., 1981. Evangelist Ch. of God in Christ, Detroit, 1965, state dean Sunday sch. dept., 1969-71, ch. lay del. Internat. Sunday Sch. Conv., 1971, internat. coord. Sunday sch. conv. pageant, 1974—, chmn. edn. com. SW Mich. dist. 9, 1982—, state chmn. scholarship com. S.W. Mich. jurisdiction 2, 1988—, mem. Gt. Lake jurisdiction and Mt. Elliott, 1989—; pub. rels. dir. Baileys Temple Ch. of God in Christ, Detroit, 1976—; owner Dorothy Dukes House de Coiffure, Detroit, 1957—. Assoc. editor Ch. of God in Christ Women's Mag., 1973. Mem. Women's Conf. of Concern, 1974, Nat. Coun. Negro Women, 1974; bd. dirs. Charles Harrison Mason Systems of Bible Coll., Detroit, 1972. Recipient Religious Workers guild honorium Ch. of God in Christ, 1982. Mem. Bus. and Profl. Women's Fedn. S.W. Mich. (state bd. dirs. 1968), Internat. Platform Soc. Democrat. Home: 4181 Burns Dr Detroit MI 48214 Office: 7414 E Canfield Detroit MI 48214 *In this life one must have an anchor. Let it be God.*

DULIN, GENE, mission executive; b. Heltonville, Ind., July 13, 1925; s. J. Fred and Emma (McCammon) D.; m. Lenora M. McDonald, Dec. 28, 1947; children: Vanita Mae, Karlita Kae. Student, Ind. U., 1942; AB, Cin. Bible Sem., 1950; postgrad., Earlham Coll., 1950. Ordained to ministry Christian Ch. Minister various Christian chs., Ind., 1946-57; pres., founder TCM, Internat., Inc., Indpls., 1957—. Editor mag. Can. Christian Harbinger; author: Faith Promise Missouri Conf.; contbr. articles to religious publs. Staff sgt. USAF, 1942-46. Office: TCM Internat Inc 6337 Hollister Dr Indianapolis IN 46224

DULLES, AVERY, priest, theologian; b. Auburn, N.Y., Aug. 24, 1918; s. John Foster and Janet Pomeroy (Avery) D. AB, Harvard U., 1940, postgrad. in law, 1940-41; PhL, Woodstock Coll., 1951, STL, 1957; STD, Pontifical Gregorian U., Rome, 1960; LLD, St. Joseph's Coll., Phila., 1969, Iona Coll., New Rochelle, N.Y., 1980; LHD, Georgetown U., 1977, Creighton U., 1983, Seton Hall U., 1989, Stonehill Coll., 1990, Loyola U., Chgo., 1990; ThD, U. Detroit, 1978; DD, St. Anselm Coll., Manchester, N.H., 1981, Jesuit Sch. Theology, Berkeley, Calif., 1984, Protestant Episcopal Theol. Sem., Alexandria, Va., 1986, Carthage Coll., Kenosha, Wis., 1991; STD (hon.), Providence Coll., 1991. Joined S.J., Roman Cath. Ch., 1946, ordained priest, 1956. Instr. philosophy Fordham U., 1951-53, vis. lectr., 1970, Laurencce J. McGinley prof. religion and society, 1988—; mem. faculty Woodstock Coll., N.Y.C., 1960-74; prof. theology Woodstock Coll., 1969-74, Cath. U. Am., Washington, 1974-88; Gasson prof. theology Boston Coll., 1981-82; prof. emeritus Cath. U. Am., Washington, 1988—; vis. lectr. Weston Coll., 1971, Union Theol. Sem., 1971-74, Princeton Theol. Sem., 1972, Pontifical Gregorian U., 1973, 90, Episcopal Theol. Sem., 1975, Luth. Sem. Pa., 1978; Martin C. D'Arcy lectr. Campion Hall, Oxford (Eng.) U., 1983; vis. John A. O'Brien prof. theology Notre Dame U., 1985; fellow Woodrow Wilson Internat. Ctr. for Scholars, 1977; mem. Commn. on Christian Unity, Archdiocese of Balt., 1962-70, Cath. Bishops' Adv. Coun., 1969-75; consultor to Papal Secretariat for Dialogue with Non-Believers, 1966-73; mem. U.S.A. Luth.-Cath. Dialogue, 1972—. Author: Princeps Concordiae, 1941, A Testimonial to Grace, 1946; (with others) Introductory Metaphysics, 1955; Apologetics and the Biblical Christ, 1963, The Dimensions of the Church, 1967, Revelation and the Quest for Unity, 1968, Revelation Theology: A History, 1969; (with others) Spirit, Faith, and Church, 1970; The Survival of Dogma, 1971 (Christopher award 1972), A History of Apologetics, 1971, Models of the Church, 1974, 2d rev. edit., 1987, Church Membership as a Catholic and Ecumenical Problem, 1974, The Resilient Church, 1977, A Church to Believe In, 1982, Models of Revelation, 1983; (with Patrick Granfield) The Church: A Bibliography, 1985, The Catholicity of the Church, 1985, The Reshaping of Catholicism, 1988; assoc. editor for ecumenism Concilium, 1963-70, adv. editorial bd., 1970—; adv. editorial bd. Midstream: An Ecumenical Jour., 1974—; contbr. column Theology for Today to America, 1967-68; contbg. editor New Oxford Rev., 1990—; cons. Theology Digest, 1985—; contbr. articles to theol. pubs. Bd. dirs. Georgetown U., 1966-68, Woodstock Theol. Center, 1974-79; trustee Fordham U., 1969-72; acad. council Irish Sch. Ecumenics, 1971-78. Served to lt. USNR, 1942-46. Decorated Croix de Guerre France; recipient Cardinal Spellman award for distinguished achievement in theology, 1970, Religious Education Forum award Nat. Cath. Edn. Assn., 1988, Campion award Cath. Book Club, N.Y., 1989. Mem. Cath. Theol. Soc. Am. (bd. dirs. 1970-72, 74-77, v.p. 1974-75, pres. 1975-76), Am. Theol. Soc. (v.p. 1977-78, pres. 1978-79), Cath. Commn. on Intellectual and Cultural Affairs (exec. com. 1991—), Phi Beta Kappa. Address: Fordham U Jesuit Community Bronx NY 10458

DUMAINE, R. PIERRE, bishop; b. Paducah, Ky., Aug. 2, 1931; student St. Joseph Coll., Mountain View, Calif., 1945-51, St. Patrick Sem., Menlo Park, Calif., 1951-57; Ph.D., Cath. U. Am., 1962. Ordained priest Roman Cath. Ch., 1957; asst. pastor Immaculate Heart Ch., Belmont, Calif., 1957-58; mem. faculty dept. edn. Cath. U. Am., 1961-63; tchr. Serra High Sch., San Mateo, Calif., 1963-65; asst. supt. Cath. schs., Archdiocese of San Francisco, 1965-74, supt., 1974-78; ordained bishop, 1978, bishop of San Jose, Calif., 1981—; dir. Archdiocesan Ednl. TV Ctr., Menlo Park, Calif., 1968-81. Mem. Pres.'s Nat. Adv. Council on Edn. of Disadvantaged Children, 1970-72; bd. dirs. Cath. TV Network, 1968-81, pres., 1975-77; bd. dirs. Pub. Service Satellite Consortium, 1975-81. Mem. Nat. Cath. Edn. Assn., Assn. Cath. Broadcasters and Allied Communicators, Internat. Inst. Communications, Assn. Calif. Sch. Adminstrs. Office: Diocese of San Jose 841 Lenzen Ave San Jose CA 95126

DUMAS, D. JUAKEN, minister; b. Eldorado, Ark., Dec. 3, 1957; s. Dewey Calvin and Carolyn Jannette (Little) D.; m. Pamela Louise Mick, Aug. 9, 1975; children: Brandy Ellen, Shana Dechet, David Juaken, Jr., Johnathon Calvin, Bethany Carolyn Denet. BA in Theology, Patriot Univ., 1986, PhD of Theology, 1989, M in Theology, 1987; DTh, Cahokia (Ill.) Bible Inst., 1988. Lic. to ministry Bapt. Ch., 1975, ordained, 1977. Founder, evangelist Christ's Cause Evangelistic Assn., Inc., Matthews, Mo., 1975-77; pastor Parklane Bapt. Ch. (now First Bapt. Ch.), Cahokia, 1977—; founder, adminstr. Parklane Bapt. Acad. (now First Bapt. Acad.), Cahokia, 1983—; founder, chancellor Cahokia Bible Inst., 1988—; advisor L.O.M.M. Devel. Corp., Inc., Cahokia, 1990—; youth camp dir. Bapt. Missionary Assn. of Ill. and Ind., Springfield, 1977-80, pres., 1978-80, missions screening com., 1978-91, missionary com., Little Rock, 1977-91. Author: Impact 2000 Church Growth, 1989, Principles of Teaching and Learning, 1988; editor: The Centurian jour., 1984-89; contbr. articles to profl. jours. Bd. dirs., founder King's Teens of Cahokia, 1983-89, The Transformer's Clubs, Cahokia, 1985-91; mem., pres. various civic orgns., 1980—. Mem. Christ's Cause Evangelistic Assn. (pres. 1977-81). Republican. Office: First Baptist Church 1771 Camp Jackson Rd Cahokia IL 62206 *Our entire purpose of being is to be an extension of God's person, to display the essence of God's presence and to exhibit God's power among mankind. We must have a cause in our life. We should be seeking the purpose that God has for us and then do it. (I Samuel 17:29).*

DUMAS, DARRELL OLEN, minister; b. Dallas, July 16, 1960; s. Hollis Olen and Janice Lurlene (Jones) D.; m. Barbara Josephine Werry, May 31, 1980; children: Lauren Michelle, Megan Danelle, Katelyn Rachelle. BS, U. Tex., Dallas, 1985; MA, Dallas Theol. Sem., 1989. Ordained to ministry Ind. Christian Ch., 1989. Min. youth Cen. Christian Ch., Covington, Tenn., 1989—; bd. dirs. Camp Christian, Burns, Tenn., 1989—; exec. com. Tenn. Christian Teen Conv., Nashville, 1990—; authorized adminstr. Taylor-Johnson Temperament Analysis, 1987—. Mem. Nat. Network Youth Mins., Evang. Tng. Assn. (tchr. 1989—). Republican. Home: 1253 Oil Mill Rd Covington TN 38019 Office: Cen Christian Ch 400 S Maple Covington TN 38019

DUMKE, BARBARA ANN, priest; b. Oshkosh, Wis., May 27, 1946; d. Robert William and Florence Rose (Seavecki) D.; m. Eugene Richard Wahl, Sept. 17, 1988. BA, U. Wis., Oshkosh, 1968; MA in Urban and Regional Planning, U. Pitts., 1970; MA in Div., United Theol. Sem., 1985; MA in Theol. Study, Ch. Div. Sch. of Pacific, 1987. Ordained priest Episcopal Ch., 1988. Pastoral cons. St. Josaphat's Roman Cath. Ch., Oshkosh, 1978-82; minister Christian Ministry in Nat. Parks, Grand Canyon, Ariz., 1984; coord. sr. citizens St. Cuthbert Episcopal Ch., Oakland, Calif., 1986-87; asst. rector St. Aidan Episcopal Ch., San Francisco, 1987-88; assoc. rector St. John Episcopal Ch., Ross, Calif., 1989—; mem. commn., mem. stewardship com. 2000 Diocese of Calif., San Francisco, 1990—; mem. Marin Deanery, San Rafael, Calif., 1990—; founding mem. spiritual formation group Lloyd Ctr. for Counseling, San Anselmo, Calif., 1990. Contbr. articles to profl. publs. Mem. instnl. rev. bd. Marin Gen. Hosp., Greenbrae, Calif., 1989—. Carnegie-Mellon fellow, 1969. Democrat. Office: St John Episcopal Ch PO Box 217 Ross CA 94957 *What is as important as eating, working, or supporting our families and people in need? Laughing is. A sense of humor tricks us into experiencing life from God's perspective: where blessing, suprise, joy come out of suffering and seriousness.*

DUMKE, MARK PAUL, minister; b. Zumbrota, Minn., June 22, 1955; s. Paul Frederick and Marilyn Lorraine (Dutcher) D.; m. Nancy Solomonson, May 30, 1981; children: Kirsten, Karin. BA in Psychology, Gustavus Adolphus Coll., 1977; MDiv, Luther Northwestern Theol. Sem, 1984. Ordained to ministry Luth. Ch., 1984. Pastor St. Luke's Luth. Ch., Cottage Grove, Minn., 1984-87, Faith Luth. Ch., Winona, Minn., 1987—; bd. dirs. Luth. Campus Ministry Minn., St. Paul, 1989—; trustee, Gustavus Adolphus Coll., St. Peter, Minn., 1991—; campus coun. Winona Luth. Campus Ministry, 1987—; mut. ministry com. S.E. Minn. Synod Evang. Luth. Ch. Am., Rochester, 1989—; sec. Metro I Dist. Minn. Synod Luth. Ch. in Am., St. Paul, 1986-87; pres. South Washington County Ministerium, Cottage Grove, Minn., 1986-87; key note speaker Ally Weekend, Alliance for Youth, Winona, 1991; publicity dir. Winona Religious Survey, 1990. Convenor Winona Coop. Youth Ministry, 1990-91; bd. dirs. Winona Area United Way, 1990—. Recipient Disting. Svc. award South Communities Youth Svcs.,

Cottage Grove, 1987. Office: Faith Luth Ch 1717 W Service Dr Winona MN 55987 *I will have lived life well if I am able to graciously, willingly and sacrificially give more than I receive. I believe such a life to be the will of God, the example of Christ and the only human source of hope for our world.*

DUMM, DEMETRIUS ROBERT, priest, educator; b. Carrolltown, Pa., Oct. 1, 1923; s. Gordon Hildebert and Esther Frances (Kirsch) D. B.A., St. Vincent Coll., Latrobe, Pa., 1945; S.T.D., Collegio di Sant'Anselmo, Rome, 1950; postgrad., Ecole Biblique Française, Jerusalem, 1950-52; S.S.L., Pontifical Bibl. Commn., Rome, 1952. Joined Order of St. Benedict, Roman Catholic Ch., 1943, ordained priest, 1947; mem. faculty St. Vincent Sem., 1952—, prof. N.T., 1952—, rector, 1963-80; master of novices St. Vincent Archabbey, 1980-83. Author: Flowers in the Desert, 1987; contbr.articles in field; contbr. New Jerome Bibl. Commentary. Mem. Soc. Bibl. Lit., Cath. Bibl. Assn. Am., East. Coast Rectors Conf. (past pres.). Address: St Vincent Archabbey Latrobe PA 15650 *If I have acquired any wisdom from my experience, it has been mainly through the ministry of other good people. They have helped me to see opportunity and promise rather than threat in the often ambiguous situations of life. Now, as my human abilities begin to decline with age, my faith indicates that the greatest promise of all is hidden in that ambiguous future where my Creator has reserved it for me.*

DUMOUCHEL, PAUL, archbishop; b. Winnipeg, Man., Can., Sept. 19, 1911; s. Joseph and Josephine D. Grad., St. Boniface (Man.) Coll., 1930; student, U. Man., 1929-300, Sem. Lebret, Sask., Can., 1931-36. Ordained priest Roman Cath. Ch., 1936; missionary to Indians of Man., 1936-50, retreat master, 1940-50, sch. prin., 1950-55; bishop of Keewatin, Can., 1955-67; 1st archbishop Le Pas, 1967-86. Author: Saulteux Grammar, 1942. Address: 204-480 Rue Aulneau, Saint Boniface, MB Canada R2H 2U2

DUNBAR, DAVID G., academic administrator. Head Bibl. Theol. Sem., Hatfield, Pa. Office: Berean Inst Tech Div 1901 W Girard Ave Philadelphia PA 19130-1599 also: Bibl Theol Sem 200 N Main St Hatfield PA 19440*

DUNCAN, CLYDE TANGLEY, pastor; b. Albuquerque, June 12, 1936; s. Claude and Mary (Brown) D.;m. Sept. 6, 1956; children: Michael, Clyde Otis, Renee. Bachelors, Internat. M.B. Sem., Little Rock, Ark., 1966, ThM, 1989. Chaplan com. ABA, 1980-91; instr. Internat. Sch. Theol., 1989—; pastor First Bapt. Ch., Alexandria, Va., 1979. Pres. Optimist, Alexandria, Va., 1987; With U.S. Army, 1953-57. Office: First Baptist CHurch 7313 Hayfield Rd Alexandria VA 22310-4602

DUNCAN, JAMES REARY, pastor, educator; b. Springfield, Mo., May 31, 1951; s. Joe R. and Helen L. Duncan; m. Kimberly Sue Davis, Nov. 7, 1981; children: Abby Joe, Whitney James. BA, Ouachita Bapt. U., 1973; MDiv, Midwestern Bapt. Theol. Sem., 1980, D in Ministry, 1986. Minister student activities First Bapt. Ch., England, Ark., 1972-74; minister of music First Bapt. Ch., Eminence, Mo., 1975-77; pastor New Liberty Bapt. Ch., Mound City, Mo., 1978-80, Urich (Mo.) Bapt. Ch., 1980-85, Noland Rd. Bapt. Ch., Independence, Mo., 1985—; ajd. prof. Midwestern Bapt. Theol. Sem., Kansas City, Mo., 1987—. Vol. chaplain to inmates program Tucker (Ark.) Intermediate Prison, 1974-76; vol. appointee Human Rels. Commn., Independence, 1987—. Mem. Rotary, Jaycees (Outstanding Young Man of Am. 1980, 85). Baptist. Avocations: sports, arts, crafts, family. Office: Noland Rd Bapt Ch 4505 S Noland Rd Independence MO 64055

DUNCAN, JOHN MALVIN, minister; b. Plainview, Tex., Aug. 29, 1934; s . Malvin Eural and Velma (Thompson) D. Banker, 1959-69; with McGavack Miller Fin. & Ins., 1973-87; min. Help Open People's Eyes (H.O.P.E.) Ministries, Plainview, Tex., 1987—. Served with U.S. Army, 1959-69. Home and Office: 2813 W 18th St Plainview TX 79072

DUNCAN, MICHAEL RAYVONNE, minister; b. Gideon, Mo., Apr. 23, 1949; s. Arthur Lamb and Juanita Vivian (Knapp) D.; m. Donna Lynn Austin, Aug. 12, 1969. BA, Union U., 1971; MDiv, So. Bapt. Theol. Sem., 1976; postgrad., Lexington Theol. Sem., 1988—. Ordained to ministry So. Bapt. Conv., 1968. Pastor Mercer (Tenn.) Bapt. Ch., 1968-70, Nashway Bapt. Ch., Jackson, Tenn., 1971-72, Utica (Ind.) Bapt. Ch., 1973-75, Mt. Moriah Bapt. Ch., Mt. Eden, Ky., 1975-79, Eminence (Ky.) Bapt. Ch., 1979—; assoc. pastor 1st Bapt. Ch., Ellendale, Tenn., 1972-73; ptnr. D.A.D. Farms Inc., Tallapossa, Mo., 1987—; mem. exec. bd. Ky. Bapt. Conv., Middletown, Ky., 1984-87, chmn. minister/ch. support com., 1987; pres. Eminence Coun. of Chs., 1981, 84; pres. Ky. Bapt. Hist. Soc., Middletown, 1984-86; mem. Religious Liberty Coun. of Bapt. Joint Com. on Pub. Affairs, Washington, 1990—. Chmn. blood program ARC, Henry County, 1981-83; chaplain Eminence Fire & Rescue, 1981—; technician Emergency Med. Svc., Eminence, 1982-89; bd. dirs. Eminence C. of C., 1981-84; mem. Foster Care Rev. Bd. for Henry and Trimble Counties, Ky., 1990—. Mem. Henry County Bapt. Assn. (bd. dirs. 1979—), Rotary. Democrat. Office: Eminence Bapt Ch PO Box 134 Eminence KY 40019-0134 *Life is a pilgrimage of faith periodically punctuated by doubt. Although sometimes disconcerting, doubt need not be an obstacle to authentic faith; it can be a door through which the pilgrim moves toward an ever deeper level of faith.*

DUNCAN, PAUL DAVID, lay worker; b. Hickory, N.C., Oct. 1, 1947; s. Zerden Billie and Verlie Estelle (Brown) D.; m. Mary Maude Smith, Feb. 02, 1974; 1 child, Elizabeth Anne. BA, Lenoir Rhyne Coll., 1969; MA in Teaching, Duke U., 1973. Cert. math. tchr. Youth adv. coun. Ch. God Abrahamic Faith, Oregon, Ill., 1967; tchr., chmn. math. dept. Hibriten High Sch., Lenoir, N.C., 1969—; elder Ch. Resurrection Hope, Lenoir, N.C., 1975—; pres. Southeast Conf. Ch. God, Pelzer, S.C., 1983-85, 88-89, youth camp dir., 1970, 75, 81, youth leader Ch. Resurrection Hope, 1969-74, Sunday sch. tchr., 1970—, youth camp tchr. Va. Conf. Ch. God, Front Royal, 1976. Organist Ch. Resurrection Hope, 1969—, speaker radio program, Berean Youth Sunday Sch. Pprgram, 1975—. Recipient Fritz Math. award, 1969. Mem. NEA, N.C. Assn. Edcuators. Republican. Home: 1044 Cottrell Hill Rd Lenoir NC 28645

DUNCAN, RICHARD CHRANE, executive director; b. N.Y.C., Mar. 11, 1946; s. Richard Davenport Duncan and Patricia Ann (Chrane) Lipps; m. Donna Lee Jennings, Dec. 27, 1967; children: Donita Noel, Richard Jennings. BA, Mo. U., 1968; MDiv, Louisville Sem., 1971; D of Ministry, McCormick Sem., 1976. Cert. fund raising exec. Pastor Okolona (Miss.) Presbyn. Ch., 1971-73, Clement United Presbyn. Ch., Cicero, Ill., 1973-78; exec. dir. Greater Birmingham Ministries, 1978-81, Corpus Christi (Tex.) Metro Ministries, 1982-89, Greater Dayton (Ohio) Christian Coun., 1989—. Author: Approach to Parish Revitalization, 1977, Guns Don't Die-People Do, 1981, Church & Child Abuse Prevention, 1987; co-author: Adopting Child Protection Workers, 1988; contbr. articles to profl. jours. Organizer Grant Works Youth Coun., Cicero, 1975, Corpus Christi Metro Ministries, 1982-83; mediator Cicero Gangs vs. Residents, 1975. Recipient Pub. Citizen award NASW, 1989. Home: 1815 Ravenwood Ave Dayton OH 45406 Office: Dayton Christian Coun 212 Belmonte Park E Dayton OH 45405

DUNGAN, SHIRLEY ANN, religious organization administrator; b. Safford, Ariz., Jan. 11, 1932; d. Guy Austin and Mabel Esther (Houck) Rhoads; m. Gerald Knox, Dec. 26, 1954 (div. Apr. 1974); children: Dirk Daniel, Kevin Knox, Delta Lynn. RN, St. Mary's Coll., Tucson, 1954; BS, St. Francis Coll., Joliet, Ill., 1986. Adminstr. St. James Presbyn. Ch., Littleton, Colo., 1985—; chaplain Swedish Med. Ctr., Englewood, Colo., 1990—. Author: Development of a Stewardship Campaign, 1989; patentee of med. equipment. Organist, choir dir., Fed. Correctional Inst., Englewood, 1965-73; reader for the blind Nat. Libr. Congress, Washington, 1970-76. Fellow Nat. Assn. Ch. Bus. Adminstrn. (v.p. Mile High chpt.); mem. WETAR Investments Club, Denver. Home: 9251 E Desert Sands Ln Tucson AZ 85710 Office: St James Presbyn Ch 3601 W Belleview Littleton CO 80123 *Mankind's first instinct is survival. Mankind's need is to find God in that survival. Mankind's hope is to add, with God's help, love, laughter, caring and grace to that survival.*

DUNHAM, RUSSELL JOHN, minister; b. Lapeer, Mich., Aug. 28, 1965; s. John C. and Judy L. (Pickett) D.; m. Lesa Marlene Keith, Apr. 11, 1987; children: Jacob Ryan, Chad Wesley. BTh, Ozark Christian Coll., Joplin, Mo., 1990. Interim minister Bornaugh (Mo.) Christian Ch., 1988-89; minister of youth Rinehart (Mo.) Christian Ch., 1989-90; assoc./youth minister First Christian Ch. of Hessville, Hammond, Ind., 1990—. Mem. Fellowship of Christian Ministers. Home: 6727 Alabama Ave Hammond IN 46323 Office: Frst Christian Ch Hessville 6733 Alabama Ave Hammond IN 46323

DUNIO, DONNA KAY, religious organization director, municipal official; b. Alexandria, La., Oct. 31, 1946; d. Robert Lowell and Cumie Violet (Wolfe) Demaree; m. Philip Michael Dunio, Feb. 5, 1966; children: Paul Brian, Cumie Carol. Student, U. Scranton, Pa., 1982—. Dist. mgr. Wm. Taylor, Inc. subs. Elaine Powers Corp., Scranton, Wilkes-Barre, Pa., 1972-74; exec. asst. Moses Taylor Hosp., Scranton, 1974-76; med. asst. Thomas H. Armstrong, M.D., Carlisle, Pa., 1976-78; mem. mgmt. team Spa Health and Fitness Ctrs., Exton, Pa., 1978-81; community liaison, dir. Allied Services, Scranton, 1982-84; exec. dir. United Chs. NE Pa., Scranton, 1984-87; exec. asst. mayor City of Scranton, Pa., 1987—; mem. church and Society com. Wyoming Conf. United Meth. Ch. Bd. dirs. Urban Ministries/St. Anthony's Shelter, Ne Pa. Goodwill Industries, SHINE, Interfaith Found., Womens's Employment Program, Moscow United Meth. Ch., local UN Assn., Scranton Interfaith Friends; mem. local PTA, ; mem. Steamtwon Bd., Downtown Scranton Bus. Assn., Deutsch Bd., Mayor's 504 Task Force, Lackawanna Arts Council, Scranton Library Bd., Leadership Lackawanna. Named NE Woman of Week The Scranton Times, 1985; recipient Women's Recognition award Scranton YWCA, 1986. Mem. Scranton C. of C. (visitors and conv. bur.), Council on Ministries, Tri-County Migrant Assn., Deutsch Inst. Sabbath, Loaned Exec. Alumni Assn., Alpha Sigma Lambda (pres.), Alpha Upsilon (Nat. Honor Soc. scholar 1987-88), Delta Tau Kappa. Republican. Avocations: sports, reading, writing, photography. Home: 16 Pen Y Bryn Dr Scranton PA 18505 Office: City Hall Scranton PA 18503

DUNKER, SANDRA S(UE), religion educator; b. Belvidere, Ill., Jan. 21, 1957; d. Robert Walter and Norenne Edwina (Pinnow) D. BA, Concordia U., 1979, MA, 1986. Tchr., youth dir. Holy Cross Luth Ch., San Diego, 1979-80; tchr. kindergarten Bethlehem Luth. ch., Aloha, Oreg., 1980-83; tchr. pre-sch. and kindergarten Christ the King Luth. Sch., Southgate, Mich., 1983-84; dir. confs. and convs. Concordia U., River Forest, Ill., 1984-86; tchr., youth dir. Zion Luth. Sch., Marengo, Ill., 1986—; early childhood cons. N.W. dist. Luth. Ch.-Mo. Synod, Portland, Oreg., 1980-82. Clown Easter Seals Soc., Portland, 1980-81. Mem. Luth. Edn. Assn., No. Ill. Dist. Early Childhood Educators. Home: 333 E Jackson Marengo IL 60152 Office: Zion Luth Sch 408 E Jackson Marengo IL 60152

DUNKERLEY, DONALD AUSTIN, minister; b. Passaic, N.J., Oct. 8, 1936; s. John Raymond and Beatrice Ethel (Chamberlain) D.; m. Eileen Joy Tomlinson, June 24, 1961; children: David, Joy Anne (dec.), Kathleen. BA, Rutgers U., 1958; MDiv, N.Y. Theol. Sem., 1961. Ordained to ministry Presbyn. Ch. in Am., 1961. Asst. pastor 2d Presbyn. Ch., Rahway, N.J., 1961-62; pastor Hope Presbyn. Ch., Tarrytown, N.Y., 1963-67; assoc. pastor 1st Presbyn. Ch., Babylon, N.Y., 1967-71; pastor McIlwain Meml. Presbyn. Ch, Pensacola, Fla., 1971-80; bd. dirs. Presbyn. Evang. Fellowship, Decatur, Ga., 1872-80, evangelist, 1980-84; dir. Proclamation Internat. Inc., Pensacola, 1984—; mem. ministerial adv. bd. Reformed Theol. Sem., Jackson, Miss., 1970, exec. com. European Missionary Fellowship, Eng., 1970-84; bd. dirs. Pensacola Theol. Inst., 1971-80; mem. adv. bd. Affirmative Evangelism, Pine Bush, N.Y., 1983—; mem. exec. com. Presbyn. and Reformed Renewal Ministries Internat., 1990—. Mem. editorial bd. Presbyn. Layman, N.Y.C., 1968-71; contbr. columns to religious publs. Founding bd. dirs. Alpha Ctr., Pensacola, 1972-76. Mem. Evang. Theol. Soc. Home: 3941 McClellan Rd Pensacola FL 32503 Office: Proclamation Internat Inc PO Box 13367 Pensacola FL 32591

DUNKIN, JONATHAN DAVID, youth music minister; b. Mobile, Ala., Feb. 14, 1963; s. Mark Mosco and Joyce Lorraine (Stevens) D.; m. Kathy Sue Kinsey, Nov. 15, 1985. Grad. high sch., St. Martin/Am. Sch. Corr. Youth music min. Cedar Lake Christian Assembly, Biloxi, Miss., 1986--; v.p. Dinotrax Inc., Biloxi, Miss., 1990--. Republican. Assembly of God. Office: Cedar Lake Christian Ass PO Box 6069 Biloxi MS 39532

DUNKLY, JAMES WARREN, theological librarian; b. Alexandria, La., Aug. 1, 1942; s. James Warren and Frances Estelle (Jones) D.; m. Nancy Rose; children: Margaret Rose, Michael Benjamin. BA, Tex. Christian U., 1963; diploma in Theology, Oxford U., Eng., 1964; MA, Vanderbilt U., 1968, PhD, 1982. Grad. fellow, tutor Episcopal Theol. Sch., Cambridge, Mass., 1969-71; libr. Nashotah (Wis.) House, 1975-83; dir. librs. Episcopal Div. Sch., Weston Sch. Theology, Cambridge, 1983—; instr. Inst. Christian Studies, Milw., 1975-83, Wis.; guest preacher Milw., Dallas, Colo., Kans., Mass., Ft. Worth; reader Gen. Ordination Exams., 1985—; mem. Cathedral Sch. Religion Com., Diocese of Mass., 1988—, Living Ch. Found., Milw., 1977-83. asst. editor N.T. Abstracts, 1971-72, mng. editor, 1972-75; editorial asst. Jour. Bibl. Lit., 1974-75; copy editor Nashotah Rev., 1975-77; mem. corp. for Anglican Theol. Rev., 1976—, asst. editor for N.T., 1976-84, editor, 1984-88; contbr. articles to profl. jours. Conant Fund grantee, Episcopal Ch., 1981-82; Henry fellow, Oxford U., 1963-64, Vanderbilt U. teaching fellow, 1967-69, Rockefeller doctoral fellow, 1969-70; Vanderbilt U. scholar, 1966-67. Mem. Soc. Bibl. Lit., Cath. Bibl. Assn., Am. Theol. Libr. Assn. (publs. com. 1977-83, bd. dirs. 1980-83, task force on structure, 1981, index bd. 1985-89, exec. com. index and preservation bds. 1988-89, v.p. 1989-90, pres. 1990—). Home: 7 Fairway Rd Acton MA 01720 Office: Episcopal Div Sch and Weston Sch Theology Libr 99 Brattle St Cambridge MA 02138

DUNLAP, CATHERINE MARY, clergywoman; b. Toronto, Ohio, Oct. 28, 1927; d. Michael Nicholas and Lena (Conti) Reale; children: Charles E., Catherine Dunlap Molinaro, Thomas Michael; m. William Freese (dec. Jan. 1980). AS in Bus., Steubenville Bus. Coll., 1947; MA in Christian Edn., Meth. Theol. Sem., Delaware, Ohio, 1983. Ordained diaconal minister United Meth. Ch., 1983. Dir. fin. assistance and ch. rels. Meth. Theol. Sem., 1983-89; diaconal assoc. minister United Meth. Ch. Kent, Ohio, 1989—; Vice pres. bd. diaconal ministry East Ohio Conf., United Meth. Ch., Canton, 1989—, v.p. NC jurisdictional program com., Detroit, 1988—, NC jurisdictional bd. ministry, Chgo., 1988—; pres. East Ohio Conf. United Meth. Women, 1975-79; v.p. bd. publ. United Meth. Ch., 1972-84, mem. bd. higher edn. and ministry, 1984-89. Trustee Ohio No. U., Ada, 1979—. Recipient Community Svc. award B'nai B'rith, 1967, nat. award United Meth. Women, 1983. Mem. Ch. Women United (pres. 1969-73), AAUW, Order Ea. Star (chaplain 1969). Avocations: travel, crewel embroidery, reading, walking. Home: 4209 Lancaster Ln Kent OH 44240 Office: United Meth Ch Kent 1435 E Main St Kent OH 44240

DUNLAP, ELDEN DALE, retired theology educator; b. Rose Hill, Kans., Nov. 1, 1921; s. Laban Christian and Ruth (Hall) D.; m. Frances Whitehead, Dec. 18, 1944; children: Margaret A., David W., Mark H. BA, Southwestern Coll., Winfield, Kans., 1943; BD, Garrett Biblical Inst., Evanston, Ill., 1945; MA, Northwestern U., 1947; PhD, Yale U., 1956. Ordained to ministry United Meth. Ch. as elder, 1945. Instr. Bible, religion, philosophy Southwestern Coll., 1951-53, asst. prof. Bible and religion, 1953-55, assoc. prof., dean of coll., 1955-59; assoc. prof. theology St. Paul Sch. Theology, Kansas City, Mo., 1959-65, prof., 1965-87, acad. dean, 1970-87, acad. dean emeritus, prof. emeritus theology, 1987—; mem. United Meth. Bd. High Edn. and Ministries, 1980-88, United Meth. Commn. Christian Unity and Interreligious Concerns, 1988—; mem. World Meth. Coun., 1986-91; chmn. com. on ministry United Meth. Ch., 1980-84, com. on baptism, 1988—. Author: Methodist Theology in Great Britain in the Nineteenth Century, 1956; contbr. articles to profl. jours., chpts. to books. Mem. Bd. Edn. Westwood (Kans.) View Elem. Dist., 1961-67, Hist. Soc. United Meth. Ch.; chmn. Johnson County (Kans.) Sch. Bds. Assn., 1963-67. Frank W. Howes scholar, 1943-45; sr. fellow Garrett Biblical Inst., 1945-46, Frank W. Howes fellow Garrett Biblical Inst., 1948-50; Yale U. fellow, 1950-51, Faculty fellow Assn. Theol. Schs., 1967-68. Mem. Am. Theol. Soc., Am. Soc. Ch. History, Am. Acad. Religion, World Meth. Historical Soc. Democrat. Home and Office: 4841 Belinder Ct Westwood KS 66205

DUNLAP, JEFFREY LEE, minister, educator; b. Washington Courthouse, Ohio, Dec. 7, 1955; s. Orville Ray and Carolyn Sue (Merritt) D. BA in Christian Ministries, Lincoln (Ill.) Christian Coll., 1980. Cert. tchr., adminstrn., supervision, Ohio. Youth minister First Christian Ch., Washington Courthouse, 1975-76; intern Westside Christian Ch., Springfield, Ill., 1978; youth minister Christian Ch., Kenosha, Wis., 1981-83; dir. community edn. Washington Courthouse City/Miami Trace Local Schs., Fayette County, 1987-89; substitute tchr. various Ohio Pub. Schs., 1990-91; vocat. counselor Pvt. Industry Coun., Circleville, Ohio, 1991—; counselor youth and adult ministry First Christian Ch., 1985—, grant writer, cons., 1986-89. Assoc. United Way, Washington Courthouse, 1986-89, Am. Heart Assn., Columbus, 1986-89; program coord. community edn. County of Fayette, Washington Courthouse, 1986-89; health coord. Fayette County Health Dept., Washington Courthouse, 1986-89. Named One of Outstanding Young Men of Am., 1987. Avocations: tennis, basketball, golf, baseball, photography. Home: 316 E Elm St Washington Court House OH 43160

DUNLOP, LAURENCE JAMES, educator; b. Adelaide, Australia, Jan. 7, 1939; came to U.S., 1980; s. Walter James and Jean Wilson (Eardley) D. Licentiate in Theology, Gregorian U., Rome, 1966; Licentiate in Scripture, Pontifical Bibl. Inst., Rome, 1967, Doctorate in Scripture, 1970. Lectr. Sacred Heart Monastery, Canberra, Act, Australia, 1964-65; lectr. St. Paul's Nat. Sem., Sydney, N.S.W., Australia, 1970-79, rector, 1975-79; asst. prof. Loyola U., Chgo., 1981-83; assoc. prof. Marymount Coll., Rancho Palos Verdes, Calif., 1983—. Author: The Happy Poor, 1975, Patterns of Prayer in the Psalms, 1981; contbr. articles to profl. jours. Roman Catholic. Office: Marymount Coll 30800 PV Dr E Rancho Palos Verdes CA 90274

DUNN, ARVIN GAIL, clergyman; b. Columbia City, Ind., Jan. 11, 1930; s. Thomas Henry Arvin and Mary Ruth (Pritchard) D.; m. Marilyn Joan Reames, Jan. 1, 1950; children—Stephen Leslie, Gaye Lynn, Karen Lou, Mark Lee. B.A., Findlay Coll., Ohio, 1952, D.D. (hon.), 1983; B.Div., Winebrenner Theol. Sem., Findlay, 1955, M.Div., 1976. Ordained to ministry Chs. of God Gen. Conf., 1952. Pastor Sugar Ridge Ch. of God, Convoy, Ohio, 1952-53; pastor Anthony Wayne First Ch. of God, Ft. Wayne, Ind., 1953-55, Anderson Bethel Ch. of God, Mendon, Ohio, 1955-60; pastor First Ch. of God, Mendon, 1955-67, Harrisburg, Pa., 1967-83; supt. East. Pa. Conf. Chs. of God, Harrisburg, 1983—; pres. Chs. of God Gen. Conf.,Findlay, Ohio, 1983-86; trustee Winebrenner Theol. Sem., Findlay, 1971—; bd. dirs. Pa. Council of Chs., Harrisburg , 1984—. Contbr. articles to profl. publs. Named Disting. Alumnus, Winebrenner Theol. Sem., 1983. Office: East Pennsylvania Conf Chs of God 900 S Arlington Ave Harrisburg PA 17109

DUNN, DAVID LEE, theology educator, administrator; b. Kitchener, Sask., Can., Feb. 13, 1948; s. Leonard and Wilma Audrey (Newhouse) D.; m. Patricia Anne Dean, July 22, 1967; children—Pamela, Debra, Sandra. B.Th., Emmanuel Bible Coll., 1973; M.Div. cum laude, Grace Theol. Sem., 1976. Acctg. clk. Massey Ferguson, Can., Brantford, Ont., 1965-69; prof. theology Briercrest Bible Coll., Caronport, Sask., Can., 1976-78, chmn. dept. theology, 1979—; dir. Creation Sci. Sask., Regina, 1977—. Soccer commr. Prairie Athletic Conf., Sask., 1978-82; referee instr. Sask. Soccer Assn., Regina, 1984. Conservative. Baptist. Club: Tennis (pres. 1982-84) (Moose Jaw, Sask.).

DUNN, EDMOND JOSEPH, priest, theology educator; b. Oxford, Iowa, Aug. 11, 1935; s. William Raymond and Kathryn Julia (McDonough) D. MA in Music, U. Iowa, 1959; MDiv, Andover Newton Theol. Sch., 1972, Pope John XXIII Nat. Sem., 1972; PhD, Boston Coll., 1978. Ordained priest Roman Cath. Ch., 1972. Assoc. prof. St. Ambrose, Davenport, Iowa, 1975-78, spiritual dir. sem. dept., 1975-77, 85—, rector sem. dept., 1978-85; prof., chmn. theology dept. St. Ambrose, Davenport, 1985—, faculty chmn., 1981-82; assoc. dir. deacon program Davenport Diocese, 1978-85, rep. pastoral coun., 1985-88. Author: Missionary Theology: Foundation in Development, 1980; contbr. column to weekly newspaper, 1984—. Mem. Am. Acad. Religion, AAUP, Cath. Theol. Soc., Am. Soc. Missiology, Western Regional Assn. Coll. Sems. (pres. 1983-84). Democrat. Home and Office: St Ambrose U 518 W Locust Davenport IA 52803

DUNN, ELWOOD, minister; b. Grant County, Ind., Jan. 8, 1906; s. Sylvester M. and Ida Belle (Ferrell) D. B.S.L. cum laude, Butler U., 1929; M.Div. cum laude, Christian Theol. Sem., 1941; postgrad., Wayne State U.; grad. student, Mich. State U. Ordained to ministry Christian Ch., 1926. Minister in Palestine, Ind., 1926-30, Etna Green, Ind., 1926-36, Medaryville, Ind., 1936-39, N. Salem, Ind., 1939-43, Wabash, Ind., 1943-46, Pontiac, Mich., 1946-49; gen. sec. Mich. Christian Endeavor Union, Detroit, 1948-85, gen. sec. emeritus, 1985—; v.p. Leadership Tng., Inc., 1952-55; minister Ferndale (Mich.) Christian Ch., 1962—; asst. dir. Neighborhood Youth Corps, Pontiac, 1967, dir., 1967-73; mgr. div. manpower Oakland Livingston Human Serves Agy., 1973-78; Mem. Ind. youth work com. Christian Ch., 1936-40, chmn. Mich. youth work com., 1947-49; pres. Ministerial Assn., Wabash, 1943-44; v.p. Great Lakes region Internat. Soc. Christian Endeavor, Columbus, Ohio, 1951-55, pres., 1967-71, mem. adv. com., 1973—. Co-author: Training for Service Senior High Department, 1966. Mem. Mayor Pontiac Com. Youth Opportunity, 1968-71, Avondale Area Youth Guidance Com., 1968-71; chmn. Oakland County Youth Assistance Com., 1971-74. Recipient scholastic honors award dept. Christian doctrine Butler U., 1929. Mem. Internat. Soc. Christian Endeavor (life), Theta Phi. Club: Exchange (Disting. Service award 1982). Home: 640 3d St Pontiac MI 48340 Office: Ferndale Christian Ch 3201 Hilton Rd Ferndale MI 48220 *Through the years those who have committed their talent and resources to promulgating the highest form of moral living thereby give stability to themselves, institutions, business, education and all forms of social living. Morality is at its strongest when it is rooted in and fostered by personal belief in God, presenting a challenge to all people.*

DUNN, JAMES MILTON, religious organization adminstrator; b. Ft. Worth, Tex., June 17, 1932; s. William Thomas and Edith (Campbell) Dunn; m. Marilyn McNeely, Dec. 19, 1958. BA, Tex. Wesleyan Coll., 1953; BD, Southwestern Bapt. Theol. Sem., 1957, ThD, 1966, PhD, 1978; LLD, Alderson-Broaddus Coll. Ordained to ministry So. Bapt. Conv. and Am. Bapt. Ch. in U.S.A., 1955. Assoc. pastor First Bapt. Ch., Weatherford, Tex., 1955-57; pastor Emmanuel Bapt. Ch., Weatherford, 1957-61; religion instr., campus minister W. Tex. State U., Canyon, 1961-66; dir. christian life commn. Bapt. Gen. Conv. Tex., Dallas, 1967-80; exec. dir. Bapt. Joint Com. on Pub. Affairs, Washington, 1981—; sec. bd. Ams. United for Separation Ch. & State, Silver Spring, Md., 1978—; bd. dirs. Bread for the World, Washington, pres., 1987; mem. ethics commn. Bapt. World Alliance, McLean, Va., 1975—. Editor, co-author: Politics a Guidebook for Christians, 1970, Endangered Species, 1976; co-author: An Approach to Christian Ethics, 1979, Teacher Renewal, 1987; author: (with others) Equal Separation, 1990, The Fundamentalist Phenomenon, 1990. Sec. Anti-Crime Coun. Tex., Dallas, 1968-80; founding mem. Dallas Dem. Forum, 1976-80; mem. Fair Campaign Practices Com., Dallas, 1972-76, Gov.'s Juvenile Coun., State of Tex., Austin, 1976-77. Recipient Disting. Svc. award Christian Life Commn. of So. Bapt. Conv., 1979, Moore-Bowman Award of Excellence, Tex. Coun. on Family Relations, 1979, Disting. Svc. award Chs. Ctr. for Theology and Pub. Policy. Mem. Soc. for the Sci. Study of Religion, Lions (pres. Canyon chpt. 1965-66). Avocation: music. Office: Baptist Joint Com 200 Maryland Ave NE Washington DC 20002 *All freedom is rooted in our being made in the image of God and is one aspect of the two-sided coin of freedom and responsibility. The two go together inextricably.*

DUNN, JESSE R., JR., minister; b. Houston, Nov. 22, 1958; s. Jesse R. and Virginia J. (Riles) D.; m. Johnnie Sylvia; children: Jesse, Quincy, Sylvia, Jason, Terra. Student, North Harris Coll., 1983-84, Tex. So. U., 1984-86. Ordained minister. Sr. pastor Greenspoint Family Worship Ctr., Houston, 1986—; organizer City Wide Food Dr., Houston Met. Ministries, 1984-85. Mem. Soc. for the Advancement of Mgmt., AICPA. Home: 4731 Geneva Dr Houston TX 77066

DUNN, LAWRENCE L., ecumenical agency administrator. Pres. Coun. Chs. of Greater Camden, Merchantville, N.J. Office: Coun Chs Greater Camden Box 1208 Merchantville NJ 08109*

DUNN, PHILLIP CLARK, music and youth minister; b. Camden, Ark., Aug. 1, 1953; s. Irvin Clark and Dorothy Jean (Graham) D.; m. Vickie Anne Lenz, June 9, 1973; children: Christopher Clark, Kori Anne. Student, Jacksonville Coll., 1971-73; B in Music Edn., East Tex. State U., 1982, BS in Elem. Edn., 1982; postgrad. in religious edn., Luther Rice Sem., 1991—. Minister of music and youth 1st Missionary Bapt. Ch., Terrell, Tex., 1972-

74, Bauman Rd. Bapt. Ch., Houston, 1976-80, Immanuel Bapt. Ch., Nashville, Ark., 1980-84, 1st Bapt. Ch., Smackover, Ark., 1984—; minister of music Cen. Bapt. Ch., Lancaster, Tex., 1974-76. 1st v.p. PTA, Smackover, 1987-89, pres., 1989-90; mem. Stirring Com. for Behavioral Objectives in Pub. Schs., Smackover, 1989-90. Mem. Liberty Bapt. Assn. (mem. youth com. 1985-89, chair 1989—).

DUNN, RICHARD WAYNE, religion educator; b. Ft. Worth, Apr. 28, 1957; s. Thomas Jesse and Hermenia Ella (Meyer) D.; m. Cynthia Lynn Davis, Dec. 30, 1977; children: Travis Justin, Chelsea Leigh. BME, Baylor U., 1978; MRE, Southwestern Bapt. Theol. Sem., 1981, EdD, 1991. Assoc. pastor First Bapt. Ch., Decatur, Tex., 1980-81; min. edn. Richmond Plaza Bapt., Houston, 1981-83; min. to single adults Casa View Bapt., Dallas, 1983-88; min. edn. West U. Bapt., Houston, 1988—. Author: (with others) Our Educational Heritage, 1985. Mem. Union Bapt. Assn. (bd. dirs. disciple tng. Houston chpt. 1990—). Home: 3409 Rice Blvd Houston TX 77005 Office: West U Bapt 6218 Auden Houston TX 77005

DUNN, RICKY ROBERT, minister; b. Windsor, Ont., Can., Mar. 7, 1948; s. Gerald Thomas and Beatrace Florence (Sherman) D.; m. Petitin Rhea Arledge, May 4, 1984; children: Todd Jeffery, Amy June, Jocelyn Christine, Joshua Allen, Emily Renay. AS, Mt. San Jacinto, 1973; postgrad., U. Calif., Riverside, 1973-77, Harding U., 1982-85. Ordained to ministry Ch. of Christ, 1982. Min. Southfork Ch. of Christ, Winston-Salem, N.C., 1985-88, Northtown Ch. of Christ, McAlester, Okla., 1989-90, Northside Ch. of Christ, Temple, Tex., 1990—. Author: (book chpt.) Rescue the Perishing, 1986. Officer Jaycees, Dearborn, Mich., 1981. With U.S. Army, 1966-69.

DUNNAM, SPURGEON M., III, minister, editor; b. Panama City, Fla., Jan. 20, 1943; s. Spurgeon M. Jr. and Thelma (Byers) D.; m. Dottie Cox, Aug. 5, 1966; children: Delilah Denise, Delayna Dawn, Daniel Spurgeon. BA, Tex. Wesleyan U., 1965, LHD, 1977; ThM, So. Meth. U., 1969. Editor, chief exec. officer The United Meth. Reporter, Dallas, 1969—; trustee Tex. Meth. Found., Austin, 1988—; chmn. bd. Religious News Svc., N.Y.C., 1984—; bd. dirs. Global Ministries, United Meth. Ch.; mem. North Tex. Conf. Bd. of Ordained Ministry, Dallas, 1984—. Office: United Meth Reporter PO Box 660275 Dallas TX 75266

DUNNAVANT, ANTHONY LEROY, religion educator; b. Hagerstown, Md., June 23, 1954; s. Ezra LeRoy and Edith Etta (Higgins) D.; m. Nancy Ruth Gragson, May 24, 1975; children: Erin Edith, Bridget Renee, Caitlin Paige, Tara Johanna. BA, Fairmont State Coll., 1974; MA, W.Va. U., 1976; MDiv, Vanderbilt U., 1979, MA, 1981, PhD, 1984. Ordained to ministry Christian Ch. (Disciples of Christ), 1980. Min. First Christian Ch., Mannington, W.Va., 1972-74, Dolls Run Christian Ch., Core, W.Va., 1974-75, First Christian Ch., Guthrie, Ky., 1976-84; assoc. prof. ch. history Lexington (Ky.) Theol. Sem., 1987—. Author: Central Christian Church, 1991; contbg. author: Case Study of Mainstream Protestantism, 1991; contbr. articles to profl. jours. Recipient postdoctoral scholarship Ctr. for Congregational Edn., Lilly Endowment, 1985-86. Mem. AAUP, Am. Acad. Religion, Assn. for the Sociology of Religion, Assn. of Profs. and Researchers in Religious Edn., Disciples of Christ Hist. Soc. Office: Lexington Theol Sem 631 S Limestone Lexington KY 40508

DUNNAVANT, EZRA LEROY, minister; b. Meherrin, Va., May 19, 1924; s. Ellis Courtney and Lena Alma (Cocke) D.; m. Edith Etta Higgins, July 24, 1943; children: Nellie June, Terry Allen, Anthony LeRoy, Kay Edith. BA, Lynchburg Coll., 1950; MDiv, Wesley Theol. Sem., 1957; D in Ministry, Lexington Theol. Sem., 1974; profl. cert. in ch. mgmt., Am. U., Washington. Ordained to ministry Christian Ch. (Disciples of Christ), 1950. Pastor First Christian Ch., Hinton, W.Va., 1950-53, Downsville Christian Ch., Williamsport, Md., 1953-61; assoc. pastor First Christian Ch., Alexandria, Va., 1961-65; pastor Suitland (Md.) Christian Ch., 1965-68, Cen. Christian Ch., Fairmont, W.Va., 1968-78, Kenbridge (Va.) Christian Ch., 1978-90; moderator-elect Christian Ch. (Disciples of Christ) in Va., 1991—. Lt. comdr. USNR, 1958-78. Ruritan. (pres. Kenbridge). Home and Office: 730 S Broad St PO Box 1050 Kenbridge VA 23944 *Life is a precious gift from the God of Creation. As we live that life, neither prejudice nor favoritism should be allowed to blind us to the fairness and justice that every person deserves, along with a measure of mercy.*

DUNNE, JOSEPH JAMES, retired rector; b. Chgo., Apr. 4, 1926; s. Joseph Patrick and Catherine (O'Malley) D.; m. Shirley Roethler, Jan. 29, 1971. BA, St. Mary's Coll., St. Mary, Ky., 1949; licentiate in theology, Cath. U. Am., 1953. Ordained priest Roman Cath. Ch., 1953, Episcopal Ch., 1972. Asst. pastor various Roman Cath. chs. Diocese of Covington, Ky., 1953-63; pastor St. Michael Ch., Paintsville, Ky., 1963-67; curate St. Thomas of Canterbury Ch., Chgo., 1968-70; priest in charge St. Luke's Episcopal Ch., Cannelton, Ind., 1972-87, St. John's Ch., Washington, Ind., 1972-75; vicar, rector St. John Episcopal Ch., Mt. Vernon, Ind., 1973-91; ret., 1991. With USN, 1946-47. Mem. Kiwanis (past pres. Mt. Vernon). Home: 35 Wyandotte Dr Cherokee Village AR 72529

DUNNE, SEAN ANTHONY, priest, editor, photojournalist; b. Trim, County Meath, Ireland, May 6, 1926; s. James and Rosemary (Hussey) D. B.A., St. Columban's, Navan, Ireland, 1951; postgrad. in journalism, Marquette U., 1952-53, Register Coll., Denver, 1953-54, cinemaphotography U. So. Calif., 1955-57. Joined Columban Fathers, Roman Catholic Ch., 1945, ordained priest, 1951. UN corr. in Korea with NC News Service, Washington, 1958-60; cameraman, editor F.E. Films, Hollywood, Calif., 1960-63; missionary Columban Fathers, Philippines, 1963-75; editor Far East Mags., Ireland and Gt. Britain, 1977—. Writer, editor numerous articles on Oriental, U.S. and European subjects; cameraman, dir. many documentary films in Orient, U.S. and Ireland. Mem. Religious Press Assn., Mission Mag. Editor's Assn., Soc. Motion Picture and Television Engrs., Delta Kappa Alpha. Avocations: fishing, photography, travel, shell-collecting.

DUNNETT, WALTER MCGREGOR, religion educator; b. Tayport, Fife, Scotland, July 5, 1924; came to U.S., 1930; s. Daniel McDougall and Jemima Kinnaird (McGregor) D.; m. Dolores Ramona Eddy ; children: Sharon, Mark. AB, Wheaton Coll., 1949, AM, 1950, BD, 1953; PhD, Case-Western Res., 1969; MST, Luther Northwestern Theol. Sem., 1980. Prof. of Bible Moody Bible Inst., Chgo., 1958-66, 72-76; asst. prof. Bible Wheaton (Ill.) Coll., 1966-69; prof. of Bible Trinity Coll. Sem., Deerfield, Ill., 1969-72, 75-76, Northwestern Coll., St. Paul, 1976—. Author: New Testament Survey, 1960, New Testament Survey, 1963, Book of Acts, 1981, Interpretaion of Holy Scripture, 1984; revising author: New Testament Survey (M.C. Tenney), 1985; contbr. articles to profl. jours. Alternate del. IR Party, St. Paul, 1988. Sgt. U.S. Army, 1943-46. Mem. Evang. Theol. Soc. (v.p., pres. 1984-87), Soc. Bibl. Lit., Inst. for Bibl. Rsch., Pi Gamma Mu. Home: 3651 N Snelling Ave Saint Paul MN 55112 Office: Northwestern Coll 3003 N Snelling Ave Saint Paul MN 55113

DUNNEVANT, EMMETT DOUGLAS, minister; b. Buckingham, Va., Dec. 7, 1924; s. Horace Eugene and Mildred Dorinda (Watson) D.; m. Betty Christine Dixon, July 12, 1947; children: Donald A., Linda G., Paul D., Douglas Lee. BA, U. Richmond, 1964; ThM, New Orleans Bapt. Theol., Seminary, 1968; ThD, Brown Seminary, Fredericksburg, Va., 1984. Minister Nicholsville (Ala.) Bapt. Ch., 1966-68, Winn's Bapt. Ch., Glen Allen, Va., 1968-84, Laurel Hill Bapt. Ch., Charlottesville, Va., 1984-87, Enon Bapt. Ch., Chester, Va., 1987—. With USN, 1944-46, PTO. Democrat. Home: 418 Bermuda Hundred Rd Chester VA 23831 Office: Enon Baptish Church 1801 Bermuda Hundred Rd Chester VA 23831

DUNNING, HUBERT RAY, religion educator; b. Slayden, Tenn., Oct. 26, 1926; s. Scott and Gussie Lee (Shelton) D.; m. Bettye J. Warren, July 10, 1952; children: William Carey, Dennis Ray, Joy Amaris. BA, Trevecca Coll., 1948; BD, Nazarene Theol. Sem., Kansas City, Mo., 1951; MA, Vanderbilt U., 1952, PhD, 1969. Ordained to ministry Ch. of the Nazarene, 1947. Pastor Ch. of the Nazarene, Tenn. and Ark., 1952-66; prof. Trevecca Nazarene Coll., Nashville, 1964—. Author: Grace, Faith and Holiness, 1988, Layman's Guide to Sanctification, 1990; co-author: Introduction to Wesleyan Theology, 1986, rev. edit., 1988; editor Biblical Resources For Preaching, 1989. Named Tchr. of Yr., Trevecca Nazarene Coll., 1971; recipient T-Award, Trevecca Alumni Assn., 1976. Fellow Oxford Soc. Scholars; mem. Wesleyan Theol. Soc. (pres. 1985-86). Office: Trevecca Nazarene Coll 333 Murfreesboro Rd Nashville TN 37210

DUNNING, JOHN WALLACE, deacon; b. Mpls., July 27, 1939; s. Wallace Theodore and Rose (Hamm) D.; m. Dianne Marie Wittman, Jan. 28, 1961; children: Thomas, Michael, Marc, Paul, William. Student, Dunwoody Inst., Mpls., 1960, St. John's Sem., L.A., 1975-79, U. Minn. Ordained deacon Roman Cath. Ch., 1979. Deacon St. Norbert's Ch., Orange, Calif., 1979-81, Immaculate Conception Ch., Dardenne, Mo., 1981-85, Assumption Cath. Ch., O'Fallon, Mo., 1985-89; regional svc. specialist Beckman Instruments, Fullerton, Calif., 1988—; mem. diaconate coun. Archdiocese St. Louis, 1984-86, 89—. Chaplain, outings chmn. Boy Scouts Am., Orange, 1978-81 (Appreciation award 1979, Bronze Pelican award 1980); chmn. Vietnamese Resettlement Orgn., Orange. Recipient Appreciation award United Cath. Conf., 1978, Speakers award Beckman Inst./Toastmasters, Fullerton, 1978. Mem. KC (chaplain 1981—). Home: 636 Lakewood Dr Lake Saint Louis MO 63367 Office: Beckman Instrumetns 2500 Harbor Blvd Fullerton CA 92634

DUNN MADDEN, ANNE MARIE, pastoral associate; b. San Antonio, Dec. 20, 1945; d. William A. and Martha L. (Mitten) Hosinski; m. Jame T. Dunn, June 8, 1968 (div. Oct. 1985); children: Laurie, Katie, Claire; m. Andrew J. Madden. BA in German, Regis Coll., 1967; MA in Theology, Mt. Angel Sem., 1985. Pastoral assoc. St. Anne's Ch., Portland, Oreg., 1985-87, Holy Trinity Ch., Beaverton, Oreg., 1987-90; nat. workshop dir. The DeSales Program, Portland, 1990—; exec. asst. Morningstar Prodns., Portland, 1990—; presenter and editor Inneraction adult faith formation video series, Morningstar Prodns., Portland, 1990—. Author, video presenter The DeSales Program, 1985-89 (Flavius award 1988). Mem. Pastoral Assocs. of Oreg. (chair 1988-90), Soc. Bibl. Lit. Democrat. Roman Catholic. Office: Morningstar Prodns 1303 SW 16th Portland OR 97201

DUNSTON, ALFRED GILBERT, JR., bishop; b. Coinjock, N.C., June 25, 1915; s. Alfred Gilbert and Cora Lee (Charity) D.; m. Permilla Rollins Flack, June 18, 1940 (div. 1947); children—Carol Dunston Goodrich, Aingred Dunston James, Armayne Dunston Pratt. A.B., Livinstone Coll., 1938; student, Drew U., 1938-39, 41-42. Ordained elder A.M.E. Zion Ch., 1938, then minister and consecrated bishop; minister Advance, N.C., 1936, Thomasville, N.C., 1937-38, Atlantic City, 1941-43, Summit, N.J., 1946-48, Knoxville, Tenn., 1948-52; minister Wesley A.M.E. Zion Ch., Phila., 1952-63, Mother A.M.E. Zion Ch., N.Y.C., 1963-64; prof. Black Ch. History Inst. for Black Ministries, 1971—; bishop 2d Episcopal area A.M.E. Zion Ch., Phila. Author: Black Man in Old Testament and Its World. Mem. Alpha Phi Alpha. Address: Executive House Ste 1117 6100 City Line Ave Philadelphia PA 19131

DUPIN, CLYDE CLEMENT, minister; b. East View, Ky., Feb. 22, 1933; s. Kendrick W. and Polly (McGuffin) D.; m. Grace E. Spencer, June 15, 1951; children: Wesley, Kenneth, Joy Beth. Student, United Wesleyan Coll., 1953, Evansville U., 1968; DD (hon.), Cen. Wesleyan Coll., 1983. Ordained elder Wesleyan Ch., 1953. Evangelist Clyde Dupin Evangelistic Assn., Indpls., 1954-59; pastor Trinity Wesleyan Ch., Evansville, Ind., 1959-69; pres. Clyde Dupin Ministries, Kernersville, N.C., 1974—; del. Internat. Wesleyan Conf., Anderson, Ind., 1964-68; speaker, del. Jerusalem Conf., 1978, Amsterdam Conf., Netherlands, 1983. Author: Wake Up America, 1976, New Life in Christ, 1979, Total Christian Living, 1986; cons. editor Evang. Rev., 1984—; columnist in 75 newspapers, 1976—. Named Outstanding Min., United Wesleyan Coll., 1964, Alumni of Yr., 1980. Mem. Delta Epsilon Chi. Avocations: golfing, reading, travel. Office: PO Box 565 840 Salisbury St Kernersville NC 27284

DUPRE, JOHN L., deacon; b. New Orleans, Dec. 6, 1953; s. Antoine Joseph and Leverne (Boutte) D.; m. Yadira Gisella McGrath, Sept. 2, 1984; 1 child, Joya Gabrielle. BS, Tulane U., 1975, MD, 1979. 7. Deacon St. Paul on the Shipwreck Ch., San Francisco, 1990—; staff psychiatrist San Quentin (Calif.) State Prison, 1983—. Mem. Am. Psychiat. Assn.

DUPRE, THOMAS L., auxiliary bishop; b. Holyoke, Mass., Nov. 10, 1933. Student, Sem. of Philosophy, Montreal, The Grand Sem., Montreal; postgrad., Cath. U. Am. ordained priest Roman Cath. Ch., 1959. Former Defender of the Bond and Pro-Synodal judge Diocese of Springfield, Mass., chancellor, 1977-90, titular bishop of Hodelm, aux. bishop, 1990—. Office: Diocese of Springfield PO Box 1730 Springfield MA 01101

DUPREE, JAMES WILLIAM, minister; b. Americus, Ga., Oct. 8, 1932; s. Charlie Jackson and Lula Belle (Weaver) D.; m. Marilyn Sue Johnson, May 31, 1955; children: Susan Dupree Nichols, Mary Lynn Dupree Matthews. BA, Asbury Coll., 1953; MA, Emory U., 1956. Pastor South Ga. Conf. United Meth. Ch., 1955—, dist. supt., 1985-88; pastor Park Ave. United Meth. Ch., Valdosta, Ga., 1988—. Author: The Eubanks of White County, Illinois, 1975, Early Georgia Collins Family Records, 1982, Glovers of Warren and Sumter Counties, Georgia, 1983, John Booth of Orange County, North Carolina, 1984. Trustee Epworth By The Sea Meth. Ctr., St. Simons Island, Ga., 1975—, Magnolia Home for Aging, Americus, Ga., 1980—, South Ga. Meth. Found., Macon, Ga., 1980—, Meth. Children's Home, 1989—. Mem. Internat. Rotary, Lions. Home and Office: Park Ave United Meth Ch 100 East Park Ave Valdosta GA 31602

DU PREEZ, RONALD ALWYN GERALD, religion educator; b. Wynberg, Republic of South Africa, Dec. 3, 1951; came to U.S., 1976; s. Alwyn George and Joyce Agnes (de Waal) du P.; m. Lynda Raye Gill, Oct. 28, 1979. BA in Religion, Helderberg Coll., Republic of South Africa, 1974; MA in Religion, Andrews U., Berrien Springs, Mich., 1978, MDiv, 1985, MA in Edn., 1987, postgrad., 1991—. Student missionary Far Ea. Div. Seventh-day Adventists, Seoul, Korea, 1978-79, lang. sch. dir., 1980-81; pastor, asst. hosp. chaplain Far Ea. Div. Seventh-day Adventists, Okinawa, Japan, 1981-82; pastor Far Ea. Div. Seventh-day Adventists, Guam, 1982, Bible tchr., 1982-83; dir. study lab. Andrews U., 1984—; tchr. religion Ea. Africa Div. Seventh-day Adventists, Zimbabwe, 1990. Initiator, coord. Ethiopia Famine Relief Project, Berrien Springs, 1984-85; vol. Maranatha Flights Internat., Puerto Rico, 1985. Named one of Outstanding Young Men Am., 1988. Mem. Adventist Theol. Soc., Am. Acad. Religion, Andrews Scholars for Religious Studies, Bibl. Archeol. Soc., Evang. Theol. Soc., Soc. Sci. Study Religion, Soc. Bibl. Lit., South African Club (pres. 1986-87), PhD/ThD Club (assoc. v.p. 1988-89), Seminary Doctoral Club (pres. 1989-90), Theta Alpha Kappa (v.p. 1989-90). Home: 4600 Dunkirk Dr Chester VA 23831 *In the conflicts and concerns of contemporary life the crucial question is whether we are willing to be people of principle and integrity who are committed to lovingly and loyally standing for the right regardless of circumstances or projected consequences.*

DURAND, GUY, theology educator; b. Dunham, Que., Can., May 30, 1933; s. Leopold and Marie (Lemieux) D.; m. Jocelyne Masse, June 10, 1961; children: Stephane, Guylaine, Isabelle. MA, U. Montreal, 1960, Licence en Droit, 1961; ThD, Faculte Cath., Lyon, France, 1967. Prof. theology U. Montreal, Can., 1968—. Author: Éthique de la Recontre Sexuelle, 1971, Sexualite et Foi, 1977, Quelle Vie?, 1978, Quel Avenir?, 1978, Choisis ta vie: lettre d'un père à ses adolescents, 1982, L'education sexuelle, 1985, La bioéthique: nature, principes et enjeux, 1989. Mem. Societe Canadienne de Theologie. Office: Universite de Montreal, Faculte de Theologie CP 6128, Montreal, PQ Canada H3C 3J7

DURBNEY, CLYDROW JOHN, minister; b. St. Louis, Sept. 27, 1916; s. Earl Elmer and Conetta Mae D.; A.B., Gordon Coll. Theology and Missions, 1950; B.D., Eden Theol. Sem., 1953; S.T.M., Concordia Theol. Sem., 1954, postgrad. 1954-59; postgrad Eden Sem., 1973-75; D.D., Am. Bible Inst., 1980; Cultural doctorate in Sacred Philosophy, World U., 1982; m. Mattie Lee Neal, Oct. 27, 1968. Ordained to ministry Nat. Bapt. Ch., 1952. Clk., U.S. Post Office, St. Louis, 1941-54; instr. Western Bapt. Bible Coll., St. Louis, 1954-67; asst. pastor Central Bapt. Ch., St. Louis, 1954, pastor, 1983; ghetto evangelist Ch. on Wheels, 1952-84; pastor, founder Saints Fellowship Ch., 1984—. Served with AUS, 1942-46; ETO. Decorated Bronze Star. Recipient Disting. World Service award Central Bapt. Ch. Prayer Aux., 1974, Home award City of Berkeley Betterment Commn., 1990. Mem. Internat. Platform Assn., Inst. Research Assn., Gordon Alumni Assn., Anglo Am. Acad., Nat. Geog. Soc., Smithsonian Instn. Republican. Author: With Him in Glory, 1955; Adventures in Soul Winning, 1966; contbr. to New Voices in Am. Poetry, 1972-87. Home: 8244 Addington Dr Berkeley MO 63134 *My personal ambition is still to be more like the Lord Jesus Christ, to do things according to His Way and in His Spirit, so to be more helpful to troubled persons of all ages in the "highways and hedges" and in the parish, that souls may be won to Christ and become His disciples.*

DUREN, LEOATIS, pastor; b. Mt. Clemens, Mich., Mar. 31, 1936; s. Leroy and Lily Mae (Moses) D.; m. Shirley Ann Hamilton, Sept. 14, 1963; children: Alicia Powell, Kevin Duren, Brian Duren. AA, Blair Jr. Coll., Colorado Springs, Colo., 1982. Pastor Gospel Svc., Okinawa, Japan, 1975-76; co-pastor Gospel Svc., Ft. Carson, Colo., 1977-79; asst. pastor Trinity Bapt., Colorado Springs, 1979-88; v.p. Pikes Peak Assn. of Chs., Colorado Springs, 1983-84; pastor Perfect Peace Bapt. Ch., Colorado Springs, 1988—; pres. Christian Ministries Fellowship, Colorado Springs, 1989—; TV Host The Ch. Game, Sta. KKTV, Colorado Springs, 1982-84. Loaned exec. AT&T to United Way, Denver, 1989. With U.S. Army, 1955-77. Office: Perfect Peace Bapt 832 S Nevada Colorado Springs CO 80903

DURFEE, HAROLD ALLEN, philosophy educator; b. Bennington, Vt., May 21, 1920; s. Lynn Stanton and Ethel (Foster) D.; m. Doris Graver, Aug. 10, 1944; children: Peter Allen, Gary Robert. Ph.B., U. Vt., 1941; B.D., Yale U., 1944; Ph.D., Columbia U., 1951; postgrad., Harvard U., 1954-55, Oxford U., 1968-69, 76. Ordained to ministry Presbyn. Ch., 1944; chmn. dept. philosophy Park Coll., Parkville, Mo., 1946-55; assoc. prof. philosophy Am. U., Washington, 1955-57; chmn. dept. philosophy and religion Am. U., 1957-73, William Frazer McDowell prof. philosophy, 1957-90, William Frazer McDowell prof. philosophy emeritus, 1990—; faculty Forum on Psychiatry and Humanities, Washington Sch. Psychiatry, 1979-80; dir. seminar contemporary European philosophy, 1963; exchange prof. Cath. U. Am., 1972; pres. Mo. Philos. Assn., 1953-54. Author: (with Harold E. Davis) The Teaching oi Philosophy in Universities of the United States, 1965, Foundational Reflections: Studies in Contemporary Philosophy, 1987; editor: Analytic Philosophy and Phenomenology, 1976; co-editor, contbr.: Explanation: New Directions in Philosophy, 1973, Phenomenology and Beyond: The Self and Its Language, 1989; assoc. editor, contbr. Psychiatry and The Humanities, Vol. II, Thought, Consciousness and Reality, 1977, Vol. V, Kierkegaard's Truth: The Disclosure of the Self, 1981; chmn. editorial bd. Am. U. Publs. in Philosophy, 1973-88; editor Am. Univ. Publications in Philosophy, 1989—. Trustee Washington Consortium of Univs., 1970-90. Recipient Scholar/Tchr. of Yr. award Am. U., 1985, Outstanding Service award Am. U., 1987; Fund for Advancement Edn. fellow, 1954-55. Mem. Am. Philos. Assn., Metaphys. Soc. Am., Am. Acad. Religion, Internat. Soc. Metaphysics, Internat. Phenomenological Research Soc., AAUP, Washington Philosophy Club (pres. 1961-62), Kappa Sigma, Phi Kappa Phi. Home: 12405 St James Rd Rockville MD 20850 Office: Am U 4400 Massachusetts Ave NW Washington DC 20016

DURFEE, JOHN B., religious organization administrator. Pres. Allegheny Wesleyan Meth. Connection, Salem, Ohio. Office: Allegheny Wesleyan Meth Connection 1827 Allen Dr Salem OH 44460*

DURHAM, BENNIE LEWIS, pastor; b. Pickens, S.C., Mar. 29, 1958; d. Kenneth Barron and Cleon Hattie (Chapman) D.; m. Loretta Carlene Aiken, Nov. 19, 1977; children: Crystal Michelle, David Matthew. Student, Dan Greer Bible Inst., Greenville, S.C., 1985-86; AA in Religion/Pastoral Ministries, Fruitland Bapt. Bible Inst., Hendersonville, N.C., 1988; student, Liberty U., Lynchburg, Va., 1990—. Ordained to ministry So. Bapt. Ch., 1987. Intern pastor Calvary Hill Bapt. Ch., Easley, S.C., 1986; pastor Saluda Hill Bapt. Ch., Cleve., 1987-91, West Greenville (S.C.) Bapt. Ch., 1991—; del. nominating com. S.C. Bapt. Conv., Columbia, 1990-91; pres. Pickens (S.C.)-Twelve Mile Ministers Assn., 1988-89. Pres. Ambler Elem. Sch. PTO, Pickens, 1990-91; mem. Pastor's Task Force for Lifeline, Easley, S.C., 1989—; chmn. bd. Tri-County Pregnancy Ctr., Easley, 1990-91. Republican. Home: 8 Sunderland Ct Greenville SC 29611 Office: West Greenville Bapt Ch 551 Perry Ave PO Box 7165 Greenville SC 29611 *I have found the best advice in life for me is to not ask why, but rather what can I do and how can I do it.*

DURHAM, JAMES STAFFORD, minister; b. Pineville, Ky., Feb. 25, 1956; s. James Stafford and Peggy Jo (Boatright) D.; m. Terresa Lucas, Oct. 28, 1978; children: Amanda Joy, Caitlin Dean. BA, U. Ky., 1981; MDiv, So. Bapt. Sem., 1985, PhD, 1991. Ordained to ministry Bapt. Ch., 1982. Pastor Long Lick Bapt. Ch., Stamping Ground, Ky., 1981-85, Woodland Bapt. Ch., Middletown, Ky., 1985-89; assoc. pastor Walnut St. Bapt. Ch., Louisville, 1989—; dir. Christian Conciliation Ministry Ky., Louisville, 1985-86. Mem. Soc. Sci. Study Religion, Sem. Consortium Urban Pastoral Edn., Eastern Jefferson County Ministerial Alliance (pres. 1986-87). Democrat. Office: Walnut St Bapt Ch 220 W St Catherine St Louisville KY 40203

DURHAM, NICOLENE ANGELA, minister; b. Kingston, Jamaica, May 9, 1947; came to U.S., 1983; d. Amy (Roberts) Kennedy; m. Elliott Durham, 1967 (div.); 1 child, Nickell Jenieve. BA, Queens U., Kingston, Ont., Can., 1983; MDiv, Interdenom. Theol. Ctr., Atlanta, 1986; ThM, Emory U., 1988. Ordained to ministry A.M.E. Ch. Assoc. pastor St. Paul A.M.E. Ch., Atlanta, 1986-89; care provider Christian Coun., Mental Health Div., Atlanta, 1986-90; pastor Graves Chapel A.M.E. Ch., Covington, Ga., 1988—; asst. vis. prof. Columbia Theol. Sem., Decatur, 1991—. Founder, dir. sr.'s program Pillars of Faith, 1986; counselor AIDS Counseling Ctr., 1986. Recipient spl. Congl. Recognition for Community Svc., Atlanta, 1988. Home: 2427 Parkland Dr Decatur GA 30032

DURMAN, KENNETH THOMAS, religious organization administrator; b. London, Sept. 22, 1920; came to U.S., 1965; naturalized, 1970; s. Thomas Joseph and Edith (Buttell) D.; m. Jessie J. Dare, Sept. 1, 1945; children: Barry K., Jeanette K., Daryl J., Frank R. Internat. dir. emeritus The Pocket Testament League, Lititz, Pa., 1978—; pres. U.S. Coun. Africa Inland Mission, Pearl River, N.Y. Mem. Evang. Free Ch. Home: 55 Brakenbury Dr Toms River NJ 08757 Office: Pocket Testament League PO Box 800 11 Tollgate Rd Lititz PA 17543 *Every individual, from a young child to the oldest adult, is entitled to their personal dignity, and to demean or shatter the self confidence of anyone is to use the cruellest weapon in th armory of power or authority.*

DURNBAUGH, DONALD FLOYD, church history educator, researcher; b. Detroit, Nov. 16, 1927; s. Floyd Devon and Ruth Elsie (Tombaugh) D.; m. Hedwig Therese Raschka, July 10, 1952; children—Paul D., Christopher S., Renate E. B.A., Manchester Coll., Ind., 1949, L.H.D. (hon.), 1980; M.A., U. Mich., 1953; Ph.D., U. Pa., 1960. Dir. program Brethren Service Commn., Austria, 1953-56; asst. prof. history Juniata Coll., Huntingdon, Pa., 1958-62, J. Omar Good disting. prof. evang. christianity, 1988-89; assoc. prof. ch. history Bethany Theol. Sem., Oak Brook, Ill., 1962-69, prof. ch. history, 1970-88; Carl W. Zeigler prof. religion and history Elizabethtown (Pa.) Coll., 1989—; dir. in Europe Brethren Colls. Abroad, France, Fed. Republic Germany, 1964-65; cons. Brethren Hist. Com., Elgin, Ill., 1982—; moderator Ch. of the Brethren, 1985-86. Author: European Origins of the Brethren, 1958, 2d edit., 1974, 4th edit., 1986, The Brethren in Colonial America, 1967, 2d edit., 1974, Guide to Research in Brethren History, 1968, The Believers' Church: The History and Character of Radical Protestantism, 1968, 2d edit., 1985, Every Need Supplied: Mutual Aid and Christian Community in the Free Churches, 1525-1675, 1974; editor: Die Kirche der Brueder: Vergangenheit und Gegenwart, 1971, The Church of the Brethren: Past and Present, 1971, To Serve the Present Age: The Brethren Service Story, 1975, On Earth Peace: Discussion on War/Peace Issues Between Friends, Mennonites, Brethren and European Churches, 1935-1975, 1978, Church of the Brethren: Yesterday and Today, 1986, Pragmatic Prophet: The Life of M.R. Zigler, 1989; editor-in-chief The Brethren Ency., Inc., 1978-84; contbr. articles, book revs. to scholarly jours., periodicals. Alternative service as conscientious objector, 1953-56. U. Pa. Scholar, 1956-57, fellow, 1957-58; NEH sr. fellow, 1976-77; fellow Assn. Theol. Schs., 1986-87; recipient Alumni award Manchester Coll., 1978. Assoc. Inst. of Mennonite Studies; mem. Am. Soc. Ch. History, Brethren Jour. Assn., Soc. German Am. Studies, Communal Studies Assn. Mem. Ch. of the Brethren. Home: 155 S Poplar St Elizabethtown PA 17022 Office: Elizabethtown Coll Elizabethtown PA 17022

DURSI, ELSIE L., ecumenical agency administrator. Exec. dir. Mahoning Valley Assn. Chs., Youngstown, Ohio. Office: Mahoning Valley Assn Chs 631 Wick Ave Youngstown OH 44502*

DURST, MOSE, religious organization administrator; b. N.Y.C., Sept. 5, 1939; s. Samuel and Lillian (Farb) D.; m. Onni Lim, Dec. 20, 1974; children: Isaac, Chaim, Yeondo. BA, Queens Coll., 1961; MA, U. Oreg., 1963, PhD, 1967. Dir. Unification Ch. of Calif., San Francisco, 1974-80; pres. Unification Ch. of Am., N.Y.C., 1980-89, chmn., 1989—; chmn. Internat. Relief Friendship Found., N.Y., 1978—, Unification Theol. Sem., Barrytown, N.Y., 1979—. Author: To Bigotry, No Sanction, 1984, Strategies of Love, 1987, Unification Culture, 1991; contbr. articles to religious jours. Pres., chmn. Project Vol., Inc., San Francisco, 1976—, Oakland (Calif.) Mayor's Small Bus. Task Force, 1977. Mem. NDEA (fellowship awardee 1961-64), Commonwealth Club. Office: Unification Ch Am 4 W 43rd St New York NY 10036

DUSMAN, PRESTON HENRY, clergyman; b. Hanover, Pa., Mar. 15, 1927; s. George Henry and Gertie (Hahn) D.; m. Virginia Florence Wentz, June 15, 1952; 1 child, Karl Wayne. BA, Gettysburg Coll., 1951; MDiv, Gettysburg Luth. Theol. Sem., 1954. Ordained to ministry Evang. Luth. Ch. in Am., 1954. Pastor Easton (Md.)-Cordova Parish, 1954-60, Christ Luth. Ch., Fredericksburg, Va., 1960-66, Williamsburg (Pa.) Parish, 1966-75, Redeemer Luth. Ch., Williamsport, 1975—; dir. Pers. Counseling Svc., Fredericksburg, 1965-66. Mem. Lions. Address: 804 Sherman St Williamsport PA 17701

DUTCHER, FRANK ALBERT, deacon; b. Cedar Falls, Iowa, May 15, 1909; s. Charles Danthing and Emily Matilda (Friedman) D.; m. Sarah Lorraine Peterson, Aug. 17, 1936; children: Richard, Anne, Mary. BA, U. No. Iowa; postgrad., Iowa State U. Ordained deacon, Roman Catholic Ch. Deacon St. Patrick's Ch., Cedar Falls, Iowa, 1979—. Democrat. Home: 1905 Madison St Cedar Falls IA 50613

DUTHOY, RAYMOND JULIUS, deacon; b. Ghent, Minn., May 7, 1929; s. Julius Peter and Everdina Margaret (Stienessen) D.; m. Patricia Ann Heinis, June 27, 1953; children: Ramona, Terance, Kevin, Brenda, Denise. AA, Rancho Santiago, 1964. Ordained deacon Roman Cath. Ch., 1979. Deacon St. Justin Martyr Ch., Anaheim, Calif., 1979—; spirituality chmn. Deaconate, Orange, Calif., 1984-87. Mem. So. Calif. Community Coll. Purchasing Assn. (chmn. 1969-78), Commercial Club (pres. 1957-59), KC (grand knight 1960-61, dist. dep. 1961-62). Home: 9672 Parade St Anaheim CA 92804 Office: Saddleback Community Coll Dist 28000 Marguerite Pkwy Mission Viejo CA 92692

DUTILE, GORDON, religious educator; b. Natchitoches, La., Apr. 1, 1941; s. Edmond Joseph and Lessie Mae (Royston) D.; m. Julia Ann Colvin, Aug. 6, 1963; children: Penny Rae Clarkson, Shonda Cherie. BEE, La. Poly. U., 1964; MDiv, Southwestern Bapt. Theol., 1973, PhD in New Testament, 1980. Pastor Dixie (Tex.) Bapt. Ch., 1971; assoc. pastor Rosen Heights Bapt. Ch., Ft. Worth, 1971-80; prof. Bible Southwest Bapt. U., Bolivar, Mo., 1980—. Mem. Assn. Bapt. Profs. Religion, Soc. Bibl. Lit. Office: Southwest Bapt U 1601 S Springfield Bolivar MO 65613

DUTILLE, HAROLD KENNETH, JR., minister; b. Lewiston, Maine, Sept. 19, 1952; s. Harold K. and Arlene M. (Carbone) D.; m. Patricia L. Witham, July 24, 1971; children: Timothy Paul, David Andrew and Melissa Joy (twins). Grad. Theology, Bapt. Bible Coll., Springfield, Mo., 1974; MA, Calif. Grad. Sch. Theology, Glendale, 1986. Ordained to ministry Ind. Bapt. Ch., 1981. Sr. min. Calvary Bible Bapt. Ch., North Whitefield, Maine, 1975-86; sr. pastor Plymouth (Mass.) Rock Bible Ch., 1989—; v.p. devel. New Eng. Bapt. Bible Coll., South Portland, Maine, 1986-87; assoc. dir. Christian Civic League Maine, Augusta, 1987-89; pres. bd. dirs. Maine Sunday Sch. Assn., Augusta, 1983-88. Mng. editor The Record mag., 1987-89; columnist Weekly News, 1980-85; host local radio sta., 1975-80. Trustee Lincoln Acad., Newcastle, Maine, 1978-80; spl. honored guest chaplain Maine State Senate, Maine Ho. of Reps., 1979-89; guest chaplain Mass. Ho. of Reps., 1991; bd. dirs. Maine Coalition on Smoking and Health, Augusta, 1988-89. Mem. Wing Family of Am., Brewsters Men's Club (tchr.). Republican. Home: 265 Carver Rd Plymouth MA 02360 Office: Plymouth Rock Bible Ch 267 Carver Rd Plymouth MA 02360 *As you travel on life's road, think on things that are "true, honest, just, pure and lovely."*

DUTTON, DENIS CHANDRARAJ, bishop; b. Kuala Lumpur, Malaysia, Feb. 26, 1935; m. Emme Kwan, 1963; children: Amanda, Lynda, Julie, Hubert. Licentiate in Theology, Trinity Theol. Coll., Singapore; BA, Ohio Wesleyan U.; MDiv, Duke U.; D in Ministry, N.Y. Theol. Sem. Ordained to ministry Christian Meth. Episcopal Ch., 1959. Pastor various Meth. chs. Singapore, 1958-61; chaplain Student Christian Movement U.S.A., 1965-68; pres. The Meth. Ch. in Malaysia, Kuala Lumpur, 1970-88, bishop, 1988—; Mem. Nat. Consultative Coun., Kuala Lumpur, 1970-72; pres. Kuala Lumpur chpt. YMCA, 1983-90; mem. exec. com. Christian Conf. of Asia, 1985-90. Mem. World Meth. Coun. (exec. com. 1989—). Office: Meth Ch in Malaysia, 23, Jalan Mayang, 50450 Kuala Lumpur Malaysia

DUVAL, LEON-ETIENNE CARDINAL, archbishop of Algiers; b. Chenex, France, Nov. 9, 1903. Ordained priest Roman Catholic Ch., 1926, bishop of Constantine, Algeria, 1947; archbishop of Algiers, Algeria, 1954-89; ret., 1989; elevated to Sacred Coll. Cardinals, 1965; titular ch. St. Balbina. Address: 4 Avenue Durak Ali, Bologhine Algeria also: Vatican City Vatican

DUVALL, CHARLES FARMER, bishop; b. Cheraw, S.C., Nov. 18, 1935; s. Henry and Elizabeth Phoebe (Farmer) D.; m. Nancy Warren Rice, June 2, 1957; children—Ann Rice, Charles Farmer, Theodore Wannamaker. B.A. with honors in History, The Citadel, 1957; M.Div., Va. Theol. Sem., 1960; D.D. (hon.), Va. Theol. Sem., 1982, DD (hon.) U. of South, 1986. Ordained priest Episcopal Ch., 1960, consecrated bishop, 1981. Served at various chs. in Diocese of S.C., 1960-70; rector Holy Trinity Ch., Fayetteville, N.C., 1970-77, Ch. of the Advent, 1977-80 bishop, Pensacola, Fla., 1981—. Address: Episcopal Diocese Cen Gulf Coast PO Box 13330 Pensacola FL 32591-3330

DUVALL, SISTER RAYMONDA, charitable organization administrator. Exec. dir. Cath. Charities, San Diego. Office: Cath Charities 349 Cedar St San Diego CA 92101*

DUY, DONALD LEWIS, minister; b. Kansas City, Mo., Dec. 25, 1950; s. H. Donald and Dorothy Emily (Nolte) D.; m. Yvonne Louise Kliewer, Dec. 29, 1973; 1 child, Nikolaus Donald. AA, St. John's Coll., Winfield, Kans., 1970; BA, Concordia Sr. Coll., Ft. Wayne, Ind., 1972; MDiv, Concordia Sem. in Exile, St. Louis, 1976. Chaplain Rockville (Conn.) Gen. Hosp., 1978-82; chaplain resident Wesley Med. Ctr., Wichita, Kans., 1976-78; chaplain resident Immanuel Med. Ctr., Omaha, 1982-83, chaplain supr., educator, 1983-85; min. 1st Luth. Ch., Omaha, 1986—; mem. exec. com. Omaha Com. for Community Organizing, 1987—; mem. consultation com. Nebr. Synod Luth. Ch., Omaha, 1986—; mem., treas. Moratorium Organizing Com., Concordia Sem. in Exile, St. Louis, 1974-76. Bd. mem. PTA, Omaha, 1987-88, Hockanum Valley Mental Health, Rockville, 1978-81. Office: 1st Luth Ch 542 S 31st St Omaha NE 68105

DVORAK, MARILYN AGNES, religious education director; b. Hopkins, Minn., Jan. 21, 1927; d. Frank Benjamin and Elizabeth Ann (Miller) D. BA in Social Work, St. Catherine's Coll., 1973; MRE, Seattle U., 1978. Group mother, counsellor Religious of the Good Shepherd, Portland, Oreg., Spokane, Wash., 1962-71; intake worker Religious of the Good Shepherd, St. Paul, Seattle, 1971-75; dir. religious edn. Christ the King Parish, Seattle, 1975-84, Immaculate Conception Parish, Everett, Wash., 1984—. Office: Immaculate Conception Parsh 2430 Hoyt Everett WA 98201

DWYER, HERBERT EDWARD, lay worker; b. Boston, Dec. 23, 1940; s. Herbert J. and Klara (Bill) D.; m. Linda C. Pepe, Aug. 23, 1962; children: Erin, Herbert D. Assoc. EE, Lowell (Mass.) Tech., 1963; BS in Mktg., Northeastern U., 1968; MBA, Boston Coll., 1972. Missionary My Father's House, Springbrook, N.Y., 1980-85, Elim Fellowship, Lima, N.Y., 1987—; founder Light of India Ministry, Mendon, N.Y., 1987—; Christian worker Elim Fellowship, Lima, 1988—; home group leader Elim Gospel Ch., Lima, 1990—; v.p. sales/mktg. AMTX, Inc., Canandaiqua, N.Y., 1988—; bd. dirs. Christ for India, Anaheim, Calif., 1988—. Editor (newsletter) News from India. Mem. Internat. Soc. Hybrid Mfrs. (pres. 1990—). Republican. Home: 4 Churchside Run Mendon NY 14506 Office: AMTX Inc 5450 Campus Dr Canandaigua NY 14425

DYAR, JAMES ERVIN, minister; b. Anderson, S.C., Dec. 23, 1959; s. James Edward and Helen Sylvene (Shaw) D.; m. Teresa Lynne Carnes; children: Hannah Brett, Jared James. AA, Anderson (S.C.) Jr. Coll., 1980; BA, Central (S.C.) Wesleyan Coll., 1982; M in Div., Erskine Theol. Sem., Due West, S.C., 1986. Mission pastor Chiquola Bapt. Ch., Honea Path, S.C., 1981-83; pastor Friendship Bapt. Ch., Honea Path, 1983-88, Antioch Bapt. Ch., Lancaster, S.C., 1988—. Bd. dirs. Palmetto Citizens Against Sexual Assault, 1989—, bd. sec., treas., 1991—; instr. Associational Vacation Bible Sch. for Older Children, Moriah Bapt. Assn., 1989-91; bd. dirs. Connie Maxwell Children's Home, Greenwood, S.C., 1990-91. Named One of Outstanding Young Men of Am., 1985. Avocations: reading, tennis. Home: Rte 2 Box 619 Lancaster SC 29720 Office: Antioch Bapt Ch Rte 2 Box 619 A Lancaster SC 29720

DYCHE, LEOLA FERN, clergywoman; b. Nevada, Mo., May 5, 1940; d. Charles Harrison and Cora Evelina (Sheat) Gamble; m. Sidney Lee Roy Dyche, Arp. 28, 1957 (div. Feb. 1981); children: Brenda, Peggy, Charles, Laura, Scott, Brian. Student, Berean Coll. Ordained to ministry Assemblies of God. Camp dir., co-dir. Evangelistic Ctr., Purcell-Alba, Mo., 1971-75; nursing home minister 1st Assembly of God, Mountain Home, Ark., 1976-81; evangelist Assemblies of God Ch., Hawaii, 1984-85; Christian edn. dir., childrens pastor 1st Assemblies of God, Iola, Kans., 1985-91, outreach ministries pastor, 1991—; sewing specialist H.L. Miller & Sons, Iola, 1987—; sales clk. Wal Mart, Iola, 1990—. Home: 920 N Washington Iola KS 66749

DYE, DWIGHT LATIMER, minister; b. Parkersburg, W.Va., Jan. 29, 1931; s. Clyde E. and Mona Pearl (Marshall) D.; m. Carolyn Sue Priest, Oct. 13, 1951; children: Linda Lee, Mark Evan. AB, Anderson Coll., 1953; MA, U. Tulsa, 1963; postgrad., U. Okla., 1966-67. Ordained to ministry Ch. of God (Anderson, Ind.), 1954. Pastor 1st Ch. of God, Pryor, Okla., 1956-59, Westridge Hills Ch. of God, Oklahoma City, 1959-69, East Side Ch. of God, Anderson, 1969-84; exec. sec . mass communications bd. Ch. of God, Anderson, 1984—; vice chmn. Nat. Bd. Christian Edn., 1970-71; state chmn. Okla Mins. of Ch. of God; exec. sec.-treas. mass communication bd. Ch. of God, Anderson; pres. Oklahoma City chpt. Nat. Assn. Evangs., 1967; speaker All-India Assembly, Kingston, 1973. Author: A Kingdom of Servants, 1979. Home: 409 Sylvan Rd Anderson IN 46012 Office: 2620 E 5th St Anderson IN 46012

DYER, GARY DON, minister; b. Killeen, Tex., Oct. 22, 1952; s. Donald Leon and Ethel Mae (Weiss) D.; m. Teena Yevonne Jones, May 25, 1973; 1 child, Brent Andrew. BA in Religion, Dallas Bapt. U., 1975; M.Th., Southwestern Bapt. Sem., Ft. Worth, 1978. Ordained to ministry, So. Bapt. Conv., 1975. Assoc. pastor Liberty Bapt. Ch., Dallas, 1972-78; pastor Lakeview Bapt. Ch., Belton, Tex., 1978-84, First Bapt. Ch., Cooperas Cove, Tex., 1984-90, Hampton Rd. Bapt. Ch., Desoto, Tex., 1990—; exec. bd. Bapt. Gen. Conv. Tex., Dallas, 1986-90; moderator Lampasas Bapt. Assn., 1988-90. Bd. dirs. Cooperas Cove Families in Crisis, 1987. Recipient Award for Acad. Excellence, Dallas Bapt. U., 1975. Home: 422 Ray Ave De Soto TX 75115 Office: Hampton Rd Bapt Ch 400 N Hampton Rd De Soto TX 75115

DYER, RAYE NELL, religious organization administrator. Dir. Assn. of Southern Baptist Campus Ministers, Galveston, Tex. Office: Assn So Bapt Campus Mins 413 8th St Galveston TX 77550*

DYKES, DAVID ORLO, pastor; b. Ruston, La., Jan. 16, 1953; s. Orlo W. and Bessie Mary (Chessnut) D.; m. Cindy Chafin, June 1, 1974; children: Jennifer Christian, Laura Grace. BA, Samford U., 1975; MDiv, So. Bapt. Sem., Louisville, 1977, D of Ministry, 1983. Pastor Tallaweka Bapt. Ch., Tallassee, Ala., 1977-80, First Bapt. Ch., Oneonta, Ala., 1980-84; sr. pastor 1st Bapt. Ch., Gardendale, Ala., 1984—. Trustee So. Bapt. Sem., Louisville, 1983—; bd. dirs. Brother Bryan Rescue Mission, Birmingham, Ala., 1987—; bd. regents Mobile (Ala.) Coll., 1987—. Republican. Lodge: Rotary (v.p. Oneonta club 1984). Avocations: flying, writing, golfing, music, racquet sports. Office: 1st Bapt Ch Box 988 Gardendale AL 35071

DYKES, DONNA STOKES, religion educator; b. Ocila, Ga., Feb. 21, 1943; d. Henry E. and Mary Ada (Williamson) Stokes; m. Ray F. Dykes Jr., Sept. 24, 1967; 1 child, David Edmond. BA, Shorter Coll., Rome, Ga., 1965; MA, Vanderbilt U., 1970, PhD, 1976. Instr. Tenn. Tech. U., Cookeville, 1971-73; prof. Cumberland U., Lebanon, Tenn., 1976-82; assoc. prof. Okla. City U., 1983—. Mem. Soc. Bibl. Lit. Republican. Office: Okla City U 2501 N Blackwelder Oklahoma City OK 73106 *I have found that the dynamism of life reveals that the secret is that there is no secret, for we live in a continuum of sacred spaces and moments which await human awareness.*

DYKES, JAMES MCKENDREE, JR., minister; b. Alexandria, La., Feb. 24, 1946; s. James McKendree and Margaret Helen (Kelly) D.; m. Cheryl Jo Wiegers, June 15, 1974; 1 child, Andrew McKendree. BS, Auburn U., 1968; MDiv, Emory U., 1978. Ordained to ministry United Meth. Ch., 1976. Assoc. pastor Clarkston (Ga.) Ch., 1978-79; pastor Redan (Ga.) Ch., 1979-84, Shiloh Ch., Carrollton, Ga., 1984-87, South Broad Ch., Rome, Ga., 1987-88, Bethel Ch., Hiram, Ga., 1988-90, Campton Ch., Monroe, Ga., 1990—; vice chair ins. com. North Ga. Conf., United Meth. Ch., Atlanta, 1980-84, vice chair health and welfare com., 1984-88; treas. Rome Urban Ministries Com., 1987-88. Vice chair Community Devel. Adv. Coun., De Kalb County, Ga., 1981-84; cubmaster Boy Scouts Am., Hiram, 1988-90, asst. scoutmaster, Monroe, 1990-91; bd. dirs. Wesley Found., West Ga. Coll., Carrollton, 1990—. Mem. Soc. Bibl. Lit., Am. Acad. Religion, Bibl. Archaeology Soc., Nat. Ry. Hist. Soc. (v.p. Atlanta chpt. 1973-74, pres. 1974-77), Am. Philatelic Soc., Walton Ministerial Assn. (v.p. 1991), Optimists (v.p. Clarkston club 1981-82, pres. 1982-83). Home: 1345 Shoal Creek Rd NW Monroe GA 30655 Office: Campton United Meth Ch 1499 Shoal Creek Rd NW Monroe GA 30655 *We live our lives as a part of the continuum of history. We each have our past, are making our present, and are looking to the future. In order to navigate successfully in life, we must know where we are by remembering how we got here. Our future is predicated upon how well we assimilate the lessons of our past.*

DYKES, JAMES TATE, religion educator; b. Bude, Miss., Nov. 1, 1948; s. James Newland and Ethel Elizabeth (McMurry) D.; m. Linda Sue Fortenberry, Aug. 16, 1969; children: James Newland, Joseph Tate, Bethany Nell Elizabeth. AA, Copiah-Lincoln Jr. Coll., Wesson, Miss., 1968; B in Music Edn., Miss. Coll., 1970; M in Music Edn., Miss. State U., 1976; MRE, Southwestern Bapt. Theol. Sem., 1985. Lic. to ministry Bapt. Ch., 1981. Min. of music Clark Venable Bapt. Ch., Decatur, Miss., 1976-82; assoc. pastor New Hope Bapt. Ch., Fox Worth, Miss., 1983, Christ Bapt. Ch., Houma, La., 1985-87; dir. Christian edn. Shalimar (Fla.) Bapt. Ch., 1987—; growth dir. Sunday sch. div. So. Bapt. Conv., Nashville, 1989—, cons. Great Commn. Breakthrough, 1991; Sunday sch. spl. worker Fla. Bapt. Conv., Jacksonville, 1989—; regional dir., state chaplain Jaycees, Meridian, Miss., 1980-81. Author: (with others) Church Publicity/Communication Strategies, 1983. Staff sgt. U.S. Army N.G., 1970-81. Mem. Fla. Bapt. Religious Edn. Assn., So. Bapt. Religious Edn. Assn., Choctaw Bapt. Assn. (ASSISTeam dir. 1991), Phi Mu Alpha (life). Home: 66 Meigs Dr Shalimar FL 32579 Office: Shalimar Bapt Ch 17 4th Ave Shalimar FL 32579

DYKSTRA, CRAIG RICHARD, theologian, educator, foundation administrator; b. Detroit, May 31, 1947; s. Richard and Pauline V. (Hollebrands) D.; m. Elizabeth Ann Hanson, June 7, 1969; children: Peter Hanson, Andrew Craig. AB, U. Mich., 1969; MDiv, Princeton Theol. Sem., 1973, PhD, 1978; DHL (hon.), Muskingum Coll., 1989. Ordained to ministry Presbyterian Ch. (USA), 1973. Asst. min. Westminster Ch. Detroit, 1973-74; instr. Princeton (N.J.) Theol. Sem., 1976-77, Synnott prof. Christian edn., 1984-89; asst. prof. Louisville Presbyn. Theol. Sem., 1977-81, assoc. prof., 1981-84; v.p. pres. religion Lilly Endowment, Inc., Inpls., 1989—; Jones lectr. Austin (Tex.) Theol. Sem.; Greenhoe lectr. Louisville Theol. Sem., 1986; Bradner lectr. Va. Theol. Sem., Alexandria, Va., 1988; Earl lectr. Pacific Sch. Religion, Berkeley, Calif., 1991. Author: Vision and Character, 1981; co-editor: Faith Development and Fowler, 1986; assoc. editor Theology Today, Princeton, 1984-87, editor, 1987-89; contbr. articles to religious jours. Practical Theology fellow Princeton Theol. Sem., 1973; recipient Grawmeyer Teaching award Kentuckiana Metroversity, 1982. Mem. Am. Acad. Religion, Assn. Profs. and Researchers in Religious Edn. (exec. com. 1984-87), Religious Edn. Assn. (bd. dirs. 1985-88), Phi Kappa Phi. Office: Lilly Endowment Inc 2801 N Meridian St Indianapolis IN 46208

DYRNESS, WILLIAM ARTHUR, religion educator, dean; b. Geneva, Ill., Jan. 23, 1943; s. Enock Christian and Grace (Williams) D.; m. Grace Strachan Roberts, Mar. 16, 1968; children: Michelle Lynn, Andrea Elisabeth, Jonathan Roberts. BA, Wheaton (Ill.) Coll., 1965; BD, Fuller Theol. Sem., Pasadena, Calif., 1968; ThD, U. Strasbourg, France, 1970; Doctorandus, Free U., Amsterdam, The Netherlands, 1975. Prof. theology Asian Theol. Sem., Manila, 1974-82; prof. theology New Coll. Berkeley, Calif., 1982-90, pres., 1982-86; dean, prof. theology and culture Fuller Theol. Sem., 1990—. Author: Themes in Old Testament Theology, 1979, Christian Apologetics in a World Community, 1983, How Does America Hear the Gospel?, 1989, Learning About Theology from the Third World, 1990. Democrat. Presbyterian. Office: Fuller Theol Sem 135 N Oakland Pasadena CA 91182

DYRUD, AMOS OLIVER, minister, educator; b. Newfolden, Minn., June 6, 1915; s. Petter Andrew and Marie (Hanson) D.; m. Ovidie Marie Evenson, June 15, 1948; children: Peter, Naomi, Rebecca, Samuel. BA, Augsburg Coll., 1949; postgrad. in Christian Theology, Luth. Free Ch. Theol. Sem., 1949; cert., L'Alliance Francaise, Paris, 1950. Ordained to ministry Free Luth. Ch., 1949. Pastor, missionary Luth. Free Ch., and Am. Luth. Ch., Madagascar, 1949-69; instr. Assn. Free Luth. Congregations Schs., Mpls., 1969—, dean theol. sem., 1971-81; chmn. World Missions Com., Assn. Free Luth. Congregations, 1982-88. With USN, 1943. Home: 4509 Jersey Ave N Minneapolis MN 55428 Office: Assn Free Luth Congregations 3110 E Medicine Lake Blvd Minneapolis MN 55441

DZIORDZ, WALTER MICHAEL, priest; b. New Bedford, Mass., Oct. 20, 1951; s. Michael Raphael and Jane (Szczepanik) D. BA, Southeastern Mass. U., 1977; MDiv, Washington Theol. Union, Silver Spring, Md., 1984. Joined Soc. Marians, Roman Cath. Ch.; ordained priest. Asst. pastor St. Joseph's Cath. Ch., Pittsfield, Mass., 1984-85; pastor Our Lady of Grace Cath. Ch., Greensboro, N.C., 1988—; dir. vocation Marian Fathers-Province of St. Stanislaus Kostka, Stockbridge, Mass., 1986-87; dir. of resident/non resident candidates Marian Fathers Scholasticate, Washington, 1987-88, councilor 1st house, 1987-88; superior local house Marian Community for Our Lady of Grace Parish, Greensboro, 1988—; 3d provincial councilor Congregation of Marians, Stockbridge, Mass., 1989—; del. provincial chpt. Marian Province of St. Stanislaus Kostka, Stockbridge, 1984, 90; chaplain pilgrimage Marian Helpers Ctr., Stockbridge, 1990. Sgt. U.S. Army, 1970-73; N.G., 1973-74. Mem. Washington Theol. Union Alumni Assn., KC (chaplain Greensboro chpt. 1988—, cert. appreciation 1989, 90). Republican. Home: 201 S Chapman St Greensboro NC 27403 Office: Our Lady of Grace Cath Ch 2205 W Market St Greensboro NC 27403

EADE, DONALD WAYNE, minister; b. Freeport, Ill., Sept. 18, 1959; s. Gordon Eugene and Nona Grace (Rose) E.; m. Cherry Lynne Hamilton, May 25, 1982; children: Chase Hamilton, Chad Edward. BA in Bible studies, Tenn. Temple U., 1981; M in Sacred Lit., Trinity Theol. Sem., Newburgh, Ind., 1989, postgrad., 1989—. Ordained to ministry Ind. Bapt. Ch., 1985. Assoc. pastor First Bapt. Ch., Ocoee, Fla., 1982; from youth dir. to pastor Colonial Bapt. Ch., Blue Ridge, VA, 1982—; dir. Proclaiming the Truth, Inc., Boulder, Colo., 1988—. Vol. chaplaincy svc., mem. instnl. rev. Community Hosp. of Roanoke Valley, 1991—. Mem. Evang. Theol. Soc. Home: 136 Hillcrest St Blue Ridge VA 24064 Office: Colonial Baptist Church 106 Hillcrest St Blue Ridge VA 24064

EADIE, DAVID ALAN, minister; b. West Frankfort, Ill., Aug. 19, 1944; s. Robert Blissfield and Nellie Mae (Horrell) E.; m. Gwendolyn Kay Holsapple, Aug. 12, 1967; children: Sarah Elizabeth, Emily Kay. BA, McKendree Coll., 1967; MDiv, So. Meth. U., 1970; Doctor of Ministry, Christian Theol. Sem., 1985. Assoc. pastor Elliott United Ch., Gibson City, Ill., 1970-73; pastor Westmer Parish, United Meth., Joy, Ill., 1973-78, First United Meth. Ch., Marshall, Ill., 1978-85; dir. pastor First United Meth. Ch., Kewanee, Ill., 1985—. Chmn. Cen. Ill. Conf. Bd. of Global Ministries, Bloomington, Ill., 1980-88, Enterprise Zone Com. Kewanee Community Devel. Corp., 1987—8; pres. Kewannee Ministerial Assn., 1988; trustee The Baby Fold, Bloomington, 1988; elder United meth. Ch. Mem. Kiwanis (Kewanee dir. 1987-89). Avocation: golf. Home: 214 McKinley Ave Kewanee IL 61443 Office: First United Meth Ch 108 E Central Blvd Kewanee IL 61443

EADS, ORA WILBERT, clergyman, church official; b. Mill Spring, Mo., Jan. 2, 1914; s. John Harrison and Effie Ellen (Borders) E.; m. Mary Ivaree Cochran, Mar. 25, 1944; children—Ora Wilbert, Wayne B., Carol Vernice, Janet Karen and Janice Inez (twins). J.D., John Marshall Law Sch., Atlanta, 1940, LL.M., 1941; postgrad., Sch. Theology, St. Lawrence U., Canton, N.Y., 1947-48. Bar: Ga. bar 1940. Practiced in Atlanta, 1940-46; ordained to ministry Christian Congregation, Inc., 1946; parish minister Sampson County, N.C., 1948-52; evangelist Charlotte, N.C., 1952-61; gen. supt. Christian Congregation, Inc., 1961—. Author numerous books of poetry, 1967—. Office: Christian Congregation Inc 804 W Hemlock St La Follette TN 37766 *A high school teacher asked her class, "What is our purpose on earth? Why are we here?" We students didn't know the answer. I now believe, some 60 years later, that the highest responsibility of any individual is to achieve his best potential.*

EAGEN, ISAAC BRENT, priest; b. Upland, Calif., Dec. 14, 1929; s. James O. and Stella E. (Powell) E. B.A., St. Francis Sem., 1951; M.A., Loyola-Marymount U., 1961; D.H.L. (hon.), U. San Diego, 1980. Ordained priest Roman Catholic Ch., 1956, rev. monsignor, 1969; assoc. pastor St. Joseph Cathedral, 1956; assoc. pastor Holy Rosary Ch., 1956-59; asst. prof. U. San Diego, 1960-65; prof. Mercy Coll. Nursing, San Diego, 1962-64, dir. sch. relations, 1965-67; chancellor Diocese of San Diego, 1968-89; pastor Mission San Diego de Alcala, 1971—; pres. Cathedral Plaza Corp., San Diego, 1971—; bd. dirs. Diocese San Diego Edn. and Welfare Corp., 1968-89; pres. Guadalupe Plaza Corp., San Diego, 1979—. Trustee, U. San Diego, 1968—; pres. Community Welfare Council, 1970; mem. Mayor's Crime Control Commn., 1981. Named Headliner of Year, San Diego Press Club, 1975; recipient Man for All Seasons-St. Vincent de Paul Good Samaritan award, 1989. Mem. NCCJ (nat. trustee, Brotherhood award 1971), Canon Law Soc. Am., Navy League U.S., Scholia, Phi Kappa Theta. Clubs: La Jolla Beach and Tennis, Kona Kai. Home: 10818 San Diego Mission Rd San Diego CA 92108 Office: PO Box 80428 San Diego CA 92138

EAGEN, L. JOHN, minister; b. Mpls., Aug. 7, 1947; s. Reginald Kenneth and Vivienne (Clark) E.; m. Phyllis L. Weisert, June 21, 1969; children: David, Deborah, Daniel, Diane. BA, Bethel Coll., St. Paul, 1970; MS in Edn., Bemidji State U., 1972; EdD, Tex. Tech. U., 1980. Ordained to ministry Christian and Missionary Alliance, 1982. Tchr. Cen. High Sch., St. Paul, 1970-74, chmn. dept. math., 1972-74; asst. to dir. admissions St. Paul Bible Coll., St. Bonifacius, Minn., 1974, asst. to dir. admissions, dir. fin. aid, 1974-76, assoc. dir. admissions, dir. fin. aid, 1976-77, dir. admissions, dir. fin. aid, 1977-79, v.p. for acad. adminstrn., 1979-81, pres., 1981-87; youth pastor Emmanuel Meth. Ch., Mpls., 1969-71, Ch. of the Open Door, Robbinsdale, Minn., 1971-74; interim pastor Bethany Alliance Ch., St. Peter, Minn., 1975, Apple Valley (Minn.) Alliance Ch., 1976, The Village Evang. Free Ch., Delano, Minn., 1977; founder, pres. H.I.S. (Home Inspirational Studies) Ministries, Mpls., 1975-81; sr. pastor Grace Ch. Edina, Edina, Minn., 1987—; speaker in various capacities throughout U.S., Argentina, Aruba, Australia, Brazil, Can., Chine, Peoples Republic of China, Colombia, Ecuador, Hong Kong, Japan, Macao, Malaysia, Mex., The Philippines, Peru, Singapore, Taiwan, V.I., 1969—; adminstrn., orgn. and planning cons. to colls. and Christian orgns., 1980—; mem. rsch. commn. Am. Assn. Bible Colls., 1981-82; mem. bd. mgrs. The Christian and Missionary Alliance, Nyack, N.Y., 1982-87; mem. and chmn. bd. dirs., Okoboji Lakes Bible and Missionary Conf. Assn., Arnold Park, Iowa, 1983-89; team mem., chmn. Accreditation Evaluation Teams, Am. Assn. Bible Colls., 1983-87; bd. dirs.

Am. Assn. Bible Colls., Fayetteville, Ark., 1984-85; bd. reference Berean League, 1984—, Assn. Ch. Missions Coms.,1987—; mem. adv. bd. Mpls. Christian Conciliation Svc., 1986-87. Author: (with Donald A. Bierle) Faith Dynamics, 1977, The Bible College in American Higher Education, 1981, The Pulpit Series, 1988-90. Legis. advisor Com. for Minn. Ho. of Reps., 1984—. Named one of Outstanding Young Men Am., 1977. Mem. Greater Mpls. Assn. Evangelicals (bd. dirs. 1990—), Phi Kappa Phi. Avocations: reading, Bible study, writing, family, athletics. Home: 9350 Hyland Creek Rd Bloomington MN 55437 Office: Grace Ch Edina 5300 France Ave S Edina MN 55410 *Truly abundant living comes from a full surrender to the Lordship of Jesus Christ as embraced and defined by the Scriptures.*

EAKIN, WILLIAM ROWLAND, college administrator, religion consultant; b. Warner Robbins, Ga., Feb. 27, 1958; s. William Leroy and Nannie Ann (Rowland) E.; m. Laura K. Wade, Dec. 27, 1983; 1 child, Benjamin Wade. BA, Hendrix Coll., 1979; MA in Philosophy, Baylor U., 1980; M. in Philosophy, U. Calif., Davis, 1984. Cert. philosophy and religion instr., Calif. Instr. philosophy and religion Solano Community Coll., Suisun, Calif., 1982-84; honors coll. asst. U. Cen. Ark., Conway, 1985-86; asst. dir. Steel Ctr. for the Study Religion and Philosophy Hendrix Coll., Conway, 1986-88, cons. Steel Ctr. for the Study Religion and Philosophy, 1988—; coord., dir. Johnson County Office of Volunteerism, Clarksville, Ark., 1989—; dialogue group leader Buddhism and Christianity, Berkeley, Calif., 1987; coord. Econs. for Community Conf., Meadowcreek, Ark., 1986, 87. Co-editor: Liberating Life, 1990, After Patriarchy, 1991; contbr. articles to profl. jours. Pres. Unified Community Coun., Clarksville, 1989, Johnson County Literacy Coun., Clarksville, 1989—, Ark. Philological Assn., Conway, 1989; chairperson Transient/Interfaith, Clarksville, 1989—. Mem. Ark. Philological Assn. (pres. 1988-89, sec.-treas. 1986-87, v.p. 1987-88), Buddhist-Christian Soc., Helping Hands. Episcopalian. Home: PO Box 261 Clarksville AR 72830 *I am convinced that each of us must assume the dangerous, radically open stance of listening to the other—all others—in order to become truly humane, in order to make justice, ecological responsibility and Christian love meaningful or possible.*

EAKINS, JOEL KENNETH, archaeology and Old Testament educator, pediatrician; b. Ozark, Mo., Feb. 22, 1930; s. Alvin Homer and Pearl Annie (Meadows) E.; m. Marian LaNette McInnes, Aug. 14, 1949; children—Douglas Gene, Nancy Lynn, Sheri Lee, Laurie Lane. B.S., Wheaton Coll., 1952; B.S., U. Ill., 1954, M.D., 1956; B.D., So. Baptist Theol. Sem., 1967, Ph.D., 1970. Diplomate Am. Bd. Pediatrics. Rotating intern Akron Gen. Hosp., Ohio, 1956-57; pediatric resident Akron Children's Hosp., 1957-59; pediatric hematology fellow Children's Hosp., Columbus, Ohio, 1961-62; practice medicine specializing in pediatrics, Thomasville, Ga., 1962-63; part-time pediatric practice Kaiser Hosp., Oakland, Calif., 1971-88 ; prof. archaeology and O.T., Golden Gate Bapt. Sem., Mill Valley, Calif., 1970—; osteologist Tell-el-Hesi expdn., Israel, 1977—. Contbr. articles to profl. jours. Flutist, Community Band, Marin County, Calif., 1977—. Served as capt. U.S. Army, 1959-61. Mem. Nat. Assn. Profs. Hebrew (v.p. 1982-89, pres. 1989—), Am. Schs. Oriental Research (ann. prof. appointment, 1983), Soc. Bibl. Lit., Paleopathology Assn. Democrat. Baptist. Home: 78 LaBrea Way San Rafael CA 94903 Office: Golden Gate Bapt Sem Mill Valley CA 94903

EAMES, ROBERT HENRY ALEXANDER, archbishop, primate; b. Belfast, Northern Ireland, Apr. 27, 1937; s. William Edward and Mary Eleanor (Alexander) E.; m. Ann Christine Daly, June 25, 1966; children: Niall William Adrian, Michael Harvey Alexander. LLB with honors, Queen's U., Belfast, 1960, PhD in Law, 1963, LLD (hon.), 1989. Ordained priest Ch. of Ireland, 1964. Priest Ch. of Ireland, 1964-75, bishop of Derry and Raphoe, 1975-80, bishop of Down and Dromore, 1980-86, archbishop of Armagh, primate of all Ireland, met., 1986—; chmn. priorities com. Ch. Ireland, 1977-79; select preacher U. Oxford, 1987; Irish rep. to Anglican Consultative Coun. and Standing Com.; chmn. commn. on communion and women in the episcopate Archbishop of Canterbury, 1988-90. Author: Form of Worship for Teenage Groups, 1965, The Quiet Revolution: The Disestablishment of the Church of Ireland, 1970, Through Suffering, 1973, Thinking Trough Lent, 1978; contbr. articles to Irish Legal Quar., Northern Ireland Legal Quar., other jours. Chmn. bd. govs. Royal Sch., Armagh. Hon. fellow Guild Ch. Musicians. Home: The See House, Cathedral Close, Armagh BT61 7EE, Northern Ireland Office: Church House, Abbey St, Armagh Northern Ireland

EARLEY, NEAL CHRISTOPHER, minister; b. Cin., Dec. 14, 1946; s. Neal Norman and Margery May (Qualheim) E.; m. Judith Ann Warner, June 16, 1973; children: Neal Howard, Joyce Ann, Nathan Warner, Bryan Christopher. BA, Columbia U., 1969; MDiv, Union Theol. Sem., 1972. Ordained to ministry, 1972. Pastor First United Presbyn. Parish, White Haven, Pa., 1972-76, Chester (N.Y.) Presbyn. Ch., 1976-80, Georgetown (Ohio) Presbyn. Ch., 1980-90; assoc. pastor Faith Presbyn. Ch., Papillion, Nebr., 1990—. Pres. Meals on Wheels, Weatherly, Pa., 1974-76. Home: 1113 S. Grandview St Papillion NE 68046 *Seeking to do the Lord's will, no matter what He requires, that is the joy that sets a person free!.*

EARL OF DUNSMERE, BARON HORAN OF ANTWERP See **HORAN, CLARK J., III**

EARLY, JEAN LESLIE HARTZ, music director; b. Durham, N.C., Sept. 5, 1945; d. John Leslie and Betty Lou (Buxton) Hartz; m. John Firman Early, Jan. 21, 1967; children: Michael, Angela. BA, So. Meth. U., 1967; postgrad., Am. Univ., 1976-78. Organist, choir dir. Fairhaven United Meth. Ch., Gaithersburg, Md., 1973-75, Trinity United Meth. Ch., Germantown, Md., 1980-87, Hopewell (N.Y.) Reformed Ch., 1989-90, Zion's Hill United Meth. Ch., Wilton, Conn., 1990—. Mem. Am. Guild Organists. Home: 9 Twixt Hills Rd Ridgefield CT 06877 Office: Zions Hill United Meth Ch 470 Danbury Rd Wilton CT 06897

EARWOOD, J. DONALD, JR., minister; b. Portsmouth, Va., May 14, 1963; s. James Donald Sr. and Rhoda Irene (Ball) E. BA, Bluefield Coll., 1985; MRE, Midwestern Sem., 1988. Ordained to ministry So. Bapt. Conv., 1989. Mem. revival team Bapt. Student Union, Bluefield, Va., 1981-85; assoc. pastor Grove Park Bapt. Ch., Portsmouth, Va., 1985-86; minister of edn. and youth Tryst Falls Bapt. Ch., Kearney, Mo., 1986-88, Villa Hts. Bapt. Ch., Roanoke, Va., 1989—; missions intern Windward Islands, 1988. Author children's witnessing tract, 1989. Pres. Bluefield Coll. Student Govt., 1984-85. Recipient Christian Edn. award Bapt. Sunday Sch. Bd., 1988; grantee Keesee Found., 1981-85. Mem. Religioous Edn. Assn., Roanoke Area Youth Assn., Roanoke Valley Assn. (dir. discipleship tng. 1990—, treas. Superweek Youth Camp 1989—). Republican. Office: Villa Hts Bapt Ch 4080 Challenger Ave NE Roanoke VA 24012 *30% of all known babies are aborted. 1,500,00 abortions last year were recorded. Drugs and alcohol abuse are at an all time high. It is time to stop trying to heal the world while at home we are killing ourselves.*

EASTBURN, JEANNETTE ROSE, religious publishing executive; b. Huntington, Ind., Mar. 18, 1916; d. Elmer Fyson and Iva Jerusha (Rose) Connett; widowed. BS, Bethel Coll., Mishawaka, Ind., 1973. ordained World Bible Way Fellowship, 1990. Mgr. Calvary Bookstore, South Bend, Ind., 1952-54; sec. Meml. Hosp., South Bend, 1954-58, Pvt. Day Christian Sch. Calvary Temple, South Bend, 1958-64; tchr. South Bend Pub. Schs., 1964-78; ednl. cons. KDSA Radio, Wichita, Kans., 1978-80; pub. Christian Communications, Inc., Wichita, 1980—. Contbr. articles to profl. jours. Mem. AUW, Order Eastern Star, Amanranth, White Shrine, Ky. Cols., Epsilon Sigma Alpha, Gamma Sigma, Phi Delta Kappa. Republican. Avocations: china painting, writing. Home: 6434 N Hillside Wichita KS 67219

EASTER, RUBY L., lay worker; b. DeKalb, Tex., July 12, 1918; d. Albert and Mary L. (Dunn) V.; children: Virgie, George, Joe, Henry, Lula, Willie, Ruby. BS, Prairie View U., 1972, ME in Edn. Youth dir. DeKalb, 1966-89, vacation Bible sch., 1980-90, YWCA dir., 1981-87, mission dir., 1988—, PTA pres., 1989—. Me. 4-H Club (pres. DeKalb chpt. 1970-89), Sch. Reunion Club (treas. 1981—), Order Ea. Star. Home: PO Box 701 DeKalb TX 75559

EASTERDAY, JAMES E., religion educator; b. Phila., Feb. 3, 1915; s. Harry and Helen (Duffy) E.; m. Adele E. Coney, Apr. 29, 1939; children: James j., Faith A., Robert H. Student, Phila. Sch. of the Bible, 1948-52, Garden State Bible Coll., 1978-81. Supt., tchr. St. John's R.E. Ch., Ventnor, N.J., 1959-65; tchr. Ocean City (N.J.) Bapt. Ch., 1967-90. Republican. Home: 104 N Bryant Ave Ventnor NJ 08406

EASTERLING, LARRY BYRON, lay worker, electrical engineer; b. Bruce, Miss., Nov. 11, 1942; s. Virgil Byron and Mary Kathryn (Ivy) E.; m. Peggy Diann Tutor, June 8, 1963; children: Shan, Connie, Ethan. BSEE, U. Miss., Oxford, 1967. Elder Community Bible Ch., Pontotoc, Miss., 1973—, sch. administr., 1980-87; mgr. Scott's Trailer Equipment, Verona, Miss., 1987—; sec.-treas. Community Bible Ch., Pontotoc, 1973-75, Faith Ministries, Inc., Pontotoc, 1973—. Mem. Miss. Hunting Dog Assn. (pres. 1986-90). Republican. Home: Rte 7 Box 120 Pontotoc MS 38863 Office: Scott's Trailer Equipment P O Box 494 Verona MS 38879

EASTLAND, JAMES HAGAN, minister; b. Augusta, Kans., Apr. 20, 1923; s. William Hagan and Nina Belle (Pampelly) E.; m. Wauletta Fern Engbrecht, July 17, 1948; children: Cynthia Donaldson, Carol Choy, Jana Ordaz, Julie Baker. BA, Baylor U., 1946; postgrad., Cen. Bapt. Theol. Sem., Kansas City, Kans., 1950-52. Pastor Palmyra Bapt. Ch., Benton, Kans., 1946-49; commd. USAF, 1952, advanced through grades to lt. col.; chaplain Alaska Pipe Line Co., Fairbanks, 1974-75; pastor Point Lookout (N.Y.) Community Ch., 1975-78, Lucas Valley Community Ch., San Rafael, Calif., 1978-83, Open Door Christian Ch., Novato, Calif., 1986—. Mem. FGBFI. Republican. Home: 228 Hahn Way Cotati CA 94931 Office: Open Door Christian Ch 720 Diablo Ave Novato CA 94947

EASTMAN, ALBERT THEODORE, bishop; b. San Mateo, Calif., Nov. 20, 1928; s. Carl John and Inette (Nordeen) E.; m. Sarah Virginia Tice, June 13, 1953; children: Sarah, Anne, Andrew. B.A., Haverford Coll., 1950; M.Div., Va. Theol. Sem., 1953, D.D., 1983; L.H.D., Episcopal Theol. Sem. Southwest, 1982. Ordained priest Episcopal Ch., 1954; vicar Trinity Ch., Gonzales, Calif., 1953-56; exec. sec. Overseas Mission Soc., Washington, 1956-68; cons. House Bishops, Washington, 1968; rector Ch. of Mediator, Allentown, Pa., 1969-73, St. Alban's Ch., Washington, 1973-82; bishop coadjutor Episcopal Diocese Md., Balt., 1982-85; bishop Episcopal Diocese Md., 1986—; co-chmn. Anglican-Roman Cath. Consultation, 1983—. Author: Christian Responsibilty in One World, 1965, Chosen and Sent, 1971, The Baptizing Community, 1982. Vis. fellow Episcopal Theol. Seminary Southwest, 1963, 80; Scholar-in-residence Coll. Preachers, 1981. Fellow Coll. Preachers. Democrat. Episcopalian. Home: 15 E Bishop's Rd Baltimore MD 21218 Office: Episcopal Diocese Md 4 E University Pkwy Baltimore MD 21218

EASTON, GLENN SCOTT, lay worker, editor; b. L.A., Feb. 10, 1959; s. David and Maxine (Schultz) E.; m. Cindy S. Easton, Nov. 24, 1984; 1 child, Lisa. Student, UCLA; BA, Calif. State U., Northridge, 1981; MPA, U. Judaism, 1984. Adminstr. Adat Ariel, North Hollywood, Calif., 1977-84; exec. dir. B'nai Israel Congregation, Rockville, Md., 1984-90; pres., editor Communal Computing News Ch. Computing News, Rockville, 1987—. Editor: The Software Bible. Fellow Nat. Assn. Synagogue Adminstrn. (sec.); mem. Greater Washington Soc. Assn. Execs. Office: Communal Computing PO Box 6599 Silver Spring MD 20916

EASTWOOD, RONALD ALAN, radio news director; b. Medina, Ohio, Sept. 2, 1961; s. Roger Ziegler and Linda Ann (White) E. BA, Geneva Coll., 1983. Announcer Sta. WSUM-AM, Cleve., 1982-84, Sta. WHLO-AM, Akron, Ohio, 1984, Sta. KTWG-AM, Agana, Guam, 1985-87, Sta. WCRF-FM, Cleve., 1987; news dir. Sta. WZLE-FM, Lorain, Ohio, 1987—. Mem. Medina County Right to Life, Medina, 1982—. Republican. Office: Sta WZLE-FM 300 Washington Ave Lorain OH 44052-1478

EATHERLY, JOHN HERSHEL, III, minister; b. Nashville, June 28, 1940; s. John Hershel and Ada Frances (Finn) E.; m. Linda Mae Thomas, Nov. 1, 1963 (div. July 1975); children: John Hershel IV, Thomas Mark. AS cum laude, Columbia State Community Coll., 1977; BS, Middle Tenn. State U., 1987; alt. degree, Memphis Theol. Sem., 1991. Ordained to ministry Presbyn. Ch., 1961. Pastor Jackson Ridge Bapt. Ch., Rockvale, Tenn., 1960-61, Rocky Fork Bapt. Mission, Smyrna, Tenn., 1961-64; pastor First Bapt. Ch., College Grove, Tenn., 1964-65, Iron City, Tenn., 1967-69; pastor Meml. Bapt. Ch., Livingston, Tenn., 1965-67, Bakers Grove Bapt. Ch., Mt. Joliet, Tenn., 1969-72, Maplewood Bapt. Ch., Nashville, 1972-74, Nolts Corner Bapt. Ch., Chapel Hill, Tenn., 1975-88, Cumberland Presbyn. Ch., Chapel Hill, 1989—. Mem. acad. coun., devel. com. Columbia (Tenn.) State Community Coll., 1977; pres. Champs PTO, 1978-79. Mem. Lions. Home: 126 Depot St Chapel Hill TN 37034 Office: Cumberland Presbyn Ch 302 N Horton Pkwy Chapel Hill TN 37034

EATON, GLENN ALAN, minister; b. North Bend, Oreg., July 15, 1917; s. Clyde Lester and Blanche Elizabeth (Howell) E.; m. Jeannette Alice Christensen, Feb. 21, 1942; children: Lillian Alice, Glenn Alan. BS, BA, U. Oreg, 1940; grad., Command and Gen. Staff Coll., 1953. Ordained deacon Episcopal Ch., 1954. Deacon Episc. Diocese of Oreg., Salem, 1954—; fin. officer Episc. Diocese of Oreg., Portland, 1960-77; dir. planned giving Episc. Bishop of Oreg. Found., Portland, 1977-83, William Temple House, Portland, 1983-89; canon Cathedral of St. John, Portland, 1991—; exec. dir. Willamette View Found., 1978—; pres. Episcopal Bishop of Oreg. Found., 1984-85. Author planned giving pamphlets: Estate Planning, 1979. Bd. dirs., trustee Good Samaritan Hosp., 1980-86; bd. dirs. Good Samaritan Hosp. Found., 1982-85, Ecumenical Ministries of Oreg., 1981-85; sr. v.p. Boy Scouts Am., Portland, 1967-69,; pres. Parkrose Lions, 1964-65. Decorated Legion of Merit, Bronze Star. Mem. Mil. Order World Wars (pres. 1973-74), Am. Legion, Res. Officers Assn., Masons. Office: Willamette View Found Portland OR 97222

EATON, JAMES EDWARD, minister, writer; b. Ann Arbor, Mich., Aug. 17, 1951; s. Edward Allen and Ruth May (Krayer) E.; m. Ellen Ann Patterson, Mar. 30, 1985; children: Amy, Jason. BA, Mich. State U., 1972; MDiv, Boston U., 1975. Ordained to ministry Nat. Assn. Congl. Christian Chs., 1975. Assoc. pastor Aldersgate United Meth. Ch., Chelmsford, Mass., 1973-75; min. Seattle Congl. Ch., 1975-79, 1st Congl. Ch., Mukwonago, Wis., 1979-81, Suttons Bay (Mich.) Congl. Ch., 1987—; mem. No. Mich. Small Ch. Task Force, 1987-89, chaplain adv. com. Munson Hosp., Traverse City, Mich., 1988-90. Author: Who Do You Say I Am?, 1977; co-author: Cross Bearing, 1989, Pray Without Crossing, 1991. Bd. dirs. Grand Traverse Habitat for Humanity, Traverse City, 1989-90, Friends of Suttons Bay, 1990—. Mem. Grand Traverse Ministerial Assn. (pres. 1991-92), Rotary. Office: Suttons Bay Congl Ch Madison & Lincoln PO Box 70 Suttons Bay MI 49682

EATON, MARILYN SUE, lay worker; b. Murphysboro, Ill., Nov. 9, 1955; d. Herbert Wanson and Opal Marie (Huppert) Vaughn; m. Robert William Eaton, June 21, 1975; children: John Robert, Michael Wade. AAS, John A. Logan Coll., 1975. Sec. 1st Evang. Luth. Ch., Murphysboro, 1984—; chair social ministry 1st Evang. Luth. Ch., 1985—, supt. Sunday sch., 1985-88, sec. coun. 1984-91, treas. women, 1979-89, leader Luth. Friendship Club, 1979—, dir. fund raising for local food pantry, 1987-90; notary pub., 1982—. Field lt. United Way, 1989; mgr. Baseball Little League, 1985-88; dir. worship Jackson County Nursing Home, 1984—. Named Mother of the Yr., 1st Evang. Luth. Ch., 1988. Mem. Beta Sigma Phi. Home: 2 Chardonnay Circle Murphysboro IL 62966 Office: 1st Evang Luth Ch 115 N 14th St Murphysboro IL 62966

EATON, TED FRANK, minister; b. Athens, Tex., Mar. 3, 1942; s. Jessie Earl and Mary Catherine (Ward) E.; m. Shriley Ann Burt, June 21, 1963; children: Trisha Lee Eaton Nolen, Shirlene Eaton Bershers. BS, U. Corpus Christi, Tex., 1968; MRE, Southwestern Bapt. Theol. Sem., Ft. Worth, 1973. Ordained to ministry, So. Bapt. Conv. Pastor Ricardo Bapt. Ch., Kingsville, Tex., 1968-71, Allendale Bapt. Ch., Wichita Falls, Tex., 1972-73; asst. pastor First Bapt. Ch., Dimmitt, Tex., 1973-75; pastor First Bapt. Ch., Leonard, Tex., 1975-82, Calallen Bapt. Ch., Corpus Christi, 1982—; exec. bd. Bapt. Gen. Conv. of Tex., Dallas, 1989—, stewardship advisor, 1978—. Contbr. articles to profl. jours.; author: Study in I John, 1986, How to Become a Christian, 1978, Bible Study #2, 1980. Bd. dirs. Instl. Rev. Bd., Meml. Med. Ctr., Corpus Christi, 1986—, United Fund, Leonard, Tex., 1979-81. Mem. Leonard C. of C. (bd. dirs. 1978-82). Office: Calallen Bapt Ch 13505 Leopard Corpus Christi TX 78410

EAVES, WILLIAM ALFRED, minister; b. Chattanooga, Nov. 25, 1962; s. William A. and Iris Shannon (Williams) E.; m. Shirley E. Jordon, May 27, 1989. BA cum laude, U. of the South, Sewanee, Tenn., 1984; postgrad., Johannes Gutenberg U., Mainz, Federal Republic of Germany, 1982-83; MDiv, Yale Div. Sch., 1987. Ordained to ministry United Meth. Ch., 1987. Student pastor United Meth. Ch., Naugatuck, Conn., 1985-87; pastor United Meth. Ch., Springfield, Ky., 1987-89; assoc. pastor Christ Ch., Louisville, 1989—; mem. Louisville Conf. Support Com. for Divorcing Clergy, 1990—; del. commn. Christian unity Ky. Coun. Chs., 1990—. Office: Christ Church 4614 Brownsboro Rd Louisville KY 40207

EBACHER, ROGER, archbishop; b. Amos, Que., Can., Oct. 6, 1936. Ordained priest Roman Cath. Ch., 1961; ordained bishop of Diocese of Baie-Comeau, Que., 1979; chevalier de Colomb du 4e degré, 1983; apptd. bishop Diocese of Gatineau-Hull, Que., 1988, archbishop, 1990—. Address: 39 Amherst St, Hull, PQ Canada J8Y 2W1

EBAUGH, DAVID PAUL, minister, school system administrator; b. Indpls., June 22, 1930; s. Paul Edward and Gladys Rachael (Ruddick) E.; m. Betty LeTourneau, Apr. 9, 1950; children—Michael, Marcellene, Diane, Rosalie. Tool and test equipment engr. IBM, Lexington, Ky., 1956-62; sr. indsl. engr. Goodyear Aerospace Corp., Akron, 1962-64; supr. mfg. methods engring. AMP, Inc., Harrisburg, Pa., 1965-67; ordained to ministry Ind. Assembly of God Ch., 1968; founder, pres. David Ebaugh Bible Sch., Harrisburg, 1968—; pastor Ch. of Revelation, 1982—. Served with USN, 1947-52. Mem. IEEE (profl. diploma 1959), Soc. Am. Value Engrs., Am. Inst. Indsl. Engrs., Am. Soc. Tool and Mfg. Engrs. Clubs: Christian Businessmen's Com. (pres. Lexington chpt. 1960), Full Gospel Businessmen's Com. (pres. Harrisburg chpt. 1967). Author, pub.: Key to Revelation, 1969, Key to Priesthood, 1970, Third Salvation, 1972, Keys to Marriage Divorce and Remarriage, 1973, Free to Live, 1976, My Daddy and Me, 1980, Daniel's 70 Weeks, 1986; pub. Monarch Monthly. Home and Office: 102 Park Terr Harrisburg PA 17111 *Bible study indicates that a group of people will not die; but the changes in human personality that are prerequisite to enter that group are enormous. My life experiences and study indicate that immortality is a goal worth pursuing.*

EBBERS, JAMES PAUL, minister, religious organization administrator; b. Oostburg, Wis., Oct. 6, 1926; s. Chester Lewis and Lavina Loretta (Zehms) E.; m. Dorothy Jean DeHaan, Dec. 28, 1949; children: Michael A., Susan K., Christopher E., Steven M. BA, Cen. Coll., Pella, Iowa, 1948; MDiv, New Brunswick (N.J.) Theol. Sem., 1951. Ordained to ministry Reformed Ch. in Am., 1951. Pastor Reformed Ch., Philmont and Mellenville, N.Y., 1951-58, Walden, N.Y., 1959-62; exec. sec. Reformed Ch. Am. Bd. World Missions, N.Y.C., 1962-69, Conf. of Chs., Akron, Ohio, 1969-78; pastor Williard United Ch. of Christ, Akron, 1978-85; exec. sec. Ill. Conf. Chs., Springfield, 1985-89, ret., 1989. Home: 1361 Northwest Dr Pella IA 50219

EBERLE, PETER RICHARD, abbot; b. Silverton, Oreg., June 29, 1941; s. Valentine Anthony and Kathryn Theresa (Moffenbeier) E. Licentiate in theology, St. Paul U., Ottawa, Can., 1972; S.T.D., Accademia Alfonsiana, Rome, 1979. Ordained priest in Roman Cath. Ch., 1968. Professed as a monk Mt. Angel Abbey, St. Benedict, Oreg., 1961—, prior of monastery, 1980-88, elected abbot of monastery, 1988—. Avocations: Portland Trailblazers basketball team, reading. Home and office: Mount Angel Abbey Saint Benedict OR 97373

EBEY, CARL FINLEY, priest, religious order superior; b. Detroit, May 31, 1940; s. Warren Edwin and Florence Evelyn (McDonald) E. BBA, U. Notre Dame, 1962, MBA, 1972; MA in Theology, Holy Cross Coll., Washington, 1968; D Bus. Adminstrn., Ind. U., 1980. Joined Congregation of Holy Cross, Roman Cath. Ch., 1962; ordained priest, 1972. CPA, Ind. Priest Congregation of Holy Cross, South Bend, Ind., 1972—, provincial treas., 1979-87, provincial superior, 1988—. Bd. dirs. King's Coll., Wilkes-Barre, Pa., 1987—; bd. regents U. Portland, Oreg., 1987—; trustee Stonehill Coll., North Easton, Mass., 1988—, U. Notre Dame, Ind., 1988—. Address: Congregation of Holy Cross 1304 E Jefferson Blvd South Bend IN 46617

EBINGER, WARREN RALPH, minister; b. Effingham, Ill., Dec. 18, 1927; s. Robert William and Florence Mabel (Sclapp) E.; m. Mary Esther Ritzman, Aug. 11, 1951; children: Lee, Lori Ebinger Lear, Jonathan. BA, North Cen. Coll., 1951; MDiv, Garrett-Evang. Theol. Sem., 1954; PhD, Am. U., 1976. Ordained to ministry United Meth. Ch., 1954. Pastor United Meth. Ch., Davis, Ill., 1954-58; mem. exec. coun. of chs. United Meth. Ch., Springfield (Ill.) and Kansas City (Mo.), 1958-64; pastor Community Ch. United Meth., Naperville, Ill., 1964-68; assoc. gen. sec. Bd. Ch. and Soc., United Meth. Ch., Washington, 1968-77; pastor Woodside United Meth. Ch., Silver Spring, Md., 1977-82; dist. supt. United Meth. Ch., Frederick, Md., 1982-88; pastor Severna Park (Md.) United Meth. Ch., 1988—. Author 4 books. Cpl. U.S. Army, 1946-47. Recipient Disting. Alumnus award North Cen. Coll. Home: 6 St Ives Dr Severna Park MD 21146

EBLING, WILLIAM LUNDER, minister; b. Barnesville, Minn., Sept. 25, 1930; s. Paul Ebling and Irine Adeline (Lunder) Crowe; m. JoAnne Mildred Erickson, Apr. 25, 1952; children—Jennifer Jo Ebling Trevithick, Melissa Milrine Ebling Ware. B.A., U. Minn., 1952; M.Div., Fuller Theol. Sem., Pasadena, Calif., 1959. Ordained to ministry Am. Baptist Ch., 1959. Vice pres. A.G. Verdolyack Co., Mpls., 1955-56; pastor Redeemer Bapt. Ch., Los Angeles, 1967-72, 1st Bapt. Ch., Burlingame, Calif., 1972-79, Bellflower, Calif., 1979—; mem. gen. bd. Am. Bapt. Chs. in U.S.A., Valley Forge, Pa., 1981—, mem. bd. internat. ministries, 1981—, v.p., 1984-85. Mem. Am. Bapt. Ministers Council, Los Angeles Bapt. Ministers Council (pres. 1963-65), Am. Bapt. Fgn. Mission Soc. (pres. 1986—). Lodge: Rotary (Bellflower). Office: First Baptist Church 9603 Belmont St Bellflower CA 90706

EBY, JOHN OLIVER, minister; b. Chgo., Aug. 28, 1940; s. John Wilbert and Gladys Anna (Palmer) E.; m. Sherrie Anne Jordan, Aug. 15, 1961; children: John Christopher, Ramona Anna-Lydia. BA, U. LaVerne, 1962; MDiv, Am. Bapt. Sem. of West, 1965. Ordained to ministry Am. Bapt. Ch., 1965. Assoc. pastor Judson Bapt. Ch., San Bernadino, Calif., 1964-68; pastor Community Bapt. Ch., Buttonwillow, Calif., 1968-74; pastor 1st Bapt. Ch., Lompoc, Calif., 1974-81, Selma, Calif., 1981—. Trustee Lompol Unified Sch, Dist., 1979-81; mem. assessment coun. Selma Unified Sch. Dist., 1982-83; chmn. sch. site coun. Selma High Sch., 1985-87, accreditation com., 1987; chmn. blood drive Cen. Calif. Blood Bank, Selma, 1982-90; mem. delinquency prevention task force City of Selma, 1989-90; co-chmn. ICU fund drive Selma Dist Hosp. Found., 1990. Recipient Svc. award Black Leaders of San Bernardino, 1968, Buttonwillow C. of C., 1974, Hon. Svc. award Buttonwillow PTA, 1974, Scouter's Key award Boy Scouts Am., Lompol, 1976, Continuing Svc. award Lompol PTA, 1977, Vocat. Svc. award Rotary Club, Selma, 1988, Outstanding Citizen award Police Chief's Assn., Fresno, Calif., 1990. Mem. Am. Bapt. Chs. of the West (moderator 1988-90, bd. mgrs. 1989-90), Am. Bapt. Chs. (mem. min. coun.), Selma Ministerial Assn. (pres. 1987-89, sec. 1990-91). Office: 1st Bapt Ch 2025 Grant St Selma CA 93662 *There is no greater recognition in life that of being seen as one who lives for Christ, with Christ, and like Christ.*

ECHOLS, TOMMY GERALD, minister; b. Braxton, Miss., Mar. 26, 1951; s. Robert J. and Cozy (Brown) E.; m. Sue Carol Smith, May 27, 1972; 1 child, Jeremy Harold. MusB, Miss. Coll., 1972; M in Ch. Music, Southwestern Bapt. Theol. Sem., Ft. Worth, 1974. Min. music Harbor City Bapt. Ch., Eau Gallie, Fla., 1974-75; min. music and youth Kosciusko (Miss.) 1st Bapt. Ch., 1976, Eastside Bapt. Ch., Pearl, Miss., 1976-81; min. edn. Ridge Ave. Bapt. Ch., West Monroe, La., 1981—. Bd. dirs. BSU, N.E. La. U., Monroe, 1990—. Mem. Nat. Bus. Adminstrs. Assn., La. Bapt. Religious Assn., N.E. Bapt. Assn. (adult specialist 1981—), So. Bapt. Religious Assn. Office: Ridge Ave Bapt Ch 1009 Ridge Ave West Monroe LA 71291

ECK, DAVID WILSON, minister; b. Pitts., Apr. 7, 1962; s. Herbert Walter Eck and Linda Joan (Pitrusu) Butera. BS in Chemistry, U. Pitts., 1984;

MDiv, Luth. Theol. Sem., Gettysburg, Pa., 1988. Ordained to ministry Evang. Luth. Ch. in Am., 1988. Assoc. pastor Mt. Zion Luth. Ch., Conover, N.C., 1988—; mem. young adult com. N.C. Synod, Salisbury, 1989-90; bd. dirs. Coop. Christian Ministry, Hickory, N.C., 1989. Mem. editorial adv. bd. Soli Deo Gloria, 1990—, also contbr. articles, poetry and music; singer, songwriter. Recipient cert. of achievement Billboard Songwriting Contest, 1990. Republican. Home: 1655 20th Ave Dr NE #94 Hickory NC 28601 Office: Mt Zion Luth Ch Rte 2 Box 785 Conover NC 28613 *Creativity is the lifeblood of the human race. If we fail to dream, to generate new ideas, to look toward the future with great hope and enthusiasm, we will surely perish from the face of the earth.*

ECKARD, RALPH EDGAR, retired clergyman; b. Alexander County, N.C., June 22, 1927; s. Frederick Lee and Vertie Veronica (Price) E.; m. Betty Jane Froehlich, June 10, 1950; children: Nancy Ellen Eckard Verderosa, Ruth Ann Eckard Anderson, Linda Jane. BD, Lenoir Rhyne Coll., Hickory, N.C., 1947; MDiv, Luth. Sch. Theology Chgo., 1950; DD (hon.), Lenoir Rhyne Coll., 1974. Ordained minister Lutheran Ch., 1950. Asst. pastor St. John's Luth. Ch., Council Bluffs, Iowa, 1950-51; pastor First Luth. Ch., Newton, Iowa, 1951-56, Trinity Luth. Ch., Kirkwood, Mo., 1956-60, Wilmette (Ill.) Luth., 1960-61; stewardship sec. Ill. Synod United Luth. Ch. Am., Chgo., 1961-62; asst. to pres./bishop Luth. Ch. Am., N.Y.C., 1962-89; ret., 1989; acting exec. dir. Office for Communications, N.Y.C., 1972-73, 77; bishop's liaison Bd. of Publication, Phila., 1982-87. Pres. PTA, Englewood, N.J., 1966. Avocation: golf. Home: 1960 12th Street Pl NE Hickory NC 28601

ECKARDT, ALICE ELIZA LYONS, religion studies educator; b. Bklyn., Apr. 27, 1923; d. Henry Egmont and Almira Blake (Palmer) Lyons; m. A. Roy Eckardt, Sept. 2, 1944; children: Paula Jean Eckardt Strock, Stephen Robert. BA, Oberlin Coll., 1944; MA, Lehigh U., 1966. Lectr. religion studies dept. Lehigh U., Bethlehem, Pa., 1972-75, asst. prof., 1976-85, assoc. prof., 1985-87, prof. emerita, 1987—, co-founder, co-dir. Jewish Studies Program, 1976-85; vis. scholar Oxford (Eng.) Ctr. for Postgrad. Hebrew Studies, 1972, 75, Maxwell fellow, 1989-90, sr. assoc. fellow, 1990—; vis. lectr. CUNY, 1973; adj. prof. Cedar Crest Coll., 1982-83; exch. prof. Muhlenberg Coll., 1984; mem. Christian Study Group on Judaism and the Jewish People, 1973—, chairperson, 1977-79; mem. United Ch. of Christ Jewish-Christian Dialogue Project, 1988—; exec. com. Nat. Christian Leadership Conf. for Israel, 1975—; spl. cons. Pres.'s Com. on the Holocaust, 1979; spl. advisor U.S. Holocaust Meml. Coun., Washington, 1981-86; exec. bd. Zachor: Holocaust Resource Ctr., 1978-82; adv. com. Holocaust Resource Ctr., Allentown, Pa., 1984—; nat. adv. coun. Scholars Conf. on Ch. Struggle and Holocaust, 1985—, chairperson 18th Ann. Conf., 1988; mem. exec. com. Remembering for the Future conf., Oxford and London, 1985-88; mem. acad. adv. bd. Berman Ctr. for Jewish Studies, Lehigh U., 1985-89, adv. bd. Inst. for Christian Jewish Studies, Balt., 1987; bd. dirs. Inst. for Jewish-Christian Understanding, Muhlenberg Coll., 1989—. Co-author: Encounter with Israel, 1970, Long Night's Journey Into Day: Life and Faith after the Holocaust, 1982, rev. and enlarged edit., 1988; contbr. introductory essay to: More Stepping Stones to Christian-Jewish Relations, 1985; editor, contbr.: Jerusalem: City of the Ages, 1987; exec. editorial bd. Holocaust and Genocide Studies, 1985—; mem. editorial bd. Holocaust Publs., Inc., 1984—; assoc. editor Jour. Ecumenical Studies, 1991—; contbr. book chpts., articles to profl. jours. Founding officer Citizens Adv. Com. for So. Lehigh Schs., 1958-60; bd. dirs. Anne Frank Inst., until 1989; nat. adv. bd. Found. to Sustain Righteous Gentiles, 1987—. Recipient Human Rels. award Am. Jewish Com., 1971, Myrtle Wreath Achievement award Hadassah, Allentown, 1971, Ea. Pa. Region, 1975, South N.J. Region, 1979; Eternal Flame award Anne Frank Inst., 1987, Righteous Person award Temple Beth El, 1987, Humanitarian award B'nai Brith, 1989. Mem. Am. Acad. Religion, Am. Profs. for Peace in Middle East, Lehigh U. Women's Club (pres. 1960-61). Democrat. Home: 6011 Beverly Hill Rd Coopersburg PA 18036 Office: Lehigh U Maginnes Hall #9 Bethlehem PA 18015

ECKARDT, ARTHUR ROY, emeritus religion studies educator; b. Bklyn., Aug. 8, 1918; s. Frederick William and Anna (Fitts) E.; m. Alice Eliza Lyons, Sept. 2, 1944; children—Paula Jean, Stephen Robert. B.A., Bklyn. Coll., 1942; M.Div., Yale, 1944; Ph.D., Columbia-Union Theol. Sem., 1947; L.H.D., Hebrew Union Coll.-Jewish Inst. Religion, 1969. Ordained to ministry United Meth. Ch., 1944. Asst. prof. religion Lawrence Coll., 1947-50, Duke, 1950-51; asso. prof., head dept. religion studies Lehigh U., Bethlehem, Pa., 1951-56; prof., chmn. dept. Lehigh U., 1956-80, prof. emeritus, 1980—; vis. prof. dept. Jewish studies CCNY, 1973; vis. scholar Oxford Centre for Postgrad. Hebrew Studies, 1982-83, 85, Maxwell fellow, 1989-90, sr. assoc. fellow, 1990—. Author: Christianity and the Children of Israel, 1948, The Surge of Piety in America, 1958, Elder and Younger Brothers, 1967, 73, (with Alice L. Eckardt) Encounter with Israel, 1970, Your People, My People, 1974, Long Night's Journey into Day, 1982, 88, Jews and Christians, 1986, For Righteousness' Sake, 1987, Black-Woman-Jew, 1989, Reclaiming the Jesus of History, 1991, Sitting in the Earth and Laughing, 1991; editor: The Theologian at Work, 1968, Christianity in Israel, 1971, Jour. of Am. Acad. Religion, 1961-69; contbr. (with Alice L. Eckardt) articles to profl. jours. Vice pres. Christians Concerned for Israel; bd. dirs. Nat. Com. on Am. Fgn. Policy; sponsor Am. Profs. for Peace in Middle East; spl. cons. Pres.'s Commn. on Holocaust, 1979—. Recipient Disting. Alumnus award Bklyn. Coll., 1963; with wife) Human Relations award Am. Jewish Commn., 1971; Jabotinsky medal, 1980; Fellow Harvard U. Fund For Advancement Edn., 1955-56; Lilly fellow U. Cambridge, 1963-64; fellow Nat. Found. for Jewish Culture, 1968-69; Rockefeller Found. humanities fellow U. Tübingen; Rockefeller Found. humanities fellow Hebrew U. of Jerusalem, 1975-76. Mem. Am. Acad. Religion (past pres.), Am. Soc. Christian Ethics, Phi Beta Kappa, Pi Gamma Mu. Research in Middle East, Europe. Home: 6011 Beverly Hill Rd Coopersburg PA 18036

ECKARDT, DOUGLAS MARSDEN, theology educator, registrar; b. Chgo., May 17, 1954; s. Robert William and Mary Louise (Youngman) E.; m. Greta Joanne Vanderhook, Aug. 1, 1981; children: Rachel Mary, Zachary John, Gabriella Lucy. BA, Dordt Coll., 1976; MAR, Westminster Theol. Sem., Phila., 1978; MA, U. Iowa, 1987. Vis. instr. in Greek Dordt Coll., Sioux Ctr., Iowa, 1980-81; tchr. Cono Christian Sch., Walker, Iowa, 1981-82; teaching asst. in religion Univ. Iowa, Iowa City, 1983-84; asst. prof. theology Trinity Christian Coll., Palos Heights, Ill., 1984—; registrar Trinity Christian Coll., Palos Heights, 1987—. Mem. Ill. Assn. Admission Officers and Registrars, Conf. on Faith & History. Avocations: computers, Marx Bros. videos, baseball books and cards. Home: 3736 Arthur Terr Markham IL 60426 Office: Trinity Christian Coll 6601 W College Dr Palos Heights IL 60463

ECKEL, MALCOLM DAVID, minister, educator; b. Albany, N.Y., Sept. 19, 1946; s. Malcolm William and Mary Constance (Winchester) E.; m. Leslie Arends, June 1, 1974; 1 child, Leslie Elizabeth. BA, Harvard U., 1968, PhD, 1980; BA, Oxford (Eng.) U., 1971, MA, 1976. Ordained to ministry Episc. Ch., 1974. Instr. Ohio Wesleyan U., Delaware, 1977-78, Middlebury (Vt.) Coll., 1978-80; asst. prof. Div. Sch. Harvard U., Cambridge, Mass., 1980-85, assoc. prof. history of religions, 1985-89; assoc. prof. religion Boston U., 1991—; priest assoc. Ch. of Redeemer, Chestnut Hill, Mass., 1980—; mem. commn. on ministry Diocese Mass., Boston, 1984-89. Author: Jnanagarbha's Commentary, 1986; contbr. articles to jours. and books of essays. Research fellow NEH, 1985. Mem. Am. Acad. Religion. Club: The Country (Brookline, Mass.). Office: Boston U Div Religious and Theol Studies 745 Commonwealth Ave Boston MA 02215

ECKENWILER, WILLIAM BRUCE, Christian education director; b. Meadville, Pa., Nov. 5, 1945; s. James William and Gretchen Louise (Thomas) E.; m. Janis Ann Palmer, Sept. 5, 1965; children: Amy Christine, Cathryn Louise. BS in Edn., Bowling Green State U., 1973; M. Christian Edn., Ref. Theol. Sem., Jackson, Miss., 1988, MEd, 1988; postgrad., U. Cen. Fla., 1990—. Grad. teaching asst. U. Cen. Fla., Orlando, 1988—; dir. Christian edn. Immanuel Presbyn. Ch., Deland, Fla., 1989—; adj. instr. Ref. Theol. Sem., Orlando, 1990—. With USAF, 1966-70. Mem. Internat. Reading Assn., Internat. Listening Assn., Phi Kappa Phi, Kappa Delta Pi. Home: 791 Monrose Ave Orange City FL 32763 Office: Immanuel Presbyn Ch 811 Orange Camp Rd De Land FL 32724

ECKERMAN, ROY EMMANUEL, clergyman; b. Grantsburg, Wis., July 12, 1921; s. Carl Adolph and Esther (Carlson) E.; m. Evelyn Mae Tarasenko, Nov. 1, 1944; children: Arva Dell Mae Eckerman Seltzer, Ginger Sue Eckerman Kent. BA, Union Coll., 1944; MEd, Ind. U., 1965. Ordained clergyman, Adventist Ch., 1948. Clegyman Iowa Conf., Spencer, 1944-49, S.D. Conf., Aberdeen, 1949-51, Mich. Conf., Pt. Huron, Escanaba, 1951-56, Ind. Conf., Bloomington, 1956-63, Upper Columbia Conf., Coeur d'Alene, Idaho, 1963-68; dir. pub. rels. Upper Columbia Conf., Spokane, Wash., 1968-73; dir. found. and corp. rels. Loma Linda (Calif.) U., 1973-84; pres., trustee Opportunity With Legacy Found., Salinas, Calif., 1977—. State conf. exec. com. Lansing, Mich., 1952-55, Spokane, 1964-69; treas. Ministeral Assn., Coeur d'Alene, 1966-67. Republican. Avocations: skiing, golf, flower gardening, library reading. Home: 25199 Casiano Dr Salinas CA 93908 Office: Opportunity With Legacy Found 25199 Casiano Dr Salinas CA 93908

ECKERT, H. CHARLES, minister; b. Mason County, Tex., May 5, 1929; s. Hilmar H. and Ruby (Marie) E.; m. Nita R.L. Gebert, Aug. 20, 1961; children: Mark, M'Liss, Michael. BA in History, Tex. Luth. Coll., 1961; MDiv, Wartburg Theol Sem., 1965; postgrad., Inst. of Religion, Houston, 1965. Ordained to ministry Luth. Ch., 1965. Pastor St. Paul's Luth. Ch., LaMesa, Tex., 1965-68, Prince of Peace Luth., Beaumont, Tex., 1969-74; instr. religion Bible dept. Lamar U., Beaumont, Tex., 1971-74; pastor St. John's Luth. Ch., Brenham, Tex., 1975—; v.p., bd. dirs. Parents Bd. of Tex. Luth., Sequin, 1989-92; chmn. Brenham Conf. Evang. Luth. Ch. in Am., 1991-92. Lion tamer Lions Club, LaMesa, 1968. Recipient Dist. Award of Merit, David Crockett Boy Scouts Am., Brenham, 1985, Silver Beaver, Sam Houston coun. Boy Scouts Am., 1987, Woodbadge Beads, Boy Scouts Am., Houston, 1989. Mem. Washington County Ministerial Assn. (sec. 1983-84, pres. 1991). Home: Rte 5 Box 72 Brenham TX 77833

ECKERT, LOWELL EDGAR, classics and religious studies educator; b. Racine, Wis., Apr. 27, 1932; arrived in Can., 1961; s. Edgar William and Florence Ida (Frickenschmidt) E.; m. Ingeborg Irma Pfau, July 12, 1964; children: Timothy, Daniel, Philip, Rebekah, Margaret. BA, Concordia Sem., St. Louis, 1952; MDiv, Concordia Sem., 1957; MA in Classics, Washington U., St. Louis, 1959; BE, U. Alberta, 1969; STM, Luth. Sch. Theology, Chgo., 1975. Cert. tchr., Alta. Instr. Concordia Sem., Springfield, Ill., 1959-61; from instr. to assoc. prof. Concordia Coll., Edmonton, Alta., Can., 1961-75; prof. Concordia Coll., 1975—, registrar, dormitory counsellor, asst. registrar, 1975-80, chmn. div. religious studies, 1989-91, acting v.p. student svcs., 1990—. Mem. Luth. Edn. Assn., Classical Assn. Can. West, Am. Philol. Assn., Can. Soc. Bibl. Studies, Soc. Bibl. Lit., N.Am. Patristics Soc. Mem. New Democratic Party. Lutheran. Avocations: photography, gardening, mountain climbing, philately. Home: 6220 III Ave, Edmonton, AB Canada T5W 0L3 Office: Concordia Coll, 7128 Ada Blvd, Edmonton, AB Canada T5B 4E4

ECKHOFF, SISTER MARY ANN, academic administrator. Supt. of Cath. schs. Archdiocese of St. Louis. Office: Schs Supt 4140 Lindell Blvd Saint Louis MO 63108*

ECKLEBARGER, KERMIT ALLEN, religion educator; b. Chgo., Dec. 10, 1935; s. Kermit Aurthur and M. Marie (Wilson) E.; m. Shirley Jean Hawkins, June 9, 1956; children: Kae Anne, Kermit Andrew. Pastor's diploma, Moody Bible Inst., Chgo., 1956; BA, Wheaton (Ill.) Coll., 1958, MA in N.T., 1961; PhD in N.T., U. Chgo., 1987. Ordained to ministry Conservative Bapt. Assn., 1960. Assoc. prof. N.T., dean students London (Ont., Can.) Coll. Bible and Missions, 1960-68; prof. N.T., dean students Ont. Bible Coll., Toronto, 1968-71, asst. to pres., 1970-72; assoc. prof. N.T. Denver Sem., 1972—, dir. extension edn., 1981—, dir. D. of Ministry Program, 1991—. Co-author: Growing Toward Spiritual Maturity, 1988; co-editor: Nelson's Illustrated Bible Dictionary, 1986; contbr. articles to profl. jours. Curriculum devel. grantee Assn. Theol. Schs., 1977-78. Fellow Inst. Bibl. Rsch.; mem. Soc. Bibl. Lit., Evang. Theol. Soc. (membership com. 1987-91). Republican. Home: 8981 S Coyote St Highlands Ranch CO 80126 Office: Denver Sem Box 10000 Denver CO 80250 *The pleasant surprise awaiting our increasingly individualistic and secular society is that the true meaning of life is found in interpersonal relationships with other people who believe in Jesus Christ.*

ECKSTEIN, YECHIEL, rabbi; b. Winthrop, Mass., July 11, 1951; s. Simon and Belle (Hirschman) E.; m. Bonnie Siegman, Sept. 2, 1974; children: Tamar, Talia, Yael. BA, Yeshiva U., N.Y.C., 1972, MA, 1975; MA, Columbia U., 1975. Ordained rabbi, 1975. Nat. co-dir. religious affairs Anti Defamation League, Chgo., 1978-84; pres., exec. dir. Internat. Fellowship of Christians & Jews, Chgo., 1984—; bd. dirs. Chgo. Bd. Rabbis, 1985-88. Author: What You Should Know About Jews and Judaism. Bd. dirs. UNICEF, Chgo., 1983-85, Am. Refugee Com., 1982-91. Office: Internat Fellowship 36 S Wabash Chicago IL 60076

ECKSTROM, VANCE LEROY, religion educator; b. Butterfield, Minn., Mar. 14, 1931; s. Carl M. and Cora V. (Madison) E.; m. Clarice J. Thorwald, Nov. 24, 1953; children: Brian, Sharon. BA, Gustavus Adolphus, 1952; MDiv, Luth. Sch. Theology at Chgo., 1956; MA, San Jose State U., 1966; ThD, Grad. Theol. Union, 1971. Ordained to ministry Evang. Luth. Ch. in Am., 1956. Pastor Evang. Luth. Ch. in Am., La Mirada, Calif., Milpitas, Calif., 1956-64; asst. prof. theology U. Portland (Oreg.), 1970-75; asst. prof. religious studies U. Santa Clara, Calif., 1975-82; prof. religion Bethany Coll., Lindsborg, Kans., 1982—; acting acad. dean Bethany Coll., Lindborg, Kans., 1990. Mem. Am. Acad. Religion, Inst. for Theol. Encounter with Sci. and Tech. Home: 511 N 3rd St Lindsborg KS 67456 Office: Bethany Coll 421 N 1st St Lindsborg KS 67456

ECONOMOU, ELLY HELEN, religion educator; b. Thessalonica, Greece, May 6, 1928; d. George and Helen (Vretopoulou) E. Diploma, Am. Coll., Thessalonica, 1946; BA, Pac. Union Coll., 1966; MA, Andrews U., 1967; PhD, U. Strasbourg, France, 1975. Prof. religion Andrews U., Berrien Springs, Mich., 1967—. Mem. Am. Acad. of Religion, Soc. of Bibl. Lit., Soc. of Bibl. Rsch., Andrews Soc. Religious Studies. Home: 8785 University Blvd Berrien Springs MI 99103 Office: Andrews U Berrien Springs MI 49103

EDELHUBER, STEPHEN WILLIAM, minister; b. Bossier City, La., Mar. 11, 1956; s. William Simon and Tennessee Lou (Crawford) E.; m. Lisa Gaye Kenney, June 5, 1976; children: April Dee, Afton Elise, Jonathan William. BA in Religion, Harding U., 1982. Ordained to ministry Chs. of Christ, 1983. Youth min. Olyphant (Ark.) Ch. of Christ, 1980-82, Hope (Ark.) Ch. of Christ, 1984-86, College Ch. of Christ, Searcy, Ark., 1986—; coun. mem. Uplift, Harding U., Searcy, 1986—. Author study guides for youth, 1986-89. Recipient Cert. of Merit USDA, Lonoke, Ark., 1977. Mem. Tag Social Club (v.p. 1981-82), Knights Social Club (sponsor 1990—). Home: 1406 Randall Dr Searcy AR 72143 Office: Coll Ch of Christ 712 E Race Searcy AR 72143

EDELMAN, KENNETH NORMAN, minister; b. Pitts., Dec. 30, 1934; s. Harry R. Jr. and Marian A. (Crooks) E.; m. Beverly Elaine Tripp. BA, U. Pitts., 1956; MDiv, Pitts. Theol. Sem., 1959. Ordained to ministry Presbyn. Ch. (U.S.A.), 1959. Asst. pastor 1st Presbyn. Ch., Bradford, Pa., 1959-61; pastor Montours Presbyn. Ch., Oakdale, Pa., 1961-64, Faith Presbyn. Ch., West Lafayette, Ind., 1964-71, Elm St. Presbyn. Ch., Alton, Ill., 1971—. Office: Elm St Presbyn Ch 101 W Elm Alton IL 62002

EDELSTEIN, JASON ZELIG, rabbi, psychologist; b. Boston, Jan. 31, 1930; s. Abraham and Anna (Freedman) E.; m. Eva Bamberger, Aug. 3, 1952; children: Philip, Sharon, Joseph. BA in Psychology, U. N.H., 1951, MA in Clin. Psychology, 1953; BHL, Hebrew Union Coll., 1956, MAHL, 1969; DMin, Pitts. Theol. Sem., 1977; DD, Hebrew Union Coll.-Jewish Inst. Religion, 1983. Ordained rabbi, 1958. Rabbi Temple David, Monroeville, Pa., 1960—; chaplain VA Med. Ctr., Pitts., 1962-90; lectr. St. Vincent Coll., Latrobe, Pa., 1968—, Seton Hill Coll., Greensburg, Pa., 1981—; nat. coord. Hotline, Cen. Conf. Am. Rabbis, N.Y.C., 1979&; pastoral psychol. cons. Sisters of Mercy, Pitts., 1990—; mem. com. Chesky Inst. on Judaism and Psychotherapy, N.Y.C., 1990—. Contbr. articles to profl. publs. Lt. USN, 1955-60. Mem. Cen. Conf. Am. Rabbis (ex-officio mem. long range planning com. 1990—, ex-officio mem. rabbi's family com. 1989—), Am. Psychol. Assn., Religious Edn. Assn., Viktor Frankl Inst. Logotherapy, Nat. Honor Soc. in Psychology. Home: 135 Mayberry Dr Monroeville PA 15146 Office: Temple David 4415 Northern Pike Monroeville PA 15146

EDGE, FINDLEY BARTOW, clergyman, religious education educator; b. Albany, Ga., Sept. 6, 1916; s. John Andrew and Daisey (Findley) E.; m. Louvenia Littleton, June 3, 1939; children—Larry Findley, Hoyt Littleton. A.B., Stetson U., 1938, D.D., 1958; Th.M., So. Bapt. Theol. Sem., 1942, Th.D., 1945; M.A., Yale, 1955; grad. study Columbia, Union Theol. Sem. Ordained to ministry Bapt. Ch., 1938; pastor in Apopka, Fla., 1938-39, Simpsonville, Ky., 1940-45, Campbellsburg, Ky., 1945-47; Basil Manly, Jr. prof. religious edn. So. Bapt. Theol. Sem., Louisville, 1947—; mem. div. Christian edn. Nat. Council Chs., 1958—, exec. com. profs. and research sect., 1967—; founder, chmn. bd. Vineyard Conf. Center, 1971—. Author: Teaching for Results, 1956, Helping the Teacher, 1959, A Quest for Vitality in Religion, 1963, The Greening of the Church, 1971, The Doctrine of the Laity, 1985; contbr. to the New Laity—Between Church and World, 1978, Modern Masters of Religious Education, 1983; mem. editorial bd. Watchman Examiner, 1964-69, Faith At Work, 1974. Bd. dirs. Opportunities Industrialization Center, Inc.; mem. com. on ch. life Bapt. World Alliance. Recipient scholarship Am. Assn. Theol. Schs., 1964-65. Mem. Religious Edn. Assn. (dir. 1967-69), So. Bapt. Religious Edn. Assn. (past pres.). Address: 527 Henkel Circle Winter Park FL 32789 *The basic question which I have faced in my life is, does this existence we call "life" have any meaning? I came to the conclusion that it does. Therefore the basic "quest" of my life has been to seek to discover and, to whatever extent possible, understand that meaning. For me, Jesus Christ has been the highest revelation of that meaning. Therefore, however inadequately, with a real sense of seriousness, I have sought to incorporate and express this meaning in my life and, where appropriate, to share it with others.*

EDGE, THOMAS LESLIE, minister; b. Detroit, Dec. 20, 1935; s. Leslie Joseph and Flora Marie (Dirksen) E.; m. Betty Ruth Maxwell, Aug. 22, 1959; children; Elizabeth Anne, Christopher Thomas Gregory, Angela Michelle Marie. BA, Concordia Sem., St. Louis, 1957, MDiv, 1960. Ordained to ministry Luth. Ch.-Mo. Synod, 1960. Founding pastor Luth. Ch. St. Ambrose, Pennsville, N.J., 1960-67; Pastor All Saints Luth. Ch., Charlotte, N.C., 1967-70, Christ the King Luth. Ch., Ringwood, N.J., 1970—; chmn. commn. on worship N.J. Dist. Luth. Ch.-Mo. Synod, 1972-74, mem. bd. adjudication, 1974-78; mem. Luth. Hour Rsch. Com., 1973-80; chaplain Fire Dept., Ringwood, 1970—. Contbr. articles to religious mags. Co-founder Charlotte Citizens for Peace in Viet-Nam, 1967; dir. Ambulance Corps, Ringwood, 1970-84. Home: 222 Skylands Rd Ringwood NJ 07456 Office: 50 Erskine Rd Ringwood NJ 07456 *In the last analysis, we are not called to be successful but to be faithful.*

EDGEMON, ROY T., JR., religious organization administrator; b. Wichita Falls, Tex., July 11, 1934; s. Leroy T. and Ruby Clara (Graham) E.; m. Anna Marie Wilson, July 23, 1954; 1 child, Lori Sue Edgemon Shepard. BS, Midwestern U., Wichita Falls, 1956; BD, Southwestern Bapt. Theol. Sem., 1959; ThD, Luther Rice Theol. Sem., 1969. Ordained to ministry So. Bapt. Conv., 1955. Pastor 1st Bapt. Ch., Throckmorton, Tex., 1959-62, Seminole, Tex., 1962-65; pastor 2d Bapt. Ch., Odessa, Tex., 1965-68, Cen. Bapt. Ch., Urasoe, Okinawa, Japan, 1968-71, Tokyo Bapt. Ch., 1971-75; dir. evangelism planning and consultation Home Mission Bd., Atlanta, 1975-78; dir. discipleship tng. dept. Bapt. Sunday Sch. Bd., Nashville, 1978—; moderator Gains, Andrews, Young Assn., West Tex., 1962-63, West Tex. Pastors Conf., 1963-67; co-moderator weekly TV program The Bible and Today's Word, Odessa, 1966-68; pres. Interdenom. Missionaries, Okinawa, 1970-71, Tokyo Ministerial Alliance, 1974-75; lectr. U.S. Army workshops, Japan and Korea, 1971-74. Author: The Doctrines Baptists Believe, 1988; editor: Evangelism Plan Books, 1976-78; editor-in-chief Disciple's Study Bible, 1988; contbr. articles to profl. jours. Chaplain Odessa Boys Club, 1966-68; pres. Burlington Home Owners Assn., Nashville, 1988-91. Roy T. Edgemon Day proclaimed by City of Nashville, 1988. Mem. So. Bapt. Religious Edn. Assn. Office: Bapt Sunday Sch Bd 127 9th Ave N Nashville TN 37234

EDGINGTON, JEFFREY WAYNE, minister; b. Cin., May 5, 1958; s. Kenneth Wayne and Helen (Corbin) E.; m. Elaine Diane Musgrove, May 18, 1979; children: Rachel, Nathan. Student, Ozark Christian Coll., Joplin, Mo., 1977-82. Ordained to ministry Ch. of Christ, 1980. Min. Dadeville (Mo.) Christian Ch., 1978-80, 1st Christian Ch., Galena, Kans., 1980-84; assoc. min. 1st Christian Ch., Rosenberg, Tex., 1984-89; min. Pleasant Grove Christian Ch., Texarkana, Tex., 1989—; pres. Galena Ministerial Alliance, 1982-84; bd. mem. Maranatha Christian Camp, 1981-84, S.W. Region Nat. Religious Broadcasters, 1988-89. Cub master Boy Scouts Am., Galena, 1984; bd. mem. Community Fund, 1983-84. Recipient Vol. Chaplain award Pinewood Hosp., 1990; named to Outstanding Young Men of Am., 1983. Mem. Texarkana Ministerial Alliance, Texarkana Christian Chs. Ministerial Fellowship (pres. 1989). Republican. Home: 9011 N Kings Hwy Texarkana TX 75501 Office: Pleasant Grove Christian Ch 6401 Pleasant Grove Rd Texarkana TX 75501 *The greatest monument a person can build for posterity is one's relationships. Only these can cross the line between physical and spiritual and remain intact.*

EDIE, JOHN MONROE, minister; b. Stella, Mo., Sept. 24, 1945; s. A.M. and Lela (Blalack) E.; m. Shirley Joan McDaniel, June 10, 1966; children: John David, Susan Beth. BA, S.W. Bapt. Coll., Bolivar, Mo., 1967; M in Religious Edn., Midwestern Seminary, Kansas City, Mo., 1969. Minister edn. 1st Bapt. Ch., North Kansas City, 1967-69; minister of edn. Highland Park Bapt. Ch., Bartlesville, Okla., 1970-71; minister youth and recreation Broadmoor Bapt. Ch., Shreveport, La., 1971-78, minister adminstrn. and edn., 1978-83; minister edn. 1st Bapt. Ch., Wichita Falls, Tex., 1983-86, assoc. pastor, 1986-89; minister edn., adminstr. Second Bapt. Ch., Springfield, Mo., 1989—. Contbr. articles to mags. including Ch. Recreation Mag., Fishing Facts Mag., La. Angler. Mem. So. Bapt. Religious Edn. Assn. (cen. v.p. 1984). Home: 3252 S Oak Springfield MO 65804 Office: Second Bapt Ch 1201 S Oak Grove Springfield MO 65804

EDIE, WAYNE PAUL, minister; b. Canton, Ohio, Feb. 3, 1942; s. Wayne Arthur and Dora Mae (Hinchliff) E.; m. Norma Jean Craddock, Aug. 21, 1965; children: Gregory Paul, Jill Renee. BA, Anderson Coll., 1968. Ordained to ministry Ch. of God (Anderson, Ind.), 1969. Pastor Ist Ch. of God, Lincoln, Nebr., 1968-70, Danville, Ky., 1970-77, Vero Beach, Fla., 1977-81, Cape Coral, Fla., 1981-82, Bloomington, Ind., 1982—; bd. dirs. City Mission, Lincoln, 1968-70; com. mem. Youth for Christ, Lincoln, 1968-70, Nebr. Coun. on Alcoholic Edn., 1968-70; mem. Ind. Evangelistic Bd., Bloomington, 1982-87. Republican. Home and Office: Ist Ch of God 1203 Matlock Rd Bloomington IN 47408 *To be seen, heard, helped and loved are still the cries of mankind. And we must realize how important this is —and then respond to those cries.*

EDIRISINGHE, ALBERT, religious organization administrator. Pres. Sri Lanka Regional Ctr. of World Fellowship of Buddhists, Colombo. Office: World Fellowship Buddists, 380 Bauddhaloka Mawatha, Colombo 7, Sri Lanka*

EDMAN, DAVID ARTHUR, priest; b. Worcester, Mass., Jan. 9, 1930; s. Victor Raymond and Edith Marie (Olson) E.; children: Sarah, Peter, Brita. BA, Wheaton Coll., 1955; MA, Columbia U., 1959; MDiv, Union Theol. Sem., 1959. Ordained priest Episcopal Ch., 1959. Assoc. rector Christ Ch., Bronxville, N.Y., 1959-62; priest-in-charge Christ the King Ch., Stone Ridge, N.Y., 1962-65; chaplain Rochester (N.Y.) Inst. Tech., 1965-69; rector Grace Ch., Scottsville, N.Y., 1969-84, St. Thomas Ch., Camden, Maine, 1984—. Author: Of Wise Men and Fools, 1972, A Bit of Christmas Whimsy, 1975, One Upon an Eternity, 1984, (with Wendell Castle)) Book of Laminations, 1979. Lt. U.s. Army, 1951-53. Address: PO Box 631 Camden ME 04843

EDMERSON, JOHN, minister; b. Grayson, Okla., Apr. 30, 1948; s. Duright E.; m. Lashelle Owens, June 27, 1969; children: Darrell, John T., Anthereca, Gamaiel. BA, U. Sci. and Arts Okla., 1976; Cert. of Preaching, Okla. Sch. Bible, 1976; postgrad., Abilene Christian U., 1981-83, Pepperdine U., 1983-85. Minister First and Ga. Ch. of Christ, Chickasha, Okla., 1971-83; assoc. minister Normandie Ch. of Christ, L.A., 1983-88; minister Inglewood Ch. of Christ, Inglewood, Calif., 1988—; lectr. in field; mem. bd.

Normandie Christian Sch.; panelist Way of Trust, others in past. Home: 19727 Leapwood Carson CA 90746

EDMISON, SUSAN KAY, lay church worker, educator; b. Nelson, Nebr., Oct. 3, 1953; d. Carroll Herbert Edmison and Elsie Ann (Knowlton) Edmison Wergin. AA in Edn., Platte Jr. Coll., Columbus, Nebr., 1973; BS in Elem. Edn., Luth. tchr.'s diploma, Concordia Coll., Seward, Nebr., 1975, MS in Edn., 1986; cert. in Spanish, Friends U., Wichita, Kans., 1990. Cert. elem. tchr., Spanish tchr., Kans. Tchr., choir dir. Cen. Luth Sch., Newhall, Iowa, 1975-82; tchr., youth dir. St. John Luth. Sch., Battle Creek, Nebr., 1982-84; tchr., chmn. playground, volleyball coach St. John Luth. Sch., Chaska, Minn., 1984-87; tchr., volleyball coach Holy Cross Luth Sch., Wichita, 1987-88, singles coord., 1987—; mem. Fellowship Commn., Holy Cross Luth. Ch., Wichita, 1988—, leader Bible study, 1989—; chmn. singles planning com. Kans. dist. Luth. Ch.-Mo. Synod, Topeka, 1990—, mem. quicentennial com., 1991—; elem. tchr. Wichita Pub. Sch., 1988—; mem., sec. Luth. Women's Missionary League, Newhall, Battle Creek, Chaska, 1975-87. Mem. Newhall Centennial Com., 1981-82; pres. Aid Assn. for Luths., Newhall, 1980-82. Mem. NEA, Luth. Edn. Assn. (pres. 1975-88), Internat. Luth. Single Adults. Office: Holy Cross Luth Ch 1018 N Dellrose St Wichita KS 67208 *As a Christian it is important to remember your faith, life, and work are Christ-centered, guided by our Father's love and empowered through the Holy Spirit. Through Jesus' death and resurrection my sins are forgiven, freeing me to encourage others, affirming each one as a person, and witnessing the servant model of Christ. This is a foundation built on prayer, the Bible, the church, and Christian friends.*

EDMISTEN, STUART ALLEN, minister; b. Boone, N.C., Aug. 1, 1960; s. Joseph Allen and Margaret Gwendolyn (Stewart) E.; m. Lisa René McKnight, June 13, 1981; children: Hunter Allen, Jacob Adam, Carissa Faith. BA in Religion, Baylor U., 1982; cert. in pastoral edn. and family counseling, Clin. Pastoral Edn. Ctr., Bapt. Hosp., Pensacola, Fla., 1986; MRE, South Ea. Bapt. Theol. Sem., Wake Forest, N.C., 1987, MDiv, 1987. Lic. to ministry So. Bapt. Conv., 1978, ordained, 1987. Min. edn. and youth 1st Bapt. Ch., Plymouth, N.C., 1987-89; min. edn. and activities Florence Bapt. Ch., Forest City, N.C., 1989—; assoc. inter-faith witness dept. N.C. Bapt. Conv., Raleigh, 1988—. Mem. ministerial bd. Gardner Webb Coll., Boiling Springs, N.C., 1989—; exec. bd. Rutherford County Mental Health Bd., Forest City, 1989—. Recipient award Ea. Star, 1984-87; Broome scholar, 1978-87, McCall scholar, 1979. Mem. So. Bapt. Religious Educators Assn., N.C. Bapt. Religious Educators Assn., Forest City Ministerial Assn. (pres. 1990—). Democrat. Home: Rte 1 Box 446 K Forest City NC 28043 Office: Florence Bapt Ch 207 S Broadway Forest City NC 28043

EDMISTON, GUY S., JR., bishop. Bishop Lower Susguehanna region Evang. Luth. Ch. in Am., Harrisburg, Pa. Office: Evang Luth Ch in Am 900 S Arlington Ave Rm 208 Harrisburgh PA 17109*

EDMISTON, REBECCA ANNE, minister; b. Richmond, Va., Jan. 30, 1953; d. Clarence Dixon and Mary Lena (Salter) E.; m. Seth A. Davidson, Aug. 20, 1978. BA, U. Va., 1975; MDiv, Union Theol. Sem., 1978; PhD, Cath. U., 1990. Cert. pastoral psychotherapist specialist; ordained to ministry Unitarian Universalist Ch., 1986. Minister Accotink Unitarian Universalist Ch., Springfield, Va., 1986—; program chair/presenter Harper's Ferry Ministers Study Group, Marriotsville, Md., 1987—; clergy chair No. Va. Religious Coalition for Abortion Rights, Annandale, Va., 1989—. Mem. planning com. Nat. Workshop on Social Justice, Washington, 1990, 91. Mem. Greater Washington Area Unitarian Universalist Ministers Assn. (v.p. 1987-89, pres. 1989-91), Alban Inst., Nat. Assn. for Preservation & Perpetuation of Storytelling. Democrat. Office: Accotink Unitarian Universalist Ch 6605A Backlick Rd Springfield VA 22150 *I believe that life is a gift and that we are called to embrace life, to celebrate and affirm life in spite of its pain and death and brokenness. Religious community helps me to do that by reminding me of the gifts I enjoy and by empowering me to work to overcome the brokenness in my own and others' lives and in my relation to the earth.*

EDMONDS, HENRY L., clergyman; b. Phila., Jan. 8, 1944; s. Jesse N. and Mary F. (Burton) E.; m. Mildred McCoy, July 9, 1966; children: Michael, Stephan. BS, Shaw U., 1966; MEd, Antioch U., 1973; postgrad., Shaw Div. Sch., 1986-88. Ordained to ministry Bapt. Ch. Pastor Ebenezer Bapt. Ch., Durham, N.C., 1987—; chaplain Wake Correction Ctr., Raleigh, N.C., 1987—; area coord. prison com. Gen. Bapt. State Conv., 1990. Dir. Paul Robeson Drama Guild, Raleigh; creator, dir. The Original Black Poet, Raleigh; prs. Minority Women's Bus. Programs Network, Raleigh, 1988. With U.S. Army, 1966-68. Recipient Human Rels. award Gov.'s Office, State N.C., 1987, Vol. award, 1988, 89, 90, Prison Ministry award Gen. Bapt. State Conv., N.C., 1990. Mem. NAACP. Democrat. Home: 104 Belcross Ct Garner NC 27529 Office: Ebenezer Bapt Ch 2200 S Alston Ave Durham NC 27707

EDRIS, PAUL MILBURN, clergyman; b. Spring Creek Twp., Iowa, July 28, 1909; s. Frank Milburn and Carrie Edith (Nichol) E.; m. Jane Alice Glascock, Sept. 8, 1930; children: James Edwin, Robert Paul. A.B., Maryville (Tenn.) Coll., 1932, D.D., 1957; B.D., Louisville Presbyn. Sem., 1935. Ordained to ministry Presbyterian Ch., 1935; pastor chs. in Ky., 1935-39; pastor First Presbyn. Ch., Daytona Beach, Fla., 1939-75; moderator Presbytery St. Johns, Fla., 1955, Synod Fla., 1956-57; moderator Gen. Assembly Presbyn. Ch. in U.S., 1975-76, chmn. operational bd. mission bd., 1976-77; trustee Fla. Presbyn. Coll. (now Eckerd Coll.), 1958-77; bd. dirs. Columbia Theol. Sem., 1974-75, 77-79. Contbr. ch. publs. Mem. Daytona Beach Interracial Adv. Bd., 1953-70; pres. Daytona Beach YMCA, 1941-46. Recipient Disting. Alumnus award Louisville Presbyn. Theol. Sem., 1986. Democrat. Club: Daytona Beach Rotary (past pres.). Address: 301 Morningside Ave Daytona Beach FL 32118 *The quality of human life is determined not by "success", whatever that is interpreted to mean, not by ease and comfort of living, but by significance. That person is a happy person who feels that his/her life is significant.*

EDWARDS, BENJAMIN THOMAS, minister; b. Dayton, Ohio, Dec. 7, 1927; s. Benjamin Thomas and Martha Alzina (Deakins) E.; m. Carolyn Lillian Pritchett, July 13, 1952; children: Daniel, Olivia, Melinda. BA, Asbury Coll., 1951; postgrad., Asbury Theol. Sem., 1951-54; BD, Wittenberg U., 1956. Ordained to ministry United Meth. Ch., 1957. Pastor Laurel Meth. Charge, New Richmond, Ohio, 1950-55, Spring Valley (Ohio) Meth. Charge, 1955-59, Trinity United Meth. Ch., Swanton, Ohio, 1959-68, Linworth United Meth. Ch., Worthington, Ohio, 1968-80; dist. supt. Athens (Ohio) Dist. United Meth. Ch., 1980-86; pastor Grace United Meth. Ch., Washington, Ohio, 1986—; del. Gen. Conf. United Meth. Ch., Balt., 1984, N.C. Jurisdictional Conf. United Meth. Ch., Diluth, Minn., 1984, DeKalb, Ill., 1988; chmn. bd. Ctr. for Town and Rural Ministries, Columbus, 1981-86. Named Rural Minister of Yr. Ohio Conf., 1958. Office: Grace United Meth Ch 301 E Market St Washington OH 43160

EDWARDS, BETTY, religious institution office manager; b. Balt., Mar. 29; d. John Robert and Janie G. (Frazier) Davis; m. Robert Lee Edwards, Oct. 26, 1966; children: Belinda Edwards. Student, Catonsville Community Coll., Balt.; stenographer, Cortez Peters Bus. Sch., Balt., 1965. Clk. typist Md. Nat. Bank, Balt., 1965-66; adminstrv. asst., sec. to dist. supt. United Meth. Ch., Balt., 1978-79; clk. New Christian Meml. Ch., 1981-89; office mgr. to dist. supt. Balt. Conf., United Meth. Ch., 1985—. sec. Cedar/Morris Hills Improvement Assn., 1970-84; treas. Cedar/Morris Hills Woman's Aux., 1975—, sec.; co-sponsor Jr. Ushers, 1983-85; mem. choir New Christian Meml. Ch., 1963—, chairperson banquet, 1975, 85, mem. Courtesy Guild, 1982—, editor ch. newsletter, 1985-89; tchr. crafts County Recreation and Pks. Dept., 1973-78. Mem. NAFE, Profl. Assn. United Meth. Ch. Secs. Avocations: crafts, travel. Office: 5124 Greenwich Ave Baltimore MD 21229

EDWARDS, BLAKE EDISON, minister; b. Dublin, Va., May 11, 1938; s. Garland Anderson and Ruby Jane (Melton) E.; m. Ann Arlayne Steinbright, May 13, 1967. BA, Eastern Coll., St. Davids, Pa., 1973; MDiv, Eastern Bapt. Theol. Sem., Phila., 1976. Ordained to ministry Bapt. Ch., 1976. Pastor Andorra Bapt. Ch., Phila., 1973-75, Taylor Meml. Bapt. Ch., Paulsboro, N.J., 1975-78, Brandywine Bapt. Ch., Chadds Ford, Pa., 1978-88, First Bapt. Ch., York, Pa., 1988—; chmn. commn. on the ministry Am. Bapt. Chs. of Pa. and Del., 1979-88; coord. Tri-County Fellowship of Christian Chs., 1979-88; moderator Riverside Bapt. Assn., 1981-84; clk. Harrisburg Assn., 1990—. With USAF, 1956-69. Mem. Mins. Coun. Am. Bapt. Chs. of Pa. and Del., Eastern Bapt. Theol. Sem. Alumni (treas. 1981-84). Office: First Bapt Ch 100 S Queen St York PA 17403

EDWARDS, BRUCE LEE, JR., minister, English educator; b. Akron, Ohio, Sept. 5, 1952; s. Bruce Lee and Betty Lou (Klever) E.; m. Joan Christine Lungstrum, Sept. 28, 1973; children: Matthew, Mary, Justin, Michael. BA, U. Mo., 1977; MA, Kans. State U., 1979; PhD, U. Tex., 1981. Ordained to ministry Chs. of Christ, 1973. Min. Ch. of Christ, St. James, Mo., 1973-77, Manhattan, Kans., 1977-79, Bowling Green, Ohio, 1981-85; asst. prof. English, Bowling Green State U., 1981-87, assoc. prof., 1987—; dir. grad. studies, elder Bowling Green Covenant Ch.; v.p. Conf. on Christianity and Lit., 1988-90; S.W. Brooks Meml. lectr. U. Queensland, Brisbane, Australia, spring 1988; Bradley resident scholar The Heritage Found., 1989-90. Author: Roughdrafts, 1985, Processing Words, 1987, The Taste of the Pineapple, 1987, A Rhetoric of Reading, 1986, Great Ideas, 1991; also articles. Ednl. dir. Right To Life, Bowling Green, 1982. Fellow U. Tex., 1980-81. Mem. MLA, Nat. Coun. Tchrs. English, N.Y. C.S. Lewis Soc. Office: Bowling Green State U Dept English Bowling Green OH 43403 *There is no more succinct philosophy of life than that expressed by Jesus: "Love God with all your heart, soul and mind, and love your neighbor as yourself".*

EDWARDS, DAVID MAURICE MICHAEL, minister; b. Ft. Thomas, Ky., Mar. 11, 1962; s. Louis Ray and Wanda Louise (Becker) E.; m. Susan Denise Smith, Oct. 20, 1990. BA in Religion, Point Loma Coll., 1985. Ordained to ministry Internat. Ch. Foursquare Gospel, 1988. Assoc. pastor Christian Faith Ctr., San Diego, 1986; founder, sr. pastor Emmaus Rd. Ch., West Chester, Ohio, 1987—; supt. Miami Valley Internat. Ch. Foursquare Gospel, Cin., 1990—. Composer songs, 1988—. Home: PO Box 86 West Chester OH 45071-0086 Office: Emmaus Rd Ch PO Box 35 West Chester OH 45071-0035

EDWARDS, HOWARD MILTON, III, minister; b. Dixon, Ill., Jan. 22, 1955; s. Howard M. Jr. and Ruth (Ganz) E.; m. Lorraine Sue Quigg, May 25, 1980; children: Benjamin, Ian. Diploma, Interlochen Arts Acad., 1973; postgrad., Ill. Wesleyan U., 1973-75; BME, U. Nebr., 1976; MDiv, Luther Northwestern Sem., St. Paul, 1985; D Ministry, Grad. Theol. Found., Notre Dame, Ind., 1990. Ordained to ministry Luth. Ch., 1985. Asst. pastor Trinity Luth. Ch., Moline, Ill., 1985-89, assoc. pastor, 1989-91; sr. pastor Gloria Dei Lutheran Ch., Rockford, Ill., 1991—. Composer numerous hymns. Mem. Hymn. Soc. U.S. and Can. Office: 4700 Augustana Dr Rockford IL 61107

EDWARDS, JAMES ROBERT, religious educator; b. Colo. Springs, Oct. 28, 1945; s. Robert Emery and Mary Eleanor (Callison) E.; m. Mary Jane Pryor, June 22, 1968; children: Corrie, Mark. BA, Whitworth Coll., Spokane, Wash., 1967; MDiv, Princeton (N.J.) Seminary, 1970; PhD, Fuller Seminary, Pasadena, Calif., 1978. Youth min. First Presbyn. Ch., Colo. Springs, 1971-78; prof. religion Jamestown (N.D.) Coll., 1978—; speaker in field. Author: (with others) The Layman's Overview of the Bible, 1987, Commentary on Romans, 1991; contbr. articles to profl. jours. Speaker N.D. Humanities Coun., 1983-85. Recipient Excellence in Teaching award Sears-Roebuck Found., 1990. Mem. Soc. Bibl. Lit., N.Y. C.S. Lewis Soc. Office: Jamestown Coll Box 6020 Jamestown ND 58401 *As I read the Bible I am continually reminded that God is not who we think he is. He disquiets those who are sure of their salvation and reassures those who think they are beyond the reach of it.*

EDWARDS, JERRY LEE, minister; b. Elkton, Ky., July 19, 1954; s. Weston Wesley and Marion Emily (Griffin) E.; m. Dianne Brotherton, Jan. 2, 1979; children: Michael David, Ronald Weston. BA in Bible, Internat. Bible Coll., 1976; BS in Speech, Abilene Christian U., 1980; MS in Psychology, San Jose State U., 1987. Ordained to ministry Ch. of Christ, 1974; cert. sch. psychologist; cert. orgnl. cons. Assoc. minister Ch. of Christ, Lawrenceburg, Tenn., 1975-77; minister Vine Ch. of Christ, Abilene, Tex., 1977-80; minister Ch. of Christ, Salinas, Calif., 1980-85, Chowhilla, Calif., 1985-91; lectr., author Ch. of Christ, Modesto, Calif., 1991—; sch. psychologist Stanislaus County Dept. Edn., Modesto, 1987—; tchr., recruiter Magnolia Bible Coll., Kosciuski, Miss., 1977-78; tchr. Hughson (Calif.) Christian Sch., 1980-82; cons., lectr. in field. Co-author: How To Preach, 1978; contbr. articles to profl. publs. Mem. Nat. Assn. Sch. Psychologists, Calif. Assn. Sch. Psychologists, Nat. Assn. Securities Dealers. Republican. Office: Stanislaus County Dept Edn County Ctr III Modesto CA 95355

EDWARDS, LONZY FITZGERALD, SR., minister; b. Sparta, Ga., Apr. 22, 1949; s. Magnolia Edwards; m. Nancy B. Roland, June 6, 1967; children: Lonzy Jr., Benjamin. BA, Knoxville (Tenn.) Coll., 1971; MDiv, Yale U., 1974; JD, Duke U., 1976; DMin, Emory U., 1988. Bar: Ga. 1977. Asst. prof. Ft. Valley (Ga.) State Coll., 1976-78; atty. Milledgeville, Ga., 1978-79, Macon, Ga., 1979-80; exec. asst. to mayor City of Macon, 1980-81; ptnr. Dozier and Edwards, Macon, 1981-86, Edwards and Williams, Macon, 1986-89; Edwards & Middleton, 1989—; pastor Mt. Moriah Bapt. Ch., Macon, 1984—; pres. L.F. Edwards and Sons, Inc., Macon, 1989—. Author: How to Manage Church Fights, 1982. Del. Nat. Rep. Conv., Detroit, 1980; pres. East-Bibb Twiggs Neighborhood Assn., Macon, 1986-87. Mem. Ga. Trial Lawyers Assn., Assn. Trial Lawyers Am., Macon Bar Assn., Ga. State Bar Assn., Nat. Assn. for Equal Opportunity in Higher Edn. (disting. alumni of yr. 1988), Kiwanis. Democrat. Avocations: fishing, woodworking, horseback riding. Office: 369 Mulberry St Macon GA 31201

EDWARDS, OTIS CARL, JR., theology educator; b. Bienville, La., June 15, 1928; s. Otis Carl and Margaret Lee (Hutchinson) E.; m. Jane Hanna Trufant, Feb. 19, 1957; children: Carl Lee, Samuel Adams Trufant, Louise Reynes. BA, Centenary Coll., 1949; STB, Gen. Theol. Sem., 1952; postgrad., Westcott House, Cambridge, Eng., 1952-53; STM, So. Meth. U., 1962; MA, U. Chgo., 1963, PhD, 1971; DD, Nashotah House, 1976. Ordained priest Episcopal Ch., 1954. Curate Episcopal Ch., Baton Rouge, 1953-54; vicar Episcopal Ch., Abbeville, La., 1954-57, Waxahachie, Tex., 1960-61; rector Episcopal Ch., Morgan City, La., 1957-60; priest in charge Episcopal Ch., Chgo., 1961-63; instr. Wabash Coll., 1963-64; asst. prof. Nashotah House, Wis., 1964-69; assoc. prof. Nashotah House, 1969-72, prof., 1972-74, sub-dean, 1973-74, acting dean, 1973-74; dean Seabury-Western Theol. Sem., Evanston, Ill., 1974-83; prof. Seabury-Western Theol. Sem., 1983—; Chmn. Coun. for Devel. of Ministry, Episcopal Ch., Coun. Sem. Deans; mem. Bd. for Theol. Edn.; mem. Gen. Bd. Examining Chaplains; vis. prof. Notre Dame, 1986—; rsch. assoc. The Newberry Libr. Author: How It All Began, 1973, The Living and Active Word, 1975 (with Robert Bennett) The Bible for Today's Church, 1979, Luke's Story of Jesus, 1981, (with John Westerhoff) A Faithful Church: Issues in the History of Catechis, 1981, Elements of Homiletic, 1982, How Holy Writ Was Written, 1989; book rev. editor Anglican Theol. Rev., 1971-76, v.p. of corp., 1975-85; contbr. articles and book revs. to various jours. and mags. Chmn. campus affairs com.; trustee Kendall Coll.; mem. Commn. on Faith and Order Nat. Council Chs.; bd. dirs. Native Am. Theol. Assn. Recipient Spl. award Mystery Writers Am., 1965; grantee The Conant Fund, Pew Foun., St. Paul's Ministry and Mission Found., Indpls. Mem. Soc. Bibl. Lit., Cath. Bibl. Assn., Am. Acad. Religion, Chgo. Soc. Bibl. Rsch., Acad. Homiletics, Mystery Writers of Am. Democrat. Home: 2127 Orrington Ave Evanston IL 60201 Office: 2122 Sheridan Rd Evanston IL 60201

EDWARDS, RICHARD ALAN, theology educator; b. West Mahanoy Twp., Pa., Dec. 31, 1934; s. Francis Reed and Helen Irene (Mates) E.; m. June Caroline Kirkhuff, Sept. 3, 1958; children: Jennifer Lynne, Emily Katharine, Jonathan Alan. BA, Princeton U., 1956; MA, U. Chgo., 1962, PhD, 1968. Instr. Susquehanna U., Selinsgrove, Pa., 1963-66; asst. to assoc. prof. Thiel Coll., Greenville, Pa., 1968-72, Va. Poly. Inst., Blacksburg, 1972-78; assoc. prof. Marquette U., Milw., 1978—. Author: The Sign of Jonah, 1971, A Theology of Q, 1976, Sentences of Sextus, 1981, Matthew's Story of Jesus, 1985. Kinsman Trust fellowship, Tonbridge, Kent, Eng., 1951-52; grantee Sears Found., 1989. Mem. Cath. Bibl. Assn., Studiorum Novi Testamenti Societas. Office: Theology Dept Marquette U Milwaukee WI 53233

EFIRD, JAMES MICHAEL, theology educator; b. Kannapolis, N.C., May 30, 1932; s. James Rufus and I. Z. (Christy) E.; m. Vivian Lee Poythress, Mar. 7, 1975; 1 child, Whitney Michelle; 1 stepchild, Anthony Kevin Crumpler. Ordained to ministry Presbyn. Ch. (U.S.A.), 1958. Asst. prof. Duke Div. Sch., Durham, N.C., 1962-68, assoc. prof., 1958-85, prof., 1985—, dir. acad. affairs, 1971-75; interim min. Westminster Presbyn. Ch., Burlington, N.C., 1987-88, St. Andrews Presbyn. Ch., Sanford, N.C., 1988-89, Glenwood Presbyn. Ch., Greensboro, N.C., 1989—. Author: How To Interpret the Bible, 1984, Marriage and Divorce, 1985, End-Times: Rapture, Anti-Christ, and Millennium, 1986, Revelation for Today, 1989, A Grammar For New Testament Greek, 1990. Duke U. scholar, 1958-62. Mem. Soc. Bibl. Lit., Phi Beta Kappa. Home: 2609 Heather Glen Rd Durham NC 27712 Office: Duke Div Sch Durham NC 27706

EFTINK, EDWARD M., academic administrator. Supt. Cath. schs. Diocese of Springfield-Cape Girardeau, Mo. Office: Cath Schs Cath Ctr 601 S Jefferson Springfield MO 65806*

EGAN, ANNE HAYS, consultant, minister; b. Montgomery, Ala., May 30, 1950; d. Thomas Patrick and Lorene (Whorton) E. BA, Converse Coll., 1972; MA, Fla. State U., 1973; MDiv, Princeton U., 1982. Ordained to ministry Prsbyn. ch., 1982. Caseworker ARC, Ft. Knox, Ky., 1973-74; caseworker, youth program dir. ARC, Seoul, Republic of Korea, 1975-76; sr. caseworker ARC, Ft. Bragg, N.C., 1976-77; casework supr. ARC, Cin., 1977-79; chaplain Riverside Home for the Aged, Phila., 1979-80; outreach coordinator East Side Parishes, Phila., 1980-82; asst. pastor Valley Forge Presbyn. Ch., Phila., 1982-84; cons. Nat. Presbyn. Ch., N.Y.C., Phila., 1984-85; regional cons. Devel. Dimensions, N.Y.C., 1985-87; cons., pres. Leadership Consortium, N.Y.C., 1987-88; pres. Leadership Consortium Cons. Firm, Louisville, 1988—; parish assoc. West Park Presbyn. Ch., N.Y.C., 1986—; pres. and pub. The Digest, N.Y.C. and Louisville, 1987—. Author: The Church and Social Welfare, 1985, Testing Your Organizational Health, 1987; contbg. author: Empowering Ministry in an Ageist Society, 1982; pub. newsletter The Digest, 1987, Success Factor Study, 1990—; editor: Nonprofit Management Strategies, 1990—. Founder, bd. dirs. Nat. Shared Housing Resource Ctr., Phila., 1981-85; chmn. bd. dirs. Interfaith Community Care Ctr., Phila., 1982-84, Human Needs Com., Phila., 1982-84; active Bread for the World, Phila., 1983—, Oxford Com., N.Y.C., 1987—; treas. Girl Scouts of Korea, Seoul, 1976. Mem. Prebyteries of N.Y. and Phila. (chmn. human needs com.), Am. Women for Econ. Devel., Am. Soc. Tng. and Devel., Nonprofit Mgmt. Assn., Soc. for Nonprofit Orgns., NOW (sec. Fayetteville, N.C. chpt. 1976-77), Nat. Assn. Female Execs., Mortar Bd. Democrat. Avocations: skiing, cycling, racquetball, symphony, theatre. Office: Leadership Consortium Starks Bldg 455 4th Ave Louisville KY 40202

EGAN, DANIEL FRANCIS, priest; b. N.Y.C., June 18, 1915; s. Thomas J. and Mary (Bierne) E. AB in Philosophy, Cath. U. Am., 1941, MA in Edn., 1945; LHD (hon.), Marist Coll., 1980, Dominican Coll., 1988. Joined Atonement Friars, Roman Cath. Ch., 1936, ordained priest, 1945. Assigned Negro mission So. U.S., 1947-49; assigned preaching missions Ea. U.S., 1949-59; founder half-way house for female drug addicts Village Haven, N.Y.C., 1963; founder live-in therapeutic community for female addicts New Hope Manor, Barryville, N.Y., 1970-78; program dir. St. Joseph's Rehab. Ctr. for Male Alcoholics, Saranac Lake, N.Y., 1978-79; assigned W.I. missions, Jamaica, 1979-81; dir. Drug Prevention Programs for Children, Youth, Adults, Graymoor, Garrison, N.Y., 1981—, Drug Rehab. and Prevention, Calcutta, India, 1989-90; mem. White House Conf. on Youth, 1960, White House Conf. on Drugs, 1960; lectr. on drug abuse to various orgns., 1960—; mem. drug task force N.Y. State, 1978-79. Contbr. articles to profl. jours.; appearances on nat. and internat. tv on drug issues; subject of: The Junkie Priest (John D. Harris). Recipient Nat. Cath. Good Samaritan award, 1974, Aquinas Humanitarian award Mt. St. Mary Coll., N.Y., 1986, Alumni award Cath. U. Am., 1991, awards from U.S. Army, USN, USMC for pioneering drug programs in armed forces. Mem. New Eng. Police Women's Assn. (hon., award 1965). Address: Graymoor Garrison NY 10524 *If we had the vision of faith, we would see beneath every behavior - no matter how repulsive - beneath every bodily appearance - no matter how dirty or deformed - a priceless dignity and value that makes all material facts and scientific technologies fade into insignificance!.*

EGAN, EDWARD M., bishop; b. Oak Park, Ill., Apr. 2, 1932; s. Thomas J. and Genevieve (Costello) E. Ph.B., St. Mary of Lake, Mundelein, Ill., 1954; S.T.L., Gregorian U., Rome, 1958; J.C.D., Gregorian U., 1963. Ordained priest Roman Catholic Ch., 1957. Sec. to Albert Cardinal Meyer Archdiocese of Chgo., 1958-60, sec. to John Cardinal Cody, 1966-68, co-chancellor, 1969-72; faculty Pontifical N.Am. Coll., Vatican City, 1960-65; judge Sacred Roman Rota, Vatican City, 1973-85; aux. bishop, vicar for edn. Archdiocese of N.Y., N.Y.C., 1985-88; bishop of Bridgeport Conn., 1988—. Office: 238 Jewett Ave Bridgeport CT 06606

EGAN, HARVEY DANIEL, theology educator, priest; b. Putnam, Conn., Nov. 6, 1937; s. Harvey Joseph and Alice Blanche (LaCroix) E. BSEE, Worcester Poly. Inst., 1959; MA in Philosophy, Boston Coll., 1965; MA in Theology, Woodstock Coll., 1969; ThD, U. Muenster, 1973. Joined S.J., 1960, ordained priest Roman Cath. Ch., 1969. Rsch. elec. engr. Boeing Airplane Co., Seattle, 1959-60, Kaman Helicopter, Moosup, Conn., 1960; lectr. Coll. of Holy Cross, Worcester, Mass., 1965-66; chaplain NATO Base, Drierwalde, Fed. Republic Germany, 1969-72; asst. prof. Santa Clara (Calif.) U., 1973-75; assoc. prof. theology Boston Coll., Chestnut Hill, Mass., 1975-88, prof., 1988—. Author: The Spiritual Exercises and the Ignatian Mystical Horizon, 1976, What Are They Saying about Mysticism?, 1984, Christian Mysticism, 1984, Karl Rahner in Dialogue, 1985, Karl Rahner--I Remember, 1986, Ignatius Loyola the Mystic, 1987, Faith in a Wintry Season, 1989, An Anthology of Christian Mysticism, 1991. Mem. Cath. Theology Soc., Cath. Theol. Soc. Am., Am. Acad. Religion, Boston Theology Soc. Office: Boston Coll St Mary's Hall Chestnut Hill MA 02167

EGAN, JOHN PATRICK, II, pastoral counselor and therapist; b. Pittston, Pa., Oct. 14, 1944; s. John Patrick Egan I and Mary Delores (Kramer) Millar; m. Judith Mitchell, May 31, 1986; stepchildren: Kimberly Ruark, Robert Ruark. BA, Seton Hall U., 1966; MS, Iona Coll., 1975. Ordained priest Roman Cath. Ch., 1971; laicized, 1984; cert. sex therapist, clin. hypnotist. Assoc. pastor Roman Cath. Archdiocese, Newark, 1971-78; dir. marriage and family counseling dept. Cath. Community Svcs., Newark, 1978-82; exec. dir. Emmanuel Cancer Found., Cranford, N.J., 1982-88, v.p., 1988—; pres. Horizon Hill Assocs., Murray Hill, N.J., 1988—; adminstr. Counseling Ctr., Bloomfield, N.J., 1975-88. Contbr. articles to profl. publs. Mem. N.J. Com. for Substance Abuse Prevention, 1989—. Mem. Am. Assn. Sex Educators, Counselors and Therapists (N.J. bd. dirs. 1987). Democrat. Avocations: film, real estate investing. Home: 17 Murray Hill Sq Murray Hill NJ 07974 Office: Horizon Hill Assocs 72 Floral Ave Murray Hill NJ 07974

EGAN, KEITH JAMES, theology educator, college administrator, author; b. Pitts., Sept. 27, 1930; s. James A. and Agnes Elizabeth (Shevlin) E.; m. Constance Kane, Aug. 8, 1976; children—Bridget G. R., Brendan K. K. B.A., Mt. Carmel Coll., 1952; M.A., Cath. U. Am., 1959; Ph.D., Cambridge U., Eng., 1965. Vice prin. Joliet Cath. High Sch., Ill., 1956-59; vis. prof. Pontifical Inst. Mediaeval Studies, Toronto, Ont., Can., 1965-67; pres. Mt. Carmel Coll., Niagara Falls, Ont., 1966-68; prof. theology Marquette U., Milw., 1968-83; adj. prof. theology U. Notre Dame, Ind., 1983—; chmn. religious studies St. Mary's Coll., Notre Dame, 1983—, dir. Ctr. for Spirituality, 1984—; co-dir. Inst. for Ecumenical Spiritual in Am., Evanston, Ill., 1970-80; mem. Carmelite Forum, Washington, 1982—, Ctr. Theol. Inquiry, Princeton, 1989. Author: What is Prayer, 1974; co-editor: (with Paul Chandler) The Land of Carmel, 1991; contbr. articles to profl. jours. Marquette U. rsch. grantee, 1972, 79-82; theologian in residence Ecumenical Lay Acad., Dubuque, Iowa, 1981; Dehon fellow Sacred Heart Sch. Theology, Hales Corners, Wis., 1983-84; Corr. fellow Institutum Carmelitanum, Rome, 1986—; Ecumenical Inst. Culture and Rsch. fellow St. John's U., Collegeville, Minn., 1980-81. Mem. Am. Acad. Religion (consultation of spirituality 1983—), Medieval Acad. Am., Coll. Theol. Soc. Am. (nat. v.p. 1978-80, pres. 1990—), Am. Cath. Hist. Assn., Coll. Theology Soc. Democrat. Roman Catholic. Avocations: swimming; hiking. Office: St Mary's Coll Dept Religious Studies Notre Dame IN 46556-5001 *Of the three transcendentals, goodness, truth and beauty, the last named, beauty has been most neglected by religious traditions and society. North America stands especially in need of heeding beauty.*

EGAN, PHYLLIS REITZ, lay worker, educator; b. Buffalo, Mar. 10, 1936; d. Gerard Herman and Diana (Henrich) Reitz; m. Gerald Richard Egan, July 2, 1955; children: Sharon Lesley, Renee Denise, Kenneth Gerard, Keith Edward. BS, Christopher Newport Coll., 1980; MEd, Coll. of William and Mary, 1984; cert. in elem. and secondary teaching, guidance counseling, N.Mex. State U., 1987. Cert. secondary tchr., guidance counselor, N.Mex. Tchr. Our Lady Mt. Carmel Cath. Sch., Newport News, 1981-84, True Cross, Dickinson, Tex., 1985-86; prin. St. Mary's, League City, Tex., 1986-87; tchr. Holy Cross Cath. Sch., Las Cruces, N.Mex., 1988-91; eucharistic min. Holy Cross Parish, Las Cruces, 1987-91; instr. summer Bible sch. program Holy Cross Sch., Las Cruces, 1987-91; liturgy planner Holy Cross Cath. Sch., Las Cruces, 1988-91. Tchr. and instr. Am. Heart Assn., Va. and N.Mex., 1967-91, Am. Red Cross, Va. and N.Mex., 1967-91. Mem. ASCD, Nat. Cath. Edn. Assn. Republican. Office: Holy Cross Cath Sch 1331 N Miranda Las Cruces NM 88004

EGENDOERFER, EUGENE ROBERT, deacon, electrician; b. South Bend, Ind., Dec. 26, 1931; s. Arthur Thomas and Mary Bernice (Blume) E.; m. Winona Rich, June 3, 1950; children: Robert Louis, Mark Allen, Kim Eugene, Jean Marie, Gregory Lee, Andrew Jon. Ed. high sch., Mishawaka, Ind., 1949. Ordained deacon Roman Cath. Ch., 1973. Pastoral assoc. Queen of Peace Ch., Mishawaka, 1973—; journeyman constrn. electrician IBEW Local 153, South Bend, 1950—. Mem. KC (fin. sec. Mishawaka club 1965-67). Democrat. Home: 1302 Cantondale Ln Mishawaka IN 46544

EGER, DENISE LEESE, rabbi; b. New Kensington, Pa., Mar. 14, 1960; d. Bernard D. and Estelle (Leese) E. BA in Religion, U. So. Calif., 1982; MA in Hebrew Letters, Hebrew Union Coll., L.A., 1985; Rabbi, Hebrew Union Coll., N.Y.C., 1988. Ordained rabbi, 1988. Rabbi Temple Beth Ora, Edmonton, Alta., Can., 1983-85; chaplain Isabella Geriatric Ctr., N.Y.C., 1986-88; Rabbi Beth Chayim Chadashim, L.A., 1988—. Contbr. articles to religious publs., chpt. to anthology. Bd. dirs. Nechama: A Jewish Response to AIDS; mem. AIDS task force S.W. coun. Union Am. Hebrew Congregations; vice chmn. spiritual adv. com. AIDS Project L.A.; mem. community adv. bd. Shanti Found.; institutional rev. bd. co-chair Search Alliance. Mem. Cen. Conf. Am. Rabbis. Avocation: guitar. Office: Beth Chayim Chadashim 6000 W Pico Blvd Los Angeles CA 90035 *I have found that in my work with the lesbian and gay community, as well as persons with AIDS, a unique resourcefulness, wellsprings of spirit and hope, in the face of death and oppression. These are truly inspirational and gifts to be shared with all humanity.*

EHLERT, ARNOLD DOUGLAS, retired librarian, minister; b. Mondovi, Wis., Apr. 22, 1909; s. Richard J. and Cora E. (Hakes) E.; m. Thelma A. Adolphs, Dec. 25, 1933; children: A. Benjamin, Susan Elizabeth Ehlert Weiss, Eunice Yvonne Ehlert Castle. BA, Fletcher Coll., 1932; ThM, Dallas Theol Sem., 1942, ThD, 1945; MSLS, U. So. Calif., 1953. Ordained to ministry Evang. Free Ch. Am., 1943. Libr. Dallas Theol. Sem., 1942-48, Fuller Theol. Sem., Pasadena, Calif., 1948-55, Biola Coll., La Mirada, Calif., 1955-69, Talbott Theol Sem., La Mirada, 1969-74; dir. librs. Christian Heritage Coll., 1974-80; dir. librs. Inst. for Creation Rsch., El Cajon, Calif., 1980-88, ret., 1988. Author: The Biblical Novel, A Checklist, 1961, Bibliographic History of Dispensationalism, 1965, Brethren Writers, A Checklist, 1969; editor: The Bible Collector, 1965-84. Mem. Internat. Soc. Bible Collectors (founder 1964, pres. 1964-87), Beta Phi Mu. Home: Town and Country Manor 555 E Memory Ln A-111 Santa Ana CA 92706

EHLINE, DAVID ALAN, clergyman; b. Mpls., Feb. 7, 1938; s. Carl Gunnar and Helen Genevieve (Hanson) E.; m. Marilyn Hansen, June 10, 1960; children: Kenneth Richard, Thomas Paul, Krista Carol. BA, Gustavus Adolphus Coll., St. Peter, Minn., 1960; MDiv, Yale U., 1963; MSW, U. Nebr., 1973. Pastor Holy Cross Luth. Ch., Pacifica, Calif., 1964-69, Village Luth. Ch., Los Angeles, 1969-70; pastoral counselor Family Service Agy., Omaha, 1973-77, Luth. Famuly Services, Omaha, 1977-81; pastor St. Matthew Luth. Ch., Omaha, 1981—; chmn. parish services com. Nebr. Synod Luth. Ch., Omaha, 1981-84, dean east dist., 1984-86. Democrat. Office: St Matthew Luth Ch 5860 Walnut St Omaha NE 68106

EHRHART, CARL YARKERS, retired minister, retired college administrator; b. Lebanon, Pa., May 11, 1918; s. Oliver Tillman and Edna (Yarkers) E.; m. Geraldine May Baldwin, Sept. 8, 1945; children: Carole Lynne Ehrhart Whittam, Constance Sue, Anne Baldwin Ehrhart Bocian. A.B., Lebanon Valley Coll., 1940; M.Div., United Theol. Sem., 1943; Ph.D., Yale, 1954. Prof. philosophy Lebanon Valley Coll., 1947-60, dean coll., prof. philosophy, 1960-67, v.p., dean coll., 1967-80, v.p., asst. to pres., 1980-83; pastor St. John's United Meth. Ch., Lebanon, Pa., 1983-90. Trustee United Theol. Sem., Dayton, Ohio. Home: 643 E Queen St Annville PA 17003

EHRLICH, LAWRENCE, retired cantor, educator; b. Bklyn., Sept. 28, 1917; s. Moses and Bella Riva Erlick; m. Pearl Barron, May 29, 1945 (dec. Dec. 1953); 1 child, Harriet Dale; m. Cecile Pincus, June 6, 1976. Grad., Hebrew Union Coll., 1952, B Sacred Music, 1955. Cantor Temple Beth Sholom, Flushing, N.Y., 1950-52; cantor educator Congregation Rodef Sholom, Youngstown, Ohio, 1952-83, cantor emeritus, 1983—; cantor/rabbi substitute for Tri-State area; nat. rep. Fedn. Temple Youth, Starlight, Pa., 1951; regional rep. Fedn. Temple Youth, Rochester, Buffalo, Cleve., 1953-58; regional rep. Am. Conf. Cantors, 1955-65; aux. cantor (hon.) Heritage Manor, Youngstown, 1970—; holiday cantor Temple Israel, New Castle, Pa., 1953—, aux. cantor/leader, 1989; aux. cantor/leader Morse Geriatric Ctr., West Palm Beach, Fla., 1990; lectr. on Jewish music; advisor to Alumni Assn., 1983. Chmn. UNICEF, 1960; pres. UN Assn. Youngstown, 1960-67, Clergy Boy Scout Camp Retreats, 1954-57, Clergy Gold Star Mothers Meml. Day, 1954-74; area chmn. Am. Heart Assn., Youngstown, 1970; chmn. Youngstown area Commn. for Jewish Edn., 1980-82. Recipient Gates of Jerusalem State of Israel Bonds, Zionist Orgn. Am., 1972, Outstanding Svc. to Congregation Rodef Sholom Lt. Gov. Richard F. Celeste, Ohio, 1972, Shiliah Tzibur award Am. Conf. Cantors, 1977, Kol Hakavod award Cantorial alumni Assn., 1977, Appreciation award Congressman Lyle Williams, 1983, Retirement award Senator Harry Meshel, 1983, Proclamation of Appreciation award Mayor George Vukovich of Youngstown, 1983m Justice Brandeis award Zionist Orgn. Am., 1987, Kfar Silver scholarship plaque, 1987; Cantor Lawrence Ehrlich Day proclaimed in his honor, May 25, Youngstown. Mem. Am. Conf. Cantors (charter), Nat. Assn. Temple Educators (charter, reform Jewish educator cert. 1989), Zionist Orgn. Am. (life), Jewish Chautauqua Soc. (life), Hadassah (life, assoc.), B'nai Brith, Congregation Rodef Sholom (life), Temple Israel (life), Rodef Sholom Brotherhood (life), Rodef Sholom Sisterhood (hon. life). Avocations: reading, collecting opera scores and records, entertaining geriatric groups, philately. Avocation: Jewish music. Home: 1530 Fisher Dr Hubbard OH 44425 *For a meaningful and happy life, share with others their sorrows and share your joys with them; and listen!.*

EHRMANN, RITA MAE, nun; b. Jersey City, N.J., Aug. 27, 1928; d. Henry Joseph and Cassandra Disbrow (Baker) E. BS in Secondary Edn., U. Dayton, 1951; MA in Math., Villanova U., 1957; PhD in Math., St. Louis U., 1969. Mem. Missionary Sisters of Sacred Heart, Reading, Pa., 1946—, coun. mem., 1989—; superior Sacred Heart Hosp. Convent, Norristown, Pa., 1987-89; assoc. prof. math. Villanova (Pa.) U., 1969-91, emeritus, 1991—; instr. U. Botswana, Africa, 1982-84; trustee Sacred Heart Hosp., Norristown, 1989—. Author: African Footprints, 1986; translator: Introduction to Finite Geometries, 1980; contbr. articles to profl. jours; producer: Discovering Minimal Surfaces, 1975. Fulbright grantee, 1982-84. Mem. Math. Assn. Am., Sigma Xi (pres. Villanova chpt. 1986-87), Pi Mu Epsilon. Home: 51 Seminary Ave Reading PA 19605 Office: MSC Provincialate Seminary Ave Reading PA 19605

EICHELBERGER, DANIEL LEE, lay worker, farmer; b. Ashland, Ohio, May 5, 1965; s. David Earnest and Diana Dee (Liston) E.; m. Katina Kay Allen, June 22, 1985; children: Colette Renea, Courtney Erin. AS in Agronomy, Ohio State U., Wooster, 1985. Song and worship leader Clear Creek Ch. of Christ, Ashland, Ohio, 1983-85; song and worship leader Greenwich (Ohio) Ch. of Christ, 1986—, Sunday sch. supt., 1987—, ch. bd. chmn., 1987-88, youth leader, 1988—, tchr. elective Sunday sch. class, 1990-91, chmn. edn. and instrn. ministry, 1990—; farmhand, Ashland, 1981—; farmer, Ashland, 1985—; instr. North Cen. Tech. Coll., Mansfield, Ohio, 1990—. Mem. Young Farmers Am., Future Farmers Am. Alumni Assn. (chmn. scholarship and awards com. 1989, 91, Am. Farmer degree 1985), Farm Bur. Fedn. Home: 5849 Olivesburg Fitchville Rd Ashland OH 44805 *There's a saying, God is rarely early but never late. How true this is. Trust in Him and when you are in despair and ready to give up, you will recognize Him. He will strengthen and deliver you.*

EICHTEN, BEATRICE MARY, pastoral psychotherapist; b. Wanda, Minn., Sept. 15, 1943; d. Everett Peter and Mary Eugenia (Beert) E. BS in Edn., BS in Home Econs., Coll. St. Teresa, 1969; M in Pastoral Studies, Loyola U., Chgo., 1983. Tchr. St. Francis High Sch., Little Falls, Minn., 1971-73; counselor, adminstr. Hope Community, Little Falls, 1973-76; v.p. Franciscan Sisters, Little Falls, 1976-80; dir., counselor Pastoral Counseling Service, Niles, Ill., 1983-85; tng. intern Pastoral Psychotherapy Inst., Park Ridge, Ill., 1982-85, sr. staff mem., 1985—. Mem. Am. Assn. Pastoral Counseling, Assn. Psychol. Type. Democrat. Roman Catholic. Avocations: gardening, pottery, knitting, crocheting, drawing. Home: 929 Lakeside Pl Chicago IL 60640 Office: Pastoral Psychotherapy Inst 1875 Dempster Ave Park Ridge IL 60048

EICK, GRETCHEN CASSEL, political advocate, religious organization director; b. Cleve., Dec. 17, 1942; d. Samuel Haag and Virginia (Cunningham) Cassel; m. Richard Norman Eick, June 26, 1965; children: Alyson Joy, Kendra Elizabeth Emily; 2d m., Michael Poage, 1991. BA, Kalamazoo Coll., 1964; MA, Northwestern U., 1965; postgrad., Howard U., 1971. Tchr. New Haven (Conn.) Pub. Schs., 1965-68, Montgomery County Pub. Schs., Kensington, Md., 1968-70, Fed. City Coll., Washington, 1972-73; lobbyist, assoc. dir. Washington Office on Africa, 1974; policy advocate United Ch. of Christ, Washington, 1977-87; dir. Interfaith Impact, Lawrence, Kans., 1987—. Democrat. Avocations: oil painting, sewing, reading. Home: 1917 Jenny Wren Rd Lawrence KS 66047

EIDE, EDWARD T., ecumenical agency administrator. Exec. dir. Community Emergency Assistance Program, Brooklyn Center, Minn. Office: Community Emergency Assistance Program 7231 Brooklyn Blvd Brooklyn Center MN 55429*

EIFRIG, GAIL MCGREW, editor, educator; b. Alhambra, Calif., May 26, 1940; d. R. Brownell and Ann (Froning) McG.; m. William F. Eifrig, May 30, 1964; children: Fritz, Ann, Karl, Katherine. BA in English with honors, Valparaiso (Ind.) U., 1962; MA, Bryn Mawr Coll., 1963, PhD, 1982. Editor The Cresset Valparaiso U., 1989—; mem. prayer staff chapel U. Valparaiso, 1985-90. Woodrow Wilson Found. fellow, 1962-63, Lilly Found. fellow, 1988-89. Fellow Soc. for Values in Higher Edn.; mem. Am. Acad. Religion, Nat. Coun. Tchr.'s of English. Democrat. Lutheran. Office: Valparaiso U The Cresset Valparaiso IN 46383

EIGENBRODT, HAROLD JOHN, religion educator; b. Peoria, Ill., June 19, 1928; s. Harold John and Mildred Geneva (Hixson) E. B.A., N. Central Coll., 1949; B.D., Yale, 1952, M.A., 1955, Ph.D., 1960; postgrad. (Lilly fellow), Oxford (Eng.) U., 1964-65. Ordained priest Episc. Ch., 1958. Instr. Berkeley Div. Sch., New Haven, 1954-55; instr. Yale Div. Sch., 1955-56; faculty DePauw U., Greencastle, Ind., 1957—; prof. religion DePauw U., 1970—; staff Westcott House, Cambridge U., 1979. Ford Found. fellow, 1970, 72. Fellow Soc. for Religion in Higher Edn.; mem. Am. Acad. Religion, Soc. Bibl. Lit. Home: 606 E Walnut St Greencastle IN 46135

EIGENFELD, ROGER CONRAD, clergyman; b. Milw., July 24, 1940; s. Otto Paul and Dorothy Anna (Wiedoff) E.; m. Carolyn Jeanne Vermazen, June 15, 1963; children: Peter, Whitney, Kirsten, Jacqueline, Lauri. BA, Carthage Coll., 1962; BD, Northwestern Luth. Theol. Sem., 1966. Developer mission Christus Victor Luth. Ch., Apple Valley, Minn., 1966-67; youth pastor Richfield Luth. Ch., Mpls., 1967-70; assoc. pastor Holy Trinity Luth. Ch., Mpls., 1970-72; sr. pastor St. Andrew's Luth. Ch., Mahtomedi, Minn., 1972—; mem. exec. bd. Minn. Synod, Mpls., 1978-80. Author: Decisions About Death, 1981. Bd. dirs. Camp Du Nord YMCA, St. Paul, 1977-80, gen. bd., St. Paul, 1980. Avocations: camping, canoeing, writing. Office: St Andrews Luth Ch 900 Stillwater Rd Mahtomedi MN 55115

EIKENBERRY, JAMES OWEN, minister; b. Decatur, Ill., Jan. 6, 1952; s. Lorrel Spencer and Nelda Maxine (Rhoades) E.; m. Susan Lynn Lampman, Aug. 11, 1973; children: David Joshua, Stephen Jonathan. AA, Christ for the Nations Inst., Dallas, 1975; BA, Evangel Coll., 1981; MA, Assemblies of God Theol., Seminary, Springfield, Mo., 1983; MDiv, Bethany Theol. Seminary, Oak Brook, Ill., 1986. Asst. pastor Freeport (Ill.) Ch. of the Brethren, 1974; minister Bethel Ch. of the Brethren, Carleton, Nebr., 1975-80, Good Shepherd Ch. of the Brethern, Springfield, 1981-83, Faith Ch. of the Brethern, Batavia, Ill., 1983-88, West Green Tree Ch. of the Brethern, Elizabethtown, Pa., 1988—; chmn. Day Seven Ministries, Elizabethtown, 1990—; coord. Brethren Renewal Svcs., Elizabethtown, 1990—; sec. Elizabethtown Ministerium, 1990—; bd. dirs. Ch. of the Brethren Gen. Bd., Elgin, Ill. Editor: Genesis: Quest for an Identity, 1987. Home: 255 Colebrook Rd Elizabethtown PA 17022 Office: West Green Tree Church of the Brethren 255 Colebrook Rd Elizabethtown PA 17022

EIKERENKOETTER, FREDERICK JOSEPH, II (REVEREND IKE), evangelist, educator, lecturer; b. Ridgeland, S.C., June 1, 1935; s. Frederick Joseph and Rema Estelle (Matthews) E.; m. Eula Mae Dent, Feb. 17, 1964; 1 son, Xavier Frederick III. B.Th., Am. Bible Coll., 1956; D.Sc. of Living, Sci. of Living Inst., 1971. Founder, pres. United Christian Evangelist Assn., 1962—, United Ch. Sci. of Living Inst., 1969—, Rev. Ike Found., 1973—; vis. lectr. dept. psychiatry Harvard Med. Sch., 1973, U. Ala., 1975, Atlanta U. Ctr., 1975; vis. lectr. dept. sociology Rice U., Houston, 1977. Served with chaplain sect. USAF, 1956-58. Recipient World Service award for outstanding contributions to mankind Prince Hall Masons, 1975. Founder of the Science of Living philosophy, church and inst. Office: 4140 Broadway New York NY 10033

EILER, DAVID RICHARD, minister, religion educator; b. Elkart, Ill., Aug. 8, 1933; s. William Linden and Cloy D. (Darr) E.; m. Rosalie May Rapp, June 20, 1954; children: Richard L., Ervin Scott, David William. BA, U. Indpls., 1956; MDiv cum laude, United Theol. Seminary, Dayton, Ohio, 1959; MA, U. Chgo., 1972. Staff counselor Interfaith Counseling and Edn. Ctr., Naperville, Ill., 1974-79, exec. dir., 1979-84; pastor Mokena (Ill.) United Meth. Ch., 1985—; instr. Worsham Coll., Des Plaines, Ill., 1984—' chair div. outdoor and retreat ministries Northern Ill. Conf., 1988—. Recognized for outstanding religious leadership in community Jaycees, 1979. Mem. Soc. for Scientific Study of Religion, Am. Acad. Religion, Soc. Bibl. Lit., Kiwanis (vice chair Naperville chpt. 1983). Home: 25 W 630 Burlington Ave Naperville IL 60563

EINERSON, RICHARD JOHN, church official; b. Montevideo, Minn., July 21, 1935; s. Raymond O. and Grace Elaine (Hegstrom) E.; m. Carolyn Jeanne Smothers, June 4, 1955; children: Stephanie, Sonia, Andrea. AB, Warner Pacific Coll., 1957; BDiv, Pacific Sch. Religion, 1961; D of Ministry, Andover Newton Theol. Sch., 1972. Intern Vandberbilt U., Nashville, 1959-60; pastor First Congl. Ch., Pelican Rapids, Minn., 1961-65, United Protestant Ch., Silver Bay, Minn., 1965-68, Sayles Meml. Ch., Lincoln, R.I., 1968-76; chaplain St. Luke's Hosp., Fargo, N.D., 1977—; supr. New Bedford (Mass.) Coun. of Chs., 1974-76. Author audio-visual counseling programs, 1983, 85. Fellow Am. Assn. Pastoral Counselors (supr. mems.-in-tng. 1974—), Coll. of Chaplains; mem. Assn. Clin. Pastoral Edn. (clin.), Mental Health Assn. Democrat. Mem. United Ch. of Christ. Avocations: photography, golf, carpentry, fishing. Home: 3250 15th Ave SW #18 Fargo ND 58103 Office: St Lukes Hosps 5th at Mills Fargo ND 58122

EINERTSON, NORRIS LEONARD, pastor, retired military officer; b. Westbrook, Minn., Aug. 6, 1930; s. Norman Hartvig and Mabel Martha Fredericka (Anderson) E.; m. Valborg Carolyn Baalson, June 7, 1958; children: Thomas Lee, John Norris, Nora Kay. BA magna cum laude, Augustana Coll., Sioux Falls, S.D., 1958; M Divinity, Luther Theol. Sem., St. Paul, 1961; MST, N.Y. Theol. Sem., 1974. Ordained pastor Am. Luth. Ch., 1961. Commd. lt. U.S. Army, 1961, advanced through grades to maj. gen., 1986; asst. div. arty. chaplain 1st Inf. Div., Arty., Ft. Riley, Kans., 1961-63; battle group chaplain 2d Battle group, 16th Inf., 1st Inf., Ft. Riley and Wildflecken, Federal Republic Germany, 1963-64; support command chaplain 1st Inf. Support Command, Ft. Riley, 1964-65; bn. command chaplain 4th Bn., 10th Inf., Ft. Davis, C.Z., Republic of Panama, 1965-68; group chaplain 34th Engr. Group, Vietnam, 1968-69; brigade chaplain 1st Basic Tng. Brigade, Ft. Ord, Calif., 1970-72; staff and faculty U.S. Chaplain Ctr. and Sch., Ft. Hamilton, N.Y., 1972-75; asst. staff chaplain VII Corps, Mohringen, Federal Republic Germany, 1975-76; div. chaplain 1st Armored Div., Ansbach, Federal Republic Germany, 1976-78; asst. installation chaplain U.S. Army Signal Ctr. and Sch., Ft. Gordon, Ga., 1978-80, installation chaplain, 1980-82; staff chaplain U.S. Forces Command, Ft. McPherson, Ga., 1985; exec. officer Office of Chief of Chaplains, The Pentagon, Washington, 1982-85, dep. chief of chaplains, 1985-86, chief of chaplains, 1986-90; comdr. U.S. Army Regiment, 1986-90; ret. U.S. Army, 1990; pastor Beaver Valley Luth. Ch., Valley Springs, S.D., 1990—; mem. Armed Forces Chaplain Bd., The Pentagon, 1985-90, chmn., 1988-89; chmn. Atlantic Area Religious Workers Assn., C.Z. and Colon, Republic of Panama, 1966-68. Mem. world-wide bd. govs., USO, Washington, 1988-89. Decorated D.S.M. with oak leaf cluster, Legion of Merit, Bronze Star, others; recipient Alumni Achievement award Augustana Coll., 1987. Mem. Mil. Chaplain Assn., U.S. Army Chaplain Mus. Assn. (pres. 1986-90), Assn. U.S. Army, 1st Inf. Div. Assn., 1st Armored Div. Assn. (bd. dirs. 1976-78). Avocations: vocal and instrumental music, running, handball.

EINSTEIN, STEPHEN JAN, rabbi; b. L.A., Nov. 15, 1945; s. Syd C. and Selma (Rothenberg) E.; m. Robin Susan Kessler, Sept. 9, 1967; children: Rebecca Yael, Jennifer Melissa, Heath Isaac, Zachary Shane. AB, UCLA, 1967; B.H.L., Hebrew Union Coll., L.A., 1968; M.A.H.L., Hebrew Union Coll., Cin., 1971. Ordained rabbi. Rabbi Temple Beth Am, Parsippany, N.J., 1971-74; rabbi Temple Beth David, Westminster, Calif., 1974-76, Congregation B'nai Tzedek, Fountain Valley, Calif., 1976—; bd. dirs. Heritage Pointe, Coll. Jewish Studies Orange County. Co-author: Every Person's Guide to Judaism, 1989; co-editor: Introduction to Judaism, 1983. Pres., trustee Fountain Valley (Calif.) Sch. Bd., 1984-90; mem. Personnel Commn. Fountain Valley Sch. Dist., 1991--. Honored for Maj. Contributions to Jewish Learning, Orange County (Calif.) Bur. Jewish Edn., 1986; recipient Micah Award for Interfaith Activities, Am. Jewish Com., 1988. Mem. Cen. Conf. Am. Rabbis (exec. bd. 1989-91), Pacific Assn. Reform Rabbis (exec. bd. 1987-91), Orange County Bd. Rabbis (pres., sec.-treas. 1974-79), Jewish Educators Assn. Orange County (pres. 1979-81), Orange County Bur. Jewish Edn. (v.p. 1982-84). Democrat. Office: Congregation Bnai Tzedek 9669 Talbert Ave Fountain Valley CA 92708

EISENBERG, FREDERICK AARON, rabbi; b. Boston, Jan. 26, 1931; s. Moses Joel and Violet (Hirshon) E.; m. Helen Louise Finer, Sept. 1, 1957; children: Matthew, Elizabeth, Rachel. Student, rabbi congregations, Petoskey and Saginaw, Mich., Marion, Ind., 1952-56; BA, Clark U., 1952; B in Hebrew Lit., Hebrew Union Coll., 1955, MA, 1958. Ordained rabbi, 1958. Ednl. dir., tchr. Muncie, Ind., 1956-58; dir. audio-visual dept. Wise Temple Religious Sch., Cin., 1956-58; asst. rabbi Temple Sholom, Chgo., 1962-64; rabbi Temple Emanuel, Grand Rapids, Mich., 1964-72, Fairmount Temple, Cleve., 1972-85, Temple Israel, Cleve., 1985—; mem. Jewish Fedn. Hunger Task Force, Task Force for Soviet Jewry; mem. broadcasting commn. Chgo. Bd. Rabbis; mem. Steering and clergy coordinating com. Lakeview Coun. Chs.; rabbinic liaison Chgo. office Jewish Welfare Bd.; mem. radio and TV commn. Grand Rapids Area Coun. Chs.; commr. cemeteries Mich., 1971; rabbinic adviser to Cleve. and Lake Erie Fedn. Temple Youth; mem. com. for continuing edn. Cen. Conf. Am. Rabbis; lectr. Jewish Chautauqua Soc. at Purdue U., Hope Coll., Aquinas Coll., Mich. State U., Calvin Coll.; Jewish chaplain Aquinas Coll., 1970; dean N.E. Lakes Fedn. Temple Youth, 1976; pres. Cleve. Bd. Rabbi's, 1987-89. Contbr. articles, sermons, film strips; recs. include What Is a Jew? What Is Judaism?. Bd. dirs. USO, Inst. Pastoral Care, Chgo., Acad. Religion and Mental Health, Mental Health Soc. Greater Chgo., Jewish Community Fund of Grand Rapids, Spectrum; mem. ministerial adv. com. Kent County Planned Parenthood Assn.; clergy chmn. United Way, 1984. Chaplain USAF, 1960-62. Recipient Nelson and Helen Glueck prize, 1956. Home: 2879 Coleridge St Cleveland Heights OH 44118 Office: Temple Israel 1732 Lander Rd Cleveland OH 44124

EISENBERG, ROBIN LEDGIN, Jewish education administrator; b. Passaic, N.J., Jan. 10, 1951; d. Morris and Ruth (Miller) Ledgin. BS, West Chester State U., 1973; M Edn., Kutztown State U., 1977. Administrv. asst. Kenesseth Israel, Allentown, Pa., 1973-77; dir. edn. Cong. Schaarai Zedek, Tampa, Fla., 1977-79, Kehilath Israel, Pacific Palisades, Calif., 1979-80, Temple Beth El, Boca Raton, Fla., 1980--. Contbr. Learning Together, 1987. Chmn. edn. info., Planned Parenthood, Boca Raton Fla. 1989. Recipient Kamiker Camp award Nat. Assn. Temple Educators, Pres.'s award for adminstrn., 1990. Mem. Nat. Assn. Temple Educators (pres. 1990-92), Coalition Advancement of Jewish Edn. Avocations:photography, master swimming. Home: 7000 Palmette Cir S 702 Boca Raton FL 33433 Office: Temple Beth El 333 SW 4th Ave Boca Raton FL 33432

EISNER, SISTER JANET MARGARET, college president; b. Boston, Oct. 10, 1940; d. Eldon and Ada (Martin) E. AB, Emmanuel Coll., 1963; MA, Boston Coll., 1969; PhD, U. Mich., 1975; LHD (hon.), Northeastern U. Joined Sisters of Notre Dame de Namur, Roman Cath. Ch. Dir. admissions Emmanuel Coll., 1967-71; lectr., teaching asst. U. Mich., Ann Arbor, 1971-73; dir. Emmanuel Coll. and City of Boston Pairings, 1976-78, asst. prof. English, 1976-78, chmn. dept., 1977-78, acting pres., 1978-79, pres., 1979—; mem. Mass. Bd. Regents, chmn. regents planning com., 1980-86; mem. adv. bd. Ctr. for Religious Devel., 1983—; mem. exec. com. Boston Higher Edn. Partnership, 1991—. Trustee Trinity Coll., 1979-85, mem. adv. coun. on enrollment planning, 1981-82; adv. coun. pres. Assn. Governing Bds., 1982-88; mem. commn. on women in higher edn. Am. Coun. on Edn., 1985-87; mem. adv. bd. Synod of Archdiocese of Boston, 1988, Anti-Defamation League Dinner Com., 1988-89; chair four-yr. coll. div. United Way Campaign, 1989; mem. NAICU/NIIC joint task force Minority Participation in Ind. Higher Edn., 1989; mem. govs. award com. Carballo Scholarships, 1989; bd. dirs. Med. Area Svc. Corp., 1989—; trustee Boston Cath. TV Ctr., 1990—. Rackham prize fellow, Ford Found. fellow, 1973-75. Mem. Nat. Assn. Ind. Colls. and Univs. (commn. on policy analysis 1991—), Assn. Ind. Colls. and Univs. in Mass. (chair 1991—), Women's Coll. Coalition (exec. com. 1991—). Office: Emmanuel Coll Office of the Pres 400 The Fenway Boston MA 02115

EITRHEIM, NORMAN DUANE, bishop; b. Baltic, S.D., Jan. 14, 1929; s. Daniel Tormod and Selma (Thompson) E.; m. Clarice Yvonne Pederson, Aug. 23, 1952; children: Daniel, David, John, Marie. BA, Augustana Coll., 1951; BTh, Luther Sem., St. Paul, 1956; LHD (hon.), Augustana Coll., 1988. Pastor 1st English Luth. Ch., Tyler, Minn., 1956-63, St. Philips Luth. Ch., Fridley, Minn., 1963-76; asst. to pres. Luther Northwestern Sem., St. Paul, 1976-80; bishop S.D. dist. Am. Luth. Ch., Sioux Falls, 1981-87; bishop S.D. Synod Evang. Luth. Ch. in Am., Sioux Falls, 1988—. Staff sgt. USAF, 1951-52. Office: Evang Luth Ch in Am SD Synod Augustana Coll Sioux Falls SD 57197

EKANDEM, DOMINIC IGNATIUS CARDINAL, bishop; b. Obio Ibiono, Nigeria, 1917; s. Paul Ino Ekandem Ubo and Nwa Ibong Umana; D.D., St. Paul's Major Sem., Enugu, 1941, Okpala, 1947; L.L.D., Loyola U., Chgo., 1989; DLitt (hon.), U. Calabar, 1990. Ordained priest Roman Cath. Ch., 1947; priest in Nigeria, 1947-54; consecrated bishop, 1954; bishop of Ikot Ekpene, Akwa Ibom State, 1963-89; chmn. Dept. Social Welfare, Cath. Secretariat of Nigeria, 1970; apostolic adminstr. of Port Harcourt, 1970-73; pres. Episcopal Conf. Nigeria, 1973-79; elevated to Sacred Coll. Cardinals, 1976; cardinal of St. Marcellus, 1976—; archbishop, 1st bishop of Abuja, 1989—; mem. Symposium of Episcopal Conf. of Africa and Madagascar; founding mem. St. Paul's Nat. Missionary Sem., Gwagwalada, Abuja. Decorated Order Brit. Empire; comdr. Order Niger, Order Fed. Republic of Nigeria; named Mission Superior of Abuja, 1981—; recipient 5 chieftancy titles in Nigeria. Mem. Assn. Episcopal Confs. of Anglophone West Africa (pres. 1977), Congregation for the Evang. of Peoples, Pioneer Total Abstinence Assn. Author: Shepherd Among Shepherds, 1979; also articles. 1st black African bishop in West Africa. Address: Bishop's Residence, PO Box 286 Garki, Abuja Nigeria *The best I have tried to do over the years, using the opportunities give to me by God and the encouragement by men, is the emulation of my eminent country-men in their dedication to nation-building.*

EKRUT, JIM, minister; b. San Antonio, Aug. 21, 1951; s. James C. and Edna C. (Fredrich) E.; divorced: children: Lauren Elizabeth, Ashley Rebekah. B Music Edn., Baylor U., 1973; MusM, Southwestern Bapt. Theol. Sem., 1978. Ordained to ministry So. Bapt. Conv., 1981. Min. music 1st Bapt. Ch., Gonzales, Tex., 1976-82, Ridglea West Bapt. Ch., Ft. Worth, 1982—; music dir. Gonzales Bapt. Assn., 1977-80, Tarrant Bapt. Assn., Ft. Worth, 1983-86. Soloist Mid-Tex. Symphony, New Braunfels, 1980. Mem. Am. Choral Dirs. Assn., Tex. Choral Dirs. Assn., Tex. Music Educators Assn., Lions, Alpha Chi. Office: Ridglea West Bapt Ch 3954 Southwest Blvd Fort Worth TX 76116

ELANDER, KELIITANE ROBERT, minister; b. Columbus, Ind., Oct. 29, 1959; s. Robert Carl and Charlotte Dianne (Calhoun) E.; m. Julie Marie Gibson, Aug. 9, 1986; children: Elizabeth Ruth, Joshua Benjamin. AA in Comml. Art, Dutchess Community Coll., 1979; BS in Communications, Ohio U., 1983; cert. Bibl. Studies, Preston Rd. Ctr. for Christian Edn., 1989. Apptd. to ministry Ch. of Christ, 1989. Min. Kingston (N.Y.) Ch. of Christ, 1989—. Office: Kingston Ch of Christ PO Box 1816 Kingston NY 12401

ELDER, ELLEN ROZANNE, editorial director, educator; b. Harrisburg, Pa.; d. B.H. and Ellen M. (Wolfe) E. AB, Western Mich. U., 1962, MA, 1964; PhD, U. Toronto, 1972. Instr. history Western Mich. U., Kalamazoo, 1968-73; dir. Inst. Cistercian Studies at Western Mich. U., Kalamazoo, 1973—; editorial dir. Cistercian Pubs., Kalamazoo, 1973—; affiliate prof. history Western Mich. U. contbr. articles to profl. jours. Mem. Episcopal Ch. (standing commn., ecumenical relations), 1980—, Anglican-Orthodox Theol. Consultation, 1981—. Mem. NADEO-EDEO (standing com. 1988—), ARCIC. Anglican. Office: Cistercian Publs WMU Sta Kalamazoo MI 49008

ELDER, ERNIE DEWEY, JR., minister; b. New Albany, Miss., Nov. 7, 1955; s. Ernie Dewey Sr. and Sarah Grace (Cox) E. BA, Memphis State U., 1979; MDiv, So. Bapt. Theol. Sem., 1983, ThM, 1987. Ordained to ministry So. Bapt. Conv., 1987. Summer youth intern North Park Bapt. Ch., Evansville, Ind., 1981; dir. children's summer program 1st Bapt. Ch., Memphis, 1983; summer youth intern Talbot Park Bapt. Ch., Norfolk, Va., 1984; pastor 1st Bapt. Ch., Cannelton, Ind., 1987; pastor Christian edn. and outreach 1st Bapt. Ch., Lafayette, Ind., 1989; mem. collaborative ministry team of Lilly Found. Ministry to Ministers Project. Adminstr. Perry County Ecumenical Choir, Tell City, Ind., 1988-89, Greater Lafayette Ecumenical Choir, 1991; active Religious Arts Festival Lafayette, 1989—. Mem. Tippecanoe Bapt. Assn. (moderator 1990-91), Bapt. Student Found., West Lafayette (exec. com. 1989—), Downtown Ministerial Assn., Tippecanoe Ministerial Assn., Perry County Ministerial Assn. (v.p. 1988-89), Lafayette Area Christian Educators. Office: 1st Bapt Ch 411 N Seventh St Lafayette IN 47901-1132 *The Holy Triune God is the dynamic reality that empowers and energizes all of life. Even the very breath we breathe finds its source in the Father, Son and Holy Spirit.*

ELDER, GOVE GRIFFITH, missionary, evangelist; b. Berea, Ohio, May 31, 1937; s. Glennard Holl and Norma (Johnson) E.; m. Barbara Broholm, June 10, 1961; children—Griffith, Elizabeth. B.A., Pa. State U., 1959; B.D., Andover Newton, 1966; M.A., U. Calif.-Berkeley, 1967; Ph.D., U. N.C., 1982. Program dir. Student Christian Centre, Bangkok, Thailand, 1960-63; student worker Vocat. Student Movement, Bangkok, 1967-71; pastor, evangelist Mahachai Bapt. Ch., Mahachai, Thailand, 1972-82; evangelist Kratumbaen Chapel, Thailand, 1983—; dir. Mahachai Christian Sch., 1972-82. Author: Ritual and Ethnicity in Mahachai Thailand, 1982. Mem. Asian Study Assn. Home: 69/2 Kratumbaen, Samutsakorn 74110, Thailand Office: TBMF, 197/1 Silom Rd, Bangkok Thailand

ELDER, JERRY MATSON, minister; b. Talladega, Ala., July 12, 1960; s. Jerry Matson and Winnie Dean (Bittle) E.; m. Pamela Renee Weakley; 1 child, Jessie Danae. BS, Freed-Hardeman Coll., 1983; postgrad., David Lipscomb U., 1991—. Youth minister Oxford (Ala.) Ch. Christ, 1981, Washington Ave. Ch. Christ, Evansville, Ind., 1982; assoc. minister W. 7th St. Ch. Christ, Columbia, Tenn., 1983—; ministers bd. Columbia (Tenn.) Acad., 1985—. Vol. tchr. Regency Health Care, Columbia, 1985—, Hillview Health Care, Columbia, 1986—; bd. dirs. Maury Christian Camp, Columbia, 1985—. Named one of Outstanding Young Men Am., 1985-86. Avocations: wood crafts, fishing, sports, music. Home: 305 Burt Dr Columbia TN 38401 Home and Office: 407 W 7th St Columbia TN 38401 *In order for this world to succeed the old must appreciate the young and the young must respect the old. Without the harmony of the two, our world will always remain in chaos.*

ELDER, JOHN WILLIAM, JR., minister; b. Lawrence, Kans., May 31, 1949; s. John William, Sr. and Bette Jean (Ellis) E.; m. Cheryl Loraine Cannady, June 12, 1971; children: Michelle, Trey, Christina. BA, S.W. Bapt. U., 1971; MDiv, Midwestern Bapt. Theol. Sem., 1973. Ordained to ministry Bapt. Ch., 1975. Assoc. pastor Oakland Bapt. Ch., Rock Hill, S.C., 1973-77; pastor Southport (N.C.) Bapt. Ch., 1977-85; pastor First Bapt. Ch., Richmond, Mo., 1985-89, Battlefield, Mo., 1989—; second v.p. Exec. Bd. Mo. Bapt. Conv., Jefferson City, Mo., 1989-90. Editor (newsletter): The Report, 1989-91. Recipient Life Svc. Disting. Alumni award S.W. Bapt. U., 1988. Mem. Mo. Bapt. Conv (second v.p. 1989-90), Caldwell-Ray Bapt. Assn. (moderator 1988-89), Rotary. Home: 4849 Gold Rd Battlefield MO 65619 Office: First Bapt Ch 5010 S FF Hwy Battlefield MO 65619

ELDER, PHILIP E. R., bishop. Bishop of the Windward Islands The Anglican Communion, Kingstown, St. Vincent and the Grenadines. Office: Bishop's House, POB 128, Kingstown Saint Vincent and the Grenadines*

ELDER, ROBERT JAY, minister; b. Birmingham, Mich., July 12, 1949; s. Charles William and Barbara Magruder (Tompkins) E.; m. Joyce Lynn Gardner, Aug. 22, 1970; children: Erin Elaine, Celia Irene. BA, Trinity U., San Antonio, 1971; MDiv, Princeton Theol. Sem., 1974; DMin, Drew U., Madison, N.J., 1983. Ordained to ministry Presbyn. Ch. (U.S.A.), 1974. Assoc. pastor First Presbyn. Ch., Corvallis, Oreg., 1974-80; sr. pastor Presbyn. Ch. of the Covenant, Port Arthur, Tex., 1980-85; sr. pastor 1st Presbyn. Ch., Amarillo, Tex., 1985-86, Salem, Oreg., 1987—; keynote speaker Synod of the Sun, Denton, Tex., 1984; commr. 197th Gen. Assembly Presbyn. Ch. (U.S.A.), Indpls., 1985, moderator assembly com. on mission program and orgn., 1985. Contbr. articles to profl. jours. Bd. dirs. United Way of Marion County, Salem, 1988-90, YMCA, Salem, 1989—, Jefferson County Mental Health, Port Arthur, Tex., 1983-85, Benton County Mental Health, Corvallis, 1978-80. Mem. Presbytery of the Cascades, Presbyns. for Renewal, Alban Inst., Blue Key, Rotary (bd. dirs. 1991—). Office: First Presbyn Ch 770 Chemeketa St NE Salem OR 97301

ELDON, MICHAEL, bishop. Bishop of Nassau and The Bahamas The Anglican Communion. Office: Addington House, PO Box N-7107, Nassau The Bahamas*

ELGERT, LOUIS GEORGE, pastor; b. Bristol, Conn., Mar. 29, 1923; s. Julius August and Ottilie Elsie (Roda) E.; m. Lillian Johanna Althaus, June 24, 1951; children: Lois Jean, John Ernest, Paul Andrew. BD, Concordia Theol. Sem., Springfield, Ill., 1952. Pastor Zion Evang. Luth. Ch., Plumas, Man., Can., 1952-55, St. Paul's Evang. Luth. Ch., McCreary, Man., Can., 1952-55, St. Luke's Luth. Ch., Putnam Valley, N.Y., 1955-67, Trinity Luth. Ch., Easthampton, Mass., 1967-88; Walther League counselor, Bronx, Manhattan, Westchester Zone, N.Y., 1956-58; cir. counselor Peekskill Cir. Luth. Ch. Mo. Synod, N.Y., 1962-67; del. to 2 Luth. Ch. convs., Detroit, 1965, Dallas, 1977; counselor Women's Missionary League West Mass., 1978-82. Unit pres. Am. Cancer Soc., Putnam, County, N.Y., 1964-65. Tech. sgt. USAAF, 1942-45, ETO. Decorated Air medal; recipient Servus Ecclesiae Christi award Concordia Theol. Sem., Ft. Wayne, Ind., 1978. Home: 1333 S Kirkwood Rd Saint Louis MO 63122-7295

ELIAHU, MORDECHAI, rabbi; b. Jerusalem, Israel, 1928; s. Ha Rau Salman Shlama E.; m. Shlita Azrani; 4 children. Ordained rabbi, 1951. Former judge religious ct. of Beersheba, Israel; then Jerusalem regional judge, 1971-83; now judge Rabbinical High Sch., Jerusalem; also Sephardi Chief Rabbi of Israel, 1983—. Served with Israeli army. Office: Sephardic Community, Chief Rabbinate, Jerusalem Israel

ELIASON, PHYLLIS MARIE, missionary, educator; b. Greenacres, Fla., Dec. 21, 1925; d. John Sylvester Underhill and Catherine (Graef) Males; m. Albert Eliason, Aug. 22 (dec. Nov. 1955); children: Phyllis, James, Nancy, Albert Jr. BA in Psychology, U. Guam, 1971, MEd, 1974. Cert. guidance counselor. Missionary dir. Child Evangelism Fellowship, Inc., Palm Beach County, Fla., 1957-62; missionary serving Guam and Micronesia Child Evangelism Fellowship, Inc., Warrenton, Mo., 1962-85; counselor Marshalls Christian High Sch., Majuro, Marshall Islands, 1976-77; mission recruiter, tchr. trainer Child Evangelism Fellowship Inc., 1985-89, Child Evangelism Fellowship of Micronesia, Inc., Guam, 1989—. Pres., v.p. Girls Scouts Guam, 1963-75; Bd. dirs. Guam Scout Council, 1967, 79-82, Simpson Bible Coll. Extension Sch., Guam. Named Hon. Citizen of Huntsville, Ala., City Council, 1966. Mem. Am. Profl. Guidance Assn. Avocations: collecting stamps, collecting shells. Office: Child Evangelism Fellowship Inc Box 348 Warrenton MO 63383 *Thru the years as I've ministered to children I've been amazed by their concepts of good and evil and challenged by their ability to accept God's word as their standard when it is presented simply to them.*

ELKINS, DOV PERETZ, rabbi; b. Phila., Dec. 7, 1937; s. Edward and Bertha (Byer) E.; m. Elaine Rash (div. June 1978); children: Hillel, Jonathan, Shira; m. Maxine Gornish, Nov. 16, 1986. Grad., Gratz Coll. for Hebrew Tchrs., 1958; BA in Lit., Temple U., 1959; MHL, Jewish Theol. Sem., 1962; doctorate degree in counseling and humanistic edn, Colgate Rochester Divinity Sch., 1976; DD (hon., Jewish Theol. Seminary, 1991. Ordained rabbi, 1964; cert. instr. of parent effectiveness tng., tchr. effectiveness tng. Mil. chaplain Ft. Gordon, Ga., 1964-66; assoc. rabbi Har Zion Temple, Phila., 1966-70; rabbi Jacksonville (Fla.) Jewish Ctr., 1970-72, Temple Beth El, Rochester, N.Y., 1972-76; pvt. practice in pastoral counseling, 1976-85; rabbi Beth El Temple, Norfolk, Va., 1985-87; sr. rabbi The Park Synagogue, Cleve., 1987—; nat. vice chmn. Rabbinic Cabinet Israel Bonds, 1986—; mem. Chancellor's Rabbinic Cabinet Jewish Theol. Sem., 1988—; co-founder Congl./Coll. Adult Inst. Jewish Studies, Cleve., 1988—; chmn. acad. and religious div. United Jewish Welfare Campaugn Jewish Community Fedn., 1988-90; lectr. in field. Author: Humanizing Jewish Life: Judaism and the Human Potential Movement, Series in Experiential Education, Clarifying Jewish Values, Jewish Consciousness Raising, Experiential Programs for Jewish Groups, Loving My Jewishness, My Seventy-Two Friends: Encounters With Refusemiks in the U.S.S.R.; contbrs. articles to Reader's Digiest, New Woman, The Christian Century, Judaism, Religious Education, The Reconstructionist and many others. Nat. chmn. Israel Bonds Rabbinic Cabinet Mission to Israel, 1991; mem. mission Jewish Community, Addis Ababa, Ethiopia. Mem. Rabbinical Assembly (com. on law and standards), United Synagogue Am. (com. on Jewish edn.), Coun. Jewish Edn., Jewish Educators Assembly, Conf. Jewish Communal Svc., Assn. Humanistic Psychology. Home: 25180 Shaker Blvd Beachwood OH 44122-2362 Office: The Park Synagogue 3300 Mayfield Blvd Cleveland Heights OH 44118-1899

ELKINS, JESSE ROY, minister; b. Houston, Aug. 5, 1955; s. Jesse Monroe and Iva Dell (Hammonds) E.; m. Sherrie Wynn Whitesel, June 16, 1978; children: Jessica Wynn, Hannah Beth. BA, Gulf Coast Bible Coll., 1983. Ordained to ministry Ch. of God (Anderson, Ind.), 1988. Asst. to music dir. First Ch. of God, Houston, 1981-84; assoc. pastor First Ch. of God, Shawnee, Okla., 1984-86; pastor McCook First Ch. of God, McCook, Nebr., 1987-90; assoc. pastor Oaklawn First Ch. of God, Hot Springs, Ark., 1991—; dist. youth coord. Ch. of God, Okla., 1985-86, youth camp evangelist, Nebr,. 1987, interim pastor, Trenton, 1990. Republican. Home: 5917 Malvern Rd Hot Springs AR 71901 Office: Oaklawn First Ch of God 2110 7th St Hot Springs AR 71913 *The writer of Ecclesiastes, in his search for meaning in life, found what so many today find and that is that all is vanity outside of God. When life is over and accomplishments are tallied, the only thing that will really matter will be "Do I know God?". It matters not what religion I am, what accomplishments I have made, or how much love I have. At the end of physical life, will I have a personal relationship with God Almighty?.*

ELKINS, KENNETH EARL, minister; b. Athens, Tenn., Sept. 25, 1945; s. Haverd Arthur and Ruby Lee (O'Daniel) E.; m. Naomi Christine Stamper, Sept. 14, 1968; children: Christi, Tonya, Kim, Joseph. BS, Tenn. Wesleyan Coll., 1972; MDiv, So. Bapt. Theol. Sem., 1977. Ordained to ministry So. Bapt. Conv., 1971. Pastor Double Springs Bapt. Ch., Athens, Tenn., 1971-74, Ellers Meml. Bapt. Ch., Harrodsburg, Ky., 1975-79, Cen. Bapt. Ch., Spring City, Tenn., 1982-85, Antioch Bapt. Ch., Athens, 1985-91, Fairfield Glade (Tenn.) Bapt. Ch., 1991—. Lt. USN, 1965-69, 79-81. Recipient Law award Athens Bar Assn., 1974. Mem. McMinn County Bapt. Assn. (moderator 1989-90), Athens Ministerial Assn. (pres. 1988-90),. Home: 1011 Lakewood Dr Fairfield Glade TN 38555 Office: Fairfield Glade Bapt Ch corner Peavine Rd and Lakeview Dr Fairfield Glade TN 38555

ELKINS, RUSSELL ALEXANDER, minister; b. Thomasville, Ga., June 25, 1948; s. Pearce Russell and Voncile (Morgan) E.; m. Deanna Lennand, Nov. 27, 1982; children: Amanda Kay, Brian Russell. BA, Mercer U., 1970; MA, West Ga. Coll., 1972; MDiv, Emory U., 1980, D of Ministry, 1987. Ordained elder, Meth. Ch. Assoc. minister Albany (Ga.) Final United Meth. Ch., 1980-82; minister Blakely (Ga.) Cir. United Meth. Ch., 1982-86; minister/chaplain Cuthbert (Ga.) United Meth. Ch./Andrew Coll., 1986—; trustee Andrew Coll., 1986—. Bd. dirs. Am. Cancer Soc., Cuthbert, 1987—. Mem. Rotary (mem. chmn.). Home: 216 E Loomis Thomasville GA 31792 Office: PO Box 499 Lumpkin St Cuthbert GA 31740

ELLAS, JOHN WAYNE, religious organization administrator; b. Birmingham, Ala., Sept. 5, 1948; s. Roy Franklin and Betty Jean (Hopkins) E.; m. Cherry Lovitt, Nov. 28, 1969; children: Tearsa, Jonathan. BS in Health and Phys. Edn., Northwestern State U., Natchitoches, La., 1970; MS in Teaching, Ga. So. Coll., 1972; MA in Religion, Harding U., Memphis, 1981; D Ministry, Fuller Theol. Sem., Pasadena, Calif., 1987; MDiv, Fuller Theol. Sem., 1988. Ordained to ministry Ch. of Christ, 1978. Min. Dodson (La.) Ch. of Christ, 1978-79, North Baton Rouge Ch. of Christ, 1979-80, Campus View Ch. of Christ, Athens, Ga., 1980-85, SW Cen. Ch. of Christ, Houston, 1985—; grad. asst. instr. Ga. So. Coll., Statesboro, 1971-72; instr. phys. edn., gymnastics coach Jacksonville (Ala.) State U., 1972-74; instr. phys. edn. Tex. A&M U., College Station, 1976-77; adj. instr. ministry Harding U. Grad. Sch. Religion, 1990; lectr. Pepperdine U., Malibu, Calif., 1986, 90, Magnolia Bible Coll., Kosciusko, Miss., 1990; participant religious workshops and seminars. Author: Church Growth through Groups: Strategies for Varying Levels of Christian Community, 1990; also articles. U.S. gymnastic rep. S.Am. Good Will Team, Ecuador, Peru, Brazil, Venezuela, 1968, Cup of Am. Team, Mexico City, 1969, Mid-West Goodwill Team, Turkey, Lebanon, Jordan, Morocco, 1970, Pan Am. Team, Cali, Colombia (gold and bronze medals, 2 silver medals), 1971. Mem. N.Am. Soc. for Ch. Growth (charter). Home: 10806 Normont Dr Houston TX 77070 Office: Ctr for Ch Growth PO Box 691006 Houston TX 77269-1006

ELLENS, J(AY) HAROLD, philosopher, educator, psychotherapist; b. McBain, Mich., July 16, 1932; s. John S. and Grace (Kortmann) E.; m. Mary Jo Lewis, Sept. 7, 1954; children: Debra, Jackie, Dan, Beckie, Rocky, Brenda. AB, Calvin Coll., 1953; BD, Calvin Sem., 1956; ThM, Princeton Sem., 1965; PhD, Wayne State U., 1970; M in Divinity, Calvin Seminary, 1986. Ordained to ministry Christian Reformed Ch., 1956. Pastor Newton (N.J.) Christian Reformed Ch., 1961-65, North Hills Ch., Troy, Mich., 1965-68, Univ. Hills Ch., Farmington Hills, Mich., 1968-78; pvt. practice psychotherapy, Farmington Hills, 1967—; religious broadcaster TV, weekly, 1970-74, periodically to date; lectr. humanities and classics Wayne State U., John Wesley Coll., 1970—; vis. lectr. Princeton U., 1977-79; lectr. U.S. and abroad. Author: Program Format in Religious Television, 1970, Models of Religious Broadcasting, 1974, Chaplain (Major General) Gerhart W. Hyatt: An Oral History, 1977, (with others) Internat. Standard Bible Encyclopedia, 1979-89, Eternal Vigilance, 1980, God's Grace and Human Health, 1982, Life and Laughter, 1983, Psychology in Worship, 1984, (with others) Baker's Encyclopedia of Psychology, 1984, (with others) Psychotherapy in Christian Perspective, 1987, (with others) Christian Counseling and Psychotherapy, 1987, Psychotheology: Key Issues, 1987, Love, Life and Laughter, 1988, (with others) Psychology and Religion, 1988, (with others) The Church and Pastoral Care, 1988, (with others) Moral Obligation and the Military, 1988, (with others) God se genade is genoeg, 1989, (with others) Counseling and the Human Predicament, 1989, (with others) Turning Points in Pastoral Care, (with others) Dictionary of Pastoral Care and Counseling, 1990, three books in Portuguese and one in Spanish; editor: CAPS Internat. Directory vols. II-V, 1976-87, Ethical Reflections, 1977, The Beauty of Holiness, 2d edit., 1985, God's Grace in Free Verse, 1987; editor in chief Jour. Psychology and Christianity, 1975-88; contbr. articles to profl. jours. Served to col. AUS, 1956-61, now Res. Created knight, Queen Juliana, The Netherlands, 1974. Mem. Christian Assn. Psychol. Studies (now exec. dir.), AAUP, Am. Psychol. Assn., Soc. Bibl. Lit., Speech Communication Assn., Mil. Chaplain Assn., Ret. Officers Assn., Archeol. Inst. Am., Am. Personnel and Guidance Assn., Mil. Order World Wars, Am. Sci. Assn., World Assn. Christian Communicators. Home and Office: 26705 Farmington Rd Farmington Hills MI 48334 *Secular and religious communities alike tend continually to shift their focus toward some orthodoxy or other, usually in the form of according ultimate authority to an aspect of the community's traditional thought or behavior, thus imposing constraints upon the quest for growth and for truth which are not responsive to reality or authenticity or relevant and wholesome freedom. Orthodoxy is always, therefore, a form of idolatry; it is a psychological phenomenon; it is the posture of arrogance in those who see themselves as "the chosen" or the elect; it is lunge for security vs. growth; it is designed to guard against the destablizing effect of change; it is, therefore inherently imperialistic, arbitrary, propagandist, and abusive.*

ELLER, RAYMON ERNEST, minister; b. Roanoke County, Va., Mar. 31, 1910; s. Christian Emory and Rebecca Martha (Henry) E.; m. Annabelle Whitmer, June 13,, 1937; children: Rebecca Ann Eller Replogle, Stanley, Jerry, Rufus. AB, Bridgewater Coll., 1937; BD, Bethany Theol. Sem., 1938; postgrad., Gettysburg Theol. Sem., 1949. Ordained to ministry Ch. of the Brethren, 1933, as elder, 1944. Pastor chs. Danville, Va., 1938-40, Bassett, Va., 1940-44, Dundalk, Md., 1944-55, Richmond, Va., 1955-59; pastor chs. Madison Ave Ch., York, Pa., 1959-63, Oakland Ch., Gettysburg, Ohio, 1963-69; pastor chs. 1st Ch., Wichita, Kans., 1969-71, Akron, Ohio, 1971-80; ret., 1980; mem. Akron Met. Interchurch Ministries Bd., 1975—; vice chmn. Campus Ministry Commn., Akron, 1975—; mem. Ea. Md. dist. bd. Ch. of the Brethren, 1948-54, chmn., 1953-54, mem. S.E. regional bd., 1949-56, chmn., 1953-56, mem. standing com. ann. conf., 1943-44; denominational rep. Balt. City Ch. Planning Commn., 1953-55, Wichita State U. Campus Ministry, 1967-69; tour host Mid-East, Europe, Hawaii and Alaska. Author: (hymns) God of the People, Lord of Glory, God of Grace, Table Grace, others; also poetry. Bd. dirs. No. dist. Ohio West View Manor Homes for Aging, 1972—, vice chmn., 1975—. Mem. Akron Ministerial Assn. (sec. 1974—), Denominational Arts and Crafts Assn., Bridgewater Coll. Alumni Assn. (founder, lst pres., Richmond, Dayton, Ohio and Ind. chpts.). Avocations: lapidary, woodworking, gardening, travel, volunteer work. Home: 303 Kohser Ave North Manchester IN 46962 *My philosophy for living: Cast your bread upon the water and it will come back to you with peanut butter on it, and what's in the peanut butter? Golden goodies, energy for the day, excitement in little things; and best of all it will stick to your ribs.*

ELLERBE, CLINTON TODD, minister; b. Big Spring, Tex., Feb. 29, 1964; s. Donald and Mary (Roger) E.; m. Jacqueline Sinclair, July 27, 1985; 1 child, Clinton Todd Jr. Pianist Hilltop Bapt. Ch., Colorado Springs, Colo., 1984-86; organist, pianist Christ Community Ch., Tampa, Fla., 1986-88; min. music Amelia Bapt. Ch., Dade City, Fla., 1988—; dep. clk. Pasco County Courthouse, Dade City, 1988—. Republican. Office: Amelia Bapt Ch 2945 Bellamy Brothers Blvd Dade City FL 33525

ELLERBRAKE, RICHARD PAUL, health care administrator, minister; b. Chgo., Dec. 14, 1933; s. George P. and Wilhelmina M. (Gluth) E.; m. Johann Lee Havenner, June 11, 1957; children—David (dec.), Stephen, Christopher, Laura (dec.). BA, Elmhurst Coll. (Ill.), 1955; BD, Eden Theol. Sem., Webster Groves, Mo., 1958; MHA, Washington U., St. Louis, 1964; DDiv (hon.), Eden Theol. Sem., 1985. Ordained to ministry United Ch. Christ, 1958. Chaplain St. Louis Juvenile Ct., Episcopal City Mission Soc., 1957-58; pastor, dir. Back Bay Mission, Biloxi, Miss., 1958-62; exec. v.p. Deaconess Hosp., St. Louis, 1963-82; pres., chief exec. officer, 1982—; adj. faculty mem. Washington U. Sch. Medicine, St. Louis, 1971—; pres., chief exec. officer Deaconess Health Services Corp., St. Louis, 1982—, Deaconess Manor, St. Louis, 1982—, Deaconess Found., St. Louis, 1982—; dir. Group Health Plan, St. Louis, 1982-85; dir. Cen. East Mo. Profl. Rev. Orgn., St. Louis, 1984-85; pres. Council Health and Human Service Ministries, Lancaster, Pa., 1985-87. Contbr. articles and poetry to profl. jours. Editor denominational ch. monthly jour. Chmn. United Way Health Services Div., St. Louis, 1984; bd. dirs. Mo. Health Plan, Health Services Group. Recipient Merit award Elmhurst Coll., 1982. Mem. Mo. Profl. Liability Ins. Assn. (bd. dirs. 1983—), Am. Protestant Health Assn. (bd. dirs. 1983—), Mo. Hosp. Assn. (bd. dirs. 1983—), Regional Transplant Assn. (bd. dirs. 1977—), Hosp. Assn. Met. St. Louis (bd. dirs. 1985—). Avocations: fishing, camping, gardening. Home: Old Enterprise Farms Ltd Route 2 Lebanon IL 62254 Office: Deaconess Health Services Corp 6150 Oakland Ave Saint Louis MO 63139

ELLINGTON, RONALD EARLE, minister, clinical family therapist; b. Dayton, Ohio, June 26, 1945; s. Claude Earle Ellington and Ruth Annette (Golightly) Rasor; m. Sharon Rose Muse, June 12, 1965; children: Brian, Brent. BA in Psychology, Wright State U., 1969; MDiv, Nazarene Theol. Seminary, Kansas City, Mo., 1972; MS in Counseling Psychology, Northwest Mo. State U., 1990. Ordained to ministry Ch. of the Nazarene, 1975. Pastor Ft. McKinley Ch. of the Nazarene, Dayton, 1972-73; asst. pastor Cen. Ch. of the Nazarene, Dayton, 1973-74; pastor Belpre (Ohio) Ch. of the Nazarene, 1974-76, Hilliard (Ohio) Ch. of the Nazarnee, 1976-80; pastor First Ch. of the Nazarene, St. Joseph, Mo., 1980-84, Hobbs, N.Mex., 1984-87; counselor Guidance Ctr. of Lea County, Hobbs, 1984-85; pastor First Ch. of the Nazarene, Farmington, N.Mex., 1987-91; clin. family therapist Counseling Assocs. Inc., Roswell, N.Mex., 1991—; dist. youth pres. Cen. Ohio Dist., Ch. of the Nazarene, Columbus, 1979-80, Kans. City Dist., 1982-83; chmn. Dist. Bd. Ministerial Studies, Kansas City, 1981-84, sec., Albuquerque, 1990—. Radio coord. Ministerial Assn., Parkersburg, W.Va., 1975-76; chaplain San Juan Regional Med. Ctr., Farmington, 1988-89; mem. Community Violence Prevention Team, Farmington, 1989—; prog. chmn. Breakfast Civitan Club, 1988-89, Knowledge award 1989. Finalist Sr. Sermon award Nazarene Theol. Seminary, 1972. Republican. Avocations: motorcycling, softball, racquetball, music, hiking. Home: 604 E Hermosa Dr Roswell NM 88201-6541 Office: Counseling Assocs Inc PO Box 1978 109 W Bland Roswell NM 88202

ELLIOTT, DARRELL KENNETH, minister, legal researcher; b. Inglewood, Calif., Apr. 19, 1952; s. Lloyd Kenneth and Marjorie (Myers) E. BA, Biola Coll., La Mirada, Calif., 1975; M Div., Talbot Theol. Sem., La Mirada, 1980; cert. in legal assistantship, U. Calif., Irvine, 1986; MS in Taxation, Northrop U., L.A., 1988; postgrad., U. Strasbourg, France, 1979, Western State U., Fullerton, Calif., 1988—, Simon Greenleaf Sch. of Law, 1990—. Ind. legal researcher, businessman Buena Park, Calif., 1970—; Simon Greenleaf U.; rep. Am. Soc. Internat. Law, 1984. Co-founder, assoc. minister Faith Community Ch., Cypress, Calif., 1972; assoc. minister Village Ch., Burbank, Calif., 1978; traveled throughout the country with Campus Crusade for Christ, 1980-81. Calif. State scholar, 1970-75, fellow 1975-80. Mem. Christian Legal Soc., Concerned Women for Am., The Rutherford Inst., Western Ctr. Law and Religious Freedom. Republican. Baptist. Avocations: jogging, tennis, baseball, basketball, volleyball. Home: 7839 Western Ave #B Buena Park CA 90620

ELLIOTT, DARRELL WAYNE, minister; b. Peoria, Ill., Oct. 22, 1955; s. Charles Westley and Sfronia Elizabeth (Powell) E.; m. Vandra Lee Buechler, May 25, 1975; children: Marcy, Jessica, Laca. BA in Theology, N.W. Bible Coll., 1977. Ordained to ministry Ch. of God. Pastor Ch. of God, Mitchell, S.D., 1977-83, Garrison, N.D., 1983—; coach, referee Garrison (N.D.) Pub. Schs., 1986—; farm laborer Farmers Arca-N.D. Orgn., McClean, Mercer Counties, N.D., 1984—; bd. dirs. North Cen. Region Youth, Bismarck, N.D., Dist. Youth and Christian Edn., Beulah Dist.; co-chmn. Gifts from the Heart, Garrison. Pres. Citizens Who Care, Garrison, 1985—; mem. N.D. Leaders, 1989-91. Recipient Children's Friend award, 1980; named one of Outstanding Young Men of Am., 1979. Mem. Fellowship Christian Athletes, Garrison C. of C. Home and Office: PO Box 434 778 Washington Dr NE Garrison ND 58541

ELLIOTT, JAMES BALLINTINE, minister; b. Phila., Mar. 14, 1936; s. James and Clara Elizabeth (Snyder) E.; m. Ruth Virginia Ehly, Mar. 5, 1955;

children: James Gregory, Vicky Lynn. Dipl., Phila. Coll. Bible, 1968; MA, Calif. Grad. Sch. Theology, N.Y. Extension, 1983; DMin, Trinity Theol. Sem., Newburgh, Ind., 1987. Ordained to ministry Bapt. Ch., 1970. Missionary BCM Internat., Upper Darby, Pa., 1968-73; min. youth and evangelism Blackhawk Bapt. Ch., Ft. Wayne, Ind., 1973-77; assoc. pastor Calvary Ch. Souderton, 1977-83; sr. pastor Halethorpe Community Ch., Balt., 1983—. With U.S. Army, 1955-57. Mem. Phila. Coll. Bible Alumni Assn. Office: Halethorpe Community Ch 1312 Francis ave Baltimore MD 21227 *God has taken a nobody and made him a somebody that he might share the Good News of Jesus Christ with anybody. Thank you, Lord.*

ELLIOTT, JAMES HENRY, clergyman; b. Aurora, Ill., Nov. 23, 1936; s. Harold Walter and Ruth (Skeen) E.; m. Lila Mae Ricketts, Dec. 22, 1957; children: Mark, Jeffry, Kathy, Julie. BA, BTh, Aurora U., 1959; MDiv, Garrett-Evang. Theol. Sem., 1961. Ordained to ministry United Ch. of Christ, 1961. Pastor 1st Congl. Ch., Lee Center, Ill., 1959-62, Union Congl. Ch., Gridley, Ill., 1962-64; min. edn. Edgebrook Community Ch., Chgo., 1964-66; pastor North Berwyn (Ill.) Congl. Ch., 1966-71, St. Paul's United Ch. of Christ, Minonk, Ill., 1971-80, St. Paul United Ch. of Christ, Hermann, Mo., 1980—; exec. bd. Ill. Conf. United Ch. of Christ, Hinsdale, 1975-76, chair stewardship com., Ill. Conf. United Ch. of Christ, 1976-79; chair stewardship com. Mo. Conf., 1982-87. Author: Confirmation Manual, 1975, A Tithing Approach, 1976. Bd. dirs. Berwyn Family Svc., 1970-71; chair Interfaith Clergy, Berwyn and Cicero, Ill., 1970-71, Families in Action, Hermann, Mo., 1985-88; chair meals-on-wheels, Fish and Young Ctr., Minonk, Ill., 1977-80; chair chaplain com. MacNeal Hosp., Berwyn, 1970; chaplain Fire Dept., Hermann, Mo., 1981, 84, 87. Republican. Home: 102 Mozart Hermann MO 65041 Office: St Paul United Ch of Christ 136 W 1st St Hermann MO 65041-0162

ELLIOTT, JOHN FRANKLIN, clergyman; b. Neosho, Mo., June 11, 1915; s. William Marion and Charlotte Jeanette (Crump) E.; m. Winifred Margaret Key, July 6, 1939; children: Paul Timothy, Stephen Marion, Andrew Daniel. Student, Maryville Coll., 1933-35; A.B., Austin Coll., 1937; postgrad., Louisville Presbyn. Sem., 1937-38, U. Tenn., 1938, Dallas Theol. Sem., 1939-40; B.D., Columbia Theol. Sem., 1942, M.Div., 1971; D.Litt. (hon.), Internat. Acad., 1954. Ordained to ministry Presbyn. Ch., 1942. Founder Emory Presbyn. Ch., Atlanta, 1941, Wildwood Presbyn. Ch., Salem, Va., 1950; pastor Wylam Presbyn. Ch., Birmingham, Ala., 1942-47, Salem Presbyn. Ch., 1947-51, Calvary Presbyn. Ch. Ind., Ft. Worth, 1952-86; founder, pastor Grace Presbyn. Ch. Ind., Roanoke, Va., 1951-52; dean, dir. Fort Worth Bible Inst., 1952-55; founder, headmaster Colony Christian Sch., Ft. Worth, 1968-86; founder dir. Grace Ministries, Ft. Worth, 1986—; ministerial adviser bd. dirs. Reformed Theol. Sem., Jackson, Miss., 1973-83; chaplain Tex. Constl. Conv., 1974; bd. dirs. Graham Bible Coll., 1966-74, Scripture Memory Fellowship Internat., 1979-84, Messianic Ministry to Israel, Inc., Chattanooga, 1989—; some-time chaplain Dallas Cowboys, Texas Rangers, Kansas City Royals. Bd. dirs., pres. Salem (Va.) Nursing Assn., 1949; charter mem. Fellowship Ind. Evang. Chs., 1951—, pres., 1967, nat. sec., 1971; founder, dir. Ft. Worth Home Bible Classes, 1954—; dir. Spanish Publs., Inc., 1969—; bd. dirs. Ind. Bd. for Presbyn. Home Missions, 1956-74; dist. committeeman Longhorn coun. Boy Scouts Am., Ft. Worth, 1960-66; bd. dirs. Union Gospel Mission, Ft. Worth, 1965-70, pres., 1968; mem. U.S. Coast Guard Aux., Ft. Worth, 1967—; pilot, chaplain, col. CAP, Ft. Worth, 1970-80, chmn. nat. chaplain com., 1979-80, chief of chaplains, 1980-82. Fellow Philos. Soc. Great Britain (Victoria Inst.), Royal Geog. Soc., Huguenot Soc. London, Ft. Worth Club, Ridglea Country Club, Ft. Worth Boat Club, Rotary (pres. 1988-89). Home: 3980 Edgehill Rd Fort Worth TX 76116 Office: Ridglea Bank Bldg 6300 Ridglea Pl Ste 420 Fort Worth TX 76116 *Neither is there salvation in any other: for there is none other Name, under heaven, given among men whereby we must be saved. (Acts 4:12).*

ELLIOTT, JOHN HALL, clergyman, theology educator; b. N.Y.C., Oct. 23, 1935; s. Charles E. and Nietta (Hall) E.; m. Dietlinde M. Kattenstroth, Dec. 28, 1962; children: Mark G., Michael S. BA, Concordia Sem., St. Louis, 1957, BD, MDiv, 1960; ThD, Westfalische Wilhelms U., Munster, 1963. Ordained to ministry Evang. Luth. Ch., 1964. Asst. prof. theology Concordia Sem., St. Louis, 1963-67; prof. theology U. San Francisco, 1967—; vis. prof. Pontifical Bibl. Inst., Rome, 1978, Notre Dame. U., South Bend, Ind., 1981; adj. prof. Grad. Theol. Union, Berkeley, Calif., 1977—; exec. bd. St. Louis Conf. on Religion and Race, 1965-67. Author: The Elect and the Holy, 1966, A Home for the Homeless, 1981, I-II Peter/Jude, 1982; author, editor: Social-Scientific Criticism of the New Testament, 1986; mem. editorial bd. Abingdon New Testament Commentary Series, 1987—. Bd. dirs. Pacific Luth. Theol. Sem., Berkeley, 1988—. Concordia Sem. rsch. grantee, St. Louis, 1965, Luth. World Fedn. exch. scholar, Geneva, 1977-78, Am. Coun. Learned Socs. travel grantee, 1981, NEH summer stipendiary, 1991. Mem. Cath Bibl. Assn. Am. (exec. bd. 1971-73, 86-88, vis. scholar 1978), Soc. Bibl. Lit. (pres. Pacific Coast region 1982-83), Studiorum Novi Testamenti Societas, The Context Group (chair). Lutheran. Home: 819 Calmar Ave Oakland CA 94610 Office: U San Francisco Ignatian Heights San Francisco CA 94117

ELLIOTT, RALPH H., educator; b. Danville, Va., Mar. 2, 1925; s. Earl A. and Consuela (Arnn) E.; m. Virginia Ellen Case, Oct. 14, 1945; children: Virginia Lee, Beverly A. AB, Carson Newman Coll., 1949; BD, Southern Bapt. Theol. Sem., 1952, ThD, 1956; LHD (hon.), Cen. Philippines U., 1987; DD (hon.), Alderson Broaddus Coll., 1989. Ordained to ministry Bapt. Ch., 1945. Prof. Old Testament Crozer-Midwestern Southern Bapt. Sems., 1956-64; sr. pastor Emmanuel Bapt. Ch., Albany, N.Y., 1964-71, 1st Bapt. Ch., White Plains, N.Y., 1971-77, North Shore Bapt. Ch., Chgo., 1977-89; v.p. acad. life, dean of faculty Colgate Rochester Div. Sch., Rochester, N.Y., 1989—; trustee, U. Chgo. Div. Sch., 1978—. Author: The Message of Genesis, 1961, Reconciliation and the New Age, 1973, Church Growth that Counts, 1982; contbr. articles to profl. jours. Mem. Internat. Bonhoeffer Soc. Home: 41 Waterford Circle Rochester NY 14618 Office: Colgate Rochester Div Sch 1100 S Goodman Rochester NY 14620

ELLIOTT, RICHARD HAROLD, minister; b. Pitts., June 1, 1953; s. John Edward Elliott and Shirley J. (Pfiester) Morgan; m. Jane R.M. Miley, June 11, 1977; 1 child, Jennifer D. BA, Thiel Coll., 1975; DivM, Luth. Sem., Gettysburg, Pa., 1979; STM, Luth. Theol. Sem., Phila., 1985. Ordained to ministry Lutheran Ch., 1981. Asst. pastor Trinity Luth. Ch., Lansdale, Pa., 1979-81; pastor Luther Meml. Luth. Ch., Blacksburg, Va., 1981-87; pastor, developer div. for mission in N.Am. Luth. Ch. in Am., Prince William County, Va., 1987-90; pastor St. James Luth. Ch., Wheeling, W.Va., 1990—; mem. Council for Luth. Theol. Edn. in the North East, Gettysburg, Pa., 1977-79, New River (Va.) Area Strategy Team, 1983-85; vice pastor Christ Luth. Ch., Radford, Va., 1982-83; dean New River Area Luth. Ch. Am., Blacksburg, 1983-87. Contbr. articles to newspapers, 1984-86. Chaplain Montgomery Regional Hosp., Blacksburg, Va., 1981-87; active Nat. Cancer Soc., Lansdale, Pa., 1980-81, North Pa. Hosp., Lansdale, 1987; mem. human services comm. City of Montgomery, 1986-87, Pa. Synod Youth Com., 1980-81, Va. Synod Lay Ministry Task Force, 1981-83; program chairperson Campus Ministry Program, West Liberty State U., 1989. Named one of Outstanding Young Men in Am., 1985; recipient scholarship Bradley Thiel, 1973, Luth. Brotherhood, 1979-85. Mem. New River Area Pastors (dean 1983-87), Blacksburg Ministerium (pres. 1983-84, v.p. 1982-83), Wheeling Clergy Coun. (treas. 1990). Democrat. Lodge: Kiwanis. Avocations: jogging, reading, weightlifting, racquetball. Office: St James Luth Ch 1409 Chapline St Wheeling WV 26003

ELLIOTT, RONALD DEAN, minister; b. Independence, Mo., Mar. 27, 1953; s. Morris Hayden and Lucille (Forman) E.; m. Deborah Ann Boehner, Dec. 30, 1977; children: Rachael Ann, Lydia Marie, Jeremiah Dean, Elizabeth Ann. BA, William Jewell Coll., Liberty, Mo., 1975; MDiv, Midwestern Sem., Kansas City, Mo., 1978. Ordained to ministry So. Bapt. Conv., 1975. Youth pastor Spring Valley Bapt. Ch., Raytown, Mo., 1977-80; assoc. pastor Southview Bapt. Ch., Lincoln, Nebr., 1981-83; pastor Calvary Bapt. Ch., Lincoln, Nebr., 1983-90, Layton Hills Bapt. Ch., Layton, Utah, 1990—; exec. bd. Kans. Nebr. Conv. So. Bapts., Topeka, 1987-89, Nebr. Coun. Alcohol and Drug Edn., Lincoln, 1987-90, Ea. Nebr. Bapt. Assn., Omaha, 1983-90. Chaplain Lincoln Police Dept., 1986-90, Boy Scouts Am., Lincoln, 1986-88; del. Lancaster County Rep. Party, 1988. Home: 1076 E 1200 N Layton UT 84040 Office: Layton Hills Bapt Ch 1332 N Hill Field Rd Layton UT 84041 *I have observed that it is only in understanding those things which are eternal that true meaning is found in the temporal.*

ELLIOTT, SUE, clergywoman; b. Dodge City, Kans., July 14, 1941; d. James William and Mary Louise (Pollock) Pickle; m. Frederick Lewis Moore, May 1, 1966 (div. 1979); children: Polly Marie, Frederick William; m. Keith R. Elliott, Nov. 4, 1988. BS, Millikin U., 1978; postgrad., U. Ill., 1978-79; MDiv, Luth. Theol. Sem., 1984. Ordained to ministry Luth. Ch., 1983. Pastor, St. Mark's Luth. Ch., Snydersburg, Md., 1982-86, St. Paul's Luth. Ch., Glasco, Kans., 1986-89; on leave, 1989— ; resident rural ministry Town and Country Ch. Inst., Gettysburg, Pa., 1983-84; chair World Hunger Task Force, Md. Synod, Luth. Ch. Am.; organizer, dir. Joyful Noise handbell choir, Snydersburg, Md., 1985-86, Snydersburg Food, Clothing, Emergency Assistance Bank, 1984-86; community service supr. Carroll County Ct. System, 1983-86; pres. Glasco Ministerial Devel. Youth Assn. Activities Ctr., Glasco, 1981-87. Emergency med. technician Glasco Ambulance Service, 1987 (cert. Kans. 1987, Glasco Ambulance Svc. 1986—, Nat. Heart Assn. CPR Inst. 1989). Recipient Millikin Dames award, Milliken U., 1978; Simon P. Eckard fellow, Gettysburg Sem. Home: PO Box 85 Glasco KS 67445 Office: St. Paul's Lutheran Ch PO Box 187 Glasco KS 67445 *We used to educate our youth to become wise, thoughtful discerning members of the community—good citizens. That was our noble dream and goal. We now educate them to get high-paying jobs. If we sow what is reaped, what harvest will those seeds produce?.*

ELLIOTT, WILLIAM EDWARD, theology educator; b. Chgo., July 9, 1942; s. Harold Guinn and Dorothy Virginia (Jilek) E.; m. Diane Katherine Brown, Oct. 17, 1964; children—David Brian, Michael Scott. B.A., Ripon Coll., 1964; B.D., San Francisco Theol. Sem., 1969, Th.M., 1971; Th.D., Grace Theol. Sem., 1981. Instr. theology Western Bapt. Coll., Salem, Oreg., 1973-75, asst. prof., 1975-78, assoc. prof., 1978-82, prof., 1982-87; prof. Dept. Gen. Sci., Oreg. State U., Corvallis, 1987—. Mem. Evangelical Theol. Assn. Republican. Baptist. Office: Oreg State U Dept Gen Sci Corvallis OR 97313

ELLIS, DONALD LLEWELLYN, retired minister; b. Crawfordsville, Ind., May 20, 1926; s. Frank M. and Bessie Retta (Llewellyn) E.; m. Ellen Elizabeth Coots, July 27, 1949; children: Dane Llewellyn, Annabeth Dee Lasky, Tonda Lee, Rebekah (dec.). Student, Purdue U., 1943-44; BSCE, Case Western Res. U., 1946; BD, Andover Newton Theol. Sch., 1956; postgrad., Ecole Coloniale, Brussels, 1957-58. Ordained to ministry Bapt. Ch., 1953. Civil engr. N.Y. Cen. R.R. Co., Indianapolis, 1948-50; pastor 1st Bapt. Ch., Methuen, Mass., 1950-56; missionary Am. Bapt. Fgn. Mission Soc., Sona Mpangu, Zaire, 1956-61; minister of mission Am. Bapt. Chs. of Mass., Boston, 1962-71; assoc. fund dir. Am. Bapts. Fund of Renewal, Valley Forge, Pa., 1971-78; dir. ch. rels. Andover Newton Theol. Sch., Newton Centre, Mass., 1978-81; dir. mission interpretation Am. Bapt. Chs. of Vt. and N.H., Hartland, Vt., 1981-88. Corporator Malden (Mass.) Hosp., 1965-82; pres. Methuen Christian League, 1955; v.p. Upper Valley Habitat for Humanity, 1989-90, pres., 1990—. With USN, 1943-47. Mem. Am. Bapt. Ministers Coun. Democrat. Avocations: photography, videotaping, travel. Home: PO Box 367 Hartland VT 05048

ELLIS, EDGAR HEB, JR., minister; b. Columbia, S.C., July 20, 1935; s. Edgar Heb Sr. and Eleanor Grace (Collins) E.; m. Iris Loraine Clardy, June 17, 1956; 1 child, Patricia Loraine. AA, Spartanburg (S.C.) Jr. Coll., 1956; BA, St. Andrews Presbyn. Coll., Laurinburg, N.C., 1964; M in Theology, Duke U., 1967; D in Ministry, McCormick Theol. Sem., 1986. Ordained to ministry United Meth. Ch. as deacon, 1965, as elder, 1967. Min. Blenheim (S.C.) Cir. United Meth. Ch., 1961-64, Leas Chapel-Warrens Grove United Meth. Ch., Roxboro, N.C., 1964-67, Laurel Bay United Meth. Ch., Beaufort, S.C., 1967-68, Bethel Meth. Ch., Spartanburg, 1968-72, Triune Meth. Ch., Greenville, S.C., 1972-75, Simpsonville (S.C.) United Meth. Ch., 1975-80, Woodland United Meth. Ch., Rock Hill, S.C., 1980-86, 1st United Meth. Ch., Bennettsville, S.C., 1986-89; sr. min. United Meth. Ch., Summerville, S.C., 1989—. Author: Growing Roses Can Be Fun, 1982. Pres. Greenville Rose Soc., 1975. With USAF, 1957-58. Mem. Civitans (bd. dirs. Spartanburg chpt. 1969-72, chaplain 1970-72, Disting. Svc. award 1970), Am. Rose Soc. (judge 1974-87), Rotary (pres. Simpsonville chpt. 1980). Republican. Home: 106 W 3d St S Summerville SC 29483 Office: Bethany United Meth Ch 118 W Third St S Summerville SC 29483

ELLIS, GORDON ELON, minister; b. Montague, Mass., Nov. 5, 1950; s. Frederick Elon and Helen Elizabeth (Ockle) E.; m. Diane Marie Deane, Aug. 11, 1973; children: Ryan Deane, Lyndsey Deane. BA, Springfield (Mass.) Coll., 1973; MDiv, Yale U., 1976; DMin, Hartford (Conn.) Sem., 1989. Ordained to ministry Congl. Ch., 1976. Asst. minister First Congregational Ch., West Haven, Conn., 1974-76; assoc. minister First Congregational Ch., Wallingford, Conn., 1976-79; sr. minister Seekonk (Mass.) Congregational Ch., 1979-90, First Congregational Ch., Southington, Conn., 1990—. Author: New Beginnings: Preparing Families for Remarriage in the Church, 1991; contbr. articles to profl. jours. Bd. dirs. Wallingford (Conn.) Community Food Bank, 1976-79, Big Bros./Big Sisters Wallingford, 1977-79, Southington YMCA, 1991; chmn. Wallingford Fuel Crisis Intervention Com., 1977-79; mem. grievance com. Seekonk Housing Authority, 1985-90; mem. Conn. Statewide Emergency Food Coun., Hartford, 1977-79. Mem. R.I. Conf. United Ch. of Christ Ministers Assn. Home: 251 Thistle Ln Southington CT 06489 Office: First Congregational Ch 37 Main St Southington CT 06489

ELLIS, HOWARD WOODROW, creative agent, evangelist, clergyman, artist, author; b. Linton, Ind., Feb. 19, 1914; s. Lee and Effie (Walraven) E.; m. Susanna Goldsmith, Aug. 27, 1942; children: Patricia Sue Ellis Beebe, Mary Lou Ellis Bordwell. Student, Art Inst. Chgo., 1944-45, Am. Art Acad., 1945-46; AB, U. Evansville, 1943, HHD hon., 1962; BD, Garrett Bibl. Inst., 1946; postgrad., Peabody Coll., 1959-60, U. Tenn.-Nashville. Ordained to ministry United Methodist Ch., 1943. Mem. nat. staff Gen. Bd. Evangelism, Meth. Ch., Nashville, 1946-66; assoc. Central Avenue Meth. Ch., Indpls., 1966-68, Main Street United Meth. Ch., Boonville, Ind., 1968-74, Wall Street United Meth. Ch., Jeffersonville, Ind., 1974-78, Gobin United Meth. Ch., 1978-79; condr. evangelist missions to Sweden, Norway, Denmark, Finland, 1957, 59, 82, Mex., 1961, 65, 87, Korea, 1961, Gt. Britain, 1982, India, 1984, also throughout U.S. Exhibited in one-man travelling exhbn., 1973; group shows include, Nashville Fine Arts Festival, 1959, 60, 61, Tenn. State Fair, Nashville, 1959-66, painting in group shows, Smithsonian Instn., Washington, 1960, U. Evansville, Ind., 1960, Ewha U., Seoul, 1962, Inst. Mexican-Am. Cultural Relations, Mexico City, 1962, Nat. Convocation Meth. Youth, Purdue U., West Layayette, Ind., 1964, retrospective show North United Meth. Ch., Indpls., 1967, represented in numerous permanent collections including U. Evansville, Upper Room Mus., Nashville; author: Sallman Interpretations, 1944, The Witnessing Fellowship, 1961, Evangelism for Teen-Agers, 1958, rev. edit., 1966, The Last Supper, 1963; (with T. McEachern) Youth Evangelism, New Reflections, The Marks of the Christian, A Study of the Beatitudes,Christian Lit. Soc., India, 1987; (latest books) Guidebook for Celebrating the Advent Story, Sourcebook for Celebrating the Nativity Story, Guidebook for Reliving the Passion Story Day by Day, Sourcebook for O Jerusalem, How Often, 1990; author, illustrator: How to Draw and Speak, 1961, He Took the Cup, 1961. Recipient Denman Evangelism award, 1984. Mem. Rotary.

ELLIS, JOHN TRACY, clergyman, educator; b. Seneca, Ill., July 30, 1905; s. Elmer Lucian and Ida Cecilia (Murphy) E. A.B., St. Viator Coll., 1927; A.M., Cath. U. Am., 1928, Ph.D., 1930, Litt.D. (hon.), 1978; student, Sulpician Sem., Washington, 1934-38; D.H.L., Mt. Mary Coll., 1954; LL.D., U. Notre Dame, 1957, Belmont Abbey Coll., 1960, Fordham U., 1972, U. So. Calif., 1983, St. Anselm Coll., 1985, Manhattan Coll., 1985; Litt.D. (hon.), Loyola Coll., Balt., 1960, U. Portland, 1969, U. Fla., 1973, Marquette U., 1974, St. Vincent Coll., 1979; LHD (hon.), Mt. St. Mary's Coll., Emmitsburg, Md., 1989. Ordained priest Roman Catholic Ch., 1938; prof. history St. Viator Coll., 1930-32, Coll. St. Teresa, 1932-34; instr. history Cath. U. Am., 1938-41, asst. prof., 1941-43, asso. prof., 1943-47, prof. ch. history, 1947-64, vis. prof., 1976—; prof. ch. history U. San Francisco, 1964-76; professorial lectr. ch. history Cath. U. Am., 1977—; vis. prof. Brown U., 1967, U. Notre Dame, 1970, Grad. Theol. Union, Berkeley, Calif., 1970-71, Gregorian U., Rome, Italy, 1974-75, Angelicum U., Rome, 1976; cons. com. for observance bicentennial Nat. Conf. Cath. Bishops, 1973-76. Author: Anti-Papal Legislation in Mediaeval England, 1066-1377, 1930, Cardinal Consalvi and Anglo-Papal Relations, 1814-1824, 1942, The Formative Years of the Catholic University of America, 1946, The Life of James Cardinal Gibbons, Archbishop of Baltimore, 1834-1921, 2 vols, 1952, American Catholicism, 1956, rev. edit., 1969, Documents of American Catholic History, 1956, rev. edit., 1962, 67, American Catholics and the Intellectual Life, 1956, A Guide to American Catholic History, 1959, John Lancaster Spalding, First Bishop of Peoria, American Educator, 1962, Perspectives in American Catholicism, 1963, Catholics in Colonial America, 1965, A Commitment to Truth, 1966, Essays in Seminary Education, 1967, Faith and Learning: A Church Historian's Story, 1988; editor, contbr.: The Catholic Priest in the United States: Historical Investigations, 1971, Catholic Bishops: A Memoir, 1983; mng. editor Cath. Hist. Rev., 1941-63; adv. editor, 1963—. Domestic prelate of Pope Pius XII, 1955; recipient John Gilmary Shea prize, 1956; Golden Jubilee medal St. Mary's Dominican Coll., New Orleans, 1960; Campion award Catholic Book Club, 1965; Bene Merenti medal Cath. U. Am., 1961; Research and Scholarship award Alumni Assn. Cath. U. Am., 1969; Laetare medal, 1978. Fellow Am. Benedictine Acad. (1969); Mem. Am. Cath. Hist. Assn. (pres. 1969), Am. Soc. Ch. History (pres. 1969), Phi Beta Kappa (hon.), Delta Epsilon Sigma (hon.), Phi Alpha Theta (hon.). Office: Catholic U Am Washington DC 20064

ELLIS, MALCOLM EUGENE, religion educator, minister; b. Greer, S.C., Oct. 15, 1929; s. Edward S. and Gertrude (Bridwell) E.; m. Virgie McCoy, Nov. 30, 1953 (de. 1969); children: David Malcolm, Deborah Sweat; m. Lois Sheridan, July 31, 1971. AB, Ind. Wesleyan U., 1952; MA, Butler U., 1954, Temple U., 1974; EdD, Ind. U., 1978. Ordained minister in Wesleyan Ch., 1953. Missionary The Wesleyan Ch., Sierra Leone, 1954-64; minister The Wesleyan Ch., Indpls., 1953—; asst. prof. philosophy and religion Houghton (N.Y.) Coll., 1969-71, Taylor U., Upland, Ind., 1971-77; prof. philosophy and religion Ind. Wesleyan U., Marion, 1978—. Author: Wesleyan Mission in Sierra Leone, 1954, Needs of International Students at Major Universities, 1978. Mem. Am. Acad. Religion, Tchrs. of Philosophy, Phi Delta Kappa. Home: 1455 Sylvan Dr Marion IN 46953 Office: Ind Wesleyan U 4201 S Washington St Marion IN 46953

ELLIS, BROTHER PATRICK (H. J. ELLIS), academic administrator; b. Balt., Nov. 17, 1928; s. Harry James and Elizabeth Alida (Evert) E. AB, Cath. U. Am., Washington, 1951; AM, U. Pa., 1954, PhD, 1960; postgrad., Barry Coll., 1963-64, Inst. Catholique, Paris, 1958; LHD (hon.), Assumption Coll., 1982; HHD (hon.), King's Coll., 1987; LLD (hon.), U. Scranton, 1988. Joined Bros. of Christian Schs., Roman Cath. Ch., 1946. Tchr. English dept. West Cath. High Sch. for Boys, Phila., 1951-60; chmn. English dept. West Cath. High Sch. for Boys, 1956-58, guidance dir., 1959-60; dir. practice teaching, sch. prin. St. Gabriel's Hall, Phoenixville, Pa., summers 1960-61, 65-66; asst. prof. English La Salle U., Phila., 1960-62; assoc. prof. La Salle U., 1968-73, prof., 1973—, dir. housing, 1961-62, dir. honors program, 1964-69, dir. devel., v.p., 1969-76, pres., 1977—; prin. La Salle High Sch., Miami, Fla., 1962-64. Condr.: series for How To Read Gt. Books, U. of the Air, WFIL-TV, Phila., 1961, 65; Contbr. articles to profl. publs. Trustee Manhattan Coll., N.Y.C., St. John's High Sch., Washington, St. Mary's Coll., Calif., St. Mary's Coll., Minn., Phila., 1981-84; bd. dirs. Roman Cath. Diocesan Coun. Mgrs., Phila., 1980-86, Phila. Cath. Charities, 1986—, Greater Phila. Urban Coalition, Police Athletic League, Phila., Free Libr. Phila., 1990—, Delaware Valley Citizens' Crime Commn.; former trustee Community Leadership Seminars, Better Bus. Bur. Recipient Lindback award for disting. teaching LaSalle Coll., Phila., 1965. Mem. Pa. Bar Assn. (com. on professionalism), Coun. on Fgn. Rels., Pa. Assn. Colls. and Univs. (past chmn.), Am. Coun. on Edn., Assn. Cath. Colls. and Univs. (past chmn.), Archdiocesan Adv. Com. on Renewal, Phi Beta Kappa. Clubs: Union League, Sunday Breakfast (Phila.), Phila. Home and Office: La Salle U 20th and Olney Ave Philadelphia PA 19141

ELLIS, RAY WENDEL, religious organization administrator; b. Salina, Kans., Dec. 5, 1938; s. Clarence Raymond and Willma Ursula (Keith) E.; m. Carollyn Jean Reid, Aug. 22, 1960; children: Timothy, Wendel, Annette, Janette. AA, Cen. Coll., 1958; BA, Greenville Coll., 1960; MDiv, Asburg Theol. Sem., 1963, D of Ministry, 1980. Ordained to ministry Free Meth. Ch., 1962; cert. ch. growth cons. Pastor Aldersgate Free Meth. Ch., Kansas City, Kans., 1963-68; founding pastor Taylor (Mich.) Free Meth. Ch., 1968-80; conf. supt. Fla. Conf. Free Meth. Ch., St. Petersburg, Fla., 1980-88; dir. evangelism Free Meth. Ch. N.Am., Indpls., 1988—; bd. dirs. Light and Life Internat., Coun. on Ethnic Affairs. Author: Strategizing for New Churches, 1989, Churches Planting Churches, 1990, Great Commission Growth Manual, 1991. Mem. Nat. Assn. Evangelists (bd. dirs. Home Missions), N.Am. Soc. Ch. Growth, Comm. on Evangelism (dir. 1988—). Office: Free Methodist Ch NAm PO Box 535002 Indianapolis IN 46253-5002

ELLIS, REID DUANE, minister; b. Esterville, Iowa, Sept. 13, 1962; s. Junior Harold and Elaine Julia (Linde) E.; m. JoAnn LaRea Masters, Aug. 11, 1984. BS in Pastoral Studies, North Cen. Bible Coll., 1985. Ordained to ministry Assemblies of God, 1988. Youth min. Detroit Lakes (Minn.) Assembly of God Ch., 1985-89; youth, evangelism min. 1st Assembly of God Ch., Marysville, Wash., 1989—. Home: 8830 67th Ave NE Apt # 2 Marysville WA 98270 Office: Marysville 1st Assembly God Ch 4705 Grove St NE Marysville WA 98270 *Knowledge is applied to one's mind by the acquiring of facts. Wisdom is applying those facts to the changing to the depths of one's heart. We must let God change our heart through applying Biblical wisdom.*

ELLIS, TERENCE BRUCE, minister; b. Mission, Tex., Feb. 13, 1958; s. William B. and Dorothy Lee (Hodgen) E.; m. Leslie Lee Buckler, May 16, 1981; 1 child, Lauren Elizabeth. BA, U. Ky., 1980; MDiv, New Orleans Bapt. Sem., 1983, ThD, 1987. Ordained to ministry Bapt. Ch., 1982. Minister of youth Bluff Creek (La.) Bapt. Ch., 1981; pastor Berwick Bapt. Ch., Liberty, Miss., 1982-87, Goodwood Bapt. Ch., Baton Rouge, 1987-90, Mulberry Bapt. Ch., Houma, La., 1990—. Contbr. articles to religious periodicals. Mem. adv. coun. Goodwood Elem. Sch., Baton Rouge, 1988-90. Mem. Am. Acad. Religion, Soc. Bibl. Lit., Rotary. Republican. Office: Mulberry Bapt Ch 2025 Bayou Black Dr Houma LA 70360

ELLIS, WALTER LEON, minister; b. McKinney, Tex., Oct. 22, 1941; s. Erwin Ballard and Mary Edra (Bray) E.; m. Susan Elizabeth Elder, Nov. 23, 1960; children: Bruce Walter, David Anthony, Patrick Durward. BA, U. North Tex., 1964, MA, 1966; MDiv, Va. Sem., 1977. Ordained to ministry Episc. Ch., 1977. Vicar St. Michael & All Angels', Longview, Tex., 1977-79, St. Mark's, Gladewater, Tex., 1977-79; rector St. Michael & All Angel's, Longview, 1979-82, St. Christopher, League City, Tex., 1982—; dean Galveston Convocation, League City, 1989—; trustee Baytown, Tex., 1983-84, 90—, Camp Allen, Navasota, Tex., 1987-90, Bishop Quin Found. Houston, 1991—. Contbr. articles to profl. jours. Bd. dirs. pres. Parents Anonymous, Longview, 1980; mem. exec. bd. Bay Area coun. Boy Scouts Am., Tex., 1983-86; pres. Rotary Club, League City, 1989-90. Paul Harris fellow Space Ctr. Rotary Club, Houston, 1989. Mem. League City Ministers' Assn. (v.p. 1989—), Clear Lake Ministerial Alliance, Brotherhood of St. Andrew. Home: 18619 Prince William Nassau Bay TX 77058 Office: St Christopher Episc Ch 2100 Saint Christopher Rd League City TX 77574 *You have been blessed by God through others. Find something you admire in each person you meet. Then bless those persons by telling them what you admire in them.*

ELLIS, WILLIAM FRANKLIN, minister; b. Shelbyville, Ky., Nov. 11, 1964; s. William Elliot and Charlotte Frances (Rohrer) E.; m. Elizabeth Ann Cummins, Aug. 16, 1986; 1 child, William Jordan Ellis. BS, Eastern Ky. Univ., 1986; MDiv, So. Bapt. Theol. Seminary, Louisville, 1989. Minister of youth/music Buck Grove Bapt. Ch., Ekron, Ky., 1987-90; minister of edn./youth First Bapt. Ch., Williamsburg, Ky., 1990—; pastor adv. com. Cumberland Coll., Williamsburg, 1990—. Mem. Ky. Bapt. Youth Minister Assn. (pres. 1990-91), Ky. Bapt. Religious Educators Assn., Ky. Bapt. Recreators Assn. Office: First Baptist Church 230 S 5th St Williamsburg KY 40769

ELLIS, WILLIAM HOMER, JR., lay worker, lawyer; b. Springfield, Mo., Feb. 15, 1932; s. William Homer Sr. and Amy Alice (Rikard) E.; m. Beverly B. Woodruff, July 28, 1962; children: Allison Ellis Baker, Nathan Woodruff. BA, Yale U., 1954; JD, Stanford U., 1957. Bar: Wash. 1958. Bd. dirs. Christian Legal Soc., Annandale, Va., 1962—, nat. pres., 1971-73; bd. fellows

Seattle Pacific U., 1985-89; bd. dirs. Evangelize China Fellowship, Monterery Park, Calif., 1987—; ptnr. Ellis & Li, Seattle, 1985—. State rep. Wash. House of Reps, Olympia, 1979-82; chmn. House Judicary Com., Olympia, 1981-82; mem. Wash. State Statute Law Com., 1971-91; bd. dirs. Western Bapt. Conservative Sem., Portland, Oreg., 1988—. Mem. Wash. Athletic Club. Republican. Home: 3527 N E 100th Seattle WA 98125 Office: Ellis & Li 3700 First Interstate Ctr Seattle WA 98104

ELLISON, CRAIG WILLIAM, psychology and urban studies educator, administrator, counselor; b. Springfield, Mass., Aug. 21, 1944; s. William Craig and Marilyn A. (Otto) E.; m. Sharon Roberta Andre, Sept. 20, 1969; children—Scott, Timothy, Jonathan. B.A., The King's Coll., 1966; M.A., Wayne State U., 1969, Ph.D. in Social Devel. Psychology, 1972. Program coordinator MacGregor Meml., Conf. Ctr., Wayne State U., Detroit, 1969-70; asst. prof. Westmont Coll. (Calif.), 1971-76, assoc. prof. psychology, 1977-78, dir. summer sessions, 1977, 78, dir. interterm, 1977-78; vis. prof. SUNY-Binghamton, 1973; prof. psychology and urban studies, chmn. dept. psychology, dir. summer inst. urban missions, adminstr. Simpson Community Counseling Ctr., Simpson Coll., San Francisco, 1978-83; prof. urban studies and psychology Alliance Theol. Sem.-Nyack (N.Y.) Coll., 1983—; bd. dirs., founder, mem. adv. council Family Research Council of Am., 1981—; western regional dir. Christian Assn. Psychol. Studies, 1973-83; cons. in urbanology Christian and Missionary Alliance, 1979-86, World Vision, 1982-84, Intervarsity, 1982-83, Evang. Presbyn. Ch., 1986. Author: The Urban Mission, 1974, 2d edit., 1983, Self-Esteem, 1976, Modifying Man: Implications and Ethics, 1978, Your Better Self, 1983, Saying Goodbye to Loneliness and Finding Intimacy, 1983, Healing for the City: Counseling for the Urban Context, 1991; host Perspective on Personal Living, nationwide radio broadcast, 1981—; series editor Urban Ministry Resource Series, Zondervan, 1990—; developer Spiritual Well-Being Scale; contbg. editor Jour. Psychology and Theology, 1989—; contbr. articles to profl. jours. Active Common Cause, 1972—, Fairmede Alliance Ch., 1978-83. Mem. Simpson Meml. Ch., 1983—. Mem. Am. Psychol. Assn., Am. Sci. Affiliation, Christian Assn. Psychol. Studies (Disting. Mem. award 1986), Soc. Psychol. Study Social Issues. Office: Alliance Theol Sem Nyack Coll Nyack NY 10960 *Choice is the most powerful dynamic in human life. As people are enabled to see that they have inner choice they are liberated and healed, in spite of external conditions which would oppress them.*

ELLISON, DAVID MORRIS, music director; b. Vermillion, S.D., Jan. 23, 1951; s. Morris Eli and Edith Margaret Lorraine (Zetterlund) E.; m. Cynthia Lee Kuehl, Dec. 23, 1979; children: Kjersti Noelle, Alexandra Nicole, Lindsay Elise, Annika Leigh. BMEd, Tex. Luth. Coll., 1973; MM, U. S.D., 1979; postgrad., U. Iowa, summers 1975,90, 91. Organist St. Peter Luth. Ch., Burbank, S.D., 1973-75, First English Luth. Ch., Lennox, S.D., 1975-78; youth dir. Trinity Luth. Ch., Vermillion, S.D., 1978-81, dir. music, organist, 1978-85; dir. music, organist First Luth. Ch., Brookings, S.D., 1985—; del. Constituting Conv. of Luth. Men in Mission, Seguin, 1988; pres. steering com. Constituting Conv. of S.D. Synod Luth. Men of Mission, Sioux Falls, 1988-89, mem. worship com., 1986—, sec. 1989-91, pres., 1991—. Arranger music for handbell and voice choir. Mem. S.D. Centennial Com. for Brookings, 1988-89; pres. Brookings Area Arts Coun., 1988-90, Rejoining Com. for Brookings Art Coun. and Community Cultural Coun., 1989-90; bd. dirs. Brookings Community Cultural Arts Coun., 1990-91. Named Outstanding Young Religious Leader, Brookings Jaycees, 1988, S.D. Jaycees, 1988. Mem. Am. Choral Dirs. Assn., Am. Guild Organists, Assn. Luth. Ch. Musicians, Choristers Guild, Am. Guild of English Handbell Ringers, Lions (bd. dirs. 1988-90). Republican. Office: First Luth Ch Box 300 8th and Main St Brookings SD 57006

ELLISON, JOHN, bishop. Bishop of Paraguay The Anglican Communion, Asuncion. Office: Iglesia Angelicana, Casilla 1124, Asunción Paraguay*

ELLOR, JAMES W., human services administrator; b. Abington, Pa., Apr. 23, 1951; s. John B. and Marjorie T. Sean (Hooper) E.; m. Janet R. Ellor, Jan. 3, 1981; children: Elizabeth Marie, Margaret Ann. BA, Kent State U., 1973; MDiv, McCormick Theol. Sem., 1978; MSW, U. Chgo., 1976; D Ministry, Chgo. Theol. Sem., 1985. Cert. social worker, Ill.; clin. dimplomate social work. Med. social worker Prebyn. St. Luke's Med. Ctr., Chgo., Augustana Hosp., Chgo.; chair dept. human svcs. Nat. Coll. Edn., Lombard, Ill.; rsch. assoc. U. Chgo. Contbr. numerous articles to profl. jours.; talk show host Nat TV.; presenter workshops nat. conf. Faculty fellow U. Chgo.; Retirement Rsch. Found. grantee. Mem. Gerontol. Soc. Am. (mem. com.), NASW, Nat. Assn. Christians in Social Work (chpt. pres.), Am. Soc. on Aging, Mid-Am. Congress on Aging (chair com.).

ELLSBERG, ROBERT BOYD, religious press editor; b. Jacksonville, N.C., Dec. 13, 1955; s. Daniel Ellsberg and Carol Cummings; m. Margaret Rizza, June 2, 1984; 1 child, Nicholas Boyd. BA, Harvard U., 1982. Mng. editor Cath. Worker, N.Y.C., 1976-78; teaching fellow Harvard U. Div. Sch., Cambridge, Mass., 1984-87; editor in chief Orbis Books, Maryknoll, N.Y., 1987—. Editor: By Little and By Little: Selected Writings of Dorothy Day, 1983, Gandhi on Christianity, 1991; co-editor: The Logic of Solidarity, 1989. Recipient Christopher award, 1984; Sheldon fellow Harvard Coll., 1982. Mem. Phi Beta Kappa. Roman Catholic. Office: Orbis Books Maryknoll NY 10545

ELLWANGER, JOHN P(AUL), minister; b. St. Louis, Nov. 7, 1931; s. Walter Henry and Jessie Lorraine (Hanger) E.; m. Jane Alice Taylor, Jan. 15, 1967; children: Jennifer Lynn, Jeremy Paul. BA, Concordia Sem., St. Louis, 1953; MDiv, Concordia Sem., 1956. Ordained to ministry Luth. Ch.-Mo. Synod, 1956. Pastor Luth. Ch. of Redeemer, Melbourne, Fla., 1956-62, Columbus, Ga., 1962-70; pastor Hope Luth. Ch., Austin, Tex., 1970—; sec. Fla.-Ga. Dist., Luth. Ch.-Mo. Synod, Orlando, Fla., 1965-70, counselor Austin Cir., 1971-73; bd. regents Concordia Coll., Austin, 1973-77; mem. Soc. Ministry Com., Tex. Dist. Luth. Ch.-Mo. Synod, 1978-88. Author: (children's devotions) My Devotions, 1964; editor: Fla.-Ga. edit. Lutheran Witness mag., 1960-65. Pres. Muscogee County Am. Cancer Soc., Columbus, 1965, vice chmn. Mayor's Com. on Fluoridation, Columbus, 1966-67, mem. Human Relations Bd., Columbus, 1968-70. Mem. Kiwanis (chpt. pres. 1985-86). Democrat. Home: 7406 Barcelona Dr Austin TX 78752 Office: Hope Luth Ch 6414 N Hampton Dr Austin TX 78723 *The great discovery in life is learning that life is to be found chiefly in giving, not getting; serving, not being served; in relationships, not in things—and then helping others make this great discovery for themselves.*

ELLWOOD, ROBERT SCOTT, JR., religious studies educator; b. Normal, Ill., July 17, 1933; s. Robert Scott and Knola Lorraine (Shanks) E.; m. Gracia Fay Bouwman, Aug. 28, 1965; children: Richard, Fay Elanor. B.A., U. Colo., 1954; M.Div., Berkeley Div. Sch., 1957; M.A. U. Chgo, 1965, Ph.D., 1967. Pastor ch. Central City, Nebr., 1957-60; chaplain USNR, 1961-62; asst. prof. religion U. So. Calif., 1967-71, assoc. prof., 1971-75, prof., 1975—, Bishop Bashford prof. Oriental studies, 1977—, dir. East Asian Studies Ctr., 1977-81, dir. Sch. Religion, 1988-91. Author: Religious and Spiritual Groups in Modern America, 1973, The Feast of Kingship, 1973, Many Peoples, Many Faiths, 1976, Words of the World's Religions, 1977, Introducing Religion, 1978, Alternative Altars, 1979, Mysticism and Religion, 1980, Eastern Spirituality in America, 1987, The History and Future of Faith, 1988. Mem. Am. Acad. Religion, Assn. Asian Studies. Office: U So Calif Sch Religion Los Angeles CA 90089

ELMS, DAVID TATUM, minister; b. Gorman, Tex., Apr. 7, 1943; s. Finley Milton and Pauline Estelle (Gressett) E.; m. Linda Marlene Benson, Jan. 8, 1943; children—Melody Lynn, David Timothy, Nathan Joel. A.A., San Diego City Coll., 1967; B.A., San Diego State U., 1971. With Naval Air Rework Facility, San Diego, 1964-73; evangelist United Pentecostal Ch. Internat., 1973-74, campus evangelism coordinator South Central States, 1974-75; ordained to ministry United Pentecostal Ch., 1978; pastor First United Pentecostal Ch., Charlotte, N.C., 1975—; dir. N.C. Dist. Youth Orgn., 1977-78. Bd. dirs. N.C. Sunday Sch. Dept., 1978-80, N.C. Dist. Fgn. Missions Div., 1982-90; dir. Dist. Home Missions, 1990—; pres. Personal Growth Inst., 1982—. Recipient Sheaves for Christ award, 1978. Author: Revival Churches for the Rapture Generation, 1977; contbr. articles to profl. jours.

ELOVITZ, MARK HARVEY, lawyer; b. Pitts., May 20, 1938; s. Meyer David and Lillian (Werner) E.; children: Rachel Aliza, Michal Aviva, Reuben Jeremiah. BA, NYU, 1960, PhD, 1973; MHL, Jewish Theol. Sem., 1964; JD, Cumberland Sch. Law, 1977. Bar: Ala. 1977, U.S. Dist. Ct. (no. dist.) Ala.; ordained rabbi, 1964. Assoc. rabbi Temple Beth El, Cedarhurst, N.Y., 1967-69; rabbi Temple Beth El, Birmingham, Ala., 1970-77; mem. Denaburg, Schoel, Meyerson, Birmingham, 1977-79; prin. Mark H. Elovitz, P.C., Birmingham, 1979—; cons., panelist NEH, 1976-78, 81-82; faculty affil. U. Ala. Sch. Nursing; 1st pres. Birmingham Area Legal Svcs. Corp., Inc., 1977-78; lectr. in field. Author: A Century of Jewish Life in Dixie, 1974; How to Handle a Lemon Case in Alabama, 1983, Alabama Lemon Law Litigation, 1986, Alabama Statutes Affecting Nursing Practice, 1986; (with others) The Right to Die: Medical Ethics, Law and Human Values, 1976; co-author Medical Malpractice in Alabama, 1986, Family Law in Alabama, 1988; contbr. chpts. to books and articles to profl. jours. Vice chmn. Ala. Com. for Humanities and Pub. Policy, 1977-78; sr. scholar Ctr. for Aging U. Ala. Birmingham., 1987—. Capt. USAF, 1964-67. Mem. ABA, Birmingham Bar Assn., Assn. Trial Lawyers Am., Ala. Trial Lawyers Assn., Rabbinical Assembly Am., Phi Beta Kappa. Democrat. Clubs: Highland Racquet (Birmingham), The Club. Home: 3728 Dover Dr Birmingham AL 35203 Office: 1919 Morris Ave Bank for Savs Bldg Ste 1420 Birmingham AL 35203

ELROD, JERRY DAVID, clergyman; b. Palestine, Tex., Dec. 31, 1938; s. Joe Regester and Hazel Louise (Fitzgerald) E.; m. Jerry Jo McNeely, Aug. 4, 1963 (div. 1971); 1 child, Joel David; m. Sharon Ann Shaw, Aug. 31, 1975. BA, Southwestern U., 1960; MDiv, So. Meth. U., 1963; DD (hon.), Nebr. Wesleyan U., 1984. Ordained to ministry Meth. Ch., 1963. Assoc. editor Tex. Meth., Dallas, 1960-62; exec. dir. United Meth. Ministries, Omaha, 1966-82; dist. supt. Omaha Dist. United Meth. Ch., 1982-85; exec. dir. Tucson Met. Ministry, 1985-88; sr. pastor Desert Skies United Meth. Ch., Tucson, 1988—; del. South Cen. Jurisdictional Conf., 1972, 80, 84; vice chmn. Conf. Coun. on Ministries Desert SW Conf., 1988—; chmn. Bd. of Communications Desert SW Conf., 1988—; del. World Meth. Conf., 1991. Producer, host TV talk show Point of View, Omaha and Tucson, 1975-87. Bd. dirs. Joint Action in Community Svcs., Washington, 1971—, mem. exec. com., 1991—; bd. dirs. Nebr. Meth. Hosp., 1982-85. Named Outstanding Citizen City of Omaha, 1976. Democrat. Avocations: collecting antique toys, whitewater rafting, swimming. Home: 5150 N Vista De Loma Segunda Tucson AZ 85715 Office: Desert Skies United Meth Ch 3255 N Houghton Rd Tucson AZ 85749

ELSE, JAMES PRENTISS, librarian; b. Pueblo, Colo., Oct. 9, 1920; s. George William and Elva Clarissa (Hillhouse) E.; m. Peggy Nicholls, Sept. 29, 1945; children: Susan, Patricia, Clara, Christopher, David. BA, U. Denver, 1946, MA, 1957; ThM, Iliff Sch. of Theology, 1949. Pastor Hanna-Medicine Bow Meth. Ch., Hanna, Wyo., 1947-48, SACO (Mont.) Hinsdale United Meth. Ch., 1950-53, Boulder (Mont.) Parish, United Meth. Ch., 1953-56; cataloger Sch. of Theology Libr., Claremont, Calif., 1957-69; cataloger, acting head tech. svcs. Grad. Theol. Union Libr., Berkeley, Calif., 1972-89, ret., 1989; ret. mem. Yellowstone Conf. United Meth. Ch. Cpl. U.S. Army, 1943-45, PTO. Mem. Am. Theol. Libr. Assn. Home: 4682 Valley View Rd El Sobrante CA 94803

ELSENER, DANIEL J., academic administrator. Supt. Cath. edn. Diocese of Wichita, Kans. Office: Edn Dept 424 N Broadway Wichita KS 67202*

ELSMAN, JAMES LEONARD, JR., lawyer, radio evangelist; b. Kalamazoo, Sept. 10, 1936; s. James Leonard and Dorothy Isabell (Pierce) E.; m. Janice Marie Wilczewski, Aug. 6, 1960; children—Stephanie, James Leonard III. B.A., U. Mich., 1958, J.D., 1962; postgrad., Harvard Div. Sch., 1958-59. Bar: Mich. 1963. Clk. Mich. Atty. Gen.'s Office, Lansing, 1961; atty. legal dept. Chrysler Corp., Detroit, 1962-64; founding partner Elsman, Young, O'Rourke, Bruno & Bunn, Birmingham, 1964—. Author: novel The Seekers, 1962; screenplay, 1976, 200 Candles for Whom?, 1973; Contbr. articles to profl. jours.; Composer, 1976, 1974. Mem. Regional Export Expansion Council, 1966-73, Mich. Partners for Alliance for Progress, 1969—; Candidate U.S. Senate, 1966, 76, 88, U.S. Ho. of Reps., 1970. Rockefeller Brothers Found. fellow Harvard Div. Sch., 1969. Mem. ABA, Am. Soc. Internat. Law, Econ. Club Detroit, World Peace Through Law Center, Full Gospel Businessmen, Bloomfield Open Hunt Club, Pres. Club (U. Mich.), Circumnavigators Club, Naples Bath and Tennis, Rotary. Republican. Mem. Christian Ch. Home: 4811 Burnley Dr Bloomfield Hills MI 48013 Office: Elsman Young O'Rourke Bruno & Bunn 635 Elm St Birmingham MI 48009 *Christianity is not a religion. It is knowing Jesus, i.e. God, personally. It does not hinge on man's works or effort. Christianity is the only way to God, as Christ is the only Mediator between God and man. Choose! You can be sincerely wrong and still go to Hell eternally.*

ELSON, EDWARD LEE ROY, minister; b. Monongahela, Pa., Dec. 23, 1906; s. Lee Roy and Pearl (Edie) E.; m. Frances B. Sandys, May 22, 1929 (dec. Dec. 1933); m. Helen Louise Chittick, Feb. 8, 1937; children: Eleanor F., Beverly L., Mary F., David Edward. BA, Asbury Coll., 1928; MTh, U. So. Calif., 1931, postgrad., 1932-33, LHD, 1954; DDiv, Wheaton Coll., 1934, Occidental Coll., 1947; postgrad. Am. sem. in Europe and Russia, 1936; LittD, Centre Coll., 1952, Lafayette Coll., 1958, Gettysburg Coll., 1960; LLD, Norwich U., 1953, Davis and Elkins Coll., 1955, Ashbury Coll., 1958, Hope Coll., 1961; STD, Coll. Emporia, 1955, Ripon Coll., 1956; DHum, Parsons Coll., 1955; LHD, Washington and Jefferson Coll., 1960, Wooster Coll., 1960; DMinistry, Salem Coll., 1974. Ordained to ministry Presbyn. Ch., 1930. Asst. minister ad interim 1st Ch., Santa Monica, Calif., 1930-31; minister 1st Presbyn., La Jolla, Calif., 1931-41; pastor Nat. Presbyn. Ch., Washington, 1946-73, pastor emeritus, 1973—; chaplain U.S. Senate, Washington, 1969-81; moderator Presbytery of Los Angeles, 1938; commr. Gen. Assembly Presbyn. Ch. U.S.A., 1933, 38, 51, 56, 67; nat. chaplain D.A.V., 1950-51; pres. Washington Fedn. Chs., 1952-54; Western Region dir. Presbyn. post-war Restoration Fund., 1946; mem. bd. pensions, 1948-57; also com. chaplains and service personnel Presbyn. Ch. 1947-57; moderator Presbytery of Washington City, 1966; lectr. Nat. Indsl. War Coll.; Mem. com. John F. Kennedy Ctr. Performing Arts. Speaker at colls. and univs.; author: One Moment with God, 1951, America's Spiritual Recovery 1954 (Freedoms Found. award 1954); And Still He Speaks, 1960; The Inevitable Encounter, 1962; Wide Was His Parish, 1986; Prayers Offered by the Chaplain the Senate of the U.S., 91st Congress, 92d-97th Congresses. Bd. dirs. Freedoms Found. at Valley Forge, Damavand Coll. Ass., Am. Near East Relief; v.p. Am. Friends Middle East 1950-73; v.p. Religious Heritage Am.; pres. bd. dirs. Am. Colony Charities Assn.; trustee Wilson Coll., 1953-73; pres. 1961-72; adv. council Ctr. Study Presidency. Chaplain U.S. Army Res., 1930, advanced through grades to col., 1944, active duty, 1941-46; ret., 1961. Decorated Legion of Merit, Bronze Star, Army Commendations medal; Croix de Guerre avec Palme, Arms City of Colmar (France); gold medal Lebanese order of Merit; Silver Star (Jordan); comdr. Order Medal of Freedom (France); recipient Freedoms Found. award, sermon category, 1951, 54, 57, 58, 59, 60, 62, 64, 72, 73, prin. sermon award, 1965-72; Clergy-Churchman of Yr. citation Ch. Mgmt. and Wash. Pilgrimage of Am. Churchmen, 1954; Edward L.R. Elson monumental wall at Nat. Presbyn. Ch. dedicated in his honor, 1971; named Disting. Citizen of Yr., Los Angeles, 1975; recipient Key to City, Knoxville, Tenn., 1976. Mem. St. Andrews Soc., Am. Friends of Middle East (chaplain), DAV, Acad. Religion and Mental Health, Am. Soc. Ch. History, Ch. Service Soc., World Alliance Ref. Chs., VFW, Am. Legion, Mil. Order World Wars (chaplain), Mil. Chaplains' Assn. (nat. pres. 1957-59), English-Speaking Union, Assn. U.S. Army, Newcomen Soc. N.Am., Internat. Platform Assn., Scottish Am. Heritage, U.S. Capitol Hist. Soc., Res. Officers' Assn. (chaplain Calif. dept. 1937-38), Phi Chi Phi, Chi Alpha, Theta Sigma. Clubs: Cosmos (Washington); Kiwanis (past pres., hon. life mem.) (La Jolla). Home: The Fairfax 9002 Belvoir Woods Pkwy Fort Belvoir VA 22060

ELSTAD, GEORGE STANLEY, minister; b. Bklyn., May 19, 1927; s. Anton and Martha Berthina (Anderson) E.; m. Laura Baldwin Randall, Nov. 7, 1953; children: Kenneth (dec.), Mildred, Molly. BA, Coll. Staten Island, 1981. Ordained to ministry Covenant Ministries, Inc., 1970. Pastor Christ Assemby, Staten Island, N.Y., 1964—; tchr. N.Y.C. Bd. Edn., 1988—; publicity dir. Staten Island com. Gospel Tent Ministries, 1990—. Contbr. articles to profl. jours. With U.S. Army, 1945-47, ETO. Home and Office: 1626 Castleton Ave Staten Island NY 10302 *We say there are 3 dimensions of space—height, depth and width. There is also a fourth—time. Most people are living in these four dimensions. In knowing Jesus Christ, one comes into a fifth dimension. We come into God's wavelength.*

ELSTON, WAYNE RALPH, JR., clergyman; b. Wilkes-Barre, Pa., Dec. 11, 1948; s. Wayne Ralph and Joan (Sutton) E.; m. Dianne Lynn Mahoney, Sept. 5, 1970; children: Michelle, Jeffrey. Student, N.E. Bible Inst., Green Lane, Pa., 1967-71, Rhema Bible Tng. Ctr., Broken Arrow, Okla., 1978-79. Lic. Rhema Bible Tng. Ctr.; ordained to ministry Ministerial Fellowship of the U.S.A.. Sunday sch. supr. Mooretown Assemblies of God Ch., Sweet Valley, Pa., 1973-77; pastor Believers Fellowship Ctr., Scotia, N.Y., 1979—. Leader The Gospel Truth, 1973-77. Mem. Internat. Conv. Faith Ministries, Rhema Ministerial Assn. Internat. Office: Believers Fellowship Ctr 304 Swaggartown Rd Scotia NY 12302

ELWELL, WILLIAM EARL, minister; b. Frankfurt, Fed. Republic Germany, June 12, 1958; (parents Am. citizens); s. James A. and Nettie M. (McKerley) E.; m. Debra Cummings, Jan. 3, 1981. BA, Huntingdon Coll., Montgomery, Ala., 1980; MDiv, Duke U., 1983. Ordained to ministry United Meth. Ch. as deacon, 1982, as elder, 1985. Pastor White Oak-Liberty United Meth. Ch., Ala., 1983-86, Glenwood (Ala.) United Beth. Ch., 1986-88, St. Francis United Meth. Ch., Mobile, Ala., 1988—; sec. Conf. of Downtown Chs., Mobile, 1989, v.p., 1990, pres., 1991. Bd. dirs. Sr. Citizen Svcs., Mobile, 1990. Office: St Francis St Meth Ch PO Box 1486 Mobile AL 36633

ELWOOD, WALTER M., ecumenical agency administrator. Pres. Christian Conf. Conn., Hartford. Office: Christian Conf 60 Lorraine St Hartford CT 06105*

ELY, DONALD JEAN, clergyman, educator; b. Frederick, Md., July 15, 1935; s. George Kline and Jennie Mabel (Boyer) E. m. Lois Jean Kirkpatrick, Aug. 27, 1967; children: Kathleen Rose, Stephen David, Yvonne Elaine. AB, Gettysburg Coll., 1955; BD, Lancaster Sem., 1958; MEd, Bloomsburg State U., 1972. Ordained to ministry Evang. and Reformed Ch., 1958. Pastor St. John Evang. and Reformed Ch., Riegelsville, Pa., 1958-61, Zion's Reformed Ch., Ashland, Pa., 1961-64, Augusta Reformed Parish, Sunbury, Pa., 1964-74, Salem United Meth. Ch., Middleburg, Pa., 1974-79, Salem Ind. Brethren Ch., Middleburg, Pa., 1979-83; tchr. social studies Shikellamy High Sch., Sunbury, Pa., 1966—. Bd. dirs. Sunbury Area YMCA, 1966—, sec., 1973-80, 88—; bd. dirs. Northumberland County unit Am. Cancer Soc., 1971-74, Snyder County unit, 1974-84; rep. candidate state legis., 1982; vice chmn. Govt. Study Commn. of City of Sunbury, 1989-91; mem. Northumberland County Rep. com., 1989—. Mem. SAR (chaplain 1971—, chpt. pres. 1981-86), Pa. Coun. Social Studies, Snyder County Hist. Soc. (pres. 1980-83, life mem.), Northumberland County Hist. Soc. (trustee 1972-83, life mem.), Union County Hist. Soc., Hist. Soc. Evang. and Reformed Ch., Hereditary Register of U.S., Ams. for Constl. Action, Am. Conservative Union, Masons. Home: PO Box 765 Sunbury PA 17801 Office: 1149 Market St Sunbury PA 17801

ELYA, JOHN ADEL, bishop; b. Maghdoucheh, Lebanon, Sept. 16, 1928; came to U.S., 1958; s. Maroun Milhim and Abla (Moussa) E. Bacalaureat Etudes Secondaires, Seminaire St. Sauveur, Saida, Lebanon, 1946; Baccalaureate in Sacred Theology, Pontifical Gregorian U., Rome, 1950, Licentiate in Sacred Theology, 1952; MA in Sociology, Boston Coll., 1966. Prof. moral theology Séminaire St. Sauveur, 1952-56; asst. pastor, prin. parish sch. Sacred Heart Ch., Zarka, Jordan, 1956-58; dean studies, prof. moral theology St. Basil Sem., Methuen, Mass., 1958-67, rector, 1963-66, co-founder, dir. Ecumenical Inst. for Religious Studies, 1964-67; aux. bishop Diocese of Newton for Melkites in U.S., Roslindale, Mass., 1986; rector Melkite Cathedral of Annunciation, Roslindale, 1985-89; regional bishop of Eastern region Melkites in U.S., Rosindale, 1989-90; regional bishop Western region Melkites in U.S., North Hollywood, Calif., 1990—; pastor Our Lady of the Cedars Ch., Manchester, N.H., 1962-63, 69-72, 80-81, St. Joseph's Melkite Ch., Lawrence, Mass., 1972-79, 82-85; local superior Basilian Salvatorian Fathers, Metheun, 1979-81; tribunal officialis Melkite Diocese, Montreal, Que., Can., 1981-82. Editor-in-chief An-Nahlah Sem. Mag., 1953-56, Du'a Al'Ajras Mission Quar., 1956-58; contbr. numerous articles to religious publs. Recipient Immigrant City award Internat. Inst. Greater Lawrence, 1986. Mem. Assn. for Soc. Religion, Greater Lawrence Clerical Fellowship (sec. 1973-78, pres. 1978-79, 84-85). Home and Office: 11246 Landale St North Hollywood CA 91602

ELZERMAN, JAMES HUBERT, minister; b. Garden City, Mich., Apr. 28, 1952; s. Ernest Eugene and Marilyn Cecelia (Hubert) E.; m. Tracie Anne York, Oct. 13, 1974; children: Jeremy James, Benjamin David, Sarah Susanne, Charity Anne. BA summa cum laude, Spring Arbor Coll., 1986; MA in Clin. Psychology, Wheaton Coll., 1990. Horticulturalist elzerman's Greenhouse, Webberville, Mich., 1970-85; pastor Conway Free Meth. Ch., Fowlerville, Mich., 1985-88, Morris (Ill.) Free Meth. Ch., 1988—; therapist Family Conseling Svc., Aurora, Ill., 1990—. Avocations: photography, architecture, computers. Home: 703 First Ave Morris IL 60450 Office: Morris Free Methodist Ch 704 Armstrong St Morris IL 60450

EMBREE, CHARLES MONROE, minister, development executive; b. Monroe County, Mo., May 26, 1935; s. Melvin R. and Dora E. (McGee) E.; m. Joyce L. Worner June 12, 1955; children—David E., Timothy C., Stephen M. B.A., Lincoln Christian Coll., 1958, M.A., 1967. Ordained to ministry, Christian Ch., 1958. Minister Akers Chapel Ch. of Christ, Plainville, Ill., 1958-63, minister Athens Christian Ch., Ill., 1963-69, First Christian Ch., Clarence, Mo., 1969-80; dir. devel. Central Christian Coll. of Bible, Moberly, Mo., 1980—, dir. 1970-80; pres., dir. Central Mo. Christian Evangelizers, Columbia, Mo., 1984—. Contbr. articles to profl. jours. Democrat. Avocation: photography. Home: Rt 3 Box 80-S Moberly MO 65270 Office: Central Christian Coll PO Box 70 Moberly MO 65270

EMERSON, ARCHIE PAUL, minister; b. Liberty, Ky., Apr. 3, 1945; s. George and Levona (Luttrell) E.; m. Linda Sue Parton, Aug. 31, 1965; children: Tammy Lynn, Paul Timothy. ThB, Bapt. Bible Coll., Springfield, Mo., 1974. Ordained to ministry, Bapt. Ch. Founder, pastor Ocean State Bapt. Ch., Smithfield, R.I., 1975—; trustee Bapt. Bible Coll. E., Boston, 1985—. Home: 19 Link St North Providence RI 02911 Office: Ocean State Bapt Ch 600 Douglas Pike Smithfield RI 02917

EMERSON, BARBARA MARIE, religion educator; b. Arcadia, Wis., Oct. 26, 1946; married; children: Derek Kim, Mindy Shin. B of Music Edn., U. Wis., 1968; MA, U. Iowa, 1973; MS in Ednl. Adminstrn., Drake U., 1991. Instrumental music dir. Newman High Sch., Mason City, Iowa, 1974-83, St. Edmond High Sch., Fort Dodge, Iowa, 1988-90; elem. prin. St. James Sch., Washington, Iowa, 1990—; lay distributor Holy Family Parish, Mason City, 1980—, scout rev. bd., 1983-85. Bd. dirs. Iowa IOOF, Mason City, 1986-88, Boy Scouts Am. award rev. bd., Mason City, 1986-88; leader Webelos, 1983-85; asst. dir. U.S. Collegiate Wind Band, Lafayette, Ind., 1976-81; musician Mason City Mcpl. Band, 1974—, Clear Lake Mcpl. Band, 1974—. Recipient Outstanding Woman of Am. award, 1979; grantee Brevard Music Ctr./Rockefeller Found., 1968. Home: 1051 Crestmore Way Mason City IA 50401

EMERY, AUSTIN H., minister, counselor; b. Central Falls, R.I., Feb. 20, 1931; s. Austin H. and Anna Elizabeth (Seaton) E.; m. Fairylee Barbara Harrison, Aug. 11, 1950; children: Timothy Austin, Mark Austin, Robin Grace. BS, MS, Abilene Christian, 1962, 63; MDiv, SWBTS, Ft. Worth, 1972; MRE, SWBTS, 1973; DMin, Brite Div., 1975. Min. Ch. of Christ, Tular, Tex., 1960-62, Kennedale, Tex., 1962, Greenville, Tex., 1962-63, Ft. Worth, 1964-66; campus min. NESC, Okal., Tahlaguah, 1966-69; min. Ch. of Christ, Hico, Tex., 1969-74, Nocona, Tex., 1974-79, Farmington, N.Mex., 1979—; hosp. chaplain, SJRMC, Farmington, 1987—; gov. com. correction, Dept. of Corrections, Farmington, 1986—; bd. sec. 4-Corners Youth Emcampment, Cortez, Cortez, Calif., 1985—. Author: The E's of Christianity, 1984. Sgt. USAF, 1947-57. Mem. Am. Assn. Christian Counselors, Internat. Assn. Christian Counselors. Avocation: photography. Office: Church of Christ 401 W 20th Farmington NM 87401

EMERY, OREN DALE, minister, religious organization executive; b. Indpls., May 30, 1927; s. Oren Wilson and Roberta Jean (Dodd) E.; m.

Ruthanne Adams, June 25, 1946; children: Steven, Paul, Deborah, David, Timothy, Elizabeth. BRE, Ind. Wesleyan U., 1950, DD (hon.), 1985; MS in Mgmt., So. Ill. U., Carbondale, 1983; LittD (hon.), Pa. Wesleyan Coll., 1970. Pastor Wesleyan chs., Ind., Wis., Mich., 1949-60; dist. supt. Ariz. Wesleyan Ch., Indpls., Marion, Ind., 1962-70; exec. sec. cen. office Christian Holiness Assn., Indpls., 1970-72; gen. sec. Christian edn. Wesleyan Ch., Indpls., 1972-80, gen. supt., 1980-92. Author: Multiple Staff-Ministries, 1974, Concepts to Grow By, 1976. Bd. dirs. Am. Family Found., 1984—, Ind. Wesleyan U., 1980-84, Houghton Coll., 1984-88. Petty officer USN, 1944-46, Guam. Mem. Am. Mgmt. Assn., Christian Mgmt. Assn., Religious Conv. Mgrs. Assn. Republican. Office: The Wesleyan Internat 6060 Castleway West Dr Indianapolis IN 46250

EMERY, ROBERT ALLAN, minister; b. Rutland, Vt., Aug. 17, 1943; s. Dexter Scott and Frances Elizabeth (Cook) E.; m. Mary Ann Whiteford, Sept. 1, 1981; children: Allan, Kimberly, Steven, Scott, Gregory. BRE, Northeastern Bible Coll., Essex Fells, N.J., 1965; MA with honors, Dallas Theol. Sem., 1976. Ordained to ministry Bapt. Ch., 1971. Assoc. pastor 1st Bapt. Ch., Foxboro, Mass., 1965-67; pastor Grace Bapt. Ch., Attleboro, Mass., 1967-69, Vance Bible Ch., Bristol, Tenn., 1970-71; assoc. pastor 1st Bapt. Ch., Wayne, Mich., 1971-78; chaplain Syracuse (N.Y.) Rescue Mission, 1979-85; assoc. pastor North Syracuse (N.Y.) Bapt. Ch., 1985—; pres. Search the Scriptures Ministries, Liverpool, N.Y., 1986—; mem. bd. reference Evang. Counseling Ctr., 1987-88; founder, pres. Greater Syracuse Singles Fellowship, 1990—. Author: (workbook) Divorce Recovery, 1985, How To Study the Bible, 1986. Chief arbitrator Wayne (Mich.)-Westland Sch. System, 1976; bd. dirs. Syracuse Rescue Mission, 1986-87. Staley Found. Disting Christian scholar, lectr., 1988. Republican. Office: North Syracuse Bapt Ch 420 S Main St North Syracuse NY 13212 *In life the only constant has been Jesus Christ. He has been Lord and friend, my source of joy and strength.*

EMINHIZER, EARL EUGENE, theologian, educator; b. Greenville, S.C., May 22, 1926; s. Eugene Lawrence and Mary Elmyra (Couch) E.; m. Lillian Marcia Downs, July 16, 1955; children: Catherine Marcia, Eugene Elwood, Eugene Lawrence II. BA, Furman U., 1948; BS in Edn., Youngstown (Ohio) Coll., 1951; BD, Chozer Seminary, Chester, Pa., 1955, ThM, 1956; ThD, Calif. Sch. Theology, 1968. Tchr. McCormick (S.C.) Schs., 1949-50, Bracevill Schs., Newton Falls, Ohio, 1950-51; instr. religion Denison U., Grandville, Ohio, 1956-57; tchr. Southington (Ohio) Schs., 1957-65; prof. Youngstown State U., 1958—. Contbr. articles to profl. jours. Bd. dirs. Lake to River Health Care Coalition, 1976, Goodwill Industries, Youngstown, 1979—, Easter Seals Soc., Youngstown, 1982—, Ohio Rehab. Svcs. Commn., Columbus, 1979—. Grantee Youngstown State U., 1978, 85. Mem. NEA, Ohio Edn. Assn., Am. Soc. Ch. Historians, So. Hist. Assn., Am. Assn. Am. Profs., Nat. Assn. Bapt. Profs. of Religion, Orgns. Am. Historians, Ohio Acad. of Religion, Ohio Philos. Assn., Masons, Phi Kappa Phi. Baptist. Avocation: photography. Home: 130 S Elm Columbiana OH 44408 Office: Youngstown State U 410 Wick Ave Youngstown OH 44555-3448

EMLER, DONALD GILBERT, college dean, minister; b. Kansas City, Mo., June 1, 1939; s. Earl Cecil and Esther Margaret (Brier) E.; m. Lenore Suzanne Plummer, Aug. 9, 1968; children: Matthew Kirk, David Earl. BA in History and Govt., U. Mo.-Kansas City, 1960; MDiv, Garrett-Evang. Theol. Sem., 1963; MS in Edn., Ind. U., 1972, EdD, 1973. Ordained to ministry Methodist Ch., 1961; minister Broadway United Meth. Ch., Kansas City, 1963-66; chaplain and instr. Cen. Meth. Coll., Fayette, Mo., 1966-68; minister Platte Woods U. Meth. Ch., Kansas City, 1968-70, Gosport-Quincy United Meth. Ch., Gosport, Ind., 1970-73, St. John's United Meth. Ch., Kansas City, 1973-76; prof. Christian edn. and chmn. religion dept. Centenary Coll. of La., Shreveport, 1976-89, dir. ch. careers program, 1980-81; dean, prof. of Christian edn. Wimberly Sch. Religion Okla. City U., 1989—; fellow, pres. Okla. Christian Educators, 1991—; cons. to local chs. in Christian edn.; video-tape instr. First Meth. Ch., Shreveport. Bd. dirs. Interfaith Com. on Human Dignity and Social Justice, 1981; bd. dirs. Lameco Credit Union, 1980-84, NCCJ, 1985-87, VAC Credit Union, 1988-89; mem. Parents Coalition, 1981-82; chmn. Shreveport Ecumenical Lecture Series, 1985-87. Mem. Christian Educators Fellowship, Religious Edn. Assn. (bd. dirs. 1991—), United Meth. Assn. Profs. of Christian Edn. (sec.-treas. 1982-84), Assn. Profs. and Researchers in Religious Edn. (exec. com. 1991—), Am. Assn. Adult and Continuing Edn., Nat. Council on Religion and Pub. Edn. Author: Revisioning the DRE, 1989; contbr. articles to religious jours. Home: 6617 Candlewood Oklahoma City OK 73132 Office: Okla City U 2501 N Blackwelder Wimberly Sch Religion Oklahoma City OK 73106

EMMERT, CHARLES MICHAEL, minister; b. South Haven, Mich., Nov. 22, 1954; s. John Price and Dorothy (Herak) E.; m. Amy Lou Plementosh, June 25, 1977; children: Craig Michael, Alison Lauren. BRE, Gt. Lakes Bible Coll., Lansing, Mich., 1978. Ordained to ministry Ch. of Christ, 1979. Youth min. Lakeshore Ch. of Christ, St. Joseph, Mich., 1974; assoc. min. Meml. Ch. of Christ, Livonia, Mich., 1975-86, Novesta Ch. of Christ, Cass City, Mich., 1986—; trustee Wolverine Christian Svc. Camp, Columbiaville, Mich., 1985-87, 89—; founding dir. statewide jr. high sch. youth rally Chs. of Christ/Christian Ch., 1980-86. Office: Novesta Ch of Christ 2896 N Cemetery Rd Cass City MI 48726

EMMONS, EARL RUSSELL, JR. (RUSTY EMMONS), minister; b. Albuquerque, Jan. 31, 1967; s. Earl R. and Sharon Ann (Shields) E. BS in Youth Ministry, Okla. Christian Coll., 1989. Min. youth Nederland (Tex.) Ch. of Christ, 1989—. Office: Nederland Ch of Christ 2300 Nederland Ave Nederland TX 77627 *Whatever happens, God is near and you keep the faith.*

EMSWILER, CHARLES E., JR., lay church worker, educator, retired information systems administrator; b. Shenandoah County, Va., Dec. 30, 1917; s. C. Edward Sr. and Ruth Irene (Pennywitt) E.; m. Catharine E. Haun, Sept. 4, 1937; children: Linda Ann, Connie Sue. Cert., Northwestern U., 1938, Control Data Inst., 1973. Tchr. Sunday sch. United Meth. Ch., Va., 1940-90, cert. lay speaker, 1948-90, edn. chairperson, 1981-85, instr., dean Christian workers sch., 1983-90; Va. infosystems adminstr. IBM Systems Sci. Inst., 1967-78. Developer Bible study courses, major computor systems. Election ofcl. Shenandoah County Bd. Elections, Woodstock, Va., 1970-88; precinct capt. Shenandoah County Reps., Woodstock, 1940's, 80's; mem. Woodstock Town Planning Commn., 1987-91; So. regional dir. Nat. Assn. for Info. Systems, 1976-79. Mem. Assn. Computer Profls. (cert. data processor). Home: 204 N Muhlenberg St Woodstock VA 22664

EMSWILER, TOM NEUFER, minister; b. Overland Park, Kans., Apr. 18, 1941; s. Thomas Clair and Velva Mae (Allmand) E.; m. Sharon Elaine Neufer; children: Evan, Elaine. BA, Emporia (Kans.) State Coll., 1963; BD, So. Meth. U., 1966; MA, Northwestern U., 1967. Pastor Trinity United Meth. Ch., Lawrence, Kans., 1967-70; assoc. pastor First United Meth. Ch., Wichita, Kans., 1970-72; co-dir. The Wesley Found. Ill. State U., Normal, 1972-86; free-lance writer Springfield, Ill., 1986—; min. of edn. Rochester (Ill.) United Meth. Ch., 1988-91; co-pastor 1st United Meth. Ch., Rock Island, Ill., 1991—; Prof. Garrett Evang. Seminary, Evanston, 1978, Iliff Sch. Theology, Denver, 1978; cons. in field, Springfield, 1986—. Co-author: Women and Worship: A Guide to Non-Sexist Hymns, Prayers and Liturgies, 1974; (cassette and guide) It's Your Wedding: A Practical Guide to Planning Contemporary Ceremonies, 1975, Wholeness in Worship, 1980; co-editor Sisters and Brothers, Sing!, 1977; author Love is a Magic Penny, 1977, The Click in the Clock, 1981, Money for your Campus Ministry, Church, or Other Non-profit Organization-How to Get It, 1981, A Complete Guide to Making the Most of Video in Religious Settings, 1985, Ten Keys: Opening the Way to a Moral Life, 1991; author, producer The Beautitudes, 1985. Guy Maier scholar Nat. Assn. Piano Tchrs., 1960; recipient Rockefeller Found. Trial Yr. in Seminary award, 1963, 1st Nat. Meth. Fellowship in Preaching award, 1966. Mem. Nat. Assn. Campus Ministers, Cen. Ill. Conf. United Meth. Ministers. Democrat. Avocations: video, coins, stamps. Home: 2507 45th St Rock Island IL 61201-5766 Office: 1st United Meth Ch 1820 5th Ave Rock Island IL 61201

ENDER, JACK LEE, minister; b. Buda, Tex., Jan. 10, 1951; s. Raymond Ernest and Virginia Lee (Felps) E.; m. Carolyn Ruth Wallis, Sept. 4, 1971; children: Valerie Michelle, Brian Keith. B in Bibl. Studies, Logos Coll., 1988, M in Theol. Studies, 1991. Ordained to ministry Faith Fellowship, 1978. Music dir. Bob Buess Ministries, Houston, 1970-71, Hill Country Faith Ministries, San Marcos, Tex., 1971-73, Faith Fellowship, Austin, Tex., 1974-78; assoc. pastor Faith Fellowship, 1978-80; sr. pastor Grace Fellowship, Georgetown, Tex., 1981—; bd. dirs., trustee, Austin Reconciliation Ctr., 1990—, Williamson County Crisis Pregnancy Ctr., Georgetown, 1991—, Youth Alive, Georgetown, 1991—; bd. dirs., Grace Fellowship Family Counseling Ctr., Georgetown, 1988-91. Author of software, Bibl. Profiles, 1985, Hostility, 1990. Chmn. nominations com. Boy Scouts Am., Williamson County, Tex., 1991. Mem. Am. Family Assn., Tex. Grassroots Coalition. Republican. Home and office: 601 Del Prado Georgetown TX 78628 *Successful living is found in those who acknowledge God's purpose which He has written in their hearts, and accomplish that purpose with enthusiasm and diligence. Jesus said it most profoundly with these words, "My meat is to do the will of Him who sent me."*

ENDRES, JOHN CAROL, priest; b. Tacoma, Wash., June 16, 1946; s. John Carol and Patricia Elizabeth (Ansley) E. BA, Holy Cross Coll., Worcester, Mass., 1968; MDiv, Weston Sch. Theology, Cambridge, Mass., 1977; PhD, Vanderbilt U., Nashville, 1982. Ordained priest Roman Cath. Ch., 1976. Tchr. Gonzaga Prep Sch., Spokane, Wash., 1971-73; prof. O.T. Jesuit Sch. Theology, Grad. Theol. Union, Berkeley, Calif., 1982—; rsch. fellow Asns. Theol. Schs., 1990. Author: Biblical Interpretation in the Book of Jubilees, 1986, Temple, Monarchy and Word of God, 1988. Trustee Holy Cross Coll., Worcester, 1981-89. Mem. Soc. Bibl. Lit., Cath. Bibl. Assn., Westar Inst. Democrat. Office: Jesuit Sch Theology 1735 LeRoy Ave Berkeley CA 94709

ENDY, MELVIN BECKER, JR., religion educator, academic administrator; b. Pottstown, Pa., Apr. 27, 1938; s. Melvin Becker and Virginia Charlotte (Myers) E.; m. Susan Halcomb Craig, Sept. 7, 1962 (div. Apr. 1983); m. Carol Deforest Moore Locke, Aug. 8, 1983; children: Michael Becker, Margaret Gordon, Nathaniel Stratton Locke, Benjamin Deforest Locke. BA, Princeton U., 1960; BD, Yale Div. Sch., 1963; MA, Yale U., 1965, PhD, 1969. Instr. religion Hamilton Coll., Clinton, N.Y., 1966-69, asst. prof., 1969-74, assoc. prof., 1974-79, prof. religion, 1979-90, assoc. dean of coll., 1979-82, dean of students, 1981-82, dean of coll., 1984-88; prof. religious studies, provost St. Mary's Coll. Md., St. Mary's City, 1991—; participant Inst. for Ecumenical & Cultural Research, Collegeville, Minn., 1977-81. Author: William Penn and Early Quakerism, 1973, also numerous articles. Sr. fellow NEH, 1975-76; recipient Best Article of Yr. award William and Mary Quar., 1985. Mem. Am. Acad. Religion, Orgn. Am. Historians, Am. Soc. Ch. History, Friends Hist. Assn. Avocations: fishing, hiking, dulcimer. Office: St Mary's Coll Md Office of Provost Saint Marys City MD 20686

ENG, CHRISTOPHER KAMUELA, minister; b. Honolulu, Mar. 13, 1949; s. Frank Harold and Joan (Mung) E.; m. Cheri M. Shimose, Feb. 14, 1988; 1 child, Skye S. T. BA cum laude, U. Hawaii, 1971, MA with honors, 1973; MDiv, Fuller Theol. Sem., 1977; D of Ministry, San Francisco Theol. Sem., 1985. Ordained to Am. Bapt. Ch., 1979. Campus min. Hawaii Conf. United Ch. Christ to U. Hawaii, Honolulu, 1975; asst. pastor Chinese United Meth. Ch., L.A., 1975-77; assoc. min. Japanese Bapt. Ch., Seattle, 1978-81, Nuuanu Congl. Ch. United Ch. Christ, Honolulu, 1981-85; sr. pastor Walpahu United (Hawaii) Ch. Christ, 1985—; tai chi instr. U. Hawaii, Leeward Community Coll., 1987—; bd. dirs. Hawaii Conf. United Ch. Christ, Honolulu, 1984—; vol. chaplain Kuakini Med. Ctr. Oncology Team, Honolulu, 1986—; pres. Oahu Assn. United Ch. Christ Mokupuni, Honolulu, 1989-90. Contbr. articles to profl. jours. Bd. mgrs. Nuuanu YMCA, Honolulu, 1986—; vol. Honolulu Jaycees and Jaycettes, 1982. Masland fellow Union Theol. Sem. N.Y., 1990; recipient Pro Deo et Patria God and Country award Boy Scouts Am., 1967, Svc. award YMCA, 1987; named legis. intern Ctr. Govtl. Devel., 1971. Mem. Hawaii Sociological Assn., Waipahu Community Assn. Democrat. Office: Waipahu United Ch Christ 94-330 Mokuola St Waipahu HI 96797 *Come join (T'ai-Chi) the Dance of Life! Mother Earth, Wind of the Spirit, and Blue Sky above...we will find harmony (Ying & Yang) in following "the Christ" when East and West meet, in Town and Country, and as relationships touch others with love and care!.*

ENGEBRETSON, MILTON BENJAMIN, retired church executive, minister; b. Grand Forks, N.D., Dec. 29, 1920; s. Hans Emil and Anna Sophie (Huss) E.; m. Esther Rhoda Hollenbeck, Dec. 12, 1945; children: Jon Philip, Donn Norman. BA, U. Wash., 1950; grad., North Park Theol. Sem., Chgo., 1954; DD, Seattle Pacific U., 1967, North Park Coll., 1975. Ordained to ministry Evang. Covenant Ch. Am., 1956. Pastor Stotler Mission Covenant Ch., Osage City, Kans., 1951-52, Mission Covenant Ch., Manakato, Minn., 1954-57, Elim Covenant Ch., Mpls., 1957-62; exec. sec. Evang. Covenant Ch. Am., Chgo., 1962-67, pres., 1967-86; chmn. conv. meeting U.S. Churchmen, 1972, U.S. Ch. Leaders, 1971-86; pres. Internat. Fedn. Free Evang. Chs., 1978-86. Decorated comdr. Royal Order Polar Star (Sweden). Office: 5101 N Francisco Ave Chicago IL 60625

ENGEL, JOHN RONALD, religious social ethics educator; b. Balt., Mar. 17, 1936; s. John August and Beatrice (McGee) E.; m. Joan Gibb, Sept. 7, 1957; children: John Mark, Kirsten Helene. AB, Johns Hopkins U., Balt., 1958; BD with highest distinction, Meadville/Lombard Theol. Sch., Chgo., 1964; MA, U. Chgo., 1971, PhD with distinction, 1977. Ordained to ministry Unitarian Universalist Assn., 1971. Intern min. All Souls Ch., Washington, 1962-63; min. Unitarian Universalist Fellowship Berrien County, 1963-65, 2d Unitarian Ch., Chgo., 1965-70; lectr. Div. Sch. U. Chgo., 1977—; prof. social ethics Meadville/Lombard Theol. Sch., Chgo., 1983—; mem. adv. bd. Beacon Press, Boston, 1985—, James Luther Adams Found., Cambridge, Mass.; mem. eco-justice working group Unitarian Universalist Assn. rep., Nat. Coun. Chs. Christ; mem. adv. bd. Internat. Ctr. for Environ. Ethics, Assisi, Italy; mem. bd. Inst. Domestic Tranquility, Washington; cons. biosphere res. project Man and the Biosphere Programme, U.S. Dept. Interior and UNESCO, Paris. Author: Sacred Sands, 1983 (Melcher award 1984); editor: Voluntary Associations, 1986; co-editor: Ethics of Environment and Development, 1990; mem. editorial bd. Am. Jour. Theology and Philosophy; contbr. articles to profl. jours. Stevens-Gessner fellow, 1960-64; recipient Cornell award Hyde Park Hist. Soc., 1985, award Chgo. Geographic Soc., 1984. Mem. Am. Acad. Religion, Am. Soc. Environ. History, Collegium: Assn. for Liberal Religious Studies, Internat. Assn. Religious Freedom, Internat. Devel. Ethics Assn. (steering com. 1988—), Social Ethics Seminar, Soc. Christian Ethics, Soc. Human Economy, Unitarian Universalist Ministers Assn., Internat. Union for Conservation of Nature and Natural Resources (chair ethics working group 1984—). Office: Meadville/Lombard 5701 S Woodlawn Chicago IL 60637

ENGELBRECHT, DAVID MICHAEL, minister; b. Woodbury, N.J., July 25, 1954; s. Joseph Anthony and Ida Rulon (Armstrong) E. BA, Asbury Coll., Wilmore, Ky., 1976; MDiv, Ea. Sem., Phila., 1985. Ordained to ministry United Meth. Ch., 1984. Pastor Barnsboro (N.J.) United Meth. Ch., 1981-84, Jackson (N.J.) United Meth. Ch., 1984-87, Trinity United Meth. Ch., Bordentown, N.J., 1987—; treas. Pastoral Counseling Ctr., Bordentown, 1987—, Ann. Crop Walk, Bordentown, 1987—; mem. So. N.J. Conf. Bd. Global Ministries. Treas. Bordentown Residents Against Drugs, 1989-90. Mem. So. N.J. Conf. Ednl. Soc. (sec. 1988—), Gloucester County Hist. Soc., Burlington County Hist. Soc. Republican. Home: 600 Farnsworth Ave Bordentown NJ 08505 Office: Trinity United Meth Ch 339 Farnsworth Ave Bordentown NJ 08505

ENGELBRECHT, ROBERT FRANK, minister; b. Watertown, Wis., Dec. 2, 1928; s. Herbert Frank and Esther Laura (Meschke) E.; m. Joan Berrel Clewell, June 3, 1956; children: Jan Edythe, Bobbi Beth, Jay Robert. BA, Moravian Coll., Bethlehem, Pa., 1953; MDiv, Moravian Theol. Sem., Bethlehem, Pa., 1956. Ordained to ministry Moravian Ch., 1956, consecrated presbyter, 1961. Pastor Hebron Moravian Ch., Altura, Minn., 1956-59, Third Moravian Ch., Phila., 1959-63, Edgeboro Moravian Ch., Bethlehem, Pa., 1963-72, Emmaus (Pa.) Moravian Ch., 1972—. Mem. long range vol. planning com. Borough of Emmaus, 1980—; Pa. consumer advocate Cen. Adv. Bd., Emmaus. Mem. Soc. for Promotion of Gospel (v.p. 1984—), Moravian Hist. Soc. (v.p., bd. dirs. 1970—), Emmaus Area C. of C. (bd. dirs. 1975—), Masons (32 deg.). Republican. Home: 136 Main St Emmaus PA 18049 Office: Emmaus Moravian Ch 146 Main St Emmaus PA 18049

ENGELSMAN, JOAN CHAMBERLAIN, religion educator; b. Mt. Vernon, N.Y.; d. William Hale and Helen (LePage) Chamberlain; m. Ralph G. Engelsman; children:Marc, Daniel. BA, Sweet Briar Coll., 1954; PhD, Drew U., 1977. Codir. Woman's Resource Ctr., Drew U., Madison, N.J., 1977-80; adj. prof. Drew U., Madison, N.J., 1985—; dir. community edn. Grace Counseling Ctr., Madison, 1983-86; dir. Peace in the Home Projects, Lawrenceville, N.J., 1986—. Author: Feminine Dimension of Divine, 1979, Clergy Manual on Domestic Violence, 1987, Peace in the Home: A Curriculum, 1991; editor Women in Ministry, 1978; contbr. articles to jours. in field. Mem. Phi Beta Kappa. Democrat. Home: 2 Green Hill Rd Madison NJ 07940 Office: Womanspace Inc 1860 Brunswick Ave Lawrenceville NJ 08648

ENGLAND, BARBARA LEE, communications executive; b. Popular Bluff, Mo., Oct. 20, 1943; d. Joseph Chester Allen and Daisy Ann (Adams) Heifner; divorced; children: Kenneth Wayde Howell, Sherri Rene Bolen, Michelle Linn Guth; m. Gary Franklin England, Nov. 18, 1989. Grad. high sch., Poplar Bluff, Mo. Cert. real estate broker, Mo. Gen. mgr. Sta. KUGT, Jackson, Mo., 1984—. V.p. Women's Aglow, Cape Giradeau, Mo., 1988-89. Mem. Am. Family Assn. (bd. advisors). Home: 116 N Henderson Cape Girardeau MO 63701 Office: Sta KUGT PO Box 546 1301 Woodland Jackson MO 63755 *Anything worth doing is worth doing to the very best of our ability. Only commit yourself to what glorifies God and what He has called you to. Sometimes we do not recognize the strength and power that rest within us, through knowing who we are in Christ Jesus, to conquer and achieve. We must do all that God has called someone else to do, someone who will do it with the fervor God has given them for the project. To know what it is God has for you, and to give that purpose He has called you to the very best you have to give, for His glory.*

ENGLAND, BOB LYLE, minister; b. Mullens, W.Va., June 24, 1946; s. Matthew Abner and Norma Louise (Lafferty) E.; m. Vivian Virginia Vandall, July 11, 1964; children: Frances Denise, Bob Lyle, Jr., Timothy Mark, Jonathan David. Ordained to ministry Wesleyan Ch., 1979. Pastor Wesleyan Ch., Mullens, W.Va., 1969-73, Terra Alta, W.Va., 1973-80, Boonville, Ind., 1980-91; pastor Washington (Ind.) Main St. Wesleyan Ch., 1991—; youth v.p. W.Va. dist., 1975-77, pres., 1977-80, sec. extension and evangelism, 1974-78; sec. leadership tng., 1988-92; dist. bd. adminstr. Wesleyan Ch., Ind. South, 1990-91, Christian edn. com., 1988-91, dist. Sunday sch. sec., 1988-91; chmn. spiritual preparation Clyde Dupin Crusade, Preston County, W.Va., 1979, Warrick County, Ind., 1984, exec. sec., 1990. EMT Terra Alta Vol. Ambulance Soc., 1976-80. Home: 622 W Main St Washington IN 47501 Office: Wesleyan Ch 624 W Main St Washington IN 47501

ENGLAND, ROBERT EUGENE, religion educator, minister; b. Bedford, Pa., June 30, 1941; s. John Clyde and Maxine Daisy (Price) E.; m. Marilyn Kay Hofacker, July 6, 1963; children—Joanna, Rebecca, Daniel, Robert, Kristin. Th.B., God's Bible Sch. and Coll., Cin., 1963; M.A., Cin. Bible Sem., 1984, postgrad., 1984—. Ordained to ministry Wesleyan Methodist Ch., 1974. Pastor, Wesleyan Meth. Ch., Murrysville, Pa., 1963-67, Beaver Falls, Pa., 1969-72, Limaville, Ohio, 1972-80; instr. Salem Bible Coll (Ohio), 1967-73, Allegheny Wesleyan Coll., Salem, 1973-80, pres., 1986—; instr. God's Bible Sch. Coll., Cin., 1980-86; bd. dirs., adviser Brinkhaven Enterprises, Inc., North Lawrence, Ohio, 1979—. Contbr. articles to religious publs. Mem. Wesleyan Theol. Soc. Avocation: Landscaping. Home: 2415 Woodsdale Rd Salem OH 44460

ENGLAND, ROBERT WALTER, minister, physician; b. Oaklyn, N.J., July 15, 1928; s. Robert Walker and Elizabeth (Jagdman) E.; m. Edna Naomi Kershaw, June 24, 1962. AB, Houghton Coll., 1949; BD, Ea. Bapt. Theol. Sem., Phila., 1952, MDiv, 1972; DO, Phila. Coll. Osteopathic Medicine, 1956, MS in Anatomy, 1961; MS in Edn. Adminstrn., U. Pa., 1964. Ordained to ministry Bapt. Ch., 1953; diplomate Am. Bd. Med.Examiners, Am. Bd. Family Practice; cert. Manupulative Med. Pastor Calvary Community Bapt. Ch., West Collingswood, N.J., 1950-54, Laurel Springs (N.J.) Community Ch., 1954-56; pastor Grace Bible Bapt. Ch., Hatboro, Pa., 1957-90, Huntingdon Valley, Pa., 1990—; assoc., cons. UFM Internat. Bala Cynwyd, Pa., 1990—.; mem. adv. com. Christ's Home, Warminster, Pa., 1980; pres., dean Bucks-Mont Sch. of Bible, Hatboro, 1961-90; dean Phila. Coll. Osteopathic Medicine, 1972-84. Author: (booklet) What The Bible Teaches About Baptism, 1990, (tract) In Case of Emergency, 1991. Fellow Am. Coll. Gen. Practitioners, 1964, Am. Academy of Osteopathy, 1966, Coll. of Physicians of Phila., 1975. Fellow Am. Sch. Assn.; mem. Southwide Bapt. Fellowship. Home and Office: Grace Bible Bapt Ch 3237 Paper Mill Rd Huntingdon Valley PA 19006-3719 *I am eternally grateful for the saving grace of our Lord Jesus Christ and for His call to a ministry as pastor and physician, enabling me to help meet the needs of the whole person. A key verse for me is Romans 1:16 and another is 1 Peter 5:7.*

ENGLE, DAVID ELBERT, religious organization administrator, consultant; b. Beaumont, Tex., July 11, 1942; s. William Edward and Celia Ann (Gibson) E.; m. Beverly Rose Alberty, Sept. 1, 1963; children: David, Todd, Marquette, Jonathan, Natalie. BS, Okla. State U., 1965. Dist. exec. Boy Scouts of Am., Oklahoma City, 1965-72; sales mgr. Logos Publs., Atlanta, 1972-79; mng. editor Solo mag., Tulsa, 1980-82; nat. accts. sales mgr. Graebel Van Lines, Tulsa, 1982-88; exec. dir. Restoration Ministries, Rogers, Ark., 1988—; apptd. adv., Tulsa, 1983-88. Author: Divorce-Count the Cost, 1988. Active speaker, seminar leader, facilitator in numerous chs., 1979—. With USMC, 1961-63. David Engle Day proclaimed by City of Tulsa, 1989. Baptist. Avocations: reading, farm work. Home: 2215 Little Flock Dr Rogers AR 72756

ENGLERT, JAMES O., religious organization administrator; b. Milbank, S.D., July 2, 1952; s. Martin I. and Mona E. (Seibel) E. BA, St. Mary's Coll., 1974; MA, The St. Paul Seminary, 1977. Assoc. pastor Sts. Peter and Paul Ch., Pierre, S.D., 1978-81; assoc. judge Cath. Marriage Tribunal, Sioux Falls, S.D., 1982-83, presiding judge, 1987-88; dir. U. S.D. Newman Ctr., Vermillion, 1989—; vis. instr. The St. Paul (Minn.) Seminary, 1984, Mt. Marty Coll., Yankton, S.D., 1985. mem. Sioux Falls Diocesan Priests' Senate, 1981-82, Personnel Bd., 1982-83. Mem. Amnesty Internat. Democrat. Home: 320 E Cherry Vermillion SD 57069 Office: U SD Newman Ctr 320 E Cherry Vermillion SD 57069

ENGLISH, JERRY BRUCE, minister; b. Hamer, S.C., June 6, 1942; s. James Sprugeon and Katherine (Singletary) E.; m. Evelyn Linton, Jan. 21, 1961; children: Kristi Lynne, Heather LeAnne. BS in Edn., East Carolina U., 1968; MDiv, Bethany Bible Coll., 1980; DD, Bethany Theol. Sem., 1982. Cert. tchr., N.C. Pastor Rock of Zion Bapt. Ch., Grantsboro, N.C., 1965-68, Antioch Bapt. Ch., New Bern, N.C., 1968-91; tchr. Pamlico County Schs., Bayboro, N.C., 1968-91; missionary Laotian Ch. in Am., cen. Calif., 1986-88. Author: It Happened in Church, 1981; composer gospel songs. Fundraiser Band Booster Club. Mem. Nat. Edn. Assn., N.C. Assn. Educators, Woodsmen of World, Craven Community Band, Lions Club, Masons. Home: 755 Antioch Rd New Bern NC 28560-9500

ENGLISH, JOHN CAMMEL, history and religion educator; b. Kansas City, Mo., Dec. 4, 1934; s. Jacob Cammel and Grace (Mortenson) E.; m. Evonne Kludas, July 29, 1966. BA, Wash. U., 1955; MDiv, Yale U., 1958; PhD, Vanderbilt U., 1965; postgrad., U. Chgo., 1969-70. Asst. prof. history Stephen F. Austin State U., Nacogdoches, Tex., 1962-65; asst. prof. history Baker U., Baldwin, Kans., 1965-66, assoc. prof. history, 1966-67, prof. history, 1968—, chair dept. history and polit. sci., 1965-73, 83—, dir. shaping of western thought program, 1977-80; chair edn. and rsch. sect. Hist. Soc. of the United Meth. Ch., 1989-90; del. 13th World Meth. Conf., Dublin, Ireland, 1976. Author: The Heart Renewed: John Wesley's Doctrine of Christian Initiation, 1967; editor: Freedom Under Grace, 1984; contbr. articles to profl. jours. Mem. Kans. Hist. Records Adv. Bd. Mem. Am. Acad. Religion, Am. Soc. Ch. History, Am. Soc. for 18th Century Studies, Am. Historical Assn. Home: 125 Santa Fe Dr PO Box 537 Baldwin KS 66006 Office: Baker U 606 8th St Baldwin KS 66006

ENGLISH, SISTER JOSEPH LOUISE, academic administrator. Supt. of Cath. Schs., Washington area Diocese of Evansville, Ind. Office: Schs Supt Cath Ctr PO Box 4169 4200 N Kentucky Ave Evansville IN 47724*

ENGLISH, VICKIE ANNE, religious organization administrator; b. Hermiston, Oreg., Oct. 11, 1959; d. Alvin Cary and Jane Anne (Vickers) Elwood; m. Gregory Albert English, June 7, 1980; 1 child, Bradford Gregory. Diploma in Music Edn., Oreg. Coll. of Edn., 1980. Tchr. Seattle Sch. Dist., 1980-87; bus. adminstr. Faith Community Ch., Covina, Calif., 1987—. Home: 2424 South Brisa Lane Rowland Heights CA 91748 Office: Faith Community Church 15906 East San Bernardino Covina CA 91722

ENGSTROM, THEODORE WILHELM, lay church worker; b. Cleve., Mar. 1, 1916; s. David W. and Ellen L. (Olson) E.; m. Dorothy E. Weaver, Nov. 3, 1939; children: Gordon, Donald, Jo Ann. AB, Taylor U., 1938, LHD, 1955; LLH, John Brown U., 1984; LittD, Seattle Pacific U., 1985. Pres. Youth for Christ Internat., Wheaton, Ill., 1957-63; chmn. Lake Ave. Congl. Ch., Pasadena, Calif., 1972—; pres., v.p. World Vision Internat., Monrovia, Calif., 1963—. Author: Managing Your Time, 1970, The Making of a Christian Leader, 1976, Strategy for Living, 1976, The Pursuit of Excellence, 1980, Your Gift of Administration, 1983, The Fine Art of Friendship, 1985. Trustee Taylor U., Upland, Ind., African Enterprise, Pasadena, Calif., Azusa Pacific U., Calif. Mem. Nat. Assn. Evangelicals, Am. Mgmt. Assn. Office: 919 W Huntington Dr Monrovia CA 91016

ENNENGA, KIRK CASTLE, minister; b. San Jose, Calif., July 3, 1964; s. Tjark John and Doris Castle (Nolan) E.; m. Mary Joy VanderHeide, Oct. 17, 1987. BRE, Reformed Bible Coll., 1987. Pastor youth and edn. 1st Reformed Ch., Edgerton, Minn., 1987-90, Waupun, Wis., 1990—; Evangelism Explosion trainer, Friendship Chapel, 1985-86; gen. dir. Inspiration Hills Camp, Inwood, Iowa, 1989-90; tchr., dir. Sunday sch., Youth sch., 1979—; founder, dir. United Youth Outreach, Waupun, 1991—. Bd. dirs. Big Bros./Big Sisters, Fond du Lac, Wis., 1991—. Office: 1st Reformed Ch 422 W Franklin St Waupun WI 53963 *If those who have too much were willing to give to those with too little, everyone would have enough.*

ENNIS, STEPHEN EUGENE, minister; b. Visalia, Calif., Sept. 18, 1933; s. Isaac Eugene and Ima Lee (Grant) E.; m. Norm June Gardner (dec. July 1988); children: Jim Holmes, Carolyn Andress, Ricky Holmes, David Holmes, Amron Lykins; m. Joy Lee Phillips, Nov. 25, 1989. BA, Abilene Christian U., 1967; MA, Pepperdine U., 1976. Ordained to ministry Chs. of Christ, 1956. Min. Ch. of Christ, Pixley, Calif., 1958-60, Estevan, Sask., Can., 1960-64, Yorkton, Sask., Can., 1967-70, Pacific Grove, Calif., 1974-89, Lapeer, Mich., 1989—; missionary to Ireland, Bahamas, Can.; fund raiser, pub. rels. Western Christian Coll., Duphine, Man., Can., 1971-72. Dir. home and sch. Estavan Region, 1963; tchr. Smile Svcs., Estevan, 1977-78. Mem. Toastmasters (pres. 1986-87), Rotary (sec. 1979—). Democrat. Home: 1937 Gardner Dr Lapeer MI 48446 Office: Ch of Christ 1680 N Lapeer Rd Box 471 Lapeer MI 48446

ENNISS, PINCKNEY C., minister; b. Jacksonville, Fla., Oct. 16, 1931; s. Pinckney Chambers and Minnie (Paschal) E.; m. Martha Jane Wiloman, June 11, 1955; children: David Pinckney, Stephen Crossley. BS, Davidson Coll., 1953, DD, 1988; BD, Columbia Sem., Decatur, Ga., 1958; ThM, Columbia Sem., 1970. Ordained to ministry Presbyn. Ch. Sr. min. Hillside Presbyn. Ch., Decatur, 1958-67, Meadowview Presbyn. Ch., Louisville, 1967-70, First Presbyn. Ch., Tallahassee, 1970-76, Cen. Presbyn. Ch., Atlanta, 1976-89, The Reformed Ch., Bronxville, N.Y., 1989—; mem. Gen. Assembly nominating com., 1977-78, com. Social Witness Policy, 1988—; moderator Atlanta Presbytery, 1985; chair. Urban (Presbyn.) Ch. Task Force, 1985. Contbr. sermons to Pulpit Digest, series of devotionals to Day by Day, articles to religious pubs. bd. trustees Eckerd Coll., St. Petersburg, Fla., 1973-76, Queens Coll., Charlotte, N.C., 1986-89; mem. Leadership Atlanta, 1977; co-chair. Civilian Rev. Bd., Atlanta, 1988. 1st lt. U.S. Army, 1953-55. Recipient martin L. King, Sr. Community Svc. award, King Ctr., Atlanta, 1988. Mem. Hudson River Presbytery, Siwandy Country Club. Democrat. Office: The Reformed Ch Box 397 Bronxville NY 10708

ENO, ROBERT BRYAN, priest, religion educator; b. Hartford, Conn., Nov. 12, 1936; s. Earl Bryan and Bernice Sarah (Landers) E. BA, Cath. U. Am., 1958, MA in Philosophy, 1959; STD, Inst. Cath., Paris, 1969. Ordained priest Roman Cath. Ch., 1963, joined Priests St. Sulpice, 1965. Lectr. patristics St. Mary's Sem., Balt., 1968-70; prof. ch. history Cath. U. Am., Washington, 1970—; mem. Nat. Luth.—Roman Cath. Dialogue, 1976—; consultor-gen. Priests St. Sulpice, Paris, 1978-90; St. Augustine lectr. Villanova U., 1985, Tuohy prof. inter-religious studies John Carroll U., 1987. Author: Teaching Authority in the Early Church, 1984, The Rise of the Papacy, 1990; translator, commentator: Newly Discovered Letters of St. Augustine, 1989. Basselin scholar Cath. U. Am., 1956-59. Basselin scholar Cath. U. Am., 1956-59. Mem. N.Am. Patristics Soc. (bd. dirs. 1980-83), Internat. Assn. Patristic Studies (mem. coun. 1983-91), Am. Soc. Ch. History, Am. Cath. Hist. Assn. Office: Cath U Am Dept Ch History Washington DC 20064

ENO, ZELLMA ANITA, lay minister; b. Bellwood, Nebr., Nov. 1, 1919; d. Zellmond Ernst and Ruth Anita (Cooper) Matheny; m. Gordon Melvin Eno, Oct. 24, 1954; children: Gene Leroy, Gordon Robert, Earl Eldon, Melodee Ruth. Student, U. Nebr., 1936-37, Pasadena (Calif.) Playhouse, 1938-39, Tchrs. Coll., Wayne, Nebr., 1939-40. Ch. clk. Cross Roads Bapt. Ch., Branson, Mo., 1985—, adult choir dir., 1986—, bd. elders, 1988—; trustee, sec. Cross Roads Bapt. Ch. Inc. Republican. Home: HCR 5 Box 1938 Branson MO 65616 *It was a great day when I surrendered to the Ministry of the Gospel of Jesus Christ. Now that I am considered retired, I am so busy serving my Lord which gives me much peace in my heart even through the testing I'm put through. The joy of the Lord is my strength.*

ENOS, RALPH GREGORY, religious writer; b. L.A., Sept. 10, 1952; s. Ralph Francis and Ruth (Hartley) E.; m. Paula Drake, Mar. 29, 1985; children: Nathan Adam, Joel Gregory. BA with honors, U. Calif., Davis, 1974; ThM, Dallas Theol. Seminary, 1982, ThD, 1989. Teaching asst. summer inst. linguistics U. Okla., Norman, 1980; instr. Dallas Theol. Seminary Lay Inst., 1981, 87; tchr. Berean Christian Acad., Irving, Tex., 1982-83; writer The Art of Family Living, Dallas, 1989—; trustee Skillman Bible Ch., Dallas, 1988—. Contbr. chpt.: Linguistics and Biblical Hebrew, 1992; contbr. articles to profl. jours. Mem. Evang. Theol. Soc., Phi Beta Kappa, Phi Kappa Phi, Phi Sigma Iota. Mem. Ind. Bible Ch. Home: 2122D Tucker St Dallas TX 75221 Office: The Art of Family Living Box 2000 Dallas TX 75221

ENRIGHT, EDWARD JOSEPH, priest; b. Medford, Mass., May 16, 1947; s. Edward Joseph and Doris Virginia (Hill) E. BA, Villanova U., 1970; STB, Cath. U., 1973, Licentiate in Sacred Theology, 1974, STD, 1991. Ordained to ministry Roman Cath. Ch., 1973. Tchr. St. Nicholas of Tolentine High Sch., Bronx, N.Y., 1974-76, Monsignor Bonner High Sch., Drexel Hill, Pa., 1976-78; asst. prof. Merrimack Coll., North Andover, Mass., 1984—; adj. lectr. Villanova (Pa.) U., 1978-80. Mem. Am. Cath. Hist. Assn., U.S. Cath. Hist. Soc., Am. Soc. Ch. History, Coll. Theology Soc., Am. Acad. Religion. Home: 300 Haverhill St Lawrence MA 01840 Office: Merrimack Coll North Andover MA 01845

ENRIGHT, WILLIAM GERALD, minister; b. Peoria, Ill., Dec. 5, 1935; s. William Gerald and Lucille Mae (Strubhar) E.; m. Edith Strai, June 13, 1959; children: Scott, Kirk. BA, Wheaton (Ill.) Coll., 1958; MDiv, Fuller Theol. Sem., Pasadena, Calif., 1961; ThM, McCormick Theol. Sem., Chgo., 1965; PhD, U. Edinburgh, Scotland, 1968; DD (hon.), Hanover Coll., 1983. Ordained to ministry Presbyn. Ch. (U.S.A.), 1963. Asst. pastor Roseland Presbyn. Ch., Chgo., 1963-65; pastor 1st Presbyn. Ch., Glen Ellyn, Ill., 1968-80, 2d Presbyn. Ch., Indpls., 1981—; prof. preaching and worship No. Bapt. Theol. Sem., Oakbrook Ill., 1970-80; trustee McCormick Theol. Sem., 1982—; dir. Lilly Endowment, Indpls., 1988—. Contbr. to ch. publs. Bd. dirs. Wishard Hosp. Found., Indpls., St. Vincent Hosp., Indpls., YMCA, Indpls., Ind. Ctr. for Advanced Rsch., Indpls; chmn. task force on ethics and values City of Indpls.; mem. Police Chief's Adv. Bd., Indpls. Mem. Soc. Am. Ch. History, Soc. for Sci. Study Religion, Rotary. Office: 2d Presbyn Ch 7700 N Meridian St Indianapolis IN 46260

ENRIQUE Y TARANCON, VICENTE CARDINAL, Spanish ecclesiastic; b. Burriana, Castellon, June 14, 1907; s. Manuel E. Urios and Vicenta T. Fandos. Ed. Seminario Conciliar Rortosa, Tarragona and Universidad Pontificia Valencia. Adminstrv. asst. Vinaroz, 1930-33, Archpriest, 1938-43; Archipriest, Villarreal, 1943-46; Bishop of Solsona, 1946-64; gen. sec. Spanish Bishopric, 1956-64; Archbishop of Ovopie, 1964-69; Archibishop of Toledo, Primate of Spain, 1969-71; Archbishop of Madrid, 1971-83; elevated to Sacred Coll. Cardinals, 1969; mem. Sacred Congregations for Bishops, Divine Worship and Reform of Canon Law; mem. Spanish Acad., 1969. Author: La Renovación Total de la Vida Cristiana, 1954, Los Seglares en la Iglesia, 1958, Sucesores de los Apostoles, 1960, La Parroquia, Hoy, 1961, El Misterio de la Iglesia, 1963, Ecumenismo y Pastoral 1964, La Iglesia en el Mundo de Hoy, 1965, El Sacerdocio a la Luz del Concilio Vaticano II, 1966, La Iglesia del Posconcilio, 1967, La Crisis de Fe en el Mundo Actual, 1968, Unidad y pluralismo en la Iglesia, 1969, Liturgia y lengua del pueblo, 1970, El magisterio de Santa Teresa, 1970. Avocations: musical composition; classical music. Address: Palacio Arzobispal, Toledo Spain

ENRIQUEZ, DIANA, religion education director; b. Pharr, Tex., Jan. 25, 1963; d. Elisandro S. and Maria del Socorro (DeLeon) E. Grad., Pharr-San Juan Alamo Pub. Schs. Dir. religious edn. St. Margaret-Mary Ch., Pharr, 1983—, Conformity of Christian Doctrine, Pharr, 1983—; treas., parliamentarian Cath. Youth Orgn., Pharr, 1980-81, sponsor, advisor, 1982-87, moderator, 1987-89. Roman Catholic. Home: 802 W Wright Pharr TX 78577 Office: St Margaret Mary 122 W Hawk Pharr TX 78577

ENSLOW, MARY BERNICE, lay worker; b. Potsdam, N.Y., Jan. 31, 1957; d. Clarence Peter and Jean Lillian (Barclay) E. AA, Mater Dei Coll., 1985; BA, Coll. of St. Rose, 1987. Catechist St. Mary's Parish, Potsdam, 1974-76, 77, 1989-90; eucharistic min. St. Francis of Assisi, Potsdam, 1978-87, lector, 1980-87, 90—; dir. religious edn. St. Agnes Parish, Lake Placid, N.Y., 1987-88, Immaculate Conception, Schenectady, N.Y., 1988-89; mother's helper Jack Locey, Potsdam, 1991—. Democrat. Roman Catholic. Home: Postwood Rd PO Box 183 Hannawa Falls NY 13647

EPLEY-SHUCK, BARBARA JEANNE, lay minister; b. Fairfield, Nebr., Nov. 28, 1936; d. Elden Claude and Clara Joan (Cornelius) Epley; m. Elmer Shuck, June 8, 1958; children; Douglas, Bruce, Michael. BA, Hastings Coll., 1957; Cert. in Journalism, U. Nebr., 1961. Lay preacher Utica (Nebr.) Presbyn. Ch., 1990—; free-lance writer Whitesboro, N.Y. Mem. Presbyn. Women of the Synod (historian Synod of Northeast, worship com. 1989—), Kappa Tau Alpha, Theta Sigma Phi. Home: 20 Vine Circle Whitesboro NY 13492

EPP, ELDON JAY, religion educator; b. Mountain Lake, Minn., Nov. 1, 1930; s. Jacob Jay and Louise (Kintzi) E.; m. ElDoris Balzer, June 13, 1951; children: Gregory Thomas, Jennifer Elizabeth. A.B. magna cum laude, Wheaton Coll., 1952; B.D. magna cum laude, Fuller Theol Sem., 1955; S.T.M., Harvard U., 1956, Ph.D., 1961. Spl. research asst. Princeton Theol. Sem., 1961-62; vis. instr. Drew U. Theol. Sch., 1962; asst. prof. religion U. So. Calif. Grad. Sch. Religion, 1962-65, assoc. prof., 1965-67, assoc. prof. classics, 1966-68; assoc. prof. religion Case Western Res. U., Cleve., 1968-71; prof. religion, Harkness prof. bibl. lit. Case Western Res. U., 1971—, dean humanities and social scis., 1977-85; acting dean Western Res. Coll., 1984, chmn. dept. religion, 1982—; Mem. Am. exec. com. Internat. Greek New Testament Project, 1968-88; N.Am. Com., 1989—; mem. accreditation rev. coun. North Cen. Assn. Commn. on Insts. Higher Edn., 1986-90, cons. evaluator corps., 1983—; Kenneth W. Clark lectr. Duke U., 1986. Author: The Theological Tendency of Codex Bezae Cantabrigiensis in Acts, 1966; co-author: Studies in the Theory and Method of New Testament Textual Criticism, 1992; co-editor: New Testament Textual Criticism: Its Significance for Exegesis, 1981, The New Testament and Its Modern Interpreters, 1989; assoc. editor Jour. Bibl. Lit, 1971-90; editor Critical Rev. of Books in Religion, 1991—, Studies and Documents, 1991—; mem. editorial bd. Soc. Bibl. Lit. Monograph Series, 1969-72, Soc. Bibl. Lit. Centennial Publs, 1975-86, Studies and Documents, 1971—, Critical Review of Books in Religion, 1987—; exec. sec.: Hermeneia: A Critical and Historical Commentary on the Bible, 1962—; mem. editorial bd., 1966—; contbr. articles, reviews to publs. Active Boy Scouts Am., 1975-78; Bd. mgrs. St. Paul's Episcopal Cathedral, Los Angeles, 1964-68, clk., 1967-68. Harvard Faculty Arts and Scis. fellow, 1958-59, Rockefeller doctoral fellow in religion, 1959-60; postdoctoral fellow Claremont Grad. Sch., 1966-68; Guggenheim fellow, 1974-75. Mem. Am. Acad. Religion (sect. pres. 1965-66), Soc. Bibl. Lit. (chmn. textual criticism seminar 1966, 71-84, mem. permanent Centennial com. 1975-80, mem. council 1980-82, 85-87, del. Council on Study of Religion 1980-82), Studiorum Novi Testamenti Societas, Cath. Bibl. Assn., Am. Soc. Papyrologists, New Testament Colloquium (chmn. 1974), Soc. Mithraic Studies, AAUP (chpt. exec. com. 1970-72), Inst. Antiquity and Christianity, Phi Beta Kappa. Office: Case Western Res U Dept Religion Cleveland OH 44106 *Personal philosophy: Integrity (in substance, incorruptibility) and maturity (basically, the capacity to tolerate ambiguity) are two essentials for the fullness of life and livelihood—integrity in every human relationship and maturity of judgment and taste in all aspects of vocation, family and civic responsibilities, and leisure. Anything less is too little.*

EPPENGER, JOHN ARTHUR, deacon, religion educator; b. Nashville, Mar. 6, 1948; s. Grant and Helen Mae (Horner) E.; m. Carolyn Faye Nation, June 21, 1968; children: John A. II, Jason A. BS in Math., Tenn. State U., 1971; postgrad., U. Tenn., 1976-77, U. Ala., 1990—. Ordained to ministry Bapt. Ch. as deacon, 1981. Mgr. S. Cen. Bell Telephone Co., Birmingham, Ala., 1971—; Sunday Sch. tchr. Galilee Bapt. Ch., Birmingham, 1980—, deacon, 1981—, youth dir., 1983-88, trustee, 1985—, Christian Edn. dir., 1988—. Coach Forest Hills Dixie Youth Baseball Team, Fairfield, Ala., 1984-85, commr., 1986-90; treas. John Carroll High Sch. PTA, Birmingham, 1985-87. Mem. IEEE. Home: 7405 Earlwood Dr Fairfield AL 35064

EPPERSON, BARBARA, missionary; b. Neosho, Mo., Jan. 2, 1921; d. Clarence Raymond and Fay Marie (Duncan) E. BS, Okla. Bapt. U., 1952. Lifetime appointee Fgn. Mission Bd. So. Bapt. Conv., Richmond, Va., 1953-86; ret. Fgn. Mission Bd. So. Bapt. Conv., 1986. Author: Tales from IRE, 1957, Out of Shango's Shadow, 1967; contbr. articles to mags. Pres. Ottawa County Rep. Women's Club, 1989-91, treas., 1992. Republican. Baptist. Avocations: writing, church, cooking, sports. Home and Office: 2525 N Elm Apt 19 Miami OK 74354 *The choices that I have made that relate to God's will and purpose for my life have been the ones that have brought joy even in adverse circumstances.*

EPPS, WILLIAM DAVID, minister; b. Jan. 15, 1951; s. William E. Epps Jr.; m. Cynthia Scott Douglas; children: Jason, John, James. B in Social Work, East Tenn. State U., 1975; ThM, Internat. Sem., 1981; D Ministry, Berean Christian Coll., 1981; postgrad., Assemblies of God Theol. Sem. Lic. to ministry Assemblies of God, 1978, ordained, 1980. Youth worker State St. United Meth. Ch., Bristol, Va., 1971-72; minister youth Wesley Meml. United Meth. Ch., Johnson City, Tenn., 1973-74; pastor Taylor Meml. United Meth. Ch., Johnston City, Tenn., 1974-75, Chuckey United Meth. Cir., Greene County, Tenn., 1975-77, Orebank Assembly of God, Kingsport, Tenn., 1978-79; minister edn. Trinity Assembly of God, Johnson City, 1979; minister outreach 1st Assembly of God, Grand Junction, Colo., 1979-83; sr. pastor Trinity Fellowship, Peachtree City, Ga., 1983—; presbyter S. Atlanta sect. Ga. Dist. Assemblies of God; chaplain Peachtree City Police Dept.; chmn. 1990 N. Ga. Intercessory Prayer Gathering, Atlanta; mem. Ga. Dist. Evangelism Com., area evangelism rep.; mem. The Acad. Parish Clergy; Assembly of God campus minister West Ga. Coll. Contbg. editor, Strategies for the 90's: A Pastoral Evangelism Handbook; contbr. articles to profl. jours. With USMC; U.S. Army N.G. Recipient Ga. Press Assn. Editorial award 1986, Cert. of Appreciation, Ga. Dist. Women's Ministries, 1989, many others. Mem. Fellowship Christian Athletes, Evang. Tchr. Tng. Assn. (honor mem.), Am. Assn. Christian Counselors, Internat. Assn. Christian Counselors, Internat. Conf. Police Chaplains, Fayette County Ministerial Assn. (past pres.). Office: Trinity Fellowship PO Box 2777 Peachtree City GA 30269-0777 *What do I want on my tombstone? What every Christian truly wishes to be said—that "he loved Jesus more than life".*

EPSTEIN, JEROME MICHAEL, religious movement executive, rabbi; b. Cleve., Apr. 27, 1943; s. Jack Hyman and Ann (Mermel) E.; m. Jane Eileen Geller, May 29, 1966; children: Efrem, Shira, Arielle. BS, U. Pitts., 1964; MHL, Jewish Theol. Sem., N.Y.C., 1969; MS, Old Dominion U., 1976; EdD, Temple U., 1980. Ordained rabbi, 1970. Rabbi Communidad Bet El, Buenos Aires, 1970, Congregation Beth Jacob, Galveston, Tex., 1971-73, Gomley Chesed Synagogue, Portsmouth, Va., 1973-76; dir. Delaware Valley region United Synagogue Am., Phila., 1976-78; dir. regional activities United Synagogue Am., N.Y.C., 1978-86, sr. v.p., 1986-89, exec. v.p., 1989—, chief exec. officer, 1986—; mem. steering com. Faith Devel. in Adult Life Cycle, Mpls., 1980-88. Editor Hamadrich, 1973-78. Named Alumnus of Yr., United Synagogue Youth, 1987. Mem. Rabbinical Assembly (exec. com. 1986—), Religious Edn. Assn. (v.p. 1986-90). Office: United Synagogue Am 155 Fifth Ave New York NY 10010

EPSTEIN, MARJORIE, communal association administrator, lay worker; b. Brookline, Mass., Feb. 5, 1952; d. George and Esther Rose (Hurwitz) E. Student, Hebrew Coll.; BA, Boston U., 1975; MA, Am. U., 1978. Dir. Jewish Family Svc., Jewish Fedn., New Bedford, Mass., 1980-81; dir. pub. policy Jewish Community Rels. Coun., Boston, 1981-88; exec. dir. Nat. Tay-Sachs, Brookline, 1988—; Israel chmn. Jewish Labor Com., Boston, 1987—; mem. coun. Na'Amat U.S.A., Boston, 1985—; chair pub. affairs Workmen's Circle, Boston, 1988—. Campaign worker Mark Draisen for State Rep., 1990; vol. Armdi. Recipient Social Action award Social Action Ministries, 1988. Mem. Assn. Jewish Communal Orgnl. Profls., Internat. Communal Workers, Hadassah (life), Women's Internat. Zionist Orgn. (life, pres. Boston chpt. 1987—), Mass. Health Action Alliance. Home: 94 Williston Rd Brookline MA 02146

EPTING, C. CHRISTOPHER, bishop; b. Greenville, S.C.; m. Pam Flagg; children: Michael, Amanda. Grad., U. Fla., Seabury-Western Theol. Sem., Evanston, Ill., 1952; STM, Gen. Theol. Sem., N.Y.C., 1984. Formerly curate Holy Trinity Ch., Melbourne; vicar Ch. of St. Luke the Evangelist, Mulberry, Fla., 1974-78; founding vicar St. Stephen's Ch., Lakeland, Fla.; canon residentiary St. John's Cathedral, from 1978; rector St. Mark's Episc. Ch. and Sch., Cocoa, Fla.; bishop coadjutor, then bishop Episc. Diocese of Iowa, Des Moines, 1988—; formerly dean Inst. Christian Studies, St. Luke's Cathedral, Orlando, Fla. Address: Episc Diocese of Iowa 225 37th St Des Moines IA 50312

ERB, CLARENCE LEIGHTON, JR., clergyman; b. Phila., Mar. 11, 1917; s. Clarence Leighton and Helen Mabel (Baker) E.; m. Maria Margarete Sticker, Feb. 19, 1949; children: Heidi Maria,,, Suzanne Helen. BS in Mil. Studies, U. Md., 1960; STB, Phila. Div. Sch., 1966, MDiv, 1971; PhD in Religious Studies, Pacific We. U., 1986. Ordained to ministry, Episcopal Ch., 1966. Curate St. Marks P.E. Ch., Frankford, Phila., 1966-67; rector The P.E. Ch. of St. John the Evangelist, Essington, Pa., 1967-87 (ret.); rector emeritus The P.E. Ch. of St. John the Evangelist, 1987—; dean Del. Deanery, Diocese of Pa., 1975-78, mem. exec. com., 1978-90, mem. com. on incorporation, 1969—; assoc. Episcopalian chaplain Taylor Hosp., Ridley Park, Pa., 1970—, mem. clergy com., 1975—. Chaplain Tinicum Twp. Police Dept., Essington, 1975-87, Essington & Lester Fire Cos., 1970-87. With U.S. Army, 1942-63, ETO, Germany, Korea, Japan and U.S. Army Europe. Named Vet. of the Year, Fox-Smith Post 4845, V.F.W., 1974; named Man of the Year, Tinicum Twp. Patriotic Assn., 1981; Disting. Svc. award, County of Del. council, 1982; citation, Ho. of Reps., Commonwealth of Pa., 1987, others. Mem. Am. Legion (chaplain 1987—), The Union League, Optimist (pres. 1987%). Republican. Episcopalian. Avocations: photography, geneology, reading. Home: 536 Sylvania Ave Folsom PA 19033

ERBES, PAUL KENNETH, minister; b. Tracy, Minn., Mar. 10, 1957; s. Gerald Clarence and Marvel Harriet (Haugen) E.; 1 adopted child, Lance; 25 foster children. BA, St. Olaf Coll., 1979; MDiv, Luther Northwestern Sem., 1983, postgrad., 1991—. Ordained to ministry Evang. Luth. Ch. Am., 1983. Pastor Our Savior's Luth. Ch., Brewster, Kans., 1983-87, Shepherd of Valley Luth. Ch., Grand Junction, Colo., 1987—; chaplain Grand Mesa Youth Svcs. Ctr., Grand Junction, 1989—. Chair Alcohol and Drug Coun., Thomas County, Kans., 1986-87, N.W. Kans. Coun. of Substance Abuse, Colby, 1986-87; bd. dirs. Ptnrs. Inc., Grand Junction, 1989—, Bethphage Community Svcs., Grand Junction, 1989—, The Jacob Ctr., 1991—. Recipient Community Svc. award Ptnrs., Inc., 1990. Home: 610 E Indian Creek Dr Grand Junction CO 81506 Office: Shepherd of Valley Luth Ch 3133 F Rd Grand Junction CO 81504

ERDAHL, LOWELL O., bishop; b. Minn., Feb. 27, 1931; s. Christian A. and Ingeborg (Fosness) E.; m. Carol Syvertsen, Jan. 15, 1955; children: Rebecca, Paul, Elizabeth. BA, St. Olaf Coll.; BD, Luther Theol. Sem.; STM, Union Theol. Sem. Pastor Farmington, Minn., 1958-68; asst. prof. Luther Theol. Sem., St. Paul, 1968-73; sr. pastor Univ. Luth. Ch. of Hope, Mpls., from 1973; former bishop S.E. Minn. dist. Am. Luth. Ch.; bishop St. Paul synod Evang. Luth. Ch. in Am., 1988—. Author: Unwitting Witnesses, 1974, Preaching for the People, 1975, (with Carol Erdahl) Be Good to Each Other, 1976, The Lonely House, 1977, Authentic Living, 1979, Pro-Life, Pro-Peace, 1986. Office: Evang Ch in Am 105 W University Ave Saint Paul MN 55103*

ERDEL, TIMOTHY PAUL, missionary; b. Decatur, Ind., Aug. 7, 1951; s. Paul Arthur and Chloetta Eileen (Egly) E.; m. Sally Elizabeth Birky, Aug. 28, 1977; children: Sarah Beth, Rachel Elaine, Matthew Robert. BA magna cum laude, Summit Christian Coll., Ft. Wayne, Ind., 1973; MDiv cum laude, Trinity Evang. Div. Sch., 1976, ThM, 1981; AM, U. Chgo., 1978; MA, U. Ill., 1986. Lic. to ministry Missionary Ch. Inc., 1973. Pastoral asst. First Missionary Ch., Chgo., 1973-76, interim pastor, 1976; pastoral intern South Shore Bible Ch., Chgo., 1976-77; asst. for collection devel. Jesuit-Krauss McCormick Libr., Chgo., 1977-78; ref. libr. and lectr. Trinity Evang. Div. Sch., Deerfield, Ill., 1978-82; vis. lectr. history of Latin Am. Trinity Coll., Deerfield, Ill., 1982; grad. teaching asst. philosophy and religious studies U. Ill., Urbana, 1982-87; missionary World Ptnrs., Ft. Wayne, Ind., 1987—; librarian and lectr. humanities Jamaica Theol. Sem., Kingston, 1987—; librarian and lectr. in hist. and philos. theology Caribbean Grad. Sch. Theology, Kingston, 1987—; sec. project coord. com. Reg. Survey of Ch. Growth in the Caribbean, 1988—; cons. to theol. librs.; lectr. in field. Editor Trinity Jour., 1975-76; co-author: Religions of the World, 2nd edit. 1988; compiler monograph: Guide to the Preparation of Theses, 2d edit., 1991; contbr. articles to profl. jours. Mem. Wesleyan Theol. Soc., Soc. Christian Philosophy, Soc. Bibl. Lit., Evang. Theol. Soc., Evang. Philos. Soc., Conf. on Faith and History, Am. Soc. Ch. History, Am. Theol. Libr. Assn., Am. Philos. Assn., Am. Acad. Religion, Coll. Libr. Info. Network, Jamaican Libr. Assn. (exec. com. 1991—), Ill. Mennonite Hist. and Genealog. Soc., Missionary Ch. Hist. Soc., Am. Sci. Affiliation, Delta Epsilon Chi, others. Home: 14 West Ave PO Box 121, Constant Spring, Kingston 8, Jamaica Office: World Ptnrs 3901 S Wayne Ave Fort Wayne IN 46807

ERDVIG, LLOYD PARKER, radio station general manager; b. Huntington, N.Y., Aug. 9, 1953; s. Oscar Gunfelt and Mabel (Stensrud) E.; m. Ellen Anderson, Nov. 17, 1979; children: Rory, Taryn. BS, Evangel Coll., Springfield, Mo. Sta. mgr. Sta. KECC-AM, Springfield, Mo., 1973-75; program dir. Sta. KLFJ-AM, Springfield, 1974; news announcer Sta. KICK-AM, Springfield, 1975; program dir. Sta. WNYG-AM, Babylon, N.Y., 1975-79; v.p., gen. mgr. Sta. WLIX, Bay Shore, N.Y., 1979—; gen. mgr. Sta. WLVX, Bloomfield, Conn., 1988—; pres., founder Gospel Spectrum, 1978-85; bd. dirs. I Care Ministries, Nashville, 1988—; exec. com. mem. Long Island Billy Graham Crusade, 1989-90. Editor (promotional newspaper) WLIX-tra, 1986—; producer Christian artist concerts, 1972—; contbr. articles to religious and trade jours. Mem. Adv. Bd. Christian Rsch. Report, Nat. Religious Broadcasters, Nat. Christian Radio Seminar (vice chmn. 1987—), Gospel Music Assn. (bd. dirs. 1983-89, v.p. 1987). Office: WLIX Radio 138 W Main St Bay Shore NY 11706

ERICKSEN, DONALD O., college president; b. Mpls., Oct. 4, 1932; s. Oscar and Gerda Henrietta (Torgerson) E.; m. Bonita J. Fenton, Jan. 7, 1956; children: Todd, Kirk, Mark. BS, St. Cloud (Minn.) State U., 1956, MS, 1967; EdD, U. Tenn., 1975. Cert. educator, Minn. Counselor Sch. Dist. 286, Brooklyn Ctr., Minn., 1967-72, dist. coord., 1972-77; dean of students Northwestern Coll., St. Paul., 1977-80, exec. v.p., 1980-84, pres., 1984—; mem. reference bd. Barnabas Internat., Rockford, Ill.; cons. para ch. ministries group, 1991. Contbr. articles to religious jours. With U.S. Naval Air Res., 1950-58. Edn. Program Devel. Act fellow State of Minn., 1973-74. Mem. Christian Coll. Coalition (bd. dirs. 1986—, chair bd. 1991—), Coun. Ind. Colls., Am. Assn. Pres. of Ind. Colls. and Univs., Internat. Assn. Univ. Pres., Nat. Assn. Ind. Colls. and Univs., Evang. Coun. for Fin. Accountability (bd. dirs. 1985-87), Gospel Assn. India (bd. reference 1988—). Office: Northwestern Coll 3003 N Snelling Ave Saint Paul MN 55113 *Being committed to a significant spiritual purpose in life is what I have found to be most satisfying and ultimately most worthwhile as we daily experience the challenges of societal change and increasing secular values.*

ERICKSON, DOUGLAS ROBERT, missionary; b. Niagara Falls, N.Y., July 17, 1956; s. Willard Edward and Evelyn Joyce (Kline) E.; m. Karen Jill Hultgren, June 17, 1978; children: Tracy, Dean, Scott, Amy. BA in Bus., Econs., Bethel Coll., 1978. Area dir. Young Life, Tinley Park, Ill., 1986—; chmn. Christian edn. bd. Salem Bapt. Ch., Orland Park, Ill., 1980-86; mem. deacon bd., 1983-86, 89—; coach V.J. Andrew High Sch., Tinley Park, 1986—. Home: 8420 W 162d Pl # 2 Tinley Park IL 60477 Office: Young Life PO Box 815 Tinley Park IL 60477

ERICKSON, JAMES HUSTON, clergyman, physician; b. Omaha, Sept. 7, 1931; s. Paul Ferdinand and Naomi Marie (Berglund) E.; m. Shirley Arlene Nordling, Dec. 26, 1959; children: Jonathan, Sonja, Ingrid. AA, North Park Coll., 1950; AB, Stanford U., 1952; MD, U. Colo., 1959; MPH, U. Minn., 1975; MS, Loyola Coll., Balt., 1982. Ordained to ministry Evang. Covenant Ch., 1985; Diplomate Am. Bd. Preventive Medicine, Am. Bd. Med. Psycho Therapy. Intern Swedish Covenant Hosp., Chgo., 1959-60; resident in surgery VA Hosp., Hines, Ill., 1963; resident in gen. practice Swedish Covenant Hosp., Chgo., 1964-65; asst. minister Bethel Covenant Ch., Orange, Calif., 1960-61; commd. USN, 1960-63, 69-70, advanced through grades to commdr.; med. missionary Christian Med. Coll., Ludhiana, India, 1965; supply pastor Covenant and Presbyn. Chs., various locations, 1965-81; commd. USPHS, 1970—, advanced through grades to asst. surgeon gen., 1976; chaplain Boy Scouts Am., Laurel, Md., 1977-81; dir. health svcs., prof. community health No. Ill. U., DeKalb, Ill., 1981-85; assoc. minister Hillcrest Covenant Ch., DeKalb, 1982-85; interim minister Community Covenant Ch., Springfield, Va., 1988-89; dir. health svcs. and pastoral care Atlantic Fleet NOAA, Norfolk, Va., 1986-88; dir. health svcs. and pastoral care hdqrs. NOAA, Rockville, Md., 1988—; med. officer USN, 1960-63, 69-70; bd. dirs. The Holmstad, Batavia, Ill.; mem. commn. Christian action Evang. Covenant Ch., Chgo., 1984-90, ministerial ethics com., 1990—. Fellow Am. Coll. Preventive Medicine, Royal Soc. Health, Am. Acad. Family Physicians; mem. Aerospace Med. Soc., Am. Assn. Counseling and Devel., N.Y. Acad. Scis., DeKalb County Epilepsy Assn. (bd. dirs. 1982-85), DeKalb Ministerial Assn., Commd. Officers Assn. U.S. Pub. Health Svc. Avocations: reading, running, bicycling. Office: Nat Oceanic and Atmospheric Adminstrn 11400 Rockville Pike Ste 505 Rockville MD 20582

ERICKSON, JOHN DAVID, minister, Bible society administrator; b. Wesleyville, Pa., Apr. 28, 1933; s. Arvid and Julia A. (Anderson) E.; m. Nancy Ann Olson, June 2, 1956; children—Alana, Julia Ann, John David, Ronald. B.A., Augustana Coll., Rock Island, Ill., 1955, B.Div., Augustana Theol. Sem., 1959; postgrad. U. Minn., 1960; D.Div., Va. Sem., 1973. Ordained to ministry Lutheran Ch. in Am., 1959. Missionary, Japan, 1960-62; asst. pastor Elim Luth. Ch., Robbinsdale, Minn., 1962-65; Asia sec. Am. Bible Soc., N.Y.C., 1965-67, exec. sec. ways and means dept., 1967-76, dep. gen. sec., 1976-78, gen. sec., 1978—; world service officer United Bible Socs., N.Y.C., 1976-88, chmn. exec. com., 1988— . Bd. dirs. Leonia (N.J.) Pub. Sch. Dist., 1974-77; pres. Leonia Civic Conf., 1969; officer Leonia Citizens for Pub. Schs., 1967-69. Mem. Nat. Soc. Fund Raisers, Augustana Coll. Alumni Assn. (Outstanding Achievement award). Home: 1 Paulin Blvd Leonia NJ 07605 Office: Am Bible Soc 1865 Broadway New York NY 10023

ERICKSON, MILLARD JOHN, dean; b. Stanchfield, Minn., June 24, 1932; s. Andrew Olaf and Ida Caroline (Sundstrom) E.; m. Virginia Nepstad, Aug. 20, 1955; children: Kathryn Sue, Sandra Lynne, Sharon Ruth. BA, U. Minn., 1953; BDiv, No. Bapt. Sem., 1956; MA, U. Chgo., 1958; PhD, Northwestern U., 1963. Pastor Fairfield Ave. Bapt. Ch., Chgo., 1956-61, Olivet Bapt. Ch., Robbinsdale, Minn., 1961-64; from asst. to assoc. prof., chair dept. bible and philosophy Wheaton (Ill.) Coll., 1964-69; from assoc. prof. to prof. theology Bethel Theol. Sem., St. Paul, 1969-84, exec. v.p., dean, 1984—. Author: Relativism in Contemporary Christian Ethics, 1974, Contemporary Options in Eschatology, 1976, Christian Theology, 1986 (Gold medallion 1987); editor: Readings in Christian Theology, 1973-79. Mem. Am. Theol. Soc. (pres. 1988-89), Am. Acad. Religion, Am. Philos. Assn., Soc. Christian Ethics, Evang. Theol. Soc., Evang. Philos. Soc. (pres. 1990-91). Home: 2677 Lake Court Cir Mounds View MN 55112 Office: Bethel Theol Sem 3949 Bethel Dr Saint Paul MN 55112

ERICKSON, RICHARD NORMAN, instructional materials director; b. Danbury, Conn., June 12, 1949; s. Raymond Arthur and Loretta Rita (Mongillo) E.; m. Elaine Joyce Osborn, Feb. 7, 1981; children: Linde Rose, Casey Frederick. BS, Western Conn. State U., Danbury, 1971, MS in communications, 1975. Cert. secondary sch. tchr. Cons. tng. Faith Venture Visuals, Lilitz, Pa., 1987—; dir. instructional materials Bapt. Bible Coll., Clarks Summit, Pa., 1978—; radio com. chmn. Heritage Bapt. Ch., Clarks Summit, Pa., 1978-81; radio com. chmn., S.S. tchr., youth leader trustee Bapt. ch. of Danbury, Conn., 1973-78. Pres. Foster Parent Assn. Lackawanna County, Scranton, Pa., 1989—; active mem. Lackawanna County Citizen's Adv. Bd., Scranton, 1990—. Mem. ASCD. Democrat. Office: Baptist Bible College of PA 538 Venard Rd Clarks Summit PA 18411

ERICKSON, ROBERT LEE, ecumenical agency administrator. Exec. dir. Met. Area Ch. Bd., Columbus, Ohio. Office: Met Area Ch Bd 760 E Broad St Columbus OH 43205*

ERICSON, CARL ERLAND, minister, newspaper columnist; b. Jacksonville, Ill., Mar. 20, 1913; s. Carl August and Ethel Jane (Plummer) E.; m. Mary Katherine Shaw, Jan. 19, 1936; children: Mary Karin, Carl Eric Jon, Helen Jane. BA, Ill. Coll., 1934, DD (hon.), 1963; MDiv, Princeton U., 1959. Ordained to ministry Presbyn. Ch. U.S.A., 1959. City editor, writer Daily Jour., Jacksonville, 1935-43; picture editor AP, Chgo., 1943-45, Washington, 1945-56; sr. pastor Knox Presbyn. Ch., Falls Church, Va., 1959-66, 6th Presbyn. Ch., Pitts., 1967-69, Beulah Presbyn. Ch., Orion, Ill., 1969-78; interim pastor in retirement Rock Island, Galesburg, and Milan, Ill., 1979—; religion columnist various newspapers, Moline, Rock Island, and Peoria, Ill., 1980—; instr. Am. U., Washington, 1951-53; moderator Presbytery of Gt. Rivers, Ill., 1974. Contbr. articles to religious publs. Dir. Jail Rehab. Program, Fairfax County, Va., 1959-66; mem. Fed. Poverty Com., Fairfax County, 1962-65. Recipient 1st prize for nonfiction Midwest Writers Conf., 1980. Democrat. Avocations: photography, gardening. Home and Office: 2668 Springer Rd Galesburg IL 61401

ERICSON, CHARLES HAYDEN, pastor; b. Hartford, Conn., Feb. 5, 1953; s. Everett Frederick and Ruth (Law) E.; m. Jane Alice Beal, Sept. 18, 1976; children: Jennifer Lee, Daniel Hayden, Amanda Jane. BS in Psychology, Trinity Coll., Hartford, 1977; MDiv cum laude, Andover-Newton Theol. Sch., 1980. Ordained to ministry United Ch. of Christ, 1980. Seminarian 1st Congl. Ch. United Ch. of Christ, Stoughton, Mass., 1977-80; assoc. pastor 1st Ch. Congl. United Ch. of Christ, Fairfield, Conn., 1980-83; pastor Bolton (Conn.) Congl. Ch. United Ch. of Christ, 1984—; pres. Bolton Ecumenical Coun., 1990—; conflict cons., instr. Bldg. Effective Youth Ministries Conn. Conf. United Ch. of Christ, Hartford, 1990—. Composer hymns and religious theme music. Office: Bolton Congl Ch United Ch of Christ 228 Bolton Ctr Rd Bolton CT 06043

ERNST, ELDON GILBERT, religion educator, seminary dean; b. Seattle, Jan. 27, 1939; s. Kenneth G. and Bydell N. (Painter) E.; m. Joy S. Skoglund, June 12, 1959; children: Michael P., David G., Peter J., Samuel F., Rachel J. BA, Linfield Coll., 1961; BD, Colgate Rochester Divinity Sch, 1964; MA, Yale U., 1965, PhD, 1968. Prof. Am. Bapt. Sem. of the West, Berkeley, Calif., 1967-82, Grad. Theol. Union, Berkeley, 1983-90; prof., dean Am. Bapt. Sem. of the West, Berkeley, 1990—; rep. No. Calif. Ecumenical Coun., 1985-88; mem. Bapt. Peace Fellowship of North Am., 1970—. Author: Moment of Truth for Protestant America, 1974, Without Help or Hindrance, 1977, 87; author: (with others) Religion and Society in the American West, 1987; contbr. articles to profl. jours. Rsch. grantee Lilly Endowment, U. Calif., Santa Barbara, 1989-92. Mem. Am. Acad. Religion (pres. West regional chpt. 1985-86), Am. Soc. Ch. History, Am. Hist. Assn., Calif. Hist. Soc., Pacific Coast Theol. Soc. Democrat. Home: 1855 San Antonio Ave Berkeley CA 94707 Office: Am Bapt Sem of the West 2606 Dwight Way Berkeley CA 94704-3029

ERNST, JOSEPH RICHARD, religious organization executive; b. Sloan, Iowa, Mar. 11, 1934; s. George John and Doris Beatrice (Miquelon) E.; m. Sara Ellen Lee, June 30, 1955; children: Joy Denise Ernst Rowland, John Richard, Jerald Lynn. AA, Miltonvale Wesleyan U., 1954, BA in Religion, 1956; BA in Philosophy, Phillips U., 1958. Ordained elder Wesleyan Ch., 1957. Asst. minister 1st Wesleyan Ch., Enid, Okla., 1956-58; sr. pastor Wesleyan Ch., Ponca City, Okla., 1958-62, Guymon, Okla., 1962-66; sr. pastor Hillside Wesleyan Ch., Cedar Rapids, Iowa, 1966-88; supt. Iowa dist. Wesleyan Ch., Charles City, 1988—; youth pres. Okla. dist. Wesleyan Ch., 1956-60, sec. 1958-64, sec. Iowa dist., 1971-73, bd. dirs., 1971—. Editor Dist. Jour., 1958-64, 71-73. Bd. dirs., vice chmn. Keys to Living, Cedar Rapids, 1982-85; bd. dirs. Linn County Jail Chaplaincy, Cedar Rapids, 1985-88; trustee Bartlesville Wesleyan Coll., 1988—. Recipient Letter of Commendation, Gov. Iowa, 1986, Congressman Tom Tauke, Senator Tom Harkin. Mem. Ministerial Assn. (pres. Ponca City 1960-61, Guymon, 1963-64, Cedar Rapids, 1967, 74, 80), Iowa Assn. Evangelicals, Toastmasters, Kiwanis (pres. Cedar Rapids 1974-76). Republican. Avocations: golfing, photography, gardening. Home and Office: 104 Hilltop Dr Charles City IA 50616

ERNSTER, SISTER JACQUELYN, college president; b. Salem, S.D., Oct. 3, 1939; d. John Ernster and Eleanor (Bie) Ingalls. B.A., Mount Marty Coll., 1965; M.A., Ind. U., 1969; Ph.D., Ohio State U., 1976. Mem. faculty Mount Marty Coll., Yankton, S.D., 1970-76, v.p. acad. affairs, 1976-83, pres., 1983—; speaker S.D. Commn. on Humanities Pub. Issues Forum, 1980-82. Corp. bd. dirs. Sisters of Sacred Heart Convent, Yankton, 1976-82; trustee Madonna Profl. Care Ctr., Lincoln, Nebr., 1977-82. Mem. editorial bd. Yankton Press and Dakotan, 1984. Bush Found. fellow, 1982-83. Mem. Am. Council on Edn. (nat. identification program 1979, nat. com. on women in higher edn. 1984—), Nat. Assn. Ind. Colls. and Univs. (bd. dirs. 1989-91), Council for Ind. Colls., S.D. Pvt. Coll. Found., Consortium for Mid-Am. (chmn. pres. 1988-89), Delta Kappa Gamma (pres. 1980-82). Club: Interchange (bd. dirs. 1985) (Yankton), Kiwanis (bd. dirs. Yankton chpt. 1990). Office: Mt Marty Coll 1105 W 8th Yankton SD 57078

ERON, LEWIS JOHN, rabbi; b. Englewood, N.J., July 26, 1951; s. Abbot and Adele Mildred (Wallach) E.; m. Gail B. Trachtenberg, Jan. 18, 1987; children: Abby, Andrew. MA, Yale U., 1975; PhD, Temple U., 1987. Ordained Rabbi, 1981. Rabbi Temple Har Zion, Mt. Holly, N.J., 1982-85; exec. dir. Reconstructionist Rabbinical Assn., Wyncote, Pa., 1986-87; rabbi Beth Israel Congregation, Woodbury, N.J., 1987-88; assoc. rabbi Temple B'nai Abraham, Livingston, N.J., 1988—. Co-author: Bursting the Bonds, 1990; contbr. articles to profl. jours. Mem. Soc. for Bibl. Lit., Assn. for Jewish Studies, Am. Acad. Religion, N.Y. Bd. Rabbis, Reconstructionist Rabbinical Assn. Office: Temple B'nai Abraham 300 E Northfield Rd Livingston NJ 07039 *In my life I have discovered that a text, particularly a religious text, does not bind its reader to a single meaning or stream of interpretation. Religious texts exhibit their power in the ways they free the reader to explore his or her soul and world. Rather than limiting discussion, they start conversations that wend their way through time and space.*

ERVIN, CRAIG LINDSAY, minister; b. Rockledge, Fla., June 8, 1961; s. Daniel Webster and Bette Rhea (Brasher) E.; m. Nancy Lynne Petty, Apr. 5, 1980; children: Daniel Joseph, Jennifer Lindsay. BA in Bibl. Edn., Lee Coll., 1984; postgrad., Ch. of God Sch. Theology, Cleveland, Tenn., 1984-87. Ordained to ministry, 1990. Pastor Bible Teaching Ctr., Chattanooga, 1990—; sec.-treas. Carol Towe Ministries, 1990-91. Lobbyist Pro-Macc, Chattanooga, 1991. Ch. of God Sch. Theology scholar, 1984. Fellow Internat. Ministerial Fellowship, Pi Delta Omicron (pres.). Home: 6032 E Brainerd Rd Chattanooga TN 37421 Office: Bible Teaching Ctr 3975 Brainerd Rd Chattanooga TN 37411

ERVIN, GEORGE, JR., minister; b. Kansas City, Mo., Jan. 2, 1957; s. George Sr. and Margaret (Joiner) E.; m. Annette Marie Ervin, May 19, 1984; 1 child, Gabrielle Marie. BA in Bus., Ottawa U., Kansas City, Mo., 1981; MDiv, Cen. Bapt. Theol. Sem., Kansas City, Kans., 1984. Ordained minister Nat. Bapt. Ch. Tchr. Western Bible Coll., Kansas City, Mo., 1983-88; pastor Park Ave. Bapt. Ch., Kansas City, Mo., 1985—; substitute tchr. Kansas City Sch. Dist., 1991—; chaplain Trinity Luth. Hosp., Kansas City, 1983; tchr., preacher Radio Ministry, On Time Ministry, 1991. Home: 7419 Campbell Kansas City MO 64131 Office: Park Ave Bapt Ch 3601 Jackson Kansas City MO 64131

ERWIN, HENRY EUGENE, JR., clergyman, radio personality; b. Birmingham, Ala., Apr. 2, 1949; s. Henry Eugene and Martha Elizabeth (Starnes) E.; m. Shelia Joyce Daniel, June 8, 1972; children: Andrew David, Jonathan Daniel. BS, Troy (Ala.) U., 1972; BA, Southeastern Bible Coll., Birmingham, Ala., 1974; MA in Bibl. Studies, Dallas Sem., 1981. Ordained to ministry Independent Ch., 1984. Pastor Christ's Fellowship Ch., Portsmouth, Ohio, 1984-85; tchr. Shades Mountain Christian Sch., Birmingham, 1985-88; youth pastor Shades Mountain Ind. Ch., Birmingham, 1988—; talk show host Sta. WDJC-FM, Birmingham, 1988—. Media advisor Ala. Pro-Life Coalition, 1990—. Named Outstanding Young Man of Am. Dallas Jaycees, 1977; recipient Eagle Eye Radio award Eagle Forum, 1990. Office: Shades Mountain Ind Ch 2281 Old Tyler Rd Birmingham AL 35226 *Life is a great adventure when lived out under the guidance of Jesus Christ! He changed my life over 20 years ago, and gave me peace, purpose and happiness!*

ERWIN, TERRY HUGH, JR., youth minister; b. Mt. Vernon, Ill., Mar. 3, 1963; s. Terry Hugh and Beverly Gail (Deitz) E.; m. Karen Sue Smith, Sept. 23, 1984; children: Sara Adrian, Timothy James, Michael David. BA, Cin. Bible, 1985. Youth ministry intern Phillips Christian Ch., Salem, Ohio, 1982; youth min. Croton (Ohio) Ch. of Christ, 1982-85, Monroeville (Pa.) Christian Ch., 1985-91; assoc., youth min. First Christian Ch., Martins Ferry, Ohio, 1991—; asst. adminstr. Martin's Ferry Christian Sch., 1991—; bd. dirs. His Place Ministry, Pitts., 1990—; exec. com. Pa. Christian Teen Conv., 1988-91, sec. 1988, v.p. 1989, pres., 1990. Author: Teen Curriculum, 1988, 89. Recipient Outstanding Achievement award Am. Bible Soc., 1985; named to Outstanding Young Men of Am., 1986, 87, Outstanding Young Minister, 1989. Home: 814 Washington St Martins Ferry OH 43935 Office: First Christian Ch Zane Hwy at Madison St Martins Ferry OH 43935

ESALA, PHILIP JOHN, minister; b. Wadena, Minn., Nov. 4, 1949; s. H. Paul and J. Lorraine (Mustonen) E.; m. Deborah Ruth Schultz, June 11, 1972; children: Nathan, Andrea, Joel, Jonathan. BA, Valparaiso U., 1971; JD, Fla. State U., 1974; MDiv, Concordia Sem., St. Louis, 1984. Bar: Mo. 1975, Ill. 1976; ordained to ministry Luth. Ch., 1984. Pres. St. Michael's Luth. Ch., Tallahassee, 1973-74; elder Our Redeemer Luth. Ch., Jacksonville, Ill., 1977-78; dir. trust svcs. Luth. Ch.-Mo. Synod Found., St. Louis, 1978-83; vicar Redeemer Luth. Ch., Rockford, Ill., 1983-84; assoc. pastor Redeemer Luth. Ch., Rockford, 1984-85; pastor Risen Savior Luth. Ch., Indian Creek, Ill., 1985-91, Emmanuel Luth. Ch., Kettering, Ohio, 1991—; com. sec. No. Ill. Dist. Ch. Extension Fund, Hillside, 1986-90; program coord. No. Ill. Dist. Peace in the Parish, Hillside, 1988—; asst. sec. No. Ill. Dist. Luth. Ch.-Mo. Synod, Hillside, 1988—; com. chmn. No. Ill. Dist. Bylaw Revision, Hillside, 1990-91; speaker Great Commn. Convocation, 1989, Conf. on Worship and Music as They Relate to Evangelism and Discipleship, 1990, Concordia Sem. Continuing Edn., 1990. Contbr. article to profl. jour. Home: 333 Blackstone Dr Centerville OH 45459 Office: Emmanuel Luth Ch 4865 Wilmington Pike Kettering OH 45440

ESARY, CHARLES RAY, minister; b. Fayette, Ala., Apr. 29, 1953; s. William Grady and Era Pauline (Bailey) E.; m. Catherine Mae Gosa, May 17, 1980. BS, U. Ala., 1975; MCM, So. Bapt. Theol. Seminary, Louisville, 1984, D of Ministry, 1988. Ordained to ministry Bapt. Ch., 1981. Minister of music First Bapt. Ch., Vernon, Ala., 1979-81, Cooke Meml. Meth. Ch., Jeffersonville, Ind., 1981, Beechland Bapt. Ch., Louisville, 1981-90; minister of music/assoc. pastor First Bapt. Ch., Shelbyville, Tenn., 1990—. Named Ministry Student of Yr., Sch. of Ch. Music, So. Bapt. Theol. Seminary, 1984. Mem. Rotary. Office: First Baptist Church 304 Depot St Shelbyville TN 37160

ESBJORNSON, ROBERT GLENDON, religious studies educator; b. Duluth, Minn., Apr. 6, 1918; s. Per Hjalmer and Victoria (Swenson) E.; m. Ruth Bernice Bostrom, May 6, 1945; children—Ruth Louise, Carl Daniel. Student, Duluth Jr. Coll., 1937-39; A.B., Gustavus Adolphus Coll., 1941; grad., Augustana Theol. Sem., 1945; S.T.M., Yale, 1954. Ordained to ministry Luth. Ch., 1945. Pastor Holy Trinity Luth. Ch., Newington, Conn., 1945-50; tchr. religion Gustavus Adolphus Coll., St. Peter, Minn., 1950-87; pastor Bethany Luth. Ch., Judson, Minn., 1960-72; fellow Center for Ecumenical and Cultural Studies, Collegeville, Minn., 1973. Author: Luther W. Youngdahl: A Christian in Politics, 1955; editor: Manipulation of Life, 1984. Pres. bd. dirs. Riverbend Assn., St. Peter, 1968-74; bd. dirs. Northwestern Theol. Sem., St. Paul, 1967-76. Mem. Am. Acad. Religion, Coll. Theology Soc. Democrat. Home: 748 Valley View Rd Saint Peter MN 56082

ESCHENBURG, FREDERICK WILLIAM, minister; b. Battle Creek, Mich., June 4, 1957; s. Elmer Frederick and Helen Page (Bohman) E.; m. Mariann Bertonaschi, Aug. 11, 1979; children: Lucas Frederick, Hillary Lynn, Emily Elizabeth. BS, Ea. Mich. U., 1979; MDiv, Gordon-Conwell Theol. Sem., 1983; postgrad., Ea. Bapt. Theol. Sem., 1989—. Youth dir. First Ch., York, Maine, 1979-80; asst. pastor Second Ch., Peabody, Mass., 1980-83; pastor Franklin (Vt.) United Ch., 1983—; chair local bike-a-thon St. Judes Hosp., Franklin, 1984-89; minister in residence Gordon Conwell Theol. Sem., South Hamilton, Mass., 1989-90. Coach, referee Franklin Sch. Basketball League, 1985—; coach, umpire Little League, Franklin, 1987—; chair pers. com. Franklin County Home Health, St. Albans, Vt., 1989—; bd. dirs. Franklin County Home Health Assn., St. Albans, 1988—; chmn. bd. dirs. Franklin County Home, 1990—. Mem. Vt. Conf. United Ch. of Christ (bd. dirs. 1985-87, preacher 1987-89). Home: Main St PO Box 84 Franklin VT 05457 Office: Franklin United Ch Main St Franklin VT 05457 *Life is not an exam to be passed or failed. It is to be experienced, to be felt, to drink in the presence of God's goodness. Life is the gift of God. As we stand in relationship to God, we are enabled to partake of life and to share this gift with those surrounding us.*

ESCRIBANO-ALBERCA, IGNACIO, theology educator; b. Criptana, Spain, Feb. 28, 1928. Lic. Philosophy, Comillas U., Spain, 1950; D in Theology, U. Munich, Federal Republic of Germany, 1956. Prof. theology Seminario, Albacete, Spain, 1956-60; from lectr. to asst. prof. dept. theology U. Munich, 1960-68; prof. theology U. Freising (Fed. Rep. Germany), 1969, U. Bamberg (Fed. Rep. of Germany), 1969—. Author: Historicism and Religion by E. Troeltsch, 1961, Salvation in coming, 1970, Faith and Knowledge of God in Patristic Time, 1974, Address to Boris Pasternak, 1976, Eschatology. From Enlightenment to 20th Century, 1987. Home: Giselastrasse 25, Munich Federal Republic of Germany Office: U Bamberg, An Der Universitat 2, Bamberg 86, Federal Republic of Germany

ESHLEMAN, DANIEL SYLVESTER, pastor; b. Hagerstown, Md., Apr. 18, 1937; s. Daniel Irvin and Grace B. (Williams) E.; m. Nancy Louise Stoner; children: Lou Ann, Carol M., Christy S., Daniel P. BA, Grace Coll., 1961; MDiv, Grace Sem., 1964. Ordained to ministry Ch. of the Brethren, 1965. Pastor Findlay (Ohio) Grace Brethren Ch., 1964-68; pastor Grace Brethren Ch., Stratford, N.J., 1968-70, Virginia Beach, Va., 1970-73; pastor Patterson Meml. Grace Brethren Ch., Roanoke, Va., 1973-78, Valley Grace Brethren Ch., Hagerstown, Md., 1978-86, Grace Brethren Ch., Elizabethtown, Pa., 1986—; moderator Mid-Atlantic Dist. Grace Brethren Ch., 1971, 76, N. Atlantic Dist. Grace Brethren Ch., 1988. Consumer rep. Bd. Examiners of Psychologists, Md., 1981-86. Mem. Rotary (sec. 1990, v.p. 1991, Man of Yr. 1986). Office: Grace Brethren Ch 305 Anchor Rd Elizabethtown PA 17022 *I believe that "outlook determines outcome" and that since man was created in the image of God, he is not 'programmed' to be satisfied with anythings less than God. Augustine said, "Thou hast made us for Thyself, and our souls are restless till they find their rest in Thee."*

ESKENAZI, DAVID, cultural organization administrator; b. N.Y.C., Apr. 23, 1929; s. Meier and Esther (Behar) E.; m. Tamara, Oct. 2, 1971; children: Willa, Elline, Michael, Joanne Cohn, David Cohn. B of Social Sci., CCNY, 1951; MSW, U. Pa., 1953. Cert. social worker. Group worker Shorefront Jewish Community Ctr., Bklyn.; br. dir. Greater Miami (Fla.) Jewish Community Ctr.; asst. dir. United Jewish Community Ctrs., San Francisco; exec. dir. Jewish Community Ctr., Denver, 1971-89. Mem. editorial com. Jour. Jewish Communal Svc., 1986—; contbr. articles to jours. Mem. Assn. Jewish Ctr. Workers (pres.), Assn. Agy. Execs. United Way, Assn. Jewish Ctr. Workers. Home: 1608 S Bentley Ave # 3 Los Angeles CA 90025

ESKEW, ELBERT WENDALL, minister; b. Mt. Hope, W.Va., Aug. 8, 1925; s. Elbert B. Eskew and Pearl (Ruby) Hylbert; m. Bonny Jean Morton, Dec. 20, 1947; children: Edward, James, Lendall, Vaughn, Jenny. AB, Asbury Coll., 1948; MDiv, Asbury Theol. Sem., 1951; DD (hon.), W.Va. Wesleyan Coll., 1978. Ordained to ministry United Meth. Ch., 1951. Pastor United Meth. Temple, Clarksborg, W.Va., 1951-57; pastor 1st United Meth. Ch., Clendenin, W.Va., 1957-62, South Charleston, W.Va., 1962-70, Fairmont, W.Va., 1974-80; dist. supt. Wheeling Dist., W.Va., 1970-74, Lewisburg Dist., W.Va., 1980-85; program dir. W.Va. Ann. Conf., Charleston, 1985-91; del. Jurisdictional Conf., United Meth. Ch., 1972, Gen. Conf., 1972, 88. With USN, 1943-47; PTO. Named Pastor of Yr., W.Va. Ann. Conf. United Meth. Ch., 1978. Mem. Northeastern Coun. Dirs. Assn. (pres. 1989-90), United Meth. Coun. on Fin. (chair episcopal svcs. 1984-92). Republican. Home: 4203 Washington Ave SE Charleston WV 25304 Office: United Meth Ctr PO Box 2313 Charleston WV 25328

ESPARZA, FRANCISCO JAVIER, minister; b. San Antonio, Aug. 10, 1967; s. Raul E. and Guillermina E. BS, Dallas Christian Coll., 1989. Ordained to ministry, Ind. Christian Ch. 1990. Assoc. minister Ridgecrest Christian Ch., Albuquerque, 1990—. Songwriter: The Lord is My Strength, 1987, You Are My Rock, 1988, His Love Endures Forever, 1988. Office: Ridgecrest Christian Ch 5300 Eastern Ave SE Albuquerque NM 87108

ESPENSHADE, KEITH LYNN, minister; b. Ephrata, Pa., Sept. 3, 1962; s. Kenneth R. and Charlotte A. (Hoover) E.; m. Linda J. Martin, June 2, 1984; children: Jeremy K., Jessica L. BA in Bible, Messiah Coll., 1984; MDiv in Pastoral Counseling, Trinity Evang. Divinity Sch., 1989. Lic. to ministry Mennonite Ch., 1987. Pastor North Suburban Mennonite Ch., Mundelein, Ill., 1987-88, Allentown (Pa.) Mennonite Ch., 1990—; mem. pastoral staff LaSalle St. Ch., Chgo., 1988-90; bd. dirs. Lehigh Valley Inter-Faith TV, Bethlehem, Pa. Mem. Alban Inst. Office: Allentown Mennonite Ch 811 S 6th St Allentown PA 18103

ESPINOZA, DANIEL ISADORE, minister; b. Salt Lake City, Mar. 29, 1951; s. Isadore and Irene (Gomez) E.; m. Marsha Ann Williams, July 8, 1972; children: Vania Lynn, Heather Ann, Danielle Reneé. Student, L.I.F.E. Bible Coll., 1969-73. Ordained to ministry Foursquare Gospel Ch., 1977. Pastor Foursquare Ch., Marinette, Wis., 1973-74; pastor youth Foursquare Ch., Glendale, Calif., 1974-75, Westminster, Calif., 1975-76, Las Vegas, Nev., 1976-78; pastor Foursquare Ch., San Bernardino, Calif., 1978—; chaplain Cops for Christ, San Bernardino, 1986—; mem. spiritual concern com. San Bernardino County Juvenile Hall, 1987—, police clergy com. San Bernardino Police Dept., 1988—. Mem. Evang. Clergy Assn. (chmn. social actions com. San Bernardino chpt. 1988-90). Office: 1st Foursquare Gospel Ch 1112 W Rialto Ave San Bernardino CA 92410

ESPREE, ELIZABETH GRACE, lay worker; b. New Orleans, Aug. 17, 1954; d. Arnold Raymond and Elizabeth (Gobert) Depass; m. Peter Steven Espree, May 23, 1972; children: Gretchen Elizabeth, John Michael Christopher. BS, U. Southwestern La., 1991. Youth dir. Diocese of Houma (La.), 1975-79, Diocese of Lafayette (La.), 1980—; nat. dir. Companions of Jesus & Mary, Opelousas, La., 1983—, retreat cons., 1983—; paralegal Paralegal Network, Opelousas, 1988—; dir. Keylight Cath. Retreat Team, 1983—. Author: Your Pet's Mission, 1988; contbr. articles to profl. jours. Bd. dirs. United Way, Opelousas, 1986-88. Mem. Data Processing Mgmt. Assn., Nat. Paralegal Assn. Democrat. Office: Companion of Jesus & Mary PO Box 84 Opelousas LA 70571 *The greatest lessons and examples on the spiritual life, I learned from my dog. The animals of this world can teach us much: patience, unconditional love, peace, total dependence. It is in being little, humble, and still that we grow to understand the eyes of God are always on us.*

ESPY, HERBERT HASTINGS, chemist, consultant; b. Rochester, N.Y., June 4, 1931; s. Herbert Graham and Blanche (Eastwood) E.; m. Sarah Davis, Sept. 5, 1953; children: Ruth, Margaret. AB, Harvard Coll., 1952; PhD, U. Wis., Madison, 1956. Rsch. chemist Hercules, Inc., Wilmington, Del., 1956-69, sr. rsch. chemist, 1969-78, rsch. scientist, 1978-83, 85-90, mgr. tech. info., 1983-84, rsch. assoc., 1990-91; ret., 1992; bd. dirs. New Castle County Coun. Chs., 1963-66, sec., 1964-66, mem. coun. Episcopal Diocese of Del., 1974-79, treas., 1976-79, standing com., 1979-83, commn. on ministry, 1979-83, dep. to gen. conv., 1979-85, alt., 1988. Author: (book chpt.) Wet Strength Resins; contbr. articles to TAPPI Jour., Jour. Am. Chem. Soc. Mem. Am. Chem. Soc., Tech. Assn. Pulp and Paper Industry. Achievements include 11 U.S. and 3 Canadian patents for additives used in paper making. Home: 35 Marsh Woods Ln Wilmington DE 19810-3942 *When one does not know what to say, "Thank you" is generally suitable.*

ESSONO, SAMUEL NANG, minister, administrator. Pres., pastor Eglise Evangélique du Gabon, Libreville. Office: Eglise Evangelique, BP 10080, Libreville Gabon*

ESTEB, ADLAI ALBERT, retired clergyman, author; b. La Grande, Oreg., Nov. 17, 1901; s. Lemuel Albert and Addretta (Koger) E.; B.Th., Walla Walla Coll., 1931; M.A., Calif. Coll., Peiping, China, 1953; Ph.D., U. So. Calif., 1944; m. Florence Edna Airey, Feb. 5, 1923; children—Adeline, Lucille. Ordained to ministry Seventh-day Adventist Ch., 1923; missionary to China, 1923-37; pastor Seventh-day Adventist Ch., Long Beach, Calif., 1938-40; sec. home missionary dept. So. Calif. Conf. Seventh-day Adventist Ch., 1940-46, Pacific Union Conf. Seventh-day Adventist Ch., Glendale, Calif., 1946-50; editor Go, Jour. for Adventist Laymen, gen. conf. Seventh-day Adventist Ch., Washington, 1950-70; vis. prof., lectr. Christian ethics Andrews U., Berrien Springs, Mich., 1955-75, ret. Cited as poet laureate of denomination by pres. World Conf., 1966; named Alumnus of Yr., Walla Walla Coll., 1979. Mem. China Soc. of So. Calif. (pres. 1946-50), Oriental Fellowship (pres. 1963), Phi Beta Kappa, Phi Kai Phi, Phi Kappa Phi. Author: Driftwood, 1947; Firewood, 1952; Sandalwood, 1955; Morning Manna, 1962; Rosewood, 1964; Scrapwood, 1967; (poetry) Redwood, 1970; Kindle Kindness, 1971; The Meaning of Christmas, 1972; When Suffering Comes, 1974; Straight Ahead, 1974. Home: 15 Oak Court Candler NC 28715

ESTEP, GERALD DOSS, minister; b. Flemmingborg, Ky., Apr. 2, 1951; s. Arnold Lee and Eula F. (Downing) E.; m. Linda Ann McElroy, June 20, 1970; children: Shannon Barry, Geoffrey Doss. AS, So. State Coll., Hillsboro, Ohio, 1977; student, Fla. Theol. Liberty U., Graceville, 1983. Ordained to ministry So. Bapt. Conv., 1983. Pastor First Bapt. Ch., Manchester, Ohio, 1983-86, Winslow Pk. Bapt. Ch., Cin., 1986—. Mem. Sharonville (Ohio) Police/Clergy, 1986—. Ky. Col. State of Ky., 1990. Mem. Cin. Bapt. Assn. (exec. bd. 1986-91). Home: 4016 Creek Rd Cincinnati OH 45241 Office: 3906 Creek Rd Cincinnati OH 45241

ESTEP, JAMES RILEY, JR., minister; b. Ypsilanti, Mich., Sept. 13, 1963; s. James Riley Sr. and Virginia Sue (Sparks) E.; m. Karen Lynn Miller, Mar. 10, 1990. BA in Christian Ministry, Cin. Bible Coll., 1985; MA in Archaeology, Cin. Bible Sem., 1986, MA in New Testament, 1988, MDiv in Apologetics, 1989. Ordained to ministry, 1985. Youth minister East Columbus Christian Ch., Columbus, Ind., 1985-88; minister edn. Ch. of Christ of Latonia (Ky.), 1988-90, Calvary Christian Ch., Swartz Creek, Mich., 1990—; part-time instr. Great Lakes Bible Coll., Lansing, Mich. Mem. Ky. Cols., Lexington, 1987. Mem. Evang. Tchr. Tng. Assn., Bibl. Archaeology Soc., Near East Archaeol. Rsch. Soc. Republican. Home: 7247 Corunna Rd Swartz Creek MI 48473 Office: Calvary Christian Ch 7315 Corunna Rd Swartz Creek MI 48473

ESTERKA, PETER, vicar, educator; b. Bojanovice, Czechoslovakia, Nov. 14, 1935; s. Paul Esterka and Anezka Sladek. STD, Lateran U., Rome, 1968. Prof. dept. theology Coll. St. Catherine, St. Paul, 1968—; episcopal vicar for Czech Caths. U.S., Can., 1986—; liasison episcopal confs. of Czechoslovakia and U.S., 1990—; pres. N.Am. Pastoral Ctr. for Czech Caths., St. Paul, 1990—; bd. dirs. St. Adalbert Found., St. Paul; nat. chaplain Catholic Workman. Lt. col. USAF Res., 1974—. Named Monsignor, Pope, 1988. Mem. Cath. Theol. Soc. Am., Coll. Theology Soc., Nat. Alliance Czech Caths. Office: Coll St Catherine Theology Dept Saint Paul MN 55116

ESTERLE, STAN, ecumenical agency administrator. Exec. dir. Highlands Community Ministries, Louisville. Office: Highlands Community Ministries 1140 Cherokee Rd Louisville KY 40204*

ESTERLINE, DAN ALLAN, minister; b. Cambria, Mich., Jan. 7, 1942; s. Blon J. and S. Belle (Abbey) E.; m. Grace Marie Harshbarger, June 16, 1962; children: Danny Jr., Mark S., Kimberly J. Diploma, Moody Bible Inst., 1962; BA, Grace Coll., 1973; MA, Wheaton Coll., 1982. Ordained to ministry Bapt. Ch., 1962. Pastor Goodrich (Wis.) Bapt. Ch., 1962-65; missionary Sudan Interior Mission, Ethiopia, East Africa, 1965-75; missionary-in-residence Calvary Bible Coll., Kansas City, Mo., 1975-76; sr. pastor Waukegan (Ill.) Bible Ch., 1976-82; prof., chmn. Christian Edn. dept. Washington Bible Coll., Lanham, Md., 1982-84; sr. pastor West Side Bapt. Ch., Rochester, N.Y., 1984-86, Suburban Bible Ch., Highland, Ind., 1986-88, Tri-Town Community Ch., Dyer, Ind., 1988-89, First Bapt. Ch., Medford, Wis., 1989—; chairperson exec. bd. Berean Mission, St. Louis, 1978-88; instr. Purdue U. Calumet, 1988-89; mem. Christian Edn. Bd. of Gt. Lakes Bapt. Conf., Wausau, Wis., 1991—. Author: Building a Biblical Philosophy of Ministry, 1985. Mem. Alcohol and Other Drugs Assn. Network CESA # 10, Chippewa Falls, Wis., Medford Clergy Assn. Republican. Home: 670 W Broadway Medford WI 54451 Office: First Bapt Ch 680 W Broadway Medford WI 54451 *My fear is that Christ will be something to everyone and everything to no one.*

ESTES, LUTHER WELDON, minister; b. Roswell, N.Mex., Aug. 22, 1954; s. Verval and Helen (Taylor) E.; m. Lorna Diane Cokely, May 24, 1974; children: Kristopher, Kyle, Kirk. Grad. in theology, Pacific Coast Bapt. Bible Coll., San Dimas, Calif., 1975; BA, Pacific Coast Bapt. Bible Coll., 1976. Ordained to ministry Bapt. Ch., 1977. Assoc. min., youth min. Gateway Bapt. Ch., Las Vegas, Nev., 1976-78; sr. pastor First Bapt. Ch., Diamond Bar, Calif., 1978—; tchr. First Bapt. Sch., Pomona, Calif., 1987—. Republican. Office: First Bapt Ch PO Box 4262 Diamond Bar CA 91765

ESTEY, KENNETH FULLER, minister; b. Fairport, N.Y., Aug. 11, 1906; s. Ralph Roswell and Florence Katherine (Fuller) E.; m. Ruth Estelle Lyon, June 11, 1935. BA, Denison U., 1929; MDiv, Colgate-Rochester Div. Sch., 1932; MEd, U. Pitts., 1939. Ordained to ministry Am. Bapt. Chs. in U.S.A., 1931. Min. Homewood Bapt. Ch., Pitts., 1935-40, 1st Regular Bapt. Ch., Indiana, Pa., 1940-43, Calvary Bapt. Ch., Williamsport, Pa., 1943-47, 1st Bapt. Ch., Penfield, N.Y., 1947-51, Fellowship Community Ch., Sao Paulo, Brazil, 1951-54; dir. pub. rels. Ricker Coll., Houlton, Maine, 1955-56; registrar Shurtleff Coll., Upper Alton, Ill., 1956-60, Keuka Coll., Keuka Park, N.Y., 1960-69; min. North Creek (N.Y.)-Minerva Bapt. Parish, 1969-77; part-time min. Magee Bapt. Ch., Seneca Falls, N.Y., 1980-90; founder, dir. Shurtleff Bapt. Found., Alton, Ill., 1956-60. Mem. Masons (chaplain 1962-69, 80-89). Home: 13 S Main St Branchport NY 14418 *I try to live positively with the help of Lord and Saviour, Jesus Christ, the son of God. I believe that, as I am accountable for the outcome of my choices, so are all others for theirs. Our youth should set goals early in life and pursue them without fear or compromise. My motto is Look Up and Never Give Up.*

ESTILL, ROBERT WHITRIDGE, bishop; b. Lexington, Ky., Sept. 7, 1927; s. Robert Julian and Elizabeth Pierpont (Whitridge) E.; m. Joyce Haynes, June 17, 1950; children: Helen Haynes Estill Foote, Robert Whitridge, Elizabeth Estill Robertson. AB, U. Ky., 1949; BD, Episcopal Theol. Sch., Cambridge, Mass., 1952; STM, U. of the South, 1960, DMin (hon.), 1979; DD (hon.), U. of South, 1984; DMin, Vanderbilt U., 1980; DD (hon.), Va. Theol. Sem., 1980. Ordained priest Episcopal Ch. Rector St. Mary's Ch., Middlesboro, Ky, 1952-55; rector Christ Ch., Lexington, Ky, 1955-63; dean Christ Ch. Cathedral, Louisville, Ky, 1963-69; rector St. Alban's Ch., Washington, 1969-73; dir. Ctr. for Continuing Edn., Va. Theol. Sem., Alexandria, 1973-76; rector St. Michael and All Angels, Dallas, 1976-80; bishop Diocese of N.C., Raleigh, 1980—; pres. N.C. Coun. of Chs., 1989-90. Chmn. Ky. Com. on Human Rights State of Ky., 1956-65. With USNR, 1946-47. Mem. Capital City Club (pres. Province IV 1990—). Democrat. Home: 3224 Landor Rd Raleigh NC 27609 Office: Episcopal Diocese NC 201 St Alban's Dr PO Box 17025 Raleigh NC 27609

ESTRELLA, JULIA, ecumenical agency administrator. Dir. Pacific and Asian Am. Ctr. for Theology and Strategies, Berkeley, Calif. Office: Pacific and Asian Am Ctr for Theology and Strategies 1798 Scenic Ave Berkeley CA 94709*

ETCHEGARAY, ROGER CARDINAL, former archbishop; b. Espelette, France, Sept. 25, 1922; s. Jean-Baptiste and Aurélie (Dufau) E. Ed. Petit Séminaire, Ustaritz, France, Grand Séminaire, Bayonne, France. Ordained priest Roman Cath. Ch., 1947; served diocese of Bayonne, 1947-60; asst. sec. then sec.-gen. French Episcopal Conf., 1961-70, pres., 1975-81; consecrated archbishop of Marseilles (France), 1970-85; prelate Mission of France, 1975-81; elevated to Sacred Coll. of Cardinals, 1979; pres. Council European Episcopal Conf., 1971-79; pres. Pontifical Coun. for Justice and Peace, 1984—; pres. Pontifical Coun. Cor Unum, 1984—; mem. Congregation for Evangelization of Peoples, Congregation for Cath. Edn., Supreme Tribunal Apostolic Signatura, Pontifical Coun. for Christian Unity, Pontifical Coun. for Social Communications, Adminstrn. of Patrimony of the Holy See. Author: Dieu à Marseille, 1976, J'avance comme une ane, 1984, L'Evangile aux couleurs de la vie, 1987. Decorated Legion of Honor (France). Mem. Congregation of Cath. Edn., Commn. of Social Communication. Address: Palazzo San Calisto, 00120 Vatican City Vatican City

ETHEREDGE, ERNEST C., minister; b. Saluda, S.C., July 4, 1946; s. Sam and Bertha Mae (Nuthridge) E.; m. Sara A. Smith (dec.); children: Anthony Tyrone, Lakicha Ann. BS in Sociology, Lander Coll., 1978; M. Div., Gammon Sem., 1981. Foreman Wisteria Mills, Saluda, S.C., 1964-66; egr. Monsanto Textile Co., Greenwood, S.C., 1966-74; minister Laurens Charge (Calvary-Mt. Carmel), S.C., 1974-79, St. James, John Wesley Trinity, Seneca, S.C., 1979-82, Silver Hill United Meth. Ch., Spartanburg, S.C., 1982-86, I. DeQuincey Newman United Meth. Ch., Columbia, S.C., 1986—; chaplain Crafts-Farrow State Hosp., Columbia. Pres. Community Assn.-Council, Spartanburg, 1982-86. Mem. Omega Psi Phi. Democrat. Lodge: Rotary. Home: 511 Torwood Dr Columbia SC 29203

ETHERIDGE, JAMES E., minister, retired civil engineer; b. Nicholsville, Ala., Mar. 15, 1921; s. Nathan P. and Lula (Tucker) E.; m. Margie Irvin, Feb. 2, 1946; children: Bruce, Ted, Danny. Grad. high sch., Sweetwater, Ala. Deacon Bapt. Ch., Sweetwater, 1964-66, pastor, 1966—. With U.S. Army, 1942-45, ETO. Democrat.

ETHINGTON, ROBERT ALLEN, minister; b. Tulsa, Nov. 8, 1954; s. James and Grethren (Larue) E.; m. Teresa Lee Keith, Dec. 30, 1977; children: Geran, Jenny, Kellie. BA in Bible, Okla. Christian Coll., 1976; MDiv in Theology, Bethel Theol. Sem., San Diego, 1986; postgrad., Abilene Christian U. Ordained to ministry Ch. of Christ, 1976. Youth minister Grand Ave Ch. of Christ, Ponca City, Okla., 1976-78, Meml. Dr. Ch. of Christ, Tulsa, 1978-82; pulpit minister Chula Vista (Calif.) Ch. of Christ, 1982-87, Westgate Ch. of Christ, Abilene, Tex., 1987—. Author: How Satan Attacks the Minds of Teens, 1981. Fundraiser United Way, Abilene, 1989; city coun. rep. PTA, Abilene, 1990. Acad. scholar Am. Airlines, 1973; faculty scholar Bethel Theol. Sem.-West, 1986. Mem. Alpha Chi. Office: Westgate Ch of Christ 402 S Pioneer Dr Abilene TX 79605 *The empowering of people to live fully human lives in union with God is not a "can we" or "should we" life thought. It is a "will we" life thought. And as part of the community of faith, I say we will.*

ETHRIDGE, GRANT COLUMBUS, minister; b. Hartwell, Ga., Dec. 30, 1964; s. Alton C. and Robbie J. (Dunn) E.; m. Tammy L. Massey, Aug. 1985; children: Taylor Grant, Lindsay Beth. AA in Religion, Emmanuel Coll., Franklin Springs, Ga., 1984; BTh, Brainard Sem., Anderson, S.C., 1985; ThM, Immanuel Bapt. Sem., Sharpsburg, Ga., 1988, MDiv, 1990. Ordained to ministry So. Bapt. Conv., 1984. Assoc. pastor Bowman (Ga.) Bapt. Ch., 1984-86; sr. assoc. pastor Morningside Bapt. Ch., Valdosta, Ga., 1986-88; pastor First Bapt. Ch., Lavaca, Ark., 1988—; 2nd v.p., sec. Ark. Bapt. Pastors Conf., 1989-90; chmn. evangelism com. Concord Bapt. Assn., Ft. Smith, Ark., 1990-91; mem. program com. and sem. extension com. for Concord Bapt. Assn. Author: A Survey of Christian Education, 1988. Mem. bd. overseers The Criswell Coll. Home: PO Box 198 Lavaca AR 72941 Office: First Bapt Ch PO Box 170 Lavaca AR 72941 *My ultimate goal in life is "that I may know Him," and the only way to know God is through His Word. The Bible is not a book about dead religion but a book about a living relationship. Everyone wants the best in life, and the only way to have it is to know Jesus. With Him, you have everything. Without Him, you have nothing.*

ETSOU-NZABI-BAMUNGWABI, FREDERIC CARDINAL, cardinal; b. Mazalonga, Zaire, Dec. 3, 1930. Titular bishop of St. Lucy, archbishop of Kinshasa, elevated to the Sacred Coll. Cardinals, 1991. Office: Archevegne, BP 8431, Kinshasa Zaire*

ETTER, DAVID SCOTT, youth pastor; b. Cin., Jan. 9, 1969; s. James Franklin and Mary Louise (Hunter) E. BS in Ch. Ministers/Youth, Liberty U., Lynchburg, Va., 1990; postgrad., Liberty Bapt. Theol. Sem., 1990—. Youth/children's pastor Connelly Meml. Bapt. Ch., Roanoke, Va., 1989—. Mem. Youth Quest Club. Home: 904 Eldon St Lynchburg VA 24501 Office: Connelly Meml Bapt Ch 3907 Hershberger Rd Roanoke VA 24017

ETTER, DOUGLAS ALBERT, minister; b. Butler, Pa., Oct. 22, 1960; s. Charles Wallace and Dorothy Yvonne (Walters) E.; m. Diane Lee Davidson, Sept. 8, 1984. BA, Grove City (Pa.) Coll., 1982; MDiv, Princeton Theol. Sem., 1987. Ordained to ministry, Presbyn. Ch. (USA). Assoc. pastor Eastminster Presbyn. Ch., Grand Rapids, Mich., 1987-90; pastor Leesburg Presbyn. Ch., Volant, Pa., 1990—; counselor Grove City Coll., 1982-84; chaplain 1/107 FA PAARNG, Pitts., 1990—; archaeologist vol. Duke U., Chapel Hill, 1989. Vol. Springfield Twp. Recycling, 1990. 1st lt. U.S. Army N.G., 1985—. Mem. Phi Theta Alpha, Omicron Delta Kappa, Pi Gamma Mu. Republican. Office: Leesburg Presbyn Ch RD 2 Box 32 Volant PA 16156

ETTINGER, CECIL RAY, church executive; b. Taylorville, Ill., July 26, 1922; s. Cecil Ray and Minnie Elizabeth (Sloan) E.; m. Betty Jean Russell, Aug. 1, 1946; children: Cecil Ray, Stephanie Lynn Ettinger Kelley, David Alexander. A.A., Graceland Coll., 1942; B.A., U. Iowa, 1948; Th.M., Am. Div. Sch., 1955, Th.D., 1957. With Reorganized Ch. of Jesus Christ of Latter-day Saints, 1947—, radio minister, 1958-60; mem. Council of Twelve Apostles, 1960-74, in charge of European mission, 1962-66; minister to Africa 1963, 67, exec. asst. to 1st presidency, 1974—; prison counselor, tchr. Leavenworth Fed. Penitentiary, also Lansing State Prison, Kans., 1958—. Served with USAAF, 1942-45, ETO. Decorated D.F.C., Air medal with 9 clusters. Lodge: Lions (pres. 1973-74, zone chmn. 1974-75, dep. dist. gov. 1975-76, dist. gov. 1976-77, internat. dir. 1983-85). Home: 2413 S Whitney Ave Independence MO 64057 Office: Winship Travel 3600 S Noland Rd Independence MO 64055

ETTLINGER, GERARD HERMAN, priest, theology educator; b. Flushing, N.Y., Sept. 30, 1935; s. Hermann Joseph and Anna (Behringer) E. BA in Classics, Fordham U., 1959, MA in Teaching, 1961, MA in Classics, 1964; Licentiate in Philosophy, Woodstock Coll., 1960, STB, 1965, Licentiate in Sacred Theology, 1967; PhD, Oxford (Eng.) U., 1972. Joined S.J., Roman Cath. Ch., 1953, ordained priest, 1966. Instr. classics Fordham Prep. Sch., Bronx, 1960-63; teaching asst. Woodstock (Md.) Coll., 1966-67; asst. prof. Pontifical Oriental Inst., Rome, 1972-74; asst. prof. classics Fordham U., Bronx, 1974-75, asst. prof. theology, 1975-77, assoc. prof., 1977-89; prof. theology and religious studies St. John's U., Jamaica, N.Y., 1989—; lectr. 10th Biennial Inst. in Pastoral Psychology, Fordham U., 1975, U. St. Michael's Coll. and Pontifical Inst. Mediaeval Studies, Toronto, Can., 1979, St. Anselm's Parish, Bklyn., 1979, Creighton U., 1980, Commemoration of 1600th Anniversary of 2d Ecumenical Coun., 1981; cons. CBS-TV; vis. chaplain Fordham, Met., Coler, Calvary hosps., 1957-60; counselor Lincoln Hall, Lincolndale, N.Y., Md. Tng. Sch., Balt., 1963-64; civilian chaplain to U.S. armed forces, Frankfurt, Fed. Republic Germany, 1970-71; chaplain Bros. of Sacred Heart, 1984—; Baronius lectr. ch. history Bklyn. Oratory, 1991. Author: Jean Chrysostome, à une jeune veuve, sur le mariage unique, 1968, Theodoret of Cyrus: Eranistes. A Critical Edition and Prolegomena, 1975, Jesus, Christ and Savior, 1987; contbr. to: The Oxford Dictionary of the Christian Church, 1974, Encyclopedia of Early Christianity, 1990; editorial cons. Theol. Studies, 1980-91; cons. Thesaurus Linguae Graecae, Thought jour., Traditio jour., Crossroad Books, Orbis Books, New Yorker mag., N.Y. Post newspaper; contbr. articles to profl. jours. Mem. Assn. Internat. d'Études Patristiques (adminstrv. coun. 1983-87), N.Am. Patristic Soc. (nominating com. 1977-80), Am. Soc. Ch. History, Soc. for Textual Scholarship (exec. com. 1984—, editor newsletter 1986-89, program com. biennial internat. conf. 1987-89), Cath. Theol. Soc. Am., Medieval Acad. Am., Am. Philol. Assn., Am. Cath. Hist. Assn., Assn. des Amis de Sources Chrétiennes, Oxford Soc. Home: 71-06 31st Ave East Elmhurst NY 11370 Office: St John's U Dept Theology and Religious Studies Jamaica NY 11439

ETTNER, DANN J., minister; b. Long Beach, Calif., Feb. 27, 1957; s. John C. and Darlene V. (Tryggeseth) E.; m. Barbara A. Bosse, June 7, 1980; children: Rebecca A., Mary K. AA, Fresno City Coll., 1977; BA, Calif. Luth. Coll., 1979; MDiv, Concordia Sem., 1983. Ordained to ministry Luth. Ch.-Mo. Synod, 1983. Asst. pastor Zion Luth. Ch. & Sch., Rapid City, S.D., 1983-86; pastor Holy Cross Luth. Ch., Atwater, Calif., 1986—; com. mem. Sierra/Nev. Program Com., 1988-90; chmn. of bd. Luth. Outdoor Ministry of No. Calif., Felton, 1990—. Author: Seven Days of Creation, 1986; asst. editor Dist. Newspaper, 1990—. Lt. USAR, 1991—. Home: 157 Center Atwater CA 95301 Office: Holy Cross Luth Ch 1495 Underwood Atwater CA 95301

EUBANKS, DAVID L., academic administrator. Head Johnson Bible Coll., Knoxville, Tenn. Office: Johnson Bible Coll Office of Pres Knoxville TN 37998*

EUDALY, NATHAN HOYT, religious education administrator, publishing company sales executive; b. Pecos, Tex., Apr. 24, 1913; s. Milton Truman and Katherine Brainerd (Barber) E.; m. Marie Saddler, Nov. 22, 1941 (dec. Oct. 1989); children: Richard Milton, Katharine Hart, Nathan Hoyt. BBA, Tex. Tech U., 1938; BD, Southwestern Bapt. Theol. Sem., 1948, MRE, 1957, DRE with honors, 1959. Mem. staff Bapt. Home Mission Bd., 1946-48; evangelist Bapt. Fgn. Missionary, So. Bapt. Conv., Morelia, Mex., 1948-49; prof. Bapt. Theol. Sem., Torreon, Mex., 1950-52; bus. mgr. Bapt. Spanish Pub. House, El Paso, Tex., 1952-60, dir. distbn. div., 1960-64, with sales-distbg. div., 1964-67, dir. sales div., 1967-73, dir. mktg. svcs. div., 1973-75, cons. market rsch. and spl. projects, 1975—; ret. sem. student counselor 1st Bapt. Ch., Crowley, Tex.; mem. Internat. Com. Christian Edn., 1952-66; participant Latin Am. Misions confs., 1956, 59; mem. religious edn. com. Bapt. World Alliance, Rio de Janeiro, 1958, 65, Christian edn. com. Mexican Bapt. Conv., 1959-62, Bapt. Youth Congress, Beirut, 1963; nat. cons. Bapt. Chs. in Spain, 1963; developer wholesale stores for Spanish gospel materials. Author: Critical Evaluation of Leadership for Baptist Churches in Spanish America, 1959; editor pedagogical and adminstrv. sect. El Promotor de Educacion Cristiana, 1966-71, assoc. editor, 1973-77; mng. editor Mundo Bautista, 1973-77; contbr. numerous articles to profl. jours. Treas. City of Grandfalls, Tes., 1938-84; parliamentarian, rep. county Dem. Convs.; active Boy Scouts Am., PTA, Am. Field Svc.; bd. govs. Am. Cancer Soc., N.E. El Paso, 1975—. Mem. Evang. Lit. Overseas, Spanish Evang. Pubs. Assn., Christian Booksellers Assn., Congreso Latinoamericano de Evangelismo. Republican. Home: 300 Huguley Blvd Apt 323 Burleson TX 76028 *In these days of marital turmoil I have observed that "couples who play and pray together stay together."*

EUGEL, JAMES FREDERICK, religion educator; b. Des Moines, Mar. 3, 1934; s. Frederick Eberhardt and Lucille Lena (Anderson) E.; m. Sharon Kay Callies, Aug. 18, 1957; children: Janet, Joanne, Susan. BS in Bus., Drake U., 1956; MS in Mktg., U. Ill., 1957, PhD in Bus., 1960. Prof. Wheaton (Ill.) Coll., 1972-90, Ea. Coll., St. Davids, Pa., 1990—; sr. assoc. Media Assocs. Internat., Bloomingdale, Ill., 1985—; sr. communication assoc. World Vision, 1991. Author: What's Gone Wrong With the Harvest?, 1977, Contemporary Christian Companion, 1979, 4 monographs, 20 secular books; contbr. articles to various jours. Trustee Latin Am. Mission, Miami, Fla., 1986—. Rsch. fellow Christianity Today mag., 1988—. Fellow Assn. for Consumer Rsch. (founder, pres. 1979-80); mem. Religious Rsch. Assn., Am. Soc. Missiologists. Episcopalian. Home: 1624 Todd Ln Chester Springs PA 19425 Office: Ea Coll Saint Davids PA 19087

EURE, JAMES L., bishop. Bishop Ch. of God in Christ, Salisbury, Md. Office: Ch of God in Christ 635 W Main St Salisbury MD 21801*

EUSDEN, JOHN DYKSTRA, theology educator, minister; b. Holland, Mich., July 20, 1922; s. Ray Anderson and Marie (Dykstra) E.; m. Joanne Reiman, June 14, 1950; children: Andrea Bonner, Alan Tolles, John Dykstra Jr., Sarah Jewell. AB, Harvard U., 1943, postgrad., 1946; BD cum laude, Yale U., 1949, PhD in Religion, 1954. Ordained to ministry United Ch. of Christ, 1949. Instr. in religion Yale U., 1953-55, asst. prof., 1955-60; assoc. prof. religion, chaplain Williams Coll., Williamstown, Mass., 1960-65; Nathan Jackson prof. Christian theology Williams Coll., Williamstown, 1970-90, vis. prof. environ. studies, 1990—; lectr., research fellow Kyoto U., 1963-64, 76; theologian-in-residence Am. Ch. in Paris, 1972; lectr. Doshisha U., Kyoto, Japan, 1976, 82; bd. dir. Associated Kyoto Program, Japan. Author: Puritans, Lawyers and Politics in Early 17th Century England, 1958, Zen and Christian: The Journey Between, 1981, (with John W. Westerhoff III) The Spiritual Life: Learning East and West, 1982; contbr. articles to profl. jours.; translator, editor, author introduction: The Marrow of Theology (William Ames), 1975; author introduction, editor: New Covenant and Saints Qualification (John Preston), 1992. Mem. adv. coun., campus ministry program Danforth Found., 1966-70; bd. dirs. Wellesley Coll. Parents Assn., 1972-75, pres., 1974-75; rsch. fellow Ctr. for Study of Japanese Religion, Kyoto, 1976-90; trustee Lingnan Found., N.Y.C., 1964—, Buxton Sch., Williamstown, Mass., 1970-83, leader trips, People's Republic of China, 1978, 81, 86, 88, 90. 1st lt. USMCR, 1943-45. Scholar Harvard U.; faculty fellow Am. Assn. Theol. Schs., 1958-59, sterling fellow Yale U., 1950-53, fellow Folger Shakespeare Libr., 1958-59, 71-72; Lilly postdoctoral grantee, 1963-64, Danforth campus ministry grantee, 1963-64; research fellow Kyoto U., Japan, 1963-64, fellow Am. Council Learned Socs., 1967-68; Fulbright research travel grantee, 1967-68; research fellow U. Utrecht, Netherlands, 1968; research grantee Williams Coll., 1976. Mem. AAUP, Am. Acad. Religion, Am. Soc. Ch. History, Am. Soc. Christian Ethics, Nat. Assn. Coll. and Univ. Chaplains, Soc. Values in Higher Edn. Clubs: Appalachian Mountain, Randolph Mountain (pres. 1973-75). Home: 75 Forest Rd Williamstown MA 01267 Office: Williams Coll Stetson Hall Williamstown MA 01267

EUSTACHE, PAUL, religious organization administrator. Pres. The Nat. Bapt. Conv. of Venezuela, Caracas. Office: Nat Bapt Conv, Apdo 61152, Chacao, Caracas 1061-A, Venezuela*

EUTSLER, STEVE DWIGHT, pastor; b. Springfield, Mo., Jan. 8, 1958; s. Dallas Wayne and Paula June (Crabb) E.; m. Jacqueline Gene Plumlee, Jan. 10, 1977. BA, Cen. Bible Coll., 1982; MA in Biblical Lit., Assemblies Theol. Sem., 1987. Ordained to ministry Assemblies of God. Asst. pastor Galena (Mo.) Assembly of God, 1979; interim pastor KirbyVille (Mo.) Community Ch., 1981; pastor West Grand Assembly of God, Springfield, Mo., 1982-87, Sparta (Mo.) Assembly of God, 1987-88, First Assembly God, Aurora, Mo, 1988—; sect. treas. Springfield Sect. Assemblies of God, 1983-87, youth rep. 1984. Contbr. book revs. to profl. publs.; freelance writer. Named one of Outstanding Young Men Am., 1983. Republican. Avocation: genealogy. Home: 215 E Walnut Aurora MO 65605 Office: First Assembly of God 211 E Walnut Aurora MO 65605

EVANGELISTA, RAMON ANTONIO, minister; b. Santo Domingo, Dominican Republic, June 15, 1952; came to U.S., 1966; s. Ramon Evangelista and Maria Dolores (Jimenez) Marti; m. Maria Estela Solis, Aug. 16, 1975; children: Yasmin Elizabet, Niurca Vernis, Ramon Antonio. BA in Psychology, CCNY, 1976; postgrad., Trinity Evang. Sem. N.Y., N.Y.C., 1976; MDiv, New Brunswick Theol. Sem., 1979; postgrad., Colgate Div. Sch., 1980, St. Bernard's Roman Cath. Sem., Rochester, N.Y., 1981; D of

Ministry, Drew U., 1988; postgrad., Buffalo State U. Coll. Ordained to ministry United Meth. Ch., 1981. With N.Y. conf., United Meth. Ch., N.Y.C., 1976-79; min. Western N.Y. conf. United Meth. Ch., Rochester, 1979-83, Buffalo, 1983-88; min. So. N.J. conf. United Meth. Ch., Camden, 1988—; del. Northeastern jurisdiction United Meth. Ch., 1988, chairperson Hispanic com. Bd. Global Ministries., chairperson conf. commn. on religion and race, tchr. So. N.J. Ann. Conf., 1989-91; instr. Ea. Bapt. Theol. Sem., 1991. Mem. exec. com. MARCHA. Mem. Acad. Parish Clergy Inc., Hispanic Clergy Phila. and Vicinity, Disciplined Order of Christ, Jurisdictional Hispanic Assn. (former pres., sec.). Office: Asbury United Meth Ch 2926 Westfield Ave Camden NJ 08105

EVANS, ABIGAIL RIAN, academic administrator, educator; b. Phila., Oct. 26, 1937; d. Edwin H. and Marian (Schall) Rian; m. Robert Maxwell Evans, Dec. 12, 1959 (div. 1976); children: Stephen Edwin, Nathanael Cameron, Matthew M.S., Thomas Evan, Rachel; m. John Richard Powers, June 25, 1988. BA, Jamestown Coll., 1958; diploma in Brazailian lang. and culture, Escola Linguas e Orientacao, Campinas, Brazil, 1960; MDiv, Princeton Sem., 1968; PhD, Georgetown U., 1984. Ordained to ministry Presbyn. Ch., 1969. Missionary United Presbyn. Ch., Santa Catarina, Brazil, 1959-64; instr. liturgy and ch. history Campinas (Brazil) Theol. Sem., 1966-67; pastor, community organizer Ebenezer Presbytery, Ky., 1968-70; dir. Broadway U. Ministries, N.Y.C., 1971-76; assoc. pastor Broadway Presbyn. Ch., N.Y.C., 1971-76; Presbyn. chaplain Columbia U., N.Y.C., 1971-76; staff assoc. in med. edn. and ethics rsch. dept. Coll. Physicians and Surgeons Columbia U., N.Y.C., 1976-79; assoc. synod exec. Synod of Vas., Presbyn. Ch. U.S., Roanoke, 1976-79; rsch. and teaching asst. Kennedy Inst. Ethics Georgetown U., Washington, 1981-84, dir. new programs, sr. staff assoc., 1984-88; founder, dir. NCP Health Ministries, sr. cons. Kennedy Inst. Ethics, Georgetown U., Washington, 1984—; assoc. prof. practical theology, dir. field edn. Princeton Theol. Sem., Washington, 1991—, 1991—; mem. Nat. Capital Presbytery, Washington, 1976—; instr. Wesley Theol. Sem., 1984; vis. prof. Theol. Consortium, Washington, 1986, Howard U., Washington, 1987, Presbyn. Sch. Christian Edn., 1988; speaker, lectr. in field; preached in over 100 chs. throughout U.S., 1983—; cons. in field, 1983—; bioethics cons. NIH, 1983—; del. World Coun. of Chs., Bangkok, 1973, Switzerland, 1988. Editor: Human Resources Catalog, 1977, Reflections, 1976-78; mng. editor Jour. Medicine and Philosophy, 1984; assoc. editor Jour. Clin. Ethics; contbr. articles to profl. publs. Member commn. on Values, D.C. Bd. of Edn., 1987—; bd. govs. Washington Ecumenical Inst., 1985—; bd. dirs., chmn. mission com. Coun. Chs. Greater Washington, 1984—; mem. ethics com. S.W. Organ Procurement Found., 1988—; mem. George Washington U. Animal Rsch. Commn., 1988, Human Genome Working Group, 1991—. Grad. fellow United Presbyn. Ch., 1982-84. Mem. Soc. for Health and Human Values. Avocations: embroidery, refinishing furniture, interior decorating, cooking. Home: 7910 Bolling Dr Alexandria VA 22308

EVANS, ANGELA MARIE, religious organization executive; b. L.A., Sept. 25, 1956; d. Frederick K.C. and Betty Ruth (Scott) P.; m. A. Michael Evans, Feb. 28, 1976; children: Alan Michael, Adrian Marie. Student, West L.A. City Coll., 1974-75; cert. in mgmt. effectiveness, U. So. Calif., 1988. Exec. sec., office mgr. Crenshaw Christian Ctr., L.A., 1977-80, exec. asst., 1980-84, exec. adminstr., 1984-88, exec. v.p., 1988—; corp. sec. Crenshaw Christian Ctr., L.A., 1983—, Employee Med. Fund/Assist Fund, L.A., 1984-85; bd. dirs. Frederick K.C. Price III Sch. Bd., L.A., 1985—. Supporter Traditional Value Coalition, Orange County, Calif., 1990—, Life Chain of So. Calif., Orange County, 1990—, Christian Legal Soc., Annandale, Va., 1988—. Reicipient Outstanding Svc. award Lung Assn., 1979, Appreciation award FKCP III Child Care Ctr., 1986; named Outstanding Young Woman of Am., 1986. Mem. Christian Mgmt. Assn. Democrat. Office: Crenshaw Christian Ctr PO Box 90000 Los Angeles CA 90009

EVANS, ANTHONY LAWRENCE, minister, educator; b. Durham, N.C., Apr. 24, 1951; s. Robert Glenn Evans and Mary LaSena (Forsyth) Polk; m. Priscilla Anne Bynum, Aug. 5, 1973; 1 child, Sean Christopher. BA, Campbell Coll., Buies Creek, N.C., 1973; MDiv., Colgate-Rochester Div. Sch., 1976, DMin., 1984. Ordained to ministry Am. Bapt. Chs. in USA, 1976. Student min., asst. pastor Greece Bapt. Ch., Rochester, N.Y., 1974-76, assoc. min., 1976-82; sr. min. 1st Bapt. Ch., Olean, N.Y., 1982-91, Colorado Springs, Colo., 1991—; adj. prof. St. Bonaventure U., Olean, 1987—; bd. dirs. Interfaith Caregivers, Olean, 1985-89; pres. Greater Olean Assn. Chs., 1985-86; moderator Allegany-Cattaraugus Bapt. Assn., Olean, 1987-88; guest chaplain U.S. Ho. of Reps., Washington, 1989. Bd. dirs. Olean YMCA, 1986—; trustee Olean Gen. Hosp., 1987—; mem. presentation team millennial celebration U.S. Congressman Amory Houghton, Moscow, 1988; pres. alumni/ae coun. Colgate-Rochester Div. Sch., 1989-90. Mem. Rotary (pres. Olean club 1990-91). Democrat. Home: 2135 Wickes Rd Colorado Springs CO 80919 Office: 1st Bapt Ch 317 E Kiowa Colorado Springs CO 80903 *Ministry involves the "bridging of the gap" between the Word and the World. Through being a genuine person as well as through authentic pastoral leadership, administrating, preaching, teaching, counseling and enablement of the laity, I seek to accomplish that to which I have been called.*

EVANS, CHARLES STEPHEN, philosophy educator; b. Atlanta, May 26, 1948; s. Charles Hinton and Pearline Billie (Prewett) E.; m. Jan Edna Walter, Sept. 6, 1969; children: Kelley Elaine, Lise Jan, Charles Stephen Jr. BA, Wheaton (Ill.) Coll., 1969; M.Phil., Yale U., 1972, PhD, 1974. Asst. prof. philosophy Trinity Coll., Deerfield, Ill., 1972-74; from. asst. prof. to prof. philosophy Wheaton Coll., 1974-84; prof. philosophy, curator Howard & Edna Hong Kierkegaard Libr., St. Olaf Coll., Northfield, Minn., 1984—. Author: Kierkegaard's Fragments & Postscript, 1982, Soren Kierkegaard's Christian Psychology, 1990, The Quest for Faith, 1986, Philosophy of Religion, 1985; editor Soren Kierkegaard Newsletter, 1989—. Fellow NEH, 1988-89, Marshall fellow Marshall Fund of Denmark, Copenhagen, 1977-78. Mem. Soren Kierkegaard Soc. (exec. com. 1989—), Soc. Christian Philosphers (exec com. 1986-89), Am. Acad. Religion, Am. Philos. Assn. Office: St Olaf Coll Northfield MN 55057

EVANS, CHARLOTTE THELMA WEAVER, religion education administrator; b. Pitts., Sept. 26, 1947; d. Charles Weaver and Delores (Ricks) Harris; divorced; children: Delores Laurann and Herbert Eldridge II (twins). BA in Elem. Edn., Wilberforce U., 1973; M. in Spl. Edn., Citadel Mil. Coll.; postgrad., Ashland Sem., Ashland U. Ordained to ministry Mt. Moriah Bapt. Ch., 1968, AME Ch. as itinerate elder, 1974. Dir. Cleve. Dist. Christian Edn. Dept., 1988—, North Ohio Ann. Conf. Christian Edn. Dept., 1989—; SBH tchr. Elyria (Ohio) City Schs. Chairperson Lorain County Urban League Edn. Task Force, Elyria, 1990. Recipient Key to the City Mayor of Fostoria, Ohio, 1989. Mem. Ohio Edn. Assn. (minority affairs com. 1988—), Elyria Edn. Assn. (election chair 1987—), Nat. Edn. Assn. Democrat. Home: PO Box 1584 Elyria OH 44035 *As God continues to use me, I feel that my life is full and complete. It is my desire to be what God would have me to be.*

EVANS, DONALD EUGENE, minister; b. Kirksville, Mo., Aug. 28, 1934; s. John Junior and Freeda Christine (Peterson) E.; m. Leilla Azelene Kelley, May 28, 1957; children: David, Douglas. BS, Northwest Mo. State U., 1959; MRE, Southwestern Bapt. Theol. Sem., 1968; Dr. of Ministries, Golden Gate Bapt. Theol. Sem., San Francisco, 1982-87. Pastor Worthington (Mo.) Bapt. Ch., 1953-55, Hamilton St. Bapt. Ch., Kirksville, Mo., 1955-57; campus minister Northwest Mo. State U., Maryville, 1957-65; minister of youth First Bapt. Ch., Natchitoches, La., Springfield, Mo., 1971-72; pastor Novinger (Mo.) Bapt. Ch., 1972-78; dir. of missions Kirksville Div., 1978-81; rural-urban dir. Mo. Bapt. Conv., 1981--.; Mo. rep. gov.'s Council on Infant Mortality and Disease, Washington, 1987—; Small Ch. Task Force Mo. Bapt. Conv., Jefferson City, 1988. Author: The Small Church Manual, 1982. Mem. Mo. Dir. of Missions, Rural-Farm Crisis Council, Jr. C. of C. (Spoke award 1964), Rotary. Lodges: Rotary Internat. Avocations: documentary video film. Office: Mo Bapt Conv 400 East High Jefferson City MO 65101

EVANS, GERALD JOHNSON, religious organization administrator, counselor; b. Warren, Ohio, Nov. 2, 1945; m. Ruth Elaine Battle, Aug. 2, 1968; children: Martha, Malcolm Marcus. Cert., Staten Island (N.Y.) Coll., 1969; BSBA, Youngstown (Ohio) State U., 1974; MA, Am. Internat. Coll., 1977. With H.K. Porter, Warren, 1964-66, 66-69; pharmacy clk. Trumbull Meml. Hosp., Warren, 1970-72; mfr. clk. Wean United Ch., Warren, 1973-74; after care therapist Child Adult Mental Health Ctr., Youngstown, 1974-78; case mgr. W.G. Nord Community Mental Health, Lorain, Ohio, 1968—; exec. dir. 1st Community Interfaith Inst., Elyria, Ohio, 1980—; 1st v.p. 1st Community Interfaith Inst., Rochester, 1984—. Founder Afro-Am. Festival, 1979—, Kanisa House II, 1980; v.p. Lorain County Habitat for Humanity, Oberlin, Ohio, 1989—; vice chmn. allocations com. United Way, Lorain, 1988—; chmn. outreach Leadership Lorain County Alumni Assn. With U.S. Army, 1966-69, Vietnam. Named to Hon. Order Ky. Col., 1988; named one of Outstanding Young Men in Am., 1978. Mem. Project Joy (trustee 1988—), Grace Community Ch. (asst. pastor 1980-88). Home: 1708 Gulf Rd Elyria OH 44035 Office: 1st Community Interfaith 142 Cleveland PO Box 1616 Elyria OH 44035

EVANS, HAYDN BARRY, social researcher, consultant, educator; b. Washington, May 3, 1936; s. Haydn Lewis and Laura Daisy (Ransom) E.; m. Polly Bercaw Williams, Apr. 11, 1964 (div. 1986); children: Michael Haydn, Lauren Trenholm. BA, Brown U., 1959; postgrad., Westcott House, Cambridge, Eng., 1961; M of Div., Va. Theol. Sem., Alexandria, 1962. Curate St. Lukes Episcopal Ch., Alexandria, 1962-63; assoc. rector St. Stephen and Incarnation Ch., Washington, 1963-70; program dir. Washington Cathedral Coll. of Preachers, 1970-83; pres. The Grubb Inst. USA, Washington, 1984—. Contbr: (book) Building Effective Ministry, 1983; editor (Jour.) Homiletic, 1975-84. Mem. Assn. for Sociology of Religion, Religious Research Assn., A.K. Rice Inst. Democrat. Episcopalian. Avocation: tennis.

EVANS, HENRY MULLEN, JR., religious educator; b. Monroe, La., May 16, 1936; s. Henry Mullen and Irma Estelle (Brown) E.; m. Mary E. Carter, Sept. 6, 1958; children: Crystal Darlene, Henry M. III. BA, Southeastern Bible Coll., Lakeland, Fla., 1967, Oral Roberts U., 1969; MA, U. Tulsa, 1974; PhD, Fla. State U., 1984; postgrad., New Orleans Bapt. Theol. Sem., 1988-89. Prof. Southeastern Bible Coll., 1969-81, Jimmy Swaggart Bible Coll., Baton Rouge, 1986-88, Oral Roberts U., Tulsa, 1989—; pastoral min., Md., 1960-66, Fla., 1979-80. Contbr. articles to profl. jours. Mem. Soc. Bibl. Lit., Am. Assn. Religion, Soc. Pentecostal Scholars. Office: Oral Roberts U Dept History Humanities 7777 S Lewis Tulsa OK 74171 *The heart is reached via the ear if we learn the art of listening so as to hear.*

EVANS, HERBERT DAVID, evangelist; b. Stockton, Calif., Apr. 27, 1944; s. Audie and Grace Mozell (Lewis) E.; m. Janis Elaine Bush, Nov. 7, 1964; children: Tina Elaine Evans Cook, Fredrick Douglas. Student, Preston Rd. Sch. Preaching, Dallas, 1977. Preacher Ch. of Christ, Elkhart, Tex., 1977-79, Diboll, Tex., 1979—; instr. South Meadows Nursing Home, Diboll, 1979—, Ron Willinham Courses, Diboll, 1978—. With U.S. Army. 1961-64. Mem. Rotary (treas. 1990—). Home: 402 Birdsong Ln Diboll TX 75941-2212 Office: Ch of Christ 100 Arrington Rd Diboll TX 75941-2211

EVANS, JOHN BORDEN, minister; b. Laurinburg, N.C., May 12, 1929; s. E. Hervey and Anne (Borden) E.; m. Margaret Thornhill Wier, June 8, 1955; children: John Borden, Alexander W., David, Margaret, Edwin C. AB, Davidson Coll., 1950; BD, Union Theol. Sem., 1954; LHD, Stillman Coll., Tuscaloosa, Ala., 1976; DD, Davis & Elkins Coll., W.Va., 1965. Ordained to ministry Presbyn. Ch. (U.S.A.), 1954. Asst. pastor Second Presbyn. Ch., Charleston, S.C., 1954-55; asst. prof. Davidson (N.C.) Coll., 1957-60; pastor First Presbyn. Ch., Auburn, Ala., 1960-64; exec. staff Bd. Christian Edn., Richmond, Va., 1964-73; gen. staff dir. Gen. Exec. Bd., Presbyn. Ch., Atlanta, 1973-78; traveler New Zealand, 1978-79; pastor Chatham, Va., 1980-87; exec. presbyter Presbytery of New Harmony, Florence, S.C., 1988—; trustee Union Theol. Sem., 1983—, Fund for Theol. Edn., N.Y.C., 1982—. Office: Presbytery of New Harmony PO Box 4025 Florence SC 29502

EVANS, JOHN F., religious organization administrator. Pres. Nat. Interfaith Coalition of Aging, Inc., Athens, Ga. Office: Nat Interfaith Coaliton Aging 98 S Hull St Box 1924 Athens GA 30603*

EVANS, LAWRENCE TIMOTHY, minister, educator; b. New Orleans, Jan. 30, 1947; s. Ernest Evans and Loretta (Smith) Anderson; m. Dorothy Pierre, Nov. 26, 1966; children: Stacey Marie, Rustin. BA in History, Fayetteville (N.C.) State U., 1976; MDiv, Duke U., 1979; ThD, Am. Theol. Sem., 1986. Chaplain Fed. Correctional Facility, Butner, N.C., 1976-77, Duke U. Med. Ctr., Durham, N.C., 1978-79, U.S. Army, 1979-89; pastor, tchr. Heritage/Fellowship United Ch. of Christ, Reston, Va., 1989—. Mem. Inst. of Logotheraphy (acad. assoc.). Democrat. Home: 1625 Sadlers Wells Dr Herndon VA 22070 Office: Heritage Fellowship United Ch of Christ 2501 Fox Mill Rd Reston VA 22091

EVANS, MARLENE JUNE, editor, dean; b. Beatrice, Nebr., Nov. 11, 1933; d. Alvin Dale and Mary Helen (Fauver) Zugmier; m. Wendell Lee Evans, Dec. 22, 1955; children: Joy Lynn Evans Ryder, David Lee. BS, Bob Jones U., 1955, MA, 1956; MEd, U. Tenn., 1962; LHD (hon.), Hyles-Anderson Coll., 1978. Dean of women, coll. activities coord. Hyles-Anderson Coll., Crown Point, Ind., 1972—; founder, editor Christian Womanhood mag., Crown Point, 1975—; dir. ann. Christian Womanhood Spectacular, Crown Point, 1975—; pres. Bus. Women's Sunday Sch. class, Chattanooga, 1962-64; dir. tng. Union Highland Park Ch., Chattanooga, 1962-63, Sunday sch. promotion coord., 1965; mem. ch. bus. ministry, 1969-72, hostess radio program Woman to Woman, 1969-70, speaker in field. Author: Through a Woman's Eyes, vols. 1 and 2, 1975-76, Redbirds and Rubies and Rainbows, Help Lord! They Call Me Mom, Comfort for Hurting Hearts. Founder, bd. dirs. Blue Beret Girls svc. group, Hammond, Ind., 1975-76. Republican. Home: 38 Risch Schererville IN 46375 Office: Christian Womanhood 8400 Burr St Crown Point IN 46307 *Without knowing the beginning from the end (Genesis to Revelation) life is nothing but a vacuum.*

EVANS, OLEN M., minister; b. Terre Haute, Ind., June 1, 1954; s. Miles W. and Lola (McCrory) E.; m. Debi Elaine DisPennet, Oct. 14, 1983; 1 child, Sara. AS, Lincoln Trail Coll., 1974; BA, Tenn. Temple U., 1976; MDiv, Temple Bapt. Theol. Sem., 1979; D. Ministry, Luther Rice Sem., 1990. Lic. to ministry Bapt. Ch., 1973, ordained, 1981; cert. in broadcasting. Pastor Prior Grove Bapt. Ch., Oblong, Ill., 1979-82, Prairie Grove Bapt. Ch., Annapolis, Ill., 1983-85, 1st Bapt. Ch., Brownstown, Ill., 1986—; owner, gen. mgr. Sta. WBFG Radio, Effingham, Ill., 1982—; dir. evangelism Rehoboth Bapt. Assn., 1990—. Chaplain Nursing Home, Oblong, Ill. Named Outstanding Young Minister of Yr., Jaycees, Robinson, Ill., 1981. Mem. Crossroads Broadcasting Corp. (pres. 1980—). Home: 206 1/2 S Willow Effingham IL 62401 Office: Sta WBFG 206 S Willow Effingham IL 62401

EVANS, VAN HOLLAND, minister; b. Danville, Ark., Feb. 18, 1924; m. Lenora Hanley, 1949; children—Linda, Joyce, Janet, Stephen. B.S. in Elec. Engring., La. Tech. U., 1949; M.R.E., New Orleans Bapt. Theol. Seminary, 1958. Dist. mgr. Cities Service Oil Co., 1949-53; ordained to ministry Baptist Ch., 1959; minister music and edn. First Bapt. Ch., Monticello, Ark., 1953-54, Sheffield, Ala. 1954-56; minister edn. and adminstrn. First Bapt. Ch., Gulfport, Miss., 1957-60; assoc. pastor in edn. and adminstrn. First Bapt. Ch., Bossier City, La., 1960-63; minister edn. and adminstrn. First Bapt. Ch., El Dorado, Ark., 1963-88; bus. mgr. Ark. Bapt. Home for Children, Monticello, 1988-91; ret., 1991; v.p. Ark. Bapt. Family and Child Care Agy., 1976, pres., 1977, chmn. personnel com., 1979-84. Bd. dirs. United Way of Union County, Ark., 1981-84, chmn. budget allocations, 1981, 1st v.p., 1982, pres., 1983, mem. agys. relation bd., 1978-80; bd. dirs. and instr. Ark. Bapt. Coll. Extension Center, 1974-80. Mem. So. Bapt. Bus. Officers Conf., Ark-La-Tex chpt. Nat. Assn. Ch. Bus. Adminstrs., Liberty Bapt. Assn. (budget, fin., personnel, stewardship coms. 1978-83). Served with USN, 1943-46. Co-author: The El Dorado Plan; contbr. to religious mags. Home: 109 Stroud St El Dorado AR 71730

EVANS, WILLIAM HALLA, minister; b. Paris, Ky., Nov. 29, 1950; s. James Hughes and Francis (Halla) E.; m. Kathleen Sue Mattingly, Aug. 25, 1973; children: James Anthony, Joshua Halla. BA in Philosophy, U. Ky., 1972; D of Ministry, Lexington Theol. Sem., 1976. Minister Paint Lick (Ky.) Christian Ch., 1970-73, Botland (Ky.) Christian Ch., 1973-76, Croften (Ky.) Christian Ch., 1976-80, Valley Christian Ch., Valley Station, Ky., 1980-84; assoc. minister Florence (Ky.) Christian Ch., 1984-86; sr. minister First Christian Ch., Pikeville, Ky., 1986-89; computer instr. Clark Mid. Sch., Winchester, Ky., 1990—; chmn. Evangelism Com. Christian Ch. in Ky., Lexington, 1984-88. Cubmaster Council Cub Scouts Am., Pikeville, 1987-89. Democrat. Lodge: Rotary. Avocations: reading, electronics, amateur radio, scouting, computer programming. Home: 3800 Pretty Run Rd Winchester KY 40391 Office: 3800 Pretty Run Rd Winchester KY 40391

EVERDING, HENRY EDWARD, JR., religion educator; b. Phila., Feb. 2, 1934; s. Henry Edward and Ruth Eleanor (Greene) E.; m. Colleen Rae Damon, Dec. 18, 1955 (div. Mar. 1976); children: Lisa Rae, Linda Kay, Kelly Ruth, Henry Edward III; m. Lee Palmer, Jan. 19, 1985. AB, Syracuse U., 1955; B.D., Drew Theol. Sch., 1958; Th.D., Harvard U., 1968. Vis. lectr. New Testament Perkins Sch. Theology, Dallas, 1965-67; from. asst. prof. to prof. New Testament Iliff Sch. Theology, Denver, 1967—, v.p., dean acad. affairs, 1982-85. Co-author: Decision Making and the Bible, 1975; contbr. articles to profl. jours. Elder United Meth. Ch., 1960—. Post-doctoral scholar Ctr. for Congregational Edn., Indpls., 1985-87. Mem. Am. Acad. Religion, Assn. Profs. and Researchers in Religion, Cath. Bibl. Assn., Religious Edn. Assn., Soc. Bibl. Lit. (coun. mem. 1973-78). Democrat. Office: Iliff Sch of Theology 2201 S University Blvd Denver CO 80210

EVERETT, ANN NEVAREZ, religious educator; b. Uvalde, Tex., Aug. 10, 1915; d. Severo Nevarez and Dorothy (Canales) N.; m. Howard Devire Everett, Oct. 16, 1947; children: Howard Devire Jr., Mary Ann, James Joseph. Student Sch. Ministry, 1974-77. Chmn. internat. affairs Archdiocesan Council Catholic Women, San Antonio, 1979-81; Western Deanery Cath. Women, San Antonio, 1976-81; chmn., counselor of Respect Life, San Antonio, 1979-85; local chmn. Telethon Navideno, San Antonio, 1983-84; instr. religious edn. Confraternity Christian Doctrine, San Antonio, 1973-85. Recipient Archbishop Francis Furey medal Archdiocese of San Antonio, 1977, Leadership Course award Our Lady of Angels Ch., San Antonio, 1982, Vol. Dedication award Elizabeth Seton Home, San Antonio, 1984. Republican. Roman Catholic. Avocations: swimming, bowling, crocheting. Home: 2034 Bronte San Antonio TX 78207

EVERETT, JAMES WILLIAM, minister, counselor; b. Belzoni, Miss., Nov. 21, 1951; s. J. P. and Willie (Fraiser) E.; m. Janet Kay Jackson, Mar. 6, 1971; children: J. Corey, Rachel Joy. BS, Miss. Coll., 1974; MRE, New Orleans Bapt. Theol. Sem., 1981; D Ministry, Internat. Sem., Plymouth, Fla., 1985. Ordained to ministry So. Bapt. Conv., 1973. Pastor Ogden Bapt. Ch., Bentonia, Miss., 1972-74, Bentonia Bapt. Ch., 1981-84, Bennington Pk. Bapt. Ch., Memphis, 1984-91; chaplain New Orleans Fairgrounds Racetract, 1980-81; coord. family life Yazoo Bapt. Assn., Yazoo City, Miss., 1982-84, Am. Family Assn., Memphis, 1985-87; leader Truthseekers Quartet, Memphis, 1974-79. Mem. Yazoo Election Com., 1983. Named one of Outstanding Young Men of Am., Jaycees, 1982. Mem. Shelby County Bapt. Assn. (various coms. 1984-91, vol. chaplain, bd. dirs. 1988-90, chmn. program com. 1989), The Shepherd's Counselors (cert. sr. counselor). Republican. Home: 1410 Elise Ave Yazoo City MS 39194

EVERETT, ROBERT ANDREW, minister; b. Middleboro, Ky., Oct. 30, 1948; s. Robert Lester and Jurl Ann (Patton) E.; m. Marie Anna Iselborn, Jan. 10, 1982; children: Amanda, Joshua, Jesse. AB, U. Ga., 1970; MDiv, Yale U., 1973, MST, 1975; MPhil, Columbia U., 1979, PhD, 1983. Ordained to ministry United Ch. of Christ, 1974. Asst. pastor Union Meml. Ch., Glenbrook, Conn., 1973-75; pastor Emanuel United Ch. of Christ, Irvingston, N.J., 1975—; mem. exec. com. Nat. Christian Leadership Conf. for Israel, N.Y.C., 1980-83; adj. prof. religion Albright Coll., 1982-83, Kean Coll., Montclair State Coll., Ramapo Coll.; vis. prof. religion Lehigh U., 1987; Protestant chaplain Fairleigh Dickenson U., Teaneck, N.J. Author: Christianity without Antisemitism, 1991; contbr. articles and book revs. to profl. publs. Advisor Youth Inst. for Peace in Mid. East, Pitts., 1982—; speaker, advisor Ams. Concerned for Peace in Mid. East, Paramus, N.J., 1983—; v.p. Am. Friends of Nes Ammim, Teaneck, N.J., 1983—; mem. Bd. of Edn., Union, N.J., 1991—. Recipient Outstanding Teaching award Albright Coll. Students, 1983; grantee Am. Friends of Tel Aviv U., 1974, NEH, 1987; Columbia U. Grad. Sch. fellow 1976-77, 77-78. Democrat. Home: 2218 Stecher Dr Union NJ 07083 Office: Emanuel United Ch of Christ Lincoln Pl and Nye Ave Irvington NJ 07111

EVERLY, DAVID NOBLE, minister; b. Evansville, Ind., May 10, 1941; s. Noble Rowe and Bernice Elizabeth (Brown) E.; m. Rebecca Sue Campbell, Aug. 19, 1967; children: David N., Timothy T. BS, Washington U., St. Louis, 1963; MDiv, Midwestern Bapt. Theol. Sem., Kansas City, Mo., 1966, DMin, 1991. Ordained to ministry, So. Bapt. Conv., 1965. Youth dir. Christ Meml. Bapt. Ch., St. Louis, 1964-78, assoc. pastor, 1978-82; pastor Chandler Bapt. Ch., Liberty, Mo., 1982—; peer group leader Midwestern Sem., Kansas City, Mo., 1989—; chmn. family ministry com. Clay-Platte Bapt. Assn., Kansas City, 1986-88, 1991—. Coach youth teams Liberty Parks & Recreation, 1983-87. Mem. Liberty Ministerial Alliance (pres. 1987). Home: 1135 Elizabeth Liberty MO 64068 Office: Chandler Bapt Ch Hwy 69 and 33 Liberty MO 64068

EVIN, ANDREW, religious organization administrator. Chmn. Union Spiritual Communities of Christ, Grand Forks, B.C., Can. Office: Union Spiritual Communities, Christ/Box 760, Grand Forks, BC Canada V0H 1H0*

EVORA, PAULINO DO LOVRAMENTO, bishop. Bishop of Santiago de Cabo Verde Roman Cath. Ch., Sao Tiago. Office: CP 46, Praia Sao Tiago, Republic of Cape Verde*

EWERS, ROGER LEONARD, minister, salesman; b. Fredericktown, Ohio, Nov. 3, 1935; s. James Leonard and Helen (Zolman) E.; m. Rosetta Dean, Oct. 21, 1987; children: Bradley, Brian, Roger II, Gina, Peggy, Angela. Grad., Mars Hill Bapt., 1977, Fruitland U., 1978, Southern Bapt., 1979; ThD, Internat. Bible Sem., 1980. Missionary Truth Bapt. Ch., Ft. Myers, Fla., 1977-80, 86-89, pastor, 1983-86; pastor Truth Bapt. Ch., Antioch Bapt. Ch., Hartsville, S.C., 1980-81, Lum Bapt. Ch., Mich., 1989—; distbr. water and air refueling Nat. Safety Assocs., Lum, Mich., 1989—. With USAF 1952-57, Korea. Home and Office: 4893 Lum Rd Lum MI 48452 *Invite Jesus into your life. Help others to invite Jesus into their lives.*

EYMAN, ROGER ALLEN, minister; b. Canton, Ill., Mar. 16, 1942; s. Silbert Lionel and Ruth Maxine (Noland) E.; m. Priscilla Ann Baker, Dec. 24, 1979; 1 child, Hans Roger. AA, Orange Coast Coll., Costa Mesa, Calif., 1969; BA in Psychology, Calif. State U., L.A., 1971; MMin, Bethany Theol. Sem., 1975, DMin summa cum laude, 1991. Ordained to ministry Am. Evang. Christian Ch./Gen. Conf., 1983. Missionary Gospel Mission Ch., Liberia, Costa Rica, 1974-76, Wadi Es Sir, Jordan, 1976-79; founder, pastor Ch. of Calvary Grace of Ariz., Tucson, 1984-89, Ch. of Calvary Grace of Alaska, Anchorage, 1989—; ins. claims cons., Anchorage, 1989—. Fellow Internat. Ministerial Fellowship, AECC Gen. Conf., Internat. Chaplains Assn., Alaska Club. Republican. Office: Ch of Calvary Grace Alaska PO Box 870915 Wasilla AK 99687-0915

EYNON, STEVEN SCOTT, minister; b. Jacksonville, Fla., July 4, 1961; s. John Jerry and Sally Ann (Stevens) E.; m. Lori Lee Hunter, June 25, 1983; children: Christopher, Steven. BA summa cum laude, Fla. Christian Coll., Kissimmee, 1984; postgrad., Ky. Christian Coll., 1990—. Ordained to ministry Christian Ch., 1984. Min. youth Winter Haven (Fla.) Christian Ch., 1982-84, 1st Christian Ch., Clearwater, Fla., 1985—; adj. instr. Fla. Christian Coll., 1988, 90; v.p. Fla. Christian Youth Conv., Orlando, 1986; bd. dirs. Christianville Mission, Haiti, 1991—. Author: (with others) Ideas, vol. 42, 1987, Good Stuff, vol. 4, 1988. Mem. Nat. Right to Life, Washington, 1983—; vol. Spl. Olympics, Clearwater, 1985—; scouting coord. Boy Scouts Am., Clearwater, 1986—; pres. Fla. Christian Coll. Alumni Assn., Kissimmee, 1987-88, v.p., 1985-87. Named Outstanding Young Min., N.Am. Christian Conv., 1989. Mem. Christ in Youth Planning Coun. (advisor 1986-87), Christian Edn. Conf. (dir. 1988). Home: 956 Wicks Dr Palm Harbor FL 34684 Office: 1st Christian Ch 2299 Drew St Clearwater FL 34625

EYRE, CHARLES GEORGE, minister; b. Belfast, No. Ireland, June 2, 1925; s. Thomas Alexander and Elizabeth McClintock (Giffin) E.; m. Betty Muriel Shier, Dec. 12, 1951; children: Maurice John, Jane Muriel Eyre Peppiatt, Ruth Elizabeth Eyre Pugh. BA, Queen's U., Belfast, 1947. Ordained to ministry Meth. Ch., 1951. Min. Meth. Ch. in Ireland, Belfast, 1947-57, sec. conf., 1977-90; supt. Meth. Ch. in Ireland, Comber, No. Ireland, 1990—; minister Meth. Missionary Soc., Jamaica, 1957-65; pres. Meth. Ch. in Ireland, 1982-83, sec.-treas. trustees, 1985—. Composer (cantata) Abraham, 1974. Chmn. Irish Coun. Chs., 1988-90. Chaplain Royal Navy res., 1953-62. Recipient svc. medal Royal Ulster Constabulary, 1975. Home: 9 Londonderry Park, Comber BT23 5EU, Northern Ireland Office: Meth Ch in Ireland, 1 Fountainville Ave, Belfast BT9 6AN, Northern Ireland

EYRING, HENRY BENNION, bishop; b. Princeton, N.J., May 31, 1933; s. Henry and Mildred (Bennion) E.; m. Kathleen Johnson, July 27, 1962; children: Henry J., Stuart J., Matthew J., John B., Elizabeth, Mary Kathleen. BS, U. Utah, 1955; MBA, Harvard U., 1959, PhD, 1963; D of Humanities (hon.), Brigham Young U., 1985. Asst., then assoc. prof. Stanford U., Palo Alto, Calif., 1962-71; pres. Ricks Coll., Rexburg, Idaho, 1972-77; dep. commr. edn., then commr. LDS Ch., Salt Lake City, 1977-85, presiding bishopric, 1985—. Co-author: The Organizational World, 1973. With USAF, 1955-57. Sloan faculty fellow MIT, 1963-64. Avocations: swimming, painting, wood carving. Office: LDS Ch Presiding Bishopric 50 E N Temple St 18th Fl Salt Lake City UT 84150

FABER, HEIJE, retired theology educator; b. Maarn, Holland, The Netherlands, Sept. 3, 1907; s. Douwe and Maria Frederika (Van der Wiele) F.; m. Muriel Ann Proctor; children: Hermine Jetske, Karin Alma, William Richard, Frances. D in Theology, Leiden U., 1933; D in Psychology, Amsterdam U., 1956; D in Divinity (hon.), Meadville-Lombard, Chgo., 1969. Min. Vrijz. Hervormden, Velsen, Holland, 1932-37; min. Ned. Prot. Bond., Schiedam, Holland, 1937-48, Wassenaar, Holland, 1948-58; from head asst. to lectr. U. Leiden, 1958-70; from prof. to prof. emeritus theology faculty U. Tilburg, Netherlands, 1970-77; ret., 1977. Author: Psychology of Religion, 1975, Striking Sails, 1984, Above the Treeline, 1989; editor: Handboek Pastoraat, 1982-85. Pres. Coun. for Clin. Pastoral Edn., Holland, 1970-85. Mem. Rotary (Schiedam). Dutch Reformed Ch. Home: Lindenlaan 2, 3951 XT Maarn The Netherlands

FABER, TIMOTHY T., minister; b. St. Louis, July 7, 1964; s. Roger A. Faber and Becky E. (Schenck) Taylor; m. Teresa J. Clements, Aug. 16, 1986; children: Isaac, Sarah. BA in Religious Studies and Psychology, S.W. Bapt. U., 1985; postgrad., Luther Rice Sem., 1990—. Ordained to ministry So. Bapt. Conv., 1986. Pastor Cedar Grove Bapt. Ch., Warsaw, Mo., 1985-88, Kidder (Mo.) Bapt. Ch., 1988—; mem. missions com. Benton County Bapt. Assn., Warsaw, 1985-88. Alderman Kidder City Coun., 1989—; coach Kidder T-Ball Team, 1988—. Mem. Caldwell-Ray Bapt. Assn. (chmn. missions com. 1988-91, sec.-treas. pastor's conf. 1989, conf. v.p. 1990, conf. pres. 1991). Republican. Office: Kidder Bapt Ch 2d and Walnut Kidder MO 64649

FABIAN, GARY LAMAR, JR., music and youth minister; b. Charleston, S.C., Sept. 2, 1966; s. Gary Lamar and Elizabeth Ann (McClellan) F.; m. Janice Marie Nettles, July 12, 1986; 1 child, Ashley Marie. MusB, Fla. State U., 1988. Lic. to ministry So. Bapt. Conv., 1989. Min. of music and youth 1st Bapt. Eutawville, S.C., 1985 (summer); min. of music Santa Clara Bapt. Ch., Quincy, Fla., 1986-88; min. of music and youth Northwood Bapt. Ch., N. Charleston, S.C., 1988—. Entertainer Civitan, Charleston, 1990, Low Country Christmas Festival, Charleston, 1990. Home and Office: Northwood Bapt Ch 2748 Donner Ave North Charleston SC 29418

FABIAN, RAYMOND FREDRICK, deacon; b. Muskogee, Okla., June 23, 1921; s. August Matthew and JuliaAnn (Munding) F.; m. Jean Ann Champlin, Jan. 23, 1943; children: Pamela Jane, Johnny Ray. Student, Muskogee Jr. Coll., 1948. Deacon Cath. Ministries of Muskogee, 1981—; retired; dir. Cath. Charities of Muskogee, 1985—. Past grand knight KC, Muskogee, 1959. Recipient Bronze Star Medal U.S. Army, 1945. Home: 712 North F Muskogee OK 74403

FACKRE, GABRIEL JOSEPH, theology educator, author; b. Jersey City, Jan. 25, 1926; s. Toufic and Mary Helen (Comstock) F.; m. Dorothy Jean Ashman, Sept. 22, 1945; children: Bonnie, Gabrielle, Judith, Skye, Kirk. Student, Bucknell U., 1942-44; BD, U. Chgo., 1948, PhD, 1962. Ordained to ministry United Ch. of Christ, 1948. Pastor Duquesne-Homestead charge United Ch. of Christ, Pitts., 1951-60; from asst. prof. to prof. theology and culture Lancaster (Pa.) Theol. Sem., 1961-70; prof. Christian theology Andover Newton Theol. Sch., Newton, Mass., 1971-80, Abbot prof., 1980—; vis. prof. religion U. Hawaii, 1970; United Ch. of Christ del. Reformed—Luth. Conversation, 1987—; lectr. numerous sems. and schs. Author: The Religious Right and Christian Faith, 1983, The Christian Story, Vol. 1, 1984, Vol. 2, 1987, others; (with Dorothy Fackre): Christian Basics, 1991; also articles; co-founder Lancaster Ind. Press, 1968, Newton Times, 1971; mem. adv. coun. Interpretation jour., 1985-90; mem. editorial bd. Living Theological Heritage, 7 vols., 1989—; editor Andover Newton Rev., 1991-92. Pres. Christian Camp Meeting Assn., Craigville, Mass., 1982-88. Recipient Judge Herbert Mellon award NAACP, 1969. Mem. Am. Theol. Soc. (v.p. 1989-90, pres. 1990-91). Democrat. Office: Andover Newton Theol Sch 210 Herrick Rd Newton Centre MA 02159

FAGAL, HAROLD EDWARD, minister; b. Ilion, N.Y., May 5, 1923; s. William and Anna Mary (Fritschler) F.; m. Ruth Ellen Smith, Oct. 15, 1944; children: Carolyn, Marilyn. BTh, Atlantic Union Coll., 1944; MDiv, Andrews U., 1964; ThM, Fuller Theol. Sem., 1969, PhD, 1975. Assoc. pastor Seventh-day Adventist Ch., Springfield, Mass., 1944-46; pastor Seventh-day Adventist Ch., Pittsfield, Mass., 1946-47, New Haven, Conn., 1947-51; pastor Prospect Ave. Ch., Hartford, Conn., 1951-53, Cleve. First Seventh-day Adventist Ch., 1953-55; dept. dir. Ohio Conf. Seventh-day Adventists, Mount Vernon, 1955-56; pastor Balt. First Seventh-day Adventist Ch., 1956-58, Miami (Fla.) Temple Seventh-day Adventist Ch., 1958-63; prof. Loma Linda U., Riverside, Calif., 1964-88; assoc. dean Coll. Arts and Sci., Riverside, Calif., 1977-86. Author (with others): Scripture, Tradition and Interpretation, 1978, The Advent Hope in Scripture and History, 1987; contbr. articles to New International Bible Encyclopedia, 1985. Mem. Soc. of Bibl. Lit., Evang. Theol. Soc., Palomar Nature Club (pres. 1983-86). Republican. Avocations: music, camping. Home: 11845 Claycroft Ln Riverside CA 92505

FAGER, CHARLES EUGENE, publisher, editor, writer; b. St. Paul, Kans., Dec. 11, 1942; s. Callistus Eugene and Alice Clare (O'Brien) F.; m. Letitia Hastings, Aug. 6, 1964 (div. 1977); children: Annika, Molly; m. Mary Lou Leonard, Jan. 26, 1980; children: Gulielma, Asa. BA, Colo. State U., 1967; postgrad., Harvard, 1968-72. Pub., editor A Friendly Letter, Falls Church, Va., 1981—; pub. Kimo Press, Falls Church, 1981—; mail handler U.S. Postal Svc., Merrifield, Va., 1985—; mem. cen. com. Friends Gen. Conf., Phila., 1988—, meeting ministries com. Friends United Meeting, Richmond, Ind., 1987—; clk. Friends Bible Conf., Phila., 1989, Emergency Quaker Peace Consultation, Washington, 1991; del. Friends World Conf., 1991. Author: Selma, 1965, 1974, 2d edit. 1985, White Reflections on Black Power, 1967, Uncertain Resurrection, 1969, Quakers Are Funny, 1984, A Respondent Spark, 1985, The Magic Quilts, 1989, Life, Death and Two Chickens, 1989; editor: Quaker Service At the Crossroads, 1988, Reclaiming a Resource, 1990. Fellow Grad. Theol. Found. Mem. Society of Friends, Langley Hill Friends Meeting. Office: A Friendly Letter PO Box 1361 Falls Church VA 22041-0361 *A journalist's job is to get the facts. But a journalist's vocation is to get the truth.*

FAGER, EVERETT DEAN, minister; b. Redkey, Ind., Apr. 6, 1947; s. Luther Von and Nola Marceil (Elliott) F.; m. Kathy Jo McKean, Mar. 17, 1973 (div. Aug. 1989); children: Holly Renee, Ryan Christopher. BA, U. Evansville, 1969; ThM, Boston U., 1972; D of Ministry, Drew U., 1981. Ordained to ministry Meth. Ch. as elder, 1973. Youth and edn. min. First United Meth. Ch., Decatur, Ind., 1972-76, St. Mark's United Meth. Ch., Decatur, 1972-76; min. Albany (Ind.) United Meth. Ch., 1976-82, Osceola (Ind.) United Meth. Ch., 1982-86; sr. pastor Taylor Chapel United Meth. Ch., Ft. Wayne, Ind., 1986-91; assoc. dir. for local ch. ministries North Ind. Conf., 1991—; ptnr. GROW Ministries, Ft. Wayne, 1983—; chaplain Jaycees, Decatur, 1975-76; mem. Area Communications Svcs. Commn. Untied Meth. Ch., 1980-86, conf. chair., 1980-86; mem. conf. program com. United Meth. Ch., 1984-90; assoc. faculty Bethel Coll., Mishawaka, Ind., 1985-86; chmn. Membership Recruitment Task Force Ch. Builders of Ft. Wayne Dist., 1987—; mem. com. on Investigation N. Ind. Conf. United Meth. Ch., 1988—; bd. dirs. Assoc. Chs. Allen County, Ft. Wayne, 1988—. Chmn. Walkathon, Adams County March Dimes, Decatur, 1973-75; mem. Publicity Com. Osceola Days, 1984-86; vice chmn. Osceola Bd. Zoning Appeals, 1985-86; mem. new ch. devel. task force North Ind. U. Meth. Ch., 1989—. Named Outstanding Young Man Am., Jaycees, Decatur, 1975; recipient Ch. Growth awards N. Ind. Conf. United Meth. Ch., 1988. Democrat. Home: 6231 Monarch Dr Fort Wayne IN 46815 *The worst of life is tolerable if one believes that the best is yet to come. The best of life is put in perspective if one believes that the best is yet to come. This is my one overeaching and unconquerable hope: the best is yet to come.*

FAGERSTROM, DOUGLAS LEE, minister; b. Duluth, Minn., June 4, 1951; s. Roy Edward and Doris Evelyn (Hedquist) F.; m. Donna Marie Feddick, May 20, 1972; 1 child, Darci. BA, Grand Rapids Bapt. Coll., 1974; postgrad., Denver Sem., 1975-77; MA in Christian Edn., Bethel Sem., St. Paul, 1984. Ordained to ministry Bapt. Gen. Conf., 1982. Min. youth Dalton Bapt. Ch., Muskegon, Mich., 1971-75, exec. pastor, 1986-90; min. youth and music Mission Hills Ch., Littleton, Colo., 1975-79; min. single adults Wooddale Ch., Mpls., 1979-86, Calvary Ch., Grand Rapids, Mich., 1990—. Author, editor: Singles Ministry Handbook, 1988, Single to Single, 1991; contbr. articles to religious mags. Mem. Nat. Assn. Single Adult Leaders (bd. dirs. 1985-87, exec. dir. 1987—). Office: Calvary Ch/NSL 777 E Beltline Ave NE Grand Rapids MI 49506

FAGGART, JONATHAN EFIRD, music pastor; b. Concord, N.C., Nov. 28, 1958; s. Parks Ray and Peggy Irene (Efird) F.; m. Janet Kay Bruner, Aug. 14, 1982; children: Katrina Elizabeth, Jonathan Ryan. B in Music Edn., Evangel Coll., 1982; MMus, Eastman Sch. Mus., 1984. Ordained minister, Assembly of God Ch. Pastor, music minstries First Assembly Ch., Concord, 1984-89; Faith Assembly, Orlando, Fla., 1990—. Named one of Outstanding Young Men in Am., 1985; recipient Collegiate Artist award Music Tchrs. Nat. Assn., 1982. Mem. Phi Mu Alpha (Orpheus award 1982). Republican. Avocation: composing music. Home: 2857 Bruckner Ct Oviedo FL 32765 Office: Faith Assembly 2008 N Goldenrod Orlando FL 32807

FAHEY, CHARLES JOSEPH, priest, gerontology educator; b. Balt., Apr. 13, 1933; s. Charles J. and M. Elizabeth (Kelly) F. AB, St. Bernard's Sem., Rochester, N.Y., 1959, MDiv, 1982; MSW, Catholic U., 1963; LLD (hon.), St. Thomas U., Can., 1983; DD (hon.), St. Bernard's Inst., 1985; LLD (hon.), D'Youville Coll., 1987. Ordained priest Roman Catholic Ch., 1959. Asst. pastor St. Vincent Ch., Syracuse, N.Y., 1959-61; asst. dir. Cath. Charities, Syracuse, N.Y., 1961-67, dir., 1967-79; dir. 3rd Age Ctr. Fordham U., N.Y.C., 1979—, Marie Ward Doty prof. of aging studies, 1980—; crw; chmn. Fed. Council on Aging, 1982; mem. faculty Salzburg Fellow Program, Austria, 1985. Contbr. articles to profl. jours. Fellow Am. Coll. Health Care Adminstrs., Gerontol. Soc.; mem. Inst. Medicine of Nat. Acad. Scis., Nat. Assn. Social Workers, Am. Pub. Health Assn., Am. Assn. Homes for Aging (pres. 1976-77), Nat. Conf. Cath. Charities (pres. 1979-81), Cath. Health Assn. (bd. mem.), Am. Fedn. Aging Rsch. (bd. dirs. 1982—), Am. Stroke Assn. (bd. mem. 1983—), N.Y. State Welfare Assn. (pres. 1975), Am. Soc. on Aging (pres.-elect 1990). Office: Fordham U 3d Age Ctr 113 W 60th St New York NY 10023

FAHY, TERRENCE GERARD, Christian broadcasting and sales executive; b. Chgo., May 31, 1955; s. Merril Jordan and Patricia (Riley) F.; m. Cynthia Sue Polley, Aug. 1, 1981; children: Brian, Garrett. BA in English Lit., U. Calif., Santa Barbara, 1977; cert. in pub. speaking, Dale Carnegie Sch., Oxnard, 1988; cert. mgmt., Dale Carnegie Sch., Woodland Hills, Calif., 1988. Cert. radio mktg. cons. Sales mgr. Stas. KTYD/KBLS, Santa Barbara, 1978-82; gen. mgr. Sta. KGFT, Santa Barbara, 1982-85, Sta. KDAR, Oxnard, Calif., 1982-86; gen. sales mgr. Sta. KKLA, L.A., 1986—; deacon Living Word Christian Fellowship, Thousand Oaks, Calif., 1989—. Editor: The Master Plan—Radio Sales Seminar, 1989. Pres. parent adv. group Hillcrest Sch., Thousand Oaks, 1989-90. Mem. Western Religious Broadcasters. Office: Sta KKLA Radio 4640 Lankershim Blvd North Hollywood CA 91602

FAILINGER, MARIE ANITA, law educator, editor; b. Battle Creek, Mich., June 29, 1952; d. Conard Frederick and Joan Anita (Lang) F.; children: Joanna, Kristina. BA, Valparaiso U., 1973, JD, 1976; LLM, Yale U., 1983; postgrad., U. Chgo., 1990. Bar: Ind. 1976, U.S. Dist. Ct. (no. dist.) Ind. 1976, U.S. Dist. Ct. (so. dist.) Ind. 1977, U.S. Ct. Appeals (7th cir.) 1979, Minn. 1984, U.S. Supreme Ct. 1980. Prof. of law Hamline U., St. Paul, 1983—. Editor: Jour. of Law and Religion, 1988—; contbr. articles, book revs. to profl. publs. Bd. dirs. Crossroads Adoption Svc., Mpls., 1986—; mem. dialogue on ministry to mil. Luth. Peace Fellowship, St. Paul, 1987. Mem. Am. Acad. Religion, Minn. Women Lawyers (bd. dirs. 1989-90), Am. Assn. Law Schs. (poverty section chair 1984-88), Nat. Equal Justice Libr. (bd. dirs. 1989—). Democrat. Mem. Evang. Luth. Ch. Am. Office: Hamline U Sch Law 1536 Hewitt Ave Saint Paul MN 55104

FAIN, JOHN WILLIAM, minister; b. Eufaula, Ala., Dec. 15, 1953; s. Kenneth E. and M. Katie Lorene (Jones) F.; m. Debbie Sue Durham, June 3, 1978; children: Melody Ruth, John Wesley. BS, U. Montevallo, 1976; MDiv, Southwestern Bapt. Theol. Sem., 1981; D in Ministry, Southwestern Bapt. Ctr. Bibl. Studies, 1985. Ordained to ministry So. Bapt. Conv. Min. of youth Montevallo (Ala.) Bapt. Ch., 1975-77; pastor Payne Bapt. Ch., Lindsey, Okla., 1978-79, Lakeview Bapt. Ch., Ft. Worth, 1979-81, Calvary Bapt. Ch., Albany, Ga., 1981-86, Dawson St. Bapt. Ch., Thomasville, Ga., 1986—; vice moderator Mallory Bapt. Ch., Albany, 1983-84; bd. dirs Christian Counseling Ctr., Thomasville, 1991—. Author: How to Build Sunday Schools. Ch. dir. United Way, Thomas County, Ga., 1990-91. Recipient Appreciation to Minister award Golden Kiwanis, Thomasville. Mem. Thomas Area Ministerial Assn. (v.p. 1988-89), Thomas County Bapt. Assn. (moderator 1991—). Republican. Home: PO Box 893 Thomasville GA 31799-0893

FAIR, FRANK THOMAS, minister; b. Clinton, S.C., Oct. 19, 1929; s. Leo and Verda (Drucilla) F.; m. Thelma Barbara Belton, Dec. 22, 1956; children: Frank II, Tamera L., Donna M., Selwyn T. BA, Benedict Coll., 1950; MDiv, Crozer Sem., 1955; MST, Gammon Sem., 1959; DMin, Ea. Bapt. Sem., 1979. Ordained to ministry Bapt. Ch., 1951. Pastor Royal Bapt. Ch., Anderson, S.C., 1955-61; tchr. religion Benedict Coll., Columbia, S.C., 1957-61; chaplain Farrow Croft State Hosp., Columbia, 1959-61; pastor New Hope Bapt. Ch., Norristown, Pa., 1961—; tchr. math, English, social studies New Life Boy's Ranch, Harleysville, Pa., 1966-67; dir. student svcs. Montco[OIC, Norristown, 1968-72, asst. to exec. dir., 1972-73, dep. exec. dir., 1973-80, exec. dir., 1980-91; chairperson Interdenominational Clergy Energy Coun., Norristown, 1984—, Black Ministerium, Norristown, 1980—, Conf. of Congregation, Norristown, 1978-80; preacher Am. Bapt. Preaching in Haiti, Valley Forge, Pa., 1966; pres. Greater Norristown Coun. of Chs., 1971-78. Mem. Mayor's Adv. Panel, Norristown, 1970-74; bd. dirs. Norristown Sch. System, 1965-71, Regional Coun. Neighborhood Orgn., 1985—, YMCA, 1978-80, Montgomery County Dept. Pub. Assistance, 1971-77, George Washington Carver Ctr., 1961-64; mem. Human Rels. Commn., 1966-71. Mem. Masons. Democrat. Avocations: reading, travel, writing, photography. Home: 1705 Johnson Rd Norristown PA 19401-2819 Office: New Hope Bapt Ch 204-206 E Oak St Norristown PA 19401

FAIR, JAMES WOODSON, minister; b. Oak Grove, La., Mar. 18, 1927; s. Iverson J. and Effie C. (Skinner) F.; m. Esther Lillian Ikast, June 19, 1949; children: Pamela Diane Fair Bagwell, James Douglas. BA, Anderson Coll., 1951; postgrad., Candler Sch. Theology, Emory U., 1964. Ordained to ministry Ch. of God (Anderson, Ind.), 1952. Pastor various chs. Cadiz, Ohio, 1951-54, Reading, Pa., 1954-57; missionary Denmark, 1957-62; pastor Ch. of God, Atlanta, 1962-65, Baton Rouge, 1965-68, Milw., 1968-74, Norfolk, Va., 1974-78; pastor Bethany Ch. of God, Sterling Heights, Mich., 1978-86; sr. pastor 1st Ch. of God, Sacramento, 1986—; cons. to exec. coun., mem. div. gen. svc. Ch. of God, 1973-78, chmn. ordination and ratification Va. region, 1976-77, pres. Va. assembly, 1977-78, vice chmn. div. ministerial credentials Ch. of God in Mich., 1981—; rep. to World Conf. Ch. of God, 1959, 70, 80; chmn. program com. Norfolk Interfaith Bicentennial Commn., 1976; ann. lectr. Fritzlar Bibelschule, Germany, 1975-62; former curriculum writer Warner Press, Inc. Contbg. editor Vital Christianity, 1963-69, Pulpit Digest, 1983-85. Active Crime Resistance Edn. Com., Norfolk, 1976-78, Norfolk Action Com. for Foster Children, 1976-78, Ad Hoc Crime Com., 1976-78, Mayor's Youth Commn., 1976-78. Home: 4427 59th St Sacramento CA 95820 Office: 4400 58th St Sacramento CA 95820 *The greatest quest of man today is for vital meaning in life.*

FAIRCHILD, PHILIP LEE, minister; b. Rittman, Ohio, May 7, 1962; s. William Harold and Mildred Irene (Hall) F.; m. Donna Joy Howard, May 8, 1982; children: Philip Daniel, Candace Lee, Bethany Joy. BS in Christian Ministry, Cin. Bible Coll., 1991. Ordained to ministry Ch. of Christ, 1985. Youth min. N. 7th St. Ch. Christ, Hamilton, Ohio, 1983-85; min. Roanoke Christian Ch., Falmouth, Ky., 1985-87, Southfork Christian Ch., Verona, Ky., 1987-88; assoc. min. Community Ch. of Christ, Hamilton, 1988-91; min. Jeffersonville (Ohio) Ch. of Christ, 1991—; del. Camp Northward, Falmouth, 1985-88, Woodland Lakes Christian Camp, Amelia, Ohio, 1988-91, Butler Spring Christian Camp, Hillsboro, Ohio, 1991—. Named Outstanding Min., Civitan Club, 1990. Mem. Evang. Teaching Assn. (cert. in standard teaching), Hamilton Ministerial Assn., Cin. Area Youth Mins. Republican. Home: 83 N Main St Jeffersonville OH 43128 Office: Jeffersonville Ch of Christ 83 N Main St Jeffersonville OH 43128

FAJEN, JOHN HERMAN, minister; b. Stover, Mo., May 26, 1929; s. Otto John and Magdalena Elise (Wittrock) F.; m. Margaret (Peggy) Thompson, June 19, 1955; children: Katherine, Elizabeth, Melanie, Barbara, Pauline. AA, St. Paul's Coll., Concordia, Mo., 1949; BA, Concordia Coll., 1952; diploma in Theology, Concordia Sem., 1955; postgrad., UCLA, 1964-65, 69-70. Ordained to ministry Luth. Ch.-Mo. Synod, 1956. Missionary to Nigeria BFMS, Luth. Ch.-Mo. Synod, St. Louis, 1956-80; sec. for pers. Luth. Ch.-Mo. Synod, St. Louis, 1980-87; pastor Trinity Luth. Ch., Glidden, Wis., 1987—; vis. prof. theology Valparaiso U., 1974, Gross Meml. lectr., 1978. Translator Bible; pub. N.T., 1980. Office: Trinity Luth Ch Lenz Rd and Hwy 13 Glidden WI 54527

FALCAO, JOSE FREIRE CARDINAL, cardinal; b. Erere, Brazil, Oct. 23, 1925. Ordained priest Roman Cath. Ch., 1949. Ordained titular bishop of Vardimissa, coadjutor of Limoeiro do Norte, 1967, bishop of Limoeiro do Norte, 1967, archbishop of Teresina, 1971, archbishop of Brasilia, 1984, created cardinal, 1988, with titular ch. St. Luke (Via Prenestina). Mem. Christian Unity, Health Care Workers (couns.). Office: QL 12-Cj12, Lote 1 Lago Sul, 71600 DF Brasilia Brazil*

FALCONE, SEBASTIAN ANTHONY, priest, academic administrator, educator; b. Rochester, N.Y., Oct. 15, 1927; s. Augustus Michael and Rose (Lanteri) F. Licentiate in Sacred Theology, Cath. U., 1961, postgrad., 1978—. Joined Capuchin-Franciscan Order, Roman Cath. Ch., 1943, ordained priest, 1951. Prof., dean St. Lawrence Sem., Beacon, N.Y., 1951-58; prof., rector Immaculate Heart Sem., Geneva, N.Y., 1961-67; prof. St. Bernard's Sem., Rochester, 1967—, acad. dean, 1972-78; acad. dean St. Bernards's Inst., Rochester, N.Y., 1981-88; pres., chief exec. officer St. Bernard's Inst., Rochester, N.Y., 1981—; regional councilor Capuchin-Franciscan Order, N.Y.C., 1955-65, vice-provincial, Newton, N.J., 1958-61; pres. Capuchin Ednl. Conf., N.Y.C., 1959-61, Franciscan Commitment Conf., Newton, 1963-72; mem. Rochester Ctr. for Theol. Studies, 1972—, co-chair, 1981—; cons. continuing edn. Diocese of Rochester. Author poetry, ency. articles, editorials; editor, contbr. various newsletters. Organizer House of Concern, Geneva, N.Y., 1966, Seneca Falls, N.Y., 1967. Mem. Am. Acad. Religion, Soc. Bibl. Lit. Office: St Bernard's Inst 1100 S Goodman St Rochester NY 14620-2545

FALCONER, ALAN DAVID, theology educator; minister; b. Edinburgh, Scotland, Dec. 12, 1945; s. Alexander and Jean Braidwood (Littlejohn) F.; m. Marjorie Ellen Walters, Aug. 6, 1968; children: David Eric, Rosalind Clare, Andrew Graham. MA, Aberdeen U., Scotland, 1967, BD, 1970; Cert. de ecumenisme, Geneva U., 1971. Ordained to ministry Ch. of Scotland. Asst. minister St. Machar's Cathedral, Aberdeen, 1972-74; J.K.L. lectr. in systemic theology Irish Sch. Ecumenics, Dublin, Ireland, 1974—, dean of studies, 1987—, dir. Irish Sch. Ecumenics, 1990—; cons. on human rights Brit. Council Chs., London, 1978—, Irish Coun. Chs., Belfast, No. Ireland, 1978—; mem. Irish and Brit. Chs. Adv. Group on Human Rights and Responsibility, London, 1985-87; cons. Reformed Roman Catholic Internat. Commn., Venice 1986—. Author: A Man Alone, 1987; co-author: Punishment and Imprisonment, 1985; editor: Understanding Human Rights, 1980, Reconciling Memories, 1988; co-editor: Freedom to Hope?, 1985; contbr. articles to profl. publs. Mem. Irish Theol. Assn. (v.p. 1977-79), Societas Oecumenica (pres. 1986-90). Home: 95 Orwell Pk, Dublin 6W, Ireland Office: Irish Sch Ecumenics, Milltown Pk, Dublin 6, Ireland

FALGOUT, WILLIAM DONALD, minister, pastoral counselor; b. Tuscaloosa, Ala., Aug. 28, 1941; s. Maurice Joseph and Ludie (Kirk) F.; m. Sheila Mathews, Nov. 11, 1972; children: Mathew David, Christopher Thomas. BS, Livingston U., 1967; ThM, New Orleans Bapt. Theol. Sem., 1972; postgrad., Columbia Pacific U., San Rafael, Calif., 1989. Ordained to ministry So. Bapt. Conv. Pastor Eoline Bapt. Ch., 1962-63, Little Sandy Bapt. Ch., 1963-74, 1st Bapt. Ch., Sandusky, Ala., 1974-79, 66th St. Bapt. Ch., Birmingham, Ala., 1979—; pastoral counselor for chief of staff St. Vincent Hosp., Birmingham, 1989—; pastoral counselor Nat. Christian Counseling Assn., Kettering, Pa., 1990—; v.p. Ala. Bapt. Pastors Conf., Birmingham, 1978-79, pres., 1979-80. Author: (religious dramas) Let Go and Let God, 1965, The Witness, 1991. Bd. dirs. Camp Tuscoba Friendship House, Tuscaloosa, 1968, Corner Stone-Hillcrest Hosp., Birmingham, 1990; mem. adv. coun., bd. dirs. ARC, Birmingham, 1988. Mem. Masons (master Mason), Alpha Chi Omega. Office: 66th Street Bapt Ch 6531 Division Ave Birmingham AL 35206

FALK, HARVEY (OSCAR), rabbi, writer, travel consultant; b. N.Y.C., Apr. 30, 1932; s. Isadore and Sadie (Eisen) F.; m. Hedy Braun, June 9, 1958; children: Sharon, Barbara, Civia. Grad., Mesivta Theol. Sem., Bklyn., 1955. Ordained rabbi, 1955. Dir. edn. Young Israel of Claremont Pkwy., N.Y.C., 1955-59; tchr. Rabbi Israel Salanter Yeshiva, N.Y.C., 1955-59; rabbi Flushing (N.Y.) Jewish Ctr., 1973-76, Congregation Ahavath Israel, Liberty, N.Y., 1976-77; travel advisor Hedy's Travel, Bklyn., 1985—. Author: Days of Judgement, 1972, Jesus the Pharisee, 1985; also articles. Mem. Rabbinical Coun. Am., N.Y. Bd. Rabbis. Office: Hedy's Travel 1274 49th St Ste 504C Brooklyn NY 11219 *The Hebrew word for truth is "emet". It consists of the first, middle and last letters of the Hebrew alphabet. The lesson would be that all our work, from beginning to end, should be a search for truth.*

FALK, NANCY ELLEN AUER, religion educator; b. Bethlehem, Pa., Sept. 3, 1938; d. Allen Archibald and Pearl Emma (Kichline) Auer; m. Arthur Eugene Falk, Oct. 28, 1967; children: Indira Joy, Amelia Marie. BA, Cedar Crest Coll., 1960; MA, U. Chgo., 1963, PhD, 1972. Asst. prof. religion Western Mich. U., Kalamazoo, 1966-72, assoc. prof. religion, 1972-79, chair religion dept., 1972-75, prof. religion, 1979—; Fulbright lectr. Coun. for Internat. Exch. of Scholars, New Delhi, 1984-85. Co-editor: Unspoken Worlds, 1981, new edit., 1989; contbr. articles to profl. jours.; contbg. author encys. A.I.I.S. sr. fellow, India, 1991-92. Mem. Am. Acad. Religion (assoc. dir. at large 1977-80), North Am. Assn. for the Study of Religion (steering com. 1989—). Office: Western Mich U Religion Dept Kalamazoo MI 49008

FALK, RANDALL M., rabbi; b. Little Rock, July 9, 1921; s. Randall Morris and Lucile (Kronberg) F.; m. Edna Unger, Dec. 21, 1952; children: Randall Marc, Jonathan David, Heidi Falk Logan. BA, U. Cin., 1943; MHL, Hebrew Union Coll., Cin., 1947; MA, Vanderbilt U., Nashville, 1966, DDiv, 1969. Ordained rabbi. Rabbi Congregation Ohabai Sholom, Erie, Pa., 1947-60; Rabbi Congregation Ohabai Sholom, Nashville, 1960-86, rabbi emeritus, 1986—; adj. faculty Sch. Theology, U. of South, Sewanee, Tenn., 1970—, Vanderbilt U. Div. Sch., 1987—. Co-author: Jews and Christians: A Troubled Family, 1990. Bd. dirs. Commn. on Social Action of UAHC, 1980—; alumni overseer Hebrew Union Coll., Jewish Inst. Religion, Cin., 1967—; exec. bd., past pres. Coun. Community Svcs., Nashville. Recipient Human Rels. Award, Nat. Coun. Christians and Jews, 1979. Mem. Cen.

Conf. Am. Rabbis (bd. dirs., sec. 1978-80). Office: The Temple 5015 Harding Rd Nashville TN 37205

FALWELL, JERRY L., clergyman; b. Lynchburg, Va., Aug. 11, 1933; s. Cary H. and Helen V. (Beasley) F.; m. Macel Pate, Apr. 12, 1958; children: Jerry L., Jeannie, Jonathan. BA, Bapt. Bible Coll., Springfield, Mo., 1956; DD (hon.), Tenn. Temple U.; LLD (hon.), Calif. Grad. Sch. Theology, Cen. U., Seoul, Korea. Founder, pastor Thomas Rd. Bapt. Ch., Lynchburg, Va., 1956—; founder Liberty U., Lynchburg, 1971, Moral Majority Inc. (now called Liberty Fedn.), 1979-89; Host: (TV show) Old Time Gospel Hour; lectr. in field. Author: Listen, America!, 1980, The Fundamentalist Phenomenon, 1981, Finding Inner Peace and Strength, 1982, When It Hurts Too Much to Cry, 1984, Wisdom for Living, 1984, Stepping Out on Faith, 1984, Champions for God, 1985, If I Should Die Before I Wake, 1986, autobiography Strength For the Journey, 1987; co-author: Church Aflame, 1971, Capturing a Town for Christ, 1973. Recipient Clergyman of Yr. award Religious Heritage Am., 1979, Jabotinsky Centennial medal, 1980, Two Hungers award Food for the Hungry Internat., 1981; named Christian Humanitarian of Yr., Food for the Hungry Internat., One of 25 Most Influential People in Am., U.S. News & World Report, 1983; Number One Most Admired Conservative Man Not in Congress Conservative Digest, 1983, 2d Most Admired Man Good Housekeeping, 1982, 84, 86; named to Nat. Religious Broadcasters' Hall of Fame, 1985. Mem. Nat. Assn. Religious Broadcasters (bd. dirs.). Address: Thomas Rd Bapt Ch Lynchburg VA 24514

FANNIN, CARL HENDRIX, minister; b. Williamson, W.Va., Feb. 24, 1955; s. Ernest and Naomi (Farley) F.; m. Janet Lynn Thayer, May 28, 1976; children: Amy K., Joshua C. BA, Malone Coll., Canton, Ohio, 1980; MDiv, Ashland (Ohio) Sem., 1984. Ordained to ministry United Meth. Ch., 1984. Pastor Dellory & Leavittsville United Meth. Ch., Ohio, 1977-80, The Northside Ch., East Liverpool, Ohio, 1980-86, Collins (Ohio) and West Hartland United Meth. Ch., 1986—. Chmn. bd. Abigail Pregnancy Svcs., Norwalk, Ohio, 1991—; coach Western Res. Little League, Collins, Ohio, 1989-91, Pee Wee Basketball, 1991—. Republican. Home: 4151 Hartland Ctr Rd Collins OH 44826

FANNING, HAROLD DEAN, minister; b. Huntsville, Ala., Sept. 3, 1952; s. Horace David and Allie Mae (Sharp) F.; m. Deborah Jo Sharpe, Aug. 11, 1973; children: Alison, Daniel. BA in Religion, Heritage Bible Coll., Huntsville, 1985; MA in Ministry, Luther Rice Sem., Jacksonville, Fla., 1990. Ordained to ministry So. Bapt. Conv., 1984. With P.P.G. Industries, 1973-90; pastor Paint Rock (Ala.) Bapt. Ch., 1983-84, Union Grove Bapt. Ch., New Market, Ala., 1985-86, Oak Park Bapt. Ch., Huntsville, 1987—; pres. Bivocat. Mins. Fellowship, Ala. Conv., 1989-90; bd. dirs. Heritage Bible Coll., 1990—. Home: 1392 Ryland Pike Huntsville AL 35811 Office: 2105 Cloys Ave NE Huntsville AL 35811 *I have learned that if a person will work hard, do their best at whatever they do, keep their eyes and thoughts on God, that person will be a success and live a happy and prosperous life.*

FANT, CLYDE EDWARD, JR., religion educator; b. Marshall, Tex., Nov. 14, 1934; s. Clyde Edward and Margaret (Moos) F.; divorced; children: Brian H., Carol E., Julie A.; m. Cheryl Hammock, Nov. 9, 1984. BA, Baylor U., 1956; BD, Southwestern Bapt. Seminary, Ft. Worth, 1960, ThD, 1964. Ordained to ministry Bapt. Ch., 1956. Pastor First Bapt. Ch., Ruston, La., 1962-66; prof. of preaching Southwestern Bapt. Seminary, Ft. Worth, 1966-75; pastor First Bapt. Ch., Richardson, Tex., 1975-82; pres. Internat. Bapt. Sem., Ruschlikon/Zurich, Switzerland, 1982-83; dean of chapel Stetson Univ., Deland, Fla., 1985—; vis. prof. of preaching Div. Sch., Duke U., Durham, N.C., Southeastern Bapt. Sem., Wake Forest, N.C., 1983-84. Author, editor: 20 Centuries of Great Preaching (13 vols.), 1971; author: Preaching for Today, 1977, Bonhoeffer: Worldly Preaching, 1991; co-author: An Introduction to the Bible, 1991; editor: Contemporary Christian Trends, 1972. Recipient Fulbright scholarship, Tubingen, Fed. Republic of Germany, 1956, Venting award/Outstanding Sr., Southwestern Bapt. Sem., 1960. Mem. Am. Acad. Religion, Soc. Bibl. Lit. Democrat. Office: Stetson U Woodland Blvd De Land FL 32720

FARGASON, EDDIE WAYNE, orchestra director, arranger; b. Lubbock, Tex., Feb. 19, 1948; s. Claude Patrick and Winnie Bertinia (Howell) F.; m. Terri Lee Rousser, Aug. 30, 1968; children: Jason Kyle, Kevin Wray. MusB, U. Tex., 1971, MusM, 1973. Arranger, orchestrator 1st Bapt. Ch., Dallas, 1978-83, orch. condr., 1983—; freelance arranger Songline Prodns., Richardson, Tex., 1975—. Composer numerous mus. works. Mem. Internat. Trombone Soc., Tex. Composer's Guild, Broadcast Music Inc., Christian Instrumental Dirs. Assn., Gospel Music Assn., Pi Kappa Lambda. Avocations: water skiing, fishing. Home: 1909 Clemson Dr Richardson TX 75081 Office: 1st Bapt Ch 1707 San Jacinto St Dallas TX 75201 *With the degrading of the moral and ethical fiber of our world, there are some things that should never change...honesty and truthfulness. The pursuit of these virtues must remain constant for our society to proceed on a positive course.*

FARLEY, MARGARET ANN, nun, philosophy educator; b. St. Cloud, Minn., Apr. 15, 1935; d. John Arthur and Mary Estelle (Mosher) F. AB, U. Detroit, 1957, MA, 1960, LHD (hon.), 1990; MPhil, Yale U., 1970, PhD, 1973; LHD (hon.), Fairfield U., 1983, Weston Sch. Theology, Cambridge, Mass., 1989. Joined Religious Sisters of Mercy, Roman Cath. Ch., 1959. Prof. ethics Yale Div. Sch., New Haven, 1971—. Author: Personal Commitments, 1986; co-author: Metaphysics of Being and God, 1966; also articles. Recipient Centennial medal John Carroll U., 1986; Danforth Found. grantee, 1967-69; Kent fellow Danforth Found., 1969-72. Mem. Soc. Christian Ethics (exec. bd. 1974-77), Cath. Theol. Soc. Am., Am. Theology Soc., Am. Acad. Religion. Office: Yale Div Sch 409 Prospect St New Haven CT 06511

FARLEY, MARY NICHOLAS, educator, nun; b. Trenton, N.J., Jan. 13, 1913; d. Nicholas Francis and Margaret E. (Henry) Farley. B.A., Georgian Ct. Coll., 1945; M.A., Villanova U., 1950; postgrad. Bowdoin Coll., 1956, Colo. U., 1958. Joined Sisters of Mercy, N. Plainfield, N.J., Roman Catholic Ch., 1931. Tchr. physics and math. Camden Cath. High Sch. (N.J.), 1935-49; prin. Star of Sea Elem. Sch., Atlantic City, 1949-55, Cathedral Grammar Sch., Trenton, N.J., 1955-61; dean women Georgian Ct. Coll., Lakewood, N.J., 1964-70, chairperson dept. physics, 1970—; pres. N.J. Cath. Round of Sci., Lakewood, 1962-64; dir. tape inst. World Book, Trenton, 1960-62; workshop dir. Georgian Ct. Coll. Author: Science and Life series K-8, 1963-67; Modern Elementary Science, 1-6, 1971. Recipient Spl. award for Outstanding Service in Sci. Edn. N.J. State Conv., 1983. NSF grantee, 1978-82. Mem. N.J. Sci. Tchrs. Assn. (elec. sci. chmn. conv. 1981, 83, middle grane chmn. 1983-84, exec. bd. dirs. 1983-84, workshop leader conv. 1979, 80), N.J. Assn. Physics Tchrs. (exec. bd. dirs. 1983-85, pres. 1985-86, 86-87), Nat. Sci. Tchrs. Assn. (workshop Boston conv. 1985). Home: Georgian Ct Coll Lakewood NJ 08701

FARLEY, WENDY LEE, lay worker, educator; b. Greencastle, Ind., Apr. 13, 1958; d. William Edward and Doris June (Kimbel) F.; m. Clifford Allen Grabhorn, Oct. 11, 1987; 1 child, Emma Elizabeth. BA, U. N.H., 1981; MA, Vanderbilt U., 1987, PhD, 1988. Sunday sch. tchr. North Decatur (Ga.) Presbyn. Ch., 1989—; asst. prof. Emory U., Atlanta, 1988—. Author: Tragic Vision and Divine Compassion: A Contemporay Theodicy, 1990. Vol. Amnesty Internat. Mid-East Coordination Group, 1986—, Bread for the World, 1986—. Mem. Am. Acad. Religion, Soc. of Phenomenology and Existential Philosophy. Office: Emory Univ Dept Religion Atlanta GA 30322 *The suffering of other people is a call to each of us to respond with compassion and justice. If we are to survive morally, spiritually, or physically, it will be because enough people respond in time.*

FARMER, DEREK MAITLAND, clergyman; b. Dillingham County, Kent, Eng., Oct. 2, 1943; s. Kenneth and Nellie Amy Elizabeth (Wooley) F.; m. Helen Ruth Palmer, June 3, 1964. Grad., Tech. Coll. Witwatersrand, Johannesburg, South Africa, Balmoral Coll. Piping, Scotland, Royal Coll., London. Ordained to ministry Salvation Army. Chaplain U.S. Dept. Prisons, Va. Dept. Corrections, N.C. Dept. Prison, 1980-87; commanding officer, minister Fredericksburg (Va.) Salvation Army, 1987—; drum major pipe major II Va. Regiment, Chesapeake, 1972-78; music instr. McPherson Sch. Piping, Norfolk, 1978-80. With USNR, 1964-76. Mem. Am. Corrections Assn., Kiwanis. Office: The Salvation Army 821 Lafayette Blvd PO Box 129 Fredericksburg VA 22404

FARMER, JEFFREY E., academic administrator. Head Eugene (Oreg.) Bible Coll. Office: Eugene Bible Coll 2155 Bailey Hill Rd Eugene OR 97405*

FARMER, MARJORIE NICHOLS, religious order administrator, educator; b. Hartford, Conn., Mar. 17, 1922; d. Edward K. and Laura (Drake) Nichols; m. Clarence Farmer, Apr. 12, 1943; children: Clarence Jr., Franklin. AB, Temple U., 1946, MA, 1954, MEd, EdD, 1958, 1975; MAR, Lutheran Theological Seminary, Phila., 1983. Cert. tchr., Pa.; prin., Pa.; supt., Pa. Asst.prof. of edn. Glassboro State Coll., Glassboro, N.J.; reading & english exec. dir. Sch. Dist., Phila.; priest-in-charge St. Matthias Episcopal Ch., Phila.; cons., prin. Clarence Farmer Assocs. Inc., Pa. Author: (with others) Composition and Grammar Grades 9-12, 1985; Consensus and Dissent, 1986. Recipient Distinguised Svc. award NCTE, 1981. Mem. Nat. Council of Tchrs. of English (past pres.). Home: 8343 Mansfield Ave Philadelphia PA 19150

FARNHOLTZ, SHARYN ANN, minister; b. Utica, N.Y., May 18, 1945; d. James Arthur and Evelyn Florence (Gurney) McCurdy; m. David Frederick Farnholtz, July 31, 1965; children: Jodee Lynn Farnholtz Cook, Nathaniel David. Student, Oneonta State U., 1963-65. Lic. to ministry Bapt. Ch., 1985. Nursery supt. Macungie (Pa.) Bapt. Ch., 1970-77; v.p. Women's Missionary Soc., Macungie, 1975-76; ch. sec. Agape New Testament Fellowship, Schnecksville, Pa., 1977-81, 91, supt. Sunday sch., 1977-84, 88, dir. youth, 1978-85, 89, elder, team pastor, 1985—. V.p. Christian Action Coun. of Lehigh Valley, Allentown, Bethlehem, Pa., 1990-91. Republican. Office: Agape New Testament Fellow 2859 Main St Schnecksville PA 18078-9622 *When trials and hardships come to us, it is the time to turn obstacles into opportunities to learn a better way, to live a better life, and to become a better person; it is God's way.*

FARNSWORTH, A. W., minister; b. Gary, Ind., Dec. 18, 1945; s. A.W. and Margaret (Bourke) F.; m. Karen Denise Richard, June 25, 1988; children: Rachelle, Aaron, Joshua Richard, Kristin Richard. BA, Culvr Stockton Coll., Canton, Mo., 1968; MDiv, Christian Theol. Sem., Indpls., 1973; DMin, McCormick Theol. Sem., Chgo., 1985. Ordained to ministry, Christian Ch. (Disciples of Christ), 1973. Minister First Christian Ch., Pontiac, Ill., 1973-78; sr. minister Cen. Christian Ch., Huntington, Ind., 1978-87, Danville (Ind.) Christian Ch., 1987—. Mem. Theta Phi, Rotary (dir. 1979-84), Masons (grand chaplain Ind. 1991). Home: 26 Round Hill Ct Danville IN 46122 Office: Danville Christian Ch 180 W Main St Danville IN 46122

FARNSWORTH, DONALD CLYDE, minister; b. Stockton, Calif., Oct. 9, 1940; s. Donald Daryl and Dollie Katherine (Fairhurst) F.; m. Jerry Ann Thormolen, June 30, 1961; children: Brian Donald, Bradley Daryl. AA in Drafting, Coll. of Sequoias, Visalia, Calif., 1960; AA in Bibl. Studies, Nazarene Bible Coll., Colorado Springs, Colo., 1977; B.Bible Theology, Internat. Sem., Plymouth, Fla., 1986, M.Bible Theology, 1987. Ordained to ministry Ch. of the Nazarene, 1979. Pastor L.A. Highland Park Ch. of the Nazarene, 1977-80, First Ch. of the Nazarene, Rolla, Mo., 1980-84, Cortez (Colo.) Ch. of the Nazarene, 1985-89, Medford (Oreg.) S.W. Ch. of the Nazarene, 1989—; adminstr. Rolla Benevolent Fund, 1981-84. Chaplain, Hospice, Cortez, 1986-88. Mem. Kiwanis. Republican. Home: 1180 S Holly St Medford OR 97501 Office: Medford SW Ch of Nazarene 1332 Mt Pitt Ave Medford OR 97501

FARNSWORTH, PHILIP WESLEY, minister; b. Caro, Mich., Apr. 12, 1947; s. Irving Melvin and Frances Catherine (Chatfield) F.; m. Roxanna Rose Ford, July 20, 1968 (dec. Mar., 1982); 1 child, Nathan; m. Donna June Decker, Aug. 7, 1982; children: Nathan, Wesley, Andrew, Stephen. BS in Bus. Adminstrn., Olivet Nazarene Univ., 1969. Ordained to ministry in Assembly of God Ch., 1970. Pastor Open Bible Standard Chs., Des Moines, Iowa, 1968-1977; prof. Open Bible Coll., Des Moines, 1972-73; pastor Assemblies of God, Mich. Dist., Dearborn, 1978-88; evangelist Phil Farnsworth Ministries, Jackson, Mich., 1988—; pres. Service Ministries, Jackson, Mich., 1982—. Office: Phil Farnsworth Ministries Svc Ministries 425 Seymour Jackson MI 49202 *Ministry is found in opportunity and choice! The opportunities are unlimited, though cloaked in the darkness of tomorrow; I choose to walk thru open doors, serving and letting God be my source for tomorrow!.*

FARQUHARSON, WALTER HENRY, minister, church official; b. Zealandia, Sask., Can., May 30, 1936; s. James and Jessie Ann (Muirhead) F.; m. Patricia Joan Casswell, Sept. 16, 1958; children: Scott, Michael, Catherine, Stephen. BA, U. Sask., Saskatoon, 1957, Diploma in Edn., 1969; BD, St. Andrew's Coll., Saskatoon, 1961, DD (hon.), 1975. Ordained to ministry United Ch. of Can., 1961. Min. Saltcoats-Bredenbury-Churchbridge Pastoral Charge, Sask., 1961—; moderator United Ch. of Can., 1990—; exec. gen. coun., pres. Sask. Conf. Contbr. numerous hymns and religious songs. Home: PO Box 126, Saltcoats, SK Canada S0A 3R0 Office: United Ch of Can, PO Box 58, Saltcoats, SK Canada S0A 3R0

FARRAKHAN, LOUIS, religious leader; b. N.Y.C., May 11, 1933; changed name from Louis Eugene Wolcott to Louis X, then to Louis Farrakhan; m. Betsy Wolcott; 9 children. Student, Winston-Salem (N.C.) Tchrs. Coll. Formerly leader of Harlem mosque Nation of Islam, N.Y.C., nat. spokesman; founder reorganized orgn. Nation of Islam, 1977. Office: Nation of Islam 734 W 79th St Chicago IL 60620*

FARRAR, MARTHA ANN, lay worker, gift shop owner; b. Victoria, Tex., July 13, 1943; d. Warrington Siebert and Byrd Lillian Bertha (Dreyer) F. Student, Victoria Coll., 1961-63; cert., Baldwin Bus. Coll., 1964; cert. in nursing, Renger Hosp. Sch. Nursing, 1966. Reporter Zion Luth Ch. Women, Mission Valley, Tex., 1970-76, sec., 1976-78, pres., 1980-82, mem. adult choir, 1957-61, 72-84, Sunday sch. tchr., 1982—, mem. altar guild, 1990—; owner Martha's Gift Shoppe, Victoria, 1972—; mem. Spirit of Zion Ch. Choir, Mission Valley, 1985—, Rebecca Circle Bible Study Group, Mission Valley, 1981—, pres. 1990-91; mem. Christian Fellowship Bowler's League, Victoria, 1990—. Democrat. Office: Marthas Gift Shoppe 4407 Lilac Ste 2 Victoria TX 77904 *I believe we could make the world better if we would treat each other like beloved brothers and sisters. We need to treat others with the same respect and compassion we expect from them, without regard for race, color, creed, or behavior. When we do so, mutual love and respect abound and overcome hate and prejudice.*

FARRELL, DAVID E., priest, religious order superior; b. June 30, 1939. Student, Williams Coll., 1957-60; BA in Philosophy, Stonehill Coll., 1964; BTh., Pontificia Universidad Catolica de Chile, 1968; MS in Sociology, U. London, 1983. Joined Congregation of Holy Cross, Roman Cath. Ch., 1961, ordained priest, 1968. Parish priest Chimbote, Peru, 1969-74; asst. superior Chile region Congregation of Holy Cross, 1975-81; parish priest Archdiocese of Santiago, Chile, 1975-82; mem. exec. com. Vicaria de la Pastoral Obrera, Archdiocese of Santiago, Chile, 1977-82; councilor Chile region Congregation of Holy Cross, 1981; parish priest Archdiocese of San Salvador, El Salvador, 1984-87; asst. provincial ea. province Congregation of Holy Cross, 1987, provincial superior ea. province, 1988—; co-founder Instituto Ferrol de Investigacion y Accion Social, Chimbote, Peru, 1970-74; cons. Oxfam-U.K., Mex., C.Am., 1984; with Salvadorean Found. for Devel. and Minimum Housing, 1984-87. Active Chilean nat. com. World Univ. Svc., 1979, Latin Am. rep. to exec. com., 1980-82. Mem. Conf. Maj. Superiors of Men (chmn. region I, nat. bd. dirs., nat. justice and peace com. 1989). Address: Congregation of Holy Cross 835 Clinton Ave Bridgeport CT 06604

FARRELL, HOBERT KENNETH, religion educator; b. Charleston, W.Va., Feb. 15, 1939; s. Kenneth Hobert and Juanita Lee (Bowling) F.; m. Irene Carol Dondit, Jan. 27, 1962; children: David Kenneth, John Douglas. BA, Wheaton Coll., 1961; MA, Wheaton (Ill.) Grad. Sch., 1964; BD, Gordon Divinity Sch., South Hamilton, Mass., 1964; ThM, Union Theol. Seminary, Richmond, Va., 1966; PhD, Boston U., 1972. Ordained to ministry Evang. Bapt. Ch., 1964. Pastor Crombie St. Congl. Ch., Salem, Mass., 1966-70; instr. in Greek Boston U., 1967-71; youth pastor Evang. Bapt. Ch., Norwood, Mass., 1970-71; prof. John Wesley Coll., Owosso, Mich., 1971-78, LeTourneau U., Longview, Tex., 1978—; pastor Chalk Hill Community Ch., Henderson, Tex., 1986-91; tchr. Sunday sch., deacon 1st Bapt. Ch., Longview, 1983—. Contbr. articles to profl. jours. Mem. Evang. Theol. Soc. (program chmn. Southwest dist. 1982-83, v.p. 1983-84, pres. 1984-85), Inst. Bibl. Rsch., Soc. Bibl. Lit. Republican. Office: LeTourneau U PO Box 7001 Longview TX 75607 *Jesus pronounced a blessing on His disciples for recognizing Him as the Messiah. I continue to thank God for the blessing of seeing Jesus as Savior and Lord.*

FARRELL, LEIGHTON KIRK, minister; b. Hillsboro, Tex., Oct. 13, 1930; s. Aubrey Lee and Lorine (Kirk) F.; m. Charlotte Ann Underwood, May 31, 1952 (div. Feb. 1986); children: Becky Ann Wilson, Scott Gregory; m. Julie Ann Yarbrough, Apr. 25, 1987. BA, So. Meth. U., 1951, MTh, 1953; ThD, Iliff Sch. of Theology, 1956; DHL, Alaska Pacific U., Anchorage, 1983. Ordained elder Meth. Ch. Pastor Edge Park United Meth. Ch., Ft. Worth, 1956-66; adminstrv. asst. to the bishop Dallas-Ft. Worth Area United Meth. Ch., Dallas, 1965-67; sr. minister First United Meth. Ch., Richardson, Tex., 1967-72, Highland Park United Meth. Ch., Dallas, 1972—; trustee So. Meth. U., Dallas, 1976—; chmn. bd. Meth. Hosps. of Dallas, 1977-83; del. to gen. conf. United Meth. Ch., 1980, 84; bd. dirs. pensions United Meth. Ch. George Washington medal of honor Freedom Founds. Office: Highland Park United Meth Ch 3300 Mockingbird Ln Dallas TX 75205

FARRIS, DONN MICHAEL, librarian, educator; b. Welch, W.Va., Nov. 4, 1921; s. Robert Coleman and Aileen Virginia (Hutson) F.; m. Joyce Gwendolyn Lockhart, Nov. 20, 1956; children: Evan Michael, Amy Virginia. AB, Berea Coll., 1943; postgrad., Northwestern U., 1944-47; MDiv, Garrett Theol. Sem., 1947; MLS, Columbia U., 1950. Libr. Duke U. Div. Sch., 1950—, asst. prof. theol. bibliography, 1959-63, assoc. prof., 1964-70, prof., 1971—. Editor: Aids to a Theological School Library, 1958, Aids to a Theological Library, Selected Basic Reference Books and Periodicals, 1969; editor book rev. sect. Duke Div. Sch. Rev., 1959—. Mem. Am. Theol. Libr. Assn. (editor newsletter 1953—, exec. com. 1953-56, v.p. 1961-62, pres. 1962-63), N.C. Libr. Assn. Home: 921 N Buchanan Blvd Durham NC 27701

FARRIS, FORREST LEVERNE, priest; b. Bicknell, Ind., Dec. 2, 1928; s. George Henry and Ethel Maud (Mahan) F.; m. Rita Ellen Dyer, Nov. 18, 1951; children: John, Susan Martin, David. BA, U. Indpls., 1952; M Div., Wesley Theol. Seminary, 1955. Ordained to ministry Episc. Ch. as deacon, 1962, as priest, 1963. Pastor Trafalgar (Ind.) Meth. Ch., 1949-51, Decatur Bethel Meth. Ch., Indpls., 1951-52, Washington Grove (Md.) Meth. Ch., 1952-56, St. Andrews Meth. Ch., Bethesda, Md., 1956-59, Hunts Meth. Ch., Riderwood, Md., 1959-61; lay reader-in-charge Mt. Johns Chapel, Relay, Md., 1961-63; asst. rector Emmanuel Episcopal Ch., Cumberland, Md., 1963-68; rector St. Margaret's Ch., Annapolis, Md., 1968-90. Democrat. Home: 9222 S Stargrass Cir Highlands Ranch CO 80126

FARSCHMAN, MARC WAYNE, minister; b. Oberlin, Ohio, Nov. 15, 1955; s. Dewayne Milton and Ruth Eleanor (Biar) F. Student, Lorain County Comml. Coll., 1974. Ordained to ministry Nondenomination Charismatic Ch., 1984. Founder, counselor New Life Thru Faith Ministries, Mesa, Ariz., 1983-86, min., 1989—; pastor Winchester Cathedral Ch., Apache Junction, Ariz., 1986-89; aux chaplain Ariz. State Prison Complex, Florence, 1987—. Author: Setting the Captives Free!, 1985. Bd. dirs. East Valley Sch. Ministry and Missions, Mesa, 1988-89. Recipient Cert. Appreciation State of Ariz. Dept. Corrections, 1988, 89, 90. Mem. Internat. Conv. Faith Ministries. Republican. Home: 898 W Calle del Norte # 2 Chandler AZ 85224 *As I go through life, I have found that the more I know, the more I know I don't know all there is to know.*

FASANARO, CHARLES NICHOLAS, religion educator; b. N.Y.C., Oct. 25, 1943; s. Charles Vincent and Edith (D'Alessandro) F. BS, Manhattan Coll., 1965; MA in Religion with distinction, Iliff Sch. Theology, 1980; PhD, U. Denver, Iliff Sch. Theol., 1983. Asst. prof. Ctr. for Study of Philosophy and Religion, Boulder, Colo., 1986; pres. Ctr. for Study of Philosophy and Religion, Santa Fe, 1985—; faculty mem. St. John's Coll., Santa Fe, 1991—. Author: Emergent Evolution in the Thought of Sri Aurobindo Ghose and Teilhard de Chardin: A Critical Analysis, 1983, (poetry) Velocities of Rage, 1991. Vol. counselor Vietnam Vets, Golden and Boulder, Colo., 1979-90. Recipient cert. teaching excellence U. Colo., 1984; named Alumni of Yr., Iliff Sch. Theology, 1989; Jonathan M. Daniel Meml. fellow U. Denver, 1983. Mem. Am. Acad. Religion, Am. Philos. Assn., Fellowship of Reconciliation, Nat. Coun. Tchrs. English, Inst. for Advanced Philos. Rsch. Home: 1867 Camino de Pabilo Santa Fe NM 87505 Office: St John's Coll Camino de Cruz Blanca Santa Fe NM 87501 *Religious symbols, if followed faithfully, give us the power, not to transcend human nature, but to become more fully human.*

FASCHING, DARRELL J., religious studies and philosophy educator, academic dean; m. Laura J. Gushin. BA in Philosophy, U. Minn., 1968; MA in Religious Studies, Syracuse U., 1971, PhD in Religious Studies, 1978. Program dir. Hendricks Chapel Syracuse U., N.Y.C., 1971-75, asst. dean, 1975-80; asst. prof. religious studies Le Moyne Coll., Syracuse, N.Y., 1980-82; asst. prof. religious studies U. South Fla., Tampa, 1982-85, assoc. prof., 1985-89, prof., 1989—, Courtesy assoc. prof. philosophy, 1988—, affiliate asst. prof. comprehensive medicine Coll. Medicine, 1983—, dir. grad. studies, dept. religious studies, 1984-89, assoc. dean for faculty devel. Coll. Arts and Scis., 1991—; cons. on corp. and mgmt. ethics Am. Can. Corp., 1979-80. Author: The Thought of Jacques Ellul, 1981, Narrative Theology After Auschwitz: From Alienation to Ethics, 1991, The Ethical Challenge of Auschwitz and Hiroshima: Apocalypse on Utopia?, 1992; contbg. author, editor: The Jewish People in Christian Preaching, 1984; editor U. South Fla. Studies in History of Judaism, U. South Fla. Studies in Religion and Soc., The Ellul Studies Forum; mem. editorial adv. bd. Martin Luther King Jr. Meml. Studies in Religion, Culture and Social Devel.; contbr. book chpts., articles to profl. jours. Mem. nat. Luth. task force on sci. and tech. Evang. Luth. Ch. in Am.; bd. dirs. Ctr. for Theol. Ethics, U. Strasbourg, France. Home: 15811 Cottontail Pl Tampa FL 33624 Office: U South Fla Dept Religious Studies Tampa FL 33620 also: U South Fla Coll Arts and Scis Office of Dean Cooper Hall Tampa FL 33620

FAST, MARION EVERETT, clergyman; b. Jonesville, Mich., Aug. 30, 1932; s. Raymond Dallas and Harriet Alta (Foust) F.; m. Sara Elizabeth Rabun, June 2, 1954; children: Rebecca, Sharon, Martha, Linda, Joanna. BA, Bob Jones U., 1953, MA, 1955; DD (hon.), Maranatha Bapt. Bible Coll., 1972. Ordained to ministry Bapt. Ch., 1953. State prison chaplain State of N.C., Tryon, 1953-55; asst. pastor Calvary Bapt. Ch., Wheaton, Ill., 1955-56; pastor Bible Bapt. Ch., New Buffalo, Mich., 1956-78, Faith Bapt. Ch., Longmont, Colo., 1978—; pres. Conservative Pastors Mich., 1968-70; trustee Bob Jones U., Greenville, S.C., 1961—; founder Heritage Christian Acad., New Buffalo, Mich., 1974l; supt. Faith Bapt. Schs., Longmont, Colo., 1978—; regional pres. Fundamental Bapt. Fellowship of Am., Rocky Mountain, 1985—; sec.-treas. Colo. Assn. Christian Schs., 1981—; v.p. Concerned Christians Colo., 1984-86; bd. mem., moderator Fundamental Bapt. Fellowship, 1985-91. Precinct committeeman Rep. party, Longmont, Colo., 1986. Recipient Alumni Achievement award Bob Jones U. Alumni Assn., Greenville, 1991. Mem. Am. Assn. Christian Schs. (bd. mem. 1990—), The Wilds Christian Camping Assn. (bd. mem. 1990). Home: 1426 Pratt St Longmont CO 80501 Office: Faith Bapt Ch and Sch 833 15th Ave Longmont CO 80501

FATORA, JOACHIM ROBERT, minister; b. Blairsville, Pa., June 7, 1928; s. John A. and Susan Elizabeth (Ritz) F. B.A., St. Vincent Coll., 1950; M.Div., St. Vincent Sem., 1976. Joined Order St. Benedict, 1948, ordained priest Roman Catholic Ch., 1954. Assoc. pastor St. Joseph Ch., Johnstown, Pa., 1954-57, Queen of the World Parish, St. Marys, Pa., 1957-59, St. Benedict Ch., Canton, Ohio, 1959-66, St. Boniface Ch., Pitts., 1966-70, St. Marys, Pitts., 1970-72; adminstrv. prin. St. Marys Sch., Pitts., 1972-73; pastor Immaculate Conception, New Germany, Pa., 1974-76, St. Vincent Basilica, Latrobe, Pa., 1976-80, Sacred Heart, Jeannette, Pa., 1980-87; St. Benedict, Marguerite, Pa., 1987—. Chaplain KC, 1962-76, 91—.

FAUPEL, DAVID WILLIAM, minister, theological librarian; b. Cass City, Mich., May 28, 1944; s. David Henry Faupel and Clara Edith (Gotts)

Wightman; m. Kathryn Clay, Dec. 8, 1978 (div. Dec. 1988); 1 stepdaughter, Sarah Kathryn. AB, Cen. Bible Coll., 1966; BA, Evang. Coll., 1967; MDiv, Asbury Theol. Sem., 1971; MLS, U. Ky., 1972; PhD, U. Birmingham, Eng., 1989. Deacon Trinity Episc. Ch., Danville, Ky., 1979; curate St. John's Episc. Ch., Versailles, Ky., 1980-83; priest in charge St. Andrews Episc. Ch., Lexington, Ky., 1985-86; asst. priest Christ Ch. Episc., Lexington, Ky., 1987-88; locum-tenuns St. John's Episc. Ch., Versailles, Ky., 1989-91; dir. libr. Asbury Theol. Sem., Wilmore, Ky., 1978—; dir. studies Episc. Theol. Sem. Ky., Lexington, 1989-90. Author: The American Pentecostal Movement, 1972; adv. editor: The Higher Christian Life, 1985. Mem. Am. Theol. Libr. Assn., Ky. Libr. Assn., Soc. Pentecostal Studies (v.p. 1989), Wesley Theol. Soc. Office: Asbury Theol Sem 1111 Lexington Ave Wilmore KY 40390

FAUR, JOSE, theology educator; b. Buenos Aires, Sept. 20, 1934; came to U.S., 1964; s. Abraham and Aurora Sofia (Joli) F.; m. Esther Faur, Apr. 3, 1963; children—Aura, Abraham, Mariane. B.A., U. Barcelona, Spain, 1957, M.A., 1961, Ph.D., 1964. Prof. rabbinics Jewish Theol. Sem., N.Y.C., 1964-84; research fellow Sephardic Heritage Found., N.Y.C., 1984—. Author: Studies in the Mishne Tora, 1978; Golden Doves with Silver Dots, 1985, In the Shadow of History, 1992.

FAVALORA, JOHN CLEMENT, bishop; b. New Orleans, Dec. 5, 1935; s. Felix J. and Leona M. (Stevens) F. BA in Philosophy and History, Notre Dame Sem., New Orleans, 1958; STL, Pontifical Gregorian U., Rome, 1962; MEd, Tulane U., 1969. Ordained priest, Roman Cath. Ch., 1962. Asst. pastor St. Theresa of the Child Jesus Ch., New Orleans, 1962-70; sec. to archbishop Archdiocese of New Orleans, 1963-65, vice chancellor, 1963-65; vice rector St. John Prep., New Orleans, 1964-67, prin., 1968-71; dir. Office of Permanent Diaconate, New Orleans, 1971-74; adminstrv. asst. Notre Dame Sem., New Orleans, 1971-73, rector-pres., 1981-86; pastor St. Angela Merici Ch., Metairie, La., 1973-79; dir. Office of Vocations, New Orleans, 1979-81; bishop Diocese of Alexandria, La., 1986-89, Diocese of St. Petersburg, Fla., 1989—; ecclesiastical notary Archdiocese of New Orleans, 1962-64, pro-synodal judge, 1973-79; dean East Jefferson Deanery, New Orleans, 1974-77; vicar Pastoral Planning, New Orleans, 1976-81; chmn. Permanent Diaconate Adv. Com., New Orleans, 1984; consultor Archdiocese of New Orleans, 1984-86. Office: Diocese of St Petersburg PO Box 40200 Saint Petersburg FL 33743

FAW, DUANE LESLIE, retired military officer, law educator, lay worker, author; b. Loraine, Tex., July 7, 1920; s. Alfred Leslie and Noma Leigh (Elliott) F.; m. Lucile Elizabeth Craps, Feb. 20, 1943; children: Cheryl Leigh, Bruce Duane, Debra Leoma, Melanie Loraine. Student, N. Tex. State Coll., 1937-41; J.D., Columbia U., 1947. Bar: Tex. 1948, D.C. 1969, U.S. Supreme Ct. 1969. Commd. 2d lt. USMC, 1942, advanced through grades to brig. gen., 1969, bn. comdr., 1959-61, staff judge adv., 1961-64, policy analyst Marine Hdqrs., 1964-67, dep. chief of staff III Marine Amphibious Force, 1967-68, judge Navy Ct. Mil. Rev., 1968-69; dir. Judge Ad. Div. Marine Hdqrs. USMC, Washington, 1969-71; ret. USMC, 1971; prof. law Pepperdine U. Sch. Law, Malibu, Calif., 1971-85; Bible tchr. So. Presbyn. Ch., Denton, Tex., 1948-50, Camp Pendleton, N.C., 1959-61, Quantico. Va., 1962-63, United Meth. Ch., Arlington, Va., 1963-71; Bible tchr. , elder Presbyn. Ch., Van Horn, Tex., 1950-52; lay speaker, Bible tchr. United Meth. Ch., Tustin and Malibu. Calif., 1972—, mem. ann. conf., 1974-81, 91. Co-author: The Military in American Society, 1978, The Paramony, 1986. Gen. councilor URANTIA Brotherhood, 1979-88; bd. dirs. Jesusonian Found., Boulder, 1988—, Touch for Health Found., Pasadena, Calif., 1988-90. Decorated Air medal with gold star, Navy Commendation medal with gold star, Legion of Merit with combat V with gold star; UN Cross of Gallantry with gold star; VN Honor medal 1st class. Mem. ABA (adv. com. mil. justice 1969-71, adv. com. lawyers in Armed Forces 1969-71), Fed. Bar Assn. (council), Judge Advs. Assn., Am. Acad. Religion, Soc. Bibl. Lit. Club: Masons. One of original 12 judges Navy Ct. Mil. Rev.; 1st gen. officer head Marine Corps Judge Advs. Address: 23301 Bocana Malibu CA 90265 *People are placed upon this planet for a purpose greater than self-maintenance and self-indulgence. True success and happiness require a personal discovery of, and commitment to, a system of values which furthers the implementation of the Divine plan.*

FAY, SISTER MAUREEN A., university president. BA in English magna cum laude, Siena Heights Coll., 1960; MA in English, U. Detroit, 1966; PhD, U. Chgo., 1976. Tchr. English, speech, moderator student newspaper, student council St. Paul High Sch., Grosse Pointe, Mich., 1960-64; chairperson English dept., dir. student dramatics, moderator student publs. Dominican High Sch., Detroit, 1964-69; co-dir. Cath. student ctr. Adrian (Mich.) Coll., 1969-71; instr. English Siena Heights Coll., Adrian, 1969-71; evaluators inst. criminal justice execs. U. Chgo., 1971-73; instr. English U. Ill., Chgo., 1971-74; dir. evaluation sch. new learning DePaul U., Chgo., 1974-75; fellow in acad. adminstrn. Saint Xavier Coll., Chgo., 1975-76, dean. grad. studies, 1979-83, dean continuing edn., 1976-83; asst. prof. No. Ill. U., Dekalb, 1980-83; pres. Mercy Coll. Detroit, 1983-90, U. Detroit Mercy, 1990—; v.p. VAUT Corp, bd. dirs. four inner city high schs., Archdiocese Chgo.; mem. exec. com. Assn. Mercy Colls.; adv. com. Adult Learning Svcs., The Coll. Bd., Met. Affairs Corp. of Detroit and S.E. Mich., cons. Nat. Assn. for Religious Women, 1974-75, North Cen. Assn. Colls. and Schs., evaluator commn. on higher edn.; trustee Rosary Coll., River Forest, Ill.; emeritus mem. div. bd. Mercy Hosps. and Health Svcs. of Detroit; bd. dirs. Nat. Bank of Detroit. Asst. editor: (book rev.): Adult Education, A Journal of Research and Theory, 1971-74. Steering com. Metro Detroit GIVES; exec. com., edn. task force Detroit Strategic Planning com., 1987; trustee Mich. Opera Theatre; bd. dirs. Greater Detroit Interfaith Round Table Nat. Conf. Christians and Jews, Inc., The Detroit Symphony. Mem. Am. Assn. Higher Edn., North Cen. Assn. (cons., evaluator commn. on higher edn.), Nat. Assn. Ind. Colls. and Univs. (bd. dirs.), Assn. Ind. Colls. and Univs. of Mich. (exec. com., chairperson), Am. Assn. Cath. Colls. and Univs., AAUW, Pi Lambda Theta. Office: U Detroit Mercy 4001 W McNichols Rd Detroit MI 48221

FEAGIN, EUGENE LLOYD, pastor; b. Hendersonville, NC, July 19, 1950; s. Eugene Lloyd and Martha (Hodges) F.; m. Anna Johnson, July 3, 1972; children: James Eugene, Travis Lee, Melissa Ann. BA, U. S.C., 1972, MEd, 1976; MDiv, Candler Sch. Theology, 1981. Ordained to ministry Methodist Ch., 1984. Pastor Fingerville (S.C.) United Meth. Ch., 1974-79, Saxon United Meth. Ch., Spartanburg, S.C., 1979-85, Cherokee Springs United Meth. Ch., Spartanburg, 1982-85, Sharon (S.C.) United Meth. Ch., 1985-91, Aldersgate United Meth. Ch., Inman, S.C., 1991—; dir. communications, Spartanburg United Meth. Dist., 1982-85; bd. dirs., Pastoral Counseling Svc., Spartanburg, 1982-85; cluster leader, York/Clover United Meth. Cluster, S.C., 1986-91. Firefighter Sharon Vol. Fire Dept., 1986-91; mem. Schs./Community Team, York, 1990-91. Mem. Western York Ministerial Assn. (pres. 1989-90). Home: 120 Pineview Dr Inman SC 29349 Office: Aldersgate United Meth Ch 4th at Park Inman SC 29349

FEATHER, MERLIN CHESTER, lay worker; b. Altoona, Pa., Feb. 3, 1929; s. Chester Michael and Lillian Willovene (Long) F.; m. Lillian Gayle McGarvey, Aug. 20, 1948; children: Dan, Elizabeth, Jane, Jonathan, Amy. Cert., Stonier Grad. Sch. Banking, New Brunswick, N.J., 1965. Treas., v.p. for fin. The Christian & Missionary Alliance, Nyack, N.Y., 1977-88; exec. v.p. Evangelism Explosion III Internat., Inc., Ft. Lauderdale, Fla., 1988—; pres., dir. Alliance Community of the C&MA, DeLand, Fla., 1985—, Wears Valley Bible Conf. Ctr., Pigeon Forge, Tenn., 1979—. Treas., dir. Town and Country Manor, Santa Ana,/Calif., 1977—, Shell Point Village, Ft. Myers, Fla., 1977—; dir., mem. United Appeal, Jr. Achievement, Am. Cancer Soc., Mcpl. Planning Bd. and Zoning Commission of Orlando, 1958-77. Mem. Nat. Assn. Evangelicals, Christian Mgmt. Assn. Home: 5761 NE 19th Ave Fort Lauderdale FL 33308 Office: Evangelism Explosion III PO Box 23820 Fort Lauderdale FL 33307

FECH, EDWARD BRUCE, educational administrator; b. East Chicago, Ind., Apr. 3, 1933; s. Edward Nicholas and Theresa Ann F.; m. Barbara Dean Krajnik, Aug. 25, 1956; children: Lynn, Julie, Bruce, Mark, Barbara, Carl. BA in Sociology, St. Joseph's Coll., Rensselaer, Ind., 1959; MS in Ednl. Adminstrn., Purdue U., 1973; PhD in Ednl. Adminstrn., Mich. State U., 1984. Mgr. Montgomery Ward, Chgo., 1960-61; tchr. Diocese of Gary (Ind.), 1961-68, prin., 1968-71, asst. supt., 1971-73; chmn. dept. edn. Diocese of Lansing (Mich.), 1973—; bd. dirs. Poverello Credit Union; cons. pub. schs. Contbr. articles to profl. jours. Mem. pub. policy adv. com. Mich. Cath. Conf., Lansing, 1990—, mem. standing com., 1973—; mem. adv. com. on profl. edn. of tchrs. St. Mary's Coll., Orchard Lake, Mich., 1990—; mem., bd. dirs. Coll. Edn. Alumni Assn. Mich. State U., 1991—; mem. $10,000,000 coun. of Greater Lansing Cath. Edn. Found., 1991—. Fellow, Inst. for Ednl. Leadership, 1981-82; grantee, Nat. Tng. Lab., Bethel, Maine, 1968, NYU, 1970. Mem. Am. Ednl. Rsch. Assn., Nat. Cath. Edn. Assn., Mich. Assn. for Distance Learning, Religious Edn. Assn., Phi Delta Kappa. Roman Catholic. Avocations: classical guitar, gardening, photography. Home: 6882 W Herbison Rd De Witt MI 48820 Office: Diocese of Lansing 300 W Ottawa St Lansing MI 48933

FECHER, VINCENT JOHN, priest; b. Wilmette, Ill., Feb. 10, 1924; s. Joseph Martin and Emilia Cecilia (Siemer) F. D. Ch. History, Gregoriana, Rome, 1954; MA in Philosophy, Cath. U. Am., 1960; PhD, Angelicum, Rome, 1974; MA in Gerontology, Trinity U., San Antonio, 1981. Ordained priest Roman Cath. Ch., 1950. Sem. prof. Divine Word Sem., Techny, Ill., 1954-59, Manila, Philippines, 1959-64; sec. gen. Soc. of Divine Word, Rome, 1968-74; parish priest San Antonio Archdiocese, 1974; pastor Sacred Heart Cath. Ch., Uvalde, Tex., 1980—; dean Uvalde deanery Diocese of San Antonio, 1980-86; sec. Diocesan Presbyteral Coun., 1980-86. Author: German National Parishes, 1955, Error, Deception, Incomplete Truth, 1974, Religion and Aging, 1982, The Lord and I, 1990; contbr. articles to profl. publs. Mem. adv. coun. Tex. Dept. Human Svcs., Austin, 1984-88; mem. Uvalde Arts Coun. Mem. Nat. Fedn. Priest's Couns. (Tex. rep. 1970s), Uvalde C. of C., Knights of Holy Sepulcher, Rotary, KC. Home and Office: 408 Fort Clark St Uvalde TX 78801-4625

FEDERMANN, BERNARD ROBERT, minister; b. Burbank, Calif., Aug. 5, 1956; s. Max Joseph and Leda Ersillia (Pomi) F.; m. Debra Linn Foss, Aug. 7, 1976; children: Jamie Linn, Brian Robert. E.T.T.A. tchr.'s diploma, L.I.F.E. Bible Coll., 1978, BA, 1978. Ordained to ministry Internat. Ch. Foursquare Gospel, 1980. Asst. pastor Santa Monica (Calif.) Foursquare Ch., 1976-78; sr. pastor Sylmar (Calif.) Foursquare Ch., 1978-86, Lompoc (Calif.) Foursquare Ch., 1986—; prin. Grace Christian Sch. Lompoc, 1986-91; mem. Sylmar Ministerial Assn., 1978-86 (pres. 1984); mem. Alumni com. L.I.F.E. Bible Coll., L.A., 1983—; div. supt. Santa Barbara County div. So. Calif. Dist. Foursquare Ch., 1988—. Mem. L.I.F.E. Bible Coll. Alumni Assn. (pres. 1985-86), Century Club (L.A. chpt.), ASCD. Office: Lompoc Foursquare Ch 117 N C St Lompoc CA 93436

FEELEY, SISTER KATHLEEN, college president, English language educator; b. Balt., Jan. 7, 1929; d. Jerome Lawrence and Theresa (Tasker) F. B.A. in English, Coll. Notre Dame of Md.; M.A. in English, Villanova U.; Ph.D. in English, Rutgers U.; student, Claremont U. Ctr. Inst. for Study of Change. Joined Sch. Sisters of Notre Dame, Roman Cath. Ch. Am. Council on Edn. intern in acad. adminstrn., to 1971; pres. Coll. Notre Dame of Md., Balt., 1971—; asst. prof. English, then assoc. prof., then prof. Coll. Notre Dame of Md.; dir. Balt. Gas and Electric Co., Md. Econ. Devel Corp.; trustee St. Vincent Coll., Latrobe, Pa., Marian House, Notre Dame Preparatory Sch.; lectured at St. John Coll., Santa Fe, Ga. State Coll., Longwood Coll., Wheaton Coll., Fairfield U.; lectr. colls., univs., Japan, 1981. Author: Flannery O'Connor: Voice of the Peacock; contbr. articles to profl. jours. Named Woman of Yr., Jewish Nat. Fund Women's Aux., 1975, Good Will Ambassador in Israel, Am.-Israel Soc., 1976; recipient Woman of Yr. award Md. Colonial Soc., 1976, J. Jefferson Miller award Greater Balt. Com., 1979, Andrew White medal Loyola Coll., Balt., 1981, Hannah G. Solomon award Nat. Council Jewish Women, 1987, Jimmie Schwartz Found. medallion, 1987. Mem. Council on Fgn. Affairs (bd. dirs.), Assn. Catholic Colls. and Univs. (trustee). Home and Office: Coll Notre Dame of Md Caroline House 4701 N Charles St Baltimore MD 21210

FEELY, MICHAEL LAMON, minister; b. Atlanta, July 15, 1963; s. Oscar Floyd and Sarah McGoogan (Carpenter) F. BA in Polit. Sci. and History, U. Ga., 1985; grad. cum laude, Wesley Theol. Sem., 1991. Legislative intern U.S. Congressman George Darden, Washington, 1985; legislative asst. U.S. Congressman Joe Kolter, Washington, 1985; legislative intern U.S. Senator Sam Nunn, Washington, 1986; campaign mgr. Steve Burns for U.S. Congress, Lincoln, Nebr., 1986; mktg. analyst Pvt. Entertainment Networks, Los Angeles, 1986; legislative assistant Preston, Thorgrimson, Ellis & Holman, Washington, 1987-88; asst. pastor Washington Street United Meth. Ch., Alexandria, Va., 1988-90; pastor Dandridge (Tenn.) United Meth. Cir., 1991—. Polit. action dir. Arlington County Young Dems., Arlington, Va., 1986-87, mem., 1987—; mem. exec. bd. Alexandria Dem. Com., 1987—. C.C. Goen History fellow Wesley Theol. Sem., 1990-91. Mem. Omicron Delta Kappa, Phi Mu Alpha, Phi Alpha Theta, Pi Sigma Alpha. *It is important that we realize that we do not exist only as individual believers. We are all God's children, and as a community of faith we should always strive in word and deed, to acknowledge that fact.*

FEGGINS, JAMES C., deacon. Deacon, sec. Ref. Zion Union Apostolic Ch., South Hill, Va. Office: Ref Zion Union Apostolic Ch 416 South Hill Ave South Hill VA 23970*

FEHENEY, JOHN MATTHEW, religion educator; b. Limerick, Ireland, Mar. 16, 1932; s. John and Bridget (Ranahan) F. B.S., Univ. Coll., Cork. Ireland, 1954, M.S., 1959; M.A., U. W.I., 1975; M.Ed., U. London, 1976, Ph.D., 1981. Lectr. Univ. Coll. Cork, 1954-55; instr. Presentation Coll., Cork, 1955-59, vice prin. Trinidad, 1959-62, prin., 1962-75; sec. gen. Presentation Bros. Inc., Cork, 1981—. Contbr. articles to profl. jours. Editor Catechectics Bulletin, 1971-74, Presentation Studies, 1981-84. Patron Chaguanas Youth Group, Trinidad, 1965-71; sec. Assn. of Prins., Trinidad, 1964-75; mem. Cath. Child Welfare Council, Eng., 1976-78. Mem. Royal Soc. Chemistry, Chem. Soc. (Eng.), Cork Hist. Soc., Congregation of Presentation Bros. Avocations: local history, genealogy. Home and Office: Mt St Joseph, Blarney St, Cork Ireland

FEINSTEIN, MORLEY TODD, rabbi; b. Chgo., May 26, 1954; s. Ralph Arnold and Muriel (Goldstine) F.; m. Nancy E. Lichtenstein, Sept. 4, 1979; children: Aaron Joshua B., Ariel Lev B. BS with highest honors, U. Calif., Berkeley, 1975; MA in Hebrew Letters, Hebrew Union Coll., 1978, MA in Hebrew Edn., 1979. Ordained rabbi, 1981. Asst. rabbi Temple Beth-El, San Antonio, 1981-83, assoc. rabbi, 1983-87; rabbi Temple Beth-El, South Bend, Ind., 1987—; mem. nat. rabbinic cabinet United Jewish Appeal, 1984—, exec. com., 1991—; lectr., instr. U. Notre Dame, Ind. U., South Bend, U. Tex. Health Sci. Ctr., St. Mary's U.; trustee Jewish Fedn. St. Joseph Valley. Author: The Jewish Law Review, 1987; creator The Jewish Values Game, 1979; contbr. articles to profl. publs. Bd. dirs. Stanley Clark Sch., South Bend; v.p. Youth Alternatives, Inc., San Antonio, 1985-87; mem. Mayor's Complete Census Count Com., South Bend, 1990. Mem. Chgo. Area Reform Rabbis (exec. com. 1990—), Phi Beta Kappa. Democrat. Home: 342 N Coquillard South Bend IN 46617 Office: Temple Beth-El 305 W Madison St South Bend IN 46601 *To be a Jew, to be a Mensch.*

FEISS, HUGH BERNARD, priest, religious educator; b. Lakeview, Oreg., May 8, 1939; s. Sherman H. and Margaret I. (Furlong) F. Licentiate in Sacred Theology, Cath. U. Am., 1967, Lic. in Philosophy, 1972; STD, Anselmianum, Rome, 1976; MA, U. Iowa, Iowa City, 1987. Ordained priest Roman Cath. Ch., 1966. Asst. dean of men Mt. Angel Seminary, St. Benedict, Oreg., 1967-72, prof. philosophy, 1967-74, prof. humanities and theology, 1976—; dir. Mt. Angel Abbey Libr., St. Benedict, 1987—. Translator: Works of Pierre de Celle, 1988, Supplement to Life of Marie d'Oignies, 1986, Hildegard of Bingen, Explanation of the Rule of Benedict, 1990; contbr. articles to profl. jours. Mem. Am. Acad. Religion, Am. Benedictine Acad., Cath. Theol. Soc. Am., Am. Cath. Philos. Assn. Home: Mount Angel Abbey Saint Benedict OR 97373 Office: Mount Angel Abbey Libr Saint Benedict OR 97373

FEKKES, JAN, III, researcher; b. Rotterdam, Netherlands, Oct. 6, 1954; came to U.S. 1957; s. Jan Jr. and Anna Cornelia (Van Dyke) F.; m. Lori Lee Weisser, June 9, 1979; children: Derek Joel, Colin Jeremy, Tobin Andrew. BA summa cum laude, Biola U., 1984; PhD, U. Manchester, Eng., 1989. Dir. music Westside Christian Ch., Long Beach, Calif., 1976-81, young adult minister, 1981-84; dir. Paperchase Rsch. Svc., Camano Island, Wash., 1990—. Mem. Soc. Bibl. Lit. Democrat. Home: 592 S Camano Ridge Rd Camano Island WA 98292

FELD, EDWARD, rabbi; b. Oct. 3, 1943; m. Merle Lizbeth Lewis, June 15, 1969; children: Uri, Lisa. BA, Bklyn. Coll., 1964; M. Hebrew Letters, Jewish Theol. Sem., 1966; postgrad., Hebrew U., 1966-67. Ordained rabbi, 1968. Founding mem. Havurat Shalom Community Sem., 1968-69; Hillel dir. B'nai Brith Hillel Found., U. Ill., Champaign, 1969-73; Hillel dir., Jewish chaplain B'nai B'rith Found., Princeton (N.J.) U., 1973—; lectr. in field; expert witness on surrogate mothers N.J. Commn. on Bio-Med. Ethics, 1988; mem. faculty Nat. Havurah Com. Summer Inst., 1980's; adj. lectr. Princeton U., 1975, 82, Jewish Theol. Sem. Am., 1968; mem. com. on law and standards Rabbinical Assembly Am., 1978-81. Author: The Spirit of Renewal: Crisis and Renewal in Jewish Life, 1991; contbr. articles to profl. publs. Fellow Danforth Found., 1973, Princeton U., 1978-79, Princeton Theol. Sem., 1983-84, Shalom Hartman Inst., 1989-90. Mem. Assn. Hillel Dirs. and Other Jewish Campus Profls. (bd. dirs. 1973-77, 88-89). Home: 2 College Rd Princeton NJ 08540 Office: B'nai Brith Hillel Found Murray-Dodge Hall Princeton NJ 08544

FELDBIN, ABRAHAM ISAAC, rabbi; b. Bklyn., Sept. 11, 1916; s. Israel Feldbin and Rebecca (Rosen) F.; m. Beatrice R. Weiner, June 28, 1941; children: Rena Perelmuter, Judith Brown, Rachelle Urist, Aliza Avital. BS, Columbia U., 1938; BJP, Jewish Theol. Sem., 1938; M in Hebrew Lit., Jewish Inst. Religion, N.Y.C., 1942; MA, Columbia U.; DD, Jewish Theol. Sem., N.Y.C. Ordained rabbi, 1942. Rabbi Congregation Bnai Israel, Auburn, N.Y., 1943-45, Congregation Shaari Israel, Bklyn., 1947-52, 69-91, Astoria (N.Y.) Ctr. of Israel, 1952-62, Shelter Rock Jewish Ctr., Roslyn, N.Y., 1962-66, Temple Bethel El of Manhattan Beach, Bklyn., 1991—; pres. Bklyn. Region, Rabbinical Assy., 1979-85, Bklyn. Region, Zionist Orgn. Am., 1978—; v.p. Bklyn. Bd. Rabbis, 1990—; nat. dep. chaplain Jewish War Vets of U.S., 1960—. Contbr. articles to profl. jours. Chaplain Sofrim Soc. N.Y., N.Y.C., 1988—; mem. N.Y.C. Community Bd. #17, Bklyn., 1975-90; exec. com. N.Y.C. Commn. of Religious Leaders, N.Y.C., 1967-88. Lt. col. U.S. Army, 1945-76. Decorated Army Commendation medal. Mem. Am. Legion (chaplain 1958-59), Assn. Jewish Chaplains of U.S. Armed Forces (pres.), K.P., Masons (chaplain N.Y. State chpt. 1954—). Home: 767 E 52 St Brooklyn NY 11203 Office: Temple Beth El 11 W End Ave Brooklyn NY 11235

FELDER, MICHAEL LEE, minister, educator; b. Charleston, S.C., May 28, 1959; s. James Carlisle Felder and Anne (Graham) Garves; m. W. Gail Dukes, Aug. 7, 1982; children: Brandon James, Sarah Marie. BA, Bapt. Coll. Charleston, 1981; MA in Religious Edn., Southwestern Bapt. Theol. Sem., Ft. Worth, 1984. Lic. to ministry So. Bapt. Conv., 1981, ordained, 1983. Summer youth dir. Highland Pk. Bapt. Ch., Hanahan, S.C., 1981; min. edn. and youth Bethany Bapt. Ch., Snellville, Ga., 1984-87; summer min. 1st Bapt. Ch., Denmark, S.C., 1982; assoc. pastor, min. edn. 1st Bapt. Ch., St. Simons Island, Ga., 1987-89; min. edn. 1st Bapt. Ch., Alpharetta, Ga., 1989—; carousel leader Bapt. Sunday Sch. Week, Ridgecrest, N.C., 1990; leader metro clinic Bapt. Sunday Sch. Bd. Atlanta Bapt. Assn., Ga., 1990; leader mins. of edn. Sunday sch. workshops Ga. Bapt. Conf. Ctr. Mem. So. Bapt. Religious Educators Assn., Metro Atlanta Bapt. Religious Educators Assn., Ga. Bapt. Religious Educators Assn., Roswell Bapt. Assn. (associational Sunday sch. dir. 1990-91, conf. leader associational Sunday sch. gen. office 1990). Office: 1st Bapt Ch PO Box 322 Alpharetta GA 30239

FELDMAN, LEONID ARIEL, rabbi; b. Kishinev, Moldavia, Russia, May 3, 1953; came to U.S. 1980; s. Moisey and Rebekkah (Aronova) F.; m. Melissa Kim Weinstein, Apr. 29, 1990. MS in Physics, Kishinev Pedagogical Inst., Russia, 1975; MA in Edn., Hebrew U., 1979; LittB in Jewish Studies, U. Judaism, L.A., 1984; MA, Jewish Theol. Sem., N.Y.C., 1987. Ordained rabbi, 1987. Dir. Russian dept. Bur. of Jewish Edn., L.A., 1981-84; faculty Wexner Heritage Found., N.Y.C., 1986—, CLAL-Nat. Jewish Ctr. for Learning & Leadership, N.Y.C., 1986—; rabbi Temple Emanu-El, Palm Beach, Fla., 1988—; vis. rabbi Jewish Cultural Assn., Kishinev, summer 1990; nat. bd. dirs. Union of Coun. for Soviet Jews, Washington, 1986—; scholar-in-residence Gen. Assy. of Coun. Jewish Fedns., San Francisco, 1990; keynote speaker Masorti Assn., London, 1987; lectr. in field; radio broadcaster to Russia, Voice of Am., 1985-86; co-chmn. Soviet Jewry Task Force of Palm Beach County, 1989—; mem. Rabbinic Cabinet of United Jewish Appeal, 1989—. Contbr. articles to profl. jours. Recipient Gates of Jerusalem medal State of Israel Bonds, 1990, Rabbinic Leadership award, Coun. Jewish Fedns., 1990; fellow Shma Mag., 1984-85; hon. fellow Bar-Ilan U., Israel, 1991. Mem. Rabbinical Assembly, World Coun. Synagogues (internat. bd. dirs.), Assn. of New Ams. (exec. com. 1990—), Cen Conf. Am. Rabbis, Bd. Rabbis of Palm Beach County (1st v.p.), Anti-Defamation League (v.p. Palm Beach County chpt.). Office: Temple Emanu-El 190 N County Rd Palm Beach FL 33480 *Ever since my childhood I have often asked myself two questions: "What will I say to myself in the last five minutes of my life?" and "What will people say at my funeral?" It gives me a perspective and an optimistic impetus to do more in my life.*

FELDMAN, YAEL S., educator, editor; b. Israel, Jan. 9, 1941; d. Jacob and Clara-Haia (Rabinowitz) Keren-Or; m. Ehud Sagiv, July 1961 (dec. 1963); m. Peter Feldman, Aug. 9, 1973. BA, Tel Aviv U., Israel, 1967; MA, Hebrew Coll., 1976; MPhil, Columbia U., 1980, PhD, 1981. Cert. tchr., Israel. Tchr. high schs. and vocat. colls., Tel Aviv, 1964-74; lectr. Boston U., Hebrew Coll., Boston and Brookline, Mass., 1974-77; instr. Jewish Theol. Sem., N.Y.C., 1977-80; teaching asst. Columbia U., N.Y.C., 1978-80, asst. prof., 1981-88, assoc. prof., 1988-89; assoc. prof. NYU, 1989—; supr. Melton Ctr., Jewish Theol. Sem., N.Y.C., 1978; cons., speaker Nat. Found. for Jewish Culture, N.Y.C., 1985—; translator, adviser 92d Y Theater, N.Y.C., 1988. Author: Modernism and Cultural Transfer, 1986, Polarity and Parallel, 1987; co-editor: Teaching the Hebrew Bible as Literature, 1989; assoc. editor Prooftexts: Jour. of Jewish Lit. History, 1984—; editor Hado'ar Hebrew Weekly, 1985—; contbr. articles to profl. jours. Mem. Nat. Assn. of Profs. for Peace in the Middle East, N.Y.C., 1988—, Friends of the Hebrew U., N.Y.C., 1985—. Recipient Rsch. fellow, Columbia U., and Littauer Found., 1987, Fulbright-Hayes fellow, Israel, 1984-85; NEH fellow, 1989; grantee ACLS, Eng., 1983. Mem. Assn. for Jewish Studies (bd. dirs. program 1983-86, 89—), Nat. Assn. Profs. Hebrew (lectr., program com. 1986-89), MLA (mem., lectr., editor 1983-89), Am. Comparative Lit. Assn., Mid. East Studies Assn. (lectr. 1988-89), Am. Coun. Learned Socs. Jewish. Avocations: dance, theater, music. Office: NYU 51 Washington South Sq S New York NY 10012

FELDSTEIN, DONALD, religious association executive, social welfare educator; b. N.Y.C., June 2, 1931; s. Ansel and Gertrude (Goldbaum) F.; m. Shirley Mintz, Sept. 5, 1954; children—Michael, Eric, Miriam, Ruth. B.A., CCNY, 1952; M.S.W., Columbia U., 1954, D. Social Welfare, 1973. Cert. social worker, N.Y. Sr. cons. Council on Social Work Edn., N.Y.C., 1967-70; prof., dir. Ctr. for Social Work and Applied Social Research, Fairleigh Dickinson U., Teaneck, N.J., 1970-76; exec. dir. for communal services Fedn. Jewish Philanthropies, N.Y.C., 1976-81; exec. v.p. Jewish Community Fedn. Met. N.J., East Orange, 1981-82, Am. Jewish Com., N.Y.C., 1982-83; assoc. exec. v.p. Council Jewish Fedns., N.Y.C., 1983—. Author: (with Ralph Dolgoff) Understanding Social Welfare, 1980, 2d edit., 1984. Vol., So. Christian Leadership Conf., Tuscaloosa, Ala., 1965; pres. Young Israel Synagogue, West Hempstead, N.Y., 1972-74; bd. dirs. Vol. Bur. Bergen County, Hackensack, N.J., 1972-76, Radius Inst., N.Y.C., 1982—. U.S. Dept. Labor research fellow, 1971-72. Mem. Nat. Assn. Social Workers, Conf. Jewish Communal Service, Acad. Cert. Social Workers. Office: Council Jewish Fedns 730 Broadway New York NY 10003

FELICI, ANGELO CARDINAL, archbishop; b. Segni, Italy, July 26, 1919. Ordained priest Roman Cath. Ch., 1942. Elected archbishop of Cesariana, Numidia, 1967; consecrated bishop, 1967, created cardinal, 1988; apostolic nuncio, France; prefect Congregation for Causes of Sts, Vatican City. Office: Congregation Causes of Sts, Office of Prefect, Vatican City Vatican City

FELIX, KELVIN EDWARD, archbishop; b. Roseau, Dominica, Feb. 15, 1933; s. Edward Mosley and Melanie (Cadette) F. Student, Sem. St. John

Vianney, Trinidad and Tobago, 1951-56; diploma in adult edn., St. Francis Xavier U., N.S., Can., 1963, LLD (hon.), 1986; MA in Sociology and Anthropology, U. Notre Dame, 1967; postgrad., U. Bradford, Eng., 1967-70. Ordained priest Roman Cath. Ch. Assoc. pastor Roman Cath. Ch., Dominica, 1956-62; lectr., tutor U. West Indies and Sem., Trinidad and Tobago, 1970-72; assoc. gen. sec. C.C.C., Trinidad and Tobago, 1975-81; archbishop of Castries St. Lucia, 1981—; chmn. commn. for ecumenism Antilles Episcopal Conf., 1981, pres., 1991; cons. Pontifical Coun. for the Family, Roman Cath. Ch., Rome, 1988, mem. Pontifical Coun. for Interreligious Dialogue, Rome, 1990. Office: Archdiocese of Castries, PO Box 267, Castries Saint Lucia

FELLHAUER, DAVID E., bishop; b. Kansas City, Mo., Aug. 19, 1939. Student, Pontifical Coll. Josephinum; D in Canon Law, PhD, St. Paul U., Ottawa, Can. Ordained priest Roman Cath. Ch., 1965. Former prof. Holy Trinity Sem., Dallas; judicial vicar Diocese of Dallas, until 1990; bishop of Victoria Tex., 1990—; bd. govs. Canon Law Soc. Am. Office: PO Box 4070 Victoria TX 77903

FELLOWS, WARD JAY, philosophy educator, minister; b. Chgo., Dec. 6, 1913; s. Norman Jay and Milfred (Myers) F.; m. Ada Louise Johnson, Sept. 18, 1937; children: Milfred L. Fellows Goodall, Catherine C. Fellows Smith, Ward J. Jr. BA, Cornell U., 1936; MDiv, Union Theol. Sem., 1939, STM, 1946, PhD, 1988; MA in Philosophy, U. Calif., Berkeley, 1964. Ordained to ministry Congregational Ch./United Ch. of Christ, 1939. Minister various Congl. chs., 1939-62; prof. in world religions and philosophy of religion Coll. San Mateo (Calif.), 1968-83, prof. emeritus, 1988—; vis. scholar Harvard U. Ctr. for Study of World Religions, Cambridge, Mass., 1982; leader study groups in field. Author: Religions East and West, 1979. Mem. bd. social action, missions Congl. Ch. of San Mateo, 1967-82. Chaplain USAAF, 1942-45, ETO. Mem. Am. Acad. Religion, AAUP. Democrat. Home: 1139 Parrott Dr San Mateo CA 94402 *There is a struggle between God's good and the evil in the world. The great religions—in spite of their imperfections—help people to stay on God's side.*

FELSON, ETHAN JOSEPH, religious organization administrator, educator; b. Hartford, Conn., Aug. 20, 1965; s. Charles Henry and Janice Barbara (Lieberman) F. Student, Am. U., 1986; BA, Lehigh U., 1987. Dir. Jewish Community Rels. Coun. of Hartford, 1987—; instr. Midrasha Jewish Community High Sch., Hartford, 1990—; mem. social justice task force Nat. Jewish Community Rels. Adv. Coun., N.Y.C., 1988—; mem. community svc. com. Nat. Conf. on Soviet Jewry, N.Y.C., 1988—. Mem. Holocaust Commemoration Com., Conn., 1987—; bd. dirs. Lesbian Gay Rights Coalition, Conn., 1987—; mem. bd. govs. Human Rights Campaign Fund, 1989—. Mem. Am. Jewish Community Orgn. Pers., Am. Jewish Community Rels. Workers, Conn. Civil Liberties Union (mem. HIV legislation network). Home: 20 Rodney St Hartford CT 06105 Office: Jewish Community Rels Coun 333 Bloomfield Ave West Hartford CT 06105

FELTNER-KAPORNYAI, DANIEL KALMAN, minister, consulting company executive; b. Hammond, Ind., Dec. 6, 1936; s. Kalman S. and Helen (Kovacs) Kapornyai; m. Nancy Rammell Agee, Jan. 23, 1960 (div. 1977); children: Phyllis, Daniel, Amy, Alan, Timothy; m. Raye Feltner, Sept. 9, 1978. AB in Religion and History, Milligan Coll., 1959; MDiv, Christian Theol. Sem., 1965; cert., Neuro-Linguistic Programming Inst. of Washington, 1985. Ordained to ministry Christian Ch. (Disciples of Christ), 1960. Pastor Buffalo Christian Ch., Blountville, Tenn., 1959-60, Bengal Christian Ch., Franklin, Ind., 1960-63, St. Paul (Ind.) Christian Ch., 1963-65, Nineveh (Ind.) Christian Ch., 1966-69, West End Christian Ch., Danville, Va., 1969-76, South Park Christian Ch., Reidsville, N.C., 1976-78, Armenia Christian Ch., Kinston, N.C., 1978-85; interm min. numerous chs. in Cen. Ind., 1985-88; min. Franklin Cen. Christian Ch., Indpls., 1988-91; pres. cons. and tng. firm Change Point, Indpls., 1991—; staff Leadership, Edn. and Devel. Cons., Reynoldsburg, Ohio, 1987—; chmn. Assoc. Billy Graham Crusade, Danville, 1975. Mem. Nat. Assn. NLP. Democrat. Home: PO Box 19167 Indianapolis IN 46219

FELTNER-KAPORNYAI, G. RAYE, religious organization administrator; b. Martinsburg, W.Va., Mar. 20, 1945; s. James I. and Mildred (Batten) Feltner; m. Daniel Feltner-Kapornyai, Sept. 9, 1978. BA, Culver-Stockton Coll., 1968; D of Ministry, Lexington Theol. Sem., 1976. Ordained to ministry Disciples of Christ, 1973. Assoc. regional min. Christian Ch., N.C., 1972-84; dir. div. homeland ministries Dept. Ch. Women, Indpls., 1984—; rep. centennial celebration Christian Ch. (Disciples of Christ), Indpls., 1982; dir. Japan tour Dept. Ch. Women, Indpls., 1991; toured African countries, 1988;. Democrat. Home: PO Box 19167 Indianapolis IN 46219 Office: Dept Ch Women PO Box 1986 Indianapolis IN 46206

FELTON, CATHERINE, nun; b. Providence, Aug. 4, 1916; d. James Joseph and Julia Adelaide (Prior) F. MEd, Cath. Tchrs. Coll., 1948. Entered Sisters of Mercy, Roman Cath. Ch., 1934. Tchr. Tyler Sch., Providence, 1937-45, St. Patrick's Sch., Providence, 1945-49, St. Catherine's Sch., Belize City, Belize, 1954-56; prin. Our Lady of Mercy Sch., East Greenwich, R.I., 1956-60; exec. sec. Instituto S. Pius XIII, Rome, 1969-72; adminstr. Eastgate Renewal Ctr., Portsmouth, R.I., 1972-74, Mt. St. Rita Health Ctr., Cumberland, R.I., 1974-83; provincial sec. Sister of Mercy, Province of Providence, 1960-69, asst. provincial, 1983-88, province archivist, 1989—; co-chmn. diocesan health consortium, Providence, 1975-79; trustee St. Joseph Hosp., Providence, 1977—. Home: 255 Mercycrest Convent Wrentham Rd Cumberland RI 02864 Office: Sisters of Mercy Provincialate RD 3 Cumberland RI 02864

FENCHAK, RICHARD, academic administrator. Supt. Dept. of Edn. Diocese of Orlando, Fla. Office: Edn Dept Supt PO Box 1800 Orlando FL 32802*

FENERTY, LAURIE DONALD, minister; b. Wolfville, N.S., Can., Nov. 14, 1936; s. Freeman Chambers and Ethel Maude Fenerty; m. Marion Mabel King, May 19, 1959; children: Marion Celeste, Laurie Shawn King, Marilee Dawn, Myria Cairine. BA, Meml. U. Nfld., St. John's, Can., 1959; BD, Acadia U., Wolfville, 1962. Ordained to ministry Bapt. Union of Western Can., 1962. Pastor First Bapt. Ch., Thompson, Man., Can., 1962-67, Brentwood United Bapt. Ch., Moncton, N.B., Can., 1967-70, Berwick (N.S.) Bapt. Ch., 1970-76, Marysville United Bapt. Ch., Fredericton, N.B., 1976-89; founder, pastor Hanwell Bapt. Ch., Fredericton, 1989—; pres. United Bapt. Conv. Atlantic Provinces, 1975-76; bd. dirs. Atlantic Bapt. Coll., 1970-76, Kingswood Camp Men's Retreats (a founder). Pioneer in new ch. devel. work for Bapt. Union of Western Can., no. Man., 1962-67. Home and Office: 50 Hollybrook St, Fredericton, NB Canada E3A 4N7

FENHAGEN, JAMES CORNER, priest, seminary president, dean; b. Nov. 4, 1929; s. Frank Donald and Mary (McLanahan) F.; m. Eulalie McFall, July 14, 1950; children: Leila, James, John. BA, U. of South, 1951; MDiv, Va. Theol. Sem., 1954, DD (hon.), 1978. Ordained priest Episcopal Ch., 1955. Rector St. Mark's Ch., Brunswick, Md., 1955-58, St. Michael's Ch., Columbia, S.C., 1958-63; dir. Christian edn. Diocese of D.C., Washington, 1963-67; dir. ch. and ministries Hartford (Conn.) Sem., 1973-78; dean., pres. Gen. Theol. Sem., N.Y.C., 1978—; dep. Gen. Conv. Episcopal Ch., 1967, 70, 77; mem. Bd. for Theol. Edn., N.Y.C., 1983—. Author: Mutual Ministry, 1977, More Than Wanderers, 1978, Ministry and Solitude, 1981; co-author: Prescription for Parishes, 1972. Mem. Assn. Theol. Schs. (coun. 1984—). Democrat. Office: Gen Theol Sem 175 9th Ave New York NY 10011

FENLASON, EDWARD JAMES, minister; b. Detroit Lakes, Minn., Mar. 13, 1937; s. Francis Skyler and Echo Ione (Elliot) F.; m. Delpha Lorraine Wittrup, June 20, 1958; children: James Jay, John Jay. BA, Macalester Coll., 1961; MDiv, Cen. Bapt. Theol. Sem., Mpls., 1965, D Ministry, 1991. Ordained to ministry Ind. Bapt. Ch., 1973. Pastor Bozeman (Mont.) Bapt. Ch., 1965-72, Belgrade (Mont.) Bapt. Ch., 1972—; pres. Homestead Land and Cattle Co., Inc., Belgrade, Inter-Mountain Bapt. Fellowship, Mont., 1987-89. Author: Chronology of the Seventy Weeks of Daniel, 1962, History of the Inter-Mountain Baptist Fellowship, 1986, How To Involve the People of the Church in the Work of the Church, 1991. Vice pres. Moral Majority Mont., 1980-81. Republican. Office: Belgrade Bapt Ch PO Box 31 Belgrade MT 59714

FENNELL, JOHN ALLISON, minister; b. Birmingham, Ala., Sept. 17, 1928; s. John Allison and Annie Laurie (Irving) F.; m. Lee Marie Garaventa, Sept. 4, 1954; children: Djina Anne, John A. Jr. MusB, U. Miami, 1952. Assoc. min. of music and youth Meth. Ch., Birmingham, Ala., 1956-57; min. music Wayside Bapt. Ch., Miami, Fla., 1960-63, First Bapt. Pompano Beach, Fla., 1963—; soloist So. Bapt. Conv. Soloist: in 25 Broadway musical comedies with The Music Circus, opening of The Marco Polo Club, symphony under Paul Whiteman, Howard Barlew and Leroy Anderson. With USAF, 1952-56. Home: 424 NE 2nd St Pompano Beach FL 33060 Office: First Bapt Ch 138 NE 1st St Pompano Beach FL 33060

FENNER, DONALD DEAN, minister; b. Fond du Lac, Wis., Apr. 25, 1929; s. Edward Benjamin and Ada Caroline (Zimmerman) F.; m. Norma Edith Oppedahl, Aug. 22, 1952; children: Bruce Steven, Caroline Grace, Kristine Ann. BA, North Cen. Coll., 1950; BD, Garrett-Evang. Theol. Sem., Evanston, Ill., 1953. Ordained to ministry Evang. United Brethren Ch., 1953. Pastor Emmanuel Evang. United Brethren Ch., Horicon, Wis., 1952-57, First Evang. United Brethren Ch., Madison, Wis., 1957-66, Evang. United Meth. Ch., Racine, Wis., 1966-73; dist. suprt. United Meth. Ch., Green Bay, Wis., 1973-79; sr. pastor First United Meth. Ch., Waukesha, Wis., 1979-86, Cargill United Meth. Ch., Janesville, Wis., 1986—; jurisdictional conf. del., gen. conf. del. United Meth. Ch., Wis., 1976, 80, 84, 88. Bd. dirs. Cedar Crest Retirement Ctr., Janesville, 1986—, Bellin Meml. Hosp., Green Bay, Wis., 1974-79. Recipient Denman Evangelism award Found. for Evangelism, 1983. Mem. Jurisdictional Coun. on Ministries, Janesville Ministerial Assn., Episcopacy Com. Office: Cargill United Meth Ch 2000 Wesley Ave Janesville WI 53545

FENNER, GARY EUGENE, minister; b. Wilmington, Ohio, Mar. 30, 1954; s. Eugene F. and Geneva P. (Salyer) F.; m. Deborah Lynn Bream, May 13, 1978; children: Joel E., Brian C., Joanna L. BA, Cin. Bible Coll., 1977; MA, Cin. Christian Sem., 1979. Ordained to ministry Ch. of Christ, 1977. Min. Bethany Ch. Christ, Foster, Ky., 1978-79; assoc. min. Fairmount Christian Ch., Richmond, Va., 1979-80, sr. min., 1980-86; founding min. Calvary Christian Ch., Sellersburg, Ind., 1986—; dir. Wonder Valley Christian Camp, Salem, Ind., 1987—; chmn. Tidewater Christian Svc. Camp, Yale, Va., 1984-86; chaplain Henrico County (Va.) Police Dept., 1980-86, Sellersburg Police Dept., 1990—. Contbr. articles to mags. Chmn. Richmond Community Easter Sunrise Svcs., 1984-86; pres. community coun. Highland Springs Elem. Sch., Va., 1984-86. Office: Calvary Christian Ch 605 Norman Dr Sellersburg IN 47172 *I've always thought the old saying, "When all else fails, read the directions" is applicable to life. For life to make sense, we must refer back to the manufacturer and His directions. Of course, the manufacturer is God and the directions are the Bible.*

FENSKE, JERALD ALLAN, minister; b. Wausau, Wis., Sept. 29, 1960; s. Martin W. and Whynona B. (Ramthun) F.; m. Kay A. Lang, Aug. 17, 1985. BA, Lakeland Coll., 1983; MDiv, United Theol. Sem. of the Twin Cities, 1988. Ordained to ministry United Ch. of Christ, 1991. Pastor St. Paul's United Ch. of Christ, Plato, Minn., 1988—. Mem. Plato Rec. Bd., 1989—. Mem. Cen. Area Clergy Cluster, Ea. Assn. Minn. Conf., Glencoe Area Ministerial Assn. (pres. 1990-91), Lions, Zeta Chi. Home: 312 1st St NE Plato MN 55370 Office: St Pauls United Ch of Christ 308 1st St NE PO Box 26 Plato MN 55370

FENTER, RANDY LYNN, minister; b. Olney, Tex., Jan. 3, 1953; s. Eugene Milton and Billie Jean (Porter) F.; m. Marta Gail Massie, Mar. 21, 1975; children: Marta Lynn, Rachel Lane. BA in Communications, Lubbock (Tex.) Christian U., 1975; postgrad., Abilene (Tex.) Christian U., 1985-87. Evangelism min. Colleyville (Tex.) Ch. of Christ, 1975-77; min. Raton (N.Mex.) Ch. of Christ, 1977-81; pulpit min. MacArthur Pk. Ch. of Christ, San Antonio, 1981—; mem. almuni bd. Lubbock Christian U., 1985—, mem. pres.'s coun., 1986—; bd. mem. Christian News of South Tex., San Antonio, 1981-89, Camp Blue Haven, Las Vegas, N.Mex., 1984—. Contbr. articles to numerous profl. mags. Chmn. troop com. Boy Scouts Am., 1978-80. Recipient K.C. Moser award Lubbock Christian U., 1987. Mem. Rotary. Home: 4615 Sunny Walk San Antonio TX 78217 Office: MacArthur Pk Ch of Christ 1907 NE Loop 410 San Antonio TX 78217

FERDON, LEE MONROE, minister; b. Dayton, Ohio, Feb. 5, 1942; s. John Monroe and Nellie Gaye (Hall) F.; m. Sandra Kay Hemming, Dec. 24, 1963 (div. 1976); m. Karen Sue Buchanan, Feb. 18, 1978. AA, Hillsborough Community Coll., Tampa, 1982; BA, Fla. So. Coll., 1984; MDiv, Emory U., Candler Sch. Theology, 1987. Ordained to ministry, United Meth. Ch., 1987. Supr. Jack's Cookie Co., Tampa, 1969-77; sales mgr. Western & So. Life, Tampa, 1977-82; pastor Cork United Meth. Ch., Plant City, Fla., 1982-84, Mt. Pleasant/Pine Chapel, Calhoun, Ga., 1984-87; assoc. pastor Plantation (Fla.) United Meth. Ch., 1987-89; pastor Gray Meml. United Meth. Ch., Tallahassee, 1989—; bd. dirs. F.A.M.U. Campus Ministry, Tallahassee, 1990—. Mem. Tampa Jaycees, Kiwanis, Masons, Phi Theta Kappa (disting. svc. award 1982, pres. 1982), Beta Phi Gamma. Democrat. Avocations: reading, fishing, canoeing, travel. Home: 2408 Tamarack Ave Tallahassee FL 32303 Office: Gray Meml Meth Ch 2201 Old Bainbridge Rd Tallahassee FL 32303

FERGUSON, BENNY WINFIELD, minister; b. Sulphur Springs, Tex., Nov. 6, 1944; s. John Henry Perry and Rosie Bell (Potter) F.; m. Sherri Lyne Blankenship, May 7, 1965; children: Benny W. II, LaDawna Lyne. Grad., Sulphur Springs High Sch., 1963. Ordained to ministry Assemblies of God, 1969. Pastor Assemblies of God Ch., Sanger, Tex., 1966-73; evangelist Assemblies of God Ch., Sulphur Springs, 1973-78; pastor Assemblies of God Ch., Sand Springs, Okla., 1978-85, First Assemblies of God Ch., Columbia, Mo., 1985-89, Praise Assemblies of God, Columbia, Mo., 1989—; sectional youth dir. Denton Sect. of Assemblies of God, Sanger, 1971-74; dist. presbyter N. Mo. Assemblies of God, Columbia, 1989—, dist. men's dir., Excelsior Springs, 1986—, dist. Light for the Lost dir., 1987—. Office: Praise Assembly of God Ch PO Box 911 Columbia MO 65205-0911

FERGUSON, DAVID L., church administrator; b. Pampa, Tex., June 6, 1947; s. Roy William and Ragina Francis (Lockard) F.; m. Teresa Jean Carpenter, June 29, 1963; children: Terri, Robin, Eric. BS, U. Tex., 1969, MS, 1972. Ordained to ministry Baptist Ch., 1981. Systems analyst J.M. Huber Corp., Borger, Tex., 1964-65; dir. info. system mgmt., dep. dir. adminstrn. Tex. Dept. Water Resources/Tex. Interagency Natural Resource Coun., Austin, 1969-81; adminstr. Allandale Bapt. Ch., Austin, 1981—. Mem. Presdl. Space Coun., 1980-81; mem. exec. bd. Alpha Omega Ministries; pres. Capitol City Community Interests. Recipient Outstanding Merit award NASA, 1979. Mem. Nat. Govs. Assn. (data coun. chmn. 1980-81), Metro Austin 2000, Leadership Austin, Bapt. Assn. (exec. bd.). Author: Meeting Your Spouse's Seven Basic Needs, 1975, Discipleship in Christ-Likeness, 1979, Discipleship in Life Issues, 1981, Family Discipleship Ministry, 1984. Office: 2615 Allandale Rd Austin TX 78756

FERGUSON, ISAAC CLYDE, religious organization administrator; b. Rock Springs, Wyoming, May 16, 1943; s. Isaac Jr. and Helen Marie (Youngberg) F.; m. Gloria Rae Bateman, Mar. 19, 1965; children: Shawn, Kiera, Devin. BS in Prephys. Therapy, Brigham Young U., 1967, MS in Health Edn., 1968; MS in Preventative Medicine, Ohio State U., 1973, PhD in Preventative Medicine, 1974. Instr. Brigham Young U., Provo, Utah, 1968-69, Ea. Ill. U., Charleston, 1969-71; asst. prof. So. Ill. U., Carbondale, 1974; mgr. health svcs. Church of Jesus Christ of LDS, Salt Lake City, 1975-77; exec. dir. Thrasher Rsch. Fund, Salt Lake City, 1977-82; adj. asst. prof. Brigham Young U., U. Utah, Provo., Salt Lake City, 1975-82; area welfare dir. Church of Jesus Christ of LDS, Indpls., 1982-86; adj. prof. health adm. Ind. U., Purdue U., Indpls., 1985-86; dir. humanitarian svcs. Church of Jesus Christ of LDS, Salt Lake City, 1986—; dir. Thrasher Rsch. Fund, Salt Lake City, 1989—. Author, editor: Personal and Family Preparedness, 1978, Mission Pres. Health Guide, 1979; contbr. author: Edn. Alcohol Intervention, Resource Study Guide & Family Discussion Plans. Chmn. Utah State Task Force on Prevention of Alcohol Problems, 1976-79; bd. dirs. Intermountain Area Cystic Fibrosis Summer Camp, Salt Lake City, 1978-80, Alcohol Rsch. Info. Svc., 1980—, Salt Lake Area United Way, 1989—. Avocations: sports, reading, family. Office: LDS Welfare Svcs 50 East North Temple 7th Fl Salt Lake City UT 84150

FERGUSON, KENNETH ALAN, pastor, educator, pastoral counselor; b. Boston, July 13, 1953; s. Oakley Alexander and Christine (Morse) F.; m. Patricia Aloisia Nydam, Apr. 1, 1978; children: Aaron Michael, Bryan Adam. BA, Gordon Coll., 1975; MDiv, Andover-Newton Theol. Sem., 1979; postgrad., Ea. Bapt. Theol. Sem. Ordained to ministry United Ch. of Christ. Dir. ednl. ministries Wesley United Meth. Ch., Framingham, Mass., 1975-77; assoc. pastor Pilgrim United Ch. of Christ, Leominster, Mass., 1977-79; pastor Southwest Harbor (Mass.) Harbor United Ch. of Christ, 1979-86; pastor, tchr. Woodridge United Ch. of Christ, Cranston, R.I., 1986—; pastoral counselor Cornerston Counseling, Cranston, 1986—; seminar dir. Prepare/Enrich Inc., Mpls., 1986—; del. Coun. for Theol. Edn. in New Eng., 1989—; pres. R.I. Conf. Clergy Assn., 1990-91. Composer songs. Mem. Am. Assn. Marriage and Family Therapists. Democrat. Office: Woodridge United Ch of Christ 546 Budlong Rd Cranston RI 02920

FERGUSON, M. DWIGHT, minister; b. Pitts., Feb. 2, 1933; s. Mark Crawford and Helen Mae (Hindman) F.; m. Donna G. Hamilton, June 26, 1959; children: Mark David, Cynthia Lynne. BA, Wheaton Coll., 1955; MDiv, Princeton Sem., 1958. Ordained to ministry Presbyn. Ch. (U.S.A.). Asst. pastor 1st Presbyn. Ch. of Bakerstown (Pa.); pastor Meml. Presbyn. Ch. of Fox Chase, Phila., 1960-68, Brentwood Presbyn. Ch., Pitts., 1968-73, Bethany Presbyn. Ch., Rochester, N.Y., 1973—. Home: 228 Apple Creek Ln Rochester NY 14612 Office: Bethany Presbyn Ch 3000 Dewey Ave Rochester NY 14616

FERGUSON, MILTON, academic administrator. Pres. Midwestern Bapt. Theol. Sem., Kansas City, Mo. Office: Midwestern Bapt Theol Sem Office of the President 5001 N Oak St Trafficway Kansas City MO 64118*

FERGUSON, NORMAN WAYNE, minister; b. Ft. Worth, Tex., May 12, 1933; s. Allie Fennel and Jessie Zeona (Van) F.; m. Mary Jane Riley, June 7, 1953 (div. 1977); children: Lori Lynette, Bradley Wayne, Nathan Riley; m. Jennifer Lay Largey, Jan. 11, 1978; children: Summer Joy, Heather Jill. BA, Bob Jones U., Greenville, S.C., 1956; MDiv, S.W. Bapt. Theol. Sem., 1959; postgrad., East Tex. State U., 1963-68; D Ministry, Bethany Sem., Dothan, Ala., 1990. Ordained to ministry So. Bapt. Conv., 1951. Pastor First Bapt. Ch., Mt. Sterling, Ill., 1953-54, Northside Bapt. Ch., Corsicana, Tex., 1959-63; Bible prof. Tyler (Tex.) Jr. Coll., 1963-68; minister, assoc. pastor Hatcher Meml. Bapt., Richmond, Va., 1968-73; minister Christ Evang. Ch., Glendale, Calif., 1981-85; pastor Bethel Bapt. Ch., Ft. Deposit, Ala., 1986—. Author: Norm's Nutty Notes, 1965; contbr. articles to profl. jours. Recipient Profl. of Yr. award, Tyler Jr. Coll., 1968. Mem. Internat. Brotherhood of Magicians, Soc. Am. Magicians, Fellowship of Gospel Magicians, Kiwanis (music com. 1990, Outstanding Citizenship award 1985). Home: PO Box 261 Fort Deposit AL 36032 Office: Bethel Bapt Ch 205 Church St Fort Deposit AL 36032 *Christian compassion comes when you quit trying to change the world and focus on changing the life of an individual.*

FERGUSON, ROBERT CARMEL, minister; b. Memphis, Oct. 30, 1938; s. Frank Ford and Bonnie (Robbins) F.; m. Diane Rosemary Hughes, July 18, 1970; children: Angela, Richard, Annette. BS, Memphis State U., 1962; MDiv, Southwestern Bapt. Theol. Sem., 1976. Ordained to ministry So. Bapt. Conv., 1960. Pastor Carey Chapel Bapt. Ch., Mt. Pleasant, 1960-63, Calvary Bapt. Ch., Augsburg, Fed. Republic Germany, 1966-69, 1st Bapt. Ch., Giessen, Fed. Republic Germany, 1970-71, Faith Bapt. Ch., Kaiserslautern, Fed. Republic Germany, 1971-86, 1st Bapt. Ch., Mandeville, La., 1986—; pres. European Bapt. Conv., Fed. Republic Germany, 1967-68, 84-85, Mandeville Ministerial Alliance, 1987-88; European coord. Internat. Congression Revival, Ft. Worth, 1976-86; mem. World Aide Com., World Bapt. Alliance, 1986—. Bd. dirs. Samaritan Ctr., Mandeville, 1987—. Home: 720 Marilyn Dr Mandeville LA 70448 Office: 1st Bapt Ch PO Box 1218 Mandeville LA 70450-1218

FERGUSON, WILLIAM EVERETT, religion educator; b. Montgomery, Tex., Feb. 18, 1933; s. William Everett and Edith Alice (Curling) F.; m. Nancy Ann Lewis, June 25, 1956; children: Everett Ray, Edith Ann Doyle, Patricia Alice. BA, Abilene Christian U., 1953, MA, 1954; STB, Harvard U., 1956, PhD, 1960. Dean Northeastern Christian Jr. Coll., Villanova, Pa., 1959-62; prof. Abilene (Tex.) Christian U., 1962—. Author: Early Christians Speak, 1987, Backgrounds of Early Christianity, 1987; editor: The Second Century, 1980—, Encyclopedia of Early Christianity, 1990. Mem. Am. Soc. Ch. History (coun. 1983-85), Ecclesiastical History Soc., Soc. Bibl. Lit., Assn. Internat. d'Etudes Patristiques, N.Am. Patristic Soc. (v.p. 1989-90, pres. 1990-92). Mem. Ch. of Christ. Home: 609 E N 16th St Abilene TX 79601 Office: Abilene Christian U Box 8402 Abilene TX 79699

FERM, DEANE WILLIAM, minister; b. Lebanon, Pa., May 22, 1927; s. Vergilius T.A. and Nellie (Nelson) F.; m. Paulie Swan, June 26, 1949 (div. 1976); children: William, Linnea, Robert, Laurie (dec.); m. Debra Campbell, Dec. 21, 1976. B.A., Coll. Wooster, 1949; B.D., Yale U., 1952, M.A., 1953, Ph.D., 1954. Ordained to ministry Presbyn. Ch., 1952. Minister Fishers Island Union Chapel, N.Y., 1952-54; dir. Sch. Religion, Mont. State U., 1954-59; asst. dir. Danforth Found., 1958; dean Coll. Chapel, Mt. Holyoke Coll., South Hadley, Mass., 1959-81; lectr. Smith Coll., 1960-63; vis. prof. St. Mary's Coll., St. Andrew's U., Scotland, 1980; adj. prof. Dickinson Coll., 1985, Gettysburg Coll., 1985-86, Colby Coll., 1987, 90—, U. Maine, Farmington, 1988-90. Author: Responsible Sexuality Now, 1971, Contemporary American Theologies: A Critical Survey, 1981, rev. edit., 1990, II: A Book of Readings, 1982, Alternative Life Styles Confront the Church, 1983, Restoring the Kingdom, 1984, Third World Liberation Theologies: An Introductory Survey, 1986, Third World Liberation Theologies: A Reader, 1986, Liberation Theology: North American Style, 1987, Profiles in Liberation: 36 Portraits of Third World Liberation Theologians, 1988, Smithfield, Maine: The Center of the Universe, A History of the Town, 1990; also articles. Served with USNR, 1945-46. Danforth Campus Ministry grantee, 1965-66; Poulson fellow Am. Scandinavian Found., 1965-66. Home: PO Box 173 Smithfield ME 04978

FERM, LOIS ROUGHAN, religious organization administrator; b. Buffalo, Feb. 5, 1918; d. Laurence Francis and Bertha Margaret Lucy (Jopp) R.; m. Robert O. Ferm, June 28, 1941; children: Lois Esther, Rebecca Ann, Paul Robert, Stephen John. BA, Houghton Coll., 1939; MA, U. Mich., 1955; PhD, U. Minn., 1972. Cert. tchr., N.Y. Tchr. Rushford (N.Y.) Cen. Sch., 1939-41; instr. library, sociology John Brown U., Siloam Springs, Ark., 1949-51; librarian Cuba (N.Y.) Cen. Schs., 1953-55; chmn. dept. edn. Houghton (N.Y.) Coll., 1955-57; instr. edn. U. Minn., Mpls., 1959-61, mgr. Coll. Edn. Library, 1961-64; personal asst. rsch., resource coord. Billy Graham Evangel. Assn., Mpls., 1973—. Pres., Riceville Property Owners Assn., Asheville, N.C., 1982, 83, 87, 88. Mem. Soc. Am. Archivists, Oral History Assn., Christian Women's Clubs, Pi Lambda Theta, Pi Alpha Theta. Republican. Baptist. Avocations: sewing, gardening, walking. Home: 27 Patriots Dr Asheville NC 28805 Office: Billy Graham Evangel Assn 1300 Harmon Pl Minneapolis MN 55403

FERM, ROBERT LIVINGSTON, religion educator; b. Wooster, Ohio, Jan. 2, 1931; s. Vergilius Ture Anselm and Nellie Agnette (Nelson) F.; m. Fleur Kinney, June 28, 1952 (div. 1968); children: Eric, Alison; m. Sonja Olson. BA, Coll. Wooster, 1952; BD, Yale U., 1955, MA, 1956, PhD, 1958. From instr. to assoc. prof. religion Pomona Coll., Claremont, Calif., 1958-67, prof., 1967-69, acting chmn. dept. religion, 1960-63, chmn. dept. religion, 1963-69; prof., chmn. dept. religion Middlebury (Vt.) Coll., 1969—, Pardon E. Tillinghast prof. religion, 1988—. Author: Jonathan Edwards The Younger 1745-1801: A Colonial Pastor, 1976, Piety, Purity Plenty: Images of Protestantism in America, 1991; editor Readings in the History of Christian Thought, 1964, Issues in American Protestantism, 1969. Mem. Am. Acad. Religion. Presbyterian. Office: Middlebury Coll Dept Religion Middlebury VT 05753

FERNANDEZ, ANTHONY SOTER, archbishop. Archbishop of Kuala Lumpur Roman Cath. Ch., Malaysia. Office: Archbishop House, 528 Jalan Bukit Nanas, 50250 Kuala Lumpur Malaysia*

FERNANDEZ, NELDA T., religious education coordinator, real estate professional; b. Bellfalls, Tex., Sept. 22, 1948; d. Lee and Ascencion Joan (Guzman) Aguilar; m. David Fernandez, Sept. 1, 1968; children: Christina

Diane, David III, Mariana Victoria. AA, Temple (Tex.) Jr. Coll., 1978; BA, U. Mary-Hardin Baylor, 1980. Grad. Realtor Inst. Catechist Our Lady of Guadalupe, Temple, 1979-91, dir., youth ministry, coord. religious edn., 1988-91, dir., lectors, 1989-91; sales agt. Coldwell Banker, LRS Properties, Temple, 1983-91; workshop presenter Diocese of Austin, Tex., 1990, deanery rep., 1990—. mem. Bell County (Tex.) Dems., 1980-91; v.p., pres. Friends of the Libr., Temple, 1984-85; del. Dem. Conv., Ft. Worth, 1990; chmn. Ways and Means Com. PTO, Temple, 1990-91; treas. Tri-County Tex. Dem. Women, Bell County, 1991. Recipient Pres.'s award Friends of the Temple (Tex.) Pub. Libr., 1985. Mem. Scott & White Meml. Hosp. Aux., The Contemporaries (Temple), Bowling League (Temple). Home: 705 Clover Ln Temple TX 76502

FERNANDEZ, RICHARD R., ecumenical agency administrator. Dir. N.W. Interfaith Movement, Phila. Office: NW Interfaith Movement Greene St at Westview Philadelphia PA 19119*

FERNÁNDEZ ARTEAGA, JOSÉ, bishop; b. Santa Inés, Mex., Sept. 12, 1933. Ordained priest Roman Cath. Ch., 1957; elevated to bishop of Apatzingán, Mex., 1974; consecrated, 1974; named bishop of Colima, Mex., 1980. Address: Palacio Episcopal Hidalgo 135, Apartado 1, 28000 Colima Mexico

FERNANDO, SUMITH D. PETER, psychotherapist, counselor; b. Colombo, Sri Lanka, Aug. 22, 1952; came to U.S., 1984; s. Samuel L. B. and Dulcie Muriel (De Silva) F.; m. Manel Chitra Dareeju, Dec. 10, 1977; 1 child, Sumali Manishka. BTh., U. Serempore, India, 1975; M in Ministry, Christian Bible Coll., Rocky Mount, N.C., 1985; DD, Trinity Valley Bapt. Sem., Ft. Worth, 1985; MEd, U. North Tex., 1990. Lic. profl. counselor, Tex. Pastor Sri Lanka Meth. Ch., 1975-84, sec. youth dept. so. dist., 1980, sr. pastor, 1981-83; missionary pastor Calvary United Meth. Ch., Flint, Mich., 1984; assoc. pastor Temple of Praise Ch., Garland, Tex., 1985; counselor, tchr. Trinity Valley Bapt. Sem., Ft. Worth, 1986-89; counselor Alpha & Omega Family Ctr. Inc., Ft. Worth, 1990—; interim pastor Liberty Congl. Meth. Ch., Aubrey, Tex., 1987-88; assoc. therapist 1st United Meth. Counseling Svc., Arlington, Tex., 1990—; presenter workshops in field. Organizer local chpt. Alcoholics Anonymous, Sri Lanka, 1982; founder med. clinic, Sri Lanka, 1983; founder, leader self-confidence support group, Tex., 1987. Mem. AACD, Internat. Assn. Marriage and Family Counselors. Baptist. Avocations: piano, walking, music, travel, humor. Home: 1930-B Shadynook Ct Bedford TX 76021 Office: 1st United Meth Counseling Svc 313 N Center St Arlington TX 76011

FERRAEZ, MARTHA ELIZABETH, religious association officer; b. Tampa, Fla., May 28, 1937; d. Warren Hudson and Martha Elizabeth (Minshew) Fulton; m. Leon R. Ferraez, Apr. 19, 1961; children: Felicia Elizabeth, Leon R., Jr., Maricarmen. BA in English, Asbury Coll., 1959; MA in Bicultural Edn., U. of the Ams., 1982. Tchr. Nicholls High Sch., New Orleans, La., 1959-60, Anchorage (Alaska) High Sch., 1960-61; officer Salvation Army, Memphis, 1963, Mex., 1964-81; officer, editor territorial newsletter Salvation Army, Atlanta, 1981-83; editor program aids Salvation Army, Verona, N.J., 1984—. Contbr. articles to profl. jours. Mem. AAUW, Montclair Hist. Soc., Glen Ridge Women's Club. Republican. Avocations: gardening, quilting. Home: 7 Astor Pl Glen Ridge NJ 07028 Office: Salvation Army Nat Hdqrs 799 Bloomfield Ave Verona NJ 07044

FERRARIO, JOSEPH A., bishop; Educator St. Charles Coll., Catonsville, Md., St. Mary's Sem., Baltimore, Catholic U., Washington, D.C., U. of Scranton, Pa. Ordained Roman Catholic priest, 1951; ord. aux. bishop of Honolulu, titular bishop of Cuse, 1978, bishop of Honolulu, 1982-. Office: Diocese of Honolulu 1184 Bishop St Honolulu HI 96813

FERRAZZETTA, SETTIMIO ARTURO, bishop. Bishop of Bissau Roman Cath. Ch., Guinea-Bissau. Office: CP 20, Bissau Guinea-Bissau*

FERRIS, RONALD CURRY, bishop; b. Toronto, Ont., Can., July 2, 1945; s. Harold Bland and Marjorie May (Curry) F.; m. Janet Agnes Waller, Aug. 14, 1965; children: Elisa, Jill, Matthew, Jenny, Rani, Jonathon. Grad., Toronto Tchrs. Coll., 1965; B.A., U. Western Ont., London, 1970; M.Div., Huron Coll., London, 1973, D.D. hon., 1982. Ordained to ministry Anglican Ch., 1970. Tchr. Pape Ave. Sch., Toronto, 1965-66; prin. Carcross Elem. Sch., Y.T., 1966-68; incumbent St. Luke's Ch., Old Crow, Y.T., 1970-72; rector St. Stephen's Ch., London, Ont., 1973-81; bishop Diocese of Yukon, Whitehorse, 1981—. Author: (poems) A Wing and a Prayer, 1990. Home: 194 Rainbow Rd, Whitehorse, YK Canada Y1A 5E2 Office: Diocese of Yukon, PO Box 4247, Whitehorse, YK Canada Y1A 3T3

FERRY, ARTHUR GEORGE, JR., minister; b. Brazil, Ind., Aug. 13, 1938; s. Arthur George and Helen Irene (Howard) F.; m. Anna Louise Ashby, May 28, 1959; children: Scott Alan, Lori Ann Garcia. BTh, Trinity Coll. of the Bible, 1987; M of Ministry, Trinity Theol., 1990. Assoc. pastor Woodville Bapt. Ch., Mitchell, Ind., 1982-85; pastor First Bapt. Ch., Williams, Ind., 1985-87, New Winchester Bapt. Ch., Danville, Ind., 1987-90; sr. pastor First Bapt. Ch., Garrett, Ind., 1991—; chaplain in field; treas., dir. Concerned Citizens for Abused Adults, Plainfield, Ind., 1987-91; moderator White Lick Bapt. Assn., Amo, Ind., 1989-91. Town chmn. Rep. Party, Staunton, Ind., 1965-72, precinct com., 1964-66; rep. Town Bd., Staunton, 1969-72. Mem. Am. Bapt. Chs., Internat. Conf. Police Chaplains, Garrett Police, Garrett Minister's Coun., Northeastern Minister's Coun., Lions (v.p. 1988-90), Masonic #264 (chair 1960-70), Eastern Star. Republican. Home: 400 S Britton St Garrett IN 46738 Office: First Bapt Ch 1357 S Randolph Box 179 Garrett IN 46738

FERWERDA, VERNON LEROY, lay worker; b. Rockford, Ill., Sept. 4, 1918; s. Benjamin LeRoy and Hildur Antonietta (Engdahl) F.; m. Martha Morse, Dec. 2, 1942 (dec. 1985); m. Anna Silva Carey, Oct. 26, 1986; children: Mark Alan, Neil Benjamin. AB, U. Mass., 1940, MS, 1941; PhD, Harvard U., 1954; D of Humanities, St. Joseph Coll., Rutland, Vt., 1985. Asst. gen. sec. Nat. Coun. Chs., Washington, 1963-66; com. min. for peace and justice United Ch. of Christ, 1981—; prof. emeritus of polit. sci. Rensselaer Polytechnic Inst., Troy, N.Y., 1968—. Editor: The Office of Technology Assessment. Moderator Town of Wardsboro, Vt., 1979-82; justice of peace State of Vt., 1979-87; chmn. Bd. Civil Authority, Wardsboro, 1984-86; mem. Simsbury (Conn.) Charter Rev. Com., 1991-92. Fellow African Studies Assn.; mem. Internat. Soc. Tech. Assessment (v.p.), Commn. to Study the Orgn. of Peace (exec. com.). Home and Office: 19 Riverside Rd Simsbury CT 06070

FESMIRE, CHARLES WAYNE, minister; b. Jackson, Tenn., Dec. 8, 1932; s. Floyd McKinley and Bonnie Wynona (Frazer) F.; m. Jayne Flatt, June 13, 1959; children: David Michael, Randal Scott, Steven Alan. BA, Lambuth Coll., 1957; MDiv, Vanderbilt U., 1960, D Ministry, 1977. Ordained to ministry United Meth. Ch. as elder, 1960. Pastor 1st United Meth. Ch., Huntingdon, Tenn., 1975-81, Paris, Tenn., 1981-84; dist. supt. Memphis Ann. Conf., Dyersburg, Tenn., 1984-89; sr. min. Broadway United Meth. Ch., Paducah, Ky., 1989—; trustee Meth. Health System, Memphis, 1986—; bd. govs., exec. com. and bldg. com. United Meth. Report, 1989—. Office: Broadway United Meth Church 701 Broadway St Paducah KY 42001-6805

FETHEROLF, FRED ARTHUR, theologian, writer, minister; b. Washington, Aug. 8, 1944; s. Mary (Facione) F.; m. Mary Larraine Fetherolf, June 20, 1970; children: Christopher John, Julie Ann. MA, U. Calif.; MDiv, Calif. Grad. Sch. Theology; PhD, Columbia Pacific U.; D of Ministry, Calif. Grad. Sch. Theology. Diplomate pub. health; lic. psychiatrist. Interim pastor So. Bapt. Conv., Calif., 1975—; pres., chief exec. officer Christian Life Evangelistic Assn., Calif., 1980—; educator Calif. Grad. Sch. Theology. Author: Answers to TOUGH Questions, 1988, How to stay Sane and Healthy in the 90's, 1990; contbr. articles to profl. jours. Coord. Cultural Arts Assn., Pleasanton, Calif., 1984; campaign mgr. No. Calif. area Pat Robertson for Pres., 1987-88, Houston for Mayor of San Jose, 1990; mem. Nat. Rep. Congl. Com., Calif. Rep. Party. With USN, 1961-65, Vietnam. Fellow Acad. Orthomolecular Psychiatry; mem. Nat. Assn. Evangelicals, Acad. Parish Clergy, Nat. Speakers Assn. Home: PO Box 1857 Pleasanton CA 94566

FETTERHOFF, CARL ELMER, minister; b. Harrisburg, Pa., Apr. 18, 1938; s. Edward Carl and Lola Inez (Gotshall) F.; m. Beverly Louise Lash, June 17, 1961; 1 child, Heather Ann. Diploma in theology, Evang. Sch., Myerstown, Pa., 1961; student, Messiah Coll., 1961-64. Ordained to ministry Evang. Congl. Ch. Minister Grace Evang. Congl. Ch., East Petersburg, Pa., 1960-61, Wiconisco, Pa., 1961-66; minister Ebenezer Evang. Congl. Ch., Williamstown, Pa., 1961-66, Bethany Evang. Congl. Ch., Allentown, Pa., 1966-70, Ebenezer Evang. Congl. Ch., Jim Thorpe, Pa., 1970-77, Bethesda Reedsville Evang. Congl. Ch., Schuylkill Haven, Pa., 1977-86, Bethany Evang. Congl. Ch., Reading, Pa., 1986-91, Trinity Evang. Congl. Ch., Shamokin, Pa., 1991—; dir. Twin Pines Youth Camp, Stroudsburg, Pa., 1970-77, treas., 1972-77; statis. sec. Eastern Conf. Evang. Congl. Ch., Myerstown, Pa., 1980—, statistician, 1986—. Ambulance technician Dilligence Vol. Fire Co., Jim Thorpe, 1970-77; care-give AIDS hospice Rainbow Home, Wernersville, Pa., 1990; pres. Salvation Army, Reading, 1991. Mem. Wesleyan Theol. Soc., Nat. Assn. Evangelicals, Masons.

FETTERS, PAUL R., academic administrator. Head Grad. Sch. Christian Ministries, Huntington (Ind.) Coll. Office: Huntington Coll Grad Sch Christian Ministries Huntington IN 46750*

FETTY, MAURICE ALLEN, minister; b. Crawford County, Wis., June 13, 1936; s. Clifford Allen and Eva Carol (Smith) F.; m. Jane Arlene Smith, Aug. 31, 1957 (dec. 1967); children: Elizabeth, Cynthia, Ellen; m. Sara Amanda Lagervall Melton, June 8, 1968; stepchildren: Scott, Susan, Stacy. BA, Minn. Bible Coll., Mpls., 1958; MDiv, Christian Theol. Sem., Indpls, 1962; STM, Union Theol. Sem., N.Y.C., 1967; MA, Butler U., Indpls., 1970. Ordained to ministry Ch. of Christ (Christian), 1959. Minister Flatbush Christian Ch., Bklyn., 1962-65; assoc. minister La Hermosa Christian Ch., N.Y.C., 1965-67; dir. La Hermosa Christian Inst., N.Y.C., 1965-67; teaching minister Colonial Ch. of Edina, Mpls., 1967-72; sr. minister Mayflower Congl. Ch., Grand Rapids, Mich., 1972-88, Congl. Ch., Manhasset, N.Y., 1988—. Author: Putting Your Life on the Line, 1977, Prayers for the New Day, 1983; contbr. articles to profl. and religious jours. Recipient Disting. Alumnus award, Christian Theol. Sem., Indpls., 1986. Mem. Manhasset Clergy Assn., Met. Assn. of United Ch. of Christ (bd. dirs. 1989—), Port Washington Yacht Club, North Hempstead Country Club, Rotary (v.p., bd. dirs. Manhasset club). Home: 90 Country Club Dr Port Washington NY 11050 Office: Congl Ch 1845 Northern Blvd Manhasset NY 11030

FEWELL, DANNA NOLAN, religion educator; b. El Paso, Tex., Jan. 10, 1958; d. Bill P. and Doris (Boney) Nolan; m. David Edwin Fewell, June 24, 1978. BA, La. Coll., 1979; MTS, Emory U., 1981, PhD, 1987. Asst. prof. Perkins Sch. Theology, Dallas, 1987—. Author: Circle of Sovereignty, 1988, (with others) Compromising Redemption, 1990; asst. editor (series) Bible and Literature, 1987-89; gen. editor (series) Literary Currents and Bible Interpretation, 1990—. Mem. Am. Acad. Religion, Soc. Bibl. Lit., Nat. Assn. Bapt. Profs. Religion. Democrat. Office: So Meth U Perkins Sch Theology Dallas TX 75275

FICHTER, JOSEPH H., priest, sociology educator; b. Union City, N.J., June 10, 1908; s. Charles J. and Victoria (Weiss) F. AB, St. Louis U., 1935, MA, 1939; PhD, Harvard U., 1947. Entered Soc. Jesus, 1930; ordained priest Roman Cath. Ch., 1942; instr. Spring Hill Coll., 1935-36, Loyola U., New Orleans, 1944-45; prof., chmn. dept. sociology Loyola U., 1947-64, 72—; vis. prof. sociology Muenster U., Germany, 1953-54; vis. prof. sociology, dir. research Notre Dame U., 1956-57, U. Chile, Santiago, 1961-62; vis. prof. sociology U. Chgo., 1964-65; Stillman prof. Harvard U., 1965-70; vis. prof. State U. N.Y. at Albany, 1971-72; Favrot prof. Tulane U., 1974-75. Author: Roots of Change, 1939, Man of Spain, 1940, Christianity, 1947, Social Relations in the Urban Parish, 1954, Sociology, 1957, Soziologie der Pfarrgruppen, 1958, Parochial School, 1958, Religion as an Occupation, 1961, Cambios Sociales en Chile, 1962, Priest and People, 1965, America's Forgotten Priests, 1968, One-Man Research, 1973, Organization Man in the Church, 1974, Catholic Cult of the Paraclete, 1975, Ardent Spirits Subdued, 1981, Religion and Pain, 1982, The Holy Family of Father Moon, 1985, The Health of American Catholic Priests, 1985, A Sociologist Looks at Religion, 1988, The Pastoral Provisions: Married Catholic Priests, 1989, The Wives of Catholic Clergy, 1991. Founder Southeastern. Region Coll. Students Interracial Commn., 1948; mem. New Orleans Commn. Human Rights, 1948, New Orleans Com. Race Relations. Mem. AAUP, Am. Sociol. Soc. (mem. exec. coun.), So. Sociol. Soc. (past pres.), Assn. for Sociology Religion, Soc. Sci. Study of Religion (past pres.), Soc. Study Social Problems, Religious Rsch. Assn., Nat. Urban League. Address: Loyola U New Orleans LA 70118 *The true believers of any religion are those who expand personal salvation to reach the needy and underpriveleged.*

FICKEY, TIMOTHY LYNN, lay church worker; b. La Fayette, Ga., Sept. 4, 1963; s. James Raymond and Theresa Linda (Johnson) F. BBA, U. Tenn., Chattanooga, 1986. Dir. music and youth Corinth Bapt. Ch., La Fayette, 1982-87, dir. music, 1987—; acct. Horizon Industries, Calhoun, Ga., 1987-88; cost acct. Fibron Co., Chattanooga, 1988-90; mgr. budget acctg. Synthetic Industries, Chickamauga, Ga., 1990—; music dir. Coosa Bapt. Assn., Ft. Oglethorpe, Ga., 1991—. Home: PO Box 117 La Fayette GA 30728 Office: Corinth Bapt Ch Rte 5 Box 277 La Fayette GA 30728

FICZERI, PAUL DANIEL, minister; b. Cleve., Feb. 16, 1946; s. Paul and Bertha Helen (Toth) F.; m. Linda Kay Auble, July 12, 1967 (div. Oct. Dec. 1970); m. Mary Elizabeth Markley, June 12, 1981; children: Susan Elizabeth , Helen Marie. BA, Tex. Christian U., 1968; M in Religious Edn., Brite Div. Sch., 1972. Ordained minister Disciples of Christ Ch., 1972. Assoc. minister First Christian Ch., Mineral Wells, Tex., 1972-73; organizing minister First Christian Ch., Coppell, Tex., 1974-75; minister First Christian Ch., Monahans, Tex., 1975-78, Mesquite, Tex., 1978-82; sr. pastor Community Christian Ch., San Antonio, 1983-87, First Christian Ch., Greenwood, Miss., 1987—; bd. dirs. Randolph Area Christian Assistance Program, Schertz, Tex. 1983-87, treas., 1985, pres., 1986; chmn. Bluebonnet Area Evangelism Dept., San Antonio, 1987; mem. Alamo Cluster Ch. Advance Now Taskforce, San Antonio, 1986-87; pres. Alamo Cluster Minister's Fellowship, San Antonio, 1986-88. Organizing dir. Footlight Players, Monahans, 1977; chaplain Optimists Club Ward County, Monahans, 1976-78; v.p. Camp Christian Bd. Dirs., San Antonio, 1987; organizer, first pres. NE San Antonio Commodore Owner's Group, 1984-85; chmn. Evangelism Commn. Christian Ch. in Miss., 1988—; mem. regional bd. Christian Ch. in Miss.; bd. dirs. Community Food Pantry of Greenwood and Leflore County, 1988—, chmn. 1989—; bd. dirs. Greenwood Salvation Army, the Children's Ctr., Lexington, Miss. and others. Republican. Mem. Disciples of Christ Ch. Lodges: Ancon, Panama Canal Bodies, Kiwanis. Avocations: computers, photography, audio and video recording, golf, bridge. Home and Office: First Christan Ch PO Box 17 Greenwood MS 38930

FIDELLOW, EDWARD ANDRE, JR., school administrator; b. Bklyn., Dec. 4, 1946; s. Edward and Jacqueline (Chauveau) F.; m. Barbara Louise Chrastina, Feb. 14, 1968; children: Charissa, Edward III, Yolande. BA, Georgetown U., 1967; MFA, So. Meth. U., 1980. Tchr. Berean Life Corps Coll., Dallas, 1967-72; with pub. rels. dept. Sta. KXTX-TV 39, Dallas, 1973-77; pres. Montessori Village Sch./Lakemont Acad., Dallas, 1977—. Contbr. articles to newspapers. Treas. Dallas Young Reps., 1980. Named Family of Yr. 23d Dist. Conservative Caucus, 1980, Quality Family Dallas Times Herald, 1978. Mem. Christian Montessori Fellowship (pres. 1983—), Rotary. Home: 1630 Oak Knoll Dallas TX 75208 Office: Lakemont Acad 3993 W NW Hwy Dallas TX 75220 *Lord, let my life be intense. Don't let me waste it on the peripheries of nothingnesses that cannot draw men to you. God, let my life be intensely yours. (Quoted from college yearbook, 1967.).*

FIEBIG, GREGORY VERNON, clergyman; b. St. Louis, Sept. 12, 1957; s. Vernon Lester and Helen Louise (Bennett) F.; m. Marilyn Sue Cage, Apr. 21, 1979; children: Jeremy, Jessica, Jeffrey. BA, S.W. Bapt., Bolivar, Mo., 1977; MA, Cen. Mo. State U., 1982; MDiv, Midwestern Bapt. Theol., 1985. Youth dir. First Bapt. Ch., Marshall, Mo., 1978-82; campus minister Bapt. Student Union, Kansas City, Mo., 1982-83; youth minister Marlborough Bapt. Coll., Kansas City, 1983-84; youth and assoc. pastor Laura St. Bapt. Ch., Maryville, Mo., 1984—; bd. dirs. Christian Civic Found., St. Louis, Drug, Alcohol, Tobacco Educator, St. Louis, educator. Contbr. articles to profl. jours. Vol. counselor High Sch., Maryville. Named Eagle Scout Boy Scouts Am., God n' Country. Mem. Mo. Bapt. Rd. Edn. Assn. (v.p. 1989—). Home: 308 S Fillmore Maryville MO 64468 Office: Laura St Bapt Ch 120 S Laura St Maryville MO 64468

FIELD, CURTIS LINCOLN, deacon; b. Troy, N.Y., Oct. 29, 1949; s. Harold Lincoln and Barbara Elizabeth (Atherton) F. AB in Polit. Sci., Grove City (Pa.) Coll., 1971; MLS, SUNY, Albany, 1979. Deacon Madison Ave. Presbyn. Ch., N.Y.C., 1986—; libr. dir. Can. Consulate Gen., N.Y.C., 1985—. Capt. USAF, 1972-75. Mem. ALA, Spl. Libr. Assn., Beta Phi Mu. Home: 136 E 208th St Apt 5D Bronx NY 10467 Office: Canadian Consulate Gen 1251 Ave of the Americas New York NY 10020

FIELD, EDWARD JOSEPH, religious organization administrator; b. L.A., Nov. 19, 1958; m. Judith Pearl Roseman. BA, Calif. State U., Northridge, 1987; M Jewish Communal Svc., Hebrew Union Coll., L.A., 1989; MPA, U. So. Calif., 1989. With Jewish Fedn., Long Beach, Calif., 1987-88, Washington, 1988-89; planning assoc. Jewish Fedn., Phila., 1989—. Mem. alumni adv. com. Hebrew Union Coll. Sch. Jewish Communal Svc., 1990—. Mem. Assn. Jewish Community Orgn. Pers., Jewish Communal Profls. Assn. of Greater Phila. (mem. exec. com. 1990—).

FIELD, KENT A., minister, publisher, career counselor; b. N.Y.C., July 12, 1952; s. Edward Kent Jr. and Joan Lydia (Koudal) F.; m. Particia Mary Fazio, June 30, 1974; children: Benjamin Kent, Tina Marie, Brian Edward. AAS in Civil Engring. Tech., Nassau Community Coll., 1973; grad., Sunset Sch. Missions, Lubbock, Tex., 1977. Ordained to ministry Ch. of Christ, 1976. Assoc. min. North Sheridan Ch. of Christ, Tulsa, 1977-78; min., missionary Huntington (N.Y.) Ch. of Christ, 1978-79; founder, missionary, corp. pres., chmn. bd. L.I. Ch. of Christ, Bay Shore, N.Y., 1979—; owner, pres. Career Advancement Cons., Kaf Amortizations, Bay Shore, 1988—; adj. campus min. SUNY, Stony Brook and Farmingdale, 1983—. Author: Test Your Salvation, 1982, A Time to Be Born; A Time to Die, 1984; patentee in field. Chaplain Southside and Good Samaritan hosps., Bay Shore and West Islip, N.Y., 1980—. Mem. Good Samaritan Clergy Assn. (bd. dirs. 1980—), L.I. Bus. Assn., Rotary (internat. exch. chmn. 1990—). Republican. Home and Office: LI Ch of Christ 1080 Martinstein Ave Bay Shore NY 11706 *It is my firm conviction that it is the truly courageous, and at once, brave and humble in heart among us who overcome shyness, insecurity and fear, thus producing an unavoidable openness and genuine spirit which paves the way for the joining of minds and hearts.*

FIELDING, DONALD HOWERTON, minister; b. Oklahoma City, Aug. 2, 1938; s. Vernon H. and Adelia (Howerton) F.; m. Minna Sharon Tannehill (div. 1982); children: Nathan, David; m. Brenda Gail Fielding, Feb. 19, 1982; 1 child, Erica. BS in Geology, U. Mo., Rolla, 1969, MS in Geology, 1971; MA in Religious Studies, U. Iowa, 1988; DMin, Meadville/Lombard Theol. Sem., Chgo., 1990. Ordained to ministry, Unitarian Universalist Ch. 1990. Minister Unitarian Universalist Fellowship of Dallas, 1990—, Denton Unitarian Universalst Fellowship, Tex., 1990—. With U.S. Army, 1959-62. Mem. Sigma Xi, Phi Kappa Phi. Democrat. Home and Office: 1206 Thomas St Denton TX 76201

FIELDS, DAVID JON, minister; b. Miami, Fla., Nov. 29, 1959; s. Samuel H. and Virginia (Swift) F.; m. Teresa Gayle Bayliss, June 27, 1981. BS, Tenn. Temple U., 1980; MRE, So. Bapt. Theol. Sem., 1982. Ordained to ministry So. Bapt. Conv., 1982. Minister youth and music Fordsville (Ky.) Bapt. Ch., 1980-82; minister edn. and youth First Bapt. Ch., Covington, Ga., 1982-84, Southside Bapt. Ch., Dothan, Ala., 1984-85, Ft. Mitchell (Ky.) Bapt. Ch., 1985-87; support trainer Bapt. Sunday Sch. Bd., Nashville, 1987-89, marketing specialist, 1989—. Guest tchr. Beechwood Sch., Ft. Mitchell, 1986-87, mem. Home Econ. Com., 1987—. Mem. No. Ky. Bapt. Assn. (exec. bd.), So. Bapt. Religious Edn. Assn., Religious Edn. Assn., Eastern Bapt. Religious Edn. Assn., Ky. Youth Ministers Assn. (found.). Democrat. Avocations: music, running, computers, writing, growing apples. Home: 305 Lawrence Ln Springfield TN 37172 Office: 127 9th Ave N Nashville TN 37234

FIELDS, DENNIS FRANKLIN, SR., university administrator, educator, minister; b. Abingdon, Va., Jan. 29, 1947; s. Joe Frank and Mabel (Overbay) F.; m. Barbara Glenna Roberts, July 6, 1965; children: Dennis Franklin II, Miriam Ruth. BS, Liberty Bapt. Coll., 1979; MA, Liberty Bapt. Theol. Sem., 1982; D Ministry, Trinity Evang. Div. Sch., 1986; DD (hon.), No. Fla. Bapt. Theol. Sem., 1990. Ordained to ministry Bapt. Ch., 1982. Dir. ch. planting Liberty U., Lynchburg, Va., 1978—, dir. Christian and community svc., 1979—; assoc. pastor Thomas Rd. Bapt. Ch., Lynchburg, 1977—; interim pastor numerous chs.; chmn. bd. dirs. Mainland China Mission Internat., Forest, Va., 1989—; bd. dirs. Unevangelized Field Missions, Inc., Bala-Cynwyd, Pa.; founding mem., exec. sec. Internat. Asian Mission Inc., Lynchburg, 1981—. Contbr. articles to religious jours. Mem. Am. Assn. Higher Edn., Va. Assn. Student Pers. Adminstrs., Nat. Assn. Student Pers. Adminstrs., Nat. Conf. Ministry to Armed Forces, Assn. Christian Svc. Pers., Liberty Bapt. Fellowship (endorsement agt., exec. sec. 1980—), Kiwanis. Home: 213 Woodville Dr Forest VA 24551 Office: Liberty U 3765 Candler's Mountain Rd Lynchburg VA 24506 *If in this life only we have hope in Christ, we are of all men most miserable. Life for me has been a challenge to give hope in despair by example and my example has been and is Jesus Christ.*

FIELDS, HANOCH MICHAEL, rabbi; b. Boston, Mar. 31, 1961; s. Edward F. and Marilyn (Posner) F. Student, Hebrew U. of Jerusalem, 1981-82; BA, Oberlin (Ohio) Coll., 1983; postgrad, Reconstructionist Rabbinical Coll., Wyncote, Pa., 1990—. Rabbi Temple B'nai Israel, Burlington, N.J., 1990-91. With Israel Def. Forces, 1986-87. Home: 4426 Fleming St Philadelphia PA 19128 *Teaching our children peace will bring us all closer to God.*

FIELDS, JAMES EDWARD, JR., evangelist; b. Oklahoma City, Sept. 22, 1963; James Edward and Kittie Lee (Hubbard) F. BA in Speech, Northestern State U., 1989. Coll. dir. First Bapt. Ch., Muskogee, Okla., 1982-1986; preacher, nursing home Grandview Bapt. Ch., 1989—. Sitting in my wheelchair faceing the millenium to come, my thoughts on life are the same as the Apostle Paul who said "I pray all who are listening to me today may become what I am, except for these chains". I desire that everyone gets to live the life I had, minus the wheelchair, and that they know the God I know who speaks and says "I am". Phone surveyer, Muskogee Reps., 1984, 86, 88; mem. Rep. Nat. Com., 1986—. Recipent Youth ward, Optimist Club, Muskogee, 1980. Mem. Ostiogenisis Imperfecta Foundation, 1988—. Baptist. Avocations: writer, illustrator. Home: 804 Grandview Blvd Muskogee OK 74403

FIELDS, SAMUEL PRESTON, JR., lay worker; b. Sparta, Mo., Oct. 2, 1918; s. Samuel Preston Sr. and Ada (Mallory) F.; m. Anna Elizabeth Yandell, June 6, 1971. On farm tng., vocat. schooling, Rogersville, Mo., 1946-50. Bible class tchr. Church of Christ, Fordland, Mo., 1948—, treas., 1960-65, sec.-treas., 1983—; trustee Ch. of Christ, Fordland, 1980—; retired farmer, woodworker. Contbr. poems to publs.; inventor no-fall bath aid, 1976. Bd. dirs. Fordland Farmers Exch., 1964-67; v.p. Fordland Cemetery Bd., 1983—. Sgt. 1st c. U.S. Army, 1942-46, ETO. Named Farmer of Yr. Kiwanis Club, Springfield, Mo., 1951. Mem. Nat. Soc. Sons Am. Revolution, Springfield, Ozarks Geneal. Soc., Springfield, Am. Legion, Springfield. Home: Rte 1 Box 169 Fordland MO 65652 *In a day and time when no one seems willing to take responsibility for anything, we need to remember that God always has, and still does, hold men responsible for their actions.*

FIELDS, WILMER CLEMONT, minister; b. Saline, La., Mar. 16, 1922; s. Felder Burkett and Eva Mae (Corbett) F.; B.A., La. Coll., Pineville, 1943; Th.M., So. Bapt. Theol. Sem., Louisville, 1946, Ph.D., 1950; m. Rebecca Elizabeth Hagan, June 22, 1946; children—Randall Hagan, Christy Alderson, Rebecca Elizabeth. Student pastor in La., 1940-43; music and ednl. dir. Carlisle Ave. Bapt. Ch., Louisville, 1943-48; ordained to ministry Bapt. Ch., 1940; pastor in Louisville, 1948-51, Yazoo City, Miss., 1951-56; editor Bapt. Record, jour. for Miss., 1956-59; pub. rels. sec., exec. com. So. Bapt. Conv., 1959-87, also press rep., dir. conv. bull. svc.; editor Bapt. Program mag., 1959-71; dir. Bapt. Press, SBC News Svc.; nat. pres. Religious Pub. Rels. Coun., 1966-67; pres. Associated Ch. Press, 1967-69. Trustee,

Coun. Religion and Internat. Affairs. Mem. Pub. Rels. Soc. Am., Bapt. Pub. Rels. Assn., Bapt. Press Assn., Evang. Press Assn., Pi Kappa Delta, Alpha Chi, Alpha Psi Omega. Author: The Chains Are Strong, 1963; Trumpets in Dixie, 1968. Editor: Religious Public Relations Handbook, 1976. Home: 2223 Woodmont Blvd Nashville TN 37215

FIENEN, DANIEL HENRY, clergyman; b. Evansville, Ind., May 14, 1952; s. Norman C. and Carolyn Marie (Becker) F.; m. Janice Lynn Bellhorn, Aug. 23, 1975; 1 child, Timothy James. AA, Concordia Luth. Jr. Coll., 1972; BA, Concordia Sr. Coll., 1974; MDiv, Concordia Theol. Sem., 1978; MA, Western Ky. U., 1980. Vicar Faith Luth. Ch., Bay City, Mich., 1976-77; pastor Prince of Peace Luth. Ch., Orlonville, Mich., 1979-88, Mt. Calvary Luth. Ch., Holdrege, Nebr., 1988—; del. Luth. Ch.-Mo. Synod Conv., St. Louis, 1983. Chaplain Holdrege Police Chaplain Corps, 1989—; chmn. Phelps County Human Resources Orgn., Holdrege, 1990—. Mem. Phelps County Ministerial Assn. (pres. 1990-91), Rotary. Republican. Office: Mt Calvary Luth Ch 1419 East Ave Dr Holdrege NE 68949 *One of the greatest challenges facing us individually as well as our society is to see individuals holistically, not just as physical creatures, or as consumers, or voters, but as people with bodies, minds, and souls with needs on all levels, and as individuals who are also part of society.*

FIETE, RICHARD WAYNE, minister; b. Chariton, Iowa, May 21, 1938; s. Claude Dean Fiete and Viola Catherine (Watkins) Brechwald; m. Kathryn Tucker, Nov. 25, 1961; children: Stephen C., Tamara L. BA, Buena Vista Coll., 1960; BD, Princeton Theol. Sem., 1966; D Ministry, McCormick Theol. Sem., Chgo., 1985. Ordained to ministry Presbyn. Ch. (U.S.A.), 1966. Pastor Trinity Presbyn. Ch., Scotia, N.Y., 1966-74; assoc. pastor 1st Presbyn. Ch., Albany, N.Y., 1974-78; pastor 1st Presbyn. Ch., Morgantown, W.Va., 1978—; moderator Presbytery of W.Va. Presbyn. Ch. (U.S.A.), 1987-88, chair theology and worship unit, 1989-91. Trustee Davis & Elkins Coll., Elkins, W.Va., 1982-88. Mem. Rotary. Office: 1st Presbyn Ch 456 Spruce St Morgantown WV 26505

FIFE, DAVID JOEL, religious association administrator; b. Elmira, N.Y., Mar. 19, 1950; s. Raymond Oscar and Clarisa Lorena (Landon) F.; m. Jeannine Joette Tice; 1 child, David Joel II. Student, Salvation Army Sch. for Officers Tng., Suffern, N.Y., 1978-80, U. Dayton, 1985. Program dir. Salvation Army, Erie, Pa., 1977-78, emergency services dir., 1978; commdg. officer Salvation Army, Sanford, Maine, 1980-83, Dayton, Ohio, 1983-86, Tarentum, Pa., 1986-89. Pres. Trotwood (Ohio)-Madison Ministerium, 1984-85, Allegheny Valley Assn. Chs., 1988-89; dep. rep. VA, Dayton, 1984-85. Salvation Army Sch. for Officers' Tng. Writer's scholar, Suffern, 1979. Republican. Lodge: Rotary. Avocations: sports cars, motor racing, collecting comic books. Home: 2015 Sunnydale Rd Pittsburgh PA 15243 Office: Salvation Army 505 Washington Ave Carnegie PA 15106

FIFE, DAVID LEE, pastor; b. Pitts., June 21, 1936; s. William Chester and Edith W. (McKean) F.; m. Barbara Judith Bubel, June 29, 1957; children: David James, Douglas Albert, Bruce William, Jenifer Lee. AB, Albright Coll., 1958; MDiv, Eastern Bapt. Theol. Sem., 1961; D of Ministry, Drew Theol. Sch., 1975. Pastor Temple United Meth. Ch., Pottstown, Pa., 1958-61, Cherry Valley United Meth. Cir., Stroudsburg, Pa., 1961-65; assoc. pastor Wesley United Meth. Ch., Bethlehem, Pa., 1965-68; pastor Schuylkill Haven (Pa.) First United Meth. Ch., 1968-73, Cen. United Meth. Ch., Reading, Pa., 1973-80; dist. supt. eastern Pa. Conf. United Meth. Ch., 1980-86; sr. pastor Lehman Meml. United Meth. Ch., Hatboro, Pa., 1986—; bd. dirs. Meth. Home for Children, Phila., Pa. Coun. of Churches. Editor: Journal of the Ea. Pa. Conf. of United Meth., 1971. Pres. Bucks Montgomery County for Human Svcs., Warring Twp., Pa., 1989. Mem. Hatboro Rotary (bd. dirs.).

FIFE, G. PATRIC, pastor; b. Harrisburg, Ill., Apr. 7, 1946; s. George William and Aileen (Chambers) F.; m. Emily Pauline Glass, Nov. 16, 1969; children: Patricia Arlene, Gretchen Eileen, Karol Elayne, Patrick Glass. BA, Belmont Coll., Nashville, 1968; MDiv, Southeastern Bapt. Theol. Sem., Wake Forest, N.C., 1972. Ordained to minsitry So. Bapt. Conv. Pastor Pontoon Bapt. Ch., Granite City, Ill., 1975-81, 1st Bapt. Ch., Elk Grove Village, Ill., 1981-83, Delano (Tenn.) Bapt. Ch., 1983-86, English Creek Bapt. Ch., Newport, 1986-90, Cen. Bapt. Ch., Altavista, Va., 1990—; trustee Harrison-Chilhowee Bapt. Acad., Seymour, Tenn., 1987-90. Office: Cen Bapt Ch PO Box 387 Altavista VA 24517

FIFIELD, RICHARD DELMAGE, lawyer; b. Elizabeth, N.J., Dec. 29, 1946; s. George Henry and Virginia Louise (Bogart) F.; m. Maureen Ann Dooley, June 10, 1978; children—Teresa, Amanda, Meghann. B.A., U. Conn., 1968; J.D., Temple U., 1971. Bar: N.J. 1971. Law sec. Hunterdon County Ct., Flemington, N.J., 1971-72; assoc. Arthur L. Alexander, Washington, N.J., 1972-83; sole practice Washington, N.J., 1983—. Committeeman Warren County Republican Com., 1982—, Washington Twp. Com., 1983—; Mayor Washington Twp., 1985. Mem. Warren County Bar Assn. Office: 142 Belvidere Ave Washington NJ 07882

FIGART, THOMAS ORLANDO, minister, religious educator; b. Altoona, Pa., July 28, 1925; s. James M. and Ellen (Horton) F.; m. Edna M. Lewis, June 9, 1945; children—Kathleen, Elizabeth, Thomas O., Jr., Phyllis. Diploma Phila. Coll. of Bible, 1946; B.S., Johns Hopkins U., 1955; Th.M., Dallas Theol. Sem., 1955; Th.D., Grace Theol. Sem., 1971. Ordained to ministry Bapt. Ch., 1950. Pastor 2d Congl. Ch., Balt., 1955-61; acad. dean, prof. Lancaster Bible Coll., Pa., 1961-72, chmn. Bible div., 1972—, interim dean, pres., 1978-79, chmn. biblical div. Author: Biblical Perspective on Race, 1973; A Legacy of Godliness, 1977; History of Lancaster Bible Coll., 1983. Mem. Ind. Fundamental Chs. of Am. Republican. Office: Lancaster Bible Coll 901 Eden Rd Lancaster PA 17601

FIGGE, CHARLENE ELIZABETH, religious organization administrator; b. Ste. Genevieve, Mo., Apr. 16, 1948; d. William Henry and Frieda Christina (Bauman) F. B in Music Edn., Fontbonne Coll., 1970; MS, U. Dayton, 1979. Joined Sisters of Divine Providence, Roman Cath. Ch., 1965; cert. elem. vocal and instrumental tchr. Tchr. Mary Queen of Universe Sch., St. Louis, 1970-71, Mt. Providence Boys; Sch., St. Louis, 1971-75, 1978-81; tchr. St. John's Sch., Imperial, Mo., 1975-76, St. Pius X Sch., Shreveport, La., 1976-78, Ascension Sch., St. Louis, 1981-85; justice coordinator, dir. devel., asst. provincial Sisters of Divine Providence, St. Louis, 1985—. Mem. Religious Involved in Social Concerns, St. Louis, 1985-91, World Peace Com., St. Louis, 1985-91, Interfaith Com. on Latin Am., St. Louis, 1985-87, Midwest Coalition on Responsible Investment, St. Louis, 1985-91, Nat. Cath. Devel. Conf., 1985-89. Mem. Nat. Soc. Fund Raising Execs. Democrat. Avocations: reading, tennis, chess. Office: Sisters Divine Providence 8351 Florissant Rd Saint Louis MO 63121

FIKE, BARRY DON, minister; b. Tuscaloosa, Ala., Sept. 5, 1955; s. W. Don and Bonnie Lee (Cropper) F.; m. Connie Beverly Fike, Sept. 10, 1977; children: Brandon, Jarrod, Whitney, Beverly. BA, Freed-Hardeman Coll., Henderson, Tenn., 1977. Ordained to ministry, Ch. of Christ. Tchr. Ga. Christian Sch., Valdosta, 1977-80; youth minister Essex Village Ch. of Christ, Charleston, S.C., 1980-82; minsiter W. Hickory (N.C.) Ch. of Christ, 1982-85, N. Park Ch. of Christ, Rockford, Ill., 1985-88, Simi Ch. of Christ, Simi Valley, Calif., 1988—. Author: Old Testament Baptism, 1988, Womens Role in the Church, 1988; contbr. articles to profl. jours. Home: 238 Callahan Ave Simi Valley CA 93065 Office: Simi Ch of Christ 1554 Sinalda Rd Simi Valley CA 93065

FILEVICH, BASIL, bishop; b. Jan. 13, 1918. Ord. priest, Roman Catholic church, 1942. Consecrated bishop Ukrainian Eparchy of Saskatoon, Sask., Can., 1984. Office: Bishop's Residence, 866 Saskatchewan Crescent E, Saskatoon, SK Canada S7N 0L4

FILHIOL, GEORGIA BLANCHARD, lay worker; b. Monroe, La., Nov. 5, 1934; d. Clyde Claude Blanchard and Christine Moore Morgan; m. John Hardy Filhiol, June 21, 1954; children: Mark, Michael, Chaterine, Therese, Paul, Charles. Operating Rm. Tech., N.E. La. U., 1978. Choir dir. St. Joseph Cath. Ch., Monroe, 1960-69; organist Our Lady of Fatima Cath. Ch., Monroe, 1975-87, music dir., 1987—, ch. sec., 1989—; mem. diocesan pastoral coun. Diocese of Shreveport, 1988—. Office: Our Lady of Fatima Cath Ch 3205 Concordia St Monroe LA 71201

FINAU, PATELISIO PUNOU-KI-HIHIFO, bishop. Bishop of Tonga Roman Cath. Ch., Nuku'alofa. Office: Bishop Tonga, POB 1, Nuku'alofa Tonga*

FINCH, KENNETH ALLEN, minister; b. Panama City, Fla., Feb. 17, 1959; s. William Dallas and Jeanette (Sewell) F.; m. Patsy Gale Money, Nov. 10, 1979; children: Dallas-Patrick, Meredith. BA, Southeastern Coll., Lakeland, Fla., 1983. Ordained to ministry Assemblies of God Ch., 1984. Youth pastor Carpenters Home Ch., Lakeland, Fla., 1981-85; exec. asst. First Assembly of God, Panama City, Fla., 1985-91; pastor 1st Assembly of God, Elba, Ala., 1991—. Mem. Nat. Assn. Ch. Adminstrn. Office: First Assemby of God PO Box 416 Elba AL 36323

FINDLAY, ALICE M., religious organization administrator. Dir. overseas div. Am. Bapt. Chs. in U.S.A., Valley Forge, Pa. Office: Am Bapt Chs USA PO Box 851 Valley Forge PA 19482*

FINDLAY, JAMES STEWART, minister; b. Bexhill-on-Sea, Sussex, Eng., Feb. 25, 1934; came to U.S., 1983; s. James Glen and Frances Mary (Brown) F.; m. Gwendoline Mary Meaden, Nov. 30, 1957; children: Christine Mary Findlay Wigg, Stephen James. Diploma in theology, U. London, 1965; BA, Open U., Eng., 1983. Ordained to ministry Anglican Ch., Eng., 1965; cert. in social work, Eng. Min. Bapt. chs. Eng., 1965-73, 77-83; interim min., probation officer Leicester, Eng., 1973-77; sr. min. United Ch. of Christ, Canton, Mass., 1983—. Chmn. Leicester Christian Aid, 1972-83; chaplain Leicester U., 1977-83; chmn., sec. Leicester Action Homeless, 1978-83. Home: 44 Wildewood Dr Canton MA 02021 Office: United Ch of Christ 1541 Washington St Canton MA 02021 *Our lives are gifts from God. We best use this gift when we give it away! Giving ourselves in love, consideration, care to all who need it.*

FINE, GREGORY MONROE, minister; b. Tulsa, Oct. 21, 1957; s. Howard Franklin and Nell (Clinton) F.; m. Melanie Jane Guest, Aug. 15, 1981; children: Matthew Ryan, Emily Michelle, Jessica Faith. BS, Tulsa U., 1979; MDiv, Southwestern Bapt. Theol. Sem., Ft. Worth, 1982; postgrad., Midwestern Bapt. Sem., Kansas City, Mo., 1986—. Youth min. Meml. Bapt. Ch., Grapevine, Tex., 1982-83; min. adminstrn. and youth 1st Bapt. Ch., Carthage, Mo., 1983—; pres. Carthage Ministerial Allinace, 1987; v.p. Christian Youth Alternative Night, Carthage, 1984-85. Mem. Nat. Assn. Ch. Bus. Adminstrn., So. Bapt Ch. Bus. Adminstrn Assn. (cert. adminstr.), Spring River Assn. (chmn. budget com. 1988—), Kiwanis. Republican. Office: 1st Bapt Ch 631 S Garrison Carthage MO 64836

FINEFIELD, SUZANNE SEIBEL, religion educator; b. Streator, Ill., Apr. 16, 1950; d. Lloyd Joseph and Winnifred (Holmes) Seibel; m. Theodore Reed Finefield, Aug. 9, 1970; children: Paige, Gavin. BS in Communication, Ill. State U., 1972. Cert. secondary edn. Dir. Christian edn. Park Presbyn. Ch., Streator, 1978-91; area counselor Synod of Lincoln Trails, 1991—; elder Park Presbyn. Ch., 1979-82. Designer: (learning game) Seek and Find, 1990. bd. dirs. Woodland Community Sch. Unit 5, Streator, 1985—.

FINFROCK, BRUCE DANIEL, religious educator; b. Upland, Calif., Oct. 24, 1950; s. Rex Marvel and Jessie Orliva (Bishop) F.; m. Sandra Jean Book, June 16, 1972; children: Candice Paige, Andrew Paul, Nathan Daniel. BA in Religious Edn., Biola U., 1972; MA in Religious Edn., Talbot Theol. Sem., 1976; postgrad. in Div., North Park Sem. Ordained to ministry Evang. Ch., 1978. Youth pastor First Bapt. Ch., Pomona, Calif., 1971-76, Rolling Hills Covenant Ch., Rolling Hills Estate, Calif., 1976-78; minister Christian edn. Peninsula Covenant Ch., Redwood City, Calif., 1978-83; interim pastor Brethern in Christ Ch., Upland, Calif., 1983-85; minister Christian edn. North Park Covenant Ch., Chgo., 1985—. Mem. Nat. Assn. Dir.'s Christian Edn., Kappa Tau Epsilon. Avocations: snow skiing, bicycling, gardening, travelling, reading. Home: 5905 N St Louis Chicago IL 60659 Office: North Park Covenant Ch 5250 N Christiana Ave Chicago IL 60625

FINK, JOYCE MCGREW, choir director, educator; b. Akron, Ohio, Feb. 24, 1942; d. Lem A. and Lorraine (Smith) McGrew; m. Philip H. Fink, Jan. 23, 1965; children: Lory, Jody, Julie. MusB in Edn., U. Miami, Fla., 1964. Soloist children's choir First Meth. Ch., South Miami, Fla., 1962-64; dir. youth choirs Old Cutler Presbyn. Ch., Miami, 1974—. Home and Office: 14700 SW 82d Ave Miami FL 33158

FINK, PHILIP H., music director; b. York, Pa., Apr. 18, 1935; s. A.R. and Hazel (Holcombe) F.; m. Joyce McGrew; children: Lory, Jody, Julie. MusB in Music Edn., U. Miami, 1957, MusM, 1958, PhD in Music, 1973. Band dir. Coral Gables (Fla.) High Sch., 1958-59; chmn. music Southwest Miami (Fla.) Sr. High Sch., 1959-67; music dir. Handel's Messiah with chorus, orch., soloists, 1960—; chmn. music 1st Meth. Ch., S. Miami, 1962-65, Miami-Dade Community Ch. S., 1968-72; assoc. prof., music coord. Fla. Internat. U., Miami, 1972-74; music dir. Old Cutler Presbyn. Ch., Miami, 1974—; prof., chmn. performing arts Fla. Internat. U., Miami, 1975-84, prof. music, 1985—; condr. country choirs, bands and orchs., 1965—; adjudicator orgns., 1972—; arranger Columbia Pictures Pubs., Miami, 1974-87; clinician ch. music workshops, Miami,. 1980—; cellist assoc. Miami Philharmonic Orch. Author: Think Guitar, Book I., 1974, Book II, 1976; author/arranger: Orchestra String Arrangements, 1974—. With USAR, 1958-64. Named to Columbia Pictures Arrangers Hall of Fame, 1980. Mem. Christian Instrumental Assn., Music Educators Nat. Conf., Am. String Tchr. Assn. (past state pres.), Nat. Sch. Orch. Assn. (past div. chmn.), Fla. Orch. Assn. (past state pres.). Republican. Presbyn. Home: 14700 SW 82d Ave Miami FL 33158 Office: Old Cutler Presbyn Ch 14401 Old Cutler Rd Miami FL 33158

FINKBEINER, OTTO KARL, church official; b. Phila., Jan. 6, 1923; s. Otto and Helen (Betcher) F.; m. Eileen Ramsay, June 10, 1944; children: Eric, Judith L., Janet L.; m. Joyce Barnes, Apr. 25, 1982. B.S., Temple U., 1947. With Westminster Press, 1947-52; with dept. adminstrn. Gen. Assembly United Presbyn. Ch. in U.S.A., 1953, mgr., 1954-67, asst. stated clk., 1967-74, asso. stated clk., treas., 1974—. Served as pilot USAAF, World War II. Mem. Adminstrv. Mgmt. Soc., Assn. Statisticians Am. Religious Bodies (pres. 1960-62, sec.-treas. 1980—), Religious Conv. Mgrs. Assn. (pres. 1980-83), Am. Soc. Assn. Execs. Republican. Home: 151 Prospect Ave Haworth NJ 07641 Office: 475 Riverside Dr Rm 1201 New York NY 10115

FINKELSTEIN, MOZES, head of religious order. Pres. Religious Union of Mosaic Faith in Poland, Warsaw. Office: Religious Union Mosaic Faith, ul Twarda 6, 00-104 Warsaw Poland*

FINKENBINDER, PAUL EDWIN, minister; b. Santurce, P.R., Sept. 24, 1921; s. Frank O. and Aura (Argetsinger) F.; m. Malinda Swartzentruber, Jan. 25, 1942; children: Paul, Gene, Sharon Finkenbinder Brown, Joan Findenbinder DeRose, Ellin Finkenbinder Sinsley. Diploma, Zion Bible Inst., East Providence, R.I., 1941; postgrad., Cen. Bible Coll., Springfield, Mo., 1941-42; diploma (hon.), Orantes Inst., El Salvador, 1971. Ordained to ministry Assemblies of God, 1948. Pastor Spanish Mission, Raton, N.Mex., 1942-43; missionary El Salvador, 1943-64; founder, pres. Hermano Pablo Ministries, Costa Mesa, Calif., 1964—; prin. syndicated radio programs worldwide. Recipient Disting. Svc. Honor citation Nat. Religious Broadcasters, 1970, Oscar award for Best Bible Story Nat. Evang. Film Found., 1971, cert. So. Calif. Coll., 1971, Angel award Religion in Media, 1980; program named Hispanic Program of Yr., Nat. Religious Broadcasters, 1983. Home: 2975 Mindanao Dr Costa Mesa CA 92626 Office: 2080 Placentia Ave Costa Mesa CA 92627 also: PO Box 100 Costa Mesa CA 92628

FINKES, BARBARA FAITH, lay worker, journalist, travel agent; b. Cin., Oct. 31, 1956; d. James Ancil and Barbara Regina (Zimmerman) Sutton; m. Milton Carl Finkes, July 2, 1977; children: Joshua Carl, Carly Noelle, Caleb Uriah. Student, U. Cin., 1975-76, TriState Travel, 1991. Tchr. Sunday sch. Faith Bapt. Ch., Richmond, Ind., 1972-74; newsletter editor Port Union Bible Chapel, Hamilton, Ohio, 1981-83, 84—, tchr. Sunday sch., 1982-89, youth leader, 1982—; reporter, photographer West Chester Press/Suburban Press, West Chester, Ohio, 1986—; travel cons. Theshipshop, Loveland, Ohio, 1988—, Apache Travel, 1991—. Mem. publicity com. West Chester Community Arts/Crafts Soc., 1986-91, West Chester YMCA, 1988-89; mem. cultural enrichment com. Freedom Elem. Sch. PTA, West Chester, 1991. Office: Port Union Bible Chapel 4756 Port Union Rd Hamilton OH 45011

FINLAY, TERENCE EDWARD, bishop; s. Terence John and Sarah (McBryan) F.; m. Alice-Jean Cracknell, 1962; 2 daus. BA, U. We. Toronto; BTh, Huron Coll., London, Ont.; MA, U. Cambridge, Eng.; DD (jure dignitatis), Huron Coll., 1987. Ordained deacon Anglican Ch., 1961, priest, 1962. Dean of residence Renison Coll., Waterloo, Can.; incumbent All Saints, Waterloo, 1964-66, St. Aidan's, London, Can., 1966-68; rector St. John the Evangelist, London, 1968-78; archdeacon of Brant, 1978-82; incumbent Grace Ch., Brantford, Can., 1978-82, St. Clement's, Eglinton, Toronto, Can., 1982-86; suffragan bishop Diocese of Toronto, 1986, coadjutor bishop, 1987; bishop Diocese of Toronto, Toronto, 1989—. Avocations: music, skiing, travel. Office: Diocese of Toronto, 135 Adelaide St E, Toronto, ON Canada M5C 1L8

FINLEY, ALLEN BROWN, religious organization administrator; b. Albermarle, Va., Nov. 11, 1929; s. William Walter and Melissa (Hoover) F.; m. Ruth Ann Goodwin, Aug. 14, 1953; children—Ruth Naomi, Catherine Ann, Gayla Melissa. B.A., Bob Jones U., Greenville, S.C., 1952; M.A., Calif. Grad. Sch. Theology, 1981. Ordained to ministry Evangelical Ch. Alliance, 1952; missionary Gospel Fellowship Assn., 1952-53; Phila. office dir. Internat. Students, Inc., 1953-54; West Coast dir. Internat. Students, Inc., 1954-60; gen. dir. Christian Nats. Evangelism Commn., San Jose, Calif., 1960-76, internat. pres., 1976—; editor World Report, 1960-72; dir. Fellowship Bible Inst. Commn., 1969—, Evang. Ch. Alliance, 1958—; del. World Congress Evangelism, Berlin, 1966; del. Lausanne Com. for World Evangelization, 1974, Thailand, 1980, Internat. Conf. Itinerant Evangelists, Amsterdam, 1983; elder Berkeley First Presbyn. Ch., 1957-60, Westminster Presbyn. Ch., San Jose, Calif., 1968—; pastor Setzer's Gap Presbyn. Ch., Lenoir, N.C., 1950-52, Beattie Meml. Presbyn. Ch., Lenoir, 1950-52; mem. internat. bd. dirs. CNEC, 1976—; cons. U.S. Ctr. for World Mission, Pasadena, Calif., 1978—; bd. dirs. CNEC Council, Sydney, Australia, Green Pastures, Inc., Mountain View, Calif., 1983—; mem. Council Advs. Presbyns. United for Mission Advance, No. Calif.; bd. dirs. ENI Mission, Sinoe, Liberia, 1972-80, Evang. Ch. Alliance, Ill., 1955—; mem. N.Am. bd. reference Nairobi Evang. Grad. Sch. Theology; mem. bd. reference Chinese for Christ Theol. Sem. Club: Commonwealth. Author: Assisting Third World Church Ministries, Vol. II, No. 3, 1980; Mission: A World-Family Affair, 1981; Is Supporting Nationals Biblical?, 1982; The Family Tie, 1983; editor CNEC Communique, 1960-72. Home: 1290 S Baywood Ave San Jose CA 95128 Office: 1470 N 4th St San Jose CA 95115

FINLEY, DOYLE CIFFORD, minister; b. Easley, S.C., June 28, 1936; s. Devoe S. and Myrtie D. (Tumblin) F.; m. Cleo Turner, Oct. 24, 1958; children: Dennis, Donna. A.Min., Fruitland Bible Inst., Hendersonville, N.C., 1972; BMin, Covington Sem., Rossville, Ga., 1988. Ordained to ministry So. Bapt. Conv., 1972. Pastor Golden Creek Bapt. Ch., Norris, S.C., 1972-84, REfuge Bapt. Ch., Pendleton, S.C., 1984-86, Calvary Bapt. Ch., Anderson, S.C., 1986, New Life Bapt. Ch., Pickens, S.C., 1989—; vice moderator Piedmont Bapt. Assn., Easley, 1980; asst. moderator Pickens Bat. Camp Mtg., 1978. With U.S. Army, 1955-58. Home: 4 Pinewood Dr Liberty SC 29657 Office: New Life Bapt Ch Hillcrest Dr Pickens SC 29671 *Life is God's created gift to man, and without Him as personal Savior it is simply void.*

FINLEY, JAMES EDWARD, minister; b. Mobile, Ala., Dec. 20, 1933; s. James Thomas and Printella Elizabeth (Stewart) F.; m. Helen Elizabeth McCoy, June 10, 1953; children: Monica, Mark, James A., Sheila. DD, Va. Sem., 1976. Ordained to ministry Pentecostal Holiness Ch. Inc., 1964. Pastor Mt. Zion Apostolic Overcoming Holy Ch. of God, Dayton, Ohio, 1964, Phillips Temple Apostolic Overcoming Holy Ch. of God, Mobile, 1973-89; bishop Apostolic Assemblies Fellowship Inc., Mobile, 1989—; bd. dirs. Commonwealth Nat. Bank, Mobile. Active Community Devel. Project Mobile County, Cystic Fibrosis Found., Mobile County Alcoholics Prevention Program. Mem. NAACP, Interracial Ministerial Alliance, Interdenominational Ministerial Alliance, Urban League Am. Office: Apostolic Assemblies Fellowship Inc PO Box 40115 Mobile AL 36640-0115 *Life is a period between two eternities in which we humans have the God-given choice of accepting the responsibility of being regenerated by the blood of Jesus Christ or being eternally lost in hell.*

FINLEY, JOHN MILLER, minister; b. St. Louis, Oct. 24, 1953; s. Miller B. and June (Malone) F.; m. Norma Kaye Vaughan, May 15, 1976; children: Nathan Vaughan, Matthew Miller, Rachel Kimble. BA, Vanderbilt U., 1976; MDiv, So. Bapt. Theol. Sem., 1979, PhD, 1984. Ordained to ministry So. Bapt. Conv., 1978. Pastor Lick Branch Bapt. Ch., Deputy, Ind., 1979-82, Scott Blvd. Bapt. Ch., Decatur, Ga., 1983—; prof. Simmons U., Louisville, 1982-83; tchr. North Ga. Ctr. of New Orleans Bapt. Theol. Sem., 1986—; bd. dirs. Christian Coun. of Met. Atlanta, 1987; sec.-treas. Ga. Bapt. Pastors' Conf., 1987-88. Author: His Blessings Upon Them, 1981. Mem. steering com. Community Appeal to Address Homelessness, Atlanta, 1990-91. Recipient scholarships Vanderbilt U., 1972-76, So. Bapt. Theol. Sem., 1976-77. Mem. Ga. Bapt. Hist. Soc. (exec. com. 1984—, v.p. 1986-88, pres. 1988-90), Atlanta Bapt. Assn. (moderator 1986-89), Ga. Bapt. Hist. Commn., So. Bapt. Hist. Soc. Office: Scott Blvd Bapt Ch 2532 N Decatur Rd Decatur GA 30033

FINLEY, ROBERT VAN EATON, minister; b. Charlottesville, Va., May 2, 1922; s. William Walter and Melissa (Hoover) F.; BA, U. Va., 1944; postgrad. U. Chgo. Div. Sch., 1946-47; LittD, Houghton Coll., 1952; m. Ethel Drummond, Dec. 23, 1949; children: Deborah Ann, Ruth Ellen. Ordained to ministry Bapt. Ch., 1957. Evangelist, Youth for Christ Internat., Chgo. and Inter-Varsity Christian Fellowship, Chgo., 1945-46, overseas, 1948-51; pastor Evang. Free Ch., Richmond, Calif., 1951-52; minister to fgn. students 10th Presbyn. Ch., Phila., 1952-55; pastor Temple Bapt. Ch., Washington, 1965-66; founder, gen. dir. Christian Aid Mission, Charlottesville, Va., 1953-70, chmn., pres., 1970—; founder, gen. dir. Overseas Students Mission, Ft. Erie, Ont., Can., 1954-68, pres., 1969-85; founder, pres. Christian Aid Mission Can., 1985-88, chmn. bd. dirs., 1989—; pres. Bharat Evang. Fellowship, Washington, 1973-87; chmn. bd. dirs. Internat. Fellowship Indigenous Missions, Harrisburg, Pa., 1988—; bd. dirs. Timber Ridge Ministries, Winchester, Va.; editor Conquest for Christ, 1954-74, Christian Mission mag., 1974—; founder, pres. Internat. Students, Inc., Washington, 1952-67, chmn., 1968-70. Mem. Omicron Delta Kappa. Republican. Office: Christian Aid Mission 3045 Ivy Rd Charlottesville VA 22901 also: Christian Aid Mission, 201 Stanton St, Fort Erie, ON Canada L2A 3N8 *To indulge myself, beyond actual need, with the benefits of material wealth leaves me the poorer. But when my surplus resources are used to uplift those who lack opportunity, I am enriched.*

FINN, DANIEL RUSH, economics and theology educator, former dean; b. Rochester, N.Y., Apr. 30, 1947; s. George Elwood and Ruth Mary (Schwenzer) F.; m. Nita Jo Rush, June 17, 1978; children: Jacob, Stephanie. BS, St. John Fisher Coll., 1968; MA, U. Chgo., 1975, PhD, 1977. Asst. prof. econs. and theol. ethics St. John's U., Collegeville, Minn., 1977-84, assoc prof., 1984-91; prof., 1991—; prof. St. John's U., Collegeville, Minn., 1991—, dean sch. of theology, 1984-89, William E. and Virginia Clemens chair econ. and liberal arts, 1989—, prof. econ. and theol. ethics, 1991; cons. on programs joining econs. and ethics, 1985—. Author: (with others) Toward Christian Economic Ethic, 1980. Mem. Assn. for Social Econs. (prs. 1986), Am. Econs. Assn., Soc. Christian Ethics (bd. dirs. 1988-92), Midwest Assn. Theol. Schs. (pres. 1985-87), Minn. Consortium of Theol. Schs. (v.p. 1987-89), Am. Acad. Religion, History of Econs. Soc., Minn. Econ. Assn. Avocations: woodworking, bridge, gardening. Office: St Johns U Dept Econs Collegeville MN 56321

FINN, JUDITH ANN FIEDLER, law educator; b. Madison, Wis., Apr. 22, 1940; d. Thomas Cameron and Naomi (Mildred) Fiedler; m. Warren Eugene Finn, Aug. 24, 1963; children: Kirstin Joanna, Arikka Kathryn. BA, U. Wis., 1962, MA in English, 1964; PhD, Tex. A & M U., 1974; MA in Urban Studies, JD, U. Tulsa, 1980. Bar: Okla. 1981, U.S. Dist. Ct. (no. dist.) Okla. 1982, U.S. Ct. Appeals (10th cir. 1982), U.S. Dist. Ct. (no. dist.) 1985. Chmn. English dept. Madison (Wis.) Area Tech. Coll., 1965-68; lectr. Tex. A & M U., College Station, 1968-75; sr. law clk. U.S. Dist. Ct., Tulsa, Okla.,

1980-85; asst. U. Tulsa, 1985-86, assoc. prof. law, 1986. Contbr. articles to profl. jours. Mem. Commn. for a New Luth. Ch., 1982-87, Commn. for Ch. and Soc., Evang. Luth. Ch. Am., 1987-91; bd. dirs. Luth. Acad., Madison, 1984-91; v.p. Ark.-Okla. synod Evang. Luth. Ch. Am., Tulsa, 1987— ; mem., chmn. environ. adv. coun., Tulsa City-County Health Dept. Mem. ABA, Okla. Bar Assn., Tulsa County Bar Assn., Tulsa Women Lawyer's Assn., Scribes. Office: 2241 E Skelly Dr Tulsa OK 74105

FINN, THOMAS MACY, religion educator; b. N.Y.C., Mar. 18, 1927; s. James Anthony and Kathleen (Macy) F.; m. Marielena Vidrio, Feb. 24, 1968; 1 child, Susannah. Ab, St. Paul's Coll., 1956, MA, 1958; Lic. in Theology, Cath. U., 1960, ThD, 1965. Asst. prof. St. Paul's Coll., Washington, 1965-67, Syracuse (N.Y.) U., 1967-69; sr. editor G.K. Hall and Co., Boston, 1969-70, editor-in-chief, 1970-73; assoc. prof. Coll. William and Mary, Williamsburg, Va., 1973-80, prof., 1980—, dean undergrad. studies, 1984-88, chmn. dept. religion, 1973-80, 88—; participant NEH seminars Yale U., 1977, Post Bibl. Inst. Jewish Theol. Sem., N.Y., 1979, Yeshiva U., 1980, Am. Acad., Rome, 1991. Author: The Liturgy of Baptism in John Chrysostom, 1967, Early Christian Baptism and the Catechumenate, 2 vols., 1991. Research fellow NEH, 1978, Coll. William and Mary, 1980, 90-91. Mem. Soc. for Values in Higher Edn., N.Am. Patristics Soc. (sec., treas. 1985-88), Am. Acad. Religion, Soc. Bibl. Lit., Cath. Bibl. Assn., Internat. Patristic Soc. Democrat. Club: Sporting (McLean, Va.). Avocation: sailing. Office: Coll William and Mary Dept of Religion Williamsburg VA 23185-8795

FINUCAN, J(OHN) THOMAS, priest, religious institution administrator; b. Eau Claire, Wis., Feb. 23, 1930; s. Edwin T. and Isabelle Genevieve (McDonald) F. A.B. cum laude, Loras Coll., Dubuque, Iowa, 1952; S.T.B., N.Am. Coll., Rome, 1954, S.T.L., 1956; M.S., U. Wis., 1964, Ph.D. in Ednl. Adminstrn., 1970. Ordained priest Roman Catholic Ch., 1955; asst. pastor St. Mary's Ch., Richland Center, Wis., 1956-58; tchr. Assumption High Sch., Wisconsin Rapids, Wis., 1958-60; prin. Assumption High Sch., 1965-70; tchr., asst. prin., guidance dir. Newman High Sch., Wausau, Wis., 1960-62; asst. to pastor St. Vincent de Paul Parish, Wisconsin Rapids, 1965-70; pres. Viterbo Coll., La Crosse, Wis., 1970-80; pastor, adminstr. St. Stanislaus Parish, Stevens Point, Wis., 1981-86; dir. div. Christian Formation and Edn. Archdiocese of St. Paul and Mpls., 1986-89; coordinator Regional Sem. Project, Milw., 1980-81; chmn. Wis. Arts Bd., Madison, 1981-85; vis. prof. grad. sch. edn. Loras Coll., Dubuque, Iowa, 1969, 70, St. Mary's Coll., Winona, Minn., Lakeland Coll., Sheboygan, Wis., 1980; exec. dir. capital programs Coll. St. Thomas, St. Paul, 1989—; mem. presbyteral council, consultor to bishop, dean Portage County, Diocese of La Crosse; vis. lectr., faculty mem., cons., evaluator colls. and high schs., speaker locally and nationally to ednl., community and religious groups. Contbr. articles to publs. including Wis. Adminstr. 3 Viterbo Coll., 1970-80, pres. bd. 1970— , St. Mary's Coll., Winona, Minn., Lakeland Coll., Sheboygan, Wis. 1980-86, Bethany-St. Joseph Home, 1972-74; mem. Acad., U. Wis.-Stevens Point; pres. Stevens Point Area Community Found., 1985-86; mem. com. on jud. ethics Wis. Supreme Ct., 1985-86; mem. com. on crisis pregnancy options Wis. Legislature, 1985; trustee Coll. of St. Catherine, St. Pau, 1987-89, Mt. St. Mary Coll., Emmitsburg, Md., 1991—; bd. dirs. St. Mary's Coll., 1980-90. Recipient Mother Seton award Lourdes Acad., Oshkosh, 1977; pres.'s award for community service La Crosse C. of C., 1979. Mem. Nat. Assn. Ind. Colls. and Univs., Nat. Cath. Edn. Assn., Council for Advancement of Small Colls. (dir. 1976-79), Wis. Assn. Ind. Colls. and Univs. (pres. 1977-79), Wis. Found. Ind. Colls., Wis. Assn. Higher Edn. (pres. 1974-78), Blue Key (hon.), Phi Delta Kappa. Lodges: K.C. Rotary. Office: St Thomas U Mail No 4097 2115 Summit Ave Saint Paul MN 55105

FIORE, JAMES PATRICK, clergyman; b. Scranton, Pa., Mar. 17, 1953; s. John Francis and Mary Marjorie (Doyle) F.; m. Susan Rybasack, May 17, 1975; childen: Bethany, Adam. BS, Temple U., 1975; diploma, Berean Coll., 1976-80; M Ministry, Internat. Sem., Orlando, Fla., 1983, PhD, 1990. Ordained to ministry Assemblies of God Ch., 1982. Adminstr. Livingston (N.J.) A/G, 1976-79; sr. minister Christian Life Ctr., West Milford, N.J., 1979—; bd. mem. Internat. Worship Symposium, Pasadena, Calif., 1987—. Author: Church Administration Vol. I, II, III, IV, 1988. Com. mem. Youth and Family Com., West Milford, N.J., 1986-89; exec. bd. mem. West Milford GAL, 1985—; mem. West Milford Little League, 1988-91, West Milford Girls Basketball League, 1985-91. Home: 19 Weedon Dr West Milford NJ 07480 Office: Christian Life Ctr 184 Marshall Hill Rd West Milford NJ 07480

FIORENZA, FRANCIS P., religion educator; b. Bklyn., Feb. 27, 1941; married, 1967; 1 child. AB, St. Mary's U., 1961, STB, 1963; ThD, U. Münster, Fed. Republic of Germany, 1972. Asst. prof. theology U. Notre Dame, Ind., 1971-77, Villanova (Pa.) U., 1977-79; assoc. prof. theology Cath. U. Am., Washington, 1979-87; now Charles Chauncey Stillman prof. Roman Cath. theol. studies Harvard U., Cambridge, Mass.; vis. scholar Union Theol. Sem., N.Y.C., 1974-75. Author: Critical Social Theory and Christology, 1975, Political Theology as Foundational Theology, 1977, Religion und Politik, Christliche Glaube, 1982; translator: Schleiermacher: Open Letters on the Glaubenslehre, 1981, Foundational Theology: Jesus and Church, 1984; editor: Systematic Theology, Roman Catholic Perspectives, 2 vols., 1991; co-editor: (with Don Browning) Habermas, Modernity and Public Theology, 1991; contbr. articles to religious jours. Fellow Div., U. Chgo., 1978-79; rsch. fellow Am. Assn. Theol. Schs., 1982-83, 89. Mem. Am. Acad. Religion, Cath. Theol. Soc. Am. (pres. 1987), Soc. Values Higher Edn., Coll. Theol. Soc., Hegel Soc. Office: Harvard U Dept Roman Cath Theology Cambridge MA 02138

FIORENZA, JOSEPH A., bishop; b. Beaumont, Tex., Jan. 25, 1931. Student, St. Mary's Sem., LaPorte, Tex. Ordained priest Roman Catholic Ch., 1954, consecrated bishop, 1979. Bishop Diocese of San Angelo, Tex., 1979-85, Diocese of Galveston-Houston, Tex., 1985—. Office: Roman Cath Ch 1700 San Jacinto Houston TX 77002

FIRESTONE, REUVEN, rabbi, educator, language and literature educator; b. Santa Rosa, Calif., Jan. 27, 1952; s. George Maurice Firestone and Betty Ann (Weiskopf) Gruberg; m. Ruth Harriet Sohn, May 21, 1983; children: Rachel, Noam. BA, Antioch Coll., Yellow Springs, Ohio, 1974; MA, Hebrew Union Coll., 1980; PhD, NYU, 1988. Ordained rabbi, 1982. Dir. coll. edn. dept. Union Am. Hebrew Congregations, N.Y.C., 1982-87; rabbi Congregation B'nai Torah, Sudbury, Mass., 1988—; asst. prof. Hebrew and Semitic lits. and langs. Boston U., 1987—; mem. Cath.-Jewish-Muslim trialogue Office Ecumenical Affairs of Cath. Archdiocese of Boston, 1989—. Author: Journeys in Holy Lands: The Evolution of the Abraham-Ishmael Legends in Islamic Exegesis, 1990; contbr. articles to religious jours. Mem. Am. Acad. Religion, Am. Oriental Soc., Cen. Conf. Am. Rabbis, Assn. for Jewish Studies, Soc. for Judeo-Arabic Studies, Middle East Studies Assn., NCCJ (exec. com. commn. of Muslims, Jews and Christians 1983-87). Office: Boston U 718 Commonwealth Ave Boston MA 02215

FISCHER, ALAN DEAN, minister; b. Oneonta, N.Y., June 19, 1947; s. Robert Lawrence and Ruth (Dean) F.; m. Carolee Nutt, Sept. 24, 1977; children: Jason, Aaron, Jordan. BBA, Lynchburg Coll., 1969; cert. dist. edn., Va. Poly. Inst. and State U., Blackburg, Va., 1973. Lic. into ministry Immanuel Bible Ch., 1982. Dir. devel. Riverdale (Md.) Bapt. Ch., 1976-78; exec. dir. Sacandaga Bible Conf., Broadalbin, N.Y., 1978-82; pastor of adminstrn. Immanuel Bible Ch., Springfield, Va., 1982—, elder, 1984—. Mem. bd. dirs. Covenant Village, Pa., 1990—. Mem. Christian Mgrs. Assn., Nat. Assn. Ch. Bus. Adminstrs. (v.p. 1985-86). Home: 13520 Carriage Ford Rd Nokesville VA 22123 Office: Immanuel Bible Ch 5211 Backlick Rd Springfield VA 22151-3604

FISCHER, DEBORAH ELENE, minister, industrial engineer; b. Tampa, Fla., June 7, 1958; d. William Joseph and Vivian Elene (Weinberg) H.; m. James Henry Fischer, Jan. 1, 1988. B in Insdl. Engring., Ga. Inst. Tech., 1981; MDiv, Luth. Sch. Theology, 1988. Ordained to ministry Evang. Luth. Ch. in Am., 1988; registered profl. engr., Fla. Vicar St. Andrew's Luth. Ch., Dover, Del., 1986-87; pastor St. Luke Evang. Luth. Ch., 1988—; youth worker, evangelist Redeemer Luth. Ch., St. Petersburg, Fla., 1985; pastor Bethlehem Evang. Luth. Ch., Lake City, Fla., 1988—; cons. engr. so. states, 1981—. Mem. Clericus, Evang. Luth. Ch. in Am. (sec. Pinelands conf., Fal. 1989—), Columbia County Ministerial Alliance (chair chaplaincy com. 1990—), Assn. for Clin. Pastoral Edn., Am. Inst. for Indls. Engrs. Home: PO Box 2916 Lake City FL 32056 Office: St Luke Evang Luth Ch 925 E Duval St Lake City FL 32055

FISCHER, JAMES ADRIAN, clergyman; b. St. Louis, Oct. 15, 1916; s. John and Agnes (Henke) F. A.B., St. Mary's Sem., Perryville, Mo., 1941; S.T.L., Cath. U. Am., 1949; S.S.L., Pontifical Bib. Inst., Rome, Italy, 1951; LL.D. (hon.), Niagara U., 1968. Joined Congregation of Mission, 1936; ordained priest Roman Cath. Ch., 1943; prof. sacred scripture St. John's Sem., San Antonio, 1943-45; prof. sacred scripture St. Mary's Sem., Houston, 1951-56, Perryville, 1958-62; provincial Western province Vincentian Fathers, 1962-71, De Andreis Sem., Lemont, Ill., 1971-81; pres. Kenrick Sem., St. Louis, 1981-86, St. Thomas Sem., Denver, 1986—. Author: The Psalms, 1974, God Created Woman, 1979, How to Read the Bible, 1981, Priests, 1987. Chmn. bd. trustees De Paul U., Chgo., 1962-71. Mem. Cath. Bibl. Assn. (pres. 1976-77). Address: St Thomas Sem 1300 S Steele St Denver CO 80210

FISCHER, JOHN D., ecumenical agency administrator. Exec. dir. Wis. Conf. Chs., Madison. Office: Wis Conf Chs 1955 W Broadway Ste 104 Madison WI 53713*

FISCHER, JOHN HANS, broadcasting engineer; b. St. Louis, Dec. 6, 1928; s. Hans and Anna Fischer; m. Wilma Wemhaner; children: Susan, Nancy, Mary. BS, Washington U., St. Louis, 1951. Engr. Sta. KFUO, St. Louis, 1959—. Mem. Soc. Broadcast Engrs. Republican. Lutheran. Office: Sta KFUO Radio 85 Founders Ln Saint Louis MO 63105 *It is important to work towards the future but not at he expense of today. Live each day in a positive way. Take time for work and play. Take time to thank the Lord and ask His care and guidance.*

FISCHER, MARILYN CAROL, nun; b. Quincy, Ill., May 23, 1936; d. Frank Carl and Marie Elizabeth (Mennel) F. BS in Nursing, U. Dayton, 1964; MA in Edn., Xavier U., Cin., 1974. Joined Franciscan Sisters of Poor, Roman Cath. Ch., 1958. Dir. formation Sisters of Poor, Cin., 1967-77; mem. leadership bd. Sisters of Poor, Bklyn., 1977-80; maj. superior Sisters of Poor, 1980-88; chmn. Franciscan Sisters of Poor Health System Inc., Bklyn., 1988. Office: Franciscan Sisters of the Poor Found 186 Joralemon St Brooklyn Heights NY 11201

FISCHER, MARK FREDERICK, theology educator; b. Bethesda, Md., May 28, 1951; s. Carl Andrew Fischer and Gloria (Scatena) Schmeder; m. Bridget Mary Lynch, Aug. 19, 1978; children: Carl, David, Paul. BA, U. Calif., Berkeley, 1973; MA, Grad. Theol. Union, 1977, PhD, 1984. Dir. office of the diocesan pastoral coun. Roman Cath. Diocese of Oakland, Calif., 1984-90; asst. prof. theology St. John's Sem., L.A., 1990—. Author: (pamphlet) Parish Pastoral Councils, 1990; reviewer Cath. Bibl. Quar., 1984—; contbr. articles to profl. jours. Fellow Thomas More and Jacques Maritain Inst., Berkeley, 1979-81. Mem. Cath. Theol. Soc. Am. (moderator ecclesiology seminar 1989—), Parish and Diocesan Coun. Network (chmn. 1988-89), Phi Beta Kappa. Democrat. Roman Catholic. Home: 1779 Ridgewood Dr Camarillo CA 93012-4216 Office: St John's Sem 5012 Seminary Rd Camarillo CA 93012-2598

FISCHER, RALPH FREDERICK, minister; b. Auburn, Mich., Sept. 1, 1924; s. Frederick Otto and Adelia Christina (Riess) F.; m. Erna Delores Lehenbauer, July 29, 1951; children: Kristi Marie, Timothy Ralph, Thomas Frederick. BA, Concordia Sem., 1947, BDiv, 1949, MDiv, 1950, MST, 1951, postgrad. Pastor St. Paul Luth. Ch., Mountain View, Calif., 1951-67, Trinity Luth. Ch., Reese, Mich., 1967-72, St. Matthew Luth. Ch., Westland, Mich., 1972—; chaplain coll. bd. U. Calif., Santa Cruz, 1968-72. Author: Evangelism Command, 1972. Vice pres. Lions, Reese, 1966-67. Mem. Calif.-Nev. Dist. LC-MS (cir. counselor Mountain View chpt. 1958-67, cir. counselor Reese chpt. 1968-72, cir. counselor Dearborn, Mich. chpt. 1976-84). Home: 7638 Flamingo Westland MI 48185

FISCUS, JACK, III, minister; b. Nashville, Apr. 13, 1967; s. Jack Jr. and Betty Geneva (Ellington) F.; m. Kasey Amacker Hendrix, May 26, 1990. BS in Mgmt. Info. Systems, La. Coll., 1989. Lic. to ministry So. Bapt. Conv., 1985, ordained, 1991. Min. to youth, activities Simpson (La.) Bapt. Ch., 1986-88; min. to students, young singles Pineville (La.) Park Bapt. Ch., 1988-91; exec. com. super summer La. Bapt. Conv., Alexandria, 1987—, exec. com. evangelism conf., 1987—, chaplain-all state, 1988—, conf. workshop leader, 1989—; asst. mgr. Itza Pizza La. Coll., 1984-85; lab instr. Bus. Computer Lab. La. Coll. Home: 4036 Sandage Fort Worth TX 76110 *Youth today are pressured by so many wordly things, because Satan knows what God can do in the lives of our youth if they give their lives to Him.*

FISH, JOHN FREDERICK, minister; b. Vinton, Iowa, June 15, 1925; s. Oscar O. and Naomi (Smouse) F.; m. Gail Marie Simmons, May 27, 1949 (dec.); children: Melody, David, Jacqueline; m. Martha Jean Gamon, Aug. 10, 1958. BTh, Dakota Bible Coll., Huron, S.D., 1953. Ordained to ministry Chs. of Christ, 1951. Min. Ch. of Christ, Highmore, S.D., 1949-53; min. Christian Ch., Burlington Junction, Mo., 1953-54, Grinnell, Iowa, 1954-59; min. 1st Christian Ch., Joliet, Ill., 1959-65, 67-71, Vandalia, Mo., 1965-67, Jacksonville, Ill., 1971-75; min. Town and Country Christian Ch., Tulsa, 1975-79, Eastview Christian Ch., Cedar Rapids, Iowa, 1979-87, Morningside Ch. of Christ, Sioux City, Iowa, 1987—; evangelist Christian Evangelistic Mission, Des Moines, 1979-87, dir., 1984—; dir. various youth camps. Staff sgt. U.S. Army, 1945-47. Home: 1702 S Lemon Sioux City IA 51106 Office: Morningside Ch of Christ 5015 Garretson Ave Sioux City IA 51106

FISH, THOMAS EDWARD, JR., clergyman; b. Greenwood, S.C., Dec. 4, 1951; s. Thomas Edward and Martha Jo (Goss) F.; m. Gerri Sue Smith, Apr. 17, 1956; children: Emily Suzanne, Gerren Thomas. BS, Lander Coll., 1980; MRE, New Orleans Bapt. Sem., 1986. Textile mgr. Milliken, Greenville, S.C., 1980-81; parts mgr. CMS Garage, Anderson, S.C., 1982-84; minister music and youth First Bapt. Ch., Folsom, La., 1984-86; minister edn. and youth First Bapt. Ch., Baxley, Ga., 1987—; music dir. Consolation Bapt. Assn., Baxley, 1987-88. Counselor Jefferson Parish Juvenile Ct., Marrero, La., 1986; vis. counselor Ga. Bapt. Children's Home, Baxley, 1987-89. Named Friend of the Ct., Jefferson Parish Ct., 1986. Mem. Ga. Bapt. Youth Ministers, Ga. Bapt. Religious Educators, Kiwanis, Masons, Shriners. Avocations: golf, walking, reading, playing guitar, family time. Home: PO Box 537 Baxley GA 31513 Office: First Bapt Ch 201 N Main St Baxley GA 31513

FISHBEIN, IRWIN HARVEY, rabbi, pastoral psychotherapist; b. Providence, Aug. 4, 1931; s. Ralph Harry and Sadie Mollie (Rich) F.; m. Barbara Tcath, June 15, 1952; children: Jonathan, Linda, David, Robert. BA, Brown U., 1952; B. Hebrew Letters, Hebrew Union Coll., 1954, M. Hebrew Letters, 1956; DMin, Andover Newton Theol. Sch., 1978. Ordained rabbi, 1956; cert. in marriage and family therapy, pastoral psychotherapy, group therapy; lic. marriage therapist, N.J. Rabbi Temple Israel of No. Westchester, Croton-on-Hudson, N.Y., 1958-60, Temple Israel, Nyack, N.Y., 1960-61; asst. rabbi Congregation Rodph Shalom, Phila., 1961-64; instr. Jewish history Gratz Coll., Phila., 1961-64; rabbi Temple Beth El, Elizabeth, N.J., 1964-70; interim rabbi Temple Emanuel, Yonkers, N.Y., 1970-71; affiliated therapist Insts. Religion and Health, N.Y.C., 1972-78; dir. Rabbinic Ctr. for Counseling, Westfield, N.J., 1970—; rabbi Rabbinic Ctr. Synagogue, Westfield, 1972—; regional resource officer Inst. Creative Judaism, Cin., 1978-84. Author: Basic Themes of Jewish History; contbr. articles to profl. jours. Lt. (j.g.), chaplain USN, 1956-58. Mem. Cen. Conf. Am. Rabbis, Am. Assn. for Marriage and Family Therapy, Am. Assn. Pastoral Counselors (diplomate), Am. Group Psychotherapy Assn., Internat. Coun. for Pastoral Care and Counseling, N.J. Assn. for Marriage and Family Therapy (treas. 1984-86).

FISHEL, DOUGLAS RAY, music minister; b. Harper, Kans., Nov. 4, 1954; s. Charles Randall and Mary Elizabeth (Latta) F.; m. Patricia Jean Hicks, Dec. 18, 1976; children: Joseph Douglas, Kelly Janelle, Kersten Geneva. MusB, Friends U., 1975; MusM, Southwestern Bapt. Theol. Sem., 1989. Youth min. of music 1st Bapt. Ch., Belle Plaine, Kans., 1973-75, South Pk. Bapt. Ch., Alvin, Tex., 1978-80; sr. adults min. of music Southside Bapt. Ch., Tempe, Ariz., 1980-83, Tyler Rd. So. Bapt. Ch., Wichita, Kans., 1983—; music leader sr. adult chautauqua Bapt. Sunday Sch. Bd., Nashville, 1983, 88, 90. Pres.-elect Singing Men of KS-NB, Topeka, 1990-93. Mem. Am. Choral Dirs. Assn., Am. Guild English Handbell Ringers, Hymn Soc. Am., So. Bapt. Ch. Music Conf., Century. Republican. Home: 11520 W Sheriac Wichita KS 67209 Office: Tyler Rd So Bapt Ch 571 S Tyler Rd Wichita KS 67209

FISHER, ALLAN EVERETT, religious publisher; b. Goshen, Ind., July 4, 1943; s. Leroy Everett F. and Naomi (Fogelsonger) Greenwalt; m. Diane A. Fisher, Sept. 14, 1968; 1 child, Jeffrey Allan. BA, Kalamazoo (Mich.) Coll., 1965; MDiv, Trinity Evang. Divinity Sch., Deerfield, Ill., 1969. Project editor Baker Book House, Grand Rapids, Mich., 1974-77, textbook editor, 1977-85, editor acad. and reference books, 1985-90, dir. publs., 1990—; bd. dirs. Wheaton (Ill.) Book Pub. Seminar, 1987—. Bd. dirs. Rockford (Mich.) Pub. Schs., 1987—. Mem. Acad. Christian Editors, Evang. Theol. Soc. (monograph editor 1983-86, assoc.), Conf. on Faith and History, Soc. Bibl. Lit., Inst. for Bibl. Rsch. (assoc.), Calvin Studies Soc. Office: Baker Book House PO Box 6287 Grand Rapids MI 49516

FISHER, ANN HOUSTON, lay worker, counselor, registered nurse; b. Knoxville, Tenn., Nov. 21, 1946; d. Robert Lockhart and Ruth Wilda (Fincannon) Houston; m. Joseph Franklin Fisher Sr.; children: Joseph Franklin Jr., Shane Houston, Britt Woodroof. BSN, U. Tenn., 1968. RN, Tenn. Tchr. Sunday sch. 1st United Meth. Ch., McMinnville, Tenn., 1983-87, mem. adminstv. bd., 1986-89, mem. coun. on ministries, 1989—, mem. pastor parish com., 1990—, jr. and sr. high youth counselor, 1986—; nurse Dr. J. Franklin Fisher, McMinnville, 1981—; patient assessment coord. McMinnville Health Care, 1991—. Nursing con. ARC, Knoxville, 1969-70, Tenn. Hosp. Assn., Nashville, 1978-81, Motlow Coll., Tullahoma, Tenn., 1977—; nursing educator Am. Diabetes Assn., McMinnville, 1978—. Recipient Vol. Svc. award ARC, Vol. of Yr. award Am. Diabetes Assn., 1982. Office: First United Meth Ch 200 W Main St McMinnville TN 37110

FISHER, BONNELL H. (BONNIE FISHER), church secretary; b. Pickens County, Ga., July 28, 1933; d. Noel Stephen and Luna Mae (Roper) Honea; m. Ernest M. Fisher, Nov. 13, 1954 (dec. May 1974); 1 child, John M. Ed. high sch., Canton, Ga., 1950. Sec. Antioch Christian Ch., Odessa, Tex., 1974—. Office: Antioch Christian Ch 4040 Maple Ave Odessa TX 79762

FISHER, CARL A., bishop; b. Pascagoula, Miss., Nov. 24, 1945. AA, Epiphany Apostolic Coll., Newburgh, N.Y., 1965; BA, St. Joseph's Sem., 1967; MA, Oblate Coll., 1970; MS, Am. U., 1974. Ordained priest Roman Cath. Ch., 1973. Titular bishop of Tlos, aux. bishop of L.A., 1987—. First African-Am. Catholic Bishop in Western U.S. Address: Archdiocese of LA 3555 St Pancratius Pl Lakewood CA 90712 *Personal philosophy: I try to do the best that I can in all things and leave the rest to God.*

FISHER, DEBORAH MAY, lay worker; b. Boynton Beach, Fla., Dec. 15, 1968; d. Samuel Phillip and Sylvia Lucille (Gustus) F. BA in History, Valparaiso U., 1991. Acolyte chmn. Trinity Luth. Ch., Delray Beach, Fla., 1984-87; altar guild chmn. Valparaiso U. chapel, Valparaiso, Ind., 1988-91. Home: 577 SW 24th Ave Boynton Beach FL 33435

FISHER, GEORGE MARK, minister; b. Mt. Vernon, Ohio, May 14, 1949; s. George Dalton and Helen Isabel (Clark) F.; m. Kathleen Ruth Russell, May 7, 1972; children: Derek, Kirk, Jana. BA, Cin. Bible Coll., 1972; MDiv, Gordon-Conwell Theol. Sem., 1975; ThM, Princeton Theol. Sem., 1981; D Ministry, So. Bapt. Theol. Sem., Louisville, 1990. Ordained to ministry Christian Chs. and Chs. of Christ, 1972. Min. Scotch Plains (N.J.) Christian Ch., 1977-82, Edmond (Okla.) Christian Ch., 1983-86, Ross (Ohio) Christian Ch., 1986—; prof. theology Ont. Christian Sem., Toronto, Can., 1975-77; vis. lectr. theology Cin. Bible Coll. and Sem., 1982-83, adj. prof., 1990—; adj. chaplain Ft. Hamilton (Ohio)-Hughes Hosp., 1989—; dir. Christian Arabic Svcs., Cin., 1991—. Office: Ross Christian Ch PO Box 39 Ross OH 45061

FISHER, NEAL FLOYD, minister; b. Washington, Ind., Apr. 4, 1936; s. Floyd Russell and Florence Alice (Williams) F.; m. Ila Alexander, Aug. 18, 1957; children—Edwin Kirk, Julia Bryn. AB, DePauw U., 1957, LHD (hon.), 1982; MDiv, Boston U., 1960, PhD, 1966; STD, MacMurray Coll., Jacksonville, Ill., 1991. Ordained to ministry United Meth. Ch., 1958; pastor 1st United Meth. Ch., Revere, Mass., 1960-63, North Andover, Mass., 1963-68; planning assoc. United Meth. Bd. Global Ministries, N.Y.C., 1968-73; dir. planning United Meth. Bd. Global Ministries, 1973-77; assoc. dean, asst. prof. theology and society Boston U. Sch. Theology, 1977-80; pres., prof. theology and society Garrett Evang. Theol. Sem., Evanston, Ill., 1980—; Mendenhall lectr. DePauw U., Greencastle, Ind., 1982; Wilson lectr., Nashville, 1983; Voigt lectr. McKendree Coll., 1984; Henry Martin Loud lectr. U. Mich., Ann Arbor, 1987; Wright lelctr. Morningside Coll., 1991; chaplain and preacher, Chautauqua, 1984, 88; mem. univ. senate United Meth. Ch.; McKendree Blair lectr. MacMurray Coll., 1986; mem. bd. ordained and diaconal ministries North Cen. jurisdiction United Meth. Ch. Author: Parables of Jesus: Glimpses of the New Age, 1979, rev. edit., 1991, The Parables of Jesus: Glimpses of God's Reign, 1990, Context for Discovery, 1980. Recipient Disting. Alumnus award Boston U. Sch. Theology, 1985; Jacob Sleeper fellow, 1960-61. Mem. Assn. United Meth. Theol. Scis., Assn. Chgo. Theol. Schs. (pres. 1985-87). Home: 3221 Hartzell St Evanston IL 60201 Office: Garrett Evang Theol Sem 2121 Sheridan Rd Evanston IL 60201

FISHER, ORVAL GEORGE, clergyman; b. Saskatoon, Sask., Can., Feb. 9, 1952; s. Kenneth George and Isabella Agnes (Shaw) F.; m. Susan Rae Barker, Jan. 6, 1973; 1 child, Nicole Marie. BS, Boise State U., 1975, MS, 1979. Tchr. Kuna (Idaho) Pub. Schs., 1975-77, Boise (Idaho) Pub. Schs., 1977-81; minister Reorganized Ch. of Jesus Christ of Latter-day Saints, Independence, Mo., 1981-82; bishop's agt. Reorganized Ch. of Jesus Christ of Latter-day Saints, Cedar Rapids, Iowa, 1982-85; bishop Reorganized Ch. of Jesus Christ of Latter-day Saints, Denver, 1985—. Democrat. Office: West Cen States Region LDS Ch 9501 Lou Dr Denver CO 80221

FISHER, RICHARD ALLEN, lay worker, physician; b. Fort Wayne, Ind., June 18, 1947; s. Richard Donald and Dorothy Jane (Adams) F.; m. Elaine Christine Enright, Aug. 7, 1976; children: Kendra, Kyle, Erin. BS in Biology, Purdue U., 1976; MD, U. Miami, 1982; MPH, Harvard U., 1990. Diplomate Am. Acad. Family Practice, Am. Bd. Preventive Medicine. Resident in family practice Halifax Med. Ctr., Daytona Beach, Fla., 1982-85, chief resident, 1984-85; med. dir. 45th St Mental Health Ctr., West Palm Beach, Fla., 1991—; missionary United Meth. Ch., Zaire, 1986-89. Sgt. USAF, 1969-73. Recipient McCarthy award, 1985. Fellow Am. Acad. Family Practice; mem. APHA, Am. Anthrop. Assn., Am. Soc. Missiology, Soc. of Med. Anthropology, Med. Ambassadors, Christian Med.-Dental Soc. (local dir. Daytona Beach chpt. 1985-86). Home: 14256 Greentree Trail West Palm Beach FL 33414 Office: 45th St Mental Health Ctr 1041 45th St West Palm Beach FL 33407

FISHER, RICHARD L., bishop. Bishop 9th Episcopal dist. A.M.E. Zion Ch., St. Louis. Office: AME Zion Ch 607 N Grand Ave Ste 701 Saint Louis MO 63130*

FISHER, ROBERT BRUCE, priest; b. Paragould, Ark., Feb. 6, 1937; s. Lawrence Bruce Fisher and Georgia M. (Paris) Kasper. BA, Divine Word Seminary, Techny, Ill., 1961, MA, 1965; STB, STL, Gregorian Univ., Rome, 1966; STD, Pont. Ateneo di Sant' Anselmo, Rome, 1969. Ordained priest Roman Cath. Ch., 1965. Adminstrv. attache Nunciature of Holy See, Accra, Ghana, 1982-83; pastor Good Shepherd Ch., Tema, Ghana, 1984-86; asst. pastor St. Matthias Ch., New Orleans, 1990-91; asst. prof. Xavier U., New Orleans, 1988—; dir. of studies A. Tolton House of Studies, New Orleans, 1991; dist. superior Divine Word Soc. of New Orleans dist., 1990-91. Editor: (liturgical ordo) Ordo for the Phillipines, 1972. Co-chmn. Cath. Returnee Crisis Com., Accra, 1982-83; dir. Food Bank, New Orleans, 1988-90. Mem. Coll. Theology Soc., Semiotic Soc. Am., Am. Acad. Religion, K.C. Democrat. Office: Xavier Univ of Louisianna Palmetto St New Orleans LA 70125

FISHER, ROBERT ELWOOD, minister, church official; b. Glendale, Calif., Aug. 29, 1931; s. Heman Harold and Anna Elizabeth (Einzig) F.; m. Mary Lena Sadler, Aug. 1, 1952; children: Robert Wesley, Cameron Michael, Loretta Lynne. BA, Fresno State U., 1964, MA, 1967; PhD, U. Hawaii, 1973. Ordained to ministry Ch. of God (Cleveland, Tenn.), 1958. Bus. mgr., v.p., supt. West Coast Bible Coll., 1952-60; pastor Ch. of God Temple, Fresno, Calif., 1960-67; state overseer Chs. of God in Hawaii, 1967-74; dir. Met. Ctr., Honolulu, 1970-74; pres. Cen. Pacific Christian Coll., Honolulu, 1970-74; state overseer Md.-Del.-Washington Ch. of God, 1974-76, nat. dir. dept. gen. edn., 1977-84, state overseer North Ga., 1984-88, mem. exec. coun., 1984, mem. Gen. Bd. Edn., 1968-74; gen. sec.-treas. Ch. of God Internat., Cleveland, 1988-90, asst. gen. overseer, 1990—. Author: The Family and the Church, The Language of Love, Quick To Listen, Slow To Speak. Chmn. bd. dirs. Lee Coll., 1984-88. Home: 3276 Chestnut Cir Cleveland TN 37312 Office: Ch of God Internat PO Box 2430 Cleveland TN 37320-2430 *The essence of life is embodied in Jesus' statement on relationships (Matthew 22:34-40). A positive relationship with God results in proper behavior toward others which, in turn, engenders a strong self-image.*

FISHMAN, BERNARD PHILIP, religious association administrator; b. N.Y.C., July 25, 1950; s. Samuel William and Rosalyn (Schachtel) F.; m. Elizabeth Andersen, Jan. 8, 1983; 1 child, Philip. BA summa cum laude, Columbia U., 1972; MA, U. Pa., 1982. Rsch. fellow Mus. Applied Sci. Ctr. for Archaeology, U. Pa., Phila., 1976-79; Egyptologist Epigraphic Survey Oriental Inst., U. Chgo., Luxor, Chgo., 1979-82; dir. Fenster Mus. Jewish Art, Tulsa, 1982-85; dir. Jewish Hist. Soc. Md. Agy. Associated Jewish Community Fedn. of Balt., 1985—; tchr., lectr. in field. Author, co-author, editor numerous books, exhibit catalogues, jours., articles; art critic World newspaper, Tulsa, 1985. Recipient award NCCJ, 1985; Applied Sci. Ctr. for Archaeology rsch. fellow, 1977-79, William Penn Found. fellow, 1976-77. Mem. Phi Beta Kappa. Home: 4815 Keswick Rd Baltimore MD 21210 Office: Jewish Hist Soc Md 15 Lloyd St Baltimore MD 21202 *Without the study of history there can be no civilization; without the cultivation of the arts there can be no immortality.*

FISKE, ARLAND ORIN, minister; b. Colfax, N.D., Apr. 11, 1927; s. Oscar Bernie and Anne Julia (Thompson) F.; m. Gerda Marie Kirkegaard, Aug. 2, 1952; children: Paul, Michael, Lisa, Daniel, Mark, John, Christopher. BA, Concordia Coll., Moorhead, Minn., 1948; BTh., Luther Sem., St. Paul, 1952, ThM, 1956. Ordained to ministry Evang. Luth. Ch. in Am., 1952. Pastor Evang. Luth. Ch. in Am., N.D., 1952-61, Webster Groves, Mo., 1961-65; tchr. Luth. Gen. Med. Ctr., Park Ridge, Ill., 1967-72; pastor Evang. Luth. Ch. in Am., Minot, N.D., 1974-89; exec. dir. deacon tng. Evang. Luth. Ch. in Am., N.D., 1989—. Author: Scandinavian Heritage, 1987, others. Bd. dirs. Luther Northwestern Sem., St. Paul, 1988—. Fellow Acad. Parish Clergy (pres. 1979-81); mem. Norsk Hosfest Assn. (sec. 1978—), Sons of Norway (pres. 1987-88). Address: HCR 70 Box 649A Laporte MN 56461

FISKO, JAMES J., ecumenical agency administrator. Exec. dir. United Religious Community of St. Joseph County, South Bend, Ind. Office: United Religious Community 2015 Western Ave South Bend IN 46629*

FITCH, GREGORY SCOTT, minister; b. Kearney, Nebr., July 21, 1962; s. Jerry Lee and Carolyn Jane (Peterson) F.; m. Martha Jean Spleth, Aug. 6, 1983; children: Mary Christine, David Lee. BA, Tex. Christian U., 1985; MDiv, Brite Div. Sch., Ft. Worth, 1988. Ordained to ministry Christian Ch. (Disciples of Christ), 1988. Youth min. Rosemont Christian Ch. (Disciples of Christ), Dallas, 1985-88; co-pastor 1st Christian Ch. (Disciples of Christ), Sterling, Colo., 1988—; v.p. Logan County Ministerial Alliance, Sterling, 1991—. Office: 1st Christian Ch (Disciples of Christ) W Main at Hall Rd Sterling CO 80751

FITCH, MARTHA JEAN, minister; b. Tulsa, May 30, 1960; d. Wallace Lee and Helen Jean (Ruth) Spleth; m. Gregory Scott Fitch, Aug. 6, 1983; children: Mary Christine, David Lee. BA, Tex. Christian U., 1982; MDiv, Brite Div. Sch., 1985. Ordained to ministry Christian Ch. (Disciples of Christ), 1986. Min. to children South Hills Christian Ch. (Disciples of Christ), Ft. Worth, 1982-88; co-pastor 1st Christian Ch. (Disciples of Christ), Sterling, Colo., 1988—; moderator elect Cen. Rocky Mountain Region of Christian Chs. (Disciples of Christ), Colo., Wyo., 1990—. Mem. AAUW, Coop. Ministry (sec., bd. dirs. 1990), vice chairperson 1991—). Democrat. Office: 1st Christian Ch 12915 County Rd 37 Rte 4 Sterling CO 80751

FITCHETT, DOROTHY MARIE, clergywoman, religious home administrator; b. Norfolk, Va., Mar. 31, 1946; d. Donald Byrd and Florence Slena (Miller) F. Grad., Salvation Army Officers' Tng. Sch., Atlanta, 1978. Cert. AIDS counselor. Officer The Salvation Army, Tex., 1978-89; officer, chaplain U. Tex. Health System, Tyler, 1989—; founder, dir. HIS House, Tyler, 1990—; pres., founder Tyler AIDS Svcs., Inc., 1990—. Recipient Pres.'s award Govt. of U.S., 1976, Seven Who Care award Tyler C. of C./Sta. KLTV, 1991. Office: HIS House PO Box 131293 Tyler TX 75713

FITTERER, JOHN ANGUS, priest, church administrator, author; b. Ellensburg, Wash., July 1, 1922; s. C.J. and Violet (McMillan) F.; m. Karen L. Guthrie, Oct. 20, 1990. AB, St. Louis U., 1945, MA, 1946, Licentiate in Philosophy, 1947; Licentiate in Sacred Theology, Gregorian U., Rome, 1954; HHD (hon.), Our Lady of the Lake U., San Antonio, 1972. Ordained to ministry Episcopal Ch., 1978. Assoc. prof. classical langs. and philosophy, dean Coll. Arts and Scis. Seattle U., 1956-64, pres., chancellor, 1965-71; pres. Assn. Jesuit Colls. and Univs., Washington, 1971-77; rector Ch. St. John Evangelist, Hingham, Mass., 1978-79; asst. to bishop Diocese of Calif., San Francisco, 1980-84; vice chmn. Episcopal Homes Found., Lafayette, Calif., 1984-86, chmn., 1986—. Translator: Thomas Aquinas Commentary on Nichomachean Ethics of Aristotle, 1965; contbr. Adminstrs. in Higher Edn., 1978; also numerous articles on higher edn., religion and life care for elderly. Chmn. Nat. Coun. on Crime and Delinquency, Wash., 1965-70; pres., chmn. bd. trustees Seattle U., 1965-70; vice chmn. Wash. Urban Affairs Coun., 1966-69; vice chmn. bd. trustees Loyola Coll., Balt., 1970-76; trustee U. Detroit, 1976-77. Recipient Disting. Civilian Svc. medal U.S. Army, 1968, 71, Disting. Citizen's award Boys' Club Am., 1972, Outstanding Svc. award Nat. Coun. on Crime and Delinquency, 1969. Mem. Bankers Club of San Francisco. Home: 640 Davis St # 26 San Francisco CA 94111 Office: Episcopal Homes Found 3650 Mt Diablo Blvd Box 1027 Lafayette CA 94549 *In order to help others, to find the way, the truth and eternal life, we must be above reproach in our own goals and become men and women of prayer.*

FITTS, R. LEWIS, minister, business administrator; b. Pontotoc, Miss., Aug. 26, 1930; s. Raymond B. and Bertha P. (Ladd) F.; m. Mary Frances Crain, Apr. 21, 1951; children: Debra D. Schaffner, Steven L., Myra F. Pullin. BS in Secondary Edn., Memphis State U., 1958; M in Religious Edn., Southwestern Bapt. Theol. Sem., 1959, MA in Religious Edn., 1983. Cert. in church adminstrn. So. Bapt. Conv. Min. edn. Carlisle Ave. Bapt. Ch., Louisville, 1966-70; min. edn. and adminstrn. First Bapt. Ch., Baton Rouge, 1970-79; ch. adminstr. Tallowood Bapt. Ch., Houston, 1979-85, Prestonwood Bapt. Ch., Dallas, 1985-89; min. bus. adminstrn. First Bapt. Ch., Wichita Falls, Tex., 1989—. Contbr. material to profl. mag. V.p. Downtown Kiwanis Club, Baton Rouge, 1978-79; pres. Spring Br. Kiwanis Club, Houston, 1983-84. Master sgt. USAF, 1950-58. Mem. Nat. Assn. Ch. Bus. Adminstrn. (v.p. 1983-85, pres. Houston chpt. 1983-84, pres. Texoma chpt. 1989-91), WAC Bapt. Assn. (fin. com. 1989-91), So. Bapt. Ch. Bus. Adminstrn. Assn. Home: 2401 Wranglers Retreat Wichita Falls TX 76308 Office: First Bapt Ch 1200 Ninth St Wichita Falls TX 76301

FITZ, JAMES FRANCIS, religious order administrator; b. Akron, Ohio, June 14, 1946; s. Raymond Leon and Mary Louise (Smith) F. BA in Philosophy, U. Dayton, 1968; MA in Hist. Theology, St. Louis U., 1973. Tchr. Monsignor Hackett High Sch, Kalamazoo, Mich., 1961-71; coord. adult religious edn. Diocese of Kalamazoo, 1975-79; dir. novices Marianist Novitiate, Dayton, Ohio, 1979-85; asst. for religious life Marianist Provincialate, Dayton, 1985-89, Marianist Provincial, Dayton, 1989—; trustee U. Dayton, 1989—, Bergamo Ctr. for Lifelong Learning, Dayton, 1988—; bd. dirs. Chaminade-Julienne High Sch., Dayton, 1985—; del. to gen. chpt. Soc. of Mary, Rome, Italy, 1986, Dayton, 1991. Contbg. author: Who Are My Brothers, 1988; contbr. articles to profl. jours. Recipient Award of Excellence U. Dayton, 1968. Mem. Conf. Major Superiors of Men. Office: Marianist Provincialate 4435 E Patterson Rd Dayton OH 45430

FITZ, BROTHER RAYMOND L., university president; b. Akron, Ohio, Aug. 12, 1941; s. Raymond L. and Mary Lou (Smith) F. B.S. in Elec. Engring., U. Dayton, Ohio, 1964; M.S., Poly. Inst. Bklyn., 1967, Ph.D., 1969. Joined Soc. of Mary, Roman Catholic Ch., 1960; mem. faculty U. Dayton, 1968—, prof. elec. engring. and engring. mgmt., 1975—, exec. dir. Center Christian Renewal, 1974-79, univ. pres., 1979—. Author numerous papers, reports in field. Bd. dirs. various civic organs. Recipient Disting. Alumnus award Poly. Inst. Bklyn., 1980. Office: U Dayton 300 College Park Dayton OH 45469

FITZGERALD, ERNEST ABNER, bishop; b. Crouse, N.C., July 24, 1925; s. James Boyd and Hattie Pearl (Chaffin) F.; m. Sara Frances Perry; children: James Boyd, Patricia Anne Poole. AB, We. Carolina U., 1947; BD, Duke U., 1951; DD, High Point Coll., 1969, Pfeiffer Coll., 1986. Ordained to ministry United Meth. Ch. Pastor Webster Circuit, N.C., 1944-47, Liberty Circuit, 1947-50, Calvary United Meth. Ch., Asheboro, N.C., 1950-55, Abernathy United Meth. Ch., Asheville, N.C., 1955-59, Purcell United Meth Ch., Charlotte, N.C., 1959-64, Grace United Meth. Ch., Greensboro, N.C., 1964-66, Centenary United Meth. Ch., Winston-Salem, N.C., 1966-82, West Market St. United Meth. Ch., Greensboro, 1982-84; bishop United Meth. Ch., Atlanta Area, 1984—; pres. United Meth. Devel. Fund; chmn. Adminstrv. Coun., Southeastern Jurisdiction; mem. Nat. United Meth. Found. for Christian Higher Edn.; chmn. bd. trustees Emory U. Author: A Time to Cross the River, 1977, How to be a Successful Failure, 1978, God Writes Straight with Crooked Lines, Diamonds Everywhere, 1983, Keeping Pace: Inspirations in the Air, 1988, others. Home: 2339 Fair Oaks Rd Decatur GA 30033 Office: United Meth Ctr 159 Ralph McGill Blvd NE Atlanta GA 30308

FITZGERALD, SISTER JANET ANNE, college president; b. Woodside, N.Y., Sept. 4, 1935; d. Robert W. and Lillian H. (Shannon) F. B.A. magna cum laude, St. John's U., 1965, M.A., 1967, Ph.D., 1971, LLD (hon.), 1981. Joined Sisters of St. Dominic of Amityville, Roman Catholic Ch., 1953; NSF postdoctoral fellow Cath. U. Am., summer 1971; prof. philosophy Molloy Coll., Rockville Centre, N.Y., 1969—; pres. Molloy Coll., 1972—; chmn. L.I. Regional Adv. Council on Higher Edn., 1981-84, trustee, 1985—; trustee Commn. on Ind. Colls. and Univs., Fellowship of Cath. Scholars, 1977—, v.p., 1977-80; Roman Cath. Ch. rep. to Nat. Congress Ch.-Related Colls. and Univs., 1979; trustee Cath. Charities, Diocese of Rockville Centre, 1979-82; invited expert Internat. Meeting on Cath. Higher Edn., Rome, 1989. Author: Alfred North Whitehead's Early Philosophy of Space and Time, 1979. Mem. bd. advisors Sem. of Immaculate Conception, 1975-80; mem. adv. bd. pre-theology program Dunwoodie Sem., Archdiocese of N.Y.; mem. adv. bd. Modern Cts. L.I., 1991; hon. chaiperson Bi-County Symposium on Bias, 1991. Recipient Disting. Leadership award L.I. Bus. News, 1988, plaque of recognition L.I. Women's Coun. for Equal Edn. Tng. and Employment, 1989, Pathfinder award Town of Hempstead, 1990, Disting. Long Islander in Edn. award Epilepsy Found. L.I., 1991; honored by L.I. Cath. League for Religious and Civil Rights, 1989. Office: Molloy Coll 1000 Hempstead Ave Rockville Centre NY 11570

FITZGERALD, JOHN THOMAS, JR., religious studies educator; b. Birmingham, Ala., Oct. 2, 1948; s. John Thomas and Annie Myrtle (Walters) F.; m. Karol Bonneaux, May 23, 1970; children: Kirstin Leigh, Kimberly Anne. BA, Abilene Christian U., 1970, MA, 1972; MDiv, Yale U., 1975, PhD, 1984. Instr. Yale Coll., New Haven, Conn., 1979, Yale Divinity Sch., New Haven, Conn., 1980-81; instr. U. Miami, Coral Gables, Fla., 1981-84, asst. prof., 1984-88, assoc. prof., 1988—; visiting assoc. prof. Brown U., Providence, R.I., 1992; dir. honors program U. Miami, 1987-91, master Hecht Residential Coll., 1987-91, chmn. Rhodes Scholarship com., 1987-91. Author: Tabula of Cebes, 1983, Cracks in an Earthen Vessel, 1988; contbr. articles to profl. jours. Judge for Silver Knight awards The Miami (Fla.) Herald, 1988, 90. Recipient Max Orovitz Summer Rsch. award U. Miami, 1985, 87, fellowship Rotary Internat., Tuebingen, Fed. Republic Germany, 1975-76, Two Bros. fellowship Yale Divinity Sch., 1974-75. Mem. Soc. Bibl. Lit. (chmn. com. 1989—), Nat. Collegiate Honors Coun., So. Regional Honors Coun., Iron Arrow Honor Soc., Omicron Delta Kappa, Golden Key Nat. Honor Soc. (chmn. scholarship com. 1990-91), Phi Kappa Phi (chpt. pres. 1988-90). Home: 15215 SW 78th Ct Miami FL 33157 Office: U Miami PO Box 248264 Coral Gables FL 33124

FITZGERALD, TIKHON (R. H. LEE), bishop; b. Detroit, Nov. 14, 1932; s. LeRoy and Dorothy Kaeding (Higgins) F. AB, Wayne State U., 1958. Enlisted U.S. Army, 1954-57; commd. 2 lt. USAF, 1960, advanced through grades to capt., 1971; air staff, 1966-71, released, 1971; protodeacon Holy Virgin Mary Russian Orthodox Cathedral, L.A., 1972-78, rector, archpriest, 1979-87; bishop of San Francisco Orthodox Ch. in Am., L.A., 1987—. Democrat. Home: 649 Robinson St Los Angeles CA 90026 Office: Orthodox Ch Am Diocese of the West 2040 Anza San Francisco CA 90026

FITZMYER, JOSEPH AUGUSTINE, theology educator, priest; b. Phila., Nov. 4, 1920; s. Joseph Augustine and Anna Catherine (Alexy) F. AB, Loyola U., Chgo., 1943, AM, 1945; Licentiate in Sacred Theology, Facultés St. Albert de Louvain, Belgium, 1952; PhD, Johns Hopkins U., 1956; Licentiate of Sacred Scripture, Pontifical Bibl. Inst., 1957. Joined S.J., 1938, ordained priest Roman Cath. Ch., 1951. Asst. prof. N.T. and Bibl. langs. Woodstock (Md.) Coll., 1958-59, assoc. prof., 1959-64, prof., 1964-69; prof. Aramaic and Hebrew dept. Nr. Ea. langs.-civilizations U. Chgo., 1969-71; prof. N.T. and Bibl. langs. dept. theology Fordham U., Bronx, N.Y., 1971-74, Weston Sch. Theology, Cambridge, Mass., 1974-76; prof. dept. Bibl. studies Cath. U. Am., Washington, 1976—; tchr. Gonzaga High Sch., Washington, 1945-48; Speaker's lectr. Bibl. studies Oxford (Eng.) U., 1974-75. Author: Essays on the Semitic Background of the New Testament, 1971, The Genesis Apocryphon on Qumran Cave I, 1966, 2d edit., 1971; editor: (with R.E. Brown and R.E. Murphy) The New Jerome Biblical Commentary, 1990; The Gospel According to Luke (Anchor Bible), vol. 28, 1981, vol. 28A, 1985. Mem. Cath. Bibl. Assn. (pres. 1970, editor Quar. 1980-84), Soc. Bibl. Lit. (pres. 1978-79, editor Jour. 1971-76), Studiorum Novi Testamenti Societas (pres.-elect 1991-92). Home: Georgetown U Jesuit Community Washington DC 20057

FITZPATRICK, ALAN JOSEPH, deacon, psychologist; b. Needham, Mass., May 16, 1937; s. Joseph Augustine and Julia (Downing) F.; m. Glenda Nadine Pinkley, Oct. 24, 1964; children: Michael, Shaun. BS in Indsl. Engring., Northeastern U., 1962; MEd in Guidance and Counseling, Shippensburg (Pa.) Coll., 1967; PhD in Ednl. Psychology, U. Mo., 1970. Ordained deacon Roman Cath. Ch., 1980; lic. psychologist, Tex. Lay missionary Soc. of Our Lady of Most Blessed Trinity, Mora, N.Mex., 1962-63; prin., psychologist Northside Ind. Sch. Dist., San Antonio, 1974—. Editor newsletter Archdiocese of San Antonio, 1980—. 1st pres. Tex. State REACT Coun., 1976; mem. exec. com. Bexar County Reps., San Antonio. Lt. col. USAR, 1963-65, 90-91. Home: 5815 Kepler Dr San Antonio TX 78228 Office: Northside Ind Sch Dist Ewing Halsell Dr San Antonio TX 78229 *God is the same, yesterday, today, and forever. We, made in His image, are not modern men, but Adam's unchanged descendants redeemed by the blood of Jesus. As such we need His Word, the Bible, and the comforter, the Holy Spirit to direct our lives.*

FITZPATRICK, DERRICK MILAS, minister, component engineer; b. Chgo., Sept. 6, 1959; s. Elbert M. and Clara (Stone) F. A in Engring. Tech., Olive-Harvey Coll., 1985; BS in Physics, Roosevelt U., 1988. Ordained to ministry Bapt. Ch., 1987. Assoc. pastor Stone Temple Bapt. Ch., Chgo., 1988—; component engr. United-Chemi-Con, Rosemont, Ill., 1987—. Mem. Bapt. Mins. Conf. Home: PO Box 813 Rosemont IL 60018 Office: Stone Temple Bapt Ch 3622 W Douglas Blvd Chicago IL 60623

FITZPATRICK, JOE ALLEN, music minister; b. Cushing, Okla., Aug. 8, 1959; s. Bill J. and G. Marilyn (Dawes) F.; m. Gwenn Marie Robertson, June 27, 1987. B. Music Edn., Okla. State U., 1982; M. Ch. Music, Southwestern Bapt. Theol. Sem., 1984. Minister of music 1st Bapt. Ch., Yale, Okla., 1976-82, Mandarin Bapt. Ch., Jacksonville, Fla., 1985-89, Park Hill Bapt. Ch., North Little Rock, Ark., 1989—; dir. music Jacksonville Bapt. Assn., 1987-89, cons. youth music, ch. music coun., 1986-87; state and associational festival adjudicator State Conventions of Ark., Ga. and Fla., 1986—; tenor The Centurymen, 1988—. Mem. So. Bapt. Ch. Music Conf., Ark. Bapt. Singing Men "MasterSingers", Am. Choral Dirs. Assn., Choristers Guild. Office: Park Hill Bapt Ch 201 E C St North Little Rock AR 72116

FITZPATRICK, JOHN J., bishop; b. Trenton, Ont., Can., Oct. 12, 1918; s. James John and Lorena (Pelkey) F. Ed., Propaganda Fide Coll., Italy, Our Lady of Angels Sem.; B.A., Niagara U., 1941. Ordained priest Roman Catholic Ch., 1942. Titular bishop of Cenae and Aux. of Miami Fla., 1968-71; bishop of Brownsville Tex., 1971—; Bd. dirs. Tex. Conf. Chs. Office: PO Box 2279 Brownsville TX 78522

FITZPATRICK, SISTER JUDE, academic administrator. Supt. Cath. schs. Diocese of Des Moines. Office: Schs Supt PO Box 1816 Des Moines IA 50306*

FITZPATRICK, RUTH MCDONOUGH, association administrator; b. Port Chester, N.Y., Mar. 10, 1933; d. Joseph Anthony Sr. and Katherine (Devereux) McDonough; m. John R. Fitzpatrick Jr., Nov. 25, 1955; children: Patricia, Michael, John. BA in Religious Studies, Georgetown U., 1975. Nat. coord. Women's Ordination Conf., 1977, 1985—, also bd. dirs.; pub. New Women, New Ch. newspaper. Bd. dirs. Guatemala Human Rights Commn/USA, Ecumenical Program on Caribbean and C.Am., Religious Task Force on C.Am., other groups. Recipient Leadership award Call to Action, 1991. Mem. Sisters Against Sexism. Roman Catholic. Office: Women's Ordination Conf Fairfax Circle Ctr 9653 Lee Hwy Ste 11 Fairfax VA 22031

FITZSIMONS, GEORGE K., bishop; b. Kansas City, Mo., Sept. 4, 1928. Student, Rockhurst Coll., Immaculate Conception Sem. Ordained priest, Roman Cath. Ch., 1961. Bishop Salina, Kans., 1984—. Office: PO Box 980 Salina KS 67402

FITZWATER, MARGARET GWEN, lay worker; b. Long Beach, Calif., Oct. 19, 1955; d. David Lee and JoAnn (Gathings) Futch; m. Roy James, June 21, 1980; children: Christopher James, Stephen Andrew. BS in Biology, Baylor U., 1978; MS in Food Sci., Tex. A&M U., 1979; MBA, So. Meth. U., 1987. Staff mktg.-devel. SonScape Ministries, Dallas, 1985—; bd. dirs. SonScape Ministries, Pagosa Springs, Colo., 1984—, Carrollton (Tex.) Nazerene Ch. Mother's Day Out, 1989—; evangelism coord., lay tchr., adult Sunday sch. tchr., Carrollton Nazerene Ch., 1987—. Patentee Frito-Lay O'Grady's Potato Chips, 1984. Vol. Crisis Pregnancy Ctr., Dallas, 1986-90. Republican. Home: 1012 Magnolia Carrollton TX 75007 Office: SonScape Ministries Pagosa Springs CO 81147

FIZER, WILLIAM J., bishop. Chief bishop Ch. of God (Which He Purchased With His Own Blood), Oklahoma City. Office: Ch of God 1907 NE Grand Blvd Oklahoma City OK 73111*

FJELD, PHYLLIS, ecumenical agency administrator. Exec. sec. Regional Coun. for Christian Ministry, Inc., Idaho Falls, Idaho. Office: Regional Coun Christian Ministry Inc PO Box 2236 Rm 10 Idaho Falls ID 83403*

FJELD, ROGER WILLARD, seminary administrator; b. Primghar, Iowa, July 13, 1933; s. Oscar Gilbert and Alice Irma (Berntson) F.; m. Marilyn E. A. Burrack, Apr. 10, 1955; children: Stuart, Karen, Douglas. BA, U. Iowa, 1955; BD, Wartburg Sem., 1959; MA, U. Colo., 1969, PhD, 1973. Ordained to ministry Luth. Ch., 1959. Pastor Christ Luth. Ch., Sedalia, Mo., 1959-65, Atonement Luth. Ch., Denver, 1965-69; asst. to bishop cen. dist. Am. Luth. Ch., Denver, 1970-71; faculty Wartburg Theol. Sem., Dubuque, Iowa, 1971-73; dir. office of support to ministries Am. Luth. Ch., Mpls., 1973-82, exec. asst. to presiding bishop, 1982-83; pres. Wartburg Theol. Sem., Dubuque, 1983—; mem., chair standing com. Div. for Svc. to Mil. Personnel, Washington, 1973-82; co-chair Luth./United Meth. Dialogue, 1983-86. Office: Wartburg Sem 333 Wartburg Pl Dubuque IA 52003

FJELLMAN, ANEL GILBERT, bishop; b. Cedar Rapids, Iowa, Apr. 27, 1917; s. Anders Gustaf and Huldah C. (Johnson) F.; m. Lorine Cecilia Hoeger, Dec. 28, 1944; children: Ruth, Jonathan. B.A., Augustana Coll., Rock Island, Ill., 1942, M.Div., 1945; D.D. hon., Pacific Luth. U., Tacoma, 1963. Ordained to ministry Lutheran Ch. in Am., 1945; pastor St. Michael's Ch., Sun Valley, Calif., 1945-51, Good Sheperd Ch., Duluth, Minn., 1952-55; dir. Bd. Am. Missions, Los Angeles, 1955-62; bishop Pacific N.W. synod. Luth. Ch. in Am., Seattle, 1963-83; dir. Pacific Luth. Sem. and Univ., 1963-83; interim pres. Luther Northwestern Theol. Sem., St. Paul, 1987—. Mem. Wash. Asn. Chs. (pres. 1965-67), Luth. Student Assn. (pres. 1941-42). Democrat. Club: Swedish (Seattle). Home: 3217 30th Ave W Seattle WA 08199

FJORDBOTTEN, ALF LEE, minister; b. Camrose, Alta., Can., Apr. 26, 1952; came to U.S., 1960; naturalized, 1987; s. Alf Lee and Helene Josephine (Hansen) F.; m. Beverly Elaine Lee, Oct. 22, 1983. BA in Religion, St. Olaf Coll., Minn., 1974; MDiv, Luther Northwestern Theol. Sem., 1978; MA in English and Comparative Lit., Fairleigh Dickinson U., 1989; postgrad., Fordham U., 1989—. Ordained to ministry Evang. Luth. Ch. Am., 1978. Vicar, chaplain Grace Luth. Ch., Good Shepherd Home, Allentown, Pa., 1976-77; pastor St. Mark's Luth. Ch., Ridge, N.Y., 1978-83, Holy Spirit Luth. Ch., Leonia, N.J., 1983—; aux. counselor Luth. Community Svcs., Hauppauge, N.Y., 1980-83; mem. Luth.-Roman Cath. Dialogue of L.I., N.Y., 1981-83; instr. ch. history and liturgics Diakonia N.Y., 1981—; mem. Worship Commn., Luths. Cooperating in Met. N.Y., 1981-87; mem. planning comms., sacristan, presenter for various worship confs., N.Y., Pa., N.J., 1984-89. Author: Light for Today, 1980; editor, contbr. parish newsletters, 1978—; contbr., mem. editorial bd. Bride of Christ mag., 1985-89; contbr. articles to profl. jours. Mem. Bass Bach Soc. Minn., 1974-78, Bach Choir of Bethlehem, 1976-77, L.I. Symphonic Choral Assn., 1979-83; bd. dirs. Camp Koinonia, Highland Lake, N.Y., 1979-84; trustee Inter-Rels. Fellowship for the Homeless of Bergen City, N.J., 1988-89. Recipient Charles J. Donahue prize Fordham U., 1990. Mem. Leonia Ecumenical Clergy, Meadowlands Cluster of N.J. Synod Evang. Luth. Ch. Am. Home: 580 Gail Ct Teaneck NJ 07666-4128 Office: Holy Spirit Luth Ch 313 Woodland Pl Leonia NJ 07605-1704 *It is never too late to set new goals. But, given life's exigencies and complications, we might never arrive at the goals themselves. It is important to enjoy also the process of setting and pursuing goals. For that, it is never too early.*

FLAANDERS, ERNEST WILLIAM, religious organization executive; b. West Palm Beach, Fla., Jan. 30, 1935; s. Ernest William and Esther Lillian (Nordstrom) F.; m. Marianne Louise Watkins, June 26, 1959; children: Kim Flanders Peacock, Louann Flanders Glover, Rebecca, Douglas. BA, Stetson U., 1959; MusB, MRE, Southwestern Bapt. Theol. Sem., Ft. Worth, 1963; DRE, Internat. Sem., Orlando, Fla., 1988. Ordained to ministry So. Bapt. Conv., 1966. Assoc. pastor 1st Bapt. Ch., Hope, Ark., 1963-66; assoc. pastor, pastor Park Avenue Bapt. Ch., Titusville, Fla., 1966-76; v.p. Arthur Davenport Assocs., Oklahoma City, 1976-79; dir. promotion MSI, Irving, Tex., 1979-81; pres. Stewardship Growth Assocs., Grapevine, Tex., 1981—. Author: God's Family Plan, 1979; composer numerous works. Office: Stewardship Growth Assocs PO Box 640 Grapevine TX 76051

FLAHERTY, DANIEL LEO, priest, editor; b. Chgo., July 29, 1929; s. Daniel Leo and Marguerite (Pauly) F. Student, Xavier U., 1950-51; A.B., Loyola U., Chgo., 1952, M.A., 1957; Ph.L., West Baden (Ind.) Coll., 1954, S.T.L., 1961; postgrad., Northwestern U., 1959-60. Joined Soc. of Jesus, 1947; ordained priest Roman Catholic Ch., 1960; book editor America, 1962-65, exec. editor, 1965-71; sec. America Press, Inc., 1965-71; mem. bd. Catholic Book Club, 1962-71; exec. dir. Loyola U. Press, Chgo., 1971-73, 79-80; dir. Loyola U. Press, 1980-89; treas. Chgo. Province Soc. Jesus, 1989—. Author: (with W.D. Ciszek) With God in Russia, 1964, He Leadeth Me, 1973; editor: National Jesuit News, 1972-73. Exec. sec. Chgo. Province Assembly, 1972-73; provincial Chgo. Province, S.J., 1973-79; mem. Chgo. Province Fin. Com., 1983—; mem. selection bd. Campion award, 1962-71; bd. dirs. John La Farge Inst., 1970-71, Appeal of Conscience Found., 1967-72; trustee Loyola U., Chgo., 1970-73, 80—, vice-chmn., 1971-73, 80-88; trustee U. Detroit, 1970-73, chmn. bd., 1972-73; trustee Loyola U., New

Orleans, 1980-86, 87—, Loyola Acad., Wilmette, Ill., 1980-86, St. Ignatius Coll. Prep., Chgo., 1988—. Address: 2050 N Clark St Chicago IL 60614

FLAHERTY, ROBERT COLEMAN, priest; b. Quincy, Mass., Aug. 22, 1917; s. Patrick Joseph and Ellen (Walsh) F. PhB, Mt. Carmelit Sem., Niagara Falls, Ont., 1944. Ordained priest Roman Cath. Ch., 1947. Dir. vocations Roman Cath. Ch., Hamilton, Mass., 1948-54; asst. novice master and prior Roman Cath. Ch., New Baltimore, Pa., 1954-68; procurator Roman Cath. Ch., Washington, 1968-70; pastor Roman Cath. Ch., New Baltimore, 1970-72, prior, 1972-79; prior Carmelite Fathers Roman Cath. Ch., Pitts., 1979—; pastor, prior St. Leo's Roman Cath. Ch., Pitts., 1981—. Address: 3113 Brighton Rd Pittsburgh PA 15212

FLAHIFF, GEORGE BERNARD CARDINAL, former archbishop of Winnipeg; b. Paris, Ont., Can., Oct. 26, 1905; s. John James and Eleanor Rose (Fleming) F. B.A., St. Michael's Coll., U. Toronto, 1926; student, U. Strasbourg, France, 1930-31; Dipl. Archiviste-Paleographe, Ecole Nat. des Chartes, Paris, 1935; Dipl. hon. degree in law, U. Seattle, 1965, U. Notre Dame, 1969, U. Man., 1969, U. Windsor, 1970, U. Winnipeg, 1972, U. Toronto, 1972, U. St. Francis Xavier, 1973, Laval U., 1974, St. Bonaventure U., 1975, U. St. Thomas, Houston, 1977. Ordained priest Roman Cath. Ch., 1930; prof. medieval history Pontifical Inst. Medieval Studies and U. Toronto, 1935-54, sec. inst., 1943-51; superior-gen. Basilian Fathers, 1954-61; archbishop of Winnipeg, Can., 1961-82; proclaimed cardinal, 1969. Mem. Sacred Congregation for Religious. Named to Coll. Cardinals, 1969; Decorated companion Order of Can., 1974. Office: 50 Stafford St, Winnipeg, MB Canada R3M 2V7

FLAKES, DENNIS, bishop. Bishop Ch. of God in Christ, Milw. Office: Ch of God In Christ 3420 N 1st St Milwaukee WI 53212*

FLAMMANG, SUSANN, author, publisher; b. Kenosha, Wis., June 2, 1950; d. Leslie James and Beatrice (Woodward) Flammang Sampe. Pres. The Family of God, Las Vegas, 1984—, World Harvest, 1985—, pub., editor The Family of God Newsletter, Poets for Africa, 1986—; pres. World Harvest, 1986—; producer, broadcaster Heart-to-Heart, Sta. KUNV-TV, Las Vegas; v.p. Art Affair. Author of 30 books, numerous works of poetry. Recipient numerous poetry awards including Calif. Fedn. of Poets award, 1983, Humanitarian award Clark County, 1986, Woman of Achievement award, 1987, Gov's Art award, 1985, 86. Mem. Internat. Women's Writing Guild, Internat. PEN Assn., Acad. Am. Poets. Office: The Family of God/World Harvest PO Box 19571 Las Vegas NV 89132

FLANAGAN, BERNARD JOSEPH, retired bishop; b. Proctor, Vt., Mar. 31, 1908; s. John B. and Alice (McGarry) F. Student, Holy Cross Coll., N.Am. Coll., Rome; JCD, Cath. U. Am., 1943. Ordained priest Roman Cath. Ch., 1931, consecrated bishop, 1953. Sec. to bishop, chancellor of diocese Burlington, Vt., 1943-53; bishop Diocese of Norwich, Conn., 1953-59; bishop Diocese of Worcester, Mass., 1959-83, ret., 1983. Home: 222 June St Worcester MA 01602

FLANAGAN, KEVIN WEST, minister; b. Providence, Sept. 19, 1958; s. Benjamin W. and Mary Jane (Coleman) F.; m. Shari L. Montgomery, Jan. 7, 1983; children: Ryan, Kean. BS in Edn., R.I. Coll., 1981; MDiv, Oral Roberts U., 1988. Ordained to ministry Bapt. Ch., 1990; cert. tchr., Okla., Kans. Youth minister First United Meth., Sand Springs, Okla., 1985, Community Bapt. Ch., Tulsa, 1988; pastor Lenexa (Kans.) New Life Fellowship, 1990; substitute tchr. Olathe (Kans.) Pub. Schs., 1991—; del. Am. Bapt. Chs. Cen. Region, Lenexa, 1990-91. Active Lenexa Arts Coun. Family Day, 1990. Mem. Lenexa C. of C., Nat. Mid. Schs. Assn., NEA (bldg. rep. 1989-90), Epsilon Pi Tau. Republican. Home: 12141 W 76th St # 102 Lenexa KS 66216

FLANAGAN, WILLIAM LEE, minister; b. L.A., Nov. 7, 1939; s. Bradford John and Annette Cleary (Stone) F.; m. Christy Pierce, July 12, 1963; 1 child, Julie Marie. BA, U. Redlands, 1961; MDiv, Princeton Theol. Sem., 1964; D of Ministry, Fuller Theol. Sem., 1986. Ordained to ministry Presbyn. Ch., 1964. Assoc. pastor youth First Presbyn. Ch., Burbank, Calif., 1964-68; assoc. pastor adult edn. for singles 1st Presbyn. Ch., Colorado Springs, Colo., 1969-81; assoc. pastor singles and missions St. Andrews Presbyn. Ch., Newport Beach, Calif., 1981—. Author: (with others) Singles Ministry Handbook, 1988; author: The Ministry of Divorce Recovery, 1991, (video series) Rebuilding the Castle That Has Come Down, 1990; contbr. articles to profl. jours. Honorary life mem. So. Calif. PTA, Burbank, Calif. 1967—. Charter mem. Nat. Assn. Single Adult Leaders (exec. dir. 1985-87, chmn. bd. dirs. 1988-89). Office: St Andrews Presbyn Ch 600 St Andrews Rd Newport Beach CA 92663

FLANARY, GARETH DEAN, minister; b. Pikeville, Ky., July 20, 1961; s. Sammy Randall and Mary Maxine (Tackett) F.; m. Deborah Lea DeLong, Aug. 15, 1981; children: Megan Rebecca, Aleithea Dawn. BA, Harding U., 1983. Ordained to ministry Ch. of Christ, 1983. Intern Kinston (N.C.) Ch. of Christ, 1981; minister DeValls Bluff (Ark.) Ch. of Christ, 1982, Uniontown (Pa.) Ch. of Christ, 1983-85; evangelist Manchester (Conn.) Ch. of Christ, 1986—; bd. dirs. Pa. Christian Camp, 1983-85; steering com. Northeastern Men's Retreat, Conn., 1988—. Vol. Am. Cancer Soc., Manchester. Recipient Evangelism award Harding U., Searcy, Ark., 1983. Republican. Home: 138 Telegraph Ave Chicopee MA 01020 Office: Church of Christ 284 Montgomery St Chicopee MA 01020 *When life is centered around God's mission, every aspect of one's life becomes glory to God and results in much fruit.*

FLANDERS, HENRY JACKSON, JR., religion educator; b. Malvern, Ark., Oct. 2, 1921; s. Henry Jackson and Mae (Hargis) F.; m. Tommie Lou Pardew, Apr. 19, 1944; children: Janet Flanders Mitchell, Jack III. BA, Baylor U., 1943; BD, So. Bapt. Theol. Sem., 1948, PhD, 1950. Diplomate: ordained to ministry Baptist Ch., 1941. Asst. prof., assoc. prof. Furman U., Greenville, S.C., 1950-55, prof., chaplain, chmn. dept. religion, 1955-62; pastor First Bapt. Ch., Waco, Tex., 1962-69; prof. religion Baylor U., Waco, Tex., 1969—, chmn. dept., 1980-83; chmn., trustee Golden Gate Bapt. Theol. Sem., Mill Valley, Calif., 1971-76; chaplain Tex. Ranger Commn., 1965—; mem. exec. com. Bapt. Gen. Conv. Tex., Dallas, 1966-68. Author: (with R.W. Crapps and D.A. Smith) People of the Convenant, 1963, 73, 88, (with Bruce Cresson) Introduction to the Bible, 1973; TV speaker: weekly program Lessons for Living, WFBC-TV, 1957-62. Trustee Baylor U., Waco, Tex., 1964-68; trustee Hillcrest Bapt. Hosp., 1963-64; chmn. Heart of Tex. Red Cross, 1967-68; narrator Waco Cotton Palace Pageant, 1970-80; chaplain Tex. Aero Commn., 1986—; pastor emeritus First Bapt. Ch., Waco, 1987; mem. grievance oversight com. Tex. Bar, 1979-87. Served to 1st. lt. USAAC, 1943-45, ETO. Named disting. alumnus Baylor U., 1986; grantee Furman U., 1960; grantee Baylor U., 1977, 82. Mem. Assn. Bapt. Profs. Religion (pres. 1958-59), AAUP (chpt. pres. 1973), Soc. Bibl. Lit., Am. Acad. Religion, Inst. Antiquity and Christianity, Waco Bapt. Ministerial Assn. (pres. 1967-68). Lodges: Rotary; Shriners. Home: 3820 Chateau St Waco TX 76710 Office: Baylor U Waco TX 76798

FLANDERS, WAYNE C., minister; b. Hutchinson, Kans., July 26, 1949; s. Clinton Wayne and Helen M. (Adams) F.; m. Linda Sue Marshall, Nov. 10, 1949. BA, Westmar Coll., LeMars, Iowa, 1971; MDiv, St. Paul Sch. Theology, Kansas City, Mo., 1974. Ordained to ministry, United Meth. Ch. 1975. Pastor Ebenezer & Hayes United Meth. Chs., Clay Center, Kans., 1972-77, Pleasant Grove United Meth. Ch., Burrton, Kans., 1977-81; assoc. pastor S. Hutchinson (Kans.) United Meth. Ch., 1977-81; pastor South Haven (Kans.) Mt. Hope United Meth. Ch., 1981-86, Cheney (Kans.) United Meth. Ch., 1986—; chmn. bd. trustees Horizon United Meth. Ctr., Arkansas City, Kans., 1983-87. Mem. Cheney Ministerial Alliance (sec. 1990-91). Home: 403 W 3d St Box 237 Cheney KS 67025 Office: Cheney United Meth Ch 406 W 3d St Box 237 Cheney KS 67025

FLAVIN, GLENNON P., bishop; b. St. Louis, Mar. 2, 1916. Grad., St. Louis Prep. Sem., Kendrick Sem. Ordained priest Roman Catholic Ch., 1941; sec. to archbishop St. Louis, 1949-57; consecrated bishop, 1957; ordained titular bishop of Joannina and aux. bishop St. Louis, 1957-67; bishop Diocese of Lincoln, Nebr., 1967—. Office: Chancery Office 3400 Sheridan Blvd PO Box 80328 Lincoln NE 68501

FLAYHART, ROBERT KEYSER, minister; b. Muncy, Pa., Aug. 30, 1959; s. Robert McCormick and Sharon (Keyser) F.; m. Laurie Legaré Kane, Apr. 28, 1984; children: Joshua James, Hannah Legaré. BS magna cum laude, Pa. State U., 1982; MDiv cum laude, Trinity Divinity Sch., 1988. Ordained to ministry Presbyn. Ch. in Am., 1989. Asst. to the pastor North Shore Presbyn. Ch., Lincolnshire, Ill., 1987-88; pastor Briarwood South Presbyn. Ch., Birmingham, 1989—; mem. presbytery com. mission to N.Am., Europe, 1990—. Republican. Office: Briarwood South Presbyn Ch 6260 Cahaba Valley Rd Birmingham AL 35242

FLEENER, ROBERT FRANCIS, minister; b. Whitinsville, Mass., May 23, 1951; s. Francis Clifton and Beatrice Cleona (Bearor) F.; m. Christine Ann Cambre, Aug. 5, 1978; children: Meredith, Paige. BA in Sociology, Furman U., Greensville, S.C., 1973; MDiv, So. Bapt. Theol. Sem., 1982; grad., Fuller Theol. Sem. Ordained to ministry Conservative Bapt. Assn. Am., 1982. Area dir. Young Life, New Orleans, 1975-78, 82-85, Lexington, Ky., 1978-80, Lafayette, La., 1985-88; singles pastor Trinity Bapt. Ch., Mesa, Ariz., 1988-90, Arcade Bapt. Ch., Sacramento, 1990—; chaplain Sacramento County Sheriff's Dept., 1990—. Book reviewer Singles Ministry Resources, 1989—. Mem. Am. Assn. Christian Counselors, Nat. Assn. Single Adult Leaders. Office: Arcade Bapt Ch 3927 Marconi Ave Sacramento CA 95821

FLEER, DAVID, clergyman; b. Sioux City, Iowa, Dec. 19, 1953; s. Arthur Ulrich and Marvelyn (Perleth) F.; m. Debra McPherren, Aug. 15, 1975; children: Joshua David, Luke Andrew, Nathan Mark. BA, Washington State U., 1976; MDiv, Abilene Christian U., 1981; D. Ministry, Fuller Theol. Sem., 1987. Ordained to ministry Ch. of Christ, 1977. Minister Vealmoor (Tex.) Ch. of Christ, 1977-81, Vancouver (Wash.) Ch. of Christ, 1982—; speaker at seminars, lectures Columbia Christian Coll., 1986, 87, Pepperdine U., 1988, 89, 90, Lubbock Christian U., 1988, Christian Scholars Conf., Malibu, Calif., 1988, 89. Mem. editorial bd. Leaven jour., 1989—; contbr. articles to profl. jours., book revs. Mem. Soc. Bibl. Lit., Am. Acad. Religion, Disciples of Christ Hist. Soc., Speech Communication Assn. Office: Vancouver Ch of Christ 800 N Andresen Rd Vancouver WA 98661 *I wish to give my life's work to the "weightier matters" issues of justice, mercy and faithfulness. All else, it seems to me, lowers ministry to the level of the mundane.*

FLEISCHER, DANIEL, minister, religious organization administrator. P-res. Ch. of Luth. Confession, Mpls. Office: Ch of Luth Confession 460 75th Ave NE Minneapolis MN 55432*

FLEISCHMANN, PAUL, youth minister; b. June 20, 1946; s. Leonard and Viola (Tyler) F.; m. Anntoinette Jordan, June 14, 1973; children: Todd Paul, Tyler Jonathan. BA, Seattle Pacific Coll., 1968; MDiv, Western Bapt. Sem., Portland, Oreg., 1975; postgrad., Internat. Christian Grad. U., San Bernardino, Calif. Ordained to ministry, Conservative Bapt. Assn., 1981. Youth pastor Ballard Bapt. Ch., Seattle, 1965-67; campus staff Seattle Youth for Christ, 1967-68; high sch. ministry staff Campus Crusade for Christ, various locations, 1968-88; exec. dir. Nat. Network of Youth Ministries, San Diego, 1982—; home missionary, 1968—; youth ministry cons., 1974—; officer Bd. Deacons, 1980-82, 88—, mem. Bd. Christian Edn., 1980-82, ch. planter, 1988—; adj. prof. Christian edn. Western Bapt. Sem., Portland, Oreg., 1981-83. Exec. editor: Insight for Student Discipleship, 1979-83; contbg. author: Working with Youth, 1982; editor: Discipling the Young Person, 1985; exec. editor Network News, 1983—; contbr. articles to profl. jours. Dir. Continental Singers Choir and Orch., 1977, Nat. Conv. on High Sch. Discipleship, 1979-83; asst. dir. Youth Congress '85, Washington. Recipient Gold Medallion, Evang. Christian Pubrs. Assn., 1986. Office: Nat Network of Youth Min 17150 Via Del Campo # 102 San Diego CA 92127

FLEMING, CAROLYN ELIZABETH, religious organization administrator, interior designer; b. Tulsa, Sept. 24, 1946; d. Jerry J. and Mary Josephine (Korten) Maly; m. Roger Earl Fleming, May 26, 1974; children—Karl Joseph, Briana Danika. Student, Texarkana Jr. Coll., 1963-65, Okla. State U., 1965-66; B.S. in Interior Design, U. Tex., 1970. Asst. to designer Planning and Design, Tulsa, 1970-72; pvt. cons., Texarkana, Tex., 1972-73; with Anchorage Neuro-Spinal Clinic, 1991—; sec. Nat. Teaching Com. Bahais of Alaska, Anchorage, 1981-85, mem., 1989—, Baha'i materials promotion com., 1987-89; chmn. Anchorage Local Spiritual Assembly, 1990-92, mem., 1980-85, 87-92; mem. Texarkana Bahai Local Spiritual Assembly, 1985, Oceanview (Alaska) Bahai Local Spiritual Assembly, 1986-87; coord. Interdenominational Cultural Unity Conf. for Anchorage Area, 1986. Vol. Rural Cap, 1986-87, Alaska Coun. on Prevention Alcohol and Drug Abuse, 1987, Spirit Days, 1987-88; trainee Parent and Youth Mediation Program, 1990; asst. aux. bd. for Bahai Oceanview Community, 1989-92. Mem. Arts Council, Valdez, Alaska, 1974-76. Mem. Assn. Interior Designers, Beta Sigma Phi. Mem. Baha'i Faith. Office: 13501 Brayton Dr Anchorage AK 99516

FLEMING, DAVID L., priest; b. St. Louis, July 4, 1934; s. Clarence C. and Emily Ann (O'Brien) F. AB, St. Louis U., 1958, MA, 1959; STD, Cath. U. Am., 1970. Joined S.J., Roman Cath. Ch., 1952, ordained priest, 1965. Assoc. prof. St. Louis U., 1970-76; founder, dir. Ministry Tng. Svcs., Denver, 1976-79; provincial superior Mo. province S.J., St. Louis, 1979-85; assoc. prof. Weston Sch. Theology, Cambridge, Mass., 1986-88; editor Rev. for Religious, St. Louis, 1988—; founder, dir. Inst. Religious Formation, St. Louis, 1971-76. Author: Spiritual Exercises, 1978; editor: Notes on the Spiritual Exercises, 1983, Christian Ministry of Spiritual Direction, 1988, Religious Life, 1990. Mem. Cath. Theol. Soc. Am. Office: Review for Religous 3601 Lindell Blvd Saint Louis MO 63108

FLEMING, EDWARD J., priest; b. Montclair, N.J., Mar. 29, 1920; s. Timothy Joseph and Agnes (Gannon) F. Student, Seton Hall Prep. Sch., South Orange, N.J., 1932-36; A.B., Seton Hall U., 1940, M.A., 1948, LL.D., 1970; student, Immaculate Conception Sem., Ramsey, N.J., 1936-40; S.T.L., Cath. U. Am., 1944; Ph.D., St. John's U., Bklyn., 1955; grad., Inst. Advanced Studies, N.Am. Coll., Rome, 1977; postgrad., Harvard Divinity Sch., 1986. Ordained priest Roman Catholic Ch., 1944, elevated to papal chamberlain, 1963, elevated to prelate to Pope John Paul II, 1983; priest St. Teresa's Ch., Summit, N.J., 1944-49; prof. ednl. psychology and religion Seton Hall U., 1949-51, dean student affairs, 1951-53, dean coll., 1953-59, exec. v.p., 1959-69, pres., 1969-70; pastor Our Lady of Blessed Sacrament Ch., Roseland, N.J., 1970—; dean Archdiocese of Newark, 1975-77, mem. bd. of consultors; vis. scholar Oxford (Eng.) U., 1987-88; dir. devel. Seton Hall U. Seminary, South Orange, N.J., 1987—; dir. Newman studies Univ. Coll., 1987—; dir. devel. Sch. Theology Seton Hall U., South Orange, 1987—; mem. exam. bd. Archdiocesan Clergy and Seminary, 1954-64; mem. Archdiocesan Commn. Parish Visitation, 1969—; Episcopal vicar Essex County Archdiocese; coordinating dean Essex County, 1975—; pres. Roseland Council Chs.; mem. ethics com. N.J. Supreme Ct., 1979—; mem. Senate of Priests, Archdiocese of Newark, 1980—, Archdiocesan Sch. Bd., 1980. Contbr. articles on higher edn. to ednl. periodicals and jours. Mem. Army Adv. Panel ROTC Affairs, 1961-70; mem. Edn. Commn. U.S.; mem. pres.'s council Caldwell Coll., N.J.; trustee Assumption Coll., Mendham, N.J., Greater Newark Black and White Opera Co., Tri-Hosp. Ecumenical Chaplaincy Council No. N.J., 1979. Recipient Alpha Epsilon Mu award, 1956; Sapientiae Christianae Humanitarian award, 1958; John J. Crecca Found. Humanitarian award, 1967; Irishman of Year award Friends of Brian Boru, Inc., 1967; Zionist Brotherhood award, 1979; named to Athletic Hall of Fame, Seton Hall U., 1986; N.Am. Coll. fellow, Rome, 1971—, fellow Weston Theol. Ctr., Cambridge, Eng., 1986-87. Mem. Eastern Assn. Coll. Deans and Advisers of Men, Nat. Cath. Edn. Assn. (pres. Eastern unit 1965-66), Middle States Accreditation Assn., N.J. Hist. Soc. (com. of 125), Cath. Theol. Soc. Am. Address: Seton Hall Univ Seminary South Orange NJ 07079 *May I never stop reaching out to others. May I never stop loving. For I should have learned long ago that love is not love 'til I give it away.*

FLEMING, JERRY ALDIN, music minister; b. Tyler, Tex., Feb. 6, 1948; s. Aldin Howard and Ernestine (Clark) F.; m. Brenda Jean Shafer, Apr. 5, 1969; children: Amy Denise, Amanda Elaine, Melodie Allison. MusB, Lamar U., 1978; MA, Southwestern Bapt. Theol. Sem., 1987. Ordained to ministry Amelia Bapt. Ch., 1977. Minister of music and youth 1st Bapt. Ch., Lindale, Tex., 1971-73, Quitman, Tex., 1973-74; minister of music and youth Amelia Bapt. Ch., Beaumont, Tex., 1974-81, Harlandale Bspt. Ch., San Antonio, 1981-83; minister of music and edn. 1st Bapt. Ch., Sanger, Tex., 1983—. Mem. Am. Choral Dir. Assn., Southern Bapt. Ch. Music Conf., Singing Men of Tex. Home: 109 Southland Sanger TX 76266 Office: 1st Bapt Ch 708 S 5th Sanger TX 76266

FLEMING, ROSE ANN, nun, former college president, lawyer; b. Cin., Aug. 23, 1932; d. Thomas John and Mary Gertrude (Sullivan) F. BA, Mt. St. Joseph-on-the-Ohio, 1954; MA in English, U. Detroit, 1964; MEd, Xavier U., Cin., 1969; PhD, Miami U., Oxford, Ohio, 1973; MBA, Xavier U., Cin., 1984; JD, Chase Coll. Law, No. Ky. U., 1988. Bar: Ohio 1989; joined Sisters of Notre Dame de Namur, Roman Cath. Ch., 1954. Tchr. Latin, social studies, English Mt. Notre Dame High Sch., Reading, Ohio, 1954-60; mem. faculty Summit Country Day Sch., Cin., 1960-75, supr., 1967-75; pres. Trinity Coll., Washington, 1975-82; acad. adminstr. Xavier U., Cin., 1982—; pvt. practice law Cin., 1989—. Mem. ABA, Ohio Bar Assn., Cin. Bar Assn., Greater Cin. Women Lawyers Assn., Internat. Assn. U. Presidents (mem. steering com. of N. Atlantic com. 1981—), Friars Club (trustee Cin. chpt.), Kappa Gamma Pi. Address: 3855 Lodgewood Dr Cincinnati OH 45207

FLEMING, STEVEN ROBERT, minister; b. San Bernardino, Calif., Apr. 30, 1951; s. Robert Ellsworth and Marie Claire (Kitzmiller) F.; m. Brenda Kay Cross, June 9, 1973. BA with honors, U. Md., 1972; D. Ministry, Union Theol. Sem., Richmond, Va., 1976. Ordained to ministry Presbyn. Ch. U.S.A., 1976. Assoc. pastor 1st Presbyn. Ch., Ft. Smith, Ark., 1976-79; pastor Shippensburg (Pa.) Presbyn. Ch., 1979-85; interim assoc. pastor Paxton Presbyn. Ch., Harrisburg, Pa., 1986-87; pastor 1st United Presbyn. Ch., Westminster, Md., 1987—; mem. Balt. Presbytery; seminar leader. Contbr. articles to profl. jours. Bd. dirs. Shippensburg U. Campus Ministry, 1979-85. Mem. Alban Inst. Republican. Avocations: photography, gardening, computers, travel, genealogy. Office: 1st Presbyn Ch 65 Washington Rd Westminster MD 21157

FLEMING, SUSAN ALICE, minister, military officer; b. Toledo, Ohio, Mar. 14, 1949; d. Max Walter and Alice Mildred (Allman) Hischke; m. Dwight Howard Fleming, Apr. 15, 1978 (dec. Nov. 1990); children: Scott Dwight, Sally Marie Forsythe, Cynthia Lynn Fleming Salyer. Student, Akron U., 1971; BA, Malone Coll., 1971; MDiv, United Theol. Seminary, Dayton, Ohio, 1977; postgrad., Miami U., Oxford, Ohio, 1987—. Tchr. Canton City Schs., Brunnerdale Sem., Canton, Ohio, 1971-74; pastor Salem United Meth. Ch., Bettsville, Ohio, 1975-77, Houcktown Cir. United Meth. Chs., Arlington, Ohio, 1977-87, St. Paul United Meth. Ch., 1988—; chaplain 9018th ARPC/HC, Denver, 1976—; dir. Fort Findlay Playhouse, Findlay, Ohio, 1983. Mem. Southern Hancock County Ministerial, Arlington, Ohio, 1977-87, Delphos Ministerial, 1988—. Capt. USAF Res. Recipient Falcon award Air Res. Personnel Ctr., Denver, Colo. Republican. Avocations: sewing, writing, acting, scuba, walking, show dogs. Home: 16536 CR 8 Arlington OH 45814 Office: St Paul United Meth Ch 335 S Main Delphos OH 45833

FLEMING, WILLIAM ROBERT (BILL FLEMING), lay church worker, utilities company administrator; b. Decatur, Ill., Apr. 13, 1960; s. Robert George and Carolyn Ann (Wilkerson) F.; m. Shari Beth Hausmann, Aug. 8, 1980; children: Robert David, William Mitchell. Grad. high sch., Atwood, Ill. Choir dir. Atwood Bapt. Ch., 1978—, deacon, 1979-84, sch. supt., 1985-86; pres. Bill Fleming Ministries Inc., Atwood, 1984—; supr. Cen. Ill. Light Co., Tuscola, Ill., 1989—; choir dir. United Ch. Atwood, 1989—; mem. adv. bd. Atwood State Bank. Soloist rec. album: Bill Fleming—Naturally, 1986. Trustee Village of Atwood, 1989—; active Atwood Econ. Devel. Corp., 1990—. Mem. Atwood C. of C. (pres. 1990-91), Am. Bus. Club (treas. Tuscola chpt. 1987-88), Lions, Tri-County Car Club. Home: 410 N Missouri Atwood IL 61913

FLESHER, HUBERT LOUIS, religion educator; b. Elyria, Ohio, Apr. 30, 1933; s. O. Jay and Armide Elizabeth (deSaulles) F.; m. Mary June Mosher, Apr. 3, 1965; children: Erika Anne, Jonathan Jay. B.A. magna cum laude, Pomona Coll., 1954; B.D., Yale U., 1958, M.A., 1960. Ordained to ministry Episcopal Ch., 1958. Asst. dean chapel Princeton U., N.J., 1956-57; instr. Episcopal Theol. Sch., Cambridge, Mass., 1963-66; chaplain Millersville State Coll., 1967-71; chaplain Lehigh U., Bethlehem, Pa., 1971-90, assoc. prof. religion, 1971-90, prof., 1980-90; dean of the chapel Smith Coll., Northampton, Mass., 1990—; vis. prof. Lancaster Theol. Sem., 1967-71; founder, 1st chmn. Lancaster Ind. Press, Pa.; mem. exec. com. Pa. Commn. United Ministries in Higher Edn., 1974-90; lectr. in field. Founding bd. dirs. Young People's Philharm. of Lehigh Valley; bd. govs. Bach Choir, 1988-90. Honnold fellow, 1954-55; NEH fellow, 1985. Mem. NEA (panelist 1991), NACU Chaplains, Am. Acad. Religion, Soc. Bibl. Lit. and Exegesis, Nat. Campus Ministers Assn., Phi Beta Kappa, Omicron Delta Kappa. Home: 16 Paradise Rd Northampton MA 01060-2907 Office: Smith Coll Helen Hills Chapel Northampton MA 01063 *Unexpectedly, the true discovery of self comes only when one is turned outward wholly in the concern for another. It is then the most arduous explorers of self will find the missing piece that rescues them from isolation.*

FLETCHER, BARBARA MILLER, lay worker; b. San Diego, Jan. 27, 1956; d. John Gordon and Bille June (Gibson) Miller; m. Craig Brian Fletcher, May 22, 1976; children: Benjamin Aaron, Stephanie Diane. AA, Southeastern State U., 1976. Sec. Berean Bapt. Ch. and Christian Sch., Humble, Tex., 1986—; sec. Garrett Corp., Houston, 1976-79; youth leader Berean Bapt. Ch., 1985-89. Office: Berean Bapt Ch 702 Atascocita Rd Humble TX 77396

FLETCHER, DAVID ROSS, minister, writer; b. Newport Beach, Calif., Oct. 8, 1959; s. John Franklin and Joan Thais (Buchholz) F.; m. Tamara Jo Shoemaker, Dec. 8, 1979; 1 child, Jason Bradford. AB, Occidental Coll., 1980; M in Theology, Dallas Theol. Sem., 1985. Ordained to ministry, 1985. Mgr. Forest Lawn Cemetery, Dallas, 1980—; minister to singles Northwest Bible Ch., Dallas, 1986-89; min. of discipleship, 1988-90, min. of communications, 1989—; pres. Fletcher Group Enterprizes, Inc., 1988—; conf. dir. Dallas Sem., 1984-85, Northwest Bible Ch., 1985-86. Author: The Ephesians Project, 1986, The Purple Thumb Sketches, 1989; contbr. articles on ch. ministries to profl. pubs. Summer worker SEND, Internat., Manila, Philippines, 1984; precinct chmn. Reps. of Dallas County, 1984—. Recipient C.I. Scofield award Dallas Sem., 1985. Club: Student Missions Fellowship Dallas Sem. (v.p. 1984-85). Home: 10977 Harry Hines Blvd Dallas TX 75220 Office: Northwest Bible Ch 8505 Douglas Dallas TX 75225

FLETCHER, DOUGLAS KIM, minister; b. Des Moines, Dec. 31, 1952; s. Robert V. and Wilma Alice (Roberts) F.; m. Wesla Liao Fletcher, July 31, 1976; children: Samuel, Matthew. AB, Drake U., 1972; MDiv, Princeton Theol. Seminary, N.J., 1975, PhD, 1982. Ordained to ministry Presbyn. Ch., 1981. Assoc. pastor First Presbyn. Ch., Tulsa, Okla., 1981-84; sr. pastor Southminster Presbyn. Ch., Tulsa, 1984—; adj. prof. Phillips Sem., Tulsa, 1989—; coun. of advisors Dubuque (Iowa) Theol. Sem., 1991. Bd. dirs. Family and Children's Svcs., 1984-90, Tulsa Met. Ministry, 1987-89, Tulsa Habitat for Humanity, 1987-89. Mem. Soc. Bibl. Lit., Rotary, Omicron Delta Kappa, Phi Beta Kappa. Home: 2459 E 23rd St Tulsa OK 74114 Office: Southminster Presbyn Ch 3500 S Peoria Ave Tulsa OK 74105

FLETCHER, HARRY EDWARD, academic administrator; b. Hamilton, Ohio, June 22, 1942; s. Orville H. and Virginia E. (Davis) F.; m. Muriel C. Graham, July 16, 1966; children: Donna J. Heindel, Mary Jo. Student, Ind. State U., 1963-64; BA, Washington Bible Coll., Lanham, Md., 1968; ThM, Capital Bible Sem., 1971; DMin, Luther Rice Sem., 1976. Ordained to ministry Bethel Bible Ch., 1968. Chaplain Good News Jail/Prison Ministry, Arlington, Va., 1966-68; pastor, tchr. Bethel Bible Ch., Boulevard Heights, Md., 1968-71, Webster (N.Y.) Bible Ch., 1971-81, York (Pa.) Gospel Ctr., 1981-84; pres. Washington Bible Coll./Capital Bible Sem., Lanham, 1984—; pastor, tchr. to missionaries Cen. and S.Am., 1968, India, 1980, Papua, New Guinea, 1988, Haiti, 1982; tchr., speaker Bible and Missionary Theol. Coll., Ikwa, Nigeria, 1990. With U.S. Army, 1960-62. Republican. Office: Washington Bible Coll Capital Bible Sem 6511 Princess Garden Pkwy Lanham MD 20706

FLETCHER, JOHN CALDWELL, bioethicist, religious studies educator; b. Bryan, Tex., Nov. 1, 1931; s. Robert Capers and Estelle Collins (Caldwell) F.; m. Adele Davis Woodall, Sept. 4, 1954; children: John Caldwell, Page

Moss, Adele Davis. B.A., U. of South, 1953; M.Div. cum laude, Va. Theol. Sem., 1956; M.Div. Fulbright scholar, U. Heidelberg, 1957; Ph.D., Union Theol. Sem., N.Y.C., 1969. Ordained priest Episcopal Ch., 1957-90. Curate St. Lukes Episc. Ch., Mountain Brook, Ala., 1957-60; rector R.E. Lee Meml. Ch., Lexington, Va., 1960-64; chaplain Cornell Med. Sch.-New York Hosp., 1964-66; assoc. prof. Va. Theol. Sem., 1966-71; dir. Interfaith Met. Theol. Edn., Inc., Washington, 1971—; pres. Interfaith Met. Theol. Edn., Inc., 1975-77; chief bioethics program Clin. Center, NIH, 1977-87; prof. religious studies, biomed. ethics U. Va., Charlottesville, 1987—; vis. fellow Inst. Med. Genetics, U. Oslo, 1984; co-investigator 2d Internat. Survey Med. Geneticists, 1990. Author: (with Celia A. Hahn) Inter/Met: Bold Experiment in Theological Education, 1977, The Futures of Protestant Seminaries, 1983, Coping with Genetic Disorders, 1982; editor: (with Mark I. Evans et al) Fetal Diagnosis and Therapy, Science Ethics and the Law, 1988, (with Albert R. Jonsen and Norman L. Quist) Ethics Consultation in Health Care, 1989; editor and author (with Dorothy C. Wertz) Ethics and Human Genetics: A Cross-Cultural Perspective, 1989; translator: Creation and Fall, 1959; assoc. editor Ency. of Bioethics, 2d edit., 1990; contbr. articles to profl. jours. Founding fellow Hastings Ctr., Hastings-on-Hudson, N.Y.; mem. Soc. of Friends, 1990—. Vis. fellow Inst. for Med. Genetics U. Oslo, 1984. Mem. Soc. Bioethics Consultation (founding, pres., bd. dirs.), Soc. Christian Ethics, Am. Soc. Human Genetics, European Soc. Human Genetics, Internat. Soc. Tech. Assessment. Mem. Soc. of Friends. Home: 1940 N Pantops Rd Charlottesville VA 22901 Office: U Va Med Ctr Box 348 Charlottesville VA 22908 *My personal philosophy is that responsibility and accountability are the highest goals for human beings. Each situation can be saved from meaninglessness by the courage not to forsake these goals.*

FLETCHER, KENNETH, minister; b. Willacoochee, Ga., Dec. 18, 1954; s. Warren Fletcher and Mattie Lorine (Sconiers) Frazier; m. Bettye Jean Williams, Aug. 22, 1974; children: Kerpasha Benite', Kenneth Benjamin. AS, South Ga. Coll., 1981; BBA magna cum laude, Albany (Ga.) State Coll., 1982. Ordained to ministry United Pentacostal Ch. Internat. as elder, 1985; cert. behavioral cons. Sr. pastor 1st United Pentecostal Ch., Albany, 1981—; sectional dir. Sunday sch. Ga. dist. United Pentecostal Internat., Albany, 1981-84; caseworker, then sr. caseworker Dept. Family and Children Svcs., 1986-87. Sgt. USAF, 1974-80. Mem. Albany/Doughtery County Ministerial Assn. (pres. 1984). Office: First United Pentecostal Ch 421 Lumpkin St Albany GA 31705-2555

FLETCHER, STEPHEN EDWIN, minister; b. Moulmein, Burma, Jan. 15, 1927; came to U.S., 1931; s. Edwin Teed and M. Virginia (Barrett) F.; m. Eva Louise Manley, Aug. 28, 1950 (dec. Jan. 1990); children: Barrett M., Rebecca A. Fletcher né Tighe, Randal W., Rodrick A. BA, Denison U., 1950; BD, Andover Newton Theol. Sem., 1954; MA, Kans. U., 1986. Ordained to ministry Am. Bapt. Assn., 1954, United Meth. Ch., 1987. Pastor Center St. Bapt. Ch., Jamaica Plain, Mass., 1952-57, Cen. Bapt. Ch., Southbridge, Mass., 1957-61, Calvary Bapt. Ch., Springfield, Vt., 1961-65, Community Bapt. Ch., Somerset, N.J., 1965-69, South Hills Community Bapt. Ch., Upper St. Clair, Pa., 1969-77, 1st Bapt. Ch., Lawrence, Kans., 1977-83, Yates Center (Kans.) United Meth. Ch., 1987-91; stewardship adv. Kans. Ea. Conf., 1991—; trustee Kans. Sch. Religion, Lawrence, 1984—; bd. dirs. Bd. Global Ministries, Kans. Ea. Conf., Topeka, 1988—; sec. Woodson County Ministerial Alliance, Yates Center, 1987-91. Riot Conf. Chair. Civil Rights Com., Franklin Twp., Somerset, 1968. Sgt. USAAF, 1945-46, ETO. Mem. Internat. Order St. Luke the Physician (convener, sec.); probationary mem. Kans. E. Annual Conf. United Meth. Ch. Democrat.

FLETCHER, WILLIAM ADRIN, minister; b. Graham, Tex., Apr. 22, 1948; s. Henry Jesse and Frances Merle (Thigpen) F.; m. Terri Lynn Hoch, June 19, 1970; children: Colin, Scott. BS, Abilene Christian U., 1970. Minister Eliasville (Tex.) Ch. of Christ, 1967-70; missionary, minister Sighthill Ch. of Christ, Edinburgh, Scotland, 1970-75; minister West 34th St./Brookhollow Ch. of Christ, Houston, 1975-83, Murray St. Ch. of Christ, Rockdale, Tex., 1983—. Bd. dirs. Cen. Tex. Area Mus., Salado, 1980, v.p., 1983-85, pres. 1986—; bd. dirs., pres. NW Christian Sch., Houston, 1983; bd. dirs. South Milam County United Way, 1988-90, pres., 1988-89; bd. dirs. Richards Meml. Hosp., Rockdale, 1989—. Named one of Outstanding Young Men Am., Jaycees, 1978. Mem. Am. Assn. Christian Counselors. Avocations: photography, swimming. Home: 1603 Sager Rd Rockdale TX 76567 Office: Murray St Ch of Christ 1301 Murray St Rockdale TX 76567

FLETCHER, WILLIAM MAHAR, minister; b. Mpls., Dec. 15, 1924; s. William David and Vera LeClare (Mahar) F.; m. Jeanette Viola Sundgaard, Sept. 3, 1948; children: Carol, Susan, David. BA in Philosophy, U. Minn., 1950; postgrad., U. Manchester, Eng., 1950-51; MA in N.T., Denver Sem., 1975, DMin, 1979. Dir. for Eng. The Navigators, 1950-54; dir. Servicemen's Work Europe, 1959-60; tchr. Missionary Internship, Detroit, 1955-58; sr. pastor Grace Bible Chapel, Grand Rapids, Minn., 1962-66, 1st Bapt. Ch., Golden, Colo., 1966-91; min. at large Rocky Mountain Conservative Bapts., Wheat Ridge, 1991—; bd. dirs. Conservative Bapt. of Am., Wheaton, Ill., 1967-73; bd. dirs., v.p., pres. Rocky Mt. Conservative Bapt., Denver, 1967-84; bd. dirs., mem. acad. affairs com. Denver Sem., 1972-84; bd. dirs. Conservative Bapt. Fgn. Mission Soc., Wheaton, 1987-91. Author: The Second Greatest Commandment, 1983, Triumph of Surrender, 1987; contbr. articles to profl. jours.; co-author Bible Study series, Studies in Christian Living, 1958. With USN, 1942-45. Republican. Home: 801 20th St Golden CO 80401 Office: Rocky Mountain Conservative Bapt Assn 10555 W 44th Ave Wheat Ridge CO 80033

FLIPPIN, KEITH ALAN, lay worker, service technician; b. Norman, Okla., Dec. 31, 1961; s. Vernon Earl and Earline Faye (Becker) F.; m. Vickie Lynn Coble, June 6, 1981. Grad. high sch., Liberal, Kans., 1990. Tchr. Sunday sch., organist Ch. of the Living God, Wichita, Kans., 1985-86; pianist, deacon, youth Sunday sch. tchr., janitor Cornerstone Pentecostal Holiness Ch., Wichita, 1989—; sr. svc. technician Bus. Systems Inc., Wichita, 1981—. Dir. concerts Lifeline Ministries, Wichita, 1986—. Home: 2945 S Euclid Wichita KS 67217

FLIPPIN, TANCREDE WAYMAN, youth minister; b. Stuttgart, West Germany, Oct. 5, 1961; s. Eddie Joe and Gail (Rutledge) F.; m. Janet Lois Reynolds, July 24, 1982; children: Reynold Andrew, Erin Leichelle. BBA, Tarleton State U., 1983; MA in Religious Edn., Southwestern Bapt. Theol. Sem., 1989. Ordained to ministry So. Bapt. Conv., 1991. Min. youth and edn. Harvey Bapt. Ch., Stephenville, Tex., 1983-87; min. youth First Bapt. Ch., Midlothian, Tex., 1987-90; min. youth and students Cook Bapt. Ch., Ruston, La., 1990—; camp staff dir. Cross-Timbers & Trinity Brazos Youth Camps, Brownwood, Tex., 1984-87, Aquilla, Tex., 1988-89; associational youth minister Ellis Bapt. Assn., Midlothian, 1987-90, Concord Bapt. Assn., Ruston, La., 1991—; speaker, seminar leader, 1984—. Contbr. articles to quarterly mag. Mem. C. of C., Stephenville, 1984-86. Office: Cook Bapt Ch 2000 Cooktown Rd Ruston LA 71270

FLIPPIN, WILLIAM EDWARD, minister; b. Nashville, May 16, 1952; s. Richard Clifton and Virginia Mae (Cole) F.; m. Sylvia Taylor, Nov. 5, 1952; children: William Edward Jr., Richard, Joseph, Joi. BA, Fisk U., 1974; MDiv, Emory U., 1982; D Ministry, McCormick Theol. Sem., 1988. Ordained to ministry Bapt. Ch. Assoc. minister Beulah Bapt. Ch., Atlanta, 1979-80; pastor Springfield Bapt. Ch., Greensboro, Ga., 1980-86, Shoal Creek Bapt. Ch., Locust Grove, Ga., 1986-90, Greater Piney Grove Bapt. Ch., Atlanta, 1990—; assoc. dir. Black Ch. Rels., Atlanta, 1982—. Bd. dirs. Gov.'s Commn. on Children and Youth, 1988-90, YMCA, Atlanta, 1988-91, Continuum, Atlanta, 1988-91. Home: 3733 Valpariso Cir Decatur GA 30034-6014 Office: Greater Piney Grove Ch 1879 Glenwood Ave SE Atlanta GA 30316

FLISS, RAPHAEL M., bishop; b. Milw., Oct. 25, 1930. Student, St. Francis Sem., Houston, Cath. U., Washington. Ordained priest, Roman Cath. Ch., 1956. Bishop Superior, Wis., 1985—. Office: Chancery Office 1201 Hughitt Ave Box 969 Superior WI 54880

FLODING, MATTHEW DUANE, minister; b. Mpls., Feb. 1, 1955; s. Duane Roy and Ardelle Dorothy (Lichtsinn) F.; m. Marcia Lynn Gannaway, Oct. 7, 1978; children: Geoffrey John Robert, Kathryn Erin, Margrethe Anne. BA, Bethel Coll., 1977; MA, Wheaton Coll., 1982; MDiv, McCormick Theol. Seminary, Chgo., 1985. Ordained to ministry Reformed Ch. in Am., 1986. Dir. sr. high ministry Park Ave. Meth. Ch., Mpls., 1977-81; assoc. pastor Bethel Presbyn. Ch., Wheaton, Ill., 1983-87; minister Christ Presbyn. Ch., Janesville, Wis., 1987-89; chaplain Northwestern Coll., Orange City, Iowa, 1989—; chaplain USNG, 1988—. Co-author: Sexuality: God's Good Idea, 1988, Who Am I: A Look in the Mirror, 1987, Relationships: Face to Face, 1986; contbr. articles to profl. jours. Named Outstanding Young Citizen, YMCA, Mpls., 1973; recipient Henry Bast Preaching fellowship Western Seminary, Holland, Mich., 1990. Mem. Am. Soc. Ch. History, Pi Gamma Mu (life). Office: Northwestern College 208 8th St SW Orange City IA 51041

FLOKSTRA, GERARD JOHN, III, missionary, librarian; b. Springfield, Mo., June 30, 1956; s. Gerard John Jr. and Ruth Marg (Barney) F.; m. Glenna Jean Crim, May 13, 1978; children: Gerard John IV, Bianca Kristine. BA in Bible, Cen. Bible Coll., 1978; MLS, U. Pitts., 1989. Libr. Asia Pacific Theol. Sem., Baquio City, Philippines, 1985—; library cons. regional office Asia Pacific Bible Schs., 1987—. Mem. Philippine Theol. Library Assn., Am. Theol. Library Assn., Assn. Christian Librs. Mem. Assemblies of God. Home: 69 Lagarda, Baguio City 2600, The Philippines Office: Asia Pacific Theol Sem, PO Box 377, Baguio City 2600, The Philippines

FLOOD, PATRICK, ecumenical agency administrator. Exec. dir. Austin (Tex.) Met. Ministries. Office: Austin Met Ministries 44 East Ave Ste 302 Austin TX 78701*

FLORES, PATRICK F., archbishop; b. Ganado, Tex., July 26, 1929. Grad., St. Mary's Sem., Houston. Ordained priest Roman Catholic Ch., 1956; ordained titular bishop of Italica and aux. bishop San Antonio, 1970; apptd. bishop of El Paso, 1978; archbishop of San Antonio, 1979. Office: Chancery Office PO Box 28410 San Antonio TX 78228 also: 2600 W Woodlawn Ave San Antonio TX 78228

FLORIAN, ROBERT BRUCE, educator, minister; b. Hartford, Conn., Jan. 17, 1930; s. Franklin Benjamin and Gertrude (Bruce) F.; m. Barbara Jean Walker, June 2, 1951; children: Linda Florian Neyhart, Laura Florian Moul, Joseph. BA, Adrian Coll., 1951; MDiv, Garrett Theol. Sem., 1956; MA, W.Va. U., 1963, PhD, 1973. Ordained to ministry United Meth. Ch. as deacon, 1953, as elder, 1957. Instr. Wesley Coll., Dover, Del., 1956-58; mem. faculty Salem (W.Va.) Coll. (now Salem-Teikyo U.), 1958—, prof. history and religion, 1974—, chmn. liberal studies dept., 1974-90, chmn. humanities and social sci. dept., 1990—; pastoral svc. W.Va. United Meth. Chs., Haywood, 1961-62, Jarvisville, 1971-73, Greenwood, 1976-79, Wallace, 1979-84; supervising pastor-in-charge, Bristol, 1984-85; interim pastor, West Milford, 1985-86, Riverside-Granville, Morgantown, 1986-90; mem. Meth. conf. Bd. Edn., 1966-69; mem. Conf. Commn. on Archives and History, 1973—, treas., 1984-88. Co-author: Melting Times: A History of West Virginia United Methodism, 1984, 2d edit., 1989; compiler: Bicentennial Historial Directory of West Virginia United Methodist Churches, 1976. Mem. Hist. Soc. United Meth. Ch. (charter), W.Va. Hist. Assn. (past pres.), Salem Ministerial Assn. (treas. 1969-76). Home: 51 Moore St Salem WV 26426 Office: Salem-Teikyo U Salem WV 26426

FLOURNOY, PHILIP JAMES, minister; b. Louisville, Oct. 25, 1955; s. Houston Marshall and Margaret LaVerne (Kirkland) F.; m. Karen Sue Rattan, Jan. 2, 1982; children: Jason Dillon, Toby Lucas. BA, Stetson U., 1978; M of Religious Edn., Southwestern Bapt. Theol., Seminary, Ft. Worth, 1982. Ordained to ministry Bapt. Ch., 1991. Fgn. missionary Fgn. Mission Bd., Richmond, Va., 1983-88; assoc. pastor youth and edn. Bulverde (Tex.) Bapt. Ch., 1988—. Coach Youth Soccer League, Bulverde, 1988-90; v.p. PTA, Bulverde, 1991. Mem. San Antonio Bapt. Assn. (mem. student union com. 1990-91). Office: Bulverde Bapt Ch 31960 Bulverde Rd Bulverde TX 78163 *For every right or privilege there is a corresponding responsibility and duty. People need to be as quick to stand up for one as for the other—starting in church!.*

FLOWER, JOSEPH REYNOLDS, administrative executive; b. Indpls., Mar. 1, 1913; s. J. Roswell and Alice Marie (Reynolds) F.; m. Mary Jane Carpenter, June 6, 1940; children: Joseph Reynolds, Mary Alice, Paul William. Diploma, Cen. Bible Coll., Springfield, Mo., 1934. Ordained to ministry Assemblies of God Ch., 1934. Pastor chs. in Pa., N.Y., Maine, Mass., 1934-54; supt. N.Y. Dist. Assembly of God, 1954-75; mem. gen presbytery Gen. Coun., Springfield, 1953—, mem. exec. presbtery, 1966—, gen. sec., 1976—; bd. dirs. Valley Forge Christian Coll., Phoenixville, Pa., Cen. Bible Coll., 1965-73, 1983-90, Assemblies of God Theol. Sem., Springfield, 1973-91, Evangel Coll., Springfield, 1979-87. Office: 1445 Boonville Ave Springfield MO 65802

FLOWERS, GLEN DALE, minister; b. Elberfeld, Ind., July 2, 1940; s. Otis Preston and Anna (Hollingsworth) F.; m. Naomi June Bruce, Aug. 13, 1943; children: Theresa Lynne Flowers Carr, Robert Preston. BA, Carson-Newman Coll., Jefferson City, Tenn., 1972; MDiv, So. Bapt. Theol. Sem., Louisville, 1976; real estate diploma, U. Indpls., 1982. Ordained to ministry So. Bapt. Conv., 1969. Driver United Parcel Svc., Evansville, Ind., 1962-69; pastor Mitchell Springs Bapt. Ch., Rutledge, Tenn., 1969-71, Broadway Bapt. Ch., Princeton, Ind., 1972-76, 1st Bapt. Ch., Mooresville, Ind., 1976-85; evangelist, Jefferson City, 1971-72; pastor Oakhill Bapt. Ch., Evansville, 1985—; dir. BSU and ISUE, U. Evansville, 1974-75; mem. nat. steering com. Festival Religion and Rural Life, Home Missions Bd., State Conv. Bapts. in Ind., 1978, mem. exec. bd. and exec. com., 1978-80, 86—, chmn. state exec. bd., 1979-80; mem. various coms. Cen. Ind. Bapt. Assn., Sunday sch. dir., 1978-79, 81-82; tchr. Boyce Bible Ctr., Monrovia, Ind., 1984-85; mem. com. on nominations So. Bapt. Conv., 1988-89; instr., ctr. dir. Extension Ctr. for Okla. Bapt. U., Evansville, 1991—; numerous others. Contbr. to Ency. So. Bapts., Vol. IV, 1980. Chmn. Vol. Probation Officers for Juvenile Delinquents, Rutledge, 1971; bd. dirs. Mooresville Sr. Ctr., 1983-84, Morgan County Sr. Svcs., Martinsville, Ind., 1983-85; chaplain Morgan County Sheriff's Office and Mooresville Police Dept., 1980-85; vol. chaplaincy program Mooresville High Sch., 1983-84; bd. dirs. Morgan County Weekday Religious Edn., 1983-84; founder Ann. Ladies' Enrichment Day, Mooresville, 1980-85. With USN, 1958-61. Mem. Southwestern Bapt. Assn. (bd. dirs. 1985—). Republican. Home: 5700 Twickingham Dr Evansville IN 47711 Office: Oakhill Bapt Ch 4615 Oak Hill Rd Evansville IN 47711 *Our generation has a need to be encouraged to express a sincere faith in God while the influences around them are teaching them to be so superficial about their feelings.*

FLOWERS, RONALD BRUCE, religion educator; b. Tulsa, Jan. 11, 1935; s. John Paul and Clara Mae (Tefertiller) F.; m. Leah Elizabeth King, Aug. 21, 1959; children: Jennifer Ruth, Philip Gregory, Ronald Paul. BA, Tex. Christian U., 1957; BD, Vanderbilt U., 1960, S.T.M., 1961; PhD, U. Iowa, 1967. Minister Crofton (Ky.) Christian Ch., 1961-63; prof. religion studies Tex. Christian U., Ft. Worth, 1966—. Author: Religion in Strange Times: The 1960s and 1970s, 1984; co-author: (with Robert T. Miller) Toward Benevolent Neutrality: Church, State, and the Supreme Court, 3d edit., 1987; contbr. religious articles to scholarly jours. Named Danforth Assoc., Danforth Found., 1971. Mem. Am. Soc. Ch. History, Disciples of Christ Hist. Soc., Nat. Coun. for Religion in Pub. Edn., Am. Acad. Religion (pres. southwest region 1988-89). Office: Tex Christian U Box 30772 Fort Worth TX 76129

FLOYD, JAMES TIMOTHY (TIM FLOYD), clergyman; b. Columbia, Tenn., Sept. 19, 1951; s. Fletcher Aubrey and Margaret Voncile (Rhodes) F.; m. Jonnel Lynn Potter, Dec. 27, 1976; children: Chandra Leigh, Stephen Cole, Natalie Rene. BA in History, BA in German, Troy (Ala.) State U., 1972; MDiv, Southwestern Bapt. Theol. Sem., Ft. Worth, 1977. Ordained to ministry So. Bapt. Conv. Assoc. pastor Heritage Bapt. Ch., Montgomery, Ala., 1978-81; pastor 1st Bapt. Ch., Oakland Park, Fla., 1982-85, Columbia, 1985—; v.p. Montgomery Bapt. Mins. Conf., 1980-81; v.p. communication Evangelism Explosion Internat., Ft. Lauderdale, Fla., 1981-85; mem. exec. bd. Tenn. Bapt. Conv., Brentwood, 1986—. Author: Welcome to the Real World, 1985; also articles. Mem. Task Force for Racial Rels., Maury County Bd. Edn., 1988-89. Republican. Avocations: swimming, weight-lifting, hiking. Office: 1st Bapt Ch 812 S High Columbia TN 38401

FLOYD, KENNETH EUGENE, minister; b. Springfield, Oh., Sept. 25, 1955; s. John W. and Doris (Eby) F.; m. Sharon Lynn McFaddin, Nov. 20, 1976; child: Allison Eloise. BA, Cedarville Coll., 1977; MDiv., Grace Theol. Seminary, 1981. Pastor Calvary Bapt., Oh., 1981-84, Perry Bapt., Canton, Oh., 1984--; chmn. trustees Skyview Ranch Ministeries 1983-90, council of 12 Oh. Assc. Regular Bapt. Ch. 1987--, chmn. Bapts. for Life Canton, Oh. 1990--, chmn. Canton Area Youth Comm. 1985-86, chmn. Educ. Comm.1987--, chmn. Oh. St. Day of Prayer 1987--. General Assc. of Regular Baptist Churches. Office: Perry Bapt Ch 2425 Perry Dr SW Canton OH 44706

FLOYD, MADGE BLACK, minister, church administrator; b. Atlanta, Sept. 23, 1935; d. William Howard and Nena Madge (Estes) Black; m. Carl M. Floyd Jr., June 14, 1958 (div. May 1981); children: Christine Elizabeth, Carl M. III. AB, Emory U., 1958; MDiv, Pitts. Theol. Sem., 1969; D in Ministry, Boston U., 1978. Ordained to ministry United Meth. Ch. Pastor 1st United Meth. Ch., Greensburg, Pa., 1971-72, Castle Shannon United Meth. Ch., Pitts., 1973-79; exec. dir. TOGETHER Program, United Meth. Ch., Pitts., 1979-84; supt. Pitts. dist. United Meth Ch., 1984—; stewardship assoc. Gen. Bd. Discipline, United Meth. Ch., Nashville, 1979—, bd. dirs. Gen. Bd. Pensions, Evanston, Ill., 1984—; mem. commn. stewardship Nat. Council Chs., N.Y.C., 1979-84. Fellow Order of St. Luke. Democrat. Avocations: walking, fishing, golf, travel. Office: United Meth Ch Pitts Dist 600 Fox Dr Pittsburgh PA 15237

FLYNN, HARRY JOSEPH, bishop; b. Schenectady, N.Y., May 2, 1933. Ed., Siena Coll., Loudonville, N.Y., Mt. St. Mary's Coll., Emmitsburg, Md. Ordained priest Roman Cath. Ch., 1960; ordained coadjutor bishop of Lafayette, La., 1986-89. Bishop of Lafayette La., 1989—. Address: PO Drawer 3387 Lafayette IN 70502

FLYNN, JAMES BERNARD, monsignor; b. Portland, Oreg., Feb. 17, 1924; s. Michael J. and Teresa (Ginty) F. BA, St. Patrick's Coll., 1944; MTh, St. Patrick's Sem., 1948; MSW, Cath. U. Am., 1952. Ordained priest Roman Cath. Ch., 1948, named Monsignor, 1964. Pastor St. Gabriel's Ch., San Francisco, St. Peter's Ch., San Francisco; faculty St. Patrick's Sem., Menlo Park, Calif., 1987—. Contbr. numerous articles to profl. jours. Gen. dir. Cath. Charities of San Francisco, Social Justice Commn., San Francisco. Named Young Man of Yr., San Francisco Jaycees, 1957. Mem. Nat. Assn. Social Workers (cert.). Home: 320 Middlefield Rd Menlo Park CA 94025-3509

FLYNN, MICHAEL FRANCIS, priest, counselor; b. Chgo., Dec. 2, 1935; s. Michael Joseph and Mary Ellen (Lydon) F. BA, St. Bonaventure U., 1958, BS, 1960; MA, De Paul U., 1966; PhD in Clin. Psychology, Loyola U., Chgo., 1974. Ordained priest Roman Cath. Ch., 1961. Diplomate Am. Bd. Med. Psychotherapists. Pastoral and marital counselor Carmel High Sch., Mundelein, Ill., 1963-70; pastoral counselor St. Athanasius Parish, Evanston, Ill., 1970-71, Nativity of Our Lord Parish, Chgo., 1971—; cons. to marriage tribunal Chancery Office, Cath. Archdiocese of Chgo., 1975—; lectr. religion and mental health to religious groups, 1961—; dir. Carmelite Inst. of Renewal, Mundelein, 1968-70; condr. workshops and retreats in various states, 1965-70, counselor, 1968-70; condr. stress mgmt. workshops in Thailand, Can., and U.S., 1986—. Mem. Am. Acad. Med. Psychotherapists (diplomate), Am. Acad. Pain Mgmt. (cert.), Am. Soc. Clin. Hypnosis (bd. govs. 1984—, faculty Ednl. and Rsch. Found. 1986—), Chgo. Soc. Clin. Hypnosis (exec. bd. 1984—), Am. Psychol. Assn., Ill. Psychol. Assn., Ill. Group Psychotherapy Soc., Assn. Psychology Internship Ctrs. (exec. com. 1980—), Assn. Chgo. Area Tng. Ctrs. in Clin. Psychology, Internat. Soc. Hypnosis, Soc. Personality Assessment (membership com. 1982—), Internat. Platform Assn. Home: 653 W 37th St Chicago IL 60609 Office: 820 S Damen Ave Chicago IL 60680

FOGARTIE, JAMES EUGENE, minister, retired; b. Brookhaven, Miss., June 20, 1924; s. Arthur Finley and Eugenia Elizabeth (Vance) F.; m. Ruth Ann Douglass, Aug. 30, 1946 (dec. 1976); children: Ann Douglass, Elizabeth Vance, Arthur Ford, James Eugene, Jr.; m. Vivian M. Reid, Feb. 18, 1978. BA, U. Tex., 1945, MA, 1948; BD, Austin Presbyn. Theol. Sem., 1948; ThM, Union Theol. Sem., Richmond, Va., 1954; DD, Austin Coll., 1969; LHD, Presbyn. Coll., Clinton, S.C., 1989. Ordained to ministry Presbyn. Ch., 1948. Minister First Presbyn. Ch., Marianna, Ark., 1948-52, Fort Smith, Ark., 1952-55; minister Myers Park Presbyn. Ch., Charlotte, N.C., 1955-74, First Presbyn. Ch., Spartanburg, S.C., 1974-90; pastor emeritus First Presbyn. Ch., Spartanburg, 1991—; supply minister St. Andrews Presbyn. Ch., Wemblen, Eng., 1952; trustee Ctr. of Theol. Inquiry, Princeton, 1986—; instnl. rev. bd. Spartanburg Regional Med. Ctr., 1978—; dir. evangelism Va. United Meth. Conf. Author: No Room, 1958, In Search of Christmas, 1959. Recipient Silver Beaver award Mecklenburg Coun. Boy Scouts, 1971, Disting. Alumni award Austin Presbyn. Theol. Seminary, 1990; named to Outstanding Young Men of Am., 1953. Mem. Spectator Club (pres. Spartanburg chpt. 1990), Rotary. Home: 138 Starline Dr Spartanburg SC 29302

FOGARTY, GERALD PHILIP, church history educator, priest; b. Balt., Jan. 7, 1939; s. Gerald Philip and Ellen Theresa (McHugh) F. Student, Loyola Coll., 1956-58, St. Mary's Sem., Balt., 1958-59, Jesuit Novitiate, 1959-62; BA, Fordham U., 1964, MA, 1966; PhL, Woodstock Coll., 1965, MDiv, 1971; MPhil, Yale U., 1967, PhD, 1969; MST, Union Theol. Sem., 1972. Ordained priest Roman Cath. Ch., 1970. Asst. prof. Woodstock Coll., N.Y.C., 1972-74; lectr. Union Theol. Sem., N.Y.C., 1972-74; asst. prof. theology Fordham U., N.Y., 1974-75; assoc. prof. U. Va., Charlottesville, Va., 1975-86; prof. U. Va., Charlottesville, 1986—; vis. prof. Cath. U. Am., Washington, 1985; participant Istituto Paolo VI, Brescia, Italy. Author: The Vatican and the Americanist Crisis: Denis J. O'Connell, American Agent in Rome, 1885-1903, 1974 (Brewer prize), The Vatican and the American Hierarchy from 1870 to 1965, 1982, Am. Catholic Biblical Scholarship: A History from the Early Republic to Vatican II; contbr. articles to profl. and scholarly jours. Trustee Loyola Coll., Balt., 1971-77, Loyola High Sch., Towson, Md., 1983-89, Fairfield (Conn.) U., 1983-89; active pastoral work Roman Cath. Ch., Diocese of Richmond, Va., 1975—. Mem. Am. Hist. Assn. (1st v.p. 1991), Am. Cath. Hist. Assn. (exec. coun. 1977-79, 1st v.p. 1991, pres. 1992), Soc. Ch. History, Cath. Theol. Soc. Home: 1847 Winston Rd Charlottesville VA 22903 Office: U Va Dept Religious Studies Charlottesville VA 22903

FOGDERUD, PATRICIA ANN, minister; b. Ashton, Ill., Sept. 30, 1938; d. Wilbur William Meister and Muriel Carreldean (Vessels) Witzel; m. Grant Hendrickson Jr., Jan. 23, 1955 (div. 1973); children: Scott Raneal Hendrickson, Diana Janeal Hendrickson, Charles Layne Hendrickson; m. David Jonathan Fogderud, June 23, 1974. GED, Beloit, Wis. Ordained to ministry Overflowing Cup Total Life Ctr., 1989. Dir. The Overflowing Cup Total Life Ctr., Beloit, 1974—, The Harbor for the Homeless, Beloit, 1985—. Mem. Nat. Christian Counselors Assn. (lic.). Republican. Office: The Overflowing Cup Total Life Ctr Inc 334 E Grand Ave Beloit WI 53512-1075

FOGEL, EDWARD, cantor; b. Turkestan, USSR, Aug. 7, 1943; came to U.S., 1964; s. Saul and Ethel (Mishevski) Shossenfogel; m. Lynne Cheryl Haber, 1967; children: Jonathan Marc, Shira Beth. B. Sacred Music, Hebrew Uion Coll., 1970; MusM, St. Louis Conservatory Music, 1983. Cantor, dir. music Congregation Shaare Emeth, St. Louis, 1970—; pres. St. Louis Circle of Jewish Music, 1980-84. Mem. Am. Conf. Cantors (pres. 1989-91). Office: Temple Shaare Emeth 11645 Ladue Rd Saint Louis MO 63141

FOGG, ERNEST LESLIE, minister, retired; b. Butte, Mont., June 4, 1920; s. Ernest L. Fogg, Sr. and Gertrude G. (Waller) Fogg-Parker; m. Margaret E., June 17, 1943 (wid. Oct. 1962); children: Judith E., Dennis M. (dec.), Stephen W.; m. Carolee Little, Sept. 1, 1965. BA, Trinity U., San Antonio, 1943; MDiv, McCormick Theol. Seminary, Chgo., 1946; DD (hon.), Mary Holmes Coll., 1981. Ordained to ministry Presbyn. Ch., 1946. Missionary Bd. of Fgn. Missions/Presbyn. U.S.A., Thailand, 1946-59; field exec. Nat. Coun. of Chs., Indonesia, 1959-65; exec. Commn. on Ecumenical Mission and Rels./Presbyn. U.S.A., N.Y.C., 1965-70, Bd. Nat. Missions/Presbyn. U.S.A., N.Y.C., 1970-72; dir., Fund for Indochina World Coun. Chs., Geneva, 1973-76; sr. minister Cen. Presbyn. Ch., Montclair, N.J., 1977-87; chmn. Am. Leprosy Mission, 1979-86. Contbr. articles to profl. jours.

Mem. World Affairs Coun., San Antonio. Mem. Rotary (pres. 1986-87). Democrat. Avocation: woodworking. Home: 10782 Oakland Rd San Antonio TX 78240

FOGG, RALPH EVERETT, JR., priest, service executive; b. Johnson City, N.Y., Jan. 29, 1932; s. Ralph Everett and Geraldine Anne (Roche) F.; m. Judith Bertha Krahmer, June 29, 1954 (div. 1974); children—Stephen Christopher Everett, Juliet Elisabeth, Allyson Margaret, Jennifer Robin; m. Ingrid Anna Lechner, Jan. 6, 1979. A.B., Hobart Coll., 1954; M.Div. Gen. Theol. Sem., N.Y.C., 1959; cert. in psychotherapy, N.Y.C., 1969. Diplomate Am. Assn. Pastoral Counselors. Ordained priest Episcopal Ch., 1960; asst. missioner Tioga Tompkins Mission, Candor, N.Y., 1959-62; rector Ch. of Divine Love, Montrose, N.Y., 1962-70; intern, resident Am. Found. Religion and Psychiatry, N.Y.C., 1965-69; clin. dir. Mid Hudson Counseling Ctr., New Paltz, N.Y., 1969—; asst. pastor St. Andrews Ch., New Paltz, 1969-85, priest-in-charge, 1986—; trustee FRMH, Inc., Briarcliff Manor, N.Y., 1985—. Served with U.S. Army, 1957-59. Democrat. Avocations: ultralight aircraft; computers. Office: Mid Hudson Counseling Ctr PO Box 355 New Paltz NY 12561

FOGGIE, CHARLES HERBERT, bishop; b. Sumter, S.C., Aug. 4, 1912; s. James L. and Mamie Foggie; m. Madeline Sharpe Swan; 1 child, Charlene Marietta. AB, Livingstone Coll., 1936, DD (hon.), 1949, LLD (hon.), 1989; AM, Boston U., 1938, MDiv, 1939, MST, 1942. Ordained to ministry AME Zion Ch., 1936; elected bishop, 1968. Pastor Wadsworth St. AME Zion Ch., Providence, 1936-39, Rush AME Zion Ch., Cambridge, Mass., 1939-44, Wesley Ctr. AME Zion Ch., Pitts., 1944-68; bishop 12th dist., Ark., North Ark., Ga., South Ga., Okla., Tex., 1968-72, 5th dist., Allegheny, Phila.-Balt., Va. Confs., 1972-76, 3d dist., 1972-80, 3d dist., Allegheny, Phila.-Balt., Ohio, Guyana, Barbados Confs., 1980-88; pres. bd. bishops AME Zion Ch.; sec., trustee Livingstone Coll., Salisbury, N.C.; mem. World Coun. Chs., Nat. Coun. Chs. Past pres. Pitts. br. NAAC, Housing Authority, City of Pitts.; mem. Leadership Conf. on Civil Rights. Recipient Congl. Record citation, 50 yrs. in pastoral ministry, 1986, 1st Ann. Svc. award Pitts. br. NAACP; fellow U. Pitts. Democrat. Home: 1200 Windermere Dr Pittsburgh PA 15218 Office: AME Zion Ch 1200 Windermere Dr Pittsburgh PA 15218

FOGGS, EDWARD J., church administrator. Exec. sec. Ch. of God (Anderson, Ind.). Office: Ch of God PO Box 2420 Anderson IN 46018*

FOGLEMAN, ALFRED, minister; b. Haw River, N.C., Mar. 9, 1937; s. Walter Parker and Jewel (Murray) F.; m. Betty Jo Cornett, July 2, 1961; children: Dianna Lynn, Leah Marie Owens, Ronald Austin. AS in Engring., U. Va., 1966; BA in Philosophy, U. Md., 1969; MDiv, Luth. Theol. So. Seminary, Columbia, S.C., 1972. Pastor Forestville Luth. Parish, Mt. Jackson, Va., 1972-76, Salem Luth. Ch., Mt. Sidney, Va., 1976-86, Redeemer Luth. Ch., McKinley, Va., 1986-87, St. Luke's Luth. Ch. and Sch., Culpeper, Va., 1988—; dist. rep. Luth. Brotherhood Fraternal Benefit Soc., Mpls., 1986—. Contbr. articles to local newspapers. Bd. dirs. Shenpaco County Sheltered Workshop, New Market, Va., 1975; asst. coach Little League Football/Baseball, Verona, Va., 1980-84; vol. chaplain Rockingham Meml. Hosp., Harrisonburg, Shenandoah County Meml. Hosp., Woodstock, 1972-76, other civic activities. With U.S. Army, 1957-59. Mem. Ruritan Club. Home: 1200 Old Roxeyville Rd Culpeper VA 22701 Office: St Lukes Church and School 1200 Old Roxeyville Rd Culpeper VA 22701

FOLEY, DAVID E., bishop; b. Worcester, Mass., Feb. 3, 1930. Student, St. Charles Coll., Catonsville, Md., St. Mary's Sem., Balt. ordained priest Roman Cath. Ch., 1952, ordained titular bishop of Octaba and Aux. bishop of Richmond, VA, 1986. Aux. bishop of Richmond Roman Cath. Ch. Va. Office: Diocese of Richmond 811 D Cathedral Pl Richmond VA 23220*

FOLEY, JOHN PATRICK, archbishop; b. Darby, Pa., Nov. 11, 1935; s. John Edward and Regina Beatrice (Vogt) F. BA summa cum laude, St. Josephs Coll., Phila., 1957; BA, St. Charles Borromeo Sem., Phila., 1958; PhL, U. St. Thomas Aquinas, Rome, 1964, PhD cum laude, 1965; MS magna cum laude, Columbia U., 1966. Ordained priest Roman Cath. Ch., 1962, bishop, 1984. Asst. pastor Sacred Heart Ch., Havertown, Pa., 1962-63; asst. editor Cath. Standard & Times, Phila., 1963, 67-70; Rome corr. Cath. Standard & Times, 1963-65, editor, 1970-84; asst. pastor St. John the Evangelist Ch., Phila., 1966; faculty mem. Cardinal Dougherty High Sch., Phila., 1966-67; assoc. prof. philosophy St. Charles Borromeo Sem., Phila., 1967-84; mem. U.S. Cath. Conf. Communications Com., 1979-82; news sec. gen. meetings Nat. Conf. Cath. Bishops, 1969-84; vice chmn. Pa. State Ethics Commn., 1979-84; apptd. pres. Pontifical Commn. for Social Communications, Vatican City, 1984; pres. Vatican TV Ctr.; bd. govs. Internat. Eucharistic Congress. Author: Natural Law, Natural Right and the Warren Court, 1965. Mem. regional bd. dirs. NCCJ, 1969-82. Named hon. prelate Pope Paul VI, 1976. Mem. Am. Cath. Hist. Soc., Am. Cath. Philos. Assn., Cath. Press Assn. Home: Villa Stritch via della, Nocetta 63, 00164 Rome Italy Office: Pontifical Coun for Social, Communications, 00120 Vatican City Vatican City *The most important reality in life is the existence of God, His love for every person exemplified in our redemption by His Son, Jesus Christ, and our eternal destiny to live with Him forever in heaven.*

FOLEY, ROBERT L., SR., ecumenical agency administrator, minister. P-res. Bronx Div. of Coun. Chs. of City of N.Y. Office: Bronx Div Coun Chs 30 W 190th St Bronx NY 10468*

FOLEY, THOMAS LESTER, minister, food retailer; b. Roanoke, Va., July 16, 1956; s. Curtis Lester and Kathryn Hope (Stultz) F.; m. Un Hwa (Yi), July 27, 1979; children: Joanna Kathryn, Rebecca Elizabeth. BS, Liberty U., 1989; postgrad., Liberty Bapt. Theol. Sem., 1989-90, Southeastern Bapt. Theol. Sem., 1990—. Buyer's asst. Kroger Food Stores, Roanoke, 1972—; min. youth Jefferson St. Bapt. Ch., Roanoke, 1989-90; pastor Riverland Rd. Bapt. Ch., Roanoke, 1991—. Researcher: The Word of the Cross: A Theology of Evangelism, 1991. With USAF, 1976-79. Republican. Office: Riverland Rd Bapt Ch 459 Riverland Rd Roanoke VA 24014 *In this era of change, man searches for stability. Christian theologians should help find stability through the Gospel of Christ, not add more variables which further destabilize life.*

FOLEY, WILLIAM E(DWARD), JR., priest, counselor; b. Washington, Oct. 8, 1952; s. William Edward Sr. and Marguerite Mary (Pratt) F. BA, St. John's U., Collegeville, Minn., 1974; MA, Christ the King Sem., 1979; MS, Loyola Coll., 1988, cert. in advanced study, 1990. Assoc. pastor Our Lady of Lourdes Cath. Ch., Bethesda, Md., 1979-83, St. John Evangelist Cath. Ch., Silver Spring, Md., 1983-90, St. Peter Cath. Ch., Olney, Md., 1990-91; pastor Our Lady of Victory Ch., Washington, 1991—. Mem. Am. Assn. for Counseling and Devel. Roman Catholic. Avocations: hiking, skiing, running, gardening. Home: 4835 MacArthur Blvd NW Washington DC 20007 Office: Our Lady of Victory Cath Ch 4835 MacArthur Blvd NW Washington DC 20007 also: Our Lady of Victory Rectory Washington DC 20007

FOLEY, WILLIAM LEONARD, minister; b. Bassett, Va., Aug. 10, 1941; s. William Albert and Mary Allie (Stultz) F.; m. Marth aLouise Ward, Nov. 25, 1961; children: Sharon Irene, William Randolph. Grad., John D. Bassett High Sch., 1960. Ordained to ministry, Christian Ch.-Disciples of Christ. Lay minister Ch. of the Brethren, Bassett, Va., 1984-87; pastor Friendly Christian Ch., Spencer, Va., 1987—; leader, singer Sounds of Faith Gospel Singers, Collinsville, Va., 1980—; personnel mgr. Am. Std. Bldg. Systems, Martinsville, Va., 1981—, asst. plant mgr., 1981—. Scoutmaster Boy Scouts Am., Collinsville, 1966-81; chmn. Va. Employment Commn. Employer Adv. Co., 1988—; mem. Blue Ridge Personnel Assn., 1981—, Patrick Henry Drug & Alcohol Coun., 1988—. Home: 205 Crestwood Rd Collinsville VA 24078 Office: Friendly Christian Ch Box 192 Spencer VA 24165

FOLLIS, ELAINE RUSSELL, biblical studies educator, Christian science practitioner; b. Quincy, Mass., Jan. 28, 1944; d. George Stanley and Celia Russell (Joy) F. A.B. summa cum laude, Tufts U., 1965, B.D., 1968; Ph.D., Boston U., 1976. Asst. prof. religion Principia Coll., Elsah, Ill., 1974-79, assoc. prof., chmn. dept. religion, 1979-83, assoc. prof., chmn. div. humanities, 1983-85, prof., chmn. div. humanities, 1985-86; editorial cons. Christian Sci. Pub. Soc., Boston, 1973—; Jeanne and George Todd Prof. Religious Studies Principia Coll., 1987; vis. scholar Harvard Div. Sch., Cambridge, Mass., 1979; reviewer NEH, Washington, 1978-82; lectr. Bibl. studies Principia Coll. Patrons Assn., Elsah, Ill., St. Louis, 1978—. Author: David King of Israel, 1979; Covenant-A Biblical Guide, 1985; editor: Directions in Biblical Hebrew Poetry, 1987; contbr. articles to religious and profl. jours. Second reader First Ch. of Christ, Scientist, Elsah, Ill., 1983-85, trustee, 1975-78, 88-91; mem. Christian Sci. Bd. Lectureship, 1991-91. Mem. Soc. Bibl. Lit. (Bibl. Hebrew poetry sect. chmn. 1983-88), Phi Beta Kappa. Clubs: Nat. Early Am. Glass (Boston); Lockhaven Country (Alton, Ill.). Lodge: Order Eastern Star (worthy matron 1974). Office: Principia Coll Dept Religion Elsah IL 62028

FOLTA, SAMUEL NATHAN, Christian religion educator; b. Chonju, Cholla Puk, Republic of Korea, Oct. 11, 1965; s. John Wesley and Ruth Claus (Humes) F.; m. Eun-soo Kim, June 25, 1988; 1 child, Johann. BA, Gordon Coll., 1987; MDiv, Gordon-Conwell Theol. Sem., 1989—. Missions course coord. Gordon Coll., Wenham, Mass., 1987; missionary trainer Ambassadors for Christ, Seoul, Korea, 1988-90; missions sch. tchr. Indianhead Primary Sch., Tongduchon, Korea, 1988-90; Christian educator youth First Presbyn. Ch., Ipswich, Mass., 1990—; evangelist, preacher for youth Korean Presbyn. Ch., Newtonville, Mass., 1990—; founder, Christian educator youth Mid. Sch. Group, 1st Presbyn. Ch., Ipswich, 1990—, Christian Edn. Program, Indianhead Sch., Tongduchon, 1988-90. Contbr. articles to profl. jours. Mem. Amnesty Internat., Wenham, 1985, Soc. For a New Politics, Wenham, 1986. Named to Pike Honors Program Gordon Coll., 1983-87, Collegian of the Yr. Gordon Coll., 1987. Mem. Phi Alpha Chi. Home: 163 County Rd Ipswich MA 01983 Office: Korean Presbyn Ch 216 Walnut St Newtonville MA 02160 *Our patchwork world is covered with peoples of every language, race, culture, and religion but they all have the same problem: sin; and they all have one answer to that problem: Jesus Christ.*

FOLWELL, WILLIAM HOPKINS, clergyman, bishop; b. Port Washington, N.Y., Oct. 26, 1924; s. Ralph Taylor and Sara Ewing (Hopkins) F.; m. Christine Elizabeth Cramp, Apr. 22, 1949; children: Ann, Mark, Susan. B.C.E., Ga. Inst. Tech., 1947; B.D., Seabury Western Theol. Sem., 1953, D.D., 1970; D.D., U. South, Sewanee, 1970. Ordained to ministry Episcopal Ch., 1952; priest Plant City and Mulberry, Fla., 1952-55; asst. chaplain St. Martin's Sch., New Orleans, 1955-56; vicar St. Augustine Ch., New Orleans, 1955-56; rector St. Gabriel's Ch., Titusville, Fla., 1956-59, All Saints Ch., Winter Park, Fla., 1959-70; bishop Diocese Central Fla., Winter Park, 1970—; asst. traffic engr. City of Miami, 1947-49. Trustee U. South; trustee Seabury-Western Theol. Sem., Evanston, Ill. Lt. j.g. USNR, 1943-46. Home: 458 Virginia Dr Winter Park FL 32789 Office: Episcopal Ch 324 N Interlachen Ave PO Box 790 Winter Park FL 32789

FONDA, DONALD ALBERT, JR., minister; b. Washington, Aug. 17, 1938; s. Donald Albert Sr. and Mary Gladys (Speaker) F.; m. Jeanne Frances Dancey, Sept. 2, 1961; children: Deborah Ann, Douw Adam. BA, Alderson Broaddus Coll., 1962; MDiv, Colgate Rochester Div. Sch., 1966. Asst. pastor Gaines-Carleton Larger Parish, Albion, N.Y., 1963-66; pastor Warrenville Bapt. Ch., Ashford, Conn., 1966-69; assoc. pastor First Bapt. Ch., Youngstown, Ohio, 1969-71; pastor First Bapt. Ch., Northampton, Mass., 1971-86, Federated Ch. of Bolton, Mass., 1986—. Pres. Mahoning County Bapt. Housing Devel., Youngstown, Ohio, 1969-71, Western Mass. Youth Orchs., Springfield, 1982-86, Decisional Tng. Vols., Northampton, 1975-86; incorporator Family Planning Western Mass. (bd. dirs. 1973-76), bd. dirs. Survival Ctr., Northampton, 1974-82. Mem. Am. Bapt. Churches (Mass. bd.dirs. 1977-83, exec. com. 1979-81, chairperson dept. of ch. and soc., 1979-81), Cen. Mass. Bapt. Assn. (exec. com. 1988—), Unitarian Universalist Assn., W.H.E.A.T. Bd. Home: 642 Main St Bolton MA 01740-0250 Office: The Federated Ch of Bolton 673 Main St Bolton MA 01740-0250

FONG, BILLY J(AW), chemist, social service organization administrator; b. Sacramento, June 28, 1955; s. Billy Jaw Sr. and June Shee (Lee) F. AA in Gen. Sci., Sacramento City Coll., 1975; BA in Chemistry, U. Calif., Davis, 1979; postgrad., Fuller Sem., Menlo Park, Calif., 1981-86; MST in Christian Ethics, New Coll., Berkeley, Calif., 1987. Agrl. chemist Calif. Dept. of Food and Agr., Sacramento, 1980—; deacon Faith Presbyn. Ch., Sacramento, 1988-90. Contbr. articles to profl. jours. Dist. coord. Bread for the World, Sacramento, 1989—. Presbyterian. Office: Calif Dept Food and Agriculture 3292 Meadowview Rd Sacramento CA 95823

FONG, BRUCE WILLIAM, minister, educator; b. Sacramento, Mar. 29, 1952; s. William G.T. And Marie Diane (Mar) F.; m. Yvonne Choy, May 28, 1977; children: Kristin Jamie, Justin Andrew, Jeremy Dustin. BS magna cum laude, Western Bapt. Coll., 1973; ThM, Dallas Theol. Sem., 1978; postgrad., U. Aberdeen, Scotland, 1988—. Ordained to ministry Ind. Bible Ch., 1978. Asst. pastor Nooksack Valley Bapt. Ch., Everson, Wash., 1973-74; high sch. pastor Grace Bible Ch., Dallas, 1977-78; pastor Chinese Bapt. Ch., Portland, Oreg., 1978-88; asst. prof. Multnomah Sch. of the Bible, Portland, 1990—. Named Preacher of Yr. Western Bapt. Coll., 1973. Mem. Delta Epsilon Chi. Office: Multnomah Sch of the Bible 8435 NE Glisan St Portland OR 97220

FONG, WILFRED WAI FAI, religion educator; b. Hong Kong, Nov. 28, 1959; s. Wing Fwong and Kor (Ngan (Young) F. BSc in Computer Sci., U. Western Ont., London, Can., 1981; postgrad., Regent Coll., Vancouver, B.C., Can., 1981, Moody Bible Inst., 1981-82; M Libr. and Info. Sci., U. Wis.-Milw., 1985. Dir. libr. London Chinese Alliance, 1979-81, dir. Christian edn., 1981-83; sec. 9th Ea .Can. Chinese Youth Winter Con., 1980; tchr. Bible Eastbrook Ch. Chinese Ministry, Milw., 1984-86, project asst. Sch. Libr. and Info. Sci., 1984; dir. Christian edn. Eastbrook Ch. Chinese Ministry, 1987—; mgr. Resource Ctr. Sch. Libr. and Info. Sci. U. Wis., Milw., 1985-88; asst. dean Sch. Libr. and Info. Sci. U. Wisc.-Milw., 1988—. Author computer software; compiler bibliographies; editor Jour. Libr. and Info. Sci.; editor at large Echo, 1983; contbr. articles to profl. jours. Mem. ALA, Fellowship of Christian Librs. and Info. Specialists, Assn. Christian Librs., Wis. Libr. Assn., Christian Edn. Fellowship, Western Chinese Christian Fellowship (exec. com.), Am. Soc. Info. Sci. (sec.-treas. 1984—, chair Wis. chpt. 1990-91, chair office info. system interest group 1991—), Chinese Am. Librs. Assn. (bd. dirs.), Christian Reader's Club (London, Ont., advisor 1982-84). Avocations: music, reading, microcomputers. Address: PO Box 11694 Milwaukee WI 53211-0694

FONTAINE, MARY ELIZABETH, lay worker; b. Kingston, N.Y., Mar. 26, 1947; d. Richard B. and Elizabeth D. (Donovan) Overbagh; m. Gregory N. Fontaine, June 23, 1979; children: Catherine Aline, Michael Richard. BS in Phys. Therapy, Ithaca Coll., 1969; MS in Allied Medicine, Ohio State U., 1973. Tchr., dir. Sunday sch. Christ Ch., Portsmouth, N.H., 1974-80, mem. vestry, 1974-77, 90—, chmn. parish life com., 1984-87, chair evangelism and renewal, 1985—; mem. Commn. on Ministry, Concord, N.H., 1984-90; pediatric phys. therapist, cons. Kittery Sch., Coastal Employment Assocs.; facilitator in parenting classes Cross Rds. House shelter, Portsmouth, 1989—; mem. Diocesan edn. com., 1975-78, Diocesan evangelism com., 1977-80, dean convocation, 198-82; del. Diocesan conv., 1974-89; mem. outreach com., 1987—, pastoral care com., 1986—. Pres. PTO, Rye, N.H., 1988—; mem. Friendship Force, Seacoast, N.H., 1985—; vol. Rye Elem. Sch., Rye Recreation, Salvation Army Soup Kitchen, 1989—. Mem. Am. Acad. Cerebral Palsy and Developmental Medicine, Am. Assn. for Mental Retardation. Home: 654 Wallis Rd Rye NH 03870

FONTENOT, WONDA LEE, religion educator; b. Grand Prairie, La., Oct. 17, 1948; d. Hayward Sr. and Emma Lou (Jacque) F.; m. Wilken Jones Jr. BA, U. Calif., Berkeley, 1972, MA, 1987, PhD, 1990; postgrad., Am. Bapt. Sem. W., 1985-86. Dir. Wonnamuse: Inst. for Study of Arts, Culture and Ethnicity, Opelousas, La., 1986—. Contbr. chpts. to books. Deaconess True Vine Bapt. Ch., Grand Prairie, 1988—, chair scholarship com., 1990; bd. dirs. Opelousas Coun. Arts and Culture, 1989, Sect. Q St. Commn. on Archives and History, Baton Rouge, 1990; mem. Nat. Bapt. Conv. Women's Aux., Baton Rouge, 1990—; lectr., presenter in field. Recipient Honorarium, Alexandria Mus. Art, 1990; Am. Soc. Newspaper Editors faculty journalism fellow, 1983. Mem. Am. Acad. Religion, Am. Anthropology Assn., Am. Sociol. Assn., Am. Folklore Soc., Phi Delta Kappa. Office: Wonnamuse Inst PO Box 7239 Opelousas LA 70571

FORBES, ALFRED DEAN, religious researcher; b. Pomona, Calif., Mar. 2, 1941; s. Paul Edward and Lela Irene (Randall) F.; m. Ada Ellen Moss, May 8, 1971. BA in Physics, Harvard Coll., 1962; MDiv, Pacific Sch. Religion, 1969. With U.S. Peace Corps, Nigeria, 1962-64; project mgr. Hewlett-Packard Labs., Palo Alto, Calif., 1971—; vis. scholar religious studies Stanford (Calif.) U., 1986-89. Author: (with F.I. Andersen) Spelling in the Hebrew Bible, 1986, The Vocabulary of the Old Testament, 1989, (with F.I. Andersen and D.N. Freedman) Studies in Hebrew and Aramaic Orthography, 1991; contbr. articles to profl. jours. Trustee, v.p. Whitney Edn. Found., Los Altos, Calif., 1981-88. Mem. Soc. Bibl. Lit., IEEE. Home: 820 Loma Verde Ave Palo Alto CA 94303 Office: Hewlett Packard Labs PO Box 10490 Palo Alto CA 94303

FORBES, BRUCE JORDAN, minister; b. Philipsburg, Pa., July 26, 1953; s. Theodore and Jane Parks (Jordan) F.; m. Shelvey Buttington, Mar. 13, 1976 (div. Mar. 1978); 1 child, Nathan; m. Helen Louise Lonsdale, June 24, 1980; 1 child, Calvin. BS, U. Pa., 1975; MDiv, Princeton Theol. Seminary, 1989. Ordained to ministry United Ch. of Christ, 1989. Pastor Orleans (Vt.) Federated Ch., 1989—; moderator Northeast assn. Vt. conf. United Ch. of Christ, 1991—, bd. dirs. Vt. conf., 1991—. Democrat. Home: 34 School St Orleans VT 05860 Office: Orleans Federated Church 24 School St Orleans VT 05860

FORBES, DANIEL MERRILL, minister; b. Savannah, Ga., June 20, 1954; s. Marion and Mary Edna (Godbee) F.; m. Wanda Iris Rosa, Sept. 25, 1977; 1 child, Daniel Felix. BA in Theology, So. Coll., Tenn., 1977; MA in Counselor Edn., U. S. Fla., Tampa, 1988; postgrad., U. S. Fla., 1989—. Cert. grief counselor. Min., pastor youth and family life Fla. Conf. of Seventh-day Adventists, Orlando, Fla., 1977—; cons. in field. Mem. Am. Assn. for Counseling & Devel., Assn. for Religious and Value Issues in Counseling, Assn. for Death Edn. and Counseling. Democrat. Seventh-day Adventist. Avocations: music, reading, nature, walking. Office: 1st Seventh-day Adventist Ch 822 W Linebough Ave Tampa FL 33612 *Life, both temporal and eternal, is a gift of God to mankind. It is in our physical life that we are to prepare to partake of the eternal life. I think that the wise man, Solomon, said it best in Eccl. 12:13 when he wrote of the purpose of man's life and said, "Let us hear the conclusion of the whole matter: Fear God keep His commandments, for this is the whole duty of man."*

FORD, ALONZO ANTHONY, minister; b. Tallahasee, Aug. 15, 1953; s. Rath Wesley Sr. and Josephine Louise (Nicks) F.; m. Chancey M. Lamb, Mar. 27, 1976; 1 child, Amanda Chanel. AD, U. Md., 1984; B, U. Md. U. Coll., 1986; Mdiv, Howard U., 1991. Lic. to ministry Greater Little Rock Missionary Bapt. Ch., 1970, ordained, 1981. Assoc. min. Greater Little Rock Bapt. Ch., Pensacola, Fla., 1970-81; lay leader, pastor Hardt Chapel, Schwaebisch, Gmuend, Fed. Republic of Germany, 1981-83; assoc. min. Bethlehem Bapt. Ch., 1983-85; youth min. 1st Mt. Zion Bapt. Ch., Dumfries, Va., 1985-89; pastor Olive Branch Bapt. Ch., Haymarket, Va., 1989-91; analyst Resource Mgmt. Directorate, Ft. Belvoir, Va., 1987—. Staff sgt. U.S. Army, 1972-84. Named to Nat. Dean's List, Howard U., 1987. Mem. Am. Soc. Mil. Comptrollers, Kiwanis (chaplain 1989-90). Home: 1811 Tilletson Pl Woodbridge VA 22191-3841 *While life is filled with potential and possibility and we are all gifted with different degrees of skills and abilities, we are all capable of becomming the best that is within us...the best is all we can be.*

FORD, CHRISTOPHER DALE, pastor; b. Wellington, Tex., Oct. 6, 1961; s. Earl Gene and Phyllis Clyde (Abernathy) F.; m. Melissa Jane Baker, Oct. 12, 1985; 1 child, Lance Jeffery. AA in Nursing, Amarillo Coll. Sch. Nursing, 1989; BS, Wayland Bapt. U., 1992. RN (vocat.), Tex. Assoc. intern Christ United Meth. Ch., Amarillo, Tex., 1988-89; youth pastor Trinity United Meth. Ch., Amarillo, 1989-90; assoc. pastor Kingswood United Meth. Ch., Amarillo, 1990—. Mem. N.W. Tex. Youth Mins. Assn. Home: 4310 Jennie Amarillo TX 79106 Office: Kingswood United Meth Ch 4801 S Austin St Amarillo TX 79110-3219

FORD, DAVID LYNN, minister; b. Springfield, Mo., Nov. 5, 1959; s. Jerry Lee Ford and Laura Carolyn (Grisham) Walters. BTh., Prairie Bible Coll., 1982; postgrad., Grace Coll. of the Bible, 1982-83. Ordained to ministry So. Bapt. Conv., 1989. Intern, assoc. to Dr. Stephen Olford Encounter Ministries, Inc., Wheaton, Ill., 1983-84; evangelist So. Bapt. Conv., Phoenix, 1986-89; pastor Trinity Bapt. Ch., Globe, Ariz., 1989—; pres. Globe for Christ Internat., Inc., 1990—. Speaker: (weekly radio) Wings of Liberty, 1990—; contbr. articles to pubs. Com. mem. Ariz. Prayer Day Rally, Nat. Day of Prayers, Phoenix, 1989; chaplain for the day Ariz. State Senate, Phoenix, 1991. Mem. San Carlos Bapt. Assn. (pres. 1989-90, dir. of evangelism 1990—). Home: 117 Hopi Ave Globe AZ 85501 Office: Globe for Christ Internat 117 Hope Ave PO Box 725 Globe AZ 85502

FORD, DONNA LOU, minister; b. Duluth, Minn., June 20, 1937; d. Louis G. Nelson and Florence M. (Touve) Rosen; m. Lynn E. Ford, July 22, 1955 (div. 1978); children: Steven R., Terri Lynn, Kristin D. BS in Psychology, Coll. of St. Scholastica, Duluth, Minn., 1980; MDiv, Bethel Sem., St. Paul, Minn., 1983. Ordained to ministry United Meth. Ch. as deacon, 1983, as elder, 1986; cert. Clinical Pastoral Edn. Chaplain U. Minn. Hosps., Mpls., 1984—; assoc. pastor Prairie United Meth. Ch., Eden Prairie, Minn., 1985—. Fellow Coll. of Chaplains. Office: Prairie Church 15050 Scenic Hts Rd Eden Prairie MN 55344

FORD, FREDERICK JAY, youth minister; b. Franklin, Ind., Aug. 11, 1960; s. William Frederick and Janice Marie (Houston) F.; m. Wendi Carol Platt, Feb. 19, 1983; children: Tonya Dawn, Clint Boone. BS in Ministry and Bible Studies, Platte Valley Bible Coll., 1988; diploma in fin. counseling, Christian Fin. Concepts, 1989; diploma in behavior analysis, Inst. for Christian Living, 1989. Ordained to ministry Christian Ch., 1987. Min. Glenrock (Wyo.) Christian Ch., 1987-88; youth min. Cen. Christian Ch., Claremore, Okla., 1988—. Town councilman City Coun., Hartman, Colo., 1987. With U.S. Army, 1979-83. Republican. Office: Cen Christian Ch PO Box 928 Claremore OK 74018

FORD, GERALD WAYNE, minister, psychotherapist; b. Shreveport, La., Apr. 20, 1948; s. Newell Orris and Lora Lucille (Graves) F.; m. Billie Fay Ritter, Apr. 16, 1986; children: Gerald, Greg; stepchildren: Scott, Chris. BA, E. Tex. Bapt. U., Marshall, Tex., 1971; MDiv, Southwestern Sem., Ft. Worth, 1984; MA in Psychology, Houston Bapt. U., 1990. Ordained to ministry So. Bapt. Ch., 1970. Pastor Wallace Bapt. Ch., Pelican, La., 1971-72, Mt. Olive Bapt. Ch., 1972-74, Pinecroft Bapt. Ch., 1974-75, Rose City (Tex.) Bapt. Ch., 1976-77, Southside Bapt. Ch., Port Neches, Tex., 1977-79, Riverview Bapt. Ch., Houston, 1979-85, Lakeside Bapt. Ch., Houston, 1988-90; therapist Houston Ctrs. for Christian Counseling, 1989—; Mem. Book Store Div., Bapt. Sunday Sch. Bd., 1985-89. Office: Houston Ctrs Christian Coun 8323 SW Freeway # 550 Houston TX 77074-4501

FORD, JAMES DAVID, clergyman; b. Sioux Falls, S.D., July 25, 1931; s. Reuben Haquin and Luella Marie (Lindquist) F.; m. Marcia Ruth Sodergren, June 25, 1954; children: Julia Ruth, Peter David, Marie Rebecca, Molly Christine, Sarah Marie. B.A., Gustavus Adolphus Coll., 1953; M.Div., Augustana Sem., 1957; postgrad., Heidelberg (Germany) U., 1957-58; D.Div., Wagner Coll., 1979. Ordained to ministry Lutheran Ch., 1958; pastor Luth. Ch., Ivanhoe, Minn., 1958-61; asst. chaplain U.S. Mil. Acad., West Point, N.Y., 1961-64; sr. chaplain U.S. Mil. Acad., 1965-79; chaplain U.S. Ho. of Reps., Washington, 1979—; speaker colls. and univs. Trustee Gustavus Adolphus Coll. Recipient Alumni Citation for disting. service Gustavus Adolphus Coll., 1965, meritorious service award U.S. Mil. Acad., 1979. Mem. Guild of St. Ansgar. Club: World Ocean Cruising. Capt. of 31 foot sailboat; sailed Atlantic Ocean, Plymouth, Eng., to N.Y. Home: 6008 Beech Tree Dr Alexandria VA 22310 Office: HB-25 The Capitol Washington DC 20515

FORD, L. H., bishop. Presiding bishop Ch. of God in Christ, Memphis. Office: Ch of God in Christ 272 S Main St Memphis TN 38103*

FORD, LEWIS STANLEY, philosophy educator; b. Leonia, N.J., Nov. 18, 1933; s. L. Stanley and Agnes (Steenland) F.; m. Anne Lide, Aug. 24, 1957;

children: Stephanie, Rachel Lynn. AB magna cum laude, Yale U., 1955, AM, 1959, PhD, 1963; postgrad., U. Muenster, Fed. Republic Germany, 1955-56; postgrad, Emory U., 1956-57. Asst. prof. MacMurray Coll., Jacksonville, Ill., 1960-62; asst. prof. U. of the Pacific, Stockton, Calif., 1963-65, assoc. prof., 1965-70; assoc. prof. Pa. State U., State College, 1970-73; prof. Old Dominion U., Norfolk, Va., 1974—; vis. prof. Baylor U., Waco, Tex., fall 1985. Author: The Lure of God, 1978, The Emergence of Whitehead's Metaphysics, 1925-29, 1984; editor: Two Process Philosophers, 1973; co-editor: (with George L. Kline) Explorations in Whitehead's Philosophy, 1983; editor Process Studies, 1971—. Danforth fellow, 1955, Sterling Pre-Doctoral fellow, 1959-60, Nat. Endowment for the Humanities Sr. fellow, 1973-74; Fulbright grantee, 1955-56. Baptist. Home: 726 Delaware Ave Norfolk VA 23508 Office: Old Dominion U Philosophy Dept Norfolk VA 23508

FORD, ROGER JULIAN, SR., clergyman; b. Esmont, Va., Oct. 2, 1934; s. Fleming Vaughn and Frances Catherine (Copeland) F.; m. Velma Lee Gray, Mar. 1, 1958; children—Lori, Nadine, Francine, Robin, Wendy, Roger Julian. D.D. (hon.), Va. Sem. & Coll., 1985. Pastor Chestnut Grove Baptist Ch., Esmont, Va., 1962-70, Mt. Zion Bapt. Ch., Greenwood, Va., 1963-69, Wake Forest Bapt. Ch., Slate Hill, Va., 1969-74, Mt. Sinai Bapt. Ch., Madison Heights, Va., 1971—; exec. dir. Monticello Community Action Agy., Charlottesville, Va., 1970-74, Opportunity Industrialized Ctr., Lynchburg, Va., 1978-80; manpower dir. Total Action Against Poverty, Roanoke, Va., 1974-78; mgr. Ebonaire Ch. Supply, Madison Heights, 1980—. Co-chmn. Amherst County Dem. Party, Va., 1980-82; pres. Va. State Conf. NAACP, 1978-80, Amherst County Br. NAACP, 1975-78, 1980—. Served to sgt. USMC, 1954-58. Recipient Community Achievement award Lynchburg Nationwide Ins. Co., 1980; named Minister of Year Community Advancement and Achievement Movement, 1977; Leader of Year Amherst County NAACP 1979. Lodge: Odd Fellows. Home: Rte 6 Box 535 Madison Heights VA 24572 Office: PO Box 707 Dixie Airport Rd Madison Heights VA 24572

FORD, WALLACE ROY, clergyman, religious organization executive; b. Walnut, Ill., Apr. 7, 1937; s. Roy Wallace and Evelyn Mary (Hand) F.; m. Valerie Laine Brown, Aug. 18, 1961; children: Tara Chantille, Christopher Wallace. BA, Tex. Christian U., 1959; BD, Brite Divinity Sch., Ft. Worth, 1962; Cert. Theologie, U. Geneva, 1963; D of Ministry, Iliff Sch. Theology, Denver, 1978. Ordanined to minstry Disciples of Christ, 1962. Pastor La Porte (Tex.) Community Ch., 1964-67, 1st Christian Ch., Boulder, Colo., 1967-83; pres. Colo. Council Chs., Denver, 1981-82; exec. sec. N.Mex. Conf. Chs., Albuquerque, 1983—; chmn. Ch. Fin. Council, Indpls., 1984-86. Author: Wise Up O Men Of God, 1981, Worship and Evangelism, 1981, Snow Melts, 1983. Mem. Nat. Assn. Ecumenical Staff, Theta Phi. Democrat. Office: NMex Conf of Chs 124 Hermosa SE Albuquerque NM 87108

FORD, WILLIAM PATRIC, minister, educator; b. Paris, Tex., Aug. 27, 1955; s. James C. and Glenna R. F.; m. Jeanie Shipp, Dec. 18, 1982; children: Amber E., Cassidy R. BS, Baylor U., 1978; MRE, Southwestern Bapt. Theol. Sem., Ft. Worth, 1980; postgrad., Southwestern Bapt. Theol. Sem., 1981, N. Tex. State U., 1984; EdD, Southwestern Bapt. Theol. Sem., 1989. Ordained to ministry Bapt. Ch., 1981. Minister of youth First Bapt. Ch., Paris, Tex., 1978-80, Saginaw, Tex., 1980-83; minister of edn. First Bapt. Ch., Mexia, Tex., 1983-84, Floydada, Tex., 1985-88, Spartanburg, S.C., 1988—; minister to youth First Bapt. Ch., Trenton, Mich. summer, 1974, 75; mission pastor Immanual Bapt. Chapel, Green Bay, Wis., (summer), 1977. Contbr. articles to profl. jours. Mem. So. Bapt. Religious Edn. Assn., Nat. Assn. of Ch. Bus. Adminstrs., S.C. Bapt. Religious Edn. Assn., Am. Mgmt. Assn. Avocations: hunting, fishing, golf, softball, tennis, tropical fish, computers. Home: 119 N Lanford Rd Spartanburg NC 29301 Office: First Bapt Ch 250 E Main St Spartanburg SC 29301

FORDHAM, WILLMON ALBERT, minister; b. West Monroe, La., Nov. 13, 1926; s. William Ether and Lura Annie (Hatten) F.; m. Ethel Hover, Dec. 22, 1946; children: Willmon Albert, Gary W. BA, William Carey Coll., 1956; BD, New Orleans Bapt. Theol. Sem., 1961, MDiv, 1975. Ordained to ministry, 1952. Pastor Napoleon Bapt. Ch., Picayune, Miss., 1952-59, Oak Hill Bapt. Ch., Poplarville, Miss., 1959-61, First Bapt. Ch., Petal, Miss., 1961—; pres. Lebanon Bapt. Pastors' Conf., 1962-63, moderator, 1972-73; mem. assembly com. Miss. Bapt. Conv. Bd., 1966-70, mem. pioneer missions com., 1970-73; pastor-advisor Tom Cox Evang. Assn., 1972; moderator Lebanon Bapt. Assn., 1989-90. Active Boy Scouts of Am., Petal, 1974-76. Recipient certs. Appreciation, Miss. Bapt. Conv. Bd., 1970, 85, Petal Middle Sch. Task Force, 1988-90. Mem. Kiwanis. Home: PO Box 318 Petal MS 39465 Office: 1st Bapt Ch 201 W Central Ave Petal MS 39465

FOREHAND, ROBERT JACKSON, education administrator; b. Goldsboro, N.C., Nov. 16, 1951; s. Loyd Jackson and Almeta Rae (Batten) F.; m. Celia Ann Marshburn, July 10, 1976; children: Samuel Aaron, Benjamin Joel. BRE, Heritage Bible Coll., 1976; BA in Religion, N.C. Wesleyan Coll., 1978. Ordained to ministry Pentecostal Holiness Ch., Falcon, N.C., 1974. Mem. Christian edn. bd. N.C. Conf. Pentecostal Holiness Ch., Falcon, 1976-82, sec.-treas. Christian edn., 1982-86, asst. dir. Christian edn., 1986-87, conf. dir. Christian edn., mem. Gen. Christian Edn. Bd., 1987—; also bd. dirs.; vice chmn. adv. bd. Sch. Christian Ministries Emmanuel Coll., Franklin Springs, Ga., 1990—. Coord. re-election com. Senator Jesse Helms, 1984. Recipient Instrumental Solo award Pentecostal Holiness Ch., 1971. Mem. Royal Rangers (comdr.). Republican. Home and Office: PO Box 60 Falcon NC 28342

FORELL, GEORGE WOLFGANG, religion educator; b. Breslau, Germany, Sept. 19, 1919; came to U.S., 1939, naturalized, 1945; s. Frederick J. and Madeleine (Kretschmar) F.; m. Elizabeth Jean Rossing, June 14, 1945; children: Madeleine Helene (Mrs. Gary Marshall), Mary Elizabeth (Mrs. Christopher Davis). Student, U. Vienna, 1937-38; BD, Luth. Theol. Sem., Phila., 1941; Th.M., Princeton Theol. Sem., 1943; ThD, Union Theol. Sem., N.Y.C., 1949; DD (hon.), Wartburg Theol. Sem., 1967; LHD, Gustavus Adolphus Coll., 1974; LLD, Luther Coll., 1983; LittD, Upsala Coll., 1983. Ordained to ministry Luth. Ch., 1941. Pastor Luth. Chs., N.J. and N.Y., 1941-47; asst. prof., then assoc. prof. philosophy Gustavus Adolphus Coll., St. Peter, Minn., 1947-54; asst. prof., then assoc. prof. theology U. Iowa, 1954-58, prof. religion, 1961-73, Carver prof., 1973-89, Carver Disting. prof. emeritus, 1989—, dir. Sch. Religion, 1965-71; prof. systematic theology Luth. Sch. Theology, Chgo., 1958-61; vis. prof. U. Hamburg, Germany, 1957-58, All Africa Theol. Seminar, Marangu, Tanzania, 1960, Japan Luth. Coll., Tokyo, 1968, Gurukul Theol. Rsch. Inst., Madras, India, 1978, Luth. Coll., Hong Kong, 1980; Eli Lilly vis. prof. Berea Coll., Ky., 1979, 86, Pacific Luth. U., Tacoma, Wash., 1987, Luth. Theol. Sem., Phila., 1988-91, Luth. Sch. Theology, Chgo., 1991—; cons. dept. studies Luth. World Fedn., Geneva, 1981-84. Author: Faith Active in Love, 1954, Ethics of Decision, 1955, The Protestant Faith, 1960, The Christian Year, 1964-65, Understanding the Nicene Creed, 1965, Christian Social Teachings, 1966, The Augsburg Confession, A Contemporary Commentary, 1968, Zinzendorf: Nine Public Lectures, 1973, The Proclamation of the Gospel in a Pluralistic World, 1973, The Christian Lifestyle, 1975, The Revolution at the Frontier: Reports from Moravian Missionaries Among the American Indians, 1976, History of Christian Ethics, Vol. I, 1979, The Luther Legacy, 1983. Mem. Ch. Coun. Evang. Luth. Ch. Am., 1987-91. Mem. Am. Philos. Assn., Am. Soc. Ch. History, Am. Soc. Reformation Research (pres. 1959), Soc. Values in Higher Edn., Omicron Delta Kappa. Democrat. Home: 10 Bella Vista Iowa City IA 52245

FOREMAN, DIANA, lay worker; b. Dunn, La., Dec. 9, 1949; d. Joseph Beaureguard and Cecelia (Fitch) Hartley; m. Ledrew B. Foreman, Oct. 19, 1974; children: Elizabeth, Joseph A. Student, Bish Mathis Inst., Monroe, La., 1969. Dir. Boarding Home Ministry, Southside Assembly, Jackson, Miss., 1980—; bookkeeper Southside Assembly of God, Jackson, 1980—; leader Children's Ch., ages 3-5, 1989-91; pres. PTA, Southside Christian Sch., Jackson, 1986-91. Republican. Home: 150 Fairway Cir Jackson MS 39212 Office: Southside Assembly of God 665 Raymond Rd Jackson MS 39204

FOREMAN, LELAND DON, minister; b. Maurice, Iowa, Nov. 7, 1943; s. Jake M. Foreman and Alice Jeannette (Cleveringa) Vander Broek; m. Jean M. Palsma, June 10, 1967; children: Joel David, Daniel Lee, Paul Aaron, Stephen Jay. BA, Northwestern Coll., Orange City, Iowa, 1965; MA, U. No. Iowa, 1973; MRE, Midwestern Sem., North Kansas City, Mo., 1980. Ordained to ministry Am. Bapt. Ch., 1982. Assoc. pastor 1st Bapt. Ch., Leavenworth, Kans., 1978-82; assoc. pastor 1st Bapt. Ch., Fremont, Nebr., 1982-91, co-pastor, 1991—. With U.S. Army, 1968-72. Mem. Nebr. Bapts. Assn. (pres. 1990-91), Fremont Mins. Assn. (sec. 1991—). Republican. Home: 749 N Nye Fremont NE 68025 Office: PO Box 422 330 E 5th St Fremont NE 68025

FOREMAN, TERRY HANCOCK, philosophy and religion educator; b. Long Beach, Calif., Mar. 12, 1943; s. Paul McElroy and Helen Margaret (Hancock) F.; m. Charlotte Leveton, June 14, 1970 (div. May 1986); children: Samuel, Alan. BA in History, Stanford U., 1964; postgrad., Union Theol. Sem., N.Y.C., 1964-66; MA in Philosophy, Pa. State U., 1968; MPhil, Yale U., 1970, MA, 1971, PhD in Religious Studies, 1975. Intern Pa. State U. campus Westminster Found./United Campus Ministry, 1966-67; assoc. prof., chair dept. philosophy and religious studies Murray (Ky.) State U., 1978—. Elder 1st Presbyn. Ch., Murray, 1985-87, 91—; active West Ky. Multiple Sclerosis Support Group, Paducah, 1985—, Murray Choral Union, 1989—. Mem. Am. Acad. Religion (steering com. 19th century theology study group 1981-84, steering com. history of study of religion group 1987—), Amnesty Internat. (corr.). Home: 1623 Sunset Dr Murray KY 42071 Office: Murray State U Dept Philosophy and Religious Studies Murray KY 42071

FORESTELL, JAMES TERENCE, theology educator, priest; b. Fort Erie, Ont., Can., Nov. 22, 1925; s. Tobias Frederick and Agnes Irene (O'Driscoll) F. B.A., U. Toronto, 1948; S.T.L., Angelicum, Rome, 1953; S.S.L., Pontifical Bibl. Inst., Rome, 1955; Eleve Titulaire, L'Ecole Biblique, Jerusalem, 1956; S.S.D., Pontifical Biblical Commn., Rome, 1974; D.Humanities (hon.), St. Michael's Coll., Winooski, Vt., 1981. Ordained priest Roman Catholic Ch., 1951. Prof., Old and New Testament, St. Basil's Sem., Toronto, 1956-68; prof. New Testament, Faculty of Theology, U. St. Michael's Coll., Toronto, 1968-88; prof. Sacred Scripture St. Joseph's U. Coll., U. Alb., Edmonton, 1988—. Author: The Word of the Cross, 1974; Targumic Traditions and the New Testament, 1979, As Ministers of Christ, 1991; contbr. articles to profl. jours. Mem. Catholic Biblical Assn. Am., Soc. Biblical Lit., Soc. New Testament Study, Canadian Biblical Soc., Assn. Des Etudes Bibliques au Canada. Roman Catholic. Avocations: swimming, walking.

FORESTER, LARRY WAYNE, minister; b. Ft. Payne, Ala., Dec. 11, 1951; s. James Harold and Mary Ellen (Hawkins) F.; m. Patricia Janes Baines, July 20, 1974; children: Katy, Abigail. Student, Belmont Coll., Nashville, 1975-77, Luther Rice, 1989—. Lic. rev.; ordained to ministry So. Bapt. Ch., 1977. Chaplain Nashville Rescue Mission, 1976-78; pastor Liberty Bapt. Ch., White Bluff, Tenn., 1979-81, Cloverdale Bapt. Ch., Rising Fawn, Ga., 1984-88, First Bapt. Ch., Hazel Green, Ala., 1988—; del. So. Bapt. Conv., Hazel Green, 1988—. Mem. Madison Bapt. Assn. (evangelism com. 1989—). Republican. Home: 105 Mandy Dr Hazel Green AL 35750 Office: First Bapt Ch 225 Hunt Dr Hazel Green AL 35750

FORLINES, FRANKLIN LEROY, minister, educator; b. Winterville, N.C., Nov. 14, 1926; s. John Leroy and Leta Nanny (Manning) F.; m. Carolyn Le Fay Gilbert, Aug. 4, 1956; children: Jonathan Gilbert, James Franklin. BA, Freewill Bapt. Bible Coll., Nashville, 1952; MA, Winona Lake Sch. of Theology, Ind., 1959; BD, No. Bapt. Theol. Sem., Chgo., 1962; ThM, Chgo. Grad. Sch. of Theology, 1970. Ordained to ministry Free Will Bapt. Ch., 1951. Pastor 1st Free Will Bapt. Ch., Newport News, Va., 1952-53; mem. faculty Free Will Bapt. Bible Coll., 1953-59, 1962—, chmn. Bible dept., 1965—, dean of men, 1953-59, 65-71, dean of students, 1971-74. Author: Biblical Ethics, 1973, Systematics, 1975, Romans, The Randall House Bible Commentary, 1987. Mem. Evang. Theol. Soc., Bible Sci. Assn. Nashville (v.p. 1988—). Home: 3801 Rolland Rd Nashville TN 37205 Office: Free Will Bapt Bible Coll 3606 West End Ave Nashville TN 37205

FORMAN, CHARLES WILLIAM, religious studies educator; b. Gwalior, India, Dec. 2, 1916; s. Henry and Sallie (Taylor) F.; m. Helen Janice Mitchell, Mar. 12, 1944; children—David, Sarah, Harriet. B.A., M.A., Ohio State U., 1938; Ph.D., U. Wis., 1941; B.D., Union Theol. Sem., N.Y.C., 1944, S.T.M., 1947. Ordained to ministry Presbyn. Ch., 1944. Prof. North India United Theol. Coll., Saharanpur, 1945-50; sec. program emphasis Nat. Council Chs., 1951-53; mem. faculty Div. Sch., Yale U., New Haven, 1953—, D. Willis James prof. missions, 1961-87, D. Willis James prof. missions emeritus, 1987—; chmn. theol. edn. fund World Coun. Chs., 1965-70, mem., 1970-77; mem. commn. ecumenical mission United Presbyn. Ch., 1962-71, chmn., 1965-71; chmn. Found. for Theol. Edn. in SE Asia, 1970-89. Author: A Faith for the Nations, 1958, The Nation and the Kingdom, 1964, Christianity in the Non-Western World, 1967, The Island Churches of the South Pacific, 1982, The Voice of Many Waters, 1986. Mem. bd. edn., Bethany, Conn., 1957-66; bd. dirs. Community Action Agy., New Haven, 1978-81, Overseas Ministries Study Center, New Haven, 1979—. Home: 329 Downs Rd Bethany CT 06524

FORMAN, WELDON WARREN, minister; b. Shelbina, Mo., Apr. 4, 1927; s. Forrest Glenn and Lula Cassie (Purdy) F.; m. Opal Ruth Poff, Aug. 25, 1945; children: Ronald Warren, Glenn Calvern, Norman Dale, James Todd. BS in Elem. Edn., S.W. Bapt. U., Bolivar, Mo., 1972; BA, Annibal LaGrange Coll., 1951. Ordained to ministry, So. Bapt. Conv. Pastor Hopewell Bapt. Ch., Thompson, Mo., 1969-76, Unity Bapt. Ch., Fulton, Mo., 1976-78; elem. sch. adminstr. Clark (Mo.) Elem. Sch., 1978-81; pastor Sturgeon (Mo.) Bapt. Ch., 1980-86, Grand Prairie Bapt. Ch., Auxvasse, Mo., 1986—. Home: Rte 2 Box 291 Auxvasse MO 65231 Office: Grand Prairie Bapt Ch N Main at Harrison St Auxvasse MO 65231

FORMHALS, DANNY LEE, religion; b. Long Beach, Calif., July 29, 1966; s. Gary Lee Formhals and Deloris Jean (Jones) Simmons; m. Michele Ann Holstein, July 7, 1990. Student, Bethany Bible Coll., Santa Cruz, Calif., 1991. With Evang. Community Ch., Sunnyvale, Calif., 1990—. Home: 798 Teatree Ct San Jose CA 95128

FORREST, EDGAR HULL, retired priest; b. London, June 23, 1916; (parents Am. citizens); s. Wilbur Studley and Floss (Springer) F.; m. Eleanor Baldwin, Oct. 4, 1947; children: Edgar Hull Jr., Marian, Richard, Patricia. BA, Yale U., 1938; MDiv, Va. Sem., Alexandria, 1964. Ordained priest Episcopal Ch., 1965. Reporter Wilmington (Del.) Morning News, 1938-40; commd. ensign USNR, 1940; advanced through grades to comdr. USN, 1952; ret., 1961; asst. rector St. John's Episcopal Ch., Wilmington, N.C., 1964-66; rector Christ Ch., North Brookfield, Mass., 1964-71; vicar St. Mark's Ch., Springfield, Mass., 1971-78; ret., 1978; mem. Christian Edn. Commn., Diocese West Mass., Springfield, 1973-86, co-chmn., 1973-75, mem. Scholarship Commn., 1978-89. Mem. East Longmeadow Rep. Town Com., 1978—, chmn., 1978-80; mem. East Longmeadow Sch. Com., 1980-83. Decorated Bronze Star, U.S. Army. Mem. Rotary. Avocations: golf, bridge, computers. Home: 15 Deerfoot Dr Springfield MA 01028 *How different our world would be if we all loved our neighbor as ourself. The impediment to this is that too many of us don't love ourselves enough to love others. The saving message is that God does love and forgives every one of us as we put our faith in Him.*

FORREST, RONNIE REED, minister; b. Centertown, Ky., Apr. 1, 1951; s. Frank Reed and Ona Rae (Ashby) F.; m. Eunice Ann Hallmark, July 30, 1971; children: Michael David, Matthew Thomas. BA, Ky. Wesleyan Coll., 1974; postgrad., So. Bapt. Theol. Sem., 1980. Ordained to ministry So. Bapt. Conv., 1969. Pastor New Hope Bapt. Ch., Moorman, Ky., 1968-70, Browder (Ky.) Bapt. Ch., 1971-73, Pellville (Ky.) Bapt. Ch., 1973-78, Temple Bapt. Ch., Owensboro, Ky., 1978-83, Mt. Pleasant Bapt. Ch., Lewisburg, Ky., 1983—; chmn. Hist. Commn. Ky. Bapt. Conv., Middletown, 1989—, mem. nominations com., 1984-85, exec. bd., 1985, adminstrv. com., 1986-88. Named Ky. Col., Commonwealth of Ky., 1983. Mem. Logan Bapt. Assn. (moderator 1987-89), Lions (pres. Lewisburg chpt. 1986-89). Home: 613 Stacker St Lewisburg KY 42256 Office: Mt Pleasant Bapt Ch 612 Stacker St Lewisburg KY 42256

FORSBERG, MARK (BISHOP MARK OF FORT LAUDERDALE), bishop. Former bishop Diocese of Boston Orthodox Ch. in Am.; now aux. bishop Orthodox Ch. in Am., Ft. Lauderdale, Fla. Office: Orthodox Ch in Am 9511 Sun Pointe Dr Boynton Beach FL 33437*

FORST, MARION FRANCIS, bishop; b. St. Louis, Sept. 3, 1910; s. Frank A.J. and Bertha T. (Gulath) F. Grad., Kenrick Sem., Webster Groves, Mo., 1934. Ordained priest Roman Catholic Ch., 1934; pastor St. Mary's Cathedral, Cape Girardeau, Mo., 1949-60; vicar gen. Diocese of Springfield-Cape Girardeau, 1956-60; bishop Dodge City, Kans., 1960-76; aux. bishop Archdiocese of Kansas City, Kans., 1976—; Kan. chaplain K.C., 1964—. Served with Chaplains Corps USNR, World War II. Office: 615 N 7th St Kansas City KS 66101

FORSTER, CORNELIUS PHILIP, priest, graduate school dean, history educator; b. N.Y.C., Oct. 27, 1919; s. Cornelius and Mary Catherine (Collins) F. A.B., Fordham U., 1941, Ph.D., 1963; M.A., Cath. U., 1951; S.T.L., S.T.Lr., Pontifical U., Washington, 1949; M.A. (hon.), Providence Coll., 1959. Joined Dominican Order, Roman Cath. Ch., ordained priest, 1948. Instr. Providence Coll., 1949-52, asst. prof., 1952-55, assoc. prof., 1955-58, prof., 1958—, chmn. dept. history, 1962—, dean Grad. Sch., 1964—, exec. v.p., 1982-85, acting pres., 1982; archivist for Dominican Province of St. Joseph, 1988—. Mem. Johannine Soc., History Club (founder, moderator), Nat. Cath. Edn. Assn., Am. Hist. Assn., Am. Cath. Hist. Assn., Am. Assn. Colls. for Tchr. Edn., Am. Assn. Univ. Adminstrs., New Eng. Assn. Grad. Schs., Delta Epsilon Sigma, Phi Alpha Theta. Office: Providence Coll Providence RI 02918

FORSTER, GARTH ANDREW, clergyman; b. Birmingham, Nov. 20, 1955; s. Roy Harold and Gloria Constance (Patterson) F.; m. Suzanne Gaie Pittman, June 21, 1980. BS in Secondary Sci. Edn., Auburn U., 1978; MDiv, Southwestern Bapt. Theol. Sem., 1985. Ordained to ministry Bapt. Ch., 1984. Pastor Pleasant Grove Bapt. Ch. #2, Boyd, Tex., 1984-87, Calvary Bapt. Ch., Gadsden, Ala., 1987—; vice-moderator Wise Bapt. Assn., Decatur, Tex., 1986-87; sec.-treas. Sch. of the Prophets, Gadsden, 1991. Republican. Office: Calvary Bapt Ch 1145 Hoke St Gadsden AL 35903 *Recently, I have formulated a five word philosophy that summarizes a Christian perspective of life: "Trust God and do right." We cannot do more, we dare not do less.*

FORSTMAN, HENRY JACKSON, theology educator, university dean; b. Montgomery, Ala., June 15, 1929; s. Joseph Carl and Kate Gertrue (Kelley) F.; m. Shirley Marie Cronk, June 3, 1950; children: David Jackson, Valerie Marie, Paul Frederick. B.A., Phillips U., 1949, D.D. (hon.), 1982; B.D., Union Theol. Sem., N.Y.C., 1956, Th.D., 1959. Asst. prof. Randolph-Macon Woman's Coll., 1958-60, Stanford, 1960-64; mem. faculty Vanderbilt U., 1964—, prof. religion, 1968—, Charles G. Finney prof. theology, 1979—, chmn. grad. dept. religion, 1969-72; acting dean Vanderbilt U. (Div. Sch.), 1970-71, dean, 1979-89; Fulbright research scholar, Germany, 1973-74, 79-80; Mem. faith and order commn. World Council Chs. Author: Word and Spirit, 1962, Christian Faith and the Church, 1965, A Romantic Triangle, 1977, Christian Faith in Dark Times, 1992. Kent fellow, 1957-58; postdoctoral fellow for cross disciplinary studies Soc. Values in Higher Edn., 1966-67. Mem. Am. Soc. Ch. History, Am. Acad. Religion, Assn. Disciples Theol. Discussion. Home: 3913 Kimpalong St Nashville TN 37205 Office: Vanderbilt U Divinity Sch Nashville TN 37240

FORSYTHE, CHARLES WAYNE, education administrator; b. Lester, Ala., Jan. 26, 1949; s. Warren J. and Marie (Evans) F.; m. Shirley Ann Forsythe, June 2, 1972; 1 child, Gregory Wayne. AA, Calhoun Coll., 1972; BS in Edn., Athens State Coll., 1982; MS, Pensacola Christian Coll., 1990. Cert. tchr., Ala., Tenn. Tchr. Athens (Ala.) city schs., 1982-83, Triana Village Sch., Huntsville, Ala., 1983-85; adminstr. Westminster Christian Acad., Huntsville, 1985-86, Highland Christian Acad., Pulaski, Tenn., 1986—. Author: (children's novel) The Midnight Stallion, 1972; (novel) Pearls from Philemon, 1990; contbr. articles to numerous profl. mags. Mem. Assn. Christian Schs. Internat. (cert. adminstr.). Republican. Baptist. Avocations: fishing, hunting, kenneling black labrador retrievers, Western art. Office: Highland Christian Acad 1827 Mill St Pulaski TN 38478 *While young people need to be taught how to make a living, they more desperately need to be taught how to make a life. The educator who can weave the threads of moral values, social graces and intellectual ascent into the tapestry of life is most worthy of his hire.*

FORT, ROBERT BRADLEY, minister; b. Portsmouth, Va., Dec. 27, 1948; s. Richard Gould and Hazel Naomi (McBride) F.; m. Esther Faith Hardin, June 10, 1967; children: Yvonne René, Nathan Michael. Ordained to ministry United Evang. Ch., 1973. Evangelist United Evang. Chs., Monrovia, Calif., 1966, nat. youth dir., 1968-70, asst. to the pres., 1970-73, Calif. dist. supt., 1973-75; evangelist Assemblies of God, Springfield, Mo., 1976-78; sr. pastor Lynden (Wash.) Assembly of God, 1978-81, County Christian Ctr., Bellingham, Wash., 1981-87, First Assembly of God, Salinas, Calif., 1988—; exec. dir. Life Mgmt. Sems., Salinas, 1989—; pres. Fort Ministries, Salinas, 1967—. Composer Love was the Color, 1980 (Grand prize 1981); singer, musician 13 records. Republican. Office: Fort Ministries 1025 Fairview Ave Salinas CA 93905

FORTIER, JEAN-MARIE, archbishop; b. Que., Can., July 1, 1920; s. Joseph and Alberta (Jobin) F. Student, Grand Sem. Que., 1940-45; L.Th., Laval U., Que., 1945; postgrad., U. Louvain, Belgium, 1946-48; Licentiate in Ch. History, Gregorian U., Rome, 1950. Ordained priest Roman Catholic Ch., 1944; sec. to bishop of Hearst, Ont., Can., 1945-46; tchr. ch. history Grand Sem. Que., 1950-60; consecrated bishop Ste. Anne de la Pocatiere, Que., 1961-65, Gaspe, Que., 1965-68; archbishop Sherbrooke, Que., 1968—; mem. Congregation for Sacraments and Divine Cult, 1975-84; v.p. Can. Cath. Conf., 1971-73, pres., 1973-75; pres. Comité Episcopal des Communications Sociales, 1976-84; v.p. l'Assemblee des Evêques du Quebec, 1981-85, pres., 1985-89. Mem. Knights Order Holy Sepulchre of Jerusalem, Assn. Evéques de Que. (pres. 1985-89), des Chevaliers de Colomb de Que. Address: 130 Rue de la Cathedrale, Sherbrooke, PQ Canada J1H 4M1

FORTNEY, DOYLE WRIGHT, minister; b. Louisville, Dec. 11, 1933; s. Karle Wright and Bertha Mae (Westerfield) F.; children: Lawrence Doyle, Kenneth Paul; m. Loretta Jean Harding, Aug. 17, 1974; children: Justin Wright, Stefani Andrea. BA with honors, Pepperdine U., 1981. Ordained to ministry; cert. sr. profl. human resources. Enlisted seaman, U.S. Navy, 1952, advanced through grades to cmdr., 1977, ret., 1981; comdr. ROTC, Louisville, 1982-83; with personnel dept. Christian Appalachian Project, Lancaster, Ky., 1983-84, dir. religious programs and planning, 1985—, dir. adminstrn. Bibles for the World; project mgr. Universal Energy Systems, Dothan, Ala., 1984-85. Crisis counselor Suicide and Crisis Intervention, Memphis, 1977. Mem. Christian Ministries Mgmt. Assn. (sec. 1984), Am. Soc. Personnel Adminstrn., Am. Assn. Tng. and Devel., Am. Assn. Counseling and Devel., Am. Mgmt. Assn. Democrat. Mem. Ch. of God. Avocation: flying. Home: 167 Pennsylvania Louisville KY 40206 Address: ON 451 Gary Ave N Wheaton IL 60187-4038

FORTUNE, MARIE M., ecumenical agency administrator. Exec. dir. Ctr. for Prevention Sexual and Domestic Violence, Seattle. Office: Ctr for Prevention Sexual and Domestic Violence 1914 N 34th St Ste 105 Seattle WA 98103*

FORTUNE, MICHAEL JOSEPH, religion educator; b. N.Y.C., Aug. 28, 1922; s. John and May (Vaughan) F.; m. Genevieve Hintz, May 27, 1945 (div. Apr. 1977); children: Michael, Patrick, Richard, Ronald, Susan, Sandra, Sharon, Laura. BS, U. Wis., Stevens Point, 1949; PhD, U. Wis., Madison, 1965; MA, U. Minn., 1952. Prof. lit. U. Wis., Stevens Point, 1956-67, chmn. comp. lit., fgn. lang., 1972-74; prof. religious lit. Mundelein Coll., Chgo., 1968-72, 74-87; sr. prof. Loyola U./Mundelein Coll., Chgo., 1987—. Author: (play) Metamorphosis, 1991; contbr. articles to jours. in field. Named Tchr. of Yr., Johnson Found., Racine, Wis., 1965. Mem. Sigma Tau Delta, Alpha Mu Gamma. Home: 1848 Balsam Rd Highland Park IL 60035 Office: Loyola U Mundelein Coll Dept Religious Studies 6363 N Sheridan Rd Chicago IL 60660

FOSCOLOS, NICOLOAS, archbishop. Archbishop Archdiocese of Athens, Roman Cath. Ch., Greece. Office: Archbishopric, Odos Omirou 9, 106 72 Athens Greece*

FOSHEE, HOWARD BRYCE, minister; b. Birmingham, Ala., May 20, 1925; s. Cornelius Howard and Audie Lucille Foshee; m. Zola Leek, June 7, 1949; children: Zola, Becky, Elizabeth. BA, Samford U., $, 1950; MDiv, So. Bapt. Theol. Sem., Louisville, 1952. Ordained to ministry, 1951. Pastor, min. edn. various chs., Ind. and N.C., 1950-56; min. edn. First Bapt. Ch., Durham, N.C., 1954-56; sec. ch. adminstrn. dept. Bapt. Sunday Sch. Bd., Nashville, 1958-79, dir. Christian devel. div., 1979-87; lectr. sems., colls. Author: Ministry of Deacon, 1968, Broadman Church Manual, 1973, Now That You Are a Deacon, 1976; also articles. Mem. ch. devel. commn. Bapt. World Alliance. Recipient Disting. Svc. award Samford U., 1975. Mem. Nat. Assn. Ch. Bus. Adminstrn., Soc. Religious Orgn. Mgmt. Home: 5629 Highland Way Nashville TN 37211

FOSHEE, HUBERT LYNN, missionary administrator, pastor; b. Paris, Ark., Jan. 28, 1941; s. Jesse Abram Foshee and Anne May (Lile) Jefferson; m. Sylvia Margaret Smith, Sept. 8, 1973; 1 child, Sara Elizabeth. BS, Ark. Tech U., 1963; MDiv, Columbia Bibl. Sem., 1975. Ordained to ministry Evang. Ch., 1983. Asst. dean men Columbia (S.C.) Bible Coll., 1975-77, dean men, 1977-78; missionary World Team, Coral Gables, Fla., 1978-85; dir. admissions/fin. aid Montreat (N.C.)-Anderson Coll., 1985-87; asst. to gen. dir. Bible Christian Union, Hatfield, Pa., 1987—. Served to capt. U.S. Army, 1963-69, Vietnam. Decorated Bronze Star with one bronze oak leaf cluster. Mem. Interdenominational Fgn. Missions Assn., Frontiers. Republican. Avocations: piano, gardening, hiking, fishing.

FOSNOUGH, LARRY WAYNE, lay worker, electrical marine designer; b. Gelnhausen, Fed. Republic Germany, Sept. 28, 1957; came to U.S., 1961; s. James Albert Fosnough and Ella Mae (Shively) Simpkins; m. Mary Ann Henry, June 24, 1989. Cert., Newport News (Va.) Shipbuilding and Dry Dock Co. Apprentice Sch., 1980. Deacon Elim Christian Fellowship, Augusta, Maine, 1990—; designer Bath Iron Works, Augusta, 1989—. Home: 18 Davenport St Augusta ME 04330 Office: Bath Iron Works 700 Washington St Bath ME 04530

FOSS, HARLAN FUNSTON, religious education educator, academic administrator; b. Canton, S.D., Oct. 10, 1918; s. Hans and Thea (Hokenstad) F.; m. Beatrice Naomi Lindaas, Sept. 2, 1943; children—Richard John, Kristi Marie, Marilyn Jean. B.A., St. Olaf Coll., 1940; B.Th., Luther Theol. Sem., 1944; Th.M., Princeton Theol. Sem., 1945; Ph.D., Drew U., 1956; postgrad., Mansfield Coll. Oxford (Eng.) U., 1967, Pontifical Inst. and Gregorian U., Rome, 1974. Ordained to ministry Luth. Ch., 1944. Pastor Mt. Carmel Luth. Ch., Milw., 1944-47; mem. faculty St. Olaf Coll., Northfield, Minn., 1947—; assoc. prof. religion St. Olaf Coll., 1954-56, prof., 1957—, v.p., dean coll., 1979-80, pres., 1980-85. Mem. Northfield Bd. Edn., 1959-66, treas., 1960-61, chmn., 1961-66. Decorated Knight 1st class Order St. Olav (Norway); Ezra Squire Tipple fellow, 1951-52. Mem. AAUP, Am. Acad. Religion, Norwegian-Am. Hist. Assn., Blue Key. Republican. Club: Lion. Home: 216 Manitou St Northfield MN 55057 *A life centered in religious faith is best lived when it is extended in love and care for other people and nature.*

FOSS, RICHARD JOHN, minister; b. Wauwatosa, Wis., Dec. 27, 1944; s. Harlan Funston and Beatrice Naomi (Lindaas) F.; m. Nancy Elizabeth Martin, June 21, 1969; children: Susan, John, Naomi, Elizabeth, Peter, Andrew. BA, St. Olaf Coll., 1966; MDiv, Luther Theol. Seminary, 1971; ThM, Luther N.W. Theol. Seminary, 1984. Ordained to ministry Luth. Ch., 1971. Pastor St. Andrews Ch. and Ch. of Christ the Redeemer, Mpls., 1971-77; assoc. pastor First Luth., Fargo, N.D., 1977-79; sr. pastor Prince of Peace Luth., Seattle, 1979-86, Trinity Luth., Moorhead, Minn., 1986—. Soloist F-M Opera Co., Fargo, 1979; coach St. James Girls' Basketball Team, Seattle, 1982-84; vol. Wash. State Patrol Crisis Chaplaincy, Seattle, 1983-86; bd. dirs. Discovery, Inc., Mpls., 1972-77, Highline Boys' and Girls' Club, Burien, Wash., 1980-81, Luth. Compass Ctr., Seattle, 1983-86, v.p., 1985-86; mem. Bio-med. Ethics Symposium, Fargo-Moorhead, 1988—, master chorale, 1987—. Avocations: racquetball, golf, reading, travel, vocal performance. Home: 1510 S 2d St Moorhead MN 56560 Office: Trinity Lutheran Moorhead MN 56560

FOSSUM, JARL EGIL, religion educator; b. Oslo, June 12, 1946; came to U.S., 1988; m. Ellen Johns, Jan. 9, 1970; 1 child, Maria Fossum Johns. MA, U. Bergen, Norway, 1972; ThD, U. Utrecht, The Netherlands, 1982. Assoc. prof. U. Mich., Ann Arbor, 1988—; vis. prof. C.G. Jung Inst., Zurich, 1990—. Author: The Name of God and the Angel of the Lord, 1985; contbr. articles to profl. jours. Mem. Soc. N.T. Studies, Soc. d'Études Samaritaines, Soc. Bibl. Lit. Office: U Mich Dept Nr Ea Studies Frieze 3074 Ann Arbor MI 48109-1285

FOSTER, ANDREW LEE, JR., pastor; b. Phila., Oct. 17, 1946; s. Andrew Lee Sr. and Blanche Marie (Brown) F.; m. Bobbi Taylor, June 23, 1968; children: Andrew III, Veronica, Brent, Karen, Vanessa, Monica, Andrea. BA, Antioch U., 1978; MDiv, MRE, Hood Theol. Sem., Salisbury, N.C., 1981; STM, Drew U., 1987, PhD candidate, 1989—. Ordained to ministry A.M.E. Zion Ch. Asst. pastor Poplar St. A.M.E. Zion Ch., Phila., 1975-77; pastor Oak Grove A.M.E. Zion Ch., Greensboro, N.C., 1977-82; sr. pastor Shrewsbury Ave. A.M.E. Zion Ch., Red Bank, N.J., 1982—; sec. N.J. Conf. and Camden Dist. Conf. A.M.E. Zion Ch., 1983—, del. Gen. Conf., 1988—; dean Camden Dist. Sch. of Prophets, 1984—; pres. Westside Ministerial Alliance, Red Bank Area, 1988—. Author: The Saying and The Doing, 1990; recording artist (tape) The Songs of Paradise, 1989. Treas. Monmouth County Arts Coun. and Red Bank Ministerium Area, 1990; pres. Count Basie Learning Ctr., Red Bank, 1991; bd. dirs. Salvation Army, Red Bank, 1990, Monmouth County Fair Housing Bd., Freehold, N.J., 1991. Recipient Outstanding Svc. award Red Bank Bd. Edn., 1989, Christian Individual of Yr. award N.J. Coun. of Chs., 1990, Pres. award Greater Red Bank NAACP, 1990, Proclamation, N.J. State Assembly, 1990. Mem. Order of St. Luke, The Physician (chaplain 1988—). Home: 84 Plum St Tinton Falls NJ 07724-2623 Office: Shrewsbury Ave AME Zion Ch 285 Shrewsbury Ave Red Bank NJ 07701-1318

FOSTER, CHARLES MATTHEWS, II, minister; b. Morgantown, Ind., Sept. 27, 1929; s. Charles Matthews and Georgia May (Barnett) F.; m. Barbara Josephine Jones, Feb. 3, 1950; children: Charles III, Stephen, Phillip, Jeffrey, Susan. Student, St. Joseph's Coll., Rensselaer, Ind., 1965-66; BTh, Purdue U., 1978. Ordained to ministry Assemblies of God, 1976. Founding pastor Assembly of God, Rensselaer, 1962-67; pastor Assembly of God, Lebanon, Ind., 1968-74, Winchester, Va., Bennettsville, S.C., 1975-78, Laurinburg, N.C.; assoc. Assembly of God, Frisco, N.C., 1978-86; pastor Assembly of God, Elwood, Ind., 1986—; dir. Christian edn., local sect. Ind. dist. Assemblies of God, Elwood, 1986-91; exec. bd. dirs. Ea. Indian Bible Sch., Shannon, N.C., 1982-86. Mem. Elwood Ministerial Assn. (treas. 1988-91). Home: 114 N 5th St Elwood IN 46036 Office: 1st Assembly of God 400 N A St Elwood IN 46036

FOSTER, DANIEL GEORGE, minister of music, organist, choirmaster, hotel executive; b. South Bend, Ind., Feb. 28, 1958; s. E. D. and Barbara Warlick (Yount) F. AA, Western Piedmont Coll., 1978; BS, U. N.C., 1980. Substitue organist Luth. Ch.-Mo. Synod, Newton and Conover, N.C., 1971-74; organist, choirmaster 1st Bapt. Ch., Claremont, N.C., 1974-78, Holy Cross Luth. Ch., Newton, 1979-85, 88—; dir. music. organist, choirmaster Concordia Evang. Luth. Ch-Mo. Synod, 1985-88; adminstr. Days Inn-Hickory, Conover, N.C., 1988—; supr. Days Inn Hickory, Conover, N.C., 1988—. Mem. Luth. Laymen's League (asst. league svcs. chmn. N.C. and S.C. dist. 1982-84, sec. local chpt. 1985—). Republican. Avocations: swimming, racquetball. Home: 210 3d St NE Conover NC 28613 Office: Holy Cross Luth Ch-Mo Synod 612 S College Ave Newton NC 28658

FOSTER, DAVID MARK, bishop; b. Fancher, Ill., Feb. 11, 1932; s. Homer Foster; m. Joy Lee Clark, Oct. 4, 1952; children: Kathleen Litton, LaDon Birk, Coleen Jeffery, David A. BA, Greenville (Ill.) Coll., 1956; MA, Azusa Pacific U., 1972; PhD, Calif. Grad. Sch. Theology, Los Angeles, 1974. Ordained to ministry Free Meth. Ch., 1955. Pastor Free Meth. Ch., 1952-79; conf. supt. Pacific Northwest Conf. Free Meth. Ch., Seattle, 1979-85; bishop Free Meth. Ch., Indpls., 1985—. Address: PO Box 535002 Indianapolis IN 46253-5002

FOSTER, DAVID WILLIAM, minister; b. Idaho Falls, Idaho, Aug. 25, 1961; s. Robert Earl Foster and Alice (Crowder) Foster-Trumblee; m. June Ann Porter, Mar. 30, 1984; children: Brandon Allen, Brittany Ann. AS, N.W. Bible Coll., Kirkland, Wash., 1981; BA, N.W. Bible Coll., 1983. Ordained to ministry Bapt. Ch., 1987. Youth intern Idaho Falls Assembly of God, 1978-82; assoc. pastor youth Neighborhood Assembly, Lake Stevens, Wash., 1983-87; min. youth Bothel (Wash.) First Bapt., 1987—; asst. dir. ACTS Drama Ministry, Kirkland, 1981-83; camp counselman Cedar Springs Com., Kirkland, 1983-87; camp dir. Cedar Springs, Lake Stevens, 1985-87; dir. mins. Mt. Pillchuck Mins. Fellowship, Lake Stevens, 1984-87; youth coord. Puget Sound Bapt. Assn., Federal Way, Wash., 1988-91; bd. dirs. Hilltop Ministries, Lake Stevens, 1990—; seminar speaker, 1990. Composer religious musicals, 1982, 85; contbr. articles to profl. jours. Co-dir. Intransit Communications, Lake Stevens, 1985-87; distributor Everett (Wash.) Rep. Party, 1986. Future Religious Leader grantee Eastern Star, 1979, 80. Mem. Nat. Right to Life Com. (presdl. commendation 1986). Office: Bothell First Bapt Ch 19527 104th Ave NE Bothell WA 98011

FOSTER, DEBRA COURTNEY, minister; b. N.Y.C., Mar. 1, 1953; d. Alexander J. and Rita Dorothy (Gollin) Courtney; m. John Courtney Foster, Nov. 3, 1978; 1 stepchild, Joy Lorraine. BS in Child Devel., U. Calif., Davis, 1976; MA in Psychology, Calif. State U., Chico, 1979; MDiv, Meth. Theol. Sch. Ohio, 1990. Ordained to ministry United Meth. Ch., 1990; cert. tchr., Calif. Coord. children's ch. Pomeroy (Ohio) United Meth. Ch., 1984-87; student pastor So. Cluster United Meth. Ch., Meigs County, Ohio, 1987-88, Cheshire (Ohio) Charge United Meth. Ch., 1988-90; pastor Fortuna (Calif.) United Meth. Ch., 1990—. Mem. adv. com. Women, Infants and Children Program, Pomeroy, Ohio, 1983-84; chair bd. dirs. Serenity House, Gallipolis, Ohio, 1984-88; chair Summer Celebration, Fortuna, 1991—. Named Outstanding Contbr. Juvenile Programs, Humboldt State U., 1991. Mem. Internat. Soc. for Study Multiple Personality and Dissociation, Fortuna C. of C., Bus. and Profl. Women, Quota Club (jr. dir. 1991—), Soroptomist Club, Kiwanis. Home: 1100 Vista Dr Fortuna CA 95540 Office: Fortuna United Meth Ch 922 N St Fortuna CA 95540

FOSTER, GARY DEAN, religious publishing management and marketing specialist; b. Van Wert, Ohio, May 24, 1944; s. Dean F. and Mildred (Bailey) F.; m. Patricia J. Sutton, July 10, 1971. BBA, Le Tourneau Coll. Bus. circulation mgr. Moody Monthly Mag., Chgo., 1968-72; asst. product mgr. David C. Cook Pub. Co., Elgin, Ill., 1972-74; agy. mgr. Am. Advt. Co., Elgin, 1974-76; publs. dir. Christian Booksellers Assn., Colorado Springs, Colo., 1976-85; pres. CBA Service Corp., Colorado Springs, 1985—, Gary D. Foster Cons., Manitou Springs, Colo., 1988—; treas. Christian Book and Lit. Inst., Colorado Springs, 1980—. Pub. Bookstore Jour., 1982-86, CBA Suppliers Directory, 1982-86, Current Christian Books, 1976-86; co-author: The Diary, 1991. Rep. precinct worker, Colorado Springs, 1983-84; deacon 1st Evang. Free Ch., Colorado Springs, 1991—. Mem. Am. Mgmt. Assn., Evang. Press Assn. (treas., bd. dirs. 1971-73, annual conv. chmn. 1978). Mem. Evang. Free Ch. Am. Office: 334 Sutherland Pl Manitou Springs CO 80829

FOSTER, JOHN BENTLEY, JR., lay worker; b. Wichita Falls, Tex., July 1, 1951; s. John Bentley and Frances (Habern) F.; m. Deborah Diane Fesmire, Nov. 17, 1973; children: Erin Michelle, Cory Eason. Student, U. Tex., Arlington, 1969-75; BS, Dallas Bapt. Coll., 1977; MRE, Southwestern Bapt. Theol. Sem., 1980. Min. edn. Monterrey Bapt. Ch., Lubbock, Tex., 1980-82; min. edn. Lamar Bapt. Ch., Wichita Falls, Tex., 1982-84; min. edn., adminstrn. North Side Bapt. Ch., Weatherford, Tex., 1984-88, First Bapt. Ch., Waxahachie, Tex., 1988-91, Hampton Rd. Bapt. Ch., De Soto, Tex., 1991—; trustee Ellis Bapt. Assn., Waxahachie, 1990-93; cons. Bapt. Gen. Conv. of Tex., 1981-91, So. Bapt. Conv., 1984-90; tchr. Sem. Extension Dept. Wichita-Archer-Clay Bapt. Assn., Wichita Falls, 1982-84. Author: (project) Selecting a Computer for the Church, 1986; contbr. articles to religious jours. Fellow Nat. Assn. Ch. Bus. Adminstrn., So. Bapt. Ch. Bus. Adminstrn. Assn. (pres. 1987-89), So. Bapt. Religious Edn. Assn., Southwestern Bapt. Religious Edn. Assn., So. Bapt. Bus. Officers Assn. (pres. 1988). Office: Hampton Rd Bapt Ch 400 N Hampton Rd De Soto TX 75115

FOSTER, LEILA MERRELL, clergywomen, lawyer, psychologist, writer; b. Richmond, Va., Feb. 27, 1929; d. George Henry and Leila Virginia (Merrell) Foster. BS, Northwestern U., Evanston, Ill., 1950; JD, Northwestern U., Chgo., 1953; PhD, Northwestern U., Evanston, 1966; MDiv, Garrett Theol. Sem., Evanston, 1964. Diplomate Am. Bd. Med. Psychotherapists. Atty. Sidley, Austin, Burgess and Smith, Chgo., 1953-61; pastor No. Ill. Meth. Ch., Maple Park, Cortland and Elsdon (Chgo.), Ill., 1963-68; postdoctoral intern Merrill-Palmer Inst., Detroit, 1968-69; vis. lectr. Garrett Theol. Sem., Evanston, Ill., 1969-70; postdoctoral intern Ill. State Psychiat. Inst., Chgo., 1970-71; clin. psychologist West Side VA Med. Ctr., Chgo., 1971-87; clin. psychologist in pvt. practice Evanston, 1972—; Co-author/coeditor: Confidentiality of Health Records, 1972, The Illinois Psychologist's Law Handbook, 1984; co-producer: (videotape) Confidentiality, 1982. Author: Bhutan, 1989, Margaret Thatcher, 1990, The Sumerians, 1990, Iraq, 1991, Rachel Carson, 1990, David Glasgow Farragut, 1991, Jordan, 1991; (with others) The Illinois Mental Health Professional's Law Handbook, 1988, At the Point of Need, 1988, Clergy Assessment and Career Development, 1990; contbr. articles to profl. jours. Fellow Am. Psychol. Assn., Am. Orthopsychiat. Assn.; mem. ABA, Ill. Bar Assn., Chgo. Bar Assn., Nat. Orgn. VA Psychologists (pres. 1982-83), Assn. for Advancement of Psychology (dir. 1980-86). Methodist. Club: Zonta (pres. 1982-83). Home and Office: 1585 Ridge Ave Evanston IL 60201

FOSTER, RICHARD JAMES, religion educator; b. Albuquerque, May 3, 1942; m. Carolynn Kerr, 1967; children: Joel, Nathan. BA, George Fox Coll., Newberg, Oreg., 1964; D. Pastoral Theology in Bibl. Studies, Fuller Theol. Sem., 1980; hon. doctorate, George Fox Coll., 1987. Min. youth Alamitos Friends Ch., Garden Grove, Calif., 1962-67; counselor Family Counseling and Rsch. Ctr., Garden Grove, 1967-68; asst. pastor Arcadia (Calif.) Friends Ch., 1968-70; pastor Woodlake Ave Friends Ch., Canoga Park, Calif., 1970-74, Newberg Friends Ch., 1974-79; assoc. prof. theology, writer in residence Friends U., Wichita, Kans., 1979—; exec. dir., The Milton Ctr. Friends Univ., Wichita, Kans.; pres. Renovaré, Wichita. Author: Celebration of Discipline: The Path to Spiritual Growth, rev. edit. 1988, Freedom of Simplicity, 1981, Study Guide for Celebration of Discipline, 1982; (booklet) Meditative Prayer, 1983, The Challenge of the Disciplined Life, 1985, Study Guide to Money, Sex and Power, 1985; producer tapes, films; contbr. articles to mags. Recipient Writer of Yr. award Warner Pacific Coll., 1978, Gold Medallion award Christian Booksellers Assn., 1982, Christy award Christian Life Mag., 1982. Office: The Milton Ctr Friends U 2100 University Wichita KS 67213

FOSTER, ROBERT LAWSON, judge, deacon; b. Putnam, Okla., Nov. 17, 1925; s. Mark M. and Jessie Marie (Gregory) F.; m. Mary Jo Hull, July 1, 1949; children—Candace Ann (Mrs. Dan Sebert), Martha Denise (Mrs. Gerald Speed), Karen Sue Greenfield, Robert L., John Michael, Cynthia Kay (Mrs. Allyn Downen Jr.). B.A., U. Okla., 1949, LL.B., 1950, J.D., 1970. Bar: Okla. 1950; ordained deacon Roman Cath. Ch., 1979. Pvt. practice Chandler, 1950-51; county judge Lincoln County, Okla., 1951-69; assoc. dist. judge 23d Jud. Dist., Chandler, Okla., 1969-87. Chmn. dist. council Boy Scouts Am., 1968-69; chmn., an organizer Chandler Combined Appeal, 1954—; sec., pres. Lincoln County Jr. League Baseball, 1960-68; county dir. Civil Def., 1953-70; mem. bd. Permanent Deacon Candidates for Okla., mem. deacon perceiver team, 1985—. Served with USAF, 1944-45. Mem. Lincoln County Bar Assn. (pres. 1965, sec. 1960-64, 67-69, 70-73), C. of C. (sec. 1964-68), Okla. Assn. County Judges (sec.-treas. 1964-67), Okla. Jud. Conf. Club: Chandler Parents. Lodge: Lion (dir. 1964-65, pres. 1967, treas. 1968-70, zone chmn. 1973-74, dep. dist. gov. 1974—). Office: Court House Square Chandler OK 74834

FOSTER, RODNEY PATRICK, personnel executive; b. San Antonio, Apr. 30, 1951; s. Cecil Glenn and Margaret Mary (Frazar) F.; m. Lynell Porritt, June 6, 1974; children—Alisa, Paul, Melinda, Emily. B.A. cum laude, Brigham Young U., 1974. Missionary to Norway, 1970-72; adminstrv. asst. First Presidency's Office, Mormon Ch., Salt Lake City, 1974-80, mgr. tng. and pre-dedication services, Temple Dept., 1980—. Mem. Mormon Youth Symphony and Chorus, 1978-81. Mem. Am. Soc. Tng. and Devel. Republican. Office: 50 E North Temple Salt Lake City UT 84150

FOSTER, STEVEN WAYNE, computer professional; b. Coldwater, Mich., July 8, 1949; s. William George and Beverly Jean (Chase) F.; m. Patricia Ann Tyson, July 15, 1973; 1 child, Jason Wayne. AS in Bus. Computer Programming, Dalton (Ga.) Jr. Coll., 1978. Programmer Coronet Carpets, Dalton, 1978-79; herdsman Lawrence Tyson & Son Dairy, Eatonton, Ga., 1979-82; programmer So. Union Conf. of Seventh-Day Adventists, Decatur, Ga., 1983—. Bd. dirs. Belvedere Seventh-Day Adventists Homeless Men's Shelter, Decatur, 1985—. Served with U.S. Army, 1969-71. Avocations: backpacking, volleyball, weightlifting. Home: 8158 Rockbridge Rd Lithonia GA 30058 Office: So Union Conf Seventh-Day Adventists 3978 Memorial Dr Decatur GA 30032

FOSTER, STILLMAN ALLEN, JR., minister; b. Pitts., Nov. 10, 1939; s. Stillman Allen and Ruth Elizabeth (Sherrard) F.; m. Miriam Marie Morris, Aug. 18, 1962; children: Stillman Allen III, Robin Wallace, Amy Ruth. BA, Westminster Coll., New Wilmington, Pa., 1961; BD, Princeton U., 1964; PhD, U. Edinburgh, Scotland, 1976. Ordained to ministry United Presbyn. Ch. in U.S.A., 1966. Instr. Am. U., Washington, 1966-67, Westminster Coll., 1970; sr. pastor Highland United Presbyn. Ch., New Castle, Pa., 1967-71, Southminster Presbyn. Ch., Dayton, Ohio, 1973-84, Pitts., 1984—; chmn. com. ministerial svcs. Miami (Ohio) Presbytery, 1975, chmn. com. on candidates, 1976; bd. dirs. United Campus Ministry, Miami U., Oxford, Ohio; chmn. Roman Cath. dialogue Pitts. Diocese and Presbytery, 1986—. Contbr. to Pittsburgh Book of Prayer, 1990. Mem. exec. bd. NAACP, New Castle, 1968-69; mem. New Castle Human Rels. Commn., 1967-71. Mem. Omicron Delta Kappa, Phi Alpha Theta. Home: 739 Pinetree Rd Pittsburgh PA 15241 Office: Southminster Presbyn Ch 799 Washington Rd Pittsburgh PA 15228 *I believe that love is the key to the meaning of human life and the cosmos. Love cannot be self-generated. It may only be received. But when love is received it transforms human personality. That is why divine love truly received, changes people radically into just, caring, giving and mature beings. This progressive loving transformation is what God is up to in dealing with us.*

FOSTER, WILLIAM SILAS, JR., minister; b. Kansas City, Mo., Nov. 5, 1939; s. William Silas and Edna LaResta (Scott) F.; m. Susan Jean Mannle, June 5, 1983; children Robert Light, Beth Light, Stacey Light; children from previous marriage, Beth Ann, Amy Lynne. BA, Mo. Valley Coll., 1962; MDiv, McCormick Sem., 1966. Ordained to ministry Presbyn. Ch. (USA), 1966. Asst. min. 1st Presbyn. Ch., Edwardsville, Ill., 1966-68; min. St. Paul's Presbyn. Ch., St. Louis, 1968-71, Moro (Ill.) Presbyn. Ch., 1971-83; min. 1st Presbyn. Ch., North Kansas City, Mo., 1983-84, Worland, Wyo., 1985—; commr. to Gen. Assembly Presbyn. Ch. (U.S.A), Omaha, Balt., 1973, 91; stated clk. Presbytery Wyo., Casper, 1990—; instr. calligraphy Synod Sch., 1982-83; pres. Presbyn. Alcohol Info. Network, 1982-83, Ill. Impact Bd., 1983. Resource person 1980 Youth Triennium, Bloomington, Ind., 1980; bd. dirs. Edwardsville Sch. Bd., 1976-83, Mental Bd. Washakie County, 1989—. Recipient M. Keith Upson award U.S. Jaycees, 1974; named Outstanding New Mem., Ill. Jaycees, 1972, Outstanding Mem., 1973. Mem. Lions (2d v.p. 1989-91). Home: 1515 Yellowstone Worland WY 82401 Office: 1st Presbyn Ch PO Box 53 Worland WY 82401 *In the 21st Century, we are called as Abraham to live on a wilderness frontier of life. This radically unique environment demands creative risks and personal ethical choices. Listening to one another's wilderness journeys, learning from each other and supporting others are the keys for genuine faith, hope and love in the future.*

FOTH, RICHARD B., academic administrator. Pres. Bethany Coll., Santa Cruz, Calif. Office: Bethany Coll Office of Pres 800 Bethany Dr Scotts Valley CA 95066*

FOUNTAIN, ANTHONY GERALD, clergyman; b. Pelzer, S.C., Nov. 14, 1963; s. Gerald Deen and Dora Lee (Fricks) F. BA, Bapt. Coll. at Charleston, S.C., 1985. Lic. minister Bapt. Ch. Asst. camp dir. Charleston Bapt. Assn., 1983; minister of youth New Hope Bapt. Ch., Pelzer, S.C., 1984; minister of youth and children Couchton Bapt. Ch., Aiken, 1985-87; tchr. Aiken County Sch. Dist., 1986-87. Vol. minister Charleston Home for Children, 1983-84; chmn. Bapt. Student Union, Charleston, 1981-85; mem. revival team Reflections, Charleston, 1982-84; staff mem. Crisis Ctr. Connie Maxwell Children's Home, Greenwood, S.C., 1987—. Republican. Avocations: singing, speaking, travel, music. Home and Office: Connie Maxwell Children's Home PO Box 1178 Greenwood SC 29648

FOUNTAIN, EDWIN BYRD, minister, educator, librarian; b. Manassas, Ga., Mar. 11, 1930; s. David Theodore and Laura Bertha (Phillips) F. BFA, U. Ga., 1951; BRE, BTh, Lexington Bapt. Coll., 1980, MRE, 1981, DD (hon.), 1990; MLS, U. Ky., 1984, ABD in Edn., 1990. Ordained to ministry Bapt. Ch., 1982. Pastor Riverview Bapt. Ch., Lexington, Ky., 1982-87; libr. asst. Lexington Bapt. Coll., 1980-81, tchr., libr., 1981-90; divisional chmn. libr. svcs. Tenn. Temple U., Chattanooga, 1990-91; librarian Statesboro (Ga.) Regional Libr., 1991—. Compiler indexes for religious books; contbr. articles to profl. jours. 1st lt. USAF, 1951-53. U. Ky. fellow, 1990. Mem. ALA, SAG, Christians Librs. Assn., Actors Equity Assn., Lexington Bapt. Coll. Alumni Assn. (pres. 1982-87, 89-90), Beta Phi Mu. Home: Rte 1 Box 152A2 Garfield GA 30425 Office: Statesboro Regional Libr 124 S Main St Statesboro GA 30425

FOURNIER, CHERYL J., campus minister, educator; b. Chgo., July 23, 1960; d. Albert Edmond and Anne Carolyn (Goerres) F. BA in Religious Studies, Mundelein Coll., Chgo., 1987, MA in Religious Studies, 1988. Cert. secondary tchr., Ill. Coord. youth liturgy St. Augustine Parish, Chgo., 1978-81, Resurrection Parish, Cin., 1981-82; tchr. religion Mater Dei High Sch., Breese, Ill., 1987—, campus min., mem. retreat team, 1988—; bd. mem. Belleville (Ill.) Diocesan Quest, 1989—; mem. adult team Belleville Quest, 1989—, Belleville Dioceasan Teens Encounter Christ, 1989—; del. Rerum Novarium coordinating com. Diocese of Belleville, 1991. Scholar Mundelein Coll., 1985-87, grad. scholar, 1988. Mem. Coll. Theology Soc. Office: Mater Dei High Sch 9th and Plum Sts Breese IL 62230 *Life's journey is continuously enhanced by the people one meets along the way. God constantly reminds me to seek God's own face in the face of those who journey side by side with me as we together go about the work of the kingdom.*

FOWLER, DAVID COVINGTON, English educator; b. Louisville, Jan. 3, 1921; s. Earle Broadus and Susan Amelia (Covington) F.; m. Mary Gene Stith, Jan. 28, 1943; children: Sandra Fowler Berryman (dec.), Caroline S. Aaron. BA in English, U. Fla., 1942; MA in English, U. Chgo., 1947, PhD in English, 1949. Prof. English U. Wash., Seattle, from 1952, now prof. emeritus. Author: The Bible in Early English Literature, 1976, The Bible in Middle English Literature, 1984; contbr. articles to profl. jours. Lt. (s.g.) USNR, 1942-46. ACLS scholar U. Pa., 1951-52; Guggenheim fellow, 1962-63, 75-76. Mem. AAR/SBL N.W. (pres. 1974), Medieval Assn. of Pacific (pres. 1980-82), Modern Lang. Assn., UW Folklore Rsch. Group (chmn. 1981-87), Calif. Folklore Soc. Home: 6264 19th Ave NE Seattle WA 98115 Office: U Wash Dept English Seattle WA 98195

FOWLER, HAROLD DOUGLAS, retired minister; b. Duluth, Minn., Apr. 18, 1927; s. Harold Douglas and Laura Anna (Schaeffer) F.; m. Dorothy Joyce Wilson, Aug. 25, 1951; children: David, Dale, Diane, Duane. BA, Macalester Coll., St. Paul, 1951; BD, San Francisco Theol. Sem., 1954. Ordained to ministry, Presbyn. Ch. (USA), 1954. Asst. pastor Calvary Presbyn. Ch., Milw., 1954-56; pastor, dir. Mayer Chapel & Ch. and Neighborhood Ctr., Indpls., 1956-62; pastor Altona (Ill.) and Oneida Presbyn. Chs., 1962-68, Presbyn. Ch., Lake Crystal, Minn., 1968-80, Horicon (Wis.) and Hustis Ford Presbyn. Chs., 1980-87, First Presbyn. Ch., Gouverneur, N.Y., 1987-91; ret.; commr. del. United Ministry Higher Edn., Minn. and Wis., 1972-86; moderator Mankato Presbytery, 1972-73; del. Presbyn. Gen. Assembly, Denver, 1972; mem. Presbytery of No. N.Y. (chmn. budget com. 1987-91). Precinct chmn. Rep. Party, Lake Crystal, 1974-78; mem. sch. bd. Horicon Sch. Dist., 1985-87. With USAAF, 1945-46. Mem. Rotary (sec. 1981-87), Kiwanis (sec. 1988-91), Lions, Masons. Republican. Home: 4390 Montezuma Ave Rimrock AZ 86335

FOWLER, JAMES WILEY, III, minister, educator; b. Reidsville, N.C., Oct. 12, 1940; s. James Wiley and Lucile May (Haworth) F.; m. Lurline Locklair, July 7, 1962; children—Joan S., Margaret. B.A., Duke U., 1962; B.D., Drew U., 1965; Ph.D., Harvard U., 1971. Ordained to ministry Methodist Ch., 1968. Assoc. dir. Interpreters House, Lake Junaluska, N.C., 1968-69; minister United Meth. Ch., 1968—; asst. prof. to assoc. prof. Harvard U. Div. Sch., Cambridge, Mass., 1969-76; assoc. prof. Boston Coll., Chestnut Hill, Mass., 1976-77; prof. theology and human devel. Emory U., Atlanta, 1977—, founder, dir. Ctr. Faith Devel., 1980—, Charles Howard Candler prof., 1987—; bd. dirs. Nat. Cath. Reporter, Zygon, 1988. Author: To See the Kingdom, 1974; (with Sam Keen) Life Maps, 1978; (with others) Trajectories in Faith, 1980; (with others) Toward Moral and Religious Maturity, 1980; Stages of Faith, 1981; Becoming Adult, Becoming Christian, 1984; (with others) Faith Development and Fowler, 1986, Faith Development and Pastoral Care, 1987, Weaving the New Creation, 1991; editor: (with others) Remembrances of Lawrence Kohlberg, 1988, Caring for the Commonweal, 1990, Faith and Religious Development, 1991. Mem. Am. Acad. Religion, Religious Edn. Assn., Assn. Profs. and Researchers in Religious Edn., Soc. Scientific Study Religion. Democrat. Home: 2740 Janellen Dr NE Atlanta GA 30345 Office: Emory U Sch of Theology Atlanta GA 30322

FOWLER, LEE (ALLAN), music and youth minister; b. Dothan, Ala., Oct. 24, 1961; s. William Buford and Betty Ruth (Beasly) F.; m. Lisa Renea Smith, Jan. 17, 1981 (div. Mar. 1989); m. Pam Denese Sizemore, Jun. 16, 1990. MusB, William Carey Coll., 1987. Lic. Grandview Bapt. Ch., 1984. Music min. Leaf River Bapt. Ch., Collins, Miss., 1983-84; min. music/youth Gulf Garden Bapt. Ch., Gulfport, Miss., 1986-87, Pleasureville Bapt. Ch., Pleasureville, Ky., 1988, Grandview Bapt. Ch., Dothan, Ala., 1989—; Rep. Columbia Bapt. Assn. Youth Comm., Dothan; music coord. Columbia Bapt. Assn. Min. Conf. Southern Baptist. Home: 1401 Summit St Dothan AL 36301 Office: Grandview Baptist Ch 1001 E Selma St Dothan AL 36301-3836

FOWLER, ROBERT M., theology educator; b. Emporia, Kans., Nov. 29, 1950; s. Robert Wayne and Jo Anne (Daily) F.; m. Mary Sue Stewart, Dec. 26, 1970; children: Geoffrey, Amanda. BA, U. Kans., 1972, MA, 1974; PhD, U. Chgo., 1978. Asst. prof. philosophy and religion Yankton (S.D.) Coll., 1978-80; from asst. to assoc. prof. religion Baldwin-Wallace Coll., Berea, Ohio, 1980—. Author: Loaves and Fishes, 1981, Let the Reader Understand, 1991; contbr. articles to profl. jours. Recipient Susan Colver Rosenberger prize, U. Chgo., 1980; fellow, NEH, 1982-83. Mem. AAUP, Am. Acad. Religion, Soc. of Bibl. Lit., Cath. Bibl. Assn., Soc. for Study of Narrative Lit., Westar Inst. Mem. United Ch. of Christ. Avocations: running, reading, computers. Office: Baldwin-Wallace Coll Dept Religion Berea OH 44017

FOWLER, TONY RAY, lay worker; b. Haines City, Fla., Mar. 17, 1961; s. Onnie and Mary Magdalene (Glass) F.; m. Vicki Tamela Moak, Aug. 13, 1981; children: Brandon Tony, Elisha Christian, Mitchell Caleb, Rebekah Ann. Worship leader, youth pastor, elder Life Church, Mc Comb, Miss., 1987—; warehouse mgr., dispatcher Brown Bottling Group, Mc Comb, 1984—. Mem. Right to Life (nat., state, county chpts.). Home: RR 4 PO Box 356H McComb MS 39648 Office: Life Ch RR 4 Box 361B McComb MS 39648

FOWLKES, DANE WINSTEAD, minister; b. New Orleans, Feb. 21, 1960; s. Henry Winstead and Lois Marie (Richey) F.; m. Gina Linette Corpier, May 30, 1981; children: Christan Joy, Jordan Ruth. BA in Missionary Studies, East Tex. Bapt. Coll., 1982; MDiv in Bibl. Studies, Southwestern Bapt. Sem., 1990. Assoc. pastor Trinity Bapt. Ch., Port Arthur, Tex., 1979; pastor Midyett Bapt. Ch., DeBerry, Tex., 1980-81, New Faith Bapt. Ch., Nacogdoches, Tex., 1981-83, Lilly Grove Bapt. Ch., Nacogdoches, 1984-85; assoc. pastor Meml. Bapt. Ch., Port Arthur, 1985-86; pastor Meml. Bapt. Ch., Channelview, Tex., 1986-88, Greenbriar Bapt. Fellowship, Ft. Worth, 1989-90, Pkwy. Bapt. Ch., Houston, 1991—; associational clk. Golden Triangle Bapt. Assn., Beaumont, Tex., 1985-86, Shelby-Doches Bapt. Assn., Nacogdoches, 1981-84; co-dir. Bible Conf. Ministries, Marshall, Tex., 1983-85. Mem. Ministerial Alliance, Channelview, 1987; v.p. ch. planting fellowship Southwestern Bapt. Sem., 1989-90. Named one of Outstanding Young Men of Am., 1985. Mem. Union Bapt. Assn. (ch. extension com. Houston chpt. 1991—), East Tex. Bapt. U. Alumni Assn., Southwestern Bapt. Sem. Alumni Assn. Avocations: hunting, fishing, painting, archery. Home: 12019 Blue Island Houston TX 77044 Office: 12818 Tidwell Rd Houston TX 77044

FOX, DOUGLAS ALLAN, religion educator; b. Mullumbimby, Australia, Mar. 20, 1927; came to U.S., 1960; s. Cecil Edwin Madison and Lilly Louise (Tucker) F.; m. Margaret Eileen Porter, Sept. 10, 1958; children—Elizabeth Rachel, Michael Glenn. B.A., U. Sydney, Australia, 1954; M.A., U. Chgo., 1957; S.T.M., Pacific Sch. Religion, Berkeley, Calif., 1958, Th.D., 1962. Minister Congl. Union of New South Wales, Wollongong, Australia, 1955-56; minister Congl. Union of New South Wales, Sydney, Australia, 1958-61; prof. religion Colo. Coll., Colorado Springs, 1963—, David and Lucille Packard prof., 1982—. Author: Buddhism, Xianity and the Future, 1972, The Vagrant Lotus, 1973, Mystery and Meaning, 1975, Meditation and Reality, 1986, The Heart of Buddhist Wisdom, 1986. Trustee Penrose Meml. Hosp., Colorado Springs, 1980-82. World Ch. fellow World Council of Churches, Chgo., 1956-57; research fellow Soc. Religion in Higher Edn., 1966. Mem. Am. Acad. Religion. Mem. United Ch. of Christ. Avocations: fishing; hiking. Home: 1413 Querida Dr Colorado Springs CO 80909 Office: Colo Coll Colorado Springs CO 80903

FOX, EDGAR LEROY, minister; b. Tulsita, Tex., Oct. 8, 1934; s. John B. and Mary (Green) F. BA, Tex. Christian U., 1957, BD, 1960; DD, Universal Bible Inst., 1975. Ordained to ministry Christian Ch., 1960. Pastor 1st Christian Ch., Gordon, Tex., 1958-59, Post, Tex., 1973-77, Quanah, Tex., 1977—; film libr. Tex. Christian U., Ft. Worth, 1958-60; pastor, bus. mgr. Valley Christian Ch., 1960-65; exec. dir. Yakima Indian Nation, 1965-70; Pres. Rolling Plains Mgmt. Corp., 1986-88. Author: (booklets) It Must Be Done, God's Gifts, God's Claims, When Suicide Comes, Is Baptism Necessary, When I go to Church. Mem. adv. coun. Ft. Simcoe Job Corp., 1965-69; scoutmaster local troop Boy Scouts Am., 1977—; bd. dirs. Sr. Citizen, 1983, v.p., 1986—; mem. cen. area bd. Christian Ch. in Tex., 1978—. Recipient Silver Beaver award Boy Scouts Am., 1987. Mem. Post Ministerial Alliance (pres. 1976-77), Quanah Ministerial Alliance (v.p. 1977-88, treas. 1989-90). Address: PO Box 356 Quanah TX 79252

FOX, LOGAN JORDAN, religion educator; b. Tokyo, Oct. 20, 1922; s. Harry R. and Pauline (Hickman) F.; m. Madeline Clark, Sept. 23, 1943; children: Ramona (dec.), Logan Lee, Violet, Katy, Matthew. BA, Pepperdine U., L.A., 1946, LLD (hon.), 1959; MA, U. Chgo., 1947; PhD, U. So. Calif., L.A., 1967. Dean Ibaraki Christian Coll., Hitachi, Japan, 1948-52, pres., 1952-60; min. Vt. Am. Ch. of Christ, L.A., 1961-63, ret., 1963. Author: Psychology as Philosophy Science and Art, 1972; editor: Christianity in Asia, 1957. Democrat. Home: 2403 W 79th St Inglewood CA 90305

FOX, MARVIN, rabbi, philosophy educator; b. Chgo., Oct. 17, 1922; s. Norman and Sophie (Gershengorn) F.; m. June Elaine Trachtenberg, Feb. 20, 1944; children: Avrom Baruch, Daniel Jonathan, Sheryl Deena. BA, Northwestern U., 1942, MA, 1946; PhD, U. Chgo., 1950. Ordained rabbi, 1942. Faculty Ohio State U., Columbus, 1948-74, instr., 1948-52, asst. prof., 1952-56, assoc. prof., 1956-61, prof. philosophy, 1961-73, Leo Yassenoff prof. philosophy and Jewish studies, 1973-74; Philip W. Lown prof. Jewish philosophy, dir. Lown Sch. Nr. Ea. and Judaic Studies Brandeis U., Waltham, Mass., 1974—; vis. prof. Hebrew Theol. Coll. Chgo., 1955, Hebrew U., Jerusalem, 1970-71, Bar-Ilan U., Ramat-Gan, Israel, 1970-71; Shoolman Disting. vis. prof. Hebrew Coll., Brookline, Mass., 1990—; mem. exec. com. Conf. Jewish Philosophy, 1963-69, Inst. for Judaism and Contemporary Thought, Israel, 1971—; mem. acad. bd. Melton Rsch. Ctr., Jewish Theol. Sem. Am., 1972—; mem. Internat. Coun. of Yad Yashem, Jerusalem, 1983—. Author: Modern Jewish Ethics—Theory and Practice, 1975, Interpreting Maimonides: Studies in Methodology, Metaphysics and Moral Philosophy, 1990; editor: Kant's Fundamental Principles of the Metaphysic of Morals, 1949; cons. editor jour. History of Philosophy, 1970-76; mem. editorial bd. Libr. of Living Philosophers, 1946—, Judaism, 1953—, Tradition, 1956-89, AJS Rev., 1976-84, Daat, 1978—, Jewish Edn. Yearbook, 1979—; bd. editors Studies in Judaism, 1986—; contbr. articles to profl. jours. With USAAF, 1942-46. Elizabeth Clay Howald Found. fellow, 1956-57, Am. Coun. Learned Socs. fellow, 1962-63, NEH fellow, 1980-81. Mem. AAUP, Am. Philos. Assn., World Union Jewish Studies (governing coun.), Assn. Jewish Studies (bd. dirs. 1970—, v.p. 1973-75, pres. 1975-78), Nat. Commn. B'nai Brith Hillel Founds. (exec. com.), Medieval Acad. Am., Metaphys. Soc. Am., Am. Acad. Jewish Rsch., Conf. Jewish Philosophy. Home: 11 Ellison Rd Newton Center MA 02159 Office: Brandeis U Dept Nr Ea and Judaic Studies Waltham MA 02254

FOX, MICHAEL VASS, Hebrew educator, rabbi; b. Detroit, Dec. 9, 1940; s. Leonard W. and Mildred (Vass) F.; m. Jane Schulzinger, Sept. 4, 1961; children: Joshua, Ariel. BA, U. Mich., 1962, MA, 1963; PhD, Hebrew U., Jerusalem, 1972. Ordained rabbi, 1968. Lectr. Haifa U., Israel, 1971-74, Hebrew U., Jerusalem, 1975-77; prof. Hebrew U. Wis., Madison, 1977—, chmn. dept., 1982-88, Weinstein-Bascom prof. in Jewish studies, 1990—. Author: The Song of Songs and the Ancient Egyptian Love Songs, 1985, Shirey Dodim Mimitzrayim Ha'atiqa, 1985, Qohelet and his Contradictions, 1988, The Redaction of the Books of Esther, 1991, Character and Ideology in the Book of Esther, 1991; contbr. articles to profl. jours. Recipient Wahrburg prize Hebrew U., 1971-72; Leverhulme fellow U. Liverpool, Eng., 1974-75; fellow Brit. Friends of Hebrew U., Liverpool, 1974-75; Vilas assoc., 1988-90. Mem. Soc. for Bibl. Lit., Nat. Assn. Profs. Hebrew (editor Hebrew Studies 1985—). Home: 2815 Chamberlin Ave Madison WI 53705 Office: U Wis Dept Hebrew Van Hise Hall 1350 Madison WI 53706

FOX, PATRICK BERNARD, religious organization administrator; b. Newark, June 22, 1948; s. Walter Thomas and Anna Teresa (Farley) F.; m. Jacqueline Anne Zick, Apr. 6, 1974. BS, Iona Coll., 1970; MS, U. Rochester, 1980. Tchr. Bishop Kearney High Sch., Rochester, 1970-72; religious educator Christ the King Ch., Rochester, 1972-74; dir. youth programs St. Louis Ch., Pittsford, N.Y., 1974-82; diocesan youth dir. Diocese of Rochester, 1982—; participant Future of Cath. Edn. Project, Washington, 1988—. Author: Life of Brother Stewart, 1971; editor: Faith Maturing, 1983. Vice-chmn. Teen Pregnancy Coalition, Rochester, 1983-90; mem. Eye Conservation Coun., Rochester, 1989—, chairperson, 1990—; mem. Cath. Family Ctr. Bd., 1989—. Mem. Nat. Fedn. Cath. Youth Ministry (bd. dirs. 1986, sec.-treas. 1987—, regional coord. 1986—), Rochester Area Youth Devel. Coun. (pres. 1985-87), Religious Edn. Assn. U.S. and Can., K.C. Democrat. Home: 201 Avondale Rd Rochester NY 14622 Office: Diocese of Rochester 1150 Buffalo Rd Rochester NY 14624

FOX, RALPH EDWARD, lay worker, dentist; b. Indpls., July 27, 1929; s. Henry Thomas and Esta D. (Delrymple) F.; m. Deloris Lavon Warford, Feb. 9, 1951; children: Brian Lamont, Bryce Edward, Brent Alan. BA, Ind. U., 1956, MA, 1957; DDS, Ind. U., Indpls., 1965. Cert. Coun. of Nat. Bd. Dental Examiners, Ind. State Bd. Dental Examiners. local trustee S.W. Ch. of Nazarene, Indpls., 1960—; trustee Olivet Nazarene U., Kankakee, Ill., 1970—; mem. adv. bd. Dist. Ch. of Nazarene, Indpls., 1975—, dir. work and witness, 1979—; dentist, Indpls., 1965—; speaker for Sunday Sch., missionary and lay retreats. Pres. Perry Manor Civic League, Indpls., 1980-82. With USN-USMC, 1951-54. Mem. Ind. Dental Assn. (nursing home cons. 1970), Nazarene Amateur Radio Fellowship. Republican. Home: 6322 Minlo Dr Indianapolis IN 46227 Office: 435 E Hanna Ave Indianapolis IN 46227 *"But if not." (Daniel 3:18) Words that bespeak a mind set, a determination to serve God regardless. If we today can exhibit that same resolution, we will make it.*

FOX, SAMUEL J., rabbi, educator; b. Cleve., Feb. 25, 1919; s. Joseph and Yetta (Mandel) F.; m. Edith Phyllis Muskin, Jan. 25, 1942; 1 child, Joseph Raphael. BA, Yeshiva U., 1940, rabbi, 1941; MA, Butler U., 1946; PhD, Harvard U., 1959. Ordained rabbi Union Orthodox Jewish Congregations Am., 1941. Rabbi United Hebrew Congregation, Indpls., 1941-51, Congregation Chevra Tehillim, Lynn, Mass., 1951—; prof. theology Merrimack Coll., North Andover, Mass., 1970—; pres. Orthodox Rabbinical Coun., Boston, 1950—, Mass. Coun. Rabbis, Boston, 1950—. Author: Hell in Jewish, 1958; profucer TV program Massachusetts Rabbis, 1960; columnist Why Because, 1942. Bd. dirs. Value of Life Com., Boston, 1952. Mem. AAUP, Coll. Theology Soc. Home and Office: Chevra Tehillim 145 Lynn Shore Dr Lynn MA 01902 *While most people think of Death as a negative, one should also think of Death as positive. It is the inevitable coming of death that makes life positive and worth while. Death is also the positive end of suffering and the arrival of final peace.*

FOX, SELENA MARIE (SUZANNE BISSET), minister; b. Arlington, Va., Oct. 20, 1949; d. Thomas Richard and Anne Elise (Fox) Bisset; m. Dennis Darrel Carpenter, June 7, 1986. BS in Psychology with honors, Coll. William and Mary, 1971; postgrad., Rutgers U., 1972, Madison Area Tech. Coll., Wis., 1973-75, U. Wis., 1991—. Min. Circle Sanctuary, Mt. Horeb, Wis., 1974—; guest min. Unitarian Universalists, Wis., others, 1980—, Meth. Ch., United Ch. of Christ, Madison, 1980—; del., speaker World Coun. of Chs. Conf., Toronto, Ont., Cand., 1988; guest speaker/tchr. various univs., 1980—. Author: Goddess Communion Rituals, 1988; cons. (Time-Life book series) Mysteries of the Unknown, 1990; founding editor: Circle Network News quarterly, 1980; founder: Circle's Worldwide Nature Spirituality Network, 1978, Wiccan Shamanism, 1979; contbr. articles, rituals to books and jours., 1975—. Recipient Feature Writing Excellence award PROCOM/WABC, Madison, 1978. Mem. Am. Assn. Counseling and Devel., Am. Mental Health Counselors Assn., Assn. for Humanistic Psychology. Mem. Circle Sanctuary/Nature Spiritualist. Office: Circle Sanctuary PO Box 219 Mount Horeb WI 53572 *The Divine is immanent in Nature. Environmental preservation is a sacred duty. Pray globally and act locally for a better environment and planetary peace and wellness.*

FOX, WILLIAM LLOYD, JR., minister; b. Takoma Park, Md., Dec. 16, 1953; s. William Lloyd Sr. and Lynn Gregory (Waters) F.; m. Lynn Smith, Aug. 1, 1981; 1 child, Harriet. AB, St. Lawrence U., 1975; MDiv, Harvard U., 1978; PhD, George Washington U., 1989. Ordained to ministry Unitarian-Universalist Assn., 1978. Min. Theodore Parker Ch., West Roxbury, Mass., 1978-79, Universalist Nat. Meml. Ch., Washington, 1979-88, First and Second Ch. in Boston, summer 1985, 86; sr. min. Pilgrim Congl. Ch., Pomona, Calif., 1988—; corp. mem. Pilgrim Pl., Claremont, Calif., 1990—; bd. dirs. Clinebell Inst., Claremont. Author: Willard L. Sperry: The Quandaries of a Liberal Protestant Mind, 1914-1939, 1991; contbr. articles to profl. jours. Advisor Salvation Army, Pomona. Mem. Am. Acad. of Religion, Am. Hist. Assn., Am. Soc. Ch. History, Pomona Valley Ministerial Assn. (pres. 1990—), Rotary. Home: 311 W 6th Claremont CA 91711 Office: Pilgrim Congl Ch 600 N Gavey Pomona CA 91767

FRAKER, BARTH LYLE, church activity director; b. Springfield, Mo., July 25, 1967; s. Donald William and Ada Lois (Rost) F. Student, S.W. Mo. State U., 1985—. Pianist United Meth., Marshfield, Mo., 1982-85; accompanist Schweitzer United Meth., Springfield, Mo., 1985-87; dir. music/youth First Bapt. Ch., Marshfield, 1987—; substitute tchr. Marshfield Reorganized Schs., 1990—; dir. "His Children" Choir, Marshfield, 1986-87. Chmn. Marshfield High Sch. Project Graduation, 1991; coord. Marshfield Community Chorale, 1987-90; chmn. Webster County Fair Queen Contest, Marshfield, 1990. Mem. Mo. Music Educators Assn., Am. Choral Dirs., Am. Guild English handbell Ringers, Webster Bapt. Assn. (music dir. 1988-90, youth dir. 1991—), Marshfield Community Events Com. Republican. Home: 530 N Elm Marshfield MO 65706 Office: First Bapt Ch 1001 S White Oak Marshfield MO 65706 *Love God-Love People!.*

FRAME, DAVID JAMES, minister; b. Phila., Aug. 9, 1941; s. James Alexander and Clara Elizabeth (Vogel) F. BA, Drew U., 1963, PhD, 1969; MDiv, Duke U., 1966. Ordained to ministry United Meth. Ch. as deacon, 1964, as elder, 1966. Assoc. pastor Morrisville (Pa.) United Meth. Ch., 1968-75; pastor Fox Chase United Meth. Ch., Phila., 1975-85, Willow Grove (Pa.) United Meth. Ch., 1985—; pres. Willow Grove Area Ministerium, 1985—; treas. N.W. Dist. Ministerium United Meth., Phila., 1988—. Bd. dirs. N.E. Phila. Meals on Wheels, 1981-85, N.E. Phila. Unit Am. Cancer Soc., 1983-85. Republican. Home: 2645 Pleasant Hill Rd Hatboro PA 19040 Office: Willow Grove United Meth Ch 34 N York Rd Willow Grove PA 19090

FRAME, JOHN TIMOTHY, bishop; b. Toronto, Ont., Can., Dec. 8, 1930; s. Duncan McClymont and Sarah Aitken (Halliday) F.; m. Barbara Alida Butters, Sept. 8, 1956; children—Alida Grace, Bronwyn Ruth, Monica Mary. B.A., Trinity Coll., Toronto, 1953, L.Th., 1957, S.T.B., 1961, D.D. (hon.), 1968. Ordained deacon, priest Anglican Ch. Can., 1957; minister Mission to Lakes Dist., Burns Lake, B.C., 1957-67; canon Diocese of Caledonia, 1965-67; bishop of Yukon, 1967-80; sr. bishop Province of B.C., 1971-80; acting metropolitan, 1973-75; dean of Columbia and rector Christ Ch. Cathedral, Victoria, B.C., 1980—. Home: 930 Burdett Ave, Victoria, BC Canada V8V 3G8 Office: 912 Vancouver St, Victoria, BC Canada V8V 3V7

FRANCIS, EVAN EUGENE, JR., lay worker; b. Cleve., Oct. 31, 1942; s. Evan E. Francis and Maryon A. (Wilson) Lachner; m. Marie E. Sikora, Jan. 16, 1964; children: Christopher, Scott, Melissa. Student, Cleve. State U., 1968-71; BA, Lake Erie Coll., 1975. Sr. warden St. Anne's in-the-Field Episcopal Ch., Madison, Ohio, 1979—, youth pastor, 1980—, treas., 1986—; materials mgr. Hubbell Indsl. Controls, Inc., Madison, 1990—. Bd. mgrs. East End br. YMCA, Madison, 1978—. 1st lt. U.S. Army, 1962-68, Vietnam. Recipient Family of Yr. award Madison Jaycees, 1985. Mem. Am. Prodn. and Inventory Control Soc., Kiwanis (pres. Madison chpt. 1986). Home: 4916 Palisade Dr Madison OH 44057 *We must be a people of prayer, seeking God's face in all that we say and do; considering others better than ourself and always with a desire to serve others as Jesus Christ served us.*

FRANCIS, JOHN L., minister; b. Indpls., Apr. 14, 1928; s. J. Lowell and Rosella Frances (Dininger) F.; m. Dorothy Jean Harper, Aug. 19, 1951; children: John Craig, Rolanda Jean. BA, Bob Jones U., 1954; BTh, Sacramento Bapt. Sem., 1971, MA, 1972, LLD (hon.), 1973; DDiv (hon.), So. Tex. Bapt. Sem., 1975; PhD, Bapt. Christian U., 1975; MS, Heritage Bapt. U., 1982. Sr. pastor Redwood Bapt. Ch., Santa Rosa, Calif., 1973-75, First Bapt. Ch., Utica, Mich., 1975-77, Peoples Bapt. Ch., Mansfield, Ohio, 1977-79; academic dean Heritage Bapt. U., Indpls., 1979-80; sr. pastor Canton Rd. Bapt. Ch., Akron, Ohio, 1980—; trustee, treas. Heritage Bapt. U., Indpls., 1989—; pres. Akron Bapt. Bible Coll., 1988—. Chmn. Summit County Moral Majority, 1979-80. Office: Canton Rd Bapt Ch 1398 Canton Rd Akron OH 44312-3998

FRANCIS, JOSEPH A., clergyman; b. Lafayette, La., Sept. 30, 1923; s. Joseph and Mabel (Coc) F. BA, Cath. U. Am., MA; postgrad., Xavier U., New Orleans, Loyola U., Mt. St. Mary's Coll. Ordained priest Roman Catholic Ch., 1950; asst. dean students St. Augustine Sem., 1951-52; asst. dir. Holy Rosary Inst., 1952-60; adminstr. Immaculate Heart of Mary Parish, 1950, Holy Cross, Austin, Tex., 1960-61; instr. Pius X High Sch., 1961-62; founder, prin. Verbun Dei High Sch., Watts, Calif., 1962-67; provincial superior, 1967-73, titular bishop of Valiposita, aux. bishop of Newark, 1976—; trustee Immaculate Conception Sem., Mahwah, N.J.; bd. overseers Harvard Div. Sch.; bd. trustees Divine Word Coll., Epworth, Iowa; bd. dirs. Am. Bd. Cath. Missions, Cath. Relief Services. Mem. Black Priests' Caucus (past pres.), Nat. Office for Black Catholics (dir.), Conf. Maj. Superiors of Men (past pres.), Nat. Cath. Conf. Interracial Justice (dir.). Address: 139 Glenwood Ave East Orange NJ 07017

FRANCIS, MOTHER MARY (MOTHER MARY FRANCIS ASCHMANN), religious order administrator; b. St. Louis, Feb. 14, 1921; d. John Wolkiewicz and Anne Marie (Maher) A. Student, St. Louis U., 1938-42. Abbess Poor Clare Monastery, Roswell, N.Mex., 1964—; fed. abbess Fedn. Mary Immaculate, Roswell, 1965-71, 1977-87; foundress Poor Clare Monastery, Newport News, Va., 1972, Alexandria, Va., 1977, Belleville, Ill., 1986, Elshout, Netherlands, 1990. Author: A Right to Be Merry, 1956, Where Caius Is, 1955; contbr. articles to profl. jours.; playwright: La Madre, 1959. Home: 809 E 19th St Roswell NM 88201-7599

FRANCIS, MICHAEL KPAKALA, archbishop. Archbishop of Monrovia, Roman Cath. Ch., Liberia. Office: Cath Mission, POB 2078, Monrovia Liberia*

FRANCIS, SISTER PATRICIA ROSE, pastoral minister; b. Chgo., Apr. 24, 1948; d. John Walter and Anna Marie (Leavey) F. BA in Elem. Edn., Quincy Coll., 1976; postgrad., So. Ill. U., 1985; MA in Christian Spirituality, Creighton U., 1987; MA in Human Devel. Counseling, Sangamon State U., 1988. Joined Dominican Sisters of Springfield-in-Ill., Roman Cath. Ch., 1966; cert. master, min. of catechesis; cert. elem. and secondary tchr. Elem. tchr. Our Saviour Sch., Jacksonville, Ill., 1969-71, Our Lady Queen of Peace, Bethalto, Ill., 1971-73, St. Dominic Sch., Quincy, Ill., 1973-76, St. Joseph Sch., Bradley, Ill., 1976-80; dir. Diocesan Office of Deaf Diocese of Springfield, Ill., 1980-86; dir. Diocesan Office for Ministry with Persons with Disabilities, 1986-90; pastoral counselor, retreat dir. Sacred Heart-Griffin High Sch., Springfield, 1990—; cons. Diocese of Joliet, Ill., 1978-80; adj. faculty So. Ill. U. Sch. Medicine, Springfield, 1991—; part-time marriage and family therapist Cath. Charities, Springfield, 1987—; part-time pastoral counselor Interfaith Counseling, Springfield, 1989—. Contbr. articles to profl. jours. Bd. dirs. Nat. Cath. Office for Persons with Disabilities, Washington, 1989—; v.p., bd. dirs. Springfield Ctr. Ind. Living, 1986-89; mem. com. on infants at high risk subcom. of med.-moral ethics com. St. John Hosp., Springfield, 1987-90; founding mem. adv. bd. Inst. for Lay Ministry Formation, Springfield, 1991—. Recipient Disting. Svc. award Springfield Ctr. Ind. Living, 1989. Mem. AACD, Am. Assn. Pastoral Counselors (cert. pastoral counselor 1990), Am. Assn. Marriage and Family Therapists (assoc.), Ill. Assn. Marriage and Family Therapists (assoc.), Ill. Assn. Counseling and Devel., Nat. Cath. Office of Deaf, Nat. Cath. Office for Persons with Disabilities (Leadership award 1989), Internat. Cath. Deaf Assn., Nat. Peer Helper Assn., Chi Sigma Iota. Avocations: writing, rsch. on spirituality of deaf people, swimming. Home and Office: 1200 W Washington St Springfield IL 62702

FRANCO, DAVID MICHAEL, religious organization administrator; b. Detroit, Mar. 14, 1948; s. Frank and Ann (Demaestri) F. BS in Commerce, Niagara U., 1971; MDiv, St. Michael's Coll., 1975; MS in Adminstrn., U. Notre Dame, 1980. Joined Oblates of St. Francis de Sales, 1966, ordained priest Roman Cath. Ch., 1976. Tchr. Bishop Duffy High Sch., Niagara Falls, N.Y., 1971-75; adminstr. Aquinas High Sch., Southgate, Mich., 1976-77, St. Francis de Sales High Sch., Toledo, 1977-81; cons. planning and devel. dept. edn. Archdiocese of Detroit, 1982-84, interim supt. schs., 1985; sec. edn. and supt. schs. Diocese of Joliet, Ill., 1986—. Mem. Nat. Cath. Ednl. Assn., U.S. Cath. Conf., Nat. Assn. Elem. Sch. Prins., Assn. Supervision and Curriculum Devel. Office: 425 Summit St Joliet IL 60435

FRANGIPANE, FRANCIS A., minister, religious organization executive; b. Lodi, N.J., Nov. 26, 1946; s. Frank and Ann (Mac) F.; m. Denise Frangipane; 5 children. Ed. high sch., Lodi, 1964. Ordained to ministry, 1971. Pastor Ch. at Hilo, Hawaii, 1972-73, Berach Chapel, Flat Rock, Mich., 1973-80, Victory Christian Ctr., Marion, Iowa, 1983-89, River of Life Ministries, Cedar Rapids, Iowa, 1989—; pres. Advancing Ch. Ministries, Cedar Rapids, 1990—; bd. dirs. Morning Star Publs., Charlotte, N.C. Author: Holiness, Truth and the Presence of God, 1986, The Three Battlegrounds, 1989, The House of the Lord, 1991. With USAF, 1965-69. Office: River of Life Ministries 3801 Blairs Ferry Rd NE Cedar Rapids IA 52402 *As I have been serving the Lord these past years, He has led me to seek for two things, and two things only: to know the heart of God in Christ, and to know my own heart in Christ's light.*

FRANK, DONALD HERBERT, minister; b. Rochester, N.Y., May 12, 1931; s. Oscar Edward and Mary Charlotte (Morgan) F.; m. Anne Sadlon, Aug. 27, 1955; children: Donna Lynn Frank Bertsch, John Edward, James David. BA, Bloomfield (N.J.) Coll., 1954; MDiv, McCormick Theol. Sem., 1957, MA, 1966; DD, Coll. of Idaho, 1980. Ordained to ministry Presbyn. Ch., 1957. Asst. pastor Hamburg (N.Y.) Presbyn. Ch., 1957-60; min. Christian edn. 1st Presbyn. Ch., Pompano Beach, Fla., 1960-63, First Presbyn. Ch., Santa Ana, Calif., 1966-69, Northminister Presbyn. Ch., Evanston, Ill., 1963-66; assoc. pastor Bellflower (Calif.) Presbyn. Ch., 1969-74; pastor Boone Meml. Presbyn. Ch., Caldwell, Idaho, 1974-87; organizing pastor Covenant Presbyn. Ch., Reno, Nev., 1987—; commr. Synod of Pacific, San Anselmo, Calif., 1977-81, 89—. Bd. dirs. Metro Ministry Interfaith Agy., Reno, 1988, Washoe at Risk Task Force on Pub. Edn., Reno, 1988. With USNR, 1948-53. Mem. Rotary. Democrat. Avocations: reading, photography. Office: Covenant Presbyn Ch 3690 Grant Dr Ste A1 Reno NV 89509

FRANK, DONALD LOUIS, minister; b. Chico, Calif., Jan. 1, 1955; s. Louis Vertran and Doris Alida (Jess) F.; m. Deanna Sue Crabb, Dec. 30, 1978. Cert., Seinan Gakuin U., Fukuoka, Japan, 1978; BA, William Jewell Coll., 1980; MDiv, Golden Gate Bapt. Theol. Sem., Mill Valley, Calif., 1983, MRE, 1984. Lic. to ministry So. Bapt. Conv., 1982; ordained, 1983. Assoc. pastor 19th Ave. Bapt. Ch., Japanese Mission, San Francisco, 1980-84; pastor Eleele (Hawaii) Bapt. Chapel, 1984—; moderator Garden Island Bapt. Assn., Kauai, 1986-91, dir. student work, 1985-87,dir. evangelism, 1986—; head evangelism team Revival, Inc., 1991—; assoc. interfaith witness Home Mission Bd., So. Bapt. Conv., 1991—. Bd. dirs. Dog Fanciers of Kauai, Inc., 1986—. Corp. USMC, 1973-75. Mem. West Kauai Mins. Assn. (pres. 1991—), Kauai Humane Soc. (sec. 1989). Home: 339 Mehana Rd Eleele HI 96705 Office: PO Box 307 Eleele HI 96705 *I have discovered that, with God at the helm of a person' life, there is no location too distant, no task too difficult, and no individual too unreachable for a believer in God's great love.*

FRANK, EUGENE MAXWELL, bishop; b. Cherryvale, Kans., Dec. 11, 1907; s. Ade W. and Emma W. (Maxwell) F.; m. Wilma A. Sedoris, June 20, 1930; children: Wilmagene Frank Noonan, Gretchen Frank Beal, Susan Frank Parsons, Thomas E. B.S., Kans. State Tchrs. Coll., 1930, Garrett Bibl. Inst., 1932; D.D., Baker U., 1947; LL.D., Central Coll., 1957; D.D., Depauw U., 1959, St. Paul Sch. Theology, Methodist, 1962. Ordained to ministry Meth. Ch., 1932; pastor Tonganoxie, Kans., 1932, Americus, Kans., 1933-36, Olathe, Kans., 1936-42, Kansas City, Kans., 1942-48, Topeka, 1948-56; consecrated bishop, 1956; bishop of Mo. St. Louis, 1956-72, Ark. Area, Little Rock, 1972-76; vis. prof. ch. ministry Candler Sch. Theology, Emory U., 1976-79; bishop-in-residence Central United Meth. Ch., Kansas City, Mo., 1979—; pres. Council of Bishops of Meth. Ch., 1968—; mem. bd. global missions, bd. ch. and soc. Mem. Kappa Delta Pi, Pi Kappa Delta, Phi Mu Alpha, Tau Kappa Epsilon. Address: 3913 W 57th Terr Shawnee Mission KS 66205

FRANK, LILY, religious organization administrator. Exec. v.p. Hadassah-WIZO Orgn. Can., Montreal, Que. Office: Hadassah-WIZO Orgn Can, 1310 Greene Ave/Ste 900, Montreal, PQ Canada H3Z 2B8*

FRANK, PHILIP MARQUIS, small business owner; b. Casper, Wyo., Jan. 12, 1924; s. Philip William and Olive Merle (Marquis) F.; m. Elizabeth Jean Beebe, June 4, 1950; children: Philip A., Meredith Jean, Margaret E., Judith E., Elizabeth E., Sarah Joyce. BA, Coll. of Wooster, 1946. Elder Westminster Presbyn. Ch., Wooster, Ohio, treas., 1974-89; elder Concordia Luth. Ch., Wooster, 1980-82, congl. chmn., 1983-85, congl. vice chmn., 1987; owner, mgr. Loaves & Fishes Christian Bookstore, Wooster, 1974—. Mem. Christian Booksellers Assn. Republican. Office: Loaves & Fishes Christian Bookstore 583 E Liberty St Wooster OH 44691

FRANKENBERG, NAOMI, religious organization administrator. Nat. pres. Hadassah-WIZO Orgn. Can., Montreal, Que. Office: Hadassah-WIZO Orgn Can, 1310 Greene Ave Ste 900, Montreal, PQ Canada H3Z 2B8*

FRANKLIN, BERNARD W., academic administrator. Pres. Livingstone Coll., Salisbury, N.C. Office: Livingstone Coll Office of Pres 701 W Monroe St Salisbury NC 28144*

FRANKLIN, CAROL BERTHA, minister; b. Paris, Tex., Apr. 5, 1947; d. Forrest Treadwell and Bertha Florence (Breazeale) F. BA, U. Wash., 1969; MDiv, Southern Baptist Theo. Sem., Louisville, 1976. Tchr. Hawaii Bapt. Acad., Honolulu, 1969-71, adminstrv. asst., 1972-73; reporter Bapt. Joint Com. on Pub. Affairs, Washington, 1976-79; min. First Bapt. Ch., Washington, 1979-82; lobbyist Am. Bapt. Chs. U.S.A., Washington, 1983—. Contbr. articles to profl. jours. Democrat. Avocations: acting, singing, sewing, reading. Home: 142 S Virginia Ave Falls Church VA 22046

FRANKLIN, MARION MCCOY, minister; b. Madisonville, Tenn., July 5, 1938; s. Christopher McCoy and Mary Alice (Steenrod) F.; m. Rebecca Jane Powell, Aug. 27, 1960; children: Elizabeth, James. BSEE, U. Tenn., 1960; MDiv, Columbia Theol. Sem., Decatur, Ga., 1964. Ordained to ministry Presbyn. Ch. (USA), 1964. Pastor Graham Meml. Presbyn. Ch., Whitesburg, Ky., 1964-68, Hermitage (Tenn.) Presbyn. Ch., 1969-74; Pastor First Presbyn. Ch., Auburn, Ala., 1974-89, Tupelo, Miss., 1989—; bd. dirs. Columbia Theol. Sem., Decatur, 1983-89; moderator John Knox Presbytery, Montgomery, Ala., 1984-85, Guerrant Presbytery, Hazard, Ky., 1966-67; chmn. Ecumenical Coord. Team of Presbyn. Ch., 1979-80. Contbr. articles to profl. jours.; editor catechism: Questions of Faith, 1985. Pres. Lee County Human Svcs., Ala., 1983-86; bd. dirs. Presbyn. Community Ministry, Auburn, 1975-89, Apalachian Reg. Hosp., Whitesburg, Ky., 1966-68. Mem. Rotary. Democrat. Office: First Presbyn Ch 400 Jefferson St Tupelo MS 38801

FRANKLIN, RONALD LEE, minister; b. Cedar Rapids, Iowa, Jan. 20, 1939; s. Clifford Oscar and Thelda Elizabeth (Sharp) F.; m. Jamie Rae Branson (div. Feb. 1977); children: Steven Scott, David Paul, Karen Sue. BS, Iowa State U., 1961; BD, Drake U., 1965; D Ministry, Tex. Christian U., 1973. Ordained to ministry Christian Ch. (Disciples of Christ), 1965. Pastor 1st Christian Ch., Ennis, Tex., 1967-72, Breckenridge, Tex., 1972-74; pastor Christian Ch. (Disciples of Christ), Kalamazoo, 1975-78, 1st Christian Ch., Eddyville, Iowa, 1978-80, Corydon (Ind.) Christian Ch., 1980-89, Cen. Christian Ch., Billings, Mont., 1989—; mem. Cath./Disciples Dialogue Team, Louisville, 1984-89, Regional Commn. on Evangelism, Ind., 1985--89; chm. Div. Nurture, Kentuckiana Disciples Area, Louisville, 1987-88, Regional Commn. on Ministry, Christian Ch. in Mont., Billings, 1991—. Mem. Community Action Program Com., Breckenridge, 1972-74; bd. dirs. Am. Cancer Soc., Corydon, 1984-89; bd. dirs. Hoosier Hills Prisoner and Community Together and Victim-Reconciliation, Corydon, 1986-89; mem. adv. bd. Fed. Emergency Mgmt. Adminstrn. Dispersements of Hoosier Valley Econ. Opportunity Corp., New Albany, Ind., 1988-89, Task Force on Homelessness, 1988-89; mem., bd. dirs. Inst. of Peace Studies affiliated with Rocky Mountain Coll. and Mont. Assn. Chs., 1990—. Mem. Billings Pastors Assn., Kiwanis. Office: Cen Christian Ch 1221 16th St W Billings MT 59102

FRANKLIN, RONALD MONROE, pastor; b. Carthage, Mo., Jan. 5, 1953; s. Earl Monroe Franklin and Ruby Frances (Forrester) Burt; stepfather, Leslie Jacob Burt; m. Cheryl Lynne Jennings, May 24, 1975; children: Aaron Monroe, Leslie Lynne. BA in Christianity and Sociology, S.W. Bapt. U., 1975. Lic. 1971; ordained to ministry, 1981. Pastor Sheldon (Mo.) Bapt. Ch., 1976-81, Elm Grove Bapt. Ch., Curryville, Mo., 1981-84, Broadway Bapt. Ch., Oak Grove, Mo., 1984-90, Union Hill Bapt. Ch., Holts Summit, Mo., 1990—; cons. brotherhood dept. Mo. Bapt. Conv., 1977—; camp dir. Salt River Bapt. Assn. Youth Camp, Troy, Mo., 1982, 83; youth dir. Nevada Bapt. Assn., Mo., 1978, 79, brotherhood dir., 1980, 81; state royal ambassador, officer, sec., v.p. brotherhood dept. Mo. Bapt. Conv., 1970, 71. Alderman City of Sheldon, 1981. Mem. Sheldon Ministerial Alliance (pres. 1974-81), Oak Grove Ministerial Alliance (pres. 1988-90). Office: Union Hill Bapt Ch 460 S Summit Dr Holts Summit MO 65043 *In my life I have found the Holy Scriptures to provide a great base for Christian living. Remember to read the Scriptures daily.*

FRANKLIN, ROOSEVELT, minister; b. Chattanooga, Aug. 30, 1933; s. James R. and Cora Ann (Ponds) F.; m. Darnell Pinkston, Sept. 30, 1972; children: Sophia, Dellazar. BS, Northeastern U., 1958; MA (hon.), Savannah State Coll., 1962. Pastor Free For All Bapt. Ch., Greenwood, S.C., 1959-61; radio min. Spiritual Ch., Aiken, S.C., 1961-63; nat. lectr. United Coun. Spiritual Ch., Raleigh, N.C., 1963-66; min. Holy Trinity House of God, Macon, Ga., 1966—; youth dir. Holy Trinity Ch., Macon, 1966-72, talent coord., 1966-73, dir. Spiritual Singers, 1966—. Organizer voters registration, Macon, 1977; pub. relations vol. Nat. Dem. Party, Atlanta, 1984; bd. dirs. Retired Persons Assn., 1980—. Capt. U.S. Army, 1951-54, Korea. Named extrovert promoter Music Workshop, 1979; recipient Hunt Bond Troop award Ft. Valley State Alumni, 1980, Afro Am. Heritage award Afro Am. Heritage Mus., 1987, Golden Eagle award Macon Courier, 1988. Mem. NAACP (life), SCLC (life), Inner Circle Congl. Aides, C. of C., Min.'s Alliance (v.p. 1966—, Citizens award 1979), Ga. Black Am. Pageant (coord. 1980—, Leadership award 1982), Direct Sellers League, Smooth Ashlar (dist. dep. 1970—), Rolls-Royce Club, Woodsmen of Am. Club, Pioneer Club, Shriners (nat. ambassador), Masons (33 deg., soveriegn grand gen. inspector), Optimist, Kiwanis, Civitan, Elks, Nat. Lodge (treas. 1987—). Democrat. Avocations: martial arts, billiards. Office: Holy Trinity House of God 280 Straight St Macon GA 31204

FRANKLIN, STEPHEN DAVID, rabbi; b. Webster, Mass., Apr. 3, 1941; s. William Maxwell and Rita (Fauer) F.; m. Karen Jeanne Spiegel, Oct. 28, 1978; children: Ross Fauer, Andrew Julian, Joshua Alexander. BA with Honors, Williams Coll., Williamstown, Mass., 1963; BHL, Hebrew Union Coll., Cin., 1965; MAHL, Hebrew Union Coll., 1969. Ordained rabbi, 1969. Asst. and assoc. rabbi Holy Blossom Temple, Toronto, Ont., 1971-77; assoc. rabbi Reform Congregation Keneseth Israel, Elkins Park, Pa., 1977-79; rabbi Riverdale Temple, Bronx, 1979—; mem. religious affairs com. United Jewish Appeal, N.Y.C., 1981—; mem. synagogue rels. coun. Fedn. Jewish Philanthropies, N.Y.C., 1981—; pres. Riverdale Clery Conf., Bronx., 1983-84. Lt. USN, 1969-71. Recipient Hurowitz award, United Jewish Appeal, 1989. Mem. Synagogue Coun. Am. (del. Cen. Conf. Am. Rabbis 1986—), Riverdale Clergy Conf. Home: 104 Franklin Ave Yonkers NY 10705 Office: Riverdale Temple 4545 Independence Ave Bronx NY 10471

FRANKLIN, WILLIAM EDWIN, bishop; b. Parnell, Iowa, May 3, 1930. Attended, Loras Coll., Mt. St. Bernard Sem., Dubuque, Iowa. Ordained priest Roman Cath. Ch., 1956. Priest Roman Cath. Ch., Dubuque, titular bishop Surista aux. bishop, 1987. Office: 320 Mulberry St Waterloo IA 50702

FRANKS, DONALD, charitable organization administrator. Vicar Cath. Charities and Social Concerns, Columbus, Ohio. Office: Cath Charities 197 E Gay St Columbus OH 43215*

FRANZ, DELTON WILLIS, religious organization administrator, minister; b. Hutchinson, Kans., Dec. 12, 1932; s. John J. and Sara (Siemens) F.; m. Marian Hilda Claassen, June 4, 1954; children: Gregory, Gayle, Coretta. BA, Bethel Coll., 1954; BDiv, Mennonite Bibl. Sem., 1958; MST cum laude, Union Theol. Sem., 1965. Ordained to ministry Mennonite Ch., 1954. Pastor Woodlawn Mennonite Ch., Chgo., 1956-68; dir. Washington office Mennonite Cen. Com., Washington, 1968—; chairperson, bd. dirs. Casa De Esperanza, Washington, 1982-86; churchman in residence Bethel Coll., North Newton, Kans., 1980-81; guest theol. ctr. Associated Mennonite Bibl. Sems., Elkhart, Ind., 1989. Contbg. author: Mennonite Encyclopedia vol. V, 1990. Recipient Disting. Achievement award Bethel Coll., 1989. Home: 6151 31st St NW Washington DC 20015 Office: Mennonite Cen Com 100 Maryland Ave NE Washington DC 20002-5625

FRANZ, FREDERICK WILLIAM, religious organization official; b. Covington, Ky., Sept. 12, 1893; s. Frederick Edward and Ida Louise (Krueger) F. Student, U. Cin., 1911-14. Ordained to ministry Jehovah's Witnesses, 1914, mem. internat. hdqrs. staff, 1920—; bd. dirs. Watchtower Bible and Tract Soc. N.Y., 1932—, v.p., 1949-77, pres., 1977—; bd. dirs. Watch Tower Bible and Tract Soc. Pa., 1943—, v.p., 1945-77, pres., 1977—. Address: Jehovah's Witnesses 25 Columbia Heights Brooklyn NY 11201 *My hope is for Jehovah's kingdom to come for the blessing of all mankind.*

FRANZ, LOUIS JOSEPH, priest; b. New Orleans, July 27, 1931; s. Valentine Joseph Jr. and Hilda (Tregre) F. BA in Philosophy, St. Mary's Sem., Perryville, Mo., 1954; MA in English, St. Louis U., 1959; PhD, U. So. Calif., 1966. Joined Congregation of Mission, Roman Cath. Ch., 1948, ordained priest, 1957. Dean students Regina Cleri Sem., Tucson, 1957-58, St. Vincent's Sem., Montebello, Calif., 1958-61; dean St. John's Sem. Coll., Camarillo, Calif., 1961-66, rector, pres., 1966-70; mem. faculty St. Mary's Sem., 1970-73, rector, pres., 1972-73; vice provincial New Orleans, vice province Vincentian Community, 1973-75; rector in residence St. Vincent's Sem., Beaumont, Tex., 1973-78; provincial So. Province, 1975-82; rector St. Mary's Sem., Houston, 1978-82; provincial dir. formation, dir. devel. So. Province, 1983-85; mem. Ark. Mission Team, Star City, 1985—; chmn. priestly formation com. Conf. Major Superiors, 1975, 76; co-dir. Office Prison Ministry, 1986—. Trustee De Paul U., Chgo., 1969-72; chmn. Franz Found., 1977—. Mem. MLA, Cath. Edn. Assn. Address: PO Box 128 Star City AR 71667

FRANZEN, CHARLES RICE, project coordinator; b. Terre Haute, Ind., June 24, 1957; s. Richard Sheaff and Edith (Eskola) F.; m. Sharon Ann Billings, Oct. 17, 1987; 1 child, Matthew David. BA, Coll. of William and Mary, 1979; MA, U. Miss., 1981. Tng. coord. Luth. World Relief, Tanzania, 1985; rehab. supr. World Vision Internat., Sudan, 1986-87; project coord. Luth. World Fedn., West Province, Zambia, 1987-89, East Province, Zambia, 1989—. Active mem. Young Dems., Williamsburg, Va., 1975-79; campaign mgr. Va. Gen. Assembly, Alexandria, 1981; vol. U.S. Peace Corps, Tanzania, 1981-85. Mem. Refugee Participation Network. Lutheran. Avocations: sports, literature, writing. Office: Luth World Fedn/ZCRS, Box 511234, Chipata Zambia

FRANZEN, LAVERN GERHARD, bishop; b. Leigh, Nebr., May 18, 1926; s. Frank L. and Addie (Korfhage) F.; m. Mary Ann Karen Langeuin, Aug. 20, 1948; children: Kathryn, Frank, Sheryl, Deborah. BS in Edn., Concordia Coll., Seward, Nebr., 1948; MA in Religion, Concordia Sem., St. Louis, 1963; D of Ministry, Columbia Sem., Decatur, Ga., 1985; DD (hon.), Newberry Coll., 1988. Ordained to ministry Evang. Luth. Ch. in Am., 1963. Tchr. St. Paul Luth. Sch., Omaha, 1948-49, Luth. High Sch., Detroit, 1949-64; pastor Messiah Luth. Ch., Saginaw, Mich., 1964-68, Our Redeemer Luth. Ch., Temple Terrace, Fla., 1969-87; bishop Fla. synod Evang. Luth. Ch. in Am., Tampa, 1988—. Author: Smile, God Loves You, 1971, Smile, Jesus Is Lord, 1973, The Good News from Luke, 1975, The Good News from Matthew, 1977. Bd. dirs. Trinity Sem., Columbus, Ohio, 1978—, Newberry (S.C.) Coll., 1988—. Mem. Kiwanis (editor, pres. local chpt.). Democrat. Home: 512 Hibiscus Dr Temple Terrace FL 33617

FRANZETTA, BENEDICT C., bishop; b. Liverpool, Ohio, Aug. 1, 1921. Attended, St. Charles Coll., Calonsville, Md., St. Mary Sem., Cleve. Ordained priest Roman Cath. Ch., 1950. Priest Roman Cath. Ch., Youngstown, Ohio; titular bishop Oderzo and aux. bishop Roman Cath. Ch., Youngstown, from 1980. Office: 144 W Wood St Youngstown OH 44503

FRANZMEIER, ALVIN HENRY, minister; b. St. Paul, Oct. 2, 1933; s. Alvin William and Thelma Ellen (Turpen) F.; m. Sylvia Rose Wenger, June 8, 1957; children: Jeffrey A., Nathan V., Cheryl Lee Swanberg. BA, Concordia Coll., St. Louis, 1955; MDiv, Concordia Theol. Sem., St. Louis, 1957; ThM, Luther Theol. Sem., St. Paul, 1965; D. Religion, Chgo. Theol. Sem., 1967. Ordained to ministry Luth. Ch., 1957. Mission developer, pastor Gethsemane Luth. Ch., Thunder Bay, Ontario, Can., 1957-62; mission developer, pastor King of Kings Luth. Ch., Roseville, Minn., 1962-67; dean of chapel, prof. Concordia Coll., St. Paul, 1968-71; mission developer, pastor Resurrection Luth. Ch., Spring, Tex., 1971-91; dir. John Howard Soc., Thunder Bay, 1960-62; cir. counselor Tex. dist. Luth. Ch. Mo. Synod, 1973-76, 91—, mem. ch. growth task force, 1982-91; chmn., presenter tng. programs for lay pastoral assts., 1985-87; seminar leader, lectr. numerous confs., retreats, 1975-88; co-founder Crossties Counseling Ministries, The Woodlands, Tex. Contbr. articles and sermons to religious jours. Mem. organizing bd. Interfaith, The Woodlands, Tex., 1971-77; mem. organizing bd., chmn. Symphony North, North Harris County, Tex., 1972-82. Mem. Am. Assn. Pastoral Counselors. Republican. Avocations: racketball, sci. fiction, skiing, camping. Address: 1922 Long Shadow Ln Spring TX 77388

FRASER, BRIAN JOHN, religion educator; b. Ft. Erie, Ont., Can., Feb. 9, 1947; s. George Alexander and Margaret Daziel (McDougall) F.; m. Joan Margaret Hambury, June 25, 1982; children: Charlene, Linda, Karen. BA with honors, U. Toronto, Ont., 1969; MA, Ont. Inst. Studies in Edn., 1971; MDiv, Knox Coll., Toronto, 1975; PhD, York U., Toronto, 1982. Ordained to ministry Presbyn. Ch. in Can. Min. Glebe Presbyn. Ch., Toronto, 1978-85; dean St. Andrew's Hall Vancouver (B.C., Can.) Sch. Theology, 1985—. Author: The Social Uplifters, 1988; co-editor: Peace, War, and God's Justice, 1989. Mem. Can. Soc. Presbyn. History (pres. 1982-85), Can. Soc. Ch. History (pres. 1983-84). Office: Vancouver Sch Theology, St Andrews Hall 6040 Iona Dr, Vancouver, BC Canada V6T 2E8

FRASER, JOHN GILLIES, retired minister; b. Glasgow, Scotland, July 5, 1914; s. John and Catherine Boyd (Gillies) F.; m. Jessie MacKenzie Mayer, June 29, 1949; children: Elizabeth Geddes, Catherine Gillies, Alexander Mayer, Janet MacKenzie. Student, Shawlands Acad., Glasgow, 1931; diploma in Pub. Adminstrn., Glasgow U., 1934; poor law diploma, 1935; diploma in Soc. Studies, Glascow U., 1936; ed., Ch. of Scotland Trinity Coll., 1950. Pub. asst., poor law insp. City of Glasgow, 1931-48; exec. officer Ministry Nat. Ins., Stranraer, Scotland, 1948; ordained missionary Ch. of Scotland, Kitwe, N. Rhodesia, 1951-54, Lubwa, Rhodesia, 1955-59; minister Ch. of Scotland Elderpark MacGregor Meml. Ch., Glasgow, 1960-86. Joint chmn. Ch. of Scotland Livingstonia Fellowship, Edinburgh, 1985-89; chmn. Ch. of Scotland Total Abstainers Assn., 1980—. Mem. Nat. Ch. Assn. (vice chmn. 1986), Scottis Assn. (chmn. Lord's Day Observance Soc. 1983-89). Home: 17 Beaufort Gardens, Bishopbriggs, Glasgow G64 2DJ, Scotland

FRASER, MICHAEL RAYMOND, minister; b. Blacktown, NSW, Australia, Mar. 13, 1960; s. Reginald John and Pauline Alice (Byrnes) F.; m. Denise Lynn Spears, June 18, 1983; children: Michael Daniel, Jacob Mark. BS in Bible, Bapt. Bible Coll., 1986. Dir. Christian edn. and youth First Bapt. Ch., Willowick, Ohio, 1986—; chmn. N.E. Ohio Pastor's Fellowship, Willowick, 1989—; mem. Ohio State Youth Com., Columbus, Ohio, 1988—, chmn. sub-com. outreach, 1989—. Author: Pastor & Assistant Relations, 1991, Poetry, 1989 (Golden Poet award 1989, 90); contbr. articles to profl. jours. Mem. Red Cross Community Bloodmobile Com., Willowick, 1990—. Recipient Vol. Svcs. award ARC, 1990. Home: 7380 Goldenrod Rd Mentor OH 44060 Office: First Bapt Ch 31433 Vine St Willowick OH 44095

FRAZIER, GREGORY CRAIG, priest; b. Savannah, Ga., June 14, 1950; s. John Asbury Jr. and Lurleen Corrie (Cureton) F.; m. Marcia Elaine Osborn, May 19, 1973; 1 child, Jonathan Gregory. BS, U. Ga., 1977; MDiv, Trinity Episcopal. Seminary, Ambridge, Pa., 1984; postgrad., U. of South, 1990. Ordained to ministry Episc. Ch., as priest. Missionary priest St. John's Anglican Ch., Eastmain, Que., 1982-84, St. Peter's Anglican Ch., Waskaganish, Que., 1982-84; rector St. Matthew's Episc. Ch., Ft. Motte, S.C., 1984-88, St. Luke's Episc. Ch., Jacksonville, Fla., 1988—; cons. in field. Ensign USN, 1968-77, Vietnam. Decorated various citiations, commendations, and medals; recipient Douglas J. Meers award U. Ga. Mem. Assoc. Parishes, Rotary (chmn. 1984-88). Avocations: gardening, scuba diving. Home: 5514 Maxine Dr Jacksonville FL 32211 Office: St Lukes Episcopal Ch 2961 University Blvd N Jacksonville FL 32211

FRAZIER, JAMES RUSSELL, minister; b. Nashville, Feb. 22, 1962; s. James Oren and Eleanor Francis (McCullough) F.; m. Carla Ann Breidenbaugh, June 2, 1984; 1 child, Rachelle Ansley. Student, Central Coll., McPherson, Kans., 1980-81; BA in Pastoral Ministries, Covenant Found. Coll., 1984; postgrad., Emmanuel Bible Coll., Nashville, 1987; MA in Religion, Trevecca Nazarene Coll., 1989. Ordained to ministry Ch. of the Nazarene, 1986, became elder, 1989. Pastor Southside Ch. of the Bible Covenant, Nashville, 1984-89; interim pastor Mt. Juliet (Tenn.) Ch. of the Nazarene, 1989-90; pastor Grand Bay (Ala.) Ch. of the Nazarene, 1990—. mem. bd. control Covenant Found. Coll., Greenfield, 1987-88; regional presiding officer Ch. of the Bible Covenant, Nashville, 1987-89. Contbr. articles to religious publs. Mem. Wesleyan Theol. Soc. (assoc.). Office: Grand Bay Ch of the Nazarene PO Box 307 Grand Bay AL 36541-0307

FRAZIER, PATRICK LOUIS, JR., minister; b. St. George, S.C., Mar. 12, 1949; s. Patrick Sr. and Cora Lee (Cohen) F.; m. Sharon Lee Douglas, Dec. 22, 1973; children: Tera Lavern, Coren Mecheré, Patrice Iola, Sharolyn Omega. BA in English, S.C. State Coll., 1971; MDiv in Bible, Interdenominational Theol. Ctr., 1974; postgrad., U. S.C., Spartanburg; DD (hon.), Fuller Normal Indsl. Inst., 1989. Lic. to ministry Fire Baptized Holiness Ch. of God of Ams., 1967, ordained, 1970. Tchr. Young People's Inst., 1973; from tchr. to prin. Fuller Normal Indsl. Inst., Greenville, S.C., 1974-81; pastor Mt. Zion Ch., Seneca, S.C., 1974-76, True Light Ch., Easley, S.C., 1976-79, Fuller Temple, Anderson, S.C., 1979-80, St. Paul Ch., Greenwood, S.C., 1980-82, Greater Macedonia Ch., Wilmington, N.C., 1982—; asst. dir. Fire Baptized Holiness Ch. of God of Ams. Min.'s Retreat, Greenville; bd. dirs. Gen. Edn. Bd.; presiding elder Greater Ea. N.C. Dist., 1986—; treas. Ch. Expansion Fund; trustee Fuller Normal Indsl. Inst., 1990. Author: Deacon's Handbook, 1978; author, editor: Introducing the Fire Baptized Holiness Church of God of the Americas-A Study Manual, 1990; contbr. symposium on the black family. Mem. adv. bd. 4-H Clubs, Greenville County, 1977-80. *In a world of irresponsible public and private behavior, Christ calls upon us to be responsible to and for our fellow man. Remember, someone wants to be like you—good, bad, or ugly.*

FRAZIER, RICHARD GLENN, minister; b. Zanesville, Ohio, Aug. 5, 1931; s. Herbert L. and Vera Z. (Steirs) F.; m. Sally Ruth Stockwell, Oct. 1, 1966; children: Anne E., Katherine, Cynthia, Jane, Daniel. BA, Wittenberg U., 1953; ThM, Trinity Sem., Columbus, Ohio, 1956; DD (hon.), Wittenberg U., 1971; LHD (hon.), Ind. Inst. Tech., 1983. Ordained to ministry Luth. Ch., 1956. Assoc. pastor Trinity Evang. Luth. Ch., Ft. Wayne, Ind., 1956-67, sr. pastor, 1967—. Co-author: What's the Good Word, 1979; contbr. articles to profl. publs. Bd. dirs. Luth. Social Svcs., Ft. Wayne, 1978—, Vincent House for the Homeless, 1989—, Tomusk Found., Ft. Wayne, 1989—; mem. chaplaincy com. Luth. Hosp., Ft. Wayne, 1980—. Mem. Quest Club, Rotary (pres. 1988-89). Home: 2717 Chichester Ln Fort Wayne IN 46815 Office: Trinity Evang Luth Ch 405 W Wayne St Fort Wayne IN 46802

FRAZIER, ROYCE ELDON, family therapist, youth superintendent; b. San Antonio, Aug. 15, 1952; s. Herbert H. and Shirley E. (Nuffer) F.; m. Carolyn Louise Binford, May 13, 1972; children: Lance, Jeremie, Shelby. BS in Religion, Friends Bible Coll., Haviland, Kans., 1975; BS in Edn., Emporia State U., 1975; MS in Marriage and Family Therapy, Friends Univ., 1991. Pastor Twin Mound Friends Ch., Olpe, Kans., 1974-75; tchr., coach Greensburg (Kans.) High Sch., 1975-77, Okla. Bible Acad., Enid, 1977-79; supt. of youth Mid-America Yearly Meeting of Friends, Haviland, 1979—; chmn. Youthquake (Nat. Friends Youth Conv.), Mexico City, 1985, Denver, 1988, asst. chmn. Burlington, Vt., 1991. Creator/dir. Family Resource Ctr., 1991. Mem. Am. Assn. Marriage and Family Therapists (assoc.), Kans. Assn. Marriage and Family Therapists, Aircraft Owners and Pilots Assn. Office: Mid-America Yearly Meeting Youth Ministries PO Box 88 Haviland KS 67059

FRAZIER, S. N., bishop. Bishop Ch. of God in Christ, Mpls. Office: Ch of God in Christ 4309 Park Ave S Minneapolis MN 55409*

FREDERICK, LARRY, clergyman; b. Orange, Tex., Oct. 14, 1957; s. Greg Arnold and Ben Irene (McDonough) F.; m. Karen Faye Martin, Aug. 9, 1986; 1 child, Amanda Faye. BA, North Tex. State U., 1980; MA in Religious Edn., Southwestern Bapt. Theol. Sem., 1985. Ordained to ministry Bapt. Ch., 1986. Minister music Hillcrest Bapt. Ch., Denton, Tex., 1977-78; minister music and youth 1st Bapt. Ch., Krum, Tex., 1979-80; minister activities Park Forest Bapt. Ch., Dallas, 1982-86; minister sr. adults, single adults and children 1st Bapt. Ch., Irving, Tex., 1986—. Mem. So. Bapt. Assn. Ministries with Aging, So. Bapt. Hist. Soc., Dallas Bapt. Assn. (sr. adult com. chmn. 1990-91), Irving Chorale. Home: 226 W 8th St Irving TX 75060 Office: First Bapt Ch 403 S Main St Irving TX 75060

FREDERICKS, DANIEL CARL, theologian, academic administrator, educator; b. Mpls., Oct. 25, 1950; s. Carl Glenn and Yvonne Emily (Dunn) F.; m. Maribeth Ann Volden, Aug. 2, 1975; children: Autumn, Ryan, Justin, Sean. BA, U. Minn., 1975; MDiv magna cum laude, Covenant Sem., St. Louis, 1978; PhD, U. Liverpool, Eng., 1983. Instr. Hebrew lang. and lit. U. Liverpool, 1979-81; assoc. prof. bibl. studies Belhaven Coll., Jackson, Miss., 1983—, v.p., dean, 1990—. Author: Qoeheleth's Language, 1987, Coping with Transcience, 1991; contbr. articles to profl. jours. Bd. dirs. Beginning Again in Christ, Jackson, Miss., 1983—, pres. 1984-87; chmn. bibl. studies Belhaven Coll., 1987-90, acad. dean, 1989—, v.p., dean, 1990—' pres. Home Educators of Cen. Miss., 1987-90. Named one of Outstanding Young Men in Am., 1985; Tyndale Fellowship grantee, 1982. Mem. Soc. Bibl. Lit., Inst.

for Bibl. Rsch. (pres. deep south chpt. 1986-87, nat. exec. bd. 1988—), Miss. Coun. Colls. of Arts and Scis. (sec., treas. 1989—), Coun. Chief Acad. Officers of Southeastern States (exec. coun. 1990—), Assn. for Student Jud. Affairs, Southern Assn. for Coll. Student Affairs, Assn. for Christians in Student Devel. Presbyterian. Avocation: travel. Home: 1242 Pinehurst Pl Jackson MS 39202 Office: Belhaven Coll 1500 Peachtree St Jackson MS 39202

FREDERIK, HENDRIK, bishop. Bishop, pres. Evang. Luth. Ch., Windhoek, Namibia. Office: Evang Luth Ch, POB 5069, Windhoek 9000, Namibia*

FREEBORN, EDMUND TIERS, III, minister; b. Phila., June 24, 1952; s. Edmund Tiers Jr. and Catherine Lynn Freeborn; m. Deborah Lee Oakes, Oct. 5, 1974; children: Charles, Thatcher, Edmund L. BA, Westminster Coll., New Wilmington, Pa., 1973; postgrad., Westminster Theol. Sem., Phila., 1973-75; MDiv, U. Dubuque, 1976; postgrad., Drew U., 1981-86. Ordained to ministry Presbyn. Ch., 1977. Asst. pastor Westminster United Presbyn. Ch., Waterloo, Iowa, 1976-77; pastor First Presbyn. Ch., Moundsville, W.Va., 1977-81, Trinity Presbyn. Ch., Butler, Pa., 1981-85, First Presbyn. Ch. & Soc., Gloversville, N.Y., 1985—; trainer Presbyn. Ch. Evangelism Cons. Svc., N.Y.C., 1980-89; moderator several presbytery com.s, Albany, N.Y., Zelienople, Pa., Wheeling, W.Va.; warden's religious adv. com. W.Va. Maximum Security Prison, chairperson, 1978-81. Bd. dirs. YMCA, Gloversville, 1990—; commr. Butler Twp. Fire Bd., 1983-85; spl. dep. sheriff Butler County Sheriff Dept., Butler, 1983-85; mem. Ohio Valley Med. Ctr. Pastoral Care Dept., chair, 1980-81 (Svc. award 1980). Major Mission Fund grantee for small ch. evangelism Presbyn. Ch., 1980-83. Mem. Gloversville Coun. Chs. (v.p. 1988-90), Fulton County Clergy Assn., Eccentric Club, Masons (officer 1983-85), Knights Templar (officer 1983-85), Rotary (pres. Gloversville club 1990-91). Home: 108 Prospect Ave Gloversville NY 12078 Office: 1st Presbyn Ch 16 W Fulton Gloversville NY 12078 *My life is a story about finding genuine joy. I find this joy in relying on the grace of God and in trying to live a life that glorifies God. Then, I try to share this joy that I've found.*

FREED, PAUL ERNEST, minister, religious broadcasting executive; b. Detroit, Aug. 29, 1918; s. Ralph and Mildred (Forsythe) F.; m. Betty Jane Seawell, Oct. 17, 1945; children: Paul David, James, Donna, Stephen, Daniel. BA, Wheaton Coll., 1940; diploma, Nyack Coll., 1943; MS, Columbia U., 1956; PhD, NYU, 1960; LHD (hon.), Immanuel Bible Sem., 1982. Ordained to ministry So. Bapt. Conv., 1949. Pastor various chs. Greenville, S.C., 1943-45; exec. dir. Youth for Christ, Greensboro, N.C., 1946-50; evangelist, 1950-52; founder, pres. Trans World Radio, Cary, N.C., 1952—. Author: Towers to Eternity, 1968, Let The Earth Hear, 1980. Recipient Alumnus of Yr. award Nyack Coll., 1982, Founders Day award NYU. Fellow Royal Geog. Soc.; mem. Nat. Religious Broadcasters Assn. (bd. dirs. 1956—, Percy award 1960), Kappa Delta Phi. Office: Trans World Radio PO Box 700 Cary NC 27511-0700

FREEDMAN, CARLA, rabbi; b. Winnipeg, Manitoba, Can., Oct. 26, 1944; d. Louis and Yetta (Hornstein) F.; m. Bernard Melman, July 2, 1963 (div. 1983); children: Deborah Melman Clement, Rena Melman Rubin. BA, U. Manitoba, 1965, MEd, 1980; MA in Hebrew Letters, HUC-JIR, Cin., 1989. Ordained rabbi, 1990. Student rabbi Temple Beth El, Traverse City, Mich., 1986-88, Temple Beth Shalom, Bloomington, Ind., 1988-89, Sinai Temple, Marion, Ind., 1989-90; rabbi Temple Beth Israel, Plattsburgh, N.Y., 1990—. Bd. dirs. No. Adirondack Planned Parenthood, Plattsburgh, 1991—. Mem. Plattsburgh Interfaith Coun. Office: Temple Beth Israel Bowman & Marcy Lns Plattsburgh NY 12901

FREEDMAN, DAVID NOEL, religion educator; b. N.Y.C., May 12, 1922; s. David and Beatrice (Goodman) F.; m. Cornelia Anne Pryor, May 16, 1944; children: Meredith Anne, Nadezhda, David, Jonathan. Student, CCNY, 1935-38; A.B., UCLA, 1939; B.Th., Princeton Theol. Sem., 1944; Ph.D., Johns Hopkins U., 1948; Litt.D., U. Pacific, 1973; Sc.D., Davis and Elkins Coll., 1974. Ordained to ministry Presbyn. Ch., 1944; supply pastor in Acme and Deming, Wash., 1944-45; teaching fellow, then asst. instr. Johns Hopkins U., 1946-48; asst. prof., then prof. Hebrew and O.T. lit. Western Theol. Sem., Pitts., 1948-60; prof. Hebrew and O.T. lit. Pitts. Theol. Sem., 1960-61, James A. Kelso prof., 1961-64; prof. O.T. San Francisco Theol. Sem., 1964-70, Gray prof. Hebrew exegesis, 1970-71, dean of faculty, 1966-70, acting dean of sem., 1970-71; prof. O.T. Grad. Theol. Union, Berkeley, Calif., 1964-71; prof. dept. Nr. Ea. studies U. Mich., Ann Arbor, 1971—, Thurnau prof. Bibl. studies, 1984—, dir. program on studies in religion, 1971-91; prof., endowed chair in Hebrew studies U. Calif., San Diego, 1987—; coord. religious studies program U. Calif., 1989—; Danforth vis. prof. Internat. Christian U., Tokyo, 1967; vis. prof. Hebrew U., Jerusalem, 1977, Macquarie U., N.S.W., Australia, 1980, U. Queensland (Australia), 1982, 84, U. Calif., San Diego, 1985-87; Green vis. prof. Tex. Christian U., Fort Worth, 1981; dir. Albright Inst. Archeol. Rsch., 1969-70, dir., 76-77; centennial lectr. Johns Hopkins U., 1976; Dahood lectr. Loyola U., 1983; Soc. Bibl. Lit. meml. lectr., 1983, Smithsonian lectr., 1984; prin. bibl. cons. Reader's Digest, 1984, 88, 89, 90; disting. faculty lectr. Univ. Mich., 1988; Stone lectr. Princeton Theol. Sem., 1989; Mowinckel lectr., Oslo U., 1991; lectr. Uppsala U., Sweden, 1991. Author: (with J.D. Smart) God Has Spoken, 1949, (with F.M. Cross, Jr.) Early Hebrew Orthography, 1952, (with John M. Allegro) The People of the Dead Sea Scrolls, 1958, (with R.M. Grant) The Secret Sayings of Jesus, 1960, (with F.M. Cross, Jr.) Ancient Yahwistic Poetry, 1964, rev. edit., 1975, (with M. Dothan) Ashdod I, 1967, The Published Works of W.F. Albright, 1975, (with L.G. Running) William F. Albright: Twentieth Century Genius, 1975, (with B. Mazar, G. Cornfeld) The Mountain of the Lord, 1975, (with W. Phillips) An Explorer's Life of Jesus, 1975, (with G. Cornfeld) Archaeology of the Bible: Book by Book, 1976, Pottery, Poetry and Prophecy, 1980, (with K.A. Mathews) The Paleo-Hebrew Leviticus Scroll, 1985, The Unity of the Hebrew Bible, 1991; others; co-author, editor: (with F. Andersen) Anchor Bible Series Hosea, 1980, Anchor Bible Series Amos, 1989; editor: (with G.E. Wright) The Biblical Archaeologist, Reader I, 1961, (with E.F. Campbell, Jr.) The Biblical Archaeologist, Reader 2, 1964, Reader 3, 1970, Reader 4, 1983, (with W.F. Albright) The Anchor Bible, 1964—, including, Genesis, 1964, James, Peter and Jude, 1964, Jeremiah, 1965, Job, 1965, 2d edit., 1973, Proverbs and Ecclesiastes, 1965, I Chronicles, II Chronicles, Ezra-Nehemiah, 1965, Psalms I, 1966, John I, 1966, Acts of the Apostles, 1967, II Isaiah, 1968, Psalms II, 1968, John II, 1970, Psalms III, 1970, Esther, 1971, Matthew, 1971, Lamentations, 1972, To the Hebrews, 1972, Ephesians 1-3, 4-6, 1974, I and II Esdras, 1974, Judges, 1975, Revelation, 1975, Ruth, 1975, I Maccabees, 1976, I Corinthians, 1976, Additions, 1977, Song of Songs, 1977, Daniel, 1978, Wisdom of Solomon, 1979, I Samuel, 1980, Hosea, 1980, Luke I, 1981, Joshua, 1982, Epistles of John, 1983, II Maccabees, 1983, II Samuel, 1984, II Corinthians, 1984, Luke II, 1985, Judith, 1985, Mark, 1986, Haggai-Zechariah 1-8, 1987, Ecclesiasticus, 1987, 2 Kings, 1988, Amos, 1989, Titus, 1990, Jonah, 1990, Leviticus I, 1991, Deuteronomy I, 1991; editor, anchor Bible Ref. Libr., Jesus Within Judaism, 1988, Archeology of the Land of the Bible, 1990, The Tree of Life, 1990, A Marginal Jew, 1991, (with J. Greenfield) New Directions in Biblical Archaeology, 1969, (J.A. Baird) The Computer Bible, 1971, A Critical Concordance to the Synoptic Gospels, 1971, An Analytic Linguistic Concordance to the Book of Isaiah, 1971, I, II, III John: Forward and Reverse Concordance and Index, 1971, A Critical Concordance to Hosea, Amos, Micah, 1972, A Critical Concordance of Haggai, Zechariah, Malachi, 1973, A Critical Concordance to the Gospel of John, 1974, A Synoptic Concordance of Aramaic Inscriptions, 1975, A Linguistic Concordance of Ruth and Jonah, 1976, A Linguistic Concordance of Jeremiah, 1978, Syntactical and Critical Concordance of Jeremiah, 1978, Synoptic Abstract, 1978, I and II Corinthians, 1979, Zechariah, 1979, Galatians, 1980, Aramaic Inscriptions, 1975, (with T. Kachel) Religion and the Academic Scene, 1975, Am. Schs. Oriental Research publs; co-editor: Scrolls from Qumran Cave I, 1972, Jesus: The Four Gospels, 1973; Reader's Digest editor: Atlas of the Bible, 1981, Family Guide to the Bible, 1984, Mysteries of the Bible, 1988; assoc. editor Jour. Bibl. Lit., 1952-54; editor, 1955-59; cons. editor Interpreter's Dictionary of the Bible, 1957-60, Theologisches Wörterbuch des Alten Testaments, 1970—; contbr. numerous articles to profl. jours. Recipient prize in N.T. exegesis Princeton Theol. Sem., 1943, Carey-Thomas award for Anchor Bible, 1965, Layman's Nat. Bible Com. award, 1978, William H. Green fellow O.T., 1944, William S. Rayner fellow Johns Hopkins, 1946, 47; Guggenheim fellow, 1959; Am. Assn. Theol. Schs. fellow, 1963; Am. Council Learned Socs. grant-in-aid, 1967, 76. Fellow Explorers Club, U. Mich. Soc. Fellows (sr., chmn. 1980-82); mem. Soc. Bibl. Lit. (pres. 1975-76), Am. Oriental Soc., Am. Schs. Oriental Research (v.p. 1970-82, editor bull. 1974-78, editor Bibl. Archeologist 1976-82, dir. publs. 1974-82), Archaeol. Inst. Am., Am. Acad. Religion, Bibl. Colloquium (sec.-treas. 1960-90). Home: PO Box 7434 Ann Arbor MI 48107 Office: U Mich Dept Religious Studies Ann Arbor MI 48109-1092 also: U Calif Dept History La Jolla CA 92093-0104

FREEHLING, ALLEN ISAAC, rabbi; b. Chgo., Jan. 8, 1932; s. Jerome Edward and Marion Ruth (Wilson) F.; children: Shira Susman, David Matthew, Jonathan Andrew. AB, U. Miami, Fla., 1953; B in Hebrew Lit., Hebrew Union Coll., 1965, MA, 1967; PhD, Kensington U., 1977. Ordained rabbi, 1967. Adminstrv. dir. Temple Israel, Miami, 1957; exec. dir. Temple Emanu-El, Miami Beach, Fla., 1960-62; assoc. rabbi The Temple, Toledo, Ohio, 1967-72; sr. rabbi Univ. Synagogue, L.A., 1972—; adj. prof. Loyola-Marymount U., St. Mary's Coll.; v.p. Westside Ecumenical Coun., 1979-81; v.p. Bd. Rabbis of So. Calif., 1981-85, pres., 1985-87; mem. com. on rabbinic growth Cen. Conf. Am. Rabbis; chair Regional Synagogue Coun., 1984-86; bd. dirs., mem. several coms. and commns. Jewish Fedn. Coun.; cons. social actions Union of Am. Hebrew Congregations, mem. nat. and Pacific-S.W. region coms. on AIDS; mem. Rabbinic Cabinet, United Jewish Appeal; bd. dirs. Israel Bonds Orgn., Nat. Jewish Fund; bd. govs. Synagogue Coun. Am. Guest columnist L.A. Hearld Examiner (Silver Angel award Religion in Media, 1987, 88); guest religion progs. Sta. KCBS, KABC. Chaplain L.A. Police Dept., 1974-86; bd. dirs., mem. exec. com., chair com. on pub. policy, chair govt. affairs com. AIDS Project L.A.; founding chair, exec. com. chairperson AIDS Interfaith Coun. So. Calif.; mem. adv. bd. L.A. AIDS Hospice Com.; apptd. mem., founding chair L.A. County Commn. on AIDS, 1987-89, chair svcs. com., 1989-91; mem. AIDS-related grants proposal rev. com. Robert Wood Johnson Found., AIDS Task Force of United Way; mem. com. on ethics, medicine and humanity Santa Monica Hosp., L.A. County Commn. on Pub. Social Svcs., 1984-86, City of L.A. Task Force on Diversity of Families, Commn. to Draft Ethics Code for L.A. City Govt.; mem. L.A. County Commn. on Juvenile Delinquency and Adult Crime, 1991—; bd. dirs. Jewish Homes for Aging of Greater L.A., NCCJ, 1989; adv. bd. Westside Children's Mus.; chmn. com. on fed. legislation commn. on law and legislation L.A. Jewish Community Rels. Com. Recipient Bishop Daniel Corrigan commendation Episcopal Diocese, 1987, Humanitarian award NCCJ, 1988, Social Responsibility award L.A. Urban League, 1988, Nat. Friendship award Parents and Friends of Lesbians and Gays, 1989, AIDS Hospice Found. Gene La Pietra Leadership award, 1989, Cath. Archdiocese's Serra Tribute award, 1989, Univ. Synagogue's Avodah award for Community Svc., 1990, Am. Jewish Congress Tzedek award for Community Leadership and Svc., 1990. Mem. Am. Jewish Congress (pres. 1977-80, 82-84), Physicians Assn. for AIDS Care (nat. adv. bd.), AIDS Nat. Interfaith Network (bd. dirs.), Sigma Alpha Mu, Omnicron Delta Kappa, Phi Mu Alpha. Office: Univ Synagogue 11960 Sunset Blvd Los Angeles CA 90049

FREELAND, CHARLES JOHNSTON, III, minister; b. Rayne, La., Sept. 8, 1940; s. Charles Johnson Jr. and Mary Alice (Wynn) F.; m. Sandra Lee Dean, May 31, 1964; children: Charles Johnston IV, Mary Kay. BA, Davidson Coll., 1962; MDiv., Austin Presbyn. Theol. Sem., 1965, D of Min., 1979. Ordained to ministry Presbyn. Ch. (U.S.A.), 1965. Pastor, First Street Presbyn. Ch., New Orleans, 1965-71, Highland Presbyn. Ch., Hot Springs, Ark., 1971-81; organizing pastor United Presbyn. Ch., Owasso, Okla., 1981-83, pastor, 1983-88; interim pastor 1st Presbyn. Ch., Sallisaw, Okla., 1990, Grace Presbyn. Ch., Grove, Okla., 1990-91; ptnr. M.A.W. Freeland Ltd., 1988—; bd. dirs. La. Irrigation & Milling Co., Crowley, La., 1975—. Pres. Irish Channel Action Found., New Orleans, 1970, Office of Econ. Adminstrn., Hot Springs, 1972-76. Fin. chmn. Ark. Presbytery, Little Rock, 1974-80, Ea. Okla. Presbytery, Tulsa, 1987-91; trustee Ark. Coll., Batesville, 1974-77, Austin (Tex.) Presbyn. Theol. Sem., 1984—. Mem. Owasso C. of C. Democrat. Avocations: sailing, scuba diving, flying, reading.

FREELAND, HERBERT THOMAS, minister; b. Rahway, N.J., Feb. 2, 1953; s. Donald Grant and Elva Margaret (Smeal) F.; m. Lynn Elizabeth McLaughlin, June 5, 1976; children: Thomas Paul, Jodie Lynn. AA, Valley Forge Mil. Jr. Coll., 1973; BA, Ramapo Coll., 1975; MDiv, Drew Theol. Sch., 1978. Min. Wesley United Meth. Ch., Belleville, N.J., 1978-80, St. John's United Meth. Ch., Hope, N.J., 1980-83, Oxford and Summerfield United Meth. Chs., Belvidere, N.J., 1983-87; assoc. min. First United Meth. Ch., Westfield, N.J., 1987-89, United Meth. Ch., Pearl River, N.Y., 1989-91; min. St. Paul's United Meth. Ch., Nyack, N.Y., 1991—; mem. Rockland Youth Adv. Coun., New City, N.Y., 1990—; founder, pres. No. N.J. Truckstop Ministries, Columbia, 1982-87; trustee Domestic Abuse & Rape Crisis Ctr., Belvidere, 1985-87, Interfaith Coun. for the Homeless, Summit, N.J., 1987-89. Named one of Outstanding Young Men of Am., Jaycees, 1984. Mem. No. N.J. Ann. Conf. (chairperson parish and community devel. 1988—). Democrat. Home: 216 S Broadway Nyack NY 10960 Office: St Pauls United Meth Ch Broadway and Division Ave Nyack NY 10960 *It is a curious fact of life that the heart which is never broken can never truly be made whole. It would certainly seem that God most greatly uses those who have been deeply hurt.*

FREELS, LARRY ELLIS, minister; b. Oliver Springs, Tenn., May 19, 1941; s. Glenn Edward and Nellie (Cook) F.; m. Barbara Ann Slack; children: Larry Allen, Teresa Elaine, Eric Kevin. BA, Frankfort Wesleyan, 1967; MDiv, Asbury Theol. Sem., 1970, D of Ministry, 1981. Ordained to ministry Wesleyan Ch., 1970. Pastor Highland Ave. Wesleyan Ch., Covington, Ky., 1970-82, Stonewall Wesleyan Ch., Lexington, Ky., 1982—; dir. Wesleyan Sem. Found., Wilmore, Ky., 1982-88; adj. prof. Asbury Theol. Sem., Wilmore, 1982—; pres. Ky. Dist. Wesleyan Youth, Lexington, 1974-78; sec. Ky Dist. Bd. Ministerial Standing, Lexington, 1984—; mem. Ky. Dist. Bd. Adminstrn., Lexington, 1988-90. V.P. Greater Lexington Ministerial Fellowship, 1990. Mem. Theta Phi, Delta Epsilon Chi. Republican. Home: 513 Cromwell Way Lexington KY 40503 Office: The Stonewall Wesleyan Ch 3353 Clays Mill Rd Lexington KY 40503

FREEMAN, ARTHUR JAMES, religion educator; b. Green Bay, Wis., Oct. 11, 1927; s. Arthur and Ethel Anita (Bins) F.; m. Roseanna Olga Jacob, Aug.18, 1958 (dec. June 1981); 1 child, David A.; m. Carole Jean Droney, July 21, 1984; 1 child, Stephen Boucher. BA, Lawrence U., 1949; BD, Moravian Theol. Sem., 1952; PhD, Princeton Theol. Sem., 1962. Ordained to ministry Moravian Ch., 1953. Founding pastor Big Oak Moravian Ch., Yardley, Pa., 1953-61; assoc. prof. Bibl. Theol. Moravian Theol. Sem., Bethlehem, Pa., 1961-66, prof. Bibl. Theology, N.T., 1966—; adminstr. Ecumenical Com. for Continuing Edn., Bethlehem, 1974-90.; leader seminars to Israel, Greece, Rome, 1969, to Europe, 1973; arranged seminar on Am. Christianity for European Moravians for Fed. Republic Germany, Switzerland, Holland, 1976; del. Moravian Ch. Faith and Order Commn., Nat. Coun. Chs., N.Y.C., 1982—; mem. Interprovincial Faith and Order Commn., Moravian Ch., 1987—; bishop Moravian Ch. (life). Contbr. articles to profl. and religious jours. Mem. Religious Coalition on AIDS, 1987—. Mem. Soc. Bibl. Lit., The Friends of Photography, Moravian Hist. Soc., Soc. for Advancement of Continuing Edn. in Ministry (rsch. com. 1979-86, bd. dirs. 1983-86, co-chair com. for internat. meeting 1984). Republican. Avocations: organ, piano, carpentry, photography, computer programming. Office: Moravian Theol Sem 60 W Locust St Bethlehem PA 18018

FREEMAN, FORSTER, clergyman; b. Paterson, N.J., Apr. 19, 1927; s. Forster Weeks and Esther (Blackwood) F.; m. Julia Parker Freeman, Sept. 4, 1948; children: Leigh, Peter, Elizabeth, Anne. BA, Princeton U., 1947; MDiv, Union Theol. Sem., 1950; postgrad., U. Edinburgh (Scotland), 1954-55; D Ministry, Weston Sch. Theology, 1984. Ordained to ministry Presbyn. Ch. Organizing pastor New Milford (N.J.) Presbyn. Ch., 1950-54, Pebble Hill Presbyn. Ch., DeWitt, N.Y., 1955-68, New Forms Community, Buffalo, 1970-73; pastor West Concord Union Ch., Concord, Mass., 1973-81; minister spiritual tng. First Congl. Ch., Berkeley, Calif., 1984—; moderator Presbytery, Syracuse, N.Y., 1968. Author: Readiness for Ministry Through Spiritual Direction, 1986. Mem. Swendonborg Found., Spiritual Dirs. Internat. Democrat. Office: First Congl Ch 2345 Channing Way Berkeley CA 94704

FREEMAN, GEORGE ROSS, JR., minister; b. Sandersville, Ga., June 27, 1945; s. G. Ross and Sara Elizabeth (Bennett) F.; m. Peggy-Ann Katherine Pillivant, Dec. 8, 1966; children: George Ross III, Betsy Ann. BS in Journalism, Ga. So. U., 1978; MDiv, Emory U., 1981. Ordained to ministry Meth. Ch., 1979. Min. Portal (Ga.) United Meth. Ch., 1975-78; assoc. min. First United Meth. Ch., East Point, Ga., 1979-81; sr. min. Simpsonwood United Meth. Ch., Norcross, Ga., 1981-88, First United Meth. Ch., Dallas, Ga., 1988—. Mem. Paulding County Hosp. Authority, Dallas, Ga., 1991, Coun. for the Arts, Inc., Dallas, 1989; pres. Paulding Meml. Med. Ctr. Chaplains Assn., Dallas, 1990. Named one of Outstanding Young Men in Am. U.S. Jaycees, 1973; Paul Harris fellow Rotary Internat., 1988; recipient Ch. of the Yr. in Evangelism award United Meth. Ch., 1984. Mem. Nat. Assn. Stewardship Leaders (exec. com. 1988—, chmn. conf. com. Atlanta 1984—, pres. Southeastern jurisdiction 1988—), Rotary (dir. Peachtree Corners and Dallas, Ga. 1981—), Exch. Club (pres. Stone Mountain, Ga. 1972-75, Exchangite of Yr. award 1975), Paulding County C. of C., Lions. Office: First United Meth Ch 141 E Memorial Dr Dallas GA 30132

FREEMAN, JAMES A., pastor; b. Arkadelphia, Ark., Mar. 16, 1950; s. James A. and Jane (Kendrick) F.; m. Brenda Sue Bell, Jan. 2, 1971; children: Jenny, Emily. BA, Ouachita Bapt. U., 1972; MDiv, New Orleans Bapt. Sem., 1976. Ordained to ministry Immanuel Bapt. Ch., 1970. Dir. Assoc. Bapt. Students, Arkadelphia, 1972-73; pastor Westgate Bapt. Ch., Kenner, La., 1974-80, Keo (Ark.) Bapt. Ch., 1980-83, 1st Bapt. Ch., Glenwood, Ark., 1983-87, Lee Chapel Bapt. Ch., Hot Springs, Ark., 1987—; dir. Trinity Assn. Ch. Camp, Kenner, 1978-79; sec.-treas. Trinity Bapt. Assn., Kenner, 1979-80; moderator Caroline Assn., Keo, 1982-83, Caddo River Assn., Glenwood, 1986. Coord. Unborn Child Amendment Com., Pike County, Ark., 1984-87; mem. Ministry of Crisis Support Adv. Com., Little Rock, 1986-89. Home and Office: Lee Chapel Bapt Ch Rte 1 Box 98 Pearcy AR 71964

FREEMAN, JAMES DARCY CARDINAL, former archbishop of Sydney; b. Sydney, Australia, Nov. 19, 1907; s. Robert and Margaret (Smith) F.; grad. St. Columba's Coll., Springwood, 1924, St. Patrick's Coll., Manly, 1927. Ordained priest Roman Catholic Ch., 1930; asst. priest in country and city parishes, 1930-37; mem. cathedral staff, Sydney, 1938-41; pvt. sec. to Archbishop of Sydney, 1941-46; dir. Cath. Info. Bur. Australia, 1946-49; pastor, Haymarket, 1949-54; parish priest, Stanmore, 1954-68; named domestic prelate, 1949, aux. bishop, 1957; bishop of Armidale, 1968-71; archbishop of Sydney, 1971-83; elevated to Sacred Coll. of Cardinals, 1973. Decorated knight Order Brit. Empire, 1977. Office: St Mary's Cathedral, Sydney NSW 2000, Australia

FREEMAN, JOEL ARTHUR, minister; b. Lewiston, Maine, July 24, 1954; s. Arthur Fickett and Katherine Ann (Schroeder) F.; m. Laurie Ann Caron, May 1, 1976; children: David Joel, Jesse Andrew. MS in Pastoral Counseling, Loyola Coll., Balt., 1986; PhD in Pastoral Counseling, Evang. Theol. Sem., Dixon, Mo., 1991. Ordained to ministry Calvary Chapel Outreach Fellowship, 1975. Pastor Glorious Gospel Ch., Friendship, Maine, 1975-77, Balt., 1977-80, Columbia, Md., 1980-88; pastor Stillmeadow Christian Fellowship, Balt., 1988—; chaplain Washington Bullets Basketball Team, 1979—; host radio talk show Sta. WABS, 1977-88; TV host Howard Cable Co., Ellicott City, Md., 1980-86; interviewer CBN Satellite Radio Network, 1988—. Author: The Doctrine of Fools, 1984, God Is Not Fair, 1987, Living with Your Conscience without Going Crazy, 1989, Kingdom Zoology, 1991. Instr. chaplain's office Johns Hopkins U., Balt., 1977-79; mem. steering com. Word Renewal Pastor's Fellowship, Balt., 1977-83, County Exec. Prayer Breakfast, Howard County, 1983-86; area coord. Washington for Jesus, 1980. Mem. Inst. in Basic Life Principles (coord. 1979-86). Republican. Home: 406 Charles Rd Linthicum Heights MD 21090 Office: Stillmeadow Christian Fellowship 5110 Frederick Ave Baltimore MD 21229 *I choose to keep the eternal perspective in clear view. I want to invest my life in that which will be important one thousand years from now. Jesus Christ is the same yesterday, today and forever.*

FREEMAN, JOSEPH MICHAEL, minister; b. Columbus, Ohio, Nov. 12, 1947; s. Joseph Boyd Freeman and Dolores (Shea) Garrettson; m. Sandra Kay Kluck, Dec. 29, 1979; children: Hannah Christine, Rachel Elizabeth. BA cum laude, Wittenberg U., Springfield, Ohio, 1970; MDiv, Yale U., 1974; student clin. pastoral edn., NIMH, Washington, 1974-75, 78-79. Ordained to ministry Luth. Ch. in Am., 1975. Asst. pastor St. Luke's Luth. Ch., Lima, Ohio, 1975-78; assoc. pastor Bethany Luth. Ch., Engelwood, Colo., 1979-81; mission pastor, parish pastor Christ the Savior Luth. Ch., Fishers, Ind., 1981—; bd. mem. Tri-County Mental Health Ctr., Indpls., 1984-91, Tri-County Mental Health Ctr. Found., Indpls., 1988-91; chairperson Congl. Mental Health Ministries Commn., Assn. Mental Health Clergy, 1985-90; religious discussion group leader Tri-County Mental Health Ctr., Indpls., 1983—. Recipient Letter of Commendation, NIMH, St. Elizabeth's Hosp., Washington, 1979,Preaching prize Yale U. Mem. Assn. Clin. Pastoral Edn., Assn. Mental Health Clergy, S.E. Lions Club (lion tamer), Fishers Ministerial Assn. (pres. 1982-87). Home: 7796 Kenetta Ct Fishers IN 46030 Office: Christ the Savior Luth Ch 11965 N Allisonville Rd Fishers IN 46038 *As a pastor, I have come to treasure precious insights: (1) One must love the Lord even more than one loves the work of ministry to avoid burnout,(2) With Christ in one's life, one will always be more than the sum total of one's life experiences.*

FREEMAN, RICHARD DWAINE, minister; b. Stockton, Calif., May 6, 1945; s. Milford Dwaine and Shirley Jean (Bourn) F.; m. Vicki Ann Jarvis, May 23, 1970; 1 child, Christina Lynn. AA, McCook Jr. Coll., 1965; BA, Hastings Coll., 1967; MDiv, United Theol. Sem., St. Paul, 1971; Doctor of Ministry, McCormick Theol. Sem., 1985. Ordained to ministry United Ch. of Christ, 1971; lic. instr. Parent Effectiveness Tng. Assoc. pastor Bath Community Ch., Akron, Ohio, 1971-72, 1st Congl. Ch., Grand Junction, Colo., 1972-73; sr. minister 1st Congl. Ch. Forest Glen, Chgo., 1974-80, St. Peter's United Ch. of Christ, Champaign, Ill., 1980-87, St. Paul's United Ch. of Christ, Rio Rancho, N.Mex., 1987—; bd. dirs. southwest conf. United Ch. Christ, 1987-91, directorate of Office for Ch. Life and leadership, 1990—; cons. Christian Edn. Shared Approaches Ch. Sch. Curriculum; exec. sec. Chgo. Met. Assn. Ill. Conf. United Ch. of Christ, Chgo., 1978-80; on-site coord. Nat. Gathering United Ch. of Christ Clergy, 1978-81. Pres. Ill. Consortium on Govtl. Concerns, Springfield, 1982-84; mem. long-range planning com. Ill. Conf. Chs., 1985-87, ann. meeting planning com. Ill. Conf. of United Ch. Christ., 1984-86; dean Prairie Mission Coun. Ill. Conf. of United Ch. Christ, 1986-87; mem. Marin Luther King, Jr. Cultural Celebration Com. for City of Albuquerque, 1990—. Recipient Alfred and Catherine Cook Meml. award United Theol. Sem., 1971. Mem. Profl. Assn. Clergy Ill. Conf. of United Ch. of Christ (sec. 1975-79), Champaign-Urbana Ministerial Assn. (pres. 1985-87, bd. dirs. SW Conf. 1988—), Rio Rancho-N.W. Albuquerque Ministerial Assn. (pres. 1990—), Kiwanis (lt. gov. Ea. Iowa Dist. 1978-79, dist. conv. chmn. 1979-80, dist. interclub chmn. 1981-82, dist. maj. emphasis chmn. 1982-83, dist. bull. editor 1983-84, pres. Forest Glen-Mayfair, Chgo. 1975-76, pres. Northwest Albuquerque 1989-90). Home: 4250 Pumice Dr NE Rio Rancho NM 87124 Office: St Paul's United Ch of Christ 3801 Rio Rancho Blvd NW PO Box 15154 Rio Rancho NM 87174

FREEMAN, ROBERT MARK, minister; b. Anniston, Ala., Aug. 30, 1961; s. Samuel Walker and Dora Elizabeth (Summerour) F. BA, Carson-Newman Coll., Jefferson City, Tenn., 1983; MDiv, So. Bapt. Sem., Louisville, 1986; Dipl. Excellence, 2nd Fgn. Lang. Inst., Beijin, China, 1986-88. Ordained to ministry So. Bapt. Conv., 1991. Lang. specialist Coop. Svcs. Internat., Richmond, Va., 1986-88; Bapt. chaplain U. Buffalo, 1989—; sec., publicist Campus Ministries Assn., Buffalo, 1990—. Named Outstanding Grad. in Religion, Carson-Newman Coll., 1983. Mem. Assn. So. Bapt. Campus Ministers, Nat. Assn. for Fgn. Student Affairs, Pi Tau Chi. Home: 1789 Eggert Rd Amherst NY 14226 Office: Bapt Conv of New York 6538 Collamer Rd East Syracuse NY 13057

FREEMAN, SIDNEY LEE, minister, educator; b. Madison, Wis., Jan. 23, 1927; s. Jack and Gertrude (Kaifetz) F.; m. Evelyn Marie Gronberg, Feb. 3, 1950 (div. 1965); children: Lynn Claire, David Eugene, Michael John; m. Gaynell Bradley, Apr. 28, 1967. BS, U. Wis., 1947; MA, Bowling Green State U., 1949; PhD, Cornell U., 1951. Ordained to ministry Unitarian Universalist Assn., 1957. Min. Unitarian Ch. Charlotte, N.C., 1957-89, min. emeritus, 1989—; instr. communication arts Cen. Piedmont Community Coll, Charlotte, part-time 1987—; chaplain Cedar Spring Hosp., Pineville, N.C., part-time 1989—; pres. So. Unitarian Coun., Atlanta, 1953, Thomas Jefferson Unitarian Dist., Charlotte, 1963-64; lectr. Albert Schweitzer Coll., Churwalden, Switzerland, summer 1959, Starr King Sch. for Ministry, Berkeley, Calif., summer 1965. Pres. Charlotte Mental Health Assn., 1978-80. Recipient Disting. Svc. award Charlotte Mental Health Assn., 1983. Mem. Unitarian Universalist Mins. Assn. (past sec.), Charlotte Area Clergy Assn. (past com.). Home: 4500 Rockford Ct Charlotte NC 28209 *I try to live by the truth that sets us free, the hope that never dies, and the love that casts out fear.*

FREEMAN, WILLIAM TAFT, JR., minister; b. L.A., Aug. 28, 1937; s. William Taft and Virginia (Sabella) F.; m. Patricia Ann Moomjean, Feb. 25, 1956; children: Renee, Jennifer, William Taft III, Desiree, Jonathan. BA, Azusa Pacific U., 1960; MA, Fuller Theol. Sem., 1979. Min. Evang. Tabernacle Ch., 1957; asst. min. Alamitos Friends Ch., Garden Grove, Calif., 1957-60; co-pastor Yorba Linda Friends Ch., 1960-64; min. Ch. in Yorba Linda, Calif., 1964-70, Ch. in Seattle, 1970-87, Ch. in Scottsdale, Ariz., 1987—; conf. speaker Ministry of Word Inc., Scottsdale, 1969—, pres., 1981—; instr. ch. history Ariz. State U., Tempe, 1988; radio Bible instr, Seattle, Scottsdale, 1981—. Author: The Testimony of Church History Regarding the Mystery of the Triune God, 1976, The Testimony of Church History Regarding the Mystery of the Mingling of God with Man, 1977, In Defense of Truth, 1981, The Dividing of Soul and Spirit, 1984, The Triune God in Experience, 1984, The Love Life of the Bride, 1990, God's Eternal Purpose, 1991, Experiential Outlines of the Old Testament Books, 1991, Experiential Outlines of the Gospel of Matthew, 1991, Experiential Outlines of the Gospel of John, 1991, The Father's Good Pleasure, 1991, (booklets) Inward and Outward Christians, 1983, How the Church Met in the New Testament, 1982, The Assurance Christ is In You, 1984; editor: How They Found Christ: In Their Own Words, 1983, Spending Time with the Lord, 1990. Mem. Am. Soc. Ch. History. Republican. Avocation: reading, computer. Home: 7561 E Sweetwater Ave Scottsdale AZ 85260 Office: Ministry of Word Inc 7135 E Sunnyside Dr Scottsdale AZ 85254 *It is wonderful to know the divine purpose of creation and human existence. Ephesians 3:10-11 reveals the purpose to be "living for Christ and the Church." My life is controlled by this eternal purpose.*

FREIDAY, DEAN, church official; b. Irvington, N.J., June 20, 1915; s. William Sidney and Ethel (Deane) F.; B.A., U. Rochester (N.Y.), 1936; m. Esther Dorothea Selke, June 27, 1946; children—Gail Freiday Crockett, William Arthur. Mem. Christian and interfaith com. Friends Gen. Conf., Phila., 1958—, chmn., 1966-72; del. 4th World Conf. on Faith and Order, World Coun. Chs., Montreal, 1963, mem. consultation on baptism, eucharist and ministry, Switzerland, 1977, mem. Nat. Faith and Order Colloquium, 1967—, FGC del. to 6th Gen. Assembly, Vancouver, B.C., 1983; observer-cons. 3d World Congress of Lay Apostolate, Vatican, Rome, 1967; ann. conf. cons. Christian World Communions Geneva, 1968, 69, 72, 73, 74, London, 1976, 86, Rome, 1977; pres. Coun. Chs., Greater Red Bank (N.J.) Area, 1965-67; mem. cen. and exec. coms. Friends Gen. Conf., 1966-72; mem. exec. com. U.S. Conf. World Coun. Chs., 1967-72, 83-87; sponsor Cath. and Quaker Studies, 1971—; mem. Faith and Order Commn., Nat. Coun. of Chs. of Christ-U.S.A., 1983—. With USNR, 1942-45. Mem. Delta Upsilon. Club: Masons (32 deg.). Author: The Bible—Its Criticism, Interpretation and Use—In 16th and 17th Century England, 1979; Nothing Without Christ, 1984; editor: Barclay's Apology in Modern English, 1967, 4th printing, 1991; The Day of the Lord, 1981; co-editor: Quaker Religious Thought, 1980-83, editor, 1984-89. Home: 1110 Wildwood Ave Manasquan NJ 08736

FREIRE FALCÃO, JOSÉ CARDINAL, archbishop; b. Ereré, Ceará, Brazil, Oct. 23, 1925; s. Otávio Freire de Andrade and Maria Falcão Freire. Lic. in Philosophy, Seminary, Fortaleza, Brazil, 1945, lic. in Theology, 1949. Priest Limoeiro do Norte, 1949-67, bishop, 1967-71; archbishop Teresina, 1971-84; archbishop Brasília, 1984—, cardinal, 1988—. Home: SHIS QL 12 conj 12, lote 1, 71 600 Brasília Brazil Office: Curia Arquidiocesana, Av L2 Sul, Q 601, 70 200 Brasília Brazil

FRENCH, HAROLD WENDELL, religion educator; b. Wichita, Kans., Jan. 14, 1930; s. Ernest Ervin and Sarah Margaret (Mason) F.; m. Rosemary Pearl Jordan, Dec. 28, 1951 (div. 1978); children: Stephen Alan, Mark Philip, Rebecca Lyn; m. Elizabeth Randylyn Barnes, May 27, 1983. BA, York Coll., 1952; MDiv, United Sem., Dayton, Ohio, 1956; MST, Boston U., 1964; PhD, McMaster U., Hamilton, Ont., Can., 1972. Ordained to ministry Evang. United Brethren Ch., 1956. Min. Evang. United Brethren Ch., Kismet, Kans., 1955-62; min. various Meth. chs. Dighton and Myricks, Mass., 1962-64; coll. chaplain Westmar Coll., LeMars, Iowa, 1964-68; asst. prof. St. Andrew's Presbyn. Coll., Laurinburg, N.C., 1971-72; prof., chair dept. religious studies U. S.C., Columbia, 1972—. Author: The Swan's Wide Waters, 1974, Adversary Identity, 1990; co-author: Religious Ferment in Modern India, 1981; editor: Annals, 1984-88. Local Dem. precinct chair, Columbia, 1986-88, del. Dem. county and state convs., 1986-90; pres. Columbia Choral Soc., 1988-89. Recipient Amoco Tchr. of Yr. award U. S.C., 1977; named Disting. lectr., Va. Consortium Asian Studies, 1988. Mem. S.C. Acad. Religion (pres. 1980-81), Assn. Asian Studies (pres. S.E. conf. 1988-89). Home: 611 LaBruce Ln Columbia SC 29205 Office: U SC Dept Religious Studies Columbia SC 29205

FRERET, RENÉ JOSEPH, minister; b. Pass Christian, Miss., Jan. 3, 1944; s. James Carroll and Pearl (Gordy) F.; m. Freda Rester; children: Katherine, Grace, Stephen, Rachel. AA, Perkinston Jr. Coll., 1964; BA, Bapt. Christian Coll., 1973; MA, Bapt. Christian U., 1978, PhD, 1984. Ordained to ministry Ind. Bapt. Ch. Pastor New Hope Bapt. Ch., McNeil, Miss., 1966-68, Cen. Bapt. Ch., Gulfport, Miss., 1968-70, Forest Hills Bapt. Ch., Benton, Miss., 1970-72; assoc. pastor Bapt. Tabernacle, Shreveport, Miss., 1972-73; pastor Temple Bapt. Ch., Gulfport, Miss., 1973—; adminstr. Temple Christian Acad., Gulfport, Miss., 1974—; pres. Temple Bapt. Inst., 1989—; trustee Bapt. Christian Coll., Shreveport, 1976-88; regional v.p. Trinity Bapt. Coll., Jacksonville, Fla., 1985—. Author: Patriotism, 1990. Chmn. Harrison County (Miss.) Fire Commn., 1990; chaplain Orange Grove Vol. Fire Dept., Gulfport, 1989. Mem. Magnolia State Assn. Christian Schs. (exec. dir. student state competition 1987—, v.p. 1988—). Home: 13092 Quail Ridge Gulfport MS 39503 Office: Temple Bapt Ch 14190 Dedeaux Rd Gulfport MS 39503 *If you will stand by the Word of the God, the God of the Word will stand by you.*

FRERICHS, ERNEST SUNLEY, religious studies educator; b. S.I., N.Y., Apr. 30, 1925; s. Ernest V. and Eva (Sunley) F.; m. Sarah Hazel Cutts, Aug. 20, 1949; children: John Allen (dec.), David Sunley, Elizabeth Ann. AB, Brown U., 1948; AM, Harvard U., 1949; STB, Boston U., 1952, PhD, 1957. Ordained to ministry Meth. Ch., 1951. Mem. faculty Brown U., Providence, 1953—, prof. religious studies, 1966—, chmn. dept., 1964-70, asst. dean. coll., 1958-59, dean grad. sch., 1976-82, dir. program in Judaic studies, 1982—; mem. Grad. and Profl. Schs. Fin. Aid Coun., 1978—; mem. Grad. Record Exam. Bd., 1980-82; mem. com. on testing Coun. Grad. Schs., 1980-82; mem. N.Am. com. Mellon Fellowship Program, 1982—; chmn. Coun. Grad. Studies in Religion, 1989—. Mem. region I and II selection com. Woodrow Wilson Found., 1959-69; trustee Am. Schs. Oriental Rsch., 1976-82, Hiatt Inst., Brandeis U., 1979-82, Roger Williams Hosp., Providence, 1981—; trustee Albright Inst. Archeol. Rsch., Jerusalem, 1974—, pres., 1976-82; bd. dirs. Assn. of Jewish Studies, 1990—. With inf. AUS, 1943-46. Recipient Disting. Alumnus award Boston U., 1987; Beebe fellow Boston U., 1952-53, Lilly postdoctoral fellow Heidelberg (Fed. Republic Germany) U., 1962-63. Mem. Soc. Bibl. Lit. (exec. com. New Eng. coun. 1977—), Am. Acad. Religion (pres. New Eng. 1970-71), Phi Beta Kappa (sec. Brown U. chpt. 1964-68, pres. 1975-77). Home: 32 Vassar Ave Providence RI 02906 Office: Brown U Program Judaic Studies Providence RI 02912-1826

FRERKING, KENNETH LEE, pastor; b. Amarillo, Tex., Feb. 22, 1932; s. Horace Robert and Lucille Magdalene (Tieman) F.; m. Ethelyn Louise Crawford, July 2, 1956; 1 child, Joanna Beth. MDiv, Concordia Sem., St. Louis, 1957; MA in Sociology, Ohio State U., 1962; PhD in Sociology, U. Mo., 1970. Ordained to ministry Luth. Ch., 1957. Campus pastor Univ. Luth. Chapel, Columbus, Ohio, 1957-64, Campus Luth. Ch., Columbia, Mo., 1965—; mem. Ohio Dist. Human Rels. Com., Columbus, 1962-64, Commn. on Ch. Lit., St. Louis, 1968-75, Mo. Dist. Bd. Youth Ministry, St. Louis, 1970-72; chmn. Western Mo. Pastoral Conf., 1972-74. Contbr. articles to numerous publs. Mem. Common Cause (Citizens' Lobby), Union of Concerned Scientists, Bread for the World. Campus Ministry Study grantee Danforth Found., 1961, 68. Home: 2102 Woodlea Dr Columbia MO 65201 Office: Campus Luth Ch 304 S College Ave Columbia MO 65201 *Good organization in one's personal and vocational life can go a long way toward accomplishing one's goals and reducing one's stress.*

FRESCONI, THERESE MARIE, church program director; b. Bklyn., Jan. 30, 1961; d. Robert and Mildred Carmela (Piccarella) Guariano; m. Daniel Joseph Fresconi, July 9, 1988. BS in Health and Phys. Edn., U. Del., 1984. Health tchr. Chesapeake Job Corp., Port DePosit, Md., 1984-86; activities dir. The Episcopal Ch. Home, Hockessin, Del., 1986—; recreation cons. Miller Recreational Svcs., Newark, 1988. Editor: (monthly newsletter) Home Happenings, 1986—. Mem. Del. Coun. Activities (sec. and edn. chmn.), 1987—, Del. Vol. Coors. (nominating com.), 1989, Am. Fitness In Bus., 1989. Roman Catholic. Avocations: jewlery design, crafts, aerobics, bowling, sewing. Home: 5 Fresconi Ct New Castle DE 19720 Office: The Episcopal Ch Home 6525 Lancaster Pike Hockessin DE 19707

FRESH, JAMES HENRY, pastor; b. Cumberland, Md., July 1, 1922; s. Frank Lee and Evelyn Manon (Lingle) F.; m. Betty M. Beem, Aug. 3, 1945; children: David L., J. Douglas, Sue A. Fresh Tasker. BA, Gettysburg Coll., 1944; MST, Chgo. Luth. Theol. Sem., 1946; MSW, Loyola U., Chgo., 1953. Ordained to ministry Evang. Luth. Ch. Am. Pastor St. Matthew Luth. Ch., Princeton, Ill., 1946-52; exec. dir. Luth. Welfare, Chgo., 1952-56; pastor 1st Luth. Ch., Galion, Ohio, 1956-66, St. Mark Luth. Ch., Dunedin, Fla., 1966-89; chmn. bd. St. Mark Village Inc., Palm Harbor, Fla., 1978—, dir. stewardship and planned giving, 1989—; pres. Social Welfare of Luth. Chs. of Ohio, Columbus, 1960-66; pres. Dunedin Ministerial Assn., 1970-73; mem. ch. bd. appeals City of Dunedin, 1975. Recipient Legion of Honor award Demolay, 1959; named Trustee of Yr., Am. Assn. of Aged, 1990. Mem. Masons, Shriners, Rotary (past-pres. Galion chpt., Paul Harris fellow 1982). Republican. Home: 2321 Watrous Dr Dunedin FL 34698 Office: St Mark Village Inc 2655 Nebraska Ave Palm Harbor FL 34684

FRESHOUR, PETER JAMES, minister; b. Columbus, Ohio, Apr. 2, 1948; s. Paul Wendel and Esther Ruth (Brandle) F.; m. Mary Kay Milligan, June 12, 1971; children: Joshua Paul, Kay Danielle, Wesley Paul. BA, Otterbein Coll., 1970; MDiv, Northwestern U., 1974. Ordained to ministry United Meth. Ch. Youth pastor Willow Ave. Presbyn. Ch., Joliet, 1970-72; intern pastor Plainfield (Ill.) United Meth. Ch., 1973-74; assoc. pastor Christ United Meth. Ch., Marietta, Ohio, 1974-77; pastor Crooksville (Ohio) Charge United Meth. Ch., 1977-83, Prospect St. United Meth. Ch., Marion, 1983-87; min. edn. Ch. of the Messiah United Meth. Ch., Westerville, Ohio, 1987—. Home: 147 Allview Rd Westerville OH 43081 Office: Ch of the Messiah United Meth Ch 51 N State St Westerville OH 43081

FRESNO LARRAIN, JUAN FRANCISCO, archbishop, university chancellor; b. Santiago, Chile, July 26, 1914; s. Luis Fresno and Elena (Hurtado) Larrain. B.Humanities, U. Chile, 1930; postgrad. Seminario Pontificio, Santiago, 1937; T.Licentiate, Gregorian U., Rome, 1939. Ordained priest Roman Cath. Ch., 1937; bishop of Copiapó, 1958; archbishop of La Serena, 1967, Santiago, 1983; elevated to cardinal, 1985. Pres. vocation and ministries dept. Consejo Episcopal Latino Americano, Bogota, 1983; great chancellor Univ. Catolica de Chile, 1983—; Cardinal cons. Sacra Congregatio pro Institutione Catholica, Rome, 1985. Named Disting. Citizen, La Serena, Chile, 1983; recipient Diego Portales award Santiago, 1985, diploma orden al merito Traders Confedn. Edn. World Council, Santiago, 1985. Office: Erasmo Escala 1822, Santiago 30-D, Chile

FRETHEIM, TERENCE ERLING, religion educator; b. Decorah, Iowa, Jan. 27, 1936; s. Erling Hartwig and Marie Olive (Langseth) F.; m. Faith Jeanne Luzum, Aug. 5, 1956; children: Tanya, Andrea. BA, Luther Coll., 1956; MDiv, Luther Northwestern Theol. Sem., 1960; PhD, Princeton Theol. Sem., 1967. Ordained to ministry Evang. Luth. Ch. Am., 1968. Asst. prof. religion Augsburg Coll., Mpls., 1961-63, 67-68; instr. of Old Testament Princeton (N.J.) Theol. Sem., 1966-67; pastor Dennison (Minn.) Luth. Parish, 1968-71; prof. of Old Testament Luth. Northwestern Theol. Sem., St. Paul, 1971—. Author: The Message of Jonah, 1977, Deuteronomic History, 1983, The Suffering of God, 1984, Exodus, 1991; assoc. editor Jour. Bibl. Lit., 1983—. Fulbright scholar U.S. Govt., 1960-61. Mem. Cath. Bibl. Assn., Soc. Bibl. Lit. Office: Luther Northwestern Sem 2481 Como Ave Saint Paul MN 55108

FREUDENBERGER, THEOBALD, church historian, educator; b. Ebern, Fed. Republic of Germany, Mar. 23, 1904; s. Michael and Ottilie Freudenberger. Student, U. Würzburg, Fed. Republic of Germany, 1923-28, ThD, 1934, habilitation, 1939. Prof. Higher Sch. Regensburg, Fed. Republic of Germany, 1945-50, U. Würzburg, 1950—. Mem. Assn. for the Encouragement of Studies. Home: Stuebenstrasse 13, D-8700 Würzburg Federal Republic of Germany

FREY, GERARD LOUIS, bishop; b. New Orleans, May 10, 1914; s. Andrew and Marie Therese (DeRose) F. DD, St. Joseph's Sem. Coll., St. Benedict, La., 1933; student, Notre Dame Sem., New Orleans. Ordained priest Roman Cath. Ch., 1938; asst. pastor Taft, La., 1938-46; asst. dir. (Confraternity Christian Doctrine, Archdiocese New Orleans); also asst. (St. James Ch.), New Oreans, 1946; dir. (Confraternity Christian Doctrine), Archdiocese New Orleans, 1946-67; also in residence Archdiocese New Orleans (St. Leo the Great Parish), 1946-54; founding pastor (St. Frances Cabrini Ch.), New Orleans, 1952-63; pastor (St. Frances de Sales Parish), Houma, La., 1963-67; clergy rep. 2d Vatican Council, 1964; dir. Diocesan Friendship Corps, New Orleans, 1966; bishop of Savannah Ga., 1967-72; bishop of Lafayette La., 1972-89; episcopal moderator Theresians Am., 1968—. Recipient Bishop Tracy Vocation award St. Joseph's Sem. Alumni Assn., 1959. Office: PO Drawer 3387 Lafayette LA 70502

FREY, TODD MATTHEW, youth worker; b. Clinton, Iowa, Dec. 21, 1962; s. Virgil Lee and Dorothy Ann (Mason) F. AA, Ill. Cen. Coll., 1990; student, Christian Bible Coll., 1991—. Camp counselor Camp Good News/ Child Evangelism Fellowship, Washington, Ill., 1978-82, 85-87, 89; assoc. staff Youth for Christ/Campus Life, Peoria, Ill., 1988-89; Sunday sch. tchr. Grace Presbyn. Ch., Peoria, 1986—; coord. Peoria Christian Ctr. Little League, 1988, 90—; store mgr. The Country's Best Yogurt, Peoria, 1990—. assoc. producer God's Rock House/Grace TV, Peoria, 1991. Sponsor Children Internat. Philippines, 1988—. With U.S. Army, 1982-84. Republican. Home: 2218 Stafford Ct Peoria IL 61614 *Because Christianity is not just something you talk about, it's something you do, my philosophy is simple but not easy: Live, love, learn, labor, and laugh. Laughter is good medicine, but I put my trust in Jesus Christ who is the Great Physician.*

FREY, VIRGINIA ANN, minister; b. Urbana, Ohio, Mar. 22, 1942; d. Levi Jasper Dooley and Martha Jane (Blake) Braley; children: Debi Lynn, Charles Jeffrey, Tamara Janell. Student in nursing, Meth. Hosp., Indpls., 1960-61; MA in Christian Psychology, Kingsway Christian Coll. and Theol. Sem., Des Moines, 1984, ThD, 1989. Cert. behavior counselor; ordained to ministry. Evangelist, 1970-85; with Praise and Worship Indpls. Christian Fellowship, 1973-80; pastor His Tabernacle, Indpls., 1981-85; founder, pastor His Tabernacle, Princeton, Ind., 1986—; tour host mission trips to Israel, Mex., Haiti, Cen. Am., 1974-90; founder, dir. New Life Homes Drug Rehab. Ctr., Indpls., 1971-81; pastor, counselor Ind. Women's Prison, 1981-84. Host, producer TV program Knowing Him, 1979-82; rec. Throne of Grace, 1981. Mem. Concerned Women Am., Women Aglow (regional sec., state pres. 1972-81), End-Time Handmaidens, Nat. Right to Life. Republican. Mem. Ind. Charismatic Ch. Home: 119 E Spruce St Princeton IN 47670 Office: HIS Tabernacle 411 N Hart St Princeton IN 47670 *True fulfillment, joy, and peace are to be found only in Jesus Christ. He is the anchor that holds us steady through the complexities of life.*

FREY, WILLIAM CARL, bishop, academic administrator; b. Waco, Tex., Feb. 26, 1930; s. Harry Frederick and Ethel (Oliver) F.; m. Barbara Louise Martin, June 12, 1952; children: Paul, Mark, Matthew, Peter, Susannah. B.A., U. Colo., 1952; Th.M., Phila. Div. Sch., 1955, D.D. (hon.), 1970. Ordained to ministry Episcopal Ch., 1955; vicar Timberline Circuit (Colo.) Missions, 1955-58; rector Trinity-on-the-Hill Ch., Los Alamos, 1958-62; missionary priest Episcopal Ch., Costa Rica, 1962-67; bishop Episcopal Ch., 1967, Diocese of Guatemala, 1967-72; chaplain U. Ark., Fayetteville, 1972; bishop Diocese of Colo., Denver, 1972-90; dean, pres. Trinity Episcopal Sch. for Ministry, Ambridge, Pa., 1990—; chmn. Epsicopal Ch.'s Joint Commn. on Peace, 1979-85. Contbr. articles to religious mags. Office: Trinity Episcopal Sch Ministry 311 11th St Ambridge PA 15003

FRIBERG, RONALD LEROY, evangelist; b. Fairview, Mont., Mar. 15, 1944; s. Clifford Roland and Rella Leah (Followwill) F.; m. Delores Marie Peters, June 4, 1966; children: Robert Lewis, Rebecca Lea, Joan Marie. AA, York (Nebr.) Coll., 1964; BA, Harding U., 1966; MA, Harding Grad. Sch. Religion, Memphis, 1972. Preacher, evangelist Ch. of Christ, Charlotte, Ark., 1965-66, Luxora, Ark., 1966-68, Albion, Nebr., 1968-72, Sublette, Kans., 1972-74, Ransom, Kans., 1974-84, Concordia, Kans., 1984-90. Active in Boy Scouts Am., Ransom, Kans., 1980. Mem. Lions (pres. Ransom club 1977, sec.-treas. 1983). Office: Ch of Christ 302 E 8th Concordia KS 66901

FRICK, FRANK SMITH, religious studies educator; b. Ponca City, Okla., Apr. 2, 1938; s. Frank K. and Faye R. (Myers) F.; m. Bonnie L. Andrews, June 3, 1961; children: Kimberly, Rachel. AB, Phillips U., 1960, MDiv, 1963; MA, Princeton U., 1969, PhD, 1970. Ordained to ministry, 1963. Campus minister United Campus Ministries Okla. State U., Stillwater, 1964-66; chaplain Albion (Mich.) Coll., 1969-72, from asst. prof. to prof. of religious studies, 1972—; dir. Ctr. for Study of Ethics, Albion Coll., 1989—. Author: (books) The City in Ancient Israel, 1977, Formation of the State in Ancient Israel, 1985; contbr. articles to profl. mags. Mem. Am. Schs. of Oriental Rsch., Soc. Bibl. Lit. Democrat. Home: 405 E Erie Albion MI 49224 Office: Albion Coll Albion MI 49224

FRICK, IVAN EUGENE, college president; b. New Providence, Pa., May 19, 1928; s. Charles George and Lillie Jane (Miller) F.; m. Ruth Hudson, July 16, 1950; children: David Alan, Daniel Eugene, Susan Marie. A.B., Findlay (Ohio) Coll., 1949; B.D., Lancaster Theol. Sem., 1952; S.T.M., Oberlin Coll., 1955; Ph.D., Columbia U., 1959; L.H.D. (hon.), Findlay Coll., 1976. Mem. faculty Findlay Coll., 1953-71, asst. to pres., 1963-64, pres., 1964-71; pres. Elmhurst (Ill.) Coll., 1971—; vice chmn. Fedn. Ind. Ill. Colls. and Univs., 1979-81, chmn., 1983-85; chmn. Associated Colls. of Ill., 1991—; chmn. West Suburban Regional Acad. Consortium, 1991—. Mem. Am. Coun. on Edn. Commn. on Govtl. Relations, 1986-89; bd. dirs. United Community Fund Findlay, 1965-71, Lizzadro Mus. Lapidary Art, Elmhurst, Elmhurst YMCA., 1971-84; chmn. non-pub. adv. com. Ill. Bd. Higher Edn., 1990—. Danforth Found. fellow, 1959, Paul Harris fellow, 1988; recipient Disting. Alumnus award Findlay Coll., 1964, Outstanding Young Man award U.S. Jr. C. of C., 1964. Mem. Am. Philos. Assn., Am. Mgmt. Assn. (President's Assn.), Am. Acad. Religion, Econ. Club Chgo., Exec. Breakfast Club of Oak Brook (sec./treas. 1986—), Rotary. Office: Elmhurst Coll 190 Prospect Ave Elmhurst IL 60126 *Mentors have played a significant role in my life; these mentors have been teachers, older friends, father figures and administrative colleagues. They have supported, challenged and stimulated me and sometimes they have presented an opposite view or role model against which I have reacted. In all, they have helped me immeasurably.*

FRICK, MURRAY ALLAN, JR., minister; b. Kansas City, Mo., Feb. 12, 1954; s. Murray Allan Sr. and Verba D. (Douglas) F.; m. Susan Elizabeth Salmon, Sept. 24, 1977; children: Erin Elizabeth, Alana Christine, Katherine Alyssa. MusB, Culver-Stockton Coll., 1976; BA in Religion and Philosophy, Culver-Stockton U., 1976; postgrad., U. Chgo., 1976-77, Drew U., 1989—. Ordained to ministry Christian Ch. (Disciples of Christ), 1986. Asst. pastor St. Charles (Mo.) Christian Ch., 1977-79; assoc. pastor Webster Groves Christian Ch., St. Louis, 1979-84, 1st Christian Ch., Cape Girardeau, Mo., 1984-87; pastor Norwalk (Iowa) Christian Ch., 1987-90; sr. min. First Christian Ch., Cheyenne, Wyo., 1990—; v.p., pres. Disciples Peace Fellowship, Iowa, 1988—. Contbr. articles, edn. materials to profl. publs. Mem. Teen Pregnancy Task Force, Cape Girardeau, 1985-87; mem. Child Protection Team Task Force, Cape Girardeau, 1986-87; treas. Civic Concert Assn., Cape Girardeau, 1986-87; pres. Norwalk Coun. on Arts, 1990—; bd. dirs. SummerTime Theater, 1989—, Cheyenne Little Theater Players, 1991—; mem. Polk County Emergency Response Team, 1990—; chaplain Laramie County Sheriff's Dept., 1991—. Named to Outstanding Young Men Am., 1986, Outstanding Religious Leader, Kiwanis, 1986. Mem. Norwalk Ministerial Alliance. Avocations: skiing, sailing, theater, music. Office: First Christian Ch 219 W 27th Cheyenne WY 82001

FRICKLAS, ANITA ALPER, religious organization administrator; b. Perth Amboy, N.J., Nov. 2, 1937; d. William and Dotty (Finkel) Alper; m. Richard Leon Fricklas, Dec. 22, 1957; children: Michael, Kenneth, Susan. A in Comml. Sci., Boston U., 1957; BBA, Upsala Coll., 1959; MA in Religion, Iliff Sch. of Theology, Denver, 1985. Reform Jewish Educator. Instr. Somerset County Coll., Somerville, N.J., 1970-72; dir. edn/programming Temple Sinai, Denver, 1973-90; prof. Iliff Sch. Theology, 1986—. Author: chpt. Jewish Principal's Handbook, 1984. Exec. dir. Am. Jewish Com., 1990—; sec. Hunter Hill Homeowners Assn., Englewood, Colo., 1973-74. Recipient Disting. Leadership award, 1989-90. Mem. LWV (pres. Somerset County chpt. 1967, Bridgewater Twnship. chpt. 1968-70), Nat. Assn. Temple Educators (cons. 1982—, bd. dirs. 1987—), Jewish Educators Coun. of Denver (pres. 1984-88), Nat. Coun. Jewish Women, Hadassah, Assn. for Supervision and Curriculum Devel. Avocations: travel, tennis, bridge, aerobic walking. *Conflict is necessary for growth. But too much conflict can hamper development. Pick your battles wisely.*

FRIEDERICH, DIANE MARIE, lay worker; b. Largo, Fla., Aug. 29, 1962; d. Paul Joseph and Janet Marie (Jaeger) F. BA in Human Resources, Eckerd Coll., St. Petersburg, Fla., 1984; postgrad., St. Thomas U., Miami, Fla., 1989—. Coord. of youth ministry St. Jerome Cath. Ch., Largo, Fla., 1984—; mem. adult rep. Diocesan Youth Coun., St. Petersburg, 1987-90. Mem. Nat. Fedn. Cath. Youth Ministry (assoc.), Fla. Parks and Recreation Assn. Office: St Jerome Ch 10895 Hamlin Blvd Largo FL 34644

FRIEDL, FRANCIS PETER, clergyman; b. Waterloo, Iowa, Nov. 26, 1917; s. Philip and Mary (Schares) F. B.A., Loras Coll., 1939; postgrad., Mt. St. Mary Sem., U. Notre Dame, summer 1947; M.A., Catholic U. Am., 1952, Ph.D., 1954. Ordained priest Roman Cath. Ch., 1943. Curate Nativity Ch., Dubuque, Iowa, 1943; instr. Loras Acad., 1947-50; asst. prof. psychology, dir. pub. relations Loras Coll., 1954, v.p., 1956, exec. v.p., 1963—, acad. dean, 1965-71, pres., 1971-77, prof., 1970—; pastor St. Joseph Parish, Elkader, Iowa, 1977-84, St. Columbkille Parish, Dubuque, 1984-87. Club: K.C. Home: 3400 Dana Dr Apt 3 Dubuque IA 52001

FRIEDLANDER, EDWARD ROBERT, lay worker; b. Evanston, Ill., Jan. 9, 1952; s. Robert and Joanne (Hiscox) F. AB, Brown U., 1973; MD, Northwestern U., Chgo., 1977. Diplomate Am. Bd. Pathology. Lay brother 3d Order Soc. of St. Francis, Mt. Sinai, 1980—; pathologist U. Mo., Kansas City, 1988—; lectr. in field. Author: (booklets) Christian Perspectives on Evolution, 1985, William Blake's Visions, 1986. Foster parent Juvenile Corrections, Johnson City, Tenn., 1984-85; bd. dirs. Tenn. Assn. Vols. Criminal Justice, 1983-86; prison vol. Yoke Fellow, Winston Salem, 1982-83. Named Tchr. of the Yr. East Tenn. State U. Sch. Medicine, 1985, U. Mo.-Kansas City Sch. Medicine, 1990. Fellow Coll. Am. Pathologists, Am. Soc. Clin. Pathologists, Lambda Chi Alpha. Home: 7909 Tauromee Rd Kansas City KS 66112 Office: Truman Med Ctr 2301 Holmes Kansas City MO 64108

FRIEDLANDER, TZVI HERSH, rabbi; b. Hungary, June 19, 1946; came to U.S., 1947; s. Joseph and Nechana (Frankel) F.; m. Malka Sternberg; children: Sholem, Ezra, Rachel. Degree of Jewish edn., 1967. Ordained rabbi, 1966. Asst. dean Ywshive Ach Pri Tevuah, Bklyn., 1968-76; rabbi Congregation Ateres Tzri Liska, Bklyn., 1971—; prin. Yeshiva Sharei Hayosher, Bklyn., 1982—. Mem. Boro Park Rabbi's Assn. (bd. dirs. 1987—). Home: 1355 45th St Brooklyn NY 11219 Office: 1334 Ocean Pkwy Brooklyn NY 11230

FRIEDMAN, ALFRED LEO, rabbi; b. N.Y.C., Jan. 14, 1917; s. Morris M. and Jenny (Myers) F.; m. Audrey Edna Green, Jan. 31, 1942; children: Stephen Hillil, Micah Robert, Ted Sylvan. BS, NYU, 1939; MA in Hebrew Lit., Jewish Inst. Religion, N.Y.C., 1943; postgrad., Mich. State Coll., 1949-

54; DD, Hebrew Union Coll., 1968. Ordained rabbi, 1943. Rabbi Temple Beth El, Benton Harbor, Mich., 1943-46; asst. rabbi Temple Isaiah Israel, Chgo., 1946-47; rabbi Congregation Shaarey Zedek, Lansing, Mich., 1947-54; dir. B.B. Hillel Found. Mich. State Coll., East Lansing, Mich., 1947-54; rabbi Union Temple Bklyn., 1954-64; rabbi Temple Beth Am, Framingham, Mass., 1964-84, rabbi emeritus, 1984; rabbi Temple Beth Am, Jupiter, Fla., 1984-86, Temple Beth Torah, Holliston, Mass., 1986-89, Temple L'Chaim, Boca Raton, Fla., 1991—. Recipient Bronze medal Nat. Freedom Found., 1958, 56. Mem. Conn. Conf. Am. Rabbis (bd. dirs. 1974, pres. northeast region 1972-74), Interfaith Clergy Assn. Greater Framingham (pres. 1970), United Rabbinic Chaplaincy Commn. (chmn. 1982), Social Action Commn. Reform Judaism, N.Y. Bd. Rabbis (v.p. 1961-63). Democrat. Home: 2924 NW 7th Ct # C Delray Beach FL 33445

FRIEDMAN, EDWARD MARC, rabbi; b. Bridgeport, Conn., Jan. 2, 1949; s. Harry Haenon and Muriel Rosalind (Smirnoff) F.; m. Sharon Marla Feinstein, Sept. 1978 (div. Apr. 1979); m. Janice Rebecca Wald Levy, Feb. 10, 1980; 1 child, Aaron Michael Levy. BA, U. Pa., 1971; MA, Jewish Theol. Sem., N.Y.C., 1973. Ordained rabbi, 1975. Asst. rabbi Congregation Shearith Israel, Dallas, 1975-82; assoc. rabbi Congregation B'nai Emunah, Tulsa, 1982-83; rabbi Congregation B'nai Israel, Northampton, Mass., 1984-89, Synagogue Emanu-el, Charleston, S.C., 1989—. Mem. Charleston Christian-Jewish Coun., 1989—, sec. 1989-91, pres., 1991—; mem. Charleston Jewish Fedn. Bd., 1989—, Charleston Jewish Community Rels. Coun., 1989—, Addlestone Hebrew Acad. Bd., 1989—; mem. Mass. Bd. Rabbis, 1984-89, Tex. Kallah of Rabbis, 1975-83; mem. Greater Dallas Rabbinical Assn., 1975-82, pres., 1978-80. Mem. Rabbinical Assembly, Greater Carolina Assn. Rabbis. Avocations: swimming, stamp collecting, piano. Office: Synagogue Emanu-el 5 Windsor Dr Charleston SC 29407

FRIEDMAN, HERBERT A., rabbi, educator, fund raising executive; b. New Haven, Sept. 25, 1918; s. Israel and Rae (Aaronson) F.; children from previous marriage: Judith, Daniel Stephen, Joan Michal; m. Francine Bensley, June 28, 1963; children—David Herbert, Charles Edward. B.A., Yale U., 1938; M.H.L., Jewish Inst. Religion, 1943; D.D. (hon.), Hebrew Union Coll., 1969. Ordained rabbi, 1944. Rabbi Temple Emanuel, Denver, 1943-52, Milw., 1952-55; exec. chmn. Nat. United Jewish Appeal, N.Y.C., 1955-75; pres. Am. Friends of Tel Aviv U., N.Y.C., 1982-85; pres. Wexner Heritage Found, 1985—. Author: Collected Speeches, 1971. Served as chaplain (capt.) U.S. Army, 1944-47, ETO. Mem. Central Conf. Am. Rabbis. Club: Yale (N.Y.C.). Home: 500 E 77th St Apt 2519 New York NY 10162 Office: Wexner Heritage Found 551 Madison Ave New York NY 10022

FRIEDMAN, JOHN STEVEN, rabbi; b. Kansas City, Mo., Dec. 11, 1949; s. Harold Bernard and Beatrice (Mackler) F.; m. Nancy Carol Eisenberg, July 2, 1977; children: Joshua, Abigail. BA cum laude, U. Kans., 1971; MA in Hebrew Letters, Hebrew Union Coll., Jerusalem, 1974. Ordained rabbi Jewish Reform, 1976. Asst. rabbi High Holidays Temple B'nai Jehudah, Kansas City, 1973; intern rabbi Temple Shomer Emunim, Toledo, 1973-74; founding rabbi Temple Kol Am, St. Louis, 1974-76; asst. rabbi Emanuel Congregation, Chgo., 1976-80; rabbi Judea Reform Congregation, Durham, N.C., 1980—; program dir. Camp Shwayder of Temple Emanuel, Denver, 1973; rabbinic advisor Chgo. Fedn. of Temple Youth, Chgo., 1978-80; lectr. NCCJ, Chgo., 1979-80. Contbr. articles to profl. jours. Pres. student body, Hebrew Union Coll., Jewish Inst. Religion, 1974, rep. bd. govs., 1975; pres. Edgewater Clergy and Rabbi Assn., Chgo., 1979-80; exec. bd. Urban Mins. Ctr., Durham, 1984-85; pres. Durham Congregations in Action, 1984-85. Recipient award of appreciation Chgo. Fedn. of Temple Youth, 1980, Better Durham Human Rels. award City of Durham Human Rels. Commn., 1989, Keeper of Dream award Martin Luther King Com., Durham, 1990. Mem. Cen. Conf. Am. Rabbis (chmn. interreligious affairs com.), Jewish Community Rels. Com., Roundtable of Blacks and Jews, Durham-Chapel Hill Jewish Fedn. (chair allocations com. 1987—). Home: 6 Womble Circle Durham NC 27705 Office: Judea Reform Congregation 2115 Cornwallis Rd Durham NC 27705 *Human redemption conceals itself amid our infinite diversity.*

FRIEDMAN, MARCIA, religious organization administrator. Exec. dir. Am. Coun. for Judaism, N.Y.C. Office: Am Coun Judaism 298 Fifth Ave Rm 301 New York NY 10001

FRIEDMAN, MARK DAVID, rabbi; b. Phila., Mar. 5, 1953; s. Bernard and Beatrice (Rafalow) F.; m. Jo Ann Kantorowitz, July 13, 1986; children: Ezra, Rebekah, Adina. BA, U. Calif., Berkeley, 1974, MA, 1976; MA, Jewish Theol. Sem., 1980. Ordained rabbi, 1981. Assoc. rabbi Temple Emanuel, Newton, Mass., 1981-86; rabbi Beth Jacob Synagogue, Norwich, Conn., 1986—; instr. Solomon Hechter Acad., Newlander, Conn., 1989—, Solomon Schecher Day Sch., Newton, Mass., 1982-86; del. Gen. Assembly of Rabbis, Miami, Fla., 1987; interim chaplain Norwich State Hosp., 1990—. Mem. Norwich Area Clergy Assn. (rep.-at-large 1987-89), Union for Traditional Judaism, Rabinnical Assembly, CLAL, Phi Beta Kappa. Home: 2 Deer Brook Rd Norwich CT 06360 Office: Beth Jacob Synagogue 400 New London Turnpike Norwich CT 06360

FRIEDMAN, MAURICE STANLEY, writer, educator; b. Tulsa, Dec. 29, 1921; s. Samuel Herman and Fanny (Smirin) F.; m. Eugenia Chifos, Jan. 1947 (div. 1974); children: David Michael, Dvora Lisa; m. Aleene Maree Wright Dorn, Sept. 29, 1986. SB in Econs. magna cum laude, Harvard U., 1943; MA in English, Ohio State U., 1947; PhD in History of Culture, U. Chgo., 1950; LLD (hon.), U. Vt., 1961; MA in Psychology, Internat. Coll., 1983; LHD (hon.), Profl. Sch. Psychol. Studies, San Diego, 1986. Prof. philosophy and lit. Sarah Lawrence Coll., 1951-54, prof. philosophy, 1954-64; prof. philosophy and religion Manhattanville Coll. of the Sacred Heart, Purchase, N.Y., 1966-67, Vassar Coll., Poughkeepsie, N.Y., 1967; prof. religion Temple U., Phila., 1966-73, also dir. PhD programs in religion and psychology and religion and lit.; prof. religious studies, philosophy and comparative lit. San Diego State U., 1973-91; tutor Internat. Coll., L.A., 1976-86, William Lyon U., 1986—; vis. prof. religious philosophy Hebrew Union Coll.-Jewish Inst. Religion, Cin., 1956, Union Theol. Sem., N.Y.C., 1965, 67; mem. faculty New Sch. for Social Research, N.Y.C., 1954-66, Pendle Hill, Quaker Ctr. for Study, Wallingford, Pa., 1959-60, 64-65, 67-73; univ. rshc. scholar San Diego State U., 1984-85; sr. Fulbright lectr. Hebrew U., Jerusalem, 1987-88; fellow com. on the history of culture U. Chgo., 1947-49; co-dir. Inst. for Dialogical Psychotherapy, San Diego. Author: Martin Buber: The Life of Dialogue, 1955, Problematic Rebel: Melville, Dostoievsky, Kafka, Camus, 1963, rev. edit. 1970, The Worlds of Existentialism, 1964, To Deny Our Nothingness: Contemporary Images of Man, 1967, Touchstones of Reality: Existential Trust and the Community of Peace, 1972, The Hidden Human Image, 1974, The Human Way: A Dialogical Approach to Religion and Human Experience, 1982, The Confirmation of Otherness: In Family, Community and Society, 1983, Martin Buber's Life and Work: The Early Years 1878-1923, 1982, The Middle Years, 1923-45, 1983, The Later Years 1945-65, 1984 (Nat. Jewish Book award for biography 1985), Contemporary Psychology: Revealing and Obscuring the Human, 1984, The Healing Dialogue In Psychotherapy, 1985 (main selection of Psychotherapy and Social Sci. Book Club, Mar. 1985), Martin Buber and The Eternal, 1986, Abraham Joshua Heschel and Elie Wiesel: "You are my Witnesses", 1987, A Dialogue with Hasidic Tales: Hallowing the Everyday, 1988, Encounter on the Narrow Ridge: A Life of Martin Buber, 1991; contbr. numerous articles to profl. jours. Recipient Outstanding Faculty award San Diego State U., 1980. Mem. Religious Edn. Assn. (past bd. dirs., past edit. bd.), Am. Philol. Assn., Am. Acad. Religion, Am. Soc. Study Religion, Fellowship of Reconciliation, Jewish Peace Fellowship, Assn. Humanistic Psychology (edit. bd. Jour. Humanistic Psychology and Person-Centered Rev.), Inst. Dialogical Psychotherapy (co-dir.). Home: 421 Hilmen Pl Solana Beach CA 92075

FRIEDMAN, RICHARD ELLIOTT, biblical literature educator; b. Rochester, N.Y., May 5, 1946; s. Alex Sandor and Reva Friedman. BA, U. Miami, 1968; M in Hebrew Lit., Jewish Theol. Sem., 1971; ThM, Harvard U., 1975, ThD, 1978. Prof. Hebrew and Comparative Lit. U. Calif. San Diego, La Jolla, 1976—. Author: The Exile and Biblical Narrative, 1981, Who Wrote the Bible, 1987; editor: The Creation of Sacred Literature, 1981, The Poet and the Historian, 1983; co-editor: The Future of Biblical Studies, 1987; contbr. articles to profl. jours. U. Calif. San Diego Rsch. grantee, 1978, 79, 84, 88; Am. Coun. of Learned Socs. Fellow, 1982. Mem. Soc. Bibl. Lit., The Bibl. Colloquium. Office: U Calif San Diego Theol Dept La Jolla CA 92093

FRIEDMANN, THELMA MAE, lay church worker; b. De Soto, Mo., Feb. 18, 1939; d. Harry E. and Viola Mae (Aders) Wideman; m. Robert E. Friedmann, June 3, 1961; children: Jeffrey, James, Daniel, Mark, Michael, Kristina. Grad. high sch., De Soto. Asst. dir. Franklin County Bapt. Assn., Union, Mo., 1987—. Baptist. Home: 61 Cedar Dr Pacific MO 63069

FRIEDRICH, CHRISTEN LOUISE, clergywoman; b. Galesburg, Ill., Sept. 20, 1963; d. Hubert Merle and Geraldine Alma (Kuster) Helmkamp; m. Keith Alan Friedrich, Nov. 18, 1989. BA, Concordia Coll., River Forest, Ill., 1985, cert. dir. Christian edn., 1986. Ordained to ministry Luth. Ch.-Mo. Synod. Dir. Christian edn. St. Matthew Luth. Ch., Lemont, Ill., 1985-87; tchr. Concordia Luth Sch., Peoria, Ill., 1987-88; dir. Christian edn. St. John's Luth. Ch., Green Valley, Ill., 1988—. Mem. Luth. Edn. Assn., Theol. Educators and Assoc. Ministries, Kappa Delta Pi. Office: St Johns Luth Ch Rte 1 Box 76 Green Valley IL 61534

FRIEDRICH, HENRY WALTER AUGUST, pastor; b. Coon Rapids, Iowa, May 26, 1928; s. Walter Henry and Alma (Thraum) F.; m. Evelyn B. Meyer, June 21, 1953; children: Barbara Elaine, Brian Lee, Mark David, Linda Diane. Student, Concordia Coll., 1945-48, Concordia Sem., 1948-53. Pastor St. Luke Luth. Ch., Oakridge, Oreg., 1953-56, Faith Luth. Ch., The Dalles, Oreg., 1956-61, Trinity Luth. Ch., Marcus, Iowa, 1961-76, Pilgrim Luth. Ch., Quimby, Iowa, 1961-76, St. John Luth. Ch., Charter Oak, Iowa, 1976-78, Concordia Luth. Ch., Jamestown, N.D., 1978—. Dist. gov. Rotary, 1972-73, team leader, 1974. Mem. N.D. Dist. Luth. Ch.-Mo. Synod (sec. 1988—, cir. counselor New Rockford, N.D. cir. 1980-88, pastoral advisor dist. Luth. Laymen's League 1982-86), Iowa West Dist. Luth. Ch.-Mo. Synod (counselor 1963-76), Luth. Home Finding Soc. (v.p. Iowa chpt. 1966-70). Office: Concordia Luth Ch 502 1st Ave N Jamestown ND 58401

FRIEDRICH, ROBERT EDMUND, JR., priest; b. Pitts., May 24, 1948; s. Robert Edmund and Mary Ellen (Forsell) F.; m. Sandra Diane Barton, June 19, 1971; children: David, Christopher. BA, Houghton Coll., 1970; MDiv, Gordon-Conwell Theol. Sem., 1974; cert. in Anglican studies, Gen. Theol. Sem., 1986. Ordained priest Episcopal Ch. Pastor Loudon (N.H.) Congl. Ch., 1975-79, 1st Presbyn. Ch., Westtown, N.Y., 1982-84; dir. pastoral svcs. Mid-Hudson Psychol. Ctr., New Hampton, N.Y., 1984-86; asst. rector Ch. of Atonement, Westfield, Mass., 1986-88; rector Ch. of the Incarnation, Penfield, N.Y., 1988—; dean Monroe dist. Diocese of Rochester (N.Y.), 1989—, rep. diocesan coun., 1989-90; v.p. Genesee Ecumenical Ministries, Rochester, 1989-90; rep. N.Y. State Coun. of Chs., Syracuse, N.Y., 1988-90. Contbr. articles to profl. publs. Mem. steering com. Goals for a Greater Rochester, 1990—; mem. Coalition for Downtown, Rochester, 1990—. Nat. Merit scholar, 1966. 010Mem. Alban Inst., Diocese of Rochester Clergy Assn., Penfield Clergy Assn., Order of St. Helena (assoc.). Democrat. Home: 1926 Jackson Rd Penfield NY 15246 Office: Ch of the Incarnation 1957 Five Mile Line Rd Box 122 Penfield NY 15246

FRIEND, JOHNNY DALE, minister; b. Lancaster, Ky., July 13, 1956; s. Hubert John and Ehha Deloris (Lewis) F.; m. Joyce Derene Rogers, Nov. 9, 1974; children: Perri Ann, John David. BA in Christian Doctrine, Clear Creek Bible Coll., Pineville, Ky., 1987. Ordained to ministry So. Bapt. Conv. Pastor Pond Bapt. Ch., Waynesburg, Ky., 1989-90, Rocky Ford Bapt. Ch., Hustonville, Ky., 1990—; with B & H Timber, Hustonville, 1991—. Mem. State Parent Adv. Coun., Frankfort, Ky., 1991. Republican. Home and Office: Rocky Ford Bapt Ch 19940 Brad Fordsville Rd Hustonville KY 40437

FRIEND, ROBERT DALE, youth minister; b. Glendale, Calif., Apr. 12, 1955; s. Martin Wyane and Bonnie (Kunkel) F.; m. Laura Maria Salazar, May 27, 1973; children: Andrew Martin, Samuel Lloyd. Assoc. Christian Edn., Boise Bible Coll., 1987. Youth minister Phoenix (Oreg.) Ch. of Christ, 1986, Redwood Christian Ch., Grants Pass, Oreg., 1986—; dir. So. Oreg. Christian Svc. Camp, 1989-91; workshop leader Grants Pass Congress on Family, 1990; speaker Boise Bible Coll., 1988. Mem. com. Task Force for Noise Abatement, Grants Pass, 1991. With USAF, 1973-77. Named Outstanding Young Minister, North Am. Christian Convention, 1989; recipient World's Greatest Youth Group Records, Group mag. Mem. VA Employment Assn. (v.p. 1983-84). Republican. Home: 455 SW I St Grants Pass OR 97527 Office: Redwood Christian Ch 4995 Redwood Ave Grants Pass OR 97527

FRIEND, WILLIAM BENEDICT, bishop; b. Miami, Fla., Oct. 22, 1931; s. William Eugene and Elizabeth (Paulus) F. Student, U. Miami, 1949-52; cert. in philosophy, St. Mary's Coll., St. Mary, Ky., 1955; cert. of ordination, Mt. St. Mary's Sem., Emmittsburg, Md., 1959; M.A. in Edn., Cath. U. Am., 1965; L.L.D., St. Leo Coll., 1986. Ordained priest Roman Cath. Ch., 1959. Parish priest, educator, counselor, adminstr., 1959-68; acting dir. ednl. research U. Notre Dame, Ind., 1968-71; vicar for edn., supt. schs. Diocese of Mobile, Ala., 1971-76, chancellor adminstrn., vicar for edn., 1976-79; aux. bishop Diocese of Alexandria-Shreveport, La., 1979-83, diocesan bishop, 1983-86; first bishop of Shreveport La., 1986—; chmn. campaign for human devel. Nat. Conf. Cath. Bishops, 1982-85, Commn. of Bishops and Scholars, chmn. sci. and human values com.; bd. dirs. La. Cath. Conf., 1986—; mem. Pontifical Coun. for Dialogue with Non-believers. Editor handbooks and study guides for Cath. edn., 1971-77; editor: (with Ford and Daues) Evangelizing the Cultures in A.D. 2000, 1990; contbr. articles on Cath. edn., Cath. ch. leadership and mgmt., theol. reflections to profl. publs. Bd. dirs. Pastoral Life Ctr., Kansas City, Mo., 1985-90, S.E. Regional Hispanic Ctr. 1986—, Schumpert Med. Ctr., Shreveport, La. Interchurch Conf.; trustee Notre Dame Sem., 1976—, St. Joseph Coll. Sem., New Orleans, 1976—. Decorated Order of Fleur de Lis K.C., 1980, knight comdr. with star Knights of Holy Sepulchre of Jerusalem, 1983; recipient Presdl. award Nat. Cath. Ednl. Assn., 1978, O'Neil D'Amour award Nat. Assn. Bds. Edn., 1982, NCCJ Brotherhood and Humanitarian award, 1987. Mem. Am. Acad. Religion, Religious Edn. Assn., Univ. Club (Shreveport), KC. Avocations: swimming; hiking; art; music; reading. Office: Diocese of Shreveport 2500 Line Ave Shreveport LA 71104

FRIESEN, MAHLON G., minister; b. Portland, Oreg., Sept. 1, 1949; s. John R. and June Maxine (Wills) F.; m. Darlene Marylyn Scofield, Sept. 6, 1975; children: Matthew, Melissa. BA, Biola Coll., 1972; MDiv, Western Conservative Bapt. Sem., 1975; DMin, Biola U., 1987. Pastor Nile Community Ch., Naches, Wash., 1975-77, Valleyford (Wash.) Community Ch., 1977-80; co-pastor Whittier (Calif.) Hills Bapt. Ch., 1980-83; co-pastor Campus Bapt. Ch., Fresno, Calif., 1984-90, sr. pastor, 1990—; tchr. part time Inland Empire Sch. of Bible, Spokane, Wash., 1978; mem. com. Christian Workers' Conf., Spokane, 1979; pres. Camp Pinecroft, Spokane, 1979-80. Chaplain fire dist. 8 Valleyford Fire Dept., 1979-80. Mem. Fresno Assn. Evangs. (v.p., pres. Fresno chpt. 1988-91). Republican. Home: 5936 E Illinois Ave Fresno CA 93727 Office: Campus Bapt Ch 4710 N Maple Ave Fresno CA 93726

FRIMOTH, BUD (E. R. FRIMOTH), clergyman, radio producer; b. June 11, 1926; s. Elmer Rytter and Stella Adeline (Simons) F.; m. Lenore Ruth Beck, Aug. 19, 1951; children: Margaret Ruth, Christen Beck, Todd Rytter, Martha Estelle (dec.). BS in Edn., Oreg. State U., 1950; BD, MA in Christian Edn., San Francisco Theol. Sem., San Anselmo, Calif., 1954. Ordained to ministry Presbyn. Ch. Pastor Federated Ch., Spearville, Kans., 1954-56; asst. pastor First Presbyn. Ch., Stockton, Calif., 1956-63; pastor Kenilworth Presbyn. Ch., Portland, Oreg., 1963-70, Sunset Presbyn. Ch., Portland, 1970-79; dir., producer Open Door Ministries, Portland, 1970—; prodn. asst. radio spls. Sandcastles Internat. Ecumenical Media Group, Portland and other cities, 1980—; asst. instr. Clown Workshops, Portland, Phoenix, Spokane, Berkeley, Calif., 1983—; instr. radio various orgns., Oreg., 1975—. Producer Insanity, 1972 (Peabody award 1972); asst. producer radio program spl. Christmas, 1981, 83 (Silver Angel award). Bd. mem. Halfway House, Stockton, Calif., 1958-60, Vis. Nurses Assn., Portland, 1983-90. With U.S. Army, 1944-46. Recipient Golden Mike Nat. award Am. Legion Aux., 1981, Gabriel awards UNDA-U.S.A., 1976, 79, 80, 81, 84, 88, 90, Silver Angel awards, Hollywood, Calif., 1982-90, award Odyssey Inst., 1981, 84, Arby award Acad. Religious Broadcasting, Seattle, 1983-90, Wilbur award Religious Pub. Rels. Coun., 1985, Gold medal Internat. Radio Festival N.Y.C., 1983-90, award Dept. Def., Armed Forces Radio, 1989, Disting. Alumnae award San Francisco Theol. Sem., 1991. Mem. World Assn. Christian Communicators (N.Am. broadcast sect. 1976—), Sandcastles Internat., Presbytery of the Cascades, Lions, Kiwanis. Republican. Avocations: photography, poetry and prose, clowning, music, stamps. Home: 10050 NW Ash St Portland OR 97229 Office: Open Door Ministries PO Box 12506 Portland OR 97212

FRINK, GEORGE MALANCTHAN DAME, clergyman; b. Ft. Pierce, Fla., Sept. 16, 1931; s. Algernon Oscar and Linnie Adelaide (Dame) F.; m. Carol Louise Hoffman, Feb. 6, 1953; children: David, Angela, Jacqueline, Arlia. BS in Bus. Adminstrn., U. Fla., 1957; B Ch. Music, Southwestern Sem., 1965, MusM, 1977. Ordained to ministry So. Bapt. Conv., 1973. Minister music First Bapt. Ch., Warner Robins, Ga., 1967-69, Marion (S.C.) Bapt. Ch., 1969-73, Hillcrest Park Bapt. Ch., Arlington, Tex., 1973-78, Emmanuel Bapt. Ch., Manassas, Va., 1978-81, Charleston Heights Bapt. Ch., Charleston, S.C., 1981—; pub., owner Carol Press, Charleston, 1982—; pres. S.C. Bapt. Singing Churchmen, Columbia, 1986-87; teaching fellow Southwestern Sem., Ft. Worth, 1975. Author: Publicity, 1991, What Do You Know About a Church Orchestra, 1991, Today's Church Orchestra, 1991. Pres. Ft. Pierce Merchants Div., 1960. Office: Charleston Heights Bapt Ch 2005 Reynolds Ave Charleston SC 29405

FRISBIE, JAMES DANIEL, minister; b. Beaver Dam, Wis., June 15, 1949; s. D. Bruce and Bernelda M. (Seefeld) F.; m. Rinya Linnette Burrill, May 31, 1975; children: Dane C., Drew B. BS, U. Wis., Oshkosh, 1971; MDiv, Iliff Sch. Theol., 1975. Ordained to ministry United Meth. Ch. as elder, 1977. Youth min. Kirk of Bonnie Brae, Denver, 1971-73, Northglenn (Colo.) United Ch. Christ, 1974-75; pastor various chs. numerous locations, 1975-86; pastor Chubbuck (Idaho) United Meth. Ch., 1986—; pres. Oreg.-Idaho United Meth. Rural Fellowship, 1986-88, legis. monitor gen. conf. team, 1984, 88. Author: (poetry) Christ Comes Running, 1989; contbr. articles to religious jours. Chair Valley Cultural Awareness Com., Milton-Freewater, Oreg., 1985-86; Rep. candidate for state senator dist. 29, Oreg., 1984. Fellow Acad. for Spiritual Formation; mem. Lions, Kiwanis (pres. Milton-Freewater club 1983-84).

FRITCH, WAYNE ALAN, minister; b. Valley City, N.D., Apr. 22, 1962; s. Dean A. and Marlene F. (Wolff) F. BA in Religious Edn. summa cum laude, Mid-Am. Nazarene Coll., 1984. Children's minister 1st Ch. of the Nazarene, Cedar Rapids, Iowa, 1984—. Named one of Outstanding Young Men Am., 1985. Mem. Linn County Evang. Assn., Child Evangelism Fellowship. Home: 1744 C Ave NE Cedar Rapids IA 52402-5228 Office: 1st Ch of the Nazarene 3113 1st Ave SW Cedar Rapids IA 52404

FRITSCHE, DAVID EMIL, SR., minister; b. Bishop, Calif., June 15, 1939; s. William E. and Thelma (Cutler) F.; m. Linda Kay Causey, Mar. 25, 1960; children: David E. Jr., Robert A., Alycia. ThB, Grace Bible Inst., L.A., 1958; ThM, Internat. Bible Sem., Orlando, Fla., 1970, ThD, 1973; cert. in advanced mgmt., GM Inst., Flint, Mich., 1974. Ordained to ministry Internat. Ch. of Foursquare Gospel, 1959. Dir. San Bernardino Bible Coll., Colton, Calif., 1967-71; pastor Life Ctr. Ch., Reno, 1976-90; supt. Sierra-Nev. div. Foursquare Chs., 1985-90; dir. Dynamic Group, Reno, 1988—. Author: (with others) Solving Ministries Greater Problems, 1983, Spiritual Reconnaissance, 1986, 7 other books; contbr. articles to profl. jours. Pres. Evang. Ministerial Fellowship, Reno, 1977-80; chaplain Reno Police Dept., 1978—, State Police Acad., Carson City, Nev., 1980—; med. ethicist Reno Woman's Clinic, U. Nev., 1980—; mem. Gov.'s Com. on Law Enforcement, Carson City, 1980—; advisor Senate Ethics Com., State of Nev., 1984. Mem. Christian Assn. for Psychol. Studies (state dir. 1988). Home: 3225 Sun Cloud Circle Reno NV 89506 *The great issue of humanity is to recover from the fall and resume the creative posture of rulership of this planet. That is our call and destiny.*

FRITTS, TOM DUFF, minister; b. Kingston, Tenn., Nov. 27, 1926; s. John Logan and Georgia Mae (Cate) F.; m. Thelma Raye Delaney, Apr. 16, 1945; children: Phyllis Diane Fritts Sampsel, Tom Duff Jr. AB, Belmont Coll., 1956; MDiv, Southwestern Bapt. Theol. Sem., 1969; DMin, Luther Rice Sem., 1978. Ordained to ministry So. Bapt. Conv. Pastor Marble City Bapt. Ch., Knoxville, Tenn., 1965-68, Walnut Hill Bapt. Ch., Harriman, Tenn., 1969-73, Calvary Bapt. Ch., Cleveland, Tex., 1973-77, First Bapt. Ch., Humble, Tex., 1977-82, Deerbrook Bapt. Ch., Humble, 1982—. Contbg. author Insights newspaper. Pres. N.E. Med. Ctr. Hosp. Chaplaincy, Humble, 1982-86; v.p. Keep Am. Beautiful, Humble, 1988. With USN, 1946-46. Mem. Mins. Alliance (v.p. Humble chpt. 1988), Rotary (v.p. Humble club 1985-88, Paul Harris fellow 1988). Republican. Home: 19902 Lions Gate Dr Humble TX 77338 Office: Deerbrook Bapt Ch 400 Main St Humble TX 77338

FRITZ, SISTER MARY THERESA, religious education director; b. Victoria, Tex., Nov. 16, 1940; d. Richard Charles and Mary Anne (Rainosek) F. AA, Annunciation Coll., 1965; BA, Incarnate Word Coll., 1972; postgrad., Univ. Houston, Victoria, 1973-76, 78-80, U. St. Thomas, Houston, 1990—. Joined Incarnate Word and Blessed Sacrament Sisters, Roman Cath. Ch., 1957; cert. coord. religious edn., cert. catechist, cert. formation toward Christian ministry, cert. computer literacy competency, high sch. tchr. life, Tex. Elem. tchr. Immaculate Conception Sch., Sealy, Tex., 1966-71; jr. high tchr., elem. prin. Sacred Heart Sch., Hallettsville, Tex., 1971-72; jr. high tchr. Saint Leo's Sch., San Antonio, 1972-73, Nazareth Acad., Victoria, Tex., 1973-76; jr. high tchr., asst. prin. Mary Immaculate Sch., Dallas, 1976-77; convent chauffeur, purchaser Incarnate Word Convent, Victoria, 1977-82; high sch. tchr., prins. sec. Saint Paul High Sch., Shiner, Tex., 1982-84; asst. treas. Incarnate Word Convent, Victoria, 1984-88; dir. religious edn. Saint Anthony Parish, Danbury, Tex., 1988-89, Our Lady of Mount Carmel Parish, Houston, 1989—; deanery rep. S.E. Deanery Dirs. Religious Edn., Houston, 1989—. Mem. Diocesan Assn. Dirs. Religious Edn., Nat. Cath. Ednl. Assn., Nat. Assn. Parish Coords./Dirs. Religious Edn., Nat. Cath. Catechists Soc. Home: 2008 Southgate Houston TX 77030-2126 Office: Our Lady Mt Carmel Parish 6723 Whitefriars Houston TX 77087-6598

FRITZ, WILLIAM RICHARD, SR., librarian, educator; b. Maywood, Ill., July 31, 1920; s. Charles Everett and Rose Margaret Leah (Stump) F.; m. Evelyn Rogers Ackerman, Feb. 1, 1945; children: Kathlyn Ann, William Richard Jr., Charles E. III, Rebecca Elizabeth. AB, Lenoir-Rhyne Coll., 1942, DD, 1966; BD, Luth. Theol. So. Sem., 1945; MS, Columbia U., 1955. Pastor Union-Whitmire (S.C.) Luth. Parish, 1945-47; asst. libr. Luth. Sem., Columbia, S.C., 1947-51, instr. in ch. music, 1952-55; dir. A capella Choir Luth. Sem., Columbia, 1949-68, libr., prof. bibliography and rsch., 1952-87, ret., 1987; co-dir. Ctr. for Religion in the South. Author: (sect. in book) History of Lutherans in S.C., 1971. Mem. Am. Theol. Libr. Ass., Am. Soc. for Ch. History, Luth. Hist. Conf., Com. on Ch. History. Democrat. Home: 29 Castle Church Rd Whiterock SC 29177

FROBE, ROGER PAUL, minister, psychiatric chaplain; b. Cin., Aug. 30, 1937; s. Paul W. and Louise W. (Smith) F.; m. Erika H. Mueller, June 11, 1963 (div. Nov. 1980); 1 child, Ruth C.; m. Mary A. Avram, July 7, 1984. BA, Concordia Coll., Ft. Wayne, Ind., 1959; MDiv, Concordia Sem., 1963, MST, 1972. Pastor St. Genevieve, St. Genevieve, Mo., 1964-68, Our Blessed Savior Luth. Ch., Alexandria, Ind., 1968-72, Peace Luth. Ch., Decatur, Ga., 1972-80; interim pastor Hope Luth. Ch., Milledgeville, Ga., 1982-84; psychiat. chaplain Moccasin Bend Mental Health Inst., Chattanooga, 1984—; affiliate, student Shalem Inst., Washington, 1990—. Bd. chmn. Luth. Social Ministry Tenn., Nashville, 1986-89. Mem. Chattanooga Ministerial Assn., Assn. Clin. Pastoral. Edn., Assn. Mental Health Chaplains. Home: 209 Stratford Way Signal Mountain TN 37377 Office: Moccasin Bend Mental Health Inst 100 Moccasin Bend Rd Chattanooga TN 37405

FROEHLE, CHARLES, academic administrator. Head St. Paul Sem. Sch. of Div. Office: St Paul Sem Sch Div 2260 Summit Ave Saint Paul MN 55105*

FROEHLICH, KARLFRIED, religion educator; b. Schmeckwitz, Germany, June 13, 1930; came to U.S., 1959; s. Karl Gottfried and Hanna Louise

(Ruttger) F.; m. Ricarda Christine Lotzin, June 29, 1961; children: Johanna R., Eberhard C., Daniel R. Student, U. Goettingen, U. Paris, 1951-58; MA, Drew U., 1961; ThD, U. Basel, Switzerland, 1963. Asst. prof. N.T. and ch. history, Drew U., 1960-66; assoc. prof. ch. history Princeton Theol. Sem., 1968-74, prof., 1974, now Benjamin B. Warfield prof. eccles. history; mem. Nat. Luth.-Roman Cath. Dialogue, 1971—; mem. ordination com. N.J. Synod. Luth Ch. Am., 1971—. Author: (with H.C. Kee and F.W. Young) Understanding the New Testament, 2d edit., 1965, 3d edit., 1973, also articles; editor: Oscar Cullman: Vortreage und Aufsaetze, 1926-62, 1966; mng. editor Jour. for Theology and the Ch., vols. 1-5, 1965-68. Fulbright travel grantee, 1959. Mem. AAUP, Soc. Bibl. Lit., Am. Soc. Ch. History Medieval Acad., Am. Bibl. Theologians. Home: 205 Moore St Princeton NJ 08540 Office: Princeton Theol Sem Princeton NJ 08540

FROELICH, KEVIN MARK, minister; b. Ortonville, Minn., Dec. 7, 1955; s. Edmund Frederick and Alta Dorthea (Ferber) F. BA, Concordia Coll., St. Paul, 1978; MDiv, Concordia Sem., St. Louis, 1982. Ordained to ministry Luth. Ch.-Mo. Synod, 1982. Pastor Our Savior Luth. Ch., Ft. Madison, Iowa, 1982-87; missionary, pastor Risen Savior Luth. Ch., Franklin, Wis., 1987—; pres. Fort Madison Ministerial Assn., 1986-87, sec.-treas., 1984-85; sec.-treas. Mt. Pleasant Cir. Pastor's Conf., Fort Madison, 1985-86, Franklin/Oak Creek Ministerial Assn., 1988-89; del. Luth. Ch.-Mo. Synod Conv., Wichita, Kans., 1986-91. Pres.-elect Am. Heart Assn., Ft. Madison, 1986; mem. Ft. Madison Hosp. Found., 1986-87. Office: Risen Savior Luth Ch 9501 W Drexel Ave Franklin WI 53132

FROHNHOFEN, HERBERT, theologian; b. Erkelenz, Fed. Republic Germany, Apr. 23, 1955; s. Hans and Ria (Esser) F.; m. Mathilde Rheinwald, July 21, 1990. MA, Hochschule für Philosophie of S.J., Munich, Fed. Republic Germany, 1978, D in Philosophy, 1981; Dip. in Theology, U. Munich, 1985, D in Theology, 1986. Sci. asst. U. Munich, Fed. Republic Germany, 1982-86; lectr. Kath. Bibelwerk, Stuttgart, Fed. Republic Germany, 1986; leader of studies Kath. Acad., Wiesbaden, Fed. Republic Germany, 1987—. Author: Structure in Mathematics, 1981, The Apathy of God in the Early Church, 1987; editor: Christlicher Antijudaismus und Jüdischer Antipaganismus, 1990. Home: Kneippstrasse 13, 6250 Limburg Federal Republic of Germany Office: Cath Acad Wilhelm-Kempf-Haus, 6200 Wiesbaden Federal Republic of Germany

FROMBERG, PAUL DAVID, priest; b. Houston, Dec. 21, 1960; s. Henry Fielding and Flora Bess (Collier) F. BA, Rhodes Coll., Memphis, 1984; MDiv, Fuller Theol. Sem., Pasadena, Calif., 1987; cert., The Episcopal Theol. Sem. S.W., Austin, Tex., 1990. Ordained priest Episcopal Ch., 1991. Cathedral priest Christ Ch. Cathedral, Houston, 1987—; mem. religious adv. com. Planned Parenthood, Houston, 1988; mem. Depart. Youth Ministries, Houston, 1989. Contbr. articles to profl. jours. Mem. Episcopal Theol. Sem. of S.W. Alumni Assn. Democrat. Office: Christ Ch Cathedral 1117 Texas Ave Houston TX 77002

FROMKNECHT, SISTER MARY, religious order superior; b. Aug. 28, 1940. BS, Villa Maria Coll., 1968; postgrad., St. Bonaventure U., 1968, 70, 71; MS IN Guidance and Counselling, Gannon U., 1977; M.T.M., Loyola U., Chgo., 1981. Joined Sisters of St. Joseph, Roman Cath. Ch., 1958. Tchr. St. Peter Cathedral, Erie, Pa., 1958-59; tchr. St. Andrew Sch., Erie, 1959-63, 65-68, adminstr., 1968-71; tchr. St. Bernard Sch., Bradford, Pa., 1963-65; supr., coord. edn. Sisters St. Joseph, Erie, 1971-72, congl. councilor, 1985-89, gen. supr. northwestern Pa. region, 1989—; adminstr. St. John the Bapt., Erie, 1972-77, pastoral min., 1977-79; min., counsellor Wholistic Health Ctr., Hinsdale, Ill., 1980-81; learning cons. Villa Maria Coll., Erie, 1981-83; parish social min., parish adminstr. St. Patrick, Erie, 1983-89; marriage, edn., career, and fin. cons. Avocations: reading, beach-combing, hiking, boating, cards. Address: 539 W 3d St Erie PA 16507

FROST, BRIAN GEORGE, religious organization administrator; b. Reigate, Surrey, England, Apr. 4, 1935; s. William Edwin and Ivy Kathleen (Jones) F. MA in English Lang. and Lit., Oxford U., 1958. Dir. London (formerly Notting Hill) Ecumenical Ctr., 1968-77; gen. sec. The Chs. Council for Health and Healing, 1978-81; staff mem. Christian Aid British Council of Chs., London, 1960-68; dir. Forgiveness and Politics Study Project British Council of Chs., 1983-88, dir. Spiritual Audit, 1991—. Author: Citizen Incognito-Meditations on the City, 1971, Glastonbury Journey-Biography of M. Milne Mowbrays, 1986; editor: The Tactics of Pressure, 1974, Dissent and Descent-Essays on Methodism and Catholicism, 1975, Celebrating Friendship, 1986, Women and Forgiveness, 1990, The Politics of Peace, 1991. Ecumenical work with World and British Councils of Chs. (hosted consultation on racism, World Council 1969) 1969—. Anglican/Methodist. Avocations: theater, Russian lit., jazz music, visiting art galleries.

FROST, ELTON TAYLOR, clergyman; b. Ft. Knox, Ky., May 30, 1957; s. Herman Elton and Laura Evelyn (Wilks) F.; m. Susan McMillan Roddey, Aug. 2, 1980; 1 child, Taylor Elizabeth. BS, Winthrop Coll., Rock Hill, S.C.; MDiv., S. Eastern Bapt. Coll., Wake Forest, N.C. Ordained to ministry Bapt. Ch., 1979. Assoc. pastor 1st Bapt. Ch., Walhalla, S.C., summers, 1979, 79, Hope Valley Bapt. Ch., Durham, N.C., 1979-81, Long Leaf Bapt. Ch., Wilmington, N.C., 1981-85; pastor Burgaw (N.C.) Bapt. Ch., 1985—; Sunday sch. campaign dir. N.C. Bapt. State Conv., 1980-81. Contbr. articles to profl. jours. Recipient Bruce E. Anderson Religious Leadership award Oconee Jaycess, 1978. Mem. Pender Ministerial Assn. (v.p.), Wilmington Bapt. Assn., Phi Eta Sigma. Republican. Lodge: Rotary (com. mem.). Avocations: reading, writing. Home: PO Box 385 Burgaw NC 28425 Office: Burgaw Bapt Ch PO Box 385 Burgaw NC 28425

FROST, JERRY WILLIAM, religion and history educator, library administrator; b. Muncie, Ind., Mar. 17, 1940; s. J. Thomas and Margaret Esther (Meredith) F.; m. Susan Vanderlyn Kohler; 1 son, James. B.A., DePauw U., Greencastle, Ind., 1962; postgrad., Yale Div. Sch., 1962-63; M.A., U. Wis.-Madison, 1965, Ph.D., 1968. Instr. Vassar Coll., 1967-68, asst. prof. history, 1968-73; assoc. prof. religion Swarthmore Coll., 1973—, prof. religion, 1979—, Howard M. and Charles F. Jenkins prof. of Quaker history and research, 1980—. Author: The Quaker Family in Colonial America, 1973, Connecticut Education in Revolutionary Era, 1974, A Perfect Freedom: Religions Liberty in Pennsylvania, 1990; co-author: The Quakers, 1988; editor: The Keithian Controversy in Early Pennsylvania, 1980, Ouaker Origins of Antislavery, 1981, Records and Recollections of James Jenkins, 1984, Seeking the Light: Essays in Quaker History, 1987; editor Pa. Mag. of History and Biography, 1981-86. Bd. dirs. Friends Hist. Assn., 1973—, Phila. Ctr. for Early Am. Studies, 1978—. John Carter Brown Library fellow, 1970; Eugene M. Lang fellow, 1980-81; NEH fellow, 1986. Quaker. Home: 3 Whittier Pl Swarthmore PA 19081 Office: Swarthmore Coll Friends Hist Libr Swarthmore PA 19081

FRUCHTENBAUM, ARNOLD GENEKOVICH, organization executive; b. Tobolsk, Siberia, USSR, Sept. 26, 1943; s. Chaim and Adele (Valentinovna (Suppes) F.; m. Mary Ann Morrow, June 29, 1968. Student, Shelton Coll., 1962-65; B.A., Cedarville Coll., 1966; postgrad. Hebrew U. Jerusalem, 1966-67, Am. Inst. Holy Land Studies, 1966-67; Th.M., Dallas Theol. Sem., 1971; postgrad. NYU, 1975—. Minister, Beth Sar Shalom Hebrew Christian Fellowship, Dallas, 1967-71; editor The Chosen People, N.Y.C., 1973-75; assoc. dir. The Christian Jew Found., San Antonio, 1975-77; pres. Ariel Ministries, Tustin, Calif., 1977—; lectr. in field. Mem. Messianic Jewish Alliance. Mem. Fundamental Chs. of Am. Author: Hebrew Christianity: Its Theology, History and Philosophy, 1974; Jesus Was a Jew, 1975; The Footsteps of the Messiah: A Study of the Sequence of Prophetic Events, 1982; Biblical Lovemaking: A Study of Sex from the Song of Solomon, 1983. Home: 21 Choate Irvine CA 92720-3320 Office: 12134 Colwick St Tustin CA 92681

FRUEH, CURT DAVID, clergyman; b. Frankfurt, Fed. Republic Germany, Oct. 26, 1959; came to U.S., 1962; s. John Curt and Gretchen (Bahr) F.; m. Elizabeth Jane Hoff, Oct. 10, 1987; 1 child, Sarah Grace. BA, Yale U., 1983; MDiv, Pitts. Theol. Sem., 1989. Ordained to ministry Presbyn. Ch., 1989. Staff, vol. East End Cooperative Ministry, Pitts., 1985-86; student minister A Christian Ministry in the Nat. Parks, Kelly, Wyo., 1986; sem. intern Hebron United Presbyn. Ch., Pitts., 1986-88; pulpit supply Pitts. Sem. Preaching Assn., 1988-89; assoc. pastor 1st Presbyn. Ch., Wausau, Wis., 1989—; mem. ednl. ministries subcom. Winnebago (Wis.) Presbytery, 1989—, ch. and soc. com., 1990—; mem. Impact Policy Bd., Wis., 1990—; founding mem. Wausau (Wis.) Youth Network, 1989—. Contbr. articles to profl. jours. Mem. Untied Way Issues Task Force, Wausau, 1989-91, fund raising com. Habitat for Humanity, Wausau, 1990—, Luth. Social Svcs. Consumer Coun., Wausau, 1990—, United Way Campaign Com., Wausau, 1990—. Mem. Assn. Presbyn. Ch. Educators. Democrat. Home: 903 Steuben St Wausau WI 54401 Office: 1st Presbyn Ch 406 Grant St Wausau WI 54401

FRY, CHARLES GEORGE, theologian, educator; b. Piqua, Ohio, Aug. 15, 1936; s. Sylvan Jack and Lena Freda (Ehle) F. BA, Capital U., 1958; MA, Ohio State U., 1961, PhD, 1965; BD, Evang. Lutheran Theol. Sem., 1962, MDiv, 1977; DMin, Winebrenner Theol. Sem., 1978. Ordained to ministry Lutheran Ch. U.S.A, 1963. Pastor St. Mark's Luth. Ch. and Martin Luther Luth. Ch., Columbus, Ohio, 1961-62, 63-66; instr. Wittenberg U., 1962-63; instr. Capital U., 1963-75, asst. prof. history and religion, 1966-69, assoc. prof., 1969-75; theologian-in-residence North Community Luth. Ch., Columbus, 1971-73; assoc. prof. hist. theology, dir. missions edn. Concordia Theol. Sem., Ft. Wayne, Ind., 1975-84; sr. minister First Congl. Ch., Detroit, 1984-85; Protestant chaplain St. Francis Coll., Fort Wayne, 1982—; interim minister First Presbyn. Ch., Huntington, Ind., 1988-89, St. Luke's Luth. Ch., Ft. Wayne, 1989-90, Mt. Zion Luth. Ch., Ft. Wayne, 1990-91; vis. prof. Damavand Coll., Tehran, 1973-74, bd. dirs. 1976—; vis. prof. Ref. Bible Coll., 1975-79, Concordia Luth. Sem. at Brock U., summer 1977, 79, St. Francis Coll., 1980—; vis. scholar Al Ain U., United Arab Emirates, 1987; theologian-in-residence Queenstown Luth. Ch., Singapore, 1991; adj.. faculty history Ind. U./Purdue U., Ft. Wayne, 1982—,other. Author books including Age of Lutheran Orthodoxy, 1979, Lutheranism in America, 1979, Islam, 1980, 2d edit. 1982, The Way, The Truth, The Life, 1982, Great Asian Religions, 1984, Francis: A Call to Conversion, 1988, Brit. edit., 1990, The Middle East: A History, 1988, Congregationalists and Evolution: Asa Gray and Louis Agassiz, 1989, Pioneering a Theology of Evolution: Washington Gladden and Pierre Teilhard de Chardin, 1989, Avicenna's Philosophy of Education: An Introduction, 1990, others. Recipient Praestantia award Capital U., 1970, Concordia Hist. Inst. citation, 1977; Regional Coun. for Internat. Edn. rsch. grantee, 1969; Joseph J. Malone post-doctoral fellow, Egypt, 1986. Fellow Brit. Interplanetary Soc.; mem. Am. Hist. Assn., Am. Acad. Religion, Middle East Studies Assn., Middle East Inst., Phi Alpha Theta. Democrat. Home: 158 W Union St Circleville OH 43113 Office: St Francis Coll 2701 Spring St Fort Wayne IN 46808

FRY, ELDON ERVIN, religious organization administrator; b. Lewistown, Idaho, Aug. 2, 1946; s. Ervin Angus and Alice May (Benjamin) F.; m. Virginia Mae Stretch, Dec. 24, 1965; children: Marla Rene, Marc Alan. BA in Religion, Bartlesville Wesleyan U., 1968; MS in Family Life Edn., Kans. State U., 1984; postgrad., Pa. State U. Ordained minister, 1968. With customer service dept. Plaza Nat. Bank, Bartlesville, Okla., 1965-68; pastor Big Bow (Kans.) Wesleyan Ch., 1968-72; credit mgr. Brookings (S.D.) Hosp., 1972-73; asst. pastor Brookings Wesleyan Ch., 1972-73; sr. pastor Westview Community Ch., Manhattan, Kans., 1973-84; dir. campus ministries Messiah Coll., Grantham, Pa., 1984—; educator Pawnee Mental Health Ctr., Manhattan, 1983; v.p. Logos Rsch. Inst., Manhattan, 1983-84, family life cons., 1983-84; adminstr. Nat. Conf. Family Well Being, Washington, 1984. Author: (with others) Now We Are Three, 1985; contbg. editor: Family Building, 1985. Chaplain Riley County Police Dept., Manhattan, 1981-83; dir. Wesleyan Youth Camp, Rock Springs, Kans., 1976; advisor 2020, Harrisburg, Pa., 1989; active Amnesty Internat., Habitat for Humanity; nat. rep. The Nat. Ctr. for Fathering, 1991. Named one of Outstanding Young Men in East, 1990. Mem. Am. Assn. Christian Counselors, Pa. Assn. Adult and Continuing Educators, Youth Service Am., Jaycees, Omicron Nu. Democrat. Avocations: refinishing furniture, camping, basketball, sports. Home and Office: Messiah Coll Grantham PA 17027

FRY, JOYCE ELAINE, minister; b. Bellville, Ohio, Nov. 25, 1943; d. Earl D. and Juanita Bell (Miller) F. BS, Ashland U., 1965; MDiv, United Theol. Sem., 1971. Ordained to ministry United Meth. Ch., 1971. Min. Hayes United Meth. Ch., Toledo, 1970-75, St. Paul - Ridge United Meth. Ch., Delphos, Ohio, 1975-78, S. Park United Meth. Ch., Dayton, Ohio, 1978-81, Ft. McKinley United Meth. Ch., Dayton, 1981-89, Cen. United Meth. Ch., Springfield, Ohio, 1989—; Dist. trustee United Meth. Ch. Housing Coalition of Dayton, 1985-89; del. United Meth. Ch. Jurisdictional Conf., Dayton, 1986; chairperson United Meth. Ch. Urban Devel. Program, Springfield, 1990—. Mem. Montgomery County Community Devel. Block Grants Com., Dayton, 1987-89. Recipient Alumni award United Theol. Sem., 1989; Merrill fellow Harvard Divinity Sch., 1989. Mem. West Ohio Ann. Conf., Zonta Club. Home: 527 Argonne Ave Springfield OH 45503 Office: Cen United Meth Ch 102 W High St Springfield OH 45502

FRY, LOWELL LAWRENCE, minister; b. Wichita, Kans., July 13, 1956; s. Lowell Lawrence and Dorothy May (Baum) F.; m. Lucinda Marie Howrey, June 15, 1976; children: Jason Matthew, Lynelle Renee, Travis Tyler. Student, Butler Community Coll., El Dorado, Kans., 1974-75; BSL, Ozark Bible Coll., Joplin, Mo., 1979; postgrad., Cin. Bible Sem., 1985—. Ordained to ministry, Christian Chs./Chs. of Christ. Minister Rose Hill (Kans.) Christian Ch., 1976-83; assoc. minister Western Hills Christian Ch., Lawton, Okla., 1983-86, sr. minister, 1986—; bd. dirs. S.W. Evangelizing Assn., Lawton, 1986—; co-dir. Shepherd's Voice Ministries, Lawton, 1989—; supervisory com. Okla. Christian Conv., Stillwater, 1988-90; area registration chmn. N. Am. Christian Conv., Cin., 1989-90. Recipient Pentecost Speech award, Ozark Bible Coll., 1976; named Outstanding Young Minister, N. Am. Christian Coun., 1989. Mem. Am. Bus. Club (bd. dirs. 1989-90). Republican. Home: 7217 NW Dogwood Ln Lawton OK 73505 Office: Western Hills Christian Ch 1401 NW 82nd St Lawton OK 73505

FRY, MALCOLM CRAIG, clergyman; b. Detroit, June 6, 1928; s. Dwight Malcolm and Josephine (Craig) F.; m. Myrtle Mae Downing, June 5, 1948; children: Pamela Mae, Malcolm Craig, Rebecca Fry Gwartney, Matthew Dwight. Student, Bible Bapt. Sem., 1950; Th.B., Am. Div. Sch., Chgo., 1959; student, McNeese State Coll., Lake Charles, La., 1958-61; B.S., Austin Peay State Coll., 1962; M.Ed., U. Ariz., 1969; D. Laws and Letters (hon.), Clarksville Sch. Theology, 1974; D.Ministry, Luther Rice Sem., 1978. Ordained to ministry Free Will Bapt. Ch., 1955. Asst. jewelery store mgr. Sonne Bros., Norwich, N.Y., 1948-50; pastor in Lake Charles, La., 1955-58, 59-61, Bryan, Tex., 1958-59, Ashland City, Tenn., 1961-62; asst. pastor in Royal Oak, Mich., 1962-64; pastor First Free Will Bapt. Ch., Tucson, 1964-71; dir. curriculum and research Bd. Ch. Tng. Service Nat. Assn. Free Will Baptists, Nashville, 1971-72; gen. dir., treas. Bd. Ch. Tng. Service, 1972-78; dir. Nat. Youth Conf., 1972-83, asst. dir. Bd. Sunday Sch. and Ch. Tng., 1978-83; pastor Unity Free Will Bapt. Ch., Smithfield, N.C., 1983-89; program writer adult and teen tng. mag. Nat. Assn. Free Will Bapts., 1963-78, clk., 1965-67, chmn. stewardship commn., 1962-67, editor-in-chief bd. Sunday Sch. and Ch. Tng., 1989—. Author: Total Involvement, 1964, Why Worry?, 1967, Precepts for Practice, 1971, Discipling and Developing, 1971, The Teacher-in-Training, 1972, Contemporary Topical Studies, 1973, rev. edit., 1991, The Ministry of Music, 1974, Balancing Christian Education, 1977, Leader's Guide Discipling and Developing, 1979, Leader's Guide the Ministry of Ushering, 1980. Served with AUS, 1946-48; with USAF, 1951-57, Korea. Mem. Evang. Philos. Soc., Phi Delta Kappa. Clubs: Kiwanis, Civitan. Office: 114 Bush Rd Nashville TN 37217

FRY, MICHAEL LYNN, minister; b. Wichita, Kans., May 22, 1951; s. Warren Moseley and Marjorie Marie (Holt) F. BA, Biola U., La Mirada, Calif., 1973; MA, Azusa Pacific U., 1977; MDiv, Claremont Sch. Theology, 1983; postgrad., Western Theol. Sem., Holland, Mich., 1989—. Ordained to ministry Presbyn. Ch. (U.S.A.), 1984. Religious educator Vinewood Community Ch., Lodi, Calif., 1973-74; religious educator, min. youth 1st Bapt. Ch., Redwood City, Calif., 1975; min. to jr. high. sch. and coll. students 1st Bapt. Ch., Pomona, Calif., 1976-81; min. youth Westminster Presbyn. Ch., Yakima, Wash., 1981-87; min. parish life 1st Presbyn. Ch., Grand Haven, Mich., 1988—; vol., club leadr Young Life, Yakima, 1983-87; moderator high edn. agy. Lake Michigan Presbytery, 1991—. Home: 17963 Mohawk Spring Lake MI 49456 Office: 1st Presbyn Ch 508 Franklin St Grand Haven MI 49417

FRY, WILLIAM EDWARD, clergyman; b. Columbus, Ohio, Mar. 29, 1954; s. Shirley Edward Fry and Maxine Wingert Evans; m. Denise June Grubb, Aug. 28, 1976 (dec. June 1979); children: Kara Denise (dec.), William Edward Jr. (dec.); m. Kathy Sue Carver, Dec. 8, 1980; children: Misty Ann, Angela Dawn. BRE, God's Bible Sch. and Coll., Cin., 1977. Ordained to ministry Wesleyan Ch., 1983. Editor Dist. Newspaper, Morgantown, W.Va., 1982-84; ednl. sec. Dist. Office, Morgantown, 1982-84; Sunday sch. sec. Dist. Office, Williamson, W.Va., 1990, dist. youth pres., 1990—; pastor Wesleyan Ch., Carthage, Ind., 1978-79, Charleston, W.Va., 1979-80, Morgantown, 1980-85, Williamson, 1987—; mem. evangelism and ch. growth dist. com., Williamson, 1990-92, leaders equipped and developed dist. mentor, Williamson, 1991-92; personal care coord. Mingo County EOC, Williamson, 1990-91; chaplain Mingo County Jail, Williamson, 1988—. Home: 522 Peter St Williamson WV 25661

FRYE, ROLAND MUSHAT, literary historian, theologian; b. Birmingham, Ala., July 3, 1921; s. John and Helen Elizabeth (Mushat) F.; m. Jean Elbert Steiner, Jan. 11, 1947; 1 child, Roland Mushat. A.B., Princeton U., 1943, M.A., 1950, Ph.D., 1952; student, Princeton Theol. Sem., 1950-52. Instr. English, Samford U., 1947-48; asst. prof. to prof. Emory U., 1952-61; research prof. Folger Shakespeare Library, Washington, 1961-65; L.P. Stone Found. lectr. Princeton Theol. Sem., 1959, vis. prof., 1963; prof. U. Pa., Phila., 1965-83; emeritus prof. U. Pa., 1983—; trustee, vice chmn., mem. adv. com. Ctr. Theol. Inquiry, 1979—, chmn., 1989—. Author: God, Man and Satan: Patterns of Christian Thought and Life in "Paradise Lost," "Pilgrim's Progress" and the Great Theologians, 1960, Perspective on Man: Literature and the Christian Tradition, 1961, Shakespeare and Christian Doctrine, 1963, Shakespeare's Life and Times: A Pictorial Record, 1967, Shakespeare: The Art of the Dramatist, 1970, Milton's Imagery and the Visual Arts: Iconographic Tradition in the Epic Poems, 1978, Is God a Creationist?: The Religious Case Against Creation-Science, 1983, The Renaissance Hamlet: Issues and Responses in 1600, 1984, Language for God and Feminist Language: Problems and Principles, 1988; editor: The Reader's Bible A Narrative: Selections from the King James Version, 1978; contbr. articles to profl. jours. Served to maj. AUS, 1943-46. Decorated Bronze Star.; Guggenheim fellow, 1956-57, 73-74; mem. Inst. Advanced Study Princeton, N.J., 1973-74, 79; grantee NEH, 1973-74, Am. Council Learned Socs., 1966, 71, 78; Am. Philos. Soc., 1968, 71, 78; vis. scholar Am. Acad. in Rome, 1971; NEH-Huntington Library fellow, 1980-81. Mem. Am. Acad. Arts and Scis., Milton Soc. Am. (pres. 1977-78, James Holly Hanford award 1979), Am. Philos. Soc. (sec. 1978-81, John Frederick Lewis prize 1979, Henry Allen Moe prize 1988), Rannaissance Soc. Am. (pres. 1984-85). Presbyterian. Clubs: Rittenhouse (Phila.); Cosmos (Washington). Home: 226 W Valley Rd Wayne PA 19087 Office: U Pa English Dept D1 Philadelphia PA 19104

FUCHS, ALAN D., rabbi; b. Paterson, N.J., May 4, 1936; s. Morris and Rose (Reines) F.; m. Carol Barnet, Dec. 27, 1964; children: Douglas S., Daniel A. BA, Trinity Coll., Hartford, Conn., 1958; BA in Hebrew Letters, Hebrew Union Coll., 1960, MA in Hebrew Letters, 1962, DD (hon.), 1988. Ordained rabbi, 1963. Rabbi Temple Beth El, Somerville, N.J., 1965-68, Reform Congregation Keneseth Israel, Elkins Park, Pa., 1968-77, Temple Sinai, Pitts., 1977-81; sr. rabbi Isaac M. Wise Temple, Cin., 1981-88, Congregation Rodeph Shalom, Phila., 1988—; trustee Am. Jewish Com., Phila., 1989—, Anti Defamation League, Phila., 1989—. Trustee Planned Parenthood, Phila., 1989—. Capt., chaplain U.S. Army, 1963-65. Mem. Cen. Conf. Am. Rabbis, Phila. Bd. Rabbis, NCCJ (trustee 1989—), Fedn. Jewish Agys. (trustee 1990—). Office: Congregation Rodeph Shalom 615 N Broad St Philadelphia PA 19123

FUCHS, STEPHEN LEWIS, rabbi; b. East Orange, N.J., Mar. 16, 1946; s. Leo and Florence (Goldstein) F.; m. Victoria Steinberg, June 9, 1974; children: Leo, Sarah Jenny, Benjamin. BA, Hamilton Coll., Clinton, N.Y., 1968; B of Hebrew Letters, Hebrew Union Coll., L.A., 1970; MA in Hebrew Letters, Hebrew Union Coll., Cin., 1974; postgrad., Vanderbilt U. Div. Sch. Ordained rabbi, 1974. Student rabbi Meir Chayim Temple, McGehee, Ark., 1971-73; rabbinic intern Temple Isaiah, Columbia, Md., 1973-74, rabbi, 1974-86; sr. rabbi The Temple, Nashville, 1986—. Contbr. articles to newspapers and mags. Bd. mem. Opportunities Industrialization Ctr., Nashville, 1986—, 2d Harvest Food Bank, Nashville, 1987—, ARC, Nashville, 1989—. Mem. Cen. Conf. Am. Rabbis (chair interreligious affairs com. 1983-89). Office: The Temple 5015 Harding Rd Nashville TN 37205 *We Jews have proven that we can withstand persecution and poverty. My hope is that our people will preserve our heritage in a time of prosperity and acceptance.*

FUDGE, DANNY HUGH, pastor; b. Wichita, Kans., Jan. 3, 1962; s. Harlan Hugh and Betty Lou (Duncan) F.; m. Penny Annette Purcell, Aug. 15, 1981; 1 child, Lindsey Ann. B of Bible Langs., Missionary Bapt. Sem., Little Rock, 1989. Ordained to ministry Am. Bapt. Ch., 1983. Pastor Marlow Bapt. Ch., Sheridan, Ark., 1983-85; assoc. pastor 1st Bapt. Ch., Cave City, Ark., 1985-88; pastor Landmark Bapt. Ch., Siloam Springs, Ark., 1988—. Mem. Kiwanis. Home: 1915 W Granite Siloam Springs AR 72761 Office: Landmark Bapt Ch 1705 1/2 S Mt Olive Siloam Springs AR 72761

FUDGE, ROY SMITH, minister; b. Athens, Ala., Apr. 4, 1920; s. Edward Benjamin Lee and Susie (Smith) F.; m. Mary Ella Norman, Aug. 18, 1948; children: Raymond, Philip, Betty, Peggy, Ellen, Kendall. Student, Abilene Christian Coll., 1945-48. Tchr. Athens Bible Sch., 1948-50; min. Ch. of Christ, Moultrie, Ga., 1951-53, Clovis, Claif., 1965-68, Laceys Spring, Ala., 1968-72, Gordon, Ga., 1986—.

FUENFHAUSEN, KENNETH LEE, clergyman; b. Liberty, Mo., Dec. 25, 1958; s. Donald Emil and Mary Lou (Roling) F.; m. Teresa Elizabeth Ryffe, May 16, 1980; children: Matthew Benjamin, Catherine Marie. BA, Rockhurst Coll., 1981; M in Pastoral Studies, Loyola U., New Orleans, 1990. Dir. religious edn. Notre Dame de Sion High Sch., Kansas City, Mo., 1981-84; pastoral assoc., youth min. Coronation of Our Lady Cath. Ch., Grandview, Mo., 1984—; dir. His Voice Liturgical Choir, Kansas City, 1980-84; coord. SEARCH Retreat Program, Kansas City, 1981-88, In Love with the Lord Contemporary Music Group, Grandview, 1984—. Cubmaster Boy Scouts Am., Lee's Summit, Mo., 1990. Mem. Nat. Assn. for Lay Ministry, Women's Ordination Conf. Home: 1803 SE 5th Lees Summit MO 64063 Office: Coronation of Our Lady Cath Ch 13000 Bennington Grandview MO 64030

FUERBRINGER, ALFRED OTTOMAR, clergyman, religion educator; b. St. Louis, Aug. 11, 1903; s. Ludwig Ernst and Anna (Zucker) F.; m. Carolyn Kuhlman, June 1, 1934; children: Kenneth Paul, Max Robert, Marian Ruth, Jane Carolyn. Student, Concordia Coll., Ft. Wayne, Ind., 1918-21; M.Div., Concordia Sem., St. Louis, 1925, S.T.M., 1927, D.D., 1953; L.H.D., Valparaiso U., 1959; Litt.D., Concordia Tchrs. Coll., Seward, Nebr., 1969. Ordained to ministry Luth. Ch., 1927; pastor Trinity Luth. Ch., Norman, Okla., 1927-34, Okmulgee, Okla., 1934-37; pastor St. Paul's Luth. Ch., Leavenworth, Kans., 1937-41; pres. Concordia Tchrs. Coll., Seward, Nebr., 1941-53, Concordia Sem., St. Louis, 1953-69; prof. Concordia Sem., 1969-74, dir. continuing edn., 1969-74; prof. Concordia Sem. in Exile (Seminex), St. Louis, 1974-77; prof. Christ Sem.-Seminex, 1977-83, matching gifts coordinator, 1979-83; commr. Luth. Church-Mo. Synod, Europe, 1948, 57, 58, 63, 66, Australia, Asia, 1957-58, Latin Am., 1957, 59, 61; mem. commn. on theology and ch. relations, 1950-69; bd. dirs. Gt. Rivers Synod, Assn. Evang. Luth. Chs., 1976-79; pres. Found. for Reformation Research, 1957-64, exec. dir., 1965-66, bd. dirs., 1967-69; v.p. Nat. Luth. Edn. Conf., 1963, pres., 1964. Editorial bd.: Concordia Theol. Monthly, 1953-74. Trustee Clayton Pub. Library, 1960-70; mem. alumni senate Luth. Sch. of Theology, Chgo., 1987-90. Recipient Disting. Alumnus award Concordia Sem., 1969, Disting. Svc. award Luth. Sch. of Theology, Chgo., 1989. Mem. Am. Mgmt. Assn. (theologians adv. council 1960-70), State Hist. Soc. Mo. (trustee 1953-85), Alumni Assn. Christ Sem. (bd. dirs. 1979-86, pres. 1979-84). Home: 4125 Quail Dr Norman OK 73072 *Gratitude is closely related to happiness. A person that takes time to think about and be grateful for the gifts, favors and privileges he has, both great and small, has little time and opportunity to grumble and complain. Many a disabled person, being grateful for the faculties he still can use, is happier than one of sound body and mind who is dissatisfied.*

FUESS, HAROLD GEORGE, retired religious organization executive; b. Belleville, Ill., Sept. 29, 1910; s. Arthur Garfield and Catherine Charlotte (Wehrung) F.; m. Lorrean W. Essenpreis, Mar. 20, 1937; 1 child, Karen Ann. BA, So. Meth. U. Profl. baseball player, 1929-32; with Kroger Co., 1934-55; mdse. mgr. Kroger Co., Little Rock, 1950-52; buyer Kroger Co.,

Cin., 1953-55; mktg. supr. Needham, Louis & Brorby, Chgo., 1956-59; sr. v.p., adminstrv. mgr., account dir. McCann-Erickson, Chgo., 1960-73; ret. McCann-Erickson, 1973; sr. v.p. Internat. Council Community Chs., Homewood, Ill., 1975-77; pres. Internat. Council Community Chs., 1977-80, pres. emeritus, 1981—; dir. printing co.; cons. Commn. on Religion in Appalachia. Chmn. drive United Fund, Park Ridge, Ill., 1969; chmn. congregation Park Ridge Community Ch., 1967-68. Served with USAAF, 1943-47, ETO. Recipient citation Chgo. Crusade of Mercy, 1972; named hon. citizen City of Sarasota, Fla., 1979. Mem. Nat. Council Chs. (governing bd.), Consulation on Ch. Union (del.), World Council Chs. (rep.), C. of C., Phi Beta Kappa. Republican. Clubs: Playboy, Mktg. Execs, Elks. Home: 31 Bray Wood Williamsburg VA 23185 Office: 900 Ridge Rd Homewood IL 60430

FUGATE, DONALD JAMES, minister, teacher; b. Oakland, Calif., May 8, 1953; s. James Duke and Doris Colleen (Norris) F.; m. Diann Georgette De Graaf, Jan. 26, 1974; children: Donald Thomas, David James. BA in Music, Calif. Bapt. Coll., Riverside, 1976; M in Ch. Music, Golden Gatge Sem., 1978. Minister of music 1st Bapt. Ch., Arlington, Calif., 1974-75, Calvary Bapt. Ch., Modesto, Calif., 1975-76; assoc. pastor Western Hills Bapt. Ch., San Mateo, Calif., 1976-83, Foxworthy Bapt. Ch., San Jose, Calif., 1983—; dir. choral music dept. Valley Chrisitan Schs., San Jose, 1988—; asst. conductor Golden Gate Sem., Mill Valley, Calif., 1977-78; bd. dirs. Destiny-Vocal Ensemble, San Jose; cons. Sound Svcs., San Jose, 1983—. Contbr. articles to profl. jours. Recipient 1st Pl. award Crescendo Music Corp., 1979; named one of Outstanding Young Men in Am., 1981, 83. Republican. Baptist. Avocations: stained glass, soccer coach, racquetball. Home: 1493 Ilikai Ave San Jose CA 95118

FUGATE, EDWARD, minister; b. Springfield, Ohio, Aug. 22, 1956; s. Claude and Arminda (Noble) F.; m. Adina Sue Campbell, Oct. 6, 1979; children: Malinda Renee, Rebecca Ellen. BA, Berea Coll., 1978; MDiv, United Theol. Seminary, 1986. Ordained to ministry Meth. Ch. as deacon, 1984, as elder 1988. Sales agt. Commonwealth Ins. Co., Springfield, Ohio, 1979-80; sales mgr. Commonwealth Ins. Co., Piqua, Ohio, 1980-82; pastor New Paris (Ohio) United Meth. Ch., 1982-86, Seaman (Ohio) United Meth. Ch., 1986-87, Piketon-Jasper United Meth. Ch., Piketon, Ohio, 1987-89, Ft. Jefferson United Meth. Ch., Greenville, Ohio, 1989—; field assoc. United Theol. Sem., 1991—. Vol. chaplain Reid Meml. Hosp., Richmond, Ind., 1982-83, Pike Community Hosp., Waverly, Ohio, 1987-89; camping coord. United Meth. Ch., Portsmouth Dist., 1988-89. Named an Outstanding Young Man of Am. 1985, 86. Mem. Kiwanis (bd. dirs. New Paris 1983-85, com. chmn. 1984-86), Lions. Home and Office: Ft Jefferson United Meth Ch 3892 St Rt 121S Greenville OH 45331 *"The secret to joy is love. The secret to love is that it is a gift not an investment. To love is to give without hope of return. To give so freely is to know joy". John 15:9-12.*

FUGLER, JON EDWARD, radio station executive; b. Rochester, N.Y., Feb. 23, 1956; s. Robert and Evelyn (Nelson) F.; m. Nancy Stoltz, Jan. 6, 1979; children: Jayna, Tommy and Travis (twins). BA in Communications and French, Ind. U., 1978. Pres. Shepherd Communications, Yucaipa, Calif., 1973—, Shepherd Communications N.W., Calimesa, Calif., 1990—; dir. radio sta. Campus Crusade for Christ, San Bernardino, Calif., 1980-83; elder Faith Bible Ch., San Bernardino, 1988-91. Bd. dirs. San Bernardino-Riverside Sunday Sch. Assn., 1987-89, Parent-Citizen Assn., Yucaipa, 1991. Office: Shepherd Communications Inc 35225 Ave A Ste 204 Yucaipa CA 92399

FUHR, ANN BARTON MOSHER, diaconal minister; b. Perham, Minn., Nov. 19, 1941; d. Thomas Robert and Gertrude Nadine (Mosher) Williams; m. Michael E. Barton (div. 1977); children: Christopher Jon, Todd Mark, Stephen Michael; m. Donald L. Fuhr, Nov. 30, 1986. BS in Music Edn., Western Ill. U., 1963; postgrad., So. Meth. U., 1985-86, Clemson U., 1990—. Consecrated to diaconal ministry Meth. Ch., 1979; cert. choirmaster. Dir. music St. Matthew's United Meth. Ch., Acton, Mass., 1966-77, Key Meml. United Meth. Ch., Sherman, Tex., 1977-79; diaconal minister music White Rock United Meth. Ch., Dallas, 1979-87; diaconal minister spl. ministries Clemson (S.C.) United Meth. Ch., 1987—; Facilitator Cen. Wesleyan Coll. Faculty Retreat, 1989; guest speaker Clemson Sr. Citizen U., 1988, 89, 90. Composer: I Hear a Drum, 1975, No Vacancy, 1976. Mem. Am. Guild Organists, Fellowship United Meth. Musicians, Choristers Guild (pres. S.C. chpt. 1988-91, guest clinician, condr. nat. festivals and workshops). Home: 2607 Ashley Oaks Ct Seneca SC 29678 Office: Clemson United Meth Ch 195 Old Greenville Hwy Clemson SC 29631

FUHRMAN, CHARLES MICHAEL, minister; b. Moberly, Mo., July 4, 1952; s. Charles Elbert and Juanita Belle (Alexander) F.; m. Branda Diane Stansifer, Aug. 5, 1978; children: Megan Elizabeth, Philip Michael, Jennifer Diane. AA, Moberly Jr. Coll., 1972; BA in History, S.W. Bapt. Coll., Bolivar, Mo., 1974; MDiv, So. Bapt. Theol. Sem., Louisville, Ky., 1977; PhD in New Testament, So. Bapt. Theol. Sem., 1981. Ordained to ministry So. Bapt. Ch., 1974. Pastor Pleasant Valley Bapt. Ch., Chilhowee, Mo., 1973-74, Markland Bapt. Ch., Vevay, Ind., 1975-78, Waddy (Ky.) Bapt. Ch., 1978-83, First Missionary Bapt. Ch., Benton, Ky., 1983-86, Northgate Bapt. Ch., Kansas City, Mo., 1986—; adj. prof. William Jewell Coll., Liberty, Mo., 1989; trustee S.W. Bapt. U., Bolivar, 1988—; pastoral field edn. supr. Midwestern Bapt. Sem., Kansas City, Mo., 1987-89. Contbr. articles to profl. jours. V.P. Marshall County Ministerial Alliance, Benton, 1984; active Lions Club, Benton, 1984-86. Recipient 1st Pl. Best Sermons award Harper & Row, 1990; Rice-Judson scholar So. Bapt. Theol. Sem., Louisville, 1974-75; Garrett fellow So. Bapt. Theol. Sem., Louisville, 1977-78. Mem. Blue River-Kansas City Bapt. Assn. (chmn. Christian Life Com. 1989-90). Republican. Home: 6904 NW Pleasantview Dr Kansas City MO 64152 Office: Northgate Bapt Church 800 NE Vivion Rd Kansas City MO 64118

FUHRMANN, BARBARA CLARA, minister; b. Gainesville, Tex., Oct. 19, 1949; d. Erwin Sylvester and Clara Catherine (Stoffels) F. BA in English, Tex. Woman's U., 1972; MA in Theology, St. Mary's U., San Antonio, 1982. Cert. catechist. Religion tchr. St. John Cath. Sch., Ennis, Tex., 1976-80; dir. religious edn. St. Andrew's Ch., Ft. Worth, 1982-83; assoc. campus minister Diocese Ft. Worth, Denton, Tex., 1983-86; dir. religious edn. Sacred Heart Ch., Muenster, Tex., 1986—; mem. bd. edn. Diocese Ft. Worth, 1982-83; leader prayer groups Ennis, 1977-80, Denton, 1980-81. Mem. Nat. Cath. Edn. Assn., Leaders in Faith Edn. Home: 513 N Cedar Muenster TX 76252

FUITEN, JOSEPH BENJAMIN, minister; b. Medford, Oreg., Nov. 21, 1949; s. John Harold and Florence (Moyer) F.; m. Linda Marie Vanden Bos, Dec. 31, 1971; children: Rosalind, Sandra, Benjamin, Zachary. BA, Willamette U., 1972. Ordained to ministry Assemblies of God Ch., 1971. Assoc. pastor Aloha (Oreg.) Assembly, 1972-73, Life Ctr., Tacoma, 1973-79; dir. Christian edn. N.W. Dist. Assemblies of God, Kirkland, Wash., 1979-81; pastor Cedar Park Ch., Kirkland, 1981—; v.p. Mainstream Ministries, Tacoma, 1976—; v.p. bd. dirs. Calcutta Mission of Mercy, Tacoma; sec. Family Broadcasting Co., Tacoma, 1979-85. Republican. Avocation: stamp collecting.

FULBRIGHT, JUNUS CYMORE, religious organization administrator, minister; b. Hickory, N.C., Nov. 18, 1942; s. Junus Cymore and Eula Mae (Leonhardt) F.; m. Barbara Gayle Harvey, June 5, 1965; children: Tanya Lejeune, Shana Ruth, Abigail Renee. BA in Bibl. Edn., Lee Coll., 1965. Ordained to ministry Ch. of God (Cleveland, Tenn.), 1962. Mission organizer Ch. of God, Chgo., 1965-66; evangelist, pastor Ch. of God, N.C., 1966-74; dir. state youth and Christian edn. Ch. of God, Ill., 1974-78, Ga., 1978-80; adminstrv. asst. evangelism and home missions Ch. of God, Cleveland, 1980-82; dir. state youth and Christian edn. Ch. of God, Fla., 1982-84; asst. internat. dir. youth and Christian edn. Ch. of God, Cleveland, 1984-88, internat. dir., 1988—; mem. faculty N.C. State Ch. of God Bible Sch., Charlotte, 1967-73; mem. state youth bd. N.C. Youth and Christian Edn., Ch. of God, 1967-74. Author: Church Growth, 1981, Sunday School in the '90's, 1990; also articles. Mem. alumni bd., officer Lee Coll., Cleveland, 1968-76. Mem. Upsilon Xi (Disting. Alumnus award 1987). Office: Ch of God Internat Offices PO Box 2430 Cleveland TN 37320-2430 *Life can be amazing. How wondrous it is to see an obscure character suddenly sparkle from individuals who once were camouflaged by the limitations of birth, education, economics or society.*

FULFER, JOHN KEITH, minister; b. Bakersfield, Calif., Feb. 2, 1959; s. Robert Wesley Fulfer and Patricia Ann (Atkerson) Rose; m. Karen Lynn Traylor, Aug. 14, 1982; children: Katherine, Benjamin. BBA, Abilene Christian U., 1981, MS, 1983. Ordained to ministry Ch. of Christ, 1989. Edn. min. dir. Sycamore View Ch. of Christ, Memphis, 1987-89; assoc. min. Glenwood Ch. of Christ, Tyler, Tex., 1989—. Pres. First Tenn. Toasmasters, Memphis, 1987, area gov. dist. 43, 1987-88. Named Outstanding Area Gov. Dist. 43 Toastmasters, 1987-88. Mem. Religious Educators Assn., Christian Edn. Assn., Toastmasters. Office: Glenwood Ch of Christ 807 W Glenwood Tyler TX 75701 *It is nice to be recognized for our accomplishments. Yet what is really important is to know who we belong to and that is what makes life worthwhile.*

FULLER, GEORGE C., academic administrator. Head Westminster Theol. Sem., Phila. Office: Westminster Theol Sem Chestnut Hill Philadelphia PA 19118*

FULLER, HORACE BARTLET, JR., minister; b. Hope, Ark., May 11, 1935; s. Horace B. and Louise (Munn) F.; m. Avis Louise Massey, Aug. 23, 1958; children: Jana Louise, Jena LeAnne, James Bartlet. BA, Baylor U., 1957; BD, Southwestern Bapt. Theol. Sem., Ft. Worth, 1960. Ordained to ministry So. Bapt. Conv., 1960. Pastor 1st Bapt. Ch., Junction City, Ark., 1960-63, Cook Bapt. Ch., Ruston, La., 1963-73, Shreve City Bapt. Ch., Shreveport, La., 1973-81, Christ Bapt. Ch., Houma, La., 1981—. Office: Christ Bapt Ch 1700 E Tunnel Blvd Houma LA 70363

FULLER, MOZELLE JAMES, clergywoman, retired nurse; b. Greer, S.C., Aug. 10, 1909; d. William and Julia (Lipscomb) James; m. James Henry Fuller, Mar. 12, 1928; 1 child, Shirley Lindsey Berkley. Diploma, Nat. Inst. Nursing; 2d semester cert., Howard U. Sch. Religion, 1968; DD (hon.), Universal Life Ch., Christ Mission, 1980, Christ's Instn. Inc., 1980. Ordained to ministry Pentecostal Bapt. Ch., 1967; Mut. Bapt. Missionary Assn., 1967. Personality Sta. WOL and Sta. WMMJ-FM, Washington; bd. dirs. Internat. Found. for the Performing Arts. Mem. D.C. Commn. on Aging; co-founder Ch. of What's Happening Now; missionary Peace Bapt. Ch., 1949—; founder Sr. Citizens United To Serve Humanity. Recieved Nat. Black Monitor Hall of Fame Community Bldg. award. Mem. Women Ministers Greater Washington, Ministers in Partnership, Am. Legion Aux. Democrat. Baptist. Home: 624 17th St NE Washington DC 20002 *I spent a great deal of time trying to find ways and means of making life better for everyone on Planet Earth. My motto is: Serve God by loving our fellow man. I intend to add to my motto: A better world must begin with me, and I intend to make it be.*

FULLER, REGINALD HORACE, clergyman, biblical studies educator; b. Horsham, Eng., Mar. 24, 1915; came to U.S., 1955; s. Horace and Cora L. (Heath) F.; m. Ilse Barda, June 17, 1942; children: Caroline Fuller Sloat, Rosemary Fuller Bazuzi, Sarah. B.A. with 1st class honours in Classics and Theology, Cambridge U., 1937, M.A., 1942; S.T.D., Gen. Theol. Sem., N.Y.C., 1960, Phila. Div. Sch., 1962; D.D., Seabury-Western Theol. Sem., Evanston, Ill., 1983. Ordained to ministry Ch. of Eng. as deacon, 1940, priest, 1941. Curate Bakewell, Eng., 1940-43, Ashbourne-w-Mapleton, Eng., 1943-46, Edgebastionshire, Birmingham, Eng., 1946-50; lectr. theology Queen's Coll., Birmingham, 1946-50; prof. theology St. David's Coll., Lampeter, Wales, 1950-55; exam. chaplain to Bishop of Monmouth, 1950-55; prof. N.T. lit. and langs. Seabury-Western Theol. Sem., Evanston, Ill, 1955-66; Baldwin prof. sacred lit. (N.T.) Union Theol. Sem., N.Y.C., 1966-72; adj. prof. Columbia U., 1966-72; prof. N.T. Va. Theol. Sem., 1972-85; prof. emeritus, 1985—, canon theologian of Brit. Honduras, also Bishop's commissary for U.S.A., 1968-72; vis. prof. Grad. Theol. Union, Berkeley, 1975, Coll. Emmanuel and St. Chad, Saskatoon, Sask., Can., 1978, 88, Episcopal Sem. of S.W., Austin, Tex., 1986, Nashotah House, Wis., 1986, 91, St. Mark's Coll. of Ministry, Canberra, Australia, 1987, Wesley Theol. Sem. Washington, 1990; mem. study commn. World Council Chs., 1957-61; mem. Episcopal-Lutheran Conversations, 1969-72, 77-80, Anglican-Luth. Conversations, 1970-72, Luth.-Cath. Dialogue (U.S.A.) Task Force, 1971-73, 75-78, Rev. Standard Version Bible Com., 1981-86. author: (with R. Hanson) The Church of Rome, A Dissuasive, 1948, The Mission and Achievement of Jesus, 1954, (with G. Ernest Wright) The Book of the Acts of God, 1957, What is Liturgical Preaching?, 1957, Luke's Witness to Jesus Christ, 1958, The New Testament in Current Study, 1962, Interpreting the Miracles, 1963, The Foundations of New Testament Christology, 1965, A Critical Introduction to the New Testament, 1966, (with B. Rice) Christianity and Affluence, 1966, Lent with the Liturgy, 1969, The Formation of the Resurrection Narratives, 1971, Preaching the New Lectionary, 1974, The Use of the Bible in Preaching, 1981, (with Pheme Perkins) Who is This Christ?, 1983, He That Cometh, 1990; contbr. books, encys.; translator: (D. Bonhoeffer) The Cost of Discipleship, 1948, Prisoner for God, 1954, (H.W. Bartsch, editor) Kerygma and Myth I, 1953, (R. Bultmann) Primitive Christianity, 1956, (J. Jeremias) Unknown Sayings of Jesus, 1957, (W. von Loewenich) Modern Catholicism, 1959, Kerygma and Myth II, 1962, (H. Flender) St. Luke Theologian of Redemptive History, 1967, (J. Moltmann and J. Weissbach) Two Studies in the Theology of Bonhoeffer, 1967, (A. Schweitzer) Reverence for Life, 1969, (T. Rendtorff) Church and Theology, 1971, (G. Bornkamm) The New Testament, A Guide to Its Writings, 1973, (E. Schweizer) The Holy Spirit, 1980; subject of book: Christ and His Communities: Essays in Honor of Reginald H. Fuller, 1990. Recipient Schofield prize and Crosse studentship, 1938; named Hon. Canon. St. Paul's Cathedral, Burlington, Vt., 1988; fellow Am. Assn. Theol. Schs., 1961-62. Mem. Studiorum Novi Testamenti Societas (pres. 1983-84, editorial com. 1978-81), Chgo. Soc. Bibl. Research, Soc. Bibl. Lit. (com. hon. membership 1978-81). Home: 5001 E Seminary Ave Richmond VA 23227

FULLER, RICKEY WAYNE, clergyman; b. Maywood, Calif., Oct. 31, 1955; s. Robert Elliott and Martha Laverne (Bossett) F.; m. Deanna F. Fuller, Dec. 19, 1983; 1 child, Laura Beth. BS in Religion, Liberty U., 1984. Ordained to ministry Bapt. Ch., 1984. Asst. pastor, min. youth and Christian edn. 1st Bapt. Ch., Apollo Beach, Fla., 1984-90; asst. pastor, min. youth, ch. sch. adminstr. Sweethaven Bapt. Ch., Portsmouth, Va., 1990—; dir. Conservative Bapt. of Fla. Youth Camp, 1987-90, chmn. Conservation Bapt. of Fla. Youth Com., 1987-90; assoc. Word of Life Fellowship, 1990—. Pres. Ga. Youth Assn. for Retarded Citizens, 1978-79. Recipient Outstanding Svc. award Macon Youth ARC, 1978. Home: 5157 Castleway Portsmouth VA 23703 Office: Sweethaven Bapt Ch 5100 W Norfolk Rd Portsmouth VA 23703

FULLER, ROBERT CHARLES, religion educator; b. Grand Rapids, Mich., May 6, 1952; s. Charles Richard and Bette Jane (De Good) F.; m. Kathy Ann Lange, Sept. 6, 1975; children: Bryan Lawrence, Matt Lawrence. BA, Denison U., 1974; MA, U. Chgo., 1975, PhD, 1978. Prof. Bradley U., Peoria, Ill., 1978—. Author: Religion and the Life Cycle, 1988, Alternative Medicine and American Religion Life, 1989, American and the Unconscious, 1986. Mem. Am. Acad. Religion, Soc. for Ch. History, Person, Culture and Religion. Office: Bradley U Peoria IL 61625

FULLER, ROBERT EARL, minister; b. Yuma, Ariz., Oct. 12, 1938; s. George Orville and Treva (Humphrey) F.; m. Aldea Rose Tharp, June 13, 1958; children: Dawn Michelle, David Earl, John Thomas, Steven Andrew. BA, L.A. Bapt. Coll., 1960; BD, Talbot Theol. Sem., La Mirada, Calif., 1964. Pastor, founder Thousand Oaks (Calif.) Bapt. Ch., 1964-79; pastor Berean Bapt. Ch., Fremont, Calif., 1980—; bd. dirs. S.W. Bapt. Home Mission, L.A., Regular Bapt. Camp, LaPorte, Calif. Mem. Calif. Assn. of Regular Bapt. Chs. (bd. dirs.). Republican. Avocations: woodworker, computers. Office: Berean Bapt Ch 2929 Peralta Blvd Fremont CA 94536

FULLMER, CHARLES WALTER, minister; b. Montoursville, Pa., Jan. 25, 1932; s. Charles Albert and Isabell Marie (Zuber) F.; m. Margare Janice Lee, Mar. 30, 1957; children: Katherine Louise, Karen Margaret. BA, Lycoming Coll., 1954; MDiv, Garrett Theol. Sem., 1958. Ordained to ministry United Meth. Ch., 1959. Pastor United Meth. Ch., Lyon Lake, Mich., 1956-59, Kalamazoo, Mich., 1959-62, Grand Rapids, Mich., 1962-66, Reed City, Mich., 1966-70, Ionia, Mich., 1970-77, Grandville, Mich., 1977-86, Petoskey, Mich., 1986—. Mem. Miinisterial Assn. (pres. 1991). Home: 900 Jennings Petoskey MI 49770 Office: United Meth Ch 1804 E Mitchell Box 477 Petoskey MI 49770

FULLMER, LEE WAYNE, minister; b. Victor, Iowa, Jan. 12, 1931; s. Joseph Jacob and Hazel Fannie (Carl) F.; m. Hazel June Shook, June 30, 1956; children: Carey Lee, Daniel Ray. Pastoral Dipl., Moody Bible Inst., Chgo., 1954; AB in History, Wheaton (Ill.) Coll., 1956; ThB in Theology, Bapt. Bible Sem., Johnston City, N.Y., 1958. Ordained to ministry Gen. Assn. of Regular Bapt. Chs., 1958. Minister Waneta Lake Bapt. Ch., Hammondsport, N.Y., 1957-61, Panama (N.Y.) Bapt. Ch., 1961-63, Shoaff Park Bapt. Ch., Ft. Wayne, Ind., 1963-69, Mt. Tabor Bapt. Ch., Beckley, W.Va., 1970-79, Norwood Bapt. Ch., Cin., 1979—; tchr. Norwood Bapt. Christian Sch., Cin., 1980—; trustee Scioto Hills Bapt. Camp, Wheelersburg, Ohio, 1982—; prof. Appalachian Bible Coll., Bradley, W.Va., part-time 1970's. Republican. Office: Norwood Bapt Ch 2037 Courtland Ave Cincinnati OH 45212 *The great need of our troubled society is a return to the Biblical Christianity based upon a renewal of a healthy fear of God.*

FULOP, ROBERT ERNEST, religion educator; b. Chgo., Oct. 21, 1926; s. Louis and Grace H. (Vencel) F.; m. Vernette F. Carlson, June 17, 1950; children: Judith Ann, James Robert, Timothy Earl. BS, Northwestern U., 1950; BD, No. Bapt. Theol. Sem., 1953; PhD, U. Edinburgh, Scotland, 1956. Ordained to ministry, Bapt. Ch., 1953. Pastor 1st Bapt. Ch., Appleton, Wis., 1955-57; prof. Kanto Gakuin U., Yokohama, Japan, 1958-73, Cen. Bapt. Theol. Sem., Kansas City, Kans., 1973—; mem. Nat. Coun. Churches (Japan), Tokyo, 1962-70, Japan Bapt. Union, Tokyo, 1963-67. Author, editor: Change and Challenge, 1985; contbr. articles to various publs. Pres. bd. dirs. Cen. Bapt. Sem. Fed. Credit Union, 1980—. With USN, 1944-46. Folger-Shakespeare Libr. fellow, Washington, 1970. Mem. Am. Hist. Soc., Midwest Assn. Profs. of Missiology (pres. 1979-80), Am. Soc. Missiology, Am. Soc. Ch. History. Republican. Avocations: gardening, book collecting, travel. Office: Cen Bapt Theol Sem Seminary Heights Kansas City KS 66102

FULTON, JAMES WAYTE, JR., clergyman; b. Stuart, Va., Feb. 23, 1911; s. James Wayte and Mary Ward (King) F.; B.A., Davidson Coll., 1933; M.Div., Union Theol. Sem., 1936; D.D., Belhaven Coll., 1956; m. Jerry Liddell, Mar. 9, 1946; children—Alyce Fulton Perkins, Christine Fulton Baldwin, Frances Anne Fulton Barnett, Jerry Virginia Fulton Mink, Kathleen Bell. Ordained to ministry Presbyterian Ch., 1937; pastor First Presbyn. Ch., Gloucester, Va., 1937-39, First Presbyn. Ch., Bishopville, S.C., 1939-41, Royal Oak Presbyn. Ch., Marion, Va., 1946-49; dir. Christian Edn., Synod La., New Orleans, 1949-52; pastor Shenandoah Presbyn. Ch., Miami, Fla., 1952-69, Meml. Presbyn. Ch., West Palm Beach, Fla., 1969-82; interim pastor First Presbyn. Ch., New Orleans, 1982-83, Hope Presbyn. Ch., Winter Haven, Fla., 1983-85, Ind. Presbyn. Ch., Savannah, Ga., 1985—; moderator Synod of Fla., 1978. Trustee Davidson Coll., 1955-75; bd. dirs. Columbia Theol. Sem., Christianity Today. Served with Chaplains' Corps, USNR, 1941-46, capt. Res. ret. Mem. U.S. Naval Inst., S.A.R. Kiwanian. Home: 711 N 5th Ave Laurel MS 39340-3412 Office: 25 W Oglethorpe Ave Savannah GA 31401

FULTON, ROBERT PAUL, minister; b. Gallipolis, Ohio, Feb. 1, 1958; s. Robert Leo and Elizabeth (Jones) F.; m. Nina Sue Sharp, May 31, 1981; children: Robert Oliver, Daniel Aaron, Hannah Lee. BS, U. Rio Grande, 1980; MDiv, Asbury Theol. Sem., 1984; postgrad., Wesley Theol. Sem., 1988; STD, Am. Bible Inst., 1991. Ordained to ministry Meth. Ch. Pastor Union United Meth. Ch., New Haven, W.Va., 1978-80, Beal Chapel United Meth. Ch., Apple Grove, W.Va., 1980-81, 1st United Meth. Ch., Owenton, Ky., 1981-83, Dillon Chapel United Meth. Ch., Huntington, W.Va., 1983-85, Oak Grove United Meth. Ch., Moorefield, W.Va., 1985-91, Brushford (W.Va.) United Meth. Ch., 1991—; mem. bd. ordained ministry United Meth. of W.Va., 1988—; mem. Romney Dist. Coun. on Ministries, Keyser, W.Va., 1988—. Leader/speaker W.Va. Clergy for Life, Morgantown, 1991. Mem. Nat. Assn. United Meth. Evangelists, Wesleyan Theol. Soc., Moorefield Ministerial Assn. (v.p. 1986-88), Rotary (chaplain Owenton club 1981-83), Phi Alpha Theta. Home: Rte 4 Box 130 Bluefield WV 24701 Office: Brushfork United Meth Ch Amory Rd Brushfork WV 24701 *During my life's travels I've discovered that there is a place where we can find rest from the storms of life. That place is the quiet closet of prayer.*

FULTON, THOMAS BENJAMIN, bishop; b. St. Catharines, Ont., Can., Jan. 13, 1918; s. Thomas Francis and Mary Catharine (Jones) F. Student, St. Augustines Sem., Toronto, 1935-41; D. Canon Law, Cath. U. Am., 1948. Ordained priest Roman Cath. Ch., 1941; asst. pastor in Toronto, 1941-51; sec. Toronto Tribunal, 1948-51; chancellor Archdiocese, Toronto, 1952-69; aux. bishop Archdiocese, 1969-78; 2d bishop of St. Catharines, 1978—; nat. dir. Soc. for Propagation Faith, 1977-83. Author: The Prenuptial Investigation, 1948. Mem. Can. Conf. Cath. Bishops (exec., treas. 1986-89, v.p. 1989-91), Ont. Conf. Cath. Bishops (pres. 1982-87). Home: 122 Riverdale Ave, Saint Catharines, ON Canada L2R 4C2

FUNDERBURK, CHARLES EDWARD (ED FUNDERBURK), clergyman; b. Nashville, Apr. 21, 1961; s. Gene and Pat (Glass) Roberts. BA in Ch. Adminstrn., East Tex. Bapt. Coll., 1984. Minister of youth Highland Park Bapt. Ch., Texarkana, Tex., 1984-85; assoc. pastor Haynes Ave. Bapt. Ch., Shreveport, La., 1985-87, Willow Point Baptist Ch., Shreveport, 1987-89, Calvary Bapt. Ch., Houston, 1989—. Named one of Outstanding Young Men Am., 1985. Mem. Bowie Assn. (youth com.), Northwest La. Bapt. Assn. (youth and music coms.). Democrat. Avocations: tennis, golf, baseball, basketball, singing. Home: 14943 Tilley St Houston TX 77084 Office: Calvary Bapt Ch 7550 Cherry Park Dr Houston TX 77095

FUNK, JOYCE ANNE, minister; b. Jacksonville, Ill., Mar. 2, 1952; d. Floyd William and Virginia Lorraine (Lackey) F. BA, Eureka Coll., 1974; M of Divinity, Yale U., 1977. Ordained to ministry Christian Ch. (Disciples of Christ). Assoc. minister West Haven (Conn.) Bapt. Ch., 1975-77, Union Baptist Ch., Mystic, Conn., 1977-79; pastor Woodward (Iowa) Christian Ch., 1979-81; assoc. regional minister Christian Ch. in the Upper Midwest, Iowa, Minn., N.D., S.D., 1979-81, Christian Ch. in Oreg., Portland, 1981—; mem. exec. com. Ecumenical Ptnrship. (nat. bd.), 1986—; bd. dirs. Ecumenical Ministries of Oreg., Portland, 1987—; rep. Consultation on United and Uniting Chs., Potsdam, Fed. Republic of Germany, 1987. Contbr. articles to denominational publs. bd. chair Groton-Stonington Youth Services, Groton, Conn., 1978-79; mem. Portland City Club, 1986—; elder Lynchwood Christian Ch. Named Outstanding Young Career Woman Bus. and Profl. Women, 1979, Outstanding Young Alumna Eureka Coll., 1984. Mem. Ecumenical Ministries of Oreg., Council on Christian Unity, Internat. Christian Women's Fellowship, Nat. Assn. Female Execs., Internat. Assn. Women Ministers (sec. 1981). Democrat. Club: YWCA. Lodge: Order Eastern Star. Avocations: contra dancing, pottery, reading, drama. Office: Christian Ch Oreg 0245 SW Bancroft Suite F Portland OR 97201

FUNK, VIRGIL CLARENCE, priest, national association director; b. La Crosse, Wis., July 25, 1937; s. Virgil Clarence and Grace Evelyn (Hundley) F. M.A., St. Mary's U., Balt., 1959, S.T.L., 1963; M.S.W., Catholic U., 1967. Ordained priest Roman Catholic Ch., 1963; lic. social worker, Va. Dir. Office of Social Ministry, Richmond, Va., 1969-74; exec. dir. Liturgical Conf., Washington, 1974-76; exec. dir., founder Nat. Assn. of Pastoral Musicians, Washington, 1976—; pres. Reliable Printing Co., Vienna, Va., 1981-88; pres. Lincoln Graphics, Washington, 1983-86. Editor: Music in Catholic Worship, 1980, NPM Workbook, 1987, Children, Liturgy and Music, 1989, Weddings, Funerals, Liturgy of the Hours, 1985; pub. mag.; Pastoral Music, 1982 (Gold Cir. award Am. Soc. Assn. Execs. 1982). Bd. dirs. Fulton Home for Aged, Richmond, 1973. Recipient Gerald Ellard award New England Liturgical Com., 1979. Fellow North Am. Acad. Liturgy. Democrat. Avocation: skiing. Home: 1525 Que St NW Washington DC 20009

FUNKA, THOMAS HOWARD, minister; b. Washington, Pa., July 14, 1946; s. Carl Thomas and Anna Rosella (Deyell) F.; m. Nancy Jane Caldwell, June 14, 1976; children: Andrew B., Gregory T. BA, Bethany Coll., 1968; MDiv, Pitts. Theol. Sem., 1974. Ordained to ministry United Meth. Ch., 1975. Pastor Anne Ashley United Meth. Ch., Munhall, Pa., 1975-79, Emerickville United Meth. Ch., Brookville, Pa., 1979-82, Grace United Meth. Ch., Meadville, Pa., 1982-91, McKean (Pa.) United Meth. Ch., 1991—; owner Funka Enterprises, Meadville, 1987—; bd. dirs. Meadville Christian Broadcasting Inc., 1987-91. Mem. Meadville Meml. Day Com., 1987-88; bd. dirs. United Meth. House, Chautauqua, N.Y., 1983-89, Wesbury United Meth. Community, Meadville, 1983-89, Am. Cancer Soc., 1989-

91. Mem. Meadville Ministerium (sec. 1990—), Lions (bd. dirs. 1987, 90-91), Masons (3d degree). Republican. Home: 5102 Cindy Ln McKean PA 16426 Office: McKean United Meth Ch 5041 N Main St McKean PA 16426 *The individual becomes great only when one realizes his or her dependence on God's power manifested through the Holy Spirit. We accomplish great things when we let God work through us, doing His will and purpose.*

FUNKHOUSER, MORTON LITTELL, JR., clergyman; b. Charlotte, N.C., Apr. 20, 1943; s. Morton Littell and Helen (Jones) F.; m. Mary Hope Moore, Sept. 6, 1969; children: Margaret Helen, Meredith Hope. BA, Asbury Coll., Wilmore, Ky., 1970; MDiv, Asbury Theol. Sem., 1973; postgrad., Chapman Coll., Orange, Calif., 1979-82. Ordained to ministry, United Meth. Ch., 1975. Minister Meth. Ch., N.C., 1973-79; commd. U.S. Air Force, 1979; advanced through grades to maj. to date chaplain Malstrom Air Force Base Chapel, Mont., 1979—. Democrat. Avocations: photography, travel, aerobics, video, tape recording. Home: 4440B Gumwood Great Falls MT 59405-6623 Office: Malmstrom Air Force Base Chapel 341 CSG/HC Malmstrom AFB MT 59402-5000

FUQUA, ROBERT VERNE, minister; b. Justin, Tex., Oct. 10, 1928; s. Henry Temple and Allene (Mays) F.; m. Eva Jean Nelson, Feb. 15, 1951; children: Sharon Christine, Douglas Verne. BS, Tex. Wesleyan U., 1951. Ordained to ministry Meth. Ch. Pastor Springtown (Tex.) Cir., 1949-52, Springtown Meth., 1952-54, Loving-Jean Cir., Loving, Tex., 1954-57, Cen. Meth. Ch., Mineral Wells, Tex., 1957-58, Ash Crescent Meth., Ft. Worth, 1958-60, 1st Meth. Ch., Wortham, Tex., 1960-64, Salem Meth. Ch., Graham, Tex., 1964-66; assoc. pastor Univ. United Meth. Ch., Ft. Worth, 1966-84; pastor St. Paul United Meth. Ch., Ft. Worth, 1984—. Home: 2005 Lipps Dr Fort Worth TX 76134 Office: St Paul United Meth Ch 920 W Hammond Fort Worth TX 76134

FURMAN, REXFORD D., minister; b. Ithaca, N.Y., Oct. 31, 1943; m. Andrea McClain, June 24, 1967; children: Dana Paul, Jonathan Mark, Loressa Jane. ThB, Bapt. Bible Coll. of Pa., 1969; MDiv, LABC, Newhall, Calif., 1971. Ordained to ministry, Gen. Assn. Regular Bapt. Chs. Pastor Bethel Bapt. Ch., Lancaster, Calif., 1967—; chmn. S.W. Bapt. Home Missions, El Monte; exec. com. Calif. Assn. Regular Bapt. Chs. Office: Bethel Bapt Ch 3100 W Ave K Lancaster CA 93536

FURMAN, WALTER LAURIE, priest; b. Charlotte, N.C., Nov. 30, 1913; s. Henry Sylvester and Edna Earl (Jenkins). BS, The Citadel, 1933; MS, U. Fla., 1941, PhD, 1961. Instr. Springhill Coll., Mobile, Ala., 1943-46, 51-53; instr. U. Fla., Gainesville, 1953-57; prof. Springhill Coll., Mobile, 1957-79; Roman Catholic priest Soc. Jesus, 1950—. Mem. Am. Math. Soc. Democrat. Home: 808 Springhill Ave Mobile AL 36602 *God controls everything.*

FURNISH, DOROTHY JEAN, retired religion educator; b. Plano, Ill., Aug. 25, 1921; d. Reuben McKinley and Mildred (Feller) F. BA, Cornell Coll., Mt. Vernon, Iowa, 1943; MA, Northwestern U., 1945, PhD, 1968. Cert. dir. Christian edn. United Meth. Ch. Dir. Christian edn. Trinity Meth. Ch., Hutchinson, Kans., 1945-52, 1st United Meth. Ch., Lincoln, Nebr., 1952-65; prof. Christian edn. Garrett-Evang. Theol. Sem., Evanston, Ill., 1968-88, adj. dir. M Christian Edn. in Ministry degree, 1988-90; ret., 1990—, freelance writer, lectr.,, 1990—. Author: Exploring the Bible with Children, 1975, DCE/MCE: History of a Profession, 1976, Living the Bible with Children, 1979, Experiencing the Bible with Children, 1990; also articles. Bd. dirs., treas. Kinheart Women's Ctr., Evanston, 1984—. Mem. Religious Edn. Assn. (steering com.), Assn. Profs. and Researchers in Religious Edn., United Meth. Assn. Profs. Christian Edn. Home and Office: 2545 Lawndale Evanston IL 60201

FURNISH, VICTOR PAUL, theology educator; b. Chgo., Nov. 17, 1931; s. Reuben McKinley and Mildred (Feller) F.; m. Jody Carmichael, May 25, 1963; children: Brianna, Rebecca. AB, Cornell Coll., Mt. Vernon, Iowa, 1952; BD, Garrett Evang. Theol. Sem., Evanston, Ill., 1955; MA, Yale U., 1958, PhD, 1960. Univ. Disting. prof. N.T. Perkins Sch. Theology, So. Meth. U., Dallas, 1959—; Alexander von Humboldt Found. rsch. fellow, Bonn, Fed. Republic Germany, 1965, Munich, 1972. Author: Theology and Ethics in Paul, 1968, The Love Command in the New Testament, 1972, The Moral Teaching of Paul: Selected Issues, 1979, 2d edit., 1985, II Corinthians, 1984 (Bibl. Archaeology Soc. award 1986); (with John H. Snow) Easter, 1975; (with Richard L. Thulin) Pentecost 3, 1981; (with Leander E. Keck), The Pauline Letters, 1984; contbr. articles to profl. jours. Mem. Soc. Bibl. Lit. (editor 1983-88), Studiorum Novi Testamenti Societas (exec. com. 1989-91), Phi Beta Kappa. Democrat. Home: 6806 Robin Rd Dallas TX 75209 Office: So Meth U Perkins Sch Theology Dallas TX 75275-0133

FURR, GARY ALLISON, minister; b. Concord, N.C., Aug. 27, 1954; s. Al W. and Shirley P. (Price) F.; m. Vickie L. Johnson, Dec. 29, 1973; children: Heather, Erin, Katie. BA (hon.), Carson-Newman Coll., Jefferson City, Tenn., 1976; MDiv (hon.), S.E. Bapt. Theol. Sem., Wake Forest, N.C., 1980; PhD, Baylor U., Waco, Tex., 1985. Assoc. pastor First United Meth. Ch., Jefferson City, Tenn., 1974-75; min. music and youth North Clinton Ave. Bapt. Ch., Dunn, N.C., 1977-79; pastor Gholson (Tex.) Bapt. Ch., 1979-80, Bruceville (Tex.) Bapt. Ch., 1986, First Bapt. Ch., Blakely, Ga., 1986—; clinical pastoral edn. Baylor U. Med. Ctr., Dallas, 1979; instr. Am. Bapt. Theol. Sem. Extension, Blakely, Ga., 1989-91; mem. rural ministry Tex. A&M U., 1988-91. Bd. dirs. Waco Bapt. Assn. Pastoral Counseling Ctr., Waco, Tex., 1981-83; pres. Early County Ministerial Assn., Blakely, Ga., 1987-88; founder Community Relations Coun., Blakely, 1988—; chair Early County Literacy Task Force, Blakely, 1989-91. Edde Dwyer scholar Baylor U., 1984. Mem. Am. Acad. Religion, Conf. of Christianity and Lit. Home: 629 McDowell Ave Blakely GA 31723 Office: First Baptist Church 130 River St Blakely GA 31723

FURUTAN, ALI-AKBAR, religious officer; b. Sabzevar, Khorasan, Iran, Feb. 28, 1905; s. Mohammad-Ali and Soghra Furutan; m. Ataieh Furutan, 1931; children: Iran Furutan Mohajer, Parvin. Degree in edn., Moscow U., 1931. Sec. Nat. Spiritual Assembly of Bahá'ís of Iran, 1934-57; mem. Body of Custodians of Baháí Faith Bahá'í World Ctr., 1957-63; mem. Body of Hands of the Cause at Holy Land Bahá'í Faith, 1963—; speaker radio program Tehran Radio. Author: Mothers, Fathers, and Children, 1980, Ali-Akbar Furutan, 1981, Stories of Bahá'u'lláh, 1986; contbr. articles to religious jours.

FUSON, RICKEY LEE, pastor; b. Crestline, Ohio, Oct. 6, 1954; s. Ernest Luther and Irene Bernice (Surgener) F.; m. Doris Aileen Henderson, June 1, 1974; children: Jennifer Nicole, Sarah Beth. BS, Lee Coll., 1978, MDiv., 1989. Ordained min. Ch. of God Internat., 1990. Min. youth and Christian edn. E. Market St. Ch. of God, Akron, Ohio, 1978-79, Mentor (Ohio) Ch. of God, 1979-85; pastor Wooster (Ohio) Ch. of God, 1986, Trinity Ch. of God, Maryville, Tenn., 1989-90, Ashland (Ohio) Ch. of God, 1990—; state youth bd. No. Ohio Ch. of God, Akron, 1980-84, 90—. Recipient Baseball scholarship Lee Coll., Cleve., 1978. Home: 1022 Masters Ave Ashland OH 44805 Office: Church of God Internat Keith at 25th St Cleveland TN 37311

FUTRAL, JAMES ROBERT, minister; b. Ft. Smith, Ark., Apr. 11, 1944; s. Guy Clemons and Mary Sue (Withers) F.; m. Shirley Fay Moore, Dec. 22, 1964; children: Melodi, Rob, Mysti. BA, Blue Mountain Coll., Miss., 1967; MDiv, New Orleans Bapt. Theol. Sem., 1977, DMin, 1980; DDiv, Blue Mountain Coll., 1989. Ordained to ministry So. Bapt. Conv., 1964. Pastor First Bapt. Ch., Verona, Miss., 1967-71, Antioch Bapt. Ch., Columbus, Miss., 1972-74, Grace Meml. Bapt. Ch., Gulfport, Miss., 1974-78, First Bapt. Ch., Amory, Miss., 1978-81, North Ft. Worth (Tex.) Bapt. Ch., 1981-85, Broadmoor Bapt. Ch., Jackson, Miss., 1985—; trustee Miss. Bapt. Children's Village, Clinton, Miss., 1979-81, 87; pres. Miss. Bapt. Conv., Jackson, 1987-89; mem. Found. bd. New Orleans Bapt. Theol. Sem., 1990—, Miss. Bapt. Conv. Bd. and Exec. Com., 1990—. Contbr. sermons to book: The Ministers Manual, 1983. Bd. dirs. Contact, Inc., Jackson, Miss.; mem. Instl. Rsch. & Rev. Bd., Miss. State Hosp., Whitfield, 1985-87, discharge adv. com., 1989—. Recipient Order of the Golden Arrow award, Miss. Coll., 1989, Disting. Alumni award, New Orleans Bapt. Theol. Sem., 1990. Office: Broadmoor Bapt Ch 787 E Northside Dr Jackson MS 39206

FUTRAL, LARRY LEE, music minister; b. Ft. Smith, Ark., Jan. 19, 1942; s. Guy Clemons and Mary Sue (Withers) F.; m. Rita Joyce Ray, Aug. 10, 1963; children: Steven Ray, Meredith Sue, Gregory Lee. BA, Miss. St. U., 1963; M. Church Music, Southwestern Bapt. Theol. Sem., 1974, M. Religious Edn., 1974. Music min. Forest Pk. Bapt. Ch., Ft. Worth, Tex., 1971-72, Henerson St. Bapt. Ch., Cleburne, Tex., 1972-74; min. music/edn. Camden Bapt. Ch., Camben, Ala., 1974-78; min. music/youth First Bapt. Ch., Ashland, Ala., 1978-82; min. music/activities First Bapt. Ch., Ocean Springs, Miss., 1983--. Staff sgt. USAF, 1967-70. Mem. Miss. Singing Churchmen, Ala. Singing Men (pres. 1980-81), Gulfcoast Mins. of Music Assn. (pres. 1987-88). Southern Baptist. Home: 139 Siowan Ave Ocean Springs MS 39564 Office: First Baptist Ch 602 Washington Ave Ocean Springs MS 39564

FYANS, THOMAS, church official. Pres. 1st Quorum of the 70 Mormon Ch. Office: 1st Quorum of the 70 50 E N Temple St Salt Lake City UT 84150

GABBERT, WILLIAM LEE, deacon, retired technical writer; b. Louisville, Mar. 13, 1915; s. Garland Lee and Helena Josephine (Kuhlmann) G.; m. Mary Lou Hermannes, Nov. 21, 1940; children: Juliet, Mary Lee, Michelle, Gabrielle (dec.), Patrick. Grad., Washington U., St. Louis, 1945. Ordained deacon Roman Cath. Ch., 1978. Permanent deacon Cath. Ch., St. Louis Archdiocese, 1978—; ret. tech. writer; mem. svc. team St. Christopher Prayer Community, St. Louis, 1975—; chmn. St. Louis sect. Soc. Automotive Engrs., 1961-62, Soc. Tech. Writers, 1974-75. Author: Appliance Service Manual, 1954; writer, performer TV show Mr. Tinker, St. Louis, 1953-54. With USN, 1942-45. Home: 4000 Stag Ct Florissant MO 63033-6648

GABER, JASON LEE, social worker; b. Boston, June 18, 1957; s. Louis L. and Anita (Shalachman) G. Student, Tel-Aviv U., 1974, Hebrew U., 1976-77; BS in Edn., Northeastern U., Boston, 1979; MSW, San Francisco State U., 1981. Ordained rabbi, 1991; cert. religious sch. tchr. Jewish program coord. San Francisco Jewish Community Ctr., 1981-84, adult svcs. dir., 1985-88, ctr.-wide program dir., 1989-91, asst. exec. dir., 1991—; rabbinical pastor, tchr., counselor Morenu, 1991—; Sun. sch. tchr. Peninsula Temple Sholom, Burlingam, Calif., 1982-85; high sch. tchr. Congregation Beth Shalom, San Francisco, 1979-81; foster care social worker Dept. Social Welfare, Boston, 1978-79; sr. svcs. rsch. analyst Dept. Elder Affairs, Boston, 1978; summer day camp counselor Young Israel Day Camp, Chelsea, 1973; field supr. San Francisco State U. Grad. Dept. Social Work Edn., 1987-91, community adv. coun., 1987-91. Contbr. articles to profl. jours. Policy planning com. Arts Edn. Focus Group, San Francisco Arts Commn., 1988-89; Jewish Community Rels. Coun., Soviet Jewry Commn., 1982-88, others. Named Louis Kraft Young Profl. Leadership awardee, Nat Conf. Jewish Communal Svcs., 1986; named Profl. of the Yr., United Jewish Community Ctrs., 1986, Program Achievement awardee, 1985, 89, others. Mem. Assn. Jewish Ctr. Profls. (nat. social action com. chpt. rep. 1990, exec. com. 1988-90, v.p., 1986-88, bd. dirs. 1983), Conf. of Jewish Communal Svc., Coalition for Alternatives in Jewish Edn., Jewish Humanists Community Fund (sec.-treas. 1983-87). Home: 700 Church St # 203 San Francisco CA 94114 Office: San Francisco Jewish Ctr 3200 California St San Francisco CA 94118 *The challenge before us today is to breath life and modern day relevancies into our rich tradition and heritage. Only if we are able to create modern day adaptations to our ancient teachings and values, will they stay alive and continue to inspire and nurture future generations.*

GABLE, DAVID LEE, priest; b. Anniston, Ala., Mar. 18, 1943; s. Carl Franklin and Lena Mae (Weems) G. BA, Jacksonville State U., 1965; MS, U. Miss., 1967; PhD, Memphis State U., 1977; MDiv, Va. Sem., 1980. Ordained priest Episcopal Ch., 1981. Deacon St. James Ch., Knoxville, Tenn., 1980-81; rector St. Andrew's Ch., Harriman, Tenn., 1981-87, Christ Ch., Chattanooga, 1987-90, St. Andrew's Ch., Edwardsville, Ill., 1991—; del. to Intramont, Appalachian People's Svc. Orgn., Blacksburg, Va., 1981-83; reader Gen. Ordination Exam, 1986—. Diocesan tutor Ciocese of Tenn., Knoxville, 1983-90, bishop and coun., 1984-90, examining chaplain, 1984-90. Mem. Rotary (chaplain Harriman chpt.). Address: 406 Hillsboro Ave Edwardsville IL 62025

GABLE, NANCY EILEEN, minister; b. Ephrara, Pa., Oct. 17, 1955; d. William Charles and Janet Lois (Zimmerman) G. BS in Edn., Indiana U. Pa., 1977; MA in Religion, Luth. Theol. Sem., Gettysburg, Pa., 1979. cert. assoc. in ministry and edn. Luth. Ch. in Am.; cert. lay profl. leader in Christian edn.; cert. nursery/kindergarten tchr., pub. sch. tchr., Pa.; cert. dir. pvt. schs, Pa. Dir. Christian edn. and youth ministry St. John's Luth. Ch., Rockville, Md., 1978-79, Trinity Luth. Ch., Waukegan, Ill., 1979-81; assoc. in ministry and edn. Grace Luth. Ch., State College, Pa., 1981-91; fir. for enrollment, fin. aid and continuing edn. Luth. Theol. Sem., Gettysburg, Pa., 1991—; mem. cons. com. growth and enrichment in ministry Evang. Luth. Ch. Am., Chgo., 1990—; coord. Mission 90, 1990—; chairperson parish ministries com. Allegheny Synod, Altocha, Pa., 1987-90; regional coord. div. for profl. leadership Lay Profl. Leaders in Northeastern Luth. Ch. Am., Phila., 1984-87; mem., rep. Alumni Coun. Gettysburg (Pa.) Sem., 1987—; treas. CROP/Ch. World Svcs., Waukegan, Ill., 1979-81; mem. Lake County Singers, Waukegan, 1979-81. Mem. Nat. Assn. for Edn. Young Children, Regional Assocs. Ministry (treas. 1987—). Republican. Office: Luth Theol Sem 61 N West Confederate Avwe Gettysburg PA 17325

GABLER, RUSSELL ALLAN, minister; b. Ann Arbor, Mich., Oct. 19, 1922; s. Joseph Walter and Caroline (Souster) G.; m. Marie Trieber, June 15, 1947; children: Grace Marie Gabler Martin, Allan Russell, Daniel Lee. Pastor's cert., Moody Bible Inst., 1945; BA, Wheaton Coll., Ill., 1948; MDiv, Fuller Theol. Sem., 1956; PhD, Calif. Grad. Sch. Theology, 1971. Ordained to ministry Independent Fundamental Chs. Am., 1946; lic. marriage, family and child counselor, Calif. Pastor Oak Park Christian Ch., Savanna, Ill., 1945-53, First Friends Ch., L.A., 1954-57, Cen. Bible Ch., Costa Mesa, Calif., 1957-62, Carson (Calif.) Bible Ch., 1963-91; Bible tchr. Cedar Lake (Ind.) Boys Camp, 1947-53; mem. ordination com. So. Calif. Independent Fundamental Chs., 1959-62, 82—; instr. in Bible Biola U., La Mirada, Calif., 1961-70; trustee Am. Missionary Fellowship Camp Wynola, Julian, Calif., 1965—; chmn. Am. Bd. Hindustan Bible Inst. Madras, India, 1984-88; chaplain Carson Sheriff Sta., 1985—. Mem. Human Resources Com., Carson, 1976-79, Carson Cares Com., 1983-85. Mem. Evangelical Theol. Soc., Carson-Wilmington Ministerial Assn. (pres. 1972-91). Republican. Home and Office: 23018 Catskill Ave Carson CA 90745 *In an age of radical changes I find stability by reading the Scriptures. Three or four chapters of God's Word each day takes me through the Bible each year. I started this habit in 1939. Now reading it through the 55th time, I can say: "Great Peace have they who love Thy law."*

GABOURY, GLEN ARTHUR, minister; b. Westfield, Mass., Oct. 24, 1957; s. Reginald Phineas and Dorothy Ann (Slate) G.; m. Donna Marie Boivin, June 12, 1982; children: Jennifer Ruth, Elizabeth Rose. AA in Music Edn., Holyoke Community Coll., Mass., 1977; MusB in Music Edn., U. Lowell, Mass., 1979; MA in Religion magna cum laude, Evang. Sch. Theol., Myerstown, Pa., 1988, Evang. Tchr. Tng. Assn. diploma, 1988; postgrad., Bethany Theol. Sem., Dothan, Ala., 1991—. Lic. to ministry Ch. of the Nazarene; cert. tchr. K-12 music, Mass. Tchr. Dayspring Christian Acad., S. Attleboro, Mass., 1982-83, Pioneer Valley Christian Sch., Springfield, Mass., 1984-86; assoc. pastor White Haven (Pa.) Free Meth. Ch., 1988-89; pastor Twin Hills Ch. of the Nazarene, Muncy, Pa., 1989—. Mem. Internat. Ministerial Fellowship. Ch. of the Nazarene. *Any definition of life that leaves out the Life-Giver is limited at best. Jesus said "I am the way, the truth, and the life..." True life, abundant life, eternal life comes only through personal faith in the Messiah, Our Lord and Saviour, Jesus Christ.*

GAERTNER, JOEL P., pastor; b. Phoenix, Sept. 1, 1964; s. John Philip and Joan LaVerne (Harting) G.; m. LuAnn Jean Siverly. BA, Northwestern Coll., Watertown, Iowa, 1986; MDiv, Wisc. Luth. Sem., 1990. Ordained to ministry Luth. Ch. Pastor Amazing Grace Luth. Ch., Florence, Ky., 1990—. Home and Office: Amazing Grace Luth Church 124 Burgess Ln Florence KY 41042

GAEWSKY, DAVID, minister; b. Bridgeport, Conn., June 23, 1960; s. Edward Francis and Veronica (Suchezski) G.; m. Sueli Alves da Costa, Aug. 17, 1985; children: Emily Alves, Lyvia Sueli. BS, U. Conn., 1981; postgrad., ISEDET, Buenos Aires, 1987-88; MDiv, Andover-Newton (Mass.) Theol. Sch., 1989. Missionary Mennonite Cen. Com., Paráiba, Brazil, 1982-85; pastor Cornwall-Weybridge Parish United Ch. of Christ, Middlebury, Vt., 1988—. Mem. Cornwall (Vt.) Vol. Fire Dept., 1989—. United Ch. Bd. for World Ministries fellow, 1987. Mem. Vt. Conf. United Ch. of Christ , Vt. Ecumenical Coun. (chairperson life and work com. Burlington, Vt. chpt. 1988—), Addison County Clergy Group (v.p. Middlebury chpt. 1989-90, pres. 1990—), Jonathon Edwards Soc., Middlebury Clergy/Mental Health Providers Assn. Home: RD 1 Box 76A Middlebury VT 05753

GAFFNEY, JAMES, religion educator; b. N.Y.C., Feb. 21, 1931; s. James G. and Lucille L. (Lynch) G.; m. Kathleen McGovern, June 30, 1970; children: Elizabeth, Margaret. BS, Spring Hill Coll., 1956; MA, Fordham U., 1965; ThD, Gregorian U., Rome, 1968; MEd, U. Tex., Houston, 1972. Instr. Fordham Prep. Sch., N.Y.C., 1956-59; assoc. prof. Gonzaga U., Florence, Italy, 1968-70; vis. prof. U. Liberia, 1971-73; chmn. dept. religion Ill. Benedictine Coll., 1973-76; prof. ethics, chmn. dept. religion Loyola U., New Orleans, 1976—; vis. prof. U. Notre Dame. Author 8 books; contbr. articles to religious jours. Malone fellow; NEH grantee. Mem. Soc. Christian Ethics (bd. dirs.), Coll. Theology Soc. (bd. dirs.), Societas Ethica, Am. Acad. Religion, Dante Soc. Office: Loyola U PO Box 193 New Orleans LA

GAGE, LELAND SCOTT, evangelist; b. Fort Smith, Ark., Jan. 29, 1952; s. Ralph Dennis and Reva O. (Walker) G.; m. La Donna Rene Maddox, Mar. 1, 1980; children: Lindsay, Megan, Kyle. BA in Edn., Cen. State U., 1974. Evangelist N.W. 50th Ch. of Christ, Oklahoma City, Okla., 1971-78, Carter Park Ch. of Christ, Del City, Okla., 1978-82, India, 1973—, E. Faulkner Ch. of Christ, El Dorado, Ark., 1982—; advisor John Abraham Christian Relief Fund, Amarillo, Tex., 1975—; chmn. India Mission Fund, El Dorado, 1977—; speaker Bible Half Hour Radio Broadcast, El Dorado, 1982—. Editor: (newsletter) India Quar., 1977—, Bread of Life, 1977—, (periodical) Basic Christianity, 1983—; contbr. articles to profl. publs. Pres. Friends of Barton Libr., El Dorado, 1989—; mem. Project Reach (Drug Program), El Dorado, 1984-88, Community Resource Forum, El Dorado, 1985-88. Home: 204 Mockingbird Ln El Dorado AR 71730 Office: E Faulkner Ch of Christ 930 E Faulkner El Dorado AR 71730 *One of the greatest contributors to human happiness is forgiveness. I can live with a few mistakes along the way but I cannot live without forgiveness. Forgiveness begins with humility and results in true charity.*

GAGE, MICHAEL LESTER, minister; b. Chico, Calif., Nov. 22, 1955; s. Lewis Charles and Dixie Lee (Dennison) G.; m. Jacqueline Rae Fish, Sept. 2, 1977; children: Aaron Mathew, Elisabeth Anne, Kathleen Marie. BSL, Ozark Christian Coll., Joplin, Mo., 1978. Ordained to ministry Christian Ch., 1976. Youth minister Cen. Christian Ch., Claremore, Okla., 1977-88; assoc. minister First Christian Ch., Lamar, Mo., 1988—; bd. dirs. FOCUS Campus Ministry, Okla. State U., Stillwater, 1981-88; treas. State Youth Conv. of Christian Chs., 1985-87. Coach Claremore Soccer Club, 1978-82. Recipient Ch. Growth award, Nat. Ch. Growth & Rsch. Ctr., 1978. Mem. Rotary (song leader 1990—). Republican. Home: Rte 1 Box 319 Lamar MO 64759 Office: First Christian Ch 1208 Walnut St Lamar MO 64759 *I believe Jesus' statement, "The greatest among you will be your servant." In our self-centered, egostistical society we must develop servant leaders who are willing to wash feet.*

GAGE, ROBERT CLIFFORD, minister; b. Beverly, Mass., Nov. 20, 1941; s. George V. and Elizabeth B. (May) G.; m. Mary Neefe, June 17, 1961; children: Joanna, Jonathan, Judith, Joshua, Joy. Student, Tenn. Temple U., 1961-62; BA, Phila. Coll. of Bible, 1964; postgrad., Ea. Bapt. Theol. Sem., 1966-67, New Sch. Soc. Rsch., 1975-76; D of Religion, Newport U., 1983. Ordained to ministry Gen. Assn. Regular Bapt. Chs., 1964. Pastor Whitehall Bapt. Ch., Phila., 1964-65, Glencroft Bapt. Ch., Glenolden, Pa., 1966-68; pastor 1st Bapt. Ch., Newfield, N.J., 1969-70, Hackensack, N.J., 1971-79; pastor Wealthy St. Bapt. Ch., Grand Rapids, Mich., 1979-88; evangelist, 1988-91; pastor Faith Bapt. Ch., Winter Haven, Fla., 1991—; radio min., 1965—. Author: The Birthmarks of the Christian Life, 1976, Our Life in Christ, 1978, The Pastor's Counseling Workbook, 1983, The PreMarriage Counseling Workbook, 1984, Discipleship Evangelism, 1985, Cultivating Spiritual Fruit, 1986, Basic Discipleship, 1987, Why Me, Lord, 1988, The Unveiling, 1990; editor Sword and Shield, 1969—; contbr. sermons to ch. publs. Home: 510 Sunny Cir Winter Haven FL 33880 Office: 2140 Crystal Beach Rd Winter Haven FL 33880 *Lord Jesus Christ, the work is Thine, not ours but Thine alone, and prospered by thy power Divine, can never be overthrown.*

GAGNE, WALTER PAUL, priest, church organization executive; b. East Providence, R.I., Aug. 18, 1944; s. Wilfred and M. Jeannette (Barrette) G. BA, St. Pius X Coll., 1967; BS in Theology, Cath. U. Am., 1970. Ordained priest Roman Cath. Ch., 1971. Assoc. pastor Ch. of Atonement, Windsor, Ont., Can., 1971-75; staff mem. Ch. of Our Saviour, Brockton, Mass., 1978-81; dir. Ch. of Our Saviour, Brockton, 1981-83; asst. dir. devel. Friars of Atonement, Garrison, N.Y., 1983-84, dir. devel., 1984—, gen. councillor, 1985-89, bd. dirs., 1985-89. Editor, author Graymoor Today monthly newsletter. Bd. dirs. Atonement Sem., Washington, 1985-89, St. Joseph's Rehab. Ctr., Saranac Lake, N.Y., 1985-89. Mem. Nat. Cath. Devel. Conf., Nat. Soc. Fund Raising Execs., Am. Mgmt. Assn., Nat. Planned Giving Inst. Alumni Assn. Democrat. Lodge: K.C. (chaplain Windsor chpt. 1974-75). Home: Graymoor Garrison NY 10524 Office: Friars of Atonement Graymoor Garrison NY 10524

GAGNON, EDOUARD CARDINAL, cardinal; b. Port Daniel, Que., Can., Jan. 15, 1918. Ordained priest Roman Catholic Ch., 1940, consecrated bishop, 1969. Bishop St. Paul, Alberta, Can., 1969-72; rector Can. Coll., Rome, 1972-77; v.p., sec. Vatican Com. for Family, 1973-80; titular archbishop of Guistiniana Prima, 1983; pro-pres. Pontifical Council for the Family, 1983-85, pres., 1985—, elevated to Sacred Coll. of Cardinals, 1985. Office: Pontifical Coun Family, Vatican City Vatican City

GAITHER, JAMES LOUIS, clergyman; b. Blocher, Ind., Nov. 6, 1931; s. Lynn Clifford and Mary Louise (Denning) G.; m. Ethel Mae Hadley, Oct. 28, 1949; children: Robert, William, Michael, Deborah, Sharon, James Louis Jr. AB, Louisville Bible Coll., 1970. Ordained to ministry Christian Ch., 1964. Minister Christian Ch., Rosiclare, Ill., 1965-69, Little York, Ind., 1969-71; promotional dir. Capstan Inc., Checotah, Okla., 1971-74; missionary CLAD, Guayaquil, Ecuador, 1974-83; minister Christian Ch., Hixson, Tenn., 1985—; pres. Am. Soc., Guayaquil, 1974-75, Am. Sch., Guayaquil, 1975-78; pres. Ministerial Alliance, Athens, Tenn., 1989-90; bd. pres. Family Life and Counseling, Knoxville, Tenn., 1990—. With USAF, 1951-55. Mem. Sale Creek 280 (chaplain 1990-91), Tellico 80. Republican. Office: North River Christian Ch 1675 Shelby Circle Hixson TN 37343 *Life is great if lived one day at a time and our eyes upon the return of our Lord. Maybe it will be today and then my tomorrow will become eternity with my precious Saviour.*

GAITHER, LEWIS JOE, religious organization administrator; b. Stillwater, Okla., Mar. 1, 1948; s. Patrick Joe and Thelma Alberta (Ishmael) G.; m. Nancy Barbara Hamilton, May 19, 1972; children: P. Josanna, Jinon N., Josiah I., Jahna P., N. Jenia, Jeremiah J., Juriah K. Student, Dallas Bible Coll., 1966-68; BA, U. North Tex., 1972; MA in Bibl. Studies, Dallas Sem., 1989; postgrad., CEF Leadership Inst., Warrenton, Mo., 1989. Dir. Child Evangelism Fellowship of East Tex.-Tarrant Chpt., Ft. Worth, 1989—. Home: Rte 2 Box 145 2075 Ottinger Rd Roanoke TX 76262 Office: CEF of East Tex Tarrant County Chpt 2075 Ottinger Rd Roanoke TX 76262 *Ministry to a child is the greatest service and hope of mankind, dealing with humanity's deepest terror, facing choices with the largest wisdom and love, and depending upon the most unobserved of all possibilities—the Grace and Spirit of God and His Word, the Lord Jesus Christ.*

GALAT, EUGENE R., religious organization administrator. Gen. sec. Apostolic Christian Ch. (Nazarene), Tremont, Ill. Office: Apostolic Christian Ch PO Box 151 Tremont IL 61568*

GALATI, MICHAEL BERNARD, lay church worker; b. Chgo., Sept. 4, 1931; s. Anthony Kenneth and Ingeborg Marie (Flugum) G.; m. Mary Jeanne Kelsey, Apr. 19, 1952; children: Anna Marie Galati Logsdon,

Anthony K., Peter M., Joseph S. BS in Edn., No. Ill. U., 1953, MS, 1956, EdD, 1985. Mem. bd. Christian social concerns Rock River Conf., United Meth. Ch., 1965-67, mem. coun. ministries No. Ill. Conf., 1971-76, 83—, vice chmn. Aurora dist. coun. ministries, 1974-76; chmn. dept. lang. arts and social scis., dir. student teaching program Lemont (Ill.) Twp. High Sch., 1956-81, head humanities div., 1981—; sr. editor Lemont Met., 1982—. Author: Love Me a Village; contbr. poems and articles to mags. and jours. Trustee Village of Lemont, 1963-69. Recipient Valley Forge Tchr. medal, 1971, Rosicrucian Humanitarian award, 1973. Mem. ASCD, Speech Communication Assn., Nat. Coun. Tchrs. English, Ill. Assn. Tchrs. English, Ill. Speech and Theatre Assn. Democrat. Home: 21 Norton Ave Lemont IL 60439 Office: 800 Porter St Lemont IL 60439 *In doing the work of the Kingdom, love and faith and caring have an efficacy that legal force and political power and the gaining of prestigious positions cannot ever equal. This applies to work done in the world as well as to work done within the church.*

GALAZKA, HELEN GORDON MACROBERT, minister, psychotherapist; b. Paisley, Scotland, June 8, 1915; came to U.S., 1953; d. John and Helen (Cunningham) MacRobert; m. Michal Galazka, Sept. 9, 1941 (dec. 1972); 1 child, Michal J. M. MA, Glasgow (Scotland) U., 1935; BD, Trinity Coll., Scotland, 1938; D. Ministry, Andover Newton, 1974. Ordained to ministry Presbyn. Ch., 1940. Pastor Montrose and Kilmarnock U.F. Chs., Scotland, 1940-53, Conant Meml. Ch., Dudley, Mass., 1953-60, 1st Ch., Glenwood, Iowa, 1960-61; exec. Mpls. Coun. of Chs., 1961-69; pastor First Ch., Ludlow, Mass., 1969-81; interim pastor Three Rivers, Mass.; psychotherapist dept. psychiatry Baystate Med. Ctr., Springfield, Mass., 1974—; mem. pastoral care dept., mem. grief com. Baystate Med. Ctr., Springfield, 1978. Contbr. articles to profl. jours. Named Woman of Achievement Women's Profl. Club, 1980, Outstanding Citizen Channel 22, 1984. Mem. Mass. Psychology Assn., Am. Assn. Marriage & Family Therapy (clin.), Women Writers Assn., Beta Sigma Phi. Home: 769 Allen St Springfield MA 01118 Office: Baystate Med Ctr 140 High St Springfield MA 01105 *I have witnessed great change in technology, morality, life styles: one thing remains unchanging, my faith in a benevolent God who will not let me down.*

GALE, FOREST MCCLURE, JR., minister; b. Morganton, NC, Mar. 20, 1940; s. Forest McClure and Marilyn Blanch (Morrow) G.; m. Linda Ann Smith, Oct. 21, 1968 (div. 1981); married, 1981; 1 child, Lewis McClure. BA in History, Frances Marion Coll., 1973; MDiv, Souteastern Bapt. Sem., 1977, ThM, 1990. Ordained to ministry So. Bapt. Conv. Interim pastor Liberty Bapt. Ch., Lake City, S.C., 1972-73; pastor Maple Springs Bapt. Ch., Louisburg, N.C., 1973-77, Stovale (N.C.) Bapt. Ch., 1977-79, Edgemont Bapt. Ch., Durham, N.C., 1982-91; int. dir. quality Nello L. Teer Co., Durham, 1991—. Chmn. United Way, Durham, 1990; recruiter Red Cross Blood Donor Program, 1986-89; pres. N. Granville EMT Svc., Stovall, 1978-79 (Outstanding Svc. award 1979); mem. North Granville Vol. Fire Dept., Stovall, 1963-66. Recipient Ch. of Yr. award Yates Bar Assn., Durham, 1987. Fellow Durham Mins. Assn. (sec., v.p., pres. 1983-86); mem. Franklin County Mins. Assn. (sec. 1977), Flat River Mins. Assn. (pres. 1979), Yates Bapt. Mins. Assn. (v.p. 1989-90). Democrat. Home: 911 Ferncrest Dr Durham NC 27705 Office: Nello L Teer Co 211 Parrish St Durham NC 27701

GALINDO, ISRAEL, school administrator, chaplain; b. Santiago, Cuba, Sept. 20, 1954; came to U.S., 1959; s. Samuel and Clara Luz (Fonseca) G.; m. Barbara Anne Kalin, July 8, 1978; children: Douglas David, Thomas Samuel. BA, Northeastern U., 1977; M Religious Edn., New Orleans Sem., 1979, MDiv, 1983, EdD, 1987. Ordained minister Bapt. Ch. Mgr. McMahon-Coburn-Briede, New Orleans, 1978-87; instr. New Orleans Bapt. Theol. Sem., 1980-86; adminstr. Horeb Christian Sch., Miami, Fla., 1988—; instr. ethnic edn. br. New Orleans Bapt. Theol. Sem., Miami, Fla., 1990; chaplain Hospice, Inc., Broward; cons. Assisteam, New Orleans, 1983-87. Contbr. articles to profl. publs. Tutor Laubach Literacy Internat., New Orleans, 1987—; mem. New Orleans Hispanic Action Com., 1978-87. Fellow New Orleans Bapt. Theol. Sem., 1985-87; recipient Excellence in Adminstrn. award Horeb Sch. Tchrs. Assn., 1988. Mem. Fla. Assn. Christian Colls. and Schs. (assoc.), Am. Assn. Family Counselors, Am. Assn. Christian Counselors. Avocations: writing, jogging, ancient coins, photography. *Processs is more important than content. True Christian vocation is answering the call of God to live a redemptive lifestyle and joining Him in His continuing acts of creation and redemption.*

GALITZ, ROBERT FREDERICK, minister, real estate professional; b. Chgo., May 24, 1931; s. Raymond Frederick and Edna M. (Poltrock) G.; m. Ramona Austin, June 27, 1955; children: Deborah Galitz Cosgrove, Rebecca Galitz Calder, Robert Austin. BA, Grinnell Coll., 1953; BD, U. Chgo., Chgo. Theol. Sem., 1956; MA, Western Mich U., 1966; postgrad., Garrett Biblical Inst., 1959. Ordained to ministry United Ch. of Christ, 1956. Minister Denmark (Iowa) Congl. Ch., 1956-60; assoc. minister First Congl. Ch., Kalamazoo, Mich., 1960-66; minister First Congl. United Ch. of Christ, Waukesha, Wis., 1966-86, St. John United Ch. of Christ, Germantown, Wis., 1986-88, First Congl. United Ch. of Christ, Rochester, Wis., 1989-90, Our Saviour's United Ch. of Christ, Germantown, 1990—; real estate broker First Realty Better Homes & Gardens, Waukesha, 1987—; chmn. bd. dirs. Wis. Conf. United Ch. of Christ, 1979-86; bd. dirs. Wis. Conf. of Chs., Madison, 1986-91. Dir. Waukesha Tng. Ctr., 1990—; mem. Waukesha Bd. Zoning Appeals, 1985—. Mem. Waukesha County Bd. Realtors, Residential Sales Coun., Rotary (pres. Waukesha club 1978-79, nominee dist. gov. 1992-93). Avocations: travel, photography, gardening. Home: 2228 Broken Hill Rd Waukesha WI 53188-1551

GALL, DONALD ARTHUR, minister; b. Edgely, N.D., Apr. 30, 1936; s. Arthur Fred and Luella Sara (Weidenbach) G.; m. Shirley Ann Stevenson, Aug. 19, 1956 (div. Aug. 1972); children: Deborah Sue, Craig Donald, Matthew Allan; m. Patricia E. deJong, Dec. 29, 1984. BA, Yankton Coll., 1958; MDiv., MA in Religious Edn., Hartford Sem., 1962; D in Ministry, Eden Theol. Sem., 1983. Ordained to ministry United Ch. of Christ. Pastor 1st Congl. Ch., Whiting, Iowa, 1962-65; assoc. conf. minister Nebr. Conf. United Ch. Christ, Lincoln, 1965-70; dir. leadership devel. Presbyns. Associated for Common Tasks, Eugene, Oreg., 1970-72; assoc. min. 1st Congrl. Ch. United Ch. Christ, Eugene, 1972-75; assoc. conf. minister Fla. Conf. United Ch. Christ, Miami, 1975-79; program exec. Bd. Homeland Ministry, N.Y.C., 1979-86; conf. minister Iowa Conf. United Ch. Christ, Des Moines, 1986—; bd. dirs. Iowa Interch. Forum, Des Moines; pres. Iowa Conf. United Chs. Christ Inc., Des Moines, 1986—; chairperson Agy. for Peace and Justice, Des Moines, 1988-91; trustee United Theol. Sem., New Brighton, Minn., 1991—. Author: THe Eleventh Hour, 1979; also articles. Bd. dirs. Mayflower Homes Inc., Grinnell, Iowa, 1986—; pres. Emergency Family Shelter House, Eugene, Oreg., 1972-74, Fla. IMPACT, Tallahassee, 1977-79; vol. Oreg. Dem. Campaign, 1974. Named a Community Leader of Am., Community Leaders of Am., Inc., 1968. Avocations: writing, skiing, golfing, wood working. Home: 7023 Oakbrook Dr Des Moines IA 50322 Office: Iowa Conf United Ch Christ 600 42d St Des Moines IA 50312

GALL, EUGENE HARVEY, minister; b. Holyoke, Colo., Apr. 10, 1946; s. Harvey Wesley and Fern Louise (Spader) G.; m. Deborah Ebel Hartman, Nov. 26, 1974; children: Seth, Kate. BA, UCLA, 1968; MA in Religion, Yale U., 1970; MA, London Sch. Econs., 1971; MDiv cum laude, Harvard U., 1976; D Ministry, Princeton Theol. Sem., 1990. Ordained to ministry Meth. Ch., 1977. Dir. chaplaincy svc. Southwester Mental Health, Luverne, Minn., 1977-83; dir. pastoral care, counseling Meml. Hosp., Cumberland, Md., 1983—; bd. dirs. Search Inst., Mpls.; sec. Mid-Atlantic Assn. for Clin. Pastoral Edn., 1988-89. Pres. Allegany County (Md.) Mental Health Adv. Com., 1988-90. Fellow Coll. Chaplains; mem. Assn. for Clin. Pastoral Edn. (supr.). Democrat. Home: 708 Dale Ave Cumberland MD 21502 Office: Memorial Hosp Memorial Ave Cumberland MD 21502

GALL, ROBERT STEPHEN, philosophy educator; b. L.A., Jan. 13, 1958; s. John Stephen and Dorothy Grace (Wyka) G. BA cum laude, U. Pa., 1978; MA, Temple U., 1980, PhD with distinction, 1984. Asst. prof. philosophy Sinclair Community Coll., Dayton, Ohio, 1988—; presenter in field. Author: Beyond Theism and Atheism, 1987; contbr. articles to profl. jours. Univ. fellow Temple Univ. Mem. Am. Acad. Religion, Ohio Acad. Religion, Am. Philos. Assn., Soc. for Phenomenology and Existential Philosophy, Internat. Assn. for Philosophy & Lit.

GALLAGHER, ANNETTE, nun, educator, librarian; b. Bevington, Iowa, Nov. 10, 1924; d. Thomas Francis and Mary Laura (Lickteig) G. A.A., Ottumwa Heights Coll., 1943; B.A., Marycrest Coll., 1948; M.A., Cath. U. Am., 1950; Ph.D., U. Ariz., 1970; M.A., U. Wis.-Madison, 1980. Joined Congregation of Sisters of Humility of Mary, Roman Cath. Ch., 1943. Tchr. St. Joseph Sch., Dunlap, Iowa, 1945-46; faculty Marycrest Coll., Davenport, Iowa, 1950—, reference librarian, 1973—. Bd. dirs. New Horizons of Faith, 1975—, Iowa Cath. Conf., 1986-89, Humility of Mary Shelter, Inc., 1991—. Office: Teikyo Marycrest U 1607 W 12th St Davenport IA 52804-4096

GALLAGHER, JOHN CLARENCE, priest; b. Yorkton, Sask., Can., Jan. 2, 1934; s. Fergal Aloysius and Mary Alberta (O'Toole) G. BA, U. Toronto, Ont., Can., 1955, MA, 1960; STB, U. of St. Michael's Coll., Toronto, 1960; STL, Angelicum, Rome, 1965; STD, Alphonsian Acad., Rome, 1967. Ordained priest Roman Cath. Ch., 1960. Tchr. Assumption High Sch., Windsor, Ont., Can., 1955-56, Aquinas Inst., Rochester, N.Y., 1957-58; lectr. St. Thomas More Coll., U. Sask., 1961-63; asst. prof. moral theology Faculty Theology, U. of St. Michael's Coll., Toronto, 1967-71, assoc. prof. moral theology, 1971-78; assoc. prof. moral theology St. Joseph's Coll., U. Alta., 1978-82; assoc. prof. moral theology U. St. Thomas, Houston, 1987-89, dean Sch. Theology, 1988-89; dir. Cardinal Carter Ctr. for Bioethics, Toronto, 1982-86; superior gen. Congregation of St. Basil, Milton, Ont., Can., 1989—; mem. task force to draft statement on conscience Can. Cath. Conf. Bishops, 1973; cons. on ethics Met. Toronto Cath. Children's Aid Soc., 1972-78; cons. on med. ethics. St. Michael's Hosp., St. Joseph's Hosp., Toronto, 1974-78; cons. to draft statement on basic Christian Moral Teaching Theology Com. of Can. Cath. Conf. Bishops, 1981-83; mem. task force to draft statement on abortion Ont. Cath. Conf. Bishops, 1982-83. Author: The Basis for Christian Ethics, 1985; co-author: A Handbook on Catholic Moral Questions, 1979; contbr. articles to religious jours. Mem. Can. Religious Conf., Soc. Christian Ethics, Unione Superiori Genarali. Home and Office: Basilwood, 15th Side Rd, Milton, ON Canada L9T 2X7

GALLAGHER, JOHN PATRICK, priest, historian, educator; b. Scranton, Pa., July 10, 1924; s. Michael J. and Beatrice (Peyton) G. AA, St. Charles Coll., Catonsville, Md., 1944; BA, U. Western Ont., London, Can., 1946; MA, Cath. U. Am., 1961, PhD in History, 1964. Ordained priest Roman Cath. Ch., 1951. Pastor St. David's Parish, Scranton, 1970-73, Holy Rosary Parish, Scranton, 1973-86, Christ the King Parish, Dunmore, Pa., 1986—; prof. history St. Pius X Sem., Dalton, Pa., 1962-73; historian Diocese of Scranton, 1964—; professorial lectr. U. Scranton, 1967-73, lectr. history Marywood Coll., Scranton, 1968-70; mem. bd. edn. Diocese of Scranton, 1976-79, pres., 1978-79; pres., exec. bd. Bishops Hannan and Klonowski High Sch., 1973-83; pres., bd. pastors West Cath. High Sch., Scranton, 1971-73, Bishop Hannan High Sch., Scranton, 1975-77. Author: Scranton, Labor and Politics, 1961, Scranton, Industry and Politics, 1964, A Century of History: The Diocese of Scranton, 1968; assoc. editor The Cath. Light, 1967-84; contbr. numerous articles to profl. jours. Bd. dirs. Scranton Pub. Libr., 1976-84, pres. bd., 1982-84. Named Reverend Monsignor Pope Paul VI, 1976. Mem. Am. Hist. Assn., Am. Ch. History Assn., Am. Cath. Hist. Assn., Am. Cath. Hist. Soc. Phila. (contbr. Dimension: A Jour. of Pastoral Concern), Lackawanna Hist. Soc., St. Peter's Alumni Assn. of London (Can.). Home: 1214 Quincy Ave Dunmore PA 18510-1182 Office: Diocese of Scranton 300 Wyoming Ave Scranton PA 18503-1279

GALLAGHER, MARY KEVIN, nun, chancellor; b. Chgo., June 1, 1926; d. James and Nellie (Boyle) G. BA, Clarke Coll., 1954; MA, Marquette U., 1963. Joined Sisters of Charity, Roman Cath. Ch.; cert. tchr., Iowa. Regional rep. Sister of Charity Blessed Virgin Mary, Dubuque, Iowa, 1968-72, v.p., 1972-76, corp. sec., 1976-80; pastoral min. St. Raphael Cathedral, Dubuque, 1981-87; chancellor, fin. commn., cabinet Archdiocese of Dubuque, 1987—; bd. dirs. Archdiocese of Dubuque (Iowa) Corp., 1987—. Editor: (history book) Seed/Harvest, 1987. Mem. Dubuque Hist. Soc., Friends of the Libr. (Dubuque). Office: Archdiocese of Dubuque 1229 Mt Loretta PO Box 479 Dubuque IA 52004-0479

GALLAGHER, THOMAS GEORGE, priest; b. N.Y.C., Jan. 20, 1941; s. Thomas John and Emma Theresa (Halek) G. BA, St. Pius X Coll., 1964; MTh, St. John Vianney Sem., 1968; MA in Edn., profl. diploma in edn., St. John's U., 1973. Ordained priest Roman Cath. Ch., 1968. Asst. pastor St. Francis Ch., Wantagh, N.Y., 1968-70; assoc. supt. schs. Diocese of Rockville Centre, N.Y., 1970-75, supt., 1975-79; rep. Cath. schs. U.S. Cath. Conf., Washington, 1979-80, sec. edn., 1980-90; assoc. pastor Sacred Heart Ch., North Merrick, N.Y., 1990—; adv. commr. Edn. Commn. of States. Monthly columnist The Catechist, 1980-90; chmn. editorial bd. The Living Light, 1980-90; contbr. articles to profl. jours. Mem. Coun. Am. Pvt. Edn. (bd. dirs.), Am. Assn. Sch. Adminstrs. (del. 1984), Nat. Cath. Edn. Assn. (bd. dirs.), Phi Delta Kappa. Home: Sacred Heart Rectory 1921 Old Mill Rd North Merrick NY 11566

GALLARDO GARCIA, RAFAEL, bishop; b. Yuriria, Mex., Oct. 8, 1927. Ordained priest Roman Cath. Ch. 1950; consecrated bishop. Named bishop of Linares Mex., 1974. Address: Obispado Apartado 70, CP 67700 Linares Nuevo Leon, Mexico

GALLEGOS, ALPHONSE, bishop; b. Albuquerque, Feb. 20, 1931; s. Jose Angel and Caseana (Apodaca) G. B.S., St. Thomas Aquinas Coll., 1971; M.S., St. John's U., Jamaica, N.Y., 1972; M.E., Loyola U., Los Angeles, 1979. Ordained priest Roman Catholic Ch., 1958. Pastor San Miguel Ch., Los Angeles, Our Lady of Guadalupe Ch., Sacramento; vicar Hispanics in Sacramento area; first hispanic bishop Sacramento; Aux. bishop of Sacramento, 1981—; pastor Guadalupe Ch., Sacramento; Vicar gen. Roman Catholic Ch., Sacramento, vicar for Hispanics; active campaign for human devel. U.S. Catholic Conf., Washington. Mem. Calif. Govs. Com.; bd. dirs. Sacramento Concilio, Boy Scouts Am.; mem. Sacramento Mayor's Hispanic Adv. Com., County of Sacramento Multi-Cultural Park Com.; mem. adv. bd. Calif. Hispanic Cath. Inst.; mem. supt. of edn.'s adv. council on Hispanic affairs State of Calif. Recipient Silver Beaver award. Home: 1119 K St Sacramento CA 95808 Office: PO Box 1706 Sacramento CA 95808

GALLEGOS, MICHEL ROSE, religious education director; b. Aberdeen, Wash., Sept. 13, 1944; d. Francis and Rosemary (Provo) Gibbons; m. Jose Ramon Gallegos, Feb. 16, 1974; children: Monica, Maria Elena, Miquela. BA, U. Wash., 1973. Cert. elem. sch. tchr. (K-12), Wash. Dir. religion edn. Holy Innocents Cath. Ch., Duvall, Wash., 1985—; tech. writer Banners Ink, Carnation, Wash., 1988—. Author: Colorado is a Far Piece, 1989; contbr. articles to mags. Leader 4-H, Woodinville, Wash., 1988—. Mem. St. Mary's Alumnae Assn. (pres. 1981-87). Home: 11233 320th NE Carnation WA 98014 *No matter how difficult life seems at times, three little words keep me up and going: "God will provide." And He always does.*

GALLIAN, LESLIE JANE, youth services administrator; b. Charleston, W.Va., Sept. 30, 1964; d. Darrell Edward Carr and Mary Lou (Knight) Lucas; m. L. David Gallian, Jr., Dec. 27, 1986. BS, U. Charleston, 1986, postgrad., 1990-92. Parish-wide youth coord. West Side Coop. United Meth. Parish, Charleston, W.Va., 1989—; temporary Manpower Temps., Charleston, 1991—. Home: 3815 Virginia Ave SE Charleston WV 25304-1507

GALLOWAY, ERNESTINE ROYAL, religious administrator; b. Newark, May 7, 1928; d. Seymour Page Galloway and Ethel (Bishop) Bigham. BA, NYU, 1957, MA, 1960; MA, NYU, 1969, EdD, 1981. Dir. edn. Concord Baptist Ch., Bklyn., 1956-60; social worker Westminster Neighborhood Assn., Los Angeles, 1962-64; field coordinator Newark Pre-Sch. Council, 1965-67, social service coordinator, 1967-69; N.Y. regional dir. Student YWCA, N.Y.C., 1970-72, co-dir., 1972-74; instr. Seton Hall U., South Orange, N.J., 1976-78; mgr. Nat. Ministries/Am. Bapt. Chs. in the U.S.A., Valley Forge, Pa., 1978—. Fellow Am. Anthropology Assn., Soc. for Intercultural Edn., Tng., and Research. Baptist. Avocations: piano, organ, singing, sewing. Home: 25 Warman St Montclair NJ 07042 Office: Nat Ministries/ABUSCA PO Box 851 Valley Forge PA 19482-0851

GALLOWAY, ROBERT GENE, minister, educator; b. East St. Louis, Ill., Aug. 10, 1949; s. Samuel Scott and June Evelyn (Powell) G. BS in Agr., So. Ill. U., 1971, postgrad., 1972-74; cert. pastoral studies, Sts. Cyril and Methodius Sem., Orchard Lake, Mich., 1979; MA in Counseling, U. No. Iowa, 1985. Lic. to ministry Universal Fellowship Met. Community Ch., 1979, ordained, 1989. Asst. camp dir. Little Grassy United Meth. Camp, Makanda, Ill., 1971-74; camp mgr., dir. Detroit Conf. of United Meth. Ch., 1974-77; acting dir. recreation ctr. City of Pontiac, Mich., 1978; interim pastor Met. Community Ch., Detroit, 1979; pastor Met. Community Ch., Knoxville, Tenn., 1985—, Ch. New Hope Met. Community, Waterloo, Iowa, 1980-85; mem. extension faculty Samaritan Coll., L.A., 1990—. d. dirs. Cedar Valley Food Bank, Waterloo, 1983-85; founder, bd. dirs. AIDS Response Knoxville, 1985; mem. Bread for World, Knoxville, 1985—. Recipient Pub. Citizen of Yr. award Knox Area chpt. NASW, 1986, Svc. to Gay and Lesbian Community award Knoxville's Ten Percent, 1986, Religious Svc. award NCCJ, 1989, Community Leadership Knoxville award Knox County Community Action Com., 1989. Mem. Knoxville Ministerial Assn. (sec. 1990—). Avocations: hiking, reading, studying Celtic christianity. Office: Met Community Ch 1316 Central Ave Knoxville TN 37917

GALT, ROBERT THOMAS, minister; b. Champaign, Ill., Nov. 1, 1953; s. Robert Allen and Susan Claire (Davidson) G.; m. LaVon Kathleen Donley, June 16, 1973; children: Phillip Andrew, Kathleen Elizabeth. ThM, Internat. Bible Inst., Plymouth, Fla., 1986. Ordained to ministry Am. Bapt. Assn., 1973. Pastor Faith Christian Ctr., Monticello, Ill., 1979-87, 1st Bapt. ch., Cambria, Ill., 1988-89, Fairview Christian Ch., Murphysboro, Ill., 1990—. Bd. dirs. Nat. Fedn. Ind. Bus., Springfield, Ill., 1986; pres. Mental Health Assn. Ill., Monticello, 1986-87, bd. dirs., 1987. Mem. Kiwanis (pres. Monticello club 1987). Home: PO Box 2502 Carbondale IL 62902 Office: Fairview Christian Ch Rte 1 Murphysboro IL 62966

GALUSZKA, MARY HELENE, religious and financial analyst; b. Chgo., Aug. 19, 1945; d. Jospeh Frank and Adeline Frances (Les) G. BS, Coll. of St. Francis, Joliet, Ill., 1969; MS, St. Mary's Coll., 1974; MBA, St. Louis U., 1986. Cert. tchr., Ill.; lic. nursing home adminstr., Ill. Elementary tchr., asst. prin. Franciscan Sisters of Chgo., 1966-74; tchr. Madonna High Sch., Chgo., 1974-84; dir. fiscal services, mem. planning com. Franciscan Sisters of Chgo. Home Office, 1986-89, treas. gen., 1989—; research sponser Ill. Jr. Acad. Sci., Chgo., 1967-84; instr. City Colls. of Chgo., 1983-84; dir. sec. bd. Madonna High Sch., Inc., Chgo., 1980-86, dept. chmn., 1982-84; dir. sec. bd. St. Joseph Home, Inc., Chgo., 1984—. NSF grantee, 1970-74; Diedrich scholar St. Louis U., 1984-85. Mem. Healthcare Fin. Mgmt. Assn. Avocation: needlework. Home and Office: Franciscan Sisters of Chgo 1220 Main St Lemont IL 60439

GALVIN, MARY ELEANOR, pastoral care director, administrator; b. Malden, Mass., Dec. 3, 1926; d. Joseph Edward and Mary D. (Downing) G. BS in Edn., St. Mary-of-the-Woods Coll., 1962; MA, St. Michael's Coll., 1970, Emmanuel Coll., 1985. Cert. elem. sch. prin., secondary/jr. high sch. prin., guidance counselor; cert. tchr. secondary English, history, social studies, gen. sci. Prin. Lady Isle Sch., Portsmouth, N.H., St. Clement Sch., Lansdowne, Md., Cheverus Centennial Sch., Malden; asst. adminstr. of health care Sisters of Providence, St. Mary-of-the-Woods, Ind. Mem. production com., editorial bd., photographer for A Journey in Love, Mercy and Justice (pictorial history of Sisters of Providence). Address: Owens Hall Saint Mary-of-the-Woods IN 47876

GAMADES, SISTER ALEXANDRA, religious organization administrator; b. St. Paul, Mar. 21, 1930; d. John and Lucetta Elizabeth (Lehmeier) G. BA in Foods and Nutrition, Cardinal Stritch Coll., Milw., 1972; MA in Religious Studies, Gonzaga U., 1981. Joined Franciscan Sisters Order, Roman Cath. Ch., 1948. Intern St. Paul Ramsey Hosp., St. Paul, 1973; founder, dir. Ecumenical Day Renewal Ctr., Spiritual Journey Ministries, Waite Park, Minn., 1985-89; dir. Spiritual Journey Ministries, St. Cloud, Minn., 1989—. Mem. Christian Ministerial Assn., Franciscan Sisters of Little Falls, Minn. Office: Spiritual Journey Ministries 316-1/2 N 7th Ave Saint Cloud MN 56303-1931 *Within each person are untapped resources of goodness, energy, and talents that are waiting to be discovered and brought forth. Each of us has the privilege of being an instrument in assisting another to be their most beautiful and talented self.*

GAMBLE, DENNIS BRUCE, I, minister, evangelist, recording production specialist; b. Memphis, Oct. 17, 1956; s. Vernice Sr. and Helen Florine (Jones) G.; m. Cynthia Taylor, Oct. 30, 1982; children: Denesia Sharde, Dennis Bruce II. Student, U. Ark., 1974-75; AS, Southwestern Christian Coll., 1976; BA, David Lipscomb Coll., 1978; postgrad., Ala. Christian Sch. of Religion, 1983-84, Internat. Bible Inst. and Sem., 1987-88, Liberty U., 1990—. Asst. minister Ch. of Christ, North Little Rock, 1975-76; stacker Baird-Ward Pub. Co., Nashville, 1978; cashier Super-X Drugs, Nashville, 1978; salesperson Radio Shack/Tandy Corp., Nashville, 1978-81; minister Ch. of Christ, Cookeville, Tenn., 1976-80; minister/evangelist Ch. of Christ, Chattanooga, 1981-88; audio cons., rec. specialist Gamble Prodns., Chattanooga, 1976-88; min., evangelist, ministry dir. Ch. of Christ, Pontiac, Mich., 1988—; asst. chmn. steering com. Tenn. Youth Conf., 1986-88; Tenn. committeeman Southeastern Lectureship Com., 1985; committeeman Tenn. Lectureship Com., 1981-88, Mich. Lectureship, 1988—, co-host min., 1989; mem. bd. Mins. Adv. Coun. Boyd-Buchannan Sch., Chattanooga, 1987-88; subs. tchr. Chattanooga Pub. Schs., 1987-88; seminar conductor family workshop, 1988—; seminar specialist youth workshop/rally, 1975—; revival crusade speaker convention/lectureship, 1975—; coord. vendors Nat. Crusade for Christ, 1990—. Nat. chaplain Nat. Shooting Stars Citizen Band Radio Club, Atlanta, Chattanooga, 1985-88; local chaplain, 1985-88, Pontiac, 1988—; chaplain Circle-K Club Southwestern Christian Coll., Terrell, Tex., 1975-76; committeeman Mich. Lectureship Com., 1989—; asst. chmn. Concerned Bros. Fellowship Breakfast of Metro Detroit Chs. of Christ, 1989-91. Named one of Outstanding Young Men of Am., 1985. Democrat. Avocations: fishing, basketball, biking, bowling, communications-electronics. Home: 77 Oak Creek Ln Pontiac MI 48340 Office: Ch of Christ 149 Martin Luther King Jr Blvd North Pontiac MI 48342

GAMBLE, RICHARD CRAIG, theology educator; b. Pitts., Jan. 12, 1955; s. Richard J. and Bettyjean (Newcomer) G.; m. Janice A. Gregory, Nov. 26, 1977; children: Lindsey, Liesl, Whitney, Hilary. BA, Westminster (Pa.) Coll., 1976; MA magna cum laude, Pitts. Theol. Sem., 1978; ThD magna cum laude, Universität Basel, Basel, Switzerland, 1983. Asst. prof. Westminster Theol. Sem., Phila., 1980-83, assoc. prof., 1983-87; assoc. prof. Calvin Theol. Sem., Grand Rapids, Mich., 1978-89, prof. hist. theology, 1989—; lectr. Freie Evangelisch-Theol. Akademi, Basel, 1979-80; adj. prof. Geneva Coll., Beaver Falls, Pa., 1982-87; dir. H. Henry Meeter Ctr. for Calvin Studies, Grand Rapids, 1987—. Home: 2111 Jefferson SE Grand Rapids MI 49507 Office: H Henry Meeter Ctr for Calvin Studies 3233 Burton SE Grand Rapids MI 49546

GAMMON, JAMES EDWIN, SR., clergyman; b. San Diego, Jan. 23, 1944; s. Jack Albert and Thalia Gammon; BA, Tex. Christian U., 1970, postgrad., 1970-72; m. Sharon Elaine Head, June 27, 1965; children: John Paul, James Edwin, Jeffrey David. Ordained to ministry Ch. of Christ, 1966; minister Carter Park Ch., Ft. Worth, 1966-69, Scotland Hills Ch., Ft. Worth, 1969-70, Northside Ch., Dallas, 1970-73, Central Ave Ch., Valdosta, Ga., 1973-78; debate coach Christian Coll. S.W., Dallas, 1971-73; pres. So. Bible Inst., Valdosta, 1977-78; minister Trinity Oaks Ch. of Christ, Dallas., 1978-80, Parkview Ch. of Christ, Sherman, Tex., 1980-85; pres. Texoma Bible Inst., 1980-85; minister Eisenhower Ch. of Christ, Odessa, Tex., 1985-86; minister, Cen. Ch. of Christ, McMinnville, Tenn., 1986—. Author: Notes on the Acts, 1983, Notes on I, II Corinthians, 1984, Thessalonians, 1985, Notes on James, 1985, Notes on Romans, 1988, Notes on the Beatitudes, 1989. With U.S. Army, 1963-66. Republican. Home: 203 S Arrowhead Dr McMinnville TN 37110 Office: Court Sq Box 536 McMinnville TN 37110

GAMMON, WILLIAM CLARENCE, clergyman; b. Williamsburg, Va., Nov. 12, 1955; s. William Johnson and Jessie (Horsman) G.; m. Lucia Elwood, June 22, 1985. AS, Bluefield Coll., 1977, BA in History, 1979, BA in Religion Philosophy, 1979; MDiv in Religious Edn., So. Sem., 1984. Ordained to ministry Bapt. Ch. Missionary Fgn. Mission Bd. So. Bapt. Ch., Botswana, Africa, 1979-81; minister edn. Olney (Ill.) So. Bapt. Ch., 1983-85; Vacation Bible Sch. dir. Fla. Bapt. Assn., Tallahassee, 1985—; minister edn. Faith Bapt. Ch., Tallahassee, 1985—; youth specialist Fla. Bapt. Assn., Tallahassee, 1985—; spl. worker Fla. Bapt. Conv., 1985—; v.p. Sch. Christian Edn., So. Sem., Louisville, 1984. Author curriculum religous tng., schs.,

Botswana, 1980. Bd. dirs. Echo, Tallahassee, 1988—. Home: 133 Dawn Lauren Ln Tallahassee FL 32301 Office: Faith Bapt Ch 3333 Apalachee Pkwy Tallahassee FL 32311

GAMWELL, FRANKLIN I., dean, educator; married; 2 children. BA in Econs., Yale U., 1959; BD, Union Theol. Sem., 1963; MA, Div. Sch., U. Chgo., 1970, PhD, 1973. Ordained to ministry Presbyn. Ch., 1963. Pastor Ch. of the Holy Trinity of West Side Christian Parish, Chgo., 1963-66; program assoc. Rockefeller Family Philanthropic Office, N.Y.C., 1975-79; research assoc. (instr.) Div. Sch. of U. Chgo., 1971-73; asst. prof. of religion Manhattanville Coll., Purchase, N.Y., 1973-75; research affiliate Yale U. Inst. for Social and Policy Studies, New Haven, 1979; asst. prof. Div. Sch., U. Chgo., 1979-80, assoc. prof. and dean, 1980-86, prof. and dean, 1986-90, prof., 1990—. Author: Beyond Preference: Liberal Theories of Independent Associations, 1984, The Divine Good: Modern Moral Theory and the Necessity of God, 1990; co-editor: Existence and Actuality: Conversations with Charles Hartshorne, 1984, Economic Life: Process Interpretations and Critical Responses, 1988; contbr. articles and revs. to religious jours. Home: 5515 S Woodlawn Ave Chicago IL 60637 Office: U Chgo Div Sch 1025 E 58th St Chicago IL 60637

GANDOLFO, LUCIAN JOHN, minister, federal official; b. Chgo., Aug. 28, 1954; s. Michael and Elda (Campi) G.; m. Lisa Mary Thornton, Aug. 24, 1985; children: Landon, Lindsay, Lauren. AA, John Jay Coll. Criminal Justice City N.Y., 1979; AS, SUNY, Albany, 1978; BS, SUNY, Briarcliff Manor, 1980; MS, L.I. U., 1982. Spl. agt. FBI, N.Y.C., 1984—; pres. ea. dist. Christ Crusaders, Christian Ch. N.Am., 1989—; min. of the Gospel, asst. pastor Italian Christian Ch., Astoria, N.Y., 1991—. *The greatest accomplishment in one's life is to be found in right relationship with his Creator. The Greatest honor and fulfillment a person can ever experience is to receive and obey the call of God in his (her) life.*

GANEFF, JOHN JOSEPH, lay worker, security guard; b. Lehigh, Iowa, Mar. 1, 1942; s. John Beeh and Velma Isabel (Nibel) G.; divorced; children: John Gregory, Peter William. BA, Simpson Coll., 1963; BD, U. Chgo., 1968, MA, 1975. Mem. Bethany Union Ch., Chgo. Mem. The Soc. Bibl. Lit., Bertrand Russell Soc., Webster County Peace Justice and Freedom Found., YMCA. Home: 1031 1/2 S 26th St Fort Dodge IA 50501

GANGEL, KENNETH OTTO, seminary professor; b. Paterson, N.J., June 14, 1935; s. Otto John and Rose Marie (Schneider) G.; m. Elizabeth Blackburn, Sept. 1, 1956; children: Jeffrey Scott, Julie Lynn. B.A. in Bus. Adminstrn, Taylor U., 1957; M.Div. cum laude, Grace Theol. Sem., 1960; M.A. in Christian Edn, Fuller Summer Sem., 1960; S.T.M., Concordia Sem., 1963; Ph.D. in Coll. Adminstrn, U. Mo.-Kansas City, 1969; postgrad. in coll. finance, Fla. State U., 1973. Ordained to ministry Christian and Missionary Alliance; mem. faculty Calvary Bible Coll., Kansas City, Mo., 1960-70; dir. Christian service Calvary Bible Coll., 1960-63, registrar, 1963-66, acad. dean, 1966-69, acad. v.p., 1969-70; adminstrv. asst. for acad. affairs Kansas City (Mo.) Regional Council for Higher Edn., 1968-69; prof., dir. Sch. Christian Edn., Trinity Evang. Div. Sch., Deerfield, Ill., 1970-74; pres. Miami (Fla.) Christian Coll., 1974-82; prof., chmn. dept. Christian edn. Dallas Theol. Sem., 1982—; Speaker, lectr. to numerous chs., schs., seminars throughout U.S. and fgn. countries, 1960—. Author: Understanding Teaching, 1968; biography of Walter L. Wilson Beloved Physician, 1970; Leadership for Church Education, 1970, The Family First, 1972, So You Want To Be A Leader!, 1973, Between Christian Parent and Child, 1974, Competent To Lead, 1974, 24 Ways to Improve Your Teaching, 1974, You and Your Spiritual Gifts, 1975, Thus Spake Qoheleth, 1983, Unwrap Your Spiritual Gifts, 1983, Toward a Harmony of Faith and Learning, 1983, Christian Education: Its History and Philosophy, 1983, Christian Education Handbook, 1985, Building a Christian Family, 1987, Personal Growth Bible Studies: Acts, 1987, Personal Growth Bible Studies: I and II Timothy, 1987; Contbg. editor: Jour. Psychology and Theology, Theology Annual; research editor: Christian Edn. Today; contbr. numerous articles to ch. publs. Bd. dirs. LeTourneau Found., Scripture Press Ministries, Evang. Tchr. Tng. Assn. Named Distinguished Alumnus of Year Grace Theol. Sem., 1973, Alumni Achievement award U. Mo. at Kansas City, 1975; Chamber of Achievement award Taylor U., 1976; Am. Assn. Theol. Schs. postdoctoral research grantee, 1972-73. Mem. NEA, Am. Assn. Higher Edn., Nat. Christian Sch. Edn. Assn., Nat. Assn. Evangelicals, Nat. Assn. Profs. Christian Edn. (past pres., 1st v.p., bd. dirs.). Office: Dallas Theol Seminary 3909 Swiss Ave Dallas TX 75204 *My life has found its meaning in the search for and communication of a distinctively Christian philosophy of higher education.*

GANN, GLENN ALAN, radio station news director; b. Houston, Miss., Sept. 27, 1955; s. William Franklin and Mable (Brassfield) G.; m. Annette Alford, Dec. 28, 1975; children: Kathryn, William Scott. BA, Miss. State U., 1977. News dir. Sta. WCPC Radio, Houston, Miss., 1986—, 1977-81; sta. mgr. Sta. WSAO Radio, Senatobia, Miss., 1981-85; sales rep. Nationwide Ins., Senatobia, 1985-86. Commr. Summer League, Houston, Miss., 1989-90; pres. Senatobia C. of C., 1985, Civitan Club, Senatobia, 1984, Jaycees, Houston, Miss., 1981. Methodist. Office: Sta WCPC Radio Houston MS 38851

GANNES, ABRAHAM P., retired educator; b. Ukraine, June 10, 1911; s. Harry and Lilly (Antonovsky) Ganapolsky; m. Miriam Jacobson, 1936; children: Judth, Howard. BA, CCNY, 1933; MA, Columbia U., 1938; PhD, Dropsie Coll., Phila., 1952. Tchr., adminstr. Bur. Jewish Edn., N.Y.C., 1930-44; dir. Bur. Jewish Edn., Miami, Fla., 1944-49, Phila. Coun. on Jewish Edn., 1949-56, Cejwin Camps, N.Y.C., 1956-67, Dept. Edn. & Culture, N.Y.C., 1968-78; lectr. Hebrew U., Jerusalem, 1979-80, San Jose State U., 1982, 83, NYU, 1972, Jewish Edn. Colloquium, Stanford U., Palo Alto, Calif., 1978-79. Author: Central Agencies for Jewish Education, 1954; editor: Selected Writings of Leo Honor, 1965, Selected Writings of A.M. Dushkin, 1980, Teaching Israel, 1981; editorial bd. Jewish Edn. Mag., 1968—, Hebrew Edn. Pedagogic Mag., 1970-88. Mem., officer Coun. on Jewish Edn., 1942—, Nat. Conf. Jewish Communal Svc., 1942—. Named Alumnus of Yr., Dropsie Alumni Assn., 1970, A.P. Schoolman award, Cejwin Camps, 1982, Dushkin Edn. award, Internat. Youth Ctr., Jerusalem, 1987, Edn. Medallion, Dept. Edn. and Culture, 1991. Democrat. Home: 10821 Northforde Dr Cupertino CA 95014

GANNETT, R. G., religious organization administrator. Moderator Associated Gospel Chs., Burlington, Ont., Can. Office: Assoc Gospel Chs, 1500 Kerns Rd, Burlington, ON Canada L7T 2M6*

GANNON, J. TRUETT, minister; b. Cordele, Ga., Apr. 5, 1930; m. Margaret Lewis, Jan. 27, 1951; children: Kenny, Karen Griffith. AB, Mercer U., 1951; B in Div., Southeastern Bapt. Theol. Sem., 1956, D in Ministry, 1975. Ordained to minister Bapt. Ch., 1948. Sec. Ga. Bapt. Conv., 1951-52; with First Bapt. Ch., 1952-76; pastor First Bapt. Ch., Avondale Estates, Ga., 1961-73, New Orleans, 1973-76; pastor Smoke Rise Bapt. Ch., Stone Mountain, Ga., 1976—; 1st v.p. Ga. Bapt. Conv., 1988, pres., 1990-91. Chmn. com. Boy Scouts Am., 1977-83, Met. Atlanta coun. Boy Scouts Am., 1977-78; trustee Midwestern Sem., 1980—, chmn. 1987—; trustee Truett-McConnell Coll., 1985—, chmn. 1985-88. Recipient Svc. to Youth award DeKalb County YWCA, 1968. Mem. Ga. Bapt. Conv. (program chmn. 1970, chmn. com. on nominations 1982, coop. program budget com., 1983, tellers com. 1985, pub. rels. com. 1981-82, med. staff com. 1983-84, search com. for dir. 1984-85, task force 1984-88, 1st v.p. 1988-89), So. Bapt. Conv. (bd. dirs. 1984), Pastor's Confs. (sec. 1962, pres. 1968, 77, chmn. nominating com. 1977, pres. elect 1985-86, 86-87). Home: 5901 Hugh Howell Rd Stone Mountain GA 30087

GANTER, BERNARD J., bishop; b. Galveston, Tex., July 17, 1928; s. Bernard J. and Marie L. (Bozka) G. Grad., Tex. A&M Coll., St. Mary's Sem., LaPorte, Tex.; D Canon Law, Catholic U. Am., Washington., 1955. Adminstr., Sacred Heart Parish, Conroe, Tex., 1955-56; ordained priest Roman Catholic Ch., 1952; sec. to Bishop W.J. Nold; asst. pastor Sacred Heart Co-Cathedral, Houston, 1956-58; rector Sacred Heart Co-Cathedral, 1969-73; officialis Diocesan Matrimonial Tribunal, 1958-64; chancellor Diocese of Houston, 1964-69, elevated to rev. monsignor, 1969; bishop Diocese of Tulsa, 1973-77, Diocese of Beaumont, Tex., 1977—; organizer Diocesan PreCana Confs.; moderator Post Cana Club Houston; chmn. Diocesan Senate Priests; trustee Cath. U. Mem. adv. bd. Seamen's Ctrs., Beaumont and Port Arthur, Tex.; mem. local govering body St. Elizabeth Hosp., Beaumont. Office: Diocesan Pastoral Office 703 Archie St PO Box 3948 Beaumont TX 77704

GANTIN, BERNARDIN CARDINAL, former archbishop of Cotonou; b. Toffo, Dahomey (now Benin), May 8, 1922. Ordained priest Roman Catholic Ch., 1951; titular bishop of Tipasa di Mauritania, also aux. bishop of Cotonou, 1953; archbishop of Cotonou, 1960-71; asso. sec., then sec. Sacred Congregation for Evangelization of Peoples, 1971-75; v.p., then pres. Pontifical Commn. Justice and Peace, 1975-76; elevated to Sacred Coll. Cardinals, 1977; deacon Sacred Heart of Christ the King; pres. Pontifical Commn. Justice; archibishop of Ernakulam of the Chaldean-Malabar Rite; mem. Congregation Oriental Chs., Secretariat of Non-Christians; mem. Commn. Revision Code of Canon Law; pres. Commn. Revision of Oriental Code of Canon Law. Address: Piazza San Calisto 16, 00153 Rome Italy

GANTT, JAMES RICHARD, minister; b. High Point, N.C., Sept. 11, 1933; s. Claude Miles Sr. and Martha Margaret (Ledbetter) G.; m. Connie L. McElveen, Aug. 30, 1958; children: Celeste, Kellie, Allison. BA, Lenoir Rhyne Coll., 1956; MDiv, Luth. Theol. So. Sem., Columbia, S.C., 1959, STM, 1970; DD (hon.), Newberry Coll., 1990. Ordained to ministry Evang. Luth. Ch. Am., 1959. Pastor St. Andrews Ch., Concord, N.C., 1959-62, Our Savior Ch., Tampa, Fla., 1962-67, Good Shepherd Ch., College Park, Ga., 1967-73; regional dir. div. for outreach Luth. Ch. in Am., N.Y.C., 1973-87; dir. mission, div. for outreach Evang. Luth. Ch. Am., Atlanta, 1987—; del. organizing conv. Evang. Luth. Ch. Am., Columbus, Ohio, 1987. Republican. Office: ELCA Div for Outreach 756 W Peachtree St NW Atlanta GA 30308

GANTT, MICHAEL DAVID, minister; b. Columbia, S.C., Oct. 21, 1951; s. Richard F. Jr. and Dolores Sybil (Hebert) G.; m. Janie Peden, May 20, 1972; children: Jennifer, Jason, Jessica, Jonathan. BBA, U. S.C., 1972; MDiv, Covenant Theol. Sem., 1986; postgrad., Fuller Theol. Sem., 1991—. Ordained to ministry Charismatic Ch., 1982; chartered property and casualty underwriter, 1976. Youth dir. Kirk of the Hills Presbyn. Ch., St. Louis, 1980-82; pastor Ch. on the Hill, Florissant, Mo., 1982-86, Established Westport Ch., St. Louis, 1986—. Author: Computers in Insurance, 1979. Home: 12424 Glencliff Dr Maryland Heights MO 63043 Office: Westport Ch 1838 Ross Ave Saint Louis MO 63146 *Jesus Christ is the King of Kings and He sits on heaven's throne speaking life to a dying world, and I'm proud to be His own.*

GANTT, REBECCA ESLER, writer; b. Phila., Sept. 14, 1909; d. Alexander Esler and Anna (Virginia) Musselman; m. Reginald Beswick Bromiley, Aug. 7, 1936 (div. 1949); m. William Andrew Horsley Gantt, Aug. 3, 1965. Student, U. B.C., Can., 1931-32, 34-36, Johns Hopkins U., 1945. Asst. Pavlovian Lab. Johns Hopkins Med. Sch., Balt., 1936-58; sec. Pavlovian Lab. Psychiat. Hosp., Perry Point, Md., 1959-65; researcher, speaker on religion and sci. at seminars. Mem. Pavlovian Soc. (W. Horsley Gantt medal 1988). Home: 7200 Third Ave Sykesville MD 21784 *Humans are endowed with three beautiful and wonderful gifts: the ability to love, the ability to reason, and an inner need to be in harmony with the Universe. These are the ingredients for grace and happiness. There is evidence that consciousness and thinking processes do not require physical energy. This suggests that humans experience two catastrophic episodes: in birth, consciousness, in its motion, is interrupted by colliding with matter, and must now learn to adapt to a materialistic environment. In death, the body disintegrates, and consciousness is released and proceeds in its motion to other experiences (without dependence on physical energy per se). Thus, if consciousness and thinking are not dependent on physical energy, could they not, like the sun when set in motion, continue through eternity, housed in some beautiful and recognizable form?.*

GANTZ, FRANK CARLTON, pastor; b. Albuquerque, Jan. 11, 1960; s. Eugene Austin and Lillie Maxine (Ussery) G.; m. Belinda Gail Pierson, Oct. 2, 1976; children: Cameron Todd, Leah Nicole, Frank Carlton Jr., Bethany Gail. BA, Okla. Bapt. U., 1985; MDiv., Mid-Am. Bapt. Theol. Sem., 1988. Ordained to Gospel Ministry, 1982. Assoc. pastor Kitzingen-Wurzburg Bapt. Ch., Kitzingen, Germany, 1980-81; pastor First Bapt. Ch., Red Rock, Okla., 1981-85, Greenfield Bapt. Ch., Harrisburg, Ark., 1986-89, West Rock Bapt. Ch., Little Rock, 1989—; vice moderator Kay Bapt. Assn., Ponca City, Okla., 1983-84. Contbr. articles to mag. Mem. Religious Leaders for Racial Justice, Little Rock, 1990-91. With U.S. Army, 1978-81. Recipient Mark Pryor scholarship Mark Pryor Found., Sapulpa, 1978; named Soldier of Yr. 66th Maintenance Co., Germany, 1980. Mem. Pulaski Bapt. Assn. (chmn. nominating com. 1990, dir. evangelism 1991—). Home: 5200 Jerry Dr Little Rock AR 72212 Office: West Rock Bapt Ch 14601 Cantrell Rd Little Rock AR 72212

GAPP, KAREN ANNE, religious education director; b. Sturgis, S.D., May 8, 1941; d. Robert Aubery and Teresa Marie (Ballmes) Lyons; m. Wilfrid John Charles Gapp, Apr. 16, 1966; children: Kimberly Clark, Kevin, Lauri, Darin, Allan. Student, Marylhurst (Oreg.) Coll., 1959-60. Sec., treas. St. Boniface Ch., Walhalla, N.D., 1972-75, organist, 1972—, tchr. religious edn., 1984—, dir. religious edn., 1987—; dir. religious edn. Fargo (N.D.) Diocese Deanery IV, 1987—. Mme. Walhalla Beautification Com., 1970, Walhalla Sch. Bd., 1985-88; leader Pembilier 4-H Club, Walhalla, 1980-90; ssec. Pembina County 4-H Coun., Cavalier, N.D., 1982-86; pres. Homemakers Club, Walhalla, 1969, 70. Roman Catholic. Home: Rte 2 Box 165 Walhalla ND 58282 Office: St Boniface Ch Box 228 Walhalla ND 58282

GARAVAGLIA, BROTHER ABDON LEWIS, retired theology educator; b. Detroit, Dec. 16, 1915; s. Amadeo and Rose (Ray) G. B.A., Cath. U. Am., 1942; M.A. in French Lit, Manhattan Coll., 1947; postgrad., St. John's U., 1947-50, Columbia, 1952-55; Litt.D., Coll. Mt. St. Vincent, 1970. Joined Brothers of Christian Schs., 1936; prof. world lit. and theology Manhattan Coll., Bronx, N.Y., 1950-62; dean Manhattan Coll. (Sch. Arts and Scis.), 1962-70, dir. grad. div., 1970-85, prof. emeritus, 1985—; Asso. univ. seminar higher edn. Columbia, 1962-71; spl. research Japanese culture and civilization. Contbr. articles profl. jours. Trustee Manhattan Coll., 1965-68; Ford Found. fellow Harvard, 1951-52. Decorated 3d Order Sacred Treasure (Japan). Mem. Cath. Renascence Soc. Am. (adv. bd. 1955-63), Am. Council Edn., Assn. Am. Colls., Assn. Higher Edn., Am. Conf. Acad. Deans, MLA, Renaissance Soc. Am., Nat. Cath. Edn. Assn., Eastern Assn. Deans, Phi Beta Kappa. Address: 4415 Post Rd Riverdale NY 10471

GARBER, CYNTHIA ANN, missionary; b. Oakland, Calif., Sept. 25, 1956; d. Gerald Gene and Lola Joanne (Sims) Houvener; m. Scott Dale Garber, July 31, 1976; 1 child, Jennifer. Student, Tenn. Temple U., 1974-76; BSBA, Grace Coll., Winona Lake, Ind., 1979. Tchr. geology labs Grace Coll., 1979; missionary Grace Brethren Bd. Evangelism, Winona Lake, 1979; counselor, dir. Kosciuszko County Juvenile Task Ctr., Warsaw, Ind., 1980; claimstaker Ind. Employment Bur., Warsaw, 1979-81; officer mgr. Hair Salons of Mel's Life Like Hair, Dayton, Ohio, 1981-83; missionary Greater Europe Mission, Wheaton, Ill., 1983—; leader numerous youth groups; speaker women's Bible study groups; aerobics instr. Spanish Bible Inst., Castelldefels, Spain, 1987—, cooking tchr., 1987-88; vol. counselor Canaan Missionary Bapt. Ch., Dayton, 1982-84. Mem. Alpha Chi. Mem. Free Ch. of Spain. Avocations: French cooking, mountain climbing, reading, traveling. Office: Spanish Bible Inst, Apartado de Correos 48, 08860 Barcelona Spain

GARBER, PAUL L., choir director; b. Lancaster, Pa., Mar. 28, 1942; m. Mary Anne Ruhl, May 2, 1964; child: Dawn M. B.M.E., Wheaton Coll., 1973; student, West Chester St. U., 1973-75. Cert. tchr. Penn. Choir dir. Warrenville Bapt. Ch., Warrenville, IL, 1971-73; choir dir. Refton (Pa.) Brethren in Christ Ch., 1973-76, min. music, 1991—; dir. Commn. on Music and Worship, Refton, 1979-88, pers. dir., 1988—. Brethren in Christ. Office: Refton Brethren in Christ PO Box 68 Refton PA 17568-0068

GARBER, REUBEN LEE, minister, church official emeritus; b. Garland, Nebr., June 21, 1929; s. Walter Joseph and Emma Anna (Sieck) G.; m. Arline Lorraine Wolf, Nov. 18, 1951; children: Phillip, David, Leslie, Joel, Kenneth, Wayne, Tamara. AA, St. John's Coll., 1949; BA, Concordia Sem., St. Louis, 1951, postgrad., 1956-58; BS in Edn., Concordia Tchrs. Coll., 1953. Ordained to ministry Luth. Ch.-Mo. Synod, 1958. Prin., tchr. St. Paul Luth. Sch., Ellsworth, Kans., 1953-56; pastor St. Paul Luth. Ch., Addison, Ill., 1958-62; founder, pastor Trinity Luth. Ch., Columbia, Tenn., 1962-70; pastor Grace Luth. Ch., New Albany, Ind., 1970-83; mission developer Ind. dist. Luth. Ch.-Mo. Synod, 1983-88, pres. Ind. dist., 1988-91, pres. emeritus Ind. dist., 1991—; sec. bd. evangelism no. Ill. dist. Luth. Ch.-Mo. Synod, Chgo., 1959-62, sec. pastoral conf., 1965-70, with youth ministry Mid-South dist., Memphis, 1968-70, mem. bd. evangelism Ind. dist., Ft. Wayne, 1972-78, v.p. Ind. dist., 1978-88; with founding staff Trinity Luth. Ch., Leitchfield, Ky., Epiphany Luth. Ch., New Salisbury, Ind., Divine Savior Luth. Ch., Shepherdsville, Ky., 1988. Author: Charting a Course in Christian Doctrine, 1968. Chmn. Maury County Assn. Retarded Children., Columbia, 1966-68; bd. dirs. Family Svc. Bur., New Albany, 1978-82. Mem. Tenn. Assn. Retarded Children and Adults (chmn. religious nurture com. 1968-70). Address: Rte 1 Box 253A Minor Hill TN 38473

GARBER, ZEV, Jewish studies educator; b. Mar. 1, 1941; s. Morris Benjamin and Pearl Garber; m. Lois Koppelman, Dec. 26, 1963 (div. Nov. 1975); children: Asher, Dorit; m. Susan Adriana Ehrlich, Oct. 4, 1985. BA, CUNY, Bronx, 1962; MA, U. So. Calif., 1970. Prof. Jewish studies La Valley Coll., Van Nuys, Calif., 1970—. Editor: Methodology in the Academic Teaching of Judaism, 1986, Methodology in the Academic Teaching of the Holocaust, 1988; editor Studies in the Shoah, 1991—. Mem. Nat. Assn. Profs. Hebrew (pres. 1988-90, Recognition award 1990), Am. Acad. Religion, Soc. Bibl. Lit., Am. Oriental Soc., Assn. Jewish Studies. Jewish Orthodox. Office: La Valley Coll 5800 Fulton Ave Van Nuys CA 91401 *Man is a word producer and language is a reciprocal tool - a window through which to discover and define our world and as a mirror through which to discover and find ourselves. What connects the mirror and window of my life is the Bible's first question, "Where are you?".*

GARCIA, GEORGE A., priest; b. Havana, Cuba, Feb. 25, 1945; s. Carlos A. and Ines (Cerqueda) G. BA, Cath. U., 1968; MA in Theology, St. Albert's, 1973. Ordained priest Roman Cath. Ch. Asst. pastor, campus min. St. Augustine Cath. Ch., Coral Gables, Fla., 1975-78, St. Agatha Cath. Ch., Miami, Fla., 1978-81; dir. religious edn. Archdiocese Miami, 1981-86; pastor St. John the Apostle Cath. Ch., Hialeah, Fla., 1986—; adj. prof. St. Vincent De Paul Sem., Boynton Beach, Fla., 1978-81; priest dir. Dade County, Miami, 1988-91; mem. Presbyn. Coun., Miami, 1991. Editor: Handbook of Religious Edn., 1986. Office: St John the Apostle Cath Ch 475 E 4th St Hialeah FL 33010

GARCIA GONZALEZ, RAFAEL, bishop; b. Guadalajara, Mex., May 10, 1926; s. Jose Garcia Calderon and Carmen Gonzalez Chavez. Ed., Marist Bros. Sch., 1931-37; license theology, Pio Latino Americano, Rome, 1949; license canon law, Gregorian U., Rome, 1952. Ordained priest Roman Catholic Ch., 1949; tchr. Guadalajara, 1952-67; founder, dir. Mex. Nat. Secs. Priestly Vocations, 1955-67; spiritual dir. Mex. Pontifical Sem., Rome, 1967-70; bishop Urbisaglia, 1972-74; residential bishop Tabasco, Mex., 1974—; mem. 6th Roman Cath. World Synod of Bishops, Rome, 1980. Mem. Paul VI Soc., Red Cross Soc. Club: K.C.

GARD, ORIN PENETON, retired physicist, lay worker; b. Tremont City, Ohio, Dec. 6, 1909; s. Clinton D. and Martha Jane (Peneton) G.; m. Bulah Lavurn Hall, June 18, 1938; children: David E., Paul E., Margaret A., Virginia M. AB, Wittenberg Coll., 1931; MS, Ohio State U., 1932. Mem. West Ohio ann. conf. United Meth. Ch., Lakeside, 1960-76; del. jursidictional conf. United Meth. Ch., Peoria, Ill., 1968; chmn. parsonnage standards com. United Meth. Ch., Columbus, Ohio, 1971-76, vice chmn. planning and rsch. com., 1980-86. Wittenberg Coll. scholar, 1927; recipient Presdl. citation Pres. Lyndon B. Johnson, 1964. Mem. Am. Physical Soc., Ops. Rsch. Soc. Am., World Future Soc., KP. Home: 2014 Ewalt Ave Dayton OH 45420

GARD, RICHARD ABBOTT, religious institute executive, educator; b. Vancouver, B.C., Can., May 29, 1914; parents U.S. citizens; s. Charles Ned and Clara Edna (Abbott) G.; m. Tatiana Ruzena Kristina Moravec, Nov. 1, 1952; children: Alan Moravec, Anita Nadine. B.A., U. Wash., 1937; M.A., U. Hawaii, 1940; postgrad. U. Pa., 1945-47; Ph.D., Claremont Grad. Sch., 1951; postgrad. Otani U. and Ryukoku U., Kyoto, Japan, 1953-54; D.H.L. (hon.), Monmouth Coll., 1963. Dir. plans dept. Asia Found., San Francisco, 1954-56, spl. adviser to pres., San Francisco and Tokyo, 1956-59, cons. Buddhist affairs, San Francisco, 1959-63; cultural affairs officer USIA, Washington, 1963-64; Buddhist affairs officer Dept. State, Washington and Hong Kong, 1964-69; librarian Inst. for Advanced Studies of World Religions, SUNY-Stony Brook, 1971-73, dir. inst. services, 1971-84, pres., 1985-89; v.p. for U.S., World Fellowship of Buddhists, Bangkok, Thailand, 1961-64, asst. sec. gen., 1971-75; vis. assoc. prof. Yale U., New Haven, 1959-63; vis. prof. Asian studies Wittenberg U., Springfield, Ohio, 1970; adj. prof. Asian studies St. John's U., Jamaica, N.Y., 1974-78; cons. Asian Buddhism Inst. Sino-Indian Buddhist Studies, Taipei, Taiwan, 1981—, Huafan Inst. Tech., Taipei, 1988—, Nova Sci. Pubs., Inc., Commack, N.Y., 1989—, Inst. for Advanced Studies of World Religions, Carmel, N.Y., 1989—. Editor-in-chief series: Great Religions of Modern Man, 1961; editor, contbg. author: Buddhism, 1961; editor Buddhist Text Info., 1974—, Buddhist Research Info., 1979-84; editor-in-chief Asian Religious Studies Info., 1987-90; contbr. articles to acad., religious jours, Asia, U.S. Sec. 3 Village Men's Garden Club, Setauket, N.Y., 1980-84. Served to lt. col. USMCR, 1941-46; PTO. Japanese Buddhist okesa Jodo-shu, Phila., 1946, Japanese Buddhist okesa Shingon-shu, Los Angeles, 1950; recipient Thai Buddhist Theravada award Mahamakuta Found., Bangkok, 1956, Burmese Buddhist Theravada award Shwedagon, Rangoon, 1957, Korean Buddhist Mahayana award Cho-gye-jong, Pom-o-sa, Republic of Korea, 1965; Rockefeller Found. research fellow U. Pa., Phila., 1946-47; Ford Found. grantee Wittenberg U., 1970. Mem. Assn. Asian Studies (pres. Mid-Atlantic region 1974-75), Tibet Soc. (bd. dirs. 1978-83, 87-89, 91—), Internat. Assn. Buddhist Studies (bd. dirs. 1982-86, 87—), Am. Soc. for Study Religion (exec. com. 1983-86). Buddhist. Avocations: landscape gardening, mountain hiking, chamber music. Home: 13 Crane Neck Rd Old Field NY 11733 Address: PO Box 2866 Setauket NY 11733

GARDNER, DAN NOBLES, church official; b. Austin, Tex., July 30, 1942; s. Dan B. and Virginia (Nobles) G.; m. Mary K. Gardner, Apr. 15, 1965; children: Ginger L., Dan B. BBA, U. Tex., 1966. Deacon Hyde Park Bapt. Ch., Austin, 1965—, bus. coord., 1975—; instr. ch. mgmt. Austin Community Coll., 1988-90; tchr. Hyde Park Bapt. Sch., Austin, 1990-81; high sch. baseball coach, 1990-92. Contbg. author: Church Administration, 1985. Lt. col. U.S. Army, Vietnam, 1966-67, mem. Res. Recipient Faith in God award Austin Jaycees, 1969, Good Shepherd award Boy Scouts Am., 1990. Mem. Nat. Assn. Ch. Bus. Adminstrs., Am. Assn. Baseball Coaches, Tex. High Sch. Coaches Assn. Home and Office: Hyde Park Bapt Ch 3901 Speedway Austin TX 78751

GARDNER, EDWARD CLINTON, religion educator; b. Columbia, Tenn., Aug. 17, 1920; s. Carl Clinton and Sarah (Berry) G.; m. Ruth Woodward Cohen, June 9, 1948; children: Edward, Marilyn, Arnold. BA, Vanderbilt U., 1942; BD, Yale U., 1945, PhD, 1952. Ordained to ministry United Meth. Ch., 1945. Asst. prof. Dept. Philosophy and Religion N.C. State Coll., Raleigh, 1949-54; from asst. prof. to prof. Christian Ethics Candler Sch. Theology, Emory U., Atlanta, 1954-90, prof. Christian Ethics emeritus, 1990. Author: Biblical Faith and Social Ethics, 1960, The Church as a Prophetic Community, 1967, Christocentrism in Christian Social Ethics, 1983; contbr. to religious periodicals. Capt. (chaplain) U.S. Army, 1945-46. Faculty fellow Am. Assn. Theol. Schs., 1962-63; visiting scholar Harvard U., 1977, Cambridge U., 1987. Mem. Soc. Christian Ethics (pres. 1961-62, exec. sec. 1964-68), Am. Assn. Univ. Profs., Phi Beta Kappa; assoc. mem. Inst. Soc., Ethics, Life Scis. Home: 2504 Tanglewood Rd Decatur GA 30033

GARDNER, LARRY ALLAN, religion educator; b. Camden, Ohio, Aug. 24, 1929; s. Myron Alonzo G. B.A., Capital U., Columbus, 1951; M.Div., Evang. Luth. Theol. Sem., Columbus, 1955; Th.M., Princeton Theol. Sem., 1956; Th.D., Boston U., 1960; postgrad. Oxford U., Eng., 1968-69. Ordained to ministry Am. Luth. Ch., 1959. Instr. practical theology Evang. Luth. Theol. Sem., Columbus, Ohio, 1958-59; asst. prof. religion and psychology Capital U., Columbus, 1959-65, assoc. prof. religion, 1965-67, prof., 1967—, chmn. dept. religion and philosophy, 1982-85 ; dean Regional Council for Internat. Edn. Summer Seminar in Japan, 1973, 75; mem. bd. publ. Am.

Luth. Ch., 1978-84. Recipient Praestantia award for disting. teaching Capital U., Columbus, 1966, faculty growth award Am. Luth. Ch., 1968. Mem. Sex Info. and Edn. Council U.S. (profl. assoc.), Alpha Phi Omega. Avocations: sports photography; travel. Office: Capital U Columbus OH 43209

GARDNER, RANDY CECIL, minister; b. Cowpens, S.C., Sept. 27, 1952; s. Troy Cecil and Inez Eleanor (Henderson) G.; m. Sara Ann Harrington, May 26, 1974; children: Randall Clayton, Clary Marie. BA in Religion, Gardner-Webb Coll., 1975; MDiv, Southeastern Bapt. Theol. Sem., 1979, DMin, 1986. Ordained to ministry Bapt. Ch. Pastor Mt. Paran Bapt. Ch., Blacksburg, 1983-87, Behtlehem Bapt. Ch., Kings Mountain, N.C., 1987-90, 1st Bapt. Ch., Franklin, N.C., 1990—. Contbr. articles on marriage enrichment to publs. Mem. Rotary. Office: First Bapt Ch 21 Iotla St Franklin NC 28734

GARDNER, RICHARD BRUCE, educator; b. Johnstown, Pa., June 8, 1940; s. Arthur Raymond and Dorothy Jean (Meloy) G.; m. Carol Jean West, Aug. 4, 1962; children: Eric, Mark. BA, Juniata Coll., 1962; MDiv, Bethany Theol. Sem., 1965; DTh, U. Würzburg, Fed. Republic of Germany, 1973. Ordained to ministry Ch. of the Brethren, 1965. Instr. Bridgewater (Va.) Coll., 1965-66; pastor Ch. of the Brethren, Wooster, Ohio, 1971-74; mem. parish ministries staff Ch. of the Brethren Gen. Bd., Elgin, Ill., 1974-88; tchr. Bethany Theol. Sem., Oak Brook, Ill., 1988—. Contbr. articles to profl. jours. Mem. Soc. Bibl. Lit., Brethren Jour. Assn. (pres. 1990—), Chgo. Soc. Bibl. Rsch. Office: Bethany Theol Sem Butterfield & Meyers Rds Oak Brook IL 60521

GARDNER, ROBERT GRANVILLE, minister, educator; b. Lima, Ohio, Apr. 26, 1924; s. Ernest Granville and Gertrude Marie (Roberts) G.; m. Anne Fargason, Dec. 18, 1947; children—Susan, David. A.B., Mercer U., 1949; B.D., Duke U., 1952, Ph.D., 1957. Minister, Reynolds Bapt. Ch., Ga., 1952-54; assoc. prof. religion Shorter Coll., Rome, Ga., 1957-58, prof. religion, 1958—, head dept. religion and philosophy, 1957—. Author: On the Hill: The Story of Shorter College, 1972; First Baptist Church, Rome, Georgia, 1835-1985, 3 vols., 1985; Baptists of Early America: A Statistical History, 2d edit., 1989; Cherokees and Baptists in Georgia, 1989; editor Viewpoints: Georgia Baptist History, 1972—; contbr. revs. and essays to profl. jours. Served with USAF, 1943-46. Recipient Disting. Svc. award Hist. Com., So. Bapt. Conv., 1986. Mem. Am. Soc. Ch. History, So. Bapt. Hist. Soc. (pres. 1982-83), Ga. Bapt. Hist. Soc. (pres. 1972-74, 75-77). Democrat. Office: Shorter Coll Box 297 315 Shorter Ave Rome GA 30165-4298

GARDNER, VICTOR F., religious organization administrator. Pres., gen. supr. Foursquare Gospel Ch. of Can., Burnaby, B.C. Office: Foursquare Gospel Ch Can, 200-3965 Kingsway, Burnaby, BC Canada V5H 1Y7*

GARINGER, LOUIS DANIEL, religion educator; b. Johnson City, Tenn.; s. Merrion X. and Hilda (Gasteiger) G.; m. Joanne Mazna, June 21, 1958. A.B., U. Tenn., 1947, J.D., 1949; M.A. in Govt, Harvard, 1957. Staff writer Christian Sci. Monitor Youth Forums, Boston, 1949-51; teaching fellow, tutor govt. Harvard, 1955-58; asso. dir. Salzburg Seminar in Am. Studies, 1958-60; editorial writer Christian Sci. Monitor, 1965-67, religious affairs editor, 1967-71; research, 1971-72; asso. prof. polit. sci. and religion Principia Coll., Elsah, Ill., 1973-86; dir. Found. Bibl. Research, Charlestown, N.H., 1987-88; vis. scholar Boston U. Sch. Theology, 1980, Grad. Theol. Union, Berkeley, Calif. Contbr. articles to profl. jours. Served with AUS, 1951-53. Recipient Religious Pub. Relations Council merit award, 1969; William E. Leidt award for religious reporting, 1970. Mem. Scarabbean, Pi Kappa Phi, Phi Kappa Phi, Phi Eta Sigma, Sigma Delta Pi, Phi Alpha Eta. Home: 624 Old Connecticut River Rd Springfield VT 05156 *Unless religion means a deep and heartfelt love for God and man expressed in very concrete and practical ways, unless it cuts to the very core of our being and radically changes our lives, it is worth little or nothing.*

GARISTO, JOHN ALBERT, religious educator; b. Harrisburg, Pa., Mar. 19, 1951; s. Samuel Joseph and Erma Jayne (Schilling) G. BA, Allentown Coll., 1974; MDiv., Loyola U., Chgo., 1982. Tchr. Cathedral Sch., Harrisburg, 1975-79, Incarnation Sch., Sarasota, Fla., 1983-88; dir. religious edn. Incarnation Parish, Sarasota, 1988—. Roman Catholic. Office: Incarnation Parish Box 5516 Sarasota FL 34239-5516

GARLAND, DAVID ELLSWORTH, religious studies educator; b. Crisfield, Md., Sept. 24, 1947; s. Edward Ellsworth and Ruth (Grey) G.; m. Diana Sue Richmond, Aug. 22, 1970; children: Sarah, John. BA, Okla. Bapt. U., 1970; MDiv., So. Bapt. Theol. Sem., Louisville, 1973; PhD, So. Bapt. Theol. Sem., 1976; postgrad., Eberhard-Karls U., Tubingen, Fed. Republic Germany, 1984-85. Ordained to ministry Bapt. Ch., 1976. Pastor Immanuel Bapt. Ch., Shepherdsville, Ky., 1973-76; asst. prof. So. Bapt. Theol. Sem., Louisville, 1977-83, assoc. prof., 1983-87, prof., 1987—. Author: Intention of Matthew 23, 1979; contbr. articles to religious publs. With USNR, 1965-71. Mem. Soc. Bibl. Lit., Assn. Bapt. Profs., Inst. Bibl. Rsch. Home: 3608 Trail Ridge Rd Louisville KY 40241 Office: So Bapt Theol Sem 2825 Lexington Rd Louisville KY 40280

GARLAND, DOUGLAS MILTON, minister; b. Washington, July 3, 1947; s. John Wesley and Anne (Williams) Baddy; m. Jocelyn Denise Watson, Nov. 22, 1980 (div. Dec. 1987); children: Douglas Milton Jr., J. Joy. BS, Howard U., 1970, MDiv cum laude, 1982. Ordained to ministry Am. Bapt. Chs. in U.S.A., 1982, eccles. endorsement, 1986. Lay min. Peoples Congl. United Ch. of Christ, Washington, 1978-79; youth min. Lincoln Congl. Temple, United Ch. of Christ, Washington, 1979-81; asst. min. Zion Bapt. Ch., Washington, 1982-85; assoc. pastor Purity Bapt. Ch., Washington, 1986—; ins. agt. Primerica/Mass. Indemnity and Life Ins. Co., Duluth, Ga., 1989—; evangelist Gospel Workshop Am., Washington, 1980-86; del. bd. ch. reps. Bapt. Home for Children, Bethesda, Md., 1982-86; mem. min.'s coun. Am. Bapt. Chs. in U.S.A., 1989—, Far NE Group Ministry, Washington, 1986—. Adult leader Boy Scouts Am., Washington, 1987; vol. St. Ann's Infant and Maternity Home, Hyattsville, Md., 1990. Chaplain USAR, 1986—. Mem. Am. Bapt. Chs. of South, Wednesday Clergy Fellowship Washington, NAACP (life). Democrat. Home: 7403 9th St NW Washington DC 20012-1701 Office: Purity Bapt Ch 1325 Maryland Ave NE Washington DC 20002

GARLAND, DOUGLAS WALTER, minister; b. Melrose, Mass., Mar. 5, 1942; s. Walter Edwin and Marion Emily (Graustein) G. BA, Cornell U., 1965; MDiv, Andover Newton Theol. Sem., 1969. Intern pastor San Miguel Parish, Naturita, Colo., 1967-68; pastor Clarion Venango Charge, Emlenton, Pa., 1969-74, St. John's United Ch. Christ, Grantsville, Md., 1974-81, Pymatuning Charge, Transfer, Pa., 1981—; del. Gen. Synod. United Ch. Christ, 1977-79. mem. participants' com. Appalachian Regional Sch. Ch. Leaders, 1981-83; treas. Grantsville Area Health Ctr., 1980-81. Mem. Lake Erie Assn. (pres. 1986-88, registrar 1983-86), Greenville Area Christian Minister's Assn. (v.p. 1990-91, pres. 1991—), Profl. Assn. Clergy (Pa. West Conf.), Rotary (pres. local club 1980-81). Home and Office: RD 1 Box 77 Church St Transfer PA 16154 *I have often found that those whom I felt needed my ministry most have in turn done the most to strengthen my faith.*

GARLAND, FLOYD RICHARD, minister; b. Ft. Wayne, Ind., Jan. 27, 1938; s. Floyd Elgie and Thlema Clara (Leasure) G.; m. Betsy Sanborn Aldrich, Sept. 7, 1963, (div. Oct. 1975); children: Craig William, Sarah Elizabeth; m. Katharine Adeline Wright, May 30, 1977 (div. Mar. 1991). BS in Hist., Purdue U., 1961; MDiv., Garrett Theol. Seminary, Evanston, Ill., 1964; MBA, Southeastern Mass. U., 1985. Ordained to ministry Meth. Ch., 1962. Student asst. Kelly Meth. Ch., Chgo., 1963-64; pastor Chester Heights Meth. Ch., Richmond, Ind., 1964-67, Hillsgrove United Meth. Ch., Warwick, R.I., 1967-75, St. Paul's United Meth. Ch., New Bedford, Mass., 1975-85, Portsmouth (R.I.) United Meth. Ch., 1985-91, Mathewson St. United Meth. Ch., Providence, 1991—; lectr., Salve Regina Coll., Newport, R.I., 1987-90; bd. dirs. Snem Fed. Credit Union, Northboro, Mass.; conf. statistician, So. New Eng. Conf. of United Meth. Ch., Boston, 1988—, pres. bd. trustees, 1979-85. Contbr. articles to profl. jours. Bd. dirs., v.p. Warwick Community Action, 1972-75; mem. Charter Rev. Commn., Warwick, 1972. Democrat. Avocations: woodworking, mountain hiking. Home: 80 Grant Dr North Kingstown RI 02852 Office: Mathewson St United Meth Ch 134 Mathewson St Providence RI 02903 *I believe that life's greatest wisdom comes with the gentle art of compassion which begins with taking care of ones's self, leads to encouraging the best in others and emerges in oneness with the source of life whom I call God.*

GARLAND, GREGORY, ecumenical agency administrator. Exec. dir. Westside Ecumenical Corp., Santa Monica, Calif. Office: Westside Ecumenical Conf PO Box 1402 Santa Monica CA 90406*

GARLAND, JAMES H., bishop; b. Wilmington, Ohio, Dec. 13, 1931. Attended, Wilmington (Ohio) Coll., Ohio State U., Mt. St. Mary's Sem., Cin., Cath. U., Washington. Ordained priest Roman Cath. Ch., 1959. Titular bishop Garriarn Garriana Roman Cath. Ch.; aux. bishop Roman Cath. Ch., Cin., from 1984, dir. pastoral svcs. dept. Address: 100 E 8th St Cincinnati OH 45202

GARLAND, WILLIAM CALVIN, JR., minister; b. Ft. Worth, Sept. 4, 1951; s. William C. and Jo Garland; m. Jenine Kimbrough, June 7, 1974; children: Joshua Ryan, Jodi Kathryn. BA, Florence State U., 1973; MDiv, Southwestern Bapt. Theol. Sem., 1977. Ordained to ministry So. Bapt. Conv., 1972. Pastor 1st Bapt. Ch., Anderson, Ala., 1971-74, DeQueen, Ark., 1977-81; pastor 2d Bapt. Ch., Hot Springs, Ark., 1981-86, 1st Bapt. Ch., Broken Arrow, Okla., 1986—; youth dir. 1st Bapt. Ch., Edgewood, Tex., 1975-76; trustee, mem. Sunday sch. bd. So. Bapt. Convention, Nashville, 1990—; chmn. budget com. Bapt. Gen. Convention Okla., Oklahoma City, 1990—, mem. state exec. bd., 1987—. Bd. dirs. Upjohn Home Health Care, Hot Springs, 1985-86, Rotary Club, DeQueen, 1979-80. Home: 113 W Yuma Broken Arrow OK 74012 Office: 1st Bapt Ch 210 E Broadway Broken Arrow AR 74012

GARLATHY, FRANK BRYAN, minister; b. Johnstown, Pa., May 6, 1946; s. Frank and Helen Rebecca (Casriel) G.; m. Mary Kay Campbell, July 27, 1968; children: Joshua, Elizabeth. BA in Philosophy cum laude, Otterbein Coll., 1967; MDiv, United Theol. Sem., Dayton, Ohio, 1970; D Ministry, Grad. Theol. Found., Notre Dame, Ind., 1988. Ordained to ministry United Meth. Ch., 1970. Pastor Christy Park United Meth. Ch., McKeesport, Pa., 1970-71, Fayette City (Pa.) United Meth. Ch., 1972-79, Riverview United Meth. Ch., Beaver Falls, Pa., 1979-83; assoc. dir. McKeesport Neighborhood Ministry, 1971-72, Trinity United Meth. Ch., Indiana, Pa., 1983-91; First United Meth. Ch., Erie, Pa., 1991—; chaplain Beaver County Jail, Beaver, Ind., 1981-83, Ind. Borough Police Dept., 1990-91; mission amb. Western Pa. Conf., Pitts., 1985-86; pres. Ind. Area Coun. Chs., 1985-87, United Campus Ministry, Ind., 1990-91. Composer, performer (record album) Sweet Release, 1978, Spirit, 1991. Mem. Belle Vernon (Pa.) Area Sch. Bd., 1977-79. Mem. Am. Acad. Religion, Bibl. Archaeology Soc., Quiz and Quill. Republican. Home: 717 Sassafras St Erie PA 16501 Office: First United Methodist 707 Sassafras St Erie PA 16501 *Our lives are a series of choices based upon the words "open" and "closed." We can extend an open hand or a closed fist. We can cultivate an open mind or a closed rationality. God gives us many choices.*

GARMATIS, IAKOVOS See **IAKOVOS, BISHOP**

GARMENDIA, FRANCISCO, bishop; b. Lozcano, Spain, Nov. 6, 1924; came to U.S., 1964, naturalized.; Ordained priest Roman Cath. Ch., 1947. Ordained titular bishop Limisa and aux. bishop. N.Y.C., 1977—; vicar for Spanish pastoral devel. N.Y. Archdiocese. Office: Chancery Office 1011 1st Ave New York NY 10022

GARNER, EDWIN LEON, JR., clergy; b. Ackerman, Miss., Dec. 30, 1959; s. Edwin Leon and Jimmie (Carroll) G.; m. Donna Lynn Langston, Nov. 22, 1959; children: Candis Grace, Drew Edwin. BS, Troy Ala.) State U., 1982; M in Divinity, Southwestern Bapt. Theol. Sem., Ft. Worth, 1985. Lic. minister, 1981, ordained minister, 1985. Assoc. pastor Calvary Chapel Bapt. Ch., Cleburne, Tex., 1982-83, interim pastor, 1984; pastor Dundee (Fla.) Bapt. Ch., 1985-88; Bapt. campus minister U. of North Ala., Florence, 1989—. Chmn. family life com. Ridge Bapt. Assn., Winter Haven, Fla., 1986—, chmn. youth com., 1987-88; vol. campus minister Polk Community Coll., 1987-88. Named one of Outstanding Young Men Am., 1982, 1985. Mem. Mortar Bd., Phi Kappa Phi, Omnicron Delta Kappa, Phi Gamma Nu. Democrat. Avocations: swimming, water skiing, tennis, golf. Home: 116 Mary Lee Dr Florence AL 35630 Office: Bapt Student Ctr 670 N Wood Ave Florence AL 35630

GARNER, KENT HOWARD, minister; b. Niagara Falls, N.Y., May 9, 1945; s. T. Howard and Eleanor L. (Milleville) G.; m. Linda L. Baird, July 3, 1971; children: Marc A., Kari L. BA, Capital U., 1966; MDiv, Trinity Luth. Sem., Columbus, Ohio, 1970, D Ministry, 1991; ThM, Pitts. Theôl. Sem., 1976. Ordained to ministry Evang. Luth. Ch. in Am., 1970. Intern 1st Luth. Ch., Fullerton, Calif., 1968-69; min. St. Paul's Luth. Ch., Canonsburg, Pa., 1970-77, Bethlehem Luth. Ch., Fairport, N.Y., 1977—; pres. Ohio River Valley Conf., Pitts., 1974-75; nat. trainer SEARCH Bible Study, 1983—; mem. synod coun. Upstate N.Y. Synod, 1987-90; rep. N.E. region Evang. Luth. Ch. in Am., 1987-90. Bd. regents Capital U., Columbus, 1983—. Osterman scholar Ea. dist. Am. Luth. Ch., 1970. Home: 19 Winding Brook Dr Fairport NY 14450 Office: Bethlehem Luth Ch 48 Perrin St Fairport NY 14450

GARNER, MILDRED MAXINE, emeritus religion educator; b. nr. Liberty, N.C., Mar. 15, 1919; d. Robert Monroe and Maize (Kimrey) G. B.A., Woman's Coll. of U. N.C. at Greensboro, 1939; M.A., Union Theol. Sem., N.Y.C., 1946; Ph.D., U. Aberdeen, Scotland, 1952. Tchr. English, history, journalism Roanoke Rapids, N.C., 1939, 41-42; asst. editor Bibl. Recorder, Raleigh, N.C., 1940; dir. religious activities Woman's Coll., U. N.C. at Greensboro, 1942-50; assoc. prof. religion Meredith Coll., Raleigh, 1952-58; prof. religion Sweet Briar (Va.) Coll., 1958—, Wallace Eugene Rollins prof. religion, 1969-84, prof. emeritus, 1984—, chmn. dept., 1961-62, 63-72, 74-78, 81-84; fellow summer seminar history and culture India U. Va., 1964, summer seminar history and culture China, 1965; summer seminar South Asia Duke U., 1966, summer seminar Banaras Hindu U., Varanasi, India, 1977; Fulbright scholar U. Aberdeen, 1950-51, 51-52; program advanced religious studies fellow Union Theol. Sem., 1955-56; Am. Inst. Indian Studies fellow, Poona, India, 1962-63, Inst. Judaism, Vanderbilt Div. Sch., Nashville, 1979; deacon Pullen Meml. Bapt. Ch., Raleigh, 1952-58. Author: First Baptist Church, Liberty, North Carolina, 1886-1986, 1986. Trustee 1st Bapt. Ch., Liberty, N.C., 1991—; grand marshal Holiday Parade, Liberty, 1991. Mem. Fulbright Alumni Assn., Phi Beta Kappa. Republican. Baptist. Lodge: Rotary (hon. Liberty chpt.). Home: 123 N Asheboro St Liberty NC 27298-0427 *My unschooled parents taught and practiced sharing and integrity. A lifetime of studying religious traditions in this country, in a Scottish university, and in India confirms what they knew without leaving our country village.*

GARNER, ROBERT F., bishop; b. Jersey City, Apr. 27, 1920. Student, Seton Hall U., Immaculate Conception Sem., N.J. Ordained priest Roman Cath. Ch., 1946. Ordained titular bishop Blera and aux. bishop Newark, 1976—. Office: Chancery Office 31 Mulberry St Newark NJ 07102

GARR, RONALD WARREN, rabbi, educator; b. Toronto, Ont., Can., July 29, 1944; came to U.S., 1949; s. Boris Max and Myne (Frankel) G.; m. Minda Gail Wolff, Aug. 29, 1971; children: Josef, Tova, Michal, Yaela. BA, UCLA, 1967; MA, Jewish Theol. Sem., N.Y.C., 1970, U. S.D., 1976. Ordained rabbi, 1972. Instr. David Yellin Tchrs. Coll., Jerusalem, 1983—; program dir. Camp Ramah in Wis. Inc., Chgo., 1979-91. Mem. Rabbinical Assembly. Home: Shalom Yehuda 16/1, Jerusalem 93395, Israel

GARRABRANDT, JOHN NEAFIE, JR., minister; b. Ocean Grove, N.J., Feb. 15, 1917; s. John Neafie and Viola (Bills) G.; m. Doris Roberson, Nov. 1, 1942; children: Theodore, Deborah, Pamela. AB magna cum laude, DePauw U., 1940; MDiv, Ea. Bapt. Theol. Sem., Phila., 1946; MST, Temple U., 1950. Ordained to ministry Am. Bapt. Conv., 1947. Exec. sec. North Phila. Bapt. Assn., 1944; pastor West Oak Ln. Bapt. Ch., Phila., 1944-47, Grace Bapt. Ch., Camden, N.J., 1947-54; pres. Camden Bapt. Assn., 1950; founder Bapt. Home for Aged of South Jersey, 1950; prof. Old Testament Bapt. Inst., Phila., 1953-54; pastor Buhl (Idaho) Bapt. Ch., 1956-59, Corona (Calif.) Bapt. Ch., 1959-61, Ustick Bapt. Ch., Idaho, 1961-62; assoc. pastor Twin Falls United Meth. Ch., 1962-65; pastor Jerome United Meth. Ch., 1965-75; coord. Fed. Emergency Mgmt. Agy., 1985-89; pres. Buhl Ministerial Assn., 1957. Chmn. Speakers Bur., Twin Falls Mental Health Soc., 1963-65; chmn. bd. Jerome Pub. Libr., 1966-70; trustee Coll. So. Idaho, 1966-75, pres. bd. trustees, 1971-73; chmn. Jerome Housing Authority, Idaho, 1967-68, GHMN Buhl (Idaho) Pub. Libr., 1980-88; founder, chmn. nominations, mem. exec. bd. St. Benedict's Hosp. Found., 1972-75; founder Buhl Emergency Food Pantry, 1982. Mem. West End Ministerial Assn. (treas. 1985—), Gold Key, Masons, Phi Beta Kappa, Phi Eta Sigma, Pi Sigma Alpha, Lambda Chi Alpha. Home: 504 13th Ave N Buhl ID 83316

GARRELS, DENNIS EARL, minister; b. Detroit, Aug. 27, 1942; s. Earl Henry Hartwick and Milda Caroline Emma (Diefenbach) G.; m. Dale Patricia Wooliver, Aug. 20, 1966; 1 child, Robin Heather. MusB, U. Mich., 1966; MDiv, Concordia Luth. Sem., 1978. Ordained to ministry Luth. Ch., 1978. Religious musician, organist, mem. choir gospel tour Detroit, 1974-76; pastor Our Savior Luth. Ch., Ft. Madison, Iowa, 1978-81; pastor St. Luke's Luth. Ch., St. Louis, 1982—, pipe organist, 1987—, min. of music, 1991—; asst. cantor Beth Hatikvah Messianic Jewish Congregation, St. Louis, 1986; trombonist, vocalist RKO Radio Hot Jazz Band, 1989—. Author: Self Identity: Buddhism and Christianity, 1976; creator, producer films include Dream and Reality-Nicholas Berdeav, 1962, Nicodemus Reborn, 197e; poetry and arts producer, 1980—; clown, improvisation comedy, 1986—. Sec. S.E. Iowa Pastors Conf., Mt. Pleasant, 1979-81; del. Clergy for Life, St. Louis, 1982—. Mem. Lions, Phi Sigma Kappa. Home: 4506 Tennessee Saint Louis MO 63111 *Daily keep life's goal in mind for self, family and their families. Thusly you can avoid trifles and witness that goal completed.*

GARRENTON, LINWOOD WILSON, priest; b. Portsmouth, Va., Apr. 1, 1941; s. Cecil Wilson and Mary Cornelia (Modlin) G. BS, Va. Poly. Inst., 1964; MDiv, Gen. Theol. Sem., N.Y.C., 1970; D in Ministry, Boston U., 1984. Ordained priest Episcopal Ch. Curate Mt. Calvary Ch., Balt., 1970-72; rector Ch. of the Holy Trinity, Balt., 1972-82, Christ Ch., Rochester, N.Y., 1982—; dean Rochester dist., 1983-89; parish cons. Diocese of Rochester, 1984—. Pres. Housing Coun., Rochester, 1988-89, bd. dirs., 1983—. Mem. Ch. and City Conf. Office: Christ Ch 141 East Ave Rochester NY 14604

GARRETT, CHARLES HOPE, clergyman; b. McKinney, Tex., Sept. 24, 1953; s. Hope and Pearlie Addine (Bevill) G.; m. Mattie Ruth Giesler, June 1, 1973; 1 child, Catherine Michelle. BS in Edn., Hardin-Simmons U., 1978. Cert. tchr., Tex. Minister youth Univ. Bapt. Ch., Abilene, Tex., 1973-78; minister youth and activities First Bapt. Ch., Vernon, Tex., 1978-82, Meml. Bapt. Ch., Baytown, Tex., 1982-83, Pioneer Dr. Bapt. Ch., Abilene, Tex., 1983-88; assoc. pastor Bapt. Temple, McAllen, Tex., 1988—; associational youth minister Abilene Bapt. Assn., 1975-77; associational youth minister Red Fork Bapt. Assn., Vernon, 1978-81, student work chmn., 1980-82; student work chmn. Rio Grande Valley Bapt. Assn., McAllen, 1988—. Author: Life Notebook, 1976, Ideas for Life and Fun, 1976, 77, 78 (Best Idea award 1977). Chmn. Am. Heart Assn., Vernon, 1979-81; bd. dirs. Boys Club Am., Vernon, 1981-82; mem. exec. coun. Palmer Drug Abuse Program, Baytown, 1982-83; mem. coun. Vernon Ind. Sch. Dist. Homemakers Am., 1981-82. Mem. Assn. Tchrs. and Profl. Educators, Tex. Assn. Phys. Health Educators and Recreators, Am. Bus. Men, Christian Magicians Am., Fellowship Christian Athletes, 1000 Mile Club (Abilene). Avocations: racquetball, furniture refinishing, audio phile. Home: 7008 N 32d St McAllen TX 78504 *When one gets ahead of God he is truly on his own. These days and times many think that the gospel isn't relevant to this day and age. If we believe, however, that God is alive and He doesn't change, then we need to make this age relevant to the gospel.*

GARRETT, DAVID, priest; b. Memphis, Oct. 9, 1951; s. James Eldon and Edna Angelene (Hall) G.; m. Virginia Ruth Shettlesworth, June 19, 1971; children: Geoffrey Reese, Arwen Eileen. BA, Southwestern at Memphis, Memphis, 1973; MDiv, U. South, 1977. Ordained priest Episcopal Ch., 1978. Deacon St. Martin's Ch., Chattanooga, 1977-78, curate, 1978; vicar Ch. of Annunciation, Newport, Tenn., 1978—; presenting couple Episcopal Marriage Encounter, 1982—; assoc. Community of St. Mary, Sewanee, Tenn., 1977—; mem. dept. of mission Diocese of East Tenn., 1984-88, bd. examining chaplains, 1985, Rural Workers Fellowship, 1981—, standing com. on Canons, 1986—. Contbr. articles to prof. jours. Bd. dirs. Boys Club of Newport, 1981-83, Rural Community Health Svcs.; del. bd. to administr. fed. grants, East Tenn. region, 1984. Mem. Cocke County Ministerial Assn. (pres.), Mid-South Aquarium Soc., Mid-South Killifish Assn. (pres. 1972-74), Smoky Mountain Striders, Knoxville Track Club. Office: Episcopal Ch of the Annunciation PO Box 337 502 Cosby Rd Newport TN 37821 *If it's true that "everything I needed to know I learned in kindergarten," it's also true that everything I need to know about God I learned in beginner Sunday school: God is everywhere, God loves me, and God wants me to share with everybody.*

GARRETT, JAMES LEO, JR., theology educator; b. Waco, Tex., Nov. 25, 1925; s. James Leo and Grace Hasseltine (Jenkins) G.; m. Myrta Ann Latimer, Aug. 31, 1948; children: James Leo III, Robert Thomas, Paul Latimer. BA, Baylor U., 1945; BD, Southwestern Bapt. Theol. Sem., 1948, ThD, 1954; ThM, Princeton Theol. Sem., 1949; Ph.D., Harvard U., 1966; postgrad. Oxford U., 1968-69, St. John's U., 1977, Trinity Evang. Divinity Sch., 1989. Ordained to ministry Baptist Ch., 1945. Pastor, Bapt. chs. in Tex., 1946-48, 50-51; successively instr., asst. prof., assoc. prof., prof. theology, disting. prof. Southwestern Bapt. Theol. Sem., Fort Worth, 1949-59, 79—, assoc. dean for PhD degree, 1981-84; prof. Christian theology So. Bapt. Theol. Sem., Louisville, 1959-73; dir. J. M. Dawson Studies in Ch.-State, prof. religion Baylor U., Waco, Tex., 1973-79, Simon M. and Ethel Bunn prof. Ch.-State Studies, 1975-79; interim pastor Bapt. chs. in Tex., D.C., Ind. and Ky.; guest prof. Hong Kong Bapt. Theol. Sem., 1988; coord. 1st Conf. on Concept of Believers' Ch., 1967; chmn. Study Commn. on Coop. Christianity, Bapt. World Alliance, 1968-75; sec. Study Commn. on Human Rights, 1980-85; theol. lectr. Wake Forest, N.C., Torreon, Mex., Cali, Colombia, Recife, Brazil, London, Queluz-Lisbon, Portugal, Montevideo, Uruguay, Oradea, Romania. Mem. Am. Soc. Ch. History, Am. Acad. Religion, So. Bapt. Hist. Soc., Conf. on Faith and History. Democrat. Author: The Nature of the Church According to the Radical Continental Reformation, 1957, Baptist Church Discipline, 1962, Evangelism for Discipleship, 1964, Baptists and Roman Catholicism, 1965, Reinhold Niebuhr on Roman Catholicism, 1972, Living Stones: The Centennial History of Broadway Baptist Church, Fort Worth, Texas, 1882-1982, 2 vols., 1984-85, Systematic Theology Vol. 1, 1990; co-author: Are Southern Baptists "Evangelicals"?, 1983; co-editor: The Teacher's Yoke: Studies in Memory of Henry Trantham, 1964; editor: The Concept of the Believers' Church, 1970, Baptist Relations with Other Christians, 1974, Calvin and the Reformed Tradition, 1980; editor Southwestern Jour. Theology, 1958-59, Jour. of Ch. and State, 1973-79. Home: 5525 Full Moon Dr Fort Worth TX 76132 Office: PO Box 22117 Fort Worth TX 76122

GARRETT, RONNIE LEE, minister; b. Exeter, Calif., June 22, 1944; s. Richard Leo and Ollie Rosie (Phillipps) G.; m. Joyce Marie Melson, May 19, 1976. Hon. D.D., Coll. of the Sequoias, 1981. Ordained min. 1980. With various constrn. cos., Tulare and Fresno, Calif., 1947-65, Snowden Sch., 1956-58; minister Ch. of Gospel Ministries, Chula Vista, Calif., 1980—. Mem. Nat Trust for Historic Preservation. Republican. Mem. Ch. of Christ. Avocations: stamp and coin collecting, fishing, hunting. Home and Office: 541 W Maple St Exeter CA 93221

GARRIS, ROBERT EUGENE, minister; b. Anderson, Ind., Apr. 2, 1930; s. William Allen and Dorothy B. (Harmenson) G.; m. Elsie Louise Tubbs, July 27, 1958; children: Rebecca, Paul, Teresa, Sharon. BA, Anderson Coll., 1956; BD, Christian Theol. Sem., Indpls., 1961; MA, Butler U., 1965. Recorded to ministry Western Yearly Meeting of the Friends Ch., 1962. Min. Gray Friends Ch., Carmel, Ind., 1955-59, Sandcreek-Azalia Friends Ch., Elizabethtown, Ind., 1959-63, 2d Friends Ch., Indpls., 1963-66; dir. Christian Edn. Western Yearly Meeting Friends Ch., Plainfield, Ind., 1966-68, gen. supt., 1968—; bd. dirs. Ind. Coun. of Chs., Indpls., 1968—, Ind. Interreligious Commn. on Human Equality, Indpls., 1968—. Mem. bd. advisers Earlham Sch. Religion, 1975-84. Office: Western Yearly Meeting PO Box 70 Plainfield IN 46168

GARRONE, GABRIEL MARIE CARDINAL, former archbishop of Toulouse; b. Aix-les-Bains, France, Oct. 12, 1901; s. Jean and Josephine (Mathieu) G.; Diploma Advanced Studies in Philosophy; Doctorate Scholastic Philosophy and Theology; licence ès lettres in Philosophie, certificat d'etudes Supérieures de Philosophie. Ordained priest Roman Catholic Ch., 1925; prof., superior Grand Sem. Chambery; archbishop-coadjutor Toulouse, 1947; archbishop of Toulouse and Narbonne, primate Gaule narbonnaise, 1956-66; v.p. Permanent Council Plenary Assembly French Episcopate, 1964-66; pro-prefect Congregation for Cath. Edn. Rome, 1966, prefect, 1968; chargé des Rapports de L'Eglise avec la Culture, 1980; created cardinal, 1967. Decorated grand cross Legion of Honor, Croix de Guerre. Author: Psalms and Prayers; Invitation to Prayer; Lessons on Faith; The Credo's Moral; The Door to Scriptures; Holy Church Out Mother; The Credo's Panorama; There is Your Mother; Catholic Action; Faith and Pedagogy; The Eucharist; Why Pray?; The Nun, Sign of God in the World; Psalms, Prayer for Today; Offers to God and to the World; Lord, Tell Me Your Name; Christian Morals and Human Values; What Must One Believe?; Le Concile, Orientations; Lumen Gentium; Gaudium et spes; Qu'est-ce que Dieu? L'Eucharistie au secours de la foi; Religieuse aujourd'hui? Oui, mais..., 1969; Prier quinze jours avec Vatican II; translations: What God Is; What Theresa of Lisieux Believed; Eucharistic and Belief; Que faut-il faire? Ce que croyait Pascal; L'Eglise 1965-72; la Foi en 1973; la Foi au fil des jours; Le Credo lu dans l'histoire; Pour vous qui su-je? Aller jusqu'à Dieu; Le Prêtre; Marie, hier et aujourd'hui; Parole et Eucharistie; La Foi tout entière; Je suis le Chemin; Ce que croyait Jeanne Jugan; Ce que croyait Anne-Marie Javouhey; 50 ans de vie d'Eglise; Synode 85; La Communion fraternelle "dernière volonté" du Seigneur: Pour une présentation sommaire et ordonnée de la foi. Address: Piazza San Pietro in Vinculi 6, 00184 Rome Italy

GARSEK, EDWARD HAROLD, rabbi; b. Ft. Worth, Apr. 13, 1946; s. Isadore and Sadye Maye (Carshon) G.; m. Sara Rivka Gold, Feb. 15, 1970; children: Cheryl Esther, Deborah Elka, William Joseph, Shoshana Ruth, Rachael Nechama, Isadore Raphael. BA, Loyola U., Chgo., 1970; B Jewish Lit., Hebrew Theol. Coll., Chgo., 1975, M Pastoral Counseling, 1980; MEd, U. Toledo, 1980. Cert. tchr., adminstr., prin., Ohio; ordained rabbi, 1972. Rabbi Congregation Etz Chayim, Toledo, Ohio, 1975—; mem. rabbinic cabinet United Jewish Appeal, 1978—. Mem. Rabbinical Coun. Am., Orthodox Coun. Rabbis Detroit, Chgo. Rabbinical Coun. Office: Congregation Etz Chayim 3853 Woodley Rd Toledo OH 43606

GARTENBERG, DOV MOSHE, rabbi; b. Honolulu, Jan. 24, 1954; s. Allan and Ina (Grouf) G.; m. Celia Cohen, Nov. 27, 1983; children: Zachary, Mariel, Fay. BA, U. Calif., Berkeley, 1972. Ordained rabbi, 1981. Asst. rabbi Adat Ariel, North Hollywood, Calif., 1981-83; rabbi Mishkin Tephilo, Venice, Calif., 1983-87, Beth halom, Seattle, 1988—; Mem. Bd. Rabbis of Seattle, pres., 1989-90. Contbr. articles to profl. jours. Coun. of Jewish Life grantee, Jewish Fedn., 1982. Mem. Rabbinical Assembly (mem. com. involvement), Phi Beta Kappa. Office: Congregation Beth Shalan 6800 35th Ave NE Seattle WA 98115

GARTON, GENA MARIE, minister; b. Menomonee Falls, Wis., Apr. 23, 1958; d. James William and Jeana Genevieve (Keagle) G. Student, U. Wis., Waukesha County, 1976-78; BS in Psychology, U. Wis., Oshkosh, 1981; MDiv, Iliff Sch. Theology, Denver, 1985. Ordained in Meth. Ch. as deacon, 1984, as elder, 1990. Minister Climax & Piedmont United Meth. Chs., Piedmont, Kans., 1983-84; chaplain Wesley Med. Ctr., Wichita, Kans., 1983-84; minister Trempealeau & Arcadia United Meth. Chs., Trempealeau, Wis., 1985-88, Marion & Wittenberg United Meth. Chs., Marion, Wis., 1988—; chaplain Shawano (Wis.) Hosp., 1988—; bd. dirs. United Ministries in Higher Edn., Oshkosh, Wis., 1978-81; horse camp dir. United Meth. Ch., Sun Prairie, Wis., 1986-90; mem. bd. ch. and soc. Wis. conf. United Meth. Ch., 1988—, bd. higher edn. and campus ministry, 1978-81. Editor (newsletters) The Link, 1985-88, Parish Visitor, 1988—, Marion Rototeller, 1989—. Songleader, guitarist Emmanuel Community Youth Group, Menomonee Falls, 1974-78; site dir. Wis. Svc. Project, Sun Prairie, 1978-79; bd. dirs. Trempealeau County 51.42 Bd., Whitehall, Wis., 1986-88. Named Hon. Mem. Lac du Flambeau (Wis.) Indian Tribe, 1979. Mem. Discerners Two, Rotary (1st v.p. Marion club 1991-92). Home: 504 NE 1st St Box 535 Marion WI 54950

GARVER, DAVID CHESTER, minister; b. Akron, Ohio, Nov. 25, 1944; s. Earl F. and Vera M. Garver; m. Carol A. Garver, Aug. 17, 1968; children: Deborah, Sarah, Elizabeth, Emily. BS in Edn., Kent State U., 1967; MDiv, No. Bapt. Sem., 1970, D of Ministry, 1982. Ordained to ministry Am. Bapt. Ch., 1970. Pastor North Towne Bapt. Ch., Rockford, Ill., 1970-75, First Bapt. Ch., Momence, Ill., 1975-82, Ridgeview Bapt. Ch., Danville, Ill., 1982—; sec. Rockford Ministerial Assn., 1973-75; bd. dirs. Ctr. for Childrens Svcs., Danville. Chmn. CROP hunger walk Ch. World Svc., Danville, 1983—; pres. bd. Habitat for Humanity of Danville, 1989—, bd. dirs., 1986—. Mem. Mins. Coun. Am. Bapt. Clergy (v.p. 1979-80, pres. 1981-82). Home: 1815 Syrcle Dr Danville IL 61832 Office: Ridgeview Bapt Ch 14 Ridgeview Bapt Ch Danville IL 61832 *As I live each day, I increasingly realize how fragile and fleeting life is. So I have come more and more to treasure the things that really matter: faith in God, love of family and friends, and making a positive difference in a hurting world for which Christ has died.*

GARVER, OLIVER BAILEY, JR., bishop; b. L.A., July 19, 1925. BS, UCLA, 1945; MBA, Harvard U., 1948; STB, Episc. Theol. Sch., Cambridge, Mass., 1962; DD, Ch. Div. Sch. Pacific, 1987. Ordained to ministry Episcopal Ch. as deacon, 1962, as priest, 1963. With Lockheed Aircraft Corp., 1948-59; curate St. Alban's, L.A., 1966-72; urban assoc. Ch. of the Epiphany, L.A., 1966-72; canon to the ordinary Staff Bishop Rusack, 1973-85; consecrated bishop suffragan Diocese of L.A., 1985-89; bishop in residence Harvard Sch., 1989—. With USNR, 1943-46. Mem. Phi Beta Kappa, Beta Gamma Sigma. Office: Harvard Sch 3700 Coldwater Cannon North Hollywood CA 91604

GARVERICK, CHARLES MICHAEL, lay worker; b. Washington, Dec. 19, 1936; s. Charles Kramer and Mae Dean (Jaynes) G.; m. Ruth Elizabeth Clark, June 6, 1959; children: Richard Michael, Karen Elizabeth, Paul David. BS, U.S. Naval Acad., 1959; MS, U.S. Naval Postgrad. Sch., Monterey, Calif., 1976. Cert. profl. logistician. Treas. Burke (Va.) Community Ch., 1982-85; exec. bd. career Impact Ministries, Washington, 1988—; counselor Christian Fin. Concepts, Gainesville, Ga., 1987—; dir. Indian Head ops. R.S. Carson & Assocs., Md., 1989—; mem. Nat. Christian Choir, Rockville, Md., 1986—. Capt. USN, 1959-83. Decorated Legion of Merit, Navy Commendation medal. Mem. Naval Submarine League (treas. 1989—), Soc. Logistics Engrs., U.S. Naval Inst. Republican. Home: 4333 Ashford Ln Fairfax VA 22032-1436

GARVEY, THOMAS JOSEPH, provincial superior; b. Chgo., Sept. 17, 1931; s. Thomas Francis and Brigid Agnes (Lenighan) G. BA, Sacred Heart Monastery, 1954; MDiv, Sacred Heart Sch. Theol., 1959; MA, Marquette U., 1963; LLD, Cardinal Stritch Coll., 1986. Dean of students Divine Heart Sem., Donaldson, Ind., 1959-65; dean of men Kilroe Sem., Honesdale, Pa., 1965-71; adminstr. Chgo. House of Studies, 1971-73; pastor Our Lady of Guadalupe, Raymondville, Tex., 1973-78; pres., rector Sacred Heart Sch. Theology, Hales Corners, Wis., 1978-86; pastor St. Matthew the Evangelist, Houston, 1987-89; provincial superior U.S. Province Priests of the Sacred Heart, Hales Corners, 1989—; pres. Bd. Dirs. Sacred Heart Sch. Theology, Hales Corners, 1989—; bd. dirs. Priests of the Sacred Heart, Chamberlain, S.D., 1990—; v.p., bd. dirs. Sacred Heart League, Walls, Miss., 1989—. Contbr. articles to profl. jours. Mem. Conf. Major Superiors of Men. Office: Box 289 Hales Corners WI 53130

GARY, JUDSON EMMET, III, international association administrator; b. Nashville, June 25, 1954; s. Laurence and Bernice Olivia (Berry) G.; m. Maria Olga Aleu, May 21, 1978; children: David Judson, Christine Elizabeth. BS of Indsl. Mgmt., Ga. Inst. Tech., 1976; MEd, Calif. State U., 1983. Campus minister Campus Crusade for Christ, Phila., 1976-78; adminstrv. dir. Inst. Internat. Studies, Pasadena, Calif., 1978-82; exec. editor World Christian Mag., Chatsworth, Calif., 1982-86; cons. tng. and communications, asst. to internat. dir. Lausanne Com. for World Evangelization, 1986-88; communications officer AD 2000 Global Svc. Office, 1989—; tng. cons. Inst. Internat. Studies, Pasadena, 1982; curriculum writer Harvest, Scottsdale, Ariz., 1985; lectr. William Carey Internat. U., Pasadena, 1983—. Author: The Countdown Has Began: The Story of the Global Consultation on A.D. 2000, 1989; editor, writer features and articles Internat. Jour. Frontier Missions, 1984, World Christian Mag., 1986. Tchr., mem. com. 1st Bapt. Ch., Pasadena, 1982-90. Mem. Nat. Soc. Performance and Instrn., World Future Soc. Republican. Baptist. Avocation: jogging. Home and Office: 1869 Galbreth St Pasadena CA 91104 *On the threshold of the Third Millennium, we are witnessing the rebirth of the human spirit through the power of the Holy Spirit. That is why I am working to see that we give the world the reason to celebrate the year 2000 as a true Bimillennium, centered around Christ.*

GARY, JULIA THOMAS, minister; b. Henderson, N.C., May 31, 1929; d. Richard Collins and Julia Branch (Thomas) G. BA, Randolph-Macon Woman's Coll., 1951; MA, Mt. Holyoke Coll., 1953; PhD in Chemistry, Emory U., 1958; MDiv cum laude, Candler Sch. Theology, 1986. Ordained to Meth. Ch. as deacon, 1986, as elder 1989. Instr. Mt. Holyoke Coll., South Hadley, Mass., 1953-54, Randolph-Macon Woman's Coll., Lynchburg, Va., 1954-55; from asst. prof. to prof. chemistry Agnes Scott Coll., Decatur, Ga., 1957-84, dean, 1969-84; pastor-in-charge St. Matthew United Meth. Ch., East Point, Ga., 1987—; bd. dirs. INSA, Atlanta. Contbr. articles to profl. jours. Recipient Alumnae Achievement award Randolph-Macon Woman's Coll., 1990. Mem. Zonta of Atlanta (pres. 1979-81, Zonta of the Yr. 1988), Phi Beta Kappa, Sigma Xi. Avocations: music, computers, gardening. Home: 117 Bruton St Decatur GA 30030

GARZA, ROSALINDA PEREZ, religion educator; b. San Antonio, Oct. 21, 1948; d. Panfilo E. and Sulema (Vielmas) Perez; m. Raymond Z. Garza, Aug. 22, 1969; children: Xanthia Isabel, Max Isidro, Naomi Beth. AA, San Antonio Coll., 1985; BA, Our Lady of the Lake U., 1989. Cert. Level II catechist, 1988. Level III catechist St. John Berchman's Ch., San Antonio, 1984-87; dir. religious edn. Divine Providence Ch., San Antonio, 1987-89, St. Gabriel's Ch., San Antonio, 1989—; mem. Western Urban Deanery of San Antonio Archdiocese, 1984—; founder parent support group Divine Providence Ch., 1988, St. Gabriel's CCD Booster Assn., exec. bd. mem., founder, 1990—. Home: 501 Pletz San Antonio TX 78226 Office: St Gabriel's Ch 747 SW 39th St San Antonio TX 78237

GASEK, STANLEY P., religious organization administrator; b. Utica, N.Y., Mar. 28, 1917; s. Albert John and Anna (Biernat) G.; m. Mary Ellen Compton, Apr. 22, 1943; children: S. Paul Jr., Shelby C., Thomas D. AB, Hobart Coll., 1939; MDiv, Gen. Theol. Sem., 1942; grad., Hobart Coll., 1966, Gen. Theol. Sem., 1967. Rector St. John's Ch., Cape Vincent, N.Y., 1942-44, Grace Ch., Utica, N.Y., 1947-87; pres. St. Margaret's Corp. Utica, 1980—; trustee, chaplain St. Luke's Meml. Hosp. Ctr., Utica, 1947-87; trustee exec. bd. Gen. Theol. Sem., N.Y.C., 1966-85; vis. fellow Anglican Ctr., Rome, 1967-68. Chmn. United Way Campaign, Utica, 1963; bd. dirs. Greater Utica C. of C., 1968-88; pres. bd. dirs. Title I Adv. Com., Utica, 1975-85. Fellow Ecumenical Inst., 1968. Mem. Associated Parishes, Conf. on City and the Ch. (sec. 1955-74), Alban Inst., Coll. of Preachers, Fort Schuyler Club, Sadaquada Golf Club. Home: 102 C Cross Keys Rd Baltimore MD 21210

GASPARD, PERRY A., minister; b. Lake Charles, La., Dec. 10, 1949; s. Albert paul and Nobie L. (Cheek) G.; m. Mary F. Kerwin, May 12, 1974; 1 child, Nicole A. Grad. high sch., Lake Charles, 1967. Ordained to ministry. Pastor Abundant Life Fellowship, Lake Charles, 1978—. Republican. Home: 4000 Lock Ln 20 Lake Charles LA Office: Abundant Life Fellowship PO Box 7700 Lake Charles LA

GASS, RICHARD BRIAN, minister; b. Pendleton, Calif., May 24, 1967; s. Richard Douglas and Nancy Caroline (Nix) G.; m. Lisa Leigh Hawkins, Feb. 13, 1987; children: Joshua Aaron, Rachel Elisabeth. BS in Edn. cum laude, U. Tenn., Martin, 1991. Lic. to ministry Bapt. Ch., 1988. Min. youth Mt. Pelia Bapt. Ch., Martin, 1990-91; Christian educator Macon Rd Bapt. Sch., Memphis, 1991—; worship chmn. Bapt. Student Union, Martin, 1990-91. Scoutmaster Boy Scouts Am., Sharon, Tenn., 199091. 1st lt. U.S. Army N.G., 1985—. Mem. Student Tenn. Edn. Assn. (sec. 1990-91). Home: 3748 Beckman Dr Memphis TN 38135 Office: Mt Pelia Bapt Ch Rte 4 Littrell Rd Martin TN 38237

GASS, SYLVESTER FRANCIS, priest; b. Milw., Dec. 31, 1911; s. Jacob and Julia (Weninger) G. BA, St. Francis Major Sem., 1936, MA, 1939; JCD, Cath. U. Am., 1942. Ordained priest Roman Cath. Ch., 1939. Parish worker Milw., 1941-45; ecclesiastical notary Milw. Archdiocesan Curia, 1940-56; sec. Tribunal Milw., 1942-56; prof. canon law and moral theology St. Francis Major Sem., 1945-47; rep. Milw., Wis. Provincial Conf., 1954-72; promoter of justice Archdiocese Milw., 1955-61, vice-officialis, 1956-61; archiepiscopal vicar Dominican Sisters of the Perpetual Rosary, 1956-83; clergy counsellor St. Michael Hosp. Family Clinic, 1948-71, spiritual dir., 1961-71; speakers' staff Cath. family life program, Milw., 1949-72, officialis, 1961-76, vicar gen., 1969-83; ret., 1983, papal chamberlain, 1954, domestic prelate, 1959. Author: Ecclesiastical Pensions, 1942. Mem. Canon Law Soc. Am. (pres. 1960-61), Can. Canon Law Soc. Home: 3501 S Lake Dr Milwaukee WI 53207

GAST, AARON EDWARD, retirement homes executive; b. Baroda, Mich., July 22, 1927; m. Beverly Shaffer (div. Mar. 1985); children: Gregory, Lisa, Brian; m. Ernestine Wingfield Lazenby, May 2, 1987. BA, Wheaton Coll., 1950; MDiv, Princeton Theol. Sem., 1953; PhD, Edinburgh U., Scotland, 1956; LHD (hon.), Davis and Elkins Coll., Elkins, W.Va., 1981; DD (hon.), Ursinus Coll., 1982; LLD (hon.), Bloomfield (N.J.) Coll., 1987. Ordained to ministry Presbyn. Ch., 1953. Dean/prof. theology Conwell Sch. of Theology, Phila., 1960-67; sr. min. First Presbyn. Ch. Germantown, Phila., 1967-81; pres./chief exec. United Presbyn. Found., N.Y.C., 1981-86; chmn., exec. officer Presbyn. Ch. (USA) Found., N.Y.C., 1986-90; exec. dir. Phila. Presbytery Homes Inc., 1990—; bd. dirs. Covenant Life Ins. Co., Premier Life Ins. Co., Phila.; trustee Charlotte Newcombe Found., Princeton, N.J., 1979—, Presbyn./U. Pa. Med. Sch., Phila., 1980—. Chmn. Nat. Com. on Self-Devel., N.Y.C., 1978-79; bd. dirs. Nat. Conf. Christians and Jews, Phila., 1972-83; chmn. Greater Germantown Alliance, Phila., 1976-78. Mem. Am. Mgmt. Assn., Presbytery of Phila., Union League Phila. Avocations: tennis, swimming, sailing. Office: Phila Presbytery Homes Inc One Aldwyn Ctr PO Box 607 Villanova PA 19085-0607 *Even Jesus himself did not pretend to have a detailed blueprint for life's pilgrimmage. The point is, rather, that through Him life is lighted up with insight and destiny.*

GASTION, HILLARY, SR., clergyman; b. N.Y.C., May 16, 1946; s. William Sr. and Ethel (Thompson) G.; m. Beatrice Terez, Sept. 11, 1965 (div. Apr. 1974); children: Desireé D., Hillary Jr., Sollemon A.K.; m. Tonya Smith, May 20, 1978; children: Kiersten R., Jennifer K. BS in Acctg., U. Balt., 1975; MDiv, N.Y. Theol. Sem., 1986. Assoc. minister Macedonia Bapt. Ch., Lakewood, N.J., 1983-85; asst. to pastro Majority Bapt. Ch., St. Albans, N.Y., 1985-88; assoc. minister Martin St. Bapt. Ch., Raleigh, N.C., 1988-90; asst. to protestant chaplain Manhattas St. Psychiat. Hosp., N.Y.C., 1984—; pastor Parkchester Bapt. Ch., Bronx, N.Y., 1990—. Community patient advocate rsch. com. Manhattan Psychiat. Ctr., N.Y.C., 1990. With U.S. Army, 1965-68, Vietnam. Mem. Nat. Assn. Notaries. Democrat. Home: 1340 Pugsley Ave Bronx NY 10462-4444 Office: Parkchester Bapt Ch 2021 Benedict Ave Bronx NY 10462

GATCH, MILTON MCCORMICK, JR., clergyman, educator, library administrator; b. Cin., Nov. 22, 1932; s. Milton McCormick and Mary (Curry) G.; m. Ione Georganna White, Aug. 25, 1956; children: Ione Waite, Lucinda McCormick, George Crosby White. AB, Haverford Coll., 1953; student, U. Cin. Sch. Law, 1953-55; BD, Episc. Theol. Sch., Cambridge, Mass., 1960; MA, Yale U., 1961, PhD, 1963. Ordained priest Episc. Ch. Chaplain Wooster Sch., Danbury, Conn., 1963-64; chaplain, chair humanities dept. Shimer Coll., Mt. Carroll, Ill., 1964-67; assoc. prof. English No. Ill. U., DeKalb, 1967-68; prof. English U. Mo., Columbia, 1968-78, chair dept., 1971-74; prof. ch. history Union Theol. Sem., N.Y.C., 1978—, acad. dean and provost, 1978-89, dir. Burke Libr., 1990—; pres. Midwest MLA, 1974; bd. dirs. Ecumenical Community Devel. Orgn., N.Y.C., 1987-89. Author: Death: Meaning and Mortality in Christian Thought and Contemporary Culture, 1969, Loyalties and Traditions: Man and His World in Old English Literature, 1971, Preaching and Theology in Anglo-Saxon England, 1977. With U.S. Army, 1955-57. NEH sr. fellow, 1974-75. Mem. Medieval Acad. Am. (del. to Am. Coun. Learned Socs. 1981—), Internat. Soc. Anglo-Saxonists (founding mem., adv. bd. 1980-85), Am. Acad. Religion, Early English Text Soc., Century Assn., Grolier Club, Yale Club. Democrat. Avocations: book collecting, gardening, running. Office: Union Theol Sem 3041 Broadway New York NY 10027

GATES, GARY LYNN, minister, religious organization executive; b. Springfield, Ill., Feb. 6, 1950; s. Harold Ross and Myra Evelyn (Love) G.; m. Rebecca Lynn Zimmerman, June 5, 1971; children: Amy, Joshua, Amber. BS, Sterling Coll., 1972; MS, Ft. Hays State Coll., 1975; M.C.M., Huntington Sch. Christian Ministry, 1984. Ordained to ministry Evang. Mennonite Ch., 1981. Bd. dirs. Christian edn. Evang. Mennonite Ch., Ft. Wayne, Ind., 1977-80, dir. ch. extension, 1979-90, asst. to pres., 1980-82, pres., 1982-90; v.p. ops. Ch. Growth Ctr., Corunna, Ind., 1990—. Mem. Nat. Assn. Evangs. (bd. dirs.), Greater Ft. Wayne Assn. Evangs. (sec. 1981-82). Office: Church Growth Ctr Corunna IN 46730

GATEWOOD, ARTHUR SMITH, minister; b. Wilmington, Del., Feb. 10, 1945; s. Jesse Harold and Mary M. (Smith) G.; m. Sarah Betts Hunter, May 31, 1969; children: Hunter, Christopher, Melissa. BA, St. Andrews Presbyn. Coll., Laurinburg, N.C., 1968; MDiv, Union Theol. Sem. in Va., 1972. Ordained to ministry Presbyn. Ch., 1972. Assoc. min. 1st Presbyn. Ch., Albemarle, N.C., 1972-75; chaplain Presbyn. Coll., Clinton, S.C., 1975-79; sr. min. Marion (S.C.) Presbyn. Ch., 1979—; commr. Presbyn. Gen. Assembly, Columbus, Ga., 1982. Founding trustee Meals on Wheels, Albermarle, 1973-75; coord. Regional Spl. Olympics, Clinton, 1975-79; founding bd. dirs. Marion Clothing Closet, 1981—; chmn. Marion County Bd. Edn., 1984—. Named Outstanding Young Profl. of Yr., S.C. Jaycees, 1981. Mem. Rotary. Office: Marion Presbyn Ch PO Box 186 Marion SC 29571

GATHERCOAL, ALLAN M., minister; b. Burtenwood, Eng., Feb. 19, 1953; s. Alfred Melvin and Mollie Genevive (Doner) G. BA, Azusa Pacific Univ., 1976; MA, Azusa Pacific U., 1978; BTh, San Bernardino (Calif.), Bible Coll.; MTh, Fuller Theol. Seminary, Pasadena, Calif., 1983. Church growth cons. Fuller Theol. Seminary, 1983-88; prof. Life Bible Coll., Christiansburg, Va., 1988-90; founder, pres. Med. Mercy Missions, Atlanta, 1990—; founder, exec. dir. Flying Doctors of Am., Atlanta. Chaplain, capt. USAF, 1991—. Office: Flying Doctors of America 1951 Airport Rd PDK Atlanta GA 30341

GATLING, RICHARD GERALD, SR., bishop, religious organization administrator; b. Waterbury, Conn., Aug. 29, 1944; s. Edward and Esther (Gatling) Burrus; m. Dolores Jones, Feb. 24, 1943; children: Richard, Alicia Ann, Dwain V., Raenette. Grad. high sch. Deacon Mt. Olive Ch. of God in Christ Internat., Waterbury, Conn., 1974-76; assoc. minister Mt. Olive Ch. of God in Christ Internat., 1976-78, Gospel Temple Ch. of God in Christ, Hartford, Conn., 1978-80; pastor, chief exec. officer Jackson Meml. Ch. of God in Christ Internat., Hartford, 1980—; commr. Chs. of God in Christ Internat., 1987—, consecrated bishop, 1990—; supt. state Sun. sch. Chs. of God in Christ Internat., Conn., 1979—, fin. sec., 1979—, chmn. nat. fin. com., 1983—. Democrat. Pentocostal Ch. Avocations: pianist, organist, singing. Address: 182 Atwood Rd Thomaston CT 06787 *My strongest desire is to help bring about a unity with people of all walks of life thru the preaching of the Gospel of Jesus Christ, because the house that is divided cannot stand.*

GATTIS, WILLIAM ANTHONY (TONY GATTIS), deacon; b. Wichita, Kans., Apr. 5, 1959; s. Billy Gene and Lounett (Faulkner) G.; m. Kim Annette Jackson, Sept. 15, 1984. BA magna cum laude, Wichita (Kans.) State U., 1984, MA, 1986; MDiv, So. Meth. U., 1990. Ordained deacon United Meth. Ch., 1988. Various positions 1st United Meth. Ch., Wichita, 1979-84, assoc. pastor, 1988-91; pastor St. Peter's and Grantville United Meth. Chs., Topeka, 1991—; grad. teaching asst. Wichita State U., 1984-86; assoc. dir single adult ministry 1st United Meth. Ch., Dallas, 1987-88; chaplain HCA Wesley Med. Ctr., Wichita, 1988-89. Active Big Bros./Big Sisters Am., Wichita, 1979-86; bd. dirs. Bread of Life Walk to Emmaus, Wichita, 1988-91. Bishop Charles C. Selecman scholar So. Meth. U., 1986. Mem. Speech Communication Assn., Alban Inst. Democrat. Avocations: racquetball, skiing, boating, reading. Office: St Peter's United Meth Ch 3737 NW 35th Topeka KS 67618

GAUCK, CARL RICHARD, minister; b. Chgo., Jan. 21, 1942; s. Carl R. and Esther Mae (Hess) G.; m. Gloria Anne Gauck, Feb. 21, 1971; children: Kenneth, Matthew, Karen. BA, N. Park Coll., 1966; MDiv, Luth. Sch. Theology at Chgo., 1970; STM, LSTC, 1975. Ordained to ministry Luth. Ch. in Am., 1970. Pastor Trinity Evang. Luth. Ch., Chgo., 1972-75, Messiah Luth. Ch., Galva, Ill., 1975-78, St. Timothy Luth. Ch., Naperville, Ill., 1978-87; coord., sr. therapist Comtrea, Festus, Mo., 1988-90; pastor St. Paul's Evang. Luth. Ch., Lohman, Mo., 1990—; mem. Region IV Evangelism Com. Evang. Luth. Ch. in Am., Lohman, 1991—, Evaluation and Structure Com., Kansas City, 1988-90; chmn. Parish Life Com. Luth. Ch. in Am., Chgo., 1974-80; pres. Ministerial Alliance, Naperville, 1981-84. Co-host (TV program) Pastors Study, 1991; contbr. articles to profl. jours. Bd. dirs. Edward Hosp. Chaplaincy, Naperville, 1980-82, Jefferson Meml. Chaplaincy, Festus, 1988-90; v.p. Contact, De Soto, Mo., 1988; chmn. Profl. Concerns Ill. Assn. Marriage and Family Therapists, Chgo., 1985-87. Mem. Am. Assn. Marriage and Family Therapists, Team Family Methods Assn. (supr. 1986-87), Ill. Assn. Marriage and Family Therapists (bd. dirs. 1985-87), Rotary (pres. Galva chpt. 1974-75). Office: St Paul Evang Luth Ch PO Box 15 Lohman MO 65053-0015

GAUGER, RANDY JAY, minister; b. Pekin, Ill., June 24, 1947; s. Wallace Earl and Opal Ellen (Berchtold) G.; m. Mary Beth Kane, Mar. 10, 1967; children: Cathy Lynn Gauger Loeppky, Christy Renee. BA, Judson Coll., 1969; MDiv, Bethel Theol. Sem., St. Paul, 1973. Ordained to ministry, Am. Bapt. Chs., 1974. Pastor Delavan (Ill.) Bapt. Ch., 1973-80; sr. pastor 1st Bapt. Ch., ElDorado, Kans., 1980-87, Topeka, 1987—; bd. dirs. cen. region Am. Bapt. Chs., Topeka, 1984-87, chmn. dept. evangelism, 1985-87, chmn. task force on regional mission statement, 1990-91, chmn. Facing Our Future campaign, 1990—; condr. workshops and preaching missions; host, phone person Your Question Please, Sta. WIBW-TV, 1989—. Trustee Ottawa (Kans.) U., 1990—. Named Best Min., Topeka Metro News, 1990. Mem. Mins. Coun. Am. Bapt. Chs., Am. Bapt. Men U.S.A. (pastor, counselor 1991—). Republican. Office: 1st Bapt Ch 3033 MacVicar St Topeka KS 66611 *I have chosen to live my life under the Lordship of Jesus Christ, who gives meaning, purpose and direction to my life. This relationship has not only brought profound satisfaction but has given me a reference point for life and helped make sense out of a sometimes confusing world.*

GAUGHAN, NORBERT F., bishop; b. Pitts., May 30, 1921; s. Thomas L. and Martha (Paczkowska) G. MA, St. Vincent Coll., Latrobe, Pa., 1944; PhD, U. Pitts., 1963; LLD, Seton Hill Coll., 1963; DD (hon.), Lebanon Valley Coll., 1980. Ordained priest Roman Cath. Ch., 1945. Chancellor Diocese of Greensburg, Pa., 1960-75, vicar gen., 1970-75, aux. bishop, 1975-84; bishop Diocese of Gary, Ind., 1984—. Author: Shepherd's Pie, 1978. Bd. dirs. Westmoreland Mus. Art, Greensburg, v.p., 1979—. Avocations: photography; silkscreens. Home: 180 W Joliet Rd Valparaiso IN 46383 Office: Diocese of Gary 9292 Broadway Merrillville IN 46410

GAUNT, JAMES JOSEPH, priest; b. Detroit, Dec. 9, 1934; s. James Joseph and Mary Johanna (Voss) G. BS, U. Windsor, 1958; STB, U. Toronto, 1964; MSc, U. Houston, 1967. Ordained priest Roman Cath. Ch., 1954; cert. tchr., Mich., Tex. Superior Basilian Fathers, Merrillville, Ind., 1973-76; prin. St. Thomas High Sch., Houston, 1976-81; superior Basilian Fathers - U. St. Thomas, Houston, 1986-90; novice master Brasilian Fathers, Sugarland, Tex., 1990—; vice chmn. bd. dirs. U. St. Thomas, Houston, 1988—; chaplain Cath. Charities, Houston, 1987-90; presbyteral coun. Houston-Galveston Diocese, 1986-90, del. NFPC, Louisville, 1988, L.A., 1990. Home and Office: 106 5th St Sugar Land TX 77478

GAUSE, NORMA NEAL, religion educator; b. St. Joseph, Mo., Sept. 21, 1920; d. Chester Abraham and Theresa Ann (Mull) Dolginoff; m. Robert Pritchard Gause, Feb. 16, 1941; children: Robert Donovan, Shannon Neal,

Rebekah Mary, Garrett Bryan. Oral Hygienist magna cum laude, Northwestern U., 1940; BA with honors, U. South Fla., 1964, MA with honors, 1967; ThD, Internat. Bible Inst. and Sem., 1983; LittD (hon.), Beacon Coll., 1977. Lic. oral hygienist, Fla. Hygienist, Van Brunt Dental, Clearwater, Fla., 1941-60; instr. U. S. Fla., Tampa, 1967-73; prof. religion Fla. Beacon Coll., Largo, 1973—; pres., lectr. Soncoat Bible Class, Inc., Tarpon Springs, Fla., 1970; pres. Norma Neal Ministries, Inc., Tarpon Springs, 1982—; v.p. Project Look Up Internat., Largo, 1982—. Author: Right Dividing Word, 1982. Author, lectr. cassette tapes: Books of the Bible, 1981; TV series: Spotlight on Israel, 1982; radio programs: Choose Life, 1982—. Mem. adv. bd. Am. Christian Trust, Washington, 1983—; mem. exec. bd. Living Ctr. Bibl. and Archeol. Studies, 1984—. Mem. Am. Assn. Univ. Profs., Mortar Bd. Republican. Methodist. Club: Hadassah (Clearwater). Avocations: travel, reading, writing.

GAUSTAD, EDWIN SCOTT, historian; b. Rowley, Iowa, Nov. 14, 1923; s. Sverre and Norma (McEachron) G.; m. Helen Virginia Morgan, Dec. 19, 1946; children—Susan, Glen Scott, Peggy Lynn. B.A., Baylor U., 1947; M.A., Brown U., 1948, Ph.D., 1951. Instr. Brown U., 1951-52, Am. Council Learned Socs. scholar in residence, 1952-53; dean Shorter Coll., 1953-57; prof. humanities U. Redlands, 1957-65; assoc. prof. history U. Calif., Riverside, 1965-67; prof. U. Calif., 1968-89, prof. emeritus, 1989—; vis. prof. Princeton Theol. Sem., 1991-92; vis. prof. Baylor U., 1976, U. Calif., Santa Barbara, 1986, U. Richmond, 1987, Princeton Sem., 1991-92. Author: The Great Awakening in New England, 1957, Historical Atlas of Religion in America, 2d edit, 1976, Religious History of America, revised edit., 1990, Dissent in American Religion, 1973, Baptist Piety: The Last Will and Testimony of Obadiah Holmes, 1978, George Berkeley in America, 1979, Faith of Our Fathers, 1987, Liberty of Conscience: Roger Williams in America, 1991; editor books, most recent being: Documentary History of Religion in America, 2 vols., 1992; editor Arno Press, 1970-79; mem. editorial bd. Jour. Ch. and State, 1970—; contbr. articles to profl. publs. Served to 1st lt. USAAC, 1943-45. Decorated Air medal; Am. Council Learned Socs. grantee, 1952-53, 72-73; Am. Philos. Soc. grantee, 1972-73. Mem. Am. Hist. Assn., Am. Acad. Religion, Am. Soc. Ch. History (pres.), Orgn. Am. Historians, Phi Beta Kappa. Democrat. Baptist. Office: U Calif Dept History Riverside CA 92521

GAUTHIER, JOSEPH DELPHIS, clergyman; b. Hartford, Conn., Aug. 23, 1909; s. Victor Adélard and Marie Alexandrine (Domingue) G. BS, Trinity Coll., Hartford, 1930; AB, Weston Coll., 1940, AM, 1941, S.T.L., 1945; D. ès L., U. Laval, 1948; D.H.L., Boston Coll., 1981. Spl. agt. Hartford Accident & Indemnity Co., 1930-35; entered Soc. of Jesus, 1935; ordained priest Roman Cath. Ch., 1944; asst. prof., chmn. Romance lang. dept. Boston Coll., 1948-52, chmn. dept., 1952-61, asso. prof. French lit., until 1966, prof., 1966—; editorial adviser, cons. Brit. World Lang. Dictionary, 1955; Mem. Mass. adv. com. fgn. lang. cons.; steering com. for Mass., Nat. Def. Edn. Act. Author: Le Canada français et le roman americain, 1948, Nouvelle Promenade littéraire, 1959, Variétés, 1960, (with Lewis A. Sumberg) Les Grands Ecrivains Francais, 1965, Douze voix Francaises, 1969, (with Vera G. Lee) La Vie des Lettres, 1970. Decorated chevalier Palmes Académiques, 1951, officer, 1958. Mem. N.E. Modern Lang. Assn. (pres. 1958), Modern Lang. Assn., Renaissance Soc. Am., Cath. Commn. Cultural and Intellectual Affairs, Am. Assn. Tchrs. French, Franco-Am. Hist. Soc., Am. Assn. Tchrs. German, Am. Assn. Tchrs. Spanish and Portuguese, Am. Assn. Tchrs. Italian. Address: Boston Coll Chestnut Hill MA 02167

GAUTHIER, ROLAND JOSEPH, priest, educator; b. Montreal, Que., Can., Oct. 2, 1915; s. Hector and Alice (Laberge) G. BA, U. Montreal, 1936, LPh, 1940; Diploma, Gregorian Chant, St. Benoit du Lac, 1945; DTh, U. St. Thomas, Rome, 1948. Ordained priest Roman Cath. Ch., 1940. Editor Cahiers Josephol St. Joseph Oratory, Montreal, 1953—, rector, pilgrimage, 1956-62; prof. theology Holy Cross Sem., Montreal, 1942-54; prof. Josephology U. Montreal, 1958-62; gen. dir. Ctr. Josephology, Montreal, 1950—; lectr. in field.; dir. internat. symposium on St. Joseph, Rome, 1970, Toledo, 1976, Montreal, 1980, Kalisz, 1985, Mex., 1989. Author: La paternite de St. Joseph, 1958, L'office de St. Joseph, 1970, Ouvrage de Jean Tritheme, 1973; (with others) Joseph et Jesus, 1975; contbr. articles to religious publs. Fellow Can. Soc. Marian Studies (counsellor 1970-76); mem. Pontifical Acad. Mariology (lectr. 1954-84), N.Am. Soc. Josephology (pres. 1962—), Ibero-Am. Soc. Josephology (cons. 1957—), Cath. Theol. Soc. Am. Home and Office: St Joseph Oratory, 3800 Queen Mary Rd, Montreal, PQ Canada H3V 1H6

GAVIN, CARNEY EDWARD, priest, museum curator, archaeologist; b. Boston, Mar. 28, 1939; s. Patrick and Grayce Ann (Carney) G.; A.B. summa cum laude in Classics, Boston Coll., 1959; postgrad. Jesus Coll., Oxford U., 1959-61; S.T.B. cum laude, U. Innsbruck, Austria, 1963, Liz. Theol., 1965; Ph.D., Harvard U., 1973; cert. of advanced research U. Damascus, Syria, 1978. Ordained priest Roman Catholic Ch. 1965. Field supv. excavations in Jordan, Araq el-Emir, Hesban, 1962, 70, 71, joint expedition to Idalion, Cyprus, 1971, 72; negotiator, planner U.S. expedition to Carthage, Tunisia, 1973, 74; asst. to curator Harvard Semitic Mus., Cambridge, Mass., 1968-73, asst. curator, 1973-75, curator, assoc. dir., 1975-86, exec. dir., 1986—; dir. Ecumenical Counselling Service, Melrose, Mass., 1979—, asst. in residence St. Columbkille's Parish, Brighton, 1965—, affiliate Harvard Univ. Winthrop House, Cambridge, 1974—, coordinator Allston-Brighton Clergy Assn. Brighton, 1968-71. Author: Image of the East, 1983, L'Heritage Lumineux, 1983, Imperial Self-Portrait, 1989, Carney Arabian Recordings, 1991. Editor book series: Readings in Theology, 1963, 64, 65. Producer, dir. exhibits and TV films on Near Eastern History. Decorated knight Equestrian Order of Holy Sepulchre; research Renovation and Archival grantee, Nat. Endowment for the Arts, 1973—; research and exhibit grantee Nat. Endowment for the Humanities, 1975—; Travelling fellow Nat. Mus. Act, 1977, 78; ednl. (poster) grantee, Internat. Fund for Promotion of Culture (UNESCO), 1981-84. Mem. Bostonian Soc. (life) 1958—, Oxford Union Soc. (life) 1959—, Effingham Club (life) 1959—, Bostin Latin Sch. Assn., Internat. Catacomb Soc (bd. dirs. 1991). Clubs: Goethe Soc. of New Eng. (dir. 1980—), Polish Cultural Heritage Soc. (dir. 1983—), Mins. of Boston (life), Coub of Old Vols. Home: St Columbkille's Rectory Brighton MA 02135 *" I believe all Thou hast revealed—because of Thy own infinite veracity. I hopein Thee above all things—because of Thy own infinite fidelity; and I love Thee above all things—with my whole heart—for Thy infinite beauty and goodness; and I am heartily sorry that ever I offended so great a God." (Last words of St. John Gavin, S.J., from court records before his execution, London, June 20, 1679.).*

GAY, CRAIG MATTHEW, religion educator; b. Pasadena, Calif., Oct. 26, 1955; s. Henry Matthew and Jan (Craig) G.; m. Julie Lane, May 31, 1980;1 child, Andrew. BS, Stanford U., 1979; diploma, Regent Coll., 1982, MTS, 1983; PhD, Boston U., 1989. Asst. prof. interdisciplinary studies Regent Coll., Vancouver, B.C., Can., 1991—. Author: With Liberty or Justice for Whom?, 1991. John M. Olin Found. fellow, 1985, 86, 87. Mem. Am. Acad. Religion, Am. Sociol. Assn., Soc. Bibl. Lit., Soc. for Sci. Study of Religion. Office: Regent Coll, 5800 University Blvd, Vancouver, BC Canada V6T 2E4

GAY, GEORGE ARTHUR, religion educator, minister; b. Niagara Falls, Ont., Can., Apr. 13, 1916; s. Robert Marshal and Marie (Copp) G.; m. Mary Thomas Bellah, May 16, 1942; children: Robert Stephen, Lloyd Thomas. BA, U. Toronto, Can., 1942; BD magna cum laude, Fuller Theol. Sem., 1952, MTh, 1958; PhD, U. Manchester, Eng., 1971. Ordained to ministry Associated Gospel Chs. Can., 1942. Sec., field rep. InterVarsity Christian Fellowship, Alta., Can., 1942-43; missionary Evang. Union of S.Am., Bolivia, 1944-49; sem. prof. Latin Am. Mission, San Jose, Costa Rica, 1953-74, Fuller Theol. Sem., Pasadena, Calif., 1974—; acting dir. Hispanic Ministries, 1974-77, 82-85. Contbr. articles to religious jours. Active YMCA, Pasadena, 1975—. Mem. Soc. Bibl. Lit., Acad. Evangelism, Tyndale Fellowship, Inst. Bibl. Rsch., Hispanic Assn. for Theol. Edn. (sec.-treas. 1973—), Alberto Mottesi Evangelistic Assn. (bd. dirs.). Home: 1259 N Hill Ave Pasadena CA 91104 Office: Fuller Theol Sem 135 N Oakland Ave Pasadena CA 91182

GAZAWAY, JAMES AUSTIN, minister; b. Decatur, Ga., Sept. 23, 1955; s. James Frank and Tinie Olena (King) G.; m. Dora Kay Allen, Apr. 23, 1977; children: Joshua Allen, James Jeremiah, Rebekah Diane. BS, Atlanta Christian Coll., 1976, BTh, 1980; MAR, Emmanuel Sch. of Religion, Johnson City, Tenn., 1989, MDiv, 1989. Ordained to ministry Christian Ch., 1976. Case worker, pastoral counselor Christian City Children's Home, College Park, Ga., 1978-79; minister of youth Snellville (Ga.) Christian Ch., 1979-83; life space therapist/house parent Grandfather Home for Children, Banner Elk, N.C., 1984-85; minister Rosspoint (Ky.) Ch. of Christ, 1985-89; minister of youth and edn. Woodstock (Ga.) Christian Ch., 1989—; vol. worker Jesus Place Inner City Missions, Atlanta, 1972-75; founding mem. Christian Youth of Ga., Atlanta, 1981-83, 89—; trustee campus ministry U. Ga., Athens, 1981-83; chaplain Appalachian Regional Hosp., Harlan, Ky., 1985-89. Author: Study of John 18:12-14, 19-24, 1989; artist religious metal sculptures, The Font, 1982 (internat. juried exhbn. 1985), Chalice 1984 (juried exhbn. 1984), The Emmanuel Cross, 1989; contbr. articles to profl. jours. Bd. dirs., chmn. Christian Family Svcs., Harlan, Ky., 1986-89. Recipient award of Arms, Soc. Creative Anachronism, Atlant, 1982, Dist. award of Merit, Boy Scouts Am., Blue Grass Coun., 1989, Whitney M. Young Svc. award Nat. Office Boy Scouts Am., 1990. Mem. NRA (field instr. 1976—, Disting. Instr. award 1987), Christian Youth of Ga. (activity coord. 1981-82, pre-teen conv. staff 1991), Religious Rels. Com. (ind. chs. rep. 1988—, God and Svc. award 1978), House of Saint Dunstan (chmn. 1986—), Fellowship of Christian Magicians, Masons, others. Office: Woodstock Christian Church PO Box 19 Hwy 92 Woodstock GA 30188 *Our life on earth is a pilgrimage. From our beginnings at conception we traveled into this world. During our lifetime we travel through this world. Then, depending on how we managed in our journey, we choose our destiny and end of our travels in the world yet to come.*

GAZOULEAS, PANAGIOTIS J., journalist; b. Thessaloniki, Greece, Oct. 3, 1927; came to U.S., 1957, naturalized, 1960; s. John Panagiotis and Eva S. (Papanastasiou) G.; m. Patricia Tuttle, Aug. 26, 1956; children—John, Edward, Mary-Elizabeth. B.A., Hunter Coll., 1964, M.A. in Soviet Affairs, 1967. Journalist Greece, 1950-56; reporter Atlantis, N.Y.C., 1957-59; editor Monthly Illus. Atlantis; editor in chief daily Atlantis, 1959-71; pub., editor Orthodox Observer, N.Y.C., 1971—. Author: (poetry) Destinies, 1956; (fiction) Chronicles 76, 1976; (biography) Breath of God, 1985. Served to 1st lt. Greek Army, 1950-53. Decorated gold cross, crusader of Holy Sepulchre, Patriarch of Jerusalem, gold cross Mount of Athos, Ecumenical Patriarchate of Constantinople. Mem. Associated Ch. Press, Overseas Press Club. Home: 10 Brooklands Bronxville NY 10708 Office: Orthodox Observer 8 E 79th St New York NY 10021

GEANEY, JOHN JOSEPH, priest, communications executive; b. Stoneham, Mass., Nov. 8, 1937; s. Denis Patrick and Hannah Mary (Barry) G. BA, St. Paul's Sem., Washington, 1960, MA in Theology, 1964; MA in Speech, UCLA, 1968. Ordained priest Roman Cath. Ch., 1964. Asst. pastor St. Paul the Apostle Ch., L.A., 1964-66; campus chaplain UCLA, 1966-68; prof. communications St. Paul's Coll., Washington, 1968-75; dir. communications Archdiocese Balt., 1975-82; pres., producer, dir. Intercommunity Telecommunications, Silver Spring, Md., 1982—, bd. dirs. com. on evangelization, 1980—; dir. Paulist Communications, 1990—. Producer radio programs Sound and Sense, Counterpoint: An Act of Thanksgiving, 1973, TV programs Share the Word, Today in Your Life, 1968-75, Counterpoint, 1971, People to People, 1973-75, Mr. Rainbow's World, 1976-82, Realities, 1978-82, Real to Reel, 1981, TV spot You Only Live Once, 1979 (Clio award 1979). Recipient Gabriel awards for religious radio programs 1973, 81, 89, Addy award for radio comml., 1978, Clio award, 1979, Proclaim award, 1982, Wilbur award for TV news feature, 1989. Mem. N. Am. Regional Assn. World Assn. Christian Communication, Unda-USA (pres. 1978-84), Unda-Internat. (mem. exec. com. 1983—), Md., D.C., Del. Broadcaster's Assn., Broadcast Pioneers, Assn. Cath. TV and Radio Syndicators, VISN (bd. dirs. mem. 1991—), Paulist Communications (bd. dirs. 1990—). Office: Intercommunity Telecommunications 818 Roeder Rd Silver Spring MD 20910

GEARY, DAVID A., pastor; b. Wilkes Barre, Pa., Jan. 1, 1943; s. Donald E. and Betty (McCaughey) G.; m. Karen A. Geary, May 20, 1965; children: Troy, Jeremy, Joshua. BS, No. State U., Aberdeen, S.D., 1965. Ordained into ministry Assembly of God, 1980. Assoc. pastor Northland Cathedral, Kansas City, Mo., 1974-75, 1st Assembly of God, Lincoln, Nebr., 1975-79; assoc. pastor Northfield Ch., Gering, Nebr., 1979-80, sr. pastor, 1980-86; sr. pastor Virginia (Minn.) Assembly of God, 1988—. Mem. Virginia Area Min. Assn. (treas. 1989—). Home: 538 11th St S Virginia MN 55792 Office: Virginia Assembly of God 1 Sunrise Dr Virginia MN 55792

GEBAUER, VICTOR EARL, music and religion educator; b. Christchurch, Canterbury, New Zealand, Oct. 13, 1938; came to U.S., 1941; s. A. Oscar and Gertrude Pauline Louise (Forster) G.; m. Marilyn Ruth Schreiber, Dec. 27, 1966; children: Amy Ruth, Christopher Earl, Aaron Paul, Hilary Paula. MDiv, Concordia Sem., St. Louis, 1964; MA, U. Minn., 1966, PhD, 1976; postgrad., U. Chgo., 1968, Free U. Berlin, 1969-70. Ordained to ministry Luth. Ch.-Mo. Synod, 1970. Prof. music and religion Concordia Coll., St. Paul, 1966—; chmn. Fine Arts div., 1978-80, 89—; gen. mgr. Festival of Worship and Witness, Luth. Chs., Mpls., 1981-83. Editor Grace Notes, 1989—, Response, 1976-78; author: Manual for Altar Guilds, 1988; contbr. articles to profl. jours., chpts. to books. Mem. N.Am. Acad. Liturgy, Hymn Soc. Am., Am. Musicol. Soc. Office: Concordia Coll 275 N Syndicate Saint Paul MN 55104

GEBERT, HERMAN JOHN, Christian radio station executive; b. Mpls., Mar. 29, 1949; s. Charlie Lewis and Pearl Evelyn (Anderson) G.; m. Margaret Ann Ray, July 3, 1971; children: Angelene Michelle, Herman John Jr. BA in Psychology, U. Minn., 1971. Cert. 1st class engr. Announcer Sta. KNOF, Selby Broadcasting, St. Paul, 1974-76, Sta. WDLM, Moody Bible Inst., East Moline, Ill., 1979-80; gen. mgr. Sta. KHEP Radio Christian Communications, Phoenix, 1980—; bd. dirs. Christian Communications, Inc., Phoenix, 1984—, v.p., 1989—; v.p., bd. dirs. Grand Canyon Broadcasters, Inc., Phoenix, 1989—. Pub. rels. chmn. Galesburg (Ill.) Exch. Club, 1979; chmn. bd. dirs., moderator Branch of Hope Ch., Phoenix, 1987-89. Mem. Nat. Assn. Broadcasters, Ariz. Broadcasters Assn., Met. Phoenix Broadcasters, Nat. Religious Broadcasters, Western Religious Broadcasters. Republican. Office: Sta KHEP Radio 3883 N 38th Ave Phoenix AZ 85019 *God has created us with the ability to choose. As a result of His divine creativity each of us can become the person we want to be. You can become the person you want to be. Christ lives within us and lives His life through us to the extent we allow Him to.*

GEDZHEV, NEDYO, head of religious order. Chief mufti of Turkish Muslim in Bulgaria, Supreme Muslim Theol. Coun., Sofia. Office: Supreme Muslim Theol Coun, Miladinovi St 27, Sofia Bratya, Bulgaria*

GEE, JAMES DAVID, minister; b. Sanger, Calif., Oct. 10, 1934; s. Arnold Bert and Myrtle Nina (White) G.; m. Diana Louis Moran, Nov. 16, 1960; children: James David Jr., Jonathon, Julie Frances. AA, Bakersfield (Calif.) Coll., 1954; BA, Fresno State Coll., 1957, Pentecostal Bible Coll., Livermore, Calif., 1967; DD (hon.), Living Faith Ministeries, Boise Idaho, 1979, ECC, Fresno, Calif., 1984; LHD (hon.), Minn. Grad. Sch. Theology, St. Paul, 1988. Ordained to ministry Pentecostal Ch. of God, 1961. Pastor Full Gospel ch., Concord, Calif., 1961-85; dist. presbyter Pentecostal Ch. of God, Citrus Heights, Calif., 1977-85; asst. gen. supt. Pentecostal Ch. of God, Joplin, Mo., 1981-85, dir. world missions, 1985-87, gen. supt., 1987-89. Editor-in-chief Pentecostal Messenger, Joplin, 1987-89. Chmn. bd. regents Messenger Coll., Joplin, 1987-89. With U.S. Army, 1952-59. Mem. N.Am. Renewal Svc. Com. (steering com. 1988-89), Nat. Assn. Evangelicals (bd. adminstrs. 1987-89), Pentecostal Fellowship of N.Am. (bd. adminstrs. 1987-89). Republican. Home: Rte 8 Box 140 Joplin MO 64804 Office: Pentecostal Ch God 4901 Pennsylvania PO Box 850 Joplin MO 64802

GEER, ANN, minister, ecumenical agency administrator. Exec. dir. Coun. of Chs. of Greater Springfield, Mass. Office: Coun Chs Greater Springfield 152 Summer Ave Springfield MA 01108*

GEER, MARY LOU, church musician, educator; b. Munich, Germany, Nov. 12, 1947; (parents Am. citizens); d. Lewis Henry and Edna Muriel (Hall) Ribble; m. John Monroe Geer Jr., May 31, 1969. BA magna cum laude, Trinity U., San Antonio, 1969, postgrad., 1970-71; BA magna cum laude, Presbyn Coll., Clinton, S.C., 1978; postgrad., Old Dominion U., 1983-84. Cert. lay profl. ch. music Evang. Luth. Ch. in Am., 1979. Organist Christ the King Luth. Ch., Universal City, Tex., 1966-67, St. John's Ch., Bayonne, N.J., 1973-75; organist, choir dir. St. John's Ch., Clinton, S.C., 1975-78; dir. worship resources Emmanuel Luth. Ch., Virginia Beach, Va., 1978-80, 82-85; organist Protestant Chapel, Kwajalein, Federated States of Micronesia, 1981-82; dir. music Bethlehem Luth. Ch., Indpls., 1985-89; dir. music, worship planner, cons. edn. Zion Luth. Ch., Deerfield, Ill., 1989-90; cantor, tchr. Park View Luth. Ch. and Sch., Chgo., 1990-91; mem. profl. preparations mng. group Va. Synod, 1979-80, coun. for ministry, 1983-85, del. congregation conv., 1983-84; chmn. worship com. Luth. Coun. Tidewater-Norfolk Area, Va., 1984-85. Author instrn. booklet, 1979, hymn text, 1982. Vol. supr. Army Community Svcs., Ft. Story, Va., 1978-80. Va. Synod Worship Com. Nat. Confs. scholar, 1983-84. Mem. Am. Guild Organists, Choristers Guild, Liturgical Conf., Hymn Soc. Am., Am. Recorder Soc., Mortar Bd., Ft. Story Women's Club (pres. 1979-80), Mu Phi Epsilon, Sigma Delta Pi, Pi Delta Phi, Alpha Chi. Home: 17650 W Julie Ln Gurnee IL 60031 Office: Zion Luth Ch 10 Deerfield Rd Deerfield IL 60015

GEERTZ, ARMIN WILBERT, religious studies writer, educator; b. Elmhurst, Ill., Feb. 25, 1948; s. Armin Martin Geertz and Audrey Grace (Blum) Jedinak. Magistrate of Art, Aarhus (Denmark) U., 1978. Asst. prof. Aarhus U., 1979-82, research fellow, 1983-84, assoc. prof., 1984—, head dept. history of religions, 1985-90. Author: Hopi Indian Altar Iconography, 1987, Children of Cottonwood, 1988; editor: Og Da Blev Jeg En Sky, 1986, Du Er Slave Ej Menneske, 1989, A Concordance of Hopi Indian Texts, 1989, Mystik-Den Indre Vej?, 1990, Religion, Tradition, and Renewal, 1991; editor Religionsvidenskabeligt Tidsskrift mag., 1982-87; assoc. editor Temenos: Studies in Comparative Religion mag., 1986—, European Rev. of Native Am. Studies mag., 1986—, Jour. for the Study of Native American Religious Traditions, 1990—; contbr. numerous articles to profl. jours. Research grantee Danish Research Council, 1978, 82, Aarhus U. Research Fund, 1986-88. Mem. Danish Assn. of History Religions (chmn. 1982—), Nordic Commn. of History Religions (chmn. 1988-89), Soc. Study Indigenous Langs. Ams., Internat. Assn. for the History of Religions (hon. treas. 1990—), Soc. for Study Native Am. Religious Traditions (bd. dirs. 1987—). Office: Aarhus U, Dept Study Religion, Hovedbygningen, Aarhus C, Denmark *Human reality is a frail ship in the seas of existence. It is constructed with the ephemeral timbers of hope and ingenuity. And yet it safely guides us wherever we will.*

GEFFEN, M. DAVID, rabbi; b. Atlanta, Nov. 1, 1938; s. Louis and Anna (Birshtein) G.; m. Rita Feld, Dec. 29, 1962; children: Avram Baruch, Elissa Kathryl, Tuvia Jeremy. BA, Emory U., 1959; M in Hebrew Lit., Jewish Theol. Sem., N.Y.C., 1963; DD (hon.), Jewish Theol. Sem., Jerusalem, 1991; PhD, Columbia U., 1970. Ordained rabbi, 1965. Rabbi Congregation Beth Shalom, Wilmington, Del., 1970-77; coord. Interreligious Coordinating Coun. in Israel, Jerusalem, 1991—; pres. Rabbinical Assn. Del., Wilmington, 1973-74. Author: 50 Year History Congregation Beth Shalom, 1972, Jewish Delaware 1655-1976, 1976, Har-El Jerusalem—A Vision Come True, 1988, American Heritage Haggadah, 1991; editor: Haggada (with Russian transl.), 1991. Mem. Del. Human Rels. Commn., Dover, 1971-75. Capt. U.S. Army, 1965-67. Named Outstanding Citizen of Del., News Jour., 1977; Woodrow Wilson fellow, 1959-60. Mem. Rabbinical Assembly, Jewish Hist. Soc. Del. (founder, hon. life bd. dirs. 1972—), Phi Beta Kappa. Home: 438/4 Bosem St, Gilo, Jerusalem 93384, Israel

GEHRES, SISTER RUTH, academic administrator; b. Evansville, Ind., Apr. 4, 1933; d. Fay Alvin and Floretta Marie (Snyder) G. BA in English, Brescia Coll., 1962; PhD in English, St. Louis U., 1968. Elem. tchr. St. Joseph Sch., Nebraska City, Nebr., 1954-57; elem. prin. Our Lady of Mercy Sch., Hodgenville, Ky., 1957-58; jr. high sch. tchr. Sts. Joseph and Paul Sch., Owensboro, Ky., 1958-62; prof. English Brescia Coll., Owensboro, 1967—, chairperson Humanities Div. and English dept., 1969-77, alumni dir., 1977-79, pres., 1986—; tchr. English Gymnasium der Ursulinen, Straubing, Fed. Republic Germany, 1984-85. Bd. dirs. Jr. Achievement, Owensboro, 1986—, Leadership Owensboro, 1986—; bd. dirs Ky. Ind. Coll. Fund, Louisville, 1986—; mem. bd. overseers St. Meinrad Sem. Mem. MLA, Nat. Assn. Ind. Colls. and Univs., Assn. Cath. Colls. and Univs., Council Ind. Ky. Colls. and Univs., C. of C. Office: Brescia Coll 717 Frederica St Owensboro KY 42301

GEIBEL, SISTER GRACE ANN, college president; b. Sept. 17, 1937. BA in Piano and Music Edn., Carlow Coll., 1961; MA in Music Edn., U. Rochester, 1967, PhD in Music, 1975. Tchr. elem. and high schs., 1959-67, ch. musician, 1972-80; assoc. prof. and co-chmn. music dept. Carlow Coll., Pitts., 1981-82, acting acad. dean, 1982-83, dean, 1983-88, v.p. acad. affairs, 1984-88, pres., 1988—; mem. pres.'s coun. Pitts. Coun. on Higher Edn., numerous other ednl. orgns. Bd. dirs. Program for Female Offenders, Girls Hope of Pitts., Pitts. Youth Symphony Orch., Pitts. Rsch. Inst., Gateway Rehab. Ctr., River City Brass Band, Oakland Cath. High Sch.; mem. adv. bd. Mom's Ho.; bd. trustees Mercy Hosp. Mem. Duquesne Club, Pitts. Athletic Assn. Office: Carlow Coll 3333 Fifth Ave Pittsburgh PA 15213-3109

GEIGER, C. EDWARD, minister, ecumenical agency administrator. Exec. dir. Met. Christian Coun. of Phila. Office: Met Christian Coun 1501 Cherry St Philadelphia PA 19102*

GEISENDORFER, JAMES VERNON, author; b. Brewster, Minn., Apr. 22, 1929; s. Victor H. and Anne B. (Johnson) G.; student Augustana Coll., 1950-51, Augsburg Coll., 1951-54, Orthodox Luth. Sem., 1954-55; BA, U. Minn., 1960; LLD, Burton Coll. and Sem., 1961; m. Esther Lillian Walker, Sept. 23, 1949; children: Jane, Karen, Lois. Grain buyer Pillsbury Mills, Inc., Worthington, Minn., 1947-48; hatchery acct., Worthington, 1949-50; night supr. Strutwear, Inc., Mpls., 1951-52; dispatcher Chgo. and North Western Ry., 1953-54; office mgr. Froedtert Malt Corp., Mpls., 1955-56, Nat. Automotive Parts Assn., 1957-60; sr. creative writer Brown & Bigelow, St. Paul, 1960-72; religious researcher, writer, 1972—; research cons. Inst. for the Study of Am. Religion; mem. panel of reference Chelston Bible Coll., New Milton, Eng.; mem. U.S. Congl. Adv. Bd., 1985. Recipient Amicus Poloniae medal Polish Ministry of Culture and Edn., 1969. Mem. Am. Acad. Religion, Acad. Ind. Scholars, Wis. Evang. Luth. Synod Hist. Inst., Augustana Hist. Soc., Ea. Territorial Hist. Soc. (charter), Wis. Acad. Scis., Arts and Letters, Can. Soc. Study of Religion, Aristotelian Soc., Hegel Soc. Am., Acad. Polit. Sci., Internat. Soc. for Comparative Study of Civilizations. Lutheran. Author: (with J. Gordon Melton) A Directory of Religious Bodies in the United States, 1977; Religion in America, 1983, Religion USA, 1989; mem. editorial bd. Biog. Dictionary of American Cult and Sect Leaders; contbr. articles to books and periodicals; cons. editor Directory of Religious Organizations in the United States, 1977. Address: 1001 Shawano Ave Green Bay WI 54303

GEISSLER, SUZANNE BURR, educator; b. Somerville, N.J., Nov. 12, 1950; d. Alfred Henry and Suzanne Judith (Golembeski) G. BA, Syracuse U., 1971, PhD, 1976; MA, Rutgers U., 1972; postgrad., Worcester Coll., Oxford U., 1973; MTS, Drew U., 1979. adj. prof. Upsala Coll., Sussex, N.J., 1979—; del. Episcopal Diocese of Newark Conv., 1989-91; mem. Diocese of Newark Com. on Constitution and Canons, Newark, 1991. Author: Jonathan Edwards to Aaron Burr, 1981, Lutheranism and Anglicanism in Colonial New Jersey, 1988. Mem. Bd. Edn., Florham Park, N.J., 1980-82. Mem. Am. Hist. Assn., Orgn. Am. Historians, U.S. Naval Inst., Navy League U.S., Aaron Burr Assn. (v.p.), Am. Soc. Ch. History, Hist. Soc. of Episcopal Ch., Chatham Club, Phi Beta Kappa. Republican. Home: 4 Midwood Dr Florham Park NJ 07932 Office: Upsala Coll 44 Compton Rd Sussex NJ 07461

GEIST, ERNEST EDWARD, minister; b. Zanesville, Ohio, Dec. 8, 1938; s. Ernest Walter and Erma Carmen (Shrake) G.; m. Ruth Elaine Keppel, July 2, 1960 (div. Feb. 1980); m. Nancy Sue Simpson, Mar. 27, 1981; children: Ernest Edwin, Douglas Alan, Daniel Jay. B Bible Philosophy, Am. Bible Inst., 1967, M Bible Philosophy, 1969, DD, 1972; BBA, Stanton U., 1969. Ordained to ministry Meth. Ch., 1965. Assoc. pastor Christ Meth. Ch., Tampa, Fla., 1963-64; pastor Hernando (Fla.) Meth. Ch., 1964-65, Hartford (Ohio) Community Ch., 1966-70, Olive Chapel United Ch. Christ, New Carlisle, Ind., 1970-71; sr. pastor Community Christian Ch, New Carlisle, 1970-75; pastor Sherman (N.Y.) Community Ch., 1975-90; sr. pastor

Evendale Community Ch., Cin., 1990—; chaplain Ind. Guard Res., 1970, N.Y. Guard Res., 1970-90; pres. United Religious Community, South Bend, Ind., 1972-74. Juvenile officer New Carlisle Police Dept., 1972, chief of police, 1974; mem. adv. bd. St. Joseph County Planned Parenthood, South Bend, 1975. Capt. USNG, 1970—. Recipient Oustanding Clergy award Hill and Dale Men's Club, New Carlisle, 1987. Mem. Acad. Parish Clergy, Police Clergy Team, Sycamore Clergy Assn., Am. Legion (Chaplains award 1975), Hamilton County Police Assn. Home and Office: 3270 Glendale Milford Rd Cincinnati OH 45241

GELDMACHER, JOAN ELIZABETH, church administrator; b. N.Y.C., Aug. 1, 1931; d. Henry William and Hazel Grace (Longstreet) Meyer; children: Cheryl, Phyllis, Dolores, David, James. BS in Edn., Elmira Coll., 1969. Dir. released time religious edn. Coun. of Chs., Elmira, N.Y., 1963-68, exec. dir., 1979—; nursing asst. St. Joseph's Hosp., Elmira, 1975-90. Active YWCA, 1969-71, Neighborhood House, 1971-74; mem. Elmira City Coun., 1975, So. Tier Regional Planning and Devel. Bd., 1975-78; chairperson Meals on Wheels; pres. Ch. Women United, 1978-82, bd. dirs.; policy coun. mem. Head Start Day Care, 1979-90; bd. dirs. Family Support Project, Elmira, 1980-84—; mem. Task Force on Children and Families, 1986—, Women in Transition Task Force, 1987—, Amerasian Resettlement Coordinating Com., 1991; sec. Coun. on Women, 1991—. Mem. Presbyn. Women in Presbytery Geneva (officer 1991). Presbyterian. Home: 621 Newton St Elmira NY 14904 Office: Coun of Chs 330 W Church St Elmira NY 14904

GELINEAU, LOUIS EDWARD, clergyman; b. Burlington, Vt., May 3, 1928; s. Leon and Juliette (Baribault) G. Student, St. Michael's Coll., Winooski, Vt., 1946-48; BA, PhB, St. Paul's U., Ottawa, Ont., Can., 1950, LST, 1954; Licentiate Canon Law, Cath. U. Am., 1959; DRE, Providence Coll., 1972. Ordained priest Roman Cath. Ch., 1954; asst. chancellor Diocese Burlington, 1959-61, chancellor, 1961-71, vicar gen., 1968-71; bishop of Providence, 1971—. Address: 1 Cathedral Sq Providence RI 02903

GELLARD, JACQUES, priest, educator; b. La Baule, France, Nov. 5, 1931; s. Gabriel and Germaine (Martin) G. M.A. in Philosophy, Jesuit Sch. Philosophy, Chantilly, France, 1957; M.A., U. Paris (Sorbonne), 1958; M.A. in Theology, Jesuit Sch. Theology, Lyon, France, 1963; Ph.D. in Sociology, U. Chgo., 1970, M.A., 1968. Joined S.J., Roman Cath. Ch., 1948, ordained priest, 1962. Asst. prof. Sociology, Jesuit Sch. Philosophy, Chantilly, France, 1968-76; prof. sociology Centre Sevres, Paris, 1974—, pres. Centre Sevres, 1979—; assoc. prof. sociology Cath. Inst., Paris, 1971—; mem. redaction com. Projet, Paris, 1971—; provincial of France of Soc. Jesus, 1985—, regional asst. to supr. gen. S.J., 1992—. Contbr. articles to profl. jours. Mem. Société Française de Sociologie, Am. Sociol. Assn., Association Française de Sociologie de la Religion, Soc. Sci. Study of Religion, Conf. Internationale de Sociologie de la Religion. Home and Office: Borgo S Spirito, 5, CP 6139, 00195 Rome Italy

GELLER, STUART M., rabbi; b. Denver, Jan. 21, 1942; s. Jack and Rose (Miller) G.; m. Ellyn Greenberg, June 9, 1963; children: David, Amy, Ari. BA, U. Colo., 1964; BHL, Hebrew Union Coll., Cin., 1968, MHL, 1970; M.Pastoral Psychology, Ashland (Ohio) Theol. Sem., 1979. Ordained rabbi. Assoc. rabbi The Temple, Cleve., 1970-80; chief rabbi Temple Emanu-el, Lynbrook, N.Y., 1980—; dir. Torah corp. UAHC/Kutz Camp, Warwick, N.Y., 1973—; bd. dirs. N.Y. Bd. Rabbis. Contbr. articles to profl. jours. Mem. N.Y. Assn. Reform Rabbis (v.p.), L.I. Assn. Reform Rabbis (pres. 1986-88), Lynbrook/E. Rockaway Clergy Assn. (pres. 1983-85, 87-89). Home: 315 Barr Ave Woodmere NY 11598 Office: Temple Emanu-el 1 Saperstein Plaza Lynbrook NY 11563

GEMAYEL, (EDMOND) BOUTROS, archbishop; b. Ain el Khar, Metn, Lebanon, June 29, 1932; s. Fares Bargis and Mathilde (Amin) G. MA in Theology, St. Joseph U., Beirut; PhD in Oriental Scis., Pontifical Oriental Inst., Rome. Archbishop of Cyprus Maronite Cath. Ch., Nicosia. Author several books. Home: Maronite Archbishop's House, 8 Faviero St, Nicosia 2249, Cyprus

GEMBALA, JOSEPH JOHN, priest; b. Ypsilanti, Mich., June 6, 1957; s. Joseph John and Irene Elsie (Bishop) G. BA, U. Mich., Ann Arbor, 1978; JD, U. Ark., Fayetteville, 1980; MDiv, St. John's Sem., Plymouth, Mich., 1987. Chmn. Pastoral Adv. Coun. Oakwood Hosp., 1989—. Mem. Down River Bar Assn. (chaplain 1988—). Democrat. Roman Catholic. Home and Office: 1531 Riverbank St Lincoln Park MI 48146

GEMEINHART, THOMAS JAMES, religion educator, minister; b. Homestead, Pa., Jan. 25, 1932; s. Charles Henry and Margaret (James) G.; m. Ruth Elaine Crawford, June 21, 1951; children: Alma Jane, Kenneth James, Bradley Jay. AB summa cum laude, Ky. Christian Coll., 1959; MA, Ind. U., 1962; postgrad., Ohio State U., 1963, U. Ky., 1966-67, Marshall U., 1989. Ordained to ministry Christian Ch., 1960. Prof. history and missions Ky. Christian Coll., Grayson, 1962—, dean students, 1972-86, asst. dean students, 1986—, asst. basketball coach, 1967-72; dir. Kyowva Missionary Rally, Grayson, 1962-83. Pres. Prichard Band Parents' Assn., Grayson, 1968-69; treas. Citizens Against State Lottery, Grayson, 1988. Named Ky. Col., State of Ky., 1969. Mem. Ind. U. Alumni Assn., Ky. Christian Coll. Alumni Assn. Avocations: model trains, gardening. Home: 213 Shady Ln Grayson KY 41143 Office: Ky Christian Coll 617 N Malone Blvd Grayson KY 41143

GENADER, ANN MARIE, church organist, educator; b. West Milford, N.J., May 28, 1932; d. Arthur John and Verina Agnes (Mathews) G. BS, Jersey City State Coll., 1954; MA, William Paterson Coll., 1969. Organist St. Joseph's Cath. Ch., West Milford, 1947-67, Our Lady Queen of Peace Cath. Ch., West Milford, 1960-84, Episcopal Ch. of Incarnation, West Milford, 1977—; tchr. West Milford Bd. Edn., 1963—; freelance writer for newspapers and mags. Named Passaic County Tchr. of Yr., 1991. Romman Catholic. Home: 1681 Union Valley Rd West Milford NJ 07480

GENDRON, ODORE JOSEPH, retired bishop; b. Manchester, N.H., Sept. 13, 1921; s. Francis and Valida (Rouleau) G. Student, St. Charles Borromeo Sem., Can., 1936-42, U. Ottawa, 1942-47. Ordained priest Roman Catholic Ch., 1947; assoc. pastor Angel Guardian Ch., Berlin, N.H., 1947-52, Sacred Heart Ch., Lebanon, N.H., 1952-60, St. Louis Ch., Nashua, N.H., 1960-65; pastor Our Lady of Lourdes Ch., Pittsfield, N.H., 1965-67, St. Augustine Ch., Manchester, N.H., 1967-71; monsignor, 1970, episcopal vicar for religious, 1972-74, episcopal vicar for clergy, 1974—; consecrated bishop of Manchester, 1975-90; ret., 1991. Office: 153 Ash St PO Box 310 Manchester NH 03105

GENEST, JEAN-BAPTISTE, priest; b. Montréal, Que., Can., Oct. 2, 1927; s. Theodore and Alice (Leclerc) G. Lic. in Theology, Grand Sem., 1954; D.E.N.S., U. Montréal, 1972. Joined Order of St. Viator, Roman Cath. Ch., 1949; ordained priest, 1954. Tchr. biology Ecole Paul-Gerin-Lajoie, Outremont, Que., 1954-89; pastoral min. parish youth Montréal, 1954-90; bd. dirs. Camp DèEcologie St. Viateur, Port-Au-Saumon, Que., 1960-91. Mem. Assn. des Camps du Que., Soc. de Botanique, l'Assn. des Biologistes du Que. (emeritus). Home: 450 Ave Querbes, Outremont, PQ Canada H2V 3W5

GENGE, KENNETH LYLE, bishop; s. Nelson Simms and Grace Winifred Genge; m. Ruth Louise Bate, 1959; three children. LTh, Emmanuel Coll., Saskatoon, Sask., 1957; BA, U. Sask., Can., 1958; BD, 1959. Parish priest The Anglican Ch. Can., 1959-85, conf. retreat ctr. dir., 1985-88; bishop Diocese of Edmonton, Alta., Can., 1988—. Office: Diocese of Edmonton, 10033 84th Ave, Edmonton, AB Canada T6E 2G6

GENN, MORDECAI HALEVI, rabbi, educator; b. N.Y.C., Dec. 6, 1946; s. Bernard and Fannie (Kusher) G. BA, BRE, MS in Ednl. Adminstrn., Yeshiva U., 1971; MA in Hebrew Lit., Brandeis U., 1975, PhD in Nr. Eastern Studies, 1978. Ordained rabbi, 1971; cert. sch. adminstr. and supr., sch. dist. adminstr.N.Y.; lic. commodities, securities broker and real estate broker. Rabbi Temple Emmanuel, Wakefield, Mass., 1971-73; asst. prin. Schechter Day Sch., Westchester, N.Y., 1973-74; prin. Hebrew Day Sch. Pelham Pkwy., Bronx, N.Y., 1975-77; rabbi Temple Israel, Daytona Beach, Fla., 1977-83; exec. dir. Bet Halevi, Inc. (nonprofit ecumenical orgn.), 1980—; account exec. Merrill Lynch, Daytona Beach, 1983-84; educator N.Y.C. High Sch. System, 1984—; guest lectr. B'nai Brith Women's Regional Conf., Bethune-Cookman Coll., Embry-Riddle Aero. U., Jacksonville Jewish Ctr., various Meth., Cath., Episc. and Unitarian instns.; adj. prof. English Mercy Coll., Dobbs Ferry, N.Y. Developer, moderator TV series Thinking Out Loud, Cen. Fla.; developer, instr. series Hebrew lang. courses for Daytona Beach Community Coll. Former activities in Volusia County, Fla. include chmn. adminstrv. bd. Community Action Agy., chmn. planning and evaluation com. bd. trustees Human Resources Ctr., mem. social services com. United Way, trustee Jewish Fedn., chmn. Interfaith-interacial Council, mem. adminstrv. bd. Jewish Social Service Council; chmn. task force studying needs of elderly for Urban Consultation, Daytona Beach, 1980; past chmn. exec. bd. Cen. Fla. O.B.T. ecumenical orgn.; past vice chmn. bd. counselors Bethune-Cookman Coll., Daytona Beach; former exec. and trustee Halifax Urban Ministries. Recipient Key to City of Daytona Beach. Mem. Nat. Coun. for Jewish Edn., Assn. Univ. Instrs. Jewish Studies, Arista, Psi Chi, Sigma Tau Delta, Pi Gamma Mu. Home: 631 N Terrace Ave # 3C Mount Vernon NY 10552

GENNADIOS, BISHOP (GENNADIOS CHRYSOULAKIS), bishop of Buenos Aires; b. Crete, Greece, Mar. 9, 1924; s. John and Evantia (Katanxsakis) Chrysoulakis. Grad. in Theology, U. Aristontelion, 1952, LLD; grad. with high honors U. Thessaloniki Sch. Theology, 1962; studied law U. Salonica. Ordained priest Greek Orthodox Church, 1944, ordained bishop, 1979. Diacono, Sitia, Crete, 1944-46, presbitero, 1946-79; obispo, N.Y., 1979; bishop of Buenos Aires (Argentina), Greek Orthodox Archdiocese of N. and S. Am., 1979—; prof. theology, Greece, Venezuela. Author: La Liberacion de Chipre, 1958; Sincronismo del Cristianismo, 1960; Los Contenidos de los Valores, 1962; Pedagogia y Moral, 1964. Served to lt., chaplain Greek Army, 1948-51. Decorated by Gen. Alexander for merit and valor, World War II, 1943. Office: Avda Figueroa Alcorta 3187, Buenos Aires 1425, Argentina

GENOVESI, VINCENT JOSEPH, religion educator, priest; b. Phila., Oct. 9, 1938; s. Dominic Vincent and Ruth Lillian (Savarese) G. BA in Sociology, Fordham U., 1962, MA in Philosophy, 1966; MDiv, Woodstock Coll., 1969; PhD in Christian Ethics, Emory U., 1973. Joined S.J.; ordained priest Roman Cath. Ch., 1969. Prof. religion St. Joseph's U., Phila., 1973—. Author: Expectant Creativity, 1982, In Pursuit of Love: Catholic Morality and Human Sexuality, 1987; contbr. articles to religious jours. Mem. Soc. Christian Ethics, Hastings Inst. Social Ethics and Life Sci., Cath. Theol. Soc. Am. Democrat. Home and Office: St Joseph's U Philadelphia PA 19131

GENTRUP, SISTER CLARICE, nun, chaplain director, administrator; b. Beemer, Nebr., Dec. 5, 1937; s. Theodore Isadore and Theresa (Spenner) G. B.S. cum laude in Pharmacy, Creighton U., 1962; postgrad. Ministry Tng. Service, 1977-78. Chief pharmacist St. Mary Hosp., Columbus, Nebr., 1963-64; dir. pharmacy and administrn. St. Anthony Hosp., Denver, 1964-77; dir. formation Sisters St. Francis, Colorado Springs, Colo., 1978-79; asst. chaplain, St. Anthony Hosp., Denver, 1979-83; chaplain dir. St. Francis Med. Ctr., Grand Island, Nebr., 1983-90; provincial councilor Sisters St. Francis, Colorado Springs, 1977-90, pres., 1990—; del. to gen. chpt. Sisters St. Francis, Olpe, W.Ger., 1984. Bd. dir. Med. Ctr. Hosps., Colo. and Nebr., 1967—; mem. adv. bd. Erhard Seminar Tng., San Francisco, 1978-81; trustee Safehouse for Battered Women, Denver, 1982-83. Recipient Merck award Merck Sharp & Dohme, 1962; E.R. Squibb Pharmacy award, 1975. Mem. Sister of St. Francis, Nat. Assn. Catholic Chaplains, sisters of Charity Healthcare System, Leadership Conf. Women Religious. Democrat. Avocations: reading, music, walking.

GENTRY, MICHAEL RAY, minister; b. El Reno, Okla., Apr. 8, 1951; s. Emmanuel Howard and Leona Drenda (Morris) G.; m. Diana Kay Sharp, Aug. 2, 1973; children: Penelope Kaye, Amy Michelle, Andrew Michael. AB in Religion, Bethany Nazarene Coll., 1973; BTh., Freelandia Inst., 1982, ThM, 1985. Ordained to ministry Ch. of the Nazarene, 1976. Dir. bus ministry Grace Ch. of the Nazarene, Kansas City, Mo., 1973-74; pastor 1st Ch. of the Nazarene, Okemah, Okla., 1974-77, Republic, Mo., 1977-79, Centralia, Ill., 1979-87, Madill, Okla., 1987-90; sr. pastor 1st Ch. of the Nazarene, Paris, Tex., 1990—; chaplain coord. Okfuskee Meml. Hosp., Okemah, 1977-79; founder, pres. Defender of the Faith, Centralia, 1981; chmn. Christian life Mt. Vernon zone Ch. of the Nazarene, Springfield, Ill., 1983-85, pres. Texoma zone, Henryetta, Okla., 1989-90, dist. treas., 1989-90; pres. Centralia Area Ministerial Alliance, 1982-83. Coord. Boy Scouts Am., Centralia, 1983-87, trainer Crooked Creek dist., Belleville, 1984-87; sec. Centralia City PTA Coun., 1984-87. Mem. Lions (bd. dirs. Centralia chpt. 1985-86, v.p. Madill chpt. 1989-90). Home: 195 20th NE Paris TX 75460 Office: 1st Ch of the Nazarene 185 20th NE Paris TX 75460 *To be successful in living the Christian life one must not merely be motivated emotionally, but changed in his heart by the Holy Spirit.*

GENTRY, SAMUEL JAMES, minister; b. Shreveport, La., June 25, 1952; s. Charles Duward and Billie Joe (Corpier) G.; m. Myra Geraldine Kampen, Jan. 29, 1977; 1 child, Laura Marie. BA, La. Coll., 1975; M of Religious Edn., So. Bapt. Theol. Seminary, Louisville, 1977, MDiv, 1983. Ordained/lic. to ministry Bapt. Ch., 1982. Missionary Home Mission Bd. So. Bapt. Conv., Atlanta, 1977-79; min. of edn. Del Norte Bapt. Ch., Albuquerque, 1980-81; minister Swallowfield (Ky.) Bapt. Ch., 1982-84, Monte Sano Bapt. Ch., Huntsville, Ala., 1984-86, Beaverdam Bapt. Ch., Fair Play, S.C., 1987—; benevolence com. Beaverdam Bapt. Ministers Conf., Seneca, S.C., 1991—; Mission Night children's speaker Beaverdam Bapt. Assn., 1988; extension tchr. Samford U., Huntsville, Ala., 1985-86; weekday early edn. com. Madison Bapt. Assn., Huntsville, 1985-86. Literacy tchr. New Orleans Coun. of Chs., 1979; v.p. Resident Men's Assn., Pineville, La., 1974-75. Named to Hon. Order of Ky. Cols., Louisville, 1984—. Mem. Athenian Literary Soc. Democrat. Home: PO Box 160 Fair Play SC 29643 Office: Beaverdam Baptist Church 328 Beaverdam Church Rd Fair Play SC 29643

GENZEN, GARY CARL, minister; b. Cleve., Feb. 18, 1944; s. Carl Henry and Lydia Caroline (Fobel) G.; m. Harriet Frieda Kretzschmar, June 28, 1969; children: David Carl, Jonathan Robert. BA, Valparaiso (Ind.) U., 1966; BD, Concordia Sem., 1970, MDiv, 1973; D Ministry, Internat. Sem., Plymouth, Fla., 1980. Ordained to ministry Luth. Ch.-Mo. Synod, 1970. Pastor Christ Luth. Ch., Southwick, Mass., 1970-77, Zion Luth. Ch., Lorain, Ohio, 1977—; pres. Greater Southwick Clergy Assn., 1973, 75. Author: Pastor, 1990; book reviewer Sharing the Practice, Concordia Theol. Quar. Mem. Westfield (Mass.) Area mental Health and Retardation Bd., 1975-77. Mem. Lorain Clergy Assn., Acad. Parish Clergy. Office: Zion Luth Ch 5100 Ashland Ave Lorain OH 44053

GEOGHEGAN, WILLIAM DAVIDSON, religion educator, minister; b. Wilmington, Del., July 16, 1922; s. Presley Downs and Mildred Alphaeus (Davidson) G.; m. Sarah Elizabeth Phelps, Oct. 5, 1946; children: Grace, Andrew, Emily, William Davidson II. BA, Yale U., 1943; postgrad., Harvard U., 1943-44; MDiv, Drew U., 1945; PhD, Columbia U., 1951. Ordained to ministry United Meth. Ch. as deacon, 1947, as elder, 1948. Pastor United Meth. Ch., Christiana, Del., 1947-50; chaplain, asst. prof. religion U. Rochester, N.Y., 1950-54; asst. prof. religion Bowdoin Coll., Brunswick, Maine, 1954-62, assoc. prof., 1962-66, prof., 1966-90, rsch. prof. religion, 1991—, chmn. dept. religion, 1954-79, 81-85, spring 1988; vis. scholar Columbia U. and Union Theol. Sem., 1964-65; dir., chmn. curriculum com., mem. exec. com. C.G. Jung Ctr. for Studies in Analytical Psychology, Inc., Brunswick, 1989—. Author: Platonism in Recent Religious Thought, 1958. Recipient Alumni award Bowdoin Coll. Alumni Assn., 1981. Mem. AAUP, Am. Acad. Religion, Hegel Soc. Am., Internat. Soc. for Neoplatonic Studies, Soc. Christian Philosophers, Town and Coll. Club, Phi Beta Kappa, Zeta Psi. Home: 40 Federal St Brunswick ME 04011 Office: Bowdoin Coll Massachusetts Hall Brunswick ME 04011

GEORGE, CARRIE LEIGH, minister; b. Winder, Ga., Sept. 28, 1915; d. Elijah James and Mattie Olian (Owens) L.; m. Domotory T. George, 1944 (dec. 1969); children: Faith Olian, Donald Tony. AB cum laude, Clark Coll., 1936; MA, Atlanta U., 1937, Ohio State U., 1943; student, Gregg Coll., 1944; MDiv, Gammon Theol. Sem., 1954; student, Hartford Sem. Found., 1956-57, Garrett-Northwestern U., 1960; EdS, NYU, 1961; PhD, Atlanta U., 1970; EdD (hon.), Burton Coll. and Sem., 1963. Min. Christian edn. Antioch Bapt. Ch., Atlanta, 1953-62; assoc. prof. religious edn., dir. field edn. Gammon Interdenom. Theol. Ctr., Atlanta, 1954-64; assoc. min. Emmanuel Bapt. Ch., Atlanta, 1963-68, K-Monumental African Meth. Episcopal Ch., Stockbridge, Ga., 1968-71; dean of edn. Mt. Hermon Missionary Bapt. Assn., Atlanta; pastor George Meml. Bapt. Ch. of Faith, Atlanta, 1981—; educator Ga. State U., Atlanta, 1970-86; instr. edn. dept. Internat. Assn. Mins. Wives and Widows, Inc., 1978-87; instr., chaplain Christian Edn. div. Atlanta Bapt. Assn., 1984—. Author: What Matters Most, 1948; columnist Atlanta Daily World, 1979-89, The Bapt. Voice, 1972; contbg. editor From the Pen of a Shepherdess, 1980; author numerous religious booklets. Pres. Urban Villa Community and Civic Orgn., Atlanta, 1963-66, 73-74, 76-78; charter mem. Presdl. Task Force, Washington, 1980; chair 33d Dist. Reps., Atlanta, 1984-87; recording sec. Nat. Black Rep. Coun., Washington, 1987-89; v.p. Black Rep. Coun., Atlanta, 1987-89; charter mem. adv. commn. Women's Rights Nat. Hist. Pk., U.S. Dept. of Interior, Seneca Falls, N.Y., 1982-87; mem. YWCA, Atlanta, 1990—, Friends of the Pub. Libr., Atlanta, 1990—; chaplain Community Savings Club, Atlanta, 1989—; pres. Friendship Uplifters, Atlanta, 1977-79. Named Woman of Yr. in Religion Iota Phi Lambda, 1957, Woman of Yr. in the Professions, 1975; recipient Most Outstanding Minister's Wife Yr. award Nat. Assn. Minister's Wives, 1956. Fellow: Anglo-Am. Acad. (Cambridge, Eng.); mem. NAACP, Am. Assn. Clin. Pastoral Women, Am. Biog. Inst. (hon., mem. editorial adv. bd.), Ga. Mental Health Assn., Bapt. Mins. Wives and Widows Coterie (pres. 1960-62, 72-73), Ch. Women United (program chair 1966-67), Societas Docta (charter), Interdenom. Theol. Ctr. Alumni Assn. (pres. 1988-90), Nat. Bapt. Women Mins. Assn. (parliamentarian 1988—), Nat. Coun. Negro Women, Atlanta U. Alumni Assn. (chaplain 1988-90), The Mayan Order, Alpha Kappa Alpha. *"I'm only human," we often hear. That's our trouble; we need more people who choose to grow Divine. Democratic government that is not girded by Christian principles spawns anarchy. If you would do away with democracy, stop teaching and living moral and spiritual values.*

GEORGE, JAMES ALFRED, music minister; b. Clinton, Mo., June 19, 1950; s. Maynard Alfred and Jean Adeline (Onwiller) G.; m. Deborah Ann Lloyd, Nov. 23, 1975; children: Christie Lynn, Jamie Ann. BS in Edn., S.W. Mo. State U., 1973; M in Ch. Music, So. Bapt. Theol. Sem., 1976. Ordained to ministry Bapt. Ch., 1979. Min. of youth and music Jefferson Ave. Bapt. Ch., Springfield, Mo., 1971-73, Shively Heights Bapt. Ch., Louisville, 1973-76, Glendale Bapt. Ch., Springfield, 1976-78; min. music First Bapt. Ch., Blue Springs, Mo., 1978—; youth music cons. Mo. Bapt. Conv., Jefferson City, Mo., 1970-85;. Named to Hon. Order of Ky. Cols.; recipient Cert. of Svc., Mayor of Shively, 1976. Mem. Blue River/Kansas City (Mo.) Bapt. Assn. (music dir. 1982-85). Republican. Office: First Bapt Ch 1405 Main St Blue Springs MO 64015

GEORGE, RANDOLPH OSWALD, bishop. Anglican bishop of Guyana; chmn. Guyana Coun. Chs., Georgetown. Office: Bishop of Guyana, Austin House, Georgetown Guyana*

GEORGE, ROY KENNETH, minister; b. Haskell, Tex., Sept. 23, 1934; s. Roy F. and Jimalee (Scott) G.; m. Patsy Sue George, May 14, 1955; children: Janis Sue, Cheryl Anne. Ordained to ministry Assemblies of God Ch., 1959. Evangelist U.S., Africa, Europe, Asia, 1954-63; pastor Highland Assembly of God Ch., Bakersfield, Calif., 1964-65, 1st Assembly of God Ch., Carlsbad, N.Mex., 1966-67, Sem. South Ch., Ft. Worth, 1968-73, Christian Ctr., Ashland, Oreg., 1974-75, 1st Family Ch., Albuquerque, 1975—; broadcaster religious radio and TV programs, including Moments with the Master, Sta. KKIM, Albuquerque, 1975-85; state exec. presbyter Assemblies of God N.Mex., 1976—; asst. dist. supt. Assemblies of God, 1981—, mem. Gen. Presbytery, 1981—. Contbr. articles to profl. jours. Bd. regents Southwestern Assemblies of God Coll. at Waxahachie, Tex., 1981—. Mem. Albuquerque Ministerial Assn., Greater Albuquerque Pentecostal Fellowship (pres. 1975-76), Rogue Valley Nat. Assn. Evangels. (v.p. 1974-75), Civitains (chaplain 1969-73), Kiwanis (pres. Albuquerque club 1982-83, lt. gov. S.W. dist. 1985-86). Office: 1st Family Ch 4701 Wyoming Blvd NE Albuquerque NM 87111 *The only way to win in the Game of Life, is to overcome evil with good. To conquer evil by being bad is folly. The Game plan that wins, is when you return Good for Evil.*

GEORGE, WILLIAM F., priest; b. Niles, Ohio, Sept. 7, 1939; s. Fanos and Rose (Borda) G.; m. Judith Ann, Jan. 7, 1968; children: Victoria Lynn, Michael David, William Jeffery. MDiv., Nashotah House. Ordained priest Episcopal Ch. Rector in charge St. James, Batavia, N.Y., 1974-75; vicar St. Andrews, Newfane, N.Y., 1975-80; assoc. rector St. Philips, Oak Bay, B.C., Can., 1981-82; exec. dir. Anglican Renewal Ctr., Victoria, B.C., 1982-86; rector St. John's, Petaluma, Calif., 1986—; chaplain Woman's Aglow, Santa Rosa, Calif., 1990—. Cpl. USMC, 1957-60. Home: 708 Glenice St Petaluma CA 94954 Office: St Johns Episcopal Ch 40 Fifth St Petaluma CA 94952

GEPFORD, WILLIAM GEORGE, minister; b. Kansas City, Mo., Jan. 12, 1927; s. Herbert John and Anna Ruth (Minckemeyer) G.; m. Barbara Joan Beebe, Dec. 28, 1952; children: David Proctor, Scott Allen, Joanna Lynn, Andrea Laine. BS in Edn. Engring., Colo. State U., 1949; MDiv., McCormick Sem., 1953; MEd, U. Colo., 1957; DSc in Theology, San Francisco Sem., 1973. Ordained to ministry Presbyn. Ch. (U.S.A.), 1953. Edn. missionary Presbyn. Ch., Lebanon, 1953-63; asst. min. First Presbyn. Ch., Boulder, Colo., 1963-65; missionary, student min. Presbyn. Ch., Hong Kong, 1965-71; chaplain, student life dir. Muskingum Coll., New Concord, Ohio, 1972-79; dir. Am./Arab Ministry Presbytery of Detroit, Mich., 1979—; dean of students Am. Univ. Beirut, Lebanon, 1961-63; dir. student ctr. YMCA (Chinese), Hong Kong, 1965-71; acting assoc. dean of students, Muskingum Coll., New Concord, 1968-69; mem. gen. assembly, adv. study com. on Islam, N.Y., 1983-86; bd. dirs. Interfaith Activities, Presbytery of Detroit; founder Muslim/Christian Dialogue Group, 1985; adv. bd. Arab Community Ctr. of Econ. and Social Svcs., Dearborn, 1983—; mem. Am. Arab Anti-Discrimination com., adv. com., Detroit, 1984—, others. mem. adv. bd. ACCESS, Dearborn, Mich., 1985—; clergy participant Interfaith Round Table of Detroit, 1985—; bd. dirs. Human Svcs., Inc., Dearborn, 1986—; mem. citizens adv. bd. WTVS Ch. 56 PBS, Detroit, 1986-89. With USN, 1945-46. Mem. McCormick Sem. Alumni Assn. (pres.-elect 1991-93), Kiwanis (pres. Dearborn 1986-87), Phi Delta Kappa. Democrat. Home: 10395 S Morrow Cir Dearborn MI 48126

GERALI, STEVEN PETER, minister; b. Chgo., Nov. 7, 1956; s. Peter A. and Ruth G. (Baldare) G.; m. Janice Blair, Oct. 22, 1983; children: Andrea Ruth, Alison Blair. BA in Pastoral Tng., Moody Bible Inst., Chgo., 1979; MEd in Counseling, Loyola U., Chgo., 1984; postgrad., Oxford Grad. Sch., U.S. Ordained to ministry, 1984. Min. music and youth Salem Bapt. Ch., Orland Park, Ill., 1977-79, Homewood (Ill.) Bapt. Ch., 1979-80; min. to youth Calvary Meml. Ch., Oak Park, Ill., 1981-87; pastor in charge student ministries Trinity Bible Ch., Phoenix, 1987—; adj. faculty Ariz. Coll. of the Bible, Phoenix, 1990—; bd. dirs. Promise House Ministries, Phoenix, 1989—; co-host radio program, Counselors Point of View, 1990—. Contbr. articles to profl. jours. Mem. AACD, Am. Mental Health Counselors Assn., Nat. Network Youth Ministries. Office: Trinity Bible Ch 3420 W Peoria Phoenix AZ 85029

GERARD, JOSEPH EUGENE, clergyman; b. Mishawaka, Ind., July 31, 1944; s. Joseph and Maxine (LaRue) G.; m. Alice Lynn Martindill, Sept. 3, 1964; children: David, Pamela, Cheri, Michael. BA, Faith Bapt. Bible Coll., 1973; postgrad., Oakland Community Coll., Pontiac, Mich., 1968, Grace Theol. Sem., Winona Lake, Ind., 1974, Moody Bible Inst., Chgo., 1985. Ordained to ministry Gen. Assn. Regular Bapt. Chs., 1975. Min. edn. Urbandale (Iowa) Bapt. Ch., 1971-72; pastor Bluffton (Ind.) Bapt. Ch., 1973-74, Calvary Bapt. Ch., Adrian, Mo., 1974-77, Portage Avenue Bapt. Ch., Portage, Ind., 1977—; Sunday sch. tchr., supt., youth sponsor, mus. evangelist various chs. Chaplain CAP. Capt. U.S. Army, 1962-73, Vietnam. Decorated Bronze Star with oak leaf cluster, Purple Heart, Air medal with two oak leaf clusters. Home: 6601 Portage Ave Portage IN 46368 Office: Portage Avenue Bapt Ch 6605 Portage Ave Portage IN 46368

GERBER, EUGENE J., bishop; b. Kingman, Kans., Apr. 30, 1931; s. Cornelius John and Lena Marie (Tiesmeyer) G. B.A., St. Thomas Sem., Denver; B.S., Wichita State U.; B.S.Th., Catholic U. Am.; S.T.L., Angelicum, Rome. Ordained priest Roman Catholic Ch., 1959; asst. chancellor Wichita Diocese, 1963, sec. to bishop, 1964, vice chancellor, 1967, mem. diocesan bd. adminstrn., 1973, diocesan cons., 1973, chancellor, 1975; chaplain, mem. governing bd. Holy Family Center for Mentally Retarded; bd. dirs. Cursillo;

bishop of Dodge City, Kans., 1976-82, Diocese of Wichita, 1982—. Office: 307 E Central Ave Wichita KS 67202 also: Diocese of Wichita 424 N Broadway Wichita KS 67202

GERBER, ISRAEL JOSHUA, rabbi, religion educator, author; b. N.Y.C., July 30, 1918; s. Marcus and Sadie Leah (Schuster) G.; m. Sydelle Reba Katzman, Jan. 9, 1943; children: Barbara Jane Gerber Parker, Sharon May, Waynes Scott. BA, Yeshiva U., 1939; MS, CCNY, 1940; PhD, Boston U., 1950. Ordained rabbi, 1939; lic. psychologist, N.C. Rabbi Beth Jacob Synagogue, Plymouth, Mass., 1943-44, Congregation Agudath Achim, Fitchburg, Mass., 1944-52, Temple Emanuel, Dothan, Ala., 1953-59, Temple Beth El, Charlotte, N.C., 1959-72; prof. Old Testament Hood Theol Sem., 1961-87; prof. psychology Johnson C. Smith U., 1972-86; former dir. S.E. coun. Union Am. Hebrew Congregations, Dothan. Author: Psychology of the Suffering Mind, 1951, Man On A Pendulum, 1955, Immortal Rebels, 1963, The Heritage Seekers, 1977, Job on Trial: A Book for Our Time, 1982; contbr. articles to The Christian Century, Jewish Heritage, Reconstructionist, others. Chmn. B'nai Brith, Dothan, 1955-57; co-chmn. NCCJ, Charlotte, 1965-66; pres. Easter Seals Soc., Charlotte, 1967-69, Halfway House, Charlotte, 1968-69; bd. dirs. Epilepsy Assn., Am. Heart Assn., Multiple Sclerosis Assn., Charlotte. Capt. U.S. Army, 1950-55. Recipient Rsch. award Ford Found., Cen. Piedmont U. Ctr., Religion award Charlotte Jr. League; Blumenthal Found. grantee. Fellow Am. Psychol. Assn.; mem. AAUP, Cen. Conf. Am. Rabbis (exec. bd.), Am. Assn. Hosp. Chaplains, VFW, Jewish War Vets., Rotary, Kiwanis. Democrat. Home: 1230 Jules Ct Charlotte NC 28226

GERBERDING, JOHN HABIGHORST, retired minister; b. Marinette, Wis., Mar. 3, 1922; s. William Passavant and Esther Elizabeth (Habighorst) G.; m. Lois Minnie Pauline Ebeling, May 21, 1948; children: Timothy John, Esther Louise, Jane Elizabeth, Paul William. Student, Macalester Coll., 1939-41; BA, Yale U., 1943; BD, Northwestern Luth. Sem., Mpls., 1948; postgrad., Iliff Sch. Theology, Denver, 1965-70, Seattle U., 1980. Ordained to ministry United Luth. Ch. in Am., 1948. Pastor Christ Luth. Ch., Lancaster, Wis., 1948-52, Holy Cross Luth. Ch., Menomonee Falls, Wis., 1952-55, Epiphany Luth. Ch., Denver, 1958-72, Grace Luth. Ch., Casper, Wyo., 1972-87; ret., 1987; news editor Grant County Ind., Lancaster, 1955-58; sec. Rocky Mountain Synod, Luth. Ch. in Am., Denver, 1960-62, chmn. worship com., 1970-80, bd. dirs., 1986-88, mem. bd. parish svcs., Phila., 1974-78; chmn. social action dept. Colo. Coun. Chs., Denver, 1964-68; exch. study Luth. World Fedn., Taize, France and Darmstadt, Fed. Republic Germany, 1968. Contbr. numerous articles to religious publs. and newspapers. Editor monthly Young Dems., Denver, 1958-63; precinct committeeman Denver Dem. Com., 1960-68, Casper Dem. Com., 1974-76; bd. dirs. Planned Parenthood Natrona County, Wyo., 1976-82, Women-Infants-Children, Natrona County, 1980-86, Wyo. Coun. for Humanities, Cheyenne, 1976-78; chmn. Paul Simon for Pres., Natrona County, 1988. 1st lt. USAAF, 1943-46, ETO, MTO. Home: 2964 S Ingalls Way Denver CO 80227-3830

GERDES, NEIL WAYNE, library director; b. Moline, Ill., Oct. 19, 1943; s. John Edward and Della Marie (Ferguson) G. A.B., U. Ill., 1965; B.D., Harvard U., 1968; M.A., Columbia U., 1971; M.A. in L.S., U. Chgo., 1975. Diplomate; Ordained to ministry Unitarian Universalist Assn., 1975. Copy chief Little, Brown, 1968-69; instr. Tuskegee Inst., 1969-71; library asst. Augustana Coll., 1972-73; editorial asst. Library Quar., 1973-74; librarian, prof. Meadville Theol. Schs., Chgo., 1973—; library program dir. Chgo. Cluster Theol. Schs., 1977-80; dir. Hammond Library, 1980—; prof. Chgo. Theol Sem., 1980—. Mem. exec. bd. Sem. Coop. Bookstore, Chgo., 1982—, Ctr. for Religion and Psychotherapy, Chgo., 1984—, Ind. Voters of Ill., 1986-89, Hyde Park-Kenwood Community Orgn., Chgo., 1988-89; pres. Hyde Park-Kenwood Interfaith Coun., 1986-90; chair libr. coun. Assn. Chgo. Theol. Sch. Libr., 1984-88. Mem. ALA, Am. Theol. Library Assn., Chgo. Area Theol. Library Assn., Unitarian Universalist Mins. Assn. (sec., treas. nat. body 1990—), Assn. Liberal Religious Scholars (sec., treas. 1975—), Phi Beta Kappa. Office: Chgo Theol Sem Hammond Libr 5757 S University Ave Chicago IL 60637

GEREBOFF, JOEL DAVID, religion educator; b. Providence, Aug. 21, 1950; s. Maurice L. and Caroline (Gordon) G.; m. Barbara Ehrenhaus, July 4, 1971; children: Arner Gvriel, Arielle Shulamit, Noah Samuel. Student, Jewish Theol. Sem., N.Y.C., 1968-71; BA, NYU, 1971; PhD, Brown U., 1977. Assoc. prof. religious studies Ariz. State U., Tempe, 1978-80; tchr. Bur. Jewish Edn., Phoenix, 1980—. Author: Rabbi Tarfor, 1979. Trustee Ariz. Peringbal Trust, Phoenix, 1989—; steering com. Ariz. Bioethics Network, Phoenix, 1989—; bd. dirs. Ariz. Jewish Hist. Soc., Phoenix, 1985—. Mem. Am. Acad. Religion, Assn. for Jewish Studies. Home and office: Ariz State U Dept Religious Studies Tempe AZ 85287

GERETY, PETER LEO, archbishop; b. Shelton, Conn., July 19, 1912; s. Peter Leo and Charlotte (Daly) G. Student, St. Thomas Sem., Bloomfield, Conn., 1934, Seminaire St. Sulpice, Paris, France, 1939. Ordained priest Roman Catholic Ch., 1939; asst. pastor New Haven, 1939-42; dir. Blessed Martin de Porres Interracial Center, 1942-56; pastor New Haven, 1956-66; coadjutor bishop Portland, Maine, 1966—; apostolic adminstr. Portland, 1967—, bishop, 1969-74; archbishop of Newark, 1974-86; archbishop emeritus, 1986—. Address: St John Vianney Residence 60 Home Ave Rutherford NJ 07070

GERGIANNAKIS, ANTHONY EMMANUEL See ANTHONY, BISHOP

GERHART, MARY J., religious studies educator; b. Stacyville, Iowa, Mar. 4, 1935; d. Karl Frederick and Mary Anna Gerhart. BA, Coll. St. Teresa, 1964; MA, U. Mo., 1968; MA, PhD, U. Chgo., 1970. Prof. religious studies Hobart & William Smith Colls., Geneva, N.Y., 1972—. Author: The Question of Belief in Literary Criticism, 1979; co-author: Metaphoric Process, 1984, Morphologies of Faith: Essays in Religion & Culture, 1991. Fulbright sr. rsch. fellow, Berlin, 1984-85; fellow NEH, 1985. Office: Hobart & William Smith Colls Dept Religious Studies Geneva NY 14456

GERICKE, PAUL WILLIAM, minister, educator; b. St. Louis, Apr. 8, 1924; s. Orville Herman and Irma Rose (Reinhart) G.; m. Jean Fisher, Feb. 18, 1953; 1 child, Michael Paul. BSEE, Washington U., St. Louis, 1949; BD, So. Bapt. Theol. Sem., 1960; ThD, New Orleans Bapt. Theol. Sem., 1964; MA, U. New Orleans, 1972. Ordained to ministry So. Bapt. Conv., 1952. Instr. electronics USAF, 1949; calibration engr. Emerson Electric Co., St. Louis, 1950; asst. pastor Calvary Bapt. Ch., St. Louis, 1951-53, Forest Ave. Bapt. Ch., Kansas City, Mo., 1954; pastor First Bapt. Ch., Marceline, Mo., 1954-56, New Hope Bapt. Ch., St. Louis, 1957, Summit Park Bapt. Ch., Louisville, 1959-60, Logtown (Miss.) Bapt. Ch., 1960-64; asst. prof., dir. libr. svcs. New Orleans Bapt. Theol. Sem., 1965-73, assoc. prof., dir. libr., 1973-91, assoc. prof. communications, dir. Communication Dept., 1991—; calibration engr. Emerson Electric Co., St. Louis, 1950; mgr. sta. WSBN-FM, New Orleans, 1979-85, chmn., 1985—; bd. dr. religious access channel REACH, New Orleans, 1985—. Author: The Preaching of Robert G. Lee, 1967, The Ministers Filing System, 1971, Sermon Building, 1973, Crucial Experiences in the Life of D.L. Moody, 1978, Pastor's Library, 1986. Served with AC USNR, 1942-46. Mem. Nat. Religious Broadcasters, Am. Radio Relay League, Theta Xi. Republican. Avocation: amateur radio. Home: 1321 Aris Ave Metairie LA 70005 Office: New Orleans Bapt Theol Sem 3939 Gentilly Blvd New Orleans LA 70126 *My life has been completely changed by a personal encounter with Jesus Christ in 1951. Through faith in Him as Savior and Lord, I received a new life, a new sense of values, a new purpose in life, and a new hope both for this life and the life to come. My purpose now is to seek first the kingdom of God and all the other things I need will be given unto me.*

GERIG, DONALD D., academic administrator. Pres. Summit Christian Coll., Fort Wayne, Ind. Office: WBCL 90.3 FM 1025 W Rudisill Blvd Fort Wayne IN 46807 also: Summit Christian Coll 1025 W Rudisill Blvd Fort Wayne IN 46807*

GERIG, JEFFREY LEE, minister; b. Ft. Wayne, Ind., June 27, 1962; s. Wesley Lee and Mary Carolyn (Steiner) G.; m. Jean Eiko Ayabe, June 22, 1985. BA, Summit Christian Coll., Ft. Wayne, 1984; MDiv, Trinity Evangel. Div. Sch., Deerfield, Ill., 1988. Assoc. pastor of Christian edn./youth Grace Missionary Ch., Celina, Ohio, 1988—; mem. Celina Ministerium, 1988—; asst. staff Campus Life/Jr. Varsity, Celina, 1991; sec./treas. East Cen. Dist. Missionary Ch./Christian Edn. Bd., Troy, Ohio, 1989-91. Mem. Nat. Network Youth Ministers. Office: Grace Missionary Church 510 Portland St Celina OH 45822

GERIG, WESLEY LEE, minister, educator; b. Ft. Wayne, Ind., Sept. 17, 1930; s. Jared Franklin and Mildred Grace (Eicher) G.; m. Mary Carolyn Steiner, Aug. 21, 1952; children—Jeanne Marie, John Wesley, Jeffrey Lee, Jared Clayton. B.A., Ft. Wayne Bible Coll., 1951; postgrad. Ind. U., Ft. Wayne, summers 1948-51; M.Div., Fuller Theol. Sem., 1954, M.Th., 1956; postgrad U. London, 1959-62; Ph.D., U. Iowa, 1965. Ordained to ministry Missionary Ch., 1957. Asst. pastor, youth dir. Faith Missionary Ch., Pomona, Calif., 1951-55; grad. asst. Sch. Religion, U. Iowa, Iowa City, 1956-57; prof. Bible and theology, chmn. div. bibl. studies Ft. Wayne Bible Coll., 1957—; prof. bibl. lang. Winona Lake Sch. Theology, Ind., 1962-69; mem. constl. com. The Missionary Ch. Contbr. Zondervan Pictorial Ency. of the Bible, 1973. Mem. Evang. Theol. Soc. (chmn. MW dist. 1969-70), Nat. Assn. Evangelicals (mem. theol. commn.), Am. Assn. Bible Colls. Republican. Avocations: trumpet playing; stamp collecting; ping pong. Home: 4030 S Wayne Ave Fort Wayne IN 46807 Office: Fort Wayne Bible Coll 1025 W Rudisill Blvd Fort Wayne IN 46807

GERKIN, CHARLES VINCENT, theology educator; b. Garrison, Kans., July 30, 1922; s. Charles Herschel and Emily Rowena (Tolle) G.; m. Mary Frances Hickox, June 10, 1945; children: Charles V. Jr., Julia M., Peter A., Kristin E., Rebecca L., Rachael A. Student, Baker U., 1942-43, DD (hon.), 1973; BA, Washburn U., 1945; postgrad., Northwestern U., 1946-47; BD, Garrett Bibl. Inst., Evanston, Ill., 1947. Ordained to ministry United Meth. Ch., 1947. Pastor 1st United Meth. Ch., Leavenworth, Kans., 1956-57; chaplain Grady Meml. Hosp., Atlanta, 1957-70; prof. pastoral psychology Emory U., Atlanta, 1970-90; asst. prof. preventive medicine and community health Emory U. Sch. Medicine, Atlanta, 1962—; Franklin N. Parker prof. pastoral theology Emory U., Atlanta, 1990—; vis. prof. Columbia Theol. Sem., Decatur, Ga., 1959-70. Author: Crisis Experience in Modern Life, 1979, The Living Human Document, 1984, Widening the Horizons, 1986, Prophetic Pastoral Practice, 1991; also articles; mem. editorial com. Jour. Pastoral Care, 1970—; mem. editorial adv. com. Pastoral Psychology, 1970—. With USNR, 1943-46. Ctr. Theol. Inquiry fellow, 1985; named Pastoral Theologian of Yr. Pastoral Psychology jour., 1987. Mem. Am. Assn. Pastoral Counselors (diplomate), Assn. for Clin. Pastoral Edn. (cert. supr., Disting. Svc. award 1986), Am. Assn. for Marriage and Family Therapy (clin.). Home: 1992 Westminster Way NE Atlanta GA 30307 Office: Emory U Candler Sch Theology Atlanta GA 30322

GERMAN, BESSIE JONES, music minister; b. Lexington, Miss., Dec. 29, 1945; d. Lewis and Bessie Mae (Ingram) Jones; m. Howard Louis German, May 18, 1968; children: Lanard, Tiffany, Courtney. BA, Miss. Indsl., 1966; MEd, U. Ala., 1973. Cert. counselor. Musician New Hope Ch., Lexington, Miss., 1955-62; choir dir. Second Bapt., Brooksville, Miss., 1966-70; counselor Elizabeth Bapt., Tuscaloosa, Ala., 1970-75; musician Elizabeth Bapt., Tuscaloosa, 1970-80, minister of music, 1980—; dir. Shelton State Coll., Tuscaloosa, 1980—; music tchr. Noxubee County Schs., Macon, Miss., 1966-70, basketball coach, 1966-68; art, music tchr. Green County Schs., Utaw, Ala., 1970-71; counselor, coord. Stillman Coll., Tuscaloosa, 1973-80. Patentee in field. Pres. PTA Tuscaloosa County High Sch., Northport, Ala., 1988; advisor Afro Am. Assn., Tuscaloosa, 1989; adv. bd. ARC, Tuscaloosa, 1985. Named Counselor of Yr. Shelton State Coll., 1981; recipient Full Music scholarship Miss. Indsl. Coll., 1962, Miss. Valley U., 1962. Mem. Ala. Edn. Assn., NEA, Phi Delta Kappa, Edn. Opportunity Program. Democrat. Home: 1103 Brierclif Northport AL 35476

GERMAN, DON EVERETT, army chaplain; b. Charleston, S.C., Jan. 8, 1959; s. Charles Bernard and Williemae (Jones) G.; m. Annell Rebecca Banner, Nov. 11, 1981; 1 child, Dana Elizabeth. BS, Clemson U., 1980; MDiv cum laude, Va. U., 1988. Community ctr. dir. Mt. Pleasant (S.C.) Recreation Dept., 1980-82; platoon leader, 2d lt. S.C. Army Nat. Guard, Charleston, 1980-82; communications officer, 1st lt. 62d Engr. Bn. U.S. Army, Ft. Hood, Tex., 1983-85; chaplain Va. Youth Correction Svcs., Richmond, 1987-88; chaplain candidate, capt. Va. Army Nat. Guard, Richmond, 1986-88; chaplain 369th Signal Bn. U.S. Army, Ft. Gordon, Ga., 1988—. Decorated Army Commendation medal, Army Svc. ribbon, 1981, Army Achievement medal, 1988, 89. Mem. Mil. Chaplains Assn. of U.S., Armed Forces Communications and Electronics Assn., Signal Corps Regimental Assn., Assn. of U.S. Army. Mem. Progressive Nat. Bapt. Conv. Avocations: coaching/playing basketball, tennis, softball, volleyball, football. Home: 830-A Ginger Ct Fort Gordon GA 30905 Office: 369th Signal Bn 15th Signal Brigade Fort Gordon GA 30905

GERMOVNIK, FRANCIS, priest; b. Vodice, Slovenija, Sept. 27, 1915; came to U.S., 1946, naturalized 1952; s. Joseph and Frances (Kosec) G. BS in Libr. Sci., Our Lade of the Lake Coll., San Antonio, 1950; MA in Libr. Sci., Rosary Coll., River Forest, Ill., 1967; JCD, Angelicum, Rome, 1945. Ordained priest Roman Catholic. Ch., 1941. Libr., prof. Canon law St. John's Sem., San Antonio, 1946-52, Assumption Sem., San Antonio, 1952-54, St. Mary's Sem., Perryville, Mo., 1954-64, De Andreis Sem., Lemont, Ill., 1964-84, St. Thomas Theol. Sem., Denver, 1984—. Contbr. articles to profl. jours. Mem. Canon Law Soc. Am., Cath. Libr. Assn. Home: 1300 S Steele St Denver CO 80210 *On the international scene small nations should have their autonomy and equal rights with the big nations. As it is, big fish are still swallowing the small one.*

GEROW, EDWIN MAHAFFEY, Indic culture educator; b. Akron, Ohio, Oct. 16, 1931; s. Adolphus Denton and Alice Corinne (Mahaffey) G.; m. Cheryl Ann Chevis, Nov. 18, 1976; children from previous marriage—Matthew, Aaron. B.A., U. Chgo., 1952, Ph.D., 1962; postgrad., U. Paris, 1954-56, 59-60, U. Madras, 1960-61. Asst. prof. Sanskrit U. Rochester, 1962-64; lectr. Sanskrit Columbia U., 1963-64; asst. prof. U. Wash., Seattle, 1964-67, assoc. prof., 1967-73, assoc. dir. Far Eastern and Russian Inst., 1969-73; Frank L. Sulzberger prof. civilizations, prof. Sanskrit dept. South Asian langs. and civilizations U. Chgo., 1973-87; vis. prof. humanities Reed Coll., Portland, Oreg., 1985-89, prof. religion and humanities, 1989—; vis. prof. history and lit. of religions Northwestern U., 1980. Author: A Glossary of Indian Figures of Speech, 1971, Indian Poetics, 1977, Theatre of Memory: The Plays of Kālidāsa 1984, The Jewel-Necklace of Argument, 1990, others; editor: (with Margery Lang) Srih: Studies in the Language and Culture of South Asia, 1974, (with Dimock and van Buitenen) The Literatures of India, an Introduction, 1974; editor in chief Jour. Am. Oriental Soc., 1987—. Ford Found. fellow, 1959-61; Am. Inst. Indian Studies fellow, 1967-68, 75; Smithsonian Instn. fellow, 1984. Mem. Am. Oriental Soc. (chair editorial bd., mem. bd. dirs., exec. com. Sanskrit council), Société Asiatique, Philol. Assn. Pacific Coast. Home: 4260 SW Council Crest Dr Portland OR 97201 Office: 3203 SE Woodstock Blvd Portland OR 97202

GERRISH, BRIAN ALBERT, theologian, educator; b. London, Aug. 14, 1931; s. Albert and Doris (King) G.; m. Dawn Ann De Vries, Aug. 3, 1990; children from previous marriage: Carolyn, Paul. B.A., Queens' Coll., Cambridge, Eng., 1952, M.A., 1956; cert., Westminster Coll., Cambridge, 1955; S.T.M., Union Theol. Sem., N.Y.C., 1956; Ph.D., Columbia U., 1958; D.D. (hon.), U. St. Andrews, Scotland, 1984. Ordained to ministry Presbyn. Ch., 1956. Asst. pastor West End Presbyn. Ch., N.Y.C., 1956-58; tutor philosophy of religion Union Theol. Sem., N.Y.C., 1957-58; instr. ch. history McCormick Theol. Sem., Chgo., 1958-59; asst. prof. McCormick Theol. Sem., 1959-63, asso. prof., 1963-65; asso. prof. hist. theology U. Chgo., 1965-68, prof., 1968-85, John Nuveen prof., 1985—; Cunningham lectr. U. Edinburgh, Scotland, 1990. Author: Grace and Reason: A Study in the Theology of Luther, 1962 (Japanese transl. 1974), reprinted, 1979, Tradition and the Modern World: Reformed Theology in the Nineteenth Century, 1978, The Old Protestantism and the New: Essays on the Reformation Heritage, 1982, A Prince of the Church: Schleiermacher and the Beginnings of Modern Theology, 1984, Korean transl., 1988; editor: The Faith of Christendom: A Source Book of Creeds and Confessions, 1963, Reformers in Profile, 1967, Reformatio Perennis: Essays on Calvin and the Reformation in Honor of Ford Lewis Battles, 1981; co-editor: Jour. Religion, 1972-85; contbr. articles to profl. jours. Am. Assn. Theol. Schs. faculty fellow, 1961; Guggenheim fellow, 1970; Nat. Endowment Humanities fellow, 1980. Mem. Am. Acad. of Arts and Scis., Am. Acad. Religion, Am. Soc. Ch. History (pres. 1979), Ernst-Troeltsch-Gesellschaft, Am. Theol. Soc. (Midwest Div.) (pres. 1973-74). Home: 1363 E 55th Pl Chicago IL 60637 Office: Swift Hall U Chgo Chicago IL 60637

GERRY, JOSEPH JOHN, priest, college chancellor, bishop; b. Millinocket, Maine, Sept. 12, 1928; s. Bernard Eugene and Blanche Agnes (McManemon) G. AB summa cum laude, St. Anselm's Coll., Manchester, N.H., 1950; postgrad., St. Anselm's Sem., 1954; MA, U. Toronto, 1955; PhD, Fordham U., 1959; LLD, Benedictine Coll., 1986, St. Anselm Coll., 1986; DD, St. Joseph's Coll., Windham, Maine, 1990. Joined Order of St. Benedict, Roman Catholic Ch., 1948 ordained priest: Roman Catholic Ch., 1954. Asst. dean studies St. Anselm's Coll., 1958-59, dean studies, 1971-72; chancellor St. Anselm's Coll., N.H., 1972-86; consecrated bishop, 1986; auxiliary bishop Manchester, N.H., 1986-89; bishop Portland, Maine, 1989—. Home: 199 Western Prom Portland ME 04102 Office: 510 Ocean Ave Portland ME 04103

GERSON, GARY STANFORD, rabbi; b. Ypsilanti, Mich., June 17, 1945; s. Bernard and Ruth Edith (Levin) G.; m. Carol Roberts, Oct. 12, 1969; children: Jordana, Jessica. BA magna cum laude, Western Mich. U., 1967; MA in Religion, Temple U., 1976; grad., Reconstructionist Rabbinical Coll., 1976; MA in Psychology, Temple U., 1977; Dr. Ministry, Chgo. Theol. Seminary, 1984. Ordained rabbi, 1976. Rsch. fellow U. Pa., 1969, teaching asst., 1972; teaching asst. Temple U., Phila., 1974-75; rabbi Temple Brith Achim, King of Prussia, Pa., 1974-78; asst. rabbi Temple Beth Israel, Chgo., 1978-79; rabbi Oak Park (Ill.) Temple B'nai Abraham Zion, 1979—; psychologist Benjamin Rush Ctr. for Mental Health and Mental Retardation Svcs., Phila., 1977-78. Contbr. articles to profl. jours. Adv. bd. Chgo. Area Jewish Hospice Assn., 1984—, Ctr. for Jewish-Christian Studies, Chgo., 1985—, Nat. Abortion Rights Action League, Ill., 1985—, Ctr. for Ch.-State Studies, Chgo., 1986—, Community Response, 1989—; chmn. Religious Coalition for Abortion Rights, Ill., 1984-88, mem. policy coun., 1980—; active Justice Campaign, 1986—, ACLU, Ill., 1979—, Jewish Fedn. Met. Chgo., 1981—. Fulbright grantee, 1967, Hebrew U. fellow, 1969-70, Dropsie U. fellow, 1970-71. Mem. Chgo. Assn. Reform Rabbis (v.p. 1987-91, pres. 1991—), Cen. Conf. Am. Rabbis (exec. bd. 1991—), Chgo. Bd. Rabbis (exec. com. 1983—), Union Am. Hebrew Congregations (exec. com. Gt. Lakes region 1991—), Olin-Sang-Ruby Union Inst. (bd. govs. 1990—, chmn. rabbinic adv. com.), United Jewish Appeal (rabbinic cabinet 1980—), Idlewild Country Club, B'nai Brith, Omicron Delta Kappa. Avocations: jogging, hiking, bicycling, travel, classical and folk music. Office: Oak Park Temple Bnai Abraham Zion 1235 N Harlem Ave Oak Park IL 60302

GERTZ, GEDALIAH, cantor, educator; b. Bklyn., Nov. 18, 1929; s. Louis and Frieda (Kamerick) G.; m. Lola Mae Waltzman; children: Susan Enid, Debbie Ann, Geoffrey Michael. AAS, SUNY, 1950; B in Sacred Music, Hebrew Union, 1957; MA in Family Ecology, Akron (Ohio) U., 1981. Cantor, educator Boro Park Progressive Synagogue, Bklyn., 1953-57, Temple Israel, Oklahoma City, 1957-60, 67—, Emanuel Synagogue, Oklahoma City, 1960-67; family counselor Temple Israel, 1980—; div. mediator By Reference, Akron, 1987—; pres., producer Audio Pathways. Artist Akron Winter Concert, 1985—; facilitator Akron Jewish Fedn., 1967—; artist, producer Akron Pub. Schs., 1967—; interfaith speaker Jewish Community Task Force, Akron, 1975—. Staff sgt. U.S. Army, 1950-52, Korea. Mem. Nat. Assn. Temple Educators, Am. Conf. of Cantors (bd. dirs. 1957—, chair nominating com. 1980), Family Mediators, Am. Ministerial Alliance (Svc. award 1990), Am. Legion. Democrat. Avocations: jewelry designing, guitars, racquetball. Office: Temple Israel 133 Merriman Rd Akron OH 44303

GERVAIS, MARCEL ANDRE, bishop; b. Elie, Man., Can., Sept. 21, 1931; s. Fredrick Pierre and Marie-Louise (Beaudry) G. B.A. in Philosophy with honors, St. Peter's Sem. U. Western Ont., London, 1954; licentiate sacred theology, Angelicum U., Rome, 1959; licentiate sacred scripture, Pontifical Biblical Inst., Rome, 1960, Ecole Biblique Jerusalem, 1961. Ordained priest Roman Catholic Ch., 1958. Prof. sacred scripture St. Peter's Sem., 1962-76; dir. Divine Word Internat. Centre of Religious Edn., London, 1974-79; aux. bishop Diocese of London; titular bishop Rosemarkie, Scotland, 1980; bishop of Sault Ste-Marie, 1985—, coadjutor archbishop of Ottawa, June-Sept. 1989, archbishop of Ottawa, 1989—; mem. adv. com. Internat. Commn. for English in the Liturgy, 1974-78; chancellor St. Paul's U. Author, gen. editor: Journey: 40 Lessons on the Bible, 1977-80, Guided Study Programs in the Catholic Faith, 1979. Mem. Episcopal Social Affairs Commn., chmn. Theology Commn., mem. Edn. Commn.; chmn. ad hoc com. Family Life Edn., Phase III. Office: 1247 Kilborn Pl, Ottawa, ON Canada K1H 6K9

GESHAY, JEFFREY JOHN, minister; b. Colorado Springs, Colo., June 17, 1952; s. John Louis and Gladys (McFarland) G.; m. Catherine Louise Geshay, June 2, 1973; children: Amy Lynn, Carrie Lynn, David Jeffrey, Katie Lynn, Laura Lynn. BS in Music, Bapt. Bible Coll., Clarks Summitt, Pa., 1974. With Heritage Bapt. Ch., Clarks Summitt, 1973-74, 1st Bapt. Ch., Butler, Pa., 1974-76; min. music 1st Bapt. Ch., Elkhart, Ind., 1976-81, 83—, Temple Bapt. Ch., Tacoma, Wash., 1981-83; dir. music Teen Leadership Conf., Clarks Summitt, 1989—, Youth Days, Gen. Assn. Reg. Bapt. Chs., Schaumburg, Ill., 1989—. Office: 1st Bapt Ch 2626 Prairie St Elkhart IN 46517-2127

GESSELL, JOHN MAURICE, minister, educator; b. St. Paul, June 17, 1920; s. Leo Lancien and Mabel Aseneth (Wing) G.; B.A., Yale U., 1942, B.D., 1949, Ph.D., 1960. Ordained priest Episcopal Ch., 1951; rector Emmanuel Episcopal Ch., Nottoway Parish, Southampton County, Va., 1951-53; assoc. rector Grace Ch., Salem, Mass., 1953-61; mem. faculty Sch. Theology, U. of South, Sewanee, Tenn., 1961—, prof. Christian edn., 1961-63, asst. prof. pastoral theology, 1963-74, prof. Christian ethics, 1974-84, prof. emeritus, 1984—, editor St. Luke's Jour. Theology, 1976-90; founder, exec. dir. Cumberland Ctr. for Justice and Peace; mem. nat. exec. com. Episcopal Pace Fellowship; bd. dirs. Absalom Jones Theol. Inst., Atlanta, Mid-South Career Devel. Center, Nashville. Bd. dirs., pres. Multi-County Comprehensive Mental Health Center, Tullahoma, Tenn., 1972-74, Sewanee Civic Assn. and Community Chest, 1967-68. Dwight fellow Yale U., 1949-50; Coll. of Preachers fellow, Washington, 1953. Mem. Am. Soc. Christian Ethics, AAUP, Am. Assn. Theol. Schs. (faculty fellow 1967-68), Phi Beta Kappa. Contbr. articles to theol. books and jours. Home: 187 Carruthers Rd Sewanee TN 37375 Office: Univ of South Sewanee TN 37375

GETTING, CAROL JEAN, religious education director; b. Sanborn, Iowa, Jan. 29, 1938; d. Harry Earl and Elbie Elizabeth (Hanefeld) Watson; m. John Jay Getting, Aug. 15, 1958; children: Janelle, Johnna, Curt, Julie. Student, No. Iowa U., 1956-58, Morningside Coll., 1959; B in Edn., Ariz. State U., 1972. Edn. dir. Faith United Meth. Ch., Phoenix, 1980—. Pres. Christian Educators Fellowship, State of Ariz., 1986-87, Phoenix, 1989—. Office: Faith United Meth Ch 8640 N 19th Ave Phoenix AZ 85021

GEWIRTZ, LEONARD BENJAMIN, rabbi; b. N.Y.C., Jan. 25, 1918; s. Henry and Leah Peshe (Greenberg) G.; m. Gladys Sarah Kerstein, Nov. 21, 1948; children: Isaac Meir, Joseph Jacob. BS cum laude, CCNY, 1941; grad., Hebrew Theol. Coll., 1945; postgrad., Dropsie Coll., 1952. Ordained rabbi, 1945. Supply rabbi Beth Shalom Congregation, Danville, Ill., 1943-45; rabbi Congregation Oir Chodosh, Chgo., 1945-47, Congregation Adas Kodesh Shel Emeth, Wilmington, Del., 1947—; dir. campus activities Hillel U. Del., Newark, 1960-63; instr. Gratz Hebrew High Sch., Wilmington, 1971-83; founder, speaker WDEL weekly radio program Rabbi Speaks, 1950—. Author: Authentic Jew and His Judaism, 1961, Authentic Jewish Living, 1977, Jewish Spirituality: Hope and Redemption, 1985; contbr. articles religious jours. Pres. Del. Citizens Conf. Social Work, Wilmington, 1954-56; bd. govs. Del. Mental Health Assn., 1967-71, Jewish Community Ctr. Mem. ACLU, Pacem En Terris, Rabbinic Assn. Del. (pres. 1967-69, 75-77, 80-82), Rabbinical Coun. Am. (chmn. social actions 1966-68, exec. com. 1960-64), Phila. Bd. Rabbis (40 Yr. Continuous Svc. award 1984), Jewish Fedn. (bd. govs.), B'nai Brith (cert. honor). Home: 26 Colony Blvd Wilmington DE 19802 Office: Adas Kodesh Shel Emeth Synagogue Washington Blvd and Torah Way Wilmington DE 19802

GHAFFARI, EBRAHIM ABE, religious organization administrator; b. Nishabour, Iran, May 7, 1945; came to U.S., 1964; s. Abolfazl and Maryam (Afkhami) G.; m. Rose Marie Hughes, Sept. 7, 1968. BS, Oreg. State U., 1968, MS, 1970; postgrad., U. Mich., 1988. Elder Grace Christ Ch., Tehran, Iran, 1975-78; exec. dir., founder Iranian Christian Internat., 1981-90, exec. dir., 1990—; bd. dirs. Iranian Christians Cen. U.S., Tulsa, 1990—. Author, editor Mojdeh mag., 1980-91. Office: Iranian Christians Internat PO Box 25607 Colorado Springs CO 80936

GHEDDO, PIERO, priest, journalist; b. Tronzano, Piedmont, Italy, Mar. 10, 1929; s. Giovanni and Franzi (Rosa) G. Diploma in missiology, Pontificia Universitas de Propaganda Fide, Rome, 1956; diploma in journalism, Luiss U., Rome, 1955. Ordained priest Roman Cath. Ch., 1953. Editor Mondo e Missione mag., Milan, 1959—, Asia News, Milan, 1987—. Author: I popoli della fame, 1982, Marcello dei Lebbrosi, 1984, Fame e Coscienza cristiana, 1985, Lorenzo Bianchi di Hong Kong, 1987, Il Vangelo delle 7, 18, 1989, Il PIME: una proposta per la missione, 1989, Quale animazione missionaria, 1990. Address: PIME, Via Mosé Bianchi 94, 20149 Milan Italy

GHOSE, JOHN ELLIOT, priest. Moderator Ch. of North India, New Delhi. Office: CNI Bhavan, 16 Bandit Pant Marg, New Delhi 110 001, India*

GIANNAKOPOULOS, PANAGIOTIS KONSTANTINE, priest; b. Keratsinion, Attica, Greese, Oct. 10, 1949; came to U.S., 1967; s. Konstantine and Poliniki (Pirintzoglou) G.; m. Paula Bounos, Sept. 2, 1979; children: Simela Nicole, Constantine Nicholas. BA, Hellenic Coll., 1972; MDiv, Holy Cross Sch. Theol., 1975; postgrad., Andover Newton Theol. Sch., 1976-79; cert., U. Geneva, Switzerland, 1975-76. Ordained priest Greek Orthodox Ch., 1979. Asst. priest Holy Trinity Greek Orthodox Ch., Chgo., 1979-81; priest St. Sophia Greek Orthodox Ch., Elgin, Ill., 1981-85, Holy Trinity Greek Orthodox Ch., Fitchburg, Mass., 1985-91, St. George Greek Orthodox Ch., Cape Cod, Mass., 1991—; chmn., Diocese Reliious Edn. Com., Oratorical Festival Com., Brookline, Mass., 1987—. Author-editor: (monthly bull.) Orthodox Witness-MAPTYPIA, 1981—. Mem. New England Clergy Syndesmos (pres. 1990-91), Archdiocean Presbyter. Coun. (treas. 1990—), Hellenic Coll. Holy Cross Alumni Assn. Office: Holy Trinity Ch 1319 Main St Fitchburg MA 01420-6922

GIANOPULOS, GEORGE A., minister; b. Jersey City, N.J., Feb. 12, 1940; s. Anthony G. and Helen M. (Parker) G.; m. O. Nancy Cook, Jan. 20, 1962; children: Gregg, Gina, Gigi, Garron. BA, Cen. Bible Coll. and Sem., Springfield, Mo., 1962. Ordained to ministry Assemblies of God Ch. Pastor various Assembly of God Chs., Tenn., S.C., Kans., 1962-75, 77-78, Batavia (N.Y.) Assembly of God Ch., 1978—; pub. relations rep. Teen Challenge, N.Y.C., 1975-77; adv. bd. Women's Aglow, Batavia, 1980-87; bd. dirs. Tenth Coin Ministry to Deaf, Batavia, 1987; lectr. on religion in Am. various coll. sems., 1973. Chmn. Citizens for Decency, Batavia, 1985; chmn. Genesee County Exec. Dave Roever Crusade, 1989; coach Little League Baseball. Mem. Gen. Council Assemblies of God (sec. youth dept. S.C. dist. 1970-73, sec./treas. N.Y. dist. western sect. 1979-81), Full Gospel Businessmen, Internat. Avocations: golf, personal computer, singing, music. Office: Batavia Assembly of God Ch 24 N Spruce St Batavia NY 14020

GIA-RUSSO, A(NTHONY) PAUL, retired minister, lawyer; b. Petrella Tifernina, Italy, Jan. 25, 1910; s. Vincenzo and Anita (Amorosa) G-R.; m. Eleanor L Bauer, Feb. 12, 1938; children: Don Paul, Mark Henry. AB in Citizenship and Pub. Affairs, Syracuse U., 1932, JD, 1936; MA, U. Chgo., 1939; MDiv, Chgo. Theol. Sem., 1940. Ordained to ministry United Ch. of Christ, 1940. Min. Congl. Ch., Oak Lawn, Ill., 1938-42, Pilgrim Congl. Ch., Milw., 1942-56; tchr. comparative religion, philosophy of religion U. Wis., Milw., 1958-65; min. Congl.-United Ch. of Christ, Brown Deer, Wis., 1969-80, ret., 1980. Speaker in field. Lilly Endowment grantee. Mem. Delta Sigma Rho. Home: 2340 Memorial Dr Brookfield WI 53045 *The fundamental forces of history are rarely comprehended or controlled. We can never return to Eden and we will never reach Utopia. There are great prices to be paid for being civilized.*

GIBBES, EMILY V., religion educator; b. N.Y.C., Aug. 14, 1915; d. George Edward and Genevieve (Anderson) G. BA, Hunter Coll., N.Y.C., 1936; MA, NYU, 1947; DHL, Mary Holmes Coll., Westpoint, Miss., 1981. Field dir. United Presbyn. Ch. USA, 1950-68; assoc. gen. sec. Div. Edn., Ministry Nat. Coun. Chs., 1972-80; prof. religious edn. N.Y. Theol. Sem., N.Y.C., 1981-88, dean religious edn. program, 1981-88; ret. Mem. Religious Edn. Assn. (pres. 1974-77). Home: 200 Veterans Ln Apt 522 Doylestown PA 18901

GIBBONS, ELIZABETH B., minister; b. Orange, N.J., June 16, 1931; d. Charles G. and Kathrina (C.) Baldwin; m. David A. Gibbons, June 20, 1953; children: Laura Emily, Kenneth Charles, Phillip Baldwin, Alan Ray. BA, Oberlin Coll., 1953; MA, U. Wash., 1960; MDiv., Meth. Theol. Sch., 1982. Ordained min. United Meth. Ch. Dir. Christian edn. 1st Bapt. Ch., Granville, Ohio, 1965-82; min. edn. 1st Bapt. Ch., Hightstown, N.J., 1983-87; min. United Meth. Ch., Browns Mills, N.J., 1987—. Office: United Meth Ch PO Box 393 Browns Mills NJ 08015

GIBBONS, GREGORY DENNIS, minister; b. Saginaw, Mich., May 23, 1953; s. Everett Durward and Doris Lorraine (Miller) G.; m. Susan Rae Schulz, Jan. 17, 1982; children: Stephanie Grace, Michael Everett, Naomi Susan, Matthew Gregory. BA, Northwestern Coll., Watertown, Wis., 1975; MDiv, Wis. Luth. Sem., 1979. Ordained to ministry Luth. Ch., 1979. Pastor Cross of Glory Luth. Ch., Baton Rouge, 1979-81, Good Shepherd Luth. Ch., West Bend, Wis., 1981-85, Mt. Zion Luth. Ch., Kenosha, Wis., 1985—; mem. S.E. Wis. Bd. of Evangelism, Milw., 1989—, mem. nominating com., 1990, chmn. So. Pastoral Conf., Kenosha, 1990—; dir., vice chmn. Shoreland Luth. High Sch., 1988—. Republican. Home: 5919 37th Ave Kenosha WI 53144 Office: Mt Zion Luth Ch 5927 37th Ave Kenosha WI 53144 *The only thing that's truly important in life is sharing Jesus Christ as our crucified and risen Savior. That makes a difference, not only for this life but for all eternity.*

GIBBONS, KEITH ALAN, minister; b. Clovis, N.Mex., Aug. 16, 1957; s. O.H. and Dorothy Alena (Kinzie) Rupe; m. Sharna Jeanne Hale, Aug. 6, 1977; children: Brenna Jeanne, Aaron Hale. BA in Religion, Eastern N.Mex. U., 1979. Assoc. minister Mountain Christian Ch., Cedar Crest, N.Mex., 1980-82; minister Coll. Heights Christian Ch., Big Spring, Tex., 1982—; bd. regents Dallas Christian Coll.; trustee Spanish Am. Evangelism, El Paso, Tex., 1983-84; bd. dirs. The Rainbow Project; mem. Howard County Ministerial Fellowship. Chmn. The Wall Com, Big Springs, Tex., 1986-87; mem. Leadership Big Spring, 1985-86. Republican. Mem Christian Ch. of Christ. Lodge: Kiwanis (pres. Big Spring chpt. 1986-87). Avocation: running. Office: Coll Heights Christian Ch PO Box 2055 Big Spring TX 79721-2055

GIBBONS, LARRY EUGENE, minister; b. Paris, Tenn., Mar. 11, 1943; m. Linda Kaye Cheek, Oct. 12, 1964; children: Scott Eugene, Lori Rene. BA, So. Ill. U., Edwardsville, 1970; MDiv, Eden Theol. Sem., 1973; D Ministry, Chgo. Theol. Sem., 1976, McCormick Theol. Sem., 1989. Ordained to ministry Christian Ch. (Disciples of Christ), 1976. Pastor st Christian Ch. (Disciples of Christ), Chicago Heights, Ill., 1976-81; fraternal worker Div. Overseas Ministeries, Leichester, Eng., 1981-82; assoc. area min. Dallas Area Christian Ch., 1982-86; area min. Southeast Gateway Area Christian Ch., Festus, Mo., 1987—; bd. dirs. Gateway Ecumenical Forum, Belleville. Bd. dirs. Gateway Homes, St. Louis, 1989-91. Mem. Nat. Soc. Fund Raising Execs. Home: 1102 Crystal Heights Rd Crystal City MO 63019 Office: Southeast Gateway Area 2d and Walnut Festus MO 63028

GIBBS, C. EARL, minister; b. Dallas, Oreg., Apr. 1, 1935; s. J. Clyde and Addie (Martin) G.; m. Laurice Dashiell, Dec. 17, 1955; children: Douglas, Barbara (dec.), Robert. B.Th., NW Christian Coll., 1957; MDiv, Phillips U., 1960; MS, U. Oreg., 1968; DMin, San Francisco Theol. Sem., 1974. Ordained to ministry Christian Ch. (Disciples of Christ), 1957. Minister 1st Christian Ch., Perry, Okla., 1959-64, Springfield, Oreg., 1964-74; sr. minister Arden Christian Ch., Sacramento, 1974-88, Woodmont Christian Ch., Nashville, 1988-91, 1st Christian Ch., Tyler, Tex., 1991—; bd. dirs., adminstrv. com., exec. com. Christian Ch. (Disciples of Christ), Indpls., 1982-89; bd. dirs. Disciples of Christ Hist. Soc., Nashville, 1989-91; pres. Christian Ch. in Oreg. Portland, 1969-71; bd. dirs. Eskaton, Sacramento, 1981-88. Author: Caring for the Grieving, 1976; contbr. articles to mags. Mem. City Coun., Springfield, 1967-70, State Bd. Funeral Dirs. & Embalmers, Sacramento, 1987-88; mem., treas. C. of C., Springfield, Oreg., 1968-74. Named Citizen of Yr. Springfield C. of C., 1970; fellow Fund for Theol. Edn., 1972. Mem. Rotary (Okla., Oreg., Calif., Tenn. club pres. 1969-70, 78-79). Office: 1st Christian Ch 4202 S Broadway Tyler TX 75701 *The most important thing in life is not what happens to us, but how we choose to respond to what happens.*

GIBBS, CHARLES KENNETH, pastor; b. Lake Charles, La., Dec. 9, 1953; s. Lloyd and Pauline (Clark) G.; m. Vanita Johnson, June 30, 1972; children: Shannon, Stephen, Jeremy, Joey. BA in Bibl. Studies, William Carey Coll., 1982; MDiv, Southwestern Bapt. Theol. Sem., 1990. Pastor Fernwood Bapt. Ch., Gulfport, Miss., 1977-82, New Hope Bapt. Ch., DeQuincy, La., 1982—. Staff sgt. USAF, 1972-78. Home: 208 Orange St De Quincy LA 70633

GIBBS, JANET ANN BENTLEY, minister; b. Gosport, Hampshire, Eng., Nov. 24, 1939; came to U.S., 1950; d. Cyril Ernest and Nan Elizabeth (Rees) Bentley; m. Kenneth Daniel Reynolds, July 23, 1966 (dec. Oct. 1972); m. Albert William Gibbs, Nov. 29, 1975; four stepchildren. BRE, Bapt. Miss. Sch., 1961; MA, Colgate Rochester Div. Sch., 1967, MDiv, 1974. Ordained to ministry Meth. Ch. as deacon, 1973, as elder, 1975; cert. elem. tchr., N.Y. Pastor United Meth. Ch., Clayton, N.Y., 1972, Scottsburg, N.Y., 1973, Harrisville and Natural Bridge, N.Y., 1974-79, Parishville and West Stockholm, N.Y., 1979-85, Sandy Creek and Orwell, N.Y., 1985—; bd. vis. Colgate Rochester Div. Sch.; bd. dirs. Folts Home, Herkimer, N.Y., 1980-90; registrar Bd. of Ordained Ministry, 1988—; pres. Pulaski/Sandy Creek Ministerial Assn., 1985—. Author numerous poems. Recipient Friendship award Girls Scouts U.S., 1973. Mem. Order of St. Luke, Zonta Internat., Outlook Club (music chair 1989). Republican. Home: RR 1 Box 149 Potsdam NY 13676 Office: United Meth Ch PO Box 158 8134 Harwood Dr Sandy Creek NY 13145

GIBBS, JOHN GAMBLE, minister; b. Asheville, N.C., Aug. 25, 1930; s. Robert Shuford and Isabella (Gamble) G.; children: Elizabeth, Suzanne, Ian, Patrick, Anne. AB in Latin and Greek, Davidson Coll., 1952; MDiv. in Systematic Theology, Union Theol. Sem., 1955, ThM in Systematic Theology, 1958; PhD in New Testament Studies, Princeton U., 1966. Ordained to ministry Presbyn. Ch. (U.S.A.), 1956. Pastor Presbyn. Ch. in U.S.A., S.C., WVa., 1956-60, N.J., 1960-64; editor Westminster/John Knox Press, Louisville, 1983-90; interim pastor United Presbyn. Ch., Keokuk, Iowa, 1990-91, Ely, Minn., 1991-92; tchr. Blake Sch., Mpls., 1965-67; prof. humanities Moorhead (Minn.) State Univ., Minn., 1967-83; adj. prof. Charis Ecumenical Inst., Moorhead, 1972-82; del. to gen. assembly of Presbyn. Ch., Balt., 1976. Author: (book) Creation and Redemption, 1971; contbr. articles and revs. to jours. Coord. Eugene McCarthy's presdl. nomination Dem. Party, 7th Congl. Dist. Minn., 1968. Fellow Inst. for Ecumenical and Cultural Rsch., Collegeville, Minn., 1973-74, Nat. Endowment for Humanities, Yeshiva Univ., 1980. Mem. Soc. Bibl. Lit. (sec. Upper Midwest region 1979-81), Cath. Bibl. Soc., Studiorum Novi Testamenti Societas, Assn. Presbyn. Interim Ministry Specialists, Phi Mu Alpha. Office: 1st Presbyn Ch 226 E Harvey St Ely MN 55731 *I am looking everywhere I go for those who love across boundaries, those at every divide between death and life their compassion whispers: You can get there from here.*

GIBBS, TONY, religion educator; b. Augusta, Ga., Sept. 12, 1953; s. Bill and Lee (Elliott) G.; m. Christine Lu Ruth, Aug. 23, 1975; children: Amber, Elliott, Tyler, Alex, Hampton. BA, Furman U., 1976; M in Christian Edn., MDiv, Ref. Theol. Sem., Jackson, Miss., 1980; postgrad., Erskin Theol. Sem., Due West, S.C., 1987—. Minister of edn. First Bapt. Ch., Ft. Valley, Ga., 1980-82; pastor Boston (Ga.) Bapt. Ch., 1982-85; pastor, founder Olive Tree Community Ch., Greenville, S.C., 1985-90; instr. Walk Thru the Bible, Atlanta, 1985—; acad. dean Phillips Jr. Coll., Greenville, 1991—; chapel coord. Baseball Chapel/Greenville Braves, 1989—; announcer WLFJ Radio, Greenville, 1990—; cons. So. Bapt. Conv. Sunday Sch. Bd., Chgo., 1984. Author: (radio devotional) Time for the Family, 1988—; editor: (newsletter) Home School Digest, 1990—. Officer precinct orgn., Greenville County, 1988; referee Swimming Assn. Invitational League, Greenville, 1986-88. Home: 1 Bermuda Ct Greenville SC 29609 Office: Phillips College 601 McBee St Greenville SC 29601 *The key to success and happiness is attitude. I am convinced that only 5 to 10 per cent of what happens to me will affect my success or happiness. Ninety to 95 per cent of my success and happiness results from how I respond to that which happens to me.*

GIBES, PATRICIA A., religious education director; b. Milw., Jan. 2, 1937; d. Ralph E. Jeske and Mary Dosta Miller; m. Robert H. Gibes, July 18, 1959 (dec. 1980); children: Paul, Mark A., Kathryn A. BA, Mount Mary Coll., Milw., 1958; MEd, Cardinal Stritch Coll., Milw., 1988. Vol. catechist St. Mary Parish, Port Washington, Wis., 1959-85, youth minister, 1986-87; dir. youth ministry St. Anthony Parish, Menomonee Falls, Wis., 1987-88; dir. religious edn. St. Mary and St. Peter Parish, Port Washington, 1988—; panel mem., workshop presentor varius parishes. Co-author course textbook: Meeting Jesus Today, 1989; co-author book: The Prophets: Showing Us the Way to Justice and Peace, 1990; contbr. articles to profl. jours. Mem. Milw. Coun. for Adult Learning, Milw. Archdiocesan Religious Edn. Dirs. Assn. (reg. bd. 1988-90, prof. devel. com. 1988—). Office: Cath Religious Edn Office 117 E Van Buren St Port Washington WI 53074

GIBSON, ANTHONY LORENZA, pastor; b. Bklyn., July 31, 1942; s. William Blueford and Catherine (Curcio) G.; m. Irene Gladys Duerr, Jan. 13, 1968; children: Stephen Todd, Jonathan Scott. BA in Bible Edn., Columbia Bible Coll., 1964; postgrad., Queens Coll., 1964-65; MDiv, N.Y. Theol. Sem., 1968; postgrad., Westminster Theol. Sem., 1991—. Ordained to ministry Bapt. Ch., 1967; cert. drug and alcohol counselor, Conn. Min. youth 1st Evang. Free Ch., Bklyn., 1964-66; asst. to pastor Valley Stream (N.Y.) Presbyn. Ch., 1966-67; pastor Christ Bapt. Ch., Bklyn., 1967-70, Grace Bapt. Ch., Bklyn., 1970-74, Calvary Bapt. Ch., Darien, Conn., 1974—; substitute tchr. Darien Pub. Schs., 1978—; chaplain Darien Fire Dept., 1975—, Darien Convalescent Ctr., 1978—; pres. Conservative Bapt. Assn. of Conn., 1985-87. Mem. Social Svc. Commn., Town of Darien, 1975—, Salvation Army Svc. Corp., Darien, 1984. Mem. Nat. Assn. Nouthetic Counselors (cert.). Republican. Office: Calvary Bapt Ch 988 Post Rd Darien CT 06820 *In this day of rapid change, I have found that my faith in Christ and the infallibility of His Word gives stability to my life.*

GIBSON, BOB DEAN, minister; b. Decatur, Iowa, July 20, 1931; s. Clyde and Hattie Mae (Dobson) G.; m. Mary Amelia Prior, Mar. 11, 1952; children: Larry, John, Wayne. BS, Grayson County Coll., Sherman, Tex., 1971; diploma in theology, Southwestern Bapt. Theol. Sem., Ft. Worth, 1976, MDiv, 1984. Ordained to ministry So. Bapt. Conv., 1971. Min. Kemp (Okla.) Bapt. Ch., 1971-73, Roberta (Okla.) Bapt. Ch., 1974-75, 1st Bapt. Ch., Bokchito, Okla., 1975-80, Southside Bapt. Ch., Lubbock, Tex., 1980-85, 1st Bapt. Ch., Kingston, Okla., 1985—; moderator Bryan Bapt. Assn., Durant, Okla., 1976-77, Johnston-Marshall Bapt. Assn., Madill, Okla., 1989-90; chmn. policy and adminstrn. Lubbock Bapt. Assn., 1982-83. With USAF, 1949-71. Home: Box 518 Kingston OK 73439 Office: 1st Bapt Ch Box 159 Kingston OK 73439

GIBSON, CHARLES RICHARD, youth minister; b. Joplin, Mo., Oct. 10, 1956; s. Charles Ray and Barbara Louise (Poor) G.; m. Carrie Lynn Smith, Aug. 26, 1978; children: Julie Janell Gibson, Courtney Lynn Gibson, Charles Ryan Gibson. BA, Ozark Bible Coll., Joplin, 1979; postgrad., Cin. Christian Sem., 1985—. Minister to youth Northside Christian Ch., Broken Arrow, Okla., 1978-82, Cen. Christian Ch., St. Petersburg, Fla., 1982-86; dir. youth ministries Christ In Youth, Inc., Joplin, 1986—; chaplain Suncoast chpt. Am. Marriage Encounter, Pinellas County, Fla., 1984-86. Author: (with others) Discipleship II, 1988, The Ministers Manual, 1982; author (mag.) Christian Standard and the Lookout. Del. Am. Legion Boys State, Tahlequah, Okla., 1973; pres. Okla. Christian Youth Conv., Oklahoma City, 1980; bd. dirs. Youth Evangelism Svc., Tulsa, 1981-82, Lake Aurora Christian Assembly, Lake Wales, Fla., 1984-86; mem. exec. bd. Columbia Elem. PTO, 1991—. Mem. Christ in Youth Conf. Planning Coun., Nat. Youth Leaders Conv. (adv. com.). Avocations: golf, basketball, home remodeling, travel. Office: Christ in Youth Inc PO Box B Joplin MO 64802

GIBSON, DAVID PAUL, minister; b. Montgomery, Ala., Aug. 2, 1946; s. James Riley and Maurine (Mount) G.; m. Janice Gail Stephens, Oct. 18, 1969; children: Keith, Timothy, Daniel. Grad., Ala. Inst. Aviation Tech., Ozark, 1970; B in Biblical Studies, Cathedral Bible Sch., Birmingham, Ala., 1978; B in Religious Edn., New Orleans Inner City Sem., 1987. Ordained to ministry, Assemblies of God Ch., 1977. V.p. Gibson Sanitation, Gulfshores, Ala., 1971-73; sta. mgr. Crawford Broadcasting Co., El Reno, Okla., 1973-75; asst. pastor Huffman Assembly of God Ch., Birmingham, 1975-80; pastor First Assembly of God Ch., Gainsville, Ga., 1980-81; asst. pastor Brownsville Assembly of God Ch., Pensacola, Fla., 1981-83; assoc. pastor Calvary Assembly of God Ch., Orlando, Fla., 1983-84, Jimmy Swaggart Ministries, Baton Rouge, 1984—; founder, pastor Soul's Harbor Assembly of God, 1987—; with Evangelistic Missions, Inc., 1988—; prof. Jimmy Swaggart Bible Coll., 1984-88; dir. personal evangelism Family Worship Ctr., Baton Rouge, 1984-88; founder, pastor Goya Family Worship Ctr. (now Resserection Life Ch.), Baton Rouge, 1986-88. Pres. Harvest Sch. Evangelism, Birmingham, 1975-80, nat. ch. growth cons., 1975—. Republican. Avocations: restoring old cars, woodworking, fishing, reading. Home: PO Box 455 Gulf Shores AL 35642 Office: 8656 St Hwt 180 Gulf Shores AL 36542-9099

GIBSON, DEWEY ELVIN, minister; b. Malakoff, Tex., Dec. 24, 1933; s. John Dewey and Margie Louise (Rogers) G.; m. Dorothy Jean Ratcliff, June 12, 1954; children: Sherry Jean, Jerry Elvin. BS, Stephen F. Austin State U., 1954; BD, Southwestern Bapt. Theol. Sem., 1957, MDiv, 1968; ThD, Luther Rice Sem., 1975. Ordained to ministry So. Bapt. Conv., 1957. Pastor various chs., Tex., 1957-68, Texas Avenue Bapt. Ch., League City, Tex., 1968-74, Hillcrest Bapt. Ch., Nederland, Tex., 1974—; Bapt. Gen. Conf. Tex. trustee Bapt. Hosp. SE Tex., 1977-87, 90-91; sec./treas. Tex. Bapt. Pastor's Conf.; cons. in discipleship tng. Contbr. articles to profl. jours. Pres. League City Elem. Sch. PTA, 1969-70. Mem. Sabine Valley Bapt. Assn. (vice moderator 1961-63), Galveston Bapt. Pastors Fellowship (pres. 1970), Clear Creek Ministerial Alliance (pres. 1971), Galveston Bapt. Assn. (clk. 1972-74). Home: 3304 Park Dr Nederland TX 77627 Office: Hillcrest Bapt Ch 3324 Park Dr Nederland TX 77627

GIBSON, EDWARD LEE, minister; b. St. Louis, July 10, 1933; s. Earlie B. and Elizabeth (Irvin) G.; m. Ida Blanche McHarg, Sept. 12, 1953; children: Glenn, Kevin. AA, S.W. Bapt. U., Bolivar, Mo., 1953; BA, William Jewel Coll., Liberty, Mo., 1955; MDiv, So. Bapt. Sem., Louisville, 1959. Ordained to ministry So. Bapt. Conv., 1957. Pastor Watson Lane Bapt. Ch., Henderson, Ky., 1963-69, Grand Rivers (Ky.) Bapt. Ch., 1969-71; Pastor First Bapt. Ch., Delta, Mo., 1971-75, Licking, Mo., 1975-80, Union, Mo., 1980—; mem. exec. com. Mo. Bapt. Conv., 1990—; founder Agape House, St. Clair, Mo., 1984; starter Grace Bapt. Chapel, Union, 1986; moderator Franklin County Bapt. Assn., 1991—. Mem. Union Ministerial Alliance, Lions, Kiwanis, Rotary. Democrat. Home: 620 S Jefferson Union MO 63084 Office: First Bapt Ch 801 E Hwy 50 Union MO 63084

GIBSON, EMMALENE, Christian education minister; b. Manchester, Ky., Dec. 17, 1944; d. Charles and Ethel (Wagers) Depew; m. Clay Michael Gibson, Jr. BS in Elem. Edn., Cumberland Coll., 1978; postgrad., Union Coll., 1990—, Lee Coll., 1990—. Cert. elem. educator. Dist. youth, Christian edn. dir. Couch Fork (Ky.) Dist., 1980-85; family tng. dir. Manchester, Ky., 1985-86; dir. Christian edn. Manchester, 1980—; asst. Kindergarten tchr. Clay County Bd. Edn., Manchester, 1985—; Christian edn. dir. Ch. of God, Manchester, 1980—; Bible sch. coord., Manchester, 1990; teen talent dir. Ch. of God, Lexington, Ky., 1980-83, 84, 85-91, jr. talent dir., 1989-90. 4-H leader 4-H Club, Manchester Elm Sch., 1984-85; leader Girl Scouts, Manchester, 1985-87. Named Counselor of Yr., 1980, Ky. Family Tng. Hour Dir. of Yr., 1980, 81, Dist. Youth and Christian Edn. Dir. of Yr., 1983, Ky. Outstanding Supt. of Sunday Sch. of Yr., 1987. Home: Rte 5 Box 230 Manchester KY 40962

GIBSON, GAYRIL, broadcasting executive; b. Laurel, Miss., Apr. 18, 1958; d. Jimmie David and Anita (Sullivan) G. BA, Okla. Bapt. U., 1980; postgrad., Southwestern Bapt. Theol. Sem., 1980. Minister of music various locations, 1978-81; acount exec. WSHO-AM Radio, New Orleans, 1981-84; mgr. Sta. WBSN-FM Radio, New Orleans, 1984-86; minister of edn. Crescent City Bapt. Ch., New Orleans, 1986—; pres. Horizon Broadcast Communications, Hattiesburg, Miss., 1986—; owner Sta. WHLV Radio, Hattiesburg, 1986—; founder Sta. WHLV Worldwide Radio, Hattiesburg, 1989—. Chmn. small bus. com. Hattiesburg C. of C., 1989. Mem. Nat. Religious Broadcasters. Republican. Baptist. Office: Horizon Broadcast Communications PO Box 17131 Hattiesburg MS 39402

GIBSON, JAMES CLARK, minister; b. Terre Haute, Ind., June 23, 1950; s. John Robert and Ellen (Holscher) G.; m. Linda McCullough, Dec. 24, 1972; children: Mark David, Peter Joseph, Paul Daniel. BA, Heritage Bapt. U., Indpls., 1972; ThM, Trinity Theol. Sem., Newburg, Ind., 1977; DMin, Faith Theol. Sem., Morgantown, Ky., 1981. Ordained to ministry, Bapt. Ch., 1973. Pastor Bethel Bapt. Ch., Linton, Ind., 1972-75; assoc. pastor Terre Haute Bible Ctr., 1975-77; pastor Horace Bapt. Ch., Chrisman, Ill., 1977-80, Bible Bapt. Ch., Beaver Dam, Ky., 1980-85, Bible Fellowship Ch., Olney, Ill., 1985—; v.p. Carib Missions, Danville, 1978-80; instr. Wabash Valley Bible Inst., Terre Haute, 1973-76; adminstr. Heritage Christian Sch., Olney, 1989—. State sec. Kentuckians for Religious Freedom, Cambelsville, 1984. Recipient Heritage Found. award, 1984. Mem. Internat Fellowship of Ind. Chs. Republican. Home: 318 N Ludlow Olney IL 62450-1441 Office: Bible Fellowship Ch 1318 Hall Olney IL 62450-1441

GIBSON, JOHN FRANK, minister; b. Delhi, LA, Jan. 7, 1959; s. John Frank and Margaret Poole (Ray) G.; m. Christina Gayle Rogers, Dec. 21, 1985; 1 child, Carolyn Elizabeth. BA, Miss. Coll., 1982; M Divinity, New Orleans Bapt. Sem., 1985, postgrad. Minister First Bapt. Ch., Greenwood, Miss. Mem. So. Bapt. Conv. Avocations: hunting, fishing, football, basketball, baseball. Home: 501 Robert E Lee # 8 Greenwood MS 38930 Office: 1st Bapt Ch 500 W Washington Greenwood MS 38930

GIBSON, LOIS NAOMI, church secretary; b. Ellijay, Ga., Aug. 4, 1933; d. Charlie Melvin and Rebecca Nellie Mae (Beavers) George; m. Tom Gibson Jr., Dec. 23, 1949; children: Linda Gail Gibson Spivey, Tommy Douglas. Grad. high sch., Cleveland, Tenn. Ch. sec. North Cleveland Bapt. Ch., 1978—. Dir. pub. rels. Cleveland Helpline; mem. Cleveland/Bradley Food Bank Bd. Home: 3800 Stephens Rd NE Cleveland TN 37312 Office: North Cleveland Bapt Ch 2815 N Ocoee St Cleveland TN 37312

GIBSON, MATTHEW LEE, minister; b. Omaha, June 22, 1957; s. Will Lee Gibson and Ida Mae (Cooper) Williams; m. Debra Annette Fitzgerald, July 27, 1984; 1 child, Matthew Lee. BA, Oakwood Coll., Huntsville, Ala., 1984; MDiv, Andrews U., Berrien Springs, Mich., 1989. Family life assoc. dir. Cen. States Conf. of Seventh-day Adventist, Kansas City, Mo., 1988-89; pastor Breath of Life Seventh-day Adventist Ch., Columbia, Mo., 1989—; del. Cen. States Conf. Seventh-day Adventist, Kansas City, 1991—. Lt. U.S. Army, 1988—. Mem. Black Sem. Assn. (pub. rels. 1988-89), Religion/Theolgy Club (del. 1982—). Democrat. Home: 101 W Alhambra Dr Columbia MO 65203 *Life's greatest pleasures become insignificant when we come face to face with the eternal.*

GIBSON, MICHAEL RAY, clergyman; b. Ft. Hood, Tex., June 29, 1954; s. Grady Ray Gibson and Darlene L. (Rodgers) Graves; m. Dellen K. Gibson, Aug. 24, 1974; children: Heather, Drew, Doug, Garrett. BA, Sul Ross State U., 1976; MA, Southwestern Bapt. Theol. Sem., 1981. Ordained to ministry, Bapt. Ch. Minister youth Champion Forest Bapt. Ch., 1977-79, F.B.C. White Settlement, 1979-81, Highland Bapt. Ch., 1981-87, So. Hills Bapt. Ch., Oklahoma City, 1987—; mem. youth com. Capital Bapt. Assn., Oklahoma City, 1988—. Home: 3134 SW 128th St Oklahoma City OK 73170 Office: So Hills Bapt Ch 8601 S Penn Oklahoma City OK 73159

GIBSON, N. S., minister, ecumenical agency administrator. Head Stratford Dist. Coun. of Chs., Ont., Can. Office: Stratford Dist Coun Chs, 20 Manning Ave, Stratford, ON Canada N5A 5M9*

GIBSON, RAYMOND EUGENE, clergyman; b. Shelbyville, Ky., Mar. 10, 1924; s. Wallace and Laura Belle (Lee) G.; m. Susan Cochran, June 29, 1945; children: Cyrus Noel, Mark Scott, Christopher Watt, Laurence Kristin, Jonathan Geoffrey. A.B. in Philosophy and History, Berea Coll., 1944; B.D., Union Theol. Sem., N.Y.C., 1947; Ph.D., Columbia U., 1963. Ordained to ministry Congl. Ch., 1947; adminstrv. asst. Inst. Religious and Social Studies, N.Y.C., 1947-48; pastor in New Lebanon, N.Y., 1948-49, Pittsfield, Mass., 1950-61; pastor in Central Congl. Ch., Providence, 1961-88; prof. religious studies Providence Coll., 1971-87; Mem. com. evangelism and devotional life R.I. Congl. Conf., 1962-65, dir., 1965-76; exec. com. R.I. br. Acad. Religion and Mental Health, 1962; Danforth Found. Kenneth Underwood fellow, 1970-71. Author: God, Man and Time, 1966, The Parables of Jesus and the Apostles Creed, 1988; editor: Conversations with God: The Devotional Journals of Myrtie L. Elmer, 1962; assoc. editor: Minister's Quar, 1958-67. Chmn. R.I. adv. com. U.S. Commn. Civil Rights; mem. mayor's com. to end de facto segregation in Providence pub. schs.; bd. dirs. R.I. Group Health Assn., Inc.; trustee Berea Coll., 1963-85; founder, vice chmn. Corp. for Hamilton House, 1972; founder, mem. exec. com. Hospice Care R.I., 1975-86. Recipient Howard prize for citizenship Berea Acad., 1941; named Man of Year in Pittsfield Area, 1959; recipient Distinguished Service award Pittsfield Jr. C. of C., 1959; named one of four outstanding young men in state Mass. Jr. C. of C., 1959. Mem. Nat. Acad. Religion and Mental Health, Nat. Geog. Soc., R.I. State Council Churches (dir.). Home: 18 E Washington Rd Hillsborough Centre NH 03244 *For me, a life lived fully requires something of the head, the heart, and the hands; thoughts, feelings, skills. Achievement is not what a person does, but what he or she is and becomes. It involves taking time for things that have meaning; contemplation, love, friendship, solitude, art, nature, dreams, doubts, poetry, philosophy, song, dance, worship, hills, plains, seas; time to live in time and time to dwell on eternity.*

GIBSON, WILLIAM EDWARD, minister; b. Alton, Ill., Oct. 23, 1921; s. Edward Leyda and Anna Catharine (New) G.; m. Julia Kistle, May 9, 1945; children: Stephen Edward, Deborah Louise, Anna Catherine. BA, U. Wis., 1942; BD, Princeton Theol. Seminary, 1949; STM, Union Theol. Sem., N.Y.C., 1951, PhD, 1972. Ordained to ministry Presbyn. Ch. (U.S.A.), 1949. Presbyn. pastor U. Ark., Fayetteville, 1950-56, U. Pa., Phila., 1956-64; dir. Bd. for Campus Ministry, Rochester, N.Y., 1964-72; United Ministries chaplain Cornell U., Ithaca, N.Y., 1972-75, coord. eco-justice project/Ctr. Religion, Ethics, Social Pol, 1975-86, staff assoc., editor eco-justice project, 1986—; cons. com. on social witness policy Presbyn. Ch., Louisville, 1988-90; mem. Presbytery of Susquehanna Valley. Author, editor: Covenant Group for Lifestyle Assessment, 1978; prin. author: Keeping and Healing the Creation, 1989, Restoring Creation, 1990; also numerous articles, chpts. to books. Lt. (j.g.) USNR, 1943-45, PTO. Democrat. Home: 101 Poole Rd Ithaca NY 14850 Office: Cornell U Eco-Justice Project Anabel Taylor Hall Ithaca NY 14853

GIDWITZ, BETSY R., aeronautics and political science educator, consultant; b. Chgo., Nov. 13, 1940; d. Joseph L. and Emily (Klein) G. BA, U. Iowa, 1962; MEd, Boston U., 1965; PhD, U. Wash., 1976. Lectr. aeros. and astronautics, also polit. sci. MIT, 1974—; cons. in air transport and USSR, Cambridge, 1976—. Author: The Politics of International Air Transport, 1980; contbr. articles to profl. jours. Exec. bd. dirs. Coun. of Jewish Fedns., N.Y., Nat. Conf. on Soviet Jewry, N.Y.C., Combined Jewish Philanthropies, Boston, Action for Soviet Jewry, Waltham, Mass., Jewish Community Rels. Coun., Boston; bd. dirs. Union Couns. for Soviet Jews, Washington, United Israel Appeal, N.Y.C. Mem. Am. Acad. Polit. and Social Sci., Am. Assn. Advancement of Slavic Studies, Am. Polit. Sci. Assn. Home: 975 Memorial Dr Cambridge MA 02138

GIEGER, LOREN GLENN, religion educator; b. Paris, Tex., Dec. 29, 1937; s. Luther Loren and Mary Ida (Stroup) G.; m. Iola Ann Gray, Dec. 26, 1959; children: Leland Loren, Gayland Glen, Shawn Alland. BA, Abilene Christian U., 1960; MDiv, Southwestern Bapt. Theol. Sem., 1973, PhD, 1981. Ordained to ministry Ch. of Christ, 1960. Pulpit minister Ch. of Christ, various locations, 1960-84; asst. prof. Bible Mich. Christian Coll., Rochester, 1981-84; prof. Bible and Greek Okla. Christian U. Sci. and Arts, Oklahoma City, 1984—; guest lectr., tchr. Namwianga Christian Schs., Kaloma, Zambia, 1987. Author Bible sch. workbooks and manuals. Mem. Soc. Biblical Lit., Evang. Theol. Soc. Republican. Home: 3500 Cheyenne Dr Edmond OK 73013 Office: Okla Christian U Sci and Arts Box 11000 Oklahoma City OK 73136

GIELOW, RICHARD WILLIAM, priest; b. Lasalle, Ill., Oct. 29, 1943; s. Robert and Virginia (Gray) G. BA in Philosophy, St. Mary's Coll., Perryville, Mo., 1966; MA in Religious Edn., Catholic U., Wash., 1976; MA in Divinity, Deandreis Inst. Theology, Lemont, Ill., 1984. Dean of students St. Johns High Sch., Kansas City, Mo., 1970-72; dir. recruitment Vincentian Fathers-Midwest Province, Chgo., 1972-76; prin. St. John's high sch., Kansas City, 1976-83; dir. preaching team Vincentian Fathers-Midwest Province, Kansas City, 1983—; dir. mission team Vincentian Parish, Kansas City, 1988—; aux. chaplain Whiteman Air Force Base Knob Lobster Mo., 1976-81; nat. spiritual dir. Ladies of Charity, Kansas City, Mo., 1976—; bd. adv. Franciscan Sisters, Independence, Mo., 1980—; bd. mem. Seton Ctr. Kansas City, 1980—. Advisor exec. Jackson County, Kansas City, 1980—; appointed nat. spiritual dir. Ladies Charity, 1987. Recipient Svc. award Serra Club, 1983. Mem. Nat. Spiritual advisor Ft. Shafter Mil. Base Honolulu, Dem. Club Kansas City. Roman Catholic. Avocations: golf, racquetball, travel, tennis. Home: 3215 Windsor Ave Kansas City MO 64123 Office: Vincentian Fathers Residence 3215 Windsor Ave Kansas City MO 64123 *Life is a gift from God. When the gift is polished it shines everywhere. And all who see it give praise and thanks to God for giving them the gift.*

GIER, NICHOLAS FRANCIS, philosophy educator; b. North Platte, Nebr., Mar. 17, 1944; s. Nicholas Francis and Verlena (McVey) G.; m. Lisbeth Bindslev, Aug. 14, 1971 (div. Feb. 1988); 1 child, Christina Bindslev. BA, Oreg. State U., 1966; MA, Claremont Grad. Sch., 1971, PhD, 1973. Prof. philosophy U. Idaho, Moscow, 1972—, coord. religious studies, 1982—. Author: Wittgenstein and Phenomenology, 1981, God, Reason, and the Evangelicals, 1987. Fellow Fulbright Found., 1970-71, Rotary, 1966-67; NEH grantee, 1980. Mem. Am. Acad. Religion. Unitarian. Home: 509 Taylor Moscow ID 83843 Office: U Idaho Dept Philosophy Moscow ID 83843 *It is imperative that we step up efforts to strengthen the study of religion at all educational levels. Ignorance in the area is one of the main causes of tension and conflict in the world.*

GIERUT, CASIMIR FRANK, priest, social issues researcher; b. Chgo., Feb. 25, 1919; s. John and Catherine (Falat) G. A.A.S., Lewis and Clark Coll., 1978; A.B. in Philosophy, Mt. Mary's Coll., Orchard Lake, Mich., 1944; B.A., So. Ill. U., 1976. Ordained priest Roman Catholic Ch., 1949; St. Patrick's Ch., Alton, Ill., 1949-54; asst. pastor Cathedral, Springfield, Ill., 1954-59, pastor St. Mary's Cath. Ch., Bunker Hill, Ill., 1959—; chmn. Nat. Com. Repeal for the Fed. Res. Act, Bunker Hill, 1972—, Pres. Citizens for Social Justice in Taxation, Bunker Hill. Author: Taxpayer's Message to Congress-Repeal the Federal Reserve Act-The Pandora's Box of Criminal Acts, 1984. Club: Legislative Research Assocs. Office: Nat Com Repeal Fed Res Act 300 S Putnam St Bunker Hill IL 62014

GIESBRECHT, HERBERT JACOB, English educator, librarian; b. Velikoknyazheskoye, Kuban, USSR, Aug. 5, 1925; arrived in Can., 1926; s. Jacob John and Katherina (Harder) G.; m. Margaret Martens, Sept. 11, 1954; children: Norman David, Victor James, John Herbert, Edward Mark. BA, U. B.C., Vancouver, Can., 1948; BTh, Mennonite Brethren Bible Coll., 1955; MA in Spl. Edn., San Francisco State U., 1956; MA in English, U. Manitoba, Winnipeg, Can., 1978; MLS, U. Minn., 1967. Cert. secondary edn. tchr., Can.; ordained to ministry Mennonite Brethren Ch., 1970. Assoc. prof. English, libr. Mennonite Brethren Coll., Winnipeg, 1955-90, ret., 1990. Editor: The Mennonite Brethren Church: A Bibliographic Guide, 1983, Moved and Seconded: Resolutions of the Canadian Conference of Mennonite Brethren Churches, 1960-90, 1991; asst. editor: Voice of the Mennonite Brethren Bible Coll., 1969-71; co-editor: People of the Way: Selected Essays and Addresses, 1981, The Bible and the Church, 1988; translator: The Kuban Settlement, 1989. Mem. selection of families com. Habitat for Humanity, Winnipeg, 1986-88. Mem. Am. Theol. Libr. Assn., Assn. Christian Librs., Can. Conf. Mennonite Brethren Chs. (hist. com. 1969-89), Beta Phi Mu. Home: 11 Pinecrest Bay, Winnipeg, MB Canada R2G 1W2

GIESBRECHT, LAWRENCE, religious organization administrator. Missions dir. Evang. Mennonite Mission Conf., Manitoba, Can. Office: Evang Monnonite Mission Conf, Box 927, Altona, MB Canada R0G 0B0*

GIESCHEN, CHARLES ARTHUR, minister; b. Tomahawk, Wis., July 6, 1958; s. Henry Carl and Lily Barbara (Brandstetter) G.; m. Kristi Lee Kienas, July 20, 1985. BS in Social Work, Univ. Wis., 1980; MDiv, Concordia Theol. Seminary, Ft. Wayne, Ind., 1984; ThM, Princeton (N.J.) Theol., Seminary, 1985; postgrad., Univ. Mich., 1990—. Ordained to ministry Luth. Ch., 1985. Pastor Trinity Luth. Ch., Traverse City, Mich., 1985—; adj. prof. Concordia Theol. Seminary, 1989—; cir. evangelism rep., The Mich. Dist. of the Luth. Ch.-Mo. Synod, Ann Arbor, 1986—; prog. coord. Western Mich. Luth. Pastors' Conf., Grand Rapids, 1988—; exec. bd. Traverse Bay Cir. Mission Coun., Traverse City, 1986-90; regional instr. Mich. Luth. Ministries Inst., Saginaw, 1988-89. Author: (Bible Study) Jesus: The Ultimate Miracle Baby, 1990; contbr. articles, revs. to prof. jours. Pastoral vol. Grand Traverse Area Hospice, 1985—. Mem. Soc. Bibl. Lit., Alpha Delta Mu. Republican. Home: 1414 Arnold Ct Traverse City MI 49684 Office: Trinity Lutheran Ch 1003 South Maple St Traverse City MI 49684 *Christians live in an eschatological tension: we interpret the present by looking back to what God did for us in Jesus Christ and forward to what will happen upon Christ's return.*

GIESE, ROBERT JAMES, minister; b. Eau Claire, Wis., Apr. 7, 1950; s. Walter H. and Doris B. (Kuhn) G.; m. Jo Ann P. Zutz, June 19, 1971; 1 child, Rachel. BS in Zoology, U. Wis., 1972; MDiv, Christ Sem.-Seminex, St. Louis, 1978; D Ministry in Pastoral Care and Counseling, Luth. Sch. Theology, Chgo., 1990. Ordained to ministry Evang. Luth. Ch. Am., 1979. Min. Christian Ministry in Nat. Pks., N.Y.C., 1974-77; chaplain Bear Creek Boys Ranch, Lodi, Calif., 1978-79; pastor Trinity Luth. Ch., Rolling Meadows, Ill., 1979—; exec. cons. Stephen Ministries, St. Louis, 1974-82; sec. Chgo.-Milw. Conf. Evang. Luth. Ch. Am., Chgo., 1983-85, v.p., 1985-86; youth adv. Luth. Social Svcs., Chgo., 1987-88. Contbr. articles to profl. jours. Bd. dirs. The Bridge Youth Svcs., Palatine, Ill., 1983-87; pres., bd. dirs. Racetrack Ministries, Arlington Heights, Ill., 1990—. Mem. Assn. of Personality Type. Home: 3203 Meadow Dr Rolling Meadows IL 60008 Office: Trinity Luth Ch 3201 Meadow Dr Rolling Meadows IL 60008 *I believe that the more I am able to know and accept myself for who I am as God knows and accepts me for who I am through Christ, the more I will be enabled to know and accept those with whom I am called to minister.*

GIESE, VINCENT, priest; b. Ft. Wayne, Ind., Oct. 19, 1923; s. Joseph John and Mae Genevieve (Yaste) G. PhB, St. Joseph's Coll., 1945; MA, Marquette U., 1948; MEd, Notre Dame U., 1950; StB, Gregorian U., Rome, 1965. Ordained priest Roman Cath. Ch., 1965. Editorial dir. Fides Pubs., Inc., Chgo., 1949-61; assoc. pastor Blessed Sacrament Ch., Chgo., 1966-72; pastor Our Lady of Perpetual Help, Chgo., 1972-78; editor Harmonizer Cath. Weekly, Ft. Wayne, 1978-80; editor-in-chief Our Sunday Vis., Inc., Huntington, Ind., 1980-84, pub., 1984—. Author: Jour. of a Late Vocation, 1966, You Got It All, 1980, Youth for Peace, 1984; editor Priest mag., Huntington, 1980—; assoc. editor New World Cath. Weekly, Chgo., 1968-78; contbr. numerous articles to religious jours. Mem. Cath. Press Assn. Democrat. Club: Ft. Wayne Press (v.p. 1980-85). Avocations: writing, jazz music, gourmet cooking. Office: Our Sunday Visitor Inc 200 Noll Pla Huntington IN 46750

GIESER, CHARLES KENNETH, minister; b. China, Nov. 26, 1939; (parents Am. citizens); s. P. Kenneth and Catherine (Kirk) G.; m. Sally Jo Hoppe, June 26, 1962; children: Carla, Jenna, Dirk. BS, Wheaton (Ill.) Coll., 1961; MDiv, Columbia Theol. Sem., Decatur, Ga., 1964; MA in Religious Edn., Hartford Sem. Found., 1967. Ordained to ministry Presbyn. Ch. (U.S.A.), 1964. Asst. pastor 1st Presbyn. Ch., Dotham, Ala., 1964-66; pastor Bakerville (Conn.) United Meth. Ch., 1966-70; Presbyn. min. Mid. Tenn. State U., Murfreesboro, 1971-71; assoc. pastor Christ Ch. Oak Brook, Ill., 1971-74; exec. dir. Sky Ranches, Inc., Dallas, 1974-81; dir. Deerfoot Lodge, Speculator, N.Y., 1981—. Home and Office: Deerfoot Lodge RD 2 Box 159B Greenville NY 12083

GIESLER, JOHN HANFORD, minister; b. Green Bay, Wis., Apr. 3, 1931; s. Carl and Laura Louise (Dickey) G.; m. Barbara Lind Gordon, Aug. 17, 1957; children: Deborah Pyatt, Christian, Rebecca Morgan, Cynthia Meier. BA, Moravian Coll., 1955; MDiv, Moravian Theol. Seminary, Bethlehem, Pa., 1958; postgrad., Escuela De Idiomas, San Jose/Costa Rica, 1959. Missionary pastor Moravian Chs., Bluefields, Bonanza, Managua, Nicaragua, 1958-69; pastor The Union Ch. of Managua, 1959-60, Friedberg Moravian Ch., Winston-Salem, N.C., 1969-75, The Moravian Ch., King, N.C., 1975-80, Bethabara Moravian Ch., Winston-Salem, 1980-90; organizing pastor New Hope Moravian Ch., Miami, Fla., 1990—; pres. Hymn Soc. Am. and Can., Ft. Worth, 1982-84, Moravian Music Found., Winston-Salem, 1976-81, Moravian Mission Soc., Winston-Salem, 1975-78; sec. Inter-provincial Hymnal Com., Bethlehem, 1985—. Author publs. in field. Recipient awards in field. Mem. Am. Guild Organists, Moravian Hist. Soc., Southwest Miami Fla. Ministers Assn. Home: 7385 SW 115 Ct Miami FL 33173 *Seeking to resolve the dissonance of this world, we try to conduct our lives in harmony with family and friends, and as far as possible live in acord with the whole creation. We search for the cantus firmus of the will of God till we achieve an authentic cadence and are transposed into the music of the spheres!.*

GIESMANN, DONALD JOHN, minister; b. Pitts., Apr. 15, 1949; s. John Weber and Harriet Elizabeth (Collingwood) G.; m. Sara Longfellow Mosher, June 2, 1974; children: Carrie Elizabeth, Alison Sara. BS, Indiana U. of Pa., 1971; MRE, Gordon-Conwell Sem., South Hamilton, Mass., 1974; EdD, Columbia Pacific U., 1980. Ordained to ministry Presbyn. Ch. in Am., 1975. Chaplain students Gordon-Conwell Sem., 1973-74; assoc. pastor Westminster Presbyn. Ch., Rock Hill, S.C., 1974-76; pastor Heritage Congl. Ch., Middletown, Conn., 1976-77; assoc. pastor discipleship South Park Ch., Park Ridge, Ill., 1977-81; pastor Community Ch., Bristol, Tenn., 1981-88; pastor 1st Presbyn. Ch., Trenton, Mich., 1988—; mem. nat. Christian edn. com. Evang. Presbyn. Ch., 1983-86; del. Ill./White House Conf. on Families, 1980; mem. world outreach com. Evang. Presbyn. Ch.; bd. dirs. William Tyndale Coll. Apptd. Ill. Selective Service System Bd. Recipient Recognition award Pa. State Student Edn. Assn., 1971; Four Way Test award Christian Workers Found., 1974. Office: 1st Presbyn Ch 2799 West Rd Trenton MI 48183

GIFFIN, MARY ELIZABETH, psychiatrist, educator; b. Rochester, Minn., Mar. 30, 1919; d. Herbert Ziegler and Mary Elizabeth (Nace) G. BA, Smith Coll., Northampton, Mass., 1939; MD, Johns Hopkins, 1943; MS, U. Minn., 1948. Diplomate Am. Bd. Psychiatry and Neurology. Cons. in neurology and psychiatry Mayo Clinic, Rochester, 1949-58; med. dir. Josselyn Clinic, Northfield, Ill., 1948-89; pvt. practice psychiatry Northfield, 1989—; mem. faculty Inst. for Psychoanalysis, Chgo., 1963-89. Contbr. numerous articles to profl. jour. Mem. Ill. Psychiat. Soc., Am. Acad. Child Psychiatry. Republican. Mem. Am. Bapt. Ch. Avocation: creative writing. Home: 1190 Hamptondale Rd Winnetka IL 60093 Office: 1 Northfield Pla Ste 300 Northfield IL 60093 *Settle into the immediate as if it were the infinite which indeed it is.*

GIFFORD, MICHAEL RICHARD, minister; b. Savanna, Ill., July 6, 1959; s. Richard Lee and Shirley Ann (McKinley) G.; m. Shannon Deneese Nolen, Dec. 30, 1979; children: Whitney Erin, Elise Ann. Student, U. Dubuque, 1977-78; BS, Freed-Hardeman Coll., 1980; MA in Religion, Harding Grad. Sch. Religion, 1982. Ordained to ministry Ch. of Christ. Minister Brooks Ave. Ch. of Christ, Raleigh, N.C., 1982-83, Commerce (Ga.) Ch. of Christ, 1983-88, Panama Street Ch. of Christ, Montgomery, Ala., 1988—. Author: The ABC's of Family Life, 1987, The Essence of Living Faith, 1988, The Greatest of These, 1990; contbr. articles to Christian mags. Named one of Outstanding Young Men in Am., 1983, 85, 86, 87, 88. Mem. Alpha Psi Omega. Republican. Avocations: golf, tennis, traveling, reading. Home: 4501 Charingwood Ct Montgomery AL 36109 Office: Panama St Ch of Christ 444 S Panama St Montgomery AL 36107

GIGEE, BRIAN KEITH, minister, evangelist; b. Youngstown, Ohio, Feb. 9, 1954; s. Howard E. and Doris M. (Hall) G.; m. Catherine L. Jacobi, July 25, 1981; children: Rachel, Nathan. BA, Tex. Luth. Coll., 1976; MDiv, Trinity Luth. Sem., Columbus, Ohio, 1981. Ordained to ministry Evang. Luth. Ch. in Am., 1981. Assoc. pastor St. Paul's Luth. Ch., Taylor, Tex., 1981-83; pastor, evangelist Prince of Peace Luth. Ch., Huntsville, Tex., 1983-88, Grace Luth. Ch., New Orleans, 1988—; mem. So. dist. Am. Luth. Ch. Outreach Commn., 1984-87; coord. region 4F Evangelism Task Force, Houston, 1988—. Contbr. articles to profl. jours. Convenor New Orleans Interfaith Com., 1990. Mem. Acad. Evangelists of Evang. Luth. Ch. in Am., Bread for the World (bd. dirs. New Orleans chpt. 1989—), Sertoma (pres. Taylor club 1982-83). Home: 607 Filmore Ave New Orleans LA 70124 Office: Grace Evang Luth Ch 5800 Canal Blvd New Orleans LA 70124 *I am inspired by those who continue to live fully in the midst of emotional and physical pain and suffering. They witness to the reality that it is not easy but that it can be done. Without being masochistic they demonstrate that suffering can be welcomed and can be a creative catalyst for life.*

GILBERT, ARTHUR JOSEPH, bishop; b. Hedley, C., Can., Oct. 26, 1915; s. George Miles and Ethel May (Carter) G. B.A., St. Francis Xavier U., N.S., Can., 1938; B.Th., Holy Heart Sem., Halifax, N.S., 1943. Ordained priest Roman Catholic Ch., 1943; curate St. Andrew's (N.B.) Parish; also sec. to bishop of St. John (N.B.), 1943-44; chancellor Diocese of St. John, 1944-49; dir. Cath. Orphanage, Saint John, 1949-55; pastor St. Pius X Parish, Saint John, 1955-69, St. Joseph's Parish, Saint John, 1969-71, St. Joachim's Parish, Saint John, 1971-74; bishop of St. John, 1974-86, bishop emeritus, 1986—. Chancellor, chmn. bd. St. Thomas U., Fredericton, N.B., 1974-86. Club: K.C. Address: 100 Villa Madonna Rd, Renforth, Saint John, NB Canada E2H 2T2

GILBERT, DAVID LEE, clergyman; b. Glendale, Calif., Oct. 10, 1956; s. Donald Leon and Marjorie (Cox) G.; m. Deborah Lu Sutliff, Aug. 25, 1979; children: Amy, Tyler. BS, Biola U., 1979; MA, Talbot Sem., 1981, MDiv, 1983. Ordained to ministry Evang. Free Ch., 1984. Youth pastor Evang. Free Ch., Orange, Calif., 1980-84, Cornerstone Ch., Mission Viejo, Calif., 1984-87; assoc. pastor Coast Hills Ch., Laguna Niguel, Calif., 1987—. Author: Dating Your Mate, 1988 (Best Seller), Romance Rekindled, 1989. Office: 26041 Cape Dr Ste 233 Laguna Beach CA 92677-1213

GILBERT, DONALD KEITH, minister, counselor; b. Parsons, Kans., Oct. 20, 1955; s. Walter R. and Dolores A. (Shepard) G.; m. Deborah-Anne Peterson, Aug. 28, 1976; children: Heather, Meghan, Bryan, Sarah. BA in Theology, Bartlesville Wesleyan Coll., Okla., 1977; MS in Counseling, Drake U., 1991. Ordained to ministry The Wesleyan Ch., 1977. Pastor Highland Wesleyan Ch., Harrison, Ark., 1977-80, Trinity Wesleyan Ch., La Porte City, Iowa, 1983-86; dir. Christian Edn. Abilene (Kans.) Brethren in Christ Ch., 1980-83; pastor Debra Heights Wesleyan Ch., Des Moines, 1986—; counselor Dr. Gary Rosberg and Assocs., Des Moines, 1990—; youth dir., Dist. Iowa The Wesleyan Ch., Des Moines, 1985, dir. youth camp, Floyd, 1985-88, sec. evangelism, Des Moines, 1989—. Com. mem. Polk County Rep. Com., 1989—. Mem. AACD, Wesleyan Men (pres. Des Moines 1986—), Internat. Assn. Marriage and Family Counselors, Nat. Christian Counselor Assn. Office: Debra Heights Wesleyan Ch 4025 Lower Beaver Rd Des Moines IA 50310

GILBERT, GEORGE CARLTON, SR., minister; b. Gretna, Va., June 2, 1947; s. George Kelly and Mamie Odessa Gilbert; m. Raba Addie Bass, July 1, 1967; children: Lisa Marshanette, George Carlton Jr. Student, Norfolk State Coll., 1965-67, Washington Bapt. Sem., 1974-78; BTh, Richmond Va. Sem., 1983, BA, 1987; postgrad., Howard U. Sch. Divinity. Ordained to ministry Bapt. Ch. 1976. Asst. to pastor Cen. Bapt. Ch., Washington, 1969-77; pastor Carolina Missionary Bapt. Ch., Washington, 1977-85, Holy Trinity United Bapt. Ch., Washington, 1985—; sec. Bapt. Conv., Washington, 1980—, pres. Missionary Bapt. Mins. Conf., Washington, 1986-88, pres. Ch. Leadership Organized For A Unified Trust, Washington, 1989—, v.p. Eastern Region Prog. Nat. Bapt. Conv., 1990—. Mem. Inst. Civil and Social Change, Washington, 1990—. Recipient Athletic scholar, Norfolk State Coll., 1965, Banjamin E. Mays Scholastic scholar, 1990. Home and Office: 2023 31st Pl SE Washington DC 20020

GILBERT, JAMES CAYCE, minister; b. Nashville, Feb. 26, 1925; s. Gettis and Delia Mae (Snyder) G.; m. Freda Mae Mitchell, Sept. 3, 1949; children—Elizabeth, Suzanne, Kathryn, Rosalie. B.A., Bethel Coll., McKenzie, Tenn., 1945, D.D. (hon.), 1976; B.D., Cumberland Presbyn. Theol. Sem., McKenzie, 1947; M.A., Scarritt Coll., Nashville, 1948. Ordained to ministry Cumberland Presbyn. Ch., 1944; asso. pastor West Nashville Cumberland Presbyn. Ch., 1947-48; pastor River Oaks Cumberland Presbyn. Ch., Houston, 1948-55, Trinity Cumberland Presbyn. Ch., Ft. Worth, 1956-64; exec. dir. Cumberland Presbyn. Children's Home, Denton, Tex., 1964-90, dir. devel., 1991—; moderator gen. assembly Cumberland Presbyn. Ch., 1979-80. Mem. Nat. Assn. Homes Children, Southwestern Assn. Children's Home (past pres.), Tex. Assn. Execs. Homes Children (past pres.), Denton C. of C. Democrat. Clubs: Lions, Masons, K.T. Home: 3720 W Biddison Fort Worth TX 76109

GILBERT, JUDITH MAY, human relations executive; b. Miami, Fla., Dec. 2, 1934; d. Stanley C. and Martha (Scheinberg) Myers; children: Robert, Carolyn, Mark. Student, U. N.C., 1952-53; BA, U. Fla., 1956. Project coord. Miami Beach Redevel. Agy., Miami Beach, Fla., 1977-78, dir. community svcs., 1978-79; dir. victim/witness svcs. Office of State's Atty., 11th Judicial Cir. of Fla., Dade County, Miami, 1980; exec. dir. S.E. region Am. Jewish Congress, Miami, 1980-83; assoc. dir. community rels. Greater Miami Jewish Fedn., 1983-90, dir. community rels., 1990—. Bd. dirs. Stanley C. Myers Community Health Ctr. Inc., Miami Beach, 1988—, Dade-Monroe Mental Health Bd., 1982-84, High Sch. in Israel, Miami, 1978-80; mem. Fla. Ednl. Equity Act Adv. Group, Dade County Schs., 1986-88; pres. Nat. Council Jewish Women, Miami, 1974-77; v.p. So. Dist. Nat. Council Jewish Women, 1976-77. Recipient Vol. Activist award Germaine Monteil, 1972, Hannah G. Solomon award Nat. Council Jewish Women, 1978. Mem. AAUW, Nat. Community Relations Dirs. Assn., Human Relations Profls. of Greater Miami, Alpha Epsilon Phi. Office: Greater Miami Jewish Fedn 4200 Biscayne Blvd Miami FL 33137

GILBERT, LARRY ALAN, religious institute administrator; b. Charleston, W.Va., Jan. 18, 1945; s. Edmond B. and Violet L. (Calahan) G.; m. Mary Louise Woodward, Oct. 15, 1965; children: Kelly, Alan, Jason. Student, Liberty U., 1981. Pres., chief exec. officer Ch. Growth Inst., Lynchburg, Va., 1983—. Author: Team Ministry, 1987, Team Evangelism, 1991. Republican. Office: Ch Growth Inst PO Box 4404 Lynchburg VA 24502

GILBERT, MICHAEL DALE, minister, consultant; b. Waynesville, Mo., Dec. 21, 1951; s. Nolan Dale and Donna Lou (Crick) G.; m. Rebecca Sue Frieze, Jan. 4, 1975; children: Kimberly Michelle, Jeffrey Ryan. BS, S.W. Mo. State U., Springfield, 1974; M in Religious Edn., Southwestern Bapt. Theol. Sem., 1977. Ordained to ministry Gospel Ch., 1980. Minister to students U. Heights Bapt. Ch., Springfield, 1971-74; minister to youth First Bapt. Ch., Cleburne, Tex., 1974-77, Northway Bapt. Ch., Dallas, 1977-79; minister to students Roswell St. Bapt. Ch., Marietta, Ga., 1979-81; prof. Gulfshore Bapt. Coll., Ft. Myers, Fla., 1981-84; minister to youth Riverside Bapt. Ch., Ft. Myers, 1981-84; minister to students First Bapt. Ch., Kenner, La., 1985-88; dir. student ministries North Phoenix Bapt. Ch., Phoenix, 1988—; pres. Nehemiah Concert Prodn. Co., Ft. Myers, 1982-84; chmn. Youth Ministers Lab Southwestern Bapt. Theol. Sem., 1976. Author: 2 chpts. Disciple Youth II Notebook, 1984; editor: La. Recreators Newspaper Jour., 1986-87, La. Youth Ministers Newspaper Jour., 1986-88; contbr. articles to profl. jours. Lay chaplain Juvenile Detention Ctr., New Orleans, 1986-87, Jefferson Parish Juvenile Detention Ctr., Harvey, La., 1986-87; speaker Morality in Media, New Orleans, 1987-89, High Sch. Assemblies/Convs., etc., nationwide, 1980—; bd. dirs. Johnson County Human Guidance Assn., Cleburne, 1977. Named one of Outstanding Young Men in Am., Jaycees, 1981. Mem. Metro Youth Ministers Assn., Religious Educators Assn., Ariz. Bapt. Youth Evangelism Com. (chmn. 1988—), Fellowship Christian Athletes, ASCAP, Nat. Youth Ministers Assn. (conf. leader 1977—), Fla. Recreators Assn. (bd. dirs. 1982-84), La. Youth Ministers Assn. (bd. dirs. 1985-88), La. Recreators Assn. (bd. dirs. 1986-88), Ariz.

Youth Ministers Assn. (chmn., bd. dirs. 1988—). Democrat. Avocations: writing, songwriting, entertaining, sports.

GILBERT, PATRICK NIGEL GEOFFREY, organization executive; b. May 12, 1934; adopted s. Geoffrey and Evelyn (Miller) Devon. Ed. Cranleigh Sch., Merton Coll., Oxford; D.Litt. (hon.), Columbia Pacific U., 1982. Lectr. in further edn. South Berks Coll., 1959-62, personal asst. to Sir Edward Hulton, 1962-64; with Oxford U. Press, 1964-69; mng. dir. in linguaphone group Westinghouse, 1970; gen. sec. Soc. for Promoting Christian Knowledge, London, 1971—. Chmn. Camden Arts Council, 1970-74, v.p., 1974-90; steward Artists' Gen. Benevolent Instn., 1971—; trustee Richards Trust, 1971—, Buxton Trust, 1973—, chmn., 1983—; trustee Overseas Bishoprics Fund, 1973—, World Assn. Christian Communication, 1975-87; gov. St. Martin's in Fields Sch., 1971—; fellow Corp. of Saints Mary and Nicholas (Woodard Schs.), 1972—, corp. exec., 1981—; chmn. bd. trustees, hon. treas. Art Workers Guild, 1976-86; chmn., founder Nat. Assn. Local Arts Councils, 1976-80, v.p., 1980—; mem. governing body SPCK Australia, 1977—; gov. Ellesmere Coll., Shropshire, 1978-87; gov. St. Michael's Sch., Petworth, 1978-88, Roehampton Inst. Higher Edn., 1978—, Pusey House, Oxford; dir. Surrey Bldg. Soc.; mem. All Saints Ednl. Trustee, chmn. fin. and investment com., 1978—; mem. Partnership for World Mission, 1979—, Church Pub. Com., 1980-84; chmn. Concord Multicultural Arts Trust, 1980-89; gov. Contemporary Dance Trust, 1981-90; mem. Exec. Anglican Centre, Rome, 1981-90; trustee Anglican Consultative Council Research Project, 1982-84; trustee Dancers Resettlement Fund, chmn. fin. com., 1982-90, Dancers Resettlement Trust, 1987-90; mem. Ct. of City Univ., 1987—; bd. dirs. SPCK, U.S., 1983—; chmn. acad. disciplinary appeals tribunal Roehampton Inst., 1983-89; parish clk. All Hallows Bread St. Decorated Lord of Manor of Cantley Netherhall, Norfolk; Order of St. Vladimir; recipient numerous awards for civic and profl. service. Mem. Greater London Arts Assn. (hon. life mem.; chmn. 1980-84), Guild of Freemen of City of London, Master Worshipful Co. of Woolmen, 1985-86, numerous others. Clubs: Athenaeum (chmn. exec. com.); Walton Heath Golf; City Livery; Bread Street Ward; Nikaean (chmn. 1984—). Address: 3 The Mount Sq, London NW3 6SU, England *To pray is to be a friend of God.*

GILBERT, SHARON MAY, music educator, choir director; b. Portage, Wis., Aug. 24, 1948; d. Ronald William and BettyLou Elizabeth (Marquardt) Wade; m. Philip Charles Gilbert, Mar. 22, 1969; children: Michelle Elizabeth, Robyn Faith, Shawn Philip. B in Music Edn., U. Wis., Stevens Point, 1970, M in Music Edn., 1981. Cert. vocal music and piano tchr., Wis. Pvt. practice tchr. piano Stevens Point, 1973—; tchr. music St. Stanislaus Sch., Stevens Point, 1984—; missionette dir. 1st Assembly of God Ch., Stevens Point, 1973—, dir. adult choir, 1980—; adjudicator Wis. Sch. Music Assn., Madison, 1976—; missionette sectional rep. Wis./North Mich. dist. Assembly of God Ch., Wanpaca, Wis., 1980—; banquet pianist Stevens Point Ch. of C., 1988—. Foster parent Portage County Social Svcs., Stevens Point, 1981—; leader Plover Clover 4-H Club, Plover, Wis., 1983—; sec. Portage County 4-H Leaders Bd., Stevens Point, 1988-89. Mem. Music Educators Nat. Conf. Avocations: reading, crafts, sewing, piano. Home: 210 Weir Blvd Stevens Point WI 54481

GILBERT, SUSAN COSBY, minister, elementary school educator; b. Ft. Benning, Ga., Apr. 4, 1964; d. Glen James and Betty Lorene (Simmons) Cosby; m. Franklin LeRoy Gilbert Jr., Mar. 18, 1989. MusB, Columbus (Ga.) Coll., 1986; postgrad., New Orleans Bapt. Theol. Sem., 1988-90. Cert. elem. tchr. (substitute), Fla. Pianist Valence St. Bapt. Ch., New Orleans, 1988-89; min. music Pine Barren Bapt. Ch., Davisville, Fla., 1989—; substitute tchr. Escambia County Sch. Dist., Pensacola, Fla., 1990—; tchr. conversational English Otsu Bapt. Ch., Otsu-Shiga, Japan, 1985, Takaishi Bible Ch., Takaishi-Osaka, Japan, 1986-87; dir. camp music Valley Rescue Mission-Camp Joy, Columbus, 1987. Democrat. Home and Office: Pine Barren Bapt Ch 5270 Pine Barren Church Rd Century FL 32535 *In this world of constant change there is one who is unchanging, steadfast in all His ways. I have chosen to make Jesus Christ Lord of my life and serve Him all my days.*

GILCHRIST, CHARLES WATERS, minister; b. Washington, Nov. 12, 1936; s. Ralph A. and Eleanor (Waters) G.; m. Phoebe Royce, July 29, 1961; children: Donald, James, Janet. MDiv, Va. Theol. Sem., 1989; AB, Williams Coll., 1958; LLB, Harvard U., 1961. Ordained to ministry Episcopal Ch., 1990. Asst. rector St. Margaret's Episc. Ch., Washington, 1989-91; exec. dir. Cathedral Shelter Chgo., 1991—; chmn. refugee com. Peace Commn. Episc. Diocese, Washington, 1989-91. Exec. Montgomery County, Md., 1978-86; senator Md. Senate, Annapolis, 1974-78; del. Dem. Conv., 1980, 84. Home: 312 N May St Chicago IL 60607 Office: Cathedral Shelter Chgo 207 S Ashland Ave Chicago IL 60607 *Our hope should be that the worship of the church will become more tightly bound with our service to humanity.*

GILCHRIST, JAY, pastoral counselor, community consultant; b. Marshalltown, Iowa, Jan. 15, 1952; s. James Gilbert and Joy Mae (Stanley) G.; m. Pamela Jean Burns, May 21, 1977; children: Matthew, Anna, Joel. BA in Religion and Letters, cert. in medieval studies, U. Iowa, 1978, MA in English, 1983; MA in Religious Studies with distinction, Mundelein Coll., Chgo., 1987. Dir. religious edn. St. John parish, Mt. Vernon, Iowa, 1978-81; instr. religion Notre Dame High Sch., Burlington, Iowa, 1981-82; houseparent, counselor Systems Unltd., Iowa City, 1982-85; pastoral assoc. St. Alexander parish, Palos Heights, Ill., 1985-86; coord. econ. devel. City of Tyler, Minn., 1986—; assoc. in pastoral care McKennan Hosp., Sioux Falls, S.D., 1988-91; project future coord. Lincoln County Minn. Extension Svc., Ivanhoe, 1991—; coord. Tyler Econ. Devel. Commn., 1987—. Writer poetry. Council of Cath. Women scholar, 1987. Mem. Nat. Assn. Cath. Chaplains (cert.), Pax Christi, Am. Diabete Assn., Amnesty Internat., U. Iowa Alumni Assn., Tyler area C. of C. (devel. com. 1987—), Country Side Coun. Avocations: poetry, photography, walking. Home: 350 Hughes Tyler MN 56178

GILDEN, GLEN GARTH, minister; b. Anacortes, Wash., Sept. 12, 1926; s. Glen Garth and Charlie (Brown) G.; m. Melba Vileen Osborn, Dec. 27, 1947; children: Sharon Christine Gilden Gayagas, Glen Jr., Sheryl Cathleen Gilden Jones, Ronald. BA, Whitworth Coll., 1948; MSW, Portland (Oreg.) State U., 1964. Ordained to ministry Salvation Army, 1949; registered social worker. Comdg. officer Salvation Army, Wash., Mont., Oreg., Ariz., 1949-67; divisional sec. Salvation Army, Denver, Phoenix, 1967-73; dir. social svc. Salvation Army, Hong Kong, 1973-82; asst. prin. Sch. for Officers' Tng., L.A., 1982-83; pub. rels. dir. Salvation Army, Mexico City, 1984-88; comdg. officer Salvation Army, Riverside, Calif., 1989—; bd. dirs. Sunday Sch. Conf., Riverside, 1990-91. Mem. NASW. Home: 26145 Goldenwood St Sun City CA 92586-3748 Office: Salvation Army 3695 First St Riverside CA 92501

GILES, JUDITH MARGARET, minister, communication educator; b. Sonora, Calif., Nov. 20, 1939; d. James Wilson and Phyllis Sue (Stafford) G. BA, Calif. State U., 1982; MA, Regent U., Virginia Beach, Va., 1986; A. Ministry, Christ for the Nations, Dallas, 1974. Real estate broker Mason McDuffie, Berkeley, Calif., 1975-77, Taylor Realty, Sonora, Calif., 1978-82; pres., adminstr., instr. Christ for the People, Pleasant Hill, Calif., 1975-77; adminstr., instr. Mt. Zion Ministries, Modesto, Calif., 1977-91; instr. Calif. Assn. Realtors, Sacramento, 1980-82; adminstrv. asst., instr. Air Force Chaplaincy, Washington, 1983-84; asst. media/press coordinator Nat. Religious Broadcasters, Washington, 1983-86; grad. teaching asst. Christian Broadcasting Network U., Virginia Beach, Va., 1984-86; instr. Global Outreach Bible Inst., Modesto, Calif., 1987—; real estate broker Re/Max Real Estate Cen., Modesto, Calif., 1987—; lectr. in field; communications cons.; radio commentator; TV guest host. Author: A Historical Overview of the Women's Movement in America, 1986; producer, dir. TV documentary: The United Jewish Fedn., 1985, What's in a Name, 1985, Chiropractic, Lutheran Council, 1984. Mgr. pub. relations dir. South Lake Tahoe Community Choir, 1971. Mem. Calif. Assn. Realtors, Nat. Assn. Realtors, Women's Club, Pres.'s Club, Rainbow Girls. Republican. Avocations: golf, history, film, Water sports, boating. Home: 1817 Scott Ave Modesto CA 95350

GILKEY, J. L., bishop. Bishop Ch. of God in Christ, Wichita, Kans. Office: Ch of God in Christ 2403 Shadybrook Wichita KS 67214*

GILKEY, LANGDON BROWN, retired religion educator; b. Chgo., Feb. 9, 1919; s. Charles W. and Geraldine (Brown) G.; divorced; 1 child, Mark Whitney; m. Sonja Weber, Jan. 26, 1963; children: Amos Welcome, Frouwkje. BA, Harvard U., 1940; PhD, Columbia U., 1954. Instr. philosophy of religion Union Theol. Sem., N.Y.C., 1949-50; lectr. religion Vassar Coll., Poughkeepsie, N.Y., 1951-54; prof. theology, Div. Sch. Vanderbilt U., Nashville, 1954-63; prof. theol., Div. Sch. U. Chgo., 1963-89, prof. emeritus, 1989—. Author: Maker of Heaven and Earth, 1959, How the Church Can Minister to the World without Losing Itself, 1964, Shantung Compound, 1966, Social and Intellectual Sources of Contemporary Protestant Theology, 1967, Naming the Whirlwind: The Renewal of God-Language, 1969, Religion and the Scientific Future, 1970, Catholicism Confronts Modernity, 1975, Reaping the Whirlwind: A Christian Interpretation of History, 1977, Message and Existence, 1979, Society and the Sacred, 1981, Creationism on Trial: Evolution and God at Little Rock, 1985, Gilkey on Tillich, 1990. Recipient Shailer Mathews Profl. award Div. Sch., U Chgo., 1978; Am. Coun. Learned Soc. fellow, 1947-49; Kent fellow, Coun. Religion Higher Edn., 1948; Guggenheim fellow, Fed. Republic German, 1960-61, Rome, 1965. Mem. Ch. Hist. Soc., Soc. Theol. Discussion, Am. Acad. Religion (pres. 1978). Research in relations between philosophical and theological discourse, history of Christian thought.

GILL, DAVID WALTER, theology educator; b. Omaha, Feb. 2, 1946; s. Walter Leonard and Vivian Erna (Wurz) G.; m. Lucia Lynn Paulson, Sept. 9, 1967; children: Jodie Lynn, Jonathan Christopher. BA in History, U. Calif., Berkeley, 1968; MA in History, San Francisco State U., 1971; PhD in Religion and Social Ethics, U. So. Calif., 1979. Co-editor Radix Mag., Berkeley, 1971-73; founder, project dir. New. Coll. Berkeley, 1977-79, dean and asst. prof. Christian Ethics, 1979-82, dean and assoc. prof., 1982-86, pres., prof., 1986-90. Author: The Word of God in the Ethics of Jacques Ellul, 1984, Peter the Rock, 1986, The Opening of the Christian Mind, 1989. Mem. Am. Acad. Religion, Pacific Coast Theol. Soc., Soc. Christian Ethics, Conf. on Faith and History. Mem. Evang. Covenant Ch. Avocations: tennis, golf, travel, music. Office: Box 5358 Berkeley CA 94705

GILL, JEFFREY HAROLD, priest; b. Muncie, Ind., May 19, 1955; s. Harold Leon and Virginia Lucille (Mock) G.; m. Carolyn Shilling, Aug. 7, 1976. BTh., Apostolic Bible Inst., St. Paul, 1976; BA, Ind. U., 1982; MDiv, Harvard U., 1985. Ordained to priesthood Episcopal Ch., 1989. Missionary assoc. United Pentecostal Ch., Tokyo, 1977-78; pastor's asst. 16th St United Pentecostal Ch., Bloomington, Ind., 1978-80; seminarian Christ Ch., Andover, Mass., 1983-84; asst. to rector Grace Ch., Lawrence, Mass., 1988-90; rector Trinity Ch., Topsfield, Mass., 1990—; chair Manchester, Eng., Linkage Com., 1990—; mem. Commn. on Wider Mission, Diocese of Mass., 1990—; bd. dirs. Greater Lawrence Ecumenical Area Ministry, 1988-90. Editor: proceedings from symposium Aspects of the Oneness Pentecostal Movement, 1984. Lilly Endowment grantee, 1984, Williams fellow Harvard U., 1982-85. Mem. Phillips Brooks Clericus, Phi Beta Kappa. Home: 114 River Rd Topsfield MA 01983

GILL, KENNETH DUANE, minister, librarian; b. Pomona, Calif., Apr. 23, 1946; s. Roy Heflin and Madelyn Ruth (Reed) G.; m. Judith Ann Haggerton, Apr. 25, 1970; children: Matthew Houston, Manola Roberta. BA, Pepperdine Coll., 1969; MA, Fuller Theol. Sem., Pasadena, Calif., 1977; MSLS, U. Ky., 1982; PhD, U. Birmingham, Eng., 1990. Ordained to ministry Ind. Pentecostal Ch., 1977. Assoc. pastor Parkview Christian Ch., Arcadia, Calif., 1976-77, missionary, 1977-84; assoc. pastor Jesus Chapel, El Paso, Tex., 1984-85; theol. libr. Billy Graham Ctr. Libr., Wheaton, Ill., 1985—; coord. CINCOMEX, Mexico City, 1979-81. Book rev. editor The Christian Librarian, 1991—. Mem. Am. Soc. Missiology (pub. 1989—), Assn. Christian Librs. (co-chair Commn. on Internat. Libr. Assistance 1989—), Chgo. Area Theol. Libr. Assn., Internat. Assn. Mission Studies, Soc. for Pentecostal Studies. Office: Wheaton Coll Billy Graham Ctr Libr Wheaton IL 60187 *It has always intrigued me that those who claim that we lack the capability to measure God's impact on the universe often posit a universe which precludes the possibility of his existence.*

GILL, MILTON RANDALL, minister; b. Cheverly, Md., Dec. 8, 1950; s. Milton Thomas and Patricia Georgiana (King) G.; m. Carroll Ann Bennett, Nov. 10, 1979; 1 child, Laura Grace. BS, U. Md., 1973; MDiv, Princeton Sem., 1977. Ordained to ministry Presby. Ch., 1979. Pastor 1st Presbyn. Ch., Theresa, N.Y., 1979-84, Weirsdale (Fla.) Presbyn. Ch., 1984-89; sr. min. 1st Presbyn. Ch., Boynton Beach, Fla., 1989—; sem. del. Gen. Assembly Presbyn. Ch. (U.S.A.), Balt., 1976; pres. Thousand Island Clergy Assn., Alexandria Bay, N.Y., 1982-83. Mem Rotary, Kiwanis (pres. Lake Weir, Fla. club 1986-87). Republican. Office: 1st Presbyn Ch 235 SW 6th Ave Boynton Beach FL 33435 *We are called to give our best to God, because God gave us His best through His Son Jesus Christ.*

GILLAM, MARSHALL ROBERT, religious organization administrator; b. Akron, Ohio, Nov. 21, 1942; s. Marshall Herbert and Hazel Annette (Miller) G.; children: Timothy Sean, Kimberly Meredith. BS, Nyack Missionary Coll., 1964; MEd, U. Ga., 1971, EdD, 1979; MPS, Alliance Theol. Sem., 1987. Cert. tchr. and ednl. adminstr., Ga., Ky. Instr., coach Toccoa Falls (Ga.) High Sch., 1965-71; grad. asst. U. Ga., Athens, 1971-73; instr., coach Toccoa Falls High Sch., 1973-75; headmaster DeKalb Christian Acad., Atlanta, 1975-84, Alliance Christian Acad., Louisville, 1984-86; asst. adminstr. Wheaton Christian High Sch., West Chicago, Ill., 1986-89; dir. adminstrn. Bibles For The World, Wheaton, Ill., 1989—; chmn. vis. com. Assn. Christian Schs. Internat. Accreditation Team, Aurora, Ill., 1988, seminar presenter assn. Tchr. and Adminstr. Conf., Ohio-Ind., Ill., 1987-88; vis. prof. edn. Grace Theol. Sem., Winona Lake, Ind., 1988-89; mem. faculty Internat. Inst. Christian Sch. Tchrs., Winona Lake, 1988-89. Mem. Kappa Delta Pi, Phi Delta kappa. Avocations: music, trombone, photography, woodworking. Office: Bibles For The World Box 805 Wheaton IL 60189 *Understanding who God is gives life purpose; seeking to live in a manner pleasing to God gives life focus; sharing God's love with others gives life enrichment; faithful service to God and His "well done!" gives life fulfillment. Nothing else matters.*

GILLAND, GINA RUTH, minister; b. Salisbury, N.C., May 15, 1955; d. Jim Conrad and Glener Musgrave (Burns) G.; m. Richard K. Osenbach, Aug. 15, 1981 (div. 1985). AB, Duke U., 1977; MDiv, Emory U., 1981. Ordained to ministry United Meth. Ch., 1987. Dir. Christian edn. Embry Hills United Meth. Ch., Atlanta, 1978-81; assoc. pastor Kemble Meml. United Meth. Ch., Woodbury, N.J., 1981-83; edn./nurture specialist S.W. Tex. conf. United Meth. Ch., San Antonio, 1983-91; assoc. pastor Laurel Heights United Meth. Ch., San Antonio, 1991—; aerobics instr. Internat. Fitness Ctr., San Antonio, 1988—; chmn. child abuse prevention task force Tex. Conf. Chs., Austin, 1983-87. Contbr. articles to various publs. Interviewer Duke U. Alumni Assn., San Antonio. Recipient Bishop's recognition for support of boy scouting United Meth. Ch., 1988. Mem. Christian Educators' Fellowship, Nat. Assn. Edn. Young Children. Office: Laurel Heights United Meth Ch Box 12867 San Antonio TX 78212

GILLCHREST, ROBERT RAYMOND, minister; b. Oakland, Calif., Dec. 25, 1946; s. Clarence Raymond and Margaret Marian (Russell) G.; m. Anita Loraine Mobley, Jan. 17, 1970; children: Russell Raymond, Andrew Lee. BA, Bapt. Coll., Charleston, S.C., 1973; MDiv, So. Bapt. Theol. Sem., Louisville, 1976. Ordained to ministry So. Bapt. Conv., 1976. Min. music and youth Woodland Bapt. Ch., Middletown, Ky., 1973-74; pastor Kaunakakai (Hawaii) Bapt. Ch., 1977-79, Olivet Bapt. Ch., Lancaster, Calif., 1979-84, 1st Bapt. Ch., Los Alamos, N.Mex., 1984-87, Kalihi Bapt. Ch., Honolulu, 1984—; chaplain Antelope Valley Med. Ctr., Lancaster, 1979-84, Hawaii Loa Coll. Kaneohe, 1989—; mem. exec. bd. Hawaii Bapt. Conv., Honolulu, 1990—. Bd. dirs. Big Bros. Big Sisters of Molokai, Kaunakaki, 1977-79, Kokua Kalihi Valley Med. Clinic, Honolulu, 1987—. With USN, 1966-70. Mem. Century Club. Office: Kalihi Bapt Ch 1888 Owawa St Honolulu HI 96819

GILLER, SISTER MOLLY, educational consultant; b. Cin., Mar. 2, 1942; d. Rowland S. and Mary E. (Cotter) G. BA, Siena Heights Coll., 1968; MA, U. Cin., 1973; EdD, U. San Francisco, 1989. Adminstr. Holy Angels Sch., Sturgis, Mich., 1968-72; reading supr. Mt. Health Pub. Sch. Dist., Cin., 1972-73; supt. Adrian (Mich.) Dominican Ind. Sch. System, 1973-78; cons. Adrian Dominican Schs., 1978-79; dir. edn. Archdiocese of Portland, Oreg., 1979-90; ednl. cons. Diocese of Boise, Idaho, 1990—; prioress, pastoral counselor Pacific West chpt. Sisters of Adrian Dominican Community. Author: The Process of Conversion to Social Justice as Perceived in the Adrian Dominican Secondary Institutions, 1989. Mem. Nat. Cath. Ednl. Assn., World Future Soc., Nat. Pastoral Planning Conf. (past sec.), Adminstrs Cath. Edn. (chief, exec. com. 1985-88), Nat. Assn. Bd. Edn. (Exec. of Yr. 1985). Avocations: traveling, walking, music, reading, sports. Home: 802 Isbel Ct Santa Cruz CA 95060 Office: Dominican Santa Cruz Rehab Svcs PO Box 2235 Santa Cruz CA 95063

GILLESPIE, ASA ISEKIAR, minister; b. Saldee, Ky., Mar. 21, 1928; s. Floyd Day and Effie Marie (Lawson) G.; m. Claudyne Lyle, Aug. 5, 1955; 1 child, Asa Lyle. Grad. high sch., Ezel, Ky. Ordained to ministry Gospel Assembly, 1966. Pastor Gospel Assembly Ch., East Prairie, Mo., 1967-69, Virginia Beach, Va., 1969-76, Paducah, Ky., 1976-77, Cin., 1977-84, Birmingham, Ala., 1984-91, Indpls., 1991—. Home and Office: Gospel Assembly Ch 5809 Bluff Rd Indianapolis IN 46217

GILLESPIE, JUDITH, religious organization administrator. Exec. World Mission in Ch. and Soc. Episcopal Ch., N.Y.C. Office: Episcopal Ch 815 2nd Ave New York NY 10017*

GILLESPIE, THOMAS WILLIAM, theological seminary administrator, religion educator; b. Los Angeles, July 18, 1928; s. William A. and Estella (Beers) G.; m. Barbara A. Lugenbill, July 31, 1953; children: Robyn C., William T., Dayle E. B.A., George Pepperdine Coll., 1951; B.D., Princeton Theol. Seminary, 1954; Ph.D., Claremont Grad. Sch., 1971; DD (hon.), Grove City Coll., 1984; ThD (hon.), Theol. Acad. Debrecen, Hungary, 1988. Ordained to ministry Presbyterian Ch., 1954. Pastor 1st Presby. Ch., Garden Grove, Calif., 1954-66, Burlingame, Calif., 1966-83; pres., prof. N.T. Princeton Theol. Sem., N.J., 1983—. Served with USMC, 1946-47. Recipient A.A. Hodge prize in systematic theology Princeton Theol. Sem., 1953; Disting. Alumnus award Claremont Grad. Sch., 1984; Disting. Alumnus award Pepperdine U., 1986. Mem. Soc. Bibl. Lit. Republican. Lodge: Rotary Internat. (Burlingame). Home: Springdale 86 Mercer St Princeton NJ 08540 Office: Princeton Theol Sem Office of Pres Box 552 CN 821 Princeton NJ 08542

GILLETTE, GEORGE FREDERICK, minister; b. Vineland, N.J., Mar. 1, 1925; s. Eugene Merle and Eva (Dise) G.; m. Jeanette Lucille Lagerfeldt, Sept. 9, 1950; children: Jean L., William M., Ann E. BA, Maryville Coll, 1948; BD, Princeton Theol. Seminary, 1951. Ordained to ministry Presbyn. Ch., 1951. Pastor First Presbyn. Ch., Ontonagon, Mich., 1954-55, First and Fraser Presbyn. Chs., Ubly, Mich., 1955-59, First Presbyn. Ch., Ithaca, Mich., 1959-66, Bethany Presbyn. Ch., Detroit, 1966-79, First Presbyn. Ch., Warren, Mich., 1979—. Mem. orgn. com. Fish NE Detroit, 1970; bd. dirs. Fish Warren Ctr. Line. Lt. USN, 1952-54. Mem. Warren Area Ministerial Assn. (sec. 1985—), Optomist (v.p. Warren club 1987—). Avocations: music, camping, boating. Office: First United Presbyn Ch 3000 E 12 Mile Rd Warren MI 48092

GILLIAM, JACKSON EARLE, bishop; b. Heppner, Oreg., June 20, 1920; s. Edwin Earle and Mary (Perry) G.; m. Margaret Kathleen Hindley, Aug. 11, 1943; children—Anne Meredith, Margaret Carol, John Howard; m. MarKatheryn Allender Brooks, Oct. 17, 1988. A.B., Whitman Coll., 1942; B.D., Va. Theol. Sem., 1948, S.T.M., 1949, D.D., 1969. Ordained to ministry Episcopal Ch., 1948; rector in Hermiston, Ore., 1949-53; canon St. Mark's Cathedral, Mpls., 1953-55; rector Ch. Incarnation, Great Falls, Mont., 1955-68; bishop Episcopal Diocese Mont., 1968-86; vicar St. Jude's Episcopal Ch., Hawaiian Oceanview Estates, 1987—; chmn. com. on pastoral devel., chmn. council on ministry, mem. program, budget and fin. com. Episc. Ch., 1978, pres. Province VI. Served to 1st lt. AUS, World War II. Decorated companion Order of Cross of Nails, companion Coventry Cathedral, Eng., 1974. Club: Rotary. Home: 390 Shoreline Dr Polson MT 59860 also: Box 6502 Captain Cook HI 96704

GILLIAM, VINCENT CARVER, religion educator, minister; b. Boston, Mar. 24, 1944; s. Wayland Westfield and Belle (Vincent) G.; m. Linda Hassan, June 22, 1970 (div. 1979); children: Halima K., Sumaiya B., Fatimah Z.; m. Nandini Vasudev Katre, Sept. 1, 1991. AB in English Lit., Stanford U., 1968; M of Religion, Claremont Sch. Theology, 1970; MA, PhD in Religious Studies and Humanities, Stanford U., 1990. Ordained to ministry United Ch. of Christ, 1982. Asst. and youth min. Lincoln Meml. Congl. Ch., L.A., 1968-69, adj. assoc. min., 1982-86; exec. dir. Coalition for Haitian Asylum, Oakland, Calif., 1983-84; rsch. asst. Martin Luther King Jr. Papers Project, Stanford, Calif., 1985-87; rsch. fellow U. Calif., Berkeley, 1990—; bd. dirs. United East Oakland Clergy, 1982-84, Am. Friends Svc. Com., San Francisco, 1983—, exec. com., 1990—. Fellow Soc. for Values in Higher Edn.; mem. Am. Acad. Religion, Soc. Bibl. Lit., Am. Hist. Assn., Am. Soc. Ch. History, Medieval Acad. Am., Renaissance Soc. Am. Democrat. Office: U Calif Dept History Berkeley CA 94720

GILLILAND, NEIL EDGAR, minister; b. Tiffin, Ohio, Oct. 25, 1943; s. Robert E. and Margaretta E. (Reuhle) G.; m. Lorene Margraf, Feb. 24, 1963; children: Tammy, Kimberly, Patrick. BS, Ky. Christian Coll., 1981; DD (hon.), Kerala Christian Bible Coll., India, 1988. Ordained to ministry Ch. of Christ, 1979. Min. Ch. of Christ, Lerona, W.Va., 1979-83, Main Street Ch. of Christ, McConnelsville, Ohio, 1983—; forwarding agt. P.V. Alexander Ministries, Kerala State, 1988—; mem. reps. bd. various Christian camps, 1979-89. Mem. McConnelsville Ch. of Christ Preachers Assn. (local pres., sec. 1979-91), Ky. Christian Coll. Alumni Assn. (coun. of 50, 1980-84). Office: Main Street Ch of Christ 9 N 4th St McConnelsville OH 43756

GILLIS, BETH MARIE, lay worker; b. Canby, Minn., Dec. 8, 1945; d. Donald Melvin and Frances Evelyn (Kruckman) Olson; m. Robert Edward Gillis, May 12, 1967 (div. Feb. 1984); children: Robert Edward Jr., Thomas Eugene. CCD tchr. U.S. Navy Chapel, Mayport, Fla., 1970-72, Virginia Beach, Va., 1977-81; CCD tchr. Our Lady of Perpetual Help Ch., Salem, Va., 1983-89, coord. youth min., 1989—. Leader Girl Scouts U.S., Virginia Beach, 1978-81. Office: Our Lady of Perpetual Help 314 Turner Rd Salem VA 24153

GILLMAN, FLORENCE MORGAN, theologian/religious studies educator; b. Utica, NY, Apr. 27, 1947; d. Wesley B. and Ann (Malone) Morgan; m. John L. Gillman, Sept. 23, 1983; 1 child, Anne Marie. BA, Catholic U. Am., Wash., 1974; MA, Catholic U. Am., 1976; PhD, U. Louvain, Belgium, 1982, STD, 1984. Asst. prof. Gonzaga U., Spokane, Wa., 1982-84; adjunct asst. prof. Mundelein Coll., Chgo., 1984-86; assoc. prof. U. San Diego, 1986—. Author: Women Who Knew Paul, 1991, Dying With Christ: Rom. 6:5, 1992; contbr. articles to profl. jours. Mem. Soc. Biblical Literature, Catholic Biblical Assn. Roman Catholic. Avocations: travelling. Office: U San Diego Dept Religious Studies San Diego CA 92110 *It is interesting to stand at life's midpoint and look back. Midst the twists and turns in my path, which I thought were merely coincidental, a pattern now is evident: everything has worked together for good. The pattern of the past becomes reassurance for the future. "On Him we have set our hope that He will deliver us again." (2 Corinthians 1:10).*

GILLMAN, JOHN LEO, hospital chaplain; b. Ind., Dec. 25, 1948; s. Carl and Georgene (Hirt) G.; m. Florence Morgan, Sept. 23, 1983; 1 child, Anne Marie. BA, St. Meinrad Coll., 1971; MA, STB, U. Louvain, Belgium, 1975, PhD, 1980. Chaplain Mercy Hosp., San Diego, 1986—; lectr. San Diego State U., 1988—. Author: Possessions and the Life of Faith, 1991; contbr. articles to profl. jours. Mem. Nat. Assn. Cath. Chaplains, Soc. Bibl. Lit., Cath. Bibl. Assn. Home: 7030 Hilton Pl San Diego CA 92111 Office: Mercy Hosp 4177 5th Ave San Diego CA 92103 *A life dedicated to the loving service of others is a life well lived. From this come joy and inner peace.*

GILLOCK, GERALD SETH, minister; b. Walla Walla, Wash., Apr. 26, 1950; s. Mahlon Seth and Lola Jesse (Bacon) G.; m. Eva-Nell Horton, Sept. 7, 1974; children: Jeremy Chad, Jolynn Eva-Nell. BA, Northwest Coll., 1972. Ordained to ministry Assemblies of God. Asst. pastor 1st Assembly of God, Grants Pass, Oreg., 1973-74; musical ministry Yakima, Wash., 1975-77; assoc. pastor 1st Assembly of God, Bend, Oreg., 1977-82; sr. pastor Goshen (Oreg.) Assembly of God, 1982-87, Life in Christ Ctr., The Dalles, Oreg., 1987—. Mem. The Dalles Ministerial Assn. Republican. Office: Life in Christ Ctr 3095 Cherry Heights Rd The Dalles OR 97058

GILLUM, PERRY EUGENE, college president, minister; b. Allen, Okla., Oct. 16, 1933; s. Perry Jefferson and Ruby Margaret (Borden) G.; m. B. Evelyn Griffin, Dec. 23, 1953; children: J. Scott, Carole Genise Gillum Dotson. B in Ministry (hon.), Tomlinson Coll., 1990. Ordained to ministry Ch. of God of Prophecy, 1964. Evangelist Ch. of God of Prophecy, Calif., 1951-53, youth dir., 1955-59; youth dir. Ch. of God of Prophecy, Tenn., 1959-60; pastor Ch. of God of Prophecy, Ridgedale (Tenn.) and Chattanooga, 1960-64; internat. youth dir. Ch. of God of Prophecy, Cleveland, Tenn., 1964-66, asst. pub., bus. mgr. White Wing Pub. House, 1966-70; Calif. state overseer Ch. of God of Prophecy, 1970-72, dir. pub. rels., 1972-74, dir. Sunday sch., lit. editor, 1974-77, dir. ministerial aid, 1978-80, ea. Can. nat. overseer, 1980-81, dir. pub. rels., lit. editor Sunday sch. div., 1981-87, dir. pub. rels., 1987-89; pres., dir. pub. rels. Tomlinson Coll., 1989—. Author: Church of God Deacon, 1970, Youth Aflame, 1970, These Stones Speak, 1974, Public Relations, 1984. Bd. dirs. YMCA, Cleveland, 1973-77, UNited Way, Cleveland, 1983—. Cpl. U.S. Army, 1952-55, Korea. Mem. Cleveland C. of C. (bd. dirs. 1983—). Republican. Office: Tomlinson Coll Office of the President PO Box 2910 Cleveland TN 37320-2970

GILMORE, CHARLES EDMUND, minister; b. Madison, Wis., Apr. 23, 1948; s. Edward Francis and Adeline (Jaedike) G.; m. Marcia Irene Smith, Aug. 17, 1974; children: Rebekah, Christopher. BA, Dana Coll., Blair, Nebr., 1970; MDiv, Wartburg Sem., Dubuque, Iowa, 1975; ThM, Pacific Luth. Sem., Berkeley, Calif., 1984; PhD, Grad. Theol. Union, Berkeley, Calif., 1991. Ordained to ministry Am. Luth. Ch., 1975. Assoc. pastor Our Savior's Luth. Ch., Lafayette, Calif., 1975-78; pastor Our Redeemer Luth. Ch., South San Francisco, 1978-84, Grace Evang. Luth. Ch., Palo Alto, Calif., 1986-88; assoc. pastor Good Shepherd Luth. Ch., Concord, Calif., 1988—; teaching asst. U. Calif., Berkeley, 1989-90; pres. Luth. Communications Commn., 1979-82; reg. rep. Inter-faith Communications Commn., San Francisco, 1975-78; dis. planning assoc. S. Pacific Dist., Am. Luth. Ch., 1982-88. Grad. Theol. Union Newhall fellow, 1989. Mem. Am. Acad. Religion, Interfaith Ministerium of So. San Francisco (pres. 1982-83). Democrat. Home: 4000 Clayton Rd Concord CA 94521 *The great discovery of learning is that moment when we first realize how much more there is to learn and discover.*

GILMORE, GLORIA LOUISE, minister; b. Big Spring, Tex., Oct. 10, 1954; d. Richard Dale and Elveta Bernice (McCoy) Foltz; m. Homer Bartholomew Gilmore, Aug. 30, 1980; children: Home Barthomew III, Matthew James. Student, Faith Leadership Bible Inst., 1987-88, Hunter Sch. Healing, 1988. Cert. evangelist, outreach coordinator Assembly of God. Youth sponsor Floral Heights Assembly of God, Wichita Falls, Tex., 1981-82, interim youth dir., 1984-85, outreach coord., 1985-90; founder, coord. Teens for Jesus, Wichita Falls, 1985-90; outreach coord. Ch. 4 Sq. Gospel, Wichita Falls, 1989-90; sales supr. Time Record News, Wichita Falls, 1990—; speaker Women's Aglow, 1991; speaker, organizer youth revivals; asst., organizer Billy Graham Revivals, 1988. Democrat. Home and Office: 8014 Carriage Ln Wichita Falls TX 76306-4114 *The most worthwhile and achievable milestones in life are those embedded in humanity. Tireless giving, forgiving and embracing achieve honors and rewards in the halls of eternity. The one opportunity that presents itself to everyone is that of touching someone with the love of Christ.*

GILMORE, MARSHALL, bishop. Bishop of 4th dist. Christian Meth. Episcopal Ch., Shreveport, La. Office: Christian Meth Episcopla Ch 109 Holcomb Dr Shreveport LA 71103*

GILPIN, W. CLARK, academic administrator. Pres. Div. Sch. U. Chgo. Office: U Chgo Disciples Divinity House 1156 E 57th St Chicago IL 60637*

GILROY, MARK KEVIN, religious organization editor, writer, minister; b. Dayton, Ohio, Aug. 14, 1958; s. J. Merrick Jr. and Margarete N. (Combs) G.; m. Jennifer Clark, June 7, 1980 (div. May 6, 1991); children: Lindsey Cecile, Merrick Austen. BA, Olivet Nazarene U., 1980; MDiv, Nazarene Theol. Sem., 1989; postgrad., U. Kans., 1990—. Ordained to ministry Ch. of the Nazarene, 1988. Youth min. Chgo. 1st Ch. of the Nazarene, Lemont, Ill., 1980-82; curriculum editor youth dept. Ch. of the Nazarene, Kansas City, Mo., 1984-86, teen program coord., 1986-89, sr. editor, 1989-91; pres., founder Life Resources, Inc., Kansas City, 1991—; project cons. Josh McDowell Ministries, San Bernadino, Calif., 1986—, Group Pub., Inc., Loveland, Colo., 1990—. Author: Spending Time With God, 1987; editor: Sharing My Faith, 1990; script writer Teaching Insights-Youth Leaders video, 1990 (Internat. TV award of merit 1990). Mem. com. Stop Violence Coalition, Kansas City, 1982-83, Crop Walk for Hunger, Kansas City, 1983-84. Mem. Religious Conv. Mgmt. Assn., Christian Camping Internat. (exec.), Evang. Press Assn. Office: Ch of the Nazarene 6401 The Paseo Kansas City MO 64131 *We are called by God to be different in a way that makes a real difference in our world.*

GILSTRAP, ROBERT EDWARD, JR. (BOBBY GILSTRAP), minister; b. Ft. Worth, Tex., Mar. 7, 1961; s. Robert Edward Sr. and Hazel (Ditsworth) G.; m. Brenda Wallace, Aug. 13, 1988. AA, Brenton-Parker Coll., 1983; BA, Okla. Bapt. U., 1985; postgrad., Southwestern Bapt. Theol. Sem. Ordained to ministry So. Bapt. Conv., 1988. Min. youth First So. Bapt. Ch., Guthrie, Okla., 1984-85; missions evangelist Gulf Coast Bapt. Assn., Angleton, Tex., 1986; assoc. pastor Fairview Bapt. Ch., Granbury, Tex., 1988-89; pastor Posey Bapt. Ch., Sulphur Springs, Tex., 1989-90, Faith So. Bapt. Ch., Ardmore, Okla., 1991—; funeral min. to 16 funeral homes Ft. Worth, 1991—; chaplain Campers on Mission, Dallas, 1989-91; preacher, worship leader Courtyards Retirement Ctr., Ft. Worth, 1988. Contbr. articles to various newspapers and mags.

GINGERICH, DENNIS DANIEL, minister; b. Portland, Oreg., Dec. 10, 1953; s. Thurlowe Frederick and Joyce Eleanor (Kropf) G.; m. Linda Estell Augsburger, Dec. 27, 1974; children: Chad Brian, Cheritt Landon, Charissa Dawn. BA, Ea. Mennonite Coll., 1976; MDiv, Ea. Mennonite Sem., 1979. Pastor Elmira (N.Y.) Mennonite Fellowship, 1979-86; pastor, ch. planter Cape Christian Fellowship, Cape Coral, Fla., 1986—; chmn. pastoral continuing edn. com. S.E. Mennonite Conf., Sarasota, Fla., 1986—; treas. Cape Coral Ministerial Fellowship, 1987-90, Lee County Evang. Assn., Ft. Myers, Fla., 1989—; mem. pastoral adv. com. Cape Coral Hosp., 1988-90. Bd. dirs. Neighborhood Justice Project, Elmira, 1979-86; coach Cape Coral Youth Soccer Assn., 1986—; mem. parent's adv. com. Caloosa Elem. Sch., Cape Coral, 1988-90, Caloosa Mid. Sch., 1991—; mem. religious task force Drug-Free Lee County Coalition, Ft. Myers, 1990—. Republican. Home: 502 SE 17th Ave Cape Coral FL 33990 Office: Cape Christian Fellowship PO Box 150777 Cape Coral FL 33915-0777

GINGRAS, FRANK EDWIN, chaplain, deacon, physician; b. Saratoga, N.Y., Sept. 28, 1919; s. Frank Patrick and Ruth Charlotte (Johnson) G.; m. Frances Marian jugenheimer, Feb. 18, 1947; children: Mary Jo, Gerald J., Ruth Ann, Frank, John, Richard, Esther, Frances. Student, Siena Coll., 1938-39, Ithaca Coll., 1939-40; D of Chiropractic, Palmer U., 1947; Ph.C. (hon.), Atlantic States U., 1966; BS, Clayton U., 1975; M (hon.), Emmerson Coll., Can., 1979. Ordained deacon Roman Cath. Ch., 1982. Extraordinary min. Epiphany Ch., Port Orange, Fla., 1974-77; extraordinary min. Our Lady of Hope, Port Orange, 1978-82, deacon, 1982—; chaplain Country Manor Rest Home, Port Orange, 1982—, CAP, 1990—; lectr., cons. in field. Author: Doctors and Deacons, 1990; editor: Gingras Clinic, 1975. Chmn. local chpt., mem. local coun. Boy Scouts Am., Glen Falls, N.Y. Sgt. U.S. Army Air Corps, 1942-45, CBI. Grantee Anglo-Am. Inst. Drugless Therapy, 1950, Chinese-Am. Inst., 1979. Mem. Am. Chiropractic Assn., Fla. Chiropractic Assn., Volusia County Chiropractic Assn. (pres. 1972, Dr. of Yr. 1973), Exchange Club (sec.), KC (chaplain 1990—), VFW (surgeon Port Orange chpt. 1978—), Am. Legion (comdr. Glen Falls post). Republican. Home: 357 Sagewood Dr Port Orange FL 32127 Office: Gingras Clinic 5085 S Ridgewood Ave Port Orange FL 32127

GINN, A(LFRED) STEPHEN, pastor; b. Greene County, N.C., Dec. 28, 1932; s. J. Alfred and Ruby (Grant) G.; m. Sharon Hazelrigg, Dec. 28, 1958; children: William Scott, Shepley James. D Ministry, Lexington Theol. Sem., 1988; BS, Barton Coll., Wilson, N.C., 1959; BD, Lexington Theol. Sem., 1962, ThM, 1974. Ordained to ministry Christian Ch. (Disciples of Christ), 1962. Pastor Div. Overseas Ministry Christian Ch., Paraguay, 1964-70, Boulevard Christian Ch., Miami, Fla., 1970-76, Cen. Christian Ch., Jacksonville, Fla., 1976—; com. mem. Week of Compassion, Christian Ch. (Disciples of Christ), Indpls., 1985—; mem. Regional Commn. on Ministry, Orlando, Fla., 1987—; mem. InterFaith Coun. Jacksonville, 1990—. Mem. NE Fla. Community Action Agy., Jacksonville, 1979-84. With USN, 1951-55, Korea. Mem. Soc. Bibl. Lit. Home: 1237 Ribault River Dr Jacksonville FL 32208 Office: Cen Christian Ch 25 W 9th St Jacksonville FL 32206

GINN, JEFFERY BYRON, minister; b. Forrest City, Ark., Aug. 9, 1961; s. Jesse Donald and Margaret Louise (Wheelington) G.; m. Nell Allein Nichols, June 21, 1986; 1 child, Anna Elise. AA, So. Bapt. Coll., 1981; BA magna cum laude, Blue Mountain Coll., 1983; MDiv summa cum laude, Mid-Am. Bapt. Theol. Sem., 1986, ThD, 1990. Ordained to ministry So. Bapt. Conv., 1988. Youth intern First Bapt. Ch., West Memphis, Ark., 1980, youth pastor, 1986-89; missionary Bapt. Student Union, Little Rock, Ark., 1981; youth pastor First Bapt. Ch., Ripley, Miss., 1981-83; pastor Pleasant Hill Bapt. Ch., Ashland, Miss., 1989—; instr. Blue Mountain Coll., 1991. Mem. Evang. Theol. Soc.

GINSBERG, HERSH MEIER, rabbi, religious organization executive; b. Vienna, Austria, July 8, 1928; s. Lazar Yonah Ginsberg and Perl Roth; m. Fradel Levy; children: Lazar Yonah, Meshulim, Chana. Dir. Union Orthodox Rabbis of U.S. and Can.; rabbinical ct. judge; dean Rabbi Jacob-Joseph Sch., N.Y.C., 1955-73. Founder Kolel Ohel Elemelech Rabbinical Coll., Jerusalem. Home: 1235 47th St Brooklyn NY 11219 Office: Union Orthodox Rabbis US & Can 235 E Broadway New York NY 10002

GINSBURG-WOLF, FRANCES RUTH, religious organization administrator; b. Troy, N.Y., Sept. 22, 1953; d. Marvin and Judith (Koscziensku) Ginsburg; m. Edwin William Wolf, Nov. 3, 1979; children: Jessica, Michael, Samuel. BA, SUNY, Albany, 1975; MA, Brandeis U., 1977. Assoc. dir. women's div. United Jewish Appeal Nat., N.Y.C., 1979-82; dir. project renewal United Jewish Appeal Fedn., N.Y.C., 1982-86, assoc. dir. major gifts div., 1986-89, exec. dir. community campaigns, 1989—; v.p. Am. Com. for the Weizmann Inst. Sci. Mem. Horstein Profl. Adv. Com. Mem. Assn. Jewish Community Orgn. Pers., Hadassah (life). Office: United Jewish Appeal Fedn 130 E 59th St New York NY 10022

GINTHER, VANCE CURTIS, minister; b. Roseburg, Oreg., Nov. 20, 1946; s. Russell Warren and Vera Marie (Waggoner) G.; m. Terralee Halane Page, Aug. 3, 1968; children: Jennifer Stacie, Bryce Randall. BTh., Northwest Christian Coll., 1970; MDiv, Emmanuel Sch. Religion, 1982. Ordained to ministry Christian Ch. (Disciples of Christ), 1969. Pastor Eastside Christian Ch., Albany, Oreg., 1968-71, Heaton Christian Ch., Elk Park, N.C., 1971-74, Taylor's Valley Ch., Damascus, Va., 1980-82, 1st Christian Ch., St. Helens, Oreg., 1982—; assoc. minister Mountainview Christian Ch., Gresham, Oreg., 1975-78; pres. Oreg. Christian Convention, Turner, 1986-87; registrar regional assembly Christian Ch. (Disciples of Christ) in Oreg., Portland, 1989-90. Founder, pres. St. Helens Teen Ctr., 1985. Mem. Toastmasters Internat. (pres. local chpt. 1988-89). Avocations: golf, hiking, reading.

GIORDANO, MICHELE CARDINAL, cardinal; b. Tursi-Lagonegro, Italy, Sept. 26, 1930. Ordained priest Roman Cath. Ch., 1953. Elected to titular Ch. of Lari Castello, 1971; consecrated bishop, 1972; prefect Matera e Irsina, 1974; transferred to Naples, Italy, 1987; created cardinal, 1988. Office: Bishop's Conf, Circonvallozione Aurelia 50, 00165 Rome Italy also: Largo Donnaregina 22, I-80138 Naples Italy

GIPSON, JAMES WILLIAM, minister, educator; b. McAlester, Okla., May 12, 1945; s. Jack Martin and Jenet Elizabeth (Turnbull) G.; m. Brenda Joyce Conner; children: Jeffrey James, Jana Joy, Jonathan Jay. BA, Tenn. Temple U., 1967; MDiv, New Orleans Bapt. Theol. Sem., 1985; ThD, North Fla. Bapt. Theol. Sem., 1990. Tchr., coach Temple Terr., Tampa, Fla., 1967-68, Trinity Bapt., Jacksonville, Fla., 1968-70; assoc. pastor Tabernacle Bapt., Orlando, Fla., 1970-73; gen. agt. Sun Life of Can., Jacksonville, 1973-76; youth dir. Univ. Bapt., Jacksonville, 1976-80; minister of music Bethany Bapt., Melbourne, Fla., 1980-82; pastor First Bapt. Ch., Venice, La., 1982-86, Plainview Bapt., Pensacola, Fla., 1986-87, Woodstock Pk. Bapt. Ch., Jacksonville, 1987—; prof. Jacksonville U., 1987-90, North Fla. Bapt. Theol. Sem., 1987-90. Author: Dearest Children, 1988. Mem. Jacksonville Minister's Conf. (pres. 1987-90), Plaqumenes Bapt. Assn. (moderator 1984-85). Republican. Baptist. Avocations: golf, snow skiing, swimming, fishing, scuba diving. Home: 3056 Commonwealth Ave Jacksonville FL 32205 Office: Woodstock Pk Bapt Ch 924 St Clair St Jacksonville FL 32205

GIRARDOT, NORMAN JOHN, religion educator; b. Balt., Apr. 19, 1943; s. Norman F. and Ruth M. (O'Leary) G.; m. Kay S. Singleton, Nov. 12, 1969; children: David, Jacob, Christopher. BS cum laude, Coll. of Holy Cross, 1965; MA, U. Chgo., 1968, PhD, 1974. Prof. Lehigh U., Bethlehem, Pa., 1980—. Fellow Woodrow Wilson Found., 1967-68, NEH, 1982-83. Mem. Am. Acad. Religion (mem. nominations comm. 1988—), Am. Soc. for Study of Religion, Soc. for Study of Chinese Religion, Folk Art Soc. Am., Assn. Asian Studies, Phi Beta Kappa. Office: Lehigh U Religion Dept Maginnes Hall Bethlehem PA 18015

GIRÓN, JUAN RENÉ (JUAN RENÉ GIRÓN T.), minister. Pastor Presbyn. Ch., Guatemala City, Guatemala. Office: Presbyn Ch, Apdo 655, 6a Avda 'A' 4-68, Zona 1, Guatemala City Guatemala*

GIRTZ, JOSEPH MICHAEL, minister; b. Fresno, Calif., Dec. 2, 1896; s. Fredrick Wilhelm and Margrethe S. (Christensen) G.; m. Mabel Hansen, Nov. 25, (dec. July 1962); children: Lois, Joseph, Albert; m. Florence Mildred Hallsten, May 30, 1964. Diploma, Dana Coll.; postgrad., Luther Sem.; DDiv, Wartburg Sem., 1959. Ordained to ministry Luth. Ch., 1924. Pastor Selma, Calif.; tchr., then supt. Kaerabani Boys' Sch., India, 1925; supt. Santal Colony, Assam; pastor Luck and North Luck, Wis., Trinity Luth. Ch., Albert Lea, Minn., Olivet Luth. Ch., L.A., Resurrection Luth. Ch., Redondo Beach, Calif., 1966—; sec., v.p. Minn. dist. United Evang. Luth. Ch., 1950's; mem. Commn. Young Chs. and Orphaned Missions; dir. Luth. World Action; v.p., mem. joint union com., bd. appeals and adjudication Am. Luth. Ch. Am. Bd. dirs. home for aged Luth. Ch. Am.; mem. bd. regents, bd. fgn. missions, bd. pensions Dala Coll.; bd. regents Calif. Luth. Coll. Home: 512 Paseo de las Estrellas Redondo Beach CA 70299

GISEL, PIERRE, theologian, educator; b. Geneva, Apr. 28, 1947; s. Charles and Nelly (Goy) G.; m. Monique Bugnion, Nov. 15, 1969 (div. 1985); children: Laurent, Irene; m. Catherine Siegenthaler, 1985; 1 child, Mathurin. Student, U. Geneva, 1966-70, 73-75, U. Marburg, U. Tubingen, 1972-73; Lic. in Theology, U. Geneva, 1970, D of Theology, 1975. Ordained to ministry Ch. of Geneva, 1977. Asst. lectr. U. Geneva, 1973-75; dir. Labor et Fides S.A., Geneva, 1976—; prof. U. Lausanne, 1976—, dean faculty, 1984-86, senate, 1990—; vis. prof. U. Fribourg, Switzerland, U. Geneva, U. Neuchatel, others. Author: Verite et Histoire, 1977, 2d edit., 1983, La Creation, 1980, 2d edit., 1987, Croyance Incarnée, 1986, Le Christ de Calvin, 1990, L'Excès du Croire, 1990; editor: Analogie et Dialectique, 1982, Karl Barth: Genese et Réception de sa Théologie, 1987, Pratique et Theologie, 1989, L'Islam: Une Religion, 1989, Albrecht Ritsch: la théologie en modernité, 1991. Home: Martinet 16, CH-1007 Lausanne Switzerland Office: U Lausanne Dept Theology, CH-1015 Lausanne Switzerland

GISH, RODNEY WAYNE, minister; b. Stockton, Kans., Dec. 7, 1946; s. Wayne Winfred Gish and Naomi Nadine (Stewart) Gish-Jones; m. Diana Gween Luckey; children: Travis K., Trina K. Student, Evang. Coll., Springfield, Mo., 1964-65; BA in History, Ft. Hays (Kans.) State U., 1969; MA in Bibl. Lit., Assemblies of God Theol. Sem., Springfield, 1988. Ordained to ministry Assemblies of God, 1974. Pastor youth 1st Assembly of God, Great Bend, Kans., 1972, Eastside Assembly of God, Tucson, 1972-74; pastor 1st Assembly of God, Sierra Vista, Ariz., 1974-76, 84—, Rock Springs, Wyo., 1979-84; dir. Christian edn. 1st Assembly of God, Garden City, Kans., 1976-79; presbyter Wyo. Assemblies of God, Rock Springs, 1982-84; asst. presbyter Ariz. Assemblies of God., Sierra Vista, 1985-90. Office: 1st Assembly of God 840 Lenzner PO Box 562 Sierra Vista AZ 85636

GITIN, SEYMOUR, rabbi; b. Buffalo, Jan. 12, 1936; s. Harry and Ida (Sterman) G.; m. Cheryl Janice Chafetz, Aug. 19, 1975; children: Michal, Adam, Talya. BA, U. Buffalo, 1956; BAHL, Hebrew Union Coll., Cin., 1959, MAHL, 1962, PhD, 1980, DD, 1988. Ordained rabbi, 1962. Rabbi Temple Beth Hillel, North Hollywood, Calif., 1964-67; rabbi, dir. edn. Temple Israel, Long Beach, Calif., 1967-68; dir. admissions Hebrew Union Coll., Cin., 1968-70; dir. and prof. archaeology W.F. Albright Inst. of Archaeol. Rsch., Am. Sch. Oriental Rs, Jerusalem, 1980—; co-dir. Tel Miqne-Ekron Excavations and Pubs. Project, 1981—; dir. Tel Dor Excavations in assn. with E. Stern, 1980; field archaeologist, Tell Gezer Excavations, 1972, 73, Jebel Qa'aqir Excavations, 1971; adj. assoc. prof. Brandeis U., 1981-82; lectr. Hebrew Union Coll., Jerusalem, 1977-78; coord. devel. Albright Artifact Collections, 1980-87; curator Nelson Glueck Study Collection, Hebrew Union Coll.-Jewish Inst. Religion, 1977-79. Author: Gezer III: A Ceramic Typology of the Late Iron II, Persian and Hellenistic Periods, 1990; contbr. to: Gezer IV: The 1969-71 Seasons in Field VI, The Acropolis, Vol. IV of the Ann. of the Nelson Glueck Sch. of Bibl. Archaeology, 1986; editor and contbr.: Recent Excavations in Israel: Studies in Iron Age Archaeology, 1989, Annual of the American Schools of Oriental Research, Vol. 49, 1989, others; contbr. numerous articles to profl. jours. Capt. USAF, 1962-64. Annenberg Rsch. Inst. fellow, 1991—. Mem. Am. Sch. Oriental Rsch. (assoc. editor 1987—), Israel Exploration Soc. (bd. dirs. 1985—), Berman Inst. Bibl. Archaeology (adv. bd. 1990—). Home and Office: WF Albright Inst, 26 Salah Ed-Din St Box 19096, 91190 Jerusalem Israel

GITTELSOHN, ROLAND BERTRAM, rabbi, writer; b. Cleve., May 13, 1910; s. Reuben and Anna (Manheim) G.; m. Ruth Freyer, Sept. 25, 1932 (dec.); children: David, Judith Fales; m. Hulda Tishler, Aug. 19, 1979. BA, Western Res. U., 1931; BH, Hebrew Union Coll., Cin., 1934, DD, 1961; ScD, Lowell (Mass.) Tech. Inst., 1961. Ordained Rabbi, 1936. Rabbi Cen. Synagogue, Nassau County, N.Y., 1936-53; Rabbi Temple Israel, Boston, 1953-77, rabbi emeritus, 1977—; Pres. Mass. Bd. Rabbis, 1958-60, Jewish Community Coun. Met. Boston, 1961-63; mem. exec. bd. Cen. Conf. Am. Rabbis, 1949-51, chmn. placement com., 1949-52, chmn. justice and peace, 1950-54, pres., 1969-71; trustee, chmn. commn. Jewish Edn. Union Am. Hebrew Congrs., 1959-68, vice chmn. 1973-75. Author: Modern Jewish Problems, 1943; Little Lower Than the Angels, 1954; Man's Best Hope, 1961; Consecrated Unto Me: A Jewish View of Love and Marriage, 1965; My Beloved Is Mine, 1969; Wings of the Morning, 1969; The Meaning of Judaism, 1970; Love, Sex and Marriage--A Jewish View, 1976; The Modern Meaning of Judaism, 1978; The Extra Dimension, 1983; Here Am I--Harnessed to Hope, 1988; How Do I Decide?, 1989; Love in Your Life, 1991. Mem. Truman Com. Civil Rights, 1947, Gov. Mass. Commn. to Survey Cts., 1955, Mass. Comn. Abolition Death Penalty,, 1957-58, Gov. Mass. Com. Migratory Labor, 1960-62, Gov. Mass. Com. to Survey Ops. in Prison, 1961-62. Mem. Assn. Reform Zionists (founding pres. 1977—). Home: Jamaicaway Tower Boston MA 02130 Office: Temple Israel Boston MA 02215

GITTELSON, ABRAHAM JACOB, educator, administrator; b. N.Y.C., Oct. 22, 1928; s. William and Libby Gittelson; m. Shirley Josephine Bakst; children: Ora, Moshe, Reva. BBS, CCNY, 1949; B in Religious Edn., Yeshiva U., 1950; MA in Hebrew Edn., CUNY Hunter Coll., 1953; EdD, U. Miami, Fla., 1985. Nat. edn. dir. B'nei Akiva, N.Y.C., 1952-54; tchr. Jewish Ctr. of University Heights, Bronx and N.Y.C., 1952-54, N.Y.C. Pub. Schs., 1950-54; ednl. dir. Temple Menorah, Miami Beach, Fla., 1954-56, Camp Ramah in Can., Toronto, 1975-76, 68-72, Beth Torah Congregation, North Miami Beach, Fla., 1958-72; assoc. exec. v.p. Cen. Agy. for Jewish Edn., Miami, 1972—; cons. Jewish edn. Cen. Agy. for Jewish Edn., Miami, 1972—. Author: (monograph) (with others) Integration in the Jewish Day School, 1970, 10 Lesson Plans for Teaching About Jerusalem, 1973. Mem. Assn. for Jewish Studies (assoc.), Jewish Educators Assembly (pres. Fla. chpt. 1970-80), Coun. for Jewish Edn. (bd. dirs. 1982—), Assn. for Supervision and Curriculum Devel., Phi Delta Kappa. Home: 970 NE 172d St North Miami Beach FL 33162

GITTLEN, BARRY M., religion educator; b. Norfolk, Va., May 21, 1943; s. Julius Leon and Ruth (Oltman) G.; m. Elaine Gaspas, June 23, 1968; 1 child, Lisa S. PhD, U. Pa., 1977. Prof. Biblical and archaeol. studies Balt. Hebrew U., 1972—; mem. edn. com. Solomon Schechter Day Sch., Balt., 1988—; mem. ritual com. Congregation Chizuk Amuno, Balt., 1987-89. Author: Tel Miqne/Ekron III SE 1984, 1985; contbr. articles to profl. publs., chpt. to book. Bd. dirs., trustee Colonial Village Neighborhood Improvement Assn., Balt., 1983—. Rsch. grantee Cohen Fund, 1984-91, NEH, 1989. Mem. Am. Schs. Oriental Rsch. (program chmn. 1988—), Israel Exploration Soc., Am. Oriental Soc., Assn. for Jewish Studies, Archaeol. Inst. Am., World Union of Jewish Studies. Office: Balt Hebrew U 5800 Park Heights Ave Baltimore MD 21215

GIUDICI, FRANCO WILLIAM, clergyman; b. San Rafael, Calif., Aug. 21, 1928; s. Enrico Luigi and Francesca Rachele (Brovelli) G.; m. Martha Verena James, Oct. 14 1968. BS in Commerce, U. Santa Clara, 1950; postgrad., Unity Sch. Ministerial Studies, 1968. Ordained to ministry Unity Sch. Christianity, 1968. Minister Unity Ch. of Christianity, Valley Stream, N.Y., 1968-69, Unity Ctr. of Pitts., 1969-73; faculty Sch. for Ministerial and Religious Studies, Unity Village, Mo., 1974-78; minister Unity Village Chapel, 1978-87; faculty, chmn. Bibl. studies Unity Sch. of Christianity, Unity Village, 1987—. Contbr. articles to profl. jours.; author Unity cassette program. With U.S. Army, 1950-52. Mem. Soc. Bibl. Lit., Am. Acad. Religion. Office: Unity Sch of Christianity Unity Village MO 64065

GIUNTA, RAYMOND, minister, administrator; b. Trenton, N.J., Nov. 21, 1960; s. Francis S. and Rosalie Giunta; m. Cathy Giunta, Dec. 26, 1983; children: Kimberlee, Kyle. BA, Calif. State U., Sacramento, 1981, Berean Coll., Springfield, Mo., 1985. Ordained to ministry Assemblies of God, 1988. Sr. pastor Cornerstone Christian Assembly, Del Paso Heights, Calif., 1987-89; sr. assoc. administrn. Capital Christian Ctr., Sacramento, 1989—. Home: 3031 Rosemont Dr Sacramento CA 95826 Office: Capital Christian Ctr 9470 Micron Ave Sacramento CA 95827-2698

GJERE, LINDA JANSSEN, communications specialist, writer; b. Mpls., July 22, 1950; d. Murel Avery and Geraldine Ella (Kohlscheen) Janssen; m. Robert Allen Gjere, Aug. 18, 1974; children: Arne, Thomas. BS, Kearney (Nebr.) State U., 1972. Freelance writer, 1964—; editor women's page Holdrege (Nebr.) Daily Citizen, 1974; tchr. Sidney (Nebr.) High Sch., 1972-74; news editor Sheridan (Wyo.) Press, 1976-84; corr. Casper (Wyo.) Star-Tribune, 1984-86; substitute tchr. Omaha Schs., 1986-89; communications dir. Nebr. Synod Evang. Luth. Ch. Am., Omaha, 1989—; instr. Sheridan Coll., 1975-86; grant writer Wyo. Arts Alliance, Women's Ctr., Sheridan, 1983-87. Mem., actress, dir. Civic Theatre Guild, Sheridan, 1977-86; bd. coord. Women's Ctr. Recipient spl. award Civic Theatre Guild, 1982, vol. award Sheriday Libr., 1982-84, Sheridan High Sch., 1981, 83. Mem. AAUW (v.p. Sheridan 1980, 3d v.p. Omaha 1987), Sigma Delta Chi. Lutheran. Avocations: theater work, hiking, walking, mountain backpacking, camping. Home: 2106 S 164th Ave Omaha NE 68130 Office: Evang Luth Ch in Am Nebr Synod 124 S 24th St Omaha NE 68102

GJERNESS, OMAR NORMAN, minister, religion educator; b. Mandal, Norway, Mar. 5, 1922; came to U.S., 1922; s. Ove Oleson and Amalie (Aaneson) G.; m. Joan Elsie Larsen, Dec. 17, 1949; children: David, Melinda, Craig, Peter. Student, Augsburg Coll., 1943-44; BA, Wagner Coll., 1950; MA, Pasadena Coll., 1970; MDiv, Luth. Brethren Sem., 1980. Ordained to ministry Ch. of Luth. Brethren Am., 1949. Pastor Luth. Brethren Ch., Malta, Mont., 1945-46, N.Y.C., 1946-47; pastor 59th St. Luth. Ch., Bklyn., 1947-54, Yellowstone Luth. Brethren Ch., Billings, Mont., 1954-57, Immanuel Luth. Ch., Pasadena, Calif., 1957-62; prof. systematic theology Luth. Brethren Sem., Fergus Falls, Minn., 1962—, pres., 1984-90; pres. Luth. Brethren Schs, Fergus Falls, 1964—; sec. Ch. Luth. Brethren, Fergus Falls, 1958-69, v.p., 1970—, dist. pres. Cen. Dist., 1970—. Author: Baptism and Related Doctrine, 1950, Knowing Good from Evil, 1980, Answers for Today, 1988. Republican. Home: Rte 1 Box 240 Fergus Falls MN 56537 Office: Luth Brethren Schs W Vernon Ave Fergus Falls MN 56537 *If men heeded the Scriptures, the world would have avoided many of the major problems we wrestle with today. I have therefore dedicated my life to the study and teaching of the Bible.*

GLASER, CHRISTOPHER ROY, religious writer; b. Van Nuys, Calif., Oct. 3, 1950; s. Arthur Wayne and Florence Mildred (Cronister) G.; life ptnr. George Franklin Lynch. BA, Calif. State U., Northridge, 1973; MDiv, Yale Div. Sch., 1977. Various youth and campus ministries Calif., Conn.,

Pa., 1971-76; dir. Lazarus Project West Hollywood Presbyn. Ch., L.A., 1977-87; author, lectr., retreat and workshop leader West Hollywood, Calif., 1987—; mem. Presbyn. Task Force to Study Homosexuality, 1976-78; founder Gay and Lesbian Peer Counseling Svc., U. Pa., 1976; nat. coord., treas. Presbyn. for Lesbian and Gay Concerns, 1977-79, newsletter editor, 1977-80; mem. exec. bd. Presbyn. Health, Edn. and Welfare Assn., 1987-89; chair. Spiritual Adv. Com. AIDS Project, L.A., 1990-92. Author: Uncommon Calling, 1988, Come Home!, 1990, Coming Out to God, 1991; contbr. articles to religious publs. Recipient Lazarus award, Lazarus Bd. Govs., 1988, Phyllis P. Hart award, Evangs. Together, Inc., 1990. Democrat. Home and Office: 7614 Hampton Ave # 3 West Hollywood CA 90046

GLASER, JOSEPH BERNARD, association executive; b. Boston, May 1, 1925; s. Louis James and Dena Sophie (Harris) G.; m. Agathe Maier, Sept. 23, 1951; children: Simeon, Meyer, Sara, John. A.B., UCLA, 1948; J.D., U. San Francisco, 1951; B.H.L., Hebrew Union Coll., 1954, M.H.L., 1956, D.Div., 1980; postgrad. (Merrill Trust grantee), Law Faculty Hebrew U., Jerusalem, 1969-70. Rabbi, 1956; rabbi Temple Beth Torah, Ventura, Calif., 1956-59; regional dir. Union Am. Hebrew Congregations, San Francisco, 1959-71; exec. v.p. Central Conf. Am. Rabbis, N.Y.C., 1971—; registrar Hebrew Union Coll., Los Angeles, 1956-59, instr. homiletics, 1956-59; instr. Bible, Hebrew Union Coll., Cin., 1954-56; vice chmn. San Francisco Conf. Religion and Peace, 1964-71, San Francisco Conf. Religion and Race, 1963-68; chmn. Clergy Com. Farm Labor Negotiation, 1967-68; chmn. bd. Religion in Am. Life, 1977-82, 87—, chmn. religious adv. coun.; v.p. Am. Friends of Oxford Centre for Postgrad. Hebrew Studies.; trustee Howard Thurman Ednl. Trust; mem., bd. dirs. Am. Jewish World Svc.; mem. exec. com. Internat. Coordinating Com. on Religion and the Earth. With inf. AUS, 1943-46. Decorated Purple heart with oak leaf cluster. Mem. Central Conf. Am. Rabbis, Synagogue Coun. Am. (exec. com.), Union Am. Hebrew Congregations (exec. com., trustee), Conf. of Presidents of Major Jewish Orgns., Jewish Law Assn. Office: 192 Lexington Ave New York NY 10016 *Religious leadership, ultimately, is example. The most eloquent preacher, the most engaging teacher, the most attentive pastor, is a functionary. One leads people to change, and to God, by example.*

GLASER, ROBERT HARVEY, SR., pastor; b. Phila., May 4, 1935; s. Harvey A. and Janet (McKechnie) G.; m. Joan Williams, Nov. 16, 1957 (div. July 1979); children: Linda Hartwell, Diane Lim Myra Ward, Linda Carrano, Robert Sr., Teresa Garcia, David Glaser; m. Virginia Sue Fischer, May 27, 1990. AB, Grove City (Pa.) Coll., 1957; MDiv, Princeton (N.J.) Theol. Sem., 1960. Pastor Smithfield Presbyn. Ch., Amenia, N.Y., 1960-64; organizing pastor Westminster Presbyn. Ch., Warner Robins, Ga., 1964-69; pastor First Presbyn. Ch., Forest Hills, N.Y., 1967-81; mem. ch. redevelopment Prospect Heights Presbyn. Ch., Bklyn., 1981-86; pastor Colcord (W.Va.) and Clear Creek Presbyn. Chs., 1987-89; interim pastor First Presbyn. Ch., Nitro, W.Va., 1989; pastor First Presbyn. Ch., Hinton, W.Va., 1989—; moderator Presbytery of N.Y.C., 1976-77; cmn. Maj. Mission Fund, N.Y.C., 1979-81; bd. sec. Edwin Gould Svcs. for Children, N.Y.C., 1987-89. Mem. Second Chance panel D.A.'s Office, Queens, 1977-81. Named Eagle Scout Boy Scouts Am., 1950. Mem. Lions (treas. 1991—), Omicron Delta Kappa, Pi Gamma Mu. Home: 1519 Fayette St Hinton WV 25951-2018 Office: First Presbyn Ch Third Ave & Ballengee St Hinton WV 25951

GLASS, JONATHAN THADDEUS, priest; b. Providence, July 22, 1957; s. John Raymond and Evangeline (Stevens) G. AB, Brown U., 1978; MDiv, Yale U., 1982; postgrad., Duke U., 1982-85. Ordained to ministry Episcopal Ch. as priest, 1982. Master St. Mark's Sch., Southborough, Mass., 1978-79; asst. to dean Cathedral of St. John, Providence, 1982; asst. to rector St. Philip's Ch., Durham, N.C., 1982-85; rector Emmanuel Ch., Powhatan, Va., 1985-89, Christ Ch., Amelia, Va., 1985-89, St. James' Ch., Cartersville, Va., 1985-89, St. Mark's Ch., Upland, Calif., 1989—; mem.. Va. Coun. Chs., 1986-89, Pomona Valley Coun. Chs., 1991—; mem. commn. on ministry, examining chaplain Diocese of So. Va., 1987-89, Diocese of L.A., 1991—. Co-editor, contbr.: The Listening Heart, 1987; also articles; translator theol. works. Pres. St. Mark's Homeless Shelter Inc., 1989—. Day fellow Yale Divinity Sch., 1982, W.B. Given Meml. fellow Episcopal Ch. Found., 1984. Mem. Richmond Episcopal Clericus (pres. 1986). Office: St Mark's Episcopal Ch PO Box 366 Upland CA 91785-0366 *I remain convinced that congregations have an unlimited opportunity to transform their members and their communities. I believe, however, that denominations and denominational structures have increasingly fewer such opportunities. I am excited to be living in this time of change.*

GLASS, JONATHAN WILSON, rabbi; b. Boston, July 22, 1957; s. MacEllis Kopel and Judith (Wilson) G.; m. Minka Gindoff, Apr. 13, 1983; children: David, Elke, Benjamin. BA, Columbia Coll., 1979. Ordained rabbi, 1986. Rabbi Civic Ctr. Synagogue, N.Y.C., 1989—; presenter invocation City Coun. of City of N.Y., 1989—. Named Assoc. Alumnus, Yeshiva U., 1989. Mem. Rabbinical Coun. Am. Home: 208 E Broadway New York NY 10002 Office: Civic Ctr Synagogue 49 White St New York NY 10002

GLASS, RICHARD LEE, pastor; b. Alliance, Ohio, May 12, 1932; s. Emmett Blaine and Anna Melissa (Weaver) G.; m. Theresa Mae Terrell, June 14, 1958; children: Anita Lynne, Eric Roneld, Nathan Scott. AB, Mt. Union Coll., 1955; MDiv, United Sem., 1958; CPE, Riverside Hosp., 1972; diploma in acctg., Medina (Ohio) Bus. Coll., 1979. Pastor Grace E.U.B. Ch., Canton, Ohio, 1958-61; youth minister Westbrook Pk. Ch., Canton, 1962-64; pastor Ch. of Our Lord, Cleve., 1964-71; chaplain Elyria (Ohio) Meth. Home, 1971-76; pastor LeRoy United Meth., Westfield Ctr., Ohio, 1976-83, Brookfield (Ohio) United Meth., 1983-87, Woodlawn United Meth., Bucyrus, Ohio, 1987—; stand-by chaplain VA Hosp., Cleve., 1970-71. Trustee East End Neighborhood House, Cleve., 1966-71; chairperson Woodhill Homes CMA Adv., Cleve., 1970. mem. United Meth. Assn. Ch. Bus. Adminstrs. (cert.), East Ohio Conf. (chmn. bd. higher edn. 1980-84), Long Range Strategy, Kiwanis (program 1966-71), Lions (treas. Westfield Ctr. chpt. 1980-83). Avocations: travel, slide photography, keyboard composition. Office: Woodlawn United Meth 1675 Hopley Ave Bucyrus OH 44820

GLASSE, JOHN HOWELL, philosophy and theology educator; b. Buffalo, June 1, 1922; s. John Alfred and Jessie Elizabeth (Howell) G.; m. Wanda Lou Howard, June 16, 1950; children: Jeffrey Howell, Paulding Howard. B.A., Williamette U., 1945; B.D., Yale U., 1948, Ph.D., 1961. Ordained to ministry Presbyterian Ch. U.S.A., 1948; dir. field work Christian Activities Council, Hartford, Conn., 1948-50; exec. dir. Christian Activities Council, 1950-52; dir. Danish program Scandinavian Seminar, Inc., 1952-53; mem. faculty Vassar Coll., Poughkeepsie, N.Y., 1956—, prof. religion, 1969-90, prof. emeritus, 1990—, Frederick Weyerhaeuser chair, 1971-90, chmn. dept. religion, 1965-67, 77-83, 87-90; vis. prof. Harvard Div. Sch., 1970, vis. scholar, 1962, 69; vis. scholar Columbia U., Union Theol. Sem., 1980-81. Contbr. articles to profl. jours. Trustee Scandinavian Seminar, 1950—. Hon. fellow Am. Scandinavian Found., 1952; grantee Am. Philos. Soc., 1964; grantee Am. Council Learned Socs., 1965, 67. Mem. Am. Acad. Religion, Am. Philos. Assn., Metaphys. Soc. Am., Soc. Values in Higher Edn., AAUP. Address: Vassar Coll Box 347 Poughkeepsie NY 12601

GLASSER, EUGENE ROBERT, religious organization administrator; b. Akron, Mich., July 11, 1925; s. Benton Albert and Leta B. Glasser; m. Kathryn Dale Schimelpfenig, May 15, 1954 (div. June 1977); children: Candace, David, Thomas, Paul; m. Jean Ann Natvick Klockow, Dec. 10, 1977; stepchildren: Kristi A. Klockow, Kevin J. Klockow. BA, Moravian Coll., 1953, MDiv, 1957; student, McCormick Seminary, Chgo., 1953-54, Luth. Seminary, Phila., 1962-67. Ordained deacon, consecrated presbyter Moravian Ch., 1957. Pastor Ephraim (Wis.) Moravian Ch., 1957-60; headmaster Moravian Prep. Sch., Bethlehem, Pa., 1960-64; assoc. gen. sec. Bd. Christian Edn., Bethlehem, 1965-66; assoc. pastor Cen. Moravian Ch., Bethlehem, 1966-68; pastor Wisconsin Rapids (Wis.) Moravian Ch., 1968-74, Lake Mills (Wis.) Moravian Ch., 1974-90; dir. Dept. Stewardship and Planned Giving, No. Province, 1990—; seminary trustee Moravian Theol. Seminary, Bethlehem, 1974-86; dist. exec. bd. Moravian Ch. Western Dist., Sun Prairie, 1982-90; bd. dirs. Ecumenical Ctr. for Stewardship Studies. Author: Facing Faith, 1971. With USN, 1943-46, ETO. Home: 398 Grove St Lake Mills WI 53551 Office: Moravian Ch Dept Stewardship/Giving PO Box 243 Lake Mills WI 53551-0243

GLEASON, FRED GENE, deacon; b. Arthur, Ill., Sept. 16, 1933; s. David Joseph and Isophenia G.; m. Sandra Janelle Insco, Nov. 21, 1954; children: Kathleen, Daniel Wayne, Janelle, Angelina. Grad. high sch., Champaign, Ill. Deacon St. Mary Magdalen, San Antonio, 1977-80, St. Gregory the Great, San Antonio, 1980-81, St. Patrick, San Antonio, 1981-84, Prince of Peace, San Antonio, 1984-89, St. Anthony Claret, San Antonio, 1989—. Sgt. U.S. Army, 1953-55. Named to Quill and Scroll, 1952. Mem. KC. Home: 2738 Ray Lieck Dr San Antonio TX 78253

GLEESON, THOMAS F., academic administrator. Pres. Jesuit Sch. Theology at Berkely, Calif. Office: Jesuit Sch Theol Office of Pres 1735 Leroy Ave Berkeley CA 94709*

GLEIM, ELMER QUENTIN, retired minister; b. Mechanicsburg, Pa., Jan. 10, 1917; s. Quentin Albert and Alverta Elizabeth (Doner) G.; m. Ruth Rishel, Apr. 5, 1942; children: Robert David, Dianne Lynne Bowders, Robin Ann Stahl. AB, Elizabethtown Coll., 1939; BD, Crozer Theol. Sem., Chester, Pa., 1945; MEd, U. Pitts., 1954. Pastor 1st Ch. of the Brethren, Phila., 1942-49, County Line Ch. of the Brethren, Fayette County, Pa., 1949-58, Madison Ave. Ch. of the Brethren, York, Pa., 1962-80; tchr. York, Pa., 1958-81. Republican. Home: 20 E Crone Rd York PA 17402

GLEMP, JOZEF CARDINAL, archbishop of Gniezno and Warsaw; b. Inowroclaw, Poland, Dec. 18, 1929; s. Kazimierz and Salomea (Kosmicka) G.; grad. Priests Sem. Gniezno, 1956; D. Canon and Roman Law, Lateran U., Rome, 1964. Ordained priest Roman Catholic Ch., 1956; sec. to Cardinal Primate Stefan Wyszynski, from 1967; bishop of Warmia, 1979-81; archbishop of Gniezno and Warsaw, 1981—, primate of Poland, 1981—, elevated to cardinal, 1983; pres. Polish Episcopal Conf.; mem. Cong. for the Eastern Ch. Author: De conceptu fictionis iuris apud Romanos, 1964, Lexiculum iuris romani, 1974, Through Justice in Charity, 1982, Czlowiek wielkiej wiary, 1983, Kosciol na drogach Ojczyzny, 1985, Chcemy z tego sprawdzianu wyjsc prawdomowni i wiarygodni, 1985, Kosciol i Polonia, 1986, W teczy Frankow orzel i krzyz, 1987, O Eucharystii, 1987, A wolanie moje niech do Ciebie przyjdzie, 1988, Boze cos Polske poslal nad Tamize, 1988, Nauczanie pasterskie, vol. I, II, 1988, Nauczanie spoleczne, 1989, Na dwóch wybrzezach, 1990, U przyjaciól Belgów, 1990, I uwierzyli uczniowie, 1990, Tysiaclecie wiary Swietego Wlodzimierza, 1991, Slowo Boże nad Łyna, 1991, Zamyślenia Maryji, 1991, Gniezno-ciagla odnowa, 1991, Poet-Priests Vis-a-Vis The New Evangelisation, 1991. Address: 17 Miodowa, 00-246 Warsaw Poland also: ul Kanclerza Jana Laskiego 7, 62-200 Gniezno Poland

GLENN, CHARLES EDWARD, pastor; b. Fordyce, Ariz., Aug. 13, 1944; s. David Edward and Willie Lee (Cooper) G.; m. Emma Lee Washington, June 23, 1967; chilldren: Charles Edward Jr., Alicia, Stephan. BRE, Marantha Bible Coll., Poulsbo, Wash., 1988, MRE, 1989; DD (hon.), Mt. Sinai Bible Sch., Kokomo, Ark., 1990; LittD, Life Sch. of Bible, Kokomo, 1991. Ordained to ministry Ch. of God in Christ. Youth pastor New Hope Ch. of God in Christs, Kokomo, 1973-75, asst. pastor, 1975-79; pastor Greater New Hope Ch., Kokomo, 1979-81, Fountain of Life Worship Ctr., Kokomo, 1981—; pres. Hope Bible Inst., Kokomo, 1976-80, Life Sch. of Bible, 1985—; dir. Life Sch. if Ministry, Kokomo, 1985—, Life Ministries, Inc., Kokomo, 1985—; pres. Minority Ministerial Coun., Kokomo, 1983. Author: The Spirits Work, 1983, False Religions and Occultism, 1985, (study guide) What Does the Bible Teach, 1990. Recipient Christian Leadership award Minority Ministerial Coun., 1983, 87. Mem. NAACPO (pres. Kokomo chpt. 1989-91), UAW. Democrat. Home: 1009 E Walnut St Kokomo IN 46901 Office: Fountain of Life Worship Ctr 611 E Jackson St Kokomo IN 46903

GLENN, CHARLES KENNETH, clergyman; b. Carlton, Ga., July 8, 1934; s. Edward Roy and Evelyn Grace (Holloman) G.; m. Beth Boroughs, July 11, 1959; children: Stephanie Grace, Richard Alan, Andrew Jacob. BA magna cum laude, Furman U., 1958; MDiv, Golden Gate Bapt. Theol. Sem., 1961, ThM, 1965; MEd in Counseling, Boston U., Munich, 1984. Cert. counselor, Va., Nebr.; ordained to ministry Bapt. Ch., 1958. Youth dir. Cen. Bapt. Ch., Alameda, Calif., 1959; asst. pastor Pacifica (Calif.) Bapt. Ch., 1959-60; pastor Peninsula Bapt. Ch., Monterey, Calif., 1960-63, First Bapt. Ch., South San Francisco, Calif., 1963-70; missionary So. Bapt. Conv., Richmond, Va., 1970-87; pastor First Bapt. Ch., Bellevue, Nebr., 1987—; mem. exec. bd. Calif. So. Bapt. Conv., Fresno, Calif., 1965-70, chmn., 1969-70, 1st v.p., 1970; pres. European Bapt. Conv., Wiesbaden, West Germany, 1974-75; moderator Ea. Nebr. Bapt. Assn., Omaha, 1989-91; student chaplain San Quentin and Soledad Prisons, Calif., 1960-63; tchr. O.T., Golden Gate Sem., Mill Valley; officer Calif. Pastors' Conf., Fresno. Pres., v.p., program chmn. PTA, Munich, 1981-85; chmn. sch. adv. bd., Munich, 1983-85. Democrat. Home: 1803 Childs Rd E Bellevue NE 68005 Office: First Bapt Ch Corner Hancock and 23d Sts Bellevue NE 68005

GLENN, DON ALLEN, minister, lay organization official; b. Columbus, Ohio, Oct. 26, 1936; s. Charles M. and Marie (Cantrell) G.; m. Ann E. Etsler, July 6, 1956; children: Pamela Ann, Scott Allen. AB, Marion Coll., 1958, MA, 1985; postgrad., Northern Baptist Theo., 1985-86. Ordained to ministry Wesleyan Ch., 1959. Pastor Wesleyan Ch., Ohio, 1958-69, Iowa, 1969-76, Ind., 1976-78, Ill., 1978-87; acting dir. ministry svcs. Dept. Edn. Ministry Wesleyan Ch., Indpls., 1987-89; interim sr. pastor Trinity Wesleyan Ch., Indpls., 1989-90; sr. pastor Westview Wesleyan Ch., Jonesboro, Ind., 1990—; Youth Enlisted Serving Wesleyan Ch., St. Croix 1970, Wesleyan Gospel Corps., 1978, 1985. Contbr. articles to profl. jour. Treas. Iowa Kidney Found., Iowa City 1971, exec. dir. Roberta Albert Kidney Transplant, Waterloo, Iowa, 1970; editor Rotary Internat., Broadview, 1980-81. Mem. Wesleyan Theol. Soc., Ministerial Assn. (pres. Waterloo chpt. 1968-70). Avocations: reading, travel, lawn garden, walking. Home: 881 E Bell Dr Marion IN 46953 Office: Westview Wesleyan Ch 1300 W 6th St Jonesboro IN 46938

GLENN, MICHAEL LEO, minister; b. Alexandria, La., Nov. 22, 1956; s. John and Barbara Glenn; m. Jeannie Powers; children: Christopher Michael and Craig Powers (twins). BA, Samford U., 1978; Clin. Pastoral Edn., Highlands Bapt. Hosp., Louisville, 1980; MDiv, So. Bapt. Theol. Sem., 1981, D Ministry, 1988. Ordained to ministry So. Bapt. Conv., 1980. Pastor Bethany Bapt. Ch., Crane Hill, Ala., 1981-82; pastor 1st Bapt. Ch., Edgefield, S.C., 1981-86, Mauldin, S.C., 1986-91; pastor Brentwood (Tenn.) Bapt. Ch., 1991—; Mem. gen. bd. S.C. Bapt. Conv., 1984-86, benevolent instns. subcom., 1984-86, Planned Growth in Giving task force, 1985, search com. for dir. Office Pub. Rels., 1985, Com. on Coms., 1989; featured speaker Ann. Retreat, Bapt. Student Union, Sunday Sch. Workshop, S.C. Bapt. Conv. Narrator, host mission film I-85 Corridor Thrust, 1989; contbr. The Bapt. Courier, 1986. Mem. Mins. Adv. Coun. Greenville Meml. Hosp.; chmn. pub. affairs com. Edgefield Assn., 1983-86; chmn. pers. com. Greenville Assn., associational strategic planning task force, chmn. Population Study Group; camp pastor S.C. High Sch. Music Week; bd. dirs. Chapel, Perry Crorrectional Ctr.; mem. Mins.' Adv. Coun., Bapt. Coll. Charleston; chmn. bd. trustees Mauldin Ednl. Found., Mauldin High Sch. Mem. Mauldin Club, Rotary Internat. Avocations: sports, reading, writing, computers. Home: 1730 Coachmans Ct Brentwood TN 37027 Office: Brentwood Bapt Ch Brentwood TN 37027

GLESSNER, GARY DAVID, lay worker; b. Lock Haven, Pa., Sept. 18, 1960; s. David Carol and Carol Lee (Homer) G.; m. Margaret Rutyh Fry, Oct. 13, 1990. BA in Bus. Adminstrn., Grove City (Pa.) Coll., 1982; MS in Computer Sys. Mgmt., U. Md., 1990. Ch. counsel United Luth. Ch., Lock Haven, Pa., 1978; Christian camp youth counselor Camp Krislund, State College, Pa., summers 1981,82, counselor, trainer, chaplain, summers 1984—; sr. high youth dir. Holy Trinity Luth. Ch., Laurel, Md., 1983—; software engr. GE, Hanover, Md., 1983—; lectr. in field. Asst. high sch. football coach Laurel High Sch., 1987-89. Mem. Info. Systems Security Assn. Home: 7615 Carissa Ln Laurel MD 20707

GLICK, GARLAND WAYNE, retired theological seminary president; b. Bridgewater, Va., Jan. 27, 1921; s. John T. and Effie (Evers) G.; m. Barbara Roller Zigler, Jan. 1, 1943; children—Martha (Mrs. Carl Barlett), John, Mary. B.D., Bethany Bibl. Sem., Chgo., 1946; M.A. in N.T, U. Chgo., 1949, Ph.D. in Ch. History, 1957; LL.D., Bridgewater Coll., 1969. Ordained to ministry Ch. of Brethren, 1942, United Ch. Christ, 1978. Pastor Lombard, Ill., 1945-48; instr., then asst. prof. Bibl. studies Juniata Coll., Huntingdon, Pa., 1948-53; mem. faculty Franklin and Marshall Coll., 1955-65, asso. prof. religion, 1958-65, prof., 1965, v.p., 1962-65, dir. research and long-range planning, 1960, asst. to dean, 1960-61, dean coll., 1961-65; pres. Keuka Coll., Keuka Park, N.Y., 1966-74; dir. Moton Center Ind. Studies, Gloucester, Va., 1975-78; pres. Bangor (Maine) Theol. Sem., 1978-86; vis. prof. Lancaster (Pa.) Theol. Sem., 1958-60, 64; coordinator of cons. Knox Seminars Ednl. Mgmt., 1963-65; seminar dir. Nat. Cath. Edn. Assn. Long-Range Planning Seminars, 1968; Bd. dirs. Empire State Found. Ind. Liberal Arts Colls., Fund for Theol. Edn. (pres. 1988—), Lancaster Guidance Ctr. Author: Maker of Modern Theology: Adolf von Harnack, 1967; Contbr. to Ency. Brit. Mem. Nat. Assn. Bibl. Instrs., Am. Soc. Ch. History, Am. Conf. Acad. Deans (treas. 1965-66), Societas Orphea, Pi Gamma Mu, Tau Kappa Alpha. Home: 1834 Ridgeview Ave Lancaster PA 17603 *Clearly, a revolution has taken place in the last generation. The meaning of that revolution is not yet clear. I believe the name of the revolution is "longing" and Augustine's "God and the soul I want to know, nothing more," demarks its direction.*

GLICKSMAN, GAIL GAISIN, rabbi; b. Phila., Dec. 12, 1956; d. Manuil and Sophia (Ostrow) Gaisin; m. Allen Glicksman, May 30, 1976. BA cum laude, Temple U., 1978; MS in Edn., U. Pa., 1982, postgrad., 1980—; MA in Hebrew Lit., Reconstructionist Rabbinical Coll., Wyncote, Pa., 1986. Ordained rabbi, 1986. Rabbi Adath Shalom Congregation, Phila., 1981-86; asst. dir. and health professions advisor U. Pa. Career Planning & Placement Svc., Phila., 1986—; chaplain Jewish Chaplaincy Svc., Phila., 1988—; lectr. YM-YWHA Sr. Adult div., Phila., 1983-85; instr. Gratz Coll. Netsky Inst., Phila., 1985-86; presenter papers at profl. meetings, confs. Mem. Am. Jewish Com., Phila., 1987—. Recipient Hebrew award Knights of Pytias, 1975; U. Pa. fellow, 1980-81; Meml. Found. for Jewish Culture scholar, 1984-85; Ida Foreman Fleisher Trust scholar, 1984-86. Mem. Assn. for Social Sci. Study of Jewry (newsletter editor 1987—). Home: 250 Beverly Blvd E107 Upper Darby PA 19082 Office: U Pa 3718 Locust Walk # 20 Philadelphia PA 19104-6209

GLIGOR-HABIAN, LISA DANIELLE, lay worker, elementary school educator; b. Youngstown, Ohio, June 16, 1964; d. John and Kathryn (Fisher) Gligor; m. John Michael Habian, July 22, 1989. BS in Edn., Youngstown (Ohio) State U., 1987, BA, 1988. Cert. elem. sch. tchr., Ohio. Mem. Holy Trinity Choir, Youngstown, 1980-86; sec. Am. Romanian Orthodox Youth, Youngstown, 1980-81, 85-86, treas., 1981-82, historian, 1982-83, pres., 1983-85; mem.-at-large Am. Romanian Orthodox Youth, U.S., Can., 1983-85; sec. Am. Romanian Orthodox Youth, Cleve., 1990-91; tchr. Cleve. Pub. City Schs., 1989—. Named Orthodox Youth of Yr., Ea. Orthodox Men's Soc., Youngstown, 1981; Goldy scholar Am. Romanian Orthodox Episcopate Am., 1984, 85, 86; Holy Trinity Romanian Orthodox Ch. scholar, Youngstown, 1985.

GLINSKI, RICHARD M., religious education director; b. Sloan, N.Y., Apr. 28, 1929; s. Michael and Elizabeth (Konopa) G. Linotypist print shop Vincentian Fathers, Erie, Pa., 1948-75; mgr. Vincentian Fathers, Erie, 1973-75; procurator, Mission House Vincentian Fathers, Utica, N.Y., 1976-90; dir. of religious edn. Our Lady of Rosary, New Hartford, N.Y., 1976-79, St. Paul's, Whitesboro, N.Y., 1987—. Home: 10475 Cosby Manor Utica NY 13502

GLISSON, JERRY LEE, minister; b. Dyer, Tenn., Mar. 15, 1923; s. Algie Lee and Mary (Keathley) G.; m. Helen Lorene Barron, July 23, 1944; children: Terrye Jan (dec.), Rickey Lee, Philip Ray, Lisa Renee Glisson Garrett. BA magna cum laude, Union U., Jackson, Tenn., 1945, DD, 1967; BD, Southwestern Bapt. Theol. Sem., Ft. Worth, 1948; ThD, Southwestern Bapt. Theol. Sem, 1951. Ordained to ministry Bapt. Ch., 1942. Pastor Allison (Tex.) Bapt. Ch., 1946-51, Acton (Tex.) Bapt. Ch., 1948-51, First Bapt. Ch., Huntingdon, Tenn., 1951-56, Leawood Bapt. Ch., Memphis, 1956-91; pres. Tenn. Bapt. Conv., 1969-70, mem. exec. bd., 1971-78; bd. dirs. Home Mission Bd. So. Bapt. Conv., Atlanta, 1982-90. Author: The Church in a Storm, Surviving or Thriving, 1983, Knowing and Doing God's Will, 1986. Trustee Union U., Jackson, 1952-91. Mem. Shelby Bapt. Pastor's Conf. (pres. 1966). Office: Leawood Bapt Ch 3638 Macon Rd Memphis TN 38122

GLISTA, JONATHAN EUGENE, minister; b. Harvey, Ill., Mar. 9, 1964; s. William E. and Sue C. (Caraker) G.; m. Cathy Elaine Henry, Aug. 11, 1985; children: Allison Christian, Devyn Jonathan. BA in Christian Ministry, Ky. Christian Coll., 1986. Ordained to ministry Ch. of Christ, 1985. Minister Carrey's Run Ch. of Christ, Portsmouth, Ohio, 1984-85, Tilton Christian Ch., Flemingsburg, Ky., 1985-86; youth minister Orrville (Ohio) Ch. of Christ, 1986—; exec. ocm. Summer in the Son Youth Conf., Grayson, Ky., 1988—; planning mem. Ohio Teen for Christ Conv., Columbus, 1987—; dir. Pastor of the Day Program, Orrville High Sch., 1988. Mem. Wayne County Ministerium, Nat. Right to Life Assn., Wayne County Drug Abuse Task Force, Orrville Ministerial Assn. Home: 1725 Meadow Ln Orrville OH 44667 Office: Orrville Ch of Christ 925 N Elm St Orrville OH 44667

GLOER, WILLIAM HULITT, religion educator; b. Atlanta, Dec. 23, 1950; s. William Talmadge and Frances (Lancaster) G.; m. Sheila Katherine Rogers; children: Jeremy Hulitt, Joshua William. BA, Baylor U., 1972; MDiv, Pitts. Theol. Seminary, 1975; PhD, So. Bapt. Theol. Seminary, Louisville, 1981. Pastor Monroeville (Pa.) Bapt. Ch., 1974-77; instr. So. Bapt. Theol. Seminary, 1979-81; asst. prof. North Am. Bapt. Seminary, Sioux Falls, S.D., 1981-83; prof. N.T. Midwestern Bapt. Theol. Seminary, Kansas City, Mo., 1983—; moderator Greater Pitts. Bapt. Assn., 1976-77; exec. bd. Bapt. Conv. Pa., 1976-77; Kerr lectr. Okla. Bapt. U., Shawnee, 1982. Editor: Eschatology and the New Testament, 1988, Jesus Christ: The Man from Nazareth and the Exalted Lord, 1987; contbr: International Standard Bible Encyclopedia, 1988, Mercer Dictionary of the Bible, Holman Bible Dictionary; contbr. articles to profl. jours. Mem. Soc. Bibl. Lit., Cath. Bibl. Assn., Nat. Assn. Bapt. Profs. Religion (pres. Midwest region 1990—), Inst. for Bibl. Rsch. Home: 616 NE 98th Terr Kansas City MO 64155 Office: Midwestern Bapt Theol Semin 5001 N Oak Kansas City MO 64118

GLOVER, GREGORY LEONARD, religion educator; b. Chgo., Apr. 25, 1966; s. Leonard Van and Carolyn Janie (Walker) G.; m. Elizabeth Faye Rix, June 13, 1987. BA, Union U., 1988; MDiv, Princeton Theol. Sem., 1991. Teaching asst., Hebrew Princeton (N.J.) Theol. Sem., 1990-91, rsch. asst., 1990-91. Recipient Benjamin Stanton prize in Old Testament, Princeton Theol. Sem., 1990; George S. Green fellow Princeton Theol. Sem., 1991. Mem. Soc. Bibl. Lit. Home: 205 Loetscher Pl 3A Princeton NJ 08540 *Our thinking in religion should not lag behind in complexity or energy our thinking in any other sphere of life.*

GLOVER, LARRY HODGES, minister; b. Sandersville, Ga., May 21, 1954; s. Thomas Eugene and Mary Elizabeth (Davis) G.; m. Susan Ragan, Dec. 13, 1975; 1 child, Margaret Christine. AA, Brewton-Parker Coll., 1974; BS in Psychology, Ga. Coll., 1986. Ordained to ministry So. Bapt. Conv., 1972. Pastor Fairmount Bapt. Ch., Sparta, Ga., 1972-73, Harrison (Ga.) Bapt. Ch., 1972-73, Brewton Bapt. Ch., Dublin, Ga., 1973-76, Macedonia Bapt. Ch., McIntyre, Ga., 1982-87; sr. pastor 1st Bapt. Ch., Centerview, Mo., 1987—; vice chmn. exec. com., dir. ch. tng. Laurens County Assn., Dublin, 1973-76. Organizer, chief Vol. Fire Dept., Alexander, Ga., 1975-76; organizer, bd. dirs. Wilkinson County Emergency Mgmt., Irwinton, Ga., 1983-87; mayor pro tem City of Centerview, 1988—. Home: 400 S Main St Centerview MO 64019 Office: 1st Bapt Ch 311 S Walnut Centerview MO 64019

GLUTH, DIANE MARIE, church lay worker; b. Hammond, Ind., Nov. 24, 1961; d. Duane Lee and Carol Sue (Reiff) G. Student, Bremen U., Fed. Republic Germany, 1983, Meiji-Gaukuin U., Tokyo, 1984; BA, Hope Coll., 1984. Coord. youth Covenant Presbyn. Ch., Hammond, 1984-88; camp dir. Presbytery of No. Ill., Elgin, 1987—; dir. recreation Presbytery of No. Ill., Lawton, Mich., 1986; dir. youth Westminster Presbyn. Ch., Elgin, 1988—. Author: Camp Counselor Manual, 1987. Mem. Sch. Improvement Program, Hammond, 1986-87, Elgin YWCA. Home: 1506 Kenneth Circle Elgin IL 60120 Office: Westminster Presbyn Ch 2700 N Highland Ave Elgin IL 60123

GNANAPRAGASASAM, JABEZ JEBASIR, bishop. Bishop of Colombo, Anglican Communion, Sri Lanka. Office: Bishop's House, 358/1 Bauddhaloka Mawatha, Colombo 7, Sri Lanka*

GNAT, THOMAS J., bishop. Bishop of the Ea. Diocese Polish Nat. Cath. Ch. of Am., Manchester, N.H. Office: Polish Nat Cath Ch Am 635 Union St Manchester NH 03104*

GNUSE, ROBERT KARL, religious educator; b. Quincy, Ill., Dec. 4, 1947; s. Karl Arthur and Margaret Elizabeth (Rupp) G.; m. Elizabeth Hammond, Dec. 30, 1982; children: Rebecca Elizabeth, John Robert, Adam Joseph. MDiv, Concordia Sem. in Exile, 1974, STM, 1975; MA, Vanderbilt U., 1978, PhD, 1980. Vis. asst. prof. religion U. Va., Charlottesville, 1978-79; asst. prof. religion N.C. Wesleyan U., Rocky Mount, 1979-80; asst. prof. religion Loyola U., New Orleans, 1980-84, assoc. prof. religion, 1984-90, full prof. religion, 1990—; campus minister Loyola U./Tulane U., New Orleans, 1989—. Author: Dream Theophany of Samuel, 1984, Authority of the Bible, 1985, You Shall Not Steal, 1985, Heilsgeschichte as a Model for Biblical Theology, 1989. Harold Sterling Vanderbilt scholar Vanderbilt U., 1975-78. Mem. Am. Schs. Oriental Rsch., Am. Oriental Soc., Soc. Bibl. Lit., Cath. Bibl. Assn., Coll. Theology Soc. (regional pres. 1985-87). Home: 7731 Wave Dr New Orleans LA 70128 Office: Loyola U 6363 St Charles Ave New Orleans LA 70118

GOATES, DONALD RAY, minister; b. Corpus Christi, Tex., Jan. 14, 1943; s. Joe Elbert Goates and Bobbie (Cochran) Goates Hammett; m. Patsy LaNetta Owens, June 7, 1963; children: Gretchen Gwyndolyn, Sunnae Millicent, Donald Ray II. BA in Music Edn., East Tex. State U., 1965; MDiv, Southwestern Bapt. Theol. Sem., 1975, DMin, 1979. Ordained to ministry Bapt. Ch., 1972. Asst. mgr. G.F. Wacker's, Commerce, Tex., 1964-65; commd. 2d lt. U.S. Army, 1965, advanced through grades to capt., 1972, served in Vietnam; pastor Water St. Bapt. Ch., Waxahachie, Tex., 1972-76, First Bapt. Ch. of Forest Hill, Ft. Worth, 1976-80, First Bapt. Ch., Sweetwater, Tex., 1980—; associational moderator Sweetwater Bapt. Assn., 1983-84; pres. Sweetwater Ministerial Alliance, 1985. Contbr. articles to profl. jours. Decorated Silver Star, Bronze Star, Hon. medal 1st class and Cross of Gallantry (Republic of Vietnam). Lodges: Rotary (bd. dirs. 1985-87, pres. 1987), Masons, Shriners. Avocations: hunting, fishing, construction. Office: PO Box 1258 Sweetwater TX 79556

GOBLE, THOMAS LEE, clergyman; b. Anderson, Ind., July 5, 1935; s. Carl Wilbur and Agnes Irene (McVey) G.; m. Esther Charlene Callaway, June 12, 1956; children: Jeffreay Mark, Jeanette Marcelle Goble Pittman. BA, Pasadena Coll., 1956; BD, Nazarene Theol. Sem., 1959; DMin, Calif. Grad. Sch. Theology, 1972. Ordained to ministry Ch. of Nazarene, 1960, deacon, 1960. Pastor various congregations Ch. of Nazarene, 1959-87; supt. Anaheim dist. Ch. of Nazarene, Orange, Calif., 1987—; prof., Point Loma Nazarene Coll., Nazarene Bible Coll.; chmn. bd. dirs., Asian Nazarene Bible Coll., Long Beach, Calif., 1987—. Trustee, Idyllwild (Calif.) Christian Camp, 1987—, Point Loma Nazarene Coll., San Diego, 1987—. Mem. Point Loma Coll. Alumni Assn., Rotary. Office: Anaheim Dist Ch Nazarene 524 E Chapman Ave Orange CA 92666

GOCHENOUR, DOUGLAS ALLEN, church worship leader; b. Harrisonburg, Va., Sept. 5, 1962; s. Garnett Glendon and Isabell Jane (Painter) G. BS summa cum laude, James Madison U., 1985; postgrad., Regent U., 1990—. Specialist wall window sales Kawneer Co. Inc., Harrisonburg, Va.; news dir. Sta. WGCM-TV, Luray, Va., 1986; mem. pastoral staff Bayview Bapt. Ch., Norfolk, Va., 1990—. Worship leader, co-youth leader, mem. bd. deacons First Assembly of God Ch., Harrisonburg, 1985-87; homecoming planning com. Town of Stanley, Va., 1986—. Named Outstanding Youth Citizen, Town of Stanley, 1984, Outstanding Young Man of Am., 1985-87. Mem. Phi Kappa Phi. Avocations: singing, counseling, tennis, cooking, speaking. Home: 5932-202 Jake Sears Cir Virginia Beach VA 23464 Office: Bayview Bapt Ch 707 E Bayview Blvd Norfolk VA 23503 *Within the realm of Christianity, no greater focus for the meaning of life can be found than in the giver of life itself - Jesus Christ. May we ever seek, as the apostle Paul said, to decrease and allow Him (Christ) to increase in our lives.*

GOCKLEY, DAVID WOODROW, ecumenical executive; b. Ephrata, Pa., Oct. 9, 1918; s. David and Elizabeth (Donner) G.; m. Olive Porter; children—Pamela, Charles, David, Sally, Stephanie, Brian. Student, Shenandoah U., Winchester, Va., 1938-40; A.B., Lebanon Valley Coll., 1942, D.D., 1978; M.Div., United Theol. Sem., Dayton, Ohio, 1945; M.A., Temple U., 1955. Ordained to ministry United Meth. Ch., 1945. Youth pastor Westminster Presbyn. Ch., Dayton, Ohio, 1943-45; dir. pub. relations and chaplain Lebanon Valley Coll., 1945-51; pastor United Meth. Ch., Phila., 1951-56; exec. sec. dept. pub. relations Greater Phila. Council Chs., 1956-61; dir. pub. relations Religion in Am. Life, N.Y.C., 1961-69; exec. v.p. Religion in Am. Life, 1969-71, pres., 1971-85, pres. emeritus, 1985—; cons. Sta. WNET, 1985-91; mem. TV Commn. Pa. Council Chs., 1959-61; bd. mgrs. broadcasting and film commn. Nat. Council Chs., 1959-62. Mem. Phila. Youth Svcs. Bd., 1958-61; chmn. Alcoholism Coun. Mid-Fairfield County, Conn., 1971-77; bd. advisors United Theol. Sem., Dayton, 1989—. Named Interreligious Clergyman of Yr.; recipient Silver Bell award Advt. Coun.; Disting. Alumnus citation Shenandoah Coll., 1986. Mem. Religious Pub. Relations Council (pres. Phila. chpt. 1960-61, nat. pres. 1964-66), Lebanon Valley Alumni Assn. (citation 1975). Lodge: Knights of Malta (Knight of grace 1985). Home: 1115 Ketch Ln Venice FL 34292 *If you want to develop a full life, don't set out to build a fortune, build a sterling character. A sterling character includes positive attitudes, affection for others and virtues such as honesty, morality, loyalty, truth, humor and piety.*

GODDARD, BURTON LESLIE, religion educator; b. Dodge Center, Minn., July 4, 1910; s. William Bliss and Myra Estella (Beckwith) G.; m. Esther Anna Hempel, July 16, 1940. Student, U. Minn., 1928-30; AB, UCLA, 1933; ThB, Westminster Theol. Sem., 1937; STM, Harvard U., 1938, ThD, 1943; SM, Simmons Coll., 1957; DD (hon.), Gordon-Conwell Theol. Sem., 1986. Pastor Carlisle (Mass.) Congl. Ch., 1937-41; asst. in Semitic langs. Harvard Divinity Sch., 1938-39, 40-41; instr. in bible and christian edn. Gordon Coll. and Divinity Sch., Wenham, Mass., 1941-44, prof. O.T., 1943-51, dean, 1944-51; dean Gordon-Conwell Theol. Sem., South Hamilton, Mass., 1951-61, prof. bibl. lang. and exegesis, 1951-75, libr. dir., 1961-73, libr. cons., 1973-75; trustee Boston Theol. Inst., 1971-74. Author: (booklet) Animals in the Bible, 1963, The NIV Story, 1989, Meet Jeremiah, 1992; editor: Encyclopedia of Modern Christian Missions, 1967; joint editor, translator: The Holy Bible, New International Version, 1978; contbr. numerous articles to profl. jours. Mem. Am. Theol. Libr. Assn. (chmn. membership com. 1970-71), Soc. Bibl. Lit., Evang. Theol. Soc. (editor 1949-54, pres. 1964). Republican. Home: PO Box 194 Quincy PA 17247-0194 *I like the perspective of the Apostle Paul: "Although he longed to leave this life and enter the presence of God, he was willing rather to forego that if to stay here would bring joy to others".*

GODDARD, DEAN ALLEN, minister; b. Ft. Morgan, Colo., Feb. 19, 1942; s. Fay Fair and Dorothy Arvilla (Suttle) G.; m. Mary Lee Leonard, May 29, 1963; children: Rebekah, Matthew. BA, Bob Jones U., Greenville, S.C., 1964; postgrad., Western Conservative Bapt.Sem., Portland, Oreg., 1964-65; DD, Maranatha Bapt. Coll., Watertown, Wis., 1980; DST, Berean Bapt. Sem., India, 1987. Ordained to ministry Bapt. Ch., 1965. Dean Pacific Coast Bapt. Coll., San Dimas, 1967-71; pastor Mid-Cities Bapt. Temple, Downey, Calif., 1971-77, Calvary Bapt. Ch., Casper, Wyo., 1977-81, Bethany Bapt. Ch., Cayce, S.C., 1981-84, Fairway Park Bapt. Ch., Hayward, Calif., 1984—; v.p. Bapt. Coll. of West, San Francisco, 1985-91; bd. dirs. Fellowship of Fundamental Bapt. of No. Calif., San Francisco, 1985—; trustee Lucerne Christian Conf. Ctr., 1985—. Mem. Wyo. Assn. Christian Schs. (pres. 1977-81). Home: 31344 Burnham Way Hayward CA 94544 Office: Fairway Park Bapt Ch 425 Gresel St Hayward CA 94544

GODDARD, HAZEL BRYAN, religious organization administrator; b. Mineral, Ill., Aug. 17, 1912; d. Thomas Benton and Maude Carrie (Riley) B.; m. John Howard Goddard; children: David Bryan, Joan Kathryn. BA, Judson Coll., 1966; MS, No. Ill. U., 1973; LittD (hon.), Calif. Grad. Sch. Theology, 1981. Lic. Marriage and family therapist, Fla., Colo. Clin. counselor Warrenville (Ill.) Med. Clinic, 1958-78; pres. Christian Counseling Ministries, Buena Vista, Colo., 1978—, lectr., cons., 1978—. Auhtor: Can I Hope Again, 1971, Somebody Else's Girl, Connie, Bob Bronson; contbr. articles to jours. Mem. Am. Assn. Marriage and Family Therapists (clin.), Nat. Assn. Social Workers, Am. Assn. Counseling and Devel. Republican. Baptist. Avocations: writing, music, hiking, fishing, travel. Home: PO Box 789 Buena Vista CO 81211

GODFREY, A. A., minister, religious organization administrator. Pastor, pres. Papua New Guinea Union Mission of Seventh-day Adventists, Lae. Office: Union Mission Seventh-day, Adventist, POB 86, Lae Papua New Guinea*

GODFREY, DARRELL DANIEL, pastor; b. Emporia, Kans., Jan. 17, 1958; s. Dan S. and Alma Laverne (Dicks) G.; m. Karen Elaine Lawrence, June 4, 1978; children: Anna Danielle, Abraham David, Arletta Dawn, Alyssa Debra, Aubrey Denaé. BFA in Rhetoric and Communication, Emporia State U., 1980, BSE in Speech, 1981; cert. in secondary edn., Calvary Bible Coll., 1984, advanced Bibl. studies cert., 1984; MA in Christian Edn., Dallas Theol. Sem., 1989. Ordained to ministry Evang. Free Ch. Am., 1987; cert. secondary elem. tchr., Nebr. Instr. speech Calvary Bible Coll., 1982-84; youth pastor Flint Hills Bapt. Ch., Osage City, Kans., 1980-82; pastor Climax (Kans.) United Meth. Ch., 1976-79, Neal (Kans.) Evang. Free Ch., 1984-87, Faith Bible Ch., North Platte, Nebr., 1989-91; co-pastor Grace Community Bible Ch., North Platte, 1991—. Mem. sch. bd. Mt. Zion Christian High Sch., North Platte, 1990—, coach basketball, 1990: coach Am. Youth Soccer Orgn., North Platte, 1989—. Mem. Evang. Free Ch. Am. Ministerial Assn., Evang. Tchr. Tng. Assn., Nat. Eagle Scout Assn. Republican. Home: 122 N Elder Ave North Platte NE 69101 Office: Grace Community Bible Ch 1021 S Buffalo Bill Ave North Platte NE 69101 *SIN Starts with an S; ends with an N. The only difference between SiN and SuN is that I am in Sin, not U. One thing I have learned in ministry is that if you don't stand up for what you believe to be true, you're going to get what you know to be false shoved down your throat.*

GODFREY, HAROLD WILLIAM, bishop. Bishop of Uruguay, Anglican Communion, Montevideo. Office: Casa Episcopal, Francisco Araucho 1287, 11300 Montevideo Uruguay*

GODFREY, JAMES MICHAEL, minister; b. Marshall, Tex., Mar. 31, 1955; s. Billie James and Mary Beth (Peden) Godfrey; m. Mary Susan Ellis, Aug. 7, 1976; children: Jonathan Michael, Lauren Elizabeth. AA, Kilgore Coll., 1975; B in Music Edn., Baylor U., 1977; MRE, Southwestern Bapt. Sem., 1981, MA in Religious Edn., 1983, D Ministry, 1991. Ordained to ministry Bapt. Ch., 1977. Minister to youth Meadowbrook Bapt. Ch., Waco, Tex., 1975-78; minister of music, youth Burton Hill Bapt. Ch., Ft. Worth, 1978-79; minister to youth Birdville Bapt. Ch., Ft. Worth, 1979-81, Fielder Rd. Bapt. Ch., Arlington, 1981-84, Mobberly Bapt. Ch., Longview, Tex., 1984—; lectr. to various colls., schs., camps, Tex., 1978—. Contbr. to publs. of Sunday Sch. Bd. , So. Bapt. Conv. Recipient Outstanding Young Man of Am. award U.S. Jaycees, 1982, 85. Mem. Nat. Network of Youth Ministries, Greater Longview Orgn. Bus. and Edn. (self-esteem com.), Gamma Beta Phi. Baptist. Avocations: reading, computers. Office: Mobberly Bapt Ch 1400 S Mobberly Ave Longview TX 75602

GODINEZ FLORES, RAMON, auxiliary bishop; b. Jamay, Jalisco, Mexico, Apr. 18, 1936; s. Ortega J. Cleofas G. and Maria del Refugio (Flores). Lic. in Philosophy, Sem. Guadalajara, (Jalisco, Mexico); theology degree, U. Gregoriana, Rome, postgrad. in canon law. Ordained priest Roman Catholic Ch., 1959, aux. bishop, 1980. Prof., superior Diocesan Sem., Guadalajara; chaplain religious communities, Templo de San Jorge, Vallarta-San Jorge, Guadalajara; pastor Parroco de Nuestra Senora de la Luz, Guadalajara; sec. Archdiocese of Guadalajara, 1972-80, aux. bishop, 1980—; secretario general del Episcopado Mexicano, 1992—. Contbr. articles to religious jours. Home: Garibaldi n 770, Guadalajara Jalisco 44290, Mexico Office: Obisop Auxiliar de Guadalajara, Liceo 17, Guadalajara Jalisco 44100, Mexico

GODSEY, JOHN DREW, minister, theology educator emeritus; b. Bristol, Tenn., Oct. 10, 1922; s. William Clinton and Mary Lynn (Corns) G.; m. Emalee Caldwell, June 26, 1943; children: Emalee Lynn Godsey Murphy, John Drew, Suzanne Godsey Douglas, Gretchen Godsey Brownley. B.S., Va. Poly. Inst. and State U., 1947; B.D., Drew U., 1953; D.Theol., U. Basel, Switzerland, 1960. Ordained to ministry United Methodist Ch., 1952. Instr. systematic theology, asst. dean Drew U., Madison, N.J., 1956-59, asst. prof., 1959-64, assoc. prof., 1964-66, prof., 1966-68; prof., assoc. dean Wesley Theol. Sem., Washington, 1968-71, prof. systematic theology, 1971-88; emeritus prof. Wesley Theol. Sem., 1988—; Fulbright scholar U. Goettingen, W. Germany, 1964-65. Author: The Theology of Dietrich Bonhoeffer, 1960, Karl Barth's Table Talk, 1963, Preface to Bonhoeffer, 1965, Introduction and Epilogue to Karl Barth's How I Changed My Mind, 1966, The Promise of H. Richard Niebuhr, 1970; co-editor: Ethical Responsibility: Bonhoeffer's Legacy to the Churches, 1981. Mem. Montgomery County Fair Housing Assn., Md. Served with AUS, 1943-46. Am. Assn. Theol. Schs. faculty fellow, 1964-65. Mem. Am. Acad. Religion, Am. Theol. Soc. (pres. 1985-86), Bibl. Theologians, Internat. Bonhoeffer Soc. (editor newsletter 1989—), Karl Barth Soc. N. Am., New Haven Theol. Discussion Group, Common Cause, Omicron Delta Kappa, Phi Kappa Phi, Alpha Zeta. Democrat. Home: 8306 Bryant Dr Bethesda MD 20817 Office: Wesley Theol Sem 4500 Massachusetts Ave NW Washington DC 20016 *My goal has been to serve others with integrity, to do every job to the best of my ability, and to respect and further the rights and welfare of my fellow creatures on planet earth. Thus should my life be a testimony to my faith.*

GODSEY, KYLE LEE, minister; b. Ponca City, Okla., Apr. 23, 1963; s. Charles Edward and Laura Belle (Hickman) G. BS, Okla. State U., 1985, MA, 1987. Youth minister First United Meth. Ch., Hugo, Okla., 1986-88; dir. youth and program Wickline United Meth. Ch., Midwest City, Okla., 1988—. Author: Object Lessons About God, 1991; contbr. articles to profl. jours. Office: Wickline United Meth Ch 417 Mid America Blvd Midwest City OK 73110

GODSIL, RICHARD WILLIAM, minister; b. Estherville, Iowa, Mar. 8, 1953; s. Richard Lee and Shirley Ann (Diamond) G.; m. Laurel Christine Webster, July 17, 1971; children: Richard II, Joshua, Rebekah. AA, Okaloosa Walton Jr. Coll., 1977; BS, Okla. Christian Coll., 1980; postgrad., Pepperdine U., 1984. Ordained to ministry Christian Ch., 1989. Youth min. Ch. of Christ, Derby, Kans., 1981-82; assoc. min. Ch. of Christ, Redlands, Calif., 1982-84; youth min. religious edn. Twin Cities Christian Ch., Oceanside, Calif., 1987-88; assoc. min. Montrose (Colo.) Christian Ch., 1988—; pres. Colo. Christian Concerts, Montrose, 1990—. V.p. Gallerya Youth Ctr., Montrose, 1990; advisor home econs. bd. high sch., Montrose, 1990—. Sgt. USAF, 1971-75. Named Young Min. of Yr. Standard Pub. Co., 1989. Mem. Mountain Area Christian Educators (v.p. Montrose chpt. 1989—), Assn. Montrose Chs. (pres. 1990), Nat. Network Youth Mins., Campus Life Club (bd. dirs. 1987 Oceanside). Republican. Home: 1030 Highland St Montrose CO 81401 Office: Montrose Christian Ch 2351 Sunnyside Montrose CO 81401 *Allowing young persons to see themselves as worthwhile beings in a confused world is the goal of my ministry. Letting them see that God loves them unconditionally, as they are now and what they can become. This pursuit keeps me up at night, causes tears to fall and brings joy to my heart. What a way to live for God!.*

GODWIN, JANICE RIVERO, clergywoman; b. N.Y.C., Sept. 24, 1953; d. Angel Vincent and Laura Choate (Quinn) Rivero; m. J. Badger Godwin, Nov. 19, 1977; children: Kristen, Ryan. BS, Coll. William and Mary, 1975; MDiv, Wesley Theol. Sem., 1980. Ordained to ministry Meth. Ch., 1981. Pastor Cedar Grove United Meth. Ch., Winchester, Va., 1980-81, Arcola (Va.)-Ryan United Meth. Ch., 1981-84, Messiah United Meth. Ch., Springfield, Va., 1984—. Mem. Va. Conf. Bd. Ordained Ministers. Avocation: music. Office: Messiah United Meth Ch 6215 Rolling Rd Springfield VA 22152

GOERGEN, DONALD JOSEPH, priest, religious organization administrator; b. Remsen, Iowa, Aug. 16, 1943; s. Julius and Sylvia (Wilhelmi) G. BA in Philosophy, French, Latin, Loras Coll., 1965; MA in Theology, Aquinas Inst., Dubuque, Iowa, 1968, PhD, 1972. Joined Dominican Order of Preachers, Roman Cath. Ch., 1971, ordained priest, 1975. Provincial Cen. Dominican Province, Chgo. Author: The Sexual Celibate, 1975, The Power of Love, 1979, A Theology of Jesus: Vol. I: The Mission and Ministry of Jesus, 1986, Vol. II: The Death and Resurrection of Jesus, 1987, Vol. III: The Jesus of Christian History, 1991. Mem. Cath. Theol. Soc. Am., Am. Acad. Religion. Address: Dominican Provincial Office 1909 S Ashland Ave Chicago IL 60608-2994

GOERING, LEONARD LOWELL, clergyman, psychotherapist, philosophy educator; b. McPherson, Kans., June 22, 1938; s. Ellis Elbert and Esther Elva (Wedel) G.; m. Imogene Helen Ediger, June 10, 1957 (div. 1969); children: Preston, Angela; m. Jane Ellen Kurtz, Dec. 15, 1979; children: David, Jonathan, Rebecca. PhB, Northwestern U., 1964; postgrad., Northeastern Ill. U., 1969-71; MDiv, McCormick Theol. Sem., 1973; postgrad., Vanderbilt U., 1975-77. Ordained to ministry Presbyn. Ch., 1977. Campus minister United Ministries in Higher Edn., Emporia, 1973-75; instr. philosophy, coll. chaplain Coll. Emporia, Kans., 1973-74, Univ. Christian Ministries, Carbondale, Ill., 1977-80; pastor United Presbyn. Ch., Trinidad, Colo., 1981—; instr. philosophy Trinidad State Jr. Coll., 1983—; pres. Family Guidance Services, Trinidad, 1985-87; exec. dir. Family Guidance Services, Trinidad, 1987—. Editorial adv. bd. Collegiate Press. Coord. congl. dist. Bread for the World, Illinois, 1979-81; chmn. local bd. Emergency Food & Shelter Program Fed. Emergency Mgmt. Agy., Las Animas County, Colo., 1983-86; behavioral specialist human rights com. So. Colo. Devel. Disabilities Svcs. Mem. Acad. Parish Clergy, Assn. Mental Health Clergy, Am. Assn. Profl. Hypnotherapists, Trinidad Ministerial Assn., Internat. Platform Assn. Lodge: Kiwanis. Avocations: sailing, hiking, wilderness camping. Home: 721 Pine St Trinidad CO 81082 Office: United Presbyn Ch 224 N Commercial Trinidad CO 81082

GOETCHIUS, EUGENE VAN NESS, clergyman; b. Augusta, Ga., Mar. 26, 1921; s. Eugene Foster and Agnes Louise (Stelling) G.; m. Ann Oliver Kirkpatrick, Dec. 17, 1955; children—Charles L.T., Nathaniel K., Edward V.N., John M. B.A., U. Va., 1941, M.S., 1947, M.A., 1948, Ph.D., 1949; B.D., Episcopal Theol. Sch., Cambridge, Mass., 1952; Th.D., Union Theol. Sem., N.Y.C., 1963; postgrad., U. Zurich, Switzerland, 1964, Mansfield Coll., Oxford, Eng., 1970-71. Master Woodberry Forest Sch., 1947-49; instr. math. Tufts U., 1950-52; instr. religion Trinity Coll., Hartford, Conn., 1952-54; fellow, tutor Gen. Theol. Sem., N.Y.C., 1954-56; ordained to ministry Episcopal Ch., 1952; asst. Grace Ch., N.Y.C., 1954-55; asst. chaplain Columbia, 1955-56; head dept. math. Am. Acad. in Athens, Greece, 1957; asst. prof. N.T. Episcopal Theol. Sch., 1957-60, asso. prof., 1960-63, prof. Bibl. langs., 1963-89, Edmund Swett Rousmaniere prof. lit. and interpretation N.T., 1978-89; emeritus, 1989; lectr. Hellenistic Greek Harvard, 1957-58, 77-81; priest assoc. Ch. of the Holy Spirit, Wayland, Mass.; dir. Inst. Bibl. Langs. and Linguistics, Vanderbilt U., summer 1968; vis. prof. Greek Andover Newton Theol. Sch., 1968; vis. prof. Hebrew Boston U., 1969; mem. heraldry com. Episcopal Ch.; instr. R.I. Diocesan Sch. for Ministry, 1989—. Author: The Language of the New Testament, 1965; co-author: Teaching the Biblical Languages, 1967, The Gifts of God, 1985; translator: Exegetical Method (by O. Kaiser and W. Kummel). Trustee Boston Theol. Inst. Mem. Studiorum Novi Testamenti Societas, Schweizerische Heraldische Gesellschaft, New Eng. Historic-Geneal. Soc. (mem. council, chmn. com. heraldry), Phi Beta Kappa, Phi Epsilon Pi (asso.). Clubs: Odd Volumes, Barnstable Yacht. Home: 4260 Main St Cummaquid MA 02637 *Belief in the importance of one's work is the basic ingredient of any kind of success.*

GOETZ, ROGER MELVIN, minister; b. Chgo., May 17, 1940; s. Charles Albert and Sidonia Helene (Heck) G.; m. Betty Jean Bokelheide, Nov. 22, 1969; 1 child, Anne Katharine. BS in Chemistry, Iowa State U., Ames, 1962, BS in Math., 1967; MDiv, Concordia Theol. Sem., 1967; STM, Luth. Theol. Sem., 1972. Asst. pastor, dir. music Gethsemane Luth. Ch., St. Paul, 1968-80; asst. pastor, minister of music St. John's Luth. Ch., Topeka, 1980—; instr. Walther Luth. Jr. High Sch., St. Paul, 1968-80; archivist Kans. Dist. Luth. Ch.-Mo. Synod, Topeka, 1985-89, chair worship com., 1985—; organ recitalist various Luth. chs., 1970—. Author: The Descendants of Johann Georg Götz, 1976, Double Cousins by the Dozens, 1982; editor: A Century of Grace: Centennial History of the Kansas District, 1888-1988, 1988. Mem. Am. Guild Organists (chpt. pres. 1983-84), Phi Mu Alpha, Alpha Chi Sigma. Office: St Johns Luth Ch 901 Fillmore Topeka KS 66606 *In my life I have found that the less I try to control things and people and rather leave things in the hands of my loving God, the more God brings gifts and joy into my life.*

GOFF, JIM, religious organization administrator. Moderator Separate Bapts. in Christ, Louisville. Office: Separate Bapts in Christ 1020 Gagel Ave Louisville KY 40216*

GOFF, KENNETH ODELL, minister; b. Kreola, Miss., Nov. 11, 1953; s. Hubert Joseph and Ella Mae (Mizelle) G.; m. Rebecca Lynn Griffin, Jan. 5, 1973; children: Dena, Dustin. BA in Religion, Mobile Coll., 1980; postgrad., New Orleans Bapt. Theol. Sem., 1989—. Ordained to ministry So. Bapt. Conv., 1975. Music min. Benndale (Miss.) Bapt. Ch., 1975-76; pastor Antioch Bapt. Ch., Leakesville, 1976-77, Cloverdale Bapt. Ch., Grand Bay, 1977-80, Antioch Bapt. Ch., Florence, 1980-83, Faith Bapt. Ch., Harrisville, 1983, Four Mile Creek Bapt. Ch., Escatawpa, 1983—; sec. Pastor's Conf., Green County Bapt. Assn., Leakesville, 1975-76; chmn. crusade prayer Jackson County Bapt. Assn., Pascagoula, Miss., 1984-85, chmn. bldg. com., 1990-91; del. So. Bapt. Conv., Nashville, 1980—, Miss. Bapt. Conv., 1980—. Author: Books of the Bible, 1990. Spiritual advisor exec. com. PTA, Escatawpa, 1987-89. Mem. Gulf Coast Jr. Coll. Alumni Assn. Republican. Home: 3801 Coventry Dr Pascagoula MS 39567 Office: Four Mile Creek Bapt Ch Hwy 613 N Escatawpa MS 39552

GOFORTH, KENNETH H., JR., minister; b. Covington, Tenn., Mar. 13, 1947; s. Kenneth H. Sr. and Verna M. (Smith) G.; m. Pamela Jo Agee, June 28, 1969; children: Leandra Joy, Amy Elizabeth. MusB, Union U., 1969; M in Ch. Music, So. Bapt. Theol. Sem., Louisville, 1976. Min. music and edn. 1st Bapt. Ch., Selmer, Tenn., 1970-74; dir. music Jeffersontown (Ky.) Christian Ch., 1974-75; min. music and youth Scottsville (Ky.) Bapt. Ch., 1975—; pres. Ky. Bapt. Mus. Assn., Middletown, 1988; mem. exec. bd. Ky. Bapt. Conv., Middletown, 1990—. Chmn. Allen County Drug Coun., Scottsville, 1980; pres. Allen County Arts Coun., 1986, Allen County Band Boosters, 1990—; bd. dirs. Community Band and Chorus, Scottsville, 1984-88. Recipient Outstanding Citizen award Scottsville Women's Club, 1980, Allen County Jaycess, 1987. Mem. So. Bapt. Ch. Music Conf., Ky. Bapt. Ch. Music Conf., Am. Guild of English Handbell Ringers, Am. Choral Dirs. Assn., Rotary. Home: 514 Hill St Scottsville KY 42164 Office: Scottsville Bapt Ch 301 E Main St Scottsville KY 42164

GOINS, JAMES ALLEN, minister; b. Pitts., Nov. 20, 1930; s. William Dorsey and Ida Marion (Washington) G.; m. Katherine Ballou, Aug. 17, 1950; children—James A., Jesse D., Pamela R., Cynthia L., Kevin L. Student U. Pitts., 1955-65; M.Div., Colgate U., 1969, M.Th., 1971. Ordained to ministry Am. Bapt. Chs. in U.S.A., 1965; cert. chaplain Council of Chs., N.Y., 1971. Asst. pastor Macedonia Bapt. Ch., Pitts., 1954-65; pastor, chaplain Second Bapt. Ch., LeRoy, N.Y., 1965-69; pastor Calvary St. Andrews Ch., Rochester, N.Y., 1970-73, Trinity Emmanuel Ch., Rochester, 73-74; nat. staff Am. Bapt. Ch. Progressive Nat. Bapt. Conv., Valley Forge, Pa., 1974-76; chaplain Monroe County Jail, Rochester, 1982—, Migrant Ministries, Rochester, 1966-69; assoc. pastor Mt. Olivet Bapt. Ch., Rochester, 1969—, min. in residence, 1990—; dir., organizer Soul Sch., Rochester, 1968-74; city ministries dir. Episcopal Diocese/Presbytery Genesee Valley, Rochester, 1970-74; Human rights specialist Exec. Dept. State of N.Y., Rochester and Buffalo, 1976-82; dir., organizer Early Childhood Edn. Ctr., Rochester, 1973-74. Active Urban League, Rochester. Recipient Superior Accomplishment award U.S. Post Office, 1965; citation, nat. dir. Am. Bapt. Ch./Progressive Nat. Bapt. Conv., 1974, 77. Mem. Genesee Ecumenical Ministries (bd. dirs. 1970-74), Rochester Area Ministers Conf. (sec. 1970-73), Black Am. Bapt. Caucus (N.Y. State), Nat. Sheriff's Assn. (charter mem. chaplain's div.), N.Y. State Sheriff's Assn. (hon.). Office: Monroe County Sheriff's Dept 130 S Plymouth Ave Rochester NY 14614 *As a minister of God in Christ Jesus I am prepared to die for what I preach and stand for—before I would let what I preach and stand for die.*

GOINS, SISTER ROSEMARIE, religious order provincial superior, artist; b. Denver, Sept. 29, 1940; d. Joe Goins and Rose Philomena (Decker) Keyes. BA, Madonna U., 1963; MA, Loyola U., L.A., 1971. Joined Felician-Franciscan Sisters of S.W., Roman Cath. Ch., 1958; cert. humanities, art, English, philosophy tchr., Calif. Tchr. St. Anne Elem. Sch., Broken Arrow, Okla., 1963-64, Pomona (Calif.) Cath. High Sch., 1964-77; vocation dir., provincial sec., coun. mem. Felician Sisters of S.W., Rio Rancho, N.Mex., 1976-89, provincial superior, 1989—; mem. justice and peace com. N.Mex. Conf. Chs., Albuquerque, 1983-89; coord. deanery A Coun. Men and Women Religious, Archdiocese of Santa Fe, 1985-88, vice-chairperson, 1987-88, chairperson, 1988-89; mem. maj. superiors' conf. in N.Mex. and Calif; gen. del. to Felician Sisters Gen. Chpt., Rome, 1988, mem. provincial superiors' conf. Mem. justice and peace com. Bread for the World, Albuquerque, 1977-89, Network, Rio Rancho, 1979—. Mem. Leadership Conf. Womem Religious (chairperson conv. 1991), Franciscan Fedn. 3d Order Men and Women Religious. Home and Office: 4210 Meadowlark Ln SE Rio Rancho NM 87124

GOKEE, DONALD LEROY, clergyman, author; b. Lansing, Mich., Aug. 8, 1933; s. Richard Alden and June Elizabeth (Colenso) G.; B.A., Mich. State U. and Temple U., 1958; postgrad. (A. Morehouse and William Walker scholar) George Washington U., 1960-64, Va. Theol. Sem., 1964-65, Columbia Theol. Sem., 1968, New Coll., U. Edinburgh (Scotland), 1975, Frankfurt U. (Germany), 1977, U. Athens (Greece), 1978, MA cum laude, 1982, PhD magna cum laude, 1983; m. Maxine Pawlik Adkins, Apr. 21, 1974; children—Douglas Richard, Charles Jeffrey, Mary Beth, Jessica Lynn. Ordained to ministry Presbyn. Ch., 1965; dir. Christian edn. Central Presbyn. Ch., Chattanooga, 1958-59, Fairlington Presbyn. Ch., Alexandria, Va., 1959-66; asso. pastor Pine Shores Presbyn. Ch., Sarasota, Fla., 1966-69; pastor Conway Presbyn. Ch., Orlando, Fla., 1969—; frequent speaker at colls. and confs.; chaplain Orange County Juvenile Ct., 1969-73; mem. council Synod of Fla., 1972-75; mem. ecumenical coordinating team as rep. Presbyn. Ch. U.S., 1977-81; 1st ann. Gingerich meml. lectr. Goshen (Ind.) Coll.; vis. prof. So. Coll. Mem. Nat. Task Force on Criminal Justice and Prison Reform, 1976-82. Author: It's a Love-Haunted World, 1985. Contbg. editor Pulpit Digest, 1986—. Recipient certificate of merit for distinguished service to Christ, ch. and community, 1970; In-God-We-Trust award Family Found. of Am., 1980; Key to City, Orlando, 1981. Mem. Ministerial Assn. (past pres.). Home: 3026 Carmia Dr Orlando FL 32806 Office: 4300 Lake Margaret Dr Orlando FL 32812

GOLD, LEONARD SINGER, librarian, translator; b. Bklyn., July 3, 1934; s. Hyman B. and Gertrude (Singer) G.; m. Stella Schmidt, June 5, 1960; children: Yael, Dalia. B.A., McGill U., Montreal, Que., Can., 1956; M.S. in Library Service, Columbia U., 1966; M.A., NYU, 1967, Ph.D., 1975. Cert. profl. librarian, N.Y. Tchr. high sch. Kiryat Hayim, Israel, 1960-61; tchr. Hugim High Sch., Haifa, Israel, 1961-63; tech. asst. N.Y. Pub. Lib., N.Y.C., 1963-66, chief Jewish div., 1971—; Dorot chief librarian Jewish div., bibliographer in Jewish studies N.Y. Pub. Library, N.Y.C., 1987—, asst. dir. Jewish, Oriental and Slavonic studies, 1980-88; chmn. Jewish and Middle East studies program com. Rsch. Librs. Group, Inc., 1989-91; curator hist. exhibit. Translator: (Nathan Shaham) The Other Side of the Wall, 3 novellas, 1983; editor: A Sign and A Witness: 2000 Years of Hebrew Books and Illuminated Manuscripts, 1988 (Nat. Jewish Book award in Visual Arts category 1989); assoc. editor Jewish Book Annual, 1979—; contbr. to bibliog. publs. Astor fellow, 1986-87. Mem. Assn. Jewish Librs. (pres. 1974-76), Coun. Archives and Rsch. Librs. in Jewish Studies (pres. 1978-80), Jewish Book Coun. (v.p. 1980-90, pres. 1990—), Assn. Jewish Studies, Rsch. Librs. Group Inc. (chair Jewish and Middle East studies program com. 1989-91, mem. programs adv. group 1991—), Jewish Publ. Soc. (mem. editorial com. 1986—). Office: NY Pub Libr Jewish Div Fifth Ave and 42d St Rm 84 New York NY 10018

GOLDBERG, ALAN SAMUEL, cultural organization administrator; b. Boston, Apr. 23, 1953; s. Herman I. and Selma (Slotnick) G.; m. Cynthia L. Block, May 29, 1976; children: Meredith H., Matthew I. BA, U. Hartford, 1975; MSW, U. Md., Balt., 1977. Cert. social worker, Ohio. Regional dir. B'nai Brith Youth Orgn., Cherry Hill, N.J., 1977-80; assoc. exec. dir. Jewish Community Ctrs. of Delaware Valley, Trenton, N.J., 1980-84, Youngstown (Ohio) Area Jewish Fedn., 1987—; exec. dir. Jewish Community Ctr., Youngstown, 1984—. Bd. dirs. Liberty Ednl. Endowment Fund, Youngstown, 1988—, Ballet Western Res., Youngstown, 1991—. Recipient Silver 3 Community Svc. award KYW-TV, Phila., 1979. Mem. Assn. Jewish Ctr. Profls. (regional pres. 1986-88, nat. treas. 1988-90), B'nai B'rith. Office: Jewish Community Ctr PO Box 449 Youngstown OH 44501

GOLDBERG, BERTRAM J., social agency administrator; b. Bklyn., Oct. 23, 1942; s. Ralph Goldberg and Geraldine Janith (Herzog) Gerber; m. Lorri Ann Schwartz, Oct. 19, 1980; children: Ilissa, Andrea, Joshua, Randi. BA, Fairleigh Dickinson U., 1964; MSW, U. Pa., 1966. Diplomate Acad. of Cert. Social Workers. Tween worker Bernard Horwich Jewish Community Ctr., Chgo., 1966-68; dir. group svcs. Seattle Jewish Community Ctr., 1968-70; chief centralized intake Eastside Mental Health Ctr., Bellevue, Wash., 1970-73; coord. coll. age youth svcs. Jewish Fedn., Chgo., 1973-74; exec. dir. Jewish Family Svc., Allentown, Pa., 1974-77, Orange County, Calif., 1977-86; exec. dir. Assn. Jewish Family and Children's Agys., Kendall Park, N.J., 1986—. Mem. Nat. Assn. Social Workers, Assn. Jewish Family and Children's Agy. Profls. (bd. dirs. 1977—), Conf. Jewish Community Svcs. (officer 1987—). Democrat. Jewish. Avocations: computers, reading. Office: Assn Jewish Family and Childrens Agys 3084 Hwy 27 Ste 1 Kendall Park NJ 08824

GOLDBERG, DAVID, religious organization administrator. Pres. Delegacion de Associaciones Israelitas Argentinas, Buenos Aires. Office: Delegacion Asociaciones, Israelitas, Pasteur 633, 5, Buenos Aires Argentina*

GOLDBERG, DON HARVEY, cantor; b. N.Y.C., Oct. 11, 1941; s. Murray Ted and Helen (Solomon) G.; m. Barbara Jane Takce, July 4, 1965; children: Andrea, Richard, Stacey. BA, Bklyn. Coll., 1968, MA, 1972. Asst. cantor Union Temple, Bklyn., 1973-76; cantor New Milford (N.J.), 1976-78, South Baldwin (N.Y.) Jewish Ctr., 1978-80, Merrick (N.Y.) Jewish Ctr., 1980-81, Beth Sholom, Amityville, N.Y., 1983—; English tchr. Abraham Lincoln High Sch., Bklyn., 1970—. With USNG, 1960-63. Mem. Jewish Ministers and Cantors Assn., Jewish Genealogy Assn. of N.Y. Office: Beth Sholom Ctr 79 County Line Rd Amityville NY 11701

GOLDBERG, HILLEL, rabbi, educator; b. Denver, Jan. 10, 1946; s. Max and Miriam (Harris) G.; m. Elaine Silberstein, May 19, 1969; children: Tehilla, Temima, Mattis, Shayna, Tiferet. BA, Yeshiva U., 1969; MA, Brandeis U., 1972, PhD, 1978. Ordained rabbi, 1976. Lectr. Machzeke Torah Inst., Brookline, Mass., 1971-71, 75, Jerusalem Coll. for Women, 1973-75, 77, The Hebrew U., 1978-85, Jerusalem Torah Coll., 1979-82; Halakhic adviser Torah MaMidbar, Santa Fe, 1986—; exec. editor Intermountain Jewish News, Denver, 1966—; bd. dirs. Rofeh Internat., Boston. Author: Israel Salanter: Text, Structure, Idea (Acad. Book of Yr. 1982), The Fire Within, 1987, Between Berlin and Slobodka, 1989, Illuminating the Generations, 1991; editor: In Honor of Walter Wurzburger, 1989; assoc. editor Tradition, 1988—; contbg. editor Jewish Action, 1987—; mem. editorial bd. Jewish Tradition, Jerusalem, 1990—. Vol. Head Start, Oakland, Calif., 1964-65, Harlem, N.Y., 1965-66; founder Torah Community Project, Denver, 1986—. Grantee Meml. Found. for Jewish Culture, 1972-74. Mem. Am. Hist. Assn., Am. Jewish Press Assn. (Rockower awards 1983, 85, 89, rec. sec. 1989-91), Rabbinical Coun. Am., Nat. Assn. Rudimental Drummers, Assn. for Jewish Studies. Office: Intermountain Jewish News 1275 Sherman St #214 Denver CO 80203

GOLDBRUNNER, JOSEF, theology educator; b. Munich, Bavaria, Germany; s. Josef and Kreszenz (Wolferseder) G. PhD, U. Munich, 1933, ThD, 1939. Ordained priest Roman Cath. Ch., 1936. Pastor, Archdiocese of Munich, 1936-58; prof. theology Paedagogische Hochschule, Berlin, 1958-62, Saarbruecken, 1962-68, prof. pastoral theology U. Regensburg State U. Bavaria, 1968-77, prof. emeritus, 1978—. Home: Groebenseeweg 4, D-8124 Seeshaupt Federal Republic of Germany Office: Univ Regensburg, State of Bavaria, D-8400 Regensburg Federal Republic of Germany *Christianity is a religion of future. This means earth and mankind are running towards the second coming of Christ. This future effects like a magnet all psychic abilities—if this prophecy is taken seriously.*

GOLDEN, GERALD SAMUEL, medical educator; b. Newark, N.J., June 8, 1935; s. Clement Harold and Jeanette (Bellat) G.; m. Deborah Ann Berlatsky, March 22, 1959 (dec. 1984); children: Leah Rachel, Ruth Naomi; m. Constance Reisa Abramson, Jan. 26, 1985. AB, Princeton U., 1957; MD, Columbia U., 1961. Diplomate Am. Bd. Pediatrics, Am. Bd. Psychiatry and Neurology. Asst. prof. of neurology and pediatrics Albert Einstein Coll. of Medicine, Bronx, N.Y., 1967-73; assoc. prof. Albert Einstein Coll. of Medicine, Bronx, 1973-77; prof. pediatrics and neurology U. Tex., Galveston, 1977-84; prof. pediatrics and neurology, dir. ctr. for devel disabl. U. Tenn., Memphis, 1984—. Author: Textbook of Pediatric Neurology; assoc. editor: Pediatric Neurology Jour., 1987—, Jour. of Devel. and Behavioral Pediatrics, 1987—, Jour. Epilepsy, 1987—; contbr. numerous articles to profl. jours. Bd. dirs. Harwood Day Tng. Ctr., Memphis, 1987— Memphis-Shelby County Assn. for Retarded Citizens, 1987—, Memphis Oral Sch. for the Deaf, 1987—, Temple Israel Memphis, 1989—. Recipient fed. grant Adminstrn. on Devel. Disabilities, 1990, Dept. of Human Svcs., 1990. Fellow Am. Acad. Pediatrics (neurology sect. head 1981-83), Am. Assn. Mental Deficiency (v.p. for medicine, 1984-86); mem. Am. Assn. U. Affiliated Programs (bd. dirs. 1987—, pres. elect 1988-89, pres. 1989-90). Democrat. Jewish. Avocations: amateur radio, travel. Office: Boling Ctr for Developmental Disabilities 711 Jefferson Memphis TN 38105

GOLDEN, JONATHAN LOHR, minister; b. Medford, Mass., Oct. 27, 1954; s. Jacob Bowles and Jane Eleanor (Lohr) G. BA, Duke U., 1977; MDiv, Duke Div. sch., 1981; MA, Holy Names Coll., 1987. Ordained to ministry United Meth. Ch. as elder, 1983. Min. Avery's Creek-Fanning Chapel United Meth. Ch., 1981-86, Mt. Vernon United Meth. Ch., 1987—; pres. Skyland (N.C.) Arden-Fletcher Emergency Assistance, 1983-84. Contbr. articles to profl. jours. Democrat.

GOLDEN, PAUL LLOYD, priest; b. San Francisco, Jan. 4, 1939; s. John Henry and Julia Lee (Clements) G. BA, St. Mary's Sem., Perryville, Mo., 1961; MDiv, De Andreis Sem., Lemont, Ill., 1965; JCL, Gregorian U., Rome, 1967; JCD, St. Thomas U., Rome, 1971. Ordained priest Roman Cath. Ch., 1965. Prof. canon law Kenrick Sem., St. Louis, 1968-77, St. Louis Univ. Div. Sch., 1968-71, 75; dir. formation Kenrick Sem., St. Louis, 1970-77; pres., rector St. Thomas Sem., Denver, 1977-84; dir. Inst. Leadership, DePaul Univ., Chgo., 1984-89; assoc. v.p. pub. svc. DePaul Univ., Chgo., 1989—; bd. dirs. St. Louis Theol. Consortium, 1970-74; mem. steering com., bishop's com. on priestly formation, Nat. Conf. Cath. Bishops, 1978-81; trustee St. Thomas Sem., Denver, 1984—. Contbg. author: The Code of Canon Law: A Text and Commentary, 1984. Mem. Canon Law Soc. Am. (pres. 1988-89), Nat. Cath. Edn. Assn. Home: 2233 N Kenmore Ave Chicago IL 60614 Office: DePaul Univ 25 E Jackson Blvd Chicago IL 60604

GOLDEN, ROBERT IRVING, minister; b. Panama Canal Zone, Sept. 15, 1947; s. Bob Irving and Julia (Kovac) G.; m. Mayr Nell Boles, July 6, 1974 (dec. Feb. 1984); m. Janet Fox Travis, May 3, 1986; stepchildren: Jeffrey Allen Fox, Todd Wayne Fox. BS, U. So. Miss., 1973; MDiv, New Orleans Bapt. Theol. Sem., 1976; D. Ministry, So. Bapt. Theol. Sem., 1985. Ordained to ministry So. Bapt. Convention, 1974. Pastor Berwick Bapt. Ch., Liberty, Miss., 1974-77, Crystal Springs Bapt. Ch., Tylertown, Miss., 1977-78, East Tipp Bapt. Ch., Lafayette, Ind., 1978—; mem. exec. bd. State Convention Bapt. in Ind., Indpls., 1986-89, 1st v.p., 1984-85. Capt. USNG, 1989. Mem. Wabach Valley Bapt. Assn. (moderator 1981-83, 89—), New Orleans Sem. Alumni Club (pres. 1984-85), Masons (sec. Lafayette chpt. 1990—), York Rite Sovereign Coll. North Am. (pres. Sagamore chpt. 1989-90, Order of Purple Cross 1989). Home: 14 N Lobo Ct Lafayette IN 47905-3616 Office: East Tipp Bapt Ch 5300 E 300 N Lafayette IN 47905

GOLDENBERG, NAOMI, religious studies educator; b. Bklyn. B.A. in Classics, Douglass Coll., 1969, Princeton U., 1970; M.A. in Jungian Psychology, C.G. Jung Inst., Zurich Switzerland, 1973; M.A. in Religious Studies, Yale U., 1974, M.Phil. in Religious Studies, 1975, Ph.D. in Religious Studies, 1976. Instr. psychology dept. Quinnipiac Coll., Hamden, Conn., 1974-75; teaching asst. in Jungian psychology Yale U., New Haven, 1973, teaching asst. in psychology, religion, world religion, 1973-76; instr. Yale Divinity Sch., 1976; temporary asst. prof. religion Central Mich. U., Mt. Pleasant, 1976-77; asst. prof. religious studies U. Ottawa, Ont., 1977-80, assoc. prof., 1980—; lectr. in field; participant numerous radio and TV talk shows; mem. Social Scis. and Humanities Research Council of Can., adjudication com., 1980-83; mem. consultative com. dept. religious studies, 1979-81; mem. faculty council Faculty of Arts, 1978-81; mem. Exec. Com. on Women's Studies, 1979-81, mem. numerous univ. coms. Author: The End of God-Important Directions for a Feminist Critique of Religion in the Works of Sigmund Freud and Carl Jung, 1982; Changing of the Gods-Feminism and the End of Traditional Religions, 1979. Author chpts. in books. Book reviewer. Consulting editor Anima, 1975—. Mem. editorial bd. Jour. Feminist Studies in Religion, 1983—. Contbr. numerous articles to profl. jours. Recipient merit increase for excellence in teaching U. Ottawa, 1980; Social Scis. and Humanities Research Council of Can. leave fellow, 1983-84, Woodrow Wilson fellow Yale U., 1975-76, Woodrow Wilson fellow Princeton U., 1969; grantee Social Scis. and Humanities Research Council of Can., 1979. Mem. Am. Acad. Religion (co-chmn. consultation on feminist theory and religion), Can. Psychoanalytic Soc. (guest), Phi Beta Kappa. Office: Univ Ottawa, Religious Studies, 177 Waller, Ottawa, ON Canada K1N 6N5

GOLDER, MORRIS ELLIS, minister; b. Indpls., Jan. 23, 1913; s. Earl and Margaret (Ellis) G.; m. Elizabeth Hall, Feb. 27, 1932; 1 child, Joanne; m. 2d, Betty Jane Golder, Mar. 25, 1973 (dec.); 1 child, Harold; m. Bobbie Ann McGlother, Feb. 11, 1989; children: Donnie, Alice, Bernice, Jean, Theron, Brenda, Yvonne. BA, Butler U., 1955; BDiv, M in Theology, Christian Theol. Sem., 1959. Ordained to ministry Pentecostal Assemblies of World, 1936. Pastor Bethesda Temple, St. Louis, 1935-48, Christ Temple, Indpls., 1948-53, Grace Apostolic Ch., Indpls., 1953—; bishop Pentecostal Assemblies of the World; diocesan Ky. Middle Tenn., 1972. Avocations: record and book collecting. Home: 7474 Holliday Dr W Indianapolis IN 46260

GOLDIE, ARCHIBALD RICHARDSON, religious administrator, clergyman; b. Annathill, Lanarkshire, Scotland, Sept. 26, 1925; came to U.S., 1981; m. Helen Jean Hands, Sept. 27, 1952; children—Nancy Goldie B. Long, Alex, Heather, Christine, Reginald. B.A., McMaster U., Hamilton, Ont., Can., 1956, BD, 1959; DD (hon.), Oakland City Coll., Ind., 1982; ThD (hon.), Theol. Acad. Reformed Ch. Hungary, 1986. Ordained to ministry Bapt. Ch. 1959. Pastor Nobles Meml. Bapt. Ch., Windsor, Ont., Can., 1959-63; pastor First Bapt. Ch., Dunnville, Ont., Can., 1963-65; sec. dept. ch. missions Bapt. Conv. of Ont. and Que., Toronto, Ont., Can., 1965-81; dir. div. Bapt. World Aid Bapt. World Alliance, McLean, Va., 1981—. Served with Brit. Royal Air Force, 1943-47; ETO. Home: 2309 Rosedown Dr Reston VA 22091 Office: Bapt World Alliance 6733 Curran St McLean VA 22101

GOLDIN, JUDAH, Hebrew literature educator; b. N.Y.C., Sept. 14, 1914; s. Gerson David and Rachel (Robkin) G.; m. Grace Avis Aaronson, June 21, 1938; children: Robin Elinor (dec.), David Lionel. BSS, CCNY, 1934; diploma, Sem. Coll., 1934; MA, Columbia, 1938; MHL, Jewish Theol. Sem., 1938, DHL, 1943, HLD, 1968; MA, Yale, 1958; DD, Colgate U., 1973; HLD, Jewish Inst. Religion, Hebrew Union Coll., 1986. Ordained rabbi, 1938. Lectr., vis. assoc. prof. Jewish lit. and history Duke, 1943-45; assoc. prof. religion U. Iowa, 1946-52; dean, assoc. prof. Agada Sem. Coll., Jewish Theol. Sem., 1952-58; adj. prof. religion Columbia, 1955-58; prof. Jewish studies Yale, 1958-62, prof. classical Judaica, 1962-73; prof. postbibl. Hebrew lit. U. Pa., Phila., 1973-85, prof. emeritus, 1985—. Author: The Two Versions of Abot de Rabbi Nathan, 1945, Hillel the Elder, 1946, The Period of the Talmud, 1949, The Fathers, 1955, The Living Talmud, 1957, The Three Pillars of Simeon the Righteous, 1958, A Philosophical Session in a Tannaite Academy, 1965, The End of Ecclesiastes, 1966, The Song at the Sea, 1971, Profile of Aqiba ben Joseph, 1976, The First Pair, 1980, Freedom and Restraint of Haggadah, 1986; editor: The Jewish Expression, 1970, The Munich Mekilta, 1980. Am. Philos. Soc. grantee, 1957, 71; Guggenheim fellow, 1958; Fulbright fellow, 1958, 64-65; Am. Council Learned Socs., 1978. Fellow Am. Acad. Jewish Research, Am. Acad. Arts and Scis.; mem. Am. Schs. Oriental Research, Conn. Acad. Arts and Scis., Oriental Club Pa., Phi Beta Kappa. Home: 405 Thayer Rd Swarthmore PA 19081 Office: U Pa Oriental Studies Dept Philadelphia PA 19104

GOLDMAN, ALEX J., rabbi; b. Drohitin, Poland, June 8, 1917; came to U.S., 1922; s. Julius David and Esther Sarah (Rubenstein) G.; m. Edith Borovay, Mar. 1, 1942; children: Robert, Pamela. JD, DePaul U., 1939; rabbi, Hebrew Theol. Coll., 1944. Rabbi Temple Israel, Tallahassee, Fla., 1944-46; dir. Hillel Found. Fla. Coll. for Women, Tallahassee, 1946, Temple U., Phila., 1946-54; rabbi Oak Lane Community Ctr., Phila., 1954-66, Temple Beth El, Stamford, Conn., 1966—. Author: Handbook for Jewish Family, 1958, Giants of Faith, 1963, JFK: The World Remembers, 1966, The Quotable Kennedy, 1967, The Truman Wit, 1968, Judaism Confronts Contemporary Issues, 1978, (novel) The Rabbi Is A Lady, 1988. Mem. Rabbinical Assembly N.Y. (editor proc. 1962, 63), Rotary Internat. Home: 564 Hunting Ridge Rd Stamford CT 06903 Office: Temple Beth El 350 Roxbury Rd Stamford CT 06902

GOLDMAN, EDWARD ARON, rabbi, rabbinic literature educator; b. Toledo, Mar. 25, 1941; s. Beryl Leonard and Ida Beatrice (Mostov) G.; m. Roanete B. Naamani, Dec. 18, 1966; children—Ariel, Dalia. A.B., Harvard Coll., 1963; M.A. in Hebrew Lit., Hebrew Union Coll., 1969, Ph.D., 1974. Ordained rabbi. Dir. B'nai B'rith Hillel Found., U. Cin., 1965-67; teaching fellow Hebrew Union Coll., Cin., 1969-72, mem. faculty, 1972—, asst. dean, 1981-85, faculty advisor to rabbinical students, 1990—. Editor: Jews in a Free Society: Challenges and Opportunities, 1978, translator and annotator: The Talmud of the Land of Israel, Vol. 16, Rosh Hashanah, 1988, contbr. articles to profl. jours. Bd. dirs. Jewish Fedn. Cin., 1975-81, mem. allocations com., edn. div., 1975-81, chmn. subcom. on nat. and overseas allocations, 1978-79. Recipient Mother Hirsch Meml. prize Hebrew Union Coll., 1966, Simon Lazarus Meml. prize, 1969. Mem. Central Conf. Am. Rabbis, Nat. Assn. Profs. Hebrew (exec. council), Assn. for Jewish Studies, AAUP, Soc. Bibl. Lit. Avocations: playing piano and organ; listening to music. Office: Hebrew Union Coll 3101 Clifton Ave Cincinnati OH 45220

GOLDMAN, THOMAS WILLIAM, JR., lawyer, religious organization administrator, educator; b. Meridian, Miss., June 20, 1944; s. Thomas William and Izola Mae (Godwin) G.; m. Sandra Snowden, July 15, 1966; children: Thomas William III, Michael Wayne. BA, U. Miss., 1965, JD, 1968; LLM, NYU, 1973. Bar: Miss. 1968, U.S. Supreme Ct. 1971, Okla. 1983, Va. 1986. Asst. prof. U. Tulsa, 1973-75; teaching fellow So. Meth. U., Dallas, 1975-76; assoc. dean, prof. law Miss. Coll., Jackson, 1976-81, O.W. Coburn Sch. Law, Tulsa, 1982-85; legal dir. Christian Fin. Planning Christian Broadcasting Network, Virginia Beach, Va., 1985—; adj. prof. Regent U., Virginia Beach, 1986—; ptnr. Frazier & Goldman, Attys., Virginia Beach, 1987—. Editor (newsletter) The Attorney's Report. Bd. dirs. Hampton Roads chpt. Alzheimers Assn., Norfolk, Va., 1990—. Dr. Thomas W. Goldman Day named in his honor, Gov. of Miss., 1986. Mem. ABA, Va. Bar Assn., Okla. Bar Assn., Miss. Bar Assn. Republican. Mem. So. Bapt. Convention. Home: 1017 Belvoir Ln Virginia Beach VA 23464 Office: Christian Broadcasting Network Inc CBN Ctr Christian Fin Planning Virginia Beach VA 23463

GOLDNER, ANNA F., religious education; b. Jersey City, N.J., June 12, 1939; d. Louis and Mary (Foglia) Celenza; m. Michael D. Goldner, May 7, 1960; children: Lori Ann, Michael L., Lisa Ann. Grad. high sch., Union City, N.J., 1957. Prin., grades 6-8, religious edn. program St. Michael's, Union City, 1972-80, asst. prin., confirmation program, religious program, 1972-80, adminstr., religious edn. program, 1980-83; sec. St. Joseph's, St. Michael's Religious Edn., Union City, 1972—, co-adminstr., religious program, 1983—, confirmation, communion programs, 1983—; parish coun. St. Michael's Ch., Union City, 1973-83, St. Joseph's Ch., Union City, 1983-85; liturgy com. St. Michael's Ch., 1974-80, eucharistic min., 1978—. Dir. Red Cross Blood Bank, St. Joseph's and St. Michael's, 1983—. Home: 819 19th St Union City NJ 07087 Office: Religious Edn Office 1500 New York Ave Union City NJ 07087

GOLDSCHEIDER, CALVIN, Jewish studies educator; b. Balt., May 28, 1941; s. A. Albert and Minnie (Kessler) G.; m. Frances K. Engeman, Aug. 18, 1983; children: Judah C., Avigaiyil L. BA cum laude, BRE cum laude, Yeshiva U., 1961; MA in Sociology, Brown U., 1963, PhD in Sociology, 1964. Asst. prof. sociology U. So. Calif., L.A., 1964-66, U. Calif., Berkeley, 1966-71; assoc. prof. demography Hebrew U., Jerusalem, 1971-78, prof. demography and sociology, 1979-85, chmn. dept. demography, 1976-78, 79-80, 82-84; adj. prof. Judaic studies and sociology Brown U., Providence, 1977-84, prof. Judaic studies and sociology, 1985—; vis. prof. contemporary Jewish studies Brandeis U., 1980-82; co-dir. R.I. Jewish Community Study, 1986-88. Author: Jewish Continuity and Change: Emerging Patterns in America, 1986, American Jewish Fertility, 1986, The American Jewish Community: Social Science Research and Policy Implications, 1986; (with Sidney Goldstein) Jewish Americans: Three Generations in a Jewish Community, 1968, The Jewish Community of Rhode Island: A Social and Demographic Study, 1987, 1988; (with Frances Kobrin) The Ethnic Factor in Family Structure and Mobility, 1978; (with Dov Friedlander) The Population of Israel: Growth, Policy, and Implications, 1979; (with Alan Zuckerman) The Transformation of the Jews, 1984; also numerous articles; editor: Brown University Studies in Population and Development, 1983—; co-editor: Chicago Studies in the History of Judaism, 1985—; (with Frances K. Goldscheider) Ethnicity and the New Family Economy: Living Arrangements and Intergenerational Financial Flows, 1989; (with Jacob Neusner) Social Foundations of Judaism, 1990; mem. editorial bd. Sociology and Social Rsch. jour., 1964-66; Brown Judaica Series, 1985—, Brown Studies on Jews and Their Societies, 1985—, Brown Classics in Judaica, 1985-90, Studies in Judaism, 1985-90, Brown Studies in Religion, 1987—; assoc. editor Pacific Sociol. Rev., 1966-70.; mem. bd. advisory editors Sociol. Inquiry, 1990—. Mem. nat. tech. adv. com. on Jewish population Coun. Jewish Fedns., N.Y.C., 1985—; bd. dirs. R.I. Bur. Jewish Edn., 1986-88, Temple Emanu-El, Providence, 1991—. With Israeli Army-Air Force Res., 1973-85. Home: 185 Taber Ave Providence RI 02906 Office: Brown U Box 1916 Providence RI 02912

GOLDSMITH, MICHAEL DAVID, minister; b. Springdale, Ark., Feb. 3, 1962; s. Jerry L. and Dorothy F. (Corter) G.; m. Deborah G. Stidham, Oct. 5, 1984; 1 child, Abigail Elizabeth. Student, Cen. Bible Coll., 1983, U. Ark., 1980-82. Lic. to ministry Assemblies of God, 1984, ordained, 1986. Youth pastor 1st Assembly of God, Conway, Ark., 1984, Pine Bluff, Ark., 1984-86, Siloam Springs, Ark., 1986-91, North Little Rock, Ark., 1991—; rep. sectional youth Assemblies of God, Ark., 1985—, youth camp speaker, Miss., Okla., 1990, 91, dist. conf. speaker, Ark., Mo., 1988, 90, 91; v.p. Ark. dist. coun. Assemblies of God, 1991—, asst. v.p. dept. youth, 1991. Republican. Office: 1st Assembly of God 4501 Burrow Dr North Little Rock AR 72120

GOLDSTEIN, MARK L., religious association administrator; b. Nashville, Aug. 31, 1958; s. Leon and Helen (Kuttig) G.; m. Shari Spark, July 1, 1984; 1 child, Carlyn Ariela. BA, U. Judaism, 1982; MA in Jewish Communal Svc., Hebrew Union Coll., L.A., 1984; MSW, U. So. Calif., 1984. Dir. youth activities Temple Aliyah, Woodland Hills, Calif., 1977-81; staff asst. Jewish Fedn. Coun. of L.A., 1983-84; dir. leadership devel. Jewish Fedn. of St. Louis, 1984-85, dir. of planning and budgeting, 1986-88, asst. exec. dir., 1988—; bd. dirs., chmn. budget com. B'nai Amoona Congregation, St. Louis, 1990—. Mem. Mayor's Task Force on Homeless, St. Louis, 1987-89. Sherman fellow Brandeis U., 1991. Mem. Conf. of Jewish Communal Svc. (Louis Kraft award 1989), Assn. Jewish Community Orgn. Pers., Nat. Assn. Social Workers, Coalition for Advancement of Jewish Edn. Office: Jewish Fedn St Louis 12 Millstone Campus Dr Saint Louis MO 63146

GOLIGHTLY, RODNEY DEAN, minister, educator; b. Flint, Mich., Aug. 24, 1962; s. Clarence Adolphus and Eva Marie (Rooker) G.; m. Jacqueline Jayne Barnes, Aug. 13, 1988; 1 child, Katharine Anne. BA, Pillsbury Bapt. Bible Coll., Owatonna, Minn., 1985; student, Cen. Bapt. Theol. Sem., Mpls., 1985-86, Detroit Bapt. Theol. Sem., Allen Park, Mich., 1988-89. Ordained to ministry Bapt. Ch., 1988. Radio announcer WCTS-FM, Mpls., 1985-86; salesperson M & R Distbrs., Burton, Mich., 1986-87; high sch. supr. Temple Christian Acad., Fremont, Ohio, 1987-88; substitute tchr. Inter-City Bapt. Schs., Allen Park, 1988-89; asst. pastor Plymouth (Mich.) Bapt. Ch., 1989, Colonial Bapt. Ch., Galesburg, Ill., 1989—; preacher Approved Workmen Are Not Ashamed (AWANA) Clubs, Internat., Owatonna, 1981-85; pres. Latin Am. Prayer Band, Owatonna, 1981-85 chaplain William's Soc., Owatonna, 1983-84; missionary Bapt. Mid-Missions, Venezuela, 1984. Author: We Won Again Men, 1974, (poetry) Down to Earth, 1980; dir.

(play) The Rivals, 1983, The Centurion, 1988. Active Rep. Nat. Com., Washington, 1986—. Mem. Evang. Tchr. Tng. Assn. (cert. 1985), Gen. Assn. Regular Bapts., Pillsbury Alumni Assn. Avocations: electronics, photography, gymnastics, swimming, travel.

GOLKA, FRIEDEMANN WALTER, theology lecturer; b. Glogau, Silesia, Germany, Apr. 5, 1942; came to U.K., 1968; s. Walter and Dorothea (Laabs) G.; Cand.Theol., U. Heidelberg, Fed. Republic Germany, 1968, Th.D., 1973. Asst. tutor Ripon Hall and Exeter Coll., Oxford, 1969-70; lect. theology U. Exeter, Devon, U.K., 1970—. Translator and editor: (C. Westermann) What Does the Old Testament Say About God?, 1979. Contbr. articles to profl. jours. Bd. mgmt. Northcott Theatre, Exeter, 1983-86. World Council Chs. scholar, (U.K.) 1968-69. Mem. Soc. Study of Theology (com. mem. 1980-83, 86—), Soc. Old Testament Study (com. mem.), Assn. Univ. Tchrs. Social Democrat. Mem. Ch. of Eng. Club: Staff Univ. Exeter. Avocations: music; drama. Home: 23 Rollestone Cres, Sylvania Park, Exeter Devon EX4 5EB, England Office: U Exeter Queen's Bldg, Dept Theology, The Queen's Dr, Exeter Devon EX4 4QH, England

GOMES, PETER JOHN, clergyman, educator; b. Boston, May 22, 1942; s. Peter L. and Orissa Josephine (White) G. AB, Bates Coll., Lewiston, Maine, 1965; STB (Rockefeller fellow 1967-68), Harvard U., 1968; DD (hon.), New Eng. Coll., 1974; LHD (hon.), Waynesburg Coll., 1978; HumD (hon.), Gordon Coll., 1985; LittD (hon.), Knox Coll., 1987; DD (hon.), U. South, 1989. Ordained to ministry Am. Bapt. Ch., 1968. Instr. history, dir. freshmen exptl. program Tuskegee (Ala.) Inst., 1968-70; asst. minister, then acting minister Meml. Ch. Harvard U., 1970-74, minister Meml. Ch., 1974—, Plummer prof. Christian morals, 1974—; nat. chaplain Am. Guild Organists, 1978-82; hon. fellow Emmanuel Coll., U. Cambridge, Eng. Author: Proclamation Series Commentaries, Lent, 1985; co-author: Books of the Pilgrims; editor: Parnassus, 1970, History of the Pilgrim Society, 1970. Pres., trustee Internat. Fund Def. and Aid in South Africa, 1977—; trustee Bates Coll., 1973-78, 80—, Pilgrim Soc., 1970—, pres. 1989, Charity of Edward Hopkins, 1974—, Donation to Liberia, 1973—, Plimoth Plantation, 1977—, Roxbury Latin Sch., 1982—, Ella Lyman Cabot Trust, 1975—, Wellesley Coll., 1985—, Boston Found., 1985—, Plymouth Pub. Library, 1985—; acting dir. W.E.B. DuBois Inst. for Afro-Am. History Harvard U., 1990—. Fellow Royal Soc. Arts; mem. Royal Soc. Ch. Music, Colonial Soc. Mass., Mass. Hist. Soc., Farmington Inst. Christian Studies, Signet Soc. (pres.), English-Speaking Union (bd. dir.), Country Day Sch. Headmasters Assn. (hon.), Phi Beta Kappa. Club: Tavern. Home: Sparks House 21 Kirkland St Cambridge MA 02138 Office: Harvard U Meml Ch Cambridge MA 02138

GOMEZ, DREXEL, bishop. Bishop of Barbados, Anglican Communion, Bridgetown. Office: Diocesan Office, Mandeville House, Bridgetown Barbados*

GOMEZ, LUIS OSCAR, Asian and religious studies educator; b. Guayanilla, P.R., Apr. 7, 1943; s. Manuel Gomez and Lucila Rodriguez; m. Ruth Cedenia Maldonado, Dec. 24, 1963; children: Luis Oscar, Jr., Miran Ruth. BA, U. P.R., 1963; PhD Asian Langs. and Lit., Yale U., 1967; MA in Clin. Psychology, U. Mich., 1991. Lic. clin. psychologist. Vis. asst. prof. U. P.R., Rio Piedras, 1967, lectr., 1969-70, assoc. prof., 1970-73; assoc. prof. dept. Asian langs. and cultures U. Mich., Ann Arbor, 1973-80, prof. Buddhist studies, dept. Asian langs. and cultures, 1980—, chmn. dept., 1981-89; vis. asst. prof. U. Wash., Seattle, 1967-68; vis. prof. Stanford U., Palo Alto, Calif., 1985. Co-editor: Barabudur, Problemas de Filosofía, Studies in the Literature of the Great Vehicle, 1989. Mem. Am. Psychol. Assn., Soc. for Sci. Study Religion, Am. Acad. Religion, Internat. Assn. Buddhist Studies (gen. sec. 1986-89), Assn. Asian Studies. Home: 3204 Lockridge Dr Ann Arbor MI 48108 Office: U Mich Dept Asian Langs & Cultures Ann Arbor MI 48108-1285

GOMEZ, MARK, pastor; b. Pico Rivera, Calif., Apr. 5, 1959; s. Vincent and Elivra (Gonzalez) G.; m. Jonnie Belinda Honeycutt, June 16, 1979; children: Corrie, Evan, Jonathan. Student, Cerritos Coll., 1986-89. Ordained to ministry. Pastor Calvary Chapel of Lakewood (Calif.), 1984—. Office: Calvary Chapel of Lakewood 4164 Woodruff Ave Lakewood CA 90713

GOMEZ, WALTER VASQUEZ, minister; b. Indiahoma, Okla., Mar. 13, 1916; s. Gabriel Joe and Anna (Hiebert) G.; m. Lois Josephine Rawlings, Nov. 14, 1936; 1 child, Lawana Norman. Student, Cameron State Coll., 1934-36; ThD, Northwestern Bible Coll., Mpls., 1943. Ordained to ministry Mennonite Brethren Ch., 1944. Co-founder, dir. Mexican dept. Plymouth Gospel Mission, Mpls., 1940-44, Lawton, Okla., 1944-45; v.p., dean Rio Grande Bible Inst., Edinburg, Tex., 1946-54; founder, chmn. Bd. Mexican Mission Ministries, Internat. Rep., Pharr, Tex., 1954—. Home and Office: Mexican Mission Ministries PO Box 636 Pharr TX 78577

GONEAU, SHERRY ANNE, lay worker; b. Virginia Beach, Va., Nov. 7, 1967; d. Paul Stephen and Karen Anne (Simpson) G. Grad. high sch., Little Silver, N.J., 1986. Youth leader Shore Christian Ctr., Wall, N.J., 1989—, drama and youth choir leader, 1991—; nurses aide Retirement Home, Ocean, N.J., 1990—. Home: 60 Virginia Dr Howell NJ 07731

GONNERMAN, DANIEL LU, minister; b. Waterloo, Iowa, May 16, 1959; s. LaVerne Virgil and Esther JoAnn (Hoffman) G.; m. Brenda Leah Capps, June 20, 1981; children: Alisha, Dana, Nicole. BS in Pastoral Studies, Faith Bible Coll. and Sem., 1983. Lic. to preach Gen. Assn. Regular Bapt. Chs., 1987. Assoc. pastor Indianola (Iowa) Regular Bapt. Ch., 1984-86; pastor Faith Bapt. Ch., Tecumseh, Nebr., 1987—; networking profl. Amway Corp., Ada, Mich., 1990—; dean Whispering Cedars Bapt. Camp, Geona, 1989—; tchr. ESL, Tecumseh. Active various community groups. Republican. Home: Rte 1 Box 55 Tecumseh NE 68450 Office: Faith Bapt Ch 491 S 11th Tecumseh NE 68450

GONZÁLES ALVAREZ, JUVENCIO, bishop; b. Matehuala, Mex., Feb. 28, 1917. Ordained priest Roman Cath. Ch., 1942, consecrated bishop, 1980. Now bishop of Ciudad Valles, Mex. Address: Apartado Postal N 170, Ciudad Valles, CP 79000 San Luis Potosí Mexico

GONZÁLES MARTÍN, MARCELO CARDINAL, archbishop; b. Villanubla, Spain, Jan. 16, 1918; ordained priest Roman Catholic Ch., 1941; formerly tchr. theology and sociology Valladolid Diocesan Sem.; founder orgn. for constrn. houses for poor; consecrated bishop of Astorga, 1961; titular archbishop of Case Medinae, also coadjutor of Barcelona, 1966; archbishop of Barcelona, 1967-71, archbishop of Toledo, Spain, 1971—; elevated to Sacred Coll. Cardinals, 1973; mem. Congregation of Evangelization of Peoples. Address: Arco de Palacio 1, Toledo Spain

GONZALEZ, LOUIS MAX, minister; b. Valparaiso, Chile, Nov. 10, 1948; s. Luis Ramon and Irma (Camus) G.; m. Annie Frances Saez, July 22, 1972; children: Anna, Carla, John. BA, Internat. Sem., Panama City, 1982; MDiv, Sch. Theology, Cleveland, Tenn., 1985. Ordained to ministry Ch. of God, 1984. Pastor Ch. of God, Panama City, 1981-82; instr. Pentecostal Bible Coll., San Juan, P.R., 1984-85, Lee Coll., Alexandria, Va., 1986-90; assoc. pastor Ch. of God, Alexandria, 1986-90; pastor Ch. of God, Arlington, Va., 1990—; lectr. in field. Author: Exegetical Refutation, Contemporary Theological Issues; contbr. articles to profl. jours. Home and Office: 6330 King Louis Dr Alexandria VA 22312

GONZALEZ, ROLANDO NOEL, religion educator, secondary education educator; b. Rio Grande City, Tex., Sept. 10, 1947; s. Ubaldo and Beulah (Gutierrez) G. BA, U. Tex., 1968; MA, Tex. A & I U., 1972. Cert. tchr. all scis., guidance and counseling. Seminarian Diocese of Brownsville, San Antonio, 1979-82; pastoral asst. Our Lady, Queen of Angels Ch., La Joya, Tex., 1982-83; coord., lay ministries Brownsville Diocese, McAllen, Tex., 1983-85; lectr., tchr. on scripture Perpetual Help Ch., McAllen, 1986-88, Holy Spirit Ch., McAllen, 1989—; tchr., dept. head Pharr (Tex.)-San Juan-Alamo High Sch., 1983—; scripture tchr., lectr. Sst. Mary Margaret Ch., Pharr, 1988. Contbr. articles to profl. jours. tchr. scripture, lectr. Sts. Mary and Margaret Ch., Pharr, 1988, Sacred Heart Ch., Mercedes, Tex., 1990. Recipient Appreciation award Sacred Heart Ch., 1990. Home: 2800 Iris Ave McAllen TX 78501-6245 *Humans are so resilient and basically optimistic. I marvel at how humans reach for the stars even though they see around them a planet full of woes.*

GONZÁLEZ-ALEXOPOULOS See CHRYSOSTOMOS OF OREOI, BISHOP

GONZALEZ ZUMARRAGA, ANTONIO JOSE, archbishop; b. Pujilí, Cotopaxi, Ecuador, Mar. 18, 1925; s. Luis González and Leonor Zumárraga. Seminario mayor, Quito, Ecuador; D in Derecho Canónico (hon.), U. Salamanca, Spain. Ordained priest Roman Cath. Ch., 1951. Bishop of Machala Ecuador, 1978; co-adjutor archbishop of Quito, 1980, archbishop of Quito, 1985—, pres. Episcopal Conf., 1987—; consejero Pontificia Comisión para América Latina, 1989—. Author: Mensaje Dominical, Vol. I, 1987, Vol. II, 1989. Mem. Junta Consultiva de Relaciones Exteriores del Ecuador. Address: Calle Chile 1140, Apartado 106, Quito Pichincha, Ecuador

GOOCH, GARY DUANE, minister; b. Avery, Okla., Mar. 28, 1936; s. George Francis and Ruby Viola (Ladd) G.; m. Donnell Kay Cooper, July 3, 1963; children: Gwendolyn Diann, Gary Duane Jr., Elizabeth Anne, Teresa Louise. BS in Chem. Engring., Okla. State U., 1957, MS in Chem. Engring., 1967; M in Div. cum laude, Nashotah House, 1974. Ordained to ministry Episcopal Ch. as deacon, 1974, as priest, 1974. Process devel. engr. Phillips Petroleum Co., Borger, Tex., 1961-66; sr. engring. analyst Phillips Petroleum Co., Bartlesville, Okla., 1966-71; curate Grace Episcopal Ch., Muskogee, Okla., 1974-76; rector, vicar St. Andrews Episcopal Ch., Broken Arrow, Okla., 1976-87; rector St. Andrews Episcopal Ch., Ft. Scott, Kans., 1988—, St. Peters Episcopal Ch., Pittsburg, Kans., 1987—; pastor All Saints Nova Cluster, Pittsburg, 1988—; vicar St. Mary's Episcopal Ch., Galena, Kans., 1988—, St. Stephen's Episcopal Ch., Columbus, Kans., 1988—; bd. dirs. examining chaplains Diocese Okla., 1977-87; chmn. Commmn. on Ministry Accountablity and Clergy Compensation, 1984-87; chmn. Continuing Edn. Com., Commn. on Ministry, 1980-82, Constn. and Canons Com., 1981-82; sec. Diocesan conv. Diocese of Kans., 1990—, mem. commn. on ministry, mem. Diocesan coun. Author: A Semi-Rigorous Method for Calculating ASTM Curves from TBP Curves, 1967. Block chmn. Rep. Com., Borger, 1964. Lt. USAF, 1958-60. Fellow Dow Co., 1957-58, Va. Theol. Sem. Continuing Edn. Program, 1987. Fellow Coll. of Preachers. Home and Office: All Saints Nova Cluster 602 W Euclid Pittsburg KS 66762-5005

GOOCH, JAMES BLANTON, minister; b. Abilene, Tex., July 13, 1947; s. Claude Blanton and Mary Ruth (Calhoun) G.; m. Nancy Eugenia South, Dec. 23, 1968; children: James Eric, Kim Hyo Eugenia. BA, Hardin-Simmons U., 1969; postgrad., Tex. Tech U., 1969-71, U. Tex., 1971-74; MDiv, Austin Theol. Sem., 1982. Ordained to ministry Presbyn. Ch. (U.S.A.), 1982. Pastor 1st Presbyn. Ch., Santa Anna, Tex., 1982-85, Mineral Wells, Tex., 1985—; del. Tex. Coun. Chs., 1984; synod del. Palo Duro Presbytery, 1982, 85; mem. com. on small ch. ministries, 1982-85, com. on representation, 1983-85, presbytery coord. coun., 1984-85; synod del. Grace Presbytery, 1989, 91, div. care of ch. profls., 1988—; bd. dirs. H.O.P.E., Inc., 1986—, chmn. bd., 1991—. W.P. Newell Meml. fellow Austin Theol. Sem., 1982. Mem. Mineral Wells Ministerial Alliance. Office: 1st Presbyn Ch 300 NW 4th Ave Mineral Wells TX 76067

GOOCH, VALERIE LYNN, minister; b. Clovis, N.Mex., June 8, 1957; d. Edward Eugene and Mary Marcelete (Trichel) Oestermyer; m. Royce Lynn Gooch, June 4, 1977; children: Trichelle Lynn, Evan Lynn. BS, Tex. Tech U, 1979. Cert. tchr. Children's min. Highland Bapt. Ch., Lubbock, Tex., 1985—; conf. leader Bapt. Gen. Conv., Tex., 1989—; children's specialist Associational AssisTeam, Lubbock, 1989—; conf. coord. Lubbock Bapt. Assn., Lubbock, 1989, 91. Developer Kids in Action mission edn. program, 1990. Mem. PTA Smith and Iles Elem. Sch., 1986—; parent vol. Lubbock Ind. Sch. Dist., 1986—. Office: Highland Bapt Ch 4316 34th St Lubbock TX 79410

GOOD, EDWIN MARSHALL, religion educator; b. Bibia, Cameroon, Apr. 23, 1928; s. Albert Irwin and Mary Rachel (Middlemiss) G.; m. Janice Aeva Sundquist, July 26, 1952 (div. 1991); children: Brian Alexander, Lawrence Marshall, John Alexander. BA, Westminster Coll., 1949; MDiv, Union Theol. Sem., 1953; PhD, Columbia U., 1958; MA, Stanford U., 1974. Instr. in religion Princeton (N.J.) U., 1954; instr. in Old Testament Union Theol. Sem., N.Y.C., 1955-56; asst. prof. religious studies Stanford (Calif.) U., 1956-61, assoc. prof., 1961-70, prof., 1970-91, prof. emeritus, 1991—; rsch. collaborator musical history Smithsonian Inst., Washington, 1988—. Author: You Shall Be My People, 1959, Irony in the Old Testament, 1965, 2d edit., 1981, Giraffes, Black Dragons, and Other Pianos, 1982 (Kinkeldey award 1983), In Turns of Tempest, 1990. Mem. Soc. for Values in Higher Edn., Am. Musicol. Soc., Am. Musical Instrument Soc., Am. Assn. Retired Persons. Avocations: chamber music, musical research. Home: 4107 N 35th St Arlington VA 22207

GOODART, ELIZABETH MAE, church secretary; b. Atlanta, June 24, 1944; d. Thomas Leo and Lucille Estelle (Scott) Nelson; married. BA, Atlanta Christian Coll., 1966. Ch. sec., youth dir. 1st Ch. of Christ, Eustis, Fla., 1966-71; ch. sec. 1st Christian Ch., Largo, Fla., 1971-90, Calvary United Meth. Ch., Largo, 1990—. Author: You're Number One, 1984. Mem. Fla. Bible Bowl Assn. (sec. Largo chpt. 1982-83, pres. 1984-87). Mem. Christian Ch. Home: 301-A Woodrow Ave NW Largo FL 34640

GOODEN, REGINALD HEBER, bishop; b. Long Beach, Calif., Mar. 22, 1910; s. Robert Burton and Alice Leonard (Moore) G.; m. Victoria Elena F. de Mendia y Miranda (dec. 1982); children: Reginald Heber, Hiram Richard; m. Sandra Marie Wojcik Roberts, July 23, 1988. A.B., Stanford U., 1931; S.T.B., Berkeley Div. Sch., New Haven, 1934, S.T.D., 1946; student, U. Madrid, 1934-35, Centro de Estudios Historicos, Madrid (Spain), 1934-35; D.D., Trinity Coll., Hartford, 1963. Ordained to ministry Episcopal Ch., 1934; hon. asst. chaplain Brit. Embassy Ch., Madrid, 1934-35; priest in charge St. Paul's Ch. and Sch., Camaguey, Cuba, 1935-39; dean Holy Trinity Cathedral, Havana, Cuba, 1939-45; bishop of missionary dist. Episc. Ch., Panama C.Z., 1945-72; also bishop in charge Episc. Ch., Ecuador, 1956-64; bishop in charge Central Central-Am., 1956-57; asst. bishop Diocese La., Shreveport, 1972-75, acting bishop, 1975-76, ret., 1976; bishop-in-residence Ch. of Holy Cross, Shreveport, 1976—. Decorated Gran Cruz Order Vasco Nunez de Balboa, Panama; recipient Distinguished Community Service award Govt. C.Z., 1972; John Henry Watson fellow Berkeley Div. Sch. Club: The Breakers (Stanford U.). Lodge: Masons. Home: The Episcopal Home 1428 S Marengo Ave Alhambra CA 91803 also: Friars 9999 Smitherman Dr #700 Shreveport LA 71115

GOODGAME, GORDON CLIFTON, minister; b. Jones County, Miss., Oct. 8, 1934; s. J. Clyde and Eloise Hertha (Smith) G.; m. Dianne Fraser, July 29, 1961; children: Gordon Clifton Jr., Gregory Carson, Cathey. BS in Law and Bus., U. Tenn., 1955; MDiv, Emory U., 1958; STM, San Francisco Theol. Sem., 1970, STD, 1974. Sr. min. 1st United Meth. Ch., Pulaski, Va., 1973-74; leader devel. cons. Holston Conf. Coun. Ministries, Johnson City, Tenn., 1974-77; sr. min. 1st United Meth. Ch., Oak Ridge, Tenn., 1977-81, 1st-Centenary United Meth. Ch., Chattanooga, 1981-90; dir. Holston Conf. Coun. Ministries, Johnson City, 1990—; del. United Meth. Gen. Conf., 1976, 80, 84, 88, Southeastern Jurisdictional Conf., United Meth. Ch., 1972, 76, 80, 84, 88; dir. United Meth. Bd. Global Ministries, N.Y.C., 1980-88; mem. World Meth. Coun., 1986—. Dir. Chattanooga United Way Bd., 1983-89, Hospice Chattanooga Bd., 1982-90; trustee Hiwassee Coll., Madisonville, Tenn., 1979—, chairperson bd., 1990; trustee Meth. Med. Ctr. Oak Ridge, 1977-81. Mem. Emory U. Alumni Assn. (bd. govs.), Candler Sch. Theology Alumni Assn. (pres.), Rotary (sgt. at arms 1989-90). Democrat. Home: 2404 Rambling Rd Johnson City TN 37604 Office: Holston Conf Commn PO Box 1178 Johnson City TN 37605 *The present day is the most fantastic of the ages. A growing sense of world interdependence is developing alongside an increased concern for justice and universal peace, while enhanced technology raises the possibility of a true world community. If we can only claim the highest truth and live faithfully by grace, humankind can become what God intends.*

GOODINGS, ALLEN, bishop; b. Barrow-in-Furness, Lancashire, Eng., May 7, 1925; s. Thomas Jackson and Ada (Tate) G.; m. Joanne Talbot, Oct. 26, 1959; children—Suzanne, Thomas. B.A., Sir George Williams U., Montreal, Que., Can., 1959; B.D., McGill U., Montreal, 1959; L.Th., Montreal Diocesan Theol. Coll., 1959, D.D. (hon.), 1978. Engr., draftsman in industry, 1941-54; ordained to ministry Anglican Ch., 1959; curate, then priest chs. in Montreal, 1959-65; rector Ch. of Ascension, Montreal, 1965-69; dean Cathedral of Holy Trinity, Quebec, 1969-77; bishop Anglican Diocese of Que., 1977-90; asst. bishop Anglican Diocese of Ottawa, 1990—; chaplain Can. Grenadier Guards, Montreal, 1966-69. Clubs: Cercle universitaire (Quebec), Officer Mess Royal 22d Regt. (Quebec), Garrison (Quebec) (hon.). Office: 71 Ave Bronson, Ottawa, ON Canada K1R 6G6

GOODLIN, GARY RUSSELL, clergyman, air force officer; b. Pitts., Aug. 28, 1953; s. Russell Edgar and Shirley Jeanne (Von Behren) G.; m. Jeanne Louise Dolinich, June 22, 1974; children: Kellie, Christina, Kathryn, Kyla. BBA magna cum laude, Nat. U., 1976; MDiv, Liberty Univ. Theol. Sem., Lynchburg, Va., 1986; MA, Liberty U., 1987. Ordained to ministry Ref. Episcopal Ch., 1988. Prodn. worker Flowers Bakery and Westover Dairy, Lynchburg, 1979-83; sales rep. Met. Ins. Cos. Inc., Lynchburg, 1983-86; asst. rector Providence Ref. Episcopal Ch., Lynchburg, 1984-89; dir. counseling ctr. Patrick Henry Boy's Plantation, Inc., Brookneal, Va., 1986-88; commd. 1st lt. USAF, 1989, advanced through grades to capt., 1990; chaplain USAF, Ft. Worth, 1989—. Mem. Eagle Scout Assn., Liberty U. Alumni Assn. Republican. Avocations: guitar, violin, reading, racquetball, softball. Home: 100 Billy Mitchell St Fort Worth TX 76114 Office: 7CSG/HC Carswell AFB TX 76127

GOODLING, JOSHUA LOREN, evangelist; b. Elgin, Ill., Feb. 4, 1966; s. Boyd Wayne and Candy Lovely (Woods) G. Grad. Theology, Pensacola Christian Coll., 1987. Evangelist, dir. Joshua Goodling Evangelistic Ministries, Knoxville, Tenn., 1989—; founder, editor Formula III Christian Paper, Knoxville, 1990—. Author: When Problems Come, 1989, It's Been a Fantastic Day, 1991. Sustaining mem. Rep. Nat. Com., Washington, 1990. *At the age of four, I was stricken with terminal cancer that almost killed me. Because of the many complications life has not been easy, but I have learned a Christian can and should always enjoy life as long as we place our complete trust in Christ and not in our circumstances.*

GOODMAN, NAN LOUISE, school administrator; b. Fort Worth, Tex., Aug. 13, 1964; d. Nelson Byron and Judy Louise (White) Baird; m. Grantlan James Goodman, May 24, 1986; 1 child, Claire Louise. BA, Tarleton State U., Stephenville, Tex., 1986. Pianist 1st Meth. Ch., Venus, Tex., 1978-82, Park St. Bapt. Ch., Dublin, Tex., 1984-85, Harvey Bapt. Ch., Stephenville, 1986-89, North Park Bapt. Ch., Sherman, Tex., 1990—; adminstr. Texoma Christian Middle Sch., Sherman, 1990—. Mem. Assn. Christian Schs. Internat. Home: 2421 N Ricketts Sherman TX 75090 Office: Texoma Christian Middle Sch 2605 Rex Cruse Sherman TX 75090

GOODMAN, PAUL FREDRICK, minister; b. Berkeley, Calif., Aug. 14, 1952; s. George Woodrow Goodman and Angelina (Caiola) Gange. BS in Spl. Edn., So. Conn. State U., 1974; MDiv, Union Theol. Sem., N.Y.C., 1983. Asst. dir. Child Adv. Office, Nat. Coun. Chs. of Christ, USA, N.Y.C., 1985-86; dir. Christian edn. 1st United Ch. of Christ, Milford, Conn., 1987-89, assoc. pastor, 1989—; del. to Nat. Synod, United Ch. of Christ-New Haven Assn., 1991—; rep. Combined Parishes Action Com., Milford, 1989—. Asst. compiler, typist: When Churches Mind the Children, 1984; info. compiler: Helping Churches Mind the Children, 1985. Treas. McGovern for Pres. campaign, Milford, 1972; pres. Milford Project Theatre, 1974-78; bd. dirs. Milford Pastoral Counseling Ctr., 1989—. Democrat. Home: 32 Winthrop Ct Milford CT 06460 Office: 1st United Ch of Christ 34 W Main St Milford CT 06460

GOODMAN, RICK EDWARD, minister; b. Lindsay, Okla., Jan. 29, 1948; s. Oran Winford and Mable Arley (Dorrell) G.; m. Rita Jean Rivers, Mar. 16, 1967; children: Rena Dian, Rusty Edward. Student, South Ea. Ky. State U., 1977-78; grad., Clear Creek Bapt. Coll., Pineville, Ky., 1978. Lic. to ministry Bapt. Ch., 1975. Pastor Mt. Zion Bapt. Ch., Mt. Vernon, 1975-76, West Pineville Bapt. (Ky.) Ch., 1976-78, Tulakes Bapt. Ch., Bethany, Okla., 1978-81, Howard Meml. Bapt. Ch., Del City, Okla., 1981-86, Calvary Bapt. Ch., Guthrie, Okla., 1986-87, Knob Hill Bapt. Ch., Oklahoma City, 1988—; mem. bd. advisors Youth for Christ, Del City, 1983-86. Contbr. articles to Bapt. Messenger. V.p. Booster club of Westmore High Sch., 1989—; active mem. Okla. Reps., 1991—. Mem. Capital Bapt. Assn. Okla. (evangelism and missions coms., advisor youth task force 1991—), Fellowship Christian Athletes. Home: 3137 SW 97th Oklahoma City OK 73159 Office: Knob Hill Bapt Ch 2700 SW 59th Oklahoma City OK 73119

GOODMAN, THOMAS HENRY, minister; b. Montgomery, Ala., May 11, 1961; s. Charles Henry and Ellen Margaret (Murphy) G.; m. Diane Dartez, May 17, 1980; children: Michael Thomas, Stephen Murphy. BA, Baylor U., 1982; MDiv, Southwestern Bapt. Theol. Sem., Ft. Worth, Tex., 1986. Ordained to ministry So. Bapt. Conv., 1982. Pastor Riverdale Bapt. Ch., Baton Rouge, 1987—; mem. Moral and Social Concerns Com. for La. Bapt. Conv., Alexandria, 1990—. Mem. Nat. Right to Life Com., Washington, 1991. Office: Riverdale Bapt Ch 2791 O'Neal Ln Baton Rouge LA 70816

GOODMAN, YITZCHAK MEIR, rabbi; b. Bklyn., Jan. 3, 1933; s. Hyman and Anna (Zucker) G.; m. Batya Gluck, June 20, 1957; children: Yisroel, Miriam, Benjamin, Bina. BA, Yeshiva U., 1954, EdD, 1978; MA, Hunter Coll., 1957. Ordained rabbi, 1956. Rabbi Congregation Sons of Israel, Astoria, N.Y., 1959-76, Young Israel of Far Rockaway (N.Y.), 1976—; mem. faculty Frisch High Sch., Paramus, N.J., 1974—; founder, prin. Hebrew Acad. of West Queens (N.Y.), 1966-67. Author Biblical commentary The Gem Collection, 1991. Mem. Rabbinical Coun. Am., Rabbinic Coun. Far Rockaway (chmn. 1990—). Home: 737 Empire Ave Far Rockaway NY 11691 Office: Young Israel Far Rockaway 716 Beach 9 St Far Rockaway NY 11691

GOODSON, CARL EDWARD, religion educator; b. St. Louis, July 31, 1917; s. Harry Edward and Clara (Cummins) G.; m. Rozelle Wordingham, May 31, 1944; children: Lynn Clark, Nancy Lea (Mrs. Dennis Mills), Margery (Mrs. Daniel Lumpkin), Charlotte Rose, Timothy Carl. A.B., William Jewell Coll., 1939; Th.M., So. Baptist Theol. Sem., 1944; Th.D., Central Bapt. Theol. Sem., 1951. Ordained to ministry Baptist Ch., 1940; pastor Baptist Ch. Smiths Grove, Ky., 1944-45, Columbia, Mo., 1945-46; mem. faculty Southwest Bapt. Coll., Bolivar, Mo., 1946-61; prof. Ouachita Bapt. U., Arkadelphia, Ark., 1961-68, 82; prof. emeritus Ouachita Bapt. U., 1982—, v.p. for acad. affairs, 1970-82; dean Mo. Bapt. Coll., St. Louis, 1968-70; fgn. expert Zhengzhou (Peoples Republic China) U., 1988-89; tchr. Boyce Sch., Little Rock, 1989—. Mem. edn. commn. So. Bapt. Conv., 1950-56; mem. hist. commn. Mo. Bapt. Conv., 1969-70; Mem. Nat. Collegiate Honors Council. Recipient Disting. Alumni award S.W. Bapt. Coll., 1977. Mem. Soc. Bibl. Lit., Am. Acad. Religion, Kiwanis. Club: Rotary. Home: 144 Evonshire Dr Arkadelphia AR 71923 *I have faced few adversities, or "hard times" in my life, but those that have come my way have invariably presented a challenge, when I was willing to take the dare. I've observed that those who don't rise to such occasions are left with little. When difficulties are faced and overcome, the risks proved to be worth the try. Fortunately, human beings are made so that the bad memories fade and the good take on a glow. The ones who refused to take the dare are left bad memories.*

GOODSON, JACK DAVID, minister; b. Gastonia, N.C., Aug. 31, 1930; s. Ferrie L. Bess; m. Frankie Elizabeth Wilson, Dec. 24, 1950; children: Bruce, Rhonda, Chris. DD (hon.), Pacific Coast Bible Coll., Sacramento, Calif., 1987. Ordained to ministry Pentecostal Holiness Ch., 1961. Pastor Pentecostal Holiness Ch., N.C., 1959-81; supt. Pentecostal Holiness Ch. Western N.C. Conf., 1982-85; gen. sec., treas. Pentecostal Holiness Ch., Oklahoma City, 1985—; bd. dirs. Community Bank, Oklahoma City, 1985—; mem. Pentecostal Holiness Ch., Oklahoma City, 1985 (dir. ch. insts., intra-ch. fund, stewardship and devel.). Editor: Minister's Handbook; contbr. articles to profl. jours. Mem. Nat. Assn. Evangs., Pentecostal Fellowship North Am., Christian Stewardship Assn. Home: 8317 NW 118th St Oklahoma City OK 73162 Office: Pentecostal Holiness Ch Box 12609 Acctg Dept Oklahoma City OK 73157-2609

GOODSON, WALTER KENNETH, retired clergyman; b. Salisbury, N.C., Sept. 25, 1912; s. Daniel Washington and Sarah (Peeler) G.; m. Martha Ann Ogburn, July 12, 1937; children: Sara Ann (Mrs. Larry M. Faust), Walter Kenneth, Nancy Craven Richey. AB, Catawba Coll., 1934, LHD; student, Duke Div. Sch., 1934-37, D.D., 1960; D.D., High Point (N.C.) Coll., 1951, Birmingham-So. Coll., Athens Coll., Shenandoah Coll., Campbell U., 1985; L.H.D., St. Bernard Coll.; LL.D., U. Ala. Ordained to ministry Methodist Ch., 1939; pastor in Western N.C. Conf., 1935-64; bishop Birmingham area, 1964-72, Richmond area, 1972-80; ret., 1980; now bishop-in-residence Duke U. Divinity Sch., Durham, N.C.; Del. World Conf. Meth. Ch., Oxford, Eng., 1951, Lake Junaluska, N.C., 1956, London, 1966, Denver, 1971, Dublin, 1977; mem. Meth. World Council; bd. dirs. Meth. Com. Overseas Relief, 1964-72; mem. (Mission Team to Gt. Britain), 1962, study team to, France and Berlin, 1962; chmn. finance com. bd. missions United Meth. Ch., 1968-72, pres. commn. on religion and race, 1968, pres. gen. bd. discipleship, 1972-80; also pres. council bishops United Meth. Ch., Southeastern Jurisdiction, 1976, pres. council on ministries, 1976. Pres. J.B. Cornelius Found., 1946-64; Trustee Duke Endowment, Brevard Coll., Duke U., Shenandoah Coll. Clubs: Rotarian, Mason (32 deg.). Home: 1244 Arbor Rd Winston-Salem NC 27104 Office: Duke U Divinity Sch Durham NC 27706

GOODWIN, B. E., bishop. Bishop ch. of God in Christ, Chgo. Office: Ch of God in Christ 296 E 16th St Chicago IL 60411*

GOODWIN, BENNIE EUGENE, II, educator, clergyman; b. Chgo., Aug. 27, 1933; s. Bennie Earl and Dessie B. (Christopher) G.; children—Bennie Eugene, Mary Ellen, Constance Marie; m. Melody Humphries, July 31, 1987. B.A., Barrington Coll., 1956; M.A., Pitts. Theol. Sem., 1973; Ph.D., U. Pitts., 1974; M.R.E., Gordon-Conwell Theol. Sem., 1965; postgrad. Eastern Nazarene Coll., 1957-58, Mass. Tchrs. Coll., 1959, Temple U., 1969, Atlanta U., 1976, Ga. State U., 1981. Ordained to ministry Ch. of God in Christ, 1955. Founder, dir. Inst. Christian Edn., Boston, 1956-66; chmn. music dept. Christian High Sch., Cambridge, Mass., 1957-64; pastor Faith Mission Ch. of God in Christ. Portsmouth, N.H., 1964-66; pres. State Youth Dept., Chs. of God in Christ, N.H. Diocese, 1965-66; dir. Bishop O.T. Jones Sch. Christian Edn., Phila., 1966-69; advisor to youth Holy Temple Ch. of God in Christ, Phila., 1968-69; chmn. Internat. Teen Conf., 1968-73; admissions counselor Pitts. Theol. Sem., 1970-74; registrar, dir. admissions Interdenominational Theol. Ctr., Atlanta, 1975-77; v.p. Nat. Black Evang. Assn., Atlanta, 1976-78; dean Soul Winners' Inst., Atlanta, 1981—; minister West End Presbyn. Ch., Atlanta, 1982-84; minister of edn. Cathedral of Faith Ch. of God in Christ, Atlanta, 1985—; dir. Friends for Missions, Inc., 1968—; chmn. Internat. Teen Conf., Southeastern Area, 1974—; state dir. Christian Edn., Ch. of God in Christ, No. Ga. Jurisdiction, 1978—; adj. prof. Morris Brown Coll., Atlanta, Beulah Heights Bible Coll., Atlanta; assoc. prof. Christian Edn., Interdominational Theol. Ctr., Atlanta, 1974—; vis. prof. Simpson Coll., San Francisco, summer 1979, 82, Alliance Theol. Sem., Nyack, N.Y., 1984; guest lectr. Bapt. Bible Inst., Pitts., 1971-74, others. Named Christian Educator of Yr., Midwest Christian Edn. Conf., 1981. Mem. NAACP, Nat. Urban League, So. Christian Leadership Conf., Religious Research Assn. Author: Speak Up Black Man, 1974, Beside Still Waters, 1973, The Emergence of Black Colleges, 1974, Pray and Grow Rich, 1974, Dr. Martin Luther King, Jr.: God's Messenger of Love, Justice and Hope, 1976, Reflections on Education, 1978, Fourteen Great Thinkers, 1980, Ten Outstanding Musicians, 1980, The Effective Leader, 1981, Play the Piano "By Ear", 1982, Sermon and Message Stimulator, 1983, The Effective Teacher, 1985, Stimulating Sermons in Series, 1986, The Effective Preacher, 1987, How to Successfully Publish Your Book, 1987, How to be a Growing Christian, 1987, The Effective Black Church, 1990; editor: The New Testament Story, 1977, An Introduction to Six Major Religions, 1978, Steps toDynamic Teaching, 19878, Steps to Successful Writing, 1979; contbr. articles to profl. jours. Office: 1137 Avon Ave Atlanta GA 30310

GOODWIN, EVERETT CARLTON, minister; b. L.A., July 28, 1944; s. Carlton Byron and Pauline (Freeman) G.; m. Jane Gray, Sept. 3, 1966; children: Elizabeth Jane, Leah Grace. BA in Polit. Sci., U. Chgo., 1966; MDiv, Andover Newton Theol. Sch., 1969; MA in History, Brown U., 1969, PhD, 1979. Ordained to ministry Am. Bapt. Chs. in U.S.A., 1971, So. Bapt. Conv., 1981. Asst. chaplain Harvard U. No. Bapt. Edn. Soc., Cambridge, Mass., 1968-69; asst. pastor Quidnick Bapt. Ch., Coventry, R.I., 1969-71; pastor Peoples Bapt. Ch., Cranston, R.I., 1971-78; pastor 1st Bapt. Ch., Meriden, Conn., 1978-81, Washington, 1981—; chmn. United Ministries in Higher Edn., R.I. State Coun. Chs., 1976-78; bd. dirs. Am. Bapt. Chs. R.I., Am. Bapt. Chs. Conn.; mem. exec. coun. D.C. Bapt. Conv., 1981—. Author: The Magistracy Rediscovered, 1980; contbr. revs. to profl. jours; revisions editor: Diary of Isaac Backus, 1974. Mem. United Way S.E. New Eng., Providence, 1974-76, chmn. appeals com., 1977; trustee Cranston Pub. Libr., 1976-78; bd. dirs. Nat. Rainbow Coalition. Recipient Religious Leadership award Order Ea. Star, Providence, 1976; Brown U. fellow, 1971, Woodrow Wilson Found. fellow, 1971-73. Mem. D.C. Bapt. Ministries Assn., Inter-ch. Club D.C. (pres. 1988-90), Am. Bapt. Mins. Assn., Bapt. World Alliance (program com. 1985-90, budget and fin. com. 1990—). Office: 1328 16th St NW Washington DC 20036 *The former structures of church and denomination are in decline. Now we come full circle to again value the significance of the individual as teacher and spiritual guide.*

GOODWIN, REX DEAN, clergyman; b. Martinsville, Mo., Nov. 30, 1909; s. Charles Morgan and Grace Leola (Pyle) G.; A.B., U. Nebr., 1932; B.D., Andover Newton Theol. Sch., 1934; D.D., Sioux Falls Coll., 1957; m. Almira Drew Wallace, June 24, 1933 (dec. Oct. 1964); 1 son, John Charles; m. Loree Presnell, June 18, 1966. Ordained to ministry Bapt. Ch., 1934; pastor chs., Oxford, Nebr., 1934-36, Oakland, Calif., 1936-37, Boston, 1941-44; dir. Christian edn. First Bapt. Ch., Oakland, 1937-38; asst. pastor Central Bapt. Ch., Hartford, Conn., 1938-41; dir. public relations Am. Bapt. Home Mission Soc., N.Y.C., 1944-51; dir. publicity Am. Bapt. Conv., N.Y.C., 1951-58, exec. dir. conv. div. communication, Valley Forge, Pa., 1958-72; public liaison exec. Am. Bapt. Chs. Bd. Ednl. Ministries, Valley Forge, 1972-74; dir. devel. Cushing Jr. Coll., Bryn Mawr, Pa., 1975-77; pastor Pughtown (Pa.) Bapt. Ch., 1977-89; chmn. communications com. Bapt. World Alliance, 1972-75, mem., 1970-76; mem. communications com. Nat. Council Chs., 1961-72; v.p. Main Line Ministerium; host TV series The Making of a Protestant, 1972. Trustee Andover Newton Theol. Sch. Mem. Religious Pub. Relations Council (pres. 1961-62), Phi Alpha. Republican. Author: Man-Living Soul, 1952; There Is No End, 1956; editor Cushing Way, 1977-78; contbr. articles to ch. jours. Home: 123 Split Rock Rd The Woodlands TX 77381 *Two thoughts fill me with awe: First God made me in His image and then called me to work with Him to make earth and people turn out as He intended. When I develop that image and work with Him I have life at its best.*

GOODWIN, SAMUEL DENNIS, minister; b. Mobile, Ala., Feb. 5, 1951; s. Nolen and Mary Eleanor (Kicker) G.; m. Susan Smith, Aug. 20, 1977; 1 child, Samuel Dennis Jr. BS, Livingston (Ala.) U., 1973; MRE, Southwestern Bapt. Theol. Sem., 1977. Ordained to ministry So. Bapt. Conv., 1978. Youth minister Seoul (Korea) Internat. Bapt. Ch. Fgn. Mission Bd., So. Bapt. Ch., 1973-75; minister of edn., youth First Bapt. Ch., Jacksboro, Tex., 1977-79; minister of edn. Capitol Heights Bapt. Ch., Montgomery, Ala., 1979-83, Second Bapt. Ch., Springfield, Mo., 1983-84, First Bapt. Ch., Plano, Tex., 1984-88, Spring Hill Bapt. Ch., Mobile, 1988-91, Dawson Meml. Bapt. Ch., Birmingham, Ala., 1991—; youth cons. Associational Assist Team, Jacksboro, 1977-78; associational Sunday sch. dir., Montgomery Bapt. Assn., 1980-83; friendship ambassador, Friendship Force, Ireland, 1982; tour leader Sr. Adult Trips, Hawaii, Can., Caribbean, 1980-88; conf. leader sr. adults, Mo. Bapt. Sunday Sch. Conf., 1984. Contbr. articles to ch. adminstrn. publs. Mem. Plano Historic Planning Commn., 1987-88. Mem. So. Bapt. Educators Assn., So. Bapt. Conv., Kiwanis. Republican. Avocations: skiing, reading, landscaping, travel, racquetball. Home: 1510 Valley Pl Birmingham AL 35209

GOODWIN, THOMAS LAROI, minister; b. Tulia, Tex., Oct. 11, 1961; s. Bob and Alfa (Crowley) G.; m. Jeanna Gayle Royal, Nov. 12, 1982; children: Andrew, Matthew, Jenna. Student, Berean Sch. Bible, Springfield, Mo., 1985. Ordained to ministry, Assemblies of God, 1985. Minister of music Calvary Temple Assemblies of God, Mesquite, Tex., 1979-81, youth pastor, 1981-85, assoc. pastor, Christian sch. adminstr., 1985-88, sr. pastor, 1990—; sr. pastor First Assembly of God, Three Rivers, Tex., 1989-90. Producer, dir. Christmas drama, Jesus Christ of Nazareth, 1984. Republican. Office: Calvary Temple Assembly of God 3150 S Beltline Mesquite TX 75181

GORDAN-FELLER, CARLA JANINE, religious psychologist, spiritual educator; b. Nettleton, Ark., July 4, 1936; d. Paul Martin and Corinne (Parrot) Neff; m. Frank Edward Gordan (div. 1975); children: Richard M., Shawn, Deborah; m. Richard A. Feller, 1975. DD, Coll. Divine Metaphysics, 1970, D Divine Metaphysics, 1972, D Religious Psychology, 1974. Assoc. minister Ch. of Universal Light, Staten Island, N.Y., 1972-75; pres. Inst. of Man, Cedar Rapids, Iowa, 1975-79, Gordan and Assocs., Dallas, 1979—; dir. curriculum Peace Valley Retreat Ctr., Caddo Gap, Ark., 1988—; pres. Soc. Universal Love, Dallas, 1988—. Author: The Prayer of Jesus, 1972, Meditation of Masters, 1973, Voice in the Wind, 1974, The Fear Factor, 1975, Benedictions of Life, 1976, A Soul Becoming, 1990; creator, narrator, lectr. audio and video tapes. Mem. Spiritual Frontier Fellowship (life). Avocations: classical music, reading, walking, crossword puzzles. Office: Soc Universal Love 1407 Braeburn Dr Richardson TX 75082 *It is not important what happens to us but what choices we make in reaction to what happens to us make our lives.*

GORDIS, ROBERT, biblical scholar, clergyman, educator, author, editor; b. Bklyn., Feb. 6, 1908; s. Hyman and Lizzie (Engel) G.; m. Fannie Jacobson, Feb. 5, 1928; children: Enoch, Leon, David. A.B. cum laude, Coll. City N.Y., 1926; Ph.D., Dropsie Coll., 1929; rabbi (with distinction), Jewish Theol. Sem. Am., 1932, D.D., 1950; D.H.L. (hon.), Spertus Coll., Chgo., 1981, Gratz Coll., Phila., 1986. Teacher Hebrew Tchrs. Tng. Sch. for Girls, 1926-28, Yeshiva Coll., 1929-30, Sem. Coll. of Jewish Studies, 1931; lectr. Rabbinical Sch. Sem., 1937-40; prof. Bibl. exegesis, 1940-60; rabbi Rockaway Park (N.Y.) Hebrew Congregation, 1931-69, rabbi emeritus, 1969—; Adj. prof. religion Columbia, 1948-57; cons. and asso. Center for Study Dem. Instns., Santa Barbara, Calif., 1960-79; vis. prof. O.T. Union Theol. Sem., 1953-54; Sem. prof. Bible Jewish Theol. Sem., 1961-69, prof. Bible, also Rapaport prof. philosophies of religion, 1974-81, prof. emeritus, 1981—; vis. prof. religion Temple U., 1967-68, prof., 1968-74; vis. prof. Bible Hebrew U., Jerusalem, 1970; Chmn. soc. justice com. Rabbinical Assembly Am., 1935-37, mem. exec. council, 1935; del. Synagogue Council of Am., 1937-40, pres., 1940-41; pres. Rabbinical Assembly, 1944-46; founder Beth-El (now Robert Gordis) Day Sch., Belle Harbor, L.I., N.Y., 1950; mem. council on religious freedom Nat. Conf. Christians and Jews; chmn. Commn. on Philosophy of Conservative Judaism, 1985-87; bd. dirs. Inst. Ch. and State, Villanova U.; Lectr. radio and TV, pub. forums speaker. Assoc. editor dept. of Bible: Universal Jewish Ency; Contbg. editor: Medical Aspects of Human Sexuality; bd. editors: Judaism (jour.), 1942-68; editor, 1969—; Contbr. to jours. and mags.; Author: over 20 books including Wisdom of Ecclesiastes, 1945, Conservative Judaism-An American Philosophy, 1945, Koheleth, The Man and His World, 1951, The Song of Songs, 1954, Judaism for the Modern Age, 1955, A Faith for Moderns, 1960, The Root and The Branch-Judaism and the Free Society, 1962, The Book of God and Man, A Study of Job, 1965, Judaism in A Christian World, 1966, Leave a Little to God, 1967, Sex and the Family in Jewish Tradtion, 1967, Poets, Prophets and Sages, Essays in Biblical Interpretation, 1970, The Biblical Text in the Making, augmented edit, 1971; Song of Songs-Lamentations, 1973, The Book of Esther, 1974, The Word and the Book: Studies in Biblical Language and Literature, 1976, The Book of Job: Commentary, New Translation and Special Studies, 1978, Love and Sex—A Modern Jewish Perspective, 1978, Understanding Conservative Judaism, 1978, Judaic Ethics for a Lawless World, 1986, The Dynamics of Judaism, 1990; editor: books including Rabbinical Assembly and United Synagogue Sabbath and Festival Prayer Book, 1946. Overseas mission War-Navy depts., investigating religious condition armed forces, Pacific, Asiatic theatres, 1946; Mem. exec. com. Nat. Hillel Commn., 1960-80; nat. adminstrv. council United Synagogue Am.; bd. govs. Nat. Acad. Adult Jewish Studies; mem. Nat. Com. on Scouting; pres. Synagogue Council of Am., 1948-49, Jewish Book Council Am., 1980-83; trustee Ch. Peace Union; cons. on religion Fund for Republic, 1957-60; asso. trustee Am. Sch. Oriental Research, 1971-73. Recipient Nat. Jewish Book award, 1979; Guggenheim fellow, 1973. Fellow Am. Acad. Jewish Research (mem. exec. com.). Home: 150 West End Ave New York NY 10023 Office: 15 E 84th St New York NY 10028

GORDON, ADELBERT M., JR., minister, educator; b. Cleve., Apr. 16, 1928; s. Adelbert M. amd Pansy (Hansen) G.; m. Minerva D. Diaz, June 6, 1953; children: Adelbert III, Victor, Rebecca, Kimberly. BS, Bluffton Coll., 1952; ThM, United Theol. Sem., 1956. Ordained to ministry Evang. United Brethren, 1956. Min. Evang. United Brethren Ch., Wellsville, Pa., 1955-57, Bryansville, Pa., 1957-64; min. Hickory Bottom Parish United Ch. of Christ, Martinsburg, Pa., 1964—; tchr. drivers and safety edn. Bedford (Pa.) Area Schs., 1964—; mem. Ch. and Ministry Com. Pa. West Conf., Juniata Assn., 1983—. Home and Office: 107 S Market St Martinsburg PA 16662-1109

GORDON, CHARLES EDWARD, minister; b. Gary, Ind., Aug. 11, 1941; s. George Charles and Glendora (Castle) G.; m. Jill Larrain Miller, Apr. 11, 1964; children: Virginia, Jennifer, Matthew, Daniel. BA, U. Dayton, 1973; postgrad., Winebrenner Theol. Sem., 1987-89. Ordained to ministry Christian Ch., 1977. Pastor Christ Fellowship, Findlay, Ohio, 1986-87, Hillcrest Christian Ch., Findlay, Ohio, 1987—. Office: 10572 Country Rd 95 Findlay OH 45840

GORDON, DANE REX, educator, minister; b. London, June 15, 1925; came to U.S., 1954; s. Leonard and Heather (Gibson) G.; m. Elizabeth May Marshall, Aug. 16, 1952 (dec. Apr. 1987); m. Judith Fisher Ward, July 6, 1991. BA, U. Cambridge, 1951, MA, 1958; BD, U. London, 1956; MA in Philosophy, U. Rochester, 1960. Ordained to ministry Presbyn. Ch., 1958. Profl. actor Eng., 1938-43; bookseller Hatchards, London, 1946-48; assoc. minister Cen. Presbyn. Ch., Rochester, N.Y., 1958-61; asst. prof. Rochester Inst. Tech., 1962-71, Danforth assoc., 1967-69, assoc. prof., then prof., chmn. dept., asst. dean, acting dean, 1976-77, assoc. dean Coll. Liberal Arts, 1976-87, prof. philosophy, 1976—. Author: New Way English, 1964, Philosophy of Religion Study Guide, 1973, (with Milford Fargo) A Family Christ Mass, 1973, Away He Run, 1976, Rochester Institute of Technology: Industrial Development and Educational Innovation in an American City, 1982: The Old Testament: a Beginning Survey, 1985, An Ethic of Basic Commitment, 1992, Thinking and Reading about Philosophy of Religion, 1992. Served with Royal Navy, 1943-46. Mem. AAUP, Am. Philos. Assn., Am. Acad. Religion, Am. Soc. Composers, Authors, Producers, Presbytery of Genesee Valley. Office: Rochester Inst Tech Coll Liberal Arts Dept of Philosophy Rochester NY 14623 *When we have faith in someone, we share in our own lives, even though slightly, the qualities of the life we trust. That I think is part of what is meant by having faith in Christ.*

GORDON, ERNEST, clergyman; b. Greenock, Scotland, May 31, 1916; naturalized, 1960; s. James and Sarah Rae (Macmillan) G.; m. Helen McIntosh Robertson, Dec. 17, 1945; children: Gillian Margaret, Alastair James. B.D., Hartford Theol. Sem., 1948, S.T.M., 1949; postgrad., U. Glasgow, 1950-51; LL.D., Bloomfield Coll., 1957; D.C.L. (hon.), Bishop's U. of Can., 1966; L.H.D. (hon.), Marshall U., 1973; D.D. (hon.), St. Andrews U., Scotland, 1976; D.Litt (hon.), Grove City Coll., 1988. Ordained to ministry Ch. of Scotland, 1950. Dep. minister Paisley Abbey, 1950-52; supply minister Amagansett and Montauk chs., 1953-54; Presbyn. chaplain Princeton U., 1954-55, dean univ. chapel, 1955-81; now pres. Christian Rescue Effort for Emancipation of Dissidents; Danforth lectr. Davis and Elkins Coll., 1968; Turnbull preacher Melbourne, Australia, 1969; Staley distinguished scholar, 1972—; tchr. in residence Presbyn. Ch., Houston, 1983; vis. prof. King Coll., Tenn., 1985; lectr. Inst. of History Princeton U., U. St. Andrews, 1987. Author: A Living Faith for Today, 1956, Through the Valley of the Kwai, 1962, Miracle on the River Kwai, 1963, Meet Me at the Door, 1969, A Guidebook for the New Christian, 1972, Solan, 1973, Islands Apart, 1977, Me, Myself & Who?, 1980. Contbr. articles to periodicals and publs. in USSR. Served as capt. 93d Highlanders, 1939-46, PTO. Recipient Amy Found. award for lit., 1986, Faith and Freedom award Presbyn. Com. for Religion and Democracy, 1987, Am. Coptic Assn. award, 1989. Fellow Victoria Inst. London; mem. Royal Inst. Philosophy (London), Ch. Service Soc. Am. (founder). Clubs: Princeton (N.Y.C.); Highland Brigade (London); Burma Star, Brit. Officers.; Nassau-Princeton. Prisoner of war, 1942-45. Home: 787 Princeton Kingston Rd Princeton Township NJ 08540 also: Bendigo Rd Amagansett NY 11850

GORDON, FORREST LYLE, minister; b. Rich Hill, Mo., Feb. 4, 1926; s. Fay Ward and Martha Blanche (Caton) G.; m. Onie Elizabeth Orr, Sept. 11, 1946; children: Carol Diane Gordon Kobe, David Ward. CLU, Am. Coll., 1977. Lic. as min. First Bapt. Ch., 1976; ordained to ministry Evang. Ch. Alliance, 1987. Capt. (ret.) L.A. City Fire Dept., 1951-62; pastor of adminstrn. and missions First Bapt. Ch., Reseda, Calif., 1986—; mem. fin. com. S.W. Bapt. Conf., West Covina, Calif., 1987-90. Author: Church Safety, 1990. chmn. Reseda Cen. Bus. Dist. Citizens Adv. com., 1987-89. With USCG, 1943-46. Fellow Nat. Assn. Ch. Bus. Adminstrn.; mem. Christian Mgmt. Assn., Reseda C. of C. Republican. Office: First Bapt Ch Reseda 18644 Sherman Way Reseda CA 91335 *For to me to live is Christ and to die is gain. (Phil. 1:21).*

GORDON, J. E., bishop. Bishop Ch. of God in Christ, Marrero, La. Office: Ch of God in Christ 6610 Chenault Dr Marrero LA 70072*

GORDON, JAMES LEE, pastor; b. Elkins, W.Va., Aug. 8, 1932; s. Preston Lee and Edith Elizabeth (Jordan) G.; m. Martha Emma Sheets, Mar. 10, 1956; children: Christena, Elizabeth, James. Grad. high sch., Elkins. Ordained to ministry Bapt. Ch., 1971. Inspector Gen. Industries, Elyria, Ohio, 1956-58; mgr. Green Thumb Products, Elyria, 1958-69; foreman Columbiana (Ohio)) Floral Co., 1969-71; assoc. pastor College Heights Bapt. Ch., Elyria, 1971-81; pastor Elyria Bapt. Ch., 1981—; dir. Jolly 60's of Lorain, Elyria, 1981—; rep. Prison Fellowship No. Ohio, 1990—. Mem. Repub. Nat. Com., Washington, 1990—; mem. Dem. State of Ohio com., Columbus, 1990. With USAF, 1953-55, Korea. Recipient cert. appreciation Lorain County Commr., 1990, Lorain County Anti-Drug award, 1982, Nat. Leadership award Am. Coalition for Traditional Values, 1985, Century Club award Bee Bee Evangelistic Ministers, 1974, cert. commendation Bible Teaching, Gospel Lite, 1988. Mem. Ohio Patrolmen's Benevolent Assn. (assoc.), Lorain County Ministerial Assn., YMCA. Avocations: photography, golf, travel. Home: 953 Wilder Ave Elyria OH 44035 Office: Elyria Bapt Ch 276 Washington Ave Elyria OH 44035

GORDON, MICHAEL GERALD FRANCIS, priest; b. Phila., June 17, 1941; s. Michael Francis and Anna Maria (O'Keefe) G. BA, St. Francis Coll., 1964; MDiv, St. Francis Sem., 1969; MA in Franciscan Studies, St. Bonaventure U., 1975. Ordained priest Roman Cath. Ch., 1969. Instr. Egan High Sch., Fairless Hills, Pa., 1969-72; dir. Franciscan Ctr. for Spl. Renewal, Winchester, Va., 1972-74; instr. St. Francis Coll. and Sem., Loretto, Pa., 1975-76; formation bd. Franciscan Third Order Regular Province, Loretto, 1975-80, dir. vocations, 1975-80, dir. fgn. missions, 1988—; adminstr. St. Francis Prep Sch., Spring Grove, Pa., 1976-77; internat. retreat dir. Retreats Internat., South Bend, Ind., 1972-76; svc. bd. Franciscan Fedn., Millvale, Pa., 1976-81. Named Padre of Yr. Cath. Youth Orgn., Diocese of Trenton, 1987, 88; recipient Outstanding Svc. award Eastern Reg. Vocation Dirs. Assn., 1980. Fellow Nat. Cath. Devel. Office, Franscican Fedn. Democrat. Home: St Francis Monastery Loretto PA 15940-0600 Office: Franciscan TOR Mission PO Box 136 St Mary St Loretto PA 15940-0136

GORDON, MORTON LAWRENCE, rabbi; b. Putnam, Conn., Oct. 17, 1924; s. Solomon Z. and Florence (Bloch) G.; m. Anna S. Lesser, Jan. 4, 1948; children: Jonathan, Sandra. BS, NYU, 1946, MA, 1971, D. Hebrew Letters, 1974; Rabbi, Yeshiva U., 1947. Ordained rabbi, 1947. Rabbi Degel Israel Synagogue, Watertown, N.Y., 1947-50, House of Peace Synagogue, Columbia, S.C., 1950-54, Sons of Zion Synagogue, Putnam, 1954-62, Jewish Ctr. of Mt. Vernon (N.Y.), 1962-68, Temple Torah, Little Neck, N.Y., 1968—; pres. L.I. (N.Y.) Commn. Rabbis, 1975-77; pres. L.I. Bd. Rabbis, 1981-83. Contbr. sermons to religious publs. Recipient Horowitz award Fedn. Jewish Philanthropies, 1980. Mem. Am. Assn. Marriage and Family Therapists (clin.), Rabbinical Coun. Am. (bd. dirs.), N.Y. Bd. Rabbis (bd. dirs.), Internat. Synagogue (bd. dirs.), Masons (chaplain). Home: 66 Bates Rd Great Neck NY 11020 Office: Temple Torah 54-27 Little Neck Pkwy Little Neck NY 11362 *Human beings are placed on this earth to serve God and other people. In this process, we will improve the world about us. When selfishness, greed and arrogance get in the way, we fail our Divine mission.*

GORDON, RYAN RUSSELL, youth minister; b. Ashland, Ohio, Aug. 25, 1965; s. Russell Carl and Sherrie Dee (Humphrey) G.; m. Vanessa Lynn Oburn, June 29, 1991. Student, Manatee Community Coll., Bradenton, Fla., 1984-86; BS in Elem. Edn., Ashland (Ohio) U., 1990. Youth advisor Brethren Ch., Bradenton, 1984-86, Touch Basic Sml. Group leader, 1985, puppet ministry leader, 1985-86; youth advisor Brethren Ch., Ashland, 1987-90; dir. youth ministries Brethren Ch., Milledgeville, Ill., 1990—; youth summer crusader Brethren Ch., Ashland, 1986-88; choral dir. Brethren Ch., Milledgeville, 1990—, children's coord., 1990—, VBS dir., Ashland, 1989-90. Mem. Rotary. Republican. Office: Brethren Ch PO Box 638 6th and Main Ave Milledgeville IL 61051

GORDON, SAMUEL NEAL, rabbi, consultant; b. Pitts., Sept. 2, 1950; s. Nathan and Rae (Segall) G.; m. Patty Gerstenblith, Jan. 29, 1977; children: Jennifer, Shira, Theodore. BA, U. Pitts., 1973; MAHL, Hebrew Union Coll., 1979, ordination, 1980; MM, Northwestern U., Evanston, Ill., 1985. Asst. rabbi Temple Beth Israel, Chgo., 1980-82; rabbi Congregation Or Shalom, Vernon Hills, Ill., 1982—; cons. Chgo. Jewish Fedn., 1986-88, Arie and Ida Crown Meml., Chgo., 1987-89, Patrick and Anna M. Cudahy Fund., Milw., 1987-89, Cen Conf. of Am. Rabbis, N.Y., 1991. Treas. Shalom Ctr., Phila.; trustee The Kiski Sch., Saltsburg, Pa.; exec. com. Ctr. for Ch./State Studies, DePaul Univ., Chgo., all current. Recipient Levinson Meml. award Hebrew Union Coll., 1985. Mem. Chgo. Bd. Rabbis (exec. com.), Chgo. Assn. Reform Rabbis (exec. com.), Cen. Conf. Am. Rabbis, Michigan Shores Club. Avocations: swimming, skiing, traveling, sailing. Home: 910 Sheridan Rd Wilmette IL 60091 Office: Congregation Or Shalom 21 Hawthorn Pkwy Vernon Hills IL 60061

GORDON, VICTOR REESE, minister; b. Ft. Dodge, Iowa, Nov. 29, 1950; s. Lyle R. and Deleina K. (Rogers) G.; m. Susan E. Sjurson, July 28, 1973; children: Joshua, Nathan, Jonathan, Joy. AB, Stanford U., 1973; MDiv, Fuller Theol. Sem., 1975, PhD, 1979. Ordained to ministry Am. Bapt. Assn., 1975. Interim pastor Geneva Rd. Bapt. Ch., Wheaton, Ill., 1985-86; sr. pastor 1st Bapt. Ch., Wichita, Kans., 1988—; chaplain, asst. prof. religious studies Sioux Falls (S.D.) Coll., 1978-83; chaplain, asst. prof. bibl. and theol. studies Wheaton Coll., 1983-88; adj. prof. N.T., No. Bapt. Sem., 1984—; bd. dirs. Christian Ministry to Offenders, Wichita, 1988—. Contbr. articles to Internat. Standard Bible Ency. and religious jours. Bd. dirs. Lawndale Community Ctr., Chgo., 1982—, Fellowship Christian Athletes, 1988—; coach Am. Youth Soccer Orgn., Wichita, 1990-91. Mem. Cath. Bibl. Assn., Soc. Bibl. Lit., Am. Acad. Religion, Inst. for Bibl. Rsch., Evang. Philos. Soc. Home: 7116 Greenbriar Cir Wichita KS 67226 Office: 1st Bapt Ch 216 E 2d Wichita KS 67202

GORE, MARTIN WAYNE, minister; b. Forest City, Ark., July 13, 1955; s. Earl and Imogene (Jones) G.; m. Robbie Billingsley, Dec. 7, 1973; children: Shane Wayne, Michelle Lynn. Student, Cen. Bible Coll., Springfield, Mo., 1986-87, Southwestern Assemblies of God, Bible Coll., Waxahachie, Tex., 1988-89. Ordained to ministry Assemblies of God, 1989. Pastor Assemblies of God Ch., Marianna, Ark., 1987-89, Magnolia, Ark., 1989—; famer, landowner, Palestine, Ark., 1973—; sec./treas. Ministerial Alliance, Marianna, 1988-89; youth rep. sect., Assemblies of God, Magnolia, 1989-90, sectional presbyter, 1990—, chaplain, 1989—. Home: 2018 N Washington Magnolia AR 71753 Office: First Assembly of God 2020 N Washington Magnolia AR 71753

GORE, TIMOTHY CLEARENCE, minister; b. Fay, N.C., Sept. 27, 1956; s. Kelly M. and Vernell H. (Turlington) G.; m. Brenda Jewell Goodwin, Aug. 15, 1981; children: Vanessa Nadine, Julie Christine. BA in Biblical Studies, East Coast Bible Coll., 1984. Ordained to ministry Ch. of God, 1987. Minister of youth and Christian edn. Ch. of God, Gastonia, N.C., 1983-84, Cumberland, N.C., 1984-85; pastor Eureka Springs Ch. of God, Fay, 1985-89; asst. pastor, dir. Christian edn. Ch. of God-Timberlake, Hope Mills, N.C., 1989—; mgr. perishable dept. Ford Lion, Inc., Hope Mills, 1985—; dist. youth dir. Hope Mills area Ch. of God, 1990—. Home: 2775-B Hope Mill Rd Fayetteville NC 28306

GORGANS, MARK THOMAS, minister; b. Miami, Fla., May 25, 1957; s. James T. and June C. (Baston) G.; m. Joy Weaver, July 12, 1980; children: Tabetha, Christiana, Matthew. BS, Toccoa Falls Coll., 1981, postgrad.; postgrad., Oxford U., England. Ordained to ministry Christian Ch., 1983. Asst. pastor Christian & Missionary Alliance, Belle Glade, Fla., 1977-81, Port Charlotte, Fla., 1981-83; pastor Christian & Missionary Alliance, Orange City, Fla., 1983-87, Elberta, Alta., Can., 1987—; bd. dirs. Save-a-life Inc., Robertsdale, Ala., 1989—; extension com. mem. Christian & Missionary Alliance, Birmingham, Ala., 1987—, dist. exec. com. mem. 1989—, new life com. for evangelism, 1991—. Contbr. articles to profl. jours. Pres. Rep. Club, Orange City, 1983-87, exec. com. 1983-87. Mem. Rotary Club, Phi Kappa Nu. Home: 110 N Main St Elberta AL 36530

GORHAM, DANIEL JOHN, priest; b. Miami, Fla., Mar. 4, 1929; s. Vincent Raymond and Ruth Leola (McSweeny) G. AA, Palm Beach Jr. Coll., Lake Worth, Fla., 1952; BA, Santa Fe (N.Mex.) Coll., 1957; BS, Fla. State U., 1959; MA, George Washington U., 1966. Ordained priest Greek Orthodox Ch., Old Calendar, 1960. Pastor St. Vincent Orthodox Ch., Fullerton, Calif., 1979—; editor, pubr. Axios, The Orthodox Jour., Fullerton, 1981—; dir. Nat. Bd. of Greek Orthodox Ch., 1985—; trustee St. Michael Fund, Fullerton, 1980—; del. Greek Orthodox Ch., Astoria, 1965—; dir. Western Am. Deanery, Orthodox Ch., 1979—. Author: St. Vincent Calendar, 1981, The Orthodox Year, 1982, Saints of the Orthodox, 1984, The Liturgical Year, 1990; contbr. articles to profl. jours. Bd. dirs. Libertarian Party, Orange County, Santa Ana, Calif., 1991—; supr. registration Palm Beach County, Fla., 1960-65. Named Outstanding Pastor, Greek Orthodox Ch., 1990. Fellow Orthodox Univ. Assn.; mem. Nat. Orthodox Clergy Assn., Assoc. Ch. Press, Santa Fe Coll. Alumni Assn. (dir. 1990), Fla. State U. Alumni Assn., Irish-Am. Soc. (dir. 1989), Alpha Phi Omega (Outstanding Alumni), Sons of Confederate Vets., Esperanto Assn., Kiwanis. Home: 800 S Euclid St Fullerton CA 92632 Office: 806 S Euclid St Fullerton CA 92632 *The closer we come to Christ the more we understand.*

GORMAN, DEBORAH EWING, minister; b. Cleve., Oct. 22, 1946; d. John Sargeant and Susan (Marquis) Ewing; m. Paul Vincent Gorman Jr., June 8, 1968; children: Rachael Carrie, Paul Vincent III. BA, Conn. Coll., 1968; M in Arts and Religion, Ashland Theol. Sem., 1981. Ordained to ministry United Meth. Ch., 1985. Dir. youth and vol. mins. Rockport United Meth. Ch., Rocky River, Ohio, 1981-83; dir. Christian edn. North Olmsted (Ohio) United Meth. Ch., 1983-86; diaconal min. Christian edn. Westlake (Ohio) United Meth. Ch., 1987—; leader tng. for ch. leaders, clergy, ch. sch. tchrs., youth workers and local chs., 1975-90; mem. East Ohio Conf. Coun. on Children's Ministries, 1980-84, chairperson, 1984-88; mem. East Ohio Youth Ann. Conf., 1981—; mem. East Ohio Ann. Conf., 1985—; mem. monitoring and evaluation coms. East Ohio Conf., 1984-88, coun. on ministries, 1984-88, mem. worship com., 1988-89, vice chairperson bd. diaconal ministry, 1988-90, chairperson lab. com., 1990—; mem. Cleve Dist. Coun. on Ministries, 1988—. Mem. Lakewood Hist. Soc., 1973-75, West Shore Concerts Bd., Cleve., 1974-75, PTA, Rocky River, Ohio, 1974-85. Recipient John Lennon Meml. award E. Ohio conf. United Meth. Ch., 1991. Mem. Religious Edn. Assn., Christian Educators Fellowship. Democrat. Office: Westlake United Meth Ch 27650 Center Ridge Rd Westlake OH 44145

GORMAN, GARY EUGENE, minister, educator, author; b. Carmel-By-The-Sea, Calif., Oct. 8, 1944; s. Eugene Wesley and Alma Gertrude (Falt) G.; m. Lynette Chaffey, June 6, 1980; 1 dau., Caroline Theresa Holmes. BA cum laude, Boston U., 1967; MDiv, Luth. Theol. Seminary, 1970; STB with honors, Trinity Coll., Toronto, Ont., Can., 1971; diploma in librarianship Univ. Coll., London, 1975; MA, U. London, 1977; ThD, Australian Coll. Theology, 1991. Chaplain, St. Hugh's Coll., Oxford, Eng., 1972-74; warden Namibia Peace Ctr., Sutton Courtenay, Berkshire, Eng., 1974-75; internat. orgns. libr. Inst. Devel. Studies, Brighton, Sussex, Eng., 1975-83; founding dir. Libr. Info. and Pub. Cons., Lewes, Eng. and Coolamon, N.S.W., Australia, 1982—; lectr. dept. librarianship Ballarat Coll. Advanced Edn., Victoria, Australia, 1984-86; sr. lectr., coord. grad. studies Sch. Info. Studies, Charles Sturt U., NSW, Australia, 1986—; cons. UNIDO, U. South Africa, IBM (France), World Vision of Australia, Sydney Coll. Div., St. John Vianney Sem., others, 1978, 80, 82, 86, 88—; hon. chaplain Anglican Bishop of Ballarat, 1984—; mem. post-ordination edn. com. Diocese of Ballarat, 1986-88; priest Anglican Ch. of Australia. Author: South African Novel in English, 1978, Guide to Third World National Bibliograpies, 1983, 2nd ed., 1987, Theological and Religious Reference Materials (3 vols.), 1984-86, Collection Development for Australian Libraries, 1988, 2d edit., 1991, Collection Development for Libraries, 1989, The Education and Training of Information Professionals, 1989, Guide to Current Indexing and Abstracting Services in the Third World, 1991; editor: (book series) Bibliographies and Indexes in Religious Studies, 1982—, Topics in Australasian Library and Information Studies, 1988—, Topics in Library and Information Studies, 1988—, The Education of Library and Information Professionals, 1991—; (serial) Index of Development Studies Literature, 1983-85; (book series) Development Studies, 1976-83; assoc. editor Jour. Libr. Acquisitions: Practice and Theory, 1983—; joint editor Australian Libr. Rev., 1987—; book rev. editor Jour. African Book Pub. Record, 1977—; cons. editor Jour. Theol. and Religious Info., 1989—; coord. editor Australasian Religion Index, 1989—; contbr. numerous articles in field to various profl. jours. Eliza Smith fellow Luth. Ch. in Am., 1971, 72; travel grantee U. South Africa, 1978. Fellow Royal Soc. Arts Eng., Libr. Assn. Eng.; mem. Am. Theol. Libr. Assn., African Studies Assn. Australia and Pacific, Internat. Assn. Agrl. Librs. and Documentalists, Australian Libr. and Info. Assn. (assoc.; conv. Distance in Edn. Spl. Interest Group 1985-88, sec. edn. for librarianship nat. com. 1986-88, sec. edn. for libr. and info. sci. sect. 1989); exec. Ctr. for Info. Studies; Standing Conf. on Libr. Materials on Africa, Assn. Brit. Theol. and Philos. Librs., Am. Theol. Libr. Assn., Australian and New Zealand Theol. Libr. Assn., Delta Mu, Phi Alpha Theta. Anglican. Office: Charles Sturt U Sch Info Studies, PO Box 588, Wagga Wagga NSW 2650, Australia *Two phrases from the Christian tradition strike me as appropriate in any age: "carpe diem" and "sin bravely". We have been blessed with the gift of life and owe our creator a positive response to this honour. We must grasp each day as a new creation and make the most of it, using our time and talents creatively, compassionately and humanely. In communion with God and the saints of our respective traditions we must have the confident humility—and humble confidence—to act, to speak out, to do, to sin bravely.*

GORMAN, JOHN R., auxiliary bishop. Ordained priest Roman Cath. Ch., 1952. Aux. bishop Roman Cath. Ch., Chgo., appointed aux. bishop, titular bishop of Catula, 1988—, consecrated, 1988—. Home: PO Box 1979 Chicago IL 60690 Office: 724 Elder Ln Deerfield IL 60015

GORMAN, LEO JOSEPH, priest; b. Far Rockaway, N.Y., June 11, 1929; s. Joseph J. and Helen Cecilia (Lally) G. BA in Philosophy, Passionist Monastic Sem., 1953, MA in Theology, 1957. Ordained priest Roman Cath. Ch., 1957. Itinerant preacher Eastern U.S. and Can., 1957-59, 61-64; assoc. pastor St. Mary's Parish, Dunkirk, N.Y., 1959-61; assoc. dir. retreats Our Lady of Fla. Monastery, North Palm Beach, Fla., 1964-67, resident retreat preacher, 1967-69; dir. Passionist Retreat House, West Springfield, Mass., 1969-74; vice rector St. Gabriel's Monastery, Brighton, Mass., 1974-76; exec. producer The Sunday Mass program WNYW-TV, Pelham, N.Y.; sec. Passionist Communications, Pelham, 1976—; v.p., sec. That's the Spirit Prodns., Inc., 1980—; substitute chaplain Kennedy Meml. Hosp. for Children, 1974-76; moderator Cath. Young Adult Club, West Palm Beach, 1963-68; vol. counselor Palm Beach County Juvenile Ct., 1963-69; panelist television program Face to Face on ABC, Palm Beach, 1968-69; mem. Springfield Clergy Task Force on Drugs, 1970-74; co-chmn. West Springfield Clergy Assn., 1971-73; founding pres. Hope Home of Western Mass., Inc., 1972-74. V.p. Big Brothers, 1968-69; pres. Community Health Commn., West Springfield, 1971-72; bd. dirs. YMCA, Palm Beach County Mental Health Assn. Mem. Nat. Assn. Broadcasters, Fla. Sheriffs Assn. (hon.). Home: 190 Mount Tom Rd Pelham NY 10803 Office: P O Box 440 Pelham NY 10803

GORMAN, MICHAEL JOSEPH, priest; b. Richland Center, Wis., Nov. 23, 1954; s. Kyrie Joseph and Susan Loretta (Nee) G. BA in Theology, St. Francis de Sales Coll., 1976; MDiv, St. Paul Sem., 1980; JCL, Pontifical Gregorian U., Rome, 1986. Ordained priest Roman Cath. Ch., 1980. Assoc. pastor Blessed Sacrament Parish, La Crosse, Wis., 1980-84; diocesan judge, defender of the bond Diocese of La Crosse, 1986—, chancellor, 1988—; prof. Latin St. Mary's Coll., Winona, Minn., 1990—. Mem. Nat. Cath. Cemetery Conf., Assn. Cath. Diocesan Archivists, Canon Law Soc. Am.

GORSKI, WILLIAM EDWARD, missionary; b. Chgo., Sept. 2, 1950; s. Arthur William and Lois Ann (Lundell) G.; m. Cynthia Helen Witt, Sept. 22, 1973; children—Amanda Elizabeth, Rebecca Christine. B.A., Augustana Coll., 1972; M.Div., Luth. Sch. Theology, Chgo., 1976. Ordained to ministry Evang. Luth. Ch. Am., 1976. Pastor, Christ the Lord Luth. Ch., Elgin, Ill., 1976-78; pastor, missionary Evang. Luth. Ch. Am., Santiago, Chile, 1978—; bd. dirs., treas. Evang. Theol. Community, Santiago, 1985—, prof. liturgics, 1978—; bd. dirs. Clinica Alemana, Santiago, 1987; sec. of ch. Evang. Luth. Ch. in Chile, 1980, bishop, pres., 1986; dir. Fundacion Ayuda Social Cristiana, Chile, 1978—; dir., pres. Fundacion Ayuda Social de las Iglesias Cristianas, 1987—. Mem. Delta Omega Nu (pres. 1972), Omicron Delta Kappa, Phi Mu Alpha. Address: Casilla 15167, Santiago Chile

GORSUCH, RICHARD LEE, graduate school educator; b. Wayne, Mich., May 13, 1937; s. Culver C. and Velma L. G.; m. Sylvia Sue Coalson, Aug. 18, 1961; children: Eric, Kay. AB, Tex. Christian U., 1959; MA, U. Ill., 1962, PhD, 1965; MDiv., Vanderbilt U., 1968. Ordained to ministry Ch. Disciples of Christ, 1968. Asst. prof. psychology Vanderbilt U., Nashville, 1966-68; asst. prof., then assoc. prof. George Peabody Coll., Nashville, 1968-73; assoc. prof. Tex. Christian U., Ft. Worth, 1973-75; assoc. prof. U. Tex., Arlington, 1975-76, prof., 1976-79; prof. Fuller Theol. Sem., Pasadena, Calif., 1979—. Author: Factor Analysis (rev. 2d edit., 1983); co-author: Nature of Man, 1976; Psychology of Religion, 1984; contbr. numerous articles to profl. jours.; cons. editor religious, ednl. and psychol. jours. Fellow NIMH, 1960-61. Fellow APA (pres. div. 36), Soc. for Sci. Study Religion; mem. Soc. Multivariate Exptl. Psychology, Religious Research Assn.

GORVEATTE, KENNETH LAYTON, minister, counselor; b. Springhill, N.S., Can., Nov. 27, 1935; came to U.S., 1975; s. Ralph Borden and Helen Francais (Layton) G.; m. Anne Louise Brittain, June 17, 1958; children: Mark, Ruth, Beth, Joel. BA, Ind. Wesleyan U., 1966; BEd, Mt. Allison U., Sackville, N.B., Can., 1971; M of Community Counseling, Miss. Coll., 1988; cert. advanced studies, Hollins Coll., 1989. Ordained to ministry Wesleyan Ch., 1960. Pastor Wesleyan chs., Maine, Can., 1958-69, Ala., Miss., Va., 1972-90; prin. Bethany Acad., Sussex, N.B., 1970-72; dir. Va. Wesleyan Counseling Ctr., Roanoke, Va., 1990—; mem. Dist. Bd. Ministerial Standing, Roanoke, 1989-91; instr. ministerial student course, Roanoke, 1990-91; dir. Christian Family Life Ministries, Martinsville, 1991; conf. speaker nationwide, Can., Haiti. Author: Project H.O.P.E. (Home Outreach Plane of Evangelism). Contact person Refugee Resettlement Com., Martinsville, 1989-91. Winner award for Fastest Growing Sunday Sch. in State of Maine. Mem. Mmartinsville Ministerial Assn. (pres. 1991). Office: Va Wesleyan Counseling Ctr 8405 Williamson Rd Roanoke VA 24019 *Strong families are the foundation on which our society rests. No adequate societal structure can long endure on any other base. Therefore the church must contribute in meaningful ways to strength this foundation.*

GOSNELL, RICKY DALE, minister; b. Spartanburg, S.C., June 4, 1958; s. Jessie James and Lillian (Spake) G.; m. Robin Ann Metts, June 11, 1983; children: Hannah Dale, Rebekah Metts. BA, Wofford Coll., 1980; MA, U. S.C., 1982; MDiv, So. Bapt. Theol. Seminary, Louisville, 1989, postgrad. Ordained to ministry Bapt. Ch., 1987. Pastor Buffalo Lick Bapt. Ch., Shelbyville, Ky., 1987—; Garrett fellow, dept. evangelism for Billy Graham/Prof. Evangelism, So. Bapt. Theol. Seminary, 1989—. Recipient full acad. scholarship Wofford Coll. via Spartan Mills, Spartanburg, S.C., 1976. Republican. Home and Office: 2761 A Grinstead Dr Louisville KY 40206

GOSS, GLENN RICHARD, religion educator; b. Columbia, Pa., Mar. 6, 1932; s. Paul A. and Emma Sauder (Shetzley) G.; m. Doris Millet, May 25, 1957; children: Stephen Dwight, Michael Andrew. BS, Pa. State U., 1954; ThM, Dallas Sem., 1958, ThD, 1966. Ordained to ministry Scofield Meml. Ch., 1958. Mem. faculty Dallas Bible Coll., 1959-66, Calvary Bible Coll., Kansas City, Mo., 1966-74, Phila. Coll. Bible, Langhorne, Pa., 1974—; mem. accrediting commn. Am. Assn. Bible Colls., Fayetteville, 1982-86. Office: Phila Coll Bible 200 Manor Ave Langhorne PA 19047

GOSS, LEONARD GEORGE, editor, marketing consultant; b. San Diego, Dec. 31, 1947; s. Joseph and Sylvia (Rosenberg) G.; m. Carolyn Stanford, June 5, 1971; children: Joseph Stanford, David Leonard. AA, Phoenix Coll., 1968; BA, Ariz. State U., 1971; MDiv., Trinity Sem., Deerfield, Ill., 1975; postgrad., U. Windsor, Ont., 1984-88. With mktg. dept. John Wiley & Sons, Inc., N.Y.C., 1975-80; with editorial, mktg. and advt. depts. Mott Media, Inc., Pub., Detroit, 1980-85; with editorial dept. Evang. Book Club, Detroit, 1980-85; with mktg. and editorial dept. Zondervan Corp. div. Harper Collins Pubs., Grand Rapids, Mich., 1985—; adj. prof. world religions Grand Rapids Bapt. Coll., 1990—. Co-author: Writing Religiously, 1984, Inside Religious Publishing, 1991. Mem. Conf. on Faith and History. Mem. Evang. Theol. Soc., Messianic Jewish Alliance, Soc. for Scholarly Pub., Pareveh Alliance. Lutheran. Home: 6134 Adacroft SE Grand Rapids MI 49546 Office: The Zondervan Corp 1415 Lake Dr SE Grand Rapids MI 49506 *Through stories the entire Bible conveys the good news that God has entered into the story of his creation. Our challenge in religious publishing is to communicate the marvelous good news. We publish for people who, like us, love and want the value of books in order to develop their own thoughts, to participate in dialogue with others, to leave something for another generation, and to build a deep foundation of faith.*

GOSSAI, HEMCHAND, minister, educator; b. Georgetown, Guyana, Apr. 11, 1954; came to U.S., 1976; m. Marie Beverly Vold, June 17, 1979; children: Nathan Paul, Chandra Michele. BA, Concordia Coll., Moorhead, Minn., 1979; MDiv, Luther Northwestern Seminary, St. Paul, 1983; PhD, U. St. Andrews, Scotland, 1986. Instr. in Old Testament Luther Northwestern Seminary, 1986-87; pastor Our Savior's Luth. Ch., New Ulm, Minn., 1987-90; exec. mem. bd. youth Southwest Minn. Evang. Luth. Ch. Am., 1988-90; adj. prof. Old Testament, St. Paul Sem., 1988-90. Contbr. articles to profl. jours. Mem. Soc. Bibl. Lit., Cath. Bibl. Assn., Sertoma. Office: Concordia Coll Moorhead MN 56562

GOSSAN, BRIAN WESLEY, clergyman, educator; b. Escanaba, Mich., Feb. 18, 1954; s. Alfred Anthony and Virginia Anne (Abraham) G.; m. Janice Diane Phillips, Feb. 5, 1983; children: Brijan Kahla, Kristopher Ryan, Philip Jemayel. AA, Bay De Noc Community Coll., 1978; BS, Andrews U., 1980; postgrad., Grand Valley State Coll. Ordained to ministry United Pentecostal Ch. Internat., 1984. Lay worker and evangelist United Pentecostal Ch., Escanaba, 1975-77; youth minister Bethel Apostolic Tabernacle, Buchanan, Mich., 1978-80; sec. Mich. United Pentecostal Ch. Internat. Conquerors, Holland, Mich., 1979-80, pres., 1979-85; pastor Holland Abundant Life Fellowship, 1980—; dir. Christian edn., youth leader sect. 6 Upper Peninsula United Pentecostal Chs., Mich., 1974-76; camp dir. jr. and sr. high sch. camps, Albion, Mich., 1980—; tchr., evangelist Fishermen's Workshop; Bible tchr. Beirut, Seoul, Republic of Korea, 1973, 88, Belize City, Belize, 1989, 91, Milan, Italy, 1990. Contbg. editor Mich. Dist. News, 1980—; contbr. articles to Life, others. Bd. dirs. Cen. Ave. Group Home of the Mich. West Shore chpt. Mich. Soc. for Autistic Children. Recipient Youth Leader Honor award sect. 4 S.W. Mich. United Pentecostal Ch. chs., 1980, sect. 5, 1982, Fishermen's Workshop award Pentecostal Ch. Kingston, Jamaica, 1983, Camp Dir. Honors award Mich. dist. Pentecostal Ch., 1983—, Outstanding Service award World Evangelism Ctr. United Pentecostal Ch. Internat., 1984. Mem. Nat. Fedn. Decency, Christian Action Council (promoter, anti-abortion com. 1984—), Travelers Protection Assn., The Attending Clergy Assn. Avocations: fishing, boating, piano, scuba diving, skiing. Home: 6471 147th Ave Holland MI 49423 Office: Holland Abundant Life Fellowship 20th and Central Holland MI 49423 *To avail oneself to all of the Word's gifts and promises bestows to mankind the same acts of the apostles to our world. To live is Jesus, to die in Him is gain.*

GOSSELIN, KENNETH STUART, minister; b. Altus, Okla., Aug. 9, 1932; s. George Clairo and Florence May (Stebbins) G.; m. P. Rodene Tayar, Sept. 8, 1962; children: Mark Alan, Kimberly Sue, Anna Jouree, Sabrina Kay. BA, Oklahoma City U., 1954; STM, Perkins Sch. Theology, 1958; MA, Claremont (Calif.) Grad. Sch., 1967. Cert. tchr., Calif. Community coll. campus minister Wesley Found., Tex. Christian U., Ft. Worth, 1958-64; minister to youth 1st Meth. Ch., Riverside, Calif., 1964-66; assoc. minister Community Meth. Ch., Sepulveda, Calif., 1967-69; minister St. Matthew's Meth. Ch., Newbury Park, Calif., 1969-71; assoc. minister Christ Ch. United Meth., Tucson, 1971-73; minister Nestor United Meth. Ch., San Diego, 1973-83, Pacific Beach (Calif.) United Meth. Ch., 1983-85; sr. minister Christ United Meth. Ch., San Diego, 1985-90; minister Lemon Grove (Calif.) United Meth. Ch., 1990—; radio announcer, editor Religion in the News, Sta. KFMB, San Diego County Ecumenical Conf., 1979-91; mem. ordained ministry com. United Meth. Dist., San Diego, 1982-91; mem. communications com. Calif.-Pacific Conf. U. Meth. Ch., Pasadena and L.A., 1988—. Entertainer, clown Muscular Dystrophy Assn. Telethon, San Diego, 1973—, Spl. Olympics, Am. Cancer Soc., Am. Heart Assn., Children's Hosp., KPBS, San Diego Symphony, etc. Danforth Found. grantee, 1956-57. Mem. Am. Acad. Religion, Clowns Am., World Clown Assn., San Diego State U. Clown Club, Mira Costa Clown Club. Democrat. Avocations: writing, cartooning, trumpet, drama. Home: 3185 Washington St Lemon Grove CA 91945 Office: Lemon Grove United Meth Ch 3205 Washington St Lemon Grove CA 91945

GOSSETT, EARL FOWLER, JR., religion and philosophy educator; b. Birmingham, Ala., Jan. 28, 1933; s. Earl Fowler Sr. and Clara May (York) G.; m. Rhoda Lois Scoates, July 17, 1956; 1 child, Amelia Gretchen. AB, Birmingham Southern Coll., 1954; BD, Vanderbilt U., 1957, PhD, 1961. Instr. in theology Scarritt Coll., Nashville, 1959-60; asst. prof. religion U. Miami, Coral Gables, Fla., 1961-65; assoc. prof. religion and philosophy to chmn. div. humanities Birmingham So. Coll., 1965—. Editor: Jour. Ecumenical Studies, 1973-76; contbr. articles to profl. jours. Mem. state bd. Nat. Conf. Christians and Jews. Recipient Excellence in Teaching award Omicron Delta Kappa, 1978. Mem. Soc. Values Higher Edn., Am. Acad. Religion (v.p. S.E. chpt. 1969-70, pres. S.E. chpt. 1970-71), Soc. Christian Ethics, Southern Soc. Psychology and Philosophy, Ala. Philos. Soc. (v.p. 1972-73), The Hastings Ctr., Phi Beta Kappa. Methodist. Office: Birmingham So Coll Box A-34 Birmingham AL 35254

GOSSMAN, FRANCIS JOSEPH, bishop; b. Balt., Apr. 1, 1930; s. Frank M. and Mary Genevieve (Steadman) G. BA, St. Mary Sem., Balt., 1952; S.T.L., N. Am. Coll., Rome, 1955; J.C.D., Cath. U. of Am., 1959. Ordained priest Roman Cath. Ch., 1955; asst. pastor Basilica of the Assumption, Balt., 1959-68; asst. chancellor Archdiocese of Balt., 1959-65, vice chancellor, 1965-68; pro-synodal judge Balt. Tribunal, 1961; vice officialis Tribunal of Archdiocese of Balt., 1962-65, officialis, 1965-68; made papal chamberlain with title Very Rev. Monsignor, 1965; elected to Senate of Priests of Archdiocese, 1967-68; adminstr. Cathedral of Mary Our Queen, 1968-70; named aux. bishop of Balt. and titular bishop of Aguntum, 1968-75, apptd. vicar gen., 1968; apptd. to Bd. Consultors, 1969; urban vicar Archdiocese of Balt., 1970-75; bishop of Raleigh N.C., 1975—; Mem. Balt. Community Relations Commn., 1969-75; mem. exec. com. Md. Food Com., Inc., 1969-75. Bd. dirs. United Fund Central Md., 1974-75. Mem. Canon Law Soc. Am., Nat. Conf. Cath. Bishops, U.S. Cath. Conf. Office: 300 Cardinal Gibbons Dr Raleigh NC 27606

GOTHONI, RENE REINHOLD, comparative religion educator; b. Helsinki, Finland, Apr. 10, 1950; s. Guido Danilo and Ulla-Britt (Carlander) G.; m. Raili Tellervo Liukku, June 2, 1973; children: Anthony, Annette, Andre. Cand. theol., U. Helsinki, 1973, Lic. theol., 1976, ThD, 1983. Asst. researcher Acad. of Finland, Helsinki, 1974-79; jr. researcher Acad. of Finland, 1984; sr. lectr. comparative religion U. Helsinki, 1980—, acting prof., 1985, 1991—. Author: Modes of Life of Theravada Monks, 1982, Patimokkha i strukturanalytisk belysning, 1985, Oletko neuvoton, 1991 ; editor: (with Mikael Tenzin Donden) Bodhipuun Juurella, 1984, (with Mahapanna) Buddhalaista viisautta, 1987, (with Juha Pentikäinen) Mythology and Cosmic Order, 1987, (with Mahapanna) Buddhalainen Sanasto Ja Symboliikka, 1990; dir., producer: (film) Buddhism in Sinhalese Culture, 1975; contbr. articles and monographs to profl. jours. Scholar World Coun. Chs., 1974, Acad. of Finland, 1974-79, 84, 85; sr. scientist grantee Acad. of Finland, 1988-89; Finnish vis. fellow Cambridge (Eng.) U., 1989-90. Mem. Finnish Soc. Anthropology (dir. 1984—), Finnish Soc. for Study of Comparative Religion (dir. 1985-89), Nordic Assn. for S. Asian Studies (bd. dirs. 1991—), Scandinavian Inst. Asian Studies, Donnerska Inst., The Finnish Ministry of Edn. Avocations: music, filmmaking. Office: U Helsinki, Dept of the Study of Religions, Meritullinkatu 1 A5, 00160 Helsinki 17, Finland

GOTT, HAROLD DEAN, minister; b. Longview, Wash., Aug. 25, 1953; s. Rex H. and Chloe B. (Adkison) G.; m. Linda G. Anderson, July 23, 1972; children: Jennifer, Robert. Ordained to ministry Ind. Christian Ch., 1984. Lay min., elder Pilot Butte Christian Ch., Bend, Oreg., 1980-84; min. Sisters (Oreg.) Ch. of Christ, 1984—; dir. jr. camp program Round Lake Christian Camp, Camp Sherman and Sisters, 1987, 88, 91. Vol. Hospice of Bend, 1987-90; mem. curriculum devel. com. Sisters Pub. High Sch., 1990-91. Home: 17325 Jordan Rd Sisters OR 97759 Office: Sisters Ch of Christ Box 70 Sisters OR 97759

GOTTLIEB, PAULA GRIBETZ, foundation administrator; b. N.Y.C., Mar. 26, 1957; d. Donald and Edith (Rubenstein) Gribetz; m. Michael Gottlieb, Aug. 28, 1978; children: Talia, Jonathan. BA, Barnard Coll., 1978. Dir. Jewish Book Coun., N.Y.C., 1986—. Office: Jewish Book Coun 15 E 26th St New York NY 10010

GOTTSCHALK, ALFRED, college president; b. Oberwesel, Germany, Mar. 7, 1930; came to U.S., 1939, naturalized, 1945; s. Max and Erna (Trum-Gerson) G.; m. Deanna Zeff, 1977; children by previous marriage: Marc Hillel, Rachel Lisa. AB, Bklyn. Coll., 1952; BHLit, Hebrew Union Coll.-Jewish Inst. Religion, 1957, MA with honors, 1957; PhD, U. So. Calif., 1965, LLD (hon.), 1976, STD (hon.), 1968; DHL (hon.), U. Judaism, 1971; DLitt (hon.), Dropsie U., 1974; LLD (hon.), U. Cin., 1976; DReligious Edn. (hon.), Loyola-Marymount U., 1977; LLD (hon.), Xavier U., 1981; LittD (hon.), St. Thomas Inst., 1982; DD (hon.), NYU, 1985; DHL (hon.), Jewish Theol. Sem., 1986, Bklyn. Coll., 1991. Ordained rabbi, 1957;. Dir. Hebrew Union Coll., Jewish Inst. Religion, L.A., 1957-59, dean, 1959-71, prof. Bible and Jewish intellectual history, 1965—, pres., 1971—; hon. fellow Hebrew U., Jerusalem, 1972; mem. Commn. on Jewish Edn. Author: Your Future as a Rabbi-A Calling that Counts, 1967, The Future of Human Community, 1967, (translator) Hesed in the Bible, 1967, The Man Must be the Message, 1968, Jewish Ecumenism and Jewish Survival, 1968, Ahad Ha-Am, Maimonides and Spinoza, 1969, Ahad Ha-Am as Bible Critic, 1971, A Jubilee of the Spirit, 1972, Israel and the Diaspora: A New Look, 1974, Limits of Ecumenicity, 1979, Israel and Reform Judaism: A Zionist Perspective, 1979, Ahad Ha-Am and Leopold Zunz: Two Perspectives on the Wissenschaft Des Judentums, 1980, Hebrew Union College and Its Impact on World Progressive Judaism, 1980, Diaspora Zionism: Achievements and Problems, 1980, What Ecumenism Means to a Jew, 1981, Introduction: Religion in a Post-Holocaust World, 1982, Tribute to Judaism, 1982, Problematics in the Future of American Jewish Community, 1982, Introduction to the American Synagogue in the Nineteenth Century, 1982, A Strategy for Non-Orthodox Judaism in Israel, Our problems and Our Future: Jews and America, 1983, The Making of a Contemporary Reform Rabbi, 1984, Is Yom Kippur Obsolete?, 1985, Ahad Ha-am: Confronting the Plight of Judaism, 1987, To Learn and To Teach, Your Future as a Rabbi, 1988, Preface to Gezer V: The Field I Caves, 1988, The American Reform Rabbinate Retrospect and Prospect, A Personal View, 1988, The German Pogrom of November 1938 and the Reaction of American Jewry, 1988, Building Unity in Diversity 1989, From the Kingdom of Night to the Kingdom of God: Jewish Christian Relations and the Search for Religious Authenticity after the Holocaust, 1983; translator: Hesed in the Bible, 1967; contbr. to Studies in Jewish Bibliography, History, and Literature, 1971, The Yom Kippur War: Israel and the Jewish People, 1974, The Image of Man in Genesis and the Ancient Near East, 1976, The Public Function fo the Jewish Scholar, 1978, The Reform Movement and Israel: A New Perspective, 1978, To Learn and to Teach, 1988; also numerous articles to profl. jours. Mem. Pres.'s Com. on EEO, 1964-66, Gov.'s Poverty Support Corps Program, 1964-66, Pres.'s Commn. on Holocaust, 1979, U.S. Holocaust Meml. Coun., 1980—, exec. com., 1980—, chmn. edn. com., 1987-88, chmn. acad. com., 1988—; chmn. N.Am. Assocs. Internat. Ctr. Univ. Teaching of Jewish Civilization, 1982-91; trustee Cin. United Appeal, Am. Sch. Oriental Rsch., Albright Inst. Archaeol. Rsch.; mem. Pres.'s Coun. Near Eastern Studies NYU. Grantee, State Dept., 1963, Smithsonian Inst., 1967; recipient award for contbns. to edn. L.A. City Coun., 1971, Tower of David award for cultural contbn. to Israel and Am., 1972, Gold medallion, Jewish Nat. Fund, 1972, Myrtle Wreath award Hadassah, 1977, Brandeis award, 1977, Nat. Brotherhood award NCCJ, 1979, Alfred Gottschalk Chair in Communal Svc., 1979, Jerusalem City of Peace award 1988, Golden Scroll award 1989, Defender of Jerusalem award honoree, 1990, Isaac M. Wise award, 1991; named Israel Bonds Man of Yr., 1982; others. Mem. AAUP, NEA, Union Am. Hebrew Congregations and Cen. Conf. Am.-Rabbis (exec. com.), Soc. Study Religion, Am. Acad. Religion, Soc.-Bibl. Lnd Exegesis, Internat. Conf. Jewish Communal Svc., Israel Exploration Soc., So. Calif. Assn. Liberal Rabbis (past pres.), So. Calif. Jewish Hist. Soc. (hon. pres.), World Union Jewish Studies (internat. Coun.), Am. Jewish Com. (exec. com., Human Rels. award 1971), World Union Progressive Judaism (v.p.), Coun. for Initiatives in Jewish Edn. (bd. dirs.), Phi Beta Kappa. Home: 17 Belsaw Pl Cincinnati OH 45220 *I value the need for the individual to feel unique and for the collective to remain hospitable to diversity. I believe in unity without uniformity and in man's capacity to redeem himself.*

GOTTSCHALK, SISTER MARY THERESE, nun, hospital administrator; b. Doellwang, Germany, June 21, 1931; came to U.S., 1953, naturalized, 1959; d. John and Sabina (Dietz) G. B.S. in Pharmacy, Creighton U., 1960; M.H.A., St. Louis U., 1970. Joined Sisters of the Sorrowful Mother, Roman Catholic Ch, 1952. Dir. pharmacy St. Mary's Hosp., Roswell, N.Mex., 1960-68; chief exec. officer St. Mary's Hosp., 1972-74; asst. administr. St. John Med. Ctr., Tulsa, 1970-72; chief exec. officer St. John Med. Ctr., 1974—; pres. Sisters of the Sorrowful Mother, U.S. Health System, 1989—. Vol. ARC, United Way. Fellow Am. Coll. Hosp. Adminstrs.; mem. Am. Hosp. Assn., Okla. Hosp. Assn. (pres. 1984), Tulsa Hosp. Council (past pres.), Okla. Conf. Cath. Hosps. (past pres.), Tulsa C. of C. Office: St John Med Ctr 1923 S Utica St Tulsa OK 74104

GOTTWALD, GEORGE J., bishop; b. St. Louis, May 12, 1914. Student, Kenrich Sem., Mo. Ordained priest Roman Catholic Ch., 1940. Ordained titular bishop of Cedamusa and aux. bishop St. Louis, 1961-88. Office: Chancery Office 4445 Lindell Blvd Saint Louis MO 63108

GOUGH, FRANK DIXON, II, youth minister; b. West Palm Beach, Fla., July 23, 1959; s. Oran Dean and Sharon Ann (Beals) G.; m. Teena Marie Berliner, Mar. 16, 1979 (div. Dec. 1982); m. Sharon Marie Nemetz, Apr. 21, 1990. Student, Palm Beach Atlantic Coll., 1977, So. Fla. Jr. Coll., 1982; Grad., Dio. Cen. Fla.'s Profl. Youth, Ministry Intern Prog., 1991. Lay youth leader St. Mark's Episcopal Ch., Palm Beach Gardens, Fla., 1983-86, Faith Luth. Ch., North Palm Beach, Fla., 1983-86; youth leader St. Matthew's Episcopal Ch., Westerville, Ohio, 1986-87; lay youth leader Holy Trinity Episcopal Ch., Melbourne, Fla., 1987-89; youth min. St. Paul's Episcopal Ch., Winter Haven, Fla., 1989-91; youth minister St. Elizabeth's Episcopal Ch., Sebastian, Fla., 1991—; mentor Edn. for Ministry, Univ. of the South Sch. of Theology Ext. ctr., 1991—; team mem. Kairos Prison Ministry, Winter Park, 1982, 91; co-dir., founder Polk County (Fla.) Assn. for Youth Ministry, 1989—; sponsor Youth Action Com., Orlando, 1990—; mem. New Beginnings Com., Orlando, 1991—. Contbr. articles to profl. jours. Advisor "Ear on Youth" Mayor's Adv. Coun., Winter Haven, 1989. Republican. Home: 8270 46th Ave Wabasso FL 32970 Office: 904 Clearmont St Sebastian FL 32958 *The three greatest things today's parents and youth workers can give to youth are Caring, Committment, and Consistancy. To give any one or two of these three, and not all of them together will only create in our youth heartache, loneliness, and confusion. We must give all three at all times, in all areas of our relationships with youth. Nothing less will do.*

GOULD, SISTER BETTE, academic administrator. Supt. of schs. Diocese of Springfield, Mass. Office: Christian Edn Ctr 625 Carew St Springfield MA 01104*

GOULD, MARTY LEON, minister, writer, composer; b. Salina, Kans., May 26, 1949; s. Aubrey Fredrick and Patricia Jolene (Johnson) G.; m. Roberta Joan Butler, May 25, 1973; children: Jeremy Alan, Brandon Matthew, Chad Austin. BA in Bible, Cen. Bible Coll., Springfield, Mo., 1972. Ordained to ministry Assemblies of God, 1976. Min. music Bethel Temple, Hampton, Va., 1972-74, Cen. Assembly, Wichita, Kans., 1974, Bethel Ch., Quincy, Ill., 1974-76, Cen. Assembly, Muskogee, Okla., 1977-78, Bethel Temple, Tampa, Fla., 1978-80, 82-89, Calvary Assembly, North Huntingdon, Pa., 1980-82, Calvary Temple, Springfield, Mo., 1989-91, Cen. Assembly, Cumberland, Md., 1991—; dist. music dir. Pa./Fla. Assemblies of God, Lakeland, Fla., 1984-86; mem. nat. music com. Assemblies of God, Springfield, 1987-89, local liaison music com., 1989—; seminar speaker Nat. Assemblies of God. Contbr. articles to religious jours.; TV producer and dir.; composer songs. Republican. Avocations: writing, photography, collecting out of print books on theater. Home: 280 National Hwy La Vale MD 21502

GOULD, WILLIAM BLAIR, religion educator; b. L.A., Apr. 22, 1924; s. Earle Albert and Marguerite Jane (Brown-Dennis) G.; m. Natalie Elaine Rosin, July 16, 1955. BA, Wesleyan U., 1948; MDiv, Union Theol. Sem., 1951; PhD, U. Edinburgh, Scotland, 1955. Pastor Community Meth. Ch., East Meadow, N.Y., 1952-55, First Meth. Ch., Middletown, Conn., 1955-59; sr. Meth. chaplain U. Nebr., Lincoln, 1959-63; dir. nat. office of campus ministry United Meth. Ch., N.Y.C., 1963-67; prof., head dept. religion Bradley U., Peoria, Ill., 1967-69; dean of coll. Washington Coll., Chestertown, Md., 1969-71; pastor Asbury Ch., Warwick, R.I., 1971-76; chair, humanities, prof. philosophy/religious studies U. Dubuque, 1976—; advisor Viktor Frank Inst., Berkeley, 1980—; trustee City of Dubuque Libr., 1980-86; advisor Inst. of Internat. Edn., London, 1976—. Author: The Worldly Christian: Bonhoeffer on Discipleship, 1967; contbr. articles to profl. jours. Globe fellow Boston Globe; Meth. scholar United Meth. Ch., 1948; vis. scholar Union Theol. Sem., 1960, 68. Mem. Am. Acad. Religion, Am. Philos. Assn. Home: 636 Loras Blvd Dubuque IA 52001 Office: U Dubuque 2000 University Ave Dubuque IA 52001

GOUNIS, PETER EDGAR, deacon; b. San Diego, Oct. 3, 1944; s. Edgar Peter and Bernice Ann (Good) G.; m. Kathleen Ann Ortmann, Aug. 7, 1970; children: Julie Ann, Elaine Ann, Kathleen Ann. Student, U. Mo., 1963-65, Paul VI Inst., Kenrick Sem., 1987. Cert. youth minister. Pastoral assoc. Sacred Heart Parish, Florissant, Mo., 1983—; retreat team mem. Pallotine Ctr., Florissant, 1985—; retreat dir. St. Louis, 1987—; youth minister St. Genevieve Parish, Ste. Genevieve, Mo., 1989-91; St. Paul Parish Fenton, Mo., 1991—; coun. mem. St. Louis Archdiocesan Pastoral Coun., 1990—; del. Synod 10, St. Louis, 1987-89; mem. Youth Com. of Priest's Coun., St. Louis, 1990; chmn. Archdiocesan Deacon Coun., St. Louis, 1989-90. Contbr. articles to profl. jours. Mem., past pres. Rotary, Florissant, 1984-85. Sgt. USMCR, 1966-72. Home: 2895 Heatherton Dr Florissant MO 63033 Office: Saint Paul Parish 15 Forest Knoll Drawer C Fenton MO 63026

GOUWENS, DAVID J., theology educator; b. South Holland, Ill., May 6, 1948; s. Paul Robert and Ruth Dena (Verduin) G. BA, Hope Coll., 1970; MDiv, Yale U., 1973, S.T.M., 1974, PhD, 1982. Ordained to ministry Presbyn. Ch., 1986. Asst. prof. theology Brite Divinity Sch., Tex. Christian U., Ft. Worth, 1983-89, assoc. prof. theology, 1989—; vis. lectr. religion Hope Coll, Holland, Mich., 1976. Author: Kierkegaard's Dialectic of the Imagination, 1989; contbr. articles to profl. jours. Mem. Am. Acad. Religion. Democrat. Office: Tex Christian U Brite Div Sch Box 32923 Fort Worth TX 76129

GOUYON, PAUL CARDINAL, archbishop; b. Bordeaux, France, Oct. 24, 1910; s. Jean-Baptiste Louis and Jeanne (Chassaing) G.; ed. in France. Ordained priest Roman Catholic Ch., 1937, consecrated bishop, 1957; bishop of Bayonne, 1957, titular archbishop of Pessinonte, 1963, archbishop of Rennes, 1964—; elevated to Sacred Coll. Cardinals, 1969. Decorated Croix de Guerre, officer Legion of Honor, comdr. Nat. Order Merit. Mem. Pax Christi (past pres. French sect.). Author several books. Address: Ma Maison, 181 rue Jadaïque, 33081 Bordeaux France

GRABER, HOWARD MELVIN, religion educator; b. Bklyn., Aug. 29, 1931; s. Samuel and Dorothy (Stempel) G.; m. Felicia Bialecki, Dec. 8, 1959; children: Sarah, Steven. BA, Bklyn. Coll., 1954; MA, Columbia U., 1957; PhD, U. Pitts., 1975. Exec. v.p. Cen. Agy. for Jewish Edn., St. Louis, 1974—. Capt. U.S. Army, 1959-63. Mem. Coun. for Jewish Edn., Rabbinical Coun. Am., St. Louis Rabbinical Assn., ASCD. Office: Cen Agy Jewish Edn 12 Millstone Campus Saint Louis MO 63146

GRABSKA, STANISLAWA HALINA, theologian; b. Lwòw, Poland, Mar. 20, 1922; d. Stanislaw Grabski and Zofia (Smolik) Grabska. MA, Acad. Fine Arts, Warsaw, Poland, 1955; grad., Cath. U. Lublin, Poland, 1969; MSc, ThD, Cath. U. Louvain, Belgium, 1973. Designer Gothern-Lesing Office, Warsaw, 1960-64; specialist theology Club Cath. Intellectuals, Warsaw, 1964-70, v.p., 1973-90, pres., 1990—; lectr. various parishes and priesthoods, Poland, 1973—. Author: The Liberty Christian, 1972, The Hope that Lies Within, 1980, Prayer in the Bible, 1983, Men in St. Trinitae, 1990, Bible in the Prayer. Served as officer with Polish Army, 1942-45. Mem. Soc. Theologique Louvain. Roman Catholic. Avocation: painting. Home: Al Niepodleglosci 71 m 86, 02 626 Warsaw Poland Office: Club Cath Intellectuals, Kopernika 34, 00 336 Warsaw Poland

GRACE, NANCY TERRELL, church official; b. Washington, Oct. 11, 1944; d. David Ralph Grace and Nancy Major (Erskine) Hussey. AA, Pine Manor Coll., 1964; BA, Wheaton Coll., Norton, Mass., 1966. Market analyst Hughes Air West, San Francisco, 1967-68; regional sales mgr. Hughes Air West, N.Y.C., 1968-71; market analyst instnl. sales G.H. Walter & Co., Inc., N.Y.C., 1971-73; investment banking mktg. analyst DuPont Walson Co., N.Y.C., 1973-74; conv. sales mgr. InterIsland Resorts, N.Y.C., 1974-76, United Airlines, N.Y.C., 1976-80; owner, mgr. Grace Resources, N.Y.C., 1980-86, 90—; dir. devel. Holy Apostles Ch. and Soup Kitchen, N.Y.C., 1986-90; mem. Direct Mail Fundraising Assn., N.Y.C.; dir. devel. Bronx Youth Ministry, N.Y.C. Contbr. articles to profl. jours. Bd. dirs. Holy Trinity Neighborhood Ctr., N.Y.C.; past bd. dirs. Greater N.Y. chpt. Meeting Planners Internat. (class treas.); treas. Wheaton Coll.; past mem. Chatham Hall Alumnae Coun.; chmn. interparish com. for St. Ann's at St. James' ch., N.Y.C. Mem. Women in Fin. Devel., N.Y. Jr. League, Manhattan Yacht Club, Blue Hill Troupe Club, Sand Bar Beach Club (past bd. dirs.). Avocations: sailing, theatre, tennis, church work, ballroom dancing. Home: 530 E 76th St Apt 26D New York NY 10021-3138

GRACIDA, RENE HENRY, bishop; b. New Orleans, June 9, 1923; s. Enrique J. and Mathilde (Derbes) G. Student, Rice U., 1942-43; B.S. in Architecture, U. Houston, 1950; postgrad., U. Fribourg, Switzerland, 1950, St. Vincent Coll., Latrobe, Pa., 1951-53, St. Vincent Maj. Sem., 1953-60. Ordained as deacon Roman Cath. Ch., 1958, as priest, 1959, as bishop, 1971. Mem. faculty Sch. Architecture, U. Houston, 1948-51; architect Donald Bartheline & Assocs., Houston, 1949-51; asst. pastor Holy Family Parish, North Miami, Fla., 1961-62, St. Coleman Parish, Pompano Beach, Fla., 1962-63, St. Matthew Parish, Hallandale, Fla., 1963-64; adminstr. St. Ambrose Parish, Deerfield Beach, Fla., 1964; asst. pastor Visitation Parish, North Dade, Fla., 1964-65; adminstr. St. Ann Parish, Naples, Fla., 1965-67; pastor Nativity Parish, Hollywood, Fla., 1967-69; rector St. Mary Cathedral, Miami, Fla., 1969-71, St. Patrick Parish, Miami Beach, Fla., 1971-72; pastor St. Kiernan Parish, Miami, 1973-75; 1st bishop Diocese of Pensacola-Tallahassee, 1975-83; apptd. 5th bishop Diocese of Corpus Christi, Tex., 1983—; mem. Liturgical Conf., 1959-72; mem. Archdiocesan Bldg. Commn., Archdiocese of Miami, 1964-73, sec., 1962-65, chmn., 1967-73, West Coast Deanery, Human Rels. Bd., 1965-67; senator Priests Senate, 1967-69, archdiocesan consultor, 1967-75; chmn. Broward Deanery, Human Rels. Bd., 1969-72, vicar gen., 1969-75; mem. steering com. Biennial Congress Worship, 1966-68; mem. Dade County Community Rels. Bd., 1972-75; aux. bishop Archdiocese Miami, 1971-75, supt. edn., 1973-75; chmn. com. on migration and tourism Nat. Conf. Cath. Bishops, 1975-80; nat. episcopal promoter of Apostleship of the Sea in U.S., 1975-89; mem. Episc. adv. bd. P.A.D.R.E.S. (Orgn. Mex.-Am. Priests), 1975—; Episc. adv. bd. Word of God Inst., 1975—; Episc. liaison for edn. Tex. Cath. Conf., 1986—; mem. Episc. adv. bd. St. Gregory Found. for Latin Liturgy, 1989—. Important archtl. works include: remodelling St. Vincent Archabbey Basilica, Latrobe, Ch. of the Nativity, Hollywood, St. Ambrose Ch, Deerfield Beach. Pres. Community Action Fund; bd. dirs. Community Act Fund, 1966-72; mem. bishop's com. liturgy Nat. Conf. Cath. Bishops, 1972-77, chmn., 1977-78, mem. policy and rev. com., 1973-77; chmn. ad. hoc. com. on migration and tourism Nat. Conf. Cath. Bishops, 1975-80; cons. Pontifical Commn. for Pastoral Care of Migrants and Tourists, 1978-83; v.p. Am. Immigration and Citizenship Conf., 1977-82; bd. dirs. Cath. Relief Services, 1981-88; trustee Nat. Shrine Immaculate Conception, Washington, 1984—; mem. adv. council South Tex. Eye Found., 1984—; hon. bd. dirs. Stop Child Abuse and Neglect, Inc., 1985—; bd. dirs. Cath. Telecommunications Network of Am., 1985-88; mem. South Tex. Regional Studies Ctr., Kingsville, 1985; mem. com. on social devel. and world peace Nat. Conf. Cath. Bishops, 1985-88; mem. Gov.'s Task Force on Border Econ. Devel., 1985-86; mem. statewide adv. com. Tex. State Aquarium, 1986—; mem. exec. com. Gulf Coast Coun. Boy Scouts Am. , 1987—; bd. dirs. Inst. Religion and Democracy, 1986, Sta. KEDT-TV, KKED-FM, 1986—, Cath. Communications Found., 1988—; trustee Cath. Mut. Relief Soc., 1989—, Tex. A&I Univ. Found., Inc., 1989—. Served with USAAF, 1943-45. Decorated Air medal with 2 oak leaf clusters; named Grand Prior So. Lieutenancy Equestrian Order Knights of the Holy Sepulchre Jerusalem, 1986. Mem. Guild for Religious Architecture, Phi Kappa Phi. Address: 4109 Ocean Dr Corpus Christi TX 78411

GRAD, ELI, retired religion educator; b. Vilno, Poland, Nov. 4, 1928; came to U.S., 1946; s. Shraga and Miriam (Lewin) G.; m. Geraldine Pescov, June 22, 1952 (dec. 1988); children: Roni, Oren, Jonathan; m. Johanna F. Perlmutter, July 2, 1989. B. Religious Edn., Jewish Theol. Sem., N.Y.C., 1950, M. Religious Edn., BD, 1955; D.J.Ped. (hon.), Jewish Theol. Sem., 1977; MA, NYU, 1951; PhD, Wayne State U., 1965. Cert. tchr., Mass. Prin. Congregation B'nai Israel, Washington, 1951-56; dir. edn. Congregation Shaarey Zedek, Detroit, 1956-65, Congregation Beth Tzedec, Toronto, Ont., Can., 1965-70; pres., dean faculty Hebrew Coll., Boston, 1970-85; retired, 1985. Home: 22 Haven Rd Wellesley Hills MA 02181-2405

GRADY, DUANE ELMER, pastor; b. Waterloo, Iowa, Nov. 25, 1957; s. Elmer Herman and Lois Jane (Gingerich) G.; m. Beverly G. Weaver, March 31, 1984; children: Jacob Weaver Grady, Anna Weaver Grady. Student, Manchester Coll., Ind., 1981; ThM, Bethany Sem., Oak Brook, Ill., 1989. Coord. Iowa Peace Network, Des Moines, Iowa, 1981-84; exec. dir. Interfaith Coun. for Homeless, Chgo., 1985-89; co-pastor Northview Ch. Brethren, Indpls., 1989—; bd. dirs. Ch. Fedn. of Greater Indpls., 1989—, Ind. Intereligious Commn. on Human Equality, Indpls., 1990—, Northside Interfaith Project, Indpls., 1989—. Author: Helping The Homeless, 1988. Home: 5535 E 46th St Indianapolis IN 46226 Office: Northview Church Brethren 5555 E 46th St Indianapolis IN 46226-3351

GRADY, M. G., clergyman. Bishop, Church of God in Christ, Southwest Tex., San Antonio. Office: Ch of God in Christ 325 Terrell Rd San Antonio TX 78209

GRADY, THOMAS J., bishop; b. Chgo., Oct. 9, 1914; s. Michael and Rose (Buckley) G. S.T.L., St. Mary of Lake Sem., Mundelein, Ill., 1938; student, Gregorian U., Rome, 1938-39; MA in English, Loyola U., Chgo., 1944. Ordained priest Roman Cath. Ch., 1938. Prof. Quigley Prep. Sem., Chgo., 1939-45; procurator St. Mary of Lake Sem., 1945-56; dir. Nat. Shrine Immaculate Conception, Washington, 1956-67; titular bishop Vamalla, aux. bishop Chgo., 1967-74; pastor St. Hilary Ch., Chgo., 1968-74, St. Joseph Ch., Libertyville, Ill., 1974; bishop of Orlando, Fla., 1974-90; Chgo. Archdiocesan dir. seminaries and post-ordination priestly tng., 1967-74; chmn. Chgo. Archdiocesan Liturg. Commn., 1968-74; dir. program Permanent Diaconate, Chgo., 1969-74; cons. Bishops' Com. on Priestly Formation, from 1967, chmn., 1969-72; mem. Ad Hoc Com. on Priestly Life and Ministry, 1971-73; chmn. Bishops' Com. on Priestly Life and Ministry, from 1973. Address: Diocese of Orlando 321 Hillman Ave PO Box 2728 Orlando FL 32802

GRAF, RICHARD BYRON, JR., minister; b. Charlotte, N.C., Sept. 27, 1939; s. Richard B. Sr. and Helen (Stillwell) G.; m. Shirley Whitley, June 10, 1961; children: Eric, Kristin. BA, Lenoir-Rhyne Coll., 1961; MDiv., Luth. Theol. Sem., 1965; DMin., Pitts. Theol. Sem., 1980. Ordained to ministry Luth. Ch., 1965. Pastor Grace Luth. Ch., Boone, N.C., 1965-67; chaplain U. Miami, Coral Gables, Fla., 1967-70; mission developer, pastor St. Thomas Luth. Ch., Miami, Fla., 1970-73; pastor St. Stephens Luth. Ch., Tallahassee, 1973-75; sec., asst. to bishop Fla. Synod Luth. Ch. in Am., Tampa, 1975-77; sr. pastor Macedonia Luth. Ch., Burlington, N.C., 1977-83, St. Paul's Luth. Ch., Wilmington, N.C., 1983—; founder, chmn. Allied Chs. of Alamance County, Burlington, 1982-83; radio, TV minister Miami, Burlington, Wilmington, 1968—; evangelist N.C. Synod, Salisbury, N.C., 1988—. Author: Re-Discovering Direction in Campus Ministry, 1965, A Radio Ministry to the Elderly, 1980; author and actor (videotape) Because You Care, Cape Fear United Way, 1986-87 (Nat. United Way award 1986-87); contbr. articles to religious and acad. jours. Pres. Community Coun. Allamance County, 1982; chmn. Gov.'s Involvement Coun., N.C., 1982; bd. dirs., planning div. chmn. United Way N.C., Raleigh, 1982-83; v.p., campaign chmn. Cape Fear Area United Way, Wilmington, 1986; bd. dirs. Thalian Assn., Wilmington Boys Club, Wilmington; Thalian Hall and City Hall commr. for City of Wilmington, 1990. Recipient Pub. Service award Community Action Program, Inc., Leon County, Fla., 1975, Outstanding Community Service award United Way N.C., 1980, 86, Gov.'s award State of N.C., 1981. Mem. Cape Fear Ministerial Assn. (pres.), Kiwanis (pres. 1989). Avocations: golf, dramatics. Office: St Paul's Luth Ch 12 N 6th St Wilmington NC 28401 *There is no more appropriate and satisfying way to express gratitude to God for the gift of life than to celebrate it to the fullest and share its joys with others.*

GRAGE, GLENN GORDON, religious organization administrator, educator; b. Milw., Aug. 28, 1956; s. Gordon Ray and Joanne Katherine (Storck) G. AA, Concordia Coll., Milw., 1976; BA, Concordia Coll., River Forest, Ill., 1978, MA, 1982. Cert. elem. tchr., Ill., Tenn.; sch. guidance couselor, Ill. Tenn. Program dir. Camp Concordia, Gowen, Mich.; tchr. N.W. Luthern Sch., Elmwood Pk., Ill.; Christian edn. dir. Luthern Ch., Elmwood Pk., Ill.; Christian edn dir., tchr. Good Shepherd Luthern Ch., Sch., Chattanooga; Christian edn. dir. Our Savior Luthern Ch., Shreveport, La. Contbr. articles to religious mags. Mem. Luthern Elem. Tchrs., Theological Educators in Assoc. Ministries. Home and Office: 13115 S Telegraph Rd Taylor MI 48180

GRAGG, DOUGLAS LLOYD, educator; b. Huntsville, Ala., Oct. 26, 1957; s. Lloyd Oliver Jr. and Amelia Jo (Harris) G.; m. Sandra Michelle Mays, Nov. 1, 1980. BA, David Lipscomb U., 1978; MA, Abilene Christian U., 1981, MDiv, 1983; PhD, Emory U., 1990. Asst. prof. Inst. for Christian Studies, Austin, Tex., 1987—; adj. instr. Abilene Christian U., 1978-79, Candler Sch. Theology, Emory U., Atlanta, 1985-87. Recipient Christian Scholarship Found. award, 1986-87. Mem. Soc. Bibl. Lit. Office: Inst for Christian Studies 1909 University Ave Austin TX 78705

GRAHAM, ALMA ELEANOR, magazine editor, writer, educational consultant; b. Raleigh, N.C., Nov. 13, 1936; d. David Robert and Irene G. (Knott) G. BA in English with honors, U. N.C., 1958; MA in Contemporary Lit., Columbia U., 1970. Exec. editor Am. Heritage Dictionary, 1970-75; editorial mgr., exec. editor McGraw-Hill, 1976-87; free-lance author, corp. cons., 1987-90; editor New World Outlook mag. United Meth. Ch., N.Y.C., 1991—; cons. in bias-free lang. and images; cons. USIA, 1978-80. Author: Our Nation, Our World, 1983, McGraw-Hill Educational Software, 1988, North Carolina: The Land and Its People, 1988, Basic Map Skills, 1991; (with others) Success With Words, 1983, Bridging Worlds Through General Semantics, 1984. Named one of 50 Extraordinary Women of Achievement, N.Y. region NCCJ, 1978; Woodrow Wilson fellow, 1958-59. Mem. Associated Ch. Press, Nat. Fedn. Bus. and Profl. Women, NAFE, NOW, ASCD, Nat. Coun. for Social Studies, Orgn. for Equal Edn. of the Sexes. Home: 380 Riverside Dr New York NY 10025 Office: New World Outlook 475 Riverside Dr New York NY 10115-0122

GRAHAM, BILLY See **GRAHAM, WILLIAM FRANKLIN**

GRAHAM, CHRIS DEAN, minister; b. Portales, N.Mex., Jan. 25, 1960; s. Earnest Harrison Graham and Adalyn Mae (Isom) Mitchell; m. Penny Lynn Russell, June 24, 1978; children: Amber Lynn, Amy Leigh. Grad., Bear Valley Sch. Bibl. Studies, Denver, 1982; AA, El Camino Coll., 1990. Min. Ch. of Christ, Bayard, N.Mex., 1982-85, Hawthorne, Calif., 1985—. Republican. Home: 12215 S Eucalyptus Ave Hawthorne CA 90250 Office: Ch of Christ 4585 W El Segundo Blvd Hawthorne CA 90250

GRAHAM, DAN DUANE, pastor; b. Mobile, Ala., May 14, 1953; adopted s. Milton Graham and Camelia Jean (Gautney) Neal; m. Claudia Denise Martin; children: Daniel Marcus, Kenneth Martin. BA in Religion, Mobile Bapt. Coll., 1981; MDiv in Pastoral Ministry, Southeastern Bapt. Sem., Wake Forest, N.C., 1986; postgrad., So. Bapt. Ctr., Jacksonville, Fla. Ordained to ministry Bapt. Ch. Pastor Scottsburg (Va.) Bapt., 1983-86, Westlawn Bapt., Mobile, 1987—; pastor conf. v.p. Minister's Conf., Mobile, 1990-91. Sgt. USAF, 1974-79. Mem. Evang. Theol. Soc. Office: Westlawn Bapt 2621 Ralston Rd Mobile AL 36606

GRAHAM, JEWEL, international religious organization administrator. P-res. World YWCA, Geneva. Office: World YWCA, 1201 Geneva Switzerland*

GRAHAM, JOHN J., bishop; b. Phila., Sept. 11, 1913. Student, St. Charles Borromeo Sem., Pa., Pontifical Roman Sem., Rome. Ordained priest Roman Catholic Ch., 1938. Ordained titular bishop Sabrata and aux. bishop Phila., 1964—. Office: Chancery Office 222 N 17th St Philadelphia PA 19103

GRAHAM, MATT PATRICK, minister, librarian; b. Colorado City, Tex., Sept. 28, 1950; s. Matt Noe and Mary Edna (Frizell) G.; m. Doris Jean Mickey, Jan. 1, 1971; children: Jennifer, Abigail, Joy, Crystal. BA, Abilene Christian U., 1973, MA, 1974, MDiv, 1976; PhD, Emory U., 1983; M in Libr. Info. Sci., U. Tex., 1990. Ordained to ministry Ch. of Christ, 1971. Min. Druid Hills Ch. of Christ, Atlanta, 1979-82; asst. prof. Columbia Christian Coll., Portland, Oreg., 1983-85, Inst. for Christian Studies, Austin, Tex., 1985-88; libr. Pitts Theology Libr., Atlanta, 1988—. Author: The Utilization of I and II Chronicles in the Reconstruction of Israelite History in the Nineteenth Century, 1990. Mem. Soc. Bibl. Lit., Am. Schs. Oriental Rsch., Am. Theol. Libr. Assn. Office: Emory U Pitts Theology Libr Atlanta GA 30322

GRAHAM, OLIVIA ELAINE, minister; b. Latrobe, Pa., Jan. 21, 1946; d. Oliver Edsall and Ruth Irene (Young) G. BA, Alderson Broaddus Coll., Philippi, W.Va., 1973; MDiv and MACE, Meth. Theol. Sem., Delaware, Ohio, 1976; DMin, United Theol. Sem., Dayton, 1988. Ordained to ministry, United Meth. Ch., 1974. Charge minister United Meth. Chs., Buffalo, 1974-76; minister Savannah United Meth. Ch., New Castle, Pa., 1976-80, Cen. United Meth. Ch., Beaver Falls, Pa., 1980-83, Beaverdale Mount Olive United Meth. Chs., 1983-89; pastor Center Ave. United Meth. Ch., Pitcairn, Pa., 1989—; alumni coun. Meth. Theol. Sch. in Ohio, Delaware, 1989—; chmn. Conf. Nominating Com., Pitts., 1990—, vice chmn. bd. edn., 1979-83. Fellow Christian Educators Fellowship, Job's Daus. Republican. Home: 412 Center Ave Pitcairn PA 15140 Office: Center Ave United Meth Ch 450 Eleanor St Pitcairn PA 15140

GRAHAM, RONALD WILLIAM, religious educator; b. Kempsey, Australia, Aug. 31, 1918; came to U.S., 1954; s. Ewan Duncan and Nella Marguerite (Espuler) G.; children: Beth Smith, Jan Easter, Kerry. BA, U. Melbourne, Australia, 1949; MA, Drake U., 1957, BD, 1958; PhD, U. Iowa, 1966. Min. various Christian chs., Iowa, Australia, 1942-60; assoc. prof. New Testament Drake U., 1960-68; prof. New Testament Lexington (Ky.) Theol. Seminary, 1968-87; ret., 1987. Author: Women in the Ministry of Jesus and in the Pauline Churches, 1983. Mem. Soc. Bibl. Lit., Am. Acad. Religion, Cath. Bibl. Assn. Home: 6118 Terrace Dr Johnson IA 50131

GRAHAM, VERNON R., ecumenical agency administrator. Exec. pastor The Associated Chs. of Fort Wayne and Allen County Inc., Ind. Office: Assoc Chs Allen County Inc 227 E Washington Blvd Ste 102 Fort Wayne IN 46802*

GRAHAM, WILLIAM ALBERT, religion educator; b. Raleigh, N.C., Aug. 16, 1943; s. William Albert and Evelyn (Powell) G.; m. Barbara Stecconi, Aug. 26, 1983; 1 child, Powell Louis. Student, U. Goettingen, Fed. Republic Germany, 1964-65; BA summa cum laude, U. N.C., 1966; AM, Harvard U., 1970, PhD, 1973. Lectr. Islamic religion Harvard U., Cambridge, Mass.,

1973-74, asst. prof. Islamic religion, 1974-79, Allston Burr sr. tutor, 1975-77; assoc. prof. Islamic religion Harvard U., Cambridge, 1979-81, sr. lectr. comparative history of religion, 1981-85, prof. history of religion and Islamic studies, 1985—, dir. Ctr. for Middle Eastern Studies, 1990—; master Currier House Harvard Coll., 1991—; Mem. Joint Com. on Comparative Study of Muslim Socs., Social Sci. Rsch. Coun., Am. Coun. Learned Socs., 1988—; mem. adv. coun. dept. religion Princeton U., 1982—, vice chmn. Coun. on Grad. Studies in Religion, 1989—; vis. lectr. Friedrich-Wilhelms U., Bonn, 1982-83. Author: Divine Word and Prophetic Word in Early Islam, 1977 (Am. Coun. Learned Socs. book prize 1978), Beyond the Written Word, 1987; co-author: Heritage of World Civilizations, 1986, 90; co-editor: Islamfiche: Readings from Islamic Primary Sources, 1987; contbr. articles and revs. to profl. jours. Woodrow Wilson Found. grad. fellow Harvard U., 1966-67, Danforth Found. grad. fellow Harvard U., 1966-73, John Simon Guggenheim Found. fellow, Germany, India, 1982-83, Alexander von Humboldt Found. fellow, Germany, 1982-83. Mem. Am. Soc. for Study of Religion, Am. Acad. Religion, Middle East Studies Assn., Am. Oriental Soc., Am. Alpine Club, Phi Beta Kappa. Democrat. Methodist. Avocations: tech. mountaineering, long distance running. Home: Currier House 64 Linnaean St Cambridge MA 02138 Office: Harvard U CMES 1737 Cambridge St Cambridge MA 02138

GRAHAM, WILLIAM FRANKLIN (BILLY GRAHAM), evangelist; b. Charlotte, N.C., Nov. 7, 1918; s. William Franklin and Morrow (Coffey) G.; m. Ruth McCue Bell, Aug. 13, 1943; children: Virginia Leftwich, Anne Morrow, Ruth Bell, William Franklin, Nelson Edman. AB, Wheaton Coll. (Ill.), 1943; ThB, Fla. Bible Sem., Tampa, 1940; ThB numerous hon. degrees, including, Houghton (N.Y.) Coll., Baylor U., The Citadel, William Jewell Coll. Ordained to ministry So. Baptist Conv.; minister First Bapt. Ch., Western Springs, Ill., 1943-45; 1st v.p. Youth for Christ, Internat., 1945-48; pres. Northwestern Coll., Mpls., 1947-52; founder World Wide Pictures, Inc., Burbank, Calif.; worldwide evangelistic campaigns, 1949—; speaker weekly Hour of Decision radio program, 1950—; also periodic Crusade Telecasts; founder Billy Graham Evangelistic Assn.; hon. chmn. Lausanne Congress World Evangelization, 1974. Author: Peace with God, 1953, World Aflame, 1965, The Jesus Generation, 1971, Angels: God's Secret Agents, 1975, How to Be Born Again, 1977, The Holy Spirit, 1978, Till Armageddon, 1981, A Biblical Standard for Evangelists, 1984, Approaching Hoofbeats, 1985, Unto the Hills, 1986, Facing Death and The Life After, 1987, Answers to Life's Problems, 1988, Hope for the Troubled Heart, 1991; also writer of daily newspaper column. Recipient numerous awards, including; Bernard Baruch award, 1955, Humane Order of African Redemption, 1960, gold award George Washington Carver Meml. Inst., 1963, Horatio Alger award, 1965, Internat. Brotherhood award NCCJ, 1971, Sylvanus Thayer award Assn. Grads. U.S. Mil. Acad., 1972, Franciscan Internat. award, 1972, Man of South award, 1974, Liberty Bell award, 1975, Templeton prize for Progress in Religion, 1982, William Booth award Salvation Army, 1989. Home: Montreat NC 28757 Office: Billy Graham Evangelistic Assn PO Box 9313 Minneapolis MN 55440-9313

GRAHAM, WILLIAM FRED, religious studies educator; b. Columbus, Oct. 31, 1930; s. William Fred and Serena (Clark) G.; m. Marjory Jean Garrett, Aug. 12, 1953; children: Terese L., Bonny, Marcy Jean Graham Murphy, Geneva S. Graham Looker. AB, Tarkio Coll., 1952; BD, Pittsburgh Theol. Sem., 1955; ThM, Louisville Presbyn. Sem., 1958; PhD, U. Iowa, 1965. Pastor Bethel Presbyn. Ch., Waterloo, Iowa, 1955-61, instr., 1963; assoc. prof. Mich. State U., E. Lansing, 1963-74, prof., 1974—. Author: The Constructive Revolutionary, 1971, reprinted, 1987, Picking up the Pieces, 1975; editor: Calvin & Calvinism, 1988, Later Calvinism, 1992. Grantee Travel to Collections Grant Nat. Endowment for the Humanities, Scotland, 1985, Fin. Grant Am. Philosophical Soc., Scotland, 1987. Mem. 16th Century Studies Soc. (pres. 1988-89), The Calvin Studies Soc., Am. Soc. for Ch. History, Phi Kappa Phi (pres. 1987, 91). Avocations: running, tennis. Office: Mich State U Dept Religious Studies East Lansing MI 48824

GRAHMANN, CHARLES V., bishop; b. Halletsville, Tex., July 15, 1931. Student, Assumption-St. John's Sem., Tex. Ordained priest Roman Catholic Ch., 1956. Ordained titular bishop Equilium and aux. San Antonio, 1981-82; 1st bishop Victoria, Tex., 1982-89; coadjutor biship Dallas, 1990—. Office: 3230 Bryan St Dallas TX 75204 also: Chancery Office PO Box 4708 Victoria TX 77903

GRAMMER, MICHAEL B., lay minister; b. Wellsburg, W.Va., Oct. 26, 1961; s. William McCready and Marjorie Ann (Boyd) G.; children: Christopher Michael, Robert William, Thomas Edward. BA in Theology, Wheeling (W.Va.) Jesuit Coll., 1984, grad. studies in religion edn., 1984-86; postgrad., U. Notre Dame, 1990—. Tchr. Mount de Chantal Visitation Acad., Wheeling, 1982-82; dir. religious edn. St. Mary and St. Ladislaus Chs., Wheeling, 1986-90; assoc. pastor Ch. of St. Boniface, Bay City, Mich., 1991—; sch. bd. pres. Wheeling Cath. Elem. Sch., 1988-91; mem. religious unity com. Diocese of Wheeling-Charleston, W.Va., 1987-91; mem. com. for ecumenism Diocese of Saginaw, Mich., 1991—; mem. planning com. Ohio Cath. Edn. Assn., Columbus, 1990-91; mem. faith and order unit W.Va. Coun. Chs., 1990-91; mem. diocesan sch. com. for Saginaw Cath. schs.; chmn. fin. com. Vicariate VIII; speaker, workshop presenter. Mem. Amnesty Internat., 1984—; cons. Holy Family Middle Sch., Bay City, 1991. Mem. Nat. Assn. Lay Mins., Religious Edn. Assn., Liturgical Conf., Nat. Assn. Diocesan Ecumenical Officers, Fedn. Diocesan Liturgical Commns. Republican. Home: 510 N Lincoln Ave Bay City MI 48708

GRAMS, BETTY JANE, minister, educator, writer; b. Lead, S.D., Mar. 13, 1926; d. Harold C. and Elizabeth Amanda (Vaughn) Haas; m. Monroe David Grams, May 1, 1949; children: MonaRe' Grams Shields, Rocky Vaughn, Rachel Jo Grams Schaible. Student, North Cen. Bible Coll., 1945-48, Diploma in Theology, 1963; BA in Edn. and Theology, Assemblies of God Theol. Sch., 1978. Ordained to ministry Assemblies of God, 1957. Asst. pastor local ch. Huron, S.D., 1948-49; co-pastor local ch. Cataract, Wis., 1949-51; missionary to Latin Am. Assemblies of God Ch., Springfield, Mo., 1951—; sec. women's orgn. Assemblies of God, various South Am. countries, 1972-77, missionary educator, Bolivia, Argentina, 1951-91; prof. North Cen. Bible Coll., Mpls., 1963-64, 68-70; speaker Pentecostal Fellowship of N.Am., 1st Hispanic Congress, Can. Author: Women of Grace, 1978, Families Can Be Happy, 1981, Solving Ministry's Toughest Problems, 1985, Familia, Fe, y Felicidad, 1985, Ministering Through Music, 1990; (music theory) Ministrando Con Musica, 1960—; contbr. articles to various publs. Home: 8613 Beekman Dr Miramar FL 33025 Office: Assemblies of God 1448 Boonville Springfield MO 65802 *God uses men and women to make miracles happen. Teaching is "being." Learning results through "seeing."*

GRANFIELD, PATRICK RICHARD, priest, theology educator; b. Springfield, Mass., Mar. 8, 1930; s. Patrick E. and Mabel (Fitzgerald) G. PhL, Pontifical Inst. St. Anselm, Rome, 1954, PhD, 1958; STL, Cath. U. Am., 1958, STD, 1963. Ordained priest Roman Cath. Ch., 1957. Mem. faculty Cath. U. Am., Washington, 1964—, prof. systematic theology, 1980—. Author: Theologians at Work, 1967, Ecclesial Cybernetics, 1973, Papacy in Transition, 1980: (with A. Dulles) The Church: A Bibliography, 1985, The Limits of the Papacy, 1987; also articles; editor: (with J. Jungmann) Kyriakon, 1970. Mem. Cath. Theol. Soc. Am. (v.p. 1982-83, pres.-elect 1983-84, pres. 1984-85, recipient John Courtney Murray award 1989), Coll. Theology Soc. Office: Catholic U Am Dept Theology Washington DC 20064

GRANGER, CHARLES FRANKLIN, minister, educator; b. Greenville, S.C., Aug. 28, 1959; s. Charles Wesley and Frankie Elizabeth (Huff) G.; m. Teresa Ann Hunt, June 26, 1982. BA, Furman U., 1981; MDiv, So. Bapt. Theol. Sem., 1985. Ordained to ministry So. Bapt. Conv., 1986. Summer youth min. Berea 1st Bapt. Ch., Greenville, 1979, 1st Bapt. Ch., Mauldin, S.C., 1981; assoc. min. youth and edn. Trinity Bapt. Ch., Seneca, S.C., 1986-89; min. edn. 1st Bapt. Ch., Athens, Ga., 1989—; sec.-treas. Oconee Chaplains Assn., Seneca, 1987-89; mem., sec.-treas. Master of Div. Coun., Louisville, 1982-84. Bd. dirs. Oconee Community Theatre, 1988-89; mem. March of Dimes Team Walk Steering Com., Athens, 1990. Mem. Ea. Bapt. Religious Educators, Christian Educators Network (steering com. 1991—). Home: 332 Cherokee Ridge Athens GA 30606 Office: 1st Bapt Ch 355 Pulaski St Athens GA 30610

GRANGER, SISTER ELEANOR (SISTER), religious organization administrator; b. Lanesboro, Minn., Apr. 16, 1938; d. Ben W. and Eleanor (Horihan) G. BS in Elem. Edn., Coll. of St. Teresa, 1962; MS in Elem. Edn., Mankato State U., 1970. Joined Sisters of St. Francis, Roman Cath. Ch., 1956. Tchr. St. Juliana's Elem Sch., Chgo., 1964-68; prin. St. Gabriel's Elem. Sch., Fulda, Minn., 1968-70, St. Mary's Elem. Sch., Winona, Minn., 1970-82; councillor Sisters of St. Francis, Rochester, Minn., 1982-88, pres., 1988—; trustee Coll. of St. Teresa, Winona, 1979-91, pres. bd. dirs., 1983-85; mem. sponsorship bd. St. Mary's Hosp., Rochester, 1988—; mem. bd. advisors Viterbo Coll., 1991—; mem. nat. bd. Leadership Conf. of Women Religious, 1989—, chairperson region XI, 1989-92. Recipient Teresa of Avila award Coll. of St. Teresa, 1988. Mem. Franciscan Fedn. Bros. and Sisters of U.S. (v.p. 1991—). Democrat. Office: Sisters of St Francis Assisi Heights Box 4900 Rochester MN 55903 *In this time of tumultuous change I am convinced we must deepen our relationship with our God and with one another. It is only by being "on fire" and committed to the mission of Jesus can our world be at peace. Courageous trust and passionate hope will need to be constant companions.*

GRANGER, PHILIP RICHARD, minister; b. Detroit, June 19, 1943; s. Myrl Richard and Alvirta May (Kling) G.; m. Karen Elizabeth Draper, Feb. 20, 1965 (div. 1972); children: Mark, Leslie; m. Susan Kay Alderfer, Mar. 4, 1973; children: Randall, Candace. AA, Jackson Jr. Coll., 1963; BA, MBA, Mich. State U., 1965, 67; MDiv, Northern Bapt. Theol. Sem., Lombard, Ill., 1978; D. Ministry, Oral Roberts U., 1986. Ordained to deacon Meth. Ch., 1977, ordained elder, 1980; CPA, Ind. Audit staff, cons. Ernst & Ernst, Detroit, 1967-71; controllers staff Assocs. Corp., South Bend, Ind., 1971-73; v.p., controller 1st Fed. Savs. and Loan, Chgo., 1973-76; pastor Mokena (Ill.) United Meth. Ch., 1976-82; dir. fin. Northern Ind. Conf. Meth. Ch., Marion, Ind., 1982-86; sr. pastor St. Lukes United Meth. Ch., Kokomo, Ind., 1986-89, Trinity United Meth. Ch., Huntington, Ind., 1989—; adj. faculty Huntington (Ind.) Coll., 1990—; new life missioner Gen. Bd. Discipleship, Nashville, 1980—; bd. dirs., sec.-treas. Bristol, Inc., Lexington, Ky.; bd. dirs. Good News, Wilmore, Ky., Samaritan Ctr., Inc., Huntington, Ind., 1989-90, Found. for Mission and Ministry, Inc., Marion, 1989-90. Author: Discerment Planning, 1986. Bd. dirs. Mental Health Assn. Ill., Chgo., 1974-75; founding mem. Tri-Village Crisis Intervention Ctr., Mokena, Ill., 1978-81; treas. Village of Mokena, 1978-82. Mem. Am. Assn. Christian Counselors, Rotary Internat., Delta Sigma Pi, Beta Gamma Sigma, Beta Alpha Psi. Avocations: reading, travel, personal computers. Home: 251 E Washington Huntington IN 46750 Office: Trinity United Meth Ch 530 Guilford St Huntington IN 46750 *To experience life requires more than experiencing the simple joys and pleasures that life provides. To really experience life is to experience the Christian community of caring and sharing that only occurs when we are truly one in Christ.*

GRANQUIST, THEODORE VERNON, minister; b. Miami, Fla., June 22, 1935; s. Verner Arnold and Lillian Anna (Peterson) G.; m. Barbara Jean Lloyd, Oct. 12, 1962; children: Timothy, Suzanne. BA, Gustavus Adolphus Coll., 1957; MDiv, Luth. Sch. of Theology Chgo., 1961. Intern pastor Salem Luth. Ch., Bridgeport, Conn., 1959-60; pastor Transfiguration Luth. Ch., Taylor, Mich., 1961-66; assoc. pastor Bethany Luth. Ch., Batavia, Ill., 1966-73; pastor Calvary-Trinity Luth. Ch., Rapid River, Mich., 1973-80, Augustana Luth. Ch., Andover, Ill., 1980—; pastoral mem. Bay de Noc Hospice, Escanaba, Mich., 1976-80; bd. dirs. Jenny Lind Chapel Commn., Andover. Bd. dirs. Bay de Noc Hospice, Escanaba, 1976-79, AACA, Orion, Ill., 1985-87; mem. Western Ill. bd. govs. Luth. Social Svcs., Moline, 1990—. Office: Augustana Luth Ch 628 6th St PO Box 157 Andover IL 61233

GRANT, BRAD WARNER, religious organization administrator; b. Rhinelander, Wis., Sept. 24, 1960; s. Vernow W. and Carol J. (Bandock) G.; m. Kelly A. Bliss, Nov. 28, 1981; 1 child, Hunter M. AA, Nicolet Coll., Rhinelander, 1981. Cert. ins. counselor. Asst. br. mgr. Thorp Fin., Niagara, Wis., 1982-84; br. mgr. U.S.A. Fin. Svc., Ladysmith, Wis., 1984-86; asst. v.p. State Bank of Medford (Wis.), 1986-89; dist. rep. Aid Assocs. for Luths., Wausau, Wis. Mem. Nat. Mgmt. Assn. (pres. Medford chpt. 1989-90), Medford Area C. of C., Medford Jaycees (bd. dirs. 1988, named Outstanding Jaycee in Region 12 1987). Republican. Avocations: outdoors, photography. Home: 1120 Woodland Dr Rhinelander WI 54501 Office: Aid Assocs for Lutherans 2600 Steart Ctr Ste 162 Wausau WI 54401

GRANT-FERRIS, PIERS HENRY MICHAEL, priest; b. Birmingham, Midlands, Gt. Britain, Apr. 9, 1933; s. Robert Grant and Florence (De Vine) Harvington. Diploma edn., Strawberry Hill, Middlesex, 1960. Novice Monastic Order St. Benedict, Ampleforth Abbey, Yorkshire, Eng., 1955, solem profession, 1959, priest, 1964; asst. priest Parish of Workington (Cumbria, Eng.), 1977-89, Parish of Leyland, Lancanshire, Eng., 1989—; form master Gilling Castle Prep Sch. Yorkshire, 1965-75; sch. chaplain St. Joseph's Roman Cath. Comprehensive Sch., Cumbria, Workington, 1979-89, St. Mary's High Sch., Leyland and Lancanshire, 1989—. Mem. sch. gov. St. Joseph's Comprehensive Sch., Workington, Cumbria, 1979-89, St. Anne's Jr. Sch. Leyalnd and Lancanshire, 1989—. Served to lt. Irish Guards, 1951-54. Recipient Gold award British Amateur Swimming Assn., 1967. Mem. Order of Malta (chaplain 1980—). Roman Catholic. Clubs: Kandahar Ski (Silver K award 1954), Alpine Ski, Achille Ratti Climbing, Alpine. Home: St Mary's Priory, Broadfield Walk, Leyland Preston PR5 1PD, England Office: Monastery of St Laurence, Ampleforth Abbey, York East Yorks YO6 4EN, England

GRASHAM, WILLIAM WESLEY, religion educator, minister; b. Phoenix, Aug. 2, 1930; s. John George and Olive Emma (Cage) G.; m. Eleanor Marie Spainhower, May 4, 1952; children: William Wallace, John Douglas, Julie Marie, Terri Lynn. BA, Pepperdine U., 1962, MA, 1968; PhD, Calif. Grad. Sch. Theology, 1970; MDiv, Abilene Christian U., 1975; PhD, U. Aberdeen, Scotland, 1985. Ordained to ministry Ch. of Christ, 1954. Min. Ch. Christ, various locations, 1952-82; instr. Religion and History McMurry Coll., Abilene Christian U., Abilene, Tex., 1982-89; religion educator Ctr. for Christian Edn., Dallas, 1990—. Contbr. articles to profl. jours. Mem. Soc. Bibl. Lit., Bibl. Archeol. Soc. Democrat. With USN, 1948-49. Office: Ctr for Christian Edn 6409 Preston Rd Dallas TX 75205

GRASSANO, THOMAS DAVID, minister; b. Greenwood, S.C., June 19, 1961; s. Thomas and Atha Elizabeth (Watts) G.; m. Lidia Angélica Minay, Aug. 20, 1983; 1 child, Gabrielle Angélica. MusB, Furman U., 1983; MusM, U. S.C., 1984; MusD, Fla. State U., 1988. Ordained to ministry Ch. of God, 1981. Evangelist Ch. of God, 1980-85; assoc. pastor Pkwy. Ch. of God, Tallahassee, Fla., 1985-86; instr. music Fla. State U., Tallahassee, 1986-88; min. youth and music Br. St. Ch. of God, Tallahassee, 1987-88; dir. worship, campus pastor Univ. Ch. of God, Tampa, Fla., 1988-89; coord. short-term missions and collegiate ministry internat. dept. youth and Christian edn. Ch. of God, 1989—; instr. music Lee Coll., Cleveland, Tenn., 1990—; lectr. Internat. Bible Schs., Mex., Guatemala, Chile, Argentina, 1981—; founder Alpha Omega Campus Outreach Ministry, Ch. of God. Mem. Soc. for Ethnomusicology, Latin Am. Ethnomusicology, Music Theory Soc., Southeastern Composers League, Coll. Music Soc. Republican. Office: Ch of God Internat Offices PO Box 2494 Cleveland TN 37320 *Success is not found through position, money or power. True success is found when selfish ambitions are pushed aside to accomplish the will of Christ.*

GRASSELLY, GILBERT, religious organization administrator. Sec. Nat. Spiritual Assembly of Baha'is of Paraguay, Asunción. Office: Nat Spitual Assembly Bahai, Eligio Ayala 1456, Apdo 742, Asunción Paraguay*

GRASSO, ANTHONY ROBERT, priest, educator; b. Boston, Feb. 23, 1951; s. Leonard Joseph and Nancy Antoinette (Solazzo) G. BA in English Lit., U. Notre Dame, 1973, MTh, 1977; MA, U. Toronto, Ont., Can., 1980, PhD in English, 1985. Joined Congregation Holy Cross, ordained priest Roman Catholic Ch., 1978. Tchr. English, Notre Dame Cath. High Sch., Fairfield, Conn., 1973-74; teaching asst. theology U. Notre Dame, South Bend, Ind., 1975-76; tchr. English, St. Mark's High Sch., Wilmington, Del., 1978-79; asst. Most Holy Trinity Ch., Saco, Maine, 1977-78; teaching asst. English, Erindale Coll. U. Toronto, 1981-82; dir. Holy Cross Sem., Toronto, 1982-85; pastoral asst., cons. St. Ann's Ch., Toronto, 1979-85; asst. prof. English, King's Coll., Wilkes Barre, Pa., 1985—, humanities rep. Faculty Coun., chmn. Bd. Student Communications Media, moderator Aquinas Soc., writing cons. ACT 101 program; mem. adv. bd. Profl. Acad. Affairs Com. and Honors Program. Author poems and articles; mem. editorial adv. bd. Collelgiate Press, Poetry. Mem. Peace Links, Washington, 1983-84. Fellow Sch. Grad. Studies, U. Toronto, 1981-82, 82-83; Charles Gordon Heyd fellow, 1984-85. Mem. MLA, Tennyson Soc., Nat. Coun. Tchrs. English, N.E. Regional Conf. on Christianity and Lit. (exec. com., chmn. N.E. region 1991—), Pa. State Poetry Soc., N.E. Pa. Writing Teachers' Conf., Delta Epsilon Sigma. *Ironically, human beings devote a good deal of time to dodging complex issues. Yet complexity is what denotes us from other creatures; it is the source of our uniqueness and diversity.*

GRATTON, JEAN, clergyman; b. Wendover, Ont., Can., Dec. 4, 1924. Ordained priest Roman Catholic Ch. 1952. Bishop of Mont-Laurier Que., Can., 1978—. Address: Bishop's House, 435 rue de la Madonne, Mont-Laurier, PQ Canada J9L 151

GRAUER, DONALD JOHN, minister; b. Chgo., Apr. 4, 1946; s. John Edward and Olive Martha (Hakala) G.; m. Brenda Jane Boyer, June 1, 1969; children: Andrew Jonathan, Benjamin Jason, Adam Jeremy. AA with high honors, Wright Jr. Coll., Chgo., 1965; BA with honors, U. Ill., 1967; MDiv with honors, McCormick Theol. Seminary, Chgo., 1971, postgrad., 1978-81. Ordained to ministry United Presbyn. Ch., 1971. Parish internship First United Presbyn. Ch., Huron, Ohio, 1969-70; asst. pastor First United Presbyn. Ch., St. Clairsville, Ohio, 1971-73, assoc. pastor, 1973-75; pastor Bethel Presbyn. Ch., White Hall, Md., 1975-83, Valley Presbyn. Ch., Chagrin Falls, Ohio, 1983—; elected presbytery del., 1982 Gen. Assembly of the United Presbyn. Ch., Hartford, Conn., 1982; adj. faculty The Ecumenical Inst. of St. Mary's Seminary and U., Balt., 1981. Contbg. writer The Bainbridge Banter newspaper, Chagrin Falls, 1990—. Bd. dirs. The Ruxton (Md.) Country Sch., 1979-80. Recipient John V. Farwell Sr. Preaching award McCormick Theol. Seminary, 1971. Mem. Chagrin Valley Ministerial Assn. (moderator 1985-87, 90—), Rotary, Phi Theta Kappa., Phi Kappa Phi. Office: Valley Presbyn Ch 17560 Chillicothe Rd Chagrin Falls OH 44022 *I have long understood life as stewardship of God's creation, gifts, and blessing. I'd like to think that in my pilgrimage and sojourn through life on earth, I would have left the "campground" in better condition than I found it.*

GRAVELINE, EDWARD PAUL, religious organization administrator; b. Long Beach, Calif., Apr. 15, 1947; s. Edwin George and Phyllis (Fordham) G.; m. Kathleen Elaine Weaver, May 18, 1968; children: Edwin George II, Nathan Allen, Peter-John, Timothy Stephen. Bus. adminstr. Valley Christian Ctr., Fresno, Calif., 1979—; acting supt. Fresno Christian Schs., 1986-87. Mem. steering com. Fresno Loves Africa/World Vision, 1984—; project chair Leadership Fresno, 1987; com. chair Leadership Fresno Alumni Assn., 1990. Mem. Christian Mghmt. Assn., Fresno C. of C. (coms. mem. 1990). Republican. Mem. Internat. Ch. of Foursquare Gospel. Office: Valley Christian Ctr 2150 N Winery Fresno CA 93703

GRAVELY, WILLIAM BERNARD, educator; b. Pickens, S.C., Aug. 19, 1939; s. W. Marvin and Artie L. (Hughes) G.; m. Cynthia Lynn McCoy, June 12, 1968 (div. Dec. 1981); m. Michele Garrison, Dec. 2, 1984 (div. Sept. 1989). BA in History, Wofford Coll., 1961; MDiv, Drew U., 1964; PhD, Duke U., 1969. Asst. prof. Dept. Religion U. Denver, 1968-72, assoc. prof., 1972-87; prof. religious studies U. Denver, 1987—, dir. joint PhD program with Iliff Sch. Theology, 1990—; instl. rep. U. Denver to Rocky Mountain United Meth. Conf. Bd. Higher Edn., 1988-90, chair bd. campus ministry, Rocky Mountain Conf., 1971-75. Author: Gilbert Haven, Methodist Abolitionist, 1973; contbr. articles to profl. jours. Recipient Jesse Lee Prize United Meth. Commn. on Archives and History, 1970; Ethnic Minorities fellow NEH, 1974-75; Univ. Tchrs. fellowship NEH, 1988-89. Mem. Am. Acad. Religion (co-chair Afro-Am. religious history group 1985-87, assoc. editor Afro-Am. Religion Documentary Project 1987—). Office: Dept Religious Studies U Denver Denver CO 80208-0206

GRAVES, ALLEN WILLIS, clergyman, educator; b. Rector, Ark., Jan. 20, 1915; s. James Henry and Anna Joyce (Keaster) G.; m. Helen Elizabeth Cannan, June 1, 1937; children: Joyce (Mrs. Carl Olney), John Raymond, Dorothy Cannan (Mrs. James Hyde), David, Virginia (Mrs. John Weisz), Thomas. B.Ed., So. Ill. U., 1935; Th.M., So. Bapt. Theol. Sem., 1939, Ph.D., 1942. Pub. sch. tchr. Herrin, Ill., 1935-36; ordained to ministry Bapt. Ch., 1935; pastor in Ill. and Ky., 1935-41; dir. young peoples work Bapt. Tng. Union Dept., Bapt. Sunday Sch. Bd., Nashville, 1941-43; pastor in Fla., 1943-45, Va., 1945-50, Okla., 1950-55; dean Sch. Religious Edn., So. Bapt. Theol. Sem., 1955-69, 76-80, sr. prof., 1980-86, dean emeritus, 1986—, adminstrv. dean, 1969-72; exec. dir. Ministry Tng. Center, also Boyce Bible Sch., Louisville, 1972-76; vis. prof. Nigerian Bapt. Theol. Sem., 1980-81. Author: Christ in My Career, 1958, Church Committee Manual, 1958, (with B.B. McKinney) Let Us Sing, 1943, Using and Maintaining Church Property, 1965, The Church at Work: A Handbook of Church Polity, 1972, How Southern Baptists Do Their Work, 1977, Principles of Administration for a Baptist Association, 1978. Mem. So. Bapt. Religious Edn. Assn. (pres. 1962-63). Home: 307 Godfrey Ave Louisville KY 40206

GRAVES, DAVID WILLIAM, minister; b. Knoxville, Tenn., Jan. 22, 1958; s. William Fred and Billie Ruth (Schumpert) G.; m. Nancy Corine Brophy, June 20, 1981; children: Casey, Gregg. BS in Bus. Adminstrn., U. Tenn., 1987; MDiv., Emory U., 1990. Ordained minister United Meth. Ch. Youth worker Fountain City United Meth., Knoxville, 1977-78; dir. sr. high/coll. Second United Meth., Knoxville, 1978-83; min. of youth Hixson (Tenn.) United Meth., 1983—; league dir. Knoxville (Tenn.) Dist. UMC Basketball, 1978-83, Hixson (Tenn.) Kiwanis Ch. Softball League, 1985-87, Hixson (Tenn.) UMC Boys Basketball League, 1991—; dist. youth coord. Chattanooga (Tenn.) Dist. United Meth., 1990—. Chaplain PTA-Ganns Middle Valley Sch., Hixson, 1990—. Mem. Nat. Youth Workers Assn. Home: 8214 Blue Spruce Dr Hixson TN 37343 Office: Hixson United Meth Ch 5301 Old Hixson Pike Chattanooga TN 37343

GRAVES, ERNEST EUGENE, minister; b. Dayton, Ohio, Oct. 7, 1947; s. Samuel Jefferson and Lottie (Whitfield) G.; m. Debra Graves, Aug. 27, 1983; children: Tasha S. Johnson, Andrea M. AS in Data Processing, Sinclair Community Coll., Dayton, Ohio, 1968; BS in Mgmt., BA in Psychology, Wright State U., 1971; MDiv, United Theol. Sem., 1981, postgrad., 1991—. Ordained to ministry Nat. Bapt. Assn., 1983, Am. Bapt. Conv., 1983. Chaplain Children's Med. Ctr., Dayton, 1981-82, on-call chaplain, 1982—; interin pastor Zion Bapt. Ch., Dayton, 1982-83; pastor Harvest Grove Bapt. Ch., Dayton, 1985-91; chaplain III Dayton Correctional Instn., 1984—; bd. dirs. Jail Chaplaincy Task Force, Dayton, Dayton Ministries in High Edn.; mem. West Dayton Mins. Alliance, 1981—. Community Rels. Com. Am. Friends Svc. Com., Dayton, 1989; ward leader Montgomery County Rep. Orgn., Dayton, 1978; del. Ohio Rep. Conv., Columbus, 1978; mem. Young Reps. West, Dayton. Named one of Outstanding Young Men of Am. U.S. Jaycees, 1980, Outstanding Advisor 7th Step Found., 1985; recipient Cert. of Appreciation Gem City Jaycees, 1984. Mem. Am. Correctional Assn., Ohio State Chaplains Assn. (treas. 1989—), Correctional Edn. Assn., Inter-Denom. Mins. Assn., Dayton Area Chaplains Assn. Republican. Home: 5274 Big Bend Dr Dayton OH 45427 Office: Dayton Correctional Instn 4104 Germantown Pk Dayton OH 45417

GRAVES, KIMBERLY ANNE, lay worker; b. Anderson, Ind., Apr. 13, 1970; d. Larry Wayne and Nancy Kay G. Student, Anderson Univ., 1989—. Minister of children's outreach Meadowbrook Bapt. Ch., Anderson, 1989—; camp dir. Am. Bapts. of Ind., Anderson, 1991—. Mem. Christian Svc. Club, Anderson U., 1990-91, team leader All Witness teams, 1989-90, mem. All Women's Chorus, 1989-91. Home: 1904 S Crosslakes Cr Apt A Anderson IN 46012 Office: Meadowbrook Baptist Church # 119 E 36th St Anderson IN 46013

GRAVES, LESTER BALDWIN, minister; b. Greenville, Miss., Apr. 23, 1958; s. Wesley Leslie and Louise (Harris) G.; m. Eugenia Defiera Neal, July 12, 1984. AA, Miss. Delta Jr. Coll., Moorhead, 1979; BA, Delta State U., 1981; MDiv, I.T.C.-Gammon Theol. Sem., 1984. Ordained to ministry Meth. Ch. Pastor Revels United Meth. Ch., Greenville, Miss., 1979-81, Chubb Chapel & Cosmopolitan United Meth. Ch., Cave Spring, Ga., 1982-84, Burns United Meth. Ch., Oxford, Miss., 1984-85, St. Mark United Meth. Ch., Cleveland, Miss., 1985-88, St. Paul United Meth. Ch., Ripley, Miss., 1988-90, Jefferson (S.C.) Parish, 1990—; del. No. Miss. United Meth. Conf.,

Grenada, 1981, Greenville, 1984, Oxford, 1986, Jackson, 1988. Mem. NAACP, Oxford, 1984, SCLC, Atlanta, 1983. Mem. Masons. Democrat. Home: 106 Mine St Jefferson SC 29718 Office: Hopewell United Meth Ch Hwy 251 Jefferson SC 29718

GRAVES, LEWIS SPOTTSWOOD, minister; b. Charlottesville, Va., Mar. 20, 1943; s. Lewis Spottswood Graves and Margarette (Eutsler) Reynolds; married, Aug. 24, 1968; children: Meredith Amanda, John Spottswood. BS, Va. Poly. Inst. and State U., 1965; MDiv, Union Theol. Sem., 1969. Ordained to ministry Presbyn. Ch. (U.S.A.), 1969. Pastor Linwood Presbyn. Ch., Gastonia, N.C., 1969-75; organizing pastor Outer Banks Presbyn. Ch., Kill Devil Hills, N.C., 1978—. Office: Outer Banks Presbyn Ch 907 S Croatan Hwy Kill Devil Hills NC 27948

GRAVES, THOMAS HENRY, seminary administrator; b. Charlottesville, Va., Oct. 11, 1947; s. Allen Willis and Helen Elizabeth (Cannan) G.; m. Wendy Lou Fowler, May 29, 1970; children: Anne Catherine, Jennifer Fowler. BA, Vanderbilt U., 1969; MDiv, So. Bapt. Sem., Louisville, 1972; STM, Yale Div. Sch., 1973; PhD, So. Bapt. Sem., 1976. Assoc. prof. religion Palm Beach Atlantic Coll., West Palm Beach, Fla., 1976-77; pastor First Bapt. Ch., Lake Park, Fla., 1977-79; prof. philosophy of religion Southeastern Bapt. Sem., Wake Forest, N.C., 1979-87; sr. pastor St. John's Bapt. Ch., Charlotte, N.C., 1987-91; pres. Bapt. Theol. Sem., Richmond, Va., 1991—. Contbr. articles to profl. jours.; editor Faith & Mission Jour., 1982-86. Recipient Founders medal, Vanderbilt U., 1966, Broadman Seminarian award, So. Bapt. Theol. Sem., 1972, Citation for Faculty Excellence, 1984. Democrat. Office: Bapt Theol Sem PO Box 9157 Richmond VA 23227

GRAVES, WILLIE I., pastor; b. Phila., June 29, 1951; s. George L. and Annie M. (Dunbar) G.; m. Lillian R. Boyd, Aug. 18, 1973; children: Tiffany B., Lillian L., Willie I. Jr., Lynet L. AAS in Computer Edn., C.E.I., 1971; BS, Phila. Coll. Bible, Langhorne, Pa., 1983. Pastor Olive Br. Bapt. Ch., Phila., 1976-80, St. Phillip's Bapt. Ch., Phila., 1980—. With U.S. Air Force, 1970-72. Mem. Inner City Faith Congress (pres.), Nat. Bapt. Conv. USA (mem. exec. bd. home mission 1986), Pa. State Bapt. Conv. (mem. exec. bd. 1990), Phila. Pastor Conf., Evenings Bapt. Min. Conf., Mins. Conf. Phila., Black Clergy Phila. (assoc.), Herbert E. Miller Lodge. Office: St Phillip's Bapt Ch 1220 N 6th St PO Box 16546 Philadelphia PA 19122

GRAWE, CAROL ANN, pastoral minister, nun; b. Quincy, Ill., Dec. 9, 1938; d. Alvin Henry and Florence Mary (Hilgenbrink) G. BA, Notre Dame Coll., St. Louis, 1960; MA, SE Mo. State U., 1974. Joined Sch. Sisters of Notre Dame, Roman Cath. Ch., 1956. Elem. tchr. Roman Cath. schs., Geneva, Nebr., St. Louis, Ft. Madison, Iowa, Kimmswick, Mo., 1959-74; elem. tchr. Hannibal, Mo.; dir. religious edn. St. Dominic Savio Parish, St. Louis, 1974-77; prin. St. Helen Sch., Fresno, Calif., 1977-81; cons. on religious edn. NE Catechitical Ctr., Diocese of Jefferson City, Edina, Mo., 1981-85; pastoral min. St. Joseph Parish, Palmyra, Mo., 1985—. Contbr. articles to religious publ. Mem. adv. bd. Palmyra Nutrition Ctr., 1988—, pres., 1990-91. Mem. Palmyra Ministerial Alliance (sec. 1987-89), Sch. Sisters Notre Dame Spiritual Dirs., Diocesan Sisters Orgn. (sec. 1971-73, diocesan pastoral coun. rep. 1983-89, 91—). Home: 202 E Hamilton St Palmyra MO 63461 Office: St Joseph Parish 411 S Lane St Palmyra MO 63461 *I believe that it is in prayer that we acknowledge, accept and freely surrender to the reality of who God is and who we are, creatures unconditionally loved by God. Prayer and Life are an attentive listening in order to do, a basic willingness to be led by God in order to bear fruit in mission.*

GRAY, BRUCE, ecumenical agency administrator. Exec. dir. Assn. Christian Chs., Sioux Falls, S.D. Office: Assn of Christian Chs 200 W 18th St Sioux Falls SD 57104*

GRAY, DANIEL FARNUM, minister, writer; b. Rocky Mount, N.C., Mar. 4, 1963; s. Farnum Moore and Wanda Jean (Davis) G.; m. Lisa Beth Cole, Feb. 15, 1986; 1 child, Daniel Stephen. BS, Bapt. U., 1984, MDiv, 1986; PhD, Christian Bible Coll., 1988. Ordained to ministry Bapt. Ch., 1984. Asst. pastor Calvary Bapt. Ch., Dunwoody, Ga., 1979-81, Forrest Hills Bapt. Ch., Decatur, Ga., 1981-84; assoc. pastor Gethsemane Bapt. Ch., Marion, Va., 1984-86; pastor Grace Bapt. Ch., Zebulon, Ga., 1986—. Author: How to Get Started Right, 1988. Pres. Flint River Right to Life, Griffin, Ga., 1987—; bd. dirs. Ga Right to Life, Atlanta, 1989—. Mem. Bapt. Bible Fellowship, Metro Bapt. Fellowship, Mid. Ga. Bapt. Fellowship (pres. 1986—). Republican. Home and Office: Grace Bapt Ch Rte 1 Box 369 Zebulon GA 30295

GRAY, DAVID FRANKLIN, minister; b. Yokohama, Japan, May 6, 1917; (parents Am. citizens); s. Franklin Hoover and Elizabeth May (Heath) G.; m. Emily Belle Butler, Nov. 22, 1936; children: Naomi May, (Mrs. John Harvey Burrows), David Samuel, Deborah Sharon (Mrs. David LeRoy Jones). Student, Citrus Coll., 1934, Morse Bible Tng. Inst., 1936; DD (hon.), Colonial Acad., 1958; DLitt (hon.), Pioneer Theol. Sem., 1958; BA (hon.), Western Apostolic Bible Coll., 1975; D Christian Lit., Christian Life Coll., 1987. Ordained to ministry United Pentecostal Ch., 1940. Founding pastor United Pentecostal Ch., Pasadena, Calif., 1937-39; pastor United Pentecostal Ch., Turlock, Calif., 1939-43; founding pastor Revival Tabernacle, San Diego, 1945—; founding pastor United Pentecostal Ch., Oakland, Calif., 1951; acting pres. Western Apostolic Bible Coll., Stockton, Calif., 1970; youth pres. Western Dist. United Pentecostal Ch., 1940-43; first gen. pres. youth dept. (nat.), 1947-50; dist. presbyter Western Dist., 1954-86; hon. presbyter Western Dist., 1986—; speaker on Hour of Power nationwide radio broadcast, 1955-67; mem. bd. Christian edn. United Pentecostal Ch., 1955-61; chmn. campus evangelism commn., 1970-74; co-founder Pentecostal Students Fellowship Internat., 1971, Forerunners, 1973; founder, chmn. bd. Christian Svc. Tng. Inst., San Diego, 1973—; mem. bd. publs. United Pentecostal Ch., 1974—. Author: The Way of Victory, 1947, The Light of Truth, 1947, The Seven Men and the Two Natures, 1957, Spiritual Temperature Chart Study, 1957, The Last Will and Testament of the Lord Jesus Christ, 1969, Our Inheritance, 1971, Questions Pentecostals Ask, 1986; assoc. editor Gospel Tidings, 1972—; contbr. articles to religious publs. Home: 3429 Boyne St Spring Valley CA 91977 Office: 1765 Pentecost Way San Diego CA 92105

GRAY, DAVID LEE, SR., minister; b. Kansas City, Kans., Feb. 8, 1931; s. James and Stella Lee (Webster) G.; m. Helen Theresa Gott, Aug. 15, 1976; 1 child, David Lee Jr. Student, U. Kans., Cen. Bapt. Theol. Sem., Kansas City; BRE, Western Bapt. Bible Coll., Kansas City, Mo., 1966. Ordained to ministry Nat. Bapt. Conv. U.S.A., Inc. Pastor Pleasant Green Bapt. Ch., Kansas City, Kans., 1959—; pres., founder Witnessing Pub. Co., Kansas City; pub. The Kansas City Voice, The Protestant mag.; founder, nat. pres. United Prayer Movement; radio and TV preacher, 1964—. Author: Jesus Christ Loves You, Does Jesus Christ Live in Your Heart?, Every Christian Is a Soul Winner, God, The Holy Spirit—Who Is He?, numerous other books. Mem. Mayor's Citizen Adv. Com., Kansas City, in 1960s; bd. dirs. YWCA; founder, exec. dir. Pleasant Green Community Sch., Kansas City, 1972—. Mem. NAACP (chmn. ch. work com. Kansas City br. 1960s), Bapt. Mins. Union (former pres. Kansas City chpt.). Office: Pleasant Green Bapt Ch 340 Oakland Ave Kansas City KS 66101

GRAY, DONALD PETER, theology educator; b. Rochester, N.Y., Mar. 29, 1937; s. Lloyd Wilfred and Rose Isabel (Pohl) G.; m. Maureen A. Lester, Aug. 26, 1961 (div. 1978); children: John, David, Ellen; m. Jeanne Anne Hull, Nov. 24, 1978; 1 child, Jessica. BA, U. Toronto, Can., 1961; MA, U. Notre Dame, 1963; PhD, Fordham U., 1968. Prof. Manhattan Coll., Riverdale, N.Y., 1962—. Author: The One and the Many, 1969, Jesus: The Way to Freedom, 1979. Danforth Found. grantee, 1965-67. Mem. Coll. Theology Soc., Cath. Theol. Assn., Am. Teilhard Assn. (v.p. 1980-88), Phi Beta Kappa. Roman Catholic. Home: 1 Shagbark Ln Woodbury CT 06798 Office: Manhattan Coll Dept Religious Studies Riverdale NY 10471

GRAY, DUNCAN MONTGOMERY, JR., bishop; b. Canton, Miss., Sept. 21, 1926; s. Duncan Montgomery and Isabel (McCrady) G.; m. Ruth Miller Spivey, Feb. 9, 1948; children: Duncan Montgomery, Anne Gray Finley, Lloyd Spivey, Catherine Gilmer. B.E.E., Tulane U., 1948; M.Div., U. South, 1953, D.D. (hon.), 1972. Ordained priest Episcopal Ch., 1953, bishop, 1974; priest-in-charge Calvary Ch., Cleveland, Miss. and Grace Ch., Rosedale, Miss., 1953-57, Holy Innocents Ch., Como, Miss., 1957-60; rector St. Peter's Ch., Oxford, Miss., 1957-65, St. Paul's Ch., Meridian, Miss., 1965-74; bishop coadjutor Diocese of Miss., Jackson, 1974; bishop Diocese of Miss., 1974—; chmn. Standing Commn. on Constn. and Canons of Gen. Conv. of Episc. Ch., 1977-83, House of Bishops' Com. Canons, 1975-89; pres. Province IV Episc. Ch., 1984-88, chmn. com. on rules, 1989—; mem. advice council to the Presiding Bishop, 1984-88; vice chmn, Bd. Archives Episc. Ch. Contbr. articles in field to religious publs. Chmn. bd. trustees All Saints Episc. Sch., Vicksburg, 1975-77; trustee U. South, Sewanee, Tenn., 1974—, regent, 1981-87, chancellor, 1991—; chmn. Miss. Religious Leadership Conf., 1977-79, So. Regional Council, 1967-73; mem. Miss. Mental Health Assn., 1968-73; bd. dirs. Miss. Council on Human Relations, 1962—, pres., 1963-67; mem. Miss. Adv. Com. to U.S. Commn. on Civil Rights, 1975—. Recipient Nat. Speaker of Year award Tau Kappa Alpha, 1962. Home: 3775 Old Canton Rd Jackson MS 39216 Office: PO Box 23107 Jackson MS 39225-3107

GRAY, EARL ERMONT, JR., minister; b. Wilmington, Del., Aug. 25, 1952; s. Earl Ermont and Rose Cecelia (Pawley) G.; m. Debra Sue Mills, June 12, 1981; 1 child, Earl Ermont III. BS, Lancaster (Pa.) Bible Coll., 1986. Ordained to ministry So. Bapt. Conv., 1987. Interim pastor Strasburg (Pa.) Bapt. Ch., 1986; missionary pastor Village Missions, Birdsall, N.Y., 1986-88; pastor Manchester (Md.) Bapt. Ch., 1988—; dir. associational brotherhood Cen. Assn., Md., 1990—; intercessor Wycliffe Bible Translators, Huntington Beach, Calif., 1990—. Editor newsletters Pastoral Perspectives, 1985-86, Equipper's Quar., 1991; contbr. poetry to various publs. Mem. pub. rels. com. Md. Spl. Olympics, 1991—. Recipient prize Acad. Am. Poets, 1980, Disting. Leadership award Lancaster Bible Coll., 1986. Mem. Pastors Who Disciple, Conservative Evang. Bapt. Fellowship. Republican. Home and Office: 2937 Manchester Baptist Church Rd Manchester MD 21102 *Anyone ready to invest all he is in knowing God will find his investment returned with the wisdom necessary to know how to live in the abundance of God's grace.*

GRAY, FRANCIS CAMPBELL, bishop; b. Manila, Apr. 27, 1940. Grad., Rollins Coll., Winter Park, Fla., 1966; BD, Nashota House, SJM, 1979; attended, St. George's Coll., Jerusalem. Ordained priest Roman Cath. Ch., 1969. Asst. St. Wilfred's Ch., Sarasota, Fla., 1969-70; chaplain Manatee Jr. Coll., 1970-74; rector St. John's Ch., Melbourne, Fla., 1979-87, Emmanuel Ch., Orlando, Fla., 1986-87; bishop co-adjutor Diocese of No. Ind., South Bend, 1986-87, bishop, 1987—. With USMC. Office: Diocese of No Ind 2502 N Twyckenham Dr South Bend IN 46614

GRAY, GEORGE MCBURNEY, clergyman, consultant, psychologist; b. Belfast, No. Ireland, Oct. 12, 1941; came to U.S., 1970; s. Charles and Wilhemina (McBurney) G.; m. Christine Irvine, Aug. 20, 1966; children—George Andrew, Charis Mary. Student Bible Tng. Inst. Glasgow (Scotland), 1963-66; diploma in theology, U. London, 1966; Th.M., Luther Rice Sem., 1973, Th.D., 1974; D.Ministry in Psychology, Fuller Theol. Sem., 1979. Ordained to ministry Baptist Ch., 1966; pastor Patrick Baptist Ch., Glasgow, Scotland, 1966-70, United Baptist Ch., Milo, Maine, 1970-74, First Baptist Ch., Gloversville, N.Y., 1974-82, Kenwood Baptist Ch., Cin., 1982-85, Grace Bapt. Ch., Westchester, Ohio, 1985—; cons. family counselor, mental health. Am. Baptist Chs. scholar, Regents Coll., Oxford U., 1981. Mem. Am. Assn. Marriage and Family Therapists, Am. Psychol. Assn., Brit. Psychol. Soc., Am. Baptist Minister's Council. Contbr. articles to psychology, religious jours. Office: Grace Baptist Ch 7983 Cox Rd Westchester OH 45069

GRAY, GORDON JOSEPH CARDINAL, former archbishop of St. Andrews and Edinburgh; b. Edinburgh, Aug. 10, 1910; s. Francis William and Angela Gray; student St. John's Sem., Wonersh; M.A. with honours, St. Andrews U., D.D. (hon.); D. Univ., Heriot-Watt U. Ordained priest Roman Cath. Ch., consecrated bishop, elevated to cardinal, 1969; asst. priest, St. Andrews, 1935-41; parish priest, Hawick, 1941-47; rector Blairs' Coll., Aberdeen, Scotland, 1947-51; archbishop of St. Andrews and Edinburgh, 1951-85, cardinal, 1969—. Mem. Congregation for Evangelization of Peoples, Congregation of the Sacraments, Congregation of Clerics. Hon. fellow Ednl. Inst. Scotland. Office: St Bennets, 42 Greenhill Gardens, Edinburgh 10, Scotland

GRAY, HELEN THERESA GOTT, religion editor; b. Jersey City, July 2, 1942; d. William E. and Cynthia B. (Williams) Gott; m. David L. Gray, Aug. 15, 1976; 1 child, David Lee Jr. BA, Syracuse U., 1963; M in Internat. Affairs, Columbia U., 1965. Editor religion sect. The Kansas City (Mo.) Star, 1971—; tchr. Bible sch. Pleasant Green Bapt. Ch., Kansas City, Kans., 1975—, counselor, 1978—. Co-author, editor several books; contbr. articles. Recipient writing award Valley Forge Freedom Found., 1967; John Hay Whitney Found. grantee, 1963-64. Mem. Religion Newswriters Assn., Kansas City Media Fellowship. Office: The Kansas City Star 1729 Grand Ave Kansas City MO 64108

GRAY, HENRY DAVID, minister, religious organization administrator; b. Antrim, No. Ireland, Jan. 18, 1908; came to U.S., 1923; s. Nathaniel and Margaret (Lawther) G.; m. Helen Katharine Lorbeer, Aug. 12, 1930; children—Mildred Ellen, David Lawther, Betsey Charisma. B.A. magna cum laude, Pomona Coll., 1930, D.D. (hon.), 1954; M. Div. summa cum laude, Hartford Theol. Sem., 1933; Ph.D., Edinburgh U., Scotland, 1935; cert. in religious edn., Boston U., 1931; Cert. Theology, Tubingen U., 1935; D. Litt. (hon.), Piedmont Coll., 1976. Ordained minister Congregational Ch., 1935. Numerous positions Congl. Chs., worldwide, 1935—; missionary Congl. Chs., Western Samoa, 1966; dir. 300th anniversary yr. program Old South Ch., Hartford, Conn., 1969-70; minister emeritus Old South Ch., Hartford, 1970—; dir. summer student study Congl. Ch., Europe, Middle East, worldwide, 1948-70; interim minister Hollywood Congl. Ch., Calif., 1971, North Hollywood Congl. Ch., Calif., 1971-72; dean Am. Congl. Ctr., South Pasadena, Calif., 1972—; founding mem. Pasadena Coun. Chs., 1947, Nat. Coun. Chs., 1950; bd. dirs. Greater Hartford Coun. Chs., 1956-60; moderator Hampshire Assn. Congl. Christian Chs., 1938-39, L.A. Assn., 1947-48, Conn. Fellowship, 1957-61, 65, Nat. Assn., 1958-59. Author: Young People In Church Work, 1940, A Theology for Christian Youth, 1941, Words For Today, 1944, Under Orders, 1946, Science and Religion, 1946, Primacy of God, 1947, Christian Doctrine of Grace, 1948 (best full length theol. book Ind. Press, London, 1948), The Christian Marriage Service, 1950, Oneonta Guide Book, 1950, 12 edit., 1985, The Upward Call, 1952, The Church Polity and Unity Report, 1954, Some Christian Convictions, 1955, A Bible Guide to the Holy Land, 1964, Blue Book of Congregational Usage #1, 1965, #2, 1967, Service Book, 1966, South Church Prayers, 1966, God's Torchbearers, 1970, Heart of Oak, Helm of Destiny, 1970, Hollywood Prayers, 1973, Congregational Usage, 1976, 6th edit., 1990, Congregational Worshipbook, 1978, 3d edit., 1990, Pilgrim Fathers Reach the Pacific, 1981, Soundings, 1980, Waymarks, 1983, Plus Ultra, Vol. 1, 1983, Vol. 2, 1985, The Mediators, 1984, The Souls Working Clothes, 1988, 26th edit. What it Means to be a Member of a Congregational Christian Church, 1991; also 8 vols. of lectures and travelog, 1948-70; editor (monthly mag.) The Congregationalist, 1962-66, (monthly mag.) The Pilgrim Highroad, 1939-42, Congregational Jour., 1975—; contbr. numerous articles to profl. jours., also pamphlets; numerous appearances on TV and radio. Active numerous civic organizations, 1924-70; mem. Hartford City Plan Commn., 1959-70, chmn., 1962-67, 70; mem. Capitol Regional Planning Coun., 1962-67, 70, Conn. Capitol Ctr. Commn., 1966-67, 69-70; organizer Ventura City Environ. Coalition, Calif., 1971; mem. exec. com. Comprehensive Planning Commn., Ventura, Calif., 1973-77; chmn. Cultural Heritage Team, Ventura, 1974-75; pres. South Village, Hartford, 1968-84; mem. Nat. Com. for Scouting, 1939-42; former parliamentarian/vice chmn. Santa Monica Mountains Nat. Commn., Nat. Park Service; founder Congl. World Assembly of Youth, 1949. Recipient numerous awards Boy Scouts Am., Hartford Theol. Sem., Congl. Chs., citation of excellence State of Conn., 1970, Resolution of Profound Appreciation City Council Hartford, 1970, Resolution Commendation award Bd. Suprs. Ventura, 1985, letter of commendation Supt. Nat. Park Service, 1985, citation Conn. Conf. United Ch. Christ, 1985, Spl. Commendation, Internat. Congl. Council, 1987; Gray Hall named in his honor, South Pasadena, Calif., 1955, Hartford, 1960, Alexandroupolis, Greece, 1962, Gray Chapel named for him, Kuzhikode, Kerala, India, 1967, Gray Student Union named for him Lady Doak Coll., Madurai, India, 1967. Fellow Am. Acad. Religion, Royal Anthropol. Inst., Am. Anthropol. Assn.; mem. Soc. Bibl. Lit., Calif. West Congl. Assn. Chs. and Ministers (cons. polity 1984—), Nat. Assn. Congl. Christian Chs. (numerous coms., chmn. coms., offices), Clerics Club, Ventura County Hist. Soc., Calif. Hist. Soc., Nat. Hist. Soc., Am. Congl. Assn. (bd. dirs. 1965-70), United Ref. Ch. History Soc., Brit. Congl. Hist. Circle, Inst. Pacific Studies, Congl. World Assembly Youth (founder, bd. dirs. 1962, chmn. 1985), Congl. Christian Hist. Soc., Congl. Fellowship Conn. (life, exec. com.), Hartford Assn. Congl. Christian Chs. and Ministers (exec. com. 1956-60, citation 1985), Nat. Pilgrim Fellowship (founder, life counselor), Nat. Eagle Scout Assn., Calif. Acad. Scis., West Coast Theol. Club, Conn. Valley Theol. Club, Congl. Mins. Club (Scotland), Pasadena Athletic Club, Wranglers Club, Oneonta Mens Svc. Club (San Gabriel), Nat. World Wildlife Fedn., Sierra Club, Ephebian Soc., Order DeMolay (hon. chevalier), Phi Beta Kappa, Delta Sigma Rho. Republican. Avocations: youth; athletics; mountaineering; swimming; crafts. Home: 298 Fairfax Ave Ventura CA 93003 Office: Am Congregational Ctr 1515 Garfield Ave South Pasadena CA 91030

GRAY, JAMES R., minister, marriage and family therapist; b. Anderson, S.C., July 31, 1953; s. Rudolph and Georgia (McCurry) G.; m. Anne Black, Aug. 19, 1977; children: Rebekah Anne, Kathyrn Leah, Cynthia Lynn. AA, Anderson Coll., 1973; BA, Central Wesleyan Coll., 1975; ThM, Luther Rice Sem, 1978, DMin, 1979; MA in Counseling, Liberty U., 1987. Cert. profl. counselor. Pastor First Baptist Ch., Central, S.C., Unity Baptist Ch., Starr, S.C., Roebuck Bapist Ch., Roebuck, S.C.; developer Marriage Enrichment Seminar-Retreat; pres. James R. Gray Ministries; bd. mem. S.C. Bapist Conv.; trustee Bapt. Courier. Author: Building An Intimate Marriage, Oneness with Healthy Separateness 1988, Will the Real Pastor Please Stand Up?, Worry: The Silent Killer, The Alarm Has Sounded. Mem. AACD, Christian Assn. for Psychol. Studies, Internat. Assn. Marriage and Family Couselors. Home: PO Box 312 Roebuck SC 29376

GRAY, TED FAY, minister; b. Broken Arrow, Okla., Aug. 30, 1942; s. James Benjamin and Faith Anna (Henegar) G.; m. Charlene Ruth Rowley, Feb. 3, 1973; children: Paul, Nick, Victoria. BA, Lee Coll., Cleve., 1967; MRE, Southwestern Bapt. Theol. Sem., Ft. Worth, 1972. Ordained to ministry Ch. of God, 1972. Dir. Christian edn. Ch. of God, Dallas, 1972-74; pastor Ch. of God, Edmond, Okla., 1974-75, Duncanville, Tex., 1975-78, Henrietta, Tex., 1978-86, Weatherford, Tex., 1990—; dir. state youth and edn. Ch. of God, Weatherford, 1986-90. Mem. Soc. for Pentecostal Studies. Republican. Home: 806 Hanover Weatherford TX 76086 Office: North Main Ch of God 803 N Main Weatherford TX 76086

GRAY, WALLACE GALE, philosophy educator; b. Palmyra, Mo., May 3, 1927; s. Wallace Gale and Marjorie (Thomas) G.; children: Toni Jo, Tara Joy. BA, Cen. Meth. U., Fayette, Mo., 1948; BD, So. Meth. U., Dallas, 1951; PhD, Vanderbilt U., 1953; postgrad., U. Hawaii, 1963-64. Ordained to ministry Meth. Ch. Assoc. pastor First Meth. Ch., Lawton, Okla., 1953-54; asst. prof. dept. religion So. Meth. U., Dallas, 1954-56; asst. prof. Southwestern Coll., Winfield, Kans., 1956-58, assoc. prof., 1958-66, chmn. div. social sci., 1960-66, prof. philosophy and religion, 1966—, Kirk chair philosophy, 1966—; vis. scholar Hiroshima (Japan) Inst. Tech., 1971-72; vis. prof. Friends U., 1986-88, Wichita State U., 1986-87; chmn. task force on effects tech. change and population growth on values and ethics Kans. Coun. Chs., 1968-77; ministerial mem., local co-chair Commn. on Status and Role of Women, Kans. West Conf., United Meth. Ch., Winfield and Wichita, 1989—; Beck lectr. on ethics Southwestern Coll., Winfield, 1990. Co-author: (with John Plott) New Keys to East-West Philosophy, 1979, Global History of Philosophy, Vol. V, 1989; contbr. articles to profl. jours. Co-chair Commn. on Celebration of the Bicentennial of U.S. Constitution, Winfield, 1987—. Mem. Am. Philos. Assn., Am. Acad. Religion, Rotary Internat. (chair vocat. svc. 1990—). Democrat. Methodist. Avocations: study of Japanese lang. and culture, kites, chess, biking. Office: Southwestern Coll Winfield KS 67156 *The sciences, particularly the social sciences, help us measure the size of our problems; the humanities illuminate the values relevant to our problems; the spirit, in one of its many forms, helps us solve our problems.*

GRAY, WILLIAM H., JR., minister; b. Waco, Tex., Sept. 13, 1927; s. William H. Sr. and Anna (Morgan) G.; m. Amy Nadine Sikes, Aug. 21; children: Bradley Steven, Anna Harriet,. BA, Baylor U., 1951; MDiv, Southwest Bapt. Theol. Sem., 1958. Pastor Dale (Tex.) Bapt. Ch., 1949-51; assoc. pastor First Bapt. Ch., Tomball, Tex., 1951-54; pastor First Bapt. Ch., Willis, Tex., 1954-60; missionary to Mexico foreign mission bd. Southern Bapt. Conv., Richmond, Va., 1960-82; partnership missions Bapt. Gen. Conv. of Tex., Dallas, 1982—. Rep. for religious edn. Rotary Internat., Willis, 1954-60. Sr. sgt. USAF, 1946-49. Mem. World Evangelism Strategy Workgroup, Bapt. World Alliance (Evangelism and Edn. div. 1990—). Avocations: reading, travel, walking. Home: 8012 Ulster Dr Fort Worth TX 76180 Office: Bapt Gen Conv 333 N Washington Dallas TX 75246 *What we are is not nearly as important as the potential of what we may become.*

GRAY, WILLIAM MARTIN, JR., minister; b. Montgomery, Ala., Dec. 15, 1962; S. William Martin and Ann (Sanders) G.; m. Mary Hill, Mar. 8, 1986; 1 child, William Martin III. MusB, Samford U., 1986. Lic. to ministry Bapt. Ch., 1981. Minister of music Blue Ridge Bapt. Ch., Wetumpka, Ala., 1982-83, Locust Fork (Ala.) Bapt. Ch., 1983-86; organist Ridglen West Bapt. Ch., Ft. Worth, 1986-88; minister of music First Bapt. Ch., Elba, Ala., 1988—. Mem. Elba Ministerial Assn., Rotary Club (sec. treas. 1990-92), Am. Guild Organists, Hymn Soc. Am., Am. Choral Dirs. Assn. Home: 967 Morrow Ave Elba AL 36323 Office: First Bapt Ch Simmons at Polka Elba AL 36323

GRAYSON, D. W., bishop. Bishop Ch. of God in Christ, Bklyn. Office: Ch of God in Christ 1237 Eastern Pkwy Brooklyn NY 11213*

GREAN, STANLEY VERNON, retired religion educator, clergyman; b. N.Y.C., Apr. 3, 1920; s. Alexandre Michael and Anna (Kurtz) G.; m. Patricia Clare Anthony, July 25, 1944; 1 child, Nicholas (dec.). BA, Columbia U., 1941; BD, Union Theol. Sem., N.Y.C., 1944; PhD in Philosophy, Columbia U., 1961. Ordained to ministry Congl. Christian Ch., 1946. Min. Universalist-Unitarian Ch., Mt. Vernon, N.Y., 1944-47; instr. philosophy U. Conn., New London, 1947-49, Storrs, 1949-53; vis. lectr. humanities Howard U., Washington, 1954; asst. prof. philosophy Ohio U., Athens, 1955-65, assoc. prof., 1965-69, prof., 1969-89, chmn. philosophy dept., 1971-76, prof. emeritus, 1989—. Author: Shaftesbury's Philosophy of Religion and Ethics, 1967; sect. editor Ultimate Reality and Meaning: Interdisciplinary Studies in the Philosophy of Understanding, Toronto, Can., 1984-88, co-editor, 1988—. Mem. Internat. Soc. for Study of Human Ideas on Ultimate Reality and Meaning (v.p. 1985-87, pres. 1987-89, excellence award 1989), Am. Acad. Religion, Am. Philos. Assn., Ohio Philos. Assn. (disting. svc. award 1989), Soc. Christian Philosophers, Phi Beta Kappa. Democrat. Episcopalian. Home: 163 B Pine Grove Heights Athens OH 45701 Office: Ohio U Dept Philosophy Gordy Hall Athens OH 45701

GREELEY, ANDREW MORAN, sociologist, author; b. Oak Park, Ill., Feb. 5, 1928; s. Andrew T. and Grace (McNichols) G. A.B., St. Mary of Lake Sem., 1950, S.T.L., 1954; M.A., U. Chgo., 1961, Ph.D., 1961. Ordained priest Roman Catholic Ch., 1954; asst. pastor Ch. of Christ the King, Chgo., 1954-64; program dir. Nat. Opinion Research Ctr., Chgo., 1961-68; dir. Ctr. for Study Am. Pluralism, from 1973; lectr. sociology U. Chgo., 1963-72; prof. sociology U. Ariz., Tucson, from 1978, now adj. prof.; cons. Hazen Found. Commn. Syndicated columnist People and Values; guest columnist Chgo. Sun Times, 1985—; Author: The Church and the Suburbs, 1959, Strangers in the House, 1961, Religion and Career, 1963, (with Peter H. Rossi) Education of Catholic Americans, 1966, Changing Catholic College, 1967, Come Blow Your Mind With Me, 1971, Life for a Wanderer: A New Look at Christian Spirituality, 1971, The Denominational Society: A Sociological Approach to Religion in America, 1972, Priests in the United States: Reflections on A Survey, 1972, That Most Distressful Nation, 1972, New Agenda, 1973, Jesus Myth, 1971, Unsecular Man, 1974, Ethnicity in the United States: A Preliminary Reconnaissance, 1974, Ecstasy: A Way of Knowing, 1974, Building Coalitions: American Politics in the 1970's, 1974, Sexual Intimacy, 1975, Denomination Society, 1975, The Great Mysteries: An Essential Catechism, 1976, The Communal Catholic: A Personal Manifesto, 1976, Death and Beyond, 1976, The American Catholic: A Social Portrait, 1977, The Making of the Popes, 1978, 79, The Magic Cup: An Irish Legend, 1979, Women I've Met, 1979, Why Can't They Be Like Us?, 1980,

The Cardinal Sins, 1981, Religion: A Secular Theory, 1982, Thy Brother's Wife, 1982, Ascent Into Hell, 1983, Virgin & Martyr, 1985, Piece of My Mind on Just About Everything, 1985, Happy are the Meek, 1985, Angels of September, 1986, Happy Are Those Who Thirst For Justice, 1987, The Final Planet, 1987, Angel Fire, 1988, Love Song, 1989, St. Valentine's Night, 1989, short stories All About Women, 1990, The Catholic Myth: The Behavior and Beliefs of American Catholics, 1990, The Cardinal Virtues, 1990, others; contbr. articles to profl. jours. Recipient Cath. Press Assn. award for best book for young people, 1965, Thomas Alva Edison award for radio broadcast, 1963, C. Albert Kobb award Nat. Cath. Edn. Assn., 1977. Mem. Am. Sociol. Assn., Soc. for Sci. Study Religion, Religious Research Assn. Office: care Warner Books Inc 666 Fifth Ave New York NY 10103

GREEN, ARTHUR, academic administrator, rabbi; b. Mar. 21, 1941; m. Kathy Held; 1 child, Hannah Leah. BA, Brandeis U., 1961, PhD, 1975; MHL, Jewish Theol. Sem., 1964. Ordained rabbi, 1967. Mem. faculty Havurat Shalom Community Sem., 1968-73; lectr. U. Pa., Phila., 1973-75, asst. prof., 1975-80, assoc. prof., 1980-87, adj. assoc. prof., 1987—; dean Reconstructionist Rabbinical Coll., 1984-86, acting pres., 1986-87, pres., 1987—; vis. lectr. Smith Coll., 1971-72, Barnard Coll., 1976, 78; vis. asst. prof. Grad. Theol. Union, Berkeley, 1977; commr. N.Am. Commn. on Jewish Edn., 1988-90. Author: Tormented Master: A Life of Rabbi Nahman of Bratslav, 1980, Devotion and Commandment: The Faith of Abraham in the Hasidic Imagination, 1989; also articles; (with others) Go and Study, Essays and Studies in Honor of Alfred Jospe, 1980, Essays in Honor of Alexander Altmann, 1981, The Other Side of God, 1981, On Being a Jewish Feminist, 1982, Take Judaism for Example, 1983, An Introduction to the Medieval Mystics of Europe, 1984, Back to the Sources: Reading the Classical Jewish Texts, 1984, Jewish Spirituality II, 1987, Contemporary Jewish Religious Thought, 1987; contbr.: Encyclopedia of Religion, 1987; cons.: Classics of Western Spirituality, 1979-86; editor: Jewish Spirituality, Vol. I, 1986; (Hebrew text) Kol ha-Neshamah, 1987—; (series) World Spirituality, 1983-87; (with Barry W. Holtz) Your Word Is Fire: The Hasidic Masters on Contemplative Prayer, 1977; editor, translator: Upright Practices, 1982, The Light of the Eyes, Homilies on Genesis, 1982; editor, author (with others): Jewish Spirituality, Vol. II, 1987; co-editor: Mysticism, Hermeneutics, and Religion: Studies in Judaism, 1984-91; contbg. editor Reconstructionist mag., 1986—; mem. editorial bd. Religion in Intellectual Life, 1987—, Tikkun, 1987—. Bd. dirs. Jewish Found. for Christian Rescuers, 1988—, Ctr. for Jewish-Christian Studies and Rels., 1990—. Recipient Lindbeck award U. Pa., 1978; NEH grantee, 1977, 79-80; Fulbright scholar, 1985. Mem. Am. Acad. Religion, Assn. for Jewish Studies, Soc. for Values in Higher Edn. (Kent fellow 1967), Rabbinical Assembly, Reconstructionist Rabbinical Assn., Fedn. Reconstructionist Congregations and Havurot (bd. dirs. 1986—). Home: 6823 Quincy St Philadelphia PA 19119 Office: Reconstructionist Rabbinical Coll Church Rd and Greenwood Ave Wyncote PA 19095

GREEN, ARTHUR SAMUEL, minister; b. Akron, Ohio, Sept. 9, 1951; s. James Samuel and Johney Evelyn (Mims) G.; m. Patricia Ann Williams, Aug. 30, 1975; 1 child, Anton DeAire'. BS in Edn., Akron U., 1973; M in Religion, Ashland (Ohio) Sem., 1988; postgrad., Inst. Holy Land, Jerusalem, 1988. Ordained to ministry Meth. Ch., 1975. Phys. dir. West Akron YMCA, 1973-75; dep. sheriff Summit County Sheriff's Dept., Akron, 1975-76; support investigator Summit County Bur. of Support, Akron, 1976-81; baliff Akron Mcpl. Ct., 1981-89; pastor Met. Christian Meth. Episcopal Ch., Cin., 1989—; pres. Interdenominational Ministerial Alliance Greater Cin., 1991—. Trustee Summit County Drug Bd., 1987-89, local coun. Boy Scouts Am., 1987-89, Better Housing League, 1989—. Recipient Youth Motivation award Nat. Alliance Bus., 1979, Svc. award East High Boosters, 1985, Achievement award Summit County Drug Bd., 1989, spl. recognition Melrose YMCA, 1991. Mem. NAACP, Christian Meth. Episcopal Ch. Ministerial Alliance (pres. 1990—), Ohio Cen. Ind. Conf., Phi Beta Sigma (Svc. award 1991). Democrat. Avocations: golf, bowling, running. Home: 1220 Paddock Hills Ave Cincinnati OH 45229 Office: Met CME Ch 2815 Melrose Ave Cincinnati OH 45206

GREEN, BERNARD DOUGLAS, priest; b. Bilbrook, Staff., Eng., Feb. 22, 1940; came to U.S., 1976; s. Edwin James and Freda May (Byatt) G. Licentiate in philosophy, Heythrop Coll., 1969; BD, London U., 1973; M in Human Devel., St. Mary's Coll., Winona, Minn., 1982. Pastor R/e Ch., Thornbury, Bristol, Eng., 1973-76; chaplain St. Mary's Nursing Home, Milw., 1976-80; psychotherapist Our Lady of Victories Rehab. Ctr., Stroud, Gloucester, Eng., 1982-84; lectr. in pastoral studies Sacred Heart Sch. Theology, Hales Corners, Wis., 1984-88; cons., rscher. Counseling Learning Inst., E. Dubuque, Ill., 1988-90; pastor St. Pius X, Wauwatose, Wis., 1990—; campus min. Mt. St. Mary Coll., Milw., 1990—. Author: (books) Counseling and Advice Giving in Pastoral Care, 1987, Learning, Values and Counseling, 1986, Education In A New Dimension, 1988. Mem. Am. Assn. Counseling & Devel., Assn. Counseling & Values. Roman Catholic. Home and Office: 2506 Wauwatosa Ave Wauwatosa WI 53213 *We can change when we have an inner sense of security about our own continued reality and significance. What perceptions, what relationships, what values will make such a sense possible, this preoccupies me. How must I be to risk transformation?.*

GREEN, BERNARD LOTHAIR, minister; b. New Castle, Ind., May 26, 1938; s. John Spencer and Mary Louise (West) G.; m. Thela Joyce Wilde, May 31, 1958; children: Brent Lothair, Quentin Sean Eamonn. AB in Religion and Philosophy, Olivet Nazarene Coll., Kankakee, Ill., 1960; BD in English Bible, Nazarene Theol. Seminary, Kansas City, Mo., 1964; D of Religion, Sch. of Theology, Claremont, Calif., 1969. Ordained to ministry United Meth. Ch., 1969. Min. Nazarene Ch., Lurgan, No. Ireland, 1964-66; assoc. min. Westchester Meth. Ch., L.A., 1967-69; min. Broadway/Pacific Meth. Ch., Glendale, Calif., 1969-71, Mesa Verde United Meth. Ch., Costa Mesa, Calif., 1971-79, Rolling Hills (Calif.) United Meth. Ch., 1979-81, Ventura (Calif.) Coll. Ch., 1982-86; minister San Carlos United Meth. Ch., San Diego, Calif., 1986—. Pres. Alumni Assn., Claremont, 1980-82. Mem. Kiwanis (pres. Costa Mesa chpt. 1976-77). Democrat. Office: San Carlos United Meth Ch 6554 Cowles Mt Blvd San Diego CA 92119 *The future is not predetermined. Neither is your life. We are shapers of both by our present choices.*

GREEN, CALVIN COOLIDGE, minister; b. Laneview, Va., July 19, 1931; s. James Herman and Consula Levallia (Deleaver) G.; m. Ella Mary Osborne, Sept. 4, 1954; children: Robert Ceasar, Carroll Anthony, Charles Conrad. BS, VA. State U., 1956; MDiv, Va. Union U., 1982; ThD, Internat. Bible Inst. and Sem., 1983; EdD, Nova U., 1987; PhD, Internat. Sem., Plymouth, Fla., 1990. Ordained to ministry Bapt. Ch., 1977. Pastor Lebanon Bapt. Ch., New Kent, Va., 1977-82, Calvary Bapt. Ch., Saluda, Va., 1979—; chairperson Sci. Thomas Jefferson Ctr., Richmond, Va., 1990—; mem. gen. bd. Bapt. Gen. Conv. Va., Richmond, 1981-85; auditor Bapt. Minister's Union, Richmond, 1986—; rec. sec. Southside Rappahannock Bapt. Assn., Saluda, 1990—. Author: Counseling: With the Pastor & CPE Student in Mind, 1984. Pres. NAACP, New Kent, Va., 1960-76; coord. New EASA Project, New Kent, 1969-70. Col. U.S. Army, 1981—. NSF grantee 1969-70; decorated Meritorious Svc. medal. Mem. NSTA, Nat. Soc. for the Study of Edn., Nat. Edn. Assn., VA ROA (chaplain 1984-88, 90-91), Phi Delta Kappa. Home: Rte 2 Box 820 Quinton VA 23141-9802

GREEN, CHARLES EDWARD, minister; b. Laurel, Miss., Feb. 27, 1926; s. Edward Henry and Mattie (Miller) G.; m. Barbara Jean Self, Feb. 11, 1950; children: Michael Edward, Cynthia Jeanne Green Crider. BA, Bob Jones U., 1949; D of Theology (hon.), Evang. Sem., Petropolis, Brazil, 1978; DLitt (hon.), Calif. Grad. Sch. Theology, 1982; LLD (hon.), Oral Roberts U., 1988. Pastor Evangelistic Tabernacle, Port Arthur, Tex., 1950-52; founder, pastor Word of Faith Christian Fellowship, New Orleans, 1953—; pres. Word of Faith Coll., New Orleans, 1970—; founder, chmn. World Fellowship of Mins., 1990—; exec. bd. dirs. Church Growth Internat., Seoul, Republic of Korea, 1983—; chmn. Network Christian Ministries, New Orleans, 1985-90; regent Oral Roberts U., Tulsa, 1987—; vice chmn. Charismatic Bible Ministries, Tulsa, 1988—. Author: God's Covenants, 1976, New Testament Church, 1979, Beginning with God, 1979. Sgt. U.S. Army, 1944-46. Republican. Office: Word of Faith 13123 I-10 Svc Rd New Orleans LA 70128

GREEN, CHARLES WAYNE, pastor; b. Cin., Apr. 6, 1948; s. Floyd and Maudie Lee (Whittymore) G.; m. Phyllis Ann Kellum, Oct. 3, 1970; children: Benjamin Duane II, Christopher Todd. AB, Morehead State U., 1970; MDiv, Emory U., 1986. Ordained to ministry Meth. Ch. as deacon, 1986, as elder, 1989. Pastor Pleasant Valley United Meth. Ch., Monroe, Ga., 1984-87, Hopewell United Meth. Ch., Gainesville, Ga., 1987—; chaplain CONTACT, Inc., Gainesville, 1988-91. Capt. U.S. Army, 1970-73. Recipient God and Svc. recognition Com. for Ch. and Youth Agy., 1990. Mem. Gainesville/Hall County Ministerial Assn. (pres. 1990). Home: 4736 Hopewell Church Rd Gainesville GA 30506 Office: Hopewell United Meth Ch 4723 Hopewell Church Rd Gainesville GA 30506 *The time has come for all of us to stop blaming our parents, our environment and our genes for the world's (and our personal) ills. We can make a difference, and with God's help, we will!.*

GREEN, CLAIRE MAGIDOVITCH, rabbi; b. Frankfurt, Federal Republic Germany, Dec. 7, 1953; d. Avshalom and Revelle Melva (Swadesh) Magidovitch; m. Steven Yale Green, June 21, 1986; children: Jacob Alexander, Daniel David. BA, Miami U., Oxford, Ohio, 1975; MHL, Reconstructionist Rabbinical, Wyncote, Pa., 1988. Ordained rabbi, 1988. Rabbi Kol Emet Reconstructionist Congregation, Yardley, Pa., 1984-85; dir. Reconstructionist Creative Liturgy Ctr., Wyncote, 1984-85; edn. dir. Congregation Beth-El Suburban, Broomall, Pa., 1985-88; dir. spl. progs. Temple Beth Emeth, Wilmingtin, Del., 1989; youth dir. Congregation Adath Jeshurun, Elkins Park, Pa., 1991. Mem. Coalition for Alternatives in Jewish Edn., Am. Jewish Congress, Am. Jewish Com., Hadassah, Reconstructionist Rabbinical Assn., Delta Phi Alpha. Home: 7503 Rowland Ave Cheltenham PA 19012

GREEN, DAVID WAYNE, minister; b. Knoxville, Sept. 7, 1954; s. William Loy and Frances Mae (Milligan) G.; m. Loyce Carol Reynolds, Dec. 22, 1979; children: Courtney, Megan. BA, U. Tenn., 1978; MDiv, So. Bapt. Theol. Sem., Louisville, 1980, DMin, 1988—. Ordained to ministry So. Bapt. Conv., 1977. Summer missionary So. Bapt. Conv. Home Mission Bd., Atlanta, 1975, 77; pastor various chs., Ind., 1977-80; resident in clin. pastoral edn. Bapt. Med. Ctr., Birmingham, Ala., 1982-83, resident in pastoral counseling, 1983-84; pastor Audubon Bapt. Ch., Louisville, 1985—; cert. field supr. So. Bapt. Theol. Sem., Louisville, 1985—; mem. So. Bapt.-Roman Cath. Dialogue Group, Louisville, 1986—. Neighborhood worker Aldermanic Campaign, Third Ward, Louisville, 1989. Recipient Christian Scholarship award, Tenn. Order Ea. Star, 1978-80. Mem. Assn. for Clin. Pastoral Edn., U. Tenn. Nat. Alumni Assn., So. Bapt. Theol. Sem. Alumni Assn., S. Cen. Ministerial Assn., Long Run Bapt. Assn. (exec. bd., vice chmn. minister's fellowship). Democrat. Home: 3108 Sunny Ln Louisville KY 40205 Office: Audubon Bapt Ch 1046 Hess Ln Louisville KY 40217

GREEN, FRANCIS J., retired bishop; b. Corning, N.Y., July 7, 1906. Ordained priest Roman Cath. Ch., 1932; ordained titular bishop of Serra and aux. bishop of Tucson, 1953; named coadjutor Tucson with right of succession, 1960. Bishop Roman Cath. Ch., Tucson, 1960-1981. Address: 192 S Stone Ave Box 31 Tucson AZ 85702

GREEN, GARRETT, educator; b. Oakland, Calif., June 1, 1941; s. Carleton and Lois (Livingston) G.; m. Priscilla Bogard, Apr. 18, 1970; children: Joshua, Abigail. AB, Stanford U., 1963; MDiv, Union Theol. Sem., 1967; MPhil, Yale U., 1970, PhD, 1971. Asst. prof. religious studies Conn. Coll., New London, 1970-76, assoc. prof., 1976-82, prof. religious studies, 1982—. Author: Imagining God: Theology and the Religious Imagination, 1989; editor: Scriptural Authority and Narrative Interpretation, 1987; translator: Attempt at a Critique of All Revelation (J. G. Fichte), 1978; contbr. articles to profl. jours. Fulbright student, 1963-64, Alexander von Humboldt rsch. fellow, 1976-77, 1979-80, Sr. Fulbright scholar, 1976-77. Mem. AAUP, Am. Acad. Religion, Am. Philos. Assn., 19th Century Theology Working Group, Karl Barth Soc. N.Am. Home: 47 Westomere Terr New London CT 06320 Office: Conn Coll Dept Religious Studies 270 Mohegan Ave Box 5525 New London CT 06320-4196

GREEN, GERALD WALKER, minister; b. Tuscumbia, Ala., Nov. 10, 1945; s. Henry Walker and Flossie Mae (McDougal) G.; m. Winnie Katherine Burgess, Aug. 27, 1965. Student, Bus. U. Tampa, 1964-65, Bible Tng. Inst., Fresno, Calif., 1971, Bible Tng. Inst., Cleve., 1977, So. Ill. U., 1979-80, Bible Tng. Inst., Cleveland, Tenn., 1990. Ordained to bishop, Ch. of God of Prophecy, 1974. Pastor Ch. of God of Prophecy, Reddick, Fla., 1965-67; pastor Leesburg, Fla., 1967-68, Casper, Wyo., 1968-69, Greybull, Wyo., 1969-74, East Peoria, Ill., 1974-77, Belleville, Ill., 1977-80, Phoenix, 1980-84, Tyler, Tex., 1984-85, Palacios, Tex., 1985-87, Houston, 1987—; youth sec. Ch. of God of Prophecy, Wyo., 1969-70, 73-74, dist. overseer, 1970-71, No. Ariz., 1980-84, Tex. Mid Coast, 1985-87, Bible Tng. Inst., Cleveland, Tenn., 1990. Contbr. articles to ch. publs. Chmn. Red Cross Funding Drive, Greybull, 1971; fund raiser Am. Cancer Soc., Phoenix, 1983. Mem. South Big Horn County Ministerial Assn. (pres. 1972-74). Republican. Avocations: guitar, coaching softball, camp counselor. Home: 14015 Muscatine Houston TX 77015

GREEN, GERARD LEO, priest, educator; b. Batavia, N.Y., July 27, 1928; s. George Leo and Marian (Powers) G.; BS, Mt. St. Mary's Coll., 1952; MA, St. Bonaventure U., 1958; postgrad. (NSF fellow) U. Notre Dame, summers 1961, 62, U. Buffalo, 1965-66; Ed.M., SUNY, 1968. Lab. technician Eastman Kodak Co., 1947-48; chemist Xerox Co., 1952; ordained priest Roman Catholic Ch., 1956; parish asst Diocese Buffalo, 1956-59; instr. chemistry Bishop Turner High Sch., Buffalo, 1959-74, dir. sci., 1959-70, 72-74; adminstr. Our Lady of the Rosary Parish, Wilson, N.Y., 1968; adminstr. St. Barnabas Parish and Sch., Depew, N.Y., 1973-75, pastor, 1976-90, prelate of honor, 1984, mem., supr., leader tng. team, 1979-90; pastor Sts. Peter and Paul Parish, Hamburg, N.Y., 1990—. Mem. sci. curriculum com. Dept. Edn. Diocese Buffalo, 1960-70, chmn. diocesan chemistry textbook evaluation com., 1961-70, mem. diocesan pastoral council for handicapped, 1976-82, sec., 1978-79, diocesan regional coordinator, 1979-80, mem. diocesan fin. com., 1984—, diocesan priests coun., 1990—; mem. Diocesan Cons. Parish Computers, 1983—, Diocesan Bd. Priests Retirement, 1985-91; diocesan bd. dirs. for TV prodn., 1986—; chaplain Hyview Fire Co., 1976-81, Cheektowaga Police PBA, 1976-90, West End Fire Co., 1977-90, Depew Village Fire Co., 1980-88; mem. Western N.Y. Sci. Congress Com., 1960-74, sec., 1968, co-chmn., 1969, chmn., 1972-73, state chmn., 1970; mem. gen. chemistry exam. com. N.Y. State Edn. Dept., 1970-73; mem. Maryvale Schs. Planning Bd., 1977-79; cons. sci. facilities in secondary schs.; mem. local IUE-AFL-CIO Scholarship Fund Com., 1968-71. Mem. dist. com. Boy Scouts Am., Buffalo, 1957-74; bd. dirs. Tifft (Conservation) Farm, 1978-82. Served with AUS, 1946-47. Recipient Disting. Service award in sci. edn., 1975. Mem. Sci. Tchrs. Assn. N.Y. (dir. 1971-73), Nat. Cath. Edn. Assn. Clubs: Order of Arrow, KC. Author articles. Address: 66 E Main St Hamburg NY 14075

GREEN, JOEL BENNETT, religion educator; b. Lubbock, Tex., May 7, 1956; s. John Wayne and Adele (Bennett) G.; m. Pamela Jane Kelley, Feb. 24, 1979; children: Aaron M.S., H. Allison. BS, Tex. Tech. U., 1978; ThM, Perkins Sch. Theology, Dallas, 1982; PhD, U. Aberdeen, Scotland, 1985. Ordained to ministry United Meth. Ch. as elder, 1987. Assoc. pastor Pleasant Mound United Meth. Ch., Dallas, 1979-82; pastor Peterhead (Scotland) Meth. Ch., 1984-85; prof., dean New Coll. for Advanced Christian Studies, Berkeley, Calif., 1985—; pres. bd. dirs. Berkeley Emergency Food Project, 1987—. Author: The Death of Jesus, 1988, How to Read the Gospels and Acts, 1987; editor: Catalyst, 1981—; contbr. articles to profl. jours. John Wesley fellow Found. for Theol. Edn., 1982-85; recipient Albert C. Outler award in theology Perkins Sch. Theology, 1981, C.T. and Jesse James Bible award, 1982. Fellow Inst. for Bibl. Rsch.; mem. Soc. Bibl. Lit. (chair New Testament gospels and acts sect. Pacific coast region 1987—), Cath. Bibl. Assn., Tyndale Fellowship. Office: New Coll Berkeley 2606 Dwight Way Berkeley CA 94704

GREEN, JOHN ROBERT, broadcasting executive, itinerant Bible teacher; b. Durant, Okla., Oct. 25, 1959; s. Jack Naler Sr. and Cathryn (McChristian) G.; m. Linda Kay Owens, June 8, 1979; children: Michael, Melissa. Student, North Star Bible Inst., Rochester, N.Y., 1981-85. Pastor New Salem Bapt. Ch., Walters, Okla., 1986-88; music dir. New Hope Bapt. Ch., Wichita Falls, Tex., 1988-89; gen. mgr. Sta. KLLF Christian Radio, Wichita Falls, 1986—; program producer, announcer Bible Truth Broadcast, Wichita, Kans., 1990—. Bd. dirs. Keep Tex. Beautiful Com., Burkburnett, Tex., 1989—; adv. bd. mem. Salvation Army, Wichita Falls, 1988-91; founder, Bible tchr. Burkburnett Bible Chapel, 1990—. Office: Sta KLLF Christian Radio 5080 Kiel Rd PO Box 1103 Wichita Falls TX 76307

GREEN, JOSEPHINE WHEELER, minister; b. Fargo, N.D., Sept. 5, 1942; d. Ernest Martin and Frieda Josephine (Erickson) Wheeler; m. Merlin George Green, Mar. 21, 1964; children: Adina, Jeffrey. BA, Macalester Coll., 1964; MDiv, U. Dubuque, 1982. Ordained to ministry United Ch. of Christ, 1982. Interim pastor First Congregational United Ch. Christ, DeWitt, Iowa, 1982, Peace United Ch. Christ, Monticello, Iowa, 1983, Immanuel United Ch. of Christ, Dubuque, Iowa, 1984, Zion United Ch. of Christ, Lowden, Iowa, 1986, 1st Congl. United Ch. of Christ, Anamosa, Iowa, 1987, Faith United Ch. of Christ, Davenport, Iowa, 1988-89, United Ch. of Christ, Maquoketa, Iowa, 1990-91, 1st Presbyn. Ch., Miles, Iowa, 1991—; facilitator Clergy Women's Group, Dubuque, Iowa, 1984—. Officer Ch. Women United, Dubuque, 1972-82; bd. dirs. Head Injury Support Group,Dubuque, 1986-89; coun. advisors U. Dubuque Theol. Sem. 1988—. Mem. Interim Ministry Network (trainer, search com. for exec. dirs. 1989, mem. div. chmn. of Capital Funds Campaign 1991), Ea. Iowa Assn. (moderator, 1989-91), U. Dubuque Alumni Assn. (bd. dirs. 1986-91, chmn. sem. com. 1988-91), Take Off Pounds Sensibly Club (leader 1987-89), Toastmasters (pres. Dubuque club 1986-87). Home: 15851 Lore Mound Rd Dubuque IA 52002

GREEN, LARRY, ecumenical agency administrator. Pres. Waterbury Area Coun. Chs. Office: Waterbury Area Coun Chs 24 Central Ave Waterbury CT 06702*

GREEN, LOWELL CLARK, minister; b. Findlay, Ohio, Nov. 29, 1925; s. Clark Frederick and Gertrude Grace (Kibler) G.; m. Violet Eleanora Handahl, July 29, 1956 (dec. 1980); children: Daniel, Katharine, Sonja, Barbara; m. Vilma Kish Dyviniak, Sept. 2, 1989. BA, Wartburg Coll., 1946; BD, Wartburg Sem., 1949; DST, Friedrich and Alexander U., Erlangen, Fed. Republic Germany, 1955. Ordained to ministry Am. Luth. Ch., 1949. Pastor various congregations, Tex., S.D., Minn., Ill., 1949-52, 52-67; prof. history Appalachian State U., Boone, N.C., 1968-80; prof. history and theology Concordia Coll., River Forest, Ill., 1978-80; prof. theology Concordia Sem., St. Catharines, Ont., Can., 1980-83; pastor Gethsemane Luth. Ch., Buffalo, 1984-89; asst. to dist. pres., Ea. Dist. Luth. Ch.-Mo. Synod, 1989-90; dean Concordia Acad., Dubuque, Iowa, 1973—; adj. prof. history SUNY, Buffalo, 1988—; cons. in ch. music; participant Luther Symposium, Acad. Sci., Mainz, Fed. Republic Germany, 1983; vis. sr. fellow Ctr. for Reformation Rsch., St. Louis, 1971. Author: How Melanchthon Helped Luther, 1980; editor Luth. Theol. Rev., 1983; translator, cons. Bach cantatas for Gregorian Inst. Am., 1984; contbr. articles to profl. jours. Mem. Am. Soc. Ch. History, 16th Century Studies Conf. (governing coun. 1974078), Am. soc. for Reformation Rsch., Concordia Hist. Inst. Home: 62 Leni Ln Buffalo NY 14225

GREEN, SISTER MARY MICHAELINE, academic administrator. Supt. of Cath. schs. Diocese of Baton Rouge. Office: Cath Life Ctr PO Box 2028 Baton Rouge LA 70821*

GREEN, MICHAEL PAUL, religion educator; b. Buffalo, Mar. 15, 1951; s. J. Paul and Margaret (Schwab) G.; m. Michele Kotarski, May 31, 1975; children: Daniel, Katherine, Rebecca, Sarah. BS, SUNY, Buffalo, 1973; ThM, Dallas Theol. Sem., 1982; PhD, U. North Tex., 1987. Mem staff Campus Crusade for Christ, Phila., 1973-74; campus dir. Pitts., 1974-75, College Park, Md., 1975-78; campus dir. Student Ministries, Dallas, 1978-82; assoc. prof. Dallas Theol. Sem., 1982-91, Moody Grad. Sch., Chgo., 1991—; interm pastor various chs.; conf. speaker various ch. retreats, college groups. Editor: The Expositor's Illustration File, 1982, Illustrations for Biblical Preaching, 1989, Green's Filing Systems, 1991; contbr. articles to profl. jours. Mem. Assn. for Theol. Field Edn., Evang. Assn. for Theol. Edn., Evang. Theol. Soc. Home: 3603 Briar Ln Hazel Crest IL 60429 Office: Moody Grad Sch 820 N La Salle Dr Chicago IL 60610

GREEN, PEARRY LEE, minister; b. Many, La., July 1, 1933; s. Pearry Olyn and Mae Mary (Samples) G.; m. Evelyn Janice Sorcy, July 12, 1954; children: Karen, Janet, Tina. Ordained to ministry. Pastor Tucson Tabernacle, 1965—. Author: Acts of a Prophet, 1969. Office: Tucson Tabernacle 2555 N Stone Tucson AZ 85705

GREEN, ROGER OSWALD, minister; b. Auckland, New Zealand, June 20, 1931; came to U.S., 1966; s. William George and Mavis (Ashby) G.; m. Marguerite Morton, June 16, 1956; m. William Alexander, Ruth Roslyn Green Mitchell, James Stewart. BTh, Toronto Bapt. Seminary, 1959; D of Ministry, Austin Presbyn. Theol., Seminary, 1986. Ordained to ministry Can. Bapt. Ch., 1959, Presbyn. Ch. (U.S.A.), 1972. Children's missionary Scripture Union, Phila., 1966-70; minister to children First Presbyn. Ch., Pitts., 1970-74; minister, head of staff Knox Presbyn. Ch., Kenmore, N.Y., 1974-78; minister to children Highland Park Presbyn. Ch., Dallas, 1978-86; assoc. minister First Presbyn. Ch., Baton Rouge, La., 1986—; founder, pres. Children's Ministries, Pitts., 1972—. Home: 4316 Claycut Baton Rouge LA 70806 Office: Childrens Ministries 250 N Highland Ave Pittsburgh PA 15206 *Plato once said, "Ye men of Athens, how is it that you vie for places of authority and yet you have no time for your children to whom you shall leave it all." Many churches could have this written over the door, "No time for their children." We need to hear the master's plea once more, "Let the children come, do not stop them."*

GREEN, RON WAYNE, music minister; b. Mayfield, Ky., June 11, 1962; s. James Orban and Mary Carlene (Davidson) G.; m. Sherry Lynn Field, June 29, 1984; 1 child, Lyndsey Nicole. MusB, U. Tenn. Martin, 1984. Music minister First Bapt. Ch., Tiptonville, Tenn., 1984-86; music, youth minister First Bapt. Ch., LaCenter, Ky., 1986-88, Southside Bapt. Ch., Princeton, Ky., 1988—. Home: 305 Bell St Princeton KY 42445 Office: Southside Bapt Ch Nichols & White St Princeton KY 42445

GREEN, RONALD ELWOOD, minister; b. Lansing, Mich., June 18, 1950; s. Virgil E. and Pauline M. (Cochran) G.; m. Winifred H. Killinger, July 14, 1974; children: P. Denee, E. Joy, C. Lynne, E.J., Ronald E. II. Student, Ferris State Coll., 1969-70, Gulf-Coast Bible Coll., 1970, 74. Ordained to ministry Ch. of God, 1984. Youth pastor 1st Ch. of God, Rocky Ford, Colo., 1974-75, LaJunta, Colo., 1975-81; pastor College Avenue Community Ch. of God, Canon City, Colo., 1981-85; pastor 1st Ch. of God, Owatonna, Minn., 1985-88, Greenfield, Ind., 1988—. Bd. dirs. ARC, Hancock County, 1990—; Rep. candidate for twp. trustee, Hancock County, 1990. Office: First Ch of God 119 N Broadway Greenfield IN 46140 *The role of the pastor is a precarious position. We are called of God and supported by mankind. We instructed to equip God's people for the work of ministry. We are not to do all the ministry by ourselves. A good leader trains others.*

GREEN, RONALD MICHAEL, ethics and religious studies educator; b. N.Y.C., Dec. 16, 1942; s. Daniel David and Beatrice (Friedlander) G.; m. Mary Jean Matthews, June 25, 1965; children—Julie Elisabeth, Matthew Daniel. A.B., Brown U., 1964; Ph.D., Harvard U., 1973. Instr. Dartmouth Coll., Hanover, N.H., 1969-73, asst. prof., 1973-79, assoc. prof., 1979-85, John Phillips prof. of religion, 1985—, chmn. dept. religion, 1980-83, 85, adj. prof. Amos Tuck Sch. Bus. Adminstrn.; vis. assoc. prof. Stanford U., Calif., 1984-85; adj. prof. dept. community medicine Dartmouth Med. Sch., 1980—. Author: Population Growth and Justice, 1975, Religious Reason, 1978, Religion and Moral Reason, 1988, Kierkegaard and Kant, 1992; assoc. editor. Jour. Religious Ethics, 1973—; mem. editorial bd. Jour. Am. Acad. Religion, 1985—. Kent fellow, 1965-69; recipient Fulbright award, 1964-65, Dartmouth Disting. Teaching award, 1978. Mem. Am. Acad. Religion, Soc. Christian Ethics (bd. dirs.), Soc. Bus. Ethics. Jewish. Office: Dartmouth Coll Dept Religion Hanover NH 03755 *I continue to believe in the ideals of the enlightenment: that human beings can use their reason to expand opportunity, freedom and community.*

GREEN, SAMUEL L., bishop. Bishop Ch. of God in Christ, Newport News, Va. Office: Ch of God in Christ 2416 Orcutt Ave Newport News VA 23607*

GREEN, TIMOTHY PAUL, minister; b. Petoskey, Mich., Sept. 7, 1949; s. Donald Lewis and Winifred (Knowlton) G.; m. Sandra Mae Green, Aug. 8, 1970; children: Jordan, Andrew, Samuel. AB, Lansing (Mich.) Community Coll, 1970; BRE, Midwestern Coll., Pontiac, Mich., 1972; BS, Bapt. Christian Coll., Shreveport, La., 1975. Ordained to ministry, Bapt. Ch., 1972. Assoc. pastor Parker Meml. Bapt. Ch., Lansing, Mich., 1972-83; evangelist Revival in Our Time, Milford, Ohio, 1983—. Office: Revival in Our Time PO Box A Milford OH 45150 *May God grant us the opportunity to leave indelible footprints in the soil of men's souls. As the gospel is only effective "good news" if it reaches others in time!.*

GREEN, WILLIAM BAILLIE, religion educator, minister; b. Mayfield, Ky., Apr. 3, 1927; s. Eben Elmer and Novella (Bailey) G.; m. Donna Harpold, Dec. 29, 1956; children: Stuart David, Ian Baillie. AB, Baylor U., 1948; BD, Louisville Sem., 1953; STM, Union Sem., N.Y.C., 1953; PhilD, U. Edinburgh, Scotland, 1955. Ordained priest Episcopal Ch., 1972. Asst. min. First Presbyn. Ch., Mt. Vernon, N.Y., 1952-54, Youngstown, Ohio, 1955-56; chaplain, assoc. prof. religion Vassar Coll., 1957-66; priest-in-charge St. Cuthbert's Episcopal Ch., MacMahan, Maine, 1972-73; prof. theology Episcopal Theol. Sem., Austin, Tex., 1970—; mem. Internat. Anglican-Orthodox Theol. Consultation, 1983—; mem. Gen. Bd. Examining Chaplains, 1977—. Author: What Is Religion?, 1969; editor/contbr.: Spirit and Light, 1982; contbr. Political Expectations, 1971. Mem. Am. Acad. Religion (chpt. v.p. 1969-70), Conf. Anglican Theologians, Am. Philos. Assn., Univ. Club (Denver), Yale Club (N.Y.C.). Office: Episcopal Theol Sem 606 Rathervue Pl Austin TX 78768

GREEN, WILLIAM RANDOLPH, music minister; b. Athens, Ga., July 26, 1959; s. Furman Nelson and Lucille (Vinson) G.; m. Twyla Lin Daugherty, Jun. 28, 1986. BME, Lee Coll., 1981; MusM, Georgia St. U., 1984. Min. music Buford Church of God, Buford, Ga., 1981-82, Morrow Church of God, Morrow, Ga., 1982-84, Mountain West Church of God, Stone Mountain, Ga., 1984--. Mem. Atlanta Symphony Orch. Chorus, 1982--, Atlanta Symphony Orchestra Chamber Ch. 1985-86. Mem. Natl. Assc. Ch. Musicians, Am. Choral Dir. Assc., N. Ga. Church of God Conf. (chmn. state music com. 1988--), Lee Coll. Music Allumni Assc. (pres. 1986--) . Church of God (Cleveland). Home: 5054 Leland Dr Stone Mountain GA 30083 *It is our personal responsibility to pass on the joys of life to those who follow after us. The simple pleasures, such as music, are best learned when handed down in love for humanity.*

GREEN, WILLIAM SCOTT, religion educator; b. Boston, May 20, 1946; s. William Segal and Joan (Jacobson) G.; m. Rebecca MacMillan Fox, Aug. 2, 1981; children: Noah Fox, Ethan Fox. AB, Dartmouth Coll., 1968; student, Hebrew Union Coll., Cin., 1968-69, Hebrew Union Coll., Jerusalem, 1969-70; PhD, Brown U., 1974. Instr. religion U. Rochester (N.Y.), 1974, asst. prof. religion, 1974-80, assoc. prof. religion, 1980-85, found. chmn. dept. religion and classics, 1983—, prof. religion, 1985—. Author: The Tradition of Joshua and Hananiah, 1981; editor: (book series) Approaches to Ancient Judaism, 1978—; editor Jour. Am. Acad. Religion, 1984—. Study fellow Am. Coun. Learned Socs., 1978-79; R.T. French vis. fellow, Worcester Coll., U. Oxford, 1981-82; recipient Disting. Achievement citation Brown U. Grad. Sch., 1986. Mem. Am. Acad. Religion (bd. dirs. 1984—, editor Jour., 1984—), Soc. for Bibl. Lit., Soc. for Sci. Study Religion. Office: U Rochester Dept Religion and Classics Rochester NY 14627

GREENAMYRE, JOHN WILLIAM, minister, religious broadcasting station executive; b. Sarasota, Fla., Nov. 30, 1929; s. Harley J. and Nellie Janet (Hildebrandt) G.; m. Emma Mae Langford, Apr. 8, 1953; 1 child, Freda Suzanne Greenamyre Yoder. BA, Fla. Bapt. Schs., 1971; M in English Bible, Gulf Coast Bapt. Coll., Mobile, Ala., 1976. Ordained to ministry Am. Bapt. Assn., 1972. Pastor Grace Bapt. Ch., Auburndale, Fla., 19971-74, 1st Bapt. Ch., Belle Fontaine, Ala., 1974-78, Union Avenue Bapt. Ch., Bogalusa, La., 1978-80, Mt. Olive Bapt. Ch., Bogalusa, La., 1980-86, Cen. Bapt. Ch., Morrow, Ga., 1986—; staff announcer Sta. WAVO, Christian broadcasting, Decatur, Ga., 1988-89, sta. mag., 1990—. Dir. chaplains group 4 Ga. wing CAP, 1988, dir. chaplain communication S.E. region, 1991. With USN, 1948-68. Mem. TI 99 Users Group (dir. spl. interest group Atlanta 1990). Home: 5333 Orchard Pl Morrow GA 30260 Office: 3589 N Decatur Rd Scottdale GA 30079

GREENAWAY, LEROY V., bishop. Mem. bd. dirs., bishoop Ch. of God of Prophecy in Can., Brampton, Ont. Office: Ch God Prophecy Can, 1st Line W/RR 2, Brampton, ON Canada L6V 1A1*

GREENBERG, IRVING, rabbi; b. Bklyn., May 16, 1933; s. Elias and Sonya G.; m. Blu Genauer, June 23, 1952; children: Jeremy, David, Deborah, Jonathan, Judith. BA summa cum laude, Bklyn. Coll., 1953; MA, Harvard U., 1954, PhD, 1960; PhD, Brandeis U., 1986. Ordained rabbi, 1953. Rabbi Riverdale Jewish Ctr., Riverdale, N.Y., 1965-72; assoc. prof. history Yeshiva U., N.Y.C., 1964-72, asst. prof. history, 1959-64; prof. dept. Jewish studies CUNY, 1972-79; pres. The Nat. Jewish Ctr. for Learning and Leadership, N.Y.C., 1974—; bd. dirs. Student Struggle for Soviet Jewry, SAR Acad., Riverdale, N.Y.C. Holocaust Meml. Commn., Mazon: A Jewish Response to Hunger, Fedn. Jewish Philanthropies, United Jewish Appeal of N.Y., CLAL - The Nat. Jewish Ctr. for Learning and Leadership, Am. Jewish World Svc., Am. Jewish Joint Distbn. Committed, Am. Assn. for Ethiopian Jewry, others. Author: The Jewish Way: Living the Holidays, 1988, Theodore Roosevelt and Labor: 1900-1918, 1988; co-editor: Confronting the Holocaust: The Impact of Elie Wiesel, 1978; contbr. articles to profl. jours. Recipient Rothberg award, Hebrew U., 1990, Smolar award, 1983, Akiba award, 1991. Mem. Am. Acad. Religion, Am. Jewish Hist. Soc., Assn. for Jewish Studies, Religious Edn. Assn., Religious Rsch. Assn., Rabbinical Coun. of Am. Office: CLAL 47 W 34th St New York NY 10001

GREENBERG, MEYER, academic administrator, educator, rabbi; b. N.Y.C., Jan. 11, 1914; s. Aaron Mordecai and Blanche Helen (Bernzweig) G.; m. Evelyn Thelma Levow, June 15, 1941; children: Saadia Reuven, Bryna Sarah, Dvora Alesa. BA, Yeshiva U., 1934; postgrad., Hebrew U. Jerusalem, 1937-38; M in Hebrew Lit., Hebrew Union Coll., 1944; PhD, U. Md., 1956; DDiv, Jewish Theol. Sem., 1975. Ordained rabbi, 1944. Dir. B'nai Brith Hillel Found. Yale U., Queen Coll., U. Md., New Haven and N.Y.C., 1944-45; mem. faculty U. Md., College Park, 1946—, dir. Hebrew program, 1968-79, acting dir. Oriental and Hebrew program, 1977-79, dir. semester in Israel at Tel Aviv U., 1970—; lectr. Tel Aviv U., 1980-85; founder, vol. head Midrasha Hebrew High Sch., Washington, 1959-61; chmn. bd. edn. Hebrew Acad. Washington, 1951-74; pres. Washington Bd. Rabbis, 1958-60. Contbr. articles to acad. jours. Pres. Am. Alumni Hebrew U., N.Y.C., 1939-41; chmn. adv. com. Juvenile Ct.Prince Georges County, Md., 1951-55. Home: 31 Hatikva St, Jerusalem Israel

GREENBERG, MOSHE, Bible educator; b. Phila., July 10, 1928; s. Simon and Betty (Davis) G.; m. Evelyn Doris Gelber, June 21, 1949; children: Joel, Raphael, Ethan. BA, U. Pa., 1949; M. Hebrew Lit., Jewish Theol. Sem., N.Y.C., 1954; PhD, U. Pa., 1954; D. Hebrew Letters, Jewish Theol. Sem., 1986. Ordained rabbi, 1954. Prof. Hebrew U. Pa., Phila., 1954-70; vis. prof. Bible Jewish Theol. Sem., N.Y.C., 1966-70; prof. Bible Hebrew U., Jerusalem, 1970—; vis. prof. Jewish Studies U. Calif., Berkeley, 1981-82; vis. prof. religious studies Yale U., New Haven, 1986-87; vis. prof. Bible Russian State U. Humanities, Moscow, 1991; mem. Bible transl. com. Jewish Publ. Soc., Phila., 1966-82. Author: Introduction to Hebrew, 1965, Ezekiel 1-20, Anchor Bible, 1983 (Bibl. Archaeology Soc. award 1984); div. editor Ency. Judaica, 1968-71; editor Bible for Israel Commentary Series, 1985—; translator, editor: Religion of Israel (Y. Kaufmann), 1960. Advisor Bible curriculum devel. Israel Ministry Edn., Jerusalem, 1971-81; mem. acad. coun. Israel Open U., Tel Aviv, 1982-87, Sem. for Judaic Studies, Jerusalem, 1983—. Recipient Harbison award Danforth Found., 1968; Guggenheim fellow, 1961. Fellow Am. Acad. for Jewish Rsch., Am. Acad. Arts & Scis.; mem. Am. Oriental Soc., Am. Soc. Bibl. Lit. Home: 29 Mitudela St, 92305 Jerusalem Israel Office: Hebrew Univ, Dept of Bible, 91905 Jerusalem Israel

GREENBERG, SIDNEY, rabbi; b. N.Y.C., Sept. 27, 1917; s. Morris and Sadie (Armel) G.; m. Hilda Weiss, Oct. 31, 1942; children: Shira Beth Ruskey, Reena Keren, Adena J. BA, Yeshiva Coll., N.Y.C., 1938, MHL, 1942, DHL, 1948. Ordained rabbi, 1942. Rabbi Temple Sinai, Dresher, Pa., 1942—; pres. Phila. br. Rabbinical Assy., 1953-55; governing bd. Commn. on Adult Jewish Edn. of United Synagogue Am., mem. exec. bd.; bd. dirs. Technion; chmn. High Holiday Appeals for Bonds for Israel; mem. nat. exec. Israel Bond Com., 1971; faculty homiletics Reconstructionist Rabbinical Coll. and Jewish Theol. Sem.; editorial bd. The Reconstructionist, The Jewish Digest; dept. editor Conservative Judaism quar. Author: Minyan of Comfort, 1990, A Treasury of Thoughts on Jewish Prayer, 1989, Light From Jewish Lamps, 1985, Lessons for Living, 1985, Say Yes to Life, 1982, The New Mahzor - for Rosh Hashanah and Yom Kippur, 1977, Teaching and Preaching the High Holy Day Bible Themes, Vol. I, 1974, Vol. II, 1975, Contemporary Junior Prayer Book for the High Holy Days, 1972, Hidden Hungers - High Holiday Sermons on the Art of Living, 1972, The New Model Seder, 1971, many others. Capt. U.S. Army, 1944-46. Mem. Rabbinical Assy. of Am., Rabbinical Assy. of Phila. (pres. 1953-55). Home: 300 Old Farm Rd Wyncote PA 19095 Office: Temple Sinai Limekiln Pike & Dillon Rd Dresher PA 19025

GREENBERG, SIMON, rabbi, education and homiletics educator; b. Horoshen, Russia, Jan. 8, 1901; came to U.S., 1905, naturalized, 1924; s. Morris and Bessie (Chaidenko) G.; m. Betty Davis, Dec. 13, 1925; children: Moshe, Daniel Asher. Student, U. Minn., 1920-21; A.B., Coll. City N.Y., 1922; Rabbi, Jewish Theol. Sem., N.Y.C., 1925; Ph.D., Dropsie Coll., Phila., 1932; D.D., Jewish Theol. Sem. Am., 1950; postgrad., Hebrew U. in Jerusalem, Am. Sch. for Oriental Research, Jerusalem, 1924-25. Rabbi Har Zion Temple, Phila., 1925-46; lectr. Jewish edn. Jewish Theol. Sem., 1932-41, asso. prof. edn., 1941-48, provost, 1946, prof. edn. and homiletics, 1947—, acting pres., 1948-49, vice chancellor, v.p. faculties, 1951; dir. U. Judaism, Los Angeles, 1948-58; pres. U. Judaism, 1958-66, pres. emeritus, 1966—; dir. Sem. Israel Project, 1973-82. Author: Living as a Jew Today, 1939, The Harishon Series, 1942, Ideas and Ideals in the Jewish Prayer Book, 1940, The First Year in the Hebrew School; A Teacher's Guide, 1945, The Conservative Movement in Judaism, 1954, Israel and Zionism, Conservative Approach, 1955, Foundations of a Faith, 1968, Words of Poetry, 1970, The Ethical in the Jewish and the American Heritage, 1977, A Jewish Philosophy and Pattern of Life, 1981, Year of the Bible: A Guide to Daily Bible Study for the Jewish Community, 1983; editor: Solomon Schechter as a Theologian, 1987, Ordination of Women as Rabbis-Studies and Response, 1988, Max Kaduskin—Explorer of the Rabbinic Universe of Discourse and Discoverer of Organic Thinking, 1989. Bd. dirs. Phila. Psychiat. Hosp.; pres. Rabbinical Assembly Am., 1937-39; past pres. Avukah-Intercoll. Zionist Orgn., Phila. br. United Synagogue, Phila. Bd. Jewish Ministers; mem. nat. exec. com. Zionist Orgn. Am., pres. Phila. br., 1941-44, chmn. nat. edn. com., 1943-45; exec. dir. United Synagogue Am., 1950-53; mem. exec. com. World Zionist Orgn., 1964-68; chmn. United Synagogue Commn. on Jewish Edn., 1962-67; mem. praesidium World Council on Jewish Edn., 1964-68; past mem. chaplains religious council U. Pa. Recipient Sam Rothberg award Hebrew U., 1977; Mordecai M. Kaplan medal U. of Judaism, 1977; Distinguished Service certificate Religious Edn. Assn. U.S. and Can.; Sem. medal, 1981; Solomon Schechter award United Synagogue, 1983; Mathilde Schechter award Women's League Conservative Judaism, 1984; hon. citation from The Seminary of Judaic Studies, Jerusalem, 1988; honored with Tur-Hebrew Festschrift, 1989. Fellow Conf. on Sci., Philosophy and Religion. Home: 420 Riverside Dr New York NY 10025 Office: Jewish Theol Sem 3080 Broadway New York NY 10027 *I have admired many, envied no one.*

GREENE, GLEN LEE, minister; b. Clarks, La., Nov. 12, 1915; s. Columbus C. and Roxie S. (Byrd) G.; m. Grace Lois Prince, Nov. 22, 1938; children: Glen Lee, Roxie Greene St. Martin, Jerry Prince. BA, La. Coll., 1939; BD, New Orleans Bapt. Theol. Sem., 1948, ThD, 1950. Ordained to ministry So. Bapt. Conv., 1934. Pastor Pollock (La.) Bapt. Ch., 1938-40, Long Leaf (La.) Bapt. Ch., 1940-42, 1st Bapt. Ch., Paris, Mo., 1942-44, Gonzales (La.) Bapt. Ch., 1944-53, Oak Ridge (La.) Bapt. Ch., 1953-87; Protestant chaplain State Colony and Tng. Sch., Pineville, La., 1938-42; ofcl. historian La. Bapt. Conv., 1973-87. Author: History of the Baptists of Oak Ridge, 1960, Masonry in Louisiana, 1962, The History of Southern Baptist Hospital, 1969, rev. edit., 1976, House Upon a Rock: About Southern Baptists in Louisiana, 1973, Louisiana Baptist Historical Atlas, 1975. Sec. Oak Ridge Dem. Exec. Com.; mem. United Fund Com. Recipient plaque La. Bapt. Hist. Soc., 1979. Mem. Lions, Masons (worshipful master Brookville lodge). Home: PO Box 203 Oak Ridge LA 71264 *Died Apr. 28, 1991.*

GREENE, JAMES YOUNG, minister, human relations consultant, administrator; b. N.C., Jan. 21, 1933; s. James Young and Myrtle Lottie (Settle) G.; m. Judith Bland Church, Nov. 22, 1956; children: Jama Bland, Jennifer Lenore, James Y. Jr. BA, Wake Forest U., 1953; BD, Southeastern Sem., Wake Forest, N.C., 1957; postgrad., Yonsei U., Seoul, Korea, 1961-63, Cen. U., Seoul, Korea, 1963-65, Yonsei U., Seoul, Korea, 1961-63; MA, U. N.C., 1969, PhD, 1975. Campus minister Bapt. State Conv., Cary, N.C., 1957-61, Cary, 1968—; univ. minister Central U., Seoul, Korea, 1962-65; campus minister Duke U., Durham, N.C., 1967-68; pvt. practice human rels. cons. Raleigh, N.C., 1969—; adj. prof. Southeastern Theol. Sem., Wake Forest, N.C., 1974-90; cons. Human Dimensions of Health Care, Raleigh, N.C., 1988—. Author: Togolese Journey, 1983, In a Different Place, 1985, Bivocational Ministry, 1989. Mem. Assn. Southern Bapt. Campus Ministers, World Future Soc. Democrat. Avocations: reading, walking. Home: 2920 Wycliff Rd Raleigh NC 27607 Office: Bapt State Conv 205 Convention Dr Cary NC 27511

GREENE, JEROME ALEXANDER, minister, public administrator; b. Welch, W.Va., Mar. 12, 1941; s. Emanuel and Savannah (Eldridge) A.; m. Aurelia Henry, Apr. 18, 1975; children: Rhonda Sobers, Russell Sobers. BA, CCNY, 1964; MA in Counseling Psychology, Bowie (Md.) State U., 1983, cert. in family counseling, 1984; postgrad., NYU, 1985-86, Billy Graham Sch. Evangelism, 1988, Moody Bible Inst., 1991—. Cert. principal/administr., N.Y. State; ordained to ministry Independent Charismatic Ch., 1983. Evangelist Bethel Gospel Tabernacle, Jamaica, N.J., 1961-63; exec. dir. People's Devel. Corp., Bronx, 1979—; founder, pastor Bronx (N.Y.) Christian Charismatic Prayer Fellowship, Inc., 1983—; prof. Touro Coll., N.Y.C., 1982-86. Composer over 120 religious songs. Pres. Morrisania Edn. Coun., Bronx, 1968—, Dist. Community Sch. Edn. Bd., Bronx, 1975-86; chairperson Community Planning Bd., Bronx 4, 1986-91; dir. funded programs Community Sch. Dist. 5, N.Y.C., 1975-77; bd. dirs., fellow mem. Morrisania Neighborhood Family Care Ctr., 1987-91; elected Dem. dist. leader 76th Assembly Dist., Bronx, 1988, 90—; coord. Bronx Project Antioch Coll., 1975-76; pres. 1071 Franklin Ave. Housing Devel. Fund Corp., 1984—. Recipient Outstanding Leadership award Morrisania Ednl. Coun., 1981, citation N.Y. State Assembly, 1985, Civic Leadership award N.Y.C. Mission Soc., 1988. Mem. Coun. Black Elected Officials, Bronx Unity Dem. Club, Inc. (pres. 1978—). Home: 1248 Teller Ave Bronx NY 10456 Office: Bronx Christian Charismatic Prayer Fellowship 3270-72 3d Ave Bronx NY 10456 *My life has been a potpourri of vicissitudinous triumphs and turbulences. I have experienced the magnificent splendor of having been permitted to help thousands in education, employmnet and aspirational uplift. The hurts and humiliations I perceive as having a redemptive outcome. In ministry, I am transcending all other priorities for the glorious call and mission of pointing scores in the inner city to the liberating transformation available in Christ Jesus. With a Christian perspective, I reflect on the good and the bad of life as a didactic experience, as I am learning to view the grand scheme of the grace of my Lord and Savior Jesus Christ, confident that He alone will balance the scales of life as He wipes away all tears and rewards according to His holy, righteous and just standard.*

GREENE, JOHN WARREN, minister; b. Camden, Ark., Mar. 25, 1950; s. Weston Henry and Alfa Jewell (Grant) G.; m. Kathryn Rose Smith, May 21, 1972; children: John Kristin, Joel Weston. BA, So. Ark. U., 1972; MDiv, Bapt. Missionary Assn. Theol. Sem., 1976. Ordained to ministry Bapt. Ch., 1972. Sr. pastor Harmony Hill Bapt. Ch., Lufkin, Tex., 1972—; trustee BMA Theol. Sem., Jacksonville, Tex., 1984-88; v.p. state conv. BMA of Tex., 1987-88, pres., 1988-90; com. mem. Bapt. Publ. House, 1990—. Office: Harmony Hill Bapt Ch 2708 S Chestnut Lufkin TX 75901

GREENE, KENNETH WAYNE, minister; b. Dayton, Ohio, May 18, 1947; s. William Henderson and Grace Ann (Parker) G.; m. Linda Irean Gibson, Nov. 13, 1965; children: Steven, Mike, Michelle, Lisa. BTh, Sch. Bible Theology, San Jacinto, Calif., 1991. Ordained to ministry Pentecostal Ch. of God. Evangelist Pentecostal Ch. of God, Joplin, Mo., 1974-76; pastor Pentecostal Ch. of God, Felton, Del., 1976-78; worker Pentecostal Ch. of God, Miamisburg, Ohio, 1078-80; pastor, State youth leader Pentecostal Ch. of God, Lawrenceburg, Ky., 1980-85, Frankfort, Ky., 1985—; pastor, dist. presbyter Pentecostal Ch. of God, Lawrenceburg, Ky., 1985—, Frankfort, Ky., 1985—; pastor Messenger Temple Pentecostal Ch. of God, Lawrenceburg, 1980—. Author: Teaching on the Holy Spirit: Power and Purpose of, 1983, Teaching on Faith: Possessing the Promises, 1983, The Uses of Music in Church History 1991; (poems) Green Pastures, 1983. Republican. Home: 78 Fawn St Frankfort KY 40601 Office: Messenger Temple PO Box 62 254 Court St Lawrenceburg KY 45342

GREENE, KEVIN THOMAS, minister; b. Lenoir, N.C., Apr. 26, 1954; s. John Stanley and Helen Mamie (Hartley) G.; m. Diana Lynn Barbour, Aug. 22, 1976; children: Kevin Thomas, John Arthur. BA, Campbell Coll., 1976; M in Divinity, Southeastern Bapt. Theol. Sem., 1980, ThM, 1983, D in Ministries, 1987; postgrad. Duke Divinity Sch., Oxford U., Wake Forest U., Union Theol. Seminary. Assoc. pastor Princeton (N.C.) Bapt. Ch., 1979-80; minister of edn. and youth Madison Ave. Bapt. Ch., Goldsboro, N.C., 1980-82, interim minister, 1981-82, sr. minister, 1982—; scholar in residence Regent's Park Coll., Oxford U., Eng., 1988; adj. prof. Mt. Olive Coll., Seymour Johnson AFB, Goldsboro, N.C.; host Madison Ave. Proclamation Series ; tchr. accredited sem. ext. Bd. dirs. Protestant Kindergarten Sch., United Ch. Ministries; adv. bd. Golden Yrs. Day Care Village; 1st v.p. Wayne Ministerial Assn.; mem. ad hoc com. Wayne Meml. Hosp., adv. com. pastoral care dept.; mem. ad hoc com. Goldsboro Bd. Edn., policy making bd. WAGES Head Start Program; pres. policy coun. Head Start Program; mem. citizens adv. com. Goldsboro City Coun.; chaplain Hospice. Mem. Internat. Platform Assn., Wayne County Ministerial Assn. (pres., officer), Wayne Oratorio Soc. (pres., co-founder). Republican. Author: Communion and Community: A Recovery of the Nurturing Aspect of the Lord's Supper in Baptist Worship, 1983, The Visible Word: A Recovery of God Through Symbolism in Worship. Home: 400 S Claiborne St Goldsboro NC 27530 Office: 1703 E Laurel St Goldsboro NC 27530

GREENE, LARRY JOE, minister; b. Spruce Pine, N.C., Mar. 25, 1949; s. Joe Taylor and Louise (Bartlett) G.; m. Margaret Collis, Dec. 17, 1971; children: Alison, Miranda. BS in Edn., Western Carolina U., Cullowhee, N.C., 1971; MDiv, Southeastern Bapt. Sem., Wake Forest, N.C., 1980, postgrad., 1980-82. Ordained to ministry So. Bapt. Conv., 1984. Pastor White Oak Bapt. Ch., Bakersville, N.C., 1984—; contr. ops. UPS, Raleigh, N.C., 1982-83; moderator Mitchell Bapt. Assn., Spruce Pine, 1990—; supply preacher in Mitchell and Yancey counties, N.C. Democrat. Home: 267 Loggy Hollow Bakersville NC 28705 Office: White Oak Bapt Ch White Oak Rd Bakersville NC 28705

GREENE, RANDALL WILLIAM, minister; b. Detroit, July 12, 1963; s. Richard William Greene and Nancy Marie (Horn) Schartz. BA in Bible and Christian Ministry, Cin. Bible Coll., 1985. Ordained to ministry Christian Ch. Intern Nashville (Ohio) Ch. of Christ, summers 1983-84; min. youth Medway (Ohio) Ch. of Christ, 1984-85; assoc. min. Christian Ch., Wyandotte, Mich., 1985-90; min. White Lake Ch. of Christ, Highland, Mich., 1990—; dir. Wolverine Christian Svc. Camp, Columbiaville, Mich., 1985— (program com. dir. 1990—); publicity chmn. Mich. Jr. High Rally, Livonia, 1985-89; leader Detroit Area Youth Rally, Highland, 1988—. Republican. Home: 48220 W Pontiac Trail #97 Wixom MI 48393 Office: White Lake Ch of Christ 3139 Oakgrove Highland MI 48031

GREENE, STEVEN SCOTT, religious organization administrator; b. Brookline, Mass., Feb. 26, 1952; s. Max Eugene and Edythe Pearl (Greenwood) G.; m. Ruth Schreiber, Oct. 13, 1974; children: Adinah Leah, Miryam Aylana. BA, Brandeis U., 1974. Dir. edn. and youth Beth David Synagogue, Greensboro, N.C., 1977-81; exec. dir. Temple Adath Yeshrun, Syracuse, N.Y., 1981-84; v.p., gen. mgr. Video Services Unltd., Syracuse, 1984-85; exec. dir. Temple Sinai, Hollywood, Fla., 1985-86; adminstr. Temple Beth Am Synagogue, Margate, Fla., 1986—. V.p. DeWitt (N.Y.) Fire Dept., 1985; vol. Guilford Coll. Fire Dept., Greensboro, 1977-81; bd. dirs. Epstein Hebrew High Sch., Syracuse, 1983-85. Mem. Nat. Assn. Synagogue Adminstrs. (bd. dirs. 1986—), United Synagogues Am. (nat. adv. council 1982-84), Fla. Assn. Synagogue and Temple Adminstrs. (program chmn.). Democrat. Avocations: computers, fire scene photojournalism, guitar. Home: 40 Byron Pl Livingston NJ 07039-3756

GREENE, STUART C., minister; b. Augusta, Ga., Mar. 22, 1955; s. Reynolds William and Saralyn (Cannon) G.; m. Becky Tucker, July 30, 1977; children: Suart Tucker, Timothy Reynolds, Tyler McNeil. AA, Reinhardt Coll., 1975; BA, Huntingdon Coll., 1977; MDiv, Emory U., 1980, D of Ministry, 1988. Assoc. pastor Frazer Meml. United Meth. Ch., Montgomery, Ala., 1976, Bostwick (Ga.) United Meth. Ch., 1977-80, Francis Asbury United Meth. Ch., Elberton, Ga., 1980-83, Moutain View United Meth. Ch., Marietta, Ga., 1983—; participant World Meth. Evangelism Inst., Atlanta, 1982. Author: Celebrate the Presence, 1984. Pres. Reinhardt Coll. Bd. Govs., Waleska, Ga., 1983-86. Home: 2019 S Cove Trail Marietta GA 30066 Office: Mountain View United Meth Ch 2300 Jamerson Marietta GA 30066

GREENFIELD, LARRY LEE, minister, educator; b. Sioux Falls, S.D., Sept. 8, 1941; s. LeRoy H. and Isabell M. (Sneiderman) G.; m. Barbara Jean Shoemaker, Aug. 31, 1963; children: Sarah Elizabeth, Jessica Christine. AB, Sioux Falls Coll., 1963; BD, U. Chgo., 1966, AM, 1970, PhD, 1978. Ordained to ministry Am. Bapt. Chs. in U.S.A., 1966. Chaplain to Bapt. students U. Chgo., 1966-67, dir. Bapt. Grad. Student Ctr., 1967-69, asst. dean students Div. Sch., 1971, acting dean students, 1972, dean students, 1972-80, asst. prof. theology, 1975-80; pres. Colgate Rochester Div. Sch.-Bexley Hall-Crozer Theol. Sem., Rochester, N.Y., 1980-90. Mem. Am. Acad. Religion, Am. Theol. Soc. Midwest. Office: 1100 S Goodman St Rochester NY 14620

GREENGUS, SAMUEL, religious educator, administrator; b. Chgo., Mar. 11, 1936; s. Eugene and Thelma (Romirowsky) G.; m. Lesha Bellows, Apr. 30, 1957; children: Deana, Rachel, Judith. Student, Hebrew Theol. Coll., Chgo., 1950-58; MA, U. Chgo., 1959, PhD, 1963. Prof. semitic langs. Hebrew Union Coll.-Jewish Inst. Religion, Cin., 1963-89, Julian Morgenstern prof. bible and near eastern lit., 1989—, dean rabbinic sch., 1979-84, dean Cin. campus, 1985-87, dean sch. grad. studies, 1985-90, dean faculty, 1987—, v.p. for acad. affairs, 1990—; vis. lectr. U. of Dayton, Ohio, 1964-69, Leo Baeck Coll., London, 1976-77; area supr. Tel Gezer Excavation, Israel, 1966-67; mem. bd. editors Hebrew Union Coll. Ann. Author: Old Babylonian Tablets from Ishchali and Vicinity, 1979, Studies in Ishchali Documents, 1986; contbr. articles to profl. jours. Mem. Cin. Community Hebrew Schs. Bd., 1970-75; mem. vis. com. Sch. for Creative and Performing Arts, Cin., 1980-82; chmn. acad. officers, Greater Cin. Consortium Colls. and Univs., 1984-85, mem. exec. com., 1989—. Am. Council Learned Socs. fellow, 1970-71, Am. Assn. Theol. Schs. fellow, 1976-77. Mem. Am. Oriental Soc., Assn. Jewish Studies, Soc. Bibl. Lit., Phi Beta Kappa. Jewish. Office: Hebrew Union Coll Jewish Inst Religion 3101 Clifton Ave Cincinnati OH 45220-2488

GREENLAW, WILLIAM ALLEN, priest; b. Alhambra, Calif., Aug. 3, 1943; s. Kenneth G. and Lois (Glassey) G.; m. Jane Veitch, Feb. 5, 1977. BA, U. Calif., Riverside, 1965; postgrad., Drew U. Theol. Sch., 1965-66; MDiv, Union Theol. Sem., 1968; PhD, Duke U., 1971. Ordained to ministry Episcopal Ch. as deacon and priest, 1971. Asst. prof. The Gen. Theol. Sem., N.Y.C., 1971-75; assoc. rector Christ and St. Stephen's Ch., N.Y.C., 1976-83; rector Ch. of Holy Apostles, N.Y.C., 1984—. Exec. dir. Holy Apostles Soup Kitchen, N.Y.C., 1984—. Office: Ch Holy Apostles 296 9th Ave New York NY 10001

GREENLEAF, ARTHUR AUSTIN, III, minister; b. New London, Conn., June 23, 1948; s. Arthur Austin Jr. and Frances Grace (Hedge) G.; m. Mae Estelle Watrous, Sep. 4, 1968; children: Heather-Mae Catherine, Arthur Austin IV, Holly-Mae Gladys, Hannah-Mae Doris. Student, Nyack Missionary Coll., 1968-71; AA, Mitchell Coll., 1973. Short-term asst. Wycliffe Bible Translators, Santa Ana, Calif., 1967-68; lay pastor Union Chapel, Fishers Island, N.Y., 1971-75; dir. N.E. Area Wycliffe Assocs., Orange, Calif., 1975-86; youth pastor Groton Heights (Conn.) Bapt. Ch., 1986—; asst. foreman Pioneer Hose Co., Groton, 1986-88. Pres. Bd. Edn., Fishers Island, 1973-76; commr. Planning and Zoning Commn., Groton, 1986-89, Youth Svc. Adv. Bd., Groton, 1989—; chaplain City of Groton Fire Dept., 1988—. Mem. Conservative Bapt. Assn. New Eng. (youth coord. 1991), Assn. Ch. Mission Coms. (assoc.), Nat. Network Youth Ministries, Fedn. Fire Chaplains, Fellowship Christian Fire Fighters, Conn. Fire Police Assn., Conservative Bapt. Assn. Nat. Youth Task Force, Wycliffe Assocs. Republican. Office: Groton Heights Bapt Ch 72 Broad St Groton CT 06340 *To sustain the church into the next generation we must minister to our youth who are the church of today, leaders of tomorrow.*

GREENSPOON, LEONARD JAY, religion educator; b. Richmond, Va., Dec. 5, 1945; s. Alvin Louis and Rose (Levy) G.; m. Eliska Rebecca Morsel, Aug. 25, 1968; children: Gallit, Talya. BA, U. Richmond, 1967, MA, 1970; postgrad., U. Rome, 1967-68; PhD, Harvard U., 1977; postgrad., U. Calif., Santa Barbara, 1978-79, Jewish Theol. Sem., 1978. Faculty adviser Hillel, 1979-81; prof. religion Clemson (S.C.) U., 1983—. Author: Textual Studies in the Book of Joshua, 1983, Max Leopold Margolis: A Scholar's Scholar, 1987; assoc. editor: Ezekiel, vols. 1 and 2, 1979, 83; contbr. book chpts., book revs., articles to Jour. Religion, Jour. Bibl. Lit., Cath. Bibl. Quar., others; also ency. articles. State pres. B'nai Brith, S.C., 1986-87, synagogue pres., 1988-90. Fulbright scholar, 1967, Danforth scholar, 1967, Woodrow Wilson scholar, 1967; grantee NEH, Am. Jewish Archives, Am. Schs. for Oriental Rsch., Am. Coun. Learned Soc., Annenberg Rsch. Inst. Mem. Internat. Orgn. for Septuagint and Cognate Studies (sec.-treas. 1982—), Am. Schs. Oriental Rsch., Assn. Jewish Studies, Cath. Bibl. Assn., Soc. for Values in Higher Edn., Soc. Bibl. Lit., S.C. Acad. Religion (pres. 1989-90). Democrat. Home: 300 Hunting Hill Circle Greer SC 29650 Office: Clemson U Dept Philosophy & Religion Clemson SC 29634-1508 *To me there is nothing more important in life than "trans lating": translating ancient texts into modern languages, translating scholarly work into commonly understood terms, translating feeling into thought, into actions, positive and constructive.*

GREENWALT, ROGER BENSON, minister; b. LaMesa, Calif., Oct. 7, 1961; s. Adolph Lee and Alice Marjorie (Bergeron) G.; m. Julie Ann Ritter, Aug. 20, 1983; children: Jennifer Leigh, Daniel Jonathan, Melissa Dawn. BA, Calif. Bapt. Coll., Riverside, Calif., 1985; MDiv, Golden GAte Bapt. Theol. Sem., Mill Valley, Calif., 1988. Ordained to ministry, So. Bapt. Conv., 1983. Youth pastor First Bapt. Ch., Rialto, Calif., 1980-81; minister youth and music First So. Bapt. Ch., Lancaster, Calif., 1982-85; youth pastor First So. Bapt. Ch., Willows, Calif., 1985-88; assoc. pastor Palms So. Bapt. Ch., 29 Palms, Calif., 1988—; dir. Campus Life, Lancaster, 1984-85; L.I.F.E. coord. Golden Gate Bapt. Theol. Sem., Mill Valley, 1984-85. Coord. 29 Palms Baccalaureate Com., 1989—. Republican. Office: Palms So Bapt Ch PO Box 442 29 Palms CA 92277

GREENWAY, DOUG, minister; b. Paragould, Ark., Sept. 6, 1954; s. Morris and Juanita (McCarroll) G.; m. Becky Mitchell, June 27, 1975; children: Stephen, Beth, Mark, David. BA in Elem. Edn., Harding U., 1975; MA in Elem. Edn., U. So. Miss., 1978; MS, Abilene Christian U., 1990. Minister Cochrum Ch. of Christ, Cardwell, Mo., 1972-76; tchr. Des Arc (Ark.) Elem. Sch., 1975-76, Beach Elem. Sch., Pascagoula, Miss., 1976-77; minister Ch. of Christ, Ocean Springs, Miss., 1977-82, Booneville, Miss., 1982—. Coach local youth soccer league; chmn. Vol. Hosp. Chaplains Bapt. Hosp., Booneville; mem. Mayor's Ministerial Com. and Mayor's Com. for Handicapped, Booneville; bd. dirs. Community Action Agy. Food Shelter. Recipient Leadership award Crowley's Ridge Coll., 1973; named one Outstanding Young Men of Am., 1982, 83, 84. Lodge: Rotary (treas., bd. dirs. Booneville club). Avocation: marathon running. Office: Booneville Ch of Christ PO Box 28 Booneville MS 38829

GREENWOOD, DRU CRIGLER, religious organization administrator; b. Balt., May 24, 1946; m. Ted Greenwood, Sept. 6, 1970; children: Daniel, Benjamin. BA, Smith Coll., 1968; MSW, Columbia U., 1990. Outreach coord. Union of Am. Hebrew Congregations, Brookline, Mass., 1981-84, Paramus, N.J., 1984-89; nat. coord. progs. for the unaffiliated Union of Am. Hebrew Congregations, N.Y.C., 1989-90, assoc. dir. outreach, 1990-91, dir. Commn. on Reform Jewish Outreach, 1991—. Co-editor: (book) Defining The Role of the Non-Jew in The Synagogue: A Resource for Congregations, 1990; contbr. articles to profl. jours. Office: Union of American Hebrew Congregations 838 Fifth Avenue New York NY 10021

GREER, ELIZABETH F., ecumenical agency administrator. Exec. dir. Lebanon County Christian Ministries, Pa. Office: Lebanon County Christian Ministries 818 Water St PO Box 654 Lebanon PA 17042*

GREER, JEAN MCDANIEL, minister; b. Griffin, Ga., June 16, 1917; s. Henry Clifford and Lillie Evelyn (Granade) G.; m. Dorothy Marie Willis, June 14, 1942; children: Priscilla Fowler, Barry Roberts, Bruce Allen. BA, Furman U., 1938; postgrad., Harvard U., 1953-54; MDiv, Andover-Newton Theol. Sch., 1955. Ordained to ministry Am. Bapt. Chs., 1938. Pastor Montgomery Community Ch., Cin., 1962-68, First Bapt. Ch., New London, Conn. and Nashua, N.H., 1968-72; pres. Ohio Bapt. Conv., 1967; mem. nat. staff Am. Bapt. Chs., 1972-76; tchr. Mohegan Community Coll., 1970-72. Founder New London (Conn.) Job Tng. Program, 1968-72; trustee No. Bapt. Edn. Soc., 1978-82. Named Man of Yr. Lynn Daily Evening Item, 1958. Democrat. Home: 414 McCormick Ave Hawkinsville GA 31036

GREER, JERRY OLIN, pastor; b. Maryville, Tenn., June 24, 1945; s. Lewis Burdine and Ada (Petty) G.; m. Lois Edna Watkins, Feb. 14, 1965; children: Nathan, Alita, Sheri, Olin. Student, E.C.J.C., Swainsboro, Ga., 1981-82; M in Bible and Theology, Internat. Bible Inst. and Sem., 1985; student, Lee Coll. Ordained to ministry Ch. of God. Pastor various chs., 1963-88, Southside Ch. of God, Warner Robins, Ga., 1988—; dist. youth and C.E. dir. Ch. of God, Tifton, Ga., 1976; mem. state evangelism and home missions bd. Ch. of God So. Ga., Tifton, 1986-88, mem. state coun., 1988—; dist. overseer Ch. of God, Warner Robins, 1990—; tchr. ministerial internship program, Statesboro, Ga. Home: 1302 Corder Rd Warner Robins GA 31088

GREER, ROWAN A., III, religious studies educator; b. Dayton, Ohio, Apr. 17, 1934. AB, Yale U., 1956, MA, 1964, PhD in New Testament, 1965; STB, Gen. Theol. Sem., 1959. Chaplain Old Testament Edinburgh Theol. Coll., 1964-66, asst. prof. New Testament, 1966-72, assoc. prof. New Testament, 1972-80, Morse fellow, 1969-70; Walter H. Gray assoc. prof. then prof. Anglican studies Divinity Sch., Yale U., 1980—. Author: Theodore of Mopsuestia, 1962, The Captain of Our Salvation, 1973, The Sermon on the Mount, ltd. edit., 1978; contbr. articles to profl. jours. Rsch. in the Nestorian controversy and the Antiochene Christology. Office: Yale U Divinity Sch Dept Anglican Studies 409 Prospect St New Haven CT 06511

GREGG, NADINE MARIE, prophet; b. Flushing, N.Y., Apr. 17, 1948; d. Joseph Martin and Estelle Marie (Andereya) Simeone; m. Thomas Gary Gregg, Aug. 2, 1969; children: Christopher, Derek, Marnie. Student, So. Calif. Sch. Prophetic Min., Carson, 1990. Sunday sch. spvr. Mission Hills Christian Ch., Laguna Hills, Calif., 1978-79; prayer coord. Faith Fellowship, Laguna Hills, Calif., 1983-84; prophet, pastor Fellowship of Jesus, Laguna Hills, Calif., 1987—; sec., co-owner Loves Alot, Laguna Hills, 1990—; counselor Saddleback Christian, Mission Viejo, Calif., 1986. Author: Derek's Story, 1990, The Truth, The Whole Truth, and Nothing But The Truth, So Help Me, God., 1991; broadcaster Sta. KLNG, 1991—, Pan Am. Broadcasting to East Africa and Israel, 1991. Home: 25103 Southport Laguna Hills CA 92653 Office: Loves Alot 25103 Southport Laguna Hills CA 92653 *Since I've met the Lord (Father, Son and Holy Spirit)—I have realized that without them, without their love, direction, power and blessings, life is surely a vanity; but with them life is surely an eternity of hope (Nadine means "Hope").*

GREGOIRE, PAUL CARDINAL, retired archbishop; b. Verdun, Quebec, Oct. 24, 1911; s. Albert and Marie (Lavoie) G. Student, Seminaire de Sainte-Therese; theol. student, Grand Sem. Montreal, Que., Can.; Ph.D., U. Montreal, Litt.L., M.A. in History, diploma in pedagogy, hon. doctorate, 1969; hon. doctorate, St. Michael's Coll., Winooski Park, Vt., 1970. Ordained priest Roman Cath. Ch., 1937; consecrated bishop, 1961. Dir. Seminaire de Sainte-Therese; prof. philosophy of edn. l'Ecole Normale Secondaire, l'Institut Pedagogique; chaplain of students U. Montreal; aux. to Archbishop of Montreal; vicar gen., dir. Office for Clergy; acting adminstr. diocese; apostolic adminstr. Archdiocese of Montreal, 1967-68, archbishop, 1968-90; elevated to cardinal, 1988, archbishop emeritus; pres. French sect. Episcopal Commn. Ecumenism, Can. Cath. Conf., 1965; presided over numerous diocesan commns., 1965—. Decorated officer Order of Can. Office: 1071 Cathédrale St, Montreal, PQ Canada H3B 2V4

GREGORIOS, PAULOS MAR, metropolitan of Delhi; b. Tripunithura, Kerala, India, Aug. 9, 1922; s. Thadikkal and Ponodath Aley (Cherian) Piely. BA, Goshen Coll., 1952; MDiv, Princeton U., 1954; STM, Yale U., 1960; ThD, Serampore U., India, 1977; ThD (hon.), Luth. Theol. Acad., Budapest, Hungary, Leningrad (USSR) Theol. Acad., Jan Hus U., Prague, Czechoslovakia. Ordained to ministry Orthodox Syrian Ch. of the East as priest, 1961, as bishop, 1975. Freelance journalist India, 1937-42; sec. Pub. Libr., Tripunithura, 1942-47; with Post and Telegraph Dept., Govt. of India, 1942-47; assoc. sec. All India Post and Telegraph Union for Travancore-Cochin, 1945-47; tchr. govt. schs. Ethiopia, 1947-50; gen. sec. Orthodox Christian Student Movement of India, 1955-57; founder Haimanote Abew Orthodox Student Assn., Ethiopia, 1957; Bible study leader 3d Assembly World Coun. Chs., New Delhi, 1961; dir. div. ecumenical action World Coun. Chs., Geneva, 1962-67; mem. cen. com. World Coun. Chs., 1968-91, mem. exec. com., 1975-91, pres., 1983-91; met. of Delhi Orthodox Syrian Ch. of the East, 1975—; prin. Orthodox Theol. Sem., Kottayam, India, 1967—; mem. Joint Working Group, World Coun. Chs.-Roman Cath. Ch., 1963-75; observer II Vatican Coun., 1963-65; v.p. Christian Peace Conf., 1970-90; joint organizer Oriental Ea.-Orthodox Unofficial Conversations, various cities, 1964-71; v.p. Kerala Philos. Congress, 1968; gen. pres. Indian Philos. Congress, 1990; Disting. vis. prof. Coll. Wooster, Ohio, 1981; vis. fellow Princeton Theol. Sem., 1986, 88; hon. lectr. Union Christian Coll. Alwaye, 1954-56, U. Coll. Addis Ababa, Ethiopia, 1956-59; Hein Meml. lectr.,U.S., 1968; Mary Louise Iliff Disting. vis. lectr., Denver, 1978; Dudley lectr. Harvard U., 1979. Author: The Joy of Freedom, 1967, 2d edit., 1987, The Gospel of the Kingdom, 1968, The Freedom of Man, 1972, Be Still and Know, 1974, Freedom and Authority, 1974, The Quest for Certainty, 1975, The Human Presence, 1978, 4th edit., 1987, Truth Without Tradition?, 1978, Science for Sane Societies, 1980, 2d edit., 1987, Cosmic Man, 1980, 2d edit., 1988, The Indian Orthodox Church, An Overview, 1982, The Meaning of Diakonia, 1988, Enlightenment—East and West, 1989, Too Bright A Light, 1992; editor, contbr.: Koptisches Christentum, 1973, Die Syrischen Kirchen in Indien, 1974, Burning Issues, 1977, Science and Our Future, 1978, Does Chalcedon Divide or Unite?, 1981; chief editor Star of the East quar., Purohitan quar.; contbr. numerous articles to profl. jours. Hon. mem. Pro Oriente Found., Vienna, Austria; hon. mem. rsch. bd. advisors Am. Biog. Inst. Decorated officer Order of St. Vladimir, 1st rank Order of St. Sergius (USSR); Order of St. Mary Magdalen, 1st class Order of St. Bishop Franciszek Hodur (Poland); recipient U.S. Hall of Fame award for extraordinary svc. for peace and human unity, Otto Nuschke Prize for Peace award German Dem. Republic, Soviet Land Nehru award India, 1988, Disting. Leadership award U.S., Bhai Param Vir Singh Internat. award India, 1990, others; Indian Inst. Advanced Study fellow, 1987, 89. Address: Orthodox Sem, Chungom PO Box 98, Kottayam Kerala 686 001, India also: Delhi Orthodox Centre, 2 Tughlakabad Institution Area, New Delhi 110 062, India

GREGORY, ANNETTE SHARP, lay church worker, educator; b. Shelbyville, Tenn., Dec. 1, 1937; d. Harrell Wilson and Katherine (Hardy) S.; m. Thomas Wayne Gregory, June 3, 1956; children: Katherine Gail Gregory Reeder, Thomas Scott. BS in Elem. Edn., Mid. Tenn. State U., 1976, MEd in Early Childhood Edn., 1979, EdS in Adminstrn. Supervision, 1983; EdD in Instrnl. Leadership, U. Ala., Tuscaloosa, 1988. Cert. elem. prin., suuprs. instrn., dir. supt. program, psychologist, Tenn. Pianist, dir. adult and childrens choirs Center Grove Bapt. Ch., Tullahoma, Tenn., 1965—, chmn. bd. ch. day care program, 1985—; elem. tchr. Franklin County Bd. Edn., Winchester, Tenn., 1976—; ednl. cons., 1980—; workshop condr. Author: Leaping into the Classroom with Music, 1980, 2d edit., 1991. Sec. Center Grove Community Club, Tullahoma, 1986. Named Tchr. of Yr., South Cen. Dist., 1988, 90, Franklin County, 1988, 90; Tchr. of Yr., Rock Creek Elem. Sch., 1988, 89, 90, 91, Disting. Tchr. of Yr., 1991; recipient State Sch. Bell award Tenn. Edn. Assn., 1991. Mem. Franklin County Edn. Assn. (exec. bd. 1981-86, Disting. Tchr. award), Kappa Delta Pi, Phi Delta Kappa (membership chmn.), Delta Kappa Gamma (state membership chmn. 1987—, achievement award 1988), Gamma Beta Phi. Home: Highland Ridge Rd PO Box 1091 Estill Springs TN 37330

GREGORY, EDWARD MEEKS, minister; b. Richmond, Va., Sept. 30, 1922; s. George Craghead and Constance (Heath) G.; A.B., U. Va., 1947; M.Div., Episcopal Theol. Sch., Cambridge, Mass., 1954; postgrad. George Washington U., 1949, Va. Commonwealth U., 1980, Harvard U., 1981; D.Min., U. of South, 1977. Ordained to ministry Episcopal Ch. as priest, 1955; instr. Staunton (Va.) Mil. Acad., 1947-48; master Episc. High Sch., Alexandria, Va., 1948-51; curate St. Mark's Episc. Ch., Richmond, 1954-69; vicar St. Peter's Episc. Ch., Richmond, 1969-79; chaplain Christchurch Sch., 1980-90, chaplain emeritus, 1990—; dean East Richmond, 1974-78; diocesan youth dir., 1956-60; diocesan del. Va. Council Chs., 1967-73; spiritual adviser Dignity-Integrity/Richmond, 1976-79; mem. Diocesan Dept. Social Relations, 1970-72, Diocesan Lit. Commn., 1973-83; pres. Religious Edn. Council, Richmond, 1961-62, Richmond Episc. Clericus, 1972-73. Bd. dirs. Vol. Service Bur., Richmond, 1960-63, Ednl. Therapy Center, 1964-79, Multiple Sclerosis, 1961-66, Va. Community Devel. Orgn., 1968-75, Va. chpt. ACLU, 1970-71, 76-77, Internat. Council; bd. dirs. Va. Council Human Relations, 1965-70, treas., 1972-73; bd. dirs. Richmond Planned Parenthood, 1969-74, Richmond chpt. ARC, 1973-79, Richmond United Neighborhoods, 1977-79, Met. Area Resources Clearing House, 1977-79, Ch. Hill Revitalization Team, 1979; bd. govs. Christchurch Sch., Va., 1978-79; pres. Richmond Council Human Relations, 1960-62; pres. Friends' Assn. for Children, 1967-70, bd. dirs., 1975-79; mem. adv. bd. Richmond Model Neighborhood, 1971-73; bd. dirs. Richmond Community Sr. Center, 1975-78, Daily Planet, 1974-79, Alcohol and Drug Abuse Prevention and Tng. Services, 1978-85, Richmond Health Center, 1981-85; vice chmn. Richmond Health Occupations, 1979. Served with Med. Dept. AUS, 1942-46. Decorated Bronze Star. Mem. Richmond Clergy Assn., Jamestown Soc. (gov. 1951-55), Mayflower Soc. (elder Va. co. 1963-81), Va. Hist. Soc., Braintree (Mass.) Hist. Soc., Episcopal Soc. Cultural and Racial Unity (chmn. Richmond 1964-66), Assn. Preservation Va. Antiquities, Valentine Mus., Va. Mus. Fine Arts, Chi Phi. Silhouettist; works exhibited Va. Hist. Soc. Clubs: James River Catfish, 2300. Home and Office: Westminster-Canterbury House 1600 Westbrook Ave # 346 Richmond VA 23227

GREGORY, JANET FAYE, principal, educator; b. Olney, Ill., July 1, 1949; d. Donald Dale and Norva Pearl (Riggs) Daubs; m. Dennis Keith Gregory, Aug. 5, 1972; children: Heidi Michelle, Darren Keith, Justin Lee. BS, So. Ill. U., 1971. Cert. tchr. Tchr. Rockford (Ill.) Christian Elem. Sch., 1981-86; prin., tchr. West County Christian Sch., St. Louis, 1986—. Mem. Assn. Christian Schs. Internat. Home: 5830 Mayberry Imperial MO 63052

GREGORY, JENNIE KANE, lay worker; b. Cin., Jan. 12, 1952; d. Richard Frank and Patricia Jean (Armintrout) Kane; m. David Kyle Gregory, Oct. 5, 1974; children: Laura Kristin, James Richard. BS in Allied Health, Ohio State U., 1974. Lic. phys. therapist. Sun. sch. sec. Immanuel Bapt. Ch., Cin., 1967-70; youth sponsor Protestant Chapel-Little Rock AFB, Jacksonville, Ark., 1974-80; sec., project chair Protestant Chapel Adv. Bd., Jacksonville, 1975-80; youth sponsor Park Hill Christian Ch., North Little Rick, 1983—, youth com. chairperson, 1987-90, Sun. sch. supt., 1988-90, edn. com. chairperson, 1990-91; asst. dir. rehab. svcs. St. Vincent Infirmary Med. Ctr., Little Rock, 1980—; guest rels. com. St. Vincent Infirmary Med. Ctr., Little Rock, 1987-90. Co-author: The Back School Manual, 1979; contbr. articles to profl. jours. Mem. St. Vincent Infirmary Med. Ctr. Aux., Little Rock, 1980—; sec., treas. Ark. Chpt. Am. Phys. Therapy Assn. Polit. Action Com., 1988—; mem. PTA, Sherwood, Ark., 1985—. Recipient Disting. Svc. award Ark. Chpt. Am. Phys. Therapy Assn., 1987, Meritorious Svc. award Chapel of Little Rock, 1981, Award of Merit Sch. Allied Health Professions, 1973. Mem. Am. Phys. Therapy Assn. Ark. Chpt. (sec. 1988—, program chair 1987-88, treas. 1979-87, chair 1976-78), Scarlet 'N Gray (pres. 1973-74), Mortarboard Soc. Home: 1002 Abercorn Pl Sherwood AR 72116 Office: St Vincent Infirmary #2 St Vincent Circle Little Rock AR 72116

GREGORY, MYRA MAY, educator, religious organization administrator; b. N.Y.C., Sept. 21, 1912; d. Thomas and Anna (Collins) G. Diploma, Maxwell Tchrs. Tng. Sch., Bklyn., 1933; BS in Edn., Bklyn. Coll., 1940, MA in History, 1952. Cert. music tchr. Tchr. N.Y.C. Bd. Edn., Bklyn., 1943-75; social worker Berean Bapt. Ch., Bklyn., 1932-48, supr., 1932—, fin. sec. Sunday sch., 1935—; bd. dir. Berean-Vacation Bible Sch., Bklyn.;tchr. Protestant Coun., N.Y.C., 1940-81; bd. dir. Recreation Bedford-Stuyvesant Area Project, Bklyn. Author poems (Golden Poet award 1988). Bd. mgrs. Bklyn. Sunday Sch. Union, 1974—, Seminar for Christian Teaching, Bklyn., 1974-86; pres. Coun. of Chs. of the City of N.Y., Bklyn., 1984-86; bd. dirs. Bklyn. Div. Coun. of Chs., 1984—. Named Tchr. of Yr. Community Sch. Bd. Dist. 14, Bklyn., 1973, Outstanding Tchr. Stuyvesant Div. of the Bklyn. Sunday Sch. Union, 1977, Educator/leader, Berean Bapt. Ch., 1977; recipient Ecumenism citation, Borough Pres.'s Office, Bklyn., 1985. Mem. Am. String Tchrs. Assn., Am. Viola Soc., Assn. Childhood Edn. Internat., Assn. for Supervision and Curriculum Devel. Democrat. Avocations: string ensemble, drama, hiking. *When one reverently and humbly acknowledges that each individual is created by God to be His "temple", then life beomes a journey exemplifying the ideals and commands of His Son. Love's banner is seen regardless of challenging self-sacrifice.*

GREGORY, PAUL RADCLIFFE, mission executive; b. Chapman Quarries, Pa., Dec. 19, 1920; s. John Thomas and Annie (Fritz) G.; m. Catherine Emmaline Hahn, May 20, 1944; children: Nancy Elizabeth, Judith Louise, Lynne Anne. BS, Lehigh U., 1940; BD, Lancaster Theol. Sem., 1944; LHD, Internat. Christian U., Tokyo, 1979; DD, Eden Theol. Sem., 1980; LLD, Tohoku Gakuin U., 1986. Ordained to ministry United Ch. Christ, 1944. Min. Trinity Reformed Ch., Mountville, Pa., 1944-45; missionary Evang. and Reformed Ch., China, 1946-48, Japan, 1949-57; East Asia sec. United Ch. Bd. for World Ministries, N.Y.C., 1957-86, gen. sec., 1972-79, 82-86; retired, 1986; pres. Japan Internat. Christian U. Found., N.Y.C., 1990—; chmn. Pa. cen. conf. United Ch. of Christ liaison with German Evang. Ch. of the Union, 1990—. Author: Mandate for Evangelism, 1987. Pres. Residents' Assn. Homestead Vill., Lancaster, Pa., 1987-89, 91—. Gregory lecture named in his honor Lancaster Theol. Sem. Democrat. Home: 1800 Village Circle #145 Lancaster PA 17603

GREGORY, RICHARD, religious organization administrator. Nat. exec. dir. Independent Fundamental Ch. Am., Byron Center, Mich. Office: Independent Fundamental Chs Am 1315 N Adams Dr Colorado Springs CO 80904*

GREGORY, TERENCE VAN BUREN, pastor; b. Atlanta, Nov. 29, 1950; s. Vic Odell and Evelyn Ora (Gardner) G.; m. Leslie Christine Lytle, July 29, 1972; children: Joshua Adam, Rachel Leigh, Matthew Jordan. BA in Bible, Antioch Bapt. Coll., 1973; MRE, Mid-Am. Bapt. Theol. Sem., 1975. Ordained to ministry So. Bapt. Conv., 1972; lic. min. Youth min. 1st Bapt. Ch., Minden, La., 1976-77, Spencer Meml. Bapt. Ch., Tampa, Fla., 1977-80; pastor Crestview Bapt. Ch., Lakeland, Fla., 1980-83; min. pastoral care 1st Bapt. Ch., Lakeland, 1983-87; pastor Seminole Bapt. Ch., Tallahassee, 1987—; del., messenger So. Bapt. Conv., Atlanta, 1990-91. Mem. Fla. Bapt. Assn. (mem. exec. com. and nominating com. 1990-91). Republican. Office: Seminole Bapt Ch 333 Ausley Rd Tallahassee FL 32304-3911

GREGORY, WILTON D., bishop; b. Chgo., Dec. 7, 1947. Student, Niles Coll., Loyola U., Chgo., St. Mary of Lake Sem., Mundelein, Ill., Pontifical Liturgical Inst., Sant'Anselmo, Rome. Ordained priest Roman Cath. Ch., 1973, ordained bishop, 1983. Aux. bishop, Chgo., 1983—. Address: PO Box 733 South Holland IL 60473

GREGORY OF SITKA, BISHOP **See ASONSKY, GEORGE**

GREIG, WILLIAM TABER, JR., publishing company executive; b. Mpls., Apr. 16, 1924; s. William Taber and Margaret Naomi (Buckbee) G.; m. Doris Jane Walters, June 23, 1951; children: Kathryn Ann Greig Rowland, William Taber, III, Gary Stanley, Doris Jane. B.Arch., U. Minn., 1945. Jr. exec. Bur. Engraving, Mpls., 1946-48; partner, mgr. Praise Book Publns., Mound, Minn., 1948-50; v.p., exec. v.p., gen. mgr. Gospel Light Publs., 1950-76; pres., owner Gospel Light Publs., Ventura, Calif., 1976—, chmn., 1983—; bd. dirs. Lighthouse Ptnrs. Bookstores, Gospel Lit. Internat. Ruling elder Presbyn. Ch. (U.S.A.); bd. dirs., chmn. Joy of Living Bible Studies, 1978—; trustee Latin Am. Mission, Concerts of Prayer Internat., 1988—; chmn. John Perkins Found., 1990—. Served to lt. (j.g.) USNR, 1943-46. Mem. Evang. Christian Pubs. Assn. (co-founder 1974, bd. dirs., pres. 1981-83). Republican. Clubs: Verdugo, Tower. Home: 347 Lupine Way Ventura CA 93001 Office: 2300 Knoll Dr Ventura CA 93003

GREIN, RICHARD FRANK, bishop, paternal theology educator; b. Bemidji, Minn., Nov. 29, 1932; s. Lester Edward and LaVina Minnie (Frost) G.; m. Joan Dunwoody Atkinson, Nov. 25, 1961; children: David, Margaret, Mary Leslie, Sara. B.A. in Geology, Carlton Coll., 1955; M. Div., Hashotah House Sem., Wis., 1959; S.T.M., Hashotah House Sem., 1970. Ordained priest Episcopal Ch., 1959; priest-in-charge Elk River mission field, Minn., 1959-64; rector St. Mathew's Ch., Mpls., 1964-69, St. David's Ch., Minnetonka, Minn., 1969-73; prof. pastoral theology Nashotah House House Theol. Sem., 1973-74; rector St. Michael and All Angel Ch., Mission, Kans., after 1974; bishop The Episcopal Ch., Topeka, Kans.; bishop co-adjutor The Episcopal Ch., N.Y.C., 1988—. Co-author: Preparing Younger Children for First Communion, 1972. Priest assoc. Order Holy Cross; pres. Guardian Angels Found., Elk River, 1963-64. Mem. Councial Assoc. Parishes. Office: 1047 Amsterdam New York NY 10025

GRELL, MARY ELLEN, lay church worker; b. Freeport, Ill., May 30, 1930; d. Clayton George and Marietta H. Bast; m. Dwain Leo Grell, Aug. 30, 1949, 1 child, Denis Lee. Student, Gt. Lakes Bible Inst., Zion, Ill., 1948. Pres. Ill. Women's Ministries Assemblies of God, Carlinville, Ill., 1955—. Home: RR 3 Lake Williamson Carlinville IL 62626 Office: P O Box 345 Carlinville IL 62626

GREMOLI, BERNARDO GIOVANI, priest. Vicar Apostolic Vicariate of Arabia, Roman Cath. Ch., Abu Dhabi, United Arab Emirates. Office: Apostolic Vicariate Arabia, POB 54, Abu Dhabi United Arab Emirates*

GRENZ, STANLEY J., religion educator; b. Alpena, Mich., Jan. 7, 1950; s. Richard A. and Clara F. (Ruff) G.; m. Edna L. Sturhahn, Dec. 29, 1971; children: Joel R., Corina D. BA, U. Colo., 1973; MDiv, Denver Conservative Bapt Sem, 1976; ThD, U. Munich, 1980. Ordained to ministry Bapt. Ch. Pastor Rowandale Bapt. Ch., Winnipeg, Man., Can., 1979-81; prof. N.Am. Bapt. Sem., Sioux Falls, S.D., 1981-90; Pioneer McDonald prof. Carey Theol. Coll., Vancouver, B.C., Can., 1990—; bd. mem. Bapt. Joint Com. on Pub. Affairs, 1983-88; ethics commn. Bapt. World Alliance, 1986—. Author: Prayer: The Cry for the Kingdom, 1988, Reason for Hope, 1990, AIDS: Ministry in the Midst of an Epidemic, 1990; contbr. articles to profl. jours.; mem. editorial bd. Perspectives in Religious Studies, 1985-88. Bd. mem. S.D. Com. on Humanities, 1986-90. Fulbright grantee, 1987. Mem. Am. Acad. Religion (regional sec. 1989-90), Nat. Assn. Bapt. Profs. Religion (pres. 1989-90), Am. Theol. Soc., Phi Beta Kappa. Home: 5992 Patrick St, Burnaby, BC Canada Office: Carey Theol Coll, 5920 Iona Dr, Vancouver, BC Canada also: N AM Bapt Sem 1321 W 22nd St Sioux Falls SC 57105 *In an age which pessimism reigns, we can derive hope from the age-old message that our lives are in the hand of the God of the future whose love is shown to us in Jesus of Nazareth.*

GRESCHUK, DEMETRIUS MARTIN, bishop; b. Innisfree, Alta., Can., Nov. 7, 1923; s. Thomas and Sophia (Stebyk) G. Student, St. Joseph's Coll., 1941-42, St. Augustine's Sem., Toronto, Ont., Can. Ordained priest, Ukrainian Cath. Ch., 1950, subdeacon, 1948-49, deacon, 1949-50, priest, 1950, consecrated bishop, 1974. Sec. Chancery Office, Edmonton, Alta., 1950-59; pastor numerous parishes, 1950-74; apostolic adminstr. Edmonton Eparchy, from 1984; aux. bishop, now bishop Archdiocese of Edmonton.

Office: Archdiocese of Edmonton, 9645 108 Ave, Edmonton, AB Canada T5H 1A3

GRESHAKE, GISBERT, theology educator; b. Recklinghausen, Germany, Oct. 10, 1933; s. August and Anna (de Hédouville) G. Lic. phil., Pontifical U. Gregoriana, Rome, 1957, Lic. theol., 1961; ThD, U. Münster, 1969. Ordained priest Roman Cath. Ch., 1960. Chaplain various parishes Diocesis of Münster, 1961-69; asst. prof. U. Münster and Tübingen, Fed. Republic Germany, 1969-74; prof. U. Vienna, Austria, 1974-85; prof. theology U. Freiburg, Fed. Republic Germany, 1985—, dean theol. faculty, 1989-90; dean of theol. faculty U. Vienna, 1979-83; cons., different commns. of German Episcopal Conf., 1985—. Author, editor 23 books; contbr. over 300 articles to theol. publs. Home: Peterbergstrasse 36, D 7800 Freiburg Federal Republic of Germany Office: Inst Theology U Freiburg, Werthmann Platz 3, D 7800 Freiburg Federal Republic of Germany

GRESSLE, LLOYD EDWARD, bishop; b. Cleve., June 13, 1918; s. Edward William and Olga I. (Hoppensack) G.; A.B., Oberlin U., 1940; B.D., Kenyon U., 1943, D.D., 1958; D.H.L., Lehigh U., 1981; m. Marguerite Louise Kirkpatrick, July 12, 1943; children—Richard L., Katherine Delia, E. Mark. Ordained to ministry Episcopal Ch., 1943; rector chs., Wooster, Ohio, 1943-48, Sharon, Pa., 1948-56; dean Cathedral St. John, Wilmington, Del., 1956-69; rector St James Ch., Lancaster, Pa., 1969-70; bishop coadjutor Diocese of Bethlehem (Pa.), 1970-72, bishop of Bethlehem, 1972-83; mem. exec. council Episcopal Ch., 1967-70; exchange priest, Portsmouth, Eng., 1965-66. Home: 5 Lincoln Dr East Quogue NY 11942

GRIBBONS, MICHAEL STANLEY, minister; b. New Castle, Ind., Oct. 11, 1953; s. Thomas Cleaver and Emma Dell (Phipps) Gribbons; m. Mary Patricia Goff, May 21, 1977; 1 child, Allison Emily. BA, Mt. Vernon Bible Coll., 1975. Ordained to ministry Evang. Ch., 1979. Pastor Foursquare Gospel Ch., Kansas City, Mo., 1975-76; pastor Foursquare Gospel Ch., Osceola, Iowa, 1976-81, Marinette, Wis., 1981—; religion edn. dir. Wis. Div. of Foursquare Chs., 1981—. Author: (booklet) Our Founders' Ministry, 1983; lectr. Foursquare History and Doctrine. Mem. Presdl. Task Force, 1984; bd. dirs. Clarke County Care Facility, Osceola, 1977-81. Recipient Vol. Recognition award, Marinette Bd. Supervisors, 1988. Mem. Nat. Assn. Evangs. (sec. Wis. br. 1990), Marinette Evang. Clergy Assn. (pres. 1985-87). Republican. Home: 627 Michaelis St Marinette WI 54143 Office: Foursquare Gospel Ch 631 Michaelis St Marinette WI 54143

GRIDER, JOE BOB, minister, hearing aid consultant; b. Russell Springs, Ky., July 4, 1936; s. Ruel E. and Mary D. (Beck) G.; m. Wilma C. Monson, Dec. 20, 1958; children: Shonda Lois Grider Judy, Sheila Kay Grider Griggs. BA, Cin. Bible Coll., 1958. Ordained to ministry Christian Ch. (Disciples of Christ), 1958. Min. Gardenside Christian Ch., Lexington, Ky., 1958—; hearing aid cons. Miracle-Ear Hearing Ctr., Lexington, 1983—. Organist, pianist, sr. citizens ministries Christian Chs., Lexington, 1958—. Mem. Cen. Ky. Christian Mins. Assn. (pres. 1980-81), Lions. Avocations: keyboard, singing, oil painting, sculpture. Home: 461 Severn Way Lexington KY 40503

GRIDER, JOSEPH KENNETH, theology educator, writer; b. Madison, Ill., Oct. 22, 1921; s. William Sanford and Elizabeth Mary (Krone) G.; m. Virginia Florence Ballard, July 4, 1942; children: Linda Lucille (dec.), Jennifer Elizabeth, Joseph Kenneth II, Carol Christine. Th.B., Olivet Nazarene Coll., Kankakee, Ill., 1944, A.B., 1945; BDiv, Nazarene Theol. Sem., Kansas City, Mo., 1947; M.Div. summa cum laude, Drew U., Madison, N.J., 1948, M.A., 1950; Ph.D., Glasgow U., Scotland, 1952; student, Oxford U., Eng., 1964. Ordained to ministry Ch. of the Nazarene, 1944; pastor Ch. of the Nazarene, Wilmington, Ill., 1944-45, Federated Ch., Kingston, Mo., 1945-47, Methodist Circuit, Colesville, N.J., 1948-50, Nazarene Mission, Glasgow, 1951-52; tutor in systematic theology, Bibl. lit. and Greek Hurlet Nazarene Coll., Glasgow, 1950-52; assoc. prof. theology Pasadena Coll., Calif., 1952-53; assoc. prof. theology Nazarene Theol. Sem., Kansas City, 1953-64, prof., 1964—. Author: books Repentance Unto Life, 1964, Taller My Soul, 1965, Commentary on Ezekiel, 1966, Commentary on Zechariah, 1969, Commentary on Daniel and Ezekial, 1968, Entire Sanctification: The Distinctive Doctrine of Wesleyanism, 1980, Born Again and Growing, 1982, Gibraltars of the Faith, 1983; translator: New International Version of the Bible, 1978; assoc. editor: Beacon Dictionary of Theology, 1984; contbr. articles to encys., jours., chpts. in books. Named Alumnus of Yr. Olivet Nazarene Coll., 1966; quinquennial citation of merit Nazarene Theol. Sem., 1985. Mem. Wesleyan Theol. Soc., Kansas City Soc. Theol. Studies, Kansas City Breakfast Club (sec.). Office: Nazarene Theol Seminary 1700 E Meyer St Kansas City MO 64131

GRIER, PATRICIA ELIZABETH WELCH, minister; b. Chissamba, Angola, Nov. 14, 1951; d. Maxwell Millard and Elizabeth Lincoln (Dorr) Welch; m. Eugene Morrison Grier, Dec. 27, 1983. BA, Upsala Coll., 1974; MDiv, Andover-Newton (Mass.) Theol. Sch., 1979. Ordained to ministry, 1979. Interim minister Preble (N.Y.) Congl. United Ch. of Christ, summer 1978; pastor Ft. Pierre (S.D.) Congl. United Ch. of Christ, 1979-83, Robbins (Tenn.) Parish United Ch. of Christ, 1984-85; co-pastor Partridge (Kans.) Community United Ch. of Christ, 1985—; co-chairperson community vitalization com. Kans. Ecumenical Ministries, 1988—. V.p. Child Protection Team, Hughes and Stanley counties, S.D., 1981-83; vol. Habitat for Humanity, Americus, Ga., 1983-84; bd. dirs., v.p. Sexual Assault and Domestic Violence Ctr., Reno County, Kans., 1988-91. Mem. S.D. Conf. United Ch. of Christ (bd. dirs. 1982-83). Democrat. *When we think of those who care often we find it is those who "have chosen...to share our pain and touch our wounds with a gentle and tender hand." (Henri Nouwen in "Out of Solitude"). So it is with God in Christ; so it is in ministry.*

GRIER, TED CHARLES, minister; b. Missoula, Mont., July 25, 1954; s. Charles Peter and Dora Minnie (Ripley) G. Student, Bethany Fellowship, Bloomington, Minn., 1972-74. Ordained to ministry, Assn. Fund. Ministers & Chs., 1989. Pastor Evang. Covenant Ch., Deer River, Minn., 1990—; office mgr. God's Answer Inc., Deer River, Minn., 1989—. With USN, 1976-81. Home: 213 1/2 Main St Deer River MN 56636 Office: 1019 Comstock Dr Deer River MN 56636 *What is life? Consider this: "Can life be compared to the chicken or to the egg? We are in the egg! This life is simply an opportunity to 1) accept our Savior, 2) prepare ourselves for the real life that is to come! Materialsism, intellectualism, mysticism are all exercises in futility!.*

GRIFFES, JAMES ELBRIDGE, pastor; b. Chgo., July 26, 1927; s. James Lincoln and Dorothy Ella (Blackwell) G.; m. Mary Elizabeth Hoyt, Aug. 30, 1952; children: Martha Hoefer, James Timothy, John Mark, Peter Hoyt. BA, Park Coll., 1949; BD, McCormick Theol. Sem., 1952; D Ministry, Chgo. Theol. Sem., 1982. Ordained to ministry Presbyn. Ch., 1952. Pastor Bethany Presbyn. & Zion Congl. Ch., Carroll, Neb., 1952-56; assoc. pastor First Presbyn. Ch., Hastings, Neb., 1956-61; pastor First United Presbyn. Ch., Red Oak, Iowa, 1961-74, Second Presbyn. Ch., Freeport, Ill., 1974-87; interim pastor Sommonack (Ill.) Presbyn. Ch., 1988; pastor Bethany Presbyn. Ch., Fort Wayne, Ind., 1988—; vis. World Coun. Chs., Evanston, Ill., 1954, Vancouver, B.C., Can., 1984; commr. Presbyn.-Gen. Assembly, L.A., 1955, Rochester, N.Y., Bloxi, Miss., 1974, 87. Mem. County Fair Bd., Red Oak, Iowa, 1962-74, Pub. Libr. Bd., Red Oak, 1969-74. Republican. Office: Bethany Presbyn Ch 1616 W Main St Fort Wayne IN 46808

GRIFFIN, BENJAMIN THEODORE, religious organization administrator, minister; b. Ogbomosho, Nigeria, Sept. 27, 1940; s. Ben Theodore and Alice Maude (Latham) G.; m. Gail VanOrmer; children: Lynne, Michael, Geoffrey, Jeremy, Brian, Jennifer. BA, Baylor U., 1961; MDiv, Andover-Newton Theol. Sem., 1964; D in Ministry, Lancaster (Pa.) Sem., 1975. Pastor First United Ch. of Christ, Mt. Pleasant, Pa., 1964-69, St. John's United Ch. of Christ, Orwigsburg, Pa., 1969-75, Trinity United Ch. of Christ, York, Pa., 1975-87; pres. United Theol. Sem. of the Twin Citis, New Brighton, Minn., 1987—; trustee Lancaster Theol. Sem., 1976-87; dir. North Cen. Career Ctr., St. Paul. Author: Americanization of a Church, 1985; editor: Jour. New Mercersburg Rev., 1985-87; contbr. articles to profl. jours. Mem. Orwigsburg Town Coun., 1972-75; pres. Mt. Pleasant Sch. Bd., 1966-69. Mem. Am. Acad. Religion, Am. Assn. Pastoral Counselors, Mercersburg Soc., Pa. Cen. Conf. United Ch. of Christ (vice moderator 1986-87). Office: United Theol Sem 3000 5th St NW New Brighton MN 55112

GRIFFIN, DONALD JAMES, minister; b. Redwood City, Calif., Apr. 8, 1958; s. John and Joan Mae (Leonard) G.; m. Martha Marie Crown, June 27, 1981; children: Annie Bricole, Aaron James. Student, Oreg. Coll. Edn., 1976-79; BA, N.W. Coll. of the Assemblies of God, 1982. Ordained minister Assembly of God Ch., 1985. Pastor Cen. Park Assembly of God, Aberdeen, Wash., 1982—; layworker Cen. Assembly of God, Seattle, 1980-82. Fellow Gen. Council Assemblies of God (pastor 1982). Avocations: archery, golfing, gardening. Home and Office: 516 7th St Hood River OR 97031

GRIFFIN, JAMES ANTHONY, bishop; b. Fairview Park, Ohio, June 13, 1934; s. Thomas Antohny and Margaret Mary (Hanousek) G. B.A., Borromeo Coll., 1956; J.C.L. magna cum laude, Pontifical Lateran U., Rome, 1963; J.D. summa cum laude, Cleve. State U., 1972. Ordained priest Roman Catholic Ch., 1960, bishop, 1979; asso. pastor St. Jerome Ch., Cleve., 1960-61; sec.-notary Cleve. Diocesan Tribunal, 1963-65; asst. chancellor Diocese of Cleve., 1965-68, vice chancellor, 1968-73, chancellor, 1973-78, vicar gen., 1978-79; pastor St. William Ch., Euclid, Ohio, 1978-79; aux. bishop Diocese of Cleve.; vicar of western region Diocese of Cleve., Lorain, Ohio, 1979-83; bishop Diocese of Columbus (Ohio), 1983—; mem. clergy relations bd. Diocese of Cleve., 1972-75, mem. clergy retirement bd., 1973-78, mem. clergy personnel bd., 1979-83. Author: (with A.J. Quinn) Thoughts for Our Times, 1969, Thoughts for Sowing, 1970, (with others) Ashes from the Cathedral, 1974, Sackcloth and Ashes, 1976, The Priestly Heart, 1983. Bd. dirs. Holy Family Cancer Home, 1973-78; trustee St. Mary Sem., 1976-78; bd. dirs., mem. pension com. Cath. Cemeteries Assn., 1978-83; bd. dirs. Meals on Wheels, Euclid, 1978-79; vice-chancellor Pontifical Coll. Josephinum, 1983—; bd. dirs. Franklin County United Way, 1984-90; chmn. bd. govs. N.Am. Coll., Rome, Italy, 1984-88; chmn. Mayor's Coun. on Youth; treas. Cath. Relief Svc. Bd. Recipient Human Rights award Anti-Defamation League B'nai B'rith, 1987. Mem. Am. Canon Law Soc., Columbus Bar Assn. (chmn. jud. advt. com. 1987—, Liberty Bell award 1989).

GRIFFIN, JERRY LYNN, minister; b. Houston, Dec. 14, 1949; s. James Arthur and Pauline Malinda (Röese) G.; m. Donna Marie Metzger, Oct. 15, 1972; children: Jenny, Jill, John. Student, North Tex. State U., 1968-69; B of Religion, Midwest Bible Coll., 1972; MDiv, Iliff Sch. Theology, Denver, 1981. Ordained to ministry Ch. of God (Seventh Day), 1973. Pastor Ch. of God (Seventh Day), Sacramento, 1973-76; instr. Summit Sch. Theology, Denver, 1976—, former bd. dirs.; former bd. dirs. Gen. Conf. Ch. of God (Seventh Day), Denver; pres. Internat. Ministerial Congress Ch. of God (Seventh Day), Denver, 1986—. Author: How We Got the Bible, 1990; also articles; editor: Making Sense of Scripture, 1987, Discovering the Gospel, 1988, Who Is Jesus?, 1989; Bible Adv. mag., 1981—. Mem. N.Am. Ministerial Coun., Summit Sch. Theology Alumni Assn. Office: Bible Advocate Press PO Box 33677 Denver CO 80233

GRIFFIN, LARRY ALLEN, minister, evangelist; b. Clark AFB, The Philippines, Dec. 22, 1949; s. Richard Eugene and Lilia (Nepomuceno) G.; m. Mary-Jane Stewart, Dec. 11, 1977; children: Lilia Adah, Leslie Ann, Caleb Andrew. BS in Secondary Edn., U. Maine, Presque Isle, 1973; MDiv, Meth. Theol. Sch., Delaware, Ohio, 1978. Ordained to ministry United Meth. Ch., 1974, Am. Bapt. Chs. in U.S.A., 1986; cert. secondary tchr., Maine, Ohio. Pastor Monticello (Maine) United Meth. Ch., 1972-73; pastor youth Sixth Ave. United Meth. Ch., Lancaster, Ohio, 1973-75; pastor Beulah United Meth. Ch., Baltimore, Ohio, 1975-76, Meadow Farm United Meth. Ch., Zanesville, Ohio, 1977-78; asst. pastor Broad St. United Meth. Ch., Columbus, Ohio, 1978-79; pastor Duncan Falls (Ohio) Bapt. Ch., 1984-86, 1st Bapt. Ch., Sunbury, Ohio, 1986—; chmn. state adv. com. for ordination Am. Bapt. Chs. Ohio, 1986-91, campus ministry task force, 1989, Commn. on Profl. Ministry, Commn. for Town/Country Ministries, 1988-91, staff coord. for evangelism and ch. growth, Am. Bapt. Ch., Ohio, 1988—; pastor, counselor Am. Bapt. Men of Ohio, 1987-91; chmn. fin. Judson Hills Camp Bd., Loudonville, Ohio, 1988-90; pres. Big Walnut Ministerial Assn., Sunbury, Ohio, 1987-88. Mem. Rep. Presdl. Task Force, 1983—, Nat. Right to Life, 1983—, Am. Bapt. Friends of Life, 1986—. Recipient Harry Manning award Town/Country Commn., Am. Bapt. Chs. Ohio, 1989. Mem. Nat. Assn. Evangelicals, Am. Bapt. Evangelism Team (steering com. 1990—). Home: 89 E Cherry St Sunbury OH 43074 Office: 1st Bapt Ch 99 E Cherry St Sunbury OH 43074 *Having been raised in a Christian home, I have always known that God loved me and had a purpose for my life. Since committing my life to Christ, my quest in life has been and shall continue to be to seek His will and strive to be faithful to His calling. I receive the advice of Colossians 3:17 and 3:23 and claim the promise of Proverbs 16:3.*

GRIFFIN, RICHARD RAY, minister; b. Topeka, Sept. 1, 1945; s. Walter O. and Ruth Marie (Gordon) G.; m. Barbara June Van DoDoeselaar, Aug. 3, 1968; children: Robert Ray, Sherilyn Sue. BA, Bob Jones U., 1968; M in Ministry, Internat. Sem., 1983, LittD, 1984; DD, Heritage Bapt. U., 1984; ThM, Fundamental Bapt. Theol. Sem., 1987. Ordained to ministry Bapt. Ch., 1970. Pastor First So. Meth. Ch., Savannah, Ga., 1968-70; assoc. pastor Faith Missionary Bapt. Ch., Easley, S.C., 1970-71; pastor First Bapt. Ch., Brown City, Mich., 1971-78; pastor, sch. adminstr. Grace Missionary Bapt. Ch., Kinston, N.C., 1978-81; pastor Calvary Bapt. Ch., Sterling, Kans., 1981-86; pastor, sch. adminstr. Grace Tabernacle Bapt. Ch., Centerville, Iowa, 1986—; former trustee Bapt. Bible Fellowship, N.C., 1981; former v.p. Iowa Bapt. Bible Fellowship, 1986-89. Mem. Gospel Fellowship Assn., Alumni Assn. Bob Jones U., Alumni Assn. Heritage Bapt. U. Republican. Home: Rock Valley Rd Centerville IA 52544 Office: Grace Tabernacle Bapt Ch N Park Ave Centerville IA 52544 *Life is what one makes of it. It is exciting or dull, fulfilling or devastating, depending on our outlook. Thankfully in Christ and with His help, we can enjoy life "abundantly."*

GRIFFIN, W. C., bishop. Bishop Ch. of God in Christ, Albuquerque. Office: Ch of God in Christ 3322 Montclaire Albuquerque NM 87110*

GRIFFIN, WILLIAM ALBERT, educator, college administrator, minister; b. Washington, N.C., Oct. 29, 1939; s. Norfleet Edward and Julia Lucille (Dunbar) G.; m. Patricia Swindell, June 9, 1962; children—Mark Alan, Carol Lynne. A.B., Roanoke Bible Coll., 1962, Milligan Coll., 1963; M.A., E. Carolina U., 1970; M.A., Cin. Christian Sem., 1979; EdS Coll. William and Mary, 1981. Prof. Roanoke Bible Coll., Elizabeth City, N.C., 1963—, dean students, 1975-86, pres. 1986—; minister Fairfield Christian Ch., N.C., 1980-86. Author: Ante-Bellum Elizabeth City, 1970; RBC-The First 25 Years, 1981. Pres. Pasquotank County Hist. Soc., Elizabeth City, 1967-70. Mem. Delta Epsilon Chi. Home: 715 First St Elizabeth City NC 27909 Office: Roanoke Bible Coll PO Box 387 Elizabeth City NC 27909

GRIFFIN, WILLIAM ARTHUR, clergyman, religious organization executive; b. Cococonk, Ont., Can., July 29, 1936; s. Arthur Campbell and Anne (Bradamore) G.; m. Patricia Rose Russell, Aug. 18, 1956; children: Kent, Wendy, Mark, Patti, Becky. Diploma, Ea. Pentecostal Bible Coll., Peterborough, Ont., 1957; BA, U. Toronto, Ont., 1960; MDiv, Luth. Theol. Sem., Saskatoon, Sask., Can., 1970; MA, U. Sask., Saskatoon, 1973. Ordained to ministry Pentecostal Assemblies Can., 1962. Pastor Pentecostal Ch., Fergus, Ont., 1960-62; dean of students Cen. Pentecostal Coll., Saskatoon, 1963-69; lectr. U. Sask., 1970-72; acad. dean Ea. Pentecostal Bible Coll., 1973-79; exec. dir. Pentecostal Assemblies Can., Mississauga, Ont., 1980—. Exec. editor Resource, 1980—, Youth Profile, 1980—, Family Talk, 1988—; contbr. articles to religious jours. Mem. Soc. for Pentecostal Studies. Office: Pentecostal Assemblies Can, 6745 Century Ave, Mississauga, ON Canada L5N 6P7

GRIFFIS, CURTIS RAYMOND, religion educator; b. Paris, Tex., Oct. 20, 1935; s. Robert Eugene and Mary Maude (Bills) G.; m. Barbara Anne Sanders, June 7, 1957; children: Sarah Reneé, Robert Curtis, Amy Elizabeth. BA, Midwestern U., 1962; MRE, Southwestern Sem., 1965. Ordained to ministry Bapt. Ch., 1969. Min. of edn. Sans Souce Bapt. Ch., Greenville, S.C., 1965-67, Far Hills Bapt. Ch., Dayton, Ohio, 1967-68; dir. of religious edn. Greater Dayton Assn. Bapts., 1968-73; dir. ch. devel. Bapt. Gen. Assn. New Eng., Northboro, Mass., 1973-79; min. edn. Mid. River Bapt. Ch., Balt., 1979-82; metro evangelism assoc. Ill. Bapt. State Assn., Springfield, 1982-87; min. of edn. Cen. Bapt. Ch., Winchester, Ky., 1987—; newspaper-pressman, stereotyper Duncan (Okla.) Banner, Wichita Falls News, Dallas News, 1953-65. Home: 214 LaMond Ruelle Winchester KY 40391 Office: Cen Bapt Ch 101 W Lexington Winchester KY 40391

GRIFFITH, DONALD NASH, minister; b. Glenwood Springs, Colo., Mar. 1, 1935; s. Paul Donal and Charlestine Louise (Nash) Tedford; m. Marilyn M. Bartlett, Aug. 26, 1956; children: Brenda, Janet, David. BA, U.Evansville, Ind., 1956; MDiv., Drew U., Madison, N.J., 1959; D in Ministry, Christian Theol. Sem., Indpls., 1977. Ordained elder United Meth. Ch., 1959. Minister Cook Meml. United Meth. Ch., Jeffersonville, Ind., 1960-64, Arlington United Meth. Ch., Bloomington, Ind., 1964-68; sr. minister St. Andrew United Meth. Ch., Indpls., 1968-75, Bradley United Meth. Ch., Greenfield, Ind., 1975-84, Irvington United Meth. Ch., Indpls., 1984—; pres. N. Cen. Commn. on Ministry, United Meth. Ch., 1985-89; bd. dirs. Bd. Higher Edn.; mem., vice chair Min. Div. Ordained Ministry United Meth. Ch., Nashville, 1985—. Mem. Indpls. City and County Council, 1972-76. Named Conf. Chairperson of Yr., Bd. Health and Welfare Ministries, United Meth. Ch., 1976; recipient Leadership award Indpls. Ch. Fedn., 1976. Republican. Lodge: Rotary. Avocations: flying, reading, travel. Office: Irvington United Meth Ch 30 N Audubon Rd Indianapolis IN 46219

GRIFFITH, MABEL MAXINE, association administrator; b. Wheeling, W.Va., Dec. 14, 1919; d. Thomas Joseph and Elizabeth Matilda (Reese) Minns; m. George William Griffith, Apr. 17, 1944 (dec.); children: Terrill Lee, Gerrill Lynn. Grad. high sch., Wheeling. Sec. Ohio County Pub. Library, Wheeling, 1940-42; addressograph clk. Wheeling Electric Co., 1942-44; mgr. office for dist. supt. United Meth. Ch., Wheeling, 1944-73; exec. dir. Greater Wheeling Council Chs., Wheeling, 1973-75. Editor Messenger newsletter. Mem. Child Study Club, past sec.; mem. W.Va. Conf. United Meth. Ch. Unity Commn., chairperson United Meth. Dist. Com. Ecumenical Concerns; dir. Greater Wheeling council Chs., 1975—. Mem. Clergy and Laity Concerned, Clergy Council Wheeling. Democrat. Avocations: crocheting, traveling, ch. work. Office: Greater Wheeling Coun Chs 110 Methodist Bldg Wheeling WV 26003

GRIFFITH, MEARLE LEE, denominational executive, pastor, futurist; b. Iowa City, Iowa, Oct. 2, 1943; s. Elbert Carl and Mary Eloise (Leuenberger) G.; m. Mary Jane Batchelder, Aug. 17, 1968; children: Maria Joy, Marci Jean. BA in Mass Communications, Drake U., 1969; MDiv, U. Dubuque, 1979; D Ministry, United Theol. Sem., Dayton, Ohio, 1991; DD (hon.), Rust Coll., 1991. Ordained to ministry United Meth. Ch., 1981. Exec. dir. Iowa United Meth. Found., Des Moines, 1976-77; pastor U. Dubuque Theol. Sem., 1977-79, United Meth. Ch., Grundy Center, Iowa, 1979-81; dir. of communications Iowa Annual Conf., United Meth. Ch., Des Moines, 1981-87; assoc. gen. sec. Gen. Coun. on Ministries, United Meth. Ch., Dayton, Ohio, 1987—; editor, gen. mgr. Express Communications, Ankeny, Iowa, 1969-71; publ. Ill. Star, Beardstown, 1971-73; dir. of community relations Des Moines Area Coll., 1973-76. Contbr. numerous articles in denominational jours. Dir. Saydel Sch. Dist., Des Moines, 1970-76, Ankeny (Iowa) Community Sch. Dist., 1985-87, Northmont Found., Englewood, Ohio, 1987—; trustee Rust Coll., Holly Springs, Miss., 1987—. Mem. Gen. Commn. Communications (dir. 1984-87). Home: 7800 Volk Dr Dayton OH 45415 Office: Gen Coun Ministries 601 W Riverview Dayton OH 45406

GRIFFITH, THOMAS HARVEY, minister; b. Burbank, Calif., Sept. 27, 1947; s. James Eli and Frances A. (Lindhorst) G.; m. Leah Jacobs, June 8, 1968; 1 child, Jacob. BA, Chapman Coll., 1969; MDiv, Garrett Theol., 1972; MBA, Chapman Coll., 1985. Contbr. L.A. Missionary and Ch. Extention Soc.; pastor Asbury United MEth. Ch., Alhambra, Calif., 1983-85; min. of adminstrn. Wilshire United MEth. Ch., L.A., 1985-87; pastor St. Paul United Meth. Ch., L.A., 1986-88, Crescent Heights United Meth. Ch., West Hollywood, Calif., 1988—; mem. Calif. Pacific Annual Conf. United Meth. Ch., Pasadena, 1971—, counsel for def. Ecclesiastical Trial, PAsadena, 1985. Mem. Social Svcs. Adv. Com., West Hollywood, 1990; treas. Human Rels. Commn., Pismo Beach, Calif., 1975-78. Mem. United Meth. Assn. Ch. Bus. Adminstrs., Christian Mgmt. Assn. Office: Crescent Heights United Meth Ch 1296 N Fairfax Ave West Hollywood CA 90046

GRIFFITH, WILLIAM DUDLEY, minister; b. Cleve., Nov. 19, 1930; s. Arthur Griffith and Marguerite (Ellis) G.; m. Tanya Hudgel, June 20, 1953; children: Mark E., Gregg H., Ginna Takacs. BA, Ohio Wesleyan U., 1952; MDiv, Garrett Evang. Theol. Sem., 1956; D Ministry, Consortium Ohio Theol. Schs., Cleve., 1977. Ordained to ministry United Meth. Ch. as deacon, 1953, ad elder, 1956. Student pastor Christ Meth. Ch., Chgo., 1953-56; pastor Zion/Union Ave. Meth. Chs., Cleve., 1956-59, Willoughby Hills (Ohio) Meth. Ch., 1959-66, Geneva (Ohio) United Meth. Ch., 1966-71; sr. pastor Macedonia (Ohio) United Meth. Ch., 1971-77, Ch. of the Savior, Canton, Ohio, 1977-84, United Meth. Ch. of Chagrin Falls, Ohio, 1984-87, Willowbrook United Meth. Ch., Sun City, Ariz., 1987—. Author: Morning Minutes, 1987, How to Pray for Some Else, 1988; radio pastor Voice of the Desert, 1988—. Founder, pres. Heart of Cleve., 1957-60. Mem. United Methodists for Ch. Renewal (chmn. Cleve. 1964-66, mem. nat. steering com. Chgo. 1965-68). Republican. Avocations: bowling, fishing, shuffleboard. Home: 10142 Saddle Ridge Dr Sun City AZ 85373 Office: Willowbrook United Meth Ch 19390 99th Ave Sun City AZ 85373 *There is no greater joy in life than to live so that Jesus Christ will rejoice in us.*

GRIGG, EDDIE GARMAN, minister; b. Shelby, N.C., Feb. 20, 1957; s. Gaston Theodore and Sylvia Evlyn (Davis) G.; m. Susan Wanda Ray, May 28, 1977; children: Mark Zolton, Jamie Ray, Steven Russell. BA, Gardner-Webb Coll., 1980; MDiv, Southeastern Bapt. Theol. Sem., 1985. Ordained to ministry So. Bapt. Conv., 1976. Pastor Victory Bapt. Ch., Kings Mountain, N.C., 1975-79, Christian Freedom Bapt. Ch., Kings Mountain, 1979-81, Sanford Meml. Bapt. Ch., Brodnax, Va., 1981-85, Pleasant Hill Bapt. Ch., Shelby, N.C., 1985-89; sr. minister Wilson Grove Bapt. Ch., Charlotte, N.C., 1989—. Mem. Mecklenburg Ministers' Conf., Mecklenberg Assn. (evangelism com. 1990—, urban ch. com. 1990—. Republican. Office: Wilson Grove Bapt Ch 6624 Wilgrove-Mint Hill Rd Charlotte NC 28227-3462

GRIGGS, CHARLES WILFRED, religion educator; b. Oct. 5, 1942; s. L.W. Jr. and Loal (Hendricks) G.; m. Karen Ann Smith, Feb. 26, 1966; children: Brian, Deborah, Stephen, Kent, Kathryn, Julie, Michael. BA in History, Music, Brigham Young U., 1966, MA in Ancient History and Greek, 1968; PhD, U. Calif., Berkeley, 1978. Univ. prof. ancient studies Brigham Young U., Provo, Utah, 1987—. Author: Early Egyptian Christianity, 1990, Excavations at Seila, Egypt, 1988, Apocryphal Writing and the Latter-day Saints, 1986, Learn Greek through the New Testament, 1984. Mem. Orem (Utah) Ednl. Adv. Coun., 1982-84. Mem. Soc. Bibl. Lit., Assn. Ancient Historians (charter), Internat. Assn. for Coptic Studies (charter), Phi Kappa Phi, Phi Alpha Theta. Mem. LDS Ch. Home: 427 E 500 S Orem UT 84057 Office: Brigham Young U Ancient Studies 4012 HBLL Provo UT 84602

GRIGSBY, PHILLIP N., ecumenical agency administrator. Urban agt., minister Schenectady Inner City Ministry, N.Y. Office: Schnectady Inner City Ministry 5 Catherine St Schenectady NY 12307*

GRIMES, KEVIN PAUL, minister; b. Silver Spring, M.D., Dec. 28, 1965; s. John Edward and Mona Gail (Ritchey) G. BA in Cross Cultural Studies, Nyack Coll., N.Y., 1988. Min. evangelism and missions Derwood Alliance Ch., Rockville, M.D., 1988—. Office: Derwood Alliance Church 16501 Redland Rd Rockville MD 20855

GRIMES, MARILYN KAY, religious educator; b. Fort Wayne, Ind., Sept. 14, 1942; d. Wayne Willis and Ruby Jeanette (Wilson) Bishop-Uore; m. Paul David Grimes, Jan. 21, 1962; children: Mark Edward, Christine Diane. Student, Reformed Bible Coll., Grand Rapids, Mich., 1981—. Edn. dir. St. Paul's United Meth. Ch., Grand Rapids, Mich., 1980—. Office: St Pauls United Meth Ch 3334 Breton Rd SE Grand Rapids MI 49512

GRIMMET, ALEX J., educator, clergyman; b. McVeigh, Ky., July 17, 1928; s. Alex A. and Edna Mae (Boyd) G.; m. Lois Jean Carter, June 24, 1949; children—Larry Bruce, Raven Alexis. A.B., Ky. Christian Coll., 1949; M.Ed., U. Cin., 1964; postgrad. in math. Washburn U., 1967, U. Cin., 1968-69, Georgetown U., 1968. Ordained to ministry Ch. of Christ, 1948. Elem.

tchr. Highland County schs., Hillsboro, Ohio, 1957-62; tchr. math. Warren County, Morrow, Ohio, 1964-67; tchr. math. Lebanon High Sch., Ohio, 1967-85, head dept., 1969-84; student minister Olympia Christian Ch., Owensville, Ky.; minister Choatville Christian Ch., Frankfort, Ky, 1949-51, Mountains Ky. and W.Va., Pike County, Ky., Mingo County, W.Va., 1951-52, Jefferson and Capella Chs. of Christ near Winston Salem, N.C., 1952-56; Danville Ch. of Christ, Hillsboro, Ohio, 1956-61, Loveland (Ohio) Ch. of Christ, 1961-66, Lerado Ch. of Christ, 1966—; adminstr. Christian Schs. of Greater Cin., 1991; chmn. math. curriculum revision com. Lebanon City Schs., 1969-70, 82-85, chmn. competency based edn. program for math., 1982-85; with IRS, 1986-89. Vol. math instr. GED program Loveland Lit. Program, 1986—, Adult Literacy Program, Loveland; precinct exec. Democrats Hamilton County, Loveland, 1980—; adminstr. Christian Schs. Cin., 1991—. Mem. NEA, Ohio Edn. Assn., Ohio Council Tchrs. Math. (dist. dir. 1981-84, v.p. 1984-87, conv. program chmn. 1986), Lebanon Tchrs. Assn. (mem. liaison com.). Club: Kiwanis (sec. local chpt., sec.-treas. 8th Ohio div.). Home: 848 Kenmar Dr Loveland OH 45140 *My life has been centered around helping my fellow man. I believe in the Bible as the inspired Word of God and accept it without change and compromise. I believe in and try to follow Matthew 6:33, "Seek you first the Kingdom of God and His Righteousness and all these things shall be added unto you." If we put Him and His church first in our lives I believe the necessities of life will be provided by our loving heavenly Father.*

GRIMSBY, KAREN (SUE), office administrator; b. Seattle, June 29, 1950; d. Keith Soren and Arjyl Pearl (Jones) Jensen; m. Lance Melvin, July 25, 1970 (div. 1987); children: Travis Melvin, Parker Chad. Student, Edmonds Community Coll., Lynnwood, Wash., 1968-70, 74, 75, Bellevue (Wash.) Community Col, 1989. Registered lay profl. Luth. Ch. Am. Parish office adminstr. Holy Spirit Luth. Ch., Kirkland, Wash., 1980—; chmn. Greater Kirkland Ecumenical Parish, 1986-87; pres. Ch. Staff Workers Assn., 1984-85. Mem. Assn. Profl. Luth. Lay Ministers. Office: Holy Spirit Luth Ch 10021 NE 124th St Kirkland WA 98034

GRINDAL, GRACIA MARIE, theology educator; b. Powers Lake, N.D., May 4, 1943; d. Harald Kivle and Jonette Torbjor (Tinseth) G. BA in English and History, Augsburg Coll., 1965; MFA in Creative Writing, U. Ark., 1969; MA in Systematics, Luther Northwestern Sem., St. Paul, 1983; LLD (hon.), Christ Sem.-Seminex, St. Louis, 1979. Assoc. prof. English, Luther Coll., Decorah, Iowa, 1968-84; assoc. prof. pastoral theology and minstry-communications Luther Northwestern Sem., 1984—; NEH vis. humanist scholar, 1972; mem. hymn text com. Luth. Book Worship, 1973-76; cons. hymn book com. United Meth. Ch., 1986-87. Author: (poetry) Pulpit Rock, 1976, Sketches against the Dark, 1983; editor newsletter Wellwoman, 1979-86. Swedish Inst. scholar, Stockholm, 1980, Aid Assn. fo Luths. travel grantee, 1987. Mem. Hymn Soc. Am. (editorial bd. 1986—), The Loft. Mem. Democrat Farmer Labor Party. Office: Luther Northwestern Sem 2481 Como Ave Saint Paul MN 55108

GRINDEL, JOHN ANTHONY, priest, educator; b. Kansas City, Mo., Sept. 14, 1937; s. Edward Anthony and Inez Elizabeth (Weber) G. STL, Cath. U. Am., 1965, MA, 1966; SSL, Pontifical Bibl. Inst., Rome, 1967. Ordained priest Roman Cath. Ch., 1964. Prof. Scripture St. John's Sem., Camarillo, Calif., 1966-78, pres., 1973-78; provincial superior Vincentian Fathers and Bros., L.A., 1978-87; vis. scholar Jesuit Sch. Theology, Berkeley, Calif., 1987-89; dir. Inst. for Leadership of Religious Orgns. DePaul U., Chgo., 1989-91; v.p., exec. asst. to pres. DePaul U., Chgo., 1990—; lectr. Mt. St. Mary's Coll., L.A., 1973—; cons. Inter-Community Cons., St. Louis, 1982—; rsch. assoc. Am. Sch. Oriental Rsch., Jerusalem, 1967. Author: I and II Chronicles, 1973, Joshua Judges, 1985, Whither the U.S. Church, 1991; contbr. articles to religious jours. Trustee DePaul U., Chgo., 1988—. Mem. Cath. Bibl. Assn. (exec. bd. 1987-90), Soc. Bibl. Lit. Avocations: golf, jogging, hiking, bicycling. Office: 25 E Jackson Blvd Chicago IL 60604

GRINDELAND, GARY ALLEN, minister; b. Ames, Iowa, Apr. 26, 1954; s. Roger Lyle and Naomi Ann (Lundberg) G.; m. Donna Jean McKeeth, Aug. 2, 1980 (div. 1987); m. Sherri Lynn Jeffery, June 11, 1988; 1 child, Joshua. BA, Luther Coll., Decorah, Iowa, 1976; MDiv, Luther Northwestern Seminary, St. Paul, 1980. Ordained to ministry Evang. Luth. Ch. in Am., 1980. Asst. pastor Bethesda Luth. Ch., Ames, 1980-81; pastor St. Peter Evang. Luth. Ch., Prairie du Chien, Wis., 1981-91, Christ the King, Evang. Luth. Ch., Brookfield, Wis., 1991—; instr. New Testament Greek Luther Northwestern Seminary, 1978. Author: A Programmed Study of Selected Readings from Matthew, 1978. Chair instnl. ethics com. Prairie du Chien Meml. Hosp., 1988-91. Mem. Soc. Bibl. Lit., Am. Acad. Religion. Office: Christ the King Evang Luth Ch 4600 N Pilgrim Rd Brookfield WI 53005

GRINDSTAFF, ROY ARTHUR, minister; b. Cambridge, Ohio, Jan. 18, 1946; s. William Roy and Hazel Mae (Barrett) G.; m. Loris Marie Caudill, Sept. 3, 1966; children: Roy Arthur II, Yolonda Grace, Benjamin Caudill. BA magna cum laude, Olivet Nazarene U., 1972, MA, 1973; MDiv, Asbury Theol. Sem., 1977; PhD in Communication, Ohio State U., 1990. Ordained to ministry Internat. Ch. of Foursquare Gospel, 1969. Pastor Foursquare Gospel Ch., Bradley, Ill., 1968-73, Royal Oak (Mich.) Community Foursquare Ch., 1973-74, Sugartree Ridge Cir., United Meth. Ch., Hillsboro, Ohio, 1974-77, New Guilford United Meth. Ch. and West Carlisle Federated Ch., 1977-80; interim pastor Interim Cardington Cir., United Meth. Ch., 1982, Mt. Vernon (Ohio) Christian Missionary Allaince, 1985; prof. Mt. Vernon Bible Coll., 1977-78, 85-86; adj. faculty Cen. Ohio Tech. Coll., 1985, Mt. Vernon Nazarene Coll., 1986, 88; adminstrv. chaplain Mt. Vernon Devel. Ctr., 1978—, program coord., 1983-88, chair human rights com., 1979—, chair resident sexuality com., 1978-80, 89—. Co-author: Chaplaincy Services, 1982. Mem. task force on ch. and handicapped Ohio Coun. Chs., 1980-83; chaplain Country Club Ctr., 1980-84; v.p. PTO, Royal Oak, 1974; mem. bus. adv. coun. Mt. Vernon Sch. Bd., 1989—. Mem. Speech Communication Assn., Religious Communication Assn., Soc. for Pentecostal Studies, Am. Acad. Religion and Study of Bibl. Lit., Knox County Ministerial Assn. (sec.-treas. 1983-85, pres. 1988-90), Ohio State Chaplains' Assn. (program com. 1988—, sec. 1991—), Theta Phi. Home: 502 1/2 N Main St Mount Vernon OH 43050 Office: Mt Vernon Developmental Ctr PO Box 762 Mount Vernon OH 43050 *We are more than we appear. We are more than our genetic code, our training, or our environment. Any limitations of our body or our mind cannot keep us from God for we are also spirit and soul.*

GRINNELL, JOHN MICHAEL, religious organization administrator; b. Eustis, Fla., Feb. 6, 1957; s. Charles Edward Sr. and Margurite Hilda (Crown) G.; m. Patricia Louise Youngblood, Dec. 31, 1977; 1 child, Michael John. BA, Freed-Hardeman Coll., 1979. Evangelist Plymouth (Fla.) Ch. Christ, 1979-85; camp dir. Cen. Fla. Bible Camp, Eustis, 1985—; co-owner Grinnell Bros. Properties, Zellwood, Fla., 1985—. Democrat. Avocations: fishing, gardening, jogging, water skiing. Office: Cen Fla Bible Camp 23713 Lake County 44A Eustis FL 32726

GRIPE, ALAN GORDON, minister; b. Indpls., Sept. 8, 1920; s. Otto Herman and Bertha (Anderson) G.; m. Elizabeth Howell, Sept. 29, 1951 (div. 1972); children: Stephen, David. BA, Lake Forest (Ill.) Coll., 1942; BD, Princeton Theol. Sem., 1946; STM, Union Theol. Sem., N.Y.C., 1953. Ordained to ministry, Presbyn. Ch. (U.S.A.), 1946. Asst. prof. Silliman U., Dumaguete City, Philippines, 1946-50; chaplain Davidson (N.C.) Coll., 1951-52; asst. chaplain U.S. Mil. Acad., West Point, 1952-55; pastor First Presbyn. Ch., Westfield, N.Y., 1955-65; exec. coord. Personnel Svcs., United Presbyn. Ch. USA, 1965-88; interim pastor Genesee Valley Presbytery, Spencerport, N.Y., 1991—. Author: The Interim Pastor's Manual, 1987. Treas. John Milton Soc. for Blind, N.Y.C., 1988-90. Mem. Assn. of Presbyn. Interim Ministry Specialists (coun. mem. 1987-90). Home: 95 Penarrow Rd Rochester NY 14618-1721

GRISANTI, MICHAEL ALAN, religion educator; b. Silver Creek, N.Y., June 26, 1957; s. Christy and Dorothy Mae (Philbrick) G.; m. Martha Ann Cahoon, July 11, 1980; children: Michael John, Mark Alan, Trisanna Marie, David Benjamin. BA, Pillsbury Coll., Owatonna, Minn., 1979; MDiv, Cen. Bapt. Theol. Sem., 1983, ThM, 1986; postgrad., Dallas Theol. Sem., 1988—. Asst. pastor 4th Bapt. Ch., Mpls., 1982-87, dean Bible inst., 1985-88; asst. prof. Cen. Bapt. Theol. Sem., Mpls., 1985-88, 91—. Editor Central Testimony, 1986-88, 91—; contbr. book revs. to profl. jours. Mem. Evang. Theol. Soc., Soc. Bibl. Lit. Home: 8625 Penn Ave N Brooklyn Park MN 55443

GRISETA, CARLO JOSEPH, minister; b. Chgo., June 12, 1960; s. Vito Onofrio and Gloria Jean (Miller) G.; m. Stephanie Renae Thomas, Feb. 15, 1986. BS, North Cen. Bible Coll., Mpls., 1984. Evangelist to Nigeria North Cen. Bible Coll., summer 1982; assoc., youth min. Family Worship Ctr., Rockford, Ill., summer 1983, 1st Assembly of God, Topeka, 1984-85, New Life Assembly of God, Janesville, Wis., 1989—; instr., prof. Christian Life Sch. of the Bible, Rockford, 1988; resident advisor North Cen. Bible Coll., 1982-83; med. aide Abbott Northwestern Hosp., Mpls., 1983-84; pre-sch. tchr. 1st Wesleyan Day Care, Rockford, 1985-86; probation officer Winnebago County Juvenile Probation Dept., Rockford, 1986-89; vol. probation officer Totem Town Juvenile Ctr., St. Paul, 1981-83; parent educator, advocate Dept. Children and Family Svc., Luth. Social Svc., Rockford, 1986. Office: New Life Assembly of God 2416 N Wright Rd Janesville WI 53546

GRISWOLD, FRANK TRACY, III, bishop; b. Bryn Mawr, Pa., Sept. 18, 1937; s. Frank Tracy Jr. and Luisa Johnson (Whitney) G.; m. Phoebe Wetzel, Nov. 27, 1965; 2 children. AB, Harvard U., 1959; attended, Gen. Theol. Sem., 1959-60; BA, Oxford U., 1962, MA, 1966. Ordained to ministry Episcopal Ch. as deacon, 1962, as priest, 1963. Bishop coadjutor Diocese of Chgo., 1985-87, bishop, 1987—; dep. to gen. conv.; former chmn. Pa. Liturgical Commn. Office: Diocese of Chgo 65 E Huron Chicago IL 60611

GROCE, HERBERT MONROE, JR., priest; b. Phila., Apr. 17, 1929; s. herbert Monroe Sr. and Gertrude Elaine (McMullin) G.; m. Marcella Groce, June 6, 1953 (div. 1974); children: Eric Herbert, Cheryl Marcella, Karen Denice; m. Linda Jane Rosenbaum, Dec. 6, 1976; children: Herbert M. III, Lauren S. Student, St. Joseph's, 1948-49, La Salle Coll., 1955-61, Gen. Theol. Sem., N.Y.C, 1972-75; AA, Thomas A. Edison State Coll., 1974. Ordained deacon, 1978; priest, 1979. Adminstr. Radio Corp. Am., Camden, N.J., 1959-63; sr. project planner Fairchild Hillar, Hagerstown, Md., 1963-64; program adminstr. Link Group, Binghamton, N.Y., 1964, personnel mgr., 1968-69; asst. dir. Delta Rehab., Greenville, Miss., 1969-70; exec. dir. Delta Found., Greenville, 1970-71; v.p. Univ. Med. and Dental of N.J., Newark, 1971-78; dir. ops. Lincoln Ctr. for the Performing Arts, N.Y.C., 1978-82; dir. Francis Halfway House, Phila., 1986-89; rector St. Andrew's Episcopal Ch., N.Y.C., 1984—; bd. dirs. Mut. Benefit Fund and affiliated networks, Newark, Council Chs. of N.Y.C. Chmn. Bd. Harlem Restoration Project, N.Y.C., 1985—. Served as sgt. USAF, 1951-55. Recipient Honorary Alumnus award Gen. Theol. Sem., 1983, St. George's medal, Episcopal Ch., 1982. Mem. Diocese of N.Y., Masons (33 degree). Republican. Avocation: making decoy ducks. Home: 875 Berkshire Valley Rd Wharton NJ 07885 Office: Saint Andrew's Ch 2067 5th Ave New York NY 10035-1219

GRODECKI, SISTER MARY REGINELLA, nun, health science facility administrator; b. Chgo., Nov. 7, 1912; d. Valentine and Victoria (Bochenek) G. Diploma in Nursing, St. Mary of Nazareth Hosp., Chgo., 1941; BS, DePaul U., 1946. Entered Sisters of Holy Family of Nazareth order, Roman Cath. Ch., 1932; RN, cert. nurse anesthetist, Ill., Tex. Nurse anesthetist, dir. Sch. Anesthesia St. Mary of Nazareth Hosp., 1941-57, adminstr., 1957-59, superior, 1959-62; vice-provincial supr. Sisters of Holy Family of Nazareth, Grand Prairie, Tex., 1962-74; adminstr. Bethania Regional Health Care Ctr., Wichita Falls, Tex., 1974-87, pres. found bd. and devel., 1987—; chmn. bd. trustees Bethania Regional Health Care Ctr., 1962-74, v.p., 1974—, bd. dirs.; chmn. bd. trustees Mother Frances Hosp., Tyler, Tex., 1962-74, bd. dirs.; mem. bd. trustees Tex. Conf. of Cath. Healthcare Facilities, 1981; ex-officio del. Sisters of Holy Family of Nazareth gen. chpt. 1966, 69, 71, elected del., 1977; mem. nominating com., sec.-treas. Chgo. Archdiocesan Conf. Cath. Hosps.; presenter, speaker in field. Contbr. articles to profl. jours. Recipient Citation award Am. Hosp. Assn., Chgo., 1950, Plaque and Recognition awards Women's Hall of Fame of North Tex., Wichita Falls, 1986. Avocations: reading, craftwork. Home and Office: Bethania Regional Health Care Ctr 1600 11th St Wichita Falls TX 76301

GROENING, LUCY COTTON, lay worker; b. N.Y.C., July 12, 1934; d. James Cosgrove and Louise Mayo (Loizeaux) B.; m. Ronald Dale Groening, Aug. 24, 1959 (div. 1972); children: Diane, Glenn, Bruce. BA, Colby Coll., Waterville, Maine, 1956. Assoc. dir. N.Y. State Coun. of Chs., Syracuse, 1978-84; dir. Thornfield Conf. Ctr., Cazenovia, N.Y., 1986—; active mem., conss. commn. Episcopal Diocese Central N.Y., Syracuse, 1986—. Mem. Internat. Assn. Conf. Ctr. Adminstrs., Episcopal Camps and Conf. Ctrs., Assn. Creative Change, Alban Inst. Episcopalian. Home: 433 Summerhaven Dr East Syracuse NY 13057 Office: Thornfield Conference Ctr 4668 West Lake Rd Cazenovia NY 13035

GROER, HANS HERRMANN CARDINAL, archbishop; b. Vienna, Austria, Oct. 13, 1919. Ordained priest Roman Cath. Ch., 1942. Elected bishop of Vienna, 1986, created cardinal,, 1988. Address: Wollzeile 2, A-1010 Vienna Austria

GROFF, RODNEY R., minister; b. Detroit, Dec. 3, 1950; s. Joseph and Elsie J. (Lamb) G.; m. Miranda L. Ford, Apr. 4, 1971; 1 child, Tara A. AA, Frontier Community Coll., 1980; AS, Wabash Valley Coll., 1981; BS, So. Ill. U., 1983; MDiv, So. Bapt. Theol. Sem., 1987. Pastor Mill Shoals (Ill.) Bapt. Ch., 1980-81, Stewart St. Bapt. Ch., Carmi, Ill., 1981-84, Mt. Pleasant Bapt. Ch., Shelbyville, Ky., 1985-87, Audubon Bapt. Ch., Henderson, Ky., 1987—. With USMC, 1970-71. Named to Honorable Order of Ky. Colonels. Mem. Green Valley Bapt. Assn. (exec. bd. 1987—, evangelism dir. 1989—, disaster relief team 1990—), Henderson Radio Controlled Airplane Club. Home: 126 S Arlington Dr Henderson KY 42420 Office: Audubon Bapt Ch 3440 Zion Rd Henderson KY 42420

GROH, LUCILLE SIDER, pastoral counselor and administrator; b. Ont., Can., June 29, 1946; d. James Peter and Ida Grace (Cline) Sider; m. Dennis E. Groh, Apr. 29, 1984; children: Jeremy, Sara, Soren Dayton. BA, Messiah Coll., 1967; postgrad., Yale U., 1969; MS, U. Ky., 1970; PhD, Northwestern U., 1981. Ordained minister Congregational Ch., 1984. Asst. dir. Urban Life Ctr., Chgo., 1972-75; founder, editor Daughters of Sarah, Chgo., 1975-78; sr. staff psychotherapist Parkside Pastoral Counseling Ctr., Park Ridge, Ill., 1980-87; exec. dir. The Samaritan Pastoral Counseling Ctr. Evanston/Wilmette, Evanston, Ill., 1987—. Contbr. articles to profl. jours. Mem. adv. bd. Samaritan Inst., Ill. Sch. Prof. Psychology. Fellow Am. Assn. Pastoral Counselors. Home: 2743 Meadowlark Ln Evanston IL 60201

GROMACKI, GARY ROBERT, minister; b. Dallas, Mar. 12, 1958; s. Robert Glenn and Gloria Gromacki; m. Kim Carol Henderson, June 13, 1981; children: Julie, Gavin. BA, Cedarville Coll., 1980; ThM, Dallas Theol. Sem., 1984. Ordained to ministry. Pastor Grace Bible Ch., Canal Winchester, Ohio, 1984—; instr. Cedarville (Ohio) Coll., 1987—. Office: Grace Bible Ch 424 S Gender Canal Winchester OH 43110

GRONER, YOSEPH Y., rabbi; b. N.Y.C., Nov. 20, 1955; s. Yehudah Leib and Yehudis (Gurevitz) G.; married June 21, 1979; children: Rachel, Esther, Ben Tzion, Leah, Mendel, Mordechai, Zalman. Ordained rabbi, 1973. Dir. Lubavitch of N.C., Charlotte, 1980—; bd. dirs. Charlotte Jewish Fedn., 1983—; del. Lubavitch Internat. Communicants, 1986—; founder Lubavitch Jewish Day Sch., 1986. Office: Lubavitch of NC 921 Jefferson Dr Charlotte NC 28270

GROOMS, JAMES TRENTON, clergyman, consultant; b. Casstown, Ohio, July 15, 1931; s. Lester Henry and Mary Francis (Gladman) G; m. Marcia Ann Malmsbury; 1 child, Sherry Norene Grooms Smith. B of Sacred Lit., Wittenberg U., 1950, Cin. Bible Coll., 1955; MDiv, Christian Theol. Sem., Indpls., 1960; D. of Ministry, St. Mary's Sem. of the West, 1977. Campus Minister St. Tchrs. Coll., Emporia, Kans., 1960-62; sr. pastor 1st. Christian Ch., Ft. Scott, Kans., 1962-66; instr. MUPL Coll. and Mercy Sch. Nursing, Ft. Scott, Kans., 1964-66, Wellington, Kans., 1966-69; sr. pastor Athens, Ohio, 1969-88; with Clergy/Cons Svcs., Athens, Ohio, 1988—; charter mem. spiritual devel. com. Christian Chs., Ohio region, 1974—, chmn. Ohio program; organizer Endowed Soviet Peace/Unity Travel Seminar; dir. Presbytery of Phila., 1989, organizing cons. Spiritual Life Covenant Group, 1989-90; dir. travel seminar to USSR, 1990; adj. prof. spirituality Ea. Bapt. Theol. Sem., Phila., 1990. Organizing pres. Joint Bd. Phys. and Mental Health, Ft. Scott, Kans., 1962-66; leader, del. peace/unity mission to USSR Nat. Coun. Chs., 1986, 87; conducted Easter pilgrimage to USSR, 1988; mem. Millennial Russian Orthodox Ch. Decorated Ky. Col. Gov. Wallace G. Wilkinson, 1991. Mem. Appalachia Old Car Club Inc., Nat. Coun. Corvette Clubs, Corvette Club Am. Lodges: Masons, Order Eastern Star. Avocation: auto restoration.

GROOTHUIS, DOUGLAS RICHARD, minister; b. Anchorage, Jan. 3, 1957; s. Harold Fred and Lillian (Cominetto) G.; m. Rebecca Merrill, Aug. 4, 1984. BS in Philosophy, U. Oreg., 1979; MA in Philosophy, U. Wis., 1986; postgrad., U. Oreg., 1990—. Instr., writer McKenzie Study Ctr., Eugene, Oreg., 1979-84; rsch. assoc. Probe Ministries, Seattle, 1986-89; campus min. Restoration Campus Ministry, Eugene, Oreg., 1989—; adv. bd. Spiritual Counterfeits Projects, 1990—. Author: Unmasking the New Age, 1986, The New Age Movement, 1986, Confronting the New Age, 1988, Revealing the New Age Jesus, 1990, New Age, New Life, 1990; contbg. editor Christian Research Jour., 1988—; contbr. articles to profl. jours. Mem. Soc. Christian Philosophers, Evang. Theol. Soc. Mem. Evang. Ch. Avocation: book collecting. Office: Restoration Campus Ministry 2880 University St Eugene OR 97405

GROOVER, GENTLE L., bishop. Bd. of apostles, bishop Ch. of Our Lord Jesus Christ of the Apostolic Faith Inc., N.Y.C. Office: Ch Our Lord Jesus Christ Apostolic Faith Inc 2081 Adam Clayton Powell Jr New York NY 10027*

GROS, JEFFREY, ecumenical theologian; b. Memphis, Jan. 7, 1938; s. C. Jefferson and Faye Elizabeth (Dickenson) G. BA, St. Mary's Coll., 1959, MEd, 1962; MA, Marquette U., 1965; PhD, Fordham U., 1973. Tchr. various high schs. and coll., Chgo., St. Louis, Memphis, 1959-69, Crhistian Bros. Coll., Memphis, 1972-81, Memphis Sem., 1976-81; dir. faith and order Nat. Coun. Chs. of Christ in U.S.A., N.Y.C., 1981-91; assoc. dir. Secretariat for Ecumenical and Interreligious Affairs, Nat. Con. Cath. Bishops, Washington, 1991—. Editor: The Search for Visible Unity, 1984, (with J. Burgess) Building Unity; contbr. articles to profl. jours. NSF fellow, 1961-64; Hebrew Union Coll. travel grantee, 1968. Mem. Cath. Theology Soc., Coll. Theology Soc., Nat. Assn. Ecumenical Officers (bd. dirs. (1979-81), Nat. Assn. Evangs. Office: Nat Coun Cath Bishops 3211 4th St NE Washington DC 20017

GROSENICK, CONRAD, ecumenical agency administrator. Pres. Evansville Area Coun. of Chs. Inc., Ind. Office: Evansville Area Coun Chs Inc 103 NW 10th St Evansville IN 47708*

GROSS, ABRAHAM, rabbi, educator; b. Bklyn., June 29, 1928; s. Joseph and Tillie (Lauer) G.; m. Hannah Leah Stern, Dec. 18, 1952; children—Israel Meyer, Elijah Moses, Vitel, Adel Binah, Hilda Mindy, Solomon Abel. Rabbi, Ch'san Sofer Rabbinical Sem., 1952; B.B.A., Coll. City N.Y., 1951; M.S. Edn, Yeshiva U., 1959; 6th yr. profl. certificate, Hunter Coll., 1968. Rabbi Young Israel of Coll. Av., Bronx, N.Y., 1953-63, Congregation Adath Jeshurum, Bronx, 1963-68, Young Israel of Vanderveer Park, Bklyn., 1968-72, Congregation Shaare Hatikvah, N.Y.C., 1972—; asst. prin. pub. schs. N.Y.C., 1966-73; prin., 1973-84; Jewish Chaplain Columbia-Presbyn. Med. Ctr., N.Y.C., 1985—. Mem. Community Planning Bd. 4, Bronx, 1966-69; active Bonds for Israel, Yeshiva, Beth Jacob movements.; Treas. Charles and Ana Elenberg Found. Mem. Rabbinical Alliance Am. (pres. 1969-71), Met. Bd. Orthodox Rabbis (treas. 1965-69). Home: 2720 Ave J Brooklyn NY 11210 Office: 711 W 179th St New York NY 10033

GROSS, DAVID CASPER, electrical engineer; b. Milw., Feb. 25, 1958; s. Frank and Ruby (Allene) G. BSEE, Northeastern U., Boston, 1985. Engr. Raytheon Co., Quincy, Mass., 1979-86; sr. engr. Philips Lighting, Lynn, Mass., 1986-90; project engr. GTE/Sylvania, Salem, Mass., 1990—. Vol. N.E. Bapt. Hosp., Boston, 1985—. Mem. Am. Phys. Soc., Optical Soc. Am., Sigma Chi. Home: 16 Iroquois St Boston MA 02120 Office: GTE/Sylvania 60 Boston St Salem MA 01970 also: 2901 Sylvan Ct Oceanside NY 11572

GROSS, EDWARD NILES, minister, missiology educator; b. Binghamton, N.Y., Jan. 26, 1954; s. Ralph James and Ruth (Sligh) G.; m. Deborah Ann Dickerson, Dec. 18, 1976; children: Charity, John, Faith, Hope. BA, Shelton Coll., 1975; MDiv, Faith Theol. Sem., 1978; D Missiology, Trinity Evang. Div. Sch., Deerfield, Ill., 1988. Ordained to ministry Bible Presbyn. Ch., 1978. Pastor Bible Presbyn. Ch., Knoxville, Tex., 1977-80; missionary Ind. Bd. for Presbyn. Fgn. Missions, Kenya, East Africa, 1980-84; asst. prof. Faith Theol. Sem., Elkins Park, Ill., 1984-88; missiologist Bibl. Theol. Sem., Hatfield, Pa., 1989—; min. Orthodox Presbyn. Ch., Phila., 1990—; dir. Word of Truth Broadcast, Phila., 1987—; bd. dirs. Whosoever Gospel Mission, Phila., 1990—. Author: Miracles, Demons and Spiritual Warfare, 1990; editor: Systematic Theology of Charles Hodge, 1988. Mem. Evang. Profs. Missiology. Republican. *No worldview is truly Christian which denies Jesus Christ his rightful place as King over and within our lives. He rules in us by His Law—the Word of God.*

GROSS, HAL RAYMOND, bishop; b. Walla Walla, Wash., Jan. 15, 1914; s. John J. and Millie (Hale) G.; m. Evelyn Blythe Kerr, July 22, 1933; 1 dau., Patricia Ann Gross Simmons. Student, Oreg. State U., 1931-36; J.D., Willamette U., 1939; student, Ch. Div. Sch. of Pacific, 1946, D.D., 1965. Bar: Oreg. bar 1939. Pvt. practice in Corvallis, 1939-42; atty. Oreg. Unemployment Compensation Commn., 1942-44; ordained to ministry Episcopal Ch., 1946; pastor U. Oreg., 1946-47; rector St. Paul's Ch., Oregon City, 1947-61; archdeacon Episcopal Diocese Oreg., 1961-65; suffragan bishop Oreg., 1965-79; ret., 1979; mem. exec. council Episcopal Ch., 1975-79; vice chmn. Ho. of Bishops, 1976-79. Trustee Ch. Div. Sch. of Pacific, 1950-55, 72-73. Mem. Oreg. Bar Assn., Phi Delta Theta. Democrat. Club: Rotary (hon.). Home: 8255 Fairway Dr Wilsonville OR 97070

GROSS, HARRIET P. MARCUS, religion and writing educator; b. Pitts., July 15, 1934; d. Joseph William and Rose (Roth) Pincus; children: Sol Benjamin, Devra Lynn. AB magna cum laude, U. Pitts., 1954; cert. in religious teaching, Spertus Coll. of Judaica, Chgo., 1962; MA, U. Tex., Dallas, 1990. Assoc. editor Jewish Criterion of Pitts., 1955-56; publs. writer B'nai B'rith Vocat. Svc., 1956-57; leader recreation program for handicapped adults United Cerebral Palsy of Greater Chgo., 1957-58; group leader Jewish Community Ctrs. of Met. Chgo., 1958-63; columnist Star Publs., Chicago Heights, Ill., 1964-80; pub. info. specialist Operation ABLE, Chgo., 1980-81; dir. religious sch. Temple Emanu-El, Dallas, 1983-86; tchr. writing Homewood-Flossmoor (Il.) Park Dist., Brookhaven Jr. Coll., Dallas, U. Tex., Dallas; advisor journalism program Prairie State Coll., Chicago Heights, 1978-80; adv. bd. The Creative Woman quar. publ. Governors State U., Governors Park, Ill. Bd. dirs., sec. Family Svc. and Mental Health Ctr. of South Cook County, Ill., 1965-71; mem. Park Forest (Ill.) Commn. on Human Rels., 1969-80, chmn., 1974-76; bd. dirs. Ill. Theatre Ctr., 1977-80, Park Forest Bus. and Profl. Assn., 1979-80, Greater Dallas sect. Nat. Coun. Jewish Women, 1981-87, Jewish Family Svc. of Dallas, 1982—, exec. com., 1987—; mem. exec. com. Jewish Community Rels. Coun. Dallas, 1983-85. Recipient Fellowship for Action Humanitarian Achievements award, 1974; Anti-Defamation League of B'nai B'rith Honor award, 1978; Dr. Charles E. Gavin Found. Community Service award, 1978, 1st Ann. Leadership award Jewish Family Svc., 1990. Mem. Nat. Fedn. Press Women, Ill. Woman's Press Assn. (named Woman of Yr. 1978), Intertel (pres. Gateway Forum of Dallas 1984-85), Nat. Assn. Temple Educators, Mensa, Sigma Delta Chi, Phi Sigma Sigma. Jewish. Developed 1st community newspaper action line column, 1966. Office: 8560 Park Ln #23 Dallas TX 75231

GROSS, JOHN BIRNEY, retired minister; b. Barbourville, Ky., Aug. 24, 1924; s. John Owen and Harriet (Bletzer) G.; m. Lois Feldkircher, July 8, 1948; children: John Birney II, Steven Louis. A.B., DePauw U., 1948; B.D., S.T.M., Drew U., 1953; Ph.D. (Kellog fellow 1956-58), George Peabody Coll., 1958. Ordained to ministry Methodist Ch., 1950; minister Mendham, N.J., 1950-53; dean chapel Centenary Coll. Women, Hackettstown, N.J., 1953-56; asst. to pres. Fla. So. Coll., Lakeland, 1958-59; dean acad. affairs Fla. So. Coll., 1959-65; dean coll. Mt. Union Coll., Alliance, Ohio, 1965-67; v.p. Mt. Union Coll., 1967-68; dean coll. Tex. Wesleyan Coll., Ft. Worth, 1968-79; prof. religion Tex. Wesleyan Coll., 1979-82; assoc. minister First

United Meth. Ch., Clearwater, Fla., 1982-85; sr. minister Druid Hills United Meth. Ch., Ocala, Fla., 1985-90. Co-chmn. membership drive Community Concerts, Alliance, 1968; mem. Crandel alumni scholarship com. DePauw U., 1967; Bd. dirs. Lakeland chpt. ARC, 1963-65, Community Concerts, Lakeland, 1963-65, Casa Manana Playhouse, Ft. Worth, 1968—. Served with AUS, 1943-46. Mem. Am. Assn. Acad. Deans, Assn. Acad. Deans, So. Assn. Schs. and Colls., Phi Delta Kappa, Kappa Delta Pi, Phi Mu Alpha. Democrat. Home: 4912 Boulder Lake Rd Fort Worth TX 76103

GROSS, MICHAEL, school system administrator; b. Omaha, Mar. 20, 1948. BA, Creighton U., 1971; MEd, U. Mo., 1972; EdD, U. Nebr., 1976. Tchr. Montessori Ednl. Ctr., Omaha, 1972-73; residence dir. U. Nebr., Lincoln, 1973-74, grad. asst., 1974-75; asst. prof. edn. Coll. of St. Mary, Omaha, 1975-79; prin. high sch. Lac Courte Oreilles Schs., Hayward, Wis., 1979-80, adminstr. K-12, 1980-83, supt., 1983-85; adminstr. Assumption High Sch., Wisconsin Rapids, Wis., 1985-87; area adminstr. Wausau Area Cath. Schs., 1987-89; supt. Cath. Schs. Diocese of Grand Rapids, Mich., 1989—; adj. instr. Mt. Senario Coll., Ladysmith, Wis., 1979-85, Buena Vista Coll., Council Bluffs, Iowa, 1975-79; reviewer Eisenhower Nat. Program for Math./Sci., 1990; presenter in field; bd. dirs. Found. for Cath. Edn.; mem. headstart policy coun. Indianhead Community Action Agy., 1983-84. Author: Kodomo to Kyoiku No Hakken, 1980, Montessori's Concept of Personality, 1978; contbr. articles to profl. jours. Vol. United Way, 1985-91; mem. adv. coun. Wausau Hosp. Ctr., 1987-89, Coll. for Kids, NCTI, 1987-89. Mem. Mich. Assn. of Non Pub. Schs. (bd. dirs. 1989-91), Mich. Non Pub. Schs. Accrediting Assn. (bd. dirs. 1989-91), Nat. Cath. Ednl. Assn., North Cen. Assn. of Colls. and Schs. (reviewing com. 1987), Assn. of Wis. Sch. Adminstrs., Nat. Ind. Edn. Assn., Nat. Vocat. Edn. Assn., Grand Rapids C. of C., KC, Serra Club. Office: Schs Supt 600 Burton SE Grand Rapids MI 49507

GROSS, PAUL STAHL, minister; b. Freeman, S.D., Jan. 15, 1910; s. Fred and Mary (Stahl) G.; widowed; children: Sarah, Barbara, Mary, William, Frank. Ed. high sch. Lic. to ministry Hutterian Brethren Ch. Am., 1949, ordained, 1951. Min. Hutterian Brethren Ch. Am. Address: Hutterian Brethren Ch Am Rte 1 PO Box 6E Reardon WA 99029

GROSS, RUTH CHAIKEN, educational administrator; b. Irvington, N.J., Mar. 22, 1941; d. Edward and Miriam (Rothman) Chaiken; m. Arnold Gross, July 4, 1960; children: Ira, Allen. BA in Edn., Newark State Coll., 1962; collateral in Judaic studies, Kean Coll. of N.J., 1987. Cert. religious tchr., cert. prin. Tchr. Temple Sinai, Summit, N.J., 1966-76, Temple Emanu-El, Westfield, N.J., 1972-77, Temple Beth-El, Cranford, N.J., 1975-78; dir. high sch. program Temple Beth Ahm, Springfield, N.J., 1975-85; dir. edn. Temple Israel of Scotch Plains (N.J.), 1985—. Co-author: Ulpan for the Afternoon Hebrew School, 1991. Recipient Chai award Jewish Edn. Assn., 1985. Mem. Coalition for Advancement Jewish Edn. (charter), Coun. for Jewish Edn., Jewish Educator's Assembly, Assn. Jewish Spl. Educators, Hadassah, Women's League for Conservative Judaism. Office: Temple Israel Scotch Plains 1920 Cliffwood St Scotch Plains NJ 07076 *It is as a Jewish educator that I have truly been able to make a difference in a child's life, for in this profession my influence transcends generations and perpetuates Hatikvah—hope.*

GROSSER, ELMER JOSEPH, priest; b. Dayton, Ky., Aug. 31, 1922; s. Albert J. and Rose Mary (Wiegand) G. BA, St. Gregory Sem., Cin., 1943; postgrad., St. Mary Sem., 1943-46; MA, U. Toronto, 1949, PhD in Philosophy, 1951. Ordained priest Roman Cath. Ch., 1946. Prof. philosophy Holy Cross Sem., La Crosse, Wis., 1951-53; rector, prof. philosophy Sem. of St. Pius X, Erlanger, Ky., 1953-73; pastor Blessed Sacrament Ch., Covington, Ky., 1973-81, St. Philip Ch., Covington, 1981-86, Holy Cross Ch., Covington, 1987—; consultor to priests' senate, mem. fin. coun. Diocese of Covington, 1955—. Home and Office: 3612 Church St Covington KY 41015

GROSSMAN, WILLIAM BERNARD STEWART, clergyman; b. Grahamsville, N.Y., Feb. 2, 1941; s. William Bernard and Marion Roberta (Williamson) G.; m. Gretta Diane Beck, Feb. 24, 1963 (div. June 1980); children: Kimberly, Dawn, William Bernard III; m. Laura Allene Cox, Apr. 4, 1981. BA, Wesleyan U., 1964; MDiv, Drew U., 1968, D Ministry, 1982. Ordained to ministry Meth. Ch., 1968. Pastor Millbrook United Meth. Ch., Dover, N.J., 1963-68, Scio, Friendship and Allentown United Meth. Ch., Scio, N.Y., 1968-72; sr. pastor First United Meth. Ch., Jamestown, N.Y., 1972-77, Williamsville United Meth. Ch., Buffalo, 1977-79, United Ch. of Livonia (N.Y.), 1979-91; founding pastor St. Andrews Ch., East Amherst, N.Y., 1991—; pres. Bd. Pensions, Buffalo, 1980-85. Allegany County legislator, Belmont, N.Y., 1970-72; pres. Romah, Inc., Jamestown, N.Y., 1973-77; trustee Livonia Cen. Sch. Bd., 1982-87; town supr. Town of Livonia, 1989. Mem. Rotary (pres. 1976-77, dist. gov. 1988-89). Home: 160 Bramblewood Lane East Amherst NY 14051 Office: St Andrews PO Box 350 East Amherst NY 14051

GROSZ, PAUL, religious organization executive. Pres. Jewish Community, Vienna, Austria. Office: Esraelitische Kultusgemeunde, Bauernfeldgasse 4, 1190 Vienna Austria*

GROTE, ROYAL U., JR., religious organization administrator. Pres. bd. of nat. ch. extension Reformed Episcopal Ch., New Province, N.J. Office: Reformed Episcopal Ch 19 Heather Ct New Providence NJ 07974*

GROUNDS, VERNON CARL, minister, seminary administrator; b. Jersey City, July 19, 1914. BA, Rutgers U., 1937; BD, Faith Theol. Sem., 1940; DD, Wheaton (Ill.) Coll., 1956; PhD in Philosophy of Religion, Drew U., 1960; LHD (hon.), Gordon Coll., 1977. Ordained to ministry Conservative Bapt. Assn. Am., 1938. Pastor Paterson (N.J.) Gospel Tabernacle, 1934-45; prof. English and philosophy King's Coll., Del., 1943-45; prof. theology, dean Bapt. Bible Sem., N.Y.C., 1945-51; prof. apologetics, dean Bapt. Theol. Sem., Denver, 1951-55, prof. ethics and counseling, pres., 1956-79, adj. prof., 1979—, chancellor, 1991—; instr. Young Life Inst., 1952—; founder, dir. Grounds Counseling Ctr., 1981—. Author: The Reason for Our Hope, 1945, Evangelicalism and Social Concern, 1968, Revolution and the Christian Faith, 1971; contbg. author: Is God Dead?, 1967, Radical Commitment, 1984; contbg. editor Christianity Today. Office: Denver Bapt Theol Sem PO Box 10000 University Park Sta Denver CO 80210

GROVE, DENISE KATHLEEN, religious organization administrator; b. Monroe, La., Aug. 10, 1957; d. Ray Marzelle and Geraldine (Hailey) Hill; m. Michael Ray Grove, July 5, 1975; 1 child, Michael Shane. A in Acctg., Grayson County Coll., Denison, Tex., 1986. Adminstr. Sherman (Tex.) Bible Ch. Mem. Nat. Assn. Ch. Bus. Adminstrs., Phi Theta Kappa. Home: Rte 1 Box 196 Bells TX 75414 Office: Sherman Bible Church Hwy 1417 and Canyon Creek Sherman TX 75090

GROVE, JEFFERY LYNN, minister; b. Chgo., Dec. 17, 1941; s. Lester and Helen (Dombrowski) G.; m. Beth J. Wilson; children: Donna, Loralyn. BA, Loyola U., Chgo., 1968; MA, Loyola U., 1972; MDiv, McCormick Theol. Sem., Chgo., 1973; DMin, McCormick Theol. Sem., 1982. Ordained to ministry Presbyn. Ch., 1973. Min. First Presbyn. Ch., Rossville, Ill., 1973-77, St. Andrews Presbyn. Ch., Waterloo, Iowa, 1977-80, Oaklawn Community Presbyn. Ch., Oak Lawn, Ill., 1980-87, North Riverside Presbyn. Ch., North Riverside, Ill., 1987-91, 1st Presbyn. Ch., Rensselaer, Ind., 1991—; chaplain Hines Hosp., Maywood, Ill., 1991—; part-time hosp. chaplain Loyola U. Hosp., Maywood, Ill., 1988—, Hines Hosp., Maywood, Ill., 1991; faculty Loyola U., Chgo., 1969-70, Moraine Valley Community Coll., Palos Hills, Ill., 1970-71, 83-88, Coll. of St. Francis, Joliet, 1988, Coll. of DuPage, Glen Ellyn, Ill., 1988—; part-time instr. St. Joseph Coll., Rensselaer, Ind., 1991—, Hiwes Hosp. Chaplain Police & Fire Dept., North Riverside, 1987—. With USCGR, 1960-68. Mem. Internat. Conf. Police Chaplains, Riverside Golf Club, Rotary, Masons, Order Easter Star, Alpha Sigma Nu. Republican. Presbyterian. Avocations: travel, writing. Home: 225 North Van Rensselaer Rensselaer IN 47978 *Preparation is everything when it comes to success.*

GROVE, TED RUSSELL, missionary; b. Houston, Mar. 26, 1961; s. Arthur Henry and Lorna (Crosswhite) G.; m. Bobetta Marie Bivens, Oct. 8, 1988. BA in Guidance Studies, S.W. Tex. State U., 1983; MA in Counseling Psychology, Trinity Evang. Divinity Sch., 1985; postgrad., Dallas Theol. SEm., 1990—. Student counselor S.W. Tex. State U., San Marcus, 1982-83; family counselor Christian Heritage Childrens Home, Hickman, Nebr., 1985-86; conf. administr. Family Ministry, Little Rock, 1986-87; researcher Campus Crusade for Christ Family Ministry, Little Rock, 1987-89, evaluation coord., 1989-90. Named Eagle Scout Boy Scouts Am., 1975. Mem. Profl. Assn. Christian Educators, S.W. Bapt. Religious Edn. Assn. Republican. Avocations: fishing, church activities, camping, reading.

GROVE, WILLIAM BOYD, bishop; b. Johnstown, Pa., Apr. 24, 1929; s. William Morgan and Elizabeth (Boyd) G.; m. Mary Lou Naylor, July 29, 1951; children: Susan Jane Grove-Jarnett, Rebecca Louise Janczewski. BA, Bethany Coll., 1951, DD (hon.), 1983; M.Div., Drew U., 1954; D.Min., Pitts. Theol. Sem., 1978; DD (hon.), Allegheny Coll., 1965; DD, W.Va. Wesleyan Coll., 1986. Pastor Friendship Park Meth. Ch., Pitts., 1954-58; pastor Oakmont Meth. Ch., Pa., 1958-62, First Meth. Ch. of Pitts., 1962-75, Christ Ch., Bethel Park, Pa., 1975-80; Bishop W.Va. Conf., United Meth. Ch., 1980—. Democrat. United Methodist. Home: 1804 Shadybrook Rd Charleston WV 25314 Office: The United Meth Ch 900 Washington St E Rm 300 Charleston WV 25301

GROVER, NORMA BENCE, church lay worker; b. Hornell, N.Y.; d. James Edwards and Florence (Lytle) Bence; m. Stephen William Grover, Aug. 2, 1980. BA, Houghton Coll., 1963; MS, SUNY, Brockport, 1967. Permanent cert. tchr., N.Y. Mem. ch. bd. Penfield (N.Y.) Wesleyan Ch., 1970-79; sec. ch. bd. Gates Wesleyan Ch., Rochester, N.Y., supt. Sunday sch., 1986—, ch. libr., 1981—; sec. Chambers Camp, Beaver Dams, N.Y., 1975—, Wesleyan Women, Rochester, 1985—; tchr. Gates-Chili Cen. Sch., Rochester, 1963—. Named Tchr. of Yr., Gates-Chili Tchrs. Assn., 1973. Mem. Christian Educators Assn. Internat., Gates Hist. Soc. Office: Gates-Chili Cen Sch 910 Wegman Rd Rochester NY 14624

GROVER, NORMAN LAMOTTE, theologian, philosopher; b. Topeka, Feb. 9, 1928; s. LaMotte and Virginia Grace (Alspach) G.; m. Anne Stottler, June 24, 1950; children: Jennifer Jean, Peter Neal, Rebecca Louise Grover Verna, Sandra Christine Grover Lacy. B. Mech. Engring., Rensselaer Poly. Inst., 1948; B.D., Yale, 1951, S.T.M., 1952, Ph.D., 1957. Mem. faculty, chaplain Hollins (Va.) Coll., 1954-57, asst. prof. religion, 1956-57; ordained to ministry Presbyn. Ch., 1952; head dept. philosophy and religion Va. Poly. Inst. and State U., 1957-75, prof. philosophy and religion, 1961-83, prof. religion, 1983-91, prof. emeritus, 1991—; mem. supervising com. So. leadership tng. project Fund for Republic, 1955-56; assoc. Danforth Found., 1958—, sr. assoc., 1962—, chmn. Va., N.C. and S.C. conf., 1962; psychotherapeutic counsellor Blacksburg Community Counselling Center, 1962-65. Mem. Amnesty Internat. Mem. AAUP (pres. Va. Poly. Inst. and State U. chpt. 1961-62, 81-82, sec.-treas. chpt. 1959-60, 77-80, v.p. chpt. 1960-61, 80-81), NAACP, ACLU, Va. Philos. Assn. (pres. 1969), So. Soc. Philosophy and Psychology, Am. Acad. Religion, United Campus Ministries of Blacksburg (bd. dirs.), Coalition for Justice in Cen. Am. (bd. dirs., v.p. 1990—), Smithsonian Assocs., Wilderness Soc., Am. Assn. Ret. Persons, New River Valley Environ. Coalition, Yale Club. Home: 705 Burruss Dr NW Blacksburg VA 24060-3205 Office: Va Poly Inst and State U Dept Religion 310 Patton Hall Blacksburg VA 24061-0135

GROVES, RANDALL D., minister; b. Bartlesville, Okla., Dec. 10, 1961; s. R.D. and Donna B. (Eyestone) G.; m. Sharon R. Suthwell, May 17, 1986; 1 child, Kristina Leigh. BA in Religion and Math., So. Nazarene U., Bethany, Okla., 1987, MA in Bibl. Studies, 1988; postgrad., Nazarene Theol. Seminary, Kans. City, Mo. Music min. Tuttle (Okla.) Nazarene Ch., 1986-88; assoc. pastor Lemay Nazarene Ch., St. Louis, 1988-89; assoc. child sponsorship Ch. of Nazarene, Kans. City, 1990—. Active Nazarene Amateur Radio Fellowship, Kans. City, 1989—. Mem. Soc. Bibl. Lit., Wesleyan Theol. Soc., Am. Acad. Religion. Home: 9302 Myrtle #216 Kansas City MO 64132 Office: Compassionate Ministries 6401 The Paseo Kansas City MO 64131

GRUBBS, FRANCIS W., academic administrator. Pres. Simpson Coll., Redding, Calif. Office: Simpson Coll Office of the President 2211 College View Dr Redding CA 96003*

GRUBBS, ROBERT DOUGLAS, minister; b. Lake Village, Ark., June 30, 1958; s. Robert Champe and Margaret Ann (Harper) G.; m. Karen Elizabeth Needham, July 9, 1982; children: Megan E., Morgan A., Miranda L., MacKenzie C. BA, U. Cen. Ark., 1981; MA in Religious Edn., Southwestern Bapt. Theol. Sem., Ft. Worth, 1984. Lic. to ministry So. Bapt. Conv., 1977, ordained, 1985. Min. youth Hebron (Ark.) Bapt. Ch., 1978-81; min. youth and edn. 1st Bapt. Ch., Troup, Tex., 1984-85; pastor Oppelo (Ark.) Bapt. Ch., 1985-88, 1st Bapt. Ch., Clarendon, Ark., 1988—; tchr. Bible, Ark. Bapt. Sch. System, Little Rock, 1985-88; brotherhood dir. Arkansas Valley Bapt. Assn., West Helena, Ark., 1988—, bd. dirs., 1988—, assn. clk., 1989—; bd. dirs. Christian Civics Found., Little Rock, 1990—. Chaplain Clarendon Vol. Fire Dept., 1988—, Monroe County Jail, Clarendon, 1989—, Monroe County Hospice Program, Brinkley, Ark., 1988—; chmn. Leukemia Thon, Leukemia Soc. Am., Clarendon, 1991; vol. Clarendon Food Bank, 1988—. Mem. Clarendon Ministerial Alliance (pres. 1988—), Kiwanis (pres. Clarendon 1989-90). Republican. Home: 232 Washington St Clarendon AR 72029 Office: 1st Bapt Ch 204 Washington St Clarendon AR 72029

GRUBBS, THOMAS WOODBURY, minister; b. Greenville, Tex., Aug. 27, 1919; s. Thomas Whitfield and Cleo Effie (Jones) G.; m. Alice Fay Boyer, Sept. 7, 1958 (dec. July 1989); children: Timothy John, Thomas Stephen, Deborah Alice. AA, Santa Monica Jr. Coll., Calif., 1938; BA in Philosophy, UCLA, 1941; BDiv, San Francisco Theol. Sem., 1944, ThM, 1968. Ordained to ministry Presbyn. Ch., 1944. Missionary Presbyn. Ch., Japan, 1948-65; pastor Sturge Presbyn. Ch., San Mateo, Calif., 1966-75; interim pastor Hillside Presbyn. Ch., Oakland, Calif., 1978-82; parish assoc. Trinity Presbyn. Ch., San Carlos, Calif., 1984—. Mem. Conf. on Race, Religion, and Social Concern, San Mateo, 1968-76. Home: 2228 Kehoe Ave San Mateo CA 94403

GRUBBS, WILLIAM EUGENE, minister, religious organization administrator; b. Foley, Ala., Dec. 4, 1924; s. Walter D. and Fbra Elizabeth (Younce) G.; B.A., Stetson U., 1949; B.D., New Orleans Bapt. Theol. Sem., 1952, Th.D., 1957; m. P. Anne Coffman, May 30, 1946; children—Walter, Paul Alan, Joseph Dennis, Laura Catherine. Ordained to ministry Baptist Ch., 1947. Pastor chs., Ala., Mo., Miss., Calif., 1948-60; mem. faculty Philippine Bapt. Theol. Sem., 1960-63; dir. dept. evangelism So. Bapt. Gen. Conf. of Calif., 1964-68; exec. dir. N.W. Bapt. Conv. (Oreg.-Wash.), 1968-71; cons. for Laymen Overseas and Relief Ministries Fgn. Mission Bd., So. Bapt. Conv., Richmond, Va., 1971-80; exec. dir. Interchurch Med. Assistance, New Windsor, Md., 1980—; cons. Church World Service, 1980—. Bd. dirs. Ch. World Service, 1976—; mem. spl. adv. com. World Hunger, 1980. Served with USN, 1943-46. Mem. IMPACT. Contbr. articles to profl. jours. Office: Interchurch Med Assistance College Ave New Windsor MD 21776

GRUDEM, WAYNE ARDEN, seminary educator, minister; b. Chippewa Falls, Wis., Feb. 11, 1948; s. Arden Elvin and Jean Calista (Sheady) G.; m. Margaret Ellen White, June 6, 1969; children: Elliot, Oliver, Alexander. BA, Harvard U., 1970; MDiv, Westminster Sem., 1973; PhD, U. Cambridge, Eng., 1979. Ordained to ministry Bapt. Gen. Conf., 1974. Asst. prof. theology Bethel Coll., St. Paul, 1977-81; asst. to assoc. to prof. Bibl. and systematic theology Trinity Evang. Div. Sch., Deerfield, Ill., 1981—; bd. pres. Christian Heritage Acad., Northbrook, Ill., 1983-85; sec.-treas. Inst. Advanced Christian Studies, Chgo., 1982-85, 88-90; bd. dirs. Mission: Moving Mountains, Eden Prairie, Minn., 1980-84; pres. Coun. on Bibl. Manhood and Womanhood, 1989-91; elder, Vineyard Christian Fellowship, Mundelein, Ill., 1990—. Author: The Gift of Prophecy in 1 Corinthians, 1982, The Gift of Prophecy in the New Testament and Today, 1988, The First Epistle of Peter, 1988; editor: Recovering Biblical Manhood and Womanhood, 1991. Mem. Evang. Theol. Soc., Tyndale Fellowship. Republican. Office: Trinity Evang Div Sch 2065 Half Day Rd Deerfield IL 60015 *"Jesus Christ is the same yesterday and today and forever"—he still answers prayer and heals broken lives today, and he still speaks to us through every word of the Bible. Through 20 years of academic study of the Bible, I have not found one word of it to be unworthy of my complete trust.*

GRUENBERG, RALPH EBERHARDT, minister, civil engineer; b. Newark, Feb. 1, 1930; s. Rudolph Alfred and Liddy (Schreiber) G.; m. Evelyn Mae Brower, Dec. 29, 1951; children: Betsy Ann, Ruth Lynn, James Ralph. BCE, N.J. Inst. Tech., 1951. Ordained to ministry Bapt. Ch., 1965; registered profl. engr., Mo., Maine. Pvt. practice as civil engr., 1950-62; dir. Christian edn. First Bapt. Ch., Johnson City, N.Y., 1962-65; pastor First Bapt. Ch., Belmont, N.Y., 1965-68, North Bapt. Ch., Rochester, N.Y., 1968-79, Tabernacle Bapt. Ch., Poughkeepsie, N.Y., 1979-83, Bethel Bapt. Ch., Jamestown, N.Y., 1983-88, North Bapt. Ch., Rochester, N.Y., 1988—; coord. for design and constrn. of med. clinic and pers. housing, Ndungu Kebbeh, The Gambia, West Africa, 1986-89; design and devel. coord. Theol. Edn. Ctr., Budapest, Hungary, 1990—. Mem. Assn. of Bapts. for World Evangelism (mem. adv. coun. 1987—), Empire State Fellowship of Regular Bapt. Chs. (chmn. Coun. of Ten 1990—). Office: North Bapt Ch 2052 St Paul St Rochester NY 14621 *The only things technology doesn't give us are the things that matter most.*

GRUITS, PATRICIA BEALL, minister; b. Detroit, Feb. 22, 1923; d. Harry Lee and Myrtle D. (Monville) Beall; m. J. Peter Guits, June 15, 1946; children—Peter, Harry, Patrick, William. Student Cen. Bible Coll., 1944-45, Bethesda Bible Inst., 1950-53, Anchor Bay Coll., 1945-46; BTh, Nat. Bible Coll., 1951; MDiv, Word of Faith Coll., New Orleans, 1990, DD, So. Calif. Bible Coll., 1990. Ordained to ministry Ch. of Christ, 1956; minister edn. Bethesda Missionary Temple, Detroit, 1955-83; founder, dean Minister Candidate Sch., Detroit, 1958-81; pres., founder RHEMA Internat. U.S.A. (Restoring Hope Through Ednl. and Med. Aid), Detroit, 1973-82, pres., 1984; founder, dir. RHEMA seminars, 1974—; founder RHEMA Hosp. and Clinics, St. Marc, Haiti, 1983—, RHEMA Med. Ctr., Bocozelle, Haiti, 1989—; cons. Christian edn. New Covenant Ch., Pompano Beach, Fla., 1987-88, Shekinah, Coral Springs, Fla, 1990, Christ Ch., Nashville, 1990-91. Author: (Bible stories) PeterPat Series, 1954, Understanding God, 1972; Understanding God and His Covenants, 1985; editor RHEMA Newsletter. Home: 1946 NW 97th Terr Coral Springs FL 33071 Office: RHEMA Internat Inc Box 9117 Fort Lauderdale FL 33310-9117

GRUMBACH, DAVID WILLIAM, minister; b. Kenner, La., Dec. 9, 1963; s. Karl Leopold and Sylvia Joy (Bullock) G.; m. Tammie Dereen Logan, May 17, 1986; 1 child, Joshua Logan. AA, Clarke Coll., 1985; BA, Miss. Coll., 1987; MDiv, New Orleans Bapt.Theol. Sem., 1991. Ordained to ministry So. Bapt. Conv., 1985. Dir. Outreach Williams Blvd. Bapt. Ch., Kenner, 1984; youth min. 1st Bapt. Ch., Collinsville, Miss., 1985-86; pastor 2d Bapt. Ch., Calhoun City, Miss., 1985-86, Rock Branch Bapt. Ch., Union, Miss., 1986-87, Standing Pine Bapt. Ch., Carthage, Miss., 1987—. Mem. Leake County Bapt. Assn. (asst. team dir. 1988-89). Republican.

GRUNLAN, STEPHEN ARTHUR, clergyman, educator; b. N.Y.C., Feb. 9, 1942; s. Magnus Arthur and Esther (Helliksen) G.; m. Sandra Jean Smits, Oct. 7, 1964; children—Stephen Arthur, Jaime C., Rebecca Sue. B.S., Nyack (N.Y.) Coll., 1970; M.A., Wheaton (Ill.) Coll., 1972; M.A., U. Ill., Chgo., 1976; D.Min., Luther Theol. Sem., St. Paul, 1981. Ordained to ministry Christian and Missionary Alliance, 1978; missionary Missionary Gospel Fellowship, Turlock, Calif., 1972-74; prof. Moody Bible Inst., Chgo., 1974-77, St. Paul Bible Coll., 1977-82; sr. pastor Minnetonka (Minn.) Community Ch., 1983-86, Appleton (Wis.) Alliance Ch., 1986—; lectr. U. Wis., Oshkosh, 1989—, seminar leader pastoral tng. Served with U.S. Army, 1960-65. Mem. Christian Assn. Psychol. Studies, Christian Sociol. Soc. Author: (with Marvin Mayers) Cultural Anthropology: A Christian Perspective, 1979, (with Milton Reimer) Christian Perspectives on Sociology, 1982, (with Daniel Lambrides) Healing Relationships, 1983, Marriage and the Family: A Christian Perspective, 1984, Serving with Joy, 1985, also numerous articles: book reviewer Alliance Life mag. Office: 3310 N Durkee St Appleton WI 54911

GRUNWALD, LINDA LISA, Christian education director; b. Munich, Aug. 16, 1956; (parents Am. citizens); d. Frank Herbert and Anne Hazel (Cheves) G. BA, Valparaiso U., 1980, Concordia U., 1987. cert. dir. Christian edn. and elem. edn. Dir. Christian edn. Immanuel Luth. Ch., Batavia, Ill., 1988—; mem. No. Ill. Dist. Dirs. Christian Edn. Conf. Office: Immanuel Luth Ch 950 Hart Rd Batavia IL 60510

GRUONER, DAVID FRANK, minister; b. Chgo., July 29, 1953; s. Arthur George and Doris Louise (Hentsch) G.; m. Karlene Lynn Carlson, June 2, 1979; 1 child, Rebecca Sue. AA, St. John's Coll., 1973; BA, Concordia Sr. Coll., 1975; MDiv, Concordia Theol. Sem., 1979. Pastor St. Paul's/Zion Luth. Parish, Fairview and Powhattan, Kans., 1979-85, Zion Luth. Ch., Linn, Kans., 1986—. Mem. Kans. Luth. Laymen's League (pastoral advisor 1983-84, 88—, cir. counselor 1984-85), LC-MS Synodial Conv. (cir. synodical del. Wichita, Kans. chpt. 1989), Linn Booster Club. Republican. Office: Zion Luth Ch 206 Church St Linn KS 66953-0343

GRZYBOWSKI, TERRY LEE, clergyman; b. Winona, Minn., Feb. 21, 1956; s. Edward Leo and Doris May (Bradley) G.; m. Nancy Barbara Brauer, Aug. 23, 1980; children: Timothy, Lindsey, Julie, Jennifer. BA, Concordia Coll., Ann Arbor, Mich., 1978; MDiv, Concordia Sem., St. Louis, 1982. Ordained to ministry Lutheran Ch., 1982. Pastor Our Savior Luth. Ch., Brinkley, Ark., 1982-85, Faith Luthe Ch., Forrest City, Ark., 1982-85, Shepherd at the Lake Luth. Ch., Garrison, Minn., 1985—. Home: Star Rte HC Box 192B Garrison MN 56450 Office: Shpherd on Lakes Luth Ch PO Box 44 Garrison MN 56450

GUDER, DARRELL LIKENS, seminary educator; b. Ventura, Calif., Nov. 12, 1939; s. Russell Otto and Eileen (Likens) G.; m. Linda Evans, Dec. 20, 1963 (div. 1978); children: Terrence Evan, Megan Claer; m. Judith Johnson Lewellen, Nov. 10, 1979. PhD, U. Hamburg, Fed. Republic Germany, 1965; DD (hon.), Jamestown (N.D.) Coll., 1988. Ordained to ministry, Presbyn. Ch. (U.S.A.), 1965. Student pastor Ch. of Schleswig-Holstein, Hamburg, 1964-67; minister Christian edn. First Presbyn. Ch., Hollywood, Calif., 1967-71; prof. theology and edn. Karlshohe Coll., Ludwigsburg, Fed. Republic Germany, 1971-75; dir. inst. youth ministries Young Life & Fuller Sem., Colorado Springs, Colo., 1976-85; v.p. for acad. affairs, dean of the faculty Whitworth Coll., Spokane, Wash., 1985-91; William A. Benfield Jr. prof. evangelism and global mission Louisville Presbyn. Theol. Sem., 1991—; mem. com. theol. edn. Presbyn. Ch. (U.S.A.), Louisville, 1987-91, chair, 1989-91; mem. ch. rels. com. Young Life, Colorado Springs, 1985—. Author: Be My Witnesses, 1985; translator: Foundations of Dogmatics (Weber, 2 vols.), 1980-84, God as the Mystery of the World (Jungel), 1984. Mem. Presbytery of Louisville. Democrat. Avocations: translating, travel, cooking, gardening. Home: 3033 Beals Branch Dr Louisville KY 40206 Office: Louisville Presbyn Theol Sem 1044 Alta Vista Rd Louisville KY 40205

GUDMESTAD, FERN LUCILLE, religious organization administrator; b. Seattle, Oct. 10, 1918; d. Emil Christian and Julia Ovidia (Olson) Hanson; m. Lawrence Maynard Gudmestad, Aug. 25, 1942 (dec. 1986); children: Julie Gudmestad Laudicina, Kim, Joan Gudmestad Sorenson, Jan Gudmestad Johnson. Student, Augsburg Coll., Mpls., 1938-39; BA, U. Wash., 1941; postgrad., U. Minn., 1973. Mem. Nat. Edn. Adv. Com., 1967-70; sec. for edn. southeastern dist. Am. Luth. Ch. Women, Mpls., 1967-70; dist. pres. Am. Luth. Ch. Women, 1974-77, nat. v.p., 1978-81, nat. pres., 1981-84; speaker various orgns., 1974—; interviewer oral history project Div. World Missions, Mpls., 1987-88; promoter "Woman to Woman" project, 1984; tchr., trainer nat. leadership seminars, 1978-84; chmn. adv. council Nat. Survey Attitudes, Mpls., 1979-81; speaker Am. Bible Soc., N.Y., 1967-70; planning com. Pan-Luth. Nat. Assembly, Mpls., 1988; del. World Coun. Chs., Vancouver, B.C., 1983, 1st Churchwide Assembly of Evang. Luth. Ch. Am., Chgo., 1989; trainer Stephen Ministry, 1990-91. Author: Act It Out-Improvise!, 1971, Ideas for Mission Event, 1972, 77, Happenings for Mothers and Daughters, 1975; contbr. to Lutheran Woman Today, 1989-90; columnist SCOPE mag., 1981-84. Active orgn. com. Ebenezer's Caroline Ctr. Aux., Mpls., 1986; speaker Community Resource Vol. for Mpls. Pub. Schs., 1973-75; bd. dirs. YWCA, Minot, S.D., 1950-52, Global Health Ministries Found., 1989-91. Mem. Women of Evangelical Luth. Ch. (presider constituting conv. 1987). Avocations: painting, collecting doll houses, travel. Home: 5321 Girard Ave S Minneapolis MN 55419 *My prayer is to be aware of God's presence and continuing creative activity manifesting itself* *in and through people. With that awareness I want to affirm and applaud the gifts I see in others. To me this is one way of living our the gospel.*

GUENTERT, PATRICK ROMAN, religious education educator; b. South Bend, Ind., Apr. 19, 1938; s. Roman Louis and Catherine Anne (Claffey) G.; m. M. Jane Taylor, Jan. 7, 1967; children: Andrea Catherine, Josua Patrick. BA, U. Notre Dame, 1962; MA, Aquinas Coll., 1971. Dir. religious edn. St. Pius X Parish, Grandville, Mich., 1970-73, St. Mary Magdalen Parish, Kentwood, Mich., 1973-81, Diocese of Great Falls (Mont.)-Billings, 1981-87, Archdiocese of San Francisco, 1987—. Mem. Nat. Conf. Diocesan Dirs. of Religious Edn. (bd. dirs. 1984-86, 91—), Calif. Cath. Conf. Dirs. of Catechatical Ministry. Office: Archdiocese San Francisco 443 Church St San Francisco CA 94114

GUENTHER, ALLEN ROBERT, minister, religious educator; b. Steinbach, Man., Can., Sept. 13, 1938; s. John Allen and Anna (Braun) G.; m. Anne Wall, Aug. 16, 1962; children: Ronald Allen, Barry Mark, Michael Bruce. ThB, Mennonite Brethren Bible Coll., Man., 1962; BA, U.B.C., Can., 1963; MA, Wheaton Grad. Sch. Theology, 1967; MDiv, Gordon-Conwell Sch. Theology, 1969; MA, U. Toronto, Ont., Can., 1971, PhD, 1978. Ordained to ministry Mennonite Brethren Ch. Gen. Conf., 1981. Instr. Mennonite Brethren Bible Inst., Coaldale, Alta., 1962-65; pastor Lakeview Mennonite Brethren Ch., Lethbridge, Alta., 1963-65; instr., dean of students Mennonite Brethren Bible Coll., Winnipeg, Man., 1967-70, asst. prof. Old Testament, 1975-81; pastor Mennonite Brethren Ch., Toronto, 1971-74; assoc. prof. Old Testament Mennonite Brethren Bible. Sem., Fresno, Calif., 1981, prof. Old Testament, 1981—; mem. editorial coun. Believer's Ch. Bible Commentary, Scottsdale, Pa., 1980-86; chmn. bd. pastoral ministries Butler Mennonite Brethren Ch., Fresno, 1983-85, moderator, 1991—. Editor Direction, 1981-89. Coach Little League, Sunnysideand Fresno, 1982-83; mem. Bd. of Reference and Counsel Pacific Dist. Mennonite Brethren, 1985—; pres. Valley Parkinson's Support Group, 1985—. Fellow Can. Council, 1971-73, Gordon-Conwell Div. Sch., 1967, Govt. Ont. Office: Mennonite Brethren Bibl Sem 4824 E Butler Ave Fresno CA 93727

GUENTHER, TIMOTHY ERIC, lay worker; b. Mansfield, Ohio, Feb. 7, 1955; s. Robert Lawrence and Bette Louise (Thompson) G.; m. Elizabeth Ann Tushingham, May 16, 1987. MusB with distinction, Eastman Sch. Music, 1977, postgrad., 1980—; MusM, U. Ala., 1979. Cert. lay profl. Luth. Ch. Am., 1987. Organist Calvary United Ch. Christ, Crestline, Ohio, 1970-72, St. Luke's Luth. Ch., Mansfield, Ohio, 1972-73; dir. music Trinity Emmanuel Luth. Ch., Rochester, N.Y., 1974-77; organist Christ Episcopal Ch., Tuscaloosa, Ala., 1977-79; organist, choirmaster First Bapt. Ch., Penfield, N.Y., 1979-80; dir. music Reformation Luth. Ch., Rochester, N.Y., 1980-89, First English Luth. Ch., Mansfield, Ohio, 1989—; mem. conf. coun. Mansfield/Ashland Conf., Evang. Luth. Ch. Am., 1990—, mem. worship subcom. Northeastern Ohio synod, Akron, 1990—, sr. examing team mem. Upstate N.Y. synod, Syracuse, 1988-89. Mem. Assn. Luth. Ch. Musicians, Am. Guild Organists (assoc., choirmaster 1980, exec. com. 1990—, S. Lewis Elmer award 1980), Hymn Soc. U.S. and Can., Am. Choral Dirs. Assn., Choristers Guild, Phi Mu Alpha Sinfonia (chpt. pres. 1975-76, chpt. treas. 1974-75). Home: 428 Shepard Rd Mansfield OH 44907-1130 Office: First English Luth Ch 53 Park Ave W Mansfield OH 44902-1698

GUENZEL, LAWRENCE MARTIN, minister; b. Phila., Apr. 18, 1947; s. Rudolph Andrew and Marion Catherine (Williams) G.; m. Virginia Lee Valerio, June 27, 1970; 1 child, Rebecca Christine. Cert., Concordia Jr. Coll., Bronxville, N.Y., 1967; BA, Concordia Coll., Ft. Wayne, Ind., 1970; MDiv., Concordia Theol. Sem., St. Louis, 1973. Ordained to ministry Luth. Ch.-Mo. Synod, 1973. Pastor Alpha Luth. Ch. of Deaf, Rochester, N.Y., 1973-77, St. Stephen Luth. Ch., Mifflintown, Pa., 1977-82; assoc. pastor Trinity Luth. Ch., Lansdale, Pa., 1982—; Protestant chaplain N.Y. Sch. for Deaf, Rome, 1973-77, Nat. Tech. Inst. for Deaf, Rochester Sch. for Deaf, 1973-77. Bd. dirs. North Pa. YMCA, 1983-86, North Pa. United Way, 1990—, North Penn Sr. Ctr., 1990—. Office: Trinity Luth Ch 1000 W Main St Lansdale PA 19446

GUERRA SORIA, ARMANDO, bishop. Bishop of Guatemala Episcopal Ch., Guatemala City. Office: Episcopal Ch, Avda, Castellana 40-06, Zona 8, Guatemala City Guatemala*

GUERRI, SERGIO CARDINAL, Vatican City official; b. Tarquinia, Italy, Dec. 25, 1905. Ordained priest Roman Cath. Ch., Mar. 30, 1929; titular archbishop of Trevi, from 1969; elevated to Sacred Coll. Cardinals, 1969; pro-pres. Congregation Pontifical Comm. for State of Vatican City; mem. Congregation Oriental Chs., Congregation Evangelization of Peoples. Address: Vatican City Vatican City

GUESS, DAVID ELWOOD, minister; b. Canton, Ohio, May 12, 1960; s. David Elwood and Juanita Jewell (Boggess) G.; m. Marcy L. Troutman, July 13, 1991. BS, Gulf Coast Bible Coll., Houston, 1982. Ordained to ministry Ch. of God, 1986. Minister of youth First Ch. of God, Nowata, Okla., 1982-83; assoc. pastor First Ch. of God, Cortland, Ohio, 1983-85; pastor First Ch. of God, Greenville, Pa., 1986-90; min. Christian edn. youth outreach, discipleship First Ch. of God, Kittanning, Pa., 1990—; vice chmn. WPA State Youth Agy., Emlenton, Pa., 1986—, mem. exec. coun., 1990—. Bd. dirs. Reg. Pregnancy Ctr., Greenville, 1990; clergy chmn. United Way, Greenville, 1986, 89; spiritual care coord. Hospice Regional Hosp., Greenville, 1988-91; advisor Reg. Hosp. Wellness Ctr., Greenville, 1990; mem. Greenville Sesquicentennial Commn., 1988-89. Home: 340 N Water St Kittanning PA 16201

GUEST, DEAN, evangelist; b. Jewitt, Tex., Aug. 8, 1929; d. Aubrey L. Carlisle and Inez Davis Skinner; m. John E. Guest, Apr. 11, 1952; children: Kelly Guest Hendrickson, Mark. BRE, Trinity Theol. Sem., 1988, M in Ministry summa cum laude, 1989. Ordained to ministry, 1976. Min., dir. Luminaire Internat. Ministry, 1972-77; co-pastor Maumelle Valley Christian Ctr., Perryville, Ark., 1979-80; pastor, adminstr. Twin Wells Indian Sch., Holbrook, Ariz., 1980-84; evangelist Dean Guest Ministries, Converse, Tex., 1984—; editor, pub. Dove Press; preacher Leroy (Tex.) Ch., 1986-88. Author: Tabernacle: A Study Guide, 1975, As The Wind Blows, 1977, The Barren Fig Tree, 1988, Hem of His Garment, 1989, Soar Like an Eagle, 1989, Women in the Church, 1991, The Other Side of Sex, 1991.. Office: Dean Guest Ministries 7326 Mystery Ridge Converse TX 78109

GUEST, JOHN, evangelist; b. Oxford, Eng., July 26, 1936; came to U.S., 1964.; s. Jack Guest and Hazel Connolly; m. Kathleen Heggar, 1967; children: Carrie Ann, Chelsea, Sarah. BDiv, Trinity Coll., Bristol, Eng., 1964; Doctorate (hon.), Geneva Coll., 1978, Grove City (Pa.) Coll., 1979. Ordained to ministry Ch. of Eng., 1961. Youth min. St. Stephens Episcopal Ch., Sewickley, Pa., 1968-71, sr. rector, 1971-90; evangelist John Guest Evangelistic Team, Sewickley, Pa., 1990—; condr. youth portion Billy Graham Crusade, Madison Sq. Garden, N.Y.C., 1969; bd. dirs. Ea. Coll. and Sem., Phila.; founder Coalition for Christian Outreach, 1970; co-founder Trinity Episcopal Sch. for Ministry, 1976; mem. bd. advisors Episcopalians United, 1987; mem. Lausanne Com. for World Evangelism; guest speaker Wheaton and Calvin Colls., Columbia Bible Coll., others; broadcaster daily radio program New Life in Christ, WPIT-FM, Pitts., 1983—. Author: In Search of Certainty, 1983, Only a Prayer Away, 1985, Knowing You Are Loved, 1987, This World Is Not My Home, 1988, Go for It!, 1988, Jeremiah/Lamentations Commentary, 1988. Avocation: golf. Office: John Guest Evangelistic Team 435 Broad St Sewickley PA 15143

GUETTGEMANNS, ERHARDT, biblical studies educator; b. Rheyolt, Germany, Mar. 6, 1935; s. Georg and Anna (Pauüluüssan) G.; m. Zsoófia Éva Toüroük, Oct. 21, 1981. ThD in Theology, U. Bonn, Bonn, Fed. Republic Germany, 1963. Prof. U. Bonn, 1980—; cons. Deutsche Gesellschaft fuür Semiotik, 1978. Author several books; contbr. essays to profl. jours. Avocations: photography, magic. Home: Dechant Kreiten Str 8, D 5309 Meckenheim Federal Republic of Germany Office: U Bonn, Evang Theol Seminar, D 5300 Bonn 1, Federal Republic of Germany

GUFFEY, LEO WESLEY, priest; b. Lewisburg, Pa., Aug. 4, 1955; s. Leo Wesley and Yvonne Carole (Mazeall) G. BA in Fgn. Langs., Pacific Coll., 1980; BA in Sacred Music, Mission Bible Inst., L.A., 1982; ThM, Stanton U., 1988, PhD, 1988. Spiritual dir. Hospice of St. John, Denver, 1983-84; priest Diocese of N.Y., Bklyn., 1984-88, Old Cath. Diocese of Chgo., 1988—. Educator Plymouth (Pa.) Pub. Libr., 1985—. With U.S. Army, 1980-82. Nominated for Humanitarian of Yr. award, The Times Leader, Wilkes-Barre, Pa., 1986. Mem. Nat. Chaplains Assn. (regional dir. 1983, adv. bd. dirs. 1983—, Legion of Honor award 1984), Pa. Soc. Advancement of the Deaf, Am. Assn. Religious Counselors, Alpha Psi Omega. Democrat. Avocations: organ, piano, accordion, tennis, reading. Home and Office: Oratory of St Casimir 50 Payne Ave Kingston PA 18704

GUFFIN, GILBERT L., clergyman, educator; b. nr. Marietta, Ga., Aug. 5, 1906; s. William Thomas and Nora (Eubanks) G.; m. Lorene Parrish, Aug. 23, 1930; children: Gilbert Truett, Orville Thomas. A.B., Mercer U., 1930, D.D., 1955; B.D., Eastern Bapt. Theol. Sem., 1935; Th.M., 1938, Th.D., 1941; LL.D., Atlanta Law Sch., 1951; L.H.D., Eastern Coll., 1972. Ordained to ministry Bapt. Ch., 1927; prin. Jr. High Sch., Mabelton, Ga., 1927-28, Elizabeth Jr. High Sch., Marietta, 1930-33; pastor various chs. in Ga., 1927-33; pastor First Bapt. Ch., Merchantville, N.J., 1935-42, Jasper, Ala., 1942-47; dean Bapt. Seminar, Walker Coll., 1942-47; dir. extension div. Christian tng. Howard Coll. (now Samford U.), Birmingham, 1947-49; dean of religion, chmn. extension div. Howard Coll. (now Samford U.), 1961-71, dean emeritus, 1971—; pres. Eastern Bapt. Theol. Sem., Phila., 1950-61, trustee, 1941-49, 1961-82, bd. dir. emeritus, 1982; pres. Eastern Coll., 1951-61, trustee, 1961-82, emeritus, 1982—; Layne lectr. New Orleans Bapt. Theol. Sem., 1958; former mem. bd. lectrs. Freedom's Found.; bd. dirs. Ala. Bapt. Conv., 1942- 47, mem. exec. com., 1945-47, chmn. Christian life and public affairs commn., 1974-82; exec. bd. N.J. Bapt. Conv., 1938-42; bd. dirs. Birmingham Council of Christian Edn., 1970-73, 75, now life mem.; bd. dirs. Ala. Baptist Ministers Benefit Soc., 1974-88, The Lord's Day Alliance U.S., 1976—; bd. advisers Bible Land Tours Assn., 1956-57; bd. dirs. Pa. Theol. Sem. Found., Inc., 1955-61; bd. dirs. Watchman-Examiner Found., N.Y., 1960-71; trustee Ala. Temperance League (now Ala. Christian Action Program), 1943-49, 61-89, hon., 1989—; bd. mgrs. Council Missionary Coop., Am. Bapt. Conv., 1953-61, pres. sem. presidents and deans, 1958-59; mem. Guatemala-Ala. Partners of Alliance, 1969-72; messenger Bapt. World Alliance, Atlanta, 1939, Copenhagen, 1947, Cleve., 1950, London, 1955, Rio de Jenario, 1960, Miami, 1965, Tokyo, 1970; tours in 45 countries; condr. European tours, 1947, Holy Land tour, 1955, 63, Around-the-World tour, 1970. Author: How To Run A Church, 1948, Called of God, 1951, Pastor and Church, 1955, El Pastor La Iglesia, 1955, The Gospel in Isaiah, 1968, El Evangelio En Isaias, 1968, The Bible: God's Missionary Message to Man, vol. I, 1973, vol. II, 1974; Editor: Walker Bapt. Herald, 1944-47, What God Hath Wrought, 1960; Writer: Monthly Bible Studies for, Royal Service, 1964-68; co-author: The Pentateuch: Joshua to Malichi; Contbr. to: religious publs. Life and Work Ann, 1966-67, 67-68, for Bapt. Sun. Sch. bd. So. Bapt. Conv. Recipient Freedoms Found. awards, 1960, 61; named Hon. Lt. Col. Aide-de-Camp, Ala. State Militia, 1986. Mem. Greater Birmingham Pastors' Assn. (exec. com. 1962-63, 67-72, 82-83), Birmingham Bapt. Assn. (exec. bd.), Birmingham Bpt. Assn. (chmn. com. on Christian life and pub. affairs 1981-85), Ala. Writer's Conclave, Birmingham-Jefferson Hist. Soc., Omicron Delta Kappa. Lodges: Masons, Rotary (past pres.). Originator Howard Plan extensive edn. Home: Kirkwood by the River 3605 Ratliff Rd Box 70 Birmingham AL 35210 *Life is a trust given to each of us, a trust to be administered with accountability to the Giver. To use it only for self is to waste it. To invest it for the good of humanity - by relieving suffering, by promoting virtue, by strengthening the home, itself the keystone of society and of civilization, and by encouraging reverence toward God - is both to preserve it and to transform it into eternal riches.*

GUHL, RICHARD DOEHRING, minister; b. Stamford, Conn., Feb. 5, 1949; s. John Lazar and Corinne Elizabeth (Doehring) G.; m. Judith Ann Frerk, Aug. 26, 1972; children: Marta Joy, Erik William. BA, Drew U., 1972; MDiv, Yale Div. Sch., 1975. Ordained to ministry United Ch. of Christ, 1975. Pastor St. John's United Ch. of Christ, Larimer, Pa., 1975-88, Coopersburg, Pa., 1988—; chair Penn West Conf. Peace and Justice Task Force, Greensburg, 1980-88; del. Gen. Synod. United Ch. of Christ, Cleve., 1987; chair Penn Northeast Conf. Ch. in Soc. Div., Palmerton, Pa., 1990-91, Hunger Task Force, 1988-91, Long-range Planning Com., 1989-91. Bd. dirs. Westmoreland County Food Bank, Greensburg, 1981-88, pres. 1986-88; mem. Westmoreland County Emergency Food and Shelter Allocation Bd., 1983-88, Westmoreland County Children's Bur. Adv. Bd., 1985-88. Democrat. Home: 1450 S Jefferson Allentown PA 18103 Office: St John's United Ch Christ 538 E Thomas Coopersburg PA 18036

GUHSE, MARY ANN, church school director; b. Freeport, Ill., Apr. 28, 1953; d. Adlai Francis and DeVere Joy (Shaffer) Hiteman; m. George Lewis Guhse Jr., Jan. 4, 1975; 1 child, Joshua George. BA in Psychology, U. N.Mex., 1975; postgrad. early childhood edn., Va. Commonwealth U., 1987. Tchr. Amity Day Care, Freeport, 1976, substitute tchr., 1977-78; child care coordinator Rockford (Ill.) Family Care Ctr., 1979; instr. family life, supr. child care YWCA, Lancaster, Pa., 1979-81; tchr. First Bapt. Ch., Richmond, Va., 1982—, coordinator curriculum and staff, 1984—; adj. instr. J. Sargeant Reynolds Community Coll., Richmond, 1986—; workshop leader early childhood groups, 1979—. Editor: (newsletter) Small Talk. Mem. Nat. Assn. for Edn. of Young Children, So. Assn. on Children Under Six, Va. Assn. for Early Childhood Edn., Richmond Area Assn. for Edn. of Young Children (treas. 1985—). Methodist. Avocations: sailing, biking, reading. Home: 9411 Greenford Dr Richmond VA 23229 Office: First Bapt Ch Monument & Blvd Richmond VA 23220

GUIDO, MICHAEL ANTHONY, evangelist; b. Lorain, Ohio, Jan. 30, 1915; s. Mike and Julia (DePalma) G.; m. Audrey Forehand, Nov. 25, 1943. Student, Moody Bible Inst., Chgo., 1933-35. Ordained to ministry So. Bapt. Conv., 1939. Min. youth and music lst Presbyn. Ch., Sebring, Fla., 1936-38, lst Bapt. Ch., Lake Charles, La., 1939; evangelist Moody Bible Inst., 1940-50; founder, pres., speaker Guido Evangelistic Assn., Metter, Ga., 1950—; writer, speaker daily telecast A Seed from the Sower, 1972—, daily broadcaster The Sower, A Seed from the Sower, Seeds from the Sower, Your Favorite Ten, 1957—. Author: (autobiography) Seeds from the Sower, 1990; editor Sowing and Reaping mag., 1957—; daily newspaper columnist Seeds from the Sower, 1957—. Named Alumnus of Yr., Moody Bible Inst., 1982, Citizen of Yr., Kiwanis Club, Metter, 1982. Home: PO Box 508 Metter GA 30439 Office: 600 N Lewis St Metter GA 30439 *Life to me is loving God and serving Him by finding a need and supplying it, and searching for a lost soul and bringing that one home to God.*

GUIDON, PATRICK, academic administrator. Pres. Oblate Sch. Theol., San Antonio. Office: Oblate Sch Theol Office of the President 285 Oblate Dr San Antonio TX 78216*

GUILBEAU, JERRY BOB, religion educator; b. Carencro, La., Feb. 22, 1935; s. Robert Edward and Enola Blanch (Broussard) G.; m. Loula Marie Thibodeaux, June 12, 1971; children: Marie, Mark, David, Paul, Timothy, Theresa. BA, U. So. La., 1957; MA, Pepperdine U., 1978. Cert. catechist/master catechist, 1991. Coord. religious edn. Carencro Cath. Sch., 1989—. With U.S. Army, 1957-85. Democrat. Home: 6708 N University Ave Carencro LA 70520 Office: Carencro Catholic School 200 W St Peter St Carencro LA 70520

GUILD-DONOVAN, ANNE LOUISE, chaplain; b. Oradell, N.J., Apr. 27, 1932; d. Russell Mansfield and Katherine Louise (Clerke) Guild; m. James Joseph Moshier, Aug. 30, 1952 (div. 1976); children: Alice M. Doxsey, Christine Weissinger, James Russell Moshier; m. Hugh William Donovan, Apr. 21, 1990. AA, Rockland Community Coll., Suffern, N.Y., 1975; BA with honors, Ramapo Coll. N.J., 1976; MDiv, Union Theol. Sem., N.Y.C., 1979; DMin, Colgate Rochester Divinity Sch, 1987. Ordained to ministry Ref. Ch. in Am., 1979. Chaplain Central Islip (N.Y.) Psychiat. Ctr., 1979-80; interim minister United Meth. Ch., Islip, N.Y., 1980; adminstrv. asst. Christianity & Crisis, N.Y.C., 1981; protestant chaplain Rochester (N.Y.) Psychiat. Ctr., 1982—. Editor (monthly newsletter) Families & Friends of Mentally Ill, 1986—. Mem. N.Y. State Assn. Chaplains (v.p.), Assn. Mental Health Clergy, N.Y. State Chaplains' Assn. (Interfaith). Office: Rochester Psychiat Ctr 1600 South Ave Rochester NY 14620 *Life, when it is good, is all too short. Jesus came that we might have life in abundance. Therefore, we should strive to live each day giving and receiving love in His name.*

GUILLERMIN, ARMAND PIERRE, university administrator; b. Buffalo, Nov. 23, 1936; s. Larry Rossolet and Apphia Adele (Gaskin) G.; m. Helen Louanne Rupp, May 27, 1959; children: Michelle, Lisa. BA, Bob Jones U., 1958, MA, 1960; postgrad., U. Va., Cen. Mich. U.; diploma, Harvard U. Inst Edn. Mgmt., 1983; LLD (hon.), Christian Heritage Coll., 1985; EdD, Nova U., 1986. Dean adminstrn. So. Meth. Coll., Orangeburg, S.C., 1963-65, pres., 1965-67; ednl. mgmt. cons., 1967-73; exec. v.p. Liberty U., Lynchburg, 1973-75, pres., 1975—; advisor Tel Aviv U., 1979-80; mem. Pres.'s Nat. Adv. Coun. on Ednl. Rsch. and Improvement, 1991—. Bd. dirs. Lynchburg Christian Acad., 1975—, United Way, Lynchburg, 1987-90, NCCJ, Lynchburg, 1986-89. Named Bicentennial Educator, Bicentennial Commn. Lynchburg, 1986. Mem. Va. State Council Higher Edn. (pvt. coll. adv. council 1975—), Am. Assn. Pres. Colls. and Univs., Assn. Evang. Sem. Pres., Am. Mgmt. Assn., Assn. Christian Schs. Internat. (bd. dirs. 1986—), Greater Lynchburg C. of C. (bd. dirs. 1987-90), Kappa Delta Pi. Lodge: Rotary (bd. dirs. Lynchburg 1987-91). Office: Liberty U PO Box 20000 Lynchburg VA 24506

GUILLORY, CURTIS J., bishop; b. Mallet, La., Sept. 1, 1943. Student, Divine Word Coll., Chgo. Theol. Union, Creighton U. ordained priest Roman Cath. Ch., Dec. 16, 1972. Ordained titular bishop of Stagno and Aux. Bishop of Galveston-Houston, 1988. Office: Chancery Office 1700 San Jacinto St Houston TX 77002*

GUINAN, MICHAEL DAMON, priest, religion educator; b. Cin., Feb. 16, 1939; s. Henry Francis and Ursula Grace (Maggini) G. BA, San Luis Rey (Calif.) Coll., 1961; STB, Old Mission Theol., Santa Barbara, Calif., 1965; STL, Cath. U. Am., Washington, 1967, MA, 1970, PhD, 1972. Ordained priest Roman Cath. Ch., 1964. Pastoral asst. St. Mary's Parish, Stockton, Calif., 1965-66; prof. theology Franciscan Sch. Theology, Berkeley, Calif., 1972—. Author: Pentateuch, 1990, (commentaries) JOB, 1986, Lamentations, 1990. Mem. Nat. Assn. Profs. Hebrew, Soc. Bibl. Lit., Cath. Bibl. Assn. (O.T. book rev. editor Cath. Bibl. Quar., 1984-90). Home: 1708 Euclid Ave #8 Berkeley CA 94709 Office: Franciscan Sch Theology 1712 Euclid Ave Berkeley CA 94709

GUINOTTE, HENRY PAUL, clergyman; b. Omaha, June 16, 1930; s. Henry P. and Pearl (Eisele) G.; m. Martha Jean Marling, June 7, 1953; children: Diana, Henry. BA, Hastings Coll., 1953; BD, U. Dubuque, 1956. Ordained to ministry United Presbyn. Ch. in U.S.A., 1956. Pastor Divide Center, Lyons, Nebr., 1955-60, Presbyn. Ch., Craig, Nebr., 1955-60, Neola (Iowa) Presbyn. Ch., 1960-66, Cedar Bluffs (Nebr.) Presbyn. Ch., 1966-72, United Protestant Ch., Palmer, Alaska, 1972-90; dir. youth caravans, Nebr. and Alaska, 1963-74; mem. NW mission evangelism com. Synod of Alaska, 1975—; mem. camp and conf. com. Synod of Iowa,1962-66; dir. Alaska youth teams Wellington Ch. Scotland, Glasgow, 1983-91. Organizer, tchr., dir. vol. rescue squads Neola Fire Dept., 1961-66, Cedar Bluffs Fire Dept., 1967-72; mem. Palmer City Coun., 1991. Named Lion of Yr., 1976; recipient joint resolution of commendation Alaska Legislature, 1986, Excellency in Ministry award Dubuque Sem., 1991. Mem. Rotary (Paul Harris fellow 1990). Address: PO Box 579 Palmer AK 99645

GUIZAR, RICARDO DIAZ, clergyman; b. Mexico City, Feb. 26, 1933; s. Antonio Barragan Guizar and Elena Pico (deGuizar) Diaz. Classic Letters and Scis. B., Instituto Angelo Secchi, Rome, 1951; Philosophy Licentiate, Pontificia Universita Gregoriana, Rome, 1954, Div. Licentiate, 1959. Ordained priest Roman Catholic Ch., 1958, bishop, 1970. Pvt. sec. Archbishop of Puebla, Mex., 1960-63; prof. theology and philosophy Seminario Palafoxiano, Puebla, Mex., 1960-70, dir. spirit, 1963-70; aux. bishop Archdiocese of Puebla, Mex., 1970-78, Diocese of Aguascalientes, Mex., 1978-84; bishop Diocese of Atlacomulco, Mex., 1984—; pres. Liturgy, Holy Musics and Arts Archdiocesan Commn. Puebla, 1970-78; advisor Cursillos de Cristiandad, Puebla, 1970-78, Diocesan Council for Laical Apostolate, Puebla, 1971-78; pres. Bishops Commn. Sems. and Vocations, Mex., 1985—. Contbr. articles to The New Catholic Ency., Revista Eclesiastica de Puebla. Contbr. Antologia Conmemorativa 450 deg. Aniversario de la Arquidiocesis de Puebla, 1977. Home: Gabriel Mancera 336, Mexico City 03100, Mexico Office: Hidalgo Sur 1, Apartado Postal 22, Atlacomulco, Estado de Mexico 50450, Mexico *I feel joyous realizing how many find now in the catholic faith the key to face the life and society challenges in the actual world. I think they deserve to find the support they need to live it intensely.*

GULBINOWICZ, HENRYK ROMAN CARDINAL, cardinal; b. Wilno, Poland, Oct. 17, 1928; s. Antoni and Waleria (Gajewska) G. Grad. Theol. Sem. Bialystok, Poland; Dr.Theology, Catholic U., Lublin, Poland. Ordained priest Roman Catholic Ch., 1950, consecrated bishop, 1970, elevated to cardinal, 1985. Titular bishop, apostolic adminstr. Archdiocese of Bialystok, 1970-76, archbishop of Wroclaw, Poland, 1976—, elevated to Sacred Coll. of Cardinals, 1985. Mem. Congregation for Eastern Churches, Congregation Clergy Affairs.

GULBIS, MODRIS KARLIS, minister; b. Tervete, Latvia, Jan. 11, 1927; came to U.S., 1950; s. Peteris and Zinaida (Zebauers) G.; m. Aina Garjanis, Dec. 23, 1950; children: Vitauts, Valda, Ingrida, Peteris. MDiv, Cen. Luth. Sem., Fremont, Nebr., 1953; MTh, Luth. Sem., St. Paul, 1972; D of Ministry, Luther Seminary, St. Paul, Minn., 1982. Ordained to ministry United Luth. Ch. in Am., 1953. Mission developer United Luth. Ch. in America, Whitehorse, Can., 1959-61; pastor Trinity Luth. Ch., Whitehorse, Can., 1961-66, Lundar Luth. Ch., Can., 1966-69; youth and edn. pastor Latvian Evangel. Luth. Ch., Mpls., 1969-72; pastor Christ Latvian Luth. Ch., Mpls., 1972. Author: Latvian Bible Handbook, five edits., 1975, Pardomu Bridi, 1985, Seras Pardzivojot, 1987; editor: Desmit Rosmes Gadi, 1982. Home: 4025 Chowen Ave S Minneapolis MN 55410

GULIANO, ALEXANDRA, clergywoman; b. Youngstown, Ohio, May 21, 1952; d. Neil Nicholas and Mary Jane (Lateana) G. BS in Edn., Ohio State U., 1973; MA in Theology, U. Notre Dame, 1985; cert spirituality, Holy Names Coll., Oakland, Calif., 1988. Tchr. music Lakeview Local Schs., Cortland, Ohio, 1974-76, Diocese of Kansas City, Mo., 1976-77; pastoral assoc., dir. worship Nativity Parish, Green Bay, Wis., 1979-86; dir. music ministries St. Augustine Parish, Oakland, Calif., 1987-88; on-call chaplain St. Mary's Hosp. Med. Ctr., Green Bay, 1988—; instr. Silver Lake Coll., Manitowoc, Wis., 1988—; field advocate Marriage Tribunal, Green Bay, 1988—. Com. mem. United Way Nominating Com., Green Bay, 1985-86, Clergy Com. for YMCA, Green Bay, 1986. Mem. Assn. Pastoral Assocs., Nat. Pastoral Musicians, Nat. Assn. Religious Women, Music Educator's Nat. Conf., RCIA Forum. Democrat. Roman Catholic. Avocations: hiking, skiing, racquetball, writing, music, reading, cooking. Home: 1021 1/2 Winford Ave Green Bay WI 54303

GULLEY, FRANK, religion educator; b. Lexington, Ky., Jan. 28, 1930; s. Frank and Agnes Opal (Stapp) G.; m. Anne Chastain Hoover, Aug. 24, 1957; children: Frank Stuart, Elizabeth Page. BA, U. Ky., 1952; BD, Emory U., 1955; PhD, Vanderbilt U., 1961. Ordained to ministry as elder United Meth. Ch., 1956. Instr., asst. to dean Vanderbilt Div. Sch., Nashville, 1960-61, libr. asst., prof. religion and ch. history, 1966-69, assoc. dean, assoc. prof. ch. history, 1969—; bd. dirs. United Protestant Edn. Bd., Urbana, Ill., 1961-62; dean, acting pres. Tenn. Wesleyan Coll., Athens, 1962-66. Mem. Am. Soc. Ch. History. Democrat. Home: 904 Robertson Acad Rd Nashville TN 37220 Office: Vanderbilt Univ Div Sch Nashville TN 37240

GULLEY, NORMAN RICHARD, theologian, educator; b. Stalbans, Herts, Eng., Sept. 22, 1933; came to U.S., 1954; s. James Richard and Norah Ellen (Wallis) G.; m. Leona Grace Minchin, June 9, 1958; children: John, Sharon, James, Sonya. BA, So. Missionary Coll., 1955; MA, Potomac U., 1956; MDiv, Seventh-day Adventist Theol. Sem., 1958; PhD, U. Edinburgh, Scotland, 1970. Tchr. Madison Acad., Nashville, 1958-60; instr. history Madison Coll., Nashville, 1958-60, chmn. religion dept., 1960-62; prof. theology Japan Missionary Coll., Tokyo, 1962-64, chmn. theology dept., 1964-69; prof. systematic theology Philippine Union Coll. Grad. Sch., Manila, 1971-73, chmn. grad. theology dept., 1973-78; acad. dean Seventh-day Adventist Theol. Sem., Manila, 1973-78; prof. systematic theology So. Coll., Chattanooga, 1978—. Author: Final Events on Planet Earth, Christ Our Substitute, Is the Majority Moral?, The Time of the End, The Holy Spirit, Christ's All-Atoning Sacrifice; contbg. author: Anchor Bible Dictionary;

contbr. articles to profl. jours. Mem. Soc. Bibl. Lit., Am. Acad. Religion, Evang. Theol. Soc., Adventist Theol. Soc. (exec. sec. 1989-91). Avocations: ham radio operator, painting, boating, gardening. Home: PO Box 192 Collegedale TN 37315

GUM, DONALD FRANCIS, clinical chaplain; b. Burlington, N.C., Nov. 24, 1946; s. Roy Morgan and Ruby Mae (Walters) Gumm; m. Brenda Faye Sawyer, Dec. 20, 1964; chidlren: Tyra Ann, Donald Mark. BA, Greensboro (N.C.) Coll., 1971; MDiv, Duke U., 1974. Cert. pastoral counselor, marriage and family therapist, chaplain. Dir. counseling svcs. Greensboro Coll., 1974-77; dir. pastoral care Wesley Long Community Hosp., Greensboro, 1977-88, Alamance Health System, Burlington, N.C., 1988—; cons. Coll. of Chaplains, Chgo., 1985—. Bd. dirs. Am. Protestant Hosp. Assn., Chgo., 1988-90. With U.S. Army, 1964-67, Korea. Fellow Coll. of Chaplains (pres. 1991—, Disting. Svc. award 1987); mem. N.C. Chaplains Assn. (pres. 1980-82), Assn. for Clin. Pastoral Edn., Am. Assn. Pastoral Counselors, Am. Assn. Marriage and Family Therapists. Methodist. Avocations: golf, reading. Office: Alamance Health Svcs PO Box 202 Burlington NC 27216

GUMBLETON, THOMAS J., bishop; b. Detroit, Jan. 26, 1930. Student, St. John Provincial Sem., Mich., Pontifical Lateran U., Rome. Ordained priest Roman Catholic Ch. 1956. Ordained titular bishop Ululi and aux. bishop Detroit, 1968—. Office: Chancery Office 1234 Washington Blvd Detroit MI 48226

GUMS, REUBEN HENRY, religious organization executive; b. Cleveland, N.D., Oct. 16, 1927; s. Fredrick and Kathrine (Vossler) G.; m. Frances Lorene Seifert, Mar. 9, 1956 (dec. 1970). BA, North Cen. Coll., Naperville, Ill., 1949; MDiv, Evang. Theol. Sem., 1952; STM, Union Theol. Sem., 1959. Ordained to ministry Evang. United Brethren Ch., 1952. Dir. radio and audio-visual commn. Philippine Fedn. Christian Chs., Manila, 1953-58; dir. radio and TV, Ch. Fedn. Greater Chgo., 1959-68, Coun. of Chs., N.Y.C., 1968-74; exec. dir. Tri-State Media Ministry, United Meth. Ch., N.Y.C., 1974—, Laymen's Nat. Bible Assn., N.Y.C., 1983—; chmn. communications com. N.Y. Conf. United Meth. Ch., 1975-79; dir., mem. exec. com. communications com. Nat. Coun. of Chs., 1960-72. Producer TV and radio programs and series on religious themes, 1953—; producer, host The Interfaith Connection, Sta. WYNY, 1973—. Mem. alumni bd. Union Theol. Sem., N.Y.C., 1964-74; bd. dirs., acting pres. Exodus House, Inc., N.Y.C., 1984-85. Mem. NATAS (bd. govs. 1976-80, Gov.'s citation 1980), Assn. Regional Religious Communicators (founder, pres. 1965-69). Democrat. Home: 224 W 75th St New York NY 10023 Office: Laymen's Nat Bible Assn 475 Riverside Dr Ste 439 New York NY 10115-0122

GUNDERSEN, BEVERLEY JOYCE, writer; b. Newton, Iowa, Jan. 9, 1936; d. Le Roy and Laura La Velma (Beal) Veenstra; m. Thomas Karl Gundersen, June 16, 1956; children: Bethann Carol, Timothy John, April Joy. Author: Junior Electives, Book 4, 1991, Book 3, 1991, Book 2, 1991, Book 1, 1991, Great Ideas for Teachers, 1991, Award Certificates for Special Achievement, 1991, Award Certificates for Children's Ministries, 1991, Window to India, 1990, Bible Stories at Your Fingertips, 1990, Let the Games Begin, 1989, King's Kids Calendar, 1989, Bible Buddies Calendar, 1989, Award Certificates for Almost All Occasions, 1989, Award Certificates for Bible Memory, 1989, Award Certificates with Bible Verses, 1989, Window to Japan, 1988, Window to Mexico, 1988, You Are There, New Testament, 1988, You Are There, Old Testament, 1988, Window to Alaska, 1988, Jesus Loves the Children of the World, 1988, Memory Verse Bulletin Boards, 1988, Egg-citing Egg Carton Games, 1987; co-author: Junior Electives: Problems in Society, Making Choices, Friendship, My Body, Divorce, Occult, Substance Abuse, Communicating with Others, Who Is Jesus?, Families, Environment, Sports and Competition, 1991. Mem. Minn. Christian Writer's Guild. Home: 7877 135th St NW Pennock MN 56279 *In my life I have observed that God cares much more about people's availability than their ability. Our willingness to carry out a project counts for much than our education or professional skills.*

GUNDRUM, DAVID EUGENE, minister; b. Reading, Pa., Jan. 9, 1952; s. David Henry and Helen Mae (Ochs) G.; m. Donna Marie Ketner, Nov. 27, 1971; children: Natalie Elizabeth, Nicole Deborah, Nina Rachel. BS, Lancaster Bible Coll., 1985; MA, Westminster Theol. Sem., 1989. Ordained to ministry Bible Fellowship Ch., 1988. Asst. pastor Grace Bible Fellowship Ch., Reading, 1985-90; sr. pastor Grace Bible Fellowship Ch., Quakertown, Pa., 1990—; past pres., bd. dirs. Berks County Christian Action Coun., Reading, 1985—; trustee candidate Internat. Missions, Inc., Reading, 1990. Chmn. steering bd. Mercy Crisis Pregnancy Ctr., Reading, 1989-90. Republican. Home: 53 Kenwood Cir Quakertown PA 18951 Office: Grace Bible Fellowship Ch 1811 Old Bethlehem Pk Quakertown PA 18951

GUNDRUM, JAMES RICHARD, retired minister; b. Muscatine, Iowa, Nov. 30, 1929; s. Otto and Margaret Isabel (Black) G.; m. Frances Ellen Lathrop, June 14, 1954; children—Cameron Michael, David William, Carolyn Anne. B.A., Iowa Wesleyan U., 1951; M.Div., Seabury Western Theol. Sem., Evanston, Ill., 1954, D.D., 1976. Ordained priest Episcopal Ch., 1954; vicar chs. in Western Iowa, 1954-58; rector St. Michael's Ch., Cedar Rapids, Iowa, 1958-69; mission cons. Episcopal Diocese Iowa, 1969-75, canon, 1976—; sec.-treas. Episcopal Gen. Conv., 1975-86, exec. officer, 1976-86, sec. exec. council, 1977-86; sec. Domestic and Fgn. Missionary Soc., 1976-86; dean Calvary Cathedral, Sioux Falls, S.D., 1986-89; trustee Seabury Western Theol. Sem., 1975-82, Ch. Pension Fund and Affiliates, 1991—; chaplain Cedar Rapids Police Dept., 1961-69. Editor jour., canons gen. conv. Bd. dirs. chmn. personnel com. Cedar Rapids chpt. A.R.C., 1960-64; bd. dirs. Cedar Rapids Mental Health Assn., 1961-65; Mem. Iowa N.G., 1946-48. Recipient Disting. Service Cross St. Michael's Ch., 1968; named Hon. Cedar Rapidian, 1969. Mem. Soc. Advancement Mgmt. Democrat. Club: Rotary (past v.p., dir. Cedar Rapids). Home: 4104 Hackberry Circle Sioux Falls SD 57103

GUNN, GILES BUCKINGHAM, English educator, religion educator; b. Evanston, Ill., Jan. 9, 1938; s. Buckingham Willcox and Janet (Fargo) G.; m. Janet Mears Varner, Dec. 29, 1969 (div. July 1983); 1 child, Adam Buckingham; m. Deborah Rose Sills, July 9, 1983; 1 child, Abigail Rose. BA, Amherst Coll., 1959; student, Episc. Theol. Sch., Cambridge, Mass., 1959-60; MA, U. Chgo., 1963, PhD, 1967. Prof. religion and lit. U. Chgo., 1966-74; prof. religion and Am. studies U. N.C., Chapel Hill, 1974-85; prof. English and Religion U. Fla., 1984-85; prof. English U. Calif., Santa Barbara, 1985—; vis. asst. prof. religion Stanford U., Palo Alto, Calif., 1973; Benedict Disting. vis. prof. Religion Carleton Coll., Northfield, Minn., 1977; William R. Kenan Disting. vis. prof. Humanities Coll. William and Mary, Williamsburg, Va., 1983-84; Humanities Disting. vis. prof. U. Colo., 1989; dir. NEH summer sems. for coll. and univ. tchrs., 1979, 81, 85, for sch. tchrs., 1987, 88, 89. Author: F.O. Matthiessen, The Critical Achievement, 1975, The Interpretation of Otherness: Literature, Religion and the American Imagination, 1979, The Culture of Criticism and The Criticism of Culture, 1987, Thinking Across the American Grain: Ideology, Intellect, and the New Pragmatism, 1992; editor: Literature and Religion, 1971, Henry James, Senior: A Selection of His Writings, 1974, New World Metaphysics: Readings on the Religious Meaning of the American Experience, 1981, The Bible and American Arts and Letters, 1983, Church, State, and American Culture, 1984; co-editor: Redrawing the Boundaries of Literary Study in English, 1992; contbr. numerous articles to profl. jours. Edward John Noble Leadership grantee, 1959-63; Amherst-Doshisha fellow, Kyoto, Japan, 1960-61, Kent fellow, Danforth Found., 1963-65, Guggenheim fellow, 1978-79, Nat. Endowment for Humanities fellow, 1990, U. Calif. Pres.'s Rsch. fellow, 1990. Mem. MLA, Am. Acad. Religion (dir. research and pubs. 1974-77), Am. Studies Assn., Soc. Religion, Arts and Contemporary Culture, Soc. Am. Phil., Nat. Critics Book Circle. Democrat. Avocations: walking, sailing. Home: Walking M Ranch 2851 Tapadero Rd Los Olivos CA 93441 Office: U Calif Dept English Santa Barbara CA 93106

GUNN, LENTON, minister; b. Greensboro, Fla., Apr. 9, 1939; s. Lenton and Essie M. G.; m. Evelyn J. Gunn, June 14, 1962; children: Jean C. III, Lisa G., Kimberly S. BA, Stillman Coll., Tuscaloosa, Ala., 1961; MDiv, Johnson C. Smith Coll., Charlotte, N.C., 1964; DHL, Stillman Coll., 1980. Ordained to ministry Presbyn. Ch. (U.S.A.), 1964. Asst. minister West Ch., St. Louis, 1964-65; pastor Phillips Ave. Presbyn. Ch., East Cleveland, Ohio, 1965-67, St. Marks Ch., Cleve., 1967-68, St. James Presbyn. Ch., N.Y.C., 1977—; moderator N.Y.C. Presbyrery, 1991; pres. Black Presbyn. United, 1983-88; mem. coun. of ch. and race Presbyn. Ch., N.Y.C., 1980-83. Chmn. bd. Home Attendant Program, N.Y.C., 1987-91; v.p. Harlem Chs. for Community Iprovement, N.Y.C., 1988—. Home: 225 Storer Ave New Rochelle NY 10801

GUNN, SANDRA JOYCE, lay worker; b. Allentown, Pa., Oct. 30, 1951; d. Hilbert Guy and Joyce Marie (Mantz) Snyder; m. Bruce Myron Gunn, Oct. 17, 1981. BS in Music Edn., Lebanon Valley Coll, 1973. Cert. instrumental and vocal music tchr. Handbell dir. Calvary Presbyn. Ch., Riverton, N.J., 1983-87; dir. choirs and orch. Broad St. United Meth. Ch., Burlington, N.J., 1987—; part-time bookkeeper Lippincott Fuel Co., Delanco, N.J., 1985—; ch. auditor Calvary Presbyn. Ch., Riverton, 1988, 91; chmn. Christian edn., elder Calvary Presbyn. Ch., Riverton, 1979-82; youth advisor Broad St. United Meth. Ch., 1987, chmn. Ann. Choir Festival, 1990—; chmn. worship com. Broad St. United Meth. Ch., Burlington, 1991—, coord. youth Sunday and Christmas Eve svcs., 1989—; asst. dir. N.J. Meth. Chorale for Gr. Britain concert tour, 1991. Treas. Porch Club, Riverton, 1983-85; sec. Riverton Rep. Club, 1985-86; mem. Riverton Improvement Com., 1989; pres. N.J. Women's Clubs, Riverton, 1985-90; instr. music appreciation course Burlington County Continuing Edn. Program, 1991. Home: 808 Main St Riverton NJ 08077 Office: Broad St United Meth Ch 36 E Broad St Burlington NJ 08016

GUNNELLS, DREW JEFFERSON, minister; b. Shreveport, La., Oct. 17, 1932; s. Drew Jefferson and Dura Lee (Hortman) G.; m. Flora Margery Noble; children: Drew Jeffrey, Lisa Gunnells Steed, Susan Lee. BA, Baylor U., 1953; MDiv., Southwestern Bapt. Theol. Sem., 1958; MA, U. So. Miss., 1966; DD, Mobile Coll., 1970. Ordained to ministry Bapt. Ch., 1953. Pastor Zion Hill Bapt. Ch., Bluffdale, Tex., 1957-58, 1st Bapt. Ch., Summit, Miss., 1958-62, Ea. Hills Bapt. Ch., Montgomery, Ala., 1962-72, Spring Hill Bapt. Ch., Mobile, Ala., 1972—; trustee Fgn. Mission Bd., So. Bapt. Conv., 1967-74, chmn. 1970-72; trustee Southwestern Bapt. Theol. Sem., 1979-89, chmn. 1985-87; pres. Ala. Bapt. State Conv., 1979-81; pres. Sunrise Rotary, Mobile, 1986-87; conf. speaker 27 countries. Contbr. articles to demon. publs. 1st lt. USAF, 1953-55. Mem. Mobile C. of C., Rotary (gov. local dist. 1991—), Pi Gamma Mu, Phi Alpha Theta. Home: 820 Regents Dr W Mobile AL 36609 Office: Spring Hill Bapt Ch 2 S McGregor Ave Mobile AL 36608

GUNNER, MURRAY, Jewish organization administrator; b. N.Y.C., Mar. 26, 1918; s. Abraham and Sadie (Schnee) G.; m. Pearl O. Katz, June 12, 1949; children: Marilyn Ruth, Janet Marie. BS, CCNY, 1938; MSW, Columbia U., 1946; cert., Hebrew U., 1971. Cert. social worker. Adminstrv. asst. Coun. House, St. Louis, 1946-50; program dir. Jewish Community Ctr., Hartford, Conn., 1950-54; exec. dir. Jewish Community Ctr., Newburgh, N.Y., 1954-62, Bklyn., 1962-66, Yonkers, N.Y., 1966-83; cons. coll. mus. Jewish Community Ctr., Jewish Fedn., 1983-89; exec. dir. Jewish Coun. of Yonkers, 1989—; co-chmn. commn. of synagogue rels. United Jewish Appeal Fedn., N.Y.C., 1980-81, co-chmn. Jewish Community Ctrs., 1981-82; co-chair adult edn. com. Greystone Jewish Ctr., Yonkers, 1980-82, bd. dirs., 1978-80. Contbr. author to various books. Mem. Charter Revision Commn., Yonkers, 1979, Mayor's Holocaust Commn., Yonkers, 1979, Mayor's Com. on Jewish Affairs, Yonkers, 1990—, Yonkers Crime Commn., 1975, Yonkers Mental Health Coun., 1978-83; bd. dirs. Yonkers United Way, 1981-83. Murray Gunner Day named in his honor City of Yonkers, 1983, County of Westchester, 1983, N.Y. State Legislature, 1983. Mem. Nat. Assn. Social Workers (Gold Care mem.), Jewish Welfare Bd. Assocs., Jewish Community Ctrs. Assn., Yonkers Assn. Social Workers, Rotary (chair pub. rels. com.). Home: 10 Gateway Rd Yonkers NY 10703 Office: Jewish Coun of Yonkers 584 N Broadway Yonkers NY 10701 *The struggle for survival we face each day, can be exhilerating or threatening. The manner, in which we handle each challenge, is dependent on the degree of our faith in God, coupled with the strength of belief in ourselves.*

GUNTHER, THOMAS REGIS, pastor; b. Union Town, Pa., Aug. 31, 1944; s. Richard Howard and Etta MaryJane (Musgrove) G.; m. Priscilla Anna Bridner, May 6, 1967; children: Thomas W., Brett D., Bethany R., Stpehen P. BS, Hyles-Anderson Bible Coll., Crown Point, Inc., 1980. Tchr. Grace Bible Bapt. Sch., Balt., 1980-81; pastor founder Grace and Truth Bible Ch., Hummelstown, Pa., 1981—; bible tchr. Harrisburg (Pa.) Sch. of the Bible, 1982-85. Republican. Office: Grace and Truth Bible Ch 62 Pleasantview Rd Hummelstown PA 17036

GUNZ, CURT GIBSON, minister; b. Corpus Christi, Tex., Oct. 20, 1964; s. Leonard Jennings and Gilda Lenora (Ackerman) G.; m. KeriAnne Marie Miller, Dec. 19, 1987. BS in Ministry and Evangelism, Abilene Christian U., 1987, postgrad., 1991—. Intern Westbury Ch. of Christ, Houston, 1986; min. Edgemere Ch. of Christ, Wichita Falls, Tex., 1988, College Ave. Ch. of Christ, El Dorado, Ark., 1989—; bd. dirs. Kurios Christian Youth Camp. Contbr. articles to profl. publs. Tutor Literacy Coun. of Union County, El Dorado, 1990-91. Home: 917 W Main El Dorado AR 71730 Office: College Ave Ch of Christ PO Box 826 El Dorado AR 71731 *Life is defined not by achievements but by relationships, both with man and with God. In an often impersonal world, we do not necessarily need to do more—we need to love more.*

GURA, CAROL ANN, diocese director; b. Cleve., Jan. 20, 1941; d. Anton F. and Ann L. (Paluf) Planicka; m. Robert John Gura, Nov. 18, 1961; children: Donald, Trisha, Robert B., Laurel. BS, St. John Coll., 1966; MA, John Carroll U., 1984. Tchr. 1st grade St. Benedict Sch., Cleve., 1961-63; dir. religious edn. St. Clare Parish, Lyndhurst, Ohio, 1977-81; religious chair person, tchr. theology 11th and 12th grades Chanel High Sch., Bedford, Ohio, 1981-83; parish facilitator, consultor for young adult ministry Urban Region Cyo Office, Cleve., 1983-84; cons. resource Youth and Young Adult Office, Cleve., 1984-86; dir. evangilization Diocese of Cleve., 1986—; cons. in field. Author: The Parish Evangelization Committiee: What Works?, 1988, Where are the Young Adults, 1988; manual Ministering to Young Adults, 1987. Mem. Nat. Coun. Catholic Evangelization (v.p. 1987-89, pres. 1989—). Roman Catholic. Avocations: knitting, design, travel. Office: Diocese of Cleve 1031 Superior Ave Cleveland OH 44114

GURVIS, ERIC STUART, rabbi; b. N.Y.C., Sept. 24, 1956; s. Alan Irwin and Judith (Pomerantz) G.; m. Laura Kizner, June 22, 1986; children: Benjamin, Sarah. BA, SUNY, Albany, 1978; MA in Hebrew Letters, Hebrew Union Coll., 1981. Ordained rabbi, 1983. Rabbi Temple Shaaray Tefila, N.Y.C., 1983-87, Beth Israel Congregation, Jackson, Miss., 1987—; vice chmn. Miss. Religious Leadership Conf., 1989-90, chmn., 1990—; mem. Commn. on Social Action of Reform Judaism, 1991—; mem. task force on youth suicide Union Am. Hebrew Congregations, 1986—. Author tchrs. guide for Why Be Different, 1990. Mem. Cen. Conf. Am. Rabbis, N.Am. Fedn. Temple Youth (life), Assn. for Reform Zionists Am. (nat. bd. dirs. 1991—). Office: Beth Israel Congregation 5315 Old Canton Rd Jackson MS 39211

GUSTAFSON, HENRY ARNOLD, New Testament and early Christianity educator; b. Mpls., Feb. 23, 1924; s. Henry Arnold and Esther Othelia (Peterson) G.; m. Joyce Edith Holmer, Aug. 2, 1946 (div. Mar. 1978; chidren: Joan Elise Cox, Mark Timothy; m. Sheila Christie, June 3, 1979. AA, North Park Coll., Chgo., 1943; BA magna cum laude, Wheaton (Ill.) Coll., 1945; BD, STM, Yale U., 1950, 52; PhD, U. Chgo., 1967. Ordained to ministry Covenant Ch. Minister Covenant Ch., Haddam Neck, Conn., 1947-51, Covenant Ch. South Chicago, Chgo., 1951-54; prof. North Park Theol. Sem., Chgo., 1954-68, U. Indonesia, Celebes, 1965, The Near East Sch. Theology, Beirut, Lebanon, 1965-66; prof. N.T. and early Christianity United Theol. Sem., New Brighton, Minn., 1968-89, prof. emeritus, 1989—; tchr. adult edn. First Presbyn. Ch., Wausau, Wis., 1989—; theologian, seminar leader denominational and local ch. groups, 1968—. Author, narrator film: Do This in Remembrance, 1981, Into All the World, 1985; author: First Corinthians, 1986; quar. guest writer Exegetical Resource, 1989—. Assn. Theol. Schs. grantee, 1976, Ctr. for Ecumenical Cultural Rsch. fellow St. John's U., Collegeville, Minn., 1979, Assn. Theol. Schs. grantee, 1984. Mem. Soc. Bibl. Lit., Chgo. Soc. Bibl. Rsch. Democrat. Mem. United Ch. of Christ. Home: 3502 Maple Hill Dr Wausau WI 54401

GUSTAFSON, JAMES M., theology educator; b. Norway, Mich., Dec. 2, 1925; s. John O. and Edith (Moody) G.; m. Louise Roos, Sept. 3, 1947; children: Karl, Greta, John, Birgitta. BS, Northwestern U., 1948; BD, Chgo. Theol. Sem. and U. Chgo., 1951; DD, Chgo. Theol. Sem., 1980, Wabash Coll., 1986, Emory U., 1987, North Pk. Coll. and Theol. Sem., 1988; PhD, Yale, 1955; DHL, Bloomfield Coll., 1972; DL, Concordia Coll., 1983; Th.D.h.c., Uppsala U., Sweden, 1985; DD, Jesuit Sch. Theology, Berkeley, 1991. Ordained to ministry United Ch. of Christ, 1951; pastor Northford, Conn., 1951-54; asst. dir. Study Theol. Edn. in Am., 1954-55; mem. faculty Yale, 1955-72; Univ. prof. theol. ethics U. Chgo., 1972-88; Henry R. Luce prof. humanities and comparative studies Emory U., Atlanta, 1988—. Author: (with H.R. Niebuhr and D.D. Williams) The Advancement of Theological Education, 1957, Treasure in Earthen Vessels: The Church as a Human Community, 1961, Christ and the Moral Life, 1968, The Church as Moral Decision Maker, 1970, Christian Ethics and the Community, 1971, Theology and Christian Ethics, 1974, Can Ethics Be Christian?, 1975, Protestant and Roman Catholic Ethics, 1978, Ethics from a Theocentric Perspective, Vol. 1, 1981, Vol. 2, 1984. Served with AUS, 1944-46. Guggenheim fellow, 1959-60, 67-68. Mem. Am. Soc. Christian Ethics (pres. 1969), Am. Acad. Arts and Scis. Home: 1358 Springdale Rd NE Atlanta GA 30306

GUSTAFSON, RALPH WENDELL, JR., minister; b. Youngstown, Ohio, Nov. 24, 1951; s. Ralph Wendell Sr. and Edith Elvira (Johnson) G.; m. Lyn Ann Ford, June 2, 1973; children: Jared Ralph, Krissa Lyn, Nathan Eric, Luke Alexander. BA with honors, Bethel Coll., 1974; MDiv with honors, Bethel Sem., St. Paul, 1978. Ordained to ministry Bapt. Ch., 1980. Youth pastor Bethany Bapt. Ch., Roseville, Minn., 1976-78; dir. youth and camping ministries N.E. Bapt. Conf., Worcester, Mass., 1978-81; assoc. pastor Bethel Bapt. Ch., Green Bay, Wis., 1981—; mem. Bapt. Gen. Conf. Youth Ministries Team, Arlington Heights, Ill., 1985-90, Youth Ministries Team, Great Lakes Bapt. Conf., Rothschild, Wis., 1988-91; youth ministries coord. Bapt. Gen. Conf., 1987—; bd. dirs., staff mem. Villa Hope Campus Ministry, N.E. Wis. Tech. Coll., 1985-89. Co-author: (book) How-to Manual for Volunteer Youth Leaders, 1986; contbr. (curriculum) Is this Missions Thing for Real?, 1990. Coach Green Bay youth soccer, 1984-90, Green Bay Christian Sch. basketball. Mem. Nat. Honor Soc., Pi Gamma Mu. Republican. Home: 1838 Aspen Ln Green Bay WI 54303 Office: Bethel Bapt Ch 1601 Libal St Green Bay WI 54301

GUSTAVSON, ERICK BRANDT, broadcast executive; b. Rockford, Ill., June 2, 1936; s. Sven Ragnar and Ruth Emelia (Johnson) G.; m. Mary Janet Gustafson, Nov. 21, 1964; children: Ruth Marie, Timothy Brandt. Student, Northwestern Coll., St. Paul, 1954-56, Cuyahoga Community Coll., Cleve., 1957-58, Loyola U., Chgo., 1962-64; LLD (hon.), Calif. Grad. Sch. Theology, 1985. Mgr. Sta. WCRF, Moody Bible Inst., Cleve., 1960-67; dir. broadcasting Moody Bible Inst., Chgo., 1968-74, v.p. devel., 1974-86; gen. mgr. Sta. KAIM-AM-FM, Billy Graham Evang. Assn., Honolulu, 1967-68; bd. dirs., exec. com. Nat. Religious Broadcasters, Morristown, N.J., 1968-89, pres., 1982-85; exec. dir. Nat. Religious Broadcasters, Parsippany, N.J., 1990—; exec. v.p. Trans World Radio, Chatham, N.J., 1986-90; pres. Evang. Christian Pubs., Chgo., 1985; charter dir. Evang. Coun. for Fin. Accountability, Washington, 1979-84, 89—. Charter mem. Rep. Presdl. Task Force, Washington, 1980—. Recipient Chinese Culture award Inst. for Chinese Culture, N.Y.C., 1989. Mem. Calvary Evang. Mission (trustee 1989—), Back to Bible Broadcast (trustee 1986-90). Home: 10 Beech Ln Morristown NJ 07960 Office: Nat Religious Broadcasting 299 Webro Rd Parsippany NJ 07054 *The Lord is good, a stronghold in the day of trouble, and He knows them who put their trust in Him. (Nahum 1:7).*

GUTERMAN, DONALD RAYMOND, minister; b. Donalsonville, Ga., Jan. 2, 1955; s. Sol A. and Nell Raymond (Wheeler) G.; m. Donna Ellen Walters, Aug. 16, 1980; children: Sarah, Anna. BS, Ga. Southwestern Coll., 1976; D in Ministry, Columbia Theol. Sem., Atlanta, 1980. Ordained to ministry Presbyn. Ch. (U.S.A.), 1980. Sr. pastor Morningside Presbyn. Ch., Columbus, Ga., 1980-89, Northwood Presbyn. Ch., Clearwater, Fla., 1989—; sec. preparation for ministry com. Presbytery of Tampa Bay, Fla., 1990—; mem. Synod of S. Atlantic Coun. Guest editorial writer Columbus Leader/Enquirer and St. Petersburg Times (Clearwater edit.; contbr. articles to profl. jours. Mem. North Pinellas Presbyn. Cluster (co-chmn. 1991—), Columbus Civic Club (pres. 1988). Office: Northwood Presbyn Ch 2875 S Rte 580 Clearwater FL 34621

GUTHRIE, BRADLEY EUGENE, music minister; b. Birmingham, Ala., Jan. 8, 1962; s. Lester Eugene and Harriet Leah (Parker) G.; m. Melissa Nabors, May 24, 1985; children: Mallory Whitney, Parker Landon, Jordan Tyler. BS in Ch. Music, Trevecaa Nazarene Coll., Nashville, 1985. Min. of music Calvary Ch. of the Nazarene, Nashville, 1985-88, Timberlake Ch. of the Nazarene, Riverdale, Ga., 1988—. Home: 160 Middling Ln Fayetteville GA 30214-3767 Office: Timberlake Ch of Nazarene 8561 Hwy 85 Riverdale GA 30296

GUTHRIE, HAROLD MADISON, minister; b. Coshocton, Ohio, Apr. 27, 1939; s. Charles Edward and Lillian Mary (Dunn) G.; m. Norma Jane Shelton, Feb. 2, 1958; Kathy Jane O'Hara, Sharon Renee Wallon, Steven Allen. BISS, Sears Ext. Inst., Chgo., 1966, Western Auto Supply Co. Inst., Kansas City, Mo., 1970; grad. in pastoral studies, Moody Bible Inst., Chgo., 1977; BTh, Internat. Sem., Orlando, Fla., 1991. Youth pastor Hope Bapt. Ch., Columbus, Ohio, 1974-75; pastor Rocky Fork Bapt. Ch., Gahanna, Ohio, 1975-78, Riley Creek Bapt. Ch., Bluffton, Ohio, 1979-89, Calvary Bapt. Ch., Tiffin, Ohio, 1989—; trustee Scioto Hills Bapt. Camp, Portsmouth, Ohio, 1973-76; youth chmn. West Moriah Fellowship, Columbus, Ohio, 1974-75; chmn., founder Mid Bethel Fellowship Bluexton, Ohio, 1979-83; mem. Coun. of Twelve, Ohio Assn. Regular Bapt., 1987-90. V.p. Foxboro Civic Assn., Gahanna, Ohio, 1971-73; pres. Fundemental Basketball League, Bluffton, 1980-87, registrar Nat. Voter Registration Week, Bluffton, 1985; founder Bapt. for Life of N.W. Ohio. Mem. Men for Missions (founder 1989), Mid Bethel Fellowship (vice moderator). Home: 369 Clinton Ave Tiffin OH 44883 Office: Calvary Bapt Ch 733 N Sandusky St Tiffin OH 44883 *God has put us here to serve Him. How we accomplish this task, shapes our eternal rewards, not merely to exist in life but amount to something for His sake.*

GUTHRIE, HARVEY HENRY, JR., clergyman; b. Santa Paula, Calif., Oct. 31, 1924; s. Harvey Henry and Emma (Aubrey) G.; m. Doris Mignonette Peyton, Dec. 29, 1945; children: Lawrence Harvey, Lynn Frances, Stephen Temple, Andrew Simpson. BA, Mo. Valley Coll., 1944; postgrad., Union Theol. Sem., N.Y.C., 1944-45; STB, Gen. Theol. Sem., N.Y.C., 1948, MST, 1953, ThD, 1958; DD, Episcopal Div. Sch., Cambridge, Mass., 1985. Ordained to ministry Episcopal Ch., 1947; vicar St. Martha's Ch., White Plains, N.Y., 1947-50; fellow, instr. Gen. Theol. Sem., N.Y.C., 1950-58; mem. faculty Episcopal Div. Sch., Cambridge, Mass., 1958-85; prof. O.T. Episcopal Div. Sch., 1964-85, asso. dean, 1967-69, dean, 1969-85; rector St. Andrew's Ch., Ann Arbor, Mich., 1985—; vis. lectr. Columbia U., 1955-56; vis. prof. Andover Newton Theol. Sch., 1966-67. Author: God and History in the Old Testament, 1960, Israel's Sacred Songs, 1966, Theology as Thanksgiving, 1981. Democrat. Home: 1230 Morehead Ct Ann Arbor MI 48103

GUTHRIE, WILLIAM ANTHONY, minister; b. Bartica, Essequibo, Guyana, May 11, 1949; came to U.S., 1980; s. Charles and Lachmin (Bridjlall) G.; m. Elizabeth Ann Feidtkou, June 24, 1977; children: Tony, Pat, Carol. BA (hon.), U. West Indies, Barbados, 1972, Licentiate in Theology, 1974; Diploma in Theology, Codrington Coll., Barbados, 1974; D Ministry, Va. Theol. Sem., 1986. Ordained to ministry Episcopal Ch. as deacon, 1973, as priest, 1974. Asst. to dean St. George's Cathedral, Georgetown, Guyana, 1974-77; rector St. Patrick's Ch., Canje, Guyana, 1977-79; priest-in-charge Berbice River Missions, Berbice, Guyana, 1977-79; vicar Trinity Episcopal Ch., Charlottesville, Va., 1980-88; dean of region Diocese of Va., Charlottesville, 1985-88; rector St. Cyprian's Episcopal Ch., San Francisco, 1989-90; mem. Diocesan Commn. on Race Rels., Richmond, Va., 1982-87, Commn. on Evangelism, Diocese of Calif., 1989-90. Mem. bd. mgmt. Trinity Child Care Ctr., Charlottesville, 1980-88, sec. 4-H Club, Barbica, 1960-62; elected clergy del. nat. conv., Diocese of Va., 1987. Named one of Outstanding Young Men Am., 1985; recipient fellowship Va. Theol. Sem., 1987, Bp. Allin Fellowship, Geneva. Mem. NAACP, Nat. Orgn. Episcopalians for Life.

Democrat. Avocations: reading, swimming, travel. Home: 1145 Elbank Ave Baltimore MD 21239 *Perhaps, the only thing worse than evil itself is to sit back and do nothing in the face of evil.*

GUTIÉRREZ, GUSTAVO, priest, educator, theologian; b. Lima, Peru, June 8, 1928; s. Gustavo Gutiérrez. Student, U. Cath. Louvain (Belgium), 1951-55, U. Cath. Lyon (France), 1955-59; PhD in Theology, U. Cath. Lyon (France), 1986; PhD in Theology (hon.), U. Nimeguen (The Nethelands), 1979, U. Tubingen (Fed. Republic Germany), 1985, King's Coll., Wilkes-Barre, Pa., 1989, U. Freiburg, Fed. Republic Germany, 1990. Prof. Cath. U., Lima, 1960—; bd. dirs. Inst. Bartholomé Las Casas, Rímac-Peru, 1982—; counselor Latin American Conf. of Cath. Bishops, 1967-78, II Gen. Conf. Catholics, Medellín, 1968; guest counselor II Gen. Conf. Catholics, Puebla, 1979; bd. dirs. Concilium, The Netherlands, Páginas, Peru, Ecumenical Assn. Third World Thelogians. Author: A Theology of Liberation, 1971, We Drink from Our Own Wells, 1983, God-talk and the Suffering of the Innocent, 1986, The Truth Shall Make You Free, 1986, Dios o el Oro en las Indias, sigla XVI, 1989, Siglo, the God of Life, 1989; contbr. articles to profl. jours. Office: Las Casas-Rímac R Bentín, 763-Rímac Ap 3090, Lima 100, Peru

GUTIERREZ, JOHN MICHAEL, religion educator, contractor; b. L.A., July 28, 1947; s. Mike Gutierrez and Anita Mary Robinson; m. Sara Jane Casaday, Apr. 17, 1971; 1 child, Jason Michael. BA, Multnomah Sch. of the Bible, 1978; MA, Western Bapt. Sem., 1981; PhD, U. Sheffield, U.K., 1990. Builder, gen. contr., 1985—; adj. prof. Fuller Theol. Sem., Pasadena, Calif., 1985—, So. Calif. Coll., Costa Mesa, Calif., 1987—. Recipient Tyndale Rsch. award Tyndale House Fellowship, 1983. Mem. Delta Epsilon Chi. Home: 229 Willow St La Habra CA 90631

GUTIERREZ, TONY, III (ANTONIO), minister; b. Laredo, Tex., Feb. 27, 1962; s. Antonio (Tony) and Rose Mary G. BS in Divinity and Christian Edn., Cen. Bible Coll., Springfield, Mo., 1985. Ordained to ministry Assemblies of God Ch., 1987. Missionary intern Campus Missions Fellowship, Calcutta, India, 1983-84; treas. Campus Missions Fellowship, Springfield, Mo., 1984-85; youth pastor Assembly of God Denomination Ch., Springfield, 1985-86; liaison officer Laredo (Tex.) Ind. Sch. Dist., 1986-87; asst. pastor and cons. Schs. and Assembly of God Chs., 1986—. Republican. Avocation: coaching baseball. Home and Office: Assemblies of God #3 Candlewood Laredo TX 78041

GUTMANN, REINHART BRUNO, clergyman, social worker; b. Munich, Bavaria, Germany, May 1, 1916; came to U.S., 1942, naturalized, 1946; s. Franz and Berta G.; m. Vivian Carol Brunke, Oct. 7, 1944; children: Robin Peter Edward, Martin Francis. Student, History Honours Sch., Manchester U., Eng., 1936-38; M.A. in Social Scis, St. Andrews U., Scotland, 1939; postgrad., Coll. of Resurrection, Eng., 1939-41, Coll. Preachers, Washington, 1948, 52, U. Wis., summer, 1951, St. Augustine's Coll., Eng., 1964. Ordained deacon Ch. of Eng., 1941, ordained priest, 1942; curate St. Michael's Parish, Golders Green, London, 1941-42; rector St. Mark's Parish, Green Island, N.Y., 1944-45, St. Andrew's Parish, Milw., 1952-54; chaplain and mem. faculty Hoosac (N.Y.) Sch., 1943-45; founder, exec. dir. Neighborhood House and Episcopal City Mission, Milw., 1945-60; part-time priest-in-charge St. Peter's Mission, North Lake, Wis., 1958-60; exec. dir. Friendship House, Washington, 1960-62; cons. Indian Social welfare Exec. Council of Episcopal Ch., N.Y.C., 1962-64; exec. sec. div. community services Exec. Council of Episcopal Ch., 1964-68, exec. for social welfare and field services, 1968-71; part-time priest-in-charge St. Thomas of Alexandria, Pittstown, N.J., 1968-75; hon. asst. priest St. Martin's Ch., Pawtucket, R.I., 1980; mgr. spl. projects Human Resources Adminstrn., N.Y.C., 1971-72, spl. asst. to asst. adminstr., 1972-73, dir. mgmt. office community services, 1973, spl. asst. to dep. adminstr. social services, 1973-75; nat. exec. dir. Foster Parents Plan, Inc., Warwick, R.I., 1975-82; pres. Cedar Brook Cons., Inc., 1982-86, ret., 1987. Chmn. dept. Christian social relations Province of Midwest, Episcopal Ch., 1954-60; chmn. social edn. and action Nat. Fedn. Settlements, 1960-62; hon. canon All Saints Cathedral, Milw., 1971. Mem. Acad. Cert. Social Workers, Nat. Assn. Social Workers. Democrat. *Personal success is not measured by wealth or public recognition. It is the knowledge that one has done everything possible to help people achieve dignity, security, and fulfillment; and in so doing has transmitted a sense of personal caring for the needs of others.*

GUTTORMSSON, STEFAN T., bishop. Bishop Evang. Luther. Ch. Am., La Crosse, Wis. Office: Evang Luth Ch Am 2350 South Ave Ste 106 La Crosse WI 54601*

GUTZ, DEBRA ANN, youth counselor; b. Yankton, S.D., Oct. 2, 1958; d. Ralph Leo and Beverly Ann (Anderson) Felber; m. Philip Norman Gutz, Oct. 24, 1981; children: Ryan, Aaron; 1 stepchild, Tricia. AA, N.E. Tech. Community Coll., Norfolk, Nebr., 1978. Ch. office sec. Luth. Ch., Osmond, Nebr., 1982-85; sec. Luth. Women's Missionary League, Osmond, 1985-86; youth counselor Luth. Youth Fellowship, Osmond, 1985—. Democrat. Home: Rte 2 Box 37A Osmond NE 68765

GUYER, (DEAN) ALLEN, JR., educator, coach; b. Memphis, Tenn., May 10, 1967; s. Dean Allen and Patricia Ann (Young) G.; m. Kristy Leigh Mitchell, Aug. 12, 1989. BME, Crichton, 1990. Min. of music Skyview Baptist Ch., Memphis, Tenn., 1986--; bible tchr. Skyview Acad., Memphis, Tenn., 1991--, coach, 1990--; choir dir. Skyview Bapt. Ch., Memphis 1990. Composer various songs. Southern Baptist. Home: 2476 Monette Memphis TN 38127 Office: Skyview Baptist Ch 2216 Clifton Memphis TN 38127

GVOZDIC, DJORDJE A., broadcast producer; b. Novi Sad, Yugoslavia, 1953. AAME, High Tech. U., Novi Sad, 1974; BA in Theology, Bible Theol. Inst., Yugoslavia, 1977; BA in Communications, So. Calif. Coll., 1984. Cert. in radio/TV communications, Yugoslavia. Dir., producer radio and TV shows AlphaVision AG, 1986-91, Gospel Media, 1991—; constructor tools Pobeda, Novi Sad, 1987-91. Producer (TV program) Zvelicanje-Boćji dar, 1990 (Silver Angel award 1991). Asst. pastor, youth leader local ch., Novi Sad, 1987-91. Address: Postfach 98, 6376 Emmetten Switzerland also: Regent U Virginia Beach VA 23464-0098 Office: Gospel Media, P.p. 53, 61107 Ljubljana Slovenia, Yugoslavia

GYSI, ANDREW TODD, minister; b. Phila., July 1, 1964; s. Charles Louis and Virginia Ethel (Eglof) G.; m. Cheryl Lynn Blades, June 7, 1986. BS in Bible, Phila. Coll. of Bible, Langhorne, Pa., 1991. Assoc. pastor student ministries Faith Community Ch., Roslyn, Pa., 1989—; computer cons. Charles E. Shoemaker, Inc., Abington, Pa., 1979—. Named to Outstanding Young Men of Am., 1988, 89,. Home: 2416 Independence Ave Roslyn PA 19001

HAAK, ROBERT DONEL, religion educator; b. Springfield, Ill., Jan. 16, 1949; s. Rudolph A. and Lenora (Becker) H.; m. G. Diane Albanito, June 7, 1969; children: Michael Andrew, Robert Aaron. BS, Concordia Coll., 1970; M in Theol. Studies, Luth. Sch. of Theol., 1974; PhD, U. Chgo., 1986. Instr. Luther High Sch. North, Chgo., 1972-77; asst. prof. Religion Augustana Coll., Rock Island, Ill., 1983—; lectr. McCormick Theol. Sem., Chgo., 1983. Contbr. articles to profl. jours. NEH Ann. Fellow, 1990, Mellon Occasional Fellow U. Chgo., 1989. Mem. Soc. Bibl. Lit., Am. Schs. of Oriental Rsch., Cath. Bibl. Assn., Chgo. Soc. of Bibl. Rsch. Democrat. Home: 4231 1/2 14th Ave Rock Island IL 61201 Office: Augustana Coll Dept Religion Rock Island IL 61201

HAAN, JAMES WARREN, lay worker, counselor; b. Grand Rapids, Mich., June 30, 1956; s. Warren John and Virginia Marie (Houskamp) H.; m. Cheryly Lynne Baugh, Oct. 6, 1990. Student, Calvin Coll., Grand Rapids, 1974-78. Leader Fellowship Christian Athletes, Holland, Mich., 1978-84; nat. conf. leader Fellowship Christian Athletes, Holland, Albion, Mich., 1980-84; leader Fellowship Christian Athletes, Grand Rapids, 1980—; youth leader Alger Pk. Christian Reformed Ch., Grand Rapids, 1988—, Christian edn. rep., 1980-86. Pres., coord. summer workshop in ministries Grand Rapids Young Calvinist League, 1988-91. Mem. Kiwanis (pres. Grand Rapids East club 1986-87, Disting. pres. 1987, internat. lt. gov. 1989-90). Home: 822 Walsh Grand Rapids MI 49507 Office: Wedgwood Acres Christian Youth Home 3300 36th Grand Rapids MI 49518

HAAS, ANDREAS MARTIN, theologian, journalist; b. Zofingen, Switzerland, June 14, 1963; s. Franz Joseph and Adelheid Dorothea (Lenggenhager) H. Diploma, U. Berne, 1987, lic. Theology, 1991; postgrad., Oxford (Eng.) U., 1988, 89; Verbi Divini Min., U. Berne, Switzerland, 1992. Dir. Svc. d'Information et de Presse, Kolliken, Switzerland, 1983—. Exec. mem. Verein Bäretatze, 1985—. Mem. Syndicat des Journalistes Ecrivains (Paris). Home: Kunzhubel 10, CH 5742 Kölliken Switzerland Office: Svc Information Presse, Kunzhubel 10, CH 5742 Kölliken Switzerland

HAAS, CLYDE PINKNEY, minister; b. Balt., May 27, 1933; s. Clyde Pinkney Sr. and Frieda Mary (Jubb) H.; m. Juanita Yvonne Wood, Oct. 3, 1935 (div. Oct. 1986); children: Eric C., Timothy A.; m. Barbara Rose Armstrong, Mar. 30, 1938. AB, Lenoir-Rhyne Coll., 1964; MDiv, Luth. Theol. So. Sem., Columbia, S.C., 1969. Ordained minister in Luth. Ch. Pastor Lebanon Luth. Ch., Cleveland, N.C., 1969-71, St. Paul Luth. Ch., Hamlet, N.C., 1971-77, Pilgrim Luth. Ch., Lexington, N.C., 1977-82, St. David's Luth. Ch., Kannapolis, N.C., 1982-88. Bd. dirs. McLaurin Ctr., Hamlet, N.C., 1973-77, CONTACT Teleministries, Lexington, 1978-81; vol. Hospice, Rowan County, 1984-87. With USNR, 1953-55, Korea. Home: 1231 Yorkshire Rd Winston-Salem NC 27106

HAAS, HAROLD, clergyman; b. Union City, N.J., Nov. 9, 1917; s. Joseph August and Magdalena (Bonin) H.; m. Evelyn Johnsen, May 23, 1942; children—Marilyn Susan, Carolyn Sandra (Mrs. Paul E. Henry, Jr.). Student, U. Jena, Germany, 1938, U. Oslo, Norway, 1947; A.B., Wagner Coll., Staten Island, N.Y., 1939, D.D., 1958; M.A., U. Pa., 1942; Ph.D., Drew U., 1952. Ordained to ministry Lutheran Ch., 1942; pastor in Rochester, N.Y., Linden, N.J. and Jersey City, 1942-57; exec. sec. bd. social missions United Luth. Ch. Am., 1957-62, bd. social ministry, 1963-66; dean of coll. Wagner Coll., 1966-70; exec. dir. div. of mission and ministry Luth. Council in U.S.A., 1971-77; pres. Tressler Luth. Service Assn., Camp Hill, Pa., 1977-85; interim pastor Trinity Luth. Ch., Camp Hill, 1989-90; Mem. gen. bd. Nat. Council Chs., 1956-65; rep. to Luth. Council U.S.A., 1967—; mem. bd. world missions Luth. Ch. Am., 1968-70; del. and visitor Luth. World Fedn. assemblies, Sweden, 1947, Germany, 1952, U.S., 1957, Finland, 1963; del. numerous confs. Nat. Council Chs.; Mem. nat. bd. Nat. Conf. Social Welfare, 1963-66; mem. bd. Nat. Assembly Nat. Vol. Health and Social Welfare Agys., 1973—. Author: Marriage, 1960, also articles, chpts. in books. Home: 121 S 27th St Camp Hill PA 17011

HAAS, PETER JEROME, religious educator; b. Detroit, Nov. 29, 1947; s. Eric and Marga (Schlamm) H.; m. Lee A. Weitzenkorn, June 27, 1971; children: Michelle, Aaron, Rebekah. BA, U. Mich., 1970; MA in Hebrew Lit., Hebrew Union Coll., Cin., 1974; PhD, Brown U., 1981. Ordained rabbi, 1974. Assoc. prof. religious studies Vanderbilt U., Nashville, 1980—. Author: History of Mishnaic Law of Agriculture: Second Tithe, 1981, Talmud of Babylonia: Meilah-Tamid, 1986, Morality After Auschwitz: The Radical Challenge of the Nazi Ethic, 1988; guest editor Semeia 34, 1985; book rev. editor Jour. Reform Judaism, 1990—. Bd. dirs. Jewish Fedn. Middle Tenn., Nashville, 1986—. Served as chaplain U.S. Army, 1974-77, with N.G., 1980—. Mem. Am. Acad. Religion, Soc. Bibl. Lit., Soc. for Sci. Study Religion, Cen. Conf. Am. Rabbis. Home: 6925 Highland Park Dr Nashville TN 37205 Office: Vanderbilt U Dept Religious Studies Box 1556-B Nashville TN 37235

HABECK, DANIEL ERNEST, minister; b. Minocqua, Wis., Mar. 25, 1932; s. Irwin John and Dorothy Bertha (Seefeldt) H.; m. Carol Mae Asp, June 14, 1957; children: Cheryl, Charis, Dania, Jana. BA, Northwestern Coll., Watertown, Wis., 1954; MST, Wis. Luth. Sem., Mequon, 1957. Ordained minister in Luth. Ch., 1957. Pastor Grace Luth., Muskegon Heights, Mich., 1957-64, Zion Luth., Toledo, 1964-71, Martin Luther Luth., Oshkosh, Wis., 1971—; bd. control Mich. Luth. Sem., Saginaw, 1963-71; chmn. No. Wis. Dist. Bd. for Parish Edn., 1982-88; cir. pastor Mich. Dist. No. Wis. Dist., 1968—. Home: 820 Viola Ave Oshkosh WI 54901 Office: Martin Luther Ch 1526 Algoma Blvd Oshkosh WI 54901

HABECKER, EUGENE BRUBAKER, association executive; b. Hershey, Pa., June 17, 1946; s. Walter Eugene and Frances (Miller) H.; m. Marylou Napolitano, July 27, 1968; children: David, Matthew, Marybeth. AB, Taylor U., 1968; MA, Ball State U., 1969; JD, Temple U., 1974; PhD, U. Mich., 1981. Bar: Pa. 1974. Asst. dean Ea. Coll., St. Davids, Pa., 1970-74; dean students, asst. prof. polit. sci. George Fox Coll., Newberg, Oreg., 1974-78; exec. v.p. Huntington Coll., (Ind.), 1979-81; pres. Huntington Coll., 1981—; exec. Am. Bible Soc., N.Y.C.; evaluation cons. North Cen. Assn., Chgo., 1982—; dir. Christian Coll. Coalition, Washington, 1982-88, ICUI Inc., Indpls., 1983-85; sec., mem. bd. Assoc. Colls. Ind., Indpls., 1983-85; bd. dirs. Community State Bank, Christian Family Fedn., Christian Mgmt. Assn. Author: Affirmative Action in Independent College, 1977, The Other Side of Leadership, 1987, Leading With A Follower's Heart, 1990; contbr. articles to profl. jours. Recipient Christian Mgmt. award Christian Ministries Mgmt. Assn., 1989. Mem. Nat. Assn. Intercollegiate Athletics (council of pres.' 1985-90), Nat. Assn. Evangs. (bd. dirs. 1985—), Christian Legal Soc., Assn. for Advancement of Higher Edn., Assn. for the Study Higher Edn., Christian Mgmt. Assn. (bd. dirs. 1989). Republican. Mem. United Brethren in Christ Ch. Office: Am Bible Soc 1865 Broadway New York NY 10023

HABERER, JOHN HENRY, JR., minister; b. Queens, N.Y., Feb. 16, 1955; s. John H. and Maureen (Hastings) H.; married; children: David, Kelly. BA magna cum laude, Roberts Wesleyan Coll., Rochester, N.Y., 1976; MDiv cum laude, Gordon-Conwell Theol. Seminary, South Hamilton, Mass., 1982; D of Ministry, Columbia Theol. Seminary, Decatur, Ga., 1989. Ordained to ministry Presbyn. Ch., 1984. Asst. mgr. Christian Ctr. Bookstore, Allendale, N.J., 1976-79; dir. of worship First United Ch., Swampscott, Mass., 1979-82; dir. of family ministries New Covenant Ch., Pompano Beach, Fla., 1982-84; sr. minister Trinity Presbyn. Ch., Satellite Beach, Fla., 1984—; bd. dirs., chmn. Spl. Gathering, Inc., Cocoa, Fla.; mem. evangelism commn. Fla. Coun. Chs., Orlando, 1989-91; chmn. Brevard-Indian River Counties Presbyn. Mission Conf., Satellite Beach, 1989—; chmn. long-range planning com. Presbytery Coordinating Coun., Cen. Fla. Presbytery, Orlando, 1985-90. Contbr. articles to profl. jours. Vol. chaplain Brevard Pub. Schs., Satellite Beach, 1984—; mgr. Little League Baseball, Satellite Beach, 1984-88; founder, dir. Mustard Seed Coffeehouse, Ramsey, N.J., 1971-79. Recipient Good Will award for 1990, City of Satellite Beach City Coun., 1990; named to Outstanding Young Men of Am., 1986. Mem. Presbyns. for Renewal, Evangel. Tchr. Tng. Assn. Republican. Office: Trinity Presbyn Church 638 S Patrick Dr Satellite Beach FL 32937 *Our northern friends are thrilled to have us living in Florida. Their way to keep in touch is to show up at the front door, arms laden with stuffed suitcases, announcing, "We're here!" God is like that, having sent the Holy Spirit into our lives. The one difference tho, is that God also says, "...and I'm staying." That's good news.*

HABERMAN, JACOB, rabbi, lawyer; b. Zurich, Switzerland, Sept. 14, 1930; came to U.S., 1941; s. Alexander S. and Esther (Liebowitz) H.; m. Henryka Korngold, Mar. 28, 1955; children: Sinclair Curtis, Brook Ariel. BA, Yeshiva U., 1950; PhD, Columbia U., 1954. Ordained rabbi, 1954. Rabbi Congregation Ramath Orah, N.Y.C., 1954-57, Congregation Torei Zohov, N.Y.C., 1964—; ptnr. Haberman & Haberman, N.Y.C., 1970—. Author: The Microcosm, 1954, Maimonides and Aquinas, 1979. Mem. Rabbinical Coun. Am., Practicing Law Inst. Office: Haberman & Haberman 2112 Broadway New York NY 10023 *All the prophets imagined they saw in a mirror dimly, but Moses looked through a clear glass and saw— nothing. "The trouble with most folks," said Josh Billings "is not so much their ignorance, as their 'knowing' so many things which 'ain't so'."*

HABERMAN, JOSHUA OSCAR, rabbi, educator; b. Vienna, Austria, Apr. 2, 1919; s. Isser Alter and Berta Beila (Berger) H.; m. Maxine Rudin, Aug. 16, 1925; children: Deborah, Judith, Daniel, Michael. BA, U. Cin., 1940; M of Hebrew Lit., Hebrew Union Coll., 1945, D of Hebrew Lit., 1966, DD, 1970. Ordained rabbi, 1945. Rabbi Govt. St. Temple, Mobile, Ala., 1944-46; asst. rabbi Beth Zion Temple, Buffalo, 1946-51; rabbi Har Sinai Temple, Trenton, N.J., 1951-69; sr. rabbi Washington Hebrew Congregation, 1969-86, sr. rabbi emeritus; founding dir. Hillel Found., U. Buffalo, 1946-47; adj. prof. dept. Hebraic studies Rutgers U., New Brunswick, N.J., 1969, dept. philosophy and religion Am. U., Washington, 1973-79, Washington Theol. Union, 1982-89, Wesley Theol. Sem., 1988—; adj. prof. Georgetown U. Law Ctr., 1989; vis. scholar Oxford Centre for Postgrad. Hebrew Studies, Eng., 1991; co-dir. summer inst. in Israel, Am. U. and George Washington U., 1974; pres. Washington Bd. Rabbis, 1982-84; founder, pres. Found. Jewish Studies, Washington, 1984—; bd. dirs. Jewish Edn. Svc. of N. Am. Author: Philosopher of Revelation: The Life and Thought of S.L. Steinheim, 1990. Co-chmn. N.Am. bd. World Union progressive Judaism, 1978-80; mem. exec. bd. Cen. Conf. Am. Rabbis, 1967-69, Ethics and Pub. Policy Ctr., Washington,1 983—; N.J. del. Children and youth White House Conf., Washington, 1960. Recipient Brotherhood award Nat. Conf. Christ and Jews, Washington, 1978, Citation of Appreciation, USIA, 1983. Clubs: Cosmos (Washington); Torch (Trenton, N.J.) (past pres.). Avocations: tennis, swimming. Home: 8604 Fenway Dr Bethesda MD 20817 Office: Washington Hebrew Congregation 3935 Macomb St NW Washington DC 20016

HABGOOD, JOHN STAPYLTON, archbishop; b. Stony Stratford, England, June 23, 1927; s. Arthur Henry and Vera (Chetwynd-Stapylton) H.; m. Rosalie Mary Ann Boston, June 7, 1961; children: Laura, Francis, Ruth, Adrian. BA, Cambridge U., 1948, MA, 1952, PhD, 1953; DD (hon.), U. Durham, Eng., 1975, Cambridge U., 1985, Aberdeen U., 1988, Huron U., 1990, Hull U., 1991. Ordained to priesthood Ch. of Eng., 1955. Demonstrator in pharmacology Cambridge U., Eng., 1950-53, fellow King's Coll., 1952-55; vice prin. Westcott House, Cambridge, 1956-62; rector St. John's Episcopal Ch., Jedburgh, Scotland, 1962-67; prin. Queen's Coll., Birmingham, Eng., 1967-73; bishop of Durham, Eng., 1973-83; archbishop Ch. of Eng., York, Eng., 1983—. Author: Religion and Science, 1964, A Working Faith, 1980, Church and Nation in a Secular Age, 1983, Confessions of a Conservative Liberal, 1988. Hon. fellow, privy councillor King's Coll., Cambridge, 1986. Club: Athenaeum (London). Home and Office: Bishopthorpe, York Y02 1QE, England

HABITO, RUBEN LEODEGARIO FLORES, religion educator; b. Cabuyao, Laguna, Philippines, Oct. 2, 1947; came to U.S., 1989; s. Celestino and Faustina (Flores) H.; m. Maria Dorothea Reis, Apr. 18, 1990. MA, Tokyo U., 1975, DLittC, 1978; STL, Sophia U., Tokyo, 1978. Ordained priest Roman Cath. Ch., 1976. Lectr. Sophia U., 1978-85, assoc. prof., 1985-89; vis. prof. Perkins Sch. Theology, So. Meth. U., Dallas, 1989—; authorized Zen tchr., 1988; dir. Maria Kannon Zen Ctr., Dallas. Author: Total Liberation, 1989. Mem. Japanese Cath. Coun. for Justice and Peace, Tokyo, 1978-89. Mem. Sanbo Kyodan Religious Found., Japanese Assn. for Religious Studies, Japanese Peace Studies Assn. (bd. dirs. 1985—), Am. Acad. Religion, Assn. Asian Studies, Japanese Assn. Indian and Buddhist Studies. Office: So Meth U Perkins Sch Theology Dallas TX 75275-0133 *The mystery of life, from moment to moment, with every breath.*

HACAULT, ANTOINE JOSEPH LEON, archbishop; b. Bruxelles, Man., Can., Jan. 17, 1926; s. Francois and Irma (Mangin) H. B.A., U. Man., 1947; theol. student, St. Boniface Maj. Sem., 1947-51; S.T.D., Angelicum U., Rome, 1954; D.C.L. honoris causa, St. John's Coll., Winnipeg, Man., 1977; D.L.L. honoris causa, U. Man., 1989. Ordained priest Roman Cath. Ch., 1951; chaplain St. Boniface Sanatorium, 1954; prof. theology St Boniface Maj. Sem., 1954-64; dir. diocesan rev. Les Cloches de Saint Boniface, 1961; former personal theologian to archbishop of St. Boniface; also council expert 2d Vatican Ecumenical Council, 1962-64; bishop titular of Media; aux. bishop of St. Boniface, 1964-72; coadjutor bishop, 1972-74; archbishop of St. Boniface, 1974—; rector Coll. St. Boniface, 1967-69; mem. Pontifical Coun. for Promoting Christian Unity, Rome, 1976-89; pres. Western Cath. Conf. Bishops. Address: 151 Ave de la Cathedrale, Saint Boniface, MB Canada R2H 0H6

HACKELMAN, THOMAS WILLIAM, youth minister; b. Richmond, Calif., June 7, 1965; s. Harry Elmer and Phyllis Elaine (Meadows) H.; m. Sharon Rose Anthony, May 4, 1985; children: David Grayson, Andrew Thomas, Jamison Bruce. BA in Marketing, Okla. Bapt. U., 1987; postgrad., Liberty U., 1989—. Ordained to ministry So. Bapt. Conv. as deacon, 1989. Youth min. S.E. Bapt. Ch., Greensboro, N.C., 1989—; corp. accts. mgr. Copier Cons., Inc., Greensboro, 1990—. Campaign asst. David Walters for Gov. Okla., 1986. Republican. Home: 3301-D Darden Rd Greensboro NC 27407 Office: S E Bapt Ch 5011 Liberty Rd Greensboro NC 27406

HACKER, HILARY BAUMANN, bishop; b. New Ulm, Minn., Jan. 10, 1913; s. Emil and Sophia (Baumann) H. Student, Nazareth Hall, St. Paul, Minn., 1928-32, St. Paul Sem., 1932-38; J.C.B., Gregorian U., Rome, Italy, 1939. Ordained priest Roman Cath. Ch., 1938; asst. pastor Ch. of Nativity, St. Paul, June-Oct. 1938; asst. pastor Ch. of Most Holy Trinity, Winsted, Minn., 1939-41; vice chancellor Archdiocese of St. Paul, June-Sept. 1941, chancellor, 1941-45, vicar gen., 1945-56; bishop Bismarck, N.D., 1956-82; asst. pastor Ch. of Christ the King, Mandan, N.D., 1982-87. Home: 1020 N 26th St Bismarck ND 58501

HACKER, JOE, minister; b. Ada, Okla., May 26, 1930; s. Joe and Doris (Shipman) H.; m. Dec. 13, 1951; children: Tim, Denise, Carol, Catherine. BA magna cum laude, Harding U., 1955, MA, 1958; MRE, Southwestern Bapt. Theol. Sem., 1961, DRE, 1966. Minister Ch. of Christ, Searcy, Ark., 1958-61; prof. religion Harding U., Searcy, 1961-75; pres. Lubbock (Tex.) Christian U., 1976-78; asst. pres. Freed Hardeman U., Henderson, Tenn., 1976-78; pres. Ouchita Christian Sch., Monroe, La., 1978-81; min. Sunset Ch. of Christ, Dallas, 1981-90, Owens Cross Roads (Ala.) Ch. of Christ, 1990—; del. Pres.'s White House Conf. on Families, Washington, 1980. Editor Pulse mag. With USN, 1948-52, Korea. Mem. Phi Delta Kappa. Office: Owens Cross Roads Ch of Christ 3229 Old Hwy 431 Owens Cross Roads AL 35763

HACKETT, EARL ALAN, clergyman; b. Jewell County, Kans., 1940. BA, Kans. Wesleyan U., 1962; MTh, So. Meth. U., 1965, STM, 1970; D Ministry, Columbia Theol. Sem., 1987. Ordained to ministry, Meth. Ch.; cert. chaplain supr.; cert. chaplain. Chaplain intern Parkland Meml. Hosp., Dallas, 1965-67; fellow The Menninger Found., Topeka, 1971-72; pastor United Meth. Congregations in Kans., 1960-62, 67-70; chaplain Brewster Pl., The Congl. Ch. Home for Aging, Topeka, 1971-72; chaplain supr. dept. pastoral care N.C. Bapt. Hosp., Winston-Salem, 1972-75; dir. dept. pastoral care Univ. Hosp., Augusta, Ga., 1975—; asst. adj. prof. dept. psychiatry and health behavior Med. Coll. Ga., Augusta, 1983—; pastoral counselor First Bapt. Ch., Augusta, 1980—, Marvin United Meth. Ch., Augusta, 1990—; mem. Forum for Death Edn. and Counseling, 1978—; mem. Hastings Ctr. Inst. Soc., Ethics and the Life Scis., 1976-89. Contbr. articles to profl. jours. Bd. dirs. St. Joseph Hosp. Home Health Care and Hospice, 1978-84, C.S.R.A. Family Svcs. Agy., 1978-81; bd. profl. advisors Augusta Area United Ostomy Assn., 1976-81; cons. St. John Towers Retirement Home, 1976-80; mem. edn. com. Augusta chpt. Am. Cancer Soc., 1984-89; bd. dirs. Augusta Burn Found., Inc., 1984-86; bd. dirs. Alzheimer's Disease and Related Disorders Assn., Inc., Augusta area chpt., 1985-89. Recipient Profl. Svc. award Am. Protestant Heath Assn., 1986; named Admiral of Ga. Navy, Gov. State Ga., 1986. Mem. Assn. Clin. Pastoral Edn. (ho. of dels. 1984-86, sec. S.E. region 1976-80), Assn. Couples for Marriage Enrichment (nat. bd. dirs. 1981-84), Ga. Hosp. Assn. Soc. Chaplains (pres. 1988-89, editor newsletter 1987-90), Coll. Chaplains (chmn. nat. cert. com. 1988-90, chmn. profl. growth and edn. com. 1990—). Home: 4221 Ivy Ln Martinez GA 30907

HACKETT, GREGORY ALAN, minister; b. Michigan City, Ind., June 25, 1961; s. Charles Eli and Dixie Marie (Cowgill) H.; m. Lisa Diane Gray, Mar. 4, 1983; children: Gregory Tyler, Katie Diane, Robert Charles. BA in Bibl. Studies, Evangel Coll., 1983. Lic. to ministry Assembly of God Ch., 1983, ordained, 1987. Youth/assoc. pastor First Assembly of God, Logansport, Ind., 1983-84; youth pastor First Assembly of God, Lafayette, Ind., 1984-91; assoc. pastor First Assembly of God, Lafayette, 1988-91, sr. pastor, 1991—; asst. youth dir. Assemblies of God, Indpls., 1988-91. Office: First Assembly of God 108 Beck Ln Lafayette IN 47905

HACKLER, ROBERT RANDOLPH, minister, pastoral consultant, educator; b. Kansas City, Mo., Dec. 2, 1935; s. Cecil Kenneth and Martha Anne (Strawsburg) H.; m. Donna Elaine Curry, July 15, 1967; children: Kenneth Colin, Elizabeth Ann. BA in Russian, Northwestern U., 1958; MDiv, Yale U., 1961; MST, Eden Theol. Sem., St. Louis, 1969, D Ministry, 1976. Ordained to ministry Presbyn. Ch. (U.S.A.), 1961; cert. cons. and tchr., Fla. Asst. pastor Webster Groves (Mo.) Presbyn. Ch., 1961-64; pastor Westminster Presbyn. Ch., Belleville, Ill., 1964-70; sr. pastor Faith Presbyn. Ch., Raytown, Mo., 1970-77, John Knox Presbyn. Ch., Florissant, Mo., 1977-82, Community Presbyn. Ch., Deerfield Beach, Fla., 1982-85, Park Lake Presbyn. Ch., Orlando, Fla., 1985-90; pastoral cons., tchr. Stepping Stones Counseling Ctr., Merritt Island, Fla., 1990—, Halifax Counseling and Family Svcs., Daytona Beach Shores, Fla., 1991—, CORE Counseling Svc. Inc., Port Orange, Fla., 1991—; prof. psychology and humanities Brevard Community Coll., Cocoa, Fla., 1991—; prof. religion Daytona Beach Community Coll., 1992—; adj. prof. religion U. Cen. Fla., Orlando, 1990; cons. evangelism S.E. Synod, Presbyn. Ch. (U.S.A.), 1983—; tchr., lectr. Belleville Area Coll., 1964-68. Contbr. articles to profl. jours. Mem. Mayor's Open Housing Com., Belleville, 1964-65; chaplain, advisor Raytown (Mo.) Police Dept., 1973-74. Recipient Wolcott Calkins award, 1961, Man in Pulpit award Belleville C. of C., 1964-65. Mem. AACD, NCCJ (interfaith coun. 1990—), Assn. for Creative Change, Presbyn. Assn. Musicians, Alban Inst. (trainee in conflict mgmt.), Internat. Transactional Analysis Assn., Cen. Fla. Jazz Soc., St. Louis Jazz Club, Kiwanis (chmn. spiritual aims 1991). Republican. Home: 8762 Belter Dr Orlando FL 32817-1632 also: Halifax Counseling and Family Svcs 101 Dunlawton Blvd Daytona Beach Shores FL 32127 also: CORE Counseling Svc Inc 610 Dunlawton Ave Ste 2 Port Orange FL 32127 *The most important thing we Christian pastors/consultants hold out to people is Hope.*

HACKMANN, STEVEN MARK, Christian education director; b. Culver City, Calif., Jan. 31, 1964; s. Paul Frederick and Jean Marilyn (Tietjen) H.; m. Rachel Lyn Skamser, July 19, 1987. BA, Christ Coll., 1987. Cert. dir. Christian edn. Dir. Christian edn. intern Grace Luth. Ch., Santa Maria, Calif., 1985-86; dir. Christian edn. practicum work St. Paul's Luth. Ch., Norwalk, Calif., 1986-87; min. Christian edn. and youth Our Savior Luth. Ch., Centereach, N.Y., 1987-90; dir. Christian edn. Messiah Luth. Ch., Cin., 1990—; project coord. Big Apple Project in Evangelism, Centereach, 1988. Mem. Theol. Educators in Associated Ministries. Republican. Luth. Ch.-Mo. Synod. Office: Messiah Luth Ch 10416 Bossi Ln Cincinnati OH 45218

HADAWAY, EILEEN, religious organization executive, nurse; b. Buffalo, Mar. 31, 1949; d. Joseph M. and Mary Evelyn (Quinlan) Klein; m. William J. Hadaway, Sept. 8, 1973; children: Shannon, Lindsay; stepchildren: William, Jeffrey, John. AAS, Trocaire Coll., 1969. R.N., N.Y., Fla. Nurse Sisters Hosp., Buffalo, 1969-71, Roswell Park Meml. Hosp., Buffalo, 1971-74, Deaconess Hosp., Buffalo, 1974-78, Lee Meml. Hosp., Ft. Myers, Fla., 1978-80; pres. World Life Scriptures, Cape Coral, Fla., 1980—. Author: Poems for the Weary, 1982. Appearing in the top ten best sellers list Spring Arbor Distbrs., 1984—. Avocations: gospel singing, song writing, poetry. Office: Word of Life Scriptures PO Box 150609 Cape Coral FL 33915

HADDAD, ROBERT MITCHELL, religion and history educator; b. Bklyn., Oct. 1, 1930; s. Nadra Abdo and Hadbo Shehadi (Trabulsi) H.; m. Helen C. Rogerson, Mar. 6, 1964; children: Emily, Leila, Josette, George. BS, U. Pitts., 1952; MA, U. Mich., 1954; PhD, Harvard U., 1965. Mem. Orthodox Theol. Soc. in Am., 1968—, pres., 1973-75; Orthodox rep. Anglican/Orthodox Theol. Consultation in U.S., 1975—, Ea. Orthodox/Roman Cath. Theol. Consultation in U.S., 1978—; Sophia Smith prof. history, prof. religion Smith Coll., Northampton, Mass., 1982—; Antiochian Orthodox rep. Task Force on Christian Muslim Rels., NCCC, 1978-84.; mem. Jewish-Christian-Muslim Trialogue, Kennedy Inst. Ethics., Georgetown U., 1979-83. Author: Syrian Christians in Muslim Society: An Interpretation, 1970; contbr. articles to religious jours. Fulbright fellow, 1954-55. Ford Found. fellow, 1958-60, Social Sci. Rsch. Coun. fellow, 1966-67. Home: 65 Kensington Ave Northampton MA 01060 Office: Smith Coll Dept Religion Northampton MA 01063

HADDON, BARBARA JENNIE, minister; b. Phoenix, Mar. 4, 1944; d. William Stephen and Claudine Lois (Black) Johnson; m. Robert Walter Haddon, Jan. 28, 1967; children: Debra H., Christina L. BA, U. Denver, 1966; MEd, U. Hawaii, 1968; MDiv, Iliff Sch. Theology, 1980. Ordained to ministry, Presbyn. Ch. (U.S.A.); cert. elem. tchr. Asst. pastor Faith Presbyn. Ch., Sun City, Ariz., 1978-80; assoc. pastor Orangewood Presbyn. Ch., Phoenix, 1980—; mem. mission coun. Presbytery of Grand Canyon, Phoenix, 1981-83, mem. com. on ministry, 1989—; pres. North Phoenix Corp. Ministry, 1985. Mem. adv. coun. Planned Parenthood, Phoenix, 1985—; pres. coun. Hospice of Sun City, 1979-80; mem. coun. Ariz. Teen. Women, Phoenix, 1989. Democrat. Office: Orangewood Presbyn Ch 7321 N 10th St Phoenix AZ 85020

HADDON, JON ROGER, rabbi; b. Chgo., June 15, 1945; s. Murray Robert and Jean (Weinert) H. B.S. in Mus. Edn., U. Ill., 1967; B in Sacred Music, Hebrew Union Coll., 1972, M in Hebrew Lit., 1978. Ordained rabbi. Cantor, Community Synagogue, Rye, N.Y., 1969-75; asst. Rabbi Jewish Community Ctr., White Plains, N.Y., 1975-80; dir. sch. of sacred mus. Hebrew Union Coll., N.Y.C., 1980-84; rabbi Temple Sinai, Newington, Conn., 1984-87. Mem. chaplaincy adv. bd. Hartford Hosp., Conn., 1985; sec. Newington Clergy Assn., Conn., 1984-85. Mem. Am. Conf. Cantors, Central Conf. Am. Rabbis, New Eng. Reform Rabbis, Ridgefield Clergy Assn. (chmn.). Democrat. Avocations: guitar, reading, music. Office: Temple Shearith Israel 46 Peaceable St Ridgefield CT 06877

HADIDIAN, DIKRAN YENOVK, librarian, clergyman; b. Aintab, Turkey, June 9, 1920; came to U.S., 1946, naturalized, 1956; s. Yenovk Haroutune and Helen (Koundakjian) H.; m. Jean Root Wackerbarth, June 9, 1948; children: Eric Dikran, Andrew Dikran. B.A., Am. U. Beirut, 1944; B.D., Hartford Theol. Sem., 1948; M.A., Hartford Sch. Religious Edn., 1949; S.T.M., Hartford Sem. Found., 1950; M.S. in L.S, Columbia U., 1960. Instr. Oak Grove Sch., Vassalboro, Me., 1950-52, Sweet Briar Coll., 1952-55; librarian Hartford Sem. Found., 1957-66; librarian Pitts. Theol. Sem., 1966-85, prof., librarian emeritus, 1985—; vis. lectr. U. Pitts., 1969-83; Mem. corp. bd. United Ch. World Ministries, 1971-77; Bd. dirs. Pitts. Chamber Music Soc. Chmn. editorial bd.: Perspective, 1967-72; editor series: Bibliographia Tripotamopolitana, 1969-85; gen. editor: Pitts. Theol. Monograph Series, 1974-82, 83—; dir., gen. editor: Pickwick Publs.; Contbr. articles to profl. jours. Mem. Studiorum Novi Testamenti, Soc. Bibl. Lit., Am. Theol. Library Assn. Home: 4137 Timberlane Dr Allison Park PA 15101

HADLEY, ARTHUR CLAYTON, minister; b. Rochester, Ind., July 8, 1938; s. Noah S. and Mary A. (Place) H.; m. Jane Ellen Keefus, June 18, 1960; children: John, Mark. BA, Purdue U., 1960; MDiv, Bexley Hall, 1963; MPA, Ball State U., 1972, D Ednl. Adminstrn., 1973; cert. program in mgmt. devel., Harvard U., 1970. Ordained priest Episcopal Ch., 1963. Rector St. Stephen's Episcopal Ch., New Harmay, Ind., 1963-68; provost St. Richard's Sch., Indpls., 1968-70; assoc. rector St. John's Episcopal Ch., Lafayette, Ind., 1973-79; canon to the ordinary Diocese of Northwestern Pa., Erie, 1979-84; bishop's dep. Diocese of Mo., St. Louis, 1984—; prof. community devel. Purdue U., West Lafayette, Ind., 1973-79; bd. dirs. St. Andrew's Found., St. Louis, 1984—. Bd. dirs. Hope House, St. Louis, 1987—, Truman Restorative Ctr., St. Louis, 1986—, Grace Hill Community Coll., St. Louis, 1989—, Ascension Housing Devel., St. Louis, 1990—, Thompson Ctr., St. Louis, 1984—. Mem. Allen Fellowship (exec. sec. 1987—), Conf. Diocesan Execs.

HAEMMELMANN, KEITH ALAN, minister; b. Billings, Mont., Jan. 5, 1956; s. Herbert Carl and Edna Francis (Pfeif) H.; m. Jeanne Louise Thorman, Dec. 28, 1978; children: Kevin, Katie, Kelli. BA summa cum laude, Whitworth Coll., 1978; MDiv summa cum laude, Andover/Newton Seminary, Boston, 1982; postgrad., McCormick Seminary, Chgo. Ordained to ministry United Ch. of Christ, 1982; cert. clin. pastoral educator. Christian edn. dir. Congregational Ch. United Ch. of Christ, Burlington, Mass., 1979-82; minister Wiggins (Colo.) Community Ch., 1982-85; sr. minister Faith United Ch. of Christ, Windsor, Colo., 1985—; moderator Northeast Assn. of Rocky Mountain Conf. United Ch. of Christ, 1991; del. Gen. Synod of the United Ch. of Christ, 1989-91; chmn. ch. and ministry com., pers. com. of the Rocky Mountain Conf., United Ch. of Christ, 1991; treas. Windsor (Colo.) Ministerial Alliance. Bd. dirs. Weld County Referral Svc. for the Homeless, Greeley, Colo., 1989—. Recipient Peace and Justice award for Parish Ministry, Office for Ch. in Soc., United Ch. of Christ, 1989. Home: 603 Buckhorn Mountain Windsor CO 80550 Office: Faith United Ch of Christ 1020 Walnut St Windsor CO 80550 *The greatest challenge of the Church in the years ahead is to cease being reactive and begin to be proactive in our ministries. Only in this way will we shape our culture rather than allowing our culture to shape us!.*

HAERLE, WILFRIED, theology educator; b. Heilbronn, Germany, Sept. 6, 1941; s. Otto and Hedwig (Reidt) H.; m. Elisabeth Pillmeier; children: Uta, Michael, Tobias. Theologiestudium, U. Heidelberg, 1963, U. Erlangen, 1965; PhD in Theology, Ruhr Universitaet Bochum, 1969. Asst. U. Erlangen, Bochum, Fed. Republic Germany, 1966-73; hab., privatdozent U. Kiel, Fed. Republic Germany, 1973-77; dozent U. Groningen, The Netherlands, 1977-78; prof. U. Marburg, Fed. Republic Germany, 1978—. Author: Theologie Barths, 1969 (U. Preis award 1969), Sein und Gnade, 1975, Annstieg aus der Kernenergie? 1986, Systemat. Philosophie, 1987, Zum Beispiel Golfkrieg, 1991; editor, co-author: Theologenlexikon, 1982, Kirche und Gesellschaft, 1989; co-author: Rechtfertigung, 1980, Lehrfreiheit und Lehrbeaustanind 1/2, 1985, ; co-editor: Theol. Realenzyklopädie, Theol. Bibliothek Toepelmann, Marburger Theol. Studien, Marburger Jahrbuch Theol., Rel. im Denken unserer Zeit. Mem. Wissenschaftliche Gesellschaft fuer Theologie, Religion in Deuken unserer Zeit, Soc. Ethica, European Conf. on Philosophy of Religion, Deytscg-0skandinav. Gers. fuer Reli. phil., Luther-Gesellschaft. Evangelisch. Avocations: reading, chess, music. Home: Tirpitzstr 1, Hessen, D-3570 Stadtallendorf Federal Republic of Germany Office: Fachbereich Evang Theol, Lahntor 3, D-3550 Marburg Federal Republic of Germany

HAERTEL, CHARLES WAYNE, minister; b. Stevens Point, Wis., May 20, 1937; s. George Henry and Eva Georgia (Kingsland) H. BA, St. Olaf Coll., 1960; BD, Luther Theol. Sem., St. Paul, 1965; STM, Wartburg Sem., 1977; D Ministry, McCormick Sem., Chgo., 1988. Ordained to min. Evang. Luth. Ch. Am., 1965. Pastor Our Saviour's Luth. Ch., Almira, Wash., 1965-68, St. Jacob's Luth. Ch., Jackson Center, Ohio, 1968-72, Immanual Luth. Ch., Salem, Ohio, 1972-76, Zion Luth. Ch., Bridgewater, S.D., 1976-85, Cedar Valley-Looney Valley Luth. Parish, Houston, Minn., 1985—; rep. nat. Am. Luth. Ch. Conv., Sioux Falls (S.D.) Conf., 1984-85; host refugee families Luth. Social Svcs., Sioux Falls, 1984. Mem. Peace and Justice Ctr., 1977-83; bd. dirs. Wellspring Wholistic Care Ctr., Freeman, S.D., 1980-85, M-2 State Penitentiary Visitation Program, 1980-85; mem. Alban Inst., Rochester Symphony Choral. Scouting scholar Luth. Brotherhood, St. Olaf Coll., 1956, McCormick scholar, 1982; grantee Shaloam Continuing Edn. Program, 1980-82. Mem. NAACP, McCook County Clergy (pres. 1982-83), So. Ea. Minn. Mission Ptnrs. (mem. com., editor mission newsletter 1988—), Amnesty Internat., Sierra Club, Nat. Geog. Soc., Toastmasters (pres. LaCrosse area club 1989-90, local area and div. gov. 1990—, Able Toastmaster-Bronze, Disting. Toastmaster award 1991), Kiwanis (pres. Jackson Center club 1969-70), Eagle Scout Assn. Office: RR 2 Box 86 Houston MN 55943

HAFFNER, KARL MARK, clergyman; b. Plentywood, Mont., Feb. 22, 1961; s. Clifford and Barbara (Peck) H.; m. Cherie Lyn Haffner, Sept. 7, 1987. BA in Bus., Walla Walla Coll., 1985, BA in Theology, 1985; MDiv, Andrews U., 1987. Ordained to ministry Seventh-day Adventist Ch. Assoc. pastor Kirkland (Wash.) Seventh Day Adventist Ch., 1988-89; sr. pastor North Creek Christian Fellowship, Bothell, Wash., 1989—. Contbr. articles to profl. jours. Home: 14211 Silver Fir Dr Everett WA 98208 Office: North Creek Christian Fellowship 2005 Bothell Way SE Bothell WA 98012

HAGAN, BARRY JOSEPH, priest, educator, archivist; b. Glendive, Mont., May 31, 1931; s. Paul Joseph and Aimee Burke (Barry) H. BA in Philosophy, U. Portland, 1953; MA in Sacred Doctrine, Holy Cross Coll., 1960; MA in History, U. Notre Dame, 1964. Instr. history U. Portland, Oreg., 1961-67, asst. prof., 1967—, univ. archivist, 1983—. Contbr. articles to profl. jours. Mem. Council on Am.'s Mil. Past (nat. pres. 1981-86), Order of Indian Wars (founding companion), Fort Phil Kearny/Boseman Trail Assn. (dir. at large 1985—). Democrat. Roman Catholic. Office: U Portland 5000 N Willamette Blvd Portland OR 97203-5798

HAGAN, JAMES FRANCIS, minister of music; b. Pittsburgh, Penn., Dec. 7, 1936; s. Thomas Theodore and Harriett Faye (Ambler) H.; m. Etta Marie Turner, Feb. 4, 1972; children: Fran, Mark, Crystal. Studied, Seminary Ext, 1979. Min. of music Sydney Bapt. Ch., Sydney, Fla., 1976-78, Northside Bapt. Ch., Plant City, Fla., 1978-80, Sydney Bapt. Ch., Sydney, Fla., 1980-82, Shiloh Bapt. Ch., Plant City, Fla., 1982--. With U.S. Army Res. Southern Baptist. Home: 2105 Parkview Dr Plant City FL 33566 Office: Shiloh Baptist Ch 905 W Terrace Dr Plant City FL 33566

HAGAN, WESLEY DILLARD, minister; b. Tompkinsville, Ky., Jan. 16, 1924; s. Bascal and Effie (Carlock) H.; m. Maxine Britt, Mar. 15, 1951; children: Michael, David, Elizabeth Ann. Student, Clear Creek Bapt. Sch., Pine Valley, Ky., 1943-44, Campbellsville Coll., 1945-46, So. Bapt. Theol. Sem., 1956. Ordained to ministry So. Bapt. Conv., 1946. Pastor 1st Bapt. Ch., Friendsville, Tenn., 1946-51, Tenn. Ave. Bapt. Ch., Knoxville, 1951-55, McPheeters Bend Bapt. Ch., Church Hill, Tenn., 1965-67, 1st Bapt. Ch., Kuttawa, Ky., 1967-68, Beaumont Ave. Bapt. Ch., Knoxville, 1968-71, 1st Bapt. Ch, Philadelphia, Tenn., 1970-73, Bufflo Trail Bapt. Ch., Morristown, Tenn., 1971-73, North Athens (Tenn.) Bapt. ch., 1973-75, Forest Hill Bapt. Ch., Maryville, Tenn., 1973-76, White Plains Bapt. Ch., Scottsville, Ky., 1975-78, Indian Creek Bapt. Ch., Flippin, Ky., 1979-87, Rogers Creek Bapt. Ch., Athens, Tenn., 1987—; moderator Chillihowee Bapt. Assn., Maryville, 1975-76, Loudon County Bapt. Assn., Philadelphia, 1977-78, Allen Bapt. Assn., Scottsville, 1981-82, Monroe Bapt. Assn., Flippin, 1983-84. Author: Philadelphia History, 1822-1973, 1978, The Joy of Being His, 1980, Looking Upward, 1982, Lord, Teach Me to Pray, 1984. Address: Kingston Hills R#4 Box 199 Athens TN 37303

HAGEMAN, HOWARD GARBERICH, clergyman, former seminary president; b. Lynn, Mass., Apr. 19, 1921; s. Howard G. and Cora E. (Derfler) H.; m. Carol Christine Wenneis, Sept. 15, 1945. Grad., Albany Acad., 1938; A.B., Harvard, 1942; B.D., New Brunswick Sem., 1945; D.D. (hon.), Central Coll., 1957, Knox Coll., Toronto, 1977; Litt.D. (hon.), Hope Coll., 1975; L.H.D., Ursinus Coll., 1975. Ordained to ministry Ref. Ch., 1945. Minister North Ref. Dutch Ch., Newark, 1945-73; pres. New Brunswick Sem., N.J., 1973-85; exchange lectr., South Africa, 1956; lectr. Princeton Sem., Drew U. Author: Lily Among the Thorns, 1952, We Call This Friday Good, 1961, Pulpit and Table, 1962, The Book that Reads You, 1962, Predestination, 1963, That the World May Know, 1965, Advice to Mature Christians, 1965, Easter Proclamation, 1974, Celebrating the Word, 1977, Two Centuries Plus, 1984, Reformed Spirituality, 1986. Pres. gen. synod Ref. Ch. Am., 1959-60; pres. Friends of New Netherland Project. Decorated knight comdr. Order of Orange-Nassau (The Netherlands). Mem. N. Am. Acad. Liturgy, Holland Soc. N.Y. (domine), Colonial Order of Acorn, Phi Beta Kappa. Address: Mt Vernon Pl New Baltimore NY 12124

HAGEN, GLENN ARTHUR, minister; b. Saline, Mich., Oct. 28, 1936; s. Arthur Enoch and Ruth Saraphia (Rosander) H.; m. Sue Ellen Klingensmith, July 30, 1966; children: Elisabeth Sue, Jill Sue Ellen. BA, Capital U., 1959; BD, Dubuque Theol. Sem., 1965, MDiv, 1972. Ordained to ministry United Ch. of Christ, 1964. Pastor 1st Reformed Ch., Pitcairn, Pa., 1964-68, Meml. Ch., York, Pa., 1968-81; assoc. pastor Trinity United Ch. of Christ, York, 1981-82; sr. pastor McGraft Congl. Ch., Muskegon, Mich., 1982-87, St. John's United Ch. of Christ, Emmaus, Pa., 1987-89; interim pastor Blue Ridge Charge, Wapwallopen, Pa., 1990-91; cons. religious, ednl. and mus. group, Ednl. Travel Inc., Bethlehem, Pa., 1991—; pres. York Assn.-United Ch. of Christ, 1975-77; chair dept. edn. devel. York Coun. Chs., 1977-79; mem. pers. com. Mich. Conf. United Ch. of Christ, East Lansing, 1985-86. Pres. Community Kindergarten Bd., Pitcairn, 1965-66; mem. South Cen. Pa. TV and Radio Bd., Harrisburg, 1978-79. With USAR, 1959-65. Mem. Optimists (chmn. respect for law com. East York club 1978-79), Kiwanis (v.p. Pitcairn club 1965-66). Republican. Home: 1030 Harris Dr Emmaus PA 18049 *One of our greatest challenges today is reducing the level of anger. Our world is filled with people who find that life isn't working very well. They turn to their Church, only to discover that their faith isn't working very well. We have tremendous resources at our disposal, we can gain the victory! How exciting it is to help people realize that.*

HAGEN, IONE CAROLYN, religion educator; b. Spring Grove, Minn., Nov. 19, 1924; d. Peter Norris and Ida Bertina (Kittelson) Wennes; m. Dean LeRoy Hagen, Oct. 19, 1954; children: Steven Dean, David Lee, Deone Marie, Susan Ilene, Daniel Paul. BA, Luther Coll., 1947. Cert. music tchr., Minn. Parish worker Glenwood (Minn.) Luth. Ch., 1947-53, Trinity Luth. Ch., LaCrosse, Wis., 1953-55; sec. Nat. ELC Hdqrs. Higher Edn., Mpls., 1955; instr. Bethel series Zion Luth., Buffalo, Minn., 1966-67; supr. Christian Sch. Rivercrest, Monticello, Minn., 1979-81, Christian Sch. New Life, Buffalo, Minn., 1981-82; adminstr. Community Christian Sch., Buffalo, 1982—. Del. State Rep. Conv., Rochester, 1988; clarinetist Assembly ofGod Orch., Buffalo, 1974—; choir mem. Assembly of God Choir, Buffalo, 1990-91. Mem. Nat. Parish Workers Assn. (pres. 1951-53), Internat. Choral Union (sec. 1951-55). Republican. Home: 409 Sigrid Dr Buffalo MN 55313 Office: Community Christian Sch 206 2d Ave NE Buffalo MN 55313 *The greatest joy of living for me has been the knowledge that I am just a vessel—a pitcher with handle and spout—filled with the results of my choices and the choices of everyone who has touched my life, sanctified by Jesus Chirst, and poured out wherever He chooses.*

HAGEN, JOHN HOLTE, minister; b. Crookston, Minn., Aug. 7, 1933; s. George T. and Evelyn Irene (Holte) H.; m. Diane Louise Reinertson, Dec. 22, 1961; children: Mark, Kristin. BA cum laude, St. Olaf Coll., 1956; JD with honors, George Washington U., 1960; BD with honors, Trinity Luth. Theol. Seminary, Columbus, Ohio, 1965; MA in Philosophy, Ohio State U., 1967. Bar: Minn., D.C.; ordained to ministry Luth. Ch., 1973. Pastor Gol Luth. Ch., Kenyon, Minn., 1973—, Grace Luth. Ch., Nerstrand, Minn., 1973—; initial interviewer for sem. candidates Evang. Luth. Ch. Am., 1989—. Pres. Kenyon Arts Coun., 1979, refugee com., Kenyon, 1978, AFS com., Kenyon, 1976. Mem. Lions (pres. 1982). Home and Office: Rte 2 Box 8 Kenyon MN 55946-9501

HAGEN, KENNETH GEORGE, theology educator; b. Mpls., July 2, 1936; s. George Walter and Eunice Evelyn (Bush) H.; m. Aldemar Ellen Johnson, June 21, 1958; children: Carolyn, Susan, Erik. AB, Augsburg Coll., 1958; STB, Harvard U., 1961, postgrad., 1961-65, ThD, 1967; postgrad., U. Bonn, 1964-65. Teaching fellow Harvard Div. Sch., 1963-65; asst. prof. religion Concordia Coll., Moorhead, Minn., 1965-67; vis. asst. prof., Calder lectr. Marquette U., Milw., 1967-68, asst. prof., 1968-71, assoc. prof., 1971-83, prof., 1983—; vis. prof. U. San Francisco, 1971; Fulbright prof. U. Oslo, 1980; with U.S. Luth./Roman Cath. Theol. Dialogue, 1981—, Coun. for Internat. Exch. of Scholars, 1982-85; Miller Meml. lectr. Valparaiso U., 1986. Author: Foundations of Theology in the Continental Reformation: Questions of Authority, 1974, A Theology of Testament in the Young Luther, 1974, Annotated Bibliography of Luther Studies, 1967-1976, Hebrews Commenting From Erasmus to Bèze, 1516-1598, 1981, The Bible in the Churches, 1985, Teologi pa tidens torg: Festskrift til Peter Wilhelm Bøckman, 1987, Introduction to Theology 001, 1990; (with Franz Posset) Annotated Bibliography of Luther Studies, 1977-1983, 1985; (with Franz Posset and Terry Thomas) Annotated Bibliography of Luther Studies, 1984-1989, 1991; also articles; editor, author: (with others) Augustine, The Harvest, and Theology (1300-1650), 1990; mem. editorial bd. Medieval Philos. Texts in Trans., 1986—. Recipient Disting. Alumnus citation Augsburg Coll., 1982; grantee Harvard Div. Sch., 1958-63, Luth. World Fedn., 1966, Newberry Libr., 1970, Am. Philos. Soc., 1977, Wolfenbüttel Libr., 1982, Marshall Fund of Norway-Am. Assn., 1982, 84, Coun. for Sci. Rsch. of Govt. of Norway, 1982-85, Bradley Inst. for Democracy, 1991, others; Rockefeller fellow, 1963-65, Newberry Libr. fellow, 1976, Fulbright-Hays fellow, 1979-80, others. Mem. Am. Soc. Ch. History (coun. 1986-89), Am. Soc. Reformation Rsch., Fulbright Alumni Assn., Luther-Gesellschaft, 16th-Century Studies Conf., Norwegian Acad. Sci. and Letters. Lutheran. Home: 2344 N 60th St Milwaukee WI 53210 Office: Marquette U Theology Dept Milwaukee WI 53233

HAGENBAUGH, MIDGE ANN, lay worker; b. Wadsworth, Ohio, Jan. 25, 1941; d. Glenn John and Helen Mary (Yergin) Williams; m. Gerald Wesley Hagenbaugh, May 4, 1963; children: Mark Wesley, Jeffery Lee, Maryann. Student secretarial sci., Kent State U., 1960-61. Editor newsletter Wooster (Ohio) dist. United Meth. Women, 1973-86; publicity mgr. E. Ohio Conf. United Meth. Women, Canton, 1985; treas. local unit United Meth. Women, Wadsworth, Ohio, 1975-79, 85-90; treas. United Meth. Ch., Wadsworth, Ohio, 1974—; sec. Bible Study Fellowship, Wadsworth, 1987-90. Bd. dirs. Wadsworth Safety Town, 1973-78; bookkeeper WHYS Thrift Shop, 1978-90; treas. Wadsworth Band Boosters, 1987-90. Named Woman of Yr., United Meth. Ch. Women, 1983, Female Citizen of Yr., Wadsworth Growth Assn., 1989. Home: 267 Simcox St Wadsworth OH 44281 Office: Wadsworth United Meth Ch 195 Broad St Wadsworth OH 44281

HAGGARD, FORREST DELOSS, minister; b. Trumbull, Nebr., Apr. 21, 1925; s. Arthur McClellan and Grace (Hadley) H.; m. Eleanor V. Evans, June 13, 1946; children—Warren A., William D., James A., Katherine A. A.B., Phillips U., 1948; M.Div., 1953, D.D. (hon.), 1967; M.A., U. Mo., 1960. Ordained to ministry Christian Ch., 1948; minister Overland Park (Kans.) Christian Ch., 1953—; pres. Kansas City Area Ministers Assn., 1959, Kans. Christian Ministers Assn., 1960; mem. adminstrn. com., gen. bd. Christian Ch., 1968-72; pres. World Conv. Chs. of Christ (Christian/Disciples of Christ), 1975—; chmn. Grad. Sem. Council, Enid, Okla., 1970; pres. Nat. Evangelistic Assn., 1972; pres. bd. dirs. Midwest Counseling Ctr., Kansas City, 1987—. Author: The Clergy and the Craft, 1970, also articles. Pres. Johnson County (Kans.) Mental Health Assn., 1962-63; mem. coun. Boy Scouts Am., 1964-69; bd. dirs. Kans. Home for Aged, 1960-65, Knas. Children's Svc. League, 1964-69, Johnson County Mental Health Ctr., 1991—; pres. bd. dirs. Kans. Masonic Home, 1974-75; bd. dirs. Kans. Masonic Found., 1970—; trustee Nat. Properties Christian Ch., 1987—. Mem. Masons (grand master Kans. chpt., chaplain gen. Grand chpt. Royal Arch Internat. 1975—, Grand Cross Supreme coun. 33d degree 1989, Disting. Svc. medal 1991). Mem. Masons (grand master Kans., chaplain gen. Grand chpt. Royal Arch Internat. 1975—, Grand Cross Supreme Coun. 33rd degree 1989). Home: 6816 W 78th Terr Overland Park KS 66204 Office: 7600 W 75th St Overland Park KS 66204 *Early confronted with a basic decision to serve myself only or others also, I determined to use time and energy as felt led by God to do. Success has had the component of personal well being and freedom as well as the feeling of being useful.*

HAGGARD, JOAN CLAIRE, church musician, piano instructor, accompanist; b. Ann Arbor, Mich., July 7, 1932; d. Clifford Buell and Bertha (Woodhurst) Wightman; m. Harold Wallace Haggard, June 30, 1956; children: Alan C., Stephen T., John A., Marian E. BA, Carleton Coll., 1954; postgrad., Ecole des Beaux Arts, Fontainebleau, France, 1954, U. Mich., 1954-55. Organist, choir dir. St. Paul's Episc. Ch., Riverside, Ill., 1955-59; dir. of music St. Andrew's Episc. Ch., Livonia, Mich., 1960-72; organist Christ Episc. Ch., Dearborn, Mich., 1973-83; dir. of music St. Philip's Episc. Ch., Rochester, Mich., 1983—; pvt. piano tchr., Livonia, 1960—; accompanist Creative & Performing Arts High Sch., Livonia, 1987-90. Editor Livonia Youth Symphony Soc. newsletter, 1972-77; contbr. articles to profl. jours. Pres. Livonia Youth Symphony Soc., 1973-76; program dir. Episcopal Diocese Mich. Jr. Choir Camp, 1981-84, 87-89; coord. daily worship Triennial Conv. Episcopal Ch., Detroit, 1988. Mem. Am. Guild Organists (dean Detroit chpt. 1976-79, gen. chmn. nat. conv. 1986, councillor Region V 1986—), Nat. Guild Piano Tchrs. (judge piano auditions 1987—), Music Tchrs. Nat. Assn., Assn. Anglican Musicians, Hymn Soc. Am., Assn. Diocesan Liturgy and Music Commns., Music Commn. Episcopal Diocese Mich. (chmn. 1980-81). Avocations: bird watching, nature, reading (especially murder mysteries). Home: 33974 N Hampshire Livonia MI 48154

HAGGE, JOHN BRADLEY, religion educator; b. Chgo., Dec. 5, 1952; s. Arthur Clarence William and Margereth (Weiss) H.; m. Betty Jane Herpolsheimer, Dec. 27, 1975; children: Nathaniel, Rebbeca, Benjamin. BS in Edn., Concordia Coll., Seward, Nebr., 1975, postgrad. Tchr./youth dir. St. Paul Luth. Sch. and Ch., Jackson, Mo., 1976-78; dir. Christian edn. Pilgrim Luth. Ch., Green Bay, Wis., 1978-81; dir. Christian edn. and youth Our Redeemer Luth. Ch., Moorhead, Minn., 1981-89; dir. Christian edn., youth and music St. Luke's Luth. Ch., Wisconsin Rapids, Wis., 1989—; youth ministry cons. Author: (Bible study) Death and Dying, 1988. Mem. Luth. Educators Assn. Office: St Lukes Lutheran Church 2011 South 10th St Wisconsin Rapids WI 54494 *Through the winding and sometimes changing road of life I am always amazed at how God watches over us as children to adults and finally with him in Heaven—especially with children. That's why I feel they are such great examples of faith to us as adults.*

HAGNER, DONALD ALFRED, biblical studies educator; b. Chgo., July 8, 1936; s. Carl Sture and Marie (Gondek) H.; m. Beverly Jean Smith, Sept. 2, 1962. BA, Northwestern U., Evanston, Ill., 1958; BD, Fuller Theol. Sem., Pasadena, 1966; ThM, Fuller Theol. Sem., 1967; PhD, U. Manchester, Eng., 1969. Instr. to assoc. prof. Wheaton (Ill.) Coll., 1969-76; assoc. prof. to prof. New Testament Fuller Theol. Sem., Pasadena, 1976—; dean summer inst. Young Life, Colorado Springs, Colo., 1977—. Author: Use of O.T. and N.T. in Clement of Rome, 1973, Jewish Reclamation of Jesus, 1984, Hebrews (Commentary), 1983; co-editor: Pauline Studies, 1980. With USN, 1958-62. Mem. Soc. N.T. Studies, Soc. Bibl. Lit., Tyndale Fellowship (U.K.), Inst. Bibl. Research (fellow), Swedish Exegetical Soc. Democrat. Presbyterian. Avocations: music, hiking.

HAGSTROM, JANE STEWART, minister; b. Searcy, Ark., Dec. 13, 1956; d. Robert Jean Stewart and Louise Wade (McHenry) Hunter; m. David Gerald Hagstrom, May 31, 1980; children: Mikhal Rebekah, James Robert. BA, Southwestern at Memphis Coll., 1979; MDiv, Union Theol. Sem., 1982. Ordained to ministry Presbyn. Ch. (U.S.A.), 1985. Stated supply pastor 1st Presbyn. Ch., Forrestburg, S.D., 1985-87; assoc. pastor St. Paul Evang. Luth. Ch., Anamosa, Iowa, 1987—; conf. del. Synod Social Ministries Bd., Iowa, 1987-90; synod del. churchwide Evang. Luth. Ch. Am., Chgo., 1989. Author: The Young Witness: Evangelism to and by Children and Youth, 1986; co-author: Your Spiritual Pilgrimage, New Journeys Confirmation series, 1991. Vol. Anamosa Community Schs., 1989-91; coord. CROP Walk, Anamosa, 1991, recruiter, 1988-89. Mem. Anamosa Ministerial Assn. (sec. 1987—). Office: St Paul Evang Luth Ch 103 E Cedar Anamosa IA 52205

HAGUE, DAVID MICHAEL, youth minister; b. Lynwood, Calif., July 30, 1963; s. David Lee and Charlotte Joy (Crandell) H. BA, Pacific Christian Coll., Fullerton, Calif., 1988. Admissions counselor Pacific Christian Coll., 1988-90; youth min. SE Christian Ch., Englewood, Colo., 1990—; mem. local arrangements com. Colo. Christian Youth Conv., Englewood, 1991. Office: SE Christian Ch 6260 S Dayton St Englewood CO 80111

HAGUE, WILLIAM, priest; b. Honolulu, Jan. 19, 1952; s. James Duncan and Henriette Catherine (Reitsma) H.; m. Jane Milliken, May 31, 1981; children: James Duncan, Christopher Hathaway. BA, U. Va., 1974; MDiv, Va. Theol. Sem., 1980; DMin, Hartford (Conn.) Sem., 1987. Ordained to ministry Episcopal Ch.,1981. Rector Christ Episcopal Ch., Kensington, Md., 1989—. Mem. City Tavern. Home and Office: 3902 Everett St Kensington MD 20895

HAHN, CELIA ALLISON, writer, editor; b. Cleve., Jan. 3, 1931; d. Latham Lee and Celia (Fisher) A.; m. Robert H. Hahn, June 24, 1961; children: David L., Allison L. BA summa cum laude, Smith Coll., 1953; postgrad., Union Theol. Sem., 1953-55, Yale Div. Sch., 1957-58; DD (hon.), Gen. Theol. Sem., 1990. Dir. religious edn. St. Andrew's Ch., Meriden, Conn., 1957-58, Grace Ch., Silver Spring, Md., 1958-63; editorial cons. Project Test Pattern, Washington, 1972-74; editor in chief Alban Inst., Washington, 1974—. Author: Lay Voices in an Open Church, 1985, Sexual Paradox, 1991; co-author: The Male-Female Church Staff, 1990, numerous others. Mem. Phi Beta Kappa. Democrat. Home: 11453 Washington Pla W Reston VA 22090 Office: The Alban Institute 4125 Nebraska Ave NW Washington DC 20016

HAHN, CHARLES GLENN, JR., minister; b. Charlotte, N.C., Nov. 25, 1949; s. Charles Glenn Sr.and Beulah Odessa (Burleson) H.; m. Shan Barta, Dec. 28, 1972 (div. Oct. 1975); m. Lawanna Deann Haddock, Dec. 30, 1977; 1 child, Katie Starling. MusB in Edn., Fla. State U., Tallahassee, 1972. Minister youth and music Hilliard (Fla.) First Bapt. Ch., 1976-80, Southside Bapt. Ch., Sarasota, Fla., 1981-83, Bee Ridge Bapt. Ch., Sarasota, 1983-88, Bunnell (Fla.) First Bapt. Ch., 1989—. Teen assoc. Sarasota Youth for Christ, 1987-89; mem. Sarasota County Teen Bd., 1980-88; cons. 4-H Clubs of Flagler County, Bunnell, 1990—. Mem. S.W. Bapt. Assn. (assoc. youth dir. Sarasota chpt. 1981-88, 85), Fla. Bapt. Conv. (del. Sarasota chpt. 1977—), Fla. Bapt. Singing Men, Christian Bus. Men's Fellowship. Home: PO Box 862 Bunnell FL 32110 Office: Bunnell First Bapt Ch PO Box 365 Bunnell FL 32110

HAHN, DANIEL BRASE, religious organization administrator; b. Flushing, N.Y., May 27, 1949; s. Alfred Otto and Irene Ruth (Brase) H.; m. Deborah Anne Davis, Sept. 6, 1975; children: David, Deirdre, Deanne. BA, Muhlenberg Coll., 1971; MDiv, The Luth. Theol. Seminary Phila., 1976; MA, SUNY, Albany, 1985. Ordained minister Luth. Ch., 1976. Pastor Trinity Luth. Ch. (West Sand Lake, N.Y.) and Evangelical Luth. Ch. (Poestenkill, N.Y.), 1976-80, Good Shepherd Luth. Ch., Loudonville, N.Y., 1980-83; dir. Luth. Office Govtl. Ministry, Albany, 1983—; lectr. SUNY, Albany, 1984—; tutor, course developer Empire State Coll., 1988—; instr. Jr. Coll. Albany, 1989—; active numerous coms. Luth. and Upper N.Y. Synod Ch. Founder Down's Syndrome-Aim High!, Inc., NE N.Y., 1982, pres., 1982-83, 85-86; chmn. N.Y. State Nutrition Consortium, 1986-87, 88—, chmn. exec. com., 1986—; bd. dirs. Statewide Emergency Network for Statewide Econ. Security, Albany, 1985—, treas., 1989—; founder, coord. Ad Hoc Health Care Proxy Coalition, 1989-90. Mem. Speech Communication Assn., Assn. for Psychol. Type, Am. Soc. for Tng. and Devel. Democrat. Avocations: karate, weightlifting, songwriting, inventing games, writing. Home: 91 Marie Pkwy Loudonville NY 12211 Office: Luth Office Govtl Ministry 160 Central Ave Albany NY 12206 *Our greatest challenge is to live in interesting times without being overcome by fear. If blinders are fear's primary instruments, our task is to broaden vision.*

HAHN, GALEN EUGENE, clergyman; b. Frederick, Md., Jan. 18, 1947; s. George John and Helen Frances (Miller) H.; m. Sandra Elizabeth Ball, July 24, 1971; children: Whitney Michelle, Mara Anne. BA cum laude, Catawba Coll., 1969; MDiv, Yale U., 1972. Ordained to ministry United Ch. of Christ, 1972. Pastor Peace United Ch. of Christ, Norfolk, Nebr., Shalom United Ch. of Christ, Norwalk, Ohio, 1st Congl. United Ch. of Christ, Mendon, Ill., Mt. Pleasant Reformed United Ch. of Christ, Frederick, Md., Sabillasville (Md.) Charge United Ch. of Christ; exec. dir., program designer Radio Ministry: Bread for the Wilderness. Exec. officer local chpt. Boy Scouts Am.; pres. chaplaincy adv. coun. Good News Jail and Prison Ministry; chaplain Victor Cullen Ctr. Recipient William T. Hornaday award Boy Scouts Am. and N.Y. Zool. Soc., God and Country award Boy Scouts Am. Mem. Catoctin Assn. Ministerium, Nat. Eagle Scout Assn., Lions (sec. Thurmont, Md. club). Democrat. Home: 17001 Sabillasville Rd Sabilasville MD 21780

HAHN, HOWARD CLAYTON, clergyman; b. Bluffton, Ohio, Sept. 20, 1930; s. Howard Clayton and Avada Bessie (Treece) H.; m. Mary Kathleen Underhill, May 31, 1952; children: Jeffrey, Elizabeth, Rebekah, Mark. BS in Edn., Bowling Green (Ohio) State U., 1952; MDiv, Wittenberg U., Springfield, Ohio, 1955. Ordained to ministry Evang. Luth. Ch. Am., 1955. Minister Christ's Evang. Luth. Ch., Cambridge, Ohio, 1955-63, First Evang. Luth. Ch., Mesa, Ariz., 1963—; chaplain Mesa (Ariz.) Luth. Hosp., 1964-88; dean Grand Canyon Synod, Rio Salado Dist. Evang. Luth. Ch. Am., Mesa, 1987-89. Editor: The Key, 1952; author: A Funny Thing Happened to Me on the Way to Heaven or My Mother Doublecrossed Me, 1990. Mem. Centennial Steering Com., Mesa, 1978; pres. Youth Guidance Com., Cambridge, 1962, Child Svc. Ctr., Cambridge, 1962; mem. bd. YMCA, Cambridge and Mesa, 1962-65; mem. bd. 7th Step Found., Phoenix, 1972-75, AIDS Referal Counseling Edn., Mesa, 1990—; hon. mem. Aux. Mesa Luth. Hosp., 1986. Recipient Svc. award Mesa Luth. Hosp., 1988. Home: 622 E 7th Dr Mesa AZ 85204

HAHN, LEO BERNARD, religious organization administrator; b. Jennings, Kans., Aug. 23, 1934; a. Leo Bernard and Rosa F. (Standfast) H. B.A., Glennon Coll., St. Louis 1956; M.A. in Counselor Edn., St. Louis U., 1971; Ed.D. in Counseling Psychology, U. No. Colo.-Greeley, 1973. Ordained priest Roman Catholic Ch., 1961. Assignments in Roman Cath. Diocese, Wichita, 1961-69; personnel psychologist Dept. Def., Fla., 1974-76; admissions counselor Parks Coll., Denver, 1976-79; dir. Cath. Instns. Program, Archdiocese of Denver, 1979-82; chaplain, Fed. Correctional Inst., Englewood, 1982—. Mem. Am. Cath. Correctional Chaplain's assn., Am. Assn. for Counseling and Devel., Am. Rehab. Counseling Assn. Home: 72 King's Rd Evergreen CO 80439 Office: 9595 W Quincy Littleton CO 80123

HAHN, SCOTT WALKER, religion educator; b. Pitts., Oct. 28, 1957; s. Fred Karl and Molly Lou (Robb) H.; m. Kimberly Kirk, Aug. 18, 1979; children: Michael Scott, Gabriel Kirk, Hannah Lorraine, Jeremiah Thomas Walker. AB in Theology, Philosophy, Econs., Grove City Coll., 1979; MDiv, Gordon-Conwell Theol. Sem., 1982. Asst. pastor Trinity Presbyn. Ch., Fairfax, Va., 1982-83; instr. Dominion Theol. Inst., McLean, Va., 1982-83; asst. to pres., guest instr. religion and philosophy Grove City (Pa.) Coll., 1983-85; asst. prof. Coll. St. Francis, Joliet, Ill., 1987-90, Franciscan U. of Steubenville, Ohio, 1990—. Roman Catholic. Home: 808 Bellview Blvd Steubenville OH 43952

HAILES, EDWARD ALEXANDER, minister; b. Petersburg, Va., Mar. 26, 1925; s. Walter Franklin and Maggie Otelia (Pierce) H.; m. Nettie Drayton, June 23, 1946; children: Edward Alexander, Gregory, Patricia. Cert., Va. State Coll., 1946; BA, Va. Union U., 1950; postgrad., Harvard U., 1952-54, Boston U., 1961; cert. adminstrn. and mgmt., Howard U., 1965. Ordained to ministry Am. Bapt. Chs., 1951. Assoc. pastor Ebenezer Bapt. Ch., New Brunswick, N.J., 1946-51; pastor Union Bapt. Ch., New Bedford, Mass., 1951-63; assoc. pastor Zion Bapt. Ch., Washington, 1964; now assoc. pastor 19th St. Bapt. Ch., Washington; dir. ops. Opportunities Industrialization Ctr., Washington, 1966-68, exec. dir., 1968—; supr. religious edn. Inter-Ch. Coun. Greater New Bedford, Mass., 1954-61, exec. sec., 1961; chmn. promotion and fin. dept. United Bapt. Conv. of Mass. and R.I., 1960-63. Vice-chmn. Project Build, Washington, 1969—, mem. Mayor's Adv. Com. on Project Home, Washington, 1973—, D.C. Citizens United for Progress, 1976—; mem. Adv. Panel for Adult Edn. Demonstration Project, Washington, 1974—; mem. Health and Welfare Coun., Washington, 1969—; bd. dirs. Housing Devel. Corp., Washington, D.C. Street Acad. Recipient Cert. of Recognition Inter-Ch. Coun., 1963, Merit award Inter-Denominational Ch. Ushers Assn., 1964, Nat. Postal Alliance award, 1966, Family award Hearts, Inc., 1966. Mem. NAACP (nat. dir. 1969—, nat. v.p. 1980—, pres. D.C. chpt. 1978—, Freedom Fund Com. award 1966), Va. Union Alumni Assn. (vice chmn. D.C. chpt. 1976—), D.C. C. of C. (bd. dirs., award 1963), Masons (pres. Charitable Found. 1984—). Home: 1439 Roxanna Rd NW Washington DC 20012 Office: 3224 16th St NW Washington DC 20010 *I have learned that happiness comes by helping others.*

HAIN, FREDERICK MICHAEL, minister; b. Lebanon, Pa., May 15, 1935; s. Adam Franklin and Rose (Sentz) H.; m. Patricia Ann Kindt, June 29, 1963; children: Frederick Michael Jr., Michael Frederick. Student, Reading Area Community Coll., 1977-78, U. Millersville, 1981-82, Evang. Sch. Theology, Myerstown, Pa., 1978-80; MDiv, Lancaster Theol. Sem., 1981; BTh., Evang. Theol. Sem., Dixon, Mo., 1990. Ordained to ministry United Ch. of Christ, 1981. Pastor, founder New Life Chapel: A New Testament Ch., Lebanon, 1982—; advisor Aglow, Lebanon, 1986—. With USN, 1953-57. Mem. Charismatic Bible Ministries, Fellowship of Christian Chs., Internat. Assn. Profl. Marriage and Family Counselors, Internat. Convention of Faith Chs. and Ministers, Inc. (area dir. 1985-86). Office: New Life Chapel New Test Ch 100 N 9th St Lebanon PA 17042

HAINES, LEE MARK, JR., clergyman; b. Marion, Ind., Dec. 9, 1927; s. Lee M. Sr. and Anna (Stevens); m. Maxine Louise Shockey, June 8, 1948; children: Mark Edward, Rhoda Lynn. B of Religion, Ind. Wesleyan U., 1950; MDiv, Christian Theol. Sem., Indpls., 1959; ThM, Christian Theol. Sem., 1973; D Ministry, Bethel Theol. Se., St. Paul, 1981; DD (hon.), Marion Coll., 1981; LittD (hon.), Houghton Coll., N.Y., 1981. Ordained to ministry Wesleyan Ch., 1950. Pastor Peru (Ind.) Wesleyan Meth. Ch., 1948-51, Blue River Wesleyan Meth. Ch., Arlington, Ind., 1951-56, Jonesboro (Ind.) Wesleyan Meth. Ch., 1956-61; editor Adult Sunday Sch. Lessons Wesleyan Meth. Ch., Marion, Ind., 1961-63; pastor Eastlawn Wesleyan Ch., Indpls., 1963-70; assoc. prof. religion Marion Coll., 1970-80; gen. sec. edn. and the ministry The Wesleyan Ch., Indpls., 1980-88, gen. supt., 1988—; historian The Wesleyan Ch., 1976-88. Assoc. editor/writer: The Wesleyan Bible Commentary; co-author: An Outline History of the Wesleyan Church; co-editor: Conscience and Commitment: History of the Wesleyan Methodist Church, Days of Our Pilgrimage: History of the Pilgrim Holiness Church. Mem. Evangelical Theol. Soc., Wesleyan Theol. Soc. (editor 1978-81). Office: Internat Ctr Wesleyan Ch PO Box 50434 Indianapolis IN 46250 *God is the divine lover of each human person, and seeks through Jesus Christ to bring about a loving relationship with each one. Our highest task is to help bring that to pass.*

HAINES, PAUL LOWELL, lawyer; b. Tokyo, Jan. 10, 1953; s. Paul Whitfield and Florence Alice (Hall) H.; m. Sherryl Ann Korfmacher, Aug. 16, 1975. BA, Taylor U., 1975; MA, Ball State U., 1977; JD, Ind. U., 1990. Residence hall dir. Taylor U., Upland, Ind., 1977-80, dir. student programs, 1980-83, dean of students, 1983-85, v.p. for student devel., 1985-87; assoc. Baker & Daniels, Indpls., 1990—; founder, co-dir. Nat. Student Leadership Conf. for Christian Colls., 1981-84, presenter Christian Artists Music Seminar, Estes Park, Colo., 1982. Editor in chief Ind. Law Jour., 1989-90. Mem. ABA, Ind. Bar Assn. Home: 8007 E 20th St Indianapolis IN 46219 Office: Baker & Daniels 300 N Meridian St Ste 2700 Indianapolis IN 46204

HAIRSTON, WILLIAM CLIFTON, clergyman, insurance professional; b. Estancia, N.Mex., Aug. 16, 1921; s. William Conway and Velma (Golden) H.; married; children: William Michael, Sharon Lynn Hairston Fuller. Student, U. N.Mex., 1939-40, U. Tenn., Martin, various yrs. Tchr. Bible sch. South Main Ch. of Christ, Roswell, N.Mex., 1946-56, Bishop St. Ch. of Christ, Union City, Tenn., 1956-72; deacon, tchr. Exch. St. Ch. of Christ, Union City, 1972-74, elder, tchr., trustee, 1974—; ins. agt. Brundige-Hairston-Durham, Union City, 1956-86, Union City Ins. Agy., 1986—; dir., sec. Reelfoot Youth Camp, Hornbeak, Tenn., 1982—. Bd. dirs. Union City C. of C., 1968-70, v.p., 1970-72. Mem. Kiwanis (sec.-treas. 1962-63, 2d v.p. 1963-64, 1st v.p. 1964-65, pres. 1965-66). Republican. Office: Union City Ins Agy 315 S 2d St Union City TN 38261 *Searching for identity ends and the guest of life's goals end when one knows who he is and whose he is. As a servant his one goal in life is to serve his Lord.*

HAKEL, EDWIN HENRY, clergyman; b. Silver Lake, Minn., June 2, 1909; s. Stephen and Emily (Zbitovsky) H.; student Macalester Coll., 1929, McPhail Sch. Music, Mpls., 1930-32, Mpls. Sch. Music, 1934-35, U. Minn., 1949, Western Pastor's Sch., 1956; m. Alice Vera Svihel, Aug. 16, 1946; adopted children—Pollyann, Richard. Ordained to ministry Congl. Ch., 1954; minister, St. Paul, 1945-54, Staples, Minn., 1954-60, 1st Congl. Ch., Sherburn, Minn., 1960-73, St. Matthew's United Ch. of Christ, Litchfield, Minn., 1973-81; dir. Oak Haven Retreat, Inc., Fairmont, Minn., 1981—. Tchr. Leadership Tng. Inst., 1961; registrar No. Pacific Assn. Congl. Chs., 1955-60, scribe Minn. Conf., 1961, youth adviser Southwestern Assn., 1962-63, registrar, 1962-63; registrar Southwestern Assn. United Ch. Christ, 1964, 65, 69, 70, 71; condr. Vesper Hour TV program, 1973-74; United Ch. of Christ rep. region Minn. Council Chs., 1976, 77, vice chmn. region 6E, also rep. theology of ecology com. Vice pres. Sherburn-Dunnell PTA, 1970, pres., 1971—; mem. Meeker County Community Adv. Council, 1976—; tenor Litchfield Area Male Chorus, v.p., 1976-77, pres., 1977—, also bd. dirs.; bd. dirs. Sherburn Civic and Commerce Assn., 1972-73; bd. dirs. Meeker County Concert Assn., 1976, 77; v.p. Meeker County unit Am. Cancer Soc., 1977—, pres.-elect 1978, pres., 1978-80; pres.-elect Meeker County Music and Arts Assn., 1978, pres., 1978-79. Served with AUS, 1942-45. Recipient Good Neighbor to NW award Radio Sta. WCCO, 1977; Certificate of Recognition for Bicentennial contbns. from Gov. Minn., 1977, Minn. Gov.'s cert. of commendation, 1980; Eastman Kodak scholar Photography Forum, 1983. Mem. Litchfield Area Ministerial Assn. (v.p. 1974-75, pres. 1975—, program com. 1978-79), Am. Legion (life mem. dist. 7; chaplain 4th dist. 1953-54, 71, chaplain 2d dist. 1972-73, chaplain 7th dist. 1976-79, state chaplain 1979—, Meritorious Service citation dist. 7, 1979), North Central Camera Club Council. Kiwanian (life mem., pres. elect Sherburn 1964, lt. gov. div. 2 Minn.-Dakotas dist. 1965, div. 5, 1977-79, v.p. Sherburn 1970, pres. 1971, dir. Litchfield 1974—, pub. relations chmn. 1975—). Clubs: Fairmont Camera (pres. 1966-67, 70-71; Gold Cup Trophy for color slide competition 1964-66, 70); Kiwanis of Fairmont (chmn. com. spiritual aims, spl. adv. to pres.; lt. gov. elect 1984-85). Address: Oak Haven Retreat Inc Route 3 Box 28K Fairmont MN 56031

HAKIM, MICHEL, religious leader. Archéparque Ea. Rite Roman Cath. Ch. in Can., Montreal. Office: Melkite Archeparchy Can, 34 Maplewood, Montreal, PQ Canada H2V 2M1*

HALBERT, JOHN K., academic administrator. Pres. Maryknoll Sch. Theology, N.Y. Office: Maryknoll Sch Theol Office of the President Maryknoll NY 10545*

HALDANE-STEVENSON, JAMES PATRICK, minister; b. Llandaff, Wales, Mar. 17, 1910; s. Graham Morton and Jane (Thomson) Stevenson; m. Leila Mary Flack, Nov. 5, 1938 (div. 1967); children: Alan, Keith, Janet; m. Joan Talbot Smith, Aug. 6, 1983. BA, U. Oxford, Eng., 1933, MA, 1941; postgrad., U. Lausanne, Switzerland, 1934. Ordained to ministry Anglican Ch., 1935. Clk. Westminster Bank, Birmingham, Eng., 1927-30; curate Anglican Ch., Lambeth, Eng., 1935-38; commissary Archbishop Ont., 1939-44; chaplain British Army, Dunkirk, France and Cassino, Italy, 1939-55; rector Anglican Ch., Wongan Hills, Australia, 1956-59; vicar Anglican Ch. of North Balwyn, Melbourne, Australia, 1959-80; founder HSC Consultancy, 1991. Author: (as J.P. Stevenson) In Our Tongues, 1944, Religion and Leadership, 1948, Crisanzio and Other Poems, 1948, Beyond the Bridge, 1973, The Backward Look, 1976; represented in anthologies including Soldiers Also Asked, 1943, Padre Presents, 1943, Poems from Italy, 1945, Songs of Australia, 1977; contbr. Australian Encyclopaedia, Australian Dictionary of Biography, Poetry Rev., Poetry Today, Guardian, New Statesman, Spectator; Australian correspondent Le Monde, 1969-73. Mem. Athenaeum Club (London), Instn. Royal Engrs. (Eng.), Melbourne Club, Nat. Press Club. Home: 3 Argyle Sq, Ainslie Ave, Canberra 2601, Australia Office: Coleg Mihangel Sant, Llandaf CF5 2YJ, Wales

HALE, AURELIA ETHEL, minister; b. Albany, N.Y., Apr. 16, 1940; d. Clarence Waters and Gertrude Mabel (Van Patten) H.; m. Donald Mason, Aug. 24, 1968 (div. June 1976); m. Peter Fabian, July 8, 1977. BA, Ea. Coll., 1963; MDiv, Ea. Bapt. Theol. Sem., 1965; cert. marriage and family therapy, Colgate-Rochester Div. Sch., 1976. Ordained to ministry Am. Bapt. Ch., 1974. Min. of edn. Am. Bapt. Ch., Ft. Collins, Colo., 1966-68; emergency svc. coord. L.I. Coun. of Chs., Valley Stream, N.Y., 1973-77; exec. dir. Deer Hill Conf. and Retreat Ctr., Wappingers Falls, N.Y., 1977-82; assoc. conf. min. Wis. Conf., United Ch. of Christ, Madison, 1982-90; dir. St. Benedict Ctr., Madison, 1990—; staff mem. Boulder County Welfare Dept., 1969-73; mem. planning team United Ch. of Christ Nat. Youth Event, Grinnell, Iowa, 1987-88, mem. nat. adv. com. on outdoor ministries United Ch. of Christ, 1978-82, 87-90, sec., 1988-90. Mem. Internat. Assn. of Conf. Ctr. Administrs., N.Am. Retreat Dirs. Assn., Spiritual Dirs. Internat. Home: 333 N Main St Oregon WI 53575 Office: St Benedict Ctr Box 5070 Madison WI 53705 *The growing edge of our spiritual life is most often nurtured in a place away from our daily routine. Jesus would go off to pray or teach the disciples. Camps, conferences and retreat centers are our "place apart" spaces today.*

HALE, JAMES RUSSELL, religion educator, minister; b. Phila., Dec. 14, 1918; s. Robert Gifford and Dorothy Emma (Graham) H.; m. Phyllis Bollinger, June 8, 1991; children from previous marriage: Douglas Graham, Dean Edward. A.B., Muhlenberg Coll., 1940; B.D., Luth. Theol. Sem., Gettysburg, Pa., 1944, S.T.M., 1950; Ed.D., Union Theol. Sem. and Columbia U., N.Y.C., 1970. Ordained to ministry Lutheran Ch. Am., 1944. Parish pastor Gethsemane and Reformation Luth. chs., Keyport and Long Branch, N.J., 1944-46, Our Savior Luth. Ch., Balt., 1946-50, Redeemer Luth. Ch., Ramsey, N.J., 1950-59, St. Paul's Luth. Ch., Collingswood, N.J., 1959-62; instr. ch. and community Luth. Theol. Sem., Gettysburg, 1962-63, asst. prof., 1963-69, assoc. prof., 1969-70, prof., 1970-84, acting pres., 1989-90, dir. continuing edn., 1990-91, editor Sem. Bull., 1965-69, dir. advanced studies program, 1975-80, dir. Town and Country Ch. Inst., 1980-85; theologian-in-residence Horthorpe Hall, Leicestershire, Eng., 1980-81; chmn. acad. com. ch. and soc. Washington Theol. Consortium, 1971-74; bd. dirs. Council on Luth. Theol. Edn. in N.E., 1975-80; vis. prof. Berea Coll., KY., Appalachian Ministries Ednl. Resource Ctr., 1986-87, Grad. Theol. Union, Berkeley, Calif, 1987, Luth. Theol. Sem., Phila., 1988; cons. Rural Ministry, Area Strategy Studies, Evangelization. Author: To Have and to Hold, 1972, Who Are the Unchurched? An Exploratory Study, 1977, rev. 1988, Lutherans and Social Action, 1979, The Unchurched: Who They Are and Why They Stay Away, 1980; contbr. articles to profl. jours. Sec., bd. dirs. Tressler Luth. Social Services, Camp Hill, Pa., 1973-77, 80-85; chmn. bd. dirs. Tressler Luth. Home for Children; bd. dirs. Adams County Office for Aging, 1989—; chmn. Adams County Com. for Family Food, Gettysburg, Pa., 1971-72; del. White House Conf. on Aging, 1981; mem. adv. coun. Luth. Social Svcs., Gettysburg Ctr., 1988—. Served with Civilian Public Service, 1943-44. Case Study Inst. fellow Cambridge, 1973-75; Gerontolgy in Sem. Tng. Program fellow Nat. Interfaith Coalition on Aging, 1979; Danforth Found. assoc., 1963-65; recipient Luth. Brotherhood Faculty Research, 1963-64, 80, award Luth. Ch. Am., 1968-70, 80-81, grants. Mem. Am. Acad. Religion, AAUP, Am. Sociol. Assn., Religious Research Assn., Soc. Sci. Study Religion, Rural Sociol. Soc. Democrat. Home: 315 Oak Ln Gettysburg PA 17325

HALE, JOE ALLEN, missionary, school administrator; b. Tupelo, Miss., May 18, 1954; s. Donzil Eugene and Hilda Mae (Pearce) Burlison; m. Annalee Carol Greiman, Dec. 10, 1977; children: Benjamin, DAniel, Jedidiah, Wesley. BS in Religion, Liberty U., 1977, MA in Fgn. Missions, 1986; MA in Ch. Growth, Calif. Grad. Sch. Theology, Anaheim, 1982. Ordained to ministry Bapt. Ch., 1977; cert. evang. tchr. Evang. Tchr. Tng. Assn. Missionary Liberty Bapt. Mission, Lynchburg, Va., 1977—; pastor Liberty Ch., Seoul, Republic of Korea, 1983—; founder Liberty Mission of Korea, Seoul, 1978—, Liberty Christian Schs., Seoul, 1983—; founder Network Internat. Christian Schs., Memphis, 1991—. Recipient Gt. Am. Family Community award Am. Family Soc., 1984, Alumnus of Yr. award Liberty U. Alumni Assn., 1987, Comdr.'s pub. svc. award Dept. Army, Korea, 1988. Mem. Internat. Christian Sch. Adminstrs. Assn., Am. C. of C. in Seoul. Office: Network Internat Christian Schs PO Box 18151 Memphis TN 38181 also: Liberty Mission, PO Box 23, Uijongbu 480-600, Republic of Korea

HALE, JOSEPH RICE, church organization executive; b. Texarkana, Tex., Mar. 25, 1935; s. Alfred Clay and Bess (Akin) H.; m. Mary Richey, June 2, 1964; 1 son, Jeffrey Glen. B.A., Asbury Coll., Wilmore, Ky., 1957; B.D., So. Methodist U., 1960; D.D., Asbury Theol. Sem., 1978. Ordained to ministry Meth. Ch., 1958; pastor Meth. Ch., Sunset, Tex., 1958-60; evangelist, 1960-66; asso. dir. dept. evangelism Bd. Evangelism, Meth. Ch., 1966-68, dir. ecumenical evangelism, 1968-74; dir. evangelization devel. Bd. Discipleship, United Meth. Ch., 1975-76; gen. sec. World Meth. Council, 1976—; mem. exec. com. Key 73, 1970-73; sec. working group evangelism Nat. Council Chs., 1972; pres. Communications Found., Inc., 1974-75; world ambassador Internat. Prayer Fellowship, 1974; exec. com. Evangelization Forum, 1973-75; registrar World Meth. Evangelism Convocation, Jerusalem, 1974; mem. Conf. Secs. Christian World Communions, 1976—, chmn. Christian World Communions, 1983-86. Author: Design for Evangelism, 1970, Christ Matters!, 1971, God's Moment, 1972, also articles, chpts. books, encys.; producer: film The Spirit is Moving, 1980; video prodns.: Roots of Faith, 1979, To Live to God, 1984, Nairobi, 1986, Singapore, 1991; editor proc. 13th-16th World Meth. Confs. Recipient Key to City of Daytona Beach Fla., 1963, 64; named Ky. col., 1977; recipient Asbury Coll. Alumni award, 1977. Home: 301 Forest Park Dr Waynesville NC 28786 Office: World Meth Coun PO Box 518 350 Lakeshore Dr Lake Junaluska NC 28745

HALE, LEONARD GERALD, pastor; b. Mt. Horeb, Wis., Jan. 13, 1939; s. Charles Samuel and Ethel Marie (Seffrood) H.; m. Shirley Mae Johnson, Mar. 15, 1960; children: Nanette, Daniel, Philip, Kimberly, Pamela. Diploma, Moody Bible Inst., Chgo., 1963; BA, Northwestern Coll., Mpls., 1966; ThM, Dallas Theol. Sem., 1970, DM, 1989. Office mgr. Racine (Wis.) Wood Products, 1956-60; maintenance supr. 1st Bapt. Ch., Mpls., 1963-66; with ins. dept. Mark IV Auto Air, Dallas, 1966-68; with personnel/pub. rels. dept. Home and Interiors, Dallas, 1968-72; pastor Fellowship Bible Ch., Shreveport, La., 1972-75, Grace Bible Ch., Mena, Ark., 1975-82; sr. pastor Sherwood Bible Ch., Kansas City, Mo., 1982—; tchr. Calvary Bible Coll., Kansas City, 1989—. Coach Sherwood Soccer Club, Kansas City, 1987—, also bd. dirs. With Air N.G., 1956-60. Mem. IFCA (bd. dirs. 1985-88), Birthright (bd. dirs. 1983-84). Republican. Avocations: tennis, coaching sports. Home: 6908 N Central Gladstone MO 64118 Office: Sherwood Bible Ch 4900 N Norton Kansas City MO 64119

HALE, ROBERT WESLEY, minister; b. Greensburg, Pa., Mar. 27, 1949; s. George Wesley and Dorothy Evelyn (Palmer) H.; m. Phyllis Ann Bacon,

June 26, 1976; children: Larissa Leanne, Chelsea Leigh, Cuyler Wesley. BA, Johnson Bible Coll., 1971. Ordained to ministry Christian Chs. and Chs. of Christ, 1971. Sr. minister Hillside Ch. of Christ, Reading, Pa., 1971-81, 1st Christian Ch., McKeesport, Pa., 1981-84, Schuylkill Ch. of Christ, Schuylkill Haven, Pa., 1984—; v.p. Eastern Christian Convention, 1972, sec., 1974, pres., 1975; treas. Pa. Christian Teen Convention, 1987-90. Contbr. articles and poems to mags. Facilitator Cancer Support Group, Schuylkill Haven, 1989—; sponsor Single Parent Support Group, 1990—. Mem. Eastern Pa. Christian Evangelizing Assn. (sec.), Delta Epsilon Chi. Republican. Office: Schuylkill Ch of Christ 44 Dock St Schuylkill Haven PA 17972 *The difference between winners and losers in life has little to do with the number of failures experienced, for winners often fail more than they succeed. The fundamental difference between winners and losers is that winners persevere through their many trials and failures while losers simply quit.*

HALE, SAMUEL WESLEY, JR., pastor; b. Chgo., Nov. 17, 1942; s. Samuel Wesley Sr. and Toledo Elizabeth (Dozier) H.; m. Gloria Marie Harris, Aug. 17, 1968; children: Samuel Wesley III, Lori Toledo, Jonathan Justin, Benjamin Prentiss. Student, U. Ill., 1960-61, Millikin U., 1961-62; BA, Am. Bapt. Theol. Sem., 1966; M of Div., So. Bapt. Theol. Sem., 1969. Ordained to ministry Bapt. Ch., 1965. Pastor Johenning Bapt. Ch., Washington, 1969-72; dir. religious activities Talladega (Ala.) Coll., 1972-73; dir. extension dept. Am. Bapt. Coll., Nashville, 1973-84; pastor Zion Missionary Bapt. Ch., Springfield, Ill., 1984—; bd. dirs. Christian Friends Ministries, Inc., Nashville; mem. adv. bd. Young Parent Support Services, Springfield, 1985. Composer religious songs. Bd. dirs. Greater Springfield Interfaith Assn., 1985; active Springfield Vicinity Misterial Alliance, 1984. Mem. Nat. Bapt. Congress of Christian Edn. (bd. dirs. 1971—), Contemporary Ministries Workshop (bd. dirs.). Democrat. Avocations: fishing, chess, badminton, basketball, softball. Office: Zion Missionary Bapt Ch 1601 E Laurel Springfield IL 62703

HALES, EDWARD JOHN, religious organization administrator; b. Pennsauken, N.J., Oct. 1, 1927; s. James Arthur and Elsa Alexandria (Almquist) H.; m. Frances June Moberg, Aug. 18, 1951; children: David, Deborah, Darlene, Diane, Donna, Daniel. Student, Moody Bible Inst., Chgo., 1945-47; BA in Theology, Gordon Coll., 1951; MA, Wheaton (Ill.) Coll., 1976. Ordained to ministry Bapt. Ch., 1951. Pastor Elim Bapt. Ch., New Britain, Conn., 1951-53, New Bedford, Mass., 1954-59; ch. extension dir. Bapt. Gen. Conf. of New Eng., 1959-63; pastor Immanuel Bapt. Ch., Kingsford, Mich., 1963-64; dir. stewardship Bapt. Gen. Conf., Chgo., 1964-71; dir. field svcs. Nat. Assn. Evangs., Wheaton, 1971-77; pastor First Bapt. Ch., Wheaton, 1977-81, Portland, Maine, 1982-88; exec. dir. Christian Stewardship Assn., South Daytona, Fla., 1988-91; regional mgr. Nehemiah Ministries, Daytona Beach, Fla., 1991—; pres. New Eng. Bapt. Bible Coll., South Portland, Maine, 1984-86, bd. dirs., 1983-84; vice chmn. of bd. Conservative Bapt. Sem. of the East, 1984-89. Author: Your Money Their Ministry, 1981, Building the Budget for the Local Church, 1965; contbr. articles to mags. Pres. HOmeowners of Fairway Estates, Daytona Beach, Fla., 1989—. Recipient Disting. Svc. award Jr. C. of C., New Bedford, Mass., 1958. Mem. Christian Mgmt. Assn., Religious Conf. Mgmt. Assn., Am. Assn. Soc. Execs., Conservative Bapt. Home Missions Soc. (rec. sec. 1986-89, v.p. 1989—), Evang. Coun. for Fin. Accountability (founding mem. standards com. 1978-86, 91—), Rotary. Home: 1320 Edgewater Rd Daytona Beach FL 32114 Office: Nehemiah Ministries 1320 Edgewater Rd Daytona Beach FL 32114 *Our lives with all of our gifts of time, talent and resources are gifts from God and we serve best when we recognize that we are called to be stewards of these gifts to use them to His glory and to the benefit of mankind and God's kingdom.*

HALEY, MICHAEL ANSLEM, minister; b. Baton Rouge, Aug. 17, 1952; s. Robert Marvin and Ann Nichols (Toler) H.; m. Dorothy Colleen Minton, June 5, 1971 (dec. Oct. 1982); children: Kara Leigh (dec.), James Eric, Melissa Ann, Lindy Michelle; m. Cheryl Lee Adams, Apr. 11, 1983 (dec. Mar. 1984); m. Carol Ruth Morgan, Nov. 10, 1984; children: Megan Lynn, Morgan Leigh. BA in Music, La. State U., 1975; BA in Theology, La. Coll., 1980; MDiv, Mid-Am. Sem., 1988; MA in Counseling, Liberty Bapt. U., 1990. Ordained to ministry Bapt. Ch., 1978. Min. of music Tri-County Bapt. Ministry, Stamford, N.Y., 1976-78; min. of music First Bapt. Ch., Jena, La., 1978-80, Bridge City, Tex., 1980-83; pastor, home missionary Floyd Bapt. Ch., Rome, N.Y., 1983-88, Fellowship Bapt. Ch., Burnham, Pa., 1988—; resident couselor Mountain View Med. Clinic, Mifflintown, Pa., 1989-91; mem. exec. bd. edn. com. Bapt. Conv. N.Y., Syracuse, 1984-87; chmn. evangelism Davin Bapt. Ch., Hartwick, N.Y., 1985-88; chmn. bd. dirs. Gospel Outreach Ministries, Lewistown, Pa., 1989—; cons. Sunday Sch. Bd. So. Bapt. Ch., 1984-89; cons. evangelism dept. Home Mission Bd., 1985-88. Contbr. articles to profl. jours. Organizer Tough Love/Students in Recovery, Burnham, 1989; pres. gymnastics YMCA, Burnham, 1991; talk show host Sta. WMRF, Lewistown, 1991. With USAF, 1970-72. Recipient Contibution of Svc. award Soc. of Disting. Am. High Sch. Students, 1984. Mem. Keystone Bapt. Assn., Christian Social Ministry. Republican. Home: 601 Chris Ave Lewistown PA 17044 Office: Fellowship Bapt Ch 22 Windmill Hill Burnham PA 17009

HALIVNI, DAVID WEISS, religion educator, rabbi; b. Romania, Dec. 12, 1928; s. Callel and Fanny (Weiss) H.; m. Tzipore Hager, Dec. 9, 1953; children: Bernard, Ephraim, Isaiah. BA, Bklyn. Coll., 1953; MA, NYU, 1956; DHL, Jewish Theol. Sem., N.Y.C., 1958. Ordained rabbi, 1943, reordained, 1952. Rector Inst. for Traditional Judaism, Mt. Vernon, N.Y.; prof. religion Columbia U., N.Y.C., 1986—; mem. Inst. for Advanced Studies, Hebrew U., Jerusalem. Author of eight books on Talmud and rabbinics. Recipient Bialik prize Tel Aviv, 1985. Mem. Am. Acad. Jewish Rsch. (pres.). Office: Columbia Univ Dept Religion 626 Kent Hall New York NY 10022

HALL, ADAM REID, JR., minister; b. Memphis, July 13, 1938; s. Adam Reid Sr. and Elise (Welch) H.; m. Patricia Ann Money, June 12, 1966; children: Adam Reid III, Dacia Dalyn. BS in Gen. Bus., U. Tenn., Martin, 1963; MA in Religious Edn., Southwestern Bapt. Theol. Sem., 1968. Ordained to ministry So. Bapt. Conv., 1976. Dir. food svcs. student store Southwestern Bapt. Theol. Sem., Ft. Worth, 1966-71; min. Bapt. campus U. Tenn., Martin, 1971—; part time dir. edn. First Bapt. Ch., Crowley, Tex., 1969-71. Mem. Assn. So. Bapt. Campus Ministries (v.p. membership 1986, 87). Home: Rte 1 Box 26 Martin TN 38327 Office: U Tenn Bapt Student Union 112 Hurt St Martin TN 38237-2999

HALL, ALFRED WAYNE, minister; b. San Juan, Utah, Aug. 9, 1947; s. Albert Leroy and Mary Ann (Gullett) H.; m. Nancy Lou Doiel; children: Calvin Leroy, Freddy Wayne. AA in Ministry, Midwest Bible Coll., Houston, 1967. Pastor Van Buren Chapel, Sarcoxie, Mo., 1967-69, Granby (Mo.) Gospel Mission, 1969-70, Keelville Ch., Baxter Springs, Kans., 1970-77; sr. pastor Decker Chapel, Magnolia, Tex., 1977-86; founding pastor Faith Restoration Ch., Tomball, Tex., 1986. Home: 14111 Limerick Ln Tomball TX 77375

HALL, ARTHUR RAYMOND, JR., minister; b. Danville, Ill., Apr. 16, 1922; s. Arthur Raymond and Hetta Ada (Wheeler) H.; m. Lou Ann Benson, Mar. 16, 1946; children: Janet Marie Hall Graff, Laura Ann Hall Scott, Nancy Marion. A.B., U. Ill., 1946, M.A., 1948; M.Div. cum laude, Union Theol. Sem., N.Y.C., 1951; D.D., Hanover Coll., 1961. Staff asst. McKinley Meml. Ch. and Found., Champaign, Ill., 1946-48; student asst. First Presbyn Ch., N.Y.C., 1948-50; ordained to ministry Presbyn. Ch., 1951; pastor First Presbyn. Ch., Monmouth, Ill., 1951-58, Cen. Presbyn. Ch., Louisville, 1958-67, Bradley Hills Presbyn. Ch., Bethesda, Md., 1967-89; pres. bd. Christian edn. United Presbyn. Ch., 1968-73; sec., bd. dirs. Louisville Presbyn. Sem., 1962-70; chmn. renewal and extension of ministry (United Presbyn. Gen. Assembly), 1965-68; mem. joint com. on Presbyn. Reunion, 1969-83; moderator Synod of Piedmont, 1974-75; trustee U.P. Ch., 1974-83; bd. dirs. U.P. Found., 1974-83; del. Uniting Assembly of World Alliance of Ref. Chs., Nairobi, Kenya, 1970; mem. com. on theol. edn. Presbyn. Ch., U.S.A., 1987, assoc. dir. 1988-90. Contbr. articles to periodicals. Pres. Citizens Met. Planning Coun., Louisville, 1962; chmn. Mayor's Adv. Com. for Community Devel., 1963-67; v.p. Louisville YMCA Downtown Bd., 1963; bd. dirs. Louisville Health and Welfare Coun., 1963-67, Greater Washington Coun. Chs., Johnson C. Smith Theol. Sem., Atlanta, 1973—, Interdenominational Theol. Ctr., Atlanta, 1974—; trustee Centre Coll. Ky., 1959-73, Union Theol. Sem., N.Y.C., 1975-84; trustee Travelers Aid Soc., Louisville, 1959-67, v.p., 1961-67. Lt. (j.g.) USNR, 1943-46. Mem. Am. Guild Organists, Washington Interchurch Club, Rotary, Beta Theta Pi, Phi Delta Phi. Democrat. Home: 8400 Whitman Dr Bethesda MD 20817

HALL, BENNETT FREEMAN, minister; b. Macon, Ga., Nov. 30, 1914; s. Charles McDonald and Mary Elizabeth (Lyon) H.; m. Mae Elizabeth Wells, June 2, 1937; children: Mari, Laura, Louise, Ben. Student, Bryan U., 1934-36; AB, Stetson U., 1938; ThM, So. Bapt. Theol. Sem., 1943; postgrad., Jewish Theol. Sem., 1968-71; ThM, Princeton Theol. Sem., 1975; DMin, Drew U., 1979. Ordained to ministry Bapt. Ch., 1936. Pastor Falmouth (Ky.) Bapt. Ch., 1942-44, First Bapt. Ch., Titusville, Fla., 1944-49, Bay Haven Bapt. Ch., Sarasota, Fla., 1950-53, Southside Bapt. Ch., Bradenton, Fla., 1954-67, Somerset Hills Bapt. Ch., Bernardsville, N.J. (Now in Basking Ridge, N.J.), N.J., 1967-79, First Bapt. Ch., Lexington, Ky., 1982-85; trustee Bapt. Bible Inst., Fla., 1949-59; mem. state mission bd. Fla. Bapt. Conv., 1957-59; dean, tchr. extention dept. Stetson U., 1960-64; evangelist Jamaica Crusade, 1966; missions com. Met. N.Y. Bapt. Assn., 1968-72, chmn. constn. and credentials com., 1972-77; tchr., sem. extension Met. N.Y. Assn., 1976-78; adv. bd. Cumberland Coll., Williamsburg, Ky., 1982-91. Chmn. ARC, Titusville, 1944-46; mem. Mental Health Orgn., Bradenton, 1964-66. Home: 293 S Main St Winchester KY 40391 *Two great statements, learned in college, have been the guiding principle of my life. The Socratic challenge: "Follow the truth wherever it leads." The other: "Learn to distinguish between the spiritual ointment and the spiritual receptacle."*

HALL, BERNICE LUCIA, music minister; b. Bronx, N.Y., Mar. 4, 1928; d. Adolphus Christopher and Ada Idalia (Cruse) Edwards; m. Edgar Waker, June 30, 1956 (dec. Sept. 1958); m. Eugene Hall, July 28, 1963. B in Music, New Eng. Conservatory of Music, 1949; cert., Longy Music Inst., Paris, 1954; AA, Annes Coll., N.Y.C., 1955; HHD, Universal Coll., 1982. Soloist New Eng. Conservatory Orch., Boston, 1951; violinist Hinton Orch., Boston, 1951-53; singer City Ctr. Opera Co., N.Y.C., 1953-54, Nat. Negro Opera Co., Washington, 1954-60; minister of music The Bapt. Temple Ch., N.Y.C., 1968-74; min. of music Caldwell African Meth. Ch. of Zion, Bronx, 1975-83, Greater Mood African Meth. Ch of Zion, N.Y.C., 1984-91; minister of music Greater Hood Meth. Ch., N.Y.C., 1986—; voice tchr. The Henry Street Music Sch., N.Y.C., 1974-84; founder, dir. youth music Besma Assn., N.Y.C., 1960—, The Luth. Ch., N.Y.C., 1984—; cons. Christian Edn., N.Y.C., 1984—; accompanist The Hodson Singers, 1989—; accompanist, dir. choir The Children's Bud Choir, N.Y.C., 1989—. Author: (poems) Seeds of Hope, 1970; edn. editor The Urban Life Newspaper, Bklyn., 1968. Cons. Republic of Liberia U., Monrovia, 1964; chmn. Ams. for Ethiopia Assn., N.Y.C., 1965; nat. supr. Girls Club NACWC, 1975-79; mem. Retired Sr. Vol. Program of Community Svc. Soc., N.Y.C., 1989-91. Recipient community service award Sachs Furniture Stores, N.Y.C., 1971, Disting. Vol. Svc. award, 1991, Paul and Esther Leith award, 1991, Disting. Artist award Ascension Luth. Ch., 1991; named Woman of Yr. 1978. Mem. Nat. Assn. Colored Women (supr. 1972, Youth Achievement award 1970), Nat. Council Negro Women, Nat. Key Women Assn., New Eng. Conservatory Alumni, Layman League (cons.). Methodist. Lodge: Zion. Avocations: writing, composing, crocheting, working with children. *To hear the truth is security; to know the truth is power; to speak the truth is reality; to live the truth is faith.*

HALL, B(LANCHE) BARBARA, biblical studies educator; b. Atlanta, June 11, 1928; d. Clarence Wilbur and Blanche Marion (Bouterse) H. BA, Bucknell U., 1949; MA, Yale U., 1951, BD/MDiv, 1961; PhD, Union Sem., N.Y.C., 1973. Exec. dir. Student YWCA, U. Ky., Lexington, 1951-54; assoc. dir. Presbyn. ministry to U. Calif., Berkeley, 1954-56; missionary Presbyn. Ch. U.S.A., Rio de Janeiro, 1956-59, Episcopal Ch., Sao Paulo, Brazil, 1961-64; prof. N.T., Gen. Theol. Sem., N.Y.C., 1978-85, Va. Theol. Sem., Alexandria, 1985—. Author: Joining the Conversation, 1985; co-editor: Christ and His Communities, 1990. Democrat. Episcopalian. Home and Office: 3737 Seminary Rd Alexandria VA 22305

HALL, CARL FRANKLIN, retired minister; b. Strong, Maine, Dec. 12, 1905; s. Frank Hosea Hall and Evelyn Kelley; m. Gretchen Von Walther Hayes, June 15, 1936; children—David Walther, Elizabeth Hall Harmon, William Douglas. B.A., Bates Coll., 1936; M.Div., Bangor Theol. Sem., 1971. Ordained to ministry Congregational Ch., 1936. Pastor Bluehill Congl. Ch., Maine, 1937-41; staff minister Maine Seaeast Missionary Soc., Bar Harbor, Maine, 1941-47; pastor Congl. Ch., Duxbury, Mass., 1948-51, Fed. Ch. North St., Norfolk, Mass., 1952-60; Congl. Ch., Gray, Maine, 1960-64, Staffordville and West Sattford, Conn., 1965-74; moderator Tolland Assn. Congl. Chs., 1972-74; ret., 1974—; exec. dir. Protestant Guild for Blind, Boston, 1951, 52. mem. Stafford Sewer Commn., 1965-74; active Casco Bay Island Devel. Assn.; pres. Peaks Island (Maine) Sr. Ctr.; mem. The Islands Health Ctr. Contbr. articles to Sea Breeze. Clk. Boston Seamans Friend Soc. Democrat. Club: 60 Plus. Lodge: Kiwanis. Avocations: photography; travel. Home: 20 A St Peaks Island ME 04108

HALL, CARSON KEITH, minister; b. Mabscott, W.Va., Aug. 5, 1945; s. Dennis and Nezra Mae (Atkins) H.; m. Charlene Kay Patrick, Sept. 17, 1968; children: Brian, Deborah. Lic. to ministry Bapt. Ch., 1982, ordained, 1988. Youth dir. Grace Bapt. Ch., Bridgeport, W.Va., 1982-83; assoc. pastor Cleve. Bapt. Ch., 1983—; counselor youth Cleve. Bapt. Ch., 1971-82, deacon 1978-82; jail chaplain Cuyahoga County Jail, Cleve., 1990—. Trustee Crisis Pregnancy Ctr., Cleve., 1989—. With U.S. Army, 1965-68. Home: 9205 Biddulph Rd Brooklyn OH 44144-2615 Office: Cleveland Bapt Ch 4431 Tiedeman Rd Brooklyn OH 44144

HALL, DAVID, minister, religious organization adminstrator; b. Augusta, Ga., Dec. 22, 1938; s. Lottie E. H. BA in Social Work, Howard U., 1964; BS in Polit. Sci., Tex. So. U., 1970; MDiv, Morehouse Coll., 1967; DD, Tex. So. U., 1978, PhD, 1979. Pastor various chs., 1972-78, Grady's Chapel Rock Bapt. Ch., San Antonio, 1976—; founder Miss Black Am., Washington, 1969-70; founder David Hall Assocs., chief exec. officer meeting planners confs. and convs., 1987; dir. pub. rels. NAACP, Washington, 1971-73; regional dir. SCLC, Washington, 1974-76; dir., founder Christian Concern for Community Action, Washington, 1970—. Chaplain CAP; coordinator Lorton Council for Progressive Action; mem. dist. adv. council Met. Police Dept. Served with U.S. Army, 1959-65, Vietnam; D.C. N.G. and USAR, ret., 1979. Decorated Meritorious Service Medal. Mem. Nat. Black Women Polit. Leadership Caucus (nat. chaplain 1977—), Acacia, Knights Kodash, Masons (32 degree), Shriners (past chaplain), Elks. Democrat. Home and Office: 1338 K St SE Washington DC 20003

HALL, DOUGLAS JOHN, minister, educator; b. Ingersoll, Ont., Can., Mar. 23, 1928; s. John Darius and Louisa Irene (Sandick) H.; m. Rhoda Catherine Palfrey, May 28, 1960; children: Mary Kate, Christopher, Sara, Lucia. BA, U. Western Ont., 1953; MDiv, Union Sem., N.Y.C., 1956; STM, Union Sem., 1957, ThD, 1963; DD (hon.), Queen's U., Kingston, 1988. Ordained to ministry United Ch. of Can., 1956. Min. St. Andrew's Ch., Blind River, Ont., 1960-62; prin. St. Paul's Coll., Waterloo, Ont., 1962-65; prof. St. Andrew's Coll., Saskatoon, Sask., Can., 1965-75; prof. Christian theology McGill U., Montreal, Que., Can., 1975—; vis. scholar Doshisha U., Kyoto, Japan, 1989. Author: Hope Against Hope, 1969, The Reality of the Gospel and the Unreality of the Churches, 1975, Lighten Our Darkness: Towards an Indigenous Theology of the Cross, 1976, Has the Church a Future?, 1980, The Canada Crisis, 1981, Ecclesia Crucis, 1979, The Steward: A Biblical Symbol Come of Age, 1982, rev. edit., 1990, God and Human Suffering, 1986, Imaging God: Dominion As Stewardship, 1986, Thinking the Faith: Christian Theology in a North American Context, 1989, The Future of the Church, 1989. Mem. Can. Theol. Soc., New Democratic Party Can. Home: 5562 Notre-Dame-de-Grace, Montreal, PQ Canada H4A 1L7 Office: McGill U, 3520 University St, Montreal, PQ Canada H3A 2A7

HALL, HAROLD ARTHUR, radio broadcaster; b. Chgo., May 13, 1938; s. Wendell Gladstone and Margaret Elisabeth (Asplund) H.; m. Marjorie Alice Neff, Jan. 16, 1960; children: Steven Arthur, Nancy Ruth, Roger Alan, Daniel Craig. AA, San Jose City Coll., 1958. Program dir., announcer Air Network, Glendale, Calif., 1965-66; announcer, bd. operator Family Stas. Inc., San Francisco, 1959-65; announcer, continuity dir. Family Stas. Inc., Oakland, Calif., 1966—; producer, host Christian Home, Life with Meaning, Radio Reading Circle; vol. cons. broadcast media Internat. Coun. Bibl. Inerrancy, Oakland, 1984—86' mem. adv. bd. Star Song Enterprises, San Jose, Calif., 1983-84, City Team Ministries, San Jose, 1990—; ch. officer Evang. Free Ch., San Jose, 1966-82, tchr., 1966—, leader home Bible study, 1978—. Republican. Avocations: gardening, writing, video recording. Office: Family Stas 290 Hegenberger Rd Oakland CA 94621 *Since heaven represents rest from the struggles of this life, now is the time to win the spiritual battles. Let us not try to retire from Christ's army too soon.*

HALL, KENNETH FRANKLIN, religion educator; b. Columbiana, Ohio, Dec. 13, 1926; s. Herbert David and Martha (Starbuck) H.; m. Arlene Stevens, Sept. 18, 1949; children: David Eric, Kenneth Douglas. BA, Anderson U., 1948; BD, Butler U., 1952; D of Ministry, Christian Theol. Sem., Indpls., 1973. Successively news editor, youth editor, book editor, dir. curriculum Warner Press, Anderson, Ind., 1948-78; prof. Christian edn., chair dept. Bible and religion Anderson U., 1978—; local affiliate Contact Teleministries USA, Harrisburg, Pa., 1971—; former nat. bd. dirs. Author books, including: They Stand Tall, 1952, On Bumping Into God, 1970, Invited to Teach, 1988, Living Leadership, 1991; curriculum writer various ch. groups. Mem. commn. Ch. of God, Anderson, 1973-78, sec. social concerns com., 1986-88. Recipient Disting. Alumnus award Anderson U., 1975. Mem. Religious Edn. Assn. (profs. and rsch. sect.), Nat. Assn. Profs. Christian Edn., Kiwanis (pres., bd. dirs. local chpt. 1975-76), Theta Phi. Home: 712 Maplewood Ave Anderson IN 46012 Office: Anderson U Anderson IN 46012

HALL, LARRY BRUCE, minister; b. Georgetown, Ky., Dec. 11, 1942; s. Bruce Browning and Juanita Ann (Patrick) H.; m. Sara Kay Yarbrough, Mar. 26, 1966; children: Larissa Kathleen, Larry Bruce Jr. BA, Georgetown Coll., 1964; grad., Lexington Theol. Sem., 1974; MDiv, Emory U., 1977, postgrad., 1978; D Ministry, Grad. Theol. Found., Notre Dame, Ind., 1990. Ordained deacon United Meth. Ch., 1974, elder, 1979. Pastor Centerville United Meth. Ch., Paris, Ky., 1972-74; assoc. pastor Sandy Springs United Meth. Ch., Atlanta, 1974-77, First United Meth. Ch., Pampa, Tex., 1977-80; pastor Agape United Meth. Ch., Lubbock, Tex., 1980-82; sr. pastor First United Meth. Ch., Dumas, Tex., 1982-84, Artesia, N.Mex., 1986—; dir. Wesley Found., W. Tex. State U., Canyon, 1978-80; chmn. evangelism Lubbock dist. United Meth. Ch., Tex., 1980-82; chmn. ethnic minority chs. N.W. Tex. Conf., 1982-86; dir. spiritual life Clovis (N.Mex.) Dist. United Meth. Ch., 1987. Editor: Services in Texas Panhandle, 1984; author, editor Theol. Thoughts, 1978—, Acad. of Faith, 1980—. Bd. dirs. Commn. on Mental Health, Dumas, Tex., 1983-86; found. dir. Com. on Volunteerism, Dumas, 1985; bd. dirs. YMCA, Dumas, 1985-86, Good Samaritan Ctrs., Artesia, N.Mex., 1987—. Capt. U.S. Army, 1965-69. Recipient Youth Leadership award United Meth. Ch., Tex., 1979-80, Evangelism Growth award, 1981, 82, 84, Leadership award Tex. Meth. Coll., 1984. Fellow Grad. Theol. Found.; mem. Am. Assn. Christian Counselors, Order St. Luke, Disciplined Order of Christ, Rotary. Democrat. Avocations: backpacking, photography. Office: First United Meth Ch 500 W Grand PO Box 499 Artesia NM 88211-0499

HALL, MILTON L., bishop. Bishop Ch. of God in Christ, Kokomo, Ind. Office: Ch of God in Christ 1404 Delphos Kokomo IN 46901*

HALL, PHILIP GEORGE, clergyman; b. Columbus, Ohio, July 18, 1946; s. George L. and Joyce (Robertson) Hall; m. Janith Ann Damron, Dec. 19, 1965; children: Chris, Aaron, Matthew, Andrew. Student, Glenville State Coll., 1964-67; MTh, Luther Rice Bible Sem., 1988, DTh, 1990. Ordained to ministry Bapt. Ch., 1978. Minister edn. Calvary Bapt. Ch., Bluefield, W.Va., 1978-81; pastor Abbs Valley Bapt. Ch., Bluefield, Va., 1981-84, Radford Bapt. Ch., Moneta, Va., 1984-87, National Ave. Bapt. Ch., New Bern, N.C., 1987—; pres. East River Pastor's Assn., Bluefield, 1983; mem. Va. Bapt. Gen. Bd., Richmond, 1984; pres. Strawberry Pastor's Assn., Bedford, Va., 1986, Atlantic Bapt. Ministers, Havelock, N.C., 1991. With USAF, 1967-70. Office: National Ave Bapt Ch 510 Watson Ave New Bern NC 28560 *The Pastor who desires to grow a great church must love Jesus, love the people and be a strong leader. His people will respond favorably to that kind of leadership.*

HALL, RANDALL STEVEN, minister; b. Cherry Point, N.C., Dec. 26, 1954; s. David Roland Gustive and Elizabeth Jean (Rice) H.; m. Kristee Leann Wollard, Nov. 25, 1981; children: Jennifer Lynn, Matthew Steven. Student, Johnson County Community Coll., 1972-73, Ozark Christian Coll., 1978-82. Ordained to ministry, Johnson County Christian Ch., 1985. Draftsman Prestige Products, Neodesha, Kans., 1984-85; minister LaFontaine (Kans.) Christian Ch., 1980-84; minister First Christian Ch., Humboldt, Kans., 1985—, radio evangelist, 1990—; bd. dirs. Preaching Christ to Millions Mission, Joplin, Mo., 1986—. Columnist This Week in the Word, 1989. Dir. fin. Hidden Haven Christian Camp, Thayer, Kans., 1988-90; organizer Humboldt Youth Ctr., 1987, All Christians Evangelizing Someone Softball Team, Humboldt, 1989; corr. Humboldt Libr. Bd., 1990—; driver Humboldt Ambulance Svc., 1988; coach Humboldt Pks. and Recreation, 1988—. Named Outstanding Young Minister, N.Am. Christian Conv., Louisville, Ky., 1989. Mem. Kans./Okla. Evagelistic Assn. (bd. dir. 1988—), Humboldt Ministerial Alliance (pres. 1990), Humboldt C. of C. Republican. Avocations: woodworking, writing, flower gardening, weight lifting, drawing. Home and Office: First Christian Ch 118 N 9th St Humboldt KS 66748

HALL, RICHARD CLYDE, JR., religious educational administrator; b. Florence, Ala., Apr. 13, 1931; s. Richard Clyde Sr. and Annie Hazel (Darrah) H.; m. Mildred Marie Denham, May 19, 1957; children: Richard Denham, Darralyn Marie, Kevin Clyde, Edward Earnest. AA, U. Fla., 1950, BA, 1953; MRE, Southwestern Bapt. Theol. Sem., 1958, DRE, 1966, EdD, 1975, MA, 1984. Ordained to gospel ministry So. Bapt. Conv., 1955. Youth dir. 1st Bapt. Ch., Miami, Fla., 1953; ednl. sec., youth dir. Ave. J Bapt. Ch., Ft. Worth, 1953-54; dir. Bapt. Student Union Fla. Bapt. Conv., Jacksonville, 1954-57; min. edn. Eastover Bapt. Ch., Ft. Worth, 1957-61; minister edn. 1st Bapt. Ch., Elizabethton, Tenn., 1961-63, Gambrell Street Bapt. Ch., Ft. Worth, 1963-65; assoc. ch. tng. dept. Bapt. Gen. Conv. Tex., Dallas, 1965-72, sec. ch. tng. dept., 1972-73; mgmt. cons. Pro., Inc., San Diego, 1973-74; cons. adult work ch. tng. dept. Bapt. Sunday Sch. Bd., Nashville, 1974-75, cons. gen. adminstrn. ch. tng. dept., 1975-76, mgr. youth sect. discipleship tng. dept., 1976—; teaching fellow religious psychology and drama Southwestern Bapt. Theol. Sem., Ft. Worth, 1960-61; instr. youth edn. Sem. Extension, 1981—. Author: Source, 1967-70, Church Training, 1970—; (cassette and workbook) The Work of the Associational Age Group Leader, 1980; (filmstrip) DiscipleLife: Training Youth in Discipleship, 1981, DiscipleLife, 1984; compiler: Youth Leadership Training Pak, 1982, DiscipleHelps: A DiscipleYouth Daily Quiet Time Guide and Journal, 1985; (with Joe Ford) DiscipleYouth I Kit, 1982, DiscipleYouth I Notebook, 1982, DiscipleYouth II Kit, 1985, DiscipleYouth II Notebook, 1985; (with Wesley Black) DiscipleHow Manual; (with Valerie Hardy) Mission Trip Administrative Manual. Trauma Center Plus,. Mem. ASTD, Internat. Religious Edn. Assn., So. Bapt. Religious Edn. Assn. (sec.-treas. 1982-83), Ea. Bapt. Religious Edn. Assn. (sec.-treas. 1975-79, pres. 1980), Southwestern Bapt. Religious Edn. Assn., Adult Edn. Assn. Office: Sunday Sch Bd of Bapt Conv 127 9th Ave N Nashville TN 37234

HALL, STUART GEORGE, ecclesiastical history educator, priest; b. London, June 7, 1928; s. George Edward and May Catherine (Whale) H.; m. Brenda Mary Henderson, Apr. 9, 1953; children—Lindsay George, Nicola Mary, Edith May, Walter Stuart. B.A., New Coll., Oxford U., 1952, M.A., 1955, B.D., Oxford U., 1973. Ordained priest Ch. of Eng., 1955. Asst. curate Ch. of Eng., Newark, Nottinghamshire, Eng., 1954-58; tutor Queen's Coll., Birmingham, Eng., 1958-62; lectr. in theology U. Nottingham, Eng., 1962-73, sr. lectr., 1973-78; prof. ecclesiastical history, King's Coll., U. London, 1978—; priest in charge St. John's, Pittenweem, and St. Michael's, Elie, 1990—. Author: Melito of Sardis, 1978, Doctrine and Practice in the Early Church, 1991; co-editor Theologische Realenzyklopadie, 1977; contbr. articles to profl. jours. Served with Brit. Army, 1947-48. Mem. Academie Internationale des Scis. Religieuses, Internat. Assn. for Patristics Studies, Ecclesiastical History Soc. Avocations: gardening; golf; music. Home: 15 High St, Elie, Leven KY9 1BY, Scotland

HALL, T. HARTLEY, IV, academic administrator. Pres. Union Theol. Sem. in Va., Richmond. Office: Union Theol Sem 3401 Brook Rd Richmond VA 23227*

HALL, THOMAS H., JR., minister; b. Springfield, Ill., June 15, 1924; s. Thomas H. Sr. and Lula (Hughes) H.; m. Thelma Smith, Oct. 3, 1959 (dec. Nov. 1989); 1 child, Kimberly Hall-Moore. BA, Wilberforce U., 1951, MDiv, 1953; LittD (hon.), Triune Bible Inst., 1984. Pastor Clinton Chapel African Meth. Episc. Ch., Montgomery, Ala., 1954-57; chaplain to migrant farm workers Montgomery, 1955-57; asst. pastor Bethel African Meth. Episc. Ch., Montgomery, 1957-59; mem. staff Conn. Assn. Ministry, Somers, Conn., 1960-75; pastor, founder Cummings Chapel African Meth. Ch., Waterbury, Conn., 1976—; counselor Conn. Prison Assn., Hartford, 1985—. Trustee Legal Aid Soc., Hartford, 1984—; dir. Nutrition for Elderly program State of Conn., Hartford, 1985-89; counselor alcohol program State of Conn., Hartford, 1989—; vol. manpower funding com. Conn. State Labor Dept., Hartford, 1972. Cpl. U.S. Army, 1943-45, ETO. Recipient cert. of Meritorious Svc. Conn. State Dept. Labor, 1971, Ofcl. citation Conn. Gen. Assembly, 1988, City of Hartford, 1988. Mem. VFW (recognition cert. 1990), Masons (past pastor 1982-83), Shriners (past potentate 1988-89, Appreciation award 1989), Elks, Phi Beta Sigma. Home: 294 Tunxis Ave Bloomfield CT 06002

HALL, THOMAS WILLIAM, religion educator; b. Portis, Kans., Sept. 20, 1921; s. Charles E. and Myrtle (DeWitt) H.; m. Ruth Helen Fisher, July 11, 1944; children: Carolyn Jane, Kristin Elaine, Douglas William. A.B., Kans. Wesleyan U., 1943; Th.M., Iliff Sch. Theology, Denver, 1946; Ph.D., Boston U., 1956. Asst. prof. Kans. Wesleyan U., 1946-48, Pittsburg (Kans.) State Coll., 1950-55; assoc. prof., chmn. dept. religion U. Denver, 1956-59; dean religion Stephens Coll., Columbia, Mo., 1959-66; chmn. dept. religion Syracuse U., 1966-74, prof., 1974-85, prof. emeritus, 1985—; Danforth tchr., 1955-56; vis. prof. Iliff Sch. of Theology, 1986, 88-89; sr. research cons. CAEL Mountains and Plains Region, 1986-87. Author: Introduction to Study of Religion, 1978, Religion: An Introduction, 1985, Leading Effectively: Men and Women of the Volunteer Boardroom, 1987. Named Alumnus of Yr., Iliff Sch. Theology, 1981, Outstanding Alumnus, Kans. Wesleyan U., 1986; travel and rsch. grantee Syracuse U., summer 1968. Mem. Am. Acad. Religion., Soc. for Values in Higher Edn. Research religious thought Europe and Asia. Home: 13631 E Marina Dr #402 Aurora CO 80014

HALL, THOR, religion educator; b. Larvik, Norway, Mar. 15, 1927; came to U.S., 1957, naturalized, 1973; s. Jens Martin and Margit Elvira (Petersen) H.; m. Gerd Hellstrom, July 15, 1950; 1 child, Jan Tore. Diploma in theology, Scandinavian Methodist Sem., 1950; postgrad., Selly Oak Colls., Birmingham, Eng., 1950-51; M.R.E., Duke U., 1959, Ph.D., 1962. Ordained to ministry Meth. Ch., 1952; minister Kongsvinger-Odal Meth. Ch., Norway, 1951-53; exec. sec. youth dept. Meth. Ch., Norway, 1953-57; minister Ansonville (N.C.) Meth. Ch., 1958-59; asst. minister 1st Presbyn. Ch., Durham, N.C., 1960-62; asst. prof. preaching and theology Duke U., 1962-68, assoc. prof., 1968-72; disting. prof. religious studies U. Tenn., Chattanooga, 1972—, LeRoy A. Martin disting. prof. religious studies, 1987—; vis. prof. Oslo U., 1977, Liberia, 1980; vis. prof. U. Copenhagen, 1984; mem. Gen. Bd. Evangelism, Meth. Ch., 1968-72, Oxford Inst. Meth. Theol. Studies, 1982—; cons. Ecumenical Prayer Seminars, 1967—, Army, Navy, Air Force Chaplains Corps, 1967, 68, 71, 72; James Sprunt lectr. Union Theol. Sem., Richmond, Va., 1970; Voigt lectr. So. Ill. Conf., United Meth. Ch., 1979; Goodson lectr. Va. Conf., United Meth. Ch., 1983; mem. Tenn. Com. for Humanities, 1978-82, chmn. subcom. on devel., mem. exec. com., 1979-82; Stahley lectr. Ferrum Coll., Va., 1987. Author: A Theology of Christian Devotion, 1969, A Framework for Faith, 1970, The Future Shape of Preaching, 1971, Whatever Happened to the Gospel, 1973, (with others) Advent-Christmas (Proclamation B), 1975, Anders Nygren, 1978, Systematic Theology Today, Part I, 1978, The Evolution of Christology, 1982, Pentecost (Proclamation 4B), 1990; editor: Var Ungdom, 1953-57, The Unfinished Pyramid (Charles P. Bowles), 1967, A Directory of Systematic Theologians in North America, 1977; translator: A Political Dogmatic (Jens Glebe-Möller) 1987, Jesus and Theology (Glebe-Möller), 1989, Forgiveness (Carl-Reinhold Bråkenhielm), 1991; contbr. articles to profl. jours. World Council Chs. scholar, 1950-51; Crusade scholar, 1957-59; Gurney Harris Kearns fellow, 1959-60; Angier Duke Meml. fellow, 1960-61; James B. Duke fellow, 1961-62; Am. Assn. Theol. Schs. faculty fellow, 1968-69; Fulbright-Hays travel grantee, 1984. Mem. AAUP, Soc. Sci. Study Religion, Am. Acad. Religion (v.p. Southeastern region 1984-85, pres. 1985-86), SE Commn. for the Study Religion (exec. dir. 1987-91), Soc. Philosophy of Religion. Home: 1102 Montvale Circle Signal Mountain TN 37377 Office: U Tenn Dept Philosophy & Religion Chattanooga TN 37403 *The greatest factor contributing to personal growth and professional development is the full utilization of opportunities available at the present and the fulfillment of one's responsibilities, whatever they are.*

HALL, WILLIAM PEMBROKE, minister; b. Clifton Forge, Va., June 26, 1929; s. Pembroke Pettit and Mary (Hannah) H.; m. Mamie Frances Barton, June 23, 1951; 1 child, Carolyn Barton. M. Accounts, Dunsmore Coll., 1946-48; postgrad., Duke U., 1970. Ordained to ministry Meth. Ch., 1972. Minister Mt. Valley Meth. Ch., Alleghany County, Va., 1964-68, Collierstown-Mt. Horeb United Meth. Chs., Collierstown, Va., 1968-72, Mt. Carmel-Mt. Pleasant United Meth. Chs., Covington, Va., 1972-85, Wesley Chapel-Mt. Zion-Ellioits Hill United Meth. Chs., Rockbridge County, Va., 1986-89, McKinley United Meth. Ch., Middlebrook, Va., 1990—; pres. men's Bible class Cen. Meth. Ch., Clifton Forge, Va. 1962. Pres. Clifton Forge Quarterback Club, 1956-57; chmn. project com. Kiwanis Club, Clifton Forge, 1966; chmn. Corrections Resources Bd., Clifton Forge, 1989—; mem. Blue Ridge Region Econ. Commn., Clifton Forge, 1990—. Mem. Masons, Shriners. Home: 1701 Ridgevue Ave Clifton Forge VA 24422 *In my ministry I have found numerous people who seemed burdened, depressed and with no sense of direction. Then there are those who have a strong belief in what they want and set goals toward it. I find they usually succeed with much happiness.*

HALLBERG, FRED WILLIAM, religion educator; b. Mpls., Aug. 15, 1935; s. Fred William Sr. and Olga M. (Heggen) H.; m. Dorothy E. Angell, Mar. 15, 1958 (div. June 1983); m. Lorraine G. Groshans, June 15, 1985; children: Cynthia Patsche, David W. BA, U. Minn., 1958, MA, 1963, PhD, 1969. Assoc. prof. philosophy U. No. Iowa, Cedar Falls, 1967—. 1st lt. U.S. Army, 1958-60. Mem. Am. Philos. Assn., Am. Acad. Religion. Unitarian Universalist. Home: 630 Main St Box 323 Janesville IA 50647 Office: U Northern Iowa 117 Baker Hall Cedar Falls IA 50614

HALLEAD, GLEN JAMES, minister; b. Detroit, June 8, 1957; s. James Edgar and Marcia June (Higgs) H.; m. Carol Diane Doelp, Sept. 1, 1984; children: Zachary James, Natalie Belle. BS, Cen. Mich. U., 1983; MDiv, Princeton Theol. Sem., 1986. Ordained to ministry Presbyn. Ch., 1987. Assoc. min. for youth ministries Westminster Presbyn. Ch., Pitts., 1986-90; pastor Waltham Presbyn. Ch., Utica, Ill., 1990—; mem. Blackhawk Presbytery Mission Stewardship and Interpretation Com., Oreg., Ill., 1991—. With USNR, 1976-81. Paul Harris fellow Rotary Internat., 1989. Office: Waltham Presbyn Ch 809 N 3450th Rd Utica IL 61373 *The great challenge to today's Christian is the same as it has always been—to perservere in the faith...The Authority of Scripture, the role of the Church in society, and the threat of assimilation into the mainstream culture are issues to which Jesus himself responded...It's good to know that there's a light which still shines in the darkness..."and the darkness shall not overcome it."*

HALLER, EVELYN HARRIS, English educator; b. Chgo., Mar. 7, 1937; d. Charles Leo and Evelyn Catherine (Qualey) Harris; m. Robert Spencer Haller, June 10, 1961; children: Scott Geoffrey, Charles Benet. AB magna cum laude, Barat Coll., 1958; MA, Emory U., 1959, PhD, 1968; postgrad., Princeton (N.J.) U., 1973. Resource humanist Women's Inst. Theology, Lincoln, Nebr., 1984-85, coordinating coun., 1985—, conf. planner, 1988-89, chair, 1989—; prof. English Doane Coll., Crete, Nebr., 1969—; mem. adv. bd. Vox Benedictina, Toronto, Ont., Can., 1984—. Contbg. editor: The Feminist Companion to Literature in English, 1990; contbr. poetry and essays to lit. periodicals and articles to profl. jours. Emory U. fellow, 1959-60, Newberry Libr. fellow, 1984; NEH grantee, 1971. Mem. AAUW, Am. Acad. Religion, MLA (regional del. 1974-77), Oriental Inst., Nebr. Commn. for the Humanities (bd. dirs. 1976-80), New Chaucer Soc., AAUP (pres. state conf. 1980-81), Amnesty Internat., Internat. Thomas Merton Soc., Virginia Woolf Soc. Democrat. Roman Catholic. Home: 1735 S 25th St Lincoln NE 68502 Office: Doane Coll Crete NE 68333

HALLER, PAMELA, ecumenical agency administrator. Pres. Ctr. City Chs., Hartford, Conn. Office: Ctr City Chs 170 Main St Hartford CT 06106*

HALLING, JENNIFER JANE, religion counselor; b. Ottawa, Kans., Mar. 19, 1962; d. Luke A. and Dolores A. (Will) H. BA, Benedictine Coll., Atchison, Kans., 1984; MS, Loyola Coll., Balt., 1989. Marketer Nat. Cath. Reporter Pub. Co., Kansas City, Mo., 1984-87; pastoral counselor Towson (Md.) State U., 1987-89; residential counselor Boys Hope, St. Louis, 1989—. Editor: (literary mag.) Loomings, 1984; author poetry. Democrat.

HALLORAN, MICHAEL JOHN, church business administrator; b. New Prague, Minn., May 6, 1957; s. Joseph Francis and Rita Ann (Cashin) H.; m. Lori Jean Pike, May 27, 1988; children: Tiffany, Joshua, Bethany, Jonathan, Timothy. Student mktg. mgmt., Willmar (Minn.) AVTI, 1978; BS, Mankato (Minn.) State Univ., 1981; student, Hyles-Anderson Bible Coll., Crown Point, Ind., 1983-84. Sales rep. A.L. Williams, Brooklyn Park, Minn., 1985—; timothy tng. program Westside Bapt. Ch., Excelsior, Minn., 1984-87; bus. adminstr., bookeeper Luth. Ch. of the Good Shepherd, Mpls., 1987—; children's program dir., Meadow Creek Bapt. Ch., Andover, Minn., 1989-90. Precinct del. Republican Orgn., Coon Rapids, Minn., Dist. 49B, 1988, '90. Mem. Berean League. Home: 9448 Flintwood St NW Coon Rapids MN 55433 Office: Luth Ch of Good Shepherd 4800 Ewing Ave S Minneapolis MN 55410

HALLOWELL, JOHN H, minister; b. L.I., Oct. 30, 1953; s. John Wentworth and Ann Marie (Burkhard) H.; m. Kathryn Margaret Allen, Dec. 30, 1978; children: David, Marke, Matthew. BA in Classical Langs., Calif. State U., Long Beach, 1979. Ordained min. Calvary Chapel, Capistrano Beach, Calif., 1985—, dir. pastoral rsch., 1985—. Mem. Am. Acad. Religion, Soc. Bibl. Lit. Home: 27251 Rosario Mission Viejo CA 92692 Office: Calvary Chapel 25975 Domingo Ave Capistrano Beach CA 92624 *It is perhaps a testimony to the subversive nature of the Christian way of life proposed in the Bible that among religious scholars near the end of the twentieth century, Christian faith is subversive.*

HALLSTRAND, SARAH LAYMON, denomination executive; b. Nashville, Oct. 25, 1944; d. Charles Martin and Lillian Christina (Stenberg) Laymon; m. John Peter Hallstrand, July 6, 1974; 1 child, Lillian Johanna. BA, Fla. So. Coll., 1966; ThM, Boston U., 1971; D of Ministry, McCormick Sch. Theol., 1985; grad., Coll. for Fin. Planning, Denver, 1990. Dir. Christian edn. Trinity United Meth. Ch., Bradenton, Fla., 1968-70, Univ. United Meth. Ch., Syracuse, N.Y., 1971-73; assoc. min. First Bapt. Ch., Syracuse, 1973-78; pastor Oneida (N.Y.) Bapt. Ch., 1978-80; midwest rep. Mins. and Missionaries Benefit Bd., Am. Bapt. Chs., Oak Park, Ill., 1981—; leader retirement planning seminars Am. Bapt. Assembly, Green Lake, Wis., 1985—; mem. rep. Midwest Commn. on the Ministry, Valley Forge, Pa., 1985—; adj. prof., pastoral care McCormick Sch. Theol., Chgo., 1986—; vis. scholar Am. Bapt. Bd. Ednl. Ministries, Valley Forge, 1986-87; v.p. Midwest Career Devel. Svc., Westchester, Ill., 1987—; bd. dirs. The Gathering Place Retreat Ctr., Gosport, Ind., 1988—; mem. program com. and women in ministry rep. Roger Williams Fellowship, 1988—; mem. nat. continuing edn. team Am. Bapt. Chs., Valley Forge, Pa., 1991—. Contbr. articles to profl. jours. Mem. Am. Bapt. Chs. Mins. Coun., Inst. Cert. Fin. Planners (cert.), Internat. Soc. Retirement Planners, Alpha Gamma Delta. Democrat. Office: Mins and Missionaries Benefit Bd PO Box 549 Oak Park IL 60303 *The church has not been called to be successful as measured by the world's standards. It has always been and will always be that the true goal of the church is faithfulness as measured by the liberating and transforming gospel of Jesus Christ.*

HALLSTROM, DAVID ERIC, clergyman; b. Chgo., Feb. 1, 1958; s. Harry Hallstrom and Shirley (Franzen) H.; m. Cindy Ann Rieckstien, Oct. 19, 1985; children: Eric, Brian. B Sacred Lit., Scottsbluff Sch. Evangelism, 1984. Ordained to ministry Ch. of Christ. Minister Ch. of Christ, Oshkosh, Nebr., 1985-88, Davenport, Iowa, 1988—. With USAF, 1976-80. Republican. Home: 1312 W 15th St Davenport IA 52804 Office: Davenport Ch of Christ 1501 Marquette St Davenport IA 52804

HALPERN, DAVID SEYMOUR, rabbi; b. N.Y.C., July 27, 1928; s. Sol and Rae (Spinner) H.; m. Sheila Ruth Lifschitz, Dec. 12, 1954; children: Neil, Risa, Beth Halpern Sitt. BA, Yeshiva Coll., N.Y.C., 1949; DDiv, Yeshiva Coll., 1984. Ordained rabbi 1952. Rabbi Flatbush Park Jewish Ctr., Bklyn., 1952—; pres. Rabbinical Bd. Flatbush, Bklyn., 1960-62. Recpient Disting. Rabbinic Alumni award, Yeshiva U., 1978, Citation of Honor, Jewish Nat. Fund, 1988. Mem. Rabbinical Coun. Am., Yeshiva U. Rabbinic Alumni Assn. (v.p. 1989-91), UOJCA. Office: Flatbush Park Jewish Ctr 6363 Avenue U Brooklyn NY 11234

HALPERN, HAROLD DAVID, rabbi; b. Providence; s. Solomon and Ethel Rachel (Eichenstein) H.; m. Sarah Selma Reinharth; children: Rena, Alita, Sharona. BA, Bklyn. Coll.; MHL, Jewish Theol. Sem., N.Y.C., 1956, DD, 1982. Ordained rabbi, 1956. Rabbi New Milford (N.J.) Jewish Ctr., 1961-86, Temple Gates of Zion, Valley Stream, N.Y., 1987—; chaplain Bergen County Instns., Paramus, N.J., 1969-72; pres. Religious Coun. of Valley Stream, 1990—. Contbr. articles to profl. jours. 1st lt. U.S. Army, 1956-58, col. USAR, 1960-90, ret. Mem. Rabbinical Assembly, L.I. Bd. Rabbis. Home: 116 Roberta St Valley Stream NY 11580 Office: Temple Gates of Zion 322 N Corona Ave Valley Stream NY 11580 *It is not incumbent upon us to complete all worthwhile tasks but we should at least begin them.*

HALPERN, LARRY J., rabbi; b. Phila., Sept. 3, 1941; s. A. Leonard and Frances (Adler) H.; children: Susan, Ari. AB, U. Pa., 1963; MAHL, Hebrew Union Coll., Cin., 1967. Asst. rabbi Temple Israel, Boston, 1967-70; rabbi to sr. rabbi Congregation of Liberal Judaism, Orlando, Fla., 1970—. Bd. dirs. Mental Health Assn., Orlando, Project 2000; bd. govs. Synagogue Council Am., 1987—; com. mem. HEAT, Help End Abuse Today, 1986—, others. Named Man of the Yr. 1975, State of Israel Bonds. Mem. Cen. Conf. Am. Rabbis (exec. bd. 1988-90), S.E. Cen. Conf. Am. Rabbis (pres. 1986-88), Jewish Fedn. Greater Orlando (pres. 1983-85), Coun. Jewish Fedns. (bd. dirs.). Office: 928 Malone Dr Orlando FL 32810

HALPIN, CHARLES AIME, archbishop; b. St. Eustache, Man., Can., Aug. 30, 1930; s. John S. and Marie Anne (Gervais) H. BA, U. Man., 1950; BTh, U. Montreal, 1956; Licentiate Canon Law, Gregorian U., Rome, 1960. Ordained priest Roman Catholic Ch., 1956; named monsignor Roman Cath. Ch., 1969, consecrated bishop, 1973; asst. St. Mary's Cathedral, Winnipeg, Man., 1956-58; vice chancellor, sec. to archbishop Archdiocese Winnipeg, 1960; officialis Archdiocesan Matrimonial Tribunal, 1962; vice-officialis Regional Matrimonial Tribunal, Regina, Sask.; archbishop of Regina, 1973—. Mem. Western Cath. Conf. Bishops (past pres.), Can. Conf. Cath. Bishops (bd. dirs.).

HALSTEAD, JOHN STANLEY, minister, religious broadcaster; b. Norfolk, Va., Apr. 22, 1958; s. John Arthur and Irma Clyde (Wilder) H.; m. Toni Lyn Pollock, Mar. 28, 1988; children: Travis Lee, Trista Inez. AA in Mass Communications, L.A. Community Coll., 1979; BA in Communications, Palm Beach Atlantic Coll., 1986; postgrad., Luther Rice Theol. Sem., Jacksonville, Fla., 1989-90. Staff announcer Sta. WYVA-FM, Yorktown, Va., 1975-76; min. youth Neptune Rd. Bapt. Ch., Kissmmee, Fla., 1982-84; min. youth, music and media 1st Bapt. Ch., Kissmmee, 1982-84; min. edn. Westview Bapt. Ch., Albany, Ga., 1984-86; min. music and youth Mercedes Bapt. Ch., Albany, 1986-88; min. music and sr. adults 1st Bapt. Ch., Ashburn, Ga., 19886; chaplain Ashburn Police Dept., 1988-91, Turner County Sheriff's Office, Ashburn, 1988-91. Author: Through It All, 1991; also articles in Children of Abuse jour.; writer, producer: (TV spl.) History of Kissimmee, 1977. Scoutmaster Boy Scouts of Am., Guantanamo Bay, Cuba, 1978, Kissimmee, 1980-81; mem. Cen. Fla. Youth Programs, Inc., Kissimmee, 1979; exec. dir. Turner County Coun. on Child Abuse, Ashburn, 1989-91, chmn., 1990-91. With USN, 1976-80. Mem. Turner Missionary Bapt. Assn. (associational dir. 1989-91), Ga. Peace Officers Assn. (chaplain), Exchange Club. Democrat. Avocations: writing, singing. Home: 306 N McLendon St Ashburn GA 31714 Office: 1st Bapt Ch 302 N McLendon St Ashburn GA 31714

HALTON, MARK ROBERT, editor; b. Pitts., Mar. 1, 1960; s. Richard John and Charlene Eugenia (Rose) H.; m. Linda Eileen Shimp, Dec. 27, 1987; 1 child, Jessica Addie. AB, Davidson Coll., 1981; MAMC, U. Fla., 1990; postgrad., Southwestern Bapt. Theol., Seminary, 1986. Religion corr. Gainesville (Fla.) Sun, 1985; asst. chaplain Lancaster Correctional Instn., Trenton, Fla., 1985-86; religion corr. Ft. Worth Star-Telegram, 1986; asst. editor The Christian Century, Chgo., 1987—; mng. editor The Christian Ministry, Chgo., 1987—; mem. profl. growth com. Assoc. Ch. Press, Ada, Mich., 1990-91, awards com., 1991—. Mem. Soc. Profl. Journalists, Am. Acad. Religion. Home: 1246 Elmwood Ave Evanston IL 60202 Office: Christian Ministry 407 S Dearborn St Chicago IL 60605

HALVERSON, RICHARD CHRISTIAN, minister; b. Pingree, N.D., Feb. 4, 1916; s. Leroy Arthur and Edna Marie (Nielson) H.; m. Doris Seaton, Feb. 6, 1943; children: Richard C., Stephen S., Deborah. Student, Valley City (N.D.) State Tchrs. Coll., 1932-35; B.S., Wheaton Coll., 1939, LL.D. (hon.), 1958; Th.B., Princeton Theol. Sem., 1942; D.D. (hon.), Gordon Coll., 1981; L.H.S. (hon.), Malone Coll., 1982; Litt. D. (hon.), Sterling Coll., 1984. Ordained to ministry United Presbyn. Ch. U.S.A., 1942; mng. dir. Forest Home Christian Conf. Grounds, 1942; asst. minister Linwood Presbyn. Ch., Kansas City, Mo., 1942-44; dir. Forest Home Christian Conf. Grounds, 1944; minister 1st Presbyn. Ch., Coalinga, Calif., 1944-47; minister leadership edn. 1st Presbyn. Ch. of Hollywood (Calif.), 1947-56; minister 4th Presbyn. Ch., Bethesda, Md., 1958-81; chaplain U.S. Senate, Washington, 1981—; assoc. Internat. Prayer Breakfast Movement, Washington, 1956—; bd. dirs. Prison Fellowship, World Vision; mem. numerous adv. bds. Author: Christian Maturity, 1956, Perspective, 1957, Man to Man, 1961, The Quiet Men, 1963, Prologue to Prison, 1964, Between Sundays, 1965, Relevance, 1968, Be Yourself ... And God's, 1971, How I Changed My Thinking About the Church, 1972, Manhood with Meaning, 1972, God's Way out of Futility, 1973, A Day at a time, 1974, A Living Fellowship—A Dynamic Witness, 1977, Somehow Inside Eternity, 1980, Gospel for the Whole of Life, 1981, The Timelessness of Jesus Christ, 1982, Walk With God Between Sundays, 1982, The Word of a Gentleman, 1983, Prayers Offered by the Chaplain of the U.S. Senate, 97th Congress, vol 2, 98th Congress, No Greater Power, 1986, We The People, 1987. Club: Kenwood Country (Bethesda, Md.). Office: US Senate Office of Chaplain Hart Senate Office Bldg Washington DC 20510

HALVERSON, WENDELL QUELPRUD, former educational association executive, clergyman, educator; b. Austin, Minn., July 11, 1916; s. Arthur Benjamin and Emma Josephine (Pederson) H.; m. Marian Lois Phypers, Aug. 3, 1940 (dec. Aug. 1985); children—Peder Quelprud, Ingrid Maud, Timothy Greenwood. B.A., State U. Iowa, 1940; M.Div., Union Theol. Sem., N.Y.C., 1943; student, Grad. Sch. Theology, Oberlin Coll., 1943-49, U. Oslo (Norway), 1949, U. Chgo., 1950; D.D. (hon.), Lake Forest U., 1956. Ordained to ministry Presbyn. Ch., 1943. Pastor in Clyde, Ohio, 1943-46; pastor in La Grange, Ill., 1949-58; asst. prof. philosophy religion Heidelberg Coll., Tiffin, Ohio, 1946-49; Chgo. corr. Christian Century, 1953; lectr. homiletics McCormick Theol. Sem., Chgo., 1957-58; gen. presbyter Presbytery N.Y., United Presbyn. Ch., 1958-61; pres. Buena Vista Coll., Storm Lake, Iowa, 1961-73, Iowa Assn. Ind. Colls. and Univs., Des Moines, 1973-80; ret., 1980; exec. dir. Wis. Assn. Ind. Colls. and Univs., Madison, 1980-84; mem. Wis. Gov.'s Adv. Council on Edn., 1980, Wis. Adv. Com. on Vocat. and Tech. Adult Edn.; dir. Iowa State Ednl. Radio and TV Broadcast, 1967-69; Sec. ch. extension bd. N.Y. Presbyn. Found., 1958-61; mem. bd. pensions Presbyn. Ch. U.S.A., 1956-58. Pres. Iowans for Better Justice, 1970-73; chmn. bd. Iowa Coll. Found., 1972-73; pres. Des Moines chpt. Am.-Scandinavian Found., 1974-75; chmn. Score, chpt. 184, Lebanon, N.H., 1990—. Mem. Ygdrasil Lit. Club (Madison), Rotary. Home: PO Box 72 Washington NH 03280 *I have not always practiced it but it has been my experience that when I have walked the second mile, I have been fully blessed.*

HAM, JAMES RICHARD, bishop; b. Chgo., July 11, 1921; s. James William and Loretta (Freely) H. B.Ed., Mundelein Maj. Sem., 1940-43; student, Maryknoll Sem. at N.Y., 1943-48, D.D. (hon.), 1968. Ordained priest Roman Cath. Ch., 1948; Maryknoll pub. relations work Chgo., St. Louis, Phila. and Mpls., 1948-58; missionary Guatemala and El Salvador region, 1958-68; ordained aux. Bishop of Guatemala, 1968, vicar gen., 1968-80; rector Asumption Cathedral, 1967-70; pastor Our Lady of Guadalupe, Guatemala, 1970-80; aux. bishop of St. Paul and Mpls., 1980—; vicargen. Vicar So. Vicariate; dir. Prelature of Esquipulas, Nat. Lay Apostolate, Nat. Maj. Sem. Aux. chaplain mil. ordinariate 1965-68, Guatemala. Club: K.C. Address: 226 Summit Ave Saint Paul MN 55102

HAMANI, AHMAD, religious organization administrator. Pres. Superior Islamic Coun., Algiers, Algeria. Office: Superior Islamic Coun, Cheik Abdalhamid ibn Badis, Algiers Algeria*

HAMBIDGE, DOUGLAS WALTER, archbishop; b. London, Mar. 6, 1927; emigrated to Can., 1956; s. Douglas and Florence (Driscoll) H.; m. Denise Colvill Lown, June 9, 1956; children—Caryl Denise, Stephen Douglas, Graham Andrew. A.L.C.D., London U., 1953, B.D., 1958, D.D., 1969. Ordained deacon Church of England, 1953, priest, 1954, consecrated bishop, 1969; asst. curate St. Mark's Ch., Dalston, London, 1953-55; priest-in-charge St. Mark's Ch., 1955-56; incumbent All Saints Ch., Cassiar, B.C., Can., 1956-58; rector St. James Parish, Smithers, B.C., 1958-64, North Peace Parish, Ft. St. John, B.C., 1964-69; canon St. Andrew's Cathedral, 1965; lord bishop of Caledonia, 1969-80, New Westminster, B.C., 1980-81; lord archbishop of New Westminster and metropolitan of B.C., 1981—. Mem. Vancouver Club, Arbutus Club. Office: 302-814 Richards St, Vancouver, BC Canada V6B 3AY

HAMBRICK-STOWE, CHARLES EDWIN, minister; b. Worcester, Mass., Feb. 4, 1948; s. Edwin Guy and Florence (Millington) Hambrick; m. Elizabeth Anne Stowe, Sept. 11, 1971; children: Anne P., Thomas W., Charles G. BA, Hamilton Coll., 1970; MA, Pacific Sch. Religion, Berkeley, Calif., 1973, MDiv, 1973; PhD, Boston U., 1980. Ordained to ministry United Ch. of Christ, 1973. Missionary United Ch. Bd. for World Ministries, Sendai, Japan, 1973-75; Christian edn. cons. Mass. Con. United. Ch. of Christ, 1976-79; pastor St. Paul's United Ch. of Christ, Westminster, Md., 1979-85, Ch. of the Apostles, United Ch. of Christ, Lancaster, Pa., 1985—; adj. prof. ch. history Lancaster Theol. Sem., 1985—; del. Luth. Reformed Dialog, N.Y.C., 1987; mem. Coun. for Ecumenism, United Ch. of Christ, Cleve., 1990—; dir. Cen. Atlanta Conf., United Ch. of Christ, Silver Spring, Md., 1982-85. Author: The Practice of Piety: Puritan Devotional Disciplines, 1982 (Jamestown prize 1980); editor: Early New England Meditative Poetry, 1988, Theology and Identity, 1990; contbr. articles to profl. jours. Mem. Downtown Devel. Com., Westminster, Md., 1980-85. Grant/fellowship Soc. of Colonial Wars, Mass., 1975-76. Mem. Am. Hist. Assn., Am. Soc. Ch. History, Am. Acad. Religion, Lancaster Assn. Ministerium. Democrat. Home: 1101 Davis Dr Lancaster PA 17603 Office: Ch of Apostles 1850 Marietta Ave Lancaster PA 17603 *Two elements make life great: Doing your best at the tasks to which you are called, and knowing that the greatest achievement is nothing compared with the gift of grace—God's love and our love for one another.*

HAMBURG, LYNN RAE, music educator; b. Chgo., Aug. 16, 1938; d. Albert Isaac and Ann Gertrude (Findelstein) Echt; divorced; children: Amy Beth, Michael Scott, Steven Edward. B. Music Edn., Ind. U., 1961. Sunday sch. tchr. Ohavey Zion, Lexington, Ky., 1965-67; dir. jr. choir Adath Jeshurun, Louisville, 1971—, music dir., Sunday sch. tchr., 1975-88; music tchr. Elaihu Acad., Louisville, 1973-81, 88-90; asst. dir. sr. adult dept. Louisville Jewish Community Ctr., 1986—. Dir. Close Harmony Project, 1985-86; vol. Heart Fund, Am. Cancer Soc., March of Dimes, 1989—. Recipient Outstanding Woman in Community award Mazrachi Women, 1986. Mem. Assn. Jewish Communal Profls., Adath Jeshurun Sisterhood, B'nai Brith Women (v.p., del. nat. convention 1970). Home: 1008 Williamsburg Ct Louisville KY 40207 Office: Jewish Community Ctr 3600 Dutchman's Ln Louisville KY 40205

HAMBY, JIM LEON, pastor; b. Pelzer, S.C., Jan. 26, 1951; s. Norman Luther and Clara Faye (Williams) H.; m. Sandra Kay Baines, June 6, 1973; children: Troy Lee, Melody Joy. BA, Lee Coll., 1973; MDiv, Luther Rice U., 1978, DMin, 1980. Ordained to ministry Ch. of God, 1978. Pastor Ch. of God, Balt., 1973-89; sr. pastor Clarksburg (Md.) Ch. of God, 1989—. Home and Office: 23900 Clarksburg Rd Clarksburg MD 20871

HAMED, NIHAD TALAAT, manufacturing executive; b. Damascus, Syria, Dec. 5, 1924; came to U.S., 1970; s. Hamed Youssef Hassanein and Mounira (Talaat) Naimee; m. Aida Rizk Hamed, June 10, 1985; children from previous marriage: Hossam, Nadia, Hazem, Hala, Lina. BS in Engring., Cairo U., 1952; MS, U. Detroit, 1978. Profl. engr., cert. mfg. engr. Mech. engr. Hedjae Railroad, Damascus, 1952-53, chief engr., 1953-54, supt. main repair shops, 1954-61; chief engr. NASR Automotive Co., Cairo, 1961-62, MISR Dredging Co., Cairo, 1962-68; dir. dept. Ministry Petroleum, Damascus, 1968-70; chief engr. Chrysler Co., Detroit, 1970-73, La Peer Mfg. Co., Detroit, 1973-88; pres. Am. Engring., Redford, Mich., 1988—; speaker Egyptian Engring. Soc., Cairo, 1974, 86. Author: Design by Welding, 1963; also posters, papers. Sec. gen. Fedn. Islamic Assns. in U.S. and Canada Inc., Redford, 1978—. Mem. Soc. Mfg. Engrs. (lectr. 1974-78), Welding Soc., Plastic Soc. Muslim. Avocation: rowing. Office: Fedn Islamic Assoc US & Can 25351 Five Mile Rd Redford MI 48329*

HAMEL, JOSEPH DONAT, minister; b. Rumford, Maine, Aug. 9, 1923; s. Donat Henry and Ethel Louise (Kennison) H.; m. Jean Marie Rowsey, Aug. 7, 1949; children: JoAnne, John, Janet. BE, Ashland U., 1949, DD (hon.), 1972; MRE, Ashland Theol. Sem., 1951. Ordained to ministry Brethren Ch., 1950. Pastor Lanark (Ill.) Brethren Ch., 1951-53, South Bend (Ind.) Brethren Ch., 1953-60; pastor Sarasota (Fla.) 1st Brethren Ch., 1960-88, pastor emeritus, 1988—. Chaplain Fla. State Fireman's Assn., 1962—, Sheriff Dept. Sarasota County, 1960—, Police Dept., Sarasota, 1960—, Fire Dept., Sarasota, 1960—. With USAAF, 1943-45; lt. col. USAF Aux., 1961-86, Ret. Recipient Freedom award Sertoma Club, 1964; named Evangelical of Yr., Manasota Ministerial, 1975, Citizen of Yr., Fraternal Order Police, Sarasota, 1980. Mem. Military Chaplains, Nat. Fellowship Christian Firefighters, Nat. Religious Braadcasters (founder, speaker The Brethren Hour), VFW. Home: 605 Caruso Pl Sarasota FL 34237 *That man never grows old who keeps a child in his heart.*

HAMELIN, JEAN-GUY, bishop; b. St.-Severin, Que., Can., Oct. 8, 1925; s. Bernard and Gertrude (Bordeleau) H. B.A., Sem. Trois-Rivieres, Que., Can., 1945; Lic. Theology, Angelicum, Rome, 1953; Lic. Social Scis., Gregoriana, Rome, 1955. Ordained priest Roman Catholic Ch., 1949; consecrated bishop, 1974. Tchr. secondary sch. Trois-Rivieres, Que., Can., 1949-52; mem. faculty Sem. Trois-Rivieres, Que., Can., 1955-58; chaplain to various social orgns. Shawinigan, Que., Can., 1958-64; dir. social action dept. Bishop's Conf., Ottawa, Ont., Can., 1964-68; gen. sec. Bishop's Conf., Montreal, Que., Can., 1968-74; bishop Diocese of Rouyn-Noranda, Que., Can., 1974—; v.p. Can. Conf. Cath. Bishops, 1983-85, 91—; ecclesiastical advisor Cooperation Internat. for the Devel. and Solidarity, Brussels, 1988. Address: 515 Cuddihy, Rouyn-Noranda, PQ Canada J9X 5W9

HAMER, JEAN JEROME CARDINAL, archbishop; b. Brussels, June 1, 1916. Ordained priest Roman Cath. Ch., 1941. Titular bishop of Lorium with personal title of archbishop, 1973, created cardinal,, 1985, deacon of San Saba, prefect of congregation for religious and secular insts., 1985—. Office: Piazza di S Uffizio 11, I-00193 Rome Italy

HAMILL, PAUL, church musician, publisher; b. Tobyhanna, Pa., June 10, 1930; s. Daniel Paul Hamill and Mildred Smith; m. M. Elinor Smith; children: Cynthia, David. MusB, Boston U., 1952; MA, Wesleyan U., 1957. Organist, choirmaster Christ 1st Presbyn. Ch., Hempstead, N.Y., 1958-70; editor music sect. Am. Book Co., N.Y.C., 1960-65, editorial dir., 1965-73; owner, pub. Gemini Press Inc., Otis, Mass., 1977—; organist, choirmaster St. James Episcopal ch., Great Barrington, Mass., 1985—; instr. Woodmere (N.Y.) Acad., 1957-64, Adelphi U., Garden City, N.Y., 1960-65; commd. by 1st Ch. United Ch. of Christ, Nashua, N.Y., 1984, Berkshire Concert Choir, Pittsfield, 1989; mem. Liturgy and Music Commn., 1985—. Pub.: Church Music Annual, 1982—; editor: (hymnals) Congregational Music for Eucharist, 1980, Introits & Responses, 1983, Sing to God, 1984. Dir. music South Ch., United Ch. of Christ, Pittsfield, Mass., 1980-85. Mem. Am. Guild Organists (dean Berkshire chpt. 1986-89), Berkshire Bach Soc. (founding mem.). Episcopalian. Home: 145 Deer Run Otis MA 01253 Office: Gemini Press Inc Box 603 Otis MA 01253

HAMILTON, DANIEL STEPHEN, clergyman; b. Cedarhurst, N.Y., Jan. 7, 1932; s. Richard Samuel and Catherine Mary (Liston) H. B.A., Cathedral Coll., 1954; S.T.B., Cath. U. Am., 1958; Ph.D., Greenwich U., 1991. Ordained priest Roman Catholic Ch., 1958; asst. pastor St. Anne's Ch., Garden City, N.Y., 1958-61; campus chaplain Adelphi U., Garden City, 1959-61; prof. St. Pius X Preparatory Sem., Uniondale, N.Y., 1961-68; campus chaplain Hofstra U., Hempstead, N.Y., 1961-66; columnist L.I. Catholic, Hempstead, 1962-85; editor L.I. Catholic, 1975-85; dir. Bur. Public Info., Diocese Rockville Centre, 1968-85; chmn. Ecumenical Commn., 1968-88; resident priest St. William the Abbot Parish, Seaford, N.Y., 1971-85; pastor Our Lady of Perpetual Help Parish, Lindenhurst, N.Y., 1985—. Named hon. papal prelate, 1980. Mem. Cath. Theol. Soc. Am., Fellowship Cath. Scholars. Home and Office: 210 S Wellwood Lindenhurst NY 11757

HAMILTON, GEORGE EDMUND, youth ministries director; b. Bangor, Maine, Feb. 9, 1961; s. Edmund Hopkins and Margarite (Conners) H. BA in Acctg., Allentown (Pa.) Coll., 1983; postgrad., Cath. Theol. Union, Chgo., 1984-87, 1991—. Dir. youth ministry St Celestine's Parish, Elmwood Park, Ill., 1987-88, St. Mary's Parish, Riverside, Ill., 1988—; mem. Cath. Youth Office Resource Group, Chgo., 1989—, Young Cath. Students Reach Out Retreat Planning, Chgo., 1990—. Mem. Lyons Twp. Networking for Youth, 1990—. Mem. Nat. Fedn. Cath. Youth Ministry (assoc. mem.). Office: St Marys Youth Office 97 Herrick Rd Riverside IL 60546-2014

HAMILTON, GEORGE WAYNE, youth pastor; b. Hendersonville, N.C., Oct. 19, 1957; s. James Clarence and Dorthy Aline (Robinson) H.; m. Kimberly Ann Marshall, June 9, 1978; children: James Michael, Christopher Jordan, Brittany Leigh. BS in Bible, Tenn. Temple, Chattanooga, 1978. Ordained to ministry, Bapt. Ch. Youth pastor Rainsville Bapt. Tabernacle Ch., Rainsville, Ala., 1976-78, Calvary Bapt. Ch., Hendersonville, N.C., 1978-84; assoc. pastor Bob's Creek (S.C.) Bapt. Ch., 1984-88; youth pastor Souside Bapt. Temple, Rock Hill, S.C., 1988-90, Southgate Bapt. Ch., Augusta, Ga., 1990—; mem. sch. bd. Southgate Christian Schs., Augusta, 1990—. Bd. dirs. Mental Health Assn., Hendersonville, 1975. Home: 2434 Yorkshire Dr Augusta GA 30909 Office: 2226 Peach Orchard Rd Augusta GA 30906-8958

HAMILTON, JACK E., academic administrator. Pres. L.I.F.E. Bible Coll., San Dimas, Calif. Office: LIFE Bible Coll Office of the President 1100 Covina Blvd San Dimas CA 91773*

HAMILTON, RONALD RAY, minister; b. Evansville, Ind., May 6, 1932; s. Floyd Ray Hamilton and Ruby Dixon (Chism) Hahn; m. Norma Jean Robertson, Mar. 25, 1956; children: Ronnetta Jean, Andrea, Robert Rae. BA, U. Evansville, 1955; BD, Garrett Theol. Sem., 1958, MDiv, 1972; PhD, Oxford Grad. Sch., Eng., Dayton, Tenn., 1989. Ordained elder United Meth. Ch. Minister Scobey (Mont.) Meth. Ch., 1958-61, St. Andrew Meth. Ch., Littleton, Colo., 1961-67; sr. minister First Meth. Ch., Grand Junction, Colo., 1967-75, Christ United Meth. Ch., Salt Lake City, 1975-80, Littleton United Meth., 1980-86, U. Park United Meth., Denver, 1986-91. Author: The Way to Success, 1972, The Greatest Prayer, 1983, A Chosen People, 1986; editor jour., 1978. Recipient Spl. award Mental Health Assn., Mesa County, Colo., 1974, Goodwill Rehab. Inc., 1975. Mem. Lions Club, Rotary Club, Civitan (chaplain 1964-67). Republican. Avocations: acting, directing, travel, chess. Home: 4509 E Frye Rd Phoenix AZ 85044

HAMILTON, RUSSELL LEE, minister; b. Cin., Mar. 6, 1936; s. Harley S. and Edna R. Hamilton; m. Marjorie Ann Chiitwood, June 13, 1958; children: Russell A., Philip L., Joy A., April D., Jennifer J. BA, Taylor U., 1958; MDiv, Grace Theol. Sem., Winona Lake, Ind., 1961. Ordained to ministry Bapt. Ch., 1973. Pastor Paul's Chapel Ch., Pulaski, Ind., 1058-61, High-Point Youth for Christ, West Liberty, Ohio, 1961-71, North Shores Bapt. Ch., St. Clair Shores, Mich., 1971-79, Bethany Evang. Free Ch., Madison, Wis., 1979-84, Faith Evang. Free Ch., Mountain Lake Park, Md., 1984—; former dir. Ohio Youth for Christ, West Liberty; former mem. internat. bd. dirs. Youth for Christ Internat.; bd. dirs. Alleghany dist. Evang. Free Ch. Am., 1986-90. Named Rural Rally Dir. of Yr., Y.F.C.I., 1965. Home and Office: 107 W 3d Ave Mountain Lake Park MD 21550

HAMILTON, W(ILLIAM) RILEY, pastor; b. Houston, Oct. 5, 1952; s. James Wallace Hamilton and Edith (Clark) Humphrey; m. Deborah Kaye Tyler, June 15, 1973; children: Misty Lynn, William Riley Jr. AA, South Plains Jr. Coll., Levelland, Tex., 1979; BA, Criswell Coll., Dallas, 1988; postgrad., Southwestern Bapt. Theol. Sem., Ft. Worth. Ordained to ministry So. Capt. Conv. Pastor Challis Bapt. Ch., Brownfield, Tex., 1975-78, Countyline Bapt. Ch., Shallowater, Tex., 1978-80, Fairview Bapt. Ch., Levalland, 1980-82, 1st Bapt. Ch., Anton, Tex., 1982-85, West Mesquite (Tex.) Bapt. Ch., 1985—; dir. River Ministry/Mex., 1980-81; vice moderator South Plains Assn., Levelland, 1981-82. Bd. overseers Criswell Coll., 1991—. Sgt. USAF, 1972-76. Home: 406 Clary Mesquite TX 75149 Office: West Mesquite Bapt Ch 2808 W Scyene Rd Mesquite TX 75149

HAMLIN, ERNEST LEE, religious organization administrator, Christian education consultant; b. Sussex, Va., Dec. 9, 1943; s. Arish Lee and Elma Roseanna (Coleman) H.; m. Pamela Diane Carter, May 6, 1978; children: Kevin, Rafael, Cherry. BA, Va. Union U., 1970, MDiv, 1974; MA, Presbyn. Sch. Christian Edn., Richmond, Va., 1976. Asst. pastor Mt. Zion Bapt. Ch., Charlottesville, Va., 1971-79; interim pastor Jerusalem Bapt. Ch., Sparta, Va., 1980; pastor Bethesda Bapt. Ch., Colonial Heights, Va., 1981-83, Union Hill United Ch. of Christ, Sedley, Va., 1986-89, Emanuel - St. Mark's United Ch. of Christ, Saginaw, Mich., 1990—; pres. Christian Edn. Ministries, Richmond, 1990—; christian edn. lectr. local chs., Richmond, 1974-90; counselor/chaplain Med. Coll. Va., Richmond, 1976-77; edn. cons./counselor Smithdeal-Massey Bus. Coll., Richmond, 1978; substitute tchr. Richmond Pub. Schs., 1979-83; admissions rep./ednl. cons. Rutledge Coll., Richmond, 1984. Counselor Janie Porter Barrett Sch. for Juvenile Delinquents, Hanover County, Va., 1973; house mgr. Offender Aid and Restoration Hospitality House, Richmond, 1979-87; active United Ch. of Christ Clergy Cluster, Elon Homes for Children campaign com., Covenant Assn., and various others. Recipient Outstanding Svc. award Richmond Va. Seminary, 1986, Merit award, World of Poetry, 1990, Golden Poet award, 1990; named Honorary Chairperson United Negro Coll. Fund, 1983. Mem. United Black Christians, acad. of Parish Clergy, Kappa Alpha Psi, Nat. Assn. Black Achievers. Home: 111 S Third Ave Saginaw MI 48607-1503 Office: Emmanuel-St Mark's United Ch of Christ 924 Lapeer Ave Saginaw MI 48607-1503

HAMLIN, GRIFFITH ASKEW, retired religion educator; b. Richmond, Va., Feb. 24, 1919; s. Charles Hunter and Mary Virginia (Griffith) H.; m. Margaret Geneva Cook, June 1, 1943; children: Griffith Askew Jr., John Charles. BA, Atlantic Christian Coll., 1939; MRE, Lexington Theol. Sem., 1942; BD, Duke U., 1946; ThD, Iliff Sch. Theology, 1952. Ordained to ministry Christian Ch., 1939. Minister First CHristian Ch., Richlands, N.C., 1942-47, Danville, Va., 1947-48; prof. religion Atlantic Christian Coll., Wilson, N.C., 1948-50; minister First Christian Ch., Hampton, Va., 1951-57, Goldsboro, N.C., 1957-61; prof. religion, chair humanities area William Woods Coll., Fulton, Mo., 1961-82, prof. emeritus religion, 1982—. Author: In Faith and History, 1964, Monticello: Biography of a College, 1976, Heritage of Frontier Discipleship, 1983, A Community and Its Schools, 1984, Remember, Renew, Rejoice, 1986, The First 30 Years: The Fulton Housing Authority, 1989, Nightingale of North Luzon, 1989; editor: Blackburn College: A History of Private Education, 1989, Duel with the Wind: The Story of Emperor Charles V, 1991. Bd. dirs. Callaway County Hist. Soc., Fulton, Mo., 1990. Mem. Am. Acad. Religion, Disciples of Christ Hist. Soc., State Hist. Soc. Mo., Masons. Home: 23 Springer Dr Columbia MO 65201

HAMLIN, (EARLE) JOHN, minister, educator; b. Iron River, Mich., Nov. 9, 1915; s. Earle Ivan and Anna Marjorie (Howes) H.; m. Frances Jane Cade, July 18, 1942. BA, Oberlin Coll., 1936, MA, 1940; MDiv, Union Theol. Sem., N.Y.C., 1941, MST, 1952, ThD, 1961. Ordained to ministry Presbyn. Ch. (U.S.A.), 1941. Asst. pastor 1st Presbyn. Ch., Auborn, N.Y., 1941-43; pastor Union Presbyn. Ch., Sauquoit, N.Y., 1943-45; tchr. Cheeloo Sch. Theology, Jinan, Shandong, China, 1946-51; prof., pres. Thailand Theol. Sem., Chiang Mai, 1954-74; prof. Trinity Theol. Coll., Singapore, 1974-80. Author: God and the World of Nations, 1972, Guide to Isaiah 40-66, 1979, Inheriting the Land. Commentary Book of Joshua, 1983, At Risk in the Promised Land Commentary. Book of Judges, 1990. Capt. U.S. Army, 1945-46. Mem. Soc. Bibl. Lit., Rotary (pres. Chiang Mai club 1965-66, Waverly, Ohio club 1990-91). Democrat. Home: 426 Robin Rd Waverly OH 45690

HAMLIN, WAYLAND, minister; b. Chillicothe, Ohio, Sept. 6, 1949; s. Woodrow and Miley (Powers) H.; m. Naomi June Grooms, Oct. 6, 1968; children: Wayland Jay, Elbert Brian, Angela Dawn. BA with honors, Circleville Bible Coll., 1978; MDiv, Wesley Bibl. Sem., 1981; postgrad., Ref. Theol. Sem., 1984—. Ordained to ministry Chs. of Christ in Christian Union, 1975. Missionary fgn. missionary dept. Chs. of Christ in Christian Union, Circleville, Ohio, 1981-84; pastor St. Paul Ind. Meth. Ch., Oxford, Miss., 1984-86, Riverside Ind. Meth. Ch., Jackson, Miss., 1986-91; prof. Circleville Bible Coll., 1983; pres. Christian Union Bible Sch., Roseau, Dominica, W.I., 1983-84; chaplain Oxford Police Dept., 1984-86; asst. coord. Fellowship Christian Athletes, Oxford, 1984-86; group leader on Campus Ministry, Oxford, 1984-86; chmn. missions Assn. of Ind. Meth. Chs., Jackson 1984—; ministerial assoc. Oxford Ministerial Assn., 1984-86. Contbr. articles to denominational jours. Relief vol. Salvation Army, Jackson, 1979. With U.S. Army, 1966-69, Vietnam.; capt. USNG, 1990—, Persian Gulf. Decorated Purple Heart, Bronze Star; named one of Outstanding Young Men Am., U.S. Jaycees, 1984. Mem. Wesleyan Theol. Soc. Avocations: reading, woodworking, tennis, other sports. Home: 206 Shenandoah Rd Brandon MS 39042

HAMLIN, WINBORNE LEIGH, church worker, educator; b. Norfolk, Va., Aug. 12, 1937; d. Southgate and Maud (Winborne) Leigh; m. Jefferson Davis Hamlin, June 27, 1959; children: Jeff, John, Frank. BA magna cum laude, Sweet Briar Coll., 1958; MAT, John Hopkins U., 1959. English tchr. pub. schs., Balt., 1958-59, Lancaster, S.C., 1959-60, 62-63; ch. sch. tchr. Christ Episcopal Ch., Lancaster, 1961-63, St. Michael and All Angels Ch., Dallas, 1974-80; adult Bible study tchr., 1981-84. Leader troop Girl Scouts U.S., Lancaster, 1961-63; tchr., dir. art program High Mus. Art, Atlanta, 1965-67; bd. dirs. St. Michael Sch., 1973-75, 89—; pres. University Park Sch. PTA, 1978-79; bd. dirs. McCulloch Middle Sch. PTA, 1981-82, Highland Park High Sch. PTA, 1981-83, 85-86; bd. dirs. Jr. League of Dallas, 1972-74, 76-78, exec. com., 1977-78; sec. Citizens' Study Com. to Recommend Best Form of Govt. for City of University Park, Tex., 1976-77; rec. sec. Dallas Mus. of Fine Arts League, 1979-80; pres. Women of St. Michael and All Angels, 1980-81, vestry mem., 1982-85, 90—, sec. Ministry with Aging, Inc., 1982-85, pres. parish council, 1983-85; del. Triennial Conv. of Episcopal Ch., 1982, 85, 88; bd. Exec. Council Diocese of Dallas, 1988-90; bd. dirs. Province VII, Episc. Ch., 1984-87; leader Camp Fire Girls, Dallas, 1970-73; pres. Friends of Libr. for Park Cities, 1988-91; bd. dirs. St. Philip's Sch. and Community Ctr., 1989-90, Child Care, Dallas, 1990—. Mem. Sweet Briar Coll. Alumnae Assn. (exec. bd. 1977-83, 85-89), Phi Beta Kappa.

HAMM, MICHAEL DENNIS, religion educator; b. Cin., Jan. 18, 1936; s. Victor Michael and Agnes (Curren) H. BA, Marquette U., 1958; MA in English and Philosophy, St. Louis U., 1964, PhD in Bibl. Langs. and Lit., 1975. Joined S.J., Roman Cath. Ch., 1958, ordained priest, 1970. Assoc. prof. Creighton U., Omaha, 1975-91, prof., 1991—; mng. editor Theology Digest, St. Louis, 1970, mem. editorial bd. 1967-71; bd. dirs. New Covenant Justice and Peace Ctr. Author: The Beatitudes in Context, 1990. Yale Sch. of Div. Rsch. Fellow, 1973-75, Hebrew Union Coll. Travel Fellow, 1970. Mem. Coll. Theology Soc., Soc. Bibl. Lit., Cath. Bibl. Assn. Democrat. *More policing and the making of new laws will not heal our violent culture. Only the conversion of hearts to justice will, with the help of God, bring that about.*

HAMMAN, REG DUANE, religious organization administrator; b. Vancouver, Wash., Dec. 23, 1945; s. Joe Leelond and Hilda (Cherry) H.; m. Glenda Fay McDowell, Aug. 17, 1968; children: Kevin Andrew, Kyle Benjamin. BA in Bus., U. Okla., 1973. Vol. Worldwide Pictures, Lawton (Okla.), Little Rock, 1975-86; premiere coord. Worldwide Pictures, Mpls., 1986-87; conf. adminstr. Dad, the Family Shepherd, Little Rock; area cochair Gothard IBYC, Little Rock, 1982-86; mem. pub. rels. com. John 3:16 Banners, Little Rock, 1984-91. Republican. Baptist. Home: 1504 Northline North Little Rock AR 72116 Office: Dad the Family Shepherd 2024 Arkansas Valley Dr Little Rock AR 72212

HAMMERLING, ROY, history educator, minister; b. Calgary, Alta., Can., June 20, 1956; came to U.S., 1958; s. Emil and Nelly (Geissler) H.; m. Margaret Ekberg, Aug. 22, 1981; children: Jeremiah, Rachel, Joshua. BA in Religion, Classics and Philosophy, Pacific Luth. U., 1978; MDiv, Wartburg Theol. Sem., 1982; postgrad. in medieval history, U. Notre Dame, 1989—. Ordained to ministry Evang. Luth. Ch. Am., 1982. Pastor Prairie Valley Luth. Parish, Williston, N.D., 1982-87; student asst. history dept. U. Notre Dame (Ind.), 1989—; v.p. Williston Ministerial Alliance, 1983-84; pres. Western N.D. Dist. Mission Support Com., 1985-86, Western N.D. Commitment to Mission Program, 1985-87; clergy rep. Am. Luth. Nat. Ch. Coun., Am. Luth. Ch. U.S.A., 1986-87. Contbr. sect. to book: Daily Readings from Spiritual Classics, 1990. Mem. staff N.W. Human Svc. Ctr., Williston, 1983-87; bd. dirs. Mercy Hosp. Recovery Ctr., Williston, 1986-87. Home: 3321 Cabot Dr South Bend IN 46635 *Our life is no dream, but it should and will perhaps become one.*

HAMMES, GEORGE ALBERT, bishop; b. LaCrosse, Wis., Sept. 11, 1911; s. August Isidore and Caroline (Schumacher) H. Student, St. Lawrence Sem., Mt. Calvary, Wis., 1925-31, St. Louis Prep. Sem., 1931-33, Kenrick Sem., St. Louis, 1933-34, Sulpician Sem., Washington, 1934-37, M.A., Cath. U. Am., 1937; L.H.D. (hon.), Mt. Senario Coll., Ladysmith, Wis., 1969. Ordained priest Roman Cath. Ch., 1937; sec. to Bishop Alexander J. McGavick, LaCrosse, Wis., 1937-43; instr. Latin and religion Aquinas High Sch., LaCrosse, 1937-42; instr. ethics and religion St. Francis Sch. Nursing, LaCrosse, 1937-46; chancellor Diocese of LaCrosse, 1943-60; pastor Parish of St. Leo the Great, West Salem, Wis., 1957-60; bishop of Superior, Wis., 1960—; Officialis Diocesan Matrimonial Tribunal, LaCrosse, 1943-60; diocesan dir. Cath. Lawyers' Guild, LaCrosse, 1956-60; pres. Tri-state Interfaith Devel. Enterprise, Superior, 1970-84. Adv. bd. Viterbo Coll., LaCrosse, from 1954-85, Cath. Social Service, La Crosse, 1954-60; trustee Mt. Senario Coll., Wis., from 1969-85; bd. dirs. Nat. Tech. Assistance Found., Mpls., 1971-84. Office: PO Box 189 Superior WI 54880

HAMMETT, EDWARD HAROLD (EDDIE HAMMETT), minister; b. Greenville, S.C., May 20, 1956; s. Harold Lloyd and Kathryn Maxine (Gillespie) H. AA, North Greenville Coll., 1974; BA, Furman U., 1976; MA, Southern Seminary, 1980; postgrad., Southeastern Bapt. Theol. Seminary, 1986-89, Duke U., 1988-89, N.C. State U., 1990—. Edn. minister Leawood Bapt. Ch., Greenville, 1980-86, Grace Bapt. Ch., Durham, 1986-90; asst. dir. dept. discipleship tng. Bapt. State Conv. of N.C., Cary, 1990—; sr. adult cons. So. Bapt. Sunday Sch. Bd., Nashville, 1981—; guest lectr. Ch. Renewal Classes So. Bapt. Theol. Sem., 1982, 84, 85, 86-89, Southeastern Bapt. Theol. Sem., 1986-89, vis. prof. Christian edn., 1988—; mem. Nat. Task Force of Home Mission Bd. So. Bapt. Conv., 1982—; workshop leader Nat. Renewal Conf., Toccoa, 1986; co-workshop leader Nat. Conf. Ministers Edn. at So. Bapt. Sunday Sch. Bd., Nashville, 1987; workshop leader for various So. Bapt. confs. and seminars; mem. marketplace ministry task force Home Mission Bd. Author: Marketplace Ministry, 1992; contbr. articles to religious pubs. Mem. Nat. Assn. Ch. Bus. Adminstrs., Eastern Bapt. Religious Assn., So. Bapt. Religious Educators Assn. Republican. Home: 104 Windward Ct Cary NC 27513 Office: Bapt State Conv PO Box 1107 Cary NC 27512

HAMMETT, RICHARD MAUPIN, minister; b. Trenton, Mo., May 22, 1947; s. Alten Ray and Dorcas Kavannaugh (Maupin) H.; m. Karen Sue Bailey, June 15, 1969; children: Sterling Allan, Chanel Renee. BS in Edn., U. Mo., 1968; MDiv, Wesley theological Seminary, Wash. D.C., 1972; postgrad., Reading U., Eng., 1968, Am. U., 1971-72. Ordained to ministry Meth. Ch., 1969. Youth min. Webster Hills United Meth. Ch., Webster Groves, Mo., 1967; dir. edn. Aldersgate United Meth. Ch., Alexandria, Va., 1969-72, Longview United Meth. Ch., Kansas City, Mo., 1972-73; sr. min. Raymore (Mo.) United Meth. Ch., 1974-84, Harrisonville (Mo.) United Meth. Ch., 1984-90, Blue Ridge United Meth. Ch., Kansas City, 1990—; conf. coord. Youth Ministries, Kansas City, 1973-75; pres. Belton-Raymore Ministerial Alliance, 1979-82, Harrisonville Ministerial Alliance, 1986-87; area coord. Ednl. Opportunities Inc., Orlando, Fla., 1988-89. Mem. Mo. West Conf. Clergy, Belton-Raymore, Harrisonville United Meth. Ch. Fellow pres. Christian Educator's, Kans. City Mo., one of the Outstanding Young Men of Am., OYM- Jaycees, 1979; Paul Harris fellow Rotary Internat. Mem. Rotary (pres. elect). Office: Blue Ridge United Meth Ch 5055 Blue Ridge Blvd Kansas City MO 64055

HAMMON, THOMAS FREDERICK, youth minister; b. Pitts., Oct. 1, 1949; s. Thomas Frederick and Mary Ellen (Pople) H.; m. Rue Hays, June 8, 1974; children: Luke, Jamie, Brett. BA, U. Pitts., 1971. Ordained to ministry Evang. Ch. Alliance. Staff rep. Young Life, Cleve., 1971-73, area dir., 1973-79; area dir. Young Life, Cin., 1979-84, Columbus, 1984-87; regional dir. Young Life, Ohio, Pa., 1986—, W.Va., 1986—; bd. dirs. Pitts. Youth Network. Coach baseball, hockey, soccer, Wheeline, W.Va., 1988—. Republican. Office: Young Life 31 Maple Ave Wheeling WV 26003

HAMMOND, BLAINE RANDOL, priest; b. Lincoln, Nebr., Oct. 30, 1946; s. Blaine Gibson and Mary Eloise (Carlson) H.; m. Elizabeth Dianne Forbes, Sept. 18, 1965; children: Dawn Marie, Sheila Dianne, Justin David. BA in English, U. Wash., Seattle, 1979; MDiv, Iliff Sch. Theology, 1982; cert. Anglican studies, Ch. Divinity Sch. of Pacific, 1988. Ordained deacon Episcopal Ch., 1988; priest, 1989. Vicar St. Irenaeus Episcopal Mission, Lyons, Colo., 1988-89; interim rector Christ Episcopal Ch., Castle Rock, Colo., 1989, curate, 1989-91; chmn., founder peace and justice com. Diocese of Colo., 1989-91; mem. world peace and global affairs com. Colo. Coun. Chs., Denver, 1988-90. Co-founder Colo. Coalition on Religion and the Environment, 1989. Home: 4000 Clayton Rd Concord CA 94521 *We have such a strong tendency to see religion as a scientific inquiry. But to me, it can only be understood as poetry—the poetry of relationship.*

HAMMOND, CHARLES AINLEY, clergyman; b. Asheville, N.C., Aug. 7, 1933; s. George Bradley and Eleanor Maria (Gantz) H.; m. Barbro Stigsdotter Laurell, July 16, 1960; children: Stig Bradley, Inga Allison. B.A., Occidental Coll., Los Angeles, 1955; B.D., Princeton Theol. Sem., 1958; D.D., Missouri Valley Coll., 1981, Wabash Coll., 1982. Ordained to ministry United Presbyn. Ch., 1958; pastor chs. in Pa. and Calif., 1958-75; exec. presbyter Presbytery Wabash Valley, West Lafayette, Ind., 1975-87, Presbytery Phila., 1987—; moderator 192d gen. assembly United Presbyn. Ch., 1980-81; chmn. Gen. Assembly Mission Council, 1982-83. Author: Newtonian Polity in an Age of Relativity, 1977, Seven Deadly Sins of Dissent, 1979. Sec. Hallam (Pa.) Borough Planning Commn., 1962-64, Westchester Community Plans, Los Angeles, 1966-68, Pasadena (Calif.) Planning Commn., 1971-75; chmn. pvt. land use com., 1972-73, chmn. public land use com., 1973-74; mem. Gen. Assembly Council Presbyn. Ch. (U.S.A.), 1983—. Recipient Disting. Alumnus award Princeton Theol. Sem., 1981. Mem. Assn. Presbyn. Ch. Educators, Friends of Old Pine. Republican. Club: Union League (Phila.). Office: 2200 Locust St Philadelphia PA 19103

HAMMOND, DEBORAH LYNN, lay worker; b. Olney, Md., Feb. 12, 1958; d. Cornelius Dennis Sr. and Beverly Laura (Dunn) H. Sec. Mt. Zion United Meth. Ch., Ellicott City, Md., 1980—. Home: 3668-B Mt Ida Dr Ellicott City MD 21043 Office: Mt Zion United Meth Ch 8565 Main St PO Box 81 Ellicott City MD 21043

HAMMOND, EARL EDWARD, clergyman; b. Mt. Vernon, Ky., June 13, 1957; s. Jack Edward and Ella Mae (Nicely) H.; m. Roxanne Hammons, May 21, 1977; children: Stuart Andrew, Heather Elizabeth. BA, Ky. Christian Coll., 1979. Ordained to ministry Christian Ch., 1979. Minister River Dr. Christian Ch., Irvine, Ky., 1979-81, Big Hill Ave Christian Ch., Richmond, Ky., 1981-84, Locust Grove Christian Ch., Keavy, Ky., 1984-86,

Shively Christian Ch., Louisville, 1986, First Christian Ch., Mt. Venron, Ky., 1986—; bd. dirs. Blue Grass Christian Camp, Lexington, Ky., 1983-84; bd. advisors Sunrise Evangelistic Mission, Grayson, Ky., 1989—; exec. coun. Ky. Teens Conv., Lexington, 1982-84. Pres. Rockcastle Emergency Assistance Program; mem. Richmond Ind. Elem. Coun., 1983-84; mem. Cumberland Valley Area Agy. on Aging Coun., Corbin, Ky., 1989—; coun. chmn. Boy Scouts Am., Mt. Vernon, 1990-91. Mem. Assn. Couples for Marriage Enrichment (v.p. Rockcastle River chpt. 1986—). Republican. *As a child I remember making a plaque at Vacation Bible School with folded hands that read, "Prayer Changes Things." I wasn't pretty, but a kind man said to me, "I like yours best, because it is true." I have found in my life that prayer does change things, mostly me!.*

HAMMOND, GUYTON BOWERS, philosophy and religion educator; b. Birmingham, Ala., Nov. 7, 1930; s. Joseph Langhorne and Fanny (Bowers) H.; m. Alice Jean Love, June 27, 1959; children—Bruce Guyton, Mitchell Love. B.A., Washington and Lee U., 1951; postgrad., U. Utrecht, Netherlands, 1951-52, So. Baptist Theol. Sem., 1952-53; B.D., Yale, 1955; Ph.D., Vanderbilt U., 1962. Grad. teaching fellow Vanderbilt U., Nashville, 1955-57; instr. Va. Polytechnic Inst., Blacksburg, 1957-58; asst. prof. Va. Polytechnic Inst., 1958-62, assoc. prof., 1962-67, prof. philosophy and religion, 1967—, head dept., 1978-85, pres. faculty senate, 1971-72, 75-76; Pres. Council on Human Relations, Montgomery County, Va., 1962-63. Author: Man in Estrangement, 1965, The Power of Self-Transcendence, 1966. Chmn. bd. advisers Va. Polytechnic Inst. chpt. YMCA, 1966-67. Mem. Am. Acad. Religion (nat. bd. dirs., pres. Southeastern region 1968-69), N.Am. Paul Tillich Soc. (pres. 1981-82), Va. Philos. Assn., Lambda Chi Alpha. Presbyterian. Home: 508 Preston Ave Blacksburg VA 24060 Office: Va Poly Inst & State U 310 Patton Hall Blacksburg VA 24061

HAMMOND, HATTIE PHILETTA, minister; b. Sharpsburg, Md., Mar. 4, 1907; d. George William and Elsie Philetta (Knode) H. Ordained to ministry Assemblies of God, 1927. Evangelist various locations including Martinsburg, W.Va., Cleve., Phila., London, Germany, Japan, numerous others. Contbr. articles to various jours. Republican. Home: 11031 Roessner Ave Hagerstown MD 21740 *No church, no person, no creed, no sect or group has a corner on truth. It is just too big. It is universal, absolute and final. It finds perfect embodiment in Jesus Christ for in Him it becomes personified. Who contracts Christ contracts truth. So we are safe intaking His Word as our guide. I choose to follow Him.*

HAMMOND, JOHN PETE, III, retired minister, consultant; b. Pulaski, Va., Mar. 13, 1936; s. John Hammond and Esther Elizabeth (Taylor) Sarner; m. Shirley Dye, Aug. 16, 1958; children: Scott, Leigh Anne, Layne. BA, Houghton Coll., 1959; MDiv, Gordon-Conwell Sem., 1962, DD, 1989. Ordained to ministry Am. Bapt. Ch., 1962. Assoc. pastor Tabernacle Ch., Norfolk, Va., 1962-66; campus staff InterVarsity, New Orleans, 1966-70; regional dir. InterVarsity, Atlanta, 1970-78; dir. marketplace dept. InterVarsity, Madison, Wis., 1979—; prof. Asian Theol. Sem., Manila, P.I., 1978-79; bd. dirs. European Sem., Boston, 1961—, Presbyns. for Renewal, Louisville, 1974—, Christianity Today, Carol Stream, Ill, 1981—; ruling elder Christ Presbyn. Ch., Madison, 1989—. Pub., editor Marketplace Networks, 1988—; host radio show Marketplace Voices, 1988. Pres. PTA, Atlanta, 1974-75. Recipient Disting. Svc. award Christian Educators Assn. Internat., Pasadena, Calif., 1988; named Alumnus of Yr., Houghton Coll., 1986. Mem. World Future Soc., Nat. Religious Broadcasters. Home: 2412 Van Hise Madison WI 53705 Office: InterVarsity Christian Fellowship 6400 Schroeder Rd Madison WI 53707-7895 *There is no such thing as full-time Christian service and secular service. Some of the world's greatest evangelists were in the seafood business. We must learn to see our work as a calling, as our own special way of serving God.*

HAMMOND, MAX DEAN, minister; b. Ypsilanti, Mich., Oct. 19, 1946; s. Max Dean Sr. and Mabel Anne (Willhite) H.; m. Rebecca Jean Swick, Nov. 1, 1969; children: Max III, Bradley. B in Sacred Lit., Great Lakes Bible Coll., 1969; postgrad., Cin. Bible Sem., 1983-86. Min. Mason (Mich.) Ch. of Christ, 1968-72, Crothersville (Ind.) Christian Ch., 1972-76; sr. min. Ripley Ch. of Christ, Big Prairie, Ohio, 1976-82, Greenford (Ohio) Christian Ch., 1982—; dir. Christian Children's Home of Ohio, Wooster, 1977-83, Round Lake Christian Assembly, Lakeville, Ohio, 1977-83, H.A.S.T.E.N. Mission, Winston-Salem, N.C., 1983—, instr. 1988—; founder, coord. High Sch. Chaplency Program South Range High Sch., North Lima, Ohio, 1984—; seminar developer and leader for ch. Leadership and Adminstrn., shepherding ministry within the ch., marriage and family life; instr. on mission fields. Vol. fireman Crothersville (Ohio) Fire Dept., 1972-76; chmn. Crothersville (Ohio) Indsl. Pk. Com., 1974-76; vol. fireman, ambulance crew mem. Green Twp. Vol. Fire Dept., Greenford, 1982-89; exec. dir. Citizens League Opposing Unwanted Trash, Greenford, 1986-90. Home: 11787 Lisbon Rd Greenford OH 44422 Office: Greenford Christian Ch 11767 Lisbon Rd Greenford OH 44422

HAMMOND, STEPHEN J., academic administrator. Supr. schs. Diocese of Nashville. Office: Schs Supt 2400 21st Ave S Nashville TN 37212*

HAMMONDS, ROGER KENT, minister; b. Naples, Tex., Jan. 11, 1948; s. Curtis Lewis Hammonds and Melba Jewell (Rogers) Edwards; m. Joan Werneking, Jan. 8, 1971; children: Susan Diane, Sharon Elizabeth. BA, East Tex. Bapt., 1971; MRE, Southwestern Bapt. Theol. Sem., Ft. Worth, 1979. Ordained minister in Bapt. Ch., 1972. With supply/revivals various chs. Tex., Ark., 1963-67; youth min. First Bapt. Ch., Kirbyville, Tex., 1967-68, Omaha, 1968-70, Jefferson, Tex., 1971-75; assoc. pastor First Bapt. Ch., Coleman, Tex., 1979—. Program dir. Royal Ambassadors/Boys Camp, Lake Brownwood, Tex., 1980—; region 15 dir. Royal Ambassadors, Bapt. Gen. Conv., Tex., 1981-86; bd. dirs. Home Health Care-Nursing, Coleman, Tex., 1987. Mem. So. Bapt. Religious Educators, Coleman Ministers Assn. (pres. 1984-85, 89-90), Coleman County (Tex.) Bapt. Assn. (moderator 1986-88, Sunday sch. dir. 1980-86, 89—), Profl. Assn. Christian Educators. Office: First Bapt Ch Box 983 Coleman TX 76834 *When our faith is shattered by unexpected results, we're okay as long as our trust remains in the God who allowed those results. Sin is choosing the less good. The maturing of wisdom is the love of God.*

HAMMONS, DENNIS ALVIN, pastor; b. Detroit, June 30, 1956; s. Herbert and Wanda Faye (Jackson) H.; m. Donna Faye Messer, Mar. 10, 1978; children: Andrea Christin, Joshua Caleb. ThB, Clear Creek Bapt. Bible Coll., 1981; EdM, Pensacola Christian Coll., 1983; ThM, Luther Rice Sem., 1987, ThD, 1988. Ordained to ministry Bapt. Ch., 1978. Assoc. pastor, minister edn. New Bethel Bapt. Ch., Crane Nest, Ky., 1977-78, 81; pastor Mt. Ararat Bapt. Ch., Crane Nest, 1978-79, Young Grove Bapt. Ch., Dewitt, Ky., 1979-80, Northside Bapt. Ch., Barbourville, Ky., 1981-83; BSU campus minister Ky. Bapt. Conv. Union Coll., Barbourville, 1982-83; pastor Walker (Ky.) Bapt. Ch., 1983-84, Turkey Creek Bapt. Ch., Flat Lick, Ky., 1985-89, 1st Bapt. Ch., Pennington Gap, Va., 1989—; chmn. finance com., devel. chmn. Powell River Camp 1st Bapt. Ch., Pennington Gap; mem. exec. bd. Ky. Bapt. Conv.; mem. exec. bd. Va. Bapt. Conv.; organizer, past dir. hosp. chaplaincy program Knox County Gen. Hosp.; prof. New Testament Heritage Bible Inst.; past tchr. 4th-6th grades Knox County Christian Sch. Named one of Outstanding Young Men in Am. Mem. Powell River Bapt. Assn. (vice moderator). Office: 1st Bapt Ch PO Box 145 Pennington Gap VA 24277

HAMPSON, THOMAS LEE, church organization executive; b. Oakdale, Calif., Nov. 17, 1948; s. Lee G. and Margaret (Crumpacker) H.; m. Anita Morano; 1 child, Thomas D. BA, U. Notre dame, 1971, MA, 1973; MA in Edn., Washington U., St. Louis, 1982. Tchr. St. Joseph's High Sch., South Bend, Ind., 1975-81; assoc. dir. Office on Global Edn., Ch. World Svc., Balt., 1982—. Co-author: Make a World of Difference, 1989, Tales of the Heart, 1990; contbr. articles to various periodicals. Mem. devel. edn. com. Interaction, 1984-89; chmn. nat. adv. com. World Food Day, Washington, 1988-89; chmn. social action com. Corpus Christi Ch., Balt., 1983-88. Recipient Tchr. of Yr. award St. Joseph High Sch., 1980, Social Justice award Midwest chpt. Order of St. Joseph, 1980, Wilber award for Make A World of Difference Religious Pub. Rels. Coun., 1990. Mem. Nat. Assn. Ecumenical Staffs, Nat. Assn. for Social Studies Edn., Nat. Assn. for Curriculum Devel. Democrat. Roman Catholic. Avocations: skiing, photography, gardening, fishing. Office: Ch World Svc 2115 N Charles St Baltimore MD 21218 *Our ruined world reflects our wounded hearts. Healing of our planetary woes and personal grief go hand in hand. Entering our broken heart links us to pain and promise of every living thing.*

HAMPTON, CAROL MCDONALD, educator, administrator, historian; b. Oklahoma City, Sept. 18, 1935; d. Denzil Vincent and Mildred Juanita (Cussen) McDonald; m. James Wilburn Hampton, Feb. 22, 1958; children: Jaime, Clayton, Diana, Neal. BA, U. Okla., 1957, MA, 1973, PhD, 1984. Teaching asst. U. Okla., Norman, 1976-81; instr. U. of Sci. and Arts of Okla., Chickasha, 1981-84; coord. Consortium for Grad. Opportunities for Am. Indians, U. Calif., Berkeley, 1985-86; trustee Ctr. of Am. Indian, Oklahoma City, 1981—; vice chmn. Nat. Com. on Indian Work, Episcopal Ch., 1986, field officer Native Am. Ministry, 1986—; coun. Native Am. Ministries, 1986—, co-chair, 1989—, sec., 1988; mem. nat. coun. Chs. Racial Justice Working Group, 1990—, co-convenor, 1991—. Contbr. articles to profl. jours. Trustee Western History Collections, U. Okla., Okla. Found. for the Humanities, 1983-86; mem. bd. regents U. Sci. and Arts Okla., 1989—; bd. dirs. Okla. State Regents for Higher Edn., mem. adv. com. on social justice; mem. World Coun. of Chs. Program to Combat Racism, Geneva, 1985-91; bd. dirs. Caddo Tribal Coun., Okla., 1976-82. Recipient Okla. State Human Rights award, 1987; Francis C. Allen fellow, Ctr. fot the History of Am. Indian, 1983. Mem. Western History Assn., Western Social Sci. Assn., Orgn. of Am. Historians, Am. Hist. Assn., Okla. Hist. Soc., Assn. Am. Indian Historians (founding mem. 1981—). Democrat. Episcopalian. Club: Jr. League (Oklahoma City). Avocation: travel. Home: 1414 N Hudson Oklahoma City OK 73103 Office: Episcopal Ch Am Indian and Eskimo Ministry 924 N Robinson Oklahoma City OK 73102

HAMPTON, GARY CALVIN, minister; b. Plymouth, Mich., Nov. 18, 1953; s. Robert Calvin and Mildred (Falls) H.; m. Teresa Allene Chester, July 28, 1973; children: Nathan James, Tabitha Allene. BA in Bible, Freed-Hardeman Coll., 1976. Minister Rose City Ch. of Christ, North Little Rock, Ark., 1976-81, Pleasant Valley Ch. of Christ, Mobile, Ala., 1981—; sec. bd. dirs. Agape of South Ala., Mobile, 1983-87; tchr. Lubagha Preacher Tng. Sch., Rumphi, Malawi, 1987-89; v.p. Mobile Christian Sch. Parents, Tchrs., Friends Assn., 1990-91. Author: Seldom Studies Scriptures, 1987; contbr. articles to religious jours. Home: 3032 Lindholm Dr E Mobile AL 36693 Office: Pleasant Valley Ch Christ 2576 Pleasant Valley Rd Mobile AL 36606 *As the Lord said, I believe the way to truly find oneself is through losing one's life in service to others.*

HAMPTON, RALPH CLAYTON, JR., pastoral studies educator, clergyman; b. Blanchard, Okla., Dec. 13, 1934; s. Ralph Clayton Sr. and Ida Lucille (Jackson) H.; m. Margaret Ann Evans, Aug. 22, 1958; children: Laura Ann, Clayton Lee, Kenneth Michael. AA, Diablo Community Coll., Pleasant Hill, Calif., 1955; BA, Free Will Baptist Bible Coll., Nashville, 1958; MA, Winona Lake (Ind.) Sch. Theology, 1961; MDiv, Covenant Theol. Sem., St. Louis, 1970; postgrad., Trinity Evang. Div. Sch., Deerfield, Ill., 1981-84. Ordained to ministry Bapt. Ch., 1962. Dir. Christian svc. Free Will Bapt. Bible Coll., Nashville, 1958-63, mem. faculty, 1958-68, 70—, chmn. dept. Christian ministries, 1975—, dean Grad. Sch., 1986—; pastor Oakwood Free Will Bapt. Ch., Woodlawn, Tenn., 1962-65, Rock Springs Free Will Bapt. Ch., Charlotte, Tenn., 1966-68, Cross Timbers Free Will Bapt. Ch., Nashville, 1975-78; asst. moderator Nat. Assn. Free Will Baptists, Nashville, 1982-87, moderator, 1987—, mem. exec. com., 1982—. Author: Adult Bible Studies in Old Testament—Teachers edit., 1971-78; contbr. articles to denominational mags. Avocations: travel, gardening. Office: Free Will Baptist Bible Coll 3606 West End Ave Nashville TN 37205

HAMRICK, LEWIS FRANKLIN, minister, publisher; b. Eden, N.C., July 11, 1938; s. Walton Dexter and Winona May (Parrish) H.; m. Judy Dare Herndon, June 9, 1962; children: Joy Ruth, Lewis Franklin Jr., Christy Leigh, Laura LeMae. BRE, Piedmont Bible Coll., 1960, ThB, 1961; DD (hon.), Northland Bapt. Bible Coll., Dunbar, Wis., 1990. Ordained to ministry Bapt. Ch., 1960. Staff evangelist Piedmont Bible Coll., Winston-Salem, N.C., 1961-66; assoc. pastor Barnhardt Bapt. Ch., Stewartsville, Va., 1966-69; assoc. pastor Falls Rd. Bapt. Ch., Rocky Mount, N.C., 1969-84, pastor, 1984—; founder, pres., chmn. bd. Positive Action for Christ, Proteens, Internat., Rocky Mount, 1969-90. Author: The Inner Man, 1978, The Christian Adventure, 1979, Behold Your God, 1980, Ancient Landmarks, 1980, Road Map to Mature Youth, 1982, Proverbs—The Fountain of Life, 1981; also booklets, articles to Christian mags.; editor Pro Maker mag. Bd. dirs. The Wilds Christian Camp, Rosman, N.C., 1972-90; trustee Piedmont Bible Coll., 1977-90. Recipient Alumnus of Yr. award Piedmont Bible Coll., 1974, Heritage award N.C. Assn. Christian Schs., 1989. Republican. Home: 558 Avent St Rocky Mount NC 27804 Office: Falls Rd Bapt Ch 722 Falls Rd Rocky Mount NC 27804

HANCE, CLIFFORD JOSEPH, minister; b. Canton, Ill., Dec. 4, 1963; s. Lawrence Robert and Marilyn Mae (Bridgewater) H.; m. Sandra Kay Burns, May 24, 1986. BA in Ch. Music, Mid-Am. Nazarene Coll., 1986. Min. of youth and music 1st Ch. of Nazarene, New Smyrna Beach, Fla., 1986-87, Ch. of Nazarene, Loveland, Colo., 1987-89, 1st Ch. of Nazarene, Ottawa, Ill., 1989—; dist. teen talent dir. N.W. Ill. Dist. Ch. of Nazarene, Eureka, 1989-90, dist. NYI v.p., 1990-91. Republican.

HANCOCK, CHARLES WILBOURNE, bishop; b. Albany, Ga., Feb. 2, 1924; s. Aubra Ernest and Mary Lois (BellP; m. Flora Mariam Crawford, Mar. 20, 1946; children: Linda Susan, Stephen Crawford, David Charles, Laura Leigh. Student, Young Harris Coll., 1944; AB, Emory U., 1946, BD, 1948. On trial So. Ga. Conf., ordained deacon United Meth. Ch., 1947, full connection, elder, 1949. Pastor United Meth. Ch., Bloomingdale, Ga., 1948-50; Butler (Ga.) charge United Meth. Ch., 1950-53, Thomasville charge, 1953-56; pastor Meml. Meth. Ch. United Meth. Ch., Albany, Ga., 1956-62; pastor Epworth Meth. Ch. United Meth. Ch., Savannah, Ga., from 1962; pres. Conf. Bd. Missions and Ch. Extension United Meth. Ch., from 1960; bishop Ala.-West Fla. Conf. United Meth. Ch., Andalusia, Ala., 1988—. Trustee Young Harris Coll., from 1960; bd. dirs. Am. Cancer Soc., from 1957. Office: United Meth Ch PO Box 700 Andalusia AL 36420

HANCOCK, JOHN, religious organization administrator. Moderator of gen. assembly Social Brethren, Harrisburg, Ill. Office: Social Brethren RR #3 Box 221 Harrisburg IL 62946*

HAND, MARCUS VERNON, minister; b. Nahunta, Ga., May 17, 1937; s. Ira J. and Rhodie B. (Johns) H.; m. Sara Jane Jarrell, Apr. 8, 1961; children: Stefani Susan, Marcus Jarrell. AB in Journalism, U. Ga., 1970, postgrad., 1971; MDiv, Sch. of Theology, 1987. lic. minister Ch. of God, 1954, ordained to ministry, 1960. Pastor Ch. of God, Lebanon, Ga., 1964-68; mem. Ga. Youth Bd. Ch. of God, 1964-72; pastor Ch. of God, Athens, Ga., 1968-70; dist. overseer Ch. of God, Athens and Alma, Ga., 1968-73; pastor Ch. of God, Alma, 1970-73; mem. Ga. State Council Ch. of God, 1972-73; editor Missions Pubs. Ch. of God, Cleveland, Tenn., 1973-78, coordinator Youth World Evangel. program, 1978-84, editor Lighted Pathway, 1984—, men. com. on social concerns, 1984-89; pastor Cornerstone Ch. of God, Athens, Ga., 1989—. Author: (books) Put Your Arms Around the World, 1978, Reaching People, 1979, I Saw a Vision, 1980, Linked Lives, 1981. Named Outstanding Young Religious Leader of the Yr., Outstanding Young Man of Yr., Athens Jaycees, 1970. Mem. Evangel. Press Assn., Internat. Pentecostal Press Assn. Home: 215 Rivermont Rd Athens GA 30606 Office: Cornerstone Ch of God 2150 Lexington Rd Athens GA 30605

HAND, MICKEY MARY, minister; b. Grand Island, Nebr., Apr. 25, 1947; d. Kenneth L. and Betty (Hart) Stone; children: Christy L., Barry H. BA in Behavior Sci., Scarritt Coll., 1969. Lic. to ministry United Ch. of Christ, 1988. Christian edn. coord. Piedmont (Calif.) Community Ch., 1969-71, Camelback United Presbyn. Ch., Scottsdale, Ariz., 1973-74, 76-81; dir. youth activities Ch. of the Beatitudes, Phoenix, 1974-76; dir. youth ministries Shadow Rock United Ch. of Christ, Phoenix, 1985-88; assoc. for youth, young adult and camping ministry S.W. Conf., United Ch. of Christ, Phoenix, 1987—; bd. dirs. Cen. Ariz. Refugee Ecumenical Svc., Phoenix, 1991—; com. mem. Interch. Resource Ctr., Phoenix, 1990—, Youth Ministry Com., 1986—, Com. on Outdoor Ministry, 1989—. Leader, neighborhood chmn. Girl Scouts U.S.A., Ft. Campbell, Ky., 1967-68, Phoenix, 1979-84; mem. speakers bur. Planned Parenthood, Phoenix, 1975-88. Democrat. Office: SW Conf United Ch of Christ 4423 N 24th St #600 Phoenix AZ 85016

HANDLEY, GEORGE E., bishop. Regional coord., bishop Evang. Luth. Ch. in Am., Phila. Office: Evang Luth Ch in Am 7 Ctr for Mission Germantown Ave Ste 7301 Philadelphia PA 19119*

HANDY, LOWELL KENT, religion educator; b. Fort Dodge, Iowa, July 18, 1949; s. Ora Addison and Doris Mary-Alice (Leamon) H. BA, U. Iowa, Iowa City, 1971, MA, 1974; MA, U. Chgo., 1980, PhD, 1987. Lectr. in Bible Loyola U., Chgo., 1987-90, vis. asst. prof., 1991-92; indexer Am. Theol. Libr. Assn., Evanston, Ill., 1988—. Contbr. articles to profl. jours. Mem. Soc. Bibl. Lit., Chgo. Soc. Bibl. Rsch. Mem. Christian Ch.

HANDY, MICHAEL HAROLD, minister; b. Nashville, Aug. 6, 1959; s. Ray Taylor and Lucille (Cook) H.; m. LuAnne Handy, Dec. 27, 1981; children: Christopher, Stephen. BMus, Middle Tenn. State U., 1982; M. Ch. Music, So. Bapt. Theol. Sem., 1989. Ordained to ministry Bapt. Ch., 1985. Minister of music Harmony Bapt. Ch., Louisville, 1983-84; minister music and youth Long Ave. Bapt. Ch., Port St. Joe, Fla., 1985-88; minister music Hillsboro Hts. Bapt. Ch., Huntsville, Ala., 1988—. Mem. A. Choral Dirs. Assns., Am. Guild English Handbell Ringers, So. Bapt. Ch. Music Conf., Port St. Joe Ministerial Assn. (sec.-treas. 1986-88), N.W. Coast Bapt. Assn. (music dir. 1986-88). Home: 2721 Hillsboro Rd Huntsville AL 35805 Office: Hillsboro Hts Bapt Ch 3614 Drake Ave Huntsville AL 35805

HANDY, ROBERT THEODORE, church historian, educator; b. Rockville, Conn., June 30, 1918; s. William Evans and Sarah (MacDonald) H.; m. Barbara Steere Mitchell, Dec. 29, 1941; children: Stephen William, Marilyn Barbara, David Robert. AB, Brown U., 1940; MDiv, Colgate Rochester Div. Sch., 1943; PhD, U. Chgo., 1949; LHD (hon.), Marietta Coll., 1977; DD (hon.), Wake Forest U., 1986. Ordained to ministry Baptist Ch., 1943; pastor South Ch., Mt. Prospect, Ill., 1943-45; instr. Bapt. Missionary Tng. Sch., 1948-49, Shimer Coll., 1949-50; instr. ch. history Union Theol. Sem., N.Y.C., 1950-51; asst. prof. Union Theol. Sem., 1951-54, asso. prof., 1954-59, prof., 1959-86, Henry Sloane Coffin prof. ch. history, 1981-86, prof. emeritus, 1986, dir. studies, 1957-63, dean, 1970-71, dean grad. studies, 1974-76, acad. dean, 1976-78; adj. prof. dept. religion, Columbia U., 1973-86. Author: We Witness Together, 1956, Members One of Another, 1959, (with others) American Christianity, 1960, 63, A Christian America: Protestant Hopes and Historical Realities, 1971, 2d edit., 1984, A History of the Churches in the United States and Canada, 1976, (with others) A History of the Christian Ch., 4th edit., 1985, A History of Union Theological Seminary in New York, 1987, Undermined Establishment: Church-State Relations in America, 1880-1920, 1991; editor: The Social Gospel in America, 1966, Religion in the American Experience: The Pluralistic Style, 1972, The Holy Land in American Protestant Life, 1800-1948: A Documentary History, 1981; co-editor: Theology and Church in Times of Change, 1970. Mem. Faith and Order Commn., World Council Chs., 1954-75. Served from 1st lt. to capt. AUS, 1945-47, PTO. Mem. Am. Soc. Ch. History (past pres.), Am. Bapt. Hist. Soc. (pres. 1974-75). Home: 20 Holly Ln Cresskill NJ 07626

HANDY, WILLIAM TALBOT, JR., bishop; b. New Orleans, Mar. 26, 1924; s. William Talbot Sr. and Dorothy Pauline (Pleasant) H.; m. Ruth Odessa Robinson, Aug. 11, 1948; children—William Talbot III (dec.), Dorothy D. Handy Davis, Stephen Emanuel, Mercedes Handy Cowley. Student, Tuskegee U., 1940-43; B.A., Dillard U., 1948, LL.D. (hon.), 1981; M.Div., Gammon Theol. Sem., 1951; S.T.M., Boston U., 1952; DD, Cen. Meth. Coll., 1991. Ordained to ministry United Meth. Ch., 1949, consecrated bishop, 1980. Pastor Newman Meth. Ch., Alexandria, La., 1952-59; pastor St. Mark Meth. Ch., Baton Rouge, 1959-68; pub. rep. Meth. Pub. House, Nashville, 1968-70; v.p. pers. svc. United Meth. Pub. House, Nashville, 1970-78; dist. supt. Baton Rouge-Lafayette dist. United Meth. Ch., 1978-80; bishop Mo. area United Meth. Ch., St. Louis, 1980—; mem. exec. com. Gen. Bd. Publ., Nashville, 1988—. Chmn. subcom. on voting rights U.S. Commn. on Civil Rights, 1959-68; mem. mayor's bi-racial adv. com. La. Adv. Com., Baton Rouge, 1965-66; life mem. NAACP, 1971—, Golden Heritage; chmn. bd. trustees Gammon Theol. Sem., Atlanta, 1990—, St. Paul Sch. Theology, Kansas City, Mo., 1980—, Interdenominational Theol. Ctr., Atlanta, 1990—. Staff sgt. AUS, 1943-46, ETO, PTO. Mem. Mo. Christian Leadership Forum. Lodge: Masons (33 degree). Avocation: collecting jazz and big band records. Office: The United Meth Ch PO Box 6039 Chesterfield MO 63006 *We are living in rapidly changing times but unfortunately our huge technological and scientific achievements have not been undergirded by maintaining our fundamental moral and ethical values and hence we are drifting into an over-indulgent society.*

HANES, CLIFFORD RONALD, religious denomination administrator; b. Vancouver, Wash., July 1, 1952; s. Keith R. and Alice M. (Stephens) H.; m. Mari Dunagan, July 8, 1972; children: Sara Lace, Benjamin, Samuel. BA, L.I.F.E. Bible Coll., L.A., 1975; DD (hon.), Internat. Ch. Foursq. Gospel, 1991. Ordained to ministry Internat. Ch. Foursquare Gospel, 1975. Assoc. pastor Ch. on Way, Van Nuys, Calif., 1975-77; pastor Ch. of Living Water, Olympia, Wash., 1977-81; Bend (Oreg.) Foursquare Ch., 1981-86; supr. NW Dist. Foursquare Chs., Bend, 1986—; mem. missionary bd., bd. regents L.I.F.E. Bible Coll., 1989—. Author: Lessons from the Mountain, 1991. Office: NW Dist Foursq Chs PO Box 7377 Bend OR 97708-7377

HANEY, GERALD LEE, minister; b. Kansas City, Kans., Sept. 25, 1925; s. Russell Simpson and Martha Ann (Williams) H.; m. Betty Marie Morse, July 20, 1947; children: Michael Lee, Jeryn Marie Scrrano-Dec, Marc Jonathan. BA, Ottawa (Kans.) U., 1950; MS, Kans. State U., 1955; MDiv, Cen. Bapt. Theol. Sem., 1978. Ordained to ministry Am. Bapt. Ch., 1978; cert. counselor. Pastor First Mex. Bapt. Ch., Topeka, 1969-74, Sabetha (Kans.) Woodlawn Bapt. Ch., 1974-76, Quindamo Bapt. Ch., Kansas City, 1976-78, Calvary Bapt. Ch., Kansas City, 1978-84, Hortonville Community Ch., First Bapt. Ch., Rhinelender, Wis., 1984-88, First Bapt. Ch., Clarinda, Iowa, 1988—; chmn. validation com. fund of renewal Am. Bapt. Cen. Region, Topeka, 1968-76, mem. ordination coun., 1981-84; chmn. camp commn. Am. Bapt. Chs. Wis., Elm Grove, 1985-88; vice moderator and mentor pastor, Mid-Am. Bapt. Chs., Des Moines, 1988—. Author: Student Relationships Ethical and Legal Implications, 1974. Chmn. Wyandotte County Crop Walk, Kansas City, 1982-83. With USCG, 1943-46. Mem. Clarinda Area Ministerial Alliance (sec., treas.), Am. Bapt. Minister Coun. Republican. Home and Office: 5317 Horsehead Lake Rd Harshaw WI 54529 *Giving of yourself in a renewable commodity, the more you give the more you have to give, to touch the untauchable, to care for the uncaring, and to reach the unreachable, and to see the joy of change in the unchangeable.*

HANGES, JAMES CONSTANTINE, editor; b. Anderson, Ind., Aug. 11, 1954; s. Constantine James and Betty Ann (Wendt) H.; m. Neila Ann Lipscomb, Nov. 17, 1973; children: Kara, Katrina, Constance. BA, Miami U., Oxford, Ohio, 1985, MA, 1988; postgrad., U. Chgo., 1988—. Editorial asst. Jour. Bibl. Lit., Chgo., 1991—. Mem. Soc. Bibl. Lit., Am. Acad. Religion.

HANIFEN, RICHARD CHARLES, bishop; b. Denver, June 15, 1931; s. Edward Anselm and Dorothy Elizabeth (Ranous) H. B.S., Regis Coll., 1953; S.T.B., Cath. U., 1959, M.A., 1966; J.C.L., Pontifical Lateran U., Italy, 1968. Ordained priest Roman Catholic Ch., 1959; asst. pastor Cathedral Parish, Denver, 1959-66; sec. to archbishop Archdiocese Denver, 1968-69, chancellor, 1969-76; aux. bishop of Denver, 1974-83; 1st bishop of Colorado Springs, Colo., 1984—. Office: 29 W Kiowa St Colorado Springs CO 80903

HANKERSON, WALTER LEROY, clergyman; b. Starke, Fla., Jan. 3, 1915; s. Avery Timothy and Johnnie Mae (Mundy) H.; D.D., Balt. Coll. of Bible, 1972; m. Bessie Mae Green, Mar. 20, 1957; children—Marion, Bette, Walter Leroy, Robert. Farmer, 1929-36; foreman Gen. Foundry & Machine Co., Fayetteville, N.C., 1937-42; moulder Wheaton Brass, Newark, 1942-44; apprentice pipefiller Bethlehem Steel Shipyard, S.I., N.Y., 1944-49, journeyman, 1950-68; heating mechanic USCG, Governors Island, N.Y., 1970-74; ordained to ministry Baptist Ch., 1928; pastor Welcome Bapt. Ch., also pres., founder Welcome Bapt. Homes, Inc., Jersey City, 1974—; bd. dirs. O.I.C., 1972-82. Candidate for N.J. State Assembly, 1966. Mem. New Hope Missionary Bapt. Assn. (sec. Quar. Union), Ministers Alliance of Jersey City and Vicinity. Republican. Club: Masons. Home: 265 Stegman St Jersey City NJ 07305 Office: 340 4th St Jersey City NJ 07302

HANKINS, DAVID JOE, clergyman; b. Reedsburg, Wis., Dec. 11, 1957; s. Hilbert Burl and Opal Mae (Martin) H. BA, Carroll Coll., 1980; MDiv, U. Dubuque, 1983. Ordained minister Presbyn. Ch. (U.S.A.), 1983. Youth dir. Emmanuel United Ch., Dubuque, Iowa, 1982-83; pastor Muscoda (Wis.) Presbyn., 1983—; youth adv. del. Presbyn Ch. Gen. Assembly, 1974 (commr. 1985); commr. Synod of Lakes and Prairies, 1989; chmn. Evangelism Com., 1987—; mem. Presbytery Coun., 1987—. Organizer/pres. Suicide Prevention Group, Muscoda, 1985; advisor Riverdale High Sch. Com., Muscoda, 1987—. Mem. Theta Alpha Kappa. Avocations: refinishing furniture, recreational sports, music. Home: 306 W Nebraska Muscoda WI 53573 Office: Muscoda Presbyn Ch 402 N Second St Muscoda WI 53573

HANKINS, LEWIS MILTON, minister; b. Hico, W.Va., Dec. 5, 1941; s. Basil and Elizabeth Agnes (Allport) H.; m. Ethel Lois Campbell, May 8, 1965 (div. 1971); children: Emily Elizabeth, Adam Lloyd; m. Deborah Anne Going, May 20, 1983. BA, Morris Harvey Coll., 1967; ThM, Trinity Sem., 1988, ThD, 1989. Ordained to ministry Bapt. Ch., 1966. Pastor First Bapt. Ch., Seville, Ohio, 1970-71; min. of music Bethel United Meth. Ch., St. Louis, 1978-82; pastor First Bapt. Ch., Rick Creek, Va., 1982-86; sr. min. Flat Creek Bapt. Ch., Lynchburg, Va., 1986-88; pastor Mineral (Va.) Bapt. Ch., 1988—; comptroller Mech. Products & Systems, Inc., St. Louis, 1972-78; bd. dirs. Goshen Bapt. Assn., Mineral, 1988-90; founder The Singin' Srs., Mineral, 1988—; del. So. Bapt. Conv., 1982—. Author: Lady in the Pink Hat, 1970; author short stories; contbr. articles to profl. jours. Mem. Ohio Devel. Bd., New Matamoras, 1968; treas., bd. dirs. Giles County Humane Soc., Rich Creek, 1988; bd. dirs. Am. Cancer Soc., Louisa County, 1989; sec. W.Va. Poetry Soc., Parkersburg, 1970. With USAF, 1960-64. Mem. Va. Bapt. Gen. Assn., Keyboard Amateur Musicians Assn. (pres. 1991), Louisa County Ministerial Assn., Goshen Ministerial Assn. Republican. Home: Rt 522 N Mineral VA 23117 *Life's greatest challenge is sustaining a dynamic faith and wit through times of adversity. A significant role of the church is nurturing such a viable, dynamic faith. I have sought to be an instrument of nurturing.*

HANKS, ELBERT WAYNE, SR., minister; b. Beaumont, Tex., Oct. 2, 1939; s. Alvie Franklin Hanks and Violet Viola (Johnson) Kendig; m. Mary Lou Wood, June 1, 1962; 1 child, Elbert W. Jr. AA, Southwestern Jr. Coll., Waxahachie, Tex., 1959; BA in Theology, Southwestern Assemblies of God, Waxahachie, Tex., 1962; BA, E. Tex. State U., 1970. Ordained to ministry Assemblies of God Ch., 1964. Pastor Lavon (Tex.) Assembly of God, 1962-64; assoc. pastor First Assembly of God, Garland, Tex., 1964-73, sr. pastor, 1974—; sec. Garland Ministerial Alliance, 1965-67, chaplaincy coord., 1970; sec. Pastor's Assn. Greater Dallas, 1966-69; sec.-treas. N. Dallas sec. Assemblies of God, 1973-1981; dist. presbyter North Tex. Dist. Assemblies of God, Dallas, 1981—. Contbr. articles to religious jours. Pres. Southwestern Assemblies of God Coll. Alumni Assn., 1971-76; mem. Mayor's Youth Commn. City of Garland, 1972; bd. dirs. Teen Challenge of Tex., Dallas, 1981— . Recipient Award of Honor, Mayor City of Garland, 1976. Mem. Assn. Pastoral Counselors, Garland C. of C. Republican. Home: 913 Wakefield Dr Garland TX 75040 Office: First Assembly of God Ch 801 W Buckingham Garland TX 75040 *All value is ultimately authenticated by relationships. I am convinced that the ultimate relationship is with God, through faith in His Son, Jesus Christ.*

HANKS, THOMAS DIXON, theologian; b. St. Louis, July 1, 1934; s. Stanley and Elizabeth (Dixon) H.; m. Joyce Main, Apr. 1, 1962; children: Stanley, Elizabeth. BS in Journalism, Northwestern U., 1956; BDiv, Princeton (N.J.) Theol. Sem., 1960, MA in Religion, 1968; ThD, Concordia Sem., 1972. Missionary Latin-Am. Mission, San Jose, Costa Rica, 1963-89; prof. O.T. Sem. Biblica Latin Am., San Jose, 1964-86; editor Latin-Am. Theol. Fraternity, 1986-89; cons. in theology Met. Community Ch., Buenos Aires, 1989—. Author: God So Loved the 3d World, 1983. Mem. Am. Acad. Religion, Latin-Am. Theol. Fraternity, Soc. for Bibl. Lit., Evang. Theol. Soc. Home: 16 Upper Ladue Saint Louis MO 63124 Office: Met Community Ch, Lavalle #376-2D, 1047 Buenos Aires Argentina

HANLEY, JOHN GERALD, clergyman; b. Read, Ont., Can., Feb. 21, 1907; s. Denis and Jessie (Bryson) H. B.A., U. Toronto, 1927; grad. theology, St. Augustine's Sem., Toronto, 1931; D.D. (hon.), Queen's U., 1973. Ordained priest Roman Cath. Ch., 1931; asst. in cathedral Kingston, Ont., 1931-32, Trenton, Can., 1934-41; editor Canadian Register, 1941-70; prof. Jr. Sem., Vancouver, B.C., Can., 1932-34; chaplain Newman Club, Queen's U., Kingston, 1941-58; vicar-gen. Archdiocese Kingston, 1969-83; nat. chaplain Canadian Newman Clubs, 1944-45, 52-55. Author: Across Canada with Newman, 1957. Chmn. Canadian Cath. Press Commn., 1958-67. Recipient Kingston award Queen's U. Alumni Assn., 1970; Queen Elizabeth II Silver Jubilee medal, 1977; Hon. Achievement award City of Kingston, 1982; Disting. Svc. award Queen's U., 1989; hon. Canon St. George's Anglican Cathedral, 1983. Mem. Cath. Press Assn. U.S. and Can. (bd. dirs. 1961-64, sec. 1962-64, 65-68), Cath. Bibl. Assn. Am. (v.p. 1944-45). Address: 279 Johnson St, Kingston, ON Canada K7L 1Y5

HANNAH, DARRELL DALE, minister; b. Bremerton, Wash., June 10, 1962; s. Harry L. and E. Grace (James) H. BA, Grand Canyon U., 1985; MDiv, So. Bapt. Theol. Sem., 1989; postgrad., Regent Coll., Vancouver, B.C., Can. Pastor Carthage (Ind.) Bapt. Chapel, 1986-87. Mem. Bread for the World, Louisville, 1981-84. Mem. Soc. Bibl. Lit. Democrat. Home: 24011 123rd St E Buckley WA 98321-9544

HANNEMANN, DANIEL PAUL, music director; b. Sioux City, Iowa, July 28, 1951; s. Norman Albert and Dorothy Luella (Moh) H. Student, Concordia Coll., Seward, Nebr., 1969-71; BMus, U. Wyo., 1974; M.Sacred Music, Wittenberg U., Springfield, Ohio, 1976. Cert. in ch. music, ELCA. Dir. music, parish worker First English Luth. Ch., Lockport, N.Y., 1976-79; dir. music Emmanuel Luth. Ch., Lincolnton, N.C., 1979—; organist, workshop leader N.C. Synod of Evang. Luth. Ch. in Am.; staff accompanist Lutheridge Sch. of Ch. Music, Arden; harpsichordist Carolina Baroque. Contbr. articles to profl. jours. Founding pres. Lincoln Community Concert Assn., Lincolnton, N.C., 1980-83; bd. dirs. N.C. symphony, Lincolnton, N.C., 1985-86; concert presenter schs., civic groups, nursing homes, clubs. Mem. Am. Guild Orgnists (dean 1987-89), Southeastern Hist. Keyboard Soc., Assn. Luth. Ch. Musicians. Home: 104 Openview Dr Lincolnton NC 28092 Office: Emmanuel Luth Ch 216 S Aspen St Lincolnton NC 28092

HANNEMANN, NORMAN ALBERT, retired pastor; b. Dimock, S.D., Sept. 15, 1924; s. Walter Frederick and Edna Pearl (Stainbrook) H.; m. Dorothy Luella Moh, June 6, 1948; children: Phillip, Daniel, Rebecca, Mark. BA, Concordia Sem., 1948. Ordained to ministry Luth. Ch., 1948. Pastor St. John Luth. Ch., Newcastle, Nebr., 1948-52, Immanuel Luth. Ch., Lidderdale, Iowa, 1952-57, Our Savior Luth. Ch., Cheyenne, Wyo., 1957-63, Faith Luth. Ch., York, Nebr., 1963-82, Christ Luth. Ch., Norfolk, Nebr., 1982-91. Mem. Iowa Dist. West Luth. Ch. Mo. Synod (youth bd. 1953-57), So. Nebr. Dist. Luth. Ch. Mo. Synod (mission bd. 1960-70), Nebr. Dist. Luth. Ch. Mo. Synod (Evangelism bd. 1970-78, constn. com. 1978—). Office: Christ Luth Ch 605 S 5th St Norfolk NE 68701

HANNEN, JOHN EDWARD, bishop; b. Winnipeg, Man., Can., Nov. 19, 1937; s. Charles Scott and Mary Bowman (Lynds) H.; m. Alana Susan Long, June 24, 1977; children—Rebecca Meghann, Meredith Alana. B.A., McGill U., 1959; G.O.E., Coll. of Resurrection, Mirfield, Eng., 1961. Ordained deacon Anglican Ch., 1961, ordained priest, 1962. Asst. curate Diocese of Birmingham, Eng., 1961-64; priest-in-charge Hart Hwy. Diocese of Caledonia, Chetwynd, B.C., Can., 1965-67; assoc. priest Diocese of Caledonia, Greenville, B.C., 1967-68; priest-in-charge Diocese of Caledonia, Port Edward, B.C., 1968-71, Kincolith, B.C., 1971-80; bishop Diocese of Caledonia, Prince Rupert, B.C., 1981—; senator Vancouver Sch. Theology, B.C., 1981-85; mem. inter ch.-interfaith relations com. Gen. Synod, Anglican Ch. of Can., 1983-89. Chmn. bd. trustees Nisgha Sch. Dist., Naas River, B.C., 1977-78; mem. exec. com. Nishga Tribal Council, Naas River, 1974—. Office: Synod Office, PO Box 278, Prince Rupert, BC Canada V8J 3P6

HANNI, PHILIP STANTON, minister; b. Washington, Kans., Apr. 28, 1932; s. Adolph and Belle Marie (Stanton) H.; m. Erin Turner, Aug. 26, 1956; children: Carl, Douglas (dec.), David (dec.). BA, U. Kans., 1955; postgrad., Drew U., 1955-57; BDiv, Kenyon Coll., 1961; MST, Yale U., 1963; D Religion, Chgo. Theol. Sem., 1971. Ordained to ministry United Meth. Ch. as elder, 1967. Campus min. Wesley Found., Valdosta, Ga., 1963-64; campus min. United Christian Fellowship, Monmouth, Oreg., 1964-67, Ellensburg, Wash., 1967-73; univ. chaplain Willamette U., Salem, Oreg., 1973-85; pastor Wesley United Meth. Ch., Milton-Freewater, Oreg., 1986—; candidacy registrar bd. ministry Conf. United Meth. Ch., Oreg. and Idaho, 1987—; instr. gt. decision program Fgn. Policy Assn., Salem and Milton-Freewater, 1984—. Bd. dirs. Walla Walla (Wash.) Area Hospice, 1987—. Recipient Human Rights award City of Salem, 1985. Mem. Am. Acad. Religion, Oreg. Coun. Humanities (bd. dirs. 1991—), Milton-Freewater C. of C. (bd. dirs. 1987-89). Democrat. Home: 142 SE 6th Milton-Freewater OR 97862 Office: Wesley United Meth Ch 816 S Main St Milton-Freewater OR 97862

HANNUM, JOHN THOMAS, evangelist; b. Portsmouth, Ohio, Dec. 4, 1948; s. Harry Francis and Katherine Elizabeth (Shanafelt) H.; m. Martha Jolene Wasson, June 10, 1970; children: Nathan Thomas, Tabitha Jo, Rebekah Elizabeth, Benjamin Ellis. BS in English Bible, Cin. Bible Sem., 1972, MA in Ch. Growth, 1989. Evangelist Brookville (Ind.) Ch. of Christ, 1971-86, Beechwood Christian Ch., Alliance, Ohio, 1986—; pres. Stark Area Mins., Canton, Ohio, 1991; dir. Round Lake Christian Assembly, Lakeview, Ohio, 1991-93. Pres. Right to Life, Brookville, 1976. Republican. Home: 13666 Easton Alliance OH 44601 Office: Beechwood Christian Ch 12950 Easton Alliance OH 44601

HANSELL, GEORGE RONALD, JR., minister; b. Jersey City, June 16, 1955; s. George Ronald and Sarah Louise (Bell) H.; m. Krista Yvonne Herr, June 24, 1978; children: Christopher George, Jennifer Adella. AA, Concordia Luth. Coll., 1975; BA, Concordia Tchrs. Coll., 1977; MDiv, Concordia Theol. Sem., Ft. Wayne, Ind., 1981. Ordained to ministry Luth. Ch., 1981; cert. police chaplaincy, fire tng. Missionary-at-large Hispanic ministry Mich. dist. Luth. Ch. Mo.-Synod, Detroit, 1981-85; vacancy pastor Berea Luth. Ch., Detroit, 1982, 84-85, Good Shepherd Luth. Ch., Sylvan Beach, N.Y., 1988-89; pastor Redeemer Evang. Luth. Ch., Oneida, N.Y., 1985—; treas., sec. Hispanic Ministries Com. Ea. Dist., Buffalo, 1985-88; sec., chmn. Urban Ministries Com. East. Dist., Buffalo, 1988—; mem, sec. Bd. for Mission Svcs. Ea. Dist., Buffalo, 1990—; pastoral del. conv. Luth. Ch. Mo. Synod, Wichita, Kans., 1989; pastoral counselor Luth. Women's Missionary League, Luth. Laymen's League, cen. N.Y., 1986-88, 89—. Contbr. sermons to Oneida Daily Dispatch newspaper, 1985—. Chaplain Detroit Police Dept., 1983-85, Oneida Fire Dept., 1987—; v.p. Oneida Area Christian Chs., 1986-87; clergy rep. AIDS com. Oneida Pub. Schs., 1989. Mem. N.Y. State Assn. Fire Chaplains. Republican. Home: 381 Earl Ave Oneida NY 13421 Office: Redeemer Evang Luth Ch Earl Ave and Oxford St Oneida NY 13421

HANSEN, ADOLF, academic administrator; b. N.Y.C., May 11, 1938; s. Adolf Sr. and Martha (Gundersen) H.; m. Naomi Leah Metzger, June 13, 1959; children: Rebecca, Rebonna. BA, Taylor U., 1959; MDiv, N.Y. Theol. Sem., 1962, STM, 1963; PhD, Northwestern U., 1968. Minister Simpson United Meth. Ch., Ft. Wayne, Ind., 1963-65, Meridian St. United Meth. Ch., Indpls., 1968-71; prof. U. Indpls., 1971-82; v.p., prof. Garrett Evang. Theol. Sem., Evanston, Ill., 1982—. Contbr. articles to profl. jours. Vice chmn. Meridian St. Preservation Commn., Indpls.; pres. Meridian-Kessler Neighborhood Assn., Indpls.; chmn. Indpls.-Marion County Bd. of Ethics, Indpls.; dir. North Cen. Jurisdictional Course of Study Sch., Evanston, 1985-89. Rockefeller Found. fellow, 1967-68. Mem. Soc. Bibl. Lit., Assn. Chgo. Theol. Schs. (treas. 1990—), Chgo. Soc. Bibl. Rsch., Lake Geneva (Wis.) Yacht Club. Home: 1516 Hinman Ave #810 Evanston IL 60201 Office: Garrett Evang Theol Sem 2121 Sheridan Rd Evanston IL 60201

HANSEN, FRANCIS EUGENE, minister; b. Underwood, Iowa, Oct. 30, 1925; s. John Alexander and Annie (Rasmussen) H.; m. Wanda Ann Hoss, Aug. 20, 1949; children: Blair, Cheryl. Student, Biarritz (France) Am. U., 1946; A.A., Graceland Coll., Lamoni, Iowa, 1948; B.S., U. Kans., 1950. Ordained to ministry Reorganized Ch. of Jesus Christ of Latter-day Saints, 1943; ordained bishop, 1956, patriarch/evangelist, 1988. Assigned bishop of Los Angeles, Calif. Stake and Hawaii Dist. Reorganized Ch. of Jesus Christ of Latter-day Saints, 1956-66, counselor to presiding bishop world hdqrs., 1966-72, presiding bishop world hdqrs., 1972-88, cons. first presidency, 1988-89; ret., sec. order of evangelists, 1989; bd. dirs., sec. HealthCare Systems, Inc.; sec. Truman-Forest Pharmacy Bd.; bd. dirs., treas. Independence Regional Health Ctr. Former mem. bd. Good Govt. League; past mem. bd. pub. Herald Pub. House; mem. community adv. com. to Councilman John Casside, L.A.City Coun., 1966—; bd. suprs. Atherton Levy Dist.; mem. Jackson County Farm Bur.; mem. Corp. bd. Mound Grove Cemetery; bd. dirs., sec. Cen. Profl. Bldg., Inc.; pres., bd. dirs. Elbert A. Smith Retirement Ctr.; bd. dirs., sec. Cen. Devel. Assn.; bd. dirs. Community Water Co.; past bd. dirs. Boatmen's Bank of Independence. With AUS, 1944-46, ETO. Decorated Purple Heart. Mem. Jackson County Hist. Soc., Order of Bishops, Rotary (bd. dirs.), Lambda Delta Sigma, Beta Gamma Sigma. Lodge: Rotary (bd. dirs.). Office: Reorganized Ch of Jesus Christ of Latter Day PO Box 1059 Independence MO 64051

HANSEN, PAUL GERHARDT, retired minister, sociology educator; b. Mpls., Sept. 17, 1914; s. Christian and Nellie (Larsen) H.; m. Darlene Ruth Werner, Sept. 14, 1939; children: Stephen P. (dec.), Karen I., Judith E., Elaine L., John M. (dec.), James R., Deborah R. BD, Concordia Sem., St. Louis, 1937; MA in Sociology, U. Denver, 1948. Ordained to ministry Evang. Luth Ch. in Am., 1937. Pastor Luth. chs., Utah, Wyo., 1937-44, St. John's Luth. Ch., Denver, 1948-72, Our Saviour Luth. Ch., Fresno, Calif., 1972-80; pastor Oakhurst-Mariposa Luth Ch., Oakhurst, Calif., 1980-88, pastor emeritus, 1988—; prof. sociology U. Denver, 1952-72, Calif. State U., Fresno, 1972-78, Fresno City Coll., 1974-79; rsch. dir. family life com. Luth. Ch.-Mo. Synod, 1952-64; mem. synod coun. Evang. Luth. Ch. in Am., Oakland, Calif., 1988—, mem. task force on human sexuality, Chgo., 1989—. Author: Lenten Sermons, 1956, 60, 82; co-author: Engagement and Marriage, 1959, Sex and the Church, 1961, Family Relationships, 1970, Newlyweds, 1972; monthly columnist Walter League Messenger, 1953-64. Bd. dirs. Planned Parenthood, Fresno, 1977—; founder Manna House, Inc., community food bank, Oakhurst, 1983, Mariposa, 1984. Chaplain AUS, 1944-46, col. Res. ret. Home: 48914 Royal Oaks Dr Oakhurst CA 93644 *In church circles we say that the seven last words of any congregation are: "We never did it that way before." It is my conviction that those are the seven last words of any society. Only Jesus is "the same yesterday, today, and forever." Change is the key to growth and glory.*

HANSEN, R. CHRISTIAN, minister; b. Mpls., Dec. 21, 1943; s. Rodney V. and Rosamund (Jorgensen) H.; Norma J. Swadner, June 4, 1966; Marcus, Jon, David. BS, Wittenberg U., 1966; MDiv, Luther Northwestern Sem., St. Paul, Minn., 1970. Ordained to ministry Luth Ch., 1970. Pastor Bethany-Elim Luth. Ch., Ivanhoe, Minn., 1970-74, Augustana Luth. Ch., St. James, Minn., 1974-82; v.p. devel. Lutheran Svc. Assn., Hartford, Conn., 1982-86; pastor Bethany Luth. Ch., Burlington, Ia., 1988—; dean Southeastern Iowa Synod, Evangelical Luth. Ch. Am., 1989—. Bd. dirs. Southeastern Iowa Mental Health, Inc., Burlington, 1987—, Hope Haven A Devel. Ctr., Burlington, 1989—, Lutheran Homes, Muscatine, Iowa, 1989—. Office: Bethany Luth Ch 2515 Madison Ave Burlington IA 52601

HANSEN, RICHARD PAUL, minister; b. North Platte, Nebr., Dec. 20, 1951; s. Paul Martin and Helen Edna (Fenton) H.; m. Marilyn Jean Werner, Sept. 14, 1974; children: Nathan, Megan, Lauren. BS, Iowa State U., 1974; MDiv, Bethel Theol. Sem., St. Paul, 1979; ThM, Princeton Theol. Sem., 1980; postgrad., Fuller Theol. Sem., Pasadena, Calif. Ordained to ministry Presbyn. Ch. (U.S.A.), 1980. Program dir. Edina (Minn.) br. Mpls. YMCA, 1974-76; assoc. pastor 1st Presbyn. Ch., Greenville, Pa., 1980-84; sr. pastor Community Presbyn. Ch., Palos Park, Ill., 1984-88, 1st Presbyn Ch., Visalia, Calif., 1988—; chmn. mission and planning com. Shenango Presbytery, Weskin, Pa., 1980-84, com. on preparation for ministry, San Joaquin Presbytery, 1990—. Author: Best Sermons I, 1988. Mem. family life com. Visalia sch. Dist., 1990—. Bethel Theol. Sem. preaching fellow, 1979. Mem. Presbyterians for Renewal, Visalia Ministerial Fellowship (v.p. 1990—), Phi Beta Kappa. Office: 1st Presbyn Ch 215 N Locust St Visalia CA 93291

HANSEN, ROBERT ARTHUR, minister; b. New Brunswick, N.J., Sept. 25, 1949; s. Robert and Dorothy (Domke) H.; m. Lynne Hodas, Jan. 16, 1981. BA, Salem Coll., 1973; MDiv, Louisville Presbyn. Sem., 1976; DMin, McCormick Sem., 1988. Ordained to ministry Presbyn. Ch. (U.S.A..), 1976. Pastor Kuhn Meml. Presbyn., Burboursville, W.Va., 1977-79, Bay View Presbyn. Ch., Cliffwood Beach, N.J., 1979-85, 1st Presbyn. Ch., Whitesboro, N.Y., 1985-90; area counselor Bicentennial Fund Presbyn. Ch. (USA), Louisville, 1990—; acting dir. Coun. of Chs., Utica, N.Y., 1988-90; chairperson Bicentennial Fund Presbyn. Ch. (USA), Utica, 1988-90, support com. Utica Presbytery, 1986-88; pres. Bayshore Assn. Ministers, Priests and Rabbis, N.J., 1981-85. Chairperson Multicultural Coalition, Utica, 1989; bd. dirs. YMCA, Utica, 1989, Presbyn. Home Control N.Y., New Hartfort, 1989. Home: 120 Conley Dr Chestertown MD 21620 Office: Bicentennial Fund 357 High St Chestertown MD 21620

HANSEN, WENDELL JAY, clergyman, gospel broadcaster; b. Waukegan, Ill., May 28, 1910; s. Christian Hans and Anna Sophia (Termansen) H.; m. Bertelle Kathryn Budman, Mar. 9, 1933 (dec. Jan. 6, 1956); 1 child, Sylvia Larson; m. Eunice Evaline Irvine, Nov. 2, 1957; 1 child, Dean. Grad. Cleve. Bible Coll., 1932; A.B., William Penn Coll., 1938; postgrad. Gletch Berg Skule, Switzerland, 1939; MA, U. Iowa, 1940, PhD, 1947. Ordained to ministry Recorded Friends, 1936, Evang. Reformed Ch., 1944; pastor chs., Grinnell, Iowa, Mpls. and Iowa City, 1934-47; evangelist with talking and performing birds, 1946—, past mgr. gospel radio stas. Two Rivers, Wis., Menomonie, Wis., Peru, Ind., Wabash, Ind., East St. Louis, Ill., Indpls., 1952—; pres., chmn. of bd. WESL Inc., East St. Louis, 1962—, cons. radio and TV, 1970—; appointed adv. com. to Indpls. Prosecutor, 1986. Dir. St. Paul Inter-racial Work Camp, 1939; chmn. Minn. Joint Refuge Com., 1940-41. Recipient honor citation Nat. Assn. Broadcasters, 1980; Boss of Yr. award Hamilton County Broadcasters, 1979, award Boys Town, 1983, award Women of Faith, St. Louis, 1984. Mem. Internat. Platform Assn., Internat. Assn. Christian Magicians, Ind. Bird Fanciers, East St. Louis C. of C. (bd. dirs. 1981-86), Pi Kappa Delta. Republican. Quaker. Club: Ind. Pigeon (best exotic bird award 1969, 75, 80). Lodge: Kiwanis. Contbr. articles to popular mags. *When unhappy people decide to trust in God, they become valuable. They find happiness in serving. Through speaking, entertaining, writing, radio and TV, without begging for money, I have tried to help people receive this happiness.*

HANSON, BRUCE LLOYD, minister; b. Lansing, Mich., Oct. 2, 1948; s. Lyle Eugene and Ruth Allen (Magruder) H.; m. Connie Ellaine, Aug. 16, 1969; children: Angela Dawn, Aaron Deon. Assoc. degree, Parkland Jr. Coll., 1969; BS, U. Dubuque, 1973; MDiv., Wartburg Sem., 1977. Ordained to ministry Luth. Ch., 1977. Pastor 1st Luth. of Arland and West Akers, Prairie Farm, Wis., 1977-80, St. Peter Luth., Benson, Ill., 1980-85, St. John's Luth., Ashton, Ill., 1985-91, St. Peter Luth. Ch., Arenzville, Ill., 1991—; v.p. bd. govs. No. Ill., Luth. Social Svcs. Ill., Dixon, 1986-90; conf. dean Cen. Conf. of No. Ill. Synod, Ashton, 1989; prison chaplain Dixon Correctional Ctr., 1988-91. Western Ill. Correctional Ctr., 1991—. Mem. Ill. Assn. Suicidologists, Ill. Ritualistic Abuse Network, Alliance for Cult and Ritual Edn. (religious dir. 1988—), Ill. Assn. for Counseling and Devel., Lions. Home: RR1 Box 91 Arenzville IL 62611 Office: St Peter Luth Ch RR1 Box 91 Arenzville IL 62611

HANSON, DONNA MCKINNEY, religious organization administrator; b. Arlington, Ky., Sept. 18, 1940; married; two sons. BA cum laude, Ursuline Coll.; MSW, St. Louis U.; postgrad., Gonzaga U., Whitworth Coll., Cath. U., Notre Dame U. Social worker Cath. Family Svc., 1964-66; sch. social worker Spokane Sch. Dist. #81, 1966-68; instr. sociology Fort Wright Coll. Holy Names, 1968; social sci./human svcs. instr. to program planner, coord. Spokane Falls Community Coll., 1968-71; assoc. dir. Cath. Charities of the Diocese of Spokane, 1974-78, exec. dir., 1978-85; sec. for social ministries Cath. Diocese of Spokane, 1981—; bd. dirs. Inst. for Pastoral Life, 1987-90, Nat. Assn. for Lay Ministry, 1989—; nat. adv. coun. mem. Nat. Conf. Cath. Bishops/U.S. Cath. Conf., 1982-87, chmn. 1986-87, addresses Pope John Paul II, San Francisco, 1987; chmn. various coms. Cath. Charities USA, 1974—, Cath. Charities of the Diocese of Spokane, 1969—; appointed to Wash. State Cath. Conf., 1977—. Bd. dirs. Assn. Jr. Leagues, 1969—, Jr. League of Spokane, 1973-74, 74-75, 76-77, Leadership Spokane, 1988-91; mem. City of Spokane Quality of Life Coun., 1974-76; chairperson Human Svcs. Com., Spokane, 1990-91, Children's Task Force, 1990—. Recipient U.S. Cath. award, 1988, Alumni Merit award, St. Louis U., 1986, fellowship grant AAUW, 1972, Angeline award Ursulines of Louisville, 1991; named Spokane Woman of Distinction, 1978, Outstanding Young Woman of Am., 1968, 72, 74, 77, others. Mem. Cath. Bus. and Profl. Women of Spokane, Spokane Area C. of C. Home: 620 West 19th Ave Spokane WA 99203

HANSON, FREDERICK DOUGLAS, minister; b. Perth, N.B., Can., Dec. 17, 1948; s. Douglas Aubrey and Mona Evelyn (Hitchcock) H.; m. Lavergne Alice Sullivan, Apr. 6, 1968; children: Darren Daniel, Darcy Elizabeth. BA, Trinity Coll., Dunedin, Fla., 1984; postgrad., Luther Rice Sem., Jacksonville, Fla., 1984. Ordained to ministry Free Will Bapt. Ch., 1970. Pastor Free Will Bapt. Ch., N.B., 1970—, moderator, 1978-90; mem. Home Missions Bd., 1989—. Contbr. numerous articles to religious jours. Gen. dir. St. John Valley Bible Camp, N.B., 1973-76, 79-81. Mem. Atlantic Can. Assn. Free Will Bapts. (exec. com. 1978—, gen. bd. Nashville 1981-89), Christian Camping Internat., Can. Camping Assn., N.B. Camping Assn., Free Will Bapts. Assn. (promotional sec. 1981—, gen. bd. 1981—), Evang. Fellowship Can. (gen. coun. 1988—). Office: Atlantic Can Assn Free Will Bapts, PO Box 355, Hartland, NB Canada E0J 1N0

HANSON, KENNETH CHARLES, biblical studies educator; b. Peoria, Ill., Oct. 11, 1951; s. Kenneth Christian and Gertrude R. (Kooy) H.; m. Deborah Ann Wyscarver, July 30, 1988. BA, Pacific Christian Coll., Fullerton, Calif., 1974; PhD., MA, Claremont (Calif.) Grad. Sch., 1983. Prof. Bibl. studies Episcopal Theol. Sch., Claremont, 1982—; elder St. John's Presbyn. Ch., L.A., 1983-85. Assoc. editor, writer: Ras Shamra Parallels, Vol. 4, 1991; contbr. articles to profl. jours. Vol. Turning Point, Santa Monica, Calif., 1985-86. Mills fellow Claremont Grad. Sch., 1976-77. Mem. The Context Group, Soc. Bibl. Lit., Cath. Bibl. Assn. Home: 1813 Morgan Ln Apt A Redondo Beach CA 90278 Office: 1325 N College Ave Claremont CA 91711

HANSON, MURRAY LYNN, minister; b. Albert Lea, Minn., May 26, 1948; s. Palmer J. and Betty (Lyle) H.; m. Mary Ann Eastwold, Dec. 26, 1970; children: Andrew, Rebecca. BA, Mankato State U., 1970; MDiv, Dubuque Theol. Sem., 1973, D Ministry, 1980. Ordained to ministry Presbyn. Ch. (U.S.A.), 1973. Intern Sunnyside Presbyn. Ch., South Bend, Ind., 1972; supply pastor Hazelton (Iowa) Presbyn. Ch., 1973; assoc. pastor Lakeside Presbyn. Ch., Storm Lake, Iowa, 1973-77; pastor 3d Presbyn. Ch., Rockford, Ill., 1977—; supr. field edn. McCormick/Dubuque Sems., Chgo., Dubuque, 1979—; commr. Gen. Assembly, Presbyn. Ch. (U.S.A.), No. Ill., 1989. Author: An Examination of the Influence of the Roman Catholic Religious Affiliation of Alfred Smith and John Kennedy in the Presidential Elections of 1928 and 1960, 1970, 71, A Self-Assessment Manual for Local Congregations, 1980, Self-Assessment Study of Third Presbyterian Church, 1980. Bd. dirs. Protestant Community Svcs., Rockford, 1985-87, Regional "For Kids' Sake), No. Ill./So. Wis., 1990—; tour organizer, host to Eng., Scotland, Jordan, Israel, Egypt, 1985—. Office: 3d Presbyn Ch 1221 Custer Ave Rockford IL 61103

HANSON, PAUL DAVID, religion educator; b. Ashland, Wis., Nov. 17, 1939; s. Hans Victor and Lydia (Thompson) H.; m. Cynthia Jane Rosenberger, Aug. 20, 1966; children. Amy Elizabeth, Mark Christopher, Nathaniel Ross. BA, Gustavus Adolphus Coll., 1961; BD, Yale U., 1965; PhD, Harvard U., 1970. Asst. prof. O.T. Harvard Div. Sch., 1970-75, prof., 1975—, Bussey prof. div., 1981-87; Lamont prof. div., master Dudley Ho. Harvard Coll., 1988—. Author: The Dawn of Apocalyptic, 1976, The Dawn of Apocalyptic, 2d edit., 1979, Dynamic Transcendence, 1978, The Diversity of Scripture, 1982, Visionaries and Their Apocalypses, 1983, The People Called, 1986, Old Testament Apocalyptic, 1987; mem. editorial bd. Hermeneia Commentary Series, 1971—. Fulbright fellow, 1961-62; Woodrow Wilson fellow, 1965-66; Kent fellow, 1966-70; Am. Council Learned Socs. fellow, 1972-74; Alexander von Humboldt fellow, 1981-82. Mem. Am Schs. Oriental Research, Soc. Bibl. Lit. Home: 27 Cushing Ave Belmont MA 02178 Office: Harvard U Divinity Sch Cambridge MA 02138 also: Dudley House Harvard Yd Cambridge MA

HANUS, JEROME, bishop; b. May 25, 1940. Attended, Conception Sem., Mo., St. Anselm U., Rome, Italy, Princeton Theol. Sem. Ordained priest

Roman Cath. Ch., 1966. Abbot Conception Abbey, 1977-87; pres. Swiss Am. Benedictine Congregation, 1984-87; bishop St. Cloud (Minn.) Ch., 1987—. Office: Box 1248 Saint Cloud MN 56302

HARAPIAK, JOHN, religious organization administrator. Pres. Bapt. Gen. Conf. Can., Calgary, Alta. Office: Bapt Gen Conf Can, 816 Canford Crescent SW, Calgary, AB Canada T2W 1L2*

HARBAUGH, GARY L., pastoral care and counseling educator, psychologist; b. Mt. Pleasant, Pa., May 20, 1936; s. Maurice Russell and Margaret Lenore (Carns) H.; m. Marlene Ellen Myton, June 1, 1957; children: Cary Christian, Heidi Kristin, Joel Jonathan. BS in Edn., Edinboro U. Pa., 1958; MDiv, Wittenberg U., 1964, MST, 1967; MA in Religion and Personality, U. Chgo., 1969, PhD in Religion and Personality, 1973; postdoctoral study, Sch. Profl. Psychology, Dayton, Ohio, 1983. Ordained to ministry Evang. Luth. Ch. Am.; lic. psychologist, Ohio, Fla. Pastor Evang. Luth. Ch. Am., Brockton, Mass., 1963-64, Heath, Ohio, 1964-67, Berwyn, Ill., 1967-70, Ashtabula, Ohio, 1970-72; prof. pastoral care and psychology Trinity Luth. Sem., Columbus, Ohio, 1976—; pvt. practice psychology, 1976—; founder Kairos Care and Counseling, Columbus, 1988—; mental health profl. Brevard County Mental Health Ctr., Rockledge, Fla., 1972-76; psychol. cons. div. for ministry Evang. Luth. Ch. Am., Chgo., 1988—; with spl. call program Fla. Synod, Tampa, 1990—. Author: Pastor as Person, 1984 (Book of Yr. award Acad. Parish Clergy 1985), The Faith-hardy Christian, 1986, God's Gifted People, 1988, expanded edit., 1990; co-author: Beyond the Boundary, 1986, Recovery from Loss, 1990. Mem. Am. Psychol. Assn., Fla. Psychol. Assn., Ohio Psychol. Assn., Am. Soc. for Clin. Hypnosis, Am. Assn. Sex Educators, Counselors and Therapists, Am. Bd. Sexology (diplomate). Office: Trinity Luth Sem 2199 E Main St Columbus OH 43209-2334

HARBER, JERRY LANCE, marriage and family therapist; b. Memphis, Nov. 6, 1940; s. Roy Jesse and Eva Elise (Wiley) H.; m. Carol Hinton, Oct. 20, 1984; children: Michael, Christopher, Lynn. BS, Memphis State U., 1965; MDiv, Vanderbilt U., 1969, DMinistry, 1975. Pres. Harber and Assocs., Memphis, 1979—; mem. regulatory bd. profl. counselors and marriage and family therapists Tenn. Bur. Health and Environ., Health Related Bds., 1990—. Mem. Am. Assn. Marriage and Family Therapy, Tenn. Assn. Marital and Family Therapy (pres. 1976-80, sec.-treas. 1989—), Univ. Club. Methodist. Avocations: golf, reading, squash. Office: Harber and Assocs Ste 150 3355 Poplar St Memphis TN 38111 *Professional helpers will do well to remember that God has not died and left you in total change.*

HARBIN, MICHAEL ALLEN, religion educator, writer; b. Vincennes, Ind., May 24, 1947; s. Hugh Allen and Norma June (Palmer) H.; m. Esther Marie Rinas, May 31, 1971; children: Athena Colleen, Heidi Elizabeth, Douglas Allen. BS, U.S. Naval Acad., 1969; ThM, Dallas Theol. Sem., 1980, ThD, 1988; postgrad., Calif. State U., Carson, 1988—. Instr. Dallas Bible Coll., 1984-86; freelance writer Garland, Tex., 1986—; fleet plans officer USN, Yokosuka, Japan, 1990—; mem. elder bd. South Garland Bible Ch., Garland, Tex., 1981—, chmn. elder bd., 1982-86. Contbr. articles to profl. jours. Del. 16th Senatorial Dist. Rep. Conv., Dallas, 1990; alt. del. State Rep. Conv., Ft. Worth, 1990. Mem. Soc. Bibl. Lit., Bibl. Archaeol. Soc., Bible Sci. Assn. (cons. speaker), Evang. Theol. Soc., Am. Legion. Home: 4806 Frontier Rd Garland TX 75043 *I owe whatever success I have achieved to the fact that I have always tried to take God and his Word seriously and apply the implications to my life.*

HARDAWAY, GREGORY SCOTT, pastor; b. Chgo., May 10, 1954; s. Albert Sr. and Priscilla (Willins) H.; m. Louvenia Ann Murry, Aug. 14, 1976; children: Gregory Sean, Gabriel Scott, Kristian Camille. Student, Bishop Coll., Dallas, 1972-76. Pastor Shiloh Bapt. Ch., Chester, Pa., 1977-83; pasor Normal Park Bapt. Ch., Chgo., 1984—; sec. Bapt. Mins. Conf. of Chgo., 1985-90, Bapt. Pastor's Conf. Chgo., 1984-87; trustee Chgo. Bapt. Inst., 1985—. Home: 131 Nanti Dr Park Forest IL 60146 Office: Normal Park Baptist Church 6948 S Stewart Chicago IL 60621

HARDEN, ROBERT NEAL, religion educator, minister; b. Lake City, Fla., Jan. 13, 1952; s. Robert Lee and Pauline (Wheeler) H.; m. Elizabeth Kane, Dec. 16, 1972; children: Bobby, Cheré, Patrick. BA, Southeastern Coll., Lakeland, Fla., 1975; MDiv, Assemblies of God Theol. Sem., Springfield, Mo., 1981; D Ministry, Concordia Theol. Sem., Ft. Wayne, Ind., 1988. Ordained to ministry Assemblies of God, 1977. Pastor 1st Assembly of God Ch., Starke, Fla., 1976-78; dir. Christian edn. Westside Assembly of God Ch., Marion, Ind., 1981-84; prof. Bible Trinity Bible Coll., Ellendale, N.D., 1984-85; prof. Jimmy Swaggart Bible Coll., Baton Rouge, 1987-88; assoc. pastor 1st Assembly of God Ch., Topeka, 1985-87; prof. religion Southwestern Coll., Waxahachie, Tex., 1989—; bd. dirs. Metroplex Children's Pastors Assn., Arlington, Tex., 1991—. Mem. Nat. Right To Life, 1991—. Recipient President's award Paul W. Davis Inc., 1977, coaching award Trinity Bible Coll., 1984, Order of the Towel Svc. award So. Assemblies of God Chs., 1991. Mem. Nat. Assn. Profs. Christian Edn., Nat. Assn. Christian Educators, Chi Epsilon Chi. Office: Southwestern Coll 1200 Sycamore St Waxahachie TX 75165

HARDENBROOK, JIM O, minister; b. Nyssa, Oreg., July 10, 1951; s. Donald Orin and Dorothy June (Bartholoma) H.; m. Pamela Sue Goodell, Mar. 27, 1972; children: Jamie Elisa, Joseph Garrett, Jay Christian. BA in Bible, Puget Sound Ch. Coll., 1973. Ordained to ministry Christian Chs. and Chs. of Christ, 1973. Min. Broadway Christian Ch., Bellingham, Wash., 1973-77, Community Christian Ch., McMinnville, Oreg., 1977-79, Anacortes (Wash.) Ch. of Christ, 1979-86, Caldwell (Idaho) Christian Ch., 1986—; pres. Oreg. Christian Evangelistic Fellowship, Springfield, 1977-79; mem. planning com. N.Am. Christian Conv., Cin., 1986-89; bd. dirs., assoc. Emmanuel Sch. Religion, Johnson City, Tenn., 1990—; chaplain West Valley Med. Ctr., Caldwell, 1987, 90—. Mem. Community Accountability Bd., Skagit County, Wash., 1980-84, Anacortes Sch. Bd., 1985-86. Mem. Kiwanis (v.p., bd. dirs. 1988). Office: 1st Christian Ch 10th and Everett Caldwell ID 83605

HARDENBROOK, WELDON MARSHALL, archpriest; b. Everette, Wash., Dec. 14, 1939; s. Marshall Victor and Marjorie (Harris) H.; m. Barbara Earlene Ramsey,June 30, 1962; children: Sheri, Todd. BA, Calif. Coll. Arts and Crafts, 1962; Cert., Inst. Bibl. Studies, San Bernardino, Calif., 1967-70. Ordained to ministry Orthodox Ch. in Am. Art dir. Campus Crusade for Christ, San Bernardino, 1967-70; min. Christian World Liberation Front, Berkeley, Calif., 1970-73; archpriest Sts. Peter and Paul Orthodox Ch., Ben Lomond, Calif., 1974—; bd. dirs. St. Athanatios Acad. Orthodox Theology, Isla Vista, Calif., Conciliar Press, Mount Hermon, Calif.; chmn. AEOM Coordinating Coun., Isla Vista, 1990—. Author: Missing from Action, 1987, Where's Daddy, 1991; editor Again mag., 1975—; contbr. articles to jours. in field. Mem. sch. bd. Sts. Peter and Paul Elem. Acad, Ben Lomond, 1990—, Nat. Right to Life Com., Washington, 1990. With U.S. Army, 1959-61. Mem. Santa Cruz (Calif.) Hist. Soc. Republican. Home: PO Box 345 Boulder Creek CA 95006 Office: Sts Peter and Paul Orthodox Ch Central and Main Ben Lomond CA 95005

HARDER, GIL J., minister; b. Salem, Oreg., June 4, 1951; s. Clarence and Laverda May (Remple) H.; m. Carol Elizabeth Chaney, June 20, 1972; children: Andrew, Daniel, Angela, Sarah. BTh, Multnomah Sch. Bible, Portland, Oreg., 1981. Ordained to ministry Greater Portland Bible Ch., 1981. Pastor Greater Portland Bible Ch., 1980—; dir. singles celebration, dir. internat. ministries; pres. Social Action Leadership Team, Portland. Author: Shepherd's Staff, 1984, Adult Ministry Guide, 1986, Mission to Mexico, 1989, Mission Intern Training, 1990. Recipient achievement award Multnomah Sch. of Bible, 1980. Office: Greater Portland Bible Ch 2374 SW Vermont St Portland OR 97219 *My faith in God means personal responsibility: my response—to God's ability. Therefore, I can do all things through Christ who empowers me.*

HARDER, JEAN, pastor; b. Douglas, Ariz., June 28, 1931; d. James Norris Barrett and Wilamet (Housel) Duncan; divorced; children: David Joseph, Pamela Jean. A in Practical Theology, Christ for the Nations, 1980. Ordained to ministry of the Gospel, 1980. Counselor Gospel Echoes Ch., Phoenix, 1978-79; asst. pastor Christ Eternity Ch., Dallas, 1980; counselor, founder, pres. Deborah House Ministries, Phoenix, 1982—; pastor, founder El Shaddai Tabernacle, Phoenix, 1989—. Author: Breaking Free, 1982, (booklets) Bound by Unforgiveness, 1983, Passivity, The Tenacious Thief, 1985. Mem. Christ Eternity Fellowship, Network of Prophetic Ministries. Office: El Shaddai Tabernacle PO Box 37756 Phoenix AZ 85069-7756 *The greatest experiences in life are the opportunity to have an intimate relationship with God, to know His character and become more like Him. The greatest wisdom is found in communion with Father God through His Son Jesus.*

HARDIN, LINDA GAY, clergywoman; b. Kankakee, Ill., Dec. 8, 1946; d. Harry Arthur and Frances Jean (Miller) H. BS in Elem. Edn., Trevecca Nazarene Coll., 1968; MS in Edn., Ind. U., 1972. Gen. coord. single adult ministries and women's ministries Internat. Ch. of Nazarene, Kansas City, Mo., 1988—; single adult ministries dir. Indpls. Dist. Ch. of Nazarene, 1982-88; dir. SoloCon Internat. Ch. of Nazarene, Kansas City, 1985-88; del. Gen. Christian Life and Sunday Sch. Conv. Ch. of the Nazarene, Anaheim, Calif., 1985. Editor: Women's Ministries Program Notebook, 1989, Faces of Single Adult Ministries, 1990. Mem. NEA, Nat. Assn. Single Adult Leaders, Women's Commn. Nat. Assn. Evangelicals (sec. 1991). Office: Ch of the Nazarene 6401 The Paseo Kansas City MO 64131

HARDIN, RODNEY EDWARD, minister; b. Lexington, Tenn., Jan. 16, 1969; s. Edward Leory and Verna Charlene (Hattachett) H.; m. Sheila Ann Smith, Dec. 2, 1990. Student, Union U., Jackson, Tenn., 1990—. Ordained to ministry So. Bapt. Ch., 1986. Min. Bapt. Ch., Lexington, 1986-88, Parsons, Tenn., 1989—; youth leader Beech River Bapt. Assn., Lexington, 1986-87; mission work Union Spl. Project Other Than Summer, Houston, (Spring) 12990, Winnipeg, Can., (Spring) 1991); chaplain Future Farmers of Am., Lexington, 1986, state farmers, 1987. Mem. North Am. Soc. Alderian Psychology. Home and Office: 78 State Rte 188 Trenton TN 38382

HARDING, GLORIA MAE, lay worker, special education educator; b. Jeanerette, La., Dec. 20, 1940; d. Nathan and Lucinda (James) Gabriel; m. William Harding, Dec. 23, 1962. BS, Grambling Coll., 1962; MA, So. U., 1966. Cert. spl. edn., elem. tchr., La. Tchr. Iberia Parish Sch. Bd., Jeanerette, 1963—; tchr. Sunday Sch. First Ch. of God in Christ, Jeanerette, 1977, dir. children's div., 1978—, dir. children's div., pres. dist. missions Franklin dist.; trustee, sec. 1st jurisdiction dept. missions First Ch. of God in Christ, Jeanerette, 1986—. Past sec. King Joseph Park Bd., Jeanerette, 1973-86; chairperson Parental Involvement Group, Jeanerette Elem. Sch., 1990-91. Mem. NEA, La. Assn. Edn., Iberia Assn. Edn. Democrat. Home: 407 Martin Luther King Dr Jeanerette LA 70544 *Life offers daily opportunities to bring about change in individuals, and we can best affect change if we despair of no man. We must see man as being a victim of sin that can become a trophy of grace through Jesus Christ.*

HARDISON, PERRY, minister; b. Kinston, N.C., Nov. 5, 1956; s. Marcellus J. and Estelle (Whaley) H.; m. Robin Stapleford, July 22, 1979. AA, Lenoir Community Coll., Kinston, N.C., 1977; MA, East Carolina U., 1979; MDiv, Southeastern Bapt. Theol. Sem., 1983. Ordained to ministry Bapt. Ch., 1983. Pastor Dover (N.C.) Missionary Bapt. Ch., 1979-84, Davis Grove Bapt. Ch., Snow Hill, N.C., 1984-85; assoc. pastor Mt. Olive Bapt. Ch., Pittsboro, N.C., 1988-89, pastor, 1989—; adj. instr. religion Campbell U., Buies Creek, N.C., 1984-89, bd. mins., 1980-92; v.p. Sandy Creek Pastors Conf., Sanford, N.C., 1990-91. Home: Rt 2 Box 361 Pittsboro NC 27312 Office: Mt Olive Bapt Ch Rt 2 Box 361 Pittsboro NC 27312

HARDON, JOHN ANTHONY, priest, research educator; b. Midland, Pa., June 18, 1914; s. John and Anna (Jevin) H. A.B., John Carroll U., 1936; M.A., Loyola U., Chgo., 1941; S.T.D., Gregorian U., Rome, 1951. Joined S.J., Roman Cath. Ch., 1936, ordained priest, 1947. Assoc. prof. fundamental theology West Baden (Ind.) Coll., 1951-62; assoc. prof. religion Western Mich. U., 1962-67; prof. fundamental theology Bellarmine Sch. Theology, North Aurora, Ill. and Chgo., 1968-73; rsch. prof. Jesuit Sch. Theology, North Aurora, 1973—; prof. advanced studies in Cath. doctrine St. John's U., Jamaica, N.Y., 1974-88; vis. prof. comparative religion St. Paul U., Ottawa, Can., 1968-74; prof. Notre Dame Inst. (a Pontifical Catechetical Inst.), Va., 1981-90; v.p. Inst. on Religious Life; dir. retreats priests and religious; chmn. bd. Cath. Voice of Am., Inc. Author: The Protestant Churches of America, 2d edit, 1968, rev. edit., 1981, Christianity in Conflict, 1959, All My Liberty, 1959, rev. edit., 1981, For Jesuits, 1963, Religions of the World, 2d edit, 1968, rev. edit., 1981, The Hungry Generation, 1967, The Spirit and Origins of American Protestantism, 1968, Religions of the Orient-A Christian View, 1970, American Judaism, 1971, Christianity in the Twentieth Century, 2d edit, 1972, rev. edit., 1978, The Catholic Catechism, 1975, Holiness in the Church, 1976, Religious Life Today, 1977, Modern Catholic Dictionary, 1980, Salvation and Sanctification, 1978, Theology of Prayer, 1979, The Question and Answer Catholic Catechism, 1981, Spiritual Life in the Modern World, 1982, Pocket Catholic Dictionary, 1985; The Treasury of Catholic Wisdom, 1987, The Catholic Lifetime Reading Plan, 1989, Pocket Catholic Catechism, 1989, The Catholic Catechist's Manual, 1989, The Catholic Answer Book, 1989, Masters of the Spiritual Life, 1990, Great Marian Writers, 1990, The Catholic Family in the Modern World, 1991; editor: Gospel Witness, 1971; contbg. editor Challenge mag., London, Can., 1987—; cons. World Book Ency. Recipient Papal medal, 1951, award outstanding work in field history Cath. Press Assn., 1973, medal Slovak World Congress, 1978, St. Maximilian Kolbe award in Mariology, 1990. Mem. Cath. Truth Soc., Soc. for Religious Vocations, Instituto Slovaco, Internat. Assn. Mission Studies, Fellowship Cath. Scholars (Cardinal Wright award 1984). Address: U Detroit Mercy Lansing-Reilly Hall Detroit MI 48221 *Conviction is the basis of courage; certitude is the foundation of peace. The secret of achievement is to have the peaceful courage of possessing the truth and acting on this conviction in everything we do.*

HARDT, JILL ANN, lay worker; b. Detroit, Nov. 26, 1959; d. Richard John and Carol Ann (Maddick) H. BA, Asbury Coll., 1988; postgrad., Asbury Sem., 1988—. Youth dir. Second Presbyn. Ch., Lexington, Ky., 1989—; assoc. pastor McDermott United Meth. Ch., McDermott, Ohio, 1989; vol. Youth for Christ, Lexington, 1989—; deacon United Meth. Ch., Detroit Conf., 1991. Vol. AIDS Vols. of Lexington, 1990—. Office: Second Presbyn Ch 460 E Main Lexington KY 40507

HARDT, JOHN WESLEY, bishop; b. San Antonio, July 14, 1921; s. Wesley W. and Ida Hardt; m. Martha Carson, Sept. 13, 1943; children—Betty Hardt Lesko, William C., John S., Joe. Student Lon Morris Coll., 1940; B.A., So. Meth. U., 1942; B.D., Perkins Sch. Theology, 1946; postgrad. Vanderbilt U., Nashville and Union Theol. Sem.; D.D. (hon.), Southwestern U., 1965; hon. degree Oklahoma City U., 1980. Pastor, Dekalb Cir., 1941, Alba Cir., 1942, Malakoff, 1943-44, Pleasant Retreat, Tyler, Tex., 1944-50, 1st United Meth. Ch., Atlanta, 1950-55, 1st United Meth. Ch., Marshall, Tex., 1955-59, 1st United Meth. Ch., Beaumont, Tex., 1959-77; dist. supt. Houston E. Dist., 1977-80; bishop Okla. United Meth. Ann. Conf., Okla. Indian Missionary Conf., 1980—. Active C. of C., Rotary Club. Author: Not the Ashes, but the Fire, 1976.

HARDWICK, JAMES RENFRO, minister; b. Quitman, Ga., Oct. 5, 1940; s. Harry Rupert and Dora (Renfroe) H.; m. Leta Karen Cunningham, Aug. 18, 1963; children: James Renfroe II, Scott William, Stephen Cary, David Ashley. AA, Norman Bapt. Jr. Coll., Norman Park, Ga., 1960; BA, Valdosta (Ga.) State Coll., 1962; MDiv, Southwestern Bapt. Theol. Sem., Ft. Worth, Tex., 1966, MEd, 1969. Ordained to ministry Foursquare Gospel Internat. Pastor First Bapt. Ch., Franklin, Tex., 1968-71, Immanuel Bapt. Ch., Valdosta, Ga., 1971-74, Emanuel Fellowship, Swainsboro, Ga., 1979-81; sr. pastor River of Life Foursquare Gospel Ch., Richmond, Va., 1981—; steering com. Pastors Intercessory Group, Richmond, 1990—, Bill Gothard Basic Youth Seminar, Richmond, 1985—; mem. S.E. Dist. Pastors Foursquare Gospel Internat. Del. Rep. Nat. Com., Richmond, 1988-90. Ky. Col., 1967. Home: 10907 Newlands Ct Richmond VA 23233 Office: River of Life Foursquare 1120 Westbriar Dr Richmond VA 23233

HARDY, CHARLES EXTER, III, minister; b. Atlanta, Dec. 22, 1960; s. Charles Exter Jr. and Loretta (Westmoreland) H.; m. Claudia Gail Barton, Jan. 11, 1986; children: Lauren Nicole, Charles Exter IV. BS in Agr., U. Tenn., 1982; MDiv, Golden Gate Sem., 1987. Youth minister Stock Creek Bapt. Ch., Knoxville, Tenn., 1981-82, Cen. Bapt. Ch., Waycross, Ga., 1982-83, Rollingwood Bapt. Ch., San Pablo, Calif., 1983-84; minister to deaf El Camino Bapt. Ch., Sacramento, 1984; youth min. Narwee (N.S.W. Australia) Bapt. Ch., 1985; asst. pastor First Bapt. Ch., El Sobrante, Calif., 1986-87; pastor First Bapt. Ch., Winters, Calif., 1987-90, First So. Bapt. Ch., Davis, Calif., 1991—. Author: (play) Cheap Show, 1990. Mem. Winters (Calif.) Ministerial Assn. (pres. 1989-90). Avocations: photography, piano, gardening. Home: 2650 Belmont Dr Davis CA 95616

HARDY, DALE DEANE, minister; b. Quincy, Mass., Dec. 25, 1947; s. Deane Reynolds and Elizabeth Joyce (Hazelton) H.; m. Diane Kay Brenneman, June 3, 1972; children: Garrick, Karri. BS in Elem. Edn., Eastern Nazarene Coll., 1972; M of Religious Edn., Nazarene Theol. Seminary, Kansas City, Mo., 1975. Ordained to ministry Nazarene Ch., 1979. Minister youth and edn. Nazarene Ch., Oxford, Pa., 1978-80; minister Nazarene Ch., Yarmouth, Maine, 1980-81; minister youth and children Nazarene Ch., New Philadelphia, Ohio, 1981-83; children's minister Nazarene Ch., Sacramento, 1983-87; minister Christian edn./sch. Nazarene Ch., Charlotte, N.C., 1987-90; minister Christian edn. Nazarene Ch., Valparaiso, Ind., 1990—; past dir. quizzing Nazarene Dist., Pa., Maine and Calif., past dir. activities, Pa., Maine, N.C. and Calif., dir. seminars, Pa. Calif., N.C., children's dir., Ind. Author: (curriculum) Lives of the Disciples, 1985. Mem. Kiwanis (mem. chmn. 1990-91). Office: 1st Ch of the Nazarene 2702 E Glendale Blvd Valparaiso IN 46383 *By working hard, reading the best of what is available, trusting God in all things, being what He intended us to be and doing it, anyone can be great in His eyes, and that is what matters.*

HARDY, DANIEL WAYNE, theological center director, theologian, educator; b. N.Y.C., Nov. 9, 1930; s. John Alexander Hardy and Barbara Wyndham Harrison; m. Kate Perrin Enyart, 1958; 4 children. BA, Haverford Coll., 1952; STB, Gen. Theol. Sem., 1955; postgrad., Oxford U., 1961-65; MST, Gen. Theol. Sem., 1963. Ordained to ministry Episcopal Ch. as deacon, 1955, as priest, 1956. Asst. min. Christ Ch., Greenwich, Conn., 1955-59; vicar St. Barnabas Ch., Greenwich, 1956-59; fellow, tutor Gen. Theol. Sem., 1959-61; lectr. in modern theol. thought U. Birmingham, Eng., 1965-76, sr. lectr., 1976-86; Van Mildert prof. div. U. Durham, Eng., 1986-90; residentiary canon Durham Cathedral, 1986-90; dir. Ctr. Theol. Inquiry, Princeton, N.J., 1990—; instr. Rosemary Hall, Greenwich, 1957-59; moderator gen. ministerial exam, Ch. of Eng., 1983-90. Author: Jubilate: Theology in Praise, 1984, Praising and Knowing God, 1985, Education for the Church's Ministry, 1986, On Being The Church, 1990, The Weight of Glory, 1991; also articles. Mem. Soc. for Study of Theology (pres.). Office: Ctr Theol Inquiry 50 Stockton St Princeton NJ 08540

HARDY, LOWELL RICHARD, church executive; b. Ann Arbor, Mich., May 6, 1953; s. Kenneth Ralph and Mary Hildegard (Thunell) H.; m. Martha Ann Ridge, Dec. 27, 1974; children: Scott Richard, Heather Marie, Robert Lowell, Alyson Suzanne, Michelle Ruth, Todd Allan. BA in Communications, Brigham Young U., 1976. Sr. profl. in human resources. Educator Latter Day Sts. Ch. Ednl. System, Salt Lake City, 1976-78; benefits mgr. Desert Mutual Benefit Assn., Salt Lake City, 1978-82; pers. dir. Latter Day Sts. Ch. Pers., Salt Lake City, 1982-88; adminstr. Latter Day Sts. First Presidency Office, Salt Lake City, 1988—; master trainer Zenger-Miller Corp., San Bruno, Calif., 1982-88; trainer Stuart Atkins Cons. Group, Beverly Hills, Calif., 1987-88. Dist. exec. Boy Scouts of Am., West Jordan, Utah, 1989—; exec. United Way-Latter Day Saints Ch., Salt Lake City, 1986—. Named Outstanding Young Man of Am., Montgomery, Ala., 1983, 87. Republican. Office: LDS Ch First Pres Office 47 E South Temple St Salt Lake City UT 84150

HARE, PETER HEWITT, philosophy educator; b. N.Y.C., Mar. 12, 1935; s. Michael Meredith and Jane Perry (Jopling) H.; m. Daphne Joan Kean, May 30, 1959; children: Clare Kean, Gwendolyn Meigs. BA, Yale U., 1957; MA, Columbia U., 1962, PhD, 1965. Lectr. philosophy SUNY-Buffalo, 1962-65, asst. prof., 1965-67, asst. chmn. dept., 1965-68, assoc. prof., 1967-71, prof., 1971—, chmn. dept. 1971-75, 85—, assoc. dean div. undergrad. edn., 1980-82. Author: A Woman's Quest for Science, 1985, (with others) Evil and the Concept of God, 1968, (with others) Causing, Perceiving and Believing, 1975; editor: Doing Philosophy Historically, 1988, (with others) History, Religion and Spiritual Democracy, 1980, Naturalism and Rationality, 1986, series Frontiers of Philosophy, Prometheus Books, 1986—; mem. editorial bds. Am. Philos. Quar., 1978-87, Philosophy Rsch. Archives, 1975—, Jour. Speculative Philosophy, 1987—. NEH fellow 1968. Mem. Peirce Soc. (editor Transactions 1974—, pres. 1975-76), N.Y. State Philos. Assn. (pres. 1975-77), Soc. Advancement Am. Philosophy (exec. com. 1977-80, pres. 1988-90), Am. Philos. Assn. (nominating com Ea. div. 1990-92), Elizabethan Club (New Haven). Avocation: sailing. Home: 219 Depew Ave Buffalo NY 14214 Office: SUNY Dept Philosophy Baldy Hall Buffalo NY 14260

HARE, ROBERT LEE, JR., evangelist; b. McKinney, Tex., Jan. 12, 1920; B.A., Harding U., Searcy, Ark., 1950, M.A., 1956; m. Ruth Bradley, June 4, 1949; children—Reggy Lynn Hare Hiller, Mary Lee, Linda Jean Glenn. Served Chs. of Christ in Ark., 1946-50; missionary, Munich, W. Ger., 1950-55; 1st missionary to Salzburg (Austria), 1952-55, Vienna, 1956-73, Wiener Neustadt, Austria, 1974-81, Yugoslavia, 1958—, Czechoslovakia, 1960—, Hungary, 1960—, Fed. Republic Germany, 1961—, Poland, 1962—, Bulgaria, 1964—, Romania, 1964—, USSR, 1965—; mem. Com. for Furtherance and Preservation Religious Freedom in Austria, 1973—; founding mem. European Christian Coll., Vienna, 1978, now trustee. Home: 307 S Harding St Breckenridge TX 76024 *I believe that every person should have the right and privilege to hear the gospel of Jesus Christ. This is why I have now spent some 45 years in spreading it, not only in Europe but in many other continents and parts of the world.*

HARGIS, BILLY JAMES, minister; b. Texarkana, Tex., Aug. 3, 1925; s. Jimmie Earsel and Laura Lucille (Fowler) H.; m. Betty Jane Secrest, Dec. 21, 1951; children—Bonnie Jane, Billy James II, Becky Jean, Brenda Jo. Student, Ozark Bible Coll., 1943-45; B.A., Pikes Peak Bible Sem., 1957; Th.B., Burton Coll., 1958; LL.D., Bob Jones U., 1961. Ordained to ministry Christian Ch., 1943; pastor Christian chs. Sallisaw, Okla., 1944-46, Granby, Mo., 1946-47, Sapulpa, Okla., 1947-50; pastor Ch. of Christian Crusade, Tulsa, 1966-86; founder, pres. Christian Echoes Nat. Ministry, Inc., Tulsa, 1948-86, Am. Christian Coll., Tulsa, 1970-74; Pub. Christian Crusade Newspaper, 1948—; speaker Christian Crusade network radio broadcasts, 1949—, syndicated TV program, 1970—; founder, chmn. bd. David Livingston Missionary Found., 1970-80, Soc., 1974-80; founder, pres. Billy James Hargis Evang. Assn., 1975—, Ch. of Christian Crusade, 1966—, Christian Ams. For Life, 1971—, Good Samaritan Children's Found., Inc., 1975—; Dir. Rose of Sharon Farm-Log Sch.-Chapel, Neosho, Mo., 1982—. Author: Communist America - Must It Be, 1960, Communism The Total Lie, 1961, Facts About Communism and Churches, 1962, The Real Extremists - The Far Left, 1964, Distortion By Design, 1965, Why I Fight For A Christian America, 1974, Thou Shalt Not Kill—My Babies, 1977, The Depth Principle, 1977, The Disaster File, 1978, Riches and Prosperity Through Christ, 1978, The National News Media, 1980, The Cross and the Sickle-Super Church, 1982, Abortion on Trial, 1982; The Federal Reserve Scandal, 1985; (autobiography) My Great Mistake, 1986, Communist America, Must It Be, vol. 2, 1986, Forewarned, 1987, Day of Deception, 1991. Home: Rose of Sharon Farm Neosho MO 64850 Office: PO Box 977 Tulsa OK 74102 *If I have achieved any success in this life, it is because I take God at His Word and act upon it, and I love the free enterprise, democratic concept of the United States with all my heart and am willing to be branded an extremist in my defense of these ideals. It is because of my love of New Testament Christianity and the United States that I have tried to add my voice in defense of "God and Country."*

HARGIS, EARL DAVID, minister; b. Phoenix, Dec. 8, 1942; s. Thomas Charles and Edith Frances (Adnerson) H.; m. Susan Kay Douglas, Dec. 8, 1967; children: Craig, Christopher, Stephen. BS, Western Bapt. Coll., 1966; postgrad., Northwestern Nazarene Coll., 1966-67, U. Ariz., 1972, U. Mont., 1985. Lic. to ministry Bapt. Ch., 1968. Asst. pastor First Bapt. Ch., Caldwell, Idaho, 1966-67; pastor Eastview Bapt. Ch., Tucson, 1969-71, First Bapt. Ch., Moses Lake, Wash., 1973-81, Florence (Mont.) Bible Ch., 1981-84, Community Bapt. Ch., Stevensville, Mont., 1985—; field cons. Accelerated Christian Edn., Lewisville, Tex., 1978-80; mem. Mont. Assn. Ch. Schs., Great Falls, 1981-84. Legis. lobbyist, Helena, Mont., 1983, 89; pro-life activist, Mont., 1981-91; parent vol. Youth Baseball, Florence, Mont., 1989, Cub Scouts, Boy Scouts Am., Stevensville, 1988-90. Home: PO Box 331 Florence MT 59833 Office: Community Bapt Ch 409 Buck St Stevensville MT 59870 *Since we can't surpass the value of God's Word, I chose to quote two Scriptures: Acts 16:31, "...Believe in the Lord Jesus, and you shall be saved, you and your household." Eccles. 12:13, "...the conclusion...Fear God and keep his commandments: for this is the whole duty of man."*

HARGROVE, ELSON PAYNE, clergyman, administrator; b. Broken Arrow, Okla., Feb. 24, 1935; s. Elson Payne and Elizabeth C. (McDowell) H.; m. Joyce Louise Agan, Aug. 30, 1958; children: Steven Neill, Belinda Gayle. BA, Oklahoma City U., 1958; BD, So. Meth. U., 1961; postgrad., Phillips U., 1971, Okla. U., 1984. Ordained to ministry, United Meth. Ch. Pastor United Meth. Ch., Valliant, Okla., 1959-61, Coalgate, Okla., 1962-63, Carnegie, Okla., 1963-66; pastor Harrison meml. United Meth. Ch., Tulsa, 1966-68; pastor United Meth. Ch., Pawnee, 1968-73, Wewoka, 1973-76, Frederick, 1976-80, Tahlequah, Okla., 1980-84; adminstr. Okla. Meth. Manor, Tulsa, 1984—. Office: Okla Meth Manor 4134 E 31st St Tulsa OK 74135

HARGROVE, JERRY EDWARD, JR., minister; b. Camden, Ark., Dec. 11, 1949; s. Jerry Edward and Fannie Lee (Blake) H.; B.A., U. Ark., 1972; postgrad. Cath. U. Am., 1972-76; M.S., Loyola Coll., 1982. Cert. nat. counselor; cert. clin. mental health conselor. Tchr., elem. secondary schs. and colls., 1955-76; ordained priest Roman Catholic Ch., 1976; assoc. pastor Nativity Ch., 1976-79; asst. pastor St. Peters Ch., Washington, 1979—; assoc. pastor Holy Name Ch., Washington, 1983-86, pastor, 1986—; chaplain Seaton High Sch., 1984; tchr./counselor St. Cecilia High Sch., Washington, 1974-78; chaplain D.C. N.G., 1978. Mem. NAACP (life), Am. Assn. for Counseling and Devel., Mil. Chaplains Assn. (pres.), Phi Mu Alpha, Alpha Phi Alpha (life). Clubs: K.C., Knights of St. John. Home and Office: 920 11th St NE Washington DC 20002

HARKE, GARY LEE, religious organization administrator; b. Utica, N.Y., Feb. 27, 1948; s. Albert Frankenfield and Lois Adele (Moser) H.; m. Judith Marie Lane, Aug. 22, 1970; children: Michael Christopher, Matthew John, Melissa Rae. BA, St. Olaf Coll., 1970; MDiv, Yale U., 1973. Ordained to ministry Moravian Ch. as deacon, 1973, consecrated presbyter, 1980. Fraternal worker Bd. World Mission, Moravian Ch., Bethlehem, Pa., 1973-79; pastor Moravian Congregation Easton, Pa., 1979-82; dir. ednl. ministries Moravian Ch., No. Province, Bethlehem, 1982—; mem. Gen. Bd., NCCC, N.Y.C., 1990—. Mem. policy bd. Wis. chpt. IMPACT, Madison, 1982—. Office: Moravian Ch No Province Dept Educational Ministries 150 Windsor St # 104 Sun Prairie WI 53590-0386

HARKNESS, BERNIE CARROLL, minister; b. Shreveport, La., July 26, 1945; s. Bernie Couston and Melba Rose (Oney) H.; m. Nancy Ann Gibbs, June 2, 1966; children: Rose Ann, Becky, Carol Jean. AA, Abilene Christian U., 1967; BA, Harding U., Searcy, Ark., 1970; MA, Ala. Christian Grad. Sch. Rel., Montgomery, 1983, MDiv, 1989. Minister Ch. of Christ, Ruleville, Miss., 1970-71, Elkhart, Ind., 1971-73; personal wk. dir. Concord St. Ch. of Christ, Orlando, Fla., 1973-75; minister S. Denver Ch. of Christ and Univ., 1975-79, Corning (Ark.) Ch. of Christ, 1979-83; Bible prof. Crowley's Ridge Coll., Paragould, Ark., 1979-83; minister Zachary (La.) Ch. of Christ, 1983-87; dir. extension campus Ala. Christian Coll., 1983-87; minister Cen. Ch. of Christ, Yuma, Ariz., 1987—; chaplain Yuma Reg. Med. Ctr., 1988—. Vol. probation officer Juvenile Ct. System, Elkhart, 1973-74. Mem. Ariz. Chaplains Assn., Assn. for Clin. Pastoral Edn. Republican. Home: 2734 S Fresno Ave Yuma AZ 85364 Office: Cen Ch of Christ 651 W 28th St Yuma AZ 85364

HARMAN, KENNETH R., counseling administrator; b. Balt., Nov. 10, 1927; s. Clarence L. and Madeline M. (Geaslen) H.; m. Linda Harman, June 5, 1965; children: Kenneth, Wendy, Jory, Jennifer, John. BD, Reformed Episcopal Sem., 1949; BS, Temple U., 1951; MA, John F. Kennedy U., 1987; MDiv, Phila. Theol. Sem., 1990. V.p. Drake Beam Morin, Walnut Creek, Calif.; dist. sales mgr. Pacific Northwest; regional adminstrv. mgr. San Leandro, Calif. Home: 9519 Davona Dr San Ramon CA 94583

HARMAN, ROBERT JOHN, religious organization administrator; b. Elmhurst, Ill., Oct. 10, 1937; s. Clifford Martin and Anna Elizabeth (Johnson) H.; m. Marcia Bornemeier, Aug. 1, 1959; children: Scott, Michael. BA, North Cen. Coll., 1959; BD, Garett Evang. Theol. Sem., 1962; postgrad., Union Theol. Sem., 1973-74, 69-72; MPA, NYU, 1975. Ordained to ministry Evang. United Brethren Ch., 1962; (merged with United Meth. Ch. 1968). Sr. pastor Community United Meth. Ch., Naperville, Ill., 1968-73; planner, nat. div. Gen. Bd. Global Ministries, N.Y.C., 1975-84; dist. supt. No. Ill. Conf. Meth. Chs., Chgo., 1984-85; dir. planning United Meth. Ch. Gen. Bd. of Global Ministries, N.Y.C., 1985-89, dep. gen. sec., world div., 1989—; unit dir. Nat. Coun. of Chs., N.Y.C., 1978-83, 89-91; del. World Coun. of Chs., Geneva, Switzerland, 1991; mem. exec. com. World Meth. Coun., 1991. Mem. editorial bd., pres. Christianity and Crisis Jour., 1982-84; contbr. articles to profl. jours. Recipient numerous fellowships. Office: Gen Bd Global Ministries United Meth Ch 475 Riverside Dr New York NY 10115

HARMAN, RONALD VERN, principal, teacher; b. Milw., July 29, 1932; s. Carl Henry and Mildred Florence (Froemming) H.; m. Evelyn Lois Krentz, June 22, 1957; children: Anthony, Gregory, Vincent, Gretchen. BS in Edn., Concordia U., 1955; MEd, U. Ill., 1962; postgrad., Ariz. State U., 1966-77. Tchr. Trinity Luth. Sch., Springfield, Ill., 1955-58; prin., tchr. Trinity Luth. Sch., Danville, Ill., 1958-61, St. Michael Luth. Sch., Ft. Wayne, Ind., 1961-62; tchr. Emmanuel-St. Michael Luth. Sch., Ft. Wayne, 1962-65; prin., tchr. Christ Luth. Sch., Phoenix, 1965—; mem., chmn. bd. for parish edn., English dist. Luth. Ch.-Mo. Synod, Detroit, 1971-76, bd. dirs., 1976-91, planning coun., St. Louis, 1990—. Mem. ASCD, Luth. Edn. Assn. Repubican. Home: 2414 N 39th Pl Phoenix AZ 85008 Office: Christ Luth Sch 3901 E Indian Sch Rd Phoenix AZ 85018

HARMELINK, HERMAN, III, clergyman, author, educator; b. Sheldon, Pa., Dec. 26, 1933; s. Herman II, and Thyrza (Eringa) H. BA cum laude, Central Coll., 1954; MA, Columbia U., 1955; postgrad. U. London, 1955; M.Div., New Brunswick Theol. Sem., 1958; World Coun. Chs. scholar U. Heidelberg, 1959; S.T.M. magna cum laude, Union Theol. Sem., N.Y.C., 1964, M.Phil., 1978; m. Barbara Mary Conibear, Aug. 11, 1959; children: Herman IV Alan, Lindsay Alexandra. Ordained to ministry Reformed Ch. Am., 1959; min. Community Ch., Glen Rock, N.J., 1959-64, Woodcliff Community Ch., Woodcliff-on-Hudson, N.J., 1964-71, Ref. Ch., Poughkeepsie, N.Y., 1971—; mem. adj. faculty in philosophy SUNY, 1993—, Marist Coll., 1990—; vice chmn. Faith and Order Commn., Nat. Coun. Chs., 1976-79, mem. Commn. on Regional and Local Ecumenism, 1981-84; pres. Synod of N.J., 1969; chmn. interch. rels. Ref. Ch. Am., 1964-71; pres. Dutchess Interfaith Coun., 1977-78, mem. development retirement community com., 1989—; del. gen. coun. World Alliance Ref. Chs., Frankfurt, 1964, Nairobi, 1970; advisor 4th Gen. Assembly World Coun. Chs., Uppsala, Sweden, 1968; U.S. del. 50th Anniversary Faith and Order Commn., Lausanne, Switzerland, 1977. Trustee St. Francis Hosp., 1979—, mem. exec. com. of bd., 1981—, joint conf. com., 1986—, chmn. planning com., 1987—; bd. dirs. Dutchess County Hist. Soc., 1974-78, also life mem.; bd. dirs. Dutchess County Arts Coun., 1976-80, Bardavon 1869 Opera House, 1978-79; mem. allocation and planning divs. United Way of Dutchess County; sec. bd. dirs. Rehab. Programs, Inc., 1977-79; bd. dirs. Collingwood Repertory Theatre, 1978-80; Mid-Hudson Meml. Soc., 1981-84; pres. Poughkeepsie Generating Community, 1974—; bd. dir. Literacy Vol. of Dutchess County, 1985—, pres. 1987-89; bd. dirs. Literacy Vols. Am., N.Y., 1989—, chmn., pers. comm., 1989—, mem. program com., 1990—; Poughkeepsie Rural Cemetery, 1986—, chmn. fin. com., 1989—; pres. Ranfurly Library Svc. of N.Y. Inc., 1982—. Lt. USNR, 1957-61. Fulbright travel grantee to Germany, 1958-59; participant U.S.-S. African Leader Exchange Program, 1971. Mem. N.Am. Acad. Ecumenists, Am. Soc. Ch. History, Presbyn. Hist. Soc., Poughkeepsie C. of C., Dutchess Interfaith Coun., Dutchess County Clergy Club, Poughkeepsie Rotary (pres. 1977-79, sec. 1979—, sec. Dist. 721, 1980-81, gov. 1982-83, chmn. World Community Svc. 1986—, Rotary Internat. Coun. on Legis., Monte Carlo, 1983, Rotary Internat. pres.'s rep. to dist. confs. 1984, 88, Paul Harris fellow), Lumanites (sec.-treas.), 251, Poughkeepsie Social Reading Club (past pres.), Circumnavigators Club (N.Y.C.), The Club, Travelers Century Club (life mem.), Fjord Club. Author: Ecumenism and the Reformed Church, 1968; The Reformed Church in New Jersey, 1969; Another Look at Frelinghuysen and His Awakening, 1969; contbg. author to Piety and Patriotism, 1976, Vision from the Hill, 1984, The Livingston Legacy, 1987. Office: 70 Hooker Ave Poughkeepsie NY 12601 *In the words of John Bunyan, "He who would valiant be 'gainst all disaster, let him in constancy follow the Master. There's no discouragement shall make him once relent his first avowed intent to be a pilgrim."*

HARMER, CATHERINE MARY, psychologist, nun; b. Philadelphia, Sept. 6, 1932; d. John Thomas and Frances Regina (Keogh) H. BA in Philosophy, Chestnut Hill Coll., 1957; MSLS, Cath. U. Am., 1962; MA in Psychology, Temple U., 1970, PhD in Psychology, 1973. Joined Med. Mission Sisters, Roman Cath. Ch., 1950. Libr. Med. Mission Sisters, Phila., 1957-62, instr., 1959-62; libr., instr. Med. Mission Sisters, Lipa City, 1963-65; sector superior Med. Mission Sisters, Phila., 1976-82, renewal dir., 1988—; bd. dirs. Med. Mission Sisters, Phila., Rome, London, 1976-82; libr., instr. Holy Family Hosp., Rawalpind, Pakistan, 1965-68; psychologist Mgmt. Design Inc., Cin., 1972-82; pvt. practice psychology Phila., 1982—; mem. program com., region III, Leadership Conf. Women Religious, Phila. 1976-82; bd. dirs. Nat. Coun. Chs., N.Y.C., 1976-82, Missionary Vehicle Assn., Washington, 1981-82, Fedn. Returned Missionaries Overseas, Detroit, 1990—. Author: Books for Religious Sisters, 1964; contbr. articles to profl. jours. NDEA Title IV fellow Temple U., Phila., 1971-73. Mem. LWV, U.S. Cath. Mission Assn. (founding), Am. Psychol. Assn., Assn. Humanistic Psychology, Network, Assn. Psychol. Type, Common Cause, Delta Epsilon Sigma, Phi Beta Mu. Democrat. Avocations: music, reading, swimming, gardening. Home: 300 W Wellens Ave Philadelphia PA 19120 Office: Med Mission Sisters 8400 Pine Rd Philadelphia PA 19111

HARMON, DANIEL PATRICK, classics educator; b. Chgo., May 3, 1938; s. Bernard Leonard and Dorothy Mildred (Lesser) H. AB, Loyola U., Chgo., 1962; MA, Northwestern U., 1965, PhD, 1968; postdoctoral, Am. Sch. Classical Studies in Athens, 1975. Acting asst. prof. U. Wash., Seattle, 1967-68, asst. prof. classics, 1968-75, assoc. prof., 1975-76, assoc. prof. classics and comparative lit., 1976-84, prof. classics and comparative lit., 1984—, chmn. classics, 1976-91. Contbr. articles and revs. to profl. jours. Mem. Am. Philol. Assn., Archaeol. Inst. Am., Société des Études Latines, County Louth (Ireland) Archaeol. and Hist. Soc., Classical Assn. Pacific Northwest (pres. 1974-75). Avocations: painting, photography, music. Home: 3149 NE 83d St Seattle WA 98115 Office: U Wash Dept Classics DH-10 Seattle WA 98195

HARMON, DAVID MICHAEL, minister, educator; b. Paducah, Ky., Aug. 13, 1947; s. David and Jennie Elizabeth (Bass) H.; m. Donna Jean Canupp, aug. 8, 1981; children, Davin Smith, Derek Smith. BS, Murray State U., 1969, MEd, 1974; MRE, So. Bapt. Theol. Sem., 1979. Math. tch. Paducah Bd. Edn., 1969-78; min. music and youth West End Bapt. Ch., Paducah, 1971-77; min. edn., youth and music Graefenburg Bapt. Ch., Waddy, Ky., 1978-83; min. edn. and music Broadway Bapt. Ch., Lexington, Ky., 1983-88; min. edn. and youth 1st Bapt. Ch., Princeton, Ky., 1988—. Del. Ky. Edn. Assn., 1976-78; treas. Paducah Edn. Assn., 1976-78. Mem. Ky. Bapt. Conv. (Sunday Sch. spl. worker 1981—), Ky. Bapt. Religious Edn. Assn. (sec.-treas. 1983-85, pres. 1989-90). Democrat. Home: 115 Canterbury Ct Princeton KY 42445 Office: 1st Bapt Ch 300 W Main Princeton KY 42445

HARMON, STEPHANIE METHVIN, lay worker; b. Ft. Benning, Ga., Nov. 2, 1951; d. Carroll Arthur and Joyce Maxine (Bedingfield) Methvin; m. Rufus Gaines Harmon, Sept. 28, 1974; children: Rachel Gaines, Caroline M'lee, Bryce Ellison. AA, Martin Jr. Coll., Pulaski, Tenn., 1971; BA in English and French, U. Tenn., Martin, 1973. Music. sec. 1st Bapt. Ch. of Donelson, Nashville, 1983—; asst. pianist Belmot Heights Bapt. Ch., Nashville; editor quarterly newsletter 1st Bapt Ch. Donelson, 1988—; actress numerous theatres, Nashville, 1973—. Home: 207 Cloverdale Ct Nashville TN 37214-3003 Office: 1st Bapt Ch Donelson 2526 Lebanon Rd Nashville TN 37214

HARMS, FORREST, ecumenical agency administrator. Exec. dir. Des Moines Area Religious Coun. Office: Des Moines Area Religious Coun 3816 36th St Des Moines IA 50310*

HARN, DOUGLAS EVANS, minister; b. Milen, Ga., July 4, 1950; s. Jessie James and Gladys (Murry) H.; m. Debra Nobles, June 28, 1970; children: Craig Anthony, Amy Michelle. MS in Ministry, Berean Coll., 1981; BA in Bible, Edn., Southea. Coll., 1984; postgrad., Southea. Sem., 1984-85; MTh, Bethany Theol. Sem., 1986. Youth pastor 1st Assembly of God, Vidalia, Ga., 1974-80; youth asst. Medulla Assembly of God, Lakeland, Fla., 1980-83; missionary Kids Camps, Abaco, The Bahamas, 1983; pastor Ebnezer Assembly of God, Aulander, N.C., 1985, Assembly of God Ch., Grandy, N.C., 1986—; camp dir. Assembly of God, Lakeland, 1984, Siler City, N.C., 1984; bd. dirs. Camp Windsor (N.C.); dir. Christian edn. Coastal (N.C.) Plains Sect.; mem. Currituck Teens for Christ, 1990. Contbr. article to profl. jour. Mem. Commn. on Aging, Currituck, N.C., P.A.S.S., Currituck; mem. campaign Evans for Re-election, 1989; sec. Lower Currituck Fire Dept., 1986-89. Recipient Appreciation award Married Students Fellowship, Lakeland, 1984, Currituck High Sch., 1989, Currituck Bd. Edn., 1990. Mem. Lower Currituck Ministerial Assn. (pres. 1987-90), Ruitian (Grandy chpt.). Office: Assembly of God Ch McHorney Rd Box 795 Grandy NC 27939

HARNAPP, HARLAN LUCINE, minister; b. Columbus, Nebr., July 3, 1932; s. Oscar Henry and Ida Wilhelmina (Behrens) H.; m. Darleen Ann Graning, June 23, 1957; children: Debra, Brian, Heidi. Student, St. Paul's Coll., 1950-51; AA, St. John's Coll., 1952; BA, Theology diploma, Concordia Sem., St. Louis, 1957, MDiv, 1986. Ordained to ministry Luth. Ch.-Mo. Synod, 1957. Min. Luth. Ch, B.C., Can., 1957-59, S.D., 1959-65; min. Our Redeemer Ch., North Platte, Nebr., 1965-80, Beautiful Savior Ch., Broomfield, Colo., 1980—; dist. steward Arapahoe Cir. So. Nebr., 1965-68; pastoral adviser Luth. Layman's League, S.D. Dist., 1960-62, Nebr. Dist., 1967-71, 2d v.p. Nebr., 1971-74, 3d v.p., 1974-75, 2d v.p., 1975-78, 1st v.p., 1978-80, Luth. Ch.-Mo. Synod Synodical Commn. on Appeals, 1983—; mem. 125th Anniversary of Synod Com., Nebr. Dist., 1972; chaplain S.D. Senate, 1964-65. Home: 960 Coral St Broomfield CO 80020 Office: 6995 W 120th Ave Box 8 Broomfield CO 80038

HARNER, VICTOR EMMANUEL, minister; b. Hagerstown, Md., June 3, 1962; s. Victor Roy and Gladys Lucille (Dillow) H.; m. Kimberly Jean Howard, Nov. 21, 1987. BSW, Shepherd Coll., 1984; MDiv, United Theol. Sem., 1987. Student assoc. pastor John Wesley United Meth. Ch., Cin., 1985-87; pastor Old Town (Md.) United Meth. Ch., 1987-90, Messiah United Meth. Ch., Taney Town, Md., 1990—. Bd. dirs. Interfaith Consortium, Cumberland, Md., Alleghany County Bd. of Social Svcs., Cumberland, Foster Care Rev. Bd., Carroll County; team mem. Suicide Prevention Ctr., Dayton, Ohio, 1984-87. Mem. Acad. Parish Clergy, Inc., Ancient Free and Accepted Masons. Home: 25 Middle St Taney Town MD 21787

HARNESS, J. HAROLD, minister; b. Crab Orchard, Ky., Jan. 5, 1941; s. John M. and Margie M. (Denny) H.; m. Virginia Belcher, Nov. 23, 1962; children: Karen S. Harness Woollard, Harold D. Assoc. in Bibl. Studies, Nazarene Bible Coll., Colorado Springs, Colo., 1977; BTh., Internat. Sem., 1985, ThM, 1986, D of Ministry, 1990; M in Sacred Lit., Trinity Sem., Newburgh, Ind., 1990. Ordained to ministry Ch. of God, 1979. Assoc. min. Ch. of the Nazarene, Cin., 1972-74; pastor Ch. of the Nazarene, Gary, Colo., 1975-77, McConnelsville, Ohio, 1977-79; pastor 1st Ch. of the Nazarene, Fairborn, Ohio, 1979-82, 1st Ch. of God, Utica, Ky., 1983—. Bd. dirs. Ohio County HELP, Hartford, 1985—, Regional Spouse Abuse Ctr., Owensboro, Ky., 1987-89. Mem. Am. Assn. Christian Counselors, Ohio County Ministerial Assn. (chmn. 1988—). Home: 3688 Boling Utica KY 42376 Office: Pleasant Ridge 1st Church of God 3690 Boling Rd Utica KY 42376

HARNOIS, MICHAEL DAVID, clergyman; b. Washburn, Wis., Apr. 14, 1956; s. Ervin Leo Harnois and Betty Lou (Brenholt) Zinski; m. Susan Kay Christensen, June 21, 1980; children: David Michael, Andrew Peter. Student, U. Wis., Madison, 1974-75; BA, U. Wis., Oshkosh, 1980; postgrad., Ind. U., 1981-82; MDiv, Luth. Sch. Theology, Chgo., 1987. Ordained min. Evang. Luth. Ch. in Am., 1988. Assoc. dir. info. mgmt. Evang. Luth. Ch. Am., Chgo., 1988; pastor Mt. Zion/St. James/St. Luke Parish, Harvel, Ill., 1988-90, St. John's Luth. Ch., Waterloo, Iowa, 1990—. Mem. ecumenical com. Cen./So. Ill. Synod Evang. Luth. Ch. in Am., Springfield, 1988-90, Northeastern Iowa Synod, Evang. Luth. Ch. in Am., Waverly, 1990—. Max Kade fellow Ind. U., Bloomington, 1981-82. Mem. Bread for the World, Alban Inst. Avocations: amateur radio, photography. Office: 4110 E Mt Vernon Rd Waterloo IA 50703-9575 *American Christianity has never recovered from Thomas Jefferson's identification of the "real Christian" as "a disciple of the doctrines of Jesus." The great challenge to the Church today is to recover discipleship to Jesus Christ, purged of sloppy sentimentality and pious blather.*

HARP, ROBERT GEORGE, JR., hospitality corporation executive; b. Balt., May 28, 1959; s. Robert George and Delores (Creutzer) H.; m. Jill Stephenson, June 4, 1983; children: Preston Robert, Natalie Joy. BA in Econs., Wheaton Coll., 1980, MA in Communications with high honors, 1981; ThM, Dallas Theol. Sem., 1985. Lic. real estate broker. Real estate broker The Swearingen Co., Dallas, 1986-87; dir. of devel., v.p. of real estate Global Hospitality Corp., San Diego, 1987—. Contbr. articles to profl. jours. Precinct capt. San Diego Count Rep. Com. Named one of Outstanding Young Men of Am., 1985. Mem. Nat. Assn. Realtors, Realtors Nat. Mktg. Inst., Calif. Assn. Realtors, San Diego Bd. of Realtors, Cert. Comml. Investment Mem. (San Diego chpt.). Republican. Avocations: travel, reading, writing. *The Bible: God's revelation. Jesus Christ: God's incarnation. God has made Himself known in word and flesh. He has spoken. Are you listening?.*

HARPER, BOBBY JOE, minister; b. Pine Bluff, Ark., Oct. 12, 1955; s. Joe Lynn and Mary Frances (McDonald) H.; m. Welda Jean Glover, Dec. 20, 1975; children: Stephanie, Lyndsey, Drew. BA in Religion, Ouachita Bapt. Coll., Arkadelphia, 1978; MDiv, So. Sem., Louisville, 1981; D Ministry, Midwestern Sem., Kansas City, Mo., 1988. Ordained to ministry So. Bapt. Conv., 1977. Chaplain intern Bapt. Med. Ctr., Little Rock, 1981-82; pastor First Bapt. Ch., Marvell, Ark., 1982-87, White Hall, Ark., 1987—; exec. bd. Ark. Bapt. State Conv., 1989—; moderator Harmony Bapt. Assn., Pine Bluff, 1989-90. Home: 303 Anderson White Hall AR 71602 Office: First Bapt Ch 8203 Dollarway Rd White Hall AR 71602

HARPER, JOE STEVEN, religious educator, minister; b. Haskell, Tex., Oct. 20, 1947; s. Joe Samuel and Martha Elizabeth (Robinson) H.; m. Jeanette Sue Waller, Apr. 10, 1970; children: John Stewart, Katrina Louise. BA, McMurry Coll., Abilene, Tex., 1970; MDiv, Asbury Sem., Wilmore, Ky., 1973; PhD, Duke U., 1981. Youth minister First United Meth. Ch., Hamlin, Tex., 1966-67; pastor First United Meth. Ch., Weinert, Tex., 1967-68; youth evangelist Ed Robb Evangelistic Assn., Abilene, Tex., 1968-70; pastor Highland-Kings Mt. Meth. Ch., Highland, Ky., 1970-72, First United Meth. Ch., Roby, Tex., 1973-75, Wesley United Meth. Ch., Borger, Tex., 1975-77; prof. dept. spiritual formation Asbury Theol. Sem., Wilmore, Ky., 1980—; dir. continuing end. Asbury Sme., 1983-84, dir. spiritual life activities, 1984—. Contbr. articles to profl. jours., books. Tutor Operation Read Literacy Prog., Lexington, Ky., 1987—. Mem. Soc. John Wesley Scholars, Wesleyan Theol. Soc., Am. Acad. Religion, Laubach Literacy Internat. Methodist. Avocations: bowling, table tennis, golf.

HARPER, KENNETH CHARLES, clergyman; b. Detroit, Aug. 31, 1946; s. Charles Burdett and Marion Anna (Pankau) H.; m. Sharon Kay Royse, June 14, 1969; children: Charles William, David Peter, Andrew Scott. BS in Edn., Ill. State U., 1969; MDiv, Trinity Evang. Div. Sch., Deerfield, Ill., 1973; ThM, Princeton (N.J.) Theol. Sem., 1976; D of Ministry, San Francisco Theol. Sem., San Anselmo, Calif., 1986; postgrad., Pepperdine U., 1989—. Ordained to ministry Presbyn. Ch., 1974. Edn. advisor Amwell Valley Commn., Reaville, N.J., 1973-74; asst. pastor 1st Presbyn. Ch., Mt. Holly, N.J., 1974-77; pastor 1st Presbyn. Ch., Herrin, Ill., 1977-82; sr. pastor 1st Presbyn. Ch., Westminster, Calif., 1982—. Contbr. book revs. and articles to religious jours. Mem. Evang. Theol. Soc., Presbyns. for Renewal, Assn. Psychol. Type. Democrat. Office: 1st Presbyn Ch 7702 Westminster Blvd Westminster CA 92683

HARPER, RONALD DEAN, religious publishing administrator; b. Peculiar, Mo., Mar. 10, 1935; s. Raymond Henry and Mildred Louise (King) H.; m. Phyliss June Zaritz, Mar. 7, 1964; children: David, Monica. Student, Cen. Mo. State U., 1953-54; AS, Cen. Tech. Inst., Kansas City, Mo., 1959. Lit. evangelist Home Health Edn. Svc., Kansas City, Mo., 1975-81, Springfield, Mo., 1981-82; asst. pub. dir. Seventh-day Adventist Ch., Springfield, 1982—. With U.S. Army, 1954-56. Home: Rte 5 Box 213 Ozark MO 65721 Office: PO Box 65665 West Des Moines IA 50265 *We seem to get what we want in life when we forget self and experience the joy of helping others. Watching them grow spiritually and mentally is one of God's greatest blessings. "The joy of the Lord is your strength," Nehemiah 8:10.*

HARPER, TERRY LAYNE, minister; b. Roanoke, Va., May 20, 1948; s. Carl Paul and Lottie Odel (Cook) H.; m. Brenda Cheryl Davis, June 1, 1974; children: Derrick Layne, Carla DeAnn, Alison Leigh. AS in Bus., Bluefield Coll., 1971; BA in Psychology, Averett Coll., 1974; MDiv, Southeastern Bapt. Theol., Seminary, Wake Forest, N.C., 1979. Ordained to ministry So. Bapt. Conv., 1972. Pastor White Rock Bapt. Ch., Hardy, Va., 1972-74, Exmore (Va.) Bapt. Ch., 1974-76, First Bapt. Ch., Alamance, N.C., 1976-79, Waverly (Va.) Bapt. Ch., 1979-84, Colonial Heights (Va.) Bapt. Ch., 1984—; mem. tellers com. So. Bapt. Conv., 1988; trustee Fgn. Missions Bd., So. Bapt. Conv., 1989-93; human rights com. Southside Va. Tng. Ctr., Petersburg, Va., 1980-86; dir. evangelism Petersburg Bapt. Assn., 1982-84; mem. faculty Eagle Eyrie Bapt. Assembly, Lynchburg, Va., 1980-83; guest lectr. coll. campuses. Vocalist, rec. artist. Moderator Meet The Candidates for Va. Legislature, Colonial Hgts., 1990, Meet The Candidates for City Coun., 1989, Meet The Candidates for City Clk., 1990; pres. North Elem. PTA, Colonial Hgts., 1986-88; mem. bd. overseers Criswell Coll., Dallas, 1991—. Recipient Friend of Edn. award Colonial Hgts. Sch. Bd., 1989. Mem. Colonial Hgts. Clergy Assn. (pres. 1987). Office: Colonial Heights Bapt Ch 231 Chesterfield Ave Colonial Heights VA 23834 *The greatest inequity in the American Society today is that of abortions. What must God think of a society that kills its children before they are even born? It is the New Holocaust.*

HARPER, WILLIAM ROBERT, minister; b. Asuncion, Paraguay, July 10, 1952; s. Leland James and Helen Elizabeth (Wicks) H.; m. Rebecca Ann Barnett, Dec. 30, 1978; children: Cynthia Nicole, Marcy Lynn. BA in Spanish, Ouachita Bapt. U., 1975; M in Div., Southwestern Bapt. Theol. Seminary, 1984. Missionary journeyman Fgn. Mission Bd. of So. Bapt. Conv., Mene Grande, Venezuela, 1975-77; oilfield equipment salesman Mid-Continent Supply Co., Odessa, Tex., 1977-78; workshop coordinator MHMR Permian Basin Community Ctr., Odessa, 1978; sales engr. NL Treating Chems., Snyder, Tex., 1978-80; drilling fluids engr. NL Baroid, Snyder, Tex., 1980-81; youth, music minister First Bapt. Ch., Peaster, Tex., 1981-82; pastor Red Springs (Tex.) Bapt. Ch., 1982-85; assoc. pastor First Bapt. Ch., Snyder, Tex., 1985—. Dir. Ministerial Alliance Scurry County Crisis Ctr., Snyder, 1986; bd. dirs. Scurry County Child Welfare, Snyder, 1987. Served as chaplain with USAF, 1983—. Mem. Southwestern Bapt. Theol. Seminary Alumni Assn., Nat. Assn. Ch. Bus. Adminstrn, Ministerial Allianc of Scurry County. Club: Postal Commemorative Soc. Avocations: reading, racquetball, tennis, stamp collecting, guitar. Home: PO Box 860 Snyder TX 79549 Office: First Bapt Ch 1701 27th Snyder TX 79549

HARPUR, THOMAS WILLIAM, writer, religious broadcaster; b. Toronto, Can., Apr. 14, 1929; s. William Wallace and Elizabeth (Hoey) H.; m. Mary Clark, June 2, 1956 (div. 1983); children: Elizabeth, Margaret, Mary Catharine; m. Susan Bette Anne Coles, Apr. 7, 1984. BA, U. Coll., U. Toronto, 1951, Oriel Coll., Oxford, Eng., 1954; MA, Oriel Coll., Oxford, Eng., 1956; MDiv, Wycliffe Coll., Toronto, 1956. Ordained deacon Anglican Ch., 1954, priest, 1956, resigned orders, 1979. Curate St. John's York Mills, Toronto, 1956-57; rector St. Margaret's-in-the-Pines, West Hill, Ont., 1957-64; lectr. introductory philosophy Trinity Coll. and Wycliffe Colls., 1959-63; assoc. prof. N.T. Greek Wycliffe Coll., 1964-68; prof. Toronto Sch. Theology, 1969-71; religion editor Toronto Star, 1971-83; freelance writer, broadcaster on religious affairs, 1983—; host radio show, 1967-71, TV show

CFTO-TV, Toronto, 1979-84, Harpur's Heaven and Hell, Vision TV Network, 1987—. Author: Road to Bethlehem, 1977, Harpur's Heaven and Hell, 1983, For Christ's Sake, 1986, Always on Sunday, 1988, Life After Death, 1991, (illustrated books for children) The Mouse That Couldn't Squeak, 1988, The Terrible Finn Mac Coul, 1990; co-editor: Jesus, 1973. Rhodes scholar, 1951; recipient Gold medal U. Toronto, 1951, Award of Merit Religious Pub. Rels. Coun., 1974. Mem. Writer's Union Can., Can. Assn. Rhodes Scholars, Assn. Can. Radio and TV Artists. Home: 5 Willowbank Sta B, Richmond Hill, ON Canada L4E 3B4 *Hope is the most revolutionary concept and attitude in the world.*

HARR, JOSEPH, religious organization administrator. Pres. Christian Union, Grower Hill, Ohio. Office: Christian Union 73 Indianhead Dr Heath OH 43056*

HARR, SHELDON JAY, rabbi; b. Youngstown, Ohio, Sept. 5, 1946; s. Aaron A. and Arlene (Levy) H.; m. Fern J. Harr, Aug. 30, 1969; children: Elizabeth (dec.), Bryan. BA, U. Cin., 1968; B. Hebrew Letters, Hebrew Union Coll., 1971, MA, 1973; postgrad., Emory U. Ordained rabbi, 1973. Asst. rabbi Temple Israel, West Palm Beach, Fla., 1973-76; sr. rabbi Temple Kol Ami, Plantation, Fla., 1976—; vice chmn. Jewish Nat. Fund, S.E. Fla., Ft. Lauderdale. Vice chmn. Urban League of Broward County, Ft. Lauderdale, 1988-90; mem. bi-racial com. Sch. Bd. of Broward County, 1987-89; chaplain Police Dept. of Davie, Fla., 1988—. Mem. Cen. Conf. Am. Rabbis (officer S.E. region), Jewish Fedn. Ft. Lauderdale (bd. dirs. Outstanding Rabbi of Yr. 1990-91), West Broward Religious Leaders Fellowship (pres. 1985-87), NCCJ (bd. dirs. 1986—), Union Am. Hebrew Congregations (bd. dirs. S.E. region). Office: Temple Kol Ami 8200 Peters Rd Plantation FL 33324

HARRELL, JAMES ANDREW, SR., lay administrator, dentist; b. Elkin, N.C., July 14, 1922; s. Roy B. and Mattie Reid (Doughton) H.; m. Isabel Jane Gibbs, June 19, 1945; children: Jim Jr., Deborah, Gavin, Stephen. Student, U. N.C.; DDS, Med. Coll. Va., 1945. Pvt. practice Elkin, 1948—; bd. dirs. United Savings and Loan, N.C. Assn. of Professions; chmn., bd. dirs. Yadkin Valley Bank and Trust. Pres. United Fund, Elkin, 1960, YMCA, 1960; scoutmaster, Elkin; mayor of Elkin 3 terms, commr. 3 terms; mem. Tar Heel 100 adv. to bd. trustees U. N.C. at Chapel Hill, v.p., bd. dirs. Gen. Alumni Assn., pres., 1986-87; Final Selection Com. Morehead Scholars in Dentistry; mem. undergrad. Morehead Slection Com., Surry County; mem. U. N.C. Com. on Dentistry; bd. dirs. Dental Found. N.C., Inc., 1972—, N.C. Blue Cross Blue Shield, 1972-73; chmn. adminstrv. bd. and fin. com. United Meth. Ch., Elkin, served all lay positions and offices, ch. sch. tchr., 1954—, cert. lay speaker, lay leader North Wilkesboro dist.; chmn. conf. Laity W.N.C. Conf. Meth. Ch., 1984-86, conf. lay leader, 1986—, chmn. coun. on Laity, 1985—, del. gen. conf., 1988. Served with USN. Recipient Torch award Western N.C. Conf., Disting. Svc. award Dental Found. N.C. and U. N.C. Sch. Dentistry, 1977, fellowship Acad. Gen. Dentistry, 1977, John C. Braurer award Dental Alumni Assn. U. N.C., 1986, Disting Svc. medal Gen. Alumni Assn. U. N.C., 1989. Fellow Internat. Coll. Dentists, Acad. Dentistry Internat., Soc. John Wesley, Am. Coll. Dentists, Royal Soc. Health London; mem. ADA (Ho. of Dels. 14 yrs., credentials com., reference coms. 1983, chmn. 1984, 2d v.p. 1985-86), United Meth. Men (life), Am. Coll. Dentists (v.p. 1986-87, pres. 1989, regent-Regency III 1982—, chmn. Carolinas sect. 1980-81), Acad. Gen. Dentistry (Ho. of Dels., chmn. coun. constitution and bylaws 1978-79, pres. 1982-83), Am. Fund for Dental Health (state chmn. 1984-87, curriculum project Nat. Adv. Com. on Dental Quality Assurance, nat. adv. com. on program planning, 1982, trustee 1986-89), World Meth. Coun. Office: 180-G Parkwood Profl Ctr Elkin NC 28621

HARRELL, ROY HARRISON, JR., minister; b. San Angelo, Tex., July 13, 1928; s. Roy Harrison and Melinda (Garza) H.; m. Iris Ann Keeton, Dec. 15, 1951 (div. Aug. 1982); children: Amy Sue Perry, Patrick Roy, Paula Ann; m. Iva Helen Odeen, Apr. 21, 1990. BA, Hardin Simmons U., 1949; MDiv, SW Bapt. Theol. Sem., 1956. Ordained to ministry So. Bapt. Conv. Campus min. Draughns Bus. Coll., Ft. Worth, 1952-53; youth min. Polytechnic Bapt. Ch., Ft. Worth, 1953-56; campus min. Tex. Wesleyan Coll., Ft. Worth, 1953-56; instr., asst. prof. Religion, campus min. Baylor U., Med. Ctr., Dallas, 1956-62; campus min. Baylor U., Waco, Tex., 1962-68; asst. pastor U. Bapt. Ch., Abilene, Tex., 1969, Pk. Cities Bapt. Ch., Dallas, 1970-82; pastor Ross Ave. Bapt. Ch., Dallas, 1983—; bd. dirs. Dallas Bapt. Assn., East Dallas Coop. Parish, pres., 1991—. Contbr. articles to profl. jours. Mem. Dallas Pastors Assn. (sec.-treas. 1990-91, v.p., pres. elect 1991—), Rotary. Home: 3521 Villanova Dallas TX 75230 *The church is the only institution dedicated to changing the lives of people at their very heart. A minister therefore has the gravest of responsibility.*

HARRELL, STEPHEN PAUL, church lay worker, university official; b. Kansas City, Mo., Oct. 26, 1947; s. Arthur Guy Jr. and Pauline Joan (Rodak) H. BS in English and Theatre, Cen. Mo. State U., 1972, MA in English, 1989; postgrad., Louisville Presbyn. Theol. Sem., 1973-75, St. Paul Sch. Theology, Kansas City, Mo., 1975-76. Student pastoral asst. West End Group Ministries, Louisville, 1973, 74; instr., dir. ch. drama Harvey Browne Meml. Presbyn. Ch., Louisville, 1974; student pastor 1st Presbyn. Ch., Elizabethtown, Ky., 1975; student asst. NE Community Ctr., Kansas City, 1972-77; playwright, actor, dir. ch. theatre Salem United Ch. of Christ, Louisville, 1983—, mem. choir, 1980—, mem. lay liturgy com., 1988—; tutor, adminstr. Office Minority Svcs., U. Louisville, 1981—. Author, player, dir. Letters of the Seven Churches, 1988, The Divine Tragedy, 1989, The Trial of Jesus of Nazareth, 1990, Pentecost!, 1991. With U.S. Army, 1967-69. Scholar Kansas City Bd. Edn., 1964-66, U. Mo. Bd. Curators, 1964-66. Mem. Gt. Alkali Plainsmen, Scion Soc. Baker Street Irregulars. Democrat. Office: U Louisville Office Minority Svcs 120 E Brandeis Louisville KY 40292

HARRELSON, LARRY EUGENE, minister; b. McLeansboro, Ill., Apr. 17, 1944; s. Willis Murrel and Jessie Verla (Buttry) H.; m. Willa Ruth Sommer, June 6, 1970; children: Christian M. Harrelson Neilson, Todd W., John P. BS, Drury Coll., 1969; MA, U. Mo., 1970, U. Okla., 1973; D in Ministry, Phillips U., 1982. Ordained to ministry Episcopal Ch. as deacon, 1976, as priest, 1976; lic. social worker, Idaho. Curate St. Matthew's Episcopal Ch., Enid, Okla., 1976-77; vicar St. John's Episcopal Ch., Woodward, Okla., 1977-79; chaplain Western State Hosp., Ft. Supply, Okla., 1977-79; vicar Holy Trinity Episcopal Ch., Wallace, Idaho, 1979-84; rector Ch. of the Nativity, Lewiston, Idaho, 1984-91; residential svc. coord. Region II Idaho Mental Health/Adult Svcs., Lewiston, 1991—; brigade chaplain 116th Calvary Brigade, USNG, Boise, 1991—; clergy del. Gen. Conv. Episcopal Ch., 1991; mem., chmn. com. on nurture Diocesan Coun., Diocese of Spokane, 1986-89; dean Clearwater Deanery, Diocese of Spokane, 1985-90; pres. East Shoshone Ministerial Assn., Shoshone County, Idaho, 1982; mem. Task Force on Human Sexuality, 1989, Diocesan Commn. on Ministry, 1988—. Contbr. articles to profl. jours. Treas. Lewiston (Idaho) City Libr. Bd., 1984—; mem. Woodward (Okla.) City Libr. Bd., 1978-79; founding chmn. Christian Aid Fund, Shoshone County, 1983; mem. region II Mental Health Adv. Bd., State of Idaho, 1989-91; mem. Idaho Housing Coalition Steering Com., 1991—. With USNR, 1973-89, USAR, 1980—, lt. col. Res. Decorated Meritorious Svc. medal, Nat. Def. Svc. medal, others. Mem. Brotherhood of St. Andrew, Order of St. Luke, NG Assn. of U.S., Rotary (Lewiston). Home: 3829 17th St C Lewiston ID 83501 Office: Idaho Mental Health/Adult Svcs PO Drawer B Lewiston ID 83501-0182

HARRELSON, WALTER JOSEPH, minister, religion educator emeritus; b. Winnabow, N.C., Nov. 28, 1919; s. Isham Danvis and Mae (Rich) H.; m. Idella Aydlett, Sept. 20, 1942; children: Marianne McIver, David Aydlett, Robert Joseph. Student, Mars Hill (N.C.) Coll., 1940-41, Litt.D. (hon.), 1977; A.B., U. N.C., 1947; B.D., Union Theol. Sem., 1949, Th.D., 1953; postgrad., U. Basel, Switzerland, 1950-51, Harvard, 1951-53; D.D. (hon.), U. of South, 1974. Instr. philosophy U. N.C., 1947; ordained to ministry Baptist Ch., 1949; tutor asst., instr. Union Theol. Sem., 1949-50; prof. Old Testament Andover Newton Theol. Sch., 1951-55; dean, assoc. prof. Old Testament U. Chgo. Div. Sch., 1955-60; prof. Old Testament Div. Sch., Vanderbilt U., Nashville, 1960-75; chmn. grad. dept. religion Div. Sch., Vanderbilt U., 1962-67, dean, 1967-75, Disting. prof. Old Testament, 1975-90, prof. emeritus, 1990—, dir. Lilly Ministry Project, 1990—; rector Ecumenical Inst. Advanced Theol. Studies, Jerusalem, 1977-78, 78-79; vice-chmn. transl. com. Rev. Standard Version of the Bible. Author: Jeremiah, Prophet to the Nations, 1959, Interpreting the Old Testament, 1964, From Fertility Cult to Worship, 1969, 80, The Ten Commandments and Human Rights, 1980, (with Rabbi R.M. Falk) Jews and Christians: A Troubled Family, 1990; co-author, editor: Teaching the Biblical Languages, 1967; editor, contbr.: Israel's Prophetic Heritage, 1962; editorial chmn. Religious Studies Rev., 1974-80; assoc. editor Mercer Dictionary of the Bible, 1990; assoc. editor Mercer Commentary on the Bible, 1991—. Dir. project to film Ethiopian Manuscripts, NEH, 1972-84. Traveling fellow Union Theol. Sem., 1949; Am. Coun. Learned Socs. fellow, 1950-51, 70; exch. fellow U. Basel, 1950-51; Fulbright rsch. scholar, Rome, 1962-63; Harvie Branscomb Disting. prof. Vanderbilt U., 1977-78, Alexander Heard Disting. Svc. prof., 1985-86; NEH fellow, Rome, 1983-84; recipient Thomas Jefferson prize, 1987-88, Alumni/ae award Vanderbilt U., 1989, Festschrift, Justice and the Holy, 1989. Mem. Soc. for Values in Higher Edn. (pres. 1972-74), Soc. Bibl. Lit. (pres. 1971-72), Am. Schs. Oriental Research, Cath. Bible Assn, Phi Beta Kappa. Home: 305 Bowling Ave Nashville TN 37205-2519

HARRIMAN, CRAIG GORDON, missionary, high school swim coach; b. Las Cruces, N.Mex., Jan. 11, 1950; s. Frank Bentley and Geraldine Minola (Gordon) H.; m. Victoria Jean Hart, June 10, 1972; children: Gretchen Rae, Gene Gordon, Kiffin Marie. BS in Animal Sci., U. Nev., 1972; postgrad., Internat. Sch. Theology, 1973-78. Animal sci. instr. Rawhide Vocat. Coll., Bonsall, Calif., 1972; coaches' chaplain Athletes in Action/Campus Crusade for Christ, Tustin, Calif., 1973-79; media events coord. Athletes in Action/Campus Crusade for Christ, Tustin, 1979-80; nat. adminstr. Athletes in Action/Campus Crusade for Christ, Fountain Valley, Calif., 1980-82; dir. of ops. Athletes in Action/Campus Crusade for Christ, Irvine, Calif., 1983-85; exec. asst. to pres. Athletes in Action/Campus Crusade for Christ, Irvine, 1985-86; sport dir. of swimming Athletes in Action/Campus Crusade for Christ, Colorado Springs, Colo., 1987—; bd. dirs., chief fin. officer Athletes in Action, Inc., Irvine, 1984-87; mgmt. cons. Black Forest Chapel, Colorado Springs, 1990. Tchr. Sunday sch. Evangelic Free Ch. of Orange, Calif., 1978-86, Black Forest Chapel, Colorado Springs, 1988-90, dir. youth, 1989-90, dir. Awana, 1991—; Awana leader Evangelic Free Ch. of Orange, 1983-87. Republican. Avocations: horseback riding, hunting, coaching, teaching. Home: 7330 Mathews Rd Colorado Springs CO 80908 Office: Athletes in Action 7899 Lexington Dr Ste 200 Colorado Springs CO 80920

HARRINGTON, DONALD JAMES, minister, university president; b. Bklyn., Oct. 2, 1945; s. John Joseph and Ruth Mary (Cummings) H. BA, Mary Immaculate Sem., Northampton, Pa., 1969, MDiv, 1972, ThM, 1973; LLD (hon.), St. John's U., 1985; postgrad., U. Toronto, 1980-82. Ordained priest Roman Catholic Ch., 1973. Instr. Niagara U., Niagara University, N.Y., 1973-80, dir. student activities, 1974-77, dean student activities, 1977-80, exec. v.p., 1981-84, pres., 1984-89; pres. St. John's U., Jamaica, N.Y., 1989—. Trustee Niagara U., 1984—, St. John's U., 1986—, Jamaica, N.Y., 1986—, De Paul U., 1988; Reserve Group, 1988; chair Western N.Y. Consortium for Higher Edn., 1987-89; bd. dirs. Sisters Hosp., Buffalo, 1987-89; chair adv. com. Love Canal Land Use, 1989; vice chair Niagara Falls C. of C., 1984-88. Office: St John's U Office of Pres Jamaica NY 11439

HARRINGTON, HANNAH KARAJIAN, religion educator; b. Berkeley, Calif., Dec. 25, 1958; d. Samuel Levon and Constance Maggie (Moore) Karajian; m. William James Harrington, June 20, 1981. BA in Biblical Studies, Patten Coll., 1978; MusB, San Francisco Conservatory Mus, 1982; MA in Near Ea. Studies, U. Calif., Berkeley, 1985, postgrad., 1988. Instr. Patten Coll., Oakland, Calif., 1983-89, asst. prof., chairperson div. bibl. studies, 1989—; ch. organist, 1989—; grad. student instr. in modern Hebrew U. Calif.-Berkeley, 1986, 87, 89-90; cellist Modesto (Calif.) Symphony, 1981—. NEH fellow, 1988. Mem. Soc. Biblical Lit. Democrat. Home: 2479 Coolidge Ave Oakland CA 94601 Office: Patten Coll 2433 Coolidge Ave Oakland CA 94601

HARRINGTON, J. B., preacher, counselor; b. Weatherford, Tex., Aug. 30, 1930; s. Joe Boyd and Ida Mae (Galbreaith) H.; m. Ruth Lenora Ferguson, Dec. 21, 1954; children: Lisa, Boyd, Alan, Dale, Elyn. BA, Abilene Christian Coll., 1950. Preacher Ch. of Christ, Texhoma, Okla., 1951-53, Elkhart, Kans., 1953-55, Loveland, Colo., 1955-63, Farmington, N. Mex., 1963-71, Big Spring, Tex., 1971-74, Albany, Tex., 1974-75, Los Alamos, N. Mex., 1975—. Mem. Kiwanis (Los Alamos pres. 1986-87), Toastmasters (Los Alamos pres. 1984). Republican. Avocations: golf, trout fishing, reading. Home and Office: PO Box 918 Los Alamos NM 87544

HARRINGTON, JEREMY THOMAS, clergyman; b. Lafayette, Ind., Oct. 7, 1932; s. William and Ellen (Cain) H. B.A., Duns Scotus Coll., 1955; postgrad., U. Detroit, 1955, Marquette U., 1961; M.A., Xavier U., Cin., 1965; M.S. in Journalism, Northwestern U., 1967. Joined Order Friars Minor, 1950; ordained priest Roman Catholic Ch., 1959; tchr. Roger Bacon High Sch., Cin., 1960-64; assoc. editor St. Anthony Messenger, Cin., 1964-66; editor St. Anthony Messenger, 1966-81, pub., 1975-81, pub., chief exec. officer, 1991—; mem. bd. Franciscan Province Cin., 1969-72, 75-81, chief exec. bd., 1981-90. Author: Your Wedding: Planning Your Own Ceremony, 1974; Editor: Conscience in Today's World, 1970, Jesus: Superstar or Savior?, 1972. Mem. Catholic Press Assn. (pres. 1975-77, dir.), Kappa Tau Alpha. Home and Office: 1615 Vine St Cincinnati OH 45210 *My success has been made by others. As a priest, as well as an editor and publisher, my challenge is to discover, recognize, encourage and make available to others the talents of authors and artists. To me, that's a parable of life. The more we can discover, appreciate and foster the good qualities and strengths of others, the more "successful" we are. Success in life is realizing how many gifts are made available to us by God and our fellow human beings.*

HARRINGTON, TIMOTHY J., bishop; b. Holyoke, Mass., Dec. 19, 1918. Ed., Holy Cross Coll., Worcester, Mass., Grand Sem., Montreal, Que., Can., Boston Coll. Sch. Social Work. Ordained priest Roman Catholic Ch., 1946, consecrated bishop, 1968. Titular bishop of Rusuca and aux. bishop of Worcester Mass., 1968-83; bishop of Worcester, 1983—. Home: 2 High Ridge Rd Worcester MA 01602

HARRIS, ANDY CLAY, minister; b. Prescott, Ark., Sept. 1, 1961; s. James Russell and Jamie Earlene (Lucas) H.; m. Sheryl Lynn Thompson, Oct. 17, 1981; 1 child, Lauren Amanda Harris. BS, Southwestern Assemblies of God Coll., 1982; postgrad., Southwestern Bapt. Theol. Sem., 1983-85. Ordained to ministry Assemblies of God, 1985. Asst. pastor Calvary Temple Assembly of God, Irving, Tex., 1981-85; adminstrv. asst. Jimmy Swaggart Ministries, Baton Rouge, 1986-88; sr. pastor Kings Corner Assemblies of God, Sarepta, La., 1988—; sec.-treas. Bossier City Sect. of the Assemblies of God, Sarepta, 1989—. Author: God's Plan for the Ages, 1986. Recipient Patriotism award Bossier City Am. Legion, 1979. Mem. SAR (Shreveport, La.), Delta Epsilon Chi. Republican. Home: Rt 1 Box 349 Sarepta LA 71071 Office: Kings Corner Assembly of God Rt 1 Box 349 Sarepta LA 71071 *Put quality and excellence into everything you do. People will notice, and God will be honored. Learn from the mistakes of others, and you will not have to learn from your own.*

HARRIS, BARBARA C(LEMENTINE), bishop; b. Phila., 1930. Grad., Charles Morris Price Sch. Advt. and Journalism, Phila.; student, Villanova U., Urban Theology Unit, Sheffield, Eng.; D in Sacred Theology (hon.), Hobart and William Smith Colls., 1981; DD (hon.), Gen. Theol. Sem., 1989, Episc. Div. Sch., 1989, Amherst Coll., 1989. Ordained to ministry Episcopal Ch. as deacon, 1979, as priest, 1980. Pres. Joseph V. Baker Assocs., Phila., 1958-68; sr. staff cons., mem. community rels. dept. Sun Oil Co.; priest-in-charge St. Augustine of Hippo, Norristown, Pa.; interim rector Ch. of the Advocate, Phila.; exec. dir. Episc. Ch. Pub. Co., 1984-88; suffragan bishop Diocese of Mass., Boston, 1989—; trustee Episc. Div. Sch. Address: Episc Diocese of Mass 138 Tremont St Boston MA 02111

HARRIS, CARLTON PHILLIP, minister; b. St. Louis, June 18, 1957; m. Carol Ann Penner, May 19, 1979; children: Carissa Marie, Candice Elise, Colin Phillip. BA, Dallas Bible Coll., 1979; ThM, Dallas Theol. Seminary, 1983. Ordained to ministry. Asst. dir. Houston Bible Inst., 1983-86; assoc. pastor Quail Valley Community Ch., Missouri City, Tex., 1986—; bible study tchr. Sta. KHCB-FM, Houston, 1985-86; chaplain Houston Rockets, 1984—; chapel leader Houston Astros, 1984-85. Editor: (newsletters) News and Views, 1983-86, The Quill, 1986-87; contbr. articles to profl. jours. Named one of Outstanding Young Men of Am., 1981, 84-85. Mem. Profl. Assn. Christian Educators. Avocations: reading, travel, sports. Office: Quail Valley Community Ch 2019 Bright Meadows Missouri City TX 77489

HARRIS, DAVID, minister; b. Dallas, Apr. 12, 1934; s. David Sr. and Annie Mae (Sanford) H. BS, Wiley Coll., 1957; BD, MA, Southwestern Sem., Ft. Worth, 1966, M in Religious Edn., 1967; LHD with honors, Teamer Sch. Religion, 1980. Ordained to ministry Bapt. Ch. Tchr. elem. sch. Elysian Field, Tex., 1952-58; prof. theology Wiley Coll. Extension, Dallas, 1960-61; rep. Black Civic Affairs, Dallas, 1961-63; program mgr. Equal Opportunity Council, Dallas, 1965-70; pastor Second Corithian Ch., Dallas, 1970—. Mem. adv. bd. Dallas Council Chs., 1970-75, Nat. Conf. Christians and Jews, Dallas, 1978-80; bd. dirs. Big Bros. Dallas, 1970-72, Dallas Crime Commn., 1971-73; sec. Dallas Voter's League. Recipient Internat. League award Southwestern Sem., 1967. Mem. NAACP (adv. bd.), Dallas Assn. Black Ministers (v.p. 1980—), Wiley Alumni Assn. Republican. Lodge: Masons. Avocations: tennis, singing, softball, jogging, football. Home: 4220 E Grand Dallas TX 75723

HARRIS, DONNELL RAY, minister; b. St. Louis, June 12, 1936; s. David Pritchard and Jewel (Mitchener) H.; m. Norma Ruth Stacy, June 1, 1959; children: Stacy Lynne, Stephen Donnell. BA, William Jewell Coll., 1958; BD, Colgate Rochester Div. Sch., 1962, ThM, 1972. Ordained to ministry Am. Bapt. Chs. U.S.A., 1962. Min. West Shore Bapt. Ch., Rocky River, Ohio, 1962-67, 1st Bapt. Ch. in Chili, Rochester, N.Y., 1967-75, Montgomery Hills Bapt. Ch., Silver Spring, Md., 1975—; clk. Am. Bapt. Chs. N.Y., 1973-75; mem. gen. bd. Am. Bapt. Chs. U.S.A., 1981-86, pres. D.C. Bapt. Conv., 1990. Contbr. articles to religious jours. Am. Assn. Theol. Schs. Sr. Honors fellow, 1962. Home: 14305 Myer Terr Rockville MD 20853 Office: 9727 Georgia Ave Silver Spring MD 20910

HARRIS, DOUGLAS ALLEN, minister; b. Kingsport, Tenn., May 25, 1954; s. William Davis and Meryl (Brooks) H. BSW, E. Tenn. State U., 1980, BS in Corrections, 1981; MA, Liberty U., Lynchburg, Va. Ordained to ministry, So. Bapt. Conv. Pastor Carters Valley Bapt. Ch., Churchill, Tenn., 1980-83, Beech Creek Bapt. Ch., Rogersmill, Tenn., 1983-84, Valley View Bapt. Ch., Church Hill, Tenn., 1985-87; evangelist Kingsport, Tex., 1987—; tchr. Ketron Middle Sch., Kingsport, Tenn., 1987—; counselor Grandfather Home for Children, Banner Elk, N.C., 1980-83. Editor: God Vs Sexual Immorality, 1982. Counselor Sullivan House, Blountville, Tenn., 1987, CCS, Kingsport, 1988; vol. probation officer Hawkins County Ct., Rogersville, 1981. Republican. Home: 3344 Lightwood St Kingsport TN 37660

HARRIS, GEORGE CLINTON, bishop; b. Dec. 19, 1925; s. Clinton George and Meta Grace (Werner) H.; m. Mary Jane Shotwell, June 27, 1953; 6 children. BSCE, Rutgers U., 1950, STB, Gen. Theol. Sem., N.Y.C., 1953, STM, 1970. Ordained to ministry Episcopal Ch. as deacon, 1953, as priest. Curate Heavenly Rest Ch., N.Y.C., 1953-55; chaplain Easter Sch.; asst. Epiphany Ch., Baguio City, The Philippines, 1956-57; priest-in-charge St. Mary the Virgin Ch., Sagada, The Philippines, 1957-62; prin. St. Francis High Sch., Upi Cotabato, The Philippines, 1963-69; rector Lower Luzerne Parish, Hazelton, Pa., 1970-74; dir. Dakota Leadership Program, 1974-81; bishop Diocese of Alaska, Fairbanks, 1981-91; ret., 1991.

HARRIS, GLEN ALAN, evangelist; b. Connersville, Ind., Feb. 28, 1960; s. Richard Lee and Margaret Kathleen (Brown) H.; m. Angela Dee Ferguson, Aug. 4, 1984; 1 child, Alex Daniel Harris. Student, Tarrant County Jr. Coll., 1982; BS, Arlington (Tex.) Bapt. Coll., 1982; BTh., DD, Great Commn. Theol. Sem., Bowling Green, Ky., 1987. Crusade evangelist Calvary Bapt. Ch., Connersville, 1972-78; with pub. relations Arlington Bapt. Coll., 1978-82; founder, evangelist Local Ch. Ministries, Connersville, 1982—; tchr. Youth Worker's Seminar, 1983; guest speaker Kansas City Youth for Christ, 1985-86, I.B.F.I., Ft. Worth, 1987; mem. World Bapt. Fellowship Internat., Bapt. Bible Fellowship Internat. Editor: (newsletter) Influence, 1983; gospel recording artist. Guest speaker Fellowship of Christian Athletes, Kearny, Nebr., 1984; host Cen. Ky. Jubilee, Lexington, Ky. Mem. Internat. Platform Assn., Southwide Bapt. Fellowship, Ind. Bapt. Fellowship Internat. Avocations: writing, drama, singing, tennis, baseball. Home: 2719 Grand Ave Connersville IN 47331 Office: Local Ch Ministries Calvary Bapt Ch PO Box 306 Connersville IN 47331

HARRIS, JAMES GORDON, religion educator, seminary administrator; b. Bunkie, La., Nov. 1, 1940; s. James G. and Tunis (Johns) H.; m. Joyce Behm, Mar. 24, 1967; children: Donna Joy, Jami Ruth. BA, Baylor U., 1962; BD, Southwestern Sem., 1965, ThM, 1967; PhD, Southern Sem., 1970. Pastor, 1963-70; theol. edn. Philippine Bapt. Sem., Bagio, Philippines, 1970-75; assoc. prof. Old Testament North Am. Bapt. Sem., Sioux Falls, S.D., 1975—, acad. v.p., 1983—; pres. bd. dirs. Kilion Community Coll., Sioux Falls, 1986-87; chaplain S.D. State Penitentiary, Sioux Falls, 1976-77. Author: Biblical Perspectives on Aging, 1987; contbr. articles to profl. jours. Major, chaplain Army Nat. Guard, 1977—. Mem. Soc. Bibl. Lit. (regional sec. and pres. 1980-86), Nat. Assn. Profs. Hebrew (v.p. 1982—), Inst. Bibl. Rsch., Lions (pres. Sioux Falls club 1987-88). Democrat. Office: North Am Bapt Sem 1321 W 22d Sioux Falls SD 57105 *God's will blows like a wind. People dedicated to this will lift up life's sails to be carried wherever God determines is best. When others resist that will it can blow more like a tornado.*

HARRIS, JOHN ARLAND, minister; b. Duluth, Minn., Aug. 12, 1946; s. Arland Lawrence and Marion Eleanor (Calverly) H.; m. Trina Joyce Mattas, Aug. 3, 1969; children: Jacqueline Renee, Joel David. BA, U. Minn., 1968; MDiv, Yale U., 1972. Ordained to ministry United Meth. Ch., 1972. Assoc. pastor Spring Glen Ch., Hamden, Conn., 1969-72; pastor Granada United Meth. Parish, Fairmont, Minn., 1972-74, Chisholm (Minn.)-Buhl United Meth. Parish, 1974-81; assoc. pastor Brooklyn United Meth. Ch., Brooklyn Ctr., Minn., 1981-82; pastor Princeton (Minn.)-Spencer Brook United Meth. Parish, 1982—. Active various ecumenical and civic activities; pres. local sch. and hosp. adv. coms., local ministerial assoc. Home: 807 1st St Princeton MN 55371 Office: 112 N 7th Ave Princeton MN 55371

HARRIS, JOHN COLIN, religion educator; b. Atlanta, Feb. 22, 1943; s. John Holder and Lydia Lorene (Grogan) H.; m. Faye Marie Gardner, Aug. 1, 1964; children: John Michael, Laura Marie. BA, Mercer U., 1965; MDiv, Southeastern Bapt. Theol. Sem., 1968; PhD, Duke U., 1974. Instr. Meredith Coll., Raleigh, N.C., 1970-73; asst. prof. Christian edn. Southeastern Bapt. Theol. Sem., Wake Forest, N.C., 1973-77; assoc. prof. religion Mercer U., Atlanta, 1977-90, chmn. div. humanities, 1981-90; assoc. prof. religion Univ. Coll. Mercer U., Atlanta, 1990—; cons. and study leader regional chs., N.C. and Ga., 1970—. Author: (with others) Equipping of Disciples, 1978; contbr. articles to profl. jours. Home: 3028 Appling Dr Chamblee GA 30341 Office: Mercer Univ 3001 Mercer University Dr Atlanta GA 30341

HARRIS, JOSEPH EUGENE, SR., minister; b. New Orleans, Aug. 25, 1942; s. Robert Dwight and Pearl Gladys (Edwards) H.; m. Yvette MArie Tyler, Sept. 6, 1964; children: Joseph Eugene Jr., Roderick Dwain. BA, Oakwood Coll., 1964. Ordained to ministry Seventh-day Adventist Ch., 1972. Pastor Southwest Region Conf., Tex., Ark., La., Okla., 1966-76, South Atlantic Conf., Wilmington, N.C., Tallahassee, 1976-81; pastor Southwestern Conf., Tallahassee, St. Petersburg, 1981-83, St. Petersburg, 1983—; mem. exec. com., Southwestern Conf., Altamonte, Fla., 1980-85, pres., Cen. Ministry Assn., 1988-91; v.p., Internat. Ministrial Assn., St. petersburg, 1984—; sec., treas., Southeast Ministrial Assn., 1991—. Coun. mem. Retired Sr. Col. Program, St. petersburg, 1983-89; chmn. bd. dirs. Southern Christian Leadership Conf., St. Petersburg, 1988—. Mem. Nat. Christian Counselors Assn. Democrat. Home: 2516 Columbus Way S Saint Petersburg FL 33712 Office: Elim Seventh Day Adventist 801 6th Ave S Saint Petersburg FL 33701 *Do all the good you can, while you can, before you can't, and live as in the presence of a holy and loving Heavenly Father.*

HARRIS, JOSEPH HENRY, minister, educator; b. Laurel, Miss., Mar. 3, 1959; s. Joe and Loretta (Parker) H.; m. Shirley Fay Ball, Dec. 28, 1984. AA, Southeastern Bapt. Coll., 1983, BS, 1985; MA, Liberty U., 1990. Ordained to ministry Bapt. Missionary Assn. Am., 1986. Pastor Pinetucky Bapt. Ch., Picayune, Miss., 1986-87, Riverside Bapt. ch., Ellisville, Miss.,

1987-90; prof. Southeastern Bapt. Coll., Laurel, 1987—; pastor Corinth Bapt. Ch., Petal, Miss., 1991—; v.p. bd. dirs. Christian Food Mission, Laurel. Mem. Big Creek Bapt. Assn. (asst. moderator 1989-91), Assn. Christian Svc. Pers. Republican. Office: Southeastern Bapt Coll 4229 Hwy 15 N Laurel MS 39440

HARRIS, LLOYD DAVID, minister, educator, journalist; b. Wichita, Kans., Apr. 28, 1940; s. Lloyd Keener and Mable Ruth (Gurwell) H.; m. Gertrude Eleanor Flothmeier, Apr. 2, 1967. BA, Lebanon Valley Coll., 1962; M in Liberal Studies, U. Okla., 1984; PhD, U. Kans., 1986; D of Ministry, Grad. Theol. Foun., Notre Dame, Ind., 1988. Lic. to ministry Evang. United Brethren Ch., 1961. Intern 1st Evang. United Brethren Ch., Cedar Falls, Iowa, summer 1959; asst. pastor 1st Evang. United Brethren Ch., Stillwater, Okla., 1959-60; pastor Grace Evang. United Brethren Ch., Steelton, Pa., 1960-61, Oak Grove Evang. United Brethren Ch. and Zion Federated Ch., Winterset, Iowa, 1961-62, Emanuel Evang. United Brethren Ch., Phila., 1962-65, Salem Evang. United Brethren Ch., Jersey City, 1965-67; interim pastor various Evang. United Brethren chs., Pa., 1967-68; pastor Manada Hill Evang. United Brethren Ch., Harrisburg, Pa., 1968-69; asst. rector Christ Episcopal Ch., Somerville, Mass., 1969-70; pastor Otterbein United Meth. Ch., Dover, Pa., 1970-74; assoc. pastor Capitol Hill United Meth. Ch., Washington, 1974-76; pastor Furley and Greenwich United Meth. Chs., Wichita, 1981-83; mem. pastoral staff Calvary United Meth. ch., Pitts., 1988—; prof. speech communication and theatre Clarion U. Pa., Pitts., 1987—; bd. dirs. The Circus Kingdom, United Meth. Ch., 1973—; instr. Police Dept., Topeka, 1984-85. Author: Sod Jerusalems: Jewish Agricultural Communities on the Kansas Frontier, 1984; contbr. articles to profl. jours. and chpts. to books; mem. World Symphony Orch., 1970. Bd. dirs. Wichita Hist. Landmark Preservation Com., 1980-84; Penn Circle Sch., Pitts., 1985-87, Goodwill Industries Inc., Pitts.,1991—; chmn. bd. publs. Washburn U., Topeka, 1984-85; mem. acad. coun. Point Park Coll., Pitts., 1985-88. Recipient 1st Pl. award Pa. Newspaper Pubs. Assn., 1969, 1st Pl. award Am. Scholastic Press Assn., 1984, Contbn. to French-Can. History award La Societe Canadienne-Francaise du Minnesota, 1987; Nat. Endowment for Arts grantee, 1975, 76; Pitts. Communications Found. grantee, 1986, Ernest Hillman Found., Pitts. grantee, 1988. Mem. Am. Acad. Religion, Religion and Intellectual Life, Soc. Bibl. Lit., Am. Journalism History Assn. (presentor nat. conv. 1986), Assn. for Edn. in Journalism and Mass Communication, Nat. Assn. Investigative Reporters and Editors, Radio-TV News Dirs. Assn., Music Critics Assn., Am. Studies Assn. (presentor nat. conv. 1986), Oral History Assn. (presentor nat. conv. 1987), Radical History Assn., Speech Communication Assn., Soc. Profl. Journalists (officer Kans. chpt. 1980-81, del. nat. conv. 1981, 84), Phi Mu Alpha. Home and Office: 951 Perry Hwy # 103 Pittsburgh PA 15237

HARRIS, MARK HUGH, priest; b. Union, S.C., Feb. 11, 1932; s. William Ernest and Iris Levonia (Craig) H.; m. Marilyn Marie Sarty, June 8, 1934; children: David Steven, Mark Elliot, Craig Matthew. BS, UCLA, 1959; diploma in theology, Oxford (Eng.) U., 1964; MDiv, Mt. Angel (Oreg.) Sem., 1976. Ordained priest, Episcopal Ch. Tchr., counselor L.A. City Schs., 1959-63; parish priest St. Cyprian's Anglican Cathedral, Kimberley, S. Africa, 1965-68; tchr. All Saints' Episcopal Sch., Carmel, Calif., 1968-69; social worker Monterey County, Monterey, Calif., 1969-73; chaplain Good Samaritan Hosp., Corvallis, Oreg., 1973-79, Arlington (Va.) Hosp., 1979—. With U.S. Navy, 1951-55, Korea. Fellow Coll. Chaplains. Democrat. Avocation: painting. Home: 10300 Bushman Dr Oakton VA 22124 Office: Arlington Hosp 1701 N George Mason Dr Arlington VA 22205

HARRIS, MARTHA ANN, lay worker; b. Elkhart, Ind., Feb. 26, 1946; d. Robert Eugene and Ruth Lillian (Lynn) H. Diploma, Moody Bible Inst., 1967. Cert. Evang. tchr. Sec., adminstrv. asst. to sr. pastor Cascades Bapt. Ch., Jackson, Mich., 1974—; mem., sec. Missionary co, 1980-91, toddler age Sunday Sch. tchr., 1977-91 Cascades Bapt. Ch. Asst. leader Lifeline Club for Girls, Elkhart, 1969-74. Republican. Home: 1608 Maguire Jackson MI 49202-3640 Office: Cascades Bapt Ch 1012 W High St Jackson MI 49203-2838 *I have discovered that life goes much more smoothly when I focus on serving others, rather than being served. I am thankful for the training I've had which has taught me Biblical principles to live by. "And He (the Lord) shall be the stability of your times. A wealth of salvation, wisdom, and knowledge. The fear of the LORD is his treasure." (Isa. 33:6).*

HARRIS, MATTIE PEARLE, minister, small business owner; b. Whatley, Ala., Aug. 29, 1938; d. John Emanuel and Annie Lou (Creighton) Raine; m. Felton Harris, July 24, 1978; children: Rhonda, Ethan, Quintin, Damita, Eucy-Ella, Feltonia. BS, Ala. State U., 1959; postgrad., U. Ala., 1966, Troy State U., 1978. Cert. secondary tchr., activity program specialist. Ala., N.Y.; lic. to ministry African Meth. Episcopal Ch., 1988. Min. African Meth. Episcopal Ch., Bklyn., 1985-87, Richmond, Va., 1987-88, Whatley, 1988—; chaplain African Meth. Episcopal Ch., Selma, Ala.; tchr. bible Wayman Chapel African Meth. Episcopal Ch., Whatley, 1988—; pres. Community Help Club, Whatley, 1991—; dir. Light a Candle Ministry, Whatley, 1988—, Madye's 2d Time Around, Whatley, 1990—; notary pub., Whatley, 1991—. Author: (song) Don't Wait Too Late, 1987; author short stories and play. Mem. NAACP, Grove Hill, Ala., 1991, Nat. Coun. Negro Women, Bklyn., 1971-87, Neighborhood Organized Workers, Whatley, 1991. Ala. State U. scholar, 1957; grad. grantee NSF, 1963, 66, Ford Found, 1969. Democrat. Home and Office: PO Box 104 Whatley AL 36482

HARRIS, MICHAEL DALE, clergyman; b. Pontiac, Mich., Jan. 31, 1963; s. Donald Eugene and Linda Beth (Mendham) H.; m. Elizabeth Ann Poole, Jun. 22, 1985; children: Caroline Nicole, Kristen Marie. BA in Pastoral Theol., Bob Jones U., 1989. Ordained to ministry. Asst. pastor Faith Missionary Bapt. Ch., Reidville, S.C., 1986-89, First Bapt. Ch., South Point, Ohio, 1990—; Sun. Sch. Dir. First Bapt. Ch., South Point, Oh., 1990-. Author various articles. Republican. Baptist. Home: 115 Meadow Ln South Point OH 45680 Office: First Baptist Church 101 Solida Rd PO Box 5 South Point OH 45680

HARRIS, NICK A., religious education director; b. Lubbock, Tex., Nov. 23, 1952; s. J.L. and N.J. (Brock) H.; m. Jana Lynn Taliaferro, Mar. 24, 1974; children: Kelli June, Jodi Lynn. BA, Tex. Tech U., 1975; MS, Abilene Christian U., 1978. Ordained to ministry Ch. of Christ, 1978. Regional sales dir. Ednl. Mktg. Svcs., Lubbock, 1975-76; missionary Chs. of Christ, Zambia, 1978-79; dir. campus ministries Chs. of Christ, Kingsville, Tex., San Angelo, Tex., 1979-83; mgr. gen. Presto Photo of San Angelo, 1983-85; fin. cons. Merrill Lynch, Lubbock, 1985-87; fin. cons., mgr. Integrated Resources Equity Corp., Lubbock, 1987-89; dir. campus ministry Christian Student Ctr., Emporia, Kans., 1989—; chaplain Meth. Hosp., Lubbock, 1988-89; pastoral counselor Hospice of Lubbock, 1988-89; pub. speaker Merrill Lynch, Lubbock, 1985-87; instr., counselor Okla. Christian U., Emporia, 1989—. Mem. Kans. Right to Life, Emporia, 1990. Mem. Nat. Christian Counselors Assn. (assoc.), Emporia State U. Religious Advisors Assn. Avocations: golf, hunting, reading. Office: CSC 1503 Merchant Emporia KS 66801 *When I finally learn to give up control of my life, then I'll be confident I can appreciate heaven.*

HARRIS, RANDY JAMES, youth services administrator; b. Winchendon, Mass., Nov. 18, 1964; s. Jerry Harlow and Priscilla Ann (Abare) H. Student, Quinsigamond Community Coll., Worcester. Youth dir. Cornerstone Assembly of God, Winchendon, 1989—; mortgage cons., loan officer Worcester (Mass.) County Instn. for Savs., 1991. Republican. Home: 6 Fessenden St Baldwinville MA 01436 Office: Worcester County Instn Savs 365 Main St Worcester MA 01608 *One of the most tragic tendencies of the human spirit is to only react to external stimuli. Only after we begin to actively enforce our ethical and moral agenda on this reactive world will we see encouraging and positive change.*

HARRIS, R(ANSOM) BAINE, philosophy educator, association executive; b. Hudson, N.C., June 5, 1927; s. Ransom Z. and Hettie L. (Crouch) H.; m. Ettie Jeanne Johnson, June 8, 1958; 2 children. A.A., Mars Hill Coll., 1946; B.A., U. Richmond, 1948, M.A., 1954; B.D., So. Baptist Theol. Sem., 1951; M.A., Emory U., 1960; Ph.D., Temple U., 1971. Instr. philosophy U. Richmond (Va.) 1953-54; instr. philosophy and social scis. Ga. Inst. Tech., 1956-60; prof. philosophy, chmn. Frederick Coll., 1960-65; asst. prof. Clemson U., 1965-70; prof., chmn. Eastern Ky. U., 1970-73; prof. Old Dominion U., Norfolk, Va., 1973—, chmn., 1973-79, eminent prof., 1981—; organizer, dir. nat. and internat. confs.; dir., host TV series. Grantee Eli Lilly Found., 1971, Dept. State, 1974-75. Mem. Am. Philos. Assn., Va. Philos. Assn., Hellenic Soc. Philos. Studies, Indian Philos. Soc., Metaphys. Soc. Am., Internat. Soc. for Neoplatonic Studies (founder, exec. dir. 1973—), So. Soc. Philosophy and Psychology, Soc. Philosophy of Religion, Soc. Study History of Philosophy. Democrat. Editor: Authority: A Philosophical Analysis, 1976; The Significance of Neoplatonism, 1976; Neoplatonism and Indian Thought, 1981, The Structure of Being: A Neoplatonic Approach, 1981; gen. editor: (series) Studies in Neoplatonism: Ancient and Modern; contbr. articles to profl. jours. Home: 4037 Windymille Dr Portsmouth VA 23703 Office: Old Dominion U Dept Philosophy Norfolk VA 23529

HARRIS, ROBERT LAIRD, minister, theology educator emeritus; b. Brownsburg, Pa., Mar. 10, 1911; s. Walter William and Ella Pearl (Graves) H.; m. Elizabeth Krugar Nelson, Sept. 11, 1937 (dec. 1980); children: Grace Sears, Allegra Smick, Robert Laird; m. Anne Paxson Krauss, Aug. 1, 1981. B.S. in Chem. Engring, U. Del., Newark, 1931; postgrad, Washington U., 1931-32; Th.B., Westminster Theol. Sem., 1935, Th.M., 1937; M.A. in Oriental Studies, U. Pa., 1941; Ph.D., Dropsie Coll., 1947. Ordained to ministry Presbyn. Ch. Am., 1936; instr. Faith Theol. Sem., Phila., 1937-43, asst. prof. Bibl. Exegesis, 1943-47, prof. Bibl. Exegesis, 1947-56; prof. Covenant Theol. Sem., St. Louis, 1956-81, dean, 1964-71, prof. emeritus, 1981—; vis. lectr. Wheaton Coll., Ill., 1957-61; prof. Winona Lake Summer Sch. of Theology, 1964, 66, 67, Near East Sch. Archaeology and Bible, Jerusalem, 1962; lectr. Japan, Korea, 1965, India, 1981, Australia, 1989; vis. prof. China Grad. Sch. Theology, Hong Kong, 1981, Freie Theologische Akademie, Giessen, Fed. Republic Germany, 1982-85, Tyndale Theol. Sem., Amsterdam, The Netherlands, 1986—; moderator Presbyn. Ch. in Am., 1982. Author: Introductory Hebrew Grammar, 1950, Inspiration and Canonicity of the Bible, 1957, Man-God's Eternal Creation, 1971, You and Your Bible, 1990; editor: Theological Wordbook of the Old Testament, 2 vols., 1981, Leviticus, Vol. 2, 1990; mem. editorial bd. New Internat. Version of Bible, 1965—, chmn., 1970-74; contbg. author various books. DuPont fellow U. Del., 1930-31; recipient first prize Zondervan Textbook Contest, 1955; Foxwell Lecture lectureship Tokyo Christian Theol. Sem., 1981. Mem. Soc. Bibl. Lit. and Exegesis, Am. Sch. Oriental Research, Evang. Theol. Soc. (pres. 1961), Tau Beta Pi, Phi Kappa Phi. Republican. Home: 9 Homewood Rd Wilmington DE 19803 *In my ministry of over 50 years I have seen a distressing erosion of national morals and decency. But there has also been a counter-resurgence of evangelical faith. As part of this movement, I am gratified to have had a part in producing the New International Version of Bible.*

HARRIS, RONALD CONRAD, minister, pharmacist; b. Itawamba County, Miss., Oct. 9, 1950; s. Conrad White and Lorene (Underwood) H.; m. Margaret Ann Oliver, Nov. 14, 1969; children: Ronald Mark, Angela Rena. BS in Pharmacy, U. Miss., 1973; MDiv, Southwestern Bapt. Theol. Sem., 1986. Ordained to ministry So. Bapt. Conv., 1978. Bivocat. pastor South Crossroads Bapt. Ch., Tishomingo, Miss.; interim pastor Wheeler Grove Bapt. Ch., Biggersville/Corinth, Miss.; pastor Trinity Bapt. Ch., Michie, Tenn.; bivocat. pastor Shiloh Bapt. Ch., Mantachie, Miss., 1989—; pharmacist, mgr. #391 Wal-Mart Stores Inc., Tupelo, Miss., 1988—; associational youth dir. Alcorn Bapt. Assn., Corinth, 1978, Itawamba Bapt. Assn., Fulton, Miss., 1990. Mem. Miss. Pharmacist Assn. (student liaison com. 1987). Republican. Home: 931 Lake Dr # 7H Brandon MS 39042 Office: Shiloh Bapt Ch PO Box 217 Mantachie MS 38855 also: Wal-Mart Pharmacy 2603 W Main St Tupelo MS 38809

HARRIS, RYLAND MICHAEL, clergyman; b. Durham, N.C., Mar. 14, 1952; s. Ryland Pett and Emogene (Gravett) H.; m. Wanda Bagbey, Aug. 15, 1971; children—Bryan Allen, Heather Lynn. B.A., Campbell Coll., 1974; M.Religious Edn., Southeastern Bapt. Theol. Sem., 1977. Ordained to ministry, Bapt. Ch., 1976. Assoc. pastor Tabernacle Bapt. Ch., Raleigh, 1985-88; pastor Greystone Bapt. Ch. Asheboro, N.C., 1988—; minister of edn. and youth First Bapt. Ch., Aberdeen, N.C., 1976-79; minister of edn. Emmanuel Bapt. Ch., Raleigh, 1980-85; Sun. sch. ch. cons. So. Bapt. Conv., Nashville, 1985—, Bapt. State Conv., Raleigh, 1976—, com. on coop. ministries with gen. bapt., 1986—; mem. mission, ministry commn. Raleigh Bapt. Assn., 1987—, chmn. family, social issues com.; sr. adult cons., 1985-88. Author: Depth Study of New Hope Baptist Church, Raleigh, 1974. Democrat. Lodge: Optimist (newsletter editor 1985—, chaplain 1984), Masons. Home: 863 Greystone Rd Asheboro NC 27203 Office: Greystone Bapt Ch PO Box 2411 Asheboro NC 27203

HARRIS, SIDNEY LEWIS, minister, sociology educator; b. Miles, Tex., Feb. 6, 1927; s. Samuel Lee and Bertha Jewell (Johnson) H.; m. Fleta Nell Lindley, June 22, 1948; children—Emily Ann, Donna Carol, Paula Karen. BA, Howard Payne Coll., 1948; MDiv, Southwest Bapt. Theol. Sem., 1952; MA, Sam Houston State Tchrs. Coll., 1961; D Arts, Western Colo. U., 1976. Ordained to ministry Baptist Ch., 1945. Pastor, Joshua and Austin, Tex., 1945-53; student dir., Bible tchr. Sam Houston State U., Huntsville, 1953-59; Tex. Tech. U., Lubbock, 1959-65; dean of students, instr. sociology Wayland Coll., Plainview, Tex., 1965-67; adminstrn. cons. Bapt. Sunday Sch. Bd., Nashville, 1967-68; counselor, assoc. prof. Tarrant County Jr. Coll., Fort Worth, 1968-77; pres. Clarke Coll., Newton, Miss., 1977-79; v.p. student affairs Howard Payne U., Brownwood, Tex., 1979-80, dean sch. social scis., 1980-84; assoc. pastor, counselor First Baptist Ch., Brownwood, 1984—; trustee Western Colo. U., Grand Junction, 1977-78, adv. bd., 1977-84; dir. Fort Worth Literacy Council, 1971-73. Author: Leadership Unlimited, 1969; Leadership Improvement Plan, 1968. Contbr. articles to profl. jours., chpts. to books. Mem. Mayor's Adv. Com. on Youth, Hurst, Tex., 1970-71; active in ch. and civic groups. Mem. Tex. Council on Family Relations, So. Bapt. Assn. Ministries with the Aging, So. Bapt. Family Life Ministries Assn., Tex. Bapt. Family Life Ministers Assn., Am. Christian Counselors Assn. Democrat. Avocation: travel. *To encourage the down-hearted, comfort the broken-hearted, and challenge the stout-hearted to achieve their God-given potential is the highest calling to which one can respond.*

HARRIS, STEPHEN DIRK, minister; b. Cambridge, Mass., Nov. 25, 1938; s. Samuel Ward Jr. and Bernice Howard (Lester) H.; m. Rebecca Caroline Barham, Feb. 24, 1968; children: Heather, Deanna. BS in Edn., Northeastern U., 1963; MDiv, Va. Theol. Sem., 1969, postgrad., 1973-74; D Ministry, Sch. Theology, U. South, 1987. Ordained to ministry Episcopal Ch. as deacon, 1969, as elder, 1970. Chaplain intern St. Elizabeths Hosp., Washington, 1972-73; chaplain, cons. NIH, Bethesda, Md., 1973-74; assoc. rector Ch. Good Shepherd, Raleigh, N.C., 1974-84; rector Christ Episcopal Ch., Binghamton, N.Y., 1984-86, St. Mary's Episcopal Ch., Waynesboro, Pa., 1987—; pres. Waynesboro Area Fellowship Chs., 1991—; convenor Waynesboro Area Ministerium, 1989-90; mem. Diocesan Coun., Harrisburg, 1988-91, chmn. worship commn., 1988-91; part-time interim rector Calvary Chapel, Beartown, Ch. Transfiguration, Blue Ridge Summit, Pa., 1990-91; part-time Protestant campus chaplain, Mont Alto Campus, Pa. State U., 1989—, part-time lectr., 1988-89. Pres. Tammy Lynn Found., Raleigh, 1979-81; chair Downtown Forum, Binghamton, 1985; vice-chairperson Mental Health/Mental Retardation Adv. Bd., Franklin County, Pa., 1989—; coord. Waynesboro Area CROP Walk, 1989, 90. 1st lt. U.S. Army, 1964-66. Mem. Hist. Soc. Episcopal Ch., Episcopal Peace Fellowship. Home: 11791 Dellwood Dr Waynesboro PA 17268 Office: St Mary's Episcopal Ch 112 E Second St Waynesboro PA 17268 *The role for the Church in the coming decade is to seek to discern and speak the mind of Christ rather than to be a mere reflector and endorser of our own culture. The call to be faithful is the struggle for any age.*

HARRIS, STEVE ROBERT, music minister; b. San Jose, Calif., Nov. 10, 1965; s. Robert Eugene and Patricia Ann (Clark) H. BS in Managerial Econs., U. Calif., Davis, 1987; MDiv, Golden Gate Sem., 1991. Acctg. specialist Apple Computer, Inc., Cupertino, Calif., 1985; credit specialist Apple Computer, Inc., Sunnyvale, Calif., 1986; teaching asst. U. Calif., Davis, 1987; profl. musicianChristian group Surrender, Davis, 1987-89; youth min. First So. Bapt. Ch., Davis, 1988-89, min. of music, 1990—; chmn. worship com. First So. Bapt. Ch., Davis, 1990; song leader neighborhood Bible study, Davis, 1989—. Composer, lyricist various songs. Avocations: composing and performing music, writing, reading. Home: 789 Solito Ct San Jose CA 95123 Office: 770 Pole Line Rd Davis CA 95616

HARRIS, W. L., bishop. Bishop Ch. of God in Christ, Detroit. Office: Ch of God in Christ 1834 Outer Dr Detroit MI 48234*

HARRIS, W(ALTON) BRYAN, minister; b. Clovis, N.Mex., Aug. 17, 1949; s. Bill and Renafaye (Reagan) H.; m. Rebecca Faye Hunt, May 26, 1972; children: Aleesa Faye, Amy Brianna, Adam Bryan, Anna Rebecca. BA, East Tex. Bapt. Coll., 1973. Cert. tchr., Tex.; ordained to Ministry Bapt. Ch., 1976. Minister of music and youth 1st Bapt. Ch., Vivian, La., 1971-73; tchr. English and Spanish Chapel Hill High Sch., New Chapel Hill, Tex., 1973-75; minister to youth Friendly Bapt. Ch., Tyler, Tex., 1973-75, Calvary Bapt. Ch., Longview, Tex., 1975-77; minister to youth 1st Bapt. Ch., Columbus, Miss., 1977-85, Texas City, Tex., 1985-87, Charlotte, N.C., 1987—; crusade preacher, Eng., 1986, Argentina, 1985, India, 1988; cons. Nat. Youth Evangelism Conf., Jackson, Miss., 1981. Author devotional guide: Youth Church Training Curriculum. Named to Outstanding Young Men Am., 1978, 81. Mem. Miss. Bapt. Religious Edn. Assn. (v.p. 1985), N.C. Bapt. Religious Educators, So. Bapt. Conf. Youth Ministers Orgn., Kiwanis. Republican.

HARRIS, WARDELL WELDON, minister; b. Madison, Ark., May 26, 1941; s. Oze Jr. and Mary E. (McDonald) H.; m. Ora Lee Davis, Oct. 5, 1963; children: Coral A., Steven C. Student, Philandes-Smich Coll., 1961, Grace Christian Coll., 1975, Moody Bible Inst., 1982, Ashland Sem., 1985. Ordained to ministry Ch. of God in Christ, 1982. Supr. Orange Sch. Dist., Cleve., 1964—; asst. pastor Jonas Temple Ch. of God in Christ, Cleve., 1978—; pastor-founder Harvard Ave. Ch. of God in Christ, Cleve., 1986—; mem. state ordination bd. Ch. of God in Christ, 1985—, state asst. dean seminars, 1987—, mem. gen. assembly, 1984, elders coun., 1984; dean State Sunday Sch., Cleve., 1975—. Pres. Street Club, Warrensville Heights, 1978; mem. Warrensville Heights Band Boosters, 1980. Home and Office: 23307 Felch St Warrensville Heights OH 44128 *We spend a lifetime on unimportant things and forget things that matter most. Happiness comes from within; you choose to be happy or sad. The choice is yours.*

HARRIS, WILLIAM DAVID, minister; b. Ft. Worth, Aug. 12, 1954; s. W.J. and Louise (Singley) H.; m. Phoebe D. Younger, Dec. 29, 1979; children: Joy, Marie, William David Jr., Ryan. BA in Speech, U. Ark., Little Rock, 1976; MDiv, Southwestern Bapt. Theol. Sem., Ft. Worth, 1980; DMin, Midwestern Bapt. Theol. Sem., Kansas City, Mo., 1990—. Ordained to ministry So. Bapt. Conv., 1980. Assoc. pastor for youth and music 1st Bapt. Ch., Bogata, Tex., 1979-81; pastor Shady Grove Bapt Ch., Kennett, Mo., 1981-83, Morton Bapt. Ch., McCrory, Ark., 1983-85, Antioch Bapt. Ch., Royal, Ark., 1985—. Contbr. articles to profl. jours. Democrat. Home: 3305 Sunshine Rd Royal AR 71968 Office: Antioch Bapt Ch 3212 Sunshine Rd Royal AR 71968

HARRIS, WILLIAM OWEN, minister, archivist; b. Petersburg, Ind., Oct. 9, 1929; s. Owen Dillon and Clara Catherine (Heldt). BA, Davidson Coll., 1951; MDiv, Princeton Sem., 1954, ThM, 1958; MLS, Ind. U., 1976. Ordained to ministry Presbyn. Ch., 1954. Chaplain USN, 1954-57; asst. pastor Presbyn. Ch., Kensington, Md., 1958-61; pastor Covenant Presbyn. Ch., St. Petersburg, Fla., 1961-67; asst. pastor 1st Presbyn. Ch., Phila., 1967-75; libr. Christian Theol. Sem., Indpls., 1976-80, Ind. State Libr., Indpls., 1980-86; archivist Princeton Sem. Libr., Princeton, N.J., 1986—. Lt. USN, 1954-57. Office: Princeton Sem Libr PO Box 111 Princeton NJ 08540

HARRIS, WILLIE GRAY, JR., religious educator; b. Carthage, N.C., May 25, 1945; s. Willie Gray and Fonnie Ann (Blake) H.; m. Joyce Louise Shipley, Mar. 24, 1948; 1 child, Heather. BA, High Point Coll., 1967; MDiv, Southeastern Bapt. Theol. Seminary, 1967-70, ThM, 1972. Mem. faculty Sandhills Community Coll., Carthage, N.C., 1972—, prof. religion, 1975—; asst. area supr. Tel Batash Archael. Excavation, Israel, 1978, 79, 83. Recipient Hays-Fulbright award U.S. Dept. Edn., 1980; Nat. Endowment Humanities Summer Seminar award Rutgers U., 1982. Mem. Soc. Bibl. Lit., Am. Acad. Religion, Community Coll. Humanities Assn., Bibl. Archeology Soc., N.C. Family Life Council. Republican. Baptist. Home: Route 2 Box 48 West End NC 27376 Office: Route 3 Box 182-C (TC-5) Carthage NC 28327

HARRISON, ALICE WILLIS, librarian; b. Milliken, Colo., Jan. 8, 1929; d. Edward S. and Alice (O'Brian) Willis; m. John Clement Harrison, Aug. 25, 1960; children: Margaret Alice, Janet Agnes. BS in Edn., Northwestern U., 1951; MLS, U. Ill., 1956; MTS, AST, Halifax, 1982. Head librarian Atlantic Sch. Theology, Halifax, N.S., 1978—; elder St. Andrew's United Ch., Halifax, 1978-88, presbyter, 1978-90; presbytery rep. Maritime Conf. of United Ch. of Can., Sackville, 1982-90; mem. Christian edn. com. St. Andrus Ch. Mem. pastoral care adv. com. V.G. Hosp., Halifax, 1990—. Alta. Letts travelling fellow, 1976; Jamaica Govt. Archives grantee, 1977; recipient Halifax Libr. Assn. Disting. Svc. award, 1979. Mem. Can. Libr. Assn., Atlantic Provinces Libr. Assn., N.S. Libr. Assn., Assn. Can. Archivists, Am. and Can. Theol. Libr. Assn., Halifax Libr. Assn., Halifax/Dartmouth Coun. Chs., Dalhousie/King's Reading Club, Epoch Reading Club, AAULC. Office: Atlantic Sch Theology Libr, 640 Francklyn St, Halifax, NS Canada B3H 3B5

HARRISON, CATHERINE LOUISE RICE, minister; b. Atchison, Kans., Sept. 18, 1945; d. Jack Byers and Bettie Catherine (Wilson) Rice; m. Shannon Marshall Harrison, July 17, 1970. BA, St. Martin's Coll., 1978; MDiv, Austin Presbyn. Theol. Sem., Austin, Tex., 1982. Ordained to ministry Presbyn. Ch., 1983. Student pastor Hyde Park Presbyn. Ch., Austin, 1975-76, 79-81; crisis counselor Ministry with Svc. People, Tacoma, 1976-79; pastor Tillicum (Wash.) Community Presbyn. Ch., 1983; stewardship cons. Western Kenya Presbytery, Eldoret, 1983-85; founding pastor Busia (Kenya) Presbyn. Ch., 1985; pastor Alupe (Kenya) Anglican Ch., 1983-85; minister for youth and fellowship New Hope Presbyn. Ch., Castle Rock, Colo., 1988-91; vol. chaplain Brooke A.M.C., San Antonio, 1976, Madigan A.M.C., Tacoma, 1977-79, 1981-83, Walter Reed Army Med. Ctr., Washington, 1980, Fitzsimons Army Med. Ctr., Aurora, Colo., 1985-86; mem. Denver Presbytery HIV Com., 1990—. Mem. Choristers Guild, Garland, Tex., 1990—. Named Vol. of Yr. State of Wash., 1983. Mem. Hi-Country Basenji Club (Colo.-Wyo., pres. 1988-90). Home: 16-1 Halloran Cir FAMC Aurora CO 80045 *In my life I am prompted to observe that preoccupation with materialism and technology in the Western world equates to a perception that God is alive and sustains us in one world and God is dead since God cannot be purchased, owned or put on display. Perhaps this is why I choose the life of the professional volunteer. I pray others will join the volunteer movement.*

HARRISON, DANIEL EDWARD, minister; b. Montgomery, Ala., Apr. 26, 1955; s. Charles Winford and Joyce Hilda (Gibbs) H.; m. Jeri Ann Baty, Sept. 8, 1979; children: Joy Elizabeth, Timothy Daniel. AS, Walker Coll., Jasper, Ala., 1978; BS, U. Ala., Tuscaloosa, 1980; MDiv, So. Bapt. Seminary, Louisville, 1983. Pastor Concord Bapt. Ch., Headland, Ala., 1983-88, 1st Bapt. Ch., Florala, Ala., 1988-90; chaplain U.S. Army, 1990—. Author: (newspaper column) Pastor's Pulpit, 1986-87. Mem. Henry County Humanitarian Resources Com., Abbeville, Ala., 1984-86. Mem. Judson Bapt. Assn. (pastor's conf., bd. dirs., royal amb.'s com. 1985—, vice moderator 1987—), Florala Area Ministerial Assn. (pres. 1988-90), Covington Bapt. Assn. (chmn. ch. minister rels. com.). Home: 4510-1 Wofford St Fort Riley KS 66442 Office: HHD 201 FSB Fort Riley KS 66442

HARRISON, DOYLE, minister, publishing executive; b. Highlands, Tex., Sept. 21, 1939; s. Ernest Doyle and Erble Daisy (Logsdon) H.; m. Patsy Guylene Hagin, Oct. 25, 1958; children: Canadas Jackson, Cookie Brothers, Damon. BBA, Golden State U., L.A., 1980, MBA, 1981, PhD, 1982; DDiv, Ind. Christian U., 1983; DHL, Bethel Christian Coll., Riverside, Calif., 1983. Dir. music and youth Mpls. Evang. Auditorium, 1964-66; bus. mgr. Kenneth Hagin Ministries, Broken Arrow, Okla., 1966-76; traveling minister Buddy Harrison Ministries, Tulsa, 1976-78; founder, pres. Faith Christian Fellowship, Tulsa, 1978—; pres., founder Harrison House Pub., Tulsa, 1975—; rep. Network Christian Ministries, New Orleans, 1985—; bd. dirs. Charismatic Bible Ministries, Tulsa. Author: Understanding Authority, (with others) County It All Joy; editor: New Concept mag., Communique mag. Mem. Rep. Presdl. Task Force, Washington. Recipient Cert. of Achievement, Robert H. Schuller Ins., 1983. Mem. Internat. Conv. Faith Chs. Avocations: stamp and coin collecting. Office: Faith Christian Fellowship 725 E 36th St N Tulsa OK 74106

HARRISON, FRANK J., bishop; b. Syracuse, N.Y., Aug. 12, 1912. Ed., Notre Dame U., St. Bernard's Sem. Ordained priest Roman Catholic Ch., 1937; apptd. titular bishop of Aquae in, Numidia; and aux. bishop of Syracuse, 1971-76, appt. bishop of, 1976; installed, 1977—. Office: PO Box 511 Syracuse NY 13201

HARRISON, H(AROLD) DONALD, priest, educator; b. Atlanta, Aug. 1, 1935; s. Harold Oliver and Hazel Katherine (Kronk) H.; m. Joan A. Bailey, June 13, 1959 (div. June 1971); children: Catherine Elaine, Michael T.; m. Barbara A. Young, Sept. 15, 1985. BA, Emory U., 1957; MDiv, U. of South, 1960; M Govt. Adminstrn., Ga. State U., 1975. Ordained priest Episcopal Ch., 1960. Rector St. Margaret's Ch., Carrollton, Ga., 1960-65, St. Dunstan's Ch., Atlanta, 1965-69; assoc. rector Atonement Ch., Atlanta, 1971-77, St. Bede's Ch., Atlanta, 1977-84; rector St. Joseph's Episcopal Ch., McDonough, Ga., 1986—; chaplain, prof. history West Ga. Coll., 1960-65; mem. exec. bd. Diocese of Atlanta, 1965-68; bd. dirs. Holy Innocents Sch., Atlanta, 1967-70; mem. adj. faculty DeKalb Community Coll., 1972-77, Mercer U., Atlanta, 1979—, Emory U., Atlanta, 1986; cons. Progressive Devel. Corp., Conyers, Ga., 1991; sr. health adminstr. region IV USPHS, 1969-90. Author: Church and Race, 1965. Office: St Joseph's Episcopal Ch 1865 Hwy 20 E McDonough GA 30253

HARRISON, JOHN PHILIP, minister; b. Covington, Ky., Apr. 28, 1949; s. Charles Philip and Thelma Petty (Sheldon) H.; m. Jenny Gastrich, July 6, 1973; children: John Philip, Amy Renea. Student, Cedarville (Ohio) Coll., 1972. Youth minister First Bapt. Ch., New Richmond, Ohio, 1971-72, asst. pastor, 1972-77, assoc. pastor, 1977-86, pastor, 1986—; organist, staff E.C. Nunne Home, New Richmond, 1971—; chaplain New Richmond, Fire, Police, 1976—, Ohio Firemen's Assn., 1988—, others. Firefighter New Richmond Fire Dept., 1976— (Fireman of the Yr. 1989); mem. New Richmond Life Squad, 1978—.

HARRISON, PAUL MANSFIELD, educator, minister; b. Phila., May 7, 1923; s. Robert Leslie and Ruth (Boyd) H.; m. Nancy Jane Romig, Sept. 11, 1948; children—Cynthia Lee, John Robert. B.A., Pa. State U., 1949; B.D., Colgate-Rochester Div. Sch., 1952; Ph.D., Yale, 1958. Ordained to ministry Am. Baptist Conv., 1952. Instr., then asst. prof. religion Princeton U., 1956-63; vis. lectr. Union Theol. Sem., N.Y.C., 1961-62; lectr. Inst. Religious and Social Studies, Jewish Theol. Sem. Am., 1961-66; mem. faculty Pa. State U., 1963-88, prof. sociology of religion and religious ethics, 1971-88, prof. emeritus, 1988—; rsch. dir. study theol. edn. United Ch. Christ, 1966-67. Author: Authority and Power in the Free Church Tradition, 2d edit., 1971. Melcancthon W. Jacobus instr. Princeton, 1958-60; Proctor Gamble fellow, 1961-62; Enoch Pond lectr. Bangor (Maine) Theol. Sem., 1969. Mem. Am. Sociol. Assn., Soc. Sci. Study Religion, Am. Soc. Christian Social Ethics Profs., New Haven Theol. Discussion Group, N. Central Assn. Colls. and Secondary Schs. Office: 1016 Liberal Arts Tower University Park PA 16802

HARRISON, PEYTON BLANCHARD, JR., minister; b. Chgo., Jan. 28, 1956; s. Peyton Blanchard Sr. and Bernice (Walker) H.; m. Jerri Elise Bender, July 18, 1981; 1 child, Brandon Blanchard. BA, Northeastern Ill. U., 1977. Itinerant deacon A.M.E. Ch., Chgo., 1982, itinerant elder, 1984; trustee, cons. Child Svcs. Lake Bluff Homes for Children, Chgo., 1986-87. Contbr. articles to profl. jours. Cons. Citizens Against Crime, Chgo., 1978-80; staff mem. Operation Challenge for Rehab. of Ex-Offenders, Chgo., 1978-80, Dem. Orgn. Twin Falls campaign, Chgo., 1988-89. Named one of Outstanding Young Man of Am., Jaycees, 1989, 90. Mem. NAIAC, Ill. Drug Edn. Alliance. Avocations: travel, reading, wind surfing, community work. Home: 1555 Dewey Ave Evanston IL 60201 Office: Wayman AME Ch 509 W Elm St Chicago IL 60610

HARRISON, RICHARD DEAN, minister; b. Gaffney, S.C., Oct. 15, 1952; s. Wiley H. and Georgia Ann (Earwood) H.; m. Sandra Kay Parris, Oct. 16, 1970; children: Kathryn Hope, Richard Dean Jr. BA, U. S.C., 1973, MAT, 1975; MDiv, So. Bapt. Theol. Sem., 1986, DMin, 1990. Ordained to ministry So. Bapt. Conv., 1985. Pastor English Bapt. Ch., Stephensport, Ky., 1985-87, Rehoboth Bapt. Ch., Gaffney, 1987—. Chaplain Gaffney Jaycees, 1977-79, Asbury-Rehoboth Vol. Fire Dept., Gaffney, 1989—; bd. dirs. Piedmont Community Action Agy., Spartanburg, S.C., 1979-81. Mem. Breckinridge Bapt. Assn. (mem. exec. com. 1985-87), Broad River Bapt. Assn. (exec. com., dir. Sunday sch. 1987—). Home: 117 Stacy Dr Gaffney SC 29340 Office: Rehoboth Bapt Ch 328 Gowdeysville Rd Gaffney SC 29340

HARRISON, ROLAND KENNETH, retired religion educator, minister; b. Lancashire, Eng., Aug. 4, 1920; s. William and Hilda Mary (Marsden) H.; m. Kathleen Beattie, Oct. 18, 1945; children: Felicity, Judith. BD, U. London, 1943, ThM, 1947, PhD, 1952; DD (hon.), Huron Coll., London, Ont., Can., 1963. Ordained to ministry Anglican Ch., 1943. Chaplain Clifton Theol. Coll., Bristol, Eng., 1947-49; prof. Bibl. Greek Huron Coll., 1949-52, Hellmuth prof. O.T., 1952-60; Bishops Frederick and Heber Wilkinson prof. O.T. Wycliffe Coll., Toronto, Ont., 1960-86, prof. emeritus, 1986—. Author: Introduction to the Old Testament, 1969, Old Testament Times, 1970, The Ancient World, 1971. Mem. Worshipful Soc. Apothecaries (faculty history medicine and pharmacy), Can. Psychiat. Assn. Office: Wycliffe Coll, Toronto, ON Canada M5S 1H7

HARRISON, TOMMY WAYNE, minister, accountant; b. Meridan, Miss., Oct. 31, 1949; s. Walter Cecil and Sibyl (Gully) H.; m. Judy Diane Webb, June 4, 1977; children: Chad, Lauren. AA, Meridian Jr. Coll., 1969; BS, U. So. Miss., 1971. Organist, children choir dir. Macedonia Bapt. Ch., Meridian, Miss., 1970-76; min. music/youth First Bapt Ch. Lauderdale, Miss., 1976-85; min. music York (Ala.) Bapt. Ch., 1985—; sr. acct. State of Miss., Meridian, 1981—. Judge local talent and beauty contests, Meridian area. Named one of Outstanding Young Men Am. Meridian Jaycees, 1971. Mem. Assn. Accountancy, Bigbee Bapt. Assn. (assoc. music dir. 1987—). Home: Rte 2 Box 262 Meridian MS 39305 Office: York Bapt Ch 330 Broad St York AL 36925 *Reaching out to others through the ministry of music has added new depth and insight to my life as I work hand in hand with other Christians.*

HARRISON DUNLAP, DEBRA LOUISE, minister of music, music educator; b. Oakley, Kans., July 20, 1956; d. Harvey H. and Louise Y. (Bertrand) Voth. Student, Manhattan (Kans.) Christian Coll., 1974-76; B in Ch. Music, Westminster Choir Coll., Princeton U., 1980. Coord. choirs, dir. handbells, vocal tchr. Riverside Bapt. Ch., Denver, 1980-83; dir. handbells Southcliff Bapt. Ch., Ft. Worth, 1984; min. music Christian Ch., Oakley, 1985—; clk. Bapt. Bookstore, Denver, 1980-82; head dept. music ARK Bookstore, Denver, 1982-83; with Pizza Hut, Inc., Oakley, 1986—. Mem. Western Plains Arts Assn. (bd. dirs., 1986—, treas. 1990). Office: Oakley Christian Ch PO Box 216 Oakley KS 67748

HARROD, HOWARD LEE, religion educator; b. Holdenville, Okla., June 9, 1932; m. Annemarie Nussbaumer; children: Lee Ann, Amy Ceil. BA, Okla. U., 1957; BD, Duke U., 1960; MST, Yale U., 1961, MA, 1963, PhD, 1965. Asst. prof. Howard U., 1964-66; assoc. prof. Drake U., 1966-68; prof. Vanderbilt U., 1968—, chair grad. dept. religion, 1972-75; lectr. Howard U., 1964, Drake U. Div. Sch., 1966, U. Mont., 1981, Vanderbilt U., 1989. Author: Mission among the Blackfeet, 1971, The Human Center: Moral Agency in the Social World, 1981, Renewing the World: Plains Indian Religion and Morality, 1987; (with others) Radical Theology: Phase Two, 1967; contbr. to: The Encyclopedia of Religion, 1987, Dictionary of Pastoral Care and Counseling, 1990; mem. editorial bd.: (series) Social World of Biblical Antiquity; newsletter editor Soc. for Study of Native Am. Religious Traditions; contbr. articles to religious jours. Yale U. fellow, 1960-62, Rockefeller fellow, 1962-63, 88, Vanderbilt U. fellow, 1981-82, 87-88, Am. Coun. Learned Socs. fellow, 1981-82; scholar Drake U., 1966, NEH, 1967, Vanderbilt U., 1969, 70, 75, Am. Assn. Theol. Schs., 1971. Office: Vanderbilt U Div Sch Nashville TN 37240

HARROP, CLAYTON KEITH, minister, educator; b. Berryton, Kans., Feb. 18, 1924; s. Joseph and Rose Belle (Fetrow) H.; m. Shirley Ann Jacobs, Dec. 24, 1944; children: Judith Ann, Joyce Elaine, Janice Louise. AB, William Jewell Coll., Liberty, Mo., 1949; BD, So. Bapt. Theol. Sem., 1952, PhD, 1956; postgrad., U. Chgo., 1964, Cambridge U, 1965, U. Gottingen, Fed. Republic Germany, 1973-74. Ordained to ministry, So. Bapt. Ch., 1948. Pastor Birmingham (Mo.) Bapt. Ch., 1947-49, New Hope Bapt. Ch., Newtonville, Ind., 1951-55; instr. Golden Gate Bapt. Theol. Sem., Berkeley, Calif., 1955-56; asst. prof. Golden Gate Bapt. Theol. Sem., Mill Valley, Calif., 1956-61, assoc. prof., 1961-68, prof., 1968—, dir. PhD studies, 1984—; acting dean acad. affairs, 1991—; vis. prof. So. Bapt. Theol. Sem., Louisville, 1986. Author: The Letter of James, 1969, History of the New Testament in Plain Language, 1984; contbr. articles to Wycliffe Bible Encyclopedia, Holman Bible Dictionary and Mercer Dictionary of the Bible. Capt. U.S. Army, 1942-46, Philippines. Recipient award of Excellence, Calif. Bapt. Found., 1986. Mem. Soc. Biblical Literature, Nat. Assn. Bapt. Profs. of Religion. Republican. Avocations: jig-saw puzzles, reading. Office: Golden Gate Bapt Theol Sem Seminary Dr Mill Valley CA 94941-3197

HARSANYI, ANDREW, bishop. Bishop Hungarian Reformed Ch. in Am. Office: Hungarian Reformed Ch Am PO Box D Hapatcong NY 07843*

HARSHMAN, JENNIFER IONE, lay worker; b. Edinburg, Tex., Mar. 18, 1959; d. William Leon III and Beverly Ione (Foedisch) Lee; m. Craig Matthew Harshman, Aug. 22, 1982; children: Matthew Foster Lee, Austin Geoffrey, Caitlin West. Student, Walla Walla Coll., 1977-79, 80-81. Supt. Sabbath Sch. Seventh-Day Adventist Ch., Edinburg, Tex., 1973-74; tchr. English Adventist English Sch., Ekamai, Bangkok, Thailand, 1979-80; supt. Sabbath Sch. Seventh-Day Adventist Ch., College Place, Wash., 1980-81; supt. Sabbath Sch. Seventh-Day Adventist Ch., Walla Walla, Wash., 1983, Sabbath Sch. tchr., 1983; Sabbath Sch. tchr. Seventh-Day Adventist Ch., Phoenix, 1984-90; del. Glass Conv., L.A., 1990, 91; dir. Vacation Bible Sch., Seventh-Day Adventist, Phoenix, 1991, wedding coord., 1990-91. Seamstress (clothing), 1988 (1st Place/Best of Show award Southeastern Wash. State Fair 1988), puppets, others; woodworker, stained glass craftsman. Democrat. Avocation: storytelling. Home: 3420 E Nisbet Phoenix AZ 85032

HART, DANIEL ANTHONY, bishop; b. Lawrence, Mass., Aug. 24, 1927; s. John J. and Susan M. (Tierney) H. B.S.B.A., Boston Coll., 1956; M.Ed., Boston State Coll., 1972; M.Div., St. John's Sem., Brighton, Mass., 1974. Ordained priest Roman Catholic Ch., 1953; asst. pastor Lynnfield, Mass., 1953-54, Wellesley, Mass., 1954-56, Malden, Mass., 1956-64; vice-chancellor (Archdiocese of Boston), 1964-70; asst. pastor Peabody, Mass., 1970-76; titular bishop of Tepelta, aux. bishop of Boston, 1976—, regional bishop S. region, 1976—, archdiocesan vicar for pastoral devel., 1976-85; pres. Boston Senate of Priests, 1972-74; mem. exec. bd. Nat. Fedn. Priests' Councils, 1973-75. Address: 235 N Pearl St Brockton MA 02401

HART, DAVID STEVEN, minister, popular music analyst, educator; b. Munich, June 13, 1950; came to U.S., 1952; s. Steven Lycurgus and Terry (Malmo) H.; m. Velva Lee Mowrey, Sept. 1986. BA in Polit. Sci., U. Colo., 1972; MA in Christian Edn., Talbot Sem., La Mirada, Calif., 1980. Ch. lay worker, 1976-84; dir. Christian concert promotion agy. Hartbeat Concerts, San Diego, 1984-87; rsch. analyst, assoc. editor Al Menconi Ministries, San Marcos, Calif., 1985—; pastor Sanctuary, San Diego, 1988—; adj. faculty mem. Drug and Alcohol Program for USN, U. Ariz., 1982-84; bd. dirs. D.I.O.S., Escondido, Calif., 1990—, Larry Bubb Evangelism Assn., Poway, Calif., 1991—. Assoc. editor Media Update mag., 1987—; columnist Youthworker Jour., 1987-90; contbr. numerous articles on music and teens to mags. With USN, 1972-76. Avocations: reading, music, racquetball. Office: Al Menconi Ministries 1635 S Rancho Santa Fe Rd San Marcos CA 92069-3621

HART, DONALD PURPLE, bishop; b. N.Y.C., Apr. 22, 1937; s. Donald Buell Hart and Ann Wentworth (Ayres) Herrick; m. Elizabeth Ann Howard, Sept. 8, 1962; children: Sarah, Thomas. BA, Williams Coll., 1959; B of Divinity, Episc. Div. Sch., Cambridge, Mass., 1962. Curate Ch. of the Redeemer, Chestnut Hill, Mass., 1962-64; priest-in-charge Good Shepherd Mission, Huslia, Alaska, 1964-69; diocesan staff Native Ministry, Anchorage, Alaska, 1969-73; rector St. Matthew's Ch., Fairbanks, Alaska, 1973-83, St. James Ch., Keene, N.H., 1983-86; bishop Diocese of Hawaii, Honolulu, 1986—. Chmn. St. Andrew's Priory Sch., Honolulu, 1986—, Seabury Hall Sch., Makawao, Hawaii, 1986—, St. John's Sch., Tumon Bay, Guam, 1986—; bd. govs. Iolani Sch., Honolulu, 1986—. Avocations: biking, hiking, jogging. Home: 3337 Niolopua Dr Honolulu HI 96817 Office: Episcopal Ch in Hawaii 229 Queen Emma Sq Honolulu HI 96813

HART, EDDIE LEE, minister; b. Eastman, Ga., Aug. 25, 1932; s. Eddie and Gertrude (Davis) H.; m. Willie Pearl Ryals, Feb. 16, 1952; children: Rose, Joyce, Delbra, Edna, Eddie, Myra, Vann. Student, Trinity Bible Coll. and Sem., 1990—. Pastor Union Bapt. Ch., Addox, Ga., 1974-77, East Light Bapt. Ch., Crescent, Ga., 1974-77, Zion Rock Bapt. Ch., Brunswick, Ga., 1977-90, First African Missionary Bapt. Ch., Kingsland, Ga., 1977—; v.p. Ministerial Alliance, Brunswick, 1974-76, pres., Kingsland, 1978-80, 89—. Pres. Kings Bay Affirmative Action com., Camden County, Ga., 1989—; mem. adv. bd. ARC, Camden, Charlton County, 1989—. Recipient Humanitarian award NAACP, 1978. Mem. Nat. Bapt. Conv. USA, NAACP (Glynn County, Camden County), Zion Assn. (exec. bd.), Gen. Missionary Bapt. Conv. of Ga. Inc., Black Bus. Assn., Bd. Realtors., Citizens CFG (pres. Glynn County chpt. 1976-78, Camden County chpt.). Home: 106 Meadow Ct Kingsland GA 31548 Office: 1st African Missionary Bapt Ch PO Box 251 Kingsland GA 31548 *In my life I have received personal joy, and inner peace by sharing love and lending a helping hand to those I come in contact with.*

HART, EUGENE C., minister; b. Kenosha, Wis., May 7, 1931; s. Delbert L. and Hilda E. (Pillegor) H.; m. Minnie Webber, Dec. 3, 1950 (div.); children: Eugene, Michael, Orpha, Dan, Hilda, Tina; m. Marilyn Bunch, June 27, 1974. Mem. Lakeshore Tabernacle Ch., Kenosha, Wis., 1980-86; pres. Full Gospel Bus. Mens Fellowship Internat., Kenosha, 1983-86; sr. pastor Kenosha United Christian Ch., 1986—; retired, 1988. Corp. U.S. Army, 1948-52. Home: 1411 74th St Kenosha WI 53143 Office: Kenosha United Christian Ch 1411 74th St Kenosha WI 53143

HART, JAMES RUSSELL, music minister, educator; b. Cleve., May 6, 1957; s. George Arthur and Shirley Mae (Russell) H.; m. Carol Lee Rinke, May 11, 1985; children: Kristin, Erika. Student, Ind. U., 1975-77; BM, Oral Roberts U., 1981; MM, U. Tulsa, 1983. Ordained to ministry United Meth. Ch., 1985. Choral and instrumental dir. Christ the Redeemer Luth. Ch., Tulsa, 1979-83; orch. dir., arranger Grace Fellowship, Tulsa, 1983-88; dir. of music and arts ministries Tyler St. United Meth. Ch., Dallas, 1989—; instr. Oral Roberts U., Tulsa, 1980-88, Christ for the Nations Inst., Dallas, 1989—, Fountaingate Bible Coll., Plano, Tex., 1990—; music dir., faculty mem. Internat. Worship Symposium, Plano, 1984—. Mem. Am. Choral Dirs. Assn., Choristers Guild, Internat. Trumpet Guild, Hymn Soc. Am., Tex. Choral Dirs. Assn. Home: 103 N Winnetka Dallas TX 75208 Office: Tyler St United Meth Ch 927 W 10th St Dallas TX 75208 *One's life takes on true meaning, personally and missionally, when it is focused on and centered around the worship of God. Only by the vicarious atonement supplied by the Lord Jesus Christ on the cross are we able to enter into the relationship with God upon which the worship is based.*

HART, JOHN WILLIAM, theology educator; b. N.Y.C., Oct. 5, 1943; s. Thomas Esmond and Veronica Frances (Merz) H.; m. Jane Helen Morell, Aug. 16, 1975; children: Shanti, Daniel. BA, Marist Coll., 1966; STM, Union Theol. Sem., 1972, MPhil, 1976, PhD, 1978. Dir. Heartland Project, Midwestern Cath. Bishops, 1979-81; asst. prof. religious studies Mt. Marty Coll., Yankton, S.D., 1981-82; assoc. prof. religious studies Coll. of Great Falls (Mont.), 1983-85; assoc. prof. theology Carroll Coll., Helena, Mont., 1985—; vis. asst. prof. religion Howard U., Washington, 1978-79; dir., founder Creation Ecology Inst., Helena, 1990—. Author: The Spirit of the Earth: A Theology of the Land, 1984; editor series Religion and Ecology, 1990—; contbr. articles to profl. publs., chpts. to books. Del. Internat. Indian Treaty Coun., UN, Geneva, 1987, 90; intern Human Rights Commn. Danforth Found. fellow, 1973-74; NEH grantee, 1985, 86. Mem. Soc. Christian Ethics, Am. Acad. Religion. Democrat. Roman Catholic. Office: Carroll Coll Theology Dept Helena MT 59625 *Humanity has been entrusted with a most sacred task: a caring responsibility for all creation. The survival of the earth and of all life depends on our fulfillment of that responsibility.*

HART, JOSEPH ANTHONY, priest, educator; b. Binghamton, N.Y., July 16, 1945; s. James Edward and Helen Katherine (Hayden) H. BA, St. John Fisher Coll., 1968; MA, U. Rochester, N.Y., 1971; MDiv, St. Bernard's Sem., Rochester, 1971, MTh, 1972; STL, Gregorian U., Rome, 1978, STD, 1981. Ordained priest Roman Cath. Ch., 1973. Assoc. pastor St. Anne's Ch., Rochester, 1973-76; assoc. prof. theology St. Bernard's Inst., Rochester, 1976—; dir. of synod Diocese Rochester, 1990—. Mem. Cath. Theol. Soc., Am. Acad. Religion. Home: 783 Hard Rd Webster NY 14580 Office: St Bernard's Inst 1100 S Goodman St Rochester NY 14620

HART, JOSEPH H., bishop; b. Kansas City, Mo., Sept. 26, 1931. Ed., St. John Sem., Kansas City, St. Meinrad Sem., Indpls. Ordained priest Roman Catholic Ch., 1956; consecrated titular bishop of Thimida Regia and aux. bishop Cheyenne Wyo., 1976; apptd. bishop of Cheyenne, 1978. Office: Bishop's Residence Box 468 Cheyenne WY 82003

HART, KATHY ANN, church secretary; b. Ft. Valley, Ga., Jan. 3, 1968; d. Glover Ivan and Mary Ann (Harrell) Hall; m. Alan Boyd Hart, Sept. 29, 1990. A.Bus., Middle Ga. Coll., 1988. Ch. sec. First Bapt. Ch., Fort Valley, 1989—. Home: PO Box 1086 Howard St Byron GA 31008 Office: First Bapt Ch College and Miller Sts Fort Valley GA 31030

HART, MARJORIE LYNN, youth ministry administrator; b. Oil City, Pa., Jan. 26, 1964; d. Earl Clifford and Irene Mae (Moore) Keefer; m. Todd Alan Hart, June 7, 1986. BS, Clarion U., 1986. Cert. tchr., Pa. Dir. youth ministries Good Hope Luth., Oil City, 1987—; mem. youth ministries com. N.W. Pa. Evang. Luth. Ch. Am., Oil City, 1987—. Home: RD 2 Box 2741 Franklin PA 16323 Office: Good Hope Luth 800 Moran St Oil City PA 16301

HART, MARK DORSEY, theology educator; b. Colfax, Wash., Feb. 14, 1956; s. Donald C. and Elizabeth M. (MacDonald) H.; m. Katherine B. Mock, Sept. 9, 1989. BA, Seattle U., 1978; PhD, Boston Coll., 1987. Asst. prof. theology Seattle U., 1987—. Mem. Am. Acad. Religion, North Am. Patristic Soc. Roman Catholic. Office: Seattle U Broadway & Madison Seattle WA 98122

HART, PHILIP RAY, religion educator, minister; b. Dendron, Va., Oct. 4, 1925; s. Edward Lee and Sarah Oceana (West) H.; m. Nancy Jean Padgett, Sept. 12, 1953; children: John Philip, Stephen Anson. BA, U. Richmond, 1945; BD, So. Bapt. Theol. Sem, Louisville, 1948; MA, Columbia U., 1952; PhD, U. Edinburgh, 1962. Ordained to ministry So. Bapt. Conv., 1948. Asst. pastor Tabernacle Bapt. Ch., Richmond, Va., 1948-51; prof. religion U. Richmond, 1956-91, prof. emeritus, 1991—; bd. dirs. Va. Bapt. Mins.' Relief Fund. Contbr. articles to religious jours. Friend Va. Bapt. Hist. Soc., 1987—; bd. dirs., treas. Richmond unit Am. Cancer Soc., 1987—. Capt. USAF, 1953-55. Mem. Soc. Bibl. Lit., Bonhoeffer Soc., Rotary, Omicron Delta Kappa. Home: 6801 Lakewood Dr Richmond VA 23229

HART, RAY LEE, religious studies educator; b. Hereford, Tex., Mar. 22, 1929; s. Albert Mann and Ruby Douglas (Bracken) H.; m. Juanita Fern Morgan, Sept. 8, 1951; children: Douglas Morgan, Stuart Bracken. B.A., U. Tex., 1949; B.D., So. Methodist U., 1953; Ph.D., Yale U., 1959. Instr., then asst. prof. Drew U. Theol. Sch., 1956-63; assoc. prof. philos. and systematic theology Vanderbilt U. Div. Sch., 1963-69; prof., chmn. dept. religious studies U. Mont., 1969-89; chmn. dept. religion, dir. div. grad. religious and theol. studies Boston U., 1989—; cons. on religious studies SUNY, 1972—. Author: Unfinished Man and the Imagination, 1968; trans. into Chinese, editor: Selections from Thomas Aquinas, 1966, The Critique of Modernity, 1986, Trajectories in the Study of Religion, 1987. Mayor, Polebridge, Mont., 1969-70. Mem. Am. Acad. Religion (editor jour. 1970-80, pres. 1983-84, del. to Am. Council Learned Socs. 1980—, mem. exec. com., bd. dirs.), Metaphys. Soc. Am., Soc. Sci. Study Religion, Soc. Values in Higher Edn., Ctr. of Study of World Religions (bd. dirs. 1986—). Home: 745 Commonwealth Ave Boston MA 02215

HART, ROBERT EDWARD, minister; b. Rochester, N.Y., Mar. 1, 1951; s. George N. and Alma A. (Anderson) H.; m. Sally Crook, Oct. 12, 1973; children: Stephen, Jonathan, Andrew. Grad. in theology, Bapt. Bible Coll., Springfield, Mo., 1973; BA, Bapt. Christian U., Shreveport, La., 1991. Ordained to ministry Bapt. Ch., 1975. Pastor youth Green Bay Bapt. Temple., 1973, 1st Bible Bapt. Ch., Green Bay, Wis., 1974-75; founder, pastor Victory Bapt. Ch., Albany, N.Y., 1975-77, Schenectady Bible Bapt. Ch., 1977-89, Sonrise Bible (Bapt.) Ch., Rotterdam, N.Y., 1989—; publicity dir. Jack Van Impe Crusade, Albany, 1977; chmmn. Jerry Falwell's I Love Am. Rally, Albany, 1984; tchr., trainer Evangelism Explosion Internat., Hampton, Va., 1988. Bd. dirs. New Yorkers for Constl. Freedoms, Albany, 1983—, New Yorker Family Rsch. Found., Albany, 1989—. Republican. Office: Sonrise Bible (Bapt) Ch 300 Dunnsville Rd Schenectady NY 12306

HART, ROBIN LEE, minister; b. Rushville, Ind., July 6, 1959; s. Lloyd James and Lois Ann (Redden) H.; m. Paula Kay Blackford; children: Crystal, Candace, Jordan. AB, Ky. Christian Coll., 1981, M in Ministry, 1985. Ordained to ministry Christian Ch. Min. Mill Springs Christian Ch., Monticello, Ky., 1981-84, Burnside (Ky.) Christian Ch., 1982-84; sr. min. Northside Christian Ch., Wadsworth, Ohio, 1984—; pres. Monticello Ministerial Assn., 1982-83, Akron Ministerial Assn., 1986-87; mem. Alumni Coun. Fifty Ky. Christian Coll., 1986-89; preaching coord. Summer in Son Summit, Ky. Christian Coll., 1988—; men's retreat chmn. Round Lake Christian Assembly, Lakeville, 1988—; chaplain Days Inn Am., Wadsworth, 1988—. Coord. short-term missionary trips Mex. Children's Home, 1990—. Mem. Lions. Avocations: basketball, hunting, fishing, whitewater rafting. Home: 2804 Greenwich Rd Wadsworth OH 44281 Office: Northside Christian Ch 1825 Reimer Rd Wadsworth OH 44281

HART, RONALD LEON, minister; b. Lodi, Calif., Feb. 6, 1937; s. John Henry Leon and Dorothy Harriet (Solkema) H.; m. Patricia Anne Pattison, Aug. 6, 1965; children: Tricia Raelyn Hart Brooks, Ryan Leon Hart. Diploma, Eugene Bible Coll., 1957; studnet, Clark Coll., 1959-61; BA, Cascade Coll., 1964, cert. tchr., 1968; MEd, U. Portland, 1971; HHD (hon.), Fla. Beacon Bible Coll., 1988. Ordained to ministry Christian Ch., 1966. Exec. dir. HiVenture Youth Outreach, Vancouver, Wash., 1966-87; pastor Walnut Grove Ch., Vancouver, 1975-91. city councilman Vancouver, 1980-91; bd. dirs. C-Tran, Vancouver, 1984-91, Intergovernmental Resource Ctr., 1981-91, Nat. Assn. Regional Couns., Washington, 1987-91. Mem. Rotary (pres. 1972-73, dist. gov. 1987-88). Mem. Open Bible Standard Chs. AvocationsL golf, photography. Home: 918 NW 50th St Vancouver WA 98663 Office: PO Box 1525 6004 NE 72d Ave Vancouver WA 98661

HART, RUSTY, minister; b. Prescott, Ark., Jan. 7, 1963; s. James L. and Carolyn (Wilson) H.; m. Lori Sue Reeves, June 21, 1985; 1 child, Laura Catherine. B, Ouachita Bapt. U., 1985, M, 1988. Ordained to minister So. Bapt. Ch., 1990. Min. of youth First Bapt. Ch., Prescott, Ark., 1984-85; min. of music, youth Crystal Valley Bapt. Ch., North Little Rock, Ark., 1985-87; min. of music First Bapt. Ch. of Gravel Ridge, Jacksonville, Ark., 1987-89, Cen. Bapt. Ch., North Little Rock, 1989—; music coord. North Pulaski Bapt. Assn., North Little Rock, 1990—; state choral adv. com. Ark. Bapt. State Conv., Little Rock, 1987—. Named Soloist Ark. Choral Soc. 1986, State Vocalist Winner Nat. Assn. Tchrs. of Singing 1985, 87, So. Regional Runner-up Vocalist, 1986. Mem. So. Bapt. Ch. Music Conf., Ark. Master Singers, Friends of the Sch. of Music, Pi Kappa Lambda. Democrat. Home: 111 Creekwood Jacksonville AR 72076 Office: Cen Bapt Ch 5200 Fairway North Little Rock AR 72116

HART, STEPHEN ALBERT, religious organization administrator; b. Chgo., Feb. 14, 1946; s. Albert Gailord and Ann (Webster) H.; m. Gail Eileen Radford, Nov. 12, 1977. BA, Harvard U., 1967; MA, U. Calif., Berkeley, 1968, PhD, 1979. Co-dir. Ecumenical Peace Inst., Berkeley, 1972-74; dir. survey studies Luth. Ch. in Am., Phila., 1982-87; dir. for rsch. Evang. Luth. Ch. in Am., Chgo., 1988—; del. diocesan conv. Diocese of Chgo., 1989-90. Democrat. Episcopalian. Home: 2824 N Richmond St Chicago IL 60618 Office: Evang Luth Ch in Am 8765 W Higgins Rd Chicago IL 60631

HART, WILLIAM FRANKLIN, pastor; b. Rochester, N.Y., Jan. 20, 1945; s. Eugene Lamont and Genevieve Francis (Dewey) H.; m. Marilyn Kay Sharp, Aug. 15, 1965; 1 child, Lori Ann Hart Wade. B Music Edn., U. Louisville, 1967. Ordained to ministry So. Bapt. Conv., 1978. Min. music Hall Street Bapt. Ch., Owensboro, Ky., 1970-77; assoc. pastor South Elkhorn Bapt. Ch., Lexington, Ky., 1977-82, lst Bapt. Ch., Seymour, Tenn., 1983—; Pres. Daviess-McLean Pastors, Owensboro, 1974-75; sec.-treas. Ky. Music Mins., Lexington, 1973-76; dir. Seymour Communityu Choir, 1989-91. Mem. So. Bapt. Music Assn., Tenn. Bapt. MMusic Assn., Chilhowee Pastors Conf., Rotary (sec. Seymour 1990-91). Home: 408 Navajo Dr Seymour TN 37865 Office: lst Bapt Ch 113 Smothers Rd Seymour TN 37865

HARTE, JOHN JOSEPH MEAKIN, bishop; b. Springfield, Ohio, July 28, 1914; s. Charles Edward and Ruth Elizabeth (Weisenstein) H.; m. Alice Eleanor Taylor, Oct. 14, 1941; children: Victoria Ruth, Joseph Meakin Jr., Judith Alice. AB, Washington and Jefferson Coll., 1936; DD (hon.), Washington & Jefferson Coll., 1954; STM, Gen. Theol. Sem., 1939, STD (hon.), 1955, D in Ministry, 1985; DD (hon.), U. South, 1955. Ordained to ministry Episc. Ch., 1939. Rector All Saints' Ch., Miami, Okla., 1939-41; curate Trinity Ch., Tulsa, 1941-42; rector St. George's Ch., Rochester, N.Y., 1942-43, All Saints' Ch., Austin, Tex., 1943-51; chaplain Episcopal students U. Tex., Austin; dean St. Paul's Cathedral, Erie, Pa., 1951-54; suffragan bishop Dioceses of Dallas, 1954-62; bishop Diocese of Ariz., 1962-80; bd. dirs. Citibank, Ariz., Gen. Conv. Episcopal Ch., 1952; chmn. St. Luke's Hosp., Tucson, 1962-80, St. Luke's Hosp. Med. Ctr., Phoenix, 1962-80; trustee Bloy Episcopal Sch. Theology; pres. Pacific Province, 1967-68. Author: Some Sources of Common Prayer, 1944, The Language of the Book of Common Prayer, 1945, The Title Page of the Book of Common Prayer, 1946, The Church's Name, 1958, The Elizabethan Prayer Book, 1959, The 1662 Prayer Book, 1962. Bd. dirs. Human Rights Commn. City of Phoenix, 1962-65. Named Man of Yr. NCCJ, Ariz., 1969, Anti-Defamation League, Ariz., 1975. Mem. Nat. Orgn. Episcopalians for Life (chmn., founder 1966—), Am. Legion, Beta Theta Pi. Lodges: Shriners (Imperial chaplain 1962-65), KT (Grand chaplain 1951-52), Masons. Office: 6300 N Central Phoenix AZ 85012

HARTER, TERRY PRICE, religion educator; b. Bluffton, Ind., July 24, 1947; s. Lee J. and Patt Ellen (Price) H.; m. Martha Jean O'Dell, Aug. 23, 1969; children: Emily, Edward. BA, Wabash Coll., 1969; ThM, Boston U., 1972, PhD, 1980. Ordained to ministry Meth. Ch. as elder. Min. of edn. St. Matthew's United Meth. Ch., Acton, Mass., 1970-75; religious edn. cons. Adventure House, Fitchburg, Mass., 1975-76; pastor Lawrence Meml. United Meth. Ch., Pepperell, Mass., 1976-77; min. of program and edn. First United Meth. Ch., Peoria, Ill., 1978—; vis. instr. of religious edn. Sch. of Theology, Claremont (Calif.) U., 1977-78; chpt. pres. Cen. Ill. Chpt. of Christian Educators Fellowship, 1988-90; bd. dirs. ordained ministry Cen. Ill. Conf. United Meth. Ch.; CPE com. Meth. Med. Ctr., Peoria, Ill., 1988—. Contbr. articles to profl. jours. Assoc. curator Fine Arts Festival Exhibits, Peoria, 1985—; bd. dirs. YMCA, Peoria, 1990—; panel mem. Heart of Ill., United Way, Peoria, 1984-88; pres. Father Sweeney Sch. for the Academically Gifted, Peoria, 1980—, v.p., 1988-90; mem. Frieds of Owens Ctr., Peoria. Lowstuter fellow Boston U., 1975, 76. Mem. Religious Edn. Assn., Ill. Valley Figure Skating Club (Peoria). Home: 2619 W Fountaindale Dr Peoria IL 61614 Office: First United Meth Ch 116 NE Perry Ave Peoria IL 61603

HARTFORD, CAROL LYNN, lay worker, advertising specialist; b. Binghamton, N.Y., July 22, 1962; d. Robert Allen and Frances Ruth (Putnam) H. Diploma, Ridley Lowell Bus. and Tech. Inst., Binghamton, 1984. Youth group leader Primitive Meth. Ch., Johnson City, N.Y., 1984—, clk., tchr. jr. high class, 1988—, Sunday sch. tchr., 1982—; sec. Advantage Realty, Endicott, N.Y., 1984-91; listing co., advt. specialist Oakwood Realty Group Inc., Vestal, N.Y., 1991—. Counselor Pocono Mountain Bible Camp, Gouldsboro, Pa., 1981, 82, 83; active Johnson City Wildcats Alumni and Friends. Republican. Home: 83 Albert St Johnson City NY 13790

HARTGROVE, BRUCE NORMAN, minister, musician; b. Greensboro, N.C., July 21, 1949; s. Leroy and Doris (Johnson) H.; m. Sara Charlcie White, June 28, 1974; 1 child, Joshua Bruce. B.Mus. Edn., Mars Hill Coll., 1971; M.Ch. Music, So. Baptist Theol. Sem., 1974. Ordained to ministry Baptist Ch., 1971. Minister of music and youth Trinity Bapt. Ch., Moultrie, Ga., 1974-76, Locust Grove Bapt. Ch., Smyrna, Ga., 1976-81; minister of music First Bapt. Ch., High Point, N.C., 1981—; v.p. Ga. Bapt. Ch. Music Conf., 1978-79; pres. Sons of Jubal, Ga., 1979-81; bd. dirs., judge choral festivals Ga. Bapt. Conv., 1981-85, 90-91. Mem. So. Bapt. Ch. Music Conf., N.C. Bapt. Ch. Music Conf. (regional bd. dirs. 1985-89, v.p. 1990—), Am. Choral Dirs. Assn., Am. Guild English Handbell Ringers, Choristers Guild, Singing Churchmen N.C. Avocations: model railroads, picture framing, photography. Home: 206 W Parkway Ave High Point NC 27262 Office: First Bapt Ch 405 N Main St High Point NC 27260

HARTLEY, GALE RAY, minister; b. Elizabethton, Tenn., May 8, 1956; s. Blaine and June (Pleasant) H.; m. Leslie Marie Lewis, July 25, 1981; children: Timothy Gale, Aaron Blaine, Asa Graham. BA, Carson Newman Coll., 1978; MDiv, So. Bapt. Theol. Sem., Louisville, 1980; MRE, New Orleans Bapt. Theol. Sem., 1982; postgrad., Luther Rice Sem., 1991—. Lic. to ministry Grace Bapt. Ch., 1974, ordained, 1981. Package handler United Parcel Svc., New Orleans, 1981-83; pastor Airport Blvd. Bapt. Ch., Pensacola, Fla., 1984-88, East Side Bapt. Ch., Elizabethton, 1988—. Recipient Citizenship award VFW, 1974; named Outstanding Religious Leader, Pensacola Jaycees, 1986. Mem. Carter County Ministerial Assn., Watauga Bapt. Assn. Pastors. Home: 1006 Walker St Elizabethton TN 37643 Office: East Side Bapt Ch 1509 Siam Rd Elizabethton TN 37643

HARTLEY, JOHN EDWARD, educator; b. Meadville, Pa., May 9, 1940; s. Walter and Mary Elizabeth (Lewis) H.; m. Dorothy Leone Robbins, June 7, 1961; children: Joyce, Johannah. BA, Greenville Coll., 1961; BD, Asbury Theol. Sem., 1965; MA, Brandeis U., 1968, PhD, 1969. Ordained to ministry. Pastor Free Meth. Ch., Eldorado, Ill., 1961-63; grad. asst. in Greek Asbury Theol. Sem., Wilmore, Ky., 1965-66; guest prof. Asbury Theol. Sem., Wilmore, 1970; prof. Azusa (Calif.) Pacific U., 1969—; vis. scholar Harvard Divinity Sch., Cambridge, Mass., 1977-78; adj. prof. Fuller Theol. Sem., 1973-82. Author, editor Wesleyan Theol. Perspectives, five vols. 1981; contbr. to book Theological Wordbook of the Old Testament, 1980, International Standard Bible Encyclopedia rev. edit., 1974 82, 86, 88, The Book of Job in NICOT, 1988. Recipient Teaching Excellence award Azusa Pacific U., 1973. Mem. Am. Sch. Oriental Research. Soc. Bib. Lit. Home: 1737 Acorn Ln Glendora CA 91740 Office: Azusa Pacific U Alosta at Citrus Azusa CA 91702

HARTMAN, BARRY DAVID, rabbi; b. Bronx, N.Y., Mar. 24, 1951; s. Gustave and Sarah (Taub) H.; m. Shoshana Turner, Oct. 8, 1975; children: Neshe Esther, Yehoshua Zev, Chava Frayde, Eliyahu Zvi, Aaron Pesach. BA, Yeshiva Coll., 1972; MS, Yeshiva U., 1975; MA, Long Island U., 1978. Ordained rabbi, 1976. Prin. Jewish Ctr. Mapleton Park, Bklyn., 1977-78; housing asst. N.Y.C. Housing Authority, 1978-79; rabbi Ahavath Achim Synagogue, New Bedford, Mass., 1979—; chaplain, mem. ethics com. St. Luke's Hosp., New Bedford, 1982—; bd. dirs. Ctr. for Jewish Culture, Southeastern Mass. U., North Dartmouth, 1982—, Jewish Fedn. New Bedford, North Dartmouth, 1979—, Providence Hebrew Day Sch., 1989—. Contbr. articles to publs. Bd. dirs. On Board Inc. Anti-Poverty Agy., New Bedford, 1982-85, U. Mass., North Dartmouth. Recipient Nat. Rabbinic Leadership award United Jewish Appeal, N.Y.C., 1990, Disting. Rabbinic Svc. award Coun. Jewish Fedns., N.Y.C., 1990. Mem. Rabbinical Coun. Am. (exec. com.), Vaad Harabonim of Mass. (v.p.), Rabbinic Ct. Justice, Am. Planning Assn., Rabbinic Alumni Yeshiva U. Office: Ahavath Achim Synagogue 385 County St New Bedford MA 02740 *I believe the best advice was stated by Micah: Do justice, love, mercy and walk humbly with God.*

HARTMAN, DORIS, retired missionary; b. Cedarville, Ohio, Nov. 2, 1913; d. George Harman and Lida Mae (Owings) H. AB, BS in Edn., Cedarville Coll., 1934; MA, Hartford Sem. Found., 1941; MDiv, Union Theol. Sem., 1963. Ordained to ministry United Meth. Ch., 1946; cert. tchr., Ohio. Pastor Union Ch., Waterville, Vt., 1942-46; min. edn. Lake Region Parish, Barton, Vt., 1946-52; missionary United Meth. Bd. of Global Ministry, Hiroshima, Japan, 1952-81; tchr. Hiroshima Girls' Sch., 1952-55. 58-81; founder, pastor Furuichi Ch., Hiroshima, 1966-81; ret., 1981; co-chair Amherst (Mass.) Martin Luther King Breakfast com., 1985-91; mem. Family Selection com. Habitat for Humanity, 1989. Vol. LWV, 1981—, Round-the-World-Women, 1981—. Home: 29 Webster Ct Amherst MA 01002

HARTMAN, EDWARD ARTHUR, church administrator, radiologic technologist; b. Harrisburg, Pa., Dec. 28, 1963; s. David Edward and Helen Virginia (Rexrode) H. AS, Harrisburg Area Community Coll., 1983. Registered radiologic technologist, Pa. Asst. youth dir. Christ Luth. Ch., Harrisburg, Pa., 1981-86, youth dir., 1987—; radiologic technologist A.Z. Ritzman Assocs., Harrisburg, 1983—; adult advisor Harrisburg Area Luth. Youth Orgn., 1984—; staff mem. Harrisburg Area Confirmation Camp, 1986—. Mem. Pa. Soc. Radiologic Technologists. Republican. Office: Christ Evang Luth Ch 1214 Crosby St Harrisburg PA 17112

HARTMAN, JEFFREY EDWARD, pastor; b. Nyack, N.Y., June 23, 1959; s. Edward Harold and Constance Ruth (Gibbs) H.; m. Cynthia Lynn Chason, Aug. 14, 1982; children: Joshua Jefferson, Jeremiah Jordan. BS, Liberty U., 1982; postgrad., Westminster Theol. Sem., 1985, Trinity Evang. Div. Sch., 1989. Ordained to ministry, 1985. Assoc. pastor Maranatha Bapt. Ch., Gainesville, Ga., 1982-84; pastor Christ Community Ch., Newfield, N.J., 1984—; baseball head coach Cumberland Christian Sch., Vineland, N.J., 1991—; chaplain Newcomb Med. Ctr., Vineland, 1989—. Bd. dir Compassion Crisi Pregnancy Cr., Clayton, N.J., 1986-90, chmn. bd. dirs. 1990—. Office: Christ Community Ch 201 Salem Ave Newfield NJ 08344

HARTMAN, STEVEN ARTHUR, minister; b. Roswell, N.Mex., Feb. 26, 1954; s. Alphonse Arthur and Barbara Jean (Clark) H.; m. Joy Louise Kissling, May 16, 1975; children: Brent Phillip, Christopher James, Ryan Greggory, Matthew Tyler. BTh., Grace Bible Coll., 1977. Ordained to ministry Grace Gospel Fellowship, 1983. Asst. pastor Berean Ch., Muskegon, Mich., 1977-86; sr./founding pastor Christ Ch., Jenison, Mich., 1986—; pres. Hosp. Chaplaincy, Inc., Muskegon, 1983-86; chmn. Grace Gospel Fellowship region 9, Grand Rapids, 1986-88; sec. ch. planting com. region 9 and 10, Grand Rapids, 1985—. Office: Christ Ch 1386 Baldwin St Ste #D Jenison MI 49428

HARTMAN, WANDA FAY, lay worker; b. Millbury, Ohio, Feb. 19, 1940; d. John Ellsworth and Verla Fay (Kurfis) Shamp; m. James Leroy Hartman, June 4, 1961; children: Lori Ann Hartman Wagner, Libby Sue Hartman Fervida, Lana Marie. BA, Manchester Coll., North Manchester, Ind., 1962; MEd, St. Francis Coll., Ft. Wayne, Ind., 1972. Bible sch. tchr. Ch. of Brethren, Nappanee and Elkhart, Ind., 1965-70; Bible Study Fellowship leader Ch. of Brethren, 1975-78; Bible sch. tchr. Missionary Ch., Wakarusa, Ind., 1977-87, Sun. sch. tchr., 1978-88; organizer, leader neighborhood Bible study group, 1979-86; v.p., pres. MWI Missionary Ch., Wakarusa, Ind., 1980-84, jr. high youth sponsor, 1988—; leader Bible Study Fellowship, 1977-80, Home Ladies' Bible Study, 1981-87; dir. Jr. High Youth, 1989-91. Author: Davey, the Shepherd Boy. Home: 63512 C R 111 Goshen IN 46526 Office: Wakarusa Missionary Ch 202 W Waterford Wakarusa IN 46573

HARTOG, JOHN, II, educator, librarian; b. Orange City, Iowa, Nov. 15, 1936; s. John and Gertrude Marie (Hofland) H.; m. Martha Griselda Nuñez, July 30, 1964; children: John III, Paul Anthony. AA, Northwestern Coll., 1956; student, Moody Bible Inst., 1956-57, Middle Coll. Langs., Middlebury, Vt., 1959; BA, Wheaton (Ill.) Coll., 1959; ThM, Dallas Theol. Sem., 1964; MS in Libr. Sci., East Tex. State U., 1970; ThD, Grace Theol. Sem., 1978; D Ministry, Cen. Bapt. Theol. Sem., 1988. Ordained to ministry Gen. Assn. Regular Bapt. Chs., 1969. Min. religious lit. Immanuel Tract Soc., Dallas, 1964-66; pastor Lipscomb (Tex.) Community Ch., 1966-67; instr. libr. Mont. Inst. Bible, Billings, 1967-68; acad. dean Mont. Inst. Bible, Lewistown, 1973-77; prof., libr. Faith Bapt. Bible Coll., Ankeny, Iowa, 1968-70, 77-84, 89—; prof., head libr. Calvary Bible Coll., 1984-89, acad. dean., 1987-89. Author: The Fall of A Kingdom, 1983, Enduring to the End, 1987, When the Church Was Young and Bold, 1988, Abounding Grace, 1991. Mem. Pi Gamma Mu, Phi Theta Kappa. Republican. Baptist. Avocation: gardening. Office: Faith Bapt Theol Sem 1900 NW 4th St Ankeny IA 50021 *It is better to help others a little each day than to pass through life waiting for the chance to be a great hero.*

HARTOKO, DICK, clergyman, writer, lecturer; b. Jatiroto, Lumajang, East Java, Indonesia, May 9, 1922; s. Mathijs Jan Willem Geldorp and Theresia Elisabeth (van't Wout Hofland) Geldorp. Grad., Canisius Coll., Batavia, N.E. Indies, 1941; BA in Philosophy, Ignatius Coll., Yogyakarta, Indonesia. Lic. theology, Canisianum, Maastricht, Holland, MO in history, 1952. Joined Soc. of Jesus, Roman Cath. Ch., Yogyakarta, Indonesia, 1942; chief editor cultural mag. Basis, Yogyakarta, Indonesia, 1957—; lectr. Weda Bhakti Theology Faculty, Yogyakarta, Indonesia, 1957—, Sanata Dharma Tchr. Tng. Coll., Yogyakarta, Indonesia, 1957—, Gadjah Mada U. Faculty of Letters, Yogyakarta, Indonesia, 1970—; chmn. Karta Pustaka Cultural Ctr., Yogyakarta. 1968—; trustee Gadjah Mada U., 1982—, Indonesian Inst. Arts, 1985—. Author: Man and Art, 1987; translator of 17 books from Engl. and Dutch into Indonesian. Home: I Dewa Nyoman 18, 55224 Yogyakarta Indonesia Office: Basis Mag, Abu Bakar Ali 14, 55224 Yogyakarta Indonesia

HARTSOCK, CHARLES PATRICK, minister; b. Washington, Aug. 20, 1945; s. Charles Fugate and Rose Helen (Duffy) H.; m. Ann Wood Squires, July 3, 1970; children: Ryan, Luke, John. BS in Bus., Am. U., 1969; MDiv, Fuller Sem., Pasadena, Calif., 1975, D of Ministry, 1984. Ordained to ministry Presbyn. Ch. Asst. pastor Cen. Presbyn. Ch., Balt., 1975-77, assoc. pastor, 1977-83; organizing pastor Covenant Presbyn. Ch., Colorado Springs, Colo., 1983-84, sr. pastor, 1984—; adj. prof. Trinity Evang. Sem. Extension, Colorado Springs, 1990—; pres. bd. dirs. Christian Lifestyle Ministries, Colorado Springs, 1985—; bd. dirs. Nehemiah Ministries, Gaithersburg, Md., 1980—. Mem. Presbyns. for Renewal, Presbyns. for Bibl. Concerns (v.p. 1987-89, bd. dirs.), Nat. Assn. Evangs., Presbyns. Pro Life. Republican. Home: 7165 Higher Ridges Ct Colorado Springs CO 80919

HARTSOE, JAMES RUSSELL, minister; b. Quarryville, Pa., Apr. 11, 1934; s. Russell E. and Laura Amanda H.; m. Mary Louise Eby, Dec. 18, 1955; children: Alison, Judith. BS, Millersville State U., 1955; MDiv, Princeton Theol. Sem., 1961; postgrad., U. Minn., 1984-87. Ordained to ministry United Presbyn. Ch., 1961; Evang. Luth. Ch., 1988. Pastor Knox Presbyn. Ch., Cedar Rapids, Iowa, 1961-66; project coord. Pa. div. Am. Cancer Soc., Harrisburg, 1966-68; pastor West Hempfield Presbyn. Ch., Irwin, Pa., 1968-77; asst. pastor House of Hope Presbyn. Ch., St. Paul, 1977-78; pastor Bethel Luth. Ch., Hudson, Wis., 1988; interim pastor Bethany Luth Ch., Mpls., 1990-91; pastor Christ Evang. Luth. Ch., Mpls., 1991—; exec. dir. Norwin Coun. of Chs., 1971-75. Bd. dirs. People, Inc., St. Paul, 1977-81. With USAF, 1957-58. Democrat. Home: 1966 Sharondale Ave Saint Paul MN 55113 *Life finds its deepest meaning in relationship—our relationship with God and with other people. In those relationship which are whole there is love.*

HARTT, JULIAN NORRIS, religion educator; b. Selby, S.D., June 13, 1911; s. Albert and Laura (Beals) H.; m. Neva Beverly Leonard, June 16, 1935; children: Beverly Ann, Susan Laura, Julian Norris; m. Elinor N. Roberts, Jan. 10, 1987. AB, Dakota Wesleyan, 1932; BD, Garrett Bibl. Inst., 1937, DD (hon.), 1973; MA, Northwestern U., 1938; PhD, Yale U., 1940; DD (hon.), St. Olaf Coll., 1982, Garrett Evang. Theol. Sem., 1983. Assoc. prof. philosophy and religion Berea Coll., 1940-43; Noah Porter prof. philos. theology Yale U., 1943-72, chmn. dept. religion, 1956-64, dir. grad. studies, dept. religious studies, 1964-67, chmn. dept. religious studies, 1967-72; William Kenan Jr. prof. religious studies U. Va., Charlottesville, 1972-81; emeritus U. Va., 1981—; Lilly vis. prof. religious studies Berea Coll., 1985; Nathaniel W. Taylor lectr. Yale U., 1983, nat. Phi Beta Kappa lectr., 1967-68. Author: The Lost Image of Man, 1963, A Christian Critique of American Culture, Theology and the Church in the University, 1969, The Restless Quest, 1975, Theological Method and Imagination, 1977; editor, contbr. The Critique of Modernity, 1986. Fulbright fellow, 1963-64; Guggenheim fellow, 1963-64. Home: 321 Harvest Dr Charlottesville VA 22901

HARTZOG, CHRISTOPHER CRAIG, minister; b. Panama City, Fla., Dec. 22, 1959; s. Grady Webster and Betty (Mullis) H.; m. Freida Jean Smith, July 29, 1978; children: Shanna Marie, Christin Leigh, Tarah Michelle. BA, Miss. Coll., 1982; MDiv, Southeastern Bapt. Sem., Wake Forest, N.C., 1985. Ordained to ministry So. Bapt. Conv., 1979. Asst. pastor 1st Bapt. Ch., Newberry, Fla., 1977-78; pastor Mt. Pleasant Bapt. Ch., West, Miss., 1979-82, Mt. Carmel Christian Ch., Franklinton, N.C., 1983-85, Mayo (Fla.) Bapt. Ch., 1985-88, Sabal Palm Bapt. Ch., Tallahassee, 1988-91, 1st Bapt. Ch., Belle Glade, Fla., 1991—; dir. evangelism Mid. Fla. Bapt. Assn., Mayo, 1986-88; brotherhood dir. Fla. Bapt. Assn., Tallahassee, 1989-90, v.p. mins. conf., 1990-91; dir. Sunday sch. Big Lake Assn., 1991—. Recipient award Billy Graham Sch. Evangelism, 1986, appreciation award Soc. Disting. High Sch. Students, 1986; grantee Order Ea. Star, 1979-81. Democrat. Home: 121 NW Ave F Belle Glade FL 33430

HARVARD, RONALD WILSON, minister; b. Lake Wales, Fla., Apr. 15, 1943; s. Burl W. and Lida (Huggins) H.; m. Linda Fay Johnson, Aug. 31, 1963; children: Melinda G., Michael W., Stephanie M., Jeffery G. (dec.). BA, Lee Coll., Cleveland, Tenn., 1965; postgrad., Barry Coll., 1969-70, U. Cen. Fla., 1973-74; MA, Ball State u., 1977. Ordained to ministry Ch. of God, 1976. Pastor Cornerstone Ch. of God, Athens, Ga., 1982-89, 91—, Countryside Cathedral, Clearwater, Fla., 1990-91; asst. prof. Lee Coll., Cleveland, 1977-82, dir. counseling, 1989-90, mem. ministerial examining bd., 1978-82, 90-91; mem. dist. overseers bd. Ch. of God, Doraville, Ga., 1982-89, 91—, edn. bd. Doraville, 1986-89, ministerial devel. bd., Tampa, 1990-91. Contbr. articles to profl. jours. Recipient Outstanding Youth Leader award Lake Wales Kiwanis Club, 1961, Outstanding Young Man of Am. award Jaycees, 1970, Outstanding Young Religious Leader award Mims-Scottsmoor Jaycees. Mem. Gen. Coun. Ch. of God. Republican. Home: 254 Wood Lake Dr Athens GA 30606 Office: Cornerstone Ch of God 2150 Lexington Rd Athens GA 30605 *In the midst of a troubled world, a peaceful life naturally unfolds when we seek to be a part of the solution and not the problem.*

HARVEY, C. FRANKLIN, JR., pastor; b. Oakland, Md., Aug. 31, 1949; s. Claude F. Sr. and Geraldine D. (Foster) H.; m. Shirley Alaine Guice, July 20, 1970; children: Catherine Marie, Miriam Elizabeth. Grad., Fruitland Bapt. Bible Coll., 1969. Asst. pastor, youth dir. Sunny Point Bapt. Ch., Canton, N.C., 1969; interim pastor Loch Lynn Heights Bapt. Ch., Oakland, Md., 1969; pastor Crestview Bapt. Ch., Canton, 1969-74, Rock Hill Bapt. Ch., Waynesville, N.C., 1974-77; sr. pastor New Covenant Ch., Waynesville, N.C., 1977—; pres. Haywood County Ministerial Assn., 1988; v.p. Haywood Bapt. Pastors Conf., 1976; exec. com. Evang. Fellowship of Mins., Spartanburg, S.C., 1986—. Exec. com. Haywood County Rep. Party, 1988—. Office: New Covenant Ch PO Box 357 Waynesville NC 28786

HARVEY, DANIEL RICHARD, minister; b. Franklin, Pa., Aug. 27, 1930; s. Richard H. and Dorothy E. (Winder) H.; m. Lois V. Meyers, Mar. 7, 1953; children: Deborah, Stephen, Rebecca, Timothy, Rachel. BA, John Brown U., 1952; postgrad., Moody Bible Inst., 1953-54, Burnside-Ott Aviation, 1970-71. Ordained to ministry Trans World Radio Ch., 1956. Pastor Christian and Missionary Alliance, Siloam Springs, Ark., 1949-52, Urbana, Ill., 1953-55; missionary Trans World Radio, various locations, 1956—; chaplain Guam Dept. Pub. Safety, Agana, 1975-82; civilian chaplain USN, Agana, 1975-82. Bd. dirs. ARC, Agana, 1976-82. Named to Ancient Order of Chammori, Govt. of Guam, 1982; recipient citation Comdr. Naval Forces Marianas, USN, 1982. Home: 4818 Leisurewood Ln Lakeland FL 33811 Office: Trans World Radio PO Box 700 Cary NC 27512-0700

HARVEY, DARREL LEE, minister; b. Flint, Mich., May 5, 1962; s. James Thomas and Joyce Hope (Davis) H.; m. Anne Marie Christiansen, June 4, 1983; children: Tyler D., Zachary James. BS in Psychology, Olivet Nazarene Univ., 1985. Youth pastor DeLand (Fla.) Ch. of Nazarene, 1985-87, Williams Lake Ch. of the Nazarene, Drayton Plains, Mich., 1987-88, First Ch. of the Nazarene, Lake Worth, Fla., 1989-90, Cen. Ch. of the Nazarene, Flint, Mich., 1990—; featured speaker North Fla. Dist. Nazarene Teen Camp, Marianna, 1986, West Flint Nazarene Jr. High Retreat, Vassar, Mich., 1991. Office: Central Ch of Nazarene 1261 W Bristol Rd Flint MI 48507

HARVEY, DAVID PAUL, missionary; b. Meadville, Pa., Oct. 4, 1932; s. Richard H. and Dorothy E. (Winder) H.; m. Margaret J. Kurlak, June 24, 1955; children: Judith James. BA, John Brown U., 1954; ThB, St. Paul Bible Coll., 1956; MA, Wheaton (Ill.) Coll., 1978; postgrad., Columbia Bibl. Sem. Missionary ch. planter Christian and Missionary Alliance, Guinea, West Africa, 1956-85; missionary educator Christian and Missionary Alliance, Ivory Coast, Africa, 1985-87; missionary prof. Telekoro Bible Inst., Guinea, West Africa, 1967-85; prof. missions Toccoa (Ga.) Falls Coll., 1987—. Mem. Rep. Task Force, Washington, 1990—, Citizens Against Govt. Waste, Washington, 1990—, The Rutherford Inst., 1990—. Office: Toccoa Falls Coll Falls Rd Rte 17 Toccoa Falls GA 30598 *Nothing is as important to an individual as his knowledge of the Creator. A person's relationships to all creatures, including those not part of his cultural world, proceed from the depth of his knowledge of the One who created all.*

HARVEY, GERALD PAUL (GARY HARVEY), education and music minister; b. Louisville, Jan. 5, 1956; s. Paul Martin and Ruth Helen (Goodson) H.; m. Carol Jane Martin, Jul. 10, 1982; children: Amy Lynn, Jennifer Leann. BS in Music, So. Bapt. U., 1981; M in Church Music, New Orleans Bapt. Theol. Sem., 1984, M in Religious Edn., 1984. Music min. First Bapt. Ch., Miller, Mo., 1978, Calvary Bapt. Ch., Jefferson City, Mo., 1980-81, Grace Bapt. Ch., New Orleans, La., 1981-84; min. of edn./music Parker Rd. Bapt. Ch., Florissant, Mo., 1984—; officer St. Louis Bapt. Rel. Educators Assn. 1985-87, officer St. Louis Bapt. Music Mins. Assn. 1989-91. Worship leader Boy Scouts of Am. St. Louis, Camp Beaumont, 1990, winter patrol New Life Evang. Assn., St. Louis, 1989-90. Mem. Mo. Bapt. Religious Edn. Assn., So. Bapt. Religious Edn. Assn.; Mo. Music Men Choir, So. Bapt. Church Music Conf., St. Louis Metro Bapt. Religious Educators Assn. So. Baptist Convention. Office: Parker Road Baptist Ch 2675 Parker Rd Florissant MO 63033

HARVEY, JOEL, chaplain, educator; b. Bklyn., Oct. 26, 1938; s. Abraham and Jenny (Miller) Smolensky; m. Patricia Moore, Mar. 21, 1970; children: Mical Sushil, Alexis Irina, Colin James. BA, Bklyn. Coll., 1968; AM, Adelphi U., 1969; PhD, Fla. State U., 1980; cert., Mercer Sch. Theology, 1984. Ordained to ministry Episcopal Ch. as deacon, 1984, as priest, 1985. Assoc. prof. Adelphi U., Garden City, N.Y., 1970-91, Episcopal chaplain, 1985-89; dir. pastoral care St. Mary's Hosp. for Children, Bayside, N.Y., 1987—; asst. chaplain St. John's Episcopal Hosp., Smithtown, N.Y., 1985-86; chaplain Village of St. John, Smithtown, 1985-86; spiritual dir. Youth Ministries Coun., Diocese L.I., 1986—; assoc. Community St. Mary, 1987—; lectr. George Mercer Sch. Theology, Garden City, N.Y., 1988—; mem. Cath. Fellowship of Episcopal Ch., 1989—. Active Arts Adv., North Shore Sch. Dist., Sea Cliff, N.Y., 1988-89. Named Bayside Clergy of Yr., Kiwanis, 1989. Mem. Coll. Chaplains, Assembly Episcopal Hosps. and Chaplains, Am. Assn. Coll. Profs., Sea Cliff Yacht Club (chaplain 1988—). Home: 5 Highland Ave Glenwood Landing NY 11547

HARVEY, JOHN FREDERICK, college dean, library and information science consultant; b. Maryville, Mo., Aug. 24, 1921; s. Abraham Frederick and Lois Ernestine (Glenn) H. BA, Dartmouth Coll., 1943; BS in Library Sci., U. Ill., 1944; PhD, U. Chgo., 1949. Prof., dean Coll. Info. Studies, Drexel U., Phila., 1958-67, dir. librs., 1958-63; chmn. dept. libr. sci., vis. prof. Faculty Edn., U. Tehran (Iran), 1967-71; founder, tech. dir. Iranian Documentation Ctr. and Tehran Book Processsing Ctr., 1968-71; dean libr. svcs. U. N.Mex., Albuquerque, 1972-74, Hofstra U., Hempstead, N.Y., 1974-76; editor, cons., writer St. Johnsbury, Vt., 1976-78; vis. prof. libr. and info. sci. Al-Zahra Woman's U., Vanak, Tehran, 1978-80; dean students Intercoll., Nicosia, Cyprus, 1984—; cons. internat. libr. and info. sci., 1960—; dean Schiller Internat. U., Cyprus Ctr., 1982; cons. Librs. Unltd., Inc., Littleton, Colo., 1983—; cons. Ea. Mediterranean Regional Office, WHO, 1976-78, Iran, 1976-77, S.E. Asian Regional Office, Indonesia, 1978-79. Author: Advances in Library Administration and Organization, Vol. III, 1984, Internationalizing Library and Information Science Education, 1987, (with others) Information Counsultants in Action, 1986; hon. contbg. cons. Internat. Libr. Rev., London, 1969-89; Cyprus corr., book rev. editor Libr. Times Internat., 1985—; contbr. numerous articles, revs. to profl. jours.

Mem. ALA (coun. 1961-67), Am. Theol. Libr. Assn., Assn. Brit. Theol. and Philos. Librs., Assn. Coll. and Rsch. Librs., Assn. Cyprus Profl. Librs., Assn. Jewish Librs., Brit. Inst. Persian Studies, Cath. Libr. Assn., Ch. and Synagogue Libr. Assn. (founder 1967, pres. 1975-76), Inst. Info. Scientists, Internat. Assn. Orientalist Librs., Libr. Adminstrn. and Mgmt. Assn. (bd. dirs. 1976-78), Libr. Pub. Rels. Assn. of Phila. and Vicinity (hon. life), Luth. Ch. Libr. Assn., Mid. East Librs. Assn., Australian and New Zealand Theol. Library Assn., Modern Greek Soc., Rotary. Avocations: swimming, walking, reading, book reviewing. Home: 605 Chanteclair House, 2 Sophoulis St, Nicosia 136, Cypros Office: 82 Wall St Ste 1105 New York NY 10005

HARVEY, LOUIS-CHARLES, minister, seminary president, religion educator; b. Memphis, May 5, 1945; s. Willie Miles Harvey and Mary Elizabeth Jones: m. Sharon Elaine Jefferson, July 10, 1976; children: Marcus-Louis, Melanee-Charles. BS, LeMoyne-Owen Coll., 1967; MDiv, Colgate Rochester Theol. Sem., 1971; MPhil, Union Sem., N.Y.C., 1977, Phd, 1978. Ordained to ministry A.M.E. Ch. as elder, 1971. Asst. prof. theology Colgate Rochester (N.Y.) Theol. Sem., 1974-78; prof., acad. dean Payne Theol. Sem., Wilberforce, Ohio, 1978-79, pres., 1989—; mem. faculty United Theol. Sem., Dayton, Ohio, 1979-89, prof., 1985-89. Contbr. articles to religious jours. Mem. Challenge 95 Leadership Com., Dayton, 1991. Mem. Soc. for Study of Black Religion (sec. 1988), Am. Acad. Religion, Urban League, Alpha Phi Alpha (sec. 1989-90). Office: Payne Theol Sem 1230 Wilberforce Clifton Rd Wilberforce OH 45384

HARVEY, MARK CHARLES, minister, social worker; b. Tokyo, Apr. 6, 1953; s. C.M. and Phyllis (Mason) H.; m. Mary Frances Baublitz, June 21, 1980; children: Bridget, Evangeline. BS in Sociology, Oklahoma City U., 1974; MS in Social Work, Columbia U., N.Y.C., 1984; MDiv, Union Theol. Sem., N.Y.C., 1984. Ordained to ministry United Meth. Ch., 1984. Dir. rsch. and advocacy Skyline Urban Ministry, Oklahoma City, 1974-76; regional dir. Ecumenical Inst.-Inst. Cultural Affairs, St. Louis, 1976-80; pastor United Meth. Chs. Wrights City, Mo., 1984-87, West Park and New Hope United Meth. Chs., Moberly, Mo., 1987-91; assoc. pastor Stephen Meml. United Meth. Ch., St. John's, Mo., 1991—; treas.-sec. Meth. Fedn. for Social Action, Mo., 1986—; mem. Area Commn. on Higher Edn., United Meth. Ch., Mo., 1987—. Mem. Raldolph County Ministerial Alliance (treas. 1988—). Democrat. Home: 2412 Pebble Beach Dr Overland MO 63114 Office: Stephen Meml United Meth Ch 2730 Watson Rd Saint John's MO 63114

HARVEY, MARK SUMNER, composer, minister, educator, musician; b. Binghamton, N.Y., July 4, 1946; s. Robert Mark and Marjorie Grace (Tolley) H.; m. Kate Matson, Aug. 14, 1983. AB, Syracuse U., 1968; ThM, Boston U., 1971, PhD, 1983. Ordained to ministry Meth. Ch. as deacon, 1970, as elder, 1975. Intern min. Old West United Meth. Ch., Boston, 1969-71, staff mem., assoc. min., 1971-73; min. with jazz and arts community Emmanuel Ch., Boston, 1974—, search and parish profiles com., 1988-90; music faculty mem. MIT, Cambridge, Mass., 1981—; founder, music dir. Aardvark Jazz Orch., 1973—, New Am. Music Ensemble, 1969—. Composer chamber, choral, jazz orch. pieces. Contbr. articles to profl. jours. Pres., founder The Jazz Coalition, inc., Boston, 1971-83; trustee Mass. Cultural Alliance, Boston, 1971-73, 81-87; mem. music adv. panel Mass. Coun. on the Arts and Humanities, Boston, 1971-75, 79-82, Meet the Composer/Reader's Digest Commissioning Program, 1989. Fellow NEH, 1987, The Whiting Found., 1986; recipient Contbn. to Cultural Activity award Mass. Cultural Alliance, 1987, City of Boston, 1980. Fellow Soc. for the Arts, Religion, and Contemporary Culture (chmn. 1991—, bd. dirs. 1986—); mem. ASCAP, Am. Acad. Religion, Am. Studies Assn., Theta Chi Beta. Office: PO Box 8721 JFK Sta Boston MA 02114

HARVEY, THOMAS J., priest, social service organization executive; b. Pitts., Jan. 5, 1939; s. James R. Harvey Sr. and Margaret E. (Gillen). BA, St. Charles Borromeo U., Phila., 1960; STB, Gregorian U., Rome, 1962, MA, Licentiate in Sacred Theology, 1964; MS, Columbia U., 1974. Ordained priest Roman Cath. Ch., 1963. Assoc. pastor Our Lady of Grace Parish, 1964-69; co-adminstr. St. Stephens Parish, Pitts., 1969-72; chaplain, instr. Carlaw Coll., Pitts., 1976-79; pastor St. Kilian Parish, Mars, Pa., 1979-82; asst. dir. Diocesean Dept. of Social and Community Devel., 1974-82; pres., chief exec. officer Cath. Charities USA, Alexandria, Va., 1982—; past mem. dean's adv. council Cath. U. Nat. Cath. Sch. of Social Svc.; bd. dirs. Am. Express Co., Project Hometown Am. Contbr. articles to profl. jours. Treas. Save our Security Coalition; v.p. Nat. Assembly; mem. adv. bd. Robert Wood Johnson Found., Interfaith Caregivers Program, Cath. Health Assn. Task Force on Health Care of the Poor; v.p. for N.Am., Caritas Internat., Carnegie Corp. Task Force on Adolescent Devel. Club: Century. Office: Cath Charities USA Office of Pres 1731 King St Ste 200 Alexandria VA 22314

HARVEY, VAN AUSTIN, religious studies educator; b. Hankow, China, Apr. 23, 1926; s. Earle Ralston and Mary Lee (Mullis) H.; m. Margaret Jean Lynn, Aug. 31, 1950; children: Jonathan Lynn, Christopher Earle. B.A., Occidental Coll., 1948, H.H.D. (hon.), 1964; B.D. (Day fellow, Kent fellow), Yale, 1951, Ph.D., 1957; postgrad., Marburg (Germany) U., 1960-61, Oxford (Eng.) U., 1966-67. Asst. prof. religion dept. Princeton (N.J.) U., 1954-58; assoc. prof. Perkins Sch. Theology, So. Meth. U., Dallas, 1958-62; prof. Perkins Sch. Theology, So. Meth. U., 1962-68, dir. grad. studies, 1965-68; prof. religious thought U. Pa., Phila., 1968-77; chmn. dept. U. Pa., 1971-76, dir. grad. studies, 1969-71; prof. religious studies Stanford U., Calif., 1977-87; chmn. dept. Stanford U., 1980-86, George Edwin Burnell prof. religious studies, 1985. Author: A Handbook of Theological Terms, 1964, The Historian and the Believer, 1966; Contbr. articles to religious and theol. jours. Served with USNR, 1943-46. Guggenheim fellow, 1966, 71; NEH sr. fellow, 1979. Mem. Am. Theol. Soc., Phi Beta Kappa. Office: Stanford U Dept Religious Studies Stanford CA 94305

HARVEY, WILLIAM DANIEL, minister; b. Florence, S.C., Jan. 9, 1958; s. William Ready and Janie Sue (Daniels) H.; m. Mary Elizabeth (Marybeth) Bass, May 29, 1982; children: Molly Elizabeth, Anna Danielle, Erin Bethany. AA, St. Johns River Community, 1978; BA, Stetson U., 1981; MDiv, So. Bapt. Theol. Sem., 1985. Ordained to ministry So. Bapt. Conv., 1984. Assoc. pastor Deltona (Fla.) Lakes Bapt. Ch., 1985-88; pastor The First Bapt. Ch. of Lake Josephine, Sebring, Fla., 1988—; vol. campus min. South Fla. Community Coll., Avon Park, Fla., 1988—; associational vacation Bible sch. dir. Orange Blossom Bapt. Assn., 1988—. Home: 1707 Lake Josephine Dr Sebring FL 33872 Office: First Bapt Ch of Lake Josephine 111 Lake Josephine Dr Sebring FL 33872

HARVEY-BELL, LINDA JEAN, music and youth director; b. Ashtabula, Ohio, Jan. 29, 1960; d. Donald Dennis and Betty Marie (Mausling) Harvey; m. Mark Alan Bell, July 18, 1981 (div. Nov. 1988). MusB in Edn., Kent (Ohio) State U., 1982. Dir. music and youth United Meth. Ch., Chardon, Ohio, 1984—; camp coord. United Meth. Ch., Chardon, 1984—, dist. youth coord., Painesville Dist., Ohio, 1986—, seminar leader, N.E. Ohio, 1988—. Coord. Local Appalachia Svc. Project Team, Chardon, 1985—; mem. Lake Erie Coll. Community Chorus, Mentor, Ohio, 1989—; bd. dirs. Chardon Ecumenical Chorus, Chardon, 1985, 86. Mem. Choirsters Guild. Home: 11717 Basswood Rd Chardon OH 44024 Office: Chardon United Meth Ch 515 North St Chardon OH 44024

HARWELL, FRANCES OLIVIA, parochial school administrator; b. Phila., Jan. 13, 1960; d. Clarence T. Jr. and Olivia Elizabeth (Lee) H.; 1 child, Sherrell Olivia. BA, Montclair State Coll., 1982; MEd, U. N. Tex., 1988. Cert. elem. tchr., Tex., mid-mgmt. adminstr., instrnl. leadership trainer, Tex. tchr. appraiser, CPR and first aid. Primary tchr. Zion Demonstration Primary Sch., Phila., 1983-84; adminstr. Oak Cliff Bible Fellowship Acad., Dallas, 1988—; tchr. appraiser Dallas schs., 1991—. Founder, dir. summer feeding program, community tutoring program, Deptford (N.J.) Twp. Bd. Edn., 1982; judge oratorical contest H.S. Thompson Sch., Dallas, 1989—; coord. community fair day, coach with basketball camp, Dallas, 1989—; mem. PTA, Dallas, 1987—; mem. Dallas Ind. Sch. Dist. Religious and Character Edn. Task Forces, 1989—. Recipient Black Alumni Recognition award, Minority Recognition award Montclair State Coll. Alumni, 1982; named Tchr. of Yr., Bayles Elem. Sch., Dallas, 1987. Mem. Assn. Christian Schs. Internat. (mem. sch. accreditation team 1989—), Internat. Fellowship Christian Sch. Adminstrs., Phi Delta Kappa. Office: Fellowship Christian Acad 1808 W Camp Wisdom Rd Dallas TX 75232 *Individuals strive for many things in life. Even after these things are obtained, they have no purpose without a true understanding of the provider. I am pleased to know the God that is the provider and creator of us all!.*

HARWELL, HUGH BLAKE, minister; b. Paducah, Ky., Jan. 17, 1964; s. Albert Brantley and Joanne (Brindley) H.; m. Dana Cozette Branton, June 25, 1988. BA, Mercer U., 1986; MDiv, So. Bapt. Theol. Sem., 1989. Ordained to ministry So. Bapt. Conv., 1988. Interim min. edn. and youth 1st Bapt. Ch., College Park, Ga., 1987; min. youth 1st Bapt. Ch., Charlestown, Ind., 1988-90; pastor Mt. Hermon Bapt. Ch., Bedford, Ky., 1990—; missionary Home Mission Bd., Anchorage, Alaska, 1983; summer min. youth 1st Bapt. Ch., Vienna, Ga., 1985, Washington, Ga., 1986. Presdl. scholar So. Bapt. Theol. Sem., 1986, Garrett fellow, 1990-91. Mem. Phi Kappa Phi. Democrat. Avocations: hunting, softball, golf, tennis. Home: SBTS Box 81921 2825 Lexington Rd Louisville KY 40280

HARWELL, PAUL LAFAYETTE, minister; b. Savannah, Ga., May 22, 1930; s. Paul Lafayette and Winifred (Chandler) H.; m. Juanita Vickery (div. 1975); children: Paula Ann, Vann, John Michael; m. Sally Wilder, Jan. 12, 1976 (div. 1989). Student, Emory U., Valdosta, 1949-51, Emory U., Atlanta, 1951-52; AB, Valdosta State U., 1959; postgrad., Ga. State U., Atlanta, 1968. Ordained to ministry United Meth. Ch. as deacon, 1960, as elder, 1962. Pastor in charge Hall County Cir. United Meth. Ch., Gainesville, Ga., 1951-53, Barwick (Ga.) Charge, 1955-59, Glenwood Hills United Meth. Ch., Macon, Ga., 1959-61, Shurlington United Meth. Ch., Macon, 1961-63, Garden City (Ga.) United Meth. Ch., 1963-66; tchr. Interdenominational Theol. Ctr., Savannah, Ga., 1964-66; pastor in charge United Meth. Ch., various locations, 1966-80; sr. pastor Jonesboro (Ga.) First United Meth. Ch., 1980-84, Sam Jones United Meth. Ch., Cartersville, Ga., 1984-85, Thomson (Ga.) First United Meth. Ch., 1985-89; Jones Meml. United Meth. Ch., Morrow, Ga., 1989—; mem. Bd. Ordained Ministry, N. Ga. Conf., 1980-88. Paul Harris fellow, Rotary, 1988, Meritorious Svc. award, United Negro Coll. Fund, 1980, others. Mem. Am. Numismatic Assn., Nat. Hist. Soc., United Meth. Vols. in Mission, Greater McDuffie County Ministerial Assn. (chmn. 1989), Rotary (prog. chmn. 1988-89), Phi Alpha Theta. Democrat. Avocations: numismatics, archaeology, antiques. Home: 216 Buena Vista Winder GA 30680 Office: 1st United Meth Ch 921 N Broad St Winder GA 30680 *We are living in a most unusual age. Children are able to read before entering a classroom, young people finish secondary school with computer literacy and the elderly are abreast of world events and much of the latest knowledge. Life is far from simple. Yet it is the simple values handed down from generation to generation that are our hopes in a bewildering and complex time in history.*

HARWELL, THOMAS L., minister; b. Akron, Ohio, May 31, 1958; s. Everett L. and Lula M. (McCutcheon) H. Student, U. Akron, 1976-81; BA in Religious Studies, Bethany Coll., 1983; MDiv, Lexington Theol. Sem., 1986; postgrad., Pitts. Theol. Sem., 1989—. Ordained to ministry Christian Ch. (Disciples of Christ). Youth minister 1st Christian Ch. (Disciples), Charleroi, Pa., 1981-82; pastor Christian Ch. United Ministry, Hazel Green, Ky., 1983-85, White Oak (Ky.) Christian Ch. (Disciples), 1985-88, Oak Hills Christian Ch. (Disciples), Butler, Pa., 1988—; bd. dirs. LOGOS System Assocs., Pitts., 1991-94; chairperson Ch. Action Div. of Pa., Christian Ch. of Pa., 1988—; bd. trustees Disciples of Christ Hist. Soc., Nashville, 1982-86; curator Alexander Campbell Mansion, Bethany, W.Va., 1982-83; mem. gen. bd. Christian Ch. (Disciples of Christ), 1991—. Mem. SPEBEQSA, Butler, 1988—; tenor Hourglass Barbershop Quartet, Butler, 1988—; sign lang. interpreter Akron Met. Housing, 1976-81; pres. Kiwanis Club, West Liberty, Ky., 1987-88. Mem. NW Dist. Christian Ch. (v.p. 1988—), Sons of Italy, Masons, Order of Ea. Star (chaplain 1987-88). Home and Office: Oak Hills Christian Ch 113 Township Line Rd Butler PA 16001

HARWICK, BETTY CORINNE BURNS, sociology educator; b. L.A., Jan. 22, 1926; d. Henry Wayne Burns and Dorothy Elizabeth (Menzies) Routhier; m. Burton Thomas Harwick, June 20, 1947; children: Wayne Thomas, Burton Terence, Bonnie Christine Foster, Beverly Anne Carroll. Student, Biola, 1942-45, Summer Inst. Linguistics, 1945, U. Calif., Berkeley, 1945-52; BA, Calif. State U., Northridge, 1961, MA, 1965. Prof. sociology Pierce Coll., Woodland Hills, Calif., 1966—, pres. acad. senate, 1976-77, pres. faculty assn., 1990-91, chair dept. for philosophy and sociology, 1990—; co-founder, faculty advisor interdisciplinary religious studies program Pierce Coll., Woodland Hills, 1988—, creator courses in religious studies in philosophy and sociology depts., Pierce Coll. Author: (with others) Introducing Sociology, 1977; author: Workbook for Introducing Sociology, 1978. faculty rep. Calif. Community Coll. Assn., Sacramento, 1977-80. Alt. fellow NEH, 1978. Mem. Am. Acad. Religion, Soc. Bibl. Lit., Am. Sociol. Assn. Presbyterian. Home: 19044 Superior St Northridge CA 91324 Office: LA Pierce Coll 6201 Winnetka Ave Woodland Hills CA 91371

HARWICK, LOIS HOOVER, religious organization administrator; b. Lancaster, Pa., Aug. 28, 1924; d. Henry Alfred and Anna Madeline (Geisler) Hoover; m. Ray Linford Harwick, Aug. 17, 1947; children: Diana, Joslyn, Nevin. BS in Edn., Millersville U., 1946; postgrad., Pa. State U., Otterbein Coll., Ohio State U.; A in Christian Edn., Hartford Sem., 1985. Cert. elem. tchr., Pa., Ohio. Interim dir. Christian edn. First. Congl. Ch., Glastonbury, Conn., 1979, Rocky Hill (Conn.) Congl. Ch., 1983-84; interim dir. Christian edn. Congl. Ch., South Glastonbury, Conn., 1984-87, dir. Christian edn., 1987—. Mem. mission projects com. Christian edn. dept. Conn. Conf., Hartford, 1987-90; coord. vols. Salmon Brook Convalescent Home; chair Glastonbury Nuclear Arms Freeze Task Force, 1982-88; bd. dirs. Literacy Vols. Am., 1986-90, tutor, 1980—, tutor trainer, 1991—. Democrat. Mem. United Ch. Christ. Office: Congl Ch in South Glastonbury Main and High Sts South Glastonbury CT 06073

HASBROUCK, NORMAN GENE, dean; b. Corry, Pa., Apr. 30, 1952; s. Gene Bennett and Anna Bell (Lucas) H.; m. Ellen Ann Kidd, Nov. 26, 1977; children: Christopher Scott, Thomas Brian. BA in Biology, Thiel Coll., 1974; MA in Guidance/Counseling, Slippery Rock U., 1979; postgrad., Ind. U. of Pa., 1987—. Admissions counselor Thiel Coll., Greenville, Pa., 1974-76, dir., summer conf., 1975; dir. admissions LaRoche Coll., Pitts., 1976-80, instr., 1978-79; dir. admissions California U. of Pa., 1980-81, dean admissions, acad. records, 1981-87, dean enrollment mgmt., acad. svcs., 1987—; bd. dirs. Thiel Coll., pres., 1984-89; cons. Cheyney U., Pa., 1983, Medialle Coll., Buffalo, N.Y., 1984; chmn.-on-site Nat. Assn. Coll.Admissions Counselors Fair, Pitts., 1978—; adv. bd. Act 101 and Upward Bound Programs, LaRoche Coll., 1977-80 and others; presentor Coun. for Advancement of Small Colls. Conf., 1978, Mid. State Assn. Collegiate Registrars and Officer of Admissions Conf., 1984 and others. Columnist Thielensian, "The Old Grad", 1976. Elder Mt. Pleasant (Pa.) Presbyn. Ch., 1978-80; talk show guest host Sta. KDKA-TV "Campus Connections", Pitts.; coach Calif. Youth Soccer Assn., 1988—. Named to Outstanding Young Men of Am., 1980; Rotary award, 1970 and others. Mem. Pa. U. Admissions Assn. (pres. 1984), Pa. Assn. Coll. Admissions Counselors (human rels. 1979-81), Admissions Commn.- Pitts. Coun. on Higher Edn. (pres. 1979), Am. Assn. Coll. Registrars and Admissions Office, Long Branch Gun Club (v.p. 1986), Calif. Gun Club, Phi Delta Kappa (v.p. 1982, pres. 1983), Delta Sigma Phi (offices 1972-74, James McGee award 1974). Republican. Avocations: photography, hunting, fishing, sports, home building. Home: 160 Quarry Lane California PA 15419 Office: California U of Pa 209 Administration Bldg California PA 15419

HASEL, FRANK M., minister; b. Wingarten, West Germany, May 13, 1962; s. Kurt H. and Berbel (Ludwig) H.; m. Ulrike Hasel, July 31, 1988; 1 child, Jonathan M. BA in Religion, Seminar Marienhohe, Darmstadt, West Germany, 1985; MA in Religion, Andrews U., Berrien Springs, Mich., 1989. Minister Seventh-Day Adventists, Penzberg, West Germany, 1985-88. Mem. Soc. of Bibl. Lit., Adventist Theol. Soc., Theta Alpha Kappa. Home: 550 Maplewood Ct F-68 Berrien Springs MI 49103

HASEL, GERHARD FRANZ, religion educator, researcher; b. Vienna, Austria, July 27, 1935; came to U.S., 1958, naturalized, 1964; s. Franz Joseph and Magdalena (Schroeter) H.; m. Hilde Schafer, June 11, 1961; children—Michael Gerald, Marlena Susan, Melissa Helen. Lic. Theol., Marienhohe Sem. (Germany), 1958; B.A., Atlantic Union Coll., 1959; M.A., Andrews U., 1960, B.D., 1962; Ph.D., Vanderbilt U., 1970. Ordained to ministry Seventh-day Adventist Ch., 1966, Minister So. New Eng. Conf., Boston, 1962-63; asst. prof. religion So. Coll., Collegedale, Tenn., 1963-67; prof. O.T. and Bibl. theology Andrews U., Berrien Springs, Mich., 1967—, chmn. O.T. dept., 1974-82, assoc. editor Sem. Studies, 1973—, dean Theol. Sem., 1982-88; dir. PhD/ThD programs, 1979—, John Nevins Andrews prof. Old Testament theology, 1992— . Author: The Remnant, 1972, Old Testament Theology, 1980, New Testament Theology, 1982, Jonah: Messenger of the Eleventh Hour, 1974, Covenant in Blood, 1982, Understanding the Living Word of God, 1983, Interpreting the Bible Today, 1985, Understanding the Book of Amox, 1991; co-editor: The Flowering of Olt Testament Theology, 1991; contbr. articles to profl. jours., dictionaries, encys. Hillel grantee Vanderbilt U., 1968, Danforth tchr. grantee, 1968-70. Mem. Soc. Bibl. Lit., Internat. Soc. for Study of O.T., Am. Acad. Religion, Mich. Acad. Sci., Arts and Letters, Am. Schs. Oriental Research, Chgo. Soc. Bibl. Studies, Adventist Theol. Soc. (pres. 1990—). Home: 9984 Red Bud Trail Berrien Springs MI 49103 Office: Andrews U Theol Sem Berrien Springs MI 49104

HASEL, MICHAEL GERALD, lay worker; b. Madison, Tenn., Sept. 19, 1968; s. Gerhard Franz and Hilde (Schafer) H. Student, Sem. Schloss Bogenhofen, Austria, 1989; BA in Religion and German cum laude and with honors, Andrews U., 1991. Sabbath Sch. supt. Village Adventist Ch., Berrien Springs, Mich., 1990-91; vol. archeaol. excavation, Gezer, Israel, 1990-92, Ashkelon, Israel, 1991, Tel Dar, Israel, 1991. Mem. Michiana Symphony Orch., Berrien Springs, 1989-92, Wind Symphony, Berrien Springs, 1990-92. Performance scholar Andrews U., 1987-91, Honors scholar, 1990-91; travel scholar Am. Sch. Oriental Rsch., Gezer, 1990. Mem. Soc. Bibl. Lit., Am. Acad. Religion, Am. Schs. Oriental Rsch. (travel scholar 1990), Am. Oriental Soc., Am. Inst. Archaeology, Theta Alpha Kappa (pres. local chpt. 1990-91), Alpha Mu Gamma. Home: 9984 Red Bud Trail Berrien Springs MI 49103

HASENOEHRL, DANIEL NORBERT FRANCIS, priest; b. Portland, July 12, 1929; s. Norbert Frank and Anna Teresa (Feucht) H. Student, U. Portland, 1947-49; BA, Mt. Angel Sem., St. Benedict, Oreg., 1951; MEd, U. Portland, 1958. Ordained priest Roman Cath. Ch., 1960. Counselor/registrar Mt. Angel Prep. Sch., Oreg., 1960-64; counselor Mt. Angel Sem., St. Benedict, Oreg., 1962-71; acad. dean/registrar Mt. Angel Sem., 1964-71, acting pres., 1969-70, instr., 1963-71; assoc. pastor Our Lady of Sorrows Parish, Portland, 1972-75; chaplain Marylhurst Coll., Lake Oswego, Oreg., 1975-81, Dammasch State Hosp., Wilsonville, Oreg., 1975—. With U.S. Army, 1952-54. Mem. Nat. Cath. Chaplains Assn., Assn. for Religious Values in Counseling, Am. Mental Health Counselors Assn., Am. Assn. for Higher Edn. Democrat. Roman Catholic. Avocations: horticulture, photography. Home: PO Box 19113 Portland OR 97280-0113 Office: Dammasch State Hosp Pastoral Services Wilsonville OR 97070

HASKELL, BENJAMIN BRUCE, minister, educational administrator; b. Attleboro, Mass., Oct. 24, 1953; s. Chester Hugh and Janet Stacia (Buck) H.; m. Margaret Ellen Devlin, Aug. 24, 1974; children: Margaret Ann, Janet Marie, Evelyn Diane. BA, U. Mass., 1975; MA, Grace Theol. Sem., 1991. Lic. to ministry Assemblies of God, 1982; cert. tchr., Mass. Christian worker Assemblies Of God, Mansfield, Mass., 1973-78; tchr., chaplain Faith Christian Acad., Hyannis, Mass., 1978-87; assoc. pastor Assemblies Of God, Dennis, Mass., 1985-87; assoc. pastor, prin. Heritage Christian Life Ctr., Assemblies of God, North Falmouth, Mass., 1987-91; prin., dir. Heritage Christian Acad., North Falmouth, 1987-91; prin. West Hills Christian Sch., Portland, Oreg., 1991—; rep., del. Heritage Christian Day Care, North Falmouth, 1990-81; assoc. pastor Mid Cape Assembly of God, Dennis, 1985-87; deacon Faith Assembly of God, Hyannis, 1979-84. Mem. Assn. Christian Schs. (cert. adminstr.), Fellowship Christian Sch. Adminstrs., Assemblies of God. Home: 7300 SW 158th Pl Beaverton OR 97007 Office: West Hills Christian Sch 7945 SW Capitol Hill Rd Portland OR 97219-2699 *To obey God in difficult and challenging times is the only course of action. To do otherwise is to cheat self and others of His reward.*

HASKELL, EVAN CHARLES, religious association executive; b. Chattanooga, Mar. 23, 1939; s. E.C. Haskell Sr. and Cleona (Brown) H.; m. Carolyn S. Shelfield, Feb. 14, 1964; children: Jonathan, Jeremy. THG, Tenn. Temple Bible Sch., 1960; BA, Temple U., Chattanooga, 1966; BRE, Temple Bapt. Sem., 1967; HHD, Okla. Bapt. U., 1980. Dir. admissions Temple U., Chattanooga, 1966-86; exec. dir. Nat. Christian Coll. Athletic Assn., Chattanooga, 1986-89; exec. adminstr. Assn. Baptist for World Evangelism, Cherry Hill, N.J., 1989—. Bd. dirs. Chattanooga Area Conv. and Visitors, 1984-89, SCORE, Chattanooga, 1985—, Chattanooga Area Mayors Prayer Breakfast, 1986-89. Republican. Baptist. Avocations: water sports, hiking. Home: 1905 Huntington Dr Cherry Hill NJ 08003 Office: Assn Baptist for World Evangelism PO Box 5000 Cherry Hill NJ 08034 *"He is no fool who gives what he cannot keep to gain what he cannot lose." (Jim Elliott).*

HASKIN, LUCILLE ARLEPHA, religion educator; b. Dixon, Nebr., Nov. 12, 1926; d. John Edward and Adeline (Harvey) McDaniel; m. Jimmie O. Haskin, Dec. 18, 1948; children: Bonnie, Betty, Dick. Grad. high sch., Creighton, Nebr. Tchr. pub. schs., 1945-49; tchr. Sunday sch. United Med. Ch., 1986-91; pres. United Meth. Women, 1991—; owner Haskin Draperies, Royal, 1977—; mem. Bible study, 1988-91; treas. United Meth. Ch., Royal, 1986-91, tchr. Sunday sch., 1989-91, lay speaker on conf., 1990—; owner Haskin Draperies, Royal, 1977—. Home: PO Box 95 Royal NE 68773 *You can do what you want to or be what you want to be as long as you keep God in the center of your life.*

HASLEY, RONALD K., bishop. Bishop Evang. Luth. Ch. in Am., Rockford, Ill. Office: Evang Luth Ch in Am 103 W State St Rockford IL 61101*

HASLING, JANIE BARRIOS, lay worker; b. Lockport, La., Jan. 21, 1959; d. Henry B. and Joyce Janie (Pepper) Barrios; children: Scott Paul, Jessica Bonnie. BA in English Edn., U. Southwestern La., 1984; postgrad., Nicholls State U., 1987; student, Moody Corr. Sch., Chgo., 1990—. Cert. tchr., La. Treas. Faith Christian Fellowship, Lockport, La., 1985-86; registered agt., sec.-treas. Victory Life, Lockport, 1988—; owner Bayou Bibles & Books Bookstore, Lockport, 1990—; music leader Faith Christian Fellowship, Lockport, 1986-88; pianist Victory Life, Lockport, 1988—. Home: 42 Comeaux Dr Lockport LA 70374 Office: Bayou Bibles & Books 211 Crescent Ave Lockport LA 70374

HASSELBRING, CHARLES M., II, youth minister; b. Grand Rapids, Mich., Sept. 26, 1963; s. Charles M. and Kathryn L. (Horner) H.; m. Margaret Lisa Tubhey, Aug. 15, 1987. BA, Olivet Nazarene U., 1985. Ordained deacon Ch. of the Nazarene, 1990. Assoc. pastor, youth West Michigan Ave. Nazarene Ch., Battle Creek, Mich., 1985-86, Venice (Fla.) Ch. of the Nazarene, 1986-90; min. of youth Coll. Ch. of the Nazarene, Bourbonnais, Ill., 1990—; mem. Mich. Dist. NYI Coun., Grand Rapids, 1985-86; v.p. So. Fla. Dist. NYI Coun., Boca Raton, 1988-90, Chgo. Cen. Dist. NYI Coun., Bourbonnais, Ill., 1990—. Mem. Chgo. Cen. Dist. Youth Coun. (v.p. 1990—). Republican. Home: 257 E Country Ct Bourbonnais IL 60914

HASSELL, JAMES THOMAS, JR. (CHUCK HASSELL), minister; b. Baldwyn, Miss., Nov. 20, 1959; s. James Thomas and Ruth Ellen (Russell) H.; m. Tammy Lyn Henderson, May 24, 1980; children: Russell Dwayne, James Thomas III, Henderson Taylor. AB in Ministries, Atlanta Christian Coll., East Point, Ga., 1981, BTh, 1988; MMin, Mid-South Christian Coll., Memphis, 1991. Ordained to ministry, Christian Ch., 1980. Youth minister First Christian Ch., Baldwyn, Miss., 1978-79, Columbus, Ga., 1979-80; youth minister E. Point (Ga.) Christian Ch., 1982-85; minister First Christian Ch., Southaven, Miss., 1985-89, Community Christian Ch., Jackson, Miss., 1989—; asst. prof. youth ministries Mid-South Christian Coll., Memphis, 1988-89; pres. Christian Youth of Ga., 1985-86; v.p. Miss. Christian Conv., Tupelo, 1991; bd. dirs. Miss. Christian Svc. Camp, 1989—, Sunbelt Christian Youth Ranch, 1990—, sec.-treas., 1990—; pres. Miss. Christian Conv., 1992. Youth coach Southaven Athletic/Brandon Athletic Assns., 1987—. Mem. Miss. Jaycees (dir., chaplain 1987-88). Home: 21 Carriage Ct Brandon MS 39042 Office: Community Christian Ch PO Box 1393 Brandon MS 39043

HASSINGER, KEITH BYRD, clergyman; b. Binghamton, N.Y., Dec. 14, 1941; s. Keith Bird and Mary (Farynyk) H.; m. Donna Johnson, Sept. 8, 1963; children: Deborah Jean, Kerri B., Holly Hope, Karla Kay. BA, Andrews U., 1963, MA, 1964; MD, Autonomour U. Guadalajara, 1978. Ordained to ministry Seventh-day Adventist Ch. Pastor Chesapeake Conf. Seventh-Day Adventists, Frederick-Towson-Waldorf, Md., 1965-68; youth dir., evangelist Far Ea. Inland Mission, Guam Island, Micronesia, 1969-72; v.p. Tex. Conf. Seventh-Day Adventists, Keene, 1984-88; sr. pastor So. Calif. Conf. Seventh-Day Adventists, Canoga Park, 1988—. Home: 10938 Key West Ave Northridge CA 91324 Office: Canoga Park Seventh-Day Adventist Ch 20550 Roscoe Blvd Canoga Park CA 91306

HASSLER, WILLIAM WOODS, lay worker; b. Cleafield, Pa., Sept. 6, 1917; s. John William and Clara (Woods) H.; m. Mary Ellen Jackson, June 12, 1941; children: Virginia, Thomas, Martha. BS in Chemistry, Juniata Coll., Huntingdon, Pa., 1939, LLD (hon.), 1974; MS in Chemistry, U. Pa., 1941, PhD, 1951. Prof., dept. chmn. Beaver Coll., Jenkintown, Pa., 1951-63, Ea. Bapt. Coll., 1958-62; religious worker, 1960—; lectr. sci. and religion, 1951-53, adult Christian edn. programs, 1970—. Author: Coping, 1990, Episcopalian, 1980, Story of "O Little Town of Bethlehem", 1984. Mem. Am. Chem. Soc. Home: 448 N Braddock St Winchester VA 22601

HASTEY, STANLEY LEROY, religious organization administrator, minister, journalist; b. Thomas, Okla., Sept. 13, 1944; s. Ervin Elmer and Ethel Ruth (Tyson) H.; m. Elizabeth Ann Baldwin, Aug. 28, 1964; children: Lisa Beth Hastey Kettlewell, Stephen Baldwin. BA, Okla. Bapt. U., 1966; MDiv, So. Bapt. Theol. Sem., 1970, PhD, 1973. Ordained to ministry Bapt. Ch., 1964. Info. asst. Bapt. Joint Com. on Pub. Affairs, Washington, 1974-75, dir. denom. svcs., 1976-78, dir. info. svcs., 1978-88; bur. chief Bapt. Press News Svc., Washington, 1978-88; exec. dir. Alliance of Bapts., Washington, 1989—; trustee Bapt. Theol. Sem., Richmond, Va., 1989—; cons. Am. Bapt. Task Force on the So. Bapt. Conv., Valley Forge, Pa., 1989—. Co-author: The Partnership Principle, 1984; contbr. articles to religious jours. Recipient Lillian R. Block award Religious News Svc., N.Y.C., 1985, Outstading Alumni Achievement award Okla. Bapt. U., 1986. Mem. Am. Bapt. Hist. Soc., So. Bapt. Hist. Soc., Va. Bapt. Hist. Soc., Okla. Bapt. Hist. Soc., Bapt. Pub. Rels. Assn. (pres. 1979-80, Frank Burkhalter award 1983, 85). Democrat. Avocations: reading, cinema, golf. Office: The Alliance of Bapts 1328 Sixteenth St NW Washington DC 20036

HASTINGS, ROBERT JEAN, minister; b. Marion, Ill., May 17, 1924; s. George Eldon and Ruby Bell (Gordon) H.; m. Bessie Ruth Emling, Apr. 1, 1945; children: Ruth Anne, Nancy Sue, Timothy Louis. BA, So. Ill. U., 1945; BDiv, Southwestern Bapt. Seminary, Ft. Worth, Tex., 1948, DTh, 1950; LLD, Judson Coll., 1977. Ordained to ministry So. Bapt. Conv., 1943. Minister Univ. Bapt. Ch., Carbondale, Ill., 1965-67; asst. dir. promotion So. Bapt. Exec. Com., Nashville, 1955-60; dir. promotion Ky. Bapt. Conv., Middletown, Ky., 1960-65; editor The Illinois Baptist, Springfield, 1967-84; author, profl. speaker, self-employed Springfield, 1984—; recording sec. Ill. Bapt. State Assn., Springfield, 1951-54; pres. So. Bapt. Press Assn., Nashville, 1983-84. Author: A Nickel's Worth of Skim Milk (award Ill. Hist. Soc. 1973, Dwight L. Moody Award for Excellence in Christian Lit. 1974), We Were There (2d place award Bicentennial competition So. Bapt. Hist. Commn. 1976, award Ill. Hist. Soc. 1977), A Penney's Worth of Minced Ham, 1984 (award Ill. Hist. Soc. 1985); author/photographer series of articles The Illinois Bapt. jour. Recipient Delta award Friends of Morris Libr., So. Ill. U., 1989. Mem. Ill. Writers. Home and Office: 98 Laconwood Springfield IL 62707

HASTRICH, JEROME JOSEPH, bishop; b. Milw., Nov. 13, 1914; s. George Philip and Clara (Dettlaff) H. Student, Marquette U., 1933-35; BA, St. Francis Sem., Milw., 1940, MA, 1941; student, Cath. U. Am., 1941. Ordained priest Roman Cath. Ch., 1941; assigned to Milw. Chancery, 1941; curate St. Ann's Ch., Milw., St. Bernard's Ch., Madison, Wis.; asst. chaplain St. Paul U. Chapel, then U. Wis.; sec. to bishop of Diocese U. Wis., Madison, Wis., 1946-52; chancellor Diocese Madison, Wis., 1952-53; apptd. vicar gen. Diocese Madison, 1953, domestic prelate, 1954, protonotary apos., 1960; aux. bishop, 1963-67, titular bishop of Gurza and aux. of Madison, 1963; pastor St. Raphael Cathedral, Madison, 1967-69; bishop Gallup, N.Mex., 1969-90, ret.; diocesan dir. Confraternity Christian Doctrine, 1946—, St. Martin Guild, 1946-69; aux. chaplain U.S. Air Force, 1947-67; pres. Latin Am. Mission Program; sec. Am. Bd. Cath. Missions; vice chmn. Bishop's Com. for Spanish Speaking; mem. subcom. on allocations U.S. Bishops Com. for Latin Am.; founder, episcopal moderator Queen of Americas Guild, 1979—; pres. Nat. Blue Army of Our Lady of Fatima, 1980—. Mem. Gov. Wis. Commn. Migratory Labor, 1964—. Club: K.C. (hon. life mem.). Home: PO Box 1777 Gallup NM 87305

HATCH, JANET MAUREEN, evangelistic minister; b. Parsons, Kans., Nov. 16, 1948; d. Jessie Cashman and Maxine Rachel (Luellen) Causey; m. George Clifford Hatch, June 18, 1972; children: Daniel Lee, Rebecca Ann. Evangelist Bible Way Assn., Donaphin, Mo., 1982—. Republican. Avocations: sewing, hand crafts, painting. Home and Office: 1052 W 6th St West Plains MO 65775

HATCH, RUTH CORDLE, religion educator; b. Atlanta, Apr. 24, 1935; d. Harry Jordan and Mary Louise (Miller) Cordle; m. Maynard F. Hatch II, July 27, 1957; children: Carolyn Ruth Hatch Myers, Keith Maynard. BA, Ea. Coll., St. Davids, Pa., 1957; MA, U. No. Iowa, 1981; PhD, Kans. State U., 1985; MDiv, Cen. Bapt. Theol. Sem., 1986. Adj. prof. family life ministries Cen. Bapt. Theol. Sem., Kansas City, Kans., 1986—, researcher Black Youth in Black Ch. project, 1987-88; adj. prof. Ottawa U., Kansas City, 1987—; researcher in field Kans. State U., Manhattan, 1989-90. Contbr. articles to profl. jours. Mem. Soc. for Sci. Study Religion, Nat. Coun. on Family Rels. (vice chair religion and family life sect. 1989-91), Kappa Omicron Nu, Phi Upsilon Omicron. Office: Cen Bapt Theol Sem Seminary Hts Kansas City KS 66102

HATCHER, BALDWIN, minister, educator; b. Chgo., Aug. 27, 1953; s. Willie James and Carmelethia (Hunt) H. BA, NYU, 1976; MDiv, Union Theol. Sem., N.Y.C., 1980. Ordained to ministry Bapt. Ch., 1980. Min. Sharon Bapt. Ch., N.Y.C., 1973-77, Greater Zion Hill Bapt. Ch., N.Y.C., 1979-87; tchr. N.Y.C. Bd. Edn., 1984—; min. Riker's Island Ho. of Detention for Men, N.Y.C., 1975; guest lectr. NYU, 1976; adj. lectr. Bronx Community Coll., 1982-83; chaplain Terence Cardinal Cook Hosp., N.Y.C., 1985-87; panelist Black studies program Taconic Correctional facility, Mt. Kisco, N.Y. Vol. fund raiser Assn. for Help of Retarded Children, N.Y.C., 1990—. Nat. Fellowship Fund fellow, 1976-80; Roothbert Fund scholar, 1976. Home: 790 Concourse Village W # 8-B Bronx NY 10451 *Oppression has many ramifications. Many times when a group of people are oppressed by a common enemy, they tend to oppress each other. However, those with scope never lose sight of the common enemy.*

HATCHER, LEANNA JEPSON, infection control practitioner; b. Camp Le June, N.C., July 31, 1954; d. George Thomas and Shirley Joy (Palmquist) Jepson. BSN, Old Dominion U., 1976. RN, Va., N.C.; cert. in infection control. Staff nurse Okla. Children's Hosp., Oklahoma City, 1976-77; nurse pub. health Okla. State Dept. Health, 1977-81, Wayne County Health Dept., Goldsboro, N.C., 1981-82; infection control practitioner Lenoir Meml. Hosp., Kinston, N.C., 1982-87, Pitt County Meml. Hosp., Greenville, N.C., 1987-90; dir. infection control Richmond (Va.) Meml. Hosp., 1990—; mem. faculty Eastern Assn. Health Ednl. Coun., Greenville, 1987-90; mem. county, hosp. and pub. sch. task force for AIDS Edn. & Policy; educator for sch., univ.and pub. health care workers on AIDS (prevention & disease). Mem. Assn. Infection Control Practitioners. Avocations: sewing, swimming, biking, gardening. Home: 6024 Wainwright Dr Richmond VA 23225 Office: Richmond Meml Hosp Richmond VA 23225

HATCHER, RICHARD D., SR., pastor; b. Mobile, Ala., Oct. 11, 1948; s. Richard Green and Mary Jane (Graves) H.; m. Patricia Ann Strickland, Dec. 20, 1969; children: Richard D. Jr., Gordon, Amanda. BTh, Gulf Coast Bapt. Inst., 1976; MTh, Internat. Bible Inst., 1980; ThD, Fla. Bapt. Sch., 1984. 1st Missionary Bapt. Ch., Pensacola, Fla., 1975-78, Village Green Bapt. Ch., 1978-83, 1st Bapt. Ch. Belle Fontaine, Theodore, Ala., 1983—; instr., registrar Gulf Coast Bapt. Inst., Theodore, 1983-85, founder, pres. Biblical Stewardship, Inst., Theodore, 1980—, v.p. Temple Bapt. Inst., Gulfport, Miss., 1989—. Author: Biblical Stewardship, 1980. Chaplain Fowl River Vol. Fire Dept., Belle Fontaine, 1990. with U.S. Army Nat. Guard, 1970-76. Republican. Home: 11170 Pioneer Rd Theodore AL 36582 Office: 1st Bapt Ch Bell Fontaine 3310 Baumhauer Rd Theodore AL 36582

HATCHETT, LLOYD RAY, minister; b. Lubbock, Tex., Jan. 23, 1937; s. Lester Preston and Fannie Belle (Wallis) H.; m. Jean Parnell, Feb. 27, 1958; children: Laurie Ann, Robert Larry. AA, Jacksonville (Tex.) Coll., 1958. Ordained to ministry So. Bapt. Conv., 1958. Pastor Landmark Missionary Bapt. Ch., Deming, N.Mex., 1963-65, Cen. Bapt. Ch., El Paso, Tex., 1965-69, Ashlan Park Bapt. Ch., Fresno, Calif., 1969-73, West Park Bapt. Ch., Fresno, 1977-83, 1st So. Bapt. Ch., Kerman, Calif., 1983—; regional mgr. Primerica Fin., Fresno, 1985—; sec. missions N.Mex. Bapt. Assn., El Paso, 1965-69. Editor N.Mex. Bapt. Messenger, 1968-69. Guest speaker Masten Towers, Fresno, 1972-91, Fresno Rescue Missions, 1983-91. Mem. CAP (maj., chaplain Fresno 1979—, Chaplain of Yr. award, Sr. Mem. of Yr. award). Republican. Office: 1st So Bapt Ch 14669 West G St Kerman CA 93630

HATER, ROBERT JAMES, priest, religious studies educator; b. Cin., Feb. 2, 1934; s. Stanley Charles and Olivia Lida (Roth) H. BA, Athenaeum of Ohio, 1957, MA, 1959; PhD, St. John's U., 1967; LHD (hon.), Ursuline Coll., 1985. Ordained priest Roman Cath. Ch., 1959. Asst. pastor Holy Angel's Ch., Cin., 1960-63; prof. philosophy Athenaeum of Ohio, Norwood, 1967-73, dir. grad. dept. philosophy, 1968-73; dir. religious edn. Archdiocese of Cin., 1973-79; prof. religious studies U. Dayton, Ohio, 1981—; tchr. high sch., Cin., 1960-64; counselor, advisor archdiocesean parishes and schs., Cin., 1960—; nat. lectr. and keynote speaker numerous religious convs. and groups. Author: Parish Catechetical Ministry, 1986, Holy Family, 1988, News That Is Good, 1990, 7 other books; contbr. numerous articles to mags., newspapers and profl. jours. Bd. dirs. Working in Neighborhoods, Cin., 1980's. Mem. Nat. Conf. Diosean dirs. Religious Edn., Cath. Theol. Soc. Am., Nat. Coun. for Cath. Evangelization. Office: U Dayton Dept Religious Studies 300 College Pk Dayton OH 45469

HATFIELD, LEONARD FRASER, retired bishop; b. Port Greville, N.S., Can., Oct. 1, 1919; s. Otto Albert and Ada (Tower) H. B.A., King's-Dalhousie U., Halifax, N.S., 1940; M.A., King's-Dalhousie U., 1943, D.D. hon., 1956, 85. Ordained deacon Anglican Ch. of Can., 1942, ordained priest, 1943; priest asst. All Sts. Cathedral, Halifax, 1942-46; rector Antigonish, N.S., 1946-51; asst. sec. council social service Anglican Ch. of Can., 1951-54, gen. sec., 1955-61; rector Christ Ch., Dartmouth, N.S., 1961-71, St. John's Ch., Truro, N.S., 1971-76; canon All Sts. Cathedral, Halifax, 1969; suffragan bishop of Nova Scotia, 1976-80; bishop of N.S. Halifax, 1980-84; chmn. Diocesan Council of N.S. Synod, corp. Anglican Diocesan Ctr.; chmn. Dean and Chpt. All Sts. Cathedral; organizing sec. Primate's World Relief and Devel. Fund; mem. Council of Chs. on Justice and Corrections; founding mem. Vanier Inst. Family, Ottawa; mem. Anglican Consultative Council; various coms. World Council Chs. and Gen. Synod; convenor Primate's Task Force on Ordination of Women to Priesthood; Anglican mem. and Can. rep. Internat. Bishops' Seminar, Rome, 1980. Author: He Cares, 1958, Simon Gibbons, 1987, Sammy-The Prince, 1990. Former chmn. bd. govs. King's Coll.; bd. dirs. Inst. Pastoral Tng. Atlantic Sch. Theology. Address: Site #31 Box #0, RR #3, Parrsboro, NS Canada B0M 1S0

HATFIELD, ROGER WILLIAM, religious educator; b. Kansas City, Mo., June 10, 1945; s. William Jackson and Lucille Elizabeth (Weaver) H.; m. Linda Dean Baker, Aug. 12, 1967; children: Angela Lynn, Melissa Ann. AA, Southwest Bapt. Coll., Bolivar, Mo., 1965, BA, 1967; MA, U. Mo., Kansas City, 1972; PhD, U. Mo., Columbia, 1991. Assoc. pastor Calvary Bapt. Ch., Jefferson City, Mo., 1975-80; minister of edn. and music Southridge Bapt. Ch., Jefferson City, 1980-82; adult assoc. Sunday Sch. Dept. Mo. Bapt. Conv., Jefferson City, 1982—; pres. Mo. Bapt. Religious Edn. Assn., Jefferson City, 1990-91; mem. com. So. Bapt. Religious Edn. Assn., Ft. Worth, Tex., 1988-89. Contbr. articles to profl. jours.; editor: (newsletter) The Assist Leader, 1989-90. Recipient Herbert Schooling scholarship Coll. of Edn., U. Mo., Columbia, 1987. Mem. Religious Edn. Assn. of U.S. and Can., Am. Assn. Adult and Continuing Edn., So. Bapt. Assn. Ministries With the Aging, Mo. Valley Adult Edn. Assn., Mo. Bapt. Religious Edn. Assn. (pres. 1990-91), Kappa Delta Pi.

HATFIELD, WILLIAM KEITH, minister; b. Detroit, Dec. 26, 1951; s. William Grant and Marquita (Ratliff) H.; m. Sharon Jean, Aug. 26, 1972; children: Sarah, Elisabeth, Matthew, Charity, Jonathan, Joshua. BA, Bapt. Bible Coll., 1976. Ordained to ministry So. Bapt. Conv., 1976. Assoc. pastor Brown Ave. Bapt. Ch., Springfield, Mo., 1974-76; pastor Bible Bapt. Ch., South Haven, Mich., 1976-79, Golden Gate Bapt. Ch., Tulsa, 1979-85, Charity Bapt. Ch., Tulsa, 1985—; prof. Old Testament Survey Mingo Bible Inst., 1987—; mem. bd. advisors Moral Majority, Tulsa, 1981—; host TV show Dynamics for Living, 1982-83, 85—. Columnist Tulsa Tribune, 1983—. Spokesman Oklahomans for Life, 1983-85, Tulsans for Life, 1983-85. Republican. Home: 5315 E 26th Pl Tulsa OK 74114 Office: Charity Bapt Ch 7301 E 15th St Tulsa OK 74112 *Never view God through your circumstances, view your circumstances through God.*

HATGIDAKIS, JOHN ANTHONY, minister; b. Bklyn., Oct. 31, 1946; s. Jack Hatgis and Marie Rose (Bescript) Root; m. Marsha Kay Anderson, Aug. 6, 1977; children: Zachary John, Samantha Christine, Anna Morning. Student, Loyola U., 1967; MDiv, Holy Order of Mans Seminary, San Francisco, 1972; BA, Met. State U., 1990. Ordination 1972. Dir. Filmore House, San Francisco, 1972-73; pastor Christian Community of San Francisco, 1973-75; seminar leader Holy Order of Mans, Denver, 1976-77; pastor Christian Community of Columbus (Ohio), 1977-83; chaplain Southwest Community Mental Health Ctr., 1978-79; chem. dependency counselor VITA, 1979-80; vocational rehab. counselor Central (Columbus) Ohio Rehab. Ctr., 1980-83; chaplain Riverside Med. Ctr., Mpls., 1984—; cons. Riverside Med. Ctr., Mpls. 1986—, MS Soc. Mpls. 1989—. Co-author: Seminar of Light, 1977; creator/dir. Video Prodn., Video Learning Ctr., 1989—; developer/facilitator Stroke Support Group, 1986—. Pres. South Mpls. Family Film Soc., 1989—. Mem. Assn. Clin. Pastoral Edn., Mpls. Ministerial Assn., Fellowship of Reconciliation, Global Edn. Assocs., Pastoral care Network for Social Responsibilty. Avocations: photography, birdwatching, video production, music, cinema. Office: Riverside Medical Ctr MS Achievement Ctr 2450 Riverside Ave S Minneapolis MN 55454

HATHAWAY, ALDEN MOINET, bishop; b. St. Louis, Aug. 13, 1933; s. Earl Burton and Margaret (Moinet) H.; m. Anna Harrison Cox, Dec. 29, 1956; children: Alden Moinet II, Christopher L., Melissa A. B.S., Cornell U., 1955; B.D., Episcopal Theol. Sch., Cambridge,Mass., 1962. Ordained priest Episcopal Ch., 1962. Rector Trinity Ch., Bellefontaine, Ohio, 1962-65; assoc. rector Christ Ch. Cranbrook, Bloomfield Hills, Mich., 1965-71; rector St. Christopher's Ch., Springfield, Va., 1972-81; bishop Diocese of Pitts., 1981—. Served to lt. USNR, 1956-59. Home: 1109 Woodland Ave Pittsburgh PA 15237 Office: Episcopal Diocese 325 Oliver Ave Pittsburgh PA 15222

HATHAWAY, VAUGHN EDWARD, JR., minister, religious school administrator; b. Corpus Christi, Tex., Dec. 10, 1937; s. Vaughn Edward Sr. and Lenora Mae (Tilton) H.; m. Alice Nell Malone, Sept. 4, 1965; children: Vaughn Eric, Bradley Farel, Joel David, Christen Elise, John Holt, Cherith Brooke. Student, So. Ill. U., 1956-57; BA in Bible, Bob Jones U., 1965; MDiv, Faith Theol. Sem., Elkins Park, Pa., 1968; postgrad., Covenant Coll., 1991—. Ordained to ministry Presbyn. Ch., 1969. Interim min. Bible Presbyn. Ch., Coatesville, Pa., 1967-68; min. 1st Bible Presbyn. Ch., Grand Junction, Colo., 1968-71; asst. min. Ind. Presbyn. Ch., Memphis, 1971-76; min. Waynesboro (Miss.) Presbyn. Ch., 1976-90; adminstr. Trinity Christian Sch., Opelika, Ala., 1990—; chmn. examining com. Grace Presbytery, S. Miss., 1977-83, stated clk., 1983-91; chmn. jud. bus. com. Presbyn. Ch. Am., Atlanta, 1981-87. Author, asst. editor: Encyclopedia of Christianity, Vol. II, 1967; contbr. articles to New Horizons mag.; inventor modification of RC1-B autoscaler. Spokesman, sec. Concerned Citizens, Grand Junction, 1969-70. With USAF, 1957-61. Named Man of Yr. (Fratres in Christo) Alpha Phi Omega, 1964. Republican. Office: Trinity Christian Sch 1010 India Rd Opelika AL 36801 *Whatever price the world seeks to exact from the person who commits himself to implicit obedience to the Word of God as it is set forth in the Bible, that price is insignificant when it is compared to the possible loss of the approbation of God for yielding to the demands of a tyrannical majority.*

HATHCOAT, RONALD ANDREW, minister, counselor, public speaker; b. Winnsboro, Tex., Aug. 27, 1949; s. David A. and Ruby Jewel (Alexander) H.; m. Patricia Ann Griffin, May 29, 1971; children: Ronnie, Michael, Stephen. BS, East Tex. State U., 1971; MDiv, Southwestern Bapt. Theol. Sem., Ft. Worth, 1975. Ordained to ministry Bapt. Ch.; cert. extension tchr. Pastor Cartwright Bapt. Ch., Winnsboro, 1971-75, N. Dixie Bapt. Ch., Tyler, Tex., 1975-77, 1st Bapt. Ch., Celina, Tex., 1977-82; extension tchr. Collin Assn. Tng. Sch., McKinney, Tex., 1981-82; pastor Greenwood Bapt. Ch., Midland, Tex., 1982-87, Rhea's Mill Bapt. Ch., Mckinney, Tex., 1987—; adminstrv. com. Collin Bapt. Assn., McKinney, 1978-80, program com., 1991-92, Lake Lavon Encampment, McKinney, 1980-81; area adminstrv. com. Midland/Odessa area, Tex., 1983-85; vol. chaplain emergency rm. Midland Meml. Hosp., 1986-87. Writer weekly religious column From the Pulpit, Celina Record, 1988—. Com. mem. Greenwood/Midland coun. Boy Scouts Am., 1987 (century mem. award 1985); active Greenwood/Midland Athletic Booster Club, 1986-87; exec. bd. Circle Six Ranch, 1986-87. Mem. Prosper Athletic Booster Club, Collin Bapt. Assn. (exec. bd., program com.), Midland Bapt. Assn. (clk. 1983-87), Southwestern Bapt. Sem. Alumni Assn. (life). Home: Rte 4 Box 167A McKinney TX 75070

HAUENSTEIN, PAUL EDWARD, minister; b. North Tonawanda, N.Y., Feb. 1, 1943; s. Edward Julius and Evelyn Ruth (Cowell) H.; m. Diane Kathi Kramer, June 26, 1965; children: Peter Robert, Lisa Diane, Kathi Ann. BA, Capital U., Columbus, Ohio, 1965; BD, MDiv, Evang. Luth. Theol. Sem., Columbus, 1969. Ordained to ministry Am. Luth. Ch., 1969. Pastor Peace Luth. Ch., Green Bay, Wis., 1969-73; co-pastor Emanuel Luth. Ch., Wasau, Wis., 1973-74; missionary to Brazil Am. Luth. Ch., Mpls., 1974-79; assoc. pastor St. John Luth. Ch., Beatrice, Nebr., 1980-84; pastor developer Christ the King Luth. Ch., Sebastian, Fla., 1984—; clergy dean Blue Valley Conf., Beatrice, 1982-84; sec. Space Coast Conf., Fla., 1987—; chmn. div. outreach Fla. Synod, Evang. Luth. Ch. Am., Tampa, 1987—; del. Evang. Luth. Ch. Am. Churchwide Assembly, Chgo., 1989. Pres. Pelican Island PTA, Sebastian, 1987-89; v.p. Fighting Indian Band Boosters, Vero BEach, Fla., 1987-88. Mem. Acad. for Evangelists, Sebastian Lions Club (sec. 1987—, Lion of Yr. 1985, 87), Beatrice Sertoma Club (1st v.p. 1983-84, Sertoman of Yr. 1983-84). Home: 933 Jamaica Ave Sebastian FL 32958-5151 Office: Christ the King Luth Ch 933 Jamaica Ave Sebastian FL 32958

HAUERWAS, STANLEY M., law educator; b. 1940. BA, Southwestern U., 1965; BD, Yale U., 1965, MA, MPhil, PhD, 1068. From asst. prof. to prof. Notre Dame U., 1970-84; prof. Duke U., Durham, N.C., 1984—, prof. divinity and law, 1988—. Author: (with W. Willimon) Resident Aliens: Life in the Christian Colony; contbr. articles to profl. jours. Mem. Am. Theol. Soc. Office: Duke U Sch Law Durham NC 27706

HAUGEN, WESLEY N., bishop. Bishop Evang. Luth. Ch. in Am., Fargo, N.D. Office: Evang Ch in Am 1703 32nd St S Fargo ND 58107*

HAUGHT, JOHN FRANCIS, theology educator; b. Buffalo, Nov. 12, 1942; s. Arthur Paul and Angela (Swint) H.; m. Evelyn L. Pellegrino, Sept. 4, 1967; children: Paul, Martin. BA, St. Mary's Sem., Balt., 1964; MA, Cath. U. Am., 1968, PhD, 1970. Prof. Georgetown U., Washington, 1970—. Author: Religion and Self-Acceptance, 1976 (named Best Book Coll. Theology Soc. 1977), Cosmic Adventure, 1984, What is God?, 1986, What is Religion?, 1990. Mem. Am. Acad. Religion, Coll. Theology Soc., Ctr. for Process Studies. Roman Catholic. Home: 1713 N Glebe Rd Arlington VA 22207 Office: Georgetown U Dept Theology Washington DC 20057

HAUSER, ALAN JON, biblical scholar, educator; b. Chgo., Oct. 15, 1945; s. Edward Frederick and Esther Caroline (Lindblade) H.; m. Gail Linda Greene, July 1, 1989; children: Stacie Nicole, Jacqueline Alese; children from previous marriage: Deborah Esther, Mary Elizabeth. BA, Concordia Tchrs. Coll., 1967; MA in Religion, Concordia Sem., 1968; PhD, U. Iowa, 1972. Asst. prof. dept. philosophy and religion Applachian State U., Boone, N.C., 1972-77, assoc. prof., 1977-82, prof. dept. philosophy and religion, 1982—, chmn. dept., 1982—, chmn. faculty senate, 1979-81; chmn. faculty assembly U. N.C. system, 1981-84. Mem. Soc. Biblical Lit. (chmn. rhetorical criticism sect. 1979-86). Lutheran. Author: From Carmel to Horeb: Elijah in Crisis, 1990; editor: Art and Meaning: Rhetoric in Biblical Literature, 1982; contbr. articles to profl. jours. Office: Appalachian State U Dept Philosophy & Religion Boone NC 28608

HAUSER, CLARENCE, ecumenical agency administrator. Head Kitchener-Waterloo Coun. of Chs., Ont., Canada. Office: Kitchener-Waterloo Coun Chs, 53 Allen St E, Waterloo, ON Canada B2J 1J3*

HAUXIKU, MONSIGNOR BONIFATIUS, bishop. Titular bishop of Traina, apostolic vicar Roman Cath. Ch., Windhoek, Namibia. Office: Apostolic Civariate, POB 272, Windhoek 9000, Namibia*

HAVEA, SIONE AMANAKI, minister; b. Nafualu, Tongatapu, Tonga, Jan. 6, 1922; s. Sione and Luisa Lakai (Valu) H.; m. Etina Feadmoetoa Finau, Jan 27, 1947; children: Salesi, Lakai, Evaline, Maata, Edwina, Tevita, Sione. BD, Drew U., 1955; DD (hon.), St. Paul's U., Tokyo, 1958. Ordained to ministry Meth. Ch. in Tonga, 1952. Ch. pres. Meth. Ch. in Tonga, 1971-76, 82—; prin. Pacific Theol. Coll., Suva, Fiji, 1977-81; chmn. Tonga Community Devel. Trust, Nukualofa, 1982—. Home: 207 Vuna Rd, Tongatapu, Nuku'alofa Tonga Office: Meth Ch in Tonga, PO Box 57, Nuku'alofa Tonga

HAWK, TIMOTHY CARL, minister; b. Indpls., Dec. 26, 1962; s. Joseph and Una Faye (Nofsinger) H.; m. Susan Jeanette Williams, May 4, 1984; children: Jason Richard, Brondon Walker, Alexandria Faye. BA, United Wesleyan Coll., Allentown, Pa., 1985. Ordained to ministry Wesleyan Ch., 1987. Asst. pastor Capital Pk. Wesleyan Ch., Salem, Oreg., 1985-87; pastor Blatchley Wesleyan Ch., Windsor, N.Y., 1987-91; substitute tchr. Windsor Cen. Sch. Dist., 1987-91; pastor New Life Wesleyan Ch., Watertown, N.Y., 1991—; pres. dist. youth Cen. N.Y. Dist. of Wesleyan Ch., Liverpool, 1990—. Republican. Home: 702 Franklin St Watertown NY 13601 Office: New Life Wesleyan Ch Watertown NY 13601

HAWKINS, CHARLES THOMAS, minister; b. Guntersvil, Ala., Jan. 4, 1965; s. Billy James and Charlene Rebecca (Hays) H.; m. Katherine Ann Kingren, Aug. 7, 1987. AB, Samford U., 1987; MDiv, So. Sem., 1990; ThM, Duke U., 1991; postgrad., So. Bapt. Theol. Sem., 1991—. With missionary dept. So. Bapt. Conv., Kimball, Nebr., 1984; min. youth Enon Bapt. Ch., Morris, Ala., 1985-86; grader Samford U., Birmingham, Ala., 1986-87; assoc. pastor Lucas Grove Bapt. Ch., Upton, Ky., 1988-89; pastor Clearspring (Ind.) Bapt. Ch., 1989-90; pres. student coun. Sch. of Theology, Southern Sem., Louisville, 1989-90. Garrett fellow So. Bapt. Theol. Sem., 1991-92. Mem. Soc. Christian Philosophy. Home: 2825 Lexington Rd Louisville KY 40280-0170

HAWKINS, ELIZABETH ANNE, clergy; b. Peoria, Ill., Apr. 24, 1957; d. William Joseph and Carol (Harper) H. BA, Millikin U., 1979; MDiv., St. Paul Sch. of Theology, Kansas City, Mo., 1982; post grad., Baptist Med. Ctr., Kansas City, Mo., 1986. Ordained to ministry Presbyn. Ch., 1985. Dir. christian edn. Emerson Park Christian Ch., Kansas City, Kans., 1979-81; asst. minister Parkville Presbyn. Ch., Kansas City, 1981-86; chaplain resident St. Luke's Hosp., Kansas City, 1982-83, Baptist Med. Ctr., Kansas City, 1983-86; supr. pastoral tng. Allegheny Gen. Hosp., Pitts., 1986-89; interim min. Rennerdale Presbyn. Ch., Pitts., 1988-89; mgr., supr. pastoral care and edn. Allegheny Gen. Hosp., Pitts., 1989—; adj. faculty Pitts. Theol. Sem., 1987—; preceptor Duquesne U. Pastoral Min., Pitts., 1989—; group facilitator Bethel Park Nursing Home, Pitts., 1989—. Mem. Internat. Assn. of Women Ministers, Soc. of Chaplains (Pa.), Assn. Clin. Pastoral Edn. Democrat. Presbyterian. Avocations: cooking, needlework, reading, attending cultural events. Office: Allegheny Gen Hosp Dept Pastoral Care 320 E North Ave Pittsburgh PA 15212

HAWKINS, GORDON LEE, clergyman, real estate broker; b. Pope, Miss., Nov. 19, 1937; s. Bennett Gordon Hawkins and Sara Lee (Carter) Hawkins Perry; m. Donna Harris, Aug. 22, 1964; children: Daphne, Suzanne, Gordon

Jr., Misty R. BS, Belmont Coll., 1968; A in Real Estate, Nashville Tech. Jr. Coll., 1976; postgrad., Luther Rice Sem., Jacksonville, Fla., 1982. Ordained to ministry Baptist Ch., 1980. Enlisted USN, 1954, served on USS Laws, served on USS Evans, resigned, 1962; prodn. planner Alladin Industries, Nashville, 1962-66; sales rep. Schering-Plough Corp., Kenilworth, N.J., 1969-76; real estate salesman Impact Properties Co., Madison, Tenn., 1976; owner real estate agy. Hawkins & Hawkins, Inc., Nashville, 1977—; real estate salesman 3M Nat., Nashville, 1977-79; assoc. pastor Temple Bapt. Ch., Old Hickory, Tenn., 1979—. Mem. adv. bd. Nashville Med. Personnel Pool, 1984—; v.p. planning Andrew Jackson Sch. Parent-Tchr. Orgn., Old Hickory, 1987-88. Recipient Presdl. "E" Excellence award, 1988. Republican. Office: Temple Bapt Ch 110 Park Circle Old Hickory TN 37138

HAWKINS, HAROLD STANLEY, pastor, police chaplain, school director; b. Santa Ana, Calif., Oct. 16, 1927; s. Henry Jesse and Susan Brown (Young) H.; m. Paula Juanita Paeschke, Feb. 19, 1949; children: Bert Stanley, Harold Paul, Kathleen Faith Mummert. Grad., L.I.F.E. Bible Coll., 1950; cert., So. Bay Regional Police Acad., 1978; DD, Hawthorne Christian Sch./Coll., 1978. Pastor Internat. Ch. of the Foursquare Gospel, Redondo Beach, Calif., 1949-58, 69—, Reseda, Calif., 1958-66; staff mem. Oral Roberts U., Tulsa, 1966-67; pastor Internat. Ch. of the Foursquare Gospel, Bell, Calif., 1967-69; chaplain Redondo Beach Police, 1978—, res. police officer, 1978-88; dir. Camp Cedar Crest, Running Springs, Calif., 1961-81, Wings of Mercy, Santa Ana, 1966-70, Hawthorne (Calif.) Christian Schs., 1973—. Mem. Redondo Beach Round Table, 1974—, pres. 1991—; commr. Harbor Commn., Redondo Beach, 1982—. With USN, 1944-46, World War II. Rotary (pres. 1982-83). Republican. Office: Internat Ch Foursquare Gospel 219 N Broadway Redondo Beach CA 90277 *We live in exciting days! The Iron Curtain has rusted through and crumbled, the Berlin Wall is gone. Many leaders are proclaiming peace is at hand. The morals of America are at an all time low..."Peace and safety, then cometh sudden destruction." Back to Biblical principals is answer.*

HAWKINS, JESSE D., minister; b. Malvern, Ark., Aug. 4, 1952; s. Jesse Sr. and Ada (Wright) H.; m. Mary Watson, May 24, 1975; 1 child, David. BE, Henderson State U., 1974; MA in Counseling, Purdue U., 1975; MDiv, Garrett Evang. Theol. Sem., 1982. Ordained to ministry A.M.E. Ch. Pastor St. John A.M.E. Ch., Aurora, Ill., 1982—. Bd. dirs. Urban League, Waukegan, Ill., 1976, Aurora, 1982. A.M.E. Ch. scholarship, 1979-82; Benjamin E. Mays fellow Fund for Theol. Edn., 1980-82. Mem. Alpha Phi Alpha. Democrat. Office: St John AME Ch 142 S 4th St Aurora IL 60505

HAWKINS, JOHN LANDRUM, pastor; b. Shelby, N.C., Apr. 9, 1954; s. John Landrum Hawkins Sr. and Ann (Byrd) Sowers; m. Janet Caveny, June 18, 1977; children: Laura, Elisabeth, Gary Ransom, William Caveny. BA in Religion, Wake Forest U., 1976; MDiv, Southwestern Bapt. Theol. Sem., Ft. Worth, 1980. Ordained to ministry Bapt. Ch., 1978. Coll. pastor Hope Bapt. Ch., Ft. Worth, 1980—; co-founder, mgr. All Clean Profl. Cleaning Svc., Ft. Worth, 1979-90; conf. speaker over 22 campuses, 1980—. Office: Hope Bapt Ch 3509 Hulen St Ste 151 PO Box 101747 Fort Worth TX 76185

HAWKINS, NANSI HUGHES, minister; b. Long Beach, Calif., Jan. 15, 1958; d. Curtis Morgan and Lisa E. M. (Humphrey) Hughes; m. Richard Thurber Hawkins, June 17, 1989. BA, U. Wash., 1984; MDiv, Princeton Theol. Sem., 1987. Ordained to ministry United Ch. of Christ, 1987. Copywriter The Crescent, Spokane, Wash., 1977, The Bon, Seattle, 1977-84; missions coord. New Covenant Evang. Free Ch., Princeton, N.J., 1984-85; prison chaplain Trenton (N.J.) State Prison, 1985-86; youth dir. Christ Congregation, Princeton, 1986-87; pastor St. Paul's United Ch. of Christ, Ft. Washington, Pa., 1987—; personnel chair Christian Concern, Inc., Norristown, Pa., 1988—, bd. dirs.; sec. bd. dirs. Christian Meml. Mission, North Hills, Pa.; facilitator lection group Phila. Ministerium, United Ch. of Christ, 1989—, vice moderator Phila. Assn., 1990—. Mem. Welsh Am. Youth. Democrat. Avocations: drawing, singing, hiking, Welsh culture. Home: 826 Pinetree Rd Lafayette Hill PA 19444 Office: St Paul's United Ch of Christ 440 Bethlehem Pike Fort Washington PA 19034 *That which we love draws the energy of our life, defines the shape of our life, describes the passion of our life. God gave us our life. I pray that I would love that which is worthy of God's gift.*

HAWKINS, RICHARD THURBER, priest; b. Walpole, Mass., Mar. 4, 1933; s. Edward Jackson and Harriet (Sherman) H.; m. Michelle Woodhouse, June 30, 1956; children: Charles Sherman, Jeffery Lee, Elizabeth J.; m. Nansi Hughes, June 17, 1989. BS, U.S. Mil. Acad., 1955; BD, Episcopal Theol. Sem., 1961. Ordained deacon Episcopal Ch., 1961, priest, 1962. Asst. min. local ch. Cin., 1961-63; rector St. Mark's Ch., Fall River, Mass., 1963-68, St. Thomas Ch., Ft. Washington, Pa., 1968—; chmn. Commn. on Ministry, 1972-78; mem. Bd. Episcopal Community Svcs., 1974-84; chaplain Pa. Army N.G., 1976—. Chmn. svc. acad. selection bd. 13th Congl. Dist., U.S. Mil. Acad., 1973—; trustee House of Rest for Aged, 1974-86; chmn. bd. All Saints Hosp., Springfield, 1979-82; mem. exec. bd. Family Svc. Phila., 1982—, chmn. pers. com., 1984-86; chmn. Project Sharing and Caring for homeless, 1990—. Mem. Mil. Order of Fgn. Wars. Home: 826 Pine Tree Rd Lafayette Hill PA 19444 Office: St Thomas Ch Fort Washington PA 19034 *A lesson from living: To truly listen and to speak the truth from the heart is to be vulnerable yet strong. It makes life significant.*

HAWLEY, BERNARD RUSSELL, clergyman; b. Ludlow, Mass., Nov. 22, 1926; s. Charles Arthur and Barbara Dickinson (Kimball) H.; m. Lois Jeanne Dick, Nov. 19, 1950; children: Steven Alan, Diane Kathleen, John Fredrick, James Russell. AB, Ottawa U., 1949; BD, McCormick Theol. Sem., 1958; DD, Sterling Coll., 1970. Ordained to ministry Presbyn. Ch., 1958. Asst. pastor, then sr. pastor Woods Meml. Presbyn. Ch., Severna Park, Md., 1958-64; head of staff First Presbyn. Ch., Salina, Kans., 1965-87; interim pastor San Marino (Calif.) Community Ch., 1987-89, Palm Desert (Calif.) Community Presbyn. Ch., 1989-91; bd. dirs., McCormick Theol. Sem., Chgo., 1969-77; trustee, Presbyn. Manors Mid Am., Newton, Kans., 1978-86, chmn. bd. trustees, 1978-79. Contbr. articles, sermons to religious publs. Republican.

HAWORTH, WILLIAM ROYAL, minister; b. Wichita, Kans., Sept. 23, 1944; s. Niles Edward and Letha Loretta (Robertson) H.; m. Diana Elizabeth Jeffries, June 6, 1964; children: William Jr., Kevin, Mark, Jason. AB, Bthany Nazarene Coll., 1969; postgrad. in ministry, So. Nazarene U., 1985, Nazarene Theol. Sem., 1989. Ordained to ministry Ch. of the Nazarene, 1972. Minister Ch. of the Nazarene, Herington, Kans., 1970-73, Hugoton, Kans., 1973-74, Elkhart, Kans., 1978-84, Meade, Kans., 1984-90, Hays, Kans., 1990—; missionary Ch. of the Nazarene, Mexico City, 1974-75, Montevideo, Uruguay, 1975-78; adj. instr. Spanish Seward County Community Coll., 1983-89; dir. IMPACT team Kans. dist. Ch. of the Nazarene, 1973-74, dir. Working Young Nazarenes, 1980-84; dir. Nazarene Bible Coll., Montevideo, 1976-78; pres. Ministerial Alliance, Meade, 1988-90. Contbr. editor: Christian Belief, 1987, How Christians Grow, 1987. Bd. dirs. Epilepsy Kans., Wichita, 1984—, Lone Tree Lodge Nursing Home, Meade, Kans., 1984-90, Kansans for Life at Its Best, Topeka, 1985—; mem. Rep. Task Force, Washington. Mem. Hays Ministerial Alliance (v.p.), Nazarene World Mission Soc. (dist. pres. 1984—). Home: 1700 Henry Dr Hays KS 67601 Office: 1st Ch of the Nazarene 400 E 7th Hays KS 67601 *God does not require us to do His will, then, tyrannically hide it from us. Rather, His will is understandable and workable in my life. Through His grace, finding His will and walking in it is the best life can offer.*

HAWTHORNE, GERALD FOSTER, religion educator; b. L.A., Aug. 16, 1925; s. Robert A. and Evelyn E. (Foster) H.; m. Jane C. Elliot, June 17, 1955; children: Stephen E., Lynn E., James R. BA, Wheaton (Ill.) Coll., 1951, MA, 1954; PhD, U. Chgo., 1969. Prof. Greek Wheaton Coll., 1954—. Author: Commentary on Philippians, 1983, Word Biblical Themes and Philippians, 1985, The Presence and the Power: The Holy Spirit in the Life and Ministry of Jesus, 1991; editor: Current Issues in Biblical and Patristic Interpretation, 1975, Traditions and Interpretation in the New Testament, 1987. Fellow Inst. for Bibl. Rsch. (treas. 1970-89, pres. 1990—, also chair); mem. Studiorum Novi Testamenti Societas, Soc. Bibl. Lit., Chgo. Soc. for Bibl. Rsch., Evang. Theol. Soc. Home: 1218 N Webster Wheaton IL 60187 Office: Wheaton Coll 501 E College Wheaton IL 60187

HAWTHORNE, HARRY DAVID, minister; b. Lancaster, Pa., Dec. 29, 1918; m. Alice Josephine Whitener, Aug. 1, 1943; children: Harry David Jr., Susan Leigh Hawthorne Cain. BA, Lenoir-Rhyne Coll., 1941, DD (hon.), 1964; BD, MDiv, Luth. Theol. Sem., 1943; postgrad., U. of the South, 1951-53; MEd, Canisius Coll., 1969; MA, SUNY, Buffalo, 1981; postgrad., Chgo. Luth. Sem., Grad. Sch. Theology, U. of South, 1951. Ordained to ministry Evang. Luth. Ch. Am., 1943; cert. secondary tchr., N.Y. Pastor St. Luke's Ch., Monroe, N.C., Beth Eden Ch., Newton, N.C.; pastor emeritus Beth Eden Ch., Newton; pastor Emmanuel Ch., High Point, N.C., 1st Eng. Luth. Ch., Lockport, N.Y.; pastor Ascension Luth. Ch. (Amherst), Buffalo, pastor emeritus; regional coord. 24,000,000 Coll. Centennial Renewal Campaign Lenoir-Rhyne Coll., 1990-91; pastor to Luth. students High Point (N.C.) Coll., 1949-63. Trustee Lenoir-Rhyne Coll., 1956-63, vice chmn. bd. trustees, 1963; vice-chmn. bd. dirs. Luth. Ch. Home, Buffalo. Mem. Lenoir-Rhyne Coll. Alumni Assn. (pres. 1948, 49), High Point Execs. Club (pres. 1958), Kiwanis (pres. Hickory, N.C. club 1990-91, pres. High Point, N.C. club 1958). Home and Office: 52 37th Ave NW Hickory NC 28601

HAWTHORNE, MINNIE BELL, minister; b. Amarillo, Tex., Dec. 30, 1945; d. Iveriee Matthew Bookman and Helen Louise (Edwards) Allen; m. Robert Hawthorne, May 23, 1969; children: Robert, Gerald, Antoine, Cheryl, Eric, Lynette, Darius. Student, Trinity Theol. Seminary, Newburg, Ind. Asst. pastor Full Gospel Holy Temple, McKinney, Tex., 1973—; conv. coord. Full Gospel, Dallas, 1985—. Author: Here We Go Again, Lord, 1985, Growing Outward, Dying Inward, 1991, Help My Parents Are Christians!. Bd. dirs. Minority Task Force, McKinney, 1989-90. Named Speaker of the Yr. Collin County Community Coll., 1988, Evangelist of Yr., Full Gospel, Dallas, 1985; recipient award for Coop Edn., Allen High Sch., 1984. Mem. Religious Meeting Assn. Home: 707 Thoreau Lane Allen TX 75002 *Every action we take, every word we speak will plant a seed for growth in our lives as well as others. We must be careful that we wont regret what we reap when the harvest is come.*

HAY, DAVID MCKECHNIE, religious educator; b. Fargo, N.D., Sept. 19, 1935; s. Donald Gordon and Esther Lillian (McKechnie) H.; m. Mary Campbell Carmichael, June 30, 1961; children: Mary Cameron, Michael David. BA, Duke U., 1957; BD, Yale U., 1960, PhD, 1965. Instr. Princeton (N.J.) Theol. Seminary, 1964-65, asst. prof., 1965-71; prof. Coe Coll., Cedar Rapids, Iowa, 1971—. Author: Glory at the Right Hand, 1973; contbr. articles to profl. jours. Mem. Soc. Bibl. Lit., Studiorum Novi Testamenti Societas. Democrat. Presbyterian. Home: 2023 Sandalwood Dr NE Cedar Rapids IA 52402 Office: Coe Coll 1220 First Ave NE Cedar Rapids IA 52402

HAY, EDWARD CRAIG, clergyman; b. Chester, S.C., Oct. 25, 1921; s. John Richards and Sara (Craig) H.; m. Mary Thomas Stockton, Nov. 28, 1947; children—Edward Craig, Robert Stockton, Thomas Douglas, Mary Sara Hay-Gwynn. A.B. cum laude, Davidson Coll., 1942; B.D., Louisville Presbyterian Sem., 1949, Th.M., 1952; D.D. (hon.), Rhodes Coll., 1966. Ordained to ministry Presbyterian Ch. U.S.A., 1949. Pastor, Nicholasville Presbyn. Ch., Ky., 1949-52, First Presbyn. Ch., Franklin, Tenn., 1952-56, St. Johns Presbyn. Ch., Jacksonville, Fla., 1956-64, First Presbyn. Ch., Birmingham, Ala., 1965-73, First Presbyn. Ch., Wilmington, N.C., 1973-84; interim exec. Presbyter, Wilmington, Presbytery, 1985-86; mem. bd. Christian Edn. Presbyn. Ch. U.S., 1960-69. Contbr. sermons to pubs. Bd. mem. St. John's Mus. of Art, Wilmington, 1985—; trustee St. Andrews Presbyn. Coll., Laurinburg, N.C., 1974-82, Davidson Coll., 1985—. Served to maj. U.S. Army, 1942-46, PTO, Japan. Democrat. Clubs: Civitan (internat. chaplain 1969-70), Cape Fear Country. Avocations: watercolor painting; golf. Home: 1422 Country Club Rd Wilmington NC 28403

HAY, GEORGE NORMAN, pastoral counseling executive; b. Tuscumbia, Ala., Jan. 1, 1928; s. Idus Linwood and Lettie Missouri (Clark) H.; m. Cecily Jack, June 10, 1950; 1 child, Laura Katheleen. BA, Stetson U., 1955; postgrad. So. Bapt. Theol. Sem., 1955-57; MDiv, New Orleans Bapt. Theol. Sem., 1962; D.Ministry, Drew U., 1981. Ordained to ministry Southern Baptist Ch., 1954; diplomate Internat. Acad. Profl. Counseling and Psychotherapy. Pastor First Bapt. Ch., Palm Bay, Fla., 1954-55; assoc. pastor, Tuscumbia, Ala., 1957-61; pastor, Grand Isle, La., 1961-64; pastor Port Sulphur Bapt. Ch. (La.), 1964-68; founding exec. dir. Gulf S. Yokefellow Ctr., New Orleans, 1968-72; ins. agt. Prudential Ins. Co., 1969-70; instr. Trinity Christian Tng. Inst., 1972-76; dir. Westbank Bible Inst., 1974-78; supr. counseling, dept. family medicine La. State U., 1980-81; founding exec. dir. George Hay Ministries, Inc., Gretna, La., 1972—; pres. Life Enhancers, Inc., 1985—; adj. faculty social sci. dept. Holy Cross Coll., New Orleans, 1984—, cons., mem. adv. com. Greenbrier Psychiat. Hosp., Covington, La., 1985—. Mem. World's Fair Chaplaincy Com., 1983—; chmn. supervision and tng. sub-com. Greater New Orleans Fedn. Chs., 1983—; mem. exec. com. Terrytown Chem. Dependency Task Force, 1983—; mem. adv. bd. Young Life New Orleans, New Orleans Family Life Ctr.; cons. Teen Challenge La. Served with USAAC, 1946-47. Fellow Am. Assn. Pastoral Counselors; mem. Am. Assn. Marriage and Family Therapy (approved supr.), Am. Acad. Psychotherapists, N.Y. Acad. Scis., Internat. Platform Assn., D.A.V. Republican. Club: Rotary. Home: 653 Fielding St Gretna LA 70053 Office: 564 Terry Pkwy Gretna LA 70053

HAY, LOUISE, lecturer, author, educator; b. L.A., Oct. 8, 1926; d. Henry Lunney and Vera Chawala; m. Andrew Mackenzie Hay, 1953 (div. 1968). DDiv, Religious Sci. Internat., L.A., 1980. Model Bill Blass Fashions, N.Y.C., 1944-53; pvt. practice counselor, tchr. N.Y.C., 1970-80; founder, lectr., author, pub. Hay House, L.A., 1980—; bd. dirs. Inside Edge, Pacific Palisades, Calif., 1980—; pres. Hay Found., Santa Monica, Calif., 1984—. Author: Heal Your Body, 1976, You Can Heal Your Life, 1984, I Love My Body, The AIDS Book: Creating a Positive Approach, Colors and Numbers; creator self-healing audio and video tapes: Conversations on Living; participant video: Doors Opening: A Positive Approach to AIDS. Bd. dirs. L.A. Ctr. for Living, 1987—; facilitator Hayride AIDS Support Group, West Hollywood, Calif., 1984—. Recipient Honoraria Brandeis U., 1988, From the Heart Found. award, 1988. Office: Hay House 501 Santa Monica Blvd Apt 602 Santa Monica CA 90401

HAYASHIDA, LARRY W., minister; b. Alamosa, Colo., Feb. 12, 1944; s. Charles T. and Sadako (Katekaru) H.; m. Bette N. Miyake, June 18, 1967; children: Charles Mark, John David. BA, Chapman Coll., 1968, MA, 1874; EdD, U. No. Colo., 1978. Cert. pub. instr., Calif. Adminstr. Faith Ministries World Outreach, Greeley, Colo., 1978-85; prin. Faith Ministries Acad., Greeley, 1982-84; founder, pastor Spectrum Christian Ctr., Sacramento, Calif., 1985—; founder, chmn. Divorce Prevention Task Force, Sacramento, 1987—; founder, pres. Spectrum Inst. Ministry, Sacramento, 1989—; Bd. drs. FACE to FACE ministries, Anaheim, Calif.; publisher Betlar Publishing Co., Rancho Murieta, Calif., 1989—; leadership coun. Integrity Leadership Ministries, Dallas, 1990—. Author: Where Do We Go From Here, 1989; producer, host: (TV prodn.) Aloha 7000, 1983-84, Divorce Prevention, 1988. Advisor Crisis Pregnancy Ctr., Sacramento, 1987. Mem. Internat. Conv. Faith Ministries, Charismatic Bible Ministries, Rotary (Spl. Svc. award 1977). Home: 6409 Rio Blanco Dr Rancho Murieta CA 95683 Office: Spectrum Christian Ctr 11415 Folsom Blvd Rancho Cordova CA 95742

HAYDEN, SISTER LAWRENCE MARIE, nun, religious order superior; b. Little Ferry, N.J., July 21, 1925; d. Charles Stanley and Lillian Marie (Kasper) H. BA in Social Studies, Ladycliff Coll., 1962; MA in Bus. Adminstrn. of Schs., NYU, 1967. Joined Franciscan Missionaries of Sacred Heart, Roman Cath. Ch., 1945. Tchr. Assumption Sch., Peekskill, N.Y., 1948-51; bookkeeper St. Joseph's Home, Peekskill, 1951-55, pres., 1986-90; tchr. Assisium High Sch., N.Y.C., 1955-57; bursar Ladycliff Coll., Highland Falls, N.Y., 1957-72; provincial treas. Franciscan Missionaries Sacred Heart, Peekskill, 1972-83, adminstr., 1985-86, provincial superior, 1986—; fin. cons. inter-parish fin. Archdiocese of N.Y., N.Y.C., 1983-85; pres. Land of God Corp., Peekskill, 1986—, Franciscan Sisters of Peekskill, 1986—. Pres. Franciscan High Sch., Mohegan Lake, N.Y., 1986—. Mem. Archdiocesan Conf. Women Religious. Home and Office: Mt St Francis 250 South St Peekskill NY 10566

HAYDEN, MARSHALL WAYNE, minister, educator; b. Canton, Ohio, June 6, 1941; s. Edwin Vincent and Hester Mabel (Weaver) H.; m. Judith Lynn Smith, Sept. 9, 1962; children: Eric Clark, Ryan Mark. AB, Milligan Coll., 1963; BD, So. Bapt. Theol. Sem., 1966, D Ministry, 1972. Ordained to ministry Ch. of Christ, 1963. Youth minister East Unaka Ch. of Christ, Johnson City, Tenn., 1961-62; minister Heaton (N.C.) Christian Ch., 1962-63, First Christian Ch., Leitchfield, Ky., 1963-67; sr. minister Converse (Ind.) Ch. Christ, 1967-73, Catlin (Ill.) Ch. Christ, 1973-76, White Oak Christian Ch., Cin., 1976-81, Worthington (Ohio) Christian Ch., 1981—; mem. pub. com. Standard Pub. Co., Cin., 1986—; recruitment chmn. Cen. Africa Mission, Zimbabwe, 1974—; pres. Worthington Christian Ch. Found., 1985—; com. mem. N.Am. Christian Com.; bd. dirs. Christian Hour, Gospel Broadcasting Mission. Author: Pete, You're God's Man, 1972, 200 Stewardship Mediations, 1984, God's Plan for Church Leadership, 1982; contbr. articles to profl. jours. Trustee Milligan Coll., Johnson City, 1984—; mem. exec. com. League for Decency, Worthington, 1987—; com. mem. Community Coordinating Bd., Worthington, 1986—. Republican. Avocations: golf, weight training, travel. Home: 404 Hinsdale Ct Worthington OH 43085 Office: Worthington Christian Ch 8145 N High St Worthington OH 43235

HAYDEN, ROY EDMUND, theologian, educator; b. Rockville, Utah, Jan. 20, 1932; s. James Edmund and Gladys (DeMille) H.; m. Mary Elizabeth Richardson, June 24, 1951; 1 child, Helen Olynda. AA, L.A. City Coll., 1952; BA, UCLA, 1953; BD, Fuller Theol. Sem., 1956, ThM, 1959; MA, Brandeis U., 1961, PhD, 1962. Assoc. prof. Bible Huntington (Ind.) Coll., 1962-67; prof. O.T. Grad. Sch. Theology and Missions, Oral Roberts U., Tulsa, 1967—, pres. faculty senate, 1972-73. Contbg. author: The Biblical World, 1966, Internat. Standard Bible Ency.; contbr. to Wycliffe Bible Ency., Zondervan Pictorial Ency. Mem. Nat. Assn. Profs. Hebrew, Inst. for Bibl. Rsch., Am. Oriental Soc., Am. Schs. Oriental Rsch., Evang. Theol. Soc., Gilcrease Inst., Nr. East Archaeol. Soc., Soc. Bibl. Lit. Home: 7805 S College Ave Tulsa OK 74136 Office: 7777 S Lewis St Tulsa OK 74171 *Success in life can be measured only in terms of obedience to God. Any other criterion falls for short of his expectation.*

HAYDUK, MICHAEL, priest; b. Cleve., Oct. 8, 1951; s. John and Laura Hannah (Rice) H. BA in Psychology, Duquesne U., Pitts., 1973; postgrad., Byzantine Cath. Sem., Pitts., 1973-77. Ordained priest Byzantine Cath. Ch., 1977. Assoc. pastor St. Mary Ch., Cleve., 1977; pastor St. George Ch., Bay City, Mich., 1977-79, Dormition Ch., Akron, Ohio, 1979-80, St. Michael Ch., Akron, 1980-85, St. Mary Magdalene Ch., Fairview Park, Ohio, 1985-87; temp. adminstr. St. Gregory Ch., Lakewood, Ohio, 1987-90; dir. communications Byzantine Cath. Diocese of Parma, Ohio, 1986—, dir. pre-cana, 1980—, judge matrimonial tribunal, 1986—. Editor newspaper Horizons, 1980-86; producer weekly radio liturgy; advisor cantor's newsletter, The Cantor's Voice, 1987-88. Mem. Cath. Press Assn., Internat. Cath. Deaf Assn., Diocesan Liturgical Commn. Home: 1900 Carlton Rd Parma OH 44134 Office: Horizons 1900 Carlton Rd Parma OH 44134

HAYES, ALAN LAUFFER, theology educator; b. Oakland, Calif., Sept. 29, 1946; came to Can., 1968; s. Lauffer Truby and Margaret (Fair) H.; m. Morar Macfarlane Murray, June 21, 1971. BA, Pomona Coll., 1967; BD, McGill U., 1971, PhD, 1975. Instr. Queen's Theol. Coll., Kingston, Ont., Can., 1972-73; asst. prof. Wycliffe Coll., Toronto, Ont. 1975-79, assoc. prof. ch. history, 1979-89, Bishops Wilkinson prof. ch. history, 1989—. Author: Little Trinity Church 1842-1991, 1992; editor: By Grace Co-Workers, 1989; contbr. articles to profl. jours. Can. Council doctoral fellow, 1972-75. Ordained priest Anglican Ch. of Can., 1989. Home: 346 Maple grove Dr, Oakville, ON Canada L6J 4V5 Office: Wycliffe Coll, Toronto, ON Canada M5S 1H7

HAYES, FATHER BONAVENTURE FRANCIS, priest; b. Buffalo, Nov. 8, 1941; s. Carl Milford and Louise Christine (Kolb) H. BA in Philosophy, St. Bonaventure U., 1964; MA in Semitics, Cath. U. Am., 1972, Licentiate in Sacred Theology, 1972; MLS, SUNY, Buffalo, 1988. Joined Franciscan Order, Roman Cath. Ch., 1961, ordained priest, 1967. Lectr. Christ The King Sem., Allegany, N.Y., 1968-70; asst. prof., then assoc. prof., libr. dir. Christ The King Sem., East Aurora, N.Y., 1976—; archivist Holy Name Province, Franciscan Order, N.Y.C., 1988—; various adv. bds. 1982—. Contbr. articles to profl. jours. Mem. Am. Theol. Libr. Assn., Western N.Y. Cath. Libr. Assn. (pres. 1989-91), Cath. Bibl. Assn., Soc. Bibl. Lit., Cath. Libr. Assn. (nat. exec. bd. 1991—), Beta Phi Mu. Republican. Home and Office: 711 Knox Rd East Aurora NY 14052

HAYES, CHARLES, religious organization executive, clergyman; b. Chgo., Aug. 4, 1950; s. Charles and Doris Yvonne (Davis) H.; children: Tammy, Beverly, Christine, Crystal, Enda. Degree in Theology, Emmaus Bible Sch., 1977; AA in Data Processing, Kennedy King Coll., 1982, AS in Acctg., 1985; BA, Chgo. State U., 1986; AA in Bus. Mgmt., Ctr. Degree Studies, Scranton, Pa., 1988. Lic. minister. Instr. Kennedy King Coll., Chgo., 1980-82; asst. coll. libr. city colls. Chgo., 1985-86; agt. IRS, Chgo., 1986; assoc. pastor St. Mary's Missionary Bapt. Church, Chgo., 1980—; nat. pres. Christians Taking Action, Inc., Chgo., 1983—; bd. dirs. Organized Urban Resource, Inc., Chgo. Contbr. articles to profl. jours. Recipient Recognition award Ch. Christ, 1977, Appreciation award U.S. Com. for UNICEF, 1985, Internat. World Leaders award. Democrat. Baptist. Avocations: horticulture, aquariums.

HAYES, CHARLES PARKER, minister, academic administrator; b. N.J., Apr. 5, 1938; s. Parker Bennett and Dorothea Sarah (Snyder) H.; m. Carolyn Ashburn, Oct. 21,1960; children: Cynthia, Candace. Student, Cen. Bible Coll., 1956-58; BS, Evang. Coll., 1961; MS, Fla. State U., 1970; EdD, U. Fla., 1980. Ordained to ministry So. Bapt. Conv., 1983. Pastor Indian Hill Bapt. Ch., Bushnell, Fla., 1983-91; v.p. adminstrn. Cen. Fla. Community Coll., Ocala, 1986-91; deacon 1st Bapt. Ch. Inverness, Fla., 1970-83. Democrat. Home: 105 S Osceola Inverness FL 32652

HAYES, FRANCIS WINGATE, JR., retired minister; b. Bristol, R.I., Mar. 20, 1914; s. Francis Wingate and Fay Scott (Harris) H.; m. Jeannette Louise Ervin, Aug. 14, 1940 (dec. Dec. 1979); children: Sara Alice, Janet Witherspoon, Helen DeWolf, Francis Wingate III; m. Elizabeth Clarke Brown-Serman MacRae, June 14, 1980. BA, U. Tex., 1936; MDiv, Va. Theol. Sem., 1939. Ordained to ministry Episcopal Ch., 1939. Priest-in-charge St. Paul's Ch., Houston, 1939-41; asst. to rector Trinity Ch., Houston, 1941-43; canon Cathedral of Incarnation, Garden City, N.Y., 1943-45; rector Falls Ch., Falls Church, Va., 1945-57, St. Timothy's Ch., Catonsville, Md., 1957-60, St. John's Ch., Hampton, Va., 1960-79; ret., 1979; mem. exec. com. Diocese of Va., Richmond, 1948-53, 55-57; mem. exec. bd. Overseas Mission Soc., Washington, 1955-63; mem. standing com. Diocese So. Va., Norfolk, 1972-74. Compiler: Elizabeth City Parish, Hampton, Va., 19th Century Parish Records, 1987. Trustee, Va. Theol. Sem., Alexandria, 1973-78; vol. St. Michaels (Md.) Library, 1988—; bd. dirs. Talbot County, Md. Free Libr. Mem. Delta Tau Delta. Democrat. Home: Conifer Point PO Box 550 Saint Michaels MD 21663

HAYES, GEOFFREY LEIGH, clergyman; b. Traverse City, Mich., June 1, 1947; s. Carl William and Shirley Margaret (Sanborn) H.; m. Sandra Lee Stricker, Dec. 27, 1969; children: Allyson Leigh, Rachel Anne. BA, Mich. State U., 1969; D in Religion, So. Calif. Sch. Theology, 1973. Ordained to ministry Meth. Ch., as deacon, 1970, as elder, 1974. Assoc. pastor First United Meth. Ch., Grand Rapids, Mich., 1973-78; pastor Asbury United Meth. Ch., Lansing, Mich., 1978-87; sr. pastor Stevensville (Mich.) United Meth. ch., 1987—; mem. bd. ordained ministry west Mich. conf. United Meth. Ch., 1978—; pres. Lansing Area Coun. Chs., 1983. Contbr. articles to profl. jours. Mem. Fellowship United Meth. Ch. in worship, music and other arts. Mem. Alban Inst., Lakeshore Ecumenical Coun. (pres. 1988-90), Twin Cities Clergy Assn. (pres. 1989—). Democrat. Avocations: singing, playing guitar, racquetball. Home: 5846 Ponderosa Stevensville MI 49127 Office: Stevensville United Meth Ch 5506 Ridge Rd Stevensville MI 49127

HAYES, GEORGE OLIVER, clergyman; b. Coon Rapids, Iowa, May 20, 1924; s. Leonard Leroy and Violet Daisy (Wright) H.; m. Ruth Viola Rayl, May 12, 1945; children: Ellen Hayes Kunkle, Lois Hayes Stoltenberg, Mark Alvin. Degree, Capital City Comml. Coll., Des Moines, 1942; student, Kletzing Coll., 1943-45, Cascade Coll., 1947; Western Evang. Sem., 1949-52, Loma Linda U., 1959. Ordained to ministry Evang. Ch. N.Am., 1954. Min. Evang. United Brethren chs., Iowa, Oreg., Wash., 1945-68; min. Evang. Ch.

N.Am., 1968—; dir. pub. rels. Peniel Missions, Sacramento, 1963-66, gen. supt., 1966-71, 72-74; exec. dir. Fairhaven Home for Unwed Mothers, Sacramento, 1969-75; regional dir. World Gospel Mission, Portland, Oreg., 1976-84. Home: 18830 S Hwy 99E Sp 20 Oregon City OR 97045

HAYES, GILES PETER, priest, educator, counselor; b. Newark, Feb. 27, 1939; s. Gerald Weldon and Florence (Auth) H. BA in Philosophy, St. John's U., Collegeville, Minn., 1961; LHD (hon.), Georgetown U., 1987. Joined O.S.B., ordained priest Roman Cath. Ch. Tchr. U.S. history, counselor Delbarton Sch., Morristown, N.J., 1964—, dean studies, 1969-75, headmaster, 1980-85, dir. Office Devel., 1987-88; cons. Coll. Bd., N.Y.C. and Phila., 1969—; mem. test devel. com. coll. bd. Ednl. Testing Svc., N.Y.C. and Princeton, N.J., 1969-75, chmn., 1973-75. Trustee, founder MORHELP, Morristown, 1967-75; co-founder RUSH (Rescue Underfed Starving Humans), Morristown and Beaufort, S.C., 1968-71; trustee Urban League, Morris County, N.J., 1986-89. Mem. Orgn. Am. Historians, Nat. Assn. Coll. Admissions Counselors. Democrat. Home: St Mary's Abbey Morristown NJ 07960 Office: Delbarton Sch 270 Mendham Rd Morristown NJ 07960

HAYES, SISTER HELEN, religious association executive director; b. Pittsfield, Mass., Dec. 21, 1923; d. Thomas William and Mary Elizabeth (Wigmore) H. BS, Coll. of St. Teresa, Winona, Minn., 1949; MS in Nursing Edn., Cath. U. Am., 1952. Joined Sisters of St. Francis, 1943; cert. clin. pastoral edn. supr. Head nurse operating room St. Mary's Hosp., Rochester, Minn., 1948-50, teaching supr. psychiatry, 1952-71, dir. chaplaincy dept., 1977-82, mem. sponsorship bd., 1986—; instr. mental health Rochester Community Coll., 1971-72; preacher Movement for Better World, Washington, 1972-75, pers. dir., 1975-77; coord. edn., cert. and accreditation Nat. Assn. Cath. Chaplains, Milw., 1983-85, assoc. dir., 1985-86, exec. dir., 1986—; mem. Joint Coun. on Rsch. in Pastoral Care and Counseling, 1984—, chmn., 1986; cons. life devel. com. Order St. Francis, Rochester, 1984—; mem. exec. com. Congress on Ministry in Specialized Settings, 1988—. Editor: Health Care Ministry, 1990; mem. editorial bd. Nursing Rsch., 1958-67, Jour. Psychiat. Nursing, 1962-65; contbr. articles to profl. publs. Mem. med. moral com. St. Francis Hosp., Milw., 1985—. Recipient Disting. Svc. award Nat. Assn. Cath. Chaplains, 1985, Cardinal Stritchaward U.S. Cath. Conf. of Diocesan Coords. of Health Affairs., 1991. Mem. Nat. Assn. Cath. Chaplains. Office: Nat Assn Cath Chaplains 3501 S Lake Dr PO Box 07473 Milwaukee WI 53207-0473

HAYES, JACKIE RHEA, public relations executive, illustrator; b. Dallas, Nov. 17, 1954; d. Johnny Ray and Rhea Sylvia (Browning) H. AA, AS, El Centro Coll., 1974. Illustrator Accelerated Christian Edn., Lewisville, Tex., 1979-89, asst. to dir. pub. rels., advt. artist, 1989-91, asst. to dir. dept. art, illustrator, 1991—. Contbr. articles to ch. jours. Recipient Fred award Westmoreland Heights Bapt. Ch., 1986-87. Republican. Home: 4241 Sexton Ln Dallas TX 75229 Office: Accelerated Christian Edn 2600 Ace Ln Lewisville TX 75067 *I'll sing with joy to Jesus. I'll sing my whole life through, I'll sing to Him forever, for I know His love is true.*

HAYES, JAMES ROBERT, deacon, retired communications administrator; b. Poughkeepsie, N.Y., Dec. 18, 1929; s. James Thomas and Irene Julia (Runk) H.; m. Barbara Edith Jaycox, May 4, 1957; children: Sharon, Felicia, Colleen, Jaime, James, Jennifer. Grad., St. Joseph's Sem., Donwoodie, N.Y., 1988, postgrad., 1988-90. Ordained deacon Roman Cath. Ch., 1988. Moderator St. Peter's Cath. Youth Orgn., Poughkeepsie, 1988-90; min. adult activity St. Peter's, Poughkeepsie, 1990—; mgr. N.Y. Telephone, Poughkeepsie. With USN, 1950-54. Mem. Telephone Pioneers Am., KC (asst. chaplain Hyde Park, N.Y. chpt. 1988—). Home: 1 Franklin Rd Hyde Park NY 12538

HAYES, JUDITH SLAYDEN, church association administrator; b. Nashville, Oct. 2, 1947; d. James Daniel and Oma Lee (Draper) Slayden; m. David Warren Hayes, Sept. 23, 1969. BS, Middle Tenn. State U., 1969; MBA, Tenn. State U., 1982, postgrad., 1990—; MA in Christian Edn., Scarritt Coll., 1987. Art manuscript asst. Sunday Sch. Bd. So. Bapt. Conv., Nashville, 1969-70, editorial asst., 1970-76, asst. editor, 1976-82, editor, 1982-87, design editor, 1987—; minister youth and edn., Eastland Bapt. Ch., Nashville, 1985-88; conf. leader Sunday Sch. Bd., Nashville, 1983—; spl. studies tchr. Bapt. Chs., Tenn., Ky., 1963—, pianist, organist, 1982—; adj. prof. Bowling Green Jr. Coll, Nashville, Scarritt Coll., 1987-88, Nashville, Midwestern Bapt. Theol. Sem., Kansas City, Mo., 1986. Vol. Nashville Zoo. Contbr. articles to profl. jours. Mem. So. Bapt. Religious Edn. Assn., Bapt. Pub. Relations Assn., Nat. League of Am. Pen Women, Mensa. Avocations: crafts; indoor gardening; piano and organ playing; travel. Home: 526 Idlewood Dr Mount Juliet TN 37122 Office: Bapt Sunday Sch Bd 127 9th Ave N Nashville TN 37234

HAYES, MARK WAYNE, youth and family minister; b. Nashville, Mar. 20, 1962; s. Owen nathaniel and Ethel Virginia (Wall) H.; m. Jennifer Lee Jent, June 14, 1986. BA, David Lipscomb, 1985, MA, 1989. Youth worker Walnut St. Ch. of Christ, Dickson, Tenn., 1983-86, West End Ch. of Christ, Nashville, 1986-88; youth and family minister Centerville (Tenn.) Ch. of Christ, 1988—; dir. Camp Muribah Christian Camp, Centerville, 1988—. Home: 4564 Elkins Dr Centerville TN 37033 Office: Centerville Ch of Christ 138 N Central Ave Centerville TN 37033

HAYES, RAYMOND LEROY, minister; b. Balt., Dec. 24, 1953; s. Wayman Waitman and Edna Mae (Tichnell) H.; m. Danita Kay McNabb, Dec. 11, 1982. BA, Campbellsville (Ky.) Coll., 1976; MDiv, So. Bapt. Sem., 1982. Ordained to ministry Bapt. Ch., 1982. Cameraman, press operator Winchester (Ky.) Sun, 1968-71; asst. to pastor Hawesville (Ky.) Bapt. Ch., 1972-75; mgr. advt. Ctl. Ky. News Jour., Campbellsville, 1975-79; assoc. pastor Kenwood Bapt. Ch., Louisville, 1979-82; bus. mgr. newspaper Western Recorder, Middletown, Ky., 1980—. Sec., treas. Young Reps., Campbellsville, 1973-76; minister, chaplain Jeffersontown (Ky.) Vol. Fire Dept., 1982-85. Served to capt. U.S. Army, 1984—, Ky. N.G. Named one of Outstanding Young Men Am., U.S. Jaycees, 1986, 89. Mem. Bapt. Bus. Mgrs. Assn., Ky. Press Assn., Bapt. Press Assn. Republican. Club: Antique Auto Am. (Louisville) (editor news 1981-85). Avocations: restoring antique autos, farming, hunting. Home: HC-89 Box 1805 Fisherville KY 40023 Office: Western Recorder PO Box 43969 Middletown KY 40243

HAYES, ROBERT CHARLES, music minister; b. Montrose, Pa., Sept. 13, 1966; s. Roger Paul and Maryann (Ellsworth) H.; m. Joyce Caroline Sparks, Aug. 19, 1989. BS, Bapt. Bible Coll., Clarks Summit, Pa., 1988; postgrad., Ithaca (N.Y.) Coll., 1989. Min. music and youth Calvary Bapt. Ch., Binghamton, N.Y., 1989-91; min. music Gospel House Ch., Walton Hills, Ohio, 1991—. Concert artist for Civic Club, Binghamton, 1990, Rep. Party, Binghamton, 1990. Mem. Independent Fundamental Chs. Am. Office: Gospel House Ch 14707 Alexander Rd Walton Hills OH 44146

HAYES, SHERILL D., religious organization administrator. Exec. dir. bd. of Christian edn. Ch. of God, Anderson, Ind. Office: Ch of God Box 2458 Anderson IN 46018*

HAYES, TERRILL GRANT, publishing executive; b. Hays, Kans., Mar. 17, 1948; s. Charles W. and Betty Jean (Schmutz) H.; m. Laureen G. Mikkelson, June 6, 1970. MusB, Ill. Wesleyan U., 1970; MusM, SUNY, Stony Brook, 1975. Asst. prodn. supr. Am. Inst. Physics, Woodbury, N.Y., 1976-79; prodn. mgr. Bahá'í Pub. Trust, Wilmette, Ill., 1979-86, gen. mgr., 1986—. Editor: Unrestrained As the Wind, 1985, Peace: More Than an End to War, 1986 (hon. mention Angel award 1987). Sec. Spritual Assembly Bahá'is of Evanston, Ill., 1981-85, treas., 1985-86, chmn., 1986—. Served with U.S. Army, 1970-73. Mem. Chgo. Book Clinic, Assn. for Bahá'í Studies, Phi Mu Alpha. Avocations: growing orchids, reading, swimming.

HAYES, ZACHARY JEROME, priest, theology educator; b. Chgo., Sept. 21, 1932; s. Robert Joseph and Elizabeth Clare (Lehman) H. BA, Quincy Coll., 1956, LittD (hon.), 1985; ThD, U. Bonn, Fed. Republic Germany, 1964; LittD (hon.), St. Bonvaventure U., 1974. Ordained priest Roman Cath. Ch., 1959. Chaplain Am. Embassy, Bad Godesberg, Fed. Republic Germany, 1960-64; lector theology St. Joseph Sem., Teutopolis, Ill., 1964-68; assoc. prof. Cath. Theol. Union, Chgo., 1968-74, prof., 1974—; mem. adv. bd. Franciscan Herald Press, Chgo., 1980—, also bd. dirs. Author: General Doctrine of Creation, 1964, What Manner of Man?, 1974, What Are They Saying About Creation?, 1980, Visions of a Future, 1989. Trustee Quincy Coll., 1984—. Assn. Theol. Schs. grantee, 1978. Mem. Cath. Theol. Soc. (J. C. Murray award 1985), Ill. Mediaeval Assn. Democrat. Home and Office: 5401 S Cornell Ave Chicago IL 60615

HAYFORD, DALE N., minister; b. Fessenden, N.D., Jan. 1, 1944; s. Chester Frend and Elizabeth (Mehloff) H.; m. Ileta Kay Garner, Aug. 2, 1963; children: Sandra Kay, Cynthia June, Connie Rae. Cert. in Theology, Bible Missionary Inst., Rock Island, Ill., 1966. Ordained to ministry Missionary Bible Ch. Pastor Bible Missionary Ch., Alamogordo, N.Mex., 1966-68, Yakima, Wash., 1968-70, Nyssa, Oreg., 1970-76, Nampa, Idaho, 1976-81; moderator Mo.-East Kans. dist. Bible Missionary Ch., 1981-85; pastor Trinity Bible Missionary Ch., Milan, Ill., 1985—; prof. theology Bible Missionary Inst., 1989-91; chmn. archives com. Bible Missionary Ch. Editor The Missionary Revivalist, 1989-91. Republican. Office: Trinity Bible Missionary Ch 1205 E 1st St Milan IL 61264

HAYFORD, JACK W., minister; m. Anna Marie Smith, 1954; children: Rebecca Hayford Bauer, Jack, Mark, Christa Hayford Andersen. Grad. with honors, LIFE Bible Coll., 1956, DD (hon.), 1977; grad., Azusa Pacific U., 1970; DD (hon.), Oral Roberts U., 1984; D of Lit. (hon.), Calif. Grad. Sch. Theology, 1985. Min. Foursquare Ch., Ft. Wayne, Ind., 1956-60; nat. youth dir. Internat. Ch. of the Foursquare Gospel, L.A., 1960-65; mem. faculty LIFE Bible Coll., L.A., 1965-73, dean students, 1965-70, pres., 1977-82; sr. pastor 1st Foursquare Ch. On The Way, Van Nuys, Calif., 1969—; bd. dirs. Every Home for Christ, Ch. Growth Internat.; speaker in field; guest TV programs including The Merv Griffin Show, Ted Koppel's Prime Time Spl.; tchr. Living Way radio broadcast. Author: Taking Hold of Tomorrow, Rebuilding the Real You, Worship His Majesty, A Passion for Fullness, 12 other books; gen. editor: Spirit Filled Life Bible. Trustee LIFE Bible Coll., L.A.; mem. internat. com. Lausanne Com. for World Evangelization. Recipient Clergyman of Yr. award Religion in Media, 1985, Calif. Community award Religious Heritage of Am., 1988, numerous others. Office: The Ch On The Way 14300 Sherman Way Van Nuys CA 91405-2499

HAYMES, DON, editor; b. Chgo., Dec. 3, 1940; s. D.J. and Margaret Blair (Law) H.; m. Betty Carolyn Hollis, Mar. 1, 1968; 1 child, Malcolm Eldridge. AA, Shelby State Community Coll., Memphis, 1977; BA, Southwestern Coll., 1979; MLS, U. Tenn., 1982; M. Theol. Studies, Harvard Divinity Sch., 1981. Min. Inner City Faith Corps, Bklyn., 1966-70; race rels. cons. NCCJ/Tenn. Roundtable, Memphis, 1974-76; editor-in-chief Mercer U. Press, Macon, Ga., 1983-86; asst. libr. pub. svcs. Libr. of Sch. of Theology U. of the South, Sewanee, Tenn., 1987-90; editor Religion Index One Am. Theol. Libr. Assn., Evanston, Ill., 1990—, dir. index programs, 1991—. Contbr. articles to profl. jours. Mem. Am. Soc. Ch. History, Am. Acad. Religion, Am. Theol. Libr. Assn., Soc. Bibl. Lit., Disciples of Christ Hist. Soc. Home: PO Box 109 Evanston IL 60204 Office: Am Theol Libr Assn 820 Church St Ste 300 Evanston IL 60201-3707

HAYMES, PEGGY A. (MARGARET ANN HAYMES), minister; b. Winston-Salem, N.C., Apr. 26, 1960; d. Joseph Albert and Edna Geraldine (Fox) H. BA, Furman U., 1982; MDiv, Southeastern Bapt. Theol. Sem., Wake Forest, N.C., 1985. Ordained to ministry So. Bapt. Conv., 1984. Interim pastor Beth Car Bapt. Ch., Halifax, Va., 1985; assoc. min. College Park Bapt. Ch., Greensboro, N.C., 1986—; mem. com. on coms. Bapt. State Conv. N.C., Cary, 1988; bd. dirs. Bibl. Recorder, Cary, 1991—. Bd. dirs. Habitat for Humanity of Greater Greensboro, 1989. Raymond Brown scholar Southeastern Bapt. Sem., 1982. Mem. So. Bapt. Women in Ministry (convener N.C. chpt. 1989, steering com. 1986-89), So. Bapt. Alliance (bd. dirs. 1987), Coop. Bapt. Fellowship (steering com., coordinating coun. 1990—), Greensboro Mins. Fellowship, SBC Friends of Missions (vice chair 1989-91). Office: College Park Bapt Ch 1601 Walker Ave Greensboro NC 27403

HAYNER, STEPHEN A., academic organization administrator. Pres., c.e.o. Inter-Varsity Christian Fellowship of the U.S.A., Madison, Wis. Office: Inter-Varsity Christian Fellowship USA 6400 Schroeder Rd Box 7895 Madison WI 53707*

HAYNES, JAMES KAY, school principal, educator; b. Harriman, Tenn., Nov. 9, 1937; s. William Kay and Edna Carmel (Harrison) H.; m. Ursula Beetz, June 19, 1957; children: James Jr., Jacqueline Yvette, Joy Elizabeth. BA (summa cum laude), U. No. Ala., 1979, MA, 1980. Cert. secondary educator in English, adminstr.; ordained to ministry Bapt. Ch., 1981. Tchr., coach Florence (Ala.) Christian Acad., 1976; prin. Lauderdale Christian Acad., 1978-81, Bible Bapt. Acad., Clarksville, Tenn., 1982—; instr. Miller-Motte Bus. Coll., Clarksville, 1987—. Author: (short stories) Lights & Shadows, 1978-79, (essays) Christian Educators, 1991; editor: Muscle Shoals Heritage, 1978. Crisis line worker United Meth. Ch., Clarksville, 1987-89. Recipient Vietnamese Cross of Gallantry, 1966-75, USAF Commendation medal USAF, 1966-75, Vietnam Svc. medal, 1966-75, Vietnam Campaign Ribbon with 9 Battle Stars, 1966-75. Mem. Nat. Coun. Tchrs. English, Freedom Alliance, Phi Kappa Phi, Sigma Tau Delta, Phi Alpha Theta. Republican. Home: 1479 Golf Club Ln Clarksville TN 37040 Office: Bible Bapt Acad 3102 Prospect Circle Clarksville TN 37043 *Teaching a child to fear God and how to live are far more important than simply teaching them how to make a living.*

HAYS, FRANKLIN ERNEST, minister, chaplain; b. Invokern, Calif., Aug. 8, 1947; s. Franklin Burley and Eileen Pauline (Munsterman) H.; m. Peggy Kay, Nov. 4, 1968 (div. Jan. 1972); m. Marsha Ann, Aug. 27, 1983; children: Noel, Robert, Shelley, Jane. BS, San Jose (Calif.) State U., 1971; MS in Divinity, Golden Gate Theology Seminary, 1977; MS of Theology, U. Chgo., 1983. Ordained to ministry Evangelical Luth. Ch., 1978. Pastor Chapel Hills, Mill Valley, Calif., 1977-78; enlisted U.S. Navy, 1978; chaplain Fleet Religious Support Actvity U.S. Navy, Norfolk, Va., 1978-80, Credo Great Lakes, Chgo., 1980-82, 3rd Marine Div., Okinawa, Japan, 1982-83, U. Chgo., 1983-84, Naval Air Sta., Alameda, Calif., 1984-86, Naval Mec Det, San Francisco, 1986-88, CNRA-8, Oakland, Calif., 1988-89, Comdr. Logistics Group One, 1989-90, Resource Bd., Norfolk, Va., 1990—. Named One of Outstanding Young Men Am. U.S. Jaycess, 1979. Lodges: Lions, Elks, Kiwanis. Home: 1492 Five Forks Rd Virginia Beach VA 23455 Office: 6500 Hampton Blvd Norfolk VA 23508

HAYS, JOHN W., minister; b. Westchester, Pa., Nov. 26, 1956; m. Pamela L. Miller, Apr. 27, 1985; 2 children. BA, Westminster Coll., 1979; MDiv, Regent Coll., Vancouver, B.C., Can., 1987. Campus minister Coalition for Christian Outreach, Pitts., 1979-82; assoc. Fellowship Found., Washington, 1982-85; pastor Washington Community Fellowship, Washington, 1987—. Bd. dirs. Neighborhood Learning Ctr., Washington, 1987—. Office: Wash Community Fellowship 907 Maryland Ave NE Washington DC 20002

HAYS, JULIAN BRITE, JR. (J. B. HAYS), minister; b. Bowling Green, Ky., Mar. 28, 1954; s. Julian Brite and Pauline (King) H.; m. Kathren Rose Goudelock, Mar. 31, 1984; children: Joel, Anna. AA, Volunteer State Community Coll., 1974; BS, Middle Tenn. State U., 1976; MDiv, Mid-Am. Bapt. Theol. Sem., 1981. Ordained to ministry So. Bapt. Conv., 1984. With workship ministry Bellevue Bapt. Ch., Memphis, 1978-81; missionary in Can. Fairwood Bapt. Ch., Reynoldsburg, Ohio, 1981; pastor First Bapt. Ch., Altamont, Kans., 1984-89, Sumner, Miss., 1990—. Author: (lesson series) Growing in Grace and Knowledge, 1991. Dir. family ministry Tallahatchie Bapt. Assn., Charleston, Miss., 1990; chaplain Altamont Fire Dept., 1986-87; sec. Community Ministries, Sumner, 1990. Home: PO Box 541 Sumner MS 38957 *Life is filled with relationships. These relationships influence our lives in many different ways. For me, the most important of all relationships is my relationship to God through Jesus Christ. This is Christianity.*

HAYS, RICHARD BEVAN, religion educator, minister; b. Oklahoma City, May 4, 1948; s. Miller Bevan and Barbara (Crick) H.; m. Judith Ann Cheek, June 21, 1970; children: Christopher Baird, Sarah Elizabeth. BA, Yale U., 1970, MDiv, 1977; PhD, Emory U., 1981. Ordained to ministry United Meth. Ch., 1980. Pastor Metanoia Fellowship, West Springfield, Mass., 1974-76; inst. Candler Sch. Theology, Emory U., Atlanta, 1978-80; asst. prof. Yale U. Div. Sch., New Haven, 1981-84, assoc. prof., 1984-91; assoc. prof. Duke U. Div. Sch., Durham, N.C., 1991—; mem. No. Ga. Conf., United Meth. Ch. Author: The Faith of Jesus Christ, 1983, Echoes of Scripture in the Letters of Paul, 1989; mem. editorial bd. Jour. Bibl. Lit., 1990—; contbr. articles to religious publs. Coach Little League and Babe Ruth League baseball, New Haven, 1981-90. Recipient Cokesbury Grad. award United Meth. Ch., 1979-80, A. Whitney Griswold award Yale-Whitney Humanities Ctr., 1982, 87; John Wesley fellow A Found. for Theol. Edn. 1978-81. Mem. Studiorum Novi Testamenti Societas, Soc. Bibl. Lit. (pres. New Eng. region 1988-89, chmn. Pauline Epistles sect. 1988—), Am. Acad. Religion, Cath. Bibl. Assn. Office: Duke U Div Sch Durham NC 27706

HAYS, RICHARD SECREST, minister; b. Warren, Ohio, Feb. 1, 1951; s. Robert Collins and Sarah Lewis (Secrest) H.; m. Paula Jeanne Barron, Dec. 27, 1975; children: Elizabeth Anne, Andrew Paul. AB, Lafayette Coll., Easton, Pa., 1973; postgrad., U. Edinburgh, Scotland, 1973-74; MDiv, Pitts. Theol. Sem., 1976. Ordained to ministry Presbyn. Ch. (USA), 1976. Student asst. to chaplain Lafayette Coll., Easton, 1971-73, Edgewood Presbyn. Ch., Pitts., 1975-76; pastor Rockford (Ohio) Presbyn. Ch., 1976-87, First Presbyn. Ch., Waverly, Ohio, 1987—; exec. sec. Rockford C. of C., 1985-87; jour. clk. Maumee Valley Presbytery, Findlay, Ohio, 1986-87; gen. assy. commr. Presbyn. Ch. (USA), Hartford, 1982. Recipient David Fowler Atkins prize, Lafayette Coll., 1973. Mem. Pike County C. of C. Democrat. Office: First Presbyn Ch 122 E North St Waverly OH 45690-1146 *When the burdens of ministry get heavy, I remember the words of a trusted mentor, "What the people need is someone to love them". That reminds me that if God loves me and I love the people, then the people will grow to love God.*

HAYWARD, RAYMOND LEE, pastor; b. Worcester, Mass., Dec. 8, 1949; s. C. Douglas and Marian (Tucker) H.; m. Linda Kay Jacobsen, Sept. 11, 1971; children: Katharine Anne, Thomas Gordon. AB, U. Calif., Berkeley, 1971; MA, MDiv, Pacific Sch. of Religion, 1974. Ordained to ministry Meth. Ch., 1972, 76. Pastor Armona (Calif.)-Laton (Calif.) United Meth. Chs., 1974-76, Sunnyhills United Meth. Ch., Milpitas, Calif., 1976-82, Grace United Meth. Ch., Stockton, Calif., 1982-88; sr. pastor Willow Glen United Meth. Ch., San Jose, Calif., 1988—; sec. Bd. of Ordained Ministry, Calif.-Nev. United Meth. Ch., 1985-88; chair div. of worship, Calif.-Nev. Annual Conf., 1980-82. Author: The Management of Interpersonal Conflict in the Local Church, 1974. Chair planning commn. City of Milpitas, 1978-81, spl. edn. com. Stockton Unified Sch. Dist., 1986-88; vice-chair County Mental Health Adv. Bd., Santa Clara County, 1981-82. Recipient Spl. Edn. Parent award Calif. State Legis., 1986; named in honor Rev. Lee Hayward Day, City of Milpitas, 1982, named for Meritorious Sv., Coun. for Exceptional Children, San Joaquin County, Calif., 1986. Mem. Ctr. for Ministry (Oakland, Calif., bd. dirs.).

HAZEL, MYRTHIE, evangelist; b. Caldwell, Tex., Sept. 30, 1959; d. R. L. and Edna B. (Bulter) Mathews; m. Darrol Hazel Sr., Mar. 14, 1980; children: Keith O. Mathews, Darrol Jr. Student, Dept. Labor Job Corps Ctr., Albuquerque, 1976-78. Ordained to ministry Ch. of God in Christ as deaconess, 1988, as evangelist 1990. V.p. Young People Willing Workers, Clovis, N. Mex., 1981-82, pres., 1982-84; pres. Young Adult Singles Fellowship, George AFB, Calif., 1984-87; pres., evangelist Sun Shine Band, Adelanto, Calif., 1988-90; pres., founder Breath of Life Ministries, Victorville, Calif., 1990—; hair stylist Victor Valley Beauty Coll., Victorville, 1990—; evangelist Ch. of God in Christ, Adelanto. Author: We Win The Victory Through Jesus Christ, 1990. With U.S. Army, 1979-80. Office: Breath of Life Ministries P O Box 2002 Victorville CA 92392 *When I Keep my eyes on Jesus, I'll know where I'm going because I know who I am following.*

HAZELETT, S(AMUEL) RICHARD, mechanical engineer; b. Cleve., July 24, 1923; s. Clarence William and Ruth (Aughe) H. BA, Oberlin Coll., 1965; MA, U. Tex., 1969, Boston U., 1973. Registered profl. engr., Vt. rsch. engr. Hazelett Strip-Casting Corp., Colchester, Vt., 1950—. Author: Benevolent Living, 1990; editor: Einstein Myth and the Ives Papers, 1979; contbr. articles to profl. jours.; patentee in metall. machinery. Sgt. USMCR, 1943-46. Mem. ASME, Am. Academy Religion, Soc. Christian Philosophers. Office: Hazelett Strip Casting Corp PO Box 600 Colchester VT 05446 *Intellectualizing about religion is a toboggan-slide to perdition, right? Wrong! "The churches hold aces and play deuces."*

HEAD, EDWARD DENNIS, bishop; b. White Plains, N.Y., Aug. 5, 1919; s. Charles W. and Nellie (O'Donahue) H. Student, Cathedral Coll. Columbia U., St. Joseph's Sem., Dunwoodie, Yonkers, N.Y.; M.A., N.Y. Sch. Social Work, 1948. Ordained priest Roman Catholic Ch., 1945; formerly tchr. Notre Dame Coll., S.I., N.Y.; asst. pastor Sacred Heart Ch., Bronx, St. Roch's Ch., S.I.; with Cath. Charities Office Archdiocese of New York, 1947-66; exec. dir. Cath. Charities, 1966-70; aux. bishop of New York, 1970-73, bishop of Buffalo, 1973—; Chmn. health affairs com. U.S. Cath. Conf. Office: Diocese Buffalo 35 Lincoln Pkwy Buffalo NY 14222

HEADLEY, BARBARA EYVONNE, minister, religion educator; b. Bklyn., Mar. 18, 1955; d. Victor Caryle and Cynthia (Jackson) H. BS, Ithaca Coll., 1977; MDiv, Union Theol. Sem., 1985; ThD with distinction, Hartford Sem., 1990. Ordained to ministry Am. Bapt. Ch. Asst. coord. worship Union Theol. Sem., N.Y.C., 1983-84; asst. dean Hartford Sem., 1988—, adj. faculty, 1989—; mem. faculty Nat. Bapt. Congress Christian Educators, 1982—; bd. dirs. Women's Advocacy Ministry Prison, N.Y.C., Hartford Campus Ministries, Conn. Women's Legal and Edn. Fund, Hartford. Contbg. author: Wise Women Bearing Gifts, 1988. Recipient Achievement In Ministry award North Manhattan Charity Guild, 1990; Bejamin E. Mays fellow Fund for Theol. Edn., 1984-85. Mem. NAACP, Nat. Coun. Negro Women, Coalition of 100 Black Women (bd. dirs. 1990—), Am. Bapt. Women in Ministry, Assn. Women Deans and Counselors, Am. Phys. Therapy Assn., Internat. Assn. Mins., Delta Sigma Theta. Office: Hartford Sem 77 Sherman St Hartford CT 06105

HEADRICK, JERRY WILLARD, minister; b. Chatsworth, Ga., Oct. 5, 1942; s. Willard M. and Frances (Keener) H.; m. Juanita Baker, Jan. 15, 1962; children: Anthony, Christopher, Jerri Lynn. Student, Bethel Coll., 1960-61, Dalton (Ga.) Coll., 1967-68; BS in Edn., U. Tenn., 1975; M in Ministry, Covington Theol. Sem., 1985, D in Ministry, 1987. Pastor Sequatchie Valley Parish, Whitwell, Tex., 1970-75; minister of christian edn. First Cumberland Presbyn. Ch., Chattanooga, 1975-76; pastor Piedmont (Ala.) Cumberland Presbyn. Ch., 1976-79; dir. new ch. devel., 1979-81; pastor East Gadsden (Ala.) Cumberland Presbyn. Ch., 1984—; cons. in Christian edn. Cumberland Presbyn. Ch., 1980-90; bd. trustees Cumberland Presbyn. Children's Home, Denton, Tex., 1988-90; family therapist Christian Counseling Ctr., Gadsden. Pres. PTO, Hokes Bluff High Sch., 1989. With U.S. Army, 1961-64, ETO. Mem. Ruritan, Kiwanis. Home: Rte 7 Box 393 Ouida Dr Gadsden AL 35903 Office: East Gadsden Cumberland Presbyn Ch 1300 Sizemore St Gadsden AL 35903

HEALEY, ANN RUSTON, church program director; b. Havana, Cuba, Dec. 29, 1939; d. Homer Max and Elizabeth Dillon (Rea) H. BA in Spanish, French, Ohio Wesleyan U., 1961; MA in Religious Studies, Mundelein Coll., 1975; cert. pastoral leadership, St. Louis U., 1982; MDiv, Assn. for Clin. Pastoral Edn., Atlanta, 1983; PhD, Columbia Pacific U., 1991. Cert. social worker, Ill. Mental health social worker Dept. Mental Health, Chgo., 1964-68; hosp. social worker St. Joseph Hosp., Chgo., 1968-73; social work progam dir. Sr. Ctrs. Met. Chgo., 1973-75; retreat and spiritual dir. Cenacle Retreat House, Chgo., 1975-80; hosp. chaplain Barnes Hosp., St. Louis, 1981-82, Mercy Med. Ctr., Bakersfield, Calif., 1982-83; chaplain tng. supr. Immanuel Med. Ctr., Omaha, 1983-84; program dir. permanent deacon formation program Catholic Diocese Ft. Worth, 1984—; resident in clin. pastoral edn. Assn. for Clin. Pastoral Edn., Atlanta, 1981-82, 83-84; exec. bd. dirs. S.W. Career Devel. Ctr., Arlington, Tex., v.p. 1990—; mem. adj. faculty Inst. for Pastoral Life, Kansas City, Kans., 1988-91, Inst. for Religious and Pastoral Studies, U. Dallas, 1989-90; chmn. 2d Ecumenical Consultation on Deacons and Diaconate, Nat. Coun. Chs., Ft. Worth, 1988; mem. exec. bd. Tarrant Area Community Chs., 1991—; retreat and spiritual dir., Il., Tex., La., Kans., 1982—; dir. Twelve Step Journey to Wholeness Workshop, 1986-91; mem. Bishop's Task Force on Women's Concerns, 1987—; mem. Tex. Cath. Conf. Task Force for Priest Shortage, 1984-85. Mem. Nat. Assn. Permanent Diaconate Dirs. (sec. 1987-89, region X rep. 1990—), Nat. Assn. Cath. Chaplains (cert.), Assn. for Clin. Pastoral Edn.

(clin.), Am. Assn. Pastoral Counsellors, Spiritual Dirs. Internat., Coll. Chaplains (assoc.), Am. Assn. Pastoral Counselors (profl. affiliate 1990—), Charles A. Lindbergh N-X-211 Collectors' Soc. (curator 1988-90, archivist 1990—, charter mem.). Democrat. Home: 210 Mountainview Dr Hurst TX 76054 Office: The Catholic Center 800 W Loop 820 South Fort Worth TX 76108 *My abilities and life come from God and are enhanced in relationships with others. Because life is precious, each person has the responsibility to develop to his or her fullest capacity. In turn, it is part of our responsibility to use these gifts on behalf of other people and the world and thus co-author and co-create with God.*

HEALEY, ROBERT MATHIEU, theologian, educator; b. N.Y.C., June 1, 1921; s. James Christopher and Catherine (Mathieu) H.; m. Edith Louise Welle, June 20, 1953; children: Christopher Leon (dec.), Paul David. AB, Princeton U., 1942; MFA, Yale U., 1947, BD, 1955, MA, 1956, PhD, 1959. Ordained to ministry Presbyn. Ch. (USA), 1956. Faculty U. Dubuque Theol. Sem., Iowa, 1956—, prof. Am. ch. history, 1966-74, prof. ch. history, 1974—, head div. history and theology, 1968-70, 81-90; interim acad. dean U. Dubuque-Theol. Sem., Iowa, 1970-71, faculty sec., 1982-85, 87-90; vis. prof. U. Paris, 1965-66, Hebrew U. and Hebrew Union Coll., Jerusalem, 1973-74, U. Edinburgh, 1980-81; theologian in residence Am. Ch., Paris, 1965-66; adminstrv. coun. Sch. Theology, Dubuque, 1968-71; coun. theol. edn. United Presbyn. Ch., 1966-69, cons. gen. coun. of gen. assembly, 1972; cons. Am.-Holy Land project Hebrew U., 1973-74; resident scholar Ecumenical Inst. Advanced Theol. Studies, Jerusalem, 1973-74; guest mem. Ecumenical Theol. Rsch. Fraternity, Jerusalem, 1973-74. Author: Jefferson on Religion in Public Education, 1962, The French Achievement: Private School Aid, A Lesson for America, 1974, A Workbook for the History of the Early and Medieval Church from Pentecost to the High Middle Ages, 1988, A Workbook for the Reformation and Modern Church: A Survey of Church History from 1300 to the Present, 1988; contbr. articles to profl. hist. and religious jours. Mem. adv. bd. Dubuque Area Sheltered Workshop, 1971; mem. Handicapped Persons, Inc., 1977—, governing bd., 1977-80; mem. Iowa Gov.'s Com. on Employment of Handicapped, 1978-82, vice chmn., 1978-80. Named Handicapped Iowan, 1977; faculty fellow Am. Assn. Theol. Schs., 1957-58, 65-66, rsch. fellow, 1980-81. Mem. Am. Acad. Religion, Am. Soc. Ch. History, Assn. Theol. Sems. Iowa (bd. dirs. 1967-71, 76—), Assn. Faculty Theol. Edn. Profls. (pres. U. Dubuque chpt. 1973, 75-77, 81-83), Dubuque County Hist. Soc., Presbyn. Hist. Soc., Sixteenth Century Studies Soc. Home: 2005 Simpson St Dubuque IA 52003 Office: U Dubuque Theol Sem 2000 University Ave Dubuque IA 52001

HEALY, BERNARD PATRICK, priest; b. Springfield, Mass., Nov. 16, 1948; s. Patrick Bernard and Margaret Mary (Ray) H. BA, Am. Internat. U., 1971; MA in ANthropology, SUNY, Buffalo, 1974; MDiv, Gen. Theol. Sem., 1986. Ordained to ministry Episc. Ch., 1987. Dir. pastoral care AIDS Resource Ctr., N.Y.C., 1986-89; chaplain Jersey City (N.J.) Med. Ctr., 1989-90; rector House of Prayer Episc. Ch., Newark, 1990—; founder, bd. dirs., Corpus Christi Ministries, Jersey City, 1989—, bd. dirs., Apostles House, Newark, 1990—. Mem. AIDS Nat. Interfaith Network (founding). Home and Office: House of Prayer Episc Ch 407 Broad St Newark NJ 07104

HEALY, MARY COLEEN QUIRK, religious organization administrator, consultant; b. St. Paul. BA, Coll. of St. Catherine, St. Paul; BS, MA, U. Minn., profl. cert.; cert., St. Thomas Coll., St. Paul. Tchr. Mpls. Area Schs.; with census dept. U.S. Govt.; adminstr. Mem. select coms. Citizens League, Mpls. Mem. Nat. Assn. Ch. Bus. Adminstrs., Archdiocese Ch. Bus. Adminstrs., Coalition Ministry Assns. (rep.). Home: 5054 Fremont Ave S Minneapolis MN 55419 *People seem to like me very much. Maybe that's because I like myself.*

HEALY, PHILIP FRANCIS, deacon; b. N.Y.C., Oct. 28, 1928; s. Maurice and Johanna (Callaghan) H.; m. Hannah Catherine Healy, Oct. 6, 1956; children: James Brendan, Mary Jo, Kathleen Anne, Joseph Francis, Teresa Marie, Joan Frances. BCE, CUNY, 1955; MS in Engring., Calif. Coast U., 1977, PhD in Engring., 1982; BA in Tech. Scis., Thomas Edison Coll., 1977, BS, 1979; MA in Social Studies, William Paterson Coll., 1977; BA in Liberal Studies, SUNY, 1979; MA in Pastoral Ministry, Immaculate Conception Sem., 1985, MDiv in Pastoral Ministry, 1987. Registered profl. engr., N.J., N.Y., Pa., Ohio, Fla.; lic. profl. planner N.J.; diploamte Am. Acad. Environ. Engrs.; ordained deacon Roman Cath. Ch., 1985. Deacon Roman Catholic Diocese of Paterson (N.J.), 1985—; prof. engr., planner, cons., Wayne, N.J., 1984—; chaplain Wayne Gen. Hosp., 1985—. With C.E., U.S. Army, 1950-52. Home and Office: 145 Laauwe Ave Wayne NJ 07470

HEANEY, JOHN JOSEPH, religious educator; b. Arklow, Wicklow, Ireland, Dec. 7, 1925; came to U.S., 1929; s. William and Caroline (Keogh) H.; m. Patricia Bree, June 2, 1971. BA, Boston Coll., 1949, MA, 1950; STL, Woodstock Coll., 1957; STD, Cath. Inst., Paris, 1963. Ordained priest Roman Cath. Ch., 1956, laicized, 1970. From assoc. prof. to prof. Fordham U., Bronx, N.Y., 1964—. Author: The Modernist Crisis: von Hugel, 1968; The Sacred and the Psychic, 1984; editor: Faith, Reason and the Gospels, 1962; Psyche and Spirit (rev.) 1984. Mem. Cath. Theol. Soc., Am. Acad. Religion, Am. Soc. for Psychical Rsch. Democrat. Home: 9 Heathcote Rd Yonkers NY 10710 Office: Fordham U Dept Theology Bronx NY 10458

HEARN, CHARLES VIRGIL, minister; b. Westport, Ind., Sept. 4, 1930; s. Forrest V. and Emma Florence (Marsh) H.; Ph.D., Thomas A. Edison U., 1972; D.D., Trinity Hall Coll. and Sem., 1977; diploma Palm Beach Psychotherapy Tng. Center, 1976; m. Linda Elmendorf; children by previous marriage—Debra Lynn, Charles Gregory, Martin Curtis. Ordained to ministry Methodist Ch., 1958; pastor various Meth. chs., Ind., Tex., Wyo., Calif., 1958-70; interpersonal minister St. Alban's Ch. of the Way, San Francisco, 1974—; clergyman and counselor Green Oak Ranch Boys Camp, Calif., 1969-70; dir. rehab. Mary-Lind Found., Los Angeles, 1970-71; med. asst. Fireside Hosp., Santa Monica, Calif., 1971-72; dir. alcoholism program Patrician Hosp., Santa Monica, 1972-74; propr., exec. dir. Consultation & Referral, Santa Monica, 1974—. Vice chmn. Western Los Angeles Alcoholism Coalition, 1974-78; pres. bd. dirs. Trinity Hall Coll. and Sem. Served with U.S. Army, 1951-53; Korea. Decorated Bronze Star; diplomate Am. Bd. Examiners in Psychotherapy, Bd. Examiners in Pastoral Counseling. Fellow Am. Acad. Behavioral Sci., Internat. Council Sex Edn. and Parenthood of Am. U.; mem. Am. Ministerial Assn. (pres. 1981—), Nat. Assn. Alcoholism Counselors, Calif. Assn. Alcoholism Counselors, Cons. on Alcoholism for Communities, Nat. Council Family Relations, Am. Coll. Clinic Adminstrs., Assn. Labor-Mgmt. Adminstrs. Democrat. Contbr. numerous articles on psychotherapy to profl. publs. Office: 1244 11th St Ste D Santa Monica CA 90401

HEARN, J(AMES) WOODROW, bishop; b. MacIntyre, La., Mar. 7, 1931; s. John Elton and Alta (Fordham) H.; m. Anne Connaughton, Sept. 24, 1952; children: John Mark, Paul Woodrow, Diana Elizabeth Smith, Bruce Charles. AB, La. Tech. U., 1952; MST, Boston U. Sch. Theol., 1955, ThD, 1965; postgrad., Harvard U., 1956; DDiv, Nebr. Wesleyan U., 1985. Ordained elder, United Meth. Ch., 1955. Exec. dir. Ft. Worth Council of Chs., 1966-69; program council dir. La. Conf. Chs., Shreveport, 1969-73; dist. supr. United Meth. Ch., Lake Charles, La., 1973-74; sr. pastor First United Meth. Ch., Baton Rouge, 1974-84; bishop United Meth. Ch., Lincoln, Nebr., 1984—. Trustee So. Meth. U., Dallas, Nebr. Wesleyan U., Lincoln, St. Paul Sch. Theology, Kansas City, Mo., Bryan Meml. Hosp., Lincoln, Meth. Hosp., Omaha; pres. bd. dirs. gen. bd. Global Ministries United Meth. Ch.; mem. advance com. African Ch. Growth and Devel. Com. Office: The United Meth Ch PO Box 4553 Lincoln NE 68504 also: NE Conf United Meth Ch 2641 N 49th St Lincoln NE 68504

HEARNE, STEPHEN ZACHARY, minister, educator; b. Burlington, N.C., Jan. 18, 1952; s. Stephen Thomas and Diana (Zachary) H.; m. Mary Gay Jaundrill, Dec. 31, 1974; children: Stephen Zachary Jr., David Phillip. BA in Religion, Elon (N.C.) Coll., 1976; MDiv, Southeastern Bapt. Theol. Sem., Wake Forest, N.C., 1979, ThM in New Testament, 1981; postgrad., Yale U., 1983, So. Bapt. Theol. Sem., 1990. Ordained to ministry So. Bapt. Ch., 1978. Interim minister Berea United Ch. of Christ, Elon Coll., N.C., 1975-77; minister of edn. Hocutt Meml. Bapt. Ch., Burlington, N.C., 1977-81; instr. (part-time) Tech. Coll. of Alamance, Haw River, N.C., 1978-81; campus minister North Greenville Coll., Tigerville, S.C., 1981-87; religion prof. North Greenville Coll., 1981—; dir. Bapt. Student Union, Tigerville, 1981-85; conf. leader various chs., North Greenville Coll. faculty, 1984-88; elected faculty marshal, 1988-89. Contbr. articles, papers, dictionary entries to various religious publs. Chief Tigerville Vol. Fire Dept., 1982-88; asst. v.p. Tigerville Dem. precinct orgn., 1989-90. Recipient faculty mini-grants, 1983, 85; Burlington-South Boston Ministerium Award, Elon Coll., 1976. Mem. S.C. Acad. Religion, Nat. Assn. Bapt. Profs. Religion, S.C. Bapt. Hist. Soc. Avocations: family outings, hunting, golf, reading, fishing. Home: PO Box 227 Tigerville SC 29688 Office: North Greenville Coll PO Box 1892 Tigerville SC 29688

HEASTON, TED R., pastor; b. Colorado Springs, Colo., May 23, 1947; s. Everett G. and Betty J. (Sinison) H.; m. Carolyn E., Aug. 16, 1968; children: Heidi A., Lindsey M. BA in Bible, Cen. Bible Coll., Springfield, Mo., 1969; MA in Bibl. Lit., Assemblies of God Theol. Sem., Springfield, Mo., 1991. Ordained to ministry Assemblies of God, 1972. Asst. pastor Dearborn (Mich.) Assembly, 1969-71; pastor Ft. Lupton (Colo.) Assembly of God, 1971-74; asst. pastor Aurora (Colo.) First Assembly, 1974-75; pastor Sisseton (S.D.) Assembly of God, 1975-78, Montrose (Colo.) Assembly of God, 1978-79, Evang. Temple, Bismarck, N.D., 1979-90, Kenosha (Wis.) Assembly of God, 1990—; asst. supt. N.D. Dist. Assembly of God Chs., Bismarck, 1981-90; gen. presbyter Gen. Coun. of the Assemblies of God, Springfield, Mo., 1981-90. Mem. Rotary. Avocations: yard work, jogging. Home: 5722 83d St Kenosha WI 53142 Office: Kenosha Assembly of God 6009 Pershing Blvd Kenosha WI 53142

HEATH, BARRY BRUCE, minister; b. Phila., July 4, 1946; s. Stanley Watson and May Sceret (Colman) H.; m. Connie Lue Gresso, Dec. 20, 1968; children: Bryn Michelle, Ashley Maye. BS in Edn., Ind. U., 1968; MDiv, San Francisco Theol. Sem., 1971; postgrad., Dominican Coll., 1970, Sch. Theology at Claremont, Calif. Ordained to ministry Presbyn. Ch. (U.S.A.), 1971. Sales profl. Westminster Press, Phila., 1969; assoc. pastor First Presbyn. Ch., Idaho Falls, Idaho, 1971-75; pastor First Presbyn. Ch., LaGrande, Oreg., 1975-81; sr. pastor Westminster Presbyn. Ch., Salem, Oreg., 1982—; moderator Ea. Oreg. Presbytery, 1981, Synod of the Pacific, 1980, moderator vocation div., 1984-86; mem. legis. commn. Ecumenical Ministry of Oreg., 1989—. Contbg. editor Presbyn. Outlook mag., 1978-79. Chmn. bd. dirs. Willamette Red Cross, Salem, 1989, 90, Blue Mountain Clin. Oncology Program, 1978-80; vice chair Salem Meml. Hosp. Bd., Lagrande, Oreg., 1978-80. Merit award Salem Hosp., 1981. Mem. Cascades Presbytery. Democrat. Office: Westminster Presbyn Ch 3737 Liberty Rd S Salem OR 97302 *Those who are vulnerable move among mysteries. It is our vulnerability which mirrors God's relationship with us. In our vulnerability with each other we finely reflect the divine image. The thousands of years of human power struggles have not defeated the power of vulnerability.*

HEATH, JAMES ERVEN, minister, air force professional; b. Cove City, N.C., May 19, 1952; s. James Nathan and Melissa (Mitchell) H.; m. Sarah Jane Boyd, Aug. 4, 1973; children: Abram Darda, Nathan Leroy. AS in Religion, Mt. Olive (N.C.) Coll., 1972; BA in Sociology, Meth. Coll., Fayetteville, N.C., 1977; AAS in Mental Health Nursing, Vernon (Tex.) Jr. Coll., 1985; AAS in Allied Health, Community Coll. Air Force, 1988, AAS in Instructional Tech., 1989. Lay leader Ch. of God in Christ Fellowship, Wiesbaden, Fed. Republic Germany, 1980-83; European serviceman rep., mission rep. Ch. of God in Christ, Fed. Republic Germany, 1981-82; founder, pastor Mission Temple Ch. of God in Christ, Mainz, Fed. Republic Germany, 1983-85; pastor Love Sanctuary, Wichita Falls, Tex., 1987—; pres. youth dept. Wichita Falls (Tex.) dist. Ch. of God in Christ, 1985—, chmn. elders, 1986—; bishop's adjutant Tex. NW Diocese, Ch. of God in Christ, Lubbock, 1987—; chmn. dept. evangelism Tex. N.W. Diocese, Ch. of God in Christ, Lubbock, 1991—; enlisted man USAF, 1974—; tech. instr. 3790th Med. Svc. Tng. Wing, Sheppard AFB, 1987—. Mem. adv. bd. East Br. YMCA, Wichita Falls, 1989—; foster parent Wichita County Family Ct. Svcs., 1990—; mentor McNiel Jr. High Sch., Wichita Falls, 1990—; pres. Sheppard Elem. Sch. PTA, Sheppard AFB, 1990. Mem. Nat. Pastors and Elders Coun., Air Force Assn. Home: 4920 Bonny Dr Wichita Falls TX 76302-4326 Office: 3790th Med Svc Tng Wing Sheppard AFB TX 76311-5465

HEATH, JEFFREY DALE, minister; b. Fayetteville, N.C., Oct. 31, 1962; s. Norman W. and Eula M. (Oakley) H.; m. Beth Landing, June 30, 1985; children: Sarah Beth, Jeffrey Scott. BA, Bob Jones U., 1985. Ordained to ministry Bapt. Ch., 1985. Tchr. Trinity Christian Sch., Greenville, N.C., 1985-87; assoc. pastor, adminstr. Grace Ch., Greenville, 1985—. Mem. Nat. Assn. Ch. Bus. Adminstrs., Greenville C. of C. Republican. Home: 313 Prince Rd Greenville NC 27858 Office: Grace Ch Rte 13 Box 60 Greenville NC 27858

HEATH, LINDEN WEIMER, minister; b. Zion, Ill., Aug. 31, 1921; s. Foster Kingsley Heath and Flossie Ione Turner; m. Janet Johnstone, Nov. 15, 1942; children: Leron Forster, Janlyn Ruth. Grad., Simpson Coll., Redding, Calif., 1942. Ordained to ministry Christian and Missionary Alliance Ch., 1944. Min. Christian and Missionary Alliance, Occidental, Calif., 1978—; dir. Youth for Christ, San Diego, 1944-45, Fresno, Calif., 1948-50; chmn. No. Calif. NAE, Piedmont, 1970-74. Contbr. articles to religious jours. Trustee Simpson Coll., 1946—; mem. Mayor's Blue Ribbon Commn., Santa Rosa, Calif., 1965. Office: Occidental Community Ch PO Box 361 Occidental CA 95465

HEATHCOCK, JOHN EDWIN, clergyman; b. Detroit, Dec. 12, 1937; s. James Richard and Laurel Viola (Manwarren) H.; m. Kathryn Iva Trexler, Aug. 31, 1958 (div. 1978); children: Jean Marie, Jeffrey Daniel, Janet Iva; m. Elizabeth Ann Porter, Dec. 12, 1978. BS, Cen. Mich. U., 1966; M Div., Duke U., 1970, ThM, 1971; PhD, Internat. Coll., 1980. Ordained priest Episcopal Ch., 1984. Dir. pastoral care SW Texas Meth. Hosp., San Antonio, 1972-80, Amarillo (Tex.) Hosp. Dist., 1980-86; adminstr. St. Luke's Hosp., Chesterfield, Mo., 1986—; cons. Perkins Sch. Theology So. Meth. U., Dallas, 1973-76, Oblate Coll., San Antonio, 1973-76; faculty Episc. Theol. Sem., Austin, Tex., 1973-78; exec. dir. Found. for Pastoral Care, Amarillo, 1980-86; faculty asst. Tex. Tech. Med. Sch., Amarillo, 1981-83. Profl. advisor Child Growth and Devel. Complex, Amarillo, 1985. Served to 1st lt. USAR, 1957-62. Fellow Coll. Chaplains, Am. Protestant Hosp. Assn.; mem. Assn. for Clin. Pastoral Edn. (supr. clin. pastoral edn., treas. 1975-78, chmn. cert. com. 1983-86), Am. Assn. for Marriage and Family Therapy, Tex. Psychotherapy Assn. (bd. dirs. 1978). Lodge: Masons (master 1969). Avocations: reading, woodworking, music, gardening, painting. Office: St Luke's Hosp 232 S Woods Mill Rd Chesterfield MO 63017

HEATON, JANE, religious educator; b. Centralia, Ill., Nov. 2? 1931; d. Wilbur Estle and Nina (Huddleston) Heaton; B.Music Edn., DePauw U., 1953; M.Religious Edn., Christian Theol. Sem., 1968. Sec., Div. Overseas Ministries, Christian Ch., Indpls., 1953-58, departmental assoc., 1958-61, dir. curriculum and edn. dept. ch. women Div. Homeland Ministries, 1961-72, dir. leadership devel., dept. ch. women, 1972-74; course adminstr. Pan-African Leadership Course for Women, Mindolo Ecumenical Centre, Kitwe, Zambia, 1975-78; asst. in curriculum and program sales Christian Bd. Publ., St. Louis, 1978-79, dir. curriculum and program sales, 1979-80, v.p. curriculum and program sales, 1980-85; dir. religious edn., Fort Belvoir, Va., 1985—; missionary in Zaire, 1959-60; ordained to ministry Christian Ch., 1970; tchr. Mindolo Ecumenical Centre, Kitwe, Zambia, 1973. Sec.-tres. Irvington Community Council, Indpls., 1972-75. Mem. Indpls. Radio Club, Zonta (pres. 1988-90), Theta Phi. Author: And What of Ourselves, Bible study guide on Hebrews, 1968; Journey of Struggle, Journey in Hope, 1983. Home: 4410-D Groombridge Way Alexandria VA 22309 Office: Office of Staff Chaplain Fort Belvoir VA 22060

HEAVILIN, JOHN KEITH, minister, educator; b. Marion, Ind., Feb. 7, 1929; s. McClellan Warren and Vera (Foster) H.; m. Beulah Mae Butcher, Aug. 12, 1952; children—Keetha Denise Heavilin Broyles, Pamela Rachelle Heavilin Holloway. A.B. magna cum laude, Marion Coll., 1951, Th.B., 1952; M.A. magna cum laude, 1982; post-grad. U. Wis., 1952-55, U. Wis.-Superior, 1957-58. Ordained to ministry Wesleyan Ch., 1954. Tchr. various high schs., Wis., 1952-72; pastor Wesleyan Ch., Wesleyan Ch., Springbrook, Wis., 1952-59, Spooner, Wis., 1955-59, Hayward, Wis., 1959-65, Wisconsin Rapids, Wis., 1965-72; pres. youth Wis. Dist. Wesleyan Ch., 1953-56, asst. supt., 1960-68, supt., 1970-77; trustee Marion Coll. Ind., 1970-77, 80, asst. prof. speech, 1982—; trustee Ind. Wesleyan U., 1988-90; assoc. Instl. Advancement, 1977-89. Editor monthly newsletter Wis. Wesleyan, 1959-70, quar. bull. The Triangle, 1980-89, Marion Coll. jour., 1950-51; cons. for coll. speech textbooks, 1987—. Mem. Assn. Instl. Advancement Officers, Ind. Council Advancement and Support Edn., Marion Area Ministerial Assn. Avocations: Gardening, hand bell player, reading, writing. Home: 4012 S Adams St Marion IN 46953 Office: Ind Wesleyan U 4201 S Washington St Marion IN 46953

HEBBARD, DON WILLIAM, minister; b. Burlington, Vt., Mar. 25, 1957; s. Wilmer E. and Catherine (Ward) H.; m. Jennifer Lee Johnson, Feb. 12, 1982; children: Angela, Jared. BS, Abilene Christian U., 1979, MS, 1980, M. MFT, 1982; EdD, Tex. Women's U., 1985. Staff internist Marriage and Family Inst., Abilene, Tex., 1981-82; instr. Communications Abilene Christian U., 1981-82; dir. Family Ctr. of the Metroplex for South MacArthur Ch. of Christ, Irving, Tex., 1982—. Contbr. articles to Single Again Newsletter, 1983-85. Clin. mem. Am. Assn. for Marriage and Family Therapy. Avocation: running. Office: South MacArthur Ch of Christ 1401 S MacArthur Irving TX 75060

HEBBARD, LEIGH G., minister; b. Bklyn., Oct. 13, 1940; s. Joseph and Myrtle (Locke) H.; m. Patricia Cratt, Sept. 1, 1962; children: Leigh Jr., Robin, Scott, James. BA, E. Carolina U., 1980; MDiv, Southeastern Bapt Theol. Sem., 1982. Ordained to ministry, So. Bapt. Conv. Asst pastor First Bapt. Ch., Robersonville, N.C., 1978-82; pastor Columbia (N.C.) Bapt. Ch., 1983-84, New Hope Bapt. Ch., Wilson, N.C., 1984—. Recipient Honors award in histroy E. Carolina U., 1980. Mem. So. Bapt. Alliance, Pi Sigma Alpha, Phi Alpha Theta, Phi Kappa Phi. Home: 5200 W Nash St Wilson NC 27893

HEBENSTREIT, JEAN ESTILL STARK, religious educator, practitioner; d. Charles Dickey and Blanche (Hervey) Stark; student Conservatory of Music, U. Mo. at Kansas City, 1933-34; AB, U. Kans., 1936; m. William J. Hebenstreit, Sept. 4, 1942; children: James B., Mark W. Authorized C.S. practitioner, Kansas City, 1955—; chmn. bd., pres. 3d Ch., Kansas City, 1952-55, reader, 1959-62; authorized C.S. tchr., C.S.B., 1964—; bd. dirs. First Ch. of Christ Scientist, Boston, 1977-83, chmn. bd., 1981-82; mem. Christian Sci. Bd. of Lectureship, Christian Sci. Bd. Edn. Bd. trustees The Christian Sci. Pub. Soc. Mem. Art of Assembly Parliamentarians (charter, 1st pres.), Internat. Platform Assn., Pi Epsilon Delta, Alpha Chi Omega (past pres.), Carriage Club. Contbr. articles to C.S. lit. Home: 310 W 49th St Kansas City MO 64112 Office: 4849 Wornall Rd Suite 104 Kansas City MO 64112

HECHT, ABRAHAM BERL, clergyman, educator; b. Bklyn., Apr. 5, 1922; s. Samuel and Sadie (Auster) H.; m. Lillian Greenhut, June 4, 1944; children: Naomi, Esther, Eli, Joseph, Isaac, Rachel, Shoshana, Samuel, Aaron, Israel. B Religious Edn., Yeshiva U., 1959, BA, 1960, MS, 1961; DD, Philathea Coll., Ont., Can., 1960. Ordained rabbi, 1942. Founder all day Yeshiva schs. in Dorchester and Worcester, Mass.; also in Newark and Buffalo, 1946-50; rabbi Bnei Magen David Congregation, Bklyn., 1946-50, Magen David Community Ctr., Bklyn., 1950-57, Shaare Zion Congregation, Bklyn., 1957—; prin. Shaare Zion Talmud Torah, 1960—, Shaare Zion Girls Sch., 1958—; instr. Bible and Jewish philosophy, Yeshiva U. High Sch., Bklyn., 1964—. Author: Spiritual Horizons, 1964. Hon. chmn., leader ann. dinner State of Israel Bond Orgn., 1961—; hon. chmn. ann. dinner United Jewish Appeal, 1964—. Recipient Honor award Israel Bond Orgn., 1959, 62, Honor award Yeshiva Magen David, 1960. Mem. Rabbinical Alliance Am. (pres. 1964-67, 85—), Rabbinical Bd. Flatbush (v.p. 1962-65, pres. from 1963), Hebrew Prins. Assn. Office: Rabbinical Alliance Am 3 W 16th St 4th Fl New York NY 10011

HECHT, MICHAEL, rabbi, lawyer, educator; b. N.Y.C., June 4, 1940; s. Jacob and Anne (Prednesky) H.; m. Sara Zimmerman; children—Judith, Jay, Esther, Shira. J.D., NYU, 1968; Rabbinic ordination, Yeshiva U., 1964, M.H.L., 1963. Prof. Talmud and polit. sci. Yeshiva U., N.Y.C., 1963—, assoc. dean, 1981—. Author: Have You Ever Asked These Questions: A Guide to Traditional Jewish Thought, 1972. Mem. N.Y. Bar Assn. Home: 147 20 77th Rd Flushing NY 11367 Office: Yeshiva Univ 510 W 185th St New York NY 10033

HECHT, SUSAN ELIZABETH, consulting executive; b. Houston, Jan. 26, 1942; d. Clarence Herbert and Mildred Bertie (Turner) Vogt; m. William Herbert Hect, July 21, 1960; children: Herbert William, Timothy Paul, James Christian. Student, Rice U., 1959, Washington U., St. Louis, 1960, U. Okla., 1964. V.p. Hecht, Spencer & Assocs., Washington, 1985—; sec. Washington adv. coun. Luth. Ch.-Mo. Synod, Washington, 1987—; chairperson commn. on orgns. Luth. Ch.-Mo. Synod, St. Louis, 1987—. Contbr. Luth. Witness mag., 1989; photographer high sch. football recruiting films, 1980-87. Office mgr. Nixon for Pres., Jefferson City, Mo., 1968; del. office George Bush for Pres., Washington, 1988; mem. White House transition team, 1988-89; mem. pres.'s adv. coun. Concordia Sem., St. Louis, 1987-91, Concordia Theol. Sem., Ft. Wayne, Ind., 1986-91. Recipient Miles Christi award Concordia Theol. Sem., 1989. Republican. Home: 2502 W Meredith Dr Vienna VA 22181 Office: 499 S Capitol St SE Ste 501 Washington DC 20003

HECKEL, DANIEL MAURICE, minister; b. Louisville, Nov. 30, 1958; s. Robert Martin and Doris Mary (Everslage) H.; m. Sheila Anne Seligman, July 7, 1984; 1 child, Benjamin Scott. Diploma, Rhema Bible Tng. Ctr., 1986. Min. children, edn. Louisville Trinity Ch., 1987—. Mem. Mid-Am. Ministries. Office: Louisville Trinity Ch 10307 Seatonville Rd Louisville KY 40291

HECKERT, L(LOYD) RANDALL, clergyman; b. Dayton, Ohio, Jan. 24, 1954; s. Lloyd Walter and Adena (Chandler) H.; m. Kathleen Ann Kibler, Aug. 24, 1974; children: Ryan, Jonathan. BA, Youngstown State U., 1976; MDiv, Trinity Evang. Div. Sch., 1979. Ordained to ministry So. of Friends, 1981. Pastor Deerfield (Ohio) Evang. Friends Ch., 1979-82; asst. pastor Sarasota (Fla.) Friends Ch., 1988-89; sr. pastor 1st Friends Ch., Salem, Ohio, 1989—. Bd. dirs. Shepherd's Heart Found., Salem, 1989—, The Way Out Prison Ministry, Columbiana County, Ohio, 1990—; mem. Little League Baseball, Salem, 1991. Capt. U.S. Army, 1982-88. Mem. Salem Ministerial Assn. (pres. 1990—). Home: 1063 Franklin Ave Salem OH 44460 Office: 1st Friends Ch 1028 Jennings Ave Salem OH 44460

HECKMAN, WARREN LESLIE, minister; b. Friend, Nebr., July 13, 1937; s. Merlin Jacob and Gladys Grace (Horner) H.; m. Donna Mae Peck, Nov. 18, 1958; children: Dawn Reneé, Cheri Suzanne, Garth Wesley. BS, Southwestern Assemblies of God Coll., Waxahachie, Tex., 1960. Ordained to ministry Fellowship of Christian Assemblies, 1961. Sr. pastor Gospel Tabernacle Ch, Madison, Wis., 1969—; founding pastor Campus for Kids Pre-Sch. Day Care, Madison, 1977—, Abundant Life Christian Sch., Madison, 1978—; bd. dirs. Fellowship Press Corp., Madison. Assoc. editor Fellowship Today, 1980—; contbr. articles to religious mags. Bd. dirs. Christian Life Coll., Mt. Prospect, Ill., 1980—, Wisdom Found. Inc., Buenos Aires, 1988—. With USNR, 1960-68. Mem. Assn. Evangelicals (treas. 1990—), Optimist Club (pres. 1980), Rotary. Office: Madison Gospel Tabernacle 4909 E Buckeye Rd Madison WI 53716

HEDGES, CHARLES EUGENE, JR., minister; b. Dayton, Ohio, May 17, 1953; s. Charles Eugene Hedges Sr. and Hazel Yvonne (Hill) Atkinson; m. Irene Helga Tschoepe, July 31, 1976; children: Charles David, Kristin Renee. BS in Secondary Edn. Music-Bible, Southeastern Coll., Lakeland, Fla., 1978. Ordained minister Assemblies of God Ch., 1983. Asst. pastor First Assembly of God Ch., Niles, Ohio, 1978-79; prin. Niles Christian Acad., 1978-79; min. Christian edn. St. Clair Shores (Mich.) Assembly of God Ch., 1979-80, min. visitation, 1981; founder, sr. pastor Living Hope Assembly of God Ch., St. Mary's, Ohio, 1981—; pres. St. Mary's Ministerial Assn., 1984-86; sec.-treas. West Cen. Sectional Coun., Ohio Dist., 1985-91; regional rep. Light for the Lost, West Region Ohio Dist., 1985—; mem. Ohio Dist. Men's Com., 1990—; presbyter West Cen. sect. Ohio Dist. Presbytery, 1991—. Co-author: Ohio Home Missions, 1983. Pres. St. Mary's PTA, 1986-88; rep. parent com. St. Mary's Supr. of Schs., 1988-90; mem. St. Mary's City Census Com., 1990. Office: Living Hope Assembly of God 1130 Indiana Ave P O Box 509 Saint Marys OH 45885

HEDMAN, BRUCE ALDEN, minister, mathematics educator; b. Seattle, Nov. 30, 1953; s. S. Alden Hedman and Patricia (Tucker) Large; m. Sandra Lee Hevenor, July 9, 1982; children: Christina Elizabeth, Jennifer Courtney. BS, U. Wash., Seattle, 1974; MA, Princeton (N.J.) U., 1976, PhD in Maths., 1979; MDiv, Princeton Theol. Sem., 1980. Ordained to Presbyn. ministry, 1980, ministerial standing United Ch. of Christ, 1989. Pastor Calvary Presbyn. Ch., Upper Darby, Pa., 1980-81; interim pastor The Congl. Ch., Union, Conn., 1985-86, The Hampton (Conn.) Congl. Ch., 1986-88; pastor Abington (Conn.) Congl. Ch., 1988—; assoc. prof. dept. maths. U. Conn., West Hartford, 1982—. J.S. Kennedy fellow Princeton U., 1974. Mem. Am. Sci. Affiliation, Math. Assn. Am., N.Y. Acad. Scis., Evang. Theol. Soc. Home: 18 Charter Oak Sq Mansfield Center CT 06250 Office: U Conn 85 Lawler Rd West Hartford CT 06117 *The Church today has slipped into a dark age, as it cares more about politics than about the truth of God. Perhaps the physical sciences can remind the Church about the power of objective truth.*

HEDRICK, CHARLES WEBSTER, religion educator, clergyman; b. Bogalusa, La., Apr. 11, 1934; s. Henry Berry Hedrick and Harriet Eva (Smith) Maki; m. Peggy Margaret Shepherd, Dec. 8, 1955; children: Charles Webster Jr., Janet Lucinda, Lois Kathryn. BA, Miss. Coll., 1958; BD, Golden Gate Sem., Mill Valley, Calif., 1962; MA, U. So. Calif., 1968; PhD, Claremont Grad. Sch., 1977. Ordained to ministry So. Bapt. Conv., 1956. Pastor Mayersville (Miss.) Bapt. Ch., 1956-58, 1st Bapt. Ch., Needles, Calif., 1962-65; dep. probation officer Los Angeles County Probation Dept., 1965-78; asst. prof. religion Wagner Coll., S.I., N.Y., 1978-80; prof. S.W. Mo. State U., Springfield, 1980—. Author: The Apocalypse of Adam: A Literary and Source Analysis, 1980; editor: (with R. Hodgson) Nag Hammadi, Gnosticism, and Early Christianity, 1986; The Historical Jesus and the Rejected Gospels, 1988, Nag Hammadi Codices XI, XII, XIII, 1990; (with J. Sanders and J. Goehring) Antiquity and Christianity. Essays in Honor of James M. Robinson, 2 vols., 1990; contbr. articles to profl. jours. With U.S. Army, 1954-56, 91, col. USAR, 1964-91. Grantee in field. Mem. Soc. Bibl. Lit., Studiorum novi testamenti societas, Egypt Exploration Soc., Internat. Assn. Coptic Studies, Soc. Archeologie Copte. Home: 963 S Delaware St Springfield MO 65802 Office: SW Mo State U Dept Religious Studies Springfield MO 65804-0095

HEDRICK, JOHN CHARLES, JR., minister; b. West Milford, W.Va., Apr. 7, 1940; s. John C. and Christine L. (Jones) H.; m. Carrie Faye Stears, June 1, 1963; children—Cindy Carole and Charles Allan (twins), Rebecca Ann. Student Ky. Bus. Coll., 1958-61; B.A., Campbellsville Coll., 1965; Th.M., New Orleans Baptist Sem., 1967, Am. Div. Sch., 1968; D.Min., Luther Rice Sem., 1975. Ordained to ministry So. Baptist Conv., 1962; pastor Rockbridge Bapt. Ch., Tompkinsville, Ky., 1962-63, Raikes Hill Mission, Campbellsville, Ky., 1963-65, Concrod Bapt. Ch., Hartford, Ky., 1966-68, Pleasant Hill Bapt. Ch., Hopkinsville, Ky., 1968-70, First Bapt. Ch., Napolean, Ohio, 1970-73, Central Bapt. Ch., Maysville, Ky., 1973-81, First Bapt. Ch., Mt. Vernon, 1981—; dir. missions Rockcastle Assoc., Mt. Vernon, 1984. Bd. dirs., treas. YMCA, Maysville, Ky., 1975-77; mem. Drug and Alcohol Abuse Com., Maysville, 1975-77. Mem. Maysville/Mt. Vernon Ministerial Assn. (pres. 1976-77). Republican. Avocations: golf; sports activities. Home: PO Box 639 Mount Vernon KY 40456 Office: First Bapt Ch PO Box 639 Main St at Craig St Mount Vernon KY 40456

HEDRICK, LAURA ANNE, lay worker, preschool educator; b. Wichita Falls, Tex., Aug. 16, 1954; d. William J. and Louise (Hinyard) Wilson; m. B. Dale Hedrick, Aug. 8, 1973; children: Anna Marie, William Karl, Lisa Michelle. Student, Kilgore Jr. Coll., 1973, Tyler Jr. Coll., 1974-75. Sunday sch. tchr. 1st Christian Ch., Kilgore, Tex., 1970—, youth sponsor, 1981, 89—, mem., officer women's group, 1980—, musician, 1981—, musician, dir. Bell Choir, 1985-90; presch. tchr. Stepping Stones Presch., Kilgore, 1989—. Leader Campfire, Kilgore, 1986-88; v.p. PTA, Kilgore, 1987-89, pres., 1988-90. Mem. Christian Ch. (Disciples of Christ). Home: 2411 Ivy Kilgore TX 75662

HEDRICK, SARAH CARMELLA, music director; b. Spartanburg, S.C., Nov. 25, 1951; d. Charles Ray and Annie Ruth (Seay) McAbee; m. Joseph Timothy Hedrick, Dec. 26, 1971; 1 child, Jason Thomas. MusB, Appalachian State U., 1973, MusM, 1974. Music dir. Cen. United Meth. Ch., Albemarle, N.C., 1980—. Rotating music dir. Stanly County Chorale, Albemarle, 1990—; music dir. Uwharrie Players Theater Orgn., Albemarle, 1982, 84, 85, 87; vol. sponsor Albemarle High Sch. Band, 1978—. Named to Outstanding Young Woman of Am., 1987. Mem. Am. Choral Dirs. Assn. Home: Rte 5 Box 633A Albemarle NC 28001 Office: Cen United Meth Ch 172 N 2d St PO Box 428 Albemarle NC 28002-0428 *As a musician, I believe that music enhances our abilities to worship, to care for one another, and to develop a positive sense of self worth. No matter how great or small our talents may be, they are magnified when we can join together and share them with others for the glory of God.*

HEEMSTRA, DANIEL CRAIG, minister; b. Sheldon, Iowa, Sept. 9, 1966; s. Calvin D. and Beverly J. (Bolkema) H. BA, Northwestern Coll., Orange City, Iowa, 1989. Youth min. Beechwood Reformed Ch., Holland, Mich., 1989—. Mem. Reformed Ch. in Am. Home: 130 E 14th St Holland MI 49423 Office: Beechwood Ch 895 Ottawa Beach Rd Holland MI 49424

HEENAN, GREG STEPHEN, clergyman; b. Phila., Apr. 14, 1950; s. William Leo and Elizabeth P. (Bergin) H.; m. Donna Marie Pluta, Aug. 31, 1972; children: Paul Stephen, Emily Elizabeth. BTh, Internat. Bible Inst., Orlando, Fla., 1987; B Bibl. Studies, Luther Rice Sem., 1988, MA in Christian Edn., 1989, postgrad., 1989—. Ordained to ministry, Bapt. Ch., 1975. Pastor Persimmon Hill Bapt. Ch., Saucier, Miss., 1975-77, Berachah Bapt. Ch., Vicksburg, Miss., 1977-79, Peninsula Bapt. Ch., Hampton, Va., 1979-83, Temple Bapt. Ch., Biloxi, Miss., 1983-86, Mt. Olive Bapt. Ch., Denham Springs, La., 1986-87, Unity Bapt. Ch., Baton Rouge, 1987—. With USAF, 1970-77, Vietnam. Mem. Bapt. Missionary Assn. Miss. (mem. state youth com. 1974-75), Bapt. Missionary Assn. La. (state missionary com. 1988). Republican. Avocations: astronomy, astrophotography, computers. Home and Office: 13238 Denham Rd Baton Rouge LA 70818

HEENAN, SISTER MARY ANNE, academic administrator. Supt. Cath. schs. Diocese of Syracuse, N.Y. Office: Cath Schs Office 240 E Onondaga St Box 511 Syracuse NY 13201*

HEERY, MICHAEL ANTHONY, lay worker; b. Allentown, Pa., July 6, 1966; s. Francis Anthony and Catherine Regina (Schwarz) H. AA, Lehigh County Community Coll., Schnecksville, Pa., 1986; BS in Elem. Edn., Kutztown (Pa.) U., 1989, BS in Early Childhood Edn., 1989. Proprietor Mauch Chunk Hobby Ctr., Jim Thorpe, Pa., 1985—; pres. Cath. Youth Orgn., Sts. Peter and Paul Parish, Lehighton, Pa. 1984—, coach, 1984—, acad. advisor, 1987—, dir. religious edn., 1990—, youth minister, 1990—. Mem. Assn. of Coords. of Religious Edn., Assn. Dirs. Religious Edn., Holy Name Soc. (marshall 1990—), KC (4th degree, 1989, 3d degree 1986). Democrat. Office: Sts Peter and Paul Ch 260 N Third St Lehighton PA 18235

HEFFNER, ELIZABETH SUMMERS, music minister; b. Rochester, Ind., Nov. 24, 1959; d. Charles Oland and Joyce Annette (Bolin) Summers; m. Dale Wayne Heffner, June 6, 1980; children: Aimee Louise, Adam Scott. BA, Garddner-Webb Coll., Boiling Springs, N.C., 1983. Min. music 1st Wesleyan Ch., Cherryville, N.C., 1981-82, East Bapt. Ch., Gastonia, N.C., 1982-86, Dover Bapt. Ch., Shelby, N.C., 1986—; ch. music clinician Gaston Bapt. Assn., Gastonia, 1983—, Kings Mountain Assn., Shelby, 1988—; assoc. music dir. Kings Mountain Bapt. Assn., Shelby, 1988-90. Office: Dover Bapt Ch 413 Polkville Rd Shelby NC 28150

HEFFNER, JOHN HOWARD, philosophy educator; b. Lebanon, Pa., Jan. 13, 1947; s. W. Howard and Marian Heffner; m. Diane M. Iglesias, Dec. 28, 1979. BS, Lebanon Valley Coll., 1968, BA, 1987; AM, Boston U., 1971, PhD, 1976. Instr. Lebanon Valley coll., Annville, Pa., 1972-76, asst. prof., 1976-80, assoc. prof., 1980-84, prof. philosophy, 1984—, chmn. dept. religion and philosophy, 1989—. Contbg. author: PSA 1976, Vol. 1, 1976, Naturalistic Epistemiology, 1987; contbr. articles to profl. jours. NSF fellow, 1978; postdoctoral fellow Northwestern U., 1978-79, U. Pa., 1986-91; Am. Philos. Assn. grantee Haverford Coll., 1976, NEH grantee Princeton U., 1977. Mem. Soc. for Advancement Am. Philosophy, Metaphysical Soc. Am. Avocation: gardening. Home: 119 E Chestnut St Cleona PA 17042 Office: Lebanon Valley Coll 101 N College Ave Annville PA 17003

HEFNER, PHILIP JAMES, theologian; b. Denver, Dec. 10, 1932; s. Theodore Godfred and Elizabeth Helen (Mittelstadt) H.; m. Neva Lamae White, May 25, 1956; children: Sarah Elizabeth, Martha White, Julia Margaret, Rebecca Mittelstadt. BA, Midland Luth. Coll., 1954, LHD, 1982; BD, Chgo. Luth. Theol. Sem., 1959; MA, U. Chgo., 1961, PhD, 1962. Ordained United Luth. Ch. in Am., 1962. Assoc. prof. systematic theology Hamma Div. Sch., Springfield, Ohio, 1962-64; prof. systematic theology Luth. Theol. Sem., Gettysburg, Pa., 1964-67; prof. systematic theology Luth. Sch. Theology, Chgo., 1967—, dir. grad. studies, 1979-88; dir. Chgo. Ctr. Religion and Sci., 1988—; vis. prof. Japan Luth. Theol. Coll. and Sem., Tokyo, 1982; rsch. lectr. Human Scis. Rsch. Coun., Republic South Africa, 1988; disting. vis. scholar Okla. scholar leader enrichment program U. Okla., 1991; lectr. religion Chautauqua Instn., 1991. Author: Faith and the Vitalities of History, 1966, Promise of Teilhard, 1970; co-author Defining America, Christian Dogmatics; editor Zygon: Jour. of Religion and Sci., 1989—; editorial assoc. Dialog: A Theol. Jour., 1982—; contbr. numerous articles to profl. jours. Fulbright scholar U. Tübingen, 1954-55; Rockefeller Found. Doctoral fellow, 1960-62, Russell fellow Ctr. for Theol. and Natural Scis., 1985; recipient Franklin Fry award for Scholarship Luth. Brotherhood, 1977-78, Susan Colver Rosenberg award U. Chgo., 1963; Nobel lectr. Gustavus Adolphus Coll., 1987. Fellow Inst. on Religion in an Age of Sci. (pres. 1979-81, 84-87), Ctr. for Advanced Study in Religion and Sci. (grantee 1985), Soc. for Values in Higher Edn.; mem. Am. Acad. Religion (chmn. cons. on theology and sci. 1986-88, chmn. theology and sci. group, 1988-90), Internat. Luth./Reformed Dialogue, Luth. World Fedn., Geneva. Office: Luth Sch Theology 1100 E 55th St Chicago IL 60615-5199 *Living through the tumultuous second half of 20th century, I have frequently been uncertain about history's direction, even as I have been very certain that I do not have the answers to many important questions. Only my deep conviction that history is in the hands of God has sustained my journey.*

HEFT, JAMES LEWIS, academic administrator, theology educator; b. Cleve., Feb. 20, 1943; s. Berl Ramsey and Hazel Mary (Miller) H. B.A. in Philosophy, U. Dayton, 1965, B.S. in Edn., 1966; M.A. in Theology, U. Toronto, 1971, Ph.D. in Hist. Theology, 1977. Prof. theology U. Dayton, Ohio, chmn. religious studies dept., 1983-89, provost, 1989—, lectr; bd. dirs. Inst. Ednl. Mgmt., Harvard U., 1989. Author: John XXII (1316-1334) and Papal Teaching Authority, 1986; contbr. numerous articles to profl. jours. Trustee U. Dayton, 1970-77. U. Toronto scholar, 1969-77; Recipient Excellence in Teaching award U. Dayton, 1983, 1st Pl. prize Cath. Press Assn., 1990. Mem. Coll. Theology Soc., Cath. Theol. Soc. Am., Mariological Soc. Am. Roman Cath. Avocations: theatre, basketball. Office: U Dayton 300 College Pk Dayton OH 45469

HEGEMIER, EUGENE EARL, minister; b. New Bremen, Ohio, July 14, 1933; s. Earl W. and Irene D. (Roettger) H.; m. June F. Hirschfeld, July 16, 1955; children: David, Jonathan, Elizabeth. BA, Heidelberg Coll., 1955, DD (hon.), 1989; MDiv, Eden Theol. Sem., 1958. Ordained to ministry United Ch. of Christ. Pastor Trinity United Ch. of Christ, McCutchenville, Ohio, 1958-65, Meml. United Ch. of Christ, Toledo, 1965-73, St. Paul United Ch. of Christ, Oak Harbor, Ohio, 1973—; assoc. coun. N.W. Ohio Assn. of United Ch. of Christ, Tiffin, 1972-76. Bd. dirs. Ottawa County Social Concerns Bd., Port Clinton, Ohio, 1980—; trustee Magruder Hosp., Port Clinton, 1989—. Mem. Oak Harbor Ministerial Assn. (pres. 1978-80), Maumee Bay Ministerial Assn. (pres. Toledo chpt. 1986-87), Lions (trustee Oak Harbor club 1981-83). Home: 138 S Toussaint-Portage Rd Oak Harbor OH 43449 Office: St Paul United Ch of Christ 165 Toussaint St Oak Harbor OH 43449

HEGGEMEIER, LYLE M., minister; b. St. Louis, Jan. 29, 1956; s. Everett and Johanna (Muelken) H.; m. Deborah Kay Koegeboehn, Jan. 1, 1983; children: Megan Elise, Melanie Kay. BS in Edn., Concordia Coll., 1978, MEd, 1991. Cert. dir. of Christian edn. Min. edn. and youth Mt. Calvary Luth Ch., Peoria, Ill., 1979-81; min. adult edn. and discipleship Ascension Luth. Ch., Wichita, Kans., 1981—; chmn. Kans. Dist. Youth Gathering, 1986-87; pres. Kans. Dist. Tchrs. Assn., 1990—; bd. dirs. Kans. Dist. the Luth. Ch.-Mo. Synod, Topeka, 1991—. Contbr. article to profl. jour. Mem. Wichita Area Com. Mem. Theol. Educators in Associated Ministries. Home: 101 S Robin Wichita KS 67209 Office: Ascension Luth Ch 842 N Tyler Wichita KS 67212 *In serving the Lord with my life, it is my personal goal to constantly make God's grace known to all people in all that I do or say. This grace was personified in His Son, Jesus Christ.*

HEIDE, GARY HOWARD, clergyman; b. Weehawken, N.J., May 29, 1940; s. Herbert Howard and Grace Vivian (Stehn) H.; m. Joan Marie Wehmueller, Dec. 29, 1965; children: Kathrine Marie, Kristin Ann, Karyl Leigh. AA, Concordia Coll., Bronxville, N.Y., 1960; BA, Concordia Coll., Ft. Wayne, Ind., 1962; MDiv., Concordia Coll., St. Louis, 1966. Assoc. pastor Immanuel Luth. Ch., Sheboygan, Wis., 1966-69; pastor Holy Cross Luth. Ch., O'Fallon, Mo., 1969-75, Peace Luth. Ch., Selah, Wash., 1975-76; asst. pastor Cen. Luth. Ch., Yakima, Wash., 1976-78; assoc. pastor St. Mark's Luth. Ch., Portland, Oreg., 1978-81; pastor 1st Luth. Ch., St. Helens, Oreg., 1981—; community minister Cen. Luth. Ch., Yakima, 1977-78; dean cluster 1 Oreg. synod Evang. Luth. Ch. Am., Portland, 1989—, mem. pub. policy commn. Oreg. synod, 1988—. Chair Adult and Family Svc. Commn., Salem, Oreg., 1988-89; mem. St. Helens Hosp. Governing Bd., 1987-90, Columbia Health Dist. Bd., St. Helens, 1990—. Lt. comdr. USNR, 1964-76. Named First Citizen, St. Helens C. of C., 1987. Mem. St. Helens Ministerial Assn., Shoe String Community Theatre (bd. dirs. 1989—), Rotary (Columbia chpt., sec. 1984-86, pres. 1986-87). Democrat. Avocations: photography, writing, golf. Office: First Evang Luth Ch 214 N 4th St PO Box 324 Saint Helens OR 97051-0324

HEIDEMAN, JOHN MARK, religious organization executive, consultant; b. Chgo., May 10, 1960; s. Donald Wayne and Bernita Ruth (Volz) H.; m. Brenda Lynn Koch, June 12, 1982; 1 child, Amber Lynn. BBA, St. John's Coll., 1982; MBA, Webster U., 1985. Acctg. clk. Gott Corp., Wichita, Kans., 1980-82; mgr. evenings Howard Johnson's, Wichita, 1982; agt. Allstate Ins. Co., Wichita, 1982-85, Am. Nat. Ins. Co., Wichita, 1982-85; bus. mgr. Holy Cross Luth. Ch. and Sch., Wichita, 1985—; coach basketball Holy Cross Luth. Sch., Wichita, 1985—, bd. dirs. endowment fund. Contbr. articles to profl. jours. Mem. Nat. Assn. Ch. Bus. Adminstrs. Republican. Avocations: golf, softball. Office: Holy Cross Luth Ch 1018 N Dellrose Wichita KS 67208

HEIDER, GEORGE CHARLES, religious educator, academic administration; b. Washington, June 13, 1953; s. George Charles Jr. and Doris Elaine (Harder) H.; m. Carolyn Elaine Wolters, May 26, 1979; children: Kristen Naomi, Matthew Aaron. MDiv, Concordia Seminary, St. Louis, 1979; MA, Yale U., 1980, MPhil, 1982, PhD, 1984. Vicar St. John Luth. Ch., Seward, Nebr., 1977-78; asst. pastor Cheshire (Conn.) Luth. Ch., 1979-84; asst. prof. theology Concordia Coll., Seward, 1984-89, v.p. for acad. affairs, 1987—, assoc. prof. theology, 1990—. Author: The Cult of Molek: A Reassessment, 1985. Mem. Soc. Bibl. Lit., Cath. Bibl. Assn., Am. Schs. Oriental Rsch., Am. Conf. Acad. Deans. Office: Concordia Coll 800 N Columbia Ave Seward NE 68434

HEIDLER, ROBERT DANIEL, minister, educator; b. York, Pa., Oct. 13, 1948; s. Robert Edwin and Gloria Elizabeth (Lloyd) H.; m. Linda Carol Dose, June 6, 1970; children: Linda Elizabeth, Michael Andrew, Joshua Daniel. BA in Psychology, U. S. Fla., 1970; ThM in N.T., Dallas Theol. Sem., 1978. Ordained to ministry, 1976. Evangelistic speaker Campus Crusade for Christ, Tampa, Fla., 1968-70; campus staff Campus Crusade for Christ, Mpls., 1970-72; pastor, tchr. Believers Fellowship, Denton, 1973—; trustee Believers Fellowship, Denton, 1975-91; bd. dirs. Baruch Ha Shem Ministries, Dallas, 1983—; curriculum coord. Internat. Ednl. Fellowship, Denton, 1989—; traveling rep. Mission Possible Found., 1990—. Author: A Layman's Introduction to New Testament Greek, 1978, Daily Time Alone with God, 1990, The Resources of the Holy Spirit, 1990; contbr. articles to profl. jours. Pres. R.E. Lee PTA, Denton, 1984-85. Republican. Office: Believers Fellowship PO Box 598 Denton TX 76202 *If we must suffer at all in this life, and one day die, why not suffer and die for the highest and the best; for the Lord Jesus Christ and His gospel.*

HEIEN, SHARON FAY CAREY, music minister, educator; b. Waldport, Oreg., May 29, 1941; d. Shirley Enslow and Lucy Irene (Skinner) Carey; m. Carl Arthur Heien, July 13, 1963; children: Carl Arthur Jr., Mark Aaron. Diploma, Mesa Jr. Coll., Grand Junction, Colo., 1961; BA, Adams State Coll., 1963. Cert. tchr., Colo. Min. music Fredonia (Kans.) 1st Christian Ch. (Disciples of Christ), 1981-87; min. music, Sunday sch. tchr. Drake Avenue Christian Ch. (Disciples of Christ), Centerville, Iowa, 1987—; tchr., counselor, workshop leader, 1960—; tchr. Plano (Iowa) Acad. Christian Edn., 1989—, Jim Bear Family, Plano, 1990—; pvt. tchr. piano and voice, Centerville, 1989—. Author: (booklet) Born Again, 1978; singer albums Tell Them, 1985, Proclaim the Glory, 1985. Mem. aux. Centerville Hosp. Mem. Music Tchrs. Nat. Assn., Iowa Music Tchrs. Assn., AAUW (v.p. Centerville 1989-90, treas. 1990-91), P.E.O. (corr. sec. Centerville 1989—), Ensemble Club, 700 Club (Virginia Beach, Va.). Home: 617 Drake Ave Centerville IA 52544 Office: Drake Avenue Christian Ch 303 Drake Ave Centerville IA 52544

HEIL, PAUL SAMUEL, radio program producer; b. Reading, Pa., June 8, 1947; s. David Paul and Virginia May (Gaul) H.; m. Shelia Kay Troyer, Dec. 19, 1982; children: Jason David, Andrew Troy. BA in English, Elizabethtown Coll., 1969. News dir. Sta. WGAL Radio, Lancaster, Pa., 1969-77; news anchor Sta. WSBA Radio, York, Pa., 1977; news dir. Sta. WGAL-TV, Lancaster, 1977-79; owner, exec. producer The Gospel Greats, Lancaster, 1979—; owner Springside Mktg., Lancaster, 1986—; producer, host weekly 2 hour nationally syndicated Gospel Greats program, 1980—. Monthly columnist Christian Music News, 1986-87, Singing News Mag., 1987—. Recipient Silver Mike award Southern Gospel Music Assn., 1983-84, Fan award Singing News, 1986, 87, 88, 89, 90, Singing News Fan award, 1991, Marvin Norcross award, 1991; named Favorite Gospel Disk Jockey, Southern Gospel Music News, 1984, People's Choice Favorite Disk Jockey Gospel Music News, 1985, 86, 87. Mem. So. Gospel Music Guild (founder 1986, pres. 1990—), Gospel Music Assn. (v.p. 1991—). Republican. Evang. Congregationalist. Office: Heil Enterprises 1519 Springside Dr Lancaster PA 17603

HEILENDAY, ANITA RICHARD, nun, home economics educator, administrator; b. Jersey City, May 6, 1927; d. Richard Arthur and Lillian Agnes (Nesbitt) H. B.S., Coll. St. Elizabeth, 1950; M.S. Simmons Coll., 1959. Joined Sisters of Charity, Roman Catholic Community, 1951; instr. dept. home econs., Coll. St. Elizabeth, Convent Station, N.J., 1953-64, asst. prof., 1965-79, assoc. prof., 1980—, chmn. dept., 1968—, responsible for establishment Nevin House, 1970; founder, dir. Ctr. for Ind. Living: Aging and Handicapped, Convent Station, 1976—; mentor ind. study students Salon of Culinary Arts, 1975-83. Mem. Downtown Devel. Com., Univ. Relations Com., Madison, N.J., 1984—. Multiple grant recipient N.J. State Dept. Edn.; recipient Disting. Educator citation Sisters of Charity, Convent Station, 1977, Kelligar award, Coll. St. Elizabeth, 1980. Mem. Internat. Fedn. Home Econs., Am. Home Econs. Assn. (state del., agy. mem., unit rep. 1950—), N.J. Home Econs. Assn. (trustee, state pres. 1970-72, Home Economics of Yr. 1983), Nat. Council Adminstrs. of Home Econs. Home and Office: Coll St Elizabeth Convent Station NJ 07961

HEILMAN, EDNA MAY, religious educator; b. New Florence, Pa., May 29, 1938; d. Evan Griffith and Edna (Hull) Williams; m. James Herman Heilman, Oct. 26, 1957; children: Susan, Kay, Judy, Beth. Licensed Practical Nurse, Allegheny Gen. Hosp., 1960. Tchr. Sun. sch. Presbyn. Ch., Kittanning, Pa., 1960-63, Greensburg, Pa., 1963-70; tchr. Sun. sch. Mt. Moriah Bapt., Smithfield, Pa., 1971-85; children's ministry coord. Calvary Bapt., Uniontown, Pa., 1986—; home health aide Albert Gallatin Vis. Nurses Assn., Uniontown, 1980—. Home: RD #1 Box 286 Smithfield PA 15478 Office: Calvary Bapt Ch Box W Uniontown PA 15401

HEIM, BRUNO BERNARD, archbishop; b. Olten, Switzerland, Mar. 5, 1911; s. Bernhard and Elizabeth (Studer) Heim-Studer. Student Benedictine Coll., Engelberg, Switzerland, 1926-31; Dr. phil., Thomas Aquinas U., Rome, 1934; BD, Fribourg U., Switzerland, 1937; DCL, Gregorian U. (Rome), 1946; grad. Pontifical Diplomatic Acad., Rome, 1947. Ordained priest Roman Cath. Ch., 1938, consecrated bishop, 1961. Curate in parishes Arbon and Basel, Switzerland, 1938-42; chief chaplain for Italian and Polish mil. internees in Switzerland, 1943-45; sec. Nuncio Roncalli, Pope John XXII in Paris, 1947-51; auditor Nunciature, Vienna, Austria, 1951-54; councillor Nunciature, Bonn, Fed. Republic of Germany, 1954-61; apostolic del., Scandinavia 1961-69; pro nuncio, Finland, 1966-69, Egypt; pres. of Caritas, Egypt, 1969-73; apostolic del. Gt. Britain, 1973-82, pro nuncio, Gt. Britain, 1982-85. Author: Coutumes et droit héraldiques de l'Eglise, 1950; Heraldry in the Catholic Church, 1978; 82; Liber amicorum, 1982. Decorated officer Acad. Legion d'honneur France, 1951, knight of honour Teutonic Order, 1961; Cross of Merit with star (Germany), 1961; gt. cross Order of Malta, 1962; Golden Cross with star (Austria), 1962; gt. officer of Merit, Italy, 1965; gt. cross of Finnish Lion, 1969; gt. cross Order of St. Maurice and Lazarus, Savoy, 1973; Gt. Cordon first class Order of Republique, Egypt, 1974; gt. cross Order of St. John, Britain, 1979; Order of Isabel la Catolica, Spain, 1982; gt. prior and bailiff gt. cross justice, decorated with the Collar of Constantinian Order of St. George, 1989; gt. officer Order of Polonia Restituta, 1985. Mem. Internat. Heraldic Acad., Soc. Suisse d'Heraldique, Accademia del Collegio Araldico, Real Acad. de la Historia, Accad. Atcheologica Italiana, Societa' Italiana di studi Araldici, French Heraldic and Geneal. Soc., Adler Vienna, Herold Berlin, Socs. Heraldica Scandinavica, Cambridge U. Heraldic and Geneal. Soc. (patron). Club: Atheneum (London). Avocations: heraldic painting; gardening; cooking. Address: Zehnderweg 31, CH 4600 Olten Switzerland

HEIM, JOEL JAMES, minister; b. Grand Island, Nebr., Nov. 12, 1958; s. E. Murry and Margaret Katherine (Haggard) H.; m. Nelia Beth Scovill, May 27, 1990. BS, U. Nebr., 1982; MDiv, Union Theol. Sem., N.Y.C., 1990; postgrad, Sch. Religion, U. So. Calif., L.A., 1991—. Ordained to ministry Christian Ch. (Disciples of Christ), 1991. Youth dir. 1st Christian Ch. (Disciples of Christ), Grand Island, 1979; youth coord. 1st Christian Ch. (Disciples of Christ), Lincoln, Nebr., 1980-81; mem. ch. camp staff Nebr. Conf., United Ch. in Christ, Burwell, 1982; tchr., debate coach Westside High Sch., Omaha, 1982-87; asst. dir. child and youth edn. Riverside Ch., N.Y.C., 1988—; mem. outdoor ministry com. United Ch. of Christ (Disciples of Christ), Nebr., 1979-87; del. Disciples Gen. Assembly, Indpls., 1989. Bd. dirs. Nebraskans for Peace, Omaha, 1985-87. Office: Riverside Ch 490 Riverside Dr New York NY 10027 *We need people of faith working on the world's problems, for only by faith can we continue to struggle knowing that there will be no improvement in the forseeable future. Faith gives hope, even when there is none. Hope is truly the gift of faith.*

HEIN, KENNETH CHARLES LAWRENCE, priest, educator; b. Longmont, Colo., June 2, 1938; s. Peter Joseph and Lena Josephine (Keller) H. BA in Latin, St. Benedict's Coll., Atchison, Kans., 1964; STB, Coll. di Sant'Anselmo, Rome, Italy, 1967; ThD, U. Tübingen, Fed. Republic Germany, 1973. Benedictine monk Holy Cross Abbey, Canon City, Colo., 1960—, bus. mgr., 1985-88, treas., 1988—; priest Roman Cath. Ch., 1969—; sem. tchr. St. Thomas Theol. Sem., Denver, 1972-74; tchr. high sch.modern langs. The Abbey Sch. Theology, Canon City, 1974-83, acad. dean, 1981-83; tchr. St. Anselm's Coll., Manchester, N.H., 1983-85; chaplain Fitzsimon's Army Med. Ctr., Aurora, Colo., 1989—; bd. dirs. Theol. Inst. Holy Cross Abbey, 1974-78; mem. Med.-Moral Bd. St. Thomas More Hosp., 1980—; presenter in Anglican Roman Cath. dialog, 1975-76, med.-moral issues, 1979—. Contbr. numerous articles to profl. jours.; translater Psalms of Bible, 1989. Founder Abbey Students Aid to Poor, 1974-83; mem. Birthright, Woodbury, N.J., 1985—. Avocations: computer sci. and programming, religious retreat master. Office: Holy Cross Abbey 2951 E Hwy 50 Canon City CO 81215-1510

HEIN, ROLLAND NEAL, English language educator; b. Cedar Rapids, Iowa, Sept. 12, 1932; s. George H. and Henrieta (Werner) H.; m. Dorothy Mae Netolicky, Aug. 31, 1954; children: Steven Ronald, Christine Lynn. BA, Wheaton Coll., 1954; BD magna cum laude, Grace Sem., Winona Lake, Ind., 1957; MA, Purdue U., 1963, PhD, 1971. Ordained to Christian Ministry, Nat. Fellowship of Brethren Ministers, Grace Brethen

Ch., Cedar Rapids, 1958. Instr. Grace Coll., Winona Lake, Ind., 1957-59; pastor Grace Brethren Ch., Flora, Ind., 1959-62; asst. prof. Bethel Coll., St. Paul, Minn., 1962-67; assoc. prof. Bethel Coll., St. Paul, 1968-70; asst. prof. Wheaton (Ill.) Coll., 1970-71, assoc. prof., 1971-78, prof., 1978—. Author: The Harmony Within, 1982; editor: (book series) The Sermons of G. MacDonald, 1974, '76, '78, '80; contbr. articles to profl. mags. Recipient Rsch. grant Wade Ctr., Wheaton, Ill., 1989. Mem. Modern Lang. Assn., Nat. Assn. Scholars, Nat. Coun. Tchrs. of English. Avocations: flower horticulture, tennis. Office: Wheaton Coll Wheaton IL 60187 *The less one is preoccupied with self and self-advantage, the happier one becomes.*

HEINE, RAYMOND ARNOLD CARL, retired bishop; b. Fort Wayne, Ind., May 28, 1922; s. William Frederick and Clara Margaretta (Gerberding) H.; m. Flora Margaretta Miller, Aug. 25, 1945; children—Ward William, Marian Ruth. A.B., Wittenberg U., 1943, D.D. (hon.), 1969; M.Div., Hamma Div. Sch., Springfield, Ohio, 1945. Pastor Whitestown-New Augusta Parish, Ind., 1945-47; asst. pastor Trinity Lutheran Ch., Fort Wayne, 1947-51; pastor Trinity Lutheran Ch., Grand Rapids, Mich., 1963-80, Christ Luth. Ch., Monroe, Mich., 1951-63; bishop Mich. Synod, Luth. Ch. in Am., Detroit, 1980-88, mem. exec.bd., 1968-78, sec., 1974-78, dean dist. 2, 1970-80, mem. cons. com. on stewardship, 1982-88. Trustee Carthage Coll., Kenosha, Wis., Luth. Sch. Theology, Chgo., bd. dirs. Luth. Social Services Mich., Detroit, 1980-88. Recipient merit award Suomi Coll., Hancock, Mich., 1982. Avocations: sailing, reading, woodworking. Home: PO Box 68 Lake Leelanau MI 49653 Office: Holy Spirit Ch 4800 Orchard Lake Rd West Bloomfield MI 48033

HEINEMANN, DAVID, rabbi; b. Hitchin, Eng., Aug. 3, 1947; came to U.S. 1949; s. Benno and Friedl (Schilo) H.; m. Judith Ann Friedman, May 2, 1972; children: Bob, Phil, Joe, Rae, Allen, Honey, Max, Abe. Ordained rabbi. Student lectr. Beth Medrosu Gouoha of Am., Lakewood, N.J., 1976-88; rabbi, dean and founder Mesivta Keser Torah of Cen. Jersey, Belmar. Office: Mesivta Keser Torah 503 11th Ave Belmar NJ 07719

HEINEN, SISTER MARY FLORITA, nun, religious order administrator; b. New Ulm, Minn., May 14, 1933; d. Arthur George and Clara Marie (Neuwirth) H. BSN, Coll. St. Catherine, St. Paul, 1958, PhD (hon.), 1991; MS in Nursing, Cath. U. Am., 1963; MA, U. Minn., 1972, PhD, 1975. Joined Sisters St. Joseph of Carondelet, Roman Cath. Ch., 1952; lic. nurse. Nurse, nursing educator various hosps. Minn. and N.D., 1958-78; assoc. prof., coord. new programs St. Mary's Jr. Coll., Mpls., 1975-78; exec. sec., adminstrv. asst. Health Care Corp.—Sisters St. Joseph of Carondelet, St. Paul and St. Louis, 1979-85; v.p. mission Health Care Corp.—Sisters St. Joseph of Carondelet, St. Louis, 1986-88; province dir. St. Paul province Sisters St. Joseph of Carondelet, St. Paul, 1988-91; mem. Minn. Bd. Nursing, Mpls., pres., 1977-81; trustee Health East, St. Paul, 1988—, Carondelet Life Care, 1988—. Trustee Coll. St. Catherine, St. Paul, 1988—, St. Joseph Hosp., St. Paul, 1988—, U. St. Thomas Sch. Div., St. Paul Sem., 1989—. Mem. Sigma Theta Tau, Pi Lambda Theta. Democrat. Home: 5101 W 70th St Apt 120 Minneapolis MN 55439

HEINING, JAMES WILLIAM, minister; b. St. Paul, June 7, 1950; s. Howard Frank and Johanna (Pritzel) H.; m. Jolene Ann Engelmann, June 11, 1972; children: Nathan, Sarah, Emily. AA, Concordia Coll., 1970; BA, Concordia Sr. Coll., 1972; MDiv, Concordia Theol. Sem., 1976. Assoc. pastor Resurrection Luth. Ch., Spring, Tex., 1976-79; pastor Zion Luth. Ch., Albert Lea, Minn., 1979—; counselor Austin Cir. Luth. Ch.-Mo. Synod, 1988—. Mem. Freeborn County Ministerial Assn. (pres. 1982-83). Home: 824 Minnie Maddern Albert Lea MN 56007 Office: Zion Luth Ch 924 Bridge Rd Albert Lea MN 56007

HEINITZ, KENNETH LAWRENCE, theology educator; b. Upland, Nebr., Nov. 13, 1926; s. Otto Richard and Minnie Augusta (Meyer) H.; m. Ione Marie Licht, June 22, 1952; children: Jacquelen, Jan, John, Mark. BA, Concordia Sem., 1947, BDiv, 1952; MA, U. Kansas City, Mo., 1951; PhD, Loyola U., 1963; STM, Luth. Sch. Theology, Chgo., 1971. Ordained to ministry Luth. Ch., 1953. Instr. in theology Concordia Tchr.'s Coll., River Forest, Ill., 1950-51, Seward, Nebr., 1952-53; jr. pastor Immanuel Luth. Ch., Twin Falls, Idaho, 1953-54; pastor Redeemer Luth. Ch., Salt Lake City, 1954-57; prof. theology Concordia U., River Forest, 1957—. Assoc. editor: Luth. Edn., 1989—. Mem. Am. Soc. Ch. History, Luth. Edn. Assn. Democrat. Office: Concordia U 7400 Augusta River Forest IL 60305 *As a Christian, I try to live as a witness to God and His grace for the benefit of other people.*

HEINRICH, JOHN JOSEPH, chaplain; b. Bklyn., Sept. 25, 1934; s. John Joseph and Genevieve (Kuperian) H.; m. Valerie Jane Schuck, Apr. 8, 1956; children: Gerald Arthur, Teresa Ann. AA, St. John's U., 1978. With Corp. Trust Co., N.Y.C., 1960-68, Hicksville (N.Y.) Post Office, 1968-79, Police Benevolent Assn., Lakeland, Fla., 1979-80; pres., chaplain Citizens Benevolent Assn., Displaced Inmates Dependents Mission, Avon Park, Fla., 1980-88; chaplain B. Flushing Hosp., Brooksville, Fla., 1988—. Served with USAF, 1953-57. Mem. Am. Assn. Retired Persons, Nat. Chaplains Assn. Democrat. Avocation: helping underprivileged. Home and Office: 9045 Cooper Terrace Dr Brooksville FL 34601

HEINZ, HANSPETER, theology educator, priest; b. Bonn, Germany, Nov. 18, 1939; s. Peter and Grete (Reuter) H. MPhil, Gregorian U., Rome, 1962, ThM, 1966; Div, U. Bonn, 1975, Habilitation, 1983. Ordained priest Roman Cath. Ch., 1965. Parish curate Diocese of Cologne (Fed. Republic Germany), 1966-70; spiritual dir. Cen. Com. German Caths., Bonn, 1970-80; prof. pastoral theology and liturgy U. Augsburg (Fed. Republic Germany), 1983—; parish priest Bachern, Diocese of Augsburg, 1983—; prof. Ecumenical Sch. Focolare-Movement, Fed. Republic Germany, 1981—, Internat. Sch. Theology of Focolare-Movement, Rome, 1982—; cons. Priests and Religious Commn., German Cath. Bishops Conf., 1984—, chmn. Pastoral Commn., Cen. Com. German Caths., 1984—. Author: Urs von Balthasar, 1975, Bonaventure and Trinity, 1985. Chmn. Commn. Jewish-Christian Dialogue, 1974—. Avocations: mountain climbing, cooking. Home: Tannenweg 1, D-8904 Friedberg Federal Republic of Germany Office: U Augsburg, Universitätsstrasse 10, D-8900 Augsburg Federal Republic of Germany

HEISER, WALTER CHARLES, librarian, priest, educator; b. Milw., Mar. 16, 1922; s. Walter Matthew and Lauretta Katherine (Kopmeier) H. AB, St. Louis U., 1945, AM, 1947, STL, 1955; MSLS, Cath. U. Am., 1959. Joined S.J., Roman Cath. Ch., 1940, ordained priest, 1953. Latin tchr. St. Louis High Sch., 1947-50; divinity libr. Saint Louis U., St. Louis, 1955—; mem. faculty dogmatic and systematic theology St. Louis U. Div. Sch., 1966—; cons. catalog Cath. supplement Wilson Sr. High Sch. Libr., 1968-77. Rev. editor Theology Digest, 1963—. Mem. Cath. Libr. Assn., Am. Theol. Libr. Assn., Cath. Theol. Soc. Am. Home: 3601 Lindell Blvd Saint Louis MO 63108 Office: 3650 Lindell Blvd Saint Louis MO 63108

HEISTAND, JOSEPH THOMAS, bishop; b. Danville, Pa., Mar. 3, 1924; s. John Thomas and Alta (Hertzler) H.; B.A. in Econs., Trinity Coll., Hartford, Conn., 1948, D.D. (hon.), 1978; M.Div., Va. Theol. Sem., 1952, D.D. (hon.), 1977; m. Roberta Crieger Lush, June 1, 1951; children—Hillary Heistand Long, Andrea Deferrier, Virginia Redmon. With Internat. Harvester Co., 1948-49; ordained to ministry Episcopal Ch., 1952; rector Trinity Ch., Tyrone, Pa., 1952-55; chaplain Grier Sch., Birmingham, Pa., 1952-55; asso. rector St. Paul's Ch., Richmond, Va., 1955, rector, 1955-69; rector St. Philip's in the Hill Ch., Tucson, 1969-76; bishop coadjutor Episcopal Diocese Ariz., Phoenix, 1976-79; bishop of Ariz., 1979—. Served with AUS, 1943-45. Decorated Bronze Star with oak leaf cluster, Purple Heart; Croix de Guerre (France). Office: Box 13647 Phoenix AZ 85002

HEITZENRATER, RICHARD PAUL, religion educator; b. Dover, N.J., Nov. 9, 1939; s. H. Clair and Ruth Naomi (Ross) H.; m. Karen Louise Anderson, June 2, 1962; children: Julia Marie, Jeffrey Paul, John Clair. AB, Duke U., 1961, BD, 1964, PhD, 1972. Ordained elder United Meth. Ch., 1964. Assoc. minister 1st United Meth.Ch., Butler, Pa., 1964-66; asst. prof., then assoc. prof. history and religion Centre Coll., Danville, Ky., 1969-77; Albert C. Outler prof. Wesley studies So. Meth. U., Dallas, 1977—. Author: The Elusive Mr. Wesley, 2 vols., 1984, Journal and Diaries of John Wesley, 7 vols., 1988—; Mirror and Memory, 1989; gen. editor Wesley Works Editorial Project, 1986—; editor: Diary of an Oxford Methodist, 1985, Oxfordnotes, 1984—, Kingswood Books, 1988—, John Wesley's Sermons: An Anthology, 1991. Mem. Gen. Commn. on Archives and History, United Meth. Ch., 1980-88, vice chmn. gen. conf. com. on doctrine, 1984-88; pres. faculty senate So. Meth. U., 1984-85. Mem. Am. Coun. Learned Socs. (fellow 1975-76), Am. Acad. Religion, Am. Soc. Ch. History, Am. Soc. for Eighteenth Century Studies, United Meth. Hist. Soc., Wesley Hist. Soc., Oxford Inst. Meth. Theol. Studies, Charles Wesley Soc. (bd. dirs. 1990—), Phi Beta Kappa, Dallas Masters Track and Field, Dallas Cross Country. Office: So Meth U Perkins Sch Theology Dallas TX 75275

HELD, HAROLD FREDERICK THEADORE, minister; b. Bridgeport, Mich., Apr. 5, 1912; s. John George and Anna (Schweikher) H.; m. Norma Edna Buetow, Oct. 5, 1941; children: Edward, Robert, Thomas. Diploma, Concordia Theol. Sem., St. Louis, 1937. Ordained to ministry Luth. Ch.-Mo. Synod, 1940. Minister Bethlehem Luth. Ch., Lewiston, Mich., 1940-43, St. John's Luth. Ch., Hillman, Mich., 1943-59, Christ Luth. Ch., New Castle, Pa., 1959—; cir. counselor Luth. Ch.-Mo. Synod, Hillman, 1957-58. Sec. Pub. Sch. Bd., Hillman, 1952-53. Republican. Home: 909 Ryan Ave New Castle PA 16101 Office: Christ Luth Ch 1302 E Washington St New Castle PA 16101

HELD, HEINZ JOACHIM, bishop, church official; b. Wesseling, Rhein, Germany, May 16, 1928; s. Heinrich and Hildegard (Roehrig) H.; m. Anneliese Novak, Aug. 22, 1959; children—Annedore, Ulrike, Beate, Joachim. Dr. Theol., U. Heidelberg, 1957; Dr. Theol. (hon.), Evang. Theol. Akademy, Budapest, Hungary, 1985. Ordained to ministry Evangelical Ch., 1957. Asst. tchr. Kirchliche Hochschule Wuppertal, 1952-56; parish pastor Friedrichsfeld Niederrhein, 1957-64; prof. theology Facultad Luterana de Teologia in José C. Paz, nr. Buenos Aires, Argentina, 1964-68, church pres. Iglesia Evangélica del Rio de la Plata, Buenos Aires, 1968-74; pres., church office for fgn. relations Evang. Ch. in Germany, Frankfurt, 1975-86, Hannover, 1986—; mem. central com. World Council of Chs., Geneva, 1968-91, moderator, 1983-91; bishop, 1991—. Office: Kirchenamt der EKD, Herrenhäuser Strasse 2, D-3000 Hannover 2, Federal Republic of Germany also: World Council of Churches, 150 route de Ferney, POB 2100, 1211 Geneva 2, Switzerland

HELD, JAY ALLEN, missionary; b. Canton, Ohio, Dec. 15, 1961; s. Earl E. and E. Jean (Robinson) H.; m. Laureen Elizabeth Allen, Mar. 19, 1988. BS in Theology, Bapt. U. Am., 1985, postgrad.; MA in Counseling, Western Sem., 1990; MA in Missions, Grace Theol. Sem., 1990. Inner-city missionary Forest Hills Bapt. Ch., Decatur, Ga., 1980-84; asst. to pastor Allgood Rd. Bapt. Ch., Marietta, Ga., 1984-85, Eastland Bapt. Ch., Orlando, Fla., 1985; tchr. high sch. Eastland Christian Sch., Orlando, 1985; inner-city missionary North Portland Bible Fellowship, Portland, 1989-91, Mt. Sinai Community Bapt. Ch., Portland, 1991—; camp counselor Camp C.H.O.F., Dalton, Ohio, summer, 1981, 82; adolescent counselor Youth Guidance Assn., Portland, 1986-88; program dir. Youth Outreach, Vancouver, Wash., 1988-89; tchr. North Portland Bible Clubs, 1989; instr. North Portland Bible Coll., 1991—. Mem. Oreg. Gang Task Force, Portland, 1989. Mem. Oreg. Mediation Assn., Portland Urban League. Home: 517 NE Morris Portland OR 97212-3160 *Empowered by the Holy Spirit, Jesus Christ was annointed to preach the Gospel to the poor and sent to heal the broken-hearted. It is my desire to live my life like the Lord Jesus Christ.*

HELFGOTT, BENJAMIN WOLF, rabbi; b. Hotin, Bessarabia, Russia, June 28, 1908; s. Moses and Chaytze Mirel (Menschel) H.; m. Hannah Stern, June 5, 1935; children: Feiga Helfgott Burnstein, Samson. Cert., Yeshiva U., 1931; MA, Western Res. U., 1947; PhD, Columbia U., 1952. Ordained rabbi, 1931. Rabbi Jewish Ctr. of Wakefield and Edenwald (N.Y.), 1928-43, 47—, Temple Emanuel, Youngstown, Ohio, 1943-47. Author: The Doctrine of Election in Tannaitic Literature, 1954; contbr. sermons to profl. publs. Mem. Yeshiva U. Alumni Assn., Western Res. U. Alumni Assn., Columbia U. Alumni Assn., Claremore Club, KP. Home: 693 E 236 St New York NY 10466

HELFRICH, BERNARD D., academic administrator. Dir., supt. of schs. Diocese of Bridgeport, Conn. Office: Edn Office 238 Jewett Ave Bridgeport CT 06606*

HELLAM, ROBERT WAYNE, lay worker, federal agency official; b. Carmel, Calif., Nov. 20, 1947; s. Franklyn John and Phyllis Ann (Forcum) H.; m. Constance Rosario Cristobal, Mar. 14, 1968; children: Charles Wayne, Brian Frank. BA, San Jose State U., 1974; postgrad., Monterey Peninsula Coll., 1964-65, 67-68, U. Calif., 1965-67. Cert. tchr., Calif. Claims rep. Social Security Adminstrn., Carmel, 1976—; Sunday Sch. tchr. Hilltop United Meth. Ch., Seaside, Calif., 1986—; chair pastor-parish rels. Hilltop United Meth. Ch., Seaside, 1985—, newsletter editor, 1983—, chmn. bd. trustees, 1991—; mem. Good News Caucus, Wilmore, Ky., 1989—. Author: Sonnets of David, 1989; weekly columnist Seaside Sentinel, 1989—; contbr. articles, revs. to jours. With USN, 1967-72. Recipient award Boy Scouts Am., 1982, City of Seaside, 1988. Mem. Nat. Taxpayers Union, Monterey Peninsula Taxpayers Assn., Mayflower Soc., Meth. Philatelic Soc. Office: Social Security Adminstrn 3785 Via Nona Marie Carmel CA 93923

HELLER, MEYER, rabbi; b. N.Y.C., Dec. 28, 1921; s. Moses Isaac and Fanny (Appel) H.; m. Esther Marcouitch, Apr. 24, 1945 (dec. Oct. 1966); m. Judy Freedman, Sept. 3, 1967; children: Marc, Joel, Judy, David, Daniel, Diane, Sherry. BA, Yeshiva U., 1941; cert. engring., U. Mo., 1943; M. Hebrew Lit., Hebrew Union Coll., 1950, D. Hebrew Lit. (hon.), 1975. Ordained rabbi, 1950. Assoc. rabbi Temple Emmanuel, San Francisco, 1950-63; rabbi Temple Solael, Woodland Hills, Calif., 1963-64, Temple Israel, Hollywood, Calif., 1964-68, Temple Emanuel, Beverly Hills, 1969—; pres. No. Calif. Bd. Rabbis, San Francisco, 1958-60. Bd. dirs. Beverly Hills YMCA, 1970-80, Found. for Jr. Blind, L.A., 1985-89, Meals on Wheels, Beverly Hills, 1988—. Lt. Sig Corps, U.S. Army, 1944-45. Named Alumnus Man of Yr. Boys High Sch. Alumni, 1990. Mem. Southern Calif. Bd. Rabbis (pres. 1978-80), Cen. Conf. Am. Rabbis (treas. 1981-84, mem. placement com. 1987—), Pacific Assn. Reform Rabbis (pres. 1971-72), Interreligious Coun. Southern Calif. (pres. 1981-83). Office: Temple Emanuel 8844 Burton Way Beverly Hills CA 90211

HELLER, WENDELL THURLO, minister; b. Berne, Ind., Apr. 11, 1930; s. Loren and Florence (Gerber) H.; m. Betty C. Elmore, Dec. 28, 1951; children: Stephen C., Wendy Jo, Pamela Sue. BA, Bob Jones U., 1952; postgrad., New Orleans Bapt. Theol. Sem., 1955-56, Grace Theol. Sem., 1959-60; DD (hon.), Ind. Bapt. Coll. Ordained to ministry Ind. Fellowship Fundamental Bapts. Pastor Pine Park (Ga.) Bapt. Ch., 1952-54, Salem Bapt. Ch., Pavo, Ga., 1954-57; pastor Colonial Hills Bapt. Ch., Indpls., 1957-89, pastor emeritus, 1989—; gen. dir. Global Bapt. Missions, Inc., Indpls., 1990—; pres. Ind. Fellowship Fundamental Bapt. Chs.; pres. bd. dirs. Mission to Cancer Patients, 1975-89; chmn. bd. Denver Bapt. Bible Coll. and Sem., 1973-85, Colonial Christian Sch., Indpls., 1970-89; mem. cooperating bd. Ind. Bapt. Coll., Indpls., 1975-85, Bob Jones U., 1985—; trustee Cen. Bapt. Theol. Sem., Mpls., 1988-90; mem. adv. bd. Regeneration Reservation; gen. dir. Global Mission. Home: 7723 S River Rd Indianapolis IN 46240 Office: Colonial Hills Bapt Ch 8140 Union Chapel Rd Indianapolis IN 46240 *The value of an action is determined by the quality of the action itself. I must therefore do what is right whether that action is understood, appreciated or incorporated.*

HELLER, ZACHARY I., religious organization administrator. Pres. World Coun. of synagogues, Bayonne, N.J. Office: World Coun Synagogues 744 Ave A Bayonne NJ 07002*

HELLMAN, URSULA SYLVIA See RADHA, SIVANANDA

HELLWIG, MONIKA KONRAD, theology educator; b. Breslau, Silesia, Germany, Dec. 10, 1929; came to U.S., 1955; d. Rudolf and Marianne (Blaauw) H.; adopted children: Ericka, Michael, Carlos. LLB, Liverpool (Eng.) U., 1949, C.S.Sc., 1951; MA, Cath. U. Am., 1956, PhD, 1968; LittD (honoris causa), St. Mary-of-the-Woods Coll., St. Mary-of-the-Woods, Ind., 1974, St. Mary's Coll., Notre Dame, Ind., 1985, Trinity Coll., Washington, 1986, St. Michael's Coll., Winooski, Vt., 1986; LLD (honoris causa), Our Lady of the Elms Coll., Chicopee, Mass., 1977, Loyola U., Chgo., 1990; STD (honoris causa), Immaculate Conception Sem., Darlington, N.J., 1980; DD (honoris causa), Jesuit Sch. Theology, Berkeley, Calif., 1987; LHD (honoris causa), Loyola Marymount U., 1989, Loyola U., New Orleans, 1989, Coll. St. Catherine, St. Paul, 1989; LHD, Fairfield U., 1990. Instr. St. Therese's Jr. Coll., Phila., 1956-62; ghostwriter, rsch. asst. Holy See, Vatican City, 1963-64; lectr. theology Georgetown U., Washington, 1967-68, asst. prof., 1968-71, assoc. prof., 1971-77, prof., 1977-90, Landegger Disting. prof., 1990—; vis. prof. DePaul U., Chgo., 1968, St. Norbert's Coll., Wis., 1974, St. Michael's Coll., Vt., 1975, U. San Francisco, 1976, Princeton (N.J.) Theol. Sem., 1977, 79, 83, St. John's U., Collegeville, Minn., 1978, 82, 85, St. Joseph's Coll., West Hartford, Conn., 1980, U. Notre Dame, 1986, U. Dayton, 1986, Boston Coll., 1987, Huntington (N.Y.) Sem., 1987-90; seminarist Ecumenical Inst. Advanced Theol. Studies, Jerusalem, 1975-76; mem. Nat. Com. on Social Justice and Peace, U.S. Cath. Conf., 1982-84, Nat. Cath.-Presbyn./Reformed Bilateral Consultation, 1982-85; theol. cons. Treehaus Publs., 1983—; mem. selection com. summer rsch. grants NEH, 1984, 86; mem. internat. selection com. Grawemeyer Award, 1991; mem. selection panel Theol. Book Award, Cath. Press Assn., 1989-91, Pax Christi Book Award, 1990-91. Author: What Are the Theologians Saying?, 1970, The Meaning of the Sacraments, 1972, the Christian Creeds, 1973, Tradition: The Catholic Story Today, 1975, The Eucharist and the Hunger of the World, 1976, Death and Christian Hope, 1978, Understanding Catholicism, 1981, Whose Experience Counts in Theological Reflection?, 1982, Sign of Reconciliation and Conversion, 1982, Jesus the Compassion of God, 1983, Christian Women in a Troubled World, 1985, Gladness Their Escort: Homiletic Reflection, Years A, B and C, 1987; also articles; author: (with others) Community of Character, 1988, Faithful Witness: Foundations of Theology for Today's Church, 1989, Catholic Perspectives on Medical Morals, 1989, The Best in Theology, Vol. 4, 1990, Handbook of Faith, 1990, Christianity and the Wider Ecumenism, 1990, Christian Uniqueness Reconsidered, 1990, The Universal Catechism Reader, 1990, Georgetown at Two Hundred, 1990, The Catholic Church and American Culture, 1990, Death or Dialogue?, 1990, The Way of Ignatius Loyola, 1991, A Spirituality for Today's World, 1991, Individuality and Cooperative Action, 1991, Systematic Theology: Roman Catholic Perspectives, 1991, others; contbr. to: Encyclopedia of Religion, 1987, The New Dictionary of Theology, 1987; gen. editor: (book series) Sacraments Series, Zachaeus Doctrinal Series; assoc. editor Jour. Ecumenical Studies, 1973—; mem. editorial bd. Theol. Studies, 1981-91; editorial cons. Religious Studies Bull., 1983—. Bd. dirs. Woodstock Theol. Ctr., 1985-91; mem. bd. visitors Sch. Religious Studies, Cath. U., 1989—; mem. disting. women's adv. coun. St. Catherine's Coll., St. Paul, 1990—. Recipient award Cath. U. Am. Alumni Assn., 1986; named D.C. Prof. of Yr., Coun. for Advancement and Support of Edn., 1988; fellow Ecumenical Inst. Advanced Theol. Studies, 1975-76, Woodrow Wilson Internat. Ctr. for Scholars, 1985-86. Mem. AAUP, Cath. Theol. Soc. Am. (v.p. 1984-85, pres.-elect 1985-86, pres. 1986-87, John Courtney Murray award 1984), Coll. Theology Soc. Democrat. Roman Catholic. Home: 8408 Galveston Rd Silver Spring MD 20910-5306 Officrgetown U 37th and O Sts NW Washington DC 20057

HELM, GARY STEWART, minister; b. Athens, Tenn., Apr. 13, 1956; s. Grant Lee and Dessie Virginia (Thompson) H.; m. Debra Y. Taylor Mayberry, July 21, 1972 (div. 1978); 1 child, Brandi Daina Mayberry; m. Debra Yvonne Taylor Helm, Dec. 22, 1986; children: Sarah Elizabeth Helm, Michael Dale Helm. BA, Mo. Bapt. Coll., St. Louis, 1980; MDiv, Southeastern Bapt. Theol. Sem., Wake Forest, N.C., 1987; postgrad., Tenn. Tech. U., 1974-77, So. Bapt. Theol. Sem., 1981-83. Ordained to ministry, 1983. Summer missionary Teton Resort Ministries, Jackson Hole, Wyo., 1979; pastoral intern Kirkwood Bapt. Ch., St. Louis, 1980; pastoral supervised minister First Bapt. Ch., Spring Hope, N.C., 1986; mission pastor Harquahala Bapt. Ch., Buckeye, Ariz., 1983-84; pastor Bethlehem Bapt. Ch., Dillwyn, Va., 1987—; participant messenger The Bapt. Fellowship, Atlanta, 1990—; mem. So. Bapt. Religious Edn. Assn., Ft. Worth, 1987-90. Literacy tutor Buckingham County Literacy Coun., Dillwyn, 1990; chaplain Harquahala Fire Dist., Buckeye, 1983. Mem. James River Bapt. Assn. (mission vol. 1990), Associated Sunday Sch. Improvement and Support Team (dir.), Bapt. Committed to the So. Bapt. Conv. Home: Route 1 Box 32 Dillwyn VA 23936-9713 Office: Bethlehem Bapt Ch PO Box 324 Dillwyn VA 23936 *Reason is reasonably reasonable to the reasoner. Therefore, being co-owners of this temporary residence we should treat each other as equals. Abandoning the alienated authorities we should avoid being domesticated domesticators.*

HELM, THOMAS EUGENE, religion educator; b. Hammond, Ind., Jan. 20, 1943; s. Eugene Thomas and Ruby Muriel Helm; m. Virginia Mae Christenson, Sept. 10, 1966; 1 child, Jonathan Eugene. AM, Earlham Coll., 1965; STB, Harvard U., 1968; AM, U. Chgo., 1972, PhD, 1977. Prof. Western Ill. U., Macomb, 1974—. Author: The Christian Religion: An Introduction, 1991; contbg. author: Classics of Christian Spirituality, 1988; contbr. articles to profl. jours. Univ. Rsch. Coun. grantee Western Ill. U., 1978-79. Fellow Soc. for Values in Higher Edn.; mem. Am. Acad. Religion (midwest chpt. pres. 1978-80). Home: 20 Hickory Bow Macomb IL 61455 Office: Western Ill U Dept Philosophy and Religious Studies Macomb IL 61455

HELM, TIMOTHY J., minister; b. Kokomo, Ind., June 3, 1957; s. Edward Arthur and Jacqueline Sue (Cassel) H.; m. Karen Lynn Kline, Jan. 1, 1982; children: Cori Lynn, Christal Danae, Matthew Joseph. BA, Asbury Coll., Wilmore, Ky., 1979; MDiv, Asbury Theol. Sem., Wilmore, 1982. Ordained to ministry Meth. Ch. Youth dir. Monticello (Ind.) United Meth. Ch., 1978; student intern pastor Mt. Zion United Meth. Ch., Winchester, Ky., 1980-81; pastor Hanfield United Meth. Ch., Marion, Ind., 1982—; chair evanglism com. Marion dist. North Ind. Conf. United Meth. Ch., 1985—, mem. dist. coun. on mins., 1985—, mem. conf. bd. of discipleship, sec. dist coun. on ministry, 1989—. Mem. North Eastbrook Ministerial Assn. (sec., treas. 1991). Republican. Office: Hanfield United Meth Ch 5391 N 500 E Marion IN 46952

HELMINIAK, DANIEL ALBERT, priest, theologian, counselor; b. Pitts., Nov. 20, 1942; s. Albert Francis and Cecelia (Ziolkowski) H. BA in Philosophy, St. Vincent Coll., 1964; S.T.B., S.T.L., Gregorian U., Rome, 1966, 68; PhD in Theology, Boston Coll., Andover Newton Theol. Sch., 1979; MA in Psychology, Boston U., 1983; postgrad. in ednl. psychology, U. Tex., 1989—. Ordained priest in Roman Cath. Ch., 1967. Assoc. pastor Sts. Simon and Jude Ch., Pitts., 1969-72; candidate Soc. of St. Sulpice, Balt., 1972-78; coord. Paulist Leadership and Renewal Project, Boston, 1978-80; asst. prof. Oblate Sch. of Theology, San Antonio, 1981-85; dir. for spiritual growth Omega Point Counseling Ctr., Austin, Tex., 1989-91; pastoral counselor Family Counseling Ctr. Episc. Theol. Sem. of the Southwest, Austin, Tex., 1991—; mental health worker McLean Hosp., Belmont, Mass., 1980-81; chaplain Dignity, Boston, 1976-81, San Antonio, 1981-85, Austin, 1985—. Author: The Same Jesus: A Contemporary Christology, 1986 (honorable mention Cath. Press Assn. 1987), Spiritual Development: An Interdisciplinary Study, 1987; editorial cons. The Collected Works of Bernard Lonergan, 1986—; editorial adv. bd. Spirituality Today, 1988-90; contbr. articles to profl. jours. Mem. AIDS task force U. Tex., Austin, 1988-90. Mem. Am. Acad. Religion, Am. Assn. Pastoral Counselors, Am. Psychol. Assn. (assoc.), Cath. Theol. Soc. Am., Soc. for the Sci. Study of Religion, Jean Piaget Soc. Home: PO Box 13527 Austin TX 78711

HELMS, J. MARK, music minister; b. Birmingham, Ala., July 3, 1955; s. Jerry F. and Joyce (Curtis) H.; m. Cynthia Amos, Sep. 17, 1977; child: Kathryn Leigh. MusB, Samford U., 1978; M. Ch. Music, New Orleans Bapt. Theol. Sem., 1982. Min. music First Bapt. Ch., Phenix, Ala., 1978-80, Airport Blvd. Bapt. Ch., Mobile, Ala., 1982-84, Jackson Way Bapt. Ch., Huntsville, Ala., 1984-88, Hilldale Bapt. Ch., Birmingham, Ala., 1988--. Music dir. Birmingham, Ala. Erwin Elem. Sch., Bapt. Campus Ministries Choir; dir. Jefferson St. Jr. Coll. Mem. Phi Mu Alpha. Southern Baptist. Home: 2320 9th Pl NW Birmingham AL 35215 Office: Hilldale Baptist Ch 533 Sunhill Rd Birmingham AL 35215

HELS, SHARON JEAN, religious organization administrator; b. Fairbanks, Alaska, Dec. 14, 1953; d. Richard Gilbert and Jean Cleveland (Lord) Hels. BA, St. Olaf Coll., 1975; PhD, Vanderbilt U., 1987. Instr. Scarritt Grad. Sch., Nashville, 1985-87; asst. prof. Sch. Theology U. of the South,

Sewanee, Tenn., 1988-90; dir. United Meth. Bd. Higher Edn. and Ministry, Nashville, 1987—; mem. faculty diaconal cert. program Scarritt U., 1986-87; mem. faculty Niobrara Summer Sem., Martin, S.D., 1991. Editor jour. Quarterly Rev., 1987—. Mem. Soc. Biblical Lit., Cath. Biblical Assn. Episcopalian. Office: United Meth Bd Higher Edn Box 871 Nashville TN 37202

HELTON, JERRY WILLIAM, minister; b. Young Harris, Ga., Oct. 22, 1950; s. Clarence William and Sarah Elizabeth (Kelly) H.; m. Barbie Ann Rogers, June 25, 1970; children: Eva Paige, Zachrey Edge. AS, Young Harris Jr. Coll., 1970; BS, North Ga. Coll., 1972, MEd, 1979. Ordained to ministry. Mem. staff His Way, San Francisco, 1977-78; pastor House of Prayer Ch., Blairsville, Ga., 1984—. Office: House of Prayer Ch PO Box 1475 Blairsville GA 30512

HELTON, MAX EDWARD, minister, consultant, religious organization executive; b. Conasauga, Tenn., Nov. 24, 1940; s. Herman Marshall and Nellie Gladys (Haddock) H.; m. Jean Bateman, June 8, 1962; children: Elaine, Melanie, Crista, Becky. BA, Tenn. Temple U., 1963; DD (hon.), Hyles-Anderson Coll., 1973. Ordained minister Bapt. Ch., 1963. Sr. pastor Koolau Bapt. Ch., Kaneohe, Hawaii, 1964-71; exec. v.p. Hyles-Anderson Coll., Crown Point, Ind., 1971-77; sr. pastor Grace Bible Ch., White Plains, N.Y., 1977-83, West Park Bapt. Ch., Bakersfield, Calif., 1983-86; pastor outreach program Grace Bapt. Ch., Glendora, Calif., 1986-88; pres. Motor Racing Outreach, Harrisburg, N.C., 1988—. Author: Thirty Qualities of Leadership, 1975; contbr. articles to profl. jours.; keynote speaker Commonwealth Youth Day, Cayman Brac, B.W.I., 1964. Mem. adv. bd. legislation N.Y., Albany, 1980-82, sch. bd. Bakersfield Christian Sch. Dist., 1985-86; dep. sheriff Lake County (Ind.) Sheriff Dept., Crown Point, 1974-77. Mem. Internat. Sports Coalition, Conservative Bapt. Assn. (cons. 1983—, chmn. fellowship com. 1985-87), Nat. Assn. for Stock Car Auto Racing. Republican. Avocations: stock car racing, basketball. Office: Motor Racing Outreach Smith Tower Ste 336 Hwy 29 N Harrisburg NC 28075 *Of all the investments in the world, none are as valuable as people. Only people will last forever.*

HELTON, ROBERT BRUCE, clergyman; b. Banner Elk, N.C., Jan. 12, 1963; s. George Frank and Shelvie Jean (Stout) H.; m. Cynthia Faye Crouse, June 25, 1982; children: Dustin, Georgia. Assoc., Fruitland Bapt. Bible Inst., 1987; BA, Gardner Webb Coll., 1991. Ordained to ministry Bapt. Ch., 1987. Youth dir. Amity Bapt. Ch., Denver, N.C., 1986-87; pastor Union Grove Bapt. Ch., Huntersville, N.C., 1987—. Democrat. Home: Rt 3 Box 485 Lincolnton NC 28092 Office: Union Grove Bapt Ch 6431 Cashion Rd Huntersville NC 28078 *I've found that the joy produced by outward circumstances is at best unstable and superficial. However, joy that results from the relationship with Christ is constant and unchangeable because he never changes. Perhaps that's why, from his prison cell, the apostle Paul instructed the Phillipians to "Rejoice in the Lord." (Phillipians 4:4).*

HELYER, LARRY RANDALL, religion educator; b. Seattle, Nov. 6, 1942; s. Robert Wilson and Hazel Margaret (Clemens) H.; m. Joyce Elaine Smith, Apr. 10, 1965; children: Alicia Ann, Nathan Randall. BA magna cum laude, Biola U., 1965; MDiv, Western Bapt. Sem., 1968; cert., Middle East Inst. Holy Land, Jerusalem, 1969; PhD, Fuller Theol. Sem., 1979. Pastor North Bapt. Ch., Portland, Oreg., 1969-73, Faith Bapt. Ch., Sun Valley, Calif., 1974-79; from asst. prof. to full prof. religion Taylor U., Upland, Ind., 1979—. Contbr. articles to profl. jours. Am. Inst. Holy Land Studies fellow, Jerusalem, 1968-69; Clyde Cook scholar, 1965, Middler scholar, 1967. Mem. Evangelical Theol. Soc. (vice-chmn. 1986-87, chmn. 1987-88), Soc. Biblical Literature, Midwest Jewish Studies Assn. Republican. Baptist. Avocation: running. Home: 11 N Shamrock Rd Hartford City IN 47348 Office: Taylor Univ Upland IN 46989

HEMEN, LEE HOWARD, minister; b. Jackson, Wyo., Mar. 20, 1953; s. Lowell S. and Virginia L. (Van Vleet) H.; m. Denise Joan Bush, Aug. 17, 1975; 1 child, Katherine. Assoc in Divinity, Golden Gate Theol. Sem., Mill Valley, Calif., 1991. Ordained to ministry So. Bapt. Conv., 1985. Assoc. pastor Evergreen Bapt. Ch., Vancouver, Wash., 1984-85; sr. pastor Grace Bapt. Ch., Vancouver, 1985—; dir. Interstate Bapt. Youth, Portland, 1986-89; chaplain Fire Dist. 5, Vancouver, 1989-91; mem. Interfaith Witness Assn. home mission bd. So. Bapt. Conv., Atlanta, 1991—. Office: Grace Bapt Ch 9400 NE 50th Ave Vancouver WA 98665

HEMENWAY, JOAN ELIZABETH, minister, clinical pastoral education director; b. Phila., Mar. 14, 1938; d. Seymour Harrison and Katherine Jayne (McKown) H. BA, Conn. Coll., 1960; MDiv, Union Sem., 1968. Ordained to ministry United Meth. Ch. Mng. editor Youth Mag., Phila., 1970-72; assoc. minister First Meth. Ch., Germantown, Pa., 1976-78; pastoral counselor Pa. Found. for Pastoral Counseling, Phila., 1974-78; chaplain Presbyn. Hosp., Phila., 1974-78; chaplain supr. Hosp. Chaplaincy, Inc., N.Y.C., 1978-84, Hartford (Conn.) Hosp., 1984—; adj. faculty Union Sem., N.Y., 1979-84, Hartford Sem., 1987—; mem. ea. Pa. conf. United Meth. Ch. Contbr. articles to jours. Bd. trustees Hartford Sem., 1987—; bd. dirs. Concern for Dying, Inc., N.Y.C., 1980-85. Fellow Coll. Chaplains; mem. Assn. Clin. Pastoral Edn. (regional dir. ea. region 1983-90), Am. Assn. Pastoral Counselors. Democrat. Office: Pastoral Services Hartford Hosp 80 Seymour St Hartford CT 06115

HEMKER, ELIZABETH JEAN, religious education director; b. Owosso, Mich., Dec. 17, 1944; d. Otto Nicholas and Willie Mae (Disspain) Yaklin; m. Donald Edwin Hemker, Sept. 11, 1965; children: Dawn, Thomas, Melissa. BA, Saginaw Valley State U., 1982, MA, 1989. Dir. religious edn. Holy Spirit Parish, Saginaw, Mich., 1982-85, St. Mary Albee Parish, St. Charles, Mich., 1985-89, Blessed Trinity Parish, Frankenmuth, Mich., 1989—; eucharistic min., lector St. Mary Albee Parish, St. Charles, 1970—, Blessed Trinity Parish, Frankenmuth, 1989—; resource person Companies on the Journey, Frankenmuth, 1989—. Tchrs. aide Albee Elem. Sch., 1973-82; park booster Albee Twp. Park Boosters, 1976—. Recipient Vol. award Chesaning Schs., 1973-82. Mem. Dirs./Coords. Religious Edn. Assn. Home: 2250 Verne Burt MI 48417 Office: Blessed Trinity Parish 958 Tuscola St Frankenmuth MI 48734

HEMPECK, MATTHEW PAUL, vicar; b. Robbinsdale, Minn., Feb. 28, 1964; s. Melvin Richard and Joan Mae (Raebel) H. BA, Western Oreg. State Coll., 1987. Vicar St. Matthew Luth. Ch., Milan, Ill., 1990—. Democrat. Office: St Matthew Luth Ch 115 W 12th Ave Milan IL 61264

HEMPEL, ELDON ROBERT, retired lay church worker; b. Hawks, Mich., Sept. 6, 1932; s. Walter Edwin and Lillian Caroline (Bade) H.; m. Ann Beatrice Claus, Sept. 19, 1964; children: Chris, Susan, David. Gen. edn. diploma, Delta Coll., 1966; grad., Mich. Luth. Ministries Inst., 1987. Cert. church planter, ins. counsellor. Chmn., zone rep. Luth. Laymans League, Alpena, Mich., 1978—; chmn. sch. bd. St. Michael Luth. Ch., Rogers City, Mich., 1978-88; cert. ch. planner Shepherd of the Lakes Luth. Fellowship, Presque Isle, Mich., 1989—; bd. dirs. Mission Devel., Ann Arbor; area, congregation rep. Ch. Extension Fund; del. Luth. Ch.-Mo. Synod Synodical Conv., St. Louis, 1980, St. Michael Luth. Ch., Rogers City, also chmn. bd. elders, 1985-89. Pres. N.E. Mich. Assn. Life Underwriters, Alpena, 1982, state legislative chmn., 1982; chmn. Life Underwriters Polit. Action Com., 1984. Cpl. U.S. Army, 1953-55. Mem. Lions, Sportsman Club. Republican. Home and Office: 8113 S Rogers Rd Hawks MI 49743 *I have discovered that hidden within unbelievers and unchurched people, there is an acre of diamonds waiting for the dust of sin to be removed-most of which was put there by self-righteous and make-believe Christians. When the dust of sin is removed by belief in The World (Jesus), they become "images of God" and priceless jewels in God's Church, and heirs of heaven.*

HEMPEL, JOHANNES, bishop; b. Zittau, Saxony, Germany, Mar. 23, 1929; s. Albert Hempel and Gertrud (Buchwald) H.; m. Dorothea Schönbach; children: Albrecht, Gabriele, Martin. Grad., Leipzig (German Dem. Republic) U., 1951, ThD, 1958, ThD (hon.), 1982; DD (hon.), Kent-Cantenbury U., Eng., 1984, Muhlenberg Coll., 1987. Ordained to ministry Evang.-Luth. Ch. of Saxony. Min. Evang.-Luth. Ch. of Saxony, 1952-56, bishop, 1971—; presiding bishop United Luth. Ch./Fedn. Evang. Chs. German Dem. Republic, 1977-91; tchr. theology Student Coll., German Dem. Republic, 1956-59, theol. dir., 1963-70; pastor for students Leipzig, 1959-63; pres. World Coun. Chs., Geneva, 1983—. Contbr. articles to religious jours. Office: Tauscherstrasse 44, 0-8027 Dresden Federal Republic of Germany

HEMSLEY, LAWRENCE E., clergyman; b. Williamsport, Pa., July 24, 1950; s. Harry E. and Esther L. (Ocker) H.; m. Sandra M. Snyder, Nov. 25, 1978; children: Joshua, Lauren. BA, Lycoming Coll., Williamsport, 1972; MDiv, Lancaster (Pa.) Theol. Sem., 1975, STM, 1976. Ordained to ministry, United Ch. of Christ. Pastor New Jerusalem Zion United Ch. of Christ, Lenhartsville, Pa., 1976—. Democrat. Home: RD 1 Kempton PA 19529 Office: New Jerusalem Zion United Ch of Christ RD 1 Krumsville PA 19534

HENDERSON, BRADLEY LAWRENCE, minister; b. Birmingham, Ala., May 23, 1963; s. Donald Carlos and Elaine (Watts) H. BS in Econs., Auburn U., 1985; MDiv, Emory U., 1988. Ordained to ministry United Meth. Ch., 1990. Min. Five Points (Ala.) United Meth. Ch. Cir., 1985-88; assoc. min. Pell City (Ala.) 1st United Meth. Ch., 1988-91, Sandusky United Meth. Ch., Birmingham, Ala., 1991—; dist. youth coord. Anniston (Ala.) Dist. United Meth. Ch., 1988-91. Clergy advisor Christian Love Pantry, Pell City, 1988-91, Troop 199 Boy Scouts Am., 1988-91. *It is refreshingly amazing to find that in this world of incredible complexity, the most absolute and eternal things are to be found in the simplest of places: a child's laughter, life-giving sun and rain, a friend's listening heart. These are the things of God.*

HENDERSON, DONALD KIRK, pastor; b. Mobile, Ala., Aug. 22, 1961; s. George Donald and Ethel Elaine (Bellman) H.; m. Lesley Ann Henderson, Dec. 20, 1986. Grad. high sch., Pearl, Miss. Pastor singles and youth Bethel Chapel, Brentwood, Tenn., 1987—. Mem. Mid-Cumberland Coun. for Children and Youth (coun. Nashville chpt. 1989—). Home: 410 English Ivy Nashville TN 37211 Office: PO Box 51 Brentwood TN 37027

HENDERSON, EDWARD HUGH, philosophy and religion educator; b. Atlanta, Apr. 21, 1939; s. David George and Lulie Speer (Harris) H.; m. Anne Atkinson, June 23, 1962 (div. 1971); children: Eleanor Atkinson Henderson Cupit, Edward Carlisle; m. Patricia Weems, Aug. 25, 1973; children: Helen Bond, Harris Weems. BA in Philosophy, Rhodes Coll., 1961; MA in Philosophy, Tulane U., 1964, PhD in Philosophy, 1967. Asst. prof. La. State U., Baton Rouge, 1966-71, assoc. prof., 1971—, chair dept. philosophy and religious studies, 1979—; mentor edn. for ministry program U. of So., Sewanee, Tenn., 1981—. Editor, author introduction: Divine Action, 1990; contbr. articles to profl. jours. Assoc. vestry St. James Episcopal Ch., Baton Rouge, 1977-80, vestry, 1980-83, lay reader, chalice bearer, 1987-90, sr. warden, 1990, lay eucharist minister, 1990; mem. exec. bd. Diocese of La., 1989—. Grantee NEH, 1977-80, La. Endowment Humanities, 1986. Mem. Am. Acad. Religion, Am. Philos. Assn., Soc. Christian Philosophers, Soc. Philosophy of Religion, Phi Beta Kappa, Omicron Delta Kappa. Home: 2928 Eastland Ave Baton Rouge LA 70808 Office: La State U Dept Phil and Religious Std Baton Rouge LA 70803

HENDERSON, EDWIN HAROLD, minister; b. Pittsburgh, Tex., Sept. 17, 1927; s. Ether Chaney and Myrtle (Davis) H.; m. Velma Jean Smith, June 2, 1948; children: Steve Edwin, Cherilyn Cheree, Sharon Leigh. BA cum laude, Tex. Christian U., 1954; BD, Southwestern Bapt. Theol. Sem., 1957, ThD, 1963. Ordained to ministry Bapt. Ch., 1945. Pastor 1st Bapt. Ch., Hydro, Okla., 1947-51, Parker St. Bapt. Ch., Mineral Wells, Tex., 1951-53, 1st Bapt. Ch. Trinity Heights, Dallas, 1953-60; chmn. dept. Bible Jacksonville (Tex.) Bapt. Coll., 1960-61; pastor Cen. Bapt. Ch., Lubbock, Tex., 1961-75, Bethel Bapt. Ch., Dallas, 1975-77; sr. pastor 1st Bapt. Ch., Red Oak, Tex., 1985—; founder Inst. Bautista Biblico de Lubbock, 1971; founder, dir. Upreach Ministries, Dallas, 1977. Author: Now Abideth Faith, 1962, Roman Dogma and Bible Doctrine, 1964, Bible Doctrines Baptists Believe, 1964, The Triumph of Trust, The Life of God in the Believer, Spiritual Warfare; contbr. articles to profl. jours.; English lang. speaker on LifeWord Broadcast Ministries (internat. religious radio broadcast). Mem. Bapt. Missionary Assn. Am. (pres. 1966-68, writer Adult Sunday Sch. Quar. 1957—), Bapt. Missionary Assn. Tex. (pres.). Home: 4838 Chilton Dr Dallas TX 75227 Office: First Bapt Ch Red Oak TX 75154

HENDERSON, EVELYN BERRY, school system administrator; b. Spartanburg County, S.C., Sept. 25, 1927; d. Claude Vetrum and Grace Kathleen (Davis) Berry; m. Wallace B. Henderson, July 16, 1948; 1 child, Amanda Gay. Degree, Warren Wilson Coll., Wofford Coll.; postgrad., U. S.C., So. Sem. Extension, Louisville. Dir. religious edn. Boiling Springs 1st Bapt. Ch., Spartanburg, S.C. Author: Missions On Our Doorsteps, 1974, Henderson History, 1988, Bi-Centennial Play, 1772-1972. Recipient Mission award S.C. Bapt. Convention, 1978, Outstanding Mission Vols., Gov. of S.C., 1986. Mem. Bapt. Religious Edn. Assn., S.C. Assn. for Children Under Six. Home: 101 Belview Dr Spartanburg SC 29303

HENDERSON, HAROLD DOUGLAS, minister; b. Tampa, Fla., Feb. 9, 1959; s. Harold Douglas Sr. and Anna (Gregory) H.; m. Donna Lee Wills, July 11, 1987; 1 child, Carolyn Marie. Cert., Coll. Albamarl, 1984; BA, Southeastern Coll., 1988. Youth pastor 1st Assembly of God, Glover, S.C., 1988—; subcontractor Blaine Goad Co., York, S.C., 1989-91. Dir. Interpretive Mime Team, 1989-91. With USN, 1977-81. Republican. Home: 229 Church St Clover SC 29710

HENDERSON, JOHN A., priest; b. Toronto, Dec. 16, 1946; came to U.S., 1980; s. Stanley Lloyd and Evelyn Ann (McNamara) H. BA, Holy Redeemer Coll., Wis., 1981; MTh, Sacred Heart Sch. Theology, Wis. Cert. Mo. Dept. Corrections. Bd. dirs. Harvest House, Cooper County Vol. Com.; founder alcohol and substance abuse groups in Wis. and Mo. Mem. Rotary Internat., K.C. (chaplain). Roman Catholic. Home: 322 7th St Boonville MO 65233

HENDERSON, MICHAEL L., minister; b. Akron, Ohio, Aug. 26, 1957; s. Elton L. Henderson and Ora (Moore) Henderson/Hicks; m. Pat, June 29, 1979. Diploma, Moody Bible Inst., Akron, 1985, Internat. Bible Inst. and, Seminary, Orlando, Fla., 1987. Minister of follow-up The House of the Lord, 1980-83, minister of evangelism, 1983-85; pastor of svc./outreach The House of the Lord, Akron, 1985—; dir. Logos Bible Inst., 1986—; trustee The House of the Lord, Akron, 1985—, adult div. dir., 1982-87, new conver class tchr., 1982-86. Named to Outstanding Young Men of Am., 1987. Office: The House of the Lord 1650 Diagonal Rd Akron OH 44320

HENDERSON, NATHAN H., bishop. Bishop Ch. of God in Christ, Houston. Office: Ch of God in Christ 15622 Rockhouse Rd Houston TX 77060*

HENDERSON, ROBB ALAN, minister; b. Wilkes Barre, Pa., Mar. 21, 1956; s. Robert Alan and Mary (Gallup) H.; m. Helen McMullan, Aug. 25, 1984; children: Jason Allyn, Gareth Kent. BA in Theology, King's Coll., Wilkes Barre, 1981; MDiv, Lancaster Theol. Sem., 1985; D Ministry, Bethany Theol. Sem., 1990. Ordained to ministry United Meth. Ch. as deacon, 1986, as elder, 1988. Pastor Luzerne (Pa.) United Meth. Ch., 1985-88, Carverton United Meth. Ch., Wyoming, Pa., 1988—; owner R&R Bus Line, Luzerne, 1990—; chmn. interreligious and ecumenical affairs com. Coun. of Chs., 1989—; bd. dirs. Wyoming Valley Coun. of Chs. Chaplain Mt. Zion Vol. Fire Dept., Mt. Zion, Harding, Pa.; mem. Wilkes Barre Dist. Coord. Coun., 1988—. Mem. Masons (chaplain Kingston lodge 1989). Home: 1633 W 8th St Wyoming PA 18644 Office: Carverton United Meth Ch 1633 8th St Wyoming PA 18644-9404

HENDERSON, ROBERT WAUGH, retired religion educator, minister; b. Evanston, Ill., May 21, 1920; s. Robert Houston and Eunice (Swain) H.; m. June E. Whamond, Dec. 15, 1945 (dec. Jan. 1978); children: Robert J., Judith L. Abernethy; m. Belva Lou Pascoe, Nov. 21, 1978; stepchildren: J. David Dickman, J. Scott Dickman, Deborah L. Henderson, Amy D. Dickman. AB, Princeton U., 1941; BD, McCormick Theol. Sem., 1949; PhD, Harvard U., 1959. Pastor First Parish Ch., East Derry, N.H., 1950-57; asst. prof. religion U. Tulsa, 1958-64, assoc. prof. religion, 1965-70, prof. religion, 1970-90, prof. emeritus religion, 1990—; mem. Christian Unity Task Force, Tulsa Met. Ministry, 1985—; mem. ordination task force Presbyn. Ch., Louisville, 1988—; mem., sub. com. chair Presbyn. Hist. Soc. Bd., Phila., 1989—; pres. Presbyn. Hist. Soc. S.W., Ark., La., Okla., Tex., 1983-89. Author: Teaching Office in Reformed Tradition, 1962; contbr. articles to profl. jours. Capt. U.S. Army, 1941-46. Mem. AAUP (pres. Okla. Conf. 1971-75), Soc. Am. Ch. History, Presbyn. Hist. Soc. Home: 2606 E 33rd Pl Tulsa OK 74105

HENDERSON, SALATHIEL JAMES, minister; b. Key West, Fla., June 15, 1944; s. James Joseph and Merlice Yvone (McIntosh) H.; m. Mary Louise Henderson, June 28, 1969; children: Salathiel James II, Shane Jamal. AA, St. Leo Coll., 1987, BA, 1988. Ordained to ministry Bapt. Ch. 1989. Deacon Antioch Bapt. Ch., Hampton, Va., 1980-87, assoc. min., 1987—; vol. chaplain VA Med. Ctr., Hampton, Va., 1987—; substitute tchr. Hampton City Schs., 1991—; fed. supply cataloger Mason & Hanger Svcs., Inc., NASA/Langley AFB, Va., 1988-91; asst. dir. Bd. Christian Edn., Antioch Bapt. Ch., 1986—, mem. fin. com., 1984—, spiritual advisor Youth Usher Bd., 1984—, sec. Ministerial Staff, 1991—; dir. Bereavement Ministry, Antioch Bapt. Ch., Hampton, 1988—; cubmaster Cub Scouts Am., Antioch Bapt.-Hampton, 1990—. Cubmaster Boy Scouts Am., Hampton, 1990—. With USAF, 1962-85. Mem. NAACP, DAV, Masons. Democrat. Home and Office: 607 Allendale Dr Hampton VA 23669 *As one views society in its present state, and before an attempt is made to criticize the actions and values of the future generation (tomorrow's leaders) it is essential and imperative to carefully scrutinize today's grotesque situations. I believe our future leaders have many goals, with every hope of attaining them (if afforded the opportunity), but it is necessary that they also have acceptable role models as examples. Not just any role model, but one who institutes integrity, while propelling a greater force toward pride, trustworthiness and a genuine love for justice to all of God's Children!.*

HENDERSON, TONY CURTIS, clergyman; b. Birmingham, Ala., May 18, 1955; s. William Henry Thomas Jr. and Doris E. Henderson; m. Paula Yvette Newton, July 11, 1981; children: Kenneth Eugene Newton, Jennifer La Shun Newton, Dormarvelyn Paulecea. BA in English, U. Ala., 1981; MDiv, Interdenominational Theol. Ctr, Atlanta, 1986; postgrad., Cen. Bapt. Theol. Sem., Kansas City, Kans., 1989—. Ordained to ministry Christian Meth. Episc. Ch., 1975. Pastor Laymen Chapel Christian Meth. Episc. Ch., Birmingham, 1974-75, St. Mark Christian Meth. Episc. Ch., Birmingham, 1975-79, 85-86, Hill's Chapel Christian Meth. Episc. Ch., Leeds, Ala., 1979-83, Greater St. Paul Christian Meth. Episc. Ch., Bessemer, Ala., 1984-85; pastor, chief exec. officer St. Peter Christian Meth. Episc. Ch., Kansas City, 1986—; instr. Ala. Leadership Sch. Christian Meth. Episc. Ch., Birmingham, 1984-86, assoc. dean, 1986; instr. Ind. Leadership Sch., Gary, 1986, Kans.-Mo. Leadership Sch., Kansas City, 1988-90; chmn. bd. fin. Kans.-Mo. Conf. Christian Meth. Episc. Ch., 1986—, mem. com. on resolutions gen. bd., 1986—, mem. gen. bd., 1990—. Mem. Martin Luther King, Jr. Celebration Commn., Kansas City, 1987—, Martin Luther King, Jr. Scholarship Com., Kansas City, 1980—. Mem. NAACP, Beta Psi (hon.). Democrat. Avocations: chess, cross-stitching, cooking, macrame, reading. Home: 3515 N 33d Terr Kansas City KS 66104 Office: St Peter CME Ch 1419 N 8th St Kansas City KS 66101

HENDERSON, VERNE EUGENE, minister; b. Paullina, Iowa, Aug. 9, 1929; s. Isaac C. and Ora Eunora (Tjossem) H.; m. Kirsten Gregersen, Sept. 5, 1953; children—Jan Mark, Lisse. B. Div., U. Chgo., 1961; M.S. in Mgmt., MIT, 1979. Ordained to ministry Congl. Ch., 1956. Dir. community service Judson Meml. Ch., N.Y.C., 1952-54; minister Congl. Ch., New Lebanon, N.Y., 1955-62; founding minister College Heights Ch., San Mateo, Calif., 1962-69; state exec. Colo. Conf., Denver, 1969-74; nat. staff United Ch. Christ, Boston, 1974-77; prof. bus. ethics A.D. Little Mgmt. Edn. Inst., Cambridge, Mass., 1979—; pres. Revehen Cons., Brookline, Mass., 1979—. Contbr. articles to profl. jours. Mem. Am. Mgmt. Assn. Republican. Home: 28 Marshal St Suite 3 Brookline MA 02146

HENDERSON, VERYL FLOYD, minister; b. Shamrock, Tex., Jan. 13, 1943; s. Lonnie Floyd and Laura Mary (Roberts) H.; m. Cheryl Lynn Owen, June 15, 1965; children: Jana Kay, Andrea Mikala. Diploma, Mesa Coll., 1963; BA, Wayland Bapt. Coll., 1965; MDiv, Southwestern Bapt. Theol. Sem., 1969; D Ministry, So. Bapt. Sem., 1981. Ordained to ministry So. Bapt. Conv., 1967. Summer pastor Lake City, Colo., 1965, Breckenridge, Colo., 1966; pastor Mildred Bapt. Ch., Corsicana, Tex., 1967-69, Lahaina Bapt. Ch., West Maui (Hawaii) Ministries, 1969-78; dir. Resort Ministries Hawaii Bapt. Conv., 1979-83; dir. of missions Hawaii Bapt. Conv., 1983—; moderator, missions and evangelism dir., camp dir., religious edn. dir. Maui County Bapt. Assn. Chs.; asst. wrestling coach Lahainaluna High Sch., 1969-76, head coach, 1977-78. Mem. Jaycees (named Jaycee of Yr. 1971, pres., sec., treas.). Home: 45-459 D Mokulele Dr Kaneohe HI 96744 Office: 2042 Vancouver Dr Honolulu HI 96822 *The reference point in one's life is how he is perceived by others. The challenge of life is for others to see the good works and glorify God as a result.*

HENDERSON, WILBURN ALLEN, religious broadcaster; b. Paducah, Ky., Oct. 19, 1953; s. Wilburn Cleff and Georgia Mae (Hayes) H.; m. Nelline Sue Perry, Feb. 15, 1975; 1 child, Amber Lynn. BA in Bible, Cen. Bible Coll., Springfield, Mo., 1979. Ordained minister, Assemblies of God, 1977. Muwsic dir. KLFJ Radio, Springfield, Mo., 1975-83; sta. mgr. WLFJ Christian Radio, Greenville, S.C., 1983—. Editor Love Letter newsletter. Mem. Gospel Music Assn., Nat. Religious Broadcasters, Nat. Assn. Broadcasters. Home: 1 S Mountain Fork Taylors SC 29687 Office: Sta WLFJ-FM 2420 Wade Hampton Blvd Greenville SC 29615 *Life is a great journey that offers many choices. I depend on God's wisdom to guide me in those choices and encourage others to do the same.*

HENDREN, ROBERT LEE, minister; b. Memphis, July 28, 1930; s. Robert Lee Sr. and Maude Evelyn (Kennedy) H.; m. Joyce Elaine Westmoreland, Dec. 22, 1955; children: Deborah, Diane, Robert L. III. BA, David Lipscomb Coll., 1964; MA, La. State U., 1966, PhD studies, 1970. Minister Donelson Ch. Christ, Nashville. Author: Chosen for Riches, 1978, Life Without End., 1981, Which Way the Church, 1985. Sgt. USMC, 1950-61. Avocations: photography, computers. Home: 3003 Fernbrook Ln Nashville TN 37214 Office: Donelson Ch of Christ 2706 Old Lebanon Rd Nashville TN 37214

HENDRICK, BRICE, academic administrator. Supt. of edn. Diocese of Birmingham, Ala. Office: Supt Edn 8133 4th Ave S PO Box 186 Birmingham AL 35201*

HENDRICK, LARRY EUGENE, JR., minister; b. Washington, Ind., Feb. 7, 1957; s. Larry E. and Esther A. (Baker) H.; m. Cathy L. Chandler, June 7, 1980; children: Nathan Lee, Aaron Scott, Leah Marie. BA in Christian Edn., Trinity Bible Coll., 1982. Youth pastor Faith Meml. Assembly of God, Toccoa, Ga., 1980-81; tchr. 4th grade West Bank Christian Acad., Marrero, La., 1982-83; assoc. pastor South Hills Assembly of God, Bethel Park, Pa., 1983-88, youth camp dir., 1984-87, youth choir tour planner, 1985-88; sr. pastor Bellwood (Pa.) Assembly of God, 1988—; planner Sectional Com., Bellwood, Pa., 1989-91; min., clergy various nursing homes, sr. citizen groups, Pitts., 1984-88. Recipient Parallel Bible award Bellwood Am. Legion, Local Vets., 1989. Home: 5361 Sandhurst Circle N Lake Worth FL 33463

HENDRICKS, CLARE JOSEPH, priest; b. East Chicago, Ind., May 5, 1938; s. Clare James and Johanna (Socha) H. AB, Atheneum of Ohio, Cin., 1960; STB, Gregorian U., Rome, 1962, STL, 1964. Ordained priest Roman Cath. Ch., 1963. Various ch. ministries Docese of Gary (Ind.), 1964-74; instr. Bishop Noll Inst., Hammond, Ind., 1964-73; lectr. Calumet Coll., Whiting, Ind., 1968-73; asst. dir CCD Sch. for Tchrs., East Chicago, Ind., 1972-74; chaplain USN, Camp Lejeune, NC., 1974—. Pub. newsletter Veritas vos liberabit. Lt. Comdr. USN, 1980—. Mem. Am. Corrections Assn. Home: PO Box 8926 Camp Lejeune NC 28542 Office: USN Office of Command Chaplain MCB Camp Lejeune NC 28542

HENDRICKS, TERENCE EUGENE, minister, church association administrator; b. St. Louis, Sept. 14, 1952; s. Oliver Carl and Elee (Allen) H.; m. Janice Franklin, Mar. 25, 1972 (div. Oct. 1978); 1 child, Terence Eugene Jr.; 1 stepchild, Lataunya; m. Wendy Freenan, Dec. 6, 1980; children: Keria Deanne, Leah JoElle. BTh, Clarksville Sch. Theology, 1983; BS in Geography, So. Ill. U., Edwardsville, 1984. Ordained to ministry Bapt. Ch., 1974; cert. tchr., Colo. Asst. pastor Straightway Bapt. Ch., East St. Louis, 1974-82; adminstrv. asst. pastor Macedonia Bapt. Ch., East St. Louis, 1982-90; assoc. min. King Bapt. Ch., Denver, 1990—; dispatcher City of East St. Louis, Ill., 1971-75; motivational therapist Child Ctr., Centreville, Ill., 1975-76; youth counselor Youth Service Bur., East St. Louis, 1976-78; urban planner City of East St. Louis, 1978-87; program coord. Luth. Child and Family Svcs., East St. Louis Father's Ctr., 1987—; tchr. Denver Pub. Schs., 1990—. Columnist Beacon Newspaper, 1984; editor Community Devel. Newsletter, 1983-85. Bd. dirs. Foster Grandparents Program, East St. Louis, 1982—, Christian Rehab. Ctr., East St. Louis, 1978-82. Recipient I Dare You Leadership award Ralston Purina Co., St. Louis, 1970; named one of Outstanding Young Men of Am., 1985; scholar Ill. State Tchrs. Assn., 1970-74, Ill. State Gen. Assembly, 1981-84. Mem. Ministerial Alliance, NAACP. Lodge: Masons (sr. deacon). Avocations: reading, speaking, bowling, fishing. Home: 21 Oakland St Apt 5 Aurora CO 80012

HENDRICKS, THOMAS LEE, II, minister; b. Norfolk, Va., Sept. 7, 1956; s. Thomas L. and Mary Jane (Peregoy) H.; m. Elizabeth Anne Noblett, June 10, 1977; children: Thomas L. III, Carolyn Elizabeth, Christina Elizabeth. BA, Bob Jones U., 1978; MDiv, Temple Bapt. Sem., Chattanooga, 1985. Ordained to ministry Bapt. Ch., 1978. Asst. pastor Bible Bapt. Ch., Chesapeake, Va., 1979; pastor Jackson Bapt. Ch., Sylvania, Ga., 1980-82, Bantam Ridge Bapt. Ch., Wintersville, Ohio, 1986—; tchr., coach Colonial Hills Christian Sch., Taylors, S.C., 1978-79; chaplain Ohio Valley Hosp., Steubenville, 1986—, Dixon Health Care Ctr., Wintersville, 1987—; co-dir. Salt Run Youth Bible Conf., Rayland, Ohio, 1986—. Mem. Southwide Bapt. Fellowship, Fellowship of Ohio Valley Ind. Pastors (pres. 1991—), Bob Jones U. Alumni Assn. (life), Tenn. Temple Alumni Assn. Republican. Home: 131 Crawford Ave Wintersville OH 43952 Office: Bantam Ridge Bapt Ch RD 2 Wintersville OH 43952

HENDRICKS, WILLIAM LAWRENCE, theology educator; b. Butte, Mont., Mar. 10, 1929; s. Homer V.H. and Ruby E. (Jennings) H.; m. Lois Ann Lindsey, June 4, 1951; 1 child, John Lawrence. BA, Okla. Bapt. U., 1950; M Div, Southwestern Bapt. Theol. Sem., 1954, ThD, 1958; MA, U. Chgo., 1965, PhD, 1972. Ordained to ministry Bapt. Ch., 1950. Assoc. min. Immanuel Bapt. Ch., Wichita, Kans., 1949-50; min. South Bapt. Ch., Dodson, Tex., 1954-57; prof. theology Southwestern Bapt. Theol. Sem., Ft. Worth, 1957-78; prof. theol. and philosophy Golden Gate Bapt. Theol. Sem., Mill Valley, Calif., 1979-84; prof. theology, dir. grad. studies So. Bapt. Theol. Sem., Louisville, 1984—; dir. Ctr. for Religion and the Arts. Author: A Theology for Aging, 1986, A Theology for Children, 1980, The Doctrine of Man, 1977, Pascal and Fenelon, 1980; (play) The Harrowing of Hell, 1977. Recipient Alumni award Okla. Bapt. U., 1985, Meritorious Service in Christian Higher Edn. award Okla. Bapt. U., 1985, Outstanding Alumni Achievement award Okla. Bapt. U., 1986. Mem. Am. Acad. Religion (pres. S.W. region), Soc. Biblical Lit., Pacific Coast Theol. Soc., Commn. on Religious Studies (pres. S.W. region). Democrat. Office: So Bapt Theol Sem 2825 Lexington Rd Louisville KY 40280

HENDRIX, WALTER NEWTON, JR., music minister; b. Atlanta, Oct. 31, 1955; s. Walter Newton Sr. and Mildred (Brown) H.; m. Kathy Diane Raughton, Aug. 7, 1976; children: Jennifer Sue, Brian Lee. B in Ch. Music, Shorter Coll., 1977; M in Ch. Music, New Orleans Bapt. Theol. Sem., 1985. Minister music and youth Fairview Bapt. Ch., Rossville, Ga., 1978-80; minister of music Fortified Hills Bapt. Ch., Smyrna, Ga., 1980-83; minister music and edn. 1st Bapt. Ch., Moss Point, Miss., 1984-88; minister of music Jefferson Ave Bapt. Ch., East Point, Ga., 1988—. Office: Jefferson Ave Bapt Ch 1150 Jefferson Ave East Point GA 30344

HENDRY, SAMUEL ALDRIDGE, JR., education minister; b. Hattiesburg, Miss., May 4, 1948; s. Samuel Aldridge and Marietta (Flynt) H.; m. Janell Sue Richardson, Oct. 10, 1975; children: Scott Samuel, Lauren Carol. MusB, Miss. Coll., 1973; MusM Ch. Music, Southwestern Bapt. Sem., 1975. Min. music (intern) Beacon Bapt. Ch., Hattiesburg, 1967-68; asst. min. music 1st Bapt. Ch., Jackson, Miss., 1972-73; music assoc. North Ft. Worth Bapt. Ch., 1973-74; min. music/youth Ferris (Tex.) 1st So. Bapt. Ch., 1974-75, Rosewood Bapt. Ch., Columbia, S.C., 1975-78; min. music/edn. 1st Bapt. Ch., Ardmore, Okla., 1978-88; min. edn./evangelism Immanuel Bapt. Ch., Shawnee, Okla., 1988—; associational music dir. Columbia Metro Music Assn., 1975-77, Enon Assn., Ardmore, 1980-84; growth cons. Bapt. Gen. Conv. Okla., Okahoma City, 1984—; tchr., trainer Evangelism Explosion, Ardmore, Shawnee, 1984—. Parade marshall City of Ardmore, 1984. With USN, 1967-73, Vietnam. Mem. Okla. Singing Churchmen, Mins. Religious Edn. Assn., Civitan, Phi Mu Alpha. Republican. Home: 5 Sunrock Dr Shawnee OK 74801 Office: Immanuel Bapt Ch 1101 E Main St Shawnee OK 74801

HENGEL, MARTIN, theology educator; b. Reutlingen, Germany, Dec. 14, 1926; s. Gottlob and Berta (Kistenmacher) H.; m. Marianne Kistler, Aug. 3, 1957. ThD, U. Tübingen, Fed. Republic Germany, 1959, Habilitation, 1967; DDiv (hon.), St. Andrew's U., Scotland, 1981; DD, Durham, 1985; DDiv (hon.), Cambridge (Eng.) U., 1989; DTheol. (hon.), U. Uppala, Sweden, 1979, U. Strasbourg, 1988. Mng. dir. Hengella GmbH, Aalen, Fed. Republic Germany, 1953-54, 57-64; prof. theology U. Erlangen (Fed. Republic Germany), 1968-72, U. Tübingen, 1972—. Author: Die Zeloten, 1961, 2d edit., 1989, Jüdentum und Hellenismŭs, 1969,2d edit., 1974, Nachfolge und Charisma, 1968, Der Solen Gottes, 1985, Studies in the Gospel of Mark, 1983, Between Jesus and Paul, 1983, The Cross of the Son of God, 1986, Earliest Christianity, 1986, The Johannine Question, 1989, The Hellenization of Judaea in the First Century after Christ, 1989, The Prechristian Paul, 1991. Fellow Brit. Acad. (corr.); mem. Heidelberger Akademie der Wissenschaften. Home: Schwabstrasse 5l, D-7400 Tübingen 1, Federal Republic of Germany

HENLEY, JANE ELLEN, religious organization administrator; b. Passaic, N.J., July 13, 1947; d. Francis Henry and Catherine Nellie (Pekaar) Ternigan; m. Robert Weldon Henley, Apr. 5, 1969; children: Jonathon Kyle, Karis Joy, Jason Kaleb. BA in Speech Communication, Calif. State U., Northridge, 1987; MA in Marital and Family Therapy, Fuller Theol. Sem., 1989. Registered marriage, family and child counselor. Internat. rep. Youth for Christ Internat., Wheaton, Ill., 1967-72; crusade guest artist Billy Graham Evangelistic Assn., Mpls., 1971-83; marriage and family therapist Family Phases Counseling Ctr., Sherman Oaks, Calif., 1988—; dir. womens ministry Bel Air (Calif.) Presbyn. Ch., 1990—. Speaker in field. Fundraiser World Vision Internat. Monrovia, Calif. 1977-79; spl. events coord. The Elmbrook Ch., Waukesha, Wis., 1973-77. Kerr Found. grantee, L.A., 1988-89. Mem. Calif. Assn. Marriage and Family Therapists, Bel Air Women. Democrat. Home: 2351 Yew Dr Newbury Park CA 91320 Office: Bel Air Presbyn Ch 16221 Mulholland Dr Los Angeles CA 90049 *Christianity is not a system of human philosophy or a code of moral ethics but a relationship with One who imparts devine truth and devine life. Apart from Christ there is no living.*

HENNEBERRY, KIRK STEPHEN, minister; b. Decatur, Ill., Feb. 22, 1960; s. Jerry Wayne and Dorothy Ann (Kierlin) H.; m. Jeanette Adelle Schenk, Sept. 15, 1984; children: Joel William, Kayla Raneé. AA of Practical Theology, Christ for the Nations, Dallas, 1980; B of Career Arts, Southwestern Assembly of God, Waxahachie, Tex., 1988. Lic. to ministry Full Gospel Fellowship of Chs. and Mins. Internat., 1980, ordained, 1981. Dir., founder End Time Harvesters, Decatur, Ill., 1980-86; assoc. pastor House of Prayers Ministries Inc., Decatur, 1984-86, Harvest Christian Ctr., Decatur, 1986—. Author: Harvesting the Field, 1983; author, editor: End Time Harvesters Skit Book #1, 1984, End Time Harvesters Skit Book #2, 1986. Mem. Evang. Min.'s Assn., Full Gospel Min.'s Fellowship (sec., treas. 1987—). Home: 2350 N Dennis Decatur IL 62526 Office: Harvest Christian Ctr 401 N College Decatur IL 62522

HENNESEY, JAMES, church history educator; b. Jersey City, Oct. 6, 1926; s. Charles Gregory and Loretta (Beggans) H. BA, Loyola U., Chgo., 1948; PhL, Woodstock Coll., 1951, STL, 1958; MA, Cath. U., Washington, 1960, PhD, 1963, LHD, St. Peter's Coll., Jersey City, 1987, LHD, Loyola Coll. of Maryland, Balt., 1987. Ordained priest Roman Catholic Ch., 1957. Prof. ch. history Fordham U., Bronx, N.Y., 1962-71, Grad. Theol. Union, Berkeley, Calif., 1971-73; pres. Jesuit Sch. Theology, Chgo., 1973-76, prof. ch. history, 1973-77; prof. Boston Coll., Chestnut Hill, Mass., 1977-87; rector, prof. ch.history, Canisius Coll, Buffalo, 1987; adj. prof. Christ the King Sem., Aurora, N.Y., 1990—. Author: the First Council of the Vatican, 1963, 63, Catholics in the Promised Land of the Saints, 1981, American Catholics, 1981; contbr. articles to profl. jours. and encys. Mem. Am. Cath. Hist. Assn. (exec. coun. 1966-68, pres. 1986-87), U.S. Cath. Hist. Soc. (dir. 1964-67), Am. Hist. Assn. Roman Catholic. Office: Boston Coll Dept Theology Chestnut Hill MA 02167

HENNESSEY, SISTER COLLEEN, academic administrator. Supt. of schs. Diocese of Galveston-Houston. Office: Schs Supt 2401 E Holcombe Blvd Houston TX 77021*

HENNESSY, BROTHER PAUL KEVIN, religion educator; b. Far Rockaway, N.Y., May 19, 1932; s. John F. and Dorothy (O'Grady) H. BA, Iona Coll., 1953; MA, St. John's U., N.Y.C., 1956; STL, Lateran U., Rome, 1962; PhD, Cath. U. Am., 1977. Ordained to ministry Congregation of Christian Bros., 1951. Headmaster Cardinal Farley Mil. Acad., Rhinecliff, N.Y., 1965-68; prof. religious studies Iona Coll., New Rochelle, N.Y., 1968-85; provinicial superior Ea. Province Congregation of Christian Bros., New Rochelle, 1985—. Contbr. articles to theol. jours. Chmn. bd. trustees Iona Coll., 1986—. Mwm. Cath. Theol. Soc. Am., Conf. Major Superiors of Men (v.p. 1988-90, pres.-elect 1990-91, pres. 1991—). Office: Congregation Christian Bros 21 Pryer Terr New Rochelle NY 10804

HENNESSY, SISTER ROSE MARIE, academic administrator. Supt. of schs. Diocese of Oakland, Calif. Office: Schs Supt 3014 Lakeshore Ave Oakland CA 94610*

HENNESSY, THOMAS CHRISTOPHER, clergyman, educator, retired university dean; b. N.Y.C., Nov. 3, 1916; s. Thomas C. and Anna E. (Regan) H. A.B., Woodstock Coll., 1940; M.A. in Latin and Greek Classics, Fordham U., 1947, M.S. in Edn., 1957, Ph.D., 1962. Joined S.J., 1934, ordained priest Roman Cath. Ch., 1947. Tchr. Fordham Prep. Sch., N.Y.C., 1941-44, 49-52, high sch. counselor, 1952-61; counselor educator Fordham U. at Lincoln Ctr., N.Y.C., 1961-81; dean, prof. counselor edn. Sch. Edn. Marquette U., Milw., 1981-85. Editor: The Inner Crusade: The Closed Retreat in the U.S., 1965, The High School Counselor Today, 1966, The Interdisciplinary Roots of Guidance, 1966, Values and Moral Development, 1976, Value-Moral Education: The Schools and the Teachers, 1979; cons. editor: Personnel and Guidance Jour., 1978-81; contbr. numerous articles to profl. jours. Mem. Am. Psychol. Assn., Am. Assn. for Counseling and Devel. Office: Fordham U Loyola Hall Bronx NY 10458

HENNESY, JAMES LEON, minister, college administrator; b. Camden, Ark., July 10, 1934; s. E.E. Hennesy; m. Margaret Louis Young, 1956; children: James Elton, Mark Edward. Diploma, Cen. Bible Coll., 1955; MA, Assemblies of God Theol. Sem., 1983; DMin., Erskine Theol. Sem., 1989; DD (hon.), Southea. Coll. Ordained to ministry Assemblies of God, 1957. Pastor 1st Assemblies of God, Camden, Ark., 1956-59, Montgomery, Ala., 1960; pastor East Highland Assemblies of God, Columbus, Ga., 1965, Crichton Assemblies of God, Mobile, Ala., 1974, Evang. Temple, Columbus, 1976; pres. Southeastern Coll., Lakeland, Fla., 1980. Avocations: golf, fishing, reading. Office: SE Coll Assemblies of God 1000 Longfellow Blvd Lakeland FL 33801

HENNIG, V., ecumenical agency administrator. Head Calgary (Alta) Inter-Faith Community Assn., Can. Office: Calgary Inter-Faith Community, Assn/7515 7th St, Calgary, AB Canada T2V 1G1*

HENNIGAR, RICHARD A., ecumenical agency administrator. Exec. dir. Worcester County Ecumenical Coun., Mass. Office: Worcester County Ecumenical Coun 25 Crescent St Worcester MA 01605*

HENNIGER, JAMES RAY, minister; b. Ft. Worth, Tex., Oct. 28, 1946; s. Harold Ray and Carmine (Sims) H.; m. Janice James, Mar. 21, 1970; children: Jennifer, Jared. BS, Liberty U., Lynchburg, Va., 1989, MA, 1991. Ordained to ministry, Bapt. Bible Fellowship, 1972. Coll. pastor Canton (Ohio) Bapt. Temple, 1972-83; sr. pastor Scott Meml. Bapt. Ch., Solana Beach, Calif., 1983-86; co-pastor Canton Bapt. Temple, 1986-90, sr. pastor, 1990—; trustee Cedarville Coll., 1986—. With Ohio N.G. 1971-77. Home: 599 Roxbury Massillon OH 44646 Office: Canton Bapt Temple 5115 Whipple Rd NW Canton OH 44708

HENNING, WILLIAM DEMMLER, JR., minister; b. Pitts., Aug. 16, 1949; s. William Demmler and Elizabeth (Kinsloe) H.; m. Molly Wright Southard, Dec. 30, 1972; children: Sara, Keira, Daniel, Matthew, Andrew. BA, Pa. State U., 1970; MDiv, Pitts. Theol. Sem., 1976. Ordained to ministry Episcopal Ch. as deacon, 1976, as priest, 1977. Asst. St. Stephen's Ch., Sewickley, Pa., 1976-77, co-rector, 1987-90, rector, 1990—; mem. faculty Trinity Episcopal Sch. for Mins., Ambridge, Pa., 1977-87; trustee Episcs. United. Office: St Stephen's Ch 405 Frederick Ave Sewickley PA 15143-1522

HENRIX, HANS HERMANN, religion educator; b. Schwalmtal-Waldniel, Germany, Nov. 21, 1941; s. Peter Matthias and Gertrud (Weuthen) H.; m. Ursula Hermans, Aug. 28, 1970; children: Mirjam, Susanne, Tobias. Diploma in Theology, U. Munster, 1969. Mgr., Kunstseiden AG, Schwalmtal, 1963-64; asst. of Directory, Episcopal Acad., Aachen, 1969-70, lectr. religion, 1970—, dep. dir., 1986-87, dir., 1988—; cons. Germans Conf. Cath. Bishops Wurzburg, 1980—; mem. theol. study circles. Author, coeditor: Jesu Jude-Sein als Zugang zum Judentum, 1976, 80; Zeitgewin Messianisches Denken nach Franz Rosenzweig, 1987; Die Kirchen und das Judentum, 1988, 2d edit., 1989; co-author, editor: Unter dem Bogen des Bundes. Christlich-jü dische Beitrage, 1981; editor: Jü dische Liturgie. Geschichte-Struktur-Wesen, 1979; Verantwortung fü r den Anderen und die Frage nach Gott-Zum Werk von Emmanuel Levinas, 1984. Cath. pres. Deutscher Koordinierungsrat, 1984-86. Home: Klemensstrasse 16, D5100 Aachen Federal Republic of Germany Office: Episcopal Acad Diocese, Leonhardstrasse 18-20, D5100 Aachen Federal Republic of Germany

HENRY, CARL FERDINAND HOWARD, theologian; b. N.Y.C., Jan. 22, 1913; s. Karl F. and Johanna (Vaethroeder) H.; m. Helga Bender, Aug. 17, 1940; children: Paul Brentwood, Carol Jennifer. B.A., Wheaton (Ill.) Coll., 1938, M.A., 1940; B.D., No. Baptist Theol. Sem., Chgo., 1941, Th.D., 1942; Ph.D., Boston U., 1949; Litt.D. (hon.), Seattle-Pacific Coll., 1963, Wheaton Coll., 1968; L.H.D. (hon.), Houghton Coll., 1973; D.D. (hon.), Northwestern Coll., 1979, Gordon-Conwell Theol. Sem., 1984; LL.D (hon.), Hillsdale Coll., 1989. Ordained to ministry Bapt. Ch., 1941; asst. prof., then prof. theology No. Bapt. Theol. Sem., 1942-47; acting dean Fuller Theol. Sem., Pasadena, Calif., 1947, prof., 1947-56, Peyton lectr., 1963, vis. prof., 1980; vis. prof. theology Wheaton Coll., Gordon Div. Sch., Columbia Bible Coll., 1977, 80, Japan Sch. Theology, 1974, systematic theology and Biblical studies Trinity Evang. Div. Sch., 1974, 87-91, Bethel Theol. Sem., W. San Diego, 1988, Denver Conservative Bapt. Sem., 1981, 83, So. Bapt. Theol. Sem., 1988; vis. prof. Eastern Bapt. Theol. Sem., 1969-70, prof.-at-large, 1970-74; lectr.-at-large World Vision, 1974-87; Disting. vis. prof. Christian studies Hillsdale Coll., 1983-84; Disting. vis. prof. systematic theology Calvin Theol. Sem., 1986; faculty mem. flying seminar to Europe and Nr. East, Winona Lake (Ind.) Sch. Theology, 1952; daily radio commentator Let the Chips Fall, Los Angeles, 1952-53; chmn. World Congress Evangelism, Berlin, 1966, Consultation Scholars, Washington, 1967; program chmn. Jerusalem Conf. Bibl. Prophecy, Israel, 1971; Latin Am. Theol. Frat. lectr., 1973; lectr. Evangelism Internat., Singapore, 1976, 78, 86, All-India Evang. Conf. on Social Action, Madras, 1979, Liberia Bapt. Theol. Sem., Monrovia, 1982, Cameroun Bapt. Theol. Coll., Ndu, 1982, Japan Christian Inst., Tokyo, 1989; vis. lectr. Asian Center Theol. Studies and Mission, Seoul, Korea, 1974, 74, 76, 78, 80, Teoloski Facultet, Matija Vlacic Illrik, Zagreb, Yugoslavia, 1977, Asian Theol. Sem., Manila, 1980, Soong Sil Univ. Inst. Christian Culture Research, Seoul, 1987, C.S. Lewis Summer Inst., Oxford, 1988, Second Bapt. Ch., Oradea, Romania, 1988, 90, Rutherford Lectures, Edinburgh, Scotland, 1989, Chavanne Scholars' Colloquium on Bibl. Principles and Pub. Policy, Baylor U., 1989, Tyndale Sem., Amsterdam, The Netherlands, 1990; bd. dirs. Inst. Advanced Christian Studies, 1976-79, 81-85, 88—, pres., 1971-74; bd. dirs. Ethics and Public Policy Center, 1979—, Inst. Religion and Democracy, 1981—, v.p., 1985—, Prison Fellowship, 1981—, lectr.-at-large, 1990—; M.E. Found., 1989—; trustee Gordon Conwell Theol. Sem., 1965-68, Elmer Bisbee Found., 1986—; bd. dirs. Ministers Life and Casualty Union, 1968-77; co-chmn. Rose Bowl Easter Sunrise Service, 1950-56; main street com. Rockford Inst., 1990—. Author: A Doorway to Heaven, 1941, Successful Church Publicity, 1942, Remaking the Modern Mind, 1948, The Uneasy Conscience of Modern Fundamentalism, 1948, Giving a Reason for Our Hope, 1949, The Protestant Dilemma, 1949, Notes on the Doctrine of God, 1949, Fifty Years of Protestant Theology, 1950, The Drift of Western Thought, 1951, Personal Idealism and Strong's Theology, 1951, Glimpses of a Sacred Land, 1953, Christian Personal Ethics, 1957, Evangelical Responsibility in Contemporary Theology, 1957, Aspects of Christian Social Ethics, 1964, Frontiers in Modern Theology, 1966, The God Who Shows Himself, 1966, Evangelicals at the Brink of Crisis, 1967, Faith at the Frontiers, 1969, A Plea for Evangelical Demonstration, 1971, New Strides of Faith, 1972, Evangelicals in Search of Identity, 1976, God, Revelation and Authority, vols. 1 and 2, 1976, vols. 3 and 4, 1979, vol. 5, 1982, vol. 6,, 1983, The Christian Mindset in a Secular Society, 1984, Christian Countermoves in a Decadent Culture, 1986, Confessions of a Theologian, 1986, Conversations with Carl Henry: Christianity for Today, 1986; Twilight of a Great Civilization, 1988, A Lifetime of Quotable Thoughts: Cary at His Best, 1990, Toward a Recovery of Christian Belief, 1990; editor: Contemporary Evangelical Thought, 1957, Revelation and the Bible, 1959, The Biblical Expositor, 1960, Basic Christian Doctrines, 1962, Christian Faith and Modern Theology, 1964, Jesus of Nazareth: Saviour and Lord, 1966, Fundamentals of the Faith, 1969, Horizons of Science, 1978; editor in chief: Baker's Dictionary of Christian Ethics, 1973; co-editor: (with Kenneth Kanzer) Evangelical Affirmations, 1990; cons. editor: Baker's Dictionary of Theology, 1964; editor: Christianity Today, 1956-68, editor-at-large, 1968-77; contbg. editor: World Vision Mag., 1976-87. Mem. Capitol Hill Met. Bapt. Ch., Washington, 1956—. Recipient Freedoms Found. award, 1954, 66, Sem. Alumnus of Yr., No. Bapt. Theol. Sem., 1971, Religious Heritage Am. award, 1975, Disting. Social Svc. award Wheaton Coll. Alumni Assn., 1961, J. Elwin Wright award Nat. Assn. of Evangelicals, 1990; honored with Carl F.H. Henry manuscript collection Syracuse U., 1975—, The Carl F.H. Henry Study and Resource Ctr., Trinity Evang. Divinity Sch., Deerfield, Ill., 1987; fellow Christianity Today Inst., 1987—. Mem. Soc. Sci. Study Religion, AAAS, Am. Soc. Christian Ethics, Am. Acad. Religion, Am. Theol. Soc. (v.p. 1974-75, pres. 1979-80), Evang. Theol. Soc. (pres. 1969-70), Conf. Faith and History, Nat. Assn. Evangelicals (bd. administrn. 1956-70), Am. Philos. Assn., Am. Soc. Ch. History, Soc. Oriental Research, Soc. Christian Philosophers, Nat. Assn. Bapt. Profs. of Religion, Evang. Press Assn. (hon. life), Soc. Bibl. Lit. Address: 3824 N 37th St Arlington VA 22207 *To know God as the ultimate Who's Who nurtures gratitude for all the days of one's years, including creation life, regenerate life, and resurrection life to come.*

HENRY, DAVID ARNOLD, minister; b. Concord, Calif., Jan. 14, 1949; s. Robert B. and Margaret A. (Blomquist) H.; m. Donna Lee Veeh, July 26, 1969; children: Trenton D., Duane D., Traci L. AA, Coll. of Sequoias, 1969; BA in Psychology, Calif. State U., Chico, 1971; MDiv, San Francisco Theol. Sem., 1978, postgrad., 1987—. Ordained to ministry Presbyn. Ch. (U.S.A.), 1978. Pastor Westminster Presbyn. Ch., Versailles, Mo., 1978-84, 1st Presbyn. Ch., Burley, Idaho, 1984—; del. Mo. Coun. of Chs., 1979-82; pres. Morgan County Ministerial Assn., Versailles, 1980-81, Lake of Ozarks Counseling Ctr., Osage Beach, Mo., 1980, Mini-Cassia Ministerial Assn., Burley, 1985-86. Contbr. articles to profl. jours.; broadcaster news program Religion in the News, 1984—. Dist. and local officer Boy Scouts Am., Mo. and Idaho, 1978-91; mem. Cassia County Child Protection Team, Burley, 1985-86; v.p. Westminster Heritage Bd., Jefferson City, Mo., 1982-84; convenor Resolving Racial Tensions, Versailles, 1984. Mem. Lions (sec. 1989-90). Office: 1st Presbyn Ch 2100 Burton Ave Burley ID 83318

HENRY, DAVID PAUL, minister; b. Atlanta, Aug. 25, 1948; s. Roland and Margaret Louise (Anderson) H. BA, Wheaton (Ill.) Coll., 1970; BD, U. London, 1975; PhD, Union Theol. Sem. in Va., Richmond, 1982. Ordained to ministry Am. Bapt. Ch., 1984. Asst. dir. Coffee House Ministers, Glen Ellyn, Ill., 1970-72; interim youth dir. Tabernacle Bapt. Ch., Richmond, 1983-84; pastor Lamoine Bapt. Ch., Ellsworth, 1984—; bd. dirs., pres. Hancock County Habitat for Humanity, Ellsworth, 1988-91. Author: The Early Development of the Hermeneutic of Karl Barth, 1985. Mem. Nat. Assn. of Bapt. Profs. of Religion. Office: Lamoine Bapt Ch RFD 2 Ellsworth ME 04605

HENRY, JAMES WILLIAM, minister; b. Worcester, Mass., Sept. 29, 1945; s. Edward J. and E. Marie (Duerr) H.; m. Paula Gouvea, June 10, 1967; children: Leslie A., J. Matthew, Jonathan D., Susanna E. BSME, Norwich U., 1967; MDiv, Asbury Sem., Wilmore, Ky., 1978. Ordained to ministry Covenant Ministries Internat., 1982. Pastor United Meth. Chs., Ky., N.J., 1975-79; area dir. The Christian Broadcasting Network, N.Y. Metro Area, 1979-86; founding pastor Agape Ch., Saddle Brook, N.J., 186-89; adminstrv. pastor Faith with Love Fellowship, Paterson, N.J., 1989—; pres., dir. Righteous Seed Ministries, Paterson, 1989—; bd. dirs., sr. v.p. Christian Aid Mission, Charlottesville, Va.; chmn. adv. bd. Christian Broadcasting Network, Bklyn., 1986—; sec., mem. exec. com. Billy Graham N. Jersey Crusade, 1987-91; mem. leadership team N. Jersey Concerts of Prayer, 1988—. Capt. U.S. Army, 1968-71. Recipient Key of City of West Orange, N.J. Office of the Mayor, 1985. Mem. Covenant Ministries Internat. Missions Commn., The Kings Fellowship, Concerned Clergy Am., Tau Beta Pi (life). Office: Righteous Seed Ministries PO Box 510 Paterson NJ 07544-0510 *Life is about people! To the degree we are able to impart to our children and those around us the values which we so highly esteem, we shall redeem the time, multiply our effectiveness, and make this world a far better and more enjoyable place to live.*

HENRY, JIMMY RUSSELL, minister; b. Malta, Mont., Nov. 7, 1943; s. John and Georgia (Gamron) H.; m. Michelle R. Cunningham, Apr. 6, 1974; children: Heidi, Joshua, Phillip, Shawn. BS, No. Mont. Coll., 1972, MS, 1975; postgrad., Trinity Evang. Coll., Ill., 1991, Ozark Christian Coll., Joplin, Mo., 1977-80. Ordained to ministry, Christian Ch./Chs. of Christ, 1974. Minister Malta (Mont.) Christian Ch., 1975-77; supt. Big Sky Christian Youth Ranch, Whitewater, Mont., 1975-77, 80-81; producer, host Internat. Forum, Kalispell, Mont., 1981-85; minister Bridgeport (Nebr.) Ch. of Christ, 1985-90, Cozad (Nebr.) Ch. of Christ, 1991—; supt. Big Sky Christian Youth Ranch, Whitewater, 1975-77, 80-81. Contbr. articles to profl. jours. Cons. Adult Basic Edn., Bridgeport, 1986-90; chaplain Morrill County, Bridgeport, 1986-90; workshop leader Compassionate Friends, Scottsbluff, 1989-90. With U.S. Army, 1964-66. Recipient Cert. of Merit, Gov. Nebr., 1990, Care award, Heritage Homes, 1990. Fellow Dawson County Ministerial Assn. Home: 1113 Ave J Cozad NE 69130 Office: Cozad Ch of Christ 22nd & Newell Cozad NE 69130

HENRY, MARION WETMORE, lay church worker; b. Durham, N.C., Aug. 9, 1925; d. Marion Dare and Durema Olivia (Watson) Wetmore; m. James Herbert Henry, May 4, 1949; children: James Watson, Nan Paterson, John Badger. BA, Duke U., 1945. Pres. bd. govs. Episcopal Ch. Home, Washington, 1976-78; dep. to Gen. Conv. Episcopal Ch., Washington, 1979, 82, 85, 88, 91; pres. standing com. Episcopal Diocese of Washington, 1982-83; bd. govs. Collington Episcopal Life Care, Inc., Mitchellville, Md., 1984—. Home: Heron Cove Box 437 Rte 2 Hollywood MD 20636

HENRY, PATRICK G., religious research administrator; b. Dallas, Apr. 22, 1939; s. Patrick and Jean Shelley (Jennings) H.; m. Nannerl Overholser, Sept. 4, 1962 (div. 1969); 1 child, Stephan Marshall; m. Patricia Anne Gillespie, June 6, 1972 (div. 1988); children: Miranda Gail, Juliet May, Brendan Wilfred; m. Patricia A. Welter, July 6, 1991. B.A., Harvard U., 1960, Oxford U., Eng., 1963; M.A., Oxford U., Eng., 1967; Ph.D., Yale U., 1967. From asst. prof. to prof. religion Swarthmore Coll., Pa., 1967-84; exec. dir. Inst. Ecumenical and Cultural Rsch., Collegeville, Minn., 1984—. Author: New Directions in New Testament Study, 1979; (with others) God on Our Minds, 1982, For the Sake of the World: The Spirit of Buddhist and Christian Monasticism, 1989; editor: Schools of Thought in the Christian Tradition, 1984; contbr. numerous articles to profl. jours. Mem. adv. coun. Marshall Scholars, 1980-86. Marshall scholar, 1960-63; Kent fellow Danforth Found., 1963-67, NEH fellow 1979-80. Mem. Am. Acad. Religion, N.Am. Acad. Ecumenists, Am. Benedictine Acad., Am. Diabetes Assn. (pres. Cen. Minn.

chpt. 1989—, bd. dirs. Minn. affiliate 1990—). Lutheran. Office: Inst for Ecumenical and Cultural Rsch Collegeville MN 56321

HENRY, PAUL EUGENE, JR., minister; b. Summit, N.J., Jan. 10, 1941; s. Paul Eugene and Arline Anita (Ferns) H; m. Carolyn Sandra Haas, July 16, 1966; children: Susan Beth, Thomas Paul, Carol Lee. BA, Gettysburg (Pa.) Coll., 1963; MDiv, Luth. Theol. Sem., Gettysburg, 1966. Ordained to ministry Luth. Ch. Am., 1966. Asst. pastor 1st Luth. Ch., Albany, N.Y., 1966-67; pastor St. John's Luth. Ch., Canajoharie, N.Y., 1967-70, Mamaroneck, N.Y., 1970-77; pastor Faith Luth. Ch., East Hartford, Conn., 1977—; chmn. Lay Workers Conf. Met. N.Y. Synod, 1974; sec. Capitol Dist., Upper N.Y. State, 1966-67; mem. worship com. Met. N.Y. State, 1975-76; mem. exec. bd. New Eng. Synod, 1979-85; mem. Common. on Budget and Fin., 1979-85, chmn., 1980-82; coord. Area V, No. Conn., 1979-85; chmn. New Eng. Synod Conv., 1991. Chaplain Mamaroneck Vol. Fire Dept, 1970-77, East Hartford Police Dept., 1982—. Mem. East Hartford Clergy Assn. (pres. 1986—), Greater Hartford Luth. Chs. (dean 1985—). Home: 22 Dartmouth Dr East Hartford CT 06108 Office: 1120 Silver Ln East Hartford CT 06118

HENRY, ROBERT JOHN, lay worker; b. Tarentum, Pa., Jan. 1, 1950; s. John Leroy and Dorothy Hazel (McLaughlin) H.; m. Patricia Ann DelVerme; children: Tricia Ann, Rebecca Kathleen. Cert., Pa. State U., 1969. Ch. sch. supt., elder East Union Presbyn. Ch., Cheswick, Pa., 1971—, youth dir., 1976—; insp. Pa. Dept. Agriculture, Gibsonia area, 1969-81, regional supr., 1981—; chmn. Integrated Pest Mgmt. Task Force, 1991. Recipient legis. citation Pa. Ho. of Reps., Harrisburg, 1989. Mem. Horticultural Inspection Soc., Bio-Integral Rsch. Ctr. Home: RD7 Box 231 Gibsonia PA 15044 Office: E Union Presbyn Ch RD1 E Union Rd Cheswick PA 15024 *There is reason to be hopeful in todays youth. In my youth work, both through the church and school activities, I see a good foundation of concerned young people that will provide great leadership for our future. I look forward to brighter tomorrows led by these young people who even today are in the forfront of concern over such issues as the environment, AIDS, and the need of a strong Christ-centered faith.*

HENRY, RODNEY, religious organization administrator. Pres. Seventh Day Bapt. Gen. Conf. U.S.A. and Can., Plainfield, N.J. Office: Sevent Day Bapt 3120 Kennedy Rd PO Box 1678 Janesville WI 53547*

HENRY-JOHN, EMMANUEL SYLVESTER, preacher, counselor; b. Ootacamund, Madras, India, Dec. 15, 1949; came to U.S., 1980; s. Isaac and Sama Thanam (Asirvatham) Henry-J.; m. Laura Elia Garza, Feb. 4, 1984; children: Sarai Samathanam, Isaac Max, Shalani Esther, Arnold Samuel. AS, Schs. for Officers Tng.; BA in Econs., U. Madras, 1970; A.C.P., Assoc. Coll. of Preceptors, 1975; postgrad., U. La Verne, 1988-89; MA, Fuller Theology Sem., 1990. Sales rep. Baba's Ice Cream Factory, Bangalore, India, 1972; tchr. Woizero Comprehensive Higher Dessie Secondary Sch., Ethiopia, 1973-77, Mopa Secondary Sch., Illorin, Kwara, Nigeria, 1977-80; fin. planner John Hancock, Cerritos, Calif., 1982; respiratory therapy technician Burbank (Calif.) Community Hosp., 1983-84; counselor The Salvation Army Rehab. Ctr., Canoga Park, Calif., 1985-86; pastor The Savlation Army, Bakersfield, Calif., 1988-89; comdg. officer The Savlation Army, Gilroy, Calif., 1989—; spiritual counselor Adult Rehab. Ctr., The Salvation Army, Canoga Park, 1980, youth minister ch. for homeless, Bakersfield, 1983, mem. adv. bd., 1988. Vol. food for homeless The Salvation Army, Bakersfield, 1988, spiritual and social work to the needy. Named Best Tchr., Wollo Province, 1974. Mem. Coun. Chs. Greater Bakersfield, Jay Strack Evangelistic Com., Soc. Internat. Missionaries, Christian Ministries Mgmt. Assn., Lions, Masons, Kiwanis. Republican. Avocations: model trains, tennis, videos, photography, play houses. Home: 781 Lawrence Dr Gilroy CA 95020

HENSELL, EUGENE MERRILL, priest; b. Logansport, Ind., Feb. 10, 1942; s. Richard and Betty (Whiteside) H. BA, St. Meinrad (Ind.) Coll., 1965, MDiv, 1969; MA, St. Louis U., 1971, PhD, 1975. Assoc. pastor Ch. of Magdalen, St. Louis, 1969-78; Benedictine monk St. Meinrad Archabbey, 1978—; pres. St. Meinrad Seminary, 1987—. Mem. Cath. Bibl. Assn., Soc. for Bibl. Lit., Am. Acad. Religion, Am. Assn. Higher Edn., Am. Benedictine Acad. Home: St Meinrad Archabbey Saint Meinrad IN 47577 Office: St Meinrad Sem Saint Meinrad IN 47577

HENSGEN, SISTER M. CAROLEEN, academic administrator. Supr. schs. Diocese of Dallas. Office: Religious Edn PO Box 190507 Dallas TX 75219*

HENSLEY, GORDON RANDOLPH, youth minister; b. San Luis Obispo, Calif., Sept. 21, 1952; s. Jimmie Clayton and Audrey Raymond (Laux) H.; m. Linda Carole Townsend, June 23, 1973. BS, Calif. Poly. State U., 1976, MS, 1983. Assoc. pastor First Ch. of the Nazarene, Glendale, Calif., 1988-90; min. to youth Ridgecrest (Calif.) Ch. of the Nazarene, 1990—; naturalist San Luis Obispo County Office of Edn., 1976-79; chmn. fin. com. El Morro Ch. of the Nazarene, Los Osos, Calif., 1977-86; sr. wildlife biologist Bowker and Hensley, Los Osos, 1978-89; substitute tchr. San Luis Coastal Unified Sch. Dist., San Luis Obispo, 1986-88; coord. teen waiters L.A. Dist. Laymen's Retreat, 1986-90; asst. dir. L.A. Dist. Jr. High Camp, 1988-90; dir. L.A. Dist. High Sch. Camp, 1990—. Mem. L.A. Dist. NYI Coun. (chmn. dist. activities com., chmn. dist. edn. and equipping com., dist. conv. com., v.p. 1991—). Democrat. Home: 400 DeWalt Ridgecrest CA 93555 Office: Ch of the Nazarene 571 N Norma Ridgecrest CA 93555

HENSLEY, JOHN CLARK, religious organization administrator, minister; b. Sullivan County, June 16, 1912; s. Truman and Ivan (Moddrell) H.; m. Margaret Sipes, Nov. 24, 1946; children: Gary, Clark, Dana. Ordained to ministry So. Bapt. Conv., 1930. Pastor Moberly and Kansas City, Mo., 1935-46, Nashville and Pulaski, Tenn., 1947-58; supt. missions Hinds County Bapt. Assn., Jackson, Miss., 1958-66; exec. dir. Christian Action Commn. Miss. Bapt. Conv., Jackson, 1966-82, exec. dir. emeritus, 1982—, cons. family life, 1982-90, rec. sec., 1982-90; assoc. prof. Cen. Bapt. Theol. Sem., 1943-46. Author: The Pastor as Educational Director, rev. edit., 1950, My Father is Rich, 1956, In the Heart of the Young, 1952, Behaving at Home, 1972, Help for the Single Parents and Those Who Love Them, 1973, Coping With Being Single Again, 1978, Preacher Behave! Pointers on Ministerial Ethics, 1978, Good News for Todays Single, 1985, The Autumn Years, 1987, The Pastor in Family Ministry, 1990. Pres. bd. CONTACT, 1973—; trustee Radio and TV Commn. So. Bapt. Conv., 1980-88; mem. Gov. Miss. Com. Alcohol Abuse and Alcoholism, 1972—; mem. bd. Am. Coun. Alcohol Problems, 1972—; trustee Hannibal, Mo. LaGrange Coll., 1939-45. Recipient Disting. Svc. award for leadership in Christian ethics Christian Life Commn., 1975, Disting. Svc. award Family Ministry Bapt. Sunday Sch. Bd., 1988. Mem. Nat. Coun. Family Problems, Southeastern Coun. Family Problems, Miss. Couns. Family Problems, Am. Judicature Soc., Am. Acad. Polit. Assn., Am. Assn. Sex Educators and Counselors. Home: 6083 Waverly Dr Jackson MS 39206 Office: PO Box 530 Jackson MS 39205 *God must have intended that we have enough of Heaven in our homes here to get us a little bit prepared for what Heaven is like. The spiritual temperature of our churches is controlled by thermostats in the homes of the members.*

HENSLEY, R. KEITH, minister; b. Penn Laird, Va., Jan. 10, 1956; s. Raymond Ray and Peggy Jean (Michael) H.; m. Teresa Eunice Snarr, Aug. 23, 1980. Student, Ea. Mennonite Coll., 1974-76; BA in History, Philosophy and Religion, James Madison U., 1979; MDiv in Pastoral Mgmt., Ashland (Ohio) Theol. Sem., 1982; postgrad., Pitts. Theol. Sem., 1986—. Ordained to ministry Ch. of the Brethren. Youth pastor Park St. Brethren Ch., Ashland, 1980-82; church planter Hickory Brethren Ch., Conover, N.C., 1982-84; pastor Pleasant View Brethren Ch., Vandergrift, Pa., 1984—; pres. Pa. dist. Mission Bd., 1987-89, 90—; past moderator Pa. Dist. Conf., 1987-88. Capt., engr. Parks Twp. Vol. Fire dept., Vandergrift, 1990. Mem. Vandergrift Ministerial Assn. (treas. 1988—), Brethren Ch. Ministerial Assn. Republican. Home: RR1 Box 429 Vandergrift PA 15690-9626

HENSON, JOHN DOUGLAS, minister; b. Nashville, Dec. 5, 1950; s. Sheridan Miller and Lorene Edna (Burnett) H.; m. Judy May Lance, May 5, 1974; children: Christina, Catherine, Scott. Student, David Lipscomb Coll., 1969, U. Tenn., 1975, Tenn. Bible Coll., 1989—. Min. Ch. of Christ, 1970—, Manchester, Tenn., 1987-89, Spencer, Tenn., 1988—; tchr., vacation Bible sch., Ch. of Christ, Manchester, 1988—; gospel meeting evangelist, 1988-90. Contbr. articles to profl. jours. Bd. dirs. Van Buren Sr. Citizens, Spencer, 1990—; vol. ARC, Spencer, 1990—, Am. Cancer Soc., Spencer, 1990—, vol. counselor Battered Women Inc., Spencer, 1990—. Home and Office: PO Box 291 Spencer TN 38585 *Of all the awards and rewards given in life, the Bible always takes note of rewarding righteousness, mercy, purity, humility and love. Such is characteristic of the Savior.*

HENSON, MICHAEL BRENT, youth minister; b. Lockney, Tex., Oct. 8, 1959; s. Virgil Lee and Margaret Ann (Walton) H.; m. Rebecca Mae Morren, Apr. 15, 1989. BBA, U. Okla., 1983; MA, Southwestern Sem., 1988. Urban staff leader Young Life, Ft. Worth, Tex., 1987-89; youth min. First Bapt. Ch., Burleson, Tex., 1989—. Republican. Home: 429 NW Wintercrest Burleson TX 76028 Office: First Bapt Ch 317 W Ellison Burleson TX 76028

HENSON, ROBERT THOMAS, retired clergyman, evangelist; b. Buffalo, W.Va., Apr. 18, 1929; s. Charles Thomas and Hazel Mirrell (Mitchell) H.; m. Nancy Lucille Stephens, Aug. 9, 1952; children: Stephen Robert, Marilyn Elizabeth. Student, Marshall Coll., 1948-49, Anderson Coll., 1949-53, Jordan Conservatory, 1954, Dana Sch. Music, 1955, Cin. Conservatory of Music, 1958-62. Unordained minister Ch. of God (Anderson, Ind.), 1954; ordained evangelist Messiah Bible Fellowship, 1974. Min. music, assoc. pastor chs., Ind., Ohio, Tex., 1952-73; founder, pres. Bob Henson Evangelistic Assn., Inc., Alexandria, Ind., 1973—; singer, preacher, evangelist all denomination chs., 1967—; singer concerts, TV,radio, sacred concerts and dramas, opera and chorales; pres. Bob Henson Travel, Alexandria, 1970—. Composer gospel music and spirituals; solo rec. artist. Address: Rte 1 Box 353 Alexandria IN 46001 *My hope is for a very important change in each person...worldwide. From personal experience, I know one can change suddenly and thoroughly by asking God to change you. I pray to Jesus Christ for this change in our world.*

HENSTOCK, THOMAS RAYMOND, minister; b. Ann Arbor, Mich., Apr. 16, 1936; s. Raymond Argyle and Zelma (Fox) H.; m. Louise Jean Henstock, Aug. 19, 1961; 1 child, Deborah Louise. BS, Mich. State U., 1958; MDiv, Pitts. Theol. Sem., 1962. Ordained to ministry Presbyn. Ch. Pastor 1st Presbytn. Ch., Centreville, Mich., 1962-66; asst. pastor Eastminister Presbyn., Grand Rapids, 1966-68, Lake Nokomis Presbyn., Mpls., 1968-71, Pk. Ave. Presbyn., Des Moines, 1971-72; assoc. pastor First Presbyn., Topeka, 1974-81; pastor First Presbyn., Sylvan Grove, Kans., 1984—; moderator Synod Div. Higher Edn., Kans., Mo., 1974-80, No. Kans. Presbytery Com. Nominations, 1984-90; intentional interim min. Synod Mid-Am. Chief exec. officer Post Rock Opportunities Found., Kans., 1991; chmn. Lincoln County Coun. on Aging, Kans., 1991; active Lincoln County Planning and Econ. Devel. Commn., 1989—, Lincoln County Com. on Tourism, 1991; pres. North Cen. Kans. Tourism Coun., 1989. Recipient Citizenship award Gov. of Kans., 1990; Presbyn. Ch. Self-Devel. People grantee, 1990. Fellow Acad. Parish Clergy; mem. Lincoln County Ministerial Assn. (pres. 1990-91), Optimist Club (com. chmn.), Kiwanis (com. chmn.), Lions Club (com. chmn.). Republican. Home: Rte 1 Box 2B 301 E 3d Sylvan Grove KS 67481-9801 Office: First Presbyterian Ch 319 E Third St Sylvan Grove KS 67481-9801

HENTE, SANDRA LORRAINE, lay worker; b. Santa Monica, Calif., Apr. 27, 1946; d. Kenneth B. and Carmen (Allen) Hasch; m. Martin Joe Hente, Dec. 26, 1971; children: Kristin, Jonathan, Derrick. AA, Santa Monica Coll., 1966; BS, Calif. State U., Fresno, 1969. RN, Calif.; cert. sch. nurse practitioner, audiometrist. Local pres. Luth. Women's Missionary League, L.A., 1978-82, v.p. mission svc. So. Calif. dist., 1982-86, dir. pub. rels., 1986-88, pres. Pacific S.W. dist., 1988—; officer Aid Assn. for Luths., Culver City, Calif., 1977—. Mem. Luth. Ch.-Mo. Synod. Home: 4111 Van Buren Pl Culver City CA 90232 *If the Lord asks you to do a job He will equip you for the task.*

HENTON, WILLIS RYAN, bishop; b. McCook, Nebr., July 5, 1925; s. Burr Milton and Clara Vaire (Godown) H.; m. Martha Somerville Bishop, June 7, 1952; 1 son, David Vasser. B.A., Kearney (Nebr.) State Coll., 1949; S.T.B., Gen. Theol. Sem., N.Y.C., 1952, D.S.T., 1972; D.D., U. of South, Sewanee, Tenn., 1972. Ordained priest Episcopal Ch., 1953; missionary St. Benedicts Mission, Besao, Mountain Province, Philippines, 1952-57; mem. staff St. Lukes Chapel, N.Y.C., 1957-58; rector Christ Ch., Mansfield, La., 1958-61, St. Augustine's Ch., Baton Rouge, 1961-64; archdeacon Diocese of La., 1964-71; bishop coadjutor Diocese N.W. Tex., 1971-72; bishop N.W. Tex., Lubbock, 1972-80, Western La., 1980-90; ret., 1990. Pres. Tex. Conf. Chs., 1978-80; pres. La. Inter-Ch. Conf., 1985-86. Served with inf. AUS, 1944-46. Decorated Bronze Star. Office: PO Box 10108 New Iberia LA 70562

HEPPNER, RICHARD ALAN, minister; b. Peoria, Ill., July 23, 1962; s. William John and Betty Jane (Polite) H.; m. Tia Renee Bolton, Dec. 17, 1988. Grad. in church family life, Lincoln Christian Coll., 1988. Ordained to ministry Christian Chs. and Chs. of Christ, 1990. Youth min. Chrisman (Ill.) Christian Ch., 1984-85; assoc. min. Auburn (Ill.) Christian Ch., 1986-87; youth min. 1st Christian Ch., Kewanee, Ill., 1989—. Office: 1st Christian Ch Dwight and Division St Kewanee IL 61443

HERBENER, MARK BASIL, bishop; b. Chgo., Jan. 2, 1932; s. Otto Berthold and Elsbeth Marie (Mueller) H.; m. Donna Fay Gergens, Apr. 25, 1958; children: Matthew, Jenny. Student, Concordia Coll., Milw., 1949-51; BA, Concordia Sem., St. Louis, 1953, theol. diploma, 1956. Ordained to ministry Luth. Ch.-Mo. Synod, 1956, Evang. Luth. Ch. in Am., 1978. Intern St. John Luth. Ch., Durand, Wis., 1954-55; pastor Messiah Luth. Ch., Richardson, Tex., 1956-61, Mt. Olive Luth. Ch., Dallas, 1961-87; bishop No. Tex.—No. La. synod Evang. Luth. Ch. in Am., Dallas, 1987—; co-chair Dallas Interfaith Task Force, 1981-86; v.p. Greater Dallas Community of Chs., 1983-85; dir. Dallas region NCCJ, 1983-86. Pres. Dallas Opportunities Industrialization Ctr., 1983-85; co-convenor Martin Luther King Jr. Inst., Dallas, 1986-87; v.p. Greater Dallas Community Rels. Commn., 1987; convenor Jewish-Christian-Muslim Dialogue, Dallas, 1990—. Recipient Disting. Ch. Svc. award Tex. Luth. Coll., 1987, A. Maceo Smith award Dallas African-Am. Mus., 1987; named Peacemaker of Yr., Dallas Peace Ctr., 1987. Mem. Dallas Com. on Fgn. Rels., Dallas Pastors Assn. (chmn. 1978-80). Democrat. Office: Evang Luth Ch in Am No Tex—No La Synod PO Box 560587 Dallas TX 75356-0587 also: 1530 River Bend Ste 105 Dallas TX 75247

HERBERT, JOHN FRANK, IV, school principal; b. Watertown, Wis., Sept. 6, 1955; s. John Frank III and Donna Belle (Slater) H.; m. Paula Jean Isaacs, Aug. 12, 1978; children: Teresa Anne, Jodi Lynn, John Frank V. BS, Maranatha Bapt. Bible Coll., 1977, MS in Ednl. Adminstrn., 1990. Tchr. Faith Bapt. Schs., Longmont, Colo., 1978-82; prin. Abilene (Kans.) Bapt. Acad., 1982—; competion coord. Kans. Assn. Christian Schs., 1983—; bd. dirs. Mid-Am. Assn. Christian Schs., Kansas City, Mo., 1987-90. Republican. Home: 1606 Wildcat Dr Abilene KS 67410 Office: Abilene Bapt Acad 410 N Van Buren Abilene KS 67410

HERDER, ROBERT H., bishop. Bishop Evang. Luth. Ch. in Am., Appleton, Wis. Office: Evang Luth Ch Am 3003 N Richmond St Appleton WI 54911*

HERGETT, H(AROLD) DOUGLAS, rector; b. Windsor, N.S., Can., Feb. 22, 1938; s. Harold Douglas and Dorothy Ruby (Sawler) H.; m. Faye Estella Thompson, Dec. 28, 1963; children: Susan, Timothy, Sarah. B of Commerce, Dalhousie U., Halifax, N.S., 1961; BST, U. King's Coll., Halifax, 1964; ThM, Atlantic Sch. Theology, Halifax, 1974. Ordained priest Anglican Ch. Can., 1964. Rector Parish of Maitland-Kennetcook, N.S., 1964-67; priest asst. Christ Ch. Parish, Dartmouth, N.S., 1967-72; rector Parish of Horton, Wolfville, N.S., 1972—; chaplain to Anglican students Acadia U., Wolfville, 1972—; archdeacon Anglican Diocese N.S., 1983—; mem., dean and chpt. Cath. Ch. of All Sts., Halifax, 1983—; formation dir. Atlantic Sch. Theology, Halifax, 1984-87. Author: Visible Faith, 1991; also articles. Sec. local group com. Boy Scouts Can., Wolfville, 1974—; bd. dirs. Interchurch Housing Soc., Kentville, N.S., 1988—; mem. provincial bd. The Lung Assn., Halifax, 1990—. Mem. Wolfville Area Inter-Ch. Coun. (exec. mem. 1972—). Home and Office: PO Box 786, Wolfville, NS Canada B0P 1X0

HERING, EBERHARD ARNULF, minister; b. Marburg on the Lahn, Hessen, Germany, Nov. 1, 1936; s. Karl F. and Eleanor W. (Friedrich) H.; m. Deloris Marie Bartling, May 30, 1936; children: Angela Marie, Tyler Bartling. BA, Midland Luth. Coll., Fremont, Nebr., 1958; MDiv, Cen. Sem., Fremont, Nebr., 1963; D Ministry, Luth. Sch. Theology, Chgo., 1977. Ordained to ministry Evang. Luth. Ch., 1963. Pastor Immanuel & Swede Valley Luth. Chs., Ogden, Iowa, 1963-69, St. Paul Luth. Ch., Mason City, Iowa, 1969-73; intern Heilig Gheist Kirche, Mexico City, Mexico, 1961-62; pastor St. John Luth. Ch., Council Bluffs, Iowa, 1973—; pres. Interfaith Response, Inc., Council Bluffs, 1988—; mem. exec. com. Western Iowa synod, Storm Lake, 1987—. Bd. dirs., v.p. Bethphage Mission Inc., Omaha, 1984-90; dir. Housing Commn., Council Bluffs, 1986—, YMCA, Council Bluffs, 1987—. Mem. Ministerial Assn. (exec. bd. 1981—). Republican. Office: St John Luth Ch 633 Willow Ave Council Bluffs IA 51501

HERION, GARY ALAN, religion educator; b. Chapel Hill, N.C., Aug. 20, 1954; s. John Carroll and Mary (MacLeod) H.; m. Carol Creath, Aug. 18, 1979; children: Melissa MacLeod, Samuel Walker, Daniel Myers. BA, U. N.C., 1976; MA, U. Mich., 1977, PhD, 1982. Asst. prof. Hartwick Coll., Oneonta, N.Y., 1991—. Assoc. editor: Anchor Bible Dictionary, 1987. James A. Gray postdoctoral fellow, 1984-86, Radcliffe-Ramsdell fellow, 1978-79. Mem. Am. Acad. Religion, Soc. Biblical Lit., Am. Schs. Oriental Rsch. Home: 31 Central Ave Oneonta NY 13820 Office: Hartwick Coll Religion Dept Oneonta NY 13820

HERLOCKER, JOHN ROBERT, priest; b. Greenville, Tex., Feb. 11, 1935; s. James Harry and Doyle Douglas (Williams) H.; m. Peggy Ann Felmet, Feb. 28, 1959; children: John Robert, James Madison, Dorsey Elizabeth, Katherine Suzannah, Douglas Reed-Bryant. BBA, U. Tex., 1956; MDiv, U. of South, 1967. Vicar St. Mary's Episcopal Ch., Winnemucca, Nev., 1969-72; rector Holy Trinity Episcopal Ch., Ukiah, Calif., 1972-74; fiscal officer Episc. Diocese of Eastern Oreg., Redmond, 1974-79; diocesan adminstr. Episc. Diocese of Idaho, Boise, 1979-82, archdeacon, 1982-90, canon to ordinary for adminstrn., 1990—. Mem., bd. dir., treas. Hogar Infantic, Inc. With USN, 1956-58. Mem. Kiwanis Club. Avocations: photography, computers. Home: 3262 Scenic Dr Boise ID 83703

HERMAN, bishop. Bishop of Phila. The Orthodox Ch. in Am., South Canaan, Pa. Office: St Tikhon's Orthodox Theol Sem Canaan PA 18459*

HERMAN, ARTHUR LUDWIG, philosophy educator; b. Mpls., Nov. 16, 1930; married; 2 children. BA in Philosophy, U. Minn., 1952, MA in Philosophy, 1958, PhD, 1970; postgrad., Stanford U., 1960-61, Harvard U., 1961-63. Instr. depts. humanities, philosophy U. Fla., Gainesville, 1957-60; instr. philosophy Hamilton Coll., Clinton, N.Y., 1963-65; asst. prof. Wis. State U., Stevens Point, 1965-71; assoc. prof. U. Wis., Stevens Point, 1971-72, prof., 1973—; vis. prof. humanities U. Minn., Mpls., 1975-76; St. Thomas Aquinas lectr. Mt. Mary Coll., Milw., 1975; lectr. Clarke Coll., Dubuque, Iowa, 1976, Western Ill. U., Macomb, 1979, U. Hawaii, Honolulu, 1984; referee for transl. grants NEH, Washington, 1987; mem. faculty, lectr. NEH Summer Inst. on Nagarjuna and Buddhist Thought, Honolulu, 1989. Author: The Bhagavad Gita, A Translation and Critical Commentary, 1973, The Problem of Evil and Indian Thought, 1976, An Introduction to Indian Thought, 1976, An Introduction to Buddhist Thought, A Philosophic History of Indian Buddhism, 1984, The Ways of Philosophy, Searching for a Worthwhile Life, 1990, A Brief Introduction to Hinduism: Philosophy, Religion and Ways of Liberation, 1991; editor, translator: Indian Folk Tales, 1968; co-editor: (with Russell T. Blackwood) Problems in Philosophy: West and East, 1975; adv. editor The Jour. Studies in the Bhagavadgita, 1980; contbr. articles to profl. jours. Recipient award Acad. Letters and Sci., 1990; So. fellow Duke U., 1960-61, Ford Found. fellow, 1962-63, Nat. Def. Fgn. Lang. fellow U. Minn., 1968-70; Danforth grantee, 1961-63, Office Rsch. and Devel. grantee, 1971; Columbia U./N.Y. State Dept. Edn. scholar, 1964-65. Mem. Phi Kappa Phi. Office: U Wis Dept Philosophy Stevens Point WI 54481

HERMAN, FLOYD LEHMAN, rabbi; b. Jackson, Miss., Dec. 13, 1937; s. Julius Lee and Phyllis (Lehman) H.; m. Barbara Jean Stricker, June 19, 1960; children: David Isaac, Beth Ann. BA, U. Cin., 1959; BA in Hebrew Letters, Hebrew Union Coll., 1962, MA in Hebrew Letters, 1964, DDiv (hon.), 1989. Ordained rabbi, 1964. Asst. rabbi Congregation Emanuel, Houston, 1966-70; rabbi Temple Emanuel, Davenport, Iowa, 1970-73, Temple Chai, Long Grove, Ill., 1973-81; sr. rabbi Har Sinai Congregation, Balt., 1981—; adj. lectr. theology Loyola Coll. Md., Balt., 1981—; trustee mid Atlantic coun. Union Am. Hebrew Congregation, Washington, 1989—; pres. Balt. Bd. Rabbis, 1989-91. 1st v.p. Jewish Family Svcs., Balt., 1990—; mem. The Leadership Greater Balt. Com., 1987. Chaplain USAF, 1964-66. Recipient Disting. Svc. award City of Davenport, 1973, Shofar award Boy Scouts Am., 1985. Mem. Cen. Conf. Am. Rabbis (exec. bd. 1989-91). Home: 2521 Farringdon Rd Baltimore MD 21209 Office: Har Sinai Congregation 6300 Park Heights Ave Baltimore MD 21215

HERMAN, STEWART WINFIELD, religion educator; b. Geneva, Sept. 25, 1948. BA, Hamilton Coll., 1970; M. Theol. Studies, Luth. Sch. Theology, 1981; PhD, U. Chgo., 1988. Instr. Concordia Coll., Moorhead, Ind., 1987-88, asst. prof., 1988—. Author: The Health Costs of Air Pollution, 1978; co-author: Energy Futures: Industry and the New Technologies, 1977; contbr. articles to profl. jours. Mem. Soc. Christian Ethics, Soc. Bus. Ethics, Am. Acad. Religion, Acad. Mgmt. Lutheran. Office: Concordia Coll Dept of Religion Moorhead MN 56562

HERMANIUK, MAXIM, archbishop; b. Nowe Selo, Ukraine, Oct. 30, 1911; emigrated to Can., 1948, naturalized, 1954; s. Mykyta and Anna (Monczak) H. Student philosophy and theology, Louvain, Belgium, 1933-35, Beauplateau, Belgium, 1935-39; ThD, Oriental Philology and History, 1943; postgrad., Maitre Agrege Theol., 1947; DD (hon.), U. St. Michael's, Toronto, Can., 1988. Joined Redemptorist Congregation, 1933, ordained priest, 1938; supr. vice provincial Can. and U.S., 1948-51; consecrated bishop, 1951; aux. bishop Winnipeg, Man., Can., 1951; apostolic adminstr., 1956, archbishop met., 1956—; first editor Logos, Ukraine Theol. Rev., 1950-51; mem. Vatican II Council, 1962-65, Secretariat for Promoting Christian Unity, Rome, 1963; prof. moral theology, sociology and Hebrew, Beauplateau, 1943-45; prof. moral theology and holy scripture Redemptor Sem. Waterford, Ont., Can., 1949-51; mem. Pontifical Commn. for Revision of Kodex of Oriental Canon Law, 1983; mem. Council Secretariat for The Synod of Bishops, Rome. Author: La Parabole Evangelique, 1947, Our Duty, 1960. Co-founder, mem. Ukrainian Relief Com., Belgium, 1942-48; co-founder 1st pres. Ukrainian Cultural Soc., 1947, organizer Ukrainian univ. students orgn., Obnova, Belgium, 1946-48, Can., 1953; mem. joint working group Cath. Ch. and World Council Chs., 1969; mem. council to Secretariat Synod of Bishops, Rome, 1977, 83. Decorated Order of Can., 1982. Mem. World Congress Free Ukrainians, Taras Shevchenko Sci. Soc., Ukrainian Hist. Assn., Mark Twain Soc. (hon.), KC. Address: 235 Scotia St, Winnipeg, MB Canada R2V 1V7

HERMAN OF PHILADELPHIA, BISHOP See SWAIKO, JOSEPH

HERMES, MOTHER THERESA MARGARET, prioress; b. Hallettsville, Tex., Sept. 30, 1906; d. Anthony Thomas and Teresa (Drysee) H. BA, U. Tex., 1930. Novice Discalced Carmelite Nuns, New Orleans, 1934-36; foundress Discalced Carmelite Nuns, Lafayette, La., 1936, directress of novices, 1936-48, prioress, 1948-82, 85—; organizer, coord. St. Teresa Assn., Lafayette, 1978; organizer, counselor Carmelite Guild, 1950—. Collaborator Satutes/St. Teresa's Assn., 1979. Recipient Papal medal Pope John Paul II, Lafayette, 1990, Jerusalem Cross, Patriarch Maximos V Hakim, Lafayette, 1991, Mission Cross Rev. Giovanni Salerno, Lafayette, 1990. Home: 1250 Carmel Ave Lafayette LA 70501-5299 Office: Discalced Carmelite Nuns 1250 Carmel Ave Lafayette LA 70501-5299 *Jesus prayed: "Father...that they may be one even as we are one...that they may be perfected in unity." John 17:22-23. As I observe the chaotic conditions prevailing in humanity today, it seems that Division (among nations, families, within Man himself) is the* *chief menace to its unity and consequent peace. May Jesus' prayer be realized through the action of the Spirit of Love in men's hearts.*

HERMS, EILERT FRANZ MARTIN, theology educator; b. Oldenburg, Germany, Dec. 11, 1940; s. Bruno-Walter and Marga (Eilers) H.; m. Elke Reuter, July 24, 1969; children—Wiebke, Fokko, Gesine, Karsten. Dr. Theol., U. Kiel, 1971, Dr. Theol. habil, 1975. Wissensch. asst. U. Kiel, Schleswig-Holstein, 1971-79; ordentl. prof. U. Munich, Bayern, 1979-85, U. Mainz, Rheinland-Pfalz, 1985—. Author: Schleiermachers System der Wissenschaften, 1974, Radical Empiricism, 1971, Theologie-eine Erfahrungswissenschaft, 1978, Theorie für die Praxis, 1982, Einheit der Christen in der Gemeinschaft der Kirchen, 1984, Luthers Auslegung des Dritten Artikels, 1987, Von der Glaubenseinheif zúr Kirschengemeinschaft, 1989, Erfahrbare Kirche, 1990, Gesellschalt gestalten, 1991. Office: Univ Mainz, Saarstrasse, 6500 Mainz Federal Republic of Germany

HERNÁNDEZ, EVELIO JOSEPH, retired priest; b. Key West, Fla., Sept. 18, 1922; s. Enrique and Inez (Parón) H.; widower; children: Charles A., Verónica. LLB, Blackstone Duarte Sch. Div., Chgo.; DD (hon.), Min. of Salvation, 1982. Ordained to ministry United Am. Orthodox Cath. Ch. Vol. tutor in Eng., Math., Spanish, Am. History Key West High Sch., 1982-83; vol. Key West Convalescent Ctr., 1990—. With USN, 1942-45, PTO. Home: 1016 Varela St (rear) Key West FL 33040

HERNÁNDEZ, GONZALEZ JOSE MARIA, bishop; b. Penjamo, Mexico, Jan. 17, 1927. Ordained priest, Roman Catholic Ch., 1950. Priest Roman Catholic Ch., 1950—; consecrated bishop Roman Catholic Ch., Chilapa, Mexico; bishop Diocese of Cuidad Nezahualcoyotl, 1990—. Address: 3a avenida #55, Col Evolucion Ap postal#89, Cuidad Nezahualcoyotl Mexico C P 57700

HERNÁNDEZ, JUAN JOSÉ, minister; b. Oshkosh, Wis., July 6, 1956; s. Ramiro and Angelica (Flores) H.; m. Erlinda Villafranco, May 25, 1985; 1 child, Josué Luis. A in Divinity, Hispanic Bapt. Theol. Sem., San Antonio, 1985; diploma in Theology, Bapt. Bible Coll., Springfield, Mo., 1979. Ordained to ministry So. Bapt. Conv., 1986. Youth dir. Primera Iglesia Bautista, Eagle Pass, Tex., 1979-80; pastor Templo Bautista Ven-A-El, Eagle Pass, 1981; assoc. pastor Iglesia Bautista, Littlefield, Tex., 1985-86; pastor Primera Iglesia Bautista, Greeley, Colo., 1986—. Chmn. Dist. 6 Sch. Lunch Adv. Coun., Greeley, 1990—; mem. Greeley Dream Team, Inc., 1991—, Cinco de Mayo-orgn. com., Greeley, 1991, Hispanic League, Colo., 1990. Mem. Longs Peak Bapt. Assn., Colo. Bapt. Gen. Conv. (bd. dirs.), Weld Assn. Evangelicals. Republican. Home: 1440 6th St Greeley CO 80631 Office: Primera Iglesia Bautista 1200 3d Ave Greeley CO 80631

HERNANDEZ ALBALATE, EMILIO J., bishop. Bishop of Cuba Anglican Communion, Havana. Office: Office of Bishop, Calle 13, # 874, Entre 4 y 6, Vedado, Havana 4, Cuba*

HERRELL, DAVID JOY, minister, social services administrator; b. Washington, Sept. 4, 1936; s. Henry Gordon and Julia Vrooman (Cookman) H.; m. Kay LaVel Moseley, June 26, 1959; children: Lori LaVel, Risa Herrell Breuonne, Joel Frederick, Jose Juan. BA, U. Pa., 1958; MSW, U. Ill., Chgo., 1964; MDiv, McCormick Theol. Sem., 1964. Ordained to ministry Presbyn. Ch., 1964; cert. ACSW. Elem. sch. tchr. St. Mary's County Pub. Schs., Meadowsville, Md., 1958-59; pastor Mt. Top Parish United Presbyn., Clearfield, Pa., 1961-62, Sisseton (S.D.) Area Associated Chs. (Presbyn.), 1964-66; dir. Neighborhood Action Western S.D. Community Action, Rapid City, 1966-67; social worker Luth. Social Svcs. S.D., Rapid City, 1967-69; rep. Ch. World Svc. Christian Coun. at Ghana, Aecra, Ghana, 1969-72; coord. western Md. Tressler-Luth. Svcs. Assocs., Woodsboro, 1972-73; program dir. Christian Children's Fund, Inc., Richmond, Va., 1973-91; exec. dir. Childhope, Rio de Janeiro, 1991; chmn. bd. dirs. Childhope, N.Y., Guatemala, U.K., Philippines, 1986—, cons., Guatemala, 1988; vice chmn. Richmond Social Svc. Adv. Bd., 1989—; moderator exec. coun. Presbytery of the James, Richmond, 1989-90. Cubmaster Pack 232 Boy Scouts Am., Richmond, 1975-76. Named Wanbli Tokahe (First Eagle) Black Hill Coun. Am. Indians, Rapid City, 1967. Home: 1504 Westwood Ave Richmond VA 23227 Office: Childhope, CP 6205 CEP 22522, Rio de Janeiro Brazil

HERRELL, JOSEPH BRETT, minister; b. Oak Ridge, Tenn., Sept. 10, 1963; s. David Oliver and Sharon Kay (Goins) H.; m. Freda Melody Drummond, June 22, 1985. MusB, Carson-Newman Coll., Jefferson City, Tenn., 1990. Ordained to ministry Bapt. Ch., 1991. Min. youth and music 1st Bapt. Ch., Andersonville, Tenn., 1988—. Home: Rte 1 Box 103 Andersonville TN 37705 Office: 1st Bapt Ch Rte 2 Box 12 Andersonville TN 37705

HERREN, DONALD RAY, minister; b. Corbin, Ky., May 2, 1930; s. Oscar K. and Viola (Shotwell) H.; m. Patricia Eads, Aug. 21, 1951; children: Thomas K., Mark R. AB, Union Coll., Barbourville, Ky., 1951, DD (hon.), 1969; BD, Lexington (Ky.) Theol. Sem., 1955; postgrad., Northwestern U., 1961—. Ordained to ministry United Meth. Ch., 1955. Min. 1st United Meth. Ch., Lexington, 1952-59; sr. min. So. Hills United Meth. Ch., Lexington, 1959—; leader groups to Middle East, USSR, Europe, Hawaii, Japan, People's Republic China. Bd. dirs. Good Samaritan Hosp., Lexington, 1964—; mem. Fayette County (Ky.) Bd. Edn., 1968-80 (steering com. for tax referendum), Ky. Bd. Edn., 1981—; vice chmn. Paul Miller Ford Found.; bd. dirs. Blue Grass Boys' Ranch, Lexington YMCA, Day Treatment Ctr. for Juveniles, Cen. Ky. chpt. ARC, Fayette United Community fund; mem. Ky. Crime Commn., Met. Pks. and Recreation Bd., Nat. Pks. and Recreation Bd., Task Force on Edn., State of Ky., Adv. Coun., Voc. Edn., State of Ky.,. Mem. NCCJ (bd. dirs. Blue Grass chpt.), Urban League (bd. dirs. Lexington chpt.), Greater Lexington Area C. of C. (bd. dirs.), Kiwanis (past pres.). Home: 667 Hill 'n Dale Rd Lexington KY 40503 Office: So Hills United Meth Ch 2256 Harrodsburg Rd Lexington KY 40503

HERRICK, IRVING WEYMOUTH, JR., minister; b. Saco, Maine, Nov. 7, 1932; s. Irving Weymouth and Florence Elizabeth (Hodgkins) H.; m. Bernice Adele Morgan, Aug. 18, 1956; children: Patricia Ann, Michael Irving. BS, U. So. Maine, 1954; MEd, U. Md., 1960, EdD, 1969; MDiv, Southeastern Bapt. Theol. Sem., Wake Forest, N.C., 1983. Ordained to ministry So. Bapt. Conv., 1981. Pastor Cornelia Ave. Bapt. Ch., Chgo., 1984-87, 1st Bapt. Ch., West Chicago, Ill., 1987-90, Cen. Bapt. Ch., Ft. Myers, Fla., 1991—; acad. dean S.W. Bapt. U., Chgo., 1984-90; dir. continuing edn. Chgo. Met. Bapt. Assn., 1987-88. Pres. Du Page Youth Svcs. Coalition, Du Page County, Ill., 1990. Staff sgt. U.S. Army, 1954-56. Danforth Found./Nat. Acad. Sch. Execs. grantee, 1976. Mem. Phi Delta Kappa. Home: 5749 Palm Beach Blvd # 30 Fort Myers FL 33905 Office: Cen Bapt Ch 3208 Central Ave Fort Myers FL 33901

HERRIN, BURLEY FRANCIS, minister; b. Clay, Ky., Sept. 9, 1944; s. William Gamon and Edna Christine (Phelps) H.; m. Martha Jane Williams, Aug. 15, 1965; children: Jeffrey David, Jennifer Layne, Deborah Gail. BA, Oakland City (Ind.) Coll., 1966; MDiv, Cen. Bapt. Theol. Sem., Kansas City, Kans., 1969. Ordained to ministry Gen. Assn. Gen. Bapts., 1964, Am. Bapt. Conv., 1968, Christian Ch. (Disciples of Christ), 1976. Pastor Wyandotte Bapt. Ch., Kansas City, 1968-69, Osburn (Idaho) Community Bapt. Ch., 1969-73; assoc. pastor 1st Christian Ch., Henderson, Ky., 1976-78; pastor Christian Ch., Beech Grove, Ky., 1980-81, Illiopolis, Ill., 1982—; regional bd. dirs. Christian Ch. in Ill. and Wis., 1986-87; pres. bd. dirs. Dove, Inc., Decatur, Ill., 1983-84, chair fin. com., 1986-87, chair pers. com., 1988—. Emergency med. technician Illiopolis Fire Dept., 1988—. Mem. Coll. Profl. Christian Mins. in Ill. and Wis. (v.p. 1990—). Democrat.

HERRING, JOSEPH DAHLET, minister; b. Englewood, N.J., Feb. 24, 1934; s. Joseph Dahlet and Alice Josephine (Westpfal) H.; m. Bonita Lynn Bender, Jan. 26, 1963; children: Julienne Marie, Jefferson Dahlet, John Foster. AB, Dartmouth Coll., 1955; STB, Gen. Theol. Sem., 1960, STM, 1971. Asst. St. Paul's Ch., Paterson, N.J., 1960-63; vicar Ch. of the Transfiguration, Towaco, N.J., 1963-68; rector St. Stephen's Ch., Millburn, N.J., 1968-83, Christ Ch., Newton, N.J., 1983—; pres. standing com. Diocese of Newark, 1984—. Mem. editorial bd. The Voice newsletter, 1980-91, chmn. editorial bd., 1991—. Served with U.S. Army, 1956-57. Recipient Polly Bond award Episcopal Communicators, 1984. Fellow The Coll. of Preachers. Lodge: Rotary. Avocations: jogging, tennis, Am. history. Home: 14 Liberty St Newton NJ 07860 Office: PO Box 146 Newton NJ 07860

HERRINGTON, BRYAN DAVID, minister; b. Fernandina, Fla., Mar. 2, 1956; s. James Bryan and Julia Faye (Thomas) H.; m. Judy Elaine Burkett, Dec. 30, 1975; children: Amber Renae, Daniel Bryan, David Paul. BBS, Trinity Coll., Newburgh, Ind., 1982; BA, Luther Rice Seminary, Jacksonville, Fla., 1984. Ordained to ministry Bapt. Ch., 1976. Pastor Pine Haven Bapt. Ch., Brunswick, Ga., 1975-77, Maranatha Bapt. Mission, Brunswick, Ga., 1977-79; sr. pastor Jamestown Bapt. Ch., Waycross, Ga., 1979—; vice-moderator Piedmont/Okefenokee Bapt. Assn., Waycross, 1986-88, evangelism chmn., 1990-91; order of bus. com., Ga. Bapt. Conv., Atlanta, 1991. Chaplain Breakfast Exch. Club, Waycross, 1990. Republican. Office: Jamestown Baptist Church 3800 ABC Avenue Waycross GA 31501

HERRINGTON, CURTIS LEO, pastor; b. Nacogdoches, Tex., Oct. 20, 1938; s. George Hampton and Lela (Honea) H.; m. Zethaleen Marshal, Apr. 16, 1965; children: Sharon, Ronnie. BA, Bethany Bapt., Dothan, Ala., 19889. Ordained to ministry Bapt. Ch. Pastor Plum Ridge Bapt., Zavalla, Tex., 1971-75, Midway Bapt., Lufkin, Tex., 1977-78, Ebenezer Bapt., Jasper, Tex., 1978—; moderator SE Tex. Bapt., Jasper, 1990—; chaplain Angelina River Fire Dept., Jasper, 1989. Mem. Zavalla Independent Sch. Dist., 1974. Sgt. U.S. Army, 1961-64. Republican. Home: Rte 1 Box 220 Zavalla TX 75980 Office: Ebenezer Bapt Ch Rte 3 Box 686 Jasper TX 75951

HERRINGTON, DALE ELIZABETH, lay worker; b. Logansport, La., Feb. 1, 1913; d. Charles Ross and Ola Delnorte (Tillery) Currie; m. Cecil Doyle Herrington, June 25, 1939; 1 child, Jo Earle Herrington Hartt. BS, Stephen F. Austin Univ., 1932, MA, 1948, MEd, 1948. Cert. tchr., Tex. Min. edn. First Bapt. Ch., Garrison, Tex., 1947-81, organist, 1947—, lay worker, 1947—, tchr. Sunday sch. Bible, 1947—, woman's missionary union dir., 1990-91; tchr., Garrison Pub. Schs., 1940-76; dir./asst. dir. Vacation Bible Sch., Garrison. Named Mother of the Yr., First Bapt. Ch., Garrison. Mem. Ret. Tchrs. Assn., Lions, Heritage Club, Eastern Star (past matron, organist), Delta Kappa Gamma. Home: PO Box 97 Garrison TX 75946 *If I should consider rewards in this life, my second blessing would be in seeing young pople whose lives I have touched and helped them to mold, taking active roles in the church and community and service to our fellowman.*

HERRMANN, SANDRA SUE, minister; b. Milw., Feb. 14, 1944; d. Jerome Joseph Hefter and Sue Rose (Newman) Koski; m. Carl F. Herrmann, Nov. 12, 1966 (div. 1977). BA, U. Wis., Eau Claire, 1974; MDiv., United Theol. of Twin Cities, 1980. Ordained to ministry Meth. Ch. as deacon, 1978, as elder, 1980; cert. clin. pastoral edn. Secretarial positions in various orgns., Milw., 1961-69; radio host Talk & Music Show Sta. WWIS, Black River Falls, Wis., 1970; feature writer Banner-Jour., Black River Falls, 1970-72; Christian edn. assoc. United Meth. Ch., Black River Falls, 1974-76; student pastor Birchwood/Exeland United Meth. Ch., Exeland, Wis., 1977-78; pastor New Hope Larger Parish, Union Grove, Wis., 1980-83, Central/Atlas United Meth. Chs., Grantsburg, Wis., 1983-85, Parfreyville United Meth. Ch., Waupaca, Wis., 1985-90; retreat leader spiritual motivation and formation and bibl. topics Milw., 1990—; tchr. Sch. of Christian Mission, Ripon, Wis., 1985, 89, Demars, Iowa, 1990. Author: (poetry) Alive Now!, 1985; editor K'tuvim, 1978-79. Chairperson Wis. Conf. Bd. Ch. and Soc., Sun Prairie, 1987-89, Union Grove (Wis.) Clergy Assn., 1982, leadership no. cen. dist. United Meth. Ch., (Stevens Point), 19087-90; pres. Burnett Area Clergy and Religions Assn., Grantsburg, 1984; mem. NOW, Waupaca, 1988—, Wis. Religious Coalition for Abortion Rights, Waupaca, 1985—; 2d v.p. Riverside Med. Ctr. Aux., Waupaca, 1987-89. Grantee Mission Ambassador Program, Wis. Conf. Mem. United Meth. Women (Mission Achievement award 1989). Avocations: weaving, photography, music. Home and Office: 2770 S Adams Milwaukee WI 53207 *I have found a great many people who are searching for someone who will love them, for a place of acceptance. But too often the message is preached NOT that God so loved us that incarnation took place, but that God was so disgusted with us that Jesus had to offer up his blood to assuage God's demand for our death. This, it seems to me, is the latest heresy we have to battle.*

HERRON, JAMES WAYNE, minister; b. Williamstown, Ky., Apr. 16, 1955; s. John Marx and Genoa (Childers) H.; m. Marjorie Ruth Simmons, May 14, 1976; children: Joshua, Rebekah, Jacob, Elizabeth. BS, Cin. Bible Coll., 1978; MA in Practical Theology, Cin. Christian Seminary, 1984; MS in Family Studies, Va. Tech. Inst., 1989. Youth minister Franklin (Ohio) Christian Ch., 1977-79, minister, 1979-84; assoc. minister Salem (Va.) Ch. of Christ, 1984-89, minister of family life, 1989—; exec. com. Blue Ridge Christian Camp, McCoy, Va., 1985-88; continuation com. So. Christian Youth Conv., 1987—, chmn. continuing com., 1990—. Co-author articles for profl. jours. Mem. Community Mental Health Bd., Warren County, Ohio, 1981-84; pres. Roanoke Valley Foster Care Assn., 1991. Named Father of the Yr., Credit Mktg. Mgmt. Assn., Roanoke, 1989. Mem. Va. Coun. Family Rels., Southeastern Coun. Family Rels., Nat. Coun. Family Rels., Rotary (sgt. of arms 1991), Delta Aleph Tau, Omicron Nu, Phi Kappa Phi.

HERSHBERGER, ERVIN N., minister, editor; b. Grantsville, Md., Apr. 17, 1914; s. Noah E. and Savilla S. (Yoder) H.; m. Barbara Beachy, May 12, 1940; 1 dau., Mildred Elizabeth Hershberger Yoder. Student pub. schs. Ordained deacon Mennonite Ch., 1964. Editor Herold der Wahrheit, 1955-69, Calvary Messenger, Meyersdale, Pa., 1970—; asst. prin., chmn. bd. Calvary Bible Sch., 1971-80, prin., 1980-88, acad. dean, asst. prin., 1989-91, acad. dean, 1991—; dairy farmer, Meyersdale, 1942-67. Mem. Mennonite Mission Bd., mem. com. mission interests, 1963-74. Address: RD 1 Box 176 Meyersdale PA 15552 *To live for Him who died for us may or may not add years to our life, but it certainly adds life to our years! And true discipleship at any cost shall in no wise lose its reward.*

HERTWECK, GALEN FREDRIC, minister; b. St. Louis, May 31, 1946; s. Vernon L. and Erma G. (Giger) H.; m. Bronte L. McGuire, July 8, 1967; children: John L., Jill R. AA, Mesa (Ariz.) Community Coll., 1967; BA, So. Calif. Coll., 1968; MDiv, Fuller Theol. Sem., Pasadena, Calif., 1972; D of Ministry, Fuller Theol. Sem., 1977. Ordained to ministry Assemblies of God Ch., 1973. Assoc. pastor Harbor Assembly of God, Costa Mesa, Calif., 1972-75, Faith Assembly Ch., Monterey Park, Calif., 1975-76; asst. min. Christian Life Ch., LaCrescenta, Calif., 1976-77; dir. adult ministries Evang. Temple Christian Ctr., Springfield, Mo., 1977-79; pastor King's Chapel Christian Ctr., Springfield, 1979—; vis. lectr. Continental Bible Coll., Brussels, 1983, Asia Pacific Theol. Sem. Baguio City, The Philippines, 1988, Asia Theol. Ctr. for Evangelism and Missions, 1984; pres. Springfield Ministerial Alliance, 1984-85; adj. faculty Assemblies of God Theol. Sem., Springfield, 1986—. Contbr. articles to publs. Pres. Child Advocacy Coun., Springfield, 1989-91. Republican. Office: King's Chapel Christian Ctr 558 S Wagner Rd Springfield MO 65809

HERTZ, RICHARD CORNELL, rabbi; b. St. Paul, Oct. 7, 1916; s. Abram J. and Nadine (Rosenberg) H.; m. Mary Louise Mann, Nov. 25, 1943 (div. July 1971); children: Nadine Hertz Urben, Ruth Mann (Mrs. Alain Joyaux); m. Renda Gottfürcht Ebner, Dec. 3, 1972. A.B., U. Cin., 1938; M.H.L., Hebrew Union Coll., 1942, D.D. (hon.), 1967; Ph.D., Northwestern U., 1948. Ordained rabbi, 1942; asst. rabbi N. Shore Congregation Israel, Glencoe, Ill., 1942-47; asso. rabbi Chgo. Sinai Congregation, 1947-53; sr. rabbi Temple Beth El, Detroit, 1953-82, rabbi emeritus, 1982—; adj. prof. Jewish Thought U. Detroit, 1970-80, disting. prof. Jewish studies, 1980—; spl. cons. to pres. Cranbrook Ednl. Community, 1983-84; del. to internat. conf. World Union for Progressive Judaism, London, 1959, 61, Amsterdam, 1978, bd. dirs. union, 1973—; Lectr. Jewish Chautauqua Soc., 1942—; former mem. plan bd. Synagogue Council Am.; past mem. chaplaincy commn., former bd. dirs. Nat. Jewish Welfare Bd.; former mem. exec. com., vice chmn. Citizen's Com. for Equal Opportunity, Am. Jewish Com.; mem. Mich. Gov.'s Com. on Ethics and Morals, 1963-69; mem. Mich. adv. council U.S. Commn. on Civil Rights, 1979-85; past mem. nat. bd. dirs. Religious Edn. Assn.; past adv. bd. Joint Distbn. Com.; former mem. nat. rabbinical council United Jewish Appeal; mem. rabbinic cabinet Israel Bonds, 1972—; pres. Hyde Park and Kenwood Council Chs. and Synagogues, Chgo., 1952. Author: Rabbi Yesterday and Today, 1943, This I Believe, 1952, Education of the Jewish Child, 1953, Our Religion Above All, 1953, Inner Peace for You, 1954, Positive Judaism, 1955, Wings of the Morning, 1956, Impressions of Israel, 1956, Prescription for Heartache, 1958, Faith in Jewish Survival, 1961, The American Jew in Search of Himself, 1962, What Counts Most in Life, 1963, What Can A Man Believe, 1967, Reflections for the Modern Jew, 1974, Israel and the Palestinians, 1974, Roots of My Faith, 1980, also articles in sci., popular publs. Dir. Am. Jewish Com., mem. nat. exec. bd., former hon. vice-chmn. Detroit chpt.; past dir. Mich. Soc. Mental Health, Jewish Family and Children's Services, United Community Services, Jewish Welfare Fedn. Detroit; v.p. Jewish Community United Council Detroit; dir. United Found., Boys Clubs, Mich. region Anti-Defamation League; chmn. bd. overseers Hebrew Union Coll.-Jewish Inst. Religion, 1968-72; bd. govs. Detroit Inst. Tech., 1955-70; trustee Marygrove Coll., Detroit, 1986—. Served as chaplain AUS, 1943-46. Recipient Histadrut award, 1984. Fellow Am. Sociol. Soc.; mem. Assn. Jewish Studies, Detroit Hist. Soc., Central Conf. Am. Rabbis (former nat. chmn. com. on Jews in Soviet orbit), Am. Jewish Hist. Soc., Am. Legion (dept. chaplain 1956-57), Jewish War Vets. (dept. chaplain 1958-59, 72—), Alumni Assn. Hebrew Union Coll.-Jewish Inst. Religion (past dir.), Nat. Assn. Ret. Reform Rabbis (pres. 1989). Clubs: Rotary (Detroit), Economic (Detroit) (dir.); Wranglers (past pres.), Great Lakes, Standard, Franklin Hills, Knollwood, Tam O'Shanter. Went on spl. mission for White House to investigate status Jews and Judaism in USSR 1959, mission for chief chaplains Def. Dept. to conduct retreats for Jewish chaplains and laymen, Berchtesgaden, Germany, 1973; mem. mission to Arab countries and Israel, Nat. Council Chs.-Am. Jewish Com., 1974; 1st Am. rabbi received in pvt. audience at Papal Palace by Pope Paul VI, 1963. Home: 4324 Knightsbridge Ln West Bloomfield MI 48033 Office: Temple Beth El 7400 Telegraph Rd/14 Mile Birmingham MI 48010 *My life has fallen in pleasant places. I have been fortunate enough and lived long enough to enjoy my life as a Rabbi and teacher. To be able to help people become better Jews and appreciate their Jewish heritage has been a source of great satisfaction.*

HERTZBERG, ARTHUR, rabbi, educator; b. Lubaczow, Poland, June 9, 1921; s. Zvi Elimelech and Nehamah (Alstadt) H.; m. Phyllis Cannon, Mar. 19, 1950; children: Linda, Susan. A.B., Johns Hopkins U., 1940; M.H.L., Jewish Theol. Sem., 1943; Ph.D., Columbia U., 1966; D.D., Lafayette Coll., 1970; D.H.L., Balt. Hebrew Coll., 1974, Jewish Theol. Sem., 1987. Rabbi, 1943; Hillel dir. Mass. State and Smith Coll., 1943-44; rabbi Congregation Ahavath Israel of Oak Lane, Phila., 1944-47, West End Synagogue, Nashville, 1947-56, Temple Emanu El, Englewood, N.J., 1956-84; rabbi emeritus Temple Emanu El, 1984—; prof. religion Dartmouth Coll., 1985-91, prof. emeitus, 1991—; lectr. Columbia U., 1961-68, adj. prof. history, 1968-90, vis. scholar Mideast Inst., 1991—; vis. assoc. prof. Jewish studies Rutgers U., 1966-68; lectr. religion Princeton U., 1968-69; vis. prof. history Hebrew U., Jerusalem, 1970-71; vis. prof. Ecole des Hautes Etudes, Paris, 1989; vis. scholar St. Antony's Coll., Oxford, 1989; pres. Conf. Jewish Social Studies, 1967-72; mem. exec. com. World Zionist Orgn., 1969-78, Jewish Agy. for Israel, 1969-71, bd. govs., 1971-78; pres. Am. Jewish Congress, 1972-78, Am. Jewish Policy Found., 1978—; v.p. World Jewish Congress, 1975—; vis. prof. humanities NYU, 1991—. Author: The Zionist Idea, 1959, (with Martin Marty and Joseph Moody) The Outbursts that Await Us, 1963, The French Enlightenment and the Jews, 1968, Being Jewish in America, 1979, The Jews in America: Four Centuries of an Uneasy Encounter, 1989; editor: Judaism, 1961, 2d rev. edit., 1991; sr. editor: Ency. Judaica, 1972; contbr.: Ency. Brit., 1975. Vice pres. bd. dirs. Meml. Found. for Jewish Culture. Served 1st lt., chaplain USAF, 1951-53. Recipient Amram award, 1967; award for Lifetime Achievement Present Tense, 1989; Inst. Advanced Studies fellow, Jerusalem, 1982. Home: 83 Glenwood Rd Englewood NJ 07631 Office: 147 Tenafly Rd Englewood NJ 07631 also: Dartmouth Coll Thornton Hall Hanover NH 03755 *I cannot even imagine improving on Hillel's dictum, nearly 20 centuries ago; what is hateful to you, don't do to your fellow man.*

HERZFELD, GARSON, rabbi; b. Cleve., May 2, 1951; s. Jacob L. Herzfeld and Lila (Bloomberg) Held. BA, Hobart and William Smith Coll., Geneva, N.Y., 1973; MA in Hebrew Letters, Hebrew Union Coll., 1979. Ordained rabbi, 1979. Rabbi Congregation Rodeph Shalom, Dollard Des Ormeax, Que., 1979-81, Temple Beth-El, Geneva, N.Y., 1981-86; campus rabbi Hobart & William Smith Colls., Geneva, N.Y., 1981-86; Jewish chaplain Willard (N.Y.) Psychiatric Ctr., 1983-86; rabbi Temple Israel, Brockton, Mass., 1986-88; rabbi, dir. B'nai Brith Hillel Found., Tampa, Fla., 1988—; adj. Hebrew instr. U. S. Fla., Tampa, 1989—; steering com. Jewish Community Rels. Coun., Tampa, 1989—, Operation Exodus task force, Tampa, 1990—; leadership v.p. Young Adults div. Tampa Jewish Fedn., 1990-91. Contbr. articles to profl. jours. Mem. Tampa Gen. Hosp. Pastoral Edn. Steering Com., 1990—; mem. Wellness Com. U.S. Fla., 1989-91. Mem. Cen. Conf. Am. Rabbis, Assn. Hillel and Jewish Campus Profls., Coalition for Advancement of Jewish Edn., Tampa Rabbinical Assn., Am. Psychol. Assn., Campus Ministry Assn. U. S. Fla., Kappa Delta Pi. Home: 13819 Lazy Oak Dr Tampa FL 33613 Office: B'nai Brith Hillel Found 14240 N 42nd St #1301 Tampa FL 33613 *As a Rabbi (or anyone, for that matter), interacts with others, he must learn, grow and mature with all those people. This means being flexible and responsive, yet standing firm in one's convictions. These are mandatory ingredients, in my opinion, to be an effective leader, facilitator, teacher and friend.*

HERZIG, CHARLES E., bishop; b. San Antonio, Aug. 14, 1929. Student, St. Mary's U., St. John's Sem., Our Lady of the Lake U., San Antonio. Ordained priest Roman Cath. Ch., 1955, consecrated bishop, 1987. Bishop, Tyler, Tex., 1987—. Address: 1920 Sybil Ln Tyler TX 75703

HESBURGH, THEODORE MARTIN, clergyman, former university president; b. Syracuse, N.Y., May 25, 1917; s. Theodore Bernard and Anne Marie (Murphy) H. Student, U. Notre Dame, 1934-37; PhB, Gregorian U., 1939; postgrad., Holy Cross Coll., Washington, 1940-43; STD, Cath. U. Am., 1945; 121 honorary degrees awarded between 1954-90. Joined Order of Congregation of Holy Cross, 1934, ordained priest Roman Cath. Ch., 1943. Chaplain Nat. Tng. Sch. for Boys, Washington, 1943-44; vets. chaplain U. Notre Dame, 1945-47, asst. prof. religion, head dept., 1948-49, exec. v.p., 1949-52, pres., 1952-87, pres. emeritus, 1987—; trustee Chase Manhattan Bank; mem. bd. overseers Harvard U.; pres bd. overseers Tchrs. Ins. and Annuity Assn. and Coll. Retirement Equities Fund. Author: Theology of Catholic Action, 1945, God and the World of Man, 1950, Patterns for Educational Growth, 1958, Thoughts for Our Times, 1962, More Thoughts for Our Times, 1965, Still More Thoughts for Our Times, 1966, Thoughts IV, 1968, Thoughts V, 1969, The Humane Imperative: A Challenge for the Year 2000, 1974, The Hesburgh Papers: Higher Values in Higher Education, 1979, God, Country, Notre Dame, 1990. Former dir. Woodrow Wilson Nat. Fellowship Corp.; mem. Civil Rights Commn., 1957-72; mem. of Carnegie Commn. on Future of Higher Edn.; chmn. U.S. Commn. on Civil Rights, 1969-72; mem. Commn. on an All-Volunteer Armed Force, 1970; chmn. with rank of ambassador U.S. delegation UN Conf. Sci. and Tech. for Devel., 1977-79 ; Bd. dirs. Am. Council Edn., Freedoms Found. Valley Forge, Adlai Stevenson Inst. Internat. Affairs; past trustee, chmn. Rockefeller Found.; trustee Carnegie Found. for Advancement Teaching, Woodrow Wilson Nat. Fellowship Found., Inst. Internat. Edn., Nutrition Found., United Negro Coll. Fund, others; chmn. Overseas Devel. Council; chmn. acad. council Ecumenical Inst. for Advanced Theol. Studies, Jerusalem. Decorated comdr. L'ordre des Arts et des Lettres. Recipient U.S. Navy's Disting. Pub. Service award, 1959; Presdl. Medal of Freedom, 1964, Gold medal Nat. Inst. Social Scis., 1969, Cardinal Gibbons medal Cath. U. Am., 1969, Bellarmine medal Bellarmine-Ursuline Coll., 1970; Meiklejohn award AAUP, 1970, Charles Evans Hughes award Nat. Conf. Christians and Jews, 1970; Merit award Nat. Cath. Ednl. Assn., 1971, Pres.' Cabinet award U. Detroit, 1971; Am. Liberties medallion Am. Jewish Com., 1971; Liberty Bell award Ind. State Bar Assn., 1971; Laetare medal Univ. Notre Dame, 1987, Pub. Welfare medal NAS, 1984; Pub. Svc. award Common Cause, 1984, Disting. Svc. award Assn. Cath. Colls. and Univs., 1982, Jefferson award Coun. Advancement and Support of Edn., 1982. Fellow Am. Acad. Arts and Scis.; mem. Internat. Fedn. Cath. Univs., Commn. on Humanities, Inst. Internat. Edn. (pres., dir.), Cath. Theol. Soc., Chief Execs. Forum, Am. Philos. Soc., Nat. Acad. Edn., Council on Fgn. Relations (trustee). Office: U Notre Dame 1315 Hesburgh Libr Notre Dame IN 46556

HESH, JOSEPH MCLEAN, minister, author; b. Macomb, Ill., July 7, 1954; s. William Leonard and Charlotte (McLean) H.; m. Claudia Sue Wallies, Aug. 9, 1975; 1 child, Corrie Elizabeth. BS, Ill. State U., 1976; RMT, Ellisville State Sch., 1976; ThM, Dallas Theol. Sem., 1981. Ordained to ministry Christian Ch., 1981. Chaplain's asst. Ellisville (Miss.) State Sch., 1977; youth worker and pastor Scofield Meml. Ch., Dallas, 1978-81, 81-86; youth pastor Pulpit Rock Ch., Colorado Springs, Colo., 1986—; recording artist Aspen Breeze Prodns. Author: Crossroads Series, 1990; composer, songwriter. Musician, speaker camps, confs., concerts. Home: 3826 Manchester Colorado Springs CO 80907 Office: Pulpit Rock Ch 301 Austin Bluffs Pkwy Colorado Springs CO 80918

HESKINS-LAZAR, SUSAN MICHELLE, social worker; b. San Antonio, Tex., July 30, 1960; d. David Michael and Sara Rebecca (Levinson) Heskins; . Howard Scott Lazar, June 25, 1989; 1 child, Shira Dina. BS in Pub. Rels. and Polit. Sci., Syracuse U., 1982; MSW, Yeshiva U., 1989. Cert. social worker, N.Y. Office mgr. Am. Zionist Youth Found., N.Y.C., 1983-84; programming asst. Coalition to Free Soviet Jews, N.Y.C., 1986-88; youth/teen dir. Shorefront YM/YWHA, N.Y.C., 1989-90; caseworker N.Y. Assn. for New Ams. (Resettle Soviet Jews), N.Y.C., 1990-91; chmn. holiday and dinner com. Kane St. Synagogue, Bklyn., 1989-91; mem. Congregation Bet Tefilla, Aberdeen, N.J., 1991—. Mem. Nat. Assn. Social Workers, Am. Jewish Communal Profls.

HESLAM, JANET VERNON, minister; b. Lynn, Mass., Feb. 17, 1940; d. John and Annie (Hatfield) Vernon; m. Charles James Heslam III, Aug. 27, 1961; children: Paul Bethany Morse, Peter David. BS in Edn., Fitchburg (Mass.) State Coll., 1961; MDiv, Bangor (Maine) Theol. Sem., 1986. Ordained to ministry, 1986. Co-pastor Waldo County Coop. Ministry, Brooks, Maine, 1983-89; pastor Gorham (N.H.) Congl. Ch., 1990—; dir., tchr. Pre-Sch. Coop., Brooks, 1973-89; owner, tchr. Dried Flowers, 1978—. Bd. dirs. Coalition for Maine's Children, Augusta, 1988-89. Mem. United Ch. of Christ Women in Mission, Ch. Women United. Home: 141 Main St Gorham NH 03581 Office: Gorham Congl Ch 143 Main St Gorham ME 03581

HESLOP, VAN CHRISTOPHER, minister; b. Salisbury, Md., Sept. 18, 1955; s. Theodore Ralph and Florence Mildred (Oakerman) H.; m. Karen Sue Freed, Aug. 7, 1976; children: Jeremy Alan, Joshua Brent, Joel Christopher. Diploma, Internat. Bible Inst. and Sem., Plymouth, Fla., 1981, BA in Theology, 1983; BA in Theology, Christian Life Coll. Theology, Salisbury, Md., 1990. Ordained evangelist Delmarva Evangelistic Ch., Salisbury, 1981. Student min. Delmarva Evangelistic Ch., 1971-81, evangelist, 1981-83, asst. pastor, worship leader, choir dir., 1985-88; assoc. pastor Life Christian Assembly, Charleston, S.C., 1983-85; sr. pastor Victory Worship Ctr., Pocomoke, Md., 1988—; nat. east coast dir. youth Full Gospel Fellowship of Chs. and Mins. Internat., Dallas, 1987-88; Md. youth coord. Washington for Jesus, Virginia Beach, Va., 1988-89. Republican. Home: Rte 1 Box 50-1 Pocomoke MD 21851 Office: Victory Worship Ctr 701 Ocean Hwy Pocomoke MD 21851 *When I sought for wisdom and peace in earthen vessels I found none, but when I placed my trust in Jesus Christ I found both wisdom and peace. I am a happy man.*

HESS, BARTLETT LEONARD, clergyman; b. Spokane, Wash., Dec. 27, 1910; s. John Leonard and Jessie (Bartlett) H.; BA, Park Coll., 1931, MA (fellow in history 1931-34), U. Kan., 1932, PhD, 1934; B.D., McCormick Theol. Sem., 1936; m. Margaret Young Johnston, July 31, 1937; children: Daniel Bartlett, Deborah Margaret, John Howard and Janet Elizabeth (twins). Ordained to ministry Presbyn. Ch., 1936; pastor Effingham, Kan., 1932-34, Chgo., 1935-42, Cicero, Ill., 1942-56, Ward Meml. Presbyn. Ch., Detroit, 1956-68, Ward Presbyn. Ch., Livonia, Mich., 1968-80, Presbyn. Ch., 1980—. Tchr. ch. history, bible Detroit Bible Coll., 1956-60, bd. dirs., 1956—; minister radio sta. WHFC, Chgo., 1942-50, WMUZ-FM, Detroit, 1958-68, 78—, WOMC-FM, 1971-72, WBFG-FM, 1972—; missioner to Philippines, United Presbyn. Ch. U.S.A., 1961; mem. Joint Com. on Presbyn. Union, 1980; adviser Mich. Synod coun. United Presbyn. Ch.; mem. com. Billy Graham Crusade for S.E. Mich., 1976; mem. adminstrv. com. Evang. Presbyn. Ch., 1980-85; mem. joint com. missions Evang. Presbyn. Ch. and the Presbyn. Ch. of Brazil. Mem., organizer Friendship and Svc. Com. for Refugees, Chgo., 1940. Bd. dirs. Beacon Neighborhood House, Chgo., 1945-52, Presbyns. United for Bibl. Concerns, 1975-80; pres. bd. dirs. Peniel Community Center, Chicago, 1945-52. Named Pastor of Year, Mid-Am. Sunday Sch. Assn., 1974; recipient Svc. to Youth award Detroit Met. Youth for Christ, 1979, Father of Evangelical Presbyn. Ch. award, 1991. Mem. Cicero Mins. Coun. (pres. 1951), Phi Beta Kappa, Phi Delta Kappa. Author: (with Margaret Johnston Hess) How To Have a Giving Church, 1974; (with M.J. Hess) The Power of a Loving Church, 1977, How Does Your Marriage Grow, 1982, Never Say Old, 1984; contbr. articles in field to profl. jours. Traveled in Europe, 1939, 52, 55, 68; also in Greece, Turkey, Lebanon, Syria, Egypt, Israel, Iraq; condr. tour of Middle East and Mediterranean countries, 1965, 67, 73, 74, 76, 78, 80, 84, 90, China and Far East, 1982; missioner, India, 1981, 89, Brazil, 85, 86, 87, 89, Argentina, 87, 89, 91. Home: 16845 Riverside Dr Livonia MI 48154 Office: 17000 Farmington Rd Livonia MI 48154 *In the increased velocity and pace of current history, the hunger for God's revelation in the Bible and in Christ is greater than at any time in my ministry of fifty-five years.*

HESS, GARY CHARLES, minister; b. Mpls., Feb. 3, 1948; s. Clifford Charles and Betty Lorrine (Merritt) H.; m. Kazuko Ueno, Oct. 7, 1972. BA, U. Colo., 1970; MDiv, Luther Northwestern Theol. Sem., 1977. Ordained to ministry Luth. Ch., 1977. Lay missionary Luth. Ch. Am., Japan, 1970-73; pastor evang. ministries Shepherd of Valley Luth. Ch., Phoenix, 1977-80; sr. pastor St. Mark's Luth. Ch., Cedar Rapids, Iowa, 1980—; Luth. Ch. Am. rep. Ariz. Ecumenical Coun., 1977-80; mem. world mission com. Pacif S.W. Synod Luth. Ch. Am., L.A., 1977-80, dist. rep. bd. outreach, Des Moines, 1982-84; chair global mission com. S.E. Iowa Synod Evang. Luth. Ch. Am., Iowa City, 1990—. Mem. spiritual adv. bd. Four Oaks Treatment Ctr. for Children and Families, Cedar Rapids, 1988—. Mem. Coun. Clergy, Luth. Pastors Assn., Ea. Iowa Exec. Club, Phi Alpha Theta. Home: 241 Brentwood Dr NE Cedar Rapids IA 52402 Office: St Mark Luth Ch 2100 1st Ave NE Cedar Rapids IA 52402 *Faith is the fount of creative energy.*

HESS, LARRY LEE, music minister; b. Akron, Oh., May 19, 1939; s. Howard O. and Florence (Weaver) H.; m. Hazel Barbara Rose, Aug. 20, 1960; children: Lisa (dec.), Linda Plum, Lori Smejkal, Lucinda Hess. BS, Bob Jones U., 1961; DD (hon.), Bapt. Bible Coll. Canada, 1990. Music min. Akron Bapt. Temple, Akron, Oh., 1965-86, Northside Bapt., Charlotte, N.C., 1986--; gospel music artist, music clinic speaker. Contrib. articles to profl.jours., recording artist/producer. Republican. Independent Baptist. Home: 11006 Bridgehampton Dr Charlotte NC 28262

HESS, MARGARET JOHNSTON, religious writer, educator; b. Ames. Iowa, Feb. 22, 1915; d. Howard Wright and Jane Edith (Stevenson) Johnston; B.A., Coe Coll., 1937; m. Bartlett Leonard Hess, July 31, 1937; children—Daniel, Deborah, John, Janet. Bible tchr. Community Bible Classes Ward Presbyn. Ch., Livonia, Mich., 1959—, Christ Ch. Cranbrook (Episcopalian), Bloomfield Hills, Mich., 1980—. Co-author: (with B.L. Hess) How to Have a Giving Church, 1974, The Power of a Loving Church, 1977, How Does Your Marriage Grow?, 1983, Never Say Old, 1984; author: Love Knows No Barriers, 1979; Esther: Courage in Crisis, 1980; Unconventional Women, 1981, The Triumph of Love, 1987; contbr. articles to religious jours. Home: 16845 Riverside Dr Livonia MI 48154 *A lifetime of teaching the Bible, mainly to women, has shown me how it meets people's needs, in the home, in the work place, in the world.*

HESSEL, KENNETH NEAL, minister; b. Buffalo, N.Y., May 7, 1960; s. Lloyd Eugene and Helen Emma (Krieger) H.; m. Theresa Ann Cotton, Oct. 8, 1961; 1 child, Kaellen N. BA, Valparaiso U., 1983; MDiv., Concordia Sem., 1987. Ordained to ministry Luth. Ch.-Mo. Synod, 1987. Assoc. pastor Immanuel Luth. Ch., Schleswig, Iowa, 1987-90, Beautiful Savior Luth. Ch., Omaha, Nebr., 1990—. Mem. Tri-City Ministerial Assn. (sec.-treas. 1991—). Republican. Luth. Ch.-Mo. Synod. Home: 5023 S 94th Ave Omaha NE 68127-2409 Office: Beautiful Savior Luth Ch 9012 Q St Omaha NE 68127-3549

HESSELFELD, HEINRICH JOSEF, missionary, physics educator, researcher; b. Lohne, Vechta, Germany, Dec. 28, 1930; emigrated to Taiwan, 1966; s. Heinrich and Josefa (Westerhoff) H. Abitur, St. Xaver's Coll., Bad Driburg, W.Ger., 1952; M.A. in Physics Catholic U., Washington, 1963, Ph.D., 1966. Ordained priest Soc. of the Divine Word, Roman Catholic Ch., 1958. Assoc. prof. physics Fu Jen U., Taipei, Taiwan, 1966-72, prof., 1972—, chmn. dept. physics, 1968-75, dir. Grad. Sch. Physics, 1972-77, dean Coll. Scis., 1973-84; sci. advisor in Tacloban, Philippines, 1984-86. Editor-in-chief: Fu Jen Studies, 1971—. Mem. Optical Soc. Am., Acoustical Soc. Am., Phys. Soc. Am., Phys. Soc. Republic of China, Sigma Xi. Home and Office: Steyler Mission, Arnold Janssen Str 26, 5205 Sankt Augustin 1, Federal Republic of Germany

HESSELINK, I(RA) JOHN, JR., theology educator; b. Grand Rapids, Mich., Mar. 21, 1928; s. Ira John Sr. and Anna (Mulder) H.; m. Etta Marie Ter Louw, Aug. 29, 1951; children: John III, Ann, Judson, Nathan, Gregory. BA, Cen. Coll., Pella, Iowa, 1950; DD (hon.), Cen. Coll., 1981; MDiv, Western Sem., 1953; ThD, Basel (Switzerland) U., 1961; LHD (hon.), Hope Coll., 1973. Ordained to ministry Reformed Ch. in Am., 1953. Missionary United Ch. Christ, Fukuoka, Japan, 1953-58; prof. hist. theology Tokyo Union Theol. Sem., 1961-73; pres. Western Theol. Sem., Holland, Mich., 1973-85, A. Van Raalte prof. systematic theology, 1986—; adj. prof. theology Meiji Gakuin U., Tokyo, 1962-66, Calvin Theol. Sem., Grand Rapids, Mich., 1988-89, Fuller Theol. Sem., 1987—. Editor: Japan Christian Quar. 1955-58; co-Translator: (of Kitamori) Theology of the Pain of God), 1965; author: On Being Reformed, 1983 book rev. edit., 1988, Christ's Peace, 1987; editorial cons. Center Jour., 1981—, Ständige Mitarbeiter, Zeitschrift für Dialektische Theologie, 1985—. Named (with wife) Alumni Couple of Yr., 1975; Postdoctoral scholar U. Chgo. Div. Sch., 1971-72, vis. scholar Free U., Amsterdam, 1985. Mem. Sixteenth Century Studies Soc., Am. Soc. Reformation Rsch., Karl Barth Soc. N. Am. (v.p. 1976—), John Calvin Studies Soc. (exec. com. 1975-77, v.p. 1989-90, pres. 1991), Mich. Acad. Theologians, Am Theol. Soc., Century Club (v.p. 1988-89, pres. 1989-90). Avocations: reading, music, sports, Japanese woodblock prints. Home: 98 W 12th St Holland MI 49423 Office: Western Theol Sem Holland MI 49423 *I am convinced that the Genevan reformer, John Calvin, still has much to say to our age with his vision of the glory of God, on the one hand, and his view that the creation is the theater of God's glory, on the other.*

HESTAND, JOEL DWIGHT, minister, evangelist; b. Henrietta, Tex., May 23, 1939; s. Dee Lathell and Jack Fern (Gamble) H.; m. Carolyn Somers, June 12, 1959; children: Paul Daniel, Joe Randall. Student, Odessa (Tex.) Coll., 1963-66; Diploma, Brown Trail Sch. Preaching, Ft. Worth, Tex., 1968-70, Sunset Sch. Missions, Lubbock, 1973; BTh, Trinity Theol. Sem., 1988. Evangelist Ch. of Christ, various locations, 1968—; missionary Tanzania, E. Africa, 1973-75; police chaplain Naperville (Ill.) Police Dept., 1977-83; ednl. dir. Rockford (Ill.) Christian Camp, 1977-82, bd. dirs., 1977-82; instr. Fishers of Men Evangelism, Frankfort, Ky., 1984—. With USAF, 1957-66. Republican. Office: Frankfort Ch of Christ 1300 Louisville Rd Frankfort KY 40601 *"Now all has been heard; here is the conclusion of the matter: Fear God and keep His Commandments, for this is the whole of man." Ecclesiastes 12:13.*

HESTER, BRUCE EDWARD, correctional facility educator, librarian, lay worker; b. Clarksville, Tenn., June 26, 1956; s. Edward Vaughan and Mabel Sarah (Chandley) H. BS, Middle Tenn State U., 1978; MEd, Trevecca Nazarene Coll., 1987. Cert. elem. tchr., cert. secondary tchr. and libr., Tenn. Correctional teacher, libr. Turney Ctr. Indsl. Prison and Farm, Only, Tenn., 1990—; choir dir. First Christian Ch., Dover, Tenn., 1983—, Sunday sch. tchr., deacon, 1988—, also chmn. bd. dirs.; dir. Stewart County Community Choir, 1987-89. Co-chmn. Stewart County Rep. Party, 1986-89. Recipient Vol. Svc. award Cystic Fibrosis Found., 1984. Mem. NEA, Tenn. Edn. Assn., Tenn. State Employees Assn. Mem. Disciples of Christ Ch. Home: 151 Lakeview Dr Dover TN 37058 Office: Turney Ctr Indsl Prison and Farm Rte #1 Only TN 37140-9709 *Our heritage is the foundation of our future. As children, our parents help to build us to be able to meet the challenge of life and embrace the future. The option is ours; to add to that foundation or remain unfinished.*

HESTER, JAMES DAVID, academic administrator; b. Paducah, Ky., Mar. 18, 1931; s. Sam T. and Mary B. (Phillips) H.; m. Barbara A. Connor, July 6, 1952; children: Dianne, Mark, Melanie, Timothy. BA, Bethel Coll., 1953; BD, Cumberland Presbyn. Theol. Sem., 1957; MA, Memphis State U., 1967; D of Ministry, Fuller Theol. Sem., 1981. Ordained to ministry Cumberland Presbyn. Ch., 1951. Pastor Cumberland Presbyn. Ch., Wingo, Ky., 1950-53, Waverly, Tenn., 1953-58; pastor Colonial Cumberland Presbyn. Ch., Memphis, 1958-70, 1st Cumberland Presbyn. Ch., Knoxville, Tenn., 1970-84; pres. Memphis Theol. Sem., 1984—; moderator Clarksville (Tenn.) Presbytery, 1955, Memphis Presbytery, 1961, West Tenn. Synod, Memphis, 1965, Gen. Assembly Cumberland Presbyn. Ch., 1969; co-creator ch. exhibit World's Fair, Knoxville, 1982. Fellow Acad. Evangelism; mem. Memphis Inst. Medicine and Religion (pres.), Rotary. Democrat. Office: Memphis Theol Sem 168 E Parkway S Memphis TN 38104

HESTER, JAMES DWIGHT, educator; b. Phila., Feb. 15, 1939; s. James Donald and Nova Louise (Pace) H.; m. Darilyn Joann Ballard, June 16, 1961; children: James David, Damon Micah. BA, Eastern Coll., 1960; MDiv, Calif. Bapt. Theol. Sem., 1963; DTh, U. Basel, Switzerland, 1966. Prof. U. of Redlands, Calif., 1967—; interim preacher Redlands United Ch. of Christ, 1981-82; chair dept. religion U. of Redlands, 1985—. Author: Paul's Concept of Inheritance, 1968; translator: Vatican Council II: New Directions, 1968. Fellow Soc. for Values in Higher Edn., Jesus Seminar-Westar Inst.; mem. Soc. Bibl. Lit. (sec. Pacific Coast chpt. 1976-79, 85-90, pres. 1980), Studiorium Novi Testamentum Societas. Democrat. Home: 736 Buckingham Dr Redlands CA 92374 Office: U of Redlands 1200 E Colton Ave Redlands CA 92373

HESTER, JAMES HERBERT, JR., minister; b. Clovis, N.Mex., July 6, 1948; s. James Herbert and Sybil Eileen (Upton) H.; m. Cynthia Rose Boal, June 6, 1969; children: Corrie Ellen, Cassie Laine. BA, U. N.Mex., 1972; MDiv, Southwestern Bapt. Theol. Sem., Ft. Worth, 1975; D Ministry, Luther Rice Internat. Sem., Jacksonville, Fla., 1978. Ordained to ministry So. Bapt. Conv., 1969. Pastor Highland Bapt. Ch., Albuquerque, 1975-78, Parkland Bapt. Ch., Clovis, 1978, Killarney Bapt. Ch., Winter Park, Fla., 1978-86, 1st Bapt. Ch., Lake Worth, Fla., 1986—; pres. So. Bapt. Pastor's Conf., Albuquerque, 1977-78; chmn. com. on order of bus. Fla. Bapt. Conv., 1982-86, Palm Lake Bapt. Assn., 1986-91; chmn. credentials com. So. Bapt. Conv., Orlando, 1985-86. Judge Mother of Yr. Award, N.Mex., 1977; chaplain football team U. Cen. Fla., Orlando, 1985-86; bd. dirs. So. Fla. Fellowship Christian Athletes, 1988-92; trustee Palm Beach Atlantic Coll., West Palm Beach, Fla., 1989-81. Republican. Home: 8300 Blue Cypress Dr Lake Worth FL 33467 Office: 1st Bapt Ch 127 South M St Lake Worth FL 33460

HESTER, JOHN EDWARD, minister; b. Topeka, June 2, 1950; s. John Edward and Lula Christine (Crouch) H.; m. Christi Lane Anderson, July 29, 1972; children: Sharla Lane, Heidi Ann, Jeffrey John. BS, Kans. State U., 1972; MDiv, Ea. Bapt. Theol. Sem., Phila., 1977. Ordained to ministry Am. Bapt. Chs. in U.S.A., 1977. Pastor Trinity Bapt. Ch., Phila., 1974-77, Chicaskia Bapt. Ch., Harper, Kans., 1977-85, 1st Bapt. Ch., Herington, Kans., 1985—; camp dir. for jrs., cen. region Am. Bapt. Chs., Kans., 1979-91, moderator Midwest area, 1980-84; pres. Ministerial Alliance-Harper, 1978-83; sec. Prairie Pantry-Non Profit Corp., Herington, 1990-91. Mem. Herington Ministerial Alliance (sec.-treas. 1985-91), Kiwanis.

HESTER, NORMAN LAWRENCE, minister, adult education educator; b. Durham, N.C., Apr. 21, 1935; s. Clinton Lee and Ruby Aline (Sessoms) H.; m. Catherine Marie Ward, Oct. 6, 1962; children: Bruce Alan, Susan Elaine, David Eugene, Diane Marie. AA, St. Leo's Coll., 1977; Diploma in Pastoral Ministry, New Orleans Bapt. Theol. Sem., 1978; BA in History, Francis Marion Coll., 1986. Ordained to ministry So. Bapt. Conv., 1978; cert. social studies tchr., S.C. Enlisted USAF, 1957, advanced through grades to tech. sgt., 1971; assigned to Castle AFB, Calif., 1957-61, Homestead AFB, Fla., 1961-64, 67-71, Naha Air Base, Okinawa, 1964-67, Cam Rann Bay, Vietnam, 1971-72, Medill AFB, Fla., 1972-77; ret. USAF, 1977; assoc. pastor Bridgedale Bapt. Ch., Metairie, La., 1978-79; pastor Napoleonville (La.) FBC, 1980-83; interim pastor Mont Clare Bapt. Ch., Darlington, S.C., 1984, FBC McColl, S.C., 1984-85; pastor FBC Clio, S.C., 1985—; adult edn. tchr. Marlboro County Sch. Bd., Bennettsville, S.C., 1989—; chmn. com. on coms. Pee Dee Bapt. Assn., Clio, 1986-87, 90-91, missions com., 1989-90, 90-91. Mem. alcohol, drug bd. Assumption Parrish, Napoleonville, La., 1981-83; chmn. exec. bd. Boy Scouts Am., Napoleonville, 1981-83. Recipient Order of the Arrow local lodge Boy Scouts Am., 1982. Mem. Marlboro Ministerial Assn. Democrat. Home: 909 Henrietta St Bennettsville SC 29512 Office: FBC Clio PO Box 218 Clio SC 29525 *Life, the miracle of birth, begins with God, our Heavenly Father. It is only through a personal encounter with God through His son, Jesus Christ, that true life can begin. This is the only way we can do our best in the mission God has for us.*

HETEBRINK, DARROW, pastor; b. Alhambra, Calif., Aug. 19, 1952; s. Harold and Eleanor Hetebrink. AA in Music and BA in Preaching, Pacific Christian Coll., 1987, postgrad. in ministry, 1987—. Ordained to ministry Christian Ch., 1988. Asst. chaplain Chino (Calif.) State Prison Calif. Dept. of Corrections, 1987; chaplain, counselor L.A. County Jail Christian Chaplain Svcs., 1989—; pastor of evangelism Cardiff Ave Christian Ch., L.A., 1988—. Cpl. USMC, 1971-73, Vietnam. Recipient Ch. Growth award Evang. Ch., 1987, Merit awards, 1987, Cert. of Merit Cardiff Ave. Christian Ch., 1991; named one of Outstanding Young Men in Am. Hollywood Street Ministry, 1987. Avocations: camping, fishing, reading, guitar, blues. Home and Office: Cardiff Ave Christian Ch 3645 Cardiff Ave Los Angeles CA 90034

HETZLER, DONALD F., retired minister, consultant; b. Fargo, N.D., Apr. 7, 1923; s. Karl Philip and Rose Elizabeth (Bergeson) H.; m. Marilyn Joyce Jens, June 10, 1950; children: Jens Timothy, John Donald, Paul Thomas. BA, U. Iowa, 1948, MFA, 1960; BTh, Luther Theol. Sem., 1952; DD (hon.), Wittenberg U., 1976. Ordained to ministry Evang. Luth. Ch. in Am., 1952. Pastor Concordia (Kans.) Luth. Ch., 1952-54; campus pastor Luth. Student Found., Iowa City, Iowa, 1954-60; regional sec. Div. Coll. and Univ. Work, Nat. Luth. Coun., Chgo., 1960-66; asst. exec. dir. Nat. Luth. Campus Ministry, Chgo., 1966-68, dir., 1968-76; exec. dir. Associated Ch. Press, Geneva, Ill., 1976-90; dir. pastoral care Luth. Social Svcs. of Ill., 1978-89; mem. youth student work com. Luth. World Fedn., Geneva, Switzerland, 1966-70, chmn., 1968-70; cons. Ctr. for Study Campus Ministry, Valparaiso, Ind., 1971-78; mem. cen. com. World Assn. Christian Communication, London, 1978-81. Chmn. Geneva (Ill.) Human Rels. Com., 1965-68; mem. Community Resources Commn., Geneva, 1977-79; pres. Fox Valley Hospice, St. Charles, Ill., 1984-86. Recipient citation Div. Coll. and Univ. Svcs., Am. Luth. Ch., 1976, citation Ministry to Blacks in Higher Edn., 1976. Mem. Religious Pub. Rels. Coun., Phi Beta Kappa. Democrat. Avocation: art. Home: 127 Ford Geneva IL 60134

HEUTGER, NICOLAUS CARL, canon; b. Rinteln, Hanover, Germany, July 1, 1932; s. Fritz Heutger and Laura (Spanuth) Klein; m. Ursula Reinhard, Feb. 8, 1964; children: Nicolaus, Viola. ThD, U. Münster, Fed. Republic Germany, 1959, Theol. Faculty Montpellier, France, 1968. Pastor St. Martin Ch., Nienburg, Fed. Republic Germany, 1961-82; hon. canon Monastery of Bassum, Fed. Republic Germany, 1973—; lectr. U. Hildesheim, 1973-89; pastor St. Lamberti Ch., Hildesheim, Fed. Republic Germany, 1982—. Author: Evangelische Konvente in den Welfischen Landen, 1961, Das Kloster Amelungsborn, 1968, Die Evangelisch-Theologische Arbeit der Westfalen, 1969, Bursfelde und Seine Reformklöster, 1975. Mem. Nienburg Town Parliament, 1968-71. Lutheran. Lodge: Lions. Home: Kaiser-Friedrich Strasse, D 32 Hildesheim Federal Republic of Germany

HEWITT, JOE B., minister; b. Grants, N.Mex., Aug. 13, 1931; s. Joseph Benjamin and Mahala Grace (Gordon) H.; m. Mary Louise Covert, Sept. 24, 1948; children: Linda E. Hewitt Edwards, Gary R., Deborah J. Hewitt Davies. BD, Arlington (Tex.) Bapt. Coll., 1965; MA, Dallas Bapt. U., 1986. Ordained to ministry, So. Bapt. Conv. Pastor Richardson (Tex.) E. Bapt. Ch., 1963-76; evangelist Joe Hewitt Evang. Assn., Richardson, 1976-80; pastor First Bapt. Ch., Fate, Tex., 1980—; coord. Rockwall County (Tex.) Jail Ministry, 1985—; chmn. interfaith witness com. Dallas Bapt. Assn., 1987-88, mem. resolutions com., 1990—, pres. pastor's conf., 1990—. Author: I Was Raised a Jehovah's Witness, 1979; editor Christian Crusader mag., 1967-73; contbr. articles to profl. jours. Mem. Tex. Alcohol Narcotics Edn. Com. and pub rels. dir., 1967-73. Mem. Tex. Conf. Bapt. Evangelists, Conf. So. Bapt. Evangelists, Tex. Bapt. Hist. Soc., So. Bapt. Hist. Soc., Rockwall Ministerial Alliance (pres. 1990—), Mensa, Rockwall Rep. Men's Club, Dallas Bapt. U. Alumni Assn., OES, Masons. Republican. Home: Prince Ln PO Box 279 Fate TX 75032 Office: First Bapt Ch 813 Holiday PO Box 346 Fate TX 75032

HEWKO, JOHN STEVEN, lay worker; b. Northampton, Pa., Nov. 16, 1954; s. Metro and Anna Mae (Voth) H.; m. Cynthia Joan Barton, June 23, 1989; children: Shanon M. Hansen, Eric R. Hansen, Sheri L. Hansen. AAS in Data Processing, Northampton County Area, Community Coll., 1984. Founder Prepare Unsaved Nihilistic Kids for Jesus, Everett, Wash., 1986—; systems analyst The Boeing Airplane Co., Everett, 1988—. Contbr. articles to jours. Office: PUNKS For Jesus PO Box 310 Everett WA 98206

HEYMANN, WERNER H., religious organization administrator; b. Oberhausen, Rhineland, Germany, July 10, 1910; came to U.S., 1936; s. Albert and Else (Klestadt) H.; m. Alice A. Sachs, May 26, 1940; 1 child, Ruth Heymann Baker. Abitur, Realgymnasium, Germany, 1928. Exec. dir. Hyde Pk. & Kenwood Interfaith Coun., Chgo., 1968—. Trustee Chgo. Sinai Congregation, 1964-72, 86—; mem. exec. bd. Nat. Fedn. Temple Brotherhoods, N.Y.C., 1972-84, chmn. coll. com., 1973-90, hon. mem. exec. bd., 1984—, co-chair coll. com. 1990—; mem. coll. com. Union Am. Hebrew Congregations, 1974—, chmn. coll. com. Chgo. Fedn., 1974. Sgt. U.S. Army, 1943-45. Home: 17 Dogwood Park Forest IL 60466 Office: Hyde Pk and Kenwood Interfaith Coun 1448 E 53d St Chicago IL 60615

HEYNS, J. A., religious organization executive. Moderator, prof. Gen. Synod, Dutch Ref. Ch., Pretoria, Republic of South Africa. Office: Gen Synod, POB 4445, Pretoria 0001, Republic of South Africa*

HEYWARD, JOHN WESLEY, JR., minister; b. Florence, S.C., Nov. 20, 1934; s. John Wayne and Wilhelmena (Wright) H.; m. Dorothy Elizabeth Thompson, Nov. 25, 1961; children: John W. III, Joy-Lynn Patrice. BA, Claflin Coll., 1956; BD, MDiv, Gammon Theol. Sem., 1959; DD (hon.), Claflin Coll., 1976, Cen. Meth. Coll., 1988. Ordained to ministry Meth. Ch. Pastor Old Bethel Meth. Ch., Charleston, S.C., 1959-62, Wesley Meth. Ch., Cheraw, S.C., 1962-65; dist. supt. Charleston Dist., S.C. Conf., 1965-71; assoc. sec. Commn. on Chaplains, Meth. Ch., Washington, 1971-76; sr. pastor Union Meml. United Meth. Ch., St. Louis, 1976-85; dist. supt. Columbia-Mexico Dist. United Meth. Ch., Mexico, Mo., 1985-89; sr. pastor St. John's United Meth. Ch., St. Louis, 1989—; trustee Gammon Theol. Sem., Atlanta, 1970—. Mem. United Svc. Orgn., St. Louis, 1991; trustee Claflin Coll., Orangeburg, S.C., 1989—, Lincoln U., Jefferson City, Mo., 1988—, Cen. Meth. Coll., Fayette, Mo., 1978-87. Col. USAR, 1972—. Crusade scholar Meth. Ch., 1956-58. Mem. Alpha Phi Alpha (chaplain 1978-85), Masons. Home: 6354 Wydown Blvd Clayton MO 63105

HEYWOOD THOMAS, JOHN, theology educator; b. Llanelli, Carmarthenshire, U.K., Nov. 9, 1926; s. David and Anne (Morris) T.; m. Mair Evans, Jan. 12, 1953; 1 child, Nicola Anne. B.A., U. Wales, Aberystwyth, 1947; D.D., 1965; B.D., U. Wales, Carmarthen, 1950; S.T.M., Union Sem., N.Y., 1953. Research fellow in philosophy U. Durham, Eng., 1955-57, reader in div., 1965-74; lectr. in philosophy of religion U. Manchester, Eng., 1957-65; prof. theology U. Nottingham, Eng., 1974—. Author: Subjectivity and Paradox, 1957; Paul Tillich-An Appraisal, 1964; Paul Tillich, 1965. Recipient Swenson-Kierkegaard prize Am. Scandinavia Soc., 1955. Mem. Gorsedd of Bards. Mem. United Reformed Ch. Avocations: gardening; riding; antiques. Home: 5 Manor Ct, Bramcote, Nottingham NG9 3DR, England Office: U Nottingham, University Park, Nottingham NG7 2RD, England

HIAPO, PATRICIA KAMAKA, lay worker; b. Honolulu, May 18, 1943; d. Ward Charles and Violet Kaopua (Nicholas) McKeown; m. Bernard Joseph Hiapo, July 9, 1960; children: Bernard Jr., Beatrice, Jacqueline, Mary-Louise. Grad. high sch., Honolulu. Cert. catechist, 1988. Area del. St. John Apostle and Evangelist, Mililani, Hawaii, 1981-84; eucharistic min. St. John Apostle and Evangelist, Mililani, 1981-88; hospice and bereavement ministry St. Francis Hosp., Honolulu, 1983, eucharistic min., 1983-88; religious edn. coord. Resurrection of The Lord, Waipahu, Hawaii, 1984-88; dir.

religious edn. St. Jude, Ewa Beach, Hawaii, 1988—; home visitor Hana Like, Honolulu, 1990—; mem. marriage encounter team Cath. Ch., Honolulu, 1981-83. Recipient award Out Lady of Peace, 1991. Office: St Jude 92-104 Leipapa Way Ewa Beach HI 96707 also: Parents and Children Together-Hana Like 45-955 Kamehameha Hwy Ste 404 Kaneohe HI 96744

HIATT, CHARLES MILTON, seminary president; b. Greeley, Colo., July 28, 1949; m. Janelle Wacker, June 20, 1969; children: Tim, Jon, Aaron. Student, U. No. Colo., 1967-69; BA, Sioux Falls Coll., 1971; MDiv, N.Am. Bapt. Sem., 1974; postgrad., Adelphi U., 1979, Warren Deem Inst. Theol. Edn. Mgmt., 1983; DD, Judson Coll., 1985; postdoctoral studies, Ariz. State U., 1989-90. Ordained to ministry N.Am. Bapt. Conf., 1974. Pastor 1st Bapt. Ch., Emery, S.D., 1974-79; v.p. for devel. N.Am. Bapt. Sem., Sioux Falls, S.D., 1979-82, pres., 1982—; speaker to various confs., retreats. Bd. dirs. Kilian Community Coll., 1975-89, Food Svc. Ctr./Food Pantry, 1985-89; div. leader local United Way, 1982, 85, 87; mem. exec. com. Sioux empire Billy Graham Crusade, 1987. Mem. Fellowship Evang. Sem. Pres., Bapt. World Alliance (com. on devel. and promotion), Rotary. Avocations: gardening, golf, computers. Office: N Am Bapt Sem Office of the President 1321 W 22nd St Sioux Falls SD 57105

HIBBS, JACK DUANE, JR., youth and music minister, educator; b. Akron, Oh., Apr. 30, 1956; s. Jack Duane and Barbara Ann (Scales)H. BS in edn., Concordia Coll., 1978. Cert. tchr., Fla. Tchr. Bethany Lutheran Ch. and Sch., Hollywood, Calif., 1978-79; tchr. Hope Lutheran Ch. and Sch., Pompano, Fla., 1979-85, min. youth and music, 1985—; Dir. music Hope Luth. sch. 1979–. Recipient Outstander Tchr., Pompano Chamber Commerce 1989. Mem. Am. Guild English Handbell Ringers, FL/GA Dist. Tchrs. Conf. Republican. Lutheran Church-Missouri Synod. Office: Hope Lutheran Church & Sch 1840 NE 41 St Pompano FL 33064

HIBBS, WILLIAM ERNEST, III, priest; b. Norfolk, Va., Sept. 28, 1950; s. William Edward Hibbs; BBA, George Washington U., 1970; ThM, U. St. Thomas, Houston, 1976; MBA, Harvard U., 1986. Ordained priest Roman Cath. Ch., 1975. Sec., treas. Interfaith Council on Human Rights, Washington, 1978—, Mandinka Village Projects, Inc., Balt., 1978; chmn., co-exec. dir. Washington based Nat. Ecumenical Coalition, Inc., 1976-88; pres. Nat. AIDS Bereavement Ctr., Arlington, Va., 1988—. Exec. producer The AIDS Digest, 1990—. Active Boy Scouts Am.; bd. dirs. Balt. Theatre Festival; bd. dirs. Balt. Performing Arts Workshop Assn. Mem. Am. Soc. Assn. Execs., Internat. Platform Assn.

HICK, JOHN HARWOOD, theologian, philosopher, educator; b. Scarborough, Yorkshire, Eng., Jan. 20, 1922; came to U.S., 1979; s. Mark Day and Mary Aileen (Hirst) H.; m. Joan Hazel Bowers, Aug. 30, 1953; children: Eleanor, Mark, Peter, Michael (dec.). MA, Edinburgh (Scotland) U., 1948, DLitt., 1975; DPhil, Oxford (Eng.) U., 1950; postgrad., Westminster Theol. Coll., 1950-53; PhD, Cambridge U., 1964; Theol.Dr. (hon.), Uppsala U., 1977. Ordained to ministry United Reformed Ch. (Eng.), 1953. Min. Belford Presbyn. Ch., Northumberland, Eng., 1953-56; asst. prof. philosophy Cornell U., Ithaca, N.Y., 1956-59; Stuart Prof. Christian philosophy Princeton (N.J.) Theol. Seminary, 1959-64; lectr./divinity Cambridge U., U.K., 1964-67; H.G. Wood prof. theology Birmingham (Eng.) U., 1967-82; Danforth prof. philosophy of religion Claremont (Calif.) Grad. Sch., 1979-92; Mead-Swing lectr. Oberlin Coll., 1962; Mary Farnum Brown lectr. Haverford Coll., 1964; James W. Richard lectr. U. Va., 1969; Arthur Stanley Eddington Meml. lectr. Cambridge U., 1972, Stanton lectr., 1974-77; Teape lectr. New Delhi U., 1975; Ingersoll lectr. Harvard U., 1977; Hope lectr. Stirling U., 1977; Younghusband lectr., London, 1977; Mackintosh lectr. East Anglia U., 1978; Riddell lectr. Newcastle U., 1979; Montefiore lectr. U. London, 1980; Brooks lectr. U. So. Calif., 1982; Nebuhr lectr. Elmhurst Coll., 1986; Gifford lectr. U. Edinburgh, 1986-87; Kegley lectr. Calif. State U., Bakersfield, 1988; Fritz Marti lectr. U. So. Ill., 1989; Birks lectr. McGill U., 1989; Resler lectr. Ohio State U., 1991; vis. prof. Benares Hindu U., Visva-Bharati U., Punjabi U., India, U. Sri Lanka, Goa U., India; vis. fellow Brit. Acad. Overseas, 1974, 90; select preacher Oxford U., 1970; Hulsean preacher Cambridge U., 1969. Author: Faith and Knowledge, 1957, 2d edit., 1966, Philosophy of Religion, 1963, 4th edit., 1990, Evil and the God of Love, 1966, 2d edit., 1977, Death and Eternal Life, 1976, An Interpretation of Religion, 1989. Chmn., pres. All Faiths for One Race, Birmingham, Eng., 1972-73, 80-85. Guggenheim fellow, 1963-64, 85-86, Leverhulme Rsch. fellow, 1976, 90, fellow Inst. for Advanced Rsch. in Humanities, Birmingham U., U.K.; recipient Grawemeyer award in religion, 1991. Mem. Am. Acad. Religion, Am. Philos. Assn., Soc. for the Study of Theology U.K. (pres. 1975-76), Royal Inst. Philosophy, Am. Soc. for the Study of Religion, West Coast Theol. Soc. Office: Claremont Grad Sch Claremont CA 91711

HICKEY, CATHERINE JOSEPHINE, school system administrator; b. N.Y.C., Mar. 14, 1936; d. John James and Delia Bridget (Finnegan) Tighe; m. Stephen M. Hickey, Mar. 30, 1959; children: Catherine, Marie, Joanne, Clare, Geraldine, Margaret. BS, Fordham U., 1958, PhD, 1983; MS, CUNY, 1974; LHD (hon.), Mercy Coll., 1991. Prin. Sacred Heart Sch., Dobbs Ferry, N.Y., 1977-89; instr., adj. prof. Mercy Coll., Dobbs Ferry, 1983-87, Long Island U., Dobbs Ferry, 1984-87, Fairfield (Conn.) U., 1984-87; supt. schs. Archdiocese of N.Y., N.Y.C., 1989—. Roman Catholic. Home: 415 Marlborough Rd Yonkers NY 10701 Office: Archdiocese NY 1011 1st Ave New York NY 10022

HICKEY, DALE EUGENE, minister; b. Nampa, Idaho, Jan. 26, 1942; s. Earl Denzil Hickey and Mary Kathryn (Smith) Kennedy; m. Suzy Mae Ayers, Aug. 10, 1963. B of Religion, Calif. Bapt. Coll., 1972; MEd, Azusa Pacific U., 1974. Tchr., vice-prin. Brethren Elem. and Jr. High Sch., Whittier, Calif., 1971-75; minister Mandaria Bapt. Ch., L.A., 1970-74; prin., asst. pastor Capastrano Valley Bapt. Ch., 1975-81; pastor Chapman Ave. Bapt. Ch., Garden Grove, Calif., 1981—; adminstr. Re-Teen Learning Ctr., Garden Grove, 1975—; dir. evangelism United Evang. Chs., Monrovia, Calif., 1966-69; dir. spl. edn. Family Enrichment Inst., Anaheim, Calif., 1976—. Author: Great Opportunities in Soul Winning, 1968, (personality test) Kingsdale Personality Profile, 1987. Police chaplain Garden Grove Police, 1982-88; hosp. chaplain Garden Grove Med. Ctr., 1981-85. Recipient Cert. of Honor Korean Am. Coun., 1991. Republican. Home: 11891 Melody Pk Garden Grove CA 92640 Office: Chapman Ave Bapt Ch 10241 Chapman Ave Garden Grove CA 92640

HICKEY, DENNIS WALTER, bishop; b. Dansville, N.Y., Oct. 28, 1914; s. Walter Morris and Aloysia (Sullivan) H. B.A., Colgate Univ., 1935; postgrad. St. Bernard's, 1941. Ordained priest Roman Catholic Ch., 1941; asst. pastor St. Mary's Ch., Auburn, N.Y., 1941-46; notary Diocesan Tribunal, Rochester, N.Y., 1946-61; pastor St. Theodore Ch., Rochester, 1961-68; consecrated bishop, 1968; aux. bishop Diocese of Rochester, 1968-89; pastor St. Thomas More Ch., Rochester, 1982-85; gen. mgr. Courier-Jour., 1985. Address: 415 Ames St Rochester NY 14611

HICKEY, GREGORY JOSEPH, priest, educational administrator; b. Darby, Pa., Aug. 10, 1947; s. Joseph Thomas and Helen Gertrude (Lockard) H. BA, Temple U., 1973; MDiv, St. Charles Sem., 1979; MA, Villanova U., 1989. Ordained priest Roman Cath. Ch., 1979. Tchr. St. Patrick Grade Sch., Norristown, Pa., 1969-74; mem. ednl. testing staff Montgomery County I.U., Norristown, 1972-73, Phila. I.U., 1974-75; asst. pastor Sts. Simon & Jude Ch., Westtown, Pa., 1979-81, St. Augustine Ch., Bridgeport, Pa., 1981-82, St. Leo Ch., Phila., 1982-87; tchr. Cardinal Dougherty High Sch., Phila., 1987-88; campus minister Bishop Conwell High Sch., Levittown, Pa., 1988-90; dir. studies St. Hubert High Sch., Phila., 1990-91; tchr. Cardinal Dougherty High Sch., 1991—. Mem. Nat. Assn. Secondary Sch. Prins., ASCD, Nat. Cath. Edn. Assn., Ancient Order Hibernians, Kappa Delta Pi. Republican. Avocations: physical fitness, music, theater, reading. Home: 3160 Gaul St Philadelphia PA 19134

HICKEY, JAMES ALOYSIUS CARDINAL, archbishop; b. Midland, Mich., Oct. 11, 1920; s. James P. and Agnes (Ryan) H. J.C.D., Lateran U., Italy, 1950; S.T.D., Angelicum U., Italy, 1951; M.A., Mich. State U., 1962. Ordained priest Roman Catholic Ch., 1946; sec. to Bishop of Saginaw, 1951-60; rector St. Paul Sem., Saginaw, Mich., 1960-68; aux. bishop Saginaw, 1967-69; chmn. bishops' com. on Priestly Formation, 1968-69; rector N.Am. Coll., Rome, 1969-74; bishop of Cleve., 1974-80, archbishop of Washington, 1980—; chancellor Cath. U. Am., 1980—; elevated to cardinal, 1988; mem. Cen. Com. for 1975 Holy Year, 1973-75; chmn. Bishop's Com. Pastoral Rsch. and Practices, 1974-77, Bishop's Com. for Doctrine, 1979-82; chmn. bd. trustees Nat. Shrine of Immaculate Conception, 1980—; chmn. Bishops' Com. Human Values, 1984-87; chmn. Bishop's Com. on N.Am. Coll., 1988—. Episcopal advisor to Serra Internat., 1981-88; Episcopal moderator Holy Childhood Assn., 1984—; chmn. N. Am. Coll. Bd. Govs., 1988—. Address: Archdiocese Washington Archdiocesan Pastoral Ctr PO Box 29260 Washington DC 20017

HICKEY, SISTER RUTH CECELIA, religious administrator; b. Erie, Pa., July 28, 1914; d. Sherman Sylvester and Nell (McKinney) H. Grad., St. Vincent's Sch. Nursing, Toledo, 1936; B.S., d'Youville Coll., U. Montreal, 1949; postgrad., Cath. U., 1950, U. B.C.; M.A., Columbia U., 1954. Head nurse medicine-surgery St. Vincent Hosp. and Med. Center, Toledo, 1936-38; nursing service and asst. adminstr. St. Vincent Hosp. and Med. Center, 1956-62, adminstr., 1962-69; nursing cons., 1969—; asso. exec. dir. St. Boniface Gen. Hosp., Winnipeg, Man., Can., 1973-79; v.p. St. Boniface Gen. Hosp., 1974-79, Taché Nursing Center, Winnipeg, 1974-79; regional sec. Can. Religious Conf., Winnipeg, 1979—; nursing instr. St. Mary's Hosp., Montreal, 1940-42; supr. obstetrics, surgery St. Peter's Gen. Hosp., New Brunswick, 1942-47; dir. sch. nursing and nursing service Regina Grey Nuns Hosp., Regina, Sask., Can., 1955-56. Bd. dirs., v.p. Bd. Catholic Hosps. Can., 1974—; bd. dirs. Canadian Council Hosp. Accreditation; bd. govs. U. Man., 1976—; bd. dirs. Sara Riel Corp., 1983—. Named Toledo Woman of Year, 1969. Fellow Am. Coll. Hosp. Adminstrs.; mem. Am. Acad. Med. Adminstrs., Canadian Hsop. Assn. (dir.), Am.), Ohio hosp. nurses assns., Am., Ohio nurses assns., Nat. Assembly Women Religious Edn., Cath. Health Assn. Man. (pres. 1974—). Address: #2 366 Enfield Crescent, Winnipeg, MB Canada R2H 1C7

HICKMAN, CAROLYN BURRELL GRANGER, lay worker; b. Denver, Jan. 30, 1920; d. Frank Rollins and Elizabeth Hall (Slattery) Chedsey Granger; m. John Everette Hickman, Jan. 12, 1943; children: Mary Elizabeth Hickman Golden, Rollins Granger. BS, U. Utah, 1941. Treas. Women's Aux., Denver, 1947-50; sec. Women's Aux., Fort Collins, Colo., 1951-56; directress Altar Guild, Fort Collins, 1956-60; treas. Episcopal Ch. Women Moscow, Idaho, 1970-72; chmn. bd. Campus Christian Ctr., Moscow, 1972-76, 76-78; diocesan treas. United Thank Offering Diocese of Spokane, 1976-79; diocesan dir. Ch. Periodical Club, 1980-85, province v.p., 1985-88, triennial del., Anaheim, 1985 ; synod del. Province 8, 1981-83, triennial province del., 1978-84; diocesan conv. del. St. Mark's, Moscow, 1974-75, 87-90, triennial del. Mpls., 1976, Denver, 1979, New Orleans, 1982—, sr. warden, 1989-91, alt. to gen. con., Phoenix, 1991; del. to electing conv. for Bishop Coajutor for Diocese of Spokane, 1990, alt. mem. diocesan nominating com., 1990, election com. for Bishop Coajutor, 1990, mem. Diocesan Task Force on Human Sexuality. Neighborhood chmn. Girl Scouts U.S.A., Greeley, Colo., 1962, leader troop, 1962-69. Mem. Am. Soc. Clin. Pathologists (registered med. technologist), Med. Technologists Faculty Women (Fort Collins, treas. 1956), Panhellenic (Greeley, sec. pres. 1956-57). Home: 807 Mabelle St Moscow ID 83843

HICKMAN, HOYT LEON, minister; b. Pitts., May 22, 1927; s. Leon Edward and Mayme (Hoyt) H.; B.A. magna cum laude, Haverford Coll., 1950; M.Div. cum laude, Yale U., 1953; S.T.M., Union Theol. Sem., 1954; D.D. (hon.), Morningside Coll., 1978; m. Martha Jean Whitmore, Dec. 16, 1950; children—Peter, John, Stephen, Mary. Ordained to ministry Meth. Ch., 1953; pastor 1st Meth. Ch., Windber, Pa., 1954-57, Claysville and Stony Point Meth. Chs., Claysville, Pa., 1957-59, Coll. Hill Meth. Ch., Beaver Falls, Pa., 1959-64, Cascade United Meth. Ch., Erie, Pa., 1964-72; dir. office local ch. worship, bd. discipleship United Meth. Ch., Nashville, 1972-78, asst. gen. sec. bd. discipleship, 1978-85, dir. resource devel. bd. discipleship, 1985—; exec. sec. Commn. on Worship, United Meth. Ch., 1968-72; mem. Commn. on Worship, World Meth. Council, 1971-81; mem. nat. program com. Christian Family Movement, 1969-73; pres. Erie County Council Chs., 1970-71. Bd. dirs. Liturgical Conf., 1973-80. Served with USN, 1945-46. Mem. Phi Beta Kappa. Democrat. Author: At the Lord's Table, 1981, Strengthening Our Congregation's Worship, 1981, United Methodist Altars, 1984, A Primer for Church Worship, 1984, The Acolyte's Book, 1985, Holy Communion, 1987, Planning Worship Each Week, 1988, Worship Resources of the United Methodist Hymnal, 1989, Workbook on Communion and Baptism, 1990, Being a Communion Steward, 1991, United Methodist Worship, 1991; co-author: Handbook of the Christian Year; contbr. numerous articles to mags. Home: 2034 Castleman Dr Nashville TN 37215 Office: PO Box 840 Nashville TN 37202

HICKMAN, RUTH VIRGINIA, Bible educator; b. Sac City, Iowa, Oct. 15, 1931; d. Ronald Minor and Ida E. (Willcutt) Wilson; m. Charles Ray Hickman, Aug. 25, 1962; children: Ronald Everett, Lisa Michelle. BS in Home Econs., Morningside Coll., 1953. Ordained to ministry Christian Ch., 1985. Staff coord., tchr. Life for Layman, Denver, 1974-77; founder, tchr. Abundant Word Ministries, Lakewood, Colo., 1980—; tchr. Bible Calvary Temple, Denver, 1980—; sales/trainer Hillestad Internat., San Jose, Calif., 1978—; bd. dirs. Morningstar Counseling, Lakewood; women's com. Billy Graham Assn., Denver, 1986-87. Author: (book) Hope for Hurting People, 1987; speaker, instr. audio and video tape series, 1980—. Mem. Rocky Mountain Fellowship Christian Leaders. Republican. Home: 3043 S Holly Pl Denver CO 80222 Office: Abundant Word Ministries 6900 W Alameda # 107 Lakewood CO 80226

HICKMAN, TIMOTHY MARK, broadcasting executive; b. Bristol, Va., Dec. 3, 1961; s. John Franklin and Peggy Faye (Cantel) H. Student, East Tenn. State U. Program dir., announcer Sta. WBCV Gospel Radio, Bristol, 1982—. Office: Sta WBCV Radio PO Box 68 26 1/2 6th St Bristol TN 37621

HICKOX, PHILIP HOMER, minister, educator; b. Jamestown, N.Y., May 25, 1949; s. Homer Charles and Hazel Evelyn (Anderson) H.; m. Diane Claudia Jaffy, Apr. 12, 1986. AA, Jamestown Community Coll., 1970; cert. in ministerial studies, Berean Sch. of Bible, 1978; D in Ministry, Internat. Bible Sem., 1985; A in Bibl. Studies, Jamestown Sch. of Theology, 1984; D in Biblical Studies, Sungrove Bible Coll., 1984. Ordained to ministry Pentecostal Ch., 1986. Sr. pastor Living Waters Open Bible Ch., Jamestown, 1987—; sectional rep. No. Allegheny Dist. Open Bible Standard Chs., 1986-91; chmn. Chautauqua County Jail Chaplaincy Com., Mayville, N.Y., 1975-84; pres. Greater Jamestown Area Pentecostal Fellowship of N.Am., 1988-89; chmn. Greater Jamestown-Warren Area Nat. Assn. of Evangs., 1987-89; advisors Jamestown Full Gospel Businessman's Internat. Chpt., 1988-89; pres. Jamestown Sch. of Theology, 1981—; founder, dir. Calvary Hotline, Jacob's Well Coffeehouse, Jamestown, 1973-78; speaker at numerous confs. Contbr. articles to profl. jours. Coord., dir. People That Care Ctr. (Food Bank), Jamestown, 1989—; registered vol. Attica (N.Y.) State Correctional Facility, 1986—; foster parent Chautauqua County Foster Parents Assn., Mayville, 1989—; trustee New Hope Ministries to Ex-Inmates, Jamestown, 1990—; bd. dirs. Haiti for Jesus (Missionary Outreach), Jamestown, 1986-88. Mem. Women's Christian Assn. Hosp. Vis. Chaplains. Republican. Office: Living Waters Open Bible Ch Rd 4 946 Southwestern Dr Jamestown NY 14701-9431 *We possess the power of life and death in the words that we speak about our physical, psychological and spiritual circumstances and those in the lives of others. If we speak words of encouragement and positive confessions then that will be the outcome.*

HICKS, BARBARA ALICE, librarian; b. Albershot, Hants, Eng., Jan. 20, 1933; came to U.S., 1956; d. Charles B. and Mary H. (Paterson) Findlay; m. Michael K. Hicks, Dec. 28, 1962; children: Jennifer, Margaret, Sarah. ALA, Sch. Librarianship, U. Loughborough, Eng., 1954; BA in Philosophy, U. Western Ont., Can., 1960; ALA, Lib. Assn . Gt. Britain. Sec. student christian movement U. Toronto, Ont., Can., 1960-62; chief libr. St. Paul U., Ottawa, Ont., Can., 1986—; convener St. Michael's Ward Sisters of St. John, 1979-81; book convenor Lay Sch. of Theology, Ottawa, 1979-85; dep. warden St. John's Anglican Ch., Ottawa, 1979-83. Mem. Canterbury House Bookrooms, Ottawa, 1978-84. Mem. Am. Theol. Libr. Assn., Can. Libr. Assn. Office: St Paul U, 223 Main St, Ottawa, ON Canada KIS 1C4

HICKS, C. J., bishop. Bishop Ch. of God in Christ, Macon, Ga. Office: Ch of God in Christ 1894 Madden Ave Macon GA 31204*

HICKS, CULLEN L., bishop. Gen. supt., bishop Congl. Holiness Ch., Griffin, Ga. Office: Congregational Holiness Ch 3888 Fayetteville Hwy Griffin GA 30223*

HICKS, DAVID GREGORY, pastor; b. Newnan, Ga., Sept. 8, 1958; s. Theron David and Shirley Fae (Frazier) H.; m. Melanie Jon Ronas, Sept. 6, 1986; children: Jonathan David, Laura Ashlyn. BS in Edn., Auburn U., 1982; MDiv, Southwestern Bapt. Theol. Sem., Ft. Worth, 1986; postgrad., Fuller Theol. Sem., Pasadena, Calif., 1990—. Ordained to ministry So. Bapt. Conv., 1988; cert. tchr., Ga. Sponsor Fellowship Christian Athletes, College Park, Ga., 1982-83; student ch. planter home mission bd. So. Bapt. Conv., Columbus, Ohio, 1985; tchr. Sheridan Hills Christian Sch., Hollywood, Fla., 1986-87; assoc. pastor ch. growth Orange Hill Bapt. Ch., Austell, Ga., 1988—. Mem. South Cobb Leadership Inst., Mableton, Ga., 1990—. Mem. Kappa Delta Pi. Home: 1492 Ashlyn Ct Austell GA 30001 Office: Orange Hill Bapt Ch 4293 Austell Rd Austell GA 30001

HICKS, HERBERT RAY, minister; b. Sardinia, Ohio, Oct. 21, 1939; s. James Blackburn and Lavina Marie (Donohoo) H.; m. Shirley McCleese, Mar. 25, 1960; 1 child, John Mark Hicks. AB, Cin. Christian Coll., 1962; BTh, Cin. Christian Sem., 1963; M in Div. with honors, Lexington Theol. Sem., 1968, D in Min., 1972. Ordained to ministry Christian Ch., 1968. Pastor 1st Chirstian Ch., Clifton Forge, Va., 1972-76; pastor Graham Christian Ch., Bluefield, Va., 1976-83, Zanesville, Ohio, 1983—. Author: An Historical Study of The Society of Friends, 1968. Lodge: Rotary, Masons, Shriners. Avocation: computer programming. Office: 1st Christian Ch 3000 Dresden Rd Zanesville OH 43701

HICKS, JOHN MARK, religion educator; b. Ft. Sumner, N.Mex., July 15, 1957; s. Mark N. and Lois Edith (Fox) H.; m. Sheila Christine Pettit, May 22, 1977 (dec. Apr. 1980); m. Barbara Elaine Adcox, Nov. 27, 1983; children: Ashley D., Joshua Mark, Rachel N. AA, BA, Freed-Hardeman Coll., Henderson, Tenn., 1976, 77; MA in Religion, Westminster Theol. Sem., Phila., 1979; MA, Western Ky. U., Bowling Green, 1980; PhD, Westminster Theol. Sem., Phila., 1985. Ordained to ministry Ch. of Christ, 1977. Minister N.E. Phila. Ch. of Christ, 1977-79, 81-82; asst. prof. Ala. Christian Sch. Religion, Montgomery, 1982-89; minister Prattville (Ala.) Ch. of Christ, 1983-89; assoc. prof. Magnolia Bible Coll., Kosciusko, Miss., 1989-91; assoc. prof. Christian Doctrine Grad. Sch. Religion, Harding U., Memphis, 1991—; dir. Rsch. Found. for Advance Bibl. Studies, DeFuniak Springs, Fla., 1987-89. Author: Woman's Role in the Church, 1978; contbr. articles to profl. jours. Mem. Am. Soc. Ch. History, Sixteenth Century, Evangelical Theol. Soc. Republican. Mem. Ch. of Christ. Avocations: racquetball, softball, computers. Home: 1838 Myrna Ln Memphis TN 38117 Office: Harding U Grad Sch Religion 1000 Cherry Rd Memphis TN 38117

HICKS, KENNETH WILLIAM, bishop; b. LaHarpe, Kans., June 18, 1923; s. Earl Franklin and Ertie Leona (Williams) H.; m. Lila Elaine Goodwin, Aug. 11, 1946; children: Linda Diane, Debra Dawn. B.A., York (Nebr.) Coll., 1947; M.Th., Iliff Sch. Theology, Denver, 1953; D.D. (hon.), Nebr. Wesleyan U., 1970, Westmar Coll., LeMars, Iowa, 1977; LL.D. (hon.), Philander Smith Coll., 1978; DD (hon.), Baker U., 1989. Ordained to ministry United Methodist Ch., 1952; pastor chs. in Nebr. and Colo., 1945-68; dist. supt. Central dist. United Meth. Ch., Kearney, Nebr., 1968-73; sr. pastor Trinity United Meth. Ch., Grand Island, Nebr., 1973-76; bishop Ark. area United Meth. Ch., Little Rock, 1976-84; bishop Kans. area United Meth. Ch., Topeka, 1984—. Trustee St. Paul Sch. Theology, Kansas City, Mo., Hendrix Coll., Conway, Ark., Meth. Hosp., Memphis, Philander Smith Coll., Little Rock; trustee Lydia Patterson Inst., El Paso, Tex.; trustee Meth. Children's Home, Little Rock; chmn. United Negro Coll. Fund Ark., 1977. Named Alumnus of Year Iliff Sch. Theology, 1977. Democrat. Clubs: Lions, Rotary, Shriners. Office: United Meth Ch 4201 SW 15th St Topeka KS 66604 *To love others, we must first have a sense of what it is to love one's self; otherwise, a fragmented self will generate a fragmented, untrusting response. The world will be helped through selfless giving of persons who know inner security.*

HICKS, MARILYN SUE, lay worker; b. Clarksville, Tenn., Mar. 21, 1949; d. Roy Davis and La Una Gertrude (Powers) Wright; m. James Ray Hicks, July 5, 1970; children: Jason, Susan, Stephen. Student, Trevecca Nazarene Coll., Nashville, Ind. U., 1991—. Children's dir. Grace Ch. of Nazarene, Nashville, 1971-72; youth dir. 1st Ch. of Nazarene, Bloomington, Ind., 1988—, sec., del., 1989—. Author song I Want To Be More Like You, 1990; contbr. articles to newsletter. Mem. Nazarene World Mission Soc. (treas. S.W. Ind. Dist. 1990-91). Home: 1105 Allendale Dr Bloomington IN 47401 Office: 1st Ch of Nazarene 700 W Howe St Bloomington IN 47403 *I always look at the positives in life and smile at whatever comes my way. God has given us each day, and if we dwell on the negatives, we will miss what He wants to give us.*

HICKS, ROBERT MICHAEL, religion educator, counselor; b. Wichita, Kans., Feb. 22, 1945; s. Charles Nehemiah and Ermagene Virginia (Riley) H.; m. Cynthia Ann Bliss, May 30, 1969; children: Charis, Ashley, Graham. BA, Emporia State U., 1968; MTh, Dallas Theol. Sem., 1976, D of Ministry, 1988; postgrad., U. Hawaii, 1979-80, Villanova U., 1991. Sr. pastor Faith Bapt. Ch., Kailua, Hawaii, 1978-81; min., counselor Ch. of the Saviour, Wayne, Pa., 1986-90; prof. Internat. Coll., Honolulu, 1976-78, Dallas Theol. Sem., 1981-86, Sem. of the East, Dresher, Pa., 1990—; exec. dir. Life Counseling Svcs., Wayne, 1987—; chaplain Air N.G., Hawaii, Tex., Pa., 1979—; dir. counseling Art of Family Living Radio, Dallas, 1982-84; coordinating chaplain Delta 191 crash Dallas-Ft. Worth Airport, Dallas, 1985. Author: Uneasy Manhood, 1991; author: (with others) Husbands & Wives, 1988; contbr. articles to mags. Disaster chaplain ARC, Dallas, 1985; researcher Family Rsch. Coun., Washington, 1985—; steering com. Govs.-Mayors Prayer Breakfast, Honolulu, 1978. Lt. col. USAFR, 1979—. Mem. AACD, Air Force Assn. (life), Soc. for Traumatic Stress Studies, Mil. Chaplain Assn., Armed Forces Communication and Electronics Assn. (chaplain 1986—), Pa. Counseling Assn., Profs. Christian Edn. Assn., Lancers Club, Officers Club. Republican. Home: 496 Black Swan Lane Berwyn PA 19312 Office: Sem of the East PO Box 611 Dresher PA 19025 *Life is but a loan...a loan from God, our Creator, Sustainer and Redeemer. What we do with the loan is our choice and our vocation. We can abuse or use the loan but we will never obtain another in the temporal. Doxa Christo.*

HICKS, ROGER ANDREW, minister; b. Joliet, Ill., Nov. 3, 1957; s. Hershal and Lela Valentine (Letterman) H.; m. Sarah Jane Haviland, Jan. 17, 1981; children: Jenny, Rachel, Glorya, Andrew, Jeremiah. BA, SE Bapt. U., Bolivar, Mo., 1982. Ordained to ministry So. Bapt. Conv. Pastor 1st Bapt. Ch., Niangua, Mo., 1979-81, West Finley Bapt. Ch., Fordland, Mo., 1981-84, Calvary Bapt. Ch., Marshfield, Mo., 1984—; farmer Oakbrook Farms Inc., Niangua. Home: RR 1 Box 237 Niangua MO 65713 Office: Calvary Bapt Ch Marshfield MO 65713

HICKS, SHERMAN GREGORY, bishop; b. Bklyn., June 22, 1946; s. Charles Sr. and Sarah Mae (Rollins) H.; m. Anna Marie Peck, Sept. 12, 1970; children: Andrea, Geoffrey, Christopher. BA, Wittenberg U., 1968; MDiv, Hamma Sch. Theology, 1973; DD (hon.), Carthage Coll., 1988, Elmhurst Coll., 1989, Wittenberg U., 1990. Ordained to ministry Luth. Ch., 1973. Pastor Concordia Luth. Ch., Buffalo, 1973-77; co-pastor Holy Trinity Luth. Ch., East Orange, N.J., 1977-79; asst. to bishop Ill. Synod, Luth. Ch. Am., Chgo., 1979-87; bishop Met. Chgo. Synod, Evang. Luth. Ch. in Am., Chgo., 1988—. Pres. Interfaith Coun. for Homeless, Chgo., 1988, AIDS Nat. Interfaith Network, 1991; trustee Carthage Coll., Kenosha, Wis., 1988; bd. dirs. Luth. Social Svcs. Ill., 1988—; mem. Coun. Religious Leaders, Chgo., 1988—. Named One of Outstanding Young Men in Am., Jaycees, 1974. Office: Evang Luth Ch Met Chgo Synod 18 S Michigan Chicago IL 60603 *In my experiences with life I have discovered that there are three very basic questions that we humans have the need to know answers for: (1) Who am I? (2) For what purpose am I here? (3) What am I going to do? Within the context of our faith we can find the answers.*

HIEB, MARIANNE, art therapist, spiritual director; b. Phila., May 7, 1946; d. John Thomas and Mary A. (Byrne) H. BA, Gwynedd-Mercy, 1971; MFA, Catholic U., 1979. Registered art therapist; cert. expressive therapist; cert. spiritual dir. Shalem Inst. Spiritual Formation. Novice Sisters of

Mercy, Merion, Pa., 1966-69; tchr. Gwynedd Mercy Acad., Gwynedd Valley, Pa., 1971-76; art therapist Mercy Cath. Med. Ctr., Darby, 1979-83, staff Mercy sponsorship, 1983—; coord. spirituality programs Our Lady of Lourdes Wellness Ctr., Camden, N.J., 1986—; mem. retreat team Our Lady of Lourdes Wellness Ctr., Camden, 1980—; cons. art therapy The Bridge, Camden, 1983-85. Represented in thesis show "Seeds", 1979. Mem. Internat. Assn. Artists-Therapists, Am. Art Therapy Assn., Nat. Expressive Therapy Assn., Internat. Registry Woman Religious Artists. Roman Catholic. Avocations: oil painting, pottery, poetry, reading. Home: 515 Montgomery Ave Merion PA 19066 Office: Our Lady of Lourdes Wellness Ctr 1600 Haddon Ave Camden NJ 08103

HIEBERT, CLARENCE ROY, religion educator; b. Winnipeg, Man., Can., July 12, 1927; came to U.S., 1940; s. Cornelius N. and Tina C. (Harms) H.; m. Ferne F. Kornelsen, Jan. 9, 1950; children: Tim, Bob, Beth, Sue. BA, Tabor Coll., 1949; S.T.B., N.Y. Theol. Sem., 1954; MA, Phillips U., 1959; PhD, Case-Western Res. U., 1971. Pastor Mennonite Brethen Ch., Enid, Okla., 1954-59; pastor, prof. Mennonite Cen. Com., Western Europe, 1959-61; prof. Tabor Coll., Hillsboro, Kans., 1962—. Author: The Holdeman People, 1972, M.B. Church, Henderson, Ne., 1979; editor, compiler: Brothers Indeed, 1973; co-editor: International Songbook, 1978. Recipient Danforth Assocs. award Danforth Found., 1990. Mem. Am. Acad. Religion. Mennonite Brethren. *Authentic Christ-faith must be expressed in a disciplined momentum toward faithful Christ-following, including those Christ-directives that move Christians in counter-stream to some of society's accepted norms.*

HIERS, RICHARD HYDE, lawyer, religious writer; b. Phila., Apr. 8, 1932; s. Glen Sefton and Mildred (Douthitt) H.; m. Jane Leslie Gale, Jan. 30, 1954; children: Peter Leslie, Rebecca Hathaway. BA magna cum laude, Yale U., 1954, BD cum laude, 1957, MA, PhD, 1959, 61; JD with high honors, U. Fla., 1983. Bar: Fla. 1984, U.S. Dist. Ct. (we. dist.) Tex. 1988, U.S. Ct. Appeals (5th cir.) 1988. Asst. prof. Coll. Liberal Arts and Scis. U. Fla., Gainesville, 1961-66, assoc. prof., 1966-72, prof., 1972—, acting chair dept. religion, 1981-82, mem. faculty doctoral rsch., 1970—; jud. law clk. U.S. Ct. Appeals, Austin, Tex., 1987-88. Author: Kingdom of God in the Synoptic Tradition, 1970, Jesus and the Future, 1981, Reading the Bible Book by Book, 1988, 2 other books; co-author/co-editor 2 books; contbr. numerous articles and book revs. to profl. jours. Mem. ABA, Fla. Bar Assn. (com. on individual rights and responsibilities 1985-87, 90—, pub. interest law sect. 1990—), Bar Assn. of 5th Fed. Cir., Am. Acad. Religion (pres. southeastern region 1969-70), Soc. Bibl. Lit. (pres. southeastern region 1982-83), Soc. Christian Ethics, AAUW (pres. U. Fla. chpt. 1972-74), Danforth Assocs. in Teaching, Order of Coif, Phi Beta Kappa (pres. U. Fla. chpt. 1975-76), Phi Kappa Phi. Democrat. Avocation: hiking. Office: U Fla 135 Dauer Hall Gainesville FL 32611 *All decisions affecting ourselves, other persons, and other living beings, are basically ethical decisions. And ethical decisions are inevitably embedded in our ultimate loyalties and convictions as to the meanings of life that are, ultimately, religious in character.*

HIESBERGER, JEAN-MARIE, religious organization administrator; b. Kansas City, Mo., Sept. 28, 1941; d. Anton August and Elizabeth V. (Nitsche) H.; m. Robert Heyer, Aug. 29, 1972; 1 child, Kristin Heyer. AB, St. Mary Coll., Leavenworth, Kans., 1963; MA in Theology, St. John's Coll., Collegeville, Minn., 1970. Religion educator, dir. St. John/St. Paul Ch., Larchmont, N.Y., 1968-70; editor Paulist Press, N.Y. and N.J., 1970-85; dir. Inst. for Pastoral Life, Kansas City, 1985—; freelance writer, cons., speaker in field, 1969—; trustee Conception (Mo.) Abbey, 1990; mem. editorial bd. Cath. World Mag., N.Y., 1975-85, Cath. Key, Kansas City, 1985-90. Author: Discovery Education, 1971, You Have Given Us Today, 1972, Let Us Pray, 1973; contbr. articles to profl. publs., chpt. to book; interviewed for various TV programs, mags. Bd. dirs. parent orgn. Pembroke Hill Sch., Kansas City, 1990—. Mem. ASTD, Am. Mgmt. Assn., Nat. Cath. Edn. Assn., Nat. Orgn. Continuing for Roman Cath. Clergy, Nat. Assn. Lay Mins. (bd. dirs. 1987-90). Home: 1216 W 60th Terr Kansas City MO 64113 Office: Inst for Pastoral Life 2015 E 72d Kansas City MO 64132

HIGDON, C. (MARK), minister; b. Birmingham, Ala., May 13, 1952; s. Clifford Ralph and Lois Evelyn (Harwell) H.; m. Sheila Lyn Phillips, May 26, 1974; children: Melody Brooke, Katie Elizabeth. BS in Pastoral Ministry summa cum laude, Mid-Am. Bible Coll., Oklahoma City, 1989. Ordained to ministry Ch. of God (Anderson, Ind.), 1987. Assoc. pastor, youth dir. CenterPoint Ch. of God, Birmingham, 1985-87, pastor, 1989—; mem. Ala. gen. assembly Ch. of God (Anderson, Ind.), sec. camp meeting programming com., mem. nat. gen. assembly. Mem. Ctr. Point C. of C. Home: 4042 Middle Ave Pinson AL 35126 Office: CenterPoint Ch of God 115 Polly Reed Rd Birmingham AL 35215

HIGGINS, DARYL CLYDE, clergyman; b. Pitts., Oct. 20, 1948; s. William James Stanley and Florence Elizabeth (Mulvey) H.; m. Ardie J. Kendig, Aug. 12, 1978. BA, Kent State U., 1970; MDiv, Ashland Coll., 1974. Ordained to ministry United Ch. of Christ, 1974. Minister Emanuel-Mt. Zwingli Parish, Doylestown, Ohio, 1972-75, Congl. ch., Hacienda Heights, Calif., 1976-81; sr. minister Brecksville (Ohio) United Ch. of Christ, 1975-76, Ch. of Valley, SSanta Clara, Calif., 1981-89, lst Protestant Ch., New Braunfels, Tex., 1989—; bd. dirs. No. Calif. Conf. United Ch. of Christ, San Francisco, 1982-85. Sustaining life mem. Nat. Rep. Com., 1985—; bd. dirs. Valley Village Retirement Homes, Santa Clara, 1981-89, chmn. policy com., 1984-89. Recipient Disting. Svc. award Wadsworth (Ohio) Jaycees, 1970, Outstanding Speak-Up award Ohio Jaycees, 1973. Mem. Masons, K.T., Kiwanis. Avocations: music, reading, travel, sports, flying. Home: 1926 Lance Circle New Braunfels TX 78130

HIGGINS, FREDERICK, deacon, funeral home director; b. New Orleans, Jan. 1, 1918; s. William and Rachel (Talbot) H.; m. Elnord Tolliver, Nov. 7, 1942; children: Katheryn D., Martin P. Student, So. U., 1938-40; grad., Ky. Sch. Mortuary Sci., 1949. Deacon St. Martin De Porres Roman Cath. Ch., Louisville; mgr. George R. Mason Funeral Home, Louisville. Address: 2605 W Chestnut St Louisville KY 40211-1310

HIGGINS, MICHAEL JOSEPH, priest; b. Boston, May 8, 1951; s. Richard Louis and Marie Therese (Pearce) H. BA, Framingham (Mass.) State Coll., 1977; MDiv, St. Michael's Coll., Toronto, Ont., Can., 1983; MST, Regis Coll., Toronto, 1985; MA, Duquesne U., 1987, postgrad., 1989-. Ordained to priesthood Roman Catholic Ch., 1985. Religious superior St. Francis Monastery, Loretto, Pa., 1987-88; provincial spiritual assistant Secular Franciscan Order, Sacred Heart Province, Newry, Pa., 1989—; novice master Franciscan Third Order Regular, 1988—. Contbg. editor: Catholic Family, 1986-87; contbr. articles to various publs. With U.S. Army, 1969-72, Vietnam. Mem. St. Clare's Fraternity Secular Franciscan Order (spiritual asst.), Sacred Heart Province. Avocation: computers. Home and Office: St Bernardine Monastery Newry PA 16665

HIGGS, CHARLES EDWARD, pastor; b. Pueblo, Colo., Jan. 30, 1950; s. Grady Lee and Audie Lee (Wright) H.; m. Nancy Lynn Lanham, Dec. 18, 1970; 1 child, Andrea Lynnette. BA, Ind. Bapt. Coll., Dallas, 1972; MA, Dallas Bapt. U., 1989. Ordained to ministry So. Bapt. Conv. Min. youth Grace Temple Bapt. Ch., Dallas, 1972-75, 1st Bapt. Ch., Dimmitt, Tex., 1975-76; pastor Forrest Park Bapt. Ch., Corpus Christi, Tex., 1976-80, Immanuel Bapt. Ch., Paris, Tex., 1980-83, 1st Bapt. Ch., Muldrow, Okla., 1983-86, Valwood Park Bapt. Ch., Farmers Branch, Tex., 1986—; moderator Red River Valley Bapt. Assn., Paris, 1982-83; pres. Dallas Bapt. Pastors Conv., 1988-89; mem. exec. bd. B.G.C.T., 1989—; mem. alumni bd. Dallas Bapt. U., 1989—. Home: 2936 Golfing Green Farmers Branch TX 75234 Office: Valwood Park Bapt Ch 2727 Valwood Pkwy Farmers Branch TX 75234

HIGHFIELD, RONALD CURTIS, religion educator, minister; b. Ft. Payne, Ala., June 1, 1951; s. Thornton Curtis and Josephine B. (Shippy) H.; m. Martha Ellen Farrar, Dec. 30, 1977; children: Nathanael Curtis, Matthew David. BA, Harding U., Searcy, Ark., 1975; ThM, Harding Grad. Sch. Religion, Memphis, 1979; PhD, Rice U., 1988. Ordained to ministry Ch. of Christ. Campus minister Coll. Ch. of Christ, Searcy, 1979-80; youth minister Bering Dr. Ch. of Christ, Houston, 1981-84; asst. prof. Pepperdine U., Malibu, Calif., 1989—. Author: Barth and Rahner in Dialogue, 1989. Mem. Am. Acad. Religion. Office: Pepperdine U Religion Dept 24255 Pacific Coast Hwy Malibu CA 90265

HIGHFILL, ROBERT STEVEN, minister; b. Albuquerque, Dec. 27, 1951; s. Robert William and Ann (Owen) H.; m. Denise Gail Sinclair, Aug. 23, 1981; children: Teagan Christine, Trevor Barton. BS, Colo. State U., 1973; MDiv, Talbot Sem., 1980; postdoctoral, Trinity Evang. Divinity Sch. Ordained to ministry Evang. Free Ch. Am., 1982. Mem. staff Campus Crusade for Christ, Internat., N.Y.C., 1973-76; pulmonary physiologist Hoag Hosp., Newport Beach, Calif., 1976-80; sr. pastor Cypress (Calif.) Evang. Free Ch., 1979-91; supt. S.W. dist. Conf. of Evang. Free Ch., Calif. and Hawaii, 1991—; chmn. bd. dirs. S.W. Conf. Evang. Free Ch., Fullerton, Calif., 1985-88, chmn. credentials com., Cypress, 1982-90, chmn. nat. conf. com., La Mirada, Calif., 1988. Mem. Aircraft Owners and Pilots Assn., Ministerial Assn. of Evang. Free Ch. Republican. Avocation: flying. Office: SW Dist Evang Free Ch Am 17918 Gridley Rd Artesia CA 90701-3945

HIGHTOWER, JAMES R(OBERT), JR., ministry director; b. El Dorado, Ark., May 27, 1954; s. James Robert Sr. and Bece (Dickerson) H.; m. Grenae Devine, June 7, 1975; children: Lydia Joy, William Marcus, Erin Lee. BA in Music, Ouachita Bapt. U., 1977; MA in Sociology, U. Ark., 1989. Program coord. First United Meth. Ch., Batesville, Ark., 1980-83; youth dir. Kingsway United Meth. Ch., Springfield, Mo., 1983-84; dir. youth, edn. and music St. Paul United Meth. Ch., El Dorado, 1984-87; dir. youth Cen. United Meth. Ch., Fayetteville, Ark., 1987—; mem. steering com. Ozark Mission Project, Ark., 1989—. Office: Cen United Meth Ch PO Box 1106 Fayetteville AR 72702

HIGI, WILLIAM L., bishop; b. Anderson, Ind., Aug. 29, 1933. Student, Mt. St. Mary of the West Sem., Xavier U. Ordained priest Roman Cath. Ch., 1959. Bishop Lafayette, Ind., 1984—. Office: 610 Lingle Ave PO Box 260 Lafayette IN 47902

HIGLE, TOMMY CHARLES, minister, religious writer; b. Concordia, Kans., Oct. 24, 1949; s. Thomas Oliver and Flona Hester (Haddock) H.; m. Virginia Lynn Bodystun, May 30, 1969; children: Monta, Jeremy, Holly. BE, Southeastern Okla. State U., 1972. Ordained to ministry So. Bapt. Conv., 1969. Pastor Banty (Okla.) Bapt. Chapel, 1968-69, Grace Bapt. Ch., Durant, Okla., 1970-73, Farris (Okla.) Bapt. Ch., 1974-76, Ridgeway Bapt. Ch., Nashville, Ark., 1976-82, 1st Bapt. Ch., Marietta, Okla., 1982—; moderator Little River Bapt. Assn., Nashville, Ark., 1981-82. Author: Journey Through The Bible, 1982, Journey To The Cross, 1984, Journey Into Discipleship, 1985, Journey Into Spiritual Riches, 1987. Mem. Lions (treas. Marietta chpt. 1985). Office: 1st Bapt Ch 402 W Main St Marietta OK 73448

HIGLEY, WILLIAM JOHN, religion educator; b. Olean, N.Y., Nov. 13, 1960; s. Vincent Arron and Doris Elizabeth (Whitemore) Acre; m. Susan Elaine Parke, May 23, 1981; children: Erin, Nathan, Andrew, Alex. BS, Bapt. Bible Coll., Clarks Summit, Pa., 1982; MA in Christian Edn., Dallas Theol. Sem., 1987. Dir. Christian edn. and youth ministries Grace Bapt. Ch., Lima, Ohio, 1987—; bd. dirs. Ohio Regular Bapt. Youth Com., 1989—; leader Bath High Sch. Fellowship of Christian Athletes, Lima, Ohio, 1990—; advisor New Directoins Campus Ministries, Lima, 1990—. Mem. Profl. Youth Workers Fellowship (sec. 1989—), Profl. Assn. Christian Educators, Fellowship of Christian Athletes. Office: Grace Bapt Ch 1097 Fett St Lima OH 45801

HIGNIGHT, SHERRILL GRANT, clergyman; b. Muskogee, Okla., Oct. 20, 1957; s. Clevas and Jo Anne (Bond) H.; m. Yolonda Marie Thurman, Dec. 31, 1982; children: Joshua Caleb, Mary Elisabeth. BA, East Tex. Bapt. U., 1979; MDiv, Southwestern Bapt. Theol. Sem., 1984. Ordained to ministry Bapt. Ch., 1983. Pastor Salesville Bapt. Ch., Mineral Wells, Tex., 1983-84, Emmanuel Bapt. Ch., Livingston, Calif., 1984-87, Brown Deer (Wis.) Bapt. Ch., 1987—; Disciples' Pathway host WKSH-AM Radio, Milw., 1988-89; sem. extension prof. Lakeland Bapt. Assn., South Milw., 1990, dir. adult ASSISTeam, 1991—; v.p. Pastors and Wives Fellowship, Minn.-Wis. So. Bapt. Conv., Rochester, 1990. Bd. dirs. Shine: Seeking to Help Inform, Notify and Educate, Milw., 1990—. Republican. Home: 7662 N 49th St Brown Deer WI 53223 Office: Brown Deer Bapt Ch 7908 N 51st St Brown Deer WI 53223

HIGUCHI, SHINPEI, clergyman; b. Los Angeles, Sept. 17, 1923; came to Japan, 1932; s. Shiro and Fuku (Saito) H; m. Fumiko Higuchi, Feb. 19, 1949; children: Nobuko, Mari, Naomi. MDiv, Fuller Theol. Sem., 1958. Ordained to ministry Japan N.T. Ch., 1963. Pastor Fujimigaoka Ch., Tokyo, 1951-66; tchr. Japan Christian Coll., Tokyo, 1958-66; pastor Makiki Christian Ch., Honolulu, 1966-74; prof. O.T., Tokyo Christian Coll., Tokyo, 1974-86, pres., 1975-86, bd. dirs., trustee, 1975-86; moderator Japan N.T. Ch., Tokyo, 1961-65; pres. Council Japanese Christian Chs., Honolulu, 1970-72; mem. exec. com. Asia Theol. Assn., Taipei, Taiwan, 1975-82. Translator 6 books of O.T., New Japanese Bible, 1966. Author: Commentary, Book of Ruth, 1969; The Fruit of the Spirit, 1981, Paul's Letter of Love, 1990; editor Ortho peridocial; contbr. articles to profl. jours. Recipient Tokinosuke Joshima award Macedonian Soc., 1983. Home and Office: 1-5 Kita 31 Nisha 4, Kita-ku, Sapporo 221, Japan

HILARION, HIS GRACE BISHOP See KAPRAL, HILARION

HILCHEY, HARRY ST. CLAIR, priest; b. N.S., Can., Feb. 12, 1922; s. Stanley Bertram and Loretta Esperance (Lawlor) H.; m. Charlotte Ruth GIbson. BA, Dalhousie U., 1941; MA, U. Toronto, Ont., Can., 1945; Licentiate in Theology, Wycliffe Coll., 1944, DD (hon.), 1972; BD, Gen. Synod, Anglican Ch., Can., 1951; DD (hon.), Montreal Diocesan Theol. Coll., Que., Can., 1979. Ordained deacon, Anglican Ch. Can., 1944, ordained priest, 1945. Incumbent Stanhope Mission Diocese of Toronto, Ont., Can., 1944-46, St. Elizabeth's Ch., Queensway, Toronto, 1946-55; rector St. Paul's Ch., Halifax, N.S., 1955-64, Ch. St. James the Apostle, Montreal, 1964-79; gen. sec. Anglican Ch. Can., Toronto, 1979—. Address: Anglican Ch House, 600 Jarvis St, Toronto, ON Canada M4Y 2J6

HILD, WILLIAM HOWARD, minister; b. Savannah, Ga., Apr. 4, 1955; s. William Howard Sr. and Mary Critchton (McKay) H.; m. Beverly Susan Glass, Aug. 18, 1979; 1 child, William Howard III. BA, Carson-Newman Coll., 1968; MDiv, Southeastern Bapt. Theol. Sem., 1982. Ordained to ministry So. Bapt. Conv. Ch., 1975. Assoc. pastor Kathleen Bapt. Ch., Lakeland, Fla.; pastor Unity Bapt. Ch., Henderson, N.C., 1980-82, Ball Camp Bapt. Ch., Knoxville, Tenn., 1982—; mem. constn. and bylaws com. Tenn. Bapt. Convention, Nashville, 1988-91; adj. faculty mem. in religion Carson-Newman Coll., Jefferson City, Tenn., 1988—; clk. Knox County Assn. of Bapts., Knoxville, 1984; bd. dirs. Yoke Youth Ministries, Knoxville, 1989—. Vol. staff mem. Tel Migne-Ekron Archaeol. Excavation, Israel, 1990. Mem. Carson-Newman Coll. Alumni Assn. (nat. pres. 1987-88). Office: Ball Camp Bapt Ch 2412 Ball Camp-Byington Rd Knoxville TN 37931

HILDEBRAND, HENRY PETER, minister, educator; b. Stonefield, Russia, Nov. 16, 1911; arrived in Can., 1925; naturalized, 1936; s. Peter and Anna (Froese) H.; m. Inger Soeyland, Aug. 12, 1937; children: Marcia (Mrs. Phillip Leskewich), Evelyn (Mrs. Robert Moore), David, Paul, Glen. BA, Winona Lake Sch. Theology, Can., 1964, MA, 1966; DD, Winnipeg Theol. Sem., Man., Can., 1975. Ordained to ministry Associated Gospel Chs., 1937. Founder, pres. Briercrest Bible Coll., Caronport, Sask., Can., 1935-77, chancellor, 1978—; provincial supt. Can. Sunday Sch. Mission for Sask., 1937-45, trustee, 1946-80. Author: In His Loving Service—Memoirs, 1985, Contemporary Leadership Dynamics, 1987, The Model of Servant Leadership, 1990. Decorated Order Can. Mem. Christian Educators Assn. (chmn. 1964-66), Assn. Can. Bible Colls. (pres. 1976-80). Address: Box 42, Caronport, SK Canada S0H OSO *My greatest discovery in life is that Jesus Christ the Saviour of the World is my Saviour and Lord.*

HILDEBRAND, RICHARD ALLEN, bishop; b. Winnsboro, S.C., Feb. 1, 1916; s. Benjamin Franklin and Agnes Luvenia (Brogdon) H.; m. Anna Beatrix Lewis, Dec. 3, 1942; 1 dau., Camille Ylonne. A.B., Allen U., 1938; B.D., Payne Theol. Sch., 1941; S.T.M., Boston U., 1948; D.D., Wilberforce U., 1953; LL.D. (hon.), Morris Brown Coll., 1975. Ordained to ministry A.M.E. Ch., 1936, elected bishop, 1972; pastor chs. Columbia and Sumter, S.C., 1936-38, Jamestown and Akron, Ohio, 1938-45, Providence, 1945-48, Bayshore, N.Y., 1948-49, Wilmington, Del., 1949-50; pastor Bethel A.M.E. Ch., N.Y.C., 1950-65, Bridge St. A.M.E. Ch., Bklyn., 1965-72; presiding bishop 6th Dist. A.M.E. Ch., Ga., 1972-76, 1st Dist., Northeastern USA and Bermuda, 1976-84; now presiding bishop 3d Dist., Western Pa., W.Va. and Ohio; pres. Atlanta N. Ga. Conf. A.M.E. Fed. Credit Union, 1972-76, Council of Bishops A.M.E. Ch., 1977-78; chmn. bd. of trustees Wilberforce Un. 1984—, A.M.E. Ch., 1980—. Chmn. Chs. for New Harlem Hosp., N.Y.C., 1957-65; pres. Manhattan Dirs. Protestant Council, 1956-60; chmn. bd. dirs. Morris Brown Coll., Turner Sem. Interdenominational Theol. Center, 1972-76, Payne Theol. Sem., from 1976. Mem. NAACP (pres. N.Y.C. br. 1962-64), Alpha Phi Alpha. Club: Masons. Office: A M E Church 700 Bryden Rd Ste 135 Columbus OH 43215 *I believe that if a person always does what he truly believes to be right, ultimately he will be victorious.*

HILDEBRANDT, THEODORE ALEXANDER, religion educator; b. Niagara Falls, N.Y., July 10, 1951; s. Theodore Frederick and Elaine (Affleck) H.; m. Annette, Jan. 25, 1974; children: Rebekah, Natanya, Zachary, Elliott. BS, U. Buffalo, 1973; MDiv, Bibl. Sch. Theology, Hatfield, Pa., 1976, STM, 1978; ThD, Grace Theol. Seminary, Winona Lake, Ind., 1985. Prof. Don Graham Bible Coll., Bristol, Tenn., 1977-79; prof., chmn. dept. Grace Coll., Winona Lake, 1980—. Translator New Living Bible, 1990; editor: Revision/Jameson, Faucett and Brown Commentary, 1989; contbr. articles to profl. jours. Prison instr. Mich. City (Mich.) Prison, 1988-90. Home: 603 Charles Dr Winona Lake IN 46590 Office: Grace College 200 Seminary Dr Winona Lake IN 46590

HILGERS, DEANNE MARIE, journalist; b. Cambridge, Minn., Mar. 20, 1965; d. Dennis Charles and Gerri Joanne (Whittlef) H. BA in Journalism, U. Minn., 1988. Reporter The Forum, Fargo, N.D., 1988—, writer religion sect., 1989-91. Com. mem. United Way Cass-Clay, Fargo, 1991. Mem. Nat. Assn. Press Women (award 1989, 90), N.D. Profl. Communicators (awards 1989, 90), F-M Media Club (program coord. 1990-91, pres. 1991-92). Office: The Forum PO Box 2020 Fargo NM 58107

HILL, CARL RICHARD, JR., minister; b. Washington, Oct. 18, 1941; s. Carl Richard and Louise H.; m. Jacqueline Daniel, Nov. 18, 1962; children: April Melanie Hill Hawkins, Carl Maxwell. AA, Emmanuel Coll., 1968; BS in Edn., U. Ga., 1970; MDiv, Emory U., 1973, D of Ministry, 1974. Pastor Shiloh United Meth., Carrollton, Ga., 1974-78, Union United Meth., Stockbridge, Ga., 1978-83; min. evangelism Peachtree Rd. United Meth. Ch., Atlanta, 1983-84, Conyers 1st United Meth. Ch., 1984-88, McDonough (Ga.) 1st United Meth. Ch., 1988—; chmn. North Ga. Bd. Global Ministries, Atlanta, 1978-82; dean North Ga. Sch. of Christian, Atlanta, 1978-82; bd. dirs. Cove Crest Renewal, Tiger, Ga. Author: Between Two Worlds, 1976, (poems) Light From Beyond the Veil, 1988, numerous others. With U.S. Army, 1958-62. Recipient Gold Poet award, 1990. Democrat. Home: 65 Dogwood Ln McDonough GA 30253 Office: First United Meth PO Box 287 151 Macon St McDonough GA 30253

HILL, CAROLYN ANN, minister; b. Kinston, N.C., Jan. 12, 1945; d. Robert Maynard and Eva Grace (Letchworth) Fader; m. Keith Edward Hill, Aug. 22, 1965; children: Paula, Kim, Christopher. Student, Mt. Oliver Coll., N.C., 1964; Dental Asst., U. N.C., 1965. Dir. activities First Bapt. Ch., Wilson, N.C., 1984—; sr. adult state planner Bapt. State Conv., Cary, N.C., 1989—; drama com. South Roanoke Assn., GVreenville, 1986-91, youth ministry com., 1985-88; pres. youth ministries Bapt. State Conv., Cary, 1989-90. Task force mem. Wilson County Youth at Risk, 1989—; bd. dirs. Meals on Wheels, Wilson, 1988—. Mem. Nat. Assn. Bapt. Sr. Adults, Sr. Adult Bapt. Ministers Assn., N.C. Bapt. Youth Ministers Assn. (pres. 1989-91). Home: 1221 Kingswood Dr Wilson NC 27893 Office: First Bapt Ch 311 W Nash St PO Box 1467 Wilson NC 27893

HILL, CHARLES EVAN, religion educator; b. Syracuse, Neb., May 15, 1956; s. Raymond Merlyn and Iris Elaine (Todd) H.; m. Marcy Ann McPheeters, Sept. 17, 1955; children: Sean Christopher, Charity Rose. BFA, U. Neb., 1978; MA in Religion, Westminster Theol. Sem., 1985; MDiv, Westminter Theol. Sem., 1985; PhD, U. Cambridge, England, 1989. Asst. prof. religion Northwestern Coll., Orange City, Iowa, 1989—; supply preacher, 1989. Contbr. articles to profl. jours. Recipient Overseas Student Rsch. award Com. of Vice-Chancellors and Prins. of the Univs. of the United Kingdom, 1985, 86, 87; Tyndale fellow, 1987; grantee Northwestern Coll., 1990, 91. Mem. Soc. Bibl. Lit., N.Am. Patristic Soc. Office: Northwestern Coll Orange City IA 51041

HILL, CHESLEY R., minister; b. St. Louis, May 4, 1934; s. Chesley A. and Mae (Hughes) H.; m. Mary E. West; children: Celecia L. Hill Cutts, Paul C. BA, Free Will Bapt. Bible Coll., Nashville, 1957; BS in Edn., Southwest Mo. State U., 1970; MA in Edn., Drury Coll., 1974. Ordained to ministry Free Will Bapt. Ch., 1954. Various pastoral positions local chs. Tenn., Mo., 1956-66; pastor Union Free Will Bapt. Ch., Success, Mo., 1967, Willow Springs Free Will Bapt. Ch., Mountain Grove, Mo., 1967-73; pastor 1st Free Will Bapt. Ch., Chipley, Fla., 1974-79, Winfield, Ala., 1979-83; pastor Harmony Free Will Bapt. Ch., Lake Butler, Fla., 1984-91, Springhill Free Will Bapt. Ch., Baconton, Ga., 1991—; substitute tchr. Union County Sch. System, Lake Butler, Springfield Pub. Sch. System; tchr. Mitchell County Sch. System, Camilla, Ga., 1991—; instr. Fla. Bible Inst., Chipley, Mo. Bible Inst./Ext. Arm of Hillsdale Free Bapt. Bible Coll., Mountain Grove, Md.; master of ceremonies Nat. Youth Conf.; condr. youth progs. and sem.; dir. youth Ga. State; mem. exec. bd. Free Will Bapt. Ch., Ala.; numerous other offices. Eidtor: Free Will Baptist Gem, Mo. Coach basketball team Mountain Grove, Mo. Mem. Fla. State Free Will Bapt. Assn. (asst. moderator), Union County Ministerial Assn. (sec.), others. Home: Rte 1 Box 534 Baconton GA 31716 Office: Springhill Free Will Bapt Ch Rte 1 Baconton GA 31716

HILL, DIANA JOAN, religious organization administrator; b. Pleasant Corner, Pa., June 17, 1936; d. Lawrence Edwin Aaron and Arlene (Wessner) Hausman; m. Bruce Handwerk Hill, June 22, 1957; children: Adrian Bruce, Anita Diann. BS in Edn., Kutztown U., 1958; postgrad., Temple U., 1958-61. Elem. tchr. Cheltenham (Pa.) Twp. Schs., 1958-62, Rockford (Ill.) City Schs., 1965-66; caseworker Lehigh County Children-Youth Services, Allentown, Pa., 1975-85; dist. rep. Luth. Brotherhood, Allentown, 1985—. Publicity chmn. LVW Rockford, 1965-66, human resources chair, Oyster Bay, N.Y. 1968-73; precinct capt. Dem. Party, Massapequa, N.Y., 1973-74. Mem. Lehigh Valley Assn. Life Underwriters. Democrat. Lutheran. Avocations: swimming, needlework, singing. Office: Luth Brotherhood 1013 Brookside Rd PO Box 3402 Allentown PA 18106-3402

HILL, DONALD V., church music director; b. Camden, N.J., Jan. 20, 1954; s. Victor Harold and Wilhelmina Falkenstein) H.; m. Janet Elton, Sept. 20, 1980; children: Jamie, Katie, Tracie. BA Music, Taylor U., Upland, Ind., 1976; AA in Bus., Crandall Coll., Macon, Ga., 1989; Dipl., Am. Sch. Piano Tech., Morgan Hill, Ga., 1986. Dir. ch. music St. Paul's Ch., Pennsauken, N.J., 1977-80, St. John's United Meth. Ch., Turnersville, N.J., 1981-84, First United Meth. Ch., Milledgeville, Ga., 1984—. Author musical compositions: Thank You Lord, 1987, New Wind Blowin, 1988, Processional for a Carillon, 1988, Hymn for Bells and Brass, 1988, Worthy, Worthy, 1990, Lord Go With Us Now, 1990. Mem. Baldwin County PTA, 1988—. Mem. Fellowship of United Meth. in Music. Democrat. Office: First United Meth Ch 300 W Hancock St Milledgeville GA 31061-3329

HILL, DOUGLAS WHITTIER, clergyman, administrator; b. Dayton, Ohio, Apr. 11, 1927; s. Eric Leslie and Helen Elizabeth (Metz) H.; m. Helen G. Kleinhenz, June 14, 1952; children—Linda E. Hill Hickok, David D., Peter D. B.S. in Edn., Miami (Ohio) U., 1949; M.Div., Colgate Rochester Div. Sch., 1952; D.D. (hon.), Alderson-Broaddus Coll., 1978. Ordained to ministry Baptist Ch., 1952. Minister Christian edn. Delaware Ave. Bapt. Ch., Buffalo, 1952-57; organizing pastor South Hills Bapt. Ch., Pitts., 1957-62; assoc. pastor Fifth Ave. Bapt. Ch., Huntington, W.Va., 1962-67; area minister, minister campus ministry W.Va. Bapt. Conv., Parkersburg, 1967-77, exec. minister, 1978—; founding dir. W.Va. Bapt. Found. for Campus Ministry, 1967-75; mem. gen. staff Am. Bapt. Ch. U.S.A., 1978—. Trustee, Alderson-Broaddus Coll., 1978—; bd. dirs. East Central region Boy Scouts Am., 1985—. Recipient Good Shepherd award Assn. Bapts. for Scouting. Mem. Regional Exec. Ministers Council (sec./treas. 1982-85). Editor W.Va. Bapt., 1978—. Office: PO Box 1019 Parkersburg WV 26102

HILL, ERIC DALE, minister; b. Beaumont, Tex., Nov. 23, 1952; s. Elvin Levelle and Velma Genevieve (Parfait) H.; m. Karen Denise McCollum, Aug. 17, 1974; children: Jeremy Dale, Christy Denise. BA Baylor U., 1978; MDiv, Southwestern Sem., 1980. Ordained to ministry So. Bapt. Conv., 1973. Pastor First Bapt. Ch., Alief, Tex., 1980-85, South Side Bapt. Ch., Abilene, Tex., 1985-89, Cen. Bapt. Ch., Clovis, N.Mex., 1989—. Home: 1604 Claremont Terr Clovis NM 88101 Office: Cen Bapt Ch 800 Hinkle Clovis NM 88101

HILL, FLOYD RANDALL, clergyman, social services administrator; b. Erick, Okla., June 30, 1941; s. Floyd Martin and Norma Jane (Cotton) H.; m. Phyllis Cannon, Aug. 21, 1963 (div. 1971); children: Cathy Jean, Chuck Allan. BA, Okla. Bapt. U., 1962; MRE, MA, So. Bapt. Theol. Sem., 1966; postgrad., Tenn. State U., 1974-75, Trevecca Nazarene Coll., 1975. Lic. tchr., adminstr., Tenn.; ordained to ministry Interdenom. Spirit-filled Ch., 1959. Editorial and info. specialist So. Bapt. Sunday Sch. Bd., Nashville, 1968-73; founder, tchr. Crockett Acad. for Emotionally Handicapped, Nashville, 1974-76; prin. Highland Rim Sch. for Girls, Tullahoma, Tenn., 1976; founder, pastor Met. Community Ch., Knoxville, Tenn., 1977-79; pastor Met. Community Ch., Saratoga, Fla., 1979-81, Tucson, 1981-83; founder, pastor Holy Trinity Community Ch., San Jose, Calif., 1985-90, Hosanna Ch. of Praise, San Jose, 1990—; founder, exec. dir. Necessities and More, Inc., San Jose, 1985—; bd. dirs. Christian Builders, Nashville, 1982-84; exec. dir. AIDS Hospice Found., Santa Clara County, 1988—; mem. various coms. Santa Clara Coun. Churches, San Jose, 1988—. Officer Campbellsville (Ky.) Rotary Club, 1972-74, Nashville Lions Club, 1974-76; founder Knoxville Gay Counsel, 1988; asst. dist. coord. South Atlantic dist. Met. Community Ch., Nashville, 1977. Mem. Ministerial Alliance Santa Clara Coun. Churches. Democrat. Avocations: stamp collecting, travel, gardening, handiwork, reading. Office: Hosanna Ch of Praise 24 N 5th St San Jose CA 95112

HILL, JIM EDWIN, clergyman, broadcasting executive; b. Chattanooga, June 9, 1969; s. James E. and Laquata P. (Chapman) H.; m. Paula Renee Moore, Mar. 24, 1990; 1 child, Justin Moore. Grad. high sch., Flintstone, Ga., 1983. Ops. mgr., disc jockey Sta. WFLI Inc., Chattanooga, 1989—. Mem. Tenn. Assn. Broadcasters. Republican. Baptist. Home: 403 Woodcreek Dr Rossville GA 30741 Office: Sta WFLI Inc 621 O'Grady Dr Chattanooga TN 37409

HILL, JOHN MILLARD, minister; b. Bristol, Tenn., Jan. 7, 1956; s. William Durward and Auda Hazel (Millard) H.; m. Mary Lenore Blanton, Sept. 1, 1979; 1 child, Corey Nathan. BA, David Lipscomb U., 1981; MA in Religion, Emmanuel Sch. Religion, 1989. Min. Lyle Lane Ch. of Christ, Nashville, 1979-82, Nor-Dan Ch. of Christ, Danville, Va., 1987—. Mem. U.S. Chess Fedn., Internat. Soc. Theta Phi. Office: Nor-Dan Ch of Christ 208 Orchard Dr Danville VA 24540

HILL, JOSEPH ALLEN, retired religion educator, minister; b. Beaver Falls, Pa., Jan. 29, 1924; s. George Dawson and May (Fullerton) H.; m. Barbara Adams, May 31, 1945; children: Robert A., Linda Hill Hughes, John Timothy. AB, Geneva Coll., 1947; BD, Ref. Presbyn. Theol. Sem., 1950; ThM, Pitts. Theol. Sem., 1971. Ordained to ministry Presbyn. Ch. (U.S.A.), 1950. Min. Ref. Presbyn. Ch., Denver, 1950-52, Walton, N.Y., 1952-56; tchr. Unity Christian High Sch., Hudsonville, Mich., 1956-64; assoc. prof. Bibl. studies and Greek Geneva Coll., Beaver Falls, Pa., 1964-88, prof. emeritus, 1989—; interim ministry specialist, 1983—. Author: A Theology of Praise, 1983; contbg. author: The Book of Books, 1978, Best Sermons, vols. 1-3, 1987-89, Pulpit Digest, 1991. Pres. Borough Coun., Patterson Heights, Pa., 1979-80; mem. adv. bd. Vocat. Tech. Sch., Beaver County, Pa., 1983. With USNR, 1943-45, PTO. Home: 410 4th St Patterson Heights Beaver Falls PA 15010 *Emerson once remarked, "We ask for long life, but 'tis deep life or grand moments that signify. Let the measure of time be spiritual, not mechanical." How true! Life cannot be measured by clock and calendar. It is the spiritual quality of our life, not its length, that is bound to give meaning to the days of our years.*

HILL, KEITH J., clergyman, educator; b. Tulsa, Sept. 1, 1925; s. Javan B. and Anna Catherine (McBroom) H.; m. Jean Bond, Sept. 1, 1946 (dec. 1978); m. Joan Van Camp Woertz, June 12, 1982; children by previous marriage—Karen Jean, Deborah Sue. Grad. Central Bible Coll./Sem., 1946. Minister, Bethel Temple, Sacramento, 1946-51, Calvary Temple, Seattle, 1951-56, Calvary Temple, Denver, 1956-62, Calvary Bible Ch., Burbank, Calif., 1962-65, Bethany Bapt. Ch., Whittier, Calif., 1965-71, Grace Community Ch., Tempe, Ariz., 1971-79, First Bapt. Ch., Lakewood, Long Beach, Calif., exec. pastor, 1979-87; assoc. exec. minister Southwest Bapt. Conf. Hdqrs., West Covina, Calif., 1987—. Contbr. articles to profl. jours. Bd. trustees S.W. Bapt. Conf., 1968-71, 80-82; mem. Bd. Christian Edn., W. Covina, Calif., 1965-71, Denomination Bapt. Gen. Conf., Arlington Hts., Ill., 1965—; charter/founder Nat. Assn. Dirs. Christian Edn., 1959, Rocky Mt. Sun. Sch. Assn., 1957, others; founder So. Calif. Dirs. Christian Edn., 1962, Phoenix Area Christian Educators, Phoenix. Mem. Nat. Bd. Christian Ednl. Bapt. Gen. conf., Arlington Heights; bd. dirs. Greater Los Angeles Sunday Schs., 1965—, Calif. Council on Alcoholic Problems; founder, charter mem. bd. dirs. Greater Long Beach Christian Schs., Inc., also sec. bd. dirs.; founder 1st Living/Singing Christmas Tree, Ariz., 1972, choral dir.; operating brethren jr. and sr. high schs. in Paramount, Calif.; v.p. exec. com. Greater Los Angeles Sunday Schs. Assn. Mem. Nat. Assn. Evangelicals (So. Calif. bd.), Nat. Assn. Dirs. Christian Edn., So. Calif. Dirs. Christian Edn., Rocky Mt. Dirs. Christian Edn., Phoenix Area Dirs. Christian Edn. Office: SW Bapt Conf Office Assoc Exec Minister 925 N Sunset Ave PO Box 728 West Covina CA 91793

HILL, KENNETH CLYDE, clergyman; b. Kingsport, Tenn., Mar. 22, 1953; s. Hubert Clyde and Erma Lee (Harless) H.; m. Janet Reynolds, Oct. 15, 1976; children: Matthew Joseph, Timothy Aaron, Lydia Rebekah. BS in Speech, History, East Tenn. State U., 1974; MS in Speech, Ind. State U., 1976; BA in Bibl. Studies, Bapt. Christian Coll., 1986; M. Religious Edn., Manahath Sch. Theology, 1989. Ordained to ministry Evang. Meth. Ch., 1982. Pastor Crestwood Bapt. Ch., Ft. Wayne, Ind., 1980-81; pres., chief exec. officer Appalachian Ednl. Communication Corp., Bristol, Tenn., 1981—; pulpit supply various ch. congregations Ind., Tenn., 1981-82; deacon Evang. Meth. Ch., Kingsport, Tenn., 1982-86, elder, 1986—; chmn. Publs. Bd. of the Evang. Meth. Ch., Kingsport, 1986—; sec. Gen. Conf. Evang. Meth. Ch., Kingsport, 1990—; bd. dirs. Bancroft Gospel Ministry, Kingsport, 1984—, Manahath Sch. Theology, Hollidaysburg, Pa., 1986—; chmn. Servant Ministries, Kingsport, 1990—; mem. Mission Field Task Force, Blantyre, Malawi, 1989. Author: Reconstructionism: Is It Scriptural, 1989; contbr. articles to profl. jours. Disaster vol. ARC, 1986—; bd. dirs. Radio Reading Svcs. Corp., Kingsport, 1989—; vol. World Reach, Inc., Honduras, 1986—. Mem. Soc. Profl. Journalists, Delta Sigma Rho, Tau Kappa Alpha. Home: 4045 Weaver Pike Bluff City TN 37618 Office: Appalachian Ednl Communication Corp PO Box 2061 Bristol TN 37621-2061

HILL, LAURETTE HURD, minister; b. Rockford, Ill., Oct. 26, 1958; d. Robert Linn and Kay (Whitney) Hurd; m. Stephen Ray Hill, Nov. 4, 1978; children: Vickie Elizabeth, Gwendolyn Anne. BA, U. Dubuque, 1980; MA, Butler U., 1986; MDiv, Louisville Presbyn. Theol. Sem., 1990. Ordained to ministry Presbyn. Ch. (U.S.A.), 1990. Assoc. pastor Newburgh (Ind.) Presbyn. Ch., 1990—; mem. evangelism com. Presbytery of Ohio Valley, 1991—; moderator Southwind Mission Coun., Evansville, Ind., 1991—; moderator nominating com. Synod of Lincoln Trails, Ind. and Ill., 1991—. Mem. NAFE (mem. nat. program). Home: 429 Eissler Rd Evansville IN 47711 Office: Newburgh Presbyn Ch PO Box 1 Hwy 662 Newburgh IN 47629-0001

HILL, MICHAEL J., religious organization administrator, consultant; b. Washington, Ohio, 1958; s. Michael and MarLynn Bell (Fioto) H.; m. Carolyn Marie Hill, Oct. 16, 1982. BS, Ohio State U., 1980. Lic. phys. therapist. Dir. pub. rels., dean of admissions Ky. Christian Coll., Grayson, 1987-90; phys. therapist, athletic trainer Harvard U., Cambridge, Mass., 1986-87; exec. dir. You Turn Ministries, Inc., Dayton, Ohio, 1990—; dir. summer in the sun Ky. Christian Coll. Mem. Fellowship Christian Athletes, Big Bros., Inc.; mem., coach Spl. Olympics. Mem. NATA. Mem. Chrisitan Ch. Avocations: reading, computers, sports, fine arts, aviation. Office: You Turn Ministries Inc 122 S Main St Miamisburg OH 45342

HILL, PAUL MARK, clergyman; b. Cin., Aug. 29, 1953; s. Paul Frederick and Helen Faith (Skeen) H.; m. Rebecca Sue Helm, Dec. 29, 1977; children: Aaron Israel Paul, Revkah Lauren Amara, Hadassah Sue Elizabeth. BA in Biology, Asbury Coll., 1975; DivM, Anderson Sch. Theology, 1981. Ordained to ministry Meth. Ch., 1984. Sr. pastor United Meth. Ch., Marion, Ind., 1978—, camp dir., 1990—; speaker and lectr. in field. Dir. TV show Offer Them Christ, 1986; partial designer grandfather clock, 1989. Actor Civic Theater, Logansport, Ind., 1981-82, Peru Civic Theater, 1981-82; coach baseball, basketball, soccer, Marion, Ind., 1986-89; organizer, dir. Stockwell Youth Orchestra, 1990. Named to Outstanding Young Men of Am., 1988. Avocations: basketball, skiing, wood working, running, baseball.

HILL, RODNEY E., religious organization administrator; b. Annandale, Minn., May 2, 1938; s. Elmer R. and Alice C. (Berg) H.; m. Arlene B. Selander, Aug. 16, 1959; children: Grier B., Marla J. BA in English Lit., Augsburg Coll., 1959; MDiv in Theology, Luth. Sch. of Theology, 1963, D of Ministry, 1981. Ordained minister Evang. Luth. Ch. in Am. Pastor Immanuel Luth. Ch., Allegan, Mich., 1963-68, Ascension Luth. Ch., Kentwood, Mich., 1968-74, Holy Trinity Luth. Ch., Flint, Mich., 1975-83; adminstr. Calvary Center Luth. Social Svcs. of Mich., Detroit, 1983-88, dir. office of quality assurance audit, 1988 . Mem. adv. bd. Detroit Area Agy. on Aging, 1984—; exec. com., bd. dirs. AIDS Consortium of Southeastern Mich. Mem. Am. Soc. for Quality Control. Office: Luth Social Svs of Mich 8131 E Jefferson Detroit MI 48214

HILL, SALLY L., ecumenical agency administrator. Exec. dir. Twin Cities Met. Ch. Commn., Mpls. Office: Twin Cities Met Ch Commn 122 W Franklin Rm 218 Minneapolis MN 55404*

HILL, STEPHANIE JEAN, minister; b. Detroit, July 9, 1956; d. Bernard Delmar and Phyllis (Longley) Strickland) H. BA in Liberal Arts, Wheaton (Ill.) Coll., 1978; MDiv, Trinity Evang. Div. Sch., Deerfield, Ill., 1985. Ordained elder United Meth. Ch., 1989. Min. Craigville (Ind.)-Lancaster Chapel Charge, 1985-87; sr. min. Norwell Parish Coop. Parish, Tocsin, Ind., 1987-89; min. Parr United Meth. Ch., Kokomo, Ind., 1989—; cons. local ch. assessment program, 1989—; trustee North Ind. Conf., United Meth. Ch., Marion, 1990—. Vol. Heifer Project Internat., Salvation Army, Kokomo, 1989—; com. mem. Habitat for Humanity Kokomo, 1990—; mem. adv. com. Mental Health Assn., Kokomo, 1991—. Mem. NAFE, Howard County Ministerial Assn. (exec. com. 1990—, sec. 1990-91), Christians for Bibl. Equality, Am. Mensa. Office: Parr United Meth Ch 1135 N Wabash Ave Kokomo IN 46901

HILL, SUSAN CHIDESTER, minister, educator; b. Auburn, N.Y., Dec. 22, 1951; d. Augustus Benjamin and Joan Gertrude (Bauer) Chidester; m. William George Hill, July 3, 1976; 1 child, Michael Chidester. BS, S.U.C., Brockport, N.Y., 1973; MA, Scarritt Coll., Nashville, 1978. Cert. christian edn. dir. and diaconal minister. Dir. christian edn. Main St. United Meth. ch., Bedford, Va., 1978-84; program dir. Raleigh Ct. United Meth. Ch., Roanoke, Va., 1984—; chairperson children's sect. Va. Conf. Council on Ave Level and Family Ministries, 1984-87. Mem. Christian Educators Fellowship, Religious Edn. Assn. Avocations: reading, swimming, walking, sewing. Home: 710 Kimball Ave Salem VA 24153

HILL, THOMAS MORGAN, minister, former army chaplain; b. Fairfax, Ala., Apr. 26, 1938; s. Thomas Joseph and Martha Ucal (Earnest) H.; m. Claudette Suzanne Clark, July 24, 1960; children: Dianne Yvonne, Dawn Elizabeth. BA, Lynchburg (Va.) Coll., 1960; BD, Lexington (Ky.) Theol. Sem., 1964; MA, Boston U., 1971; cert. in advanced profl. studies, Pacific Sch. Religion, Berkeley, Calif., 1973. Ordained to ministry Christian Ch. (Disciples of Christ), 1963. Pastor 1st Christian Ch., Bartow, Fla., 1964-65; commd. 2nd lt., staff specialist U.S. Army Reserve, 1961; commd. chaplain (1st lt.) U.S. Army, 1966, advanced through grades to lt. col., 1979; chaplain, 1966-85; pastor 1st Christian Ch., Black Mountain, N.C., 1986-91, Eastway Christian Ch., Charlotte, N.C., 1991—; chair SHALOM Task Force, Christian Ch. in N.C., Wilson, 1987-90, pres. western dist., Black Mountain, 1989-91; pres. Ministerial Fellowship, Black Mountain, 1988-90; past mem. Am. Assn. Pastoral Counselors, Assn. Clin. Pastoral Edn., Internat. Transactional Analysis Assn. Contbr. articles to Mil. Chaplain's Rev., The Disciple mag. Class chair Alumni Fund, Lynchburg Coll., 1974-81, mem. alumni bd. dirs., 1976-79; pres. PTA, Ft. Sam Houston, Tex., 1977-78, Parent-Tchr.-Student Orgn., Owen High Sch., Swannanoa, N.C., 1990-91; mem. Community Energy Campaign, Black Mountain, 1988-90, Black Mountain Pairing Project, 1988-91. Decorated Bronze Star, Meritorious Svc. medal with 2 oak leaf clusters, Joint Svcs. Commendation medal. Mem. Optimists (treas. Bartow club 1964-65). Office: Eastway Christian Ch 1825 Eastway Dr Charlotte NC 28205 *Some people who consider themselves positive thinkers sugarcoat problems—others merely overlook or deny them. For me, the most powerful tool of one who takes a positive approach to life is to identify strengths—in self and others—then build on them! Such an approach overcomes the problems others only seek to avoid.*

HILL, WILLIE RAY, minister, evangelist; b. San Bernardino, Calif., Mar. 8, 1962; s. Willie Dee and Betty Joyce (Brown) H.; m. Patricia Ann Jones, Feb. 17, 1990; 1 child, Brittani Patrice. AA, San Jose City Coll., 1981; AA in Bible, Southwestern Christian Coll., Terrell, Tex., 1985, BA in Bible, 1987; postgrad., Harding U., 1987-88. Ordained to ministry Chs. of Christ, 1985. Assoc. min. Berkeley Heights Ch. of Christ, St. Louis, 1985-86; min., evangelist Johnson Street Ch. of Christ, Benton, Ark., 1987-88, Dublin Street Ch. of Christ, Urbana, Ill., 1988—; speaker area lectureships, youth confs., gospel meetings, and workshops. Home: 1903 Blackthorn Dr Champaign IL 61821 Office: Dublin Street Ch of Christ 1402 W Dublin St Urbana IL 61801

HILLER, MICHAEL JAMES, minister; b. Greeley, Colo., May 9, 1952; s. Bruce Frederick and Elva Ann (Obermeier) H.; m. Janet Kay Sylwester, Aug. 21, 1976; children: Robert, Timothy. BA, U. No. Colo., 1974; MDiv, Concordia Theol. Sem., 1975; postgrad., Fuller Theol. Sem., 1988—. Assoc. pastor Peace Luth. Ch., Arvada, Colo., 1978-81; pastor Peace with Christ Luth. Ch., Aurora, Colo., 1982—. Mem. Profl. Workers Conf. (chmn. Rocky Mountain dist. chpt. 1989—), Denver Area Pastors Conf. (chmn. 1986-87), Rocky Mountain Dist. LC-MS (chmn. youth com. Aurora chpt. 1979-83). Office: Peace with Christ Luth Ch 3290 S Tower Rd Aurora CO 80013 *I believe that life lived by faith in Christ is the only way to find true happiness, peace, and joy.*

HILLER, THOMAS CARL, pastor; b. Monte Vista, Colo., July 22, 1950; s. Carl Otto Albert and Ruth Caroline (Terrass) H.; m. Lisa Marie Moore, June 28, 1980; children: Alexandra Moore, Victoria Moore. AA, St. John's Coll., Winfield, Kans., 1970; BA, Concordia Sr. Coll., Fort Wayne, Ind., 1972; MDiv, Concordia Seminary, St. Louis, 1976. Chaplain Luth. Compass Ctr., Seattle, 1977-83; pastor Pilgrim Luth. Ch., Portland, 1983-87, Colton (Oreg.) Luth. Ch., 1987—; dist. and state coord. Bread For the World, Seattle, Portland, Oreg., 1977-87; bd. dirs. Operation Nightwatch, Portland, 1988—. Chaplain Colton Rural Vol. Fire Dept., 1987—; active Colton Community Edn. Adv. Bd., 1987—. Mem. Fellowship Fire Chaplains. Home and Office: Colton Luth Ch 20808 S Hwy 211 PO Box 16 Colton OR 97017

HILLIARD, DONNIE RAY, minister; b. Athens, Tenn., July 23, 1950; s. Bennie and Sarah Grace (Haskins) H.; m. Sherrie Kaye McFarlin, Mar. 3, 1979; children: David Ray, Sarah Ann. AA, Ala. Christian Coll., Montgomery, Ala., 1970; BS in Religious Edn., Ala. Christian Coll., 1972; MS in Guidance & Counseling, Troy (Ala.) State U., 1975. Ordained to ministry, Ch. of Christ. Youth minister Homewood Ch. of Christ, Birmingham, 1981-85; assoc. minister Coll. Ch. of Christ, Montgomery, 1985—; Bible prof. Faulkner U., Montgomery, 1985—; deacon Coll. Ch. of Christ, Montgomer, 1986—; counselor Maywood Christian Camp, Hamilton, Ala., 1986—. Author: Upon That Rock I Stand, 1972. Mem. Nat. Family Life Inst. (bd. dirs., sec. 1990-91), Christian Family Devel. Ministries (co-founder, treas.), Kiwanis (v.p. 1984-85). Home: 5007 W George Green Dr Montgomery AL 36109 Office: Coll Ch of Christ 5315 Atlanta Hwy Montgomery AL 36109

HILLIARD, THOMAS EUGENE, lay worker, exterminator; b. Butler, Pa., Dec. 23, 1948; s. Charles Anthony and Genevieve Rita (Kriley) H.; m. Janie Diane Gardener, Jan. 16, 1971 (dec. Jan. 1974); m. Linda Grace Cartwright, Dec. 27, 1975; children: Bambi LeAnn, Katrina Noelle. AS, Butler County Community Coll., 1975. Lay leader, chmn. coun., chmn. fin. com., dir. youth group United Meth. Ch., Chicora, Pa., 1988—; mem. cast and choir Sing Hosanna Contata Choir, Butler, 1991; sr. technician J.C Ehrlich Co., New Bethlehem, Pa., 1985—. With U.S. Army, 1966-69, Vietnam. Home: Box 1000 Chicora PA 16025

HILLMAN, PEARL ELIZABETH, minister; b. Lincoln, Kans., Sept. 2, 1907; d. Isaiah Marine and Estelle Bella Elizabeth (Mastersen) Turner; m. Lester Robert Turner Hillman (dec. July 1973); children: Bernice, Lois, Robert, Roberta, Dunward, Donald. BS, Nazarene Bible Coll., 1980; MDiv, Asbury Theol. Sem., 1985. Lic. to ministry Ch. of the Nazarene, 1980. Min. Ch. of Nazarene, Crockett, Tex., 1987—; tchr., bd. dirs. Mt. Hope Ch. of Nazarene, Jacksonville, Tex., 1973-75, steward, del., 1973-79; pres. missionary West of Colorado Springs, Colo., 1976-79; tchr. asst. Nicholasville (Ky.) Nazarene, 1982-85. Author: (devotions) Oral Roberts, 1960. Mem. Ministerial Assn. Home and Office: Ch of Nazarene 505 S 4th St Crockett TX 75835 *Age has little to do with achievement and nothing to do with committment.*

HILT, THOMAS HARRY, minister; b. Phila., May 19, 1947; s. Francis Joseph and Alice Elizabeth (Flanagan) H.; m. Carolyn Louise Poulsen, Aug. 23, 1969; 1 child, Tamara Leah. BA, Tusculum Coll., Greeneville, Tenn., 1969; grad., Missionary Tng. Sch., Long Beach, Calif., 1974; M Ministry, Internat. Bible Inst. and Sem., Plymouth, Fla., 1983, D Ministry, 1984. Ordained min. of Gospel, Okinawa, Japan, 1979. Mem. staff Christians in Action, Long Beach, 1974-77; missionary Christians in Action, Okinawa, Japan, 1977-79; founder Christians in Action Evang. Ch., Guam, 1979-81; founder, dir. Micronesian Evang. Mission, Barrigada, Guam, 1981—; founder, adminstr. Evang. Christian Acad., Chalan Pago, Guam, 1982—; founder, dir. Family Counseling Ministries, 1990—; mem. Nat. Bible Week-Guam Com., 1988—; advisor Guam chpt. Women's Aglow Fellowship Internat., 1987—. Mem. Guam Gov.'s Social Svcs. Adv. Bd., 1981-83; mem. standards of licensing com. child welfare task force Guam Dept. Pub. Health and Social Svcs., 1982-83; mem. Blue Ribbon Commn. on Edn., 1991—. With U.S. Army, 1970-73. Recipient award Ancient Order of Chamorri, 1983, 1st place award Guam Press Club, 1985. Mem. Guam Ministerial Assn. (sec.-treas. 1980-81, pres. 1983-84, 86-88, v.p. 1991—), Bible Soc. Micronesia (pres. bd. dirs. 1989-90, v.p. bd. 1991—), Nat. Christian Counselor Assn. (lic., area rep. 1989—). Home: 211 Clara St Toto GU 96927 Office: PO Box 23998 GMF Barrigada GU 96921-3998 *It has been my experience that God does not grant us special favors, but rather special grace.*

HILTON, CLIFFORD THOMAS, clergyman; b. St. Paul, June 2, 1934; s. Bernard Moll and Winifred (Lockwood) H.; m. Janet Corine Fylling, Aug. 31, 1956; children: Lynn Ann, Jean Marie, Karin Elizabeth, Clifford Thomas, Jr. BA, Macalester Coll., 1957; MDiv, Princeton Sem., 1960; D of Ministry, Drew U., 1980. Ordained minister Presbyn. Ch., 1960. Asst. minister House of Hope Presbyn. Ch., St. Paul, 1960-62; minister Bethany Presbyn. Ch., Bridgeton, N.J., 1962-67; sr. minister Lewistown (Pa.) Presbyn. Ch., 1967-73, Irvington Presbyn. Ch., Indpls., 1973-83, 1st Presbyn. Ch., Pompano Beach, Fla., 1983—; chaplain Chautauqua Instn., N.Y., 1988; Royster Bible lecture preacher Henderson, N.C., 1991. Author: Be My Guest, 1991; homiletics editor Clergy Jour., 1979—; contbr. articles to mags., chpts. to books. trustee Princeton Seminary, 1983—, Eckerd Coll., St. Petersburg, Fla., 1984—. Recipient Freedoms Found. award, 1962, 85. Office: First Presbyn Ch 2331 NE 26th Ave Pompano Beach FL 33062 *All of God's grace that I have experienced in the past, gives me strength in the present, and hope for the future.*

HIMMELFARB, MILTON, editor, educator; b. Bklyn., Oct. 21, 1918; s. Max and Bertha (Lerner) H.; m. Judith Siskind, Nov. 26, 1950; children: Martha, Edward, Miriam, Anne, Sarah, Naomi, Dan. B.A., CCNY, 1938, M.S., 1939; B.Hebrew Lit., Jewish Theol. Sem. Coll., 1939; diplôme, U. Paris, 1939; postgrad., Columbia U., 1942-47. Dir. information and research Am. Jewish Com., N.Y.C., 1955-86; editor Am. Jewish Year Book, N.Y.C., 1959-86; contbg. editor Commentary mag., N.Y.C., 1960-86; vis. prof. Jewish Theol. Sem., N.Y.C., 1967-68, 71-72; vis. lectr. Yale, 1971; vis. prof. Reconstructionist Rabbinical Coll., Phila., 1972-73. Author: The Jews of Modernity, 1973. Mem. U.S. Holocaust Meml. Council, 1986-89.

HINCKLEY, GORDON B., church official; s. Bryant S. and Ada (Bitner) H.; m. Marjorie Pay, Apr. 29, 1937; children: Kathleen Hinckley Barnes, Richard G., Virginia Hinckley Pearce, Clark B., Jane Hinckley Dudley. Asst. to Council of Twelve Apostles, Church of Jesus Christ Latter Day Saints, 1958-61, mem. council, 1961-81, now mem. First Presidency. Office: First Presidency LDS Ch 47 E S Temple St Salt Lake City UT 84150 also: Bonneville Internat Corp Broadcast House 55 N 3d W Salt Lake City UT 84110

HIND, STEPHEN ROBERT, minister; b. Peekskill, N.Y., Nov. 11, 1952; s. Robert and Claudia (Bunney) H.; m. Lucie Tissot, Aug. 18, 1973; children: Matthew Robert, Aimee Jacqueline. BS, Lancaster Bible Coll., 1980; MA, Wheaton Grad. Sch., 1984; diploma, Word of Life Bible Inst., 1971. Ordained to ministry Bapt. Ch., 1990. Youth pastor Peekskill and Lancaster, Pa., 1970-80; mem. staff Youth for Christ, Wheaton, Ill., 1980-82; dean men Phila. Coll. Bible, 1982-86; dir. programs New Life Camp, Raleigh, N.C., 1986-88; asst. pastor for single adults Calvary Bapt. Ch., Winston-Salem, N.C., 1989—. Office: Calvary Bapt Ch 5000 Country Club Rd Winston-Salem NC 27104 *The glow of every success in my life dims in comparison to the joy I find each day as I walk with my best friend and Lord, Jesus Christ.*

HINDMAN, LLOYD STEPHENSON, retired minister; b. Cross Creek, Pa., Apr. 3, 1914; s. Audley Oliver and Ada Myrtle (Newcomer) Hindman; m. Bertha Wilhelmina Wigman (dec. Aug. 1964); children: Carolyn L. Brown, Lloyd S. Jr., Elizabeth A. Foster, Paul W., Amy S. Hindman-Roney; m. Billie Fern McReynolds, July 14, 1966. BS, Washington and Jefferson Coll., 1935; MDiv, Princeton Theol. Sem., 1938; DD, Washington and Jefferson Coll., 1948. Ordained to ministry Presbyn. Ch., 1938. Pastor Manokin Presbyn. Ch., Princess Anne, Md., 1938-40; chaplain (capt.) USN, 1940-47; pastor Vance Meml. Ch., Wheeling, W.Va., 1947-51, First Presbyn. Ch., Davenport, Iowa, 1951-58; missionary Presbyn. Ch., Korea, 1958-61; pastor St. Andrew Presbyn. Ch., Denton, Tex., 1961-66; missionary Presbyn. Ch., Thailand, 1966-70; assoc. pastor First Presbyn. Ch., Ft. Collins, Colo., 1970-75; interim pastor First Presbyn. Ch., Akron, Colo., 1975-76, Ridglea Presbyn. Ch., Ft. Worth, 1980, Cumberland Presbyn. Ch., Denton, Tex., 1985-86, 89; bd. dirs. The Vintage Retirement Ctr., Denton, Tex., 1990—; pres., bd. dirs. Ret. Srs. Vol. Program, Denton County, 1984-90; bd. dirs. Denton Good Samaritan Village, 1983-89, chaplain, 1977-84; trustee Dubuque Theol. Sem. and Univ., Dubuque, Iowa, 1954-56. Bd. dirs. Davis and Elkins Coll., W.Va., 1949; chaplain Good Samaritan Village, Denton, 1977-83. Home: 2313 Vanderbilt Ct Denton TX 76201

HINKLE, JAMES ALTON, religious educator, foreign language educator; b. Athens, Ala., Dec. 8, 1940; s. F. Samuel and S. Neva Hinkle; m. Harriett Ann Walker, Nov. 28, 1963; children; Keith, Maribeth, Jim. BA in Communication, David Lipscomb U., Nashville, 1963; MA in Greek, Harding U., Memphis, 1969; DMin, Fuller Theol. Seminary, Pasadena, Calif., 1986. Tchr. Hickman County Schs., Centerville, Tenn., 1963-64; min. Ch. of Christ, Parsons, Tenn., 1964-70, Janesville, Wis., 1970-78; prof. York (Nebr.) Coll., 1978—, dept. chmn., 1987-90; cons. Living in Harmony, York, 1983—; cons. in marriage in family. Author: Among Friends, 1989, (videos) Living in Harmony, 1987; editor: Wisconsin Challenge, 1974-78; contbr. articles to profl. jours. Cons. Nebr. Dist. Ct. Clks., 1989; v.p. York Booster Club, 1987-88. Named one of Outstanding Young Men Am., 1973. Mem. Bibl. Archaeol. Soc., York Coll. Forum (pres. 1984-85), Lectureship Com. (chmn. 1985-90), Nat. Christian Counselors Assn. Avocations: fishing, travel, sports, reading. Home: 828 Iowa St York NE 68467 Office: York Coll York NE 68467

HINKLE, JILL ELAINE, religion educator, counselor; b. Santa Rosa, Calif., Dec. 30, 1956; d. Edward Ben and Rosalie Bertha (Jacoby) H. BA in Psychology, Westmont Coll., 1978; MA in Marriage and Family Ministry,

Biola U., 1986, postgrad., 1990—; MA in Coll. Student Affairs, Azusa Pacific U., 1987; cert. in theology, The Julian (Calif.) Ctr., 1988. Cert. secondary tchr., Calif. Tchr., coach Calvary and South Bay Christian high schs., Mountain View, Calif., 1979-82; career and personal alumni counselor Azusa (Calif.) Pacific U., 1984-87; counselor, speaker Ministry Assocs., Orange County, Calif., 1985-86; vocat. dir. Julian Ctr., 1988-89; mem. faculty Biola U., La Mirada, Calif., 1991—; mem. adv. bd., dir. seminars Summit Expeditions, West Covina, Calif., 1987-88; dir. mktg. and personality, career cons. Personality Devel. Inst., Anaheim, Calif., 1989—. Author: (study guide) Holy Sweat, 1987. Counselor Girls Club, Santa Barbara Area YMCA, 1976-77; facilitator City of Long Beach Adminstrs., Dana Point, Calif., 1988; instr. Probation Dept., L.A., 1989-91. Coll. Scholarship Program, Biola U. grantee and fellow, 1990-91. Mem. Assn. Christians in Student Devel., Christian Assn. for Psychol. Studies. Republican. Home: 22295 Vista Verde Dr Lake Forest CA 92630

HINLICKY, PAUL RICHARD, minister; b. Portchester, N.Y., Sept. 4, 1952; s. William Paul and Marie Maxine (Novotny) H.; m. Ellen Irene Christiansen, Aug. 17, 1974; children: Sarah Ellen, William Alfred. BA, Concordia Coll., Fort Wayne, Ind., 1974; MDiv, Seminex, St. Louis, 1978; PhD, Union Theol. Sem., 1983. Ordained to ministry Evang. Luth. Ch. Am., 1978. Asst. pastor Mount Zion Luth. Ch., Harlem, N.Y., 1978-80; resch. assoc. Dept. Ch. in Soc. Luth. Ch. in Am., 1982-85; pastor Immanuel Luth. Ch., Delhi, N.Y., 1985—; editor, exec. dir. Luth. Forum Am. Luth. Publicity Bur., 1988—. Contbr. articles to jours. in field. Office: Am Luth Pub Bur PO Box 327 Delhi NY 13753

HINOJOSA, LUIS SAINZ, archbishop. Archbishop of La Paz, Roman Cath. Ch., Bolivia. Office: Roman Cath Ch, Casilla 259, Calle Ballivian 1277, La Paz Bolivia*

HINOJOSA BERRONES, ALFONSO, bishop; b. Monterrey, Mex., Oct. 7, 1924; s. Emilio Hinojosa and Guadalupe Berrones. ThD, Gregorian U., Rome, 1951. Ordained priest Roman Cath. Ch., 1949, ordained bishop, 1974. Prof. theology Seminario de Monterrey, 1951-52, 59-74; bishop of Ciudad Victoria Mex., 1974; aux. bishop Roman Cath. Ch., Monterrey, Mex., 1985—. Address: Apartado Postal 7, 64000 Monterrey Mexico

HINSHAW, VERLIN ORVILLE, minister; b. Wichita, Kans., Nov. 15, 1925; s. Orval L. and Ethel Charlotte (Craft) H.; m. Annabelle Bowers, Aug. 26, 1945; children: Daryl, Kathleen. AB, Friends U., 1948; BD cum laude, Nazarene Theol. Sem., 1951; PhD, Vanderbilt U., 1964. Ordained to ministry Religious Soc. of Friends, 1948. Pastor various chs., Kans. and Mo., 1945-48, 51-52; assoc. prof. religion William Penn Coll., Oskaloosa, Iowa, 1953-58; prof. of religion and Greek Friends U., Wichita, 1958—. Regional editor, contbg. editor Evang. Friend, 1967; contbr. articles, ednl. materials to profl. publs. Bd. dirs. Inter-Faith Ministries, Wichita, 1987—. Fellow Inst. Biblical Rsch.; mem. Soc. Biblical Lit. and Exegesis. Home: 9900 Bekemeyer Wichita KS 67212 Office: Friends U 2100 University Wichita KS 67213

HINSON, ROBERT EVANS, pastor; b. Richmond, Va., July 13, 1945; s. Garnett Lyell and Leafie Virginia (Bell) H.; m. Evelyn Carrah Harrison, June 21, 1969; children: Stephen Kyle, Christa Dominique, Michelle Elizabeth. BA, Lee Coll., Cleveland, Tenn., 1968; MA, Hartford Sem., 1970; MDiv, Yale U., 1972. Ordained to ministry Ch. of God (Cleveland, Tenn.), 1971. Co-pastor Springfield (Mass.) Ch. of God, 1972-74; pastor Spring Valley Ch. of God, Reading, Pa., 1974—; bd. dirs. Local 700 Club, Reading, 1980-88, Peniel Ministries, Somerset, Pa., 1982—, State Coun. Pa. Chs. of God, Somerset, 1982-86, 88—, Ch. of God of Theology, 1990—. Contbr. rticles to Ch. of God Evangel. Mem. Pi Delta Omicron. Republican. Home: 2101 Mayo Dr Reading PA 19601 Office: Spring Valley Ch of God 2727 Old Pricetown Rd PO Box 14143 Reading PA 19612 *The greatest challenge in life is to unselfishly serve others with the attitude of a servant with the goal to elevate the misery and suffering of my fellow man. I am enriched when I empty myself in service.*

HINTON, ANITA MARIE, church secretary; b. Wallace, Idaho, Feb. 8, 1946; d. Charles Fredrick and Charlotte Christina (Krasin) Stephens; m. Jimmy Dwayne Hinton, May 21, 1976; children: Stephen, Eric. BA in Edn., Arizona State U., 1974. Pres. Luther League group Grace Luth. Ch., Amarillo, Tex., 1958-60; vol. office profl., libr. Paramount Terr. Christian Ch., Amarillo, 1983-85, music sec., 1985—; costume chmn. Christmas pageant Paramount Terr. Christian Ch., Amarillo, 1983-85, 89, adminstrv. coord., 1987—, supr. vacation Bible sch., 1984, officer Women in God's Svc., 1984-85, sponsor ch. youth choir, 1986—, rep. ch. choir officers, 1985—; mem. Pinetop (Ariz.) Presbyn. Choir, 1974-75. Author: (melodrama) Choir at the OK Corral, 1987. Mem. Avondale Elem. Sch. PTA, Amarillo, 1984-85; pres. band and orch. parents Houston Jr. High Sch., Amarillo, 1984-85; cub master local pack Boy Scouts Am., Amarillo, 1986-87, chmn. com. local Boy Scouts troop women's aux., 1988-91; mem. cast Amarillo Little Theatre, 1988, 89; assoc. N.W. Tex. Choristers Guild, Amarillo Ch. Music Secs. Guild, also organizer. Office: Paramount Terr Christian Ch 4000 Mays St Amarillo TX 79109

HINZ, GERALD, religious organization administrator. Rec. sec. The Protes'tant Conf. (Lutheran), Inc., Shiocton, Wis. Office: Protes'tant Conf PO Box 86 Shiocton WI 54170*

HINZ, LEO, minister. Head Humboldt Clergy Coun., Saskatchewan, Can. Office: Humboldt Clergy Coun, Box 1989, Humboldt, SK Canada S0K 2A0*

HIPKINS, JAMES RICHARD, minister; b. Leipsic, Ohio, July 13, 1927; s. Thomas C. and Dorotha M. (Cruickshank) H.; m. Charlotte E. Wahl, Aug. 27, 1949; 2 children: Jill Elaine, Thomas Corwin. BA, Ohio Wesleyan U., 1951; MDiv, Boston U., 1954; cert. in Chinese, Yale U., 1964. Pastor Saviour Meth Ch., Cin., 1957-63; tchr., missionary Bd. of Missions United Meth. Ch., Sarawak and Singapore, 1963-72; pastor United Meth. Chs., Dayton, Zanesville, Ohio, 1972-79; exec. sec. Am. Friends Svc. Com, Dayton, 1979-80; pastor Hope United Meth. Ch., Whitehouse, Ohio, 1980-86, Mt. Washington United Meth. Ch., Cin., 1986-90; chmn. Commn. on Peace, Ohio Coun. Chs., Columbus, 1987—; bd. dirs. Interfaith Ctr. for Peace, Columbus, 1988—. Chmn. Willshire (Ohio) Devel. Corp., 1955; pres. Montgomery (Ohio) PTA, 1959; chmn., bd. dirs. Parkside Community Ctr., Dayton, Ohio, 1978-79, Bond Drive for Schs., Zanesville, 1975; founder Pierce St. Community, Zanesville, 1974. Sgt. US Army, 1944-47. Mem. Assn. for Type, Kiwanis (pres. Montgomery 1963), Lions Club (tail twister 1967). Democrat. Avocations: art, gardening, golf. Home: 348 Reed School House Rd Sevierville TN 37862

HIPPS, DIANA L., lay worker; b. Kokomo, Ind., Dec. 22, 1951; d. William C. and Betty M. (Calveard) Spencer; m. John Hipps, June 7, 1970; children: Ryan C., Steven D., Andrew M. Sec. diploma, Ind. Bus. Coll., Kokomo, 1970; student, Ind. U., Ft. Wayne, 1990—. Sunday sch. tchr. Trinity United Meth. Ch., Kokomo, 1972-76, ch. sec., 1974-76; Sunday sch. tchr. Taylor Chapel United Meth. Ch., Ft. Wayne, 1978—, jr. high youth leader, 1987—; mem. various coms. Taylor Chapel United Meth. Ch., Ft. Wayne, 1978—, choir, 1980—, trustee, 1988-89; payroll adminstr., adminstrv. asst. The Med. Protective Co., Ft. Wayne, 1989—. Bd. dirs. St. Joseph's Little League, Ft. Wayne, 1986. Mem. Am. Payroll Assn.

HIPPS, LARRY CLAY, clergyman, evangelistic association executive; b. Huntsville, Ala., Aug. 11, 1953; s. William B. and Clara M. (Yance) H.; m. Cathy Ann Dees, Mar. 22, 1975; children: Betsy Ann, Allison Renee, Jonathan Clay. BS, Ala. A&M U., 1975; MinM, Internat. Bible Inst. and Sem., 1983, MinD, 1984. Ordained minister Bapt. Ch., 1975. Dir. ministry Flint River Bapt. Ch., Huntsville, 1973-76; assoc. pastor West Rome Bapt. Ch., Rome, Ga., 1976-80, Broadway Bapt. Ch., Memphis, 1980-87; pres. Bring Them In Evangelist Assn., Inc., Memphis, 1976-88, Houston, 1988—; pres. BTI Home Bus. Dirs. Inst., Memphis and Houston, 1984-89. Author: Bring Them in Sunday School Lesons, 1980, BTI Bus Director Manual, 1981, BTI Bus Captain's Handbook, 1987; pub., editor Bring Them In Mag., 1975—; pub. Puppet UpDate mag., Tulsa, 1978. Mem. Nation Wide Bus Ministry Assn. (pres. 1978-79). Republican. Avocation: Disneyana collector. Office: Bring Them In 11323 Hughes Rd Houston TX 77089

HIRBE, RICHARD ANDREW, JR. (BROTHER), pastoral care director, counselor; b. Culver City, Calif., Jan. 11, 1952; s. Richard Andrew Sr. and Dorothy (Stadler) H. Student, U. St. Thomas, 1976-78, Allan Hancock Coll., 1984-86; MA in Religious Studies/Pastoral Couns., Mt. St. Mary's Coll., 1990. Hospice chaplain Mercy Med. Ctr., Redding, Calif., 1981-83; religious brother Franciscan Friars, Arroyo Grande, Calif., 1983-86; spiritual asst. Secular Franciscan Order, Arroyo Grande, 1984-86; asst. provincial minister Secular Franciscan Order, Ventura, Calif., 1985-87; chaplain St. Francis Med. Ctr., Lynwood, Calif., 1986-87; assoc. pastor Little Co. of Mary Hosp., Torrance, Calif., 1987-88; dir. pastoral care St. Francis Med. Ctr., Lynwood, Calif., 1988—; co-founder Calif. Task Force, 1983-86; founder AIDS Task force, San Luis Obispo, Calif., 1984-86; cons. Pacific Inst. for Bioethics, Solvang, Calif., 1984—; internat. communication coord. Bros. for Christian Communication, 1991—. AIDS minister Monterey Diocese Calif., Arroyo Grande, 1985; active AIDS Task Force, Bros. for Christian Community; bd. dirs. South Bay AIDS Being Alive, 1985—. Mem. Nat. Assn. Cath. Chaplains. Democrat. Avocation: running. Home: PO Box 604 Hermosa Beach CA 90254-0604

HIRNBOCK, AUGUST, minister, religious organization administrator. P-res. Bapt. Union of Austria, Vienna. Office: Bapt Union, 1160 Vienna Austria*

HIRSCH, CHARLES BRONISLAW, religion educator; b. Bklyn., Jan. 23, 1919; s. Hugo G. and Mary (Romanowicz) H.; m. Patricia Parsons, June 1, 1941; children: Judith Rae, Susan Kathryn, Cynthia Jean. B.A. in History, Atlantic Union Coll., Mass., 1948; M.A. in History and Polit. Sci, Ind. U., 1949, Ph.D., 1954. Instr. State Tchrs. Coll., New Britain, Conn., 1950-51; assoc. prof., chmn. dept. social scis., dir. pub. relations La Sierra Coll., Arlington, Calif., 1951-57; prof. history, chmn. dept. Columbia Union Coll., Washington, 1957-59; pres. Columbia Union Coll., 1959-65; v.p. acad. adminstrn. Andrews U., Berrien Springs, Mich., 1965-66; sec. dept. edn. Gen. Conf. Seventh-day Adventists, Washington, 1966-74; dir. office edn. Columbia Union Conf., Takoma Park, Md., 1974-75, N.Am., 1975—; dir. Office Edn., World Hdqrs. Seventh-day Adventists Ch., 1980; gen. v.p. Gen. Conf. Seventh-day Adventists, Washington, 1981-85; dir. Internat. Ins. Co., Takoma Park, Md., Gen. Conf. Risk Mgmt. Services. Trustee Loma Linda U., Calif., Corona Community Hosp., Calif.; chmn. Andrews Univ., Mich., Home Study Internat., Washington, Seventh Day Adventist Bd. Edn., Washington. With AUS, 1941-45, ETO. Decorated Bronze Star with oak leaf cluster. Mem. Am. Hist. Assn., Orgn. Am. Historians, Am. Assn. Sch. Adminstrs., Am. Polit. Sci. Assn., Phi Alpha Theta. Club: Rotary. Home: 10974 Applewood Ln Yucaipa CA 92399 *The stability of the person depends much on strong spiritual leanings, family support, and true friendships. These are enhanced by integrity, fairness, and an outreaching loving attitude.*

HIRSCH, JUNE SCHAUT, chaplain trainee; b. Green Bay, Wis., Sept. 30, 1925; d. Clifford Charles and Eleanor Josephine (Arts) Schaut; m. Marshall E. Gilette, Jan. 23, 1946 (div. 1974); children: Ronald Leigh, Patrick Allen, Vicki Jeanne Baumann; m. Hubert L. Hirsch, Nov. 7, 1975. Student, St. Mary's Sch. Nursing, Rochester, Minn., 1943-45, U. Wis., Sheboygan, 1974-75. Cert. med. asst., 1966. Med. asst. James W. Faulkner, M.D., Phoenix, 1953-56; med. office mgr. Edward E. Houfek, M.D., Sheboygan, Wis., 1956-75; med. office cons. Profl. Mgmt. Inc., Milw., 1975-77; office mgr., adminstrv. asst. Schroeder & Holt Architects Ltd., Milw., 1977-90; vol. chaplain Camilles Health Ctr., Milw., 1991—; instr. med. asst. program Lake Shore Tech., 1975-76. Mem. Am. Assn. Med. Assts. (nat. trustee 1963-66), Wis. Soc. Med. Assts. (life, exec. bd. 1960-81), Greater Milw. Med. Assts. (life, exec. bd. 1975-89), Lake Shore Med. Assts. (exec. bd. 1959-75). Republican. Roman Catholic. Home: 10200 W Bluemound Rd # 918 Wausatosa WI 53226

HIRSCH, RICHARD GEORGE, rabbi; b. Cleve., Sept. 13, 1926; s. Abe and Bertha (Gusman) H.; m. Bella Rosencweig, Sept. 5, 1954; children—Ora Hirsch Pescovitz, Raphael, Ammiel, Emmet. B.A., U. Cin., 1947; B.H.L., Hebrew Union Coll.-Jewish Inst. Religion, Cin., 1948, M.H.L., 1951, D.D., 1976. Rabbi Temple Emanuel, Chgo., 1951-53, Denver, 1953-56; regional dir. Union Am. Hebrew Congregations, Chgo., 1956-61; dir. Union Am. Hebrew Congregations Religious Action Center, Washington, 1962-73; exec. dir. World Union Progressive Judaism, Jerusalem, 1973—; vis. lectr. Hebrew Union Coll. Jewish Inst. Religion; mem. exec. com. World Zionist Orgn., elected chmn. Zionist gen. coun., 1987; mem. exec. bd. Cen. Conf. Am. Rabbis. Author: Judaism and Cities in Crisis, 1961, There Shall Be No Poor, 1964, The Way of the Upright, 1967, Thy Most Precious Gift, 1969. Sec. Citizens Crusade Against Proverty, 1964-68. Office: 13 King David St, Jerusalem Israel

HIRSCHFELD, WILLIAM JACOB, minister; b. N.Y.C., Apr. 6, 1938; s. William Maximilian and Katharine (Geyer) H.; m. Lorraine Rose Gesser, Apr. 18, 1958 (div. 1976); children: William, Elliott, Matthew, Eric; m. Julia Moore Daugharty, Aug. 7, 1983. BA, NYU, 1959, MS in Biology, 1960, PhD in Biology, 1964; MDiv, Chgo. Theol. Seminary, 1979. Ordained to ministry United Ch. of Christ, 1979. Pastor Davies Meml. United Ch. of Christ, Potosi, Wis., 1978-79, Christ Ch. of Chgo., 1980-81, First Congregational United Ch. of Christ, Cadillac, Mich., 1981-85, Pilgrim United Ch. of Christ, Cuyahoga Falls, Ohio, 1985—. Contbr. articles to profl. jours. Bd. dirs., trustee Taylor Meml. Libr., Cuyahoga Falls, 1990; pres. Minister's Assn., 1991. Recipient Founder's Day award NYU, 1964, postdoctoral traineeship, USPHS, 1966-68; Carl S. Patton fellow Chgo. Theol. Seminary, 1977, 78. Mem. Soc. for Math. Biology (charter). Democrat. Home: 845 Broad Blvd Cuyahoga Falls OH 44221 Office: Pilgrim United Ch of Christ 130 Broad Blvd Cuyahoga Falls OH 44221

HIRSCH-FIKEJS, JUDITH ANN, minister; b. Macon, Ga., Aug. 17, 1939; d. Alvin and E. Jo (Vaughn) Hirsch; m. George Arthur Fikejs, Mar. 20, 1959; children: Ann-Laureen, Jeffrey, Allison, Tracy. BA, Stephens Coll., 1982; MDiv, Fuller Theol. Seminary, Pasadena, Calif., 1985. Ordained to ministry, Presbyn. Ch. (USA), 1986. Studio musician Word, Sacred and RCA Records, Chgo., 1958-65; nursing asst. Good Samaritan Hosp., San Jose, Calif., 1966-69; pvt. music instr. various, 1966-82; high sch. tchr. Linfield Sch., Temecula, Calif., 1977-82; jr. high tchr. Pacific Christian High Sch., L.A., 1983-85; interim dir., Christian edn. Pasadena Presbyn. Ch., 1984-85; pastor Community Presbyn. Ch., Acton, Calif., 1985—; mission study coord. Presbytery of San Fernando and L.A., 1986-90; chair Sta. Clarita New Ch. devel. steering com., 1989—, com. on reps., San Fernando Presbytery, 1990—; chaplain Antelope Valley Rehab. Ctrs., Acton and Castiac, Calif., 1987—; vol. chaplain VA Hosp., Sepulveda, Calif., 1989—. Author religious column, Acton News, 1985—; conf. reviewer, The Presbyterian, 1987. Bd. dirs. Antelope Valley Rehab. Ctrs., L.A. County, 1988-89; bd. dirs., pres. Agape Home for Women Alcoholics, Lancaster, Calif., 1986-89; chmn. Com. for Nat. Am. Ministries, L.A., 1987-88. Recipient Vol. award, L.A. Assessor, Acton Rehab. Ctr., 1988. Mem. Nat. Assn. Female Execs., Rotary. Democrat. Home: 23137 Magnolia Glen Dr Valencia CA 91354 Office: Community Presbyn Church 32142 Crown Valley PO Box 177 Acton CA 93510

HIRSH, RICHARD ALLAN, rabbi; b. Bayshore, N.Y., Feb. 22, 1953; s. Ira L. and Mae H.; m. Barbara Furman; children: Shira Tova, Nadav Yaron. BA, Hofstra U., 1975; MA, Temple U., 1981. Ordained rabbi, 1981. Rabbi Congregation Darchei Noam, Toronto, Can., 1981-83; exec. dir. B'Nai Brith Hillel, Toronto, 1982-83; dean admissions Reconstructionist Rabbinical Coll., Phila., 1983-87; dir. internat. concerns Jewish Community Rels. Coun., Phila., 1987-88; exec. dir. Bd. Rabbis Jewish Chaplaincy Svc., Phila., 1988—. Mem. Cen. Con. Am. Rabbis., Reconstructionist Rabbinical Assn. Home: 32 Lodges Ln Bala Cynwyd PA 19004 Office: Bd Rabbis/Jewish Chaplaincy 1616 Walnut St Ste 909 Philadelphia PA 19103

HIRSLEY, MICHAEL, religion writer; b. N.Y.C., Nov. 8, 1942; s. Erwin and Marian Hirsley; m. Kathleen Hirsley, July 25, 1970; children: Suzanne, Elizabeth, Quentin, Nolan. BS in Journalism, U. Wis., 1964. Reporter Waukegan News-Sun, 1965-69, Chgo. Today, 1969-74; mem. staff Chgo. Tribune, 1974—, nat. corr. for South, 1982-87, religion writer, 1988—. Recipient investigation award Ill. AP, 1971, 1st pl. award, 1978; 1st pl. award for investigative series Am. Soc. Planning Officials, 1973. Office: Chgo Tribune 435 N Michigan Ave Chicago IL 60611

HISEK, DENNIS DALE, religious organization administrator; b. Tyndall, S.D., Apr. 14, 1949; s. Leo J. and Meta V. (Finck) H.; m. Jeannette Marie Vanecek, June 12, 1971; children: RosMery, Jennifer, Bradley. BS, S.D. State U., 1972; MS, U. Mo., 1979. Recreation therapist Butterfield Youth Svcs., Marshall, Mo., 1976-86; mgr./dir. Wilderness Camp United Meth. Ch., Lawson, Mo., 1986-89; dir. programming Mo. west conf. United Meth. Ch., 1989. Vol. Peace Corps U.S. Govt., Ibague, Columbia and S.Am., 1973-76; mem. Bd. Diaconal Ministry; co-founder Adoption Support Group for Western Cen. Mo.; cluster coord. YMCA/YPUM, 1981-86; organizer recycling ctr. City of Lawson, 1990-91; chairperson, mem. ch. coms., 1980—; lay spaker; mgr., dir. Wilderness Camp, 1989—; tchr. Sunday sch., 1989—.

HITCHCOCK, JOHN LATHROP, physics educator, author; b. Chgo., June 18, 1936; s. Bonver Ridgeway Hitchcock and Elizabeth (Mack) Munger. BS in Physics, U. Mich., Ann Arbor, 1954-59; MA in Astronomy, U. Calif., Berkeley, 1966; PhD, Grad Theol Union, Berkeley, 1975. Lectr. physics U. Wis., LaCrosse, 1984—; leader Guild for Psychol. Studies, San Francisco, 1968—; lectr., workshop presenter; mem. adv. bd. Ctr. for Studies in Sci. and Spirituality, San Francisco. Author: Atoms, Snowflakes and God, 1986, Web of the Universe: Jung, the New Physics and Spirituality, 1990; contbr. articles to profl. jours. Lt. USNR, 1959-63. Mem. Am. Acad. Religion, Am. Assn. Physics Tchrs. Democrat. Office: U Wis Physics Dept 1725 State St La Crosse WI 54601

HITCHENS, ROBERT JOSEPH, minister, college president; b. Milford, Del., Mar. 2, 1942; s. Bradford and Pearl Elizabeth (Scott) H.; m. Charlotte Roberta Shiflett, Feb. 1, 1964. Bible diploma, B.R.E., Prairie Bible Inst., Three Hills, Alta., Can., 1971; MA in Theology, Immanuel Baptist Coll., Atlanta, 1979; D Ministry, Clarksville Sch. Theology, 1982. Ordained to ministry Baptist Ch., 1971; cert. Evang. Tchr. Tng. Assn. Assoc. pastor Maranatha Bapt. Ch., Elkton, Md., 1971—; acad. dean Md. Bapt. Bible Coll., Elkton, 1973-90, pres., 1990—. Served with U.S. Army, 1959-67. Mem. Fundamental Bapt. Fellowship Am., Archaeol. Inst. Am., Md. Coalition of Bible Insts., Colls. and Seminaries (pres. 1985), Smithsonian Assocs., Citizens for Republic, U.S. Senatorial Club, NRA. Republican. Home: 3228 Old Elk Neck Rd Elkton MD 21921 Office: PO Box 66 Elkton MD 21921

HITE, JOSEPH PIERCE, minister, consultant; b. Wenatchee, Wash., Aug. 16, 1957; s. James Edward and Clarice Ann (Shotwell) H.; m. Robin Mae Grissom, Dec. 9, 1978; children: Chelsea Lynn, Austyn Michele, Pierce Jameson Mitchell. AA, Wenatchee Valley Coll., 1978. Mgr. prodn. Spokane (Wash.) Parks, 1978-80; mktg. Clarklift of Wash., Seattle, 1980-83, Keebler Corp., Seattle, 1983-84; pastor Puget Sound Christian Ch., Tacoma, 1984—; dir. Messenger Northwest, Tacoma, staff cons. Messenger Internat., San Jose, Calif. Producer (video) Kingdom Session, 1986, Messenger in Action, 1986; producer, engr. (record) Spirit of Truth Singers, 1979. Named Eagle Scout Boy Scouts Am., Cashmere, Wash., 1973. Republican. Avocations: reading, hiking, sailing, fishing, golf. Home: PO Box 9503 Tacoma WA 98409 Office: Puget Sound Christian Ctr 5446 S Birmingham Tacoma WA 98409

HITTINGER, RAYMOND CLAYTON, minister; b. White Haven, Pa., July 9, 1942; s. Henry Grant and Grace Catherine (Warg) H.; m. Joyce Alice Herbener, June 10, 1967; children: Tammy Jo, Jeffrey Alan, Matthew David, Jessica Ann. BA, Gettysburg Coll., 1964; MDiv, Luth. Theol. Sem., Phila., 1968. Ordained to ministry Luth. Ch. in Am., 1968. Pastor Friedens Luth. Ch., Hegins, Pa., 1968-75, Rosemont Luth. Ch., Bethlehem, Pa., 1975—; mem. justice and social change com. Northeastern Pa. Synod, Luth. Ch. in Am., 1973-76, mem. exec. bd., 1982-85, sec. Bethlehem-Easton dist., 1980-86, dean of dist., 1986-88; dean Bethlehem-Easton Mission Dist., Northeastern Pa. Synod, Evang. Luth. Ch. Am., 1988—; bd. dirs. Greater Bethlehem Area Coun. Chs., 1989—, v.p., 1991—; chmn. migrant ministry com. Pa. Coun. Chs., Harrisburg, 1974-78; chmn. com. on seasonal farm workers Pa. Conf. interchurch Cooperation, 1974-79; bd. dirs. Bethlehem Area Luths. in Mission, 1978—; pres. Luth. Manor of Lehigh Valley, Inc., Bethlehem, 1979-82; del. Luth. Ch. in Am. Biennial Conv., 1984, Constituting Conv. of Evang. Luth. Ch. in Am., 1987, Biennial Assembly, 1989. Bd. dirs. Tri-Valley Can Do, Hegins 1970-75; mem. Schuylkill County Child Welfare Adv. Com., 1972-75; pres. Hegins Area Ambulance Assn., 1973-75; mem. com. on seasonal farm workers Pa. Dept. Environment Resources, 1978-79; pres. Rosemont Family Health Ctr., Bethlehem, 1983-88; chaplain City of Bethlehem Police Dept., 1988—. Mem. Bethlehem Ministerial Assn., Bethlehem Luth. Pastors Assn. Office: Rosemont Luth Ch 1705 W Broad St Bethlehem PA 18018 *The greatest joy in life for me is the satisfaction of knowing that another person's life has been affected positively because I was there responding to God's call to love.*

HIVELY, NEAL OTTO, clergyman; b. Williamsport, Pa., Aug. 19, 1950; s. Otto Ezra and Mildred Ruth (Mizener) H.; m. Lee Codd; children: Christopher Stephen, Beth Ellen. BA in Classics, Thiel Coll., 1972; MDiv, Gettysburg (Pa.) Seminary, 1976, MST, 1984; D.Ministry, Phila. Sem., 1990. Ordained to ministry Luth. Ch., 1976. Pastor Upper Bermudian Luth. Ch., Gardners, Pa., 1976-82, Bethlehem Coop. Parish, Glen Rock, Pa., 1982-90, St. John Luth. Ch., Columbia, Pa., 1990—; chmn. Conf. for Evangelism to the Inactive Mem., Cen. Pa. Synod, Luth. Ch. Am., 1978-88, Evangelism to the Unchurched task force, Cen. Pa. Synod, 1977-81; adj. instr. Gettysburg Seminary, 1977-82; chmn., bd. dirs. Luth. Social Svcs. Author: The History of the Upper Bermudian Lutheran Church, 1984, Codorus Township, York County, 1988, West Manheim (Pa.) Township, York County, 1989, Manheim/Heidleberg Township, York County, 1989. Mem. Evang. Luth Ch. Am. (lower Susquehanna synod), Luth. Hist. Soc. (editor Gettysburg newsletter 1989—), Upper Adams County Ministerium. Home: 187 Ridings Way Lancaster PA 17601 Office: St John Evang Luth Ch 616 Locust St PO Box Columbia PA 17512

HIXSON, KEITH EVAN, pastor; b. Walla Walla, Wash., Oct. 14, 1945; s. Fred Cunningham and Erma (Kempton) H.; m. Susan Lorrie Turner, July 5, 1969; children: Kevin, Patricia. Student, So. Calif. Coll., 1964-66; BA in Bibl. Lit., NW Coll., Kirkland, Wash., 1973. Lic. minister Assemblies of God, 1973, ordained to ministry, 1976; cert. first aid and CPR instr. Pastor Winthrop (Wash.) Assembly of God Ch., 1973-75, Tenino (Wash.) Assembly of God Ch., 1975-87, Newport (Wash.) Assembly of God Ch., 1987—; chaplain Thurston County Sheriff's Dept., Olympia, Wash., 1983-87, Newport Community Hosp., 1989—; past pres. Methow Valley Ministerial Assn.; past pres. and sec.-treas. Tenino Ministerial Assn.; past chaplain Tenino Fire Dept.; instr. first aid and CPR, South Community Coll., 1977-87. Vol. fireman, EMT, Tenino Fire Dept., 1975-84; mem. Tenino Town Coun., 1978-84, mayor, 1984-87; Bd. dirs. Mason-Thurston County br. ARC, Olympia, 1984-87, Pend Oreille County Hosp. Dist. 1, Newport, 1988—; past memt. Thurston County Emergency Med. Svcs. Bd., Thurston County Regional Planning Bd., Thurston County Animal Control Bd. With U.S. Army, 1967-69. Mem. Newport Ministerial Assn. (pres. 1990-91). Home: 900 W 5th St PO Box 1318 Newport WA 99156 Office: Newport Assembly of God Ch 1428 W 1st St Newport WA 99156

HNAT, MARSHA ANN, youth and young ministry director; b. Perth Amboy, N.J., June 11, 1950; d. Joseph Frank and Helen Marie (Tkach) H.; m. Joda Edward Maynard Jr., May 25, 1972 (div. Aug. 1977). BS, Fla. State U., 1973, MS, 1980; postgrad., Loyola U., New Orleans, 1991—. Catechist St. Thomas More Parish, Tallahassee, 1975-85; pastoral assoc. St. Columba Parish, Conception Junction, Mo., 1988-89; assoc. dir. of religious edn. Diocese of Orlando, Fla., 1989—. Mem. Nat. Cath. Young Adult Ministry Assn., Nat. Fedn. Cath. Youth Ministry. Roman Catholic. Office: Diocese of Orlando 408 E Ridgewood St Orlando FL 32803 *The essence of life to me is the love I share—in friendship, in service, in compassionate presence. This love unites me with both divinity and humanity providing the source of my joy and peace.*

HO, CHEE SIN, minister, bishop, administrator; b. Singapore, Oct. 1, 1935; s. Choy Kian Ho and Ah Djin Sak; m. Phaik Cheng Ooi, Aug. 14, 1965; children: Mark, Boon Kin, Gail, Mae Choo, Luke, Boon Choong. GCE, Anglo-Chinese Sch., Singapore, 1954; BTh., Trinity Theol. Coll., Singapore, 1963, M of Ministry, 1978. Pastor Wesley Meth. Ch., Kampar/Telok Intan, Malaysia, 1964-65, Seremban, Malaysia, 1966-69; pastor Trinity Meth. Ch., Petaling Jaya, Malaysia, 1970-72, Penang, Malaysia, 1973-76; dist. supt. Meth. Ch., Perak Dist., Malaysia, 1976; pastor Faith Meth. Ch., Singapore,

1977-84; dist. west. supt. Meth. Ch., Singapore, 1980-84, pres. Trinity Annual Conf., 1984-88, 88—, bishop, 1984-88, 88—; chair Ch. Growth Ctr, Petaling Jaya, 1970-73, Regional Bd. Meth. Pvt. Schs., Perak Dist., 1976, Coun. on Worship and Liturgy, 1980-84, Singapore, Coun. on Trustees, 1984-88, Coun. on Edn., 1984-88, bd. govs. Trinity Theol. Coll., 1987-88; sec. Coun. Evangelism, 1980-84; mem. exec. coun. Nat. Coun. Chs., 1984-90, adv. coun. Lausanne Com. World Evangelization 2, 1988-89. Home: 50 Barker Rd, Singapore Singapore 1130 Office: Meth Ch, 10 Mount Sophia, Singapore Singapore 0922

HO, PAK TAE, religious organization administrator. Chmn. cen. com. Korean Buddhists Fedn., Pyongyang, Dem. People's Republic Korea. Office: Korean Buddhists Fedn, Pyongyang Democratic People's Republic of Korea*

HOADLEY, WALTER EVANS, economist, financial executive, lay worker; b. San Francisco, Aug. 16, 1916; s. Walter Evans and Marie Howland (Preece) H.; m. Virginia Alm, May 20, 1939; children: Richard Alm, Jean Elizabeth (Mrs. Donald A. Peterson). A.B., U. Calif., 1938, M.A., 1940, Ph.D., 1946; Dr.C.S., Franklin and Marshall Coll., 1963; LL.D. (hon.), Golden Gate U., 1968, U. Pacific, 1979; hon. degree, El Instituto Technologico Autonomo de Mexico, 1974. Collaborator U.S. Bur. Agrl. Econs., 1938-39; rsch. economist Calif. Gov.'s Reemployment Commn., 1939, Calif. Gov.'s State Planning Bd., 1941; rsch. economist, teaching fellow U. Calif., 1938-41, supr. indsl. mgmt. war tng. office, 1941-42; econ. adviser U. Chgo. Civil Affairs Tng. Sch., 1945; sr. economist Fed. Res. Bank Chgo., 1942-49; economist Armstrong World Industries, Lancaster, Pa., 1949-54, treas., 1954-60, v.p., treas., 1960-66, dir., 1962-87; sr. v.p., chief economist, mem. mng. com. Bank of Am. NT & SA, San Francisco, 1966-68, exec. v.p., chief economist, mem. mng. com., mem. mgmt. adv. council, chmn. subs., 1968-81; ret., 1981; sr. research fellow Hoover Inst., Stanford U., 1981—; dir. Levolor Corp., PLM Internat., Transcisco Industries, Inc., Selected Funds; dep. chmn. Fed. Res. Bank, Phila., 1960-61, chmn., 1962-66; chmn. Conf. Fed. Res. Chairmen, 1966; faculty Sch. Banking U. Wis., 1945-49, 55, 58-66; adviser various U.S. Govt. agys.; Wright Internat. Bd. Econ. and Investment Advisors, 1987—; spl. adviser U.S. Congl. Budget Office, 1975-87; mem. pub. adv. bd. U.S. Dept. Commerce, 1970-74; mem. White House Rev. Com. for Balance Payments Statistics, 1963-65, Presdl. Task Force on Growth, 1969-70, Presdl. Task Force on Land Utilization, Presdl. Conf. on Inflation, 1974; gov. Com. on Developing Am. Capitalism, 1977—, chmn. 1987-88. Mem. Meth. Ch. Commn. on World Service and Fin. Phila. Conf., 1957-64, chmn. investment com., 1964-66; bd. dirs., exec. com. Internat. Mgmt. and Devel. Inst., 1976—; trustee Pacific Sch. Religion, 1968-89; adviser Nat. Commn. to Study Nursing and Nursing Edn., 1968-73; trustee Duke U., 1968-73, pres.'s assoc., 1973-80; trustee Golden Gate U., 1974—, chmn. investment com., 1977—; trustee World Wildlife U.S.-Conservation Found., 1974-87; mem. periodic chmn. adminstrv. bd. Trinity United Meth. Ch., Berkeley, Calif., 1966-84; mem. adminstrv. bd., advisor Lafayette (Calif.) United Meth. Ch., 1984—; mem. bd. overseers vis. com. Harvard Coll. Econs., 1969-74; chmn. investment com. Calif.-Nev. Meth. Found., 1968-75, mem., 1976-91; mem. Calif. Gov.'s Council Econ. and Bus. Devel., 1978-82, chmn., 1980-82; trustee Hudson Inst., 1979-84; co-chmn. San Francisco Mayor's Fiscal Adv. Com., 1978-81, mem. 1981—; chmn. Bay Area Econ. Advisers, 1982—; spl. adviser Presdl. Cabinet Com. Innovation, 1978-79; mem. Calif. State Internat. Adv. Com., 1986—; regent U. Calif., 1990-91; mem. nat. coun. World Wildlife Fund/The Conservation Found., 1987-901. Fellow Am. Statis. Assn. (v.p. dir. 1952-54, pres. 1958), Nat. Assn. of Bus. Economists, Internat. Acad. Mgmt.; mem. Am. Fin. Assn. (dir. 1955-56, pres. 1969), Conf. Bus. Economists (chmn. 1962), Atlantic Coun. of U.S. (dir. 1985—), trustee, U.S. Coun. for Internat. Bus., 1977—, Commonwealth Club of Calif. (pres. 1987), Internat. Conf. Comml. Bank Economists (chmn. 1978-81), Am., Western Econ. Assns., Am. Marketing Assn., Fin. Analysts San Francisco, Conf. Bd. (econ. forum), Am. Bankers Assn. (chmn. urban and community affairs com. 1972-73, mem. econ. adv. council 1976-78), Nat. Bur. Econ. Rsch. (dir. 1965-81), Western Fin. Assn., dir., mem. steering com., U. Calif. Alumni Assn. (pres. 1989-91, chmn. investment com. 1983-89), U.S. Nat. Com. on Pacific Econ. Cooperation (vice chmn. 1984-89, mem. exec. com. 1989—), Caux Internat. Roundtable, St. Francis Yacht Club, Commonwealth Club, Pacific Union Club, Bankers Club, Silverado Country Club, Phi Beta Kappa (dir. 1986—), Kappa Alpha. Office: Bank of Am Dept 3001-B PO Box 3700sco CA 94137 *From long observation and living, I've concluded that faith in a Supreme Being is the most powerful force enabling an individual to deal with the ongoing challenges of human existence.*

HOBBS, HERSCHEL HAROLD, minister; b. Coosa County, Ala., Oct. 24, 1907; s. Elbert Oscar and Emma Octavia (Whatley) H.; m. Zula Frances Jackson, Apr. 10, 1927 (dec. 1984); children: Jerry Marlin, Harold Elbert. BA, Howard Coll., 1932; ThM, So. Bapt. Theol. Sem., 1935, PhD, 1938; DD (hon), Howard Coll., 1941; LittD (hon.), William Jewell Coll., 1963; LHD (hon), Oklahoma City U., 1968; LLD (hon), John Brown U., 1970; DD (hon.), La. State Coll., 1985, Okla. Bapt. U., 1986. Ordained to ministry Bapt. Ch., 1929. Pastor various Bapt. congregations, Ala., Ky. and La., 1929-49, First Bapt. Ch., Oklahoma City, 1949-72; pastor emeritus First Bapt. Ch., 1973—; pastor syndicated radio program Bapt. Hour, 1958-76; Mem. exec. com. So. Bapt. Conv., 1951-63, pres., 1961-63, pres. pastors' conf., 1951-52; past pres., bd. trustees Okla. Bapt. U.; mem. Fgn. Mission Bd., So. Bapt. Conv.; trustee New Orleans Bapt. Theol. Sem.; v.p. Bapt. World Alliance, 1965, mem. exec. com., 1965-70; missionary tours, 1959, 62, 68. Author over 133 books including Great Passages of the Bible, 1977, The Axioms of Religion, 1978, Preacher Talk, 1979, Galatians, 1979, Hebrews, 1981, Studying Adult Life and Work Lessons, 92 vols., 1969—. Recipient E.Y. Mullins Denominational Service award So. Bapt. Theol. Sem., 1964, Disting. Communications medal So. Bapt. Radio and TV Commn., 1967, 76, Disting. Alumnus award for service to denomination Samford U., 1970, Spl. Citation Didtinctive Service So. Bapt. Radio and TV Commn., 1976; knight gt. band Order of African Redemtion, Govt. of Liberia, 1968. Democrat. Avocation: football. Home: 2509 NW 120th St Oklahoma City OK 73120

HOBBS, LYNDEL ERIN, minister; b. Tulsa, Sept. 23, 1958; s. Lowell Earl Hobbs and Clydel (Weatherly) Cheatham; m. Pamela Sue Estep, May 1, 1981; 1 child, Lindsay Elise. BA, Okla. State U., 1981; postgrad., Southwestern Bapt. Theol. Sem., 1982. Min. of music Southside Bapt. Ch., Stillwater, Okla., 1977-81, B.H. Carroll Bapt. Ch., Ft. Worth, 1982-85; min. of music and edn. Oak Cliff Bapt. Ch., Fort Smith, Ark., 1985—; assn. music dir. Concord Bapt. Assn., Fort Smith, 1986-89, assn. sunday sch. dir., 1988—. Home: 3420 Hendricks Blvd Fort Smith AR 72903 Office: Oak Cliff Bapt Ch 3701 S Gary Fort Smith AR 72903

HOBSON, JOHN RICHARD, minister; b. Clover, S.C., May 3, 1931; s. Patrick Henry and Lena (Clarke) H.; m. Hilda Plecker, July 20, 1956; children: John Richard Jr., Paul Thomas, Carl Patrick. AB, Davidson Coll., 1953; BD, Union Theol. Sem., 1957, MDiv., 1959; DMin., Columbia Theol. Sem., 1989. Ordained to ministry Presbyn. Ch., 1957; min. of the word and sacraments. Pastor Oakboro-Ridgecrest Presbyn. Ch., Stanfield, N.C., 1957-61, Shiloh Presbyn. Ch., Grover, N.C., 1961-65, Squires Meml. Presbyn. Ch., Norfolk, Va., 1965-71; sr. pastor First Presbyn. Ch., Sanford, N.C., 1971—; chmn. budget com. Synod of N.C., Raleigh, 1963-65; chmn. coun. Fayetteville (N.C.) Presbytery, 1974-77; trustee Coastal Carolina Presbytery, Fayetteville, 1988-89, chmn. preparation for ministry, 1991—. Author: (book) Care Takers Into Care Givers, 1989. Chmn. Lee-Harnett Mental Health Bd., Sanford, 1976-80; pres. Lee County Ministerial Fellowship, Sanford, 1980. Mem. Rotary (Sanford). Democrat. Home: 212 Hawkins Ave Sanford NC 27330 Office: First Presbyterian Ch 203 Hawkins Ave PO Box 477 Sanford NC 27330

HOBUS, ROBERT ALLEN, minister; b. Milw., Apr. 11, 1924; s. Herbert Walter and Clara (Hass) H.; m. Alice Olinda Jacobsmeyer, July 10, 1949; children: Paul Alan, David Andrew, Steven Robert, Michael Jon. MST, So. Meth. U., 1970; MDiv, Concordia Theol. Sem., St. Louis, 1971; DMin, Luth. Sch. Theology, Chgo., 1988. Ordained to ministry Luth. Ch.-Mo. Synod., 1949; cert. secondary tchr., Wis., Kans. Pastor 1st Luth. Ch., Rosebud, Tex., 1949-52; assoc. pastor Mt. Olive Luth. Ch., Milw., 1952-56; pastor Peace Luth. Ch., Antigo, Wis., 1956-58, Our Shepherd Luth. Ch., Greendale, Wis., 1958-65, Hope Luth. Ch., Friendswood, Tex., 1970-73; pastor Redeemer Luth. Ch., Wichita, Kans., 1973-78, Arkansas City, Kans., 1980-89; assoc. pastor Hope Luth. Ch., Des Moines, 1989—; dir. pilot project Young Adult/Apt. Ministry, Dallas, 1965-70; chaplain VA Hosp., Temple, Tex., 1949-52; exec. dir. Inter-Faith Ministries, Wichita, 1978-80. Editor (South Wis. dist. supplement) Luth. Witness, 1959-65. Chaplain Wichita Police Dept., 1974-79. Home: 477 Christie Ln Pleasant Hill IA 50317 Office: Hope Luth Ch 3857 E 42d St Des Moines IA 50317

HOCK, ROBERT LEROY, JR., minister; b. Richmond, Va., July 8, 1933; s. Robert L. Sr. and Josephine (Fletcher) H.; m. Mary Quaid McLean, July 17, 1954; children: Deborah Carol Hock Byorick, Robert Daniel, Donna Eliz Hock Wall. BA, Roanoke Coll., 1955; MDiv, Luth. Theol. S. Sem., Columbia, S.C., 1958; D Ministry, McCormick Sem., 1977; DD (hon.), Newberry Coll., 1981. Ordained to ministry Luth. Ch., 1958. Pastor Grace Luth. Ch., Waynesboro, Va., 1958-63; sr. pastor Ebenezer Luth. Ch., Columbia, S.C., 1963-72, St. John Luth. Ch., Winter Park, Fla., 1972—; mem. coun. Fla. Synod Evang. Luth. Ch. Am., Tampa, 1987—; mem. exec. coun. Luth. Ch. in Am., N.Y.C., 1984-87, mem. Fla. Synod exec. bd., 1980-87, dir. evang. outreach, 1979-82. Author: Human Chain, 1985, An Easter Song, 1987. Bd. dirs. Christian Svc. Ctr., Orlando, Fla., 1987—; pres. Columbia Urban Svc. Ctr., Columbia, 1968-72, Lowman Home for Aged, White Rock, S.C., 1971-72; trustee, bd. dirs. Luth. Theol. So. Sem., 1989—. Named Outstanding Young Man Am., Jaycees, 1960. Office: St John Luth Ch 1600 S Orlando Ave Winter Park FL 32789

HOCK, RONALD FRANCIS, religion educator, historian; b. Elmhurst, Ill., June 15, 1944; s. Francis Allen and Grace Magdalen (Hiltenbrand) H.; m. Carol Elenore Erlandson, June 11, 1966; children: Jennifer Lynne, David Ronald. BA, No. Ill. U., 1966; BD, So. Meth. U., 1969; MPhil, Yale U., 1972, PhD, 1974. Asst. prof. religion U. So. Calif., L.A., 1975-81, assoc. prof., 1981—. Author: The Social Context of Paul's Ministry, 1980; co-author: The Chreia in Ancient Rhetoric, 1986. Mem. Soc. Biblical Lit., Inst. Antiquity and Christianity. Democrat. Congregationalist. Avocations: jogging, reading mysteries, travel. Office: U So Calif Sch Religion THH 328 Los Angeles CA 90089-0355

HOCKLE, SISTER M. HENRIETTA, academic administrator. Supt. of Schs. Diocese of Little Rock. Office: Diocesan Schs Supt 2500 N Tyler St PO Box 7565 Little Rock AR 72217*

HODAPP, LEROY CHARLES, bishop; b. Seymour, Ind., Nov. 11, 1923; s. Linden Charles and Mary Marguerite (Miller) H.; m. Polly Anne Martin, June 12, 1947; children: Anne Lynn Hodapp Gates, Nancy Ellen Hodapp Wichman. AB, U. Evansville, Ind., 1944, DD (hon.), 1961; BD, Drew Theol. Sem., Madison, N.J., 1947; LHD (hon.), Ill. Wesleyan U., 1977; DD (hon.), McKendree Coll., 1978; D.D., Wiley Coll., 1980. Ordained to ministry Methodist Ch., 1947; pastor chs. in Ind., 1947-65; supt. Bloomington (Ind.) Dist. Meth. Ch., 1965-67, supt. Indpls. West Dist., 1967-68, supt. Indpls. N.E. Dist., 1968-70; dir. S. Ind. Conf. Council, 1970-76; bishop Ill. area United Meth. Ch., Springfield, 1976-84, Ind. area United Meth. Ch., Indpls., 1984—; pres. United Meth. Gen. Bd. Ch. and Soc., 1980-84, United Meth. Coun. Bishops, 1990-91. Co-editor: Change in the Small Community, 1967. Democrat. Office: The United Meth Ch 1100 W 42d St Indianapolis IN 46208

HODGE, JANICE CONSTANCE, pastoral psychotherapist, minister; b. Chgo., Dec. 3; d. James C. and Bebe Y. (Duncan) h. BA, Roosevelt U., Chgo., 1973, MA, 1980; MDiv, Chgo. Theol. Sem., 1986, D Ministry, 1988. Ordained to ministry United Ch. of Christ, 1987, ecclesiastical endorsement, 1989. Primary tchr. Chgo. Pub. Schs., 1975-83; sr. staff pastoral psychotherapist Parkside Pastoral Counseling Ctr., Park Ridge, Ill., 1990—; assoc. pastor Bryn Mawr Community Ch., Chgo., 1991—; co-chmn. Bd. Svcs. to Chs. and Mins., Chgo., 1985-87; mem. bd. Ill. Conf. Women's Team, Chgo., 1985-87. Ward asst. Office Congressman Harold Washington, Chgo., 1979-81; chmn. Women's Resource Team, Chgo., 1985-87. Black studennt fellow Chgo. Theol. Sem., 1983-84, William J. Faulkner fellow, 1984-86; Carroll Wise clin. fellow Parkside Pastoral Psychotherapy Inst., 1988-89. Mem. Am. Assn. Pastoral Counselors, Prof. Assn. Clergy (bd. dirs. 1989-90). Office: Parkside Pastoral Counseling Ctr 1875 Dempster Rd Ste 365 Park Ridge IL 60068 *Hope, which arises out of resurrection faith, is the most important attribute of my life. No matter how despairing the circumstance, hope extends her hands in the promise of renewal.*

HODGE, JESSE LYNN, minister; b. Tahoka, Tex., Aug. 28, 1942; s. Joe and Myrtle Ellen (Hammond) H.; m. Elizabeth Luccille Dorn, Jan. 10, 1963; children: Jesse Lynn Jr., Radonda Raschelle, Thaddaeus Paul, Rebecca Erlene. BA, West Tex. U., 1979. Pastor St. Luke's United Meth. Ch., Colorado City, Tex., 1972-75, Wesley United Meth. Ch., Hereford, Tex., 1976-84; pastor 1st United Meth. Ch., Adrian, Tex., 1975-76, Raton, N.Mex., 1984—; mem. N.Mex. Conf. Bd. Evangelism, 1989, N.Mex. Conf. Bd. Ch. Revitalization, 1989; chmn. Dist. Bd. Evangelism, N.Mex., 1989. Pres. Youth Sports Bd., Raton, 1986, Am. Cancer Soc., Raton, 1989, C. of C. Ambs., Raton, 1990; mem. Sierra Grande Cowboy Camp Meeting, Des Moines, 1986, Community Correction Bd., Raton, 1989. Mem. Kiwanis (mem. bd. 1985-90). Democrat. Office: 1st United Meth Ch PO Box 547 Raton NM 87740

HODGE, JIMMY L., minister; b. Loudon, Tenn., Oct. 9, 1947; s. James R. and Lillian B. (Long) H.; m. Teresa Johnson, Aug. 27, 1970; children: Brent, Brad. BS, Trevecca Coll., 1969; M of Sacred Lit., Trinity Sem., 1986; D of Ministry, Trinity Theol. Sem., 1987. Ordained to ministry Ch. of the Nazarene, 1971. Pastor White Wing Ch. of Nazarene, Lenoir City, Tenn., 1970-73; pastor First Ch. of the Nazarene, Fayetteville, Tenn., 1973-76, Tullahoma, Tenn., 1976—; youth pres. East Tenn. Dist., 1977-79; chmn. EastTenn. Christian Life., 1987-90. Chaplain Tullahoma Police Dept., 1990—. Office: First Nazarene Ch PO Box 687 Tullahoma TN 37388

HODGE, RALPH WAYNE, minister, editor, consultant; b. Balt., Oct. 26, 1943; s. Virginia Viola (Wells) H.; m. Delores June Jones, Feb. 7, 1963; 1 child, Christy Lynne Blackwell. BS, Cumberland Coll., 1968; MDiv, So. Bapt. Sem., 1974; D of Ministry, Luther Rice Sem., 1978. Ordained to ministry So. Bapt. Conv., 1967. Pastor Bethlehem Bapt. Ch., Louisville, 1972-85, 1st Bapt. Ch., Hopkinsville, Ky., 1985-87, Bluegrass Bapt. Ch., Hendersonville, Tenn., 1987-88; editor, cons. Bapt. Sunday Sch. Bd., Nashville, 1988—. Editor, contbr. Discipleship Tng. mag., 1988—. With U.S. Army, 1961-64. Mem. Kiwanis (spiritual activities chmn. Hopkinsville club 1986). Democrat. Home: 366 Eastland Ave Gallatin TN 37066 Office: Bapt Sunday Sch Bd 127 9th Ave N Nashville TN 37234

HODGE, RAYMOND DOUGLAS, minister; b. Charlotte, N.C., Dec. 5, 1951; s. George Washington Hodge and Mary (Allen) Maloy; m. Gale Lynn Baldwin, Aug. 11, 1972; children: Raymond Douglas Jr., Randolph Daniel. Student, Carson-Newman Coll., 1968, Lee Coll., 1970-71, Ch. of God Sch. Theology, 1989—. Ordained to ministry Ch. of God., 1979. Evangelist Ch. of God in S.C., Mauldin, 1972-73; pastor Chs. of God, N.C. and Tenn., 1974-79, Dandridge (Tenn.) Ch. of God, 1979-84, Paragon Mills Ch. of God, Nashville, 1984-85, South Haven Ch. of God, Maryville, Tenn., 1985—; bd. dirs. State Bd. Evangelism, Chattanooga, Tenn., 1990—, State Bd. Youth and Christian Edn., Chattanooga, 1984; chmn. Ministerial Examination Bd., Nashville, 1984-85; speaker on daily radio program Life In the Spirit, 1978. Recipient Merit award Vision Found., 1978. Mem. Blount County Ministerial Assn. Republican. Home: 909 Willow Dr Maryville TN 37801 Office: South Haven Ch of God 228 Calderwood Hwy Maryville TN 37801 *One must stand on the Scriptures, lead by serving others, pray without failing, love sincerely, understand if at all possible, be joyful in Christ always. Then life will be a pleasure and not a task.*

HODGE, REGINA HAZEL, minister; b. Charlotte, N.C., Apr. 9, 1963; d. Gary Jerome and Patricia (Walters) Peele; m. Eric Samuel Hodge, June 16, 1991. BA in Psychology, Mars Hill Coll., 1985; MRE, New Orleans Sem., 1989. Youth, children's minister Camden (N.C.) Bapt. Ch., 1989—; counselor Camp Mundo Vista, Asheboro, N.C., summer 1981; youth/children's minister various chs., summers 1982-88; mem. day care com. Camden Bapt. Ch., 1989—, puppet/drama dir., 1989—. Republican. Home: Rt 2 Box 13A Camden AL 36726 Office: 300 Broad St Camden AL 36726-1504

HODGEN, MATHEW EARL, minister; b. Tulsa, Sept. 9, 1964; s. Earl Wayne and Patricia Ann (Hamner) H.; m. Cheryl Ann Peters, Oct. 21, 1989. BA in Christian Ministry, Lincoln (Ill.) Christian Coll., 1990. Assoc. min. 1st Christian Ch., Joliet, Ill., 1989-91; min. Attica (Ind.) Christian Ch., 1991—. Republican. Home anf Office: 411 Sycamore Attica IN 47918 Office: 1st Christian Ch Joliet 1701 Laraway Rd Joliet IL 60433

HODGES, JOHN OLIVER, religious studies educator; b. Greenwood, Miss., Jan. 26, 1944; s. Tommy James and Samantha (Wilson) H.; m. Carolyn Ruth Richardson, Apr. 8, 1972; 1 child, Daniel. BA, Morehouse Coll., Atlanta, 1968; MA, Atlanta U., 1971; AM, U. Chgo., 1972, PhD, 1980. Dir. lang. lab. Morehouse Coll., Atlanta, 1969-70; lectr. English Barat Coll., Lake Forest, Ill., 1970-72, dir. Afro-Am. studies, 1972-75; asst. to dean students U. Chgo., 1977-80, asst. dean, 1980-82; asst. prof. U. Tenn., Knoxville, 1983-88, assoc. prof. religious studies, 1988—, acting head religious studies, 1989-90. Program com. Knoxville Urban League, 1987—. Merrill Overseas fellow Morehouse Coll., Atlanta, 1966, U. Chgo. fellow, 1974, Ford Found. fellow, 1978, NEH fellow, 1984. Mem. Am. Acad. Religion, Modern Lang. Assn., Coll. Lang. Assn., South Atlantic Modern Lang. Assn., The Langston Hughes Soc. Democrat. Baptist. Avocation: table tennis. Home: 4815 Skyline Dr Knoxville TN 37914 Office: U Tenn 501 McClung Tower Knoxville TN 37996

HODGES, LOUIS WENDELL, religion educator; b. Eupora, Miss., Jan. 24, 1933; s. John Calvin and Lorene (Phillips) H.; m. Helen Elizabeth Davis, June 6, 1954; children: John David, George Kenneth. BA, Millsaps Coll., 1954; BD, Duke U., 1957, PhD, 1960. Ordained to ministry Meth. Ch., 1958. Asst. prof. religion Washington and Lee U., Lexington, Va., 1960-64, assoc. prof., 1964-67, prof., 1967-87, Fletcher Otey Thomas prof. Bible, 1987—; vis. prof. U. Va., 1967-71; vis. Disting. prof. applied and profl. ethics Ohio U., 1990. Co-author: The Christian and His Decisions, 1969; editor Social Responsibility: Bus., Journalism, Law, Medicine, 1974—; mem. editorial bd. Jour. Mass Media Ethics, 1988—; producer, anchor TV program series, 1984. Chmn. Coun. on Human Rels., Lexington, 1965-68; mem. Va. adv. com. U.S. Commn. on Civil Rights, Richmond, 1968-74; founder, pres. Rockbridge Area Housing Corp., Lexington, 1968-74; 1st v.p. bd. dirs. Lexington-Rockbridge United Fund, 1972. Gurney Harris Kearns fellow Duke U., 1958-60, Univ. Ctr. in Va. fellow, 1965-66, The Hastings Ctr. fellow, 1985—. Mem. Soc. Profl. Journalists (nat. ethics com.), Assn. for Edn. in Journalism and Mass Communication (chmn. profl. freedom and responsibility com. mass communications and soc. div.), Investigative Reporters and Editors, Assn. for Moral Edn. Democrat. Home: Rte 1 Box 235C Lexington VA 24450 Office: Washington and Lee U Dept Religion Lexington VA 24450

HODGSON, PETER CRAFTS, theology educator; b. Oak Park, Ill., Feb. 26, 1934; married; 2 children. AB in History summa cum laude, Princeton U., 1956; BD cum laude, Yale U. Div. Sch., 1959; MA, Yale U., 1960, PhD in Religion, 1963. Ordained to ministry Presbyn. Ch. (U.S.A.), 1961. Asst. prof. religion Trinity U., San Antonio, 1963-65; asst. prof. Vanderbilt U. Div. Sch., Nashville, 1965-69, assoc. prof., 1969-73, prof., 1973—, chair grad. dept. religion, 1975-80, 90—. Author: The Formation of Historical Theology: A Study of Ferdinand Christian Baur, 1966, Jesus—Word and Presence: An Essay in Christology, 1971, Children of Freedom: Black Liberation in Christian Perspective, 1974, New Birth of Freedom: A Theology of Bondage and Liberation, 1976, Revisioning the Church: Ecclesial Freedom in the New Paradigm, 1988, God in History: Shapes of Freedom, 1989; (with others) The New Day: Catholic Theologians of the Renewal, 1968, Nineteenth Century Religious Thought in the West, 1985; editor, translator: Ferdinand Christian Baur: On the Writing of Church History, 1968, (with W.F. Hegel) Lectures on the Philosophy of Religion, 3 vols., 1984-87; editor: The Life of Jesus Critically Examined (David Friedrich Strauss), 1972; co-author, co-editor: Christian Theology: An Introduction to Its Traditions and Tasks, 1982; co-editor: Readings in Christian Theology, 1985; co-translator (with Michael Stewart): Reason in Religion: The Foundations of Hegel's Philosophy of Religion (Walter Jaeschke), 1990; gen. editor (book series) Hegel Lectures: Selected Texts; mem. bd. cons. The Owl of Minerva, 1983-88, mem. editorial adv. bd., 1988—; editor theology and philosophy of religion Religious Studies Rev., 1986—, editorial chair, 1987—. Danforth fellow, 1956-62, Woodrow Wilson fellow, 1956-57, Am. Assn. Theol. Schs. fellow, 1968-69, Guggenheim fellow, 1974-75, Univ. fellow Vanderbilt Rsch. Coun., 1980-81, 86-87, Hooker fellow Yale Div. Sch.; grantee Deutscher Akademischer Austauschdienst, 1980, Assn. Theol. Schs., 1980-81, 86-87, NEH, 1981-87, Fritz Thyssen Stiftung, 1983-86; Fulbright scholar, 1981. Mem. soc. for Values in Higher Edn., Am. Acad. Religion (chair theology and religious reflection sect. 1979-82, sect. steering com. 82-85), Coun. on Grad. Studies in Religion, 19th-Century Theology Group, Workgroup on Constructive Christian Theology (chair 1975-77, 89—), Hegel Soc. Am., Phi Beta Kappa. Home: 1742 Kingsbury Dr Nashville TN 37215 Office: Vanderbilt Div Sch Nashville TN 37240

HODGSON, STEVEN SARGEANT, minister, counselor; b. Evanston, Ill., Feb. 15, 1956; s. Richard S. and Lois Hodgson; m. Cheryl Dee Richards, Dec. 30, 1989. BS, Cornell U., 1978; MDiv cum laude, Trinity Evang. Div. Sch., 1990. Lic. to ministry Bapt. Gen. Conf., 1989. Communications asst. The Navigators, Bonn, Fed. Republic Germany, 1980-84; youth pastor Calvary Bapt. Ch., Mundelein, Ill., 1988-90; admissions counselor Trinity Evang. Div. Sch., Deerfield, Ill., 1990—. Office: Trinity Evang Div Sch 2065 Half Day Rd Deerfield IL 60015

HOEFAKKER, GILBERT, JR., minister, educator; b. Grand Rapids, Mich., June 9, 1933; s. Gilbert Sr. and Margret Marie (Dunn) H.; m. Ruth Alice Williams, May 3, 1957; children: Dale Donald, Tawnya Jean, Jane Anne, Jon Richard. BRE, Grand Rapids Bapt. Coll. and Sem., Mich., 1965; MDiv, Grand Rapids Bapt. Coll. and Sem., 1968; DPhil, Dayton, Tenn., 1989. Youth pastor Waukesha (Wis.) Bible Ch., 1971-86, adult pastor, 1986-88, interim pastor, 1988-89, dir. of christian edn. and music, 1989—; bd. dirs. Crescent Lake Bible Camp, Rhinelander, Wis. V.p. Wis. chpt. Ind. Fundamental Chs. Am., 1987-89; mem. Wis. Sunday Sch. Assn. (bd. dirs., 1980-85). With USN, 1951-57. Avocations: hunting, fishing. Home: W26153319 Genesee Rd Waukesha WI 53188 Office: Waukesha Bible Ch S53 W24079 Glendale Rd Waukesha WI 53186

HOEFFE, DIETMAR, priest; b. Beuthen, Germany, June 10, 1942. D paed., Pädagogische Hochschule, Dortmund, Fed. Republic Germany, 1972, Habilitation, 1975. Full prof. for practice theology Landau, Fed. Republic Germany, 1976-80; full prof. U. Koblenz, 1980-87, full univ. prof., 1987-90; univ. prof. U. Koblenz, Fed. Republic Germany, 1990—; dean Landau, 1979-80, Fachbereich 2: Philologie, 1990—. Author: Curriculare Forschungen und Neuorientierungen schulischen Religionsunterrichts, 1973, Problemorientierter Religionsunterricht und Systematik, 1975; contbr. articles to profl. jours. Mem. Arbeitsgemeinschaft Katholischer Katechetikdozenten, Deutscher Katechetenverein. Roman Catholic. Avocation: reading. Office: U Koblenz, Rheinau 3, D 5400 Koblenz 1, Federal Republic of Germany

HOEFLINGER, NORMAN CHARLES, clergyman; b. Hawthorne, N.Y., Dec. 19, 1925; s. Herman George and Mabel Magdalena (Stenstrom) H.; m. Virginia Louise Murphrey, June 12, 1950; children: Laurel (Mrs. Robert Clausing), Fern (Mrs. Gary Vander Hart), Sara (Mrs. William Drennon), Heidi (Mrs. David Brauning). Student, U. Colo., 1948-50; B.A., U. Denver, 1951; B.D., Westminster Theol. Sem., Phila., 1955. Ordained to ministry Ref. Ch. in U.S., 1955; pastor Odessa Ref. Ch., Artas, S.D., 1955-61, Salem-Ebenezer Ref. Ch., Manitowoc, Wis., 1961-73; pastor Minot (N.D.) Ref. Ch., 1973-76, Menno, S.D., 1976-82; pastor Hope Ref. Ch., Kansas City, Mo., 1982-89, Grace Ref. Ch., Mitchell, S.D., 1989—; stated clerk Ref. Ch. in U.S., 1957-61, pres., 1966-78; Trustee Westminster Theol. Sem., 1964-84, Hope Haven, Rock Valley, Iowa, Mid-Am. Reformed Sem., Orange City, Iowa. Editor: Ref. Herald, 1956-59, 61-74. Served with USNR, 1944-46. Address: 420 E 14th Ave Mitchell SD 57301

HOEHNER, HAROLD WALTER, theology educator; b. Sangerfield, N.Y., Jan. 12, 1935; s. Walter Jacob and Marie (Siegel) H.; m. Virginia A. Bryan, June 7, 1958; children: Stephen, Susan, David, Deborah. BA, Barrington Coll., 1958; ThM, Dallas Theol. Sem., 1962, ThD, 1965; PhD, Cambridge U., 1968. Asst. prof. of Bible exposition Dallas Theol. Sem., 1968-73, assoc.

prof. in New Testament, 1973-77, prof., chmn. dept. New Testament, 1977—, dir. ThD studies, 1975—; chmn. bd. dirs. Evantell Inc., Dallas. Author: Herod Antipas, 1972, Chronological Aspects of Life of Christ, 1977; contbr. articles to profl. jours. William Anderson scholar, 1965. Mem. Studiorum Novi Testamenti Soc., Soc. Biblical Lit., Evang. Theol. Soc., Inst. Biblical Rsch., Tyndale Fellowship Biblical Rsch. Home: 6538 Ridgemont Dr Dallas TX 75214 Office: Dallas Theol Sem 3909 Swiss Ave Dallas TX 75204

HOEHNS, KENNETH WAYNE, clergyman; b. Smithton, Mo., Dec. 27, 1927; s. Leo Herman and Grace Iola (Payne) H.; m. Esther Marita Rosbrugh, Aug. 30, 1951; children: Anita Elizabeth, Kristin Kay. BA, Cen. Mo. State U., Warrensburg, 1950; ThM, Perkins Sch. Theology, Dallas, 1953. Ordained to ministry United Meth. Ch., 1952. Pastor Meth. Ch., Mt. Vernon, Tex., 1952-53, Seymour, Iowa, 1953-56, Attica, Iowa, 1956-60, Birmingham, Iowa, 1960-64, Fremont, Iowa, 1964-68, Adair, Iowa, 1968-74; sr. pastor Meth. Ch., Creston, Iowa, 1974-82, Knoxville, Iowa, 1982-92; chmn. Iowa Conf. Bd. Pensions, Des Moines, 1983-88; bd. dirs. Iowa United Meth. Found., 1981-89. Mem. Lions (sec. 1987-91), Masons. Democrat. Avocations: camping, canoeing, travel, stone crafting, rock hounding. Home: 802 W Merna Dr Knoxville IA 50138 Office: First United Methodist Ch 313 E Montgomery Box 288 Knoxville IA 50138

HOENE, ROBERT EDWARD, pastoral care director; b. Duluth, Minn., Mar. 21, 1920; s. Arthur C. and Vera Katherine (Vollmer) H. AB, St. Louis U., 1944, MA in Classics, Licentiate in Philosophy, 1947, Licentiate in Theology, 1955; MS in Biology, Marquette U., 1958; MS in Psychology, Loyola U., 1962, PhD in Psychology, 1963. Joined S.J., Roman Cath. Ch., 1940; ordained priest Roman Cath. Ch., 1953; lic. psychologist, Wis. Instr. St. John's Coll., Belize, 1947-50; asst. prin. Campion High Sch., Prairie du Chien, Wis., 1955-56; asst. prof. Marquette U., Milw., 1963-80; dir. pastoral care St. Joseph Ctr. Mental Health, Omaha, 1984—; research assoc. (baseline study in human genetics for U.S. gene-pool) Argonne Nat. Lab., 1956-60; cons. Good Shepherd Sisters, St. Paul, 1961-86, Misericorde Sisters, Milw., 1964-80; research assoc. Child Welfare League Am., N.Y.C., 1966-68. Author: (book) The Unadjusted Delinquent Girl, 1986; contbr. articles to profl. jours. Mem. Am. Psychol. Assn., Nat. Assn. Cath. Chaplains (dir. region IX 1984-86), Nebr. Psychol. Assn., Wis. Acad. Arts, Scis., Letters. Avocations: oil painting, tennis, skiing. Home: Creighton U Jesuit Community Omaha NE 68178 Office: St Joseph Ctr Mental Health 819 Dorcas Omaha NE 68108

HOERZ, BARRY SCOTT, minister; b. Sheboygan, Wis., Sept. 6, 1956; s. Richard Henry and Nelva Grace (Finger) H.; m. Ingrid Birgitta Wallestad, Apr. 18, 1982; 1 child, Kenneth Richard Philip. BS, U. Wis., Eau Claire, 1985; MDiv, Luth. Sch. Theology, Chgo., 1989. Ordained to ministry Evang. Luth. Ch. Am., 1989. Pastor St. Stephen Evang. Luth. Ch., Edgar, Wis., 1989—; mem. Synod Task Force on World Hunger, Appleton, Wis., 1990—, sec., task force on companion synod, 1990—, mem. synod Christian edn. com., 1991—. Vol., chaplain Edgar Vol. Fire Dept., 1990—. Mem. Rotary, Lions. Office: St Stephen Evang Luth Ch 424 N Third Ave Edgar WI 54426-9009 *I John 3:18 says it best: "Little children, let us love, not in word or speech, but in deed and truth." We need to talk less, and do more. Soli Dei Gloria!.*

HOFF, MARVIN DEAN, theology educator; b. Sioux Ctr., Iowa, Oct. 3, 1936; s. Arend and Nellie Mildred (Dykstra) H.; m. Joanne B. Rozendaal, June 4, 1958; children: Jean Marie, David John, Mary Elizabeth. BA, Cen. Coll., Pella, Iowa, 1958; DD, Cen. Coll., 1987; BD, Western Theol. Sem., Holland, Mich., 1961; ThM, Princeton (N.J.) Sem., 1965; Doctorandes, Kampen Sem., The Netherlands, 1975. Ordained to ministry Ref. Ch. in Am., 1961. Min. Rea Ave. Ref. Ch., Hawthorne, N.J., 1961-65, Ref. Ch., Palos Heights, Ill., 1965-69, 81-85; sec. for Asian Ministries Ref. Ch. in Am., N.Y.C., 1969-71, sec. for ops., then sec. for ops. and fin., 1971-81; pres. Western Theol. Sem., Holland, Mich., 1985—; exec. dir. Found. for Theol. Edn. in S.E. Asia, Ref. Ch. Am., 1977—; cons. Programme for Ecumenical Theol. Edn., World Coun. of Chs. Author: Structuring for Mission, The Reformed Church in America: 1945-80, 1985. ; contbr. articles to profl. jours. Chaplain Bd. of Edn., Hawthorne, N.J., 1961-65; bd. dirs. United Way, Holland, 1986-90. Mem. Internat. Assn. Mission Studies, Am. Soc. Missiology, Soc. Bibl. Lit. Office: Western Theol Sem 86 E 12th St Holland MI 49423

HOFFMAN, DAN CLAYTON, religious organization administrator; b. Denver, June 19, 1943; s. Clayton Pershing and Doris Bernice (Adle) H.; m. Josenilda Correia de Araujo, July 8, 1971; children: Marcelo Iraja Araujo, Nelia Berenice. BA, Phillips U., 1966; MA in Religion cum laude, Christian Theol. Sem., 1970, D Ministry, 1982; MDiv, Iliff Sch. Theology, 1975; STM, Union Theol. Sem., N.Y., 1976. Ordained to ministry Christian Ch. (Disciples of Christ), 1974. Vol. Peace Corps, Timbauba, Brazil, 1966-68; min. edn. Meadlawn Christian Ch., Indpls., 1968-69; missionary to Evang. Congl. Ch. Brazil, Rio Grande do Sul, 1970-74, Ref. Ch. France, 1976-81; exec. sec. dept. Africa, Christian Ch. (Disciples of Christ), Indpls., 1982—; missionary to Mindolo Ecumenical Foun., Kitwe, Zambia, 1981; bd. dirs. Washington Office on Africa; chmn. Africa com. Nat. Coun. Chs., mem. exec. unit and fin. coms. div. overseas ministries. Contbr. articles to religious jours. Home: 2712 Constellation Dr Indianapolis IN 46229 Office: PO Box 1986 Indianapolis IN 46206 *Believing strongly in the unity of God's creation and in the global human family, I have committed my life's work to the objectives of peace, justice and the integrity of creation. I do this in the name of Jesus Christ.*

HOFFMAN, DAVID POLLOCK, pastor; b. Lansing, Mich., Feb. 8, 1934; s. Donald Alonzo and Cecile Louise (Pollock) H.; m. Loretta Virginia Shoemaker, Feb. 8, 1955; children: Donald David, James Lawrence, Cheryl Bertha Reynolds. BS, San Diego State Coll., 1957, MS in Chemistry, 1960; MS in Pastoral Counseling, Calif. Christ Inst., Orange, 1984; MA in Marriage, Family, Child Counseling, Calif. Christ Inst., 1985. Neuropsychiat. technician U.S. Army, Fort Sam Houston, Texas, 1954-56; research asst. General Atomic, San Diego, 1956-58; sr. chemist General Dynamics (Astro), San Diego, 1958-65; project engr., supr. National Cash Register, Hawthorne, Calif., 1965-69; sr. staff engr. Hughes EDD, Torrance, Calif., 1969-78; adminstr. pastor The Harbor Church, Harbor City, Calif., 1978—; pvt. practice Torrance, 1987—; bd. dirs. Psychol. and Spiritual Integrations, Wilmington, Calif., 1988-91. Precinct Sect. leader Calif. Rep., Escondido, Calif., 1964; sect. leader The John Birch Soc., North San Diego County, 1964-65; with U.S. Army, 1954-56. mem. Am. Chem. Soc., Calif. Assn. Marriage Family Therapists. Avocation: music. Home: 22949A Nadine Circle Torrance CA 90505-2627 *In each situation of life, as I exchange my thoughts, plans, feelings, words and actions for His, then walk rejoicing in His in obedience by faith, I am fruitful, blessed, fulfilled, victorious and powerful.*

HOFFMAN, GEORGE HENRY, JR., retired minister; b. Lebanon County, Pa., July 2, 1924; s. George Henry and Lillie May (Eberly) H.; m. Evelyn Mae Krall, Mar. 27, 1948; children: Bryan George, David Michael, Susan Marie, Rebecca Ann. Grad., Lancaster Theol. Sem., 1965. Ordained to ministry United Ch. of Christ, 1965. Mission pastor Twin Valley Charge United Ch. of Christ, Halifax, Pa., 1965-69; pastor The Valley United Ch. of Christ, Halifax, 1969-72; pastor Emmanuel Reformed United Ch. of Christ, Export, Pa., 1972-90, pastor emeritus, 1990—; bd. dirs. Penn West Conf. United Ch. of Christ, Greensburg, 1976-81, spl. asst. Appalachian affairs; cons. ch. affairs Bishop's Resource Team, Luth. Ch. in Am. Bd. dirs. St. Paul Homes, Greenville, 1981—. Mem. Alban Inst. Republican. Home: 3820 Windover Rd Murrysville PA 15632

HOFFMAN, JAMES R., bishop; b. Fremont, Ohio, June 12, 1932. Ed., Our Lady of Lake Minor Sem., Wawasee, Ind., St. Meinrad Coll., Mt. St. Mary Sem., Norwood, Ohio, Cath. U. Am. Ordained priest Roman Cath. Ch., 1957; ordained titular bishop of Italica and aux. bishop of Toledo, 1978, apptd. bishop of Toledo, 1980. Office: Bishop's Residence 2544 Parkwood Ave Toledo OH 43610 also: 1933 Spielbush Toledo OH 43624

HOFFMAN-LADD, VALERIE JON, religion educator; b. Rockville Centre, N.Y., Apr. 27, 1954; d. Robert Edward and Dolores Muriel (Ogren) H.; m. Steven James Ladd, May 26, 1984; children: Rachel, Michael. BA in Anthropology, U. Pa., 1975; postgrad., Am. U., Cairo, Arab Republic of Egypt, 1975-76; MA in Islamic Studies, U. Chgo., 1979, PhD in Islamic Studies, 1986. Vis. lectr. U. Ill., Urbana, 1983-86, asst. prof., 1986—. Fulbright rsch. fellow, Cairo, 1987-88, rsch. fellow Am. Rsch. Ctr. in Egypt, Cairo, 1980-81, NDEA Title VI fellow U. Chgo., 1976-79. Mem. Am. Acad. Religion (steering com. study of Islam sect.), Middle East Studies Assn., Assn. for Middle East Women's Studies, Am. Rsch. Ctr. in Egypt, Am. Inst. Maghrebi Studies. Office: U Ill Program for Study Religion 3014 FLB 707 S Mathews Ave Urbana IL 61801

HOFFMANN, ANDREW W., religious education axecutive. Exec. dir. bd. edn. Diocese of Sioux City, Iowa. Office: Office of Diocesan Edn 1821 Jackson St PO Box 3379 Sioux City IA 51102*

HOFFMANN, OSWALD CARL JULIUS, minister; b. Snyder, Nebr., Dec. 6, 1913; s. Carl John and Bertha (Seidel) H.; m. Marcia Rosalind Linnell, June 23, 1940; children: Peter, Paul, John, Katharine Ann. Student, Luther Inst., Chgo.; grad., Concordia Coll., St. Paul, 1932; MA, U. Minn., 1935; BD, Concordia Sem., St. Louis, 1936, DD (hon.), 1952; LLD (hon.), Valparaiso U., 1952; LHd (hon.), Philippine Christian U., 1982. Ordained to ministry Luth. Ch., 1939. Instr., dean of men, dir. music, head English dept. Bethany Luth. Coll., Mankato, Minn., 1936-40; pastor English Luth. Ch., Cottonwood, Minn., 1939-40; instr. linguistics and classical langs. U. Minn., 1940-41; prof. Greek and Latin, dir. publicity and promotions Concordia Collegiate Inst. (now Concordia Coll.), Bronxville, N.Y., 1941-48; dir. pub. rels. dept. Luth Ch. Mo. Synod, 1948-63; asst. pastor St. Matthew Luth. Ch., N.Y.C., 1948-63; with Internat. Luth. Laymen's League, St. Louis, 1963—; bd. dirs. Aid Assn. for Luths.; pres. Luth. Coun. in U.S., 1970-73; speaker Internat. Luth. Hour, 1955-88, hon. speaker, 1989—; sec. Luth. Ch. Prodns.; chmn. Minn. Jr. Coll. Con. Forensic Festival; mem. nat. religious adv. com. Fed. Civil Def. Adminstrn.; pres. Nat. Religious Publicity Coun., 1953-55. Author: The Passion Journey, 1956, The Joyful Way, 1958, Life Crucified, 1959, God Is No Island, 1969, Hurry Home Where You Belong, 1970, God's Joyful People—One in the Spirit, 1973, The Lord's Prayer, 1983, There is Hope, 1985; supr. prodn. films Question Seven and Martin Luther; editorial assoc. Am. Luth. mag.; mem. bd. nat. TV program This is the Life; narrator, host 5-hour TV mini series Yeshua, 1984. Bd. dirs. Wheat Ridge Found., Found. Reformation Rsch. Named Clergyman of Yr. Religious Heritage Am., 1973; recipient Sec. Def. award, 1980, Gutenberg award Chgo. Bible Soc., 1980, Gold Angel award as Internat. Clergyman of Yr. Religion in Media, 1982, William Ayer Disting. Svc. award NAt. Religious Broadcasters, 1989, Aeterna Moliri award Concordia Coll., 1990. Mem. Am. Philol. Assn., Am. Bible Soc. (life, bd. mgrs., 1st ann. award 1987), United Bible Socs. (pres. 1977-88, hon. pres. 1988—), Religious Pub. Rels. Coun. (life). Home: 586 Oak Valley Dr Saint Louis MO 63131 Office: 2185 Hampton Ave Saint Louis MO 63139

HOFFMANN, ROBERT MILLARD, minister; b. Phila., July 29, 1946; s. Blaird M. and Lillie M. (Ward) H.; m. Alice Joy Rogers, Aug. 29, 1965; children: Angela, Alice, Honey, Judith. BA, Mercer U., 1968; MDiv, Southeastern Bapt. Theol. Sem., 1971; D Ministry, So. Bapt. Theol. Sem., 1979. Ordained to ministry So. Bapt. Conv., 1965. Pastor Calvary Bapt. Ch., Brunswick, Ga., 1971-73; pastor First Bapt. Ch., McRae, Ga., 1973-81, Thomaston, Ga., 1981—; trustee Brewton-Parker Coll., Mt. Vernon, Ga., 1973-85; evangelistic cons. Ga. Bapt. Conv., 1984—; mem. Ga. Bapt. Conv. Adv. Bd. for Mercer U., Macon, Ga., 1990—; mem. radio and TV commn. Ga. Bapt. Conv., 1983-85. Mem. Am. Cancer Soc., Thomaston chpt., 1986—, Upson Drug and Alcohol Coun., 1986—. Mem. Ga. Bapt. Conv., Centennial Ministers Conf., So. Bapt. Sem. Alumni, 1979-91. Home: 108 Kennesaw Dr Thomaston GA 30286 Office: First Bapt Ch PO Box 751 Thomaston GA 30286

HOFMAN, LEONARD JOHN, minister; b. Kent County, Mich., Jan. 31, 1928; s. Bert and Dora (Miedema) H.; m. H. Elaine (Ryskamp) H., Aug. 19, 1949; children: Laurie, Janice, Kathleen, Joel. BA, Calvin Coll., 1948; BTh, Calvin Sem., 1951, MDiv, 1981. Pastor Wright Christian Reformed Ch., Kanawha, Iowa, 1951-54, Kenosha Christian Reformed Ch., Kenosha, Wis., 1954-59, North St. Christian Reformed Ch., Zeeland, Mich., 1959-65, Ridgewood Christian Reformed Ch., Jenison, Mich., 1965-77, Bethany Christian Reformed Ch., Holland, Mich.; pres. bd. trustees Christian Reformed Ch., Grand Rapids, Mich., 1977-82; gen. sec. Christian Reformed Ch. in N.Am., Grand Rapids, 1982—. Sec. bd. trustees Calvin Coll., Grand Rapids, 1970-76. Recipient Oustanding Service award Calvin Alumni Assn., 1978. Mem. Nat. Assn. Evangelicals (mem. bd. adminstrn., exec. com.). Home: 2237 Radcliffe Circle Dr SE Grand Rapids MI 49546 Office: Christian Reformed Ch in N Am 2850 Kalamazoo Ave SE Grand Rapids MI 49560

HOFMANN, HANS, theology educator, author; b. Basel, Switzerland, Aug. 12, 1923; came to U.S., 1951, naturalized, 1956; s. Oscar and Henriette (Burbiel) H.; m. Emilie Scott Welles, Oct. 15, 1955; children—Elizabeth Scott, Mark Lawrence, David Hans, Scott Cluett. A.B., Thurg. Kantonsschule, 1943; B.D., U. Basel, 1948; Th.D., U. Zurich, 1953. Mem. faculty Princeton Theol. Sem., 1953-57, asso. prof., 1956-57; mem. faculty Harvard Div. Sch., 1957-62, prof. theology, 1961-62, Ingersoll lectr. at univ., 1956-57; leader Danforth seminar religion and bus. ethics Grad. Sch. Bus. Adminstrn., 1958, dir. project religion and mental health at univ., 1957-61; inaugural Thorp lectr. Cornell U., 1955-56; exec. dir. Center Study Personality and Culture, Inc., Cambridge, Mass., 1964-66; pres. Inst. for Human Devel., Cambridge, 1966—; ordained to ministry United Ch. Christ, 1957; cons. dept. internat. affairs Nat. Council Chs. Author: The Theology of Reinhold Niebuhr, 1955, Religion and Mental Health, 1961, Incorporating Sex, 1967, Breakthrough to Life, 1969, Discovering Freedom, 1969; Editor: Making the Ministry Relevant, 1960, The Ministry and Mental Health, 1960, Sex Incorporated, 1967. Mem. bd. overseers Shady Hill Sch., Cambridge. Mem. Internat. Platform Assn., Nat. Cum Laude Soc. (hon. mem.), Nat. Inst. Arts and Letters, English-Speaking Union, Soc. Sci. Study Religion, Am. Soc. Christian Social Ethics, Fedn. Am. Scientists, AAUP, Signet Soc. Home: 110 Evening Glow Pl Sedona AZ 86336 *It is simply amazing how much more can be achieved when one learns to flow with the life forces, participate rather than obstruct the inevitable life development, and to infuse with understanding enlightenment all that cannot be dealt with constructively through confrontation and mere power play. Human development through growth in awareness, understanding, and creative self-expression in union with natural development represents therefore the most needed and promising breakthrough for all of us in our immediate future and the very goal to which I have dedicated myself fully and with great joy.*

HOFRENNING, JAMES BERNARD, religion educator; b. Harvey, N.D., Feb. 10, 1926; s. Bernt M. and Anna Hofrenning; m. Ingeborg Skarsten, June 18, 1955; children: Kathryn Hofrenning Cooper, Daniel, Peter. BA, Concordia Coll., Moorhead, Minn., 1950; BTh, Luther Theol. Sem., St. Paul, 1953; MST, Union Theol. Sem., N.Y.C., 1962; PhD, NYU, 1964. Ordained to ministry Evang. Luth. Ch. Am., 1953. Sr. pastor Zion Luth. Ch., 1954-63; prof. religion Concordia Coll., 1964-77, 84—, Reuel and Alma Wije Disting. prof., 1991—; prof. Luth. Theol. Sem., Shatin, Hong Kong, 1979-80; rep. com. to Africa Evang. Luth. Ch. Am., 1986, theologian of ch. com., 1990—. Editor: Continuing Quest: Opportunities, Resources & Program in Post Seminary Education, 1970. Founder, dir. F-M Communiversity, 1965-83; co-founder, dir. CHARIS Ecumenical Ctr., 1979-83. Tech. sgt. cav. U.S. Army, 1944-46, Phillipines and Japan. Recipient Founders Day award NYU, 1964, Humanitarian award Temple Beth El, Fargo, N.D., 1984. Mem. Am. Acad. Religion, Soc. Christian Ethics. Home: 1508 S 3rd St Moorhead MN 56560 Office: Concordia Coll 901 S 8th St Moorhead MN 56562

HOGAN, WILLIAM LEGRANGE, homiletics educator; b. Little Rock, Mar. 31, 1934; s. Marvin Lester and Elizabeth (Lee) H.; m. Jane Kee, June 11, 1959; children: Marion Elizabeth Hogan Larson, Amy Barton Hogan Hartman. BA, Rice U., 1955; ThM, Dallas Theol. Sem., 1959, Columbia Theol. Sem., 1960; D of Ministry, Westminster Theol. Sem., 1981; DD (hon.), Ea. Coll., 1984. Ordained to ministry Presbyn. Ch. in Am., 1961. Asst. pastor Trinity Presbyn. Ch., Montgomery, Ala., 1960-63, 10th Presbyn. Ch., Phila., 1963-65; area dir. Campus Crusade for Christ, Mpls., 1965-68; regional dir. Campus Crusade for Christ, Phila., 1968-72; pastor Ch. of the Saviour, Wayne, Pa., 1972-88; organizing pastor Proclamation Presbyn. Ch., Bryn Mawr, Pa., 1989-90; assoc. prof. homiletics Reformed Theol. Sem., Jackson, Miss., 1990—. Home: 131 Royal Lytham Dr Jackson MS 93211 Office: Reformed Theol Sem 5422 Clinton Blvd Jackson MS 39209-3099

HOGE, JAMES CLEO, priest, school administrator; b. Charleston, W.Va., Nov. 28, 1916; s. James Cleo and Theresa (Bohnert) H. BA, Benedictine Coll., 1940; MA, St. Leo Coll., 1980. Joined Order St. Benedict, Roman Cath. Ch., 1938; ordained priest, 1943. Priest in charge Henando County Missions, Brooksville, Fla., 1944-48, 54-55; pastor Our Lady of Fatima Ch., Inverness, Fla., 1962-65, St. Benedict's Ch., Crystal River, Fla., 1969-89; pres. Cen. Cath. Sch. of Citrus County, Lecanto, Fla., 1989—. Trustee St. Leo Coll., 1965-78; mem. sch. bd. Diocese St. Petersburg, Fla., 1983—. Mem. North Suncoast Mins. Assn. (pres. 1974-75, 83-84), Rotary (pres. 1982-83, 90-91). Democrat. Home and Office: 4340 W Homosassa Dr Lecanto FL 32661 *What is the most important reflection man can have on life? The Greek philospher Socrates said it first: "Knothe sou"—"Know thyself."*

HOGGARD, JAMES CLINTON, clergyman; b. Jersey City, Aug. 9, 1916; s. Jeremiah Matthew and Symera (Cherry) H.; m. Eva Stanton, Dec. 10, 1949; children: James Clinton, Paul Stanton. B.A., Rutgers U., 1939; M.Div., Union Theol. Sem., 1942; D.D., Livingstone Coll., 1956. Ordained to ministry African Meth. Episcopal Zion Ch., 1939; pastor St. Francis A.M.E. Zion Ch., Mt. Kisco, N.Y., 1940-42, Instnl. A.M.E. Zion Ch., Yonkers, N.Y., 1942-51, Little Rock A.M.E. Zion Ch., Charlotte, N.C., 1951-52; sec., treas., bd. fgn. missions, editor The Missionary Seer (A.M.E. Zion Ch., Washington), 1952-60, N.Y.C., 1960-72; bishop A.M.E. Zion Ch., Indpls., 1972—. Contbr. articles to ch. publs. Vice chmn. Mcpl. Housing Authority, Yonkers, 1945-51; mem. governing bd. Nat. Council Chs. U.S.A., 1950-72; mem. exec. com. World Meth. Council, 1948—; pres. Ind. Interreligious Commn. Human Equality, 1975-76. Mem. Commn. Ecumenical Studies, ACLU, Alpha Phi Alpha, Sigma Pi Phi. Clubs: Kiwanis, Elks, Masons. Office: 1100 W 42nd St Indianapolis IN 46208 *From childhood, with Christian parents motivating me, I have tried to live and let live; to love God and serve Him and to love my neighbor as I would love myself.*

HOGUE, JAMES LAWRENCE, clergyman; b. Wellsburgh, W.Va., June 9, 1923; s. Dewey Talmadge and Mary Inez (Lawrence) H.; m. Ethel Florence Park, Sept. 15, 1945; children: James Lawrence, Kelsey Graham, Kerrilee, Janiel Louise. B.D., Louisville Presbyn. Sem., 1951; B.S. in Bus. Adminstrn. (Bank of Maryville Econ. award 1948), Maryville (Tenn.) Coll., 1948. Ordained to ministry United Presbyn. Ch., 1951; pastor chs. in Ind., 1951-52, 60-64; dir. Washington County Student Tng. Parish, Salem, Ind., 1953-59; field adminstr. Synod Colo.; Bd. Nat. Missions United Presbyn. Ch., 1964-68; exec. dir. Synod of Sierra, Sacramento, 1968-72; dir. Council Adminstrv. Services, N.Y.C., 1972-80; v.p. Hogue and Assos. (accountants), Steamboat Springs, Colo., 1980—; moderator Synod Rocky Mountains, 1984-86; interim pastor Delta (Colo.) Presbyn. Ch., 1984; interim sr. pastor Immanuel Presbyn. Ch., Albuquerque, 1985-87; interim exec. presbyter Presbytery of Wabash Valley, 1987-88; interim minister Westminster Presbyn. Ch., Cin., 1988—. Served as aviator USNR, 1942-46. Mem. Am. Mgmt. Assn., Am. Philatelic Soc., Aircraft Owners and Pilots Assn. Republican. Clubs: Rotary (charter dir. Salem), Masons, Odd Fellows. Home: 5034 Cleves Pike Cincinnati OH 45238 Office: 4991 Cleves Pike Cincinnati OH 45238

HOKE, DONALD EDWIN, clergyman, educator; b. Chgo., June 18, 1919; s. Edwin Floyd and Edith Mary (Dingle) H.; m. Martha Cowan, July 20, 1945; children: Donald Edwin Jr., Steven T. BA, Wheaton Coll., 1941, MA, 1944, DD (hon.), 1959. Ordained ministry, 1942. Founding pastor South Park Ch., Park Ridge, Ill., 1941-47; asst. to pres. Columbia (S.C.) Bible Coll. and Sem., 1947-52; missionary Evangelical Alliance Mission, Wheaton, Ill., 1952-73; founding pres. Tokyo Christian U., 1955-73; co-founder Japan Bible Sem., Tokyo, 1955-73; exec. dir. Internat. Congress for World Evangelization, Lausanne, Switzerland, 1973-74, Billy Graham Ctr., Wheaton, 1974-78; sr. pastor Cedar Springs Presbyn. Ch., Knoxville, Tenn., 1978-89; treas. Lausanne Com. World Evangelization, Charlotte, N.C., 1975—; trustee World Radio Missionary Fellowship, Quito, Ecuador, 1986—; bd. dirs. Mission to World, Presbyn. Ch. Am., 1983-87. Author, editor: The Church in Asia, 1975; editor: Refugee, 1971, Evangelicals Face the Future, 1977; contbg. editor Christian Life, 1943-75. Trustee Columbia Bible Coll., 1987—, Mafraqu Sanitarium, Jordan, 1985—, Christ Ccoll., Taipei, Taiwan, 1988—, Spiritual Leadership Knoxville, 1987—; mem. adv. coun. Knoxville Juvenile Ct., 1987-91. Mem. Evang. Theol. Soc. Republican. Avocations: travel, book collecting. Home: 604 Villa Crest Dr Knoxville TN 37923 Office: Cedar Springs Presbyn Ch 9123 Kingston Pike Knoxville TN 37923 *In this day, when traditional values are being abandoned and society is adrift, now as never before we need to return to the Bible for truth, moral guidance, hope and eternal life.*

HOKE, KENNETH OLAN, minister; b. Jamalpur, India, Nov. 5, 1949; (parents Am. citizens); s. William Robert and Mary (Hess) H.; m. Carolyn Louise Thuma, Jan. 3, 1970; children: Bryan, Steven, Julie. BA in Psychology, Messiah Coll., 1970; MDiv in Psychology and Pastoral Care, Ashland Theol. Sem., 1973. Ordained to ministry Brethren in Christ Ch., 1978. Assoc. pastor Sippo Brethren in Christ Ch., Massilon, Ohio, 1971-72; pastor Ashland (Ohio) Brethren in Christ Ch., 1972-75; assoc. pastor Carlisle (Pa.) Brethren in Christ Ch., 1975-87, sr. pastor, 1987—; pres., sec. Carlisle Ministerial Assn., 1977-83; ministerial tng. com. Brethren in Christ Ch., 1980-84, mem. ministerial credentials bd., 1980-84, mem. commn. ednl. instns., 1984-90, bd. adminstrn., 1990—; lectr. Ch. Edn. Messiah Coll., Grantham, Pa., 1977—. Mem. Kiwanis (pres. Carlisle chpt. 1983-84). Republican. Home: 101 Clarindon Pl Carlisle PA 17013 Office: Brethren in Christ Ch 1155 Walnut Bottom Rd Carlisle PA 17013 *Humanity seeks to find out who we are and what exists beyond us. Interestingly, I find the answer to both of these questions found in the person of Jesus Christ and God's revelation as recorded in the Christian Bible. Most liberating is the fact that before I ever realized my questions, God was already providing and searching for me.*

HOKE, STEPHEN TURNER, minister, educator; b. Columbia, S.C., Dec. 31, 1949; s. Donald Edwin and Martha (Cowan) H.; m. Eloise Ann Achterberg, Aug. 19, 1972; children: Stephenie Ann, Christopher Stephen. BA, Wheaton Coll., 1971, MA, 1972; MDiv, Trinity Evang. Div. Sch., 1975; PhD, Mich. State U., 1977. Ordained to ministry Evang. Free Ch. Am., 1977; cert. secondary sch. tchr., Ill. Asst. prof. Seattle Pacific U., 1977-85, dir. campus ministries, 1980-85; assoc. dir. field tng. World Vision Internat., Monrovia, Calif., 1985-88; pres. LIFE Ministries, San Diego, 1988-90; v.p. tng. Ch. Resource Ministries, Fullerton, Calif., 1991—; bd. dirs. CALEB Project, Denver; elder Westminster Chapel, Bellevue, Wash., 1983-85; part-time prof. Azusa Pacific U., 1991—; assoc. for younger leaders Lausanne Commn. for World Evangelization, 1988-90; bd. dirs. Singapore Conf. for Younger Leaders, 1987. Contbr. articles to jours. in field, chpts. to books; photographer for book: Coping with Christmas, 1975. Mem. site com. Upland, Calif. Unified Sch. Dist., Pepper Tree Sch. PTA, 1990—; coach, referee Am. Youth Soccer Orgn. Mem. ASCD, Am. Soc. Trainers and Developers, Assn. Evang. Profs. Mission, Assn. Profs. Missions, Soc. Intecultural Thinking and Rsch. Republican. Home: 1709 Coolcrest Ave Upland CA 91786

HOLBEN, DOUGLAS ERIC, minister; b. Barberton, Ohio, Jan. 30, 1946; s. Conrad E. and Gladys E. (Parkinson) H.; m. Joyce E. Goldwood, June 22, 1968; children: Thomas G., David P. BA, Baldwin Wallace Coll., 1968; BD, MDiv, Pitts. Theol. Sem., 1971, DMin, 1991. Ordained to ministry Presbyn. Ch. (USA), 1971. Asst. min. First United Presbyn. Ch., Houston, Pa., 1971-73; min. Clinton (Pa.) United Presbyn. Ch., 1973—; vice chair bd. mgrs. New Wilmington Missionary Conf., 1986-90; trustee Pitts. Presbytery, 1987—, moderator, 1983. Named Citizen of Yr. Findlay Twp., Pa., 1990. Mem. Presbyn. Assn. Musicians, West Allegheny Ministerial Assn. (pres. 1988). Republican. Home and Office: Box 175 Wilson Rd Clinton PA 15026-0175 *I believe the future provides the church with the continuing opportunity to be intentional about its mission and ministry. In order to fulfill its mandate to go, to make disciples, to baptize, and to teach, the church seeks to equip itself appropriately. I believe the church is called to set goals, determine priorities, establish its direction, and identify its strengths in order to move faithfully into the future.*

HOLBERT, JOHN CHARLES, religious educator; b. New Castle, Ind., July 8, 1946; s. Harold Laverne and Martha May (Zink) H.; m. Diana Brown, Aug. 23, 1969; children: Darius Anthony, Sarah Elizabeth. BA, Grinnell (Iowa) Coll., 1968; ThM, Perkins Sch. Theology, Dallas, 1971; PhD, So. Meth. U., 1975. Pastor Univ. United Meth. Ch., Lake Charles, La., 1974-76; tchr. Tex. Wesleyan U., Ft. Worth, 1976-79; prof. Perkins Sch. Theology, Dallas, 1979—. John M. Moore fellow United Meth. Ch., 1973. Mem. Acad. Homiletics. Democrat. Home: 7325 Haverford Dallas TX 75214 Office: Perkins Sch Theology So Meth U Dallas TX 75275

HOLBROOK, A. C. (BUDDY HOLBROOK), evangelist; b. Atlanta, Jan. 16, 1938; s. Ree and Sallie H.; m. Becky Berry; children: Sallie, Jonathan. AA, Truett-McConnell Coll., 1963; BA, Grand Canyon Coll., 1971; MRE, Southwestern Seminary, 1976. Pastor First Southern Bapt. Ch., Taft, Calif., 1978-85; pres. Good News Internat., DeSoto, Tex., 1985—; founder Taft Sem. Ctr.; adminstrv. dir. Am. Renewal Foundn., Richardson, Tex.; Com. on Coms. So. Bapt. Conv., 1982, Com. on Bds., 1984; chmn. bd. servants Christ Internat., 1990—. Contbr. column to newspaper. Coordinator disaster relief Calif. Men's Ministries, 1982. Served with USN, 1955-58. Lodge: Masons (32 degree).

HOLBROOK, STEVEN CHARLES, clergyman; b. Kenton, Ohio, Dec. 2, 1952; s. Sherman Charles and Opal Jean (Poe) H.; m. Kayleen Marie Waugh, June 16, 1984; children: Steven Cody, Lindsey Marie. Lic., Radio Engring. Inst., 1971; BS, Ky. Christian Coll., 1986. Lic. engr.; ordained to ministry Christian Ch./Chs. of Christ, 1985. Minister Nashville (Ohio) Ch. of Christ, 1986-88, Worthington (Ind.) Christian Ch., 1988—; chmn. bd. Adventures in Missions, Bloomfield, Ind., 1990-91. Recipient Faithful Tchr. award Standard Pub. Co., Cin., 1991. Mem. Am. Assn. Christian Counselors, Fellowship Christian Ministers, Ky. Christian Alumni Assn. Home: 24 N Edward St Worthington IN 47471 Office: Worthington Christian Ch 105 E Main St Worthington IN 47471

HOLCK, FREDERICK H. GEORGE, priest, educator, counselor; b. Neuenburg, Germany, June 6, 1927; came to U.S., 1963, naturalized, 1968; s. Edward W. and Elizabeth L. (Luger) H.; m. Miriam I. Ahlgren, Jan. 23, 1954; children: Mark, Christopher, Thomas, David, Timothy. Student, U. Heidelberg, 1947-49, U. Tuebingen, 1949-52; Lic. Phil. in Philosophy summa cum laude, U. Salzburg, 1953, Ph.D. in Comparative Religion summa cum laude, 1954. Ordained to priesthood Anglican Ch. Diplomate Am. Bd. Counselors. Tutor Helsinki, 1954-56; sr. lectr. Peshawar U., Pakistan, 1957-59; parish minister in Can., 1960-62; prof. theology and history of religions Luth. Theol. Sem., Saskatoon, Sask., Can., 1962-63; asst. prof. religion and human devel. Lake Erie Coll., Painesville, Ohio, 1963-66; asst. prof. religion and Oriental philosophy Cleve. State U., 1966-68, assoc. prof., acting chmn. dept. philosophy and religion, 1968-70, prof., chmn. dept. religion, 1970-80, dir. Asian Studies Program, 1969-80, dir. Extended Campus Coll., 1982-85, prof. emeritus, 1987—; acad. v.p., dean coll. N.C. Wesleyan Coll., Rocky Mount, N.C., 1980-82. Editor: Ohio Jour. Religious Studies, 1972-80; Co-author, editor: Death and Eastern Thought, 1974, Ethics in World Religions: Systems and Sources, 1987; co-editor internat. editorial bd.: Ency. Hinduism, 1979-82; contbr. articles to profl. jours. and encys. Mem. Archtl. and Zoning Bds., Kirtland Hills, Ohio, 1970-72; bd. dirs. Greater Cleve. Counseling, Inc., 1978-80, v.p., 1982-87; mem. adv. bd. World Fellowship Religions, 1978-82; bd. dirs. Polk County Hospice, 1991. Fellow Nat. Acad. Counselors and Family Therapists, Am. Coll. Counselors (founding); mem. Am. Acad. Religion, Ohio Acad. Religion (pres. 1974-75), Am. Philos. Assn., Nat. Alliance for Family Life (clin. mem., pres. S.E. region 1981-82), Rotary. Home: PO Box 1372 Tryon NC 28782 Office: Cleve State U Cleveland OH 44115

HOLCOMBE, GEORGE ROLAND, clergy, consultant; b. Houston, Tex., Mar. 11, 1933; s. Horace Chester and Elma (Waltz) H.; m. Wanda Gay Batchelor, May 5, 1940; children: Christopher, Sara. BA, Southwestern U., 1955; MDiv, So. Meth. U., 1959. Ordained elder, United Meth. Ch. Pastor United Methodist Ch., Baton Rouge, La., 1959-66; staff mem. Inst. Cultural Affairs, Chgo., 1966-69, Kuala Lumpur, Malaysia, 1969-70, Derby, Australia, 1970-72, Majuro, Marshall Islands, 1975, JeJuDo, Korea, 1975; staff mem. Inst. of Cultural Affairs, Hong Kong, 1980; cons. East Dallas Cooperative Parish, Dallas, 1981-84, GRH Planning Systems, Dallas, 1984—; bd. dirs. Dallas-Ft. Worth Refuse Agy., Restart, Inc. Dallas. Home: 2618 Sharpview Dallas TX 75228

HOLDCROFT, LESLIE THOMAS, clergyman, educator; b. Man., Can., Sept. 28, 1922; s. Oswald Thomas and Florence (Waterfield) H.; student Western Bible Coll., 1941-44; BA, San Francisco State Coll., 1950; MA, San Jose State Coll., 1955; postgrad. Stanford, 1960, 63, U. Cal., 1965-67; DDiv., Bethany Bible Coll., 1968; m. Ruth Sorensen, July 2, 1948; children: Cynthia Ruth, Althea Lois, Sylvia Bernice. Instr. Western Bible Coll., 1944-47; instr. Bethany Bible Coll., 1947-55, dean edn., 1955-68, v.p., 1967-68; pres. Western Pentecostal Bible Coll., 1968-87; acad. cons., researcher, Clayburn, B.C., 1991—; pastor Craig Chapel, 1959-68; dir. Can. Pentecostal Corr. Coll., Clayburn, 1985-90. Pres., Assn. Canadian Bible Colls., 1972-76. Author: The Historical Books, 1960, The Synoptic Gospels, 1962, The Holy Spirit, 1962, The Pentateuch, 1951, Divine Healing, 1967, The Doctrine of God, 1978, The Four Gospels, 1988, Anthropology: A Biblical View, 1990, Soteriology: Good News in Review, 1990. Home: 34623 Ascott Ave, Abbotsford, BC Canada V2S 5A3 Office: Box 123, Clayburn, BC Canada V0X 1E0

HOLDEN, DAVID POWELL, minister; b. Chgo., Dec. 23, 1927; s. David Powell and Ann Mary (Walker) H.; m. Gwendolyn Joy Huff, Oct. 23, 1948; children: David III, Daniel, Dorcas, Dennis, Donald, Douglas. BA, William Jewell Coll., Liberty, Mo., 1954; BD, Cen. Bapt. Sem., Kansas City, Kans., 1957, MDiv, 1969; DMin, Golden Gate Bapt. Sem., Mill Valley, Calif., 1983. Ordained to ministry, So. Bapt. Conv., 1951. Pastor Spanish Lake Bapt. Ch., St. Louis, 1956-65, First Bapt. Ch., St. Clair, Mo., 1966-68, Calvary Bapt. Ch., Clinton, Iowa, 1968-76; dir. missions Iowa So. Bapt. Fellowship, Des Moines, 1976-80; dir. Puget Sound Bapt. Assn., Seattle, 1980—; Chmn. Mo. Bapt. Exec. Bd. Missions Co., 1978-80; pres. N.W. Conv. DOM, 1985-86. Bible tchr. YMCA, Clinton, Iowa, 1972-76; mem. Mayor's Blue Ribbon Com., City of Clinton, Iowa, 1972-76. Home: 6522 25th St NE Tacoma WA 98422 Office: Puget Sound Bapt Assn 32924 Pacific Hwy S Federal Way WA 98003

HOLDEN, MARK RAYMOND, minister; b. Syracuse, N.Y., Dec. 10, 1956; s. Edwin Kenneth and Dorothy Jean (Henderson) H.; m. Pamela June Ross, Apr. 23, 1977; children: Jeremy, Bethany, Joanna, Micah, Elise. BRE, Bapt. Bible Coll. Pa., 1980. Ordained to ministry Gen. Assn. Regular Bapt. Chs., 1986. Pastor West Smyrna (N.Y.) Bapt. Ch., 1985—; bd. dirs. Christian Family Ministries Inc., Smyrna, 1988—; chmn. bd. dirs. N.Y. Bapts. for Life, Inc., 1991—. Home and Office: RD 1 Box 80 Smyrna NY 13464

HOLDER, ARTHUR GLENN, religious educator; b. Atlanta, Sept. 6, 1952; s. C. Glenn and Mary Ruth (Craig) H.; m. Sarah Noble Henry, Oct. 21, 1978; 1 child, Charles. AB magna cum laude, Duke U., 1973; MDiv, Gen. Theol. Sem., 1976; PhD, Duke U., 1987. Ordained to ministry Episcopal Ch. as priest, 1977. Asst. to rector St. James Episc. Ch., Hendersonville, N.C., 1976-78; vicar Holy Cross Episc. Ch., Valle Crucis, N.C., 1978-82, rector, 1982-85; asst. prof. pastoral theology, dir. field edn. Ch. Divinity Sch. of the Pacific, Berkeley, Calif., 1986-91, assoc. prof. religion and edn ., dir. field edn., 1991—. Contbr. articles to profl. jours. Angier B. Duke scholar Duke U., 1970-73; Medieval & Renaissance fellow Duke U., 1980-83. Mem. Assn. for Theol. Field Edn., Religious Edn. Assn., Assn. Profs. & Researchers in Religious Edn., Am. Soc. Ch. History, Phi Beta Kappa. Democrat. Office: Ch Divinity Sch of the Pacific 2451 Ridge Rd Berkeley CA 94709

HOLDER, DAVID HUGH, religious broadcaster; b. Scottsville, Ky., Feb. 3, 1964; s. John Hugh and Wanda Sue (Borders) H.; m. Debra Ann Lee, Aug. 28, 1982; children: Brandon Hugh, Bridgett Lee. Student, Western Ky. U. Gospel music singer and instrumentalist Westmoreland, Tenn., 1969—; religious broadcaster Sta. WLCK Radio, Scottsville, Ky., 1983—; S.S. asst. supt. New Hope Ch., Westmoreland, 1989—. Mem. Allen County (Ky.) Singing Conv. (pres. 1989—). Republican. Baptist. Home: 1866 Brownsford Rd Scottsville KY 42164 Office: Sherandan Broadcasting 104 1/2 Public Sq Scottsville KY 42164

HOLDER, DOUGLAS RICHARD, minister; b. West Reading, Pa., Feb. 15, 1959; s. Richard Charles and Sally Ann (Robison) H.; m. Ellyn Louise Spence, Dec. 23, 1984; children: Laura, Abigale, Ryan. AB in Religion, Albright Coll., 1980; MDiv, Lancaster (Pa.) Theol., Seminary, 1986. Pastor Mount Bethel United Ch. of Christ, McClure, Pa., 1987—; del. Gen. Synod-United Ch. of Christ, Norfolk, Va., 1991; pres. parish life com. Cen. Assn., Sunbury, Pa., 1988—. Pres. McClure (Pa.) Community Chest Fund; mem. elem. sch. lay adv. com., McClure. Mem. Choristers Guild. Democrat. Home: PO Box 136 McClure PA 17841-0136 Office: PO Box 136 McClure PA 17841-0136

HOLDERNESS, SUSAN RUTHERFORD, religious education administrator, convention planner, tour guide; b. Cherokee, Iowa, Nov. 5, 1941; d. Parker William and Ruth Elvera (Peterson) Rutherford; m. Michael Aaron Holderness, Aug. 12, 1961; children: Lauren, Lisa, Jennifer, Joshua. BA in Edn., Wayne State U., Nebr., 1964; student, Iowa State U., 1960-61, Vocat. Cert., 1973. Tchr. various high schs. including Norwalk (Iowa) High Sch., 1968-78; hist. site interpreter Salisbury House, Des Moines, 1971-78, 84-88, Minn. State Hist. Soc., St. Paul, 1978-84; cons. Profl. Match Cons., Des Moines, 1985-90; tour guide and conv. planner Des Moines Tour and Conv. Svcs., 1987—; also dir. Christian edn. Douglas Ave. Presbyn. Ch., Des Moines; owner gourmet food shop, 1973. Vice pres. fund raising Des Moines Symphony Guild, 1990—; bd. dirs., treas., sec. playground bldg. project Greenwood Sch. PTA, Des Moines, 1986-89; co-chmn. Civic Music Assn., Des Moines, 1987; pres., v.p., tour dir. St. Paul New Residents, 1980-83, others in past; bd. dirs. Ramsey County Friends of the Libr., 1981-83, Symphony Assn., mem. steering com. showhouse and ball. Mem. Iowa Victorian Soc., Compass Club (internat. pres. 1986-87), Kappa Delta Phi, Gamma Phi Beta. Republican. Presbyterian. Avocations: tennis, water sports, gourmet cooking, volunteer work, art and theater. Home: Owl's Head Hist Dist 2900 Forest Dr Des Moines IA 50312 Office: Douglas Ave Presbyn Ch 4601 Douglas Ave Des Moines IA 50310

HOLIFIELD, E. BROOKS, theology educator; b. Little Rock, Jan. 5, 1942; s. E. J. and Irene (French) H.; m. Vicky Lee Thompson, June 22, 1963; children: Erin, Ryan. BA, Hendrix Coll., 1963, DLitt (hon.), 1985; BD, Yale U., 1966, MA, 1968, PhD, 1970. Asst. prof. Candler Sch. Theology, Emory U., Atlanta, 1970-75, assoc. prof., 1975-80, prof., 1980-83, Charles Howard Candler prof., 1983—. Author: The Covenant Sealed, 1974, The Gentlemen Theologians, 1978, A History of Pastoral Care in America, 1983, Health and Medicine in the Methodist Tradition, 1986, Era of Persuasion, 1989. NEH fellow, 1976, 83, 91. Mem. Am. Acad. Religion, Am. Soc. Ch. History, Orgn. Am. Historians. Democrat. Methodist. Home: 3300 Old Mill Ct Decatur GA 30033 Office: Emory U Bishops Hall Atlanta GA 30322

HOLIMAN, WILLIAM JESS, minister; b. Little Rock, Mar. 10, 1958; s. William Jess Holiman and Joyce Rogers Graham; m. Loralee Lyn Hight, May 19, 1979; children: Graham, Alan, Madeline. BA, U. Ark., 1981; MDiv, Ref. Episcopal Sem., 1984; DD, Cummins Meml. Theol. Sem., 1991. Ordained deacon Ref. Episcopal Ch., 1984, presbyter, 1985. Min. in charge Resurrection Ref. Episcopal Ch., Rochester, N.Y., 1984-85; rector 1st Ref. Episcopal Ch., N.Y.C., 1985—; pres. bd. fgn. missions, chmn. state of ch. com. Ref. Episcopal Ch., Phila., 1987—. Author: (booklet) The Church Year, 1987. Office: 1st Ref Episcopal Ch 317 E 50th St New York NY 10022

HOLLADAY, JAMES FRANKLIN, JR., minister; b. Meridian, Miss., May 23, 1951; s. James Franklin and Anne (Wedsworth) H.; m. Patricia Ann Martin, June 18, 1977; children: Meredith Anne, Emily Jean. BA, Samford U., 1973; MDiv, So. Bapt. Sem., Louisville, 1976, D Ministry, 1983. Ordained to ministry So. Bapt. Conv., 1976. Summer youth min. 1st Bapt. Ch., Chatsworth, Ga., 1972; campus min. Ky. Bapt. Conv., Middletown, 1974-76; program coord. East Bapt. Ch., Louisville, 1976-79, pastor, dir., 1979—; bd. dirs. Office Ecumenical Affairs, Archdiocese of Louisville, 1985-91; mem. pub. affairs com. Ky. Bapt. Conv., 1987-89. Chmn. Louisville Full-Employment Task Force, 1976-78; sec. Kentuckiana Interfaith Community, Louisville, 1979-80, v.p., 1980-81, pres., 1981-82, now bd. dirs.; mem. Jefferson County Anti-Freeze Com., Louisville, 1980-81; pres. Phoenix Hill Assn., Louisville, 1981-83, now bd. dirs.; mem. steering com. Met. Louisville Interreligious Coalition on Civil Rights, 1987—. Recipient Peace and Justice award Peace and Justice Commn., Archdiocese of Louisville, 1990, Vol. of Yr. award Phoenix Hill Assn., 1990. Mem. Interdenominational Ministerial Coalition of NAACP, Cen. Dist. and Long Run Bapt. Assns. (chmn. Bapt. joint com. 1989—), Fedn. Ch. Social Agys. (pres. 1979-84), Omicron Delta Chi. Democrat. Home: 2817 Grinstead Dr Louisville KY 40206 Office: East Bapt Ch 809 E Chestnut St Louisville KY 40204 *The prophet Micah reminds us that God desires three things of us: that we love mercy, do justice, and walk humbly with God. I suspect I will spend the rest of my life seeking to understand and practice those three simple admonitions.*

HOLLADAY, KENNETH RICHARD, clergyman; b. Louisville, Oct. 31, 1952; s. Kenneth Reed and Jean (Carothers) H.; m. Deborah Ann Bennett, Aug. 21, 1976; children: Benjamin, Andrew, Geoffrey. BA in Religion and Philosophy, Ky. Wesleyan U., 1974; MDiv, Asbury Theol. Sem., 1978, MA of Religion in Christian Edn., 1978. Ordained deacon Meth. Ch., 1975; elder, 1979. Assoc. pastor Epworth United Meth. Ch., Lexington, Ky., 1978-80; founding pastor Bethany United Meth. Ch., Mt. Vernon, Ky., 1980-83; assoc. pastor program devel. First United Meth. Ch., Winchester, Ky., 1983-84; pastor Mt. Tabor United Meth. Ch., Centerfield, Ky., 1984-86; assoc. pastor membership care Centenary United Meth. Ch., Lexington, Ky., 1986-89; pastor First United Meth. Ch., Corbin, Ky., 1989—; chair Barbourville Dist. Coun. on Ministries, Corbin, 1989—; mem. Conf. Coun. on Ministries, Lexington, 1981—. Mem. Corbin Ministerial Assn., Wesleyan Theol. Soc., Corbin C. of C., Kiwanis (pres. elect 1991). Office: First United Meth Ch 220 N Main St Corbin KY 40701

HOLLAMON, ELIZABETH ERSKINE, headmistress; b. Seguin, Tex., Aug. 9, 1930; d. Thomas Henry and Elizabeth Humphreys (Erskine) H.; m. Bert A. Perry, Jr., Aug. 7, 1954 (div.). BA, U. Tex., 1952; MS, Fla. State U., 1967; EdD, Kennedy We. U., 1989. Lic. elem. and secondary tchr., Tex. Headmistress Trinity Episc. Sch., Galveston, Tex., 1970—; mem. bd. Nat. Assn. Episcopal Schs., 1976-81; life bd. mem. Southwestern Assn. Episcopal Schs., 1973—. Bd. mem. William Temple Found., Galveston, 1981-86; bd. pres. Salvation Army, Galveston, 1991. Grantee Fla. State U., 1966-67, NSF, 1966-67. Mem. Ind. Sch. Assn. S.W. (exec. com., treas. 1986-88), Philos. Soc. Tex., DAR, Daus. Rep. Tex., Colonial Dames, Kappa Kappa Gamma. Office: Trinity Episcopal Sch 720 Tremont Galveston TX 77550

HOLLAND, ANITA CAROL, religious education administrator; b. Oxford, Miss., Aug. 23, 1963; d. Wayne Dennis and Martha Evelyn (Roney) H. BS in Christian Edn., Tenn. Wesleyan Coll., 1985. Dir. youth and music 1st United Meth. Ch., Richlands, Va., 1985-86; dir. Christian edn. Jones Meml. United Meth. Ch., Chattanooga, 1986-88; dir. program and Christian edn. 1st United Meth. Ch., Greenville, Miss., 1988—; chmn. edn. leadership devel., dist. coun. on ministries Cleve. Dist. United Meth. Ch., 1990—; dist. youth coord., dist. coun. on ministries Chattanooga Dist. United Meth. Ch., 1987-88. Named Youth Dir. of the Yr., Chattanooga Roundtable, 1988. Mem. Christian Educators Fellowship. Home: Rte 3 Box 759A Greenville MS 38701 Office: 1st United Meth Ch 402 Washington Ave Greenville MS 38701

HOLLAND, DARRELL WENDELL, newspaper religion editor; b. Charleston, W.Va., Apr. 30, 1932; s. Ray E. and Esther (Dean) H.; m. Ann Holland, Nov. 25, 1971; 3 children. AB, Olivet Coll., 1954; BD, Nazareth Theol. Sch., 1957; MS in Journalism, Boston U., 1970. Ordained to ministry United Ch. of Christ. Dir. communications Mass. Conf. United Ch. of Christ, Bostonn, 1966-74; religion editor PLain Dealer Pub. Co., Cleve., 1974—. Home: 12900 Lake Ave Lakewood OH 44107 Office: The Plain Dealer 1801 Superior St Cleveland OH 44114

HOLLAND, DAVID VERNON, minister; b. L.A., June 21, 1954; s. Walter Vernon H. and Wilma (McKenzie) Cowles; m. Dianne Sheri Cooper, July 17, 1976; children: Jessica, Lisa, Melinda, Justin. BTh, LIFE Bible Coll., 1979; postgrad., Gordon Conwell Sem., 1988—. Ordained to ministry, 1981. Youth pastor Angelus Temple, L.A., 1977-79; asst. pastor Bradford (Pa.) Foursquare Ch., 1979-81; pastor Easton (Mass.) Foursquare Ch., 1981—; div. supt. Northeast Div. Foursquare Chs., 1986—; pres. Emmaus Ministry Inst., Easton, 1983—; nat. cabinet mem., Internat. Ch. of Foursquare Gospel, L.A., 1990—; bd. dirs., Greater Boston Christian Alliance, 1990—; coun. mem., Boston Oper. Rescue, 1990—. Contbr. articles to profl. jours. Office: Foursquare Ch 140 Main St North Easton MA 02356

HOLLAND, JACK HENRY, educator, lecturer, clergyman; b. San Diego, Oct 31, 1922; s. Henry Joseph and Hazel M. (Mitchell) H.; student U. So. Cal., 1940-41; A.B., San Diego State U., 1943; grad. student Harvard, 1943; M.B.A., Stanford, 1948; Ph.D. in Theology, Fla. State U.; D.D., Divine Sci. Ednl. Center; hon. degree Faith Sem. Prof., San Jose (Calif.) State U., 1948-79, emeritus, 1979—, head mgmt. dept., 1956-68; sometimes prof. Stanford, summers; sr. assoc. Saratoga Inst.; lectr. on human motivation. Ordained minister Ch. Divine Sci.; founder, pres. Inst. Human Growth and Awareness, now lectr., cons., minister; v.p. Internat. New Thought Alliance, Divine Sci. Fedn. Internat.; co-founder, dir. Sci. of Mind Inst. Sch. Ministry, San Jose; minister Divine Sci. Ch. Served from ens. to lt. USNR, 1943-46; PTO. Decorated Purple Heart, Presdl. Unit Citation. Mem. Am. Mktg. Assn., Acad. of Mgmt., Nat. Assn. Purchasing Mgmt., Purchasing Mgmt. Assn. No. Calif., Soc. Advancement Mgmt. (nat. exec. v.p. univ. chpts. 1963-69), Bay Area Bus. Edn. Forum (pres. 1956), Am. Inst. Banking, Beta Gamma Sigma, Phi Kappa Phi., Alpha Tau Omega Alumni Assn. (dir. 1952). Club: Commonwealth of Calif. Author: Outline of Materials Management; An Annotated Bibliography for Parapsychology; Man's Victorious Spirit; The Healing Image, 1976; Love: The Scientific Evidence, 1976; Your Freedom To Be, 1977; Divine Energy, 1979; The Healing Image, 1980; the 'Well' and the 'Will', 1981; Patience: An Aspect of Healing, 1982; You Are Not the Guilty Party, 1984. Office: PO Box 6695 San Jose CA 95150

HOLLAND, JEFFREY R., religious organization administrator; b. St. George, Utah, Dec. 3, 1940; s. Frank D. and Alice (Bentley) H.; m. Patricia Terry, June 7, 1963; children: Matthew, Mary, David. BS, Brigham Young U., 1965, MA, 1966; PhD, Yale U., 1973. Dean religious instrn. Brigham Young U., 1974-76; commr. Latter Day Saints Ch. Ednl. System, 1976-80; pres. Brigham Young U., 1980-89; gen. authority, mem. 1st Quorum of the 70 LDS Ch., 1989—; dir. Deseret News Pub. Co., Key Bank of Utah, Key Bancshares of Utah, Inc. Mem. Am. Assn. Presidents of Ind. Colls. and Univs. (past pres.), Nat. Assn. Ind. Colls. and Univs. (former bd. dirs.), Am. Council Edn., Phi Kappa Phi. Office: LDS Church 47 E South Temple St Salt Lake City UT 84150

HOLLAND, JOHN RAY, minister; b. Fisher County, Tex., June 3, 1933; s. John Ramsey and Josephine Pearce (Cooper) H.; m. Doris Jean Hines, Jan. 1, 1953; children: Bradley Ray, Johnnea Lee, John Barton, Joanna Joy. Grad., L.I.F.E. Bible Coll., 1953; LLD (hon.), Oral Roberts U., 1989. Ordained to ministry Internat. Ch. of Foursquare Gospel, 1980. Pastor Internat. Ch. of Foursquare Gospel, 1954-77; pres. L.I.F.E. Bible Coll., Can., 1969-75; supr. S.W. dist. Internat. Ch. of Foursquare Gospel, 1977-89; pres. Internat. Ch. of Foursquare Gospel, L.A., 1989—; supr. Western Can. region Internat. Ch. of Foursquare Gospel, 1969-75, mem. internat. bd., L.A., 1975-77, pres. L.I.F.E. Inc., 1989—, chief exec. officer internat. bd., 1989—; pastor Angelus Temple, 1975-77. Editor Advance, 1988—. Bd. dirs. Madge Meadwell Founds., 1970-75. Mem. Am. Bible Soc. (bd. dirs. 1989—), World Pentecostal Fellowship (bd. dirs. 1989—), Nat. Assn. Evangs. (bd. dirs. 1989—). Office: Internat Ch of the Foursquare Gospel 1910 W Sunset Blvd Los Angeles CA 90026

HOLLAND, RICHARD EUGENE, minister; b. Coral Gables, Fla., Apr. 15, 1951; s. Jimmie Eugene and Jean (Coggin) H.; m. Betty Jean Huckabee, Nov. 26, 1971; children: Michael, Susan, Daniel. BBA, Fla. Atlantic U., 1985; MDiv., So. Bapt. Theol. Sem., 1989. Pastor 1st Bapt. Ch. of Alton, Pleasant View Bapt., Alton, Ind., 1986-89, Eastview Bapt. Ch., Paoli, Ind., 1989—. Sgt. USMC, 1969-77. Mem. Lions (Paoli). Home: 310 Elm St Paoli IN 47454 Office: Eastview Bapt Ch PO Box 316 Hwy 56E Paoli IN 47454

HOLLAND, TIM RAY, minister; b. Denver, Sept. 9, 1959; s. Lee Roy Holland and Geneva Doris (Hemphill) Woods. BA, Stetson U., 1981; M in Divinity, So. Bapt. Sem., 1984. Minister of youth First Bapt. Ch., Sanford, Fla., 1979-81, Hurstbourne Bapt. Ch., Louisville, 1981-82, Beechmont Bapt. Ch., Louisville, 1983-85; assoc. minister First Bapt. Ch., Myrtle Beach, S.C., 1985—; bd. dirs. Helping Hand, Myrtle Beach; outreach chmn. Bapt. Student Union, Deland, 1979-81. Vol. Spouse Abuse Prevention Program, Louisville, 1981-84; coach YMCA-Girls Softball, Deland, 1980-81. Named one of Outstanding Young Men of Am., 1985. Mem. Grand Strand Ministerial Assn., Waccamaw Bapt. Assn. (dir. student ministries 1986—), Ch. Atheletic Assn. (commr. 1985—), Resort Ministries Subcom. Democrat. Avocations: golf, tennis, basketball, softball, photography. Home: 1009 Indian Wells Ct Murrells Inlet SC 29576 Office: First Bapt Ch 500 4th Ave N Myrtle Beach SC 29577

HOLLAS, ERIC M., priest, educator; b. Oklahoma City, Sept. 22, 1948; s. Lawrence Joseph and Lenora Celeste (Schumacher) H. BA, Princeton U., 1971; MDiv, St. John's U., Collegeville, Minn., 1975; MA, Yale U., 1976, PhD, 1985. Ordained priest Roman Cath. Ch., joined Benedictine Monks, 1971. Benedictine monk St. John's Abbey, Collegeville, 1971—; asst. prof. St. John's U., Collegeville, 1980—. Office: St John's U Collegeville MN 56321

HOLLE, REGINALD HENRY, bishop; b. Burton, Tex., Nov. 21, 1925; s. Alfred W. and Lena (Nolte) H.; m. Marla C. Christianson, June 16, 1949; children: Todd, Joan. BA, Capital U., 1946, DD (hon.), 1979; MDiv, Trinity Luth. Sem., 1949; D. Ministry, Ohio Consortium Religious Stdy, 1977; DD (hon.), Wittenberg U., 1989. Ordained minister Evang. Luth. Ch. Am., then bishop. Assoc. pastor Zion Luth. Ch., Sandusky, Ohio, 1949-51; sr. pastor Salem Meml. Luth. Ch., Detroit, 1951-72, Parma Luth. Ch., Cleve., 1973-78; bishop Mich. dist. Am. Luth. Ch., Detroit, 1978-87; bishop NW Lower Mich. Synod Evang. Luth. Am., Lansing, 1988—; chmn. bd. dirs. Inst. for Mission in U.S.A. Columbus, Ohio, 1982—; bd. dirs. Wittenberg U., Springfield, Ohio, 1988; chmn. bd. life and mission in congregation Am. Luth. Ch., Mpls., 1973-76, chmn. colloquy com., 1981-87. Author: Planning for Funerals, 1978; contbr. to Augsburg Sermon Series. Recipient Pub. Svc. citation Harper Woods City Coun., 1976, Recognition for Community Svc., Detroit Pub. Schs., 1974. Office: Evang Luth Ch Am 801 S Waverly Rd Lansing MI 48917

HOLLEMAN, SANDY LEE, religious organization administrator; b. Celina, Tex., June 6, 1940; d. Guy Lee and Gustine (Kirby-Sheets) Luna; m. Allen Craig Holleman, June 5, 1959. Cert., Eastfield Coll., 1979. With Annuity Bd., So. Bapt. Conv., Dallas, 1958—; mgr. personnel So. Bapt. Conv., Dallas, 1983-85, dir. human resources, 1985—. Mem. Am. Mgmt. Soc. (dir. salary surveys local chpt. 1986—, v.p. chpt. svs. 1987—), Soc. Human Resource Mgmt., Dallas Personnel Assn., Diversity Club Dallas (program chmn. 1976, v.p. 1977), Order Ea. Star, Daus. of Nile. Baptist. Avocations: needlepoint, genealogy, decorating, doll collecting, square dancing. Home: 4524 Sarazen Dr Mesquite TX 75150 Office: Annuity Bd So Bapt Conv 2401 Cedar Springs Rd Dallas TX 75221-2190

HOLLEMAN, WARREN LEE, medical ethics educator; b. Raleigh, N.C., Oct. 20, 1955; s. Carl Partin and Annie Ruth (Warren) H.; m. Marsha Carol Cline, June 18, 1978; children: Annie Dillon, Thomas Carlos. AB, Harvard U., 1977; MA, Rice U., 1984, PhD, 1986; postgrad., Baylor Coll. Medicine, 1988. Instr. Houston Grad. Sch. Theology, 1983-86, asst. prof., 1986-87; asst. prof. Baylor Coll. Medicine, Houston, 1988—; vis. asst. prof. U. Houston, 1986-88; interim pastor Houston Friends Ch., 1982-83; convener nominating, overseers and religious edn. coms. Live Oak Friends Meeting, 1985—; founder, dir. Compassion and the Art of Medicine lectureship. Author: The Human Rights Movement: Western Values and Theological Perspectives, 1987; contbr. articles to profl. jours.; contbr. Houston Cath. Worker newspaper, 1987—. Vol. Ben Taub Gen. Hosp., Houston, 1988-89; adv. panelist Perceptions of Human Rights by Young Ams. coordinated by Rothko Chapel, Houston, 1988. Rsch. grantee Am. Acad. of Family Physicians, 1989, residency tng. grantee USPHS, 1989-90, med. tng. grantee Community Hosp. Fund, 1989-91. Mem. Am. Acad. Religion, Soc. for

Health and Human Values, Am. Maritain Assn., Soc. Tchrs. Family Medicine. Democrat. Office: Baylor Family Practice Ctr 5510 Greenbriar Houston TX 77005 *I screamed at God for allowing children to starve until I realized that the starving children were God screaming at me. (Author unknown).*

HOLLENBACH, MARK HAROLD, minister; b. Allentown, Pa., June 9, 1954; s. Charles Revere and Margaret Stella (Honsel) H.; m. Deborah Christine May, Aug. 25, 1985; children: Erin Lynn, Christina Joy. BA, U. Ill., 1976; MDiv, Lincoln Christian Sem., 1983. Ordained to ministry Christian Ch. Assoc. campus min. Christian Campus Found., Urbana, Ill., 1976-77; assoc. pastor Souderton (Pa.) Brethren In Christ Ch., 1978-79; campus min. Christian Campus Ministry, Tempe, Ariz., 1983-85; assoc. pastor Cen. Christian Ch., Mesa, Ariz., 1985—; pres. U. Ill. chpt. Fellowship Christian Athletes, Champaign, Ill., 1976-77. Republican. Office: Cen Christian Ch 933 N Lindsay Rd Mesa AZ 85213

HOLLENBACH, SISTER RUTH, college president. BS in Math. and Sci., Webster Coll., 1952; MA in Philosophy, U. Notre Dame, 1958, PhD, 1960; postgrad., Cath. U., 1964, U. Notre Dame, 1971. Joined Sch. Sisters of Notre Dame, Roman Cath. Ch. Tchr. math., sci. St. Joseph High Sch., Conway, Ark., 1952-55; chairperson dept. philosophy Notre Dame Coll., St. Louis, 1958-65; prof. Am. studies Nanzan U., Nagoya, Japan, 1966-78, adminstr. internat. div., 1974-78; fin. dir., dir. devel. Maria Ctr., St. Louis, 1978-84; adminstr. St. Mary's Spl. Sch., St. Louis, 1984-87; pres. Mt. Mary Coll., Milw., 1987—. Office: Mt Mary Coll 2900 N Menomonee River Pkwy Milwaukee WI 53222

HOLLER, ADLAI CORNWELL, JR., minister; b. Orangeburg, S.C., Mar. 21, 1925; s. Adlai Cornwell and Miriam (Fair) H.; m. Elizabeth Cobb, June 4, 1949; children: Suzanne Elizabeth, Adlai Stephen, Stephanie Elwood. AB, Wofford Coll., 1947; MDiv, Duke U., 1952; D of Ministry, Columbia Sem., 1987. Lic. marriage and family therapist, profl. counselor. Mil. pilot USAAF, 1943-46; chaplain USAF, various cities, 1952-82; minister of counseling Bethany United Meth. Ch., Summerville, S.C., 1982—; bd. dirs. Medicine and Ministry Conf., Kanuga, N.C., 1983—; dir. Charleston (S.C.) Dist. Pastoral Counseling Ctr., 1987—; mem. Bd. Ordained Ministry, Columbia, 1980-88. Author: Ministry to Flying Students, 1957, Training Laity for Counseling, 1987. Mem. Disable Am. Vets., Rotary. Methodist. Avocations: antique automobiles, travel. Home: 112 Old Dominion Dr Charleston Heights SC 29418 Office: Pastoral Counseling Ctr 118 W Third St S Summerville SC 29483 *God comes to others through us, therefore God who is Love in me greets God who is Love in you. We are thereby both used as God's loving agents in the ministry of reconciliation.*

HOLLER, ROBERT KEATH, minister; b. Mendota, Ill., Sept. 11, 1931; s. Howard Jay and Helen Frances (Littlewood) H.; m. Carol Lynn Wurtz, Nov. 4, 1962; children: Kathryn Holler Herzog, Sarah Holler Suddeth, Nancy. BA, Carroll Coll., 1953; MDiv, McCormick Theol. Sem., 1956, ThM, 1957, D of Ministry, 1977. Ordained to ministry Presbyn. Ch. (U.S.A.), 1956. Min. 1st Presbyn. Ch., Litchfield, Ill., 1957-69, Canton, Ill., 1969—. Office: First Presbyn Ch 275 Linden Canton IL 61520

HOLLERAN, SHEILA, development officer; b. Irvington, N.J., May 1, 1939; d. Thomas Jerome and Loretta Dorothea (Griffin) Holleran. BA, Dunbarton Coll. Holy Cross, Washington, 1961; MA, Jersey City State Coll., 1969. Joined Sisters of Charity of St. Elizabeth, 1961; cert. sch. adminstr., N.J. Tchr. Sisters of Charity of St. Elizabeth, Convent Station, N.J., 1963-68, Ridgewood, N.J., 1968-70; elem. sch. prin. Sisters of Charity of St. Elizabeth, Tenafly, N.J., 1970-78, Montclair, N.J., 1978-86; grant dir. for aged Sisters of Charity of St. Elizabeth, Convent Station, N.J., 1986—, spl. events dir. for maj. fund raisers, 1986—, dir. direct mail program, 1990—. Mem. Nat. Cath. Devel. Conf., N.J. Soc. Fund Raising Execs. Avocations: writing, reading. Home: 158 High St Passaic NJ 07055 Office: Sisters of Charity Convent Station NJ 07961

HOLLEY, GREGORY LEE, pastor; b. Wichita Falls, Tex., Aug. 5, 1954; s. Ernest Lee and Verba Joy H.; m. Gayla Joyce Latta, Dec. 27, 1975; 1 child, Angela Joy. Student, Tex. Bible Coll., 1970-73. Traveling evangelist Am., Can., Europe, 1975-78; missionary overseer Ptnrs. in Missions, Zimbabwe, South Africa, 1978-81; pastor, founder New Life Ministries, Bloomington, Ill., 1983—; assoc. pastor Life Tabernacle, Houston, 1973; asst. pastor Peace Tabernacle; co-pastor New Life Tabernacle, Harare, Zimbabwe, 1981. Founder New Life Community Action, Bloomington, 1984—, New Life Rehab. Ctr., New Life Recycling Svcs.; co-dir. Youth Outreach for Am., 1990—; youth camp dir. Youth for Christ-U.S.A., 1975—. Home: PO Box 3642 Bloomington IL 61702 Office: New Life Ministries PO Box 3642 Bloomington IL 61702

HOLLIDAY, PATRICIA RUTH MCKENZIE, evangelist; b. Jacksonville, Fla., Nov. 17, 1935; d. Robert Irving and Leona Adele (Bell) McKenzie; student Massey Bus. Coll., 1969, Luther Rice Sem., 1976; D.D., Southeastern Sem., 1986; m. Jan. 20, 1965; children—Connie, Katheryn, Alexander. Sec., Delta Drug Corp., Jacksonville, 1965—; pres. Microfilm Center, Jacksonville, 1974—; pres. Miracle Outreach Ministry, Jacksonville, 1974—. Sec.. Four Found., Inc.; Republican candidate for Fla. Ho. of Reps., 1972; mem. Fla. Republican. Com., 1976-80; lobbyist Fla. Legislature, 1978-80; hostess Pat Holliday TV Show, Jacksonville. Clubs: Minutewomen of Fla. (founder), Univ., Women, Ponte Vedra Women's. Author: Holliday for the King, 1978; Be Free, 1979; Only Believe, 1980; Born Anew, 1981; The Walking Dead, 1982; Anointing Power, 1982; Signs, Wonders and Reactions, 1984; AIDS, 1985; Dealing with Heresies, 1986; columnist Christian Courier. Home: 9252 San Jose Blvd Apt 2804 Jacksonville FL 32217 Office: Miracle Outreach Ministry PO Box 10126 Jacksonville FL 32207

HOLLIES, LINDA HALL, minister, educator, author, publisher; b. Gary, Ind., Mar. 29, 1943; d. James Donald and Doretha Robinson (Mosley) Adams; m. Charles H. Hollies, Oct. 14, 1962; children—Gregory Raymond, Grelon Renard, Grian Eunyke. B.S. in Adminstrn., Ind. U., 1975; M.A. in Communications, Gov. State U., 1980; M.Div., Garrett-Evang. Theol. Sem., 1986—. Tchr. Hammond Public Schs., Ind., 1975-77; supr. Gen. Motors Corp., Willow Springs, Ill., 1977-79; gen. supr. Ford Motor Co., East Chicago Heights, Ill., 1979-82; coord. Women in Ministry, Evang. Theol. Sem., Evanston, Ill., 1984-86; pastor New Life Community Fellowship United Methodist Ch., Lansing, Mich., 1983-86; clin. pastoral edn. intern supr., 1986-88; sr. pastor Richards St. United Meth. Ch., 1988—; founder, dir., cons. Wonder Woman Seminars, Discovery Unltd., Joliet, Ill., 1989—, Woman to Woman Ministries, Inc. Exec. dir. Discovery Unlimited Prevention Program, 1989; appointee Mayor's Coomn. on Role and Status of Women, Gary, 1982-83. Ford fellow, 1975, Benjamin E. Mays fellow, 1984; Crusade scholar United Meth. Ch., 1984; Lucy Ryder Myer scholar, 1985-86, Dr. Martin L. King scholar, 1989. Mem. Zonta Profl. Women's Assn., Nat. Assn. Pastoral Educators, Zonta Internat., Internat. Toastmistress Club (pres. 1976-77). Author, pub.: Innner Healing for Broken Vessels, Womanist Rumblings, Womanistcare: Tending the Souls of Women, Restoring Wounded Warriors. Democrat. Avocations: reading, preaching, creative writing, latch hook. Home: 212 Sherman St Joliet IL 60433 Office: The Richards St United Meth Ch 212 Richards St Joliet IL 60433

HOLLINGSWORTH, DAVID ROYCE, minister; b. Terre Haute, Ind., Aug. 3, 1946; s. Wilbur Royce and Betty Jane (Maddox) H.; m. Kathleen Lula Mahan, Dec. 15, 1967; children: William Scott, Laura Melinda, Andrew Morgan. BS, Western Bapt. Bible Coll., El Cerrito, Calif., 1969, ThB, 1969. Ordained to ministry Gen. Assn. Regular Bapt. Chs., 1970. Christian edn. dir. First Bapt. Ch., Pleasant Hill, Calif., 1968-71; asst. pastor Trinity Bapt. Ch., Sunnyvale, Calif., 1971-74; pastor Grace Bapt. Ch., Morgan Hill, Calif., 1974-76; asst. pastor Trinity Bapt. Ch., Sunnyvale, 1976-77; pastor First Bapt. Ch., Cambria, Calif., 1977—; treas. Calif. Assn. Regular Bapt. Chs., 1981-88, presiding chmn., 1988-90. Republican. Office: First Bapt Ch 2120 Green St Cambria CA 93428-5035

HOLLINGSWORTH, DEVON GLENN, organist, minister of music; b. Boone, Iowa, Dec. 5, 1946; s. Walter Delbert and Gwendolyn Elaine (Mayer) H.; m. Carol Ruth Bethke, Jan. 19, 1980; 1 child, Mark William. MusB, Wheaton (Ill.) Coll., 1968; MusM, Northwestern U., 1970. Organist, choirmaster Trinity Luth. Ch., Evanston, Ill., 1968-77; min. music, organist Christ Ch. Oak Brook, Ill., 1977—. Home: 5802 S Washington St Hinsdale IL 60521-4959 Office: York Rd and 31st St Oak Brook IL 60521

HOLLINGSWORTH, MARY CAROLYN, author, editor; b. Dallas, Oct. 18, 1947; d. Clyde E. and Thelma G. (Hargrave) Shrode. BS in Edn., Abilene Christian U., 1970, MA in Communication, 1972. Adminstr. Ouachita Christian Sch., Monroe, La., 1980-82; assoc. editor Sweet Pub. Co., Ft. Worth, 1984-86; mng. editor Worthy Pub., Ft. Worth, 1986-88, Teach Newsletter, Ft. Worth, 1985—; freelance writer Creative Enterprises, Ft. Worth, 1988—; ministry leader spl. music Richland Hills Ch. of Christ, Ft. Worth, 1987—, pres. Richland Hills Family Singers, 1985—. Mem. Ft. Worth Arts Coun., 1989—. Mem. Nat. Writers Assn., Tex. Music Educators Assn., Tex. Choral Dirs. Assn. Office: Creative Enterprises 3950 Fossil Creek Blvd Ste 203 Fort Worth TX 76137

HOLLIS, ALLEN, clergyman; b. Concord, N.H., Jan. 8, 1932; s. Franklin and Eleanor (Slaker) H.; m. Susan Tower, Nov. 10, 1962 (div. June 1975); children: Deborah, Harrison; m. Joanna Phillips, Aug. 30, 1975; children: Deborah Shell, Cynthia Shell. BA, Harvard Coll., 1953; STB, Harvard U., 1956. Ordained to ministry United Ch. of Christ, 1959. Pastor First Congl. Ch., Millers Falls, Mass., 1957-64; pastor Cen. Congl. Ch., Fall River, Mass., 1964-71, Lynn, Mass., 1971-80; pastor Union Congl. Ch., West Palm Beach, Fla., 1980—; co-host TV program Perspectives in Faith, WPEC, West Palm Beach, Fla., 1984—; religious columnist Palm Beach Post, West Palm Beach, 1985—. Author: The Bible and Money, 1975. Dir., v.p. Planned Parenthood of Palm Beaches, 1988-91. Mem. Ministerial Fellowship of the Palm Beaches (pres. 1984-86). Avocations: duplicate bridge, tennis. Home: 7424 Clarke Rd West Palm Beach FL 33406 Office: Union Congl Ch 2727 Georgia Ave West Palm Beach FL 33405

HOLLIS, LANNY KEITH, theology educator; b. Loretto, Tenn., Dec. 17, 1957; s. Samuel Edward and Maxine Hazel (Monnett) H. BA in Psychology, St. Meinrad Coll., 1980; MST, St. Meinrad Sch. of Theology, 1986; MA in Religious Studies, Ind. U., 1989. Vocat. counselor Goodwill Industries of Toledo, 1980-81, Vocat. Guidance Svcs., Cleve., 1981-82, 86-87; instr. theology and history, retreat coord. Erieview Cath. High Sch., Cleve., 1987—; instr. in history St. Edward High Sch., Lakewood, Ohio, summer 1988, 89. Orphanage dir. Christian Found. for Children, Barquisimeto, Venezuela, 1985. Cleve. Diocese Edn. Fund grantee, 1989. Mem. Diocesan Campus Ministers. Democrat. Roman Catholic. Avocations: racquetball, chess, languages. Office: Erieview Cath High Sch 1736 Superior Ave Cleveland OH 44107

HOLLIS, REGINALD, archbishop; b. England, July 18, 1932; emigrated to Can., 1954; s. Jesse Farndon and Edith Ellen (Lee) H.; m. Marcia Crombie, Sept. 7, 1957; children—Martin, Hilda, Aidan. B.A., Cambridge U., Eng., 1954; M.A., Cambridge U., 1958; B.D., McGill U., Montreal, 1956; D.D. (hon.), U. South, 1977, Montreal Diocesan Theol. Coll., 1975. Ordained to ministry Anglican Ch. as deacon, 1956, as priest, 1956. Chaplain Montreal Diocesan Theol. Coll.; also chaplain to Anglican students McGill U., 1956-60; asst. St. Matthias Parish, Westmont, Que., 1960-63; incumbent St. Barnabas Ch., Roxboro, Que., 1963-66; rector St. Barnabas Ch., 1966-71, Christ Ch., Beaurepaire, Que., 1971-74; dir. parish and diocesan services Diocese Montreal, 1974-75, bishop, 1975-89; archbishop of Montreal Met. of the Ecclesiastical Province of Can., 1989-90; episcopal dir. Anglican Fellowship of Prayer, 1990—. Author: Abiding in Christ, 1987. Home: 5553 Jessamine Ln Orlando FL 32839 Office: PO Box 31 Orlando FL 32802

HOLLIS, SUSAN TOWER, religion educator; b. Boston, Mar. 17, 1939; d. James Wilson and Dorothy Parsons (Moore) Tower; m. Allen Hollis, Nov. 10, 1962 (div. Feb. 1975); children: Deborah Durfee, Harrison. AB, Smith Coll., 1962; PhD, Harvard U., 1982. Asst. prof. Scripps Coll., Claremont, Calif., 1988-91; prof. Coll. of Undergrad. Studies The Union Inst., L.A., 1991—. Author: The Ancient Egyptian "Tale of Two Brothers", 1990; asst. editor: Working With No Data, 1987; mem. adv. bd. KMT, A Modern Jour. of Ancient Egypt, 1991—; contbr. articles to profl. publs. Music vol. Open Readings, Belmont, Mass., 1982-88; vol. Sierra Club, 1988—. Mem. Am. Acad. Religion, Am. Folklore Soc., Am. Oriental Soc., Am. Rsch. Ctr. Egypt, Internat. Egyptolog. Soc., Nat. Women's Studies Assn., Soc. Biblical Lit., Appalachian Mountain Club (co-leader 1987—). Democrat. Home: 1233 Woodbury Ct # D Upland CA 91786 Office: The Union Inst Coll Undergrad Studies 4801 Wilshire Blve Ste 250 Los Angeles CA 90010-3813

HOLLORAN, LORI JEAN, lay church worker; b. Mpls., Oct. 21, 1956; d. Ellis Wendell and Marilyn Marcella (Muehlberg) Pike; m. Michael John Halloran; children: Tiffany Jean, Joshua John, Bethany Ann, Jonathan Joseph, Timothy Michael. AA, Grand View Coll., Des Moines, 1976; BS in Elem. Edn., BS in Bible, Pillsbury Bible Coll., Owatonna, Minn., 1981; cert. deaf edn., Temple Deaf Bible Coll., Peoria, Ill., 1983. Cert. nurse asst. Counselor girls' camp Child Evangelism Fellowship, Mpls., 1973-75; leader jr. high sch. girls Hospitality House, Mpls., 1976; Sunday sch. tchr. Crosstown Bapt. Ch., Eden Prairie, Minn., 1978-81; coord. childrens' ch. Meadow Creek Ch., Andover, Minn., 1988-90; dir. children's choir West River Road Bapt. Ch., Brooklyn Park, Minn., 1991—. Precinct del. Coon Rapids (Minn.) Pub. Com., 1989; del. Iowa Gov.'s Prayer Breakfast, Des Moines, 1976, 77. Home: 9448 Flintwood St NW Coon Rapids MN 55433

HOLLOWAY, CARLTON LAWRENCE, minister, consultant; b. Jarratt, Va., Aug. 22, 1938; s. Sidney Taylor and Blanch Lee (George) H.; m. Joan Elswick, Oct. 27, 1956; 1 child, Carlton Lawrence Jr. Diploma, Hargrave Mil. Acad., 1956. Ordained to ministry Bapt. Ch.; cert. counselor. Pastor Samaritan Mission, Emporia, Va., 1987-90; evangelist Va., N.C., 1985—; owner ins. agy. Emporia, Va., 1978—; Pres. United Meth. Men, Jarratt, Va., 1988-89; cons., chaplain ICM Ministries, correctional ctr., Emporia, 1985-91, chaplain hosp., industry, 1985-90. Author monthly mission newsletter. Min. Prison Ministries, Emporia, 1986—; active in fundraising for homeless emergency shelter. Mem. Gideons Internat. (sec. 1988-89), Woodsmen of World (chmn.). Home: 417 Harding St PO Box 1229 Emporia VA 23847

HOLLOWAY, GARY NELSON, religion educator; b. Griffin, Ga., Aug. 18, 1956; s. Raliegh Nelson and Mary Alice (Perkins) H.; m. Deborah Fay Rogers, Aug. 15, 1977. BA, Freed-Hardeman, 1976; M.A.R., Harding U., 1979; PhD, Emory U., 1987. Tchr. Harding Acad., Memphis, 1977-83, Greater Atlanta Christian Sch., Norcross, Ga., 1983-89; asst. prof. Inst. for Christian Studies, Austin, Tex., 1989—. Author: Saints, Demons, and Asses, 1989. Mem. Am. Acad. Religion, Am. Theol. Librs. Assn., Am. Folklore Soc. Office: Inst for Christian Studies 1909 University Ave Austin TX 78705

HOLLWEG, ARND, clergyman; b. Moenchengladbach, Germany, Mar. 23, 1927; s. Ernst and Henriette (Voswinckel) H.; m. Astrid Blomerius, Aug. 30, 1961; children—Heike, Uta, Karen. Student U. Bonn, 1946-48, U. Goettingen, 1948-50, U. Tuebingen, 1952-53, U. So. Calif., 1953-54, U. Muenster, 1955-56; Dr. theol., U. Bonn, 1967. Ordained to ministry United Chs. Rhineland, 1958. Tchr. religion Gymnasium and Berufsschule, Lobberich, Germany, and asst. minister ch., Essen, Germany, 1955-57; lectr. Inst. Theology and Edn. of Rhineland Protestant Ch. (W.Ger.) and regional pastor Rhineland for Christian Edn., 1958-63; researcher Ecumenical Inst., U. Bonn (W.Ger.), 1964-65; pastor, ch., Bad Honnef, W.Ger., 1966-72; dept. head, hdqrs. diaconical relief ctr. German Protestant Ch., Stuttgart, 1973-76; pastor Ch. of Bethlehemsgemeinde, Berlin, and chmn. German Reformed Ch. of West Berlin, 1976-90; freelance writer and scientist, 1991—; lectr. Free U., Berlin, 1978-79, Kirchliche Hochschule, Berlin, 1979-84. Author: Theologie und Empirie, 3d edit., 1974; Gruppe-Gesellschaft-Diakonie, 1976; (with others) Obdachlosenhilfe, 1981; contbr. numerous essays to profl. publs.; editor Innere Mission and Diakonie, 1973-76. Served with German Army, 1943-44, German Inf., 1945. Mem. Deutsche Gesellschaft fü r Pastoralpsychologie, Gemeinschaft Evangelischer Erzieher, Christliche Presseakademie. Home: Hähnelstr 7, D-1000 Berlin 41, Federal Republic of Germany *The knowledge of God, ourselves and reality, on which we live, belongs together in Jesus Christ. What does that mean for thinking and science today?.*

HOLM, DUANE, minister. Dir. Met. Area Religious Coalition of Cin. Office: Met Area Religious Coalition 1055 Enquirer Bldg 617 Vien St Cincinnati OH 45202*

HOLMER, MARK EDWIN, minister; b. Creston, Iowa, July 21, 1942; s. J. Erik and Anita Rae (Wahlen) H.; m. Linnea Louise Allen, July 2, 1966; children: Krista, Kaia. BA, Augustana Coll., Rock Island, Ill., 1964; MDiv, Luth. Sch. Theol. Chgo., 1968. Ordained to ministry Evang. Luth. Ch. Am., 1968. Pastor All Sts. Luth. Ch., Fox Lake, Ill., 1968-73, St. Matthew Luth. Ch., Davenport, Iowa, 1973—; dean Ea. Cen. dist. Iowa Synod, Luth. Ch. Am., 1982-88; bd. dirs. Manor Scott County, Inc., Bettendorf, Iowa; tchr. Geneva Summer Sch. Missions, Williams Bay, Wis., 1969-72; pres. parish life coun. Iowa Synod, Luth. Ch. Am., Des Moines, 1984, 85, del. 13th biennial conv., Milw., 1986. Producer, creator slide program Life in the Land of Lenin, 1983. Mem. instnl. rev. bd. Palmer Coll. Chiropractic, Davenport, 1983—; mem. adv. bd. Salvation Army, Davenport, 1987—. Mem. Kiwanis (pres. Davenport chpt. 1985-86, lt. gov. Ill.-Ea. Iowa dist. 1986-87, chair spiritual aims com. 1988-89). Home: 2640 W 37th St Davenport IA 52806 Office: St Matthew Luth Ch 1915 W Kimberly Rd Davenport IA 52806

HOLMES, ALFRED, minister; b. Aiken, S.C., Oct. 14, 1939; s. Bright Ridge and Glwillie (Corbitt) H.; m. Gladys Folks, Dec. 19, 1959; children: Catharine, Annette, Jeannette, Telford, Rebecca, Stephanie. BA in Bible, Bible Sem., Plymouth, Fla., 1985. Ordained to ministry, Bapt. Ch. Pastor Mt. Anna Bapt. Ch., Aiken, S.C., 1978—, Carey Hill Bapt. Ch., Edgefield, S.C., 1978—; moderator Storm Br. Assn., Aiken, 1985—, Macedonia Assn., Barnwell, S.C., 1975-83; bd. dirs. ACT Clergy Bd., 1990—, mem. homeless com., 1990—; bd. dirs. Bapt. State Conv., Columbia, 1976—. Home and Office: Mt Anna Bapt Ch 685 Edrie St Aiken SC 29801

HOLMES, MICHAEL WILLIAM, religion educator; b. Delano, Calif., Dec. 14, 1950; s. William Robert and Shirley May (Rasmussen) H.; m. Mary Patricia Bergwall, June 24, 1972. BA with honors, U. Calif., Santa Barbara, 1973; MA magna cum laude, Trinity Evang. Div. Sch., Deerfield, Ill., 1976; PhD cum laude, Princeton Theol. Sem., 1984. Instr. Princeton (N.J.) Theol. Sem., 1981-82; asst. prof. Bethel Coll., St. Paul, 1982-85, assoc. prof., 1985-90, prof., 1990—. Editor, revisor: The Apostolic Fathers, 1989; contbr. articles, revs. to profl. publs., chpts. to books. Fellow Inst. Biblical Rsch.; mem. Soc. Biblical Lit., Internat. Greek New Testament Project (mem. exec. com., Am. editor 1989—). Baptist. Office: Bethel Coll 3900 Bethel Dr Saint Paul MN 55112

HOLMES, PAUL, minister; b. Louisville, Miss., Aug. 2, 1954; s. Jimmie T. and Martha (Triplett) H.; 1 child, Adesola. BBA, Ea. Mich. U., 1976. Missionary Pan-African Orthodox Christian Ch., Detroit, 1973-86, minister, 1986—; fin. dir. Pan-African Orthodox Christian Ch., Detroit, 1986—, dir. Bible Studies, 1987—. Home and Office: 700 Seward Detroit MI 48202

HOLMES, REED M., clergyman, former religious organization administrator; b. Mansfield, Wash., June 17, 1917; s. Lawrence Earl and Emma Virginia (Reed) H.; m. Dorothy Lois Carter, Aug. 3, 1943; children: David, Carol (Mrs. Leslie T. Flowers), Joy Holmes Soper, Jewell (Mrs. Andrew Bolton), Lawrence. AA, Graceland Coll., 1937; BA, State U. Iowa, 1939; MA, Calif. State Coll., Los Angeles, 1959; postgrad., U. Wash., 1939-40, Boston U., 1948, U. Iowa, 1967-70; PhD, Haifa U., 1990. Ordained to ministry Reorganized Ch. of Jesus Christ of Latter Day Saints, 1940; missionary So. New Eng. and Maine, 1940-42; pastor Attleboro, Mass., 1942-44, Boston, 1945-48; dist. pres. So. New Eng., 1942-48; ordained apostle, 1948; gen. dir. religious edn. World Hdqrs., Independence, Mo., 1948-54; field dir. Southwest states and Alaska, 1954-59, Australia, N.Z., French Polynesia, 1959-64; dir. communications and program services div., 1964-73, assoc. dir. field ministries, 1973-74, presiding patriarch, 1974-82; founder, chmn. bd. View Pax Mondiale, 1982; co-founder, bd. govs. Keshet haShalom, Israel, 1989. Author: Seek This Christ, 1952, Israel-Land of Zion, 1978, The Patriarchs, 1978, Kendra, 1979, The Forerunners, 1981, The Church in Israel, 1983, Hanachshonim, 1985; co-author: editor: Exploring the Faith, 1970; Contbg. editor: Saint's Herald, 1964-74. Chmn. Human Rights Commn., Independence, 1971, 72, Independence Personnel Com., 1974-76; bd. dirs. Restoration Trail Found., 1970-76. Mem. John Whitmer Hist. Assn., Maine Hist. Soc. (James Phinney Baxter prize 1981). Democrat. Home: PO Box 1234 Gardiner ME 04345 *Most of us grow up being quite provincial, more local than global. Now, more than ever, we need a global outlook. We need to break out of our cultural cocoons and recognize our interdependence.*

HOLMES, THOMAS EWEN, minister; b. Whitehead, Northern Ireland, Oct. 1, 1954; s. Alexander and Dorothy (Cowan) H.; m. Holly Gruber, Sept. 20, 1986; children: Patrick Colin, Oliver Barret. BA, Coll. Wooster, Ohio, 1976; MDiv, Princeton (N.J.) Tehol. Sem., 1981; D Ministry, Pitts. Theol. Sem., 1989. Ordained to ministry, Presbyterian Ch., 1982. Asst. to moderator Gen. Assembly of United Presbyn. Ch. in U.S.A., Houston, 1981; asst. minister E. Liberty Presbyn. Ch., Pitts., 1982-86; minister First Presbyn. Ch., Henderson, N.C., 1986—; mem. Pitts. Presbytery, 1982-86, com. on shared and extended ministry, 1983-86, task force on housing, 1985-86; Orange Presbytery, Durham, 1986-88, New Hope Presbytery, Rocky Mount, N.C., 1989—, pers. com., 1989—, Family Violence Intervention Program, region K, N.C., 1988-90; v.p. Vance Co. Ministerial Assn., 1990—, Maria Parham Chaplain Hosp., 1989—, charter mem. Hospice of Vance-Warren, 1991—. Bd. dirs. East End Coop. Ministry, Pitts., 1982-86; bd. dirs., exec. com. Area Christians Together in Svc., Henderson, 1986—; bd. dirs., chmn. bd. Family Violence Intervention Prog. for Region K of N.C., 1988—. Republican. Presbyterian. Office: First Presbyterian Ch PO Box 726 Henderson NC 27536 *Life is often burdensome because we have not been willing to expend the energy that is necessary for happiness.*

HOLMES, WESLEY C., clergyman; b. Vaiden, Miss., Apr. 25, 1916; s. Wess and Mary Jane (Brooks) H.; m. Erline Towns, Dec. 24, 1950; children: Lynn Renee, Jan Michele. BS, Rust Coll., 1959; MDiv, Memphis Theol. Sem., 1969; DD (hon.), Ea. Nebr. Chrisitan Coll., 1971; ThD, Trinity Theol. Sem., Evansville, Ind., 1979. Ordained to ministry Bapt. Ch. Minister Elcanaan Bapt. Ch., Whiteville, Tenn., 1939-43, St. John Bapt. Ch., Memphis, 1943-48, Mt. Vernon Bapt. Ch., Memphis, 1948-54, Beulah Bapt. Ch., Memphis, 1955—; pres. Sardis (Miss.) Coll., 1945-48; chmn. bus. com. Tenn. B.M. and E. Conv., Nashville, 1968-72, pres., 1972-76. Chmn. Non-Partisan Voters League, Memphis, 1965; mem. Orange Mound Day Care Ctr., Memphis, 1980—; vice chmn. Housing Opportunity Bd., Memphis, 1983-84; pres. bd. dirs. Lemoyne-Owen Coll., Memphis, 1984-86. Recipient achievement award Rust Coll., 1974, Trustee's award Memphis Theol. Sem., 1976, spl. recognition Lemoyne-Owen Coll., 1982, Inter-religious award NCCJ, 1988. Mem. Am. Bapt. Ministers Coun., Met. Interfaith Assn. (bd. dirs. 1979—), NACCP. Office: Beulah Bapt Ch PO Box 240472 Memphis TN 38124

HOLMGREN, FREDRICK CARLSON, religion educator; b. Cadillac, Mich., Apr. 1, 1926; s. Charles Olaf and Freda Natalia (Teelander) H.; m. Betty Jean Margaret Carlson, June 12, 1948; children: Mark, Margaret. AB, Calvin Coll., 1949; BD magna cum laude, Union Theol. Sem., 1955, MST summa cum laude, 1957, ThD, 1963. Prof. Biblical lit. North Park Theol. Sem., Chgo., 1960—. Author: With Wings As Eagles, 1973, The God Who Cares, 1979, Israel Alive Again, 1987; editor Internat. Theol. Commentary, 1982—; contbr. articles to profl. jours. Rockefeller Found. fellow, 1960; Deutscher Akademischer Austauch scholar, 1991. Mem. Soc. Biblical Lit., Chgo. Soc. Biblical Lit. Office: North Park Theol Sem 3225 W Foster Ave Chicago IL 60625

HOLMGREN, LATON EARLE, clergyman; b. Mpls., Feb. 20, 1915; s. Frank Albert and Freda Ida (Lindahl) H. Student, U. Minn., 1934-35; A.B. cum laude, Asbury Coll., 1936; M. Div. summa cum laude, Drew U., 1941; postgrad., Edinburgh (Scotland) U., 1947; D.D., Ill. Wesleyan U., 1956, Asbury Theol. Sem., 1972. Ordained to ministry United Methodist Ch., 1942; assoc. minister Calvary Meth. Ch., East Orange, N.J., 1940-42, Christ Ch. Meth., N.Y.C., 1943-48; minister Tokyo (Japan) Union Ch., 1949-52; lectr. internat. dept. Tokyo U. Commerce, 1950-52; adviser Japanese Fgn. Office, Tokyo, 1951; sec. for Asia Am. Bible Soc., N.Y.C., 1952-54; exec. sec. Am. Bible Soc., 1954-62, gen. sec., rec. sec., 1963-78, cons., 1978—; mem. exec. com. United Bible Socs., Stuttgart, Germany, 1957-78, chmn., 1963-72, spl. cons., 1978-88. Recipient Gutenberg award, 1975, Disting. Alumni award Asbury Coll., 1981, Baron von Canstein award, 1982, Disting. Svc. award United Bible Socs., 1990. Mem. Asia Soc., Japan Soc., Metropolitan Club, Monday Club. Home: 328 Desert Falls Dr E Palm Desert CA 92260 Office: 1865 Broadway New York NY 10023

HOLMSTROM, GUSTAF WERNER, clergyman; b. Malmberget, Sweden, July 13, 1923; s. Alfred and Amalia (Larsson) H.; m. Sonja Viola Lundmark; children: Robert Kerstin, Astrid, Lennart, Torbjörn. Degree in ministry, U. Stockholm; student, N.K.I., 1966; PhD (hon.), U. Malta, 1988. Ordained to ministry Pentecostal Ch., 1948. Evangelist Pentecostal Bapt. Ch., Sweden, 1942-45, pastor, 1945-66; founder Christian Cons. Union, Sweden, 1973—. Moderator, Christian Conservative Party, Stockholm, 1977. Chaplain Swedish armed forces, 1944-45. Mem. ABI (dep. gov. 1987, chmn. 1988, grand amb. 1990, Fellow of Yr. award 1987), ABIRA, WIA. Roman Catholic. Home: Syrengatan 10, 15145 Södertälje Sweden

HOLSOPPLE, CURTIS ROYER, college program director; b. Huntington, Ind., Oct. 23, 1951; s. Donald Galen and Mary Etta (Stinebaugh) H.; m. Edith Mabel, May 4, 1974; 1 child, James Joseph. BA in Edn., Manchester Coll., 1973; MA in Edn., Ball State U., 1985. Lic. 1st. class radiotelephone, 2nd class comml. telegraph, ship radar endorsement. Youth sponsor Ridgeway Mennonite Ch., Harrisonburg, Va., 1987-89; dir. communications Ea. Mennonite Coll. and Sem., Harrisonburg, 1987—; gen. mgr. Sta. WEMC-FM religious radio, Harrisonburg, 1987—. Author: Skills for Radio Broadcasters, 1988; co-author: Handbook of Radio Publicity, 1990. Mem. Coun. for Advancement in Higher Edn., Massanutten Amateur Radio Assn. (newsletter editor 1987—), Am. Radio Relay League (asst. dir. 1987—). Mennonite. Office: Ea Mennonite Coll 1200 Park Rd Harrisonburg VA 22801

HOLST, ERNST FREDERICK, minister; b. Bklyn., Mar. 18, 1934; s. Ernst John and Anna Kathryn (Meyer) H.; m. Barbara Ann Christman, Sept. 7, 1957; children: Diane, Susan, Beth. BA, Wagner Coll., 1955; MDiv, Luth. Theol. Sem., Phila., 1958; MA, Union Coll., Schenectady, N.Y., 1969. Ordained to ministry Evang. Luth. Ch. Am., 1958. Mission developer Redeemer Luth. Ch., Orangeburg, N.Y., 1958-61; pastor various chs., N.Y., 1961-72, Augustana Luth. Ch., Tonawanda, N.Y., 1972-78; campus pastor The Luth. Assn. Cornell U., Ithaca, N.Y., 1978-87; pastor Gloria Dei Luth. Ch., Lakewood, N.Y., 1987—; dir. Luth. Social Svcs., Jamestown, N.Y., 1988—, Pastoral Counseling Svcs., Lakewood, 1988—; dean Southwestern Conf. Upstate N.Y. Synod, Evang. Luth. Ch. Am., Lakewood, 1989—. Author: Devotional Book, 1985, Exegetical Study, 1986. Mem. Alumni Assn. Luth. Theol. Sem. (pres. 1986-89). Office: Gloria Dei Luth Ch 39 W Fairmount Ave Lakewood NY 14750 *Success is not so much a measurement of accomplishments as it is the sustaining of relationships.*

HOLST, MARY-ELLA, religion educator; b. Detroit, Oct. 12, 1934; d. Spencer and Ruth Catherine (McCullough) Holst; B.A., U. Toledo, 1959; M.A., N.Y.U., 1970; m. Bert Zippel, Jan. 18, 1969 (dec. May 1985); children: Patricia Hall, Darcy Hall. Sr. counselor, employment specialist N.Y. Dept. Labor, 1962-75; religious edn. dir. Unitarian Ch. of All Souls, 1976-87, dir. emerita, 1987—; mem. Unitarian Universalist Hist. Scholarship Com. Bd. mgrs. Pres. Annie Eaton Soc., 1974—; bd. dirs. Yorkville Common Pantry, 1982-88—. Contbg. editor Conversations. . . Journal of Women and Religion; contbr. poetry to lit. jours. Mem. Unitarian Universalist Svc. Com. (major gifts com.), Booker T. Washington Learning Ctrs. (N.Y.C., devel. com.). Home: 340 E 80 St New York NY 10021 Office: Unitarian Ch of All Souls 1157 Lexington Ave New York NY 10021

HOLSTEIN, JAY ALLEN, Judaic studies educator; b. Phila., Mar. 22, 1938; s. Jules B. and Belle (Kellman) H.; m. Roberta Lynn Pope, Apr. 16, 1967; children: Sarah Abigail, Joshua Saul. AB, Temple U., 1960; B in Hebrew Lit., Hebrew Union Coll., N.Y.C., 1962, M in Hebrew Lit., 1966; PhD, Hebrew Union Coll., Cin., 1970. Ordained rabbi, 1966. J.J. Mallon prof. Judaic studies Sch. Religion U. Iowa, Iowa City, 1970—, endowed chair Judaic studies, 1976. Author: The Jewish Experience, 1989; contbr. articles to profl. publs.; mem. editorial bd. Counseling and Values, 1984—. Mem. B'nai B'rith Internat. Democrat. Avocations: marathon running, tae kwon do. Home: 1 Rapid Creek Dr Iowa City IA 52240 Office: U Iowa Sch Religion 404 Gilmore Hall Iowa City IA 52242

HOLSTON, JAMES EUGENE, minister; b. Terre Haute, Ind., Jan. 4, 1951; s. James W. and Marie Agnes (Kern) H.; m. Kathleen Karr, Aug. 6, 1977; children: James Steven, Marianne. AA, Freed-Hardeman U., 1971; BA, Harding U., 1974, ThM, 1980; postgrad., Trinity Evang. Divinity Sch., 1990—. Min. Westside Ch. of Christ, Ames, Iowa, 1979-86, Eastside Ch. of Christ, East Syracuse, N.Y., 1986—. Contbr. articles and book reviews to profl. theology jours. Republican Home: PO Box 74 East Syracuse NY 13057-0074 Office: Eastside Ch of Christ PO Box 743 East Syracuse NY 13057-0743

HOLT, BERTHA MARIAN, international adoption agency executive; b. Des Moines, Feb. 5, 1904; d. Clifford Ai and Eva Eda (Sherman) H.; m. Harry Spencer Holt, Dec. 31, 1927 (dec. Apr. 1964); children: Stewart, Wanda, Molly, Barbara, Suzanne, Linda, Joseph, Robert, Mary, Christine, Nathaniel, Helen, Paul, Betty. BSN, U. Iowa, 1926; hon. doctorate, Choong Ang U., Seoul, 1968, Linfield Coll., 1977. Pvt. duty nurse, Des Moines, 1926-27; self-employed farmer, Firesteel, S.D., 1927-37, Creswell, Oreg. 1937-56; co-founder, pres. bd. Holt Internat. Children's Services, Creswell, 1956—. Author: Seed From the East, 1956; Outstretched Arms, 1956; Created for God's Glory, 1982; Bring My Sons from Afar, 1986. Named U.S. Mother of Yr., Am. Mothers Com., 1966, Woman of Yr., Soroptimist Internat., 1973, Moran medal for civil merit Republic of South Korea, 1974, Decade of the Child medallion Republic of Philippine Islands, 1981. Mem. Oreg. Mother's Assn. Organized passage of spl. Congl. bill for Korean orphans, 1955. Avocations: writing, traveling to visit children adopted through Holt Internat., gardening. Office: Holt Internat Children's Services 1195 City View PO Box 2880 Eugene OR 97402 *I am most grateful that our holy, holy, holy God became Human Being so He could die for my sins.*

HOLT, EARL KENDALL, III, minister, writer, lecturer; b. Providence, Dec. 31, 1945; s. Earl Kendall Jr. and Priscilla Carolyn (Rowe) H.; m. Joan Burton Scott, Aug. 10, 1969 (div. 1983); children: Alicia Shallcross, Julia Payne; m. Marilyn Miner Hall, Dec. 11, 1987. AB, Brown U., 1967; MDiv, Starr King Sch for Ministry, Berkeley, Calif., 1972. Ordained to ministry Unitarian Ch., 1972. Asst. min. North Shore Unitarian Ch., Plandome, N.Y., 1972-74; min. First Unitarian Ch. of St. Louis, 1974—; min. on loan Unitarian Ch., Kingsport, Tenn., 1980; vis. prof. Starr King Sch. for the Ministry, Berkeley, 1982; minister in residence Meadville Theol. Sch., Chgo., 1982; guest lectr. Dept. of English Duke U., Durham, N.C., 198 8. Author: William Greenleaf Eliot; Conservative Radical, 1985; contbr. articles to profl. jours. Bd. dirs. Joint Community Ministries, Inc., St. Louis, 1974—; steering com. Eighth Nat. Workshop on Jewish-Christian Rels., St. Louis, 1984; trustee Starr King Sch., 1990—. Recipient Sermon prize Soc. for Alcohol Edn., Boston, 1984. Mem. Interfaith Clergy Coun. Greater St. Louis (pres. 1988—), T.S. Eliot Soc. (treas. 1985-88), Unitarian U. Ministry Assn. (chpt. pres. 1977-79), Brown Club, Chi Alpha. Republican. Office: First Unitarian Ch 5007 Waterman Blvd Saint Louis MO 63108

HOLT, EDGAR JOE, JR., marriage and family therapist; b. Mesa, Ariz., Feb. 13, 1955; s. Edgar Joe and Frances Louise (Dobbs) H.; m. Jan Carol Righten, Apr. 11, 1981; children: Jason, Jarod. BA, Okla. Bapt. U., 1977; MA in Religious Edn., Southwestern Sem., 1980, EdD, 1984. Minister edn. Meadowbrook Bapt. Ch., Ft. Worth, 1980-82, Riverside Bapt. Ch., Miami, 1982-84, 1st Bapt. Ch., North Augusta, S.C., 1984—. Named one of Outstanding Young Men Am. 1985. Mem. Am. Psychol. Assn., Am. Assn. Marriage and Family Therapists (clin.). Lodge: Lions. Avocations: woodworking, photography, computers. Office: Charter Hosp of Augusta 3100 Perimeter Pkwy Augusta GA 30909

HOLT, EDWARD JAMES, Episcopal priest, rector; b. Columbia, Tenn., Oct. 2, 1942; s. James Gaston and Effie Rose (McKowan) H.; m. Linda Joyce Smith Holt, Apr. 10, 1964; children: Richard Robert Holt, James Edward Holt. BA, Northeast La. U., 1969; MDiv, Episc. Theol. Sem. S.W., Austin, Tex., 1979. Spl. agt. FBI, Tampa, Fla., 1969-70, Little Rock, Ark., 1970-76; canon St. Paul's Cathedral, Oklahoma City, 1979-81, priest-in-charge, 1982; rector St. Mary's Episc. Ch., El Dorado, Ark., 1982-90, St. John's Episc. Ch., Decatur, Ill., 1990—; dean S.W. Convocation, Diocese of Ark., 1985-89, mem. exec. com. 1985-90, pres. standing com., 1987-90; dep. gen. conv. Episcopal Ch., N.Y.C., 1988; chmn. dept. nat. and world mission Diocese of Springfield, Ill., 1991—, mem. diocesan coun., 1991—; mem. Congregations of Decatur Area Bd., 1990—. Mem. adv. bd. Salvation Army, El Dorado, 1986-90; bd. dirs. Habitat for Humanity. Mem. Assn. for Psychol. Type, El Dorado C. of C. Avocations: cooking, computers. Home: 57 Montgomery Pl Decatur IL 62522-2654 Office: St John's Episc Ch 130 W Eldorado St Decatur IL 62522-2111

HOLT, GREGORY ALLAN, minister; b. Louisville, Aug. 21, 1956; s. Clarence E. and Norma Jean (Waters) H.; m. Sherry Gale Rodgers, June 17, 1978; 1 child, Jonathan Gregory. Diploma, Rhema Bible Tng. Ctr., 1977; BA, Spalding U., 1982. Ordained to ministry Assemblies of God, 1982. Assoc. pastor Evang. Christian Life Ctr., Louisville, 1977—; asst., administr. Bethesda Manor Nursing Home, Louisville, 1982-85; pres. Evang. Schs. Inc., Louisville, 1986—; pres. Sta. WJIE-FM, Louisville, 1982—; owner, pres. Autotronics Inc., Louisville, 1989. Republican. Office: Evang Christian Life Ctr 5400 Minors Ln Louisville KY 40219

HOLT, JEFFERY THOMAS, clergyman; b. Rochelle, Ill., Aug. 21, 1959; s. Jerry T. and Betty J. (Childers) H.; m. Sherle Marie Groover, July 27, 1979; children: Brandon Thomas, Nicholas Jordan. BS in Bibl. Studies, Lee Coll., 1980. Ordained to ministry Ch. of God, 1990. Youth pastor Ch. of God, Calhoun, Ga., 1979-80, Forrest City, Ark., 1980-82; assoc. pastor Ch. of God, Daisey, Tenn., 1982-83; pastor Ch. of God, Decatur, Ill., 1983-86; assoc. pastor Ch. of God, Jesup, Ga., 1986-88; pastor Ch. of God, Chester, Ga., 1988—; trustee Ch. of God in Ill., Decatur, 1983-86; dist. youth and Christian edn. dir. Ch. of God, Dublin, 1988—. Named Dist. Youth and Christian Edn. Dir. of Yr., Ch. of God in South Ga., 1990. Mem. Lee Coll. Alumni Assn. South Ga. (bd. mem. 1989—). Republican. Home and Office: Main St Chester GA 31012 *The greatest good that man can do is to perform the will of his Creator. Once that is accomplished, everything else will fall in place.*

HOLT, JOHN B., theologian; b. Abilene, Tex., June 15, 1915; s. Holland and Emma Cleora (Morriset) H.; m. Margaret Ann Buster, Feb. 14, 1940; children: John Michael, Stephen Lee, Paul Holland. B.S., McMurry Coll., 1937, D.D. (hon.), 1954; postgrad., U. Tex., 1938-39, U. Chgo., 1958; M.Th., So. Meth. U., 1945; D.D. (hon.), Paul Quinn Coll., 1962. Youth dir. Central Tex. Conf., United Meth. Ch., 1941-43; ordained to ministry United Meth. Ch., 1944; exec. sec. (Bd. Edn.), 1944-46; assoc. pastor Austin Ave. Meth. Ch., Waco, Tex., 1946-48; pastor Knox Ch., Manila, 1948-58; assoc. dean Perkins Sch. Theology, So. Meth. U., Dallas, 1958-82; sec. Gen. Conf. United Meth. Ch., 1973-85. Author: Our Methodist Heritage, 1952, A Study Guide for the Book of Acts, 1956, Financial Aid for Seminarians, 1966; Editor: Perkins Perspective, 1958-72; Contbr. articles to mags. and jours. Trustee Mary Johnston Hosp., Union Theol. Sem., Am. Bible Soc., Philippine Christian Coll. Clubs: Kiwanis, Masons. Home: 4130 San Carlos Dallas TX 75205 Office: So Meth U Perkins Sch Theology Dallas TX 75275

HOLT, NOEL CLARK, minister; b. Cape Girardeau, Mo., Dec. 8, 1935; s. Archie N. and Dorothy G. (Shaw) H.; m. Rosalee Powell, Feb. 27, 1955; children: Sidney Clark, Jennifer Lee, Julie Powell. BA, Cen. Coll., Fayette, Mo., 1959; MDiv, Garrett Theol. Sem., 1963; DMin, Princeton Sem., 1983. Founding minister Kingswood Ch., Buffalo Grove, Ill., 1963-71; sr. minister Faith Ch., Dolton, Ill., 1971-77, First Ch., Park Ridge, Ill., 1977-80, Trinity Ch., Wilmette, Ill., 1980-85, Baker Meml. Ch., St. Charles, Ill., 1985—. Mem. ACLU. Club: Union League. Avocations: sailing, travel, photography. Home: 307 Iroquois Ave Saint Charles IL 60174 Office: Baker Meml United Meth Ch 307 Cedar Ave Saint Charles IL 60174

HOLT, NORMAN BARRY, radio executive, church representative; b. Canton, Ga., Aug. 9, 1949; s. James Taylor and Gladys (Goss) H.; m. Patsy Dean Pendley, Sept. 18, 1970; children: James, Melody. BBA, Rienhardt Coll., 1990. Bd. dirs. Chapel Christian Acad., Jasper, Ga., 1984-88; mem. pastoral staff Mt. Paran Ch. of God, Atlanta, 1987—; sec.-treas. Sawnee Communications, Atlanta, 1987—. With USMC, 1967-70. Republican. *God provides for the birds of the air, true. But, to find food they must land on the ground and subject themselves to the possibility of being eaten by a cat. "Pie in the sky" attitudes must be balanced by an empty plate.*

HOLTER, DON WENDELL, retired bishop; b. Lincoln, Kans., Mar. 24, 1905; s. Henry O. and Lenna (Mater) H.; m. Isabelle Elliott, June 20, 1931; children: Phyllis (Mrs. Robert Dunn), Martha (Mrs. Robert Hudson), Heather (Mrs. Lee Ellis). B.A., Baker U., 1927, D.D., 1948; postgrad., Harvard U., 1928; B.D., Garrett Theol. Sem., 1930; Ph.D., U. Chgo., 1934; LL.D., Dakota Wesleyan U., 1969; D.D., St. Paul Sch. Theology, 1973. Ordained to ministry Meth. Ch. as elder, 1934. Asst. minister Euclid Meth. Ch., Oak Park, Ill., 1930-34; missionary in Philippines, 1935-45; minister Central Ch., Manila, 1935-40; interned with family by the Japanese, Santo Tomas Internment Camp, Manila, 1942-45; prof. Union Theol. Sem., Manila, 1935-40; pres. Union Theol. Sem., 1940-45; minister Hamline Meth. Ch., St. Paul, 1946-49; prof. Garrett Theol. Sem., 1949-58; founding pres. St. Paul Sch. Theology, 1958-72; bishop Nebr. area United Meth. Ch., 1972-76; del. Internat. Missionary Conf., India, 1938; spl. study mission, Africa, 1958; rep., mem. pers. com. Meth. Bd. of Global Ministries, 1964-72; chmn. commn. ministry United Meth. Ch., 1968-70, mem. gen. bd. higher edn. and ministry, 1972-76, chmn. div. ordained ministry, 1972-76, del. gen. and jurisdictional confs., 1964, 66, 68, 70, 72. Author: Fire on the Prairie, Methodism in the History of Kansas, 1969, Flames on the Plains, A History of United Methodism in Nebraska, 1983, The Lure of Kansas, The Story of the Evangelicals and United Brethren, 1853-1968, 1990. Trustee St. Paul Sch. Theology. Home: 7725 Briar Dr Prairie Village KS 66208

HOLTGREWE, KAREN JUNE, church organist, choir director, junior high school educator; b. Belleville, Ill., Jan. 29, 1952; d. Oliver Frederick and Carmen Aileen (Stocks) Buescher; m. Gary Wynn Holtgrewe, Aug. 24, 1974; children: Alan, Angela. BS in Edn., Ea. Ill. U., 1973; MS in Early Childhood Edn., So. Ill. U., Edwardsville, 1987. Cert. home econs., early childhood and elem. tchr., Ill. Organist, choir dir. St. Peter's United Ch. of Christ, Addieville, Ill., 1984—, tchr. Sunday sch., 1980-83, tchr. vacation bible sch., 1984-85, co-dir., 1988—; tchr. home econs. Mascoutah (Ill.) Jr. High Sch., 1974—; dir. youth St. Peter's United Ch. of Christ-Stone Ch., Addieville, 1990—; camp counselor, DuBois (Ill.) Ctr., 1990, dir., 1991. Recipient Creative Nutrition award Nutrition Edn. and Tng., 1990. Home: Rte 1 Box 133 Okawville IL 62271 Office: St Peters Ch-Stone Ch Rte 1 Box 49 Addieville IL 62214 *Whenever a challenge seems overwhelming, I remember that I am not alone. If God has helped others achieve success, then He will help me do the same.*

HOLTROP, PHILIP CORNELIUS, religion and theology educator; b. Cleve., Mar. 23, 1934; s. Elton John and Ella (Veen) H.; m. Marie Greenfield, Aug. 12, 1958; children: Stephen Dean, Philip Alan, Daniel Charles, Peter Grant. AB, Calvin Coll., 1955; BD, Calvin Theol. Sem., 1958; ThDoctorandus, Free U., Amsterdam, the Netherlands, 1963; PhD, Harvard U., 1988. Instr. Philosophy Trinity Christian Coll., Palos Heights, Ill., 1963-65; pastor North Haledon (N.J.) Christian Reformed Church, 1971-77; prof. Calvin Coll., Grand Rapids, Mich., 1977—; assoc. minister Eastern Ave. Christian Reformed Ch., Grand Rapids, 1977—; preacher, adult edn. classes western Mich., 1977—; reporter, sec. Belgic Confession Translation Com. Christian Reformed Ch., Grand Rapids, 1977-85; sec. Calvin and Calvinism Study, Grand Rapids, 1978-82; adjunct prof. Calvin Theol. Sem., Grand Rapids., 1990—. Author Theologia Pietatas: Notes on Selected Passages in Calvin's Insts., 1981; contbr. articles to profl. jours. Mem. Bread for the World, Evangelicals for Social Action, Just Life, Right to Life, Amnesty Internat. (Urgent Action), 1982—; Citizen's League of Grand Rapids. Recipient Alumni scholarship Calvin Coll. Alumni Assn., Grand Rapids, 1951-52, Fulbright scholarship, 1958-59, Centennial Mission scholarship, Christian Reformed Ch., Grand Rapids, 1959-60, various Harvard scholarships, 1965-69, Rockefeller Doctoral fellowship, 1969-70. Mem. Am. Acad. Religion, Calvin Study Soc., Internat. Congress on Calvin Rsch. (sect. leader 1990), Sixteenth Century Studies Soc. Home: 1223 Calvin Ave SE Grand Rapids MI 49506 Office: Calvin Coll Religion & Theology Dept Grand Rapids MI 49546

HOLTZ, ALAN EDWARD, minister; b. Evansville, Ind., July 27, 1932; s. Edward Henry and Huldah Emile (Fellwock) H. BTh, Concordia Sem., Springfield, Ill., 1963. Ordained to ministry Luth. Ch., 1963. Minister Luth. Ch. of Our Redeemer, Cushing, Okla., 1963-69, Grace English Evang. Luth. Ch., Jersey City, 1969-73, Faith Luth. Ch., Derby, Kans., 1973-85, Grace Luth. Ch., El Dorado, Kans., 1985—. Home: 338 Hunton Rd El Dorado KS 67042

HOLTZMAN, JEROME JOSEPH, priest; b. Highmore, S.D., Nov. 5, 1930; s. Victor Henry and Ellen (Brady) H. BA, St. John's U., 1952; MA, U. S.D., 1960; MAT, U. San Francisco, 1971; M Div., St. Paul Sem., 1957. Ordained priest, Roman Cath. Ch., 1957. Sec. Allied Secretariat, Vienna, Austria, 1951-52; held pastoral positions Sioux Falls (S.D.) Diocese, 1957-86; lang. instr. Cath. high schs., S.D., 1958-69; dean of students Inst. European Studies, Vienna, 1972—; mem. pastoral staff Diocesan Cathedral, Udon Thani, Thailand, 1987; asst. field dir. Hmong Refugee Camp Cath. Orgn. Relief and Refugees, Ban Viani, Thailand, 1988—; dir. Thailand tourism apostolate Nat. Cath. Bishops Conf., 1990—; dir., Permanent Deacon Formation Program, Sioux Falls, 1979-85; co-dir., Buddhist/Christian Dialog, N.Y.C., 1986, 89. Co-author: Liberation Theology in Latin America, 1982; editor refugee camp publ., 1988-89. Democrat. Avocations: skiing, canoeing, mountain hiking, photography.

HOLWERDA, DAVID EARL, religion educator; b. Grand Rapids, Mich., Aug. 26, 1932; s. Peter G. and Edith (Banninga) H.; m. Gayla Fern Kortman, Aug. 19, 1954; children: Marigay, Faith Anne, Sondra Sue, Lynn Ellen. AB, Calvin Coll., 1953; BD, Calvin Sem., 1956; ThD, Free U., 1959. Prof. Bibl. Studies Trinity Christian Coll., Palos Heights, Ill., 1959-62; prof. Religion and Theology Calvin Coll., Grand Rapids, 1963-84; prof. New Testament Studies Calvin Theol. Sem., Grand Rapids, 1984—. Author: Holy Spirit & Eschatology, 1959; editor: Exploring the Heritage of John Calvin, 1976; contbr. articles to profl. jours. Mem. Soc. Bibl. Lit., Chgo. Soc. Bibl. Rsch., Inst. Bibl. Rsch., Calvin Studies Soc. Home: 1652 Gorham SE Grand Rapids MI 49506 Office: Calvin Theol Sem 3233 Burton St SE Grand Rapids MI 49506

HOLYER, ROBERT KENT, theologian, educator; b. Sioux Falls, S.D., Mar. 31, 1946; m. Karen Elizabeth Steinbinder, Sept. 5, 1970; children: Christiana Elizabeth, James Bentley Bringhurst, John Michael Milford, Margaret Alexandra. BA summa cum laude, Bethel Coll., 1968; postgrad. Westminster Theol. Seminary, 1968-69; BD, Yale U., 1971; Ph.D., U. Cambridge (Eng.), 1978. Asst. prof. religion dept. religious studies U. Va., Charlottesville, 1976-79; asst. prof. dept. religion Converse Coll., Spartanburg, S.C., 1979—, chmn. spl. events and lectures com.; freshman advisor, honors com., founder, chmn. Converse Film Soc., pre-law adv. com., chmn. humanities div. com. on curriculum revision, 1982-83, chmn. dept. religion. Bethel Coll. Honors scholar, 1966-68; Cambridge U. (Eng.) Pembroke Coll. Bethune-Baker fellow, 1974-75; U. Va. Dean's List of Disting. Tchrs., 1979. Mem. Am. Acad. Religion, Soc. Christian Philosophers, Soc. Philosophy Religion. Democrat. Lutheran. Contbr. to theol. publs. Office: Converse College Dept Religion Spartanburg SC 29301

HOLZ, ANTHONY DAVID, rabbi; b. Cape Town, South Africa, May 1, 1942; came to U.S., 1964; s. Erich and Ursula (Kassel) H.; m. Judith Devine, Nov. 27, 1966; children: Meiera, Jessa, Dara. MA in Hebrew Lit., Hebrew Union Coll., 1970, postgrad., 1970-72, 77-81. Ordained rabbi, 1970. Hillel advisor Miami U., Oxford, Ohio, 1970-72; rabbi Progressive Jewish Congregation, Pretoria, South Africa, 1972-77, Temple Israel, Paducah, Ky., 1977-81, Cong Beth Tikvah, Columbus, Ohio, 1981-83, Temple Israel, Duluth, Minn., 1983—; v.p. Institute of Creative Judaism, Cin., 1971—; chaplain Fed. Prison Camp, Duluth, 1985—. Author: (with others) Funeral & Memorial Services, 1979. Sec. Lake Superior Chamber Orch.; bd. dirs. NAACP, Duluth, 1984—. Mem. Cen. Conf. of Am. Rabbis, Mid-Western Assn. Reform Rabbis. Lodge: Rotary. Home: 2614 E Superior St Duluth MN 55812 Office: Temple Israel 1602 E 2d St Duluth MN 55812

HOLZBAUER, DALE LEE, minister; b. Cin., May 21, 1947; s. Albert Henry and Clydella Margaret (Waters) H.; m. Elizabeth Scott Foster, Oct. 24, 1969; children: Jeff, Amy, Sherry. AB, Cin. Bible Coll., 1969; MA, Cin. Bible Sem., 1988; postgrad., Cin. Christian Sem., 1988—. Ordained to ministry Ch. of Christ, 1970. Youth minister/counselor 1st Ch. of Christ/Osso Home, Xenia, Ohio, 1971-78; sr. minister Branch Hill Ch. of Christ, Cin., 1978-83, Franklin (Ind.) Meml. Ch., 1983-91, Fortville (Ind.) Christian Ch., 1991—. Head instr. Franklin Christian Karate Club, Franklin, 1983-91, Fortville Christian Karate Club, 1991—, Branch Hill Christian Karate Club, Cin., 1979-83. Named Nat. Weightlifting Champion class I AAU, 1979. Mem. Kyokushinkai Karate-Do (3 degree black belt). Republican. Home: PO Box 205 Fortville IN 46040 Office: Fortville Christian Ch PO Box 205 Fortville IN 46040

HOMAN, BENJAMIN KEITH, theological seminary official; b. Burbank, Calif., Nov. 17, 1959; s. Franklin Keith and Margaret Glee (Pratt) H.; m. Annette Kay Bonness, May 28, 1988. BA magna cum laude, Biola U., 1980; postgrad., U. Nebr., 1980-82. Grad. teaching asst. speech dept. U. Nebr., Lincoln, 1980-82, asst. instr., 1982; instr. speech Chaffey Coll., Alta Loma, Calif., 1983, Biola U., La Mirada, Calif., 1983-85; dir. speech and debate U. Calif., Irvine, 1983-85; dir. for East Asia, Campus Crusade for Christ, San Bernardino, Calif., 1986-87, asst. dir. communication, 1987-88; dir. devel. Covenant Theol. Sem., St. Louis, 1988—, editor Inside Covenant Sem. newsletter, 1988—; communication cons.-auditor Office of Mayor, City of Lincoln, 1981-82, Lincoln Edn. Assn., 1982. Editor newsletters Insider Report, 1986, Dialog with U.S. Ministry Leaders, 1987-88; writer, dir. slide-tape Medicaid and You, 1982. Deacon Foothills Presbyn. Ch., San Bernardino, 1987-88; mem., deacon Presbyn. Ch., St. Louis, 1989—. Mem. Christian Ministries Mgmt. Assn., Christian Stewardship Coun. Republican. Avocations: swimming, photography, writing, travel. Office: Covenant Theol Sem 12330 Conway Rd Saint Louis MO 63141-8697

HOMAN, KENNETH B., theology educator; b. Harvey, Ill., June 28, 1953. BA with highest honors, Quincy Coll., 1976; postgrad., Vanderbilt U., 1976-77; MA, U. Iowa, 1985, PhD summa cum laude, 1990. Instr. theology Quincy (Ill.) Coll., 1977-78; pastoral counselor Homan Pastoral Svcs., St. Louis, 1984-86; asst. prof. theology Quincy Coll., 1986—; cons. Cath. Hosp. Assn., St. Louis, 1988; workshop leader Homan Pastoral Svcs., St. Louis, 1983—. Acad. scholar Vanderbilt U., 1977; rsch. grantee Lily Found./Am. Acad. Religion, 1991-92. Mem. Am. Acad. Religion, Coll. Theology Soc., Soc. for Sci. Study of Religion. Office: Quincy Coll 1800 College Ave Quincy IL 63139

HOMAN, MARTIN J., minister; b. Hammond, Ind., Oct. 12, 1953; s. Marten and Beverly (Jane) H.; m. Lisa C. Loeffler, Aug. 13, 1964. BA, Concordia Sr. Coll., Ft. Wayne, Ind., 1976; MDiv, Concordia Sem., St. Louis, 1980, MST, 1982, postgrad., 1986—; ThM, Luth. Sch. Theology, Chgo., 1986. Ordained to ministry Luth. Ch.-Mo. Synod, 1981. Instr. Concordia Coll., River Forest, Ill., 1981-84, asst. prof., 1984-87; pastor Grace Luth. Ch., Del Rio, Tex., 1988-90; in-house Hebrew specialist God's Word to the Nations Bible Soc., Cleve., 1990—; pastoral asst. St. Thomas Luth. Ch., Rocky River, Ohio, 1990—. Mem. Evang. Theol. Soc., Soc. Bibl. Lit., Internat. Orgn. Septuagint and Cognate Studies. Home: 5568 Decker Rd North Olmsted OH 44070 Office: God's Word to the Nations Bible Soc 22050 Mastick Rd Cleveland OH 44126-0343

HON, JACKSON P., minister; b. Rockford, Ill., Aug. 23, 1932; s. Jackson and Jane (Piersen) H.; m. Janet J., Dec. 28, 1953; children: Nina Jane Paselk, Michael Kevin, Jill D'Ann Giallanza. BBA, Tex. Tech. U., 1954. Minister, sch. prin., elder, founder Jesus Chapel, El Paso, Tex., 1972—; bd. dirs. Oral Roberts U. Ednl. Fellowship. Del. Rep. Party, Houston, 1988. With U.S. Army, 1954-56. Home: 8701 Catalpa El Paso TX 79925 Office: Jesus Chapel 10555 Edgemere El Paso TX 79925

HONEYCUTT, ROY LEE, academic administrator. Pres. So. Bapt. Theol. Sem., Louisville. Office: So Bapt Theol Sem Office of Pres 2825 Lexington Rd Louisville KY 42080*

HONG, FRANCIS, bishop. Bishop Diocese of Pyongyang, Roman Cath. Ch., Dem. People's Republic Korea. Office: Cath Mission, Pyongyang Democratic People's Republic of Korea*

HONIG, EMANUEL M., rabbi; b. Bklyn., Feb. 1, 1915; s. Louis and Minnie (Metzger) H.; m. Muriel Bette Mosler, June 13, 1942; children: Madalyn, Jeffrey, Sheila. BS, Bklyn. Coll., 1935; MD, U. Oreg., Portland, 1950; PhD, So. Calif. Psychoanalytic Inst, Beverly Hills, Calif., 1972. Ordained rabbi, 1939. Rabbi Congregation Beth-El, Binghamton, N.Y., 1939-41; psychiatrist, psychoanalyst Beverly Hills, Calif., 1954—; bd. govs. U. Judaism, L.A., 1982-89; mem. L.A. Bd. Rabbis, 1987—; bd. govs. Sinai Temple, L.A., 1982—. Contbr. articles to profl. jours. Bd. dirs. Jewish Fedn. Coun. L.A., 1984—. Maj. USAAF, 1941-46. Fellow Am. Psychiat. Assn. (life); mem. Am. Psychoanalytic Assn. (life), Cen. Conf. Am. Rabbis (life), Alpha Omega Alpha. Democrat. Office: 300 S Beverly Dr Beverly Hills CA 90212

HOOBING, STANLEY CARL, pastor; b. Boise, Idaho, July 2, 1942; s. Carl Alfred and Marian Walter (Cleare) H.; m. Carol Jane Kinzle, June 24, 1972; children: Rachel Elizabeth, Matthew David. AA, Boise State U., 1962; BA, Pacific Luth. U., 1965; MTh, Pacific Luth. Theol. Sem., 1968. Ordained to ministry Luth. Ch. Parish pastor Cen. Luth. Ch., Morton, Wash., 1969-73, Good Shepherd Luth., Richland, Wash., 1973-76; interim/parish pastor Faith Luth. Ch., Junction City, Oreg., 1977-82; parish pastor Grace Luth. Ch., Spokane, 1982-86, Gethsemane Luth. Ch., Tacoma, 1986-89, Hope-Valby Luth. Parish, Heppner, Oreg., Ione, Oreg., 1990—; synod youth com. mem. Pacific NW Synod Evang. Luth. Ch. in Am., Morton, Wash., Richland, Wash., 1970-76, parish life com. mem., Junction City, 1978-82; mem. parish life com. Intermountain dist., Spokane, Wash., 1982-86. Vol. Operation Nightwalk, Spokane, Tacoma, 1983-89; pres. Neighborhood Ctr., Heppner, 1990—; convenor Oreg. Together, Heppner, 1990—. Named Vol. of Yr., Operation Nightwatch, 1987. Mem. Rural Pastors of Oreg. Synod. Democrat.

HOOD, KREGG RUSSELL, minister; b. Dallas, Nov. 18, 1956; s. Billie Joe and Esta Marjorie (Mullican) H.; m. Karen Lynn Hahn, May 23, 1981; children: Kalah Michelle, Kyle Joel. BA, Harding Coll., Searcy, Ark., 1978; MA, Abilene Christian U., 1982, M.Missiology, 1983; EdD, Tex. Tech. U., 1987. Ordained to ministry Chs. of Christ, 1982. Minister Culpepper Mt. Ch. of Christ, Clinton, Ark., 1978-79; missionary Mil. Pkwy. Ch. of Christ, Limerick, Ireland, 1979-80; assoc. min. Broadway Ch. of Christ, Lubbock, Tex., 1982-86; instr. Lubbock Christian Coll., 1984-86; min. College Ch. of Christ (now Meml. Rd.), Oklahoma City, 1986-89, South MacArthur Ch. of Christ, Irving, Tex., 1989—; mem. pres.'s coun. Harding U., Searcy, 1991—; co-host TV program The Way of Truth, Dallas, 1990-91; circulation mgr. 21st Century Christian, Nashville, 1990—; cons. Sweet Pub. Co., Ft. Worth, 1983-85; bd. visitors Abilene Christian U., 1990—. Assoc. editor TEACH newsletter, 1984—; contbr. articles to profl. jours. Recipient Christian Edn. award, Sweet Pub. Co., 1989. Mem. Christian Edn. Assn., Speech Communication Assn., Rotary, Phi Delta Kappa. Home: 1205 Cross Bend Irving TX 75061 Office: South MacArthur Ch Christ 1401 S MacArthur Blvd Irving TX 75060

HOOD, LESLIE LYNN, publishing executive; b. Indpls., June 24, 1948; s. John Marquis and Gloria (Bennett) H.; m. Jean Marie Rawlings, Dec. 12, 1969; children—Derek, Heath, Brecka, Shamene. B.S., Mo. Valley Coll., 1970; degree in Ministrial Studies, Berran Coll., 1985; postgrad., So. Calif. Theol. Sem. Student personnel adminstr. Mo. Valley Coll., Marshall, 1969-71; ordained to ministry, 1985. Dist. dir. Crossroads of Am. council Boy Scouts Am., Indpls., 1971-74, fin. dir. Dan Beard council, Cin., 1974-83; v.p. Lay Leadership Internat., Christian lit. pub. co., Fairfield, Ohio, 1983-91; pres. C.C.S. Cons., Cin., 1980—; bd. dirs. Santa Marie Neighborhood, Cin., 1976-80, H.I.P. Inc., Cin., 1977-79. Author: Financing Local Institutions, 1981; Baptist Church in Scouting, 1983. Kansas City Council Higher Edn., 1969. Mem. Nat. Assn. Ch. Adminstrs. (pres. 1987—), Nat. Soc. Fund Raising Execs. (cert.; Honors scholar 1983; mem. exec. bd. 1980-90, del. Lusanne II, 1989), Cin. Soc. Fund Raisers, Advt. Council. Republican. Mem. Assemblies of God. Clubs: Hamilton (Ohio); Kiwanis (Cin.). Lodge: Elks. Avocations: hiking; camping; canoeing. Home: 5841 Gilmore Dr Fairfield OH 45014 Office: Lay Leadership Internat 1267 Hicks Blvd Fairfield OH 45014 *The quality of indigenous leadership is the essential catalyist allowing an exposion of Christ-centered values on our emerging world.*

HOOD, THOMAS GREGORY, minister; b. Stamford, Conn., Mar. 26, 1948; s. George E. and Shirley W. (Brundage) H.; m. Esther A. Whitcomb, July 1, 1967; children: Thomas G., Sarah D. BA, Johnson State Coll., 1984; MDiv, Covington Sem., Rossville, Ga., 1986, PhD in Counseling, 1988. Ordained to ministry Fellowship of Christian Assemblies, 1969, Am. Bapt. Chs. in U.S.A., 1984. Asst. pastor Bethel Full Gospel Ch., Barton, Vt., 1968-71; pastor Lyndonville (Vt.) Full Gospel Ch., 1969-71, Sheffield (Vt.) Fed. Ch., 1971-74, Sutton (Vt.) Bapt. Ch., 1972-84, Adams Center (N.Y.) Bapt. Ch., 1984—; del. Am. Bapt. Conv., N.Y., 1984—; presenterAdams, N.Y. pub. schs., 1986—. Author: The Lord's Prayer, 1986, A Theology of Victory, 1987, Biblical Principles, 1988; composer religious songs. Mem. Am. Bapt.Mins. Coun. Republican. Home: 4023 Church St Adams Center NY 13606 *It is impossible to forgive ourselves for our failures if we are unwilling to forgive others theirs. The rule we use to judge others will always reflect back on ourselves.*

HOOKER, MORNA DOROTHY, theology educator; b. Croydon, Surrey, Eng., May 19, 1931; d. Percy Francis and Lily (Riley) H.; m. Walter David Stacey, Mar. 30, 1978. BA, U. Bristol, Eng., 1953, MA, 1956; PhD, U. Manchester, 1966; MA, U. Oxford, Eng., 1970, U. Cambridge, Eng., 1976. Research fellow U. Durham, Eng., 1959-61; lectr. N.T. studies King's Coll., London, 1961-70; lectr. theology U. Oxford, 1970-76, Keble Coll., Oxford, 1972-76; Lady Margaret's prof. divinity U. Cambridge, 1976—; fellow Linacre Coll., Oxford, 1970-76, hon. fellow, 1980—; fellow Robinson Coll., Cambridge, 1976—, King's Coll., London, 1979—; vis. prof. McGill U., 1968, Duke U., N.C., 1987, 89; vis. fellow Clare Hall, Cambridge, 1974. Author: Jesus and the Servant, 1959, The Son of Man in Mark, 1967, Pauline Pieces, 1979, Studying the New Testament, 1979, The Message of Mark, 1983, Continuity and Discontinuity, 1986, From Adam to Christ, 1990, A Commentary on The Gospel According to St. Mark, 1991; co-editor: What about the New Testament?, 1975, Paul and Paulinism, 1982, Jour. Theol. Studies, 1985—; also articles. Mem. Studiorum Novi Testamenti Societas (pres. 1988-89), Soc. Old Testament Study. Methodist. Avocation: molinology. Office: Divinity Sch, St John's St, Cambridge CB2 1TW, England

HOOKWAY, HUGH EATON, JR., minister; b. Marion, Ohio, Oct. 2, 1944; s. Hugh Eaton and Althea (Ballinger) H.; m. Judith E. Goetter, Jan. 28, 1967; children: Branden H., Ian C. BA, Bowling Green U., 1967, MA, 1970; MDiv, Meth. Theol. Sch. Ohio, 1978. Ordained to ministry United Meth. Ch., 1980. Pastor Chesterville (Ohio) United Meth. Ch., 1975-78, Grace United Meth. Ch., Willard, Ohio, 1985-89, Otterbein United Meth. Ch., Navarre, Ohio, 1989—; assoc. pastor Mentor (Ohio) United Meth. Ch., 1981-84. Mem. East Ohio Evang. Fellowship (bd. dirs. 1990—), Internat. Order of St. Luke, Phi Sigma Tau. Office: Otterbein United Meth Ch 6025 Shepler Church Ave SW Navarre OH 44662

HOON, PAUL WAITMAN, retired theologian, minister; b. Chgo., Feb. 11, 1910; s. Clarence Earl and Fannie Ruth (Waitman) H.; m. Grace Nichols, Nov. 23, 1938 (dec. June 1943); children: Peter Waitman, David Nichols; m. Alice Emerson Blodgett, Oct. 14, 1950. Student, U. Cin., 1926-28; BA, Yale U., 1931; MDiv, Union Theol. Sem., N.Y.C., 1934; postgrad., U. Marburg, Germany, 1934, U. Cambridge, Eng., 1935; PhD, U. Edinburgh, Scotland, 1936; DDiv, Ursinus Coll., 1948. Ordained to ministry United Meth. Ch., 1933. Student min. Madison Ave. Presbyn. Ch., N.Y.C., 1931-32; asst. pastor Chester Hill Meth. Ch., Mt. Vernon, N.Y., 1932-34; pastor New Milford (Conn.) Meth. Ch., 1936-38, Summerfield Meth. Ch., Bridgeport, Conn., 1938-41, First Meth. Ch., New Rochelle, N.Y., 1941-43, First Meth. Ch.Germantown,, Phila., 1943-53; Henry Sloane Coffin prof. pastoral theology Union Theol. Sem., N.Y.C., 1953-75; adj. prof. Drew Theol. Sem., Madison, N.J., 1948-50, 75-77; ret., 1977; lectr. Woodstock Coll., N.Y.C., 1972-74; cons. Am. Assn. Theol. Schs., 1970-72. Author: The Integrity of Worship, 1971; co-author: Interpreters Bible, Vol. XII, Exposition: Johannide Epistles, 1951, Death and Resurrection: The Church's Ministry at Death, 1979, Voyage, Vision, Venture: A Report on Spiritual Development; contbr. articles to religious jours. Named Steven Green lectr. Andover Newton Theol. Sem., Phillips U. Theol. Faculty, Scott lectr. Phillips U., Zimmerman lectr. Gettysburg Theol. Sem., Div. Sch. lectr. Duke U., Orr lectr. Huron Coll., Nyvall lectr. North Park Sem., others; vis. scholar Ecumenical Inst. Adavnced Theol. Studies, Jerusalem, 1974. Fellow N.Am. Acad. Liturgy; mem. Phila. Coun. Chs. (pres. 1946-48), Am. Assn. Profl. Edn. Ministry (pres. 1958-59). Home: Pennswood Village Fell 101 Newton PA 18940

HOOPENGARDNER, STANLEY JOSEPH, music director; b. Frostburg, Md., Oct. 20, 1947; s. Joseph Luther and Loretta Joy (Ashby) H.; m. Ingritt Pauline Johnson, July 25, 1970; children: Kimberly, Angela, Stacie, Michael. BS with Honors, U. Md., 1970; postgrad., George Washington U., Towson State U., U. Md. Dir. music Hollywood (Md.) Ch. of Nazarene, 1962-65, 70-87; min. youth Lexington Park (Md.) United Meth. Ch., 1987—, dir. music, 1990—; choral dir. Spring Ridge Mid. Sch., Lexington Park, Md., 1974—; adminstrv. bd. Lexington Park United Meth. Ch., 1988-91; dir. The Witness, musical, 1971; dir. choir St. Mary's City Hist. Pageant, 1980. Trio arranger Hollywood Harmoneers. Campaign mgr. t. Mary's County Commr., 1986. Mem. NEA, Friends of the Kennedy Ctr., So. Md. Music Conf., Nat. Fedn. Interscholarstic Coaches of Am. Republican.

HOOPER-TODD, NITA LAVONE, pastor; b. Sant Monica, Calif., Feb. 17, 1952; d. Velmer Eugene and Bernita Leone (Lester) Hooper; m. David Wheaton Hooper-Todd, Nov. 7, 1981. BA in English and Creative Writing, Calif. State U., Long Beach, 1975; MDiv., Fuller Tech. Theol. Sem., Pasadena, 1984. ordained pastor, United Meth. Ch., 1984. Youth pastor, dir. Christian edn. various United Meth. Chs., Calif., 1980-84; assoc. pastor Yorba Linda (Calif.) United Meth. Ch., 1984-86; sr. pastor San Jacinto (Calif.) United Meth. Ch., 1986—. Asst. editor: Pearl mag., 1974, contbr. editor, 1975; news editor: Paradeigma newspaper, 1979-80. Bd. dirs. Ctr. Against Sexual Assault, San Jacinto, Calif., 187-88; vol. for abused children, 1978-88. Mem. Women's Law Ctr., Clergywomen's Assn. of United Meth. Chs. (participant Calif.-Pacific annual conf., 1984—). Democrat. Avocations: writing poetry and fiction, reading.

HOOPS, CHRISTOPHER RORY, minister; b. Hawthorn, Calif., Jan. 29, 1950; s. Wilbert Charles and Elizibeth Alice (Roberts) H.; m. Gail Milinda Hoops, Apr. 29, 1977; children: Erin Christine, Christopher Rory Jr., Michael Charles. BTh., San Bernardino Bible Coll., 1975; postgrad., Whitefield Theol. Sem. Lic. to ministry Revival Fellowship of Chs., 1974, ordained, 1984. Prin. Christian Ctr. Acad., Colton, Calif., 1979-80; tchr. No. Ariz. Bible Coll., Holbrode, 1980-81, Mayflower Inst., Thousand Oaks, Calif., 1983-85; founding pastor Am. Heritage Christian Ch., Camarillo, Calif., 1984—; founding com. mem. So. Calif. Constn. Edn. Com., 1987—; founding exec. com. mem. So. Calif. Coun. Pastors and Leaders, 1988—; exec. mem. Coalition on Revival, Ventura County, Calif., 1989-91; founder, pres., dean Emanual Coll., Colville, Wash. Mem. Calif. Rep. Assn. Address: 669 Lindsay Rd Colville WA 99114

HOORNSTRA, PAUL ZENAS, priest; b. Pontiac, Mich., May 3, 1920; s. David Charles and Augusta Wilhelmina (Wickstrom) H.; m. Bertha Elisabeth Wysong, Dec. 24, 1939 (dec. 1987); children: Charles David, Jonathan Dennis, Betha Lee Jeanne; m. Mary-Nelson Coleman Campbell, Jan. 23, 1988. Cert., Cen. Mich. U., 1942; ThB, Olivet Nazarene U., 1943; D Ministry, Galilean Sem., 1949; postgrad., Somerset U., 1991—. Ordained to ministry Episcopal Ch. as deacon, 1952, as priest, 1953. Pastor Ch. of the Nazarene, Mich., 1943-52; canon pastor St. Paul's Episcopal Cathedral, Detroit, 1952-55; dean Diocese of No. Mich., 1955-58; asst. Grace Ch., Madison, Wis., 1958-59, rector, 1959-75; missioner Diocese of Ga., Savannah, 1975—; judge marital ct. Diocese of Mich., Detroit, 1953-55, ct. of array, Diocese of Ga., 1990—; mem. standing com. Diocese of No. Mich., 1955-58; pres. standing com. Diocese of Milw., 1960-70; pres. associated parishes, U.S.and Can., 1968-70; chmn. com. on alcoholism edn., Ga., 1977-82. Book reviewer The Living Ch., Milw., 1962-90. Pres. Madison Area Coun. of Chs., 1962-75; pastoral counseling advisor U. Wis., Madison, 1960-75, Wilmington Island, Savannah, 1976-83. Mem. Am. Med. Soc. on Alcoholism, Mensa, Rotary, Lions. Home and Office: 108 Talbot Rd Wilmington Island Savannah GA 31410-4016 *Memory is our human ability to readjust past events in order to serve our present need. The greater our need, the more we adjust. Therefore, I must be careful of what I say happened in the past. The greater the consequence of the moment, the greater the caution I must exercise.*

HOOSEINNY, LLOYD MICHAEL, minister; b. Guyana, S.Am., Dec. 2, 1949; came to U.S., 1984; s. Majeed and Rosaline Hooseinny; m. Heather Ann MacLean, July 17, 1982; children: Tracey, Kim. AA in Broadcasting, ITT Tech. Inst., Tucson, 1985; postgrad., Pacific Bible Coll., 1991—. Ordained to ministry Pentecostal Holiness Ch., 1976. Pres. coll. ministries Youth for Christ, Georgetown, Guyana, 1966-68; pastor Full Gospel Fellowship, Georgetown, 1968-71; nat. evangelist Pentecostal Holiness Ch. Can., 1975-84; pastor Pentecostal Holiness Ch., Tucson, 1984-87; news dir., talk show host Sta. KVOI, Tucson, 1985—; lectr. in field. Editor Editor and Columnist, 1988-90. Office: Sta KVOI 3425 E Grant Rd Ste 202 Tucson AZ 85716 *The Church is the spiritual and moral conscience of any society. While its foremost responsibility is evangelistic, its voice and presence must be distinctly represented in all aspects of life.*

HOOVER, HERBERT ALLEN, youth services administrator; b. Auburn, Ind., Apr. 20, 1957; s. Robert Allen and Janet Rosé (Brown) H.; m. Tori von Butler, Nov. 7, 1981; children: Krystal Ranae, Kimberly Ruth. A in Biblical Studies, Christian Tng. Ctr., 1987. Youth worker Campus Life, Auburn, Ind., 1980-81, 85-87; youth worker Calvary Chapel of Auburn, 1981-86, deacon, 1983-86; youth dir. Calvary Chapel in Waterloo (Ind.), 1989—; deacon, bd. dirs. Calvary Chapel in Waterloo, Ind., 1990—; lead welder Vulcraft div. Nucor, St. Joe, Ind., 1978—. Home: 900 Ruth St Auburn IN 46706

HOOVER, KENNETH EDWARD, retired pastor; b. West Union, Iowa, Feb. 2, 1907; s. Louis Edward and Agnes (Smith) Hoover; m. Irene Witner, Aug. 5, 1934; children: Rollin L., Barbara L., Noel E., Charlotte J., James E. AB, Taylor U., 1931; STB, Bibl. Sem., 1934. Ordained to ministry United Meth. Ch., deacon, 1934. Pastor United Meth. Ch. N.Y. Annual Conf., Poughkeepsie, 1934-72; dist. supt. United Meth. Ch. N.Y. Annual Conf., 1949-55. Pres. Upper Nohave County Improvement Assn., Bullhead City, Ariz., 1975-77. Mem. Rotary (pres. 1971-72). Home: 10639 Saratoga Cir Sun City AZ 85351

HOOVER, ROY WILLIAM, religion educator; b. Everett, Mass., Jan. 1, 1932; s. Virgil Merritt and Ruth Bevere (White) H.; m. Elizabeth Arnn Killgore, June 12, 1952; 1 child, Richard Roy. BA, Pasadena (Calif.) Coll., 1953; BDiv, Nazarene Theol. Sem., 1956; ThD, Harvard U., 1968. Ordained to ministry United Ch. of Christ (Congl.), 1962. Prof. religion Whitman Coll., Walla Walla, Wash., 1967—. Co-editor: Five Gospels, One Jesus. What Did Jesus Really Say?, 1992. Fellow The Jesus Seminar; mem. Am. Acad. Religion, Westar Inst., Soc. Bibl. Lit., Polebridge Press. Mem. United Ch. Christ. Home: 1406 S Division St Walla Walla WA 99362 Office: Whitman Coll 345 Boyer Ave Walla Walla WA 99362

HOPE, JIMMY MILTON, minister; b. Gainesville, Ga., Nov. 12, 1944; s. Jerry Homer and Inez (Dean) H.; m. Judy Carol Skinner, June 19, 1965; children: Lisa Michelle Hope Thrift, Carol Anne, John Michael. BA, Gainesville Coll., 1967; BBA, U. Ga., 1969; ThM, Internat. Sem., 1985, ThD summa cum laude, 1988. Cert. state and nat. Recreation and Parks Adminstr. Sr. pastor Praise Fellowship, Gainesville, 1988—; pres. New Life Ministry, Gainesville, 1988-91, Praise Coll., 1989-91; co-founder Host Christian Ministry, 1989-91. Author: The Trinity, Is Jesus God?, 1986, Once Saved, Always Saved?, 1987, Can A Christian Have A Demon?, 1988. Delegate Rep. Party, Gainesville, 1989-90; vol. N.E. Ga. Med. Ctr., chaplain program, 1988-91. Mem. Evangel Fellowship of Chs., Christian Businessmen's Com., Phi Kappa Phi. Home: 3320 Partridge Ln Gainesville GA 30501 Office: Praise Fellowship PO Box 2932 Gainesville GA 30503

HOPKINS, A. R., bishop. Bishop Ch. of God in Christ, Portland, Oreg. Office: Ch of God in Christ 1705 NE Dekum Portland OR 97211*

HOPKINS, DAVID ROGER, academic administrator; b. Wilington, N.C., Sept. 15, 1941; s. William Paul and Dorothy D. (Dalton) H.; m. Claudia Dale Fountain, Aug. 19, 1962; children: Christine Michele, David Mark. AA, Emmanuel Coll., 1961; BS, Towson State U., 1963, MEd, 1968; EdD, U.Ga., 1974. Tchr. English Edgewood (Md.) High Sch., 1963-67, East Mecklenburg High Sch., Charlotte, N.C., 1967-69; instr. English Emmanuel Coll., Franklin Springs, Ga., 1969-73, acad. dean, 1973-83, pres., 1983—. V.p. Royston (Ga.) PTA, 1976, pres. 1977; pres. Franklin County High Sch. Band Boosters, Carnesville, Ga., 1981. Mem. Assn. Pvt. Colls. and Univs. Ga. (treas. 1988—), C. of C. (v.p. 1983), Rotary, Phi Delta Kappa. Office: Emmanuel Coll Office Pres Franklin Springs GA 30639*

HOPKINS, DWIGHT NATHANIEL, religion educator; b. Richmond, Va., Feb. 22, 1953; s. Robert Roosevelt and Dora Hopkins; m. Nancy Diao, July 5, 1986; children: William, Eva. BA, Harvard U., 1976; MDiv, Union Theol. Sem., 1984, M in Philosophy, 1987, PhD, 1988. Ordained to ministry Progressive Nat. Bapt. Conv., 1984, Am. Bapt. Chs. U.S.A., k1989. Assoc. minister Bethany Bapt. Ch., Bklyn., 1982-87; asst. prof. religion and ethnic studies Santa Clara (Calif.) U., 1988—. Author: Black Theology USA and South Africa, 1989; editor: We Are One Voice, 1989, Black Theology in the Slave Narratives, 1991. Ford Found. fellow, 1990—. Mem. Am. Acad. Religion (chair black theology consultation 1990—), Pacific Coast Theol. Soc., Soc. for Study of Black Religion. Home: 8180 Hansom Dr Oakland CA 94605 *To be at peace with oneself, one has to aid those who cannot speak for themselves.*

HOPKINS, HAROLD ANTHONY, JR., clergyman; bishop, Episcopal Ch., Fargo, N.D.; dir. Office Pastoral Devel., presiding bishop of staff. Office: Episcopal Ch 815 2nd Ave New York NY 10017 also: Office Pastoral Devel 2 Fox Run Rd Cumberland ME 04021

HOPKINS, JAMES MELVIN, II, youth pastor; b. Frankfurt, Germany, Aug. 29, 1954; s. James M. and Pat H.; m. Nina Wrenn, June 22, 1974; children: Phil, Paul. Student, Arlington Bapt. Coll., Midwestern Bapt. Coll. Ordained to ministry Bapt. Ch., 1984. Coll., career dir. Faith Bapt. Ch., Dearborn Heights, Mich., 1979-87; youth dir. Faith Bapt. Ch., Dearborn Heights, 1987-89, singles dir., 1989; youth dir. 1st Bapt. Ch., Washington, Mich., 1989—; treas. Detroit area So. Mich. Youth Fellowship, 1990-91, pres., 1991—. Home: PO Box 22 55754 Van Dyke Washington MI 48094

HOPKINS, JERRY BERL, clergyman, educator; b. Mt. Vernon, Ky., Nov. 18, 1945; s. Berl V. and Anna Ruth (Stanley) H.; m. Lucyann Mitchell Hopkins, Dec. 27, 1968; children: Joseph David, Sarah Elizabeth, Hannah Marie. BA, Ea. Ky. U., 1968, MA, 1969; PhD, U. Ky., 1986; postgrad., Southwestern Bapt. Sem., Ft. Worth, 1969-72, Oxford U., Tex. Christian U. Ordained to ministry Bapt. Ch., 1964. Pastor Cen. Bapt. Ch., Italy, Tex., 1970-72, Temple So. Bapt. Ch., Little Stukeley, Eng., 1972-74, Mt. Freedom Bapt. Ch., Wilmore, Ky., 1975-81, Reidland Bapt. Ch., Paducah, Ky., 1982—; campus minister Bapt. Student Union, Murray (Ky.) State U., 1981-82; grad. asst. Ea. Ky. U., Richmond, 1968-69, Southwestern Bapt. Sem., 1969-72; grad. asst. U. Ky., Lexington, 1975-78, instr. history, 1978-81; prof. Midcontinent Bapt. Coll., Mayfield, Ky., 1981—. Contbr. articles to profl. publs. Mem. Orgn. Am. Historians, Conf. on Faith and History, So. Hist. Soc., Ky. Bapt. Hist. Soc., So. Bapt. Hist. Soc., Pi Tau Chi, Phi Alpha Theta. Democrat. Avocations: amateur radio, hiking, writing. Home: 210 Edwards Dr Paducah KY 42003 Office: Reidland Bapt Ch 5559 Benton Rd Paducah KY 42003

HOPKINS, KENNETH ARTHUR, JR., minister; b. Lisbon, N.D., Nov. 6, 1962; s. Kenneth Arthur Sr. and Judith Ann (Maurer) H.; m. Christine Louise Bisping, June 22, 1985; children: Tharemy James, Thaddeus Roy, Trevor Jordan. BA, Concordia Coll., St. Paul, 1985; MDiv, Concordia Sem., St. Louis, 1989. Ordained to ministry Luth. Ch., 1989. Pastor Trinity/Immanuel Luth. Chs., Holloway, Minn., 1989—; edn. rep. Appleton Circuit, Minn. No. Dist. Luth. Ch. Mo. Synod, 1989—. Home: Rte 1 Box 29 Holloway MN 56249 Office: Trinity/Immanuel Luth Chs Rte 1 Box 29 Holloway MN 56249

HOPKINS, PAUL JEFFREY, educator, author, translator; b. Providence, Sept. 30, 1940; s. Charles Edwin and Ora Ruth (Adams) H. BA, Harvard U., 1963; PhD, U. Wis., 1973. Asst. prof. U. Va., Charlottesville, 1973-77, assoc. prof., 1977-89, prof., 1989—; vis. assoc. prof. U. B.C., Vancouver, 1983-84; dir. U. Va. Ctr. for South Asian Studies, 1979-82, 85—. Author or translator of 18 books on Indo-Tibetan Buddhism; contbr. articles to profl. jours. Fulbright scholar, India and Germany, 1971-72, 82. Mem. Am. Inst. Buddhist Studies (trustee 1984—), Internat. Assn. Buddhist Studies (bd. dirs. 1986-89), Am. Acad. Religion, Tibet Soc., Tibetan Studies Inst. (pres. 1987—). Office: U Va Dept Religious Studies 104 Cocke Hall Charlottesville VA 22903

HOPKINS, THEODORE MARK, minister, guidance counselor; b. Vermontville, Mich., Jan. 2, 1926; s. Donald James and Alice (Truman) H.; m. Ruth Ann Allspaw, Oct. 10, 1954; children: Sarah, Phoebe, Martha, Rebekah. BA, Taylor U., 1954; MRE, No. Bapt. Theol. Sem., Lombard, Ill., 1957; BD, No. Bapt. Theol. Sem., 1958; MDiv (converted from BD), 1971. Ordained to ministry Bapt. Ch., 1958; cert. tchr., high sch. counselor. Pastor First Bapt. Ch., Darlington, Wis., 1958-60, Lexington, Ill., 1960-61; pastor Killdeer (N.D.) Bapt. Ch., 1961-65, First Bapt. Ch., Hardin, Mont., 1965-66, Centerville (S.D.)-Wakonda Bapt. Chs., 1966-68; interim pastor Meml. Bapt. Ch., Chambers, Nebr., 1969-70; bi/voacat. pastor First Bapt. Ch., Mercer, Mo., 1976-78, Blythedale, Mo., 1979-90; guidance counselor public schs., Lineville, Iowa, 1976—; pastor-counselor to Am. Bapt. Men Janesville Bapt. Assn., 1959-60, Am. Bapt. Men of Mont., 1965-66; chmn. Christian edn. N.D. Bapt. Conv. 1962-64, leadership edn., 1964-65; rep. N.D. Bapt. Conv. Open Theol. Conf., Greenlake, Wisc. 1964, S.D. Bapt. Conv., 1968; chmn. Fergus Falls, Minn. Child Evangelism Com., 1972-73. Sec. Centerville Ambulance Svc., 1967-68; served two terms pres. Lineville Edn. Assn.; vol. Centerville chpts. Alcoholics Anonymous; dir. of music North Grand River (Mo.) Bapt. Assn., 1986—. With USN, 1944-46, PTO, 1951-52, Korea; with USNR, 1946-51, 52-54. Republican. Avocations: music, walking, photography, reading. Home: Box 68 303 Brown St Lineville IA 50147 *I have found the greatest satisfaction and happiness in life comes through being of service to others, even when that service is not always appreciated.*

HOPPE, LESLIE JOHN, religion educator; b. Chgo., Sept. 22, 1944; s. Daniel John and Florence Martha (Kapuscinski) H. BA, St. Francis Coll., 1966; MA, Aquinas Inst., 1971; PhD, Northwestern U., 1978. Instr. St. Mary's High Sch., Burlington, Wis., 1971-73; asst. prof. Aquinas Inst., Dubuque, Iowa, 1976-79; assoc. prof. St. Mary's of the Lake Sem., Mundelein, Ill., 1979-81, Cath. Theol. Union, Chgo., 1981—; provincial councilor Assumption Province, Order Of Friars Minor, Pulaski, Wis., 1983—, provincial vicar, 1990—. Author: Joshua-Judges, 1983, What Are They Saying About Biblical Archaeology, 1984, Deuteronomy, 1985, Being Poor, 1986. Mem. Cath. Bibl. Assn. (cons. 1979-81), Soc. Bibl. Lit., Chgo. Soc. Bibl. Rsch., Am. Schs. of Oriental Rsch., Nat. Assn. of Profs. of Hebrew. Democrat. Roman Catholic. Office: Cath Theol Union 5401 S Cornell Ave Chicago IL 60615-5698

HOPPER, DAVID HENRY, religion educator; b. Cranford, N.J., July 31, 1927; s. Orion Cornelius and Julia Margaret (Weitzel) H.; m. Nancy Ann Nelson, June 10, 1967 (div. June 1984); children: Sara Elizabeth, Kathryn Ann, Rachel Suzanne. BA, Yale U., 1950; BD, ThM, Princeton Theol. Sem., 1953, ThD, 1959. Asst. prof. Macalester Coll., St. Paul, 1959-67, assoc. prof., 1967-73, James Wallace prof. of religion, 1973—. Author: Tillich: A Theological Portrait, 1967 (N.J. Authors award 1968), A Dissent on Bonhoeffer, 1975, Technology, Theology, and the Idea of Progress, 1991. With USN, 1945-46. Mem. Am. Acad. Religion, Internat. Bonhoeffer Soc., Hist. of Sci. Soc., Kierkegaard Soc. Home: 1757 Lincoln Ave Saint Paul

MN 55105 Office: Macalester Coll Dept Religious Studies 1600 Grand Ave Saint Paul MN 55105

HOPPER, GEORGE DREW, minister; b. Paterson, N.J., July 19, 1950; s. George Raymond and Alice Grace (Plavier) H.; m. Cathleen Louise Moen, May 13, 1972; children: Jacob, Candace. BS in Bible, Phila. Coll. of Bible, 1972. Youth pastor 1st Bapt. Ch., Little Falls, N.Y., 1973-75; pastor 1st Bapt. Ch., W. Edmeston, N.Y., 1975-82; exec. dir. Sacandaga Bible Conf., Broadalbin, N.Y., 1982—; pres. N.Y. State Div., Christian Camping Internat., Wheaton, Ill., 1983-86. Mem. Braodalbin Vol. Ambulance Group, 1985—, pres., 1989—. Republican. Baptist. Avocation: running. Home: Lakeview Rd Broadalbin NY 12025

HOPPER, STEPHEN RAYMOND, education and administration minister; b. St. Louis, Aug. 21, 1951; s. Raymond and Margie Fern (Keith) H.; m. Toby Rae Berger, Aug. 3, 1974; children: Stephen Jr., Christopher, David. BS in Edn., Greenville Coll., 1974; M of Religious Arts, Asbury Sem., 1977. Ordained to ministry Evang. Free Ch., 1990. Minister edn. Warm Beach Free Meth. Ch., Standwood, Wash., 1977-80, Deerflat Ch., Caldwell, Idaho, 1980-82; minister edn., adminstrn. Calvary Ch., St. Charles, Mo., 1982—. Author (curriculum): Youth Sunday School, 1978. Named Outstanding Young Men Am., 1985; recipient Pres.'s award for Excellence in Christian Edn., 1977, Eagle Scout award Boy Scouts Am., 1968. Mem. Am. Philatelic Soc., Phi Alpha Theta. Home: 3817 Lexington Saint Charles MO 63304 Office: Calvary Ch 1310 Mid River Mall Dr Saint Peters MO 63376 *I have learned that when everything has been evaluated in the light of God's Holy Word, the Bible, we see a clear picture of life. Whether we are rich or poor in material possessions, fame, or relationships, if we can face God on his terms and be found right in His eyes then we have found the secret of life, real life.*

HOPPERT, EARL W(ILLIAM), minister, educator, pastoral counselor; b. Duluth, Minn., Nov. 14, 1939; s. Glenn A. and Margaret J. (Server) H.; m. Candice N. Leuthold, Dec. 26, 1974; children—Lesley, Kelly. A.A. with honors, N.D. State Sch. Sci., 1959; B.A. magna cum laude, Yankton Coll., 1961; M.Div., Andover Newton Theol. Sch., 1965; postgrad. Trinity Coll., Glasgow U., 1965-68; D.Min. in Pastoral Care and Counseling, Christian Theol. Sem., Indpls., 1982. Ordained to ministry United Ch. Christ, 1965. Asst. pastor The Tron Ch., Balornock, Glasgow, Scotland, 1967-68; pastor 1st Congl. Ch., Eastlake, Colo., 1968-72, United Ch. Christ Westminster (Colo.), 1968-72; chaplain resident Methodist Hosp., Rochester, Minn., 1972-73; chaplain intern/resident St. Luke's Hosp., Milw., 1973-75; chaplain educator Central State Hosp., Indpls., 1975—, head dept. pastoral care, 1975—, founder, chmn. patient advocacy com., 1979-84, chmn. specially constituted com., 1991—; clin. pastoral edn. supr., mem. faculty Christian Theol. Sem., Indpls., 1976—, counselor Pastoral Counseling Services, 1980—; family therapist Ctr. for Rational Living, 1990—. Leader Kick the Habit Clinics, Wis. Lung Assn., 1974-75. Turner fellow, 1965; Ind. Dept. Mental Health grantee, 1976-82; recipient numerous scholarships; recipient Dist. Service award DeMolay. Mem. Assn. Clin. Pastoral Edn. (cert. chaplain supr.; life mem.), Am. Assn. Marriage and Family Therapy (clin.), Am. Assn. Pastoral Counselors (cert., mem. profl. concerns com. 1987-89, fin. com. 1990-91, theol. and social concerns com. 1991—), Assn. for Humanistic Psychology, Council Health and Human Services Ministries (assoc.), Internat. Preview Soc. Lodge: Masons. Contbr. to profl. publs. Office: Cen State Hosp 3000 W Washington St Indianapolis IN 46222 *As Plutarch noted, "A mind is not a vessel to be filled, but a fire to be lighted." In education we bring a spark of flame to fire the imagination of our students, who then blaze their own trails into the future. This same principle applies in therapy, where we do not solve the problems of others but assist them in eductive ways to find new pathways through life's maze.*

HORAN, CLARK J., III (EARL OF DUNSMERE, BARON HORAN OF ANTWERP), priest, corporate executive; b. Syracuse, N.Y., Feb. 3, 1950; s. Clark James Horan Jr. and Joan Roumage (Kelsey) Bergin. BA, U. Waterloo, Ont., Can., 1972, LLD (hon.), 1982; STB, BTh, St. Peter's Sem., London, Ont., Can., 1975; MDiv, U. Western Ont., London, 1975. Ordained priest Roman Cath. Ch., 1976. Priest Diocese of Honolulu; chief exec. officer Abercrombie & Waterhouse, Del., Can. Air Travellers; v.p. The Checkley Found., Can.; chmn. bd. dirs. Horan, Macmillan, Bache & Chapman, Ottawa, Ont., Can.; cons. Wardair Internat., Calgary, Alta., Can., 1978-82; bd. dirs. Horan-in-Trust, N.Y.C. Decorated Order of Can., officer Order Brit. Empire, Knight Bachelor (Eng.), Knight and Knight Comdr. of Holy Sepulchre; ascendency 5th Earl of Dunsmere and Baron Horan of Antwerp, 1988. Fellow Royal Commonwealth Soc., Can. Commonwealth Council (chancellor, editor Can. Commonwealth newsletter 1978-84), Monarchist League Can. (editor Monarchy Today mag. 1979-81), Circumnavigators Club. Clubs: Plaza, Honolulu; Ottawa Hunt and Golf, Albany (Toronto, Can.), Empire, Confederation. Lodges: Elks, KC. Address: PO Box 3939 Syracuse NY 13220-3939 also: PO Box 38016 Honolulu HI 96837-1016

HOREVAY, DUANE JOSEPH, minister; b. Cumberland, Md., Dec. 13, 1955; s. Joseph and Helen Virginia (Marple) H.; m. Lisa Lynn Lockard, July 3, 1976; children: Aaron, Jared, Joshua, Anna. AA, Alleghany Community Coll., Cumberland, Md., 1976; BA, Bapt. Christian Coll., Shreveport, La., 1989. Ordained to ministry Christian Cathering Ch., 1984. Dir. Living Light Youth Ministries, Cumberland, Md., 1972-76; pastor Christian Gathering, Cumberland, Md., 1978—; pres. Tri-State for Jesus, Cumberland, 1989-90; trustee Christian Gathering, 1984—; pres. Penn Ave. Christian Sch., Cumberland, 1985-91. Contbr. articles to profl. jours. Troop sponsor Boy Scouts Am., Cumberland, 1989-91. Mem. Cumberland Ministerial Assn. (v.p. 1990-91, bd. dirs. 1988-90). Republican. Home: 921 Bedford St Cumberland MD 21502 Office: Christian Gatherine 130 Pennsylvania Ave Cumberland MD 21502

HORINE, PAUL ARLINGTON, minister; b. Ridgon, Ind., Mar. 1, 1921; s. Cornelius Frank and Wrennie Olive (Downs) H.; m. Helen Ilene Horine, Feb. 14, 1941 (div. 1970); children: Larry, Marvin, Dennis; m. Dorotha Jene Jacoby, Oct. 7, 1971. Grad., Garret Bibl. Coll., Evanston, Ill., 1953. Ordained to ministry United Meth. Ch., 1951. Minister Dunkirk (Ind.) Community Ch., 1950-54, Cowan (Ind.) Meth. Ch., 1954-57, Cammack (Ind.) Meth. Ch., 1954-63, Roann (Ind.) Meth. Ch., 1963-70, Pennville (Ind.) Meth. Ch., 1970-72, Atwood (Ind.) United Meth. Ch., 1978-82, Somerset (Ind.) United Meth. Ch., 1982-86, Ch. of Saviour, Wabash, Ind., 1986—. Mem. Order Eastern Star, Masons. Republican. Office: Church of Our Saviour RR 2 Wabash IN 46992-9802

HORLANDER, WALTER FRANKLIN, religious organization administrator; b. Jeffersonville, Ind., Feb. 11, 1932; s. Herman Graham and Grace (Reichle) H.; m. Joann Scott, Aug. 1, 1954; children: Nancy, Shelly, Scott. AB, Heidelberg Coll., Tiffin, Ohio, 1954; BD, Eden Theol. Sem., Webster Groves, Mo., 1957; MS, Ind. U., 1979. Pastor St. Peter United Ch. of Christ, Dubois, Ind., 1957-59, Bethany United Ch. of Christ, Louisville, 1960-64, Evang. United Ch. of Christ, Portsmouth, Ohio, 1964-66; assoc. exec. dir. Ind. Coun. of Chs., Indpls., 1966-83; exec. dir. Fla. Coun. of Chs., Orlando, 1983—; v.p. Nat. Coun. on Religion and Pub. Edn., Lawrence, Kans., 1981-83; mem. adv. bd. Sta. WMFE-TV, Orlando, 1983-90; accredited visitor 7th World Assembly, Canberra, Australia, 1991. Home: 2459 Sunderland Rd Maitland FL 32751 Office: Fla Coun of Chs 924 N Magnolia Ave Ste 236 Orlando FL 32803

HORN, CHRIS WAYNE, minister; b. Grundy, Va., Apr. 15, 1965; s. Amos and Marie (Trent) H. Student, Ky. Christian Coll. Ordained minister in Ch. of Christ. Minister Northside Ch. of Christ, Mavisdale, Va., 1985-87; youth minister Kelsa Ch. of Christ, Mavisdale, 1988-89. Home: Box 39 Mavisdale VA 24627

HORN, FRIEDEMANN HANS CHRISTIAN, minister; b. Oppeln/Upper Silesia, Poland, Apr. 30, 1921; came to Switzerland, 1950, naturalized, 1972; s. Johannes Rudolf and Gertrud (Muller) H.; ed. U. Jena; Dr. Religious Sci., U. Marburg, 1952; m. Hella Merseburger, Dec. 29, 1948; children—Christiane, Beate, Johannes. Ordained to ministry Swedenborgian Ch., 1952; asst. minister Swedenborgian Ch., Zurich, 1952-56, minister, 1956-77, gen. pastor European field, 1977—, pres. Theol. Sem., Newton, Mass., 1977-79. Served with German Air Force, 1940-45. Mem. Swedenborg Gesellschaft, German Swedenborg Gesellschaft, Swedenborg Found., Swedenborg Soc. London, Schweizer Akademie fur Grundlagenstudien. Author: Schelling und Swedenborg, 1954; Der innere Sinn des Alten Testaments, 1972; Der innere Sinn der Bergpredigt, 1965; Wie dachte Jesus uber Tod und Auferstehung, 1970; Reinkarnation-Ja oder Nein, 1988; editor: Offene Tore, Beitrage zu linem neuen christl Zeitalter, 1957—, Neukirchenblatt, 1963—; translator from Latin and English. Home: 2 Apollostr, CH 8032 Zurich Switzerland

HORN, GILBERT, minister. Exec. dir. Colo. coun. of Chs., Denver. Office: Colo Coun Ch 1370 Pennsylvania Ste 100 Denver CO 80203*

HORN, JAMES CHARLES, minister; b. Abington, Pa., July 26, 1950; s. Charles Haubert and Patricia (Allen) H.; m. Ann Ellen Glabau, May 5, 1973; children: Emilie, Crystal, David, Justin, Jacob. BS, Muskingum Coll., 1972; MDiv, Princeton Theol. Sem., 1977; postgrad., Columbia Theol. Sem., Decatur, Ga., 1991—. Ordained to ministry Presbyn. Ch. (USA), 1977; cert. cons. evangelism. Pastor 1st & Westminster Presbyn. Chs., Manchester, N.H., 1977-82; Meml. Presbyn. Ch., Dayton, Ohio, 1982-87, Penn Wynne Presbyn. Ch., Wynnewood, Pa., 1987—; founder, chmn. bd. Advanced Sem. Studies of Evangelism in Reformed Tradition, Phila., 1988—; chair rev. and audit coms. Presbytery Phila., 1988—. Bd. dirs. Urban Gardening Project, Dayton, 1983-86, Wynnewood Valley Civic Assn. Grantee Neighbor to Neighbor, 1984, Outreach Found. Presbyn. Ch., 1988, Pittcairn Crabbe Found., 1988. Republican. Home: 1514 Powder Mill Ln Wynnewood PA 19096 Office: Penn Wynne Presbyn Ch Haverford & Manoa Rds Wynnewood PA 19096

HORN, JERRY EUGENE, priest; b. Roseburg, Oreg., Dec. 5, 1938; s. Jerry E. and Catherine E. (Matthews) H.; m. Diane L. Bailey, Aug. 23, 1974; children: Zara S., Rebeka D. BS in Organic Chemistry, Portland State U., 1966; student, Ch. Divinity Sch. of Pacific, Berkeley, Calif., 1969-72, Grad. Theol. Union, Berkeley, Calif., 1969-72. Ordained to ministry Episcopal Ch. as deacon, 1972, as priest, 1981. Asst. St. Paul's Episcopal Ch., Sacramento, 1976-79, St. George's Episcopal Ch., Roseburg, 1979-82; vicar St. Mathias' Episcopal Ch., Cave Junction, Oreg., 1982-85; rector Ch. of the Holy Spirit/Diocesan Renewal and Tng. Ctr., Albany, Oreg., 1985—; interim pres. and sec. Episcopal World Mission, Inc., Forest City, N.C., 1985—. With U.S. Army, 1961-63, Fed. Republic Germany. Recipient rsch. grant NIMH, Berkeley, 1973-74. Mem. Order of St. Luke, Episcopal Renewal Ministries. Republican. Home: PO Box 743 Albany OR 97321 Office: Church of the Holy Spirit PO Box 743 Albany OR 97321 *When all is said and done, nothing else matters but the truth that Jesus is Lord.*

HORN, SISTER JOANNE GABRIELLE, nun; b. Sheboygan, Wis., May 9, 1929; d. Oscar Emil and Verona Barbara (Pfister) H. BA, Mt. Mary Coll., 1960; MEd, Marquette U., 1968. Joined Sch. Sisters of Notre Dame, Roman Catholic Ch., 1948. Tchr. various schs., Ind., Wis., 1946-79; prin. various schs., Tex., Wis., 1970-74; receptionist, switchboard provincial Motherhouse, Sch. Sisters of Notre Dame, Milw., 1990—. Home: Convent Hill 1325 N Jefferson St #403 Milwaukee WI 53202-2631 Office: Sch Sisters Notre Dame 1233 N Marshall St Milwaukee WI 53202

HORN, PAUL ERVIN, minister; b. Grinnell, Iowa, Mar. 24, 1919; s. Harry Edgar and Florence Henrietta (Bump) H.; m. Elvis Devlin, Dec. 21, 1940; children: Sandra, Larry, Cynthia. BA, San Jose State U., 1942; MDiv, Berkeley Bapt. Div. Sch., 1945; PhD, Calif. Grad. Sch. Theology, 1973. Ordained to ministry Conservative Bapt. Assn. Am., 1945. Pastor Elmhurst Bapt. Ch., Oakland, Calif., 1945-55, Bell Bapt. Ch., Cudahy, Calif., 1955-66, 1st Bapt. Ch., Montclair, Calif., 1966-77, Calvary Bapt. Ch., Hemet, Calif., 1977-83, 1st Bapt. Ch., Wrightwood, Calif., 1984-90; bd. dirs. Conservative Bapt. Assn. So. Calif., Anaheim, 1956-88, pres., 1959-60, min. at large, 1990—; bd. dirs. Conservative Bapt. Home Mission Soc., Wheaton, Ill., 1960-66; parliamentarian Conservative Bapt. Assn. Am., Wheaton, 1950-85, v.p. western chpt., 1967-74. Mem. Conservative Bapt. Fgn. Mission Soc. (sec. 1988—). Republican. Avocation: photography. Address: PO Box 162 Wrightwood CA 92397

HORNE, ALVIN MATTHEW, clergyman; b. Gainesville, Fla., June 12, 1947; s. Calvin Matthew and Annie Lee (Eason) H.; m. Catherine Susan Oakley, May 2, 1970; children: Matt, B.J., Josh. BS, N.C. Wesleyan Coll., Rocky Mount, 1969; MA in Edn., East Carolina U., Greenville, 1973; MDiv, Duke U., 1982. Ordained to ministry Meth. Ch., 1983. Admissions counselor N.C. Wesleyan Coll., 1969-71, dir. fin. aid and placement, 1971-74, dean of students, 1974-78; pastor Rock Creek United Meth. Ch., Snow Camp, N.C., 1978-82, Friendship United Meth. Ch., Burlington, N.C., 1982—; mem. Equitable Salary Commn., N.C. Ann. Conf., United Meth. Ch., 1986—; mem. Burlington Dist. Bd. Ordained Ministry, 1986—. Trustee N.C. Wesleyan Coll., 1986—. Named Coach of Yr., Dixie Intercollegiate Athletic Conf., 1974, 77. Mem. N.C. Wesleyan Coll. Alumni Assn. (pres. 1987—). Republican. Lodge: Civitan. Avocation: fishing. Home: Route 6 Box 119 Burlington NC 27215 Office: Friendship United Meth Ch Route 6 Box 379-D Burlington NC 27215

HORNE, DENNIS LAFON, minister; b. Erwin, N.C., May 22, 1954; s. Junius LaFon and Delano Elaine (Stewart) H.; m. Kerry Jeanne Snyder, Aug. 21, 1976; children: Joel Matthew, Jonathan Andrew. BA, Bob Jones U., 1976, MA, 1980. Ordained to ministry Bapt. Ch., 1977. Youth pastor Marquette Manor Bapt. Ch., Downers Grove, Ill., 1976-77, Granite Bapt. Ch., Glen Burnie, Md., 1980-84, Grace Bapt. Ch., Decatur, Ala., 1984-85, Tabernacle Bapt. Ch., Virginia Beach, Va., 1985-87; pastor Mountain Home (N.C.) Ind. Bapt. Ch., 1987—; counselor The Wilds Camp and Conf. Ctr., Rosman, N.C., 1975, 76; asst. dir. Md. Ind. Bapt. Camp, Glen Burnie, 1982, 83; mem. The Rugherford Inst., Charlottesville, Va., 1991. Coach, Henderson County Cap League, Hendersonville, N.C., 1988-90; state rep. Rep. party, dist. 2, Va., 1982. Recipient Spark Plug award The Wilds Camp and Conf. Ctr., Rosman, N.C., 1976. Mem. Smithsonian Assoc., Bob Jones U. Alumni Assn. Home: 14 Hunters Ridge Rd Horse Shoe NC 28742

HORNE, MILTON PARNELL, religion educator; b. Antlers, Okla., Mar. 19, 1956; s. Cleveland Reid and Virginia (Gnann) H.; m. Karen Elizabeth Rogers, May 31, 1975; children: Robert, Jared. BA, U. Mo., 1979; MDiv, Midwestern Bapt. Sem., 1983; D.Phil., Oxford U., 1990. Ordained to ministry Bapt. Ch., 1977. Pastor Harrisburg (Mo.) Bapt. Ch., 1975-81, McFall (Mo.) Bapt. Ch., 1981-83; asst. prof. William Jewell Coll., Liberty, Mo., 1986—. Recipient Keatley award-archaeology, Keatley Found., 1983; Francis Found. Mentor grantee, 1989. Mem. Soc. Bibl. Lit. Office: William Jewell Coll College Hill Liberty MO 64068

HORNER, EVAN WAYNE, minister; b. Burwell, Nebr., Dec. 27, 1950; s. Loren Charles and Julia Rose (Smith) H.; m. Linda Kathleen Jensen, June 14, 1975; children: Dane Martin, Kelsey Lauren. BA, Puget Sound Christian Coll., 1973; MDiv, Lincoln Christian Sem., 1984; postgrad., Inst. Holy Land Studies, Jerusalem, 1974. Ordained to ministry Christian Ch. Minister Grandview (Wash.) Christian Ch., 1975-78, Witt (Ill.) Christian Ch., 1979-85; minister of pastoral care and counseling Dodge City (Kans.) Christian Ch., 1985—, singles minister, 1985—; adj. chaplain Meml. Med. Ctr., Springfield, Ill., 1982-84; vol. chaplain Meml. Hosp., Prosser, Wash., 1977-78, Humana Hosp., Dodge City, 1986—. Eastern Star scholar, 1972, 78-82. Mem. Am. Assn. Pastoral Counselors. Avocations: photography, jogging. Home: 1706 6th Ave Dodge City KS 67801 Office: 1st Christian Ch 711 5th Ave Dodge City KS 67801

HORNER, JERRY WADE, religion educator; b. Miston, Tenn., Apr. 30, 1936; s. Tommie Boyd and Bessie Delana (Bartlett) H.; m. Annie Nelle Moore, May 25, 1956; children: Tamara, Bart, Thad. BA, Union U., Jackson, Tenn., 1957; BD, Southwestern Bapt. Theol. Sem., Ft. Worth, 1960; ThD, Southwestern Bapt. Theol. Sem., 1964, MDiv, 1966. Ordained to ministry Bapt. Ch., 1954. Pastor Emmanuel Bapt. Ch., Finley, Tenn., 1954-56, Middleburg Bapt. Ch., Bolivar, Tenn., 1956-57, First Bapt. Ch., Woodson, Tex., 1958-62; prof., chmn. theology Southwest Bapt. U., Bolivar, Mo., 1962-73, Oral Roberts U., Tulsa, 1973-82; dean Regent U. Coll. Theology, Virginia Beach, Va., 1982—; advisor Tulsa area Women's Aglow, 1979-82, Chaplaincy Full Gospel Chs., Dallas, 1983—; regent Bahamas Faith Ministries Internat., Nassau, The Bahamas, 1984—; exec. dir. New Creation, Inc., Virginia Beach, 1985—; bd. dirs. African Christian Mission, Accra, Ghana, 1988—; mem. Christian Sch. Bd., Virgina Beach, 1988, 89. Author: (books) An Outline of New Testament Survey, 1967, Seven Portraits of Christ, 1971, Living in the Family: Fellowship in the New Testament, 1982, Daughter of Destiny, 1988; contbr. articles to various publs., 1965—. area capt. Am. Heart Assn., Virginia Beach, 1990—. Mem. Evang. Theol. Soc., Soc. Pentecostal Studies. Republican. Home: 1400 Chartfield Ct Virginia Beach VA 23456 Office: Regent U Centerville Turnpike Virginia Beach VA 23464

HORNER, NADINE DAWN, lay worker; b. Monett, Mo., Oct. 6, 1940; d. Wilbur Deleo and Oma Loraine (Morlan) Dawn; m. James Ted Horner, Dec. 9, 1960; children: James Robert, Wilma Deanne, John Lee. BS in Edn., So. Mo. State U., 1961; MS in Edn., Mo. U., 1968. Cert. elem. educator, prin., counselor, spl. edn. dir., sch. psychol. examiner. Elem. prin. Forsyth (Mo.) Elem. Sch., 1969—; jr. youth camp dir. White River Assn. Gen. Bapts., Taneysville, Mo., 1973—; children's missions coord., Gen. Bapts., 1987-91; children's ch. dir. New Vision Gen. Bapt. Ch., Taneyville, 1980—. Named Outstanding Prin. Sub-Dist. D Princs., 1988, 2d Runner-Up to Mo. Nat. Disting. Prin., 1988. Mem. NAESP, Mo. Assn. Elem. Sch. Prin., S.W. Dist. Elem. Sch. Prin. (v.p.), Mo. State Tchrs. Assn., Sub-Dist. D Princ. (sec., pres.), Alpha Psi Delta Kappa Gamma (treas. 1980-83), Forsyth Tchrs. Assn., White River Assn. Gen. Bapt. (treas. 1977-91). Home: Rte 3 Box 90 Taneyville MO 64759

HORNER, NORMAN ASTE, minister; b. Denver, Sept. 6, 1913; s. John Willard and Lillian Rose (Aste) H.; m. Esther May Daniels, Dec. 16, 1940. BA, Coll. Emporia, 1935; BD, Louisville Presbyn. Theol. Sem., 1938; MA, Kennedy Sch. Missions, Hartford, Conn., 1950; PhD, Hartford Sem. Found., 1956. Ordained to ministry, 1938. Missionary, tchr. Cameroun, 1938-49; dean, prof. mission and ecumenics Louisville Presbyn. Theol. Sem., 1949-68; cons. ecumenical relationships in Mid. East United Presbyn. Ch. in U.S.A., Beirut, 1968-76; prof. Near East Sch. Theology, Beirut, 1974-76; assoc. dir. Overseas Ministries Study Ctr., Ventnor, N.J., 1976-82. Author: Cross and Crucifix in Mission, 1965, Protestant Crosscurrents in Mission, 1968, Rediscovering Christianity Where It Began, 1974, A Guide to Christian Churches in the Middle East, 1989. Mem. Am. Soc. Missiology, Internat. Assn. Mission Studies, Assn. Profs. Missions. Home: 2520 Glenmary Ave Louisville KY 40204

HORNIBROOK, (WILLIAM) WALLACE, music ministries director; b. Goldendale, Wash., Apr. 22, 1925; s. William Franklin and Elizabeth Caywood (McMahon) H.; m. Donna Mae Carlson, Dec. 10, 1952; child: Lisa Klare H. Marte. MusB, Ariz. St. U., 1965; DM Conducting, Ind. U., 1973. Choir dir. Westside Episc., Seattle, Wash., 1947-48; organist/dir. Shawnee Presbyn., Shawnee, Pa., 1953-55; organist/min. music E. Stroudsburg Meth., E. Stroudsburg, Pa., 1955-59; min. music Crossroads Meth., Phoenix, Ariz., 1959-66; dir. music ministries St. Marks United Meth., Bloomington, Ind., 1967--; prof. music Ind. U., Bloomington, 1966--. Composer/arranger, Shawnee Press, 1955--. Pianist Bible Study Fellowship, 1975--; mem. Pi Kappa Lambda. Republican. United Methodist. Home: 1005 Nota Dr Bloomington IN 47401 Office: Indiana U Sch of Music Bloomington IN 47405

HORNYAK, EUGENE AUGUSTINE, bishop; b. Kucura, Backa, Yugoslavia, Oct. 7, 1919; emigrated to U.S., 1948, naturalized, 1955, emigrated to Eng., 1961; s. Peter and Juliana (Findrik) H. Ph.B., Pontifical U., Rome, 1941, S.T.D., 1947; J.C.B., Gregorian U., Rome, 1947. Ordained priest Roman Catholic Ch. (Byzantine rite), 1945; asst. priest Struthers and Warren, Ohio, 1948-49; adminstr. St. Michael's Ch., Newton Falls, Ohio, 1949-50; prof. moral theology, canon law, liturgy, also spiritual dir. Sts. Cyril and Methodius Byzantine Seminary, Pitts., 1950-55; spiritual dir. St. Basil's Ukrainian Minor Seminary, Stamford, Conn., 1958-61; entered Order St. Basil the Great, Can., 1956-57; master novices, also superior St. Josaphat's Monastery, Glen Cove, L.I., 1961; apptd. titular bishop Hermonthis; also aux. to Cardinal Godfrey (for Ukrainian Catholics in Eng. and Wales), London, 1961-63; bishop-apostolic exarch for Ukrainian Catholics in Eng. and Wales, 1963-87, for Ukrainians in Scotland, 1968-87. Mem. Pontifical Commn. of Eastern Code of Canon Law, Rome, 1977-90; consultor Sacred Congregation for Eastern Cath. Chs., Rome, 1978—. Home and Office: St Olga's House, 14 Newburgh Rd, Acton, London W3 6DQ, England *Our earthly life comes, grows and fades away; it has God's support, it has its aims and its destiny. As a Christian, a monk and a Catholic bishop, I am endeavouring to attain those aims, reach that destiny, and be instrumental in helping and guiding my fellowmen to do likewise, according to the teachings and example of Christ, God incarnate, as faithfully transmitted to us by his Church.*

HOROWITZ, DAVID MORRIS, rabbi; b. N.Y.C., Aug. 18, 1942; s. Russell and Grace (Williams) H.; m. Theodora Ellen Kessler, Dec. 22, 1963; children: Wendy Ilene, Daniel Jonathan. BA, Tulane U., 1964; B in Hebrew Letters, Hebrew Union Coll., 1966, MA in Hebrew Letters, 1969, rabbi, 1969. Ordained rabbi, 1969. Assoc. rabbi Indpls. Hebrew Congregation, 1969-72; rabbi Temple-Beth-El, Hammond, Ind., 1972-83, Temple Israel, Akron, Ohio, 1983—; adj. prof. Calumet Coll., East Chicago, Ind., 1978-84; instr. U. Akron, 1984-85; lectr. Kent (Ohio) State U., 1986-88; chmn. Rabbinic adv. bd. Olin Sang Ruby Camp, Oconomowoc, Wis., 1978-82. Contbr. articles to profl. jours. Pres. regional bd. Anti-Defamation League, Indpls., 1974-78; bd. dirs. Planned Parenthood, Gary, Ind., Akron, 1976-88; instr. rev. bd. Children's Hosp. Med. Ctr., Akron, 1985—, ethics com., 1987—; Rabbinic advisor N.E. Lakes Fedn. Temple Youth, Cleve., 1985—; bd. dirs. ARC, Akron, 1985—; pres. Akron Area Interfaith Coun., 1988—. Recipient Century Club Mem. award Jewish Chautauqua Soc., 1989, Outstanding Svc. award City Hammond, Ind., 1983, Shofar award State Israel Bonds, 1974, Community Rels. Achievement award Jewish Fedn., 1983. Mem. Assn. Reform Zionists, Cen. Conf. Am. Rabbis, Cleve. Bd. Rabbis, Great Lakes Ohio Valley Assn. Reform Rabbis (v.p. 1986-87), Akron Jewish Community Fedn. (bd. dirs.), B'nai B'irth. Democrat. Avocation: collecting yo-yo's. Home: 1267 Lisa Ann Dr Akron OH 44313 Office: Temple Israel 133 Merriman Rd Akron OH 44303

HORRIGAN, ALFRED FREDERIC, clergyman; b. Wilmington, Del., Dec. 9, 1914; s. William James and Anna (Kienle) H. Student, St. Joseph Coll., Collegeville, Ind., 1928-34; B.A., St. Meinrad (Ind.) Sem., 1940; M.A., Cath. U. Am., 1942, Ph.D., 1944; LL.D., Belmont Abbey Coll., 1961, St. Joseph's Coll., 1966, U. San Diego, 1971, Bellarmine Coll., 1975, Centre Coll., 1976. Ordained priest Roman Catholic Ch., 1940; asst. pastor Louisville, 1940-41, 44-49; head dept. philosophy Nazareth Coll., Louisville; also part-time prof. philosophy Ursuline Coll., U. Louisville, 1944-49; editor The Record (newspaper), 1946-49; first pres. Bellarmine Coll., Louisville, 1949-72; chmn. bd. Bellarmine Coll., 1972-73; exec. asst. to Archbishop of, Louisville, 1973; exec. dir. Commn. on Peace and Justice, Archdiocese Louisville, 1974-75; pastor St. James Ch., Louisville, 1976-84, sr. assoc. pastor, 1984—. Author: Metaphysics as a Principle of Order in the University Curriculum, 1944; Editor: Roots of a Catholic College, 1955. Chmn. Louisville-Jefferson County Commn. on Human Relations, 1965-68. Named founding pres. emeritus Bellarmine Coll., 1989. Mem. English Speaking Union. Club: Filson. Home: 1826 Edenside Ave Louisville KY 40204

HORSCH, JAMES EVERETT, editor; b. McClean County, Ill., Nov. 1, 1939; s. Henry L. and Esther (Litwiller) H.; m. Ruth Amelia Emerson, July 11, 1958; children: James Anthony, Janet Renee, Jon Emerson. AA, Hesston Coll., 1960; BA, Goshen Coll., 1962; BD, Goshen Bibl. Sem., 1966; MEd, U. Pitts., 1974. Ordained to ministry Mennonite Ch., 1966. Interim pastor Albany (Oreg.) and Logsden (Oreg.) Mennonite Ch., 1963-64; summer pastoral intern Blooming Glen (Pa.) Mennonite Ch., 1965; asst. pastor Hesston (Kans.) Mennonite Ch., 1966-68; editor Mennonite Pub. House, Scottdale, Pa., 1968-82, 84—; former bd. dirs. Laurelviile Mennonite Ch. Ctr., Mt. Pleasant, Pa.; exec. dir. Laurelville Mennonite Ch. Ctr., Mt. Pleasant, Pa., 1982-84; chmn. bd. Pa. Mennonite Credit Union, Scottdale. Congl. chair, elder Menonite Ch. Scottdale, 1974—; bd. dirs. Southmoreland Civic Assn., Scottdale, 1976-78. Mem. Assn. Statisticians of Am. Religious Bodies (v.p. 1984-88, pres. 1988-90), Laurelville Mennonite Ch. Ctr. Assn. (v.p. 1980-82). Democrat. Home: Rte 1 Box 634 Scottdale PA 15683 Office: Mennonite Pub House 616 Walnut Ave Scottdale PA 15683

HORSEMAN, BARBARA ANN, church musician, educator; b. Clinton, Iowa, Nov. 29, 1935; d. Ted Rex and Lillian Mae (Bean) Smith; m. William F. Horseman, Dec. 26, 1963; children: Megan, Jill. Diploma, Cottey Jr. Coll. for Women, Nevada, Mo., 1955; MusB, U. Mo., Kansas City, 1957, MusM, 1958, postgrad., 1958-61. Dir. chancel choir Zion United Ch. of Christ, Kansas City, Kans., 1957—, dir., founder 4 handbell choirs, 1989—, founding mem., officer 3-C Circle, 1981-83, mem., past pres. adult fellowship, 1963—, co-sponsor youth group, 1981-83, dir. jr. and sr. high sch. choirs, 1979-80, supt. Sunday sch., 1986-88; pvt. tchr. voice and piano, Kansas City, 1963—; pre-school tchr., Kansas City, 1991—. Pres. Philharm. Aux., Kansas City, 1975-76; pres. Creative Experiences, Kansas City, 1983; pres. PTA, 1970-72, bd. dirs., 1976-81, now life mem. Mem. Am. Guild English Handbell Ringers, Choristers Guild, Cottey Coll. Alumnae Assn. (bd. dirs. 1963-75, nat. pres. 1973-74), Mozart Music Club, P.E.O. (pres. Kansas City 1975-77), Mu Sigma Epsilon, Delta Psi Omega, Sigma Alpha Iota. Home: 3233 N 85th Pl Kansas City KS 66109 Office: Zion United Ch of Christ 2711 N 72d St Kansas City KS 66101

HORTON, DAVID ALAN, evangelist; b. Thomasville, Ga., Feb. 8, 1957; s. Willis Moorman and Vivian Jerolene (Norris) H.; m. Cherie Dawn Bonnema, Apr. 10, 1982; children: Christopher, Nicholas. Diploma, Rhema Bible Tng. Ctr., Broken Arrow, Okla., 1982. Pianist, organist Klaudt Indian Family, Atlanta, 1975-76; healing instr. Kenneth Hagin Ministries, Tulsa, 1977-84; pres. David Horton Ministries, Tulsa, 1984—; v.p. Have a Heart Crusades/Rosey Grier Ministries, L.A., 1986—. Editor, Miracle Harvest mag., 1987—. Minority affairs asst. Jimmy Carter for Pres. campaign, 1976. Mem. Rhema Ministerial Assn. Internat. Republican. Avocations: antique collecting, sailing, swimming. Office: David Horton Ministries Inc 1331 E 58th St Tulsa OK 74146

HORTON, JERRY SMITH, minister; b. Columbus, Miss., Oct. 6, 1941; s. William Robert and Sarah Elizabeth (Smith) H.; m. Patricia Jan Taylor, May 30, 1964; children: Thomas Christian, William Andrew. AA, Wood Jr. Coll., 1963; BA in Edn., U. Miss., 1968; MDiv, Emory U., 1972. Ordained to ministry United Meth. Ch., 1973. Min. various chs. in Miss. and Ga., 1962-72; assoc. min. Southaven (Miss.) 1st United Meth. Ch., 1972-74; min. Minor Meml. United Meth. Ch., Walls, Miss., 1974-81; parish dir. Iuka (Miss.) 1st United Meth. Ch., 1981-84; min. Belzoni (Miss.) 1st United Meth. Ch., 1984-91, Fulton (Miss.) 1st United Meth. Ch., 1991—; mem. bd. diaconal ministries No. Miss. Conf., United Meth. Ch., 1972-74, mem. commn. on equitable salaries, 1981-90, conf. ins. com., 1990—; head chaplain vol. chaplaincy program in local hosp. Mem. Vol. Chaplaincy Program in local hosp., North Miss. chpt. Emmaus Walk Community in Miss. Named one of Outstanding Young Men of Am., Internat. Jaycees, 1976, Top Evangelistic Pastor of Conf., 1981; honored with Spl. Proclamation, Mayor of Iuka; Estaral scholar. Mem. Rotary. Avocations: hunting, scuba diving, fishing, youth work, writing devotions. Home: 414 E Sheffield Dr Fulton MS 38843 Office: 1st United Meth Ch PO Box 279 Fulton MS 38843 *The real test of a truly great minister is not that his members will think about him, but that will be lead to remember what he said and will think more about Jesus.*

HORTON, O. CHARLES, pastor; b. Palatka, Fla., Nov. 18, 1937; s. Alva E. and Estelle (Minton) H.; m. Carolyn DeLoach, Sept. 6, 1957; children: Holli Suzanne, Vincent Charles. BA, Stetson U., 1959; MDiv, Southwestern Bapt. Theol. Sem., 1962; MTh, New Orleans Bapt. Theol. Sem., 1967, D of Ministry, 1975. Ordained to ministry So. Bapt., 1956. Student pastor First Bapt. Ch., Oakland, Fla., 1956-59, Enterprise Bapt. Ch., Whitewright, Tex., 1960-62, Maurepas Bapt. Ch., Baton Rouge, 1963-64; pastor First Bapt. Ch., Lake Alfred, Fla., 1964-66, Flagami Bapt. Ch., Miami, Fla., 1966-77, Coll. Park Bapt. Ch., Orlando, Fla., 1977—; tchr. Mid-City Jr. High Sch., New Orleans, 1962-63; adj. tchr. Stetson U. Extension Div., 1963-80; mem. budget allocations com. State Bd. Missions, Fla. Bapt. Conv., 1969-72, vice chmn. nomination com., 1970-71, chmn. constn. and by-laws com. Miami Bapt. Assn., 1970-72, chmn. fin. com. 1972-74, moderator, 1975-76; program chmn. Miami Pastors Conf., 1973-74; mem. fin. com. Greater Orlando Bapt. Assn., 1978-80, personnel com., 1984-85. Author: (with others) What Christ Means to Me, 1988; contbr. articles to religious publs. Pres. Polk County Mental Health Assn. 1963-65; mem. campus ministry proposal com. Fla. Internat. U., Miami, 1968-70; mem. civic righteousness com., 1969-71, chmn. Bapt. campus ministry com., 1970-74; trustee Bapt. Hosp., Miami, 1975-77, Southeastern Bapt. Theol. Sem., Wake Forest, N.C., 1975—, vice chmn. bd. 1984-85, chmn. bd. dirs. 1985—. Named Min. of Yr. Stetson U., 1988. Mem. Kiwanis. Democrat. Avocations: golf, hunting, fishing, jogging. Home: 3913 Lake Sarah Dr Orlando FL 32804 Office: College Park Bapt Ch 1914 Edgewater Dr Orlando FL 32804

HORTON, PATRICIA SANDRA, priest; b. Asheville, N.C., Oct. 3, 1947; d. Charles Dwight and Edith (Greer) H. BS in Edn., Western Carolina U., 1969; MEd, U. Ga., 1973; MDiv, U. of the South, 1986. Ordained to ministry Episcopal Ch. as priest, 1987. Asst. to rector St. David's Ch., Roswell, Ga., 1986-90; rector St. Francis Episcopal Ch., Macon, Ga., 1990—; mem. commn. on ministry Diocese of Atlanta, 1987-90, mem. liturgy and music com., 1986-90, mem. consultation commn., 1989—, gen. conv. dep., 1991, Macon (Ga.) convocation dean, 1990—. Mem. Nat. Episcopal Clergy Assn. Democrat. Office: St Francis Episcopal Ch 432 Forest Hill Rd Macon GA 31210-4824

HORTON, STANLEY MONROE, educator; b. Huntington Park, Calif., May 6, 1916; s. Harry Samuel and Myrle May (Fisher) H.; m. Evelyn Gertrude Parsons, Sept. 11, 1945; children: Stanley Jr., Edward, Faith. BS, U. Calif., Berkeley, 1937; MDiv, Gordon Div. Sch., 1944; MST, Harvard U., 1945; ThD, Cen. Bapt. Sem., 1959. Ordained to ministry Assemblies of God, 1946. Instr. Met. Bible Inst., North Bergen, Mo., 1945-48; prof. Cen. Bible Coll., Springfield, Mo., 1948-78; disting. prof. Assemblies of God Theol. Sem., Springfield, 1978—. Author: What the Bible Says About the Holy Spirit, 1976, Acts Commentary, 1991, The Ultimate Triumph, 1991. Mem. Am. Sci. Affiliation, Nat. Assn. Profs. Hebrew, Nat. Assn. Evangs., Near East Archeol. Soc., Soc. Pentecostal Studies (pres. 1979-8), Evang. Theol. Soc. Republican. Home: 615 W Williams St Springfield MO 65803 Office: Assemblies of God Theol Sem 1445 Boonville Ave Springfield MO 65803

HOSINSKI, THOMAS EDMUND, priest; b. South Bend, Ind., Oct. 9, 1946; s. Edmund Joseph and Martha Mary (Drajus) H. AB in Geology, U. Notre Dame, 1969, MTh, 1972; MA in Theology, U. Chgo., 1976, PhD in Theology, 1983. Ordained priest in Roman Cath. Ch., 1973. Mem. Congregation of Holy Cross, South Bend, Ind., 1965—; assoc. prof. U. Portland (Oreg.), 1978—. Contbr. articles to profl. jours. Mem. Am. Acad. Religion. Office: U Portland 5000 N Willamette Blvd Portland OR 97203

HOSMAN, GLENN B., JR., minister; b. Chillicothe, Mo., Mar. 17, 1937; s. Glenn Burton and Ethel Keo (Brott) H.; m. Judith Ann Williams, June 24, 1962; children: Donna Elaine, Glenn Michael F. BA, Cen. Meth. Coll., Fayette, Mo., 1959; BD, St. Paul Sch. Theology, Kansas City, Mo., 1962; PhD, Drew U., 1970. Ordained to ministry United Meth. Ch. Campus min. Wesley Found., Emporia, Kans., 1962-65; state dir. United Meth. Campus Ministry, Madison, N.J., 1967-70; dir. campus ministry nat. office United Meth. Ch., Nashville, 1970-76; campus min., bd. dirs. Toledo Campus Ministry, 1976—; regional dir. S.E. United Ministries in Higher Edn., Nashville, 1974-76; trustee Crittendon Svcs., Toledo, 1977-83; interim dir. Toledo Area Coun. Chs., 1980-82; chair career planning and counseling com. United Meth. Ch., Columbus, Ohio, 1985-89, chair peace and world order, 1989—; bd. dirs. United Health Svcs. Inc., Toledo. Mem. editorial bd. Peace Adv. newsletter, 1989—. Mem. Nat. Campus Mins. Assn., Ohio Ecumenical Campus Mins. Assn. (sec./treas.), Press Club, Univ. Club. Home: 2416 Barrington Toledo OH 43606 Office: Toledo Campus Ministry PO Box 2558 Toledo OH 43606

HOSTETTER, WILLIAM WALLACE, minister; b. Chgo., Dec. 18, 1945; s. Gordon William and Betty (Lowe) H.; m. Linda J. Wilson, May 25, 1967 (div. Nov. 1972); 1 child, Electa Laren; m. Linda Joan Schurman, Nov. 27, 1974; children: Katherine Elisabeth, Emma Leigh Susannah. BS, Ga. State U., 1971; MDiv, Reformed Theol. Seminary, Jackson, Miss., 1979, D of Ministry, 1985; D of Ministry, Westminster Seminary, Escandido, Calif., 1990. Sr. pastor Helena (Miss.) Presbyn. Ch., 1979-81; minister of evangelism Ward Presbyn. Ch., Livonia, Mich., 1981-85; sr. pastor Faith Ch., Rochester, Mich., 1985—; chmn. church devel. Evangelical Denomination, Redford, Mich., 1989—; guest lectr. Ch. Planting Ctr., Orlando, Fla., 1990, Reformed Seminary, Jackson, Orlando, 1988—. Home: 2648 Orbit Dr Lake Orion MI 48360 Office: Faith Church 1000 W University Dr #108 Rochester MI 48063

HOTCHKIN, JOHN FRANCIS, church official, priest; b. Chgo., Feb. 3, 1935; s. John Edward and Sarah Jane (Cure) H. BA, St. Mary of Lake Sem., Mundelein, Ill., 1954; STL, Pontifical Gregorian U., Rome, 1960, STD cum laude, 1966. Ordained priest Roman Cath. Ch., 1959. Assoc. pastor Christ the King Parish, Chgo., 1960-64, St. Therese Parish, Chgo., 1966; assoc. dir. bishop's com. for ecumenical and interreligious affairs Nat. Conf. Cath. Bishops, Washington, 1967-71, exec. dir., 1971—; consultor Pontifical Coun. for Promoting Christian Unity, 1972—, Vatican Secretariat for Non-Christians, 1985-90. Recipient award Cath. Press Assn., 1969. Mem. Cath. Theol. Soc. Am., N.Am. Acad. Ecumenists, Ecumenical Officers Assn. Office: Nat Conf Cath Bishops 3211 4th St NE Washington DC 20017

HOTCHKISS, DANIEL DELOS, minister; b. Rockford, Ill., Mar. 23, 1955; s. Hilton Delos and Katherine Ruth (Huffer) H.; m. Frances Luellen Stephenson, June 21, 1976; children: Carolyn Kay, Samuel Stephenson. BA, Oberlin Coll., 1976; MDiv, Harvard U., 1980. Ordained to ministry Unitarian Universalist Assn., 1980. Min. Unitarian Universalist Fellowship, Boca Raton, Fla., 1980-87, Unitarian Soc., Hamden, Conn., 1987-90; dir. ministerial settlement Unitarian Universalist Assn., Boston, 1990—; pres. Unitarian Universalist Assn., Fla. Dist., 1985-87. Chmn. Youth Programs Rev., 1987-89 (editor report 1989), Fla. Religious Coalition Abortion Rights, 1985-87. Mem. Unitarian Universalist Mins. Assn. (pres. Conn. chpt. 1990). Office: Unitarian Universalist Assn 25 Beacon St Boston MA 02108

HOTCHKISS, WESLEY AKIN, clergyman, educator; b. Spooner, Wis., Jan. 26, 1919; s. Fay W. and Codie L. (Akin) H.; m. Mary Ellen Fink, Sept. 16, 1941; 1 child, Tannia Hotchkiss. B.A., Northland Coll., Wis., 1944, Th.D., 1958; M.S., U. Chgo., 1948, Ph.D., 1950; D.D., Yankton Coll., 1956; LL.D., Pacific U., 1965; L.H.D., Ill. Coll., 1979, Talladega Coll., 1981; LL.D., Hawaii Loa, 1983; Litt.D., Ripon Coll., 1982. Ordained to ministry, Congl. ch., 1944. Research asso. Chgo. Theol. Sem., 1947-49; research dir. Greater Cin. Council Chs., 1949-50; research dir. United Ch. Bd., 1950-55, sec., 1955-58, gen. sec. for higher edn., 1958-82; ret., 1982. Trustee Affiliate Artists, Inc. Served as chaplain AUS, 1945-47. Fellow Assn. Am. Geographers; mem. Nautical Research Guild, Internat. Soc. Folk Harpers and Craftsman, Nature Conservancy, People for the Am. Way. Home: 134 Martinique Ln Ramrod Key FL 33042

HOUCK, JOHN ROLAND, clergyman; b. Balt., Apr. 15, 1923; s. Walter Webb and Wilhelmina Anna (Pfaff) H.; m. Minerva Arline Wiessinger, Nov. 28, 1947; children—John Roland, James Michael, David Walter, Paul Harold. B.A. cum laude, Capital U., Columbus, Ohio, 1947, D.D. (hon.), 1976; B.D., Evang. Lutheran Sem., Columbus, 1950. Ordained to ministry Am. Luth. Ch., 1950; pastor St. Michael Luth. Ch., Perry Hall, Md., 1950-60; regional dir. bd. Am. missions Am. Luth. Ch., Washington, 1960-67; exec. dir. bd. Am. missions Am. Luth. Ch., Mpls., 1970-73; dir. div. service and mission in Am. Am. Luth. Ch., 1974-79; asso. exec. sec. div. mission service Luth. Council U.S.A., N.Y.C., 1967-70; gen. sec. Luth. Council U.S.A., 1979-87; visitation pastor St. Michael's Luth. Ch., Perry Hall, Md., 1988—. Democrat. Home: 4100 N Charles St #408 Baltimore MD 21218 Office: St Michael's Luth Ch Perry Hall MD

HOUCK, WILLIAM RUSSELL, bishop; b. Mobile, Ala., June 26, 1926. Student, St. Bernard Jr. Coll., Cullman, Ala., St. Mary's Sem. Coll., St. Mary's Sem., Balt., Cath. U. Ordained priest Roman Cath. Ch., 1951. Titular bishop of Alessano and auxiliary bishop Jackson, Miss., 1979-84, bishop, 1984—. Address: PO Box 2248 Jackson MS 39225-2248

HOUGAN, CAROLYN AILEEN, writer; b. New Iberia, La., Dec. 16, 1943; d. Samuel Arvid and Elisabeth (Case) Johnson; m. James Richard Hougan, Dec. 17, 1966; children: Daisy Case, Matthew Edwards. BA, U. Wis., Madison, 1966. Writer, 1980—. Author: Shooting in the Dark, 1984, The Romeo Flag, 1989. Mem. Wash. Ind. Writers.

HOUGH, BRUCE HAROLD, minister; b. Centralia, Ill., Aug. 8, 1944; s. Shirley Harold and Bess Fern (Wilson) H.; m. Jean Elizabeth Baylor, Aug. 8, 1965; children: Cheryl Lynn, Kimberly Ann, Rebecca Sue. AS, Centralia Jr. Coll., 1964; BA in Ministry, Lincoln (Ill.) Christian Coll., 1968; BA in Christian Edn., Lincoln Christian Coll., 1968. Ordained to ministry Christian Ch. Min. Bethany Chapel Christian Ch., Fowler, Ind., 1967-69, Alma (Ill.) Christian Ch., 1969-72, Falmouth Christian Ch., Newton, Ill., 1972-75, Boyd Christian Ch., Dix, Ill., 1975—; bd. dirs. Oil Belt Christian Svc. Camp, Flora, Ill., 1970—, So. Ill. Christian Counseling Ctr., Mt. Vernon, Ill., 1988—.

HOUGH, THOMAS BRYANT, minister; b. Anson County, N.C., Nov. 7, 1903; s. Robert Andrew and Janie (Simpson) H.; B.A., Duke U., 1937, postgrad. theology Emory U., 1930-34, U. Iowa, 1950; Th.M., Am. Bible Sch., 1950, Th.D., 1952, D.D., 1952; m. Mary Garnett Martin, June 15, 1928; 1 dau., Mary Jane (Mrs. Thoroughgood Fleetwood Hassell). Ordained to ministry United Methodist Ch., 1929; pastor various chs., N.C., 1929-62; supt. Burlington (N.C.) dist., 1962-67; pastor First Ch., Rockingham, N.C., 1967-71; mem. bd. ministerial tng. United Meth. Ch., 1958-62. Del., Jurisdictional Conf., 1964, World Conf. United Meth., London, 1966. Vol. chaplain Richmond County Meml. Hosp., 1967-71, civilian adviser to 3d Army, 1958-70; dist. commr. Cherokee Council Boy Scouts Am., 1948-49. Bd. trustees N.C. United Meth. Conf., 1960-72, Meth. Retirement Homes, 1962-76. Named Citizen of Yr., Rockingham, 1979. Democrat. Lodge: Kiwanis. Author: Steeple Tones, 1958-62. Contbr. articles to religious jours. and lodge mags. Home and Office: 430 Curtis Dr Rockingham NC 28379

HOUSE, JAY WESLEY, minister. Pres. Christian Chs. United of Tri-County Area, Harrisburg. Office: Christian Chs United Tri-County Area Rm 128 900 S Arlington Ave Harrisburg PA 17109*

HOUSE, MARK AARON, minister; b. Sioux City, Iowa, Sept. 22, 1953; s. Richard Vernon House and Joy Jeannine (Green) Slauter; m. Sharon Diane Grey, July 19, 1975; children: Jessica, John, David. BA, Biola U., 1976; MDiv, Westminster Theol. Sem., Phila., 1980; magna cum laude (hon.), Biola U., 1980. Ordained to ministry Presbyn. Ch. Assoc. pastor Cerritos Valley Orthodox Presbyn. Ch., Artesia, Calif., 1980-83; pastor New Life Presbyn. Ch., Manhattan Beach, Calif., 1983—; chaplain Manhattan Beach Police Dept., 1987—; chmn. Com. on Mission in North Am., Pacific Presbytery, 1990—. Contbr. articles to profl. jours. Republican. Office: New Life Presbyn Ch 500 Manhattan Beach Blvd Manhattan Beach CA 90266

HOUSER, ROBERT ERLE, minister; b. Fairbury, Nebr., July 15, 1947; s. Edward Erle and Lois Charlotte (Dux) H.; m. Theadra Jean Schaaf, Feb. 17, 1979; children: Jason West, Jennifer West, Jerrod Houser. BA, Tarkio (Mo.) Coll., 1968; MDiv, Dubuque Theol. Sem., 1970; DMin, McCormick Theol. Sem., Chgo., 1989. Ordained to ministry Presbyn. Ch. (USA). Assoc. pastor First United Presbyn. Ch., Atlantic, Iowa, 1970-76; pastor United Presbyn. Ch., Griswold, Iowa, 1970-76, United Ch. of Avoca (Iowa), 1976—; mem. leadership devel. work group Synod of Lakes and Prairies, 1990—; chmn. ministry com. Presbytery of Mo. River Valley, 1989, mem. exec. search com., 1984-85, com. on ministry, 1984-86; commr. Gen. Assy. of Presbyn. Ch., 1983, others in past. Pres. Avoca Promotions, Inc., 1985; dir., v.p. Western Iowa Devel. Assn., 1986; cons. Elderberry Sr. Citizens Ctr., 1987; bd. dirs. I CARE, 1987, Circle West Incubator, Des Moines Area Community Coll., 1988; mem. Avoca Mus. Com., 1989; dir. Pub. Policy Edn. project, Iowa State U., 1989. Recipient Iowa CROP Leadership award, 1974, Avoca Econ. Devel. award, 1987, Iowa Gov.'s Leadership award, 1990. Home: 106 W Wool Avoca IA 51521

HOUTEPEN, ANTON WILLEM JOSEPH, theology educator; b. Etten-Leur, Netherlands, Apr. 1, 1940; s. Adrian J. and Johanna P. (Ossenblok) H.; m. Eelkje De Boer, June 29, 1970; children: Wibo, Arjan. ThD, U. Nijmegen, 1969, U. Nijmegen, 1973. Staff mem. Diocesan Pastoral Ctr., Breda, Netherlands, 1970-75; dir. Diocesan Pastoral Ctr., 1975-79; staff mem. Interuniversity Inst. Missiology and Ecumenical Rsch., Utrecht, Netherlands, 1979-86; dir. Interuniversity Inst. Missiology and Ecumenical Rsch., 1986—; prof. fundamental theology Erasmus U., Rotterdam, Netherlands, 1984—; sec., v.p. Dutch Found. for Acad. Rsch. in Theology and Religion, Den Haag, 1986—. Author: Theology of the Saeculum, 1976, People of God, 1983, In God is Geen Geweld, 1985. Mem. St. Willebrord Assn. (bd. dirs. 1971-83), Soc. Ecumenica (bd. dirs. 1986-88, pres. 90—), Dutch Coun. Churches (advisor 1977-87). Roman Catholic. Avocations: chess, swimming, canoeing. Office: IIMO, Heidelberglaan 2, 3584 GS Utrecht The Netherlands

HOVESTOL, MARK, academic administrator. Pres. Oak Hills Bible Coll., Bemidji, Minn. Office: Oak Hills Bible Coll 1600 Oak Hills Rd SW Bemidji MN 56601*

HOVEY, RALPH WAYNE, minister; b. Kooskia, Idaho, June 12, 1926; s. Ralph Winfield and Marie (Rose) H.; m. Mary Ellen Wakefield, Feb. 28, 1947; children: Wayne, David, Terry, Cynthia. Student, North Idaho Tchrs. Coll., Lewiston, 1947-48, Linfield Coll., 1950, Wayland Bapt. Coll., 1951-52, Memphis State U., 1954-55; diploma in theology, Southwestern Bapt. Theol. Sem., Ft. Worth, 1958. Ordained to ministry So. Bapt. Conv., 1950. Pastor Brooks Road Bapt. Ch., Memphis, 1952-55, First Bapt. Ch., Colleyville, Tex., 1955-56, Bellevue Bapt. Ch., Hurst, Tex., 1956-58, First Bapt. Ch., Whitesboro, Tex., 1958-59, Northside Bapt. Ch., San Antonio, 1959-62; pastor First Bapt. Ch., South Houston, Tex., 1962-66, Clovis, N.Mex., 1966-69; sales rep. Church Bond & Fund Raising, Memphis, 1969-76; pastor Woodland Place Bapt. Ch., Magnolia, Tex., 1976-82, 1st Bapt. Ch., Mobeetie, Tex., 1982—. Sgt. USAF, 1944-54. Mem. Masons (chaplain). Republican. Home: PO Box 160 Mobeetie TX 79061

HOVINGH, MORRIS FRANK, mission executive; b. Grand Rapids, Mich., July 27, 1928; s. Frank and Eleanor (Stevens) H.; m. Phyllis Van Puffelen, June 15, 1950; children: Ronald, Cheryl, Marcia. BA, Bob Jones U., 1952. Dir. ministries Ind. Bible Mission, Constock Park, Mich., 1978-90, supr. bldg. projects, 1990—. Editor of profl. jours. Pres. Am. Bus. Club, 1972. with U.S. Army, 1946-48, Korea. Office: Ind Bible Mission 749 Lamoreaux Comstock Park MI 49321

HOVSEPIAN, VATCHE, clergyman; b. Beirut, Lebanon, June 11, 1930; s. Krikor and Ovsanna (Tchakerian) H. Diploma, Armenian Theol. Sem., Lebanon, 1951; postgrad., Coll. Resurrection, York, Eng., 1953-54, U. Edinburgh, Scotland, 1954-56; B.Div., New Brunswick Theol. Sem., 1960. Ordained priest Armenian Apostolic Ch., 1951; instr. Armenian Theol. Sem., Lebanon; priest Holy Cross Ch., Union City, N.J., 1956-67; bishop of Can., 1967-71; elevated to archbishop, 1976; primate of Western Diocese, Armenian Ch. of Am., Hollywood, Calif., 1971—. Mem. Nat. Council of Chs. (past mem. central bd.). Clubs: Riviera Country (Pacific Palisades, Calif.); Knights of Vartan. Address: Armenian Ch Am 1201 N Vine St Hollywood CA 90038

HOWARD, BARRY C., minister; b. Anniston, Ala., Jan. 13, 1960; s. Cecil C. Howard and Sandra (Ginn) McKleroy; m. Amanda Marie Nance, Sept. 7, 1985. BA, Jacksonville State U., 1983, MA, 1990; postgrad., New Orleans Bapt. Theol. Sem., 1990—. Ordained to ministry So. Bapt. Conv., 1982. Assoc. min. youth activities West Anniston Bapt. Ch., 1981-82; pastor Post Oak Spring Bapt. Ch., Jacksonville, Ala., 1982-85; assoc. pastor 1st Bapt. Ch., Weaver, Ala., 1986-87; pastor 1st Bapt. Ch. of Williams, Jacksonville, 1987—; mem. teller's com. Ala. Bapt. Convention, Montgomery, 1988. Recipient Outstanding Young Men of Am. award Jaycees, 1981, 86. Mem. Calhoun Bapt. Assn. (mem. evangelism com. 1986-89, dir. youth ministry 1986-89), Jacksonville Ministerial Assn. (coord. chaplain ministry 1988—), Pleasant Valley Booster Club. Home: 6331 Nisbet Lake Rd Jacksonville AL 36265-9802

HOWARD, CLYDE THOMAS, III, minister; b. Columbia, S.C., Nov. 7, 1959; s. Clyde Thomas and Phyllis Anne (Griffin) H.; m. Sandra Rebecca Aho, July 11, 1981. BMus, Furman U., Greenville, S.C., 1981; MDiv in Ch. Music, So. Bapt. Theol. Sem., Louisville, 1985. Ordained to ministry, So. Bapt. Conv., 1984. Minister music First Bapt. Ch., Olar, S.C., 1981-82; minister music and youth Dover Bapt. Ch., Shelbyville, Ky., 1983-84, Rolling Fields Bapt. Ch., Jeffersonville, Ind., 1984-85, Reidsville (Ga.) Bapt. Ch., 1985-89, First Bapt. Ch., Hapeville, Ga., 1989—; associational music dir. Tattnall-Evans Bapt. Assn., Reidsville, 1987-89; v.p. Tattnall-Evans Ministers Conf., Reidsville, 1986-89. Mem. Tattnall County Coalition on Aging, Reidsville, 1987-89, Reidsville Crisis Fund, 1986-89, Travelers Protection Agy., Hapeville, 1989—. Mem. So. Bapt. Assn. Ministries with Aging, Atlanta Bapt. Associational Youth Ministers, Choristers Guild, So. Bapt. Ch. Music Conf., Ga. Bapt. Ch. Music Conf., Sons of Jubal (section leader 1987). Home: 741 Oak Dr Hapeville GA 30354-1062 Office: 1st Bapt Ch 612 College St Hapeville GA 30354-1797

HOWARD, DAVID MORRIS, missionary; b. Phila., Jan. 28, 1928; s. Philip E. Jr. and Katharine (Gillingham) H.; m. Phyllis Gibson, July 1, 1950; children—David, Stephen, Karen Elisabeth, Michael. A.B., Wheaton Coll., 1949, M.A. in Theology, 1952; LL.D., Geneva Coll., 1974; L.H.D., Taylor U., 1978. Ordained to ministry, 1952; asst. gen. dir. Latin Am. Mission, Colombia S.Am., Costa Rica, C.Am., 1953-68; missions dir. Inter-Varsity Christian Fellowship, Madison, Wis., 1968-76, asst. to pres., 1976-77; dir. Urbana Student Missionary Convs., 1973, 76; dir. Consultation on World Evangelization, Pattaya, Thailand, 1977-80; gen. dir. World Evangel. Fellowship, Wheaton, Ill., 1982—. Author: Hammered as Gold, 1969, reprinted as The Costly Harvest, 1975; Student Power in World Missions, 1979; How Come, God?, 1972, By the Power of the Holy Spirit, 1973; Words of Fire, Rivers of Tears, 1976, The Great Commission for Today, 1976, The Dream That Would Not Die, 1986, What Makes a Missionary, 1987. Adv. life trustee Wheaton Coll. Office: World Evang Fellowship PO Box WEF Wheaton IL 60189

HOWARD, DONALD RAY, religious organization administrator, educator; b. Petersburg, Ind., Oct. 29, 1945; s. Stanley Rupert and Mary Jane (Curry) H.; m. Candace Stacey Katterman, Oct. 4, 1969; children: Brody J., Barth Trevor. BS, Concordia Coll., 1973. Prin. St. John's Luth. Sch., Vernon Center, Minn., 1973-76, St. Matthew's Luth. Sch., New Britain, Conn., 1976-79; dir. Christian edn. Trinity Luth. Ch., Daytona Beach, Fla., 1979-81; prin. Hope Luth. Sch., Austin, Tex., 1981-87; dir. Christian edn. Holy Cross Luth. Ch., Lawton, Okla., 1987—; bd. dirs. Holy Cross Learning Ctr., Lawton, Okla. Dist. Bd. Parish Edn., Oklahoma City, 1988—; pres. adminstrs. conf. Tex. dist. Luth. Ch.-Mo. Synod, 1985; presenter in field. Co-chmn. religious subcom. Citizens for Drug Free Lawton, 1989-91; mem. Friends of the Lawton Libr., 1989-91; bd. dirs. Cameron campus ministry Cameron U., 1988-91. Mem. Luth. Edn. Assn., Assn. for Supervision and Curriculum Devel. Home: 4805 NE Winfield Circle Lawton OK 73507 Office: Holy Cross Luth Ch 2105 NW 38th St Lawton OK 73505 *May it be our goal in life to not only see Christ in others but also to have them see Christ in us.*

HOWARD, DONAVAN CRAIG, broadcasting executive; b. Lubbock, Tex., Dec. 5, 1967; s. August Jesse and Carolyn Ann (Johnson) H. BS in Journalism, Stephen F. Austin U., 1988. Promotion dir. Sta. KWWJ AM, Baytown, Tex., 1988—; min. music Powerhouse Ch. of God In Christ, 1989—; musician Tex. N.W. Jurisdiction, 1988—. Bd. dirs. Operation PUSH, Houston, 1990. Named Youngest Lic. Minister (7 yrs. old) Ch. of God in Christ, 1974. Mem. Gospel Announcers Guild of Am., Tex. Announcers Guild. Democrat. Home: 6300 W Bellfort Houston TX 77035 Office: Sta KWWJ 1360 AM 4638 Decker Dr Baytown TX 77520

HOWARD, GEORGE EULAN, religion educator, academic administrator; b. Clinton, Okla., June 3, 1935; s. Frances Sterling and Ann (Turner) H.; m. Teresa Ann Ingram, Aug. 22, 1983; children: Cecile Elizabeth Allison, Lindsey Ann Paige, Georgia Mandy Gail, Harrington Heath. BA, David Lipscomb Coll., 1957; MA, MTh, Harding Grad. Sch., 1961; PhD, Hebrew Union Coll., 1964. Asst. prof. religion David Lipscomb Coll., Nashville, 1964-67, assoc. prof. religion, 1967-68; asst. prof. classics U. Ga., Athens, 1968-70, 1970-72, assoc. prof. religion, 1972-78, prof., 1978—, head religion dept., 1983—; acting head of philosophy, religion 1979-80. Author: Paul,

Crisis in Galatia, 1979, The Teaching of Addai, 1981; The Gospel of Matthew According to Ancient Hebrew Text, 1987; contbr. numerous articles and papers to profl. and scholarly jours. Grantee in Nat. Found. Humanities, 1969—, Am. Council Learned Socs., 1974. Mem. Internat. Orgn. for Septuagint and Cognate Studies (treas. 1972-74, bulletin editor, 1973-79), Soc. Bib. Lit. (sect. chmn. 1977-79; editorial bd. 1979-81, 82-84, v.p. Southeastern chpt. 1979-80, pres. Southeastern chpt. 1980-81). Office: Univ of Ga Dept of Religion Athens GA 30602

HOWARD, GERALD KENNETH, minister; b. Cleve., May 25, 1938; s. Fred Joseph and Thelma Josephine (Johnson) H.; m. Donna Ashmore, Nov. 26, 1977 (div. Dec. 1990); children: Charles, Tyrone Mayo-Howard, Keisha Mayo-Howard. BS in Sociology, Southeastern U., 1978; MDiv, Nat. Theol. Sem., Balt., 1982; DD, Nat. Theol. Sem., 1982; PhD, Cornestone Sem., Jerusalem, Israel, 1991; DD (hon.), Kashi Dharma Peetha, Varanasi, Calcutta, India, 1981; DHL (hon.), Teamer Sch. Religion, 1983. Lic. to ministry Bapt. Ch., 1970, ordained, 1972; lic. pastoral counselor. Diplomate Am. Bd. Examiners Psychotherapy. Asst. pastor Abyssinian Bapt. Ch., Phila., 1973-77, 1980-89; new pastor Gibson Temple Bapt. Ch., Phila., 1977-80; pastor Unity Bapt. Ch., Chester, Pa., 1989—; casework supr. Commonwealth Pa. Dept. Pub. Welfare, Phila., 1971—; del. Nat. Bapt. Conv., USA, Inc., Baton Rouge, 1969—; commd. chaplain, Nat. Chaplain's Assn., Gatlinburg, Tenn., 1975—; corr. sec. New Hope Bapt. Assn., Chester, 1989—; clergy to police, 35th Dist, Broad St., Phila. Police Dept., 1974; v.p., rep. Cornerstone U. and Sem., 1990. With U.S. Army, 1961-64, Korea. Recipient Outstanding Svc. award Nat. Chaplain's Assn., Gatlinburg, 1976, Legion of Honor The Chapel of Four Chaplains, Phila., 1978, 83, Martin Luther King award Defense Pers. Support Ctr., Phila., 1987, Dedicated Christian Svc. award, Pa. Bapt. State Conv., Phila., 1990, Disting. Person and Outstanding Citizen awards Phila. City Coun., 1991. Fellow Am. Coll. Clinic Adminstrs.; mem. Masons. Democrat. Home: 1552 E Upsal St Philadelphia PA 19150 Office: Unity Bapt Ch Inc 600 W 6th St Chester PA 19013 *All of my life I've strived to be somebody, whether good or bad I strived. If I become somebody, let that somebody be an ambassador for Christ and a keeper of my brother.*

HOWARD, MARK EDWIN, minister; b. Memphis, Apr. 17, 1954; s. Durwood and Jane (Gilliland) H.; m. Rebecca Joy Pitt, Feb. 7, 1975; 1 child, Joshua Mark. BA, Union U., Jackson, Tenn., 1976; MDiv, Southwestern Bapt. Theol. Sem., 1979; DMin, New Orleans Bapt. Theol. Sem., 1984. Ordained to ministry, So. Bapt. Conv., 1975. Sr. pastor First Bapt. Ch., Trenton, Tenn., 1981-84, Portage, Mich., 1984-86; Sr. pastor Ch. on the Rock, Kalamazoo, 1986-87; assoc. pastor Woodland Bapt. Ch., Jackson, 1987—; trustee Union U., 1982-84. Exec. producer recording: You Are Faithful, Lord, 1989, Now Unto The King Eternal, 1990. Mem. Rotary. Republican. Office: Woodland Bapt Ch 365 Wallace Rd Jackson TN 38305

HOWARD, M(OSES) WILLIAM, JR., minister; b. Americus, Ga., Mar. 3, 1946; s. M. William and Laura (Turner) H.; m. Barbara Jean Wright, July 11, 1970; children: Matthew Weldon, Adam Turner, Maisha Wright. B.A., Morehouse Coll., 1968, L.H.D., 1984; M.Div., Princeton Theol. Sem., 1972; D.D., Miles Coll., 1979, Central Coll., 1980. Ordained to ministry Am. Baptist Ch., 1974; exec. dir. Black Council, Ref. Ch. in Am., N.Y.C., 1972—; bd. dirs. Nat. Conf. Black Churchmen, 1975-80; moderator Commn. of World Council Chs. Program to Combat Racism, 1976-78; bd. dirs. Nat. Media Found.; pres. Nat. Council Chs., 1979-81; condr. Christmas services for hostages Am. embassy, Tehran, 1979; chmn. UN Seminar on Bank Loans to South Africa, Zurich, 1981; chmn. ecumenical delegation to Syria, 1984, instrumental (with Rev. Jesse Jackson) in obtaining release of Lt. Robert O. Goodman, USN; chair religious com. to welcome Nelson Mandela to U.S.A., 1990. Researcher: Born to Rebel - Autobiography of Benjamin Elijah Mays, 1967; editor: monthly newsletter Black Caucus RCA, 1973—; pub., producer ann. lectureship, 1975—. Active YMCA; trustee Trenton State Coll., 1981-82, Nat. Urban League; bd. dirs. Children's Def. Fund, The Independent Sector, founding mem. People for Am. Way; pres. Am. Com. on Africa, 1987—. Recipient Disting. Service award as chmn. Commn. on Justice, Liberation and Human Fulfillment, Disting. Alumnus award Princeton Theol. Sem., 1984; decorated comdr. Order Knights of Holy Sepulchre. Mem. NAACP, Sigma Pi Phi. Office: 18th Fl 475 Riverside Dr New York NY 10027 *Perhaps the greatest challenge to humanity today is to see that our moral and ethical development catches up, and keeps pace with, our advances in technology.*

HOWARD, RONALD EUGENE, chaplain; b. Fairfield, Ala., Aug. 5, 1955; s. Forney Talent and Merry Alma (Grubbs) H.; m. Deborah Sue Tennyson, June 7, 1975; children: Melissa Diane, Jonathan Blake. BA, Samford U., Birmingham, 1977; MDiv, Southeastern Sem., Wake Forest, N.C., 1981. Chaplain resident Bapt. Med. Ctrs., Birmingham, 1981-82; dir. pastoral care and social svc. BMC Cherokee, Centre, Ala., 1982-86; chaplain Golden Triangle Reg. Med. Ctr., Columbus, Miss., 1986-88; chaplain/pastoral counselor DCH Reg. Med. Ctr., Tuscaloosa, Ala., 1988—. Bd. dirs. Cherokee-Etowah-DeKalb Reg. Alcoholism Coun., Gadsden, Ala., 1984-86; pres. Coun. Community & Health Svcs., Centre, 1983-86; advisor County Multidisciplinary Child Protective Team, Centre, 1984-86; dir. Camp Bluebird Adult Cancer Camp, Tuscaloosa, 1989—; chmn. Rural Devel. Com., Centre, 1985. Lt. USN, 1987—. Mem. Civitans Internat., Am. Assn. Clin. Pastoral Edn. Democrat. Baptist. Avocations: electronics, reading, music. Office: DCH Regional Med Ctr 809 University Blvd E Tuscaloosa AL 35401

HOWE, DOUGLAS PAUL, lay worker; b. Alton, Ill., Dec. 28, 1959; s. William Joseph and Norma Jean (Saxby) H.; m. Roseanne Lynn Hickman, Dec. 21, 1985. AAA in Ministerial Tng., Bob Jones U., 1985. Elem. supr. Coll. Lakes Bapt. Ch., Fayetteville, N.C., 1985-86; minister of music/youth Coll. Lakes Bapt. Ch., Fayetteville, 1985-86; Sun. sch. tchr. Cornerstone Bapt. Ch., Fayetteville, 1986-88; minister of youth/music Maranatha Bapt. Ch., Orlando, Fla., 1988-89; Sun. sch. supt., music dir. Maranatha Bapt. Ch., Orlando, 1990—; retail electronics dept. mgr. Wal-mart Discount Store, Orlando, 1989-91; Sun. sch. supt. Maranatha Bapt. Ch., Orlando, 1990—, minister, dir. music, choir, 1988—, vacation Bible sch. dir., 1990—, children's ch. leader, 1989—. Recipient Retail Volume Producing Item of the Yr. Wal-mart Stores, Inc., 1990, Retail Volume Producing Item of the Month, Wal-Mart, 1990. Mem. Assn. Christian Tchrs., Bob Jones U. Alumni Assn., Awana Youth Assn. Club (leader 1975-80). Republican. Home: 4641 Stag Horn Dr Apt 230 Orlando FL 32808-5074 Office: Maranatha Bapt Ch 5601 Santa Anita St Orlando FL 32808-6242

HOWE, E. MARGARET, Middle Eastern studies educator; came to U.S., 1976; BA in Bibl. History and Lit., U. Sheffield, England, 1960; postgrad., U. London, 1960-61; PhD, U. Manchester, England, 1964. High sch. tchr. religion and history Manchester, 1964-69; tchr. Am. and Can. lit., local high sch. and coll. Man., Can., 1969-72; asst. prof. religious studies Western Ky. U., Bowling Green, 1972, full prof. dept. philosophy and religion, 1981—, mem. grad. faculty, 1978—; lectr. Ky. Humanities Coun./NEH, 1981-83, Calvin Coll., Mich., 1982, Ind. U., Bloomington, 1983, others; resident scholar Ecumenical Inst. for Theol. Studies, Jerusalem, 1979-80, 87, participant in regional study tour of Israel, 1990. Author: Women and Church Leadership, 1982; contbr. articles to profl. jours.; producer audio-visual teaching programs; host radio talks, TV programs. Mem. Bibl. Archaeology Soc., Am. Schs. Oriental Rsch. Home: 526 Claremoor Dr Bowling Green KY 42101 Office: Western Ky U Dept Philosophy and Religion Bowling Green KY 42101

HOWE, IRVING, author, historian, critic; b. N.Y.C., June 11, 1920; s. David and Nettie (Goldman) H.; m. Ilana Wiener; 2 children. Grad., CCNY. Tchr. English Brandeis U., 1953-61, Stanford U., 1961-63; prof. English City U. N.Y. at Hunter Coll., 1963-86, Distinguished prof., 1970-86; Christian Gauss seminar chair prof. Princeton U., 1954. Author: Politics and the Novel: A World More Attractive, 1963, Steady Work, 1966, Thomas Hardy, 1967, The Decline of the New, 1969, The Critical Point, 1973, World of Our Fathers, 1976 (Nat. Book award), A Margin of Hope, 1982, Socialism & America, 1985, Socialism and America, 1985, The American Newness, 1986; co-author: The Radical Papers, 1966; editor: periodical Essential Works of Socialism, 1971, The Penguin Book of Modern Yiddish Verse, 1987; co-editor: A Treasury of Yiddish Poetry, 1971; contbr. to N.Y. Times Book Rev. Served with AUS, World War II. Recipient Longview Found. prize for lit. criticism; Nat. Inst. Arts and Letters award; Nat. Book award for history, 1976; Kenyon Rev. fellow for lit. criticism, 1953; Bollingen Found. fellow; Guggenheim fellow, 1971, MacArthur fellow, 1987.

HOWE, JOHN WADSWORTH, bishop; b. Chgo., Nov. 4, 1942; s. John Wadsworth Howe and Shirley Anita (Hansen) Packer; m. Karen Louise Elvgren, Sept. 1, 1962; children: Katherine Janet Howe Rickwald, John Wadsworth III, Jessica Ruth Howe. BA, U. Conn., 1964; MDiv, Yale U., 1967; DD (hon.), Berkeley-Yale, 1989, U. of the South, Tenn., 1990, Naskota House, 1991. Ordained to ministry Episcopal Ch. as deacon, 1967, as priest 1968, as bishop, 1989. Chaplain Loomis Sch., Windsor, Conn., 1967-69, Miss Porter's Sch., Farmington, Conn., 1969-72; assoc. rector St. Stephen's Episcopal Ch., Swickley, Pa., 1972-76; rector Truro Episcopal Ch., Fairfax, Va., 1976-89; bishop coadjuter Diocese of Cen. Fla., Orlando, 1989-90, bishop, 1990—; founder Sharing of Ministries Abroad. Author: Which Way? 1972, Our Anglican Heritage, 1976, Sex: Shall We Change the Rules, 1991; contbr. articles to mags; co-author Resolution and the Sanctity of Human Life adopted by 69th Gen. Conv. Episcopal Ch., Detroit. Mem. Nat. Orgn. of Episcopalian for Life (chmn. bd.), Fellowship of Witness (former pres.). Home: 5583 Jessamine Ln Orlando FL 32839

HOWE, MARY JANE, youth ministry director; b. Medford, Oreg., May 15, 1964; d. William J. Jr. and Lillian Anne (Loschicky) H. BA in Theol., U. Portland, 1986. Cert. religious edn., U. Portland. Youth min. Holy Trinity, Beaverton, Oreg., 1984-86; dir. religious edn. St. Anthony's, Tigard, Oreg., 1986-88; dir. youth min. Tri-Youth, St. Luke's, Woodburn, Oreg., 1988-90, St. Pius X Youth Min., Portland, Oreg., 1990—; co-chmn. Archdiocese Youth & Young Adult Commn., Portland, Oreg., 1989—. Recipient Appreciation award Rosemont Sch., Portland, Oreg., 1988. Mem. Christ & Co. (co-dir. 1990—). Office: St Pius X Church 1280 NW Saltzman Rd Portland OR 97229

HOWE, REUEL LANPHIER, JR., minister; b. Phila., Mar. 9, 1943; s. Reuel Lanphier and Marjorie Martin (Stryke) H.; m. Eileen Estelle Segar, Feb. 25, 1967 (div. 1980); children: Sara Constance, Douglas Reuel; m. Sara Stark Barclay, Apr. 13, 1985. BA, Olivet (Mich.) Coll., 1966; MEd, Temple U., 1968; MDiv, Lancaster (Pa.) Sem., 1980. Ordained to ministry Presbyn. Ch., 1982. Youth min. First Presbyn. Ch., Belaire, Md., 1978-80; assoc. pastor Kennett Sq. (Pa.) Presbyn. Ch., 1982-86; pastor Makemie Meml. and Gunby Meml. Presbyn. Chs., Snow Hill, Md., 1986—; recorder Synod of the Mid-Atlantic, Richmond, Va., 1989—; founder Pathfinders Support Ministry, Kennett Sq., 1983-86; pres. Snow Hill Ministerial Assn., 1989—. Pres. Life Lines Worcester County Youth Suicide Prevention, Newark, Md., 1990-91; tchr., vol. Worcester County AIDS Prevention Program, Newark, 1989-91. Democrat. Home and Office: 101 W Market St Snow Hill MD 21863

HOWE, RONALD EVANS, minister; b. Charles City, Iowa, Feb. 17, 1945; s. Evans R. and Elizabeth (Atchison) H.; m. M. Kristin Petersmith, Aug. 16, 1970; children: Sarah Elizabeth, Rachel Ellen, Michael Evans. Cert., Moody Bible Inst., 1966, AB, 1969; AB, U. Iowa, 1968, JD, 1972; ThM, Dallas Theol. Sem., 1975. Lic. to ministry Ind. Mission Ch., 1966, ordained Evang. Free Ch. Am., 1990. Bar: Iowa 1972, Tex. 1973, U.S. Tax Ct. 1974. Sr. min. Elim Chapel, Winnipeg, Man., Can., 1975-85, Evang. Free Ch., Fresno, Calif., 1985—; adj. prof. Winnipeg Theol. Sem., 1975-85, Briercrest Grad. Sch., Caronport, Sask, Can., 1985-87; bd. dirs. Haggai Inst., Winnipeg, 1977-85, Link Care Ctr., Fresno, 1985—; bd. govs. Winnipeg Bible Coll. and Sem., 1982-85; mem. exec. com. Fresno Christian Sch., 1985—; lectr. in field. Author: (booklet) Breakfast of Champions, 1984. Republican. Home: 889 E Portland Ave Fresno CA 93710 Office: Evang Free Ch 3438 E Ashlan Ave Fresno CA 73726-3597 *The greatest challenge of my life is to be alert daily to the struggle of maintaining integrity between what I preach and what I practice. What an impact this authenticity or lack thereof will have upon my personal, family and professional life.*

HOWELL, DAVID BRIAN, religion educator, academic administrator; b. Wichita, Kans., Mar. 12, 1956; s. James Garner and Betty Rae (Warner) H.; m. Gloria Jean Whitworth, Aug. 19, 1978: 1 child, Andrew James. AB, William Jewell Coll., 1978; MDiv, So. Bapt. Theol. Sem., Wake Forest, N.C., 1981, ThM, 1982; DPhil, U. Oxford, Eng., 1988. Instr. religion, sr. assoc. dean students William Jewell Coll., Liberty, Mo., 1988—. Author: Matthew's Inclusive Story: A Study in the Narrative Rhetoric of the First Gospel, 1990. Mem. Soc. Bibl. Lit., Nat. Assn. Student Pers. Adminstrs. Mem. So. Bapt. Conv. Democrat. Home: 411 E Mississippi Liberty MO 64068 Office: William Jewell Coll Liberty MO 64068

HOWELL, DAVID DWIGHT, JR., minister; b. Pasadena, Calif., Mar. 30, 1965; s. David Dwight and Caroline May (Simons) H. BA, Houghton Coll., 1987; MA, Trinity Evang. Div. Sch., Deerfield, Ill., 1990. Lic. to ministry Wesleyan Ch., 1990. Min. youth and young adults 1st Wesleyan Ch., Bossier City, La., 1990-91; asst. pastor Debra Heights Wesleyan Ch., Des Moines, 1991—; pres. Fgn. Missions Fellowship, 1986-87; vol. Wesleyan Gospel Corps., Magelang, Indonesia, 1987-88; sec. Trinity Missions Fellowship, Deerfield, 1989-90; sec., treas. Delta Dist. Wesleyan Youth, Bossier City, 1990-91. Office: Debra Heights Wesleyan Ch 4025 Lower Beaver Rd Des Moines IA 50310

HOWELL, HONOR SHARON, minister; b. Seguin, Tex, Oct. 12, 1947; d. Joe Milam and Mary Elizabeth (McKay) H. BA, Austin Coll., 1970; MDiv, St. Paul Sch. Theology, 1973. Youth minister Key Meml. United Meth. Ch., Sherman, Tex., 1969-71, Second Presbyn. Ch., Kansas City, Mo., 1971-72; pastor Edwardsville United Meth. Ch., Kans., 1972-75; assoc. program dir. Council on Ministries, Topeka, 1975-80; v.p. St. Paul Sch. Theology, Kansas City, 1980-85; sr. pastor St. Mark United Meth. Ch., Overland Park, Kans., 1985-87; exec. program dir., Council on Ministries, Topeka, 1987—; pres. Commn. on Status and Role of Women in United Meth. Ch., Evanston, Ill., 1984-88; chmn. personnel com. Council on Ministries, Topeka, 1984-87. Mem. NOW, ACLU, Greenpeace, LWV, NAFE, Smithsonian Assocs., Internat. Assn. Women Ministers, Amnesty Internat., Nat. Mus. Women in Arts (charter), Women's Action for Nuclear Disarmament. Democrat. Home: 3012 Tutbury Town Rd Topeka KS 66614 Office: 4201 SW 15th St Topeka KS 66604

HOWELL, JOHN PAUL, minister; b. Boise, Idaho, June 23, 1952; s. Charles Dickson and Lena Beth (Waitley) H.; m. Nancy Jean Hart, Aug. 7, 1978; children: Timothy Paul, Joshua Rodney, Sarah Beth. B of Religion, Maranatha Bible Coll., 1974; BA in Religion, N.W. Nazarene Coll., 1978. Ordained to ministry Chs. of God (7th Day), 1974. Pastor Ch. of God (Old Time), Maryville, Mo., 1979-82, Ch. of God (7th Day), Meridian, Idaho, 1982-86; chaplain intern Western State Hosp., Steilacoom, Wash., 1987-88; pastor Ch. of God (7th Day), Tulsa, 1988—; mem. lic. and credential com. N. Am. Ministerial Coun. Gen. Conf. Ch. of God (7th Day), 1990—, mem. internship com., 1990—; chmn. Ministerial Coun., 1982-86. Chmn. Mayor's Prayer Breakfast, Meridian C. of C., 1983-86. Mem. N. Am. Ministerial Coun. Gen. Conf. Ch. of God (7th Day). Office: Ch of God (7th Day) 13902 E 11th St Tulsa OK 74108

HOWELL, LEON, editor; b. Copperhill, Tenn.; s. Francis Leon Sr. and Mary Lee (Haney) H.; m. Barbara Smith, June 26, 1965; children: Leah Ruth, Marya Lee. BA, Davidson Coll., 1957; MDiv, Union Theol. Sem., N.Y.C., 1962. Communications sec. Univ. Christian Movement Nat. Coun. Chs., N.Y.C., 1965-69, United Ministries in Higher Edn., N.Y.C., 1969-70; editor Christianity and Crisis, N.Y.C., 1985-90; communications cons. World Coun. Chs., Geneva, 1977-85; ruling elder Chevy Chase Presbyn. Ch., Washington, 1983—; bd. dirs. Associated Church Press, Nat., 1991—; mem. communication com. Presbyn. Ch. (USA), Louisville, 1988—. Author: Freedom City, 1968, People Are the Subject, 1980, Acting in Faith, 1982; co-author: Asia, Oil Politics and the Energy Crisis, 1974, Southeast Asians Speak Out: Between Hope and Despair, 1975; editor: Ethics in the Presence Tense, 1991. Mem. Bi-Nat. Servants, Nat., 1980—, Parent's Coun. Davidson (N.C.) Coll., 1988-91. 1st lt. U.S. Army, 1958-60, Korea. Recipient Best News Story award, Associated Church Press, 1983, Best Editorial award, 1988. Democrat. Home: 1436 Holly St N W Washington DC 20012 Office: Christianity and Crisis 537 W 121st St New York NY 10027

HOWELL, MARIBETH ANNE, educator; b. Chgo., Oct. 9, 1949; d. Hubert Charles and Marion Therese (Lavin) H. BS in Spl. Edn., Wayne State U., 1972; STB, St. Paul U., 1977, Sacred Theology Licentiate, 1979; PhD, Cath. U. Leuven, Belgium, 1986, STD, 1988. Instr. adult religion edn. Kino Inst., Phoenix, 1979-81; asst. prof. Spring Hill Coll., Mobile, Ala., 1986-88, Kenrick Sem., St. Louis, 1988—. Mem. Cath. Theol. Soc. Am., Cath. Bibl. Assn., Soc. Bibl. Lit. Office: Kenrick Sem 5200 Glennon Dr Saint Louis MO 63119

HOWES, ALLAN JOHN, minister; b. North Charleroi, Pa., July 1, 1916; s. George Edward and Orthelia Mae (Layton) H.; m. Sara Ann Keibler, Nov. 25, 1943; children—Ruth Ann, Stanley Allan. A.B., Washington and Jefferson Coll., 1938; M.Th., Westminister Sem., 1943; D.D., Allegheny Coll., 1951. Ordained to ministry Methodist Ch., 1943. Sr. minister Asbury United Meth. Ch., Uniontown, Pa., 1954-59, South Avenue United Meth. Ch., Wilkinsburg, Pa., 1959-65; exec. dir. Meth. Ch. Union, Pitts., 1965-72; assoc. minister 1st Bethel United Meth. Ch., Bethel Park, Pa., 1977—. Pres. Howes Animation, Inc., Bethel Park, 1981—; pres. Srs. Residential Care, Inc., 1985—, Concerned Care Mgmt. Co., Inc., 1984—. Author, producer TV Christmas spl. A Star for Jeremy, 1982—. Recipient bronze medal Internat. Film and TV Festival, 1983. Republican. Avocations: reading; boating; walking. Home: 3699 Ashland Dr Bethel Park PA 15102 Office: First Bethel United Meth Ch 5901 Library Rd Bethel Park PA 15102

HOWES, BRUCE BECKER, minister; b. Evanston, Ill., Mar. 24, 1953; s. Allen Hudson and Connie (Becker) H.; m. Patricia Ruth Howes, Sept. 12, 1981; children: Kenneth Allen, David Becker. BS, So. Ill. U., 1975, BA, 1978; MAR, Westminster Theol. Sem., 1980, MDiv, 1981. Ordained to ministry Presbyn. Ch. in Am., 1982. Stated clk. Delmarva Presbytery Presbyn. Ch. Am., Balt., 1985-90, Heritage Presbtery Presbyn. Ch. Am., New Castle, Del., 1990—; recording clk. Gen. Assembly of the Presbyn. Ch. Am., 1987—; v.p. Evang. Mins. Fellowship of New Castle County, Del., 1986-88. Pres. Christian Action Coun. of New Castle County, Inc., Wilmington, Del., 1985-88, treas., 1988-90. Office: Heritage Presbyn Ch 140 Airport Rd New Castle DE 19720 *Through Jesus Christ I have peace with God, assurance of acceptance with God and eternal life. "Whoever believes in Him as Savior can have eternal life" (John 3:16).*

HOWZE, JOSEPH LAWSON EDWARD, bishop; b. Daphne, Ala., Aug. 30, 1923; s. Albert Otis and Helen Artamesa (Lawson) H. B.S., Ala. State U., 1948; postgrad. in bus. mgmt., Phillips Coll., Gulfport, Miss., 1980; LL.D. (hon.), U. Portland, 1974, St. Bonaventure U., 1977, Manhattan Coll., N.Y.C., 1979; H.H.D. (hon.), Sacred Heart Coll., Belmont, N.Y., 1977; HHD (hon.), The Lift Bible Crusade Coll., 1987. Ordained priest Roman Catholic Ch., 1959; pastor chs. Charlotte, Southern Pines, Durham, Sanford, Asheville, all N.C., 1959-72; aux. bishop of (Diocese of Natchez-Jackson), Miss., 1972-73; bishop (Diocese of Natchez-Jackson), 1973-77; bishop of Biloxi, 1977—. Trustee Xavier U., New Orleans; mem. Miss. Health Care Commn.; mem. adminstrv. bd., vacation com. NOCB/USCC; mem. edn. com. USCC, mem. social devel. and world peace com.; liaison com. to Nat. Office of Black Catholics, NCCB.; bd. dirs. Biloxi Regional Med. Ctr. Democrat. Clubs: K.C, Knights of St. Peter Claver. Address: PO Box 1189 Biloxi MS 39533

HOY, GEORGE PHILIP, clergyman, food bank executive; b. Indpls., Feb. 5, 1937; s. Clarence Augustus Hoy and Margaret Louise (Etter) Wooley; m. Barbara J. Turpen, Aug. 11, 1957 (dec. Feb. 1987); children: Rene Hoy Riegle, Sherri Hoy Haas, Matthew Philip; 1 foster child, Richard H. Johnson. BA, Ky. Wesleyan Coll., 1958; MDiv, So. Bapt. Theol. Sem., Louisville, 1962. Ordained to ministry United Ch. of Christ, 1962. Pastor Union United Ch. of Christ, Evansville, Ind., 1962-72, Faith United Ch. of Christ, Ft. Wayne, Ind., 1975-80, St. Matthew's United Ch. of Christ, Evansville, 1981-87; dir. Youth Svc. Bur., Evansville, 1972-75; pastor St. Peter's United Ch. of Christ, Evansville, 1988—; mem. faculty Brescia Coll., Owensboro, Ky., 1970-72; chaplain Evansville State Hosp., 1966-72, Fraternal Order Police, Evansville, 1982—; dir. Tri-State Food Bank, Evansville, 1987—; del. gen. synod Ind.-Ky. Conf., United Ch. of Christ, 1978-81. Religion columnist Evansville Press, 1983—. Vol. Habitat for Humanity, Americus, Ga., 1980-81; mem. City-County Human Rels. Commn., Evansville, 1984—; bd. dirs. Leadership Evansville, 1987—, Outreach Ministries, Evansville, 1987—; mem., regional bd. advisors Ch. World Svc., 1987—; mem. Ill. And Ind. Hunger Coalitions, mem. vol. and outreach svcs. Com. United Way, gifts-in-kind com.; mem. Bread for the World, Amnesty Internat., Food Rsch. and Action FRAC, Police Athletic League; sec. United ch. of Christ Day Shelter Bd. Recipient ecumenical award Evansville Area Coun. of Chs., 1987, Native Am. award Coun. of Bear, Evansville, 1988. Mem. NAACP, ACLU, Southwestern Ind. Psychol. Assn., Tri-State Pastors Circle (pres. 1984-85), Northside Ministerial Assn., Evansville Tri-State Assn. (pres. 1972-75), Greenpeace. Republican. Avocations: music, art, drama, dance performing, model railroading. Home: 217 Cherry St Evansville IN 47713

HOY, MICHAEL CHARLES, minister; b. Lewiston, Maine, Dec. 11, 1953; s. Charles Herman and Florence Ernestine (Brown) H.; m. Dawn Elizabeth Riske, Dec. 12, 1981; children: Martin Charles, Philip Robert. BA cum laude, Concordia Sr. Coll., Fort Wayne, Ind., 1975; MDiv, Christ Seminary-Seminex, St. Louis, 1979; ThM, Luth. Sch. Theology, Chgo., 1988, ThD, 1990. Ordained to ministry Luth. Ch., 1982. Vis. instr. theology Valparaiso (Ind.) U., 1979-80; chaplain Luther Coll. U. Regina, Sask., 1980-81; pastor St. John Luth. Ch., Snow Lake, Manitoba, 1981-83; visitation pastor St. James Luth. Ch., Chgo., 1986-88; interim pastor St. John's Luth. Ch., Wilmette, Ill., 1986-87; assoc. pastor Zion Luth. Ch., Wausau, Wis., 1990—. Theol. advisor Denominational Ministry Strategy, Pitts., 1985-87; active INFACT, Chgo., 1984-86. Mem. Jour. Bibl. Lit., Am. Acad. Religion. Home: 624 Grand St Wausau WI 54401

HOY, WILLIAM GLENN, pastor; b. Baton Rouge, Sept. 23, 1961; s. Edwin Willis and Lillie Mae (Coleman) H.; m. Debra Kay Coffey, July 23, 1988. BS in Social Scis., La. State U., 1984; MDiv, Golden Gate Sem., 1990. Minister coll. and single adults First So. Bapt. Ch., Long Beach, Calif., 1985-86, assoc. pastor, 1986-88; pastor Pacific Breeze Community Ch., Seal Beach, Calif., 1988—. Author: When You Have to Say Goodbye, 1991. Mem. Long Beach Bapt. Assn. (bd. dirs.), Found. of Thanatology. Avocation: gardening. Home: 21329 Rossford Ave Lakewood CA 90715 Office: Pacific Breeze Community Ch 6475 Pac Coast Hwy Ste 248 Long Beach CA 90803

HOY, WILLIAM IVAN, minister, educator; b. Grottoes, Va., Aug. 21, 1915; s. William I. and Ileta (Root) H.; student Lees-McRae Coll., 1933-34; BA, Hampden-Sydney Coll., 1936; BD, Union Theol. Sem., 1942; S.T.M., Bibl. Sem. N.Y., 1949; PhD, U. Edinburgh, 1952; m. Wilma J. Lambert, Apr. 29, 1945; children: Doris Lambert Hoy Bezanilla, Martha Virginia. Tchr. high sch., Va., 1936-39; interim pastor Asheboro (N.C.) Presbyn. Ch., 1948, 52-53; asst. prof. Bible, Guilford Coll., 1947-48; asst. prof. religion U. Miami, from 1953, prof., 1963—, chmn. dept. religion, 1958-79; cons. World Coun. Christian Edn., Lima, Peru, 1971. Moderator, Presbytery of Everglades, 1960-61, stated clk., 1968-73, 78-79; temporary stated clk. Presbytery of Tropical Fla., 1991—; moderator Synod of Fla., 1985-86; pres. Greater Miami Ministerial Assn., 1964, 80-82; mem. bd. Christian edn. Presbyn. Ch. U.S., 1969-73, mem. Gen. Assembly Mission Bd., 1978-88; bd. dirs. Met. Fellowship Chs., 1970—, v.p., 1972-73, exec. sec., 1974-76, mem. Task Force on World Hunger, 1978-81; trustee Davidson Coll., 1975-87; bd. dirs. South Fla. Ctr. for Theol. Studies; participant profl. internat. confs., Barcelona, Lausanne, Rome, Sydney, Goettingen, others, and three White House confs. for religious leaders. Served to comdr. USNR. Decorated Purple Heart; given keys to Cities of Miami Beach (twice) and Coral Gables, 1987; named to Honorable Order of Ky. Colonels. Mem. Soc. Bibl. Lit., Am. Acad. Religion, Am. Soc. Ch. History, Studiorum Novi Testamenti Societas, Scottish Ch. History Soc., Soc. for Sci. Study Religion, Religious Rsch. Assn., Internat. Assn. Historians of Religion, Internat. Conf. Sociology of Religion, Am. Oriental Soc., Internat. Sociol. Assn., Res. Officers Assn. (past nat. chaplain, nat. councilman 1965-66, pres. Fla. dept. 1965-66, v.p. for navy dept. Fla.), Seabee Vets. Am., Iron Arrow, Tiger Bay Club, Rotary (pres. S. Miami club 1991—), Phi Kappa Phi, Omicron Delta Kappa (province dep., mem. gen. council 1971-76, Disting. Service Key 1976, Robert L. Morlan Faculty Sec. nat. award 1990), Lambda Chi Alpha, Alpha Psi Omega, Theta Delta, Omega. Co-author: History of the Chaplains

Corps, USN, Volume 6; also articles and book revs. in various publs. Home: 5881 SW 52d Terr Miami FL 33155 Office: PO Box 248348 Coral Gables FL 33124 *It is better to fail at a worthy cause than to succeed at an unworthy one.*

HOYE, DANIEL FRANCIS, priest, organization administrator; b. Taunton, Mass., Jan. 18, 1946; s. Charles E. and Virginia (Cleary) H. BA, St. John's Sem., Brighton, Mass., 1968, ThM, 1972; licentiate in canon law, Cath. U., 1975. Ordained priest Roman Cath. Ch. Assoc. pastor Diocese of Fall River, Mass., 1972-73, vice officialis, 1975-77; assoc. gen. sec. Nat. Conf. Cath. Bishops, U.S. Cath. Ch., Washington, 1978-82, gen. sec., 1982—; bd. dirs. Cath. Relief Services, N.Y., 1982—, Cath. Telecommunications Network Am., 1982—. Mem. Canon Law Soc. Am., Canon Law Soc. Gt. Britain and Wales. Office: Nat Conf Cath Bishops 1312 Massachusetts Ave NW 6th Fl Washington DC 20005

HOYLAND, JANET LOUISE, clergyman; b. Kansas City, Mo., July 21, 1940; d. Robert J. and Dora Louise (Worley) H.; B.A., Carleton Coll., 1962; postgrad. in music (Mu Phi Epsilon scholar 1966), U. Mo. at Kansas City, 1964-67; M.L.A., So. Meth. U., 1979; MDiv, St. Paul Sch. Theology, 1986. Policy writer Lynn Ins. Co., Kansas City, 1963-64; music librarian U. Mo. at Kansas City, 1966-68; benefit authorizer Social Security Adminstrn., Kansas City, Mo., 1969-75, tech. specialist, 1976-79, claims authorizer, 1980-83; pastor Mercer United Meth. Ch., 1986-88, Adrian (Mo.) United Meth. Ch., 1988—; piano tchr. Leta Wallace Piano Studio, Kansas City, 1963, 68; piano accompanist Barn Players, Overland Park, Kans., 1972-75, Off Broadway Dinner Playhouse, Inc., Kansas City, 1973. Co-chmn. Project Equality work area, 1971; work area chmn. on ecumenism Council on Ministries, 1969-70; sec. fair housing action com. Council on Religion and Race, Kansas City, 1968; chmn. adminstrv. bd. Kairos United Meth. Ch., 1982; active ward and precinct work Democratic Com. for County Progress, 1968. Mem. Baton Soc. Kansas City Symphony, Friends of Art Kansas City, Fellowship House Assn. Kansas City, Internat. Platform Assn., Kansas City Mus. Club (chmn. composition dept. 1967-68), Lions Club (treas.), Mu Phi Epsilon (v.p. Kansas City 1968, sec. 1971, pres. 1975-76), Pi Kappa Lambda. Mailing Address: Adrian United Meth Ch 802 N Houston Adrian MO 64720

HOYT, JAMES EDWARD, church administrator, real estate broker; b. Chgo., Aug. 6, 1955; s. William Francis and Anna Marie (Hynes) H.; m. Patricia Marguerite Therese O'Mahony, Jan. 31, 1981; children: Christopher, Melissa, Michael, Rebecca. BA, Loyola U., Chgo., 1977; postgrad., Regis U., 1990—. Summer coord. St. Mary of the Lake Ch., Chgo., 1974-76; educator Sts. Peter and Paul Sch., Chgo., 1977-78; vol. Jesuit Community, Arequipa, Peru, 1978-79; parish adminstr. Christ the King Ch., Mesa, Ariz., 1985—; broker Hoyt Realty, Mesa, Ariz., 1988—. Mem. Nat. Assn. Ch. Bus. Adminstrs., Nat. Assn. Ch. Pers. Adminstrs., Adminstrs. Diocese of Phoenix (co-founder 1986), KC. Roman Catholic. Office: Christ the King Ch 1551 E Dana Ave Mesa AZ 85204

HOYT, SAMUEL LEROY, pastor; b. Jackson, Mich., Feb. 18, 1947; s. Malvern L. and Lois P. (Reynolds) H.; m. Elaine M. Lathrop, Aug. 15, 1969; children: David, Sarah, Paul. BS in Math., Mich. State U., 1969; MDiv, Western Conservative Bapt. Sem., Portland, Oreg., 1972, ThM in Bibl. Studies, 1973; ThD, Grace Theol. Sem., Winona Lake, Ind., 1977. Ordained to ministry, 1975. Youth pastor South Bapt. Ch., Lansing, Mich., 1974-77, asst. pastor, 1977-82; sr. pastor 1st Bapt. Ch., Romeo, Mich., 1982—. Contbr. articles to religious jours. and mags. Mem. Romeo Health Edn. Com., 1988—. Republican. Home: 68254 Wingate Dr Romeo MI 48065 Office: 1st Bapt Ch 7800 W Thirty Two Mile Rd Romeo MI 48065 *I find great satisfaction in doing the best I can with the gifts God has given me, in the time available. My motto is "Do a little thing in a fine way for a great God."*

HOYT, WILLIAM RUSSELL, III, religion and philosophy educator; b. Falling Springs, Va., Mar. 20, 1924; s. Samuel Browne and Virginia Carlisle (Brown) H.; m. Sara Ann Lippard, June 15, 1954; children: Nancy C., Jane Hoyt Leidlein, Harriette Russell Hoyt. AB, Davidson Coll., 1949; MDiv, Columbia Theol. Seminary, 1952; PhD, Duke U., 1962. Ordained to ministry Presbyn. Ch., 1954. Pastor North Gadsden and Rainbow Presbyn. Chs., Gadsden, Ala., 1952-54; minister to students Duke U., Durham, N.C., 1954-57; asst. to full Dana prof. of religion and philosophy Berry Coll., Rome, Ga., 1957—, head dept. religion and philosophy, 1957-86; moderator Cherokee Presbytery, Northwest Ga., 1971, 83; chmn. Synod of Ga. Guidance Coun., 1966-71; commr. to Presbyn. Gen. Assembly, 1963, 73; mem., chmn. various coms., Cherokee Presbytery; mem. campus ministry Synod of South Atlantic, 1991—. Contbg. author: Encyclopedia of Southern Religion, 1984; contbr. revs., articles to profl. jours. Vice-chmn. human rels. coun., Rome, 1973-78, bd. dirs. 1977-84; bd. dirs. Floyd County Unit Am. Cancer Soc., 1964-68. Sgt. U.S. Army Air Corp, 1943-46. Named Staff Mem. of Yr., Berry Coll. Student Body, 1963, Joseph J. Malone Fellow, Duke U., Cairo, 1984, Fulbright-Hayes Fellow, U.S. Dept. Edn., Beijing, Xian, Kunming, Shanghai, China, 1988; Lilly Found. grantee, Berry Coll., Kyoto, Japan, 1975. Mem. Am. Acad. Religion, AAUP, Am. Soc. Ch. History, Southeast Region Middle East and Islamic Seminaries, Danforth Assocs. Democrat. Avocations: jogging, automobiles, astronomy. Office: Dept Religion/Philosophy Mount Berry Sta Box 550 Rome GA 30149

HROMATKO, WESLEY VINTON, minister; b. Slayton, Minn., Oct. 2, 1947; s. Annel Jay and Maybelle (Moffatt) H. BA cum laude, U. Minn., 1969; MA, Meadville Theol. Sch., Chgo., 1971, D of Ministry, 1973. Ordained to ministry Unitarian Universalist Assn., 1973. Asst. min. 3d Unitarian Ch., Chgo., 1972-73, Unity Temple, Oak Park, Ill., 1972-73; min. Abraham Lincoln Fellowship, Springfield, Ill., 1972-73, Oaklandon (Ind.) Universalist Ch., 1973-75, 1st Unitarian Ch., Hobart, Ind., 1975-82, All Souls Ch., Braintree, Mass., 1982-85; bd. dirs., chmn. rligious edn. Ch. of the Larger Fellowship, Boston, 1983-86; assoc. min. Ch. of Larger Fellowship, Boston, 1985—; min. 1st Congl. Parish, Unitarian, Petersham, Mass., 1987-90; chaplain Oaklandon Vol. Fire Dept., 1973-74; mem. ind. justice project Unitarian-Universalist Svc. Com., 1973-74; mem. Ind. Unitarian-Universalist Legis. Conf., 1973-75; trustee Chgo. area Unitarian Universalist Coun., 1976-78. Co-editor: Appeal of the Irreligious, 1980. Mem. adv. coun. Religious Coalition for Abortion Rights, 1974-75; mem. Orgn. for Better Austin, Chgo., 1972, Braintree Hist. Soc., 1983-85, Protestant Social Svcs. Bur., 1983-85, North Braintree Civic Assn., 1984-85, Petersham Arts Coun., 1987-90, Hist. Soc. & Craft Ctr., Petersham Ecumenical Commn., Athol/Orange Food Bank, 1988-89; bd. dirs. Oaklandon Civc Assn., 1974-75, Ea. Lawrence Twp. Planning Commn., 1974-75; mem. Prairie Group program com. Save the Dunes Coun., 1973-82, Hobart Am. Revolutionary Bicentennial Commn. Recipient Entemann Ohanian award, 1975. Mem. ACLU (legal panel N.W. Ind. chpt. 1982-83), Unitarian-Universalist Mins. Assn., Cen. Midwest Unitarian Universalist Min.'s Assn. (sec. 1976, 83-85), Conn. Valley Dist. Mins. Assn., Prairie Star Dist. Mins. Assn., Meadville Theol. Sch. Alumni Assn. (life, treas. 1973-75), U. Minn. Alumni Assns. (life), Hobart Ministerial Assn. (past v.p.) Internat. Assn. Religious Freedom, Unitarian-Universalist Advance (former bd. dirs., v.p.), Universalist Hist. Soc., Indpls. Mental Health Assn., Ams. United (teas. Indpls. 1974-75), New Eng. Hist. Geneal. Soc., Unitarian-Universalist Geneal. Soc., Unitarian-Universalist Hist. Soc., North Quabbin Interfaith Clergy Assn. (past sec. 1988-90), others. Address: RR 1 Lake Wilson MN 56151 *The best advice I ever received was to hope for the best, prepare for the worst and take whatever comes.*

HUANG, KAI-LOO, religion educator emeritus; b. Indonesia, 1909; came to U.S., 1938; BA, Tsinghua, Beijing, 1934; MA, U. Wis., 1936, PhD, 1938. Prof. emeritus Moravian Coll., Bethlehem, Pa., 1965-84; lectr. comparative religions, Chinese religions. Contbr. articles to profl. jours. Home: PO Box 55788 Riverside CA 92517

HUBBARD, DAVID ALLAN, minister, educator, religious association administrator; b. Stockton, Calif., Apr. 8, 1928; s. John King and Helena (White) H.; m. Ruth Doyal, Aug. 12, 1949; 1 child, Mary Ruth. BA, Westmont Coll., Calif., 1949; BD, Fuller Theol. Sem., Pasadena, Calif., 1952, ThM, 1954; PhD, St. Andrews U., Scotland, 1957; DD (hon.), John Brown U., 1975; LHD (hon.), Rockford Coll., 1975, Hope Coll., 1990; DLitt (hon.), King Sejong U., Korea, 1985; EdD (hon.), Friends U., 1990. Ordained to ministry Conservative Bapt. Assn., 1952, Am. Bapt. Chs. in the U.S.A., 1984. Lectr. Old Testament studies St. Andrews U., 1955-56; asst. prof. Bibl. studies Westmont Coll., 1957, chmn. dept. Bibl. studies and philosophy, 1958-63; interim pastor Montecito (Calif.) Community Ch., 1960-62; pres., prof. Old Testament Fuller Theol. Sem., 1963—; exec. v.p. Fuller Evangelistic Assn., 1969—; Tyndale Old Testament lectr., Cambridge, Eng., 1965, Soc. Old Testament Studies lectr., London, 1971, lectr. numerous U.S. univs., 1973—. Speaker: internat. radio broadcast The Joyful Sound, 1969-80; author: With Bands of Love, 1968, (with others) Is God Dead?, 1966, Is Life Really Worth Living?, 1969, What's God Been Doing All This Time?, 1970, What's New?, 1970, Does the Bible Really Work?, 1971, Psalms for All Seasons, 1971, Is The Family Here To Stay?, 1971, The Practice of Prayer, 1972, Spanish edit., 1974, Chinese edit., 1979, How To Face Your Fears, 1972, The Holy Spirit in Today's World, 1973, Church—Who Needs It?, 1974, They Met Jesus, 1974, More Psalms for All Seasons, 1975, An Honest Search for a Righteous Life, 1975, Colossians Speaks to the Sickness of Our Time, 1976, Happiness: You Can Find the Secret, 1976, Beyond Futility, 1976, Chinese edit., 1982, Themes from the Minor Prophets, 1977, Strange Heroes, 1977, Galatians: Gospel of Freedom, 1977, Thessalonians: Life That's Radically Christian, 1977, Why Do I Have to Die?, 1978, How to Study the Bible, 1978, What We Evangelicals Believe, 1979, Book of James: Wisdom That Works, 1980, Right Living in a World Gone Wrong, 1981, German edit., 1982, Parables Jesus Told, 1981, (with Bush and LaSor) Old Testament Survey, 1982, The Practice of Prayer, 1982, The Second Coming, 1984, Proclamation 3: Pentecost 1, 1985, Unwrapping Your Spiritual Gifts, 1985, Holy Spirit in Today's World, 1986, Tyndale Commentary: Joel, Amos, 1987, Tyndale Commentary: Hosea, 1989, Communicator's Commentary: Proverbs, 1989, Ecclesiastes, Song of Solomon, WORD 1991; contbg. editor: Eternity mag.; mem. editorial bd. The Ministers' Permanent Library, 1976—; adv. bd. Evang. Book Club, 1977-86; contbr. articles to dictionaries, mags. Chmn. Pasadena Urban Coalition, 1968-71; mem. Calif. Bd. Edn., 1972-75; bd. dirs. Nat. Inst. Campus Ministries, 1974-78. Mem. Nat. Assn. Bapt. Profs. Religion, Nat. Assn. Profs. Hebrew, Am. Acad. Religion, Soc. Bibl. Lit., Soc. for Old Testament Study, Inst. Bibl. Rsch., Assn. Theol. Schs. in U.S. and Can. (exec. com. 1972—, pres. 1976-78), Fuller Evang. Assn. (trustee 1969—, exec. v.p. 1969-82), Twilight Club of Pasadena, Univ. Club of Pasadena, Rotary (hon. mem. Pasadena club). Office: Fuller Theol Sem 135 N Oakland Ave Pasadena CA 91182

HUBBARD, HOWARD JAMES, bishop; b. Troy, N.Y., Oct. 31, 1938; s. Howard James and Elizabeth D. (Burke) H. B.A., St. Joseph's Sem., Yonkers, N.Y.; S.T.L., Gregorian U., Rome; D.D. (hon.), Siena Coll., 1977; L.H.D. (hon.), Coll. St. Rose, 1977. Ordained priest Roman Catholic Ch., 1963; bishop of Albany N.Y., 1977—; former parish priest St. Joseph's Ch., Schenectady; parish priest Cathedral Parish, Albany; asst. dir. Cath. Charities, Schenectady; chaplain Convent of the Sacred Heart, Kenwood, Albany; dir. Providence House, Albany; vicar gen. Diocese of Albany; dir. Cath. Interracial Council; coordinator Urban Apostolate. Pres. Urban League. Address: 465 State St Box 6297 Quail Sta Albany NY 12206

HUBBARD, ROBERT LOUIS, JR., religion educator; b. Reedley, Calif., July 3, 1943; s. Robert Louis and Verna Alexander (Carlson) H.; m. Pamela Joan Iverson, June 28, 1969; children: Matthew, Benjamin. AB in Psychology, Wheaton (Ill.) Coll., 1965; BD, Fuller Seminary, Pasadena, Calif., 1969; MA in Religion, Claremont (Calif.) Grad. Sch., 1977, PhD in Religion, 1980. Ordained to ministry Evang. Free Ch., 1970. Youth pastor Evang. Free Ch., Covina, Calif., 1969-70; dir. publs. Gospel Broadcasting Assn., Pasadena, 1969-70; pastor Evang. Free Ch., Hemet, Calif., 1974-76; prof. Old Testament Denver Seminary, 1976—; mem. Chaplain Resource Bd., Washington, 1990—; bd. dirs. Urban Acad., Denver, 1987—; editorial bd.: Theol. Students Fellowship, Madison, Wis., 1976-87. Author: The Book of Ruth, 1988 (critics award 1989); contbr. articles to profl. jours. Chaplain USNR, 1970-74. Mem. Soc. Bibl. Lit., Inst. for Bibl. Rsch. (exec. bd. 1980-83, 85-87), Evang. Free Ch. Ministerial Assn. Republican. Home: 6837 S Birch Way Littleton CO 80122 Office: Denver Seminary 3401 S University Blvd Englewood CO 80110 *Life's best treasures are faith, family, friends and meaningful work. And nothing beats receiving a warm smile, firm hug, or "Well done." I love to give and receive them all.*

HUBER, DONALD LESTER, theology educator; b. Columbus, Ohio, Sept. 19, 1940; s. Lester William and Lillian Virginia (Dierker) H.; m. Shirley Ann Lemke, Aug. 22, 1965; children: Michael Stuart, Melinda Sue, Mark Stephen. AB, Capital U., 1962; BDiv, Evang. Luth. Theol. Sem., 1966; PhD, Duke U., 1971; MLS, U. Mich., 1973. Instr. in ch. history Evang. Luth. Theol. Sem., Columbus, 1969-72, libr., 1973-78; libr. Trinity Luth. Sem., Columbus, 1978-91, prof. ch. history, 1991—; vis. lectr. Luth. Sem., Adelaide, South Australia, 1986-87; bd. div. for ministry Evang. Luth. Ch. in Am., Chgo. Author: Educating Lutheran Pastors in Ohio, 1830-1980, 1989; contbr. articles to profl. jours. Danforth Found. apprentice teaching fellow Duke U., 1967-69. Mem. Am. Soc. Ch. History, Am. Theol. Libr. Assn. (conf. host 1989), Luth. Hist. Conf. (treas. 1978-82). Office: Trinity Luth Sem 2199 E Main St Columbus OH 43209

HUBER, SISTER MARGARET ANN, college president; b. Rochester, Pa., July 27, 1949; d. Francis Xavier and Mary Ann (Socash) H. B.S. in Chemistry, Duquesne U., 1972; M.S.A., U. Notre Dame, 1975; Ph.D., U. Mich., 1979. Joined Sisters of Divine Providence of Pittsburgh, Pa.; jr. high tchr. St. Martin Sch., Pitts., 1971-72; asst. to acad. dean LaRoche Coll., Pitts., 1972-75; research assoc. U. Mich., Ann Arbor, 1978; dir. planning LaRoche Coll., 1978-80, exec. v.p., 1980-81, pres., 1981—. Mem. Am. Assn. for Higher Edn. Democrat. Roman Catholic. Office: LaRoche Coll 9000 Babcock Blvd Pittsburgh PA 15237-5828

HUBERT, BERNARD, bishop; b. Beloeil, Que., Can., June 1, 1929. Ed., U. Ottawa, Columbia U. Ordained priest Roman Catholic Ch., 1953; bishop of St. Jerome, 1971-77; coadjutor bishop Saint-Jean-de-Que., 1977-78; bishop of St.-Jean-de-Que., now St.-Jean-Longueil, 1978—; pres., Can. Conf. Catholic Bishops. Address: 740 Boul Ste Foy CP 40, Longueuil, PQ Canada J4K 4X8

HUBIAK, DANIEL, clergyman; b. Akron, Ohio, Dec. 29, 1926; s. Athanasius and Susan (Wanchishen) H.; m. Evelyn Martynuk, Sept. 16, 1951; children—Larice, Annice. B.S., Columbia U., 1952; B.S. diploma grad. studies theology, St. Vladimir's Orthodox Theol. Sem., N.Y.C., 1956. Ordained priest Orthodox Ch. in Am., 1952; asst. pastor Holy Trinity Ch., Detroit, 1952-53; pastor St. Mary Ch., Marblehead, Ohio, 1953-55; asst. pastor Holy Transfiguration Ch., Bklyn., 1956-58; pastor Holy Trinity Ch., East Meadow, N.Y., 1958-70; treas. Orthodox Ch. Am., Syosset, N.Y., 1963-70; sec.-treas. Orthodox Ch. Am., 1970-73, chancellor, 1973—. Trustee St. Vladimir's Orthodox Theol. Sem., Crestwood, N.Y., St. Tikhon's Theol. Sem., South Canaan, Pa. Served with AUS, 1945-46. Office: PO Box 675 Syosset NY 11791

HUBLER, MYRON J., JR., religious educator; b. Columbus, Ohio, Feb. 29, 1928; s. Myron J. and Alice (Lockwood) H.; m. Sarah Ramsey, Mar. 14, 1953; children: Myron III, Leigh Alice, Lynn Helen, William Ramsey. BS in Acctg., Ohio State U., 1952; MBA, Case Western Res. U., 1968; postgrad., U. Akron; cert. ministry, Berean Coll., Springfield, Mo., 1987. CPA, Ohio. With audit and tax depts. Ernst & Ernst, Cleve., 1955-62; various positions Reliance Electric Co., Cleve., 1965-70; project mgr. AICPA, N.Y.C., 1970-74; chief div. fin. statistics bur. econs. FTC, Washington, 1974-75; asst. prof. acctg. Cleve. State U., 1975-82, Akron U., 1982-85; assoc. prof. acctg. Houghton Coll., N.Y., 1989; chmn., founder Agape Sch., Inc., Sta. WCVJ-FM, Jefferson, Ohio, 1974; adj. prof., lectr. Am. U., Washington, Columbia U., N.Y.C., Cuyahoga Community Coll., Cleve., Ohio State U., Columbus, Pace U., N.Y.C., Seton Hall U., Orange, N.J.; adv. coun. Salvation Army, Cleve., 1974-80; communications com. Cleve. Inner Ch. Coun., 1978-80. Contbr. articles to profl. jours. Active Right to Life, Ashtabula, Ohio, Washington for Jesus, 1980, 88. Martha Holden Jennings Found. grantee, 1982-83. Mem. Nat. Religious Broadcasters Assn., Regional Religious Broadcasters Assn., NAB, Am. Acctg. Assn., Ohio Soc. CPAs. Home: PO Box 244 Jefferson OH 44047 Office: Agape Sch Inc Jefferson OH 60089

HUBNER, DAVID PETER, minister; b. New Brunswick, N.J., Aug. 22, 1940; s. George Christopher and Sara Johnson H.; m. Michael Mary Kehoe; 1 child, Benjamin. AB, Rutger's U., 1962; MDiv, Harvard U., 1974. Ordained with fellowship status Unitarian Universalist Assn., 1974. Min. Unitarian Universalist Ch., Hudson, Mass., 1974-80, First Ch. in Dedham, Mass., 1980-88; dir. ch. staff fins. Unitarian Universalist Assn., Boston, 1988—. Lt. USNR, 1962-65. Democrat. Home: 45 Sheridan Rd Wellesley MA 02181 Office: Unitarian Universalist Assn 25 Beacon St Boston MA 02108

HUCKABA, JAMES ALLEN, pastor; b. Missoula, Mont., Sept. 1, 1946; s. Marion Allen and Edith (Giesel) H.; m. Linda G. Grafmiller; children: Paul David, Thomas Matthew, Jonathan Michael. BTh, N.W. Christian Coll., 1969; MDiv, Western Bapt. Sem., 1972; ThD, So. Bible Sem., 1977. Ordained to ministry Christian Ch., 1972. Youth min. Hillsboro (Oreg.) Christian Ch., 1969-72; pastor First Christian Ch., Coquille, Oreg., 1972-76, Buhl, Idaho, 1977-80; pastor Dinuba (Calif.) Christian Ch., 1981—; assoc. in edn. Emmanuel Sch. Religion, Johnson City, Tenn., 1977-90, trustee, 1990—, N.W. Christian Coll., Eugene, 1984—, trustee, 1984. Author: After You Dry Off, 1982, (with others) Lifting Up Jesus, 1989. Scoutmaster Boy Scouts Am., Mt. Whitney Coun., 1982—; mem. adv. com. to dist. supt. Dinuba Pub. Schs., 1983-87. Mem. Dinuba Ministerial Assn. (sec. 1986-90, pres., 1991—). Office: Dinuba Christian Ch 355 Saginaw Box 726 Dinuba CA 93618

HUCKABEE, MICHAEL DALE, minister; b. Hope, Ark., Aug. 24, 1955; m. Janet McCain, May 25, 1974; children: John Mark, David, Sarah. BA in Religion magna cum laude, Ouachita Bapt. U., Arkadelphia, Ark., 1976; postgrad., Southwestern Bapt. Theol. Sem., Ft. Worth, 1976-77. Ordained to ministry So. Bapt. Conv., 1974. Pastor Walnut Street Bapt. Ch., Arkadelphia, 1974-75; with James Robison Evangelistic Assn., other ministries, 1975-80; pastor Immanuel Bapt. Ch., Pine Bluff, Ark., 1980-85; evangelist various Christian ministries; dir. communications James Robison Evangelism Assn.; pastor Beech Street 1st Bapt. Ch., Texarkana, Ark., 1986—; founder, past pres. Am. Christian TV System, Pine Bluff, Texarkana, pres., Ark., 1985; pres. Ark. Bapt. Conv., 1989—, pres. Pastor's Conf., 1985-86; mem. com. on coms. So. Bapt. Conv., 1987, chmn. program com., 1988-89; chmn. evangelism SW Ark. Bapt. Assn.; past vice moderator Hramony Bapt. Assn., also past chmn. evangelism com., mem. nominating and bldg. coms.; mem. promotion com. Fgn. Mission Bd. Appointment Svc.; mem. adv. bd. So. Bapts. for Life; numerous others. Weekly newspaper columnist Positive Alternatives. Former bd. govs. Ark. Boys State; former county coord. Unborn Child Amendment Com., Pine Bluff; former pres., bd. dirs. Jefferson County unit Am. Cancer Soc.; former participant, bd. dirs. Leadership Pine Bluff; bd. dirs. B.O.N.D., bus. orgn. for new downtown, Texarkana, Friendship Ctr., Texarkana; mem. allocations com. United Way Texarkana; mem. citizen's adv. com. Texarkana Sch. Bd.; mem. adv. com. Wadley Regional Med. Ctr., Texarkana; speaker to numerous chs., schs. and bus. orgns. Mem. Nat. Religious Broadcasters, Texarkana Ministerial Alliance (TV chmn.), Texarkana C. of C. Home: 2 Cambridge Dr Texarkana TX 75502 Office: Beech Street 1st Bapt Ch 601 Beech St Texarkana TX 75502 *It's my hope that Christians of America could rediscover that our faith is based on a relationship with God instead of a mere ritual about God. We are malnourished on grace and overfed on selfish sainthood.*

HUCKABY, TERI LYNN, minister; b. Frankfurt, Fed. Republic Germany, Feb. 7, 1962; d. Irvin Glen and Carolyn Louise (Hiatt) Blevins; m. Timothy Carl Huckaby, Sept. 3, 1988. BS in Pub. Adminstrn., U. Ariz., 1985; MDiv, Golden Gate Sem., 1988. Ordained to ministry Am. Bapt. Chs. in U.S.A., 1990. Youth intern Casas Adobes Bapt. Ch., Tucson, 1983-85; dir. Christian edn. Am. Canyon Bapt. Ch., Vallejo, Calif., 1985-88, assoc. pastor, 1988-89; assoc. pastor 1st Bapt. Ch., Lemoore, Calif., 1989-90, interim pastor, 1990-91; pastor Reno Community Bapt. Ch., 1991—; mem. bd. women in ministry Am. Bapt. Chs., Oakland, Calif., 1991. Mem. Minister's Coun., Lemmore Minister's Assn. (spl. program dir. 1989-91), Inst. for Biblical Preaching, Am. Kennel Club. Republican. Office: Reno Community Bapt Ch 1001 Wheeler Ave Reno NV 89502

HUDDLESTON, DAVID WINFIELD, minister; b. Harrodsburg, Ky., Oct. 15, 1943; s. James Irvin Sr. and Lucile (Gabhart) H.; m. Edie Combs, Aug. 5, 1972; children: Sean Jameson, Heather Anne, Amy Elizabeth. BA, U. Ky., 1971; MDiv, Trinity Theol. Sem., 1988. Ordained to ministry Am. Evang. Christian Ch., 1991. Interim pastor Willow Springs United Meth. Ch., Liberty, Ky., 1984; dir. evangelism and youth First United Meth. Ch., Naples, Fla., 1985-86; asst. min. Lely Presbyn. Ch., Naples, Fla., 1986-88; ind. evang. min. Naples, Fla., 1989-91; founder Maranatha Ministries Internat., Naples, 1991—; del. Stephen Ministries Leadership Tng., Leesburg, Fla., 1986; officer Naples Ministerial Assn., 1987; mem. Naples Pro-Life Coun., Naples Evang. Ministerial Fellowship. Candidate for state rep. Dist. 75 Rep. Orgn., Naples, 1990; organizer Ecumenical Mission, Jamaica, W.I., 1987. Mem. Nat. Right to Life, Fla. Right to Life, Rotary. Home and Office: 3533 Balboa Circle Naples FL 33942 *I believe that the task of proclaiming the Gospel is more vital and critical today than at any time in history. The turbulent events unfolding in the Middle East are taking place in that part of world where history began and where history, as we know it, will end. God is calling all (who are willing) to sow the seeds of Christianity and reap His harvest with a renewed sense of urgency.*

HUDDLESTON, JOSEPH WAYNE, minister; b. East Chicago, Ind., July 9, 1948; s. LaVerne Wright Huddleston and Helen Irene (Richey) Peters; m. Janet Elaine Huey, June 19, 1971; children: Jonathan, Jadon. BA in Religion cum laude, Olivet Nazarene U., 1970; MDiv cum laude, Nazarene Theol. Sem., 1975. Ordained to ministry Ch. of Nazarene, 1987. Asst. pastor 1st Ch. of Nazarene, Hutchinson, Kans., 1976-79; mgr. of communication and info. Bd. Pensions and Benefits Ch. of Nazarene, Kansas City, Mo., 1979—. Contbr. articles to profl. jours. Mem. Phi Delta Lambda. Avocations: reading, carpentry, computers. Office: Ch of the Nazarene 6401 The Paseo Kansas City MO 64131

HUDGENS, RICHARD WAYNE, minister; b. Charlotte, N.C., Feb. 13, 1955; s. Paul Richard and Dora Mae (Cooke) H.; m. Sharron Marie Wiltshire, June 9, 1978; children: Danielle Marie, Stephanie Nicole. BA, Cen. Wesleyan Coll., 1977; postgrad., Bethany Sem., 1984—. Ordained elder Wesleyan Ch., 1980. Assoc. pastor St. Paul Wesleyan Ch., Charlotte, N.C., 1977-81; min. of youth Christian Fellowship Ch., Vienna, Va., 1981-84, div. pastor, teaching ministries, 1984, exec. pastor, 1985—; evangelist, workshop leader for youth, interdenomination ministries, U.S., Can., 1977—; youth camp evangelist, workshop leader, U.S., Can., 1977—. Contbr. articles to profl. jours. Mem. clergy task force Wesleyan Ch., Charlotte, 1978; pres. Wesleyan Youth, Washington, 1982-83; mem. exec. com. Christian Ams. for Republic of South Africa. Recipient Outstanding Leadership award DAR, 1973; named one of Outstanding Young Men Am., U.S. Jaycees, 1980, 83, 85, 86, 87. Office: Christian Fellowship Ch 10237 Leesburg Pike Vienna VA 22182

HUDGINS, DUDLEY RODGER, pharmaceutical company official; b. Chgo., Nov. 4, 1937; s. Dudley Wallace and Helen (Sterling) H.; BA in Psychology, Kans. U., 1959; m. Pegge Resch, Aug. 8, 1975; children: Brian, Randy; stepchildren: Todd Woods, Mianne Woods. With Marion Labs., Inc., 1961—, tng. mgr., also bids and contracts mgr., 1970-72, dir. pharm. div., 1972-82, dir. sales tng. and devel. for entire co., Kansas City, Mo., 1982-89; dir. sales tng. and devel. prescription div. Marion Merrell Dow U.S.A (merger Marion Labs and Merrell Dow Pharms.), 1989—; cons. in field. Pres. Zion Luth. Ch., 1980; condr. chapel svc. City Union Mission, Kansas City; chaplain U.S. Naval Sea Cadets, Prairie Schooner Squadron, Olathe, Kans. With AUS, 1960. Recipient Nat. Builder's award Marion Labs., 1979, 85, Marion Presdl. award, 1985. Mem. Nat. Soc. Pharm. Sales Trainers (hon. life, chpt. pres. 1978-79, nat. pres. 1979-80). Home: 511 W 123d Terr Kansas City MO 64145 Office: Marion Merrell Dow 10236 Bunker Ridge Rd Kansas City MO 64137

HUDLEY, JAMES C., minister; b. Albany, Ga., Nov. 23, 1943; s. James Jones (stepfather) and Corine (Johnson) J.; m. Sandra Lorraine Chislom, Aug. 22, 1969; 1 child, Sheerah Lorraine. AA, Freed-Hardeman Coll., 1970; BA, Union U., Jackson, Tenn., 1972; postgrad., Harding Grad. Sch. Religion, Memphis, 1978-79. Ordained to ministry Ch. of Christ, 1972. Min. Ch. of Christ, Baumholder, Fed. Republic Germany, 1965-67, Selmer, Tenn., 1969-70, Bolivar, Tenn., 1970-72, Memphis, 1972—; aux. probation officer Memphis Juvenile Ct., 1975—. Bd. dirs. Whitehaven SW Mental Health Ctr., Memphis, 1973-82, Mid-South Christian Nursing Home, Memphis,

1984-89, West Tenn. AGAPE, child placement agy., Memphis, 1983-89, Exch. Club Child Abuse Prevention Ctr., Memphis, 1991—; elections officer, Memphis, 1975-82, election insp., 1982—; mem. alumni bd. dirs. Freed-Hardeman Coll., Henderson, Tenn., 1978-80. Sgt. U.S. Army, 1964-67. Recipient Officer of Yr. Juvenile Ct., 1984. Home: 385 Byron Dr Memphis TN 38109

HUDNUT, ROBERT KILBORNE, clergyman, author; b. Cin., Jan. 7, 1934; s. William Herbert and Elizabeth (Kilborne) H.; m. Janet Lee Morlan; children by previous marriage—Heidi, Robert Kilborne, Heather, Matthew. B.A. with highest honors, Princeton, 1956; M.Div., Union Theol. Sem., N.Y.C., 1959. Ordained to ministry Presbyn. Ch., 1959; asst. minister Westminster Presbyn. Ch., Albany, N.Y., 1959-62; minister St. Luke Presbyn. Ch., Wayzata, Minn., 1962-73, Winnetka (Ill.) Presbyn. Ch., 1975—; exec. dir. Minn. Pub. Interest Research Group, 1973-75; Co-chmn. Minn. Joint Religious Legis. Coalition, 1970-75. Author: Surprised by God, 1967, A Sensitive Man and the Christ, 1971, A Thinking Man and the Christ, 1971, The Sleeping Giant: Arousing Church Power in America, 1971, An Active Man and the Christ, 1972, Arousing the Sleeping Giant: How to Organize Your Church for Action, 1973, Church Growth Is Not the Point, 1975, The Bootstrap Fallacy: What The Self-Help Books Don't Tell You, 1978, This People-This Parish, 1986, Meeting God in the Darkness, 1989. Pres. Greater Met. Fedn. Twin Cities, 1970-72; chmn. Citizens Adv. Com. on Interstate 394, 1971-75; nat. chmn. Presbyns. for Ch. Renewal, 1971; Chmn. Democratic Party 33d Senatorial Dist. Minn., 1970-72, Minnetonka Dem. Party, 1970-72; fusion candidate for mayor, Albany, 1961; Bd. dirs. Minn. Council Chs., 1964-70; trustee Princeton U., 1972-76, Asheville (N.C.) Sch., 1979—. Rockefeller fellow, 1956; named Outstanding Young Man Minnetonka, 1967; recipient Distinguished Service award Minnetonka Tchrs. Assn., 1969. Mem. Phi Beta Kappa. Home: 1078 Elm St Winnetka IL 60093 Office: 1255 Willow Rd Winnetka IL 60093

HUDSON, HILLIARD CLYDE, minister; b. Brownsville, Tenn., Feb. 22, 1954; s. Clyde and Gessana (Minor) H.; m. Mirta Angelita Gibbs, Dec. 29, 1979; children: Shayla, Brandon, Saunya, Christopher, Kristina. BA in Acctg., Millikin U., 1976; AB in Christian Edn., La. Theol. Sem., 1979; postgrad., No. Bapt. Theol. Sem., Lombard, Ill., 1991—. Ordained to ministry Nat. Bapt. Conv., U.S.A., 1983. Assoc. pastor St. Paul's Bapt. Ch., Decatur, Ill., 1975-80; asst. pastor Canaan Bapt. Ch., Urbana, Ill., 1980-84; pastor Pilgrim Bapt. Ch. South Chgo., 1985—; mem. Greater Era Dist. Chgo., 1985—, auditor, 1990—; mem. Bapt. Gen. State Conv. Ill., 1975—; instr. GNE Congress Christian Edn., Chgo., 1985—; state instr. Bapt. Gen. State Congress Christian Edn., 1985—; lectr. Bapt. Mins. Conf., Chgo., 1991—. Trustee SE Chgo. Housing Orgn., 1986-87. Recipient Religious Leader award South Chgo. Orgnized People Efforts, 1988. Democrat. Home: 9340 S Essex Ave Chicago IL 60617 Office: Pilgrim Bapt Ch South Chgo 3235 E 91st St Chicago IL 60617

HUDSON, LES EUGENE, minister; b. Mattoon, Ill., Sept. 12, 1961; s. David Richard and Mary Ina (McPherson) H.; m. Michelle Lynn Schraer, July 9, 1988. BS, Ea. Ill. U., 1984; postgrad., So. Bapt. Theol. Sem., 1987-88, Ky. Christian Coll., 1990—. Ordained to ministry Indiana Ind. Christian Ch., 1990. Dir. program and Christian edn. 1st United Meth. Ch., Henderson, Ky., 1986; dir. youth and Christian edn. Zion United Ch. of Christ, Louisville, 1987-88; min. youth Greenville (Ind.) Christian Ch., 1989-91; assoc. min. Franklin Hts. Christian Ch., Vincennes, Ind., 1991—; exec. dir., pres. Henderson Community Outreach Ministries, 1986; v.p. Scenic Hills Christian Camp, Mitchell, Ind., 1990, pres., 1991. Bd. dirs. Am. Cancer Soc., Henderson, 1986, Christian Campus House, Vincennes (Ind.) U., 1991—. Campbell scholar, 1990. Home: 205 State Rd 67 # 57 Vincennes IN 47591 Office: Franklin Hts Christian Ch 1509 Franklin Dr Vincennes IN 47591

HUDSON, REBEKAH JANE (BEKI HUDSON), religious organization officer; b. Clinton, Okla., Feb. 23, 1962; d. John H. and Juanita Lee (McFarland) Tharp; m. Stephan R. Hudson, Feb. 28, 1981; children: Jacob Lee, Adam Garbiel. Ordained to ministry Salvation Army, 1986. Asst. corps officer The Salvation Army, Huntsville, Ala., 1986-87; corps officer The Salvation Army, Birmingham, Ala., 1987-89, Biloxi, Miss., 1989-91, Lake Charles, La., 1991—. Vol. 12 Days of Christmas, Sta. WLOX-TV, Biloxi, 1990. Office: The Salvation Army 4200 Kirkman St Lake Charles LA 70605

HUDSON, RICHARD LLOYD, retired educator, clergyman; b. Watertown, N.Y., Dec. 1, 1920; s. Milo Alfred and Marion (Davidson) H.; AB, Syracuse U., 1944; BD, Yale U., 1947, STM, 1950; PhD, Syracuse U., 1970; m. Beatrice Evalin Olson, Apr. 23, 1955; children: Margery Elise, Pamela Kristine. Ordained to ministry United Methodist Ch., 1947; asst. minister Rome (N.Y.) Meth. Ch., 1946-48, Meth. Ch., Parish, N.Y., 1950-54; dir. pub. rels. Syracuse Area United Meth. Ch., 1954-56; minister Meth. Ch., Carthage, N.Y., 1956-58; Cokesbury fellow, grad. asst. Syracuse U., 1958-61; mem. faculty Wyoming Sem., Kingston, Pa., 1961-64; mem. faculty New Eng. Coll., Henniker, N.H., 1964-83, prof., 1971-83, prof. emeritus, 1983—, acting dean div. humanities, 1970-71, chmn. Am. studies, 1972-79, coord. liberal studies, 1981-83, prof. emeritus, 1983—; adj. prof. history Post Coll., Waterbury, Conn., 1985-91, Quinnipiac Coll., Hamden, Conn., 1987—; resident mgr. The Old Homestead, North Haven, Conn., 1983—. Chmn., Henniker Historic Dist. Commn., 1976-83; docent Canterbury Shaker Village, 1975-83, New Haven Colony Hist. Soc., 1984—, bd. dirs., 1988-90. Author: A Burden for Souls, 1950; A Student's Guide to the New Testament, 1963; The Challenge of Dissent, 1970; editor: The Only Henniker on Earth, 1980. Home and Office: 44 Cloudland Rd North Haven CT 06473

HUDSON, WINTHROP STILL, minister, history educator; b. 1911; s. Grant Martin and Mildred (Gilchrist) H.; m. Mildred Lois Austin, June 23, 1934; children: Judith Ann, Susan Camille. BA, Kalamazoo Coll., 1933, DD (hon.), 1958; BD, Colgate Rochester Divinity Sch., 1937; PhD, U. Chgo., 1940; DD (hon.), Franklin Coll., 1978, McMaster U., Hamilton, Ont., Can., 1982. Ordained to ministry Bapt. Ch., 1937; minister York (N.Y.) Ch., 1935-37, Normal Park Ch., Chgo., 1937-42; instr. Colgate Rochester Divinity Sch., 1942-44, adminstrv. assoc., 1947-48, James B. Colgate prof. history of Christianity, 1948-77, Disting. Sem. prof., 1977-80; prof. history U. Rochester, 1970-77; asst. prof. U. Chgo., 1944-47; vis. scholar U. N.C., 1979-80, adj. prof., 1980—. Author: John Ponet-Advocate of Limited Monarchy, 1942, The Great Tradition of the American Churches, 1953, The Story of the Christian Church, 1958, Understanding Roman Catholicism, 1959, American Protestantism, 1961, Religion in America, 1965, 4th rev. edit., 1986, Nationalism and Religion in America, 1970, Baptists in Transition, 1979, The Cambridge Connection and the Elizabethan Settlement, 1980; editor: Christian Leadership in a World Society, 1946, Henry Scougal's Life of God in the Soul of Man, 1948, Roger Williams Experiments of Spiritual Life and Health, 1951, Baptist Concepts of the Church, 1959, Walter Rauschenbusch: Selected Writings, 1984; subject of work: In the Great Tradition, Essays in Honor of Winthrop S. Hudson on Pluralism, Voluntarism and Revivalism, 1982, Foundations: Essays in Honor of Winthrop S. Hudson, 1980. Recipient Susan Colver Rosenberg award for meritorious research, 1940; Nat. Endowment for Humanities sr. fellow, 1975; named Alumnus of Yr. U. Chgo. Divinity Sch., 1981. Mem. Am. Soc. Ch. History (pres. 1948, sec. 1955-60), Am. Bapt. Hist. Soc. (pres. 1955-66), Am. Hist. Assn. Home: 211 Second St NW Apt 1117 Rochester MN 55901

HUDSON, YEAGER, philosophy educator, minister; b. Meridian, Miss., Aug. 14, 1931; s. William Ernest and Effie (Yeager) H.; m. Margaret Louise Hight, Dec. 20, 1953; children: Paul Brinton, Gareth Yeager. A.B., Millsaps Coll., 1954; S.T.B., Boston U., 1958, Ph.D., 1965; M.A. (hon.), Colby Coll., 1977. Ordained to ministry United Methodist Ch., 1963. Instr. Colby Coll., 1959-65, asst. prof. philosophy, 1965-70, assoc. prof., 1970-77, prof., chmn. dept. philosophy, 1977-89; Fulbright lectr. Ahnednager Coll., (India), 1967-68. Author: Emerson and Tagore: The Poet as Philosopher, 1988, Philosophy of Religion, 1990; editor: Profile of a College, 1972, Philosophy of Religion: Selected Readings, 1991; co-editor: Revolution, Violence and Equality, 1990, Philosophical Essays on the Ideas of a Good Society, Terrorism, Justice and Social Values, 1991. Mem. Am. Philos. Assn., N.Am. Soc. for Social Philosophy (bd. officers), Am. Inst. Indian Studies (trustee 1980—), Assn. Asian Studies. Office: Colby Coll Dept Philosophy and Religion Waterville ME 04901 *There is widespread agreement among the thinkers and seers of nearly every society concerning the highest ideals according to which humans should live. The tregedy is that we still lack the moral will to put our ideals into effect in practical international affairs.*

HUDSON-KNAPP, MARSHALL RALPH, minister; b. Bennington, Vt., July 16, 1949; s. Ronald Ralph and Frances Evelyn (Marshall) Knapp; m. Lucinda Jean Hudson, June 23, 1973; children: Naomi Ruth, Moses James. BA cum laude, Lone Mountain Coll., 1973; MDiv, Pacific Sch. Religion, 1975. Ordained to ministry United Ch. of Christ, 1975. Chaplain intern Med. Ctr. Hosp. Vt., Burlington, 1973; asst. pastor Rockland Area Ministry, Roscoe, N.Y., 1974; pastor Orleans Federated Ch., Vt., 1975-80, Brownington Congl. Ch., Vt., 1975-80, 1st Congl. Ch. United Ch. of Christ, Fair Haven, Vt., 1980—; founding mem. com. on healing ministry Vt. conf. United Ch. of Christ, 1976-85, alt. del. gen. synod United Ch. of Christ, 1985-88; cert. trainer Calling and Caring Ministry, Princeton Sem., 1984—. Author: Clothes for Celebrating Good News, 1974. V.p. Orleans County Coun. Social Agys. Newport, Vt., 1975-80; pres. Fair Haven Concerned, Inc., 1983—; bd. dirs. Apple Tree Children's Ctr., Castleton, Vt., 1981-83. Mem. Order St. Luke (chaplain 1982-88), Bros. and Sisters of the Way (able brother), Greenpeace, Nat. Resource Def. Coun. Democrat. Home: 19 West St Fair Haven VT 05743 Office: First Congl Ch United Ch of Christ North Park Pl Fair Haven VT 05743 *To think about God is wonderful. To experience Jesus and to allow the Holy Spirit to work through you can transform you and the world around you.*

HUEBNER, KATHLEEN MARY, foundation executive; b. Easthampton, Mass., Apr. 26, 1945; d. Herbert J. and Mary Ann (Stepnowski) H. MusB, Seton Hill Coll., Greensburg, Pa., 1967; MEd, U. Pitts., 1970, PhD, 1980. Cert. tchr., Pa. Tchr. orientation and mobility Greater Pitts. Guild for Blind, Bridgeville, Pa., 1967-78; sr. teaching fellow U. Pitts., 1978-80; substitute tchr. Westren Pa. Sch. for Blind, Pitts., 1978-80; asst. prof. SUNY, Geneseo, 1980-83; nat. cons. in edn. Am. Found. for Blind, N.Y.C., 1983-85, asst. dir. nat. cons., 1986-87, dir. nat. cons., 1987—; guest lectr. numerous colls. and univs., 1980—, including Pa. Coll. Optometry, Calif. State U., L.A., U. Tex., Austin, U. Ariz., San Jose State U.; mem. adv. com. tchr. preparation program Boston Coll., 1983-85; mem. adv. com. spl. edn. program vision program U. Tex., 1983-90; reviewer grant awards March of Dimes, 1986; mem. adv. com. VA Med. Ctr., Atlanta, 1989; chmn. Coalition for Info. Access for print-handicapped Readers, 1988-90; peer reviewer Spl. Net, 1989—. Editor: Skills To Thrive Not Just Survive, 1987; co-editor: Program Planning and Evaluation for Blind and Visually Impaired Students: National Guidelines for Educational Excellence, 1989; contbr. numerous articles to profl. jours. Mem. chorus Pitts. Opera Co., 1967-78. Grantee U.S. Office Edn., 1980, U.S. Dept. Edn., 1983-86, 90-94, Fla. Dept. Edn., 1984-85, Delta Gamma Found., 1988-90. Mem. Assn. for Edn. and Rehab. Blind and Visually Impaired, Assn. Persons with Severe Handicaps, Nat. Assn. for Parents Visually Handicapped, Coun. for Exceptional Children, Assn. for Retarded Citizens, Am. Coun. Rural Spl. Edn., Sigma Alpha Iota. Democrat. Home: 445 E 14th St Apt 4D New York NY 10009 Office: Am Found for Blind 15 W 16th St New York NY 10011

HUEBSCHMAN, PAULA JOANN, Christian education director; b. Detroit, Aug. 21, 1964; d. W. James and Carol Joyce (Bremer) Le Borious; m. Timothy Paul Huebschman, Aug. 15, 1987. BS in Secondary Edn., Concordia Coll., 1989. Intern in christian edn. Our Savior Luth. Ch., Corpus Christi, Tex., 1986-87; dir. christian edn. Our Savior Luth. Ch., St. Paul, 1989—. Mem. Theol. Educators in Associated Ministries, Luth. Educators Assn. Office: Our Saviors Luth Ch 674 Johnson Pkwy Saint Paul MN 55106

HUEGEL, WILLIAM A., minister; b. Erie, Pa., Mar. 29, 1943; s. Pearl (Holden) H.; m. Deborah Karen Reichel, Sept. 4, 1972; 1 child, Gregory; adopted children: Robert, Renee, Jeremy, Tony, Jason. BS, Nyack Coll., 1968; MDiv., Gordon-Conwell, 1972. Ordained to ministry Am. Bapt. Chs. in U.S.A., 1974. Asst. pastor Danvers (Mass.) 1st Bapt. Ch., 1974; pastor Peabody (Mass.) 1st Bapt. Ch., 1975-82, Winchester (Mass.) 1st Bapt. Ch., 1982—; pres. Peabody (Mass.) Clergy Assn., 1978-79, Winchester (Mass.) Interfaith Assn., 1988-89; mem. Judson Com. on Ministry, 1980-82; com. on evangelism Am. Bapt. Ch. of Mass., 1991—. Mem. Winchester Interfaith Assn., Mins. Coun. Am. Bapt. Ch., No. Bapt. Edn. Soc., Interfaith Wichita Coun. (pres. 1991-92). Home: 10 Lawrence St Winchester MA 01890 Office: 1st Bapt Ch 90 Mt Vernon St Winchester MA 01890 *I hope my life will be something like a basement window that let's some light in to an otherwise darkened place.*

HUENEMANN, EDWARD MARTIN, theologian; b. Curtiss, Wis., Feb. 18, 1920; s. William Arthur and Mary Sophia (Hansmeier) H.; m. Gladys Frances Oesau, June 23, 1946; children: Kathryn, Joan, Jonathan. BA, Lakeland Coll., 1943; BD, McCormick Sem., 1946; ThD, Princeton Sem., 1961. Ordained to ministry Presbyn. Ch. (U.S.A.), 1946. Pastor Ottowa Presbyn. Ch., Dousman, Wis., 1946-48, 1st Presbyn. Ch., Cedar Grove, Wis., 1948-52, East Trenton Presbyn. Ch., Trenton, N.J., 1952-56; asst. pastor 1st Presbyn. Ch., Trenton, 1956-58; prof. theology Hanover (Ind.) Coll., 1958-67; dir. theol. studies Presbyn. Ch. (U.S.A.), N.Y. C., 1967-86; dir. Theology in Global Context Assn., N.Y. C., 1986—; lectr. chs. and univs. in 7 countries and 31 states, 1962—. Contbr. articles to jours. in field. Mem. Am. Acad. Religion, Duodecim (hon.). Democrat. Home: 22 Tenakill St Closter NJ 07624 Office: Theology in Global Context Assn 475 Riverside Dr New York NY 10115

HUENEMANN, JOEL, ecumenical agency administrator. Exec. dir Arrowhead Coun. of Chs., Duluth, Minn. Office: Arrowhead Coun Chs 230 E Skyline Pkwy Duluth MN 55811*

HUENEMANN, RUBEN HENRY, clergyman; b. Waukon, Iowa, Jan. 15, 1909; s. William and Mary (Hansmeier) H.; m. Clara James, Aug. 19, 1936; children: Robert Gilchrist, Ralph William, Carol Ruth, Grace Noel. A.B., Luther Coll., Decorah, Iowa, 1933; B.D., Mission House Sem., Plymouth, Wis., 1936; postgrad., Washington U., also Pacific Sch. Religion, Berkeley, Calif.; D.D., Franklin and Marshall Coll., 1954; LL.D., Heidelberg Coll., 1960. Ordained to ministry Evang. and Ref. Ch., 1936. Tchr. rural schs. S.D., 1927-29; pastor St. Stephen's Ch., Juneau, Wis., 1936-38, Salem Ch., St. Louis, 1938-44, Zion Ch., Lodi, Calif., 1944-54, Grace Ch., Milw., 1954-58, Faith Ch., Milw., 1958-60; pres. United Theol. Sem. of Twin Cities, Mpls., 1960-70, pres. emeritus, 1970—; conf. exec. Central Pacific Conf. United Ch. Christ, Portland, Oreg., 1970-76; interim pastor various chs. United Ch. of Christ, 1976-86; pres. Calif. Synod Evang. and Ref. Ch., 1950-54; moderator Gen. Synod, Tiffin, Ohio, 1953. Contbr. articles to denominational periodicals. Mem. Nat. Council Chs. (gen. bd. 1966-69). Address: 12705 SE River Rd Portland OR 97222

HUESCA PACHECO, ROSENDO, archbishop; b. Ejutla, Mex., Mar. 1, 1932. Ordained priest Roman Cath. Ch. 1956; consecrated bishop 1970. Archbishop of Puebla de los Angeles, 1977—. Address: Calle 2 Sur N 305, Puebla Mexico also: Apartado 235, CP 72000 Puebla de los Angeles, Puebla Mexico

HUESMANN, LOUIS MACDONALD, minister; b. Indpls., Mar. 28, 1957; s. Louis Cass and Margaret Simpson (Bateman) H.; m. Laurie Schumacher, May 29, 1982; children: Louis Cass III, Nathan William. BS, Ohio State U., 1979; MDiv, Grace Theol. Sem., 1984. Lic. to ministry Brethren Ch., 1982, ordained, 1991. Intern pastor Grace Brethren Ch. of Columbus, Worthington, Ohio, 1983-84; pastor Grace Brethren Ch., London, Ohio, 1984-85, N.W. Chapel, Dublin, Ohio, 1985-86, Grace Brethren Ch., Hartford, Conn., 1986-90; sr. pastor Grace Brethren Ch., Long Beach, Calif., 1990—; ch. planter Grace Brethren Home Missions, London, 1984-85, Hartford, 1986-90. Office: Grace Brethren Ch 3590 Elm Ave Long Beach CA 90807

HUETER, RICHARD GEORGE, minister; b. Mt. Clemens, Mich., Feb. 17, 1935; s. George Leonard and Anna Katharina (Henkelmann) H.; m. Evelyn Laura Mueller, Aug. 23, 1959; children: Mark R., David M., Paul A. BA, Capital U., 1956; MDiv, Wartburg Theol. Sem., Dubuque, Iowa, 1960; MA, Duquesne U., 1969. Ordained to ministry Am. Luth. Ch., 1960. Tchr. Mission Sem., Neuendettelsau, Fed. Republic Germany, 1958-59; missionary Luth. Mission, Madang, Papua New Guinea, 1960-70, dist. supr., 1970-79; pastor Cen. Luth. Ch., Menominee, Mich., 1980-85, Community Luth. Ch., McAllister, Wis., 1980—; svc. counsellor Luth. Brotherhood Br. 8051, Menominee, 1985—. Active Menominee Dist. Schs., 1983-85, Wausaukee Schs. Student Assistance Program, 1987—; driver Wagner Fire Dept., McAllister, 1986—. Mem. Am. Assn. Luth. Chs. (trustee 1989-91, mem. Western Commn. for Am. Missions, 1990—, chmn. Great Lakes region 1990—). Home and Office: Community Luth Ch N9945 Hwy 180 Wausaukee WI 54177 *Wise people learn from the mistakes of others. God gives us wisdom to see ourselves as we truly are—in desperate need of God's mercy. He gives us all we need through His Son, Jesus, our Lord.*

HUEY, F. B., JR., minister, theology educator; b. Denton, Tex., Jan. 12, 1925; s. F.B. and Alma Gwendolyn (Chambers) H.; m. Nonna Lee Turner, Dec. 22, 1950; children: Mary Anne Huey Lisbona, Linda Kaye Huey Miller, William David. BBA, U. Tex., 1945; MDiv, Southwestern Bapt. Theol. Sem., 1958, PhD, 1961. Ordained to ministry So. Bapt. Conv., 1956. Pastor Bolivar Bapt. Ch., Sanger, Tex., 1956-59, Univ. Bapt. Ch., Denton, 1959-61; prof. Old Testament So. Brazil Bapt. Theol. Sem., Rio de Janeiro, 1961-65; prof. Old Testament Southwestern Bapt. Theol. Sem., Ft. Worth, 1965—, chmn. D in Ministry program, 1978-79, assoc. dean for PhD program, 1984-90; guest prof. Bapt. Theol. Sem., Ruschlikon, Switzerland, 1971-72. Author: Exodus: Bible Study Commentary, 1977, Chinese edit., 1983, Yesterday's Prophets for Todays' World, 1980, Jeremiah: Bible Study Commentary, 1981, Chinese edit., 1982, Numbers: Bible Study Commentary, 1981, Ezekiel-Daniel, 1983, (with others) Student's Dictionary for Biblical and Theological Studies, 1983, Helps for Beginning Hebrew Students, 1981; translator: (with others) New American Standard Bible, 1971, New International Version Bible, 1978; editor Southwestern Jour. Theology, 1975-78; contbr. articles to profl. jours. Mem. Soc. Bibl. Lit., Nat. Assn. Profs. Hebrew, Nat. Assn. Bapt. Profs. Religion, Delta Sigma Pi, Beta Gamma Sigma, Theta Xi. Home: 6128 Whitman Ave Fort Worth TX 76133 Office: Southwestern Bapt Theol Sem Box 22000 Fort Worth TX 76122-0148

HUFF, BRETT EUGENE, administration executive; b. Biloxi, Miss., Jan. 29, 1960; s. Carroll Geroge and Ellen Kay (Spurrier) H.; m. Elizabeth Lee Lamb, June 1, 1985; children: Katie Lee, Mark William. BS, Oreg. State U., 1982. CPA. Dir. adminstrn. 1st Assembly God, Albany, Oreg., 1988—; acct. Donaca, Battleson, Kerkoch & Co., Bend, Oreg., 1982-87. Recipient Bing Crosby scholar, 1981-82. Mem. AICPA, Nat. Assn. Ch. Bus. Adminstrs. (past pres. Willamette Valley chpt.), , Oreg. Soc. CPAs (past pres. Cen. Oreg. chpt.), Phi Kappa Phi. Republican. Home: 1921 Breakwood Circle SE Albany OR 97321 Office: 1st Assembly God 2817 Santaim Hwy SE Albany OR 97321

HUFF, DAVID LAWRENCE, minister; b. Augusta, Ga., Sept. 20, 1957; s. Norman Lawrence and Martha Ruth (Simmons) H.; m. Pamela S. Hagen, Oct. 7, 1978; children: Heidi, Noel, Brenna. BA magna cum laude, Ill. State U., 1985; MDiv magna cum laude, Emory U., 1989. Ordained to ministry United Meth. Ch. as deacon, 1988, as elder, 1991. Assoc. student pastor Bondville Charge, Seymour, Ill., 1982-86; student pastor Center Point United Meth. Ch., Temple, Ga., 1986-89; pastor 1st Federated Ch., Clayton, Ill., 1989-91; assoc. pastor Wesley United Meth. Ch., Macomb, Ill., 1991—; trustee Sunset Home, Quincy, Ill.; mem. Dist. Coun. on Ministry, Galesburg, Ill., 1990—. Rep. Algonquin dist. Boy Scouts Am., Camp Point, Ill., 1990-91. Mem. Theta Phi, Alpha Chi, Sigma Tau Delta. Home: 1209 W Adams St Macomb IL 61455 Office: Wesley United Meth Ch 1212 W Calhoun Macomb IL 61455 *What we all want more than anything else is to feel valued and esteemed. What we need more than anything else are leaders who value and esteem without crushing and bruising those around them.*

HUFF, JOHN DAVID, church administrator; b. Muskegon, Mich., Nov. 20, 1952; s. Lucius Barthol and Marian (Brainard) H.; m. Diane Lynn Church, May 17, 1975; children: Joshua, Jason, Jessica. B in Religious Edn., Reformed Bible Coll., 1977; MA in Sch. Adminstrn., Calvin Coll., 1983; postgrad., Western Mich. U. Cert. ch. educator. Dir. edn. 1st Christian Reformed Ch., Visalia, Calif., 1977-79, Bethany Reformed Ch., Grand Rapids, Mich., 1979-83; dir. edn. Haven Reformed Ch., Kalamazoo, 1983-90, exec. dir. ops., 1990—; cons. David C. Cook Pubs., 1988-90, Office Evangelism Reformed Ch. in Am., 1987—; tchr. trainer, mem. renewal forum Synod of Mich. Reformed Ch. in Am., 1987-90. Author: Effective Decision Making for Church Leaders, 1988, Leader's Guide for Out of the Saltshaker and into the World, 1988. Vice chmn. Youth Com. Bill Glass Crusade, Visalia, 1978, chmn. Cen. Valley Ch. Workers Conf., Visalia, 1978; mem. Youth Com. City-Wide Easter Svcs., Visalia, 1979; trustee Reformed Bible Coll., Grand Rapids, 1984-91, mem. exec. com., 1985-91, asst. sec. bd. dirs., 1986-87, sec. bd. dirs., 1987-90; chmn. S.W. Mich. Christian Discipleship Com., 1984-85. Recipient DeVos award Reformed Bible Coll., 1977; Mich. State scholar, 1970. Mem. Bibl. Archeol. Soc., Christian Educators-Reformed Ch. Am., Inst. for Am. Ch. Growth (cons. 1986—), Christian Mgmt. Assn., Cen. Valley Youth Ministers (sec. 1978-79), Alban Inst., Delta Epsilon Chi. Republican. Avocations: reading, racquetball, golf, civil war info. Home: 5150 Simmons Kalamazoo MI 49004 Office: Haven Reformed Ch 5350 N 25th St Kalamazoo MI 49004 *Half of being smart is knowing what you're dumb at!.*

HUFF, LARRY WALDO, minister; b. Pensacola, Fla., Dec. 3, 1953; s. Clyde Vernal and Frances Adele (Flowers) H.; m. Susan Loretta Roberts, Aug. 9, 1974; children: Christopher Lee, Amanda Angeline. AA in Music, Jefferson Davis Jr. Coll., 1974; MusB, Cumberland Coll., 1976; BA, U. West Fla., 1983; M in Religious Edn., New Orleans Bapt. Theol. Sem., 1983. Ordained to ministry, Bapt. Ch., 1983. Music and youth edn. minister Main St. Bapt. Ch., Bogalusa, Ala., 1983-86; minister edn. and outreach Ridgecrest bapt. Ch., Tuscaloosa, Ala., 1986—. Mem. Ala. Bapt. Edn. Music Assn., Tuscaloosa County Bapt. Assn., Nat. Geographic Soc., Phi Mu Alpha. Democrat. Avocations: fishing, hunting, tennis, softball, golf. Office: Ridgecrest Bapt Ch 912 31st St E Tuscaloosa AL 35405

HUFF, NORMAN LEROY, minister; b. Tucumcari, N.Mex., Jan. 26, 1921; s. Otto Andrew and Addie May (Holley) H.; m. Lurline McGregor, Sept. 20, 1944; children: Shirley, Bruce, Dale. BS in Bus., Abilene Christian U., 1942; postgrad., Tex. Tech U., 1946-47. CPA, Tex. Deacon Univ. Ch. of Christ, Abilene, Tex., 1952-64, elder, 1964—; elder coord. Univ. Ch. of Christ, 1985—; pres. Christian Village of Abilene, Inc., 1985-88, mem. exec. com., 1988—; treas. Restoration Quarterly, 1985—. Master sgt. USAF, 1942-46, PTO. Mem. AICPA, Tex. Soc. CPA's, Kiwanis (Golden K-Abilene chpt., treas. 1988-90, pres. 1990-91). Republican.

HUFFMAN, DAVID CURTIS, minister; b. Burlington, N.C., Mar. 28, 1950; s. Donald Tyson and Merle (Walker) H.; m. Elaine Janine Wolf,June 25, 1988; 1 child, Katherine Elizabeth Wolf. BA, U. N.C., 1972; MDiv, Princeton Theol. Sem., 1976. Ordained to ministry Presbyn. Ch. (U.S.A.), 1976. Student asst. min. Franklin Lakes (N.J.) Presbyn. Ch., 1973-76; asst. min. Old South Ch., Boston, 1976-79, assoc. min., 1979-81; pastor Trinity Presbyn. Ch., Raleigh, N.C., 1981—; bd. dirs. Boston-Cambridge Campus Ministry Bd., 1976-80, Mass. Campus Ministry in Higher Edn., Worcester, 1976-81; chmn. profl. devel. com. Orange Presbytery, Durham, N.C., 1982-84, chmn. peacemaking com., 1982-85, mem. com. on ministry, 1983-87; chmn. com. on ministry New Hope Presbytery, Rocky Mount, N.C., 1988-90; pres. Presbyn. Urban Coun., Raleigh, 1988. Merrill fellow Harvard Div. Sch., 1986. Mem. Raleigh Ministerial Assn., Phi Beta Kappa, Beta Theta Pi. Democrat. Home: 8705 Mansfield Dr Raleigh NC 27613 Office: Trinity Presbyn Ch 3120 New Hope Rd Raleigh NC 27604

HUFFMAN, D(AYON) L(EE), clergyman; b. Center, Wis., Dec. 22, 1944; s. Dale W. and June M. (Klock) H.; m. Connie Jean Gluck, June 3, 1967; children: Amy, Elizabeth, David. BA in Religion, Olivet Nazarene U., 1968. Ordained to ministry Nazarene Ch., 1970. Pastor Ch. of the Nazarene, Brookhaven, Miss., 1969-71, First Ch. of the Nazarene, Dexter, Mo., 1971-74, Ch. of the Nazarene, Bryan, Ohio, 1974-79, Oreg. Ch. of the Nazarene, Toledo, Ohio, 1979-81, Community Ch. of the Nazarene, San Antonio, 1981-85, St. Paul's Ch. of the Nazarene, Kansas City, Mo., 1985—. Home: 12113 E 62d St Kansas City MO 64133 Office: St Paul's Ch of the Nazarene 8500 E 80th Terr Kansas City MO 64138

HUFFMAN, GORDON SETH, JR. (TIM HUFFMAN), clergyman, religion educator; b. Pitts., Mar. 26, 1943; s. Gordon Seth and Janet Kathryn (Koster) H.; children: Todd Andrew, Kevin Scott. BA, Captal U., 1964;

BD, Luth. Theol. Sem., Columbus, Ohio, 1968; PhD, U. St. Andrews, Scotland, 1977. Ordained to ministry Am. Luth. Ch., 1972. Assoc. pastor Div. Luth. Ch., Parma Heights, Ohio, 1972-75; prof. systematic theology Luth. Theol. Sem., Hong Kong, 1976-79; Kuder chair Christian mission Trinity Luth. Sem., Columbus, 1979—; mem. governing bd. Inst. Mission in U.S.A., Columbus, 1984—. Mem. Internat. Assn. Mission Studies, Am. Soc. Missiology, Assn. Profs. Mission. Democrat. Office: Trinity Luth Sem 2199 E Main St Columbus OH 43209

HUFFMAN, JOHN ABRAM, JR., minister; b. Boston, May 24, 1940; s. John A. and Dorothy (Bricker) H.; m. Anne Mortenson, June 19, 1964; children: Suzanne Marie (dec.), Carla Lynne, Janet Leigh. BA, Wheaton (Ill.) Coll., 1962; MDiv, Princeton Theol. Sem., 1965, DMin, 1983; MA, U. Tulsa, 1969. Ordained to ministry Presbyn. Ch. (U.S.A.), 1965. Sr. pastor Key Biscayne (Fla.) Presbyn. Ch., 1968-73, 1st Presbyn. Ch., Pitts., 1973-78, St. Andrew's Presbyn. Ch., Newport Beach, Calif., 1978—; moderator Everglades Presbytery, Presbyn. Ch., Fla., 1972, Presbytery of Los Ranchos, 1988; bd. dirs. Gordon-Conwell Theol. Sem., S. Hamilton, Mass., 1969—, Christianity Today, Inc., Carol Stream, Ill., 1976—, World Vision, Inc., Monrovia, 1986—. Author: "Joshua" vol. of The Communicator's Commentary, 1986, Who's in Charge Here? Foundations of Faith From Romans 1-8, 1981, Liberating Limits--A Fresh Look at the Ten Commandments, 1980. Named Man of the Yr. in Religion, Jr. C. of C., 1977. Office: St Andrew's Presbyn Ch 600 St Andrews Rd Newport Beach CA 92663

HUFFMAN, JOHN WILLIAM, JR., pastor; b. Memphis, Aug. 27, 1953; s. John W. Huffman Sr. and Sharon Lee (Braaten) Warning; m. Olivia Lynn Martinez, June 23, 1973; children: Brandon, Jeremy, Alyse, Natalie. BA, Life Bible Coll., L.A., 1975; postgrad., Azusa Pacific, 1976-77, 89, U. Calif., Santa Barbara, 1990. Ordained to ministry Internat. Ch. Foursquare Gospel, 1977. Youth pastor Foursquare Ch., Ventura, Calif., 1975-79; chaplain Baseball Chapel, Ventura, 1985; sr. pastor South Coast Fellowship, Ventura, 1980—; pres., founder World Reaching Faith Inc., Ventura, 1980-91; pastor, founder South Coast Fellowship, Ventura, 1980-91. Author: Declaring War on Hell, 1984, Fitting into the Kingdom, 1985. Office: South Coast Fellowship 1711 Wood Pl Ventura CA 93003

HUFFMAN, MARGARET ANN, minister; b. Alamosa, Colo., Apr. 15, 1955; d. Walter Vincent and Frances Esther (Nickelson) H. BA, Adams State Coll., 1977; MDiv, Iliff Sch. Theology, Denver, 1983. Ordained minister, United Methodist Ch. Elem. sch. tchr. Valley Christian Sch., Alamosa, 1978-79; pastor First United Meth. Ch., Las Animas, Colo., 1988—, United Meth. Ch., Siebert/Stratton, Colo., 1985-88; mem. com. on retreats and camping, Rocky Mountain Conf., also dist. camping coord. Chmn. Buggsville Revitalization Com., Las Animas, 1988—; leader Brownie Troop, Las Animas, 1988-90. Recipient scholarships Iliff Sch. Theology, Denver, 1979-84. Mem. AAUW, Rocky Mountain Hist. Soc. (bd. dirs.), Lions Club, Las Animas C. of C. (bd. dirs. 1988-89). Democrat. Avocations: history, reading, camping, hiking. Home: 516 6th St PO Box 186 Las Animas CO 81054 Office: United Methodist Church 546 6th St PO Box 186 Las Animas CO 81054

HUFFMAN, TED E., minister; b. Big Timber, Mont., June 15, 1953; s. Walter Eli and Margaret (Lewis) H.; m. Susan Kay Ricketts, June 22, 1973; children: Isaac Ross, Rachel Eve. BA, Rocky Mountain Coll., 1974; MDiv, Chgo. Theol. Sem., 1977, D of Ministry, 1978. Ordained to ministry United Ch. of Christ, 1978. Co-pastor Adams County Parish United Ch. of Christ, Hettinger, N.D., 1978-85, Wright Congl. United Ch. of Christ, Boise, Idaho, 1985—; chmn. Christian nurture Cen. Pacific Conf. United Ch. of Christ, Portland, Oreg., 1986—; moderator Idaho Assn. Untied Ch. of Christ, Boise, 1989—. Mem. Assn. United Ch. Educators. Office: Wright Congl Ch 4821 Franklin Rd Boise ID 83705 *In this world of powerful changes and often painful choices it is easy to see oneself as a victim. Who am I amid the movement of history? In truth, I am not much. In order for my life to have meaning, I must serve a cause which has greatness.*

HUFFMAN, WILLARD KEITH, minister; b. Marquand, Mo., Nov. 16, 1939; s. George Henry and Ruby Alma (Gipson) H.; m. Jacquelyn Zeldara Upchurch, June 2, 1962; 1 child, Becki Lyn. AA, SW Bapt. Coll., 1960; BA, Union U., Tenn., 1962; MDiv, Midwestern Bapt. Theol. Sem., 1965. Ordained to ministry So. Bapt. Conv., 1959. Pastor lst Bapt. Ch., Clarkton, Mo., 1965-66, Elvins, Mo., 1966-74, Ironton, Mo., 1974—; moderator Mineral Area Bapt. Assn., 1968-70, dir. ch. tng., 1967; mem. exec. bd. Mo. Bapt. Conv., 1974-78; pres. Bates Creek Camp Bd., 1976, Mineral Area Bapt. Pastors Conf.; mem. mission trips to Rep. China, 1982, Australia, 1989, Paraguay, 1991; trustee New Orleans Bapt. Theol. Sem., 1986—. Mem. Child Welfare Abuse Com. Iron County, 1975-77. Home: HCR 69 Box 1695 Ironton MO 63650 Office: lst Bapt Ch Madison and Knob Sts Ironton MO 63650

HUFFSTUTLER, EDGAR LANE, retired minister; b. Denison, Tex., Oct. 8, 1920; s. Tracy Lee and Monta Louisa (Morris) H.; m. Dorothy Wheatley Schrader, June 4, 1944; children: Stephen Lee, Susan Ann. BA, East Tex. State Tchrs. Coll., 1939; BD, So. Meth. U., 1942, MA, 1942. Ordained deacon Meth. Ch., 1942, ordained elder, 1943. Probationary mem. North Tex. Annual Conf., Dallas, 1941-42; full mem. Mo. Annual Conf., St. Joseph, 1942-44, Ala. Conf., Montgomery, 1944-45; full mem. North Tex. Annual Conf., Dallas, 1945-90, retired, 1990; mem. youth commn. The Meth. Ch., 1940-44, gen. bd. edn., 1940-44. Mem. Rotary (pres. Lewisville, Tex. chpt. 1967, Whiterock, Tex. chpt. 1972). Home: 3156 Ramona Palo Alto CA 94306

HUGEL, PHILIP RUDOLPH, IV, pastor; b. White Plains, N.Y., Oct. 9, 1940; s. Philip Rudolph Hugel III and Clara Caroline (Bennett) Brummer; m. Susan Appler, June 10, 1967; 1 child, Susan Elizabeth. BA, Newberry (S.C.) Coll., 1962; MDiv, Luth. Theol. So. Sem., 1966. Ordained minister to Evang. Luth. Ch. in Am., 1966. Pastor 1st Luth. Ch., Pascagoula, Miss., 1966-67, Shepherd of the Hills Luth. Ch., Rome, Ga., 1967-73, Jerusalem Luth. Ch., Rincon, Ga., 1973-82, Bethany Luth. Ch., Memphis, 1982—. Office: Bethany Luth Ch 501 N Mendenhall Memphis TN 38117

HUGHART, THOMAS ARTHUR, minister; b. Morgantown, W.Va., Feb. 21, 1932; s. Joseph Marvin and Helen Hood (Williams) H.; m. Gloria Joyce Wiley, Feb. 1, 1958; children: Andrew William, Heidi Ellen, Bradford David. BA, Coll. of Wooster, 1953; MDiv, Union Theol. Sem., N.Y.C., 1956; STD, San Francisco Theol. Sem., San Anselmo, Calif., 1982. Ordained to ministry Presbyn. Ch. (U.S.A.), 1956. Assoc. min. Watchung Presbyn. Ch., Bloomfield, N.J., 1956-59; pastor Bedford (N.Y.) Presbyn. Ch., 1959-89, co-pastor, 1989—; pres. Presbyn. Conf. Assn., N.Y.C., 1985—; moderator Presbytery of Hudson River, 1975. Democrat. Home: 459 Old Post Rd Box 447 Bedford NY 10506 Office: Bedford Presbyn Ch Village Green Box 280 Bedford NY 10506

HUGHBANKS, ROBERT ALLEN, minister; b. Maxwell, Nebr., Sept. 28, 1944; s. Albert Allen and Alice Margarete (Miller) H.; m. Sherrylyn Rae Adkins, Sept. 12, 1965; children: Shane, Kellie Jo, Matthew. DD, Pioneer Bapt. Bible Coll., Cheyenne, Wyo., 1981; ThD, Internat. Sem., Orlando, Fla., 1986; PhD, Patriot U., Colorado Springs, Colo., 1988. Ordained to ministry Bapt. Ch., 1976. Pastor North Park Bapt. Ch., Walden, Colo., 1976-80, Bible Bapt. Ch., Rangely, Colo., 1978-80; tchr. Pioneer Bapt. Bible Coll., Cheyenne, 1980-81; pastor Holbrook Bapt. Ch., Swink, Colo., 1981-86, Lynn Gardens Bapt. Ch., Pueblo, Colo., 1987—; discipleship tng. cons. So. Bapt. Conv., Nashville, inter-faith witness assoc., Atlanta; vice modrator Royal Gorge Assn., Pueblo. Author: Counseling Manual, 1988; contbr. articles to profl. jours. With Nebr. N.G., 1961-67. Republican. Home: 3939 Lancaster Pueblo CO 81005 Office: Lynn Gardens Bapt Ch 3804 Pueblo Blvd Pueblo CO 81005

HUGHBANKS, WOODARD MONROE, educator, minister; b. Attica, Kans., Dec. 20, 1928; s. James Frank and Vivian Esther (Hunt) H.; m. Avis Corinne Neubauer, Sept. 2, 1948; children: Stephen Bryce, Melody Ann, Vincent Monroe. AB, Asbury Coll., 1952; postgrad., Asbury Theol. Sem., 1958; MS, Emporia (Kans.) State U., 1964; EdD, U. Nebr., 1971. Ordained to ministry Evang. Meth. Ch., 1953. Pastor chs., Kans. and Ky., 1949-64, Monitor Community Ch. of Brethren, Conway, Kans., 1969-70, 72—; missionary World Gospel Mission, McAllen, Tex., 1953-58, Saltillo, Mex., 1959-61; tchr. Sunnyvale Elem. Sch., Harper County, Kans., 1950-51, Pleasant Valley Elem. Sch., Jessamine County, Ky., 1952-53, Taylor Inst., McAllen, Tex., 1953-55; tchr. secondary edn. Escuela Evangelica Mundial, Saltillo, Mex., 1959-61, Union Valley Elem. Sch., Hutchinson, Kans., 1961-64; prof. edn. McPherson (Kans.) Coll., 1964—; vis. prof. Universidad Evangelica Boliviana, Santa Cruz, Bolivia, 1987; leader Teen Missions Internat. teams to Finland, 1985, Bolivia, 1986, Poland, 1989. Contbr. numerous articles to profl. jours. Bd. dirs. Deer Creek Christian Camp, Pine, Colo. Mem. Nat. Assn. Evangs., Kans. Ministerial Alliance (pres. McPherson chpt. 1990-91), Assn. Tchr. Educators (bd. dirs., state pres. 1985-86), Phi Delta Kappa (pres. 1974-75, del. 1975). Methodist. Avocations: genealogy, gardening, reading, volunteer, travel. Home: 1204 Glendale Rd McPherson KS 67460 Office: Mc Pherson Coll Mc Pherson KS 67460 *To live life to the fullest is to live not somehow but triumphantly. I can do all things through Christ which strengtheneth me.*

HUGHES, ALFRED CLIFTON, bishop; b. Boston, Dec. 2, 1932; s. Alfred Clifton and Ellen Cecelia (Hennessey) H. A.B., St. John's Sem. Coll., 1954; S.T.L., Gregorian U., Rome, 1958, S.T.D., 1961. Ordained priest Roman Cath. Ch., 1957, ordained bishop, 1981. Asst. pastor St. Stephen's Parish, Framingham, Mass., 1958-59, Our Lady Help of Christians, Newton, Mass., 1961-62; lectr. St. John's Sem., Brighton, 1962-65, spiritual dir., 1965-81, rector, 1981-86; aux. bishop Archdiocese of Boston, 1981—; regional bishop of Merrimack Region, 1986-90; vicar for adminstrn. Archdiocese of Boston, 1990—. Author: Preparing for Church Ministry, 1979; contbr. articles to profl. jours. Mellon and Davis Founds. grantee, 1976. Mem. Catholic Theol. Soc. Am. Office: Chancery Bldg 2121 Commonwealth Ave Brighton MA 02135

HUGHES, C. DON, minister; b. Martin County, Tex., Oct. 8, 1935; s. Elmer Roscoe and Bobbie (Perkins) H.; m. Sonya Karrel, Feb. 2, 1957; children: Don Jr., Renee, Kevin, Lori. Student, Moody Bible Inst., Chgo.; DD (hon.), Ind. Christian U., 1987. Ordained to ministry So. Bapt. Conv. Pastor So. Bapt. Ch., Tulsa, 1960-63, Assemblies of God, Rockford, Mich., 1969-71; ind. evangelist Tulsa, 1971-87; ind. pastor Stockton, Calif., 1988—; pastor Covenant Faith Fellowship, Stockton, 1991—; pres. Zoe Bible Inst., Stockton, 1988-90. Author 14 books. Mem. Rep. Task Force, Washington, 1988—. With USN, 1953-61. Mem. Rep. Task Force, Washington, 1988—. Home: 5923 Mustang Pl Stockton CA 95210 Office: Covenant Faith Fellowship 1800 Marshall Ave Stockton CA 95209

HUGHES, CHARLES RICHARD, minister; b. Phila., Apr. 17, 1955; s. Robert Lane and Mary Lou (Eddins) H.; m. Katherine Carol Allen, Nov. 2, 1976; children: Sarah, Rachel, Rebecca. BS, Liberty U., 1977, MA in Religion, 1989, MRE, 1990, postgrad., 1990—. Ordained to ministry Bapt. Ch. Asst. pastor Temple Bapt. Ch., Titusville, Fla., 1983-87; pastor Glen Fork (W.Va.) Bapt. Temple, 1987-88; single adult pastor Thomas Rd. Bapt. Ch., Lynchburg, Va., 1988—. Home: 1901 Pocahonta St Lynchburg VA 24501 Office: Thomas Rd Bapt Ch Lighthouse Dept Lynchburg VA 24514-0001

HUGHES, DAVID MICHAEL, minister; b. Indpls., June 29, 1952; s. John Bruce and Ruth Ann (Ashburn) H.; m. Joan Elizabeth Ray, Aug. 17, 1974; children: Timothy Ryan, Molly McLain, Kevin Austin. BA, Wake Forest U., 1974; MDiv, Princeton Theol. Sem., 1977; PhD, So. Bapt. Theol. Sem., 1984. Ordained to ministry Bapt. Ch., 1977. Youth minister Covenant United Presbyn. Ch., Cinnaminson, N.J., 1975-77; assoc. pastor Woodbrook Bapt. Ch., Balt., 1977-80; Garrett fellow So. Bapt. Theol. Sem., Louisville, 1981-84; pastor Bagdad (Ky.) Bapt. Ch., 1982-84, 1st Bapt. Ch., Elkin, N.C., 1984-91; sr. pastor 1st Bapt. Ch., Winston-Salem, N.C., 1991—; adj. prof. Gardner-Webb Coll., Boiling Springs, N.C., 1987-88; exec. com. mem. Bapt. State Conv. N.C., Cary, 1989—, pres. coun. on Christian higher edn., 1989—; pres. Tri-County Ministerial Alliance, Elkin, 1988-89; exec. dir. Shelby County Hospice, Inc., Shelbyville, Ky., 1983-84. Author: Youth Alive, 1990-91, 92-93, The Biblical Recorder, 1988; monthly columnist The Tribune, 1986-89. Co-chmn. Human Rels. Task Force, Elkin, 1990-91; chair steering com. local chpt. Habitat for Humanity, Elkin, 1988; mem. steering com. Elkin Centennial Celebration, 1989; vol. Great Books Program, Elkin Primary Sch., 1990-91; mem. bd. advisors Div. Sch., Wake Forest U., 1991. Named Ky. Col. Gov. Martha Layne Collins, State of Ky., 1984. Mem. Wake Forest U. Ministerial Alumni Coun. (exec. com. 1989—), Phi Beta Kappa, Omicron Delta Kappa, Sigma Chi (Regional Balfour award). Democrat. Mailing Address: 260 Gloucestershire Rd PO Box 618 Winston-Salem NC 27104 Office: 1st Bapt Ch Fifth and Spruce Sts Winston-Salem NC 27101

HUGHES, EDWARD T., bishop; b. Lansdowne, Pa., Nov. 13, 1920. Student, St. Charles Sem., U. Pa. Ordained priest Roman Catholic Ch. 1947. Ordained titular bishop Segia and aux. bishop Phila., 1976-86; 2d bishop Diocese of Metuchen, N.J., 1986—. Office: Chancery Office PO Box 191 Metuchen NJ 08840

HUGHES, H. HASBROCK, JR., bishop. Bishop The United Meth. Ch., Lakeland, Fla. Office: United Meth Ch PO Box 3767 Lakeland FL 33802*

HUGHES, HAROLD HASBROUCK, JR., bishop; b. Richmond, Va., June 12, 1930; s. Harold Hasbrouck and Mildred Virginia (Powers) H.; m. Mera Ann Gay, June 17, 1950; children: Christine Gay Hughes Layman, Harold H. III, Kathryn S. Hughes Wise, Laura Ann Hughes Saltzer. BA, Randolph-Macon Coll., 1955, DD (hon.), 1982; BD, Duke U., 1959; DD (hon.), Fla. So. Coll., 1988, Bethune-Cookman Coll., 1989. Pastor Lawrence Meml. Meth. Ch., Bent Mountain, Va., 1951-52, Walmsley Boulevard Meth. Ch., Richmond, Va., 1952-55, Mt. Olivet Meth. Ch., Danville, Va., 1955-59, Stanleytown (Va.) Meth. Ch., 1959-62, Cokesbury Meth. Ch., Woodbridge, Va., 1962-67, Front Royal (Va.) United Meth. Ch., 1967-71, Asbury United Meth. Ch., Harrisonburg, Va., 1971-77, Reveille United Meth. Ch., Richmond, 1982-88; dist. supt. United Meth. Ch., Lynchburg, Va., 1977-82; bishop Fla. area United Meth. Ch., Lakeland, 1988—. Trustee Fla. So. Coll., Lakeland, 1988—, Bethune-Cookman Coll., Daytona Beach, Fla., 1988—, Wesleyan Coll., Macon, Ga., 1988—. Home: 130 Lake Hollingsworth Dr Lakeland FL 33801

HUGHES, HERSCHEL AUSTIN, pastor; b. Grant County, Ind., July 13, 1921; s. Cleftie Aaron and Rachel Ioma (Todd) H.; m. Lorene Lester Whited, June 6, 1942 (div. 1967); m. Carmen Lou Gray, June 27, 1971; children: Charles Evans, Dianne Kaye Hendricks. BS, Owosso (Mich.) Coll., 1942; MS, Fresno (Calif.) State U., 1956; ThM, Chgo. Theol. Sem., 1964. Pastor Wesleyan Ch., Rising Sun, Ind., 1942-44, Terre Haute, Ind., 1944-48; chaplain VA Hosp., Fresno, 1954-57; exec. dir. Community ACtion P., Columbia, Mo., 1968-72; pastor Peace United Ch. of Christ, Hartsburg, Mo., 1968—; bd. dirs. Evang. Children's Home, St. Louis. Mem. Gateway Com. Boone County, Mo., 1990—; pres. South Boone County Schs., Boone County, 1980-86. Mem. Western Assn. Mo. Conf. United Ch. of Christ (pres. 1986-88), Lions (bd. dirs. Hartsburg chpt. 1980-90). Home: PO Box 100 Hartsburg MO 65039 Office: Peace United Ch of Christ PO Box 100 Hartsburg MO 65039 *One can accomplish any thing, if he doesn't care who gets the credit.*

HUGHES, JONATHAN PHILIP, minister, contractor; b. Hastings, Mich., Nov. 26, 1947; s. Ralph Philip and Margaret Lucille (Covill) H.; m. Esther Elise Beckdahl, May 26, 1967; children: J. Forrest, Byron P., Fryth E., Nathan E. BA in Bible, Cen. Bible Coll., Springfield, Mo., 1970. Ordained to ministry Christian and Missionary Alliance. Lay min. of youth and assimilation Lakeland Reformed Ch., Vicksburg, Mich., 1975-77; pastor Reynoldsburg (Ohio) Alliance Ch., 1977-79; founding pastor Northwood Alliance Ch., Blaine, Wash., 1979-90. Home: Blaine WA *Died Feb. 6, 1991.*

HUGHES, LISA LYNN, lay church worker; b. Pinehurst, N.C., Apr. 16, 1964; d. Rollow Hershel and Annie Ruth (McIntosh) H. Student, U. N.C., 1982-87. Youth leader Brownson Meml. Presbyn. Ch., Southern Pines, N.C., 1987—, elder, 1988—, Sunday sch. tchr., 1988-89, dir. Christian growth, youth dir., 1991—; youth advisor Coastal Carolina Presbytery, Presbyn. Ch. (U.S.A.), 1989—; exec. dir. Drug-Free Moore County, Inc., Carthage, N.C., 1990—. Mem. Moore County Youth Svcs. Commn., 1990-91; publicity chmn. Moore County Rep. Women, 1991—. Home: 1440 E Hedgelawn Way Southern Pines NC 28387 *Man has a way of turning something (life) very simple and beautiful into something complicated and ugly by wanting instant-gratification, among the other things. Let's rejoice in the world God created.*

HUGHES, PAUL ANTHONY, minister, musician, writer; b. Tulsa, Sept. 14, 1957; s. James Barrie and Naomi Ruth (Kinard) H. BS in Indsl. Distbn., Tex. A&M U., College Station, 1980; MDiv in Christian Edn., Assemblies of God Theol. Sem., Springfield, Mo., 1986; postgrad., Baylor U., 1987. Ordained to ministry Assemblies of God, 1989. Pastoral asst., adult tchr., asst. supt. Magnolia Hill Assembly of God, Livingston, Tex., 1988-90; tchr. Bible, musician, 1990—; founder, dir. Accuracy in Religion. Contbr. articles, book revs. Mem. Soc. Bibl. Lit., Am. Acad. Religion, Soc. Pentecostal Studies. Home and Office: Rte 4 Box 469 Livingston TX 77351 *When it comes to ministry, talent and education and hard work are insufficient for the task. There is no replacement for the power of God through the Holy Spirit, and no way to fake it.*

HUGHES, RAY HARRISON, minister, church official; b. Calhoun, Ga., Mar. 7, 1924; s. J.H. and Emma Hughes; m. Euverla Tidwell; children—Janice, Ray H., Donald, Anita. B.A., Tenn. Wesleyan Coll.; M.S., Ed.D., U. Tenn.; Litt. D., Lee Coll., Cleveland, Tenn. Ordained to ministry Ch. of God, 1950. Pastor, Fairfield Ch. of God (Ill.), 1945-46, North Chattanooga Ch. of God, 1948-52; organized churches in Spain, Md., Ill., Tenn., Ga.; pres. Lee Coll., Cleveland, Tenn., 1960-66, 82-84; pres. theol. seminary Ch. God Sch. Theology, 1984-86, 1st asst. gen. overseer, 1986-90; Md.-Del.-D.C. overseer Ch. of God, 1956-60, mem. exec. council 1956-60, 62-82, nat. Sunday Sch. and youth dir., 1952-56, exec. dir. gen. bd. edn., 1st asst. gen. overseer, 1970-72, gen. overseer, 1972-74, 78-82, Ga. overseer, 1974-76; speaker for convs., preaching missions, ministers retreats. Chmn. Pentecostal Fellowship of N.Am.; chmn. Pentecostal World Conf., 1990—. Mem. Nat. Assn. Evangelicals (pres.), Pi Delta Omicron, Phi Delta Kappa. Author: Planning for Sunday School Programs, 1960; Order of Future Events, 1962; What is Pentecost?, 1963; The Effect of Lee College on World Missions, 1963, The Transition of Church Related Junior Colleges To Senior Colleges, 1966; Church of God Distinctives, 1968; The Outpouring of the Spirit; Dynamics of Sunday School Growth, 1980; Pentecostal Preaching, 1981; editor the Pilot; contbr. in field. Address: Pentecostal World Conf PO Box 4815 Cleveland TN 37320-4815

HUGHES, RICHARD THOMAS, religion educator; b. Lubbock, Tex., Feb. 21, 1943; s. Howard Hair and Rosalee (Knox) H.; m. Janice Wright, Sept. 8, 1963; 1 child, Christopher. BA, Harding U., 1965; MA, Abilene Christian U., 1967; PhD, U. Iowa, 1972. Min. Chs. of Christ; assoc. prof. religious studies S.W. Mo. State U., Springfield, 1977-82; prof. history Abilene (Tex.) Christian U., 1982-88; asst. prof. religion Pepperdine U., Malibu, Calif., 1972-76, prof., 1988—; mem. corp. bd. Restoration Quar., 1986—. Co-author: Illusions of Innocence, 1988, The Wordly Church, 1988, Discovering Our Roots, 1988; editor: American Quest for the Primitive Church, 1988; mem. editorial bd. Religion and Am. Culture: Jour. Interpretation, 1989—. Mem. Inst. for Study Am. Evangelicals (adv. bd. 1988—).

HUGHES, ROBERT DAVIS, III, theology educator; b. Boston, Feb. 16, 1943; s. Robert Davis and Nancy (Wolfe) H.; m. Barbara Brunn, June 12, 1965; children: Robert David, Thomas Dunstan. BA, Yale U., 1966; MDiv, Episcopal Divinity Sch., 1969; MA, St. Michael's Coll., U. Toronto, Ont., Can., 1973, PhD, 1980. Ordained deacon Episcopal Ch., 1969, priest, 1970. Assoc. rector Good Shepherd Ch., Athens, Ohio, 1969-72; vicar Epiphany Ch., Nelsonville, Ohio, 1969-72; asst. curate St. Anne's Ch., Toronto, 1972-75; instr. Sch. of Theology, U. of the South, Sewanee, Tenn., 1977—, assoc. prof. systemic theology, 1984-91, prof., 1991—; bd. dirs. Anglican Ctr. Christian Family Life, Sewanee, Tenn., 1981—; mem. Dept. Christian Edn. Ecumenical Commn. Alcohol and Drug Commn., Diocese Tenn., 1981—. Contbr. articles to various publs. Soloist Toronto Chamber Soc., 1975-77; pres., soloist Sewanee Chorale, 1977—; vol. Community Chest, Boy Scouts Am., Sewanee, 1979—; pres. Sewanee Chem. Dependency Assn., 1982. Episcopal Ch. Found. fellow, 1972—, Kent fellow Danforth Found., 1975-77; Sabbatical grantee Mercer and Conant funds., 1984, 91. Mem. AAUP (v.p. chpt. 1982-83, pres. 1985-87, v.p. state conf. 1990—), Conf. Anglican Thelogicans, E.Q.B. Club (bd. dirs. 1981-83), Crystal Lake Yacht Club (Frankfort, Mich.), Phi Beta Kappa. Office: U of the South Sch Theology Sewanee TN 37375

HUGHES, STEPHEN PHILLIP, evangelist, minister; b. Oakland, Calif., Mar. 13, 1948; s. Walter Ren and Iris (Hyslop) H.; divorced; children: Stephen Phillip Jr., Michelle Hughes Gavosto. Grad. high sch., Walnut Creek, Calif., 1966; student, Rhema Bible Tng. Ctr., Tulsa, 1990—. Deacon Tahoe Faith Fellowship, Tahoe City, Calif., 1988-90; founder Teddy Bear Ministries, Tahoe Vista, Calif., 1988—. Home: Rte 1 Box 1133 Broken Arrow OK 74011-9110 Office: Teddy Bear Ministries Box 463 7486 N Lake Blvd Tahoe Vista CA 95732

HUGHES, THOMAS CLAYTON, minister; b. Forrest City, Ark., Mar. 16, 1962; s. Thomas Elmer and Lillian Virginia (Jones) H.; m. Janett Lea Davis; 1 child, Timothy Caleb. BA, Cen. Bapt. U., 1987; MDiv, So. Sem., Louisville, 1990. Ordained to ministry, So. Bapt. Conv. Pastor Naylor (Ark.) Bapt. Ch., 1985-87, Providence Bapt. Ch., Campbellsburg, Ky., 1987-90, Moreland (Ky.) First Bapt. Ch., 1990—; evangelism dir. Faulkner Assn., Conway, Ark., 1986-87, stewardship dir. Sulphur Fork Assn., LaGrange, 1989-90. Vol. Human Devel., Conway, 1984-86. Mem. Hustonville Ministerial Alliance (pres. 1990—). Democrat. Office: Moreland First Bapt Ch 501 Old Danville Pike Hustonville KY 40437-9439 *My thought on life, especially the Christian life, is much like a line in a chorus which states, "Try living your life on the edge of your faith." I believe for God to be a reality in one's life, then He must be a reality in that life's existence.*

HUGHES, THOMAS RUSSELL, religion educator; b. Beaumont, Tex., Nov. 8, 1940; s. Charles Samuel and Electra (Phillips) H.; m. Nancy Henderson, Apr. 2, 1966; children: Christopher Alan, Todd Ryan. BA, Wayland Bapt. U., 1966; MRE, Southwestern Bapt. Theol. Sem., 1969. Minister of edn. Calvary Bapt. Ch., Borger, Tex., 1971-73; minister edn. Maize Rd. Bapt. Ch., Columbus, Ohio, 1973-75, Mt. Carmel Bapt. Ch., Cin., 1975-78, 1st Bapt. Ch., Calvert City, Ky., 1978-80, Cen. Bapt. Ch., Port Arthur, Tex., 1980-83, Skycrest Bapt. Ch., Clearwater, Fla., 1983-88, Tampa Bay Bapt. Assn., Tampa, Fla., 1988-90, Fla. Bapt. Conv., Jacksonville, 1990—; spl. worker, cons. Fla. Bapt. Conv., Jacksonville, 1983—; growth cons. Ky. Bapt. Conv., Middletown, 1978-80, State Conv. of Bapt. in Ohio, Columbus, 1973-78. Asst. coach Little League Baseball, Calvert City, 1977, 78. Recipient Campus Leadership Favorite award Wayland Bapt. U., 1966. Mem. Fla. Bapt. Religious Edn. Assn., Southwestern Bapt. Religious Edn. Assn., So. Bapt. Religious Edn. Assn., Lions. Republican. Home: 7925 Belleméade Blvd S Jacksonville FL 32211 Office: Fla Bapt Conv 1230 Hendricks Ave Jacksonville FL 32207

HUGHES, WILLIAM ANTHONY, bishop; b. Youngstown, Ohio, Sept. 23, 1921; s. James Francis and Anna Marie (Philbin) H. Degree, St. Charles Sem., Balt., St. Mary's Sem., Cleve.; M.A. in Edn, Notre Dame U., 1956. Ordained priest Roman Catholic Ch., 1946; pastor chs. in Boardman and Massillon, Ohio, 1946-55; prin. Cardinal Mooney High Sch., Youngstown, 1956-65; supt. schs. Diocese of Youngstown, 1965-72, episcopal vicar of edn., 1972-73, vicar gen., 1973-74; aux. bishop, 1974-79; bishop of Covington, Ky., 1979—. Office: Diocese of Covington PO Box 18548 Covington KY 41018-0543

HUGHEY, MARK WILLIAM, youth minister; b. Madison, Wis., Oct. 22, 1957; s. William Wade and Janet Grace (McFarlane) H.; m. Connie Ruth DeRosa, Aug. 15, 1981; children: John Mark, Alyssa. BA in Bibl. Studies, Trinity Coll., Deerfield, Ill., 1984; postgrad., Olivet Nazarene Coll., Kankakee, Ill., 1989—. Ordained to ministry Fellowship of Christian Assemblies, 1989. Dir. Christian edn. Christian Life, Mt. Prospect, Ill., 1983-85; dir. Christian edn., youth min. First Presbyn. Ch., Newark, Ohio, 1985-88; youth min. Northminster Presbyn. Ch., Cin., 1988-89, Prairie Creek Community Ch., Sun Prairie, Wis., 1989—; tchr. Crisis Pregnancy Ctr., Newark, Ohio pub. schs., 1987-88, Curriculum Pregnancy Info. Ctr., Christian schs., Madison, 1991—; counselor College Hill Presbyn. Ch., Teleios

Counseling Ctr., 1988-89. Nat. Network Youth Ministries. Home: 243 E Main St Sun Prairie WI 53590 Office: Prairie Creek Community Ch 707 Davis St Sun Prairie WI 53590

HUGHEY, WILBUR LEWIS, clergyman; b. Canon, Colo., Jan. 22, 1925; s. Douglas Patterson and Molly Olive (Buck) H.; m. Rae Belle Town, Jan. 30, 1949 (div. June 1979); children: Donna Earline, Stanley Douglas, Kenneth Warren, Peggy Jo Ann, David Paul; m. Ann Elizabeth Knapp, June 26, 1980. BS, N.W. Christian Coll., Eugene, Oreg., 1953; MDiv, Christian Theol. Sem., Inpls., 1960; MS, Butler U., 1963. Ordained to ministry Christian Ch. (Disciples of Christ), 1953. Student pastor Christian Ch., Noti, Oreg., 1951-53; pastor Christian Ch., Hazelwood, Ind., 1954-59, Union Christian Ch., Franklin, Ind., 1959-61, Westside Christian Ch., Indpls., 1961-64; chaplain LaRue D. Carter Meml. Hosp., Indpls., 1962-65; dir. chaplaincy svcs. A.L. Bowen Children's Ctr., Indpls., 1965-77; chaplain, assoc. dir. Iowa Meth. Med. Ctr., Des Moines, 1977-91, retired; rsch. asst. dept. pastoral care Christian Theol. Sem., 1962-63; clin. trainer Askelepion-Internat. Transactional Analysis Assn., Carbondale, Ill., 1967-69. Active various ministerial assns. and community orgns. Sgt. USAAF, 1943-46, ETO, MTO. Recipient Cert. of Superior Achievement award Governor State of Ill., 1972. Fellow Am. Protestant Hosp. Assn. (profl. hosp. chaplain Coll. Chaplains); mem. Assn. for Clin. Pastoral Edn. (mem. standards and accreditation com. north cen. region 1977-89, mem. cert. com. north cen. region 1989-90, accreditation chair south cen. region 1970-91). Democrat. Avocations: woodworking, winemaking, hunting, fishing, gardening. Home: 5372 NE 9th Des Moines IA 50309 Office: Iowa Meth Med Ctr 1200 Pleasant St Des Moines IA 50309

HUGIN, ADOLPH CHARLES EUGENE, lawyer, engineer, inventor, educator; b. Washington, Mar. 28, 1907; s. Charles and Eugenie Francoise (Vigny) H. BS in Elec. Engring., George Washington U., 1928; MS in Elec. Engring., MIT, 1930; JD, cert. in patent law and practice Georgetown U., 1934; Cert. Radio Communication (electronics) Union Coll., 1944; Cert. Better Bus. Mgmt. III GE, 1946; LLM, Harvard U., 1947; SJD, Cath. U. Am., 1949; Cert. in Christian Doctrine and Teaching Methods, Conf. of Christian Doctrine, 1960; Cert. in Social Svcs. and Charity Ozanam Sch. Charity, 1972. Bar: D.C. 1933, U.S. Ct. Customs and Patent Appeals 1934, U.S. Supreme Ct. 1945, Mass. 1947, U.S. Ct. Claims, 1953, U.S. Ct. Appeals (fed. cir.) 1982; registered U.S. Patent and Trademark Office Atty. Bar, 1933; registered U.S. Treasury Dept. Atty Bar, 1934; registered profl. elec. and mech. engr., D.C.; tchr. french McKinley Tech. High Sch., Washington, 1923-24; examiner U.S. Patent and Trademark Office, 1928. With GE, 1928-46, engr. Instruments R&D Lab., West Lynn Works, Mass., 1928, engr.-in-charge Insulation Lab. River Works, Lynn, 1929, Engine-Electric Drive Devel. Lab., River Works, 1929-30, patent legal asst., Schenectady, 1930, patent investigator, Washington, 1930-33, patent lawyer, Washington, 1933-34, Schenectady, N.Y., 1934-46; engr.-in-charge section aeros. and marine engring. div., Schenectady, 1942-45; organizer, instr. patent practice course GE, 1945-46; pvt. practice law, cons. engring., Cambridge and Arlington, Mass., 1946-47; vis. prof. law Cath. U. Am., Washington, 1949-55; assoc. Holland, Armstrong, Bower & Carlson, N.Y.C., 1957; pvt. practice law, cons. engr. Washington and Springfield, Va., 1947—. Author: International Trade Regulatory Arrangements and the Antitrust Laws, 1949; editor-in-chief Bull. Am. Patent Law Assn., 1949-54; editor notes and decisions Georgetown U. Law Jour., 1933-34, staff, 1930-34; contbr. articles on patents, copyrights, antitrust, radio and air law to profl. jours.; inventor dynamoelectric machines, insulation micrometer calipers, ecology and pollution controls, musical instruments, dynamometers, heavy-duty inherent constant voltage characteristic generators, water-cooled eddy-current clutches, brakes, and others, granted 12 U.S. patents, several fgn. patents. Mem. Schenectady com. Boy Scouts Am., 1940-42, North Springfield Civic Assn.; charter mem., 1st bd. mgrs. Schenectady Cath. Youth League, 1935-38, hon. life mem., 1945; mem. adv. bd. St. Michael's Parish, Va., 1974-77, lector, commentator, 1969-80; bd. dirs. St. Margaret's Fed. Credit Union, 1963-67, 1st v.p., 1965-67; chmn. St. Margaret's Bldg. Fund, 1954; lector St. Margaret's Parish, Md., 1966-69, retreat group capt., 1965-68, Parish Coun., 1969-71; mem. legis. com. Schenectady C. of C., 1940-46. Recipient Dietzen Drawing prize George Washington U., 1926, Aviation Law prize Cath. U. Am., 1948, Radio Law prize, 1949, Charities Work award St. Margaret's Ch., 1982; elected to GE Elfun Soc. for Disting. Exec. Svc., 1942. Mem. Am. Intellectual Property Law Assn. (life, cert. of Honor for 50 Yrs. Svc. 1980), ABA (life), John Carroll Soc. (life), Nat. Soc. Profl. Engrs., D.C. Soc. Profl. Engrs., St. Vincent de Paul Soc. (St. Margaret's parish conf. v.p. 1949-65, pres. 1965—, pres. Prince Georges County, Md. dist. coun. 1958-61, founding pres. Arlington, Va. Diocesan cen. coun., 1975-77, nat. trustee 1975-77, Frederick Ozanam Top Hat award 1991), Nocturnal Adoration Soc., St. Margaret's Parish Confraternity Christian Doctrine (pres., instr. 1960-61), Washington Archdiocesan Coun. Cath. Men (pres. So. Prince George's County Md. deanery, 1956-58, 65-68), Holy Name Soc. (pres. St. Margaret's parish soc. 1950-52, Prince George's County section 1953, Washington Archdiocesan Union 1953-55), Nat. Retired Tchrs. Assn., Men's Retreat League (Wash. exec. bd. 1954-58), Delta Theta Phi (E.D. White Senate 1931, mem. emeritus 1974, scholarship key award Georgetown U. Law Sch. chpt. 1934). Avocationstravel, photography, sketching, horticulture. Address: 7602 Boulder St North Springfield VA 22151-2802

HULL, GRETCHEN GAEBELEIN, lay worker, writer, lecturer; b. Bklyn., Feb. 5, 1930; d. Frank Ely and Dorothy Laura (Medd) Gaebelein; m. Philip Glasgow Hull, Oct. 24, 1952; children: Jeffrey R., Sanford D., Meredyth Hull Smith. BA magna cum laude, Bryn Mawr Coll., 1950; postgrad., Columbia U., 1950-52. Major presenter Internat. Coun. on Bibl. Inerrancy, Chgo., 1986; guest lectr. London Inst. on Contemporary Christianity, 1988; lectr. at large Christians for Bibl. Equality, St. Paul, 1988—; major presenter Presbyn. Ch. (U.S.A.) Nat. Abortion Dialogue, Kansas City, Mo., 1989; disting. scholar lectr. Thomas F. Staley Found., Stony Brook, N.Y., 1991; elder Presbyn. Ch. (U.S.A.); mem. session Madison Ave. Presbyn. Ch., N.Y.C. Author: Equal to Serve, 1987; (with others) Women, Authority and the Bible, 1986, Applying the Scriptures, 1987; editor Priscilla Papers 1989—; contbr. articles to religious mags. Trustee Cold Spring Harbor Village Improvement Soc., 1966-69, Soc. of St. Johnland, Kings Park, N.Y., 1972-75. Mem. Woman's Union Missionary Soc. Am. (bd. dirs. 1954-71), Presbyns. United for Bibl. Concerns (bd. dirs. 1973-75), L.I. Presbytery (gen. coun. 1981-83), Christians for Bibl. Equality (bd. dirs. 1987—), Latin Am. Mission (trustee 1989—), Evangelicals for Social Action (bd. dirs. 1991—), Cosmopolitan Club. Home and Office: 45 E 62d St Apt 4B New York NY 10021

HULL, JAMES ERNEST, religion and philosophy educator; b. Laurel, Miss., June 30, 1928; s. Tillette Reyphord and Gladys Evelyn (Reeves) H.; m. Jo Welch, July 7, 1956; children: Alan Walter, Timothy Olen, Richard James. AB, So. Meth. U., 1950, MDiv cum laude, 1952; PhD, U. Edinburgh (Scotland), 1959; postgrad., Yale U., 1968, U. Oxford, U. Cambridge, Eng. Ordained to ministry Meth. Ch., 1953. Preacher Ch. of Scotland and Meth. chs., Scotland, 1956; assoc. pastor St. Mary's Parish Kirk, Haddington, Scotland, 1957-58; minister Scarsdale (N.Y.) Congregational Ch., 1958-60; prof., chmn. dept. religion and philosophy Lambuth Coll., Jackson, Tenn., 1960-66; prof., chmn. dept. religion and philosophy Greensboro (N.C.) Coll., 1966—, Jefferson-Pilot prof. religion and philosophy, 1976—; cons. various denominations throughout the South, 1966—, various sems., 1966—, S.E. jurisdiction United Meth. Chrs., 1968-78; cons., tchr. chs., Miami, Fla., 1972-80; mem. World Theol. Conf., Oxford U., Eng., 1969, Piedmont Colls. Archaeol. Dig, Beersheba, Israel, 1973. Author: Beyond the Dream, Live Justuce-Love Peace, Symphony of Spirit and Stone, On the Way, 1976, Ecumenical Celebrations—Interfaith Resources, 1991; contbr. articles to profl. jours. Assoc. minister Grace United Methodist Ch., Greensboro, 1978-79; gen. coun.. U. Edinburgh, del., 1976—. Lt. USN, 1953-56. Recipient commendation 11th Workshop Christian-Jewish Rels., Charleston, S.C., 1989; named one of 10 Most Outstanding Citizens, Greensboro News & Record, 1985; Lilly scholar Duke U., 1976; Bryan Found. grantee, 1991. Mem. AAUP, N.C. Assn. Profs. of Religion, Piedmont Interfaith Coun. (co-founder), Civitan Club. Avocations: gardening, music, travel. Home: 5409 Southwind Rd Greensboro NC 27405 Office: Greensboro Coll 815 W Market St Greensboro NC 27401

HULL, ROBERT RICHARD, JR., minister; b. Mattoon, Ill., Dec. 4, 1944; s. Robert Richard and Sara Elizabeth (Chuse) H.; m. Carole Irene Pocza, Nov. 28, 1970; children: Aaron Paul, Joshua Dwyer. BA in Psychology with honors, Ind. U., 1966; MDiv, Goshen Bibl. Sem., 1974. Ordained to ministry Mennonite Ch., 1990. Sec. for peace and justice Gen. Conf. Mennonite Ch., Newton, Kans., 1979—; chairperson Christian Peacemaker Teams, Chgo., 1989— Nat. Campaign for a Peace Tax Fund, Washington, 1982-89; bd. dirs. Parenting for Peace and Justice, St. Louis, 1986-91; mil. conscientious objector counselor Cen. Com. for Conscientious Objectors, Phila., 1979—. Author: As Conscience and Church Shall Lead, 1990, Justice and the Christian Witness, 1982; co-author: Fear God and Honor the Emperor, 1988. Capt. USAF, 1967-71. Mem. Assn. for Psychol. Testing. Democrat. Office: Gen Conf Mennonite Ch 722 Main St Newton KS 67114-0347 *In my experience, when someone searches within himself or herself for the courage to stand up for their conscience, others are often empowered to stand up for their conscience also.*

HULL, WILLIAM EDWARD, theology educator, provost; b. Birmingham, Ala., May 28, 1930; s. William Edward and Margaret (King) H.; m. Julia Wylodine Hester, July 26, 1952; children: David William, Susan Virginia. BA, Samford U., 1951; MDiv, So. Bapt. Theol. Sem., Louisville, 1954, PhD, 1960; postgrad., U. Gottingen, Germany, 1962-63, Harvard U., 1971. Ordained to ministry Bapt. Ch., 1950. Pastor Beulah Bapt. Ch., Wetumpka, Ala., 1950-51, Cedar Hill Bapt. Ch., Owenton, Ky., 1952-53, 1st Bapt. Ch., New Castle, Ky., 1953-58; from instr. to assoc. prof. So. Bapt. Theol. Sem., Louisville, 1954-67, prof., 1967-75, dean theology and provost, 1969-75; pastor 1st Bapt. Ch., Shreveport, La., 1975-87; provost Samford U., Birmingham, Ala., 1987—; bd. dirs. Corporators Covenant Life Ins. Co., Phila., 1981—. Author: Gospel of John, 1970, Broadman Bible Commentary, 1970, Beyond the Barriers, 1981, Love in Four Dimensions, 1982, The Christian Experience of Salvation, 1987; (with others): Professor in the Pulpit, 1963, The Truth That Makes Men Free, 1966, Salvation in Our Time, 1978, Set Apart for Service, 1980, Celebrating Christ's Presence Through the Spirit, 1981, The Twentieth Century Pulpit, Vol. II, 1981, Biblical Preaching: An Expositor's Treasury, 1983, Preaching in Today's World, 1984; contbr. articles to profl. publs. Mem. Futureshape Shreveport (La.) Commn., 1985-87. Recipient Denominational Svc. award Samford U., 1974, Liberty Bell award Shreveport Bar Assn., 1984, Brotherhood and Humanitarian award NCCJ. Mem. Nat. Assn. Bapt. Profs. Religion (pres. 1967-68), Am. Acad. Religion, Soc. Bapt. Lit., The Club (Birmingham), Univ. Club (Shreveport), Vestavia Country Club (Birmingham), Rotary, Phi Kappa Phi, Phi Eta Sigma, Omicron Delta Kappa. Home: 435 Ves Club Way Birmingham AL 35216 Office: Samford U Office of Provost 800 Lakeshore Dr Birmingham AL 35229

HULSEY, SAM BYRON, bishop; b. Ft. Worth, Feb. 14, 1932; s. Simeon Hardin and Ruth (Selby) H.; m. Linda Louise Johnson, Oct. 3, 1959. B.A., Washington and Lee U., 1953; M.Div., Va. Theol. Sem., 1958. Ordained to ministry Episcopal Ch. Am., Asst. St. John's Ch., Corsicana, Tex., 1958-60; rector, 1960-63; dean So. Deanery, 1961-63; asst. dir. Christian edn. St. Michael and All Angels Ch., Dallas, 1963-66; rector St. Matthew Ch.; headmaster parochial sch. Pampa, Tex.; priest-in-charge All Saints Ch., Perryton, 1966-73; rector St. David Ch., Nashville, 1973-78, Holy Trinity Ch., Midland, Tex., 1978-80; bishop of N.W. Tex., 1980—. Address: 1314 K Ave Ste 506 PO Box 1067 Lubbock TX 79408

HULSEY, WILDA JEAN, religious organization administrator; b. Dongola, Ill., Aug. 7, 1937; d. Ora Carl and Alice Augusta (Buckles) Hughes; m. Albert Lonney Hulsey, Dec. 28, 1957; children: Angelia, Janice, Cindy, Kent. AA, Hannibal-LaGrange Coll., 1955-57; BSE, Ouachita Bapt. Univ., 1959. Dir. Woman's Missionary Union Benton County Assn., Windsor, Mo., 1965-67, Iowa So. Bapt., Des Moines, 1977-82, Iowa So. Bapt. Fellowship, Des Moines, 1986—. Recipient For Inc. award Woman's Missionary Union mag., Birmingham, Ala., 1991, Second Century Fund grant, 1991. Home: 302 Fairview Dr Glenwood IA 51534 Office: Iowa So Bapt Fellowship 2400 86th St Westview #27 Des Moines IA 50322

HULTBERG, DAVID GODFREY, minister; b. Columbus, Ohio, Apr. 19, 1951; s. Norman M. and Virginia Pauline (Scott) H.; m. Belinda Lea Schoby, Feb. 3, 1973; 1 child, Liberty Lea. BA, Capital U., Columbus, 1973; MDiv, No. Bapt. Theol. Sem., Lombard, Ill., 1976; DMin, Garrett Evang. Sem., Evanston, Ill., 1986. Ordained to ministry, United Meth. Ch. Pastor Tiskilwa (Ill.) Yoked Parish, 1976-81; assoc pastor Pekin (Ill.) Grace United Meth. Ch., 1981-84; pastor Elmwood (Ill.) United Meth. Ch., 1984-88, Hopedale (Ill.) Yoked Parish, 1988—; del. Specialized Ministries, Peoria, Ill., 1990—, Ann. Conf. United Meth. Ch., MaComb, Ill., 1976—, Peoria Coun. Ministries, 1983-84, Conf. Worship Task Force, 1983-84. Author: Conflict Management Training, 1986; contbr. articles to profl. jours. Rep. Friends of the Libr., pekin, 1983, Olympia Adv. Com., Hopedale, Ill., 1990—. No. Bapt. Theol. Sem. scholar, 1973. Mem. Mackinaw Valley Ministry Coun. Office: Hopedale Yoked Parish PO Box 386 Hopedale IL 61747-0386

HULTGREN, ARLAND JOHN, religion educator; b. Muskegon, Mich., July 17, 1939; s. Arnold Edward and Ina Lucille (Wold) H.; m. Carole Ruth Benander, June 26, 1965; children: Peter, Stephen, Kristina. BA, Augustana Coll., Rock Island, Ill., 1961; MA, U. Mich., 1963; MDiv, Luth. Sch. Theology Chgo., 1965; ThD, Union Theol. Sem., N.Y.C., 1971. Asst. pastor Trinity Luth. Ch., Tenafly, N.J., 1966-68; instr. to assoc. prof. religious studies Wagner Coll., Staten Island, N.Y., 1969-77; assoc. prof. N.T. Luther Northwestern Theol. Sem., St. Paul, 1977-86, prof. N.T., 1986—. Author: I-II Timothy, Titus, 1984, Paul's Gospel and Mission, 1985, Christ and His Benefits, 1987; editor Word and World, 1981-88. Trustee Gustavus Adolphus Coll., St. Peter, Minn., 1990—. Mem. Soc. Bibl. Lit., Studiorum Novi Testamenti Societas, Phi Beta Kappa. Office: Luther Northwestern Theol Sem 2481 Como Ave Saint Paul MN 55108

HULTSTRAND, DONALD MAYNARD, bishop; b. Parkers Prairie, Minn., Apr. 16, 1927; s. Aaron Emmanuel H. and Selma Avendla (Liljegren) H.; m. Marjorie Richter, June 11, 1948; children—Katherine Ann, Charles John. B.A. summa cum laude, Macalester Coll., 1950; B.D., Kenyon Coll., 1953; M.Div., Colgate-Rochester Theol. Sem., 1974; D.D. honoris causa, Nashotah Divinity Sch., 1986. Ordained priest Episcopal Ch., 1953, consecrated bishop, 1982. Vicar St. John's Episcopal Ch., Worthington, Minn., 1953-57; rector Grace Meml. Ch., Wabasha, Minn., 1957-62, St. Mark's Episcopal Ch., Canton, Ohio, 1962-68, St. Paul's Episcopal Ch., Duluth, Minn., 1969-75; assoc. rector St. Andrew's Episcopal Ch., Kansas City, Mo., 1968-69; exec. dir. Anglican Fellowship of Prayer, 1975-79; rector Trinity Episcopal Ch., Greenley, Colo., 1979-82; bishop Episcopal Diocese of Springfield, Ill., 1982-91; exec. bd. Episcopal Radio (TV Found.), Atlanta, 1982-87, Anglican Fellowship of Prayer, Winter Park, Fla., 1968—; adv. bd. Episcopal Boys' Homes, Salinas, Kans., 1983-91; com. of execs. Ill. Conf. Chs., 1982-91; mem. House of Bishops, 1982—, Minn. Standing Com., 1970-73; chmn. Minn. Examining Chaplains, 1954-61; chaplain Pewsaction Fellowships U.S.A., 1983—; advisor Diocesan Youth of Minn., 1956-60. Author: The Praying Church, 1978, And God Shall Wipe Away All Tears, 1968, Intercessory Prayer, 1972, Upper Room Dialogues, 1980. Bd. dirs. Sr. Citizens Housing, Duluth, 1972-75, St. Luke's Hosp., Duluth, 1969-75; pres. Low-Rent Housing Project, Greenley, 1979-82. Served with USNR, 1945-46. Recipient Disting. Service award Young Life Minn., 1974; named hon. canon Diocese of Ohio, Cleve., 1967. Mem. Pi Phi Epsilon. Lodge: Rotary. Address: 1701 S Lake le Homme Dieu Dr Alexandria MN 56308

HUMBERGER, FRANK EDWARD, pastoral counselor; b. Troy, Ohio, July 10, 1914; s. Frank Longfellow and Myrtle May (McDowell) H.; BS, Case Inst. Tech., 1935; BD, San Francisco Theol. Sem., 1959; ThD, Pacific Sch. Religion, 1967; m. Jackeline H. Armstrong, Apr. 14, 1973; children by previous marriage: Sallie Marshall, Edward McDowell, Janet Lolov. Diplomate Inst. Logotherapy. Owner, mgr. Tech. Metal Processing, Inc., Cleve., 1945-57, Aerobraze Corp., 1953-57; ordained teaching elder, United Prebyterian Ch. U.S.A., 1959; pastor Presbyn. Ch., Turlock, Calif., 1960-68; dir. Logos West Tng. Ctr., Lafayette, Calif., 1968-78; pres. Interpersonal Relations, Inc., Calif. and Wash., 1964-83, Exec. Services Assocs., Bellevue, 1978-83; IPR, Inc., 1983-86, new ch. devel. Palm Springs (Calif.) Presbyn. Ch., 1985-87; assoc. prof. mgmt. dept. San Francisco State U., 1967-70; assoc. prof. psychology John F. Kennedy U., Moraga, Calif., 1967-70; pres. Calif. Health Group, 1974-78; lectr. Sch. Edn., U. Pacific, Stockton, Calif., 1965-67. Chmn. Grower-Worker Reconciliation Task Force, United Presbyn. Ch. U.S.A., San Joaquin Valley, Calif., 1970. Fellow Am. Assn. Pastoral Counselors; mem. Am. Assn. Marriage and Family Therapists (cert. supr., clin. mem.), Blue Key, Tau Beta Pi. Republican. Clubs: Wash. Athletic, Orcas Island Yacht, Orcas Tennis. Author: Your Personal Career, 1978, Developing Effective Communication Styles, 1979, Outplacement and Inplacement Counseling, 1984; contbr. articles to profl. jours. Home: PO Box 789 Eastsound WA 98245

HUME, BASIL CARDINAL (GEORGE HALIBURTON), archbishop; b. Newcastle-upon-Tyne, Eng., Mar. 2, 1923; s. William Errington and Marie Elisabeth (Tisseyre) H.; M.A. in History, Oxford U., 1947, S.T.L., Fribourg (Switzerland) U., 1951; D.Div. (hon.), U. Newcastle-upon-Tyne, 1979, Cambridge U., 1979; D.D. (hon.), Manhattan Coll., 1980, Cath. U., 1980, U. London, 1980, Oxford U., 1981, U. York, Eng., 1982, U. Kent, Eng., 1983, U. Durham, Eng., 1987, Benedictine Internat. Athenaeum St. Anselm, 1988, U. Hull, Eng., 1989, U. Keele, Eng., 1990. Professed Benedictine monk, 1942, ordained priest Roman Cath. Ch., 1950; abbot of Ampleforth, 1963-76; consecrated archbishop of Westminster, 1976; created cardinal priest San Silvestro in Capite, 1976; chmn. Benedictine Ecumenical Commn., 1972-76; v.p. Episcopal Conf. Eng. and Wales, 1976-79, pres., 1979—; mem. Sacred Congregation for Religious and Secular Insts.; mem. Pontifical Secretariat Ch. Unity; mem. council for secretariat for Synod of Bishops, 1978-87; pres. European com. of Bishops Confs., 1979-87; mem. Pontifical Commn. Revision of Code of Canon Law; mem. Synod Council for Internat. Synod. Author: Searching for God, 1977, In Praise of Benedict, 1981, To Be a Pilgrim, 1984, Towards a Civilization of Love, 1988. Named Hon. Bencher of Inner Temple, 1976, Hon. Freeman of London and Newcastle-Upon-Tyne, 1980. Address: Archbishop's House, Westminster, London SW1P 1QJ, England

HUMMEL, FREDERICK EUGENE, minister; b. N.Y.C., May 28, 1935; s. John Clarence and Helene (Hodges) H.; m. Ellen Gruber, May 18, 1957; children: David H., Diana Claire, Cynthia Jean. BS, N.Y.U., 1960; MDiv, New Brunswick Theol. Seminary, N.J., 1963; cert. psychotherapist, Alfred Adler Inst., N.Y.C., 1978; D of Ministry, Drew U., 1981. Assoc. minister Reformed Protestant Dutch Ch. of Flatbush, Bklyn., 1963-65; minister St. Paul's Reformed Ch., Babylon, N.Y., 1965-71; sr. minister Mattituck (N.Y.) Presbyn. Ch., 1971-83; minister, head of staff Church By the Sea Presbyn. Ch. (U.S.A.), Ft. Lauderdale, Fla., 1983—; chmn. Presbyn. Nominating Com., Presbytery of Fla., 1988—. Author: 28 Days to Better Christian Stewardship, 1984. Chm. Shinnecock (N.Y.) Reservation Counseling Task Force, 1971-83, Narcotic Guidance Council of Babylon Twp., 1968-71. Ltjg. USN, 1953-56. Named Kentuck Colonel, Commonwealth of Ky., 1984; honored by City of Babylon, N.Y., 1971. Mem. Rotary (bd. dirs. Ft. Lauderdale 1988—), Kappa Phi Kappa. Republican. Avocations: golf, tennis, oil painting, wood carving, woodworking. Home: 2728 Mayan Dr Fort Lauderdale FL 33316-3240 Office: Ch By the Sea Presbyn Ch 2700 Mayan Dr Fort Lauderdale FL 33316-3240

HUMMEL, GENE MAYWOOD, bishop; b. Lancaster, Ohio, Nov. 12, 1926; s. Ivan Maywood and Anna Mildred (Black) H.; m. R. Jeannine Lane, June 17, 1950; children: Gregory L., G. Michael. Student, Miami U., Oxford, Ohio, 1944, Dartmouth Coll., 1944-45; BS in Agr, Ohio State U., 1949, BS in Agrl. Engring, 1950. Supr. North Am. Aviation Inc., Columbus, Ohio, 1951-57; prodn. control chief Martin Co., Orlando, Fla., 1957-61; ordained to ministry Reorganized Ch. of Jesus Christ of Latter Day Saints, 1961; ministerial asst. to Center Stake bishop, Independence, Mo., 1961-63; bishop San Francisco Bay Stake, 1964-70, Hawaii, 1968-70; bishop Center Stake, 1970-72; bishop, mem. Presiding Bishopric Internat. Ch., 1972-88, presiding bishop, 1988—; dir. Health Care Systems, Inc., 1983—, Ctr. Place Improvement Inc., Independence, Cen. Profl. Bldg., Inc., Independence, E.A. Smith Retirement Ctr., Inc., Cen. Devel. Assn., Inc., Boatmans Bank of Kansas City, Mo.; dir., v.p. Systems Communication, Inc., Independence, 1975—. Mem. corp. body Independence Sanitarium and Hosp., 1972—; bd. dirs. Mid-Am. Health Network, Kansas City, 1983—. With USNR, 1944-45. Mem. Independence C. of C., Rotary. Office: Box 1059 221 W Lexington St Independence MO 64051

HUMPHREY, LLOYD RAY, pastor; b. Mare Island, Calif., Mar. 7, 1951; s. Raymond Lloyd and Margie Marie (Evans) H.; m. Patricia Ann Ellington, June 10, 1973; children: Angela, Laura Ann. BA, Ouachita Bapt. U., 1973; MDiv, Southwestern Bapt. Theol. Sem., 1976; DMin, New Orleans Bapt. Theol. Sem., 1989. Ordained to ministry Bapt. Ch., 1976. Pastor Hickory Ridge Bapt. Ch., Memphis, 1976-82, North Oxford (Miss.) Bapt. Ch., 1982-87, Wildwood Bapt. Ch., Kennesaw, Ga., 1987—; bd. dirs. NewSong, Kennesaw, 1987—. Chaplain Ole Miss. Football Team, Oxford, 1986; advisor Ole Miss. Chpt. Fellowship Christian Athletes, 1982-85; vol. mgr. Sandy Plains Softball Assn., Marietta, Ga., 1990-91. Named Outstanding Young Men Am. U.S. Jaycees, 1977, 79, 86. Home: 5012 Shallow Ridge Kennesaw GA 30144 Office: Wildwood Bapt Ch PO Box 218 Kennesaw GA 30144

HUMPHREY, N. JEAN, lay worker; b. Kansas City, Mo., Dec. 18, 1933; d. Lloyd A. and Mary (Quay) Lawson; m. Edward F. Humphrey, June 4, 1955; children: Sue Ann, Lisa Marie, Mark Edward, Nancy Louise, Shelly Frances, Ann Elizabeth, Jeanne Maureen. Student, Johnson County Community Coll.; MA, Loyola U., New Orleans. Dir. Johnson County region Family Life, Archdiocese of Kansas City (Kans.), Overland Park; assoc. dir. Family Life, Archdiocese of Kansas City (Kans.). Author: Newly Married Ministry Manual, Widowed Ministry Manual; editor archdiocesan newsletter. Mem. Nat. Assn. Lay Ministry, Nat. Assn. Cath. Dirs. of Family Life Ministry (editorial bd. newsletter), Nat. Assn. Separated and Divorced Catholics. Home: 7018 Broadman Ophelia KS 66204

HUMPHREY, WILLARD EDWARD, JR., pastor; b. San Angelo, Tex., Apr. 2, 1945; s. Willard Edward Sr. and Hazel Fern (Parks) H.; m. Karen Jane Kiesling, June 11, 1966; children: Paul Edward, Jason Andrew. BA, U. Corpus Christi, 1968; MRE, Southwestern Bapt. Sem., 1970. Ordained to ministry So. Bapt. Ch. Assoc. youth min. Riverside Bapt. Ch., Ft. Worth, 1970-71; min. youth and youth edn. 1st Bapt. Spring Br., Houston, 1971-76, min. edn. and adminstrn., 1976-78; assoc. pastor edn. and adminstrn. Harlandale Bapt. Ch., San Antonio, 1978-80; sr. pastor 1st Bapt. Wells Br., Austin, Tex., 1980—. Author cassettes Dreaming New Dreams, 1989, Pathway to Armaggedon, 1991; contbr. articles to profl. jours. Bd. dirs. Half Way House, Inc., San Antonio, 1979-82. Recipient Outstanding Ministerial Dedication award Southwestern Bapt. Sem., 1990. Mem. Austin Bapt. Assn. (mem. exec. bd. 1980—, v.p. pastor's conf. 1981-83), So. Bapt. Conv. (mem. pastor's conf.), Phi Upsilon Pi (pres. 1966-67), Circle K. Club (pres. 1968), Lake Pointe Club. Republican. Office: 1st Bapt Wells Br 2013 Wells Branch Pkwy Ste 310 Austin TX 78728

HUMPHREYS, BEVERLEY JOAN, religious organization administrator; b. Nelson, New Zealand, July 19, 1939; d. Kenneth Douglas and Dorothy Elsa (Hay) Wood; m. Eric Michael Humphreys, Jan. 15, 1963; children: Michael John, Susan Joan, Kathryn Anne. Teaching Diploma, Christchurch (New Zealand) Tchrs.' Coll., 1961; B.Sc., Canterbury U., Christchurch, 1962. Cert. postprimary tchr., New Zealand. Nat. sec. New Zealand Bapt. Women's Missionary Union, 1977-83; nat. pres. New Zealand Bapt. Missionary Fellowship, 1987; pres. New Zealand Bapt. Union and New Zealand Bapt. Missionary Soc., 1990-91. Home: 16 Fergusson St, Nelson New Zealand Office: Bapt Union, POB 23-242, 53 Rangitoto Rd, Papatoetoe New Zealand

HUMPHREYS, KENT JACK, small business owner; b. Oklahoma City, June 29, 1946; s. Jack C. and Bonita Gene (Mahaffy) H.; m. Davidene P. Stuart; children: Lance, Kenda, Kami. BA, U. Okla., 1968. Co-owner Jacks Svc. Co., Oklahoma City, 1972—; bd. dirs. The Navigators, Colorado Springs, Colo.; cons.-speaker Billy Graham Amsterdam (the Netherlands), 1986; speaker Lausanne II, Manila, the Philippines, 1989, Navigators African Leaders Conf., Nigeria, 1990, Lausanne Leadership '88, Washington. Counseling dir. Kelly Green Evangelistic Assn., Mobile, Ala., 1987-90. Capt. U.S. Army, 1968-72, Vietnam. Mme. Am. Health & Beauty Assn. Internat. (founder 1983), Barbar Beauty Supply Internat., Nat. Assn. Svc. Merchandisers, Beta Gamma Sigma. Baptist. Avocations: travel, public speaking, family sports. Office: Jacks Svc Co 4401 SW 23rd Oklahoma City OK 73108

HUMPHRIES, MICHAEL LAWRENCE, religion educator; b. Bakersfield, Calif., Sept. 26, 1953; s. Richard Laurence and Joy (Carr) H.; m. Robin Ann

Logsdon, June 19, 1982; children: Megan Ariel, Erin Nicole. BA magna cum laude, Pacific Christian Coll., 1979; MA, Sch. Theology, Claremont, Calif., 1982; PhD, Claremont Grad. Sch., 1990. Lectr. Mount St. Mary's Coll., L.A., 1984-86, The U. Judaism, L.A., 1989. Grad. fellowship Claremont Grad. Sch., 1982-84. Fellow The Jesus Sem.; mem. Soc. of Bibl. Lit., Internat. Q Sem., Phi Beta Sigma. Home: 272 W Fourth St Apt 4 Claremont CA 91711

HUNEKE, JOHN GEORGE, minister; b. Bklyn., Aug. 6, 1931; s. John Jacob and Adelaide (Peper) H. BA, Columbia U., 1953; MDiv, Luth. Theol. Sem., 1956; ThM, Harvard U., 1958. Ordained to ministry Luth. Ch., 1958. Asst. pastor Holy Trinity Luth. Ch., Bklyn., 1957-59, Trinity Luth. Ch., Middle Village, Queens, N.Y., 1959-60; pastor St. John's Luth. Ch., Greenpoint, Bklyn., 1960-73, Luth. Ch. of the Reformation, Bklyn., 1973—; instr. religion Wagner Coll., S.I., 1957-58; stewardship com. Met. N.Y. Synod Luth. Ch. Am., 1966-73. Author: Our Church 1867-1967, 1967. Bd. govs. Greenpoint Br. YMCA, Bklyn., 1963-73. Mem. Ordained Clergy Evang. Luth. Ch. Am. (Timotheans). Avocation: fishing. Home: 6016 Palmetto St Ridgewood Queens NY 11385 Office: Luth Ch Reformation 105 Barbey St Brooklyn NY 11207 *As a Pastor for more than thirty years, I have found satisfaction in my endeavor to be compassionate, to be present (to be there) where people hurt, and to have vision of the mission and message of justification by God's grace through faith. As the years go by, life becomes more meaningful to see other people realize that God loves all of us.*

HUNLEY, JEARL DEAN, minister; b. Cedar Grove, Tenn., Jan. 8, 1938; s. Oscar Nathaniel and Hattie (Baucum) H.; m. Charlotte Graves; children: David Jearl, Terry Michael, Melanie Dawn. BS, Bethel Coll., McKenzie, Tenn., 1963; MDiv, Memphis Theol. Sem., 1967. Ordained to ministry, Cumberland Presbyn. Ch., 1963. Minister New Salem Cumberland Presbyn. Ch., Arlington, Tenn., 1966-71, Lexington (Tenn.) Cumberland Presbyn. Ch., 1971-78, Parkway Cumberland Presbyn. Ch., Nashville, 1978-80, Manchester (Tenn.) Cumberland Presbyn. Ch., 1980-88, Firest Cumberland Presbyn. Ch., Columbus, Miss., 1988—; moderator Grace Presbytery, 1990-91; chaplain Tenn. Army N.G., 1972-88, Miss. Army N.G., 1988—. Chaplain Civitan, Columbus, 1989—. Lt. col. USNG, 1972—. Mem. Miss. Army N.G. Assn., Nat. Field Artillery Assn., Rotary (v.p. 1987). Home: 2618 Canterbury Rd Columbus MS 39701 Office: First Cumberland Presbyn Ch 2698 Ridge Rd Columbus MS 39701

HUNSBERGER, KEN DUANE, minister; b. Memphis, Feb. 4, 1953; s. Carl K. and Maurine (Childs) H.; m. Sherree McLemore, May 16, 1975; children: Christopher, Alicia, Chad. BS in Edn., Memphis State U., 1977; MA in Communication, Southwestern Bapt. Theol. Sem., 1986. Ordained to ministry Bapt. Ch., 1975. Minister music/youth Scenic Hills Bapt. Ch., Memphis, 1976-80; minister music/edn. LaBelle Haven Bapt. Sch., Memphis, 1980-84; regional dir. Am. Christian TV System, Ft. Worth, 1985-86; assoc. pastor Carmel Bapt. Ch., Charlotte, N.C., 1986-90, Briarlake Bapt. Ch., Decatur, Ga., 1990—. Mem. Nat. Assn. Single Adult Leaders. Home: 789 Bruxton Woods Ct Lilburn GA 30247 Office: Briarlake Bapt Ch 3715 LaVista Rd Decatur GA 30033

HUNSBERGER, RUBY MOORE, electronics manufacturing corporation executive, religious organization representative; b. Nappanee, Ind., Feb. 28, 1913; d. Clinton Clarence and Irene Mae (Moyer) Clyde; m. Clarence Cecil Moore, Dec. 21, 1933 (dec. Jan. 1979); children: Clyde W., Edwin C., Kay E. Moore Branch; m. Lowell Harold Hunsberger, Feb. 1, 1982 (dec. Aug. 1988). Student, Presbyn. Hosp., Chgo., 1932. Missionary Sta. HCJB, Quito, Ecuador, 1939-45, spl. rep., 1945—; v.p. Crown Internat., Inc., Elkhart, Ind., 1950-79, chmn. bd., 1979—; pres. Stas. WCMR and WFRN, Elkhart, 1979—. Del. Missionary Ch., Nappanee, 1980, 82, 89-90. Mem. Elkhart C. of C. Republican. Home: 502 Maple Ln Nappanee IN 46550 Office: Crown Internat Inc 1718 W Mishawaka Rd Elkhart IN 46517

HUNSINGER, EDWARD EUGENE, clergyman; b. Gaffney, S.C., July 12, 1945; m. Mary Margaret Thomas, June 3, 1967; children: David Scott, Kristina Renee. AA, Gardner Webb Coll., 1965; BA, Limestone Coll., 1967; MDiv, Southeastern Sem., 1972, D of Ministry, 1973. Ordained to ministry So. Bapt. Conv., 1966. Pastor El Bethel Bapt. Ch., Gaffney, 1966-69, Olive Grove Bapt. Ch., Creedmoor, N.C., 1969-73, 1st Bapt. Ch., Wadesboro, N.C., 1973-81; sr. minister 1st Bapt. Ch., Concord, N.C., 1981—. Pres. Am. Heart Assn., Wadesboro, 1980; dist. comdr. Boy Scouts Am., Wadesboro, 1981; trustee Wingate (N.C.) Coll., 1988; bd. dirs. gen. bd. N.C. Bapt. St. Conv., Cary, N.C., 1977-81. Recipient God and Country award Boy Scouts Am. Mem. Greater Concord Ministerial Assn. (pres. 1986), Rotary (Paul Harris fellow 1988), Masons. Democrat. Avocation: coin collecting. Home: 441 Claymount St SE Concord NC 28025 Office: 1st Bapt Ch 200 Branchview Dr Concord NC 28026

HUNT, BARNABAS JOHN, priest, religious order administrator; b. Sayre, Pa., Jan. 6, 1937; s. Clarence Elmer and Margarite Frances (Bennett) H. BS in Edn., Pa. State U., 1958; postgrad., Elmira Coll., 1960-61, Portland (Oreg.) State U., 1969-70, Clackamas Community Coll., 1970-71, Mt. Hood Community Coll., 1973-74. Ordained priest Episcopal Ch., joined Soc. St. Paul, Episcopal Ch. Headmaster St. Luke's Sch., Soc. St. Paul, Gresham, Oreg., 1961-64; lic. adminstr. St. Jude's Nursing Home, Inc., Portland and Sandy, Oreg., 1964-73; supr. Soc. St. Paul, Palm Desert, Calif., 1975-89, prior, 1989—; brother-in-charge St. Paul's Press, Sandy, 1969-76. Pres. adv. bd. The Carlotta, 1985—. Mem. Tri-County Bd., Oreg. Agy. on Aging, 1971-76; pres. Sandy C. of C., 1972; mem. Sandy City Coun., 1975-76, candidate for City Coun., City of Palm Desert, 1986; pres. St. Jude's Home, Inc., Palm Desert, 1989—. Fellow Am. Coll. Nursing Home Adminstrs. (fellow Found. 1984-87); mem. Nat. Guild Churchmen (pres. 1982—), Conf. on Religious Life in Anglican Communion, Nat. Episcopal Coalition on Alcohol and Drugs. Home and Office: 44-660 San Pablo Ave Palm Desert CA 92260

HUNT, DANIEL STEVENSON, SR., minister; b. Williamson, W.Va., Oct. 7, 1947; s. Carl Bryson and Carrie Frances (Hammond) H.; m. Sharon Elaine Morrison, May 23, 1968; children: Daniel Jr., Marci Elizabeth, Joshua Carl. BA, Campbellsville Coll., 1977; postgrad., Criswell Coll., 1983-84. Ordained to ministry Bapt. Ch. Pastor Beechgrove Bapt. Ch., Campbellsville, Ky., 1974-78, The Chapel in West Park, Cleve., 1978-83; assoc. pastor Windsor Park Bapt. Ch., DeSoto, Tex., 1984-86; pastor First Bapt. Ch. Greenup, Ky., 1986-87, Austintown (Ohio) Bapt. Ch., 1987—; trustee Brotherhood Commn. So. Bapt. Ch., Memphis, 1990—. Scoutmaster Boy Scouts Am., Russell, Ky., 1967-68. Republican. Home: 2279 Birch Trace Austintown OH 44515 Office: Austintown Bapt Ch 1180 S Raccoon Rd Austintown OH 44515

HUNT, ERNEST EDWARD, III, minister; b. Oakland, Calif., May 23, 1934; s. Ernest Edward and Maselia (Carter) H.; m. Elsie Beard, Aug. 23, 1958; children: Ernest Edward IV, Elizabeth Hunt Blanc. BA, Stanford U., 1956; MDiv, Episcopal Sem. S.W., Austin, Tex., 1959; MA, Stanford U., 1965; DMin, Princeton Sem., 1981. Ordained to ministry Episcopal Ch., 1959. Vicar Trinity Ch., Gonzales, Calif., 1959-63; asst. rector St. Paul's Ch., Salinas, Calif., 1963-66; rector St. Timothy's Ch., Creve Coeur, Mo., 1966-72, Ch. of the Epiphany, N.Y.C., 1972-88; dean St. Matthew's Cathedral, Dallas, 1988—; mem. ministries com. Diocese of Dallas, 1988—, exec. coun., 1991—, dep. gen. conv. Episcopal Ch., 1990—; instr. Anglican Sch. Homilectics, Dallas, 1988—; vis. lectr. homiletics Union Theol. Sem., N.Y.C., 1987; bd. dirs., exec. com. Anglican Sch. Theology, Dallas, 1988—. Author: Sermon Struggles, 1982; contbr. articles to profl. jours. Bd. dirs. Epiphany Community Ctr., Manhattan, 1972-88, Common Pantry of Dallas, 1988—. Capt. USAR, 1961-71. Fellow Coll. Preachers, Episcopal Sem. S.W. Alumni Assn.; mem. Union Club, Onteora Club, Lansdowne Club (London), Lakewood Country Club (Dallas), Masons. Office: St Matthews Episcopal Ch 5100 Ross Ave Dallas TX 75206 *I believe the challenge for our society today is to balance individual self-interest with the common good of all.*

HUNT, GEORGE NELSON, bishop; b. Louisville, Dec. 6, 1931; s. George N. and Jessie Mae (Alter) H.; m. Barbara Noel Plamp, June 18, 1955; children: Susan, Paul, David. B.A., U. South, Sewanee, Tenn., 1953; M.Div., Va. Theol. Sem., Alexandria, 1956; D.D., Yale U., 1980. Ordained to ministry Episcopal Ch., 1956; vicar Holy Trinity Ch., Gillette, Wyo., 1956-60; priest in charge St. John's Ch., Upton, Wyo., 1957-60, St. Francis Ch., Reno Junction, Wyo., 1959-60; asst. St. Paul's Ch., Oakland, Calif., 1960-62; rector St. Alban's Ch., Worland, Wyo., 1962-65, St. Anselm's Ch., Lafayette, Calif., 1965-70, St. Paul's Ch., Salinas, Calif., 1970-75; exec. officer Episcopal Diocese Calif., 1975-80; bishop Episcopal Diocese R.I., Providence, 1980—; mem. nat. council ministry, 1973-79. Episcopalian. Club: University (Providence, R.I.). Office: Episcopal Ch 275 N Main St Providence RI 02903

HUNT, GEORGE WILLIAM, priest, magazine editor; b. N.Y.C., Jan. 22, 1937; s. George Aloysius and Grace Winifred (Jordan) H. AB, Fordham U., 1961, MA, 1963; PhL, Woodstock Coll., 1961, STL, 1967; STM, Yale U., 1968; PhD, Syracuse U., 1974; DHL (hon.), Spring Hill Coll., 1991. Joined S.J., 1954; ordained priest Roman Cath. Ch., 1967. Asst. prof. St. Peter's Coll., Jersey City, 1968-70; assoc. prof. Le Moyne Coll., Syracuse, N.Y., 1973-81; vis. prof. Georgetown U., Washington, 1983-84; pres., editor in chief Am. mag., N.Y.C., 1984—. Author: (literary criticism) John Updike and the Three Great Secret Things, 1980 (Christianity lit. award 1981), John Cheever: The Hobgoblin Company of Love, 1983.Y. Trustee Boston Coll., 1985—, Carnegie Coun. on Ethics and Internat. Affairs, 1986—, Holy Cross Coll., Worcester, Mass., 1990—; trustee emeritus U. Detroit, 1984—. Home and Office: 106 W 56th St New York NY 10019

HUNT, GREGORY LYNN, minister; b. Bartlesville, Okla., Oct. 8, 1954; s. Joe H. and Adeanya June (Standridge) H.; m. Priscilla Lee Prince, July 10, 1976; children: Michelle Leanne, Ethan Standridge. BA, Baylor U., 1977; MDiv, So. Bapt. Theol. Sem., 1981, PhD, 1985. Ordained to ministry Bapt. Ch., 1979. Coll. minister First Bapt. Ch., Knoxville, Tenn., 1978-79; pastor Sanders (Ky.) Bapt. Ch., 1979-82, Graefenburg (Ky.) Bapt. Ch., 1982-84; assoc. pastor First Bapt. Ch., Shreveport, La., 1985-89; pastor Holmeswood Bapt. Ch., Kansas City, 1989—; chmn. mission com. Shelby County (Ky.) Bapt. Assn., 1983-84, refugee relocation and support com. White's Run Bapt. Assn., Carroll County, Ky., 1980-82. Contbr. articles to profl. jours. Mem. Bapt. Assn. (long-range planning com. Kansas City, Mo., chmn. Christian social ministries com. Shreveport 1988-89). Home: 14135 W 113th Terr Lenexa KS 66215 Office: Holmeswood Bapt Ch 9700 Holmes Rd Kansas City MO 64131

HUNT, HARRY BASS, JR., biblical studies educator; b. Marshall, Tex., July 16, 1944; s. Harry Bass and Annie Beverly (Ross) H.; m. Patricia Lou Blackwell, Jan. 23, 1965; children: Patrick Douglas, Amy Carol. BS, Stephen F. Austin Coll., Nacogdoches, Tex., 1966; MDiv, Southwestern Bapt. Sem., Fort Worth, 1968, ThD, 1972, PhD, 1978. Ordained to ministry So. Bapt. Ch., 1965. Pastor Pleasant Valley Bapt. Ch., Jonesboro, Tex., 1965-70, Friendship Bapt. Ch., Gladewater, Tex., 1971-73; deacon South Hills Bapt. Ch., Ft. Worth, 1978—. Contbr. articles and book revs. to profl. jours. Mem. Nat. Assn. Profs. Hebrew, Soc. Bibl. Lit., Assn. Bapt. Profs. Religion (v.p. 1983-84, pres. 1984-85). Office: Southwestern Bapt Theol Sem PO Box 22388 Fort Worth TX 76122-0388

HUNT, JAMES DENNIS, religion educator; b. Springfield, Mass., Mar. 28, 1931; s. Richard Hunt and Elizabeth Frances (Dennis) Daneker; m. Jane Amelia Henry, Apr. 16, 1955; children: Sarah, Nathaniel, Priscilla, Jennifer. AB, Tufts Coll., 1952; S.T.B., Boston U., 1955, S.T.M., 1958; PhD, Syracuse U., 1965. Ordained to ministry Unitarian Universalist Ch., 1955. Minister Unitarian Univeralist Assn., Mass., N.Y., 1953-61; prof. Crane Theol. Sch., Medford, Mass., 1966-68, Shaw U., Raleigh, N.C., 1968—. Author: Gandhi in London, 1978, Gandhi & the Nonconformists, 1986; co-author: Gandhi's Editor, 1989. Active ACLU, Amnesty Internat., Witness for Peace. Younger Humanist fellow NEH, 1972. Mem. Am. Acad. Religion, Assn. for Asian Studies, Soc. for Christian Ethics. Democrat. Avocations: hiking, dance. Home: 120 Pineland Circle Raleigh NC 27606 Office: Shaw U Raleigh NC 27611

HUNT, KENTON LLOYD, minister; b. Goshen, Ind., July 22, 1960; s. Edgar Franklin and Sharon Adele (Brant) H.; m. Kelli Lyn Oglesby, May 21, 1983; children: Joseph, William, Haley, Joy. B in Ch. Music, Shorter Coll., 1983; MDiv in Ch. Music, So. Bapt. Theol. Sem., 1988. Lic. to ministry So. Bapt. Conv., 1990. Min. music and youth Spring Creek Bapt. Ch., Rome, Ga., 1981-84; min. youth, dir. choir Deer Park Bapt. Ch., Louisville, 1987-88; assoc. pastor of music, youth 1st So. Bapt. Ch., Williamsport, Pa., 1989—; mem. state youth com., chmn. program and arrangements com. Bapt. Conv. of Pa., S. Jersey, 1990-91. Bd. dirs. Am. Rescue Workers Women's Ctr., Williamsport, 1990—. Mem. N.E. Pa. Bapt. Assn. (associational music dir. 1989—, youth ASSIST leader 1990—), Loyalsock Ministerium, Hymn Soc. Am. and Can. Home: 1635 Andrews Pl Williamsport PA 17701 Office: 1st So Bapt Ch RD 1 Box 43 Williamsport PA 17701

HUNT, STEVEN JAMES, minister; b. Fort Collins, Colo., Jan. 24, 1954; s. James Wayne and Arlene Julia (Willeke) H.; m. Melodee Elaine Lewis, Aug. 31, 1973; children: Amy Arlene, Courtney Nicole. AA, Northwest Coll., Kirkland, Wash., 1974, BA, 1976; cert. Grad. Studies, Fuller Theol. Sem. Ordained to ministry Assemblies of God, 1978. Youth pastor Redmond (Wash.) Assembly of God, 1976-78; minister of adult edn. Life Center, Tacoma, Wash., 1979-84; assoc. pastor First Assembly of God, San Diego, Calif., 1984-89; pastor Bethel Assembly of God, Tulare, Calif., 1989—; mem. adv. bd. Ch. Care Network, Bakersfield, Calif., 1990—; mem. sectional adminstrn. com. Assemblies of God, Central, Calif., 1990—; adult workshop coord. Central Valley Christian Edn. Conv., Fresno, Calif., 1990; sec. Tulare Assn. Chs., 1991—. Author: (devotional guide) Family Affair, 1984. Mem. Kiwanis, Tulare C. of C. Home: 2165 North M St Tulare CA 93274 Office: Bethel Assembly of God 358 North E St Tulare CA 93274

HUNT, T(HOMAS) W(EBB), religion educator; b. Mammoth Spring, Ark., Sept. 28, 1929; s. Thomas Hubert and Ethel Clara (Webb) H.; m. M. Laverne Hill, July 22, 1951; children: Melana Claire Hunt Monroe. MusB, Ouachita Bapt. U., 1950; MusM, N. Tex. State U., 1957, PhD, 1967. Mem. faculty Southwestern Bapt. Theol. Sem., Ft. Worth, 1963-87; life cons. for prayer Bapt. Sunday Sch. Bd., Nashville, 1987—. Author: The Doctrine of Prayer, 1986, Music in Missions, 1986, Prayer Life, 1988. Mem. Assn. Mins. and Coords. Discipleship. Home: 1150 Vultee F-103 Nashville TN 57217 Office: Bapt Sunday Sch Bd 127 Ninth Ave N Nashville TN 37234 *In a rapidly changing world, we rely on a God who does not change.*

HUNT, TIMOTHY JON, youth minister; b. Eden, N.C., Mar. 12, 1968; s. Thomas Jefferson and Mary Ann (Taylor) H. BS, Roanoke Bible Coll., 1990. Youth min. Union Grove Ch. of Christ, Pantego, N.C., 1987-88, Horsepasture Christian Ch., Ridgeway, Va., 1990—; mem. music groups NOMAD, 1986-87, Men's Trio, 1989, Noble Theme, 1989-90, all Roanoke Bilbe Coll., Elizabeth City, N.C. Home: Rt 2 Box 771 Ridgeway VA 24148 Office: Horsepasture Christian Ch Rt 2 Box 769A Ridgeway VA 24148

HUNT, WILLIAM H. (SKIP HUNT), religious organization administrator; b. Athens, Ga., Mar. 30, 1942; s. Dock Leon and Era Ruth (Jones) H.; m. Cornelia Anne Lester, Jan. 10, 1963; children: Jannie Cornelia, James Howard. BBA, U. Ga., 1964. Founder, chmn. Tampa (Fla.) Helpline, 1978—, Christian Helplines Internat., Tampa, 1987—. Author: Organizing & Operating a Christian Helpline, 1988, How Can I Help?, 1990. Named Outstanding Religious Leader Tampa Jr. C. of C., 1975; recipient People of Dedication award Salvation Army Women's Aux., Tampa, 1989. Mem. Nat. Assn. Christian Social Workers. United Methodist. Office: Christian Helplines Internat 611 Willow Tampa FL 33606

HUNT, WILLIE WAYNE, minister; b. Greenville, Tex., Sept. 28, 1943; s. Clifford B. and Rose J. (Billnitzer) H.; m. Laura Mae Eisen, Aug. 12, 1967; children: Aaron M., Jacob M. BA, Tex. Luth. Coll., 1966; MDiv, Wartburg Theol. Sem., 1970. Pastor Christ Luth. Ch., La Porte, Tex., 1978-84; pastor developer Tree of Life Luth. Ch., Ft. Worth, 1984-86; dir. Urban Ministries, Ft. Worth, 1987-90; pastor Christ the King Luth. Ch., Ft. Worth, 1989—; technician J&S Communications, Ft. Worth, 1986—; mem. communications com. No. Tex.-No. La. Synod, Evang. Luth. Ch. in Am., 1989—; chaplain La Porte Internat. Seamen's Ctr., 1982-84. Co-founder La Porte Police Chaplains Corps, 1983-84; chmn. Community Rels. Commn., La Porte, 1983; bd. dirs. La Porte-Bayshore Neighborhood Ctr., La Porte, 1979-83. Office: Christ the King Luth Ch 4200 Denton Hwy Fort Worth TX 76117-2013

HUNTER, ALEXANDER WATSON, minister; b. Camden, N.J., Sept. 5, 1950; s. Alexander Watson and Frances Jester (Reeves) H.; m. Rachel Anne Rasmussen, Dec. 19, 1976 (div. May 1982); m. Joan Elizabeth Robin, June 26, 1982; 1 child, Robin Lynn. BA, U. Mass., 1973; MDiv, Nazarene Theol. Sem., Kansas City, Mo., 1977; D of Ministry, Austin (Tex.) Presbyn. Sem., 1990. Assoc. pastor Cypress (Tex.) United Meth. Ch., 1982-85; assoc. pastor Westminster United Meth. Ch., Houston, 1985-88; campus min. United Ministry at Pa. State U., State Coll., 1988—; vice chair Task Force on Alcohol and Other Drugs, Harrisburg, Pa., 1990—; lectr. Sci., Tech. and Soc. Dept., Pa. State U., 1989—. Mem. Interfaith Coalition Affirming Diversity, 1989—. Mem. Cen. Pa. Conf. of the United Meth. Ch., MENSA. Democrat. Office: United Ministry at Pa State 256 E College Ave State College PA 16801

HUNTER, CAROL MARGARET, religion educator; b. Cobleskill, N.Y., Apr. 27, 1948; d. Avery Victor and Helen Emma (Stephenson) DeLuca; m. Robert Frederick Hunter, Sept. 4, 1976; children: Rachel Carol, Daniel Robert. BS, Cornell U., 1970; MS, SUNY, Buffalo, 1973; MA, SUNY, Binghamton, 1985, PhD, 1989. Instr. Religion Ithaca (N.Y.) Coll., 1986-87, SUNY, Oswego, 1988-89; prof. Social, Cultural, Religious History Ark. State U., State University, 1989-90; prof. history Earlham Coll., Richmond, Ind., 1990—. NEH grantee, 1990. Mem. Am. Acad. Religion, Am. Hist. Assn., Am. Studies Assn. Home: 1621 Capri Ln Richmond IN 47374

HUNTER, CHARLES ALVIN, religious organization administrator; b. Longview, Tex., May 7, 1926; s. Wallace Alvin and Ivernia Charlot (Fleming) H.; m. Annie Mary Alexaner, June 5, 1950; children: Alpha A., Rhonda F., Rhashell D., Byron C., Rosalyn A. BA in Sociology/Religion, Bishop Coll., 1947; BD, Howard U., 1950; MTh, ThD in O.T., Div. Sch. Phila., 1954, 58; MS in Sociology, U. North Tex., 1971. Tchr. social studies Trinity High Sch., Athens, Ala., 1950-52; pastor Trinity Congl. Ch., Athens, 1950-52, Trinity Presbyn. Ch., Tallahassee, 1959-61; prof. sociology Bishop Coll., Dallas, 1961-88; tchr. Dallas Police Acad., 1965-69; pastor Hope Presbyn. Ch., Dallas, 1962-68; assoc. pastor St. Luke Presbyn. Ch., Dallas, 1969-80; dir. ch. and community Greater Dallas Community Chs., 1989—; moderator N.E. Presbytery, Dallas, 1966; vice moderator Synod Tex., Dallas, 1971; moderator Grace Presbytery, Dallas, 1985; moderator Synod of the Sun, Tex., Okla., La., Ark., 1991—. Named Alumni of the Yr., Bishop Coll. Alumni Assn., Dallas, 1966; recipient Fair Housing award Greater Dallas Housing Opportunity Ctr., 1972. Democrat. Home: 2329 Southwood Dr Dallas TX 75224 Office: Greater Dallas Community Ch 2800 Swiss Ave Dallas TX 75204

HUNTER, CLARENCE CAL, minister; b. Ft. Smith, Ark., Feb. 2, 1927; s. Clarence and Mary Adline (Brammar) Snow H.; m. Wilma Jean Jamison, Oct. 8, 1958; children: Michael, Rickey. BA, Okla. Bapt. U., 1950; postgrad., Baylor U., 1952-54; D.C., Carver Chiropractic Coll., Okla. City, Okla., 1958. Chiropractic physician pvt. practice, Minco, Okla., 1958-66; pastor Eastisde Bapt. Ch., Marlow, Okla., 1967-69; pastor First Bapt. Ch., Tipton, Okla., 1968-79, Mooreland, Okla., 1979-87; missions dir. Northwestern Bapt. Assn., Woodward, Okla., 1987—; dir. Bapt. Gen. Convention, Okla., 1978-82. Contbr. numerous articles to Bapt. periodicals. 2nd Lt. U.S. Army, 1945-54. Avocations: pilot, ham radio operator. Home: 2819 Edgewood Woodward OK 73801 Office: Northwestern Bapt Assn 2801 Maple Woodward OK 73801

HUNTER, DAVID GEORGE, theology educator; b. Del Rio, Tex., July 8, 1954; s. Richard B. and Evangeline (Fell) H.; m. Lynn Joyce Hunter, Aug. 4, 1984; children: Gregory John, Robert William. BA, MA, Catholic U., 1976; MA, St. Michael's Coll., Toronto, 1980, Notre Dame U., 1983; PhD, Notre Dame U., 1986. Asct. prof. Coll. St. Thomas, St. Paul, Minn., 1984—. Author, translator: John Chrysostom: Comparison Between a King and a Monk, 1988; editor: Preaching in the Patristic Age, 1989. Recipient Charlotte W. Newcombe dissertation fellowship, 1983-84, fellowship for Coll. Tchr., Nat. Endowment for the Humanities, 1990-91, Leverhulme Commonwealth/USA vis. fellowship, U. Nottingham, 1990-91. Mem. Am. Acad. Religion, N. Am. Patristic Soc. (sec.-treas. 1988-90). Office: Univ of St Thomas 2115 Summit Ave Saint Paul MN 55105

HUNTER, GEORGIA L., clergywoman; b. Wiergate, Tex., June 14, 1938; d. George Clavert and Leria (Thomas) Spikes; m. LeRoy Hunter, Feb. 2, 1967; children—Balenda M. Spikes, Maria A. Spikes. Student Bible Moody Bible Inst. Ordained to ministry Christian Meth. Episcopal Ch., 1983. Counselor Ill. Dept. children and Family Services, Freeport, 1970-74; food service dir. Retirement Inc., Freeport, 1978—; pastor Christian Meth. Episcopal Ch., Madison, Wis., 1983-91; asst. pastor Miles Meml. Christian Meml. Episcopal Ch., Rockford, Ill.; corr. Jour. Standard, Freeport, 1982-83; chairperson expansions and missions sect. Milw. dist. Christian Meth. Episcopal Ch. V.p. Freeport Bd. Edn., 1977—; pres. Ch. Women United, Freeport, 1970-83; asst. dir. youth Rockford and Vicinity Dist. Assn., 1980-82; sec. Freeport Good Samaritan Refuge House. Recipient Human Relations award City Council Freeport, 1974, Spiritual Achievement award Martin Luther King Ctr., Freeport, 1983, Good Neighbor award Freeport Jour. Standard, 1983, Achievement award Ch. Women United, 1983. Mem. Fully Gospel Women Assn. (bd. dirs., coord.), Young Adult Christian Women (pres.). Democrat. Avocations: bowling; researcher; reading; sewing; writing poetry. Home: 846 E Pleasant St Freeport IL 61032 *Being a woman of color in the ministry has been an experience of determination, dedication, overcoming obstacles, isolation and gratification.*

HUNTER, JAMES PAUL, lay minister, investment banker; b. Birmingham, Ala., Aug. 9, 1963; s. Jean Paul Hunter III and Ann White (Tulles) Pearce. BA in Religion, Rhodes Coll., 1985; MBA, Auburn (Ala.) U., 1988. Alloyte Ind. Presbyn. Ch., Birmingham, 1975-81; head counselor, counselor Camp McDowell Ch. Camp for the Episcopal Diocese of Ala., Navvoo, 1985-87; youth dir., mem. choir St. Mary's Episcopal Ch., Birmingham, 1985-87; song leader, guitarist St. Dunsman's Episcopal Student Ctr., Auburn, 1987-88; lay min., vestryman St. Francis of the Point, Pt. Clear, Ala., 1989—; investment banker Shearson-Lehman Bros., Birmingham, 1990—. Mem. Pi Kappa Alpha (chmn. social com. 1984). Home: 148 The West Green Birmingham AL 35243 Office: Shearson Lehman Bros 3800 Colonnade Pkwy Ste # 600 Birmingham AL 35243

HUNTER, RODNEY JOHN, theology educator; b. Detroit, Oct. 8, 1940; s. William Clarence Hunter Jr. and Mabel Florence (Murphy) McCutchan; m. Ann Covington, May 16, 1970; 1 child, David William. BA, Yale U., 1962; BD, Princeton Theol. Sem., 1965, PhD, 1974. Ordained minister Presbyn. Ch. (U.S.A.), 1971. Chaplain Youth Reception-Correction Ctr., Yardville, N.J., 1969-71; instr. pastoral theology Candler Sch. Theology, Emory U., Atlanta, 1971-72, asst. prof., 1972-78, assoc. prof., 1978-89; prof. Candler Sch. Theology, Emory U., Atlanta, 1989—; tutor Inman Sch., Atlanta, 1988-90. Gen. editor: Dictionary of Pastoral Care and Counseling, 1990; book editor Pastoral Psychology, 1975-83; contbr. numerous articles to religious jours. and books. Presbyn. grad. fellow, 1967-70; Assn. Theol. Schs. rsch. grantee, 1978-79, 86-87. Mem. Assn. for Clin. Pastoral Edn., Am. Acad. Religion, Soc. for Pastoral Theology, Assn. for Practical Theology, Soc. for Sci. Study Religion. Democrat. Avocations: carpentry, swimming, classical piano. Office: Emory U Candler Sch Theology Atlanta GA 30322

HUNTER, WILLIAM HAL, pastor; b. Live Oak, Fla., May 29, 1919; s. William Archibald and Elma Stella (Brenan) H.; m. Esther Lena Strange, Aug. 17, 1942; children: Elaine Marie, William Hall Jr., Thomas Brenan. BA, Stetson U., 1942; ThM, S.W. Bapt. Theol. Sem., 1945; ThD, New Orleans Theol. Sem., 1975. Pastor various churches, Fla., 1947-75; missionary pastor So. Bapt. Ch. fgn. Missionary Bd., Zama, Japan, 1975-77; pastor First Bapt. Ch., Pelham, Ga., 1977-85; pastor emeritus First Bapt. Ch., Pelham, 1985—; tchr. S.W. Ga. Bapt. Bible Inst., Norman Park, 1980-85, Ga. Bapt. Conv., 1984-87. Contbr. articles to profl. jours. Bd. dirs. ARC annual campaign, Pahokee, Fla. Lt. U.S. Army, 1945-46. Mem. Fla. Bapt. Conv. (assoc. dir. 1946-47), Rotary, Kiwanis, Civitan. Home: 223 Tennyson St NE Pelham GA 31779-1352

HUNTHAUSEN, RAYMOND GERHARDT, archbishop; b. Anaconda, Mont., Aug. 21, 1921; s. Anthony Gerhardt and Edna (Tuchacherer) H. A.B., Carroll Coll., 1943, St. Edward's Sem., 1946; M.S., Notre Dame U., 1953; LL.D., DePaul U., 1960; postgrad. summers, St. Louis U., Cath. U., Fordham U. Ordained priest Roman Cath. Ch., 1946. Instr. chemistry Carroll Coll., 1946-57, football, basketball coach, 1953-57, pres., 1957-62; bishop Helena Diocese, Mont., 1962-75; archbishop of Seattle, 1975-91. Recipient Martin Luther King Jr. award Fellowship of Reconciliation, 1987. Mem. Am. Chem. Soc. Office: Chancery Office 910 Marion St Seattle WA 98104

HUNTING, WESLEY JAY, minister; b. Pittsfield, Mass., June 17, 1958; s. Joseph L. and Mabel E. (Grimes) H.; m. Diane R. Atwell, June 14, 1980; children: Chadwick W., Nathaniel J. BTh, God's Bible Sch. and Coll., Cin., 1981. Ordained to ministry Pilgrim Holiness Ch. of N.Y., Inc., 1985. Min. music Hephzibah Holiness Ch., Dixon, Mo., 1981-82; pastor Pilgrim Holiness Ch., Russell, N.Y., 1983-85, Pierrepont Manor, N.Y., 1985-87, Fostoria, Ohio, 1988—; prin. Pilgrim Learning Ctr., Marshall, Ill., 1982-83; adminstr. Pilgrim Holiness Acad., Fostoria, 1988—. Editor Spirits of '76 newspaper, 1976. Home: 289 W 4th St Fostoria OH 44830

HUNTLEY, HARVEY LEWIS, JR., minister; b. Sewickley, Pa., May 19, 1945; s. Harvey Lewis and Lucy Olga (Tompkins) H.; m. Cristy Catherine Fossum, Aug. 4, 1969; children: Elizabeth Marie, Georgia Catherine. BA, Emory U., Atlanta, 1967; ThM, U. Chgo., 1969, DMin, 1971; CASE, Johns Hopkins U., 1989. Ordained to ministry Evang. Luth. Ch. in Am., 1971. Pastor Greene County Luth. Parish, Greeneville, Tenn., 1971-76, Emmanuel Luth. Ch., Atlanta, 1976-78, Luth. Ch. of Our Saviour, Albany, Ga., 1978-81; assoc. dir. for leadership support Div. Profl. Leadership, Luth. Ch. Am., Phila., 1981-87; pastor Messiah Luth. Ch., Knoxville, 1987—; pres. Luth. Social Ministries of Tenn., Nashville, 1989—, Luth. Community Svcs., 1988-90, United Proclamation Ministries, Knoxville, 1989-90; steering com. Evang. Luth. Ch. in Am. Appalachian Coalition, 1988—. Author: Lutherans in Greene County, 1976. Chmn. Christian Unity Svc. Com., Knoxville, 1988—; ELCA rep. Assn. Christian Denominations, Knoxville, 1988—. Rockefeller Theol. fellow, 1967-68. Mem. Nat. Career Devel. Assn., Phi Beta Kappa. Democrat. Lutheran. Avocations: bridge, travel, antique automobiles, tennis, singing. Office: Messiah Luth Ch 6900 Kingston Pike Knoxville TN 37919

HURAS, WILLIAM DAVID, bishop; b. Kitchener, Ont., Can., Sept. 22, 1932; s. William Adam and Frieda Dorothea (Rose) H.; m. Barbara Elizabeth Lotz, Oct. 5, 1957; children—David, Matthew, Andrea. BA, Waterloo Coll., Ont., 1954; BD, Waterloo Sem., Ont., 1963; MTh, Knox Coll., Toronto, Ont., 1968; MDiv, Waterloo Luth. U., 1973; DD (hon.), Wilfred Laurier U., Waterloo, 1980, Huron Coll., London, Ont., 1989. Ordained to ministry Luth. Ch. in Am., 1957. Pastor St. James Luth. Ch., Refrew, Ont., 1957-62, Advent Luth. Ch., Willowdale, 1962-78; bishop Eastern Can. Synod Luth. Ch. in Am., Kitchener, 1978-85, Eastern Synod Evangel. Luth. Ch. in Can., 1986—; mem. exec. com. Can. sect. of Luth. Ch. in Am., 1969-79; mem. exec. com. Luth. Merger Commn., Can., 1978-85; pres. Luth. Council Can., 1985-88. Bd. govs. Waterloo Luth. U., 1966-75, Waterloo Luth. Sem., 1973-75, 78—. Mem. Can. Assn. Pastoral Edn., Order of St. Lazarus of Jerusalem (Ecclesiastical Grand Cross 1985). Office: Eastern Synod Evang Luth Ch in Can, 50 Queen St N 3d Fln, Kitchener, ON Canada N2H 6P4 *We are called by God and God covets on affirmative response. To say "yes" to God is to say "yes" to all of life and to all of God's people.*

HURD, ALBERT EDWARD, administrator; b. Goodrich, Mich., Dec. 12, 1940; s. Edward H. and Majorie (Campbell) H.; m. Julieanne MArie Borromey, June 17, 1961. AB, Mich. State U., 1964; MDiv, Chgo. Theol. Sem., 1967. Libr. dir. Chgo. Theol Sem., 1968-80; exec. dir. Am. Theol. Libr. Assn., Evanston, Ill., 1985—. Mem. Am. Theol. Libr. Assn., ALA. Office: Am Theol Libr Assn 820 Church St Ste 300 Evanston IL 60201

HURLEY, FRANCIS T., archbishop; b. San Francisco, Jan. 12, 1927. Ed., St. Patrick Sem., Menlo Park, Calif., Catholic U. Am. Ordained priest Roman Cath. Ch., 1951; with Nat. Cath. Welfare Conf., Washington, asst. sec., 1958-68; assoc. sec. Nat. Cath. Welfare Conf., now U.S. Cath. Conf., 1968-70; consecrated bishop, 1970; titular bishop Daimlaig and aux. bishop Diocese of Juneau, Alaska, 1970-71; bishop of Juneau, 1971-76, archbishop of Anchorage, 1976—. Office: Chancery Office PO Box 2239 Anchorage AK 99510

HURLEY, MARK JOSEPH, bishop; b. San Francisco, Dec. 13, 1919; s. Mark J. and Josephine (Keohane) H. Student, St. Joseph's Coll., Mountain VIew, Calif., 1939, St. Patrick's Sem., Menlo Park, Calif., 1944; postgrad., U. Calif., Berkeley, 1943-45; PhD, Cath. U. Am., 1947; JCB, Lateran U., Rome, 1963; LLD, U. Portland, 1971. Ordained to priest Roman Cath. Ch., 1944. Asst. supt. schs. Archdiocese, San Francisco, 1944-51; tchr. Serra High Sch., San Mateo, Calif., 1944; prin. Bishop O'Dowd High Sch., Oakland, Calif., 1951-58, Marin Cath. High Sch., Marin County, Calif., 1959-61; supt. schs. Diocese, Stockton, Calif., 1962-65; chancellor, diocesan counsultor Diocese, 1962-65; asst. chancellor Arcdiocese, San Francisco, 1965-67; vicar gen. Arcdiocese, 1967-69; titular bishop Thunusuda; aux. bishop Thunusuda, San Francisco, 1967-69; bishop Santa Rosa, Cal., 1969—; pastor St. Francis Assisi Ch., San Francisco, 1967—; Prof. grad. schs. Loyola U., Balt., 1946, U. San Francisco, 1948, San Francisco Coll. Women, 1949, Dominican Coll., San Rafael, Calif., 1949, Cath. U. Am., 1954; prof. theology Beda Coll. Rome, 1987—, Angelicum U., Rome, 1989—; Del. Conf. Psychiatry and Religion, San Francisco, 1957; mem. bd. Calif. Com. on Study Edn., 1955-60; cons. Congregation for Cath. Edn., 1986—; del.-at-large Cal., White House Conf. on Youth, 1960; Cath. del., observer Nat. Council Chs., Columbus, Ohio, 1964; del. edn. conf. German and Am. educators, Nat. Cath. Edn. Assn., Munich, Germany, 1960; mem. commns. sems., univs. and schs. II Vatican Council, Rome, 1962-65; mem. commn. Christian formation U.S. Cath. Conf. Bishops, 1968; asst. archdiocesan coordinator Campaign on Taxation Schs. Calif., 1958, Rosary Crusade, 1961; adminstr. Cath. Sch. Purchasing Div., 1948-51, St. Eugene's Ch., Santa Rosa, Calif., 1959, St. John's Ch., San Francisco, 1961; mem. U.S. Bishops' Press Panel, Vatican Council, 1964-65, U.S. Bishops' Com. on Laity, 1964, U.S. Bishops' Com. Cath.-Jewish Relationships, 1965—, U.S. Bishops' Com. on Ecumenical and Interreligious Affairs, 1970, Conf. Maj. Superiors of Men, 1970; chmn. citizens Com. for San Francisco State Coll., 1968—; mem. adminstrn. bd. Nat. Council Cath. Bishops, 1970, mem. nominating com., 1971; mem. Internat. Secretariat for Non-Believers, Vatican, 1973; chmn. Secretariat for Human Values, Nat. Conf. Cath. Bishops, Washington, 1975; mem. Secretariat for Non-Believers, Vatican, 1986—; Vatican del. World Intellectual Properties Orgn., Washington, 1990. Syndicated columnist, San Francisco Monitor, Sacramento Herald, Oakland Voice, Yakima (Wash.) Our Times, Guam Diocesan Press, 1949-66, TV speaker and panelist, 1956-67. Author: Church State Relationships in Education in California, 1948, Commentary on Declaration on Christian Education in Vatican II, 1966, Report on Education in Peru, 1965, The Church and Science, 1982, Blood on the Shamrock, 1989. Trustee N.Am. Coll., Rome, 1970, Cath. U. Am., 1978—, Cath. Relief Services, 1979; cons. Congregation for Edn.; mem. Secretariat for Non-Belief, Vatican City; bd. dirs. Overseas Blind Found. Address: 273 Ulloa St San Francisco CA 94127

HURN, RAYMOND WALTER, religious order administrator; b. Ontario, Oreg., June 27, 1921; s. Walter H. and Bertha Sultana (Gray) H.; m. Madelyn Lenore Kirkpatrick, Dec. 30, 1941; children: Constance Isbell, Jacqueline Oliver. BA, Bethany (Okla.) Nazarene Coll., 1943, DD (hon.), 1967; postgrad., U. Tulsa, 1946-47, Fuller Sem., Pasadena, Calif., 1978-81. Ordained to ministry Ch. of Nazarene, 1943. Pastor Ch. of Nazarene chs., Kans., Okla., Ga., Oreg., 1943-59; dist. supt. Ch. of Nazarene, Tex., 1959-68; dir. home missions and ch. extension Internat. Hdqrs. Ch. of Nazarene, Kansas City, Mo., 1968-85, gen. supt., 1985—. Author: Mission Possible, 1973, Black Evangelism, Which Way from Here, 1973, Spiritual Gifts Workshop, 1977, Finding Your Ministry, 1980, Mission Action Sourcebook, 1980, Unleashing the Lay Potential in the Sunday School, 1986. Recipient Exec. award Am. Inst. Ch. Growth, 1980, B award Bethany Nazarene Coll., 1982.

HURON, JAMES RAYMOND, clergyman, educator; b. Chesapeake, Ohio, July 16, 1936; s. Raymond Clarence and Minnie Opal (Williams) H.; m. Judith Anne Cooper, May 21, 1960 (div. 1982); children: Laura Anne, Elizabeth Susan, Mary Lynn, Rebekah Jane; m. Darlene Patricia Kane, Aug. 5, 1983. AB, Ky. Christian Coll., 1958; BA, Milligan Coll., Tenn., 1959; MDiv, Emmanuel Sch. Religion, Milligan College, 1970; MA, Ashland (Ohio) Theol. Sem., 1976. Ordained to ministry Christian Ch. (Disciples of Christ), 1958. Youth min. Lakeview Ch. of Christ, Akron, Ohio, 1959-60; min. Greenup (Ky.) Christian Ch., 1960-66, Lily Dale Ch. of Christ, Erwin, Tenn., 1966-68, West Akron Ch. of Christ, 1971-77, North Royalton (Ohio) Christian Ch., 1983-88; asst. min. 1st Christian Ch., Columbus, Ind., 1968-71; chaplain, counselor Western Res. Psychiat. Hosp., Sagamore Hills, Ohio, 1977—; assoc. dir., mem. faculty NE Clergy Tng. Inst., Sagamore Hills, 1978—; tchr. Greenup High Sch., 1960-66; mem. faculty Bible dept. Milligan Coll., 1967-68; counselor, cons. Am. Cancer Soc., Akron, 1982-85. Contbr. articles to religious jours. Mem. Chautauqua Assn. Disciples of Christ (trustee 1990—, pres. 1991—). Avocations: farming, travel, arts, music, literature. Home: 293 Houghton Rd Sagamore Hills OH 44067 Office: Western Res Psychiat Hosp PO Box 305 Northfield OH 44067

HURON, RODERICK EUGENE, religious organization administrator; b. Chesapeake, Ohio, Dec. 5, 1934; s. Raymond Clarence and Minnie Opal (Williams) H.; m. Autumn June Hostetter, July 24, 1956; children: Lila Kay Huron Albinger, Eric Scott, Sara Lynn Huron Myers. BA, Ky. Christian Coll., 1956; MEd, U. Pitts., 1967; postgrad., U. Akron, 1968-70. Ordained to ministry Christian Chs. and Chs. of Christ, 1958. Min. Highlawn Ch. of Christ, Huntington, W.Va., 1956-57; youth min. 1st Christian Ch., Canton, Ohio, 1957-62; min. LaBelle View Ch. of Christ, Steubenville, Ohio, 1962-67, West Akron (Ohio) Ch. of Christ, 1968-71; missionary Toronto (Can.) Christian Mission, 1971-75; sr. min. North Industry Christian Ch., Canton, 1976-84; dir.-elect N.Am. Christian Conv., Cin., 1984-86, conv. dir., 1986—; guest on various TV and radio programs. Author: Do You Know Who You Are, 1976, Checkpoint, 1979 (Sherwood E. Wirt award Billy Graham Evangelistic Assn.), Christian Minister's Manual, 1984, Say Hellow to Life, 1984; also numerous articles to religious jours. Republican. Office: NAm Christian Conv PO Box 39456 Cincinnati OH 45239

HURT, HUBERT OLYN, religous demonination executive, minister; b. Louisville, Miss., May 30, 1925; s. Benjamin Clinton and Amanda Pearl (Cockrell) H.; m. Eva May White, Aug. 18, 1949; children: David Louis, Sharon Lynne Hurt Strickland. BA, Miss. Coll., 1947; MA, U. Southern Miss., 1950; M Div., New Orleans Baptist Seminary, 1950, D. Min., 1978. Tchr. Ellisville Jr. High Sch., Miss., 1950-51; pastor Sand Hill Baptist Ch., Ellisville, Miss., 1950-54; dean, prof. Shady Grove Negro Seminary, Collins, Miss., 1954; tchr. Talbot County High Sch., Talbotton, Ga., 1954-57; missionary, prof. Baptist Seminary, Havana, Cuba, 1957-61; dean, prof. Panama Baptist Sem., Arrijan, Panama, 1961-65; language missions dir. Home Mission Bd., SBC, Miami, 1965-73; dir., transcultural outreach Home Mission Bd., SBC, Atlanta, 1980-81; dir. language missions Fla. Bapt. Conv., Jacksonville, 1974-80, 81-90; refugee resettlement Home Mission Bd., SBC, Atlanta, 1980-81; Cuban refugee resettlement, Southern Baptist Conv., Miami, 1965-70. Author: (book) Transcultural Outreach, 1978; Establishing Hispanic Congregations, 1978. Mem. Southern Baptist Historical Soc. Democrat. Home: 9030 Warwickshire Rd Jacksonville FL 32257 Office: Fla Bapt Conv 1230 Hendricks Ave Jacksonville FL 32257

HURT, LARRY EMERY, minister; b. Paint Lick, Ky., July 6, 1944; s. Augustus and Bernice Low (Combs) H.; m. Jan Marie Traywick, Oct. 11, 1974; childrren: Larry Jr., Jeri Marie, Christopher Jack. Student, Rhema Bible Sch., Tulsa, 1982-83, Word of Faith Bible Sch., Dallas, 1983-84. Ordained to ministry Faith and Joy Fellowship, 1982. Founder, pastor Faith of God Fellowship Ch., Savannah, Ga., 1982; founder, pres. Faith of God Ministries, Savannah, 1983—; advisor Women's Aglow Fellowship, Savannah, 1987—; tchr. Faith of God Christian Acad., 1987-89; pres. Chatham Clergy Conf., Savannah, 1989—; marriage counselor; speaker Christian Life seminars.. Author: (tract) St. Patrick, 1985. Chmn. 7th dist. Chatham County Rep. Com., Savannah, 1989—; vol. Chatham County Jail system, vol. chaplain in State Prison system. With U.S. Army, 1962-69, Vietnam. Home and Office: 118 Mark Circle Savannah GA 31405 *In our search for solutions and a better way of life during these troubled times, we must seek the guidance of the Creator of life. There is no greater service I can do for a man than to lead him to Jesus Christ.*

HUSBAND, J. D., bishop. Bishop Ch. of God in Christ, Atlanta. Office: Ch of God In Christ PO Box 824 Atlanta GA 30301*

HUSTON, STERLING WENDELL, religious organization administrator; b. Perham, Maine, May 19, 1936; s. Walter E. and Florence M. (Tupper) H.; m. Esther Volonino, June 12, 1965; children: Todd Wendell, Alissa Joy. BS, U. Maine, Orono, 1958, MS, 1959; DD (hon.), Roberts Wesleyan Coll., 1984. Asst. dir. Rochester (N.Y.) Youth for Christ, 1961, exec. dir., 1961-66; assoc. evangelists' crusade coord. Billy Graham Evangelistic Assn., Mpls., 1966-69, asst. pers., dir. assoc. crusades, 1969-73, dir. Billy Graham N.Am. crusades, 1974—. Author: The Billy Graham Crusade Handbook, 1983, Crusade Evangelism and the Local Church, 1984. Bd. dirs. Bethany Home, Inc., Rochester, 1980; trustee Roberts Wesleyan Coll., North Chili, N.Y., 1985, Dave Roever Evangelistic Assn., Ft. Worth, 1988, Evangelism Explosion III Internat., Ft. Lauderdale, Fla., 1989. Office: Billy Graham Evangelistic Assn PO Box 9313 Minneapolis MN 55440-9313

HUTCHESON-TIPTON, DAVID QUINN, seminarian; b. Pampa, Tex., Dec. 18, 1962; s. John Mullen and Mary (Melugin) Hutcheson; m. Michelle Tipton, Nov. 19, 1988. BA, U. Denver, 1985; MDiv, Iliff Sch. Theology, 1990. Seminarian intern St. John's Cathedral, Denver, 1988-90; bookseller Tattered Cover Book Store, Denver, 1985—. Recipient Skaggs scholar Iliff Sch. Theology, 1987. Democrat.

HUTCHINGS, WILLIAM A., lay worker; b. Sandersville, Ga., Mar. 9, 1952; s. William Alonzo and Lavin (Hodges) H.; m. June Elton Hutchings, May 2, 1976; 1 child, William Jarrod. BS in BA, Ga. Southwestern Coll., 1976. Sec. Giddens Internat., Sandersville, 1984-87; chmn. bd. Deepstep (Ga.) United Meth. Ch., 1984-87, chmn. pastor/parish, 1987-88, trustee, 1989—; owner Hutchings Store/Hutchings Cattle Farm, Deepstep, 1986—; tchr. Deepstep United Meth. Ch., 1979—. Vice pres. Am. Heart Assn., Sandersville, 1989, pres., 1990; mayor Town of Deepstep, 1987-91; active Ch. of the Larger Fellowship. Mem. The Jesus Seminar, Ga. Cattlemen's Assn., Am. Cattlemen's Assn., Men's Club (v.p. 1987-88). Democrat. Home: Route 2 Box 76 Sandersville GA 31082 Office: Hutchings Store General Delivery Deepstep GA 31082 *We are on the threshold of acknowledging that God is working salvifically through other religious faiths. Because they are genuine faiths, we can learn from them as they can learn from us.*

HUTCHINS, GREGORY RAY, record and concert promoter; b. Kingsport, Tenn., Feb. 5, 1955; s. Ray Pitzer and Mildred Maxine (Tiller) H.; m. Tami Renee Taylor, Apr. 7, 1984; children: Gregory Ray II, Taylor Renee. AAS, Va. Highlands Coll., Abingdon, 1980. Program dir. Sta. WZAP Radio, Bristol, Va., 1982—; owner, pres. Rejoice Records, Bristol, Va., 1989—. Staff drummer Classic Recording Studio, Bristol, 1982—; producer several Top 80 records in So. Gospel Music. Recipient Golden Mic award Singing News Mag., 1991, Named DJ Yr. The Eddie Croock Record Co., 1988, 91. Office: Rejoice Promotions PO Box 1441 Bristol VA 24203

HUTCHINSON, ALAN BRADFORD, minister; b. Fall River, Mass., Sept. 19, 1927; s. William and Doris (Hart) H.; student Bowdoin Coll., 1945; A.B., Brown U., 1949; B.D., Andover Theol. Sem., 1952; M.A., Columbia, 1959; M.S., Danbury State Coll., 1964; M.S.W., Boston Coll., 1970; Ph.D., Tenn. U., 1975; m. Jean Caryl Cobb, Feb. 14, 1953; m. 2d, Muriel S. Johnson, Sept. 22, 1972; 1 child, Julianna Edith. Ordained to ministry Congl. Ch., 1951; dir. youth work Park Pl. Congl. Ch., Pawtucket, R.I., 1948-51; minister of youth United Ch., Walpole, Mass., 1951-52; pastor Congl. Ch., New Fairfield, Conn., 1952-66; dir. social services Blackstone Valley Community Action Program, Pawtucket, R.I., 1966-72; clin. psychotherapist Providence Mental Health Center, 1972-76, adminstr. outpatient services, 1976-82, adminstr. community support svcs., 1982—; pastor 1st Universalist Ch., Burrillville, R.I., 1972—;instr. U. R.I., 1975—; chaplain Fed. Correctional Instn., Danbury, Conn., 1957-58. Fellow Am. Orthopsychiat. Assn.; mem. Ballou-Channing Unitarian-Universalist Ministers Assn., No. R.I. Clergy Assn., Am. Correctional Chaplains Assn., Soc. Mayflower Descs. (elder Conn.), Am. Group Psychotherapy Assn., Register Clin. Social Workers, Nat. Assn. Social Workers (clin. diplomate), Acad. Certified Social Workers, Phi Delta Kappa. Clubs: Community (past pres.), Brown University, Bristol Yacht. Home: 3 Brookwood Rd Bristol RI 02809 Office: 520 Hope St Providence RI 02906

HUTCHINSON, ARNO MERTON, JR., minister, writer; b. Spokane, Wash., July 9, 1924; s. Arno Merton Sr. and Floy Virginia (Atkinson) H.; m. Anna Caroline Ogburn, Aug. 23, 1947; children: Amanda Kay Hutchinson Cosat, John Mark. BA, U. Wash., 1949; BD, Garrett-Evang. Theol. Sem., 1954; MA, Northwestern U., 1961, U. Ill., 1966. Ordained to ministry United Meth. Ch., 1954. Pastor Meth. Ch., Plymouth and Altona, Ill., 1950-54, Allen and Eatonville, Wash., 1954-58, Ogden, Seymour and Kansas, Ill., 1958-70; pastor United Meth. Ch., Williamsville, Buda, Raymond, Illinois City and Joy, Ill., 1970-87; pastor, ret. United Meth. Ch., Edgar and Metcalf, Ill., 1987—; freelance writer, Chrisman, Ill., 1987—. Contbr. articles to profl. jours. Sgt. USAAF, 1943-46, PTO. Mem. Am. Acad. Religion, Soc. Bibl. Lit., Linguistic Soc. Am., Assn. Computational Linguistics, Chgo. Soc. Bibl. Rsch., Kiwanis (sec. Muscatine club 1983-84). Home and Office: United Meth Ch 114 E Monroe Chrisman IL 61924 *We must live each day as it comes. Planning can be helpful but it is not as important as really living our present moments.*

HUTCHINSON, ORION NEELY, JR., minister; b. Charlotte, N.C., Sept. 20, 1928; s. Orion Neely Sr. and Elsie Winstead (Petty) H.; m. Mary Louise Conrad, June 23, 1950; children: Carolyn Louise Hutchinson Coram, Frances Grace Hutchinson Oldenburg, Florence Christian, Catherine Anne Hutchinson Dieter. BA, Davidson (N.C.) Coll., 1949; BD, Duke U., 1952; Merrill fellow, Harvard Div. Sch., 1965-66; DD (hon.), High Point (N.C.) Coll., 1976. Ordained to ministry United Meth. Ch. as deacon, 1951, as elder, 1952. Pastor various Meth. chs., N.C., 1940-62, Love's United Meth. Ch., Walkertown, N.C., 1962-66; sr. min. Ardmore United Meth. Ch., Winston-Salem, N.C., 1966-70, First United Meth. Ch., Brevard, N.C., 1970-72, Cen. United Meth. Ch., Asheville, N.C., 1975-79, Wesley Meml. United Meth. Ch., High Point, N.C., 1979-83; supt. Greensboro (N.C.) Dist. United Meth. Ch., 1972-75, Salisbury (N.C.) Dist. United Meth. Ch., 1983-87; editor ch. sch. publs. United Meth. Bd. Discipleship and Publs., Nashville, 1987-89; sr. min. Meml. United Meth. Ch., Thomasville, N.C., 1989—; spl. instr. in religion, Brevard Coll., 1970-72; del. World Meth. Confs., Dublin, Honolulu, Nairobi, Singapore, 1976, 81, 86, 91, Southeastern Jurisdictional Conf., Lake Junaluska, N.C., 1972, 76, 80, 84, 88, 91, gen. conf., 1976; sec. World Meth. Family Life Com., 1978-92; exec. com. mem. World Meth. Coun., 1986—; mem. Conf. Com. on Episcopacy, Charlotte, 1988—, Bible Translation and Utilization Com. Nat. Coun. Chs., N.Y.C., 1988—; vice-chmn. Conf. Commn. on Religion and Race, Charlotte, 1990—. Author: The Cross in 3-D, 1975, 4 Adult Bible Studies booklets, 1982, 84, 87, 90, student's and tchr's. books on The Gospel of Mark, 1985, Gospel of Luke, 1989; editor: Happy If With My Latest Breath, 1966; contbr. Prayers and Devotions for Teachers, 1989. Recipient Sheldon Communication award N.C. Coun. Chs., 1968, Gold Key award Nat.Mental Health Assn., 1974, Speaker's award Babcock Sch. Mgmt. Wake Forest U., 1985. Mem. Western N.C. Conf. United Meth. Ch., So. Furniture Club (hon.), Lake Junaluskans, Biltmore Forest Country Club, Rotary. Democrat. Home: 216 W Colonial Dr Thomasville NC 27360 Office: Meml United Meth Ch PO Drawer 428 Thomasville NC 27361-0428 *The tasks and privileges of writing, teaching, and preaching, I look upon as forms of the stewardship of words and the Word. I speak to myself as I prepare to share with others. Much of what I share is born out of my own felt need. My prayer is 'Lord, speak through me to those who wait upon me that the Word might become flesh again, even our own flesh'.*

HUTCHISON, KATHRYN LEE, religion educator; b. Holdenville, Okla., Sept. 10, 1945; d. Maurice Leroy and Cecelia (Rhoades) Filson; m. Joe Ed Hutchinson, June 9, 1967; children: Timothy Ryan, Holly René. BS in Edn., E. Cen. U., 1967. Church nursery coord. Castle Hills 1st Bapt. Ch., San Antonio, 1971-79, tchr. Mothers' Day Out, 1979-80, tchr. day care and pre-sch., 1980-82, tchr. 1st grade, 1982-86, dir. pre-sch., kindergarten, 1986-90. Mem. Assn. Christian Sch. Adminstrs. Home: 19098 Redland Rd #1 San Antonio TX 78259 Office: Castle Hills 1st Bapt Ch Day Care Kindergarten 2220 NW Military Hwy Dallas TX 78213

HUTCHISON, RICHARD CONNOR, minister; b. Orbisonia, Pa., Nov. 17, 1933; s. Lewis Maxwell and Lois Vandalia (Conner) H.; m. Marian Veals, Sept. 11, 1955 (div. 1971); children: Richard L., Thomas, Beth, Janet, John; m. Patricia Ann Olsen, Jan. 28, 1973. AB, Juniata Coll., 1955; MRE, Princeton Theol. Sem., 1958; D Ministry, San Francisco Theol. Sem., 1987; DD (hon.), Hanover Coll., 1991. Ordained to ministry Presbyn. Ch. (U.S.A.). Asst. pastor Highland Park (Ill.) Presbyn. Ch., 1962-64; assoc. pastor 2d Presbyn. Ch., Indpls., 1964-69; co-pastor Montview Blvd. Presbyn. Ch., Denver, 1969-80; sr. pastor Westminster Presbyn. Ch., Sacramento, 1980-88, 1st Presbyn. Ch., Ft. Wayne, Ind., 1988—; del. Gen. Assembly, Presbyn. Ch. (U.S.A.), 1973, 77; moderator Presbytery of Denver, 1977; chmn. Maj. Mission Fund Synod of Rocky Mountains, Denver, 1976-78. Author: Theodicy in Process Perspective, 1987; editor Patchwork mag., 1973-78. Pres. Pine Springs Camp, Jennerstown, Pa., 1960-62; mem. Rotary, Sacramento, 1980-86; trustee Smock Found., Ft. Wayne, 1988—, Peabody Retirement Ctr., North Manchester, Ind., 1990—. Mem. Assn. Presbyn. Ch. Educators, Presbytery of Whitewater Valley. Democrat. Home: 1725 Ardmore Ave Fort Wayne IN 46802 Office: 1st Presbyn Ch 300 W Wayne St Fort Wayne IN 46802

HUTCHISON, RICHARD DAVID, minister; b. Albuquerque, Oct. 29, 1957; s. George David and Ella Faye (Sanders) H.; m. Susan Holly Waddington, Nov. 29, 1980; children: Shannon Denae, Brandon David. BA, Bethany (Okla.) Nazarene Coll., 1979. Ordained Nazarene Ch., 1982. Assoc. pastor First Ch. of the Nazarene, Clovis, N.Mex., 1979-81; pastor Ch. of the Nazarene, Shattuck, 1981-85; assoc. pastor Ch. of the Nazarene, Woodward, Okla., 1985-86; pastor La Vista Ch. of the Nazarene, Los ALamos, N.Mex., 1986—; sec. n.w. Okla. Dist. Nazarene Youth Internat., 1983-85, v.p. n.w. Okla., 1985-86. Pres. City-Wide Youth Orgn., Clovis, 1980-81. Religion scholar Broadhurst Found., 1976-79; named One of Outstanding Young Men of Am., 1985. Mem. Ministerial Alliance (sec. 1983-84, v.p. 1984-85), N.Mex. Dist. Ch. Nazarene. Republican.

HUTCHISON, WILLIAM ROBERT, history educator; b. San Francisco, May 21, 1930; s. Ralph Cooper and Harriet (Thompson) H.; m. Virginia Quay, Aug. 16, 1952; children: Joseph Cooper, Catherine Eaton, Margaret Sidney, Elizabeth Quay. BA, Hamilton Coll., 1951, DHL (hon.), 1991; BA (Fulbright scholar), Oxford U., 1953, MA, 1957; PhD, Yale U., 1956; MA (hon.), Harvard U., 1968. Instr. history Hunter Coll., 1956-58; assoc. prof. Am. studies Am. U., 1958-64, prof. history and Am. studies, 1964-68; Charles Warren prof. history of religion in Am. Harvard U., 1968—; master Winthrop House, 1974-79; vis. asso. prof. history U. Wis., 1963-64. Author: The Transcendentalist Ministers, 1959, The Modernist Impulse in American Protestantism, 1976, Errand to the World: American Protestant Thought and Foreign Missions, 1987; editor: American Protestant Thought, the Liberal Era, 1968; co-editor: Missionary Ideologies in the Imperialist Era, 1982; editor and joint author: Between the Times: The Travail of the Protestant Establishment in America, 1900-1960, 1989; contbr. articles to profl. jours. Recipient Brewer prize Am. Soc. Ch. History, 1957; Guggenheim fellow, 1960-61; fellow Charles Warren Ctr. for Studies in Am. History, Harvard, 1966-67; Fulbright Sr. Research scholar Free U., Berlin, 1976; Fulbright Disting. lectr. in Am. history India, summer 1981; Fulbright Western European Regional Research grantee, 1987. Mem. Am. Hist. Assn., Orgn. Am. Historians, Am. Studies Assn., Am. Soc. Ch. History (pres. 1981), Unitarian Universalist Hist. Soc., Mass. Hist. Soc., Phi Beta Kappa. Democrat. Mem. Soc. of Friends. Home: 4 Ellery Sq Cambridge MA 02138

HUTSON, ANNMARIE, religious education director; b. DeKalb, Ill., June 20, 1965; d. Thomas George and Frances Ann (Sullivan) H. BA, Coll. of St. Benedict, 1987. Youth minister Sacred Heart Ch., Waseca, Minn., 1987-89; dir. religious edn. St. Stephen Parish, Stevens Point, Wis., 1989—; pres. bd. dirs. Diocese of LaCrosse, Wis., 1989—; pres. LaCrosse T.E.C. Diocesan Coun. of Cath. Women scholar, 1990. Mem. Diocesan Area Religious

Educators. Home: 435 N West St Stevens Point WI 54481 Office: St Stephen Parish 1335 Clark St Stevens Point WI 54481

HUTSON, RONALD ALAN, minister; b. Indpls., Nov. 27, 1942; s. Harold Edward and Valda Lenore (Russom) H.; m. Elaine Joan Kolb, Dec. 28, 1963; children: Jeffrey Alan, Anthony Duane, Eric David. BS in Edn., Ind. U., Indpls., 1976; MDiv, McCormick Theol Sem., 1978, D in Ministry, 1983. Ordained to ministry Presbyn. Ch., 1978. Min. First Prebyn. Ch., London, Ky., 1978-86; min., head of staff James Island Presbyn. Ch., Charleston, S.C., 1986—; Ordained to ministry Presbyn. Ch. Home: 892 Joe Rivers Rd Charleston SC 29412 Office: James Island Presbyn Ch 1632 Ft Johnson Rd Charleston SC 29412

HUTTON, LEWIS JOSEPH, minister, Hispanic studies educator; b. N.Y.C., July 26, 1921; s. Louis Francisco and Clemencia Olimpia (Castro de Pontevedra) H.; m. Irene Catherine Daroczy, Oct. 2, 1948; children: Elaine Christine, Paul Christopher, Jane Elizabeth, Peter Alexander. AB, Columbia Coll., 1942; MA in History, Columbia U., 1946; MDiv, Princeton Theol. Sem., 1944; MA, Princeton U., 1948, PhD, 1950; STM, Union Theol. Sem., 1950. Pastor First Presbyn. Ch., Gowanda, N.Y., 1951-55; min. First Presbyn. Ch., Kirksville, Mo., 1962-64; sr. min. The Capitol Hill Presbyn. Ch., Washington, 1955-62; asst. prof. Spanish Drake U., Des Moines, 1964-66; assoc. prof., then prof. U. R.I., Kingston, 1966-89, prof. emeritus Hispanic studies, 1989—; moderator Presbytery of Providence, 1972-73. Author: Teresa de Cartagena, 1966, The Christian Essence of Spanish Literature, 1988, (chpt.) Spain: Church-State Relations, 1983. Princeton Theol. Sem. fellow, 1944. Mem. AAUP, Am. Assn. Ch. History, Am. Assn. Tchrs. Spanish and Portuguese (chpt. pres.), Modern Lang. Assn., Nat. Fedn. Fgn. Lang. Tchr. Assn. (pres.). Republican. Home: PO Box 96 Kingston RI 02881

HWANG, EVELYN, religious organization executive; b. Nanking, China, June 5, 1935; came to U.S. 1958; d. Hwan-chang and Chin (Hsiang) Wu; m. Ming C. Hwang, Aug. 15, 1959; 1 child, Stephen. MS, Rutgers U., 1962; MEd, Columbia U., 1988; postgrad., Columbia U. Tchrs. Coll., 1988—. Asst. coord. dept. program svcs. Presbyn. Ch. U.S.A., N.Y.C., 1971-73; mgr. Ins. Mgmt. Office, 1973-75; assoc. mgr. info. svcs. for pers., 1975-83, mgr. pers. referral svcs., 1983-88; coord. pers. referral svcs. Louisville, 1988—; pres. Interch. Fed. Credit Union, N.Y.C., 1980-86, consulting com. mem. Ethnic Minority Ministry, Professional Ch. Leadership, Nat. Council of Churches of Christ in U.S.A., 1984-87. Pres. Chinese Christian Fellowship Inc., N.Y.C., 1979, 81; v.p. N.Y.C. Council of Chs., 1984-86, chmn. bd., 1987-88. Mem. Minority Women Exec. Group of Presbyn. Ch. U.S.A. (convener 1979-82), Nat. Assn. Female Execs. Office: Presbyn Ch USA 100 Witherspoon St Louisville KY 40202

HWANG, TZU-YANG, minister; b. Kaohsiung, Taiwan, Republic of China, Sept. 21, 1953; came to U.S., 1985; d. Chi-Chou and Iu-Chih (Tsai) Huang; m. Wei-Chih Shih Hwang, Sept. 6, 1980. MD, Tainan Theol. Sem., 1980; ThD, Princeton (N.J.) Theol. Sem., 1986; PhD, Chinese for Christ Theol. Sem., Rosemead, Calif., 1990. Ordained to ministry Presbyn. Ch. Chairperson, min. Presbytery's Zrhlin Dists. Ch., Champhua, Taiwan, 1981-83; min., lectr., sr. editor Tainan Theol. Sem., 1983-85; founder, min. The Youth Fellowship of Kingston Presbyn. Ch., Princeton, 1985-86; head of religion edn., lectr. Good Shepherd Formosan Presbyn. Ch., Monterey Park, Calif., 1987-88; head of religion edn., lectr. Chinese for Christ Theol. Sem., 1987-88, dir. theology and philosophy, dean students, sr. editor, 1990—; Vis. Scholar, Harvard U. Div. Sch., Duke U. Div. Sch., Emory U. Candler Sch. Theol., 1991-92. Contbr. articles to profl. jours. With Chinese Def., 1972-74. mem. Am. Acad. Religion, Soc. Biblical Literature. Home: 11768 Roseglen St Rosemead CA 91732 Office: Chinese for Christ Theol 3342 Del Mar Ave Rosemead CA 91770

HYATT, JAMES LEWIS, JR., minister; b. Lancaster, S.C., May 4, 1938; s. James Lewis and Loree (McManus) H.; m. Julia Bowers, Dec. 30, 1956; children: James III, Don, Luanne Hyatt Hendricks. BA, Wofford Coll, 1960; BD, Chandler Sch. Theol., 1966; MDiv., Emory U., 1972. Ordained deacon United Meth. Ch., 1964. Owner, mgr. Hyatt Theatres, Lancaster and Spartansburg, S.C., 1960-63; pastor Lebanon United Meth. Ch., Honea Path, S.C., 1963-66, Adnah-Antioch United Meth. Ch., Rock Hill, S.C., 1966-71, Pacolet (S.C.) United Meth. Ch., 1971-76, Duncan Acreas United Meth. Ch., Union, S.C., 1976-78; sr. pastor Broad St. United Meth. Ch., Clinton, S.C., 1978-81, First United Meth. Ch., Bennettsville, S.C., 1981-86, Woodland United Meth. Ch., Rock Hill, 1986-91, Main Street United Meth. Ch., Columbia, S.C., 1991—. Chmn. S.C. United Meths. Active in Disaster, 1984-87; mem. adv. bd. S.C. United Meth. Found.; chmn. Ann. Conf. on Worship; chmn. bd. trustees Palmetto Health Care, Inc., Spartanburg, 1974-90, Spartanburg Area Mental Health Ctr., 1975-81, Marlboro Citizens for Better Edn., Bennettsville, 1983-86; chmn. bd. trustees James L. Belin, 1980-87; bd. dirs. Wesley Found. of Winthrop Coll., Rock Hill, 1986-91. Served to 1st lt., chaplain U.S. Army, 1970-75. Mem. So. United Meth. Fond. (chmn. ann. conf. com. of worship 1972-80), Am. Therapeutic Cons. (pres. 1989—). Democrat. Lodges: Lions, Rotary (v.p. Bennettsville club, 1984-86), Masons, Shriners (chaplain, 1972-75), SCMH Assn. (pres. Spartanburg 1971-81). *The nineties will bring many of the world's troubles to our door and our pews. We must fully appropriate our Lord's peace as we accept these challenges without allowing these troubled times to alter ours or His direction, or, our personal peace.*

HYDE, MARK ANTHONY, youth minister; b. Meriden, Conn., Dec. 18, 1952; s. William J. and Katherine T. (Beier) H. BA in Philosophy, Don Bosco Coll., 1975; MDiv., Pontifical Coll. Josephinum, 1981. Deacon St. Matthew Parish, Gahanna, Ohio, 1980-81; youth pastor St. Anthony of Padua Parish, Elizabeth, N.J., 1981-82; vocation dir. Salesian Jr. Sem., Goshen, N.Y., 1982-86; dir. religious activities Mary Help of Christians Sch., Tampa, Fla., 1986-88; chaplain, youth min., dir. youth svcs. Salesian Ctr. and Boys Club, Columbus, Ohio, 1988—; supr. pastoral field edn. Pontifical Coll. Josephinium, Columbus, Ohio, 1988—; instr. field edn. Ohio State U. Coll. of Social Work, Columbus, 1990—. Recipient English award Columbus Found., 1989; named Salesian Boys Club Staff Mem. of Yr., 1990-91, Outstanding New Field Instr., Coll. Social Work, Ohio State U., 1991. Mem. Salesians of Don Bosco, Nat. Fedn. for Catholic Youth Ministry, Vols. Adminstrs. Network, Callvac Youth Vols. (adv. bd.), Nat. Religious Vocation Conf. Office: Salesian Boys Club 80 S 6th St Columbus OH 43215 *Happiness and holiness in life comes from relationship with God and with neighbor. Recognize and affirm the goodness of all.*

HYERS, CONRAD, religion educator; b. Phila., July 31, 1933; s. A. Melvin and Miriam Demaris (Soper) H.; m. Geraldine Ruth Ort, Sept. 6, 1955; children: Jon Winston, Dean Lincoln, Laurilyn. BA, Carson-Newman Coll., 1954; MD, Ea. Sem., Phila., 1958; ThM, Princeton Theol. Sem., 1959, PhD, 1965. Assoc. prof. Beloit (Wis.) Coll., 1966-77; prof. Gustavus Adolphus Coll., St. Peter, Minn., 1977—. Author: The Comic Vision and the Christian Faith, 1981, The Meaning of Creation, 1984, The Bible As Divine Comedy, 1987, Once-Born, Twice-Born Zen, 1989, The Laughing Buddha, 1990. NEH Younger Humanist fellow, 1970, Sr. Humanist fellow, 1976, Blandin Found. fellow, 1990. Mem. Am. Acad. Religion. Presbyterian. Home: Box 277A Rte 1 Saint Peter MN 56082 Office: Gustavus Adolphus Coll College Ave Saint Peter MN 56082

HYMAN, ROBERT SCOTT, religious association administrator; b. Denver, Aug. 14, 1953; s. Jerome and Estelle Mae (Davis) H.; m. Nancy Lynn Bier, July 30, 1972; children: Binyamin, Yakir. BA, Memphis State U., 1975; MSW, Columbia U., 1977. Asst., then assoc. exec. dir. Memphis Jewish Fedn., 1977-82; community cons. Coun. Jewish Fedns., N.Y.C., 1982-84; exec. dir. Jewish Community Fedn. Richmond (Va.), 1985—. Mem. Assn. Jewish Community Orgn. Pers., Nat. Assn. Social Workers, Acad. Cert. Social Workers, Leadership Metro Richmond. Office: Jewish Community Fedn PO Box 17128 Richmond VA 23226

HYMERS, ROBERT LESLIE, JR., pastor; b. Glendale, Calif., Apr. 12, 1941; s. Robert Leslie Sr. Hymers and Cecelia Juanita (Flowers) McDonell; m. Ileana Patricia Cuellar, Sept. 27, 1982; children: Robert Leslie Hymers III, John Wesley Hymers (twins). BA, Calif. State U., L.A., 1970; MDiv, Golden Gate Bapt. Theol. Sem., 1973; DMin, San Francisco Theol. Sem., 1981; ThD, La. Bapt. Theol. Sem., 1989. Ordained to ministry Bapt. Ch., 1972. Pastor Ch. of the Open Door, San Rafael, Calif., 1973-75, Fundamentalist Bapt. Tabernacle, L.A., 1975—; guest TV programs. Author: Holocaust II, 1978, The Ruckman Conspiracy, 1989, Inside the Southern Baptist Convention, 1990; contbr. articles to profl. jours. Republican. Office: Fundamentalist Bapt 1329 S Hope St Los Angeles CA 90015 *At the age of twenty I had no hope. Life had no meaning. I turned to Jesus. Jesus has forgiven me and has given me the strength to do God's work. My life is centered in Jesus.*

IAKOVOS, BISHOP (IAKOVOS GARMATIS), bishop; b. Athens, Greece. Grad., Sch. Theology Athens U.; postgrad., Boston U., Harvard Div. Sch. Ordained deacon Greek Orthodox Ch., 1952, priest, 1954; named Archimandrite, 1954. Pastor Assumption Ch., Somerville, Mass., 1957; svc. in Boston area, until 1968; archdiocesan vicar Detroit Diocese, 1968; consecrated bishop of Apameia, 1969; dist. bishop Detroit Diocese, 1969; also pres. Hellenic Coll./Holy Cross Sch. Theology, 1971-76; also bishop N.Eng. area, 1971-76; aux. bishop of Archbishop Iavakos of Greek Orthodox Archdiocese in the Ams., from 1969; bishop Diocese of Chgo., 1979—; former mem. faculty Holy Cross Greek Orthodox Sch. Theology, Brookline, Mass. Office: Greek Orthodox Archdiocese 40 E Burton Pl Chicago IL 60610

IAKOVOS, ARCHBISHOP (DEMETRIOS A. COUCOUZIS), archbishop; b. Imvros, Turkey, July 29, 1911; s. Athanasios and Maria Coucouzis. Grad., Theol. Sch. of Halki, Ecumenical Patriarchate, 1934; S.T.M., Harvard, 1945; D.D., Boston U., 1960, Bates Coll., 1970, Dubuque U., 1973, Assumption Coll., 1980; L.H.D., Franklin and Marshall Coll., 1961, Southeastern Mass. Tech. Inst., 1967, Am. Internat. Coll., 1972, Cath. U., 1974, Loyola Marymount U., 1979, Queen's Coll., 1982; LL.D., Brown U., 1964, Seton Hall U., 1968, Coll. of Holy Cross, 1966, Fordham U., 1966, Notre Dame U., 1979, N.Y. Law Sch., 1982, St. John's U., 1982; H.H.D., Suffolk U., 1967, Stonehill Coll., 1980; D.S.T., Berkeley Div. Sch., 1962, Gen. Theol. Sem., 1967, Thessalonica U., 1975; Lit.D., PMC Colls., 1971; others. Ordained deacon Greek Orthodox Ch., 1934; archdeacon Greek Orthodox Ch., Met. Derkon, 1934-39; prof. Archdiocese Theol. Sch., Pomfret, Conn., 1939; ordained priest, 1940; parish priest Hartford, Conn., 1940-41; preacher Holy Trinity Cathedral, N.Y.C., 1941-42; parish priest St. Louis, 1942; dean Cathedral of Annunciation, Boston, 1942-54; dean Holy Cross Orthodox Theol. Sch., Brookline, Mass., 1954, now pres.; bishop of Holy Cross Orthodox Theol. Sch., Melita, Malta, 1954-56; rep. Ecumenical Patriarchate, World Council Chs., Geneva, 1955-59; then co-pres. council Ecumenical Patriarchate, World Council Chs., 1959-68; elevated to Metropolitan, 1956; archbishop, N. and S. Am., Holy Synod of Ecumenical Patriarchate, 1959—; chmn. Standing Conf. Canonical Bishops in the Americas; mem. adv. bd., v.p. Religion in American Life. Author works in Greek, French, English, German. Pres. St. Basil's Acad., Garrison, N.Y.; chmn. trustees Hellenic Coll., Brookline; trustee Anatolia Coll., Salonika, Greece. Recipient Man of Yr. award B'nai B'rith, 1962; recipient Nat. award NCCJ, 1962, Clergyman of the Yr. award Religious Heritage Am., 1970, Presdl. Citation as Disting. Am. in Voluntary Service, 1970, Man of Conscience award Appeal of Conscience Found., 1971, Presdl. Medal of Freedom, 1980, Interreligious award Religion in Am. Life, 1980, Clergyman of Yr. award N.Y.C. Council Churches, 1981, others. Mem. Am. Bible Soc. (bd. mgrs.). Address: Greek Orthodox Archdiocese 10 E 79th St New York NY 10021

IBACH, DOUGLAS THEODORE, minister; b. Pottstown, Pa., July 23, 1925; s. Hiram Christian and Esther (Fry) I.; B.S. in Edn., Temple U., 1950, postgrad. Sch. Theology, 1950-52; M.Div., Louisville Presbyn. Theol. Sem., 1954; m. Marion Elizabeth Torok, Sept. 2, 1950; children—Susan Kay, Marilyn Lee, Douglas Theodore, Grace Louise. Ordained to ministry Presbyn. Ch., 1953; pastor, Pewee Valley, Ky., 1952-55, West Nottingham Presbyn. Ch., Colora, Md., 1955-61, Irwin, Pa., 1961-67, Knox Presbyn. Ch., Falls Church, Va., 1967-72, United Christian Parish Reston (Va.), 1972-87; exec. dir. Camping Assn. of the Presbyteries of Northwestern Pa., Mercer, Pa., 1986-90; pastor Pulaski (Pa.) Presbyn. Ch., 1990—. Youth ministry cons. Nat. Capital Union Presbytery, 1967-86; ecumenical officer Nat. Capital Presbytery, chmn. stewardship com., 1986—; mem. ecumenical relations com. Synod of Virginias, also mem. Interfaith Conf. of Metro Washington; bd. dirs. Reston Inter-Faith, Inc.; dir. Presbyn. Internat. Affairs Seminars. adv. bd. Christmas Internat. House; mem. ch. devel. and redevel. com., Christian edn. com. Lake Erie Presbytery, stated supply Pulaski (Pa.) Presbyterian Ch.; sec. New Wilmington Mininsterium; exec. dir. Camping Assn. of Presbyteries of No. Pa., 1986-90. With USNR, 1943-44. Mem. Council Chs. Greater Washington (pres., chmn. instl. ministry commn.), Piedmont Synod U.P. Ch. (dir. youth, camping), Acad. Parish Clergy Assn. Presbyn. Christian Educators, Fairfax County Council Chs. (pres.), Com. 100 Fairfax County, Mercer Fun Club (bd. dirs.). Home: RD 1 Box 584 New Wilmington PA 16142 Office: Pulaski Presbyn Ch Liberty St and Shenango Ave Pulaski PA 16143

IBACH, ROBERT DANIEL, JR., library director; b. Lynch, Nebr., Dec. 31, 1940; s. Robert Daniel Sr. and Mabel Bertine (Selstad) I.; m. Paula Joanne Hubbling, June 11, 1977. B.R.E., Detroit Bible Coll., 1963; BD, Grace Theol. Sem., Winona Lake, Ind., 1966, ThM, 1969; MLS, Ind. U., 1975. Ordained minister, 1989. Libr. Grace Coll. and Sem., Winona Lake, 1969-86; library dir. Dallas Theol. Sem., 1986—; archaeologist Heshbon (Jordan) Expedition, 1971-76; library cons. Inst. of Holy Land Studies, Jerusalem, 1989. Author: Archaeological Survey of the Hesban Region, 1987; consulting editor Jour. Religious & Theol. Info., 1991—; contbr. articles to profl. jours., 1972-91. Mem. Soc. Bibl. Lit., Am. Theol. Library Assn. Home: 3229 Colby Circle Mesquite TX 75149 Office: Dallas Theol Sem 3909 Swiss Ave Dallas TX 75204

IBANEZ, RAMON MEDINA, religious organization administrator. Pres. Bapt. Conv., Medellin, Colombia. Office: Bapt Conv, Apdo Aereo 61988, Medellin Colombia*

IBRAHIM, IBRAHIM N., bishop; b. Telkaif, Mosul, Iraq, Oct. 1, 1940; came to U.S., 1978; s. Namo Ibrahim and Rammo Yono. Grad., Mosul Sem., Iraq, 1951, St. Sulpice Sem., Paris, 1962; D.S.T., Rome, 1975. Dir. sem. Baghdad, Iraq, 1964-68; assoc. pastor St. Joseph Ch., Baghdad, 1975-78; pastor Chaldean Ch., Los Angeles, 1979-82; bishop Chaldean Church of U.S.A., Southfield, Mich., 1982—; first Bishop Eparch Eparchy of St. Thomas the Apostle - Chaldean Cath. Diocese of Am., 1985—. Home: Our Lady of Chaldeans Cathedral 25585 Berg Rd Southfield MI 48034

ICE, RICHARD EUGENE, minister, retirement housing company executive; b. Ft. Lewis, Wash., Sept. 25, 1930; s. Shirley and Nellie Rebecca (Pedersen) I.; m. Pearl Lucille Daniels, July 17, 1955; children: Lorinda Susan, Diana Laurene, Julianne Adele. AA, Centralia Coll., 1950; BA, Linfield Coll., 1952, LHD (hon.), 1978; MA, Berkeley Bapt. Div. Sch., 1959; grad. advanced mgmt. program Harvard U., 1971. Ordained to ministry Am. Bapt. Ch., 1954; pastor Ridgecrest Community Bapt. Ch., Seattle, 1955-59; dir. ch. extension Wash. Bapt. Conv., 1959-61; dir. loans Am. Bapt. Extension Corp., Valley Forge, Pa., 1961-64; assoc. exec. minister Am. Bapt. Chs. of West, Oakland, Calif., 1964-67; dep. exec. sec., treas. Am. Bapt. Home Mission Socs., Valley Forge, 1967-72; pres. Am. Bapt. Homes of the West, Oakland, 1972—; dir. Minister's Life Ins. Co., Mpls., 1975-87, chmn. bd. dirs. 1986-87; bd. dir. Bapt. Life Assn., Buffalo, 1988—; pres. Am. Bapt. Homes and Hosps. Assn., 1978-81. v.p. Am. Bapt. Chs. U.S.A., 1990-91; Ministers and Missionaries Benefit Bd.; mem. Bapt. Joint Com. on Pub. Affairs; trustee, chmn. com. fin. affairs Linfield Coll., 1972—; trustee Calif./Nev. Methodist Homes, 1975—, Bacone Coll., 1968-77, Grad. Theol. Union, Berkeley, Calif., 1982—; trustee Am. Bapt. Sem. of West, Berkeley, 1975—, chmn. bd. trustees, 1987—. Recipient Disting. Baconian award Bacone Coll., 1977, Disting. Alumnus award Centralia Coll., 1981, Meritorious Service award Am. Assn. Homes for Aging, 1982, Merit citation Am. Bapt. Homes and Hosp. Assn., 1985, Award of Honor Calif. Assn. Homes for the Aging, 1988. Mem. U.S. Assn. for UN, Am. Assn. Homes for Aging, Calif. Assn. Homes for Aging, Harvard Bus. Sch. Assn. No. Calif., The Oakland 100, Pi Gamma Mu. Democrat. Clubs: Harvard of San Francisco, Lakeview, Athenian Nile (Oakland). Office: 400 Roland Way Oakland CA 94621

ICENOGLE, PHILLIP LEE, pastor; b. Astoria, Ill., Aug. 19, 1943; s. Loren Eugene and Dollie (Gruber) I.; m. Judith Ann Roby, Aug. 15, 1965; children: Wesley Arron, Christian Lee, Buffie Jo. AA, Hannibal LaGrange Coll., 1968; BA, Quincy Coll., 1970; MDiv, Garrett-Evang. Theol. Sem., 1973, DMin, 1989. Assoc. pastor Morton (Ill.) United Meth. Ch., 1973-78; pastor Manteno (Ill.) United Meth. Ch., 1978-82; assoc. pastor First United Meth. Ch., Springfield, Ill., 1982-85; pastor Casey (Ill.) United Meth. Ch., 1985—; vice-chair Conf. Rules of Order, 1979-82, chairperson, 1983-86; sec. Dist. Com. on Ministry, 1987—; mem. Conf. Bd. of Ordained Ministry, 1989—. Mem. East Cen. Ill. Agy. on Aging, Bloomington, Ill., 1987-90. Named Outstanding Young Religious Leader Ill. Jaycees, 1976. Mem. Casey Ministerial Assn. (pres. 1989), Morton Jaycees, Casey Lions Club (3d v.p. 1987-88, 1st v.p. 1988-89, pres. 1989-90). Methodist. Avocations: stain glass crafting, biking, photography, camping. Home: 706 E Washington Casey IL 62420 Office: Casey United Meth Ch 700 N Central Casey IL 62420

IDLEMAN, KENNETH DARRELL, college president; b. Champaign, Ill., Aug. 18, 1947; s. Kenneth F. and Lois R. (Collins) I.; m. Kaylene Ruth Conover, Aug. 17, 1968; children—Karissa Marie, Kyle David, Kamille Joy. A.B., Lincoln Christian Coll., Ill., 1969; M.Div., Lincoln Christian Sem., 1973. Ordained to ministry Christian Ch., 1968. Pastor, Broadwell Christian Ch., Ill., 1968-70, Mt. Pulaski Christian Ch., Ill., 1970-72; adminstr. Lincoln Christian Coll., 1972-73; prof. Ozark Bible Coll., Joplin, Mo., 1973-77, v.p., 1977-79, pres., 1979—, trustee, 1979—; bd. dirs. Am. Rehab. Ministry, Joplin, 1979-81, Christ in Youth, Joplin, 1980-82. Republican. Office: Ozark Christian Coll 1111 N Main St Joplin MO 64801

IGLEHART, T. D., bishop. Bishop Ch. of God in Christ, San Antonio, Tex. Office: Ch of God in Christ 325 Terrell Rd San Antonio TX 78209*

IGNATIOS, PATRIARCH IV, international religious organization official. Mem. presidium World Coun. Chs., Geneva. Office: care World Coun Chs, 150 Rte de Ferney, POB 2100, 1211 Geneva 20, Switzerland*

IGRAS, HENRY, minister; b. Niagara Falls, N.Y., June 16, 1952; s. John and Helen (Jankowski) I.; m. Carlene Marie Hyla, Nov. 12, 1977; 1 child, Elizabeth Anne. BAmagna cum laude, SUNY, Buffalo, 1974; MDiv summa cum laude, Grace Theol. Sem., 1989. Ordained to ministry Bapt. Ch., 1990. Sr. pastor Immanuel Bapt. Ch., Marion, Ind., 1989—; elder Niagara Frontier Bible Ch., Lewiston, N.Y., 1983-85; intern. tchr. Pleasant View Bible Ch., Warsaw, Ind., 1988-89. Active Grant County Right to Life, Marion. Republican. Home: 2 Valley Ct Marion IN 46953 Office: Immanuel Bapt Ch 1321 E 39th St Marion IN 46953

IIDA, JOHN, church administrator; b. Inglewood, Calif., Aug. 7, 1962; s. Harry Tatsuo and Florance Kimiyo (Wada) I. BBA, Linfield Coll., 1984; MBA, Oral Roberts U., 1986. Grad. asst. Oral Roberts U., Tulsa, 1984-85, grad. fellow Sch. Bus., 1985-86; adminstr. Harvest Fellowship Inst., Tustin, Calif., 1989—; office mgr. U.S. Lifestyles, Orange, Calif., 1990. Mem. Christian Ministries Assn.

IKE, REVEREND See EIKERENKOETTER, FREDERICK JOSEPH, II

ILANGYI, BYA'ENE AKULU, bishop. Free Meth. Ch. of N. Am. Indpls. Office: Free Meth Ch N Am PO Box 535002 Indianapolis IN 46253-5002*

ILAO, TOM JAVATE, religious organization official, deacon; b. Cabanatuan, Nueva Ecija, The Philippines, Mar. 7, 1941; came to U.S., 1971; s. Agapito De Guzman and Feliza (Javate) I.; m. Lolita Reyes, Aug. 12, 1972; children: Francis Thomas R., Margaret Mary R., Jeremiah R. BSBA, Far Ea. U., Manila, 1963. Ordained deacon Roman Cath. Ch., 1990; lic. ins. agt., Calif. Lector, eucharistic min. St. Finn Barr Ch., San Francisco, 1974-89; deacon, homilist, coord. baptism, spiritual dir. St. Vincent de Paul Soc., Corpus Christi Ch., San Francisco, 1990—; instr. Confraternity Christian Doctrine, San Francisco, 1984-87; guest homilist Immaculate Conception Ch., San Francisco, 1990—; guest speaker San Francisco Bus. League, San Francisco Press Club, Tenn. Mental and Health Depts., Chattanooga, others. Author: America Under Siege: The Drug Invasion, 1989 (Benjamin Franklin award Pubs. Mktg. Assn. 1990). Workshop leader Calif. Pro-Life Orgn., Oakland, 1974; speaker San Francisco Right to Life, 1975. Recipient Dist. Speech Champion award Livermore (Calif.) Jaycees, 1977; named one of the Most Outstanding Asians of Calif., Asian Voice/Victor Roberts Publs., 1990. Mem. Nat. Writers Club, Nat. Press Club-U.S.A. (cert. of achievement Philippine chpt. 1990), Pubs. Mktg. Assn., Com. Small Mag. Editors and Pubs., Calif. Lawyers for Arts, KC (past grand knight), Toastmasters (past pres. West Portal, Calif. club, Internat. Area Speech champion (2) 1976). Home: 634 Joost Ave San Francisco CA 94127 *The death of communication—nothing can prevent it from happening when we start building walls so thick around us that we prevent others from coming into our lives. And the tragedy is: we may not be able to get out anymore.*

ILIYA, II, religious leader. Catholicos-Patriarch of All Georgia The Georgian Orth. Ch., Tbilisi, Georgia, USSR. Office: Ch of Georgia, Catholicos, Patriarch of Georgia, Tiflis Georgia, USSR*

ILOGU, EDMUND CHRISTOPHER ONYEDUM, priest; b. Ihiala, Anambra, Nigeria, Apr. 25, 1920; came to U.S., 1986; s. Nwaku and Agnes Ugboego (Asuzu) I.; m. Elizabeth Chineze Obiago, Apr. 25, 1946; children: Ikechukwu, Chidi, Gordon, Dennis, Noel, Comfort, Rosemary, Ezinne. BD, London Coll. Div., 1953; STM, Union Theol. Sem., N.Y.C., 1958; MA, Columbia U., 1959; PhD, State U. Leiden, The Netherlands, 1974. Ordained priest Anglican (Episcopal) Ch., 1950. Prof. religion, head dept. U. Nigeria, Nsukka, 1967-76; commr. pub. complaints Anambra State Nigeria, Enugu, 1980-86; Episcopal chaplain Howard U., Washington, 1988-90; priest-in-charge Calvary Episcopal Ch., Washington, 1990—; hon. canon St. Bartholomew's Cathedral, Enugu, 1972—; mem. Washington Diocesan Conv., 1988—; adj. prof. ch. history and mission Wesley Theol. Sem., Washington, 1987-91; adj. prof. African philosophy U. D.C., 1991. Author: West Meets East, 1956, Social Philosophy for the New Nigerian Nation, 1962, Christianity and Ibo Culture, 1974, Igbo Life and Thought, 1988. Pres. Washington br. Nigeria World Network, 1990—. Mem. Internat. Assn. for Sociology of Religion (exec. com. for Africa 1974), Rotary Internat. (news editor Enugu 1980-81, Paul Harris fellow). Home: 8025 New Riggs Rd Hyattsville MD 20783 Office: Calvary Episcopal Ch 820 6th St NE Washington DC 20002 *Best things of life are nearly always shared, at least between two persons, signifying the communality of life. We share stories, we share joys, laughter, love, sorrow, success and failure. Attainment of the most important aspects of life, I think, is in the communality human beings share with the Spiritual Plurality of Being that Creates, Saves and Inspires. How much we miss in life when we neglect the fellowship our essential nature of communality demands of us! To live in this fellowship is, in a nutshell, what love of God and of neighbors means.*

IMATHIU, LAWI, bishop. Presiding bishop Methodis Ch. in Kenya, Nairobi. Office: Meth Ch in Kenya, POB 47633, Nairobi Kenya*

IMBLER, JOHN MARK, church executive, clergyman; b. Kokomo, Ind., Mar. 27, 1945; s. Chester and Jeanette (Ferguson) I.; m. Toni Wine, Sept. 3, 1967; children: Andrew, Bethany, Catherine. BA, Butler U., 1967; MDiv., Christian Theol. Sem., 1971, STM, 1981; DD, Columbia Coll., 1987. Ordained to ministry Christian Ch. (Disciples of Christ), 1974. Counselor Indpls. Skills Ctr., 1971-74, asst. dir., 1974-76; dir. vocat. services State of Ind., Indpls., 1976-79; dir. instl. services div. higher edn. The Christian Ch. (Disciples of Christ), 1979-81; v.p. div. higher edn. The Christian Ch. (Disciples of Christ), St. Louis, 1981—; Mem. Task Force on Ministry, The Christian Ch. (Disciples of Christ), 1984—, study task group Assn. Theol. Sch., 1981; treas. ADTD, St. Louis, 1979—; project dir. Advancing the Quality of Ordained Leadership, 1989-91. Assoc. editor Disciples Theol. Digest, 1986-88, editor, 1989—; contbr. articles to ch. jour. Active Lindbergh Sch. Dist. Citizen's Adv. Council, St. Louis, 1983-85, 87. Named one of Outstanding Young Men Am, 1980. Mem. Am. Acad. Religion, Soc. For Advancement Continuing Edn. for Ministry, Disciples Christ Hist. Soc. (life). Avocations: sports, reading. Office: Christian Ch (Disciples of Christ) Div Higher Edn 11780 Borman Dr Ste 100 Saint Louis MO 63146

IMESCH, JOSEPH LEOPOLD, bishop; b. Grosse Pointe Farms, Mich., June 21, 1931; s. Dionys and Margaret (Margelisch) I. B.S., Sacred Heart

Sem., 1953; student, N.Am. Coll., Rome, 1953-57; S.T.L., Gregorian U., Rome, 1957. Ordained priest Roman Cath. Ch., 1956; sec. to Cardinal Dearden, 1959-71; pastor Our Lady of Sorrows Ch., Farmington, Mich., 1971-77; titular bishop of Pomaria and aux. bishop of Detroit, 1973-79; asst. bishop N.W. Region, 1977-79; bishop of Joliet Ill., 1979—. Office: Chancery Office 425 Summit St Joliet IL 60435

IMPELLIZZERI, RICHARD, minister; b. Hollywood, Fla., Aug. 4, 1950; s. Frank and Ann (Motto) I.; m. Roseanne Pagliarulo, Aug. 12, 1978; children: David, Jonathan, Nathan, Angela Rose. BA, Evangel. Coll., Springfield, Mo., 1975. Ordained minister Gen. Coun. Assemblies of God, 1985. Asst. pastor Full Gospel Christian Ch., Copiague, N.Y., 1980-84; sr. pastor First Assembly of God, Hollywood, Fla., 1984—; men's sect. rep. Assemblies of God Chs. Section XV, Broward, Dade Counties, Fla., 1990—. Lyricist: (song) Praise You, Jesus, 1971. Office: Assembly of God Ch 1019 N 24th Ave Hollywood FL 33020

IMPERIALE, MICHAEL JAMES, pastor; b. Wood Ridge, N.J., Mar. 29, 1952; s. Petr Fabiano and Alice Teresa (Schreiber) I.; m. Dorothy Leitzell Mosher, Aug. 27, 1978; children: Michael Charles, Elisabeth Brown, Sarah Ruth. MusB, Westminster Choir Coll., Princeton, N.J., 1974; MDiv, Gordon-Conwell Theol. Sem., South Hamilton, Mass., 1984. Ordained to ministry Presbyn. Ch. (U.S.A.), 1984. Dir. music and youth United Presbyn. Ch., New Wilmington, Pa., 1978-80; choir dir. North Shore Community Bapt. Ch., Beverly Farms, Mass., 1981-83; assoc. pastor 1st Presbyn. Ch., Greenlawn, N.Y., 1984-89; pastor Covenant Presbyn. Ch., Cinnaminson, N.J., 1989—; chaplain Area II, Am. Guild English Handbell Ringers, 1989; mem. Presbytery of L.I., 1984-89, Presbytery of West Jersey, 1989—. Author: (sermons) The Promise of Life, 1989, Power for the Church Today, 1990, Faith that Works, 1990, Letters to the Church, 1991. Mem. alumni coun. Westminster Choir Coll., 1991. Mem. Tri Boro Ministerial Assn. Republican. Office: Covenant Presbyn Ch 2618 New Albany Rd Cinnaminson NJ 08077

INADA, MINORU, clergyman; b. Taihoku, Japan, Sept. 5, 1930; s. Inajiro and Yuri (Kato) I.; m. Mitsuko Yamazaki, July 25, 1961; children: Mika, John Mitsuru, Marika. BA in Econs., Rikkyo (St. Paul's) U., 1953; BA in Theology, Japan Missionary Coll., 1959; MA in Edn., Andrews U., 1966. Cert. secondary tchr. Ordained to ministry Seventh-Day Adventist Ch. Instr. Japan Missionary Coll., Chiba, 1959-67; editor-in-chief Japan Publ. House, Yokohama, 1967-74; dir. edn. Japan Union Seventh-day Adventists, Yokohama, 1974-79; pastor-in-chief Amanuma Ch. Seventh-day Adventists, Tokyo, 1979-85; counselor Path-finders Club, Tokyo, 1979-85; assoc. dir. Ch. Ministries, Dept. for Eastern Div., Seventh Day Adventists, 1985-87, assoc. sec. Ministerial Assn. for Far Ea. Div., 1988—; dir. Pub. Affairs and Religious Liberty Dept.; exec. sec. Adventist Laymans; Svcs. and Industries. Author: Human Relations for Your Success, 1974. OECD grantee, Tokyo, 1964; recipient Minister of Edn. award Japan Times Inc., 1970. Mem. Japan Soc. Rel. Edn., Parent Effectiveness Tng. Assocs. Inc. (instr. 1982—). Home and Office: 800 Thomson Rd, Singapore 1129, Singapore *Unless and until we come to know the Invisible superceding and subsuming in all the visible, our lives cannot be viable in this vexed and vicious world.*

INAMINE, GAIL TAMAE, religion educator; b. Hilo, Hawaii, June 25, 1951; d. Joseph Hiroshi and Patsy Tomiko (Oshiro) I. BS, Colo. State U., 1973; MRE, Southwestern Bapt. Theol. Sem., Ft. Worth, 1976. Mission coord. Puna Bapt. Mission Kinoole Bapt. Ch., Hilo, Hawaii, 1977-78; from dir. edn. to min. edn. Kinoole Bapt. Ch., Hilo, Hawaii, 1979—; com. conf. arrangment Hawaii Bapt. Conv., 1988-91; youth cons. Big Island Bapt. Assn., 1987— (youth dir. 1991—). Baptist. Office: Kinoole Baptist Church 1815 Kinoole St Hilo HI 96720

INBODY, TYRON LEE, minister, educator; b. Goshen, Ind., Mar. 21, 1940; s. Orville Charles and Lavon Evelyn (Wideman) I.; m. Frances Elaine Reger, June 25, 1961; children: Mark, David. BA, U. Indpls., 1962; MDiv, United Theol. Sem., Dayton, Ohio, 1965; AM, U. Chgo., 1967, PhD, 1973. Prof. religion Adrian Coll., 1969-76, United Theol. Sem., Dayton, 1976—. Editor: Changing Channels, 1990, United Theol. Sem. Jour. Theology, 1985, Am. Jour. Theology and Philosophy, 1991—; contbr. articles to profl. jours. Grantee NEH, 1974. Mem. Am. Acad. Religion, Ohio Acad. Religion, Highlands Inst. (bd. dirs.). Methodist. Avocation: photography. Home: 8020 Paragon Rd Dayton OH 45458 Office: United Theol Sem 1810 Harvard Dayton OH 45406

INCH, MORRIS ALTON, theology educator; b. Wytopitlock, Maine, Oct. 21, 1925; s. Clarence Sherwin and Blanche (Mix) I.; m. Joan Parker, Dec. 16, 1950; children: Deborah, Lois, Thomas, Joel, Mark. AB, Houghton Coll., 1949; MDiv, Gordon Div. Sch., 1951; PhD, Boston U., 1955. Ordained to ministry Baptist Ch., 1951; pastor South Boston Bapt. Ch., 1951-55, Union Sq. Bapt. Ch., Somerville, Mass., 1955-61; prof., dean students, dean of coll. Gordon Coll., Wenham, Mass., 1955-62; prof., chmn. dept. Biblical, religious and archeol. studies Wheaton (Ill.) Coll., 1962-86; pres. The Inst. of Holy Land Studies, 1986-90. Author: Psychology in the Psalms, 1969, Christianity Without Walls, 1972, Paced by God, 1973, Celebrating Jesus as Lord, 1974, Understanding Bible Prophecy, 1977, The Evangelical Challenge, 1978, My Servant Job, 1979, Doing Theology Across Cultures, 1982, Saga of the Spirit: A Biblical, Systematic and Historical Theology of the Holy Spirit, 1985, Making the Gospel Relevant, 1986; editor: (with Samuel Schultz) Interpreting the Word of God, 1976, (with C. Hassell Bullock) The Literature and Meaning of Scripture, 1981, (with Ronald Youngblood) The Living and Active Word of God, 1983; contbr. articles to profl. jours. Served with USAAF, 1943-46. Named Sr. Tchr. of Year Wheaton Coll., 1971; recipient Centennial award Houghton Coll., 1983; ann. lectureship established Wheaton Coll., 1986. Mem. Evang. Theol. Soc. Home: 348 Fairview Ave West Chicago IL 60185 *Life consists for me in practising an openness to God, an availability to others and for their ministry to me. In these relationships I rely on the sustaining grace of Jesus Christ.*

INGALL, CAROL KREPON, religion educator; b. Boston, Apr. 15, 1940; d. Harry and Olla (Davis) Krepon; m. Michael A. Ingall, June 18, 1961; children: Marjorie Beth, Andrew Morris. BA, Barnard Coll., 1961; BHL, Jewish Theol. Sem., N.Y.C., 1961; MA in Teaching, U. Chgo., 1963; MLS, U. R.I., 1973. Synagogue educator Temple Emanu-El, Providence, 1973-80, trustee, 1989—; cons. Bur. Jewish Edn., Providence, 1980-83, assoc. dir., 1983-86, exec. dir., 1986-90; curriculum writer Melton Rsch. Ctr., N.Y.C., 1980—; dir. continuing edn. Horstein program Jewish communal svc. Brandeis U., Waltham, Mass., 1991—. Contbr. articles, monographs to profl. publs. Recipient Sidney Hillson prize for contbns. to Jewish edn. Hebrew Coll., 1988. Fellow Coun. for Jewish Edn.; mem. Conf. for Advancement of Jewish Edn. Home: 150 Upton Ave Providence RI 02906

INGBER, ABIE I(SAAC), rabbi; b. Montreal, Quebec, Can., Mar. 30, 1950; s. Wolfe and Fania (Paszht) I.; m. Shelley Sandra Nadler, Aug. 19, 1973; children: Avital Nadler, Dorit Peck, Tamar Sorkin. BS, McGill U., Montreal, 1971; MA in Hebrew Letters, Hebrew Union Coll.-Jewish Inst. Religion, 1976. Ordained rabbi, 1977. Exec. dir., rabbi Hillel Found., Cin., 1977—; homiletics instr. Hebrew Union Coll.-Jewish Inst. Religion, Cin., 1984—; bible instr. Xavier U., 1988-90; moderator Dialogue, weekly interfaith TV program. Author: (books) Cook Unto Others, 1983, Assessing the Significance of the Holocaust, 1987; advice columnist "Dear Abie" Clifton Town Meeting Bulletin, Cin., 1987-88. bd. dirs. Cin. Coun. for Soviet Jews, 1980—, Clifton Town Meeting, Cin., 1985-90, Gov. Celeste's Holocaust Com., Columbus, Ohio, 1986; v.p. Interfaith Holocaust Found., Cin., 1983-89; active human svcs. adv. com. City of Cin., 1989—. Recipient Key to the City of Cin., 1991; named to Honorable Order of Ky. Colonels. Mem. Cen. Conf. Am. Rabbis, Campus Ministries Assn. (chmn. 1984-85), Assn.Hillel Jewish Campus Profls. (pres. 1984-86), Am. Jewish Com., Jewish Agy. Execs. Group (pres. Cin. chpt. 1988, Cin. Bd. Rabbis, v.p. 1990-91, pres. 1991—). Avocations: cooking, urban archaelogy. Office: Hillel Found 2615 Clifton Ave Cincinnati OH 45220

INGIBERGSSON, ASGEIR, minister, librarian; b. Alafoss, Iceland, Jan. 17, 1928; arrived in Can., 1968; s. Ingibergur and Sigridur Olga (Kristjansdottir) Runolfsson; m. Janet Smiley, June 27, 1959; children: David, Ragnar, Elisabet, Margret. Candidatus theologiae, U. Iceland, 1957, teaching diploma, 1967; postgrad., Trinity Coll., Ireland, 1958; MLS, U. Alta., Can., 1980. Ordained to ministry Evang. Luth. Ch. Iceland, 1958. Pastor Hvamms Parish, Iceland, 1958-66; chaplain, youth dir. Keflavik, Iceland, 1966-68; pastor Grace Luth. Ch., Man., Can., 1968-71, Bawlf Luth. Ch., Alta., 1971-78; head libr. Camrose (Alta.) Luth. Coll., 1978—. Chmn. bd. trustees Stadarfell Home Econs. Sch., Iceland, 1958-66, Bethany Aux. Hosp., Camrose, 1974-82. Mem. ALA, Can. Libr. Assn., Assn. Coll. Librs. Alta., Libr. Assn. Alta. Home: 6213 42d Ave, Camrose, AB Canada T4V 2W8 Office: Camrose Luth Coll, Camrose, AB Canada T4V 2R3 *A quest for meaning for my own life has been the basis for my study of theology. As my life progressed so have my points of view. It has been a spiritual pilgrimage and still is.*

INGRAHAM, KIMBERLEE D(EANN), youth ministry director; b. Downey, Calif., June 16, 1955; d. Dean Marshall and Roberta I. (Hayes) I. BA, Azusa Pacific U., 1977; colloquy, Concordia Coll., 1988. Cert. Dir. Christian Edn., 1988. Dir. of youth and Christian Edn. Grace Luth. Ch., Eugene, Oreg., 1988—; mem. Oreg. Conf. Youth Bd., Portland, 1989—; bd. dirs. Greater Eugene Educators Assn.

INGRAM, BARBARA AVERETT, minister; b. Decatur, Ga., May 8, 1960; d. Charles Cole and Avarilla Gleen (Caldwell) Averett; m. George Conley Ingram IV, Nov. 7, 1987; 1 child, Martha Elizabeth. AS, Montreat-Anderson Coll., 1981; BA, Pfeiffer Coll., 1983; MDiv, Emory U., 1986. Ordained to ministry United Meth. Ch. as deacon, 1986, as elder, 1988. Assoc. min. 1st United Meth. Ch., Lenoir, N.C., 1986-87, Cen. United Meth. Ch., Mt. Airy, N.C., 1987-88; sr. min. Ogburn Meml. United Meth. Ch., Winston-Salem, N.C., 1988—. Republican. Office: Ogburn Meml United Meth Ch 651 Akron Dr Winston-Salem NC 27105

INGRAM, OSMOND CARRAWAY, JR., minister; b. Birmingham, Ala., Sept. 5, 1952; s. Osmond Carraway and Frances Elizabeth (McReynolds) I.; m. Ann Lochamy, Dec. 21, 1973; children: Joshua Carraway, Jared Scott. BS, U. Ala., Birmingham, 1973; M in Religious Edn., Southwestern Sem., Ft. Worth, 1977. Ordained to ministry Bapt. Ch., 1978. Min. music and youth First Bapt. Ch., Elkhart, Tex., 1976-78; assoc. pastor youth and outreach Bethel Bapt. Ch., Houston, 1978-80; min. edn. and youth Vinesville Bapt. Ch., Birmingham, 1980-81; min. youth Calvary Bapt. Ch., Scottsboro, Ala., 1981-85, First Bapt. Ch., Minden, La., 1985-89; assoc. pastor youth Immanuel Bapt. Ch., Lexington, Ky., 1989—; mem. Pregnancy Aid Ctr., Minden (bd. dirs. 1986-89, sec. and treas. 1988-89). Author: Youth in Discovery, 1991; contbr. articles to profl. jour. Mem. La. Bapt. Youth Mins. Assn. (sec. and treas. 1987-88, v.p. 1988-89), Ky. Bapt. Religious Edn. Assn., Ky. Bapt. Youth Mins. Assn. Home: 3900 Crosby Dr # 2504 Lexington KY 40515 Office: Immanuel Bapt Ch 3100 Tates Creek Rd Lexington KY 40502 *In a society that is on the brink of moral decay, and filled with hopelessness and uncertainty, I find that it is possible to have peace, joy, and hope. Thankfully, the Savior in whom I trust, provides peace and joy for today, and hope for tomorrow.*

INNES, DAVID CHARLES, minister; b. Kenosha, Wis., Feb. 6, 1940; s. Delbert Charles and Ferne Elizabeth (Shattuck) I.; m. Edith Joy Yunk, July 14, 1962; children: Delbert, David Jr., Deborah, Dorothy. BA, Bob Jones U., 1961, BD, 1964; DD (hon.), San Francisco Bapt. Theol. Sem., 1978. Ordained to ministry Bapt. Ch., 1964. Founder, pastor Tabernacle Bapt. Ch., Morganton, N.C., 1962-65; asst. pastor Cen. Bapt. Ch., Anaheim, Calif., 1965-68; pastor Calvary Bapt. Ch., Yucca Valley, Calif., 1968-76, Hamilton Sq. Bapt. Ch., San Francisco, 1977—; pres., chmn. bd. trustees San Francisco Bapt. Coll and Grad. Sch. of West ; pres. bd. dirs. No. Calif. Fellowhip Fundamental Bapts.; mem. adv. bd. Internat. Bapt. Missions, Tempe, Ariz., 1982—; mem. exec. bd. No. Calif.-We. Nev. Assn. Christian Schs., San Francisco, 1981—; bd. dirs. Fundamental Bapt. Fellowship Am., Virginia Beach, Va. Trustee, pres., v.p. Morongo Unified Sch. Dist., San Bernardino Couty, Calif., 1969-77; trustee, pres. San Francisco Christian Schs., 1978-84. Office: Hamilton Sq Bapt Ch 1212 Geary St San Francisco CA 94109

INNES, RICHARD WILSON (DICK INNES), religious organization administrator; b. Brisbane, Queensland, Australia, Mar. 15, 1933; came to U.S. 1959; s. Richard Mervyn and Edina Mavis (Wilson) I.; m. Muriel Edna Lynn, Nov. 29, 1964 (div. Apr. 1989); children: Brent Richard, Mark Sean. BA, Greenville Coll., 1964; MA, Wheaton (Ill.) Coll., 1983. Ordained to ministry ACTS (A Christian Teaching Svc.) Internat., 1967. Pastor Maple Grove Bapt. Ch., Lansing, Mich., 1965-67; dir. Youth for Christ, Adelaide, Australia, 1968-69; internat. dir. ACTS Internat., Adelaide, 1970-80, Upland, Calif., 1980—. Author: I Hate Witnessing, 1983, How To Mend A Broken Heart, 1991; editor, pub. Encounter mag., 1979-91; contbr. articles to various jours.; author over 200 brochures/leaflets. Mem. Am. Assn. Christian Counselors, Christian Assn. for Psychol. Studies. Office: ACTS Internat 280 N Benson Ave #5 Upland CA 91786 *The purpose of my life is to discover truth—about God, life and myself—and empower others to do likewise. This, as the Master Teacher taught, is the power that sets men free.*

INNOCENTI, ANTONIO CARDINAL, Italian ecclesiastic; b. Poppi, Fiesole, Tuscany, Aug. 23, 1915. ordained Roman Cath. Ch., 1938. Consecrated bishop Titular See Aeclanum, 1968; archbishop of Eclano; then archbishop Apostolic Nuncio Spain; proclaimed cardinal, 1985; prefect Congregation for the Clergy. Address: Congregation for Clergy, Vatican City Vatican City

IOZZO, ANNE MARIE WILCHEK, religious educator; b. Yonkers, N.Y., Apr. 17, 1945; d. Stephen Bernard and Mary Anna (Ridzik) Wilchek; m. Richard J. Iozzo, Feb. 10, 1968; children: Michael Rudolph, Angela Marie. BA, Coll. New Rochelle, 1967; MA, St. Joseph Sem., Dunwoodie, N.Y., 1985. Dir. religion edn. Immaculate Conception Parish, Tuckahoe, N.Y., 1983-85; tchr. Monsignor Scanlan High Sch., Bronx, N.Y., 1985-90, Aquinas High Sch., Bronx, 1990—; tchr. Catechetical Inst., St. Joseph Sem., 1987-88; mem. curriculum com. Archdiocese of N.Y. Dept. Edn., N.Y.C., 1988-90, liturgy-spirituality com. St. Ursula Parish, Mt. Vernon, N.Y., 1989—. Contbr. articles on architectural histories to mags. Com. worker Conservative Party of Mt. Vernon, 1968—. Recipient Bronze and Extraordinary prizes Advt. Club Westchester, 1980. Mem. Nat. Cath. Ednl. Assn. Home: 25 Sheridan Ave Mount Vernon NY 10552 Office: Aquinas High Sch Belmont and E 182d St Bronx New York NY 10457

IPEMA, WILLIAM BERNARD, clergyman; b. Worth, Ill., Mar. 14, 1938; s. Benjamin and Gertrude Frederika (Ven Huizen) I.; m. Donna Kay Huizenga, Sept. 10, 1960; children: Garland Chole Ipema Wilks, Benjamin Todd, Bradley Jon. BA, Calvin Coll., 1965; BD, Calvin Theol. Sem., 1969. Ordained to ministry Christian Reformed Ch., 1975. V.p. I.V.I. Constrn. Corp., Worth, Ill., 1957-62; pastor, founder Lakeside Community Ch., Campau Lake, Mich., 1966-68; pastor to teen gangs Young Life, Chgo., 1969-73; faculty in youth ministry North Park Theol. Sem., Chgo., 1973-78; ops. dir. Chgo. Orleans Housing Corp., 1977-79; dir. multicultural devel. The Christian Reformed Ch., Grand Rapids, Mich., 1979-86; pres. Mid Am. Leadership Found., Chgo., 1986—; assoc. pastor Lawndale Christian Reformed Ch., Chgo., 1969—; dir. John M. Perkins Found., Pasadena, Calif., 1985—, Young Life Found., Colorado Springs, Colo., 1987—, Chgo. Cities in Schs., 1989—; cons. World Vision, Monrovia, Calif., 1989—; team mem. housing experiment in cultural and econ. mix Atrium Village, 1978. Mem. Mayor's Multicultural Task Force, Village of Oak Park (Ill.), 1983; cons., founder Chgo. cities in schs., 1988—. Avocations: flying, woodworking, boating. Home: 721 W Ontario Apt 108 Oak Park IL 60302 Office: Mid Am Leadership Found 122 S Michigan Ave Ste 1220 Chicago IL 60603

IRESON, ROGER WILLIAM, religious organization administrator, minister, educator; b. Saratoga, N.Y., June 2, 1939; s. Orrin Francis and Elisabeth (Hempel) I.; m. Judith Ann Marsh, Aug. 17, 1963. BA, De Pauw U., 1962; MDiv, Garrett Theol. Sem., 1966; PhD, Manchester U., Eng., 1974; DD (hon.), Iowa Wesleyan U., 1988; LittD (hon.), Fla. So. U., 1989. Ordained to ministry United Meth. Ch. as elder, 1966. Assoc. pastor Franklin (Mich.) Community Ch., 1970-75; pastor St. Paul Ch., Bloomfield Hills, Mich., 1975-79; sr. pastor St. Timothy Ch., Detroit, 1979-88; gen. sec. bd. higher edn. and ministry United Meth. Ch., Nashville, 1988—; chmn. bd. Ecumenical Theol. Ctr., Mich., 1980-88; lectr. humanities Lawrence Technol. U., Southfield, Mich., 1977-87; adj. prof. history and theology, Vanderbilt U., Nashville, 1990—. Contbr. to acad. publs. Trustee Am. U., Washington, 1990—; mem. Community Affairs Forum, Detroit, 1980-88, World Meth. Coun., 1981—. Univ. studentship Manchester U., 1967-69; recipient medallion Meth. Coll., 1989; honored by proclamation Mayor of Detroit, 1989. Mem. Am. Acad. Religion, Soc. Bibl. Lit., Oxford Inst. Meth. Studies, Wesley Hist. Soc., World Meth. Hist. Soc., Econ. Club Detroit, Detroit Athletic Club. Office: Bd Higher Edn and Ministry 1001 19th Ave S Nashville TN 37212

IRISH, JERRY ARTHUR, academic administrator, religion educator; b. Syracuse, N.Y., Nov. 25, 1936; s. Frank Leonard and Dorothy (Fries) I.; m. Patty Lee Williams; children: Lee Douglas, Jeffrey Scott, Mark Steven. BA in English and Philosophy, Cornell U., 1958; BD, So. Meth. U., 1964; PhD, Yale U., 1967. Instr. religion Stanford (Calif.) U., 1967-68, asst. prof. religious studies, 1968-75; assoc. prof. religion, dept. chmn. Wichita (Kans.) State U., 1975-80; provost, prof. religion Kenyon Coll., Gambier, Ohio, 1980-86; v.p., dean coll., prof. religion Pomona Coll., Claremont, Calif., 1986—; Stauffacher vis. prof. Pomona Coll., 1980. Author: A Boy Thirteen: Reflections on Death, 1975, The Religious Thought of H. Richard Niebuhr, 1983; contbr. articles to jours. and chpts. to books. Served to capt. USMC, 1958-61. Fellow Soc. for Values in Higher Edn.; mem. Am. Acad. Religion(sec. 1975-78). Office: Pomona Coll Office of Dean Summer Hall 201 Claremont CA 91711

IRISH, TERRY LEE, minister; b. Nampa, Idaho, Oct. 18, 1951; s. Carl Orville and Miriam Ivis (Eastly) I.; m. Carol Frances Helliwell, June 21, 1974; children: Jeremy Ryan, Jonathan Kyle, Jennifer Erin Frances. BA, N.W. Nazarene Coll., Nampa, Idaho, 1970-74; MDiv, Nazarene Theol. Sem., Kansas City, 1978. Ordained elder Ch. of Nazarene, 1981. Assoc. pastor First Ch. of Nazarene, Roseburg, Oreg., 1978-80; pastor Ch. of the Nazarene, Cle Elum, Wash., 1980-84; sr. pastor Crestline Ch. of Nazarene, Spokane, Wash., 1984-86; assoc. pastor First Ch. of Nazarene, Baker, Oreg., 1986-88; pastor Ch. of the Nazarene, Crescent City, Calif., 1988—; del. Gen. Christian Life Conv., Anaheim, Calif., 1985. Contbr. articles to profl. jours.; author original drama: He's Alive, 1980; drama script author, producer: King of Love, 1979. Chmn. Spokane County Sexual Abuse Team, Spokane, 1985-86; chmn. Year Round Edn. Task Force, Crescent City, 1991—. Mem. Del Notre Evang. Ministerial Assn. (pres. 1990—), Kiwanis (spiritual aims chmn. 1985-86, 87-88, 89-90). Republican. Home: 177 7th St Crescent City CA 95531 Office: Crescent City Ch Nazarene 224 F St Crescent City CA 95531 *Life is too short to invest it in those things that do not have the proper return. The very best way to live life is to glorify God. If we give ourselves to this task for life, we can bank on the fact that God will bless our efforts and investment for eternity. Truly, for me to live is Christ. (Philippians 1:21a).*

IRMER, DOUGLAS DARYL, pastor; b. Lincoln, Nebr., May 6, 1959; s. Daryl Lloyd and Constance Louise (Mitchell) I.; m. Carol Sue Heininger, May 25, 1980. BS in Edn., Concordia Tchr.'s Coll., 1981; MDiv, Concordia Theol. Sem., 1985. Vicar Community Luth. Ch., South Burlington, Vt., 1983-84; pastor Christ Luth. Ch., Dudley, Mass., 1985-87, Cairo, Nebr., 1987—. Mem. Hall County Leadership Tomorrow, Grand Island, Nebr., 1988, Cairo Vol. Fire Dept., 1988—. 1st lt. Mass. Air N.G., 1987, capt. Nebr. Air N.G., 1988—. Mem. Nebr. Dist. Luth. Ch.-Mo. Synod, Cairo Ministerial Alliance (treas. 1990—). Republican. Home: 501 W Medina St Cairo NE 68824-0347 Office: Christ Luth Ch 503 W Medina St Cairo NE 68824-0347

IRONS, MARK WILLIAM, minister; b. Chillicothe, Mo., Feb. 23, 1962; s. Norman Lee and Miriam Patricia (Morton) I.; m. Margaret Ann Crick, July 6, 1985. BA, Tex. Christian U., 1984; MDiv, Brite Div. Sch., Ft. Worth, 1988. Ordained to ministry. Christian Ch. (Disciples of Christ), 1988. Ministerial apprentice First Christian Ch., Wichita Falls, Tex., summer 1982; inner-city minister to children First United Meth. Ch., Ft. Worth, 1983-84; assoc. minister First Christian Ch., Athens, Tex., 1984-87; youth dir. Trinity Episcopal Ch., Ft. Worth, 1987-88; minister Park Pl. Christian Ch., Wichita Falls, 1989—. Chaplain Wichita Falls Police Dept., 1990—. Christian Ch. scholar, 1988-89; recipient book award, Brite Div. Sch., 1986, 88. Home: 4131 McGaha Wichita Falls TX 76308 Office: Park Pl Christian Ch 4400 Call Field Rd Wichita Falls TX 76308

IRONS, NEIL L., bishop; b. Elkins, W.Va., Oct. 1, 1936; s. E. Leon and Greta (Lipscomb) I.; m. Inez Rossey, July 24, 1958; children: Andrew Leon, Anne Kirsten. BA, Davis and Elkins Coll., 1958, DD (hon.), 1986; MDiv, U. Theol. Sem., 1963; MA, Vanderbilt U., 1971, PhD, 1973. Ordained to ministry Meth. Ch. Pastor Evang. United Brethren, Belington, W.Va., 1958-60, Huntington, W.Va., 1963-67; pastor United Meth. Ch., Franklin, Tenn., 1967-71; asst. prof. U. Ill., Urbana, 1971-74; pastor United Meth. Ch., Buckhannon, W.Va., 1974-81, dist. supt., Romney, W.Va., 1981-84, bishop, N.J. area, 1984—; pres. Coll. Bishops, 1986-87. Author: (Bible study) Profits of Judgment and Hope, 1974. Pres. Gen. Commn. on Archives and History, Madison, N.J., 1985—; trustee W.Va. Wesleyan Coll., Buckhannon, 1982-84, Drew U., Madison, 1984—. Mem. Rotary (Buckhannon chpt., scholarship com. 1978-80). Avocations: music, tennis, hiking. Office: United Meth Ch NJ Area care Pennington Sch 112 W Delaware Ave Pennington NJ 08534

IRVIN, MAURICE RAY, editor, minister; b. Louisville, Dec. 14, 1930; s. Mitchell and Venus (Crosier) I.; m. Darolyn O'Bryant, Sept. 1, 1951; children: Timothy, Rebecca, Leeann. Diploma, Nyack Coll., 1951; BA, Taylor U., 1952; MA, U. Ky., 1960; PhD, Case Western U., 1972. Ordained to ministry Christian and Missionary Alliance, 1955. Pastor Christian and Missionary Alliance, various cities, 1952-83; editor Alliance Life mag., Colorado Springs, Colo., 1983—. Author: Eternally Named, 1975, Consider This, 1989. Mem. bd. regents Oxford Grad. Sch., Dayton, Tenn., 1983—. Named Alumnus of Yr. Nyack Coll., 1990. Mem. Evang. Press Assn. Office: Christian & Missionary Alliance 8595 Explorer Dr Colorado Springs CO 80920

IRWIN, DARLENE MURIEL, lay worker; b. Mpls., Sept. 23, 1946; d. Jonus Sylvester and Mary Elizabeth (Turcotte) Johnson; m. Brian Thomas Irwin, Aug. 5, 1967 (dec. Jan. 1974); children: Robie Jon, Kelley Jo. Christian worker diploma, Wesley Bible Coll., Mpls., 1967. Treas. missions Evang. Ch. North Cen. Conf., Mpls., 1977-91, exec. sec. missions, 1986-91; program dir. missions Evang. Ch. of N.Am., Mpls., 1989-90, office mgr. missions, 1991—; pres. Women-Evang. Ch. North Cen. Conf., Mpls., 1977-81, 82-85, v.p., 1981-82, 89—; lay mem. coun. Evang. Ch. N.Am., Portland, Oreg., 1982-90, lay mem. exec. coun., 1982-90, lay mem. commn. on the discipline, 1983-91, sec. commn. on the discipline, 1983-89; conf. sec. Evang. Ch. North Cen. Conf., Mpls., 1984-89, dir. Christian social concerns, 1989—. Del., alt. del. Ind. Reps. of Minn., 1980—. Office: Evang Ch Missions 7733 W River Rd Minneapolis MN 55444 *During all the tragedies and stresses of life the choice is ours whether to be happy or sad, thankful or ungrateful, etc., but the most important choice we make not only affects life here but hereafter and that is to accept Jesus Christ as our personal Savior and Lord of all areas of our life. That makes life worth living. (Proverbs 3:5-6).*

IRWIN, PAUL GARFIELD, minister, humane society executive; b. Brantford, Ont., Can., Apr. 3, 1937; came to U.S., 1956; s. Wesley G. and Evelyn (Shelby) I.; m. Jean Rose Hathaway, Sept. 5, 1960; children—Christopher, Jonathan, Craig. B.A., Roberts Wesleyan U., N.Y., 1960; M.Div., Colgate Rochester Theol. Sem., 1964; S.T.M., Boston U., 1967; LL.D. (hon.), Rio Grande Coll., Ohio, 1981. Ordained to ministry United Meth. Ch., 1962. Pastor chs. in Boston, 1962—; v.p. Humane Soc. of U.S., Washington, 1976—; v.p. Nat. Assn. Advancement of Humane and Environ. Edn., 1980—; dir. World Soc. Protection of Animals, London, 1984—. Mem. Asia Soc. (bd. dirs.), Am. Bible Soc. (bd. dirs. 1985—). Office: Humane Soc US 2100 L St NW Washington DC 20037

IRWIN, RONALD GILBERT, minister; b. Pitts., Aug. 4, 1933; s. Ronald Eli and Gertrude Marie (Gilbert) I.; m. Pauline Ann Laipply, Oct. 21, 1967; 1 child, Christopher Bryce. BS in Edn., Rutgers U., 1955; postgrad., Temple U., 1955-56; MA, Columbia U., 1967. Ordained to ministry The Salvation Army, 1957. Divisional comdr. western N.Y. The Salvation Army, Buffalo, 1978-79; tng. prin. Sch. for Officer's Tng. The Salvation Army, Rancho Palos

Verdes, Calif., 1979-81; divisional comdr. N.W. The Salvation Army, Seattle, 1981-84; field sec. for pers. western terr. The Salvation Army, Rancho Palos Verdes, 1984-89, chief sec., 1989—; mem. nat. pers. commn. The Salvation Army, 1984-89, mem. nat. planning and devel. commn., 1981-84, 86—, mem. nat. conf. commrs., 1989—. Contbr. articles to Salvation Army publs. Trustee Azuza Pacific U., 1979-81. Mem. Phi Delta Kappa. Office: The Salvation Army 30840 Hawthorne Blvd Rancho Palos Verdes CA 90274

ISAACS, DAMON LYNN, minister; b. Wichita, Kans., June 11, 1962; s. Carl D. and Latricia L. (Lankford) I.; m. Janet A. Milne, May 12, 1984; 1 child, Caleb A. Student, Wichita State U., 1982-87. Lic. to ministry Assemblies of God, 1987, ordained, 1991. Pastor youth Assembly of God, Mustang, Okla., 1988—; vol., youth worker, evangelist Pentecostal Holiness, Okla., Kans., Ark., Mo., 1981-85; vol., youth worker Assembly of God, Wichita, 1985-88; instr. Okla. Youth Leadership Inst., 1990—; dir. Mustang (Okla.) Youthfest, 1990—. Recipient award Mayor/Mustang City Coun., 1990. Republican. Office: Mustang Assembly of God PO Box 207 1116 N Hwy 152 Mustang OK 73064 *In a world where second chances are few, our greatest challenge is show teenagers that God is god of second chances. When a teenager is saved not only is a soul saved, but also an entire life. I choose to accept these challenges.*

ISAACSON, CLIFFORD EDWIN, minister; b. Floodwood, Minn., May 17, 1934; s. Richard Emil Isaacson and Allie Marie (Nissila) Thomas; m. Kathleen Mae Myre, Apr. 18, 1953; children—Duane, Mary, Shirley, Linda, Kevin. B.A., Northwestern Coll., Mpls., 1958; B.Div., U. Dubuque, 1961. Pastor United Presbyterian Ch., Waukon, Iowa., 1961-64, United Presbyn. Ch., Keokuk, Iowa, 1964-70; assoc. pastor First United Methodist Ch., Clinton, Iowa, 1970-72; pastor First United Meth. Ch., Ida Grove, Iowa, 1972-79; Algona, Iowa, 1979-86; dir. Upper Des Moines Counseling Ctr., Algona, 1986—; originated Therapeutic Question Counseling Method; facilitator Large Ch. Pastors Fellowship, Spencer, Iowa. Author: Understanding Yourself Through Birth Order, 1988, The Birth Order Challenge, 1991. Pres., bd. dirs. Northwest Iowa Mental Health, Ida Grove, 1978; v.p. Algona Area Substance Prevention, 1984. Mem. Algona Area Clergy Assn. (pres. 1983), Mensa. Democrat. Lodge: Kiwanis. Home: 931 E Oak Algona IA 50511 Office: Upper Des Moines Counseling Ctr 403 E Nebraska St Algona IA 50511

ISAKSEN, ROBERT L., bishop; b. Bklyn.; m. Beverly Isaksen; children: Elisabeth, Lois. Grad., Concordia Coll., Moorhead, Minn., 1957, Luther/Northwestern Sem., St. Paul, 1961; MST, N.Y. Theol. Sem., 1971; PhD (hon.), Upsala Coll., 1990. Ordained to ministry Am. Luth. Ch. Vicar St. Timothy Luth. Ch., Chgo., 1960; pastor various chs. N.Y.C.; mission dir. Am. Luth. Ch.; bishop New Eng. synod Evang. Luth. Ch. in Am., Worcester, Mass., 1987—; former mem. staff Luth. Immigration and Refugee Svcs., N.Y.C. Address: Evang Luth Ch in Am New Eng Synod 90 Madison St Worcester MA 01608-2030

ISBELL, CHARLES LESTER, minister; b. Galveston, Tex., Oct. 10, 1936; s. Frank Lester and Elba Versilla (Goodyear) I.; m. Carol McBride, Jan. 23, 1958; children: Elizabeth Rene, Ian, Sara. BA, Tex. Christian U., 1958; MDiv, Brite Divinity Sch., 1961, D. Ministry, 1978. Ordained to ministry Christian Ch. (Disciples of Christ), 1961. Pastor 1st Christian Ch., Marfa, Tex., 1961-62, Uvalde, Tex., 1962-66; pastor Northwood Christian Ch., Beaumont, Tex., 1966-72, Irving (Tex.) North Christian Ch., 1972-81, 1st Christian Ch., Denton, Tex., 1981-91; area minister coastal plains area Christian Ch. (Disciples of Christ) in S.W., Houston, 1991—; chair com. for design North Tex. Area Christian Ch. (Disciples of Christ), 1988-89, mem. search com. for assoc. area minister; mem. ch. advance not task group Christian Ch. (Disciples of Christ) in S.W., mem. camp and conf. com. Chair chaplaincy bd. Denton County Hosp., 1986-87; founding mem. H.O.P.E. inc., 1984—, sec., bd. dirs., 1989-90. Mem. Dallas Area Assn. Christian Chs. (chair search com. for area minister 1986, pres. 1986-88, chair dept. of ch. extension 1984-86), DAO (Thrice Lustrious Master, pender chpt. # 50), Kiwanis (pres. Denton club 1990). Office: Coastal Plains Area 5404 Cherokee Houston TX 77005

ISENBERG, PETER JAMES, religion educator, minister; b. Washington, July 16, 1966; s. Dilworth Duran and Katherine Ann (McCorkle) I.; m. Ann Marie Brisson, May 23, 1987; 1 child, Michal. BA, Roanoke Bible Coll., 1987; postgrad., Lincoln Christian Sem., 1987—. Youth min. Berea Christian Ch., Hertford, N.C., 1986-87, Auburn (Ill.) Christian Ch., 1987-90; instr. Greek, Lincoln (Ill.) Christian Coll., 1989—; assoc. min. 1st Christian Ch., Mt. Pulaski, Ill., 1991—. Named one of Outstanding Youth Mins. of Am. N.Am. Christian Conv., Louisville, 1989. Mem. Imago Dei (pres. Lincoln 1989-91). Home: 103 Thompson Dr Lincoln IL 62656 Office: 1st Christian Ch 115 Washington St Mount Pulaski IL 62548 *The only possible resolution of the abortion issue rests in the acceptance of Gods's definition of humanity as the "Imago Dei."*

ISMAEL MANIGRA, SHEIKH ABOOBACAR, religious organization head. Leader Islamic Coun. of Mozambique. Office: Islamic Coun, Maputo Mozambique*

ISOM, DOTCY IVERTUS, JR., bishop; b. Detroit, Feb. 18, 1931; s. Dotcy and Laura (Scales) I.; m. Esther L. Jones, Jan. 30, 1955; children—Dotcy, III, Jon Mark, David Carl. B.S., Wayne State U., 1956; grad. Eden Sem., 1967, M.Div., 1968; D.D., Miles Coll., 1982, Balt. Bible Coll., 1976. Ordained to ministry Methodist Ch., 1957. Pastor Allen Temple, Christian Meth. Epis. Ch., Paris, Tenn., 1957-58, St. Luke Christian Meth. Epis. Ch., Saginaw, Mich., 1958-67, Carter Chapel, Gary, Ind., 1961-62, Pilgrim Temple, East St. Louis, Ill., 1962-68, St. Paul Ch., Chgo., 1968-82; bishop Christian Meth. Epis. Ch., Birmingham, Ala., 1982—; dir. Christian Edn., Southeast Mo. and Ill. Conf., 1978-82. Mem. Human Relation Commn., East St. Louis, 1964-68; mem. Mayor's Task Force on Hunger; bd. dirs. Greater Birmingham Ministries; chmn. bd. dirs. Miles Coll., Birmingham. Served with U.S. Army, 1948-52. Mem. NAACP, So. Christian Leadership Conf. (vice chmn. 1976-80), Fla. Council of Chs.

ISRAEL, RUCKER L., minister; b. Edwards, Miss., Mar. 10, 1927; s. Whitney E. and Luberta (Jones) R.; m. Velma L. Brandon, Sept. 12, 1950; children: Edward E., Debra A.R. Bunkley. AB, Rust Coll., 1950, DD (hon.), 1973; MDiv, Gannon Theol. Sem., Atlanta, 1956; D Ministry, ITC, Atlanta, 1973. Ordained to ministry United Meth. Ch. Pastor Pickens (Miss.) Charge, 1950-53, Asbury United Meth. Ch., Rust Coll., Holly Springs, Miss., 1956-60, Wesley United Meth. Ch., Greenwood, Miss., 1960-68; dist. supt. Starkville (Miss.) dist. United Meth. Ch., 1968-73; assoc. exec. dist. SEJ adminnstrv. coun. United Meth. Ch., Lake Junalaska, W.Va., 1973—; mem. Gulfside Assembly, Miss., 1960—, Hinton Rural Life Ctr., Hayesville, N.C., 1973—. Chmn. bd. trustees Rust Coll., 1972—. Recipient Healing for Spirtual Formation award The Upper Room, 1985, Call to Ministry award Gen. Bd. Edn., 1990. Mem. NAACP, Kiwanis. Democrat. Home: 2541 Elkhorn Dr Decatur GA 30034 Office: 159 Ralph McGill Bldg Atlanta GA 30365

ISRAEL, WARTHEN TALMADGE, college president, minister; b. Tampa, Fla., Jan. 30, 1932; s. Travis Braxton and Sarah Francis (Long) I.; m. Anna Bell Louthan, Aug. 9, 1952; children: Stephen, David, Deborah, Priscilla, Elizabeth. BA, Vennard Coll., 1953, William Penn Coll., 1954; MDiv, Iliff Sch. Theology, Denver, 1962; D of Ministry, San Francisco Theol. Sem., San Anselmo, Calif., 1981. Ordained to ministry United Meth. Ch., 1962. Pastor various chs. United Meth. Ch., Nebr., 1956-87; dist. supt. Nebr. conf. United Meth. Ch., 1977-81; pres. Vennard Coll., University Park, Iowa, 1987—; bd. dirs. World Gospel Mission, Marion, Ind. Author: Alcoholism Among United Methodist Clergy, 1981. Trustee Westmar Coll., LeMars, Iowa, 1978-81. Named Alumnus of Yr., Iliff Sch. Theology, 1977, Vennard Coll., 1985. Home: 901 Bethel University Park IA 52595 Office: Vennard Coll University Park IA 52595

ISSA, ASWAD HASHIM ASIM, minister, educator; b. Detroit, Feb. 19, 1948; s. Roscoe Conquering and Flora Dell (Sanders) Johnson; m. Diane Christine Gray, Aug. 6, 1978; children: Jamila Bahati Safiya, Bomani Akil Omari, Akilah Sauda Nailah. BS, Wayne State U., 1971, MEd, 1977; M of Div., Interdenominational Theol. Ctr., 1981. Ordained to ministry, 1978; cert. tchr., drug edn. cons. Instr. Detroit Bd. Edn., 1971—; ministerial asst., advisor to youth advisor council, ch. sch. instr. New Calvary Bapt. Ch., Detroit, 1982-87, instr. bibl. analysis and exegesis, 1989—, instr. African-Am. manhood tng. program, 1990—; pastor Greater Macedonia Bapt. Ch., Detroit, 1987-89; tchr. social studies Osborn High Sch., Detroit, 1985—; adminstrv. aid to pres. Progressive Nat. Bapt. Conv., Washington, 1983-85, v.p. task force on preparation and initiation of youth into black Christian adulthood, 1983-86, instr., 1985—; adminstrv. asst. Christian Temple Bapt. Ch., Detroit, 1981-83, chmn. civic action com., 1968-78, 81-83, youth marriage counselor, 1977-78, 81-83; rep. adminstrn. governance task force Interdenominational Theol. Ctr., Atlanta, 1980-81, treas. Bapt. Fellowship, 1979-80, asst. dir. Children's Ministries, 1978-80; chmn. Morehouse Sch. Religion's Children Recreational Resources and Activities, Atlanta, 1979-80; prin. Christian Temple Freedom Sch., Detroit, 1973. Author: My Dear Ebony Rose. Distbr., dispatcher Richard Austin for Sec. of State com., Detroit, 1971, Coleman Young for Mayor com., Detroit, 1973; chmn. polit. action com. Eastside Detroit Concerned Citizens, 1973-74; del. Mich. Dem. Party, 1973-76; asst. supr. employment and tng. dept. cen. records Summer Youth Employment Program, 1980-81; contract worker Detroit Sr. Citizens Dept., 1982; chaplin Ga. Regional Hosp. Devel. Learning Ctr., 1980; pastor Meml. Dr. Bapt. Ctr. Children's Ch., Atlanta, 1979; dir. Black Applied Cultural Ctr., Detroit, 1972-73; chmn. interviewing com. C.T.B.C. Ebony Rose Debutante Balls, 1974-78, Osborn High-Detroit Fedn. Tchrs. Election Commn., 1986-90, social studies curriculum devel. and instr. in Basic Law and Practical Skills for Living Osborn High Sch., 1991—; supr., instr. nat. summer youth sports program Wayne State U., 1968-79; mem. coun. Bapt. Pastors Detroit, 1987—; coord. Osborn High-United Negro Coll. Fund Drive, 1990—; mem. history pilot program African and African-Am., 1989-90, coord. African-Am. history programs and contest, 1986—; coord. Osborn High-Detroit Urban League Salute to Disting. Warriors Youth Seminars and Banquet, 1987—; dep. registrar Voter Registration Drive, 1987-90; mem. Detroit chpt. of U.S. Dept. Edn. Drug Free Schs., 1991—. Recipient Disting. Svc. award Detroit City Coun., 1985, Cert. of Merit award Mich. Edn. Assn., Lansing, 1985, Spl. Tribute award State of Mich., 1987, Cert. of Appreciation Wayne County Commn., 1987, Cert. Recognition Mich. State Legis., 1987, Testimonial Resolution Detroit City Coun., 1987, Booker T. Washington Educator's Achievement award, 1989; finalist Wayne County Regional Outstanding Tchr. award, 1991. Fellow Fund for Theol. Edn. (Benjamin E. Mays award 1980-81), Dr. Charles W. Butler-New Calvary Bapt. Disting. Ministers (scholarship, award 1979-81); mem. NAACP, Interdenominational Theol. Ctr.-Morehouse Alumnus (treas. 1979-80, Service award 1980), State Bar Mich. (young lawyers pub. service announcement team, 1987), Wayne State U. Alumnus, Kappa Alpha Psi (lt. strategist 1979-81). Avocations: hist. investigations, handicrafts, fixing and repairing, sports, music. Office: Osborn High Sch 11600 E Seven Mile Rd Detroit MI 48205 also: New Calvary Bapt Ch 3975 Concord Detroit MI 48207

ISSAYI, YOUHANNAN SEMAAN, archbishop. Archbishop of Teheran, Roman Cath. Ch., Iran. Office: Archeveche, Forsat Ave 91, Tehran 15819, Iran*

IVERSON, JANICE, nun, physical education and cardiac rehabilitation educator; b. Miranda, S.D., Mar. 3, 1941; s. Marvin W. and Viola D. (Gebhart) I. Teaching cert. Mt. Marty Coll., 1961, B.A., 1968; postgrad. Dickinson State Coll., spring 1968; M.S., S.D. State U., 1972, postgrad., 1974-75; M.S., Va. Poly. Inst. and State U., 1981. Joined Benedictine Sisters, Roman Catholic Ch., 1959; tchr. fourth grade St. Joseph's Cath. Sch., Piere, S.D., 1962-63, elem. grades St. Mary's Cath. Sch., Aberdeen, S.D., 1963-67; tchr. 5th and 6th grades, phys. educator all grades, high sch. girl's basketball coach, girl's dorm matron St. Mary's Grade and High Sch., Richardton, N.D., 1967-70; phys. educator, coach, adviser fgn. students Harmony Hill High Sch., Watertown, S.D., 1970-74; phys. educator, tchr. religion grade 6, tchr. math. grades 5 and 6, boy's basketball coach grades 5 through 8, Cath. sch., Richardton, 1975-76; asst. prof. phys. edn., head women's volleyball coach, asst. women's basketball coach Mary Coll., Bismark, N.D., 1976-77; athletic dir., tchr. phys. edn. and health grades 9 to 12, head women's volleyball coach, asst. women's basketball coach, head maintenance personnel Sacred Heart High Sch., East Grand Forks, N.D., 1977-78; phys. educator elem. grades, tchr. religion grades 5 and 6, tchr. mat grades 4 through 6, boys' basketball coach St. Bernard's Indian Mission Sch., Ft. Yates, N.D., 1978-79; intern, exercise technician dept. health, phys. edn. and recreation Va. Poly. Inst. and State U., Blacksburg, 1980; grad. student intern St. Catherine Hosp. Rehab. Ctr., East Chicago, Ind., 1981; instr. in health, phys. edn. and recreation, head women's softball coach S.D. State U., Brookings, 1981-83, instr. in health, phys. edn. and recreation, dir. cardiac rehab. program, phase II and III, 1983—; speaker on cardiac rehab. and phys. fitness to various civic orgns. Tennis Singles and Doubles City champion Watertown (S.D.) Recreation Dept., 1973; named Most Valuable Softball Player, Clark (S.D.) Invitation 8 Team Tournament, 1973. Mem. AAHPERD, Am. Coll. Sport's Medicine, Am. Volkssport Assn. Democrat. Home: Benedictine Sisters Mother of God Priory Watertown SD 57201 also: 602 3d St Brookings SD 57006 Office: 261 Health Phys Edn Recreation Ctr SD State U Brookings SD 57007

IVERSON, MARLOWE WENDELL, church administrator, management consultant; b. Mpls., Mar. 7, 1925; s. Elmer and Emma (Fister) I.; m. Bethel Ann Locke, Sept. 4, 1948; children: Robert, Thomas, Marilyn, Kathy. BEE, BBA, U. Minn., 1950. Registered profl. engr., Minn. Bus. adminstr. Richfield Luth. Ch., Mpls., 1989—. Chmn. ch. coun. Richfield Luth. Ch., 1984-85. With USNR, 1943-46, Europe, 1950-52, Korea. Mem. Nat. Assn. Ch. Bus. Adminstrn. Republican. Home: 7313 Wooddale Ave Edina MN 55435 Office: Richfield Luth Ch 8 W 60th St Minneapolis MN 55419

IVES, ROBERT BLACKMAN, minister; b. Bryn Mawr, Pa., Nov. 9, 1936; s. Robert B. and V. Grace (Harpster) I.; m. Nancy Draper, Aug. 4, 1962; children: Karen, Brian Daniel, Jeffrey Nathan. BS, Drexel U., 1959; BD, Fuller Sem., 1962; ThM, Princeton Sem., 1963; PhD, U Manchester, Eng., 1965. Ordained to ministry Presbyn. Ch., 1965. Min. to students Park St. Ch., Boston, 1965-69; asst. min. Tenth Presbyn. Ch., Phila., 1969-71; sr. pastor Brethren in Christ Ch., Grantham, Pa., 1971—; coll. pastor, lectr. in religion Messiah Coll., Grantham, 1971—; chmn. music and worship com., Brethren in Christ Ch., 1974-84, asst. chmn. hymnal com. 1980-84; asst. moderator, Brethren in Christ Ch., 1988-90; mem. editorial coun. Beliver's Ch. Commentary Series, 1989—. Author: (with others) Within the Perfection of Christ, 1990; contbr. articles to profl. jours. Mem. C. S. Lewis Soc. N.Y.C. Office: Grantham Ch Grantham PA 17027 *I admire people who have read all of War and Peace, The Divine Comedy, and Karl Barth's Church Dogmatics. I have often begun them again, but never finished any of them; so I see them as an analogy of all of life.*

IVES, S. CLIFTON, minister; b. Farmington, Maine, Nov. 13, 1937; s. Alfred H. and Alice (Smith) I.; m. Jane P. Ives, June 6, 1959; children: Bonnie, Stephen, Jonathan. BA, U. Maine, 1960; STB, Boston U., 1963, D in Ministry, 1983. Pastor Cape Elizabeth (Maine) United Meth. Ch., 1962-68, First United Meth. Ch., Bangor, Maine, 1968-73; dir. Maine Conf. Coun. on Ministries, Winthrop, Maine, 1973-77; sr. pastor Waterville (Maine) United Meth. Ch., 1977-86; dist. supt. So. Dist. United Meth. Ch., Portland, Maine, 1986—; gen. conf. del. United Meth. Ch., 1972, 74, 80, 84, 88. Mem. Assn. Couples for Marriage Enrichment, World Meth. Coun. Maine Coun. of Chs. (exec. com. 1981—).

IVEY, CHARLES WRAY, religious organization administrator; b. Atlanta, May 8, 1936; s. Claude W. and Kathleen (May) I.; m. Glenda Simons; children: Chris, Cheryl, Steve. AB, Ga. State U., 1965; BD, Southeastern Sem., 1966, MDiv, 1973; DD (hon.), Mercer U., 1984. Ordained to ministry Bapt. Ch., 1963. Programmer, supr. Plantation Pipe Line, Atlanta, 1954-63; pastor Plainview Bapt. Ch., Durham, N.C., 1963-66, Pine Lake (Ga.) Bapt. Ch., 1966-74; pastor 1st Bapt. Ch., Swainsboro, Ga., 1974-79, Macon, Ga., 1979-85; dir. ch. svcs. div. Ga. Bapt. Conv., Atlanta, 1985—. Chmn. Heart Fund, Swainsboro, 1975. Club: Exchange. Avocations: woodwork, sports. Office: Ga Bapt Conv 2930 Flowers Rd S Atlanta GA 30341

IVEY, RACHEL SHOAF, lay worker; b. Cicero, Ind., Dec. 29, 1908; d. Ithiel and Ada Luella (Jessup) Shoaf; m. John Milton Ivey, Nov. 17, 1934 (dec. Aug. 1990); children: Mitty Ann Ivey Courtoy, Donna Ivey Ard. Student, Tampa Bus. Coll., Union Bible Sem., Ind., Fla. So. Coll. Mem. choirs, organist, evangelism chair in 7 United Meth. chs., Fla.; society writer for Noblesville (Ind.) Ledger. Mem. Ch. Women United (lit. sec. 1961-68), U. Meth. Women (pres. 1970-74), Fed. Woman's Club (entertainment 1954-58), Eastern Star (chaplain 1944-48). Address: 1175 S Lake Reedy Blvd Frostproof FL 33843

IWANSKI, RUTH ANN, nun, school administrator; b. Wisconsin Rapids, Wis., Aug. 22, 1946; d. Adam John and Mary Elizabeth (McNamee) I. BA, Alverno Coll., 1969; MA in Teaching, Webster Coll., 1974; MA, Tex. Woman's U., 1977. Professed nun Roman Cath. Ch., 1965. Grade sch. tchr. St. Monica Sch., Whitefish Bay, Wis., 1969-70; primary tchr. St. John Nepomuk Sch., Racine, Wis., 1970-74; adapted phys. edn. cons. St. Francis and St. Vincent Schs., Freeport, Ill., 1976-84; adminstr. St. Francis Sch., Freeport, Ill., 1984—; pres. Freeport Sacred, 1977—; rep. Liturgy Com., Racine, 1970-72, Freeport Area Ch. Coop., 1977-79; instr. Highland Community Coll., 1990—. Choreographer liturgical dance. Researcher NAACP, Milw., 1967; advisor Sect. 504 Adv. Com., Freeport, 1984, Northwest Ill. Spl. Olympics, Rockford, 1982-87, Freeport Rehab. Enrichment Enterprises, 1988—. Named Outstanding Young Woman, Jaycees, 1977. Mem. Internat. Platform Assn., Ill. Pk. and Recreation Assn., Nat. Recreation and Pk. Assn., Am. Alliance Health, Phys. Edn., Recreation and Dance, Sacred Dance Guild. Avocations: quilting, landscaping, arts and crafts, bicyling, lighting design for Winneshiek Community Theatre. Home and Office: St Francis Sch for Exceptional Children 1209 S Walnut Ave Freeport IL 61032 *Life is not fair, and God is always there answering our prayers. The important thing is not counting our accomplishments but persisting at striving to ease the apparently insurmountable pain around us by reaching out in love to those our 20th century society would judge unloveable, attempting to mirror God's unconditional love without asking what's in it for me.*

JABERG, EUGENE CARL, theology educator, administrator; b. Linton, Ind., Mar. 27, 1927; s. Elmer Charles and Hilda Carolyn (Stuckmann) J.; m. Miriam Marie Priebe; children: Scott Christian, Beth Amy, David Edward. BA, Lakeland Coll., 1948; BD, Mission House Theol. Sem., 1954; MA, U. Wis., 1959, PhD, 1968. Ordained to ministry, United Ch. of Christ, 1959. Staff announcer WKOW-TV, Madison, Wis., 1955-58, 67-68; minister Pilgrim Congl. Ch., Madison, 1956-57; assoc. prof. speech Mission House Theol. Sem., Plymouth, Wis., 1958-62; asst. prof. communications United Theol. Sem., New Brighton, Minn., 1962-76; prof. communications United Theol. Sem., New Brighton, 1976-91, dir. admissions, 1984-87, dir. MDiv program, 1988-90, prof. emeritus, 1991—; bus. ptnr., Dimension 3 Media Svcs., Mpls., 1988—; vis. scholar Cambridge U., England. Author, editor: A History of Lakeland-Mission House, 1962; author: The Video Pencil, 1980; contbr. articles, revs. to various publs.; producer films, videotapes. Artistic dir. Interfaith Players, Mpls., 1965-73; TV producer, moderator Town Meeting of Twin Cities, Mpls., 1967-70; producer, writer, host various radio and TV series, Mpls., 1970—; mem. Ctr. Urban Encounter, Mpls., 1972-74, New Brighton Human Rights Commn., 1975-77; bd. mem. office communications United Ch. Christ, N.Y.C., 1975-81; mem. North Suburban System Cable Access Commn., 1986-91. Corr. U.S. Army, 1949-50. Kaltenborn Radio scholar, 1957; grantee Assn. Theol. Sems., 1983. Mem. Religious Speech Communication Assn. (co-chmn. 1972-74), World Assn. Christian Communication. Democrat. Avocations: travel, hiking, spectator sports, film. Home: 1601 Innsbruck Dr Fridley MN 55432 Office: United Theol Sem 3000 5th St NW New Brighton MN 55112

JACK, HOMER ALEXANDER, minister; b. Rochester, N.Y., May 19, 1916; s. Alexander and Cecelia (Davis) J.; m. Ingeborg Kind, June 14, 1972; children: Alexander, Lucy Jack Williams. B.S., Cornell U., 1936, M.S., 1937, Ph.D., 1940; B.D., Meadville Theol. Sch., 1944, D.D., 1971. Ordained to ministry Unitarian Universalist Assn., 1949; minister Universalist Ch., Litchfield, Ill., 1942, Unitarian Ch., Lawrence, Kans., 1943; exec. dir. Chgo. Council Against Racial and Religious Discrimination, 1944-48; minister Unitarian Ch., Evanston, Ill., 1948-59; assoc. dir. Am. Com. on Africa, 1959-60; exec. dir. Nat. Com. for Sane Nuclear Policy, 1960-64, mem. nat. bd., 1965-84; chmn. Non-Govtl. Orgn. Com. on Disarmament, UN Hdqrs., 1973-84; dir. Div. Social Responsibility, Unitarian Universalist Assn., 1964-70; sec.-gen. World Conf. Religion and Peace, N.Y.C., 1970-84, emeritus 1984—; minister Lake Shore Unitarian Soc., Winnetka, Ill., 1984-87; pres. Unitarian Fellowship for Social Justice, 1949-50; vice chmn. Ill. div. ACLU, 1950-59. Editor: Wit and Wisdom of Gandhi, 1951, To Albert Schweitzer, 1955, The Gandhi Reader, 1956, Religion and Peace, 1966, World Religion and World Peace, 1968, Religion for Peace, 1973, Disarmament Workbook: The UN Special Session and Beyond, 1978, World Religion/World Peace, 1979, Religion in the Struggle for World Community, 1980, Disarm: Or Die, 1983, Albert Schweitzer on Nuclear War and Peace, 1988. Bd. dirs. Dana Greeley Found. for Peace and Justice, 1986—; bd. dirs. Albert Schweitzer Fellowship, 1974—. Recipient Thomas H. Wright award City of Chgo., 1958; Niwano Peace prize, 1984, Adlai Stevenson award, 1985, Minns Lectrs., 1987, Defender of Peace award Sarvodhaya Peace Movement, India, 1988, Holmes/Weatherly award, 1989. Home: 139 Rutgers Ave Swarthmore PA 19081

JACKS, BENJAMIN BAREND, religious educator; b. Cape Town, Republic of South Africa, Oct. 11, 1939; came to U.S., 1972; s. William Charles and Jane (Augustine) J.; m. Olive Marks, Mar. 9, 1968; children: Eleanor Cecilia, John William, Cheryl Roseanne, Paul Barend. Dipl. in Christian Edn., Johannesburg Bible Inst., 1965; BA, Northeastern Bible Coll., Essex Fells, N.J., 1974; M.R.E., Southwestern Bapt. Theol. Sem., 1976, grad. specialist in Religious Edn., 1980; diploma in Theology, Bapt. Coll. So. Africa, 1977. Preacher, Nashville Bapt. Ch., Gwelo, Zimbabwe, 1968-72; tchr. Fort Worth Ind. Sch. Dist., 1980—; minister of edn. Mt. Olive Missionary Bapt. Ch., Fort Worth, 1983—; mem. com. Fort Worth Social Studies Coun., 1983-84; mem. Bldg. Rep., Fort Worth, 1983—. Mem. Cable TV Adv. Bd., Forest Hill, 1985. Mem. NEA, Tex. State Tchrs. Assn., Fort Worth Classroom Tchrs. Assn. (mem. by-laws com.), Phi Alpha Theta. Address: 3229 Centennial Fort Worth TX 76119

JACKSON, ALTHEA, nun, writer, retired bookstore executive; b. Taunton, Mass., June 27, 1922; d. Harold Robinson Hall and Jeannette (Cahoon) Tingwall; m. John E. Jackson, June 15, 1945 (dec. Aug. 1974); children—Jean, Paul. B.A., Middlebury Coll., 1944; M.S., Simmons Coll., 1965. Cert. profl. librarian. Librarian, Mass., 1959-74; propr. Agape Bible & Book Store, St. Augustine, Fla., 1982-88. Mem. ALA (life). Roman Catholic.

JACKSON, ARCHIE KIM, minister; b. Jacksonville, Fla., Aug. 22, 1954; s. Frank Charles and Vivian Irene (Johns) J.; m. Lisa Joy Durall, Mar. 6, 1982; 1 child, Kimberly Joy. AA, Fla. Jr. Coll., 1975; BA, U. N. Fla., 1979. Ordained to ministry So. Bapt. Conv., 1882. Min. music and youth Macedonia Bapt. Ch., Jacksonville, 1976-77; singer Promise Gospel Group, Jacksonville, 1977-78; min. music and youth Hyde Park Bapt. Ch., Jacksonville, 1978-79; music evangelist Jerry Drace Evang. Assn., Jacksonville, 1980-81; min. music Hillcrest Bapt. Ch., Jacksonville, 1981—; tchr. voice Hillcrest Sch. Music, Jacksonville, 1981—; host Morning Praise WROS Radio, Jacksonville, 1986087; dir. crusade music Jerry Dance Evang. Assn., South Korea, Hong Kong,1978, 81. Rec.: All I Ever Have to Be, 1980. Mem. mus. group River City Kids' Day, Jacksonville Landing, 1988-90, Christmas Spl., 1988-90. Republican. Home: 1275 Avondale Ave Jacksonville FL 32205 Office: Hillcrest Bapt Ch 1176 LaBelle St Jacksonville FL 32205

JACKSON, BOBBY RAND, minister; b. Wilson, N.C., Dec. 14, 1931; s. Joel John and Bessie Francis (Mayo) J.; m. Martha Jane Ketteman, May 30, 1953; children: Stephen Rand, Philip Wayne. B.A., Free Will Baptist Bible Coll., Nashville, 1954; M.A., Bob Jones U., Greenville, S.C., 1955. Ordained to ministry Free Will Baptists Ch., 1951; evangelist Free Will Baptists Ch., Nashville, 1955—; asst. moderator Nat. Assn. Free Will Baptists, Nashville, 1972-77; moderator Nat. Assn. Free Will Baptists, 1978-87, mem. exec. com., 1972-87, chmn. exec. com., 1978-87; presiding officer of gen. bd. Nat. Assn. Free Will Baptists, Nashville, 1978-87. Author: Messages That Matter, 1960, Six Steps to Successful Living, 1962, Awakening in the Wilderness, 1965, Beyond the Stars, 1966; soloist: record albums Softly and Tenderly, 1968, Then Sings My Soul, 1969, Fill My Cup, Lord, 1970, My God and I, 1978, Songs from Two Generations, 1985. Mem. Free Will Baptist Bible

Coll. Alumni Assn., Bob Jones U. Alumni Assn. Home: 1412 E 14th St Greenville NC 27858

JACKSON, BYRON HADEN, religion educator; b. Lexington, Va., Dec. 25, 1943; s. Jack Lee and Lillian Vaden (Snyder) J.; m. Beverly Diane Fortson, Aug. 29, 1967; 1 child, Rachel Lynn. BA, Randolph-Macon Coll., Ashland, Va., 1966; MDiv, Union Theol. Sem., Richmond, Va., 1971; EdD, Columbia U., 1980. Asst. pastor First Presbyn. Ch., Rocky Mount, N.C., 1968-70; assoc. pastor Harvey Browne Meml. Presbyn. Ch., Louisville, 1974-78; staff assoc. Gen. Assembly Mission Bd., Atlanta, 1978-83; coord. Gen. Assembly Coun., Atlanta, 1983-86; asst. prof. Pitts. Theol. Sem., 1986-91, assoc. prof., 1991—; trustee Presbyn. Sch. Christian Edn., Richmond, 1974-80. Mem. ASCD, Assn. Presbyn. Ch. Educators, Religious Edn. Assn., Assn. Theol. Field Edn. (rsch. coord. 1989-91). Democrat. Office: Pitts Theol Sem 616 N Highland Ave Pittsburgh PA 19206

JACKSON, CEDRIC DOUGLAS TYRONE, SR., minister; b. Amarillo, Tex., Feb. 8, 1962; s. Ervin Vester and Claudine (Brown) Chatman; m. Linda Jeannine Parker, July 1, 1989; children: Jeanniece LeeAnna Lynn, Cedric Douglas Tyrone, Jr. BA in Pastoral Ministries, ThB in Bibliology, Am. Bapt. Theol. Sem., 1991. Ordained to ministry Bapt. Ch. Assoc. min. Union Bapt. Ch., Atlanta, 1980-81; presiding min. Cosmopolitan Gospel Ministries, Cleve., 1981—; assoc. min. Olivet Instl. Bapt. Ch., Cleve., 1982—, St. James Missionary Bapt. Ch., Nashville, 1987-89, Mt. Olivet Missionary Bapt. Ch., Hendersonville, Tenn., 1989-91; proprietor CNL Enterprises, 1990—; pres. Clark Atlanta U. Christian Fellowship, 1981-82. Counselor Nashville Union Rescue Mission, 1987-88; deputy registrar Cuyahoga County Bd. Elections, Cleve., 1986-89; active Operation PUSH. L.H. Woolfolk Mem. scholar Am. Bapt. Theol. Sem., Nashville, 1988-89; recipient Meritorious Svc. award Clark Atlanta U. Campus Ministries, 1981-82. Mem. NAACP, Progressive Nat. Bapt. Conv., Inc., Nat. Bapt. Conv., USA, Inc., Am. Bapt. Chs., USA, Bapt. Ministers Conf. Cleve. and Vicinity, Inc. Home and Office: Cosmopolitan Gospel Ministries 13016 S Parkway Dr Garfield Heights OH 44105 *Attempting to reform the soul of society without regenerating the souls of individuals, is like composing a musical symphony with no concept of rhythm, harmony or melody. One will make a catastrophic mess long before one makes a masterpiece.*

JACKSON, CHARLES BENJAMIN, minister; b. Columbia, S.C., July 16, 1952; s. Thomas and Ezella (Rumph) J.; m. Robin Lynn Hoefer, Apr. 21, 1953; children: Charles B. Jr., Candace Celeste. BS, Benedict Coll., 1974; MDiv, Morehouse Sch. of Religion, of Interdenominational Theol. Ctr., Atlanta, 1977; DD, Morris Coll., 1985. Ordained to ministry Bapt. Ch., 1965; cert. clin. counselor. Pastor Brookland Bapt. Ch., West Columbia, S.C., 1971—; gospel announcer WOIC Radio AM, Columbia, S.C., 1984—; pres. S.C. Bapt. Congress of Christian Edn., 1983-86; v.p. Gethsemane Bapt. Sunday Sch. Congress, 1975—; bd. dir. Edn. and Publ. Bd. Progressive Nat. Bapt. Conv. Recipient James H. Clark Meml. Preaching award, Protestant Fellowship, Fund for Theol. Edn., others. Mem. NAACP, Rotary, Kappa Alpha Psi. Democrat. Home: 6727 Valleybrook Rd Columbia SC 29206 *Life is made up of little decisions and big decisions, and how a person decides determines the direction of his or her life.*

JACKSON, CHARLES LEWIS, minister; b. Livingston, Tex.; s. Charlie and Irene (McCardell) J.; m. Bettie Joyce Edmond, June 30, 1954; children: Sheldon Lewis, Bridgette Cheri. BTh, Moody Coll.; cert. of Christian achievement, Fla. State U.; hon. degree, Union Bapt. Theol. Sem. Ordained to ministry Bapt. Ch. Pastor Pleasant Grove Missionary Bapt. Ch., Houston, 1970—; speaker Prayer Movement, Kansas City, Houston, 1987; inst. tchr., Israel; preacher, tchr. in Ethiopia, Kenya, Senegal, other places; participant fact finding mission to Republic of South Africa; traveled worldwide. Author: The Pleasant Grove Membership Hand Book, From Jerusalem to Jericho, I Am The Door, The Promise, The Pleasant Grove Way, Spiritual Oasis in the Wilderness, Memories Cultivated, The Hidden Enemy, No Substitute For Jesus; also 6 albums, 700 tapes recorded. Bd. dirs. disaster team ARC, Tex. Funeral Commn., 1988. Recipient cert. of appreciations from Harris County, City of Houston, 1990, others; inducted into Archives of Union Bapt. Bible Coll., 1989. Office: Pleasant Grove Missionary Bapt Church 2801 Conti St PO Box 15256 Houston TX 77220

JACKSON, CHRISTOPHER PAUL, school principal; b. Logan, W.Va., June 1, 1949; s. Phyllis (Riffe) Bashaw; m. Nancy J. Jackson, June 11, 1972; 1 child, Joshua Paul. Student, So. W.Va. Community Coll.; BA, Bluefield (W.Va.) State Coll.; MRE, Bethany Bible Coll., Dothan, Ala., DRE summa cum laude, 1990. Ind. ins. salesman Logan, 1977-84; prin. Beth Haven Christian Sch., Chauncey, W.Va., 1984—. Sgt. USAF, 1969-77. Mem. Am. Assn. Christian Schs., Kiwanis (chmn. spiritual aimes com.). Baptist. Avocations: golf, basketball, volleyball. Home: Rte 44 Box 280 Switzer WV 25638 Office: Beth Haven Christian Sch Rt 44 Box 620 Omar WV 25638

JACKSON, CLEO EUGENE, III, minister; b. Atlanta, Oct. 26, 1961; s. Eugene Jackson and Margie Nell (Burdette) Taylor; m. Vickie Denisha Brackin, June 11, 1983; children: Andrea Danile, John Caleb, Micah Paul. BA, Mercer U., 1983; MDiv, Princeton Theol. Sem., 1986; D of Ministry, So. Bapt. Theol. Sem., 1989—. Ordained to ministry Bapt. Ch., 1985. Minister to youth Shadnor First Bapt. Ch., Union City, Ga., 1982-83; assoc. pastor West Monmouth Bapt. Ch., Freehold, N.J., 1983-86; minister to youth Northside Bapt. Ch., Fitzgerald, Ga., 1986-88; assoc. pastor First Bapt. Ch. Avondale Estates, Ga., 1988—. Named Outstanding Young Men Am., 1989. Mem. Am. Assn. Christian Counselors, Atlanta Bapt. Assn. Home: 732 Stratford Rd Avondale Estates GA 30002 Office: First Bapt Ch 47 Covington Rd Avondale Estates GA 30002 *There is no greater pattern for the development of the human person than that established by Christ: "And Jesus increased in wisdom and stature, and in favor with God and man" (Luke 2:52).*

JACKSON, DAVID GORDON, religious organization administrator; b. Derby, N.Y., Nov. 5, 1936; s. Peter Thomas and Sarah (Staubitz) J. BS, SUNY, Buffalo, 1960; MDiv, Huntington Coll. Theol. Sem., 1964. Ordained elder Ch. of the United Brethren in Christ, 1969. Dir. youth work Ch. United Brethren in Christ, Huntington, Ind., 1966-73, adminstrv. asst., treas., 1973-79; exec. sec., treas. Internat. Soc. Christian Endeavor, Columbus, Ohio, 1979-84, exec. dir., 1981—; exec. dir. World's Christian Endeavor Union, Columbus, 1984—. Office: 1221 E Broad St PO Box 1110 Columbus OH 43216

JACKSON, DAVID HENRY, priest; b. Smackover, Ark., June 5, 1917; s. Henry Clay and Susie Jane (Bilyeu) J.; m. Ann Thornton, June 26, 1942; 1 child, Murray Clay. BSEE, U.S. Naval Acad., 1941, cert. Marine Engring., 1944; cert. Internat. Rels., Naval War Coll., Newport, R.I., 1958; MDiv, Va. Theol. Sem., 1977. Ordained to ministry Episcopal Ch., 1977. Commd. ensign USN, 1941, advanced through grades to rear adm., 1974; assisting priest St. Paul Episcopal Ch., Alexandria, Va., 1977-81; assisting priest, assoc. rector Epiphany Episcopal Ch., Seattle, 1981-87, priest in charge, 1987-89; assisting priest Emmanuel Episcopal Ch., Mercer Island, Wash., 1989—; vestryman St. Anne's Ch., Annapolis, Md., 1960-62; lay reader in charge Ch. of the Holy Cross, Middletown, R.I., 1963-66; lay reader, chalicist St. George's Ch., Pearl Harbor, Hawaii, 1968-71. V.p. King County Youth Chaplaincy Bd., Seattle, 1984. Decorated Legion of Merit with two gold stars, Commendation medal; recipient Commendation medal Eaton, Ohio Kiwanis Club, 1975. Mem. Am. Soc. Naval Engrs. (pres. 1973), Clergy Assn, Diocese of Olympia, Civil War Roundtable Club, Mil. Order of World Wars. Home: 13820 NE 65th St Apt 540 Redmond WA 98052 Office: Emmanuel Episcopal Ch 4400 86th St SE Mercer Island WA 98040 *The world is full of conflict between individuals, groups and nations. The answer for this is love and reconciliation. And our Lord has given each of us the ministry of reconciliation.*

JACKSON, DERRAH EUGENE, counseling educator; b. Dallas, Jan. 25, 1948; s. James E. and Pauline (Hundley) J.; m. Pamela Elizabeth Holton, Sept. 2, 1968; 1 child, Joshua James. BS in Psychology, North Tex. State U., 1969, MS in Psychology, 1970; postgrad., U. Tex., 1988—. Lay dir. edn. Grace Covenant Ch., Austin, Tex., 1975-78, minister of edn., 1978-88; mem. field staff Internat. Students, Inc., Colorado Springs, Colo., 1988-90, dir. tng., 1990—; dir. Helping Aging Parents Conf., Austin, 1989; co-founder Austin Christian Counseling Ctr., 1977; founder Austin Area Christian Educators, 1979; co-coord. Tex. Law for Tex. Clergy Conf., Austin, 1984. Editor newsletter Update (Christian Counselors), 1989-90, International Friends, 1990—. Outreach dir. Gladney Aux., Austin, 1977-78. Mem. Christian Counselors Tex., Greater Austin Area Christian Counselors, Phi Kappa Phi, Kappa Delta Pi. Office: Internat Students Inc PO Box C Colorado Springs CO 80901

JACKSON, DON EDWARD, minister, religion educator; b. Jasper, Ala., Oct. 9, 1954; s. Donald W. and Billie Jean (Myers) J.; m. Donna Jo Dill, May 31, 1973; children: Michael, Mandy, Matthew. AA, Freed-Hardeman U., 1973; BA, Harding U., Searcy, Ark., 1975; MA, Harding Grad. Sch. Religion, Memphis, 1980, MTh, 1982, DMin, 1984; PhD, U. So. Miss., 1988. Ordained to ministry Ch. of Christ. Min. Ch. of Christ, Cuba, Mo., 1976-77, Looxahoma Ch. of Christ, Senatobia, Miss., 1977-81, Ch. of Christ, Kosciusko, Miss., 1982-88, Quince Road Ch. of Christ, Memphis, 1989—; instr. Magnolia Bible Coll., Kosciusko, 1979-89; adj. prof. Harding Grad. Sch. Religion, 1989—. Author: Churches of Christ in Mississippi, 1986. Recipient Alumni Appreciation award Magnolia Bible Coll., 1990. Mem. Evang. Theol. Soc., Soc. Bibl. Lit., Religious Rsch. Assn., Soc. for Sci. Study Religion, Acad. Homiletics. Office: Quince Road Ch of Christ 6384 Quince Rd Memphis TN 38119

JACKSON, DONALD, minister. Head Atlantic Bapt. Fellowship, Wolfville, N.S., Can. Office: Atlantic Bapt Fellowship, Tideways/Apt 207, Wolfville, NS Canada B0P 1X0*

JACKSON, FRANK, pastor; b. Chgo., Mar. 11, 1941; s. Frank Raymond and Dorothy (Swoul) J.; m. Jimmye Wilkes, Sept. 30, 1967; 1 child, Rachel. B in Humanities, Simpson Coll., 1972; MDiv, Fuller Theol. Sem., 1976; M in Non-Profit Adminstrn., U. San Francisco, 1990. Interim pastor Light House Full Gospel Ch., Pasadena, Calif., 1974-75, Faith United Presbyn. Ch., L.A., 1976-79; assoc. pastor Menlo Park (Calif.) Presbyn. Ch., 1979-83; pastor Faith Presbyn. Ch., Oakland, Calif., 1983—; mem. mission team Faith Equador Missions, Haiti and Jamaica, 1968-69, Kenya, 1975; bd. dirs. Women's Refuge of Oakland/Berkeley, Calif., 1986-89, Harbor House, Oakland, 1990—; trainer, seminar leader San Quentin (Calif.) State Penitentiary, 1987. Voter registrar Interdenominational Ministrial Alliance of L.A., 1976; bd. dirs. Black Leadership Coalition, L.A., 1976-77. Sgt. U.S. Army, Korea. Recipient Community Svc. award Exch. Club of Pasadena, Calif., 1974, Exch. Club of Daly City, Calif., 1983. Mem. Interdenominational Ministrial Alliance of Oakland (fin. sec. 1987-90), Black Presbyn. Caucus of No. Calif. (fin. sec. 1990—). Avocation: judo (black belt). Home: 4142 Maynard Ave Oakland CA 94605 Office: Faith Presbyn Ch 430 49th St Oakland CA 94609

JACKSON, FREDA LUCILLE, minister, church administrator, editor; b. Sikeston, Mo., Sept. 15, 1928; d. Jesse Freda and Ruby Lucille (Carter) Andres; student Three Rivers Jr. Coll., 1969, Central Bible Coll., Springfield, Mo., 1973; B.S., Drury Coll., 1980; M.A. in Bibl. Lit., Assemblies of God Theol. Sem., 1986; m. Thomas Lowell Jackson, Oct. 2, 1947; children—Stephen Andres, Elizabeth Ann, Thomas Dean. Bookkeeper, Aduddel Wholesale Auto Parks, Sikeston, 1947-48; pvt. sec. to v.p. So. Ice & Coal Co., Memphis, 1948-49; sec. firm Bailey & Craig, Sikeston, 1950-56, firm Blanton & Blanton, 1956-57; ordained to ministry Assemblies of God Ch., 1983; promotions coordinator, editor deferred giving and trusts dept., gen. council Assemblies of God, Springfield, Mo., 1974—; tchr. English, Central Bibl. Coll., 1986—. Mem. Women's Ministries, Maranatha Aux., Springfield Christian Writers Club (v.p. 1991), Alpha Sigma Lambda. Editor: New Dimensions, 1979—, Maranatha newsletter, 1977; contbr. articles to denominational publs. Home: 2407 W Atlantic St Springfield MO 65803 Office: 1445 Boonville Ave Springfield MO 65802

JACKSON, GREGORY ALLEN, minister; b. Kansas City, Mo., June 4, 1956; s. Lester Allen Jr. and Janet Lou (Door) J.; m. Paula Sue Epperson, June 11, 1977;. BA in Religion, William Jewell Coll., 1978; MRE, Midwestern Bapt. Theol. Sem., 1980, postgrad., 1980-81, 82—. Min. youth and edn. High Point Bapt. Ch., Kansas City, 1977-81; min. edn. and adminstrn. Cen. Bapt. Ch., North Little Rock, Ark., 1981—; state spl. worker Children's Sunday Sch., Kansas, 1979-81, Adult and Gen. Officer Sunday Sch., Ark., 1981—; Sunday sch. growth cons. Mem. census com. North Little Rock, 1990. Homer and Augusta Jones scholar Midwestern Bapt. Theol. Sem., Kansas City, 1979, 80, 81. Mem. Nat. Assn. Ch. Bus. Adminstrs. (pres. Ark. chpt. 1990-91), Ark. Bapt. Religious Edn. Assn., So. Bapt. Religious Edn. Assn. Office: Cen Bapt Ch 5200 Fairway North Little Rock AR 72116

JACKSON, HERBERT CROSS, religion educator; b. War, W.Va., May 13, 1917; s. John Henry and Sara Martha (Cross) J.; m. Mary Caroline London, Aug. 30, 1941; children: Charlotte, Carolyn Jackson Angell, Bruce, Stephen. BA, William Jewell Coll., 1939; ThM, So. Bapt. Theol. Sem., 1942; MA, Yale U., 1944, PhD, 1954. Prin. Coles Meml. High Sch., India, 1945-47; prof. history Andhra (India) Christian Coll., 1947-49; asst. prof. comparative religion Cen. Bapt. Theol. Sem., 1950-51; prof. comparative religion Ea. Bapt. Theol. Sem., 1951-54, registrar, 1953-54; assoc. prof. comparative religion So. Bapt. Theol. Sem., 1954-59, prof. comparative religion, chmn. hist. div., dean summer sch., 1959-61; dir. Missionary Rsch. Libr., N.Y.C., 1961-66; prof. religious studies Mich. State U., East Lansing, 1966-85, prof. emeritus, 1985—; adj. prof. history of religions Union Theol. Sem., N.Y.C.; rsch. sec. div. overseas ministries Nat. Coun. Chs. of Christ in USA, 1961-66. Mem. Internat. Assn. History of Religions, Assn. Asian Studies, N.Am. Assn. Profs. Missions, Am. Soc. Missiologists, Deutsche Gesellschaft für Missionswissenschaft, Internat. Assn. Mission Studies, Am. Acad. Ecumenists, Am. Acad. Religion. Home: 201 Disosway St Black Mountain NC 28711-3805

JACKSON, HOPE ERNA, minister; b. Waterloo Twp., Ont., Can., Oct. 2, 1922; d. Norman and Mildred Viola (Becker) Weber; m. Arthur Jackson (dec. May 1978). BA in Gen. Arts, U. Western Ont., 1948; cert. in Christian edn., Ctr. for Christian Studies, Toronto, Ont., 1950; MDiv, Victoria U., Toronto, 1958. Ordained to ministry United Ch. of Can., 1966. Missionary Women's Missionary Soc., United Ch. of Can., Gypsumville, Man., Can., 1950-56; pres. Manitou conf. United Ch. of Can., Ont., 1985-86, chmn. vision com. Manitou conf., 1987—; sec. Sudbury (Can.) Presbytery United Ch. of Can., 1989—; chmn. Inter-Ch. Coun., Massey, Ont., 1978—; commr. to Gen. Coun., United Ch. of Can., 1980, 84. Active Massey Players, 1986—. Mem. Massey Agrl. Soc. (sec. 1990—), Women's Inst., Hort. Soc. (dist. bd. dirs.). Address: Government Rd, Massey, ON Canada P0P 1P0

JACKSON, JAMES LARRY, recreation educator; b. California, Mo., Nov. 27, 1940; s. James Taylor and Ruby Catherine (Steenbergen) J.; m. Catherine Galloway, July 27, 1974. BS in Edn., Lincoln U., 1962; MS in Recreation, U. Mo., 1977, EdS in Higher Edn., 1980, PhD, 1983. Ordained to ministry So. Bapt. Conv., 1965. Min. recreation 1st Bapt. Ch., Jefferson City, Mo., 1960-65, Pompano Beach, Fla., 1965-69; min. activities Walnut Street Bapt. Ch., Louisville, 1969-74; instr. ch. recreation So. Sem., 1970-73; sr. prof. recreation, chmn. dept. recreation-leisure studies SW Bapt. U., Bolivar, Mo., 1974—. Contbr. to Ch. Recreation mag., 1960—. Fellow Nat. Recreation and Park Assn.; mem. Soc. Park and Recreation Educators, Mo. Park and Recreation Assn. Home: 1303 S Oakland Dr PO Box 607 Bolivar MO 65613 Office: Southwest Bapt U 105 Taylor Ctr Bolivar MO 65613

JACKSON, JAMES WESLEY, minister; b. Ennis, Tex., Aug. 18, 1952; s. Wesley Pearson and Ollie Dean (Searcy) J.; m. Mary Deane Tolar, June 22, 1973; children: Laura Elizabeth, James Thomas. BMus, U. Mary Hardin-Baylor, 1988; MMus, Baylor U., 1989. Minister music Fairway Bapt. Ch., Wichita Falls, Tex., 1973-74, Bellevue Bapt. Ch., Colorado Springs, Colo., 1981-82; minister music, edn., coord. deaf wk. Meml. Bapt. Ch., Killeen, Tex., 1983-88; interim minister music First Bapt. Ch., Waco, Tex., 1988-89; minister music First Bapt. Ch., Uvalde, Tex., 1989—; vocal supr. USAF Acad. Band, 1975-81. Composer, arranger more than 150 songs, poems, 1981—; author poetry pub. several deaf periodicals, articles in ch. music periodicals. With USAF, 1972-81. Mem. Am. Guild English Handbell Ringers, Singing Men of Tex., So. Bapt. Ch. Music Conf., Am. Choral Dirs. Assn., Hymn Soc. U.S. and Can., Alpha Chi. Home: #3 Birch Circle Uvalde TX 78801 Office: First Bapt Ch 220 N High Uvalde TX 78801 *The greatest experience in my life is to know Jesus Christ. The second greatest experience is to love my wife and family.*

JACKSON, JESSE LOUIS, civic and political leader, clergyman; b. Greenville, S.C., Oct. 8, 1941; s. Charles Henry and Helen Jackson; m. Jacqueline Lavinia Brown, 1964; children: Santita, Jesse Louis, Jonathan Luther, Yusef DuBois, Jacqueline Lavinia. Student, U. Ill., 1959-60; B.A. in Sociology and Economics, N.C. A&T State U., 1964; postgrad., Chgo. Theol. Sem., D.D. (hon.); hon. degrees, N.C. A&T State U., Pepperdine U., Oberlin U., Oral Roberts U., U. R.I., Howard U., Georgetown U. Ordained to ministry Baptist Ch., 1968; founder (with others) Operation Breadbasket joint project So. Christian Leadership Conf., Chgo., 1966; nat. dir. Operation Breadbasket joint project So. Christian Leadership Conf., 1967-71; founder, exec. dir. Operation PUSH (People United to Serve Humanity), Chgo., 1971—; candidate for Democratic nomination for Pres. U.S., 1983-84, 87-88; nat. pres. Nat. Rainbow Coalition Inc., Chgo.; founder PUSH-Excel and PUSH for Econ. Justice; lectr. for high schs., colls., prof. audiences in Am., Europe. Interviewer TV program Jesse Jackson, 1990—. Active Black Coalition for United Community Action, 1969. Recipient Presdl. award Nat. Med. Assn., 1969; Humanitarian Father of Year award Nat. Father's Day Com., 1971; Third Most Admired Man in Am. Gallup Poll, 1985; named one of six new leaders on the rise U.S. News World Report. Address: 1110 Vermont NW Ste 410 Washington DC 20005 also: care Operation PUSH 930 E 50th St Chicago IL 60615

JACKSON, JESSE LUTHER, III, pastor; b. Kinston, N.C., Jan. 15, 1947; s. Jesse Luther Jr. and Iris Elizabeth (Cauley) J.; m. Carol Ann Vest, Aug. 24, 1968; children: Jesse Luther IV, James Joshua. BS in Aerospace Engring., N.C. State U., 1968; MME, U. So. Calif., L.A., 1976; MDiv, Mid-Am. Bapt. Theol. Sem., Memphis, 1979. Ordained to ministry So. Bapt. Conv. Systems engr. Garrett AiResearch, Torrance, Calif., 1968-76; sem. asst. Bellevue Bapt. Ch., Memphis, 1976-79; sr. pastor Williston (Tenn.) Bapt. Ch., 1979-82, Marble City Bapt. Ch., Knoxville, Tenn., 1982-87, Westwood Hill Bapt. Ch., Virginia Beach, Va., 1987—; pres. Fayette County Pastors' Conf., Somerville, Tenn., 1981-82; tchr., trainer Evangelism Explosion Internat., Ft. Lauderdale, Fla., 1987—. Recipient Hudgin's award Tenn. Bapt. Conv., Brentwood, 1981, Eagle award So. Bapt. Sunday Sch. Bd., Nashville, 1985, Top Ten in Evangelism Bapt. Gen. Assn. Va., Richmond, 1988-91. Avocations: golf, personal computers. Home: 1645 Lola Dr Virginia Beach VA 23464 Office: Westwood Hill Bapt Ch 865 Woodstock Rd Virginia Beach VA 23464 *God forbid that I should glory, save in the cross of our Lord Jesus Christ (Galations 6:14).*

JACKSON, JOHN JAY, minister; b. Chula Vista, Calif., July 13, 1961; s. E. Marvin and Mildred (Welch) J.; m. Pamela Harrison, Aug. 19, 1979; children: Jennifer Lynn, Dena Michelle, Rachel Elizabeth. BA, Chapman Coll., 1981; MA, Fuller Theol. Seminary, Pasadena, Calif., 1983; MA, PhD, U. Calif., Santa Barbara, 1986. Ordained to ministry Bapt. Ch., 1984. Min. youth 1st Bapt. Ch., Buena Park, Calif., 1979-81, min. youth and edn., 1981-83, assoc. pastor, 1984-87; sr. pastor 1st Bapt. Ch., Oxnard, Calif., 1988—. Chmn. integration adv. com. Oxnard (Calif.) Sch. Dist., 1987-90; pres. Pastor's Cluster of Buena Ventura, Calif., 1987-88. Mem. Am. Bapt. Chs. of the Pacific Southwest (1st v.p. 1989-90, pres. 1990-91, chmn. new ch. devel. div. 1989-90), Oxnard C. of C. (chmn. edn. com. 1986-88, Leadership Oxnard 1990—). Republican. Office: 1st Bapt Ch-Oxnard 936 W 5th St Oxnard CA 93030-5270

JACKSON, JOHNNY W., minister; b. Shamrock, Tex., Aug. 4, 1933; s. John W. and Faye Leota (Gregory) J.; m. Nancy Jean Howdeshell, June 26, 1953; children: Danny Michael, Stephen Mark, Faye Luanne, Lauree Sue. BA, Abilene Christian U., 1974. Ordained to ministry Chs. of Christ, 1954. Min. Ch. of Christ, Pottsboro, Tex., 1954-55, Morton St. Ch. of Christ, Denison, Tex., 1955-58, Abrams Ch. of Christ, Richardson, Tex., 1958-64, Southside Ch. of Christ, Amarillo, Tex., 1964-66, Cen. Ch. of Christ, Houston, 1966-69, So. MacArthur Ch. of Christ, Irving, 1969-79, Eldridge Rd. Ch. of Christ, Sugar Land, 1979-82, De Soto (Tex.) Ch. of Christ, 1982—; bd. dirs. Cedar Green Living Ctr., DeSoto. Contbr. articles to profl. jours. Mem. Rotary (sec. De Soto chpt. 1986-87). Home: 1408 Richards Circle De Soto TX 75115 Office: De Soto Ch of Christ 115 W Belt Line De Soto TX 75115 *I have found that living up to my responsibility depends not as much upon my ability as it does to my response to God's ability!.*

JACKSON, JULIAN CURLEY, minister, marriage and family counselor; b. Sylvania, Ga., May 5, 1933; s. Sonny Jose and Iola (Reason) J.; m. Thelma Phronetta Watson, Mar. 14, 1953; children: Barbara Jackson Murray, Julian D., Mary Brigham. AA, Miami-Dade Community Coll., 1971; BS, Fla. Internat. Coll., 1974; MA, Biscayne Coll., 1983; postgrad. N.Y. Theol. Sem., 1984—. Owner Jackson's Cleaner, Miami, Fla., 1962-67; mail courier Dade County Schs., Miami, 1965-74; social worker Miami Mental Health Ctr., 1975-78; project dir. New Horizons Mental Health Ctr., Miami, 1978-82; minister Ch. of God in Christ, Miami, 1960—, trustee, Memphis, 1972-80, dist. supt., Miami, 1971—. Home: 6890 NW 19th Ave Miami FL 33147 Office: Gamble Meml Ch of God in Christ 1898 NW 43rd St Miami FL 33142

JACKSON, JULIUS LEE, clergyman; b. Beaumont, Tex., July 13, 1938; s. Oscar and Mary (Crochett) Green J.; m. JoAnn Bostic, Aug. 21, 1958 (div. Nov. 1977); children—Julius Lee, Jr., L'Tonya, Randy; m. Reda Jo Monroe, Sept. 12, 1981; stepchildren—Willis, Kelley, Keisha. Student Lamar U., 1964-67; A.D., Southwestern Theol. Sem., 1972; B.Th., Conroe Coll., 1973; D.D., New World Bible Inst., 1985, postgrad., 1987; postgrad. Tarrant County Jr. Coll., 1976-77, Tex. Wesleyan Coll., 1982, Princeton Theol. Sem., 1983, 85, Arlington Bible Coll., 1974-77, Bishop Coll., 1985. Ordained to ministry Baptist Ch., 1966. Pastor Lilly of the Valley Baptist Ch., Beaumont, 1968-70, Macedonia Bapt. Ch., Fort Worth, 1972—; bd. dirs. New World Bible Inst. Blytheville, Ark., 1985—, provost to pres., 1985—. Mem. adv. bd. Fort Worth State Sch.; mem. adv. bd. distributive edn. program Dunbar High Sch., Fort Worth; juror Grand Jury, Criminal Justice Tarrant County, Fort Worth, 1974, 84; mem. mgmt. com. Morningside Middle Sch., Fort Worth, 1985—; advisor Concerned Citizens for Quality Edn., 1985. Served to cpl. USMC, 1956-62. Recipient Nobel award F. Brooks and Gray, Fort Worth, 1977; Psycho Cybernetics award Dr. Maxwell Malt Miller Seminar, Houston, 1977; Progress award Ecclesiatical Christian awards, Atlanta, 1982. Mem. Bapt. Minister Alliance (courtesy com. 1983—), Black Pastor Assn. Tex. (exec. treas. 1983—), Zion Rest Dist. Assn. (1st vice moderator 1985—). Democrat. Baptist. Lodge: Masons. Avocations: tennis; running. Home: 7113 Kildee Ln Fort Worth TX 76133 Office: Macedonia Bapt Ch 2712 S Freeway Fort Worth TX 76104

JACKSON, KELVIN PURNELL, music minister; b. Augusta, Ga., July 30, 1959; s. Purnell Jackson and Irene (Edwards) O'Bryant. Student, Aladdin Beauty Coll., 1986, Augusta Coll., 1990—. Musician Lackland AFB (Tex.) Chapels, 1981-82, Holloman Gospel Voices, Alamogordo, N.Mex., 1982-83; minister of music Antioch Bapt., Midland, Tex., 1983-88; musician Augusta (Ga.) Masonic Choir, 1988—; minister of music Galilee Bapt., Augusta, 1988—; data processing mgr. Trooper, Inc., Augusta, 1988—. Recipient Marksmanship award USAF, 1982. Mem. James Cleveland Gospel Music Workshop of Am., Masonic Choirs of Ga. Home: 281 E Wynngate Dr Martinez GA 30907 Office: Galilee Bapt Ch 918 Cedar St Augusta GA 30901

JACKSON, KENT PHILLIPS, religious educator; b. Salt Lake City, Aug. 9, 1949; s. Richard W. and Hazel (Phillips) J.; m. Nancy P. Jackson, June 18, 1975; children: Sarah, Rebecca, Jennifer, Jonathan, Alexander. BA, Brigham Young U., 1974; MA, U. Mich., 1976, PhD, 1980. Prof. ancient scripture Brigham Young U., Provo, Utah, 1980—. Editor: Studies in Scripture, Vols. I-8, 1984-90; contbr. articles to profl. jours. Mem. Soc. Bibl. Lit. (regional pres. 1985-86). Office: Brigham Young U Provo UT 84602

JACKSON, KEVIN GRAY, clergyman; b. Nashville, Dec. 25, 1962; s. Billy Gray and Shirley Dean (Gaskins) J.; m. Debra Dianne Gardner, Aug. 7, 1981; children: Jessica Sue, Emily Dean. Grad. high sch., Jacksonville, N.C. Ordained to ministry Bapt. Ch., 1982. Pastor Lakeside Free Will Bapt. Ch., Norman, Okla., 1983-85; asst. pastor Cardinal Village Free Will Bapt. Ch., 1985-88; pastor Hatfield (Ark.) Free Will Bapt. Ch., 1988-89, Harmony Free Will Bapt. Ch., Kansas City, Mo., 1989—; mem. search com. Little Mo. River Assn., Kirby, Ark., 1988-89; mem. exec. bd. Kansas City Assn. Free Will Bapts., Kansas City, Mo. Organizer Muscular Dystrophy Dr., Jacksonville, 1986. Republican. Home: 5001 NW Northwood Kansas City MO 64152 *It takes more than one success to make a man happy. It is the constant day to day living which makes us a success.*

JACKSON, MICHAEL SCOTT, minister; b. Milw., May 3, 1952; s. Steven and Gwendolyn (Temple) J.; m. Gail Marie Oehrlein, May 24, 1980; 1 child, Amanda Gail. BA, Luther Coll., 1974. Lay min. Green Pastures Christian Ctr., St. Cloud, Minn., 1977-81, adminstr., 1981-84, sr. pastor, 1984—; bd. dirs. St. Cloud Christian Sch., 1988-90; advisor Women's Aglow Bd., 1988-90. Contbr. articles to publs. Precinct officer, conv. del. Senate Dist. 17, Minn., 1984-90. Mem. Assn. Faith Chs. and Ministries. Home: 875 Pearl View Dr Sauk Rapids MN 56379 Office: Green Pastures Christian Ctr 7242 Old Hwy 52 Saint Cloud MN 56303

JACKSON, SISTER MICHELE, religion educator; b. Buffalo, N.Y., Feb. 18, 1945; d. Delbert Wilson and Mary Ellen (Moriarity) J. BS in Elem. Edn., Medialle Coll., 1976. Cert. elem. tchr., N.Y. Religion educator Diocese of Buffalo, 1960-75; dir. religion edn. St. Stephen's Ch., Middleport, N.Y., 1975—; cons. William H. Sadlier Co., 1974-76, 90—, mem. Parish Pastoral Coun., Middleport, 1985—, Parish Bereavement Team, Middleport, 1985—; dir. Baptismal Prep. Team, Middleport, 1976—, Marriage Prep. Team, Middleport, 1988—, Parish High Sch. Retreat Team, Middleport, 1975—; employment counselor Ctr. for the Study of Aging, U. Buffalo, 1985-86. Fellow Diocesan High Sch. Curriculum Com., Diocesan Jr. High Curriculum Com. Democrat. Home: 6380 Main St Williamsville NY 14221 Office: St Stephens Cath Ch 21 S Vernon St Middleport NY 14105

JACKSON, PAUL HOWARD, librarian; b. Topeka, Nov. 10, 1952; s. Dwight Stover and Janice Ilona (Woeltje) J.; m. Elizabeth Ann McGhghy, July 23, 1977; children: Christopher, Jeremy, Catherine, Johanna, Caleb. BA, Washburn U., 1973; MLS, Emporia (Kans.) State U., 1974; MDiv, Concordia Sem., Clayton, Mo., 1979. Ordained to ministry Luth. Ch.-Mo. Synod, 1979. Pastor St. Paul's Luth. Ch., Wakefield, Nebr., 1979-81, 1st Trinity Luth. Ch., Wayne, Nebr., 1979-81; libr., tchr. Luth. High. Sch. Indpls., 1981-82; libr., prof. St. John's Coll., Winfield, Kans., 1982-85; pastor 1st Luth. Ch., Pond Creek, Okla., 1986-88; libr. Concordia Theol. Sem., Ft. Wayne, Ind., 1988—; counselor Wayne cir. Luth. Women's Mission League, 1981. Organizer musical group Celebration, 1982; contbr. articles to religious jours. Bd. dirs. Trinity Ch. S.E. Asian Mission, Winfield, 1984-86; co-chair Winfield Com. for Commemorating the Bicentennial of the Constn., Winfield, 1987-88; chmn. Coalition for Purchase and Renovation, St. John's Coll., Winfield, 1988; sec. exec. com. Area 3 Libr. Svc. Authority, Ft. Wayne, 1990—. Mem. Ohio Computing Libr. Ctr. Theol. Users Group of Am. Theol. Libr. Assn., Chgo. Area Theol. Libr. Assn., Phi Kappa Phi, Mu Alpha Pi. Democrat. Home: 7 Wycliffe Pl Fort Wayne IN 46825 Office: Concordia Theol Sem 6600 N Clinton St Fort Wayne IN 46825

JACKSON, RANDON HOWARD, minister; b. Murfreesboro, Tenn., Nov. 17, 1951; s. Melvin Moore and Gracie Ruth (Sherer) J., m. Cathleen Vernelle Pidgeon, June 29, 1974; children: Sarah Elizabeth, James Howard, Stephen Edward. BS, Presbyn. Coll., 1974; MDiv, Union Theol. Sem., Richmond, Va., 1977; D Ministry, Union Theol. Sem., Rcihmond, Va., 1978. Ordained to ministry Presbyn. Ch., 1978. Assoc. pastor 1st Presbyn. Ch., Greenville, S.C., 1978-80, Idlewild Presbyn. Ch., Memphis, 1980-86; pastor Covenant Presbyn. Ch., Decatur, Ala., 1986—; chmn. Com. on Ministry N. Ala. Presbytery, 1989—; mem. Nat. Presbyn. Youth Coun., Presbyn. Ch. (U.S.A.) Gen. Assembly, 1989—. Bd. dirs. Big Brothers/Big Sisters of Morgan County, Decatur, 1988—; pres., bd. dirs. Presbyn. Home, Decatur, 1989—. Recipient Clergy Appreciation award Civitan Internat., Decatur, 1991. Office: Covenant Presbyn Ch 2002 Westmeade St SW Decatur AL 35601

JACKSON, TIMM C., minister; b. Memphis, Mar. 16, 1945; s. Roy R. and Alice Rachel (Hada) J.; m. Karen Lea Cox; children: Jennifer Rachelle, Jina Chanelle. BA in Theology, Miltonvale Wesleyan Coll. Youth min. Richardson (Tex.) Ch. of Nazarenes; single adults min. Ward Presbyn. Ch., Livonia, Mich., Grace Community Ch., Tempe, Ariz.; assoc. min. Second Presbyn Ch., Memphis, 1988—; exec. dir., bd. dirs. Nat. Assn. Single Adult Leaders. Republican. Home: 8523 Bazemore Rd Cordova TN 38018 Office: Second Presbyn Ch 4055 Poplar Ave Memphis TN 38111

JACKSON, WALTER COLEMAN, III, minister, marriage therapist, educator; b. Chester, Pa., Mar. 21, 1933; s. Walter Coleman and Elsie Irene (Watson) J.; m. Jacqueline Jean Rhoads, Aug. 17, 1957; children—Jerri Leigh, Jeffrey Walter, Nanci Carol. B.A., U. Richmond, 1955; B.D., So. Baptist Theol. Sem., 1959, Th.M., 1961, Ph.D., 1968. Ordained to ministry, Baptist Ch., 1955; pastor chs., Va., Ky., 1954-64; chaplain Ky. Bapt. Hosp., Louisville, 1964-77, instr. sch. of Nursing, 1964-72; clin. instr. Louisville Presbyterian Theol. Sem., 1971-72; chaplain Bapt. Med. Ctr. Okla., Oklahoma City, 1977-81; prof. ministry So. Bapt. Theol. Sem., Louisville, 1982—, acting dean Sch. Theology, 1991—. Diplomate Am. Assn. Pastoral Counselors; mem. Am. Assn. Marriage and Family Therapy (clin.; supr. 1981), Assn. Clin. Pastoral Edn. (supr. 1974), Coll. Chaplains, Am. Protestant Hosp. Assn., Louisville Assn. Mental Health (dir. 1976-77), Jefferson County Med. Soc. (physician clergy com.), Ky. Med. Assn. (com. religion and medicine, clergy cons.). Author: Codependence and the Christian Faith, 1990. Office: So Baptist Theol Sem 2825 Lexington Rd Louisville KY 40280

JACKSON, WILLIAM JOSEPH, religion educator; b. Rock Island, Ill., Aug. 31, 1943; s. Laverne Charles and Roselle (Conwell) J.; m. Marcia Plant; 1 child, Rose. BA, Lyndon State Coll., 1975; MTS, Harvard U., 1977, MA, 1979, PhD, 1984. Asst. prof. Ind. U.-Purdue U., Indpls., 1985—. Author: Walk Through a Hill Town, 1977, Saikrishnalila, 1980, Tyagaraja-Life and Lyrics, 1991. Mem. Am. Acad. Religion. Home: 5750 Broadway Indianapolis IN 46220-2570 Office: Ind U-Purdue U 425 University Blvd Indianapolis IN 46202

JACO, JAMES HAROLD, JR., minister; b. Warren County, Tenn., June 11, 1941; s. James Harold and Margaret Louanne Jaco; m. Frances Juanita Smithson, June 20, 1963; children: James Harold III, Jina F., Jeffery Y. Student, Union U., 1959-61, Conquerors Bible Coll., 1961-63; BTh, BA, Pentecostal Bible Inst., 1975. Ordained to ministry United Pentecostal Ch. Internat., 1965. Pastor various chs. Tenn., Ont., Can., Miss., 1963-75; pastor East Dyersburg Pentecostal Ch., Dyersburg, Tenn., 1975—; head counselor Pentecostal Children's Retreat, Perryville, Tenn., 1976—; past pres. Apostolic Missionary Inst. Author: The Tabernacle, 1974; editor Pentecostal Voice Tenn., 1975—, Ont. Dist. News, 1968-73; contbr. articles to religious jours. Mem. Dyersburg Ministerial Assn. (v.p. 1982-83). Home: 908 Lewis Ave Dyersburg TN 38024 Office: East Dyersburg Pentecostal Ch 922 Lewis Ave Dyersburg TN 38024

JACOBS, ANTHONY BECKET, minister; b. Portland, Oreg., Jan. 24, 1965; s. Helmut Arno and Brigitte Ingrid (Hedges) J.; m. Christina Marie Moore, Apr. 15, 1989. BS in Bibl. Edn., Multnomah Sch. of Bible, 1989. Campus leader InterVarsity Christian Fellowship, Vancouver, Wash., 1983-84; staff overseer, discipleship dir. Crossroads Community Ch., Vancouver, 1984-89, pastoral intern, 1987-89, dir. discipleship and staff tng., 1990-91; assoc. pastor Calvary Chapel, Boise, Idaho, 1989-90. Composer music: Early Winter, 1989. Bd. mem. King's Korner St. Ministries, Vancouver, 1984-85; dir. Rock Christian Concert Promotions, Boise, Vancouver, 1989—; bd. mem. Treasure Valley Youth Network, Boise, 1990. Recipient Recognition Christian Leadership, Am. Christian Leadership Coun., 1989. Mem. Nat. Network Youth Ministries. Home: 207 SE 156th Ave Vancouver WA 98684 *Knowledge is the pride of youth and wisdom is the jewel of the aged, but it is love and humility which give glory to God.*

JACOBS, DONALD GUSTAVUS, minister; b. Chelsea, Mass., Aug. 24, 1916; s. Burchell Gustavus and Melissa Jane (VanDerZee) J.; m. Maxine Lanell Sides, June 11, 1942; children: Donald Albert, Burchell Lewis. AB, Wilberforce U., 1939; BD, Payne Theol. Sem., 1943; postgrad. Bucknell U., 1943-44, Duquesne Coll., 1946-47, Oberlin Sch. Theology, 1950-52; DD (hon.), Payne Sem., 1955; LLD, Monrovia Coll., 1957, Edward Waters Coll., 1965. Ordained to ministry African Meth. Episc. Ch., 1940. Pastor, AME chs., Pa. and Ohio, 1940-88; pastor community AME Ch., Cleve., 1989—. exec. dir. Interch. Coun. Greater Cleve., 1968-82, gen. minister, 1983—; nat. dir. Ptnrs. in Ecumenism, Nat. Coun. Chs., N.Y.C., 1981—; tchr. Cleve. Theology Ctr., Ashland Coll., 1972-81. Sec., Wilberforce Bd. Trustees (Ohio); co-chmn. Stokes for Mayor Com., 1965, Operation Black Unity, 1969. Mem. Cleve. Ministerial Assn. (pres. 1961), NAACP (pres. Cleve. chpt. 1964-66), Nat. Assn. Ecumenical Staff, Cleve. Urban League, Connectional Coun. AME Ch. Democrat. Office: 2230 Euclid Ave Cleveland OH 44115 also: AME Church 5805 Lexington Ave Cleveland OH 44103

JACOBS, GARY WAYNE, minister; b. Cin., Aug. 7, 1961; s. Eugene William and Mary Emily (Shoemaker) J.; m. Cynthia Ann Groves, June 16, 1984; children: Amy Katherine, Gary Steven. BA, Cedarville Coll., 1983; MDiv, Grace Theol. Sem., 1987. Ordained to ministry Gen. Assn. of Regular Bapt. Chs., 1990. Youth dir. 1st Bapt. Ch., Athens, Ohio, 1979-80; youth pastor 1st Bapt. Ch., Rittman, Ohio, 1983; pastor Eel River Community Ch., Pierceton, Ind., 1986-87; asst. youth pastor Christian edn. Calvary Bapt. Ch., Byesville, Ohio, 1987—; counselor Scioto Hills Bapt. Camp, Wheelersburg, Ohio, 1981-82. Founder, bd. dirs. Cedar Cliff Elderly Housing Team, Cedarville, Ohio, 1981-83; v.p. Cedarville Coll. Swordbearers, 1982-83. Mem. Ohio Assn. Regular Bapt. Chs. (mem. Ohio state youth com. 1990—). Home: 313 S 7th St Byesville OH 43723 Office: Calvary Bapt Ch 245 S 6th St Byesville OH 43723

JACOBS, WALTER W., clergyman; b. Louisville, May 8, 1932; s. Walter Wallace and Dolla (Carter) J.; m. Jean Brooks, June 21, 1958; children: Emily, Alicia, Rita, Patricia. AB, Berea Coll., 1952; MRE, So. Bapt. Theol. Sem., 1955. Minister music/edn. Front St. Bapt. Ch., Statesville, N.C., 1955-59, North Main Bapt. Ch., High Point, N.C., 1959-62, North Trenholm Bapt. Ch., Columbia, S.C., 1962-74; minister edn. First Bapt. Ch., Jackson, Tenn., 1974-76, Union Ave. Bapt. Ch., Memphis, 1976-79, Edwards Rd. Bapt. Ch., Greenville, S.C., 1979—; chmn. pub. affairs/Christian life com. S.C. Conv., 1968, chmn. govt. fund evaluation com., 1989. Contbr. articles to profl. jours. Mem. So. Bapt. Religious Edn. Assn. (v.p. 1988), Ea. Religious Edn. Assn. (pres. 1974), S.C. Religious Edn. Assn. , S.W. Religious Edn. Assn., Masons. Home: 305 Roberts Rd Taylors SC 29687 Office: Edwards Rd Bapt Ch 1050 Edwards Rd Greenville SC 29615

JACOBSEN, JACK ELLSWORTH, clergyman; b. Racine, Wis., July 20, 1923; s. Holger Swend and Lydia Marie (Christiansen) J; m. Edith Marjorie Rosvold, June 20, 1948; children: Paul, Sandra, Thomas, Sharon, Larry. BA, Augsburg Coll., 1946; MDiv, Northwestern Sem., Mpls., 1949; ThD, Citadel Bapt. Sem., Brycus, Ohio, 1981. Ordained to ministry Luth. Ch., 1949. Mgr. News Realty, Mpls., 1978-80; pastor St. Andrews Luth. Ch., Mpls., 1959-65, Kingsway Luth. Ch., Wayzata, Minn., 1965-68, St. John Luth. Ch., Rushmore, Minn., 1978-80, Eternal Hope Luth. Ch., Mpls., 1980—; pres. Kings Outreach, Wayzata, 1968-72. Author: Human Destiny, 1989. Sec., treas. Golden Valley Luth. Coll., Mpls., 1987-90. Home: 9200 Lakeside Trail Champlin MN 55316 Office: Eternal Hope Luth Ch 10508 Douglas Dr Minneapolis MN 55443

JACOBSEN, THORKILD, Assyriology educator emeritus; b. Copenhagen, June 7, 1904; s. Christian Laurits and Gerda (Jensen) J.; m. Rigmor Schroll, Sept. 16, 1927 (dec. 1947); m. Joanne Poole, 1949 (dec. 1964); m. Katryna Hadley Parmenter, June 21, 1966; children: Dana Perrone, Pamela Pastacaldi, Caroline Apfel, Katryna Lockwood. MA, U. Copenhagen, 1927, D.Phil. (hon.), 1939; PhD, U. Chgo., 1929; MA (hon.), Harvard U., 1962; D.Phil. (hon.), Hebrew U., Jerusalem, 1988. Prof. emeritus Harvard U. Author: The Treasures of Darkness: A History of Mesopotamian Religion, 1976, The Harps That Once Sumerian Poetry in Translation, 1987; author: (with Frankfort and others) Before Philosophy, 1949. Recipient George Foot Moore award The Soc. of Bibl. Lit., 1980. Mem. Am. Soc. for the Study of Religion, Am. Philos. Soc., Am. Acad of Arts and Scis, Royal Danish Acad. Scis. (corr.), British Acad., Deutch Archeol. Inst. Home: E Washington Rd Bradford NH 03221

JACOBSON, ARLAND DEAN, religion educator; b. Mitchell, S.D., Sept. 25, 1941; s. Olaf Johannes and Ruth Amelia (Gjesdal) J. m. Wilhelmine Treadwell, Aug. 4, 1964; children: Erik Eugene, Karin Inga. BA, Augustana Coll., 1963; student, Div. Sch., U. Chgo., 1964-65; BD, Luther Theol. Sem., St. Paul, 1967; PhD, Claremont Grad. Sch., 1978. Ordained to ministry Evang. Luth. Ch. Am., 1967. Pastor Scranton (N.D.) Luth. Parish, 1967-71, St. Paul Luth. Ch., Humboldt, S.D., 1974-76; vis. prof. Loyola Marymount U., L.A., 1978-79; asst. prof. Concordia Coll., Moorhead, Minn., 1979-83; exec. dir. Charis Ecumenical Ctr., Fargo-Moorhead Communiversity, Moorhead, 1983—; chair bd. Great Plains Inst. Theology, Bismarck, N.D., 1969-71; mem. Faith and Order Commn., Minn. Coun. Chs., Mpls., 1985—. Author: Wisdom Christology in Q, 1978, The First Gospel, 1991; also numerous articles. Chair conf. planning com. Internat. Coalition for Land-Water Stewardship in the Red River Basin, Moorhead, 1983-85, chair edn. com., 1985-87. Scholar Luth. Theol. Sem., 1966, scholar in residence Inst. for Ecumenical and Cultural Rsch., 1990. Mem. Soc. Bibl. Lit., Cath. Bibl. Assn., Soc. for Advancement Continuing Edn. for Ministry, The Jesus Seminar, Westar Inst., Kiwanis (bd. dirs. Moorhead club 1989—). Home: 1915 12th Ave S Moorhead MN 56560 Office: Concordia Coll CHARIS Ecumenical Ctr Moorhead MN 56562

JACOBSON, DAVID, rabbi; b. Cin., Dec. 2, 1909; s. Abraham and Rebecca (Sereinsky) J.; m. Helen Gugenheim, Nov. 6, 1938; children: Elizabeth Anne, Dorothy Jean Jacobson Miller. A.B., U. Cin., 1931; Rabbi, Hebrew Union Coll., 1934, D.D., 1959; Ph.D., St. Catherine's Coll., U. Cambridge (Eng.), 1936; LL.D., Our Lady of Lake Coll., 1964. Instr. Hebrew Union Coll., 1933-34; rabbi West Central Liberal Congregation, London, 1934-36, Indpls. Hebrew Congregation, 1936-38, Temple Beth-El, San Antonio, 1938-76; emeritus Temple Beth-El, 1976—; rabbi Temple Mizpah, Abilene, Tex., 1981-86; aux. chaplain, area mil. installations; chaplain Audie Murphy VA Hosp., 1973—; chmn. Rabbinical Placement Commn., 1973-78; chmn. discussion program KSAT-TV, 1956-80, KLRN-TV, 1983. Author: Social Background of the Old Testament, 1942, The Synagogue Through the Ages, 1958; contbr. articles to profl. and gen. publs.; also contbr. to: Universal Jewish Ency, 1939-43. Mem. Tex. Senate Com. Welfare Reform, 1970, Tex. State Ethics Commn., 1971, Tex. State Medicaid Task Force, 1977; mem. com. nursing homes Tex. Dept. Human Resources, 1978-80; pres. San Antonio Soc. Crippled Children and Adults, 1963-66, Goodwill Industries San Antonio, 1956-60, Bexar County chpt. Nat. Tb Assn., 1955-57, Community Welfare Council San Antonio, 1951-53, San Antonio Area Found., 1965-69, Research and Planning Council San Antonio, 1966-67, Tex. Social Welfare Assn., 1967-69, San Antonio Manpower Devel. Council, 1968-76, S.W. region Central Conf. Am. Rabbis, 1969-70, Multiple Sclerosis Soc. San Antonio, 1975-78, Nat. Conf. Social Welfare, 1976-77, Am. Inst. Character Edn., 1976-78, Prevent Blindness Soc., San Antonio, 1980-82; mediator San Antonio Printing Trades and Employers, 1968—; mem. nat. labor panel Am. Arbitration Assn., 1977—, Fed. Mediation and Conciliation Service, 1981—; commr. Housing Authority San Antonio, 1954-58; bd. dirs. Our Lady of Lake U., 1966-76, hon. bd. dirs., 1977—; also chmn. adv. bd. Worden Sch. Social Service of coll., 1958-67; founder U. Ind. Hillel Found., 1938, San Antonio Vis. Nurses Assn., 1952, Community Welfare Council San Antonio, 1944; bd. dirs. S.W. Tex. Meth. Hosp., 1956-84, San Antonio Med. Found., 1962—, Alamo council Boy Scouts Am., 1950—, Children's Hosp. Found., 1964—, Keystone Sch., San Antonio, 1960-80, Ecumenical Center for Religion and Health, 1968—, Alamo chpt. Am. Cancer Soc., 1975-83, Hospice of St. Benedict's Hosp., 1977-81, Tex. Council Higher Edn., 1969—, Nat. Jewish Welfare Bd., 1964-72, Alamo chpt. Assn. U.S. Army, 1964-71, Hemis Fair, 1968; chmn. scholarship com. City, County Martin Luther King Commn., 1967—, Child Advocates, 1968—; life mem. bd. Tex. United Community Services, 1970—; co-chmn. community relations council San Antonio Jewish Fedn., 1978-79; chmn. religion com. United San Antonio, 1980-81, vice chmn. public sector, 1981—; chmn. Bexar County Community Corrections Commn., 1979-81; mem. nat. bd. Goodwill Industries Am., 1965-78; bd. overseers Hebrew Union Coll.-Jewish Inst. Religion, 1966-88, bd. govs., 1966-68; mem. Commn. on Social Action of Reform Judaism, 1978-88; mem. nat. bd. Nat. Council on Crime and Delinquency, 1972-88, Florence G. Heller-Jewish Welfare Bd. Research Center, 1966-70; bd. dirs. Army Med. Dept. Mus. Found., 1985-88. Served as chaplain with USNR, 1944-46. Recipient Silver Beaver award Boy Scouts Am., 1958; Aristotle-Aquinas award Cath. Coll. Found. S.A., 1959; Golden Deeds award Exchange Club San Antonio, 1959; Keystone award Boys' Club Am., 1962, Lifetime Achievement award B'nai B'rith, 1964, Nat. Humanitarian award, 1975, Edgar Helms award Goodwill Industries, 1972, leadership award San Antonio Transcendental Meditation Soc., 1977, Shofar award, 1984, Outland award Tex. Soc. Prevent Blindness, 1988; named Outstanding Jew NCCJ, 1961, Citizen of Year Sembradores de Amistad, 1971, Martin Luther King Disting. Achievement award, 1979; honoree S. Tex. chpt. Prevent Blindness as Persons of Vision, 1 Central Conf. Am. Rabbis (chmn. com. Judaism and health 1967-72, chmn. nominating com. 1979), Kallah of Tex. Rabbis (pres. 1950-51, chancellor-historian 1977—), Am. Social Health Assn. (dir. 1969-75), Tex. Congress Parents and Tchrs. (hon. life), Sigma Alpha Mu, Pi Tau Pi. Clubs: Rotary (San Antonio), B'nai B'rith (San Antonio) (hon. chmn. 1974), Torch (San Antonio) (pres. 1961), Argyle (San Antonio). Home: 207 Beechwood Ln San Antonio TX 78216

JACOBSON, GILBERT H., lawyer; b. Memphis, Feb. 6, 1956; s. Irvin and Edith (Shainberg) J.; m. Shauna Brown, Aug. 23, 1983; children: Yisroel, Esther C., Nechama F. BBA, Memphis State U., 1980; JD, Touro Coll. Sch. Law, Huntington, N.Y., 1983. Bar: N.Y. 1984, Tenn. 1985, Colo. 1986. Tax cons. Rooney, Pace, Inc., N.Y.C., 1983-84; chief fin. officer Denton Mills, Inc., New Albany, Miss., 1984-85; endowment cons. Coun. of Jewish Fedns., N.Y.C., 1986-90; assoc. dir. endowment devel. Coun. of Jewish Fedns., 1990—. Contbr. articles to profl. jours. Founding pres. Torah Community Project, Denver, 1985-86; officer Congregation Adas Israel, Passaic, N.J., 1987—. Mem. Am. jewish Community Orgn. Personnel, N.Y. State Bar Assn. Avocation: Talmudic study. Office: Coun of Jewish Fedns 730 Broadway New York NY 10003

JACOBSON, SVERRE THEODORE, retired minister; b. Loreburn, Sask., Can., Sept. 20, 1922; s. Sverre and Aline Tomina (Joel) J.; m. Phyllis Lorraine Sylte, Sept. 14, 1948; children—Katherine Ann, Paul Theodore. B.A., U. Sask., 1946; B.D., Luther Theol. Sem., Sask., 1947; postgrad., Luther Theol. Sem., St. Paul, Minn., 1952-53; Th.D., Princeton Theol. Sem., 1959. Ordained to ministry Evang. Lutheran Ch., Can.; pastor Lomond, Alta., 1947-53; lectr. Luther Theol. Sem., Saskatoon, Sask., 1956-57; pastor Torquay, Sask., 1958-63; asst. to pres. Evang. Luth. Ch. Can., Saskatoon, 1963-70; pres. Evang. Luth. Ch. Can., 1970-85; interim parish pastor Saskatoon, 1987-91; lectr. Luth. Theol. Sem., Saskatoon, 1987-88. Home: 53 Moxon Crescent, Saskatoon, SK Canada S7H 3B8

JACOBSON, WAYNE LEE, minister, writer; b. Selma, Calif., Mar. 21, 1953; s. Eugene William and Joanne Celeste (Williams) J.; m. Sara Jo Fought, May 17, 1975; children: Julie Ann, Andrew John. BA in Bibl. Lit., Oral Roberts U., 1975. Ordained to ministry Ind. Charismatic Ch., 1976. Assoc. pastor Valley Christian Ctr., Fresno, Calif., 1975-80; co-pastor The Savior's Community, Visalia, Calif., 1980—; vis. instr. U. of the Nations, Kona, Hawaii, 1988—. Author: The Naked Church, 1989, A Passion for God's Presence, 1990; contbr. articles to religious jours.; contbg. editor Leadership Jour., 1984—. Mem. Family Life Edn. Subcom., Visalia, 1985—, Coalition to Prevent Teen Pregnancies, 1989—, Supt.'s Adv. Com. for Visalia Unified Sch. Dist., 1990—. Mem. Oral Roberts U. Alumni Assn. (trustee 1982-85). Republican. Office: The Savior's Community 2043 S Court Visalia CA 93277 *There is nothing more needful in our Christian experience than to cultivate our ongoing friendship with Jesus; and there is nothing easier to be distracted from, than that same friendship!.*

JACOBSON-WOLF, JOAN ELIZABETH, minister; b. Flint, Mich., July 15, 1949; d. William and Helen Wolf; m. Don M. Jacobson, May 27, 1978; children: Lara Heather, Heidi Kirsten, Joan Noel. AA, Concordia Coll., 1969; BA in Theology, Valparaiso U., 1972; postgrad., Luth. Sem., Mexico City, Phila. and Columbus, Ohio, 1974-76; M in Div., Luth. Sch. Theology, Chgo., 1978; D in Ministry, McCormick Theol. Seminary, 1986. Ordained minister Luth. Ch., 1979; cert. psychiatric chaplain. Community organizer Cleve. Hispanic Murals, Centro Juvenil de Puertoriqueña; deaconess, missionary Hispanic ministry Trinity Luth., Cleve., 1972-75; intern, asst. minister Berwyn (Ill.) United Luth. Ch., 1977-78; chaplain Tenn. Women's Prison, Nashville, 1978-79, Spencer Youth Ctr., Nashville, 1979-81; minister St. Paul's Luth. Ch., Nashville, 1979-81; chaplain Edison Park Home, Park Ridge, Ill., 1982; minister in residency Riverside Presbyn. Ch., Chgo., 1982-85; assoc. minister First Congl. Ch., Owosso, Mich., 1985-87; pvt. practice as pastoral psychotherapist Owosso, 1988—; assoc. minister 1st Congl. Ch., Grand Blanc, Mich., 1991—. Author: When to Counsel, When to Refer, 1989; violinist Flint Summer Theater Orch., 1965-67, Ann Arbor (Mich.) Symphony, 1967-69, Valparaiso (Ind.) U. Orch., 1969-72, Cherokee String Quartet, Iowa, 1971, Cleve. Women's Symphony, 1973-75, Oak Park (Ill.) Symphony, 1977, Nashville Symphony, 1978-80. Home: 785 Riverbend Dr Owosso MI 48867 Office: 802 W King Ste 0 Owosso MI 48867

JACOBY, LEO PETER, religion educator; b. St. Louis, June 2, 1949; s. Paul Joseph and Virginia (Harbison) J.; m. Janet Ruth Bender, Aug. 6, 1977; children: Tobias, Joyana. BA in English and Philosophy, Boston Coll., Chestnut Hill, Mass., 1971; postgrad., St. Mary's Coll., Winona, Minn., 1976-79. Dir. religious edn. Blessed Sacrament Cathedral, Greensburg, Pa., 1971-73; dir. religious edn./youth minister St. Joseph Ch., St. Johns, Mich., 1974-76; dir. religious edn. Sacred Heart Cathedral, Winona, 1976-79, St. Joseph Ch., Stevens Point, Wis., 1979—; coord. for adult formation Stevens Point Deanery, 1988—; preparatory commn. Fourth Synod Diocese of La Crosse, Wis., 1984-86; mem. Sacred Worship Comm./Diocese of La Crosse, 1984-86; mem. RCIA Study Group Diocese of La Crosse, 1988—; group facilitator Loyola U., New Orleans, Inst. for Ministry Extension, 1991—; mem. adv. coun. on evangelization and adult catechesis, Diocese of La Crosse, 1989—; mem. pastoral planning com., Diocese of La Crosse, 1991—. Mem. Wis. Dirs. Religious Edn. Fedn. (conv. co-chmn. 1986-88, Stephen C. Gilmour award for Outstanding Leadership in the Catechetical Ministry 1988. Office: Deanery Office for Adult Formation 1901 Lincoln Ave Stevens Point WI 54481-3719

JAD AL-HAQ, JAD AL-HAQ ALI, head of religious order. Grand sheikh of al-Azhar, Islam Faith, Cairo. Office: Grand Sheikh of Al-Azhar, Cairo Arab Republic of Egypt*

JADOT, JEAN LAMBERT OCTAVE, clergyman; b. Brussels, Belgium, Nov. 23, 1909; s. Lambert Paul and Gabrielle Marie (Flanneau) J. D.Philosophie Thomiste, U. Catholique Louvain, Belgium, 1930. Ordained priest Roman Catholic Ch., 1934, consecrated bishop, 1968; parish asst., 1934-39; nat. chaplain Jeunesse Etudiante Catholique, 1939-45; chaplain Ecole Royale Militaire, 1945-52; chief chaplain Force Publique Belgian Congo, 1952-60; nat. dir. Propagation of Faith for Belgium, 1960-68; apostolic pro nuncio in Thailand; also apostolic del. in Laos, Malaysia and Singapore, 1968-71; apostolic pro nuncio in Cameroun and Gabon, also apostolic del. in Equatorial Guinea, 1971-73; apostolic del. to U.S., 1973-80; permanent observer of Holy See to OAS, 1978-80; pro pres. Secretariat for Non Christians at Vatican, 1980-84; titular arch-bishop of, Zuri, 1968. Served as chaplain Belgian Army, 1945-52. Decorated Order Leopold. Address: Ave de l'Atlantique 71B12, Brussels Belgium 1150

JAECKS, LENARD DALE, clergyman; b. Wausau, Wis., Mar. 21, 1932; s. Lawrence and Leona (Goede) J.; m. Lois Iattoni, June 7, 1953; children: Steven, Ronald. BA cum laude, Andrews U., 1955, MA, 1961, D Ministry, 1976. Ordained to ministry Seventh-Day Adventist Ch., 1961. Pastor Wis. Conf. Seventh-Day Adventists, Madison, 1955-67, S.E. Calif. Conf. Seventh-Day Adventists, Riverside, 1967-70, 78-79, Ill. Conf. Seventh-Day Adventists, Brookfield, 1970-74, Potomac Conf. Seventh-Day Adventists, Staunton, Va., 1974-78; v.p., ministerial dir. Wash. Conf. Seventh-Day Adventists, Bothell, 1979-86, pres., 1986—; mem. Nat. Ministerial Tng. Adv. Coun. Seventh Day Adventists; sponsor, tchr. seminars on ch. growth and ch. adminstrn. Author: (seminar program) Walking with Christ. Office: Wash Conf Seventh Day Adventists 20015 Bothell Way SE Bothell WA 98012

JAEGER, VERNON PAUL, minister, church official; b. St. Paul, Apr. 17, 1906; s. Paul Harry and Mathilda (Hirt) J.; m. Alice Harriet Cole, July 16, 1928; children: Wendell F., Charles P., Jane L. Jaeger Polly. AB, U. Redlands, 1928; BD, No. Bapt. Theol. Sem., 1931, DD, 1952; postgrad., U. Chgo. Ordained to ministry Am. Bapt. Chs. in USA, 1931. Pastor local ch. Wash., 1931-32; commd. 1st lt. chaplain U.S. Army, 1932, advanced through grades to col., 1954, retired, 1963; state missionary Oreg. Bapt. Conv., 1963-69, interim exec. min., 1970, state missionary, bus. mgr., 1971-73; asst. pastor Mountain Park Ch., Lake Oswego, Oreg., 1974-89, ret., 1989—.

Mem. Portland USO Com., 1969-76; bd. dirs. Portland Campus Christian Ministry, 1968-84; Oreg. state chaplain DAV, 1976-77; mem. adv. com. Oreg. Dept. Vets. Affairs, 1977-91, chmn. 1978-79, 84-85; DAV vol. svc. rep. to Portland VA Med. Ctr., 1976—. Named Hon. Rabbi Jewish Welfare Bd., 1962. Mem. Oreg. Coun. Chs. (treas. 1970-73), Ret. Officers Assn., Am. Bapt. Mins. Coun. Home: 13505 SE River Rd Portland OR 97222-8038 *Helping others brings both satisfaction and significant meaning to one's life.*

JAFFE, HOWARD LAWRENCE, rabbi; b. N.Y.C., Nov. 7, 1955; s. Nathaniel Herbert and Eleanor Gerogine (Arkow) J. BA, CUNY, 1978; MA in Hebrew Lit., Hebrew Union Coll.-Jewish Inst. Religion, 1981. Ordained rabb. 1983. Ast. rabb. Temple Israel, Mpls., 1983-85, assoc. rabb., 1985-88; rabb. Mountain Jewish Community Ctr., Warren, N.J., 1988—; bd. dirs. Assn. Reform Zionists Am., N.Y.C., chmn. Watchung Hills Ministry Assn., Warren, 1988—; chmn. privilege card com. Union Am. Hebrew Congregation, 1989—, trustee United Israel Appeal, N.Y.C., 1989—. Bd. dirs. Sumerset Coun. Alcoholism, Sommerville, N.J., 1990, Jewish Family Svcs., Sommerville, 1990. Mem. Cen Conf. Am. Rabbs. Office: Mountain Jewish Community Ctr 104 Mt Horeb Rd Warren NJ 07059

JAFFE, MARLYN BLOCH, religious organization administrator; b. Cleve., Sept. 15, 1964; d. Kurt Michael and Susan (Fast) Bloch; m. Ari H. Jaffe, Dec. 28, 1986. BA, Yale U., 1986; M in Non-Profit Orgns., Case Western Res. U., 1992. Communications assoc. Jewish Community Fedn., Cleve., 1987-90, community svcs. planning assoc., 1990—. Mem. Assn. Jewish Community Orgn. Profls. (Yale Book award 1981, alumni interviewer 1986—). Office: Jewish Community Fedn 1750 Euclid Ave Cleveland OH 44115

JAFFE, SAMUEL ZELMEN, rabbi, educator; b. N.Y.C., Dec. 15, 1922; s. Morris and Toby (Sharlin) J.; m. Edythe Judith Golin, Aug. 1952; children: Arvin, Joshua, Michele. BA, Yeshiva U., 1943; MA, Columbua U., 1946; M. Hebrew Lit., Hebrew Union Coll., 1948, DD (hon.), 1973; ThD, Burton Sem., 1962. Ordained rabbi, 1948. Dir. B'nai Brith Hillel Found., U. Fla., Gainesville, 1949-52; rabbi Congregation Beth Sholom, Park Forest, Ill., 1954-58, Temple Beth El, Hollywood, Fla., 1958-91; assoc. prof. Barry U., Miami Shores, Fla., 1975—; v.p. Holacaust Documentation and Edn., Miami, Fla., 1982—; bd. dirs. Jewish Family Svc., Broward County, Fla., 1990. Bd. dirs. Henderson Mental Health Ctr., Ft. Lauderdale, Fla., 1985—; pres. Jewish Nat. Fund, Miami Beach, 1989—. 1st lt. U.S. Army, 1952-54. Rabbi Samuel Z. Jaffe Chair in Jewish Studies named in his honor Bar Ilan U., Israel, 1990; recipient Appreciation award City of Hollywood. Mem. Greater Miami Rabbinical Assn. (past pres.), South Broward Coun. Rabbis (past pres.), S.E. Assn. Cen. Conf. Am. Rabbis (past pres., exec. bd.), Zionist Orgn. Am., B'nai Brith. Home: 1237 Wiley St Hollywood FL 33019 Office: Temple Beth El 1351 S 14th Ave Hollywood FL 33020 *I find that people are far better in terms of character than the words they speak. Language instead of serving as a vehicle of communication often becomes a facade masking our true feelings, either to provoke or startle or to cover up our insecurities.*

JAGGER, PETER JOHN, religious organization administrator, executive; b. Leeds, Yorkshire, England, Jan. 31, 1938; s. Willie and Annie (Pullen) J.; m. Margaret Thompson, Mar. 12, 1960; children: Mark, Catherine. MA, Lambeth, 1971; M. of Philosophy, U. Leeds, Eng., 1976; PhD, U. Leeds, 1987. Ordained priest, 1969. Curate All Saints Ch., Leeds, 1968-71; vicar Bolton cum Redmire, Yorkshire, 1971-77; warden, chief librarian St Deiniol's Libr., Hawarden, Deeside, Clywd, Wales, 1977—. Author: Christian Initiation 1552-1969: Rites of Baptism and Confirmation since the Reformation Period, 1970, Being the Church Today: A Collection of Sermons and Addresses by Bishop Henry de Candole, 1974, The Alcuin Club and its Publications: An Annotated Bibliography 1897-1974, 1975, Bishop Henry de Candole: His Life and Times 1895-1971, 1975, A History of the Parish and People Movement, 1978, Clouded Witness: Initiation in the Church of England in the Mid-Victorian Period, 1850-1875, 1982, Gladstone: Politics and Religion A Collection of Founder's Day Lectures delivered at St. Deinol's Library, Hawarden, 1967-1983, 1984, Gladstone, The Making of A Christian Politician: The Personal Religious Life and Development of William Ewart Gladstone, 1809-1832, 1991; contbr. articles to various periodicals. Dir. ministry tng. course St. Deiniol's Libr.; regional rep. Lambeth Diploma of Theology; mem. Brit. Libr. Nat. Preservation Adv. Com., 1985-88, Archbishop of Canterbury's Lambeth Diploma com. Fellow Royal Hist. Soc.; mem. Alcuin Club, Theol. Coll. Prins. Conf. Conservative. Anglican. Avocations: gardening, walking, music, sailing, shooting. Home and Office: St Deiniol's Library, Hawarden Deeside, Clwyd CH5 3DF, Wales

JAGGERS, STEVEN BRYAN, minister; b. Frankfort, Ind., Mar. 7, 1962; s. Winston Churchill and Karen Sue (Hitch) J. BA, Purde U., 1984; BA summa cum laude, Tenn. Bible Coll., Cookeville, 1988, MA summa cum laude, 1991. Youth minister Sycamore Ch. of Christ, Cookeville, 1985-87, Monterey Ch. of Christ, Cookeville, 1987-88; assoc./youth minister Livingston (Tenn.) Ch. of Christ, 1988—. Author/illustrator: (books) God, Are You Really Up There? 1989, Tell Me about Jesus Church, 1990, What Must I Do To Be Saved? 1990, Creation or Evolution: What's The Big Deal? 1991, Does The Bible Really Have The Answer to Today's Questions 1991; author: Christian Science: From God or Man? 1991, A Ready Reference Dictionary of Non-Christian Religions, 1988. Named to Outstanding Young Men of Am., 1985. Mem. Rotary. Home: Rte 1 PO Box 295-A Livingston TN 38570 Office: Livingston Ch of Christ 215 East Main St Livingston TN 38570 *In the words of Solomon, "Fear God, and keep His commandments: For this is the whole duty of man" (Eccles. 12:13).*

JAKOBOVITS, BARON IMMANUEL, rabbi; b. Feb. 8, 1921; s. Julius and Paula (Wreschner) J.; m. Amelie Munk, 1949; 6 children. BA, U. London, PhD, 1955; diploma, Jews' Coll. and Yeshivah Etz Chaim, London, 1944; DD (hon.), Yeshiva U., 1975; DLitt (hon.), City U. London, 1986. Ordained rabbi. Assoc. Jews' Coll.; rabbi Brondesbury Synagogue, 1941-44, S.E. London Synagogue, 1944-47, Gt. Synagogue, London, 1947-49; chief rabbi of Ireland, 1949-58; rabbi 5th Ave. Synagogue, N.Y.C., 1958-67; chief rabbi United Hebrew Congregations of Brit. Commonwealth of Nations, 1967-91. Author: Jewish Medical Ethics, 1959, Jewish Law Faces Modern Problems, 1965, Journal of a Rabbi, 1966, The Timely and the Timeless, 1977, If Only My People...Zionism in My Life, 1984; also articles. Decorated knight (U.K.); recipient Templeton prize in religion, 1991; U. London fellow, 1984—, hon. fellow, 1987. Office: United Hebrew Congregations, Adler House, Tavistock Sq, London WC1H 9HN, England*

JAKUBOWSKI, THAD J., bishop. Ordained priest Roman Cath. Ch., 1950, bishop, 1988. Apptd. aux. bishop Roman Cath. Ch., Chgo., 1988—; apptd. titular bishop Plestia Roman Cath. Ch., 1988—, consecrated, 1988—. Address: 6002 W Berteau Chicago IL 60634

JAMES, A. LINCOLN, SR., minister, religious organization executive; m. Clara Rose Thompson (dec. 1987); children: A. Lincoln Jr., Alexandria Linda, Clara Rose James-Thornton, Clayton Ronald, Andrea Lori; m. Wilma Cotten. BA, Va. Union U., DD (hon.), LLD (hon.); MDiv, Va. Union Theol. Sem. Ordained to ministry Nat. Bapt. Conv. U.S.A. Pastor 1st African Bapt. Ch., Richmond, Va., 1st Bapt. Ch., Suffolk, Va., Greater Bethesda Bapt. Chgo., Chgo., 1954—; v.p., then pres. Nat. Bapt. Congress Christian Edn., Nat. Bapt. Conv. USA, Inc., bd. dirs. Nat. Bapt. Conv. USA, Inc., 1982—; former editor Va. Jour. and Guide; prof. Va. Theol. Sem. and Coll., Lynchburg; former instr. Chgo. Bapt. Inst.; religion editor Chgo. Courier Newspaper, 1961-67; chmn. bd. dirs., organizer Chgo. Bldg. Maintenance Corp., 1973; mem. governing bd. Nat. Coun. of Chs. of Christ in U.S.A., 1983—; exec. dir., coord. Nuture for Bapt. Ch. series Sunday Sch. Pub. Bd. Former pres. Suffolk chpt. NAACP; former chair Mayor's Coun. Youth Activities, City of Suffolk; former v.p. Chgo. chpt. NAACP; former pres. Mins.' Coop. Civic League; apptd. by Pres. of U.S. to Ill. Civil Rights Commn.; apptd. by Mayor of Chgo. to Youth Commn., City of Chgo.; bd. dirs. Chs. United, Inc., 1968. Office: Greater Bethesda Bapt Ch 5301 S Michigan Ave Chicago IL 60615

JAMES, ALLIX BLEDSOE, university chancellor; b. Marshall, Tex., Dec. 17, 1922; s. Samuel Horace and Tannie Etta (Judkins) J.; m. Sue Nickens, Feb. 14, 1945; children: Alvan Bosworth, Portia Veann. AB, Va. Union U., 1944, MDiv, 1946; ThM, Union Theol. Sem. Va., 1949, ThD, 1957; postgrad., Boston U., summer 1951, Pa. State U., summer 1957; LLD, U. Richmond, 1970; DD, St. Paul's Coll., 1980. Ordained to ministry Bapt. Ch., 1942; moderator No. Neck Bapt. Assn., 1950-52; minister Union Zion Bapt. Ch., Gloucester, Va., 1944-53, Mt. Zion Bapt. Ch., Downings, Va., 1945-57, 3d Union Bapt. Ch., King William, Va., 1953-70; dean students Va. Union U., Richmond, 1950-57; dean Va. Union U. (Sch. Theology), 1957-70, Henderson-Griffith prof. pastoral theology, v.p., 1960-70, pres., 1970-79, pres. emeritus, 1979-85, chancellor, 1985—. Author: Calling a Pastor in a Baptist Church; Contbg. editor: The Continuing Quest, 1970. Chmn. Richmond City Planning Commn., 1969-75; dir. Va. Electric and Power Co., Dominion Resources, Inc. Consol Bank and Trust Co.; Mem. Commn. on Ch. Family Fin. Planning; mem. scholarship selection com. Philip Morris, Inc.; mem. Mayor's Commn. on Human Relations, 1963-65; pres. Norrell Sch. PTA, 1963-65; mem. exec. com. Central Va. Ednl. TV; mem. Richmond Independence Bicentennial Commn., Richmond Downtown Econ. and Devel. Commn.; co-chmn. Northside Community Assn., 1964-68; chmn. Univ. Center in Va.; mem. State Bd. Edn. Va., 1975-85, pres. 1980-82; bd. dirs. NCCJ, Va. Inst. Pastoral Care, Task Force for Renewal Urban Strategy and Tng., Richmond chpt. ARC, 1974-75, Better Richmond, Inc., Richmond Downtown Devel. Unltd., Am. Council on Edn., 1970-72, Fund for Theol. Edn., 1970-72, Richmond Renaissance, Inc., Met. Richmond Leadership ; mem. adv. bd. Inst. for Bus. and Community Devel., U. Richmond; bd. fellows Interpreters House, Lake Janaluska, N.C.; Trustee Richmond Meml. Hosp., Nat. Assn. for Equal Opportunity in Edn. (v.p.); pres. Richmond Gold Bowl Sponsors, Inc., Nat. Conf. Richmond and Jews, Inc., 1987-90. Recipient Disting. Svc. award Links, Inc., 1971, Alpha Phi Alpha achievement award, 1981, 85, Alpha Kappa Alpha Ednl. Achievement award, 1985, Good Govt. award Richmond First Club, 1985, Brotherhood award NCCJ, 1975, Outstanding Svc. award Met. Bus. League, 1991, Outstanding Leadership award Va. Legislature Black Caucus, 1991; named Citizen of Yr., Astoria Beneficial Club, 1971, Citizen of Yr., Omega Psi Phi, 1972, Citizen of Yr., Richmond Urban League, 1974; Va. Union U. Chapel named in his honor, 1991. Mem. Clergy Assn. Richmond Area (pres.), Am. Assn. Theol. Schs. (pres. 1970-72), Am. Bapt. Conv. (pres. coun. on theol. edn. 1969-72), Bapt. Gen. Conv. Va. (exec. bd.), Soc. for Advancement Continuing Edn. for Ministers (exec. bd.), Greater Richmond C. of C. (bd. dirs.), NCCJ (chmn. Va. chpt., pres., nat. exec. bd.), Alpha Kappa Mu, Alpha Phi Alpha (Black Caucus, Gen. Assembly Commonwealth of Va. Achievement award 1991). Club: Kiwanis. Office: Va Union U 1500 N Lombardy St Richmond VA 23220

JAMES, CONNIE SUE, Christian education educator; b. Newark, Ohio, Mar. 8, 1947; d. Marvin Kenneth and Ethel Marie (Walters) Jacks; m. George Merton James, Feb. 12, 1977; children: Jeremy J., Monica R., Ginger M. Processing clk. to comml. underwriting asst. State Farm Ins., Newark, 1965-77; asst. Natchez (Miss.) Christian Learning Ctr., 1985-87; asst. North York (Pa.) Christian Learning Ctr., 1987-88, supr., 1988-90. Mem. Chattanooga Home Edn. Assn. Avocations: cooking, walking, travel, reading, country handcraft. Home: 5107 Stony Brook Dr Louisville KY 40291

JAMES, EDDIE WILLIAM, minister; b. Kansas City, Mo., Jan. 2, 1939; s. Jimmy G. and Margaret E. (Pine) J.; m. Betty Jean Broaddrick, May 29, 1959; children: Sharon, Eddie James Jr., David Andrew, Paul Timothy. Student, Okla. Bapt. U., 1958-61, Tulsa U., 1958, Kansas City Bible Coll., 1957-58. Ordained to ministry Sheridan Rd. Bapt. Ch., 1960. Pastor Immanuel Bapt. Ch., Maysville, Ark., 1962-66, Liberty Bapt. Ch., Dutch Mills, Ark., 1966-69, Calvary Bapt. Ch., Hughes, Tex., 1969-71, Falfa Bapt. Ch., Talihina, Okla., 1971-72, Union Hill Bapt., Purcell, Okla., 1972-75, Meadowview Bapt. Ch., Owasso, Okla., 1975-86, Hillcrest Bapt. Ch., Tulsa, 1986-88, Immanuel So. Bapt. Ch., Wagoner, Okla., 1988—; evangelist Eddie James Ministries, Okla., 1980—; evangelism com. Muskogee (Okla.) Bapt. Assn., 1988—. Recipient Pace Setter award Bapt. Conv. Okla., 1976. Mem. Tulsa Bapt. Assn., Rogers Bapt. Assn. Home: 601 N Gertrude Wagoner OK 74467 Office: Immanuel So Bapt Ch 611 N Gertrude Wagoner OK 74467

JAMES, EDGAR C., Bible and theology educator; b. Bryn Mawr, Pa., Jan. 6, 1933; s. Edgar Jefferson and Dorothy (Cutler) J.; m. Barbara R. Gill, July 21, 1956; children: Sharon Louise, Brenda Kathleen. BA, Wheaton (Ill.) Coll., 1955; ThM, Dallas Sem., 1959, ThD, 1962; AS, Tex. Inst. Tech., Dallas, 1958. Prof. Calvary Bible Coll., Kansas City, Mo., 1961-73; prof. Bible and theology Moody Bible Inst., Chgo., 1973—. Author 25 books; contbr. articles to profl. jours. Avocations: golf, tennis, swimming. Office: Moody Bible Inst 820 N LaSalle Dr Chicago IL 60610

JAMES, FREDERICK CALHOUN, bishop; b. Prosperity, S.C., Apr. 7, 1922; s. Edward and Rosa Lee J.; m. Theressa Gregg, Dec. 30, 1944. A.B., Allen U., 1943; M.Div., Howard U., 1947. Ordained to ministry A.M.E. Ch.; pastor Friendship A.M.E. Ch., Irmo, S.C., 1945; bishop Meml. A.M.E. Ch., Columbia, S.C., 1946, Wayman A.M.E. Ch., Winnsboro, S.C., 1947-50, Chappelle Meml. A.M.E. Ch., Columbia, 1950-53, Mount Pisgah A.M.E. Ch., Sumter, S.C., 1953-72; elected 93d bishop A.M.E. Ch., Dallas, from 1972; bishop 7th dist. A.M.E. Ch., Columbia, S.C., 1984—; dean Dickerson Theol. Sem., 1949-53; bishop in, Botswana, Lesotho, Swaziland, Mozambique, South Africa, Namibia, 1972-76, presiding bishop in, Ark. and Okla., 1976-81; chmn. Commn. on Missions, A.M.E. Ch., 1976—; mem. World Conf. Ch. and Soc., Geneva, 1966, Nat. Council Chs. Christ, U.S.A., 1979—; hon. consul-gen. representing Lesotho, in, Ark. and Okla., 1979—; del. World Meth. Council, Honolulu, 1981, Nairobi, 1986, Singapore, 1991; sec. Am. Meth. Episc. Coun. of Bishops, 1981, pres., 1982-83; pres. Gen. Bd. Am. Meth. Episc. Ch. Author social action bill, A.M.E. Ch., 1960, African Methodism in South Carolina, bicentennial edit., 1989; builder James Sq. Shopping Ctr., Columbia, 1989. Pres. Sumter br. NAACP, 1959-72, S.C. Coalition of Black Ch. Leaders, 1986—; chmn. Wateree Community Actions Agy., 1969-72; bd. dirs. Greater Little Rock Urban League, Palmetto Project of S.C., 1988, Palmetto Partnership Found., 1989; chmn. bd. Shorter Coll.; founder Mt. Pisgah Apts., Sumter, James Centre, Maseru, Lesotho; chmn. bd. trustees Allen U., Columbia, S.C.; co-chmn. re-apportionment com. S.C. Legis. Black Caucus, 1989; gov's appointee commn. on econ. recovery State of S.C., 1989; mem. adv. bd. Habitat for Humanity, S.C., 1988. Mem. Nat. Interfaith Com., Fund for Open Soc., World Meth. Coun., Alpha Phi Alpha. Democrat. Clubs: Odd Fellows, Masons, Shriners. Office: African Meth Episcopal Ch 370 Forest Dr Suite 402 Landmark East Columbia SC 29204

JAMES, HOWARD OLAND, SR., minister, automobile mechanic; b. Ft. Worth, Oct. 27, 1941; s. Oland Fleet and Vera Wynelle (Cruce) J.; m. Helen May McBee, May 27, 1961 (div. Sept. 1967); children: Margaret Ann, Howard Oland Jr., Cynthia Deniece; m. Barbara Jean Ort, Aug. 30, 1969 (dec. Nov. 1990); m. Della Marie Anderson, Mar. 16, 1991. B in Ministry, Bapt. Bible Inst., 1984. Pastor Ballew Springs Bapt. Ch., Weatherford, Tex., 1985-87, Cen. Bapt. Ch., Weatherford, 1987—; freelance auto repairman, Weatherford, 1985—. SSgt. USAF, 1961-81. Mem. IOOF (sec. Weatherford chpt. 1985—), Lions (treas. Penster, Tex. chpt. 1989—). Democrat.

JAMES, JERRY LEE, minister, state official; b. Marion, Ohio, July 28, 1945; s. Leroy Henry and Ruth Ellen (Miller) J.; m. Ruth Ellen Woods, Aug. 1, 1965; 1 child, Jeneen Lynette. BTh, Circleville (Ohio) Bible Coll., 1968. Ordained to ministry Chs. of Christ in Christian Union, 1968. Coord. printing State of Ohio, Columbus, 1968—; pastor Ch. of Christ in Christian Union, Londonderry, Ohio, 1967-69, Clarksburg, Ohio, 1969-71, Carey, Ohio, 1976-77; tape min. Ch. of Christ in Christian Union, Circleville, 1979—; pastor Ch. of Christ in Christian Union, Jeffersonville, Ohio, 1977-83, New Holland, Ohio, 1984-86; asst. pastor Ch. of Christ in Christian Union, Georgesville, Ohio, 1987-90. Pres. Miami Trace Schs. PTO, Washington Court House, Ohio, 1978; chaperone, min. Spirit Am. Band, European tour, 1987-91. Home: 8692 US 62 NE Washington Court House OH 43160

JAMES, LAURENCE JOSEPH (FATHER ANDREW JAMES), priest, educator; b. Enterprise, Ky., July 24, 1934; s. Jesse M. and Edith Dowdy J.; m. Suzanne Jordre, Jan. 19, 1963; children: Elizabeth Ann James Brubaker, Ian Andrew Stephen, Alexandra Marie. BA, Ea. Ky. U., 1956; MDiv, Episcopal Theol. Sem., Lexington, Ky., 1962; MA, Miami U., Oxford, Ohio, 1968; MEd, Xavier U., 1971; PhD, Ohio U., 1976. Ordained to ministry Episcopal Ch., 1962; ordained priest Greek Orthodox Ch., 1977. Episcopal clergyman Trinity Ch., Covington, Ky., 1962-64, St. James Ch., Pittston, Pa., 1964-66; asst. chaplain Tyson House U. Tenn., Knoxville, 1968-71; Orthodox chaplain Chillicothe (Ohio) Correctional Inst., 1985—; Ea. Orthodox chaplain Ohio U., Athens, 1977—; curator Packard Libr. Columbus (Ohio) Coll. Art and Design, 1987—; instr. art history Ohio U., Zanesville, 1977-79, 81-82, French Art Colony, Gallipolis, Ohio, 1984; instr. speech London Correctional Inst. Urbana (Ohio) U., 1990—; editorial assoc. Writer's Digest Mag., Cin., 1972-74; instr. Ohio U., Athens, 1979-80, 80-81; dir. Christian Edn. Commn. Western Rite Vicariate Antiochian Orthodox Christian Archdiocese N.Y. and N. Am., 1977-81; columnist Christianity and Crisis, N.Y.C., 1989—; instr. English, speech, drama Knoxville Coll., 1968-71. Contbr. articles to profl. jours. Recipient Gold medal John Carson, Lord Mayor of Belfast, No. Ireland, 1986. Democrat. Home: 32 Franklin Ave Athens OH 45701 Office: Columbus Coll 107 N Ninth St Columbus OH 48216

JAMES, MARIE MOODY, clergywoman, musician, vocal music educator; b. Chgo., Jan. 23, 1928; d. Frank and Mary (Portis) Moody; m. Johnnie James, May 25, 1968. B Music Edn., Chgo. Music Coll., 1949; MusM, Roosevelt U., 1969, MA, 1976; DD, Internat. Bible Inst. and Sem., Plymouth, Fla., 1985. Ordained to ministry Pentecostal Ch., 1976; cert. vocal music tchr., Ill. Key punch operator Dept. Treasury, Chgo., 1950-52; tchr. Posen-Robbins Bd. Edn., Robbins, Ill., 1952-59; tchr. vocal music Englewood High Sch., Chgo., 1964-84; music counselor Head Start, Chgo., 1965-66; exec. dir. House of Love DayCare, 1983, 88, Mary P. Moody Christian Acad., 1989, supt., 1989; dir. Handbell Choir for Srs. Maple Park United Meth. Ch., 1988—. Composer, arranger choral music: Hide Me, 1963, Christmas Time, 1980, Come With Us, Our God Will Do Thee Good, 1986, The Indiana House, 1987, Behold, I Will Do a New Thing, 1989. Organist Allen Temple A.M.E. Ch., 1941-45; asst. organist Choppin A.M.E. Ch., 1945-49; organist-dir. Progressive Ch. of God in Christ, Maywood, Ill., 1950-60; missionary Child Evangelism Fellowship, Chgo., 1955-63; unit leader YWCA, New Buffalo, Mich., 1956-58; min. of music God's House of All Nations, Chgo., 1960-80; pastor God's House of Love, Prayer and Deliverance, Robbins, 1982—; chmn. Frank and Mary Moody Scholarship Com., 1984—; dir. music Christian Women's Outreach Ministry, 1984-88; mem. Robbins Community Coun., 1987—; camp counselor Abraham Lincoln Ctr., 1951-53. Coppin A.M.E. Ch. scholar, 1946. Mem. Music Educators Nat. Conf., AFT. Democrat. Club: Good News (tchr. 1987—Robbins, Ill.). Home: 8154 S Indiana Chicago IL 60619

JAMES, WILLIAM, bishop. Bishop Ch. of God in Christ, Toledo. Office: Ch of God in Christ 3758 Chippendale Ct Toledo OH 44320*

JAMESON, RICHARD P., ecumenical agency administrator. Exec. dir. Coun. of Christian Communions of Greater Cin. Office: Coun Christian Communions Greater Cinn 2439 Auburn Ave Cincinnati OH 45219*

JAMESON, VICTOR LOYD, magazine editor emeritus; b. Clayton, N.Mex., Sept. 4, 1924; s. Earl Percy and Juna Dorothy (Kephart) J.; m. Barbara Oswald, July 13, 1947 (div. Dec.. 1982); children: Ronald Wallace, Michael Loyd; m. Frances Russell Furlow, Nov. 8, 1986. BA, East N.Mex. Univ., 1949. Tchr. Hobbs (N.Mex.) Mcpl. Schs., 1949-51; reporter, editor Hobbs Daily News-Sun, 1951-64; journalist, writer United Presbyn. Ch., N.Y.C., 1964-73, dir. info., 1973-83; editor, pub. Presbyn. Survey mag., Louisville, 1983-91, editor emeritus, 1992—. Co-author: Bull at a New Gate, 1964; editor: What Does God Require of Us Now, 1971; editor The Main Trail, 1974; contbr. articles to profl. jours. Served to sgt. OSS Army, 1943-46. Recipient E.H. Shaffer award N.Mex. Press Assn., 1955, Editorial writing award Religious Pub. Relations Council, 1986. Mem. Assoc. Ch. Press. Democrat. Presbyterian. Avocations: reading, travel, geneology.

JAMIESON, JOHN EDWARD, JR., social services administrator, minister, bioethicist; b. Phila., Mar. 5, 1945; s. John Edward and Frances (Hayes) J.; m. Marilyn T. Haws, June 8, 1968; children: Douglas Stuart, Heather Lynn, Mark Stuart. BA, U. Pa., 1967; MDiv, Ref. Episcopal Sem., Phila., 1970; PhD, Christian Bible Coll., Rocky Mount, N.C., 1990. Ordained to ministry Ref. Episcopal Ch., 1970, Bapt. Ch., 1978. Pastor Trinity Ref. Episcopal Ch., Phila., 1970-73, St. Mark's Ref. Episcopal Ch., Miami, Fla., 1973-75, Hammonton (N.J.) Bapt. Ch., 1978-81; supr. Nepaug Christian Acad., New Hartford, Conn., 1976-78; coord. ops. emergency med. svcs. div. AID Ambulance Svc., Atlantic City, 1982-83; paramedic mobile ICU, West Jersey Health, Camden, N.J., 1983-88; dir. pastoral care Atlantic City Med. Ctr., 1988—; pastor Grace Bible Chapel, Ocean City, N.J., 1988—; vice chmn. instnl. med. ethics com. Atlantic City Med. Ctr., 1988—. Editor Bibl. Bioethics, 1990. Chaplain Somers Point (N.J.) Vol. Rescue Squad, 1987—; bd. dirs. Atlantic County unit Am. Cancer Soc., Northfield, N.J., 1988-90, program coord. Cansurmount support program, 1988-90. Mem. Nat. Christian Counselors Assn., Coll. Chaplains, Atlantic-Cape May Pastor's Fellowship (pres. 1990—), Delaware Valley Bioethics Com. Network, Jersey Cape Ethics Consortium. Republican. Avocations: travel, photography, reading. Office: Atlantic City Med Ctr 1925 Pacific Ave Atlantic City NJ 08401 *When we concentrate our thoughts on that which is true, noble, right, pure, lovely, admirable and excellent we are lifted above the drudgery of life and open ourselves to the possibility of true greatness.*

JAMISON, JOSEPH VANJAMIN, lay worker; b. Callaway, Va., June 18, 1933; s. Joe B. and Ella (Helms) J.; m. Joyce Ann Sowder, Dec. 22, 1954; children: Joseph Benjamin IV, Jennifer Lynn Jamison Stults. BA, Lynchburg Coll., 1954; MEd, Va. Poly Inst. & State U., 1963; postgrad., U. Va. Cert. sch. administr., counselor, tchr. Deacon, elder Peidmont Presby. Ch., Callaway, Va., 1958—; lay preacher Rocky Mt. (Va.) Presby. Ch., 1989—; dir. lit., STEP Inc. (community action), Rocky Mt., 1989—. Exihibited in one man shows, 1960-70. Pres., Young Dems., Rocky Mt., 1964-65. With USN, 1954-58. Mem. 300 Club, Ruvitan Club (pres.). Democrat.

JAMISON, MICHAEL HOWARD, minister; b. Sylva, N.C., Feb. 15, 1950; s. Vernon Jacob and Joan (Dillard) J.; m. Elizabeth Clark, Aug. 4, 1973; 1 child, Matthew Lyndon. BA, Gardner-Webb Coll., 1973; MDiv, Southern Bapt. Theol. Sem., 1977, D Ministry, 1985. Ordained to ministry So. Bapt. Conv., 1975. Pastor Beech Fork Bapt. Ch., Gravel Switch, Ky., 1975-77; asst. pastor Shamrock Bapt. Ck., Charlotte, N.C., 1977-81; pastor College Park Bapt. Ch, Greensboro, N.C., 1981—. Mem. bd. execs. YMCA, Charlotte, 1978-80, CROP Walk Hunger Com., Greensboro, 1983-86; coach City Baseball Leagues, Greensboro, 1981—. Mem. N.C. Bapt. Assn. (pres. com. on Christian Life and pub. affairs 1989—, mem. exec. com. 1989—), Greensboro Mins. Fellowship (pres. 1990—), So. Bapt. Sem. Alumni Assn. (pres. N.C. chpt. 1990—). Democrat. Home: 602 Beckwith Dr Greensboro NC 27410 Office: College Park Bapt Ch 1601 Walker Ave Greensboro NC 27403 *I have discovered that one of the keys to a fulfilled life is to understand that life comes back to us as we give ourselves away.*

JANETZKE, DOUGLAS KIRK, clergyman; b. Lansing, Mich., Dec. 2, 1948; s. Reinhold Herman and Mary Lou (Jolliff) J.; m. Marguerite Ellen Zerbst, Feb. 28, 1970; children: Joshua Douglas, Andrew William. AA, Concordia Jr. Coll., 1969; BA, Concordia Tchrs. Coll., 1970; MDiv, Concordia Theol. Sem., Springfield, Ill., 1974; D Ministry, Concordia Theol. Sem., Ft. Wayne, Ind., 1983. Ordained to ministry Luth. Ch., 1974. Asst. pastor Bethlehem Luth. Ch., Roseville, Mich., 1974-78; pastor Christ Luth. Ch., Boyne City, Mich., 1978-82; head adminstrv. pastor St. Paul's Luth. Ch., Fairmont, Minn., 1982—; zone counselor Luth. Women's Missionary League, Roseville, Boyne City and Fairmont, 1974-78, 79-82, 84-86; cir. counselor Fairmont Cir. Luth. Ch.-Mo. Synod, 1986—; del. Synodical Conv., Wichita, Kans., 1989. Mem. Martin County Ministerial Assn., Fairmont Cir. Forum (chmn. 1986—). Office: St Paul's Luth Ch 211 Budd St Fairmont MN 56031-2999

JANKE, ROGER ALVIN, minister; b. Milw., July 22, 1938; s. Alvin Henry and Ruth Elisa (Plautz) J.; m. Nancy L. Strobel, June 7, 1964 (dec. 1974); children: Paul, Joel, Naomi; m. Marva Lou Fedderson, June 15, 1975; children: Jonathan Kugath, Nathaniel Kugath, Melissa Kugath. BA, Concordia Sr. Coll., Ft. Wayne, Ind., 1960; BD, Concordia Sem., St. Louis, 1964, MDiv, 1964, MST, 1965. Ordained to ministry Luth. Ch.-Mo. Synod, 1965. Pastor Grace Luth. Ch., Hastings, Mich., 1965-68, Oberlin, Ohio, 1968-75; asst. pastor St. John's Luth. Ch., West Bend, Wis., 1975-82; sr. pastor Our Father's Luth. Ch., Greenfield, Wis., 1982—; counselor Luth. Women's Missionary League, N.Y.C., 1967; synodical del. Luth. Ch.-Mo. Synod, St. Louis, 1983; nat. chaplain Luth. Rangerettes, 1985—; nat. chmn. Luth. Life

Enrichment, singles ministry; cir. counselor. Mem. Hastings Ministerial Alliance (pres. 1967), Oberlin Ministerial Assn. (pres. 1971). Office: Our Father's Luth Ch 6025 S 27th St Greenfield WI 53221 *It is humbling to see the power of Jesus Christ in the lives of his believers today as volunteers do mighty works, as the sick are healed or held by their faith and as the mourners receive hope to continue. Christ is the only Lord to follow.*

JANN, DONN GERARD, minister; b. Eau Claire, Wis., July 17, 1929; s. August William and Dorothy Olive (Nuesse) J.; m. Alice Joan Hartwell, Aug. 29, 1949 (div. 1974); children: Patricia, Scott, Lucinda, Susanna, Todd, Gregg; m. Nancy Ruth Hearn, June 22, 1985. Student, U. Minn., Duluth, 1947-48; BA, Whitworth Coll., 1951; MDiv, Theol. Sem., Princeton, N.J., 1955. Ordained to ministry Presbyn. Ch. (U.S.A.), 1955. Assoc. pastor 1st Presbyn. Ch., Bartlesville, Okla., 1955-59; pastor 1st Presbyn. Ch., Lexington, Nebr., 1960-67, Santa Rosa, Calif., 1967-73; v.p. Presbyn. Ch. Found., N.Y.C., 1973-88; pastor New Hempstead Presbyn. Ch., New City, N.Y., 1988—; moderator Platte Presbytery, Hastings, Nebr., 1965-66; commr. Presbyn. Gen. Assembly, Portland, Oreg., 1967; chairperson presbytery Christian edn. com. Presbyn. Ch. (U.S.A.), Nebr., 1965-66, presbytery stewardship com., Nebr., 1966-67, synod ch. world interaction com., Calif., 1969-70, presbytery com. on minority candidates, Calif., 1970-71, synod regional budget com., Calif., 1971-72, presbytery com. on spl. gifts, 1989—; chairperson Community Ministries Corp., Lexington, 1966, Profl. Counseling Svcs., Lexington, 1966, County Protestant Community Svcs., Calif., 1969-70; area rep. Ch. Nat. Emergency Convocation on War, Washington, 1968; adj. prof. San Francisco Theol. Sem., San Anselmo, Calif., 1971-72; lectr. Santa Rosa Community Coll., 1972; mem. commn. on stewardship Nat. Coun. Chs., N.Y.C., 1975-88, v.p., chairperson commn. on stewardship, 1984-87, chairperson theol. resource ctr., N.Y., 1986-87. Pres. Coun. Social Svcs., Santa Rosa, 1971. Bd. dirs. Sonoma County (Calif.) chpt. People for Econ. Opportunity, 1968-70; mem. adv. coun. Santa Rosa Sch. Bd.; pres. Coun. Social Svcs., Santa Rosa, 1971; chairperson Interfaith Week of Christian Unity, Calif., 1971-72; active No. Am. Conf. on Christian Philanthropy, N.Y., 1974-87, chair, 1987-88. Mem. Presbytery Hudson River, Area Clergy Assn. (pres. 1990—). Democrat. Home: 3 Glen Haven Dr New City NY 10956 Office: New Hempstead Presbyn Ch 484 New Hempstead Rd New City NY 10956 *It is not what happens to us that necessarily controls our life. The determative factor is what we do with those happenings. And that is what a vibrant faith is all about.*

JANNING, MARY BERNADETTE, nun, association executive; b. Custer City, Okla., May 20, 1917; d. Frank R. and Mary Elizabeth (Kreizenbeck) J. R.N., St. Francis Hosp. Sch. Nursing, Wichita, Kans., 1942; B.S. in Nursing Edn, Marquette U., 1951, M.S., 19S2; postgrad., George Washington U., 1972. Joined Sisters of Sorrowful Mother, 1935; asst. dir. St. Johns Sch. Nursing, Tulsa, 1952-56; dir. St. Francis Sch. Nursing, Wichita, 1956-65; provincial superior Tulsa Province, Sisters of Sorrowful Mother, 1965-70; asso. adminstr. St. Francis Hosp., Wichita, 1972-73; pres., chief exec. officer, dir. St. Francis Hosp., 1973-79; exec. dir. Franciscan Villa, Inc., Broken Arrow, Okla., 1979-80, Okla. Cath. Health Conf., 1980—. Author: Life of a Student Nurse, 1961. Chmn. bd. Kans. affiliate Am. Diabetes Assn., 1974; sec. bd. dirs. Midway Kans. chpt. ARC, 1974—, pres., 1979; chmn. Mid-Central Kans.; adv. bd. KBEZ Stereo 93, Tulsa, Okla., 1982-83. Recipient Twenty-Year Pin award ARC, 1962; Alumni Nurse of Year award St. Francis Sch. Nursing, 1972. Fellow Am. Coll. Health Care Execs.; mem. Am. Hosp. Assn., Kans. Hosp. Assn. (dir.), Catholic Hosp. Assn., Nat., Kans. leagues nursing, Kans. Hosp. Assn., Kans. Conf. Cath. Health Affairs (pres. 1977), Hosp. Council Met. Wichita, Wichita Hosp. Adminstrs. Office: 17600 E 51st St Box J Broken Arrow OK 74012

JANSEN, E. HAROLD, bishop; b. Bklyn., Aug. 3, 1930; s. Herman Nicholai and Gesine (Olsen) J.; m. Patricia Hughes, May 29, 1954; children: Daniel, Elizabeth, Nathanael, Mark. BCE, CCNY, 1952; MDiv, Luther Sem., St. Paul, 1957; DD, Capital U., Columbus, Ohio, 1980, Wagner Coll., 1982; DD (hon.), Roanoke Coll., 1991. Ordained to ministry Evang. Luth. Ch. in Am. Pastor Eltingville Luth. Ch., S.I., N.Y., 1957-70; ecumenical dir. St. Francis Sch., S.I., 1970-72; dean ea. dist. Am. Luth. Ch., 1972-78, bishop ea. dist., 1978-88; bishop Evang. Luth. Ch. in Am., Washington, 1988—. Office: Met Washington DC Synod 224 E Capitol St Washington DC 20003

JANSON, SISTER MARILYN, religion educator; b. Columbia, Ill., Dec. 12, 1936; d. Alfred Barnard and Anna Marie (Bequette) J. AB, St. Louis U., 1967, MA, 1974; postgrad., Duquesne U., 1979-82. Joined Adorers of the Blood of Christ, Roman Cath. Ch., 1955. Assoc. dir. Diocese of Jefferson City, Mo., 1974-82; cons. Diocese of Springfield, Ill., 1982-84; dir. religious edn. St. Mary's Ch., Belleville, Ill., 1984-87; religious edn. cons. Diocese of Columbus, Ohio, 1989—; assoc. Nat. Conf. Diocesan Dirs., 1984—, Nat. Assn. Catechetical Media Pers. Author: Catechetical Handbook, 1982. Home: Box 115 Red Bud IL 62278 Office: Religious Edn Dept 197 E Gay St Columbus OH 43215

JANSSEN, ORVILLE HENRY, priest; b. Appleton, Wis., Mar. 7, 1926; s. Henry Edward and Rose Marie (O'Barski) J. BA, Pontifical Coll. Josephinum, Worthington, Ohio, 1948; MA, Register Coll. Journalism, Denver, 1957. Ordained priest Roman Cath. Ch., 1952. Assoc. pastor Holy Innocents Parish, Manitowoc, Wis., 1952-56; founder, pastor St. Bernard's Parish, Appleton, Wis., 1966—; first chmn. Diocesan Ecumenical Commn., 1968; mem. Priest Senate, 1968-74, Presbyteral Coun. and Coll. Consultors, Diocese of Green Bay, Wis., 1984—, Bishop's Planning Coun., Diocese of Green Bay, 1988-90; diocesan dir. of evangelization, 1979-84. Founding editor Green Bay Register, 1957-66. Pres. Community Alcoholism Svcs., 1970-73, Family Svc. Assn., 1974-75; bd. dirs. Xavier High Sch., 1966—, pres. 1989-91; bd. dirs. United Fund, Vis. Nurses Assn., Epilepsy Found., Valley Packaging Inc., Outagamie County Jail Rehab. Com., 1974, St. Elizabeth Hosp., 1979-85, Wheaton Franciscan Svcs., Fox Valley, 1989—, Fox Valley Pastoral Counseling Ctr., 1991—; mem. inst. rev. bd. St. Elizabeth Hosp., 1988—. Named Man of Yr. U. Notre Dame Club, 1974; recipient Fox Valley Brotherhood award, 1972. Home: 1600 Orchard Dr Appleton WI 54914 Office: 1617 W Pine St Appleton WI 54914

JANTZ, HAROLD DAVID, minister, editor; b. Laird, Sask., Can., Jan. 8, 1937; s. Henry A. and Helena (Penner) J.; m. Neoma Hinz, Aug. 19, 1961; children: Constance, Andrea, Ruth. BTh., Mennonite Brethren Bible Coll., 1960; BA, Waterloo Luth. U., 1961. Ordained to ministry Gen. Conf. Mennonite Brethren Chs., 1964. Tchr. Eden Christian Coll., Niagara-on-the-Lake, Ont., Can., 1961-64; min. Gen. Conf. Mennonite Brethren Chs., 1964—; editor Mennonite Brethren Herald, Winnipeg, Man., Can., 1964-85; editor, pub. ChristianWeek, Winnipeg, 1987—; bd. dirs. faith and life commn. Mennonite World Conf., Bd. Christian Lit., Mennonite Brethren Conf. Editor: Looking Back in Faith. Mem. Can. Ch. Press. Office: ChristianWeek, 507-228 Notre Dame, Winnipeg, MB Canada R3B 1N7

JANZEN, JOHN GERALD, Old Testament educator; b. Meadow Lake, Sask., Can., Aug. 9, 1932; s. John Daniel and Agnes (Zacharias) J.; m. Eileen Rose Calder, June 20, 1959; children: Holly Rachel, John Daniel. BA, U. Sask., 1958; Licentiate in Theology, Emmanuel Coll., Saskatoon, Sask., 1959; PhD, Harvard U., 1965; DD (hon.), Coll. Emmanuel and St. Chad, Saskatoon, Sask., 1987. Prof. Old Testament Coll. Emmanuel and St. Chad, Saskatoon, Sask., 1965-68; assoc. prof. Old Testament Christian Theol. Sem., Indpls., 1968-73, prof. Old Testament, 1973-89, MacAllister-Petticrew prof. Old Testament, 1989—; vis. prof. Harvard U., Cambridge, Mass., 1985-86. Author: Studies in the Text of Jeremiah, 1973, Job, 1985; contbr. articles to profl. jours. R.H. Pfeiffer fellowship Harvard U., 1963-64, Rockefeller fellow Fund for Theol. Edn., Harvard U., 1964-65; grantee Am. Coun. of Learned Socs., 1985-86, Assn. of Theol. Schs., 1985-86. Mem. Am. Acad. Religion, Soc. Bibl. Lit., Colloquium for Bibl. Rsch. Home: 5335 Graceland Ave Indianapolis IN 46208 Office: Christian Theol Sem 1000 W 42nd St Indianapolis IN 46208

JARBOE, ROBERT STEVEN, minister; b. Auburn, Ind., Nov. 30, 1951; s. Evelyn Lucille (Hartman); m. Bonnita Lou Howe, July 20, 1974; children: Elizabeth Erin, Rebekah Louise. BS, Manchester Coll., 1977; MDiv, United Theol. Sem., 1980. Ordained to ministry United Meth. Ch. as deacon, 1981. Pastor Gilead, Ebenezer, Pleasant Hill United Meth. Chs., Macy, Ind., 1973-76, Hobbs (Ind.) United Meth. Ch., 1976-80, Greentown (Ind.) North United Meth. Ch., 1976-78, Beaver Dam United Meth. Ch., Akron, Ind., 1986-91, Lincolnville (Ind.) United Meth. Ch., 1991—; bd. dirs. Camp Lakewood, South Milford, Ind.; exec. dir., chaplain Friendship Haven Retirement Community, Kokomo, Ind., 1980-86; chaplain Together We Help Each Other Cope, Kokomo, 1985-86; advisor Singles with a Vision. Mem. Tippecanoe Valley Sch. Corp. AIDS Coun., 1990. Named one of Outstanding Young Men of Am., 1982. Mem. Wabash Ministerial Assn., Lions Club. Home and Office: R 4 Box 221 Wabash IN 46992

JARMUS, STEPHAN ONYSYM, priest; b. Lidychiv, Ukraine, May 25, 1925; s. Onysym J. and Eufrosynia (Chuchmay) J.; m. Constance E. Houghton, Feb. 12, 1955; 1 child, Andrew O. Diploma in pastoral tng., London, Eng., 1955; licentiate in theology, St. Andrew's Coll., Winnipeg, Can., 1962; BA, U. Man., 1974; MDiv, St. Andrews Coll., 1974; STM, U. Winnipeg, 1978; D Ministry, San Francisco Theol. Sem., 1981. Ordained priest Ukrainian Greek Orthodox Ch. Can., 1956. Pastor Ukrainian Greek Orthodox Ch., London, 1955-60, Sheho, Sask., Can., 1967-69; lectr. homiletics and pastoral theology St. Andrew's Coll., 1970—. Author: Freemasonry and Orthodoxy, 1966, Ecclesiastic Economy, 1967, A Contribution to Thoughts on Contemporary Pastorship, 1975, Charismatism-A Complex Religious Phenomenon, 1975, Spirituality of the Ukrainian People, 1983, On the Issues of Aging, Sickness and Dying, 1989, Selected Works, 1991; asst. editor The Herald, Visnyk, 1963-67, editor in chief, 1969-75, 85—. Mem. Order of St. Andrew, Volynia Rsch. Inst., Ukrainian Hist. Soc. Home: 9 St John's Ave, Winnipeg, MB Canada Office: Ukrainian Greek-Orthodox Ch Can, 9 St John's Ave, Winnipeg, MB Canada R2W 1G8

JARRETT, MITZI MARIE, librarian; b. Salisbury, N.C., Aug. 7, 1961; d. James Curtis and Donna Lee (Kluttz) J. BA, Lenoir-Rhyne Coll., 1982; MA, Luth. Theol. Sem., 1984; M in Librarianship, U. S.C., 1985. Asst. libr. Luth. Theol. So. Sem., Columbia, S.C., 1985-87, libr. dir., 1987-91; libr. Va. Theol. Sem., Alexandria, 1991—. Sec. Luth./Meth. Campus Ministry, U. S.C., Columbia, 1988-91. Mem. ALA, Am. Theol. Libr. Assn., Luth. Hist. Conf., S.C. Libr. Assn., Beta Omega chpt. Beta Phi Mu (pres. 1989-90). Office: Va Theol Sem Seminary Post Office Alexandria VA 22304

JARVIS, GARY LEE, religious orgainzation administration; b. Oakland City, Ind., Apr. 21, 1949; s. Gilbert Ray and V. Winifred (McCandless) J.; m. Jennifer Lynn Baki, Mar. 10, 1972; children: Rachel Christine, Amanda Lee, Mitchell Steven. Student, U. Evansville, 1967-69, Moody Bible Inst., 1969, U. Northern Colo., 1973-76. Ordained to ministry Tri-State Bapt. Fellowship, 1969. Assoc. pastor Bethel Bapt. Ch., Greeley, Colo., 1972-76; dir. ministries Grace Bapt. Ch., Newhall, Calif., 1976-81; exec. v.p. Nehemiah Ministries, Longmont, Colo., 1981-87; pres. Nehemiah Ministries, Burnsville, Minn., 1987—. Office: Nehemiah Ministries 14300 Nicolett Ct #301 Burnsville MN 55337 *God sees things - life, ministry, people - as they can be, not simply as they are. We would benefit greatly by adopting His perspective.*

JARVIS, HAROLD LEWIS, minister, religious administrator; b. Waterloo, N.Y., Aug. 3, 1930; s. Lewis Edmund and Jennie Marie (Hannah) J.; m. Janet Ruth Robb, Aug. 16, 1952; children: Lois Ellen Jarvis Gillette, David Robb, Ruth Louise Jarvis Jenkins, Paula Ann Jarvis Chamberlain. Grad., Practical Bible Tng Sch., Bible Sch. Pk., N.Y., 1952; ThB, Am. Bible Coll., 1953; postgrad., Santa Rosa (Calif.) Jr. Coll.; degree, Am. Inst. Banking, Orange County, Calif., 1962. Ordained Gen. Assn. Regular Bapt. Chs., 1954. Pastor Prattsburg (N.Y.) Bapt. Ch., 1952-55; pastor Calvary Bapt. Ch., Huntingburg, Ind., 1955-57, Garden Grove, Calif., 1957-62; pastor Grace Bapt. Ch., Sonoma, Calif., 1962-65; comml. RE officer Bank Am., San Francisco, 1965—; office mgr. Berean Bapt. Ch., Rohnert Park, Calif., 1984—; bd. dirs. Western Bapt. Home Mission, Sacramento, 1990—. Contbr. articles to Philately and Genealogy; editor ch. newsletter Lamb Chowder, 1984—. Commr. Airport, Willits, Calif., 1970; chaplain Calif. CAP, 1974-83 (Comdr.'s Spl. award 1977), Pacific region, 1983-91 (Chaplain of Yr. award 1984). Mem. Assn. Profl. Genealogists, Am. Philatelic Soc., Calif. Ornament Collectors Club (founder, pres.), Applepickers Computer Club (co-founder). Office: Berean Bapt Ch PO Box 1206 Rohnert Park CA 94927

JARVIS, POLLY STEVENS, church secretary; b. Bakersville, N.C., Mar. 25, 1939; d. Lawrence L. and Etta (Gortney) Stevens; m. Ronald Clark Jarvis, Jan. 23, 1960; children: Tammy Jarvis Wyatt, STeven George. Student, Blanton Jr. Coll., Asheville, N.C., 1959. Sec., bookkeeper Victory Bapt. Ch., Asheville, N.C., 1969—; treas. Victory Bapt. Ch., Asheville, 1975-90, library com., 1987-90, chairperson history com., 1980-90; mem. Women's Missionary Union, 1965-90. Democrat. Home: 5 Macedonia Dr Asheville NC 28804 Office: Victory Bapt Ch 80 Olivette Rd Asheville NC 28804

JASPER, DAVID, minister, educator; b. Stockton, Eng., Aug. 1, 1951; s. Ronald Claud Dudley and Ethel (Wiggins) J.; m. Alison Elizabeth Collins, Oct. 29, 1977; children: Hannah Elizabeth, Ruth Christine, May Sannah. BA, Jesus Coll., 1972, MA, 1976; BA, St. Stephens House, 1975, MA, 1979; BD, Keble Coll., 1980; PhD, Hatfield Coll., 1983. Oxford cert. in theology, 1976. Curate, Buckingham Parish Ch., Diocese of Oxford, Buckingham, Eng., 1976-79; chaplain, Harris fellow Hatfield Coll., Durham U., Eng., 1979-87, prin. St. Chad's Coll., Durham U., 1988-91; sr. lectr. lit. and theology Glasgow U., 1991—; dir. Centre Study of Lit. and Theology, 1987—; tutor English lit. U. Buckingham, part-time 1978; dir. Ctr. Study of Lit. and Theology, U. Glasgow, 1991—. Author: Coleridge as Poet and Religious Thinker, 1985; editor: Images of Belief in Literature, 1984; contbr. articles to profl. and religious pubs. Joyce of Exmoor scholar Hatfield Coll., 1984. Mem. MLA, Conf. on Lit. and Religion (sec. 1980—), Brit. Comparative Lit. Assn. Mem. Ch. of Eng. Avocations: photography, reading, music. Office: Glasgow U Centre for Study Lit and Theology, Dept English, Glasgow G12 8QQ, Scotland

JASPERS, LOUIS J., priest; b. Nerem Tongeren, Limburg, Belgium, Apr. 8, 1928; came to U.S., 1969; s. Hubert and Irma (Portugaels) J. MDiv, CICM Coll., Louvain, Belgium, 1953. Assoc. pastor Archdiocese Inongo, Belgian Congo, Azire, 1953-54, Archdiocese Westminster, London, Eng., 1958-69, Archdiocese L.A., 1969-80; assoc. pastor Archdiocese San Antonio, 1980-84, pastor St. Gabriel Parish, 1984—. Home: 747 SW 39th St San Antonio TX 78237

JASTRAB, KATHLEEN MARIE, religious librarian; b. Oak Park, Ill., Sept. 12, 1958; d. Casimir Anthony and Elizabeth Anne (Oleksa) J. BA in History, Marquette U., 1980; MLS, Rosary Coll., River Forest, Ill., 1981; MA in Theology, Marquette U., 1989. Assoc. libr. Sacred Heart Sch. Theology, Hales Corners, Wis., 1982—. Mem. Cath. Libr. Assn. (pres. Wis. chpt. 1989—, chair acad. sect. 1991—), Am. Theol. Libr. Assn. Office: Sacred Heart Sch Theology Leo Ochon Libr 7335 S Hwy 100 Hales Corners WI 53130-0429

JASTRAM, DANIEL NORMAN, Greek and biblical studies educator; b. Shibata, Japan, Nov. 26, 1955; s. Robert and Phyllis (Matthies) J.; m. Joan Maria Parkhurst, Aug. 20, 1977; children: Brian, Eleanor, Hannah. BA, U. S.D., 1979; MDiv, Concordia Theol. Sem., Ft. Wayne, Ind., 1983; MA, U. Wis., 1985, PhD, 1989. Asst. prof. Greek and N.T. Concordia Coll., St. Paul, 1989—. Mem. Am. Acad. Religion, Soc. Bibl. Lit., Am. Philol. Assn. Office: Concordia Coll 275 N Syndicate Saint Paul MN 55104

JAVALERA, ELIZABETH RICO, religion educator; b. Manila, Oct. 8, 1934; d. Ireneo Topacio and Salome Villamina (Rico) J. Tchr.'s cert. with honors, Philippine Normal Coll., 1953; AB in Psychology cum laude, Far Ea. U., 1968; MA in Christian Edn. cum laude, Trinity Evang. Div. Sch., 1973; PhD in Edn., Mich. State U., 1984. Instr. Far Ea. Bible Inst. and Sem., Bulacan, The Philippines, 1960-61; instr. Christian edn. Philippine Missionary Inst., Cavite, 1961-65; editor Christian edn. Crusader mag., 1966-71; nat. missionary Philippine Crusades, Manila, 1969-76; instr. and dir. Christian edn. Asian Theol. Sem., Quezon City, 1974-80; dir. tng. women's tng. sessions Haggai Inst., Singapore, 1984-86, instr., 1979—; dir. PACE Grad. Sch. Christian Edn., Quezon City, 1991—; bd. dirs. Philippine Sunday Sch. Publs., 1968-76, World Vision, The Philippines, 1985-88; mem. Christian edn. com. Asian Theol. Assn., Taiwan, 1979-87. Author: National Sunday School Convention...How to Conduct it Successfully, 1971, Training for Competence, 1973, Christian Education and Its Correlated Educational Agencies, 1977, Train to Multiply, 1979, What Can Christian Women Do?, 1987, Designing Programs for Training Volunteer Workers, 1988. Mem. Philippine Assn. Christian Edn. (bd. chmn. 1967-69, 72-74, publ. editor 1969—, gen. sec. 1974—), Philippine Bible Soc. (bd. dirs. 1985—). Home: 623 Sto Niño St, Mandaluyong Metro Manila The Philippines Office: ACPO, Box 301, Cubao Quezon City The Philippines *Give God top priority in every area of your life and He will provide everything you need in this life and in the life to come.*

JAVIERRE ORTAS, ANTONIO MARIA CARDINAL, archbishop, writer, educator; b. Sietamo, Huesca, Spain, Feb. 21, 1921. Grad. theology studies, U. Salamanca, U. Louvain, Belgium, U. Pontificia Gregoriana, Rome. Ordained priest Roman Cath. Ch., 1949, joined Order of Salesian Monks, 1951; consecreated archbishop titular Meta, 1976; created cardinal 1988. Prof. theology Ateneo Pontificio Salesiano, Rome, 1959-71, dean faculty theology, 1971, vice chancellor, 1976; libr., archivist Holy Roman Ch., Vatican City; libr., archivist S.R.E.; mem. Congregation for Doctrine of Faith, Congregation for Cath. Edn. and Pontifical Cons. for Promoting Christian Unity. Author: Sucesión apostólica en la I Clem, 1958, Sucesión apostólica en Mt., 1958, El tema literario de la sucesión, 1963, Diálogo ecuménico, 1966, Promoción, conciliar fel diálogo ecuménico, 1966, Il padre tuo che è nel segreto, 1974, Christo Parola e parola di Christo, 1975, La Unión de las Iglesias, 1977, La Educación Universitaria Católica, 1988. Office: Vatican City Vatican City

JAWORSKI, ROSANNE, youth minister; b. Cleve., Nov. 17, 1952; d. Joseph Patrick and Betsy (Blythe) Dragga; m. James S. Jaworski, Sept. 4, 1971; children: James Steven Jr., Joseph Scott. BA, Ursuline Coll., 1990; postgrad., John Carroll U., 1990—. With Diocese of Cleve., 1982—; youth min. St. Jude Ch., Cleve., 1986—, dir. religious edn., 1990—; advisor Cath. Youth Orgn., Cleve., 1986—. Mem. Warrensvile Ministerial Assn., Am. Psychol. Assn., Cleve. Orgn. Religious Edn., Youth Mins. Support Group. Home: 10114 Greenview Cleveland OH 44128 Office: St Jude Parish 4761 Richmond Rd Cleveland OH 44128

JAY, CHARLES DOUGLAS, religion educator, college administrator, clergyman; b. Monticello, Ont., Can., Oct. 10, 1925; s. Charles Arthur and Luella Gertrude (McPherson) J.; m. Ruth Helen Crooker, Jan. 30, 1948; children—David, Ian, Garth. B.A., Victoria Coll., U. Toronto, Ont., 1946; M.A., U. Toronto, Ont., 1948; M.Div., Emmanuel Coll., 1950; Ph.D., U. Edinburgh, 1952; D.D. (hon.), Queen's U., 1971, Wycliffe Coll., 1976, Regis Coll., 1980, U. St. Michael's Coll., 1983. Ordained to ministry United Ch. of Can., 1951. Lectr. dept. philosophy Queen's U., 1946-47; pastor Elk Lake-Matachewan Ch., Ont., 1952-54, Trafalgar-Sheridan Ch., Oakville, Ont., 1954-55; asst. prof. philosophy of religion and Christian ethics Emmanuel Coll. U Toronto, 1955-58, assoc. prof., 1958-63, prof. philosophy of religion and ethics, 1963-91, registrar, 1958-64, prin., 1981-90; founding dir. Toronto Sch. Theology, 1969-80; R.P. McKay meml. lectr., various univs., colls. across Can., 1966-67; spl. lectr. Hankuk Theol. Sem., Seoul, Korea, 1978, Fed. Theol. Sem., Pietermaritzburg, Republic of South Africa, 1981, Union Sem., Manila and Nanjing Theol. Sem., Nanjing, People's Republic of China, 1991; mem. working group Dialogue with People of Living Faith and Ideologies, World Council Chs., 1970-83; chmn. div. world outreach United Ch. of Can., 1975-82; mem. commn. on accreditation Am. Assn. Theol. Schs., 1962-68. Contbr. chpts. to various books. Served with Can. Officers Tng. Corps, 1953-54, as chaplain Royal Can. Navy Res., 1956-59. Decorated Order of Can. Fellow Am. Theol. Schs., 1963. Mem. Assn. Theol. Schs. U.S. and Can. (v.p. 1976-78, pres. 1984-86), Am. Soc. Christian Ethics, Can. Theol. Soc. Office: Emmanuel Coll, 75 Queen's Park Crescent, Toronto, ON Canada M5S 1K7

JAYNES, MARLIN SANDERS, JR., clergyman; b. Kingsport, Tenn., Nov. 28, 1942; s. Marlin Sanders and Frances Lee (Dodson) J.; m. Karen Fern Lindsey, June 14, 1963; children: Brenda Lynn, Sandra Marlene. Student, Anderson Coll., 1960-61; BTh, Gulf Coast Bible Coll., 1964; postgrad., Midwestern Sem., 1966. Ordained to ministry Ch. of God, 1965. Asst. pastor lst Ch. of God, Texas City, Tex., 1961-63; pastor lst Ch. of God, Farmington, Mo., 1964-66, Narrow Lane Community Ch. of God, Montgomery, Ala., 1967-69, lst Ch. of God, New Boston, Ohio, 1969-73; co-pastor lst Ch. of God, Ft. Myers, Fla., 1973-74; pastor Anderson Ch. of God, Bristol, Va., 1974—; mem. bd. conservation and evangelism Ch. of God in Ohio, 1970-73; dir. camping in Ala., Ch. of God, 1968; v.p. evangelism Christian Sch., Ft. Myers, 1973-74; lectr. in field; speaker daily radio broadcast In the Word, Bristol, Tenn., 1983—. Contbr. Pathways to God mag., 1969—; contbg. editor The Gospel Outreach, 1986—. Exec. dir. Bristol Children's Acad., 1974—; div. advisor Practical Nurses Ohio, 1969-73; election judge Sullivan County, Tenn., 1987-90, election officer, 1990—. Recipient award Kiwanis Internat., 1972, Ohio dist. award, 1972. Home: 229 Woodway Circle Hartwood Addition Bluff City TN 37618 Office: Anderson Ch of God 1075 Wagner Rd Bristol VA 24201 *Each of us are given an opportunity in this life to know and serve God. What we do with these opportunities determines our quality of life on this earth—and where and how we will spend eternity.*

JAYROE, AUBREY L., minister; b. Forrest City, Ark., July 23, 1952; s. J. Cecil and Mattie Ruth (Reynolds) J.; m. Brenda Kay Ruff, Aug. 19, 1971; 1 child, Trenton A. BDiv, Twin City U., W. Monroe, La., 1990; Mgmt. Cert., E. Ark. Community Coll., Forrest City, 1980. Ordained to ministry First United Pentecostal Ch., 1981. Sect. youth pres. Ark. United Pentecostal Ch. Internat., 1971-73, youth sec. State of Ark., 1981-85, youth pres. State of Ark., 1985-89; reg. pres. Nat. Youth Dept. Ark. United Pentecostal Ch. Internat., St. Louis, 1987-88; dir. fgn. missions div. Ark. United Pentecostal Ch. Internat., 1989—; pres. Jayroe & Co., Pub. Acct., Forrest City, Ark., 1981—; chaplain Forrest City Police Dept., 1990—; instr. seminars in field; del. Govs.' Rural Devel. Conf., 1991. Author: Tax Regulations for Church and Minister, 1990; contbr. articles to profl. jours. Adv. bd. E. Ark. Community Coll., forrest City, 1981-85, computer bd., 1983-86; mem. Crowley Ridge Vo-Tech., Bus. Adv. Bd., Forrest City, 1978—. Mem. Ark. Soc. Pub. Accts., Nat. Soc. Pub. Accts., Nat. Assn. Acctg. Svcs., Forrest City C. of C. (bd. dirs. 1990—). Home: Route 1 Box 87B Forrest City AR 72335 Office: Jayroe & Co 1338 N Washington Forrest City AR 72335 *Life in itself is a challenge, but it is a challenge worth facing. The beauty of this challenge is to live to your fullest potential and give God the glory for allowing you to enjoy everything life gives.*

JEAN, SYLVIO HERVE, priest; b. Nashua, N.H., Nov. 27, 1926; s. Thomas Noel and Elise (Archambeault) J. BA, U. Mo., 1950, BTh, 1954. Ordained priest Roman Cath. Ch. 1955. Tchr. St. Laurent Coll., Que., 1954-57; missionary Bangla Desh, East Pakistan, 1958-70; priest, pastor West Island, Dollard Des Ormeaux, Que., 1971-88; mission preacher Montreal, Que., 1988—. Home and Office: 4901 Piedmont, Montreal, PQ Canada H3V 1E3

JEANBLANC, DEAN BAYLOR, clergyman; b. Amboy, Ill., July 13, 1933; s. Charles Welsey and Justina Kate (Baylor) J.; m. Nelly Jean Walters, Feb. 1, 1953 (div. 1980); children: William Dean, Deborah Lynn, Wesley; m. Anne Willis, Mar. 10, 1982; children: Michael Timothy Lockwood, Joshua Willis Lockwood. AA, Blackburn Coll., Carlinville, Ill., 1953; BS, Ill. Wesleyan U., 1955; MDiv, Drew U., 1960; MS, Syracuse U., 1968. Ordained to ministry Presbyn. Ch. USA. Dir. pub. info. Ocean Grove Assn., N.J., 1956-60; pastor First Meth. Ch., Asbury Park, N.J., 1956-58, Simpson Ch., Old Bridge, N.J., 1958-62, Trinity Ch., Albany, N.Y., 1962-64, First Presbyn. Ch., Utica, N.Y., 1964-66; prof. Mohawk Valley Community Coll., Utica, 1966-88; pastor First Presbyn. Ch., Little Falls, N.Y., 1988—; bd. dirs. United Ministries in Higher Edn., N.Y. State, 1970-82, chmn., 1978-80, 89; commr. Synod of N.E. Author: The Plain People in New York, 1987. Mem. Phi Delta Kappa, Lions, Yanandasus Golf Club, Kiwanis, Sadaquada Golf Club. Republican. Presbyterian. Avocations: tennis, golf, travel, skiing. Office: First Presbyn Church 16 Jackson St Little Falls NY 13365

JEANES, SAMUEL ARTHUR, retired minister; b. Phila., June 16, 1912; s. Arthur H. and Marguerite Pearl (Smyth) J.; m. Harriette Swope, Dec. 21, 1935. ThB, Ea. Bapt. Coll. and Sem., 1938, AB, 1940, BD, 1941, ThM, 1945, DD, 1966. Ordained to ministry Am. Bapt. Conv., 1938. Pastor Trinity Bapt. Ch., Phila., 1935-42, lst Bapt. Ch., Merchantville, N.J., 1942-

90; pres. Internat. Reform Fedn., Merchantville, 1990—; editor Progress mag., Merchantville, 1990—; pres. Internat. Reform Fedn. Inc., Washington, also editor Progress monthly pub.; gen. sec. Lord's Day Alliance N.J., 1951—; exec. sec. Coun. Chs. Greater Camden, N.J., 1957—; chaplain Gen. Assembly N.J., 1970. Contbr. articles to religious jours. Mem. Camden County Com. on Aging, Camden County Ethics in Govt. Office: Coun Chs Braddock Bldg Ste 200 205 Tuckerton Rd Medford NJ 08055

JEFFCOAT, CLEATIES HARRIEL, minister; b. Grandfield, Okla., Mar. 15, 1948; s. Clarence L. and Imogeen O. (Kuykendall) J.; m. Esther Ellen Finney, Aug. 30, 1968; children: Melody Joy, Angela Joy. BS, Southwestern Assemblies of God Coll., Waxachie, Tex., 1975. Ordained to ministry Assemblies of God, 1977. Pastor 1st Assembly of God, Alamosa, Colo., 1975-79, Glenrock (Wyo.) Assembly of God, 1980—; substitute tchr. Converse County Sch. Dist. 2, Glenrock, 1984—; sectional youth dir. Rocky Mountain Assemblies of God, Grand Junction, Colo., 1976-79; sectional youth dir. Wyo. Assemblies of God, Casper, 1981-84, sectional Sunday sch. dir., 1984—, treas. state youth, 1990—. Treas. Glenrock Community Svcs., 1986—; advisor Wyo. Area Women's Aglow Fellowship, Casper, 1989—; bd. dirs. Converse County Group Home, Douglas, Wyo., 1991. With U.S. Army, 1969-71. Home: 232 N 3d St PO Box 357 Glenrock WY 82637 Office: Assembly of God 201 N 3d St PO Box 357 Glenrock WY 82637

JEFFCOAT, MARK RANDALL, religious organization executive; b. Columbia, S.C., Nov. 4, 1950; s. Alex Hoyt and Doris Elizabeth (Joyner) J.; m. Barbara Lynn Hamby, June 12, 1971; children: Lisa Lynn, Jonathan Mark. BA in Journalism, U. S.C., 1973, postgrad., 1983-87. Minister of music and youth Siloam Bapt. Ch., Easley, S.C., 1974-76; minister of youth and adminstrn. Northside Bapt. Ch., West Columbia, S.C., 1976-81; assoc. office pub. rels. Gen. Bd. of S.C. Bapt. Conv., 1981-86, dir. pub. rels., 1986—; condr. various workshops and clinics in youth ministry, recreation and communications. Mem. Pub. Rels. Soc. Am., Bapt. Pub. Rels. Assn. (honors competition award 1982, 89, 90), S.C. Bapt. Communicators Network, Assn. Edn. in Journalism and Mass Communication, Religious Pub. Rels. Coun., Kappa Tau Alpha. Home: 114 Vale Dr Lexington SC 29073 Office: 907 Richland St Columbia SC 29201

JEFFERS, RONALD JOSEPH, music minister; b. Floreffe, Pa., Sept. 29, 1939; s. Joseph Barlow and Vera Adeline (Crownover) J.; m. Carolyn Sue Higgins, Aug. 1, 1963; children: Rebecca Lynn, Rhonda Sue, Rachel Marie. BS in Bus., U. Tampa (Fla.), 1972; MS in Personnel Mgmt., Troy State U., Dothan, Ala., 1980, MS in Found. of Edn., 1981. cert. commercial pilot. Music minister First Free Will Bapt. Ch., Enterprise, Ala., 1985-88, Ch. of the Nazarene, Ozark, Ala., 1989—; flight comdr. Burnside-Ott U. N.C., Ft. Rucker, Ala., 1977—; music coord. Enterprise Nursing Home, 1990—. Maj. U.S. Army, 1956-77, Vietnam. Mem. Soc. for Preservation of Barbershop Quartet Singing in Am. (v.p. 1988—). Home: Rt 1 Box 357 Daleville AL 36322 Office: Sta WRDJ Gospel Radio Box 81 Daleville AL 36322

JEFFORD, CLAYTON NANCE, religion educator; b. Greenwood, S.C., Sept. 23, 1955; s. Jack Duane and Beth (Nance) J.; m. Susan Sanders, July 1, 1978; children: Dustin S., Ashley L., Logan N. BA, Furman U., Greenville, S.C., 1977; MDiv, Southeastern Bapt. Sem., Wake Forest, N.C., 1980, ThM, 1983; MA, Claremont (Calif.) Grad. Sch., 1986, PhD, 1988. Ordained, 1978. Chaplain, counselor Camp Dogwood for the Blind, Sherrill's Ford, N.C., 1976; assoc. pastor Lawtonville Bapt. Ch., Estill, S.C., 1978; asst. dir. Inst. for Antiquity and Christianity, Claremont, 1985-89; asst. prof. St. Meinrad (Ind.) Sch. Theology, 1989-91, assoc. prof., 1991—; adj. asst. prof. Long Beach (Calif.) State U., 1988-89. Author: The Sayings of Jesus in the Teaching of the Twelve Apostles, 1989; editor: Occasional Papers of IAC, 1986-89, Bull. Inst. for Antiquity and Christianity, 1985-89. Recipient award Am. Bible Soc., 1983; Fellner archaeol. grantee Hebrew Union Coll., 1985, Avery rsch. grantee Claremont Grad. Sch., 1984. Mem. Am. Acad. Religion, Internat. Assn. for Coptic Studies, Nat. Assn. Bapt. Profs. Religion, North Am. Patristics Soc., Soc. Bibl. Lit., Archaeol. Inst. Am. Office: Saint Meinrad Sch Theology Saint Meinrad IN 47577

JEFFRESS, ROBERT J., minister; b. Dallas, Nov. 29, 1955; s. Robert J. Sr. and Julia (Fielder) J.; m. Amy Lyon Renard, June 29, 1956. BA magna cum laude, Baylor U., 1977; ThM, Dallas Theol. Sem., 1981; D in Ministry, Southwestern Bapt. Theol. Sem., 1983. Ordained to ministry Bapt. Ch., 1979. Youth minister, asst. pastor First Bapt. Ch., Dallas, 1978-85; pastor First Bapt. Ch., Eastland, Tex., 1985—; pres. Discovery Bible Ministries, Dallas, 1985—. Author: Gods Pattern for the Church, 1985, Faith at the Crossroads, 1987, Choose Your Attitudes...Change Your Life, 1991; star video series. Mem. com. Majestic Theatre, Eastland, 1987, Indsl. Relations Com., 1986—. Named one of Outstanding Young Men in Am., 1984, 85, 86. Baptist. Avocations: writing, accordion playing. Home: 100 W Plummer Eastland TX 76448 Office: First Bapt Ch 405 S Seaman Eastland TX 76448

JEFFREY, JAMES E., minister; b. Norwalk, Conn., Nov. 21, 1953; s. Clarence E. and Marjorie (Lyons) J.; m. Alberta Dart, July 14, 1973; children: Daniel, Amy, Rachel. BRE, Bapt. Bible Coll., Clarks Summit, N.Y., 1979; MRE, Grand Rapids (Mich.) Bapt.Sem., 1985. Ordained to ministry, Bapt. Ch. Asst. pastor Grace Bapt. Ch., Binghamton, N.Y., 1975-79; sr. pastor Calvary Bapt. Ch., Sandusky, Ohio, 1979-84, Bible Bapt. Ch., Auburn, Ind., 1985-89, Calvary Bapt. Ch., Grand Rapids, 1989—. Office: Calvary Bapt Ch 1200 28th St SE Kentwood MI 49508

JEGEN, SISTER CAROL FRANCES, religion educator; b. Chgo., Oct. 11, 1925; d. Julian Aloysius and Evelyn W. (Bostelmann) J. BS in History, St. Louis U., 1951; MA in Theology, Marquette U., 1958, PhD in Religious Studies, 1968; hon. degree, St. Mary of the Woods, Terra Haute, Ind., 1977. Elem. tchr. St. Francis Xavier Sch., St. Louis, 1947-51; secondary tchr. Holy Angels Sch., Milw., 1951-57; coll. tchr. Mundelein Coll., Chgo., 1957-91; prof. pastoral studies Loyola U., Chgo., 1991—; adv. coun. U.S. Cath. Bishops, Washington, 1969-74; trustees Cath. Theol. Union, Chgo., 1974-84. Author: Jesus the Peace Maker, 1986, Restoring Our Friendship with God, 1989; co-author: (with Byron Sherwin) Thank God, 1989; editor: Mary According to Women, 1985. Participant Nat. Farm Worker Ministry, Fresno, Calif., 1977—; mem. Pax Christi, U.S.A., 1979—, Jane Addams Conf., Chgo., 1989. Recipient Loyola Civic award Loyola U., Chgo., 1981; named one of 100 Women to Watch Today's Chgo. Woman, 1989. Mem. Cath. Theol. Soc. Am., Coll. Theology Soc., Cath.-Jewish Scholars Dialog, Liturgical Conf. Democrat. Roman Catholic. Avocations: music, gardening. Home: Wright Hall 6364 N Sheridan Rd Chicago IL 60660 Office: Loyola U Inst Pastoral Studies 6525 N Sheridan Rd Chicago IL 60626

JEILLISON-KNOCK, RANDY WAYNE, minister; b. Watertown, S.D., Sept. 26, 1959; s. Marvin francis and Arlys Jean (Rislov) K.; m. Sandra Sue Jellison,, Jan. 26, 1986. BA in Music, Yankton (S.D.) Coll., 1981; MDiv, St. Paul Sch. Theology, Kansas City, Mo., 1987. Ordained to ministry, S.D. Ann. Conf. United Meth. Ch., 1989. Musician Knock-Abouts, Watertown, S.D., 1981-83; choir dir. Trinity Presbyn. Ch., Independence, Mo., 1983-84; youth dir. Neighborhood Youth Prog., Kansas City, Mo., 1984-87; pastor Lincoln/Hickory Chapel, Lincoln, Mo., 1987-90, Selby and Lowry (S.D.) United Meth. Ch., 1990—. Author poetry and short stories. Active Dakota Rural Action, Brookings, 1990—, United Meth. Rural Fellowship, 1990—. Mem. Amnesty Internat., Selby Area Ministerial Assn. (treas. 1990), Lions. Democrat. Home: 3305 4th Ave Selby SD 57472-0174 Office: Selby United Meth Ch 3301 4th Ave Selby SD 57472-0174

JELINEK, JAMES L., minister; b. Milw., May 9, 1942; s. James F. and Ruth Dorothy (Seaman) J.; m. Marilyn Kay Wall, June 18, 1988; 1 child, Mark Anthony Barreto. BA cum laude, Carthage Coll., Kenosha, Wis., 1964; MDiv, Gen. Theol. Sem., N.Y.C., 1970; postgrad., Vanderbilt U., 1964-67. Ordained to ministry Episcopal Ch., 1971. Asst. rector St. BArtholomew's Ch., Nashville, 1971-72; program developer Youth Svc. in Memphis, Inc., 1972-73; assoc. recotr Ch. of the Holy Communion, Memphis, 1972-77; rector St. Michael & All Angels, Cin., 1977-84, St. Aidan's Episcopal Ch., San Francisco, 1985-91; alt. dep. to gen. conv. Episcopal Ch., 1988, 91;/ mem. diocesan coun. Diocese of Calif., San Francisco, 1986-90, pres., 1989-90, mem. Ethnic Ministries Commn., 1986—. Vice pres. Mental Health Assn. Ohio, 1983-84; pres. Coalition of Citizens Adv. Bds., Dept. Mental Health, Ohio, 1981-84, Avondale Community Redevel. Corp., Cin., 1981-84; trustee Mental Health Assn. San fRancisco, 1985-89; bd. dirs., Am. Israel Friendship League, 1989—. Grantee, Koret Found., 1988, Oomoto Found., Japan, 1991. Mem. Gen. Theol. Sem. Alumni Assn., Dakota Club. Office: St Aidan's Episcopal Ch PO Box 31526 San Francisco CA 94131

JELINEK, SUSAN LYNN, minister; b. Oak Park, Ill., June 23, 1960; d. Richard and Marilyn Ruth (Larsen) J. BS in Edn., Valparaiso U., 1982; MDiv, Eden Theol. Sem., 1989. Chaplain resident St. Luke's Hosp., St. Louis, 1989—. Mem. Am. Acad. Religion, Soc. Bibl. Lit. Office: St Lukes Hosp Pastoral Care 232 S Woods Mill Rd Chesterfield MO 63017

JEMELIAN, JONI LEE, lay worker, sales consultant; b. Arcadia, Calif., Dec. 18, 1964; d. John Nazar and Rose (Melkonian) J. AA in Gen. Edn., Pasadena City Coll., 1984; BS in Home Econs., Calif. Poly. State U., San Luis Obispo, 1986. Prin. 1st grade Sunday sch. Lake Ave Congl. Ch., Pasadena, Calif., 1981-82, coord. Bible study study support group, 1989-90; coord. spl. events Lake Ave Congl. Ch., Pasadena, 1990-91, small group leader Jr. High, 1991—; sales cons., pres. customer svc. bd, fundraising, spl. events Nordstrom Dept. Store, Glendale, Calif., 1988—; mem. single adult com., Lake Ave. Congl. Ch., Pasadena, 1988-89, nominating com., 1988; founder, organizer 7:45 Network, Pasadena, 1987-89; speaker in field. Congregationalist. Home: 261 Sharon Rd Arcadia CA 91007 Office: Nordstrom Dept Store 200 W Broadway Glendale CA 91204

JEMISON, THEODORE JUDSON, religious organization administrator; b. Selma, Ala., Aug. 1, 1918; m. Celestine C. Catlett,, 1945; childrne: Bettye Jane, Dianne Frances, Theodore Judson Jr. BS, Ala. State Coll., 1940; MA in Div., Union U., 1945; DD, Natchez Coll., 1953, Union U., 1971. Ordained to ministry Bapt. Ch., 1945. Pastor, minister Mt. Zion Bapt. Ch., Staunton, 1945-49, Mt. Zion 1st Bapt. Ch., Baton Rouge, 1949—; gen. sec. Nat. Bapt. Conv. U.S.A., Inc., 1953-87, pres., 1987—; mem. bd. cen. Nat. Council Chs. in U.S. Pres. Nat. Bapt. Convention, U.S.A., Inc., 1982—; v.p. Bapt. World Alliance, 1985—; active La. Rights Commn., Baton Rouge Commn. on Rels, NAACP; pres. Frontiers Internat. Baton Rouge chpt. Named Minister of Yr. Nat. Beta Club, 1973, Citizen of Yr. for Outstanding Contbns. in Civics, Recreation, Edn. City of Baton Rouge; recipient Disting. Service award East Baton Rouge Edn. Assn., 1973. Mem. Alpha Phi Alpha. Lodges: Shriners, Masons. Office: Nat Bapt Conv USA Inc 915 Spain St Baton Rouge LA 70802

JENKINS, AGNES ELIZABETH, lay worker; b. Bethlehem, Pa., Jan. 22, 1947; d. Erwin Charles and Elizabeth Catherine (Stankius) Wirth; m. Thomas Aloysius Cassidy, Apr. 12, 1969 (div. Nov. 1979); children: Shawn T., Colleen E.; m. Harry Alexander Jenkins, Dec. 29, 1979. RN. Coord. assimilation ministry Ch. of the Good Samaritan, Paoli, Pa., 1988—, computer sec. ch. office, 1989—; aspirant to diaconate Diocese of Pa., Paoli, 1990—; mem. diocesan lay coord. of lay ministry Diocese of Pa., 1988—. Home: 75 Devon Rd Paoli PA 19301

JENKINS, BARBARA ALEXANDER, pastor; b. Ft. Bragg, N.C., Oct. 13, 1942; d. Archie Herman Alexander and Hattie Elizabeth (Thigpen) Truitt; m. Warren Keith Jenkins, Aug. 22, 1964 (div. Sept. 1980); children: Pamela, Eric, Jason. BS, Ea. Mich. U., 1964, postgrad., 1964-66; postgrad., Duke U., 1978; DD (hon.), Ch. of Christ Bible Coll., Madras, India, 1988. Ordained to ministry, World Faith Clinic Inc., 1983, African Meth. Episcopal Zion Ch., 1984. Min. World Faith Clinic Inc., Fayetteville, N.C., 1981-83, A.M.E. Zion Ch., Fayetteville, 1982-84; pastor Noah's Ark Ministry, Fayetteville, 1985-86; founder, pastor Rainbow Tabernacle of Faith Ministries, Inc., Winston-Salem, N.C., 1984—; founder Rainbow Raleigh (N.C.) Outreach Ministries, 1986—, Rainbow Tabernacle of Faith, Charlotte, N.C., 1987—; dir. Spotlight on Truth Internat. Radio Ministries, Winston-Salem, 1985—; founder Rainbow Internat. Crusade Ministry, Winston-Salem, 1986—; dean Rainbow Inst. Commensurate Studies, Winston-Salem, 1985—; mem. Internat. Conv. Faith Ministries, Tulsa, 1989—. Contbr. articles to religious jours. Concert vocalist N.C. Black Repertory Co., Winston-Salem, 1987, 88; youth coord. Jerry Lewis Muscular Dystrophy Telethon, Raleigh, 1987, 88; guest speaker Wake Forest U., Winston-Salem, 1991. Recipient Outstanding Svc. award Rainbow Tabernacle Faith, Inc., 1987; scholar March of Dimes-Easter Seals, 1960-64. Mem. N.C. Women in Ministry (bd. dirs.), NAFE, Delta Sigma Theta (project coord. 1979-80). Democrat. Office: Rainbow Tabernacle Faith Ministries Inc 4091 New Walkertown Rd Winston-Salem NC 27105 *Life is the culmination of ascending and descending movements through time and space. A journey to reach the ultimate equilibrium that permits us to control and maintain order as it is perceived. Of course, many fail the Divine Assignment...which is: to share and to enjoy the fullness and richness of this precious experience—regardless of the gains and losses. There is a secret for Peace through it all: To Surrender the Control of it back to God!.*

JENKINS, C(ARLE) FREDERICK, religious organization executive, minister, lawyer; b. Orange, N.J., Nov. 18, 1931; s. Carle Brong and Euphemia (Repp) J.; m. Jane Shearer, Sept. 15, 1956; children: Elizabeth Ruth, Timothy Carle, Jeffrey Anson, Katharine Ann. AB, Amherst Coll., 1953; MDiv, Yale U., 1956; MA, Case Western Res. U., 1972; JD, Cleve. State U., 1982. Ordained to ministry Presbyn. Ch. USA, 1960; bar: Ohio, 1982, N.J., 1985. Urban min., community worker Inner City Protestant Parish, Cleve., 1956-65; pastor Phillips Ave. Presbyn. Ch., East Cleveland, Ohio, 1965-69; exec. presbyter Presbytery of Monmouth, Tennent, N.J., 1984-90; dir. constl. svcs. Presbyn. Ch. (USA), Louisville, 1990—; interim pastor Northminster Presbyn. Ch., Lorain, Ohio, 1972; stated clk. Presbytery of Western Res., Cleve., 1973-83; interim min. Westlake (Ohio) Presbyn. Ch., 1978-79, East Side Presbyn. Ch., Ashtabula, Ohio, 1982-83; sec. com. on reorgn. of presbytery Greater Cleve. Coun. Chs., 1972-73, bd. dirs. 1969-70; sec. Gen. Coun. Presbytery, 1973-83. Trustee Winding Brook Condominium Assn., 1986-88, Wessex Pl. Community Assn., Louisville. Recipient Resolution of Appreciation Cleve. City Coun., 1965. Mem. ABA. Democrat. Home: 9520 Wessex Pl Louisville KY 40222-5043 Office: Presbyn Ch (USA) 100 Witherspoon St #4416 Louisville KY 40202-1396

JENKINS, EDWIN FRED, minister; b. Birmingham, Ala., Aug. 21, 1948; s. Warren Frederick and Johnnie Louise (Milstead) J.; m. Joan Evans, Dec. 21, 1969; children: Andrew Edwin, Matthew Russell, Amanda Elyese. Student, U. Ala., 1966-67; BA, Samford U., 1970; MDiv, Southwestern Bapt. Theol. Sem., 1973, DMin, 1976. Ordained to ministry So. Bapt. Conv., 1972. Pastor Lone Willow Bapt. Ch., Cleburne, Tex., 1972-73, First Bapt. Ch., Milford, Tex., 1973-75, Calvary Bapt. Ch., Rosenberg, Tex., 1975-79, First Bapt. Ch., Katy, Tex., 1979-84, Hilldale Bapt. Ch., Birmingham, Ala., 1984—; instr. religion Jefferson State Community Coll., Birmingham, 1987-90, Samford U. Ext., Birmingham, 1985-86. Fund raising chmn. Salvation Army, Rosenberg, 1976; trustee Bapt. Home for Sr. Citizens, Birmingham, 1987-89; mem. State Bd. of Mission, Ala. Bapt. Conv., 1990—. Mem. Birmingham Bapt. Assn. (vice moderator 1990—, vice chmn. campus ministries 1986-87), Pastors for Life, Birmingham Bapt. Mins. Conf. (pres. 1989-90), Birmingham Brasilia Partnership (chmn. steering com. 1989—), Richmond-Rosenberg C. of C., Rosenberg-Richmond Optimist Club (bd. dirs. 1977-78), Rotary (Katy, Tex.). Home: 534 24th Ave NW Birmingham AL 35215 Office: Hilldale Bapt Ch 533 Sun Hill Rd NW Birmingham AL 35215 *The opportunity to make a difference in our world is available to each of us. Yet, only those who are willing to press beyond the barriers of mediocrity to the blessings of excellence in Christ will ultimately impact our society.*

JENKINS, ERNEST ALFRED, religion educator, minister; b. Detroit, Aug. 10, 1926; s. Ernest F. and Zoey (Bramall) J.; m. Katherine Dean Griffin, Aug. 27, 1948; children: Judith Lynn, Sandra Beth, Joan Carol. BA, Wheaton (Ill.) Coll., 1948; BD, No. Bapt. Theol. Sem., 1951; MA, U. Chgo., 1953, PhD, 1967. Ordained to ministry Am. Bapt. Ch., 1951. Min. edn. St. Paul's Union, Chgo., 1951-63, Morgan Pk. Bapt. Ch., Chgo., 1963-66, 1st Bapt. Ch., Oak Park, Ill., 1966-68; assoc. prof., dir. admissions No. Bapt. Theol. Sem., Lombard, Ill., 1964-75, prof. Christian edn., 1972—, dir. doctoral studies, 1976-90, dean of sem., 1990; mem. nat. com. Pastor as Tchr. Convocation, Am. Bapt. Assn., Green Lake, Wis., 1984; pres. Soc. Profl. Ch. Leaders, Chgo. Bapt. Assn., 1980-81; dir. Chgo. Bapt. Credit Union, 1982—. Author study guides; contbr. articles to profl. jours. With USAAF, 1944-45. Mem. Religious Edn. Assn., Assn. Profs. and Researchers in Religious Edn., Am. Bapt. Educators, Phi Delta Kappa. Home: 1139 Aurora Way Wheaton IL 60187 Office: No Bapt Theol Sem 660 E Butterfield Rd Lombard IL 60148

JENKINS, HOWARD J., church education administrator. Supt. of edn. Archdiocese of New Orleans. Office: Office of Schs Supt 7887 Walmsley Ave New Orleans LA 70125*

JENKINS, JOHN AKINS, pastor; b. Atlanta, Nov. 12, 1953; s. John A. III and Mary Louise (Akins) J.; m. Donna Gray, June 7, 1985; children: Brent Alan, Christopher Scott, Stacie Lynn. BA, Mercer U., 1985; student, Mid-Am. Bapt. Sem., 1986-90. Ordained to Gospel ministry, 1990. Min. to youth Prays Mill Bapt. Ch., Douglasville, Ga., 1976-78; pastor Oakland Bapt. Ch., McDonough, Ga., 1979-80; assoc. pastor Westside Bapt. Ch., Mableton, Ga., 1980-81; min. of edn. New Hope Bapt. Ch., Fayetteville, Ga., 1981-85; assoc. pastor Colonial Hills Bapt. Ch., Southaven, Miss., 1985-88; pastor Southcrest Bapt. Ch., Southaven, 1988-90, Corinth Bapt. Ch., Jonesboro, Ga., 1990—. Co-author: The Vine Life Ministry, 1981. Home: 5374 Pear Dr Southaven MS 38671 Office: Corinth Baptist Church 398 Corinth Rd Jonesboro GA 30236

JENKINS, JOHN CLACK, minister; b. Waxahachie, Tex., Sept. 7, 1951; s. Warwick H. and Barbara (Clack) J.; m. Patty Gail Holmes, Aug. 14, 1971; children: Cassidy, Speight, Allison, Brett. B in Religion, Baylor U., 1973; MDiv, Southwestern Bapt. Theol. Sem., 1977; DST, Bethany Theol. Sem., 1989. Ordained to ministry So. Bapt. Conv., 1981. Dir. youth edn. Henderson St. Bapt. Ch., Cleburne, Tex., 1976-77; min. evangelism 1st Bapt. Ch., Longview, Tex., 1979-81; pastor Ebenezer Bapt. Ch., El Dorado, Ark., 1981-84, Lake Hamilton (Ark.) Bapt. Ch., 1984—; mem. tellers com. Ark. Bapt. State Conv., 1983. Mem. Cen. Bapt. Assn. (mem. mission com. 1984), Lakeside Athletic Booster Club (pres. 1989-91). Home and Office: PO Box 305 Lake Hamilton AR 71951 *With no transcendant moral foundation, America has no social, political or even economic foundation. The result is chaos. Man will always sacrifice his liberty for order. Order must begin with a moral foundation.*

JENKINS, JOYCE L., minister; b. Cleve., Aug. 20, 1953; d. John William and Mary Louise Freiling; m. Dan E. Jenkins, Aug. 10, 1974; children: Michael, Matthew, Christopher, Amber, Ashley, Mark. BA, Baldwin-Wallace Coll., 1982; MA, Ashland (Ohio) Theol. Sem., 1986, MDiv, 1987. Ordained to ministry United Meth. Ch. Pastor West Lebanon United Meth. Ch., 1991—. Clergy rep. to Dist. Bd. Missions, Ohio, 1988-91, mem. health and welfare com.; camp dean Rolling-Y Ranch (YMCA camp), Carrolton, Ohio, 1991—. Mem. Quota Club, Teen Consorsium. Office: Apple Creek United Meth Ch Apple Creek OH 44606

JENKINS, KEVIN LYNN, minister; b. Portsmouth, Ohio, Nov. 26, 1955; s. Therron Chaney and Joan Naomi (Askin) J.; m. Donna Jean Montavon, July 3, 1976; children: Benjamin, Joshua, Christian. Assoc. in Applied Bus., Shawnee State Coll., Portsmouth, 1976; ministerial degree, Sunset Sch. Preaching, 1982. Asst. controller Mobile Homes Acceptance Corp., Portsmouth, 1976; asst. v.p. McGinnis, Inc., South Point, Ohio, 1976-80; minister Queen St. Ch. of Christ, Mt. Sterling, Ky., 1982—. Pres. PTO, Mt. Sterling, 1986-87; pres.-elect Ky. Assn. Gifted Edn., Orgn., Mt. Sterling, 1987—; ambassador Pres.'s Ambassadors Christian Edn., Ohio Valley Christian Coll., Parkersburg, W.Va., 1984—; coach Ky. Youth Soccer Assn., Montgomery County, 1982—, Youth Baseball League, Montgomery County, 1984—. Named Outstanding Young Man of Am., 1983-85. Mem. Alumni Assn. Sunset Sch. Preaching (pres. Ky. chpt. 1986—), Rotary (bd. dirs. 1986-88, v.p. 1989-90, pres.-elect 1990-91). Democrat. Lodge: Rotary (bd. dirs. 1986—). Avocations: sports, historical pursuits. Home: 1412 Greenleaf Ct Mount Sterling KY 40353 Office: Ch of Christ PO Box 194 Mount Sterling KY 40353

JENKINS, O. RANDALL, education minister; b. Jackson, Miss., Feb. 10, 1964; s. Otis Raymon and Catherine Elizabeth (Donald) J.; m. Susan Elise Heath, June 6, 1987; 1 child, Forrest Randall. AA, Hinds Jr. Coll., Raymond, Miss., 1984; BS, U. So. Miss., 1986; MRE, New Orleans Bapt. Theol. Sem., 1990. Lic. to ministry Bapt. Ch., 1989, ordained, 1990. Student intern home mission bd. So. Bapt. Conv., New Orleans, 1989-90; clk. Missionary Expediters, New Orleans, 1989-90; min. edn. and activities 1st Bapt. Ch., Phila., Miss., 1990—. Program chmn. Neshoba County Brotherhood Mission Project '91, Phila., 1991. Office: 1st Bapt Ch 414 Pecan Ave Philadelphia MS 39350 *A Christian's reasonable service to the Savior, Jesus Christ, and his fellow men is to live the Gospel daily in such a way to lead men to the throne of Almighty God.*

JENKINS, ORVILLE WESLEY, retired religious administrator; b. Hico, Tex., Apr. 29, 1913; s. Daniel Wesley and Eva (Caldwell) J.; m. Louise Cantrell, June 29, 1939; children—Orville Wesley, Jannette (Mrs. John Calhoun), Jeanne (Mrs. David Hubbs). Student, Tex. Tech U., 1929-34; B.A., Pasadena Coll., 1938; student, Nazarene Theol. Sem., 1946-47; D.D., So. Nazarene U., 1957. Ordained to ministry Ch. of Nazarene, 1939; pastor Dinuba, Calif., 1938-42, Fresno, Calif., 1942-45, Topeka, 1945-47, Salem, Oreg., 1947-50, Kansas City, Mo., 1959-61; supt. West Tex. Dist. Ch. of Nazarene, 1950-59, Kansas City Dist., 1961-64; exec. sec. dept. home missions Ch. of Nazarene, Kansas City, 1964-68; gen. supt. Ch. of Nazarene, 1968-85. Former trustee So. Nazarene U. Home: 2309 W 103d St Leawood KS 66206 Office: 6401 Paseo Kansas City MO 64131 *The Christian life has brought meaningful and purposeful existence and has led to a wonderful sense of fulfillment in living. It is a joy to follow the day-to-day excitement of this life.*

JENKINS, WILLIAM FERRELL, minister; b. Huntsville, Ala., Jan. 3, 1936; s. B. M. and Vera Elizabeth (Mann) J.; m. Elizabeth Ann Williams, Dec. 16, 1954; children: William Ferrell Jr., Stanley Eugene. AA, cert., Fla. Christian Coll., 1957; student, Western Ky. U., 1957, 62-63; MA, Harding Grad. Sch., 1971. Min. various Chs. of Christ, Fla., Ky., Mo., Tenn., Ind., Ohio, 1953-82, Carrollwood Ch. of Christ, Tampa, Fla., 1983—; mem. Bible faculty Fla. Coll., Temple Terrace, 1969-84, chmn. Dept. Bibl. Studies, 1991—; dir. study tours to Bible lands, 1967—; mem. edn. staff Lachish Archeol. Expdn. to Israel, 1980. Author: The Old Testament in Book of Revelation, 1973, The Finger of God, 1984, Studies in Revelation, 1984, Better Things, 1988, Introduction to Christian Evidences, 1989, God's Eternal Purpose, The Theme of the Bible, Biblical Authority, 1990; assoc. editor: Cogdill Found., Marion, Ind., 1969-76, study materials; contbr. articles to New Smith's Bible Dictionary, 1966. Am. Schs. Oriental Rsch., Evang. Theol. Soc., Soc. Bibl. Lit., Near East Archaeol. Soc. Republican. Home: 9211 Hollyridge Pl Tampa FL 33637 *I make it my aim to do always those things which are pleasing to the One who called me, thus providing the proper motivation for my relation to man and God.*

JENNE, CAROLE SEEGERT, minister, marriage and family therapist; b. Ypsilanti, Mich., Nov. 22, 1942; d. Ellsworth Noah and Ruby Loretta (Stetter) S.; m. Eugene Erven Jenne, Feb. 25, 1961; children: Jeanne-Marie Segler, Philip John. AS, Monroe Co. Community Coll., 1972; BS, Eastern Mich. U., 1974; MSW, U. of Mich., 1979; PhD, Intl. Sem., 1986. Lic. marriage counselor, cert. social worker, ordained elder/pastor. Pastoral counselor Lambertville Christian, Lambertville, Mich., 1985--, elder/pastor, 1990--; seminary inst. Intl. Sem., Plymouth, Fla., 1989--; family therapist, 1980--, retreat/conf. speaker. Mem. Natl. Assn. Social Workers. Interdenominational. Office: Lambertville Christian Fell 11100 Summerfield Rd Box 354 Lambertville MI 48144

JENNESS, EUGENE RAY, JR., youth minister; b. Jacksonville, N.C., Feb. 17, 1966; s. Eugene Ray and Ovaline Virginia (Holt) J. Student, U. N.C., Wilmington, 1991. Youth leader Heritage Fellowship, Wilmington, 1983-84, Glad Tidings Assembly, Toccoa, Ga., 1984-85; youth dir. New Covenant Ch., Wilmington, 1986-87; jr. high youth min., bulletin bd. com., youth adv. bd. Freedom Bapt. Ch., Wilmington, 1990—, Sunday sch. tchr., ch. coun., 1990—. Author: (booklet) Satan in the Cinema, 1987, (book) What the Devil's Wrong With Movies?, 1989. County organizer N.C. Right-to-Life Com., New Hanover County, 1987. Republican. Baptist. Home: 4101 Lynbrook Dr Wilmington NC 28405

JENNEY, TIMOTHY PAUL, religious educator; b. Erie, Pa., Sept. 15, 1956; s. Theodore and Ramona Ann (Hagerty) J.; m. Gloria Jean Combs, May 7, 1976; 1 child, Zechariah John. BA in Bible, Cen. Bible Coll., Springfield, Mo., 1978; MA in History, S.W. Mo. State U., 1980; MA in Bibl. Lang., O.T., Assemblies of God Theol. Sem., Springfield, Mo., 1980; MA in Near Eastern Studies, U. Mich., 1985. Ordained to ministry Assemblies of God Ch., 1983. Pastor Olivet First Assembly of God Ch., Olivet, Mich., 1980-87, Bethel Assembly of God Ch., Lincoln Park, Mich., 1987-89; assoc. prof. N. Cen. Bible Coll., Mpls., 1989—. Assoc. editor Bible Dictionary, The Eerdmans Bible Dictionary, 1987; contbr. Greek dictionary, The Complete Bibl. Libr., bd. rev. Commr. Human Rights Commn., Roseville, Minn., 1990—. Mem. Soc. Bibl. Lit. Office: N Cen Bible Coll 910 Elliot Ave S Minneapolis MN 55404

JENNINGS, SISTER VIVIEN ANN, academic administrator; b. Jersey City, May 18, 1934; d. Eugene O. and Alice (Smith) J. BA, Caldwell Coll., 1960; MA in English, Cath. U. Am., 1966; MS in Telecommunications, Syracuse U., 1980; PhD in English, Fordham U., 1972; EdD (hon.), Providence Coll.; LittD (hon.), Caldwell Coll. Assoc. prof. English Caldwell Coll., 1960-69; instr. broadcasting writing Syracuse U., 1979-80; with community affairs dept. Sta. WIXT TV, Syracuse, N.Y., 1980; dir. telecommunications Barry U., 1982-83; dir. pub. affairs Cath. Telecommunications Network Am., 1983-84; pres. Caldwell Coll., 1984—; originator, designer campus TV studios Caldwell Coll., Barry U.; curriculum planner, coord. new grad.-level curriculum in telecommunications Barry U.; lectr. on ednl. and media issues. Producer: Centenary Journey, 1981, Advent Vesper Chorale, 1981, American Immigrant Church, 1982; co-producer The Boat People, 1980. Founder, dir. Children"s TV Experience; founder Project Link Ednl. Ctr., Newark; bd. trustees Las Casas Fund for Cheyenne and Arapaho Indians. Mem. Assn. Cath. Colls. (coord. nat. teleconf.), Assn. Ind. Colls. (pres.'s group), Cath. Telecommunications Network Am. (bd. trustees), Providence Coll. (bd. trustees). Office: Caldwell Coll 9 Ryerson Ave Caldwell NJ 07006

JENSEN, HERLUF MATTHIAS, bishop; b. Cordova, Nebr., July 12, 1923; s. Alfred and Milda Hanna (Schmidt) J.; m. Dorthea Lund, July 3, 1948; children—Tezanne, Lance, Cynthia, Peter, Roslind. A.B., Harvard U., 1949; M.A., U. Minn., 1951; M.Div., Union Theol. Sem., 1964; DD (honoris causa), Grand View Coll., 1989; DLitt (honoris causa), Upsala Coll., 1990. Ordained to ministry Lutheran Ch. in Am., 1968, consecrated bishop, 1978. Pres. Luth. Student Assn. in Am., Chgo., 1951-53; exec. sec. United Student Christian Coun., N.Y.C., 1954-59; gen. sec. Nat. Student Christian Fedn., N.Y.C., 1959-62; lay staff ofcl. Bd. Social Ministry, Luth. Ch. in Am., 1963-68; pastor St. Matthew Luth. Ch., Moorestown, N.J., 1968-78; bishop N.J. Synod Luth Ch. in Am. (merged into Evang. Luth. Ch. in Am. 1988), 1978—; pres. Coalition of Religious Leaders, N.J., 1983-85. Pres. Human Relations Council, East Brunswick, N.J., 1965-68; trustee Neighborhood House, New Brunswick, 1965-68, Luth. Theol. Sem., Phila., 1975-91, Upsala Coll., East Orange, N.J., 1978-90. Served with U.S. Army, 1943-46, ETO. Decorated Purple Heart; recipient Disting. Service award Human Relations Council, 1968. Mem. Liturgical Soc. Am., Luth. Human Relations Assn. Am., Luth. Soc. for Worship, Music and the Arts. Democrat. Office: NJ Synod Luth Ch in Am 1930 State Hwy 33 Hamilton Sq Trenton NJ 08690

JENSEN, JOSEPH (NORMAN), priest, educator; b. Mannheim, Ill., Nov. 22, 1924; s. Harry and Annette (Gerbing) J. BA, Cath. U. Am., 1951, STD, 1971; S.T.L., Collegio San Anselmo, Rome, 1955; S.S.L., Pontifical Bibl. Inst., Rome, 1968. Joined Benedictine Order, Roman Cath. Ch., 1948, ordained priest, 1954. Assoc. prof. Cath. U. Am., Washington, 1961—; prior St. Anselm's Abbey, Washington, 1981-85. Author: The Use of Tora by Isaiah, 1977, God's Word to Israel, 1982, Isaiah 1-39, 1984; mng. editor Old Testament Abstracts, 1977—. 2d lt. USAAF, 1943-45. Mem. Cath. Bibl. Assn. (exec. sec. 1970—), Soc. Bibl. Lit., Cath. Learned Socs. (sec. joint com. 1977-82, del. 1974—), Coun. on Study of Religion (treas. Waterloo, Can. chpt. 1970-77, del. 1970—, sec. 1985—). Home: St Anselm's Abbey 4501 S Dakota Ave NE Washington DC 20017 Office: Cath Bibl Assn 415 Adminstration Bldg Catholic U Am Washington DC 20064

JENSEN, PAUL TIMOTHY, philosophy educator; b. Stambaugh, Mich., Aug. 3, 1950; s. Louis Frederick and Iris Maxine (Davis) J.; m. Rebecca Jo James, Aug. 1, 1981 (div. 1986); m. Sharon Lynn Kleinhuizen, Aug. 5, 1989. BA, North Park Coll., Chgo., 1972; MDiv, Trinity Div. Sch., Deerfield, Ill., 1976, ThM, 1979; PhD, U. Va., 1988. Asst. pastor Nat. Evang. Free Ch., Annandale, Va., 1977-81; pulpit supplier First United Presbyn. Ch., Moline, Ill., 1991—; asst. prof. philosophy Augustana Coll., Rock Island, 1988—. Govs. fellowship U. Va., 1982-83. Mem. Am. Phil. Assn., Soc. Christian Philosophers, Calvin Studies Soc., Univ. Faculty for Life. Home: 2824 21 1/2 Ave Rock Island IL 61201 Office: Augustana Coll Rock Island IL 61201

JENSEN, TIMOTHY WARD, minister; b. Seattle, Oct. 22, 1956; s. Gerald Frederick and Betty Jo (Krause) J.; m. Margaret Florence Weddell, June 21, 1985; children: Jacob Ryan Sullivan, Stephanie Jon Sullivan. BA, U. Wash., 1978; MDiv, Harvard U., 1981; MA, We. Wash. U., 1983. Ordained to ministry, First and Second. Ch. Boston, 1981. Residence hall advisor U. Wash., Seattle, 1976-78; chaplancy intern Va. Mason Hosp., Seattle, 1979; theol. student intern First and Second Ch. in Boston, 1978-81; residence hall dir. We. Wash. U., Bellingham, 1981-82; intern minister Univ. Unitarian Ch., Seattle, 1983-84; lectr. Midland Coll., Tex., 1986; minister Unitarian Universalist Ch., Midland, 1984-88, Unitarian Universalist Community Ch., Aloha, Oreg., 1988—; bd. dirs. S.W. Unitarian Universalist Conf., 1988, Midland Assn. Chs., 1988. Treas. Midland CROP Walk, 1988; emergency rm. chaplain Midland Mcpl. Hosp., 1985-88. Mem. Unitarian Universalist Ministers Assn., Prairie Group. Office: Unitarian Universalist Ch PO Box 5190 Aloha OR 97006

JENSEN-REINKE, CLEMENS IMMANUEL, minister; b. Hamburg, West Germany, Jan. 3, 1961; s. Otfried and Marie Luise (Jaehne) R.; m. Kristina Vibeke, Oct. 15, 1988; 1 child, Hannah Luise. BA, U. Hamburg, 1983; MDiv, Luth. Theol. Sem., 1989. Ordained to ministry Luth. Ch., 1989. Pastor St. Luke's Evang. Luth. Ch., Bklyn., N.Y., 1988—; chaplain Pratt Inst., Bklyn., 1988—. Chairperson Community Adv. Bd. Heights Hill Mental Health Svc., Bklyn., 1989—. Home: 450 67th St Brooklyn NY 11220 Office: Saint Luke Evang Luth Ch 259 Washington Ave Brooklyn NY 11205

JENSON, RONALD ALLEN, religious executive, educator; b. Bremerton, Wash., Apr. 15, 1948; s. Robert C. and Maxine (Mitchell) J.; m. Mary Kunz, Dec. 27, 1969; children: Matthew Robert, Mary Rachael. BA cum laude in Speech Communications, Lewis and Clark Coll., 1969; MDiv, summa cum laude, Western Conservative Bapt. Sem., 1972, DMinistry, 1974. Ordained Ch. of the Saviour, 1976. Pastor, Ch. of the Saviour, Wayne, Pa., 1973-79; pres. Ch. Dynamics, San Bernardino, Calif., 1978-79, Internat. Sch. Theology, San Bernardino, 1978-86; vice chancellor Internat. Christian Grad. U., San Bernardino, 1983-86; pres. High Ground, 1987—. Mem. nat. exec. com. Reagan's Yr. of the Bible; mem. bd. govts. Council Nat. Policy. Named Outstanding Young Man in Am., U.S. Jaycees, 1976. Mem. Am. Assn. Higher Edn. Author: How to Succeed the Biblical Way, 1981, Dynamics of Church Growth, 1981, Together We Can, 1982, Always Advancing, Always Planning, 1984, Kingdoms at War, 1986. Home: 12989 Abra Dr San Diego CA 92128 Office: PO Box 270001 San Diego CA 92128

JENT, GLENN ALVIN, minister; b. Neosho, Mo., Apr. 27, 1944; s. Charles Jonathan Jent and Laura Josephine (Watson) Thomas; m. Mary Jane Simmons, Mar. 1, 1968; children: Jon Leland, Jason Thomas. AA, S.W. Bapt. Coll., 1964; BSE magna cum laude, Ouachita Bapt. U., 1966; MDiv summa cum laude, Midwestern Bapt. Sem., 1978; EdD, New Orleans Bapt. Sem., 1983. Ordained to ministry So. Bapt. Conv., 1965. Pastor Liberty Bapt. Ch., Lincoln, Ark., 1970-71; pastor 1st Bapt. Ch., Jenny Lind, Ark., 1972-74, Welch, Okla., 1974-78; min. of edn. 1st Bapt. Ch., Amite, La., 1978-82; pastor 2d Bapt. Ch., Poplar Bluff, Mo., 1982—; bd. dirs., past pres. South Mo. Bapt. Assembly, Van Buren, 1983—, Christian Civic Found., Bridgeton, Mo., 1987—; pres. S.E. Mo. Pastors/Wives Fellowship, 1986; tchr. Sem. Ext. for Coll. Credit-Bapt. Student Ctr., Hayti, Mo., 1989—. Mem. Poplar Bluff Ministerial Alliance, 1982-89; organizer Save Our Sundays Com., Poplar Bluff, 1988, Christian Athletic League, Poplar Bluff, 1983; chmn. Gen. Assembly of a Twp., Jenny Lind, 1974. Named Charles Haddon Spurgeon fellow William Jewell Coll., Liberty, 1990. Mem. Lions. Office: Second Bapt Ch 503 W Pine Poplar Bluff MO 63901

JERDAN, WILLIAM H. S., JR., bishop. Bishop Reformed Episcopal Ch., Summerville, S.C. Office: Reformed Episcopal Ch 414 W Second South St Summerville SC 29483*

JERGE, MARIE CHARLOTTE, minister; b. Mineola, N.Y., Dec. 26, 1952; d. Charles Louis and Helen Marie (Scheld) Scharfe; m. James Nelson Jerge, Aug. 27, 1977. AB, Smith Coll., 1974; MDiv, Luth. Theol. Sem. of Phila., 1978. Pastor St. Mark Evang. Luth. Ch., Mayville, N.Y., 1978-88; co-pastor Zion Evang. Luth. Ch., Silver Creek, N.Y., 1983-88; asst. to the bishop Upstate N.Y. Synod, Buffalo, 1988—; bd. dirs. Acad. Preachers, Phila., 1982—. Chairperson Chautauqua County Commn. of Family Violence and Neglect, Mayville, 1981-82, bd. dirs., 1978-88. Named one of outstanding Young Women in Am., 1980. Avocations: needlework, aerobics, tennis, golf. Home: 370 Borden Rd West Seneca NY 14224 Office: Upstate NY Synod 49 Linwood Ave Buffalo NY 14209

JERGENS, ANDREW MACADIDH, minister; b. Omaha, July 16, 1935; s. Andrew N. Jergens (stepfather) and Edna May (Walker) Richardson; m. Virginia Hawn, June 20, 1962 (div. Nov. 1976); m. Linda Busken, Feb. 21, 1977; children: Andrew W.M., Peter Hawn. BS, Yale U., 1957; MBA, U. Pa., 1962. Pres. The Andrew Jergens Found., Cin., 1967—; assoc. rector Ch. of Redeemer, Cin., 1973-89; interim rector Christ Ch. of Glendale, Ohio, 1990—. Trustee emeritus Cin. Playhouse, 1975. With U.S. Army, 1959-60. Mem. Caledonian Soc. of Cin., Clergy Assn. of So. Ohio (treas. 1988—), Cin. Country Club, Univ. Club of Cin., Order of the Holy Cross. (assoc.). Episcopalian. Avocations: bird watching, tennis, hill walking. Home: 2374 Madison Rd Cincinnati OH 45208

JERNIGAN, HOMER LARGE, religion educator; b. Longmont, Colo., Mar. 6, 1922; s. Virgil Jackson and Mary Ethel (Large) J.; m. Margaret Jane Belinfante, June 19, 1949; children: Daryl Beth, Catherine, Margaret Ann, David, Christopher. BA, U. Denver, 1943; BD magna cum laude, Union Theol. Sem., N.Y.C., 1946; PhD, Northwestern U., 1959; postgrad., Harvard U., 1964-65, 78-79. Ordained deacon United Meth. Ch., 1947, elder, 1949. Layreader St. Johnn's Chapel, Greenwich, Conn., 1944-46; pastor chs., St. Albans, N.Y., 1946-49, Amityville, N.Y., 1949-51; chaplain Cook County Hosp., Chgo., 1951-53, Western State Hosp., Staunton, Va., 1953-57; mem. faculty Boston U. Sch. Theology, 1957-91, asst. prof. pastoral psychology, 1957-64, Albert V. Danielsen assoc. prof. pastoral care and counseling, 1964-67, Danielsen prof., 1967-91, prof. emeritus, 1991—; dir. Danielsen Pastoral Counseling Svc., Boston, 1963-71; vis. prof. Trinity Tehol. Coll., Singapore, 1971-72. Robbins fellow, 1965, Assoc. Theol. Schs. fellow, 1971-72, Whiting fellow, 1985. Fellow Pastoral Inst. Washington, Am. Assn. Theol. Schs.; mem. APA, Am. Assn. Pastoral Counselors (diplomate), Assn. Clin. Pastoral Edn. (supr.). Office: Boston U 745 Commonwealth Ave Boston MA 02215 *As an aging person in an aging society, I am increasingly impressed with the importance of organizing the life of the individual and society around meanings, values, and relationships which cannot be lost.*

JERRETT, NATHANIEL, minister. Pres. The Ch. Fedn. of greater Chgo. Office: Ch Fedn Greater Chgo 18 S Michigan Ave Ste 900 Chicago IL 60603*

JERVING, JOHN WESLEY, minister; b. Sheboygan, Wis., June 11, 1950; s. Wesley Keneth and Arlene (Jurk) J.; m. Diane Lee Davis, July 28, 1974; children: Nicole, Kristine. BS, Lakeland Coll., 1980; MDiv, Garrett-Evangelical Theol. Sem., 1984. Deacon United Meth. Ch., Springfield, Ill., 1984-86, elder, 1987, youth coord., 1987, mem. coun. youth, 1987—. Chaplain local troop Boy Scouts Am., 1985; directing pastor Pioneer Parish, 1989; mem. exec. com. Conf. of Higher Edn., 1990, Dist. Coun. of Ministries, 1990, Project Equality, 1991—, subdist. group leader. Mem. Phi Alpha Theta. Republican. United Methodist. Home: 200 Bissel Jacksonville IL 62650 Office: Pioneer Parish United Meth Ch 200 Bissel Jacksonville IL 62650

JESCHKE, MARLIN, philosophy and religion educator; b. Waldheim, Sask., Can., May 18, 1929; s. Ernest and Eva (Schmidt) J.; m. Charmaine S. Shidler, Dec. 30, 1955; children: Eric, Margaret, David. BA, Tabor Coll., 1954; BD, Garrett Theol. Sem., 1958; PhD, Northwestern U., Evanston, Ill., 1965. Lectr. North Park Coll., Chgo., 1959-61; prof. Goshen (Ind.) Coll., 1961—. Author: Believers Baptism, 1983, Discipling the Church, 1988; book review editor Mennonite Quar. Review, 1979—. Recipient Susan B. Wise Theology prize Garrett Sem., 1957, 58; fellowship i Asian Rels. Soc. for Rels. in Higher Edn. Mem. Mennonite Hist. Soc. (sec.), Am. Theol. Soc. Office: Goshen Coll Goshen IN 46526

JESSUP, LYNNE KATIE, minister; b. Ithaca, N.Y., Sept. 14, 1951; d. John Fitzgerald and Ruth Elizabeth (Hoerber) Dixon; m. Robert Keith Jessup, Sept. 14,1985. BA, Wittenberg U., 1973; BTh, Gulf Coast Bible Coll., 1978. Ordained to ministry Ch. of God, 1981. Pastor Ch. of God, Saratoga, Ind., 1978-90; del. Ch. of God Gen. Assembly, Anderson, Ind., 1978—; forwarding agt. Friends of Turkey, 1984-86; alumni recruiter Gulf Coast Bible Coll., 1982-86; bd. dirs. Haven Ministries, 1984-85; chaplain Randolph County Hosp., 1985-90. Columnist From the Chaplain's Desk, local newspaper, 1985-86. Pres. R.E.A.C.H. Svcs., Inc., Winchester, Ind., 1982-82; chmn. Cystic Fibrosis Bike-a-thon, Saratoga, 1981, 82. Mem. Winchester Area Ministerial Assn. (pres. 1981-82, sec.-treas. 1983-85, 91), Randolph County Hosp. Chaplains Assn. (pres. 1982-83), Youth Explosion, Alumni in Action, Mid-Am. Bible Coll. Republican. Home: P O Box 11 Washington St Saratoga IN 47382 Office: Saratoga Ch God P O Box 11 Saratoga IN 47382 *Living in this world can keep us so busy "doing" things that we fail to take time to develop who we "are". God calls us first to "be" His people and to "be" the kind of people He desires, and if we will seek after this, the "doing" will take care of itself.*

JESSUP, RICHARD EDWARD, minister; b. San Francisco, Nov. 4, 1932; s. Abraham Edward and Florence Ellan (Hickey) J.; m. Shirley Mae Book, June 18, 1954; children: Judy, Richard, Stephen. BA, So. Calif. Coll., 1955, La Verne (Calif.) U., 1960; MA, Calif. Poly. State U., 1974. Ordained to ministry Assemblies of God, 1958; cert. elem. and secondary tchr., adminstr., Calif. Pastor Assembly of God Ch., Shandon, Calif., 1963-75; tchr., adminstr. Atascadero (Calif.) Jr. High Sch., 1967-75; assoc. pastor Calvary Community Ch., San Jose, Calif., 1975-78; min. Christian edn. Bethel Assembly of God, Tulare, Calif., 1978-80; prin. Mountlake Christian Sch., Mountlake Terrace, Wash., 1982-86; pastoral assoc. Spanaway (Wash.) Assembly of God, 1987-89, Neighborhood Ch., Bellevue, Wash., 1989—; cons. Mountlake Christian Sch., 1990; cons., adminstr. Vacaville (Calif.) Christian Acad., 1986-87. Contbr. poetry to Pentecostal Evangel mag. Fellow Christian Schs. Commn. Northwest Dist. Assemblies of God; mem. Northwest Assn. Christian Sch. Adminstrs., Prins. Assn. Christian Schs. (pres. 1990-91, v.p. 1991—), Internat. Fellowship Christian Sch. Adminstrs. Office: Neighborhood Christian Sch 625 140th Ave NE Bellevue WA 98005 *Whether change or challenge comes from man-made or natural events, survival depends on our willingness to take risks. Try new ideas. So what if you fail. Learn from the failure. Change and move on.*

JESTER, JOHN SELBY, minister; b. Barnesville, Ga., Oct. 29, 1942; s. John Lee and Regina (Britt) J.; m. Cheryl Jean Sims, Mar. 14, 1966 (div. Oct. 1985); children: Andrea Jester Wheeler, Jennifer Jester Tillirson, R. Jane, Laurie Jester Brown; m. Pushpika Priyadarshani Fernando, Feb. 22, 1990 (div. Oct. 1991). Degree in Mortuary Sci., John A. Gupton Coll., Nashville, 1963; BBA, N.Am. U., 1980, MBA, 1982; PhD, Golden State U., 1984; postulant, Buddhist Theosophical Soc., LaFayette, La., 1985-90; JD, LaSalle U., Mandeville, La., 1990; D Law Letters, Meridian U., 1991. Ordained to ministry Buddhist Theosophical Soc., Kandy, Sri Lanka, 1990; lic. embalmer, funeral dir., Ga., health care administr., Ga. Mortician various firms, Ga., 1963-70; health care adminstr. Charter Med. Corp., Macon, Ga., 1970-72; adminstr. Meml. Med. Ctr., Dublin, Ga., 1972-73; mgmt. cons. J.S. Jester and Assocs., Dublin, 1973-74; regional dir. Carex Internat., C.A., 1974-76; adminstr. Spring Valley Ctr., Jeffersonville, Ga., 1976-78; chief exec. officer Free Enterprise Systems Inc., Dublin, 1978-85; priest Buddhist Theosophical Soc., Lafayette, La., 1990—; founder, pres. Meridian U., Lafayette, 1990—; post-mortem surgeon Lions Eye Bank, 1973-76; coroner Laurens County, Dublin, 1969-73, Houston County, Perry, Ga., 1975-76. Sculptor: Tobac indian, 1974 (1st pl. award 1974); contbr. poems to mags. in field. Chmn. Salvation Army Svc. Unit, Dublin, 1970; mem. Republican Task Force, Ga., 1982. Sgt. USAFNG, 1965-71. Mem. Internat. Soc. Jurists (chmn. 199—), Theosophical Soc. in Am., Pali Text Soc. (Eng.), Buddhist Theosophical Soc., Order of Shilelagh (charter), Brit. Inst. Embalmers (Eng.). Avocations: sculpture, poetry, short stories, Tai Chi. Office: Buddhist Theosophical Soc PO Box 31436 Lafayette LA 70593-1436 *Doom's henchmen—ignorance, apathy and greed—I see everywhere. I hear Chief Seattle's final heartrending plea. It echoes through the garbage dump mountains on the now spoiled wind, "Have compassion for our mother (Earth) and all her children or face the end of existence."*

JETER, JOSEPH ROSCOE, JR., religious educator, minister; b. Ft. Worth, Oct. 5, 1943; s. Joseph Roscoe Sr. and Helen Virgina (Reams) J.; m. Brenda Mable Sargent, July 11, 1975; 1 child, Justin Beau. BA, Tex. Christian U., 1965; BD, Union Thol. Sem., N.Y.C., 1971; MA, Claremont (Calif.) Grad. Sch., 1983, PhD, 1983. Ordained to ministry Christian Ch. Various pastorates N.Y. and Calif., 1967-84; asst. prof. Brite Divinity Sch., Ft. Worth, 1984—; lectr. in field. Author: Alexander Procter: The Sage of Independence, 1984; contbr. articles to profl. jours. Mem. Acad. Homiletics. Democrat. Office: Brite Divinity Sch PO Box 32923 TCU Station Fort Worth TX 76129

JETT, STEVEN ADRIAN, minister; b. Knoxville, Tenn., Aug. 2, 1952; s. Lowell Adrian and Lucy Lee (Galyon) J.; m. Susan Kay Drake, Oct. 23, 1976; children; children: Elizabeth Ashleigh, Steven Matthew. BA in Religion, Cumberland Bapt. Coll., 1977; MDiv, Southwestern Bapt. Theol. Sem., 1982; PhD, Oxford Grad. Sch., 1986. Ordained to ministry, Bapt. Ch., 1977. Minister of music youth Main St. Bapt. Ch., Williamsburg, Ky., 1974-78; minister Renner Bapt. Ch., Dallas, 1978-79; assoc. pastor Western Park Bapt. Ch., Dallas, 1979-82; pastor French Broad Valley Bapt. Ch., Kodak, Tenn., 1982-84, Stock Creek Bapt. Ch., Knoxville, Tenn., 1984—. Mem. Sevier County Bapt. Assn. (asst. ch. tng. dir., asst. moderator 1982-83, moderator 1983-84), Chilhowee Bapt. Assn. (mem. Bapt. student union com. 1986—), Oxford Soc. Scholars (bd. govs., Grail award 1986). Republican. Avocations: flying, guitar, banjo, antiques. Home: 2425 Stock Creek Rd Knoxville TN 37920 Office: Stock Creek Bapt Ch 8106 Martin Mill Pike Knoxville TN 37920

JEWETT, ROBERT, biblical studies educator; b. Lawrence, Mass., Dec. 31, 1933; s. Walter Leroy and Elizabeth (Bailey) J.; m. Janet Miller, June 11, 1956; 1 child, Ellen Elizabeth. BA, Neb. Wesleyan, 1955; BD, U. Chgo., Chgo. Theol. Sem., 1958; ThD, U. Tübingen, Fed. Republic Germany, 1966; DD (hon.), Morningside Coll., 1985, Kalamazoo Coll., 1989. Ordained to ministry United Meth. Ch. as deacon. Min. Meth. Chs., Dakota City, Homer, Nebr., 1964-66; prof. religious studies Morningside Coll., Sioux City, Iowa, 1965-80; Harry R. Kendall prof. New Testament Garrett Evan. Theol. Sem., Chgo., 1980—; bd. higher edn. Nebr. Conf., 1975-79; trustee Morningside Coll., 1973-75, Garrett-Evang. Theol. Sem., Evanston, Ill., 1986-88. Author: Paul's Anthropological Terms, 1971, The Captain America Complex, 1973, 84, The American Monomyth, 1977, 88, A Chronology of Paul's Life, 1979, Jesus Against the Rapture, 1979, Letter to Pilgrims: A Commentary on The Epistle to the Hebrews, 1981, Christian Tolerance, 1982, Thessalonian Correspondence, 1986. Recipient Melcher Book award Unitarian-Universalist Assn., 1974. Mem. Soc. Bibl. Lit. (chair Pauline Epsitles 1974-81, chair social scis. and new testament interpretation sect. 1982-84, chair Pauline theology group 1985-89), Semeia (editorial bd. 1980-85), Am. Acad. Religion, Midwest Soc. Bibl. Lit. (pres. 1988-89). Home: 729 Emerson St Evanston IL 60201 Office: Garrett-Evang Theol Sem 2121 Sheridan Rd Evanston IL 60201

JIPSON, EUGENE EDWARD, minister; b. Lincoln, Maine, Mar. 29, 1955; s. Edward Harrison and Francena Gladys (Harvey) J.; m. Katherine Marie Welch, May 30, 1981; 1 child, Jeffrey Allen Edward. Student, Husson Coll., 1973-75; BA in Religion, Ea. Nazarene Coll., Quincy, Mass., 1978; MDiv, Nazarene Theol. Seminary, Kansas City, Mo., 1984. Ordained to ministry Ch. of the Nazarene, 1989. Pastor Ch. of the Nazarene, Lacona, Iowa, 1984-86, Boone, Iowa, 1988—; robot operator Constrn. Products, Inc., Des Moines, 1986—. Home: 417 State St Boone IA 50036 Office: 1427 Story St Boone IA 50036

JOB, REUBEN PHILIP, bishop; b. Jamestown, N.D., Feb. 7, 1928; s. Philip and Emma (Schock) J.; m. Beverly Nadine Eilerbeck, Aug. 20. 1953; children: Deborah, Ann, Philip, David., A.B., Westmar Coll., 1954, D.D., 1975, B.D. Evang. Theol Sem., Naperville, Ill., 1957; DSc (hon.), Dakota Wesleyan U., Asbury Theol. Sem., U. Dubuque Theol. Sch. Ordained to ministry Meth. Ch., 1957; pastor chs. Tuttle, N.D., 1957-60, Minot, N.D., 1960-61,. Fargo, N.D., 1962-65, Calvary Ch., Fargo, 1962-65; chaplain USAF, France, 1961-62;, elected asst. sec. evang. United Brethren Bd. Evangelism, Dayton, Ohio, 1965-67; asst. gen. sec. Bd. Evangelism, United Meth. Ch., Nashville, 1967-74; elected assoc. gen. sec. div. evangelism, worship and stewardship, Bd. Discipleship, Nashville, 1974-84; bishop, Des Moines, 1984—; tchr. young adult Sunday sch. class. Editor, compiler: A Guide to Prayer for Ministers and Other Servants, A Guide to Prayer for All God's People; co-author student and tchrs. books in Living Bible Series, 1974. Office: United Meth Ch 1019 Chestnut St Des Moines IA 50309

JOBE, ROBERT WELTY, minister; b. Latrobe, Pa., Jan. 23, 1951; s. Frank Edward and LaVerne K. (Klingensmith) J. BA in Elem. Edn., Alderson-Broaddus Coll., 1973; MDiv, So. Bapt. Sem., Louisville, Ky., 1976; MRE, So. Bapt. Sem., 1979; MSW, U. Louisville, 1980; postgrad., Pitts. Presbyn. Sem., 1986, 90—. Ordained to ministry United Ch. of Christ, 1980; cert. practitioner neuro-linguistic programming. Asst. pastor Christ Evang. and Ref. United Ch. of Christ, Louisville, 1979-80; pastor First Trinity United Ch. of Christ, Youngwood, Pa., 1981-91, Grace United Ch. of Christ, Jeannette, Pa., 1991—; Registrar Westmoreland Assn. church and ministry com., Greensburg, Pa., 1985-90; Del. to Gen. Synod Penn West Conf. United Ch. of Christ, Ft. Worth, 1989, Norfolk, Va., 1991. Mem. Profl. Assn. Clergy (bd. dirs. 1986-89), Lions (pres. 1990-91). Democrat. Home: 119 N Second St Jeannette PA 15644-3399 Office: Grace United Ch of Christ 119 N Second St Jeannette PA 15644-3399

JOB OF HARTFORD, BISHOP **See OSACKY, JOHN**

JODOCK, DARRELL HARLAND, minister, religion educator; b. Northwood, N.D., Aug. 15, 1941; s. Harry N. and Grace H. (Hansen) J.; m. Janice Marie Swanson, July 8, 1972; children: Erik Thomas, Aren Kristofer. BA summa cum laude, St. Olaf Coll., 1962; BD with honors, Luther Theol. Sem., 1966; postgrad., Union Theol. Sem., N.Y.C., 1966-67; Phd, Yale U., 1969. Ordained to ministry Am. Luth. Ch., 1973, Luth. Ch. in Am., 1978. Instr. Luther Theol. Sem., St. Paul, 1969-70, asst. prof., 1970-73, 75-78; asst. pastor Grace Luth. Ch., Washington, 1973-75; prof., head dept. religion Muhlenberg Coll., Allentown, Pa., 1978—, Class of 1932 rsch. prof., 1989; mem., chmn. various coms. N.E. Pa. Synod Evang. Luth. Ch. in Am., 1979—; mem. adv. bd. Berman Ctr. for Jewish Studies, 1985—; founder, chmn. bd. Inst. for Jewish-Christian Understanding, 1988—. Author: The Church's Bible: Its Contemporary Authority, 1989; translator: Luther and the Peasant's War (Hubert Kirchner), 1972; contbr. articles to profl. jours. Del. Dem. Farm Labor Party, Rochester, Minn., 1972, St. Paul, 1976. Recipient Paul C. Empie Meml. award Muhlenberg Coll., 1987; Danforth Found. fellow 1962-69, Inst. for Ecumenical and Cultural Rsch. fellow, 1982-83. Mem. Am. Acad. Religion (pres. 19th century theology group 1981-86), Am. Soc. Ch. History, Soc. for Values in Higher Edn., Phi Beta Kappa, Omicron Delta Kappa (campus leadership 1985—). Office: Muhlenberg Coll Dept Religion Allentown PA 18104

JOFFE, HAL, ecumenical agency administrator. Pres. Calgary (Alta.) Jewish Community Coun., Can. Office: Calgary Jewish Community, Coun/ 1607 90th Ave SW, Calgary, AB Canada T2V 4V7

JOFFE, WILLIAM IRVING, priest, educator; b. Oak Park, Ill., Mar. 24, 1931; s. Irving B. and Minna (Coia) J. A.B., Loras Coll., 1953; M.A., Mt. St.

Bernard Sem., 1957; M.A. in Journalism, Marquette U., 1959; D.Ministry, St. Mary U., Balt., 1983. Ordained priest Roman Catholic Ch., 1957; tchr. high sch. Aurora, Sterling and Woodstock, Ill., 1960-82; asst. editor diocesan newspaper The Observer, Rockford, Ill., 1959-62; dir. vocations Diocese of Rockford, 1959-61; pastor St. Joseph Ch., Harvard, Ill., 1983; chmn. bd. Cath. edn. McHenry County; owner, mgr. horse farm. Mem. Nat. Psychology Assn., Nat. Priests Senate, Am. Quarter Horse Assn. Author: The Triple Way, 1956; contbr. articles to profl. jours. Office: St Joseph Ch 206 E Front St Harvard IL 60033

JOHANSSON, ROBERT JOHN, minister; b. Queens, N.Y., Jan. 4, 1936; s. Paul Edward and Catherine Elizabeth (Williams) J.; m. Janice Marie Hicks, Aug. 5, 1961; children: Brian Robert, Carolyn, Steven John. BA, Roberts Wesleyan Coll., N. Chili, N.Y., 1962; MDiv, NYU, 1984. Ordained to ministry Assemblies of God, 1959. Pastor Glad Tidings Ch., 1956-61; asst. pastor Bethel Assembly of God, Rochester, N.Y., 1961-66; pastor Evangel Ch., Long Island City, N.Y., 1966—; v.p. N.Y. Sch. Urban Ministry, L.I.C., 1984—; bd. dirs. Here's Life New York, N.Y.C., 1985-91; trustee N.Y. Ctr. for Urban Ministry, Bklyn., 1991—. Named Alumni of the Yr., Elim Fellowship, 1990.

JOHN, K. K. (JOHN KURUVILLA KAIYALETHE), minister; b. Erath, India, May 24, 1936; came to U.S., 1962; s. Kuruvilla Korula and Rachel (Yohannan) K.; m. Tamara Fogel, Sept. 3, 1963; children: Nava, David, Michal. Diploma in Theology, Zion Bible Coll. and Sem., Mulakuzha, India, 1957; ThD, Kingsway Coll. and Sem., 1986; DD (hon.), Jameson Christian Coll. Nat. dir. Christian edn. and youth Ch. of God, India, 1957-61; sr. pastor Ch. of God, Bombay, 1960-61; free-lance journalist Jerusalem, 1961-62; pres. Internat. Student Fellowship, 1966-71; founder-dir., dir. Assemblies of God Campus Ministries, 1967-74, min., conf. speaker, ch. growth cons., 1974—; evangelist, conf. speaker; nat. dir. edn. and Sunday schs. India; v.p. U. Minn. Council Religious Advisors. Mem. U.S. presdl. adv. com. Commn. Campus Unrest; mem. Parent Adv. Commn., Mpls. Pub. Schs., 1986—; active pioneered adult edn., active participant in internfaith movements. Avocations: photography, travel. *The Bible reveals God thru every day life and experiences of the Hebrews. The loving God is the caring parent of us all. We must keep on searching, seeking, and learning thru our own personal relationship with God and all humans - regardless of race, color, nationality or even religion - we are one as humans in this planet - our destiny is one - for we are intertwined.*

JOHN PAUL II, HIS HOLINESS POPE (KAROL JOZEF WOJTYLA), bishop of Rome; b. Wadowice, Poland, May 18, 1920; s. Karol and Emilia (Kaczorowska) W. Student, Jagiellonian U., Krakow, 1937-39; studied in underground sem., Krakow, 1942-46; D. ethics, Pontifical Angelicum U., Rome, 1948; ThD, Jagiellonian U., Cracow, Poland, 1949; Dr. (hon.), J. Guttenberg U., Mainz, Fed. Republic Germany, 1977. Ordained priest Roman Cath. Ch., 1946; pastor St. Florian's Parish, Krakow, 1948; student chaplain Jagiellonian U., 1949; prof. moral theology Krakow, 1953; prof. ethics, then chmn. dept. philosophy Cath. U. of Lublin, 1954-58, dir. ethics inst., 1956-58; aux. bishop of Krakow, 1958, archbishop of Krakow, 1964-78; great chancellor Pontifical Theol. Faculty, Krakow; created cardinal by Pope Paul VI, 1967; elected Pope, Oct. 16, 1978, installed, Oct. 22, 1978. Author of: books, poetry, plays, including The Goldsmith's Shop; Play Easter Vigil and Other Poems, 1979, Love and Responsibility, 1960, The Acting Person, 1969, Foundations of Renewal, 1972, Sign of Contradiction, 1976; encyclicals: The Redeemer of Man, 1979, On Human Work, 1981, The Apostles of the Slavs, 1985, The Lord, the Giver of Life, 1986, Redemptoris Mater, 1987, Sollicitudo Rei Socialis, 1987, Dives in Misericordia, 1989; contbr. articles on philosophy, ethics and theology to various jours. Mem. Polish Acad. Scis. Address: Palazzo Apostolico, Vatican City Vatican City

JOHNS, DONALD ARVID, Bible translator; b. Springfield, Mo., Feb. 19, 1953; s. Donald F. and Dorothy (Lindgren) J.; m. Kathleen Joy Fenton, May 26, 1972; children: Pamela, Donald, David, Ginger, Kelly. BA in Bible, Cen. Bible Coll., 1974; MA in Bibl. Studies New Testament, Trinity Evang. Divinity Sch., 1977; PhD in Bibl. Langs. and Lit., St. Louis U., 1983. Asst. prof. Bible Cen. Bible Coll., Springfield, Mo., 1982-85; assoc. prof. in Bibl. Studies Assemblies of God. Theol. Sem., Springfield, 1985-90; translator Am. Bible Soc., N.Y.C., 1990—; treas. cen. states region Soc. Bibl. Lit., 1989—; convenor Hebrew Bible Colleagues of Springfield Area, 1986-88. Contbr. to Dictionary of Pentecostal and Charismatic Movements, 1988; translator: (with others) Contemporary English Version. Mem. Soc. Bibl. Lit., Inst. for Bibl. Rsch., Evang. Theol. Soc., Nat. Assn. Profs. of Hebrew. Mem. Assemblies of God. Home and Office: 2107 E Camorene Springfield MO 65803

JOHNSON, ALICE ELAINE, retired academic administrator; b. Janesville, Wis., Oct. 9, 1929; d. Floyd C. and Alma M. (Walthers) Chester; m. Richard C. Johnson, Sept. 25, 1948 (div. 1974); children: Randall S., Nile C., Linnea E. BA, U. Colo., 1968. Pres., administrator Pikes Peak Inst. Med. Tech., Colorado Springs, Colo., 1968-88; mem. adv. com. to Colo. Commn. on Higher Edn., 1979-80, State Adv. Council on Pvt. Occupational Schs., Denver, 1978-86; mem. tech. adv. com. State Health Occupations, 1986-88; bd. dirs. All Souls Unitarian Ch., Colorado Springs, 1990—, mem. celebration team, 1990-91, pres. bd. trustees, 1991—. Mem. Colo. Pvt. Sch. Assn. (pres. 1981-82, bd. dirs. 1976-88, Outstanding Mem. 1978, 80), Phi Beta Kappa. Democrat. Unitarian. Avocations: writing, travel, reading. *We must review and renew our committment, as a nation, to true freedom of religion, and resist current tendencies to mix church and state.*

JOHNSON, SISTER ANDREA, Hispanic liturgical music specialist; b. Pittsburg, Kans., May 21, 1947; d. Andrew E. And Lillian Katherine (Hansen) J. BA cum laude, Kans. Newman Coll., 1972; M in Mus. Edn., Wichita State U., 1975. Parish minister St. Mark's Ch., Eugene, Oreg., 1966-68; instr. music Holy Savior Sch., Wichita, Kans., 1972, St. Mary's Sch., Derby, Kans., 1972-74, St. Patrick's Sch., Wichita, 1972-74; asst. prof. music St. Mary of the Plains Coll., Dodge City, Kans., 1975-80; parish minister of Spanish, music and youth Blessed Sacrament Ch., Hollywood, Calif., 1981-87, co-dir. Spanish choir, 1981-87; dir. music and liturgy St. John's Coll. Sem., Camarillo, Calif., 1982-86; coordinator Hispanic lituriqal music Archdiocese of L.A., 1987—; dir. Spanish choir St. Philip the Apostle Ch., Pasadena, Calif., 1987—; asst. dir. Maranatha choir (Spanish) St. Emytius Ch., Lynwood, Calif., 1988—; mem., cons. music and liturgy commn. Archdiocese of Los Angeles, 1981—; planner, dir. Archdiocesan Choir for Celebration of Our Lady of Guadalupe, 1982—; workshop conductor in liturgy and Spanish church music, 1982—; coordinator Cantors and Foreign language singers for Papal visit of John Paul II, Los Angeles, 1987. Asst. editor (Spanish songbook) La Familia De Dios Celebra, 1981; editor (Spanish songbook) Cantos for Carisma en Misiones, 1982, Flor and Canto, 1989. Mem. Nat. Assn. Pastoral Musicians, Wichita Choral Soc. (bd. dirs. 1969-75). Avocations: vocal and choral music, hiking. Home: 2911 Idell St Los Angeles CA 90065 Office: Office for Worship 1530 W 9th St Los Angeles CA 90015

JOHNSON, ARNOLD GORDON, clergyman; b. Albert Lea, Minn., June 30, 1936; s. Arnold Clifford and Georgia (Godtland) B.; m. Mary Lou Zemke, Mar. 26, 1960; children: Dawn Marie, Eric Blair, Tanya Leigh, Mija Leah. BA, St. Olaf U., Northfield, Minn., 1958; MDiv., Luther Sem., St. Paul, 1968; MA, Liberty U., 1990. Ordained to ministry, Luth. Ch. Commd. 2d lt. USAF, 1958, pilot, 1959-65, pilot Minn. Air N.G., 1965-68, chaplain, 1968, advanced through grades to col., 1981, ret., 1984; parish evangelist The Am. Luth. Ch., Seattle, 1978—; stewardship counselor Evang. Luth. Ch., Spokane, 1984—; interim pastor Luth. Ch. of The Master, Coeur d' Alene, Idaho, 1991—. Author: The Chaplain's Role as a Transcendant Symbol in the Military, 1974. Fundraiser United Way, Lubbock, Tex., 1979. Mem. Red River Valley Fighter Pilots Assn., Rotary, Lions (v.p. 1985—), Daedalians (v.p. 1985-86). Avocations: flying, golf, skiing, fishing. Home: S 1815 Koren Rd Spokane WA 99212-3264 Office: Luth Ch of the Master 4800 Ramsey Rd Coeur d'Alene ID 84814

JOHNSON, ARNOLD HJALMER, minister; b. Simrishamn, Sweden, Feb. 29, 1920; came to U.S., 1920; s. John Anton and Anna (Trozell) J.; m. Gertrude Warner (dec.); m. Doris Johnson, June 30, 1972; children: Betty Johnson Tomlinson, Ruth Johnson Coburn, Arnold Hjalmer Jr. AA, North Park Sem., 1941; grad., North Cark Sem., 1945; BA, East Tenn. State U., 1964. Ordained to ministry Evang. Covenant Ch. Am., 1947. Missionary Covenant Mountain Mission, Jonesville, Va., 1945-54; tchr. Hancock County Pub. Schs., Sneedville, Tenn., 1962-72; pres., Ministrial Assn., South Chgo. Area, 1974-77; leader, enabling disabled project, Evang. Covenant Ch., Chgo., 1986-89. Pastor, exec. sec. Jonesville C. of C., 1954-56. Home: 8134 Dinsmore St Brooksville FL 34613

JOHNSON, AUDREY JACKSON, minister; b. New Orleans, Oct. 7, 1936; d. Solomon Neal Jackson Sr. and Dorothy (Hudson) Jones; m. Felix Joseph Johnson Jr., Sept. 7, 1957; children: Felix Joseph III, Troy Tyrone, David Joel. BA in Psychology, So. U., 1959; BSN, Dillard U., 1963; MRE, New Orleans Bapt. Sem., 1976. Ordained to ministry Bapt. Ch.; cert. vocat. edn., clin. pastoral edn., curriculum devel. Community ch. educator Sunday sch. New Orleans Bapt. Sem., 1974-76; dir. youth dept. Gloryland Mt. Gillion Bapt. Ch., New Orleans, 1975-78; dir. Christian edn. Beacon Lights Bapt. Ch., New Orleans, 1982-84; asst. to pastor Christian Unity Bapt. Ch., New Orleans, 1989—; nurse educator Children's Hosp. Pediatric AIDS Program, New Orleans 1989—; minister edn. Christian Unity, New Orleans, 1989—, women ministry, 1989; past nursing instr.; mem. ommunity workshops, music, edn. work. Contbr. articles to profl. jours. Mem. NAACP, Nat. Coun. Negro Women, Assoc. of Clin. Pastoral Edn., Nurses Assn., Women for Women with AIDS, Nat. Urban Leage. Office: Christian Unity Bapt Ch 1700 Conti St New Orleans LA 70112-3606 *All of the people in a community do not belong to the neighborhood church but the neighborhood church belongs to all of the people of that community. Therefore, the church's agenda should reflect and embrace the needs of that community.*

JOHNSON, BENJAMIN EDGAR, clergyman; b. Sterling, Colo., Oct. 30, 1921; s. A. Judson and Elsie Lydia (Marks) J.; m. Kathryn May Pierret, Feb. 8, 1944; children: Lois Louise Johnson Van Hooser, Janet Elizabeth Johnson Bonstrom. B.A., Pasadena Coll., 1943, D.D., 1965. Ordained to ministry Ch. of Nazarene, 1943; pastor Los Angeles, 1943-46, Whittier, Calif., 1946-58, Santa Ana, Calif., 1958-62, Upland, Calif., 1962-64; dist. sec. Ch. of Nazarene, 1950-64; gen. sec. Ch. of Nazarene, Kansas City, Mo., 1964-90; dir. Nazarene Pub. House, Central Am. Holding Corp., N.J. Hispanic Nazarene Corp. Editor: Nazarene Manual, 1964, 68, 72, 76, 80, 85, 89, Quadrennial Denominational Jour., 1964, 68, 72, 76, 80, 85, 89. Trustee Pasadena Coll. Mem. Am. Soc. Assn. Execs., Mid Am. Soc. Assn. Execs. (pres.), Assn. Statisticians Am. Religious Bodies (pres.), Religious Conv. Mgrs. Assn. (pres.), A.I.M., Nat. Assn. Evangelicals (pres. 1990—), Am. Bible Soc. (bd. dirs. 1990), World Relief Corp. (bd. dirs. 1990), Christian Holiness Assn.

JOHNSON, CAROL ANN, book editor; b. Seattle, Aug. 19, 1941; d. Jack Rutherford and Marian Frances (Cole) Schisler; m. Gary L. Johnson, Sept. 8, 1962; children: Deborah Carol Johnson Erickson, Barbara Ann Johnson Lilland. Grad., Bethany Coll. of Missions, Mpls., 1962. Typesetter Bethany Printing Div., Mpls., 1960-69; librarian Bethany Coll. of Missions, Mpls., 1969-79; mng. editor Bethany House Pubs., Mpls., 1980-84, editorial dir., 1984—. Avocations: sewing, tennis, bicycling, cooking. Office: Bethany House Pubs 6820 Auto Club Rd Minneapolis MN 55438

JOHNSON, CHARLES BIRKERY, priest; b. Manchester, Conn., Nov. 8, 1932; s. Charles Hjalmar and Rosalie (Riordan) J. BA, Cath. U. Am., 1954, MLS, 1965; MA, Trinity Coll., Hartford, Conn., 1972. Ordained priest Roman Cath. Ch., 1960. Instr. St. Thomas Sem., Bloomfield, Conn., 1963-75, dean of studies, 1975-80, rector, 1980-86; rector, pastor Cathedral of St. Joseph, Hartford, 1986-91; vicar for priests Archdiocese of Hartford, 1991—. Vice chair, bd. dirs. St. Francis Hosp. and Med. Ctr., Hartford, 1980—. Address: Office of Vicar for Priests 467 Bloomfield Ave Bloomfield CT 06002

JOHNSON, CHARLES CLINTON, minister; b. Rome, Ga., Oct. 3, 1946; s. Albert Jesse and Doris Imogene (Gresham) J.; m. Lynn Brown, Aug. 16, 1966; children: Sara Lynn, Rachel Ann. AS, Kennesaw Jr. Coll., 1972; BBA in Mgmt., Ga. State U., 1974; MDiv in Religious Edn., Southeastern Sem., 1980, D in Ministry, 1989. Ordained to ministry So. Bapt. Conv., 1978. Assoc. pastor Durham (N.C.) Meml. Bapt. Ch., 1977-80; assoc. pastor, min. edn. adminstrn. Temple Bapt. Ch., Raleigh, N.C., 1980—; guest dir. metro clinics So. Bapt. Conv., 1986-91; conf. leader, Ridgecrest, N.C., 1991. Contbr. articles to religious jours. Bd. dirs. Family Svcs. Wake County, Raleigh, 1989. Sgt. USAF, 1966-69. Mem. Raleigh Bapt. Assn. (assoc. assist team 1980—). Home: 7325 Shellburne Dr Raleigh NC 27612 Office: Temple Bapt Ch 1417 Clifton St Raleigh NC 27604

JOHNSON, CHARLES EMIL, minister; b. Denver, Apr. 28, 1959; s. Robert Edward and Marylee (Harbacheck) J.; m. Evelyn Eileen Brown, June 29, 1985; 1 child, Michael. BS, Colo. Sch. of Mines, 1981; MA, St. Thomas Seminary, Denver, 1986; Advanced Cert. in Youth Ministry, St. Thomas Univ., Houston. Youth minister St. Joan of Arc Cath. Ch., Arvada, Colo., 1977-85; dir. religious edn. St. Edwards Cath. Community, Spring, Tex., 1985-87; youth minister St. Thomas Aquinas Parish, Sugarland, Tex., 1987-88; dir. youth ministry St. Ambrose Cath. Community, Houston, 1988—; advisor Parish Svcs. Adv. Bd., Denver, 1983-85; coord. San Jancito Deanery Youth Ministers, Spring, 1985-87. Mem. Nat. Fedn. Cath. Youth Ministry, Nat. Cath. Ednl. Assn., Assn. Dirs. of Religious Edn. Roman Catholic. Office: St Ambrose Cath Community 4213 Mangum Rd Houston TX 77092

JOHNSON, CHARLES REGINALD, clergyman; b. Huntsville, Tex., May 20, 1965; s. Homer Harry Jr. and Lois Jean (McMahon) Hill. BA in Polit. Sci., U. So. Calif., 1988; postgrad., Southwestern Bapt. Theol. Sem., Ft. Worth, 1988—. Ordained to ministry Bapt. Ch. 0min. Mt. Zion Missionary Bapt. Ch., L.A., 1985—; med. researcher VA Med. Ctr., L.A., 1984-86; pres. Young Peoples Conv., Calif. State Bapt. Conv., 1986-87; mem. Nat. Bapt. Conv. U.S.A. Named Outstanding Christian Young Man A.C.C. newspaper, 1985; scholar State of Calif., 1985. Mem. SCLC, NAACP, Urban League. Republican. Avocations: football, bowling, reading, basketball. Home: 8904 Mettler St Los Angeles CA 90003

JOHNSON, CHARLIE JAMES, minister; b. Barnesville, Ga., Sept. 24, 1923; s. Emory Moses and Ruth B. (Traylor) J.; m. Mary Ellen Upton, June 7, 1957; children: Marcus Anthony, Michael A. (dec.). Student, Ft. Valley (Ga.) State Coll., 1940-42; BA, Morehouse Coll., 1956; BD, Morehouse Sch. Religion, 1960, MDiv, 1973; ThD summa cum laude, Trinity Theol. Sem., Newburgh, Ind., 1980, D Ministry summa cum laude, 1982. Ordained to ministry Bapt. Ch., 1949; joined United Presbyn. Ch. in U.S.A., 1961. Pastor New Hope Bapt. Ch., Dalton, Ga., 1951-61, Bethesda Presbyn. Ch., Johnson City, Tenn., St. James Ch., Kingsport, Tenn., Tabernacle Ch., Greeneville, Tenn., 1951-61, 1st United Presbyn. Ch., Athens, Tenn., St. Paul United Presbyn. Ch., Sweetwater, Tenn., 1966-82; ret. Presbytery of East Tenn., 1983; adj. prof. Cedine Bible Inst., Spring City, Tenn., 1983-85; treas. Athens Ministerial Assn., 1975-76. Weekly columnist Daily Post-Athenian, 1967—, Monroe County Adv., 1989—. Mem., counselor CONTACT McMinn-Meigs-Monroe Counties, Tenn., bd. dirs., 1989-90. Fellow Trinity Theol. Sem., 1986. Mem. Kiwanis (bd. dirs. Sweetwater club 1989-90). Home and Office: Rte 3 Box 216 Sweetwater TN 37874 *I have tried to do my best, where I am, with what was available to me. Nobody can do more than that.*

JOHNSON, CLARENCE RAY, minister; b. Port Arthur, Tex., Jan. 31, 1943; s. Ervin Ray and Mina Frances (Cox) J.; m. Betty Olene Mears, Nov. 22, 1962; children: Gregory Clarence, Garemy Kevin, Darren Kendall, Sherry Lynn. Ordained to ministry Ch. of Christ, 1962. Min. Hwy. 29 Ch. of Christ, Liberty Hill, Tex., 1962-63, Jonestown Ch. of Christ, Leander, Tex., 1963-70, Springhill (La.) Ch. of Christ, 1970-75, La Porte (tex.) Ch. of Christ, 1975-84, Exton (Pa.) Ch. of Christ, 1984-91, Shiloh Ch. of Christ, Mexia, Tex., 1991—; tchr., counselor Sabinal (Tex.) Bible Camp, 1978-80. Author: (with others) Is It Lawful, 1989, series of tracts, 1983-91; news editor Gospel Guardian, 1971-73; contbr. articles to profl. jours. Trustee Liberty Hill Ind. Sch. Dist., 1968-70; panel mem. life issues seminar La. State U. Med. Coll., Shreveport, 1973. Republican. Home: 819 E Commerce Mexia TX 76667 Office: Shiloh Ch of Christ Hwy 39 S Mexia TX 76667 *Your child's first concepts of his heavenly Father are almost certain to be based on what he has seen, heard, and experienced at the hand of his physical father. May God help us strike that delicate balance between strictness and mercy, and provide a loving, secure atmosphere where our children may properly grow "in wisdom and stature, and in favor with God and men."*

JOHNSON, DALE ARTHUR, religion educator; b. Duluth, Minn., Mar. 13, 1936; s. Arthur B. and Luella D. Johnson; m. Norma Freeman, Sept. 23, 1958; children: Eric, Kristin, Stephanie. BA, Colgate U., 1957, Oxford U., Eng., 1959; MA, Oxford U., Eng., 1963; MDiv, Luth. Sch. Theology, Chgo., 1962; ThD, Union Theol. Sem., N.Y.C., 1967. Asst. prof. religion Luther Coll., Decorah, Iowa, 1965-69; prof. ch. history Vanderbilt U. Div. Sch., Nashville, 1969—. Editor: Women in English Religion, 1700-1925, 1983; co-editor: Moral Issues and Christian Response, 4th edit., 1988; contbr. articles to profl. jours. Mem. Am. Soc. Ch. History, Am. Acad. Religion, Eccles. History Soc., Conf. Brit. Studies. Office: Vanderbilt U Div Sch Div Sch Nashville TN 37240

JOHNSON, DALE BAKER, minister; b. Sacramento, Calif., Nov. 16, 1935; s. George Randolf and Mildred Irene (Baker) J.; m. Ann Justice, Dec. 16, 1961; 1 child, Jeffrey Jones. BA, Sacramento State U., 1958; BD, Pacific Luth. Theol. Sem., 1962. Ordained to ministry Luth. Ch. Am., 1962. Pastor various congregations, Calif., Utah and Hawaii, 1962-86, Mt. Calvary Luth. Ch., Cypress, Calif., 1986—; bd. dirs. Pacificia Synod, Evang. Luth. Ch. Am., Yorba Linda, Calif., 1988—, mem. cabinet Orange Conf., 1988—. Head chaplain Buena Park (Calif.) Police Dept., 1985—. Mem. Internat. Conf. Police Chaplains, Rotary (pres. Cypress chpt. 1990—). Office: Mt Calvary Luth Ch 7251 Garden Grove Blvd Bldg 11 Garden Grove CA 92641

JOHNSON, DAVID ELLIOT, bishop; b. Newark, Apr. 17, 1933; s. Theodore Eames and Frances Lysett (Wetmore) J.; m. Joyce Joanne Evans, Feb. 24, 1958; children: Stephanie Johnson Duensing, Elizabeth Johnson, Scott Johnson. BA, Trinity Coll., 1955; MDiv, Va. Theol. Coll., 1961; postgrad., Coll. Preachers, 1970, 74, 78, 81, 83; DD, Va. Theol. Sem., 1986, Trinity Coll., 1986. Ordained to ministry Episcopal ch., 1962. Rector Ch. Good Shepherd, Little Rock, Ark., 1961-65; vicar St. Martin's, Fayetteville, Ark., 1965-72; chaplain, instr. humanities U. Ark., 1965-72; rector Calvary Ch., Columbia, Mo., 1972-76, St. Boniface Ch., Sarasota, Fla., 1976-85; bishop coadjutor Diocese of Mass., Boston, 1985-86, bishop, 1986—; chair Dovemass. Bd. trustees Kent (Conn.) Sch., Berkeley Div. Sch. Yale U. Capt. USAF, 1955-58. Office: Episcopal Diocese Mass 138 Tremont St Boston MA 02111

JOHNSON, DAVID L., religion educator; b. Mpls., Jan. 25, 1941; s. F. Maurice and Elizabeth A. (Martinson) J.; m. Rebecca Ann Johnson, Aug. 17, 1963; 1 child, Nicole C. AB, Augsburg Coll., 1966; PhD, U. Iowa, 1972. Asst/ !Prof. Ind. Sate U., Terre Haute, 1970-75, assoc. prof., 1975-83, prof., 1983—. Author: Religious Roots of Indian Nationalism, 1974, Technology Change and Society, 1978, 2d edit., 1983, A Reasoned Look at Asian Religions, 1985. Mem. YMCA, Terre Haute. Mem. Am. Acad. Religion, Phi Kappa Phi. Home: 810 S Center St Terre Haute IN 47807 Office: Ind St U Terre Haute IN 47809

JOHNSON, DON ROBERT, religious organization leader, administrator; b. Salina, Kans., Oct. 8, 1942; s. Ben Henry and Bertha Lucile (Armstrong) J.; m. Judith Mae Skelton, Apr. 12, 1980; children: Jennifer, Monica, Anaise, Rebekah. AA, S.W. Bapt. Coll., 1962; BA, East Tex. Bapt. Coll., 1964; MDiv, Midwestern Theol. Sem., 1968; postgrad., U. Iowa, 1969-70. Ordained to ministry So. Bapt. Conv., 1966, United Meth. Ch., 1970. Pastor various Meth. chs., Iowa, 1968-74, Calvary United Meth. Ch., Waterloo, Iowa, 1974-82; chaplain Stephens Coll., Columbia, Mo., 1982-86; sr. leader N.Y. Soc. for Ethical Culture, N.Y.C., 1986—; dir. Metzger Price Fund, N.Y.C., 1987—; advisor Ctr. for Urban Well-Being, Carmel, Calif., 1988—; speaker. Contbr. articles to jours. Chmn. multi-cultural com. Mid Mo. Assn. of Colls. and Univs., Columbia, 1984-86; pres. Neighborhood Housing Svcs., Inc., Waterloo, Iowa, 1978-82; chmn. People's Community Health Clinic, Waterloo, 1978-80. Mem. Nat. Leaders Coun., Am. Ethical Union (cert.), Internat. Humanist and Ethical Union. Avocations: walking, reading, music, travel, geography. Office: Ethical Culture Soc 2 W 64 St New York NY 10023 *I believe in the centrality of ethics in human life, the uniqueness of each individual and their right to dignity, the significance of relationships, and the human responsibility to create a better world.*

JOHNSON, DONNA MAE, nun; b. Stockton, Calif., Sept. 11, 1931; d. Ralph Wesley and Elizabeth Louise (Pucci) Johnson. BA, Calif. State U., Fullerton, 1976; MSA, U. Notre Dame, Ind., 1982. Entered Dominican Sisters, Roman Catholic Ch. Tchr. St. Elizabeth High Sch., Oakland, Calif., 1963-65; sch. treas. St. Catherine Mil. Sch., Anaheim, Calif., 1965-75; dir. devel. Immaculate Conception Acad., San Francisco, 1975-86; treas. gen. Dominican Sisters of Mission San Jose, Fremont, Calif., 1986—; bd. dirs. St. Catherines Mil. Sch., 1986—, Dominican Sisters of Mission San Jose Found., 1986—; trustee Religious Trust, San Francisco, 1986-91; treas. Queen of Holy Rosary Coll., Fremont, 1986—. Mem. Conf. Religious Treas. (sec.-treas. 1987-91, co-chair 1991—), Nat. Assn. Treas. of Religious Insts. Avocations: sailing, reading, cooking. Home: PO Box 3908 Fremont CA 94539 Office: Dominican Sisters of Mission San Jose 43326 Mission Blvd Fremont CA 94539

JOHNSON, DOROTHY ALMYRA, pastor; b. Seattle, July 11, 1916; d. Otis Willis and Safrona Almira (McGarvey) Cady; m. Charles James Hancock, Nov. 29, 1939 (div. Aug. 1950); m. Harold F. Johnson, Aug. 5, 1950 (dec. Sept. 1980); children: Sandra Johnson Feldman, Susan Leigh Montoya, Sally Ann Eustice. DD (hon.), Ministry of Salvation, Chula Vista, Calif. Co-founder Christ's Community Ch., Carson, Calif., 1974, pastor, 1980—; mgr. apt. complex, Harbor City, Calif. Mem. Carson-Wilmington Ministerial Assn. Office: Christ's Community Ch 225 W Torrance Blvd Carson CA 90745

JOHNSON, DOUGLAS WAYNE, church organization official, minister; b. nr. Carlyle, Ill., Aug. 21, 1934; s. Noel Douglas and Laura Margaret (Crocker) J.; m. Phyllis Ann Heinzmann, June 8, 1956; children: Kirk Wayne, Heather Renee, Kirsten Joy, Tara Carlynne. Student, So. Ill. U., 1952-53; BA, McKendree Coll., 1956; STB, Boston U., 1959, MA, 1963; PhD, Northwestern U., 1968. Ordained to ministry as elder United Meth. Ch., 1959. Pastor Pullman Meth. Ch., Chgo., 1960-64; dir. rsch. No. Ill. conf. United Meth. Ch., Chgo., 1964-66; assoc. for planning and rsch. Nat. Coun. Chs. in Christ in the USA, N.Y.C., 1968-75; exec. dir. Inst. Ch. Devel., 1975-85; dir. rsch. Gen. Bd. Global Ministries United Meth. Ch., N.Y.C., 1985—; mem. faculty Western Conn. State Coll., Danbury, 1969-73; mem. rsch. adv. com. United Meth. Ch. Author: Managing Change in the Church, 1974; (with George Cornell) Punctured Preconceptions, 1972; The Care and Feeding of Volunteers, 1978; (with others) Religion in America, 1978; The Challenge of Single Adult Ministry, 1982, Computer Ethics, 1984, Growing Up Christian in the Twenty-First Century, 1984, The Tithe: Challenge or Legalism, 1984, Lets Be Realistic About Your Church Budget, 1984, Ministry to Young Couples, 1985, Secretary's Guide to Church Office Procedures, 1985, Using Computers in Mission, 1985, Finance in the Church, 1986; (with Alan K. Waltz) Facts and Possibilities, 1988; Vitality Means Church Growth, 1989, Empowering Lay Volunteers, 1991; contbr. articles to ch. periodicals. Teaching fellow Garret Theol. Sem. Northwestern U., 1967-68; recipient Svc. award Nat. Coun. Chs., 1973. Mem. Soc. Sci. Study of Religion, Religious Rsch. Assn., Am. Sociol. Assn. Office: 475 Riverside Dr New York NY 10115

JOHNSON, EDNA RUTH, editor; b. Sturgeon Bay, Wis., Dec. 23, 1918; d. Charles Frederick and Georgina (Knutson) J.; m. Al Larson Johnson, 1955. BA, U. So. Fla., 1971. With The Churchman (now The Human Quest), 1950—; editor The Human Quest (formerly The Churchman), St. Petersburg, Fla., 1986—. Editor Ghe Friendship News (USA-USSR), N.Y.C., 1975-88; editorial bd. The Humanist, Amherst, N.Y., 1980—. Bd. Dirs. ACLU, Nat. Emergency Civil Liberties Com., N.Y.C. Named Fla. Humanist of Yr. Am. Humanist Assn. Fla., 1975. Mem. Am. Soc. Sr. Profls. ad Eckerd Coll. Avocation: ballroom dancing, ballet, painting. Home and Office: 1074 23d Ave N Saint Petersburg FL 33704

JOHNSON, FRANCIS WILLARD, clergyman; b. Haxtun, Colo., Mar. 13, 1920; s. Aaron William and Lettie Victoria (Lindgren) J.; m. Ruth Marian Palm, Sept. 11, 1945; children—Christine Louise Johnson Sleight, Roland

Wayne. B.A., Augustana Coll., 1943; B.D., Augustana Theol. Sem., 1946; M.Div., Luth. Sch. Theology, 1971; D.Min. summa cum laude, 1977. Ordained to ministry Lutheran Ch. Am., 1946. Pastor Bethany Luth. Ch., Laurens, Iowa, 1946-50, Mamrelund Luth. Ch., Stanton, Iowa, 1950-69; sr. pastor St. Mark's Luth. Ch., Washington, Ill., 1969—; sec. Iowa Conf. Stewardship Com., Des Moines, 1951-59, stewardship dir., 1953-58, chmn. commn. on social action, 1956-62; dir. Luth. World Action, Des Moines, 1955-59; dist. supr. Christian Rural Overseas Program, Stanton, Iowa, 1958; exec. bd. Iowa Synod Luth. Ch. Am., Des Moines, 1962-68. Chmn. library bd. Pub. Library, Laurens, Iowa, 1948-50; chmn. bd. trustees Pub. Hosp., Laurens, 1949-50; mem. Montgomery County Farm Bur., Red Oak, Iowa, 1951-69; bd. dirs. Luth. Social Services, Chgo., 1973-76, Luth. Home for Aged, Peoria, Ill., 1978-83, 85—, Sr. Center, Washington, 1982—. Mem. Washington Ministerial Assn. (pres. 1974, 76, 77, 82), Ill. Synod Ministerium (Service award 1981), Ministerium of Luth. Ch. Am., Peoria Dist. Ministerium (dean 1973-83). Republican. Home: 606 Yorkshire Dr Washington IL 61571 Office: St Mark's Luth Ch 101 Burton St Washington IL 61571

JOHNSON, FRANK, bishop. Bishop Ch. of God in Christ, Aurora, Colo. Office: Ch of God in Christ 12231 E Arkansas Pl Aurora CO 80014*

JOHNSON, FRANK ARTHUR, minister; b. Salmon Arm, B.C., Can., Oct. 29, 1938; s. Frank Alba and Ada Florence (Astleford) J.; m. Muriel Yvonne Critchley, June 27, 1960; children: Richard Frank Alfred, Rosalie-Ann Blize. BS in Edn., Atlantic Union Coll., 1970. Ordained to ministry Seventh-day Adventists, 1978. Tchr., prin. Seventh-day Adventist Ch. Schs., various locations, Can., 1960-74; pastor Seventh-day Adventist Ch., Bonavista, Nfld., Can., 1969-73; ship missionary, B.C. Coast Seventh-day Adventist Ch., 1974-75; pastor, evangelist Seventh-day Adventist Ch., B.C., Alta., Can., 1975-84, Edson, Alta., 1982-85, Edmonton, Alta., 1985—; operator, announcer Voice of Adventist Radio, St. John's, Nfld., 1961-63; dir., speaker TV program Profiles of Faith, Revelstoke, B.C., 1980-82; speaker radio program Sounds of Praise, Edson, 1984-85; contract chaplain Edmonton Instn., 1984—. Pres. Clarenbridge br. Nfld. Tchrs. Assn., 1971-74; bd. dirs. Sherwood Park (Alta.) Nursing Home, Coralwood Jr. Acad., Edmonton, 1985—. Mem. Ministerial Assn. Home: 13 Hillcrest Dr, Edmonton, AB Canada T6P 1J1 Office: Seventh-day Adventist Ch, 2018 Brentwood Blvd, Sherwood Park, AB Canada 18A 2A6 *When one looks up, he sees even the silver in the clouds; and in looking up he sees beyond—to the blue of the clear sky beyond—to the warmth of the Sun—and ultimately to his Creator and God. That makes me happy! The happiness is catching because the people around me want to be happy too. God is good! Life is good! Although there are difficulties, problems—I enjoy life! Keep smiling!.*

JOHNSON, GARY ALLEN, minister, pastoral counselor; b. Denver, May 18, 1954; s. Donald Duane and Joan Lou (Reynolds) J.; m. Cynthia Carol Ozman, June 2, 1979; children: Erin Elizabeth, Zachary Allen. B Environ. Design, U. Colo., 1976; MDiv with honors, Denver Sem., 1988. Staff mem. Campus Crusade for Christ, Colo.,Oreg, 1977-84, Student Ministries, Inc., Aurora, Colo., 1984-88; pvt. practice psychotherapy Aurora, 1988-91; chaplain Care Unit Colo., Aurora, 1988-89, dir. outpatient svcs., 1989-90; min. of counseling 1st Presbyn. Ch., Boulder, Colo., 1990—; counselor, cons., Faith Counseling Ministries. Author marriage preparation course materials. Mem. Christian Assn. Psychol. Studies, Am. Assn. for Counseling and Devel. Avocations: fishing, duck hunting, basketball, reading, golf. Home: 529 W Arrowhead St Louisville CO 80027 Office: 1820 15th St Boulder CO 80302

JOHNSON, GARY LEE, minister; b. Troy, Ohio, Feb. 1, 1955; s. Russell Hurbert Johnson and Iona Marie Berry Minx; m. Joyce Larue Jackson, Aug. 8, 1981; children: Jenna, Julie, Garrett. AA, Pensacola Jr. Coll., Fla., 1977; BA, Luther Rice Bible Coll., Jacksonville, Fla., 1981; MRE, Luther Rice Sem., Jacksonville, Fla., 1983; DMin, Internat. Sem., Independence, Mo., 1991. Ordained to ministry, So. Bapt. Conv. , 1981. Youth evangelist Fla. Bapt. Conv., Jacksonville, 1980; youth minister Springfield Bapt. Ch., Jacksonville, 1980-82; asst. pastor First Bapt. Ch., MacClenny, Fla., 1982-84; pastor First Bapt. Ch., Winthrop Harbor, Ill., 1984-88, Vale Bapt. Ch., Bloomington, Ill., 1988—; Sun. sch. leader E. Cen. Ill. Bapt. Assn., Champaign, 1988—, Lake County Bapt. Assn., Waukegan, 1984-88; v.p. Zion Benton Ministerial Assn., 1986-87; chaplain Police and Fire Depts. of Bloomington, Ill., 1989—; growth cons. Bapt. Sun. Sch. Bd., 1990—. Author: Hidden Hurdles in Church Growth, 1991. With USN, 1974-80. Recipient Heroism award, City of Jacksonville, 1979, Bravery award, Mayor Jake Godbold, Jacksonville, 1979. Republican. Home: 5 Yew Ct Bloomington IL 61701 Office: Vale Bapt Ch 1304 Morrissey Dr Bloomington IL 61701 *Church growth is built upon personal relationships. A pastor must motivate his people to make an impact in this world, one soul at a time. This is our mission.*

JOHNSON, GARY LEROY, publisher; b. Mpls., Aug. 19, 1938; s. Maurice Fred and Alta Elizabeth J.; m. Carol Ann Schlisler, Sept. 8, 1962. Diploma, Bethany Coll. of Missions, Mpls., 1959; student, Augsburg Coll., 1960-63. Mgr. Bethany Book Shop, Mpls., 1960-63, Bethany Printing Div., Mpls., 1963-76; pub. Bethany House Pubs., Mpls., 1963—. Writer songbooks: Come Songbook, 1979, Thanks Songbook, 1979, Reminded of His Goodness Songbook, 1981. Avocations: songwriting, photography. Office: Bethany House Pubs 6820 Auto Club Rd Minneapolis MN 55438

JOHNSON, GEORGE WILFRED, minister; b. Portland, Oreg., Oct. 16, 1956; s. Wayne MacLaren and Laura Agnes (Mendum) J.; m. Linda Gail Burris, June 18, 1977; children: Alisha, Melyssa, Christina. BA, Puget Sound Christian Coll., 1978; MA, Pepperdine U., 1985. Ordained to ministry Christian Ch., 1978. Youth min. College Way Christian Ch., Lacey, Wash., 1974-76; youth min. Shoreline Christian Ch., Seattle, 1976-78; sr. min. Cen. Christian Ch., Snohomish, Wash., 1978—; trustee Christian Evangelistic Assn., Seattle, 1988-90, Pleasant Valley Christian Camp, Mineral, Wash., 1988—. Chmn. bd. dirs. Snohomish Community Food Bank; chaplain Everett (Wash.) Gen. and Providence Hosps., 1980-84, Snohomish County Fire Dist. 4, 1985-90, Snohomish City Police Dept., 1985-90. Office: Cen Christian Ch 126 Cedar Ave Snohomish WA 98290 *We are all of us creatures of commitment. What we give ourselves to pursuing is what we become—for better or worse.*

JOHNSON, GORDON GILBERT, religion educator, minister; b. St. Paul, Nov. 19, 1919; s. Gilbert Oliver and Myrtle Isabel (Bjorklund) J.; m. Alta Fern Borden, May 21, 1945; children: Gregg A., Gayle E. Johnson Boyd. Cert., Moody Bible Inst., 1941; AA, Bethel Coll., St. Paul, 1943; student, Harvard U., 1944, 45; BA, U. Minn., 1945; BD, Bethel Theol. Sem., 1946; ThM, Princeton Theol. Sem., 1950; ThD, No. Bapt. Theol. Sem., 1960. Ordained to ministry Bapt. Gen. Conf., 1946. Pastor 1st Bapt. Ch., Milltown, Wis., 1946-48, Bethel Bapt. Ch., Montclaire, N.J., 1948-51, Central Ave. Bapt. Ch., Chgo., 1951-59; v.p., dean, prof. preaching Bethel Theol. Sem., St. Paul, 1959-84; assoc. pastor, intrim sr. pastor College Ave. Bapt. Ch., San Diego, 1984-89; interim dean Bethel Sem. West, San Diego, 1990—; moderator Bapt. Gen. Conf., Chgo., 1957-58, 85-86; mem. gen. coun. Bapt. World Alliance, Washington, 1965-85. Author: My Church; contbr. articles to various jours. With USN, 1944-45. Rsch. scholar Yale U. Div. Sch., 1969. Mem. Acad. Homileticians, Religious Speech Assn. Office: Bethel Sem West 6116 Arosa St San Diego CA 92115 *In a capricious and sometimes explosive world an underlying confidence in the gracious providence of a loving God gives peace and wholeness of life. That makes possible an optimism about life.*

JOHNSON, HAROLD HAZEN, religious organization administrator; b. Flint, Mich., Feb. 7, 1936; s. Ernest Robert and Alta Mae (Gillam) J.; m. Fe. Jeanne Johnson, May 24, 1980; children: Tammi, Todd, Timothy, Tyler; stepchildren: Douglas, Karelle. BA cum laude, Union Sch., 1958; MDiv, Iliff Sch. Theology, 1961; postgrad., St. Paul Sch. Theology, 1986—. Assoc. minister Montclair Meth. Ch., Denver, 1958-61, Cent. Meth. Ch., Pontiac, Mich., 1961-63; minister Davisburg (Mich.) Meth. Ch., 1963-67; assoc. minister First Meth. Ch., Warren, Mich., 1967-68; minister Holly (Mich.) Presbyn. Ch., 1968-73; minister First Presbyn. Ch., Ionia, Mich., 1973-75, Alamogordo, N.Mex., 1975-77; minister Unity in Pontiac, Mich., 1979-84; dir. Mich. Assn. Youth Service Bur., Pontiac, Mich., 1979-80, Parent to Parent Coop. Extension, Pontiac, 1980-82; counselor Oakland County Jail, Pontiac, 1982-84; chairperson pastoral studies and skills Unity Sch. Christianity, Unity Village, Mo., 1984—. Club: Toastmasters (Lees Summit, Mo.) (v.p. 1987). Lodge: Lions (dir. 1987—). Avocations: travel, landscaping, golf. Home: PO Box 1571 Lee's Summit MO 64063 Office: Unity Sch Christianity Unity Village MO 64065

JOHNSON, HAROLD STEPHENS, minister; b. Newport, Ky., Feb. 11, 1928; s. Oren Glessner and Loretta (Stephens) J.; m. Marjorie Ethel Connell, Aug. 17, 1953 (dec. 1976); children: Stephen Walten, Karen Winetta; m. Harriet Elsie Dinsmore, Aug. 8, 1976. Diploma in edn., So. Missionary Coll., Collegedale, Tenn., 1952; BS in Elem. Edn. and Religion, So. Missionary Coll., 1958; BD, Immanuel Bapt. Coll., 1965, MA in Edn., 1969, DD (hon.), 1975. Ordained to ministry Seventh-Day Adventist, 1969; cert. tchr. Ky., Tenn. Pastor, tchr., prin. Seventh-Day Adventist Ch. Schs., Fla., Tenn., Ky., Ga., 1953-60; missionary pastor, tchr. Middle East div. Seventh-Day Adventists, Beirut and Iran, 1960-70; chaplain, tchr., v.p. Laurelbrook Sanitarium and Sch., Dayton, Tenn., 1970-77; missionary South East Africa Union Seventh-Day Adventists, Blantyre, Malawi, 1977-83; assoc. chaplain Meml. Hosp., Manchester, Ky., 1984-85; chaplain Meml. Hosp., Manchester, 1985-90, Walker Meml. Med. Ctr., Avon Park, Fla., 1991—. Editor: SEAU Tidings, 1981-83. Chaplain, maj. CAP USAF Aux. Sgt. USAAF, 1945-51. Mem. Seventh-day Adventist Chaplains Assn., Ky. Chaplains' Assn., Malawi Bible Soc. (life), Maranatha Flights Internat., The Mil. Chaplains' Assn. of the USA (life). Home: 2735 Avocado Rd Avon Park FL 33825 Office: Walker Meml Med Ctr Highway 27 N Avon Park FL 33825 *My greatest desire is to reach out to those who suffer through sickness and the loss of loved ones, and to help them, by faith, in the Lord Jesus Christ, to see that beyond the shadows of this old world of sin there is something far better awaiting them.*

JOHNSON, INA PHAY ROBERTS, lay church worker, educator; b. Homestead, Fla., May 2, 1944; d. Edgar Allen and Ina Maude (Phay) Roberts; m. Allen Byers Johnson, Jr., Aug. 9, 1969; children: Jennifer Phay, Rebecca Grace. BS, Fla. State U., 1966. Cert. elem. and early childhood tchr., Fla. Elder 1st Presbyn. Ch. USA, Homestead, Fla., 1986-90; chmn. task force, eldr Village Presbyn. Ch. USA, Homestead, 1990—; mem. new ch. devel. com. Tropical Fla. Presbytery, Pompano, 1990—; tchr. preschool, elem. and jr. high grades St. John's Episcopal Ch. Sch., Homestead, 1984—. Leader Girl Scouts U.S., Homestead, 1982-90. Democrat. Home: 1885 NW 6th Ave Homestead FL 33030 Office: Village Presbyn Ch-USA 1541 SE 12th Ave Ste 14-15 Homestead FL 33035 *Pray from the depth of your heart and soul to the Lord several times daily. Read the Holy Bible, study commentaries and take classes. This is the preparation for the Lord's call. Accept His call with prayer for it is awesome!.*

JOHNSON, J. M., minister; b. Kanniya Kumari, Tamil Nadu, South India, Feb. 27, 1940; s. Mascilamani and Nesammal J.; m. Thangam, Jan. 22, 1969. Grad. 8th standard, MathiCode, Kanniya Kumari. Ordained to ministry World Wide People's Salvation Prayer Mission. Pastor, pres. World Wid People's Salvation Prayer Mission, Bangalore, India, 1983—. Home: 140 Avalahalli Mysore Rd, Bangalore 560026, India Office: World Wide People's Salvation Prayer Mission, PO Box 2607, Bangalore 560026, India

JOHNSON, JAMES A., bishop. Bishop Pentecostal Assemblies of the World Inc. Office: Pentecostal Assemblies of the World Inc 12643 Conway Downs Dr Saint Louis MO 63141

JOHNSON, JAMES DWIGHT, religious music educator; b. Benson, N.C., May 29, 1932; s. Samuel Dwight and Mildred Polly (Stephenson) J. BA, Furman U., 1954; postgrad., So. Bapt. Theol. Sem., 1954-56, U. Chgo., 1956-59, Sherwood Music Sch., 1964-67. Organist, choirmaster First Bapt. Ch., Coats, N.C., 1955-56; asst. min. Millard Congl. Ch., Chgo., 1956-57, organist, choirmaster, 1957-78; organist, choirmaster Ch. of the Redeemer, Chgo., 1958-67; asst. organist U. Chgo., 1960-62; organist Disciples Div. House, Chgo., 1964-67; organist, choirmaster St. Paul's By-the-Sea, Jacksonville Beach, Fla., 1967-90; dir., chmn. Beaches Fine Arts Series, Jacksonville Beach, 1973—; music dir. Titular Parish Day Sch., Jacksonville Beach, 1967-90; chmn. publicity com. Jacksonville Music Tchrs. Assn., 1968-80. Active Diocese Fla. Music and Liturgy Commn., Jacksonville, Fla., 1967-90; chmn. Jacksonville Coordinating Coun. of the Arts, 1968-70. Mem. Am. Guild Organists (dean, 1969-85), Assn. Anglican Musicians, Am. Coll. Musicians, Jacksonville Symphony Assn. Democrat. Episcopalian. Home and Office: 821 Penman Rd Neptune Beach FL 32266

JOHNSON, BROTHER JAMES G., librarian; b. Philipsburg, Pa., Mar. 5, 1935; s. George Bernard and Ruth Naomi (Askey) J.; widowed; children: Alberta, Eugene, Jerome, Ruth, James, Joan. BS, SUNY, 1980; MLS, St. John Univ., Jamaica, N.Y., 1984. Staff Retreat House Passionist Community, West Springfield, Mass., 1965-72; libr. Passionist Community, Jamaica, 1980—. Mem. Gay Men's Health Crisis, N.Y.C., 1989—, Literacy Prog., Jamaica, 1986—, Children with AIDS, N.Y.C. Harlem Hosp., 1988—, Task Force for AIDS, 1990—. Mem. Cath. Libr. Assn., ALA, Bklyn. Diocese Bros. (sec. 1989—), K.C. Home and Office: Passionist Community 86-45 178th St Jamaica NY 11432

JOHNSON, JAMES WILSON, pastor; b. Benson, N.C., Apr. 11, 1942; s. Roy Allen and Edna Mavoreen (Allen) J.; m. Charlotte Marie Smith, Aug. 15, 1964; children: Donna Marie, Johnnie Allen. BA in History and Edn., Meth. Coll., Fayetteville, N.C., 1964; postgrad., East Carolina U., 1964, Southeastern Bapt. Sem., Wake Forest, N.C., 1964—. Lic. to ministry So. Bapt. Conv., 1964, ordained, 1987. Interim pastor 15 chs., N.C., 1964-86; pastor Albertson (N.C.) Bapt. Ch., 1986—; driver edn. specialist N.C. Div. Motor Vehicles, Raleigh, 1968—; dir. brotherhood Ea. Bapt. Assn., Warsaw, 1987-91, chmn. nominating com., 1988-90, vice moderator, 1989-91, moderator, 1991—, mem. numerous coms., 1968—. Bd. dirs. Duplin County Assn. for Retarded Citizens, 1969—, v.p., 1975-77, pres., 1977-79. Mem. N.C. State Employees Assn. Home and Office: Albertson Bapt Ch 515 W Boney St Wallace NC 28466-1830

JOHNSON, JEFFREY ALLAN, minister; b. Lock Haven, Pa., Jan. 16, 1956; s. William Sherman and Doris Virginia (Frable) J.; m. Debbie Elaine Hurst, Aug. 6, 1988; 1 child, Sarah Elaine. BS, Cin. Bible Coll., 1987. Ordained to ministry Christian Ch., 1987. Minister New Liberty Christian Ch., Lawrenceburg, Ky., 1987-88, Bowersville (Ohio) Ch. of Christ, 1988—. Office: Bowersville Ch of Christ 3138 Maysville St Bowersville OH 45307

JOHNSON, JERALD D., religious organization administrator. Gen. supt. Ch. of the Nazarene, Kansas City. Office: Ch Nazarene 6401 The Paseo Kansas City MO 64131*

JOHNSON, JEROME, minister. Supt. The Evang. covenant Ch. of Can., Prince Albert, Sask. Office: Evang Covn Ch Can, 245 12st St E, Prince Albert, SK Canada S6V 1L9*

JOHNSON, JERRY CARL, minister; b. Tifton, Ga., Mar. 17, 1951; s. Waldemar Carl and Mary Louise (Edmondson) J.; m. Norma Jean Luke, Sept. 22, 1973 (div. Dec. 1979); m. Susan Elaine Padgett, Apr. 28, 1984; children: Kristen Louise, Hannah Grace and Wesley Carl (twins). AA, North Fla. Jr. Coll., 1971; BA, U. So. Fla., 1973; MDiv cum laude, Emory U., 1989. Ordained to ministry United Meth. Ch., 1988. Pastor in charge Lee (Fla.) United Meth. Ch., 1989—; chair communications com. Tallahassee Dist. Coun. Ministries, Fla. Conf., United Meth. Ch., 1990—, mem. conf. coun. on ministries, 1990—, publicity chair Claim the Flame capital funds drive, 1991. Sherman scholar, 1990. Republican. Office: Lee United Meth Ch PO Box 38 Lee FL 32059 *One of the greatest gifts God has given to humankind is the gift of story. Through the mutual sharing of stories we are provided with memories that link us to the past in a meaningful way, and give us hope and a vision for the future.*

JOHNSON, JOHN RANDALL, SR., religious organization administrator; b. Marion, Va., July 26, 1945; s. Marvin Roy and Ida Alice (Roe) J.; m. Margaret Mae Sullivan, Aug. 8, 1965; children: John Jr., Brian, Joanna. BS in Mgmt., Va. Poly. Inst. and State U., 1971; MS in Mgmt., So. Nazarene U., 1984. Sec., treas., Christian edn. dir. Stoneville (N.C.) Internat. Pentecostal Holiness Ch., 1970-75; Sunday Sch. tchr. Bloomfield Dr. Internat. Pentecostal Holiness Ch., Macon, Ga., 1975-77, deacon, 1975-77, assoc. pastor, 1977-78; pastor Warner Robins (Gas.) Internat. Pentecostal Holiness Ch., 1978-79; contr. Internat. Pentecostal Holiness Ch., Oklahoma City, 1979—; adj. prof. Southwestern Coll. Christian Ministries, Bethany, Okla., 1985-90. Mem. Nat. Assn. Evangelicals (mem. at large affiliate Christian Stewardship Assn., 1981—), Nat. Assn. Accts. Republican. Office: Internat Pentecostal Holiness Ch 7300 NW 39th Expwy Bethany OK 73008

JOHNSON, JOHNNIE, bishop. Bishop Ch. of God in Christ, Goose Creek, S.C. Office: Ch of God in Christ 649 Liberty Hall Rd Goose Creek SC 29445*

JOHNSON, JOSEPH LESLIE, retired minister; b. Lakeland, Fla., May 27, 1925; s. Boen Colon and Amy Mae (Darley) J.; m. Mary Hazel Jones, Dec. 23, 1946 (div. 1982); 1 child, Joseph Leslie Jr.; m. Grace Windella Moll, July 10, 1982; 1 child, Josean Lovelle. BA, Stetson U., DeLand, Fla., 1949; ThM, New Orleans Bapt. Theol. Sem., 1956; DDiv, Otay Mesa, L.A., 1976. Ordained to ministry So. Bapt. Conv., 1946. Pastor Eastside Bapt. Ch., Haines City, Fla., 1946-53, Pleasant Grove Bapt. Ch., Brookhaven, Miss., 1954-56, First Bapt. Ch., Land O Lakes, Fla., 1956-60, Forest Hills Bapt. Ch., Tampa, Fla., 1960-66, New Hope Bapt. Ch., Tampa, 1966-67; assoc. pastor Northgate Bapt. Ch., Tampa, 1967; pastor Castle Hts. Bapt. Ch., Tampa, 1969-81, Trinity Bapt. Ch., Tampa, 1985-91; ret.; mem. State Bd. Missions, Fla. Bapt. Conv., Jacksonville, 1980-83. With USNR, 1943-46; PTO. Recipient ARC award, 1952, Appreciation award State Bd. Missions, 1983, Career award Dept. Labor, State of Fla., 1989. Mem. Am. Legion, Lions. Home: 825 Strawberry Ln Brandon FL 33511 *Wisdom is doing the right thing in the right way at the right place at the right time for the right reason with the right motives.*

JOHNSON, KAREN BROWN, minister; b. Worcester, Mass., Nov. 2, 1943; d. Chester Woodbury and Dorothy Antoinette (Bates) Brown; m. Bernard B. Johnson, Aug. 5, 1967 (div. 1978); children: Susan, Sarah, David. BS, Bates Coll., Lewiston, Maine, 1965; MDiv, Yale U., 1980. Ordained to ministry Episcopal Ch. as priest, 1981. Chaplain St. Catherine's Sch., Richmond, Va., 1980-83; asst. rector Ascension Ch., Gaithersburg, Md., 1983-85; rector St. Anne's Ch., Damascus, Md., 1985—; program chmn. Damascus Clergy Assn., 1985—, Washington Episcopal Clergy Assn., 1985-90, pres., 1990—. Mem. Washington Episcopal Clergy Assn. (pres. 1990—). Office: St Anne's Ch 25100 Ridge Rd Damascus MD 20872

JOHNSON, KEITH EDWIN, religious organization director, industrial psychologist; b. Chgo., Feb. 21, 1948; s. Edwin Anderson and Margeret Jeanette (Jennings) J. BA, Judson Coll., 1969; postgrad., Career Acad. Broadcasting, 1970; MA, No. Ill. U., 1971; ThM, MDiv., ThD, Luther Rice U. Dir. admissions Judson Coll., 1968-69; host TV show Sta. WXJT-TV, Aurora, Ill., 1969-70; host radio show Impact, LaGrange, Ill., 1970-71; speaker seminar Nationwide Lifestream Program, 1970-72; exec. dir. Teens for Christ, Jacksonville Beach, Fla., 1971-84; bus. psychologist Johnson & Assoc., Atlantic Beach, Fla., 1986—; cons. tchr. U. North Fla., 1978-80, Fla. Jr. Coll., 1978—; indsl. psychologist, bus. cons. Bray & Singletary, P.A. Author: God's Policeman, 1979, Family Guidance Series, 1978-82, How to Overcome Stress, 1981, Can We Save Our Children, 1982, Knowing Our Temperaments, 1985, God's Plan for Stress Management, 1985, (video series) Knowing Your Temperament, 1985. Probation supr. Jacksonville Beach. Am. Legion grantee, 1976-80, Kiwanis Club grantee, 1979-80. Mem. Internat. Christian Edn. Assn. (advisor), Greater Internat. Teen Challenge Assn. (cons.). Office: 645 Mayport Rd Ste 4E Atlantic Beach FL 32233 *I have found that regardless of our progress in technological advance, we only truly progress as we place our emphasis on the importance of the individual and his faith in God.*

JOHNSON, KENNETH RAY, minister; b. Dunlap, Tenn., Oct. 9, 1941; s. Raymond and Wilma Bessie (Heard) J.; m. Mary Louise Kilgore, July 28, 1961; children: Kimberly Colleen, Brenda Renee, Kristi Louise. Student, U. Chattanooga, So. Bapt. Conv., Ga. Bapt. Conv. Ordained to ministry So. Bapt. Conv., 1975. Evangelist Bapt. Ch., Soddy-Daisy, Tenn., 1970-73; pastor Sale Creek (Tenn.) Bapt. Ch., 1975-78, Gateway Bapt. Ch., Rossville, Ga., 1978-82, Falling Water Bapt. Tabernacle, Hixson, Tenn., 1983-85, Subligna Bapt., Summerville, Ga., 1986—; moderator Chattooga Bapt. Assn., Summerville, 1990—; chaplain Chattooga High Athletics, Summerville, 1987—. Charter leader Fellowship Christian Athletes, Summerville, 1990—; pres. PTO-Soddy Elem., 1984-85; charter rep. Subligna Cub Scouts, Boy Scouts Am., Summerville, 1988—; chaplain Athletic Assn. of Cattooga County, 1987—. Home: Rte 4 PO Box 91 Gore-Subligna Rd Summerville GA 30747 Office: Subligna Baptist Church Rte 4 PO Box 91 Gore-Subligna Rd Summerville GA 30747 *The world needs a more positive attitude about life, and I as a Christian feel that the church and God will provide this if we will allow it to do so.*

JOHNSON, KENT LAUREL, religion educator, clergyman; b. Rockford, Ill., Nov. 18, 1934; s. Earl Alfred and Geneva Marie (Quist) J.; m. Shirley Constance Breen, Aug. 27, 1955; children: Karen Marie, Steven Kent. BA, Luther Coll., 1955; BD, Luther Theol. Sem., 1961; MA, U. Wyo., 1965, EdD, 1970. Ordained to ministry Evang. Luth. Ch. in Am., 1961. Tchr. pub. schs., Hurley, S.D., 1955-56, Barrows, Alaska, 1956-57; tchr. Augustana Acad., Canton, S.D., 1957-60; pastor St. Paul Luth. Ch., Lynwood, Calif., 1964-66, 70-74; asst. prof., dean men Augustana Coll., 1966-70, campus pastor, 1974-76; asst. prof., assoc. prof. pastoral theology and ministry Luther Northwestern Theol. Sem., St. Paul, 1976-85, prof., 1985—, chmn. dept., 1982-86, acting dir. continuing edn., 1986-87. Author: Decisions about Death, 1981, Called To Teach, 1984, Review and Evaluation of the Affirm Confirmation Series, 1986, Paul the Teacher, 1986, Evaluating Education Programs in the Congregation, 1988, Growing with God's Child, Parenting the 20-29 Year-Old, 1988; contbr. numerous articles and revs. to religious jours. Maj., Chaplain Corps, U.S. Army, 1961-64, Korea. Mem. Relgious Edn. Assn., Phi Kappa Phi, Phi Delta Kappa. Office: Luther NW Theol Sem 2481 Como Ave Saint Paul MN 55108

JOHNSON, KENWIN N. (BILL JOHNSON), religious organization administrator. Gen.-treas. Pentecostal Fire-Baptized Holiness Ch., Laurinburg, N.C. Office: Pentecostal Fire-Baptized Holiness Ch PO Box 1528 Laurinburg NC 28352*

JOHNSON, KERMIT DOUGLAS, minister, retired military officer; b. Mpls., Sept. 2, 1928; s. J. Anton Uno and Anna Judith (Goranson) J.; m. Carolyn Marie Johanson, Dec. 22, 1951; children: Karin Joy, Christopher Douglas. BS, U.S. Mil. Acad., 1951; MDiv, Princeton Theol. Sem., 1960; grad., Command Gen. Staff Coll., 1969, U.S. Army War Coll., 1976. Commd. 2d lt. U.S. Army, 1951; infantry co. comdr. U.S. Army, Korea, 1952-53; resigned U.S. Army, 1955, recommd. as chaplain, 1960, advanced through ranks to maj. gen., 1979, served in Vietnam, two tours Federal Republic of Germany; dep. chief of chaplains U.S. Army, Washington, 1978-79, chief of chaplains, 1979-82, ret., 1982; assoc. dir. Ctr. for Def. Info., Washington, 1983-86. Author: Realism and Hope in a Nuclear Age, 1988, chpts. in 5 books on mil. ethics, nuclear issues and just war; contbr. articles to various periodicals. Decorated Bronze Star with oak leaf cluster. Home: 1216 Bishopsgate Way Reston VA 22094 *In this world so full of tragedy, I believe the only cure for an inhuman aloofness from suffering is in our attempt to discern the good news and join with it.*

JOHNSON, LARRY DEAN, religious organization executive, minister; b. Alexandria, Minn., Jan. 4, 1943; s. Olaf M. and Marilynn Elizabeth (Nelson) J. BA, Concordia Coll., 1965; MDiv, Luther Theol. Sem., 1969; ThM, Princeton U., 1970. Ordained to ministry Evang. Luth. Ch. in Am., 1971. Youth evangelist Commn. on Evangelism, Am. Luth. Ch., Mpls., 1968-70; assoc. pastor 1st Luth. Ch., Columbia Heights, Minn., 1971-72; pres. Luth. Youth Encounter, Mpls., 1973—; bd. dirs. Tentmakers, 1978-84, Affiliation Luth. Movements, 1980—, Luth. Bible Inst. Seattle, 1986—, Youth Leadership, 1984—. Author: Institutions and Movements, 1983; editor, contbr. Encounter paper, 1973—. Home: 2901 NE 31st Ave Minneapolis MN 55418 Office: 2500 39th Ave NE Minneapolis MN 55421

JOHNSON, LARRY WILSON, priest, pastoral counselor; b. Raleigh, N.C., Jan. 24, 1938; s. Lewis Marvin and Della (Wilson) J.; m. Sondra Elizabeth Baker, Nov. 29, 1974; children: Elizabeth Anne, John, Robert, Patricia, Larry Jr., James. AA, Campbell U., 1958; AB, U. N.C., 1960; MEd, N.C. State U., 1965. Tchr. indsl. edn. pub. schs. Cary, N.C., 1960-63; asst. state supr. State Bd. Edn., Raleigh, 1963-65; founder, hon. life mem., chief exec. officer Vocat. Indsl. Clubs of Am., Leesburg, Va., 1965-87, ret., 1987; priest Anglican Cath. Ch., 1983—, mem. diocesan ct. Mid-Atlantic states; rector Christ Ch., Warrenton, Va., 1987-90; chief exec. officer Christian Guidance and Counseling Inst., Inc., Leesburg, Va., 1990—; rector St. Paul's Anglican Ch., Leesburg, Va. Founder, chmn. Loudoun County Pub. Nominating Fedn., 1970-71; mem. Loudoun County adv. com. on vocat. edn., Leesburg, Va., 1974; U.S. del. Internat. Skill Olympics Organizing Coun., Madrid, 1973-84; chmn. nat. coordinating coun. for Vocat. Student Orgn., Washington, 1972, 77; chmn. bus. edn. adv. com. Fairfax County Bd. Edn., 1972, mem. adult edn. adv. com., 1972-73. Mem. Am. Soc. Assn. Execs. (cert.), Nat. Assn. for Trade and Indsl. Edn. (founder, bd. dirs. 1973—), Am. Vocat. Assn. (life, policy and planning com., nat. adv. coun. trade and indsl. edn. 1974-87). Home: Scarlet Oak Farm Rte 1 Box 193 Purcellville VA 22132 Office: Christian Guidance and Counseling Inst Inc Rte 1 Box 193 Purcellville VA 22132

JOHNSON, LOVELL, SR., minister; b. Moffat, Ala., May 12, 1925; s. James and Amanda (Frierson) J.; m. Marguerite Jane DeSleet, June 10, 1953; children: Lovell Jr., Muriel Johnson Eckert. BA, Wilberforce U., 1951; BDiv, Payne Theol. Seminary, Wilberforce, Ohio, 1952; postgrad., Drake U., 1955; DD, Shorter Coll., 1968. Assoc. pastor, dir. Christian edn. Bethel African Meth. Episcopal Ch., Detroit, 1953-54; minister Bethel African Meth. Episcopal Ch., Des Moines, 1954-56, St. Paul African Meth. Episcopal Ch., Springfield, Ill., 1956-60, St. Peter African Meth. Episcopal Ch., Mpls., 1960-64, ST. Mark African Meth. Episcopal Ch., Milw., 1964—; pres. 4th Dist. Self-Perpetuating Fund, Milw., 1980—; chmn. Chgo. Com. on Admissions, 1978—, Evangelism Com., Chgo., 1968—; mem. Payne Theol. Seminary Bd., Wilberforce, 1980—; del. African Meth. Episcopal Conf., 1972, 76, 80, 84. Author: Handbook on Evangelism, 1972. Chmn. Milw. City Plan Commn., 1967-88; vice-chmn. Opportunities Industrialization Corp., Milw., 1968—; bd. dirs. 1st Wis. Bank Community Investment Corp., Milw., 1981—, Garfield Found., Milw., 1968—. Sgt. U.S. Army, 1943-46, ATO. Recipient Disting. Svc. award Wilberforce U., 1974, A. Rphillip Randolph award A. Phillip Randolph Assn., Milw., 1984, B'nai B'rith Community award, Milw., 1984, Black Role Model Gallery, Milw. Pub. Lib., 1989. Mem. NAACP, Milw. African Meth. Episcopal Ministerial Assn. (pres. 1975-80, treas.). Home: 2477 N Palmer St Milwaukee WI 53212 Office: St Mark African Meth Episcopal Church 1616 W Atkinson Ave Milwaukee WI 53206

JOHNSON, MARK STEPHEN, minister; b. Kingsport, Tenn., Apr. 4, 1960; s. Howard and Willa Dean (Hood) J.; m. Janell Anne Cook, Dec. 28, 1985; children: Jessica Nicole, Tory Rebecca. BS, E. Tenn. State U., 1982; MDiv, Southwestern Bapt. Theol. Sem., 1987. Ordained to ministry So. Bapt. Conv., 1983. Summer missionary Sullivan Bapt. Assn., Kingsport, Tenn., 1980; minister of music, youth Judson Bapt. Ch., Cayuga, Tex., 1983-84; supply preacher chs. in Tenn., Tex., 1984-87; pastor First Bapt. Ch., Honaker, Va., 1987—; mem. com. on bds. and coms. Bapt. Gen. Assn. Va., Richmond, 1991—, chmn. credentials com., 1991; exec. com. Bapt. Com. of Va., 1990—. Mem. Russell County Youth Svcs. Bd., Lebanon, Va.; del. Tarrant County Dem. Conv., Ft. Worth, 1984; coord. St. Jude Hosp. Bike-a-thon, Honaker, 1990; mem. phys. edn. adv. bd. E. Tenn. State U., 1982. Order Easter Star scholar, 1984. *When the search for financial security makes us compromise our convictions, we have become poor indeed.*

JOHNSON, MARSHALL DUANE, religious publisher; b. Middle River, Minn., Nov. 15, 1935; s. Ingvald and Bertha Sylvia (Maijala) J.; m. Alice Joy Peterson, May 31, 1959; children: Nathan Erick, Catherine F., Jennifer B. BA, Augsburg Coll., Mpls., 1957; ThB, Augsburg Seminary, Mpls., 1961; ThD, Union Seminary, N.Y.C., 1966. Pastor Bronx (N.Y.) Luth. Ch., 1961-63; vis. instr. Luth. Seminary, Phila., 1965-66; prof. religion Wartburg Coll., Waverly, Iowa, 1966-84; acad. editor Augsburg Fortress, Mpls., 1984-90; editorial dir. Fortress Press, Mpls., 1990—. Author: The Purpose of the Biblical Genealogies, 1989; contbr. articles to profl. jours. Fulbright lectr., 1976; Rockefeller fellow, 1963-65. Mem. Soc. Bibl. Lit., Am. Acad. Religion, Studiorum Novi Testamenti Societas. Office: Fortress Press Box 1209 Minneapolis MN 55440

JOHNSON, MARTIN, evangelist; b. Memphis, July 4, 1962; s. Robert Louis and Elaine Elizabeth (Rhodes) J.; m. Marissa Rayne Holly, Aug. 31, 1985; 1 child, DeShaye Emmanuel. Degree in bus. mgmt., Am. U., 1986; lic. in radio broadcasting, Columbia Sch. Broadcasting, 1983. Ordained to ministry Ch. of God in Christ, 1987. Nat. evangelist Chs. of God in Christ, 1991—; rsch. analyst in news and media Video Monitoring Svcs. Am., Washington, 1989—; instr. religious edn. Faith Progressive Sanctified Ch., Washington, 1990—; sec. elders coun. Ch. of God in Christ, 1989—, sec. evangelist dept., 1991—. Editor newleteer New Horizon Ministries, 1989 (Creative Writing award); author poems Special Dream, 1980 (Creative Writing award). Organizer, leader anti-drug march, Young Ministers Alliance, 1989; spokesperson Young Dems., U.S.A., Washington, 1984. Mem. Religious Edn. Assn. U.S.A. Home: 6500 Ronald Rd Ste 204 Capital Heights MD 20743

JOHNSON, MARY BEATRICE, religious organization administrator; b. Beckley, W.Va., Sept. 1, 1942; d. Samuel Arthur Jr. and Virginia Nellie (Miller) Boatman; m. Arnold Erik Johnson, Mar. 26, 1963; children: Jon Erik, William Scott. BS cum laude, Black Hills State Coll., 1972; ThM cum laude, Boston U., 1978; DMin, Andover Newton, 1983. Ordained to ministry; cert. pastoral counselor. Exec. dir. Green Pastures Counseling Assocs., Dover, N.H.; clin. chaplain, supr. Tewksbury (Mass.) State Hosp.; clin. dir. Good News Christian Counseling Svc., North Swanzey, N.H. Mem. AACD, Am. Assn. Pastoral Counselors (cert. pastoral counselor), Assn. for Clin. Pastoral Edn. (clin. mem.), Assn. for Counselor Edn. Supervision, Assn. for Religious Values in Counseling. Home: 103 Old Homestead North Swanzey NH 03431

JOHNSON, MARY LOU, lay worker; b. Moline, Ill., July 15, 1923; d. Percy and Hope (Aulgur) Sipes; m. Blaine Eugene Johnson, May 30, 1941; children: Vivian A. Johnson Sweedy, Michael D., Amelia H. Johnson Harms, James Michael (dec.). Grad. high sch., Moline. Chmn. Christian edn. 1st Christian Ch., Moline, 1971-73, 77-79, elder, 1973-76, 77-80, chmn. official bd., 1979-81, dir. Christian edn., 1988—; Sunday sch. tchr. 1st Christian Ch, Moline, 1958-84; cluster del. Christian Chs. Ill. and Wisc., Moline, 1988-89. Author: (poem) What Is A Mother?, 1965. Officer (various) PTA, Moline, 1952-75 (hon. life mem. State of Ill. 1972); leader, dist. dir. Girl Scouts U.S. Moline, 1955-65; skywatcher USAF Ground Observer Corps, Moline, 1955-57; vol. telethon coord. Muscular Dystrophy Assn., Moline, 1971— (numerous appreciation awards 1964-90); del. It. gov.'s Commn. on Aging, Springfield, Ill., 1990. Republican. Home: 2014 9th St Moline IL 61265 Office: First Christian Ch 1826 16th St Moline IL 61265 *Life hands us many challenges. I find them interesting and always have been willing to accept them. Not all my efforts have been successful; however, each attempt has helped me grow to be a better person.*

JOHNSON, MERWYN STRATFORD, minister, theology educator; b. Annapolis, Md., Oct. 27, 1938; s. John Edward and Lila Miree (Thomas) J.; m. Beverly Meade Neale, July 25, 1964; children: Neale, Sarah, Carlysle. BA, U. Va., 1960; BD cum laude, Union Theol. Sem., Va., 1963, ThM, 1964; ThD summa cum laude, U. Basel (Switzerland), 1973. Ordained to ministry Presbyn. Ch. Asst. minister 1st Presbyn. Ch., Staunton, Va., 1964-66; evangelist Birmingham (Ala.) Presbytery, 1966-69; prof. religion and philosophy Stephens Coll., Columbia, Mo., 1973-74; asst. prof. theology Austin (Tex.) Presbyn. Theol. Sem., 1974-80; prof. hist. and systematic theology Erskine Theol. Sem., Due West, S.C., 1980—. Author: Locke on Freedom, 1978; contbr. articles to profl. jours. Presbyn. Theologians Work Group grantee Lilly Endowment. Mem. Calvin Studies Soc., Am. Acad. Religion, Soc. for Bibl. Lit. Home: PO Box 368 Due West SC 29639 Office: Erskine Theol Sem Due West SC 29639

JOHNSON, MICHAEL JAY, minister; b. Ellensburg, Wash., Aug. 30, 1961; s. Stanley Morris and Beverly Mae (Enloe) J.; m. Tamara Faye McCreary, Sept. 21, 1985. BA in Youth Ministry, Northwest Coll., 1983; student, Liberty U., 1989—. Ordained to ministry Assemblies of God Ch., 1985; lic. to preach, 1983. Assoc. min. of youth Calvary Temple, Auburn, Wash., 1980-83, min. of youth, 1985-88; assoc. pastor Bethlehem Chapel Assembly of God, Ephrata, Wash., 1983-85; min. of youth and coll. Kings Circle Assembly of God, Corvallis, Oreg., 1988-91; assoc. pastor Kings Cir. Assemblies of God, Corvallis, 1991—; sect. youth rep. Northwest Dist. Coun. Assembly of God, Grand Coulee Sect., Wash., 1984-85, Silver Lake Camp Commn., Cheney, Wash., 1983-85, Cedar Springs Camp Commn., Lake Stevens, Wash., 1986-88; Camp David Jr. Camp Commn., Grand Coulee Sect., 1983-85. Contbr. articles to profl. jours. Mem. Nat. Network of Youthworkers, Albany-Corvallis Youthworkers Roundtable, Oreg. Dist. of Assemblies of God Campus Min. Com., Oreg. State U. Campus Min. Consortium. Office: Kings Circle Assembly God 2110 NW Circle Blvd Corvallis OR 97330

JOHNSON, NORBERT EDWIN, retired clergyman; b. Gladstone, Mich., Apr. 6, 1925; s. Edwin Reinhold and Elsie Marie (Lindahl) J.; m. S. Elaine Larson, June 17, 1950; children: Don Norbert, Carolyn Christel, Timothy Burton. AA, North Park Coll., 1948; BA, Wheaton (Ill.) Coll., 1950; AA, North Park Theol. Sem., 1953; ThM, Union Theol. Sem., Richmond, Va., 1970. Ordained to ministry Covenant Ch., 1955. Pastor Evang. Covenant Ch., Lafayette, Ind., 1953-61; pastor 1st Covenant Ch., St. Paul, 1962-76, Omaha, 1976-84; pastor North Park Covenant Ch., Chgo., 1984—; chmn. Denominational Bd. Publ., Chgo., 1958-63; mem. Exec. Bd. Denomination, Chgo., 1977-83, Bd. of Ministry, Chgo., 1977-83. Mem. Met. Coun., Mpls.-St. Paul, 1967-84; bd. dirs. North Park Coll., Chgo., 1970-75. With U.S. Army, 1943-46, ETO. Avocations: reading, music, woodwork. Home and Office: 4263 Pond View Ct White Bear Lake MN 55110

JOHNSON, ORA J., clergyman; b. Oakland City, Ind., Aug. 31, 1932; s. Ora F. and Thelma Pauline (Julian) J.; B.S., Oakland City Coll., 1971; m. Wanda Mae Lockamy, Aug. 11, 1952; children—David Russell, Kent Alan, Vicki Jeanne. Ordained to ministry Baptist Ch., 1966; sales rep., staff sales mgr. Western & So. Ins. Co., Evansville, Ind., 1956-70, also pastor Corydon (Ky.) Gen. Bapt. Ch., 1965-68, Wadesville (Ind.) Gen. Bapt. Ch., 1968-70, North Haven Gen. Bapt. Ch., Evansville, 1970-75; nat. dir. evangelism and ch. growth Gen. Bapt. Hdqrs., Poplar Bluff, Mo., 1976-82; pastor 1st Gen. Bapt. Ch., Malden, Mo., 1982-88, Howell Gen. Bapt. Ch., Evansville, Ind., 1988-90; asst. v.p. for denomination rels. Oakland City Coll., 1990—; moderator Gen. Assn. of Gen. Bapts. Nat. Conv., 1991; producer, dir. weekly TV program Moments of Worship, 1973-74; pres. Greater Evansville Sunday Sch. Assn., 1975; pres. Gen. Bapt. Home Mission Bd., 1972-73, Gen. Bd. Gen. Bapts., 1972-73; pres. Evansville Clergy Assn., 1975-76. Named Outstanding Theolog of 1971, Gen. Bapt. Brotherhood; recipient Good Shepherd award Boy Scouts Am., 1980. Mem. Christian Resource Assoc., Evangelization Forum, Nat. Assn. Evangelicals, Malden Ministerial Alliance (pres. 1983), Malden C. of C. (pres. 1985-86). Club: Malden Optimist. Lodge: Kiwanis (bd. dirs. Evansville club 1975, Poplar Bluff club 1981-83). Home: 1521 N St James Blvd Evansville IN 47711 Office: Oakland City Coll Devel Office Ste 206 Oakland City IN 47660

JOHNSON, PEARL M., evangelist, Christian family consultant; b. St. Louis, Mar. 25, 1942; d. Nicolis James and Lula Mae (Stewart) Johnson. BS, Lindenwood Coll., St. Charles, Mo., 1983; MSW, Washington U., St. Louis, 1984; PhD summa cum laude, Lael Sem., St. Charles, 1987. Adminstrv. asst. St. Louis Community Coll., 1972-85; clin. social worker Dept. Social Svcs., St. Louis, 1985—. Author: Pentecostal Catholics: A New Outpouring of the Holy Spirit, 1989; co-author religious study guide: Feed My Sheep, 1987. Religious edn. advisor Cath. Ch., St. Louis, 1971—; dir. Christian Family Counseling, St. Louis, 1990—. Named Employee of the Yr., St. Louis Community Coll., 1984; Washington U. scholar, 1981. Mem. Linwood Coll. Alumni Assn., Washington U.-St. Louis Alumni Assn., Lael Theol. Sem. U. Alumni Assn. Democrat. Roman Catholic. Avocations: sewing, reading, free lance writing, volunteer work. Home: 2800 Olive St Saint Louis MO 63103

JOHNSON, PHYLLIS MARIE, clergywoman; b. Snohomish, Wash., Apr. 21, 1918; d. Arthur Abel and Alta Campbell (Cochran) J. BA, U. Wash., 1941; M Religious Edn. cum laude, San Francisco Theol. Sem., 1950. Commd. Christian educator Presbyn. Ch., 1950; ordained minister Presbyn. Ch., 1978. Dir. Christian edn. First Presbyn. Ch., Aberdeen, Wash., 1950-55, Northminster Presbyn. Ch., Seattle, 1955-56, United Chs. of Olympia (Wash.), 1956-65, Millwood Presbyn. Ch., Spokane, Wash., 1966-69; dir. Christian edn. Pullman (Wash.) Presbyn. Ch., 1969-77, assoc. pastor, interim, 1978; interim pastor Community Presbyn. Ch., Rigby, Idaho, 1979; interim assoc. pastor Emmanuel Presbyn. Ch., Spokane, Wash., 1980-81; ednl. cons. Presbyn. Ch. U.S.A., Covenant Christian Ch., Spokane, 1988-89; Horizons rep. Presbyn. Women Inland Empire, Spokane, 1988-90; chaplain Ecumenical Ch. Secretarial Group, Spokane, 1980-90. Author, illustrator: Trees for Sharing, 1984, Christmas Cache: A Storehouse of Christmas Treasures, 1990; editor newsletter Com. on Women, Presbytery of Inland Empire, Spokane, 1982-89. Mem. Proclaim Liberty Day Care and Low Cost Housing Unit Bd. Named Hon. life mem. Pullman Presbyn. Ch. Women, 1978, Millwood Community Presbyn. Ch.-Presbyn. Women, Spokane, 1989. Mem. UN Assn., Spokane Valley Ch. Women United (pres.), Spokane Valley Minister's Fellowship, Nat. Assn. Presbyn. Ch. Educators, Nat. Assn. Presbyn. Clergywomen, Internat. Assn. Women Ministers. Avocations: writing, gardening.

JOHNSON, RALPH GLASSGOW, lay worker, retired English language professional; b. Pitts., Mar. 22, 1913; s. William Henry and Rhoda (Williams) J.; m. Bettye Lois Smith, June 11, 1955; children: Gloria, Goldiaree, Ralph Jr. and Adrienne (twins). AB, Duquesne U., 1948; MA, U. Pitts., 1950, PhD, 1961. Sunday sch. tchr. Wesley Ctr. African Meth. Episcopal Zion Ch., Pitts., 1934-42, violinist ch. choir, 1934-43; assoc. prof. English Rust Coll., Holly Springs, Miss., 1951-56, acad. dean, 1968-69; assoc. prof. English Dillard U., New Orleans, 1956-61; prof. English LeMoyne Coll., Memphis, 1961-68; assoc. prof. English Memphis State U., 1969-79, prof. emeritus, 1979—; Sunday sch. tchr. New Phila. Bapt. Ch., Memphis, 1960-70, treas., trustee, 1983—. Author: (poetry) Duke Ellington, 1934 (1st prize Pitts. Courier). Sgt. U.S. Army, 1942-45, ETO. Recipient George Washington Carver prize Achievement Clubs, Pitts., 1970, Dr.Martin Luther King Jr. award Memphis State U., 1981. Mem. White Sta. Colored Civic Club (pres., v.p., sec. 1955-65). Democrat. Home: 4958 William Arnold Rd Memphis TN 38117

JOHNSON, RICHARD E., lay minister; b. Webster, Mass., Aug. 7, 1945; s. Axel T. and Olga K. (Kallgren) J.; m. M. Kristen VanDyke, Dec. 21, 1968; children: Karin, Sara, Erica. BS, Wheaton (Ill.) Coll., 1967; MD, U. Colo., Denver, 1971. Diplomate Am. Bd. Surgery. Elder Christ's Ch., Amherst, N.H., 1985—; surgeon The Hitchcock Clinic, Nashua, N.H., 1978—; mem. com. on oversight of Christian edn. Christ's Ch., Amherst, 1985-91. Contbr. articles to profl. jours. Maj. USAF, 1973-75. Named Physician of the Yr., Hitchcock Clinic, Nashua, 1990. Fellow ACS; mem. Am. Sci. Affiliation, Christian Med., Dental Soc., Soc. Am. Gastrointestinal Endoscopic Surgeons, Evang. Theol. Soc. Republican. Home: 31 Holt Rd Amherst NH 03031 Office: Hitchcock Clinic 21 E Hollis St Box 2064 Nashua NH 03061

JOHNSON, RICHARD WAYNE, minister; b. Indianola, Iowa, Apr. 30, 1933; s. Walter Faye and Grace Truman (Catlin) J.; m. Beverly Ann Collins, July 31, 1954; children: Mary Grace Johnson Mowry, Sara Johnson Ostransky. BA, Cedarville Coll., 1959. Ordained to ministry Gen. Assn. Regular Bapt. Chs., 1960. Pastor 1st Bapt. Ch., New Hartford, Iowa, 1960-66, Kasson, Minn., 1966-75; sr. pastor Temple Bapt. Ch., Lincoln, Nebr., 1975—; mem. adv. bd. Bapt. Mission N.Am., Elyria, Ohio, 1975-90. Trustee Denver Bapt. Bible Coll., Broomfield, Colo., 1978-85, Grand Rapids Bapt. Coll. and Sem., 1991—. Republican. Office: Temple Bapt Ch 4940 Randolph Lincoln NE 68510

JOHNSON, RICKY LEON, theology educator; b. Houston, Mar. 18, 1952; s. J.W. and Meta Fay (Whitman) Johnson; m. Martha Ann Clampitt, June 12, 1976; children: Cherise, Victoria. BA, La. Coll., 1974; MDiv, Southwestern Bapt. Theol. Sem., 1977, PhD, 1983. Instr. Wayland Bapt. U., Plainview, Tex., 1982-84, asst. prof., 1984-87, assoc. prof., 1987-90; prof. Wayland Bapt. U., Plainview, 1990—; interim pastor 1st Bapt. Ch., Quitague, Tex., 1983-84, Calvary Bapt. Ch., Floydada, Tex., 1986-88, 1st Bapt. Ch., Kress, Tex., 1990-91, 1st Bapt. Ch., Matador, Tex., 1991. Fellow NEH, 1988, Andrew Mellon Found., 1989. Mem. Soc. Biblical Lit., Nat. Assn. Bapt. Profs. of Religion. Home: 3601 W 11th St Plainview TX 79072 Office: Wayland Bapt U 1900 W 7th St Plainview TX 79072

JOHNSON, ROBERT CLYDE, theology educator; b. Knoxville, Tenn., Aug. 17, 1919; s. Robert Clyde and Lucille (Davis) J.; m. Elizabeth Childs, June 26, 1942; children—Robert Clyde III, Richard Albert, Catherine Barton, Anne Elizabeth. B.S., Davidson Coll., 1941, D.D., 1963; postgrad., Princeton Theol. Sem., 1941-43; B.D., Union Theol. Sem., N.Y.C., 1944, S.T.M., 1953; M.A., Columbia U., 1947; M.A. (hon.), Yale U., 1963; D.D., Tusculum Coll., 1953; Ph.D., Vanderbilt U., 1957. Ordained to ministry Presbyterian Ch., 1943; minister in Shrewsbury, N.J., 1943-47, Greeneville, Tenn., 1947-55; asst. prof. theology Pitts. Theol. Sem., 1955-57, prof., 1957-63; Noah Porter prof. theology Yale Div. Sch., 1963-90, Noah Porter prof. theology emeritus, 1990—, dean, 1963-69; fellow Ezra Stiles Coll., Yale, 1963-83. Author: The Meaning of Christ, 1958, Authority in Protestant Theology, 1959, The Church and Its Changing Ministry, 1962. Served as chaplain USNR, 1944-46. Home: 141 Garfield Ave North Haven CT 06473 Office: Yale Div Sch 409 Prospect St New Haven CT 06510

JOHNSON, ROBERT EDWARD, theology educator; b. Farmville, Va., Nov. 5, 1950; s. Clyde Thompson and Margaret Ann (Denton) J.; m. Celia Claycomb, June 4, 1976; children: Rebekah Ann, Robert William. BA in Religion, U. Richmond, 1973; MDiv, Southwestern Bapt. Theol. Sem., Ft. Worth, 1977, PhD in Ch. History, 1984. Ordained to ministry So. Bapt. Conv., 1970. Pastor Chestnut Grove Bapt. Ch., Appomattox, Va., 1970-73; prof. ch. history Faculdade Teológica Batista, São Paulo, Brazil, 1980-91, dean grad. studies, 1988-89; prof. ch. history Baptistische Theologische Hochschule Rüschlikon, Zurich, Switzerland, 1991—; missionary Fgn. Mission Bd., So. Bapt. Conv., São Paulo, 1979-91; guest prof. Southwestern Bapt. Theol. Sem., Ft. Worth, 1989-90. Author: Uma Breve História da Reforma Protestante, 1989; contbr.: O Enciclopédia Evangélica de Teologia; also articles. Bd. dirs. Inst. Bapt.-Anabaptist Studies, Rüschlikon. Mem. Am. Soc. Ch. History, Sixteenth Century Soc., Conf. on Faith and History, So. Bapt. Hist. Soc., Associação Batista de Institutos Bíblicos e Teológicos. Home: 811 19th St Plano TX 75074 Office: Baptistische Theologische, Hochschule, CH-8803 Rüschlikon Zurich, Switzerland *The search for truth repeatedly demands that familiar but culturally-bound viewpoints yield ground to those perspectives which, while sometimes threatening, are more inclusive and global.*

JOHNSON, ROBERT HOYT, minister; b. Crawford, Ga., July 7, 1939; s. Sanford George and Sue Lene (Hardeman) J.; m. Dorothy Sparks, Oct. 20, 1962; children: Robert A., Gina Kay. Student, Johnson Bus. Coll., Athens, Ga., 1960-61; grad., Edn. Extension Ctr., 1990. Ordained to ministry So. Bapt. Conv., 1979. Deacon Johnson Dr. Bapt. Ch., Athens, 1971-78; pastor Freeman Creek Bapt. Ch., Farmington, Ga., 1978-86, Boldsprings Bapt. Ch., Monroe, Ga., 1987—; dir. Royal Ambs., Sapeptu Bapt. Assn., Athens, 1972-77; with sales dept. Ivy-Coile Mfrs. Inc., Athens, 1978—; vice moderator Appalachee Bapt. Assn., Monroe, 1984, moderator, 1985-86, dean extension ctr., 1986—, dir. Sunday sch., 1989—. With USAR, 1958-64. Democrat. Home: 0244 Doster Ave NW Monroe GA 30655 Office: Boldspring Bapt Ch Rte 3 Boldsprings Rd Monroe GA 30655 *Since Jesus Christ came into my life and helped me get my priorities right, my one goal in life is to live and work in such a way that this world will be a better place to live.*

JOHNSON, ROBERT L., minister. Head Halifax-Dartmouth Coun. of Chs. and Queen's County Coun. of Chs., N.S., Can. Office: Halifax-Dartmouth Coun Chs, 2021 Oxford St, Halifax, NS Canada B3L 2T3 also: Queen's County Coun Chs, PO Box 394, Milton, NS Canada B0T 1P0*

JOHNSON, ROBERT ROSS, minister; b. Spokane, Wash., June 26, 1920; s. John J. and Metta (Nickleberry) J.; m. Ernestine Norwood, June 3, 1943; children: Michelle Johnson Tompkins, Stephen, John E. BA, Whitworth Coll., 1943; BDiv, Colgate-Rochester Divinity Sch., 1946, MDiv, 1946. Ordained to ministry United Ch. Christ, 1945. Pastor 2d Bapt. Ch., LeRoy, N.Y., 1947-48, South Congl. Ch., Chgo., 1948-52, Bklyn. Nazarene Congl. Ch., 1952-56; pastor, founder St. Albans (N.Y.) Congl. Ch., 1953—; moderator State Conf. United Ch. Christ, 1968-69, conf. chaplain, chmn. ch. extension; bd. dirs. Queens Fedn. Chs.; bd. cooperators, founder, past bd. dirs. Queens Interfaith Clergy Coun.; guest speaker Rotary, Kiwanis, other orgns. Bd. dirs. YMCA (svc. award 1988); chmn. Arthur Ashe Vols. com. United Negro Coll. Fund; mem. N.Y.C. Bd. Higher Edn., 1968-77 (citation mayor of N.Y.C. 1973); bd. dirs. NAACP; mem. Jamaica Queens Dist. 15 Sch. Bd.; bd. dirs. Neighbors Houses; founder Amistad Child Day Care and Family Ctr. (award 1982); supporter Queens Assn. for Edn. Exceptionally Gifted Children Inc., 1973, Self Help Program, Queens. Recipient Scroll of Honor Omega Psi Phi, 1959, Outstanding Contbns. award Nat. Coun. Negro Women Inc., Bklyn., 1963, cert. for outstanding svc. Jamaica C. of C., 1975, Outstanding Svc. award Epsilon Pi Omega chpt. Alpha Kappa Alpha Sorority, 1975, Disting. and Exceptional award Friends of Sr. Citizens, Disting. Svc. award Nu Omicron chpt. Omega Phi Psi, 1979, Disting. Merit citation NCCJ, 1980, Resolution honoring 35th anniversary of ordination as min., Coun. of City of N.Y., 1980, N.Y. Urban League award 1980, Disting. Svc. citation United Negro Coll. Fund, 1980, Religion award NAACP, 1981, Outstanding Leadership to ch. and community award, Jamaica Seventh-day Adventist Ch., 1983, Martin Luther King Jr. Meml. award Congl. Ch. of South Hempstead, 1986, Congratulatory Letter Mayor of N.Y.C. on St. Albans ribbon cutting ceremony, 1987, Roy Wilkins award Rickey Prodn. Caribbean Cultural Assn., 1988, Community Svc. award Jewish War Vets. U.S., 1989, Liberty Bell award Queens County Bar Assn., 1989, Community award Black Tennis and Sports Found., 1989, Outstanding Svc. award Congressman F.H. Flake, 1990, award Black Am. Heritage Found. Inc., 1990, citation of honor Borough of Queens, 1990, Retirement award St. Albans C. of C., 1990; named Clergyman of Yr., NACCJ, Queens Region, 1973, Outstanding Churchman of Yr., Queens Fedn. Chs., 1981. Mem. The Fellas (pres. 1975-80, citation 1980), 100% Right Club, Rotary (award 1982, 88-89), Alpha Phi Alpha. Office: St Albans Congl Ch 172-17 Linden Blvd Saint Albans NY 11434 *The unsolicited blessings of life carry the greatest meanings.*

JOHNSON, ROGER LEE, minister; b. Anniston, Ala., Dec. 6, 1941; s. Paul Lee and Margie Ree (Malone) J.; m. Virginia Ruth Grubb, June 3, 1947; children: Sheri Leigh, Stephanie Michelle. BA, Harding U., 1964; MA in religion, Harding Grad. Sch., Memphis, 1987. Min. Ch. Christ, Lebanon, Va., 1964-65, Northwest Ch. Christ, Durant, Okla., 1965-67, Ch. Christ, Caledonia, Miss., 1967-68, Garden Ridge Ch.Christ, Lewisville, Tex., 1972-77, Sharpstown Ch. Christ, Houston, 1977-83, Union Ave Ch. Christ, Memphis, 1983—; speaker weekly TV program He Lives!, Memphis. Book rev. editor The Christian Observer; contbr. articles to religious jours. Mem. Evang. Theol. Soc. Republican. Home: 5390 McElroy Cove Memphis TN 38120 Office: Union Ave Ch Christ 1930 Union Ave Memphis TN 38104 *To live honorably is to live with dignity. To treat others kindly is to live compassionately. To live in faith and love for God is to live supremely.*

JOHNSON, SOLOMON TILEWA, bishop. Bishop of Gambia, Anglican Communion, Banjul. Office: Bishop's Ct, POB 51, Banjul The Gambia*

JOHNSON, STEPHEN MONROE, pastor; b. Columbus, Ga., July 16, 1949; s. Nolan Lewis and Dorothy Mae (Kamm) J.; m. Meredith Elaine Vedder, May 24, 1975; children: Lindsey Erin, Matthew Stephen. BS, Ga. Inst. Tech., Atlanta, 1971; ThM, Dallas Theol. Sem., 1976; PhD, Westminster Theol. Sem., Phila., 1988. Ordained to ministry Northwest Bible Ch., 1976. Min. edn. and evangelism Community Bible Ch., Marietta, Ga., 1976-78, min. singles, 1980-86; exec. pastor N.W. Bible Ch., Dallas, 1986-90; sr. pastor Christ Community Ch., Tampa, Fla., 1990—. Mem. Dallas Ind. Sch. Dist. Religious Task Force, 1988-90. 1st lt. U.S. Army, 1972. Mem. Dallas Theol Sem. Alumni Assn. (pres. Tampa Bay chpt. 1991—), Delta Sigma Phi. Republican. Home: 5612 Piney Lane Dr Tampa FL 33625 Office: Christ Community Ch 6202 N Himes Ave Tampa FL 33614

JOHNSON, STEPHEN RANDALL, minister; b. Lansing, Mich., May 17, 1957; s. James Theodore and Juanita Elizabeth (Wall) J.; m. Zane Elizabeth Alkhas, June 20, 1987; children: Stephen James, Faith Elizabeth. BTh, Berean Bible Coll., San Diego, 1984; MST, Bethel Bible Coll., Riverside, Calif., 1985, ThD, 1989. Ordained to ministry Shield of Faith Ministries, 1984, Living Word Internat., 1985. Assoc. pastor Shield of Faith Ministries, Escondido, Calif., 1983-85; founder, sr. pastor His Ch. Christian Fellowship, Escondido, 1985—; instr. Berean Bible Coll., San Diego, 1985-89; pres. north campus Berean Bible Coll., Escondido, 1989-91; founder, pres. Word Bible Coll. and Grad. Sch. Theology, 1991—; conv. speaker His Internat. Ministries, Escondido; founder, missionary statesman His Ch. Christian Fellowship; founder several local chs. Broadcaster KPRZ Radio, 1986—; writer Times Advocate, Times Mirror, Good News Pub., 1984-87; guest TV programs. Office: His Ch Christian Fellowship 600 S Andreasen Dr Ste B Escondido CA 92029

JOHNSON, STEPHEN WENDELL, prison chaplain; b. Evansville, Ind., Feb. 10, 1947; s. Ora F. and Thelma J.; m. Janet S. Burger, Sept. 1, 1968; children: Paul H., Peter J. BS, Oakland City Coll., 1969; MDiv, So. Theol. Sem., 1973. Ordained to ministry United Meth. Ch., 1971; cert. chaplain. Min. So. Ind. Conf., United Meth. Ch., Cory, 1973-76; chaplain Fed. Bureau Prisons, Wis., W.Va, 1976—; bd. dirs., Jour. Pastoral Care, 1989—. Mem. Am. Protestant Correctional Chaplains Assn. (pres. 1988-90). Home: 1003 Ridgewood Cove S Niceville FL 32578 Office: Fed Prison Comp PO Box 600 Elgin AFB FL 32542-7606

JOHNSON, TED H., minister; b. Zeeland, Mich., Apr. 19, 1948; s. Theodore Starks and Jeanette (Berghorst) J.; m. Laura Ellen Willis, June 22, 1974; children: Michelle Lynn, Mary Jeanette. BA, Spring Arbor Coll., 1970; MDiv, Asbury Theol. Sem., Wilmore, Ky., 1980. Ordained to ministry Free Meth. Ch., 1983. Sr. pastor Lakeview (Mich.) Free Meth. Ch., 1980—; chmn. social action/moral issues com. North Mich. Conf., Big Rapids, 1984—. Chmn. local fund raisig United Way, Lakeview, 1985-89; trustee Spring Arbor (Mich.) Coll., 1985—. Mem. Lakeview Ministerial Assn. (chmn. 1987—). Home: 112 Edgar St 1 Lakeview MI 48850 Office: Free Meth Ch 110 Edgar Lakeview MI 48850 *Life like the weather is constantly changing. Our Creator is our climate control, who provides the stabilty we creatures need to remain in His image.*

JOHNSON, THOMAS FLOYD, college president, educator; b. Detroit, June 1, 1943; s. Edward Eugene and Adella Madeline (Norton) J.; m. Michele Elizabeth Myers, Mar. 26, 1965; children: Jason, Amy, Sarah. BPh, Wayne State U., 1965; BD, Fuller Theol. Sem., 1968; ThM, Princeton Sem., 1969; PhD, Duke U., 1979. Pastor Presbyn. Ch. U.S.A., Pa., Mich., 1969-76; asst. prof. Sioux Falls (S.D.) Coll., 1978-83, acad. dean, 1981-83, pres., 1988—; prof. N.Am. Baptist Sem., Sioux Falls, 1983-88. Contbr. 9 articles to Internat. Standard Bible Ency., 1988. Bd. dirs. Children's Home Soc. S.D., Sioux Falls, 1980-86, S.D. Symphony Orch., 1988, Carroll Inst., 1989—. Mem. Soc. Bibl. Lit., Rotary (bd. dirs. Downtown club, Sioux Falls 1991—). Office: Sioux Fall Coll 1501 S Prairie Sioux Falls SD 57105 *Every day, in all its tasks and relationships, is a gift from God. Our response is to live thankfully, in service to God and God's world.*

JOHNSON, TIMOTHY ALLEN, minister; b. Princeton, W.Va., July 16, 1948; s. Robert Eugene and Mary (Thompson) J.; m. Susan Manning Britton Johnson, Dec. 5, 1970; children: Crissie Jane, Susan Elizabeth. AB, Ky. Christian Coll., Grayson, Ky., 1970, Master of Ministry, 1985; ThD, Southern Seminary, Birmingham, Ala., 1986. Youth min. Cherry Ave. Christian Ch., Charlottesville, Va., 1970-73; sr. min. First Christian Ch., Paintsville, Ky., 1973-76; chaplain Eastern Ky. Comprehensive Rehab. Ctr., Thelma, Ky., 1974-76; sr. min. Capital City Ch. of Christ., Raleigh, N.C., 1976-90; pres. Brown Found., Inc., Raleigh, 1990—; Trustee Howell's Mill Christian Assembly, Ona, W.Va., 1974-76; trustee Raleigh chpt. Sudden Infant Death Syndrom & Found.; mem. N.C. Christian Conv., Raleigh. Panel chmn. United Way Allocations Com., Raleigh, 1990; commr. Cary Cultural Arts Commn., 1990. Recipient Gov's. Vol. Award, State of N.Car. 1985; Ky. Col. Commn., State of Ky., 1974. Avocations: profl. graphic artist, photography, racquetball. Office: Brown Found Inc 4048 Barrett Dr Raleigh NC 27609

JOHNSON, TIMOTHY NEIL, pastor; b. Elyria, Ohio, Oct. 9, 1959; s. Otis Clyde and Mildred Maxzine (Farrell) J.; m. Julia Jane Cottrell, Aug. 30, 1978; children: Joshua James, Jill Joyce, Jeremiah, Jennifer Jane. Student, Cedarville Coll., 1978-79, Lorain County Community, Elyria, 1979-80. Ordained to ministry Bapt. Ch. Asst. bus. dir. Faith Bapt. Ch., Morefelden, Fed. Republic Germany, 1983-85; youth pastor Independent Bible Ch., Montezuma, Ind., 1985-87; pastor Tenn. Valley Bapt. Ch., Clinton, Ind., 1987-89, Greenwood Bapt. Ch., Terre Haute, Ind., 1990—; sr. officer U.S. Penitentiary, Terre Haute, 1987—. With U.S. Army, 1980-85. Republican. Home: RR4 Box 237 Rockville IN 47872 Office: Greenwood Bapt Ch 2431 S 1st St Terre Haute IN 47802

JOHNSON, WALTER STANLEY, clergyman, educator; b. Chgo., Feb. 22, 1945; s. Walter Henry and Virginia Phyllis (White) J.; m. Carol Littlejohn, Aug. 18, 1966; children—David Stanley, Jennifer Mae. B.A., Seattle Pacific U., 1967; M.Divinity, Western Evang. Sem., Portland, Oreg., 1970; Ph.D., St. Louis U., 1982. Ordained to ministry Free Methodist Ch. N.Am., 1970. Asst. pastor Greenville Free Meth. Ch., Ill., 1970-73; pastor Pittsburgh Free Meth. Ch., Ill., 1973-75; prof. Christian theology Western Evang. Sem., 1975—, chmn. div. Christian history and thought, 1977—; retreat speaker and evangelist; mem. bd. ministerial edn. and guidance Free Meth. Ch., Turner, Oreg., 1977—. Editor: Kardia: A Journal of Religious Thought, 1984—. Contbr. articles to religious publs. Mem. edn. com. Wesley Christian Acad., Portland, 1982—; mem. Oreg. Right to Life Edn. Found., 1982-83. Research fellow Yale U. Divinity Sch., 1982. Mem. Am. Philos. Assn., Wesleyan Theol. Soc., Am. Acad. Religion, Pacific NW Theol. Soc. (chmn. 1985—). Home: 4911 SE Meldrum St Portland OR 97222 Office: Western Evang Sem 4200 SE Jennings Ave Portland OR 97222

JOHNSON, WAYNE GUSTAVE, religion educator, minister; b. Odebolt, Iowa, Dec. 31, 1930; s. John Gust and Ruth Helen (Hanson) J.; m. Jeanne Marie Kaiser, Jan. 1, 1984; children from previous marriage: Susan, Scott, Jeffrey, Jonathan. BSCE, Iowa State U., 1954; BDiv, Andover Newton Theol. Sem., 1960; PhD, U. Iowa, 1966. Ordained to ministry Am. Bapt. Ch., 1959. Pastor Savona (N.Y.) Federated Ch., 1959-62; asst. prof., then assoc. prof. Carthage Coll., Kenosha, Wis., 1966-70; assoc. prof., then prof. U. Wis.-Parkside, Kenosha, 1970—, chair philosophy dept., 1988—. Mem. Am. Acad. Religion, Am. Philos. Assn., Assn. Christian Philosophers, Tau Beta Pi. Democrat. Home: 1107 4 1/2 Mile Rd Racine WI 53402 Office: U Wis Box 2000 Kenosha WI 53141 *To understand human beings is, in depth, to gain a sense of our terror of death and of the fragility of our self-esteem. Thus the quest of all profound religions.*

JOHNSON, WESLEY EARL, religious organization administrator, minister; b. Mpls., June 21, 1931; s. Earl R. and Evelyn Johnson; m. Carol A. Sandberg, June 28, 1952; children: Larry E., Rick, Tamara Johnson VanDixhorn. BA, Northwestern Coll., Mpls., 1954; MDiv, Trinity Evang. Div. Sch., Derrfield, Ill., 1957, M Ministry, 1985. Ordained to ministry Evang. Free Ch. Am., 1960. Youth pastor Crystal Free Ch., New Hope, Minn., 1950-55, 1st Evang. Free Ch., Chgo., 1955-59; pastor Calvary Evang. Free Ch., Rochester, Minn., 1959-63, Evang. Free Ch., Thief River Falls, Minn., 1963-67, Liberty Bible Ch., Chesterton, Ind., 1968-76; supt. Gt. Lakes dist. Evang. Free Ch. Am., Fox River Grove, Ill., 1977—; bd. dirs. North Cen. Dist., Evang. Free Ch. Am., Thief River Falls, 1964-67, sec., chmn., Gt. Lakes dist., Chesterton, 1968-77; nat. pres. Free Ch. Youth Fellowship, Mpls., 1957-59; bd. dirs. Minn. Sunday Sch. Assn., Rochester, 1961-632. Office: Gt Lakes Dist Evang Free Ch Am 960 Rte 22 Ste 201 Fox River Grove IL 60021

JOHNSON, WILLIAM ALEXANDER, clergyman, philosophy educator; b. Bklyn., Aug. 20, 1934; s. Charles Raphael and Ruth Augusta (Anderson) J.; m. Carol Genevieve Lundquist, June 11, 1955; children—Karin Ruth, Karl William, Krister Frederick. B.A., Queens Coll., City U. N.Y., 1953; B.D. (Univ. fellow, Morrow Meml. fellow, Daniel Delaplaine fellow), Union Theol. Sem., 1956; Teol. Kand., Lund U., 1957, Teol. Lic., 1958, Teologie Doktor, 1962; M.A., Columbia U., 1958, Ph.D. (Univ. fellow, Rockefeller Bros. fellow), 1959. Ordained deacon Meth. Ch., 1955, priest Episcopal Ch., 1968. Profl. baseball player N.Y. Giants, 1949-51; dir. Boys Club, Salvation Army, Jamaica, N.Y., 1952-54; minister Mt. Hope and Teabo Meth. chs., Wharton, N.J., 1954-56; elder Meth. Ch., 1956; minister Immanuel and Union Meth. chs., Bklyn., 1957-59; asst. in instrn. Columbia U., N.Y.C., 1957, Union Theol. Sem., N.Y.C., 1958; instr., asst. prof. religion Trinity Coll., Hartford, Conn., 1959-63; lectr. philosophy and theology Hartford Sem. Found., 1961-62; assoc. prof. religion, chmn. dept. religion Drew U., Madison, N.J., 1963-66; research prof. religion NYU, N.Y.C., 1966; vis. lectr. Union Theol. Sem., N.Y.C., 1966; vis. prof. religion Princeton (N.J.) U., 1966-68; prof., chmn. dept. religion Manhattanville Coll., Purchase, N.Y., 1967-71; vis. prof. Christian ethics Gen. Theol. Sem., N.Y.C., 1970; Albert V. Danielsen prof. Christian thought, prof. philosophy and history of ideas Brandeis U., Waltham, Mass., 1971—; canon residentiary Cathedral Ch. of St. John The Divine, N.Y.C., 1973—; vis. prof. Protestant theology N.Am. Coll., Vatican City, 1969-75, Bryn Mawr Coll., 1976, U. Strasbourg, France; vis. scholar MIT, Cambridge, 1974-75; vis. prof., Tokyo, Japan, Stockholm, Sweden, 1979, U. Gothenburg, 1979; examining chaplain Diocese of the Arctic, 1982; prof. nr. ea. and Jewish studies Brandeis U., 1988. Author: The Philosophy of Religion of Anders Nygren, 1958, Christopher Polhem: The Father of Swedish Technology, 1963, Nature and the Supernatural in the Theology of Horace Bushnell, 1963, On Religion: A Study of Theological Method in Schleiermacher and Nygren, 1964, Problems in Christian Ethics, 1965, (with Nels F.S. Ferré) Swedish Contributions to Modern Theology, 1966, The Search for Transcendence, 1974, The Christian Way of Death, 1974, Invitation to Theology, 1979, Philosophy and the Gospel, 1979, (with Moorhead Kennedy) Christianity and Terrorism, 1986, O Boundless Salvation, 1987; debut as Popolo in Aida Met. Opera, 1989; contbr. articles to profl. jours.; lectr., Europe, Asia, Africa, South Am., Australia, Caribbean., Arctic. Democratic committeeman Hartford, 1960-63; mem. exec. com. Am. Friends Service Com., Coll. Div., 1966-70; bd. dirs. Queens Coll. CUNY. Recipient David F. Swenson-Kierkegaard Meml. award, 1964, Harbison award for Tchr. of Yr. Danforth Found., 1965; named Outstanding Young Man in Am. Jr. C. of C., 1964; Disting. Alumnus Queens Coll., 1980; Scandinavian-Am. Found. fellow, 1956, 85; Fulbright scholar U. Copenhagen, 1957-58; Dempster Grad. fellow Meth. Ch., 1958; Am. Philos. Soc. fellow, 1971, 85. vis. rsch. fellow Princeton, 1972; Guggenheim fellow for study in Rome, Italy, 1972; NSF grantee, 1978; Rockefeller fellow Aspen Inst., 1978, fellow Aspen Inst., Jerusalem, 1982; Nat. Endowment Humanities grantee, 1978, 86; grantee Arthur Vining Davis Found., 1981; grantee Trinity Ch. of N.Y.C., 1982, 84; grantee Tauber Inst. Study of European Jewry. Mem. Am. Acad. Religion, Asia Soc., Japan Soc., Scandinavian-Am. Heritage Soc., Am. Philos. Assn., Danforth Assos., Soc. for Sci. Study Religion, Soc. for Religion in Higher Edn. (Kent fellow 1959), Soc. Anglican Theologians, Vasa Order Am., Am. Soc. Christian Ethics, Swedish Pioneer Hist. Soc., Soc. for Scandinavian Study, Willa Cather Pioneer Meml. Found., Authors Guild, Episcopal Churchmen for S.Africa, New Haven Theol. Group, Westchester Inst. Psychiatry and Psychoanalysis (dir.), Ecumenical Found. for Christian Ministry, English Speaking Union, Ch. Soc. for Coll. Work, Columbia University Club, Met. Opera Club, The Pilgrims, The Coffee House, Lotos Club, Century Club, Explorer's Club, Phi Beta Kappa, Pi Gamma Mu, Phi Sigma Tau. Home: 27 Fox Meadow Rd Scarsdale NY 10583 also: 44 Pascal Ave Rockport ME 04856 Office: Brandeis U Rabb Grad Ctr Waltham MA 02154 *I have attempted in my life to fulfill the simple prayer of St. Francis: Lord, make me an instrument of your peace/Where there is hatred . . . let me sow love/Where there is injury . . . pardon/Where there is doubt . . . faith/Where there is despair . . . hope/Where there is darkness . . . light/Where there is sadness . . . joy. For it is giving that we receive; it is pardoning that we are pardoned; and it is dying that we are born to eternal life.*

JOHNSON, WILLIAM C. (BILL JOHNSON), religious press editor, minister; b. Eudora, Ark., July 10, 1940; s. Robert Sisro and Edrie Catherine (Smith) J.; m. Rita D. Rankin, June 8, 1962; 1 child, Reba Lynn. B in Bible Lang., Missionary Bapt. Sem., Little Rock, 1970; BA, U. Ark., 1973; DD, Okla. Missionary Bapt. Sem., 1984. Ordained to ministry Am. Bapt. Assn., 1964. Chmn. missionary com. Friendship Bapt. Assn., Star City, Ark., 1970-77, vice moderator, 1978; dir. pub. rels. Am. Bapt. Assn., Texarkana, Tex., 1979-86, dir. meeting arrangements, 1980-86, editor in chief publs., 1986—. Author: Pastor, Have a Talk With Keith, 1982; editor Christian Edn. Bull., 1979; contbr. articles to religious jours. Active Dem. Cen. Com., Dumas, Ark., 1971; chaplain CAP, Texarkana, Ark., 1982—. With USN, 1958-61. Mem. Optimists (sec./treas. Dumas chpt. 1970-71). Home: 7 Country Estates Texarkana AR 75502 Office: Bapt Sunday Sch Com 4605 State Line PO Box 502 Texarkana TX 75503

JOHNSON, WILLIE EARMAN, minister; b. Fairfax, Ala., June 16, 1933; s. Chester Earman and Willie Edith (Carroll) J.; m. Clarice May Hubbard, Dec. 23, 1952; children: Willie Jr., Joseph H., Judy K. AS, So. Union Jr. Coll., 1974; BA, Auburn U., 1975; MRE, New Orleans Bapt. Theol. Sem., 1977; Edn. Specialist degree, Miss. State U., 1982. Ordained to ministry Bapt. Ch., 1971; lic. pastoral counselor. Commd. USN, 1951, advanced through grades to chief petty officer, retired, 1971; pastor Midway Bapt. Ch., Riverview, Ala., 1972-73, Shiloh Bapt. Ch., Roanoke, Ala., 1974-75, New Sardis Bapt. Ch., Mt. Olive, Miss., 1975-78, Bethel Bapt. Ch., Brandon, Miss., 1978-84, Friendship Bapt. Ch., Newark, Del., 1985—. Mem. Nat. Christian Counselors Assn., Del. Pastors' Conf. (pres. 1989—), Del. Bapt. Assn. (vice moderator 1990—), Rankin County Bapt. Assn. (moderator 1982-83, tng. dir. 1982-84). Republican. Home: 404 Blackstone Rd Newark DE 19713 Office: Friendship Bapt Ch 2200 S College Ave Newark DE 19702

JOHNSTON, DOUGLAS SCOTT, minister; b. Elgin, Ill., May 13, 1947; s. Douglas Becker and Mary Dow (Thomas) J.; m. Deborah Langland, June 25, 1971. BA, Judson Coll., Elgin, 1973; MDiv, Bethel Theol. Sem., St. Paul, 1976. Ordained to ministry Am. Bapt. Chs. in U.S.A., 1978. Pastor 1st Bapt. Ch., Sullivan, Ill., 1978-82; sr. pastor Maryvale Bapt. Ch., Phoenix, 1982-86, Market St. Bapt. Ch., Zanesville, Ohio, 1986—; mem. exec. bd. Am. Bapt. Chs. Ohio, Granville, 1989—. Trustee Shurtliff Found., U. Ill., Champaign, 1978-82, Judson Coll., 1978-84, Southeastern Ohio Hospice, Zanesville, 1989—; cons. Ohio U., Zanesville, 1988—. Recipient Life Survivor Achievement award Am. Cancer Soc., 1990. Mem. Rotary. Office: Market St Bapt Ch 140 N 6th St Zanesville OH 43701 *I am convinced that the purpose of our existence is to serve God, serve others and serve ourselves.*

JOHNSTON, GEORGE, retired religion educator, minister; b. Clydebank, Scotland, June 9, 1913; arrived in Can., 1952; s. William George and Jenny Connolly (McKeown) J.; m. Alexandra Gardner, Aug. 6, 1941; children: Christine Johnston Griffin, Ronald, Janet Johnston Campbell. MA, Glasgow U., 1935, BD, 1938, DD (hon.), 1960; PhD, Cambridge U., 1941; LLD (hon.), Mt. Allison U., 1974; DD (hon.), United Theol. Coll., Montreal, 1974, Montreal Diocesan Theol. Coll., 1975. Ordained to ministry Ch. of Scotland, 1940, received as min. of United Ch. Can., 1953. Min. Martyrs' Ch., St. Andrews, Scotland, 1940-47; assoc. prof. Hartford (Conn.) Theol. Sem., 1947-52; prof. N.T., Emmanuel Coll., Toronto, Ont., Can., 1952-59; prof. religious studies McGill U., Montreal, Que., Can., 1959-81, dean Faculty Religious Studies, 1970-75, prof. emeritus, 1982—; prin. United Theol. Coll., 1959-70; commr. United Ch. Gen. Coun., 1958, 66, 68; acting chaplain 7th Black Watch 51st Div., Germany, 1945; mem. assembly New Delhi World Coun. Chs., 1961, Humanities Rsch. Coun., Can., 1974-75. Author: The Church in the New Testament, 1943, The Secrets of the Kingdom, 1954, The Church in the Modern World, 1967, The Spirit-Paraclete in the Gospel of John, 1970; contbr. to New Century Bible, Peake's Commentary, The Interpreter's Dictionary of the Bible. Mem. Port Credit (Ont.) Pub. Libr. Commn., 1958-59; bd. govs. McGill U., 1971-75. Black theol. fellow, Glasgow, 1938, Brown Downie fellow, 1937, Am. Assn. Theol. Schs. fellow, 1967, Can. Coun. fellow, 1975. Mem. Can. Bibl. Soc. (pres. 1963), Can. Theol. Soc. (pres. 1966), Soc. Bibl. Lit. (coun.). Office: McGill U Faculty Religious, Studies, 3520 University St, Montreal, PQ Canada H3A 2A7 *Modern life presents a host of problems to young and old alike. As an educator in Religion I am privileged to help young people to find ground on which to stand and find some meaning. It is an exciting and rewarding task.*

JOHNSTON, GORDON HOWARD, minister, educator; b. Long Island, N.Y., Mar. 15, 1959; s. Hugh L. and Eileen B. (Boerrigter) J.; m. Danielle Louise Damoude, Dec. 20, 1960. BA, U. Nebr., 1981; ThM, Dallas Theol. Sem., 1985, postgrad., 1985—. Teaching asst. Dallas Theol. Sem., 1983-88, instr. Lay Inst., 1988-89; assoc. pastor First Bapt. Ch., Carollton, Tex., 1990—; tchr. Community Bible Chapel, Richardson, Tex., 1981-84, Trinity Fellowship Ch., Richardson, 1984-90, Grace Bible Ch., Dallas, 1987; pastoral intern Community Bible Chapel, Dallas, 1983, Indian Hills Community Ch., Lincoln, Nebr., 1984, tchr., 1980-81; dir. font designing Paraclete Software, Plano, Tex., 1988-90; font designer Gamma Software, Portland, Oreg., 1990—. Relief dir. Rotary Club of Dallas: Half-Way House for Juvenile Delinquents, 1981-84. Mem. Soc. Bibl. Lit., Evang. Theol. Soc. Home: 3560 Country Sq Dr # 202 Carrollton TX 75007

JOHNSTON, JAMES KIRKLAND, minister; b. Dallas, Feb. 15, 1956; s. Wendell Graham and Martha Bright (Lamb) J.; m. Gayle Marie Timm, July 28, 1979; children: Blaine, Trevor. BRE, William Tyndale Coll., 1978; ThM, Dallas Sem., 1982; D of Ministry, Talbot Sch. Theology, 1990. Ordained to ministry, 1983. Min. North Highlands Bible Ch., Dallas, 1982-85; sr. min. Harmony Bible Ch., Danville, Iowa, 1985—; bd. dirs. Gust Bass Evang. Assn., Hudsonville, Mich. Author: Why Christians Sin, 1992. Mem. Lamb Found. (bd. dirs. 1979—). Home: 107 E Seymour Danville IA 52623 Office: Harmony Bible Ch RR1 Geode Park Rd Danville IA 52623 *Religion should enrich one's life and make it full and complete. If religion stifles or gives no additional meaning to life, then it is a certainty that one's religion has not put one in touch with the true and living God.*

JOHNSTON, JOHN ALEXANDER, minister; b. Edmonton, Alta., Can., Nov. 3, 1927; s. Joseph Samuel and Marion Halley (Leslie) J.; m. Heather Erika Elizabeth Johnston, Feb. 20, 1957; children: Andrew, Ian, Mary. BA with honors, U. Western Ont., Can., 1950; MA with honors, McGill U., Can., 1951, PhD, 1955; BD, Presbyn. Coll., Can., 1954, DD (hon.), 1980; ThM with honors, Princeton Sem., 1956. Ordained to ministry Presbyn. Ch. Dir. ch. extension Presbytery of Ottawa, Ont., 1956-58; min. St. Timothy's Presbyn. Ch., Ottawa, 1958-64, Lagos (Nigeria) Presbyn. Ch., 1964-66, MacNab St. Presbyn. Ch., Hamilton, Ont., 1966—; lectr. Christian edn. Immanuel Coll., Ibadan, Nigeria, 1964-66; moderator Synod of Hamilton-London, Presbyn. Ch. in Can., 1979-80, Presbyteries of Ottawa, Hamilton. Author: Strong Winds Blowing, 1979 (History prize Presbyn. Ch. in Can. 1980). Pres. Boys Brigade Can., 1961-64, Planned Parenthood Assn. Hamilton, 1978—, Leprosy Mission Can., 1984—; mem. race rels. com. Office of Mayor of Hamilton, 1987—, pks. and recreation com. City of Hamilton, 1990—; trustee Bd. Edn., City of Hamilton, 1988—. Mem. Social Planning and Rsch. Coun. Hamilton, Masons (grand chaplain Grand lodge 1985-86, 91—). Home: 147 Chedoke Ave, Hamilton, ON Canada L8P 4P2 Office: MacNab St Presbyn Ch, 116 MacNab St S, Hamilton, ON Canada L8P 4P2

JOHNSTON, JOHNIE EDWARD, JR., minister; b. Albertville, Ala., Aug. 25, 1946; s. Johnie Edward and Aleta Elizabeth (Evans) J.; m. Linda Faye Taylor, May 5, 1967; children: David, Jonathan. AA, Snead Jr. Coll., 1966; BA, U. Ala., Tuscaloosa, 1978; postgrad., Samford U., 1971-73, Southwestern Bapt. Theol. Sem., Ft. Worth, 1978-82. Ordained to ministry So. Bapt. Conv., 1979. Assoc. pastor Happy Home Bapt. Ch., Leeds, Ala., 1973-74; houseparent Tuscoba Friendship Home, Northport, Ala., 1976-78; dir. childhood edn. Ridglea Bapt. Ch., Ft. Worth, 1979-82; pastor Alapaha (Ga.) Bapt. Ch., 1982-86, Edgewood Bapt. Ch., Gadsden, Ala., 1986—; v.p. Etowah Bapt. Assn. Min.'s Conf., Gadsden, 1987-89; cons. Bapt. Viewpoint, Nashville, 1986-88; moderator Mell Bapt. Assn., Tifton, Ga., 1985-86. With U.S. Air Force, 1967-71. Named Centennial Pastor, Woman's Missionary Union of the So. Bapt. Conv., 1988. Home: 1729 Mount Zion Ave Gadsden AL 35901 Office: Edgewood Bapt Ch 1727 Mount Zion Ave Gadsden AL 35901

JOHNSTON, LLOYD ALLAN, minister; b. Ft. Morgan, Colo., Oct. 28, 1953; s. Glenn Grandville and Annabelle Ruth (McIlvanie) J.; m. Cynthia Parry, May 24, 1975; children: Jessica Lynn, Tiffany Desiree, Jarrod Parry. BA, Ottawa U., 1976; MDiv., Cen. Bapt. Sem., 1980. Ordained to ministry Bapt. Ch., 1980. Interim pastor First Bapt., Sublette, Kans., 1976; assoc./youth minister First Bapt., Paola, Kans., 1976-84; minister First Bapt., Wamego, Kans., 1980-84, Ruhamah Bapt., Rantoul, Kans., 1984-88, First Bapt. "Brick" Ch., Walworth, Wis., 1989—; camping comm. mem. Wis. Am. Bapt. Chs., 1990—. Mem. Central Heights Sch. Bd., Richmond, Kans., 1988-89; res. policemen chaplain Wamago (Kans.) Police Dept., 1981-84. Republican. Home: RR 1 Box 225 Walworth WI 53184 Office: First Bapt Brick Church RR 1 Box 227 Walworth WI 53184

JOHNSTON, MARYANN, religious organization administrator; b. Phila., Sept. 24, 1939; d. Rudolph John and Frances (McGinley) Seppy; m. William James Johnston Jr., Feb. 20, 1965; 1 child, Christopher. BEd, Seattle U., 1978, M of Religious Edn., 1979, EdD, 1990. Adminstrv. asst. Cath. Archdiocese of Seattle, 1979-83, asst. to dept. dir., 1983-84, adminstrv. mgr., 1984-85, dir. cen. and adminstrv. svcs. Faith and Community Devel. Dept., 1985-90; dir. Phinney Ridge Luth. Child Care and Kindergarten, Seattle, 1991—. Mem. Child and Family Resource Ctr, Seattle, 1986—; officer Ecumenical Interfaith, 1989—. Mem. ASTD, NAFE, Lay Mins. Assn. of Western Wash. (past pres.), Nat. Assn. Edn. of Young Children, Alpha Sigma Nu, Kappa Delta Pi, Phi Delta Kappa. Office: Phinney Ridge Luth Child Care and Kindergarten 7500 Greenwood N Seattle WA 98103

JOHNSTON, NORMAN LLOYD, pastor; b. La Porte, Ind., Dec. 15, 1933; s. Loran Raymond and Ivy (Hinshaw) J.; m. Mary Lou Crane, Dec. 18, 1954; children: Deborah Sue Johnston Miller, Sharon Diane Johnston Davis. Student, Kansas City (Mo.) Bus. Coll., Drury Coll., Springfield, Mo.; Diploma of Theology, Southwestern Bapt. Theol. Sem., Ft. Worth, 1973. Asst. pastor 1st Bapt. Ch., St. Clair, Mo., 1977-79; pastor 1st Bapt. Ch., Dexter, N.Mex., 1973-75, Oak Grove Bapt. Ch., Lonedell, Mo., 1975-77, 1st So. Bapt. Ch., Portage, Ind., 1979—; dir. Christian Coalition of Ind., 1991—; advisor religious matters Mayor of Portage, 1989—. Bd. dirs. Family Christian Svc. Inc., Portage, 1989—, Bill Costas 1st Dist. Congressman, Ind., 1990. With U.S. Navy, 1952-60. Mem. N.W. Ind. Bapt. Assn. (brotherhood dir. 1981-84, dir. vol. builders 1986—), Am. Family Assn. N.W. Ind. (pres. 1988-91), Lions (pres. 1956-57). Home: 2666 Elm St Portage IN 46368 Office: 1st So Bapt Ch 5785 Mulberry Ave Portage IN 46368

JOHNSTON, ROBERT KENT, provost, seminary dean, educator; b. Pasadena, Calif., June 9, 1945; s. Roy Gunnar and Naomi Mae (Harmon) J.; m. Catherine M. Barsotti; children: Elizabeth Amy, Margaret Nell. A.B., Stanford U., 1967; B.D., Fuller Theol. Sem., Pasadena, 1970; postgrad., North Pk. Theol. Sem., Chgo., 1970-71; Ph.D., Duke U., 1974. Ordained to ministry Evang. Covenant Ch., 1975. Youth pastor Pasadena, 1967-69; asst. min. Edgebrook Covenant Ch., Chgo., 1970-71; asst. prof. Western Ky. U., Bowling Green, 1974-78, assoc. prof., 1978-82; dean, assoc. prof. theology North Pk. Theol. Sem., Chgo., 1982-85, dean, prof. theology, 1985—; provost North Pk. Coll. and Theol. Sem., Chgo., 1988—; vis. prof. New Coll., Berkeley, Calif., 1980-81; mem. bd. of the ministry, pastoral rels. commn., exec. com. of ministerium Evang. Covenant Ch., 1982—. Author: Evangelicals at an Impasse, 1979, Psalms for God's People, 1980, The Christian at Play, 1983; editor: The Use of the Bible in Theology: Evangelical Options, 1985; co-editor: The Variety of American Evangelicalism, 1991. Mem. North Suburban Spl. Edn. Dist. Governing Bd., 1987-89; mem. sch. bd. Dist. 39, Wilmette, Ill., 1987-91; bd. dirs. Centro de Estudios Teologicos del Pacto Evangelico, L.A., 1988—. James B. Duke fellow Duke U., 1971-74. Mem. Am. Acad. Religion (co-chair evang. theology group 1986-90), Am. Theol. Soc. (east coast and midwest sects.), Assn. Theol. Schs. in U.S. and Can. (commn. on accrediting 1988—), Bonhoeffer Soc., Phi Beta Kappa. Democrat. Avocations: contemporary fiction, tennis. Office: N Park Coll & Theol Sem 3225 W Foster Ave Chicago IL 60625

JOHNSTON, ROBERT MORRIS, religious educator; b. Palo Alto, Calif., May 8, 1930; s. Arthur Martin and Mary Elizabeth (Butler) J.; m. Madeline Steele, July 29, 1956; children: Paul Martin, Robert Thomas, Elizabeth Ann, Margaret Kathryn. Student, Stanford U., 1948-49; BA, Pacific Union Coll., Angwin, Calif., 1954; BD, Andrews U., Berrien Springs, Mich., 1966; PhD, Hartford (Conn.) Seminary, 1977. Secondary tchr. Fresno (Calif.) Union Acad., 1956-58; prof. theology Korean Union Coll., Seoul, 1958-69; Philippine Union Coll., Manila, 1969-70, Seventh-day Adventist Theol. Seminary, Berrien Springs, 1974-84; prof. New Testament Seventh Day Adventist Theol. Seminary, Berrien Springs, 1984—; pres. Andrews Soc. for Religious

Studies, 1981; del. Gen. Conf. Seventh Day Adventists, 1990. Contbr.: Seventh-day Adventist Bible Dictionary, 1979, Sabbath in Scripture and History, 1982; co-author: They Also Taught in Parables, 1990; contbr. articles to profl. jours. Recipient Moses Bailey prize Hartford Seminary, 1971. Mem. Soc. Bibl. Lit., Chgo. Soc. for Bibl. Rsch., Am. Acad. Religion. Home: 8742-1 N Ridge Ave Berrien Springs MI 49103 Office: Andrews U Berrien Springs MI 49104

JOHNSTON, ROBIN W., academic administrator. Pres. Barclay Coll., Haviland, Kans. Office: Barclay Coll Office of Pres PO Box 288 Haviland KS 67059-0288*

JOHNSTON, TERRY L., minister, religious orgainization administrator; b. Eclectic, Ala., Nov. 11, 1946; s. Aubrey and Annie J.; m. Sherry Johnston, June 7, 1968; children: Shella, Jeremy, Nancy, Holly. BA, Samford U., 1969; MEd, Auburn U., 1987; cert., Inst. for Reality Therapy, 1987. Ordained to ministry Bapt. Ch. Practicum supr. Inst. for Reality Therapy, Canoga Park, Calif.; minister Bethlehem East. Bapt. Ch., Kent, Ala.; coord. Ingram State Tech. Coll., Deatsville, Ala. Mem. AACD, ASGW, ALASGW, Ala. Assn. Counseling and Devel. Home: Rt 3 Box 28 Eclectic AL 36024

JOINER, C. RAYMOND, JR., religious administrator; b. Birmingham, Ala., July 7, 1952; s. Clyde Raymond Sr. and Evelyn Grace (Eaves) J.; m. Vicky Sharlene Stamm, Jan. 5, 1977; children: Timothy Issac, Matthew Benjamin, Sarah Elizabeth. BA, U. Montevallo, 1975; MRE, Social Work, The So. Bapt. Theol. Sem., Louisville, 1984. Dir. childrens activities Phoenix Baptist Ctr, 1975-77; assoc. dir. Rio Vista Bapt. Ctr., Phoenix, 1977-79, dir., 1979-81; asst. dir. Carver Bapt. Ctr., New Orleans, 1984-86; dir. The Bapt. Ctr., Birmingham, Ala., 1987—; minister of edn. So. Temple Bapt. Ch., Phoenix, 1975-77. Community organizer, Friendship House, Louisville, 1983-84. Republican. Avocations: natural scis., geneology, creative writing. Office: Birmingham Bapt Assn 2501 12th Ave N Birmingham AL 35234

JOINER, EDWARD EARL, religious studies educator, minister; b. Colquitt, Ga., Apr. 25, 1924; s. John B. Sr. and Nancy Lula (Harrison) J.; m. Geraldine McCarty Rouse, July 21, 1946; children—Edward Earl Jr., Paul Allen, Ann Eileen, John Andrew. A.B., Stetson U., 1949; B.D., So. Bapt. Theol. Sem., 1953, Th.M., 1954, Th.D., 1960. Ordained to ministry So. Bapt. Conv., 1947. Prof. religion Stetson U., DeLand Fla., 1955—. Author: A History of Florida Baptists, 1972; A Christian Considers Divorce and Remarriage, 1983; contbr. to Holman Dictionary of the Bible, Mercer Dictionary of the Bible, Ency. So. Bapts., vols. III-IV, Issues in Christian Ethics; contbr. articles to profl. jours. Curator Fla. Bapt. Hist. Soc., DeLand, 1975—. Served with U.S. Army, 1944-46. Mem. Am. Acad. Religion. Democrat. Baptist. Lodge: Rotary. Avocations: backpacking; photography; fishing. Home: 735 N Sans Souci DeLand FL 32720 Office: Stetson U N Woodland Blvd De Land FL 32720

JOINER, STEVEN CRAIG, minister; b. Midland, Tex., Sept. 5, 1958; s. Herbert Lloyd and Bonnie Jean (Williams) J.; m. Linda Marie Wright, May 12, 1984; 1 child, William Craig. BA, Lubbock (Tex.) Christian Coll., 1980; postgrad., Harding Grad. Sch., Memphis, 1980-81; MS, Abilene (Tex.) Christian U., 1987. Intern minister Southside Ch. of Christ, Ft. Worth, summer 1980; minister to adolescents Harvey Drive Ch. of Christ, McAllen, Tex., 1981-84; minister to adolescents and families Hillcrest Ch. of Christ, Abilene, 1984—; lectr. Abilene Christian Family Conf., 1985, adj. prof.; lectr. Lubbock Christian Coll., 1986, Pepperdine U. Internat. Family Conf., Malibu, Calif., 1987. Bd. dirs. Pregnancy Counseling Service, Abilene, 1986. Avocation: cross training. Home: 1409 Friars Abilene TX 79602 Office: Hillcrest Ch of Christ 650 E Ambler Abilene TX 79601

JOKERST, CAROL ANN, religious group leadership team member; b. St. Louis, Mar. 28, 1939; d. Oliver W. and Mary Virginia (Prendergast) J. BA, Incarnate Word Coll., 1964; MA, St. Louis U., 1971, Duquesne U., 1974. Cert. jr./sr. high sch. tchr. Tchr. St. Dismas Sch., Florissant, Mo., 1962-63, Incarnate Word Acad., St. Louis, 1964-71; dir. formation Sisters of Charity of Incarnate Word, San Antonio, 1974-80, gen. adminstrv. team, 1984-90, gen. superior, 1990—; exec. dir. Religious Formation Conf., Washington, 1980-83; dir. mission effectiveness Incarnate Word Health System, San Antonio, 1983-84; chmn. bd. Spohn Health Care System, Corpus Christi, Tex., 1985—; bd. dirs. Santa Rosa Health Care System, San Antonio, Incarnate Word Health System, San Antonio, Incarnate Word Coll., San Antonio. Tchr. G.E.D. Program, St. Louis, 1967-69; vol. chaplain Med. Ctr. Hosp. (County), San Antonio, 1977-80. Mem. Religious Formation Conf. (bd. dirs. 1976-78), World Future Soc., Nat. Vocation Conf., Tex. Conf. Catholic Health Care Facilities. Democrat. Roman Catholic. Avocations: reading, cooking, listening to music, writing.

JOLLEY, RONALD SWAPP, religious organization executive; b. Ogden, Utah, Aug. 11, 1936; s. Leonard and Farris (Swapp) J.; m. Joette Fern Rogers, June 13, 1959; children: Jay Ronald, Jeffrey Leonard, Jon Rex, James Bruce. BS, Oreg. State U., 1962; JD, Willamette U., 1965; postgrad., Brigham Young U., 1970. Area coordinator ch. ednl. system Ch. of Jesus Christ of Latter-day Saints, Salem, Oreg., 1965-67; dist. coordinator cen. Oreg. Ch. of Jesus Christ of Latter-day Saints, Salem, 1967-68, area dir. Pacific northwest, 1968-89; stake pres. Ch. of Jesus Christ of Latter-day Saints, Salem, 1971-80, bd. dirs. social svcs., 1971-89, regional rep., 1980-87; sealer Seattle Temple, 1984-89. Mem. exec. bd. Cascade Area coun. Boy Scouts Am., 1967-74, 83—, mem. adv. bd., 1974-81, v.p., 1987-89. Recipient Silver Beaver award, 1987, Scouter's tng. award, 1970. Mem. Assn. Mormon Counselors and Psychotherapists, Mormon History Assn. Republican. Avocation: fishing. Home: 1696 Aerial Way SE Salem OR 97302

JOLLIFFE, RONALD LYNN, religion educator; b. Walla Walla, Wash., May 22, 1949; s. Robert Lynn and Edolene Mae Jolliffe; m. Glenda Fae Witt, Aug. 30, 1970; children: Melissa C., Kara Michele. BA, Walla Walla Coll., 1971; MDiv, Andrews U., Berrien Springs, Mich., 1974; MPH, Loma Linda (Calif.) U., 1979; PhD, Claremont (Calif.) Grad. Sch., 1990. Ordained to ministry Adventist Ch., 1980. Asst. prof. religion Southwestern Adventist Coll., Keene, Tex., 1984-89; assoc. prof. Bibl. studies Walla Walla Coll., College Place, Wash., 1989—; mem. Internat. Q Project, Claremont, 1987—; interim chair humanities majors Walla Walla Coll., 1990—. Author: Collegiate Quarterly, 1985-90, Spectrum, 1988; contbr. revs. to profl. jours. Mem. Soc. Bibl. Lit., Assn. Adventist Forums (chpt. pres. 1981-82). Office: Walla Walla Coll College Place WA 99324

JOLSON, ALFRED JAMES, bishop; b. Bridgeport, Conn., June 18, 1928; s. Alfred James and Justine Elizabeth (Houlihan) J. BA, Boston Coll., 1951, MA, 1952; BTh., Weston Coll., 1958; MBA, Harvard U., 1962; PhD, Gregorian U., Rome, 1970; LHD (hon.), Wheeling (W.Va.) Jesuit Coll., 1990. Joined S.J., Roman Cath. Ch., 1946, ordained priest, 1958, bishop, 1988; lic. psychologist, Zimbabwe. Tchr. Baghdad (Iraq) Coll., 1952-55; prof., dean Al-hikma U., Baghdad, 1962-64; dean Boston Coll., Newton, Mass., 1964-68; dean, prof. Sch. Social Workers, Salisbury, Rhodesia, 1970-76, St. Joseph U., Phila., 1976-86, Wheeling (W.Va.) Jesuit Coll., 1986-87; bishop Reykjavik, Iceland, 1987—. Chmn. bd. dirs. St. Joseph's Prep Sch., Phila., 1979-84; bd. dirs. St. Joseph's U., Phila., 1978-79. Mem. Knights of Holy Sepulcher. Democrat. Home and Office: Diocese Reykjavik, Havallagata 14, 101 Reykjavik Iceland

JONES, ALAN WILLIAM, dean; b. London, Mar. 5, 1940; s. Edward Augustus and Blanche Hilds (Hunt) J.; m. Josephine Morris Franklin, June 8, 1966; children: Madeleine, Charlotte, Edward. BA, U. Nottingham, Eng., 1963; postgrad., Gen. Theol. Sem., 1965, 67; PhD, U. Nottingham, Eng., 1971. Ordained priest Episcopal Ch. Chaplain, lectr. Lincoln (Eng.) Theol. Coll., 1968-81; asst. dir. Trinity Inst., N.Y.C., 1971-73; dir. Ctr. for Christian Spirituality, prof. Gen. Theol. Sem., N.Y.C., 1973-85; dean Grace Cathedral, San Francisco, 1985—. Author: Living in the Spirit, 1979, Exploring Spiritual Directions, 1982, Soul Making, 1985, Passion for Pilgrimage, 1988. Mem. Univ. Club. Office: Grace Cathedral 1051 Taylor St San Francisco CA 94118

JONES, ALLAN BARRY, clergyman, religious association executive; b. Liverpool, Eng., June 25, 1936; came to U.S., 1968; s. Alfred William and Ethel May (Sumner) J.; m. Christine A. Lidster, Oct. 17, 1959; children—Glyn, Owen. Diploma, Skerry's Coll., Liverpool, 1953, Cliff Coll., Calver, Eng., 1957; B.Th., Toronto (Ont., Can.) Bible Coll., 1964; M.A., Calif. Grad. Sch. Theology, 1980. Ordained to ministry Congl. Christian Conf., 1962; pastor Murray Hall Ch., Liverpool, 1958-60, Ringwood (Ont.) Congl. Christian Ch., 1960-65, Univ. Ave. Congl. Ch., St. Paul, 1968-73, Carlsbad (Calif.) Community Ch., 1973—; pres. Conservative Congl. Christian Conf., Carlsbad, 1972-75; Tchr. Northwestern Coll., St. Paul, 1971-73. Mem. St. David's Soc. of San Diego. Home: 3760 Catalina St Carlsbad CA 92008 Office: Carlsbad Community Ch 3175 Harding St Carlsbad CA 92008

JONES, BOB GORDON, bishop; b. Paragould, Ark., Aug. 22, 1932; s. F.H. and Helen Truman (Ellis) J.; m. Judith Munroe, Feb. 22, 1963; children: Robert Gordon, Timothy Andrew. B.B.A., U. Miss., 1956; M.Div., Episcopal Sem. S.W., 1959, D.D. hon., 1978. Asst. to dean Trinity Cathedral, Little Rock, 1959-62; vicar St. George-in-Arctic, Kotzebue, Alaska, 1962-67; rector St. Christopher's Ch., Anchorage, 1967-77; bishop Episcopal Diocese Wyo., Laramie, 1977—; chmn. bd. Cathedral Home Children, Laramie, 1977—; mem. exec. com. Provence N.W., Helena, Mont., 1980-83, Coalition 14, Phoenix, 1982-84. Pres. Arctic Circle C. of C., Kotzebue, 1966; mem. exec. com. Alaska C. of C., Juneau, 1967; chmn. allocations com. United Way, Anchorage, 1973-75; pres. United Way Anchorage, 1975-76. Served with USN, 1950-55, Korea. Republican. Lodges: Lions; Elks. Home: 3207 Alta Vista Dr Laramie WY 82070 Office: Episcopal Diocese of Wyo 104 S 4th St Box 1007 Laramie WY 82070

JONES, BRIAN KEITH, minister; b. Gary, Ind., Apr. 21, 1943; s. Cleo Herbert and Marion Esther (Braatz) J.; m. Emily Scott Borst, May 2, 1981; children: Rita Faye, Thomas F., William N. BS in Edn., N.E. Mo. State U., 1965; MDiv, Wartburg Theol. Sem., Dubuque, Iowa, 1970; postgrad., St. Francis Coll., W.Va. U. Ordained to ministry Evang. Luth. Ch. in Am., 1970. Pastor Emmanuel Luth. Ch., LaOtto, Ind., 1970-72, Grace Luth. Ch., Elkhart, Ind., 1972-74, Our Savior Luth. Ch., Gatlinburg, Tenn., 1974-85, Bethany Luth. Ch., South Bend, Ind., 1985-87; pastor, developer Holy Spirit Luth. Ch., Pikeville, Ky., 1987—; mem. Evang. Luth. Coalition Ministry in Appalachia, Luth. Appalachia Ministry in Ky., East Ky. coun. Ind.-Ky. synod Evang. Luth. Ch. in Am. Bd. dirs. United Helping Hands Pikeville, Inc., Pikeville Area Family YMCA, Family Resource Ctr. Mem. Pikeville Area Ministerial Assn. (pres.), Pike County C. of C. Home: 140 Green Meadow Ln Pikeville KY 41501

JONES, BURTON IRA, minister; b. Flint, Mich., Apr. 2, 1934; s. Ira William and Ursle Azalea (Hogsten) J. AB, Wheaton (Ill.) Coll., 1956; MDiv, No. Bapt. Sem., Chgo., 1959; MA, U. Mich., 1967. Ordained to ministry Bapt. Ch., 1959; cert. elem. tchr., sch. adminstr., Mich. Dir. Christian edn. Berean Bapt. Ch., Flint, Mich., 1959-60; pastor Birch Run (Mich.) Bapt. Ch., 1962-77; asst. to pastor North Bapt. Ch., Flint, Mich., 1989—; sec. Victorious Christian Youth/chpt. Youth for Christ, Internat., Flint, 1989—. Pres. United Way Mt. Morris (Mich.) and Genesee, 1981—; mem. president's coun. United Way, Flint, 1981—. Mem. Christian Mgmt. Assn., Kiwanis (past pres. Mt. Morris). Republican. Home: 1044 W Stanley Rd Mount Morris MI 48458 Office: North Bapt Ch 2001 N Saginaw Flint MI 48505

JONES, CAROLYN JANE, minister; b. Grove City, Pa., Jan. 28, 1937; d. Hester Clark and Winifred Eleanor (Hoag) J.; m. Thomas Woodward Golightly. BA, Westminster Coll., 1958; MA in Edn., Syracuse U., 1963; MDiv, Pitts. Theol. Sem., 1977, D Ministry, 1989. Ordained to ministry Presbyn. Ch. (U.S.A.), 1977. Tchr. Am. Coll. for Girls, Cairo, 1958-61, Bethel Park High Sch., Pa., 1963-68; asst. dean women Syracuse U., N.Y., 1968-71, dir., asst. dir. activities and orgns. Office Student Affairs, 1971-74; assoc. in Christian edn. Pebble Hill Presbyterian Ch., DeWitt, N.Y., 1971-74; dir. Christian edn. Newlonsburg United Presbyn. Ch., Murrysville, Pa., 1975-77; assoc. pastor Glenshaw Presbyn. Ch., Pa., 1977-84; interim minister at large Pitts. Presbytery, 1984-90; exec. presbyter Washington Presbytery, Presbyn. Ch. (U.S.A.), 1990—; bd. dirs. Pitts. Theol. Sem.; bd. mgrs. New Wilmington Missionary Conf. Recipient Thomas Jamison scholar, 1977; Sylvester S. Marvin Meml. fellow, 1977. Mem. Cleric of Pitts., Internat. Assn. Women Ministers, Interim Network, Assn. Presbyn. Interim Ministry Specialists, Presbyn. Clergywomen's Assn. Home: 106 Farmview Pl Venetia PA 15367 Office: PO Box 146 Eighty Four PA 15330

JONES, CHARLES EDWARD, religion educator; b. Mobile, Ala., Jan. 18, 1956; s. Willie L. and Mary (Davis) J.; m. Sandra Hayward, Aug. 4, 1979; children: Michael Hayward Davis Jones, Maria Faith. BA, U. Ala., 1978; MDiv, Va. Union U., 1982; D of Ministry, Howard U., 1986. Ordained to ministry Bapt. Ch., 1982; cert. clin. pastoral counselor. Pastor Ebenezer Bapt. Ch., Staunton, Va., 1982-84, Gravel Hill Bapt. Ch., Richmond, Va., 1984-88, Mount Tabor Bapt. Ch., Richmond, 1988—; prof. of religion Va. Union Univ., Richmond, 1986—, chmn. dept. of religion, 1986—; instr. Bapt. Gen. Conv. of Va.; prof. Sch. of Theology, Va. Union U., 1991; instr. Church Leadership Inst., Richmond, 1991, Ebenezer Bapt. Assn., Petersburg, 1987-91. Trustee Averett Coll., Danville, Va., 1988—. Named Tchr. of Yr. Va. Union U., 1989, 90; named to Outstanding Young Men of Am., 1988. Mem. East End Ministers Conf. (treas. 1989-91), Howard Univ. Alumni, Va. Union Univ. Alumni, Univ. of Ala. Alumni, Alpha Phi Alpha. Home and Office: 1808 Leslie Lane Richmond VA 23228 *The challenge and call of clergy is to become professional teachers bringing to fruition a more informed society. The truth that comes through education will truly set us all free.*

JONES, CHARLES EDWIN, minister, historian, bibliographer; b. Kansas City, Mo., June 1, 1932; s. Dess Dain and Dove (Barnwell) J.; m. Beverly Anne Lundy, May 30, 1956; 1 child, Karl Laurence. BA, Bethany-Peniel Coll., 1954; MALS, U. Mich., 1955; MS, U. Wis., 1960, PhD, 1968; postgrad., Episcopal Div. Sch., Cambridge, Mass., 1975-76. Ordained to ministry Reformed Episcopal Ch. as deacon, 1990. Lay min., edn. Episcopal Ch. of Resurrection, Oklahoma City, 1980-83; chaplain-in-residence Westlake Nursing Ctr., Oklahoma City, 1989—. Author: Perfectionist Persuasion, 1974, Guide to the Study of the Holiness Movement, 1974, Guide to the Study of the Pentecostal Movement, 1983, Black Holiness, 1987; contbr. articles to scholarly jours. With U.S. Army, 1956-58. Mem. Am. Theol. Libr. Assn., Can. Ch. Hist. Soc. Democrat. Mem. Reformed Episcopal Ch. Home: 12300 Springwood Dr Oklahoma City OK 73120

JONES, CHARLES IRVING, bishop; b. El Paso, Tex., Sept. 13, 1943; s. Charles I. Jr. and Helen A. (Heyward) J.; m. Ashby MacArthur, June 18, 1966; children: Charles I. IV, Courtney M., Frederic M., Keith A. BS, The Citadel, 1965; MBA, U. N.C., 1966; MDiv, U. of the South, 1977, DD, 1989. CPA. Pub. acctg. D.E. Gatewood and Co., Winston-Salem, N.C., 1966-72; dir. devel. Chatham (Va.) Hall, 1972-74; instr. acctg. U. of the South, Sewanee, Tenn., 1974-77; coll. chaplain Western Ky. U., Bowling Green, 1977-81; vicar Trinity Episcopal Ch., Russelville, Ky., 1977-85; archdeacon Diocese of Ky., Louisville, 1981-86; bishop Episcopal Diocese of Mont., Helena, 1986—; bd. dirs. New Directions Ministries, Inc., N.Y.C.; mem. standing com. Joint Commn. on Chs. in Small Communities, 1988—; v.p. province VI Episcopal Ch., 1991—, mem. Presiding Bishop's Coun. Advice, 1991—. Author: Mission Strategy in the 21st Century, 1989; bd. editors Grass Roots, Luling, Tex., 1985—; contbr. articles to profl. jours. Founder Concerned Citizens for Children, Russelville, 1981; bd. dirs. St. Peter's Hosp., Helena, 1986—. With USMCR, 1961-65. Mem. Aircraft Owners and Pilots Assn. Avocations: running, flying, writing. Office: Diocese Mont 515 N Park Ave Helena MT 59601

JONES, CHARLES LEONARD (CHUCK JONES), religious organization administrator; b. Santa Monica, Calif., Mar. 30, 1949; s. Johnny W. and Alice Billie (Robinson) J. BA in Humanities, U. So. Calif., 1971, MA in Drama and Cinema, 1973, MFA, 1974; postgrad., Candler Sch. Theology, Emory U., Sch. of Theology, Claremont. Cert. ch. bus. adminstr. Asst. mgr. The Wherehouse, Santa Monica/Westwood, Calif., 1972; press agt./act rep. Gene Shefrin Entertainment, Beverly Hills, Calif., 1973; dispatcher, supr. Yellow Cab Co., L.A., 1973-75; owner Express Transp. Svc., L.A., 1975-77; ops. mgr. Baggage Master Delivery, El Segundo, Calif., 1978; dir. communications United Ind. Taxi, Hollywood, Calif., 1979; gen. mgr. Extran Inc., Westchester, Calif., 1980-86; ind. ch. cons. L.A., 1987; exec. dir. So. Calif. Ecumenical Council, L.A., 1987—; bd. dirs. Gen. Bd. Discipleship United Meth. Ch., 1984—, nat. chmn. UMMENS div., 1989—, pres. W St, 1984—; bd. dirs. Calif. Ch. Council, So. Calif. Interreligious Council. Mem. Canterbury Trust Fund in Am., Washington, 1986—, Williamsburg (Va.) Trust, 1987—; bd. dirs. AIDS Interfaith Task Force, L.A., 1988, United Meth. Men's Found., 1988—, life mem., 1986; del. United Meth. Ch. Gen. and Juris Conf., 1988, 92; active Boy Scouts Am. Named Layman of Yr. United Meth. Ch. Calif.-Pacific Ann. Conf., 1987, John Wesley fellow, 1988; recipient Torch award United Meth. Ch., 1986. Mem. Nat. Assn. United Meth. Scouters (bd. dirs. 1988—), Nat. Assn. Ch. Bus. Adminstrn., United Meth. Assn. Ch. Bus. Adminstrn., U. So. Calif. Gen. Alumni Assn. (life), U.S.C. Cinema/TV Alumni Assn., Cinema Circulus, The Am. Film Inst., Pi Soc., Alpha Phi Omega (life mem., dir. alumni rels., disting. svc. award). Democrat. Avocations: reading, directing community theatre, history. Home: 15917 Kittridge St Van Nuys CA 91406 Office: So Calif Ecumenical Coun 1010 S Flower St #403 Los Angeles CA 90015

JONES, CHARLES S., minister; b. Orlando, Fla., July 31, 1941; s. Walter Brannen and Susie Jane (Rose) J.; m. Judy Palmer Thompson, June 26, 1961; children: Charles S. Jr., Timothy, Deborah, Walter, Karen, Amanda. BA in Music, Asbury Coll., Wilmore, Ky., 1972. Ordained to ministry So. Bapt. Conv.; cert. K-12 tchr. music, Ky. Evangelist, Lesington, Ky., 1972-74; min. music and youth Wrens (Ga.) Bapt. Ch., 1974-77; min. music 1st Alliance Ch., Mansfield, Ohio, 1978-81; pastor San Pablo Bapt. Ch., Jacksonville, Fla., 1988—; staff musician Bill Glass, Evangelist, Tex., 1972-74; advisor Sta. WVCF, Christian radio, Mansfield, 1979-81; mem. Stark Ministries, Internat., Jacksonville, 1988—. Composer gospel song We Have A Strong City, 1973. Mem. Jacksonville Bapt. Assn. (Christian life com. 1989-90). Home: 3126 Courtney Woods Ct Jacksonville FL 32224 Office: San Pablo Bapt Ch 3044 San Pablo Rd Jacksonville FL 32224

JONES, DAVID ALAN, music minister; b. Hartford, Conn., Oct. 26, 1954; s. Harold Byron and Edith (Hubbard) J.; m. Betty Southerland, Mar. 29, 1987. BA, U. Ga., 1978; M of Ch. Music, Southwestern Bapt. Theol. Sem., 1981; MusM in Vocal Performance, U. Ga., 1991. Asst. music dir. Watkinsville First Bapt. Ch., 1973-77; minister music Lakeview Bapt. Ch., Fort Worth, 1978-80; minister music and youth Southside Bapt. Ch., Wichita Falls, Tex., 1980-82, Oconee Heights Bapt. Ch., Athens, Ga., 1982-86; minister music Moon's Grove Bapt. Ch., Colbert, Ga., 1987—; asst. supr. D&B Jones Health Products, Athens, 1990—. Appeared in various operas; roles in Verdi's Rigoletto, 1990, The Mikado, 1991, The Marriage of Figaro, 1991, Evita, 1990. Mem. Clarke County Adoption Resource Exchange, Athens, 1991. Recipient First Pl. winner Nat. Assn. Tchrs. Singing, 1990; named grad. asst. U. Ga. Sch. Music, 1988-90. Mem. Nat. Assn. Tchrs. Singing, Am. Choral Dirs. Assn., Ga. Bapt. Ch. Music Conf., So. Bapt. Ch. Music Conf., Athens Area Music Ministers Assn. (pres. 1982-85), Ch. & Civic Choral Orgns. (soloist 1978—). Home and Office: 309 Providence Rd Athens GA 30606

JONES, DAVID COLIN, priest; b. Youngstown, Ohio, June 20, 1943; s. John Henry and Jean (Clark) J.; m. Mary Kennedy Biddle, June 5, 1965; children: David Colin Jr., Elizabeth. AB, W.Va. U., 1965; MDiv, Va. Sem., 1968, DMin, 1991. Ordained to ministry Episcopal Ch. as diaconate, 1968, as priest 1968. Vicar St. James' Episcopal Ch., Lewisburg, W.Va., 1968-72; rector St. Stephen's Episcopal Ch., Beckley, W.Va., 1972-77, Ch. of the Good Shepherd, Burke, Va., 1978—; dean West Fairfax region Episcopal Diocese of Va., 1981-85; dep. Gen. Conv. Episcopal Ch., 1973, 88, 91; founder St. Peter's in the Woods Episcopal Ch., Fairfax, 1989. Office: Ch of the Good Shepherd 9350 Braddock Rd Burke VA 22015

JONES, DAVID LEE, minister; b. Newark, Feb. 18, 1956; s. Morgan R. and Mildred Claire (Zahner) J. BA, Messiah Coll., Grantham, Pa., 1978; MDiv, Princeton Theol. Sem., 1982; AAS, Valedicbrian-Sullivan County Community Coll, 1987; STD, Emory U., Atlanta, 1988—. Ordained to ministry Presbyn. Ch., 1982. Asst. pastor First Presbyn. Ch., Southampton, N.Y., 1982-83; pastor First Presbyn. Ch., Jeffersonville, N.Y., 1983-87; chaplain Grady Meml. Hosp., Atlanta, 1987-88; staff counselor Harmony Grove Meth. Ch., Lilburn, Ga., 1988—; pastoral counselor in tng. Ga. Assn. for Pastoral Counselors, Atlanta, 1988-91; pastor Kelley Presbyn. Ch., Lithonia, Ga., 1991—; mental health cons. Newton County Mental Health, Covington, Ga., 1990—, Newton County Mental Health, 1991—. Bd. dirs. Sullivan County Coun. on Alcoholsim, Monticello, N.Y., 1984-87; chaplain Sullivan County Sheriff's Dept., Monticello, 1984-87. Recipient Disting. Grad. award, Sullivan County Community Coll., 1987. Mem. Am. Assn. Pastoral Counselors, Jeffersonville Clergy Assn. (pres. 1983-87). Democrat. *I have long believed the true value of people's lives would be best assessed if you first removed all their earthly possessions.*

JONES, DAVID LEIGH, religious organization administrator, journalist, minister; b. Buffalo, Apr. 25, 1954. BA, U. Minn., 1976. Ordained to ministry Bapt. Gen. Conf., 1990. Mng. editor Comml. West, Mpls., 1976-79; dir. publs. Luis Palau Evangelistic Assn., Portland, Oreg., 1979-82, dir. print media, 1982-86, v.p. communications, 1986-88, v.p. adminstrn., 1988—. Mem. Soc. Profl. Journalists, Evang. Press Assn., Nat. Religious Broadcasters, Christian Ministries Mgmt. Assn. Office: Luis Palau Evangelistic Assn 1100 NW Murray Rd Portland OR 97229

JONES, DEE R., pastor; b. Danville, Ill., July 13, 1939; s. M. Richard and Estella R. (Davis) J.; m. R. Diane, July 3, 1961 (div. 1983); m. Deborah J., August 11, 1984; children: Kim, Charles. BSBA, Olivet Nazarene U., 1963. Tchr., coach Bethalto (Ill.) Sch. Dist., 1963-68, Roosevelt Sch. Dist., Phoenix, 1970-73; pastor, tchr. West Milton Ch. of the Nazarene, Ohio, 1973-74, Manhattan Blvd. Ch. of the Nazarene, Toledo, 1974-75, Globe 1sr Ch. of the Nazarene, Globe, Ariz., 1975-76; pastor, tchr. 1st Ch. of the Nazarene, McAllen, Tex., 1976-85, La Mirada, Calif., 1985—; dir. chaplain services Rio Grande Radiation Treatment Ctr., McAllen, Tex., 1977-84. Bd. dirs. Gila County Mental Health Clinic, Globe, Ariz., 1975, Vol. Ctr., La Mirada, Calif., 1986-88; active Leadership McAllen, 1983. Republican. Avocations: softball, skiing, boating, hiking.

JONES, DENNIS NEIL, deacon; b. St. Petersburg, Fla., Oct. 15, 1946; s. Charles Senator and Carmel Mary (Colcolough) J.; m. Carolyn Poole, July 19, 1975; children: Ellen, Susan, Anne, Thomas. BA, U. S.C., 1972. Ordained deacon Roman Cath. Ch., 1985. Min. to sick Cath. Ch., Columbia, S.C., 1977-89, counselor to divorced, 1985-89; tchr. classes for premarriage Our Lady of the Hills, Columbia, S.C., 1985-89; field agt. KC, New Haven, 1989—. Active Pro-Life, Indialantic, Fla., 1990—. With U.S. Army, 1967-70. Mem. Life Underwriters (bd. dirs. 1990-91). Office: Holy Name of Jesus Ch 3050 A1A Indialantic FL 32903

JONES, DERWYN DIXON, bishop; b. Chatham, Ont., Can., Aug. 5, 1925; s. Walter and Mary Rosalie (Dixon) J.; m. A. Carole DiLamarter, Apr. 18, 1960; children—Paula, Evan. B.A., U. Western Ont., London, Can., 1946; L.Th., Huron Coll., London, Ont., Can., 1946, D.D.(hon.), 1983. Ordained to ministry, Anglican Ch. Can., 1946. Rector St. Andrew's Ch., Kitchener, Ont., Can., 1949-52; rector Canon Davis Meml. Ch., Sarnia, Ont., Can., 1955-58, St. Barnabas Ch., Windsor, Ont., Can., 1958-66, St. Peter's Ch., Brockville, Ont., Can., 1966-69, St. James Westminster Ch., London, Ont., Can., 1969-82; bishop Diocese of Huron, London, Ont., Can., 1982—; broadcaster Sta.-CBE, Windsor, Ont., Can., Sta.-CFPL-FM, London, Ont., Can. Contbr. editorials to London Free Press. Hon. sr. fellow Renison Coll., Waterloo, Ont., Can., 1983. Avocations: piano; organ. Home: 25 Cherokee Rd, London, ON Canada N6G 2N7 Office: Diocese of Huron, 4-220 Dundas St, London, ON Canada N6A 1H3

JONES, DONALD BARRY, pastor; b. Suffern, N.Y., Apr. 20, 1939; s. Donald Ellsworth and Lillian (Close) J.; m. Kathleen Rigolosi, Nov. 17, 1962; children: Donald Ellsworth, Matthew Paul, Holly Michelle, Anthony Timothy. BA, Tenn. Wesleyan Coll., 1961; MDiv., Drew U., 1965. Ordained to minister Meth. Ch., 1962. Pastor Wesley Chapel Circuit Meth. Ch., Suffern, 1962-65, Madison Park-Simpson Meth. Ch., Paterson, N.J., 1965-69; urban pastor Grace Meth. Ch., Wyckoff, N.J., 1969-72; pastor Pearl River (N.Y.) Meth. Ch., 1972-77, Trinity Meth. Ch., Rahway, N.J., 1977—; founder, adminstr. Monsignor Wall Social Service Ctr., Hackensack, N.J., 1969-70; dir. Narcotic Edn. County Bergen, Hackensack, N.J., 1970-72; chaplain Rahway (N.J.) Geriatric Ctr., 1983—; bd. dirs. Meth. Homes N.J, Neptune, 1986—; active Rahway Bd. Edn. Contbr. numerous articles on alcoholism and drug abuse to profl. jours. Founder, bd. dirs. Community Blood Bank Program, Pearl River, Rahway; trustee Union County ARC, chaplain Tallman (N.Y.) Fire Dept., Rahway First Aid Squad Bldg. Com., Rahway Adult Basic Edn.; counselor hospice program Rahway Hosp.; police chaplain County of Bergen, Rahway, N.J.; mem. Rahway Local Bd. Assistance, 1987—, Rahway Bd. Edn., 1986-87; counselor N.J. Council on Alcohal Problems, Youth Guidance Commn., Paterson, others. Recipient Humanitarian Service, Rahway Geriatirc Center, 1984, Key to the City City of Athens, Tenn., 1985. Mem. Am. Assn. Suicidology, Internat. Narcotic Enforcement Officers Assn., Am. Soc. Aging, Gerontological Soc. N.J., N.J. Council on Alcohol Problems (trustee), N.J. Pub. Health Service, Sigma Phi Epsilon. Avocations: deep sea fishing, gardening. Home: 790 Bryant St Rahway NJ 07065 Office: Trinity United Meth Ch 1428 Main St Rahway NJ 07065

JONES, EDDIE, JR., minister, educator; b. Opelika, Ala., Jan. 19, 1950; s. Eddie Sr. and Gertrude (Calloway) T.; m. Mary Ann Nix, Dec. 26, 1973; children: Dexter, Carlos, Edkenjunta. AA, Selma U., 1972; BS, Jarvis Christian Coll., 1975; MEd, Ala. State U., 1989. Ordained to ministry African Meth. Episcopal Zion Ch. as elder, 1978; cert. elem. sch. tchr., Ala. Pastor Pleasant Grove African Meth. Episcopal Zion Ch., Evergreen, Ala., New Hope African Meth. Episcopal Zion Ch., Burnt Corn, Ala., Spring Hill African Meth. Episcopal Zion Ch., Prattville, Ala., Popular Spring African Meth. Episcopal Zion Ch., Prattville; tchr. Conecuh County Schs., Evergreen, 1989-91; musician S. Ala. Conf., Brewton, Cahaba Conf., Prattville. Named Outstand Young Man Am., Montgomery Jaycees, 1977. Mem. Jr. Beta Club (sponsor 1989-91), Ala. Edn. Assn., Nat. Eng. Coun., Epsilon Delta Chi. Home: Rte 2 Box 241-I Evergreen AL 36401 Office: African Meth Zion Ch Charlotte NC 28203 *Life is a gift from God. We can use our life to help create positive things for people who have lost hope. I try to let my life be a good example for others to follow.*

JONES, EDMUND SAMUEL PHILIP, minister; b. Belfast, No. Ireland, Mar. 1, 1934; came to U.S., 1983; s. Thomas Edmund and Charlotte (Rowe) J.; m. Dorene Esther Taylor, Aug. 23, 1969; children: Jennifer, Jeremy, Jonathan. BA, Trinity Coll., Dublin, Ireland, 1955; BD, Fitzwilliam Hall, Cambridge, Eng., 1958; postgrad., Edinburgh (Scotland) U., 1961; PhD, St. Andrews (Scotland) U., 1965. Ordained to ministry Ch. of Scotland, 1961. Sr. minister Queen's Cross Ch., Aberdeen, Scotland, 1965-83, N.Y. Ave. Presbyn. Ch., Washington, 1983-87; interim minister Irvington (N.Y.) Presbyn. Ch., 1987-91; sr. minister Abington (Pa.) Presbyn. Ch., 1991—; religious adviser BBC, Glascow, Scotland, 1980-83, Independent Broadcasting Authority, London, 1981-83; Warrack lectr. in preaching Ch. of Scotland, Edinburgh, Aberdeen, Glasgow, St. Andrews Univs., 1982-83. Editor: Worship and Wonder, 1971; author: (booklet) Christian Engagement in Politics, 1975; author: (with others) Blueprint, 1976. Home: 2310 Fairway Rd Hungtindon Valley PA 19006 Office: Abington Presbyn Ch Abington PA 19001

JONES, EDWARD WITKER, bishop; b. Toledo, Mar. 25, 1929; s. Mason Beach and Gertrude (Witker) J.; m. Anne Shelburne, July 13, 1963; children: Martha, Caroline, David. BA, William Coll., 1951; BD, Va. Theol. Sem., 1954, DD, 1978. Ordained to ministry Episcopal Ch., 1954. Rector Christ Ch., Oberlin, Ohio, 1957-68; exec. asst. to bishop and planning officer Diocese of Ohio, Cleve., 1968-71; rector St. James' Ch., Lancaster, Pa., 1971-77; bishop Episc. Diocese of Indpls., 1977—; lectr. homiletics, 1963-67. Bd. dirs. Ohio Chpt. ACLU, 1964-67, Lorain County Child Welfare Dept., Ohio, 1964-68, Lancaster Tomorrow, 1975-77, Indpls. United Way, 1978-83, Indpls. Urban League, 1982—; bd. visitors DePauw U., 1982-85. Mem. Urban Bishops Coalition. Democrat. Home: 5008 Derby Ln Indianapolis IN 46226 Office: Diocese of Indpls 1100 W 42nd St Indianapolis IN 46208

JONES, ELIZABETH SELLE, minister; b. L.A., May 15, 1926; d. Raymond Martin Louis and Claire (Holley) Selle; m. James Latimer Jones, Dec. 22, 1945; children: Stephen, Nancy, David, Susan. BA, U. Calif., Santa Barbara, 1970; MDiv, Starr King Sch. for Ministry, Berkeley, Calif., 1980. Ordained to ministry Unitarian Universalist Ch., 1980. Minister Unitarian Universalist Ch. in Livermore (Calif.), 1981—; trustee Starr King Sch. for the Ministry, Berkeley, 1989—; del. gen. assembly Unitarian Universalist Assn. of Congregations, 1974-91. Pres. Glendale (Calif.) PTA, 1958-60. Mem. Unitarian Universalist Ministers Assn. (exec. com. 1987-89), Amnesty Internat., NOW, Greenpeace, Nat. Peace Inst., LWV, Habitat for Humanity, Neighbor to Neighbor, Planned Parenthood. Democrat. Office: Unitarian Universalist Ch 1893 N Vasco Rd Livermore CA 94550

JONES, ERNEST EDWARD, minister, religious organization administrator; b. DeRidder, La., May 3, 1931; s. David Jesse and Daisy (Hatcherson) J.; m. Leslie Alexander, Aug. 31, 1952; children: Beryl J., Ernest E. Jr., Carolyn Jones Haygood, Donna J. Winston. BS, Grambling (La.) Coll. (now Grambling State U.), 1952; BA in Religion and Philosophy, Bishop Coll., Dallas, 1961; DD (hon.), United Theol. Sem., Monroe, La., 1966; LHD (hon.), Va. Sem., Lynchburg, 1986. Ordained to ministry Bapt. Ch., 1951. Tchr., coach, prin. Morehouse Parish Sch. System, Bastrop, La., 1952-58; pastor St. John's Bapt. Ch., Homer, La., 1953-56, Mt. Zion Bapt. Ch., Dubach, La., 1953-56, Macedonia Bapt. Ch., Rayville, La., 1956-58, Mt. Harmony Bapt. Ch., Ruston, La., 1951-58, Galilee Bapt. Ch., Shreveport, La., 1958—; Pres. Nat. Bapt. Conv. of Am., Inc., 1985—; former chmn. social justice commn. of Nat. Bapt. Conv. of Am., Inc.; affiliated with Bapt. World's Alliance, Congress of Nat. Black Chs., Nat. Council of Chs. of Christ, La. Interchurch Conf. Former mem. NCCJ, Police Jury Caddo Parish, Shreveport, La. Gov.'s Commn. on Race Rels. and Civil Rights; former membership chmn. United Dem. Campaign Com., Shreveport; bd. suprs. La. State U., Baton Rouge; past trustee Morehouse Sch. Religion, Atlanta; bd. dirs. Grambling State U. Found. Recipient Brotherhood Citation NCCJ, 1987, Friend of Edn. award Caddo Assn. Educators, 1986, Grambling State U. Hall of Fame award, 1986; local nominee Nat. MLK Meml. award NEA, 1987. Mem. Alpha Phi Alpha (outstanding alpha award 1986). Democrat. Baptist. Avocation: gardening. Office: Galilee Bapt Ch 1540 Pierre Ave Shreveport LA 71103

JONES, FRANKLIN ALLAN, minister; b. Mason City, Iowa, July 25, 1932; s. Randall Franklin and Lydia (Moen) J.; children from previous marriage: Eric Hodges, Lydia Jo, Keith Fairbanks, Ingrid Sonia; m. Carol Sue Silverman, Nov. 30, 1974; 1 child, Rachel Sarah. BA cum laude, Augustana Coll., Sioux Falls, S.D., 1954; MDiv, Luth. Sch. Theology, 1959. Ordained to ministry Luth. Ch. in Am., 1959. Vicar local ch. Phila., 1957-58; founding pastor St. Philip Luth. Ch., Trenton, Mich., 1959-64; pastor Advent Luth. Ch., Arlington, Va., 1964—; founder, coord. Christianity-Recreation-Edn. Workshop, Washington, 1967-71. Vol. Exec. sec. Arlington Community Action Program, 1965-66. Fulbright scholar Eberhard-Karls U., Tubingen, Fed. Republic Germany, 1954-55. Home: 515 N George Mason Dr Arlington VA 22203 Office: Advent Luth Ch 2222 S Arlington Ridge Rd Arlington VA 22202

JONES, FREDERICK STANLEY, theologian, educator; b. Paducah, Ky., Jan. 19, 1953; s. Malcolm David and Catherine (Neuman) J.; m. Britt Waltraud Halvorsen-Kamm, May 20, 1988. BA, Yale U., 1975, U. Oxford, Eng., 1978; MA, U. Oxford, Eng., 1982; Dr. Theology, U. Göttingen, Fed. Republic Germany, 1987; PhD, Vanderbilt U., 1989. Instr., researcher U. Göttingen, 1984-88; asst. prof. Calif. State U., Long Beach, 1988—; guest prof. religion École Pratique des Hautes Études, Paris, 1990. Author "Freiheit" in den Briefen des Apostels Paulus, 1987, Pseudo-Clementine Recognitions, 1.27-71, 1989; contbr. articles to profl. jours. Mem. Soc. Bibl. Lit., Am. Acad. Religion, Inst. for Antiquity and Christianity, Internat. Assn. Manichaean Studies, Assn. pour l'Étude de la Littérature Apocryphe Chrétienne. Office: Calif State U 1250 Bellflower Blvd Long Beach CA 90840

JONES, G. DANIEL, minister; b. Norfolk, Va.; s. George Raymons and Estelle (Campbell) J.; m. Geraldine Estelle Saunders, Nov. 27, 1965; 1 child, Bryant Daniel. BS, Va. Union U., 1962; MDiv, Andover Newton Theol. Sch., 1966; D of Ministry, Howard U. Sch. Religion, 1978. Ordained to ministry, Bat. Ch., 1964. Pastor St. John's Bapt. Ch., Woburn, Mass., 1965-67, Messiah Bapt. Ch., Brockton, Mass., 1967-73, Zion Bapt. Ch., Portsmouth, Va., 1973-82, Grace Bapt. Ch. Germantown, Phila., 1982—; instr. Norfolk (Va.) State U., Dept. Religion, 1974-82; chmn., Nat. Commn. Ministry Am. Bapt. Chs., Valley Forge, Pa., 1988—, mem. gen. bd., 1988—; exec. com., bd. dirs., Phila. Bapt. Assn., 1987—, Lott Carey Bapt. Fgn. Mission Conv. Contbr. articles to profl. jours. Pres., bd. dirs. Family Svc. Personal Counseling, Brockton, 1969-73; chmn. fin. com. Portsmouth Pub. Sch. Bd., 1974-80; bd. mgrs. YMCA Germantown Branch, Phila, 1984-, Effingham St. Branch, 1975-82. Recipient Key to City, Brockton, Mass., 1985. Mem. Nat. Mins. Coun., Am. Bapt. Ch. (v.p. 1974-80, exec. com. 1980-82, 88-92), Am. Bapt. Ch. Pa., Del., (exec. com. 1986-90), Am. Bat. Chs. of South (1st pres., founder, 1974-76), Phila. Bapt. Assn. (1st pres., founder 1987-90), Portsmouth Clergy Assn. (pres. 1979-80), Omega Psi Phi (Man of Yr. 1978), Masons. Office: Grace Bapt Ch Germantown 25 W Johnson St Philadelphia PA 19144

JONES, G. MARCUS, church officer; b. Cuyahoga Falls, Ohio, Nov. 24, 1919; s. Mark B. and Nellie R. (James) J.; m. Mildred G. Rayburn, Oct. 4, 1946; children: Sandra Jones Smith, Lee J., Mark B. II. BBA, U. Miami, Coral Gables, Fla., 1946. Lic. gen. contractor, Tenn. Tchr. adult Sunday sch. 1st Presbyn. Ch., Morristown, Tenn., 1958-82; ruling elder 1st Presbyn. Ch., Morristown, 1960-81; ruling elder Gatlinburg (Tenn.) Presbyn. Ch., 1983-89, tchr. adult Sunday sch., 1983-91, treas., 1986-91. Mem., chmn. Hamblen County Planning Coms., Morristown, 1963-65, Morristown Bd. Zoning Appeals, 1965-68. Capt. USAF, 1942-45. Decorated Bronze Star; Order of Flying Cloud (China). Mem. Morristown C. of C. (pres. 1970), Rotary (past chmn.), Kiwanis (pres. Gatlinburg chpt. 1985-91), Masons, Shriners, Elks. Republican. Home: PO Box 709 Gatlinburg TN 37738

JONES, GEORGE WILLIAM, student development educator, administrator; b. Macon, Mo., Apr. 14, 1930; s. Lyndell Walker and Florence (Myers) J.; m. Garnell Hamilton, May 2, 1953; children: Lynette, Daniel, Andrew, Wendy. BS, U. Mo., 1951; MRE, Southwestern Bapt. Theol. Sem., 1953; MA, Vanderbilt U., 1960; EdD, Columbia U./ Union Theol. Sem., 1965. Dir. Bapt. student activities at colls. Mo. Bapt. Conv., Springfield, 1953-56, Tenn. Bapt. Conv., Nashville, 1956-64; dir. religious programs, prof. higher edn. Ball State U., Muncie, Ind., 1964—; sec. Coun. Student Personnel Assns. in Higher Edn., 1971-74; bd. dirs. Southwestern Bapt. Theol. Sem., Ft. Worth, 1972-82; cons., trainer Assn. Governing Bds., 1981—. Contbr. to religion and edn. publs. Delaware County Dem. precinct committeeman, Muncie, 1978—; pres. Delaware County Bd. Pub. Welfare, Muncie, 1985-88; v.p. Delaware County Airport Authority, Muncie, 1987—. Mem. Assn. for Coordination of Univ. Religious Affairs (sec.-treas. 1977—), Nat. Assn. Student Personnel Adminstrs., Ind. Coll. Personnel Assn. Avocations: gardening, reading. Home: 2216 Euclid Ave Muncie IN 47304 Office: Ball State U Religious Programs 400 N McKinley St Muncie IN 47306

JONES, HAROLD CALVERT, II, minister; b. Munich, Sept. 3, 1949; came to U.S., 1950; s. Harold Calvert and Doris (Pipes) J.; m. Vicky Shove, Dec. 1, 1984. BA in Religion, Baylor U., 1971; MDiv, Southwestern Bapt. Sem., Ft. Worth, Tex., 1975; D of Ministry, Midwestern Bapt. Sem., Kansas City, Mo., 1988. Asst. pastor Haynes Ave. Bapt. Ch., Shreveport, La., 1975-76; pastor Valley Bapt. Ch., Winona, Minn., 1976-79, Albert Lea (Minn.) Bapt. Chapel, 1979-80, Emmanuel Bapt. Ch., Topeka, Kans., 1980—; chaplain Police Dept. City of Topeka, 1981-84, City Council, 1986—. Bd. dirs. Indian Hills Mental Health Clinic, Topeka, 1988—; vol. counselor drug treatment unit St. Francis Hosp., Topeka, 1988—; chmn. com. Mayor's Task Force on Literacy, Topeka, 1987—. Recipient City Medallion award City of Topeka, 1987. Mem. Kaw Valley Baptist Assn. (chmn. com. social ministry 1985—), Kans./Nebr. Conv. Bapt. (bd. dirs. 1984-87), Greater Topeka C. of C. (Leadership Tng. award 1984), Kiwanis. Republican. Avocations: photography, motorcycling, canoeing, hunting. Home: 3124 SE Granger Topeka KS 66605 Office: Emmanuel Bapt Ch 1329 SW 37th Topeka KS 66611 *Second only to the relationship we have with Christ, the most important relationship we have is to ourself. How we feel and act towards ourself dictates how we relate to all people.*

JONES, HAWATTHIA, minister; b. Rapid City, S.D., Feb. 25, 1960; s. Cynthia (Trice) J. Student, Internat. Bible Coll., 1978-81. EMT. Youth min. Ch. of Christ, Hahn, Fed. Republic of Germany, 1985-88, Riverside, Calif., 1988—; med. dermatologist USAF, March AFB, Calif., 1988—; bd. dirs. Christian Employment Agy., Riverside. Office: Magnolia Ctr Ch of Christ PO Box 2346 Riverside CA 92516-2346

JONES, HOMER DANIEL, JR., academic administrator; b. Oak Park, Ill., Apr. 27, 1917; s. Homer Daniel and Jessie Louise (Whaley) J.; m. Helen Louise Cornwell, Sept. 6, 1941; children: H. Daniel III, Jonathan C., Lawrence A. BA, Washington & Lee U., 1940; cert. in advanced mgmt., Harvard U., 1946. Tchr. Bryn Mawr (Pa.) Presbyn. Ch., 1956-60; dir. of devel. Princeton (N.J.) Theol. Sem., 1960-63; dir. devel. bd. nat. missions Interch. Ctr., Presbyn. Ch. U.S.A., N.Y.C., 1963-75, dir. devel. Project Forward, 1975-76; v.p. Marry Holmes Coll., West Point, Miss., 1975-78; asst. to pres. Warren Wilson Coll., Asheville, N.C., 1976—. Elder Nassau Presbyn. Ch., Princeton, 1970-75. Lt. USNR, 1942-45. Mem. Nassau Club, Princeton Club, Skytop Club. Home: 188 Carter Rd Princeton NJ 08540

JONES, J. WILLIAM, minister; b. Maroa, Ill., Dec. 25, 1929; s. Roy Orville and Esther Estelle (Burris) J.; m. Eliza Anne Snyder, June 11, 1950; children: Cynthia Anne, Deborah Diane, Jan Ellen. BA, Ill. Wesleyan U., 1951; MDiv, Garrett Evang. Theol. Inst., Evanston, Ill., 1955; DD (hon.), Wiley Coll., Marshall, Tex., 1975. Ordained to ministry United Meth. Ch., 1955. Pastor Meth. Ch., Hammond, Ill., 1950-54, Vermont St. Assn. Meth.Ch., Quincy, Ill., 1955-56; pastor Meth. Ch., Ashland, Ill., 1957-61, Clinton, Ill., 1962-65, Monmouth, Ill., 1966-68; pastor First Meth. Ch., Moline, 1969-77, Grace Meth. Ch., Decatur, Ill., 1978-88, First United Meth. Ch., Peoria, Ill., 1989—; trustee Sunset Home, Quincy, 1956-81, The Baby Fold, Normal, Ill., 1958-64, MacMurray Coll., Jacksonville, Ill., 1970-80; trustee, chmn. Bio-Ethics Com. Meth. Med. Ctr., Peoria, 1989—; del. World Coun. Evangelism, Miami, Fla., 1978, World Meth. Conf., Honolulu, 1981; mem. exec. com. World Meth. Coun., 1991—. Co-chmn. Inter-racial Unity Task Force, Peoria, 1990; bd. dirs. Channel 36 TV, Peoria, 1990. Recipient Blue Key Ill. Wesleyan U., 1951. Mem. Rotary. Home: 515 W Altorfer Ln Peoria IL 61615 Office: First United Meth Ch 116 NE Perry Peoria IL 61603

JONES, JACK E., clergyman; b. Indpls., Mar. 3, 1919; s. Ralph Levi and Anna Clara (Evans) J.; m. Gladys Lucile Scudder, Aug. 27, 1940; children: Arthur, Omar (dec.), James. BSL, Butler Sch. Religion, Indpls., 1943; MA, U. Chgo., 1948. Ordained minister Bapt. Ch. of Acton, Ind. and Indpls. Bapt. Assn., 1943. Pastor various Ind. chs., 1938-44; pastor 1st Bapt. Ch., Woodstock, Ill., 1944-48, Greensburg, Ind., 1948-54, Berwyn, Ill., 1954-63, Shelbyville, Ind., 1963-71, Superior, Wis., 1971-75; pastor Immanuel Bapt. Ch., Brookfield, Wis., 1976-84; mgr. Cambridge Apts. (for Srs.), Milw., 1984-89; interim pastor Ch. of the Hill, Oak Creek, Wis., 1989—; vis. prof. Christian edn. Bapt. Missionary Tng. Sch., Chgo., 1957-60. Bd. dirs. Edna Martin Christian Ctr., Indpls., 1968-71, Project Focal Point, Milw., 1979-89. Recipient various awards. Mem. Nat. MInisters Coun. of Am. Bapt. Chs., Wis. Conf. Chs. (bd. dirs.), kiwanis. Avocations: travel, photography, reading, writing devotionals. Home: 4617 N 76th St #1 Milwaukee WI 53218

JONES, JAMES ALONZO, educator, minister; b. Jonesboro, Ark., Aug. 9, 1933; s. Armour Otto Jones and Arelia Juanita (Phillips) Chambers; m. Esther Ruth Jenkins, Aug. 13, 1955; 1 child, Crystal Lynne. BA, Ark. State U., 1953; diploma in theology, Pentecostal Bible Inst., 1955; MS in Edn., Ind U., 1959, EdD, 1967. Ordained to ministry United Pentecostal Ch., 1956; cert. tchr., Ind. Bus. mgr. publs. Ark. State U., Jonesboro, 1952-53; min. United Pentecostal Ch., Hazelwood, Mo., 1953—; pastor United Pentecostal Ch., Camden, Tenn., 1955; instr. Pentecostal Bible Inst., Tupelo, Miss., 1953-55; from tchr. to adminstr. Ind. Pub. Schs., Salem, Bedford and Indpls., 1956-69; prof. U. Indpls., 1969-90; pastor Apostolic Bible Ch., Brownsburg, Ind., 1969—; editor, ch. sch. dir. Camp Dean, United Pentecostal Ch., Hazelwood, 1953—. Bd. dirs. South Cen. Edn. Unit, Bedford, Ind., 1966-69. Mem. Assn. Tchr. Educators, Nat. Assn. Elem. Sch. Prins., Nat. Middle Sch. Assn. Republican. Avocation: domestic and foreign travel. Home: 627 Locust Ln Brownsburg IN 46112 Office: 621 Locust Ln Brownsburg IN 46112

JONES, JAMES EDWARD, minister; b. Birmingham, Ala., Dec. 2, 1934; s. Fred S. and Annie (Dews) J.; m. Martha Elizabeth Bell, Feb. 4, 1956; children: Angela, Darlene, Byron. BA, Samford U., 1957; BD, So. Bapt. Theol. Seminary, Louisville, 1961, D of Ministry, 1982. Various pastoral positions to Valley View Bapt., Louisville, 1964-73; pastor Eastern Hills Bapt., Montgomery, Ala., 1973-81, Campbellsville (Ky.) Bapt. Ch., 1981—; pres. Ky. Bapt. Conv., 1989-90; exec. com. So. Bapt. Conv., Nashville, 1983-91, chmn. budget com., 1990-91. Author: The Implementation of a Perennial Program of Evangelism, 1982. Chaplain Rescue Squad, Campbellsville/ Taylor, Ky., 1982—. Named Man of Yr., C. of C., Campbellsville, 1986. Mem. Kiwanis (bd. dirs. 1986), Mason. Office: Campbellsville Bapt Church 424 N Central Ave Campbellsville KY 42718

JONES, JERRY D., editor, publisher, writer; b. Syracuse, Kans., Feb. 17, 1951; s. Paul Henry Franklin and Violet Fern (Mueller) J. BS in Communication, U. Tulsa, 1979. Dir. coll. and single adult ministries First Wesleyan Ch., Bartlesville, Okla., 1976-80; editor Solo Mag., Bartlesville and Tulsa, 1979-82, Solo & Spirit Mags., Sisters, Oreg., 1983-86, Sml. Group Letter, Colorado Springs, Colo., 1987-89; editorial team Discipleship Jour., Colorado Springs, Colo., 1987-89; editor, pubr. Single Adult Ministries Jour., Colorado Springs, Colo., 1986—; chmn. Evang. Press Assn. Nat. Conv., 1990. Author: First Person Singular, 1981, Beating the Break-Up Habit, 1985 (with Dick Purnell), Singles Ministry Handbook (with others), 201 Great Question, 1988, Baby Boomers and The Future of World Missions (with Jim Engel), 1989. Recipient Book of Yr. award, Campus Life Mag. for Beating the Break-Up Habit, 1985, Interview of the Yr. award, Evang. Press Assn., 1981. Mem. Nat. Assn. Single Adult Leaders (founding bd. dirs.). Office: Singles Ministry Resources PO Box 60430 Colorado Springs CO 80960

JONES, KATHRYN CHERIE, pastor; b. Breckenridge, Tex., Nov. 26, 1955; d. Austin Thomas and Margaret May (Mohr) J. BA, U. Calif., San Diego, 1977; MDiv, Fuller Theol. Sem., 1982. Assoc. pastor La Jolla (Calif.) United Meth. Ch., 1982-84; pastor in charge Dominguez United Meth. Ch., Long Beach, Calif., 1984-88, San Marcos (Calif.) United Meth. Ch., 1988—; coord. chaplains Pacific Hosp., Long Beach, 1986-88. Bd. dirs. So. Calif. Walk to Emmau Community, L.A., 1987-88, San Diego chpt., 1988—. Mem. Christian Assn. Psychol. Studies, Evangs. for Social Action. Democrat. Office: San Marcos United Meth Ch PO Box 126 San Marcos CA 92069

JONES, KATHY RAMBUS, lay worker, legal secretary; b. Detroit, Oct. 16, 1950; d. Emmitt and Leola (Sanders) Rambus; m. Freddie Louis Jones Jr., Feb. 20, 1982; children: Toya, Katrina, Frederick. Sec. 36th Dist. Ct., Detroit, 1973—; trustee, youth dir. People's Missionary Bapt. Ch., Detroit, 1986—. Home: 17360 Steel Detroit MI 48235 Office: People's Missionary Bapt Ch 3000 McDougall Detroit MI 48207

JONES, KELVIN SAMUEL, minister; b. Hornell, N.Y., Dec. 22, 1947; s. Wendell Homer and Dorothy (Isaman) J.; m. JoAnne Marie DeSerio, June 20, 1970; 1 child, Keely. BS, U. Rochester, 1970; postgrad., Houghton Coll., 1974-76; MDiv, Asbury Theol. Sem., 1979; D Ministry, Drew U., 1991. Ordained to ministry Wesleyan Ch., 1981. Sr. pastor Bentley Creek Wesleyan Ch., Gillett, Pa., 1979-91; pastor Community Wesleyan Ch., Kirkville, N.Y., 1991—; leader, Crisis Support Group, Gillett, Pa., 1989-91. Author: Support Ministry for Emotionally Distressed Persons Through A Unified Small Group in the Local Church, 1991, (with others) And They Shall Prophesy, 1978. Lt. USN, 1971-74. Mem. Wesleyan Theol. Soc. *Love for God and humanity leads responsive souls to see the needs of others and to strive to meet those needs. But the challenges we find are bigger than our abilities. So the only ultimately successful philosophy of life is dependence upon God's wisdom, strength and love.*

JONES, KEN WAYNE, minister; b. Denison, Tex., June 26, 1951; s. Noel Albert and Flora Ellen (Powell) J.; m. Deborah Lee Dudley, June 5, 1970; children: Kristi Lee, Ashley Gail. Cert. in paramedicine, Grayson Community Jr. Coll., Denison, Tex., 1978; BA in Theology, Pacific Coast Bapt. Bible Coll., 1988. Assoc. pastor, fin. dir. Puente Hills Bapt. Ch., Walnut, Calif., 1985—. Home: 1010 Alyeska Pl Walnut CA 91789 Office: Puente Hills Bapt Ch 18901 Amar Rd Walnut CA 91789

JONES, KENNETH C., minister. Head West Prince Christian Coun., Ellerslie, P.E.I., Can. Office: West Prince Christian Coun, Box S, Ellerslie, PE Canada C0B 1J0*

JONES, LARRY DAVID, minister; b. Somers Point, N.J., July 4, 1956; s. Marion Harold and Miriam Emma (Beck) J.; m. Cynthia Anne Davies, May 29, 1976; children: Joshua, Jonathan. A in Biblical Studies, Nazarene Bible Coll., Colorado Springs, Colo., 1980; BA in Religion magna cum laude, Mid-Am. Nazarene Coll., Olathe, Kans., 1981; postgrad., Memphis State U., 1985-86. Pastor Mt. Pleasant Community Ch., Lyndon, Kans., 1981-84, First Ch. of the Nazarene, Jackson, Tenn., 1984—. Mem. Ministerial Assn. (pres. Lyndon chpt. 1983, Jackson chpt. 1986-87), Am. Assn. Bible Colls. Avocations: camping, athletics.

JONES, LARRY E., clergyman; b. Greenfield, Ind., Nov. 27, 1938; s. Cleo Avery and Mildred May (Curry) J. Student, Ozark Bible Coll.; B Bible Theology, Internat. Bible Inst. and Sem., 1979, M Bible Theology, 1980, D Bible Theology, 1981. Ordained to ministry Christian Ch. (Disciples of Christ). Minister Christian Ch., Kansas City, Kans., 1957—; del. Christian Ch., Kansas City, 1983—. Author Bible study lessons for home and classroom use. Mem. Optimist Club, Masons. Home: 1811 N 73d Terr Apt 5 Kansas City KS 66112 Office: Grandview Christian Ch 1916 Central Ave Kansas City KS 66102

JONES, LAWRENCE NEALE, university dean, minister; b. Moundsville, W.Va., Apr. 24, 1921; s. Eugene Wayman and Rosa (Bruce) J.; m. Mary Ellen Cooley, Mar. 29, 1945; children: Mary Lynn (Mrs. Gary C. Walker), Rodney Bruce. B.Ed., W. Va. State Coll., 1942, LL.D., 1965; M.A., U. Chgo., 1948; B.D., Oberlin Grad. Sch., 1956; Ph.D., Yale U., 1961; LL.D., Jewish Theol. Sem., 1971. Ordained to ministry United Ch. Christ, 1956; student Christian Movement Middle Atlantic Region, 1957-60; dean chapel Fisk U., 1960-65; dean students Union Theol. Sem., N.Y.C., 1965-71; prof. Union Theol. Sem. (Afro-Am. ch. history), 1970; dean Union Theol. Sem., 1971-74, acting pres., 1970; dean Sch. Div. Howard U., Washington, 1975-91, ret., 1991; Pres. Civil Rights Coordinating Council, Nashville, 1963-64. Bd. dirs. Sheltering Arms and Children's Svc., 1970-75, Inst. Social and Religious Studies Jewish Sem., United Ch. Bd. for World Ministries, 1969-75; bd. dirs., sec. exec. com. Assn. Theol. Schs. U.S. and Can.; chmn. exec. com. Fund for Theol. Edn., 1978—. With AUS, 1943-46, 47-53. Rockefeller Doctoral grantee; Lucy Monroe scholar; Rosenwald scholar; Am. Assn. Theol. Schs. Study grantee. Mem. Am. Ch. History Soc., Am. Acad. Religion, Soc. Study Black Religion (pres. 1973-75), Nat. Com. Black Churchmen.

JONES, LEWIS BEVEL, III, bishop; b. Gracewood, Ga., July 22, 1926; s. Lewis Bevel Jr. and Gertrude Kathryn (Carson) J.; m. Mildred Hawkins, Aug. 12, 1949; children: David Bevel, Mark Edward, Sharon Jones Brewer. BA, Emory U., 1946; MDiv, Candler Sch. Theology, Atlanta, 1949; DD (hon.), LaGrange (Ga.) Coll., 1964; LHD (hon.), High Point (N.C.) Coll., 1987. Min. Audubon Forest United Meth. Ch., Atlanta, 1949-59, 1st United Meth. Ch., LaGrange, Ga., 1959-63, St. Mark United Meth. Ch., Atlanta, 1963-67; min. 1st United Meth. Ch., Decatur, Ga., 1967-76, Athens, Ga., 1976-82; min. Northside United Meth. Ch., Atlanta, 1982-84; bishop United Meth. Ch., Charlotte, N.C., 1984—; del. Southeastern Jurisdictional Conf. United Meth. Ch., 1960-84; del. Gen. Conf. United Meth. Ch., 1968-84, 12th World Meth. Conf., Denver, 1971, 14th World Meth. Conf., Honolulu, 1981, 15th World Meth. Conf., Nairobi, Kenya, 1986; mem. bd. mgrs. Gen. Bd. Global Ministries, UMCOR, 1972-80; pres. Ga. Meth. Commn. Communications, 1966-70; pres. Ga. United Meth. Commn. Higher Edn., 1972-76; vice chair United Meth. Ch. Gen. Commn. on Religion and Race, 1984-88; mem. exec. com. United Meth. Gen. Commn. Communications, 1988—; vice chair United Meth. Appalachian Devel. Com., 1985-88, chair, 1989—; pres. S.E. Jurisdiction Coll. Bishops, United Meth. Ch., 1988. Contbr. articles to religious jours.; columnist local papers; host daily radio program, Atlanta, 1970-75, Athens, 1980-82. Mem. Met. Atlanta Commn. on Crime, 1964-68; mem. exec. com. Mecklenburg Ministries, N.C. Coun. Chs., 1985—; pres. Christian Coun. Met. Atlanta, 1966-68; bd. dirs. Met. Atlanta YMCA, 1965-76, Met. Atlanta Boys' Clubs Inc., 1965-75, Fellowship of Christian Athletes, 1967-76, YMCA, Charlotte/Mecklenburg, 1984—, Boy Scouts Coun., Charlotte/Mecklenburg, 1988—, United Way Charlotte/Mecklenburg, 1985—; trustee Emory U., 1971—, vice chmn., 1988—; trustee Wesleyan Coll., Macon, Ga., 1972—, Young Harris Coll., 1974—, Brevard Coll., 1985—, Bennett Coll., 1985—, Greensboro Coll., 1985—, High Point Coll., 1985—, Pfeiffer Coll., 1985—; bd. visitors, Duke U., 1986—. Mem. World Meth. Coun. (pres. N.Am. sect. 1988—), Internat. Svc. Assn. for Health (bd. dirs. 1972—), Charlotte Area Clergy Assn., Common Cause, Ctr. Study Dem. Instns., Charlotte City Club, Rotary (Paul Harris fellow 1988), Omicron Delta Kappa. Democrat. Avocations: golfing, bicycling, spectator sports. Office: United Meth Ch Western NC Conf 3400 Shamrock Dr Charlotte NC 28218

JONES, MAJOR J., chaplain; b. Rome, Ga., Dec. 24, 1918; s. Pleas and Bertha (Freeman) J.; m. Mattie Parker, June 1956; 1 child, Chandra M. Jones Foster. AB and DD, Clark Coll., 1941, 85; BD, Gammon Theol. Sem., 1944; PhD, Boston U., 1957; D of Ministry, Vanderbilt U., 1974. Ordained to ministry, Meth. Ch. Pastor, dist. supt., pres. Gammon Theol. Sem., Atlanta, 1967-85; chaplain Atlanta U. Ctr., Robert W. Eoodruff Libr., 1986—; bd. dirs., Concerned Black Clergy, Atlanta; treas., bd. dirs., Southern Christian Leadership Conf. Contbr. articles to profl. jours. Mem. bd. trustees Clark Atlanta U.; mem. Adv. Coun. Cancer. Reecipient Disting Alumnus award, Boston U., 1971. Mem. Am. Acad. Religion, Soc. Christian Ethics (past pres.). Democrat. Home: 930 Burnt Hickory Dr SW Atlanta GA 30311

JONES, MARK ALLEN, minister; b. Brownwood, Tex., Oct. 28, 1953; s. Clarence Alfred Jones and Betty Jane (Bedingfield) Abell; (stepfather George Lyman Abell); m. Beth L. Eason, Feb. 5, 1981; children: Kristee Dawn, Misty Kay, Keith Allen. BBA, McClennan Coll., 1979. Lic. to ministry Bapt. Ch.; cert. EMR; cert. nursing home adminstr. Evangelist Assembly of God Ch., Lubbock, Tex., 1980-85; founder Lifeline Ministries, Roanoke, Tex., 1985—; pastor youth Shiloh Ch., Flower Mound, Tex., 1989-91, min. music, 1991—; producer/announcer Lifeline Radio Prog., Dallas, 1988-90; dir./minister Lifeline Prison Ministry, Roanoke, 1987—; exec. dir. Lifeline Acad., Lewisville, Tex., 1990—. Editor: (newsletter) The Lifeline, 1988-90, The Prison Lifeline, 1980-91. Initiator Lake Cities Youth Network, Lewisville, 1989; bd. dirs. Evangel. Alliance of Greater Dallas, 1989; mem. Mid-Cities Youth Pastor's Network, Euless, Tex., 1990—; mem. Denton County Parent/Educators Conf., 1991. Grantee James Robison Ministries, Ft. Worth, 1990-91. Home: 409 West 3040 Apt 206 Lewisville TX 75067 Office: Lifeline Academy 331 Church St Lewisville TX 75057

JONES, MARK WILLIAM, minister; b. Oklahoma City, Feb. 10, 1960; s. Wight William and Joyce (Tontz) J.; m. Diane Jennings, June 9, 1984; children: Sierra Nicole, Garrett Jennings. BS in Mktg., Okla. State U., 1982; MDiv in Religious Edn., Golden Gate Bapt. Sem., 1987. Ordained to ministry Presbyn. Ch., 1988. Min. to youth St. Andrew Presbyn. Ch., Sonoma, Calif., 1985-87; min. to youth and children Boiling Springs (N.C.) Bapt. Ch., 1987-89; min. to youth and coll. Cen. Bapt. Ch., North Little Rock, Ark., 1989—; assoc. youth min. North Pulaski Assn., North Little Rock, 1990—. Republican. Home: 805 Autumnbrook Circle Sherwood AR 72120 Office: Cen Bapt Ch 5200 Fairway North Little Rock AR 72116

JONES, MATTHEW LINCOLN, minister; b. Snow Lake, Ark., Feb. 20, 1945; s. Joe and Gertrude (George) J.; m. Maxine White, Apr. 6, 1969; children: Ramona, Monica, Monique. Student, Chgo. State U., 1969-70; BA, U. Ark., Pine Bluff, 1969; MDiv, Va. Union U., 1973; D Ministry, Union Theol. Sem., Richmond, Va., 1974. Ordained to ministry Bapt. Ch., 1972. Pastor Macedonia Bapt. Ch., Heathsville, Va., 1971-77, Greater Mt. Moriah Bapt. Ch., Richmond, 1979-87; assoc. pastor Oak Grove Bapt. Sch., Richmond, 1978; pastor Concord Bapt. Ch., Balt., 1987—; dir. family counseling program House of Happiness, Richmond, 1974-78; mem. adj. faculty Va. Union U., Richmond, 1975-77, 81-84; staff mgr. So. Aid Life Ins. Co., 1979-82; dist. mgr. Va. Mut. Benefit Life Ins. Co., Richmond, 1982-84; pres. 1001 Safe Developers, Richmond, 1983-85; chief exec. officer Concord Found. for Urban Devel., Balt., 1988—; mem. Mins. Conf., Balt., Nat. Bapt. Conv., Balt., United Bapt. Missionary Conv., Balt., Nat. Bapt. Congress Christian Edn., Balt. Author: The Church in the Valley, 1978. Advisor Sch. Suspension Prevention Program, Richmond; precinct capt. Richmond Dem. Com., 1984; coord. Jessie Jackson Presdl. Campaign, Va., 1984; mem. Legal Aid, Richmond; mem. tchrs. adv. coun. Operation Bread Basket, Chgo.; former mem. exec. bd. PTA; bd. dirs. Greater Balt. Opportunities Industrialization Ctrs., 1991—. Recipient Outstanding Leadership award City of Pine Bluff, 1968, Outstanding Pastor award Macedonia Bapt. Ch., 1977. Mem. NAACP, Alpha Phi Alpha. Home: 3910 Grierson Rd Randallstown MD 21133 Office: Concord Found Urban Devel 5204 Liberty Heights Ave Baltimore MD 21207

JONES, MCKINLEY, minister. Moderator 2d Cumberland Presbyn. Ch. in U.S.A., Huntsville, Ala. Office: 2d Cumberland Presbyn Ch in USA 2914 Broadview Huntsville AL 35810*

JONES, MEDFORD HERBERT, minister, educator; b. Silver Lake, Oreg., July 1, 1919; s. Richard F. and Gertrude (Durall) J.; m. Vinnie R. Oliver, Oct. 6, 1940; children: Medford H. II, Bob O., Terry Dale. BTh, N.W. Christian Coll., 1942; MDiv, Christian Theol. Sem., 1946; MS, Butler U., 1949; DD (hon.), Milligan Coll., 1960. Ordained to ministry Christian Chs. (Ind.), 1940. Minister Christian Ch., Eugene, Oreg., 1938-42, Gosport, Ind., 1942-46; minister Fleming Garden Christian Ch., Indpls., 1946-49; evangelist Christian Chs., nationwide, 1949-65; prof. Emmanuel Sch. Religion, Johnson City, Tenn., 1965-69; pres. Pacific Christian Coll., Fullerton, Calif., 1969-81, prof., 1981—; condr. ch. growth consultations, 1959—, multiple ch. diagnoses and program projection seminars, 1988—. Author: Building Dynamic Churches, 1990, (manuals) Festival of Faith Crusade, 1955, Fund Raising Guide, 1960, Church Diagnosis and Program Growth Guide, 1988. Mem. N.Am. Soc. Church Growth, Theta Phi. Republican. Home: 2219 Belford Placentia CA 92670 Office: Pacific Christian Coll 2500 Nutwood Fullerton CA 92631

JONES, MICHAEL ROY, minister; b. Portsmouth, Va., Oct. 20, 1958; s. Roy Vando and Mary Elizabeth (Rea) J.; m. Robyn Lynn Bunch, May 3, 1986; 1 child, Lauren Elizabeth. BA, Bridgewater Coll., 1981; MDiv, Union Theol. Sem., Richmond, Va., 1990. Ordained to ministry Presbyn. Ch., 1990. Assoc. min. Second Presbyn. Ch., Oil City, Pa., 1990—. Office: Second Presbyn Ch 111 Reed St Oil City PA 16301

JONES, MILTON LEE, minister; b. Big Spring, Tex., July 13, 1953; s. James William and Helen (Francis) J.; m. Barbara Perkins, Aug. 23, 1975; children: Patrick, Jeremy. BBA, Tex. Tech. U., 1974; MA, Ea. N.Mex. U., 1976; DMin, Calif. Grad. Sch. Theology, 1984. Ordained to ministry, Ch. of Christ. Campus minister Broadway Ch. of Christ, Lubbock, Tex., 1974-78; Campus minister N.W. Ch. of Christ, Seattle, 1978-80, preaching minister, 1980—; vis. faculty Pepperdine U., Malibu, Calif., Puget Sound Christian Coll. Editor Campus Jour.; author: Discipling: The Multiplying Ministry, 1982, Upward, Inward, Outward, 1984, The Brothers, 1986, Grace - The Heart of the Fire, 1991. Home: 19623 20th St NW Seattle WA 98177 Office: Northwest Ch of Christ 15555 15th Ave Seattle WA 98155

JONES, NANCY GLEN, religion educator; b. Plainfield, N.J., Jan. 17, 1944; d. Harvey Roydon and Florence (Dobbs) J. BA, Waynesburg Coll., 1966; MA, U. Northern Colo., 1975. Cert. tchr., Fla., N.J. Tchr. Bridgewater (N.J.)-Raritan Pub. Schs., 1966-69, Dade County Pub. Schs., Miami, Fla., 1969-79; dir. christian edn. Sunrise Presbyn. Ch., Hialeah, Fla., 1979—. Mem. ASCD, Nat. Assn. Edn. Young Children, Assn. Presbyn. Edn. Office: 18400 NW 68th Ave Hialeah FL 33015

JONES, NATHANIEL, bishop. Bishop Ch. of God in Christ, Barstow, Calif. Office: Ch of God in Christ 630 Chateau Barstow CA 92311*

JONES, O. T., bishop. Bishop Ch. of God in Christ, Phila. Office: Ch of God in Christ 363 N 60th St Philadelphia PA 19139*

JONES, ODELL, minister; b. Stephens, Ark., Nov. 21, 1932; s. Roy and Alleotha (Lawson) J.; m. Martha B. Jones, Dec. 25, 1963; children: Alletha U., Yvette S. BS, Ark. Bapt. Coll., 1956; MDiv, Union U., 1960; D Ministry, Drew U., 1982; DD (hon.), Cen. Miss. Coll., 1966, Ark. Bapt. Coll., 1970. Ordained to ministry Nat. Bapt. Conv. Pastor New Bethel Bapt. Ch., Hampton, Va., 1957-60, Bapt. Ch., Church Road, Va., 1958-60, Stephens Bapt. Ch., 1960-65; dean religion Ark. Bapt. Coll., Little Rock, 1960-65; pastor Pleasant Grove Bapt. Ch., Detroit, 1965—. With USAF, 1950-53. Recipient Detroit Top Citizen award Weekly Newspaper, 1978. Mem. Masons. Democrat. Home: 19458 Littlefield Detroit MI 48235

JONES, OSCAR CALVIN, minister; b. San Antonio, Sept. 1, 1932; s. Oscar Sr. and Nonnie Lee (Cunningham) Jones Simpson; m. Peggy Ann Helm, June 12, 1967; children—Dennis Ray, Shawntelle Janora. B.Th., Am. Sch. Divinity, 1968, Th.M., 1971; Ph.D., Trinity Theol. Sem., 1981, D. Min., 1982, postgrad., 1982—. Ordained to ministry Am. Bapt. Chs., 1952. Pastor, counselor St. John Bapt. Ch., Long Beach, Calif., 1965-69; exec. dir. M.A.T.E. Inc., Los Angeles, 1969-71; area rep. ABC, N.Y.C., 1971-83; pastor, counselor Shiloh Bapt. Ch., Sacramento, 1983—; prof. Calif. State U., Sacramento, 1985; western rep. M&M benefit bd. Am. Bapt. Churches U.S.A., N.Y.C., 1986—; mem. supr. Com. Am. Bapt. Credit Union, 1986—; mem. Western Commn. on Ministry, Oakland, 1986—. Author: The Preachers Dilemma, 1978: The 10 Crowns of the Bible, 1974: The Psychological View-Point on Counseling The Black American, 1982; Motifs for Ministry, The Call to the Ministry. Exec. com. Am. Bapt. Black Chs., Valley Forge, Pa., 1969-84; exec. bd. Inter-Faith Service Bur., Sacramento, 1983-84; trustee Am. Bapt. Sem. West, Oakland, Calif., 1985—Am. Bapt. Homes of West. Pastoral clin. edn. Fellow, 1982-84. Mem. Alpha Phi Alpha, Democrat. Office: Shiloh Bapt C 3565 9th Ave Sacramento CA 95817

JONES, PAUL GRIFFIN, II, clergyman, lobbyist, denominational executive; b. Waynesville, Mo., Oct. 12, 1942; s. Paul Griffin and Era Frances (Foley) J.; m. Sandra Lee Poe, July 2, 1966; children: Stephanie Noel, Paul Griffin III, Mark David, Heather Elizabeth. BA, Baylor U., 1964; MDiv, Southwestern Bapt. Theol. Sem., 1967, ThD, 1976, PhD, 1978. Ordained to ministry So. Bapt. Ch., 1967; coordinator 4th St. Bapt. Mission, Waco, Tex., 1961-64; dir., instr. extension dept. So. Bapt. Conv. Sem., Ft. Worth, 1965-66; pastor Pleasant Valley Bapt. Ch., Olney, Tex., 1967-68; chaplain St. Francis Retirement Village, Crowley, Tex., 1968-70; dir. Bapt. Student Union, Tex. Christian U., Ft. Worth, 1970-80; dir. Bapt. Student Union, dir., chmn. dept. bibl. studies East Tex. State U., Commerce, 1980-81; exec. dir., treas. Christian Action Commn., Miss. Bapt. Conv., Jackson, 1982—; mem. Nat. Inst. Campus Ministry, 1978-82; Miss. Religious Leadership Conf., Jackson, 1982—; mem. adv. bd. Christian Life Commn., Nashville, 1982—. Author: Comprehensive Family Planning, 1975, Handbook for Group Leaders, 1981, Bible Speaks on Sex, Love and Marriage, 1982; numerous articles to profl. pubs. Bd. dirs. Family Planning Soc., Ft. Worth, 1971-77, chmn. bd., 1973-77; mem. North Central Tex. Council Govts., Arlington, 1975, Bi-Racial Council, Ft. Worth, 1976-80, Am. Council on Family Relations, 1982, Am. Council on Alcohol Problems, 1982; mem. adv. bd. Middle Miss. council Girl Scouts U.S.A., 1982—. Scholar-in-ministry Southwestern Bapt. Theol. Sem., Ft. Worth, 1977-82; named Outstanding Young Man Am., U.S. Jr. C. of C., 1979; Good Shepherd award Boy Scouts Am. Mem. 8th Air Force Hist. Soc. Home: 3 Dove Way Circle Clinton MS 39056 Office: Miss Bapt Conv Christian Action Commn 515 Mississippi St Jackson MS 39201

JONES, PHILLIP C., minister; b. Shelbyville, Ky., June 16, 1950; s. Walter L. and Norma L. (Harrell) J.; m. Ann Hughey, June 10, 1972 (dec. Feb. 1985); children: Amy Renee, Audrey Susan, Amanda Anne; m. Cynthia M. Lovell, July 3, 1986. BS, Trevecca Nazarene Coll., 1978; M of Ministry, Trinity Theol. Sem., Newburg, Ind., 1983, MDiv summa cum laude, 1986, ThD summa cum laude, 1986. Ordained to ministry Ch. of Nazarene. Pastor Sunflower Ch. of Nazarene, Merigold, Miss., 1972-75, 1st Ch. of Nazarene, Hattiesburg, Miss., 1975-79, Meridian St. Ch. of Nazarene, Indpls., 1979-80; pastor 1st Ch. of Nazarene, Winslow, Ind., 1980-85, Monterey, Tenn., 1985-89, Bicknell, Ind., 1989—; dean grad. studies, prof. Caribbean Coll. of Bible and Sem., Sunbright, Tenn., 1986-90. Author: (with others) Faces of Single Adult Ministries, 1991. Fellow Trinity Theol. Sem., 1986. Republican. Office: 1st Ch of the Nazarene 1125 Durbin St Bicknell IN 47512

JONES, RAYMOND EDWARD, minister; b. Abilene, Tex., Mar. 5, 1949; s. Edward Raymond and Lodema (Watts) J.; m. Norma Jo Eubank, Sept. 22, 1973; children: Raymond Edward Jr., Darla Kay, Danna Jo. Grad. high sch., Santa Anna, Tex., 1967. Ordained to ministry Bapt. Ch., 1988. Music dir. Harmony Bapt. Ch., Fisk, Tex., 1989—, deacon, 1990—; pres. Bapt. Men, Santa Anna, 1989—; asst. mgr. Harvey Shipp Tire Store, Brownwood, Tex., 1989—. Trustee City Coun., Santa Anna, 1979; pres. Coleman (Tex.) County Little League, 1984-87, umpire, 1982-89, Brownwood Tex. Teenage League, 1990-91; trustee sch. bd. Santa Anna Ind. Sch. Dist., 1989-90. With USN, 1968-72. Democrat. Home: Rte 1 Box 87A Santa Anna TX 76878 Office: Harvey Shipp Tire St 706 W Commerce Brownwood TX 76801 *America was founded through faith in the one and only true God, and I am convinced that we must return to that same faith; then and only then will we be able to interpret our constitution as it was intended to be interpreted.*

JONES, RAYMOND JACKSON, JR., minister; b. Birmingham, Ala., Nov. 10, 1959; s. Raymond J. and Dessie (Wineman) J.; m. Alison Payne, Dec. 27, 1981; 1 child, Karis Rae. Student, Samford Bapt. U.; BA, Dallas Bapt. U., 1982. Ordained to ministry So. Bapt. Conv., 1981. Youth pastor various chs., Ala., Tex. and Fla., 1979-86; assoc. pastor Calvary Bapt. Ch., Clearwater, Fla., 1987—; youth pastor Bapt. jr. colls., Ala., 1984-85; traveling speaker Insight Prodns., 1982—; marriage counselor Prepare/Enrich, 1988—. Author: (manual) S.M.A.R.T., 1981; contbg. author: The Lordship of Christ, 1989; writer Bapt. Sunday Sch. Bd., 1985—. Mem. Metro Youth Mins. Assn. (rep. S.E. region 1986, 87), Fellowship Christian Athletes (bd. dirs. St. Petersburg/Tampa chpt. 1987). Office: Calvary Bapt Ch 331 Cleveland St Clearwater FL 34615

JONES, RICHARD MERRITT, minister; b. Atchinson, Kans., Sept. 12, 1958; s. Eugene Jack Owen and Camillia (Marsh) J. BSBA, U. Ill., 1980; ThM, Faith Sch. Theology, Urbana, Ill., 1983. Ordained to ministry Crusaders Ch. U.S.A., 1986. Assoc. pastor Crusaders Ch., Urbana, 1983—; producer The Crusaders Pulpit Radio Broadcast, Urban, 1988—. Editor Faith in the Future mag., 1986—. Founder Champaign County Citizens for Decency, Champaign, Ill., 1984; co-founder Coalition for Traditional Values East Cen. Ill., Champaign, 1989. Home: 1808 Golfview Dr Urbana IL 61801-1113 Office: Crusaders Inc 2111 Willow Rd PO Box 321 Urbana IL 61801-0321

JONES, RICHARD NELSON, clinical laboratory scientist, Arabist; b. Oakland, Calif., Nov. 12, 1950; s. Norman Beecher and Marcia Ruth (Nelson) J.; m. Kathryn Johnson, May 20, 1979; 1 child, Nicholas Richard. BSc, Utah State U., 1976; MA, U. Utah, 1981, PhD, 1991. Registered med. technologist. Scientist dept. trace metals Assoc. Regional and Univ. Pathologists, Inc., Salt Lake City, 1985—; dir. Nr. East Antiquity Cons. Group, Inc., Sandy, Utah, 1991—. Contbr. articles to profl. jours. and dictionaries. Mem. Am. Schs. Oriental Rsch., Soc. Bibl. Lit., Soc. Coptic Archaeology, Paleopath. Soc., Sigma Chi. Home: 9231 Stone Ridge Circle Sandy UT 84093 Office: Assoc Regional and Univ Pathologists Inc 500 Chipeta Way Salt Lake City UT 84108

JONES, ROBERT CALVIN, minister, secondary school educator; b. Clarksdale, Miss., Aug. 8, 1958; s. Paul Jr. and Sarah Dean (McCain) J.; m. Jane Montgomery Guinn, Dec. 13, 1986; 1 child, Robert Montgomery. BSE in Speech/Drama, English, Delta State U., 1979; MRE in Adminstrn., New Orleans Bapt. Theol. Sem., 1989. Ordained to ministry So. Bapt. Conv., 1986; cert. secondary sch. tchr., Miss. Min. music Morrison Chapel Bapt. Ch., Cleveland, Miss., 1982-87, First Bapt. Ch., Gulport, Miss., 1987-88; min. music and youth Broadmoor Bapt. Ch., Gulfport, 1988—; music evangelist various chs., 1982—; coach music/drama, Gulfport, 1989-91. Contbr. poetry to Confidante Literary Jour., 1978-79. City coord. Gerald Ford Presdl. campaign, Cleveland, 1976, Young Reps. Senatorial campaign, Cleveland, 1978; dir. Whistlestop Playhouse, Cleveland, 1980-86; mem. Delta Playhouse, Cleveland, 1976-79. Mem. So. Bapt. Conv. (del. 1986—), So. Bapt. Religious Edn. Conv. (del. 1989—), Kiwanis (officer Cleveland club 1979-82), Alpha Psi Omega, Pi Kappa Delta. Home: 1124 1/2 E Beach Blvd Gulfport MS 39501 Office: Broadmoor Bapt Ch 1902 Kelly Ave Gulfport MS 39501 *If you can hurt with people when they hurt, and give them help when they have needs; then, and only then, can you comprehend the depth of their rejoicing when they turn to the Lord in worship.*

JONES, ROBERT GEAN, religion educator; b. Magnolia, Ark., Feb. 17, 1925; s. Emless Bunyan and Eunice (Gean) J.; m. Marian Laverne Alexander, July 23, 1946; 1 dau., Carolyn Ann. B.A. cum laude, Baylor U., 1947; B.D. cum laude, Yale, 1950, M.A., 1957, Ph.D., 1959. Ordained to ministry Bapt. Ch., 1946; minister Deep River (Conn.) Bapt. Ch. and; First Bapt. Ch. of, Saybrook, 1950-59; asst. prof. religion George Washington U., Washington, 1959-61; asso. prof. George Washington U., 1961-64, prof., 1964-91, prof. emeritus, 1991—, chmn. dept. religion, 1963-79, univ. marshal, 1969-89. Author: The Rules for the War of the Sons of Light With the Sons of Darkness, 1957, The Manual of Discipline (1QS), The Old Testament and Persian Religion, 1964. Mem. Soc. Bibl. Lit. and Exegesis, Am. Acad. Religion, Alpha Chi, Omicron Delta Kappa. Home: 307 Amohi Ln Loudon TN 37774 Office: George Washington U Washington DC 20052

JONES, ROBERT LEE, religion educator; b. Sapulpa, Okla., June 17, 1920; s. Clyde William and Arminia (Harris) J.; m. Mary Claire Collingsworth, June 12, 1948; 1 child, Mary Lee. B.A, Oklahoma City U., 1948; B.D., So. Methodist U., 1951; M.A., 1952; Ph.D., St. Mary's Coll., U. St. Andrews, Scotland, 1961. Ordained to ministry Meth. Ch., 1952; asso. pastor Wesley Meth. Ch., Oklahoma City, 1947-48, Dallas, 1948-52; pastor Grove (Okla.) Meth. Ch., 1952-54, Ch. of Scotland, 1954-56; pastor, dir. Wesley Found. Meth. Ch., Goodwell, Okla., 1956-57; asst. prof. religion Oklahoma City U., 1957-61, assoc. prof., 1961-65, prof., 1965—, Ollie Bell prof. ecclesiastical history, 1979—, dean of men, 1960-62; assoc. dean Oklahoma City U. (Coll. A. and S.), 1962-63, dean, 1963-70, v.p. acad. affairs, 1970-79; dir. Oklahoma City U. (Ch. Leadership Center); del. 3d Oxford Inst. Meth. Theol. Studies, 1965; Internat. Conf. on Higher Edn., Oxford, Eng., 1965; Chmn. com. on edn. Community Relations Commn., Oklahoma City, 1966-70, vice chmn. Commn., 1970. Serve with F.A. U.S. Army, 1941-45. Decorated Bronze Star. Mem. Am. Soc. Ch. History, Am. Acad. Religion. Home: 3240 NW 18th St Oklahoma City OK 73107 Office: NW 23d at Blackwelder Oklahoma City OK 73106

JONES, ROGER EUGENE, religious organization administrator; b. Hordville, Nebr., Mar. 24, 1928; s. Hilmer Gilbert and Bertha (Johnson) J.; m. Alice Marie Rodine, June 26, 1948; children: Cynthia Jean, Christine Marie, Connie Ann, Craig Dean. Announcer, communication mgr. Radio Station KJSK, Columbus, Nebr., 1948-53; mgr. sales, svc. Cen. Elec. and Gas, Columbus, 1953-54; auditor First Nat. Bank, Columbus, 1954-76; cons. stewardship Evang. Free Ch. Am., Columbus, 1976-78; exec. dir. in bus. affairs Evang. Free Ch. Am., Mpls., 1978-85, exec. dir. stewardship, 1985—; bd. dirs. Christian Ministries Mgmt., Mpls., 1980-83. Councilmen City of Columbus, 1971-74. With USN, 1946-48. Mem. Christian Stewardship Coun. (bd. dirs. 1985-88), Nat. Assn. Evangs. (stewardship commn. bd. dirs. 1986—). Republican. Avocations: woodworking, gardening. Home: 723 E 130th St Minneapolis MN 55337 Office: Evang Free Ch of Am 1515 E 66th St Minneapolis MN 55423

JONES, ROLAND MANNING, minister; b. Washington, Jan. 30, 1932; s. Roland E. and Rachael (Manning) J.; m. Marcia Wiebe, Dec. 26, 1953; children: Katherine, roland, Susan. BS, U. Md., 1953; MDiv, Va. Sem., 1958. Ordained to ministry Episcopal Ch., 1958. Rector St. John's Parish, Accokeek, Md., 1958-67, Sligo Parish, Silver Spring, Md., 1967-74, St. Francis Parish, Greensboro, N.C., 1974-84, St. Mark's Parish, New Canaan, Conn., 1984—; pres.-founder The Canterbury Sch., Accokeek, 1961-67; mem. standing com. Diocese of Washington, 1973-74; staff Va. Sem., Alexandria, 1967-74. Trustee Wavney Care Ctr., New Canaan, 1987—, Greensboro Hosp., 1983-84, New Canaan Inn. (Sr. Home), 1984—; pres. Silver Springs Citizens Assn., 1973. 1st lt. USAF, 1953-55. Mem. Washington Clergy Assn. (pres. 1972-74). Office: St Marks Ch 111 Oenoke Ridge New Canaan CT 06840

JONES, RONALD EDWARD (EDDY JONES), minister; b. Orlando, Fla., Aug. 18, 1958; s. Charles Edward and Barbara Jean (Walker) J. BA, Fla. Christian Coll., 1981; MA, Cin. Bible Sem., 1983. Ordained to ministry Christian Ch. Youth min. 1st Christian Ch., Dunnellon, Fla., 1979-80, Clermont, Fla., 1980-81; houseparent East Tenn. Christian Home, Elizabethton, Tenn., 1984-85; prin. 1st Christian Ch. Sch., Clermont, 1986-88; assoc. min. Fairburn (Ga.) Christian Ch., 1988—. Pres. Ga. Jr. Bible Bowl League, 1990—. Home: 50 Clay St B2 Fairburn GA 30213 Office: Fairburn Christian Ch 154 Fayetteville Rd Fairburn GA 30213

JONES, RUSS L., minister; b. Rogers, Ark., Sept. 21, 1963; s. Jimmy Don and Helen (Hyden) J.; m. Betty Lynn Engstrom, May 3, 1984. BA in bible, Central Bible Coll., 1985. Ordained to ministry Gen. Coun. Assemblies of God. Music/youth pastor Faith Temple Assembly of God, Jacksonville, Fla., 1985-88; assc. pastor First Assembly of God, Crystal River, Fla., 1988-89; pastor Fountain of Life Assembly of God, Coral Springs, Fla., 1989—; sectional youth rep. Peninsular Fla. Dist. Coun. Assemblies of God, Jacksonville, Fla. 1987-88, sectional sec., Christian dir. Coral Springs, 1991—. Author: A Family of God, The Blessings of God 1990; co-author: P.O.W.E.R. School 1986. Mem. Youth Wave, Coral Springs Mus. Assc. Mem./founder Citrus County Youth Fellowship. Republican. Assemblies of God. Home: 6538 NW 70th Ave Tamaroc FL 33321 Office: Fountain of Life Assembly of God 3300 University Dr # 210 Coral Springs FL 33065 *We measure life by numbers and statistics, God measures by faith. I have learned that God's standards are fairer and easier to comprehend. Also I can live with myself and enjoy life.*

JONES, SAMMY RAY, pastor; b. Grant, Ala., July 6, 1941; s. Gordon Ray and Vessie Mae (Evans) J.; m. Donna Jo Morehead, June 17, 1961; children: Stephen Ray, Paul Kevin, Mary Ann. BA, Belmont Coll., 1964; MDiv, So. Bapt. Theol. Sem., 1970, D Ministry, 1980. Ordained to ministry So. Bapt. Conv., 1961. Pastor Immanuel Bapt. Ch., Portland, Tenn., 1961-64, Calvary Bapt. Ch., Franklin, Tenn., 1964-67, Mt. Olive Bapt. Ch., Winchester, Ky., 1967-70, Antioch First Bapt. Ch., Nashville, 1970-77, Harvest (Ala.) Bapt. Ch., 1977-84, First Bapt. Ch., Camden, Tenn., 1984—; growth cons. So. Bapt. Sun Sch. Bd., Nashville, 1981—. Treas. Project Help, Camden, 1988—; bd. dirs. Literacy Coun., Camden, Hosp. Hospitality House, Huntsville, Ala., 1981-84. Mem. Tenn. Bapt. Conv. (constn. and bylaws com. 1990—, coop. program regional advisor, 1988—), West Tenn. Bapt. Pastors Conf. (pres. 1990-91), Benton County Ministerial Alliance, Carroll-Benton Bapt. Assn. (moderator 1990—), Rotary (sec. Camden club 1991—). Home: 193 Eastview Camden TN 38320 Office: First Bapt Ch PO Box 545 Camden TN 38320

JONES, SAMUEL, JR., minister; b. Nassau, The Bahamas, Oct. 16, 1944; came to U.S., 1944; s. Samuel and Harriet (Taylor) J.; m. Margaret Ann Woodard, Aug. 23, 1964; children: Cynthia Demetrice, Katrina Elaine, Cassandra H., Samuel III, Timothy Lael. Student, F. A&M U., 1966, Fuller Sem. Inst., 1978, Bill Gother Inst., 1974-91. Pastor Open Door Bapt. Ch., Gainesville, Fla., 1975—; pres. Open Door Bapt. Ch. Corp., 1975—; treas. Full Gospel Mins. Assn., 985. Bd. dirs. Pregnancy Crisis Ctr., Gainesville, 1982—; mem. Harbor House Orgn., Gainesville, 1986. Home: 915 S E 19th St Gainesville FL 32601

JONES, SPENCER, minister; b. Poplar Bluff, Mo., Mar. 24, 1946; s. Frank Jesse and Evelina (Louis) J.; m. Kathy A.E. Drake, Sept. 1, 1973; children: Daliz, Trayon, Shemen, Melinet. BA in Theology, Cen. Bible Coll., 1972. Ordained to ministry Assemblies of God, 1974. Sr. pastor Southside Tab, Chgo., 1972—; dir. Inner City Ministries, Chgo., 1980—; pres. Inner City Workers Conf., Chgo., 1980—. Contbr. religious articles to publs. Pres. local sch. coun., Chgo., 1989—; community rep. 21st ward, 1990—. With U.S. Army, 1966-67, Vietnam.

JONES, STEPHEN RICHARD MAURICE, minister; b. St. Thomas, Ont., Can., Aug. 20, 1950; s. Maurice Baldwin and June Mae (Williams) J.; m. Kim Colleen Stemmler, Oct. 2, 1976; children: Mark Douglas, Erin Leigh, Robyn Lynn. BRE, Ont. Bible Coll., 1973; BA, U. Windsor, Ont., 1975; MTS, Ont. Theol. Sem., 1987. Ordained to ministry Bapt. Conv. of Ont. and Que., 1976. Pastor Brooker Bapt. Ch., Cottam, Ont., 1973-77, Mimico Bapt. Ch., Toronto, Ont., 1977-83, Lakefield (Ont.) Bapt. Ch., 1983-89, 1st Bapt. Ch., Smiths Falls, Ont., 1989—; mem. assembly program com. Bapt. Conv. of Ont. and Que., 1983-90. Mem. Bapt. Min.'s Fellowship (v.p. Ont.-Que. chpt. 1984-85, pres. 1985-86). Home: 195 Andrews Ave, Smiths Falls, ON Canada K7A 4R9 Office: 1st Bapt Ch, 73 Beckwith St N, Smiths Falls, ON Canada K7A 2B6

JONES, STEVEN MATTHEW, minister; b. Shickshinny, Pa., July 4, 1950; s. James Albert and Mary Rose (Belles) J.; m. Andrea Elizabeth Pastuszak, May 17, 1980; children: Krystal Leigh, Ryan Matthew. BA in English, Wilkes Coll., 1973. Commd. to ministry Vols. of Am. Ch., 1983. Pres., chief exec. officer, min. Vol. of Am., Harrisburg, Pa., 1982—; sec. Full Gospel Bus. Mens Fellowship, Wilkes-Barre, Pa., 1977-82; chmn. David Wilkerson Crusade Com., Wilkes-Barre, 1981; promoter, coord. various Evangelistic community events, Wilkes-Barre, 1976-82; coord. in field. Reporter: Country Impressions New, 1973-74. Bike hike coord. Luzerne Assn. for Retarded Citizens, Wilkes-Barre, 1981; coord. Capitol Egg Hunt, Harrisburg, Pa., 1982—. Named Boy of Mo. Shickshinny Rotary, 1967; recipient All-Am. Partnership award City of Harrisburg, 1990, Outstanding Svc. Orgn. at Christmas award Office of the Gov., Harrisburg, 1988. Mem. Pa. Assn. Adult Continuing Edn., Full Gospel Bus. Men, Outreach, Sigma Delta Chi. Republican. Office: Volunteers of America 2112 Walnut St Harrisburg PA 17103

JONES, T. DALE, minister; b. Birmingham, Ala., Nov. 18, 1965; s. Lloyd and Emily (Hicks) J.; m. Tonya D. Hill, Nov. 14, 1987; children: Prentice Evar, Kayla René. Min. music and youth Hopewell 1st Bapt. Ch., Bessemer, Ala., 1985-87, Seventh St. Bapt. Ch., Bessemer, 1987-88; min. youth Cross Rds. Bapt. Ch., Hueytown, Ala., 1988-89; min. music and youth Glenn Meml. Bapt. Ch., Bessemer, 1989-90, 1st Bapt. Cottage Hill, Cantonment, Fla., 1990—; mem. Fla. Singing Men, 1991—. Recipient merit recognition Fla. Bapt. Conv., 1991. Avocations: softball, basketball. Home: 1847 Chavers Rd Cantonment FL 32533 Office: 1st Bapt Cottage Hill 230 William Ditch Rd Cantonment FL 32533

JONES, THOMAS FRANKLIN, JR., minister; b. Steubenville, Ohio, Feb. 28, 1955; s. Thomas F. and Naomi Burke (Sinnett) J.; m. Deborah Arlene Fralish, Sept. 7, 1977; children: Melanie Noel, Thomas F. III. BA, Milligan Coll., 1977; MDiv., Emmanuel Sch. Religion, 1982; D of Ministry, United Theol. Sem., 1992. Youth min. West Side Christian Ch., Elizabethton, Tenn., 1979-81; asst. min. First Ch. of Christ, Painesville, Ohio, 1981-83; min. of evangelism First Christian Ch., Springfield, Ohio, 1983-85; founding pastor Centerville Christian Ch., Dayton, Ohio, 1985-91, Princeton (N.J.) Project, 1992—; bd. dirs. Double Vision, Miami Valley Evangelism, Dayton; pres., bd. dirs. 1993 Nat. New Ch. Conf.; pres. Centerville Clergy Assn., 1989-90. Editor: (periodical) Visionary, 1988—. Bd. Fight Against Drug Epidemic, Centerville, 1988-91, Choices in Community Living, Dayton, 1989-91. Mem. Rotary Club (Centerville). Office: Centerville Christian Ch PO Box 303 Centerville OH 45459

JONES, THOMAS FREDERICK, minister; b. Jerseyville, Ill., Apr. 26, 1936; s. Frederick Theodore and Mary (Alice) J.; m. Jeannette Walker, Mar. 19, 1960 (div. Sept. 1972); children: Bradley T., Kristina R., Jon A.; m. Reidun Marie Knaust, Aug. 24, 1985. BA, So. Ill. U., 1961; BD, Covenant Theol. Sem., 1965; MA, U. Ga., 1973. Ordained to ministry Presbyn. Ch., 1965. Pastor 1st Reformed Presbyn. Ch., Lookout Mountain, Tenn., 1965-72, Concord Presbyn. Ch., Waterloo, Ill., 1973-76; coord. ch. planting Commn. on Ch. Extension, Carbondale, Ill., 1977-85; pastor Immanuel Presbyn. Ch., Belleville, Ill., 1985-90; adj. prof. Covenant Theol. Sem., St. Louis, 1974-76, 80-82; coord. male discussion group Belleville Area Coll., 1983-87; co-dir. Fresh Start Divorce Recovery Seminars, Wayne, Pa., 1984-89, v.p., 1990—. Author: Sex and Love When You're Single Again, 1990; contbr. ministry articles to profl. jours. and newsletters. Served with USNR, 1953-61. Avocations: guitar, singing and songwriting recordings, mountain climbing. Home and Office: 116 N Ferkel St Columbia IL 62236

JONES, THOMAS LAWTON, minister, educator; b. Dearborn, Mich., Feb. 28, 1947; s. David Bevan and Dorothy Elaine (Lawton) J.; m. Linda Eve Critchfield, Sept. 16, 1967; children: Jason Alun, Amy Ruth, Bryn Thomas. AA, Henry Ford Community Coll., Dearborn, Mich., 1972; ThB, Tyndale Coll., 1975; postgrad., Detroit Bapt. Sem., 1980-82; MA, Ea. Mich. U., 1990. Ordained to ministry Bapt. Ch., 1976. Missionary Bapt. Mid-Missions, Taylor, Mich., 1976-83, Rome and Foligno, Italy, 1983-87; missionary pastor Village Bapt. Ch., Dearborn, 1989—; tchr. ESL Henry Ford Community Coll., Dearborn, 1990—; bd. dirs. Centro per Studi Biblici, Am. Lang. Clinic. Contbr. articles to profl. jours. With USN, 1967-71. Mem. Tchrs. of English to Speakers of Other Langs., Mich. Tchrs. of English to Speakers of Other Langs. Home: 13538 Irene Southgate MI 48195 Office: Village Bapt Ch 2630 Village Rd Dearborn MI 48124

JONES, THOMAS WILLIAM, priest; b. St. Paul, Oct. 27, 1955; s. William Trevor and Kathryn Cecelia (Garvey) J. BS, U. Minn., 1977; postgrad., Cath. U., 1978-81; MA in Religious Studies, Mt. St. Mary's, L.A., 1991. Ordained to Roman Cath. Ch., 1982. Assoc. pastor St. Nicholas Cath. Ch., North Pole, Alaska, 1981-86; assoc. dir. U. Cath. Ctr. U. Calif., L.A., 1986-88, dir., 1988—; cons. Missionary Soc. of St. Paul the Apostle, N.Y.C., 1990—. Mem. Univ. Religious Conf. (pres. L.A. chpt. 1989-91). Democrat. Avocations: hockey referee, tennis, downhill skiing. Home: 10750 Ohio Ave Los Angeles CA 90024 Office: 840 Hilgard Ave Los Angeles CA 90024

JONES, TOM L., minister; b. Okmulgee, Okla., Aug. 5, 1954; s. Clarence Jones and Myra D. (Goolsby) Reed; m. Connie R. Jones, Nov. 2, 1974; children: Adam, William. AA in Psychology, Oklahoma City Community Coll., 1985. Ordained to ministry Ch. of God. Pastor Ch. of God of Prophecy, Enid, Okla., 1975-78, Porter, Okla., 1978-81; pastor youth Ch. of God of Prophecy, Oklahoma City, 1981-89, Cleveland, Tenn., 1989-90; pastor youth Heartland Worship Ctr., Kissimmee, Fla., 1990—; pastor rep. Youth for Christ of D.C., Washington, 1988; instr. workshops, youth confs., dir. youth camps. Contbr. articles to Heartland Mag. Mem. Osceola County Youth Mins. Assn. (founder, del. 1990—). Home: 1681 Starfish St Kissimmee FL 34741 Office: Heartland Worship Ctr 2875 E Irlo Bronson PO Box 1421459 Kissimmee FL 34744

JONES, TRACEY KIRK, JR., minister, educator; b. Boston, Mar. 16, 1917; s. Tracey Kirk and Marion (Flowers) J.; m. Martha Clayton, Sept. 12, 1942 (dec. June 1975); children: Judith Grace Watson, Tracey Kirk Jones, III, Deborah Anita Jones Breitenbach; m. Junia K. Moss, July 1, 1978. B.A., D.D., Ohio Wesleyan U.; B.D., Yale Div. Sch., 1942. Ordained to ministry Meth. Church, 1945; missionary Meth. Ch., China, 1946-50, Malaya, 1952-55; exec. bd. mission Meth. Ch., 1955; exec. sec. S.E. Asia, 1955-62; assoc. gen. sec. div. world missions, 1962-64, assoc. gen. sec. world div., 1964-68, gen. sec. bd. missions, 1968-72, gen. sec. bd. global ministries, 1972-80; adj. prof. Drew Theol. Sch., Madison, N.J., 1980-89; mem. governing bd. Nat. Coun. Chs., 1st v.p., 1978-80. Author: Our Mission Today, 1963. Home: 3649 Aster Dr Sarasota FL 34233

JONES, VIVIAN, minister; b. Garnant, Dyfed, Wales, Jan. 3, 1930; came to U.S., 1980; s. Daniel and Dorothy (Daniel) Jones; m. Mary Williams, Mar. 28, 1958; children: Anna Vivian, Heledd Mair. BA with honors, U. Wales, Bangor, 1952, BD, 1958; MTh, Princeton (N.J.) Sem., 1970; DD, United Sem. of the Twin Cities, 1990. Min. Union of Wealth Inds., Onllwyn, Wales, 1955-62; min. ch. Swansea, Wales, 1962-65, Allt-Wen, Wales, 1965-80; sr. min. Plymouth Congl Ch. of Mpls., 1980—; vice chairperson Inst. Ecumenical and Cultural Rsch., Collegeville, Minn., 1984-90. Mem. Mpls. Club, Minikahda Club. Home: 400 Groveland Ave # 409 Minneapolis MN 55403 Office: Plymouth Congl Ch 1900 Nicollet Ave Minneapolis MN 55403

JONES, WALTER, archbishop. Met., archbishop Anglican Ch. of Can., Winnipeg, Man. Office: Anglican Ch Can, 935 Nesbitt Bay, Winnipeg, MB Canada R3T 1W6*

JONES, WILBUR L., bishop. Bishop Ch. of Our Lord Jesus Christ of the Apostolic Faith, Inc., N.Y.C. Office: Ch Our Lord Jesus Christ Apostolic Faith Inc 2081 Adam Clayton Powell Jr New York NY 10027*

JONES, WILLIAM AUGUSTUS, JR., bishop; b. Memphis, Jan. 24, 1927; s. William Augustus and Martha (Wharton) J.; m. Margaret Loaring-Clark, Aug. 26, 1949; 4 children. B.A., Southwestern at Memphis, 1948; B.D., Yale U., 1951. Ordained priest Episcopal Ch., 1952; priest in charge Messiah Ch., Pulaski, Tenn., 1952-57; curate Christ Ch., Nashville, 1957-58; rector St. Mark Ch., LaGrange, Ga., 1958-65; asso. rector St. Luke Ch., Mountainbrook, Ala., 1965-66; dir. research So. region Assn. Christian Tng. and Service, Memphis, 1966-67; exec. dir. Assn. Christian Tng. and Service, 1968-72; rector St. John's, Johnson City, Tenn., 1972-75; bishop of Mo. St. Louis, 1975—. Office: Diocese of Mo 1210 Locust St Saint Louis MO 63103

JONES, WILLIAM JENIPHER, pastor; b. Spring Hill, Md., Oct. 27, 1912; s. Richard Edward and Margret Sadie (Brown) J.; m. Pauline Payne, Oct. 30, 1946; children: William Edward, William David. AA, Tenn. Christian Coll., 1975; BD, Tenn. Christian U., 1977; MA, Fla. State Christian Coll., 1980. Ordained to ministry Internat. Coun. Community Chs., 1961; cert. notary pub., Ill. Asst. min. St. John Community Ch., Robbins, Ill., 1969-86, pastor, 1986—; former operator, sta. transp. clk. Chgo. Transit Authority; del. United Coun. Community Chs., Birmingham, Ala., 1991; mem. conf. unification ministry Internat. Religious Found., Korea and Japan, 1987; mem. Pioneer Orgn., Martin Luther King Coll. Mins., Morehouse Coll., Atlanta, 1986-89. Pres. Better Govt. Party, Chgo., 1986; former trustee Village or Robbins, also former police and fire commr.; bd. dirs. Family Health Ctr. Clinic; former chmn. South Suburban Mayors Planning Group. Staff sgt. U.S. Army, 1944-46. Mem. Internat. Religions Assn. Am. Christian Ministry, Ill. Sheriffs Assn., Ill. Police Assn., Ill. Fire and Police Commrs. Assn., Am. Legion (post comdr. Robbins 1965-68), Elks (exalted ruler Robbins 1957-58), Masons (master Robbins 1952-54), Alpha Psi Omega (bd. dirs. 1977—). Democrat. Home: 3702 W 135th St Robbins IL 60472 Office: St John Community Ch 13434 S Harding Ave Robbins IL 60472

JONGEWAARD, DAVID LAWRENCE, minister; b. Jefferson, Iowa, Sept. 9, 1946; s. Lawrence Harold and Grace Elizabeth (Kapp) J.; m. Faith Charlene Dow, June 8, 1968; children: Nathan, Rebekah, Matthew. BA, Wheaton (Ill.) Coll., 1968; MDiv, McCormick Theol. Sem., Chgo., 1973; cert. phys. edn., Luth. Gen. Hosp., Park Ridge, Ill., 1972. Ordained to ministry Presbyn. Ch. (U.S.A.), 1973; cert. C.P.E. Intern San Juan Larger Parish, Bayfield, Colo., 1970-71; youth dir. 1st Presbyn. Ch., Deerfield, Ill., 1971-72; pastor Latta Meml. Presbyn. Ch., Christiana, Pa., 1973-77; pastor, head staff Chestnut Grove Presbyn. Ch., Phoenix, Md., 1977-87, 1st Presbyn. Ch., Ottumwa, Iowa, 1987—; mem. Des Moines Presbytery, 1987—; chmn. Christian svc. Ottumwa Area Fellowship Chs., 1988—. Chmn. Ottumwa Area Betterment and Beautification Coun., 1988—; bd. dirs. Regional Retirement Living, Inc., Ottumwa, 1988—; chmn. strategic planning Wapello County United Way, Ottumwa, 1990—. Mem. Rotary. Democrat. Home: 161 W Alta Vista Ottumwa IA 52501 Office: 1st Presbyn Ch 228 W 4th St Ottumwa IA 52501 *Conscious that I am a person for whom Christ died, I am committed to a life that manifests the grace and peace of God through Jesus Christ, our risen Lord.*

JONSSON, JOHN NORMAN, religion educator, minister; b. Paulpietersburg, Natal, Republic of South Africa, Mar. 20, 1925; came to U.S., 1980; s. Erik Jonsson and Sarah Magdelena Hagemann; m. Gladys Crankshaw, Aug. 9, 1952; children: Lois Bertha, Sylvia Lynn, David Erik (dec.), Sven Thomas. BA with honors, U. Natal, MA, 1963, PhD, 1966; diploma in theology, Spurgeons Coll., U.K., 1952; BD, U. London, 1959. Ordained to ministry Brit. Bapt. Ch. Asst. min. Rosebank Union Ch., Johannesburg, Republic of South Africa; min. Lambert Rd. Bapt. Ch., Durban, Natal, Cen. Bapt. Ch., Pietermaritzburg, Natal, 1961-65; prin. Bapt. Theol. Coll. So. Africa, Johannesburg, 1966-71; lectr. history of religions U. Witwatersrand, Johannesburg, 1972-75; sr. lectr. U. Natal, Pietermaritzburg, 1976-81, acting head dept. div., 1981; W. O. Carver prof. missions and world religions So. Bapt. Theol. Sem., Louisville, 1982—; prof. world religions Baylor U., Waco, Tex., 1992—. Author: The Spirit of the Matter, 1983, Not Benevolence But Atonement, 1987, The Crisis of Missions in the Bible: A Literary-Critical Socio-Human Hermeneutic of Scripture, 1987, Worlds Within Religion: A Phenomenological Approach to the Study of Religion, 1987, Calabash Religion: The Ethos and Kerygma of Africa. The Poetry of Africa's Collective Sufferings, 1990; also articles; editor: World Strategy Resource Manual: 1986-87, 1988, Witness to Life in Judaism, 1990, Exploring the Ethos of Africa, 1990, Existence, Language and Religion, in the Thoughts of Alfred G. Rooks, 1991. New Republic Party candidate for Parliament, Natal, Republic of South Africa, 1977. Named to Hon. Order of Ky. Col., 1985. Mem. Soc. for Old Testament Study (assoc.), Am. Acad. Religion, Internat. Assn. for Mission Study. Home: 200 Guittard Ave Waco TX 76706 Office: Baylor U Dept Religion Waco TX 76798

JOOSTENS, M., minister. Stated clk. Protestant Ref. Chs. in Am., Grand Rapids, Mich. Office: Protestant Ref Chs in Am 2016 Teconsha SE Grand Rapids MI 49506*

JOPP, HAROLD DOWLING, JR., deacon, lawyer, academic administrator; b. Balt., Oct. 20, 1946; s. Harold Dowling and Violet Stella (Karpinski) J.; m. Margaret Carole Wallace, Dec. 20, 1967; children: Harold Dowling III, Devin Alexander. MA, U. Del., 1970, EdD, 1988; ThM, St. Mary's Sem., Balt., 1979; MA, Cen. Mich. U., 1983; JD, U. Md. Ordained deacon Roman Cath. Ch., 1980; bar: Md. 1976, U.S. Supreme Ct. 1980. Deacon St. Benedict's and St. Elizabeth's, Ridgely, Md., 1980—; dir. continuing edn. Md. State Bd. for Community Colls., Annapolis, 1989-91; dir. grad. studies Coll. Notre Dame Md., Balt., 1991—; mem. coun. St. Benedict's Parish Coun., Ridgely, 1978—; bd. mem. United Concerned Christians, Denton, Md., 1977-80. Co-author, editor: (anthology) Shoremen, 1974; (books) The Last Hotel, 1986, Rediscovery of Eastern Shore, 1987; editor: Chesapeake Seasons. Basselin fellow Cath. U., 1966. Office: Coll Notre Dame Md 4701 N Charles St Baltimore MD 21210 *Although contemporary theories of evolution suggest that we human beings have developed enormously, we continue to grapple with fundamental questions of meaning in life. I believe that our individual existence is purposeful but, in company with Job and Ecclesiastes, I struggle toward certainty.*

JORALEMON, BARBARA GAIL, health care administrator, minister; b. Salt Lake City, Apr. 10, 1951; d. Peter and Barbara Ann (Hayward) J.; m. Brian Kanne Hansen, Feb. 25, 1984; 1 child, David Winston Joralemon Hansen. Student, Beaver Coll., 1969-71; BA cum laude, Boston U., 1974; MDiv., Pacific Sch. Religion, 1976. Ordained to ministry United Ch. Christ, 1977. Coord. TV monitoring project United Meth. Women, Berkeley, Calif., 1975-76; coord. counseling Reproductive Health Services, Columbia, Mo., 1977-78; program dir., chaplain United Ecumenical Ministry, Columbia, 1977-79; coordinator service and edn. Sudden Infant Death Syndrome Project, Jefferson City, Mo., 1979-80; exec. dir. Abortion and Pregnancy Testing Clinic, Albuquerque, 1980-88; co-founder, pres. N.Mex. Health Decisions, Albuquerque, 1989—; bd. dirs., exec. council United Campus Ministries, Albuquerque, 1980-89, v.p. bd. dirs., 1986-87, pres., 1988-89; tchr. ESL, Kaohsiung, Taiwan, 1984-85. Author: Adolescents and Abortion: Choice and Loss, Adolescents and Death; co-author (booklet) Sex Role Stereotyping in Prime Time TV, 1976. State coord. policy action com. Nat. Abortion Fedn., Washington and Albuquerque, 1982-88; mem. N.Mex. Right to Choose; mem. bio-ethics com. U. N.Mex. Hosp.; mem. instnl. rev. bd. St. Joseph's Hosp., 1990—; mem. pastoral care adv. com. Presbyn. Hosp., 1989—; mem. sub-com. on prioritization Gov.'s Health Care Adv. Com., 1990, N.Mex. Dept. Human Svcs. Task Force on Implementing Nat. Health Care Reform, 1991—; mem. S.W. conf. com. on ch. and ministry United Ch. of Christ, 1990—. Mem. Religious Coalition for Abortion Rights (bd. dirs. 1980-89, pres. N.Mex. chpt. 1987-88), Profl. Orgn. Women (co-chmn., 1982-87), Clergy Women Orgn. (convener 1985—). Democrat. Avocations: bicycling, camping, hiking, gardening.

JORDAHL, RONALD IVAN, librarian, educator; b. Buffalo Ctr., Iowa, May 29, 1936; s. George Harry and Leota Eola (Yost) J.; m. Faye Lorraine Bixby, Aug. 29, 1964; children: Philip, Ronald, Rebekah. BA, Luther Coll., 1958; MLS, U. S.C., 1988. Librarian, tchr. Prairie Bible Inst., Three Hills, Alta., Can., 1966—. Contbr. articles to profl. jours. Editor, The Christian Librarian, 1978—. Mem. ALA, Can. Library Assn., Assn. Christian Librarians (pres. 1981-82, bd. dirs. 1975—). Home: Box 4317, Three Hills, AB Canada T0M 2A0 Office: Prairie Bible Inst, Three Hills, AB Canada T0M 2A0

JORDAN, CARL EDWARD, minister; b. Greenville, Miss., Aug. 6, 1935; s. Lawrence Jonathan and Bessie Pearl (Phillips) J.; m. Maxine Hughes, May 11, 1969; children: Carl Edward, Yolunda, Ervin, Chauncy. BS, Tougaloo Coll., Miss., 1962; Dipl. in Christian Edn., Miss. Bapt. Sem., Jackson, 1965; ThB, Miss. Bapt. Sem., 1979, ThM, 1982. With Singer Sewing Machine Co., Inglewood, Calif., 1956-58; tchr., coach Bolivar County Sch. Dist. #5, Rosedale, Miss., 1962-63; recreation supr. Greenville Park Commn., Greenville, Miss., 1963-65; work supr. Neighborhood Youth Corp., Greenville, 1965-66; adminstrv. asst. Mid-Delta Edn. Assn., Greenville, 1966-67; letter carrier U.S. Postal Svc., Greenville, 1967-80; pastor New Jerusalem M.B. Ch., Ruleville, Miss., New Hope M.B. Ch., Lake Village, Ark., Chapel Hill M.B. Ch., Clarksdale, Miss.; bd. dirs. Gen. Missionary Bapt. State Conv. of Miss.; instr. Miss. Bapt. Congress of Christian Edn.; bd. dirs. Fgn. Mission Bd., Nat. Bapt. Conv. U.S.A., Inc. With U.S. Army, 1958-60. Mem. Washington County Gen. Bapt. Assn., Interdenominational Ministers Alliance, Masons. Democrat. Baptist. Address: PO Box 4342 Greenville MS 38704

JORDAN, CECILE BLANK, educational administrator; b. Newark, N.J., Aug. 27, 1937; d. Robert and Adele (Schechner) Blank; m. Earl A. Jordan, May 26, 1956 (div. 1977); children: Philip, Ruth Ellen. BA, Case Western Res. U., 1968; MS, U. Bridgeport, 1972; EdD, U. Houston, 1983; MA, NYU, 1986. Tchr. Fox Run Sch., Nowalk, Conn., 1969-72; tchr. math. Plumfield Sch., Noroton, Conn., 1972-73; tchr. Beth Yeshurun Day Sch., Houston, 1975-78, prin., 1978-86; exec. dir. Agy. for Jewish Edn., San Diego, 1986—; mem. Com. on Jewish Edn., Houston, 1979-80; sec.-treas. Bur. Dirs. Fellowship, 1991—. Contbg. editor Private Sch. Monitor, 1981-83; contbr. articles to profl. publs. Mem. Nat. Assn. Elem. Sch. Prins., Nat. Assn. Temple Educators, Am. Ednl. Research Assn., Jewish Edn. Assn., Ind. Schs. Assn. SW (chair minority affairs com.), Tex. Assn. Non-Pub. Schs. (bd. dirs. 1981-86).

JORDAN, CHARLES WESLEY, minister; b. Dayton, Ohio, May 28, 1933; s. David Morris and Naomi Azelia (Harper) J.; m. Margaret May Crawford, Aug. 2, 1959; children: Diana, Susan. BA, Roosevelt U., 1956; MDiv, Garrett Evangel. Theol. Seminary, Evanston, Ill., 1960. Ordained to ministry United Meth. Ch., 1960. Pastor Woodlawn United Meth. Ch., Chgo., 1960-66; dir. of urban ministries Rockford, Ill., 1966-71; prog. staff No. Ill. Con./United Meth. Ch., Chgo., 1971-82; dist. supt. Chgo./So. Dist. United Meth. Ch., 1982-87; sr. pastor St. Mark United Meth. Ch., Chgo., 1987—; del. United Meth. Gen. Conf., 1976, 80, 84, 88, 92, Gen. Bd. Global Ministries, 1972-80, Gen. Coun. on Ministries, 1980-88; trustee Garrett Evangel. Theol. Sem., 1982—. Commnr. Rockford Housing Authority, 1969-71; bd. dirs. Community Mental Health Coun., Chgo., 1989—, Project Image, Inc., Chgo., 1987—. With AUS, 1953-55. Named to Hall of Fame Wendell Phillips High Sch., Chgo., 1989. Mem. NAACP (chmn. religious affairs 1990—). Home: 8101 S Eberhart Chicago IL 60619 Office: St Mark United Methodist Ch 8441 S St Lawrence Chicago IL 60619

JORDAN, DAN W., minister; b. Harrison, Ga., Dec. 14, 1946; s. Isadore and Willie Mae (Roberts) J.; m. Emma Jean Jordan, Dec. 22, 1968; children: Daniel, David, Kimberly, Jonathan, Emma J. Douglas Jordan. Student, St. Louis U., 1970, Lael U., 1976, Concordia Sem., 1971-73, Eden Theol. Sem., 1974-75. Ordained to ministry Metro Bapt. Assn. Pastor Green Chapel Bapt. Ch., Clarkville, Mo., 1970-73, Mt. Airy Bapt. Ch., St. Louis, 1978-80; pastor, founder The Hist. Christ Bapt. Ch., St. Louis, 1982-87, Christian Tabernacle Bapt. Ch., Webster Grove, Mo., 1987—; owner, mgr. Jordan's Exec. Barber Shop, University City, Mo., 1972—; exec. sec. Mo. State Conv., 1968-71; pres. Berean dist. St. Louis Street Ministry, 1977-78. Author: The Struggle of the Church, 1990. Active Oper. Brite Side. Home: 119 Robins Song Dr Ellisville MO 63021 Office: Christian Tabernacle Bapt Ch 412 Oaktree Dr Webster Groves MO 63119

JORDAN, DAVID M., minister; b. Washington, Mar. 19, 1960; s. Adiel Moncrief and Diane (Owen) J.; m. Elizabeth Ann Jackson, Jan. 4, 1986. BA in History, Furman U., 1982; student, Rüschlikon Bapt. Seminary, Zürich, Switzerland, 1983-84; MDiv, So. Bapt. Theol. Seminary, Louisville, 1986. Ordained to ministry Bapt. Ch., 1986. Assoc. minister Riverside Bapt. Ch., Washington, 1986-91; pastor Twinbrook Bapt. Ch., Rockville, Md., 1991—; mem. exec. com., minister's fellowship D.C. Bapt. Conv., 1986—. Composer/guitarist original songs. Coord. Inner City Boy's Club, Louisville, 1985-86; participant S.W. Ch. Big Bros., Washington, 1987—; chmn. Com. on Pub. Affairs and Social Concerns, Washington, 1986—. Named one of Outstanding Young Men of Am., 1985. Mem. S.W. Clergy Assn., Bapt. Peace Fellowship, Amnesty Internat., Intereligious Human Rights Group. Democrat. Avocations: music, sports, reading, writing. Office: Twinbrook Bapt Ch 1001 Twinbrook Pkwy Rockville MD 20851

JORDAN, GREGORY DOTY, academic dean, religion educator; b. Jackson, Miss., Dec. 19, 1951; s. Wallace Doty and Nell (Kirkland) J.; m. Sally Bruce Franze, Sept. 2, 1973; children: Benjamin, Samuel, Jonathan. BA, Belhaven Coll., 1973; MA, Trinity Evang. Div. Sch., 1976, MDiv, 1977; PhD, Hebrew Union Coll., 1986; postgrad., Am. Inst. Holy Land Studies, Jerusalem, 1976-77, Albright Inst. Archtl. Rsch., Jerusalem, 1977. Grad. asst. Trinity Evang. Divinity Sch., Deerfield, Ill., 1975-76; prof. King Coll., Bristol, Tenn., 1980—, dean of faculty, 1990—; adj. prof. Inst. Holy Land Studies, Jerusalem, 1985. Recipient Erna & Julius Krouch scholarship Hebrew Union Coll., 1977-78, Joseph & Helen Regenstein fellowship, 1978-80, S.H. Scheur fellowship, 1982-83, Ilse Hitchman fellowship, 1983-85. Presbyterian. Home: 100 Tadlock Rd Bristol TN 37620 Office: King Coll 1350 King College Rd Bristol TN 37620-2699

JORDAN, JAMES ELGIE, clergyman, computer consultant; b. Hattiesburg, Miss., July 19, 1949; s. William F. and Mary F. (Shows) J.; m. Yvonne Winfield, Apr. 8, 1951; 1 child, William Chad. BS, U. So. Ala., 1972; MDiv, MidAm. Bapt. Theol. Sem., 1984. Ordained to ministry Baptist Ch., 1980. Systems analyst Daniel Internat. Corp., Greenville, S.C., 1972-76, Neco Elec. Products, Laurel, Miss., 1976, Morrison's, Inc., Mobile, Ala., 1976-79; office mgr. Green Vet. Clinic, Memphis, 1979-82; cons. computers Mobile, 1982-84; pastor Friendly Tibbie (Ala.) Bapt. Ch., 1984—. Vol. chpt. St. Joseph Charity Hosp., Memphis, 1980-82; counselor Union rescue Mission, Memphis, 1980-82; leader Boy Scouts Am., Mobile, 1962; counselor Evangel. Crusade, Dothan, Ala., 1974-76. Named one of Outstanding Young Men Am., 1985. Southern Baptist. Avocations: poultry, trapping, tennis, fishing, reading. Home: Hwy 17 PO Box 21 Tibbie AL 36583 Office: Friendly Tibbie Bapt Ch Gen Delivery Tibbie AL 36583

JORDAN, JOHN W., school system administrator. Supt. of schs. Diocese of Scranton, Pa. Office: Office of Schs Supt 300 Wyoming Ave Scranton PA 18503*

JORDAN, MORRIS LEE, minister; b. Crossville, Ala., Sept. 23, 1939; s. George Lamar and Lyda Mae (Wilkinson) J.; m. Marjorie Ann Hamrick, Nov. 26, 1966; 1 child, Michael Lee. BA in Ch. Music, Carson-Newman Coll., 1961; MA in Music Edn., Appalachian State, 1966. Ordained to ministry Bapt. Ch., 1979. Minister music and religious edn. Dover Bapt. Ch., Shelby, N.C., 1961-67; minister music and youth 1st Bapt. Ch., New Bern, N.C., 1967-69; minister music 1st Bapt. Ch., Canton, N.C., 1969-79, music minister, assoc. pastor, 1979-87; music minister, sr. adults minister 1st Bapt. Ch., Kings Mountain, N.C., 1987—; regional music dir. N.C. Bapt. Music Dept., Cary, 1964-82; adjudicator for festivals Tenn. Bapt. Music Dept., Nashville, 1980-82. Bd. dirs. East Haywood United Way, Canton, 1984-86, pres., 1985-86; mem. Kings Mountain Sr. Ctr. Adv. Coun., 1990—; bd. dirs. Cleveland County Community Concert Assn., 1991—. Mem. Centurymen, N.C. Singing Churchmen (charter mem.), Kings Mountain Inter-

Denominational Ministers Assn. (spl. svcs. com. 1988-90). Office: First Bapt Ch 605 W King St Kings Mountain NC 28086

JORDAN, NERIUS FRED, JR., minister; b. Salisbury, N.C., Sept. 30, 1945; s. Nerius Fred and Katherine (Wagoner) J.; m. Katherine Parker, July 27, 1974; children: David McLeod, Robert Frederick, Margaret Ann. BA, Catawba Coll., 1967; MDiv, Duke Div. Sch., 1970; postgrad., Trinity Coll., U. Glasgow, Scotland, 1971. Ordained to ministry United Meth. Ch. as deacon, 1969, as elder, 1971. Pastor Merrylea Parish Ch., Glasgow, 1970, Concord (N.C.) United Meth. Ch., 1971-75, Salem United Meth. Ch., Albemarle, N.C., 1975-80, Bethany United Meth. Ch., North Wilkesboro, N.C., 1980-84, Morris Chapel United Meth. Ch., Winston-Salem, N.C., 1984-91, Elkin (N.C.) 1st United Meth Ch., 1991—; chmn. com. continuing edn. Western N.C. Conf. United Meth. Ch., 1980-83, bd. mgrs. N.C. Pastors' Sch., 1980-84, bd. of ordained ministry, 1983-84, dist. coun. on ministries, Albemarle and Winston-Salem Dists., dist. com. on ordained ministry, Albemarle and N. Wilkesboro Dists.; registrar N. Wilkesboro Dist. com. on ordained ministry; chairperson higher edn., N. Wilkesboro Dist.; mem. Western N.C. Conf. Ins. Com.; v.p. Western N.C. Conf. Brotherhood/Sisterhood; chmn., registrar Western N.C. Conf. Backpacking Program; mem. Commn. on Evangelism and Ch. Growth; cons. Growth Plus; supervising pastor candidacy studies; chief clergy teller Gen./Jurisdiction election, 1991. Author: (with others) Methodism Alive in North Carolina, 1976; writer monthly column for Elkin Tribune, contbr. articles to Winston-Salem Jour. Bd. dirs. Tri-County Christian Crisis Ministry; soccer coach, Elkin Recreation Program; mem. Laurel Dist. Com. Boy Scouts Am.; pres. Concord Civitan Club, 1983, lt. gov. N.C. Dist. West Civitan, 1974; capt., chaplain Millingport Vol. Fire Dept., 1975-80, Fleetwood Vol. Fire Dept. 1980-84. Avocations: camping, microcomputers, woodworking, travel. Home: 206 Hawthorne Rd Elkin NC 28621-3019 Office: 1st United Meth Ch PO Box 69 Elkin NC 28621-0069

JORDAN, PHILIP DEAN, history educator, lay church worker; b. Copaigue, L.I., Nov. 23, 1940; s. Arthur Mason and Emily (Denton) J.; m. Kay Irene Kirkpatrick, June 22, 1968; children: Anne Katherine, Mead Mason. BA, Alfred U., 1963; MA, U. Rochester, 1965; PhD, U. Iowa, 1971. Elder Mt. Calvary Luth. Ch., Gunnison, Colo., 1977-79, v.p., 1979-80, pres., 1980-81; prof. history Hastings (Nebr.) Coll., 1985—; mem. Episcopal Diocesan Ecumenical Coun., Colo., 1985, 1st St. Paul's Luth. Ch., Hastings, 1987—; vis. assoc. prof. dept. history and Sch. Religion, U. Iowa, 1979, 87. Author: Evangelical Alliance for the U.S.A., 1983; contbg. author: The Social Gospel: Religion and Reform in Changing America, 1976; contbr. articles to profl. jours. Trustee Campus Ministry, Western State Coll. Colo., Gunnison, 1972; del. State Dem. Conv., Colo., 1972, 74. N.Y. State Regents scholar, 1959-63, tuition scholar U. Rochester, 1963-65; Teaching fellow N.Y. State Coll., 1963-65, All Univ. Teaching Rsch. fellow, 1968-69, NEH fellow, 1980, 86—; Western State Coll. Found. grantee, 1984. Mem. Am. Acad. Religion (treas. Rocky Mountain-Gt. Plains regional conf. 1979-85), History Sci. Soc., Colo. Assn. Univ. Press (trustee), Orgn. Am. Historians, Am. Hist. Assn., Am. Soc. Ch. History, Phi Alpha Theta. Democrat. Office: Hastings Coll Dept History Hastings NE 68901 *Although science and technology transforms even nature itself, wise use of such immense power derives not from science but rather our humane tradition rooted in religious and philosophical values, ethics and systems of logic.*

JORDAN, PRESTON LEROY, JR., minister; b. Jamaica, N.Y., May 11, 1954; s. Preston LeRoy Sr. and Jennie Mae (Folds) J.; m. Josephine Elaine Coleman, June 26, 1976; children: Jason, Vincent, Lauren. BA in History, King's Coll., Briarcliff Manor, N.Y., 1976; MDiv, Va. Union U., 1979. Ordained to ministry Bapt. Ch., 1979. Pastor Mt. Olive Bapt. Ch., Essex County, Va., 1979-86, Trinity Bapt. Ch., Newport News, Va., 1986—; counselor Va. Dept. Youth and Family Svcs., Hampton, 1979—. Mem. Peninsula Bapt. Assn., Bapt. Gen. Conv. Va., Phi Beta Sigma. Democrat. Home: 102 Onancock Turning Yorktown VA 23693 Office: Trinity Bapt Ch 29th St and Chestnut Ave Newport News VA 23607

JORDAN, RANDALL BRYANT, clergyman; b. Florence, S.C., Nov. 27, 1951; s. Julius Bryant and Jeanette (Hinson) J.; m. Mary Paulla Morris, Feb. 8, 1952; children: Christopher Bryant, Bethany Faith. AA, Wingate Jr. Coll., N.C., 1972; BS, U. S.C., 1974; MDiv, So. Bapt. Theol. Sem., Louisville, 1978; DMin, So. Bapt. Theol. Sem., 1990. Ordained to mininstry, So. Bapt. Ch. With various cos., 1971-75; children's chaplain St. Matthews Bapt. Ch., Louisville, 1975-76; assoc. minister First Bapt. Ch., Eastwood, Ky., 1976-78; minister/pastor Bethel Bapt. Ch., Monetta, S.C., 1978-81, First Bapt. Ch., Walhalla, S.C., 1981-84, Reedy Creek Bapt. Ch., Marion, S.C., 1984—; nominating com. S.C. Bapt. Conv., Marion, 1986—; vice moderator Marion Bapt. Assn., 1985, Marion Pastors Conf., 1985. Chmn. Multiple Schlerosis Soc., Marion, 1984-85; chaplain Lions Club, 1982-83. Mem. S.C. Bapt. Hist. Soc., S.C. Christian Action Council, Lions. Democrat. Baptist. Avocations: tennis, photography, fishing, swimming, book collecting, sports. Home: Route 4 Box 317 Marion SC 29571 Office: Reedy Creek Baptist Church Route 4 Box 317 Marion SC 29571

JORDAN, RANDY WAYNE, radio station manager, programmer, air personality; b. Okalahoma City, Dec. 16, 1952; s. Marvin Wayne Jordan and Dolores Francis (Harper) Taliaferro; m. Mary Louise Eldredge, Dec. 28, 1972; children: Lael Eve, Abigail Hope, Gabriel Asher. Program dir. Sta. KCNW Radio, Universal Broadcasting, Kansas City, Kans., 1978-79, 86-88, Sta. KTOF Radio, Young Broadcasting, Cedar Rapids, Iowa, 1979-83; pastor, elder Fellowship Christian Ch., Cedar Rapids, 1981-85; program dir. Sta. WTOF Radio, Mortenson Broadcasting, 1985-86; sta. mgr. Sta. KNRB Radio, Marsh Broadcasting, Ft. Worth, 1988—. Home: 4302 Maple Springs Dr Arlington TX 76107 Office: Marsh Broadcasting Sta KNRB 3001 W 5th St Fort Worth TX 76017

JORDAN, RICHARD ALAN, minister; b. Oakland, Calif., June 21, 1953; s. John Carrol and Dana Patricia (O'Connell) J.; m. Susan Jane Garmatz, June 5, 1981. BS, St. Mary's Coll., Moraga, Calif., 1975; MDiv, Concordia Sem., St. Louis, 1981. Ordained to ministry Luth. Ch., 1981. Pastor Emanuel Luth. Ch., Sisseton, S.D., 1981-91, Zion Luth. Ch., Ocheyedan, Iowa, 1991—; mem. adv. bd. Shalom Ctr., Sioux Falls, S.D., 1986-90; del. Luth. Ch. Mo. Synod Conv., Indpls., 1986. Contbr. articles, ednl. materials to profl. publs. Chmn. Roberts County chpt. ARC, Sisseton, 1986-91, mem. resolutions com. nat. conv. 1992; chmn. Roberts County Health Fair, Sisseton, 1984, 86, Aid Assn. for Luths. Br., Sisseton, 1982-91; pastor advisor Lake region zone Luth. Layman's League, S.D., 1983-88. Recipient Clara Barton award Roberts County ARC, 1991. Mem. Soc. Biblical Lit., Cath. Biblical Assn., Concordia Hist. Inst., Guild of Am. Luthiers, Sisseton Ministerial Assn. (treas. 1982-91), NRA. Republican. Home and Office: RR 2 Box 218 Ocheyedan IA 51354

JORDAN, RICHARD WINSLOW, minister; b. Vacaville, Calif., Sept. 10, 1958; s. Roger Winslow and Marcia Zenda (Lantz) J.; m. Susan Gail Bodamer, Aug. 7, 1982; children: Todd Nathaniel, Benjamin Thomas. BA, King Coll., 1980; MDiv, Midwestern Bapt. Theol. Sem., Kansas City, Mo., 1984. Ordained to ministry So. Bapt. Conv., 1984. Youth min. Second Bapt. Ch., Liberty, Mo., 1981-84; assoc. pastor Viewmont Bapt. Ch., Hickory, N.C., 1986—; dir. Sun. Sch. of Bapt. Assn., Hickory, N.C., 1986-91, Pastoral Ministries of Bapt. Assn., 1991—; spl. worker Sun. Sch. Bd. of N.C., Cary, 1987—; chmn. CROP Walk publicity com., Hickory, 1986-88; co-chair United Way profls. subcom., 1989. Author newspaper cols. for Hickory Daily Record. Co-chmn. profl. com. United Way, Hickory, 1989; facilitator Parent to Parent Drug Awareness workshops, 1991—; bd. dirs. Furniture Crisis Ministry, 1991—; vice-chmn. Search Com. for Associational Dir., 1990; chmn. pastoral care adv. com. Frye Hosp., Hickory, 1991. Mem. Greater Hickory (N.C.) Ministerial Assn. (pres. 1990, treas. 1991), Christian Coop. Ministry (bd. dirs. 1990), N.C. Bapt. Religious Educators Assn. (sec. 1991—), So. Bapt. Religion Educators Assn., N.C. Youth Ministers Assn. Democrat. Office: Viewmont Bapt Ch 1246 2nd St NE Hickory NC 28601 *I heard once of a very short commencement address that went as follows: "Love God. Love people. Bring the two together." When I combine that with Paul's wordds in Colossians 2:2-3, I find the meaning and purpose of my life.*

JORDAN, WALTER FANT, minister; b. Xenia, Ohio, May 13, 1938; s. Walter Fant and Gladys Myona (Payne) J.; m. Janice Marie Morgan, Jan. 30, 1960; children: Lisa Marie Jordan Scott, Jennifer Kay Jordan Barrett. BA cum laude, Wittenberg U., 1976; MDiv, Trinity Luth. Sem., Columbus, Ohio, 1979. Ordained to ministry Evang. Luth. Ch. Am., 1979. Chaplain intern St. John's Ctr., Springfield, Ohio, 1978-79; min. St. Timothy Luth. Ch., Columbus, 1979-87, Augsburg Luth. Ch., Orrville, Ohio, 1987—; chairperson Orrville Ch. World Svc./CROP Walk, 1991—. Bd. dirs. United Way, Orrville, 1992. With USAF, 1958-62. Mem. Northeastern Ohio Synod. of Evang. Luth. Ch. in Am. (min. 1979—, chairperson evangelism com. 1989—), Orrville Ministerial Assn. (publicity chmn. 1989—, v.p. 1991—), Wayne Area Luth. Pastor's Assn., Wayne United Ministries (bd. dirs.), Phi Eta Sigma. Home: 524 S Main St Orrville OH 44667 Office: Augsburg Luth Ch 140 W Water St Orrville OH 44667 *In the decade of the 1990s I think that our greatest challenge will be developing and equipping religious leaders who are tuned to a rapidly changing high tech society and yet sensitive to the continued human need for meaningful community.*

JORDON, ROBERT MARK, pastor; b. Jackson, Miss., Oct. 13, 1950; m. Donna Marie Gressett, Aug. 18, 1972. AA, Meridian (Miss.) Jr. Coll., 1970; BA, U. So. Miss., 1972; MDiv, So. Bapt. Theol. Sem., Louisville, 1975; D of Ministry, Southeastern Bapt. Theol. Sem., Wake Forest, N.C., 1986; clin. pastoral edn. tng., Louisville, 1975; pastoral counseling tng., Washington Pastoral Counseling Svc., 1978-81. Ordained to ministry Bapt Ch., 1972, lic. to ministry, 1966. Preacher Lauderdale Bapt. Assn., 1968-72; youth dir. Enterprise (Miss.) Bapt. Ch., summer 1972; pastoral intern Crescent Hill Bapt. Ch., Louisville, fall 1972; chaplain Jewish Hosp., Louisville, summer 1975, Louisville Gen. Hosp., fall 1975; assoc. pastor Parkwood Bapt. Ch., Annandale, Va., 1976-81; pastor Pleasant Ridge Bapt. Ch., Frankfort, Ky., 1972-75, Beth Car Bapt. Ch., Madison, Va., 1981-87, Rapidan Bapt. Ch., Wolftown, Va., 1981-87, 1st Bapt. Ch., Front Royal, Va., 1987—; regional rep. So. Bapt. Alliance. Bd. mem. Rappahannock Rapidan Community Support Svcs.; mem. Madison County Task Force, Front Royal Coun. of Chs., Community Action Team; active Madison Emergency Svcs. Assn., Aging Svcs.; mem. planning com. area youth summer camp, 1978, dir., 1979. Mem. Mount Vernon Va. Bapt. Assn. (mem. mutal care commn. and leader workshops, mem. ordination com.), Shiloh Assn. (chmn. stewardship com.), Shenandoah Bapt. Assn. (mem. Christian life com.), Madison Ministerial Assn., Front Royal Ministerial Assn. (pres.), Rotary. Home: 1035 Northview Ave Front Royal VA 22630

JORGENSEN, GERALD THOMAS, psychologist, educator; b. Mason City, Iowa, Jan. 15, 1947; s. Harry Grover and Mary Jo (Kollasch) J.; m. Mary Ann Reiter, Aug. 30, 1969; children—Amy Lynn, Sarah Kay, Jill Kathryn. B.A., Loras Coll., Dubuque, 1969; M.S., Colo. State U., Ft. Collins, 1970, Ph.D., 1973. Lic. psychologist, Iowa; ordained to ministry Roman Cath. Ch. as deacon, 1979. Psychology intern Counseling Ctr., Colo. State U., Ft. Collins, 1971-72, VA Hosp., Palo Alto, Calif., 1972-73; psychologist Loras Coll., 1973-76, Clarke Coll., Dubuque, 1973-76; asst. prof. psychology, Loras Coll., 1976-80, assoc. prof., 1981—, dir. Ctr. for Counseling and Student Devel., 1977-86, assoc. dean of students, 1985-86, dean of students, v.p. for student devel., 1986—; cons. and supervising psychologist Dubuque/Jackson County Mental Health Ctr., 1977—; asst. dir. for formation Office of Permanent Diaconate, Archdiocese of Dubuque,1979—; chairperson Iowa Bd. Psychology Examiners, Des Moines, 1984-90, continuing edn. coordinator, 1983. Contbr. articles to profl. jours. Treas. Dubuque County Assn. Mental Health Inc., Dubuque, 1975-82. NDEA fellow, 1969-72. Mem. Am. Coll. Pers. Assn. (chmn. com. VII 1980-82), Am. Assn. Counseling Devel., Am. Psychol. Assn., Iowa Psychol. Assn. (mem. exec. coun., highest honors 1990), Am. Assn. State Psychol. Bds. (exec. com. 1986-89, pres. 1989—), Nat. Assn. Permanent Diaconate Dirs. (sec. 1983-85, treas. 1985-90, award 1991), Iowa Student Pers. Assn., Delta Epsilon Sigma, Phi Kappa Phi, Sigma Tau Phi. Democrat. Roman Catholic. Home: 2183 St Celia St Dubuque IA 52002 Office: Loras Coll 1450 Alta Vista St Dubuque IA 52004-0178 *Perhaps the greatest challenge in my life has been to not only see a natural tension built into Christianity but also to accept that its resolution is remaining faithful to the struggle, not necessarily dissipating the tension. The struggle is to preserve the purity of the Gospel in the light of a changing world; to integrate human truth—wherever it is found—with the revealed truth that comes from God through Scripture and the Church.*

JORGENSON, WAYNE JAMES, priest; b. Evanston, Ill., Sept. 1, 1943; s. Wayne W. and Kathleen J. (Conroyd) J.; m. Patricia Ellen Guzy, June 7, 1969; children: Daria, Michael. BA, St. Meinrad Coll., 1966; MDiv, St. Vladimir Sem., 1969; PhD, Boston U., 1979. Ordained to priest Orthodox Ch. in Am., 1969. Pastor Holy Assumption Ch., Lublin, Wis., 1969-71; asst. pastor St. Mary's Ch., Mpls., 1971-74; pastor Nativity of Virgin Mary Ch., Chelsea, Mass., 1974-79, St. Seraphim Ch., Dallas, 1979-81, All Sts. Ch., Detroit, 1981—; adj. prof. ch. history St. John Provincial Sem., Plymouth, Mich., 1983-88; assoc. prof. ch. history Sacred Heart Major Sem., Detroit, 1988—; with Faith and Order Commn., NCCC, 1983—, Luth. Orthodox Bilateral Dialogue, 1984—. Mem. Orthodox Theology Soc. Am. Home: 35240 Joy Rd Livonia MI 48150 Office: All Saints Ch 2918 E Hendrie Detroit MI 48211

JOSEPH, KENNETH ROBERT, clergyman, missionary; b. Chgo., Oct. 30, 1928; s. Samuel Noah Joseph and Martha (Adams) Joseph Assyrian; m. Lila May Finsaas, Aug. 24, 1955; children—Kenneth Phillip, Robert Samuel, James Orvin, Mark Scott. B.A., Bob Jones U., 1950; M.A., Fuller Theol. Sem., 1959. Ordained to ministry Evang. Ch. Alliance, 1955, So. Bapt. Conv., 1951; Dir. Hendersonville Youth for Christ, N.C., 1947-51; with The Evangel. Alliance Mission, Japan, 1951-66; with Reinforcing Evangelists and Aiding Pastors Mission, Tokyo, 1966—, also dir.; vice chmn. Japan Evang. Missionary Assn., 1959; internat. coordinator Japan Christian Council Chs., 1967—; pres. Japan Bible Christian Council, 1965-66; bd. dirs. Holy Land Research Soc., 1967—; internat. coordinator World Christian Lay Assn., 1967—, World Christian Anti-Communism Assn., 1967—; chmn. bd. World Gospel Chs., 1975—; Asian rep. Second Coming, 1977—. Author: Missionary Language Handbook, vol. 1, 1955, vol. 2, 1957; Combined (Eng.) Evangelism-Theory and Practice, Personal Evangelism I and II, 1960. Editor: REAP-Ketsudan Quar., 1961-66, Japan Harvest, 1959-65; assoc. editor Japan Jour., 1982—. Mem. Japan Evangelists Fellowship, Assoc. Missions. Republican. Clubs: Stamp, Tokyo Am., Million Mile. Office: REAP Mission, 7-39-6 Higashi Oizumi, Nerima Ku, Tokyo 178, Japan also: PO Box 488 La Mirada CA 90637-0488

JOSEPH, METROPOLITAN BISHOP See BOSAKOV, JOSEPH BLAGOEV

JOSEPH, PAUL, rabbi; b. Miami, Fla., July 19, 1944; 1 child, Rachel. BA in History magna cum laude, SUNY, Binghamton, 1972; MA in Hebrew Lit., Hebrew U. Coll., 1975. Ordained rabbi, 1977. Dir. edn. Congregation Rodeph Sholom, N.Y.C., 1973-77, The Temple, Cleve., 1980-82; rabbi Congregation Beth Israel, Monterey, Calif., 1977-80, Cen. Synagogue, Rockville Centre, N.Y., 1982-88; dir. Jewish edn. 92d St Y, N.Y.C., 1988—; adj. assoc. prof. Hofstra U., Uniondale, N.Y., 1988, Cleve. Coll. Jewish Studies, Beachwood, Ohio, 1980-82; adj. prof. Molloy Coll., Rockville Centre, N.Y., 1984-88, 91-92; v.p. No. Calif. Bd. Rabbis, 1978-80, Monterey Peninsula Ministerial Assn., 1978-80. Bd. dirs. Monterey Peninsula Salvation Army, 1978-80. Named Man of Yr. United Jewish Appeal, Rockville Centre, 1986. Mem. Am. Acad. Religion, Soc. Bibl. Lit., Am. Schs. Oriental Rsch., Am. Soc. Law and Medicine, Jewish Peace Fellowship. Home: 12 Addison Pl Rockville NY 11570 Office: 92d St Y 1395 Lexington Ave New York NY 10128

JOSEPH, RONALD EVANS, priest; b. Dover, Del., Feb. 5, 1936; s. Ronald Franklin and Helen Fosque (Lofland) J.; m. Ruth Baker, June 18, 1960; children: David Thomas, Elizabeth Anne. BSEd, Temple U., 1958; MDiv., Phila. Div. Sch., 1961; DMin., Internat. Sem., 1979; cert. pastoral psychotherapy, Pa. Found. Pastoral Counseling, 1980. Ordained priest Episcopal Ch., 1961. Curate Trinity Meml. Ch., Phila., Pa., 1961-65; rector Ch. of St. James the Less, Phila., 1965-70, St. Martin's Ch., Boothwyn, Pa., 1970—; Ecclesiastical triers Episcopal Diocese of Pa., Phila., 1985—, dean Delaware Deanery, 1987—; bd. dirs. Little Lambs Christian Day Care Ctr., Boothwyn, 1984—; Diocesan spiritual dir. Episcopal Cursillo Movement, Diocese of Pa., Phila., 1986-88. Contbr. articles to publs. Mem. Am. Assn. Pastoral Counselors. Home: 726 Meetinghouse Rd Boothwyn PA 19061 Office: St Martins Episcopal Ch 700 Meetinghouse Rd Boothwyn PA 19061

JOSEPH, SAMUEL KENNETH, educator, rabbi; b. Phila., Aug. 15, 1949; s. Arthur W. and Judith (Brandes) J.; m. Dori Matje; children: Rachel, Bethami. BS, U. Cin., 1971; MA in Hebrew Letters, Hebrew Union Coll., Cin., 1974; PhD, Clayton U., 1979. Ordained rabbi, 1976. Rabbi Temple Israel, Dayton, Ohio, 1976-79; nat. dir. admissions Hebrew Union Coll., 1979-81, asst. to pres., 1980-81, asst. prof. edn., 1981-84, assoc. prof. edn., 1985-91, prof., 1991—; vis. prof., scholar-in-residence Australia (Monash U.), New Zealand, Hong Kong, 1988, 90. Author: Jews and The Founding of the Republic, 1985, How to be a Jewish Teacher: An Invitation to Make a Difference, 1987, The Madrikhim Handbook: A Training Program fpr Teenagers Working in Jewish Schools, 1989; editor Compass Jour., 1986—; contbr. articles to profl. jours. Bd. dirs., religious edn. assoc. Metro Area Religious Coalition Cin., Jewish Community Rels. Coun., Black-Jewish Coalition, Interfaith Roundtables. Recipient Tchr. of Yr., Kohl Edn. Found., 1985. Fellow Internat. Ctr. Univ. Teaching Jewish Civilization; mem. Religious Edn. Assn., Assn. Supervision and Curriculum Devel. (nat. supervision commn. 1984-86), Nat. Assn. Temple Educators, Cen. Conf. Am. Rabbis. Avocations: travel, music. Home: 4047 Beechwood Cincinnati OH 45229 Office: Hebrew Union Coll 3101 Clifton Cincinnati OH 45220

JOSLIN, DAVID BRUCE, bishop; b. Collingswood, N.J., Jan. 8, 1936; s. Sheppard and Elizabeth (Andrews) J.; m. Kathrine E. Brockett, June 15, 1958; children: Paul Gregory, Suzanne Marie. BA, Drew U., Madison, 1958; M of Divinity (hon.), Drew U., 1961; Assoc. in Anglican Studies, Episcopal Div. Sch., 1965. Assoc. rector St. Paul's Ch., Montvale, N.J., 1965-67; rector St. David's Ch., Wilmington, Del., 1967-74, Christ Ch., Westerly, R.I., 1974-87, Ch. of St. Stephen the Martyr, Edina, Minn., 1987-91; Episcopal bishop Cen. N.Y., 1991—; keynote speaker for retreats and confs., cons. liturgies and ch. design, chmn. bd. various state and nat. ch. bds. Author: Apostle in Our Midst-the Office of Bishop, 1982. Mem. Downtown Revelopment Task Force, Westerly, 1983-87; Citizen's Adv. Bd. Westerly, 1982-87; deputy gen. conv. Episcopal Ch., 1985. Mem. Fellowship of Sts. Alban and Sergius, Anglican Soc. of the U.S.A. (v.p. 1980-87), Rotary. Avocations: traveling, collector of antique autos.

JOSLIN, JAMES E., religious organization administrator; b. White River, S.D., Jan. 10, 1932; s. Virgil Newton and Mary Matilda (Hutcheson) J.; m. Kathryn Joan Anderson, Nov. 27, 1953; children: Mary Kathryn, Linda Carol. AA, S.W. Bapt. Coll., 1952; BA, William Jewell Coll., 1954; MS in Div., So. Bapt. Sem., 1958, PhD in Ministry, 1981; DD (hon.), S.W. Bapt. Coll., 1975. Ordained to ministry So. Bapt. Ch., 1954. Pastor Mt. Gilead Bapt. Ch., Clinton, Mo., 1953-54, Peach Creek Bapt. Ch., Como, Miss., 1958-59; dir. missions Panola Bapt. Assn., Batesville, Miss., 1959-63, Greene County Bapt. Assn., Springfield, Mo., 1964—; recording sec. Mo. Bapt. Conv., Jefferson City, 1978, 86, 1st v.p., 1987-88, sec./editor dir. missions. Mem. Mo. Bapt. Dir. Missions Orgn. (pres. 1985-86, dir. missions yr. 1982). Republican. Avocations: softball, reading, travel. Office: Green County Bapt Assn 2029 E Grand Springfield MO 65804

JOSSI, STEVEN MICHAEL, church administrator; b. Portland, Oreg., Dec. 21, 1957; s. Henry Albert and Evelyn Jean (Elde) J.; m. Sara E. Mann, Dec. 8, 1985; 1 child, Alex. BA in Econs., Bus., Jourism, cum laude, U. Portland, 1980. Adminstr. Sunnyside Foursquare Ch., Clackamas, Oreg., 1981—. Republican. Home: 12498 SE Ashley Clackamas OR 97015 Office: Sunnyside Foursquare Ch 13231 SE Sunnyside Rd Clackamas OR 97015

JOVANOVIC, ROBERT PAUL, priest; b. St. Louis, July 18, 1935; s. Paul Gregory and Agatha Valentine (Durbin) J. BA, Kenrick Sem., 1957; MEd in Adminstrn., St. Louis U., 1971. Ordained priest Roman Cath. Ch., 1961. Assoc. pastor various parishes, St. Louis, 1961-83; tchr. St. Pius X High Sch., Festus, Mo., 1961-67; tchr., asst. adminstr. Bishop DuBourg High Sch., St. Louis, 1967-75; adminstr. Duchesne High Sch., St. Charles, Mo., 1975-83; pastor Sacred Heart Ch., Crystal City, Mo., 1983—. Mem. support group, Dealing with Feelings Club, Barnes Hosp., St. Louis, 1982. Mem. Nat. Cath. Edn. Assn., Optimists. Address: 555 Bailey Rd Crystal City MO 63019

JOYCE, JAMES DANIEL, clergyman; b. Spencer, Va., Jan. 12, 1921; s. James Garfield and Mary (Taylor) J.; m. Dorothy Beatrice Campbell, Aug. 2, 1946; 1 son, Kevin Campbell. AB in Religion, Johnson Bible Coll., 1945, Lynchburg Coll., 1946; BD, Butler U., 1949; MA in Biblical Theology, Yale U., 1952, PhD, 1958. Ordained to ministry Disciples of Christ Ch., 1943. Pastor Hanover Ave. Christian Ch., Richmond, Va., 1954-59; sr. student leader ecumenical inst. World Council Chs., Geneva, 1960; prof. New Testament and Bible theology Christian Theol. Sem., Indpls., 1961-62; dean grad. sem. Phillips U., Enid, Okla., 1962-74; pastor Bethany Christian Ch., Houston, 1974-80, Covenant Christian Ch., Houston, 1980—; W.E. Garrison lectr. Disciple students Yale U., 1963; Jesse M. Bader lectr. evangelism Drake U., 1968; columnist Christian Jour., 1962-80; bass soloist rec. Joy-ce Sounds, 1977; pres. World Conv. Chrs. of Christ, 1970-74, mem. exec. com., 1974—; lectr. for armed forces in Far East, 1968; adj. prof. speech and creative writing U. Houston and Houston Community Coll., 1981-82; prof. speech and writing Houston Community Coll., 1982—, also head dept. speech; mem. bd. mgrs. Pension Fund Disciples of Christ. Author: The Living Christ in Our Changing World, 1962, The Place of the Sacraments in Worship, 1967. Recipient cert. of merit Methodist Bishop of Korea, 1972. Mem. Am. Assn. Theol. Schs. (exec. com. 1966-72), Theta Phi. Home: 5211 Carew St Houston TX 77096

JOYE, AFRIE SONGCO, minister; b. Guagua, Pampanga, Philippines, Aug. 8, 1942; came to U.S. 1968; d. Emilio Lelay and Elmerita (Atienza) Laus Songco; m. Charles James Joye, Aug. 28, 1971. BA in Christian Edn., Harris Meml. Coll., Manila, 1963; MA in Christian Edn., Scarritt Grad. Sch., Nashville, 1970; PhD in Theology and Religious Edn., Claremont Sch. Theology, Calif., 1990. Dir. Christian edn. First United Meth. Ch., Naga, Philippines, 1963-66; dist. Christian Edn. coord. Bicol-Palawan Region of United Meth. Ch., 1963-66; dir. Christian Edn. Cen. United Meth. Ch., Manila, 1966-68; dir. youth ministry and student ctr. Cen. United Meth. Ch., 1970-71; instr. psychology and Christian edn. Philippin Christian Coll./Harris Meml. Coll., Manila, 1970-71; dir Christian Edn. Aldersgate United Meth. Ch./John Wesley United Meth. Ch., Charleston, S.C., 1971-74; instr. Palmer Coll., Charleston, S.C., 1972-74; nat. dir. Christian edn. in Asian and Native Am. chs. Gen. Bd. Discipleship, Nashville, 1976-79, nat. dir. Christian edn. in small membership chs., 1979-83; minister Christian edn. Community United Meth. Ch., Huntington Beach, Calif., 1987-90; assoc. minister Laguna Hills (Calif.) United Meth. Ch., 1990—; cons./trainer in Christian edn. Editor: Program Ideas and Training Designs for Pacific and Asian American Church Schools, 1981; contbr. articles to profl. jours. Nat. mem. Bread for the World, Fellowship of Reconciliation, Amnesty Internat. Coolidge Colloquium fellow, Assn. for Religion and Intellectual Life, 1989. Mem. AAUW (life), Nat. Christian Educators Fellowship, Am. Acad. Religion, Assn. of Profs. and Researchers of Religious Education, Nat. Fedn. Asian Am. United Meth., Religious Edn. Assn. Avocations: reading, psychology, theology, organ playing, gardening, Christian education. Office: 24442 Moulton Pkwy Laguna Hills CA 92653 *The ethical responsibility of human beings to love, as embodied in the covenant between the Creator and the people, evokes a paradigm of a mature faith response. Such response entails the nurture of life—enhancing relatedness and responsible caring to God, oneself, others and the world.*

JOYNER, ALBERT LEWIS, JR., minister; b. Lexington, N.C., Sept. 3, 1946; s. Albert Lewis Joyner and Myrtle (Hardy) Miller; m. Gaynelle Garwood, Apr. 27, 1969; children: Christi Michele, Chadwick Lewis. AB, Pfeiffer Coll., 1983; MDiv, Duke U., 1987. Mgmt. Burlington Industries, Greensboro, N.C., 1967-78, Springs Mills Corp., Lancaster, S.C., 1978-80; minister United Meth. Ch., Asheboro, N.C., 1980—. Mem. Phi Alpha Theta, Phi Delta Sigma. Democrat. Methodist. Lodge: Lions (pres. Franklinville, N.C. club 1985). Avocations: offshore fishing, golf. Home: 1663 Plantation Circle Asheboro NC 27203 Office: Brower's Chapel Rt 4 Browers Chapel Rd Asheboro NC 27203

JUAREZ, MARTIN, priest; b. Kansas City, Kans., Mar. 23, 1946; s. Martin Huerta and Hermelinda (Rocha) J. AS, Colby Community Coll., 1971; BA in sociology, U. Mo., Kansas City, 1974; MDiv, St. Thomas Sem., Denver, 1985; cert. in Hispanic ministry, Oblate Sch. of Theology, San Antonio, 1991, Mexican-Am. Cultural Ctr., 1991. Ordained priest Roman Cath. Ch., 1981. Adminstr. St. Aloysius Parish, Meriden, Kans., 1982; assoc. pastor various parishes, 1981-86; pastor Sacred Heart Parish, Paxico, Kans., 1986-89, St. John Vianney, Eskridge, Kans., 1986-89; co-pastor Our Lady of Guadalupe, Topeka, 1989-90; assoc. pastor St. Joseph/St. Benedict, Kansas City, Kans., 1991—; Cath. priest Archdiocese of Kansas City, Kans., 1981—. Bd. dirs. Pioneer Village, Topeka, 1983-88; co-dir. El Centro, Topeka, 1989. Mem. Kans. Registered Animal Hosp. Techs. Assn., North Am. Veterinary Techs. Assn., Nat. Hispanic Priests Assn., U. Mo. Alumni Assn., KC. Office: PO Box 410695 Kansas City MO 64141

JUBANY ARNAU, NARCISCO CARDINAL, archbishop of Barcelona; b. Santa Coloma de Farnes, Spain, Aug. 12, 1913. Ordained priest Roman Cath. Ch., 1939; formerly prof. law Barcelona Sem.; served on Ecclesistical Tribunal; titular bishop of Ortosia, also aux. of Barcelona, 1956; bishop of Gerona, 1964-71; archbishop of Barcelona, 1971—; elevated to Sacred Coll. of Cardinals, 1973; pres. Com. of Def. of the life of the Spanish Episcopate; episcopate archbishop dimissionary, 1990. Mem. Congregation per il Culto Divino e la Disciplina dei Sacramenti. Address: Calle Sales y Ferrer 60, Barcelona 08026, Spain

JUDAH, JAY STILLSON, historian, educator; b. Leavenworth, Wash., July 7, 1911; s. Stillson and Maude Alice (Cannon) J.; m. Lucile Elaine Baker, Dec. 2, 1935 (dec. Mar. 1987); children: Jay Stillson Jr., Elaine Judah Keller, Diane Judah Moore; m. Helen Janin Nov. 24, 1987. AB, U. Wash., 1934; Libr. cert., U. Calif.-Berkeley, 1941; Litt.D., Chapman Coll., 1955. Head libr. Pacific Sch. Religion, 1941-69, prof. history of religion, 1955-69; libr. dir. Bibliog. Ctr., Grad. Theol. Union, Berkeley, 1966-69; head libr. Common Libr. Grad. Theol. Union, Berkeley, 1969-76; prof. history of religion Grad. Theol. Union, 1969-76; adj. prof. Pacific Sch. Religion, 1974-79; field faculty Vt. Coll., Norwich U., 1984-85; nat. v.p. Alliance for Preservation of Religious Liberty, 1978-79. Author: Jehovah's Witnesses, 1964, History and Philosophy of the Metaphysical Movements in America, 1967, Hare Krishna and the Counterculture, 1974; compiler, editor: Index to Religious Periodical Literature, 1949-52, 1952. Lt. USNR, 1944-46, ETO. Guggenheim fellow, 1934; Sealantic Fund fellow, 1957-58. Fellow Internat. Inst. Arts and Letters; mem. Am. Theol. Library Assn. (v.p. 1962-63, pres. 1963-64), Western Theol. Library Assn. (pres. 1954-55), Internat. Assn. Theol. Libraries (sec.-treas. 1955-60). Republican. Mem. Christian Ch. N.Am. Clubs: El Cerrito (Calif.); Tennis (pres. 1958-65); Rossmoor Tennis (pres. 1985-86). Home: 2711 Saklan Indian Dr #2 Walnut Creek CA 94595 *My goal and motivation as a Christian have been to practice to the best of my ability my belief in a sacrificial love for God and humanity without any reservations, and to contribute whatever possible toward the furtherance of justice and truth.*

JUDAY, DAN, religious publications administrator. Dir. office publ. and promotion svcs. Roman Cath. Ch., Washington. Office: Roman Cath Ch 3211 4th St Washington DC 20017*

JUDD, JERRY GORDEN, minister; b. Greensburg, Ky., July 19, 1946; s. Dwight Edward and Zella (Reynolds) J.; m. Martha Dale O'Banion, June 13, 1964; children: Jacqueline Patrice, Jimmy Gorden. Youth dir. to evangelist/pastor various, various, Ky., 1965—; pastor Liberty Bapt. Ch., Mt. Sherman, Ky., 1982—. Recipient various awards So. Bapt. Assn. Democrat. Home: 7060 Hwy 88 Greensburg KY 42743

JUDD, RAYMOND EARL, JR., chaplain; b. Sherman, Tex., Aug. 27, 1934; s. Raymond Earl and Glenna Charlyn (Robinson) J.; m. Mary Jane Grafton, Sept. 12, 1959; 1 child, Jane Charlyn. BA, Trinity Univ., 1956; MDiv, Princeton Theol. Seminary, 1959; DD, Coll. of Ozarks, 1985. Ordained to ministry Presbyn. Ch., 1959. Minister First Presbyn. Ch., Clarksville, Tex., 1959-64, Hemphill Presbyn. Ch., Ft. Worth, 1964-67; univ. chaplain Trinity Univ., San Antonio, 1967—. Home: 139 Oakmont Ct San Antonio TX 78212 Office: Trinity University 715 Stadium Dr San Antonio TX 78212

JUDSON, BETTY DORSEY, ecumenical agency administrator. Dir. Wilkinsburg Community Ministry, Pitts. Office: Wilkinsburg Community Ministry 710 Mulberry St Pittsburgh PA 15221*

JULIAN, CHARLES WILLIAM, clergyman; b. Athens, Tex., Aug. 20, 1954; s. William H. and Helen (Gist) J.; m. Cindy Laine, Dec. 28, 1976; children: Charles Laine, Linda Gayle. BA, Baylor U., Waco, Tex., 1976; MDiv, So. Bapt. Theol. Sem., Louisville, 1980. Ordained to ministry Bapt. Ch., 1984. Pastor River Ave. Bapt. Ch., Indpls., 1980-86, Riverside Ave. Bapt. Ch., Muncie, Ind., 1986—; instr. religious studies and philosophy Ball State U., Muncie, 1990—; bd. dirs. Christian Ministries Delaware County, Muncie, 1985-90, mem. social justice commn., 1988—; chair div. higher edn. Am. Bapt. Chs. Ind., 1989—; pres. Am. Bapt. Chs. Campus Ministry, Muncie, 1988—. Bd. mem. Madison/Delaware Counties AIDS Task Force, Muncie, 1988—; bd. dirs. Planned Parenthood of East Cen. Ind., Muncie, 1990—, Ind. Office of Campus Ministry, 1991—. Mem. Am. Bapt. Ministers Coun., Delaware County Ministerial Assn. (pres. 1987-88). Office: Riverside Ave Bapt Ch 3700 W Riverside Ave Muncie IN 47304-3760

JULIAN, DENNIS WAYNE, music minister; b. Dallas, Oct. 8, 1952; s. Alvie Ray and Mary Lou (Adams) J.; m. Darlene Carroll Van Houten, Jan. 4, 1975; children: Deanna Elaine, Daniel Adams, David Wayne. MusB, West Tex. State U., 1980. Min. music, youth, edn. Blodgett St. Bapt. Ch., Carlsbad, N.Mex., 1976-77; min. music, youth Bykota Bapt. Ch., Amarillo, Tex., 1977-80, Hillcrest Bapt. Ch., Nederland, Tex., 1980-82; min. music, youth Fairview Bapt. Ch., Sherman, Tex., 1982-84, min. music and media, 1984-87, min. music, 1987—; associational music dir. Grayson Bapt. Assn., Sherman, 1985-88. Composer: Ye Must Be Born Again, 1976, O Come, O Come Emmanuel, 1978. Mem. Am. Choral Dirs. Assn. (life), So. Bapt. Ch. Music Conf. (life), Tex. Choral Dirs. Assn., Delta Chi Alpha, Lambda Chi Alpha. Republican. Avocations: computers, softball, working out. Home: 227 W McGee Sherman TX 75090 Office: Fairview Bapt Ch 222 W Taylor Sherman TX 75090

JULIAN, TIMOTHY RAY, minister, music educator; b. Kokomo, Ind., Oct. 3, 1956; s. John Franklin and Nancy Ann (Hostetler) J.; m. Melody Ann Romack, Dec. 31, 1976; children: Aaron Timothy,, Jonathan Allen. BA, Anderson (Ind.) Coll., 1980; M of Music Edn., Wichita (Kans.) State U., 1984. Cert. music tchr., Ind., Ohio. Music tchr. Eastern Howard Sch., Greentown, Ind., 1981-82; minister of music and youth East Foulke Church of God, Findlay, Ohio, 1984—. Home: 712 Charles Ave Findlay OH 45840

JULIOT, VIRGIL F., minister; b. Lake City, Minn., Sept. 22, 1925; s. William F. and Lydia J. (Hedberg) J.; m. Marilyn Lee Culver, May 14, 1955; children: Kathleen, Karen, Keith, Kevin, Mark. BA, Gustavus Adolphus Coll., 1949; BD, Augustana Luth. Sem., Rock Island, Ill., 1954. Ordained to ministry Luth. Ch. Pastor Ruston Luth. Ch., Tacoma, 1954-57, Saron Luth. Ch., Hoquaim, Wash., 1957-60, Gethsemane Luth. Ch., Dassel, Minn., 1960-68, Bethesda Luth. Ch., Moorhead, Minn., 1968-69, Trinity Luth. Ch., Canton, Ill., 1969—. 1st lt. USAF, 1943-46, PTO. Home: 235 Lincoln Rd Canton IL 61520 Office: Trinity Luth Ch 301 E Chestnut St Canton IL 61520

JUMP, CHESTER JACKSON, JR., clergyman, church official; b. Covington, Ky., Mar. 31, 1918; s. Chester Jackson and Inez (Moore) J.; m. Margaret Elizabeth Savidge, Sept. 5, 1942; children—Karen Jane, Richard Alan, Catherine Louise, Robert Jon. A.B., Albright Coll., 1938; M.A., Columbia, 1940; B.D., Union Theol. Sem. N.Y.C., 1943; postgrad., Ecole Coloniale, Brussels, Belgium, 1950-51; D.D., Eastern Bapt. Theol. Sem., 1965. Ordained to ministry Bapt. Ch., 1943. Pastor N.E. Larger Parish, Lyndon Center, Vt., 1943-44; missionary Belgian Congo, Republic of Congo, 1945-62; regional rep. Am. Bapt. Fgn. Mission Socs., Valley Forge, Pa., 1961-64; exec. dir. Am. Bapt. Fgn. Mission Socs., 1965-83; assoc. gen. sec. Am. Bapt. Chs., 1965-83, dir. world relief, 1983-88, interim gen. sec., 1987-88; mem. gen. bd. Nat. Council Chs., 1965-75, mem. program bd., exec. com. div. overseas ministries, 1965-83, mem. gov. bd., 1965-75, 87-88; mem. exec. com. Bapt. World Alliance, 1965-85, 87-88, v.p., 1980-85; bd. dirs., exec. com. Am. Bapt. Chs., Pa., Del., 1989—; chmn. budget com. Commn. on New Ch. Planting and Adminstrv. Svcs., 1989—; Trustee Eastern Bapt. Theol. Sem.; mem. Ch. World Service Commn., 1983-88, fin. com., 1983-88; mem. Bapt. World Aid, 1970-85. Author: (with wife) Congo Diary, 1950, Coming, Ready or Not, 1959. Mem. Pi Gamma Mu. Home and Office: K 2 Delta Pl Lewisburg PA 17837

JUMP, DONALD WAYNE, lay church worker, firefighter; b. Corbin, Ky., Apr. 25, 1954; s. Wayne Wesley and Joann (Roaden) J.; m. Nancy Irene Lange, June 21, 1975; children: Amy Irene, Amanda Ann. Grad. high sch., Wapakoneta, Ohio. Treas. Hillsdale Bapt. Ch., St. Marys, Ohio, 1979—, discipleship tng. dir., 1987-90; treas. West Cen. Bapt. Assn., Jackson Center, Ohio, 1985—, stewardship dir., 1985—; capt. Wapakoneta (Ohio) Fire Dept., 1989—; enrolled agt. IRS, 1990—. CPR coord. Am. Heart Assn., Auglaize County, Ohio, 1981-82. Mem. Nat. Assn. Tax Practitioners, Ohio Soc. Enrolled Agts., N.W. Ohio Fire Prevention Assn., Auglaize County Fire Investigators Assn., Apollo Career Ctr. Pub. Safety Adv. Commn. Republican. Home: 604 Erie St Wapakoneta OH 45895

JUMPER, ANDREW ALBERT, minister; b. Marks, Miss., Sept. 11, 1927; s. William David and Irma Belle (Nason) J.; m. Sydney Kay Dicken, Nov. 20, 1974 (dec. Dec. 1973); children: Mark Andew, Peter Sharpe, Kathryn Elizabeth, Carol Ann, Amy Elizabeth. BA, U. Miss., 1951; MDiv, Austin (Tex.) Sem., 1954, ThM, 1960; DD (hon.), King Coll., Bristol, Tenn., 1971, Belhaven Coll., 1971, Westminster coll., 1980. Ordained to ministry Evang. Presbyn. Ch. Pastor Christ Presbyn. Ch., Houston, 1954-58, West Shore Presbyn. Ch., Dallas, 1958-62, 1st Presbyn. Ch., Lubbock, Tex., 1962-70, Cen. Presbyn. Ch., St. Louis, 1970—; moderator Evang. Presbyn. Ch., 1989. Author manuals. Petty officer 1st class USCG, 1945-48. Father of the Ch. award Evang. Presbyn. Ch., 1991. Home: 14585 Harleston Village Dr Chesterfield MO 63017 Office: Cen Presbyn Ch 770 Davis Dr Saint Louis MO 63105

JUNG, JAY JOSEPH, priest, religious organization administrator; b. Evanston, Ill., May 31, 1950; s. John Peter and Dorothy Rose (May) J. BA, St. Mary's Sem., 1973; MA, S.E. Mo. State U., 1976; MDiv, DeAndreis Inst. Theology, 1977. Ordained priest Roman Cath. Ch., 1977. Dir. vocations Vincentian Fathers and Brothers, Chgo., 1977-83; dir. vocations Midwest Province Vincentian Fathers and Brothers, 1991—; dir. campus ministry DePaul U., Chgo., 1983-88, dir. human resources, 1988—, religious superior of Vincentian Residence, 1990—; mem. provincial coun. midwest province Congregation of the Mission, Chgo., 1987—. Mem. Cath. Campus Ministry Assn., Assn. Vincentians (chmn. 1984). Home: 2233 N Kenmore Chicago IL 60614 Office: DePaul U 25 E Jackson St Chicago IL 60604 *Because life is ultimately a gift, freely given, use the gift by living fully. As much as this might sound like pop psychology, it is firmly based in the Judeo-Christian scriptures and allows me to enjoy the best of times and people and learn from my brokeness and mistakes.*

JUNG, LOYLE SHANNON, religion educator; b. Baton Rouge, July 23, 1943; s. Jean Baptiste and Frances Ellen (Shannon) J.; m. Patricia Jeanne Beattie, Sept. 21, 1949; children: Michael, Robert, Nathan. BA, Washington and Lee U., Lexington, Va., 1965; BD, Union Sem., Richmond, Va., 1968; STM, Yale U., 1969; PhD, Vanderbilt U., Nashville, 1973. Ordained to ministry Presbyn. Ch. (U.S.A.), 1973. Prof. sociology and religion Virginia Intermont Coll., Bristol, Tenn., 1972-79; prof. Christian ethics Concordia Coll., Moorhead, Minn., 1979-87; prof. Christian ethics, dir. rural ministry program U. Dubuque (Iowa) Theol. Sem., 1987—; dir. rural ministry program Wartburg Theol. Sem., Dubuque, Iowa, 1987—; mem. rural ministry support team Presbyn. Ch. (U.S.A.), Dubuque, 1989—. Author: Identity and Community, 1980; contbr. articles to religious jours. Mem. Am. Acad. Religion (pres. upper Midwest region 1985-86), Soc. Christian Ethics. Office: U Dubuque Rural Ministry Program 2000 University Ave Dubuque IA 52001

JUNG, PATRICIA BEATTIE, theology educator; b. Great Falls, Mont., Sept. 21, 1949; d. Arthur S. and June (Swab) Beattie; m. L. Shannon Jung, June 1, 1974; children: Michael, Robert, Nathan. BA, U. Santa Clara, 1971; MA, Vanderbilt U., 1974, PhD, 1979. Assoc. prof. religion Concordia Coll., Moorhead, Minn., 1979-87; assoc. prof. social ethics Wartburg Theol. Sem., Dubuque, Iowa, 1987—; adv. bd. Loras Bioethics Resource Ctr., Dubuque, 1987—. Co-editor: Abortion & Catholism: The American Debate, 1988; editorial com. Chs. Ctr. for Theology and Pub. Policy, 1989—; editorial bd. Jour. Religious Ethics, The Annual; contbr. articles to profl. jours. Bd. dirs. LWV, Dubuque, 1989-92. Exxon fellow in ethics and medicine, Houston, 1985. Mem. Cath. Theol. Soc. Am., Soc. Christian Ethics, Am. Acad. Religion. Office: Wartburg Theol Sem 333 Wartburg Pl Dubuque IA 52003

JÜNGEL, EBERHARD, theology educator; b. Magdeburg, Germany, Dec. 5, 1934; s. Kurt and Margarete (Rothemann) J. ThD, Kirchliche Hochschule, Berlin, 1961; DD, U. Aberdeen, Scotland, 1985. Lectr. for N.T. Sprachenkonvikt, Berlin, 1961-63, lectr. in systematic theology, 1963-66; minister Evangelische Kirche of Berlin-Brandenburg, East Germany, 1963; prof. in systematic theology and history of dogma U. Zürich, Switzerland, 1966-69; prof. in systematic theology and philosophy of religion U. Tübingen, Fed. Republic of Germany, 1969—, dean Evangelisch-Theologische Fakultät, 1970-72; dir. Inst. for Hermeneutics, Tübingen, 1969—; ephorus Evangelisches Stift, Tübingen, 1987—; guest prof. systematic theology U. Halle-Wittenberg, 1990—. Author: Geistesgegenwart, 2d edit., 1978, Barth-Studien, 1982, Schmecken und Sehen, 1983, Glauben und Verstehen, 1985, Entsprechungen, 2d edit., 1986, Gott als Geheimnis der Welt, 5th edit., 1986, Unterwegs zur Sache, 2d edit., 1988, Tod, 8th edit., 1985, Gottes Sein ist im Werden, 4th edit., 1986, Paulus und Jesus, 6th edit., 1986, Unterbrechungen, 1989, Wertlose Wahrheit, 1990; editor: Zeitschrift für Theologie und Kirche Jour.; co-editor: Evangelische Kommentare Jour.; contbr. numerous articles to profl. jours. Chmn. Theologischer Ausschuss of the Evangelische Kirche der Union, 1981—; substitute judge Constnl. Ct. Baden-Württemberg, 1985—. Fellow Acad. Scis. Heidelberg, Acad. Scis. Oslo. Lutheran. Office: Inst für Hermeneutik, Hölderlinstr 16, 7400 Tübingen Federal Republic of Germany

JUNIEL, EUNICE KIMBROUGH, clergywoman; b. Magnolia, Ala., Sept. 12, 1931; d. Joseph and Emma Lee (Jenkins) Kimbrough; B.A. in Sociology, Calif. State U., 1969, M.A., 1974; D. Metaphysical Sci., U. Metaphysics, Los Angeles, 1981; children—Josephus, Cheryl, Michael, Kathleen. Psychiat. technician State of Calif., Walnut, 1962-64; tchr. Los Angeles public schs., 1971-81; founder, dir. weekly program Patterns for Living, Sta. KTYM, Los Angeles, 1982—. Founder, pres. Universal Truth Found., 1982—. Mem. Los Angeles Urban League, Phi Delta Kappa, Psi Gamma Mu. Democrat. Office: PO Box 11088 Marina Del Rey CA 90295

JUNKINS, BILLY EUGENE, minister; b. Noble, Ill., Feb. 14, 1925; s. Bert Leland and Bessie (Cleo) J.; m. Frances Edna Lewis (div. Jan. 1975); m. Patricia Ruth Mullen, Sept. 18, 1941; children: Larry, Nancy, Jay Sheffield, Jodi, Mark Sheffield. AB, Lincoln (Ill.) Bible Inst., 1949; BD, Lincoln Christian Sem., 1955; LittD (hon.), Midwest Christian Coll., 1968; MDiv, Lincoln Christian Sem., 1969; PhD, Calif. Grad. Sch. Theol., Glendale, 1971. Pastor Christian chs., Clinton, Ill., 1951-62, 1st Christian Ch., Long Beach, Calif., 1963-65; pres. Midwest Christian Coll., Oklahoma City, 1965-68; pastoral counselor Christian chs., San Diego, 1968-75, Cen. Christian Ch., St. Petersburg, Fla.; founder, mgr. L.G.C.A. Youth Camp, Clinton, 1952-62. Contbr. numerous articles to mags. Trustee Lincoln Christian Coll., 1957-62, Pacific Christian Coll., 1963-65. 1st lt. U.S. Army, 1943-45. Republican. Home: 5925 5th St S Saint Petersburg FL 33705

JUPIN, J. MICHAEL, ecumenical agency administrator. Exec. dir. South Louisville Community Ministries. Office: South Louisville Community Ministries 801 Camden Ave Louisville KY 40215*

JURGENSEN, BARBARA, religious educator; b. Excelsior, Minn., Nov. 22, 1928; d. W.H. and Ethel E. (Nesbitt) Bitting; m. L. Richard Jurgensen, Aug. 28, 1949; children: Janet, Marie, Peter. BA, St. Olaf Coll., Northfield, Minn., 1950; MA, U. Chgo., 1975, DMin, 1982. Ordained minister 1978. Freelance writer, 1955—, writer, editor, 1969-73; pastor First Luth. Ch., Chgo., 1978-84; prof. Trinity Luth. Sem., Columbus, Ohio, 1984—. Author 15 books, numerous articles and stories. Office: Trinity Luth Sem 2199 E Main St Columbus OH 43209

JURISTA, DIANA MAE, church official; b. Sheboygan Falls, Wis., May 9, 1940; d. Roman Valentine and Arline Eileen (Young) Brown; m. Edward John Jurista, June 29, 1985. BA in Sociology and Religious Studies, Alverno Coll., Milw., 1972; MA in Religious Studies, Loyola U., Chgo., 1981. Dir. religious edn. Our Lady of Humility Parish, Zion, Ill., 1979—. Mem. Nat. Parish Coords. and Dirs., Ill. Parish Coords. and Dirs., Lake County Dirs. Religious Edn., Chgo. Assn. for Religious Educators (sec. 1981-83), Alverno Coll. Alumni Assn. (historian 1973-75). Home: 500 Forest View Rd Lindenhurst IL 60046 Office: Our Lady of Humility Parish 10601 Wadsworth Rd Zion IL 60099 *Pursuing truth and dignity for all is an up hill battle. Belief in a higher power is often all we have to hang onto.*

JUSTER, DANIEL CALVIN, minister, writer; b. River Edge, N.J., Oct. 26, 1947; s. Myron and Edith (Christensen) J.; m. Patricia Ann Ludington; children: Benjamin, Becca, Simcha, Samuel. BA in Philosophy, Wheaton (Ill.) Coll., 1969; student, Trinity Evang. Div. Sch., Deerfield, Ill., 1969071; M Div., McCormick Coll., 1973. Ordained to ministry Presbyn. Ch., 1974. Pastor Adat Hatikvah Synagogue, Chgo., 1972-77, Beth Messiah Congregation, Rockville, Md., 1978-86; founder, pres. Union of Messianic Jewish Congregations, Gaithersburg, Md., 1979-86; gen. sec. Union of Messianic Jewish Congregations, Gaithersburg, 1985-88, 88—; sr. pastor Beth Messiah Congregation, Gaithersburg, 1988—; vis. prof. philosophy Trinity Coll., 1971-74; pres. Messiah Bibl. Inst. and Grad. Sch. Theology, Gaithersburg, 1982—; exec. bd. Messianic Jewish Alliance, Phila., 1977-81. Author: Jewishness and Jesus, 1978, Growing to Maturity, 1983, Dynamics of Deception, 1985, Jewish Roots, 1986, Israel, The Church and The Last Days, 1990, Revelation: The Passover Key, 1990, Due Process: A Plea for Biblical Justice in the Church, 1991. Exec. bd. Montgomery Acad. High Sch., Gaithersburg, 1983-87; bd. dirs. Citizens for Decent Govt., Rockville, 1985. Mem. Phi Sigma Tau. Republican. Home: 21 Grantchester Pl Gaithersburg MD 20877 Office: Messianic Life Ministries 13-15 E Deer Park Rd 9057B Gaither Rd Gaithersburg MD 20877

JUSTICE, EUNICE MCGHEE, missionary, evangelist; b. Fairchance, Pa., Feb. 13, 1922; d. Felix McGhee and Clara May Chavous; divorced; children: Rebecca L. Brothers, William Wood. Ordained to ministry Evang. Ch., 1969. Youth leader dir. Avalon Zion Foursquare Ch., L.A., 1969-71; missionary, prayer warrior Pentecostal Faith Ch. for All Nations, N.Y.C., 1972-77, missionary, evangelist, 1979—; prophetess, pres. Missionary Evang. Tng. Ctr., Inc., Tampa, Fla., 1977—, Dorcas House Ministries, Tampa, 1986—; producer Dorcas House childrens Workshop, Jones Intercable Pub. Access TV. Editor: Untitled, 1970; paintings exhibited Fla. and Ga., 1980—. Advocate for the poor, 1980—. Recipient Nat. Achievement award Nat. Assn. Negro Bus. and Profl. Womens Clubs, N.Y.C., 1956, Excellence in Gov. Publs. award Nat. Advt. Couns. Colo., Ohio, 1962. Mem. Nat. Fedn. Local Community Producers, Glorious Cogic. Home: 101 E Amelia Ave Tampa FL 33602 Office: Dorcas House Ministries PO Box 664 Tampa FL 33602 *The greatest challenge to humanity today is to get hold of the abundant life that Jesus came and showed us to be in the Kingdom of God that is within.*

JUSTICE, ORA LYNN, corporate executive, former church official; b. Milan, Ind., Aug. 6, 1942; s. Leo Edgar and Sarah Edna (Stacy) J.; m. Bonita Hedrick, June 30, 1963; children: Chrissan, Jennifer, Vanessa, Rebecca, Aaron, David, Sarah, Florence. BA, Ind. U., Bloomington, 1966. Store mgr. Western Auto Supply Co., Ponce, Puerto Rico, 1965-67; mgr. Argentine div. Nat. Chemsearch Corp., Buenos Aires, 1967-74; owner, mgr. Equity Labs., Fairfield, Ohio, 1974-77; gen. mgr. Arco de Centro Am., S.A., Tegucigalpa, Honduras, 1977-81; dir. temporal affairs, Cen. Am. Ch. of Jesus Christ of Latter-day Saints, Salt Lake City, 1981-90; gen. mgr. Equilab, S.A., Guatemala City, 1990—; franchiser cons., Equity Labs., Mex., Cen. Am., Uruguay, 1981—. Inventor aerosol can adaptor. Scoutmaster, Guatemala area Boy Scouts Am., 1988—. Avocation: woodworking. Office: Equilab SA, 42 Calle 12-38, Zona 8, Guatemala City Guatemala

JUSTUS, THOMAS CLYDE, clergyman; b. Hendersonville, N.C., Aug. 26, 1964; s. Clyde L. and Doris M. (Orr) J.; m. Tanya D. Thomas, Aug. 18, 1984; 1 child, Victoria Lorin. BA, Appalachian State U., 1986; MDiv, So. Bapt. Theol. Sem., 1990. Ordained to ministry So. Bapt. Conv., 1985. Minister of youth Refuge Bapt. Ch., Hendersonville, N.C., 1980-82, First Bapt. Ch., Boone, N.C., 1983-87; activities dir. Christ Ch. United Meth., Louisville, Ky., 1987-89; minister to youth Broadway Bapt. Ch., Louisville, 1989-90; minister with youth Porvidence Bapt. Ch., Charlotte, N.C., 1990—; mem. Ky. Bapt. Youth Ministries Assn., Middletown, 1989-90; regional coord. N.C. Bapt. Youth Ministries Assn., Cary, 1985-87; youth dir. Three Forks Bapt. Assn., 1984-87. Canoeing instr. ARC, Charlotte, N.C., 1986—. Presdl. Preaching and Congregational Leadership scholar So. Bapt. Theol. Sem., 1987. Mem. So. Bapt. Alliance. Democrat. Office: Providence Bapt Ch 4921 Randolph Rd Charlotte NC 28211

KABERLE, WILLIAM JOSEPH, minister; b. Austin, Tex., Mar. 26, 1951; s. Joseph Ernest and May Bell (Willis) K.; m. Cynthia Dianne Jaroszewski, Aug. 25, 1984; 1 child, Hanz Joseph. BS in Religious Edn., Am. Bible Coll., 1980; ThM, Empire Bible Coll., 1990, ThD, 1991; DST, Am. Bible Inst., 1991. Ordained to ministry So. Bapt. Conv., 1973. Pastor Murray Hill Bapt. Ch., Three Rivers, Tex., 1973-74; bus ministry pastor Forrest Pk. Bapt. Ch., Corpus Christi, Tex., 1974; ch. starter Community Bapt. Ch., Millburg, Mich., 1980-81; pastor Second Bapt. Ch., New Braunfels, Tex., 1982-85; assoc. pastor outreach Eastside Bapt. Ch., New Braunfels, 1985-89; pastor, tchr. 1st Bapt. Ch., Knott, Tex., 1989-91; pastor Mineral (Tex.) Bapt. Ch.; fellow Wessex Theol. Coll., Dorset, Eng., 1990. Contbr. articles to local newspapers. Recipient Missionary Svc. award San Maros Bapt. Assn., 1987. Mem. Big Spring Bapt. Assn. (del., exec. bd. 1989—, royal ambassador dir. 1989-90), Blanco Bapt. Assn. (prayer thrust com., chmn. evangelism com.), Acad. Parish Clergy, United Assn. Christian Counselors, Am. Assn. Family Counselors (cert. masterlife leader, pastoral ministries and advanced pastoral ministries diploma Aunday Sch. Bd.), Guild of Clergy Counselors. Home and Office: PO Box 47 Mineral TX 78125 *The greatest need of our world today is that all persons be who they really are and be truthful to themselves as well as others. Then in that mind set obey the golden rule—"treat others as you want to be treated."*

KADING, DELORES RUTH, school educator; b. Crookston, Minn., Jan. 20, 1944; d. Frederick William and Mable Natalie (Anderson) Ulrich; m. Marvin Lee Kading, July 24, 1966; children: Melanie Ann, Brian Ray, Angela Lynn. BA, Concordia Coll., St. Paul, 1966; postgrad., Accelerated Christian Edn., Lewisville, Tex., 1989. Tchr. Trinity Luth. Sch., Waconia, Minn., 1966-71; tchr. Our Saviour's Christian Acad., Thief River Falls, Minn., 1989—, prin., 1988—; choir dir. St. John's Luth. Ch., Red Lake Falls, Minn., 1981—, dir. music, 1982—, tchr. teen Bible class, 1982—, Sunday sch. music dir., 1983—. Contbr. articles to profl. jours. Bible study tchr. Hillcrest Nursing Home, 1990. Republican. Lutheran. Avocations: writing, reading, cooking, baking, gardening. Office: Our Saviours Christian Acad Box 269 Sorteberg Dr Thief River Falls MN 56701

KAFFER, ROGER LOUIS, bishop; b. Joliet, Ill., Aug. 14, 1927; s. Earl Louis and Helen Ruth (McManus) K. BA, St. Mary of the Lake, Mundelein, Ill., 1950, STB, 1952, MA, 1953, licentiate in sacred theology, 1954; licentiate of canon law, Pontifical Gregorian U., Rome, 1958; D of Pastoral Ministry, St. Mary of the Lake, Mundelein, Ill., 1983; MEd, DePaul U., 1965; LHD (hon.), Felician Coll., 1986; hon. doctorate, Coll. of St. Francis, 1990, Lewis U., 1990. Ordained priest Roman Cath. Ch., 1954; cert. K-14 supr., Ill. Eccles. notary Roman Cath. Diocese of Joliet, 1954-56; asst. chancellor Roman Cath. Diocese Joliet, 1958-65; aux. bishop Roman Cath. Diocese of Joliet, 1985—, vicar gen., vicar for clergy, 1985—; rector St. Charles Borromeo Sem., Lockport, Ill., 1965-70; prin. Providence High Sch., New Lenox, Ill., 1970-85; rector Cathedral of St. Raymond, Joliet, 1985; consecrated bishop, 1985; past. mem. Marriage Tribunal, Diocesan Sem. Bd., Diocesan Bd. Religious Edn. Recipient DeLa Salle medallion, Lewis U., 1984; named Cleric of Yr., KC, 1973, Citizen of Yr., New Lenox Assn. Commerce, 1976, Man of Yr. Joliet Cath. High Alumni Assn., 1978. Mem.

Nat. Conf. Cath. Bishops, Cath. Conf. Ill. (sec.). Avocations: youth work, retreat work. Address: 425 Summit St Joliet IL 60435

KAFITY, SAMIR, bishop. Bishop, pres. Episcopal Ch. in Jerusalem and Mid. East, Jerusalem. Office: St George's Close, PO Box 1248, Jerusalem Israel*

KAGAN, DAVID DENNIS, priest, communications administrator; b. SpringGrove, Ill., Nov. 9, 1949; s. Louis Leigh and Catherine Ruth (Hoffman) K. B.A. summa cum laude, Loras Coll., 1971; St.B. magna cum laude, Pontifical Gregorian U., Rome, 1975, J.C.L. magna cum laude, 1979. Ordained priest Roman Catholic Ch., 1975; assoc. pastor St. Patrick Parish, Dixon, Ill., 1975-77; instr. Newman Cath. High Sch., Sterling, Ill., also campus minister Sauk Valley Coll., 1975-77; advocate, judge and vice officialist Diocesan Tribunal, Rockford, Ill., 1976-78, 79—, diocesan dir. office communications, 1982—; instr. Boylan Central Cath. High Sch. Mem. Canon Law Sc. Am., Cath. Theol. Soc. Am. (assoc. mem.). Office: 850 N Church Suite 300-301 Rockford IL 61103

KAGEDAN, TOM ELLIOT, religious association administrator; b. Montreal, Que., Can., Apr. 15, 1960; s. Joseph and Miriam (Weiner) Kage; m. Marcia Linda Leigh, Aug. 2, 1983; children: Adina, Noam, Eitan. BA, Jewish Theol. Sem., 1981, Columbia U., 1981; MA, Brandeis U., 1985. Asst. dir. N.Y. region United Synagogue Am., N.Y.C., 1985-87, dir. spl. projects, 1987-88, program dir., 1988—. Editor, writer various publs. in field. Mem. Phi Beta Kappa.

KAHAN, NORMAN, rabbi; b. Mozyr, USSR, Jan. 2, 1922; came to Can., 1923; s. Shaia and Fannie (Grand) Kahanowitch; m. Shirley Segal: children: Sylvia, Judith Kahan Rowland, Eric. Student, Hebrew Theol. Coll., 1936-38, Coll. Jewish Studies, 1938, Western Res. U., 1943, Telshe Yeshiva, 1943, Hebrew U., 1951; BA in Hebrew Lit., Hebrew Union Coll., 1950, DD, 1977; MA in Hebrew Lit., Jewish Inst. Religion, 1952. Ordained rabbi, 1952. Rabbi Temple Beth Israel, Lima, Ohio, 1952-55; Jewish chaplain U.S. Mil. Acad., West Point, N.Y., 1956-61; rabbi Temple Beth Jacob, Newburgh, N.Y., 1955-68; sr. rabbi Temple Sinai, Roslyn Heights, N.Y., 1968-86, rabbi emeritus, 1986—; past pres. N.Y. Bd. Rabbis; bd. overseers Hebrew Union Coll.-Jewish Inst. Religion, United Israel Appeal; mem. nat. rabbinic cabinet Israel Bonds; trustee Fedn. Jewish Philanthropies N.Y.; del. Jewish Agy. Assembly; mem. various coms. Cen. Conf. Am. Rabbis; rep. Synagogue Coun. Am.; past pres. Newburgh Ministerial Assn.; nat. dir. small congregations dept. UAHC, N.Y.C. Past v.p. Orange County (N.Y.) Mental Health Assn., past mem. city of Newburgh Human Rels. Commn.; bd. overseers Hebrew Union Coll.-Jewish Inst. Religion. Served as acting chaplain and ednl. cons. USAAF, 1946. Recipient Hon. Palatine award Newburgh City Coun., 1967, Tzedakah award Commn. on Synagogue Rels. Fed. Jewish Philanthropies, awards and honors United Jewish appeal, State of Israel Bonds Orgns., awards from Jewish, Christian, cultural and civic orgns.; Hebrew U. fellow, 1950. Mem. Hebrew Union Coll.-Jewish Inst. Religion Rabbinic Alumni Assn. (past pres.), Rotary (past pres. Newburgh chpt., dist. gov. 1966-67). Office: Temple Sinai 425 Roslyn Rd Roslyn Heights NY 11577

KAISER, BYDUS FRANCIS, minister; b. Vincennes, Ind., Jan. 10, 1931; s. Gay Field and Hattie Ann (Boley) K.; m. Beverly Fay Bramblett, Aug. 10, 1952; children: Gail, Nancy, David. BS, U. Ill., 1952; STB, Boston U., 1957, ThD, 1962. Ordained to ministry United Meth. Ch. as deacon, 1957, as elder, 1959. Pastor Helen L. Lawrence Meml. Meth. Ch., East Pepperell, Mass., 1957-68, Community United Meth. Ch., Wayland, Mass., 1968-72, 1st United Meth. ch., Westborough, Mass., 1972-82; supt. Conn.-Western Mass. Dist., So. New Eng. United Meth. Conf., 1982-88; pastor Rockville (Conn.) United Meth. Ch., 1988—; chairperson Bd. of Ordained Ministry, So. New Eng. Conf., 1974-80; res. del. Gen. Conf., United Meth. Ch., 1984-88, del., 1988—. 1st lt. U.S. Army, 1952-54, Fed. Republic Germany. Democrat. Home: 22 Elizabeth St Rockville CT 06066 Office: Rockville United Meth Ch 142 Grove St Rockville CT 06066

KAISER, RICHARD ALLEN, minister; b. Marshall, Minn., Oct. 3, 1954; s. Joseph and Mona (Caron) K.; m. Beth Newton, Aug. 13, 1977; children: Joshua, Jonathan. BA, Open Bible Coll., Des Moines, 1980. Ordained to ministry Assemblies of God, 1983. Assoc. pastor Glad tidings Assembly of God, Des Moines, 1981-84; sr. pastor Afton (Iowa) Assembly of God, 1984—; sect. 4 youth rep. Iowa Dist. Assemblies of God, Des Moines, 1987—. Councilman Afton City Coun., 1985—. Office: Afton Assembly of God 105 S Browning PO Box 335 Afton IA 50830

KAISER, WALTER CHRISTIAN, JR., academic administrator; b. Folcroft, Pa., Apr. 11, 1933; s. Walter Christian and Estelle Evelyn (Jaworsky) K.; m. Margaret Ruth Burk, Aug. 24, 1957; children: Walter Christian III, Brian Addison, Kathleen Elise, Jonathan Kevin. BA, Wheaton Coll., 1955, BD, 1958; MA, Brandeis U., 1962, PhD, 1973. Instr. bible Wheaton (Ill.) Coll., 1958-61, asst. prof., 1961-65; assoc. prof. Old Testament Trinity Evang. Div. Sch., Deerfield, Ill., 1966-73, prof. Old Testament, 1973-80, academic dean, v.p. edn., 1980-89, sr. v.p. edn., 1989—. Author: Toward Old Testament Ethics, 1983, Malachi: God's Unchanging Love, 1984, The Uses of the Old Testament in the New, 1985, Quest For Renewal: Personal Revival in the Old Testament, 1986, Quality Living, 1986, Toward Rediscovering the Old Testament, 1987, Have You Seen the Power of God Lately?, 1987, Hard Sayings of the Old Testament, 1988, Back Toward the Future: Hints for Interpreting Biblical Prophecy, 1989, Exodus: A Commentary, 1990, other books. Bd. dirs., trustee Wheaton Coll., 1983—. Faculty fellow Wheaton Coll., 1957-58; Danforth Tchr. Study grantee, 1961-62, 62-63. Mem. Evang. Theol. Soc. (pres. 1977), Near East Archaeol. Soc. (bd. dirs. 1975—), Soc. Bibl. Lit., Inst. Bibl. Rsch., Commn. Accreditation of Assn. Theol. Schs. Home: 1150 Linden Deerfield IL 60015 Office: Trinity Evang Div Sch 2065 Half Day Rd Deerfield IL 60015 *The strength and joy of life is to be found in the service and in the comfort of the presence of the living God.*

KAITSCHUK, JOHN PAUL, bishop; b. Red Bud, Ill., Dec. 31, 1937; s. Walter E. and Bine (Nielsen) K.; m. Janet Nay, June 18, 1965; children: Jennifer, James. BA, Carthage Coll., 1959, DD (hon.), 1988; MDiv, Northwestern Luth. Theol. Sem., Mpls., 1962; D of Ministry, Drew U., 1980. Ordained to ministry Luth. Ch. in Am., 1962. Missionary Luth. Ch., Madison, Ind., 1962-65; pastor Resurrection Luth. Ch., Madison, 1965-70, Salem Luth. Ch., Indpls., 1970-76, Trinity Luth. Ch., Olney, Ill., 1976-87; bishop Cen./So. Ill. synod Evang. Luth. Ch. in Am., Springfield, 1987—; mem. death penalty task force Evang. Luth. Ch. in Am., Chgo., 1990; chair judicatory execs. Ill. Conf. Chs., Springfield, 1990—. Pres. adv. com. Mayor's Commn. on Youth, Madison, 1965-70; vice-chair bd. dirs. Opportunity Ctr. Southeastern Ill., 1978-84; mem. East Richland Bd. Edn., Olney, 1985-87; exec. dir., bd. dirs. Luth. Social Svcs. Ill., Des Plaines, 1987—; bd. dirs. Luth. Sch. Theology, Chgo., 1991—. Office: Evang Luth Ch in Am Cen/So Ill Synod 1201 Veterans Pkwy Ste D Springfield IL 62704

KAIUEA, PAUL EUSEBIUS MEA, bishop. Bishop of Tarawa and Nauru, Roman Cath. Ch., Republic of Kiribati. Office: Bishop's House, POB 79, Bairiki, Tarawa Republic of Kiribati*

KAIYALETHE, JOHN KURUVILLA See JOHN, K. K.

KAKAC, CARROLL CONRAD, minister; b. Cresco, Iowa, July 24, 1929; s. Victor Otto and Blanche (Frazier) K.; m. Karen Joyce Corbin, Sept. 22, 1961; children: Kim Annette Kakac Skaggs, Kevin Carroll, Kyle Douglas. BA, Lincoln Bible Inst., 1955. Ordained to ministry Christian Ch., 1952. Pastor chs. Benton City, Mo., 1952-55, Novelty, Mo., 1955-63, Shelbina, Mo., 1963-70, Fairfield, Ill., 1970—; pres. So. Ill. Christian Conv., 1974; mem. plan com., continuation com., workshops, prayer chmn. Nat. Missionary Conv., 1975; mem. plan com., workshops N.Am. Christian Conv., 1989—. Chmn. Shelby County chpt. ARC, 1968-69; bd. dirs. Cen. Christian Coll. Bible, Moberly, Mo., 1956-57, Shelby County Christian Camp, Lincoln (Ill.) Christian Coll., South India Ch. of Christ Mission, Christian Hosp. of South India, Fellowship of Assocs. of Med. Evangelists, 1975—, Slavic Mission, Bel Aire, Md., 1980—, Christian Ch. Found. for Handicapped, Knoxville, Tenn., 1987—; bd. dirs. Zambia Christian Mission, pres., 1985—; tchr. Sunday Sch., Ch. Camp, Vacation Bible Sch. With USNG, 1949-51. Mem. Modern Woodmen Am. (Svc. award 1991), Lions, Masons. Home: 18 Park Ln Fairfield IL 62837 Office: Center at 1st St Fairfield IL 62837 *I would like to be remembered as a preacher of the Gospel of Jesus Christ.*

KAKALEC, JOSEPH MICHAEL, priest; b. McAdoo, Pa., Feb. 23, 1930; s. Peter and Mary (Pensock) Kakalec. BS in Fgn. Svc., Georgetown U., 1953; PhL, MA in Polit. Sci., St. Louis U., 1962; MDiv, Woodstock Coll., 1968; postgrad., U. Pa., 1968-70. ordained priest, Roman Catholic ch., 1967. Founder, counselor North Cen. Community Orgn., Phila., 1970-74; exec. dir. Phila. Coun. Neighborhoods, 1974-82; tchr. West Catholic High Sch. Girls, Phila., 1974-82; exec. dir. Regional Coun. Neighborhood Orgns., Phila., 1982—; instr. politics St. Joseph's U., Phila., 1989—; cons., organizer Met. Christian Coun. Phila.; instr. polit sci. and regionalism, Temple U., Phila., 1988—. Contbr. articles on urban problems to numerous publs. Past bd. dirs. Cedar Park Neighbors, Women in Transition, Phila. Coun. Neighborhood Edn., Phila. Century Four Celebration Com., Phila. City-Wide Devel. Corp., others; mem. Cardinal's Urban Affairs Commn. on Human Rels., Phila., Urban Affairs Partnership, For the People, Inc., Chester, Pa. Mem. Soc. of Jesus. Office: Regional Coun Neighborhood 5600 City Ave Philadelphia PA 19131

KAKOS, PETER JOHN, minister; b. Somerville, Mass., Sept. 12, 1946; s. Leonides and Mary (Parker) K.; m. Linda Lacour, Dec. 20, 1969; children: Vanessa, Peter, Aaron. BA, Columbia U., 1968; MDiv, Gordon-Conwell, 1975; postgrad., Hartford Sem., 1989—. Pastor Wilson Congl., Windsor, Conn., 1975-77, 2d Congl., Douglas, Mass., 1978-81, United Ch. Christ 2d Congl., Westfield, Mass., 1982—; intermin pastor Wananalua Congl., Hana, Maui, Hawaii, 1990; chaplain Westfield State Coll., 1983—. founder, pres. Com. for Homeless, Westfield, 1987—; founder The Samaritan Inn (shelter for homeless), Westfield, 1988—. Recipient Tomorrow's Min. award United Ch. Christ, New England Region, 1988; named Citizen of Yr. City of Westfield, 1989. Mem. Westfield Clergy Assn. (pres. 1989—). Home: 8 Overlook Dr Westfield MA 01085 *God has given us the sacred, precious gift of life so that individually and collectively we may, in turn, love God, every neighbor and ourselves, and so live most the fulfilling life imaginable.*

KALAF, WALTER NADEEM, retired clergyman; b. Bklyn., Jan. 30, 1925; s. Nasib Khalil and Mabel (Shehadi) K.; m. Janie Grace Hollis, Jan. 1, 1953; children: Leila Elizabeth, John Walter, Peter Andrew. AB, Emory U., 1945, MDiv, 1948; DD (hon.), Fla. So. Coll., Lakeland, 1972. Founding pastor, sr. minister St. Luke's United Meth. Ch., St. Petersburg, Fla., 1948-63; sr. minister Southside United Meth. Ch., Jacksonville, Fla., 1963-70, Palma Ceia United Meth. Ch., Tampa, Fla., 1970-76, First United Meth. Ch., Coral Gables, Fla., 1976-81, Trinity United Meth. Ch., Tallahassee, 1981-88; ret.; pres. The Scarritt Found., 1988—; trustee Piedmont Coll.; bd. dirs. Scarritt-Bennett Ctr.; mem. governing bd. Nat. Coun. Chrs. of Christ in Am., 1976-87, mem. unit com. div. edn. and ministry, 1965-87, del. gen. conf., 1972-76, del. Southeastern jurisdictional conf., 1968, 72, 76, 80; chmn. bd. trustees Scarritt Grad. Sch., 1980-86. Bd. dirs. Tallahassee Opera Guild, Sr. Soc. Planning Council, United Way of Leon County, Wesley Found., Fla. State U., Fla. A&M U. United Meth. Campus Ministry, others in past. Mem. Sigma Chi, Omicron Delta Kappa, Rotary (chmn. community welfare com., chaplain 1984-85, 86-87). Address: 1048 N Shore Dr NE #3 Saint Petersburg FL 33701

KALBERER, AUGUSTINE ANTHONY, clergyman, educator; b. Portland, Oreg., Mar. 8, 1917; s. August and Helen (Gall) K. B.A., Mt. Angel Coll., 1939; M.A., U. Toronto, 1944, Ph.D., in Philosophy, 1946; Lic. Med. Studies, Pont. Inst. Med. Studies, Toronto, 1945. Ordained priest, Roman Catholic Ch., 1942. Prof. philosophy, Sem. of Christ the King, Mission, B.C., Can., 1946—, dir. of studies, 1955-69, pres., rector, 1969—; subprior Westminster Abbey, Mission, 1953—. Author: Lives of the Saints, 1975; contbr. articles to profl. jours. Home: Westminster Abbey, Mission, BC Canada V2V 4J2 Office: Seminary of Christ the King, Mission, BC Canada V2V 4J2

KALISZEWSKI, CHARLES STANLEY, clergyman, international evangelist; b. Houston, July 18, 1950; s. Stanley Edward, Jr. and Charlene (Jackson) K.; m. Mary Suzanne Pierce, Jan. 8, 1972; children: Elizabeth Mary, Christopher Nathan, Catherine Renee. Student South Tex. Jr. Coll., 1969, Phillips U., 1970-71. Ordained to ministry Trinity Christian Ch., 1980, Jesus Hour Ministries, 1982, Full Gospel Evangelistic Assn., 1982. Internat. prophetic min., Houston, 1970—; pres., founder Jesus Hour radio programs, Nacogdoches, Tex., 1975-76, Jesus Hour Ministries, Houston, 1982—, Jesus Hour Ministerial Conv., 1982-91, World Ministry Fellowship, 1990, 91; ch. cons. Jesus Hour Ministries, Tex., 1970—, Costa Rica, 1983-84, 86, 91, Mex., 1981, Guatemala, 1984, Spain, 1984-85, 87-90, Ghana, 1985, Portugal, 1989-90; founder Jesus Hour Ministerial Alliance, 1990. Pub. The Prophetic Chronicles mag.; contbr. religious articles to jours. Avocations: writing, travel, flying. Office: Jesus Hour Ministries 8524 Hwy 6 N Ste 107 Houston TX 77095 *Our function is to equip this generation to face the unveiling of coming prophetic events.*

KALKWARF, LEONARD V., minister; b. Parkersburg, Iowa, Mar. 17, 1928; s. John Jr. and Helen (Haats) K.; m. Beverly Jane Hardy, May 22, 1954; children—Deborah Joy, Cynthia Sue, Scott Craig. B.A., Central Coll., Pella, Iowa, 1950; B.D., New Brunswick Sem., 1953; M.A., NYU, 1957; S.T.M., Luth. Sem., Phila., 1973; D.Min., Princeton Sem., 1980; D.D. (hon.), Central Coll., 1983. Ordained to ministry Ref. Ch. in Am., 1953. Assoc. pastor Bellevue Ref. Ch., Schenectady, N.Y., 1953-55; assoc. pastor Levittown (N.Y.) Community Ch., 1955-57; pastor Ref. Ch., Willow Grove, Pa., 1957-64, 65-91, Nat. Evang. Ch., Kuwait, Kuwait, 1964-65; pres. Particular Synod of N.J., 1969-70, 70-71, Gen. Synod of Ref. Ch. in Am., 1983-84. Author: History, 1st Reformed Church of Philadelphia, 1960, God Loves His World, Book I, 1963, Book II, 1964; contbr. articles to religious jours. Served as chaplain CAP, 1960-62. Republican. Lodge: Rotary.

KALLAND, LLOYD AUSTIN, minister; b. Superior, Wis., Aug. 8, 1914; m. Jean Williams, July 20, 1945; children—Doris Jean Kalland McDowell. A.B., Gordon Coll., 1942; B.D., Phila. Theol. Sem., 1945; M.A., U. Pa., 1945; M.Th., Westminster Theol. Sem., 1946; Th.D., No. Bapt. Theol. Sem., 1955. Ordained to ministry Am. Bapt. Chs. in U.S.A., 1947. Pastor ch. Slatington, Pa., 1946-49, Calvary Bapt. Ch., Chgo., 1949-55; lectr. N.T., No. Bapt. Theol. Sem., Chgo., 1949-51; exec. v.p. Gordon-Conwell Theol. Sem., South Hamilton, Mass., 1973-81, prof. contemporary theology, 1955-70, prof. Christian ethics, 1971-86; ret., 1986, interim min. in chs., 1955—. Cons. editor The Bible Newsletter; book rev. editor Christian Life mag., 1949-61; contbr. articles to religious jours. Mem. Evang. Theol. Soc., Dietrich Bonhoeffer Soc. (Eng.). Home: 102 Chebacco Rd South Hamilton MA 01982

KALLAS, JAMES GUS, JR., minister; b. Chgo., Dec. 15, 1928; s. James G. and Lillian C. (Pulaski) K.; m. Darlean P. Kallas, June 3, 1950; children: James III, Paris, Jacqueline, Kingsley. BA, St. Olaf Coll., 1950; MDiv, Luther Sem., St. Paul, 1955; PhD, U. So. Calif., 1967; DD (hon.), U. Redlands, 1975. Ordained to ministry Luth. Ch., 1955. Dir. primary schs. Mission Protestante, Cameroun, 1955-60; prof. in religion Calif. Luth. U., Thousand Oaks, 1961-78; pres. Dana Coll., Blair, Nebr., 1978-84; sr. pastor Mt. Olive Luth. Ch., Santa Monica, Calif., 1985—. Author: The Significance of the Synoptic Miracles, 1960, The Satan Ward View, 1963, Jesus and Power of Satan, 1965, The Story of Paul, 1967, The Book of Revelation, 1969, Satan: A Portrait Through the Ages, 1973. Knighted Order of Dannebrog, Queen Margrethe of Denmark. Mem. Phi Beta Kappa. Home: 3259 Pioneer Ave Thousand Oaks CA 91360 Office: Mt Olive Luth Ch 1343 Ocean Park Blvd Santa Monica CA 90405

KALLHOFF, SISTER KATHERINE, school system administrator. Supt. schs. Diocese of St. Cloud, Minn. Office: Pastoral Ctr Bur Edn 305 N 7th Ave Saint Cloud MN 56301*

KALLMYER, JERRY DOANE, minister, activist, foundation executive; b. Balt., Nov. 19, 1955; s. Carl Bertram and Bertha Mae (Creek) K.; m. Jill Scott Shrimpton, June 24, 1989. BA in Polit. Sci., Frostburg (Md.) State U., 1985; postgrad., St. Mary's Sem., Balt., 1989—. Lic. minister So. Bapt. Conv., 1990. Chief exec. officer Nat. Workers Network, Balt., 1979-87; project asst. to physician-in-chief The Johns Hopkins Hosp., Balt., 1986-90; exec. dir. Metanoia Ministries, Riderwood, Md., 1989—; asst. pastor for ch. adminstrn. Belvedere Bapt. Ch., Towson, Md., 1991—; pres. Kallymer Enterprises, Towson, Md., 1981—. Editor: Prison Voices, 1990; (newsletter) The Cristian Connection, 1989. Pres. Citizens for Better Sci. in Edn., 1990—; pres. Families Against Drug Abuse, Inc., 1990—. With USAR, 1975-77. Home and Office: 2721 Merrick Way Abingdon MD 21009-1162 Office: Belevedere Bapt Ch 1301 Cheverly Rd Towson MD 21204 *Ministry is often a seemingly solitary struggle against the powers and principalities of darkness; one man living out his convictions in a thankless and merciless world. In that respect, ministry is truly Chrisikeness.*

KALSHOVEN, THOMAS N., ecumenical agency administrator. Exec. dir. Chs. United of the Quad Cities Area, Rock Island, Ill. Office: Chs United Quad Cities Area 630 9th St Rock Island IL 61201*

KALTENBAUGH, PETER CHARLES, JR., minister; b. Johnstown, Pa., Sept. 16, 1948; s. Peter Charles and Grace Louise (Jacobs) K.; m. Janice Ruth Brougher, Apr. 11, 1970; children: Apryle Elizabeth, Lance Peter. BS, U. Pitts., 1974; MDiv, Bethany Theol. Sem., 1982. Ordained to ministry Ch. of the Brethren, 1974. Pastor Oakdale Ch. of the Brethren, New Bethlehem, Pa., 1967-68, Karamusel (Turkey) Ch. of Christ, 1969-70, Rummel Ch. of the Brethren, Windber, Pa., 1973-77, Marley Community, Mokena, Ill., 1977-84; sr. pastor Hartville (Ohio) Ch. of the Brethren, 1984—; field staff for evangelism Ch. of the Brethren, Elgin, Ill., 1988—; pres. Ohio Ch. of the Brethren Pastors Assn., Columbus, 1989-91, Lake Area Clergy Assn., Hartville, 1991—; moderator of No. Ohio Dist. Ch. of the Brethren, Hartville, 1987-89. With U.S. Army, 1968-70. Home: 13629 Sunflower Ave NW Mogadore OH 44260 Office: Hartville Ch of Brethren 353 Crestmont Ave SW PO Box 775 Hartville OH 44632 *Christianity cannot be adequately defined with words. Our life defines the meaning with which others must live.*

KALTHOFF, JAMES W., clergyman; b. Marshall, Mo., Feb. 13, 1938; s. James William Sr. and Elsie (Osborn) K.; m. Vickie Kaye Jump, July 20, 1961; children: John Martin, Kassandra Kaye, James Paul. BTh, Concordia Sem., Springfield, Ill., 1963. Ordained to ministry Luth. Ch. Mo. Synod. Pastor Our Savior Luth. Ch. and St. Paul's Ch., Muscatine and Wapello, Iowa, 1963-66, Our Savior Luth. Ch., Sedalia, Mo., 1966-71, Faith Luth. Ch., Jefferson City, Mo., 1971-91; cir. counselor Luth. Ch. Mo. Synod, 1968-71, 81-85, pres., 1991—, Luth. Ch. Mo. Synod Coun. Presidents, 1991—, 1st v.p. Mo. dist., 1988-91, 2d v.p. Mo. dist., 1985-88, bd. dirs. Mo. dist., 1985—, chmn. Family Life com., 1973-75, chmn. Mo. dist. Pastor's Conf., 1977-83; pastoral counselor Mo. dist. Luth. Women's Missionary League, 1984-88; mem. bd. regents Concordia Sem., 1991—; speaker (radio program) Word of Faith, 1975-91. Contbr. articles to profl. jours. Recipient Effective Ministry award Concordia Sem., 1978. Mem. Nat. Right to Life, Mo. Lutherans for Life (bd. dirs.), St. Louis Clergy for Life (bd. dirs.), Meml. Hosp. (bd. govs.). Avocations: reading, writing, tennis. Office: Mo Dist Luth Ch Mo Synod 3558 S Jefferson Ave Saint Louis MO 63017

KAMALESON, SAMUEL THEODORE, religious organization administrator; b. Vellore, Madras, India, Nov. 18, 1930; came to U.S., 1974; s. Job and Lily Sundaresan; m. Adela Balraj, May 27, 1953; children: Sunderraj Mark, Nirmala Ruth, Manoharan Paul. B in Vet. Sci., U. Madras, India, 1957; MDiv, Asbury Sem., Wilmore, Ky., 1960, ThM, 1971, DD, 1971; STD, Emory U., Atlanta, 1971. Pastor Emmanuel Meth. Ch., Madras, 1961-68, 1971-74; evangelist-at-large Meth. Ch. So. Asia, India, 1963-74; v.p. at large World Vision Internat., Monrovia, Calif., 1974-79, v.p. pastor's conf., 1980-84, v.p. evangelism/leadership, 1985-90, v.p. at large, 1990—; pres. Bethel Agrl. Fellowship, Salem, South India, 1961—, Friends Missionary Prayer Band Hqtrs., Madras, India, 1961—; adj. prof. Fuller Theol. Sem., Pasadena, Calif., 1979; Staley lectr. Asbury Theol. Sem., 1983, bd. dirs.; mem. council Azuza Pacific U. Sch. Theology, 1983. Author: Christ Alive is Man Alive, 1973, Happy: Married or Single, 1975, Transforming Power of Jesus, 1980. Recipient Philip award Nat. Assn. United Meths. Fla., 1980. Mem. Theta Phi. Avocations: reading, fish aquarium, exercise. Office: World Vision Internat 919 W Huntington Dr Monrovia CA 91016

KAMIN, BENJAMIN ALON, rabbi, author; b. Kfar-Saba, Israel, Jan. 11, 1953; came to U.S., 1962; s. Jeff Israel K. and Ruth (Flek) Nizar; m. Cathy Jill Rosen, June 8, 1975; children: Sari Judith, Debra Eve. BA with honors, U. Cin., 1974; MAHL, Hebrew Union Coll., Cin., 1977. Ordained rabbi, 1978. Asst. rabbi Temple Sinai Congregation, Toronto, Ont., Can., 1978-81; rabbi Sinai Reform Temple, Bay Shore, N.Y., 1981-82; N.Am. dir. World Union for Progressive Judaism, N.Y.C., 1982-85; rabbi The Temple, Cleve., 1985-90, sr. rabbi, 1990—; program unit head Union Camp Inst., Zionsville, Ind., 1977; rabbinic dean Can. Fedn. Temple Youth, Toronto, 1979-81; admissions com. Hebrew Union Coll., Cin., 1977-78; instr. Hebrew Union Coll., N.Y.C., 1983, 84; polit. columnist News Record, Cin., 1970-73. Author: poetry series Everything is Falling Into Place, 1970; Be Glad You Can Feel Enough, 1978 (Kahn oratory prize 1978); Stones in the Soul: One Day In The Life Of An American Rabbi, 1990; contbr. editorials to newspaper and periodicals. Pres. Cin Council World Affairs, 1969-70. Named Young Citizen of Week City of Cin., 1969; recipient citation for pub. svc. Ohio Gen. Assembly, 1987. Mem. Central Conf. Am. Rabbis (com. on overseas jewry), Assn. Reform Zionists of Am. (bd. dirs.). Democrat. Office: The Temple Univ Circle at Silver Park Cleveland OH 44106

KAMMAN, HAROLD WILLIAM, minister; b. Cin., Nov. 8, 1924; s. Louis William and Bertha Elizabeth (Miller) K.; m. Thelma Dorothea Dittmer, Apr. 21,1957; children: Ruth Elizabeth Kamman Murphy, Lois Margaret Kamman Buesser. AA, Concordia Jr. Coll., Ft. Wayne, Ind., 1945; AB, Concordia Sem., St. Louis, 1948, Diploma, 1950. Ordained to ministry Luth. Ch.-Mo. Synod, 1950. Pastor Faith Luth. Ch., Abilene, Kans., 1950-57, St. Paul Luth. ch., Texhoma, Okla., 1957-64, Hope Luth. Ch., Boise City, Okla., 1957-64, Trinity Luth. Ch., El Reno, Okla., 1964-75, Good Shepherd Luth. Ch., Duncan, Okla., 1975-91; del. nat. convs. Luth. Ch.-Mo. Synod, 1962; pub. rels. staff, 1967, 69, 71, 73, 77, 79, 83, 86, 89; cir. counselor Luth. Ch.-Mo. Synod, Kans., 1955-57, Okla., 1963-74, 77-82; dist. dir. pub. rels., Okla., 1967-70, 76—; mem. Dist. Commn. on Adjudication, Okla., 1974-78, 85—. Editor Luth. Witness, Okla. edition, 1959—. Bd. dirs. Duncan community Residence, 1979-82. Mem. Mental Health Assn. Stephens County (pres. 1990). Republican. Home and Office: 10113 S Carter Ct Oklahoma City OK 73159-7029 *In all the world there is no higher calling than the ministry of the Gospel, leading people to know Chirst as their personal Savior. All other honors and tasks are secondary to serving as a Christian pastor.*

KAMRASS, LEWIS HOWARD, rabbi; b. Atlanta, Oct. 29, 1959; s. David Paul and Anna Lee (Goldman) K.; m. Renee Slotin, Aug. 14, 1983; children: Jenna, Micah, Jared. AB, U. Ga., 1980; MHL, Hebrew Union U., Cin., 1984. Ordained rabbi, 1985. Asst. rabbi Isaac M. Wise Temple, Cin., 1985-88, assoc. rabbi, 1988-89, sr. rabbi, 1989—; lectr. theology Xavier U., Cin., 1986—; adj. faculty Hebrew Union Coll., Cin., 1988—. Bd. dirs. Jobs for People, 1985-89, ARC, Cin., 1989—, Cin. Jewish Community Rels. Coun. (bd. dirs. 1986—), Hospice of Cin. (bd. dirs. 1987—). Mem. Cen. Conf. Am. Rabbis (com.), Cin. Bd. Rabbis (pres. 1989—), Cin. Jewish Fedn. (bd. dirs. 1989—), Alpha Epsilon Pi. Office: Wise Temple 8329 Ridge Rd Cincinnati OH 45236

KAMSLER, HAROLD MILTON, rabbi; b. N.Y.C., Dec. 10, 1911; s. Samuel S. and Annie (Levy) K.; m. Etta Seymans, Dec. 5, 1937; children: Joel, David. BA, NYU, 1932, MA, 1935; MHL, Jewish Inst. Religion, 1936; DD (hon.), Jewish Theol. Sem., 1975. Ordained rabbi, 1936. Rabbi Hillside Hollis Hebrew Ctr., N.Y., 1936-43, Oyster Bay (N.Y.) Jewish Ctr., 1980-85, Bnai Jacob Congregation, Phoenixville, Pa., 1985—; rabbi, exec. dir. Jewish Community Ctr., Norristown, Pa., 1943-80; chmn. Nat. Youth Commn., United Synagogue Am., N.Y., 1960-65. Contbr. articles to profl. publs. Pres. Norristown Pub. Libr.; mem. Norristown Human Rels. Commn., Montgomery County TB Soc., Norristown Community Chest. Recipient Chapel of Four Chaplains award, 1977. Mem. Rabbinical Assembly (exec. com. 1958-61), N.Y. Bd. Rabbis, Phila. Bd. Rabbis, B'nai Brith, Masons. Home: 512 Reeves Dr Phoenixville PA 19460 Office: Bnai

Jacob Congregation Starr & Manavon Sts Phoenixville PA 19460 *"Give unto God what is His, for you and what is yours are His. For all things come of Thee and of Thine own have we given Thee." (King David).*

KAMUYU, JACQUELINE LEVERNE, lay worker; b. Detroit, Feb. 16, 1947; d. Robert Jacques and Lee Delia (Douglass) Anderson; m. Michael Muturi Kamuyu, Sept. 14, 1968; children: Melissa, Magdalena, MaKena, Kimani. BS, Wayne State U., 1972. Tchr. Sunday sch. Detroit Unity, 1982-87, youth lay min., 1987—; prin. acct. City of Detroit, 1972—; owner Mail Order Religious Books. Leader Camp Fire Girls, Detroit, 1977-80, Girl Scouts, 1982-90; sec. PTA, Detroit, 1989-91. Mem. Assn. Mcpl. Profl. Women, Premier Investment Club (pres. 1988—). Office: City of Detroit 1220 City County Bldg Detroit MI 48235 *Life is an inward as well as an outward journey. The inward journey reveals truths about ourselves and the universe.*

KANE, RICHARD JAMES, principal; b. Rochester, N.Y., June 4, 1950; s. Francis Joseph and Sylvia Elizabeth (Brundage) K.; m. Lois Schildwachter, June 10, 1972; children: Richard James Jr., Sara, Erin, Seth, Leah. BS in Edn., Concordia Tchrs. Coll., 1973; MA in Ednl. Adminstrn., Sangamon State U., 1979. Cert. sch. adminstr., supr. Tchr., athletic dir., youth dir. Martin Luther Sch., Buffalo, 1973-75; dir. Christian edn. Salem Luth. Ch., Buffalo, 1975; tchr., minister youth, ednl. agys. Trinity Luth. Ch., Springfield, Ill., 1975-80; tchr., prin., athletic dir. Trinity Luth. Sch., West Seneca, N.Y., 1980-84; prin. St. Paul Luth. Ch., Hilton, N.Y., 1984—; mem. prin. cabinet ea. dist. Luth. Ch.-Mo. Synod, 1981—; adj. prof. edn. Concordia Coll., Bronxville, N.Y., 1982—; site visitation team N.Y. State Div. Sch. Registration, Albany, N.Y., 1986; bd. regents Concordia Coll., Bronxville, 1989—; author/cons. instructional material Faith Alive, 1991; tchr. del. Ea. Dist. Educators, Luth. Ch., 1983. Oratorial judge Optimist Internat., Springfield, Ill., 1974-79; dir. Gymnastics Summer Camp, Hilton, N.Y., 1989—. Named Educator of Yr., Jaycees, West Seneca, N.Y., 1982. Mem. ASCD, Coun. Ednl. Facility Planners, Luth. Edn. Assn.-Dept. Luth. Elem. Sch. Prins. Republican. Home: 63 Little Tree Ln Hilton NY 14468 Office: St Paul Luth Sch 130 East Ave Hilton NY 14468

KANG, BENJAMIN TOYEONG, clergyman; b. Republic of Korea, Mar. 30, 1931; came to U.S., 1963; naturalized, 1979; s. Tae-Un and Kumjoo (Lee) K.; m. Katherine Chungcha Chung, Apr. 29, 1955; children: Jennifer, Mira, Gregory. BA, Yonsei U., Republic of Korea, 1954; MA, Kyungbuk U., Republic of Korea, 1959; BD, Temple U., 1967; ThD, Internat. Sem., 1981. Ordained to ministry Christian Ch., 1970. Instr. Yonsei U., Republic of Korea, 1956-58; exec. dir. Kyungju YMCA, Republic of Korea, 1958-59; asst. prof. Keimyoung U., Republic of Korea, 1959-61; pastor Korean Ch. of Lower Bucks, Levittown, Pa., 1974-84; pres. Korean Sch. of Lower Bucks, 1980-82; pastor Korean Gloria Ch., Phila., 1984-89; parish assoc. 1st Presbyn. Ch. Levittown, Pa., 1990—. Trustee Presbytery of Phila., Presbyn. Ch. (USA), 1982-88, Met. Christian Coun. Phila., 1984-88, Coun. Korean Chs. in Phila., 1985-89 Home: 3128 Benjamin Rush Ct Bensalem PA 19020

KANG, CHIN HUAT, minister; b. Taiping Perak, Malaysia, Oct. 12, 1953; s. Chooi Tit and Siew Mooi (Chong) K.; m. Wai Chee Muck, May 20, 1982. BA, William Jewell Coll., 1982; MDiv, MA, Golden Gate Bapt. Theol. Sem., 1983-84; D Ministry, San Francisco Theol. Sem., 1986. Ordained to ministry Gashland Bapt. Ch., 1982. Assoc. pastor Ipoh Bapt. Ch., San Jose, Calif., 1975-76; student pastor Sik Aun Bapt. Ch., George Town, Penang, 1977; pastor Grace Bapt. Ch., Kuala Lumpur, 1978-79; assoc. pastor Southbay Chinese Bapt. Ch., San Jose, 1982-83; pastor Chinese Mission, 1st Bapt. Ch., Rancho Cordova, Calif., 1983-84; lectr. Bapt. Theol. Sem., Penang, 1986-88; adv. pastor Penang Bapt. Ch., 1986-88, Emmanuel Bapt. Ch., Petaling Jaya, 1988; chaplain Hong Kong Bapt. Coll., 1989—; sr. pastor Acad. Community Ch., Hong Kong, 1989—; speaker Malaysia Bapt. Conv. Ann. Messagers' Conf., Port Dickson, Malaysia, 1986, Malaysia Bapt. Conv. Youth Conf., Port Dickson, 1987. Contbr. articles to profl. jours. Mem. Pi Gamma Mu. Baptist. Club: Chinese Swimming. Avocations: swimming, classical music, table tennis. Office: Hong Kong Bapt Coll, 224 Waterloo Rd, Kowloon Hong Kong

KANG, WI JO, religion educator, writer; b. Jinju, Kyungsang, Korea, Mar. 10, 1930; came to U.S., 1954; s. Pan Joon Kang and Bong Sun Shin; children: John, Sueliann, Miliann, Martin. BA, Concordia Sem., St. Louis, 1957, MDiv, 1960; MA, U. Chgo., 1962, PhD, 1967. Ordained to ministry Luth. Ch., 1968. Instr. religion dept. Columbia U., N.Y.C., 1964; asst. prof. theology dept. Valparaiso (Ind.) U., 1966-68; assoc. prof. Concordia Sem., St. Louis, 1968-74, Christ Sem., St. Louis, 1974-80; Wilhelm Loehe prof. Wartburg Sem., Dubuque, Iowa, 1980—. Author: Religion and Politics in Korea 1910-1945, 1987; editor: Christian Presence in Japan, 1981, Future of Christian Mission, 1972; contbr. scholary articles to profl. jours. Bd. dirs. Iowa Humanities Bd., Iowa City, 1988—. Mem. Assn. Profs. Mission (pres. 1989-90), Internat. Assn. Mission Studies (exec. com. 1982-85), Am. Soc. Missiology, Am. Acad. Religion, Assn. for Asian Studies. Home: 870 Valentine Dr Dubuque IA 52001

KANGAS, CARLTON WARREN, minister; b. Detroit Lakes, Minn., July 31, 1952; s. Leonard S. and Hilma Maria (Yoki) K.; m. Jane Marie Belmas, June 20, 1981; children: Kara, Katria, Kristen. BA, Concordia Coll., Moorehead, Minn., 1973; MDiv, Concordia Theol. Sem., Ft. Wayne, Ind., 1980. Ordained to ministry Luth. Ch.-Mo. Synod, 1980. Pastor Holy Cross Ch. and Faith Ch., Seely Lake and Condon, Mont., 1980-82, Immanuel Luth. Ch., Mellen, Wis., 1982-85, Grace Luth. Ch. and St. Peter's Luth. Ch., Augusta, Wis., 1985—; cir. counselor north Wis. Luth. Ch., Wausau, 1988—, chair program com., 1986—. Editor: (hymnal) The Hill Country Sings, 1988. Presentor Guidance Clinic, Eau Calire, Wis., 1986-90. Republican. Home: 819 Hudson Augusta WI 54722 Office: Grace Luth Ch RR 3 Box 102 Augusta WI 54722

KANIECKI, MICHAEL JOSEPH, bishop; b. Detroit, Apr. 13, 1935; s. Stanley Joseph and Julia Marie (Konjora) K. BA, Gonzaga U., 1958, MA in Philosophy, 1960; MA in Theology, St. Mary's, Halifax, Can., 1966. Ordained priest, 1965; consecrated bishop, 1984. Missionary Alaska, 1960-83; coadjutor bishop Diocese of Fairbanks, Alaska, 1984-85, bishop, 1985—. Address: 1316 Peger Rd Fairbanks AK 99709

KANNADY, DONALD JOE, clergyman, nurse; b. Covington, Ky., Feb. 8, 1949; s. Joe Albert and Mary Katherine (Brashear) K.; m. Donna Sue Williams, Jan. 24, 1973; children—Donald Matthew, Mary Elizabeth. B.A., Cumberland Coll., 1972; M. Div., So. Baptist Sem., 1976; R.N. diploma Jewish Hosp., Cin., 1980. Ordained to ministry Baptist Ch., 1980. Pastor Pleasant Hill Bapt. Ch., Williamsburg, Ky., 1970-72, Madison Fellowship, Hamilton, Ohio, 1975-76, Oakland Bapt. Ch., Sparta, Ky., 1979-84, Stewartsville Baptist Ch., 1984—; attendant Grant County Hosp., Williamstown, Ky., 1976-79; nurse Booth Hosp., Florence, Ky., 1981—. Mem. exec. bd. Ten Mile Assn., Warsaw, Ky., 1979-84, brotherhood dir., 1980-84; pres. Glencoe PTA (Ky.), 1983-84, Gallatin County PTA, 1985-86; pres. Ministerial Assn. Cumberland Coll., 1971-72. Democrat. Home: Route 1 Box 242-B Glencoe KY 41046

KANNENGIESSER, CHARLES A., theology educator; b. Alsace, France, May 24, 1926; came to U.S., 1981; ThD, Inst. Cath., Paris, 1976; D Classics, U. Sorbonne, Paris, 1982. Prof. Inst. Cath., Paris, 1964-82; Catherine Huisking prof. theology U. Notre Dame (Ind.), 1982—. Author: Athanasius of Alexandria, 1973, Origen, 1988. Mem. N.Am. Patristic Soc. (pres. 1989-90), Cath. Theol. Soc. Home: 6166 N Sheridan Rd Chicago IL 60660 Office: U Notre Dame Hesburgh Libr 715 Notre Dame IN 46651

KANODE, ROY EDGAR, pastor; b. Roanoke, Va., Jan. 8, 1960; s. Lewis Eugene and Bessie Inez (Hudgins) K.; m. Mary Jane Crawford, June 21, 1986; 1 child, Amanda Michele. AS in Bus., Lancaster Community Coll., Clifton Forge, Va., 1991. Ordained to ministry, Bapt. Ch. Dir. spl. ministries Covington (Va.) Bapt. Ch., 1983—; dir. The Gathering Place, Covington, 1983—. Mem. Youth Min. Assn., Phi Theta Kappa. Home: 2808 S Carpenter Dr Covington VA 24426 Office: Covington Bapt Ch 280 W Riverside Covington VA 24426

KANSFIELD, NORMAN J., theological librarian, church history educator; b. East Chicago, Ind., Mar. 24, 1940; s. Orval Russel and Margaret (Norman) K.; m. Mary L. Klein, June 25, 1965; children: Ann Margaret, John Livingston. AB, Hope Coll., 1962; BD, Western Theol. Sem., 1965; STM, Union Theol. Sem., 1967; MA, U. Chgo., 1970, PhD, 1981. Ordained to ministry Ref. Ch. in Am., 1965. Pastor 2d Reformed Ch., Astoria, N.Y., 1965-68; asst. libr. Western Theol. Sem., Holland, Mich., 1970-74, libr., prof. theol. bibliography, 1974-83; assoc. prof. church history, dir. Ambrose Swasey Libr. Colgate Rochester Div. Sch.—Bexley Hall—Crozer Theol. Sem., Rochester, N.Y., 1983—. Author: (with others) Evangelism: The Church's Proclamation, 1988; also articles; mem. editorial bd.: (hymn book) Rejoice in the Lord, 1979-85. Mem., treas. Dutch Am. Hist. Commn., 1970-83; chair Holland Area Hist. Adv. Coun., Holland, 1970-83. Sealantic fellow Rockefeller Found., 1968-70, Conant Fund fellow, 1989-90. Mem. ALA, Am. Theol. Libr. Assn. (bd. dirs. 1978-81, 91—, chmn. index bd. 1983-89, joint program bd. 1988-89), N.Y. Libr. Assn., N.Y. Libr. Assn., Rochester Regional Libr. Coun. (adv. bd.). Home: 15 Summit Dr Rochester NY 14620 Office: Ambrose Swasey Libr 1100 S Goodman St Rochester NY 14620

KANTER, SHAMAI, rabbi; b. Boston, Mar. 27, 1930; s. David Coleman and Celia (Wexler) K.; m. Jeannette Elizabeth Fink, Jan. 27, 1957; children: Raphael, Elana, Ethan. AB, Boston U., 1951; MHL, Rabbi, Jewish Theol. Sem., N.Y.C., 1955, DD (hon.), 1980; PhD, Brown U., 1974. Ordained rabbi, 1955. Rabbi Congregation Beth Am, Toronto, Ont., Can., 1958-62, Temple Israel, Sharon, Mass., 1962-76, Congregation Beth El, Rochester, N.Y., 1976—; vis. prof. Brown U., Brandeis U., U. Rochester, Hobart and William Smith Colls., St. John Fisher Coll., SUNY, Brockport, 1970—. Author: Rabban Gamaliel II The Legal Traditions, 1980; editor Conservative Judaism jour., 1989—. 1st lt. Chaplain Corps, USAF, 1955-57. Coolidge Rsch. Colloquium fellow, 1989. Mem. Rabbinical Assembly, Am. Acad. Religion. Office: Congregation Beth El 139 W Winton Rd Rochester NY 14610

KANTNER, HELEN JOHNSON, religion educator; b. Chgo., Oct. 22, 1936; d. Wilbert E. and Edna M. (Benson) Johnson; m. Robert O. Kantner, Aug. 22, 1959; children: Robert O. Jr., Sheryl Jackson. BA, Wheaton Coll., 1958; MS in Education, Youngstown State U., 1987. Asst. to prin. 1st Bapt. Day Sch., West Palm Beach, Fla., 1970-72; elem. tchr. Am. Heritage Schs., Ft. Lauderdale, Fla., 1973-76; social studies tchr. Champion High Sch., Warren, Ohio, 1977-88; edn. dir. Ocean Dr. Presbyn. Ch., North Myrtle Beach, S.C., 1988—. Bd. dirs. Horry County (S.C.) Arts Coun. Youngstown State U. scholar. Mem. NEA, Ohio Edn. Assn., Champion Classroom Tchrs. Home: 3610 Golf Ave Little River SC 29566 Office: 410 6th Ave S North Myrtle Beach SC 29582

KANTNER, ROBERT OBURN, minister; b. Altoona, Pa., Apr. 15, 1934; s. Robert Clifford and Ruth (Irwin) K.; m. Helen Johnson, Aug. 22, 1959; children: Sheryl Jackson, Robert Oburn Jr. AB, Wheaton (Ill.) U., 1956, MA, 1960; MDiv, Gordon-Conwell Sem., South Hamilton, Mass., 1959; D Ministry, Fuller Theol. Sem., Pasadena, Calif., 1980. Ordained to ministry Presbyn. Ch. (U.S.A.), 1959. Min. Countryside Chapel, Glen Ellyn, Ill., 1960-70, 1st Presbyn. Ch., North Palm Peach, Fla., 1972-73, Champion Presbyn. Ch., Warren, Ohio, 1976-88; assoc. min. Meml. Presbyn. Ch., West Palm Beach, Fla., 1970-72; min. Ocean Drive Presbyn. Ch., North Myrtle Beach, S.C., 1988—. Bd. dirs. Trumbull County Children's Svcs., Warren, 1976-88; chmn. sch. levy Champion Schs., Warren, 1982. Recipient 5 medals of honor for sermons Freedoms Found., 1967-85. Mem. North Grand Strand Ministerial Assn. (v.p.), Rotary. Republican. Home: 3610 Golf Ave Little River SC 29566 Office: Ocean Drive Presbyn Ch 410 6th Ave S North Myrtle Beach SC 29582

KANTZER, KENNETH SEALER, clergyman; b. Detroit, Mar. 29, 1917; s. Edwin Frederick and Clara (Sealer) K.; m. Ruth Forbes, Sept. 21, 1939; children: Mary Ruth Wilkinson, Richard Forbes. AB, Ashland Coll., 1938; MA, Ohio State U., 1939; BD, Faith Theol. Sem., 1942, MST, 1943; PhD, Harvard U., 1950; postdoctoral, U. Goettingen, Fed. Republic Germany, 1954-55, Basel U., Switzerland, 1955; DD (hon.), Gordon Coll., 1979; HHD (hon.), John Brown U., 1981; DD (hon.), Ashland Theol. Sem., 1981; DLitt (hon.), Wheaton Coll., 1987. Ordained to ministry Evang. Free Ch., 1948. Instr. Bible, history Kings Coll., New Castle, Del., 1941-43; instr. Hebrew Gordon Coll./Sem., Boston, 1944-46; instr. Bible, prof. bibl. and systematic theology, chmn. div. Bible, philosophy and religious edn. Wheaton (Ill.) Coll., 1946-63; dean, v.p. grad. studies, prof. bibl. and systematic theology Trinity Evang. Div. Sch., Deerfield, Ill., 1963-78, prof. bibl. and systematic theology, 1984—; dir. PhD program Trinity Evang. Div. Sch., Deerfield, 1987-91; editor in chief Christianity Today, Carol Stream, Ill., 1978-82, sr. editor, dean research inst., 1984—; pres. Trinity Coll., Deerfield, 1982-83, chancellor, 1983-91; bd. dirs. Columbia (S.C.) Bible Coll., John Brown U., Siloam Springs, Ark., The Evang. Alliance Mission, Wheaton; bd. dirs. Inst. Advancement of Christian Scholarship, 1978—, sec. 1979-83, pres. 1986-88. Editor: Evangelical Roots, 1978, Perspectives in Evangelical Theology, 1979, Applying the Scriptures, 1987; contbr. numerous articles to profl. jours., chpts. to books. Bd. dirs. Heritage Christian Sch., Northbrook, Ill., 1984—, Pioneer Ministries, Carol Stream, 1980—. Named Tchr. of Yr., Wheaton Coll., 1962; Hopkins scholar Harvard U., 1944-46. Mem. Evang. Theol. Soc. (pres.), Evang. Philos. Soc. Republican. Home: 1752 Spruce Highland Park IL 60035 Office: Trinity Evang Divinity Sch 2065 W Half Day Rd Deerfield IL 60015

KAPACINSKAS, DIANE, lay worker; b. Kewanee, Ill., Mar. 30, 1955; d. Albert Joseph and Aldona Isabela (Sutkaitis) K. MusB, Ill. State U., 1976; cert. in Youth Ministry, Ctr. for Youth Ministry Devel., Nagatuck, Conn. Cert. youth ministry, 1987. Dir. youth ministries St. Mary's Ch., Kewanee, 1983-87; staff mem. Woodlands Acad. of Sacred Heart, Lake Forest, Ill., 1987-88; dir. youth ministries St. Peter's Ch., Geneva, Ill., 1988—; coord. youth rally Diocese of Rockford, 1990; coord. region 7 Interim Summer Inst., 1987. Mem. Geneva In Touch, Regional Prevention Group, 1988—. Mem. Nat. Fedn. for Cath. Youth Ministry. Office: St Peters Ch 1891 Kaneville Geneva IL 60134-1801

KAPALIN, JERMAN (THE MOST REVERENT BISHOP OF SERPUKHOV CLEMENT), bishop. Consecrated bishop, Russian Orthodox Ch. Moscow Patriarchate, 1982, as archbishop, 1989. Bishop of Serpukhov; adminstr. patriarchal parishes Russian Orthodox Ch. U.S.A.; vicar bishop of His Holiness Patriarch of Moscow and all Russia. Office: St Nicholas Cathedral 15 E 97th St New York NY 10029

KAPLAN, ALLEN STANFORD, rabbi; b. Chgo., Mar. 26, 1939; s. Nathan and Belle Sarah (Levin) K.; m. Jane Gruber, July 22, 1967; children: Walter H., Sarah N., David J. BA, U. Cin., 1960; BHL, MAHL, Hebrew U. Coll.-Jewish Inst. Religion, 1965; DD, N.Y., 1990. Ordained rabbi, 1965. Rabbi Temple Beth Sholom, N.Y.C., 1970-78; assoc. dir. N.Y. Bd. Rabbis, N.Y.C., 1978-82; assoc. dir. N.Y. Fedn. Reform Synagogues, N.Y.C., 1982-91, dir., 1991—; v.p., bd. dirs. JACS Found., N.Y.C.; advisor on religious matters Gay Men's Health Crisis, N.Y.C., 1988—. Contbr. articles to profl. jours. Comdr. USNR, 1980—. Mem. Cen. Conf. Am. Rabbis, Internat. Psychology Assn., Naval Res. Assn., Assn. N.Y. Reform Rabbis (treas. N.Y.C. chpt. 1987—). Avocation: photography. Home: 445 E 86th St New York NY 10028 Office: Union Am Hebrew Congregations 838 Fifth Ave New York NY 10021

KAPLAN, DANIEL LEE, rabbi; b. Balt., Aug. 24, 1934; s. Louis Lionel and Etta (Jenkins) K.; m. Arleen Kulin, Dec. 23, 1962 (div. Mar. 1990); children: Jennifer, Jonathan; m. Barbara Susan Litchman, June 24, 1990. Acad. cert., Balt. Hebrew Coll., 1953; BA, Johns Hopkins U., 1954; DD (hon.), Hebrew Union Coll.-Jewish Inst. Religion, 1983. Asst. rabbi Temple Emanuel, Worcester, Mass., 1959-62; rabbi Temple Beth Shalom, Needham, Mass., 1962-70, Melrose, Mass., 1970-72; rabbi Temple Sinai, Sharon, Mass., 1972-86; founding rabbi Congregation Klal Yisrael, Stoughton, Mass., 1986—; instr. sch. edn. Boston Coll., 1971-72, Providence Coll., 1984; pastoral care coord. New Eng. Sinai Hosp., Stoughton, 1988—; dean Acad. Jewish Studies, Boston, 1971-80. Author: A New Haggadah, exptl. edits. 1985—; contbr. articles to profl. publs. Mem. Cen. Conf. Am. Rabbis (pres. New Eng. region 1968-70), Mass. Bd. Rabbis (pres. 1984-86). Home: 1296 Pleasant St Canton MA 02021 Office: Congregation Klal Yisrael 1819 Central St Box 503 Stoughton MA 02072

KAPLAN, PHILIP, retired rabbi; b. Albany, N.Y., Dec. 28, 1918; s. Abraham Moses and Anna Dina (Wepner) K.; m. Esther Koffler, Oct. 21, 1945; children: Andrea Dina, Allan Saul. BA, Yeshiva U., 1939, MA, 1961. Ordained rabbi, 1942. Rabbi Congregation United Sons of Jacob, Fall River, Mass., 1943-47, Congregation Ahavas Isaac, Sarnia, Ont., Can., 1953-60; rabbi Congregation Agudas Achim, Colchester, Conn., 1960-65, Attleboro, Mass., 1965-78; retired, 1978; inspector Rabbinical Coun. of New Eng., Boston, 1965—. Office: Vaad Harabonim 65 Wilcox Ave Pawtucket RI 02860

KAPNEK, ABRAHAM BRUCE, rabbi; b. Phila., Dec. 18, 1947; s. Bertram Harry and Betty (Kingan) K.; m. Jacqueline Iris Naftelberg, May 31, 1970; children: Shoshana, Aliza, Ilan. BA, Pa. State U., 1969; MA in Edn., Dropsis U., 1971. Ordained rabbi, 1975. Rabbi, Hillel counselor Temple Beth-El, Newark, Del., 1973-77; rabbi Congregation Beth Torah, Willingboro, N.J., 1977-84, Beth Ahm Israel, Hollywood, Fla., 1984—; chaplain Pembroke Pines (Fla.) Police Dept., 1991—. Mem. Interfaith Coun. of Greater Hollywood (v.p. 1990-91), South Broward Coun. Rabbis (v.p. 1989-91), Rabbis and Educator's Coun. (chmn. 1989-91), Rabbinical Assembly. Office: Beth Ahm Israel 9730 Stirling Rd Hollywood FL 33124

KAPP, RAY, clergyman; b. Ashley, N.D., June 18, 1925; s. Konrad and Mary (Eisenbeis) K.; m. Esther Eslinger, Aug. 12, 1945; children: Cheryl, Carole, Paulette, Joy. Student, Lincoln Barber Coll., 1949-50, Grace Bible Inst., Omaha, 1958-60. Ordained to ministry. Evangelist Lincoln, Nebr., 1956-58; missionary Christians in Action, Long Beach, Calif., 1960-63; dir. ministry New Life Ednl. Found., Brookings, S.D., 1973-75; pastor Beaver Crossing (Nebr.) Christian Fellowship, 1979-85, Faith in Christ Fellowship, Seward, Nebr., 1985—; v.p. New Life Ednl. Found., Brookings, 1972-75; asst. dir. trip to USSR, Youth With a Mission, London, 1973; bicentennial outreach Team Ministries, Sioux Falls, S.D., 1975-76. Author 30 sonnets. With USN, 1943-45. Mem. Evang. Pastor Fellowship. Republican. Home: 315 Lindell Seward NE 68434

KAPRAL, HILARION (HIS GRACE BISHOP HILARION), bishop; b. Spirit River, Alta., Can., Jan. 6, 1948; came to U.S., 1977, permanent resident; s. Alex and Euphrosyne (Kasaniuk) K. BTh, Holy Trinity Orthodox Sem., Jordanville, N.Y., 1972; MA, Syracuse (N.Y.) U., 1981. Professed monk Holy Trinity Russian Orthodox Monastery, Jordanville, 1974-84; bishop of Manhattan Synod of Bishops of Russian Orthodox Ch. Outside Russia, N.Y.C., 1984—; pres. Russian Youth Com., Baldwin Pl., N.Y., 1987—; dir. Orthodox Palestine Soc. in U.S.A., 1986—. Mng. editor (bi-monthly) Orthodox Life, Jordanville, 1970-89. Home and Office: Synod of Bishops Russian Orthodox Ch 75 E 93d St New York NY 10128

KARABAN, ROSLYN ANN, ministry studies educator, pastoral counselor; b. Waterbury, Conn., June 27, 1953; d. William John and Regina Rita (McGinn) K.; m. Devadasan Nithya Premnath, May 15, 1982; children: Deepa Lynn Premnath, Micah Reyan Premnath. BA summa cum laude, Stonehill Coll., 1975; MDiv, Harvard Div. Sch., 1978; PhD, Grad. Theol. Union, 1984. Instr. pastoral counseling United Theol. Coll., Bangalore, India, 1985-87; instr. St. Bernard's Inst., Rochester, N.Y., 1987-88; asst. prof. St. Bernard's Inst., 1988-91, assoc. prof., 1991—; assoc. counselor Samaritan Pastoral Counseling Ctr., Rochester, 1990—. Contbr. articles to profl. jours. Claretian Social Justice grantee Mex.-Am. Cultural Ctr., San Antonio, 1980. Mem. AAUW, Soc. for Pastoral Theology, Theol. Commn. Diocese Rochester, Rochester Women's Ordination Conf. (mem. steering com. 1988—, coord., pres. 1990—), Phi Alpha Theta, Delta Epsilon Sigma. Democrat. Roman Catholic. Avocations: reading novels, walking, travel. Office: St Bernard's Inst 1644 Denton Green Hempstead NY 11350

KARAKAS, RITA S., community services association executive. Former v.p. United Way/Centraide Can.; former program dir. Alliance Que.; now chief exec. officer YWCA of/du Can.; bd. dirs. Greenshield Prepaid Svcs. Inc. Bd. dirs. , corp. advisor Inst. for Prevention Child Abuse; mem. children's svcs. adv. com., Premier of Ont.; mem. adv. com. Dept. Health and Welfare, Govt. Can. Office: YWCA of/du Canada, 80 Gerrard St E, Toronto, ON Canada M5B 1G6

KARAMPELAS, NAPOLEON DEMETRIOS, priest; b. Varympope, Menastereon Messeneas, Greece, Dec. 31, 1904; came to U.S., 1938; naturalized, 1944; s. Demetrios Panteles and Georgia (Kalampokes)P K. m. Panagoula Lontos, July 20, 1929; children: Angelos, Panagiotis. Diploma in Theology, Theol. and Ecclesiastical Sch., Corinth, Greece, 1932. Ordained deacon Greek Orthodox Ch., 1934, priest, 1934. Pastor Greek Orthodox Ch., Greece, 1934-38, Calif., 1938-39, Colo., 1939-41, Little Rock, 1941-42, Ill., 1942-45, Kans., 1945-49; pastor Ch. of the Assumption Holy Trinity Greek Orthodox Ch., Grand Rapids, Mich., 1949-52; archpriest Upper Peninsula Greek Orthodox Ch., Marquette, Mich., 1963—; pastor Greek Orthodox Ch., Nebr., 1952-55, 59-63, Wyo., 1955-56, Idaho, 1956-59; Mem. Marquette Ecumenical Coun., 1963. Author: (with others) The Oxford Dictionary of Byzantium, 1991; contbr. over 300 articles on theology and Greek history to Jour. Hellenic Am. Soc., Am. Rev. Ea. Orthodox Ch. and various newspapers. Served with Greek Army, 1924-26. Mem. Hellenic Profl. Assn. Am., Clergy Assn. Marquette. Home: 237 W Ridge Marquette MI 49855 *Because always in my life I took into consideration that every priest must live for his church and for his people, I have lived for our church and for our beloved spiritual children, and now my church and my children live for me. Then and always, and especially in my rainy days and difficult days of my life, our church and Orthodox Christians have helped me morally and financially during those rainy and difficult days.*

KAREKIN, II, religious leader. Leader Armenian Apostolic Orthodox Ch., Beirut. Office: Armenian Apostolic Chs, Catholicos, Cilicia Antelias Lebanon*

KARES, KAARLO OLAVI, bishop; b. Mikkeli, Finland, Mar. 24, 1903; s. K.R. and Sigrid (Koskinen) K.; m. Aili Mattila; 1 child, Leena. D in Theology (hon.), U. Helsinki, Finland, 1942. Ordained to ministry Luth. Ch., 1928; qualified for prof. eccles. history U. Helsinki;. Curate Lapua, 1928-30; headmaster Christian People's Ednl. Inst., Turku, 1930-60; dean Turku, 1960-62; bishop Diocese of Kuopio, 1962-74. Author: Palava kyntilä, 1936, Heränneen kansan vaellus I-V, 1942-52, Luther, 1945, Päiväkirja, 1958, Kierros auringon Ympäri, 1961, Kallaveden rannalta, 1965, Seuratkaa tähteä, 1974, Olavi Kares kertoo elämästään, 1976, Pohjanmaan lakeusilla ja Auran rannoilla, 1977, Myrskyä ja tyventä, 1978, Värikäs elämän kausi, 1980, Tervaa ja palsamia, 1984. Address: 49 A Linnank, Turku Finland

KARFF, SAMUEL EGAL, rabbi, religious studies educator; b. Phila., Sept. 19, 1931; s. Louis and Reba (Margalit) K.; m. Joan Gabriel Mag, June 29, 1959; children: Rachel Weissenstein, Amy Halvey, Elizabeth Kampf. BA, Gratz Coll., 1949; AB magna cum laude, Harvard U., 1953; MA in Hebrew Letters, Hebrew Union Coll., 1956, DHL, 1961, DD (hon.), 1981. Ordained rabbi, 1956. Rabbi Temple Beth El, Flint, Mich., 1960-62; sr. rabbi Chgo. Sinai Congregation, 1962-75, Congregation Beth Israel, Houston, 1975—; adj. prof. religious studies Rice U., Houston. Author: Agada: The Language of Jewish Faith, 1981; contbg. author: Religions of the World, 1982, 2d edit., 1988; editor: History of Hebrew Union College at 100 Years, 1975; contbr. articles to various publs. V.p. Chgo. Conf. on Rels. and Race, 1967-69; pres. Cen. Conf. Am. Rabbis, N.Y.C., 1989-91; bd. dirs. Inst. Religion Tex. Med. Ctr., Houston, 1980; officer Houston Met. Ministries, 1982. 1st lt. USAF, 1956-58. John Harvard Scholar Harvard U., 1951-52. Mem. Kiwanis, Forum Club, Phi Beta Kappa. Avocations: tennis, walking. Home: 5343 Paisley Houston TX 77096 Office: Congregation Beth Israel 5600 N Braeswood Houston TX 77096

KARIKA, MARK, minister; b. Ft. Benning, Ga., Dec. 5, 1952; s. Charles and Mary Catherine (Booten) K.; m. Karen Joy Weaklend, June 7, 1975; children: Kimberly Ann, Charles, Michelle Kristine, Jonathan Mark. BS, Liberty Bapt. Coll., 1979. Ordained to ministry So. Bapt. Conv. Pastor Victory Blvd. Bapt. Ch., Portsmouth, Va., 1979—; security guard Portsmouth Police Dept., 1986-87. Mem. Portsmouth Police Chaplains (treas. 1989—). Office: Victory Blvd Bapt Ch 3014 Victory Blvd Portsmouth VA 23702

KARIVALIS, DAMIANOS GEORGE See DIODOROS I

KARJIAN, HOVHANNES, religious organization head. Moderator Union of Armenian Evang. Chs. in Nr. East, Beirut. Office: Union Armenian Evang Chs, The Near E, POB 110-377, Beirut Lebanon*

KARMONOCKY, LORRAINE MARGARET, lay church worker; b. Bronx, Jan. 19, 1941; d. Michael Joseph Lemmick and Beatrice Matilda Olson Swartz; m. Karl Joseph Karmonocky, June 9, 1962; children: Karl Joseph, Michael Joseph, Heather Mary. BBA, N.C. Cen. U., 1991; AB, Latin Am. Inst., N.Y.C., 1960. Dir. edn. St. Bernadette's Roman Cath. Ch., Butner, N.C., 1978-85; eucharist min. Holy Infant Roman Cath. Ch., Durham, N.C., 1987—; adminstrv. asst. Duke Meml. United Meth. Ch., Durham, N.C., 1990—. Editor newsletter, Insights, 1990-91. Pub. rels. dir. S.G.S.H. Band Parents Assn., creedmoor, N.C., 1981—; coord. N.C. Easter Seal Soc., Raleigh, 1976-80; chmn. bd. dirs. ACCEPT, Greensboro, 1985-88; reg. rep. IMPAC, N.C. State Employees Assn., Chapel Hill, 1985-90. Home: Route 3 Box 298 Creedmoor NC 27522 Office: Duke Meml United Meth Ch 504 W Chapel Hill St Durham NC 27701

KAROL, LAWRENCE PAUL, rabbi; b. Kansas City, Mo., Oct. 3, 1954; s. Joseph G. and Ruth Harriet (Glazer) K.; m. Rhonda Phyllis Marks, Aug. 8, 1982; 1 child, Adam. AB in Liberal Arts and Sociology, U. Ill., 1976; MA in Hebrew Letters, Hebrew Union Coll., 1980. Ordained rabbi, 1981. Asst. rabbi Temple Israel, Dayton, Ohio, 1981-84; rabbi Temple Beth Sholom, Topeka, 1984—; pres. Interfaith of Topeka, 1989-90; mem. Reform Commn. on Synagogue Music, Paramus, N.J., 1989—. Sec. Brown Found. for Ednl. Equity, Topeka, 1990—; mem. multicultural task force Topeka Pub. Schs., 1988—; mem. ethics com. Stormont-Vail Hosp., Topeka, 1990—; mem. Kans. State Holocaust Commn., Topeka, 1987—. Recipient Civil Rights award Living the Dream Com., 1991, Emma P. Cohen award Greater Hartford (Conn.) Jewish Hist. Soc., 1981. Mem. Cen. Conf. Am. Rabbis, Coalition for Advancement of Jewish Edn., Guild Temple Musicians, Topeka Area Clergy (pres. 1989-90). Office: Temple Beth Sholom 4200 Munson Topeka KS 66604 *The rabbis of Jewish tradition said, "Find yourself a teacher and get yourself a colleague (friend)." In serving my congregation and community, I have tried to be open to the possibility that anyone could be my teacher, my colleague, or my friend.*

KARP, ABRAHAM JOSEPH, Jewish studies educator; b. Indura, Poland, Apr. 5, 1921; came to U.S., 1930, naturalized, 1930; s. Aaron and Rachel (Schor) K.; m. Deborah Burstein, June 17, 1945; children:Hillel J., David J. BA magna cum laude, Yeshiva U., 1942; Rabbi, Jewish Theol. Sem. of Am., 1945, MHL, 1949, DD, 1971; DHL (hon.), Gratz Coll., 1985. Rsch. prof. Jewish Theol. Sem. Am.; rabbi Beth Shalom Synagogue, Kansas City, Mo., 1951-56; Rabbi Beth El, Rochester, N.Y., 1956-72; prof. history and religious studies U. Rochester, 1972-91, Philip S. Bernstein prof. Jewish studies, 1976-91; vis. prof. Dartmouth, 1967, Hebrew U., Jerusalem, 1970, Jewish Theol. Sem. Am., 1967-71, 75-76; corr. mem. Inst. Contemporary Jewry, Hebrew U., 1973—. Author: The Jewish Way of Life, 1962, The United Synagogue of America-A History, 1963, The Jewish Experience in America, 1971, Golden Door to America, 1976, To Give Life, 1980, The Jewish Way of Life and Thought, 1981, Hayyei Haruah shel Yahadut Amerika (Hebrew, in Israel), 1984, Haven and Home: A History of the Jews in America, 1985, From the Ends of the Earth: Judaic Treasures of the Library of Congress, 1991; editor: Conservative Judaism-The Legacy of Solomon Schechter, 1965, Beginnings-Early American Judaica, 1976, Mordecai Manuel Noah-The First American Jew, 1987; translator: Five from the Holocaust, 1975; contbg. author: Jewish Art and Civilization, 1972; mem. editorial bd. Midstream; curator exhbn. From the Ends of the Earth: Judaic Treasures of the Library of Congress, 1991. Mem. Am. Jewish Hist. Soc. (pres., chmn. publs. com., Lee M. Friedman medal 1976), President's Historians Circle Jerusalem, Rabbinical Assembly, Assn. Jewish Studies, Conf. on Jewish Social Studies (v.p.), Phi Beta Kappa. Home: 3333 Henry Hudson Pkwy Apt 22E Riverdale NY 10463 *On April 5, 1921, I was granted a loan: my life. On February 18, 1930, I was given a gift: life in America, which has been for me a land of freedom and opportunity. All my family, all the friends of my youth who remained behind in Europe perished in the Holocaust. Years have been granted me to repay the loan. I seize each opportunity to return the gift.*

KARSTENSEN, ELMER LELAND, lay worker; b. Lincolnville, Kans., May 18, 1934; s. Karl John and Ernestine Mathilda (Westphal) K.; m. Bernice Thelma Fry, July 3, 1960 (div. July 1982); children: Brian Paul, John Philip; m. Linda Reichenau, July 29, 1989. BS in Tech. Journalism, Kans. State U., 1956; M. Urban Affairs, Wichita State U., 1979. Bus. mgr. Holy Cross Luth. Ch., Wichita, Kans., 1983-85, Kans. Dist. Luth. Ch.-Mo. Synod, Topeka, 1985—; mem. handbook com. Kans. Dist. Luth. Ch.-Mo. Synod, Topeka, 1974—, bd. dirs., 1979-85. Maj. U.S. Army, 1956-79, Vietnam. Mem. Luth. Bus. Mgrs. Assn. (chmn. 1990—). Republican. Home: 3318 SW Skyline Dr Topeka KS 66614 Office: Kans Dist Luth Ch Mo Synod 2318 W 10th St Topeka KS 66604

KASEROW, JOHN MARION, priest; b. Chgo., May 6, 1938; s. Joseph Stanley and Rose Agnes (Urban) K. BA in Philosophy, Maryknoll Sem., Glen Ellyn, Ill., 1964; MDiv, Maryknoll Sem., Maryknoll, N.Y., 1968, ThM in History, 1969; MA in Liturgy, U. Notre Dame, 1969; PhD in Hist. Theology, U. St. Michael's Coll., Toronto, Can., 1977. Joined Maryknoll, Roman Cath. Ch.; ordained priest, Roman Cath. Ch., 1969. Missionary priest Maryknoll Fathers and Bros., N.Y., 1969—; prof. theology Maryknoll Sch. Theology, Ossining, N.Y., 1973-75, 79-88, chief exec. officer, acad. dean, 1979-82, dir. inst., 1980-88; prof. mission studies Cath. Theol. Union, Chgo., 1988—, dir. world mission program, 1991—. Mem. N.Am. Acad. Liturgy, Midwest Fellowship Missions, Cath. Theol. Soc. Home: 5508 S Cornell Ave Chicago IL 60637 Office: Cath Theol Union 5401 S Cornell Ave Chicago IL 60615

KASEY, GARY LEONARD, minister; b. Louisville, July 1, 1955; s. Ernest Leonard and Evangeline (Miller) K.; m. Vicky Regina Smith, Dec. 10, 1976; children: Karen Kay, Rebecca Gayle, Kyle Andrew. BS in Religion, Cumberland Coll., Williamsburg, Ky., 1978; postgrad., So. Bapt. Theol. Sem., Louisville, 1978-81. Ordained to ministry, So. Bapt. Conv. Minister of edn. High St. Bapt. Ch., Somerset, Ky., 1979-81; pastor Buena Vista Bapt. Ch., Somerset, Ky., 1981-85; campus minister Somerset Community Coll., 1982-85; pastor Calvary Bapt. Ch., Harrodsburg, Ky., 1985-87, New Salem Bapt. Ch., Vine Grove, Ky., 1987—; summer missionary Arcade Bapt. Ch./Home Mission Bd., Louisville, 1975, youth dir., 1977-79; ch. missions com. Salem Bapt. Assn., 1989—; del. Ky. Bapt. Conv., 1981-91, So. Bapt. Conv., 1985-91. Basketball coach Radcliff Recreation Dept., 1991—; mission trip evangelist Fgn. Mission Bd., So. Bapt. Conv., Nigeria, 1981. Mem. Salem Bapt. Assn. (exec. bd. 1987—), Meade County Ministerial Assn., N. Hardin Ministerial Assn. Home: 4252 Berrytown Rd Rineyville KY 40162 Office: New Salem Bapt Ch 632 New Salem Ch Rd Vine Grove KY 40175

KASHUCK, CLAIRE, ecumenical agency administrator. Exec. dir. Coop. Met. Ministries, Newton, Mass. Office: Coop Met Ministries 474 Centre St Newton MA 02158*

KASSOUF, JOHN FRED, minister; b. Bklyn., Sept. 30, 1954; s. Fred and Caroline Rose Kassouf; m. Francine Fruscillo, June 4, 1978; children: Andrew, Timothy, Mark. BA, Concordia Coll., Bronxville, N.Y., 1976; postgrad., Iona Coll., New Rochelle, N.Y., 1976-77; MA, Towson (Md.) State U., 1982; M Theol. Studies., Brock U., St. Catharines, Ont., Can., 1991. Ordained to ministry Luth. Ch.-Mo. Synod; cert. tchr., N.Y. Min. Christian edn. Calvary Luth Ch., Balt., 1977-87, St. Paul Luth. Ch., Catonsville, Md., 1987-89; pastor 1st Luth. Ch. Calvert County, Sunderland, Md., 1989—. Chaplain Kiwanis Club, Towson, 1982-87. Republican. Office: 1st Luth Ch PO Box 129 Sunderland MD 20689

KASSOVER, JEFFREY ABRAHAM, religious organization administrator, fund raiser; b. N.Y.C., Nov. 16, 1947; s. Benjamin Max and Helen (Wisen) K.; m. Kathleen Mechanik, Mar. 17, 1991. BA, Queens Coll., CUNY, 1970; postgrad., Sch. Visual Arts, N.Y.C., 1971-72; cert. in Fund Raising Mgmt., NYU, 1984. Dir. New Leadership Manhattan Israel Bonds Orgn., N.Y.C., 1981—; dir. Young Mens Div. Albert Einstein Coll. Medicine, Bronx, N.Y., 1983-85; dir. devel. South Shore YM-YWHA, Oceanside, N.Y., 1985-86; v.p. Joel S. Friedman & Assocs. Inc., Harrison, N.Y., 1987—; campaign dir. Mountain Jewish Community Ctr., Warren, N.J., 1987-88, YM-YWHA of Greater Morris City, N.J., 1988-89, Midway Jewish Ctr., Syossett, N.Y., 1989-90, Pomona (N.Y.) Jewish Ctr.,1990, Temple Sholom, Bridgewater, N.J., 1990-91. Mem. Assn. Jewish Community Orgns. Pers., Coun. Jewish Fedns. Home: 201 Bridge Plaza N A5F Fort Lee NJ 07024 Office: Joel S Friedman & Assocs 99 Woodlands Rd Harrison NY 10528

KASTEL, KASRIEL B., rabbi; b. Balt., Dec. 15, 1943; s. Joshua T. and Golda (Pattashnick) K.; m. Nechomo Blau, June 22, 1967; children: Mendel, Zalman, Leah, Dina, Shmuel. Grad., United Lubavitcher Yeshivos, Bklyn. Ordained rabbi. Program dir. Lubavitch Youth Orgn., Bklyn., 1967—; lectr. Lincoln Sq. Synagogue, N.Y.C., 1980—. Pubr. Wellsprings mag. Office: 770 Eastern Pkwy Brooklyn NY 11213

KASTENS, ROBERT WILLIAM, clergyman; b. N.Y.C., Apr. 23, 1942; s. Ernst and Elsie (Soderberg) K.; m. Etta Lee Raulston, June 22, 1962; children: Robert Lee, Ronald Earl, Sherry Ann, Judy Lee. BA, Johnson Bible Coll., 1970. Ordained to ministry Christian Ch., 1968. Minister Bethel and Keenersville Christian Ch., Hot Springs, N.C., 1967-68, Sullivan Rd. Christian Ch., Knoxville, Tenn., 1968-72, Belvue Christian Ch., Kingsport, Tenn., 1972-84, Havendale Christian Ch., Winter Haven, Fla., 1984-87, Hickory Valley Christian Ch., Chattanooga, 1987—; clk. U. Tenn. Hosp., Knoxville, 1964-68; chmn. Tyner-Silverdale Ministries, 1990-91; mem. Statewide Ministers Com., 1987-91; mem. coun. Johnson Bible Coll., 1990-93. With USAF, 1960-64. Home: 2301 David Ln Chattanooga TN 37421 Office: Hickory Valley Christian Ch 6605 Shallowford Rd Chattanooga TN 37421

KATZ, DAVID ARTHUR, rabbi; b. Rochester, N.Y., Mar. 20, 1953; m. Nancy Katz; children: Emily, Benjamin. BS in Theater, Northwestern U., 1974, MA in Theater, 1975; MA in Hebrew Letters, Hebrew Union Coll., 1978, MA in Hebrew Edn., 1979. Ordained rabbi, 1981. Temple educator Temple Israel, Boston, 1981-83; asst. dir. Leo Baeck Day Sch., Toronto, Ont., Can., 1983-85; rabbi Temple Beth Sholom, Fredericksburg, Va., 1985-88, Temple Israel Reform Congregation of Staten Island (N.Y.), 1988—. Contbr. articles to profl. publs. Founding mem. Crimesolvers, Anonymous, Fredericksburg; co-chair Staten Island Ruman Rights Coun.; bd. dirs. Staten Island Mental Health Soc.; mem. adv. bd. Supt. Schs., Staten Island; mem. adv. bd. Retired Sr. Vol. Program, N.Y.C.; mem. edn. policy com. Staten Island Acad. Mem. Cen. Conf. Am. Rabbis (mem. reform Jewish practise and liturgy coms., mem. spl. task force), Nat. Assn. Temple Educators (bd. dirs. 1984-90, chair social action com., liaison, mem. commn. on Jewish edn.). Home: 24 Gregg Pl Staten Island NY 10301 Office: Temple Israel 315 Forest Ave Staten Island NY 10301

KATZ, M., religious organization administrator. Pres., prof. South African Jewish Bd. Deps., Johannesburg. Office: South African Jewish Bd Deps, PO Box 1180, Johannesburg Republic of South Africa*

KATZ, SOLOMON HERTZ, anthropologist, educator; b. Beverly, Mass., July 22, 1939; s. Max and Rose (Hefferon) K.; m. Judith Kapustin, June 21, 1964; children: Noah, Rachel. B.A., Northeastern U., 1963; M.A. (NIH fellow), U. Pa., 1966, Ph.D., 1967. Research asst. Harvard U.-Mass. Gen. Hosp., Boston, 1961-63, Bermuda Biol. Sta., St. Georges, West Bermuda, 1963; NIH fellow U. Pa., 1968, asst. prof. anthropology, depts. pediatric dentistry and anthropology, 1968-72, asso. prof., 1972-76, prof., 1976—, curator phys. anthropology Univ. Museum, 1968—; sr. med. research scientist, dir. div. psychoendocrinology Eastern Pa. Psychiat. Inst., Phila., 1972-80; research prof. preventive and community medicine Med. Coll. Pa., Phila., 1981—, dir. perinatal div. Eastern Pa. Psychiat. Inst. div., 1981-85; dir. W.M. Krogman Center for Research in Child Growth and Devel., Children's Hosp. of Phila.-U. Pa., 1972—; pres. Inst. Continuous Study of Man, 1974—, Ctr. for Advanced Studies in Religion and Sci., 1989—. Editor: Biological Anthropology, 1975, (series) History and Anthropology of Food and Nutrition; corr. editor Comments on Contemporary Psychiatry, 1972-74; asso. editor, co-chmn. joint publs. bd. Zygon, 1975—; asso. and founding asso. editor Human Ecology, 1972-74. Mem. Narberth Home and Sch. Bd., 1976-77. NIH-Nat. Inst. Dental Research grantee, 1963-67; Nat. Inst. Environ. Health Scis. grantee, 1975-79; Nat. Heart, Lung and Blood Inst. grantee, 1976-81, 82-85; NSF grantee, 1968-69; Smithsonian Instn. grantee, 1978-79; Grant Found. grantee, 1974-78; Internat. Research Exchange grantee, 1978; Wenner Gren Found. grantee, 1979. Mem. Am. Assn. Phys. Anthropologists, AAAS, Am. Heart Assn., Phila. Acad. Scis., Am. Anthrop. Assn. (sec.-treas. biol. anthropology sect. 1984—), Am. Mammologist Soc., Inst. on Religion in an Age of Sci. (pres. 1977-79, 81-84). Home: 519 N Wynnewood Ave Narberth PA 19072 Office: U Pa Krogman Growth Ctr 4019 Irving St Philadelphia PA 19104

KATZ, STEVEN THEODORE, religious educator; b. Jersey City, Aug. 24, 1944; s. Abraham and Mary (Bell) K.; m. Rebecca Anne Horwich, Jan. 5, 1969; children: Shira, Tamar, Yehuda. BA, Rutgers U., 1966; MA, NYU, 1967; PhD, Cambridge U., 1972; DHL, Gratz Coll., 1987; BD, Cambridge U., Eng., 1991. From asst. to assoc. to full prof. Dartmouth Coll., Hanover, N.H., 1972-84; prof., chmn. Cornell U., Ithaca, N.Y., 1984-88; vis. prof. Hebrew U., Jerusalem, 1971, U. Lancaster, Eng., 1974, U. Toronto, Can., 1978, 80, U. Calif., Santa Barbara, 1981, Harvard U., Cambridge, Mass., 1982-84, Brandeis U., Waltham, Mass., 1983, Yale U., New Haven, 1983; Mason prof. Coll. William and Mary, 1983, Meyerhoff prof. U. Pa., 1989—. Author: Jewish Philosophers, 1975, Jewish Ideas and Concepts, 1977, Mysticism and Philosophical Analysis, 1978, Mysticism and Religious Traditions, 1983, Post-Holocaust Dialogues, 1984 (Natl. Jewish Book award 1984), Historicism, The Holocaust and Zionism, 1992, The Holocaust in Historical Context, 3 vols., 1992, Mysticism and Language, 1992 ; editor: Modern Jewish Masters Series, 1984—, Johns Hopkins Studies in Judaica Series, 1987—; editor Modern Judaism, 1981; mem. editorial bd. Ency. of Holocaust, 1986—, Ency. of Spirituality, 1986—. Recipient Lakrits prize Hebrew U., 1978; NEH fellow, 1981, David Baumgardt fellow Am. Philos. Assn., 1984. Fellow Am. Soc. Study Religion, Am. Acad. Jewish Philos., Assn. Jewish Studies (v.p. 1980-86), Am. Acad. Religion; mem. Internat. Metaphysical Soc. Avocations: book collecting, travel, photography. Home: 92 Riverside Dr Binghamton NY 13905 Office: Cornell U Dept Nr Eastern Studies 360 Rockefeller Hall Ithaca NY 14853

KAUFFMAN, JEFFREY LAYNE, SR., minister; b. Plymouth, Ind., Sept. 3, 1961; s. Ronald Lynn and Sara Leah (Blackford) K.; m. Barbara Carol Hendricks, June 30, 1984; children: Jeffrey Layne Jr., Elyse Joy, David Raymond. Diploma, Moody Bible Inst., 1980, Word of Life Bible Inst., 1983. Ordained to ministry Bapt. Ch. Student staff evangelist Open Air Campagners, N.Y.C., 1980-83, Chgo., 1980-83; dir. student outreach Moody Bible Inst., Chgo., 1981-83; youth pastor Tippecanoe (Ind.) Community Ch., 1984-85; asst. pastor El Dorado Bapt. Ch., Phoenix, 1985-86; sr. pastor El Dorado Bapt. Ch., 1986-88, Cactus Bapt. Ch., Phoenix, 1988—; mem. Southwest Conservation Bapt. New Ch. Com., Phoenix, 1988—; mem.-at-large Conservative Bapt. Pastor's fellow, Phoenix, 1990; mem. Conservative Bapt. Ordination Com., Phoenix, 1991—. Coach Paradise Valley Parks Recreation, Northeast Phoenix, 1990-91. Mem. Nat. Assn. Evangelicals, Greater Phoenix Assn. Evangelicals. Republican. Avocations: reading, horseback riding, hunting. Home: 3932 E Captain Dreyfus Phoenix AZ 85032 Office: Cactus Bapt Ch 13244 N 21st Pl Phoenix AZ 85022

KAUFFMAN, LUKE EDWARD, minister; b. Hummelstown, Pa., Dec. 19, 1941; s. Jeremiah Martin and Mary Elizabeth (Kreider) K.; m. Sandra Jean Garber, Aug. 1, 1964; children: Kurt Alan, Kent David, Kristen Lyn. AA, Hershey (Pa.) Jr. Coll., 1961; BA, Grace Coll., Winona Lake, Ind., 1963; MDiv, Grace Theol. Sem., Winona Lake, Ind., 1966; DMin, Luther Rice Sem., Jacksonville, Fla., 1989. Ordained to ministry Fellowship of Grace Brethren Chs., 1969. Pastor Grace Brethren Ch., Beaverton, Oreg., 1966-69; sr. pastor Grace Brethren Ch., Myerstown, Pa., 1969—; founder Grace Christian Sch., Myerstown, 1974; trustee Brethren Missionary Herald Co. Winona Lake 1974-77; pres. Grace Brethren Home Mission Coun., 1982—, Grace Brethren Investment Found. 1982—, Northern Atlantic Dist. Mission Bd. of Fellowship of Grace Brethren Chs.; speaker Grace Brethren Hour (radio) 1976-88, The Message of Grace (TV) 1983-88; dir. Grace Christian Sch. Myerstown 1974—; founder, dir. Grace Community, Inc. (retirement community) 1987—. Author: Eldership Church, 1978, Church Planting Principles and Policies That Produce, 1989. Chaplain Pa. State Senate 1983. Mem. Pa. Counseling Ctr (v.p. 1970-76). Republican. Avocations: reading, horticulture. Home: 613 Hilltop Rd Myerstown PA 17067 Office: Grace Brethren Ch 430 E Lincoln Ave Myerstown PA 17067 *The two guideposts that I choose to direct my life are honesty, and discretion.*

KAUFFMANN, DEBORAH LYNN, lay ministry administrator; b. Cleve., Dec. 27, 1954; d. Myron John and Rose Virginia (Hill) K. BA, Wittenberg U., 1977. Chmn. cabinet Luth. Social Ministry of S.W., Tucson, 1985—. Libr. Community Chorus, Green Valley, 1985—; past pres. Community Transp. Vols., Green Valley. Mem. Assn. Luth. Ch. Musicians (assoc.). Republican. Home: 1976 S Abrego Dr Green Valley AZ 85614 Office: Luth Svc Ctr 1222 N Campbell Ave Tucson AZ 85719-4608

KAUFFMANN, NANCY LEE, minister; b. Wooster, Ohio, Apr. 25, 1948; d. Warren Roger and Phyllis Ann (Greenbank) Geiser; m. Joel Dean Kauffmann, Apr. 15, 1972; children: Justin Quinn, Julian Clay. BA in Edn., Goshen Coll., 1973; MDiv, Assoc. Mennonite Bibl. Sems., Elkhart, Ind., 1982. Ordained to ministry Mennonite Ch., k1981. Assoc. min. College Mennonite Ch., Goshen, Ind., 1981—; mem. chaplaincy com. Goshen Gen. Hosp., 1984-86, 89-91, mem. pastoral care adv. com., 1989-91; mem. Ch. Life Commn., Ind.-Mich. Conf., Mennonite Ch., Goshen, 1986—. Project leader Goshen High Sch., 1991. Democrat. Office: College Mennonite Ch 1900 S Main St Goshen IN 46526

KAUFMAN, GERALD JULIUS, minister; b. Bronx, N.Y., Aug. 29, 1935; s. Fred and Julia (Weiss) K.; m. Juanita Lazarus, Apr. 16, 1966; children: Jerry, April, Joshua. Diploma, Zion Bible Inst., 1965; B in Sacred Lit., Vision Christian U., 1980, ThM, 1981, D of Ministry, 1982, PhD, 1991. Ordained to ministry non-denom. Pentecostal Ch., 1967. Bishop Love Gospel Assembly, Bronx, 1970—; chaplain Fed. Protective Bur., Manhatten, N.Y., 1989; bd. dirs. Youth Challenge, Hartford, Ct. Author: Cry for The Cities, 1982, It's Time for War, 1985, God's Treasure in Earthen Vessels, 1990. Mem. community adv. bd. for James A. Thomas Ctr. Office: Love Gospel Assembly 2315 Grand Concourse Bronx NY 10468

KAUFMAN, GORDON DESTER, theology educator; b. Newton, Kans., June 22, 1925; s. Edmund George and Hazel (Dester) K.; m. Dorothy Wedel, June 11, 1947; children: David W., Gretchen E., Anne Louisa, Edmund G. A.B. with highest distinction, Bethel (Kans.) Coll., 1947, L.H.D. (hon.), 1973; M.A. in Sociology, Northwestern U., 1948; B.D. magna cum laude, Yale, 1951, Ph.D. in Philos. Theology, 1955. Ordained to ministry Mennonite Ch., 1953; asst. prof. religion Pomona Coll., 1953-58; asso. prof. theology Vanderbilt U., 1958-63; prof. theology Harvard Div. Sch., 1963—, Edward MallincKrodt Jr. prof. div., 1969—; vis. prof. United Theol. Coll., Bangalore, India, 1976-77, Doshisha U., Kyoto, Japan, 1983, U. South Africa, Pretoria, 1984; vis. lectr. Oxford U., 1986, Chinese U. Hong Kong, 1991. Author: Relativism, Knowledge and Faith, 1960, The Context of Decision, 1961, Systematic Theology: a Historicist Perspective, 1968, God the Problem, 1972, An Essay on Theological Method, 1975, rev. edit., 1979, Nonresistance and Responsibility and other Mennonite Essays, 1979, The Theological Imagination: Constructing the Concept of God, 1981, Theology for a Nuclear Age, 1985. Mem. Am. Acad. Religion (pres. 1981-82), Am. Theol. Soc. (pres. 1979-80). Democrat. Home: 6 Longfellow Rd Cambridge MA 02138 Office: 45 Francis Ave Cambridge MA 02138

KAUFMAN, LESTER ROBERT, social services administrator; b. Bronx, N.Y., Feb. 3, 1946; m. Susan Debora Katz, July 3, 1966; children: Michael H., Shani Lynn. BA in Sociology, Yeshiva Coll., 1967, MSW, 1969. Caseworker Jewish Community Services of L.I., Rego Park, N.Y., 1969-71; dir. profl. services Ohel Childrens Home and Family Services, Bklyn., 1971-74, exec. dir., 1974—; bd. dirs. N.Y. State Coun. of Voluntary Family and Child Care Agys., Interagy. Coun. of Mental Retardation Agys. of N.Y.C., treas.; chmn. bd. dirs. Herbert G. Birsch Sch. for Spl. Children; past. chmn. bd. Health Systems Agy. of N.Y.C. Dist. I. Nat. Inst. Mental Health fellow, 1966. Mem. Acad. Cert. Social Workers, Nat. Assn. Social Workers, Assn. Human Svcs., Conf. Jewish Communal Svcs., Assn. of Orthodox Jewish Scientists of Am. (past. pres., past chmn. bd.). Democrat. Office: Ohel Children's Home & Family Svcs 4423 16th Ave Brooklyn NY 11204

KAUFMAN, WILLIAM ELLIOT, rabbi; b. Phila., Dec. 28, 1938; s. Harry and Elizabeth (Sladovsky) K.; m. Nathalie L. Kaufman, June 20, 1965; children: Ari, Beth. BA, U. Pa., 1959; MHL, Jewish Theol. Sem., 1964, DD, 1991; PhD, Boston U., 1971. Ordained rabbi, 1964. Asst. rabbi Congregation Kehillath Israel, Brookline, Mass., 1964-67; rabbi Congregation B'nai Israel, Woonsocket, R.I., 1967-80, Congregation Agudas Achim, San Antonio, 1980-82, Temple Beth El, Fall River, Mass., 1982—; adj. prof. R.I. Coll., Providence, 1984, 91—; sec. R.I. Bd. Rabbis, Providence, 1970-72. Author: Contemporary Jewish Philosophies, 1976, Journeys, 1980, The Case For God, 1991; contbr. numerous articles to profl. jours. Bd. dirs. No. R.I. Mental Health Clinic, Woonsocket, Inter-Faith Counseling Ctr., Greater Fall River. Mem. Am. Acad. Religion, Am. Philos. Assn., Assn. for Jewish Studies, Woonsocket Clergy Assn. (v.p. 1974-80), Greater Fall River Inter-Faith Coun. Home: 404 Langley St Fall River MA 02720 Office: Temple Beth El 385 High St Fall River MA 02720

KAULUMA, JAMES HUMAPANDA, bishop. Bishop of Namibia, Anglican Communion, Windhoek. Office: Coun Chs, 8 Mont Blanc St, POB 41, Windhoek 9000, Namibia*

KAUNITZ, RITA DAVIDSON, religious organization official; b. N.Y.C., Apr. 18, 1922; d. David and Bessie (Golden) Davidson; B.A. magna cum laude, N.Y. U., 1942; M.A., Columbia U., 1946; Ph.D., Radcliffe Coll., 1951; m. Paul E. Kaunitz, Aug. 10, 1947; children—Victoria Moss, Jonathan Davidson, Andrew Moss. Adminstrv. asst. OPA, Washington, 1943-44; columnist planning and housing Progressive Architecture mag., N.Y.C., 1944-46; editor Plan for Rezoning, 1st year's studies, N.Y.C., 1948-49; asso. editor bull. housing and town and country planning UN Secretariat, 1950-52; cons. Center Housing, Bldg. and Planning, UN Secretariat, 1960-66; research asso. grad. program in city planning Yale U., 1955-57; policy and program specialist Model Cities Program, Bridgeport, Conn., 1969; project dir. Conn. Issues and Answers, Regional Plan Assn., N.Y.C., 1976-78; sci. adv. L.I. Sound Regional Study, New Eng. River Basin Commn., New Haven, 1972-75; asst. to dir. N.Y. chpt. Am. Jewish Com., N.Y.C., 1980-85; adv. bd. adminstrv. council Jacob Blaustein Inst. for Advancement Human Rights, Am. Jewish Com., 1980-85; vis. lectr. U. R.I., 1967-69; cons. in field, condr. seminars, planning cons., 1965—. Mem. Conn. Clean Air Commn., 1969-71; chmn. reorgn. task force Conn. Public Utilities Control Authority, 1976-77; chmn. com. housing and urban affairs Nat. Council of Women, N.Y.C., 1968-70; active Commn. Soc. Action (cons. South Africa, 1985—), bd. dirs. Woman's Place, Darien, 1976-80. Recipient service citation Fulbright-Hayes Fellowships, 1975. Mem. Am. Soc. Planning Ofcls. (dir. 1973-76), Union Am. Hebrew Congregations. Democrat. Club: Lower Fairfield County Radcliffe. Author articles. Address: 9 Marine Ave Westport CT 06880

KAVANAGH, AIDAN JOSEPH, priest, university educator; b. Mexia, Tex., Apr. 20, 1929; s. Joseph Gerard and Guarrel Dee (Mullens) K. A.B., St. Meinrad Sem., Ind., 1956; S.T.L., U. Ottawa, Ont., Can., 1958; S.T.D., Theologische Fakultat, Trier, Fed. Republic Germany, 1963; M.A. (hon.), Yale U., 1974. Ordained priest Roman Cath. Ch., 1957. Asst. prof. St. Meinrad Sem., 1962-66; assoc. prof. U. Notre Dame, Ind., 1966-1971, prof., 1971-74; prof. Yale U. Div. Sch., New Haven, Conn., 1974—, acting dean, 1989-90; founding mem. N.Am. Acad. Liturgy, 1975; lectr. schs. and colls. Author: The Shape of Baptism, 1978; Elements of Rite, 1982; On Liturgical Theology, 1984; Confirmation: Origins and Reform, 1988, also articles. Assoc. editor Worship, 1968-87. Fellow Woodrow Wilson Internat. Ctr. Scholars, 1981. Mem. Liturgical Conf. (dir. 1964-68), N.Am. Acad. Liturgy, Societas Liturgica. Club: Mory's. Office: Yale Div Sch 409 Prospect St New Haven CT 06510

KAVANAGH, DECLAN MARY, religious music company executive, media consultant; b. Hollywood, Calif., Oct. 29, 1956; s. Joseph and Anne (Dowdall) K.; m. Mara Sue Rosenberg, July 24, 1982; children: André Megan, Craig Joseph, Mathew J. BA in Acctg., San Francisco State U., 1979; MBA, JD, U. So. Calif., 1983. CPA, Calif. Asst. contr. Universal

Studios, L.A., 1977-79; contr. Motion Pictures, Inc., L.A., 1979-81; v.p. Video Assocs., L.A., 1981-83, Media Home Entertainment, L.A., 1983-84, Active Home Video, L.A., 1984-85, Vanguard Home Video, Tulsa, 1985-87; pres. Legacy Entertainment, Beverly Hills, Calif., 1987—; chmn., chief exec. officer Bread'n Honey Music Ministry, Van Nuys, Calif., 1991—; media cons. Scott Newman Found., L.A., 1987—, Partnership for a Drug Free Am., 1987—, Just Say Know, Internat., Walnut Creek, Calif., 1991. Co-producer: (TV program) Drug Free Kids, 1990; (home video) Jane Fonda Workout, 1982, The Bruce Jennen Workout, 1984. Group leader St. Elisabeth's Youth Group, Van Nuys, 1973—. Mem. Nat. Assn. Record Mchts., Christian Booksellers Assn., Motion Picture and TV Contrs. Assn., Video Software Dealers Asn., San Francisco State U. Alumni Assn. Republican. Roman Catholic. Office: Bread'n Honey Music PO Box 3391 Ventura CA 93003

KAVANAUGH, PATRICK T., religious association executive; b. Nashville, Oct. 20, 1954; s. Edward Joseph and Anne (Nichols) K.; m. Barbara Lee Beeler, Aug. 23, 1975; children: Christopher Beeler, John Patrick, Peter Andrew, David Edward. MusB, Cath. U., 1976; MusM, U. Md., 1978, D of Mus. Arts, 1980. Dir. music Fairfax (Va.) Christian Sch., 1980-82; minister of music Christian Assembly Ctr., Vienna, Va., 1982-87; exec. dir. Christian Performing Artists' Fellowship, Vienna, 1985—. Author: The Spiritual Lives of the Great Composers, 1992; composer songs, symphonic music, chamber and choral music, opera, ballet music; classical guitarist. Condr. Asaph Ensemble. Home: 106 Battle St SW Vienna VA 22180 Office: Christian Performing Artists Fellowship 10523 Main St Ste 31 Fairfax VA 22030 *My greatest responsibility and most sublime challenge is to each day bring everyone with whom I have contact—including myself—closer to Christ.*

KAY, JAMES FRANKLIN, religion educator; b. Kansas City, Mo., May 18, 1948; s. Bob Burton and Mary Lenore (Branstetter) K. BA, Pasadena (Calif.) Coll., 1969; MDiv, Harvard U., 1972; MPhil, Union Seminary, N.Y.C., 1984, PhD, 1991. Pastor No. Lakes Parish, Beltrami County, Minn., 1974-78; campus minister United Ministries, Bemidji, Minn., 1977-79; cons. PHEWA, N.Y.C., 1980-82; instr. Princeton (N.J.) Theol. Seminary, 1988-91, asst. prof., 1991—. Book rev. editor The Princeton Sem. Bull., 1991—; contbr. articles to profl. jours. Vice-pres. Bemidji Home Loan Improvement, 1978. Mem. Am. Acad. Religion, Acad. Homiletics, Karl Barth Soc. of N.A., Phi Delta Lambda. Office: Princeton Theol Seminary CN 821 Princeton NJ 08542

KAY, JUDITH WEBB, ethics educator; b. Cedar Rapids, Iowa, Dec. 19, 1951; d. James Maddux and Martha Louise (Lindsay) Webb; m. Joshua M. Kay, Aug. 27, 1972; 1 child, Jeremy N. BA, Oberlin Coll., 1973; MA, Pacific Sch. Religion, 1978; PhD, Grad. Theol. Union, 1988. Instr. Chapman Coll., Vallejo, Calif., 1979, Am. Coll. Traditional Chinese Medicine, San Francisco, 1981-88, San Francisco Theol. Sem., San Anselmo, Calif., 1987, Starr King Sch. for Ministry, Berkeley, Calif., 1987; asst. prof. ethics Wake Forest U., Winston-Salem, N.C., 1988—; rsch. cons. Ctr. for Ethics and Social Policy, Berkeley, 1975-78, 85-86; mem. ethics com. Bowman Gray Sch. Medicine, Winston-Salem, 1988, rsch. humanist, 1989-91. Author book revs. Pacific Theol. Rev., 1985. community mem. com. for protection human subjects U. Calif., Berkeley, 1985-88; mem. Speaker's Bur. N.C. Humanities Coun., Winston-Salem, 1990—; bd. dirs. Calif. Food Policy Project, Berkeley, 1980-82. Fellow Roothbert Fund, 1987. Mem. Nat. Assn. Bapt. Profs. Religion, Am. Acad. Religion, Soc. Christian Ethics, Ctr. for Women and Religion (bd. dirs. 1986). Office: Wake Forest Univ PO Box 7212 Winston-Salem NC 27109

KAYE, STEVEN E., rabbi, educator; b. Queens, N.Y., Feb. 23, 1956; s. Philip R. Kaye and Leona H.; 1 child, Sam. BA, SUNY, Albany, 1978; MSW, Wurzweiter Sch. Social Work, N.Y., 1982; MA in Hebrew Lit., Reconstructionist Rabbinical Coll., 1983. Ordained rabbi, 1983. Rabbi Colo. Jewish Reconstructionist, Denver, 1983—; host/moderator House of the Lord KMGH-TV, Denver, 1985—; instr. Metropolitan State Coll., Denver, 1987—; chaplain Greenwood Village (Colo.) Police Dept., 1990—; free-lance lectr. Bio-Medical Ethics, Denver, 1983—. Editor Jewish Bio-Medical Ethics, 1982. Pres. Rocky Mountain Rabbinical Coun. 1988-90; active Exec. Com. Allied Jewish Fedn., 1988-90, Clergy Task Force Mt. Airy Hosp., 1988—, Human Subjects Com. U. Scis. Ctr., 1989—. Avocations: Golfing, skiing. Office: Colo Jewish Reconstructionist Fdn 644 E Ohio Ave Denver CO 80224

KAYLOR, ROBERT DAVID, religion educator; b. New Market, Ala., Oct. 1, 1933; s. Lemuel Jefferson and Johnnie (Hanson) K.; m. Dorothy Henning, Dec. 28, 1956; children: Marilyn Lee, Cathryn Ann, David William, Charles Henning, Marion Hanson. Student, So. Ill. U., 1951-53; AB, Southwestern U., Memphis, 1955; BD, Louisville Presbyn. Sem., 1958; PhD, Duke U., 1964. Ordained to ministry Presbyn. Ch. Pastor Montevallo (Ala.) Presbyn. Ch., 1958-61; asst. prof. Davison (N.C.) Coll., 1964-68, assoc. prof., 1968-80, prof., 1980—. Author: God Far, God Near, 1980, Paul's Covenant Community, 1988. Bd. dirs. Davidson chpt. Habitat for Humanity, 1987—. Recipient Thomas Jefferson award Davidson Coll., 1987; James B. Duke fellow Duke U., 1962, Am. Inst. Indian Studies fellow, 1977, Ecumenical Inst. fellow, 1984. Mem. Am. Acad. Religion, Soc. Bibl. Lit. Democrat. Home: 740 Virginia Rd Davidson NC 28036 Office: Davidson Coll Davidson NC 28036

KAZAN, FREDRIC, rabbi, educator; b. Phila., Oct. 30, 1933; s. George and Betty (Richter) K.; m. Marian Rena Axelrod, Mar. 1, 1955; children: Liebe E. Kazan Gelman, Rachel, Adam, Faith, Linda. BA in Philosophy with honors, Temple U., 1954; B of Hebrew Lit., Gratz Coll., 1955; cert., Hebrew U., Jerusalem, 1955; postgrad., White Inst., 1956-59; M of Hebrew Lit., Jewish Theol. Sem., 1959; postgrad., UCLA, 1960-63, Dropsie Coll., 1964-67. Ordained rabbi, 1959. Rabbi Temple Ner Tamid, Los Angeles, 1959-63, Melrose B'nai Israel, Cheltenham, Pa., 1963-68; dir. adult edn. Gratz Coll., Phila., 1968-69; dean Recon Rabbinical Coll., Phila., 1969-77; planning exec. Fedn. Jewish Agys., Phila., 1977-82; rabbi Adath Israel, Merion, Pa., 1982—; instr. U. Judaism, Los Angeles, 1960-63, Gratz Coll., Phila., 1964-68; cons. Nat. Jewish Study, N.Y.C., 1975-77. Contbr. articles to profl. jours.; TV moderator in Calif., Phila. Chaplain bicentennial prayer City Council of Phila.; Ner Tamid advisor Boy Scouts Am., 1968. Recipient Jerusalem award Israel Bonds, 1967, City of Phila. award, 1974, Merit award Israel Bonds, 1980. Mem. Rabbinical Assembly Phila. (v.p. 1988—, nat. exec. council), Bd. Rabbis (exec. bd. 1980—, radio and TV chmn. 1980—). Republican. Club: Golden Slipper (Phila.) (chaplain 1971—). Home: 429 N Highland Ave Merion Station PA 19066 Office: Adath Israel Old Lancaster Rd Merion PA 19066

KAZEMZADEH, FIRUZ, history educator; b. Moscow, Oct. 27, 1924; came to U.S., 1944, naturalized, 1955; s. Kazem and Talieh (Yevseyev) K.; children: Tatiana, Allegra, Monireh. B.A., Stanford U., 1946, M.A., 1947; Ph.D., Harvard U., 1951. Research fellow Hoover Inst., Stanford, Calif., 1949-50; cons. publs. State Dept., 1951-52; head Soviet affairs unit, information dept. Radio Free Europe, 1952-54; research fellow Russian Research Center, Center Middle Eastern Studies, Harvard U., 1954-56, instr. history and lit., 1955-56; mem. faculty Yale U., 1956—, prof. history, 1967—, chmn. council Russian and East European studies, 1968-69, chmn. com. Middle Eastern studies, 1979-84, dir. grad. studies in history, 1975-76, dir. grad. studies in the Soviet Union and East Europe study program, 1987-89; master Davenport Coll., 1976-81. Editor: World Order, Baha'i Mag, 1966—; Author: The Struggle for Transcaucasia, 1917-1921, 1952, Russia and Britain in Persia, 1864-1914; A Study in Imperialism, 1968. Morse fellow, 1958-59; Ford fellow internat. studies, 1966. Mem. Baha'i Faith and Nat. Spiritual Assembly Baha'is of U.S. Office: Yale U Dept History New Haven CT 06520

KAZMAREK, LINDA ADAMS, secondary education educator; b. Crisfield, Md., Jan. 18, 1945; d. Gordon I. Sr. and Annie Ruby (Sommers) Adams; m. Stephen Kazmarek, Jr., Aug. 2, 1981. B of Music Edn., Peabody Conservatory of Music, 1967; postgrad., Morgan U., Towson U. Cert. advanced profl. tchr., K-12, Md. Organist, choir dir. Halethorpe United Meth. Ch., Balt., Olive Branch United Meth. Ch., 1973-77; min. music Halethorpe United Meth. Ch., Balt., 1978—; piano tchr. Modal Cities Program, Balt., Balt. Community Schs; tchr. vocal music Balt. City Schs., 1967—; pvt. tchr. piano and organ. Composer: A Family of Care (award). Concert performer for Meth. Bd. Child Care, 1989, Balt. Southwest Emergency Svcs., 1991; guest performer Balt. City Tchrs. Appreciation Banquet, 1991. Recipient vol. award for music enrichment summer program, 1973, award for voluntarism Fund. for Ednl. Excellence, 1985; Fund for Ednl. Excellence grantee, 1988. Mem. NAFE, NEA, Md. State Tchrs. Assn., Balt. City Tchrs. Assn., Md. Music Educators Assn., Music Educators Nat. Conf., Md. State Music Tchrs. Assn., Nat Music Tchrs. Assn., Peabody Alumni Assn.

KEA, PERRY VERNON, biblical studies educator; b. Florence, S.C., Aug. 24, 1953; s. James Harvey and Barbara Ann (Hatchel) K.; m. Jana Ellen Lane, June 6, 1987. BA, U. S.C., 1975; MA, Vanderbilt U., 1977; PhD, U. Va., 1983. Assoc. prof. U. Indpls., 1983—. Contbr. articles to profl. publs. NEH summer seminar fellow, 1984. Mem. Westar Inst. (regent), Soc. Bibilcal Lit., Am. Acad. Religion, AAUP. Office: U Indpls 1400 E Hanna Ave Indianapolis IN 46227

KEAR, MICHAEL R., minister; b. Clayton, N.Mex., July 12, 1960; s. James Kenneth and Patricia Kay (LeCrone) K.; m. Latrecia Jean Bowers, Aug. 24, 1978; children: Michael II, Miles. Assoc. of Bible, Christian Bible Sem., 1986. Ordained to ministry Bapt. Ch. Assoc. pastor Ch. of Abundant Life, Colorado Springs, Colo., 1983-85, Faith Fellowship Free Will Bapt. Ch., Roswell, N.Mex., 1987-89; founding pastor Friendship Bapt. Ch. Inc., Ponca City, Okla., 1989—; pres. Blessed Hope Evangelistic Fellowship, Ponca City, Okla., 1990—. Author: Stories of a Little Boy, 1987; editor Midnight Cry, 1990. Recipient Cert. Merit Maranatha Bapt. Ministries, 1988. Home: PO Box 3 Ponca City OK 74602 Office: Blessed Hope Evang Fellowship PO Box 3 Ponca City OK 74602

KEARBY, PAUL DOYLE, minister; b. Oklahoma City, Nov. 30, 1955; s. John C. and Elaine F. (Pollard) K.; m. Teresa A. Smith, Dec. 31, 1977; children: Laura Beth, Stephen Paul. BS in Bibl. Studies, Okla. Christian Coll., 1979. Assoc. minister Mayfair Ch. of Christ, Oklahoma City, 1978-79; minister Wayne (Okla.) Ch. of Christ, 1979-81, Ch. of Christ, Alva, Okla., 1981-82, Cherry Hill Ch. of Christ, Joliet, Ill., 1982-84; chaplain Joliet Correctional Ctr., 1982-84; minister Ch. of Christ, Valparaiso, Ind., 1984—; chaplain Westville (Ind.) Correctional Inst., 1985-86; missionary work Austria, Hungary and Yugoslavia, 1977-78; tchr., co-dir. Lariet Creek Christian Camp, Okla., 1979-82; tchr, counselor Rockford (Ill.) Christian Camp, 1982—; teaching house parent Shults-Lewis Child and Family Care Agy., Valparaiso, 1984-86. Author: Historical Outlines of Old Testament Characters, 1979, Accepting God's Power, 1981, Detours, Dead Ends and Dry Holes, 1982, Marriage, Divorce and Remarriage, 1985; co-host radio program, 1981-82; featured columnist The Paul's Valley Dem., 1980, The Alva Rev. Courier, 1981-82. Named one of Outstanding Young Men of Am., 1982, 83. Club: Exchange (Joliet). Lodge: Rotary (bd. dirs. Alva club 1982). Avocations: writing, golfing, softball. Home: 397 S 195 E Valparaiso IN 46383 Office: Valparaiso Ch of Christ 1155 Sturdy Rd Valparaiso IN 46383

KEARLEY, F. FURMAN, minister, religion educator, magazine editor; b. Montgomery, Ala., Nov. 7, 1932; s. John Ausban and Zelma Olene (Suggs) K.; m. Helen Joy Bowman, July 18, 1951; children: Janice Gail Kearley Mink, Amelia Lynn Kearley Johnson. BA, Ala. Christian Coll., 1954; MA, Harding U., 1956; MEd, Auburn U., 1960; MRE, ThM, Harding U., 1965; PhD, Hebrew Union Coll.-Jewish Inst. Religion, 1971. Min. of the Gospel. Evangelist Chs. of Christ, various cities, 1951—; chmn., bible dept. Ala. Christian Coll., Montgomery, 1956-64; chmn., humanities div. Lubbock (Tex.) Christian Univ., 1970-75; dir., grad. studies in religion Abilene (Tex.) Christian Univ., 1975-85; sec., treas. S.W. Region Evang. Theol. Soc., 1982-85; adv. bd. Gospel Svcs., Houston, 1985-91; pres.' coun. Lubbock (Tex.) Christian Univ., 1986-91. Author: (book) God's Indwelling Spirit, 1974; editor: (book) Biblical Interpretation, 1986, (religious periodical) Gospel Advocate, 1985—; contbr. over 400 articles to jours. Named Alumnus of Yr. award Harding Univ., Searcy, Ark., 1985, Harding Grad. Sch. of Religion, Memphis, Tenn., 1986. Mem. Soc. Biblical Lit., Evang. Theol. Soc., Nat. Assn. Tchrs. Hebrew, Rotary (Monahan, Tex. dir.). Home: 1406 S James Monahans TX 79756 Office: Editor Gospel Advocate 500 E Third St PO Box 167 Monahans TX 79756

KEARNS, ALBERT OSBORN, minister; b. Shattuck, Okla., Apr. 15, 1920; s. Arthur Alexander and Grace Mae (Booth) K.; m. Maria Metlova, Oct. 18, 1947; 1 child, Alscot. Student, U. Redlands, 1948-52. Ordained to ministry Lighthouse Gospel Fellowship of Mins. and Chs., 1984. Evangelist L.A., 1971-75, Simi Valley, Calif., 1975-84; pastor Somis (Calif.) Christian Ch., 1984-89, Simi Valley, 1989—; advisor, counselor Women's Aglow Fellowship, Thousand Oaks, Calif., 1987—; pub. A.O.K. Books, 1991. Petty officer 2d class USN, 1940-46, PTO. Republican. Home and Office: 1621 Patricia Simi Valley CA 93065

KEARNS, FRANCIS EMNER, bishop; b. Bentleyville, Pa., Dec. 9, 1905; s. George Verlinda and Jennie Mae (McCleary) K.; m. Alice Margaret Thompson, Sept. 1, 1933; children—Rollin Thompson, Margaret (Mrs. Richard E. Baldwin), Francis Emner II. A.B., Ohio Wesleyan U., 1927, D.D., 1954; S.T.B., Boston U. Sch. Theology, 1930; postgrad., U. Berlin, Germany, U. Edinburgh, Scotland, 1930-31; Ph.D., U. Pitts., 1939; LL.D., Mt. Union Coll., 1965; L.H.D., Ohio No. U., 1965; Pd.D., Baldwin-Wallace Coll., 1966. Ordained to ministry Meth. Ch., 1931. Pastor Dravosburg, Pa., 1931-32; asso. pastor Christ Meth. Ch., Pitts., 1932-35, Ben Avon Meth. Ch., 1935-40, Asbury Meth. Ch., Uniontown, Pa., 1940-45, Wauwatosa (Wis.) Meth. Ch., 1945-64; bishop United Meth. Ch., 1964—; mem. gen. bd. evangelism, 1965-68, vice chmn. gen. bd. edn., 1968-72, chmn. div. curriculum resources, 1968-72, mem. program council, 1968-72; mem. Meth. Corp., 1968-72; mem. gen. assembly Nat. Council Chs.; pres. Ohio Council Chs., 1969-71; mem. gen. bd. Global Ministries of United Meth. Ch., 1972-76, vice-chmn. div. health and welfare ministries, 1972-76; mem. gen. bd. Ch. and Soc. of United Meth. Ch., 1972-76; chmn. Meth. Interbd. Com. on Christian Vocations, 1964-68, Faith and Order Commn., Ohio Council Chs., 1965-69; mem. Meth. Interbd. Commn. on Town and Country, 1964-68, North Central Jurisdictional Council, 1972-76; vis. prof. Meth. Theol. Sch., Ohio, 1976-78. Author: The Church is Mine, 1962; Contbr. articles profl. jours. Trustee Baldwin-Wallace Coll., Mt. Union Coll., Ohio No. U., Ohio Wesleyan U., Meth. Theol. Sch. in Ohio, Otterbein Coll., United Theol. Sem. Mem. Phi Beta Kappa. Clubs: Mason (33 deg.), Rotarian. Home: 800 S 15th St 1-629 Sebring OH 44672 *In early life I had an experience of Christ. I have sought to be a faithful servant of his. This has enabled me to set high goals and to give myself wholeheartedly to their realization. The central motivation for my ministry has been love and concern for persons kindled by the love and compassion of Christ.*

KEARNS, JACQUES MERLIN, music minister; b. Mobile, Ala., July 18, 1930; s. Rhett Goode and Susan Elizabeth (Crabtree) K.; m. Jean Hennesy, Aug. 25, 1950; children: Martin Edward, David Alan, Robert Jacques. M Sacred Music, No. Bapt. Theol. Sem., New Orleans, 1956; BMus, U. Ala., Tuscaloosa, 1954. Min. music and youth First Bapt. Ch., Biloxi, Miss., 1956-59, Alta Woods Bapt. Ch., Jackson, Miss., 1959-65; min. music and youth First Bapt. Ch., Augusta, Ga., 1965-84, Sylvania, Ga., 1984—. Composer, arranger Handbells, 1970—; contbr. articles to profl. jours. Mem. Am. Guild English Handbell Ringers Inc. (nat. treas. 1983-87, pres.-elect 1991—), Rotary. Home: 2448 Apricot Ln Augusta GA 30904 Office: First Bapt Ch PO Box 149 Sylvania GA 30467 *Music is the balm that calms the troubled heart, stimulus which challenges the reticent to action and avenue which provides the easiest access to Almighty God, for Whose praise music is made and Whose Author it is.*

KEATHLEY, NAYMOND HASKINS, clergyman, educator; b. Memphis, Sept. 25, 1940; s. Maurice Franklin and Rubye Geneva (Haskins) K.; m. Carolyn Jeannine Griffin, Aug. 4, 1962; children: Kevin, Craig, Kristen. BA cum laude, Baylor U., 1962; BD, So. Bapt. Sem., 1966, PhD, 1971. Ordained to ministry Bapt. Ch., 1966. Asst. prof. religion Palm Beach Atlantic Coll., West Palm Beach, Fla., 1972-76; asst. prof. N.T. Golden Gate Bapt. Sem., Mill Valley, Calif., 1977-79, assoc. prof. N.T., 1979-81; assoc. prof. religion Baylor U., Waco, Tex., 1981-89, prof. religion, 1989—. Author: Discovering Romans, 1985; editor: With Steadfast Purpose, 1990; contbr. articles to religious publs. Mem. AAUP, Soc. Bibl. Lit., Nat. Assn. Bapt. Profs. of Religion (nominating com. 1983), Alpha Chi. Democrat. Baptist. Avocation: skiing. Home: 310 Trailwood Dr Waco TX 76712 Office: Baylor U PO Box 97294 Waco TX 76798-7294

KEATING, JOHN RICHARD, bishop; b. July 20, 1934; s. Robert James and Gertrude Helen (Degen) K. BA, St. Mary of the Lake Sem., 1955; STL, Gregorian U., Rome, 1959; JCD, Gregorian U., 1963. Ordained priest Roman Catholic Ch., 1958, consecrated bishop, 1983. Asst. chancellor Archdiocese of Chgo., 1963-70, co-chancellor, 1970-83, mem. clergy personnel bd., 1971-83, bd. consultors, 1975-83; judge Chgo. Met. Tribunal, 1968-83; bishop of Arlington Va., 1983—; cons. canon law com. Nat. Conf. Cath. Bishops, from 1969; mem. Chgo. Presbyteral Senate, 1972-83; mem. com. human subjects ADA, 1976—. Author: The Bearing of Mental Impairment on the Validity of Marriage, 1964, 2d edit., 1973; also articles. Mem. Am. Canon Law Soc., Can. Canon Law Soc. Office: 4600 N Carlin Springs Rd Arlington VA 22203

KEATON, THEODORE, academic administrator. Pres. Am. Bapt. Sem. of the West, Berkeley, Calif. Office: Am Bapt Sem Office of Pres 2606 Dwight Way Berkeley CA 94704*

KECK, DAVID RHODES, minister; b. Sterling, Ill., Nov. 24, 1938; s. Albert H. Jr. and Virginia Elizabeth (Rhodes) K.; m. Rachel Diana Rudisill, June 10, 1961; children: David R. Jr., Charlotte Elizabeth, Frances Diana. BA, Lenoir-Rhyne Coll., 1960; BD, Luth. Theol. So. Sem., Columbia, S.C., 1964. Ordained minister in Luth. Ch. Intern. St. Luke Luth. Ch., Charlotte, N.C., 1962-63; pastor Luth. Ch. of Our Father, Greensboro, N.C., 1964-67; pastor, campus pastor Grace Luth. Ch., Boone, N.C., 1967-76; pastor Kimball Meml. Luth. Ch., Kannapolis, N.C., 1976—; bd. dirs. N.C. Synod Coun. Evang. Luth. Ch. in Am., Salisbury, 1988—, del. from N.C., Columbus, Ohio, 1987, Chgo., 1989; bd. dirs. N.C. Synod Exec. Com. Luth. Ch. in Am., Salisbury, 1983-88, del. from N.C., Toronto, Can., 1984, Columbus, 1987, sec. so. dist. N.C. Synod, Salisbury, 1982-86, dean so. dist. N.C. Synod, Salisbury, 1986-88, com. mem. N.C. Synod Parish Edn. Com., Salisbury, 1966-67. Bd. dirs. Cabarrus County chpt. ARC, Concord, N.C., 1988-90. Mem. Rotary (treas. Kannapolis club 1988-89, v.p. 1989-90, pres. 1990-91, Paul Harris fellow 1991). Home: 909 Nance St Kannapolis NC 28083 Office: Kimball Meml Luth Ch 101 Vance St Kannapolis NC 28081

KECK, DURWIN JULIUS, minister; b. Alexandria, Va., Aug. 3, 1953; s. Alton Monroe and Beatrice Lucille (Marlette) K.; m. Beverlee Gail Buller, May 28, 1983; 1 child, Molly Christina. BA, Calif. State U., Bakersfield, 1976; MDiv summa cum laude, Biola U., 1989. Lic. to ministry Bapt. Gen. Conf., 1989. Mem. staff San Diego State U. Campus Crusade for Christ, 1976-80, dir. Sacramento State U. campus, 1980-83; area adminstr. Campus Crusade for Christ, Walnut Creek, Calif., 1983-85; campus rep. Student Ministries, Inc., Long Beach, Calif., 1985-87; minister, singles and evangelism 1st Bapt. Ch. of Lakewood, Long Beach, 1987—. Mem. Kappa Tau Epsilon. Home: 18003 Ibex Ave Artesia CA 90701 Office: 1st Bapt Ch Lakewood 5336 Arbor Rd Long Beach CA 90808

KECK, LEANDER EARL, theology educator; b. Washburn, N.D., Mar. 3, 1928; s. Jacob and Elizabeth (Klein) K.; m. Janice Osburn, Sept. 7, 1956; children: Stephen Lee, David Alderson. BA, Linfield Coll., McMinnville, Oreg., 1949, DLitt (hon.), 1980; BD, Andover Newton (Mass.) Theol. Sch., 1953; PhD, Yale U., 1957; STD (hon.), Bethany Coll., 1975; DHL (hon.), Atlantic Christian Coll., 1980; DD (hon.), Tex. Christian U., 1980; LLD (hon.), Davison Coll., 1987. Ordained to ministry Christian Ch. (Disciples of Christ), 1952. Instr. Wellesley Coll., 1957-59; from asst. prof. to prof. N.T. Vanderbilt U. Div. Sch., Nashville, 1959-72; prof. N.T. Candler Sch. Theology Emory U., Atlanta, 1972-79; Winkley prof. Bibl. theology Yale U. Div. Sch., New Haven, 1979—, dean, 1979-89. Author: Taking The Bible Seriously, 1962, Mandate to Witness, 1964, Future For the Historical Jesus, 1975, The Bible in the Pulpit, 1978, Paul and His Letters, 1979, rev. edit., 1988; co-author: Interpreting the Pauline Letters, 1984; translator, editor D.F. Strauss, The Christ of Faith and the Jesus of History, 1977; editor numerous books; editorial coun. Interpretation, 1976-82; mem. editorial bd. Quar. Rev., 1980-88; convenor editorial bd. New Interpreter's Bible, 1990—; contbr. articles, essays to profl. publs. Rsch. fellow Assn. Theol. Schs., 1964-65, 76. Mem. Soc. Bibl. Lit. (editor monograph series 1972-78), Assn. Theol. Schs. (exec. com. 1980-86), Studiorum Novi Testamenti Societas. Democrat. Office: 409 Prospect St New Haven CT 06510

KECKLEY, E. WELDON, minister; b. Licking County, Ohio, Jan. 8, 1921; s. Arthur Carl and Mae Deborah (Hoover) K.; m. Betty Marion McIntyre, Aug. 27, 1944; 1 child, Thomas Weldon. AB, Bethany Coll., W. Va., 1943; MDiv, Yale U., 1946; MA, Washington U., St. Louis, 1951; DDiv, Piedmont Coll., $, 1977. Ordained to ministry, 1942. Min. edn. Union Ave. Christian Ch., St. Louis, 1946-49, Country Club Christian Ch., Kansas City, Mo., 1949-53; sr. min. 1st Community Ch., Joplin, Mo., 1953-60, Bethany Union Ch., Chgo., 1960-85; mem. adj. faculty Bethany Theol. Sem., Oak Brook, Ill.; co-founder, dir. Beverly Hills/Morgan Park Protestant Cluster, Chgo; observer, mem. exec. com., del. Consultation Ch. Union; rep. Nat. Coun. Community Chs. to Vatican Ecumenical Coun. II, Rome, 1963; pres. Nat. Coun. Community Chs., 1962-64. Author: The Church School Superintendent, 1961. Mem. Inst. Humane Studies (Midwest dir. 1985-87), Phi Delta Kappa, Kappa Delta Pi. Home: PO Box 1822 Tabor Woods Joplin MO 64802

KEE, BERTHINIA, minister; b. Suffolk, Va., June 9, 1940; d. Clarence and Berneathia (Thompson) H.; m. Frank Kee, Nov. 2, 1958; children: Frank Jr., Anita Marie, George Eric, Randy Antonio, Sybrella Nanette, James Randolph, Collette Verita. Student, Mattatuck Coll., 1979, Hartford Sem., 1985. Ordained to ministry Penecostal Ch., 1981. Deaconess True Holiness Ch., Waterbury, Conn., 1979-80, asst. pastor, 1980-82; founder, pastor Macadonia Ch., Waterbury, 1982—; jr. choir dir., Sunday sch. and Bible tchr. Mt. Olive Ch., Waterbury, 1965-79. Bd. dirs. Prison Fellowship, Peace Dale, R.I., 1990. Mem. Charismatic Bible Ministries. Office: Macadonia Ch 769 N Main St Waterbury CT 06704 *Life itself is aimless without a goal, and that goal is not obtainable if we do not work toward it. But we must look to the Lord for guidance in this direction.*

KEE, HOWARD CLARK, religion educator; b. Beverly, N.J., July 28, 1920; s. Walter Leslie and Regina (Corcoran) K.; m. Janet Burrell, Dec. 15, 1951; children: Howard Clark III, Christopher Andrew, Sarah Leslie. A.B., Bryan (Tenn.) Coll., 1940; Th.M., Dallas Theol. Sem., 1944; postgrad., Am. Sch. Oriental Research, Jerusalem, 1949-50; Ph.D. (Two Bros. fellow), Yale, 1951. Instr. religion and classics U. Pa., 1951-53; from asst. prof. to prof. N.T. Drew U., 1953-68; Rufus Jones prof. history of religion, chmn. dept. history of religion Bryn Mawr (Pa.) Coll., 1968-77; William Goodwin Aurelio prof. Biblical studies Boston U., 1977-89, chmn. grad. div. religious studies, 1977-86; sr. rsch. fellow U. Pa., 1987—; vis. prof. religion Princeton U., 1954-55, Brown U., 1985; mem. archaeol. teams at Roman Jericho, 1950, Shechem, 1957, Mt. Gerizim, 1966, Pella, Jordan, 1967, Ashdod, Israel, 1968; chmn. Coun. on Grad. Studies in Religion; cons. for transls. Am. Bible Soc., 1989—. Author: Understanding the New Testament, 4th edit., 1983, Making Ethical Decisions, 1958, The Renewal of Hope, 1959, Jesus and God's New People, 1959, Jesus in History, 1970, 2d edit., 1977, The Origins of Christianity: Sources and Documents, 1973, The Community of the New Age, 1977, Christianity: An Historical Approach, 1979, Christian Origins in Sociological Perspective, 1980, Miracle in the Early Christian World, 1983, The New Testament in Context: Sources and Documents, 1984, Medicine, Miracle and Magic in New Testament Times, 1986, Knowing the Truth: A Sociological Approach to New Testament Interpretation, 1989, What Can We Know About Jesus?, 1990, Good News to the Ends of the Earth: The Theology of Acts, 1990, Christianity: A Social and Cultural History, 1991; editor: Biblical Perspectives on Current Issues, 1976-83, Understanding Jesus Today, 1985—; librettist: New Land, New Covenant (Howard Hanson), 1976; contbr.: Interpreter's Dictionary of the Bible, 1962, supplement, 1976, Harper's Bible Dictionary, Dictionary of Bible and Religion, The Books of the Bible. Bd. mgrs. Am. Bible Soc., 1956-89, chmn. transls. com., 1985-89; chmn. transls. com. United Bible Socs., 1985—; bd. dirs. Mohawk Trail Concerts, Inc., Charlemont, Mass.; mem. adv. bd. Yale U. Inst. Sacred Music. Am. Assn. Theol. Schs. fellow Germany, 1960; Guggenheim fellow Israel, 1966-67; Nat. Endowment Humanities grantee Eng., 1984. Mem. Soc. Values in Higher Edn., Columbia U. Seminar in N.T., Am. Acad. Religion, Soc. Bibl. Lit., Bibl. Theologians, Studiorum Novi Testamenti

Societas, New Haven Theol. Discussion Group, Assn. for Sociology of Religion. Presbyterian. Home: 220 W Rittenhouse Sq Philadelphia PA 19103 *Life is a gift from the Creator. It is mediated to us through parents, family, friends, teachers. It is conveyed through love and learning, through challenge and conflict, through accomplishment and disappointment. The gift must be shared, not jealously guarded or proudly prized. By sharing life, we can approach others with candor and honesty, with joy and sympathy, with wonder and understanding. The shared gift brings gratitude and fulfillment.*

KEEFE, DONALD JOSEPH, religion education, theological consultant; b. Hamilton, N.Y., July 14, 1924; s. Donald John and Frances Katherine (Balmes) K. BA, Colgate U., 1949; JD, Georgetown U., 1951; PhL, Fordham U., 1958; STL, Woodstock Coll., 1963; STD, Gregorian U., Rome, 1967. Bar: D.C., N.Y., U.S. Supreme Ct.; ordained priest Roman Cath. Ch. Asst. prof. Canisius Coll., Buffalo, 1966-70; asst. prof. St. Louis U. Div. Sch., 1970-73, assoc. prof., 1973-76, prof., 1976-78; prof. theology Marquette U., Milw., 1978-91; theol. cons. Archdiocese of Denver, 1991—. Author: Thomism and the Theological Ontology of Paul Tillich, 1971, Covenantal Theology: The Eucharistic Ordering of History, 2 vols., 1991. Lt. USNR, 1942-46, 51-54. Mem. Fellowship of Cath. Scholars, Cath. Bibl. Assn., Cath. Mariological Soc., Nat. Assn. Scholars.

KEEFE, JEFFREY FRANCIS, priest, psychologist; b. Syracuse, N.Y., June 11, 1926; s. Francis M. and Mary M. (Kulas) K. BA, St. Anthony on Hudson, 1948; STL, then MA in Edn., Cath. U., 1952, 55; MA in Psychology, Fordham U., 1961, PhD in Clin. Psychology, 1965. Ordained priest Roman Cath. Ch., 1952; lic. psychologist, N.Y. Tchr. Trenton (N.J.) Cath. Boys High Sch., 1952-56, St. Francis Sem., Staten Island, N.Y., 1956-58; staff mem. Staten Island Mental Health, 1965-70, St. Vincent Outpatient Svc., Staten Island, 1965-70; assoc. prof. Notre Dame U., South Bend, Ind., 1966-71; staff mem. Onondaga Pastoral Counseling Ctr., Syracuse, N.Y., 1975-84; cons. marriage tribunal Diocese of Syracuse, 1975-84; dir. Personal Resource Ctr., Syracuse, 1989—; cons. on candidate selection Diocese of Syracuse, other religious orders, 1970—; cons., pastoral adv. bd. Hutchings Psychiat. Hosp., Syracuse, 1979—. Mem. Am. Psychol. Assn., Psychologists Interested in Religious Issues. Avocations: travel, photography. Home: 812 N Salina St Syracuse NY 13208 Office: Personal Resource Ctr 257 E Onondaga St Syracuse NY 13202

KEEFER, ROBERT ALAN, minister; b. Harrisburg, Pa., Nov. 10, 1956; s. Paul Daniel and Anna Mae (Mullen) K. AB, Dartmouth Coll., 1979; MDiv, Princeton (N.J.) Theol. Sem., 1982. Ordained to ministry Presbyn. Ch., 1982. Dir. admissions Princeton Theol. Sem., 1982-84; pastor Divine Grace Presbyn. Ch., Miami, Ariz., 1984—, Presbyn. Ch. of Superior, Ariz., 1989—; stated clk. Presbytery de Cristo, Tucson, 1987—. Sec. The Caring Pl., Inc., Globe, Ariz., 1989—, pres., 1985-89. Recipient Globe-Miami award Salvation Army, 1989. Mem. Nat. Assn. R.R. Passengers, Soc. for Creative Anachronism, Am. Mensa, Gila County Ministerial Assn. (officer Globe chpt. 1984—), Rotary (pres. Miami chpt. 1984—). Democrat. Office: Divine Grace Presbyn Ch 305 Live Oak St Miami AZ 85539

KEEFER, YVONNE JUNE KELSOE, religious organization administrator; b. Gotebo, Okla., Oct. 2, 1935; d. Carl Clifford and Zelma Phoebe (Bond) Kelsoe; m. James Albert Keefer, June 8, 1956; children: Steven Dale, Brian Lee. BS in Home Econs., Okla. State U., 1966. Ednl. dir. 1st So. Bapt. Ch., Lawrence, Kans., 1969-70; dir. campus ministries U. Kans., Lawrence, 1969-82; exec. dir. Woman's Missionary Union, Family Ministry, Partnership Missions Kans. Nebr. Conv. So. Bapts., Topeka, Kans., 1983—; chmn. 1990-91 dated plan Woman's Missionary Union So. Bapt. Conv., Birmingham, Ala., 1987-88. Assoc. editor The Campus Minister, 1980-82. Chaplain Lawrence Police Dept., 1976-83; mem. Friends of Art, Lawrence; exec. bd. Kaw Valley Assn., Topeka, 1970-82; bd. dirs. Wellspring Found., Prairie Village, Kans., 1984—, Douglas County Mental Health Assn., Lawrence, 1979-82. Mem. Assn. So. Bapt. Campus Ministers (nat. v.p. 1982-83), Exec. Dirs. Woman's Missionary Union, Phi Kappa Phi, Omnicron Nu, Phi Upsilon Omnicorn, Pi Zeta Kappa (Outstanding Mem. award, nat. v.p.). Republican. Club: PEO (Lawrence) (pres. 1981-82). Avocation: travel. Home: 4011 W 13th Lawrence KS 66049 Office: Kans Nebr Conv So Bapts 5410 W 7th Topeka KS 66606

KEELAN, KEVIN ROBERT, priest; b. Elizabeth, N.J., Mar. 4, 1921; s. Patrick Joseph and Ellen Cecelia (McNesby) K. Student, Seton Hall U., 1940-42; BA, St. Francis Coll., 1945; STL, Cath. U. Am., 1949; PhL, St. Thomas U., Rome; HHD (hon.), U. Steubenville, 1987; D Pedagogy (hon.), St. Francis Coll., 1991. Joined Third Order Regular of St. Francis, Roman Cath. Ch., 1942, ordained priest, 1949. Instr. philosophy, dean students St. Francis Coll., Loretto, Pa., 1951-53; pres. St. Francis Coll., 1956-59; asst. prof. philosophy, dean U. Steubenville, Ohio, 1953-56, pres., 1959-62, chmn. bd. trustees, exec. v.p., 1966-69, pres., 1969-74; minister provincial Province Most Sacred Heart Jesus, 1962-66; pastor St. John the Evangelist Ch., Pitts., 1977-86, St. Francis Sem., Toronto, Ont., Can., 1986-88; parochial vicar St. Gabriel Parish, Marlboro, N.J., 1988-91; chaplain St. Francis Convent Motherhouse, Sisters of St. Francis, Pitts., 1991—; bd. trustees St. Francis Coll., 1984—. Recipient Porter W. Averill award Thomas Jefferson High Sch., 1955, Poverello medal Founders Assocs. Coll. of Steubenville, 1975. Lodges: K.C., Ancient Order Hibernians. Address: St Francis Convent Motherhouse Grove and McRoberts Rd Pittsburgh PA 15234

KEELER, RANDALL SCOTT, minister; b. Sellersville, Pa., May 27, 1958; s. Harvey Noah and Anna Ruth (Landis) K.; m. Karen Joan Simmons, June 23, 1979; children: Matthew, Philip, Andrew. BA, Bluffton (Ohio) Coll., 1980; MDiv, Ea. Mennonite Sem., 1986. Ordained to ministry, Mennonite Ch. and Gen. Conf. Mennonite Ch. Program assoc. Bluffton Br. YMCA, 1979-81; dir. Boys Club of Fresno (Calif.), 1981-83; youth pastor Waynesboro (Va.) Ch. of Brethren, 1983-85; conf. youth and young adult minister Mennonite Ch., Souderton, Pa., 1986—; commn. mem. Commn. on Edn., Newton, Kans., 1989—; bd. trustees Bluffton Coll., 1989—, Ea. Pa. Mediation Svc., Souderton, 1987—. Author: Weathering the Storm, 1991; author youth ministry jour. Youthguide, 1990. Home: 327 Jefferson St East Greenville PA 18041 Office: Franconia and Ea Dist Conf PO Box 116 Souderton PA 18964

KEELER, WILLIAM HENRY, archbishop; b. San Antonio, Mar. 4, 1931; s. Thomas Love and Margaret T. (Conway) K. BA, St. Charles Sem., Phila., 1952; STL, Pontifical Gregorian U., Rome, 1956, JCD, 1961; DD (hon.), Lebanon Valley Coll, Pa., 1984, Gettysburg Coll., 1986, Susquehanna U., 1989; LHD (hon.), Mt. St. Mary's Coll., 1985. Ordained priest Roman Catholic Ch., 1955, consecrated bishop, 1979. Sec. diocesan tribunal Diocese of Harrisburg, Pa., 1956-58, defender of the bond, 1961-66, vice-chancellor, 1965-69, chancellor, 1969-79, aux. bishop and vicar gen., 1979-83, bishop of Harrisburg, 1984-89; archbishop of Balt., 1989—; chmn. Md. Cath. Conf., 1989—; co-chmn. Pa. Conf. Inter-Ch. Cooperation, 1981-89; pres. Pa. Cath. Conf., 1983-89; chmn. com. ecumenical and inter-religious affairs Nat. Conf. Cath. Bishops, 1984-87, mem., 1987—, Episcopal moderator for Cath.-Jewish Rels., 1988—, sec., 1988-89, v.p., 1989—; mem. Internat. Joint Com. for Cath.-Orthodox Theol. Dialogue, 1986—. Mem. Interreligious Forum Greater Harrisburg, 1969-89; mem. exec. bd. Keystone Area coun. Boy Scouts Am., 1979-89. Recipient Gold medal Pope John XXIII, 1961; named papal chamberlain Pope Paul VI, 1965; prelate of honor Pope Paul VI, 1970; recipient John Baum Humanitarian award Dauphin County unit Am. Cancer Soc., 1984, Anti-Defamation League Americanism award, 1985, De Tocqueville Soc. award, 1988. Mem. Canon Law Soc. Am., Am. Cath. Hist. Soc.

KEELEY, RICHARD CHARLES, minister; b. Indpls., June 22, 1951; s. Charles William and Hilma Ann (Williams) K.; m. Brenda Joyce Storm, Feb. 23, 1974; children: Sara Louise, Richard Scott, Mary Frances. BA, Nazarene Sem., Kansas City, 1976; BTh, Internat. Bible Sem., Orlando, Fla., 1982, ThM, 1984, ThD, 1986. Pastor Brownsburg (Ind.) Nazarene Ch., 1977-81, Shirley (Ind.) Nazarene Ch., 1981-84, Plainfield (Ind.) Nazarene Ch., 1984—; analyst Chrysler Corp., Indpls., 1971—. Avocations: fishing, camping, weight lifting. Home: 149 Vestal Rd Plainfield IN 46168

KEELY, KENNETH LEE, JR., minister; b. Bklyn., July 27, 1960; s. Kenneth Lee Sr. and Lorrain Grace (Thorgersen) K. AA, Edison Community Coll., Fort Myers, Fla., 1980; student, Palm Beach Atl. Co., West Palm Beach, Fla., 1980-82; BA, U. So. Fla., 1985; MRE, New Orleans Bapt. Theol. Sem., 1987. Min. music, youth, sr. adults Russell Park Bapt. Ch., Fort Myers, 1982-85; min. music, children Enon Bapt. Ch., Jayess, Miss., 1985-87; min. music, youth First Bapt. Ch., Punta Gorda, Fla., 1987—; music chmn. Peace River Bapt. Assn., Punta Gorda, 1988—, evangelism com., 1990—, youth com., 1987—, exec. com. 1987—; youth com. Royal Palm Bapt. Assn., 1982-85, chmn. 1985, music com. 1982-85, singles com. 1982-85; mem. Fla. Bapt. Singing Men, 1982-85; Revival Music com. Whalthal County (Miss.) Bapt. Assn., 1986. Music 24 Handbell arrangement used in local churches. Mem. County Youth Mins. Roundtable, Charlotte County, 1989—, Evang. Ministries, Charlotte County, 1989—. Mem. Fla. Bapt. Religious Educators, Fla. Bapt. Recreation Assn., Fla. Bapt. Music Dir. Assn., SMENC, Min. Fellowship. Republican. Office: First Bapt Ch 459 Gill St Punta Gorda FL 33950-4811 *Christians have the greatest honor, presenting the greatest story, of the only salvation from the one and only Lord and Saviour, Jesus the Christ.*

KEENAN, DENNIS, charitable organization administrator. Exec. dir. Cath. Charities, Archdiocese of Portland, Oreg. Office: Cath Charities Inc 2838 E Burnside St Portland OR 97214*

KEENEN, HOWARD GREGORY, minister; b. Arkadelphia, Ark., Jan. 17, 1960; s. Marvin Dean and Shirlene (Finn) K.; m. Sami Tara Cathey, Sept. 21, 1984; children: Gregory Taylor-Dean, Jennifer Elizabeth. Student, Okla. State U., 1979-80, Criswell Coll., 1985-87; diploma, Immanuel Bapt. Sem., 1988. Ordained to ministry Southern Bapt. Conv., 1982. Min. music First Bapt. Ch., Verdigris, Okla., 1979; assoc. pastor Trinity Bapt. Ch., Moore, Okla., 1980-85, Meadowbrook Bapt. Ch., Irving, Tex., 1985-87; assoc. pastor, min. music Morningside Bapt. Ch., Valdosta, Ga., 1987-88; sr. pastor 1st Bapt. Ch., Chelsea, Okla., 1988-91, Tuttle, Okla., 1991—; pres. Pastors' Conf., Rogers Bapt. Assn., Claremore, Okla., 1991—. Republican. Home: 8 W Main Tuttle OK 73089 Office: 1st Bapt Ch PO Box 307 Tuttle OK 73089

KEERAN, KEITH PETER, academic administrator; b. Marion, Ohio, June 21, 1943; s. Melvin Forest and Ruth (Armintrout) K.; m. Nancy Lee Fleischman, June 12, 1964; children: Keith L., Shannon D., Angela R. BA, Ky. Christian Coll., 1966, ThB, 1967; MA, Abilene Christian U., 1976; PhD, Mich. State U., 1978. Prof. Great Lakes Bible Coll., Lansing, Mich., 1971-82; Prof. Ky. Christian Coll., Grayson, 1982-87, pres., 1987—; exec. dir. Am. Ctr. for Leadership Studies, Grayson, 1978-91; cons. ch. orgns., 1978—; speaker in field. Mem. Am. Assn. Bible Colls. (pres. elect 1990-91, pres. 1992—). Office: Ky Christian Coll Office Pres 617 N Carol Malone Blvd Grayson KY 41143

KEGLEY, JACQUELYN ANN, philosophy educator; b. Conneaut, Ohio, July 18, 1938; d. Steven Paul and Gertrude Evelyn (Frank) Kovacevic; m. Charles William Kegley, June 12, 1964; children: Jacquelyn Ann, Stephen Lincoln Luther. BA cum laude, Allegheny Coll., 1960; MA summa cum laude, Rice U., 1964; PhD, Columbia U., 1971. Asst. prof. philosophy Calif. State U., Bakersfield, 1973-77, assoc. prof., 1977-81, prof., 1981—; vis. prof. U. Philippines, Quezon City, 1966-68; grant project dir. Calif. Council Humanities, 1977, project dir. 1980, 82; mem. work group on ethics Am. Colls. of Nursing, Washington, 1984-86. Author: Introduction to Logic, 1978; editor: Humanistic Delivery of Services to Families, 1982, Education for the Handicapped, 1982; mem. editorial bd. Jour. Philosophy in Lit., 1979-84; contbr. articles to profl. jours. Bd. dirs. Bakersfield Mental Health Assn., 1982-84, Citizens for Betterment of Community. Recipinet Outstanding Prof. award Calif. State U., 1989-90, Golden Roadrunner award Bakersfield Community, 1991. Mem. N.Y. Acad. Scis., Philosophy of Sci. Assn., Soc. Advancement Am. Phil. soc. (chmn. Pacific div. 1979-83, nat. exec. com. 1974-79), Philosophy Soc., Soc. Interdisciplinary Study of Mind, Am. Philosophical Assn., Dorian Soc., Phi Beta Kappa. Democrat. Lutheran. Avocations: music, tennis. Home: 7312 Kroll Way Bakersfield CA 93309 Office: Calif State U Dept Philosophy & Religious Studies Bakersfield CA 93311

KEHOE, RICHARD J., academic administrator. Pres. Mary Immaculate Sem, Northampton, Pa. Office: Mary Immaculate Sem 300 Cherryville Rd Box 27 Northampton PA 18067*

KEHRES, DONALD WAYNE, minister; b. Homestead, Pa., Oct. 17, 1951; s. Paul William and Dorothy Virginia (Pesch) K.; m. Ruth Ellen Dumroese, June 24, 1972; children: Jennifer Collette. BA, Concordia Coll., River Forest, Ill., 1973; postgrad., Luth. Sch. Theo., Chgo., 1980. Pastor Prince Peace Luth. Ch., Grandview, Mo., 1980--; pres. Grandview Ch. Alliance, 1981-83, 1987; v.p. Community Services League, Independence 1985--. Bd. dirs. v.p. Am. Cancer Soc., Grandview 1988. Mem. Grandview Kiwanis Club (pres. 1984-85, 1987-88). Democrat. Avocations: photography, gardening. Home: 13001 Crystal Grandview MO 64030 Office: Prince of Peace Luth Ch 13031 Winchester Ave Grandview MO 64030

KEHRWALD, LEIF JOSEPH, church organization official; b. Salmon, Idaho, Dec. 8, 1957; s. Richard Joseph and Caroline Marie (James) K.; m. Rene Marie Mehlhaff, Aug. 25, 1979; children: Nicolo, Luke. BA, Gonzaga U., Spokane, Wash., 1980; MA, Regis U., Denver, 1989. Coord. youth ministry St. Thomas More Ch., Spokane, 1978-79, St. Patrick Ch., Spokane, 1979-82; cons. family life and youth ministry Roman Cath. Diocese of Spokane, 1982-85, cons. family life and adult edn., 1985-89; dir. family life Roman Cath. Archdiocese of Portland, Oreg., 1989—; trainer, cons. Nat. Fedn. for Cath. Youth Ministries, Washington, 1987-89; cons., speaker nat. families project Ctr. for Youth Ministry, Naugatuck, Conn., 1988—. Author: Caring that Enables: A Manual for Parish Family Ministry, 1991; also numerous articles to Roman Cath. jours. Mem. Nat. Assn. Cath. Family Life Mins. (bd. dirs. 1986-89, chmn. family perspective com. 1986—). Office: Family Life Office 2838 E Burnside St Portland OR 97214

KEILLER, JAMES BRUCE, college dean, clergyman; b. Racine, Wis., Nov. 21, 1938; s. James Allen and Grace (Modder) K.; diploma Beulah Heights Bible Coll., 1957; B.A., William Carter Coll., 1963, Ed.D. (hon.), 1973; LL.B., Blackstone Sch. Law, 1964; M.A., Evang. Theol. Sem., 1965, B.D., 1966, Th.D., 1968; M.A. in Ednl. Adminstrn., Atlanta U., 1977; EdS in Ednl. Adminstrn., Ga. State U., 1987; grad. Nat. Tax Tng. Sch., Monsey, N.Y., 1986; postgrad. Atlanta Law Sch.; m. Darsel Lee Bundy, Feb. 8, 1959; 1 dau., Susanne Elizabeth. Ordained to ministry Internat. Pentecostal Assemblies, 1957; pastor Maranatha Temple, Boston, 1957-58, Midland (Mich.) Full Gospel Ch., 1958-64; v.p. acad. dean Beulah Heights Bible Coll., Atlanta, 1964—, trustee, 1964—; nat. dir. youth and Sunday sch. dept. Internat. Pentecostal Assemblies, 1958-64, dir. world missions, Atlanta, 1964-76, youth commn., 1958-64, missions com., 1964-76, exec. bd., 1964-76, missionary editor Bridegroom's Messenger, 1964—; dir. global missions Internat. Pentecostal Ch. of Christ, 1976—, mem. exec. com., 1976—; mem. exec. bd. Mt. Paran Christian Sch. Mem. Republican Presdl. Task Force; mem. Nat. Rep. Senatorial Com., Am. Tax Reduction Movement, So. Ctr. Internat. Studies. Named Alumnus of Year, William Carter Coll., 1965. Fellow Coll. of Preceptors; mem. So. Accrediting Assn. Bible Colls. (exec. sec.), Christian Mgmt. Assn., Soc. Pentecostal Studies, Acad. Polit. Sci., Ind. Order Foresters, Am. Inst. Parliamentarians, Am. Bd. Master Educators (cert.), Evang. Theol. Soc., Nat. Assn. Tax Practitioners, Nat. Fedn. for Decency (bd. dirs.), Intercollegiate Studies Inst., Econometrics Rsch. Group, Kiwanis (lt. gov. Ga. dist. 1986-87, chmn. human values state com. Ga. dist. 1989-90). Republican. Home: 892 Berne St SE Atlanta GA 30316 Office: Beulah Heights Bible Coll 906 Berne St SE Atlanta GA 30316

KEIP, FRED FRANK, minister; b. Two Rivers, Wis., July 29, 1930; s. Fred Frank and Evelyn Helene (Klatt) K.; m. Margaret Ada Johnson, Jan. 27, 1958; children: David, Jeffry, Kristen. BA, Carthage Coll., 1958; MA, Purdue U., 1960; MDiv, Starr King Sch., 1971. Ordained to ministry Unitarian Universalist Ch., 1972. Co-minister Monterey Peninsula Unitarian Ch., Carmel, Calif., 1971—; mem. conflict resolution team Pacific cen. dist. Unitarian Universalist Assn., No. Calif., 1985—. Bd. dirs. Personal Empowerment Ctr., Monterey Peninsula, 1982-87. Cpl. USMC, 1951-53. Mem. Unitarian Universalist Ministers' Assn., Monterey Peninsula Ministerial Assn. Democrat. Office: Monterey Peninsula Unitarian Ch 490 Aguajito Rd Carmel CA 93923 *I believe that there is intentionality throughout creation, and that every human being experiences the numinous, that many of us may not recognize it when we do, that all sincere religious questing results in glimpses of portions of divine truth. At the deepest level of being, we are one with all that is.*

KEIP, MARGARET ADA, minister; b. Chgo., Sept. 24, 1938; d. John Hinrich and Margaret Elizabeth (Siegel) Johnson; m. Fred Frank Keip, Jan. 27, 1958; children: David Mikhail, Jeffry Lowell, Kristen Elizabeth. BS in Art, Purdue U., 1960; MDiv, Starr King Sch., 1976. Ordained to ministry Unitarian Universalist Ch., 1975. Co-minister Monterey Peninsula Unitarian Ch., Carmel, Calif., 1976—; trustee Starr King Sch. for Ministry, Berkeley, Calif., 1982-92, chair bd. dirs., 1989-91. Sec. bd. dirs. Planned Parenthood of Monterey County, 1988-89. Mem. Unitarian Universalist Ministers Assn. (good offices person Pacific cen. dist. 1988-89), Monterey Peninsula Ministerial Assn. (pres. 1981-82, sec. 1988-89). Democrat. Office: Monterey Peninsula Unitarian Ch 490 Aguajito Rd Carmel CA 93923

KEISS, SISTER ISABELLE, academic administrator; b. N.Y.C., Dec. 11, 1931; d. Walter and Sara (Boyle) K.; B.A., Villanova U., 1960; M.A., Cath. U., 1966; Ph.D., Notre Dame U., 1972; postgrad. Harvard U. Grad. Sch. Edn., 1972. Joined Religious Sisters of Mercy, 1952; tchr. English, Bishop Egan High Sch., Levittown, Pa., 1960-63; chmn. English dept. Walsingham Acad., Williamsburg, Va., 1963-65; teaching asst. U. Notre Dame (Ind.), 1967-71; pres. Gwynedd-Mercy Coll., Gwynedd Valley, Pa., 1971—. Author: Tender Courage, 1988, Preferential Option for the Poor, 1988; contbr. Dictionary of Christianity in Am., 1989. Bd. dir. North Penn Hosp., 1975&, Redeemer Hosp., 1991—, Assn. Cath. Colls. and Univs., 1990—; mem. exec. com. Commn. for Ind. Colls. and Univs, 1990—; bd. dirs. Mercy Cath. Med. Center, 1975—, Coll. Misericordia, 1979—. Recipient award Rotary Club, 1980. Home and Office: Gwynedd-Mercy Coll Sumneytown Pike Gwynedd Valley PA 19437

KEITH, JAMES MELVIN, clergyman; b. Jackson, Miss., June 22, 1943; s. Hardy Melvin and Mary Frances (Walton) K.; B.A., Miss. Coll., 1966; M.Div., Southwestern Bapt. Theol. Sem., 1969, Th.D., 1975; m. Saundra Elaine Gordon, Aug. 20, 1966; children—James Scott, Gordon Todd, Kristin Elaine. Ordained to ministry So. Baptist Conv., 1967; pastor Antelope Bapt. Ch. (Tex.), 1967-69, 1st Bapt. Ch., Blum, Tex., 1970-71, 1st Bapt. Ch., McGregor, Tex., 1971-72, 1st Bapt. Ch., San Marcos, Tex., 1972-74, 1st Bapt. Ch., Laurel, Miss., 1974-77, 1st Bapt. Ch., Gulfport, Miss., 1977—; chaplain U.S. Ho. of Reps., 1981; grad. asst. dept. preaching Southwestern Bapt. Theol. Sem., 1970-72; adj. prof. O.T., William Carey Coll., 1977; adj. prof. homiletics William Carey Coll., 1978, preaching New Orleans Baptist Theol. Sem., 1982; pres. Jones County Bapt. Pastors Conf., 1975-76. Trustee, William Carey Coll., 1976-79, 79-82, chmn. bd. trustees, 1980, 81. Mem. Miss. Bapt. Conv. (chmn. order of bus. com. 1978, mem. com. on coms. 1980), Miss. Coll. Ministerial Alumni Assn. (pres. 1977-78), Southwestern Bapt. Theol. Sem. Alumni (pres. 1980). Office: PO Drawer 70 Gulfport MS 39501

KEITH, RAYMOND J., church treasurer, high school educator; b. Barnesboro, Pa., Dec. 23, 1942; s. Raymond B. and Mazel A. (Lamer) K.; m. Gloria F. Whited, June 6, 1970; children: Rae-Anne, Tammy. BS in Edn., Indiana U. Pa., 1964, MS in Edn., 1976. Youth leader, Sunday sch. tchr., treas. North End Assembly of God, Barnesboro, Pa., 1965—, also bd. dirs.; tchr. Purchase Line High Sch., Commodore, Pa., 1967—. Mem. NEA, Pa. State Edn. Assn., Pa. Bus. Edn. Assn. Home: RD 1 Box 395 Barnesboro PA 15714

KEITH, SEAN PAUL, education and youth minister; b. Hattiesburg, Miss., Sept. 13, 1961; s. J.C. Sr. and Doris Mae (McPhail) K.; m. Pamela Jean Randle, Aug. 23, 1986. BSBA, U. So. Miss., 1984; MA in Religious Edn., Southwestern Bapt. Theol. Sem., 1987. Ordained to ministry So. Bapt. Conv., 1987. Youth dir. First Bapt. Ch. Glendale, Hattiesburg, 1983-84; youth min. Matthew Rd. Bapt. Ch., Grand Prairie, Tex., 1985-87; assoc. pastor youth and edn. Clarksdale (Miss.) Bapt. Ch., 1987-89; min. edn. and youth 1st Bapt. Ch., Corinth, Miss., 1989—; conf. leader Miss. Bapt. Conv. Bd., Jackson, Miss., 1988—. Mem. Miss. Bapt. Religious Edn. Assn. Office: First Baptist Church 501 Main St Corinth MS 38834

KEITHLEY, THOMAS WILLIAM, Christian education director; b. Evergreen Park, Ill., Feb. 20, 1958; s. Robert Lee and Corinne Edith (Landeck) K.; m. Deborah Lynn Ledebuhr, June 23, 1979; children: Joshua John, Erinn Lynn, Sara Elizabeth. BA, Concordia U., River Forest, Ill., 1980, MA in Theol. and Edn., 1988. Cert. dir. christian edn., 1988. Tchr. level 6 athletics youth min. Peace Luth., Ft. Lauderdale, Fla., 1980-82; from athletics youth tchr. to family min. Redeemer Luth., Stuart, Fla., 1982—; epsilon region rep. Adv. Coun. Youth Min., Orlando, Fla., 1982—; workshop leader Youtn Min. & Family Life Conf. Mem. Nat. Christian Counselors Assn., Luth. Edn. Assn. Home: 5943 SE Pine Dr Stuart FL 34997 Office: Redeemer Lutheran 2450 E Ocean Blvd Stuart FL 34996

KELBER, WERNER HEINZ, religious educator; b. Burghausen, Fed. Republic of Germany, Sept. 13, 1935; came to U.S., 1962; s. Karl and Mathilde (Bucher) K.; m. Mary Ann Long, Mar. 24, 1962. BD, U. Erlangen, 1962; ThM, Princeton Theol. Seminary, 1963; MA, U. Chgo., 1967, PhD, 1970. Asst. prof. religious studies U. Dayton, Ohio, 1970-73; from asst. to assoc. prof. religious studies Rice U., Houston, 1973-81, Turner chair in Bibl. studies, 1981—, chmn. dept. religious studies, 1989—; vis. prof. U. des Scis. Humaines, Strasbourg, France, 1985-86; editorial bd. Oral Tradition, 1986—, Mercer Univ. Press, 1987—; reader Fortress Press, Mpls., 1975—. Author: The Kingdom in Mark, 1974, Mark's Story of Jesus, 1987, The Oral and the Written Gospel, 1983; editor: The Passion in Mark, 1976; contbr. articles to profl. jours. Mem. Soc. Bibl. Lit. (editorial bd. monograph series 1980-83, editorial bd. jour. 1988-91, chmn. nat. seminar gospel Mark 1977-80, pres. Southwest region 1978-79, coun. 1990—), Cath. Bibl. Assn. Am., Studiorum Novi Testamenti Societas, Ctr. for Study Religion in Greco-Roman World (assoc.). Lutheran. Office: Rice U Dept Religious Studies Houston TX 77251

KELEHER, JAMES P., bishop; b. July 31, 1931. BA, St. Mary of the Lake Sem., Mundelein, Ill., 1954; DST, St. Mary of the Lake Sem., 1961; Licentiate in Sacred Theology, 1968; MA in Ednl. adminstrn., Loyola U., Chgo., 1967; PhD, Gregorian U., Rome. Ordained priest, Roman Catholic ch., 1958. Rector Quigley Sem. South, Chgo., 1976-78; pres., rector St. Mary of the Lake Sem., Mundelein, Ill., 1978-84; bishop Belleville, Ill., 1984—; Mem. Papal Visitation Com. for Sems.; chmn. bishop's com. on priestly formation, mem. com. migration, mem. com. econ. concerns of the Holy See Nat. Conf. Cath. Bishops. Mem. Nat. Cath. Edn. Assn. (sem. dept.), Midwest Assn. Theol. Schs. Office: Chancery Office 222 S Third St Belleville IL 62220

KELLAR, GERALD DEAN, minister; b. Springfield, Ark., Oct. 14, 1916; s. Marcus William and Lily Mae (Brown) K.; m. Mary Lou Nunn, June 19, 1938; children: Sandra Kay, Jerrie Sue, Chas Mark, Mary Ann, Joseph. AA, Jacksonville (Tex.) Bapt. Coll, 1938; BA, Baylor U., Waco, Tex., 1940; ThM, Southwestern Theol. Sem., Ft. Worth, 1944; ThD, Bapt. Missionary Assn., Jacksonville, 1960. Ordained to ministry Bapt. Ch., 1937. Pres. Jacksonville Coll., 1944-56, Bapt. Missionary Assn. Sem., Jacksonville, 1956-67, Central Bapt. Coll., Conway, Ark., 1967-70; pastor First Bapt. Ch., Galena, Kans., 1970-83; v.p. Southwestern Bapt. Coll., Laurel, Miss., 1983-90, pres., 1990—. Author: In the Midst of the Years, 1948, Bound for the Promised Land, 1959, The Church Attending God's Business, 1961, Pulpit Treasures, 1975; editor Bapt. Herald, 1970-83; contbr. articles to profl. jours. Home: 4229 Hwy 15 N Laurel MS 39440

KELLEHER, SISTER MARY ANNUNCIATA, nun, hospital administrator; b. Buffalo, Apr. 4, 1926; d. James and Julia Marie (Hyde) K. RN, Mercy Hosp. Sch. Nursing, 1948; BS, D'Youville Coll., 1958. Joined Religious Sisters of Mercy, Roman Cath. Ch., 1949. Tchr. various schs., Buffalo, 1949-51; mem. staff St. Jerome Hosp., Buffalo, 1952-54, Kenmore (N.Y.) Mercy Hosp., 1954-66; mem. staff Mercy Hosp., Buffalo, 1966-68, adminstr., 1968-76; superior gen. Sisters of Mercy, Buffalo, 1976-84; pres. Mercy Health Systems of Western N.Y., Kenmore, 1984—. Bd. dirs. Kenmore Mercy Hosp., 1970—, St. jerome Hosp., 1970—, Mercy Hosp. of Buffalo, 1967—, Trocaire Coll., Buffalo, 1967-84; mem. adv. com. nursing curriculum Erie (N.Y.) Community Coll., 1969-82. Mem. Am. Coll. Healthcare Execs., Western N.Y. Hosp. Assn., Cath. Health Assn. Office: Marian Profl Ctr 515 Abbott Rd Buffalo NY 14420

KELLER, CARL ALBERT, retired religion educator; b. Guntur, India, Aug. 2, 1920; s. Albert and Elisabeth (Kleiner) K.; m. Marianne Wille, July 21, 1945; children: Ulrich, Peter, Samuel. ThD, U. Basel, Switzerland, 1946. Ordained to ministry Reformed Ch. Zurich, 1944. Prof. theology Ch. of South India, Trivandrum, 1947-52; pastor Reformed Ch. Zurich, Ossingen, Switzerland, 1952-56; prof. Old Testament, sci. of religions U. Lausanne, Switzerland, 1956-86; ret., 1986. Author: Communication avec l'Ultime, 1986, Approche de la Mystique, 2 vols., 1989, 90. Home: Morettes 14, CH 1052 Le Mont sur Lausanne Switzerland

KELLER, CHRISTOPH, JR., bishop; b. Bay City, Mich., Dec. 22, 1915; s. Christoph and Margaret Ely (Walter) K.; m. Caroline P. Murphy, June 22, 1940; children: Caroline, Cornelia, Cynthia, Kathryn, Christoph, Elisabeth. Grad., Lake Forest (Ill.) Acad., 1934; B.A., Washington and Lee U., 1939, D.D., 1973; student, Grad. Sch. Theology, U. South, 1954, D.D., 1968; certificate spl. work, Gen. Theol. Sem., N.Y.C., 1957; S.T.D. (hon.), Gen. Theol. Sem., 1968. Planter Alexandria, La., 1940—; pres. Deltic Farm & Timber Co., El Dorado, Ark., 1948-51; exec. v.p. Murphy Corp., El Dorado, 1951-54, dir., 1948-89; ordained priest P.E. Ch., 1957; rector Harrison, Ark.; also charge missions in Eureka Springs and Mountain Home, Ark., 1957-61; rector St. Andrews Episcopal Ch., Jackson, Miss., 1962-67; dean St. Andrews Cathedral, Jackson, until 1967; bishop coadjutor Diocese of Ark., 1967-70, diocesan bishop, 1970-81; exec. council Episc. Ch., 1976-82; chmn. Episcopal Ch. Bldg. Fund, 1982-87; dep. Gen. Conv. P. E. Ch., 1958, 61, 64, 67. Pres. La. Aberdeen Angus Breeders Assn., 1947, La. Delta Council, 1950; chmn. United Fund, El Dorado, 1952; mem. Madison Parish (La.) Sch. Bd., 1952-53; Trustee All Saints Jr. Coll., Vicksburg, Miss., 1949-51, 67-81, U. South, 1973-77; bd. dirs. Washington and Lee U., Lexington, Va., 1981-86, Gen. Theol. Sem., N.Y.C., 1981-89, The Living Ch., 1988-90. Served as officer USMCR, World War II. Mem. Phi Kappa Alpha (bd. dirs. 1989-90). Home: Inglewood Plantation Po Box 5443 Alexandria LA 71307-5443

KELLER, DIANE CECELIA, religious organization administrator; b. Queens, N.Y., Sept. 23, 1955; d. John G. Sr. and Cecelia M. (Welsh) Wall. BA in Human Relations, Marian Coll., 1978; MSW, U. Denver, 1982. Cert. drug and alcohol counselor, Colo. Family therapist Ctr. Creative Living, Denver, 1983; dir. br. office Crossroads Counseling, Denver, 1983-84; mktg. dir. Raleigh Hills Hosp., Denver, 1984-85; parish adminstr. Christ the King Ch., Denver, 1985—. Served with U.S. Army, 1974. Mem. Nat. Assn. Social Workers, Nat. Assn. Ch. Bus. Adminstrn. (com. chairperson for Nat. 1988 Conv., chpt. pres. 1988-89). Democrat. Roman Catholic. Avocations: tennis, cross country skiing, downhill skiing, running, racquetball. Office: Christ The King Cath Ch 845 Fairfax St Denver CO 80220

KELLER, F. ANNETTE, religion educator; b. Warsaw, Ind., Jan. 7, 1951; d. John Phillip and Lois Frances (Williamson) Aebersold; m. Stephen Lewis Keller, June 5, 1971; children: Scott Lewis, Sherilyn Anne. BA in Christian Edn., Taylor U., 1972. Asst. to editor Wesley Press, Marion, Ind., 1972-74; ch. sec. 1st United Meth. Ch., Eaton Rapids, Mich., 1975-76; tchr. presch. Litchfield, Mich., 1978-80; clerical worker Sunday Publs., Lake Worth, Fla., 1984-85; adminstrv. sec. Good Shepherd United Brethren Ch., Huntington, Ind., 1986-87; adminstrv. asst. Morningstar United Meth. Ch., Valparaiso, Ind., 1987-90; asst. pastor Vineyard Christian Fellowship, Merrillville, Ind., 1991—; del. No. Ind. Annual Conf. United Meth. Ch., Lafayette, Ind., 1989-90; dist. mission sec. West Mich. Conf., Lake Odesa, Mich., 1981-83; tchr. Bible, 1975—. Speaker Valparaiso Women's Club, 1990. Named to Outstanding Young Woman of Am., 1990. Home: 1955 Beanblossom Ct Valparaiso IN 46383 Office: Vineyard Fellowship PO Box 10607 Merrillville IN 46411 *In these fast changing and perilous times God's Word to us in the Bible is a light to our path and an anchor to our soul.*

KELLER, JACK ARTHUR, JR., religious publisher; b. Kansas City, Mo., June 5, 1952; s. Jack Arthur and Bernice Karleen (Martin) K.; m. Cherie Lynn Parker, June 14, 1980; children: Juliana, Joshua. BA, U. Puget Sound, Tacoma, Wash., 1974; MA, Sch. Theology, Claremont, Calif., 1979, Vanderbilt U, Nashville, 1982; PhD, Vanderbilt U, Nashville, 1988. Instr. U. of South, Sewanee, Tenn., 1981-82; editor Ch. Sch. Publs., United Meth. Pub. House, Nashville, 1984-89; project dir. New Interpreter's Bible commentary series, Abingdon Press, Nashville, 1989—; ref. editor Abingdon Press, Nashville, 1990—. Contbr. articles to profl. jours. Mem. Am. Acad. Religion, Soc. Bibl. Lit., Soc. Christian Ethics. Office: Abingdon Press 201 8th Ave S PO Box 801 Nashville TN 37202

KELLER, ROBERT M., bishop. Bishop Evang. Luth. Ch. in Am., Spokane, Wash. Office: Synod of Ea Washigton-Idaho S 314-A Spokane WA 99204*

KELLER, RON L., minister; b. Morenci, Mich., Mar. 14, 1936; s. Orin W. and Verlah Charlotte (Evers) K.; m. Patricia Jane Reppert, June 22, 1958; children: Paul Matthew, Laurel Ann, Bradley David, Brent Earl. BA, Albion Coll., 1958; MDiv, Oberlin Grad. Sch. Theology, 1962. Ordained to ministry United Meth. Ch., 1962. Pastor Washington Heights Meth. Ch., Battle Creek, Mich., 1956-58, Republic (Ohio) Meth. Ch., 1958-62, Union City (Mich.) Meth. Ch., 1962-66, Birchwood United Meth. Ch., Battle Creek, Mich., 1966-70, Rockford (Mich.) United Meth. Ch., 1970-73; prog. staff dir. West Mich. conf. United Meth. Ch., Grand Rapids, 1973-81; pastor Milwood United Meth. Ch., Kalamazoo, Mich., 1982-88; sr. pastor Cen. United Meth. Ch., Muskegon, Mich., 1988—; clergy del. gen. conf. United Meth. Ch., Indpls., 1980, Balt., 1984, dir. gen. bd. discipleship, chmn. sect. on Christian edn., 1980-88. Pres. Battle Creek Ministerial Assn., 1969, Rockford Ministerial Assn., 1972, Kalamazoo Ministerial Assn., 1987-88. Mem. U.S. Lighthouse Soc., Internat. Guild of Candle Artisans, Masons (organist). Home: 1707 Ritter Dr Muskegon MI 49441 Office: Cen United Meth Ch 1011 2d St Muskegon MI 49440 *In the true Wesleyan tradition, I have pledged myself to a balanced ministry of personal salvation and social redemption. Of utmost importance is commitment to the person of Jesus Christ and the urgency of inviting others to follow him as Christian disciples. The result is that we be positive, outgoing, winsome persons.*

KELLER, WALTER ARTHUR, clergyman; b. Detroit, Dec. 16, 1954; s. Raymond Richard and Marguerite (Lucille) K.; m. Robyn Susan Karbach, Apr. 8, 1979; children: Daniel Joseph, Joshua David, Joanna Michal. AA, Concordia Coll., Ann Arbor, Mich., 1975; BA, Concordia Sr., Ft. Wayne, Ind., 1977; MDiv, Concordia Sem., St. Louis, 1981; postgrad., Luth. Sem., Gettisburg, Pa., 1989—. Ordained to ministry Luth. Ch.-Mo. Synod. Vicar St. John's Luth. Ch., Sayville, N.Y., 1979-80; pastor Bethel Luth. Ch., Du-Quoin, Ill., 1981-84, Messiah Luth. Ch., Waldorf, Md., 1984; substitute tchr. Charles County Pub. Schs., LaPlata, Md., 1989—; del. Luth. Ch.-Mo. Synod Conv., Indpls., 1986. Republican. Home: 5022 Nicholas Rd Waldorf MD 20601

KELLER, WALTER ERIC, theology educator; b. Milw., Feb. 20, 1929; s. Erick Martin and Mathilda (Forster) K.; m. Gloria Elaine Evanson, July 18, 1954; children: Cynthia Marie, Martin Eric, Christen Evanson, Rebekah Jean, Karl Walter. M Div., Concordia Sem., St. Louis, 1955, MST, 1956; PhD, Cambridge U., 1968. Ordained to pastor Lutheran Ch., 1956. Pastor St. John Luth. Ch., Columbia, S.D., 1956-59; prof. theology Valparaiso (Ind.) U., 1959—. Ecumenical Inst. fellow, 1979-80. Mem. Rotary. Office: Valparaiso Univ Valparaiso IN 46383

KELLEY, ARLEON LEIGH, religious organization administrator; b. Cass City, Mich., May 5, 1935; s. Harley L. and L. Elna (Aurand) K.; m. Jacqueline A. Wisel, Aug. 29, 1959; children: Erin, Timothy; m. Donna J. Meinhard, Mar. 19, 1985. AB, Taylor U., Upland, Ind., 1956; MDiv, Christian Theol. Sem., Indpls., 1961; ThD, Boston U., 1970. Ordained to ministry Meth. Ch. Pastor United Meth. Ch., Ind., R.I., 1955-63; dir. rsch. and planning Ind. Coun. Chs., Indpls., 1963-69; assoc. exec. dir. Ohio Coun. Chs., Columbus, 1967-72; asst. gen. sec. Nat. Coun. Chs., N.Y.C., 1972-84; co-regional repr. for Bangladesh, Nepal and India Ch. World Svc./Overseas Ministries, Dhaka, 1984-87; exec. dir. N.Y. State Coun. Chs., Albany, 1987—. Author: Your Church, 1982; contbr. articles to profl. jours. Mem. Nat. Assn. Ecumenical Staff, N.Am. Acad. Ecumenists, Internat. Sociol. Soc., Am. Sociol. Assn. Democrat. Methodist. Office: NY State Coun Chs 362 State St Albany NY 12210

KELLEY, CAROLYN AGNES, educator; b. Council Bluffs, Iowa, Dec. 30, 1958; d. Alvin Oliver and Anna Christiani (Nielsen) Short. BA in Bus. Edn., U. No. Iowa, 1983. Lay vol. Immanual Luth. Ch., Harlan, Iowa, 1983-89; dir. youth Trinity Luth. Ch., Webster City, Iowa, 1989-91; substitute tchr. Webster City, 1991—. Lutheran. Home: Rte 3 Box 216 Webster City IA 50595

KELLEY, DEAN MAURICE, clergyman, church association administrator; b. Cheyenne, Wyo., June 1, 1926; s. Mark M. and Irena (Lancaster) K.; m. Maryon M. Hoyle, June 9, 1946; 1 child, Lenore Hoyle. A.B., Denver U., 1946; Th.M., Iliff Sch. Theology, Denver, 1949; postgrad., Columbia U., 1949-50. Ordained to ministry Methodist Ch., 1946; pastor in Oak Creek, Colo., 1946-49, East Meadow, N.Y., 1950-52, Westhampton Beach, N.Y., 1952-55, Queens, N.Y., 1955-56, Bronx, N.Y., 1957-60; exec. dir. religious liberty Nat. Coun. Chs., 1960-90, councilor on religious liberty, 1990—; Co-dir. project on ch., state and taxation NCCJ, 1980-83. Author: Why Conservative Churches Are Growing, 1972, Why Churches Should Not Pay Taxes, 1977; editor: Government Intervention in Religious Affairs, 1982, Government Intervention in Religious Affairs II, 1986. Home: Melville NY 11747 Office: 475 Riverside Dr New York NY 10115

KELLEY, DIANA LYNN, lay worker; b. Clinton, Ind., Apr. 3, 1958; adopted d. Bill and Rosemary (Golden) Sills; m. Mark Allen Kelley, Sept. 1, 1976; children: William Wesley, Andrew Preston. Musician Faith Mountain Ch., Rosedale, Ind., 1988—, youth group Bible tchr., 1989—; owner Diana's Day Care, Terre Haute, Ind., 1978—. Mem. Community Coordinated Child Care, 1978—. Home: Rte 21 PO Box 240 Terre Haute IN 47802

KELLEY, EDWARD ALLEN, publisher; b. Clinton, Mass., June 28, 1927; s. Edward Francis Kelley and Lillian Marion (Keigwin) French; m. Margaret Jordan Talbott, Feb. 24, 1962; children: Catherine, Edward, Michael. BA, Trinity Coll., Hartford, Conn., 1950; STM, Gen. Theol. Sem., N.Y.C., 1953. Mgr. bookstore Morehouse-Barlow Co. Inc., N.Y.C., 1957-61, v.p., editorial dir., 1961-74; sr. v.p. Oxford U. Press, N.Y.C., 1974-83; pres. Kelley Assocs., Ridgefield, Conn., 1983-87; pres., pub. Morehouse Pub. Co., Ridgefield, 1988—. Editor The Episcopal Ch. Annn., 1967-74, 87—. With USNR, 1945-47, World War II. Democrat. Episcopalian. Home: 345 North St Ridgefield CT 06877 Office: Morehouse Pub Co 871 Ethan Allen Hwy Ste 204 Ridgefield CT 06877

KELLEY, FRANCIS H., priest; b. Boston, Sept. 9, 1941; s. Francis James and Margaret Elizabeth (Reid) K. AB in History, Holy Cross Coll., 1963; postgrad., St. John's Sem., 1963-68; MA in Pastoral Theology, Notre Dame U., 1976. Ordained priest Roman Cath. Ch., 1968. Assoc. pastor St. Ambrose Parish, Dorchester, Mass., 1968-75, St. John's Parish, Peabody, Mass., 1976-83; team ministry St. Boniface Parish, Quincy, Mass., 1983-91; pastor Sacred Heart Ch., Roslindale, Mass., 1991—; cons. Ctr. Pastoral and Social Ministry, U. Notre Dame, South Bend, Ind., 1976-82; participant Yr. of Learning Archdiocese of Boston, 1977-78; pres. Pine St. Inn Inc., Boston, 1970—. Contbr. articlesto religious jours. Chmn. Dorchester House Health Ctr., 1973-74; mem. Quincy Human Rels. Com., 1987-91.

KELLEY, H. C. TED, minister; b. Montclair, N.J., Sept. 5, 1931; s. Haven C. Sr. and Natalie I. (Bennett) K.; m. Linda L. Boers, Feb. 28, 1960; children: Philip H., Christopher S. B. Music, Otterbein Coll., 1953; MDiv, McCormick Sem., 1960; MA in Liberal Studies, Valparaiso U., 1973; DMin, Drew U., 1980. Ordained to ministry Presbyn. Ch. (U.S.A.), 1960. Pastor Mahoning Presbyn. Ch., Danville, Pa., 1960-64, Ogden Dunes (Ind.) Community Ch., 1968-71, Sunnyside Presbyn. Ch., South Bend, Ind., 1971—; moderator Presbytery of Wabash Valley, Ind., 1989; chaplain Ind. State Police, 1976—; pres. Clergy Assn. of St. Joseph County, Ind., 1974; del. gen. assembly Presbyn. Ch. (U.S.A.), 1978, 89. Bd. dirs. Meml. Hosp., 1981-87, ARC, 1973-78; v.p. Mental Health Assn., 1978-79. Comdr., chaplain USNR, 1953-83. Mem. Res. Officers Assn. (life, pres. 1981-82), Ret. Officers Assn. (life), Naval Res. Assn. (life), Navy League of U.S. (life), Am. Legion, Rotary (pres.-elect South Bend club 1991-92), Elks, Masons. Office: Sunnyside Presbyn Ch 115 S Frances St South Bend IN 46617-3195 *Instead of attempting to secularize, neutralize or eradicate religion, it is high time we affirm and become supportive of a transcendent religion as that social mucilage apart from which human life cannot hope to have longevity.*

KELLEY, JAMES KEVIN, religious organization administrator; b. Houston, Tex., Dec. 10, 1961; s. James Stanley and Judith Kay (Jacks) K.; m. Kathryn Anne Stirling, Jan. 3, 1962. BS in Wildlife Sci., Tex. A&M U., 1984; MA in Counseling, Denver Sem., 1988. Dir. of children/youth Elizabeth Sullivan Meml. United Meth. Ch. First Presbyn. Ch., Bogalusa, La., 1988—; vol. Young Life, College Station, Tex., 1983-85, South Fellowship, Englewood, Colo., 1986-88. Bd. mem. Washington Habitat for Humanity, Bogalusa, 1989—, Campfire Inc., Towazi Coun., Bogalusa, 1990—, Bogalusa (La.) Mental Health Clinic, 1990—. Mem. Christian Assn. for Psychol. Studies. Home: 502 Avenue B Bogalusa LA 70427 Office: ESM United Meth Ch 510 Avenue B Bogalusa LA 70427

KELLEY, LARRY DEAN, minister; b. Akron, Ohio, July 22, 1954; s. Earl and Monie (Reip) K.; m. Brenda Carol Hay, Dec. 27, 1975; children: Lorrel Deann, Timothy Michael, Joshua Alan. BA, Bryan Coll., 1976; MDiv, Grace Theol. Sem., 1979. Ordained to ministry N.Am. Bapt. Ch. Pastor Tippecanoe Christian Ch., Winamac, Ind., 1977-79; asst. pastor Chapel in University Park, Akron, 1979-82; pastor Highland Bapt. Ch., Junction City, Kans., 1984—. Writer, narrator devotional radio spots KHCA-FM. Mem. Evang. Ministerial Fellowship Geary County (pres. 1987-88), Crossroads of Leadership/C. of C.. Home: 324 Kiowa Ct Junction City KS 66441

KELLEY, ROBERT W., bishop. Bishop Evang. Luth. Ch. in Am., Akron, Ohio. Office: Evang Luth Ch Am 282 W Bowery 3rd Fl Akron OH 44307*

KELLEY, WILLIAM GEORGE, chaplain; b. Spokane, Wash., Oct. 11, 1959; s. Trueman Orville and Beverly Anne (Derr) K.; m. Betty Marion Cammack, Sept. 8, 1984; children: Joel Edwin, Mark Lucas. BA in Religion, George Fox U., 1984; MA in Bibl. Studies, Western Evang. Sem., 1988; cert., Caperniora/Bodenseehof, Friedrichshafen, Germany, 1980. Dir. Radio Cristã do Brasil, Saõ Paulo, Brazil, 1979-80; assoc. prof. Rosedale Friends Ch., Salem, Oreg., 1984-87; dir. Wyandotte (Okla.) Friends Ctr., 1988-89; presiding clk. South Salem Friends Ch., 1989—. John Sarrin scholarship, Western Evang. Sem., 1987. Mem. Coll. of Chaplains (affiliate), Assn. of Clin. Pastoral Edn., Am. Acad. Religion, Soc. Bibl. Lit. Republican. Home: 406 Madrona S Salem OR 97302

KELLOGG, CHARLES PEZAVIA, SR., religious organization executive; b. Steubenville, Ohio, Jan. 3, 1927; s. William Pitt and Fannie Laura (Gassaway) K.; m. Nora Lee Spotts, Aug. 23, 1948; children—Brenda C. Kellogg Jones, Saundra A. Kellogg Green, Charles Pezavia. BS, Wittenberg U., 1949; MA, Kent State U., 1950, Vt. Coll. of Norwich U., 1987; LLB, Blackstone Sch. Law, 1952; LLD (hon.), Bethune Cookman Coll., 1968; postgrad. John Carroll U., 1951-52, United Theol. Coll., 1970-71, U. West Indies; HHD (hon.) Rust Coll., 1986. Instr. polit. sci. Elizabeth City (N.C.) State Coll., 1949-52; tchr. Turtle Mountain Indian Sch., Belcourt, N.D., 1952-54; instr. Glenville High Sch., Cleve., 1955-64; mem. exec. staff Gen. Bd. of Laity, United Methodist Ch., Evanston, Ill., 1964-72, Gen. Bd. Discipleship, Nashville, 1972-74; exec. dir. health and welfare div. Bd. Global Ministries, United Meth. Ch., Evanston, Ill. and N.Y.C., 1974—. Served with USAAF, 1945-46. Mem. NEA. Home: 10 Olin Dr Spring Valley NY 10977 Office: Bd Global Ministries United Meth Ch 475 Riverside Dr New York NY 10115

KELLOGG, EDWARD SAMUEL, III, deacon; b. Pasadena, Calif., Feb. 13, 1933; s. Edward Samuel Jr. and Dorothy Emily (Griggs) K.; m. Margaret Anne Wagner, June 26, 1954; children: Stephen Edward, Joyce Margaret, Carolyn Gay. BS, U.S. Naval Acad., 1954; BTh, Sch. for Deacons, 1984. Cert. nuclear engr. Deacon Cathedral Ch. St. Paul, San Diego, 1984-86, Ch. of Good Samaritan, San Diego, 1987-89, St. Bartholomew's Episcopal Ch., Poway, Calif., 1989—; vol. chaplain San Diego Med. Ctr., 1985—; diocean coun. Episcopal Diocese, San Diego, 1986-88; bd. dirs. Episcopal Community Svcs., San Diego, 1986—; clergy adv. bd., Sharp Hosps., San Diego, 1986—. Vol. San Diego Hospice, 1984—. capt. USN, 1954-84, decorated Legion of Merit, 1974, 81, 84. Home: 3407 Larga Circle San Diego CA 92110-5335 Office: St Bartholomew's Episcopal Ch 16275 Pomerado Rd Poway CA 92604-1826

KELLOUGH, DOUGLAS ROBERT, minister; b. Edmonton, Alta., Can., Mar. 6, 1951; s. Gordon Vincent and Sarah Jane (Cheshire) K.; m. Laura Lee MacFarlane, Aug. 16, 1975; children: Christopher, James, Kevin. Cert. with honours, Bapt. Leadership Tng. Sch., Calgary, Alta., 1970; BSc, U. Alta., Edmonton, 1973; MDiv, So. Bapt. Theol. Sem., 1976; MTh, Acadia Div. Coll., 1985. Ordained to ministry Bapt. Ch., 1977. Student pastor Lavoy Bapt. Ch., Lavoy, Alta, 1972-73; pastoral intern Highland Bapt. Ch., Louisville, 1973-74, Beechwood Bapt. Ch., Louisville, 1975-76; pastor Bethel First Bapt. Ch., Prince Rupert, B.C., Can., 1976-79, South Rawdon (N.S., Can.) Bapt. Ch., Can., 1979-85; chaplain Halifax (N.S., Can.) Hosps., 1985—; teaching asst. clin. tng. Acadia Div. Coll., Wolfville, N.S., 1988—. Contbr. articles to various publs. Active Bapt. Youth Fellowship, Western Can., 1967-70; publicity dir. Gull Lake Bapt. Camp, Lacombe, Alta., 1970-73; del. People's Law Conf., Ottawa, Ont. Can., 1984; commr. Ea. Valley Assn. United Bapts., 1984-85; ministerial rep. Inter-Agy. Coun. Prince Rupert, 1977-79. Mem. Can. Assn. Pastoral Edn. (cert. specialist in instnl. ministry, regional admitting com. 1989—), Inst. Pastoral Tng. (com. 1989—). Office: Pastoral Care Dept, Victoria Gen Hosp, 1278 Tower Rd, Halifax, NS Canada B3H 2Y9 *Among the many possible meanings of Christian love and service there stands one which seems so insignificant that it is often overlooked—listening. It is the beginning of ministry.*

KELLY, BILLIE MARION, JR., music educator, conductor; b. Wilmington, N.C., Sept. 7, 1959; s. Billie Marion Kelly Sr. and Evelin Lucille (Stanley) Faulkenberry; m. Sheila Gaye Dobbs, Aug. 22, 1981; 1 child, Stephen Craig. MusB, Tenn. Temple U., 1981; MusM, U. Tenn., 1990. Tchr., head dept. Tenn. Temple High Sch., Chattanooga, 1981-86; orch. condr. Highland Park Bapt. ch., Chattanooga, 1981-87, Cadek Conservatory of Music, Chattanooga, 1989—; tchr., head dept. Grace Acad., Chattanooga, 1989—; condr. Chattanooga Community Orch., 1989—. Mem. Nat. Educators Music Conf. (tchr.), Chattanooga Music Tchrs. Assn. (instrumental music chmn.). Republican. Avocations: water skiing, bike riding, camping. Home: 9408 B Bennie Ln Ooltewah TN 37363 Office: Grace Acad 7815 Shallowford Rd Chattanooga TN 37421

KELLY, DAVID FRANCIS, theology educator; b. Somerville, Mass., Dec. 5, 1940. BA in English magna cum laude, Coll. Holy Cross, 1962; BA in Theology summa cum laude, Cath. U. Louvain, Belgium, 1964, MA in Theology magna cum laude, 1966, STB magna cum laude, 1966; MRE, Loyola U., Chgo., 1971; PhD in Theology, U. Toronto, Ont., Can., 1978. Teaching asst. dept. religious studies U. St. Michael's Coll. Toronto, 1972-74, 75-76; asst. prof. religious ethics St. Thomas Sch. Theology, Kenmore, Wash., 1974-75; instr. religious studies Cleve. State U., 1976; asst. prof. moral theology and systematic theology St. Bernard's Sem., Rochester, N.Y., 1976-77, 78-80, assoc. prof., 1980-81; vis. assoc. prof. U. Rochester, 1981; asst. prof. theology Duquesne U., Pitts., 1981-83, assoc. prof., 1983-87, prof., 1987—; vis. lectr. St. Vincent's Sem., Latrobe, 1983-84; vis. assoc. prof. U. Pitts., 1985, mem. assoc. faculty Ctr. Med. Ethics, 1990—, mem. panel med. ethics, 1986—; cons., lectr. health care ethics Mercy Hosp., Pitts, 1982—; cons., lectr. St. Francis Med. Ctr., Pitts., 1986—, resident ethicist, 1989-90, mem. com. ethics, 1986—; assoc. pastor St. Luke's Parish, Westboro, Mass., 1966-72; chaplain Westboro State Hosp., 1966-69. Author: The Emergence of Roman Catholic Medical Ethics in North America, 1979, A Theological Basis for Health Care and Health Care Ethics, 1985, Critical Care Ethics, 1991; contbr. articles to profl. jours.; presenter numerous talks and papers to health care instns., orgns. health care pers., community groups; appeared on TV and radio. Holy Cross scholar, 1958-62, St. Michael's scholar, 1973-74; NEH grantee, 1983. Mem. Am. Acad. Religion, Cath. Theol. Soc. Am., Soc. Christian Ethics, Coll. Theol. Soc., Hastings Ctr. Inst. Soc., Ethics, and Life Scis, Soc. Critical Care Medicine. Office: Duquesne U Pittsburgh PA 15282

KELLY, SISTER DOROTHY ANN, college president; b. Bronx, N.Y., July 26, 1929; d. Walter David and Sarah (McCauley) K. BA in History, Coll. New Rochelle, 1951; MA in Am. Ch. History, Cath. U., Washington, 1958; PhD in Am. Intellectual History, U. Notre Dame, 1970; LittD (hon.), Mercy Coll., Dobbs Ferry, N.Y., 1976; LLD (hon.), Nazareth Coll. of Rochester, N.Y., 1979; DHL (hon.), Coll. St. Rose, 1981, Manhattan Coll., 1979, LeMoyne Coll., 1990, St. Thomas Aquinas Coll., 1990. Joined Order of St. Ursula, Roman Cath. Ch., 1952. Assoc. prof. history Coll. New Rochelle, N.Y., 1957—, chmn. dept. history, 1965-67, acad. dean, 1967-72, acting pres., 1970-71, pres., 1972—; mem. Interreligious Coun. New Rochelle, 1974—, exec. com., 1974-79, v.p., 1980-84, pres., 1984-88; trustee, vice chmn. Commn. Ind. Colls. and Univs. State of N.Y., 1977-78, chmn. bd. trustees, 1978-80, mem. govt. rels. com., 1980—; chmn. Com. Higher Edn. Opportunity, 1977; mem. commr. of edn. Adv. Coun. on Higher Edn. for N.Y. State, 1975-77, subcom. on postsecondary occupational edn., 1975-77; exec. com. Empire State Found. Ind. Liberal Arts Colls., 1975—, vice chmn., 1977-81, chmn., 1981—; trustee, mem. exec. com. Assn. Colls. and Univs. State of N.Y., 1976-80; mem. com. on purpose and identity Assn. Cath. Colls. and Univs., 1975-80; mem. steering com. Neylan Conf., 1978—, mem. bishops and pres. com., 1979—; mem. adv. coun. on fin. aid to students Office Edn., HEW, 1978—; chmn. Women's Coll. Coalition, 1981-83; chmn. govt. rels. adv. com. Nat. Assn. Ind. Colls. and Univs., 1981-82, chair, 1987-88. Chair City-wide Confs., New Rochelle, 1977-79; bd. dirs. United Way Westchester, 1977-84, mem. planning, allocations, evaluation com., 1977-80, nominating and campaign coms., 1990—; bd. dirs. Westchester County Assn., 1980—, New Rochelle Community Action Program, 1982-83, New Rochelle Community Fund, 1989—; mem. steering com. Westchester County Women's Hall of Fame, 1984-85; bd. dirs. Vis. Nurse Svcs. in Westchester, Inc., 1985-86, chair nominating com., 1985-86; trustee LeMoyne Coll., 1982-88, vice chairperson, 1984-87; mem. bd. govs. New Rochelle Hosp. Med. Ctr., 1987—; trustee United Student Aid Funds, 1980—, Ursuline Sch., New Rochelle, 1988—, Cath. U. Am., 1988—, Am. Coun. on Edn., 1990—. Recipient Medallion award Westchester Community Coll., 1978, Leadership award Am. Soc. Pub. Adminstrn., 1986; inducted into Westchester County/Avon Women's Hall of Fame, 1989. Mem. AAUP, AAUW, NCCJ (trustee 1989—), Am. Hist. Assn., Nat. Fedn. Bus. and Profl. Women, Am. Assn. Higher Edn., Nat. Assembly Women Religious, Am. Coun. Edn. (bd. dirs. 1990), Assn. Am. Colls. (bd. dirs. 1983-86), Tchrs. Ins. and Annuity Assn. Am. (trustee 1987—, fin. com. 1987-88, exec. com. 1988—, audit com. 1990—, products and svcs. com. 1990—, nominating and pers. com. 1991), Assn. Colls. Mid-Hudson Area (pres. 1979-81, exec. com. 1982—). Address: Coll New Rochelle New Rochelle NY 10801

KELLY, GEORGE ANTHONY, clergyman, author, educator; b. N.Y.C., Sept. 17, 1916; s. Charles W. and Bridget (Fitzgerald) K. M.A. in Social Sci., Catholic U Am., 1943, Ph.D. in Social Sci., 1946. Ordained priest Roman Cath. Ch., 1942, elevated to monsignor, 1960. Priest St. Monica's Parish, N.Y.C., 1945-56; dir. Family Life Bur., 1955-65, Family Consultation Service, 1955-65; dir. dept. edn. Archdiocese N.Y.C., 1966-70; pastor St. John's Ch., N.Y.C., 1970-74; dir. Inst. Advanced Studies in Cath. doctrine, St. John's U., Jamaica, N.Y., 1975-81; exec. sec. Fellowship of Cath. Scholars, 1976, pres., 1986-88; consultor Archdiocese N.Y., Congregation for the Clergy, Rome, 1984; sec. bd. trustees St. Joseph's Sem.; sec. adv. bd. Pastoral Life Conf.; co-chmn. Archdiocesan Parish Councils, 1966-70. Author: Who Should Run the Catholic Church?, 1976, The Battle for the American Church, 1979, The Crisis of Authority: John Paul II and the American Bishops, 1981, The New Biblical Theorists: Raymond E. Brown and Beyond, 1983, Inside My Father's House, 1989, Keeping the Church Catholic with John Paul II, 1990, others. Recipient 1st Cardinal Wright award Friends of Fellowship of Cath. Scholars, 1979, Faith and Family award Women for Faith and Family, 1988. Mem. AAUP, Am. Sociol. Assn., Am. Cath. Sociol. Soc., Assn. for Sociology of Religion, Am. Cath. Hist. Soc., Am. Cath. Theol. Soc. Office: St John's U Jamaica NY 11439

KELLY, H. ANDREW, minister; b. Ithaca, N.Y., Sept. 11, 1956; s. Harry Earl and Mae Grant (MacIntosh) K.; m. Amelia Margaret Abernathy, June 5, 1978; children: Sarah Elizabeth, Laura Rebekah, Andrew James, Abby Catherine. BS in Music Edn., Asbury Coll., Wilmore, Ky., 1979. Ordained to ministry The Salvation Army, 1985. Officer Dallas Temple Corps, The Salvation Army, 1985-89; officr Tex. and Ark. dist. The Salvation Army, Texarkana, Ark., 1989—. Office: The Salvation Army 400 E 4th St Texarkana AR 75502

KELLY, JANET KIMBALL, educator; b. Kingsville, Tex., Jan. 25, 1964; d. Milton Solon and Susan Etta (Smith) Kimball; m. John Patrick Kelly, Jan. 11, 1986; children: Patrick Christian, Daniel Christopher. BA in Biology, Tex. A&M U., 1986. Cert. sci. educator, Tex. Vice-moderator Presbyn. Women, Kingsville, Tex., 1990-91; outreach coord. Presbyn. Women, Kingsville, 1989-90; contact Presbyn. Lay Com., Kingsville, 1989—; tchr. Presbyn. Pan Am. Sch., Kingsville, 1987—. Newspaper chmn. Charity Dept. Women's Club, Kingsville, 1990-91; regent DAR, Kingsville, 1990-92; mem. Concerned Women for Am., Washington, 1990—. Mem. Tex. Sci. Tchrs. Assn., Kappa Kappa Gamma. Home: PO Box 1578 Kingsville TX 78364 Office: Presbyn Pan Am Sch PO Box 1578 Kingsville TX 78364

KELLY, JOSEPH FRANCIS, theology educator; b. N.Y.C., Aug. 13, 1945; s. James Patrick and Marion Rita (Gleason) K.; m. Ellen Marie Murray, Aug. 17, 1968; children: Robert, Amy, Alicia. BA, Boston Coll., 1967; MA, Fordham U., 1970, PhD, 1973. Instr. theology Molloy Coll., Rockville Ctr., N.Y., 1969-72; from asst. to assoc. prof. John Carroll U., Cleve., 1972-82, prof., 1982—, chmn., 1985—. Author: Why There Is A New Testament, 1986; editor: Scriptores Hiberniae Minores, 1974, Perspectives on Scripture, 1976. NEH fellow, Andrew W. Mellon Found. fellow. Mem. N.Am. Patristic Soc., Medieval Acad. Am., Am. Soc. Ch. History. Democrat. Roman Catholic. Avocations: piano playing, running, gardening. Office: John Carroll U University Heights OH 44118

KELLY, JOSEPH R., deacon, systems analyst; b. Collingdale, Pa., Jan. 21, 1943; s. Eugene C. and Irene E. (Collins) K.; m. Margaret A. Hearn, Jan. 25, 1964; children: Joseph Jr., Shawn P., Mary D. BA in History, Villanova U., 1964; grad., St. Mary's Sem., Houston, 1978; MS in Computer Sci., Houston Bapt. U., 1987. Ordained deacon Roman Cath. Ch., 1978. Deacon St. Theresa Ch., Sugarland, Tex., 1978-80, St. Thomas Aquinas Ch., Meadows, Tex., 1980—; sr. systems analyst Unisys Corp., Houston, 1984—. Address: 2803 N Blue Meadow Circle Sugar Land TX 77479-1530

KELLY, KENNETH WILLIAM, minister; b. Anderson, S.C., June 17, 1953; s. John Butler and Doris (Madden) K.; m. Anita Bishop, July 10, 1976; children: Kenny, Kevin, Tyler. BS, Clemson U., 1975; MDiv, Southwestrn Bapt. Theol. Sem., Ft. Worth, 1979, PhD, 1986. Ordained to ministry So. Bapt. Ch., 1980. Pastor 1st Bapt. Ch., Melissa, Tex., 1980-86, Chapin (S.C.) Bapt. Ch., 1986—; dir. Collin Bapt. Tng. Ctr., McKinney, Tex., 1985-86; mem. missions devel. coun. Lexington (S.C.) Bapt. Assn., 1990—. Home: 235 Caro Ln Chapin SC 29036 Office: Chapin Bapt Ch PO Box 205 Chapin SC 29036

KELLY, LEONTINE T. C., clergywoman; b. Washington; d. David D. and Ila M. Turpeau; m. Gloster Current (div.); children: Angella, Gloster Jr., John David; m. James David Kelly (dec.); 1 child, Pamela (adopted). Student W.Va. State Coll.; grad. Va. Union U., 1960; MDiv, Union Theol. Sem., Richmond, Va., 1976. Formerly sch. tchr.; former pastor Galilee United Meth. Ch., Edwardsville, Va.; later mem. staff Va. Conf. Council on Ministries; pastor Asbury United Meth. Ch., Richmond, 1976-83; mem. nat. staff United Meth. Ch., Nashville, 1983-84; bishop Calif.-Nev. Conf., San Francisco, 1984-88. Vis. prof. evangelism and witness Pacific Sch. Religion, Berkeley, Calif., 1988—. Office: 316 N El Camino Real # 112 San Mateo CA 94401

KELLY, ORRIS EUGENE, former army chaplain; b. Montrose, Kans., July 28, 1926; s. Herman Albertis and Theodora Viola (Pacak) K.; m. Phyllis Louise Goodenow, July 2, 1948; children—Jeffrey Robert, Joel Craig, Karen Colleen, Collette Maureen. Student, U. Kans., 1944; A.B., Kans. Wesleyan U., Salina, 1950, D.D. (hon.), 1976; B.D., Garrett Theol. Sem., Evanston, Ill., 1953; M.S., Shippensburg (Pa.) State Coll., 1973. Ordained to ministry Methodist Ch., 1953. Commd. 2d lt. U.S. Army, 1945, advanced through grades to maj. gen., 1975; mem. staff U.S. Army Chaplain Sch., Ft. Hamilton, N.Y., 1962-66; dir. U.S. Forces Religious Retreat Center, Berchtesgaden, Fed. Republic Germany, 1966-69; div. chaplain 4th Inf. Div., Pleiku and An Khe, Vietnam, 1969; dir. plans, programs and policies directorate Office Chief of Chaplains, 1970-72, exec. officer, 1973-75, chief of chaplains U.S. Army, 1975-79; assoc. gen. sec. div. chaplains Bd. Higher Edn. and Ministry, United Methodist Ch., 1979-85; v.p. pastoral services Hosp. Corp. Am., Nashville, 1985—. Decorated D.S.M., Legion of Merit with 2 oak leaf clusters, Army Commendation medal with 2 oak leaf clusters, Bronze Star with 2 oak leaf clusters, Air medal with 2 oak leaf clusters; recipient Four Chaplains awards B'nai Brith, 1977. Office: United Meth Parrish 2415 Timberlane Manhattan KS 66502

KELLY, ROBERT SNOWDEN, clergyman; b. Wooster, Ohio, Sept. 17, 1932; s. Paul Snowden and Ada Miriam (Zufall) K.; m. Gloria Elaine Albright, Nov. 23, 1956; children: Sharon Elizabeth, David Paul, Cynthia Ellen. AB, Wittenberg U., Springfield, Ohio, 1954; MDiv, Luth. Sem., Phila., 1957. Ordained to ministry Luth. Ch., 1957. Pastor Doylestown (Ohio) Luth. Parish, 1957-64, St. Jacob's Luth. Ch., North Canton, Ohio, 1964-70, Our Saviour Luth. Ch., Toledo, 1970—; chaplain St. Luke Luth. Home, North Canton, 1964-66, bd. dirs., 1967-70; chaplain Edwin Shaw Saniitarium, Akron, Ohio, 1966-70; bd. dirs. Good Shepherd Luth. Home, Ashland, Ohio, 1962-64; dean Toledo dist. Luth. Ch. in Am., 1979-82. Bd. dirs. St. Luke's Luth. Home, North Canton, Ohio, 1968-70. Avocations: genealogy, travel, tennis. Home: 4745 Monac Dr Toledo OH 43623 Office: Our Saviour Luth Ch 2820 Alexis Rd Toledo OH 43613

KELLY, RONALD DAVID, religious organization administrator, minister; b. Lewes, Del., June 25, 1943; s. William and Hazel (Ickles) K.; m. Tana Lynn Rittinger, Aug. 28, 1965; children: Mark David, Jeremy Sean. BS, ThB, United Wesleyan Sem., 1966; MDiv., Asbury Theol. Sem., 1969. Ordained to ministry Wesleyan Ch., 1970. Sr. pastor Wesleyan Ch., Allendale, Mich., 1969-80, Washington St. Wesleyan Ch., Owosso, Mich., 1980-84; supt. western Mich. dist. The Wesleyan Ch., Hastings, Mich., 1984—. Contbr. articles to religious jours. Mem. alumni bd. dirs. Asbury Theol. Sem., Wilmore, Ky., 1985—; trustee Ind. Wesleyan U., Marion, 1980—. Mem. Wesleyan Theol. Soc. Republican. Home and Office: 1993 Campground Rd Hastings MI 49058

KELLY, THOMAS CAJETAN, archbishop; b. Rochester, N.Y., July 14, 1931; s. Thomas A. Kelly and Katherine Eleanor (Fisher) Conley. A.B., Providence Coll., 1953; S.T., Dominican House of Studies, Washington, 1959; D.Canon Law, U. St. Thomas, Rome, 1962; S.T.D. (hon.), Providence Coll, 1979; D.H.L. (hon.), Spalding Coll., 1983. Sec. Dominican Province, N.Y.C., 1962-65; sec. Apostolic Del., Washington, 1965-71; assoc. gen. sec. Nat. Conf. Cath. Bishops-U.S. Cath. Conf., Washington, 1971-77; gen. sec. U.S. Cath. Bishops Conf. Washington, 1977-82; archbishop Archdiocese of Louisville, 1982—; chmn. Catholic Conf. Ky., Louisville, 1982—; bd. dirs. Cath. Health Assn., 1985—. Chancellor Bellarmine Coll.; bd. dirs. St. Luke Inst. Recipient Veritas medal St. Catharine Coll., 1984. Mem. Canon Law Soc. Am., Nat. Cath. Edn. Assn. (chmn. bd. dirs.). Home and Office: 212 E College St Louisville KY 40203

KELMAN, STUART LAURANCE, rabbi, religious organization administrator, educator; b. Bridgeport, Conn., Feb. 13, 1942; s. Wilson and Esther (Levin) K.; m. Victoria Koltun, Dec. 20, 1964; children: Navah Michal, Ari Yitzchak, Etan David, Elana Tamar. BS, Columbia U., 1964; B in Hebrew Letters, Jewish Theol. Sem., 1964, MRE in Hebrew Letters, 1967; MA, Calif. State U., L.A., 1973; PhD, U. So. Calif., 1974. Ordained rabbi, 1969. Prin. Herzl Schs., L.A., 1973-74; asst. prof. Hebrew Union Coll., L.A., 1974-84; exec. dir. Agy for Jewish Edn., Oakland, Calif., 1984—; chair Coalition for Advancement of Jewish Edn., N.Y.C., 1983-86, Conf. on Alternatives in Jewish Edn., 1979, 80. Contbr. articles to religious jours. Recipient Weinberg-Chai award Jewish Fed. Coun., 1980, award United Synagogue Am., 1987. Mem. ASCD, Cen. Conf. Am. Rabbis, East Bay Coun. Rabbis (chair 1987), Assn. for Jewish Studies, Rabbinical Assembly, Jewish Edn. Assembly, Phi Delta Kappa. Office: Agy for Jewish Edn 401 Grand Ave 5th Fl Oakland CA 94610

KEMMETER, MARK C., Christian formation director; b. Appleton, Wis., Sept. 22, 1949; s. Peter John and Mary Therese (Suess) K.; m. Kathleen Therese Tessmer, Aug. 2, 1986; children: Kristin, Elizabeth. BA, St. Francis DeSales, Milw., 1971; M in Theol. Studies, St. Francis Sem., Milw., 1982; D in Ministry, U. St. Mary of Lake, 1988. Dir. of formation St. Veronica Parish, Milw., 1978-87, Blessed Sacrament Parish, Milw., 1987—; adj. faculty Mount Mary Coll., Milw., 1990—, Sacred Heart Sh. Theology, Hales Corners, Wis., 1991—; planning cons. Office of Parish Couns., Milw., 1985-88; staff assoc. Office of Rsch. and Planning, Chgo., 1988-90. Editor: (book) Ecumenism: Striving for Unity Amid Diversity, 1985; author: (planning manual) Transforming People, Mission, Structure, 1987. Developer Youth Ctr. for City Wide Teens, Shawano, Wis., 1970-72; officer Cudahy (Wis.) Jaycees, 1973-79 (disting. svc. award 1977). Mem. Milw. Archdiocesan Religious Edn. Dirs. Assn., Archdiocese Milw. Planning and Collaboration Commn., Collaboration Com. (chair 1988-89). Roman Catholic. Home: 3651 S 3rd St Milwaukee WI 53207 Office: Blessed Sacrament Parish 3100 S 41st St Milwaukee WI 53215 *Despite all of the rapid advances of this century, it still seems that the need for people to experience hope and to recognize a power to change and grow is as evident as ever. My mission is to be a witness of hope and of the power of transformation.*

KEMP, JAMES WALKER, minister; b. Lexington, Ky., July 5, 1955; s. James Dillon and Helen Gertrude (Walker) K.; m. Barbara Carol Abbott, June 12, 1976; children: Jennifer E., Cynthia S., Emily K. BS, U. Ky., 1976; MDiv, Duke U., 1979. Ordained to ministry Meth. Ch. as deacon, 1977, as elder, 1981. Assoc. minister Epworth United Meth. Ch., Lexington, 1980-81; pastor Mead Meml. United Meth. Ch., Russell, Ky., 1981-87, Mt. Tabor United Meth. Ch., Crestwood, Ky., 1987-89; sr. pastor Trinity United Meth. Ch., Winchester, Ky., 1989—; mem. Coun. on Finance and Adminstrn., Lexington, 1987—; adu. faculty Asbury Theol. Sem., Wilmore, Ky., 1991—; del. Ky. Coun. of Chs., 1981-86; mem. Ky. Conf. United Meth. ch. Trustee Community Svc. Ctr., Winchester, Ky., 1991; v.p. Multiple Sclerosis Support Group, Winchester, 1991, founder, 1988; founder The Country Kitchen, Russell, 1986. Named Papa Chief, Camp Fire, Ashland, Ky., 1987. Mem. Winchester Assn. of Chs. (pres.-elect 1991, pres. 1991-92). Home: 36 Milwood Winchester KY 40391 Office: Trinity United Meth PO Box 701 Winchester KY 40392-0701 *Multiple sclerosis has taught me two things: 1) The most important question is not, "Why did this happen?" but, "What do we do now?" 2) What one cannot do is not important. Doing what one can is all essential. We can do all things through Christ who gives true strength.*

KEMP, STEPHEN JAMES, religion educator; b. Omaha, June 13, 1962; s. James Carson and Mabel Dorothy (White) K. BA, Moody Bible Inst., Chgo., 1985; MDiv, Trinity Evang. Divinity Sch., Deerfield, Ill., 1990. Teaching fellow Trinity Evang. Div. Sch., 1990—, asst. dir. Extension and Continuing Edn., 1990—; with Moody Bible Inst. Extension Studies, Chgo., 1990—; pastor Lawrence House Congregation, Chgo., 1982-86. Mem. Evang. Theol. Soc., Soc. Bibl. Lit., Oriental Inst., Soc. for Study Old Testament. Home: 1508 Glencoe Ave Highland Park IL 60015 *What does God think of what I have done, what I am doing and what I intend to do?.*

KEMPER, DAVID SCOTT, minister, educator; b. Alhambra, Calif., Mar. 20, 1956; s. Donald Eugene and Lucy Elizabeth (Tuff) K.; m. Cheryl Ann Drozd, Nov. 11, 1974; children: David Scott Jr., Nathan Allen, Jonathan Steven, Jeremy James. Diploma, N.E. Inst., 1975, Gordon Conwell Sem., 1989; MRE, Gordon Conwell Sem., 1990; postgrad., Oxford Grad. Sch., 1991—. Ordained to ministry, 1988. Assoc. pastor Fellowship Bible Ch., Burlington, Mass., 1987—; adj. prof. Gordon Conwell Sem., Boston, 1991—; tchr. Assoc. Tech. Inst., Worburn, Mass., 1989—. Mem. New Eng. Network Youth Workers (coord. New Eng. region 1991—). Office: Fellowship Bible Ch 71 Center St Burlington MA 01803

KEMPSKI, RALPH ALOISIUS, bishop; b. Milw., July 16, 1934; s. Sigmund Joseph and Cecilia Josephine (Chojnacki) K.; m. Mary Jane Roth, July 30, 1955; children—Richard, Joan, John. B.A., Augsburg Coll., 1960; M.Div., Northwestern Luth. Theol. Sem., 1963; D.Div., Wittenberg U., Springfield, Ohio, 1980. Pastor Epiphany Luth. Ch., Mpls., 1963-68; pastor St. Stephen Luth. Ch., Louisville, Ky., 1968-71, Our Saviour Luth. Ch., West Lafayette, Ind., 1971-79; bishop Ind.-Ky. Synod Luth. Ch., Am., Indpls., 1979-87, Ind.-Ky. Synod Evang. Luth. Ch. Am., 1987—; bd. dirs. Luth. Sch. Theology Chgo., 1979-88 , Wittenberg U., Springfield, Ohio, 1979—; governing bd. Nat. Coun. Chs. Christ U.S.A., N.Y.C., 1981-88, Luth. Theol. So. Sem., 1988—; v.p. Ind. Coun. Chs., 1991—. Avocations: gardening, reading, camping, travelling, flying. Office: Evang Luth Ch in Am 9102 N Meridian St Indianapolis IN 46260

KEMPTON, TODD DANIEL, minister; b. Daly City, Calif., June 16, 1968; s. John Howard and Sandra Kay (Schirer) K. BA, Harding U., 1990. Asst. youth minister Coll. Ch. of Christ, Searcy, Ark., 1986-90; assoc. minister/youth minister Nash (Tex.) Ch. of Christ, 1990—; campaigner internat. campaigns/Harding U., Poland, Austria, Switzerland, others, summer 1988, 90. Hosp. clergy area hosps., Texarkana, Tex., 1990—. Recipient Bible scholarships Harding U., Searcy, 1988-90. Mem. Area-wide Youth Ministers Assn. (sec. 1990—). Republican. Home: 4615 Summerhill Rd PO Box 76 Texarkana TX 75503 Office: Nash Church of Christ PO Box 524 Nash TX 75569

KENDALL, CHARLES TERRY, librarian; b. Chambersburg, Pa., Aug. 13, 1949; s. Guy William and Virginia Mae (Naugle) K.; m. Alice Marie Bienz, Aug. 21, 1971; children: Terri, Anita, Kendra. BA, Huntington (Ind.) Coll., 1971; MLS, George Peabody Coll., 1972; postgrad., Asbury Theol. Sem., 1982-83; MA in Religion, Anderson (Ind.) U., 1990. Dir. Byrd Meml. Libr. Anderson Sch. Theology, Anderson U., 1983-89; theol. studies libr. Anderson U. Libr., 1989—. Mem. Am. Theol. Libr. Assn. Office: Anderson U Libr Anderson IN 46012

KENDALL, DAVID WALTER, minister; b. Flint, Mich., May 17, 1954; s. Walter B. and Shirley (Warner) K.; m. Lavone Renee Kendall, Aug. 16, 1975; children: Charis, Rachel, Katrina. BA, Spring Arbor (Mich.) Coll., 1976; MDiv, Asbury Theol. Seminary, Wilmore, Ky., 1979; PhD, Union Theol. Seminary, Richmond, Va., 1984. Ordained to ministry Free Meth. Ch. as elder, 1982. Teaching fellow in Greek Asbury Theol. Seminary, 1979-81; pastor Charlotte (Mich.) Free Meth. Ch., 1984-87; sr. pastor Ferndale (Mich.) Free Meth. Ch., 1987-91, Mc Pherson (Kans.) Free Meth. Ch., 1991—; del. Gen. Conf. Free Meth. Ch., 1989—; mem. editorial com. Illustrated Bible Life, 1985—; mem. study Commn. Doctrine of Free Meth. Ch., 1989—. Contbr. articles to profl. jours. Mem. Soc. Bibl. Lit.

KENDRICK, JAMES ERVIN, minister; b. Memphis, Dec. 13, 1948; s. James and Effie Mae (Lane) K.; m. Yvonne Deloris Thrill, Oct. 13, 1972; children: Tanarsha Nichole, J. Michael, Ebony Michelle. BS in Theology and Psychology, Crichton Coll., 1988. Ordained to ministry Bapt. Ch., 1980. Interim pastor Geeter Pk. Bapt. Ch., Memphis, 1980-81; pastor Enon Springs Bapt. Ch., Hernando, Miss., 1981-84, Oakgrove Bapt. Ch., Memphis, 1985—. Bd. dirs. Memphis Literacy Coun., 1990—, Justice Ministries, 1991—; chmn. mins. adv. com. Memphis Housing Authority, 1991—; founder, dir. United Leaders Against Crime, Memphis, 1991—. With U.S. Army, 1968-70, Vietnam. Mem. Union Progressive Assn. (vice moderator 1989—). Home: 3240 Crete Ave Memphis TN 38111 Office: Oakgrove Bapt Ch 183 Joubert Ave Memphis TN 38109

KENNA, JOHN THOMAS, priest; b. N.Y.C., July 19, 1919; s. John Joseph and Nadja Louise (Leahy) K. AB, St. Mary's Sem., Balt., 1943; MDiv, Holy Apostles Sem., Cromwell, Conn., 1987. Ordained priest Roman Cath. Ch., 1988. Assoc. pastor St. Patrick's Ch., Corpus Christi, Tex., 1988—; dir. NCCJ, Kans. region, 1948-50, Ky. region, 1950-56; assoc. dir., Chgo. region, 1956-58; founding dir., Religious Activities Div., Nat. Safety Coun., 1958-60; instr. St. Basil's Coll., Stamford, Conn., 1945-47. Author: Safety in the 60's, 1959, Latinization of the U.S., 1983 (for 1983 Yearbook, Encyclopedia Britannica). Co-founder, bd. dirs. Nat. Cath. Conf. for Interracial Justice, Chgo., 1959-80; bd. dirs. Safer Found, Chgo., 1980-83; regional dir. Nat. Easter Seals Soc., 1966-68; dir. info. svcs., Pres. Kennedy's Com. on Youth Employment, 1961-63; dir. leadership devel., Nat. Coun. Cath. Men, Washington, 1960-61. With U.S. Merchant Marine, 1943-44. Mem. Corpus Christi Ministerial Alliance (pres. 1990—). Democrat. Home and Office: St Patricks Ch 3350 S. Alameda Corpus Christi TX 74811 *Too many people think life is over at 60 or 65. Wrong, if you have health and ability and self-confidence. I was ordained at 68 and am still enjoying a fruitful ministry!.*

KENNARD, ELIZABETH, pastor; b. Boston, July 7, 1947. BA, U. Conn., 1972; MA, U. Hartford, Conn., 1975; MDiv, Yale U., 1983. Pastor First Congl. Ch., Plymouth, Conn., 1983-89, Coventry, Conn., 1989—. Vol. tutor Literacy Vols. of Am., Mansfield, Conn., 1990—. Mem. Am. Psychol. Assn. (assoc.). Home: 70 Lynwood Rd Storrs CT 06268 Office: First Congl Ch Box 355 Coventry CT 06238

KENNEDY, ARTHUR LEO, priest; b. Boston, Jan. 9, 1942; s. Arthur L. and Helen I. (O'Rourke) K. BA, St. John's Coll., 1963; MST, Gregorian U., 1967; PhD, Boston U., 1978. Ordained priest Roman Cath. Ch., 1966. Assoc. pastor St. Monica's Ch., Methuen, Mass., 1967-69, St. Joseph's Ch., East Boston, Mass., 1969-74, Holy Trinity Ch., South St. Paul, Minn., 1974-82, Assumption Ch., St. Paul, 1982—; assoc. prof., chair dept. theology U. St. Thomas, St. Paul, 1985-90; chair com. on ecumenism and interreligious affairs Archdiocese of St. Paul and Mpls., 1987—; vis. fellow Inst. für die Wissenschaften von Menshen Vienna, Austria, 1991. Editor: Collected Works of Bernard Lonergan; contbr. articles to profl. jours. Councillor Lonergan Trust Fund, Toronto, Ont., Can., 1981—. Mem. Am. Acad. Religion, Cath. Theol. Soc. Am., Am. Philos. Assn., Boston Theol. Inst., Jaspers Soc. N.Am. Home: 47 Crehore Rd Chestnut Hill MA 02167 Office: The Coll St Thomas 2115 Summit Ave Saint Paul MN 55105

KENNEDY, BERNARD PETER MEL, priest; b. Dublin, Ireland, May 20, 1952; s. William Augustine and Alice (Hughes) K. Student, De LaSalle Coll., 1963-72. Lab. asst. Cheeseborogh Ponds, Dublin, 1970-72; deacon Good Shepherd Ch. Churchtown, Dublin, 1978-79; religious educator Community Coll. Sallyvoggin, Dublin, 1979-83, Balbriggan Community Coll., Dublin, 1983—; youth ministry coord. Sallynoggin Ch., Dublin, 1979-83; spiritual counsellor St. Garbriels Hosp., Dublin, 1982-83; chaplain Loreto Convent Balbriggan, Dublin, 1983—; spiritual adviser North Dublin Charismatic Movement, Dublin, 1983-88, Balbriggan Coun. Against Bloodsports, Dublin, 1988—; chaplain Balbriggan Renewal Group, Dublin, 1983—. Contbr. articles to Intercom mag., and poetry to Stet mag., Rainbows & Stone. V.p. Bracken Boxing Club, Balbriggan, 1986—; group leader 75th Troop Scout Assn., Dublin, 1979-83. Cert. in Philos. Studies Nat. Coun. for Ednl. Awards, 1978. Mem. Poetry Ireland, Leopardstown Club. Avocations: rugby, moutaineering, poetry, ballet, drama, music. Home and Office: Dublin St, Balbriggan, Dublin Ireland

KENNEDY, CALVIN FREDRICK, minister; b. Russellville, Ark., Dec. 7, 1933; s. Calvin Estes and Vida Mae (Williams) K.; m. Carole G. Bellar, July 22, 1956; children: Kimberly, Cara Lee, Julie Beth. BA, Western State Coll. Colo., 1958; MDiv, Phillips U., 1984; DD (hon.), Brownell U., 1981. Ordained to ministry Christian Ch. (Disciples of Christ), 1984. Math. tchr. Lordsburg (N.Mex.) High Sch., 1958-59; math., sci. tchr. La Junta (Colo.) High Sch., 1959-63; min. 1st Christian Ch., Mannford, Okla., 1973-76; min., tchr. Colo. Christian Sch., Denver, 1976-78; min. 1st Christian Ch., Las Animas, Colo., 1979-81, Billings, Okla., 1982-88, Anadarko, Okla., 1988—; del. Internat. Conv. Chs. of Christ, Jamaica, 1984, Gen. Assembly (Disciples of Christ), Indpls., 1990; dist. treas. Christian Ch. in Okla., Hobart, 1990—; dir. sec. sch. Colo. Christian Sch., Denver, 1975-77; math., English tchr., sr. tchr. Manzanola (Colo.) High Sch., 1977-82; math., English tchr. Billings (Okla.) Sch., 1984-88. Author: Military Word and Phrase Finder, 1980; writer, actor local TV show The Ultimate Gift, 1990. Mayor City of Manzanola, Colo., 1979-82; founder Billings Sr. Citizens Ctr., 1984-88; mem. Organ Donation Hot Line, 1989—; bd. dirs. Okla. Eye Bank, 1991—. Capt. U.S. Army, 1963-72; Vietnam. Decorated Air medal, Purple Heart, Bronze Star (2); Vietnamese Staff Svc. medal 1st class (Republic of Vietnam). Mem. Lions (v.p., pres. Manzanola club, 2d v.p. Anadarko club), Masons (32 degree). Republican. Home: 3014 S Mission Blvd Anadarko OK 73005 Office: 1st Christian Ch 212 SW 2d St Anadarko OK 73005 *Perhaps the greatest challenge facing Americans today is trying to be happy. Too many people depend on the wife or husband to make them happy. The key to remember is that the mate cannot make the other mate happy. The decision to be happy, must be made by each person.*

KENNEDY, DAVID LAURENCE, deacon; b. Racine, Wis., Jan. 17, 1936; s. Laurence Frank and Margaret Cecelia (Degrand) K. BS in Indsl. Tech., U. Wis.-Stout, Menomonie, 1965. Ordained deacon Roman Cath. Ch., 1975. Permanent deacon Sts. Edward and Rose Cath. Chs., Racine, Wis., 1975-91; sr. tech. writer Eaton Corp., Kenosha, Wis., 1966—. Scoutmaster Boy Scouts Am., Racine, 1965-74. With USNR, 1954-62. Mem. Deacon Senate Assn. Home: 1316 Russet St Racine WI 53405-2843

KENNEDY, EARL WILLIAM, religion educator; b. L.A., July 20, 1932; s. Earl Carleton and Eleanor Harris (Gregg) K.; m. Cornelia Breugem, Sept. 10, 1960; children: James Carleton, David Harris. AB, Occidental Coll., L.A., 1953; BD, Fuller Theol. Sem., Pasadena, Calif., 1956; ThM, Princeton Theol. Sem., 1958, ThD, 1968. Ordained to ministry United Presbyn. Ch. in U.S.A., 1963, transferred to Reformed Ch. in Am., 1970. Assoc. prof. religion Northwestern Coll., Orange City, Iowa, 1963-71, prof., 1971—, chmn. dept., 1987—; chmn. Commn. on History, Ref. Ch. in Am., 1990—. Contbr. articles and book revs. to religious publs. Mem. Phi Beta Kappa. Republican. Avocations: genealogy, music. Home: 321 Albany Ave NE Orange City IA 51041 Office: Northwestern Coll Dept Religion Orange City IA 51041

KENNEDY, FRANCIS BARRETT, priest; b. Cin., Aug. 10, 1915; s. Joseph James and Helen Marie (Taylor-Barrett) K. BA, Atheneum, Ohio, 1936; STL, Pontifical Gregorian U., Rome, 1940. Ordained priest Roman Cath. Ch., 1939, monsignor, 1957. Asst. pastor Archdiocese Cin., 1940-52; tchr., librarian Elder High Sch., Cin., 1946-52; asst. nat. sec. Cath. Nr. East Welfare Assn., N.Y.C., 1952-57; asst. dir. Papal mission to Palestinians, Beirut, 1954-56; rector St. Peter in Chains Cathedral, Cin., 1957-70; pastor St. William Ch., Cin., 1970-90, emeritus, 1990—; sec. Archdiocesan Priest Senate, 1966-72; dean St. Lawrence Deanery, Cin., 1972-75. Pres. HOPE Cin., 1967-72; chmn. trustees Sr. Chateau on the Hill, Cin., 1972—; mem. West End Task Force, 1967, Cin. Restoration, 1974-76. Lt. comdr. USNR, 1944-57. Named domestic prelate by Pope Paul VI, 1967; decorated knight comdr. with star Order Knights Holy Sepulchre, 1957. Mem. KC. Democrat. Address: 382 Liberty Ave Hamilton OH 45013

KENNEDY, KIRBY KENNETH, minister; b. Sidney, Nebr., Mar. 13, 1958; s. Martin Travis and Bessie Louvene (Brittain) K.; m. Debra Susan Klein, Aug. 10, 1985. BA in Religion, Wayland Bapt. U., Plainview, Tex., 1980; MDiv, Southwestern Bapt. Theol. Sem., Ft. Worth, 1984, D Ministry, 1991. Ordained to ministry So. Bapt. Conv., 1982. Min. music and youth Concord Bapt. Ch., Chandler, Tex., 1980-82; pastor 1st Bapt. Ch., Las Lunas, N.Mex., 1982-87, Calvary Bapt. Ch., Roswell, N.Mex., 1987—; pres. Ministerial Fellowship, Cen. Bapt. Assn., Albuquerque, 1984-86, chmn., mem. various coms., 1985-87; mem. associational coun. Pecos Valley Bapt. Assn., Artesia, N.Mex., 1987—, also chmn. stewardship coun., Christian life com.; mem. edn. com. Bapt. Conv. N.Mex., Albuquerque, 1986—, mem., sec. exec. bd., 1986-90, mem. Christian Life Commn., 1990—, convenor Evangelism Conf., 1991; mem. faculty Southeastern N.Mex. Congress on Family Living, Artesia, 1988, 89; chmn. upward 90 campaign Southwestern Bapt. Theol. Sem., N.Mex., 1985-90; nummerous others. Mgr. Valencia County Little League, Los Lunas, 1985; mem. disting. tchr. awards com. Los Lunas Sch. Dist., 1986-87. Mem. Southwestern Bapt. Theol. Sem. Alumni Assn. (pres. N.Mex. 1990-91). Home: 3501 Mission Arch Dr Roswell NM 88201 Office: Calvary Bapt Ch 1009 W Alameda PO Box 127 Roswell NM 88201 *The greatest knowledge and achievement is to know and experience God and His will. This not only brings peace and joy in the inner person in this life but also in the life to come. The beginning of this knowledge I experience is accepting Jesus Christ, God's Son, as Savior and Lord.*

KENNEDY, MARY ELIZABETH, missionary sister, educational administrator; b. New Castle, Pa., Aug. 14, 1926; d. Thomas G. and Mary Ann (Holloway) Lee; m. Charles Cunningham Kennedy, June 25, 1949; children—Charles Cunningham, Mary Ann, Elizabeth Rose, Grace Lorraine. B.A., Temple U., 1948; M.Bible Theology, Internat. Bible Inst., Fla., 1981. Lic. tchr., adminstr., clergywoman; lic. midwife. Missionary sister Ch. of God in Christ, Memphis, 1949—; co-founder, prin. Community Country

Day Sch., Erie, Pa., 1968—; co-founder, exec. dir. Community Drop-In Ctr., Erie, 1973-78; co-founder, dir. Community of Caring, Erie, 1982—; founder, dir. Project Hunger, 1984—; assoc. mem. Benedictine Sisters, Erie, 1982—; mem. internat. mission bd. Ch. of God in Christ, 1980—. Author: Love Therapy in Classroom Management, 1982; Teach Me, Lord, 1983. Bd. corporators Gannon U., Erie, 1980—; mem. Sta. WQLN, 1986—. Recipient Outstanding Educator award Mercyhurst Coll., Erie, 1973, Humanitarian award, 1980; Outstanding Educator award Gannon U., 1977, Nat. Faith and Svc. award Kappa Gamma Pi, 1991; named Church Mother, House of Prayer, 1975—; Kennedy Day proclaimed in her and spouse's honor Erie City and County, 1983. Mem. Internat. Assn. Psycho-Social Rehab. Services, Pi Gamma Mu. Democrat. Avocations: writing; singing; sports. Home: 2108 German St Erie PA 16503 Office: 5800 Zuck Rd Erie PA 16506 *Love is the most dynamic power on earth; it is capable of effecting tremendous changes in those we meet. Love can change the world. We simply have to let God's love flow through us to others.*

KENNEDY, RUSTY LANE, minister; b. Dallas, Jan. 13, 1964; s. William Arlis and Dixie Jean (Brunkow) K.; m. Michelle Renee Wilson, May 31, 1986. BA, Okla. Bapt. U., 1986; MQA, Southwestern Bapt. Theol. Sem., 1988. Ordained to ministry So. Bapt. Conv., 1989. Youth assoc. First Bapt. Ch., Tulsa, 1984-85; recreation intern Park Cities Bapt. Ch., Dallas, 1986-88; minister of activities, youth Northside Bapt. Ch., Indpls., 1989—; assoc. youth dir. Met. Bapt. Assn., Indpls., 1989-91, youth asst. dir., 1990-91. Counselor Listening Post, Lawrence Twp.-Lawrence Cen. High Sch., Indpls., 1989-91. Mem. Reflections Club (dir. 1989-91). Republican. Home: 6811 Wild Cherry Dr Fishers IN 46038 Office: Northside Bapt Ch 3021 E 71st St Indianapolis IN 46220 *Your life is worth as much as you invest in it.*

KENNEDY, SANDRA GAIL, minister; b. Midville, Ga., Nov. 2, 1943; d. Harry Pybus Kennedy and Martha Ann (Hurst) Chandler. BS in Edn., Ga. So. U., 1965; M of Religious Edn., Southwestern Bapt. Theol., Seminary, Ft. Worth, 1969, Grad. Specialist in Edn., 1972. Cert. pub. mgr., chaplain. Youth dir. First Bapt. Ch., Brunswick, Ga., 1965-67; GA and Acteens dir. Md. Bapt. Conv., Balt., 1969-72; asst. to minister Midville (Ga.) First Bapt. Ch., 1974-82, Woodlawn Bapt. Ch., Augusta, Ga., 1982-83; pastor Whole Life Ministries, Augusta, 1987—; tchr. Glynn County Bd. Edn., Brunswick, 1965-67; youth/children's dir. Md. Bapt. Conv., 1969-72; dist. dir. Mental Health/Mental Retardation, Waynesboro, Ga., 1973-87. Mem. Salvation Army, 1989-91, Sr. Citizens Assn., 1989, The Encouragers, 1988-91, Women in Leadership, 1989-91, Charismatic Bible Ministries, 1986-91. Named to Outstanding Young Women of Am., 1971. Office: Whole Life Ministries 1929 Walton Way Augusta GA 30904 *In my walk with the Lord, I have discovered that it really doesn't matter where one has been, only where one is going.*

KENNEDY, WILLIAM BEAN, theology educator; b. Spartanburg, S.C., Oct. 18, 1926; s. Leland McDuffie and Elizabeth Fleming (Bean) K.; m. Frances Barron Harris, July 9, 1952; children: Katharine Fleming, William Bean, Jane Harris, Emily Pou. B.A., Wofford Coll., 1947, LL.D. (hon.), 1970; M.A., Duke U., 1948; B.D., Union Theol. Sem., Richmond, Va., 1954; Ph.D., Yale U., 1957. Ordained to ministry Presbyn. Ch. (U.S.A.), 1954. Tchr. Spartanburg High Sch., 1948-49; instr. Emory U. at Oxford, 1949-51; minister of edn. First Congl. Ch., West Haven, Conn., 1954-57; asst. prof. Christian edn. Union Theol. Sem., Richmond, 1957-59, assoc. prof., 1959-65; sec. edn. Bd. Christian Edn., Presbyn. Ch. U.S., Richmond, 1965-69; dir. office edn. World Council Chs., Geneva, 1969-75; dir. Atlanta Assn. Internat. Edn., 1976-79; prof. religion and edn. Union Theol. Sem., N.Y.C., 1979-81, Skinner and McAlpin prof. practical theology, 1981—; mem. task force on world hunger Presbyn. Ch. U.S., Atlanta, 1976-82; cons. hunger program Nat. Council Chs., N.Y.C., 1981; cons. pilot immersion project for globalization of theol. edn., Plowshares Inst., 1988—. Author: Into Covenant Life, 1963, Shaping of Protestant Education, 1965; author, editor: (with others) Pedagogies for the Non-Poor, 1987; contbr. numerous articles, revs. to profl. jours. Served with USN, 1945-46. Moore fellow, 1954; recipient issues research grant Assn. Theol. Schs., Vandalia, Ohio, 1982. Mem. Nat. Council Chs. (pres. profs. and research sect. 1961-62, div. edn. and ministry unit com.), Religious Edn. Assn. (bd. dirs. 1981—, chmn. bd. dirs. 1984-89), Assn. Profs. and Researchers in Religious Edn. (bd. dirs. 1983-85, pres. 1990-91), Am. Acad. of Religion, Soc. for the Scientific Study of Religion, Phi Beta Kappa. Democrat. Presbyterian. Home: 99 Claremont Ave Apt 501 New York NY 10027 Office: Union Theol Sem 3041 Broadway New York NY 10027

KENNELLY, SISTER KAREN MARGARET, college administrator; b. Graceville, Minn., Aug. 4, 1933; d. Walter John Kennelly and Clara Stella Eastman. BA, Coll. St. Catherine, St. Paul, 1956; MA, Cath. U. Am., 1958; PhD, U. Calif., Berkeley, 1962. Joined Sisters of St. Joseph of Carondelet, Roman Cath. Ch., 1954. Prof. history Coll. St. Catherine, 1962-71, acad. dean, 1971-79; exec. dir. Nat. Fedn. Carondelet Colls., U.S., 1979-82; province dir. Sisters of St. Joseph of Carondelet, St. Paul, 1982-88; pres. Mt. St. Mary's Coll., L.A., 1989—; cons. N. Cen. Accreditation Assn., Chgo., 1974-84, Ohio Bd. Regents, Columbus, 1983-89; trustee colls., hosps., Minn., Wis., Calif., 1972—. Editor, co author: American Catholic Women, 1989; author: (with others) Women of Minnesota, 1977. Fulbright fellow, 1964, Am. Coun. Learned Socs. fellow, 1964-65. Mem. Am. Hist. Soc., Am. Cath. Hist. Soc., Medieval Acad., Am. Assn. Rsch. Historians on Medieval Spain. Roman Catholic. Avocations: skiing, cuisine. Home and Office: 12001 Chalon Rd Los Angeles CA 90049

KENNETT, COLETTE ANN, religious organization administrator; b. Breese, Ill., May 2, 1951; d. John Franklin and Virginia Mary (Micheel) K. BA, Park Coll., 1971; MS, So. Ill. U., Edwardsville, 1980; postgrad., Loyola U., Chgo., 1986—. Clk., stenographer U.S. Treasury Dept., St. Louis, 1969-72, U.S. Dept. of Def., Scott AFB, Ill., 1972-79; assoc. dir. Cath. Youth Orgn. Belleville (Ill.) Diocesan, 1979-83, dir., 1983—; legal sec. Listeman, Bandy & Hamilton, New Baden, Ill., 1969-72; coll. instr. Kaskaskia Jr. Coll., Centralia, Ill., 1983-86; bd. dirs. Diocesan Cath. Newspaper, Belleville, Ill., 1980-82; chairperson Diocesan Youth Ministry Coalition, Belleville, 1985-86, assoc. coord., 1990; vice chairperson region VII of Youth Ministry Coalition, 1990—; mem. Guatemalan Mission Soc. Bd., 1991—, ad hoc com. Teens Encounter, Christ/Residents Encounter, Christ Com., Nat. Teens Encounter Christ Conf., 1990; mem. Guatemalan Mission Soc. Bd., 1991—; assoc. coord. Region VII Youth Ministry Coaliation, 1991—. Vol. Clinton Manor Shelter Care, New Baden, Ill., 1969-76, Menard Correctional Ctr., Chester, Ill., 1984—, Centralia (Ill.) Correctional Ctr., 1983—, Vienna Correctional Ctr., 1975—, Ill. Youth Ctr., Dixon Springs, Ill., 1980-82, Harrisburg, 1983; campaign chairperson, Cystic Fibrosis Found., St. Louis, 1985-89, Teens Encounter Christ, Belleville, 1978-82; vice chairperson Diocesan mem. Cath. div. Girl Scouts U.S., 1983— (medal 1987, 88); mem. Nat. Cath. Com. for Campfire and Girl Scouts, 1988—; sec. Residents Encounter Christ, Belleville, 1984-85, Clinton County Assn. for Spl. Persons, Breese, 1982-84, Nat. Teens Encounter Christ, Belleville, 1977-81; exec. com. Region VII Youth Coalition, Chgo., 1979-86; bd. dirs. Clinton County Mental Health Bd., Breese, 1970-72; mem. Boy Scouts Am., 1986—, Area 12 Spl. Olympics, 1979—. Recipient voice scholarship So. Ill. U., Edwardsville, 1969, Ill. Tchrs. scholarship, 1969, Spirit of St. Francis award St. Francis Coll., 1987, cert. of achievement A World of Difference, 1991; named Outstanding Am. Woman for State of Ill. Lady Stetson Cologne, 1987. Avocations: writing, singing, photography. Home: 305 E Cedar St New Baden IL 62265 Office: Cath Youth Orgn 2620 Lebanon Ave Belleville IL 62221

KENNEY, BRAD THOMAS, minister; b. Dayton, Ohio, Oct. 19, 1956; s. Thomas Marion and Elizabeth (McKinley) K.; m. Teresa Lynn Nelms, Dec. 31,1981. BSBA, U. Dayton, 1978; MBA, Hardin Simmons U., 1981; MDiv, Southwestern Bapt. Theol. Sem., Ft. Worth, Tex., 1987; postgrad. studies, Southwestern Bapt. Theol. Sem., 1988—. Ordained to ministry Bapt. Ch., 1987. Home parent Paul Anderson Youth Homes, Lewisville, Tex., 1984-85; pastor Mission of First Bapt. Ch., Waxahachie, Tex., 1985-87, Verona Bapt. Ch., Blue Ridge, Tex., 1987-90; assoc. pastor Legacy Dr. Bapt. Ch., Plano, Tex., 1991—; Bapt. student dir. Collin Bapt. Assn., McKinney, Tex., 1990; mem. Big Country So. Bapt. Assn. Coll. Coms., Abilene, Tex., 1982-83; chmn. Collin Bapt. Assn. Student Com., McKinney, Tex., 1988-90. Staff sgt. USAF, 1979-81. Mem. Soc. of Bibl. Lit., Nat. Assn. Bapt. Profs. Religion. Republican. Home: 618 Willow Oak Allen TX 75002 Office: Legacy Dr Bapt Ch 4501 Legacy Dr Plano TX 75024

KENNEY, DEBORAH CHRISTINE, lay worker; b. N.Y.C., Jan. 10, 1956; d. Christian Peter Magnussen and Louvinia (Tipton) Thiel; m. Dennis Sundquist, June 10, 1980 (div. Aug. 1984); 1 child, Karli Sundquist; m. Michael Stanton Kenney, Apr. 25, 1986; 1 child, Melissa. Med. asst. diploma with honors, Health Careers, Merchantville, N.J., 1976. Cert. religious educator; cert. master catechist. Lector St. Joe's Pro Cathedral, Camden, N.J., 1986—, religion educator, 1988—, environ. coord., youth group advisor, mem. liturgy com., 1989—, centennial environ. coord., 1990—. Scenery designer, creative cons., dir. ch. plays including Tales of Wonder, 1990. Prodn. coord. Burlington PTA, Pennsauken, N.J., 1989-90, rec. sec., 1990—, drug, health, and environment officer, 1990—. Home: 2308 48th St Pennsauken NJ 08110-2046

KENNEY, LAWRENCE JAMES, bishop; b. New Rochelle, N.Y., Aug. 30, 1930; s. Alexander Lawrence and Madeleine Rose (O'Gorman) K. BA, Cathedral Coll., N.Y.C., 1952; MS in Edn., Iona Coll., 1971. Ordained priest Roman Catholic Ch., 1956. Asst. pastor St. Lawrence O'Toole Ch., Brewster, N.Y., 1956, Holy Cross Ch., N.Y.C., 1956-59; mem. N.Y. Apostolate Mission Band, 1959-67; asst. pastor St. Stephen Ch., N.Y.C., 1967, St. Barnabas Ch., Bronx, N.Y., 1967-69; asst. chancellor Archdiocese of N.Y., 1969-71, vice chancellor, dir. priest personnel, 1971-73, sec. to Terence Cardinal Cooke, 1973-83; chaplain to His Holiness, 1971, prelate of His Holiness, 1974; consecrated bishop Roman Catholic Ch., 1983; titular bishop of Holar, aux. bishop mil. svcs. Silver Spring, Md., 1983—.

KENNY, MICHAEL H., bishop; b. Hollywood, Calif., June 26, 1937. Ed., St. Joseph Coll., Mountain View, Calif., St. Patrick's Sem., Menlo Park, Calif., Cath. U. Am. Ordained priest Roman Cath. Ch., 1963; ordained bishop of Juneau, Alaska, 1979—. Office: Diocese of Juneau 419 6th St Juneau AK 99801

KENSEY, CALVIN D., bishop. Bishop Ch. of God in Christ, Jacksonville, Fla. Office: Ch of God in Christ 9462 August Dr Jacksonville FL 32208*

KENSKY, ALLAN DAVID, rabbi; b. N.Y.C., July 17, 1946; s. Samuel R. and Ada (Leinwand) K.; m. Tikva Simone Frymer, Oct. 20, 1974; children: Meira, Eitan. BA, Queens Coll., 1967; MA, NYU, 1971; M. Hebrew Letters, Jewish Theol. Sem. Am., 1969, PhD, 1990. Ordained rabbi, 1971. Rabbi Beth Israel Congregation, Ann Arbor, Mich., 1971-88; scholar-in-residence Har Zion Temple, Penn Valley, Pa., 1988-91; vis. asst. prof. Jewish Theol. Sem., N.Y.C., 1989—, assoc. dean Rabbinical Sch., 1991—; bd. dirs. United Synagogue Am., Mich., 1972-73. Mem. Rabbinical Assembly, Assn. Jewish Studies.

KENT, CLIFFORD EUGENE, priest; b. Butler County, Kans., Oct. 11, 1920; s. Oris Glee and Lucy (Sillin) K.; m. Elizabeth Rue, Oct. 3, 1942; children: Jane Durose, Peter Reeves, Richard Dennis. BS, Purdue U., 1942; BTh, Diocesan Sch. for Ministry, San Francisco, 1980. Ordained deacon Episcopal Ch., 1982, priest, 1984; registered profl. engr., Wash., Calif. Engr., scientist various energy devel. cos., space industries, nuclear power plants, 1942-83; priest assoc. St. Andrew's Episcopal Ch., Saratoga, Calif., 1983-86; assisting priest Trinity Episcopal Ch., Sonoma, Calif., 1987-90; interim rector St. Patrick's Episcopal Ch., Kenwood, Calif., 1990-91; assisting priest St. Patrick's Episcopal Ch., Kenwood, Calif., 1991—; camp dir. St. Andrew's Epis. Ch., 1978-86; mem. coun. Diocese of El Camino Real, Seaside, Calif., 1984, 85. Contbr. articles to engrng. jours.; patentee air-depolarized batteries. Mem. Am. Chem. Soc.

KENT, HARRY ROSS, lay church worker, construction executive; b. Upland, Pa., Oct. 17, 1921; s. Bernard Cleveland and Edith Mary (Johnson) K.; m. Aurelia Naomi Canady, Jan. 15, 1945; children: Jennifer Gayle, Edith Marie. BS in Physics and Chemistry, Coll. William and Mary. Instr. physics The Citadel, 1947-51; with Canady Constrn. Co., 1951-78, sec.-treas., 1960-74, pres., 1974-78; v.p. K.C. Stier & Co., Inc., 1974-78, Stier, Kent and Canady, Inc., 1978—; mem. exec. coun. World Meth. Coun., 1991—. Mem. Asbury Meml. Meth. Ch., Charleston, S.C., 1946—, mem. commn. on stewardship and fin., 1949—, treas., 1951-58, 68—, lay mem. ann. conf., 1959-70, 80—, trustee, 1963-74, chmn. long-range planning com., 1957-70, tchr. ch. sch.; mem. bd. bldg. and ch. location Charleston dist. United Meth. Ch., 1958—, pres. bd. missions and ch. extension, 1958—, dist. trustee, 1960—, chmn. bd. dist trustees, 1974—, chmn. bd. missions, 1975—; mem. bd. lay activities S.C. ann. conf. United Meth. Ch., 1957—, mem. coordinating coun., 1960—, vice-chmn. continuing com. on merger, conf. lay leader, 1970-80, chmn. equitable salary commn., 1984-88, mem. coun. on fin. and adminstrn., 1988—; conf. pres. United Meth. Men, 1980-84; del. southeastern jurisdiction conf. United Meth. Ch., gen. conf., 1966, 68, 70, 72, 76, 80, 84, 88, gen. coun. on ministries, 1980-88, chmn. Africa sect. of advance com., mem. gen. bd. discipleship, 1988—; mem. exec. bd. Coastal Carolina coun. Boy Scouts Am., 1960—, chmn. Charleston dist. bd., 1967; various exec. positions St. Andrew's schs. PTA, 1963-68; bd. dirs. Piedmont Nursing Ctr., 1967-82, treas., 1970-82; vice-chmn. civil engrng. adv. bd. Trident Tech. Coll., Charleston, 1969-71, chmn., 1971-80; pres. Charleston Boys Coun., 1982-86, v.p., 1987—. Lt. comdr. USN, World War II, Res. Recipient God and Country award, Scouters award, Scoutmasters Key, 50-Yr. Vet. award, Silver Beaver award Boy Scouts Am., God and Svc. award United Meth. Ch./Boy Scouts Am. Mem. ASTM, Associated Gen. Contractors, Am. Phys. Soc., Am. Assn. Physics Tchrs., Charleston Trident C. of C., Country Club Charleston. Home: 2935 Doncaster Dr Charleston SC 29414

KENT, ODA ALLEN, pastor, clinical psychologist; b. Stilwell, Okla., Dec. 21, 1945; s. John Benton and Ella Mae (Heustis) K.; m. Ava Lynn Smith, Mar. 25, 1983. BA, MA, Pepperdine U., 1969, 71; MS, Calif. State U., 1986; PhD, U. Calif., Berkeley, 1988; D in Ministry, Bethany Sem., 1989. Lic. clin. psychologist. Assoc. pastor Lodi (Calif.) Community, 1981-87; sr. pastor Community Ch. of God, Capitola, Calif., 1988—; pres. Santa Cruz (Calif.) Ministerial Fellowship, 1989—; vice-chmn., trustee Warner Pacific Coll., Portland, Oreg., 1989—, regent, 1990—; regent Asbury Theol. Sem., Wilmore, Ky., 1990—. Author: The Christian at Home, 1987, Revelation, 1990; contbr. articles to profl. publs. Mem., advisor Govs. Task Force on Alcohol and Drug Abuse, Sacramento, Calif., 1989—; bd. advisors Interfaith Disaster Recovery Project, Santa Cruz, 1987—. Capt. U.S. Army, 1965-68, Vietnam. Named one of Outstanding Young Men of Am. Jaycees, 1970, Outstanding Community Leader City of Chandler, Ariz., 1981. Mem. APA, Am. Assn. Christian Counselors, Am. Assn. Family Counselors (adv. bd. 1989—), Nat. Rehab. Assn., Nat. Psychiatric Assn. Democrat. Home: 1963 Catalina Dr Santa Cruz CA 95062 Office: Community Ch of God 1255 41st Ave Capitola CA 95010

KENT, PAUL J., religion educator; b. Shreveport, La., June 23, 1955; s. Keith C. and Louise (Goode) K.; m. Lyn Brown, Aug. 9, 1980; children: Andrew Lee, Collin Lyle. BS in Edn., Baylor U., 1977; MDiv, Southwestern Bapt. Theol. Sem., Ft. Worth, 1981; postgrad., So. Bapt. Sem., Louisville, 1988—. Ordained to ministry So. Bapt. Conv., 1981. Chaplain intern Baylor U. Med. Ctr., Dallas, 1981-82; min. edn. and adminstrn. 7th and James Bapt. Ch., Waco, Tex., 1983-90; min. edn. Willow Meadows Bapt. Ch., Houston, 1990—. Bd. dirs. Ctr. for Action Against Sexual Assault, Waco, 1988-90, Family Counseling and Children's Svcs., Waco., 1989-90, Evangelia Settlement Day Care, McLennan County, 1989-90; mem. Waco-McLennan County Teen Pregnancy Steering Com., 1985-87. Fellow Nat. Assn. Ch. Bus. Adminstrn. Democrat. Office: Willow Meadows Bapt Ch 4300 W Bellfort Houston TX 77035

KENZY, JOHN QUINTON, minister; b. Morrill, Nebr., Nov. 29, 1941; s. Eugene Edward and Opal Edna (Fees) K.; m. Carol Ann Young, June 20, 1964; children: Renee Lynne, Rachelle Genee, Ronda Kay Kenzy Richards, Raelene Joy. BA, Cen. Bible Coll., Springfield, Mo., 1964; DD (hon.), Gt. Commn. Theol. Sem., Rossville, Ga., 1986. Cert. in Christian counseling United Assn. Christian Counselors. Dir. Teen-Age Evangelism, Springfield, 1963-64; dir. edn. Teen Challenge, Bklyn., 1964-65; acad. dean Teen Challenge Inst. Missions, Rhinebeck, N.Y., 1965-68; pres. Youth Challenge Internat. Bible Inst., Sunbury, Pa., 1968—; founding pastor New Creation Chapel, Sunbury, 1983-91; bd. dirs. Teen Challenge, 1966-72; sec. Youth Challenge Internat., Hartford, Conn., 1984-90; sec., pres. Susquehanna Valley Assn. Evangelicals, Hummels Wharf, Pa., 1985-87; com. chmn. So. Accrediting Assn. of Bible Colls., Atlanta, 1987. Author: (recs.) I've Been New-Born, 1969, It Depends on You, 1974, God Speaks to Me, 1983; (books) Reversing Deviate Behavior, 1981, Youth Challenge Staff Instructional Manual, 1984. Republican. Home and Office: Youth Challenge Internat Bible Inst RD 2 Box 33 Sunbury PA 17801

KEOUGH, JAMES GILLMAN, JR., minister; b. Reading, Pa., June 2, 1947; s. James Gillman Sr. and Nora (Deturck) K.; m. Dawn Eileen Wiest, Sept. 17, 1976; children: Cynthia Ann, James Michael, Wendy Sue, Danielle Lynn, Erin Mae, Bevin Leigh. BA in History Edn., Messiah Coll., Grantham, Pa., 1970; MDiv, Lancaster (Pa.) Theol. Sem., 1973; D of Ministry, Ashland (Ohio) Theol. Sem., 1980. Ordained to ministry United Ch. Christ, 1973. Minister St. Luke's United Ch. Christ, Kenhorst, Pa., 1972-75, Congl. Ch., Winchester, Va., 1975-78, 1st Congl. Ch., Newton Falls, Ohio, 1978-82, Cen. Congl. Ch., Middleboro, Mass., 1982-85; sr. minister 1st Congl. Ch., Pontiac, Mich., 1985—. Author: Teaching Prayer in the Local Parish, 1980. Bd. dirs. Clinton Valley coun. Boy Scouts Am.; bd. dirs. Boys Clubs Am., Pontiac; pres. Somebodycares, Pontiac, 1983—; active Dem. Century Club. Mem. Nat. Assn. Congl. Christian Chs., S.E. Mich. Congl. Ministerium, Pontiac Ministers Assn. Lodge: Kiwanis. Avocations: reading, hiking, fishing. Home: 3062 St Jude Dr Waterford MI 48329 Office: 1st Congl Church Clarkston Rd at Pine Knob Rd PO Box 221 Clarkston MI 48347-0221

KEOWN, WILLIAM ARVEL, minister; b. Clinton, Ind., June 4, 1920; s. James and Lula (Jackson) K.; m. Jewel Cook, Mar. 25, 1950; children: Evelyn, Deborah, William, Duane, Wayne. ThB, God's Bible Sch., Cin., 1949; MA, Butler U., 1956; cert., Ind. State U., 1961. Ordained to ministry Ch. of God (Anderson, Ind.), 1957. Dean of men God's Bible Sch. and Coll., Cin., 1948-49; pastor ch. Evansville and Clinton, Ind., 1950-52; tchr. Frankfort (Ind.) Coll., 1954-57, dean of men, 1954-55; tchr. jr. high sch. Clinton, 1957-79; pastor 1st Ch. of God, Terre Haute, Ind., 1970-80, interim pastor, 1980-81, assoc. min., 1981—; instr. Ind. State Dept. Corrections, Anderson, 1979-82. Fellow Internat. Platform Assn.; mem. Nat. Ret. Tchrs. Assn, Ind. Ret. Tchrs. Assn., Ind. Ministerial Assembly. Home and Office: Rte 2 Box 47 Clinton IN 47842 *Applying singularity of purpose by enjoying each thing in itself in life makes apparently complex things open up to the simplicity of understanding necessary for enjoyable comprehension. I find in all disciplines (religion, science, philosophy, etc.) the interrelatedness of each to the other. That which at first appears to be totally incomprehensible responds to this view of relationships; consequently learning is fun, not drudgery.*

KERBER, WALTER JOSEF, Jesuit priest; b. Karlsruhe, Baden, Germany, Mar. 28, 1926; s. Josef and Rosa (Zimmermann) K. Lic.phil, Berchmanskolleg, 1950; S.T.L., Loyola U., Chgo., 1956; PhD, Pontifical Gregorian U., 1961; PhD in Econs., U. Freiburg, 1966. Lectr. Berchmanskolleg, Pullach, Federal Republic of Germany, 1960-67; prof. Berchmanskolleg, Pullach, 1967, Hochschule fuer Philosophie, Munich, Federal Republic of Germany, 1971—; dir. Institut fuer Gesellschaftspolitik, Munich, 1976-86, Rottendorf Forschungsprojekt, Munich, 1984—. Author: Ethos und Religion bei Fuehrungskraeften, 1986; contbr. articles to profl. jours. Editor: Rottendorf-Schriften, 1985—. With German Air Force, 1944-45. Mem. Am. Econ. Assn., Internat. Gesellschaft fuer Rechts und Sozialphilosophie, Allgemeine Deutsche Gesellschaft fuer Philosophie, Groupe Européen des Jésuites en Sciences Sociales, Arbeitskreis fuer Fuehrungs Kraefte. Roman Catholic. Avocation: chess. Home and Office: Kaulbachstrasse 33, D 8000 Munich Federal Republic of Germany

KERBY, CLEVE LOY, minister; b. Denver City, Tex., June 12, 1953; s. Deward H. and Odell G. (Jenkins) K.; m. Sharon Fay MacGregor, July 26, 1974; children: Christopher Loy, April Dawn. AA, South Plains Coll., 1973; BA, Hardin-Simmons U., 1978; MDiv, Southwestern Bapt. Theol. Sem., Ft. Worth, 1981, D of Ministry, 1990. Ordained to ministry So. Bapt. Conv., 1975. Pastor 1st Bapt. Ch., Carrizozo, N.Mex., 1981-83, Ruidoso, N.Mex., 1983-87; pastor Blodgett St. Bapt. Ch., Carlsbad, N.Mex., 1987—; leader critical incident stress debriefing team State of N.Mex., 1988-91; chaplain Carlsbad Police Dept., 1987-91, Ruidoso Police Dept., 1983-87; sec. exec. bd. Bapt. Conv. N.Mex., Albuquerque, 1983-87. Mem. Internat. Conf. Police Chaplains, Hardin-Simmons Alumni (pres. 1988-89), Kiwanis (bd. mem. 1986-87). Republican. Office: Blodgett St Bapt Ch 1500 W Blodgett Carlsbad NM 88220

KEREKES, JOSEPH JOHN, evangelist; b. Toledo, Oct. 28, 1949; s. Joseph John and Zelpha Fay (Hayes) K.; m. Sarah Helene Marantha, May 15, 1970; children: Jennifer, Constance, Melanie. Ordained to ministry Pentecostal Ch., 1980; cert. home health technologist. Pastor Ministry of Life Pentecostal Ch., Toledo, 1975-82; founder, sr. elder Shepherd of the Dove Ministries, Toledo, 1983—; home health technologist, Dove Health Care, Toledo, 1987—. Usher Ministry of Life Pentecostal Ch., 1970-72, elder 1972-75. With USAF, 1969-70. Recipient Christian Patriot Leadership award Am. Christian Leadership Coun., 1989-90. Office: Shepherd of the Dove 2008 Oakwood Toledo OH 43607-1548

KERLEY, OTTIE RAY, II, minister; b. Burlington, Iowa, May 30, 1949; s. Loren Clarence and Betty Lou (Timberlake) K.; m. Erlene Grace Shoesmith; children: Elizabeth Grace, Deborah Rae, Clara Eilene, Ottie Ray III. BS, Ottawa U., 1971; MA, Ea. Bapt. Theol. Sem., 1974, MDiv, 1975. Ordained to ministry Am. Bapt. Chs. in U.S.A., 1976. Student traffic supr. Am. Bapt. Chs. in U.S.A., Valley Forge, Pa., 1971-75; pastor youth 1st Bapt. Ch., Oaklyn, N.J., 1973-75; pastor 1st Bapt. Ch., McKees Rocks, Pa., 1975-82, Bethel Bapt. Ch., Powers Lake, N.D., 1982-90, Murray (Utah) Bapt. Ch., 1990—; mem. gen. bd. Am. Bapt. Chs. USA, Valley Forge, 1984-90, bd. of nat. ministries, 1984-90, chmn. world relief com., 1987-90; bd. dirs. N.D. Bapt. Conv., Bismarck, 1984-90; chmn. budget and fin. com., bd. dirs. Shared Ministry of Utah, 1990—. Dir. Meals on Wheels, McKees Rock, Pa., 1978; bd. dirs. Disaster Preparedness Com., McKees Rock, 1977. Mem. Am. Bapt. Ministers Coun., N.D. Bapt. Mins. Coun. (sec.-treas. 1984-90), Utah Bapt. Mins. Coun. (convenor 1990—), Soc. of Bibl. Lit., Nat. Assn. Radio and Telecommunications Engrs. (sr.), Rotary (McKees Rocks chpt., bd. dirs., bull. editor 1978-80). Republican. Home: 5745 S 700 W Murray UT 84123 Office: Murray Bapt Church 184 E 5770 S Murray UT 84107 *The secret to a happy and successful life is learning to love God, others, and one's self.*

KERN, STEPHEN DOUGLAS, pastor; b. San Diego, July 25, 1946; s. Geroge Edward and Mildred Lourane (Harris) K.; m. Sally Rogers, Jan. 23, 1970; children: Jesse Aaron, Nathan Daniel. BS, Palm Beach Atlantic Coll., 1975; MDiv, Southwestern Bapt. Theol. Sem., 1980, D of Ministry, 1987. Pastor, tchr. Lone Star (Tex.) Bapt. Ch. Sgt. USMC, 1965-69. Mem. Christian Life Svc. Ctr. (exec. bd.).

KERN, TINA JOY, lay worker; b. Falls Church, Va., Aug. 9, 1969; d. Kenneth L. and Faith I. (Hunter) K. Student, Ea. Nazarene Coll., 1991. Counselor, compassionate min., program dir. Quincy (Mass.) Crisis Ctr., 1988—. Republican. Mem. Ch. of the Nazarene. Home: 231 Fayette St Quincy MA 02170 Office: 98 Philips St Quincy MA 02170

KERNS, JANET MARTHA, services manager; b. Yakima, Wash., Oct. 5, 1954; d. Charles Lloyd and Frances Lorraine (Peabody) K. BA in Secondary Edn., Cen. Wash. U., 1981. Guest svcs. mgr. Cannon Beach (Oreg.) Conf. Ctr., 1982—. Mem. Christian Camping Internat. U.S.A. (sectional planning com. Cannon Beach chpt. 1989—).

KERR, BARRY JACK, lay church worker, elementary school educator; b. Grass Valley, Calif., Nov. 16, 1949; s. Robert Dean and Virginia Beesley Kerr; m. Frances Christine Martin, Aug. 3, 1974; children: Bradley Martin, Rosemary Anna. BA, U. Calif., Davis, 1971; teaching credential, Sacramento State U., 1971; MEd, administrv. credential, U. Laverne, 1978. Youth worker, mem. choir, Sunday sch. coms. United Meth. Ch., Grass Valley, Calif., 1964-87; youth worker Univ. Covenant Ch., Davis, Calif., 1968-71; tchr. Grass Valley Sch. Dist., 1972—; youth worker, mem. choir Sierra Presbyn. Ch., Nevada City, Calif., 1987—; chair edn. com. United Meth. Ch., Grass Valley, 1983-84, chair coun. mins., 1984-86. Bd. dirs. ARC, Grass Valley, 1980-84; treas. N.U. High Sch. Choir Boosters, 1985—.

Mem. Calif. Tchrs. Assn. Presbyterian. Home: PO Box 744 Grass Valley CA 95945 Office: Hennessy Sch 225 S Auburn St Grass Valley CA 95945

KERR, DONALD CRAIG, retired minister; b. Pitts., July 29, 1915; s. Hugh Thomson and Olive (Boggs) K.; m. Nora Minetta Lloyd, Sept. 12, 1942; children: Donald Jr., Elizabeth, Douglas. BA, Princeton U., 1937; MDiv, Princeton Theol. Sem., 1940; ThD, U. Toronto, Ont., Can., 1942. Ordained to ministry Presbyn. Ch. (U.S.A.). Min. East Kiskacoguillas Presbyn. Ch., Reedsville, Pa., 1942-47, 1st Presbyn. Ch., New Haven, 1947-48; min. Roland Pk. Presbyn. Ch., Balt., 1948-80, ret., 1980; pastoral assoc. Presbyn. Ch., Sarasota, Fla., 1980-87; chaplain Plymouth Harbor, Sarasota, 1982-91; moderator Presbytery of Balt., 1960-61, mem. bd. pensions, exec. com., 1963-66. Author: How the Church Began, 1953, What the Bible Means, 1954, History of Religion in America, 1975; editor: Design for Christian Living, 1952. Recipient 50-yrs. in ministry plague Lake Joseph Community Ch., 1989. Mem. St. Andrew's Soc. (trustee, chaplain 1980-91, cert. appreciation 1990), Ivy League Club (v.p. 1991), Princeton Club (pres. 1988-90), Univ. Club Sarasota, Sarasota Yacht Club, Sara Bay Club, Shriners, Masons (32 degree). Home: 97 Sunset Dr Sarasota FL 34236

KERR, HUGH THOMSON, editor, emeritus theology educator; b. Chgo., July 1, 1909; s. Hugh Thomson and Olive May (Boggs) K.; m. Dorothy DePree, Dec. 28, 1938; 1 child, Stephen T. A.B., Princeton U., 1931; B.D., Western Theol. Sem., Pitts., 1934; M.A., U. Pitts., 1934; Ph.D., U. Edinburgh, Scotland, 1936. Ordained to ministry Presbyn. Ch., 1934. From instr. to prof. doctrinal theology Louisville Presbyn. Theol. Sem., 1936-40; prof. systematic theology Princeton Theol. Sem., 1940-74, Benjamin B. Warfield prof. theology emeritus, 1974—; mem. univ. chapel com., 1960-63, nat. council com. on ch. architecture, 1960-62; dir. Gallahue Conf. Quo Vadis, 1968, Westminster Found., 1954-65; Del. for N.Am., World Alliance Reformed Chs., 1945-60; mem. commn. on women World Council Chs., 1950-54, del. faith and order conf., 1957; chmn. com. curriculum Council Theol. Edn., 1949-53; mem. coms. marriage and divorce, ordination of women Presbyn. Ch., 1955-57. Editor: Theology Today quar., 1944—, Sons of the Prophets, 1963; author: A Compend of Calvin's Institutes, 1938 (in Japanese 1958), Compend of Luther's Theology, 1963, Positive Protestantism: An Interpretation of the Gospel, 1960 (in Japanese 1954), Mystery and Meaning in the Christian Faith, 1958, What Divides Protestants Today, 1958, By John Calvin, 1960, Readings in Christian Thought, 1966, rev. edit., 1990, Our Life in God's Life, 1979, Protestantism, 1979, (with J.M. Mulder) Conversion, 1983, Calvin's Institutes: A New Compend, 1989, The Simple Gospel, 1991; multi-media presentations, articles, chpts. in books. Guggenheim fellow, 1960. Mem. Am. Acad. Religion. Office: Theol Today PO Box 29 Princeton NJ 08542

KERR, JAMES R., minister. Exec. dir. W.Va. Coun. Chs., Charleston. Office: WVa Coun Chs 1608 Virginia St E Charleston WV 25311*

KERR, NANCY KAROLYN, pastor, mental health consultant; b. Ottumwa, Iowa, July 10, 1934; d. Owen W. and Iris Irene (Israel) K. Student Boston U., 1953; AA, U. Bridgeport, 1966; BA, Hofstra U., 1967; postgrad. in clin. psychology Adelphi U. Inst. Advanced Psychol. Studies, 1968-73; m. Richard Clayton Williams, June 28, 1953 (div.); children: Richard Charles, Donna Louise. Ordained pastor Mennonite Ch., 1987. Pastoral counselor Nat. Council Chs., Jackson, Miss., 1964; dir. teen program Waterbury (Conn.) YWCA, 1966-67; intern in psychology N.Y. Med. Coll., 1971-72; rsch. cons., 1972-73; coord. home svcs., psychologist City and County of Denver, 1972-75; cons. Mennonite Mental Health Svcs., Denver, 1975-78; asst. prof. psychology Messiah Coll., 1978-79; mental health cons., 1979-81; called to ministry Mennonite Ch., 1981, pastor Cin. Mennonite Fellowship, 1981-83, coord. campus peace evangelism, 1981-83, mem. Gen. Conf. Peace and Justice Reference Council, 1983-85; instr. Associated Mennonite Bibl. Sems., 1985; teaching elder Assembly Mennonite Ch., 1985-86; pastor Pulaski Mennonite Ch., 1986-89; v.p. Davis County Mins.' Assn., 1988-89; pastoral counselor Bethesda Christian Counseling Ctr., Prince George B.C., 1989—; bd. dirs. Tri-County Counselling Clinic, Memphis, Mo., 1980-81; spl. ch. curriculum Nat. Council Chs., 1981; mem. Cen. Dist. Conf. Peace and Justice Com., 1981-89; mem. exec. bd. People for Peace, 1989—. Mem. Waterbury Planned Parenthood Bd., 1964-67; mem. MW Children's Home Bd., 1974-75; bd. dirs. Boulder (Colo.) ARC, 1977-78; mem. Mennonite Disabilities Respite Care Bd., 1981-86. Mem. Am. Psychol. Assn. (assoc.), Soc. Psychologists for Study of Social Issues, Davis County Mins. Assn. (v.p. 1988-89), Prince George Ministerial Assn. (chmn. edn. and Airport chapel coms. 1990—).

KERSHAW, JOHN WILLIAM, minister; b. Salt Lake City, Sept. 4, 1943; s. Douglas H. and Joan E. (Weenig) K.; m. Jacqueline Elaine Holdsworth, May 23, 1983; children: John M., Paul, Joel. BA, U. Denver, 1965; MDiv, St. Paul Sch. Theology, 1969. Ordained deacon United Meth. Ch., 1966, elder, 1970. Pastor Riverbank United Meth. Ch., Wyandotte, Mich., 1969-70; pastor Elmwood-Aldersgate United Meth. Chs., Pontiac, Mich., 1970-75; pastor First United Meth. Ch., Marine City, Mich., 1975-79, Berkley, Mich., 1979-89, Wayne, Mich., 1989—; chairperson Mich. Area Sem. Grant Fund, 1972-80; sec. Detroit Conf. Standing Roles, 1980-88; chairperson Detroit Conf. Vols. in Mission, 1989—; bd. dirs. Intersharing, 1989—, Eastside Ministry of Social Svc., 1985—. Mem. Detroit Annual Conf. United Meth. Ch. Office: First United Meth Ch 3 Town Sq Wayne MI 48184

KERTELGE, KARL, theology educator; b. Selm, Germany, Apr. 28, 1926; s. Hubert and Anna (May) K. D.Theology, U. Muenster, Westfalen, 1967. Acad. lectr. U. Munster, 1969-76, prof. theology, 1976—; prof. theology Theologische Fakultaet Trier, 1969-76. Author: Rechtfertigung bei Paulus, 1967; Die Wunder Jesu im Mk-Ev,1970, Gemeinde und Amt in NT, 1972, Grundthemen paulinischer Theologie, 1991. Contbr. articles on Bibl. theology to profl. jours. Mem. Studiorum Novi Testamenti Societas, Soc. N.T. Scholars in German Speaking Countries (pres. 1971-89), Deutscher Oekumenischer Studienausschuss (pres. 1987—), Rheinisch-Westfaelische Akademie der Wissenschaften, Domkapitular in Muenster. Roman Catholic. Home: Isolde-Kurz-Strasse 19, D-4400 Münster Federal Republic of Germany Office: Fachbereich Kath Theologie der Universitat, Johannisstrasse 8-10, D-4400 Münster Federal Republic of Germany

KERZE, MICHAEL ANTHONY, religion educator; b. Hollywood, Calif., July 20, 1948. PhD in History, UCLA, 1983. Lectr. Calif. State U., Northridge, 1985-91; vis. prof. Loyola Marymount U., L.A., 1989-91; dir. Herrick Meml. Chapel and Interfaith Ctr. Occidental Coll., L.A., 1991—; dir. Circle of History of Religions, L.A., 1990; mem. Buddhist-Cath. Dialogue, L.A., 1989—. Mem. Am. Acad. Religion, N.Am. Assn. for Study of Religion, So. Calif. Collogium on Religion and Scis. Office: Occidental Coll Herrick Meml Chapel and Interfaith Ctr 1600 Campus Rd Los Angeles CA 90041

KERZNER, ROBYN PATRICIA, religious organization administrator; b. New Haven, Mar. 19, 1964; d. Elliott Jay and Sandra Ruth (Kovener) K. BS in Edn., U. Miami, Coral Gables, Fla., 1986; MSW, Yeshiva U., 1988. Dir. youth and young adults Jewish Community Ctr., New Haven, 1987-90; staff assoc. Jewish Fedn. of Greater New Haven, 1990—; youth group leader Temple Beth Tikvah, Madison, Conn., 1987-90, Temple Judea, Coral Gables, 1983-86. Mem. Nat. Orgn. Social Workers, Coun. Jewish Communal Profls. Democrat. Office: Jewish Fedn Greater New Hav 419 Whalley Ave New Haven CT 06511

KESLER, JAY LEWIS, university administrator; b. Barnes, Wis., Sept. 15, 1935; s. Elsie M. Campbell Kesler; m. Helen Jane Smith; children: Laura, Bruce, Terri. Student, Ball State U., 1953-54; BA, Taylor U., 1958, LHD (hon.), 1982; Dr. Divinity (hon.), Barrington Coll., 1977; DD (hon.), Asbury Theol. Sem., 1984; HHD (hon.), Huntington Coll., 1983; LHD, John Brown U., 1987. Dir. Marion (Ind.) Youth for Christ, 1955-58, crusade staff evangelist, 1959-60, dir. Ill.-Ind. region, 1960-62, dir. coll. recruitment, 1962-63, v.p. personnel, 1963-68, v.p. field coordination, 1968-73, pres., 1973-85, also bd. dirs.; pres. Taylor U., Upland, Ind., 1985—; bd. dirs. Christianity Today, Associated Colls. Ind., Brotherhood Mut. Ins. Co., Ind. Colls. and Univs. Inc., Christian Coll. Consortium, Ints. for Nonprofit Orgns. Nat. Assn. Evangelicals, Youth for Christ Internat., Youth for Christ U.S.A.; mem. bd. reference Christian Camps. Inc, , Christian College Coalition, Nat. Educators Fellowship; mem. adv. bd. Christian Bible Soc.; co-pastor First Bapt. Ch. Geneva, Ill., 1972-85; mem. faculty Billy Graham Schs. Evangelism; lectr. Staley Disting. Christian Scholar Lecture Program. Speaker on Family Forum (daily radio show and radio program); mem. adv. com. Campus Life mag.; author: Let's Succeed With Our Teenagers, 1973, I Never Promised You a Disneyland, 1975, The Strong Weak People, 1976, Outside Disneyland, 1977, I Want a Home with No Problems, 1977, Growing Places, 1978, Too Big to Spank, 1978, Breakthrough, 1981, Parents & Teenagers, 1984 (Gold Medallion award), Family Forum, 1984, Making Life Make Sense, 1986, Parents and Children, 1986, Being Holy, Being Human, 1988, Ten Mistakes Parents Make With Teenagers (And How to Avoid Them), 1988, Is Your Marriage Really Worth Fighting For?, 1989, Energizing Your Teenagers' Faith, 1990, Raising Responsible Kids, 1991; contbr. articles to profl. jours. Bd. advisors Prison Fellowship Internat., Boys JIM Club Am., Christian Camps Inc., Christian Educators Assn. Internat., Pine Cove Camping, Project Ptnr., Christian Bible Soc., Discovery Network Inc., Evangelicals for Social Action, Love and Action, Venture Middle East, Internat. Com. of Reference for New Life 2000. Recipient Angel award Religion in Media, 1985, Outstanding Youth Leadership award Religious Heritage Am.. 1989. Office: Taylor U Office Pres 500 W Reade Ave Upland IN 46989-1001

KESNER, GARY M., chief engineer; b. Lima, Ohio, July 27, 1961; s. John William and Patricia Ann (Kriegel) K.; m. Lori Ann Nesler, Dec. 30, 1982; children: Sarah, Matthew G., Andrea, Jordon. Chief engr. Sta. WTGN, Lima. Home: 954 Richie Ave Lima OH 45805 Office: Sta WTGN 1600 Elida Rd Lima OH 45805

KESSELRING, GLORIA JEAN, religious education administrator; b. Waltham, Mass., Jan. 18, 1950; d. Paul Arthur and Marion Louise (Marshall) Hooper; m. Frank Eddy Kesselring III, Dec. 17, 1982; children: Charmaine, Jean. BS in Christian Edn., Nyack Coll., 1973. Adminstrv. asst. World Wide Prodns., Manchester, N.H., 1975; team staff assoc. Billy Graham Assocs., Youngstown, Ohio, 1976; exec. adminstrv. asst. Campus Cusade, Parkersburg, W.Va., 1976; min. christian edn. Emmanuel Bapt. Ch., Parkersburg, 1977-88, Calvary Bapt. Ch., Charleston, W.Va., 1989—; com. chmn., Assn. Christian Edn., Parkersburg, 1977-78, 80-82; coord., Youth Leader Core-W.Va. Bapt. Ch., Parkersburg, 1979-80; curriculum cons., W.Va. Bapt. Conv., Parkersburg, 1978-87. Office: Calvary Bapt Ch 510 Maryland Ave Charleston WV 25302

KESSLER, DIANE COOKSEY, religious organization administrator, minister; b. Jan. 8, 1947. BA in Religion, Oberlin Coll., 1969; MA in Religion and Soc., Andover Newton Theol. Sch., 1971, postgrad., 1979—; postgrad., Boston U., 1979—, Ecumenical Inst., World Coun. Chs., Bossey, Switzerland, 1983. Ordained to ministry United Ch. of Christ, 1983. Lobbyist Civil Liberties Union Mass., Boston, 1972; substitute tchr. Harwood Union High Sch., Duxbury, Vt., 1973; reporter The Valley Reporter, Waitsfield, Vt., 1973-74; assoc. dir. for strategy and action Mass. Coun. Chs., Boston, 1975-88, exec. dir., 1988—; del. to XV-XVI Gen. Synod, United Ch. of Christ, assoc. del. XVII-XVIII Gen. Synod; ind. preacher; speaker in field. Author: Parents and the Experts, 1974, God's Simple Gift: Meditations on Friendship and Spirituality, 1988; also articles; mem. editorial adv. bd. Theology and Pub. Policy, 1989—. Apptd. mem. Gov. of Vt.'s Commn. on Status of Women, 1974-75; former mem. adv. bd. Mass. Dept. Revenue; active Newton Highlands Congl. Ch.; mem. coun. for ecumenism United Ch. of Christ, 1984—, chairperson coun., 1988-89, 90-91; mem. Atty. Gen.'s Adv. Com. on Pub. Charities, 1988—; mem. adv. group to Commr. of Corrections, Mass., 1988—; bd. dirs. Howard Benevolent Soc., 1989—, New Eng. Holocaust Meml. Com., 1st Ch. Legacy Fund; corp. bd. dirs. City Mission Soc., Boston; bd. dirs. edn. fund TEAM, 1991; mem. adv. bd. Mass. Housing Partnership, 1990—; mem. exec. com. Dove Mass, 1990—. Recipient Outstanding Woman award Coll. Club, 1990. Mem. Nat. Assn. Ecumenical Staff, Ch. Women United (exec. bd. mem.-at-large Mass. chpt., Valiant Woman award 1991), Boston Min.'s Club, Am. Congl. Assn. (bd. dirs., nominating com.). Office: Mass Coun Chs 14 Beacon St Rm 416 Boston MA 02108

KESSLER, GEORGE AARON, seminary official, lawyer; b. Somerville, Mass., Mar. 13, 1928; s. Myer and Celia (Waldman) K.; m. Harriet Kendall, May 11, 1975; children: Michael Laurence, Wendy Kessler Bruslins. AA, Boston U., 1949, LLB, 1953. Atty. Brandeis U., Waltham, Mass., 1965-75; exec. vice chmn. Assoc. Jewish Charities and Welfare Fund-Endowments, Balt., 1975-85; nat. dir. endowment dept. Coun. Jewish Fedns., N.Y.C., 1985-90; dir. major gifts Jewish Theol. Sem. Am., N.Y.C., 1990—. Author, editor: Basics of Endowment Law, 1976; dir. videotape Endowment Giving, 1988; producer TV and videotape Charitable REmainder Trusts, 1989; editor: Handbook-Split Interest, 1988. Mem. Nat. Soc. Fund Raising Execs. (bd. dirs. Balt. 1982-85). Office: Jewish Theol Sem 3080 Broadway New York NY 10027 *In an age dominated by skeptics, meaningless social disasters and cyclical violence, both individually and corporately, the younger generation's recognition of the place of the Almighty in their lives brings hope to us all.*

KESSLER, JAMES LEE, rabbi; b. Houston, Dec. 10, 1945; s. Harry Samuel and Ruthe (Aron) K.; m. Shelley Gail Nussenblatt, Aug. 20, 1977; children: Andy, Jenny. BA, U. Tex., 1967; MA in Hebrew Letters, Hebrew Union Coll., 1972, D Hebrew Letters, 1988. Ordained rabbi, 1972. Hillel dir. B'nai B'rith Hillel Founds., Austin, Tex., 1972-75; rabbi Temple B'nai Israel, Galveston, Tex., 1976-81, 89—, Victoria, Tex., 1981-88; rabbi Jewish Temple, Alexandria, La., 1988-89; 1st chmn. ch. rels. adv. bd. Tex. Dept. Human Resources, 1976-77; mem. cen. conf. Am. Rabbis Bd., 1977-79; mem. alumni bd. overseers Hebrew Union Coll., 1980-86. Editor: Deep in the Heart, 1990; contbr. articles to profl. jours. Chmn. Lipson Scholarship Fund, Galveston; mem. Siebel Loan Fund, Galveston; advisor Handbook of Tex., Austin; mem. instnl. rev. bd. U. Tex. Med. Br., Galveston. Mem. Cen. Conf. Am. Rabbis, Tex. Jewish Hist. Soc. (founder, pres. 1980-82), Kallah of Tex. Rabbis, B'nai B'rith, Masons. Office: Temple B'nai Israel 3008 Ave O Galveston TX 77550

KESSLER, SILAS GEORGE, minister; b. St. Louis, Aug. 29, 1911; s. Jacob George and Lena (Hoffman) K.; m. Ruth Margaret Schap, July 3, 1935; children: Eleanor, Stanley. BA, U. Dubuque, 1932, MDiv, 1934, DD, 1941, LLD, 1964. Pastor Sharon Presbyn. Ch., Farmington, Iowa, 1934-37; pastor First Presbyn. Ch., Fullerton, Nebr., 1937-40, Hastings, Nebr., 1940-76; ret.; chmn. organizing com. Synod of Lakes and Prairies, Mpls., 1969-72; pres. Nebr. Coun. Chs., Lincoln, 1966-68; moderator Gen. Assy. of Presbyn. Ch. USA, 1963-64, Synod of Lakes and Prairies, 1972-74; bd. trustees Hastings Coll., 1941—; mem. Omaha Presbyn. Sem. Found., 1974—; sec. Nebr. Welfare Found., 1983—. Home and Office: 219 University Hastings NE 68901

KESSLERING, RALPH NICHOLAS, religious practitioner; b. Chgo., Jan. 8, 1938; s. Nicholas Jr. and Imogene (Gunderson) K. Cert. specialist in philosophy of religion. Initiated Babalocha Obatala, 1985, espinardo, 1986, Iyewa, 1989; specialist in philosophy of religions. Mem. Cabildo Yoruba Omo Orisha Assn. Mem. Loucomi (Santaria) Ch. Home: 1216 Camp St New Orleans LA 70130 *All religions are spiritual prisons for those who have not risen above them.*

KESTENBAUM, JEROME, rabbi; b. N.Y.C., Apr. 20, 1919; s. Alexander and Sarah (Herskovitz) K.; m. Roslyn Weisser, Jan. 25, 1942; children: Sherry Grossman, Lenny. BA, Yeshiva U., N.Y.C., 1939; MA, U. Ill., 1943; DD, Vanderbilt U., Nashville, 1970. Ordained rabbi, 1947. Rabbi Lincoln, Nebr., 1947-49, Orlando, Fla., 1949-52; Hillel dir. Gainesville, Fla., 1952-59; rabbi Nashville, 1959-70; ret. Home: 2117 S Flagler West Palm Beach FL 33467

KESTER, SHERYL MARIE, minister; b. Ft. Campbell, Ky., Oct. 21, 1961; d. Jack Russell and Annette Grace (Carpenter) K. BA, Dana Coll., 1983; MDiv, Wittburg Theol. Sem., 1987. Minister St. Peter's Luth. Ch., Bassett, Nebr., 1987—; Mem. Call Assistance Team, Nebr., 1988—; sec. Rock County Ministerial Alliance, Bassett, 1987—; mem. youth com. Nebr. Synod of ELCA, 1988-90; mem. coun. Nebr. Synod Evang. Luth. Ch. Am., 1990—; youth clergy dean Nebr. Synod Youth Com., 1988—. Mem. Community Choir, Bassett, 1987—, Project Access Adv. Com., Norfolk, Nebr., 1988-90; mem., sec. Bassett Fine Arts Coun., 1988—; bd. dirs. Rock County Literacy Program, Bassett, 1990—. Office: St Peters Luth Ch Box 474 Bassett NE 68714

KESTNER, CHARLES PHILLIP, minister; b. Kingsport, Tenn., July 7, 1949; s. William Franklin and Dosha Mae (Burnette) K.; m. Stephanie Sandra Shaffer, Aug. 21, 1982. BA cum laude, King Coll., Bristol, Tenn., 1971; DMin, Union Theol. Sem., Richmond, Va., 1975, ThM, 1976. Ordained to ministry Presbyn. Ch., 1975.; cert. adminstr. Taylor Johnson Temperament Analysis. Pastor Oakdale and Westminster Presbyn. Chs., Norfolk, Va., 1976-83, Vaughn Meml. Presbyn. Ch., Fayetteville, N.C., 1983-84; minister-at-large, pulpit supply Charlotte (N.C.) Presbytery, 1988-91; pastor Fairfield (Va.) Presbyn. Ch., 1991—; instr. U. N.C., Charlotte, 1989-91; supervisory chaplain Naval Hosp. Camp Lejeune 307 Naval Res. Ctr., Charlotte, 1990-91; command chaplain Sierra Det 107; mem. peacemaking and social justice com. Charlotte Presbytery, 1988-91; hosp. chaplain Charlotte Meml. Hosp., 1988; ch. camp pastor and counselor Charlotte Presbytery, Camp Grier, Old Fort, N.C., 1988. Mem. Charlotte-Mecklenberg Clergy Assn., Charlotte, 1989, YMCA, Charlotte, 1990, Mint Mus. Patron, Charlotte, 1990, N.C. Pub. TV, Charlotte, 1988-91; contbg. and working mem. Habitat for Humanity, Charlotte, 1988. Lt. USNR, 1985-87, lt. comdr., 1991. Decorated Navy Unit Commendation ribbon, Fleet Marine Force ribbon, Navy Sharp Shooter ribbon. Mem. Lexington Area Ministerial Assn., Presbyn. Peacemaking Fellowship, Ctr. Def. Info., Res. Officer's Assn., Naval Res. Assn. Democrat. Office: Fairfield Presbyn Ch US Hwy 11 PO Box 155 Fairfield VA 24435-0155 *No greater evidence for God exists than in the extraordinary compassion human beings have toward one another no matter how rarely exhibited in every generation since recorded history.*

KETSENBERG, JULIUS T., minister; b. Marion Country, Mo., Aug. 10, 1949; s. Julius Turner and Opal Lee (Berry) K.; m. Carolyn Rose Bender, June 17, 1969; children: Debra, Curtis, Jonathan. Student, Perkins, Dallas, 1984, Wesley, Washington, 1985-86, St. Paul Sch. Theology, 1988. Ordained to ministry Meth. Ch. Pastor, parish chairperson United Meth. Ch., Taylor, Mo., 1980-82; pastor United Meth. Ch., Alton, Mo., 1984-88, Owensville, 1988—; model maker Monogram Industries, Quincy, Ill., 1969-74; lay speaker United Meth. Ch., Taylor, 1978-84, ch. sch. tchr., 1979-82; mem. Ministerial Alliance, Owensville, 1990—. Local chairperson Crytic Fibroas, 1985. With U.S. Army, 1969-71. Home: 106 W Washington St Owensville MO 65066

KETTINGER, BURTON EDWARD, JR., clergyman, musician; b. Zanesville, Ohio, Nov. 19, 1944; s. Burton Edward and Mary Jane (Probst) K.; m. Sharon Rose Meads, June 22, 1968; children: Shauna Rae, Burton III. B.A., Spring Arbor Coll., Mich., 1967; M.A., Am. Conservatory Music, Chgo., 1978. Ordained to ministry Free Methodist Ch. N.Am., 1975. Tchr. Turner Jr. High Sch., Warren, Ohio, 1967-69, Wheaton Christian High Sch., West Chicago, Ill., 1972-74; minister youth and music Free Methodist Ch., Indpls., 1969-71, Winona Lake, Ind., 1971-72; free lance musician, minister, Wheaton, Ill., 1974—; pres. Sound Servant Ministries, Wheaton, 1986; vocal soloist Moody Bible Inst., Chgo., 1974-87; dir., cons. Free Spirit Music Ministry, Winona Lake, 1971-76; mem. Ill. State Bd. Nat. Assn. Evangelicals; chaplain-minister Fellowship of Christian Peace Officers, Chgo., 1977—; mem. parent adv. coun. Luth. Gen. Hosp., Park Ridge, Ill. Named Young Leader of Yr., Spring Arbor Coll., 1976. Mem. Evang. Free Ch. Ministerial Assn., West Suburban Ministerial Fellowship. Republican. Avocation: golfing. Home: 1523 Gainesboro Dr Wheaton IL 60187 Office: PO Box 1098 Wheaton IL 60189

KETTINGER, LEROY WILLIAM, minister; b. Mansfield, Ohio, Mar. 5, 1942; s. Burton Edward and Mary Jane (Probst) K.; m. Wilma Jean Lawson, June 8, 1963; children: Kirk, Kevin, Valerie, Janelle. Student, Roberts Wesleyan Coll., 1960-63; AB, Youngstown U., 1966; MDiv, Asbury Theol. Sem., 1971; postgrad., Kent State U., 1969-70; D of Ministry, United Theol. Sem., 1989. Ordained to ministry Free Meth. Ch., 1965. Steel worker Ohio Corrugating Corp., Warren, Ohio, summers 1960-63; sr. pastor Free Meth. Community Chapel, New Middletown, Ohio, 1963-67; salesman Sears & Roebuck, Lexington, Ky., 1967-68; min. of music Nicholasville (Ky.) Bapt. Ch., 1968-69; sr. pastor 1st Free Meth. Ch., Cleve.; dir. youth ministries Free Meth. Ch. N.Am., Winona Lake, Ind., 1970-74; sr. pastor First Free Meth. Ch., Columbus, Ohio, 1974-80, Seattle, 1980-82; v.p., dean of chapel Roberts Wesleyan Coll., Rochester, N.Y., 1982-91; sr. pastor Dearborn (Mich.) Free Meth. Ch., 1991—; cons. in field student svcs. Author: (with others) Arnold's Commentary, 1972-75, Youth As Learners, 1983, A Faith Journey, 1989; editor in chief Youth in Action, 1970-74; editor: God and Country series, 1974. Chmn. Ch. Commn. for Youth Serving Agys., St. Louis, 1974080, Ch. Commn. on Scouting, North Brunswick, N.J., 1976-80, Protestant Orthodox Rels. Com. Boy Scouts Am., Rochester, 1987-91; chaplain gen. internat. and nat. jamborees, Boy Scouts Am., 1976-77. Seattle Pacific U. fellow, 1981—, Roberts Wesleyan Coll., 1983—. Mem. Am. Assn. for Higher Edn., Nat. Assn. Student Pers. Adminstrs., Assn. Christians in Student Devel., Nat. Assn. Evangelicals (bd. adminstrn., pres.'s club). Home: 23870 Princeton Dearborn MI 48124 Office: Dearborn Free Meth Ch 2801 S Telegraph Rd Dearborn MI 48124 *Life is a journey with the intended partner being the God who created us all. The goal, intensity, duration, and effectiveness of our journey is determined by our willingness to be inextricably and personally linked with the God who controls all of life's vastitudes.*

KEUCHER, WILLIAM FREDERICK, minister; b. Atlantic City, June 6, 1918; s. Otto Ernest Rudolph and Margaret (Wilson) K.; m. Edith Warnick Kimber, Nov. 28, 1940; children: Margaret Valerie, Louise Sherilyn. AB, ThB, Eastern Coll., 1942; BD, Eastern Bapt. Theol. Sem., 1946, DD, 1971; DD, Ottawa U., 1953, Kalamazoo Coll., 1971; HHD, Alderson Broadds Coll., 1980. Pastor Allegheny Ave. Bapt. Ch., Phila., 1942-48, 1st Bapt. Ch., El Dorado, Kans., 1948-52; exec. minister Kans. Bapt. Convention, Topeka, 1953-70; sr. minister Covenant Bapt. Ch., Detroit, 1971-81, pastor emeritus, 1982—; prof. pastoral theology Cen. Bapt. Theol. Sem., Kansas City, Kansas, 1982-87, pres., 1983-87, pres. emeritus, 1987—; pres. Am. Bapt. Chs. USA, 1980-81, gen. bd., 1972-83, mem. exec. com., 1978-83; pres. Bd. Internat. Ministries, 1971, mem. exec. com., 1972-79, chmn. budget com., 1976-79, ministers and missionaries benefit bd., 1975-79; trustee Kalamazoo Coll., 1979-82, Ottawa U. (life); nat. chmn. Bd. Nat. Ministries Bicentennial Fund, 1982-83; vice chmn. Bapt. Joint Com. Pub. Affairs, Washington, 1974, mem. exec. com., 1974-82, chmn. pers. rels. 1978-82; bd. govs. Nat. Coun. Chs., 1976-81; adj. staff Ohio Bapt. Conv., 1989-91; interim minister First Bapt. Ch., Dayton, 1990-91; bd. dirs. Bapt. Peace Fellowship N.Am., 1990—; mem. Religious Liberty Coun., Washington, 1990—; pres. Kans. Bapt. Conv., 1952; chair nat. program com. Am. Bapt. Chs. in U.S.A., 1953, 63, pres. exec. mins.' coun., 1956, ann. preacher, 1973; pres. Am. Bapt. Fgn. Mission Soc., 1971. Author: An Exodus for the Church, 1973, Main Street and the Mind of God, 1974, Good News People in Action, 1975; contbr. articles to profl. jours. Sec. Detroit Christian Communication Council, 1977-78, chmn. div. fin. & bus., 1978-79; pres. Detroit Urban League, 1976-78, adv. bd. 1979-82; profl. div. group chmn. United Found. Torch Drive, 1976-77, clergy rep. 1976-82; bd. dirs. Met. Fund Detroit, 1976-82; clergy mem. Econ. Club Detroit, 1977-82; citizen's adv. council united Community Services, 1978-82. Recipient Award of Merit Am. Bapt. Chs. USA, 1960, Resolution of Merit Mich. Ho. and Senate, 1981. Past mem. Am. Acad. Religion, Acad. Polit. Sci., Menninger Found., Internat. Platform Assn., Wranglers Club, Rotary. Avocations: gardening, writing poetry. Home and Office: 1526 Londondale Pkwy Newark OH 43055

KEY, THOMAS DONNELL SPORER, minister, biology educator; b. Marshall, Tex., Aug. 4, 1928; s. Harry Hayden and Sophia Bain (Sporer) K.; m. Frances Jane Blackburn, Jan. 3, 1954 (dec. 1976); children: Carolyn, Martha; m. Mary Ann Miller, Mar. 3, 1983 (dec. 1991). BA, MA, So. Meth. U., 1952; EdD in Biology, Ball State U., 1969; ThD and PhD, Antioch Sem., 1984, 86; ScD, Immanuel Coll., 1978. Ordained to ministry Congl. Meth. Ch. as elder, 1984. Pastor Wesleyan Congl. Ch., Citronelle, Ala., 1982-85, 1st Ind. Meth. Ch., Bainbridge, Ga., 1985-86, 1st Congl. Meth. Ch., Magee, Miss., 1986-89, Skyview Congl. Meth. Ch., Laurel, Miss., 1989-90, Springridge Bible Ch., Raymond, Miss., 1990—; biology instr. Hinds Community Coll., Raymond, 1990—; bd. dirs. Immanuel Bapt. Sem., Sharpsburg, Ga., Meth. Bible Hour Caribbean Mission. Co-author: Evolution and Christian Thought Today, 1959; contbr. articles to profl. jours. Mem. Govs. Adv. Com. on the Environment, Atlanta, 1972-74; vol. chaplain

Magee (Miss.) Gen. Hosp., 1986-89; chaplain Community Work Ctr. of Miss. Dept. of Prisons, Magee, 1987-89. Fellow Am. Sci. Affiliation; mem. Grace Gospel Fellowship, Grace Evang. Soc. Address: ECCC Biology Dept # 43 Decatur MS 39327-0129 *As both a professional biologist and pastor, I have had the privilege of knowing the works of God and the Word of God. My life goal is to help sinners come to the Creator who is our Savior and Lord.*

KEYES, CHARLES FENTON, anthropology educator; b. Hyannis, Nebr., Oct. 3, 1937; s. A. Marshall and Geraldine (Fleming) K.; m. E. Jane Godfrey, June 17, 1962; children—Nicholas, Jonathan. B.A. with high distinction, U. Nebr., 1959; Ph.D., Cornell U., 1967. Successively asst. prof., assoc. prof., prof. anthropology U. Wash., Seattle, 1965—, chmn. dept., 1981-90; vis. prof., Chiang Mai U., Thailand, 1972-74; vis. asst. prof. SUNY Binghampton, 1965; chmn. Indochinese studies com. Social Sci. Research Council, N.Y.C., 1983-88, mem. Com. on Southeast Asia, 1980—, chmn. 1987-88, me. Indochina Scholarly Exch. Program com., 1988-90; bd. dirs. N.W. Regional Consortium for S.E. Asia Studies, 1989—. Author: The Golden Peninsula, 1977, Thailand, 1987; editor: Ethnic Adaptation and Identity, 1979, Ethnic Change, 1981 (with others) Karma: An Anthropological Inquiry, 1983. Ford Found. fellow, 1972; Social Sci. Research Council fellow, 1978-79; NSF grantee, 1966-71; Guggenheim fellow, 1984-85. Fellow Am. Anthrop. Assn., Royal Anthrop. Inst. (fgn.); mem. Assn. for Asian Studies (book rev. editor jour. 1980-83), Am. Ethnol. Soc. (assoc. editor jour. 1981-84), Siam Soc. Office: U Wash Dept Anthropology Seattle WA 98195

KEYLOCK, LESLIE ROBERT, Bible and theology educator; b. Islay, Alta., Can., Dec. 7, 1933; came to U.S., 1959; s. Mervyn Leslie and Daisy Louise (Keast) K.; m. Adrienne Todd, June 16, 1962; children: Rebecca Louise, Kerry Todd, Melissa Joy. BA, U. Alta., Edmonton, 1956, BE, 1958; AM, Wheaton Coll., Ill., 1964; postgrad., U. Iowa, 1962-65, Gen. Theol. Sem., N.Y.C., 1972-75, Trinity Evang. Div. Sch., 1991—. Prof. religious studies St. Norbert Coll., West De Pere, Wis., 1965-70; prof. religions studies Coll. Mt. St. Vincent, N.Y.C., 1970-75; editor book div. Christian Herald, Chappaqua, N.Y., 1977-80; editor Religious Thought, Christianity Today, Carol Stream, Ill., 1982-84; prof. Bible and theology Moody Bible Inst., Chgo., 1984—; dir. Moody Write-to-Publish Conf., Chgo., 1986—; founder, pres. Fox Valley Bible Inst., Elgin, Ill., 1990. Author: Leader's Guide to Bible Study, Book 2, 1983, Why Me, Lord? Leader's Guide, 1983; co-author: Victor Handbook of Bible Knowledge, 1982; author, editor: Encyclopedia of Christian Parenting, 1982; transl.: L'Egypte et la Bible (Pierre Montet), 1968. Pres. Green Bay Area Voluntary Com. on Human Rights, 1965. Mem. Inst. for Bibl. Rsch., Soc. Bibl. Lit., Evang. Theol. Soc. (sec.-treas. 1988-89, v.p., 1989-90, pres. Midwest chpt. 1990—). Democrat. Mem. Willow Creek Community Ch. Home: 34 Green Ridge Elgin IL 60120-3120 Office: Moody Bible Inst 820 N La Salle Chicago IL 60610

KHAMIS, MAR APRIM, bishop. Bishop Apostolic Cath. Assyrian Ch. of the East, N.Am. Diocese, Morton Grove, Ill. Office: Apostolic Cath Assyrian Ch E N Am Dioceses 8908 Birch Ave Morton Grove IL 60053*

KHAN, ABRAHIM HABIBULLA, philosophy of religion educator; b. Albion, British Guiana, Apr. 13, 1943; arrived in Can., 1968; s. Habibulla and Delasia K.; m. Pamela Anne O'Neill, Oct. 11, 1969; children: Tariq, Roshan, Laith. BS, Howard U., 1965; BD, Yale U., 1968; MA, McGill U., Montreal, Can., 1971, PhD, 1973. Asst. prof. religious studies U. Man., Can., 1975, U. Toronto, 1975-78; asst. prof. philosophy McGill U., 1979-81, Trent U., 1983; researcher, lectr., faculty religious studies Trinity Coll., U. Toronto, Can., 1984—; lectr. McMaster U., Hamilton, Ont., Can., 1985—; vis. assoc. prof. dept. religion Concordia U., Montreal, 1991—. Author: Salighed As Happiness?, Kierkegaard on the Concept of Salighed, 1985; contbr. articles to theol. and philos. jours. Fellow McGill U., summer 1971, summer 1972; grantee Que. govt., 1973, Can. Fed. Humanities, 1982, Soc. Sci. and Humanities Rsch. Coun., 1979-80, 85, 86, 88-90. Mem. Am. Acad. Religion (chmn. Kierkegaard seminar 1985-90), Can. Theol. Soc. (newsletter editor 1985-90, pres.), Can. Soc. Study of Religion, Soren Kierkegaard Soc. U.S.A., Kierkegaard Cir. in Can. (convener 1985—), Can. Philos. Assn., N.Am. Assn. for Study Religion (mem. exec. com.). Office: U Toronto Trinity Coll, 6 Hoskins Ave, Toronto, ON Canada M5S 1H8

KHAN, SARDAR FEROZE, school principal, religious organization administrator; b. Sialkot, Punjab, Pakistan, Feb. 20, 1941; s. Feroz and Hakam (Bibi) K.; m. Zarina Sardar, Nov. 12, 1965; children: Suhail Sardar, Neena Khan, Rina Khan, Davis. BA with honors, Gordon Coll., Rawalpindi, Pakistan, 1963; MA in Psychology, Punjab U., 1964; BTh., Theol. Sem., Gujranwal, India, 1990. Elder 1st United Presbyn. Ch. Pakistan, Rawalpindi, 1968—; moderator synod United Presbyn. Ch. of Pakistan, Rawalpindi, 1979-85; mgr., prin. Solomon Standard Secondary Sch.; v.p. Nat. Coun. Chs. Pakistan, 1979-81, mem. exec. com., 1990—, chmn. nat. affairs commn., 1991—, chmn. fin. com., 1991—; moderator Rawalpindi presbytery United Presbyn. Ch. Pakistan, 1985-86. Pres. Christian Aid & Rehab. Endeavour, Rawalpindi, 1979—; chief organizer Christian Dem. Alliance, Lahore, Pakistan, 1991—. Office: United Presbyn Ch, PO Box 395, Rawalpindi 46000, Pakistan

KHANJIAN, JOHN, religion educator, academic dean; b. Aleppo, Syria, Dec. 3, 1932; came to U.S., 1966; s. Georges Khanjy Ekmekji and Sayyoud (Zevart) Garikian; m. Pauline Lucy Alexanian, July 28, 1963; children: Tanya Joy, Jonathan Alex. BA, Am. U. Beirut (Lebanon), 1962, MA, 1968; BD, Near East Sch. Theology, Beirut, 1963; PhD, Claremont Grad. Sch., 1974. Lic. min., 1971. Chair dept. religion Aleppo Coll., 1963-66; assoc. prof. Old Testament, libr. Nr. East Sch. Theology, 1971-76; assoc. prof., chair dept. religion and philosophy Kans. Wesleyan U., Salina, 1977-87; assoc. prof., chair dept. religion U. LaVerne (Calif.)/Am. Armenian Internat. Coll., 1987—, acad. dean, 1987—. Trustee Armenian Cilicia Congl. Ch., Pasadena, Calif. 1988—, chair Christian edn. dept., 1989—. Cpl. Syrian Army, 1951-54. Mem. Soc. Biblical Lit. Home: 1825 Rosemount Claremont CA 91711 Office: U La Verne/AAIC 1950 3d St La Verne CA 91750

KHOARAI, PAUL, bishop. Bishop of Leribe, pres. Lesotho Cath. Bishops' Conf., Maseru. Office: Lesotho Cath Bishop's Conf, Cath Secretariat, POB 200, Maseru 100, Lesotho also: PO Box 1, Saint Monica 390, Lesotho*

KHORAICHE, ANTOINE PIERRE CARDINAL (HIS BEATITUDE ANTHONY PETER), patriarch of Antioch for Maronites; b. Ain-Ebel, Lebanon, Sept. 20, 1907. Ordained priest Roman Catholic Ch., 1930; consecrated titular bishop of Tarsus and aux. bishop of Sidon of Maronites, 1950; bishop of Sidon, from 1957; elected patriarch of Antioch for Maronites, Beirut, Lebanon, 1975; elevated to Sacred Coll. of Cardinals, 1983. Mem. Congregation of Oriental Chs., Commn. for Revision of Code of Oriental Canon Law. Advocate reconciliation among various Lebanese ethnic and religious groups and withdrawal fgn. troops from Lebanon. Office: Patriarcat Maronite, Dimane Lebanon

KHOURY, ELIA, bishop. Asst. bishop in Amman, Anglican Communion, Khaury, Jordan. Office: POB 598, Amman Jordan*

KHUMALO, S. A., religious congregation administrator. Chief clk. Presbyn. Ch. of Africa, Umlazi, Republic of South Africa. Office: Presbyn Ch, PO Box 54840, Umlazi 4031, Republic of South Africa*

KIBLER, RAY FRANKLIN, III, minister; b. Columbus, Ohio, Sept. 9, 1951; s. Ray F. Jr. and Evelyn B. (Wiehe) K.; m. Victoria Louise Bergstrom, June 30, 1973; children: Jonathan, Joanna. MusB, Calif. State U., Long Beach, 1974; MDiv, Luther Theol. Sem., 1977; ThM, Luther Northwestern Theol. Sem, 1987; D Ministry, Sch. Theology Claremont, 1990. Ordained to ministry Am. Luth. Ch. (now Evang. Luth. Ch. Am.), 1979. Pastor Grace Luth. Ch., Redway, Calif., 1979-83, Miranda (Calif.) Presbyn. Ch., 1979-81, Holy Redeemer Luth. Ch., Bellflower, Calif., 1984-86; interim pastor Highland Ave. Luth. Ch., San Bernardino, Calif., 1986-87, Peace Luth. Ch., Corona, Calif., 1987-88; pastor Good Shepherd Luth. Ch. and Sch., L.A., 1988-91; interim pastor Prince of Peace Luth. Ch., La Mirada, Calif., 1991-92; mem. faculty Luth. Bible Inst., Anaheim, Calif., 1992—; chaplain Eel River Conservation Ctr., Redway; part-time interim pastor 1st Luth. Ch., Compton, Calif., 1986; mem. So. Calif. West Synod Evang. Luth. Ch. Am. Interim Ministry Task Force, 1989—, ch. coun. retreat leader, 1989—, mem. congregation conflict mgmt. team, 1989; vice dean Rosecrans Conf., 1984-86, Redwood Conf., 1981-83; corr. mem. Presbytery of Redwoods, 1979-81, vice chmn., Six Rivers Federated Dist., 1980-81. Author: At the Crossroad: A Lutheran Confessional response to the question of what it means to believe in Jesus in today's religiously pluralistic world, 1990; contbr. articles to profl. publs. Bd. dirs. Solheim Luth. Home, L.A., 1988—, chair chaplain call com., 1990; chmn. region 2 archives adv. group, dir. Evang. Luth. Ch. Am. Region 2 Archives, Berkeley, Calif., 1989—; bd. dirs. Luth. History Ctr. of the West, 1980—, Luth. Hist. Conf., 1990—. Mem. Am. Soc. Ch. History, Luth. Hist. Conf. Home: 4249 N La Junta Dr Claremont CA 91711 *If it will speak a word of hope for the world, the community in Christ must base its proclamation upon Scripture and upon the witness of what the historic Creeds call "the one holy catholic and apostolic Church". If it ignores its past, it lacks an authoritative word for the future.*

KIDD, JAMES LAMBERT, minister; b. Fall River, Mass., June 12, 1933; s. Thomas W. and Elizabeth Ann (Buckley) K.; m. O. Joann Hamilton, Sept. 12, 1953; 1 child, Pamela Elizabeth. BA, U. Mass., 1955; MDiv, Andover Newton Theol. Sem., Mass., 1959; DDiv, Chgo. Theol. Sem., 1969. Ordained to ministry United Ch. of Christ, 1958. Pastor First Congl. Ch., Pelham, N.H., 1957-61, Wellington Ave. United Ch. of Christ, Chgo., 1961-69, First Congl. Ch., Wilmete, Ill., 1969-79; sr. pastor Asylum Hill Congl. Ch., Hartford, Conn., 1979—; vice pres. bd. dirs. Chgo. Theol. Sem., 1969-79; bd. dirs. Andover Newton Theol. Sem., 1986—, pres. alumni/ae, 1984-85. Author: Good News from Growing Churches, 1990; contbr. articles to profl. jours. Pres. Nat. Cystic Fibrosis Rsch. Found., Chgo., 1968-70; host TV talk show Wonderful World, Chgo., 1968-70. Recipient Ch. Growth award, UCC Ann. Synod, 1985, 89. Mem. Hartford Citywide Clergy Assn. (v.p. 1990-91). Office: Asylum Hill Congl Ch 814 Asylum Ave Hartford CT 06105

KIDD, JOHN S., minister. Exec. dir. Coun. Chs. of Greater Bridgeport (Conn.), Inc. Office: Coun Chs Greater Bridgeport 126 Washington Ave Bridgeport CT 06604*

KIDD, KATHERINE ASHBY, lay worker, church administrator; b. Jasper, Ala., May 13, 1941; d. George Dewey and Pauline Elizabeth (Williams) Ashby; m. Clarence Alton Martin, Oct. 3, 1958 (div. June 1977); children: Benjamin C., Janice S. Martin Cook, Jeffrey D., Jennifer L. Martin Rief; m. George William Kidd, May 27, 1989. AAS, Jefferson State U., 1980; postgrad., U. Ala., 1990—. Cert. in ch. bus. administrn., Ala. Dir. food svc., housekeeping, hostess Ind. Presbyn. Ch. U.S.A., Birmingham, Ala., 1978-82, dir. ops., elder, 1982—, adminstrv. asst. to pastor, 1991—. Mem. Parents without Ptnrs. (sec. 1986-88), Ch. Adminstrs. (pres. Ala. chpt. 1983-85), Nat. Assn. Ch. Bus. Adminstrs. (sec. Ala. chpt. 1989—). Home: 2625 Highland Ave S #410 Birmingham AL 35205 Office: Ind Presbyn Ch 3100 Highland Ave S Birmingham AL 35256

KIDD, WILLIAM B., minister. Head Ecumenical Com., Sault Sainte Marie, Ont., Can. Office: Ecumenical Comm, 76 Eastern Ave, Sault Sainte Marie, ON Canada P6A 4R2*

KIDDER, S. JOSEPH, minister; b. Baghdad, Iraq, Nov. 18, 1953; s. Norie Joseph and Sue (Salak) K.; m. Denise Kay Loffius, July 26, 1981; children: Jason Andrew, Stephanie Rachel. BSCE and BA in Religion, Walla Walla (Wash.) Coll., 1980; MDiv in Theology, Andrews U., 1984, postgrad., 1984—. Assoc. pastor Spokane (Wash.) Valley Seventh-day Adventist Ch., 1980-81, Spokane Cen. Seventh-day Adventist Ch., 1984; pastor Colfax/Endicott Seventh-day Adventist Ch., Colfax, Wash., 1984-88, East Wenatchee/Chelan Seventh-day Adventist Ch., East Wenatchee, Wash., 1988—. Contbr. articles to profl. jours. Vice pres. Kiwanis, Colfax, 1987-88. Mem. Ministerial Alliance (v.p. treas. Colfax chpt. 1985-88). Home: 704 Gormley East Wenatchee WA 98802 Office: Valleyview Seventh-day Adventist Ch 1201 10th St East Wenatchee WA 98802

KIECKHEFER, RICHARD, religion educator; b. Mpls., June 1, 1946. BA in Philosophy, St. Louis U., 1968; MA in Philosophy, U. Tex., 1970, PhD in History, 1972. Instr. history U. Tex., Austin, 1973-74, extension lectr., 1974; asst. prof. Phillips U., 1975; asst. prof. Northwestern U., Evanston, Ill., 1975-79, assoc. prof., 1979-84, prof., 1984—, chair dept., 1981-84, 90, acting chair dept., 1989-90; lectr. Dickinson Coll., 1976, Princeton (N.J.) U., 1976, Internationaler Kongress über Spiritualität Heute und Gestern, Lilienfeld, Austria, 1982, U. Wis., Madison, 1985, St. James Episcopal Cathedral, Chgo., 1985, Sts. Peter and Paul Greek Orthodox Ch., Glenview, Ill., 1986, St. Xavier Coll., Chgo., 1986, St. Mark Episcopal Ch., Evanston, 1986, Harvard Div. Sch., 1987, St. Athanasius Ch., 1987, Brown U., 1987, U. St. Mary of the Lake, 1987, Barnard Coll., 1987, U. London, 1988, U. Notre Dame, Ind., 1989, Newberry Libr., 1990, U. Chgo., 1991. Author: European Witch Trials: Their Foundations in Popular and Learned Culture, 1300-1500, 1976, Repression of Heresy in Medieval Germany, 1979, Unquiet Souls: Fourteenth-Century Saints and Their Religious Milieu, 1984, Magic in the Middle Ages, 1989; co-author, co-editor (with George D. Bond): Sainthood: Its Manifestations in World Religions, 1988. Recipient citation Coun. for Advancement and Support of Edn.; NEH fellow, 1987-88, Guggenheim fellow, 1991; grantee NDEA, 1968-71, Deutscher Akademischer Austauschdienst, 1971-72, Am. Coun. Learned Socs., 1981, Alumnae of Northwestern, 1982. Mem. Phi Beta Kappa, Eta Sigma Phi, Alpha Sigma Nu. Home: 2314 Hastings Ave Evanston IL 60201 Office: Northwestern U Dept Religion 1940 Sheridan Rd Evanston IL 60208

KIEHL, ERICH HENRY, educator; b. Lone Elm, Mo., Aug. 27, 1920; s. Henry G.H. and Clara Dorothy (Kuecker) Kiehl; m. Dorothy L. Krone, July 21, 1946; children: David, Kathryn, Sharon, Daniel, Mark, Thomas. BA, Concordia Sem., 1942, MDiv, 1945, STM, 1951, ThD, 1959; postdoctoral, Cambridge U., 1975-76. Dir. planning and rsch. Ch.-Craft Pix., St. Louis, 1946-60; asst. to pastor Timothy Luth. Ch., St. Louis, 1946; editor of weekday mat. Luth. Ch. Mo. Synod, St. Louis, 1960-65; prof. Concordia Coll., Ann Arbor, Mich., 1965-74, Concordia Sem., 1974—. Author: God and His Covenant People, 1965, Jesus, The Messiah, 1966, The Gospel in Paul's World, 1965, Building Your Biblical Studies Library, 1988, The Passion of Our Lord, 1990, and others. Recipient John W. Behnken award Aid Assn. for Luths., 1975. Mem. Soc. of Bibl. Lit., Evang. Theol. Soc., Cath. Bibl. Soc., Archaeol. Inst. Am. Office: Concordia Sem 801 De Mun Saint Louis MO 63105

KIENER, RONALD CHARLES, religion educator; b. Mpls., May 28, 1954; s. Harold and Marian (Goldish) K.; m. Andrea S. Cohen, Oct. 13, 1974; children: Samuel, Sara, Isaac, Ariana. BA, U. Minn., 1976; PhD, U. Pa., 1984. Vis. instr. Dartmouth Coll., Hanover, N.H., 1981-83; assoc. prof. religion Trinity Coll., Hartford, Conn., 1983—; vis. lectr. Smith Coll., Northampton, Mass., 1989. Co-author: The Early Kabbalah, 1986; contbr. articles to scholarly jours. NEH grantee, 1987. Mem. Assn. for Jewish Studies, Am. Acad. Religion, World Union for Jewish Studies. Home: 134 St Charles St Hartford CT 06119 Office: Trinity Coll Dept Religion Hartford CT 06106

KIENZLER, KLAUS, theology educator; b. Triberg, Baden-Wurttenberg, Fed. Republic Germany, May 28, 1944; s. Fritz and Josephine (Worz) K.; Bacc.-Philos., Pont U. Gregor, Rome, 1967, Lic.Theol., 1971; Dr.Theol., Univ., Freiburg, Fed. Republic Germany, 1975, Dr.Theol.Habil., 1979. Prof. fundamental theology University Augsburg, Bayern, Fed. Republic Germany, 1980—. Author: Auferstehung, 1976, Anselm v. Canterbury, 1981; co-author: Einladung, 1979, Sein und Schein, 1983, Mythos und Glaube, 1985, Spuren der Erlösung, 1986, Verborgener Gott, 1987, Religionsphilosophie, 1988, Versöhnung in der jüdischen und christlichen Liturgie, 1990, Der neue Fundamentalismus, 1990, Max Josef Metzger, 1991. Roman Catholic. Office: Univ Augsburg, Universitatsstr 10, D-8900 Augsburg Federal Republic of Germany

KIEPURA, SALLY, religious organization administrator; b. Harvey, Ill., Mar. 1, 1938; d. Stephen and Frances (Golab) K. BS in Edn., De Lourdes Coll., Des Plaines, Ill., 1964; MS, U. Okla., 1970; postgrad., Loyola U., Chgo., 1982—. Cert. elem. sch. tchr., adminstr., Ill. Elem. tchr. various Cath. schs., Chgo., 1962-64, 68-71, Dallas, 1964-68, Irving, Tex., 1971-74; sci. instr. St. Ann High Sch., Chgo., 1974-76; prin. St. Andrew the Apostle Sch., Calumet City, Ill., 1976-79; dir. tchr. edn. De Lourdes Coll., 1979-86, acting pres., 1986-88; province adminstr., dir. pers. and ministries Sisters of Holy Family of Nazareth, Des Plaines, Ill., 1989—; trustee Holy Family Coll., Phila., 1987—. Active Clergy and Householders Opposed to Petroleum Profiteering, Chgo., 1976. NSF grantee, 1966, 67, 68-70, 73. Mem. Nat. Assn. Ch. Personnel Adminstrs., Nat. Cath. Edn. Assn., Nat. Assn. on Aging. Avocations: reading, travel, crocheting. Home and Office: Sisters Holy Family 353 N River Rd Des Plaines IL 60016

KIESCHNICK, JOHN HENRY, clergyman; b. Walburg, Tex., Mar. 5, 1942; s. Oscar Henry and Lina (Doering) K.; m. Carol Elaine Trimble, July 4, 1970; children: Jonathan, Kimberly, Jason. BS in Edn., Concordia Tchrs. Coll., River Forest, Ill., 1964; BD, Concordia Sem., Springfield, Ill., 1970; MDiv, Concordia Sem., Ft. Wayne, Ind., 1985. Ordained to ministry Luth. Ch., 1970. Tchr., prin. Calvary Luth. Ch., Havertown, Pa., 1964-66; pastor Our Redeemer Luth. Ch., Irving, Tex., 1970-74; sr. pastor Gloria Dei Luth. Ch., Houston, 1974—; bd. dirs. Parish Svcs. for Tex. Dist., Austin, 1972-82; dir. anniversary thankoffering for Tex. dist. of Mo. Synod Luth. Ch., St. Louis; mem. Ch. Growth Task Force, Austin, 1986, Luth. Ch. Extension Fund, St. Louis, 1987—. Mem. Luth. Edn. Assn. Office: Gloria Dei Luth Ch 18220 Upper Bay Rd Houston TX 77058

KIESCHNICK, MELVIN MARTIN, religion educator; b. Walburg, Tex., Dec. 10, 1927; s. Oscar H. and Lina Emma (Doering) K.; m. June Anne Scheimann, July 14, 1951; children: David A., Margareth M., Timothy P., Elizabeth L., John H. BS in Edn., Concordia U., River Forest, Ill., 1950; MA in Psychology, U. Pacific, 1954; LlD (hon.), Concordia U., 1973. Supt. of schs. Luth. Ch. Mo. Synod Mich. Dist., Ann Arbor, 1968-72; exec. dir. Bd. of Parish Edn. The Luth. Ch., St. Louis, 1972-76; exec. v.p. Effectiveness Tng. Inc., South Beach, Ga., 1976-84; resource person to bishop for schs. Evang. Luth. Ch. in Am. Metro N.Y. Synod, 1987; exec. dir. Luth. Schs. Assn., Eastchester, N.Y., 1984—; advisor div. for edn. Evang. Luth. Ch. in Am., Chgo., 1987—; dir. projects Ctr. for Urban Edn. Concordia, Bronxville, N.Y., 1984—. Author: The Pastor & teh Lutheran School, 1985, Perspective on Effective Parenting, 1979; contbr. articles to Luth. Edn., 1954—. Mem. N.Y. State Coalition for Non-Pub. Edn., Albany, 1986—, Commr. Adv. Com. N.Y., Albany, 1984—, Citizens for Ednl. Freedom, Washington, 1970-72; v.p. Mich. Assn. Nonpub. Schs., Ann Arbor, 1969-72; trustee Head Start San Diego, 1974-80. Recipient Cristus Vivet award Concordia Sem., 1975, Cristus Magistra award Concordia U., 1966, Ivan Zylstra award Mich. Assn. Nonpub. Schs., 1989, Spiritus Christi medalion Concordia U., 1973. Mem. Evang. Luth. Edn. Assn., Luth. Edn. Assn., Assn. for Supervision & Curriculum Devel. Democrat. Home and office: Luth Schs Assn 35 Deerfield Ave Eastchester NY 10707

KIESELBACH, JOSEPH LEO, priest; b. Fargo, N.D., Nov. 20, 1931; s. Leo John Kieselbach and Ann Catherine Hilgers. BA, St. John's U., Collegeville, Minn., 1953. Ordained priest Roman Cath. Ch., 1961. Assoc. pastor various parishes, 1961-71; pastor St. Joseph's Ch., Oslo, Minn., 1971-77, Sacred Heart Ch., Frazee, Minn., 1977, St. Mary's Ch., Fosston, Minn., 1977-86, St. Michael's Ch., Mahnomen, Minn., 1986—; dir. Spanish edn. program Diocese of Crookston (Minn.), 1969-86. Mem. U.S. Army, 1953-55. Office: St Michaels Ch Rte 1 Box 22 Mahnomen MN 56557 *(Quoted from some place and thus not original: "Much can be accomplished if one does not care who receives the credit."*

KIEWE, JEROME MARK, religious organization administrator, educator; b. Balt., Aug. 2, 1961; s. Bernhard and Marlene (Shulman) K. BA in Sociology and Social Work, U. Md., Baltimore County, 1983; MA in Jewish Studies, Balt. Hebrew U., 1985; MSW, U. Md., Balt., 1985. Asst. regional dir. Fla. region B'nai B'rith Youth Orgn., Ft. Lauderdale, Fla., 1985-89; regional dir. Greater Jersey-Hudson River region B'nai B'rith Youth Orgn., Linden, N.J., 1989—; religious sch. tchr. Temple Emanu-El, Westfield, N.J., 1990—. Mem. B'nai B'rith, Conf. Jewish Communal Svc. (trustee). Democrat. Office: B'nai Brith Youth Orgn 411-A N Wood Ave Linden NJ 07036

KIFFMEYER, JAMES GEORGE, priest, pharmacist, educator; b. Cin., Mar. 2, 1957; s. James Costello and Patricia Mary (Fessler). B.S., U. Cin., 1980; M.A., Athenaeum of Ohio, 1985, M. Div., 1985. Registered pharmacist, Ohio; cert. secondary tchr. Ohio. Ordained priest Roman Catholic Ch., 1985. Pharmacist, St. George Hosp., Cin., 1980-81, Moore's Pharmacy, Cin., 1981-84; tchr. McNicholas High Sch., Cin., 1983-84; Roman Catholic deacon Archdiocese of Cin., 1984-85; chaplain Carroll High Sch., Dayton, Ohio, 1984-85, tchr., chaplain Fenwick High Sch., Middletown, Ohio, 1985—. Mem. Hamilton County Pharm. Assn., Ohio State Pharm. Assn., Catholic Pharmacist Guild. Avocations: photography, racketball. Home: 462 Considine Ave Cincinnati OH 45205 Office: St Mary Ch 3917 Central Ave Middletown OH 45044

KIK, FRANK NICHOLAS, minister; b. Dalhousie, N.B., Can., Nov. 17, 1935; came to U.S, 1952; naturalized, 1957; s. Jacob Marcellus and Evelyn Winona (Reid) K.; m. Phyllis Ann Savage, June 1, 1957; children: Scott Douglas, Heather Jean, Daryl Andrew. BA, Gordon Coll., 1959; MDiv, Gordon Conwell Sem., 1963, DD, 1976. Ordained to ministry United Presbyn. Ch., 1963. Pastor Queens Village Presbyn. Ch., N.Y.C., 1963-68; sr. pastor Knox Presbyn. Ch., Buffalo, 1968-73, Eastminster United Presbyn. Ch., Wichita, 1973—; lectr. Gordon-Conwell Sem., Mass., Wichita State U.; chmn. adv. bd. World Impact Inc., Wichita; former chmn. bd. Sterling (Kans.) Coll.; founder Ellicott Ministry, Buffalo, Wichita Christian Counseling Ctr. V.p. Presbyns. United for Bibl. Concerns, 1974—. Mem. Kiwanis (past pres. Wichita Downtown club). Home: 232 Lochinvar Rd Wichita KS 67207 Office: 1958 N Webb Rd Wichita KS 67206

KIKAWADA, ISAAC MITZURU, Oriental studies educator, priest; b. Sendai, Miyagi, Japan, Apr. 16, 1937; came to U.S., 1956; s. John Seiki and Sarah Katsuko (Ito) K.; m. Heidi Gerster, 1989. BS, Baldwin-Wallace Coll., 1962; BD, Kenyon Coll., 1965; PhD, U. Calif., Berkeley, 1979. Cert. secondary tchr., Ohio; ordained to priesthood Episcopal Ch., 1966. Tchr. Cain Pk. Youtheatre, Cleveland Heights, Ohio, 1958-59; chaplain, tchr. St. Ann's Sch. for Girls, Boca Raton, Fla., 1965-66; dir. summer sch. St. James Episcopal Ch., Painesville, Ohio, 1967-68; instr. Nr. Ea. studies U. Calif., Berkeley, 1972-84, vis. lectr., 1972-89, asst. specialist, 1989—; vis. assoc. prof. Oriental studies U. Ariz., Tucson, 1984-85; cons. LENANTE, Inc., Osaka, Japan, 1983—. Co-author: Before Abraham Was, 1985; contbr. articles to profl. jours. and the Anchor Bible Dictionary. Advisor St. Luke's Ch., Osaka, 1969-90. Baldwin-Wallace scholar, 1959-62, Firestone scholar Kenyon Coll., 1962-65, Grad. Theol. Union scholar, 1968-69; Ford grantee U. Calif.-Berkeley, 1972-73. Fellow Ctr. Mid. Eastern Studies; mem. Am. Oriental Soc. (exec. com. 1976-80), Soc. Biblical Lit. (pres. West Coast chpt. 1984-85), Soc. of Palaeology Japan, Japanese Biblical Inst. (contbg. mem.), World Union Jewish Studies of Jerusalem, San Francisco Mycological Soc. Episcopalian. Avocation: tea ceremony. Home: 1787 Sonoma Ave Berkeley CA 94707 Office: U Calif Dept Nr Ea Studies Berkeley CA 94720

KIKER, HENRY ROGER, minister; b. Monroe, N.C., Jan. 5, 1949; s. John Henry and Ruby Jane (Rushing) K.; m. Sheila Gail Helms, Jan. 18, 1969; children: Thomas Henry, Rhonda Lynn, Donna Marie. Student, Cen. Piedmont Coll., Wingate Coll.; Assoc. Div., Southeastern Sem., 1981; ThB, Empire Bible Coll. and Sem., 1989. Ordained to ministry So. Bapt. Conv., 1981. Pastor Eureka Bapt. Ch., Keysville, Va., 1981-83, Reedy Creek Bapt. Ch., Freeman, Va., 1983—; mem. Concord Mins. Conf., South Hill, Va., 1984—, Greensville Mins. Conf., Emporia, Va., 1984—. Active in Charlotte County Rescue Squad, Keysville, 1982-83. With U.S. Army, Vietnam. Recipient Leadership and Guidance award Community Youth Ctr., Emporia, 1989. Mem. Va. Bapt. Pastors Conf. (sec., treas. 1984—), Am. Christian TV System Concord Bapt. Assn. (cons. 1984—). Republican. Avocations: golf, fishing, hunting. Home: RR 1 Box 220 Freeman VA 23856 Office: Reedy Creek Bapt Ch RR 1 Box 220 Freeman VA 23856

KILBOURN, LAWRENCE WINFORD, minister; b. Hartford, Conn., Mar. 31, 1956; s. John H. and Rhoda (Janes) K.; m. Deidre Ann Smith, June 14, 1980; children: Lauren Michelle, Emily Kristen, Charlotte Joy. B of Music Edn., Fla. State U., 1978; MDiv, Emory U., 1982. Ordained to ministry

United Meth. Ch. as deacon, 1984, as elder, 1984. Assoc. pastor First United Meth. Ch., Jacksonville, Fla., 1982-84, Trinity United Meth. Ch., Bradenton, Fla., 1984-86; pastor Faith United Meth. Ch., Bradenton, 1986—; vice-pres. to pres. Manatee Ministerial Assn., Bradenton, 1985-89; v.p. Greater Manatee Area Outreach 91, Bradenton, 1990-91, Christian Community Coun., Bradenton, 1990-91. Bd. dirs. Downtown Ctr. for Children, Inc., Bradenton, 1990-91. Marcy Preaching scholar Fla. Conf. United Meth. Ch., 1984. Mem. Sertoma (chaplain 1990-91). Democrat. Office: Faith United Methodist Ch 7215 1st Ave W Bradenton FL 34209 *There are very few problems facing folks today that a smile, a kind word or a warm embrace can not make easier. These may not solve problems, but they make them easier to bear.*

KILBURN, S. COLLINS, minister. Exec. dir. N.C. Coun. Chs., Raleigh. Office: NC Coun Chs 1307 Glenwood Ave Ste 162 Raleigh NC 27605*

KILGORE, L(EROY) WILSON, minister; b. Elmira, N.Y., Feb. 25, 1917; s. Roy Dunning and Bertha Pearl (Bush) K.; m. Ursula Dunbar, June 27, 1940 (wid. 1960); children: Keith, Sharon, Paul, Debra; m. Lois Morse Bell, Feb. 14, 1961; 1 child, Kristie. BA, Colgate U., 1939; MDiv, Colgate-Rochester Div. Sch., 1942; DD (hon.), Colgate U., 1964. Ordained to ministry Presbyn. Ch. (U.S.A.), 1942. Pastor 1st Presbyn. Ch., Hartford, Conn., 1943-53; sr. pastor Lakewood Presbyn. Ch., Cleve., 1953-64, Cherry Hill Presbyn. Ch., Dearborn, Mich., 1964-72, Valley Presbyn. Ch., Scottsdale, Ariz., 1972-86; interim minister 3d Presbyn. Ch., Rochester, N.Y., 1987-88, 1st Presbyn. Ch., Tulsa, 1990-91; trustee San Francisco Theol. Seminary, San Anselmo, Calif., 1978-90; mem. support agy. Presbyn. Ch. USA, 1978-86; chmn. com. on communication Presbyn. Ch. USA, 1980-82; moderator Grand Canyon Presbytery, 1986-87. Author: What a Way to Live, 1977, When the River Runs Backward 1983, 2nd edit. 1989. Mem. Acad. of Parish Clergy, Cleve., 1976—; trustee, pres. Westminster Village Retirement Ctr., Scottsdale, Ariz., 1990—. Mem. Rotary. Home and Office: 7800 N 65th St Scottsdale AZ 85253

KILGORE, WILSON ROY, religion educator; b. Louellen, Ky, Aug. 14, 1949; s. Wilson Roy and Stella Mae (Searcy) K.; m. Patsy Gail Kornegay; 1 child, Kristian Andrew. BS, Lee Coll., 1971; MA, Ch. of God Sch. of Theology, 1987. Tchr. Palm Vista Christian Sch., Ft. Pierce, Fla., 1971-73; youth, Christian edn., outreach dir. Palm Vista Ch. of God, Ft. Pierce, Fla., 1974-76, Okeechobee (Fla.) Ch. of God, 1976-78; Christian educator, outreach dir. Dayton (Tenn.) Ch. of God, 1978-79, Eastland Temple Ch. of God, Orlando, Fla., 1979-84; minister of Christian edn. Broadmoor Ch. of God, Nashville, 1986-91; minister of Christian edn. and evangelism Tremont Ave. Ch. of God, Greenville, S.C., 1991—; Chmn. Family Restoration Ministries, Nashville, 1986-87, Ch. of God State Laymen's Bd., Tampa, Fla., 1976-78, mem. 1972-76, Chattanooga, 1978-79, Cleveland, Tenn., 1972-78. Team leader Pioneers for Christ, Cleve., 1968-69, v.p., 1970-71; minister of christian edn. Evangelism Tremont Ave Ch. of God, Greenville, S.C., 1991—. Named one of Outstanding Young Men of Am., 1985; Louis Cross Scholar, Ch. of God Sch. of Theology, Cleveland, 1984-85. Mem. Ch. of God Sch. of Theology Alumni Assn. (pres. 1990—). Republican. Avocations: reading, softball, travel. Home: 15 Best DR # 907 Greenville SC 29611

KILIMNICK, SHAYA M., rabbi, educator; b. Bklyn., June 19, 1947; s. Harry and Evelyn (Gerstein) K.; m. Nichele Wernick, Oct. 13, 1969; children: Yosef, Shifron, Zipora, Dovid, Avi. B.Talmud, Ner Israel Rabbinical Coll., Balt., 1969; MS, U. Cen. Ark., 1973. Ordained rabbi. Rabbi Congregation Agutat Achim, Little Rock, 1970-77, Congregation Beth Sholom, Rochester, N.Y., 1977—; religious dir. Jewish Home of Rochester, 1980—; chmn. Rochester Orthodox Rabbinical Coun., 1983—; chmn. UpState N.Y. Youth Commn., 1985—, Rabbinic Israel Bonds, Rochester, 1984—. Civilian chaplain USAF, 1970-77. Mem. Jaycees, B'nai B'rith. Office: Beth Sholom Synagogue 1161 Monroe Ave Rochester NY 14620

KILLEN, PATRICIA O'CONNELL, religion educator; b. Portland, Oreg., Nov. 30, 1951; d. William Leo and Florence Delores (Duyck) O'Connell; m. David Patrick Killen, May 28, 1975. BA in Religious Studies, Gonzaga U., 1974; MA in Religious Studies, Stanford U., 1976, PhD in Religious Studies, 1987. Asst. prof. religion Pacific Luth. U., Tacoma, 1989—; instr. in theology U. of S., Sewanee, Tenn., 1978-85; adj. prof. Loyola U., Chgo., 1985-87, asst. prof., 1987-89. Editor: Journeys in Ministry, 1989; contbr. articles to profl. publs. Whiting fellow, 1978, CBS Bicentennial Narrators fellow, 1978; Mellon grantee, 1988; recipient Profl. Achievement award Burlington No., 1990. Mem. Am. Acad. Religion, Cath. Theol. Soc. Am., Coll. Theology Soc. Office: Pacific Luth U Tacoma WA 98447

KILLIAN, DAVID ALLEN, priest; b. Mondovi, Wis., Aug. 16, 1940; s. Alphonse Peter and Helen (Sosalla) K.; m. Barbara Ann O'Neil, June 23, 1984; children: Brendan Hyun, Meeya Ann. AB, St. Paul's Coll., 1964; MA, New Sch. for Social Rsch., 1984; DMin, Andover-Newton, 1990. Ordained priest Roman Cath. Ch., 1967, to ministry Episcopal Ch. as priest, 1988. Asst. dir. Paulist Ctr., Grand Rapids, Mich., 1967-71; assoc. dir Paulist Ctr., Boston, 1971-78; mem. presdl. bd. Paulist Fathers, Scarsdale, N.Y., 1978-83; exec. dir. Interfaith Counseling Svc., Newton, Mass., 1985—; interim pastor St. Dunstan's Ch., Dover, Mass., 1989-90, St. Michael's Ch., Marblehead, Mass., 1990, Ch. of the Good Shepherd, Watertown, Mass., 1991—; mem. diocesan coun. Episc. Ch., Boston, 1991—, mem. diocesan evangelism com., 1989—; chmn. Jovenes Catolicos En Accion, Lawrence, 1984-91. Treas. Wide Horizons for Children Inc., Waltham, Mass., 1989—. Mem. Mass. Episc. Clergy Assn. (editor newsletter 1991—). Home: 42 Eldredge St Newton MA 02158 Office: Interfaith Counseling Svc 60 Highland St West Newton MA 02165

KILLIAN, NATHAN RAYNE, clergyman; b. Shickshinny, Pa., Jan. 8, 1935; s. Howard Elmer and Helen Marie (Hontz) K.; m. Jeanette Eaves, Sept. 17, 1936; children: Sheri Jean, Brian James. Student, Bloomsburg (Pa.) U., 1952-53, Valley Forge Christian Coll., Phoenixville, Pa., 1953-56; MA, Internat. Sem., Plymouth, Fla., 1981, ThD, 1982, PhD in Religious Psychology, 1990. Ordained to ministry Assemblies of God Ch.; diplomate Assn. Christian Clin. Counselors. Nat., internat. lectr. Assemblies of God, Camp Hill, Pa., 1956-74; sr. minister Abundant Life Assembly of God, Lithia, Fla., 1974-75, Treasure Coast Cathedral, Vero Beach, Fla., 1975-78; sr. minister First Assembly of God, Wilmington, Del., 1978-85, DeLand, Fla., 1985—; radio-TV lectr. First Assembly of God, Wilmington, 1980-85; behavioral counselor First Assembly of God, Deland, 1984—;pres. Abundant Life Ministries, Inc., Deland, 1981—, Christian Bible Inst. Deland, 1985-86; chmn. bd. First Assembly of God, 1985—. Author: The Holy Spirit Now, 1977, Your Questions Answered, 1981, Theological Government, 1982, Those Golden Moments, 1989. Adminstr. "We Care" Assistance Program, Wilmington, 1980-85. Recipient Nat. Growth awards Gen. Coun. Assemblies of God, Springfield, Mo., 1974, 75, First Place Growth award Peninsular Fla. Dist., Lakeland, 1978, Div. award Pa.-Del. Dist., Camp Hill, 1981. Mem. Nat. Christian Counselors Assn., Gen. Coun. Assemblies of God. Republican. Avocations: jogging, swimming, golf. Home: 2731 Charleston Pl De Land FL 32720 *The concrete existence of God is undoubtedly verified through the wondrous splendor of the universe—with its hidden mysteries, unchartable immensity, celestial regions and myriad galaxies.*

KILLIAN, TIMOTHY WAYNE, religion educator; b. Hickory, N.C., Aug. 11, 1961; s. Robert Wayne and Judy Gilbert (Huffman) K.; m. Karen Meredith (div.); 1 child, Brandon; m. Lora Sue Davis, May 7, 1982; 1 child, Seth. Grad. high sch., Hickory, N.C., 1979. Youth pastor Word of Life Christian Ctr., Newton, N.C., 1982-90; elder New Horizon Ministries, Newton, 1990—; supr. Christian Sch., Newton, 1990—. Home: Rt 3 Box 202B Newton NC 28658 Office: New Horizon Christ Road Rt 2 Box 427 Newton NC 28610

KILLORAN, MARGARET MAUREEN, minister; b. Toronto, Ont., Can., Aug. 29, 1944; d. John Henry and Margaret Glenrose (Long) K.; m. Gerald Schwartz, 1966 (div. 1977); 1 child, Andrea Jayne; m. Peter Channing Hyatt, Aug. 30, 1987. BA in Sociology with honors, McMaster U., Hamilton, Ont., 1980, MA in Sociology, 1982; MDiv, Victoria U., Toronto, 1986. Ordained to ministry Unitarian Universalist Ch., 1986. Pastoral cons. Can. Unitarian Coun., Toronto, 1981-86; min. 1st Unitarian Soc. of Salem, Oreg., 1986-91, Unitarian Universalist Ch., Asheville, N.C., 1991—; chmn. Commn. on Gen. Resolutions, Unitarian Universalist Assn., Boston, 1990—; mem. steering com. Oreg. Meml. Assn., Portland, 1990-91; chaplain Women's Crisis Ctr., Salem, 1986-91; del. Gen. Assemblies of Unitarian Universalist Assn., 1985—. Contbr. articles and poems to various jours. Mem. ethics com. City of Salem, 1990-91; mem. Internal Rev. Bd., Salem Hosp., 1990-91. Unitarian Universalist Women's History Project study grantee, 1991. Mem. Salem Ministerial Assn. (pres. 1989-90), Unitarian Universalist Ministers Assn., Unitarian Universalist Hist. Assn., Alban Inst. Office: Unitarian Universalist Ch Asheville One Edwin Pl Asheville NC 28801

KILLOUGH, REGINALD ALLEN, minister; b. Marion, N.C., Dec. 29, 1945; s. James Allen and Ruth Lillian (Erwin) K.; m. Shirley Anne Wilkerson, Sept. 19, 1965; 1 child, Zachary. BTh., Internat. Sem., 1984, postgrad., 1980. Ordained to ministry Bapt. Ch., 1969. Founder, dir., 24 hr. crisis line Christ Team, Asheville, N.C., 1968-75; dir. Christ Team, Miami, Fla., 1975-85; dir., youth outreach Christ Team, Daytona Beach, Fla., 1985—; speaker various civic clubs, schs. and colls. Producer: (tv) The Beach Preach, 1980-82; editor: (newsletters) Fathers' Business, 1975-89, The Sandpaper, 1989—; speaker, producer: (audio/video show) I.O.U. Love, 1975—; contbr. articles to newspapers. With U.S. Army, 1966-68. Home: 242 Treeline Ln Ormond Beach FL 32174 Office: Christ Team Inc PO Box 3456 Daytona Beach FL 32118 *The combination of a happy heart, a positive mind and a life of love can conquer anything set before one's life.*

KILMARTIN, EDWARD JOHN, theologian, educator; b. Portland, Maine, Aug. 31, 1923; s. Patrick Joseph and Elizabeth Gertrude (Sullivan) K. A.B., Boston Coll., 1947, M.A. in Philosophy, 1948, S.T.L., 1955; M.S. in Chemistry, Holy Cross Coll., 1950; S.T.D., Gregorian U., Rome, 1958. Joined S.J., Roman Catholic Ch., 1941; ordained priest Roman Cath. Ch., 1954; tchr. chemistry Fairfield (Conn.) Prep. Sch., 1950-51; prof. sacramental theology Weston Coll., Sch. Theology, Boston Coll., 1958-77, dean sch., 1960-62; prof. liturg. theology U. Notre Dame, 1977-84, dir. grad. program in liturg. studies, 1980-84; prof. liturgical theology Pontifical Oriental Inst., Rome, 1985—. Assoc. editor New Testament Abstracts, 1959-67; author numerous books and articles on N.T. and Christian worship. Mem. Cath. Theol. Soc. Am., Cath. Bibl. Assn. Avocation: mountain climbing. Office: Pontifical Oriental Inst, Maggiore 7 Piazza S Maria, 00185 Rome Italy

KILPATRICK, ROBERT EDWARD, minister, musician; b. Louisville, Oct. 25, 1952; s. August Christian and Mary Delores (Gardner) K.; m. Cynthia Rae Shively, Nov. 13, 1971; children: Joel Seth, Ian Philip, Andrew Michael, Kyle Robert, Brittany Mary-Elizabeth. Grad. high sch., Wheatland, Calif. Pres. Bob Kilpatrick Ministries, Inc., Fair Oaks, Calif., 1976—; cons. dir. Messenger Internat., San Jose, Calif., 1986—. Composer, pub. (album) It's So Simple, 1985, Won by One, 1987, The Long March, 1990, Through the Kinder Day, 1991. Grantee Bethesda Found., 1991. Mem. ASCAP. Republican. Avocations: downhill skiing, tennis, racquetball, international travel, swimming. Office: Bob Kilpatrick Ministries PO Box 2383 Fair Oaks CA 95628

KILPATRICK, STEPHEN PAUL, minister; b. Waterloo, N.Y., Dec. 2, 1959; s. George Frederick and Helen Oneida Jane (Gleason) K.; m. Lynn Suzanne Gunderson, Sept. 8, 1960; 1 child, Stephen Paul II. BS in Systems Analysis and Design, Elmira (N.Y.) Coll., 1985; BS in Bible and Theology, United Wesylan Coll., Allentown, Pa., 1988. Ordained to ministry Wesleyan Ch., 1988. Factory worker Thatcher Glass Mfg. Co., Elmira Heights, N.Y., 1978-80; mental hygiene therapy aide Elmira Psychiat. Ctr., 1982-86; youth pastor Pulaski (N.Y.) Wesleyan Ch., 1986-89; asst. pastor Bethany Wesleyan Ch., Cherryville, Pa., 1989—. Mem. Pa.-Jersey Dist. Exec. Youth Bd.; dir. N.E. Area Teens-N-Talent, 1988—. With U.S. Army, 1980-82. Mem. Nat. Assn. of Evangelicals, Nat. Right to Life Com., Am. Family Assn. Republican. Wesleyan. Avocations: sports, mechanics, carpentry. Home: 675 Blue Mountain Dr Cherryville PA 18035 Office: Bethany Wesleyan Ch PO Box 793 675 Blue Mountain Dr Cherryville PA 18035

KIM, DAVID SANG CHUL, seminary president, publishing executive; b. Seoul, Korea, Nov. 9, 1915; came to U.S., 1959; m. Eui Hong Kang, Jan. 6, 1942; children: Sook Hee, Sung Soo, Hyun Soo, Young Soo, Joon Soo. BA in English Lit., Chosen Christian Coll., Seoul, 1939; postgrad., U. Wales, 1954-55, Western Conservative Bapt. Sem., 1959-61, U. Oreg., 1962-63; MA, U. Oreg., 1965; postgrad., Pacific Sch. Religion, Berkeley, Calif., 1965-66; PhD, Columbia Pacific U., 1988. Mem. staff Chosen Rubber Industry Assn., Seoul, 1939-45; fin asst. U.S. Mil. Govt., Kunsan City, Korea, 1945-48; govt. official Ministry of Fin., Ministry of Social Affairs and Health, Ministry of Fgn. Affairs Govt. of Republic of Korea, Seoul, 1948-59; charter mem. Unification Ch., Seoul, 1954; 1st missionary to Eng., 1954-55; missionary, evangelist Unification Ch., U.S., 1959-70; supr. counseling Clearfield Job Corps Ctr., Clearfield, Utah, 1966-70; founder, pres., owner The Cornerstone Press (name change to Rose of Sharon Press), 1978; supr. counseling Clearfield (Utah) Job Corps Ctr., 1966-70; founder, pres., trustee Internat. Relief Friendship Found., Inc., 1974—; pres. Internat. One World Crusade Inc., 1975—; charter mem., trustee Nt. Coun. Chs. and Social Action, 1976—; advisor, fin. supporter Global Congress of World Religions, Inc., 1978—; charter mem. INternat. Religious Found., Inc., 1982—; v.p. Unification Thought Inst., 1989. Author: Individual Preparation for His Coming Kingdom: Interpretation of the Principle, 1964; Victory Over Communism and the Role of Religion, 1972; editor: (book series) Day of Hope in Review, Part I-1972-74, 1974, Part 2-1974-75, 1975, Part 3, Vol. 1-1976-1981, 1981. Office: Unification Theol Sem 10 Dock Rd Barrytown NY 12507

KIM, EDWARD SUNG-MAN, pastor, academic administrator; b. Naju, Korea, Mar. 9, 1930; s. Heung Soon and Soon Dan (Park) K.; m. Grace Seung-Hie Choi, Oct. 30, 1955; 1 child, David C. Student, Chong Shin Coll., Seoul, Korea, 1952; BD, Chong Sin Theol. Sem., Seoul, 1956; BA, Won-Kwang U., Iri, Korea, 1971; ThM, Tex. Christian U., Ft. Worth, 1977. Chaplain Soongil High Sch., Kwangju, Korea, 1956-59; pastor Soekwang Presbyn. Ch., Kwangju, 1959-64, Iri Sun Nack Presbyn. Ch., 1964-71, Korean Presbyn. Ch. Houston, 1977—; pres. Korean Bible Inst. Houston, 1987—, prof., 1987—; moderator Korean S.W. Presbytery Presbyn. Ch. in Am., Calif., 1984-85, Korean So. Presbytery, Houston, 1988-90, stated clk. Southwestern Presbytery, Calif., 1986-88; chmn. Korean Christian Chs. Fedn. Greater Houston, 1987-88; pub. ch. paper Korean Presbyn. Ch. Herald, 1990. Recipient Cert. Appreciation award Korean Sr. Citizens Assn. Houston, 1984, Korean-Am. Assn. Houston, 1987. Home: 11234 Ivyridge Houston TX 77043 Office: Korean Presbyn Ch 9002 Ruland Rd Houston TX 77055

KIM, HA-KYUNG CHO, minister, pharmacology consulant; b. Seoul, Korea, Sept. 22, 1938; came to U.S., 1961; d. Wan and Uhnshin (Kim) Cho; m. Kyuha Kim, Mar. 9, 1962; children: Mary M., Eugene H. BS in Pharmacy, Ewha Women's U., 1961; MS in Pharmacology Chemistry, Duquesne U., 1965; PhDin Pharmacognosy, U. Pitts., 1969; MDiv., Pitts. Theol. Sem., 1985. Registered pharamcist; ordained min. United Meth. Ch. Assoc. pastor United Meth. Ch., Mars, Pa., 1985-87; pastor Christ Community Ch., McKees Rocks, Pa., 1987—; clin. pharmacologist Children's Hosp., Pitts., 1980—. Author: (book) The Way of Life, 1984. Mem. Am. Pharm. Assn., West Pa. Conf. United Meth. Ch., Kims Martial Arts. Office: 900 Chartiers Ave McKees Rocks PA 15136

KIM, HEE-JIN, religious studies educator; b. Masan, Kyongsang-do, Korea, Apr. 8, 1927; came to U.S., 1952; s. Young-Ho and Um-Chon (Kim) K.; m. Kyue-In Lee, June 4, 1957 (dec. 1963); children: Sun-Chul, Hae-Sil; m. Jung-Sun Kim, Feb. 7, 1965; 1 child, Yeong-Jue. BA, U. Calif., Berkeley, 1957, MA, 1958; PhD, Claremont Grad. Sch., 1966. Mem. faculty U. Oregon, Eugene, 1973—, prof. religious studies, 1983—. Author: Dogen Kigen-Mystical Realist, 1975, rev. edit. 1987, Flowers of Emptiness: Selections from Dogen's Shobogenzo, 1985. Mem. Assn. for Asian Studies, Soc. for Asian and Comparative Philosophy, Internat. Assn. Buddhist Studies, Am. Acad. Religion. Home: 570 Ful Vue Dr Eugene OR 97405 Office: U Oreg Eugene OR 97403

KIM, STEPHAN SOU-HWAN CARDINAL, cardinal, archbishop; b. Taegu, Korea, May 8, 1922. BTh, Sophia U., Tokyo, 1944; ThM, Cath. Coll., Seoul, Republic of Korea, 1950; D Sociology, Münster U., Fed. Republic Germany, 1964; hon. doctorate, Sogang U., Seoul, 1974, U. Notre Dame, 1977, Sophia U., Tokyo, 1988, Korea U., Seoul, 1990, Seton Hall U., 1990. Ordained priest Roman Cath. Ch., 1951, consecrated bishop, 1966. Pastor Andong (Republic of Korea) Parish, Archdiocese of Taegu, 1951-53; sec. to archbishop Archdiocese of Taegu, 1953-55; pastor Hwangkeumdong parish, Archdiocese of Taegu, Kimcheon, Republic of Korea, 1955-56; pres. Cath. Shibo weekly newspaper, Taegu, 1964-66; bishop Diocese of Masan, Republic of Korea, 1966-68; archbishop Archdiocese of Seoul, 1968—, cardinal, 1969—; pres. Bishop's Conf. Korea, Seoul, 1971—, del. to synod, Vatican City, 1967, 71, 74, 80, 83-86; pres. Follow-up Com. for Fedn. Asian Bishop's Conf., 1970-73. Home and Office: Archdiocese of Seoul, 1 2ka Myong-dong/Chung-ku, Seoul 100, Republic of Korea

KIM, STEPHEN S., religion educator; b. Seoul, Republic of Korea, Mar. 29, 1943; m. Sung P. Kim, May 13, 1972; 1 child, David. BA, Yonsei U., Seoul, 1969; MDiv, U. Dubuque, 1973; PhD, Drew U., 1987. Asst. prof. Sch. of Theology Claremont (Calif.) Grad. Sch., 1987—. Mem. Am. Acad. Religion, AAUP. Office: Sch of Theology at Claremont 1325 N College Ave Claremont CA 91711

KIMBALL, CHARLES ALVAH, III, minister, religion educator; b. Manchester, N.H., Aug. 29, 1962; s. Charles Alvah Jr. and Sandra Ann (Campbell) K.; m. Connie Lee Mund, May 28, 1983. BA in Religion and Psychology, Southwest Bapt. U., Bolivar, Mo., 1983; MDiv, Southwestern Bapt. Theol. Sem., Ft. Worth, 1986, PhD in N.T., 1991. Ordained to ministry So. Bapt. Conv., 1983. Assoc. pastor Highland Bapt. Ch., Arlington, Tex., 1985-91; pastor Calvary Bapt. Ch., Kingsville, Tex., 1991—; teaching fellow Southwestern Bapt. Theol. Sem., 1987-88, tchr.'s asst., 1986-91. Named one of Outstanding Young Men Am., 1986, 87; Pres.' scholar Southwestern Bapt. Theol. Sem., 1983, Univ. scholar, 1981-83. Mem. Soc. Bibl. Lit., Inst. Bibl. Rsch., Alpha Chi. Home: 1427 E Warren Kingsville TX 78363 Office: Calvary Bapt Chh 1500 E Caesar Kingsville TX 78363

KIMBALL, LES LEWIS, minister; b. Spencer, Iowa, Jan. 1, 1941; s. Herman Jacob and Edith Rosalina (Hendricksen) K.; m. Diane Michele Harcourt, Aug. 7, 1965; children: Kimberly, Karen, Michael, Paul, Tamara. BA in Religion, Concordia Sr. Coll., Ft. Wayne, Ind., 1964; MDiv, Concordia Sem., Springfield, Ill., 1968. Ordained to ministry Luth. Ch.-Mo. Synod, 1968. Pastor Good Shepherd Luth. Ch., Lansing, Mich., 1968-71, St. John Luth. Ch., Columbia City, Ind., 1971-74; missionary Luth. Bible Translators, Sierre Leone, 1975-86; pastor St. Matthew Luth. Ch., Mapleton, Iowa, 1986-89; sr. pastor St. Luke's Luth. Ch., Montgomery, Ill., 1989—; bd. dirs. Luth. Bible Translators, Inc., Aurora, Ill., 1988—. Office: St Luke's Luth Ch 11 Pembrooke Rd Montgomery IL 60538

KIMBLE, MARCUS ALLEN, minister, religious organization administrator; b. Sussex, N.J., Oct. 30, 1920; s. Marcus Lynn and Wilhelmena (McConnell) K.; m. Sara Elizabeth Rogers, Aug. 28, 1945; children: Carolyn, Beverly. BA, Wheaton (Ill.) Coll., 1943; BD, Princeton Theol. Sem., 1946, MDiv, 1972; DD (hon.), Lake Forest (Ill.) Coll., 1976; LHD (hon.), Nat. Coll. Edn., Evanston, Ill., 1976. Ordained to ministry United Presbyn. Ch. in U.S.A., 1946. Asst. min. 1st Presbyn. Ch., Westfield, N.J., 1946-47; min. Presbyn. Ch., Lawrenceville, N.J., 1947-59; master of religion Lawrenceville Boys Sch., 1947-52; min. Calvary Presbyn. Ch., Wyncote, Pa., 1959-72; dir. devel. Presbyn. Home, Evanston, 1972-81, chmn., chief exec. officer, 1981—. Trustee Presbytery of Chgo.; mem. div. fin. and resource devel. Synod of Lincoln Trails. Home: 6 Calvin Circle Evanston IL 60201 Office: Presbyn Home 3200 Grant St Evanston IL 60201

KIMSEY, RUSTIN RAY, bishop. s. Lauren Chamness K.; m. Gretchen Beck Rinehart, 1961; 2 children. BS U. Oreg., 1957, BD Episcopal Theol. Sem., 1960. Ordained priest, Episcopal Ch., 1960; vicar, St. John Ch., Hermiston, 1960-61; priest in charge, St. Paul NYSSA, 1961; vicar, St. Albany, 1961-67; rector, St. Stephen, Baker, 1967-71, St. Paul, the Dalles, 1971-80; consecrated bishop of Eastern Oreg., 1980; bishop, Episcopal Diocese Eastern Oreg., The Dalles, 1980—. Office: Episcopal Diocese Ea Oreg PO Box 620 The Dalles OR 97058

KINCL, RICH LOUIS, minister; b. Sacramento, Jan. 31, 1953; s. Jerry J. and Vinola R. (Hunziker) K.; m. Kay G. Owens, May 14, 1978; children: Sarah Vi, Barry Richard. BA, U. Ark., 1975; MDiv, Southwestern Bapt. Theol. Sem., 1978; D of Ministry, Midwestern Bapt. Theol. Sem., 1986. Ordained to ministry, 1978. Youth min. First Bapt. Ch., North Little Rock, 1975-76, Mineola, Tex., 1977-78; assoc. pastor Watson Chapel Bapt. Ch., Pine Bluff, Ark., 1978-80; pastor First Bapt. Ch., Berryville, Ark., 1980-87, Cen. Bapt. Ch., Magnolia, Ark., 1987—; exec. bd. Ark. Bapt. State Conv., 1984; mem. Associational Sunday Sch. Improvement Support Team No. Ark. Bapt. Assn., 1980-84. Dir. Citizens United Against Gambling, Berryville, 1984, mem. Health Bd., Berryville. Mem. Pastors Conf. Ark. Bapt. State Conv. (2nd v.p. 1985), Berryville C. of C. (v.p. 1983), Rotary (bd. dirs.), Sigma Pi. Home: 1711 Gean Magnolia AR 71753 Office: Cen Bapt Ch 207 W Union Magnolia AR 71753

KINEMAN, LANIS EUGENE, minister; b. Brookport, Ill., Oct. 2, 1926; s. Charles and Ida (Harris) K.; m. Kathryn Winton Turnbull, June 5, 1948; children: Larry, David, Kathryn Jean Ralph, Janet Ruth Windlan. AB, Johnson Bible Coll., Knoxville, 1948; BD, Butler U., 1956. Ordained to ministry Christian Ch./Chs. of Christ, 1946. Min. Shepherdsville (Ky.) Christian Ch., 1947-48, Mt. Vernon (Ky.) Christian Ch., 1948-52, Normanda Christian Ch., Tipton, Ind., 1952-57, Carlisle (Ky.) Christian Ch., 1957-62, Bethany Christian Ch., Anderson, Ind., 1962—; mem., past bd. trustees, sec. Johnson Bible Coll., Knoxville, 1970—, Alexander Christian Found., Stae Ch. Safety Net Program; vice chmn. bd. Barnabas Ctr. Project, Anderson, 1991—. Past chmn. Citizens for Community Values, Anderson. Mem. Exchange Club (pres. 1983-84). Home: 2705 Catalina Anderson IN 46012

KING, ARNOLD KIMSEY, JR., clergyman, nursing home executive; b. Durham, N.C., May 7, 1931; s. Arnold Kimsey and Edna May (Coates) K.; m. Marjorie Jean Fisher, June 22, 1952; children: Leslie Diane, Carole Jean, Arnold Kimsey III, Julia Paige. BA, U. N.C., 1955; M in Divinity, Duke U., 1959; DD, Am. Bible Inst., 1971. Ordained deacon Methodist Ch., 1956, elder, 1959; lic. hotel adminstr., nursing home adminstr. N.C. Enlisted U.S. Air Force, 1951, served as staff sgt., various assignments in psychol. training, bus. adminstrn., mgmt.; minister, organizer Aldersgate Methodist Ch., Chapel Hill, N.C., 1955-61; assoc. pastor Edenton St. Methodist Ch., Raleigh, N.C., 1961-64; pastor Ahoskie (N.C.) United Methodist Ch., 1964-70; pastor Woodland (N.C.) United Methodist Ch., 1970-74; sec. N.C. Annual Conf., United Methodist Ch., Raleigh, 1972-74; asst. adminstr. Methodist Retirement Homes Inc., Durham, 1974-75, adminstr., Durham, 1975-88; statistician N.C. Ann. Conf. of United Meth. Ch., 1988—; bd. dirs. Equity Homes Inc., Equity Retirement Housing, Marriott Vacation Resorts, Marriott's Swallowtail at Sea Pines; vis. prof. Methodist studies Southeastern Bapt. Theol. Sem., Wake Forest, N.C. Mem. N.C. Commn. on Health Services Mem. Young Democrats Club, N.C. Gov.'s Com. on Aging, United Fund, Am. Cancer Soc.; councilman Town of Woodland, 1972-74; trustee, mem. exec. com. Goodwill Industries, Durham, 1974-78; theol. adv. to UN Internat. Yr. of Handicapped. Named Tar Heel of Week, Raleigh (N.C.) News and Observer, 1969. Mem. N.C. Bd. Examiners of Nursing Home Adminstrs., N.C. Hist. Assn. (past pres. United Methodist Conf.), Am. Acad. Med. Adminstrn., Am. Coll. Health Care Adminstrs., Am. Assn. Non-Profit Homes for Aging, N.C. Assn. Non-Profit Homes for Aging, Am. Hotel and Motel Assn., Paralyzed Vets. Am., Disabled Am. Vets, Am. Legion Found., N.C. Conf. Bd. Evangelism (past pres., v.p.), Mensa, Lambda Chi Alpha. Lodges: Kiwanis, Rotary, Optimists, Masons, Shriners. Contbr. to U.S. Air Force manuals; contbr. articles to profl. jours.; contbr. N.C. Christian Advocate Weekly, 1973—; lectr. to profl. confs. Home: 5315 Yardley Terr Durham NC 27707-9740

KING, BARBARA DE ANNE, missionary, secretary, writer; b. Huntington Park, Calif., Feb. 14, 1941; d. Grant Cooke Ferguson and Olive Mae (Gale Ferguson) Baldwin; children: Sherryl DeAnne Burres Amihan, Jeremias, Joshua. Student, U. of the Nations, 1978-81, San Antonio Coll., 1987. Lic. foster mother, Hawaii. Sec. Bendix Corp., Burbank, 1959-67; exec. sec. Semtech Corp., Newbury Park, Calif., 1968-78; founder/dir. Agape Children's Home, The Philippines, 1985-88; adminstrv. sec. Youth With A Mission, Kailua Kona, Hawaii, 1978-84, 89—; Reporter, editor Village Times,

1978-83, YWAM Philippine News, 1983-85, Agape Children's Home News, 1985-87; contbr. articles to profl. jours. Republican. Avocations: writing, reading, water sports, plants, children.

KING, BARBARA LEWIS, minister, lecturer; b. Houston, Aug. 26, 1930; d. Lee Andrew Lewis and Mildred Marie (Jackson) Shackelford; m. Moses King, Sept. 8, 1966 (div. Sept. 1970); 1 child, Michael. BA, Tex. So. U., 1955; MSW, Atlanta U., 1957, postgrad.; DDiv, Bethune Cookman Coll., 1988. Exec. dir. South Chgo. Community Svc. Assn., Chgo., 1966-68; dean community rels. Malcolm X campus Chgo. City Coll., 1967-69; instr. Sch. Social Work Atlanta U., 1970-71; dir. South Cen. Community Mental Health Ctr., 1971-73; dean students Spelman Coll., 1973-74; founder, minister Hillside Internat. Truth Ctr., 1971—; founder, pres. Barbara King Sch. Ministry, 1977—; host Sta. WVEU, Atlanta, 1987—, WXIA, Atlanta, 1980-85, Channel 8, Atlanta, 1980-85. Author: What is a Miracle?, 1973, Do I Need a Flood, 1983, Transform Your Little Book, 1989. Mem. nat. rules com. Dem. Nat. Conv., Ga., 1984; mem. State Com. on the Life and History of Black Georgians, Atlanta, 1986, Ethics Bd. Met. Atlanta, 1986, Joint Bd. Family Practice, Atlanta, 1986. Mem. Am. Mgmt. Assn., Internat. New Thought Alliance (v.p. 1972), Christian Coun. Met. Atlanta (trustee 1985), Internat. Congress Women Ministries (internat. pres. 1975), Acad. Cert. Social Workers, Nat. Assn. Social Workers, Women's C. of C. in Atlanta, Zeta Phi Beta. Office: Hillside Internat Truth Ctr 2450 Cascade Rd SW Atlanta GA 30311

KING, CHARLES BENJAMIN, minister; b. Gasburg, Va., Oct. 20, 1942; s. James Skelton and Frances (Walton) K.; m. Patsy Mitchell, Sept. 11, 1965; children: James A., Katherine A. BA, Randolph-Macon Coll., 1964; MDiv, Duke U., 1967; cert. clin. pastoral edn., Med. Coll. Va., 1969. Ordained to ministry Meth. Ch. as deacon, 1965, as elder, 1969. Student pastor Bethel United Meth., Hanover, Va., 1963-64; youth dir. Noland Meml. United Meth. Ch., Newport News, Va., 1964; student minister 1st United Meth. Ch., Graham, N.C., 1965-67; minister St. Peter's United Meth. Ch., Montpelier, Va, 1967-70; minister of evangelism Trinity United Meth. Ch., Richmond, Va., 1970-72; minister Courtland (Va.) United Meth. Ch., 1972-76; sr. minister Westover Hills United Meth. Ch., Richmond, 1976-80, Christ United Meth. Ch., Norfolk, Va., 1980-84; assoc. dir. leadership devel. Va. United Meth. Conf., Richmond, 1984-89, dir. evangelism, 1989—. Author: Jesus the Christ, 1978; co-author: Revealing Christ: Sharing the Faith. Recipient Lifetime Membership award United Meth. Women, 1976, Growth Plus award Bd. of Discipleship, 1990. Office: Va United Meth Conf PO Box 11367 Richmond VA 23230 *The great challenge of Christian evangelism: "Where there is vision...there is risk. Where there is risk...there is witness. Where there is witness...there is Gospel (Good News of Jesus Christ). Where there is Gospel...there is hope."*

KING, CHARLES LARRY, minister; b. Houston, Sept. 27, 1950; s. Walter Lee and Lois (Warren) King; m. Ethel Mae Haggerty, June 6, 1970; children: Michael Jermaine, Teneka Kenyatta. BA, U. Houston, 1978; MA, Tex. So. U., 1991. Cert. tchr., Tex.; ordained to ministry Ch. of God in Christ. Youth minister New Jerusalem Ch. of God in Christ, LaPorte, Tex., 1977-81; asst. pastor Christway Ch. of God in Christ, Houston, 1982-85; pastor Gospel Temple Ch. of God in Christ, La Marque, Tex., 1985-89, Bethel Temple Ch. of God in Christ, Nacadoches, Tex., 1989—; dir. pub. rels. Tex. South Cen. Ch. of God in Christ, Houston, 1984—, liaison to Gov. Mark White, Houston, 1982, liaison to nat. aux. conv. chmn., 1986; drug counselor VA Hosp., Houston, 1980-83. Author play: Changed, 1983; contbr. articles to profl. publs. Staff sgt. USAF, 1971-75, 90—. Mem. Am. Fedn. Tchrs., Houston Fedn. Tchrs. (union steward 1990—), Nat. Assn. Social Studies Tchrs. Democrat. Office: Bethel Temple Ch of God in Christ 1716 Butt St Nacogdoches TX 75961 *Life is a constant flow of ups and downs. We must be able, with the help of God, to adjust and adapt to the ever changing circumstances and situations in life.*

KING, DAVID MICHAEL, minister; b. Grosse Pointe, Mich., Dec. 10, 1960; s. Clarence Eugene and Barbara Elizabeth (Ferry) K.; m. Nora Jane Krajewski, May 25, 1985; 1 child, Jonathan Edward. BA, U. Mich., Dearborn, 1981; MDiv, Ashland (Ohio) Theol. Sem., 1991; postgrad., Wycliffe Hall, Oxford, Eng., 1991—. Ordained to ministry Healing For the Nations Christian Ch., 1983. Asst. pastor Healing For the Nations Christian Ch., Roseville, Mich., 1983-91; instr. Ashland Theol. Sem., 1989-91, guest lectr., 1990. Mem. Evang. Theol. Soc., Soc. Bibl. Lit., Am. Acad. Religion, Eta Beta Rho. Office: Healing For The Nations 17350 Wellington Roseville MI 48066

KING, DIANE WALKER, lay worker; b. Danville, Va., Mar. 19, 1941; d. Herman Herbert and Ruth Mildred (Riley) Walker; m. McLeroy King, July 11, 1964; children: Aaron Walker, Kevin Bennett. Student, Executrain, Tampa, Fla., 1990-91. Ch. sec. Palma Ceia Presbyn. Ch., Tampa, 1980—. Mem. Adminstrv. Personnel Assn., Winterset (pres. 1984-85), Caliandria Garden Club. Home: 4702 San Rafael Tampa FL 33629 Office: Palma Ceia Presbyn Ch 3501 W San Jose St Tampa FL 33629-7022

KING, FELTON, bishop. Bishop Ch. of God in Christ, Phoenix. Office: Ch of God in Christ PO Box 3791 Phoenix AZ 84030*

KING, FRANCIS EDWARD, priest, religion educator; b. San Francisco, Nov. 19, 1931; s. Francis A. and Helene B. (Johnson) K. BA, Gonzaga U., 1955, MA, 1956; STL, Alma Coll., 1963; STM, Santa Clara U., 1963; STD, Pontifical Gregorian U., Rome, 1972. Ordained priest Roman Cath. Ch., 1962. Asst. prof. theology U. San Francisco, 1964-66, 69—. Author: The Institutional Aspects of the Church According to William Law (1686-1761), 1971; contbr. articles to profl. jours. Democrat. Home and Office: U San Francisco San Francisco CA 94117

KING, JOHN KENNETH, minister; b. Shelbyville, Tenn., Jan. 20, 1958; s. Allen Benton Jr. and Mary Louise (Hood) K.; m. Debra Lin Hastings, Aug. 21, 1981; children: John Kenneth II, Rachel Leigh. AA, Freed-Hardeman U., 1978, BA, 1980; MA, Ala. Christian Sch. Religion, 1984; postgrad., Luth. Theol. Seminary, Gettysburg, Pa., 1985—. Min. Richmond (Tenn.) Ch. of Christ, 1978-79, Lone Oak Ch. of Christ, Richmond, 1979, 80-85, Rockville (Md.) Ch. of Christ, 1985—; lectr. in field. Contbr. articles to profl. jours. Office: Rockville Church of Christ 1450 West Montgomery Ave Rockville MD 20850-3109 *While sound bytes are incomplete in the realm of faith, a few statements are vast enough to give insight into God'a glory—e.g., "God is love." God, trust Him again, for the first time!.*

KING, JOHNNY, bishop. Dist. supt. Can. Plains Dist., United Pentecostal Ch. in Can., Calgary, Alta. Office: United Pentacostal Ch, 1840 38th St SE, Calgary, AB Canada T2B 0Z3*

KING, LESLIE RAE, JR., church construction consultant; b. Mendota, Ill., Oct. 29, 1944; s. Leslie Rae and Lois (Mellott) K.; m. Gayle Minter, Dec. 20, 1970; 1 child, Leslie Rae III. AS in Design and Drafting, So. Ill. U., Carbondale, 1965; cert. in structural steel, Tulsa Pub. Adult Edn., 1969. Cert. Inst. for Cert. Engring. Technicians, Am. Inst. Design and Drafting. Constn. cons. for N.C., Ky. and Mich. dist. Wesleyan Ch.; with Vols. in Missions, United Meth. Ch., Assembly of God, Assn. Nazarene Bldg. Profls., Gideons Internat., Asheboro, N.C.; draftsman Indsl. Air Inc., Greensboro, N.C., 1976—; mem. adv. coun. John Wesley Coll., High Point, N.C.; with Engring. Ministries Internat., Colorado Springs, Colo., Pilgrim Tract Soc., Randleman, N.C., Fla. Evangelistic Assn., Hobe Sound. Mem. So. Ill. U. Alumni Assn. Home: 101 Magnolia Dr Randleman NC 27317

KING, LOUIS BLAIR, minister; b. Dec. 31, 1925; m. Freya Synnestvedt; children: Khary Allen, Steven, Alan C., Janne Odhner, Cedric, Bronwin Cooper, Aileen Synnestvedt, Blair, Wendy Walter, Kristin Bibler, Dag. P., Bradley, John Cairn, Tamar. BA, U. Pa.; BTh, Acad. of New Ch.; postgrad., Acad. of New Ch. Theol. Sch. Ordained to ministry Gen. Ch. in Can., 1951. Min. Sharon Ch., Chgo., 1952, pastor, 1952-54; pastor Pitts. Soc., 1955-62; pastor, headmaster ch. sch. Immanuel Ch., Glenview, Ill., 1963-72; asst. bishop Gen. Ch., 1973-75, bishop, gen. pastor, 1976—; pastor Bryn Athyn Ch., 1976-80; dean Bryn Athyn (Pa.) Ch., 1973; exec. v.p. Acad. Corp., Bryn Athyn, 1974, pres., 1975, chancellor, 1976—; vis. pastor South Ohio Circle, 1954, Erie Circle, Pa., 1960, North Ohio Circle, 1961; pres. Midwestern Acad., 1963-72; pres. Gen. Ch. in Can., 1976—, Gen. Ch. Internat., Inc., 1976—. With U.S. Army, 1944. Mem. Rotary. Avocations: golf, fishing, playing violin. Address: PO Box 278 2744 Alnwick Rd Bryn Athyn PA 19009

KING, MALCOLM MONTGOMERY, minister; b. Tuxedo Park, N.Y., Apr. 15, 1954; s. Joseph Montgomery and Doris Harmony (Corbett) K.; m. Katherine Bibb Berry King, June 26, 1976; children: Leah Elizabeth, David James Montgomery. Student, Westminister Choir Coll., 1976-77; BA in Church Music, Pfeiffer Coll., 1978; M of Church Music, New Orleans Bapt. Theol., Seminary, 1987. Ordained to ministry Bapt. Ch., 1989. Dir. music ministries Lake Osborne Presbyn. Ch., Lake Worth, Fla., 1979-82; interim minister of music Oak Park Bapt. Ch., New Orleans, 1989-90, assoc. minister of music, 1985-91, minister of youth, 1987-91; assoc. minister Shenandoah Heights Bapt. Ch., Waynesboro, Va., 1992—. Physics Honor scholar, U. Miami, Coral Gables, Fla., 1972, Nat. Merit scholar, 1972. Mem. Chorister's Guild, Am. Guild of English Handbell Ringers, Presbyn. Assn. Musicians (CACM award 1980), Phi Mu Alpha Sinfonia. Office: Shenandoah Heights Bapt Ch 901 Shenandoah Ave Waynesboro VA 22980

KING, MARK EDWARD, minister; b. Lexington, Ky., Oct. 10, 1959; s. Donald Edward and Dixie Davis (Wagner) K.; m. Phyllis Jean Lile, Aug. 9, 1986. BA, Georgetown Coll., 1981; MDiv, So. Bapt. Theol. Sem., 1987. Ordained to ministry Bapt. Ch., 1987. Pastor Underwood (Ind.) Bapt. Ch., 1987-88, Scottsville (Va.) Bapt. Ch., 1988—. Mem. ethics com. Martha Jefferson Hosp., Charlottesville, Va., 1991. Mem. Albemarle Bapt. Assn. (chairperson edn. coun. 1990—). Home: PO Box 175 Scottsville VA 24590 Office: Scottsville Bapt Ch Harrison St Scottsville VA 24590

KING, MARY EVELYN MARKS, minister; b. Pitts., Apr. 23, 1954; d. Charles Hale and Gloria Rowene (Armitage) Marks; m. William Edward King, Aug. 29, 1981; children: Timothy Cochran, Gloria Grace. BS, Pa. State U., 1976; MDiv, Pitts. Theol. Sem., 1979. Min. Union 1st Presbyn. Ch., Cowansville, Pa., 1979—; pres. bd. dirs. Presbyn. Media Mission, Pitts., 1983-86. Mem. Coll. Arts and Architecture Alumni Soc. of Pa. State U. (bd. dirs. 1980-86). Home: PO Box 217 Cowansville PA 16218

KING, NOEL Q., history and comparative religion educator; b. Taxila, Punjab, Pakistan, Dec. 26, 1922; s. William Henry and Mary (McCarthy) K.; m. Evelyn Collard, June 23, 1946 (dec. Mar. 1972); children: Francis, Clare, Naomi, Jeremey; m. Laurie Richardson, Nov. 11, 1977; children: Zoe Q., Nathan Adderley. BA, Oxford (Eng.) U., 1946, MA, 1947; PhD, Nottingham (Eng.) U., 1954. Prof. history and comparative religion U. Calif., Santa Cruz, 1968—. Author: Theodosius and the Establishment of Christianity, 1961, Religions of Africa, 1970, Christian and Muslim in Africa, 1972; editor: Mtoro Bin Bakari: Desturi Za Waswahili, 1981. Lt. U.S. Army, 1940-46, ETO, CBI. Home: 350 Primrose Ln Watsonville CA 95076 Office: U Calif Merrill Coll Santa Cruz CA 95064

KING, PRISCILLA, lay worker, church musician; b. Phila., Dec. 14, 1950; d. William Shellrow and Patricia Ann (Gumby) K. B in Human Svcs., Antioch U., 1982, M in Adminstrn., 1984. Patient accounts rep. Meth. Hosp., Phila., 1979—; recreation leader Phila. Recreation Dept., 1980—; min. of music Lombard Cen. Presbyn. Ch., Phila., 1981—, ruling elder, 1988—, clk. of session, 1989—; music tchr. Pa. Synod./ Phila., 1983-86; music cons. Presbytery. Writer, producer: This Train of Mine, 1989; rec. Commit Thy Way Unto The Lord, 1972; toured Europe with John Thompson Singers, 1973-75. Settlement Music Sch. scholar, Phila., 1982. Mem. Order Eastern Star (Queen Helena chpt. fin. sec. 1990—). Democrat. Home: 2319 Mountain St Philadelphia PA 19145

KING, RACHEL HADLEY, religious studies educator; b. Leavenworth, Kans., Apr. 27, 1904; d. Frank Campbell and Georgianna May (Brackett) King; B.A., Smith Coll., 1926; M.A., U. Chgo., 1927, U. Colo., 1931; Ph.D., Yale, 1937, Bible tchr., then head dept. Northfield (Mass.) Sch. Girls, 1928-31, 35-66; tchr. English, Kobe Coll., Japan, 1937-38; adj. prof. Bibl. studies Barrington (R.I.) Coll., 1972-85; vol. tchr. underprivileged children N.Y.C. Pub. Schs., summers 1969-71. Mem. Kobe Corp., 1960—; alumni council Yale Div. Sch., 1968-75. Recipient citation Council Religion in Ind. Schs., 1967. Mem. Am. Acad. Religion, Nat. Assn. Bible Instrs. (chmn. curriculum com. 1946-64), Am. Sch. Oriental Research, So. Bibl. Lit. Presbyterian. Author: George Fox and The Light Within 1650-1660; 1940; God's Boycott of Sin, 1946; Theology You Can Understand, 1956; The Omission of the Holy Spirit from Reinhold Niebuhr's Theology, 1964; The Creation of Death and Life, 1970. Home: The 60 Broadway Providence RI 02903

KING, ROBERT HENRY, minister, church denomination executive, former educator; b. Sunny South, Ala., Apr. 1, 1922; s. Henry C. and Della S. (Bettis) K.; m. Edna Jean McCord, June 1, 1949; children: Jocelyn, Jann, Roger. BD, Immanuel Luth. Sem., Greensboro, N.C., 1949; MEd, U. Pitts., 1956; MA, Ind. U., 1968, PhD, 1969. Ordained to ministry Luth. Ch.—Mo. Synod, 1949. Pastor Victory Luth. Ch., Youngstown, Ohio, 1949-57, St. Philip Luth. Ch., Chgo., 1957-65; asst. prof. Concordia Tchrs. Coll., River Forest, Ill., 1968-70; prof. edn. Lincoln U., Jefferson City, Mo., 1970-87; v.p. Luth. Ch.—Mo. Synod, St. Louis, 1986—; pastor Pilgrim Luth. Ch., Freedom, Mo., 1979—; dir. lay ministry Concordia Coll., Selma, Ala., 1987-90; vis. instr. Concordia Sem., St. Louis, 1989, 91; dir. workshop Obot Idim Sem., Nigeria, 1990. Contbr. articles to religious jours. Mem. Jefferson City Sch. Bd., 1973-76. Lilly Found. fellow, 1965. Mem. Am. Assn. Adult Continuing Edn., Mo. Assn. Adult Continuing Edn., Phi Delta Kappa. Home: 901 Roland Ct Jefferson City MO 65101

KING, ROY D., religious organization administrator. Pres., gen. supt. Pentecostal Assemblies of Nfld., St. John's, Can. Office: Pentacostal Assemblies, 50 Brownsdale St, Saint John's, NF Canada A1E 4R2*

KING, SALLIE BEHN, philosophy and religion educator; b. Washington, Mar. 22, 1952; d. James Forrest and Carolyn (Prout) K.; m. Steven Lynn Keffer, Dec. 17, 1977; children: Leslie, Sarah. BA, Smith Coll., Northampton, Mass., 1973; MA, U. Brit. Columbia, Vancouver, Can., 1975; PhD, Temple U., 1981. Assoc. prof. dept. philosophy So. Ill. U., Carbondale, 1983—. Author: Passionate Journey: The Spiritual Autobiography of Satomi Myodo, 1987, Buddha Nature, 1990. Profl. fellow Japan Found., 1983-84. Mem. Am. Acad. Religion (steering com. consultation on mysticism group 1987—, steering com. Buddhism sect. 1991—), Assn. for Asian Studies, Soc. for Buddhist-Christian Studies (bd. dirs. 1989—), Internat. Assn. Buddhist Studies, Soc. for Asian & Comparative Philosophy, Phi Beta Kappa. Mem. Soc. of Friends. Buddhist. Office: So Ill U Dept of Philosophy Carbondale IL 62901

KING, SUSAN MARIE, minister; b. Jackson, Mich., Nov. 13, 1956; d. Russell Chapman and Flora Jean (McKee) K. BA in Psychology with honors, BA in Biology with highest honors, U. Calif., Santa Cruz, 1978; MPH, U. Hawaii, 1981; MDiv, San Francisco Theol. Sem., 1988. Ordained to ministry United Ch. of Christ, 1989. Intern pastor Plymouth Congl. Ch., New Plymouth, Idaho, 1986-87; chaplain intern Queen's Med. Ctr., Honolulu, 1988; pastor Ewa (Hawaii) Community Ch., 1989—; campus ministry asst. Hawaii Conf., United Ch. of Christ, Honolulu, 1980-81; bd. dirs. Hawaii Coun. Chs., Honolulu, 1982-84, Hawaii Conf., 1989-90. Mem. adv. bd. Friends for Ewa, 1989—, sch. community coun. Ewa Elem. Sch., 1989—. USPHS grantee, 1980. Mem. Ewa Ministerial Assn. (pres. 1990-91), Oahu Assn.-Hawaii Conf. United Ch. of Christ (bd. dirs. 1989—, v.p. 1990-91), Hawaii Soc. for Pub. Health Edn., U. Hawaii Sch. Pub. Health Alumni Assn. (sec. 1983-84). Democrat. Address: Ewa Community Ch PO Box 1148 Ewa HI 96706 *A key breakthrough in my own spiritual development has been recognizing my own capacity for denial and self-deception. I believe we need God's Holy Spirit, often speaking through a fellowship of those committed to spiritual growth, to truly know ourselves, both as we are and as God is calling us to become.*

KING, WILLIAM CHARLES, pastor; b. Davenport, Iowa, Mar. 8, 1957; s. George Joseph and Eileen Catherine (Hart) K.; m. Glenda Renae Cook, July 31, 1976; children: Bridget Renae, Lydia Amber, Rebecca Noel. Student, Northland Bapt. Bible Coll., 1979-80; BS (with honors), Faith Bapt. Bible Coll., 1986-88. Ordained to ministry Bapt. Ch., 1989. Trustee, asst. treas. New Testament Bapt. Ch., Davenport, Iowa, 1977-79; jr. ch. dir. Faith Bapt. Ch., Pembine, Wis., 1979-80; asst. pastor Family Bapt. Ch., Kingsford, Mich., 1980-86, First Bapt. Ch., Norwalk, Iowa, 1987-89; pastor Grace Bapt. Ch., Moweaqua, Ill., 1989—; camp rep. Camp Manitoumi, Low Point, Ill., 1989—; league dir. Scott County Christian Fellowship League, Davenport, 1975-79, league v.p., 1977-79. Republican. Office: Grace Bapt Ch 230 N Main St Moweaqua IL 62550

KING, WILLIAM MCGUIRE, religion educator, minister; b. Chgo., Mar. 27, 1947; s. Edward Ernst and Ione Dorothy (McGuire) K.; m. Janet Lynn Schulz, Aug. 31, 1968; children: Jeremy, Eleanor, Gregory. BA summa cum laude, Cornell Coll., 1968; BD cum laude, Harvard U., 1971, PhD, 1978. Ordained to ministry United Meth. Ch., 1980. Asst. prof. religious studies U. Va., Charlottesville, 1976-83; assoc. prof. Albright Coll., Reading, Pa., 1983—; mem. bd. higher edn. and campus ministry Va. Ann. Conf., United Meth. Ch., Richmond, 1981-83; sesquicentennial assoc. Ctr. for Advanced Study, U. Va., 1982. Mem. Am. Soc. Ch. History, Am. Hist. Assn., Am. Acad. Religion, Phi Beta Kappa. Home: 1610 N 15th St Reading PA 19604 Office: Albright Coll PO Box 516 Reading PA 19603

KING, WINSTON LEE, minister, retired religion educator; b. Avilla, Ind., Aug. 30, 1907; s. Alfred Hiram and Alberta (Bodenhafer) K.; m. Jocelyn Asbury Brownlee, June 2, 1931; children: Carroll, Christopher, Jonathan. AB, Asbury Coll., 1929; BD, Andover Newton Theol. Sch., Newton Ctr., Mass., 1936; STM, Harvard U., 1938, PhD, 1940. Pastor Meth., Congl. parishes various New Eng. states., 1930-43, Congl. Parish, Waterville, Maine, 1945-49; dean of chapel, prof. philosophy and religion Grinnell (Iowa) Coll., 1949-64; prof. history of religion Vanderbilt U., Nashville, 1964-73; prof. philosophy Colo. State U., Ft. Collins, 1973-77; book review editor Jour. Am. Acad. Religion, 1968-71. Author: (books) The Holy Imperative, 1949, Introduction to Religion, 1954, Buddhism and Christianity, 1962, In the Hope of Nibbana, 1964, A Thousand Lives Away: Buddhism in Contemporary Burma, 1964, reprint 1990, Introduction to Religion: A Phenomenological Approach, 1968, Theravada Meditation: The Buddhist Transformation of Yoga, 1980, Death Was His Koan: The Samurai-Zen of Suzuki Shosan, 1986; contbr. numerous articles to profl. jours. Capt. US Army (chaplain), 1943-45, ETO. Named Sr. Project Advisor Ford Found., Rangoon, Burma, 1958-60, Fulbright Lectr., Fulbright Fellowships, Japan, 1965-66. Mem. Am. Acad. Religion, Assn. for Asian Studies, Am. Soc. for Study of Religion. Democrat. Home: 518 Caldy Pl Madison WI 53711

KINGMA, P., religious organization administrator. Head Am. Ref. Chs., Caledonia, Mich. Office: Can and Am Ref Chs 3167-68th St SE Caledonia MI 49316*

KINKEL, GARY STEVEN, clergyman; b. St. Paul, Apr. 19, 1956; s. Merlyn Riley and Patricia Anne (Holmquist) K; m. Karen Lee Thompson, Aug. 16, 1980; children: Nikolas Steven, Monika Claire. BA, U. Minn., Duluth, 1978; MDiv, Moravian Sem., Bethlehem, Pa., 1981; ThM, Union Sem., Richmond, Va., 1982; PhD, U. Iowa, Iowa City, 1988. Ordained to ministry Moravian Ch. Pastor Redeemer Moravian Ch., Richmond, Va., 1981-82. Author: Our Dear Mother the Spirit: An Investigation of Count Zinzendorf's Theology and Praxis, 1990. Mem Am. Acad. Religion, Soc. Christian Ethics. Democrat. Home: 213 E Oak St Lake Mills WI 53551-1352

KINLAW, DENNIS FRANKLIN, college chancellor; b. Lumberton, N.C., June 26, 1922; s. Wade Hampton and Sally (Burney) K.; m. Elsie Blake, Dec. 31, 1943; children: Elizabeth Kinlaw Coppedge, Dennis Franklin Jr., Katherine Kinlaw Key, Susan Kinlaw Masters, Sally Kinlaw Babcock. BA, Asbury Coll., 1943, LHD (hon.), 1980; MDiv, Asbury Theol. Sem., 1946; MA, Brandeis U., 1961, PhD, 1967; LLD (hon.), Houghton Coll., 1971; DD (hon.), 1990. Ordained deacon N.C. Conf. United Meth. Ch., 1949, ordained elder, 1951; transferred to Ky. Conf., 1969, ret., 1984. Pastor Meth. Ch., Faison, 1949-53, Loudenville (N.Y.) Community Ch., 1955-61; assoc. prof., prof. Old Testament langs. and lit. Asbury Theol. Sem., Wilmore, Ky., 1963-68, prof. bibl. theology, 1982-83; pres. Asbury Coll., Wilmore, 1968-81, 86—; pres. Francis Asbury Soc., Wilmore, 1982—; vis. prof. Seoul (Republic of Korea) Theol. Coll.; bd. dirs. Christianity Today, Carol Stream, Ill., Ludhiana Christian Med. Bd., N.Y.C., Am. Security Life Ins. Co., San Antonio; mem. Lausanne Commn. on World Evangelism, Theol. Commn. of World Evang. Fellowship; chmn. bd. OMS Internat., Greenwood, Ind. Author: Preaching in the Spirit, 1985; contbr. commentaries in bibl. publs., others; mem. editorial bd. Francis Asbury Press. Recipient Alumnus award Asbury Theol. Sem., 1961. Fellow Christianity Today Inst.; mem. Soc. Bibl. Lit. and Exegesis, Wesley Theol. Soc., Evang. Theol. Soc. Home: 404 Akers Dr Wilmore KY 40390 Office: Asbury Coll 1 Macklem Dr Wilmore KY 40390

KINLOCH, DONALD EDMONDS, minister; b. Hawick, Scotland, Dec. 16, 1941; came to U.S., 1974; s. Alexander McDonald Edmonds and Catherine Maria (Balfour) Kinloch; m. Susan Dandridge Phillips, Dec. 9, 1974; children: Gordon Hadley, Graham Balfour. MA, U. Edinburgh, Scotland, 1963, BD, 1967; STM, Union Theol. Sem., N.Y.C., 1968; D Ministry, Union Theol. Sem., Richmond, Va., 1978. Ordained to ministry Ch. of Scotland, 1967. Asst. min. Astoria Presbyn. Ch., Long Island City, N.Y., 1967-68; assoc. pastor Rutherglen Road Parish Ch., Glagow, Scotland, 1986-69; min. St. Christopher's Parish Ch., Glagow, 1969-74; sr. pastor Calvin Presbyn. Ch., Norfolk, Va., 1974-81, Gaithersburg (Md.) Presbyn. Ch., 1981—; mem. moral welfare com. Ch. of Scotland Gen. Assembly, Edinburg, 1971-74; mem. Makemi Woods bd. Norfolk Presbytery, 1978-81; chmn. new ch. devel. Nat. Capital Presbytery, Washington, 1984-90. Fulbright scholar, 1967. Office: Gaithersburg Presbyn Ch 610 S Frederick Ave Gaithersburg MD 20877

KINLOCH, GREGORY JAMES, religious organization administrator; b. Honolulu, June 24, 1946; s. James Thomas and Emily Edith (Barhorst); m. Barbara Jean Borton, June 15, 1968; children: Jason, Jon. BA, Seattle Pacific U., 1968; MRE, Denver Sem., 1970. Various adminstrn. positions Firs Bible Missionary Conf., Bellingham, Wash., 1970-84, exec. dir., 1984—. Contbr articles Jour. Christian Camping. Named Regional Alumni of Yr. Seattle Pacific U., 1991. Mem. Am. Camping Assn. (mem. conf. ctr. standards adv. com.), Christian Camping Internat. (bd. dirs. 1988—). Home and Office: 4605 Cable St Bellingham WA 98226

KINNAMON, MICHAEL KURT, religious educator; b. Ottumwa, Iowa, Apr. 15, 1949; s. Robert Jack K. and Gretta Louise (Osborn) deGroot; m. Katherine Gayle Newman, Apr. 8, 1979; children: Anna-Kapila Elaine, Leah Margery. Student, Tel Aviv U., 1969-70; BA magna cum laude, Brown U., 1971; MA, U. Chgo., 1976, PhD, 1980. Ordained to ministry Christian Ch., 1976. Exec. sec. Commn. on Faith and Order World Coun. of Chs., Geneva, Switzerland, 1980-83; asst. prof. Christian Theol. Sem., Indpls., 1983-88; dean, assoc. prof. theology Lexington (Ky.) Theol. Sem., 1988—; nominee gen. min. and pres. Christian Ch. in U.S. and Can.; mem. Disciples Gen. Bd. and Adminstrv. Com., 1988—; mem. Disciples United Ch. Christ Ecumenical Partnership Com., 1985—; mem. Gen. Commn. on Christian Unity, United Meth. Ch., 1988—; lectr. in field; vis. prof. United Theol. Coll., Bangalore, India, 1987. Author: Truth and Community: Diversity and Its Limits in the Ecumenical Movement, 1988; co-author: (with Katherine Kinnamon) Thankful Praise: a Resource for Christian Worship, Every Day We Will Bless You: a Book of Daily Prayer, 1990; editor: report from World Coun. Chs. 7th Assembly Signs of the Spirit, 1991; editor: Disciples of Chirst in the 21st Century, 1988. Div. Sch. fellow U. Chgo. Div. Sch., 1975-77. Mem. Am. Acad. Religion, North Am. Acad. Ecumenists, Disciples Peace Fellowship, Bread for the World. Avocations: sports, travel. Office: Lexington Theol Sem 631 S Limestone Lexington KY 40508

KINNEY, JOHN FRANCIS, clergyman; b. Oelwein, Iowa, June 11, 1937; s. John F. and Marie B. (McCarty) K. Student, St. Paul Sem., 1957-63, N.Am. Coll., Rome, 1968-71; J.C.D., Pontifical Lateran U., 1971. Ordained priest Roman Catholic Ch., 1963. Assoc. pastor Ch. of St. Thomas, Mpls., 1963-66; vice chancellor of St. Paul and Mpls. Diocese, 1966-73; assoc. pastor Cathedral, St. Paul, 1971-74, chancellor, 1973; pastor Ch. of St. Leonard, St. Paul, from 1974; titular bishop of Caorle and aux. bishop Archdiocese of St. Paul and Mpls., 1977-82; bishop Diocese of Bismark,

N.D., 1982—. Mem. Canon Law Soc. Am. Roman Catholic. Office: Chancery Office 420 Raymond St PO Box 1575 Bismarck ND 58501

KINNEY, WILLIAM LEE, minister, religious writer; b. Akron, Ohio, Jan. 12, 1955; s. William Austin and Violette Myrtle (Smith) K.; m. Marguerite Elizabeth Ross, May 9, 1976; children: Daniel Lee, Elizabeth Anne. AB in Religion, Drew U., 1988; MDiv, Princeton Theol. Sem., 1991; postgrad., Drew U., 1987-88. Dir. youth ministries First Presbyn. Ch., New Vernon, N.J., 1983-84; asst. pastor-intern Meml. Ch., Dover, N.J., 1985-87; sem. intern Livingston (N.J.) Presbyn. Ch., 1988-89; cons. for evangelism and young adult ministries St. Mark United Meth. Ch., Hamilton Square, N.J., 1989-90; editor Testament Mag. Princeton Theol. Sem., Princeton, 1989-91; assoc. pastor 1st Presbyn. Ch., Hilton Head, S.C., 1991—; editor, curriculum writer The Mason Early Edn. Found., Princeton, 1990-91; elder, commr. Presbyn. Ch. USA, New Vernon, 1982-86; trustee The Madison Day Care Ctr., 1985-88; ethics cons., Ethics Consulting Inc., Morristown, N.J., 1986-87; researcher and adminstrv. asst. Citizens' Com. on Biomedical Ethics, Summit, N.J., 1986-87. Author: Human Rights and Islam, 1991; editor-at-large: The Presbyterian Outlook; contbr. articles to periodicals. Mem. Rockaway, N.J. Young Reps., 1973; den leader Cub Scouts Am., West Windsor, N.J., 1989-91; pres. The Munger Chapel Soc. and Social Club, Princeton, 1988—. Recipient Cert. of Merit Am. Song Festival, 1979, ThD (hon.) Munger Chapel Soc. and Social Club, 1991. Assoc. mem. Nat. Christian Counselors Assn.; mem. Am. Acad. Religion, The Presbyn. Writers Guild, The Nat. Writers Club, Santa Clara U. Ctr. for Applied Ethics. Office: 1st Presbyn Ch 540 William Hilton Pkwy Hilton Head SC 29926 *The heart of the Gospel for me is not liberation, but in liberating; not in safety, but providing sanctuary; not in claiming rights, but in securing them for others. And if we can become what this Gospel calls us to be, then the heart of the Gospel has become our heart, and the God whom we all proclaim truly does rule our lives.*

KINSEY, KIMBERLY DAWN, minister; b. El Paso, Tex., Mar. 25, 1966; d. Charles Hanson and A. Carolyn (Baxter) K. BA, McMurry U., Abilene, Tex., 1988; MDiv, Garrett-Evang. Sem., Evanston, Ill., 1991. Ordained to ministry United Meth. Ch., 1990. Asst. pastor Ingalls Park United Meth. Ch., Joliet, Ill., 1989-91, 1st United Meth. Ch., Clovis, N.Mex., 1991—; student trustee Garrett Evang. Theol. Sem., 1989-90. Vol. Abilene State Sch. for Retarded, 1985-88; pres., sec. Rotaract, Abilene, 1984-88. W.F. McMurry scholar, 1984-88, Cal C. Wright scholar, 1987, 88, W. Hutchison scholar, 1988-91. Home: 1000 Uano Estacado # 3 Clovis NM 88101

KINTZI, GREG JAMES, minister; b. Waco, Tex., Aug. 2, 1958; s. James Edward and Lynn Joan (Gornitzka) K.; m. Dona Hue Robbers, May 31, 1980; children: Corey Anders, Kendra Michelle, Kristin Taylor. BA, San Francisco State U., 1982; MDiv, Luther Northwestern Sem., St. Paul, 1987. Ordained to ministry Luth. Ch., 1987. Min. Trinity Evang. Luth. Ch., Santa Barbara, Calif., 1987-90, King of Glory Luth. Ch., Tempe, Ariz., 1990—. Office: King of Glory Luth Ch 2085 E Southern Ave Tempe AZ 85282

KINYON, BILL OLIVER, youth pastor; b. Seattle, Aug. 22, 1956; s. Norman Oliver and Betty Jean (Falconer) K.; m. Virginia Marie Root, July 9, 1976; children: Christopher Michael, Katie Lynn, David Oliver, Scott Alan. AA, Highline Community Coll., Seattle, 1976; BA, Seattle Pacific U., 1978; postgrad., Western Evang. Sem., Portland, Oreg., 1978-80. Ordained deacon Free Meth. Ch. in N.Am., 1982, elder, 1985. Youth pastor Salem (Oreg.) Free Meth. Ch., 1978-80, Pleasant Hill (Calif.) Free Meth. Ch., 1980-81; sr. pastor Ione (Calif.) Free Meth. Ch., 1981-85; youth pastor Glasgow (Mont.) Evang. Ch., 1985-87, Pendleton (Oreg.) Free Meth. Ch., 1987—; dir. Campus Christian Fellowship, Pendleton, 1987—; dir. youth ministries Columbia River Conf., Free Meth. Ch., Pendleton, 1988—; dir. follow-up Free Meth. Powersurge, Anaheim, Calif., 1989; dir. spiritual devel. Free Meth. Internat. Youth Conv., Ft. Collins, Colo., 1991. Rep. supt.'s adv. coun. Pendleton Schs., 1989—, mem. supt. search com., 1990-91. Mem. Pendleton Ministerial Assn. (sec. 1990—). Office: Free Meth Ch 1711 SW 44th St Pendleton OR 97801 *Youth ministry is the most strategic movement in our day for transforming the future of the world. I want to invest my life in discipling youth and so build the kingdom of God.*

KIO, STEPHEN HRE, minister; b. Haka, Chin State, Burma, Mar. 19, 1937; came to U.S., 1979; s. Sang and Kawl (Dong) Fen; m. Klem Kyin Kio, Apr. 26, 1964; children: Van, Zalal, Lal, Dede. BA, U. Rangoon, Burma, 1960; BD, Serampore Coll., West Bengal, India, 1963; MA, Emory U., 1980, PhD, 1984. Lectr. Zomi Bapt. Theol. Sem., Falam, Burma, 1963-64; sr. pastor Falam (Chin State) Bapt. Ch., 1964-73; prin. Zomi Bapt. Theol. Sem., Falam, Burma, 1977-78; bible translator old testament Falam Bapt. Assn., 1973-78; bible translator new testament Falam Bapt. Assn., Atlanta, 1979-85; translations cons. United Bible Socs., Guam, 1986—; com. mem. Asia-Pacific Reg. Translation Com., Hong Kong, 1980—; treas. Zomi Bapt. Conv., 1964-77; sr. pastor Haka Bapt. Ch., 1978-79. Author: Church History, 1974, Pastoral Works 1966, N.T. Introduction, 1976. Mem. Bible Soc. Micronesia (bd. dirs. 1986—), United Bible Socs. (com. new readers selection 1987—), Soc. Bibl. Lit. Home: 129-25 Gollo Ct Perez Acres Yigo GU 96929 *I have never applied for or desired to hold high position. Rather I aimed at little jobs and yet do it well. If I make a difference in small things, life would be worthwhile.*

KIPNIS, JUDITH ROBISON, deacon, religious administrator; b. Bklyn., July 14, 1931; d. Richard Porteous and Doris (Turney) Robison; m. Igor Kipnis, Jan. 6, 1953; 1 child, Jeremy Robison. BA, Radcliffe Coll., 1952; MA, Columbia U., 1953; MA in Religion, Yale U., 1983; grad., Shalem Inst. for Spiritual Formation, Nat. Ctr. for Death Edn., Mt. Ida Coll. Lay reader Christ Ch. Parish, West Redding, Conn., 1979—, chalice bearer, 1980—, also lector, 1976-79, mem. vestry, 1981-84, staff sec., 1978-79, parish del. to Danbury Deanery, 1977-78, 79—, subdean, 1981-83, guest preacher, 1982—, del. exec. coun., 1983-86; pastoral care coord., bereavement coord. Regional Hospice of Western Conn.; chaplain chem. dependency unit Danbury Hosp., mem. pastoral care com; conv. del. Diocese of Conn., 1977-78, 83—, exec. coun. 1983-86, various coms.; free-lance writer, educator, counselor West Redding, 1954—. Asst. editor: The Encyclopedia of Twentieth-Century Music, 1974. Mem. Redding (Conn.) Bd. Edn., 1973-89, chmn., 1977-81; mem. Park Ridge Ctr. Recipient William E. Downes prize Yale U., 1983; Grammy award nominee Nat. Acad. Recording Arts and Scis., 1976; grantee Martha Baird Rockefeller Found., 1969-70, Ford Found., 1970-71. Mem. Religious Edn. Assn., Am. Acad. Religion (assoc.), Nat. Ctr. for Diaconate. Democrat. Home: 20 Drummer Ln West Redding CT 06896

KIRBY, FRANKLIN HUGH, minister; b. Spartanburg, S.C., Feb. 13, 1939; s. Joe Charles and Vernie (Davis) K.; m. Deane Rae Owen, Apr. 28, 1964; children: Kelly Denise, Cory Owen. AA, North Greenville Coll., 1959; BA, Furman U., 1962; BDiv, So. Bapt. Theol. Sem., 1966, MA, 1967; DMin, Columbia Theol. Sem., 1982. Ordained to ministry So. Bapt. Conv., 1963. Assoc. pastor, min. edn. Grace Bapt. Ch., Richmond, Va., 1967-70, First Bapt. Ch., Raleigh, N.C., 1970-71, Dunwoody Bapt. Ch., Atlanta, 1971-80; pastor Calvary Bapt. Ch., West Lafayette, Ind., 1980-87, First Bapt. Ch., Hartwell, Ga., 1987—. Author, producer children's films including How Big is Big?, 1975, Are Any Two Alike?, 1977; contbr. articles to religious journs. mem. N.E. Ga. adv. bd. Emanual Coll., Franklin Springs, Ga., 1988—; bd. visitors Truette-McConnel Coll., Cleveland, Ga., 1991—; mem. adv. bd. N.E. Ga. Counseling Ctr., Royston, Ga., 1988—; bd. dirs. Hart County Clothes Closet, Hartwell, Ga., 1987—, Hart County Salvation Army, Hartwell, 1987—. Mem. Optimists, Masons. Home: 114 Smith St Hartwell GA 30643 Office: First Bapt Ch 404 W Howell St Hartwell GA 30643

KIRBY, H(ARRY) SCOTT, priest; b. Richmond, Va., May 6, 1938; s. William Alphus and Lucille Viola (Patterson) K.; m. Heather Patricia Roberts, June 22, 1963; children: Cheryl Christine Kirby, Robert Bruce. BA, U. Richmond, 1960; MDiv, Gen. Theol. Sem., N.Y.C., 1963. Ordained priest Episcopal Ch., 1963. Asst. to rector Cathedral of St. Luke and St. Paul, Charleston, S.C., 1963; curate Ch. of the Advent, Kenmore, N.Y., 1963-66; rector Ch. of St. John the Bapt., Dunkirk, N.Y., 1966-73, Ch. of St. John on the Mountain, Bernardsville, N.J., 1973-79; canon Christ Ch. Cathedral, Salina, Kans., 1979-89; dean Christ Ch. Cathedral, Eau Claire, Wis., 1989—; devel. cons. St. Francis Acad., Salina, 1991; chmn. long range planning Diocese of Eau Claire, 1989—, mem. 1991—, dean Chippewa Valley, 1990—. Contbr. articles to mags. Recipient Bishop's Svc. award Diocese of Western Kans., 1980. Mem. Anglican Soc. Home: 1712 Lehman St Eau Claire WI 54701 Office: Christ Ch Cathedral 510 S Farwell St Eau Claire WI 54701

KIRBY, JAMES EDMUND, JR., theology educator; b. Wheeler, Tex., June 24, 1933; s. James Edmund and Mamie (Helton) K.; m. Patty Ray Boothe, July 22, 1955; children: David Edmund, Patrick Boothe. B.A. cum laude, McMurry Coll., 1954; B.D., Perkins Sch. Theology, 1957, S.T.M., 1959; Ph.D., Drew U., 1963; postgrad., Cambridge (Eng.) U., 1957-58. Ordained to ministry United Meth. Ch., 1959; pastor First Meth. Ch., Roby, Tex., 1958-59, Milford (Pa.) Meth. Ch., 1960-61; asst. prof. Bible, McMurry Coll., Abilene, Tex., 1959-60; asst. prof. religion Sweet Briar Coll., Va., 1963-67; prof. religion, head dept. religion Okla. State U., Stillwater, 1967-70; head Sch. Humanistic Studies, 1970-76; dean, Prof. Ch. History Sch. Theology, Drew U., Madison, N.J., 1976-81; dean Perkins Sch. Theology, So. Meth. U., Dallas, 1981—, prof. ch. history; teaching asst. Drew Theol. Sem., Madison, N.J., 1960-61; cons. bd. missions United Meth. Ch., South Africa, 1968. Contbr. articles to profl. jours.; bd. dirs. Wesley Works Editorial Project. John M. Moore fellow, 1957-58; Dempster fellow, 1962. Mem. Am. Acad. Religion, Soc. Values in Higher Edn., Am. Soc. Ch. History, Assn. United Meth. Theol. Schs., Alpha Chi, Omicron Delta Kappa. Home: 9235 Windy Crest Dallas TX 75243 Office: Perkins Sch Theol Kirby Hall Southern Meth U Dallas TX 75275

KIRBY, RODNEY NIEL, school administrator; b. Christiansburg, Va., Dec. 5, 1953; s. Ernest Wilson and Dorothy Mildred (Farmer) K.; m. Martha Ellen Bowe, May 23, 1975; children: Benjamin Forrest, Jonathan Farmer, David Michael. MusB, Jacksonville U., 1975; M. Christian Ed., Ref. Theol. Sem., 1978. Headmaster Grace Christian Sch., Louisville, Miss., 1978-85, Providence Christian Sch., Sugarland, Tex., 1985-88, Cherokee Christian Sch., Woodstock, Ga., 1988--; pres. Westminster Assc. Christian Schs., Sugarland, Tx. 1984-88. Author numerous religious articles; editor The Westminster Educator, 1984-88. Del. Cherokee County Rep. Conv. Recipient award in organ performance Fla. State Music Tchrs. Assc. 1974-75. Mem. Assc. Christian Sch. Adminstr. Presbyterian Church in America. Office: Cherokee Christian School PO Box 913 Woodstock GA 30188

KIRINDA, MARGARET B., religious organization administrator; b. Kampala, Uganda, Nov. 22, 1946; came to U.S., 1973; d. Yoweri Buswandii and Vena Nalwoga Nsubuga; m. Adoniya Kirinda, June 21, 1963 (dec. Oct. 1988); children: Susan Ayouglan, Becky Njuki, Jennifer, Ruth, Timothy. Adminstrv. asst. Every Home Crusade, Kampala, 1969-73; office asst. World Lit. Crusade, Woodland Hills, Calif., 1973-79; missionary Internat. Gospel League, Pasadena, Calif., 1979-84; exec. dir. Africa Village Outreach, Sun Valley, Calif., 1988—. Office: Africa Village Outreach 12501 Chandler Blvd Ste 205 North Hollywood CA 91607

KIRK, DAVID ARNEIL, evangelist; b. Marlin, Tex., Feb. 16, 1948; s. Onnie Isaac and Mary Jane (McGauder) K.; m. Eva Yvonne Scott, Sept. 26, 1969 (div. Sept. 1978); children: Onnie, David; m. Patricia Ann Harden, Dec. 24, 1980; children: Kevin, Nedra, Shawn. BBA in Bus., U. Tex., 1972; AA in Real Estate, El Paso (Tex.) Community Coll., 1981. Mktg. rep. Shell Oil Co., Dallas, 1972-73, Am. Tng. Svcs., Memphis, 1973-75, Southwestern Pub. Co., Nashville, 1976-80; real estate agt. Kaufmann Realtors, El Paso, 1980-83, A D Realtors, El Paso, 1983-88; sta. mgr. KZOL Radio 860, El Paso, 1987-88; real estate agt. Century 21 Paul Barry Realtors, El Paso, 1988-89; pres. Video Bible Co., Houston, 1989—; asst. dir. Lovely Sunset Orgn., Sweetwater, Tex., 1985-89; cons. Greentree Street Ministry, El Paso, 1983-89. Pub. (newspaper) Good Neighbor, 1977. Chmn. Dawson Bullard Polit. Com., El Paso, 1987, founder Vietnam Vets at Home, El Paso, 1987; chmn. Krystiel Found., 1986—, co-dir. Children Pageants. With USNR, 1966-72. Recipient Achievement award USN, 1971, Sales Leadership award A.D. Realty, El Paso, 1983; named Top Recruiter, Am. Tng. Services, 1975, #1 Sales Producer, Southwestern Co., 1978. Mem. Am. Mktg. Assn., Alpha Phi Alpha. Democrat. Baptist. Lodge: Masons. Avocations: photography, travel, reading, pub. speaking. Home: 3101 Spencer # 8 Pasadena TX 44504 Office: Video Bible 950 Echo Lane # 170 Houston TX 77024

KIRK, EDGAR S., minister. Pres. R.I. Conf., Gen. Six Principles Bapts., North Kingstown. Office: Gen Six Principle Baptists 350 Davisville Rd North Kingstown RI 02852*

KIRK, JAMES ALBERT, religious studies educator; b. L'Anse, Mich., Jan. 20, 1929; s. Orman Albert and Gladys E. (Tremaine) K.; m. Lois Eileen Grubaugh, Aug. 19, 1956; children: Robert A., Aletha K., Ann L. BA, Hillsdale Coll., 1951; ThM, Iliff Sch. of Theology, 1954, ThD, 1959. Ordained to ministry Congregationalist Ch., 1954. Minister 1st Congregational Ch., Arriba, Colo., 1951-59; instr. U. Denver, 1959-60, asst. prof., 1960-68, assoc. prof., 1968-77, prof., 1977—; dir. PhD's Iliff/Denver U., 1982-85; vis. faculty U. Pitts., 1989. Author, compiler: Stories of the Hindus, 1972; co-author: Religion and the Human Image, 1977. Rsch. fellow U. Madras (India), 1967-68, Doshisha U., Kyuto, Japan, 1968. Mem. Am. Acad. Religion (pres. Rocky Mountain Region 1969-70), Assn. for Asian Studies, Internat. Assn. Buddhist Studies, The Asia Soc. Mem. United Ch. of Christ. Home: 1919 E Cornell Ave Denver CO 80210 Office: U Denver Dept Religious Studies Denver CO 80208

KIRK, JAMES GRAHAM, pastor; b. Alameda, Calif., Jan. 9, 1937; s. Roy and Helen Graham (Thomson) K.; m. Sandra J. Killam Aug. 24, 1958 (div. 1985); m. Elizabeth Juliana Dittmer, Sept. 26, 1987; children: John Graham Kirk, Eric William Villegas, James Keith Kirk. AB, Lewis & Clark Coll., 1958; BD, San Francisco Theol. Seminary, 1961; postgrad., Heidelberg U., 1961-64; STD, San Francisco Theol. Seminary, 1980. Ordained to ministry Presbyn. Ch., 1964. Pastor St. Mark Presbyn. Ch., Newport Beach, Calif., 1968-73; dir. adv. coun. Discipleship and Worship, N.Y.C., 1973-85; co-pastor First Presbyn. Ch., Kalamazoo, Mich., 1985-86; interim pastor Cen. Presbyn. Ch., Lafayette, Ind., 1986-88; pastor Harundale Presbyn. Ch., Glen Burnie, Md., 1988—; del. Conf. on Renewal of Congregations, World Coun. of Chs., Crete, Greece, 1981. Author: When We Gather (3 vols.), 1983-86, Meditation for Lent, 1988, Meditations for Advent, 1989. Trustee Bd. of Edn., Cresskil, N.J., 1977-85. Mem. Rotary (trustee Glen Burnie chpt. 1990-91), F&AM (chaplain 1965-67). Office: Harundale Presbyn Ch 1020 Eastway Glen Burnie MD 21060 *Life is a journey along faith's trail. Led by God's Spirit we seek to avoid the pitfalls, detours and hazards that hinder our faithful response to Christ's call, "come, follow me!".*

KIRK, KEVIN LEE, college administrator; b. Logan, Utah, June 13, 1950; s. Lee K. and LaRue (Monson) K.; m. Jan Nuttall, Aug. 3, 1973; children: Tyler, Landon, Carson, Emily. BS, Brigham Young U., 1975, M degree, 1976, EdD, 1990; postgrad., Harvard U., 1989. Dir. community edn. Nebo Sch. Dist., Spanish Fork, Utah, 1975-76; dir. continuing edn. Dodge City (Kans.) Community Coll., 1976-78; dean, continuing edn. Colby (Kans.) Community Coll., 1978-80; dir. evening sch., ind. study Utah State U., Logan, 1980-88; asst. dean Fla. Community Coll., Jacksonville, 1988—. Contbr. articles to profl. jours. Asst. scoutmaster Boy Scouts of Am., Jacksonville, 1988—; council mem. Jacksonville Community Council, 1988—; chmn. United Heart Fund Drive, Colby, 1979; promotion chmn. United Way campaign, Jacksonville, 1988. Fellow Mountain Plains Adult Edn. Assn., 1987, C.S. Mott Found., 1975-76; recipient 1st place nat. award Nat. U. Continuing Edn. Assn., 1986; named to Outstanding Young Men of Am., 1987. Mem. Fla. Assn. Community Colls. (1st place award 1988), Mountain Plains Adult Edn. Assn. (bd. dirs. 1986-87), Adult Edn. Assn. of Utah (bd. dirs., pres. 1984-88), Western Community Coll. Consortium (pres., sec. 1977-79). Republican. Mem. LDS Ch. Avocations: tennis, fishing, hunting. Home: 2495 Castaway Dr Jacksonville FL 32224 Office: FCCJ 101 W State St Jacksonville FL 32202

KIRKEBY, OLIVER MURLE, counselor, religion educator, sociologist; b. Henning, Minn., Sept. 14, 1930; s. Ole B. and Wilhelmena Kirkeby; children from previous marriage: Paul, Beth, Jayne; m. Judith Dixon Hillestad, June 9, 1987. BA, Concordia Coll., 1953; MA, U. Windsor, Can., 1972; D of Ministry, Trinity Sem., 1980; PhD, Wayne State U., 1982. Ordained to ministry Am. Evang. Luth. Ch. Assoc. pastor First Luth. Ch., Stoughton, Wis., 1958-60; pastor Trinity Luth. Ch., Chgo., 1960-63; dir. Metro-Luth. Campus Ministry, Detroit, 1963-74; pastor Salem Luth. Ch., Detroit, 1974-80; lay assoc. Zion Luth. Ch., Ferndale, Mich., 1980-90; internat. counselor Wayne State U., Detroit, 1985-90; researcher various Luth. Chs., Mich., 1963—; with Global Mission Com. S.E. Mich. Synod, Detroit, 1989—. Contbr. articles to profl. jours. Trustee Scandinavian Symphony Soc. Mich., 1980—; sec., v.p. Highland Park (Mich.) Libr. Commn., 1972-87; pres. Rotary Internat., Highland Park, 1979-80. Recipient Paul Harris award Rotary, 1980. Mem. Soc. Bibl. Lit., Nat. Assn. of Fgn. Student Advisors, Mich. Coun. Social Studies, World Futurist, Am. Coll. Nursing Home Adminstrs., People to People, Sons of Norway. Home: 8619 Centralia Dearborn Heights MI 48127 Office: Wayne State U 5454 Cass Ave Detroit MI 48202 *The greatest treasure is a life that is shared and passed on to grandchildren who in turn can share with their parents when they are not too busy.*

KIRKLAND, BRYANT MAYS, clergyman; b. Essex, Conn., May 2, 1914; s. Henry Burnham and Helen Josephine (Mays) K.; m. Bernice Eleanor Tanis, Aug. 19, 1937; children: Nancy Tanis (Mrs. Tom L. Thompson), Elinor Ann Hite , Virginia Lee (Mrs. Laird James Stuart). AB, Wheaton Coll., 1935; ThB, Princeton Theol. Sem., 1938; ThM, Eastern Bapt. Theol. Sem., Phila., 1946; DD (hon.), Beaver Coll., 1949, Lafayette Coll., 1962, Denison U., 1964; LLD (hon.), U. Tulsa, 1962; STD (hon.), Parson Coll., 1966, Hastings Coll., 1989; LittD (hon.), Washington and Jefferson Coll., 1968; LHD (hon.), Lebanon Valley Coll., 1983. Ordained to ministry Presbyn. Ch., 1938; pastor Pa., 38-46, N.J., 1946-57, Tulsa, 1957-62; pastor Fifth Ave. Presbyn. Ch., N.Y.C., 1962-87, elected minister emeritus, 1987—; pres., chief exec. officer Am. Bible Soc., N.Y.C., 1989-91; interim min. Nat. Presbyn. Ch., Washington, 1991—; vis. lectr. homiletics Princeton Theol. Sem., 1951-56, 64-85, 87—; overseas guest lectr. U.S. Armed Forces, U.S. Army Chaplain Sch., 1965, 68, 71, 74, 81, 87, 88—; Berger lectr., 1968, Swartley lectr., 1969, T.J. and Inez Raney lectr., 1969, Logan lectr., 1974, Royster lectr., 1976, 80, Staley lectr., 1978, 81, B. Cobb lectr., 1982, George A. Buttrick lectr., 1983, 85, Otis lectr., 1984, B. Cobb lectr., 1982; disting. adj. prof. Ea. Bapt. Theol. Sem.; mem. Commn. Ecumenical Mission and Relations, Presbyn. Ch., 1949-62, Commn. on Continuing Edn., 1967; mem. council Nat. Presbyn. Ch. Center, Washington, 1962-65. Author: Growing in Christian Faith, 1963, Home Before Dark, 1965, 1986, Living in a Zig Zag Age, 1972, Experiencing God in Unexpected Ways, 1978, Pattern For Faith, 1982; contbg. author: Evangelical Sermons of Our Day, 1959, Year of Evangelism in Local Church, 196O. Trustee Beaver Coll., U. Tulsa; pres. bd. trustees Princeton Theol. Sem. Recipient Disting. Alumni award Princeton Theol. Sem., 1988, Legion of Merit Chapel Four Chaplains, 1989; named Clergyman of Year Religious Heritage Am., 1975. Mem. Am. Bible Soc. (trustee), Princeton Club (N.Y.C.), Nassau Club. Home: Rydal Park Apt 540 Rydal PA 19046 Office: 4101 Nebraska Ave NW Washington DC 20016

KIRKLAND, WILLIAM DENNIS, minister, missionary; b. Blakley, Ga., Dec. 16, 1961; s. William Horace and Kathrine (Dyson) K.; m. Lora Shereen Makemson, July 19, 1986; children: William Daniel, Paul Alexander. BA in Missions, Southeastern Bible Coll., 1988. Ordained to ministry Bapt. Ch., 1988. Missionary Ind. Fundamental Chs. Am., 1987; pastor Grace Bible Ch., Ceiba, P.R., 1988—. With USMC, 1980-84. Home: PO Box 1119 Ceiba PR 00735

KIRKMAN, MICHAEL EUGENE, minister; b. Newport, Oreg., Aug. 23, 1954; s. Ashley Arden and Opal Joan (Rauch) K.; m. Carol Elaine Hoyle, June 23, 1979; children: Kelli Elese, Kristin Elizabeth, Timothy James. Student, Clackamas Community Coll., Oregon City, Oreg., 1972-73; BS in Biology, George Fox Coll., Newberg, Oreg., 1975; MDiv in Christian Edn., Western Bapt. Sem., Portland, Oreg., 1980. Ordained to ministry N.Am. Bapt. Conf., 1985. Summer staff Portland Campus Crusade for Christ, 1973; youth dir. United Meth. Ch., Newberg, 1974-75; intern 1st Bapt. Ch., Gladstone, Oreg., 1979-80; assoc. pastor Trinity Bapt. Ch., Portland, 1980-85, 1st Bapt. Ch., Redmond, Oreg., 1986—. Editor CenPac Courier, newsletter, 1983-85. Mem. budget com. City of Redmond, 1988-91. Mem. Redmond Ministerial Assn. (treas. 1987-88, pres. 1988-90, sec. 1990-91—), Kiwanis (treas. 1988-89, 2d v.p. 1989-90, 1st v.p. 1990-91, pres. 1991—). Home: 309 NW 9th St Redmond OR 97756 Office: 1st Bapt Ch 936 NW Cedar Ave Redmond OR 97756

KIRKPATRICK, FRANK GLOYD, minister, religion educator; b. Washington, Aug. 4, 1942; s. George Gloyd and Amy Mary (Cook) K.; m. Elizabeth Alden Murray, June 11, 1966; children: Amy, Daniel. BA, Trinity Coll., 1964; MA, Columbia U., Union Theol. Sem., N.Y.C., 1966; PhD, Brown U., 1970. Ordained to ministry Episcopal Ch., 1973. Prof. religion Trinity Coll., Hartford, Conn., 1969—; parish assoc. Trinity Ch., Hartford, 1973-79; chair Peace and Justice Commn., Diocese of Conn., 1980-82, examining chaplains com. Common Ministry, 1982-88, Commn. on Ministry, 1988-91; bd. dirs. Episcopal Ch., Yale U., New Haven, 1985-87. Author: Community, 1986; co-author: Living Issues in Ethics, 1982; contbr. articles to profl. jours. mem. Conn. Freeze Campaign, Hartford, 1980—. Mem. Am. Acad. Religion (pres. New Eng. chpt. 1990-91), Christian Conf. Conn., Episcopal Peace Fellowship. Democrat. Home: 154 Clearfield Rd Wethersfield CT 06109 Office: Trinity Coll 300 Summit St Hartford CT 06106

KIRLIN-HACKETT, SUSAN KAYE, minister; b. Roseburg, Oreg., Feb. 4, 1949; d. John Linden and Marian Jeanette (Hansen) Kirlin; m. Gary Michael Stillwell, Dec. 13, 1969 (div. 1977); m. William George Hackett, July 16, 1977; 1 child, Micah Joseph Kirlin-Hackett. BA in Speech-Communication, Calif. State U., Long Beach, 1979; MDiv, Pacific Luth. Theol. Sem., 1984. Co-pastor Holy Redeemer Luth. Ch., San Jose, Calif., 1985-89; assoc. pastor St. Olaf Luth. Ch., Garden Grove, Calif., 1989—; vice-pastor Santa Clara County (Calif.) Cluster, Evang. Luth. Ch. Am., 1985-87. Bd. dirs. Body & Soul Dance Co., Berkeley, Calif., 1984-85. Home: 1012 E Mayfair Ave Orange CA 92667

KIRMSE, SISTER ANNE-MARIE ROSE, nun, educator, researcher; b. Bklyn., Sept. 23, 1941; d. Frank Joseph Sr. and Anna (Keck) K. BA in English cum laude, St. Francis Coll., 1972; MA in Theology with honors, Providence Coll., 1975; PhD in Theology, Fordham U., 1989. Joined Sisters of St. Dominic, Roman Cath. Ch., 1960; cert. elem. tchr., N.Y. Tchr. elem. sch. Diocese Bklyn., 1962-73; instr. adult edn. Diocese Rockville Centre, N.Y., 1974—; dir. religious edn. St. Anthony Padua Parish, East Northport, N.Y., 1975-83; dir. spiritual programs Diocese of Rockville Centre, 1979—; demonstration tchr. Paulist Press, N.Y.C., 1968-70; cons. Elem. Sch. Catechetical Assocs., Bklyn., 1971-73; mem. adj. faculty grad. program Sem. Immaculate Conception, Huntington, N.Y., 1979-80; adj. instr. Molloy Coll., Rockville Centre, 1985, St. Joseph's Coll., Patchogue, N.Y., 1990—; asst. to Rev. Avery Dulles, Fordham U., Bronx, 1988—, rsch. assoc. Laurence J. McGinley chair in religion and soc., 1989. Recipient Dominican scholarship Providence (R.I.) Coll., 1973, Kerygma award Diocese Rockville Centre, 1980, Presdl. scholarship Fordham U., 1988; McGinley fellow Fordham U., 1988. Mem. L.I. Women's Ordination Conf. Democrat. Roman Catholic. Avocations: swimming, needlework, cooking, traveling, reading. Office: Fordham U Keating Hall 322 Laurence J McGinley Chair in Religion and Soc Bronx NY 10458 *With Saint Irenaeus, I believe that "the glory of God is a person fully alive!" Life is meant to be lived to the full, with passion and extravagance, with commitment and the courage of one's convictions. As with love, the more of our lives we give away, the more life we find we have.*

KIRSCH, CHARLES DEE, clergyman; b. Portsmouth, Ohio, Feb. 4, 1928; s. Paul Francis and Thelma Irene (Fannin) K.; m. Janice Erlene Croteau, July 3, 1954; children: Marilyn Sue, Diane Louise. AB, Ohio U., 1950; MDiv, Boston U., 1953; DD, Otterbein Coll., Westerville, Ohio, 1982. Minister Trinity Ch., Boston, 1950-53, Hyde Park Community Meth. Ch., Cin., 1953-56, Sabina United Meth. Ch., Ohio, 1956-62, Reynoldsburg Meth. Ch., Ohio, 1962-68, Christ United Meth. Ch., Kettering, Ohio, 1968-78; dist. supt. Columbus United Meth. Ch., 1978-82, North Broadway United Meth. Ch., Columbus, 1982—; chmn. bd. Meth. Theol. in Ohio, 1988—; trustee Riverside Meth. Hosp., Columbus, 1982—; bd. dirs., div. chmn. Gen. Council on Ministries, United Meth. Ch., 1980-88; mem. investment com. United Meth. Ch., Chgo., 1980-88. Chmn. bd. dirs. Travelers Aid, Columbus, 1966-68; bd. dirs. United Way, Dayton, 1970-78; bd. dirs. Family Svc., Dayton, 1974-78, Florence Crittenden Svcs., Columbus, 1963-68. Avocations: stamps, coins, investments, travel, music. Office: North Broadway Meth Ch 48 E North Broadway Columbus OH 43214

KIRSCH, ELMER EDWIN, academic administrator; b. Gillett, Wis., Mar. 5, 1927; s. Paul and Mathilda (Miller) K.; m. Alice Martha Wood, Aug. 11, 1951; children: Norman Lee, William Alan. Diploma, Cen. Bible Coll., 1952; BS, Taylor U., 1954; MEd, U. Toledo, 1960; EdD, U. So. Calif., 1972. Cert. tchr. Calif., Wis., Ohio. Tchr. Clinton (Wis.) High Sch., 1956-59, Libby High Sch., Toledo, 1959-61; dean of students Bethany Coll., Scotts Valley, Calif., 1961-67, dean of edn., 1968-74; dean of edn. Cen. Bible Coll., Springfield, Mo., 1974-77; div. chmn. Bethany Coll., Scotts Valley, Calif., 1977-82; v.p. acad. Cen. Bible Coll., Springfield, Mo., 1982—. Contbr. articles to religious jours. Chmn. Planning Commn., Scotts Valley, 1969-74, 78-82. Mem. Phi Delta Kappa, Delta Epsilon. Assemblies of God. Home: 1075 W Lyons Springfield MO 65803 Office: Cen Bible Coll 3000 N Grant Springfield MO 65803 *A life is always a seed planted but the harvest varies.*

KIRSCHE, EDWARD GEORGE, seminary dean, minister, educator; b. Phila., Aug. 12, 1949; s. Edward Joseph Kirsche and Beverly Jane (Branyan) Derbyshire; m. Loraine Jeanette Bates, Dec. 8, 1970; children: Wendy, Melissa, Shannon, Dana, Edward Jr. Theology diploma, Antioch Bapt. Coll., Marietta, Ga., 1976; BD, Luther Rice Sem., Jacksonville, Fla., 1978; MTh, Immanuel Sem., Peachtree City, Ga., 1980; ThD, Antioch Sem., Marietta, 1989; D of Religious Edn. (hon.), Trinity Sem., 1982. Lic. to ministry So. Bapt. Conv., 1973, ordained, 1983. Dean of acad. affairs Antioch Sem., 1978-89, dean of external affairs, 1989—; tchr. Landmark Christian High Sch., Fayetteville, Ga., 1990—; pastor Antioch Bapt. Ch., Fayetteville, 1988—; bd. mem. Shiloh Bible Coll., Inc., Marietta, 1979—, Rock of Ages Prison Ministry, College Park, Ga., 1986—, Antioch Bapt. Ch., Inc., Fayetteville, 1990—. With USMC, 1966-69, Vietnam. Mem. Evang. Tchrs. Tng. Assn. (cert. tchr.). Home: 602 Antioch Rd Fayetteville GA 30214 Office: Antioch Bapt Ch 144 Woolsey Brooks Rd Fayetteville GA 30214

KIRSCHNER, ANTHONY, priest; b. Eichstaett, Ger., June 12, 1910; came to U.S. 1938; s. BArtholomy and Mary Ann (Weindl) K. BA, U. Wuerzburg, 1935. Ordained priest Roman Cath. Ch., 1937. Pastor St. Raphael Ch., Garden City, Mich., 1938-44, Our Lady of Grace Parish, Dearborn Hts., Mich., 1944-53, Navismaster, Brighton, Mich., 1953-57; provincial superior Am. Can. Province of Marionhill Fathers, 1957-63; procurator and editor-in-chief Leaves Mag., 1963-89; procurator Our Lady of Grace Monastery, Dearborn Hts., 1989—; chaplain K.C., 1954—. Home and Office: Marionhill Mission Soc 23715 Ann Arbor Trail Dearborn Heights MI 48127

KIRSTEIN, JOHN AUDELBERT, retired minister; b. Fruitland, N.C., May 27, 1925; s. Martin Luther and Aleatha Vera (Garren) K.; m. Myrl Baxter, Dec. 28, 1949; children: Janis Adrian, Mark Noel. BA, Maryville Coll., 1945; BD, Columbia Theol. Sem., 1948; ThM, Louisville Presbyn. Sem., 1957. Pastor various churches, various cities, 1948-78; assoc. editor Presbyn. Survey Mag., 1960-65; info. dir. Presbyn. Bd. Christian Edn., Richmond, Va., 1965-69; exec. adminstr. Synod of Mid-South, Nashville, 1978-79; pastor Cen. Presbyn. Ch., Jackson, Miss., 1979-86; organizing pastor Community Stewpot and Sims House for Women, 1979-86. Contbr. numerous articles to religion mags. Committeeman Dem. Party, Henrico County, Va., 1968. Named Alumnus of Yr. Louisville Presbyn. Sem., 1982. Democrat. Home: 7 Starling Sq Clinton MS 39056 *The greatest gift is life, to have it and use it wisely. My ministry has centered in empowering others with life through development and keeping count only of the joy and privilege.*

KIS, MIROSLAV MIRKO, minister, religion educator; b. Miklusevci, Croatia, Yugoslavia, Nov. 6, 1942; came to U.S., 1974; s. Andrija and Natalija (Pap) K.; m. Brenda Starr Bond, Aug. 22, 1971; children: Richard Andrej, Adam Daniel. BA, Seminarie Adventiste, France, 1973; MDiv, Andrews U., Berrien Springs, Mich., 1976; PhD, McGill, Montreal, Que., Can., 1983. Ordained to ministry Seventh-day Adventist Ch., 1979. Pastor, intern Seventh-Day Adventist Ch., France, 1972-73; assoc. pastor Seventh-Day Adventist Ch., San Pedro, Calif., 1973-74; pastor Seventh-Day Adventist Ch., Montreal, 1976-79, 81-83; asst. prof. Can. Union Coll., College Heights, Alta., Can., 1979-81; assoc. prof. Christian ethics Andrews U., Berrien Springs, 1983—, chmn. dept. theology and Christian philosophy, 1984—; trustee Loma Linda (Calif.) Bioethics Com., 1985—. Sgt. Yugoslavia mil, 1961-63. Mem. Soc. Christian Ethics, Am. Acad. Religion, Andrews Soc. Religious Studies. Office: Seventh-day Adventist Theol Sem Andrews U Berrien Springs MI 49104-1500

KISER, HOWARD WAYNE, minister, writer, publisher; b. Springfield, Ill., May 18, 1939; s. Russell and Dorothy (Cummings) K.; m. Ruth Ann Lemcool, June 7, 1958; children: Daniel Wayne, Debra Jean, Timothy David. BA in English and Bible, Grace Coll., Winona Lake, Ind., 1962; MA in Communications, Wheaton (Ill.) Coll., 1977. Ordained to ministry Ind. Fundamental Chs. Am., 1964. Interim pastor various chs., Tenn., Ind., Ill., 1959-72; min. Zion Bethel Ch., Monticello, Ind., 1963-68; missionary editor Christian Svc. Brigade, Wheaton, 1968-70; pres. Graphic and Editorial Svcs., Glen Ellyn, Ill., 1972—; adj. faculty Wheaton Coll., 1972—, Moody Bible Inst., Chgo., 1987—; judge design Religious Pub. Rels. Coun., Chgo., 1985; leader seminar Latin Am. Mission, Lima, Peru, 1987. Author: From Manuscript to Printed Piece, 1972, Getting More Out of Church, 1986; also articles; co-author: (audio course) Introduction to Design for Desktop Publishing. Recipient Christiansen Excellence award Moody Monthly Mag., 1978-79, Golden Quill award Old Cars Weekly, 1988. Mem. Evang. Press Assn. (conv. steering com. 1983, 91), Studebaker Drivers Club (editor newsletter 1984-89, 1st pl. award 1988, 89), Amateur Radio Club. Office: Graphic and Editorial Svcs 1N410 Eastern Ave Glen Ellyn IL 60137

KISER, RAYMOND DOUGLAS, minister; b. Welch, W.Va., Feb. 3, 1951; s. Raymond Erving and Helen (Murin) K. BA, Duke U., 1973; MDiv, Yale U., 1976; PhD, Claremont Sch. Theology, 1991. Ordained to ministry United Meth. Ch., 1975. Assoc. pastor Meml. United Meth. Ch., Austin, Tex., 1976-79; chaplain Baylor U. Med. Ctr., Dallas, 1979-80; assoc. pastor Sierra Madre (Calif.) United Meth. Ch., 1980-83, Travis Park United Meth. Ch., San Antonio, 1983-88; sr. pastor NW Hills United Meth. Ch., Austin, 1988—; resident counselor Pomona Valley Pastoral Counseling Ctr., Claremont, Calif., 1980-83; bd. dirs. Bexar County Detention Ministries, San Antonio, 1983-85; chmn. human welfare div. bd. ch. and society SW Tex. Conf., United Meth. Ch., 1983-89; vice chmn. bd. dirs. New Life Inst., Austin, 1988-91; sec. Austin Dist. Bd. Missions, 1990-91; editorial asst. Basic Types of Pastoral Care and Counseling (Howard Clinebell), 1981-83; mem. AIDS task force SW Tex. Conf., 1986-89. Contbr. articles to religious publs. Vol. counselor Christian Assistance Ministry, San Antonio, 1983-88; vol. SAMM Shelter for Homeless, San Antonio, 1983-88; mem. United Meth. Bishops' Task Force Against Gambling, Tex., 1987-89; mem. bd. ch. and society Tex. Conf. Chs., 1988-89. Mem. Am. Assn. Pastoral Counselors (counselor-in-tng.), Phi Beta Kappa. Home: 4006 Edgefield Ct Austin TX 78731 Office: NW Hills United Meth Ch 7017 Hart Ln Austin TX 78731

KISHKOVSKY, LEONID, religious organization administrator. Pres. Nat. Coun. Chs. of Christ in U.S.A., N.Y.C. Office: Nat Coun Chs 475 Riverside Dr New York NY 10115*

KISSINGER, H. P., religious organization administrator. Pres., chmn. commn. on chaplains Associated Gospel Chs., Tallahassee. Office: Associated Gospel Chs 3209 Norfolk St Hopewell VA 23850*

KISSINGER, WARREN STAUFFER, minister; b. Akron, Pa., Sept. 8, 1922; s. Howard Elmer and Anna Adams (Stauffer) K.; m. Jean Thelma Young, Sept. 1, 1951; children: John Howard, David Charles, Ann Constance, Adele Marya. AB, Elizabethtown Coll., 1950; BD, Yale Divinity Sch., 1953; MST, Luth. Theol. Sem., Gettysburg, Pa., 1964; MLS, Drexel U., 1968. Pastor Windber Ch. of Brethren, Pa., 1953-57, Carlisle Ch. of Brethren, Pa., 1957-60; asst. prof. religion, philosophy Juniata Coll., Huntingdon, Pa., 1960-64, Drexel Hill Ch. of Brethren, 1964-70; subject cataloger religion Libr. Congress, Washington, 1968—. Author: The Sermon the Mount, 1975, the Parables of Jesus, 1979, The Buggies Still Run, 1983, The Lives of Jesus, 1985; editor Brethren Life and Thought, 1981-90. Mem. Am. Theol. Libr. Assn. Democrat.

KITAGAWA, JOSEPH MITSUO, religion educator, university dean; b. Osaka, Japan, Mar. 8, 1915; s. Chiyokichi and Kumi (Nozaki) K.; m. Evelyn Mae Rose, July 22, 1946; 1 child, Anne Rose. BA, Rikkyo U., 1937; PhD, U. Chgo., 1951. Assoc. prof. history of religion U. Chgo., 1959-64, prof., 1964—, dean Div. Sch., 1970—. Author: Religions of the East, 1969, rev. edit. , 1968, Gibt es ein Verstehen fremder Religionen, 1963, Religion in Japanese History, 1965, Gendai-Sekai to Shukyo-gaku, 1985, On Understanding Japanese Religion, 1987, The Quest for Human Unity, 1990; co-editor: The History of Religions: Essays in Methodology, 1959, Folk Religion in Japan, 1968, Myths and Symbols: Studies in Honor of M. Eliade, 1969, Introduction to the History of Religions, 1987, Essays in the History of Religionss, 1987, Buddhism and Asian History, 1989, Gendai Meicho-Zenshue, 8 Vols., 1060-66, Ency. Religion, (16 vols.), 1987; translator: The Great Asian Religions; editor: The Comparative Study of Religions, 1858, Modern Trends in Worls Religions, 1959, The History of Religions: Essays on the Problem of Understanding, 1967, Understanding and Believing, 1968, Understanding Modern China, 1969, American Refugee Policy: Ethical and Religious Reflections, 1984, The History of Religions: Retrospect and Prospect, 1985, The Religious Traditions of Asia, 1989, Religious Studies, Theological Studies and the University-Divinity School, 1991. Mem. Am. Coun. Learned Socs., Am. Soc. Study Religions (pres. 1969-72), Am. Acad. Religion, Internat. Assn. History Religions (v.p. 1975—), Assn. Religious Studies in Japan, Fund for Theol. Edn. Home: 5512 Woodlawn Ave Chicago IL 60637 Office: U Chgo Div Sch Chicago IL 60615

KITBUNCHU, MICHAEL MICHAI CARDINAL, archbishop of Bangkok; b. Samphran, Thailand, Jan. 24, 1929. Ordained priest Roman Catholic Ch., 1959; rector minor sem., Bangkok, 1965-72; consecrated archbishop of Bangkok, 1973; elevated to Sacred Coll. of Cardinals, 1983 (1st cardinal from Thailand); titular ch., St. Laurence in Panisperna. Mem. Congregation for Evangelization of Peoples. Address: 51 Assumption Cathedral, Bangrak, Bangkok 10500, Thailand

KITTS, ELBERT WALKER, minister; b. Knoxville, Tenn., Apr. 12, 1939; s. Robert Theodore and Armanda (VanDerGriff) K.; m. Ellen Abner, May 11, 1956; children: David, Donna, Timothy, Ronald, Daniel, Paul, Jonathan, Angela. Ordained to ministry Bapt. Ch., 1965. Evangelist Tex. Valley Bapt. Ch., Knoxville, 1961-65; pastor Centerview Bapt. Ch., Knoxville, 1965-68, Valley Grove Bapt. Ch., Maynardville, Tenn., 1968-70, Emory Valley Bapt. Ch., Knoxville, 1970-74, Pleasant Hill Bapt. Ch., Powell, Tenn., 1974-84, Grace Missionary Bapt. Ch., Knoxville, 1985—; founder, dir. TV and radio ministry Old Time Bapt. Hour, Knoxville, 1976-90; exec. dir. Bapts. United in Missions, Knoxville, 1982-89; founder, bd, dirs. Proclaiming Jesus to the World, St. Christopher and Nevis, 1982-90. Editor, pub. Bapts. United in Missions News Jour., 1982-90. Mem. bd. advisors Nat. Home Health, Inc., Knoxville, 1983; chmn. Midland Assn. for Endowment, Jefferson City, 1983-86, Midland Assn. Tenn. Bapt. Children's Home Endowment, 1990-91. Republican. Home: Knoxville TN Office: PO Box 5873 Knoxville TN 37928 *We have an unequivocal salvation through the Gospel. Let us approach the moral decay of this generation with this sword of the Lord. God never gives us a dream without giving us the ability to accomplish it.*

KIWIET, JOHN JOHANNES, religion educator; b. Wildervank, The Netherlands, Apr. 1, 1925; came to U.S. 1962; s. Hindrik and Jacoba G. (Blaauw) K.; m. Margaret E. Barendregt, Dec. 19, 1951; children: Eva Marie, Hendrik, Talitha, Peter, Nicoline. BTh, U. Utrecht, The Netherlands, 1950, ThD, 1952; BD, Bapt. Theol. Sem., Rüschlikon, Switzerland, 1954; PhD cum laude, U. Zürich, Switzerland, 1956. Tchr., vice-prin. Dutch Bapt. Sem., Utrecht, 1957-62; assoc. prof. Ch. History No. Bapt. Theol. Sem., Oakbrook, Ill., 1962-64, prof. Hist. Theology, 1964-67; prof. Theology Southwestern Bapt. Theol. Sem., Ft. Worth, 1968—. Author: Pilgram Marbeck, 1958, Hans Kung, 1985; contbr. articles to profl. jours. Mem. Am. Soc. Religion, Cath. Seminar an 2d Century. Office: Southwestern Bapt Theol Sem 2001 W Seminary Dr Fort Worth TX 76122-0128 *Love is creative. We should, therefore, trust the ultimate outcome of world events as well as engage constructively in our individual challenges.*

KIZER, CHARLES ANDREW, evangelist; b. Huntington, Tenn., July 17, 1949; s. Charles Freddie and Mackey Ruth (Cole) K.; m. Mary Jane Colvett, Aug. 2, 1969; children: Drew, Ashley, MacKenzie, Barton. BS, U. Tenn., 1971; cert. Brown Trail Sch. Preaching, 1979. Evangelist, Bedford Ch. of Christ, Tex., 1979-82, Howe Ch. of Christ, Tex., 1982—; dean, instr. Brown Trail Sch. of Preaching, Hurst, Tex., 1979-82. Mem. Bd. Parks and Recreation, Howe, 1983-84; com. chmn. Grayson County Lectrs. Com., Grayson County, Tex., 1984-85. Served with USAR, 1971-77. Club: Lions (pres. 1984-85, chmn. rodeo com. 1985, 86, 87). Avocations: music, guitar, voice. Home: PO Box 1094 Howe TX 75059 Office: Ch of Christ PO Box 275 Howe TX 75059

KJOLLER, JOHN KAI, minister; b. Holyoke, Mass., June 2, 1936; s. Kai Emil and Ruth Olga (Zaumseil) K.; m. Elizabeth Mehrtens, Dec. 27, 1959; children: John Kai Jr., Catherine Elizabeth, Marie Louise, Andrew Charles. BA, Valparaiso U., 1958; MDiv, Concordia Sem., 1973. Ordained to ministry Evang. Luth. Ch. Am., 1962. Min. Trinity Ch., St. Francis, Kans., 1962-64, Resurrection Ch., Cairo, N.Y., 1964-68; sr. min. St. Andrew's Ch., Ridgefield, Conn., 1968—; coord. pastoral care Ridgefield Hospice, 1983—; commr. Christian Conf. of Conn., 1979—. Contbr. articles to religious periodicals. Bd. dirs. Mid-Fairfield Hospice, Inc., Norwalk, Conn. Mem. Ridgefield Clergy Assn. (pres. 1977-82), Toastmasters, Lions. Home: 40 Ivy Hill Rd Ridgefield CT 06877 Office: St Andrews Ch 6 Ivy Hill Rd Ridgefield CT 06877

KLAASEN, MARY GREEN, management consultant; b. Dallas, June 18, 1942. BS, U. Houston, 1963; MA, Mich. State U., 1967; postgrad., Tulane U., 1969-70, U. New Orleans, 1979-81. Sales clk. Laufman's Jewelers, Houston, 1959-60; sales person Liberty's, London, 1963-64; instr. Mich. State U., East Lansing, 1966-69; owner, mgr. Logos Bookstore, New Orleans, 1971-81; mgmt. cons. M. Klaasen & Co., New Orleans, 1981—; Mgmt. trainer Mgmt. Tree Systems, Dallas, 1984—; bd. dirs. Galilean Bookstore, Houston, 1986—. Editor The Logos, 1983-84, Mgmt. Tree Systems newsletters, 1986-87. Mem. Am. Soc. Tng. and Devel., Assn. of Logos Bookstores (dir. mktg and advt. 1983-85, bd. dirs. 1977-80, 87—), Women's Bus. Owners of Am., New Orleans-Gulf South Booksellers (sec. 1986-87). Home: 1728 Cadiz New Orleans LA 70115 Office: 1728 Cadiz New Orleans LA 70115

KLADIAS, NIKOLAOS ANTONIOS, priest, school teacher; b. Chios, Greece, Jan. 4, 1964; s. Antonios Nikolaos and Evanthia (Skandalis) K.; m. Kalliope Fitousis, Aug. 31, 1986; children: Antonios, Aggeliki. Degree in teaching and religion, Ecclesiastici Pediagogiki Acad, Thessalonki, Greece, 1984. Sch. tchr. various schs., Chios, 1985-87; chanter Constantine and Helen Greek Orthodox Cathedral, Merrillville, Ind., 1987-88; priest, Village of Pitios, Chios, Greece, 1989—, also sch. tchr. Home: Pitios, 82300 Chios Greece

KLAFEHN, RICHARD KARL, minister; b. Clarkson, N.Y., Mar. 30, 1957; s. Karl Wayne and Barbara Ann (Hays) K.; m. Judith Lynn Romzek, July 30, 1983; children: Zachary Richard, Joshua Luther. BA in Philosophy, Valparaiso U., 1979; postgrad., Yale U., 1979-80; MDiv, Trinity Luth. Sem., Columbus, Ohio, 1983; ThM in Systematic Theology, Luth. Sch. Theology, Chgo., 1986. Ordained to ministry Luth. Ch., 1983. Pastor Bethany and Bethel Luth. Chs., Olean and Portville, N.Y., 1990—; asst. pastor Edison Park Luth. Ch., Chgo., 1983-84; pastor St. Paul Luth. Ch., Pontiac, Ill., 1985-90; v.p. Greater Olean (N.Y.) Assn. Chs., 1990-91; pres. Pontiac Area Ministerial Assn., 1986-89; mem. Bd. for Life Mission in Congregation, Ill., Am. Luth. Ch., Chgo., 1985-87; me. com. on ch. in soc. Upstate N.Y. Synod, Evang. Luth. Ch. in Am., 1991—; bd. dirs. Lake Chautauguz Luth. Camp, Bemus Point, N.Y., 1991—. Asst. translator: Martin Luther: His Road to Reformation, 1985; contbr. articles to newspapers and jours. Bd. dirs. Inst. for Human Resources, Pontiac, 1987-90, Pastoral Counseling Svcs., Jamestown, N.Y., 1990—; mem. Bread for the World, Washington, 1983-90. Home: 1105 W Washington St Olean NY 14760 Office: Bethany/Bethel Luth Parish 106 S 6th St Olean NY 14760

KLAIMAN, MIRIAM HOLLY, educator; b. Washington, Feb. 8, 1953; d. Maurice Hirst and Rose (Axelrod) K. BA summa cum laude, U. Pitts., 1974; MA, U. Chgo., 1976, PhD, 1980. Rsch. fellow U. Minn., Mpls., 1990—. Translator, annotator: Singing the Glory of Lord Krishna: Baru Candidasas Srikrsnakirtana, 1984; contbr. articles to profl. publs. Fulbright fellow, 1975-76; Am. Inst. Indian Studies grantee, 1974, 78, 91. Mem. Am. Acad. Religion, Linguistic Soc. Am. Home: 1653 Frost Ave Maplewood MN 55109 *Success in passing courses unfortunately doesn't entail success in passing life.*

KLAPERMAN, GILBERT, rabbi, comparative law educator, religious organization administrator; b. N.Y.C., Feb. 25, 1921; s. Louis and Frieda (Rubenstein); m. Libby Mindlin, Aug. 23, 1942 (dec. 1982); children: Judith Reena Goldman, Joel Simcha, Frieda Lisa, Carol Nechama Morrow; m. Susan Cacher Alter, Dec. 29, 1985. BA, Yeshiva Coll., 1940; rabbi, Yeshiva U., 1941; MA, State U. Iowa, 1946; DHL, Yeshiva U., 1955, DD, 1971; JD, Hofsta U., 1978. Rabbi and Hillel dir. Queens U., Kingston, Ont., Can., 1942-43; prof. Sch. Religion and Hillel dir. State U. Iowa, 1943-45; rabbi West New York, N.J., lectr. Yeshiva U., 1945-47; rabbi Congregation Brith Shalom, Charleston, S.C., 1947-50, Congregation Beth Sholom, Lawrence, N.Y., 1950—; prof. sociology Yeshiva U., 1957-67; prof. Judaic studies Lehman Coll., N.Y., 1973-75; prof. sociology Stern Coll., Yeshiva U., from 1979; prof. comparative law Hofstra U., from 1989; pres. Synagogue Coun. Am., N.Y.C., 1988—. Author: (with Libby Klaperman) The Story of the Jewish People, 4 vols., 1961, How and Why Wonder Book of the Old Testament, 1964, The Story of Yeshiva University, 1969, Programmed Instruction Course in Jewish History, 1970, numerous articles and revs. Chmn. bd. trustees Yad Harav Herzog, Israel, 1969—; pres. Nat. Jewish Book Coun., 1962-66; pres. N.Y. Bd. Rabbis, 1968-70; chmn. Greater N.Y. Conf. on Soviet Jewry, 1970-72; pres. Yeshiva Coll. Alumni; chmn. Nat. Rabbinical ORT Com.; mem. first rabbinical del. to countries behind iron curtain, 1958. Ret. Res. capt. Can. Chaplaincy. Mem. Rabbinical Coun. Am. (v.p. 1978-82, pres. 1982-84), Synagogue Coun. Am. (pres. 1987-89), Rabbinical Alumni Yeshiva U. (v.p. from 1978). Office: Synagogue Coun of Am 327 Lexington Ave New York NY 10016

KLARENBEEK, HENRIETTA, minister; b. Rock Rapids, Iowa, Jan. 30, 1955; d. Cebus Martin and Johanna Christina (Wildeman) K.; m. Terry Van Kolk (div. 1973); children: Kandice Leigh, Kristin Mare. BA in Music and Edn., Westmar Coll., 1979; MDiv in Religious Edn., St. Paul Sch. of Theology, 1985. Ordained to ministry Methodist Ch. as deacon, 1984, as elder, 1988. Student asst. Crossroads Reformed Ch., Overland Park, Kans., 1983-84; student pastor Daugherty United Meth. Ch., Harrisonville, Mo., 1984-86, East Lynne (Mo.) United Meth. Ch., 1984-86; chaplain trainee Osawatomie (Kans.) State Hosp., 1985-86; assoc. pastor Spirit Lake (Iowa) United Meth. Ch., 1986—. Guest lectrs. Iowa Lakes Community coll., Estherville, 1987, Northwest Iowa Tech. Sch., Sheldon, 1988; alternate del. Dickinson County Jackson for Pres., Spirit Lake, 1988. Fellow AAUW, Iowa Chpt. Christian Educator, Iowa Women in Ministry, Northwest Cluster Iowa Christian Educators (chmn. 1987—); mem. Dickinson County Ministerial Assn. (pres. 1986-87). Democrat. Avocations: sewing, walking. Office: Spirit Lake United Meth Ch 1812 Gary St PO Box 253 Spirit Lake IA 51360

KLASSEN, ELMER GLEN, religious publishing executive; b. Hillsboro, Kans., July 2, 1929; s. David S. and Anna (Friesen) K.; m. Leonore Grace Friesen, Mar. 27, 1988. Pub. Herold-Verlag, Frankfurt, Fed. Republic Germany, 1957-83, Herald of His Coming, Newton, Kans., 1988—; pres. Gospel Revivals, Inc. Republican. Office: Herald of His Coming 304 N Main St Newton KS 67117-0886 *The right message at the right time has eternal values.*

KLASSEN, JACOB M., retired church administrator; b. Steinfeld, Sagradowka, Ukraine, USSR, Feb. 12, 1929; arrived in Can., 1930; s. Jacob and Aganetha (Martens) K.; m. Katherine Thiessen, July 2, 1950; children: Martha, Lorna. BA, U. Man., Can., 1969, BE, 1970; LLD (hon.), U. Waterloo, 1989. Dir. Mennonite Cen. Com., Taegu, Republic of Korea, 1958-61; asst. dir. overseas Mennonite Cen. Com., Akron, Pa., 1961-63; exec. dir. Mennonite Cen. Com. Can., Winnipeg, Man., 1963-70, 76-84, ret., 1984; moderator River East Mennonite Brethren Ch., Winnipeg, 1966-75, Mennonite Brethren Conf., 1972-74, asst. moderator, 1970-72, 80-81. Home: 102-1880 Henderson Hwy, Winnipeg, MB Canada R2G 1P2 *Whoever wants to be great, must be your servant, and whoever wants to be first must be the willing slave of all. Matthew 20: 26-27 (NEB).*

KLAUBER, MARTIN INNIS, religion educator; b. N.Y.C., Dec. 19, 1956; s. Martin Arthur and Virginia Ellen (McInnis) K.; m. Barbara J. Branson, May 30, 1987. BA, U. Buffalo, 1978; MA, MDiv, Trinity Divinity Sch., Deerfield, Ill., 1981; MA, PhD, U. Wis., 1987. Lectr. Trinity Coll., Deerfield, 1988—; asst. prof. U. Iowa, Iowa City, 1987; instr. Trinity Divinity Sch., Deerfield, Ill., 1987-88. Contbr. articles to profl. jours. Mem. Am. Hist. Assn., Am. Acad. Religion, Am. Soc. Ch. History, Conf. on Faith & History. Mem. Evang. Covenant Ch. Home: 34230 N Birch Ln Gurnee IL 60031 Office: Trinity Coll 2077 W Half Day Rd Deerfield IL 60015

KLAUS, KENNETH SHELDON, church musician; b. Baton Rouge, La., Oct. 1, 1952; s. Kenneth Blanchard and Marian Ida (Fyler) K.;m. Phebe Darlene Arceneaux, Aug. 16, 1975; children: Christopher Fyler, Michael Calvin. MusB, La. State U., 1974, MusM, 1976, PhD, 1983. Bass soloist St. James Episcopal Ch., Baton Rouge, summer 1972; dir. music Blackwater United Meth. Ch., Baker, La., 1972-79; interim dir. music Goodwood Bapt. Ch., Baton Rouge, summer 1980; dir. music First United Meth. Ch., Brookhaven, Miss., 1981-84, Houma, La., 1985—; violist Baton Rouge Symphony Orch., 1971-79; dir. choral music Nicholls State U., Thibodaux, La., 1979-84, dir. choral activities, 1984—; vocal soloist New Orleans Opera, Miss. Opera, Baton Rouge Symphony, Concert Choir New Orleans, Choral Acadienne, Jefferson Performing Arts Soc., Copiah-Lincoln Community coll., Wesson, Miss., others; choral music clinician various high schs. and jr. high schs. in La. and Miss., ch. music workshops; adjudicator dist. and regional choral festivals in La. and Miss., solo/ensemble festivals in La. and Miss.; conductor various choirs. Author: Chamber Music for Solo Voice and Instruments since 1960, 1992; author book and music revs. The Choral Jour., 1985—. Bd. mem. Thibodaux Playhouse, Inc., 1987-89. Mem. Fellowship United Meths. in Worship, Music and Other Arts (rep. La. conf. Acadiana dist.), Nat. Assn. Tchrs. Singing (Miss. artist award 1980), Am. Choral Dirs. Assn. (La. student activities chmn. 1985—), Music Educators Nat. Conf., La. Music Educators Assn., Music Tchrs. Nat. Assn. (nat. cert. voice tchr.), La. Music Tchrs. Assn. Home: 410 Winder Rd Thibodaux LA 70301 Office: Nicholls State U Dept Music Thibodaux LA 70310 *As we go through this life, God help us not to become prisoners of our own minds.*

KLAVEN, LOUISA ANNE, pastoral counselor; b. Bklyn., July 16, 1953; d. Karl A. and Tally (Addonizio) K.; m. David Allen Naugle, Sept. 19, 1981. BA, Wagner Coll., 1975; M in Arts and Religion, Luth. Theol. Sem., 1979. Cert. lay profl. Student tchr. Brentwood (N.J.) Pub. Schs., 1980; English tutor Luth. Service Assn., Bloomsburg, Pa., 1980-81; dir. Christian edn. St. Matthew Luth. Ch., Bloomsburg, 1980-81; ski chaplain Luth. Theol. Sem., Gettysburg, Pa., 1981; supply pastor Cen. Pa. Synod/Luth. Ch., Pa. and Md., 1981-83; pastoral asst. Emanuel Luth. Ch., Worchester, Mass., 1983-89; assoc. in ministry, supply pastor New eng. Synod, 1989—; dir. Christian edn. Bethel Luth. Ch., Auburn, Mass., 1990—. Group leader Crop Walk for Hunger, Worchester, 1984-85. Mem. New Eng. Lay Profl. Orgn., Alpha Tau Mu. Avocations: dollhouse making, knitting, aerobics, gardening, raising birds.

KLEIN, ANNE CAROLYN, religious studies educator; b. N.Y.C., June 20, 1947; d. Ludovic and Isabelle Leslie (Duscinsky) K.; m. Harvey B. Aronson, Jan. 9, 1976. BA in English with highest honors, SUNY, Binghamton, 1969; MA in Buddhist Studies, U. Wis., 1971; PhD in Religious Studies, U. Va., 1981. Lectr. rsch. assoc. woman's studies Harvard U., Cambridge, Mass., 1982-83, vis. scholor, Ctr. Study of World Religions, 1983-84; acting asst. prof. Stanford (Calif.) U., 1984-89; asst. prof. Rice U., Houston, 1989-91, assoc. prof., 1991—; mem. adv. bd. women and religion programs Harvard U. Div. Sch., 1988—; mem. adv. com. Rockefeller Found., N.Y.C., 1990. Author: Knowledge and Liberation, 1986; author, trans: Knowing, Naming and Negation, 1991; editor: Tantric Practice in Nyingma, 1984, The Tantric Distinction; edit. bd. Pacific World, 1989—, Jour. Feminist Studies in Religion, 1988—; contbr. articles to profl. jours. Grantee NEH, 1987, Fulbright Found., 1980. Mem. Am. Acad. Religion (steering com. Buddhist studies sect. 1984—). Office: Rice U Dept Religious Studies Box 1892 Houston TX 77251

KLEIN, BARRY PHILLIP, clergyman; b. Litchfield, Minn., Oct. 5, 1956; s. H. Phillip and Shirley Ann (West) K.; m. Cynthia Ann Cary, Aug. 11, 1979; children: Renee, Erick, Samuel. BA, Minn. Bible Coll., 1978; MA, Lincoln Christian Sem., 1983; M of Ministry, Ky. Christian Coll., 1987; postgrad., Northwest Grad. Sch. Ministry, 1991—. Ordained to ministry Christian Ch., Ch. of Christ, 1978. Youth minister Ch. of Christ, Janesville, Wis., 1977, 79; pastor Ch. of Christ, Truman, Minn., 1981-85, Clarksville, Iowa, 1985-87, Nevis, Minn., 1987—; alumni pres. Minn. Bible Coll., Rochester, Minn., 1983-85; treas. Park Rapids (Minn.) Ministerial Assn., 1990-91; chmn. pornography Task Force Park Rapids Ministerial, 1989-90. Chmn. Cystic Fibrosis Bike-A-/Thon, Nevis, 1989; scoutmaster Boy Scouts Am. Troop 56, Nevis, 1988-91. Named Outstanding Young Minister North Am. Christian Conv., 1989, Outstanding Young Men Am., 1989. Mem. Comml. Club (treas. 1983-85). Republican. Home: 443 W Main Nevis MN 56467 Office: Ch of Christ 101 E Pleasant Nevis MN 56467 *An all pervasive (moment by moment) sense of wonder can and should permeate our lives as we realize what it means to have God bother with us at all. When Christian Scripture tells us that "all things hold together in Him," that is as far reaching as the expanse of the universe to relationships to the chair I sit on.*

KLEIN, DIXIE E., religious education administrator; b. Watertown, S.D., May 9, 1950; d. Mancel Arthur and Marvel (Catherine) Lee; m. Gerry Anthony Klein, Apr. 8, 1970; children: Kristifir, Susan, Brock. BA, Valley City State U., 1973; MEd, U. N.D., 1988. Cert. elem. edn. adminstr., tchr. elem./secondary music, spl. edn., pre-sch. handicapped. Elem. tchr. St. Rose Cath. Sch., Great Bend, Kans., 1980-84; tchr. St. Anthony's Ch., Linton, N.D., 1985-86, lay eucharistic minister, 1985-87; elem. prin. St. Alphonsus Sch., Langdon, N.D., 1989—; dir. religious edn., St. Alphonsus Sch., 1989-91. Recipient scholarship N.D. Bd. Higher Edn., Univ. N.D., Grand Forks, 1988, awards Govs. Com. on Children and Youth, Bismarck, N.D., 1990, others. Mem. N.D. Assn. for Edn. of Young Children, Nat. Assn. Edn. of Young Children, Nat. Assn. Elem. Sch. Prins., Nat. Assn. Elem. Sch. Prins., Nat. Cath. Edn. Assn., N.D. Coun. Sch. Adminstrs. Home: Rte 1 Po Box 123 Langdon ND 58249 Office: St Alphonsus Catholic Sch 209 10th Ave Langdon ND 58249

KLEIN, ELIZABETH ARCHER, clergywoman; b. Richmond, Calif., Oct. 15, 1963; d. George William and Donna (Garman) Archer; m. Jeffrey Marshal Klein, Feb. 14, 1987. AB, Stanford U., 1985; MDiv, Fuller Theol. Sem., Pasadena, Calif., 1989. Ordained to ministry Presbyn. Ch. as reverend, 1990. Intern Knox Presbyn. Ch., Pasadena, 1988-89; pastor San Martin (Calif.) Presbyn. Ch., 1990—. Mem. San Jose Prebyn. Assn., The Fellowship (assoc.). Avocations: environmental action, apologetics, poetry, sports, horse-back riding. Office: San Martin Prebyn Ch 13200 Lincoln Ave San Martin CA 95046 *Many, many people today willfully choose to live in darkness—it is somehow comforting. I will choose to approach the light, however harsh, for it is only in light that one sees truth clearly.*

KLEIN, JAMES EDWIN, minister; b. Oakes, N.D., Jan. 11, 1951; s. Albert Franklin and Frances (Long) K.; m. Patricia Renee, Aug. 10, 1974; children: Jason, Katrina. BA, Vennard Coll., University Park, Iowa, 1973. Ordained elder in the Ch. of the Nazarene. Assoc. minister Evang. Meth. Ch., Cudahy, Calif., 1973-75; sr. pastor Evang. Meth. Ch., Lake Elsinore, Calif., 1975-79; asst. to the pres. World Gospel Crusades, Upland, Calif., 1979-80; field coordinator Energy Mktg., Inc., Tustin, Calif., 1981; regional v.p. A.L. Williams, Garden Grove, Calif., 1982—; minister Ch. of the Nazarene, Anaheim, Calif., 1985-89; asst. dist. supt. Evang. Meth. Ch., Stockton, Calif., 1979-81; bd. dirs. Azusa Pacific U. Scoutmaster Boy Scouts of Am., Garden Grove, Calif., 1983-85, com. chmn. Troop 1340, Anaheim, 1987—; named Eagle Scout, 1969. Mem. Inland Soc. Tax Cons., Christian Ministries Mgmt. Assn. Republican. Avocations: computers, sailing, camping. Home: 224 S Ashford Pl Fullerton CA 92631 Office: Focus Fin Svcs 2555 E Chapman Ave Ste 300 Fullerton CA 92631

KLEIN, JERRY LEE, religion educator; b. Walters, Okla., Oct. 25, 1947; s. Rudolf Anton and Mable Eula (Elliott) K.; m. Jane Ellen Keeth, Apr. 20, 1969; children: Jerry, Jr., John. AA, Cameron U., 1967; BA, Okla. Christian Univ. of Sci. and Arts, 1969; MA, Harding U., 1974; postgrad., N.Y. Inst., 1988-91. Instr. in Bible Henderson State Coll., Arkadelphia, Ark., 1970-71; pulpit minister Ch. of Christ, Comanche, Okla., 1971-75; instr. in Greek Prairie Hill Sch. of Bible, Comanche, 1974-75; pulpit minister Main St. Ch. of Christ, Lockney, Tex., 1975-82; prof. of religion Amarillo (Tex.) Coll., 1982—; dir. Amarillo Bible Chair, 1982—; edn. dir. Mountain Terrace Ch. of Christ, Memphis, Tenn., 1969-70, San Jacinto Ch. of Christ, Amarillo, 1984-89; campus coun. Amarillo Coll., 1982—, chaplain, 1990-91; steering com. Amazing Grace Campaign, Amarillo, 1990. Author: Leadership in Christ, 1976, True Worship, 1989, (children's songs) Bible Teachers Mailbox, 1988; contbr. articles to religious jours. Dir. vols. Ark. Children's Colony, Arkadelphia, 1970-71; bd. dirs. VICA, Tuscosa High Sch., 1983—; city chmn. Heart Fund and Kidney Found., Comanche, 1974-75; cubmaster Boy Scouts Am., Lockney, 1978-82; coach Little League Baseball, Lockney, 1978-82; mem. child welfare bd., Floyd County, Tex., 1980-82. Recipient spl. citation Ark. Children's Colony, 1971, certs. appreciation Tex. Dept. Health, 1982, Tex. Dept. Human Resources, 1983; named Favorite Prof. Bapt. Student Union, Amarillo Coll., 1989. Mem. Soc. Bibl. Lit., Tex. Jr. Coll. Tchrs. Assn., Bibl. Archaeol. Soc., Lions (pres. Comanche chpt. 1974-75), Rotary, Kappa Chi (sponsor 1982-91). Republican. Home: 5614 Purdue Amarillo TX 79109 Office: Amarillo Coll 2501 S Jackson Amarillo TX 79109 *Life itself can't give me joy—unless I really will it. Life just gives me time and space—it's up to me to fill it.*

KLEIN, JOEL TIBOR, psychotherapist; b. Megyaszo, Hungary, Jan. 1, 1923; came to U.S., 1957; s. Jeno and Serena (Reich) K.; m. Anna Berkovits, June 28, 1949; children: Leslie M., Judy K. PhD, U. Sci., Budapest, Hungary, 1947. Cert. pastoral counselor, N.H.; cert. sex counselor. Psychiatric chaplain VA, Downey, Ill., 1962-64, White River, Vt., 1964-77; assoc. Silverman and Assocs., Haverhill, Mass., 1973-77; pvt. practice Manchester and Bedford, N.H., 1977—; bd. examiners N.H., 1979-83; mem. Interdisciplinary Team on Child Abuse and Neglect Div. Children and Youth, Manchester, 1983. Fellow Am. Assn. Pastoral Counselors (regional membership com., legis. com.), Am. Assn. Marriage and Family Therapy (approved supr., pres. N.H. unit 1984-86), Am. Assn. Sex Educators, Counselors and Therapists; mem. Am. Psychol. Assn., N.H. Psychol. Orgn. (exec. bd.). Home: 562 Fairfield St Manchester NH 03104-2857 Office: 51 Riverway Pl Bedford NH 03110-6748 *As long as I am able to keep my two eyes open, my two ears sensitive to perceive changes and to remain able to adopt to them, I feel young, vigorous and alive. If you ever see me, please, don't greet me, "I had not seen you for years, you haven't changed." If you do, I take it not as a compliment, but as an insult.*

KLEIN, SISTER LORRAINE MARGARET, religious school administrator, nun; b. Woodbury, N.J., Jan. 9, 1955; d. Norbert H. and Theresa H. (Paul) K. AAS in Med. Technology, Camden County Coll., 1975; BA in Life Sci., Glassboro State Coll., 1978; MA in Religious Studies, St. Charles Borrameo Sem., 1987; MA in Elem. Adminstrn., Glassboro State Coll., 1992. Joined Franciscan Missionary Sisters of Infant Jesus, Roman Cath. Ch., 1977. Med. technologist Our Lady of Lourdes Hosp., Camden, N.J., 1975-77; tchr. St. Margaret's Sch., Woodbury Heights, N.J., 1980-81, Holy Cross Sch., Rumson, N.J., 1981-88; prin. St. Margaret's Sch., Woodbury Heights, N.J., 1988—. Mem. ASCD, Nat. Coun. Tchrs. Math., N.J. State Sci. Tchrs. Assn. Office: St Margarets Sch 3rd St Woodbury Heights NJ 08097

KLEIN, MARY KAY, academic administrator. Pres. Swedenborg Sch. Religion, Newton, Mass. Office: Swedenborg Sch Religion 48 Sargent St Newton MA 02158*

KLEIN, WILLIAM WADE, religious educator; b. Weehawken, N.J., Feb. 11, 1946; s. William Carl and Eleanor (Kinkel) K.; m. Phyllis Gail Merritt, June 29, 1968; children: Alison, Sarah. BS, Wheaton (Ill.) Coll., 1967; MDiv, Denver Seminary, 1970; PhD, U. Aberdeen, Scotland, 1978. Ordained pastor Bapt. Ch., 1974. Assoc. pastor Calvary Bapt. Ch., Los Gatos, Calif., 1970-74; instr. Columbia (S.C.) Bible Coll., 1977-78; assoc. prof. Denver Seminary, 1978—. Author: The New Chosen People, 1990; contbr. articles and book revs. to profl. jours. Named one of Outstanding Young Men Am., 1978; King William scholar U. Aberdeen, 1976. Fellow Inst. for Bibl. Rsch., Tyndale Fellowship for Bibl. Rsch.; mem. Soc. Bibl. Lit., Evang. Theol. Soc. Democrat. Office: Denver Seminary Po Box 10000 Denver CO 80210

KLEINERT, HENRY BERNHARD, minister; b. Keyeser, Wis., May 5, 1917; s. Bernhard Haakon and Olena Rokne (Anfinson) K.; m. Helen Rose Peck, Aug. 2, 1940; children: Gary Bernhard, Linda Marlene Kleinert Cole. BA, Midland Coll., 1952; BD, Cen. Luth Theol. Sem., 1955. Ordained to ministry Luth. Ch. Am., 1953. Asst. pastor Luth. Meml. Ch., Madison, Wis., 1953-55; pastor Luth. chs., Black Earth, Wis., 1955-57, West Middleton, Wis., 1955-57; sr. pastor Mt. Carmel Luth. Ch., Mpls., 1961-68, 1st Luth. Ch., Ottumwa, Iowa, 1968-70, Grace Luth. Ch., Deephaven, Minn., 1971-83; pastor Vision of Glory Luth. Ch., Mpls., 1983—; adviser to Luth. Student Assn., U. Wis., Eau Claire, 1957; chaplain Midland Coll., Fremont, Nebr., 1957-61; mem. exec. bd. parish edn. com. Minn. Synod, Luth. Ch. Am., 1962-65; pres. Mpls. Ch. Athletic Assn., 1965-66; bd. dirs. Greater Mpls. Coun. Chs., sec, 1968; chmn. bd. Social Ministry, Iowa Synod, Luth. Ch. Am., 1968-70; bd. dirs. United Prayer Tower, Mpls., 1976—, New Hope Ctr., Mpls, 1984-90, pres. bd., 1988-89. Pres. Am. Bethesda Found., 1970-71; mem. Capital Long Range Improvements Com., Mpls., 1973-75, Mpls. Bd. Ethics, 1967; bd. dirs. Minn. Group Homes, chmn. 1974-75, YMCA, Mpls., 1963-67, YMCA, Ottumwa, Iowa, 1968-70, Vols. Am., Mpls., 1973-75. Home: 12300 Marion Ln Minnetonka MN 55343 Office: 13200 Highway 55 Minneapolis MN 55441

KLEM, HERBERT VIELE, religion educator; b. N.Y.C., Jan. 9, 1937; s. Arthur Christian and Jessie Mable (Fisher) K.; m. Barbara Hellen Gustavson, July 8, 1961; children: Jonathan H., Daan A., C. Kristen. BA, Gordon Coll., Wenham, Mass., 1959; MS in Edn., Hofstra U., 1963; MDiv, Gordon-Conwell Theol. Sem., South Hamilton, Mass., 1971; D Missions, Fuller Theol. Sem., Pasadena, Calif., 1977. Ordained to ministry Bellerose Bapt. Ch., 1965. Tchr. East N.Y. Tech. and Vocat. High Sch., Bklyn., 1960-62, 65-66; missionary, lectr. Titcombe Coll., Sudan Interior Mission, Egbe, Nigeria, 1966-68, Igbaja (Nigeria) Sem., Sudan Interior Mission, 1968-73; edn. cons., project dir. Daystar Communications, Naibori, Kenya, 1973-78; vis. prof. cross-cultural communications Wheaton (Ill.) Grad. Sch., 1978-80; prof. dept. missions Bethel Sem., Arden Hills, Minn., 1980—; Africa adminstr. Living Bibles Internat., 1973-78; communications cons. Pattaya Conf. on World Evangelism, 1981; active confs. throughout U.S.; cons., seminar leader for chs. and outreach orgns. in areas world missions and ch. communications, African oral art and evangelism in Africa and U.S.; cons. bd. world missions Bapt. Gen. Conf., Arlington Heights, Ill., 1982—, also cons. to Mex. missionaries, mem. advanced planning com., com. on devel. ministries, Commn. on Evangelism. Author: Toward the Oral Communication of Scripture, 1982; contbr. articles to religious publs. Bd. dirs. Mission: Moving Mountains, Mpls., 1983—, pres., 1985-86, v.p. 1986-90; bd. dirs. Kenya Children's Fund, Mpls., 1986—. Mem. Am. Soc. Missiology, Evang. Theol. Soc., Religious Speech Communication Assn., World Assn. for Christian Communications, Fellowship Evang. Profs. Mission. Avocations: skiing, sailing, automobile repair, carpentry. Office: Bethel Theol Sem Dept Missions 3949 Bethel Dr Saint Paul MN 55112

KLEM, STEVEN MICHAEL, lay worker; b. Chgo., Apr. 2, 1959; s. Joseph Frederick and Barbara Elaine (Pezzino) K.; m. Laurie Kathleen Widener, June 9, 1990. Lay youth worker St. Peters Episcopal Ch., Jacksonville, Fla., 1986-87; asst. youth leader St. Mark's Episcopal Ch., Jacksonville, 1987-88; youth dir. St. Margarets Episcopal Ch., Green Cove, Fla., 1988—; clerical supr. Univ. of Fla. Bookstore, Gainesville, 1989—. With USN, 1977-82. Republican. Home: 1694 NW 19th Lane Gainesville FL 32605

KLEMM, DAVID EUGENE, religion educator; b. Dekalb, Ill., Apr. 15, 1947; s. Eugene W. and Pamela (Mawdsley) K.; m. Joyce Rush (div. 1975); 1 child, Matthew; m. Gretchen Peden, Dec. 23, 1978; children: Hannah, Stephen. Student, Williams Coll., Williamstown, Mass., 1965-67, Marlboro (Vt.) Coll., 1970-72; PhD, U. Iowa, 1980. Assoc. prof. Religion U. Iowa, Iowa City, 1982—. Author: Hermeneutical Theory of Paul Ricoeur, 1983; author, editor: Hermeneutical Theory, 1987. Mem. Am. Acad. Religion. Democrat. Home: 128 Columbia Dr Iowa City IA 52245 Office: Sch Religion 310 Gillmore Hall U Iowa Iowa City IA 52242

KLEMM, LOWELL ERWIN, parochial school educator, principal; b. Chgo., Nov. 11, 1940; s. Erwin Adolph and Ruth Ann (Fasse) K.; m. Karen Anne Stoppenhagen, June 13, 1964; children: Bryan David, Sheryl Lynn. BA, Concordia Tchrs. Coll., River Forest, Ill., 1963, MA, 1971. Cert. elem. sch. tchr. Tchr., youth dir. St. Paul's Luth. Ch., Aurora, Ill., 1963-76, prin., tchr., 1983—; prin., tchr. Trinity Luth. Ch., Elkhart, Ind., 1976-83. Bd. regents Concordia U., River Forest, 1989—. Mem. Luth. Edn. Assn., Dept. Elem. Luth. Sch. Prins., ASCD,. Home: 725 Bangs St Aurora IL 60505

KLEMPNAUER, CRAIG STEPHEN, clergyman; b. Kansas City, Mo., Mar. 31, 1956; s. Richard Gordon and Beverly Jean (Lobaugh) K.; m. Christi Lynn Price, Aug. 24, 1979; children: Chad Stephen, Courtney Lynn. BA, Hardin-Simmons U., 1980; MRE, Southwestern Sem., 1982. Lic. to ministry Bapt. Ch., 1976, ordained, 1983. Assn. youth dir. Palo Pinto Assn., Mineral Wells, Tex., 1980-81; youth minister First Bapt. Ch., Amarillo, Tex., 1986—. Mem. Youth Ministers Metro Assn., Alpha Phi Omega (life). Republican. Home: 6228 Belpree Amarillo TX 79106 Office: First Bapt Ch Tyler at 13th St Amarillo TX 79101

KLENICKI, LEON, civic organization administrator; b. Buenos Aires, Sept. 7, 1930; came to U.S., 1959; s. Isaias and Inda (Kuzewika) K.; m. Ana Raquel Klenicki, Aug. 1959 (div. 1983); m. Myra Cohen, Nov. 30, 1985; children: Ruth Sharon, Daniel Raphael. BA in Philosophy, U. Cin., 1963; BA in Rabbinics, Hebrew Union Coll., Cin., 1964; MA in Hebrew Letters, Hebrew Union Coll., 1967. Ordained rabbi, 1967. Dir. World Union for Progressive Judaism, Argentina, 1968-73; dir. dept. interfaith affairs Anti-Defamation League of B'nai B'rith, N.Y.C., 1973—; prof. Jewish theology, Immaculate Conception Sem., Seton Hall U., N.J.; v.p. Stimulus Found., 1985. Author: Passover Celebration; editor: In Our Time: The Flowering of Jewish-Catholic Dialogue, A Dictionary of the Jewish-Christian Dialogue; contbr. to religious publs. Office: Anti Defamation League B'nai Brith 823 UN Pla New York NY 10017

KLEPAL, DWAYNE MICHAEL, minister; b. Mc Kees Rocks, Pa., Nov. 21, 1959; s. Ronald Lee and Gerri (Cokus) K.; m. Kimberly Ann Whaley, Sept. 7, 1983; children: Ashlee Elizabeth, Taylor Dwayne. B of Religious Edn., Great Lakes Bible Coll., Lansing, Mich., 1983. Ordained to ministry Ch. of Christ, 1984. Youth min. Allen Park (Mich.) Christian Ch., 1980-82; student advisor Great Lakes Bible Coll., Lansing, 1981-83; youth min. Westhills Christian Ch., Corapolis, Pa., 1984-90, assoc. min., 1990—; sec.-treas. Greater Pitts. Ministerial Assn., 1987-89; com. chair. Pa. Christian Teen Conv., Hershy, 1987-89; dean Camp Christian, Mill Run, Pa., 1987—; youth dir. Ea. Christian Conv., 1987; seminar leader N. Am. Christian Conv., 1987-89; chair. bd. dirs. His Place, Pitts., 1989—. Coach Moon High Sch., Coraopolis, 1986-89. Recipient Cert. Appreciation Am. Assn. Ret. Persons, Mc Kees Rocks, 1986. Home: 1316 Main St Coraopolis PA 15108 Office: West Hills Christian Ch 965 Thorn Run Rd Coraopolis PA 15108

KLETT, DENNIS R., clergyman, school administrator; b. Massilon, Ohio, Mar. 10, 1952; s. Louis V. and Grace E. (Venables) K.; m. Kathy Lou Rinehart, June 6, 1970; children: Julie Ann, Jennifer Lynn. BDiv, Arlington (Tex.) Bapt. Coll., 1973; M Christian Edn., Uniontown (Pa.) Bapt. Coll., 1981, D Christian Ministries, 1983. Asst. pastor Victory Bapt. Ch., West Portsmouth, Ohio, 1973-74, Sycamore Bapt. Ch., Jackson, Mich., 1974-76, Reimer Rd. Bapt. Ch., Wadsworth, Ohio, 1976-77; pastor Fundamental Bapt. Ch., St. Petersburg, Pa., 1977-79; pastor, adminstr. Calvary Bapt. Ch. and Acad., Pitts., 1979-84; pastor Pensacola (Fla.) Bapt. Temple, 1984-85; pastor, adminstr. Temple Bapt. Ch. and Temple Christian Sch., 1985—; v.p. N.E. Ohio Youth Fellowship, Akron, 1976-77; pres. Calvary Bible Inst., Pitts., 1980-82, Temple Bible Inst., Pensacola, 1986—. Author: Action Life Youth, 1975. Mem. Am. Assn. Christian Schs., Fundamental Bapt. Pastor's Fellowship, Fla. Assn. Christian Colls. and Schs., South Wide Bapt. Fellowship. Republican. Baptist. Avocations: walking, weight lifting, motorcycles. Office: Temple Bapt Ch Sch 398 N Navy Blvd Pensacola FL 32507

KLEWIN, THOMAS WILLIAM, minister; b. Sheboygan, Wis., Jan. 31, 1921; s. Emil Hyman and Whilamina (Gottowske) Klewin; m. Jean Shirley McDaniel, Feb. 8, 1947; children: Michael, Diana, Leslie Ellen, Matthew, Shelley. BA, Concordia Sem., St. Louis, 1943, BD, 1945; MA in European History, Washington U., St. Louis, 1946; MST, Drew Sem., Madison, N.J., 1951; BS in Anthropology, Stockton State Coll., Pomona, N.J., 1977. Ordained to ministry Luth. Ch., 1946. Missionary-at-large Mo. Synod, N.J., N.Y., 1946-47; min. Trinity Luth. Ch., Morristown, N.J., 1947-51; commd. 1st lt., chaplain USAF, 1951; exec. dir. P.E.I. Human Rights Commn., Charlottetown, Can., 1979-88; advanced through grades to lt. col. USAF, 1966, ret., 1973. Author: Love Thy Teenager, 1971, Thinking of Drinking, 1972, (with Jean Klewin) When the Man You Love is an Alcoholic, 1980; contbr. numerous articles to profl . jours. Chaplain Kiwanis Club, Morris Plains, N.J., 1948-51; pres. Civil Liberties Assn., Charlottetown, 1977-79. Recipient award Valley Forge Freedom Found., 1963, 68, St. Martin of Tours medal Luth. Ch. Mo. Synod, 1973. Home: Box 58, Crapaud, PE Canada COA 1JO

KLIEBHAN, SISTER M(ARY) CAMILLE, academic administrator; b. Milw., Apr. 4, 1923; d. Alfred Sebastian and Mae Eileen (McNamara) K. Student, Cardinal Stritch Coll., Milw., 1945-48; B.A., Cath. Sisters Coll., Washington, 1949; M.A., Cath. U. Am., 1951, Ph.D., 1955. Joined Sisters of St. Francis of Assisi, Roman Catholic Ch., 1945; legal sec. Spence and Hanley (attys.), Milw., 1941-45; instr. edn. Cardinal Stritch Coll., 1955-62, assoc. prof., 1962-68, prof., 1968—, head dept. edn., 1962-67, dean students, 1962-64, chmn. grad. div., 1964-69, v.p. for acad. and student affairs, 1969-74, pres., also bd. dirs., 1974-91, chancellor, 1991—. Bd. dirs. Goals for Milw. 2000, 1980-83, treas. Wis. Found. Ind. Colls., 1974-79, 87-90, v.p., 1979-81, pres., 1981-83; bd. dirs. DePaul Hosp., 1982-91, Sacred Heart Sch. Theology, 1983—, Viterbo Coll., 1990—, Milw. Cath. Home, 1991—, Wis. Psychoanalytic Fedn., 1991—; mem. adv. bd. St. Camillus Campus, 1989—; bd. dirs. Internat. Inst. of Wis., 1984—, Mental Health Assn. Milwaukee County, 1983-87, Pub. Policy Forum, 1987-90, Better Bus. Bur. of Wis. Inc., 1989—; mem. TEMPO, 1982—, bd. dirs., 1986-89; bd. govs. Wis. Policy Rsch. Inst., 1987—. Mem. Am. Psychol. Assn., Rotary Club of Milw., Phi Delta Kappa, Delta Epsilon Sigma, Psi Chi, Delta Kappa Gamma, Kappa Delta Pi. *It is because of my faith that I can meet every condition with courage.*

KLIETZ, SHELDON HENRY, minister; b. Chgo., Feb. 26, 1935; s. George Henry and Edna Bertha (Neumann) K.; m. JoAnne Marie Thomas, June 7, 1959; children: Mark Thomas, Beth Jeannine, Todd Stephen. AA, Concordia Coll., 1954; BA, Concordia Theol. Sem., St. Louis, 1960. Ordained to ministry Luth. Ch.-Mo. Synod, 1960. Pastor St. Paul's Luth Chs., Campbell-Nashua, Minn., 1960-65, Grace Evang. Luth. Ch.., Hazel Crest, Ill., 1965-74, Trinity Evang. Luth. Ch., Marseilles, Ill., 1974-83, Faith Evang. Luth. Ch., Oak Lawn, Ill., 1983-91, Grace Luth. Ch. and Sch., El Centro, Calif., 1991—. Part-time chaplain Tinley Park (Ill.) Mental Health Ctr., 1965-88, Howe Developmental Ctr., Tinley Pk., Ill., 1974-91; dist. bd. dirs. Standing Com. for the Retarded, Hillside, Ill., 1978-88; contact campus pastor Morraine Valley Community Coll., Palos Hills, Ill., 1983-88; bd. dirs. Marseilles Nursing Svc., 1975-78, 82-83. Mem. Marseilles Ministerial Assn. (sec. 1978-82). Office: Grace Luth Ch and Sch 768 Holt Ave El Centro CA 92243 *If a person prioritizes his life with God first, family second and church third, he will be a blessing to others. Therefore, I am committed to sharing the saving Gospel of Jesus Christ as Lord with concern, compassion and care.*

KLIEVER, LONNIE DEAN, religion educator; b. Corn, Okla., Nov. 18, 1931; s. David R. and Amanda W. Kliever; m. Arthiss Marie Laughman, Aug. 14, 1964; children: Launa Natale, Marney. BA, Hardin-Simmons U., 1955; MDiv, Union Theol Sem., 1959; PhD, Duke U., 1963. Prof. philosophy U. Tex., El Paso, 1962-65; prof. religion Trinity U., San Antonio, 1965-69; prof. religious studies U. Windsor (Ont., Can.), 1969-75, So. Meth. U., Dallas, 1975—. Author: H. Richard Niebuhr, 1978, The Shattered Spectrum, 1981, The Terrible Meek, 1987, Dax's Case, 1989. Mem. Am. Acad. Religion, Soc. for Sci. Study of Religion, Can. Soc. for Study of Religion, Am. Cultural Assn., AAUP. Methodist. Home: 9549 Spring Branch Dallas TX 75238 Office: So Meth U Dept Religious Studies Dallas TX 75275

KLIMKOWSKI, SISTER ANN FRANCIS, college president; b. Wyandotte, Mich., Jan. 1, 1931; d. Alexander and Mary (Koncki) K. BS in Edn., Bowling Green (Ohio) U., 1961, MEd, 1967; PhD, U. Toledo, 1983. Joined Sisters of St. Francis, Roman Cath. Ch. Tchr. elem. schs. Cin., 1954-59, Detroit, 1961-62; tchr. St. Ladislaus High Sch., Mpls., 1962-72; with faculty and staff devel. sect. Lourdes Coll., Sylvania, Ohio, 1981—, pres., 1983—, trustee, 1983—; del. Sisters of St. Francis, Sylvania, 1991—; bd. dirs. Mid-Am. Bank, Sylvania. Active Com. of 100—Toledo, 1989—, Flower Hosp. Bd., Sylvania, 1990—, Humanities Inst., U. Toledo, 1990—, Toledo Symphony Bd., 1990—. Mem. Toledo C. of C., Rotary. Office: Lourdes Coll 6832 Convent Blvd Sylvania OH 43560

KLINCEWICZ, JOHN GREGORY, deacon, mathematician; b. Bkyln., Mar. 4, 1954; s. John James and Matilda Sophia (Gerlowski) K.; m. Kristine Ann Zagrobelny, Sept. 20, 1986. SB, MIT, 1975; MA, Yale U., 1979, PhD, 1979. Disting. mem. tech. staff AT&T Bell Labs., Holmdel, N.J., 1979—; deacon Our Lady Star of the Sea Roman Cath. Ch., Long Branch, N.J., 1990—. Office: AT&T Bell Labs Crawfords Corner Rd Holmdel NJ 07733

KLINE, CLAIRE BENTON, JR., theological educator; b. Pitts., May 13, 1925; s. Claire Benton and Wilma S. (Huot) K.; m. Mary C. Hicks, June 6, 1950; children: John B., Mary M. B.A., Coll. Wooster, 1944; B.D., Princeton Theol. Sem., 1948, Th. M., 1949; Ph.D., Yale U., 1961. Ordained to ministry Presbyn. Ch. (U.S.A.), 1948. Asst. instr. philosophy Yale, 1950-51; interim supply pastor Bklyn., 1950-5l; asst. prof. philosophy Agnes Scott Coll., 1951-61, assoc. prof., 1961-62, prof., 1962-68, chmn. dept., 1957-63, dean faculty, 1957-68, vis. prof., 1969-71, 76-83; vis. prof. theology Columbia Theol. Sem., Decatur, Ga., 1964-65; prof. theology Columbia Theol. Sem., 1969-86, adj. prof., 1987-89, vis. prof., 1989—, dean faculty, 1969-71, pres., 1971-76, pres. emeritus, 1986—; vis. asst. prof. philosophy Emory U., summers 1952-54, 56; sr. assoc. Westminster Coll., Cambridge U. (Eng.), 1981-82; acting dir. Council on Theology and Culture, Presbyn. Ch. (U.S.A.) 1984-86; vis. prof. theology Union Theol Sem., Va., 1990-91. Author: Study Guide to the Directory for Worship, 1990. Mem. Decatur Bd. Edn., 1972-80; bd. dirs. Pastoral Counseling Service, Ga. Assn. Pastoral Care. Mem. Am. Acad. Religion, Calvin Soc., Phi Beta Kappa. Democrat. Home: 717 Lake Dr SW Lithonia GA 30058

KLINE, ROBERT REEVES, clergyman, educator; b. Williamsport, Pa., Dec. 27, 1918; s. George F. and Gertrude (Thibodeau) K. B.A., Mt. St. Mary's Coll., Emmitsburg, Md., 1941; student, Mt. St. Mary's Sem., Emmitsburg, 194l-45; M.A., Georgetown U., 1951, Ph.D., 1959. Ordained priest Roman Catholic Ch., 1945, created domestic prelate, 1962; parish priest Diocese of Scranton, Pa., 1945-47; asst. dean mem. Mt. St. Mary's Coll., 1947-53, chaplain, 1953-57; chaplain St. Joseph Coll. Women, Emmitsburg, 1957-61; lectr. St. Joseph Coll. Women, 1947-73; chmn. dept. philosophy Mt. St. Mary's Coll. and Sem., 1952-62, pres., 1961-67, pres. emeritus, 1983—, ret., 1987, prof. emeritus philosophy an psychology, 1987—, chmn. dept. psychology and sociology, 1969-80, trustee, 1951-68, chmn. bd. trustees, 1961-67; Prosynodal judge Matrimonial Tribunal, Archdiocese of Balt., 1971-77. Author: The Present State of Axiology in the United States, 1959; contbr. Cath. Ency. Recipient Pres.'s medal Mt. St. Mary's Coll. Mem. Am. Cath. Philos. Assn., Monsignor Tierney Honor Soc., Delta Epsilon Sigma. Address: Mt St Mary's Coll and Sem Emmitsburg MD 21727

KLINGSPORN, GARY WAYNE, minister; b. Granby, Mo., Mar. 25, 1951; s. Urban Paul and Esther M. (Doss) K.; m. Debra Holliday, Sept. 20, 1980; children: Laura Kathryn, Kari Elizabeth. AA, St. Paul's Coll., Concordia, Mo., 1971; BA, Oral Roberts U., 1973; PhD, Baylor U., 1985. Min. 1st Presbyn. Ch., Teague, Tex., 1979-85; interim min. St. Matthew Luth. Ch., Waco, Tex., 1986-87; teaching min. Colonial Ch. Edina, Minn., 1988—; instr. dept. religion Baylor U., 1978-80; faculty dept. religious studies Met. State U., Minn., 1991—; with Word Pub., Waco, 1986-88. Bd. dirs. Sabathani Community Ctr., Mpls., 1990. Mem. Soc. Bibl. Lit., Phi Beta

Kappa. Lutheran. Home: 6028 Kellogg Ave Edina MN 55424 Office: Colonial Ch 6200 Colonial Way Edina MN 55436

KLINK, WILLIAM RICHARD, minister; b. Fontana, Calif., Dec. 31, 1933; s. William Richard and Ora Agnes Dode Gamble; m. Barbara Marie Smith, Feb. 20, 1954; children: William Richard, Susan Louise, Robert Derrell. MDiv, U. Dubuque, 1973; PhD, Columbia Pacific U., San Rafael, Calif., 1989. Ordained to ministry, Presbyn.Ch. (USA). Student pastor Cascade (Iowa) Community Ch., 1971-74; pastor First Presbyn. Ch., Stapleton, Nebr., 1974-77, Fairfield (Nebr.) Community Ch., 1977-80; sr. pastor Sequim (Wash.) Presbyn. Ch., 1980—; dept. chaplain Clallam County Sheriff's Dept., Port Angeles, Wash., 1987—; chmn. nominations Presbytery of N. Puget Sound, Everett, Wash., 1990, com. on ministry, 1989—; moderator Presbytery of Cen. Nebr., Kearney, 1978; chmn. youth ministry Synod of Lakes and Prairies, Bloomington, Minn., 1977. Author: Lighten Up, 1991; contbr. articles to profl. jours. Mem. Sequim Planning Commn., 1986; commr. police City of Fairfield, 1978-79. Recipietn Herbert E. Manning Award for excellence in parish ministry, U. Dubuque, 1991. Mem. Sequim C. of C. (bd. dirs. 1991—), Rotary (pres. 1987-88), Masons (32 deg.). Home: 362 Port Williams Box 669 Sequim WA 98382-0669 Office: Sequim Presbyn Ch 1010 N Fifth Ave PO Box 456 Sequim WA 98382-0456

KLINKSICK, CHARLES THEODORE, minister; b. Toledo, Ohio, June 12, 1916; s. Theodore George and Alma Marie (Kuhlman) K.; m. Lois Julia Jahnke, Jan. 10, 1945; children: James E., Carolyn R. Kaylor, Dale E., Joann M. Peters. BA, Capital U., Columbus, Ohio, 1938; MDiv, Trinity Luth. Sem., Columbus, Ohio, 1942; DMin, Josephinum Sem., Worthington, Ohio, 1976. Ordained to ministry Am. Luth. Ch., 1943. Founding pastor Christ Meml. Luth. Ch., Detroit, 1943-55; co-pastor Univ. Luth. Ch., E. Lansing, Mich., 1955-62; sr. pastor Clinton Hts. Luth. Ch., Columbus, Ohio, 1962-78; pastor Hope Luth. Ch., Hubbard lake, Mich., 1978-82; interim supply pastor chs. Grace Luth., 1st Presbyn., Alpena, Trinity Luth., Barton City, Mich., 1984-91; min. N.W. Mich. Synod, Evang. Luth. Ch. Am., Lansing, 1982—; chmn. Luth. Housing Corp. of Alpena, Mich., 1983-91. Writer newspaper religious column, Life Lines, 1985—; author sermons in Selected Sermons, 1974, 75, 76; contbr. International Lesson Annual, 1991-92. Grantee, Ohio Synod of Am. Luth. Ch., 1942, 73, 75. Mem. Kiwanis (bd. dirs. 1962, v.p., prog. chmn. 1975). Republican. Home and Office: 1805 Jewell Lake Dr Barton City MI 48705-0323 *Your past is always ahead of you. My future continues to confront me with people, doings, and places from my past. I find myself increasingly accountable for what I did, whom I was with, and what I was in the past. One's past is an awesome responsiblility.*

KLISIEWICZ, SISTER JEANNE MARIE, nun, religious organization administrator; b. Altoona, Pa., Jan. 12, 1947; d. John Florian and Catherine Ann (Bem) K. AA, St. Aloysius Jr. Coll., 1967; BA in English, St. Francis Coll., Loretto, Pa., 1969; ThM, Villanova U., 1974. Joined Sisters of St. Ann, 1964. Dir. religious studies Bishop Carroll High Sch., Ebensburg, Pa., 1969-74; founding mem. Carmelite Community of the Word, Ebensburg, 1971—, formation dir., 1973-79; gen. adminstr. Carmelite Community of the Word, Ebensburg, Pa., 1982-89; lectr., field educator St. Francis Sem., Loretto, 1975-79; dir. Diocesan Pastoral Ctrs. Altoona, Johnstown Ctrs., 1989—; dir. MA Lay Ministry Program, St. Francis Coll., 1979-82, trustee, 1987-90; mem. lay ministry com. Altoona-Johnstown Diocese, 1989-91, 1990—, fin. coun., 1989—; vice chmn. peace and justice commn., 1990—. Co-author: Community Constitutions. Mem. Western Pa. Christians for Corp. Responsibility. Named Disting. Alumna St. Francis Coll., 1990. Address: 401 5th St Huntingdon PA 16652

KLITZKY, BRUCE R., bishop. Bishop Evang. Luth. Ch. in Am., Dallas. Office: Evang Luth Ch in Am 1210 River Bend Dr Ste 108 Dallas TX 75247*

KLOEPFER, JOHN WARNER, clergyman, educator; b. Emporia, Kans., July 12, 1947; s. Henry Warner and Ruth Elizabeth (McCoy) K.; m. Margery Lucille Coon, Aug. 9, 1975; children: Karen Jean, Kristen Elizabeth, Kendra Grace. BA, U. Ill., Chgo., 1969; MDiv, Colgate Rochester Div. Sch., 1976; PhD, Duquesne U., 1990. Ordained to ministry United Presbyn. Ch. in the U.S.A., 1976. Religious edn. cons. Ecumenical Inst., Chgo., 1966-70; dir. religious studies Ecumenical Inst., Denver, 1970-71; exec. dir. Ecumenical Inst., Cin., 1971-73; program dir. Univ. Presbyn. Ch., Buffalo, 1973; asst. pastor Eastside Meml. Presbyn. Ch., Rochester, N.Y., 1974-75; interim pastor West Avenue Presbyn. Ch., Buffalo, 1975-76; pastor Bovina Center (N.Y.) Presbyn. Ch., 1976-84, McGinnis Presbyn. Ch., Pitcairn, Pa., 1984—; mem. nat. faculty Ecumenical Inst.; mem. adj. faculty Duquesne U., Pitts., 1985-91, assoc. prof., 1991—. Contbr. articles to religious jours. Home: 410 3d St Pitcairn PA 15140 Office: McGinnis Presbyn Ch Pitcairn PA 15140 *The greatest need in our time is not for greater moral or ethical knowledge, but the courage to do what we already know is right and to live as we know we must.*

KLOOS, EDWARD JOHN MICHAEL, JR., minister; b. N.Y.C., Jan. 26, 1951; s. Edward John Michael Sr. and Marjorie May (Needham) K. BA, Wagner Coll., 1973; MDiv, New Brunswick (N.J.) Seminary, 1982; STM, N.Y. Theol. Seminary, 1984; PhD, Clayton (Calif.) Seminary, 1984. Ordained to ministry Christian Ch., 1985. Chaplain New Brunswick Seminary, 1981-82; vicar St. John's Luth. Ch., Lindenhurst, N.Y., 1981-83; pastor United Christian Ch., Copiaoue, N.Y., 1984-86; theologian/pulpit supply United Christian Ch., Wading River, N.Y., 1986-90; pastor First Congregational Ch., Woodbridge, N.J., 1990—; bd. dirs. Deer Hill Conf. Ctr., Wappinger Falls, N.Y.. Contbr. articles to publs. in field. Chaplain Woodbridge Learn Ctr., 1991, Berkshire Nursing Home, Babylon, N.Y., 1984, N.Y. State Senate, Albany, 1986; spokesperson 79 St Assn., N.Y.C., 1985. Recipient music dept. award Horace Greely, 1969, Wagner Coll., 1973, L. W. Wheeler award Wheeler Found., 1978; Lanberchter scholar Concordia Coll., 1971. Mem. Woodbridge Ministerium (treas. 1990—), Woodbridge Youth Coun., Am. Assn. Counselors, Am. Assn. Family Counselors, Am. Organist Assn., Suffolk Assn. United Ch. of Christ (pub. rels. mem. 1986-90, stewardship mem. 1984-86), others. Home: 58 Grove Ave Woodbridge NJ 07095 Office: First Congregational Ch 539 Barron Ave Woodbridge NJ 07095 *Life is not a struggle of good vs. evil. Rather it is the tension between what one is and what one aspires to be.*

KLOSTERMAIER, KLAUS KONRAD, philosophy and indology educator, writer; b. Munich, June 14, 1933; arrived in Can., 1970; s. Mathias and Therese (Blaimayr) K.; m. Doris Maria Wenzel; children: Cornelia Susanne, Evelyn Christine. Abitur, Domgymnasium, Freising, Fed. Republic Germany, 1952; Licentiate Phil., P. U. G., Rome, 1955, Dr. Phil., 1961; PhD, U. Bombay, 1969. Rsch. guide Inst. Oriental Philosophy, Vrindaban, India, 1962-64; dir. Inst. Indian Culture, Bombay, 1965-70; prof. dept. religion U. Man., Winnipeg, Can., 1970—, chmn. dept. religion and Asian studies com., 1986—; vis. prof. Tata Inst. for Social Sci., Bombay, 1964-65, Radhakrishnan Inst. Advanced Study in Philosophy, Madras, India, 1977-78; bd. dirs. Shastri Indo-Can. Inst., Calgary/New Dehli, 1988—. Author: In the Paradise of Krishna, 1971, Mythology and Philosophy of Salvation in the Theistic Tradition of India, 1984, A Survey of Hinduism, 1989. Mem. Am. Oriental Soc., Can. Soc. for Study of Religion, Am. Acad. Religion., Am. Soc. for Study of Religion, Inst. Religion in Age of Sci. Avocations: reading, music, gardening. Home: 1018 Kilkenny Dr, Winnipeg, MB Canada R3T 5A5 Office: U Manitoba, Dept Religion, Winnipeg, MB Canada R3T 2N2

KLOTZ, JOHN WILLIAM, seminary educator, author, minister; b. Pitts., Jan. 10, 1918; s. John William and Anna Mathilde (Kauffmann) K. MDiv, Concordia Sem., 1941; PhD, U. Pitts., 1947. Ordained to ministry, 1943. Instr. Concordia Tchrs. Coll., Bronxville, N.Y., 1941-43, Bethany Luth. Coll., Mankato, Minn., 1943-45; prof. religious studies Concordia Tchrs. Coll., River Forest, Ill., 1945-59; prof. and acad. dean Concordia Sr. Coll., Ft. Wayne, Ind., 1959-74; prof. practical theology, dean acad. affairs Concordia Sem., St. Louis, 1974-78, dir. grad. studies, 1978—; Sec. Com. Rsch. Luth. Ch.-Mo. Synod, 1955—, mem. Commn. Constl. Matters, 1974-81. Author: Genes, Genesis and Evolution, 1955, The Challenge of the Space Age, 1961, Modern Science in the Christian Life, 1961, Abortion, 1973, Ecology Crisis, 1973, Studies in Creation, 1985, Men, Medicine and Their Maker, 1991. Pres. Friends of Our Native Landscape, Chgo., 1954-59, ACRES, Inc., Ft. Wayne, 1960-70; bd. dirs. Merry Lea Environ. Ctr., Wolf Lake, Ind., 1970-74. Mem. AAAS, Am. Inst. Biol. Sci., Izaak Walton League, Nature Conservancy. Office: 801 De Mun Ave Saint Louis MO 63105

KLUESNER, SISTER MARIAN, charitable organization administrator. Dir. Cath. Charities, El Paso, Tex. Office: Cath Charities 408 Park El Paso TX 79901*

KLUGE, RALPH WILLIAM, retired minister; b. Black Creek, Wis., Jan. 2, 1926; s. Walter Carl and Ella Helen (Behl) K.; m. Bernadine Constance Pearce, June 24, 1950; children: Timothy Ralph, Mark William, Nancy Aileen Armstrong, Marsha Elaine Bortolussi. BA, Elmhurst Coll., 1947; BD, Eden Theol. Sem., 1950, MDiv, 1978; student, Bradley U., 1969-71. Ordained to ministry United Ch. of Christ, 1950; cert. elem. tchr., Ill. Pastor Peace Ch., Brillon, Wis., 1950-56, Friedens Ch., Reedsville, Wis., 1950-56, Midland Community Ch., Nickerson, Kans., 1956-60, Bethel Meml. Ch., Creve Coeur, Ill., 1960-68; tchr. Parkview Sch., Creve Coeur, 1968-88; pastor Christ Ch., Germantown Hills, Ill., 1972-79, St. Paul's Ch., Minonk, Ill., 1970-71, 80, First Congl. Ch., Canton, Ill., 1981-82, Congl. Ch., Lacon, Ill., 1982-83; pastor emeritus Christ Ch., Germantown Hills, Ill., 1990—; pres. Appleton Region United Ch. of Christ, Appleton, Wis., 1953-55; dean Pioneer Mission Coun. United Ch. of Christ, Peoria, Ill., 1975-76. Hon. life mem. Ill. Congress of Parents and Tchrs., 1970; vol. chaplain Galena Park Home, Peoria Heights, Ill., 1988—. Named Creve Coeur Tchr. of Year, Sch. Dist. 76, 1988. Mem. Profl. Assn. Clergy, Internat. Assn. Lions Clubs (key mem. 1971, pres. Creve Coeur 1982-83, 87-88), Nat. Geographic Soc., Nat. Wildlife Fedn., Santa Fe Trail Assn., Soo Line Hist. and Tech. Soc., Appalachian Trail Conf. Republican. Avocations: philatelist, railfan, camper-hiker. Home: 320 Illini Dr East Peoria IL 61611 *As I have matured, I have found that not only does life seem to be more complex, and have more challenges, but it is more exciting, and more rewarding. Therefore, I always feel as though the best is yet to come.*

KMIEC, EDWARD URBAN, bishop; b. Trenton, N.J., June 4, 1936. Ed. s. John Kmiec and Thecla (Czupta) St. Charles Coll., Catonsville, Md., 1956; St. Mary's Sem., Balt., 1958; S.T.L. Gregorian U., Rome. 1962, Ordained priest Roman Cath. Ch., Dec. 20, 1961; ordained titular bishop of Simidicca and aux. bishop of Trenton, 1982—. Address: Diocese of Trenton St Catharine Rectory 215 Essex Ave Spring Lake NJ 07762

KNABENSHUE, EDWIN MARK, minister; b. Waynesburg, Pa., Nov. 3, 1954; s. Morris Carl and Edna Blanche (McElroy) K.; m. Debra Sue Ross, Apr. 7, 1978; children: Lisa Anne, Daniel Ross. AA in Bus. Adminstrn., Pa. Comml. Coll., 1974. Ordained to ministry Free Meth. Ch., 1986. Pastor Free Meth. Ch., Apollo, Pa., 1983-90, United Meth. Ch., Wheeling, W.Va., 1990—; sec. Gideons Internat., Nashville, 1981-83; dir. Dist. Youth Ministries, Apollo, 1983-85; pres. Conf. Ministerium, Apollo, 1986-87; area liaison to supt. Pitts. Annual Conf., Apollo, 1989-90; dir. Light & Life Campground, Fairchance, Pa., 1989-90; crisis residential technician Hancock-Brooke Mental Health Svcs., Weirton, W.Va., 1991—. Contbr. articles to profl. jour. Recipient Ch. Growth award Pitts. Annual Conf., 1984, 88. Republican. Home: RD # 1 Box 447 Wellsburg WV 26070 *Life is but a vapor. How imperative it is that we find to know both true happiness and peace within.*

KNAPP, GARY ALAN, minister, psychotherapist; b. Jackson, Miss., Feb. 2, 1951; s. George Shellie and Ivy Mae (Warren) K. BA, Miss. Coll., 1977, M in Community Counseling, 1983; MDiv, New Orleans Bapt. Theol. Seminary, 1979. Lic. profl. counselor, Miss.; lic. mental health counselor, Fla.; nat. cert. counselor; cert. counselor, Washington. Pastor Knoxo Bapt. Ch., Tylertown, Miss., 1978-80; sr. min. Griffith Meml. Bapt. Ch., Jackson, 1980-87; psychotherapist Clin. Counseling Assocs., Jackson, 1983-87; family counselor Family Svc. Ctr., Cecil Field, Fla., 1987-90; sr. couselor Family Svc. Ctr., Yokosuka, Japan, 1990-91; dep. dir. Family Svc. Ctr., Atsugi, Japan, 1991, dir., 1991—; psychotherapist Assocs. for Evaluation & Therpay, Jacksonville, Fla., 1989. Mem. AACD, Mil. Educators and Counselors Assn., Am. Assn. Profl. Hypnotherapists, Hinds-Madison Bapt. Assn. (vice-moderator 1986-87). Lodge: Lions (pres. Jackson chpt. 1982-83). Avocations: fishing, music. Office: Family Svc Ctr NAF Atsugi Japan PSC 477 Box 32 FPO AP CA 96306-1232

KNAPP, GEORGE WERNER, minister; b. New Lenox, Ill., July 14, 1916; s. George William and Kathryn Elizabeth (Werner) K.; m. Virginia Louise Mallinckrodt, Sept. 14, 1940; children: Barry, Joan, Keith, Cheryl, Gayle. 2 yr. cert., Joliet (Ill.) Jr. Coll., 1936; AB, Elmhurst Coll., 1938; BD, Eden Sem., 1941. Ordained to ministry United Ch. of Christ, 1941. Pastor St. Peter Trinity, Lenzburg-Fayetteville, Ill., 1961-43, Nazareth Ch., St. Louis, 1945-48, Community Ch., Blue Island, Ill., 1948-52, Zion Ch., Dyer, Ind., 1952-65, Peace Ch., Bellwood, Ill., 1965-81; chaplain Plymouth Pl. Retirement Home, La Grange Park, Ill., 1981—; gen. synod del. United Ch. of Christ, Denver, 1963, Chgo., 1965, Cin., 1967, Norfolk, Va., 1991. Capt. Chaplain Corps U.S. Army, 1943-45, ETO. Mem. Kiwanis (spiritual advisor Westchester, Ill. chpt. 1985-91), VFW. Home: 2237 Mayfair Westchester IL 60154 Office: Plymouth Pl Retirement Home 315 La Grange Rd La Grange Park IL 60525

KNAPP, KENNETH R., religious organization administrator; b. Haubstadt, Ind., Mar. 18, 1937; s. Henry J. and Katherine (Gastenveld) K. BA, St. Mehrad, 1959; MS, Ind. State U., 1968; MSW, Cath. U., 1970. Cert. ACSW. Dir. Cath. Charities, Evansville, Ind., 1970-81, Ctr. for Human Devel., Washington, 1981-84; vicar gen. Diocese of Evansville, 1984—. Office: PO Box 4169 Evansville IN 42724-0169

KNAPSTEIN, JOHN WILLIAM, psychologist; b. New London, Wis., June 20, 1937; s. John Joseph and Irene Frances (Poepke) K.; m. Betty Ann Wilhelm, Nov. 25, 1966; John Karl, Susan Elise, Eric Steven. BA, St. John's U., Collegeville, Minn., 1959; MA, Marquette U., 1961; PhD, Tex. Tech U., 1970. Tchr. Hortonville (Wis.) High Sch., 1959-60; counselor Vocat. and Adult Sch., Racine, Wis., 1961-62; psychologist VA Hosp., St. Louis, 1970-72, Hines, Ill., 1972—. Deacon Diocese of Joliet, Ill., 1982—; bd. dirs., officer Community Service Council of No. Will County, Romeoville, Ill., 1979—. Served to capt. USAF, 1962-66. Marquette U. scholar, 1960. Mem. Am. Psychol. Assn., Nat. Rehab. Assn., Am. Assn. for Counseling and Devel., Nat. Career Devel. Assn., Nat. Rehab. Counseling Assn. Roman Catholic. Lodge: KC. Avocations: gardening, reading, computers. Home: 120 Pamela Dr Bolingbrook IL 60440-1347 Office: Psychology Svc VA Hosp Hines IL 60141

KNAVEL, CHRISTOPHER CHARLES, clergyman; b. Fairfield, Ill., Jan. 24, 1958; s. Lee Albert and Ruth (French) K.; m. Barbara Sue Thompson, June 8, 1991. BA, Lincoln Christian Coll., 1980, postgrad., 1980-82; postgrad., Sangamon State U., 1981-83. Ordained to ministry Christian Ch., 1984. Min. youth No. Highlands Ch. of Christ, Ft. Wayne, Ind., 1983-89; min. singles West Side Christian Ch., Springfield, Ill., 1989—; alumni coun. rep. Lincoln (Ill.) Christian Coll., 1990—; nat. singles leader Nat. Single Adult Leaders, Grand Rapids, Mich., 1989—. Named Outstanding Young Minister Standard Pub. Co., 1989.

KNEEBONE, LEON RUSSELL, lay worker, educator; b. Bangor, Pa., May 28, 1920; s. Russell Joseph and Dorothy Edwina (Tucker) K.; m. Elizabeth Costen Morgan, May 5, 1945; children: Patricia Anne, Stephen Brooks, Eileen Elizabeth. BS, Pa. State U., 1942, PhD, 1950. Prof. Pa. State U., University Park, 1950-78, prof. emeritus, 1978—; chmn. bd. Wesley Found., University Park, 1964—; cons. in field. Contbr. numerous articles to profl. jours. Chmn. bd. State College (Pa.) Coun. Chs., 1960-61, Mt. Nittany Home, State College, 1962-64, Centre County United Way, State College, 1974-75. Capt. U.S. Army, 1942-46, PTO. Mem. World Meth. Coun., Am. Phytopathol. Soc., Am. Mycological Soc., Bot. Soc. Am., World Meth. Conf. (del. Lake Juna Luska, N.C. chpt. 1981, 86, 91), Sigma Xi (pres.), Gamma Sigma Delta (pres.). Republican. Home: 628 Fairway Rd State College PA 16803

KNIGHT, ALLAN RUNYON, minister; b. Plainfield, N.J., July 28, 1912; s. John Marcus and Edith Maria (Leonard) K.; m. Pearl Prescott, Sept. 18, 1937; children: Phyllis Marie Rinehart, Douglas A., Rolf T., Karl W. Diploma, Practical Bible Tng. Sch., Bible School Park, N.Y., 1932; BA, Wheaton (Ill.) Coll., 1935; ThM, So. Bapt. Theol. Sem., Louisville, 1937; ThD, Eastern Bapt. Theol. Sem., Phila., 1946. Ordained to ministry Am. Bapt. Chs. in U.S.A., 1938. Pastor Mansfield Bapt. Ch., Port Murray, N.J., 1937-41, Meml. Bapt. Ch. and Summer Hill Bapt. Ch., Cortland, N.Y., 1941-48, Moulton Meml. Bapt. Ch., Newburgh, N.Y., 1948-53, First Bapt. Ch., Council Bluffs, Iowa, 1953-65; exec. minister Am. Bapt. Chs. Nebr., Omaha, 1965-77; mem. Gen. Coun., Am. Bapt. Ch. in U.S.A., Valley Forge, Pa., 1956-62, 65-77; pres. Am. Bapt. Chs. N.Y. State, Syracuse, 1952-53, Iowa Bapt. Conv., Des Moines, 1960-61. Co-author: New Life, 1947; editor Nebr. Bapt Messenger, 1965-77. Chairperson Mayor's Com. on Human Rels., Council Bluffs, 1959-65; co-chmn. Billy Graham Greater Omaha-Council Bluffs Crusade, 1964; bd. dirs. Omaha Opportunities Industrialization Ctr., Omaha, 1968-77; chairperson Bentonville (Ark.) Ednl. Enrichment Program Adv. Coun., 1982-88. Recipient Effective City Ch. Citation, Am. Bapt. Home Mission Soc., Valley Forge, 1957, Medal of Merit, Relief Project Bentonville-Bella Vista Rotary Club, 1981-82; named Alumnus of Yr., So. Bapt. Theol. Sem., Louisville, 1975, Pastor Emeritus South Broadway Bapt. Ch., Pittsburg, Kans., 1987. Mem. Soc. Bibl. Lit., Mins. Coun. Am. Bapt. Chs. U.S.A. (life), Coun. Retired Execs. Am. Bapt. Chs. in U.S.A. (coord. 1981-91, editor Esprit de C.O.R.E. 1981-91), Rotary.

KNIGHT, ARUMAINAYAGAM JOHN, lay worker, former institute administrator; b. Bangalore, Karnataka, India, May 24, 1927; s. Abraham Perianayagam Gell and Grace Clara Pushpammal (Suviseshamuthu) K.; m. Sarojini Sonabai Aaron, Jan. 26, 1955; children: Samuel, David. BS in Agr., Agrl. Coll., Coimbatore, India, 1949, diploma in horticulture, 1954; MS, Cornell U., 1961; PhD, Indian Agrl. Rsch. Inst., New Delhi, 1973. Cert. agrl. extension educator, India. Pres. Indian Missionary Soc., Coimbatore, 1976-84; dean spiritual affairs Karunya Inst. Tech.—Alandurai, Coimbatore, 1986-87; chmn. Far East Broadcasting Assocs. India, Bangalore, 1981-87, bd. dirs. Mem., pres. Coimbatore br. Gideons Internat., 1968-87; treas. World Cassette Outreach India, 1988—. Recipient Best Rsch. Paper awards, 1965, 66; named Best Debator, Nat. Soc. Co-operation for Debating, 1970, 71. Mem. Indian Soc. on Extension Edn. (life), Bible Soc. India (co-opted). Mem. Ch. South India. Home: 3, Magarath Rd, Bangalore Karnataka 560 025, India Office: Far East Broadcasting Assocs India, 7, Commissariat Rd, Bangalore Karnataka 560 025, India

KNIGHT, DOUGLAS ALLAN, Hebrew Bible educator; b. Cortland, N.Y., May 1, 1943; s. Allan Runyon and Pearl (Prescott) K.; m. Evelyn Irene Hofstad, May 29, 1965 (div. Dec. 1981); 1 child, Lisa Irene; m. Catherine Whitehead Snow, Feb. 29, 1984; 1 stepchild, Jonathan Whitehead Snow. BA, Ottawa U., 1965; MDiv cum laude, Calif. Bapt. Theol. Sem., 1968; postgrad., U. Oslo, 1967; ThD magna cum laude, Georg-August U., Göttingen, Fed. Republic Germany, 1973. Asst. prof. Old Testament Div. Sch., Vanderbilt U., Nashville, 1973-78, assoc. prof., 1978-86, prof. Hebrew Bible, 1986—; adj. prof. Old Testament Am. Bapt. Sem. of the West, Covina, Calif., 1973; vis. prof. or scholar Georg-August-U., 1976, U. Mont., Missoula, 1977, The Iliff Sch. Theology, Denver, 1980, Hebrew U. of Jerusalem, 1981-82, Ecumenical Inst. for Theol. Rsch., Tantur, Jerusalem, 1981-82, Eberhard-Karls-U., Tübingen, Fed. Republic Germany, 1987-88; trustee Scholars Press, Chico, Calif., 1981-82. Author: Rediscovering the Traditions of Israel, 1973, rev. edit., 1975; editor, contbr.: Tradition and Theology in the Old Testament, 1977, Julius Wellhausen and His Prolegomena to the History of Israel, 1982, Humanizing America's Iconic Book,1982, The Hebrew Bible and Its Modern Interpreters, 1985, Justice and the Holy, 1989; gen. editor: (series) The Bible and Its Modern Interpreters, 1985-89, The Library of Ancient Israel, 1990—; co-editor: (series) Issues in Religion and Theology, 1980-87; mem. editorial bd. Jour. Bibl. Lit., 1991—; contbr. articles, book revs. to profl. jours. Vol. Aphek-Antipatris Archaeol. Expdn., Tel Aviv, 1984; mem. area adv. com. of Mid. East, Coun. for Internat. Exch. Scholars, Washington, 1984-86; co-chair Holocaust Lectures Com., Nashville, 1989-91. Recipient Fulbright award Fulbright-Hays Program, 1981-82; Deutscher Akademischer Austauschdienst postgrad. study grantee, 1976; scholar, rsch. grantee Assn. Theol. Schs. in U.S. and Can., 1976; Univ. fellow Vanderbilt U., 1981-82, NEH fellow, 1987-88. Mem. Am. Acad. Religion, Am. Schs. of Oriental Rsch. (editorial bd. Dissertation Series 1990—, corp. rep. 1991—), Soc. for Bibl. Lit. (editor Dissertation Series 1974-78, co-chair Centennial Com. 1979-80, dir. NEH grant 1980-85, treas. 1981-82), Cath. Bibl. Assn. Am. Democrat. Home: 2106 19th Ave S Nashville TN 37212 Office: Vanderbilt U Div Sch Nashville TN 37240

KNIGHT, FLOYD, JR., minister; b. Indpls., Jan. 11, 1959; s. Floyd Sr. and Tani (Nitta) K.; 1 child, Floyd III. BA, Ind. U., 1984; MDiv, Boston U., 1988; postgrad., U. Chgo. Ordained to ministry Christian Ch. (Disciples of Christ). Chaplain assoc. Boston U., 1985-86; acting interim-assoc. minister 1st Christian Ch., Lynn, Mass., 1987-88; assoc. minister 1st Freewill Bapt. Ch., Chgo., 1989—; ednl. con. Park Manor Christian Ch., Chgo., 1990; mem. sub-com. racial ethnic incluriveness and empowerment Christian Ch. (Disciples of Christ), 1990, mem. steering com. African-Am. Network, 1988—, mem. hymnal com. Black Min.'s Fellowship Nat. Convocation, 1988—. Treas. Hyde Park Pre-sch. Ctr., Chgo. Henry Barton Robison scholar, 1988-90, Martin Luther King Jr. scholar, 1984-87. Mem. Phi Lambda Theta. Democrat. Home: 1338 E Hyde Park Blvd #1 Chicago IL 60615 *My time is spent on fulfilling the requirements of intimacy in its reflexive, passive, and active manifestations, I strive to explore the intimate reaches of my own mental, affective, physical and religious selves to passively allow others to be fully intimate with me; and to be actively engaged in the intimate exploration of others. This pursuit is not just psychological or individualistic. It is also communal, even triunal. For this pursuit must involve the self, community, and God.*

KNIGHT, GEORGE LITCH, minister; b. Rockford, Ill., Jan. 2, 1925; s. Bradley Jay and Grace (King) K. BA, Centre Coll. Ky., 1947, DD, 1968; BD, Union Theol. Sem., N.Y.C., 1951. Ordained to ministry Presbyn. Ch., 1951. Asst. min. West Side Presbyn. Ch., Ridgewood, N.J., 1951-56, copastor, 1956-57; min. Lafayette Ave. Presbyn. Ch., Bklyn., 1957-67, 68-89, Old 1st Presbyn. Ch., Newark, 1967-68; lectr. in Christian edn., evangelism and music, 1975—; tchr. New Brunswick (N.J.) Sem., 1957-63, Bibl. Sem., N.Y.C., 1960-63, Union Sem. Sch. Sacred Music, N.Y.C., 1967-71; moderator Presbytery of N.Y.C., 1963; founder Clarence Dickinson Libr. Sacred Music and Art, William Carey Coll., Hattiesburg, Miss., 1970. mem. editorial com.: 1955 Presbyterian Hymnal; contbr. articles to religious jours. Co-founder Clergy Concerned for a Better Ft. Greene, Bklyn., 1964. Fellow Hymn Soc. Am. (founder The Hymn quar.); mem. Am. Guild Handbell Ringers (founder 1954).

KNIGHT, GEORGE R., church history educator; b. Ross, Calif., Oct. 16, 1941; s. George Creighton and Betty Adele (Rice) K.; m. Betty Lou Birky, Aug. 28, 1960; children: Bonnie Jean Scull, Jeffrey Scott. BA, Pacific Union Coll., 1965; MA, Andrews U., 1966, MDiv, 1967; EdD, U. Houston, 1976. Lic. min. Seventh-day Adventist Ch. Pastor Tex. Conf. of Seventh-day Adventists, Ft. Worth, 1967-69; prin. Houston Jr. Acad., Tex. Conf. of Seventh-day Adventists, 1971-76; prof. ednl. founds. Andrews U., Berrien Springs, Mich., 1976-85, prof. ch. history, 1985—. Author: Myths in Adventism, 1985, From 1888 to Apostasy, 1987, Angry Saints, 1989, My Gripe with God, 1990; co-editor Andrews U. Sem. Studies, 1988—; rsch. editor Jour. Adventist Edn., 1980—. Trustee Adventist Hist. Properties, 1985—. With U.S. Army, 1960. Mem. Am. Acad. Religion, Am. Hist. Assn., Am. Soc. Ch. History, Wesleyan Theol. Soc., Phi Kappa Phi. Home: 3001 Lakeshore Dr Apt 231 Saint Joseph MI 49085 Office: Andrews U Berrien Springs MI 44103

KNIGHT, HENRY FLOYD, religion educator, chaplain; b. Alexander City, Ala., June 25, 1948; s. H. Floyd and Wanda (Rawls) K.; m. Pamela Damron, May 25, 1974; children: Paul, Laura. BA in English, U. Ala., Tuscaloosa, 1970; MDiv, Emory U., 1973, D Ministry, 1975. Ordained deacon United Meth. Ch., 1973, elder, 1975. Assoc. min. West End United Meth. Ch., Nashville, 1974-79; assoc. dir. field edn. Vanderbilt U. Div. Sch., Nashville, 1978-79; chaplain Baldwin-Wallace Coll., Berea, Ohio, 1979-91, asst. prof. religion, 1979-85, assoc. prof., 1985-91; chaplain, assoc. prof. U. Tulsa, 1991—; mem. Faith and Order Commn., Interch. Coun., 1984-91. Contbr. essays to religious publs. Mem. Ohio Peacemaking Edn. Network, 1983-87, Performers and Artists for Nuclear Disarmament, 1984-89. Recipient Bishop James C. Baker Grad. award Bd. Higher Edn. and Ministry, 1988. Mem.

Assn. Coords. Univ. Religious Affairs, Assn. for Religion and Intellectual Life, Nat. Assn. Coll. and Univ. Chaplains. Home: 2264 E 37th St Tulsa OK 74105 Office: U Tulsa Sharp Chapel 600 S College Tulsa OK 74104

KNIGHT, JOHN LOWDEN, JR., religion educator; b. Beverly, N.J., Nov. 4, 1915; s. John Lowden Sr. and Elizabeth (Mac Burney) K.; m. Alice O. Kingston, Aug. 9, 1941; children: Merrie E. Knight Crawford, Wendy L. Knight Carpenter. AB, Drew U., 1939; AM, Boston U., 1941, STB, 1942; MA, Vanderbilt U., 1943; DD (hon.), Kans. Wesleyan U., 1947; LLD, Willamette U., 1949. Ordained to ministry Meth. Ch., 1945. Asst. prof. Willamette U., Salem, Oreg., 1943-46; pres. Nebr. Wesleyan U., Lincoln, 1946-49, Baldwin-Wallace Coll., Berea, Ohio, 1949-54; sr. pastor Trinity United Meth. Ch., Columbus, Ohio, 1954-61, First United Meth. Ch., Syracuse, N.Y., 1961-67; pres. Wesley Theol. Sem., Washington, 1967-82, pres. emeritus, 1982—. Home: 4114 E Mandan St Phoenix AZ 85044

KNIGHT, LINDA JEAN, minister; b. Bellows Falls, Vt., Feb. 5, 1942; d. Charles Russell and Muriel Edith (Barnjum) K.; m. D. David Nuss, Oct. 6, 1973 (div. 1980); children: Charles, Christopher. BS, U. Vt., 1964, MA, 1967; MDiv, Boston U., 1987. Ordained to ministry United Ch. of Christ, 1988. Dir. Christian edn. North Beverly (Mass.) 2d Congl. Ch., 1987; min. Christian edn. West Parish United Ch. of Christ, Andover, Mass., 1987-88; assoc. min. Congl. Ch. of Littleton (Mass.), 1988-91; sr. pastor Broadway Winter Hill Congl. Ch., United Ch. of Christ, Somerville, Mass., 1991—; mem., Interfaith Group, Somerville, 1991—. Home: 15 Normandy Rd Lexington MA 02173 Office: Broadway Winter Hill Congl United Ch of Christ 404 Broadway Somerville MA 02145 *I am constantly surprised by God—not only my call to the ministry, but the continual and unexpected invitations to a deeper relationship.*

KNIGHT, NORMAN LEROY, minister; b. Baldwin, Kans., Apr. 11, 1934; s. Clifford C. and Elsie L. (Hoefer) K.; m. DeRonda Clark, Oct. 23, 1954 (div. 1969); m. Doris Jean Holden, Jan. 29, 1970; children: Terilyn, Kathy, Kaye, Karen, Kelli, Karl. BA, U. Puget Sound, 1958; BD, Garrett Evang. Sem., 1967. Ordained to ministry United Meth. Ch. as deacon, 1967, as elder, 1968. Pastor United Meth. Ch., West Burlington, Iowa, 1967-70; pastor Minburn (Iowa) United Meth. Ch., 1973-77, Epworth United Meth. Ch., Council Bluffs, Iowa, 1977-83, Valley United Meth. Ch., West Des Moines, Iowa, 1983—; mem. Iowa Conf. Bd. of Ordained Ministry, Des Moines, 1982-88, registrar, 1984-88. Chair Human Svcs. Adv. Com., Council Bluffs, 1980-83. Mem. Fellowship of United Meths. in Worship. Home: 1042 Belle Mar Dr West Des Moines IA 50265

KNIGHT, PAUL FORD, pastor; b. Greenwood, Miss., Feb. 9, 1960; s. James P. and Annie Lou (Tucker) K. BA, Miss. Coll., 1982; MDiv, So. Bapt. Theol. Sem., 1985, ThM, 1991. Ordained to ministry Bapt. Ch., 1985. Assoc. pastor Lower Burrell Bapt. Ch., Pitts., 1985-86; interim pastor St. Louis Crossing Ind. Meth. Ch., Columbus, Ind., 1986-87; pastor St. Louis Crossing Ind. Meth. Ch., Columbus, 1987—. Vol. Am. Cancer Soc., Columbus, 1990-91; mem. steering com. Community Revival, Hope, Ind., 1991; mem. Community Chem. Abuse Task Force, Hope, 1989-90. Recipient U.T. Owen scholarhip Miss. Coll., 1981, Carrier scholarship U. Miss., 1978-79; named Nat. Merit Scholar, 1978. Mem. Soc. Biblical Lit., Am. Acad. Religion, Chess Club. Home and Office: 6535 E Richard Ct Columbus IN 47203 *It is through loving others that we come to know God.*

KNIGHTON, JEFFREY HOLMES, pastor; b. Canyon, Tex., Nov. 17, 1952; s. Thomas Eugene and Ellen Yvonne (Sanders) K.; m. Linda Darlene Parrish, July 5, 1980; children: Joshua, Kaleb. BS in Edn., Tex. Tech U., 1976; MDiv, Phillips Grad. Sem., Enid, Okla., 1988; DMin, Covington Theol. Sem., Rossville, Ga., 1990. Ordained to ministry Christian Ch. (Disciples of Christ), 1988. Pastor lst Christian Ch., Hunter, Okla., 1985-88, Scott City, Kans., 1988—; del. Christian Ch. Gen. Assembly, Indpls., 1987, Louisville, 1989, Tulsa, 1991; rep. Kans. Region Recommendations Com., Manhattan, 1989—; mentor Edn. for Ministry, Scott City, 1990—. Contbr. poetry to religious publs., also devotions. Recipient award Tex. Assn. Broadcasters, 1984, Investigative News award AP, Tex., 1985. Mem. Scott County Ministerial Alliance (pres. 1990-91), Fellowship Merry Christians, Renovaré, Lions. Office: 1st Christian Ch 701 Main St Scott City KS 67871

KNIJFF, HENRI W. DE, theologian, educator; b. Enschede, Overijssel, The Netherlands, June 23, 1931; s. Henri J. and Antje M. (Ormeling) de Knijff; m. Magdalena D. de Jong, July 4, 1936; children: Johannes, David, Hermina, Rudolf. Ch. exam, U. Amsterdam (The Netherlands), 1956; D in Theology, U. Leiden (The Netherlands), 1970; cert, U. Basel (Switzerland), 1955; hon. degree, Debrecen Theol. Inst., Hungary, 1988. Ordained minister Ref. Ch., 1959. Vicar Ref. Ch. Basel-Stadt, Basel, 1958-59; min. Ref. Ch. Netherland, 1959-64, 69-74, Protestant Ch. Belgium, 1964-69; prof. theology U. Utrecht (The Netherlands), 1981—. Author: Exegesis and Interpretation in O. Noordmans, 1970 (award U. Groningen 1975), A Short History of Biblical Hermeneutics, 1980, European Erotic Culture and Christian Sexual Ethics, 1987, Collected Studies in Theology and Culture, 1989. Pres. Protestant dept. Dutch Labour Party, Amsterdam, 1979—. Mem. Soc. for Theology (Berlin, sect. system theology), European Soc. for Study Rels. Between Theology and Sci. (sect. system theol.), Soc. for Study Sci. and Theol. (Atomium, pres.), Theol. Commn. Dutch Ref. Ch. (pres. 1978-91). Avocations: history of culture, history of science. Home: 5 M H Trompstr, 3572 XS Utrecht The Netherlands Office: Theol Inst, 2 Heidelberglaan, 3584 CS Utrecht The Netherlands

KNIPE, DAVID MACLAY, religion educator; b. Johnstown, Pa., Nov. 25, 1932; s. Donald M. and Hazel H. (Heacock) K.; m. Monica E. Setterwall, Nov. 12, 1959 (div. 1973); children: Nicola, Viveka, Jennifer; m. Susan T. Stevens, June 22, 1980. BA, Cornell U., 1955; MA, Union Theol. Sem., 1958, U. Chgo., 1965; PhD, U. Chgo., 1971. Prof. U. Wis., Madison, 1967—, chair religious studies program, 1976—, chair dept. S. Asian studies, 1987—, dir. South Asian Area Ctr., 1987-90. Author: In the Image of Fire, 1975, Hinduism, 1990; co-author: Focus on Hinduism, 1977, 2d edit., 1981; dir., producer ednl. TV series Exploring the Religions of South Asia, 1975. Fellow Social Sci. Rsch. Coun., 1984, sr. rsch. fellow Am. Inst. Indian Studies. Mem. Am. Soc. Study of Religion, Am. Acad. Religion, Internat. Assn. History of Religion, Assn. Asian Studies, Internat. Assn. Study of Traditional Asian Medicine. Home: 6217 Roselawn Ave Madison WI 53716 Office: U Wis 1252 Van Hise Madison WI 53706

KNITTER, PAUL FRANCIS, theology educator; b. Chgo., Feb. 25, 1939; s. Paul Lewis and Rose Georgiana (Dolezal) K.; m. Catherine Mary Cornell, Dec. 31, 1982; children: John, Moira. Lic. theology, Pontifical Gregorian U., Rome, 1966; ThD, U. Marburg, Fed. Republic Germany, 1972. Asst. prof. Cath. Theol. Union, Chgo., 1972-75; assoc. prof. Xavier U., Cin., 1975-78, prof. theology, 1978—; bd. dirs. Christians for Peace in El Salvador, San Antonio, 1988—. Author: Toward A Protestant Theology of Religions, 1974, No Other Name?, 1985, The Myth of Christian Uniqueness, 1987; (with others) Faith, Religion, and Theology, 1990; editor: Pluralism and Oppression, 1990; gen. editor Faith Meets Faith Series, 1987—. Rsch. grant Xavier U., 1986, 88. Mem. Am. Acad. Religion, Cath. Theol. Soc. Am., Coll. Theology Soc. (bd. dirs. 1985-88), Am. Soc. Missiology. Home: 2636 Marlington Ave Cincinnati OH 45208 Office: Xavier U Cincinnati OH 45207

KNOTT, ELIZABETH B., clergywoman; b. Phila., July 29, 1927; d. Harry Gustus and Lillian (Leapson) B. BA, Maryville Coll., 1957; BD, McCormick Sem., 1963; MS, Okla. State U., 1970. Bookkeeper Sun Oil Co., Phila., 1946-53; dir. of Christian Edn. Roosevelt Dr. Presbyn. Ch., Milw., 1958-63; assoc. pastor First Presbyn. Ch., Littleton, Colo., 1963-66; pastor First Presbyn. Ch., Tonkawa, Okla., 1966-73; assoc. synod exec. mission funding Synod of Lincoln Trails, Indpls., 1973-80; organizing pastor New Creation Presbyn. Ch., Altoona, Iowa, 1980-83; interim pastor Grace Presbyn. Ch., Springfield, Va., 1984-85, Lewistown (Pa.) Presbyn. Ch., Va., 1986; interim exec. Presbytery of Detroit, 1986-87; synod exec. Synod of Alaska-Northwest, Seattle, 1987—; Mem.-at-large Consultation on Ch. Union, Princeton, N.J., 1975-76; bd. trustees McCormick Sem., Chgo., 1980-83, Sheldon Jackson Coll., Sitka, Ala., 1987—, Whitworth Coll., Spokane, Wash., 1987—; organizing bd. Creative Futures Ctr., Seattle, 1989; vice-moderator Churchwide Coordinating Cabinet, Louisville, 1989; mem. Wash. Assn. of Chs., Seattle, 1987. Organizer of intergenerational arts and crafts fair, City Council, Tonkawa, 1972, organizer of year-round recreation, City Council, Tonkawa, 1971; chairwoman Ch. Employed Women, 1975-76. Recipient Alumni citation Maryville Coll., 1989. Mem. Alban Inst., Assn. for Creative Change, Witherspoon Soc., Presbyn. Health, Edn. and Welfare, Women Execs. Democrat. Avocations: travel, gardening, photography, racquetball, tennis. Home: 106 SW 299th Pl Federal Way WA 98023

KNOTT, ESTHER RAMHARACKSINGH, minister; b. San Fernando, Trinidad, W.I., May 17, 1959; d. Ramnarine and Alice (Henry) Ramharacksingh; m. Ronald Alan Knott, June 10, 1990. BA in Religion, Andrews U., 1980, MA in Religious Edn., 1987. Campus chaplain Broadview Acad., Lafox, Ill., 1980-83; asst. chaplain Andrews U., Berrien Springs, Mich., 1985-87; dir. Adventist Heritage Project N.Am. Div. Edn. Dept. Seventh-day Adventist Ch., Silver Spring, Md., 1987-90; assoc. pastor Sligo Seventh-day Adventist Ch., Takoma Park, Md., 1990—. Contbr. articles to Adventist jours. Coord. Family Life Workshop, Berrien Springs, 1983-87; vol. Maranatha Vols. Internat.ch. builder, Belize, 1988, Mex., 1989. Office: Sligo Seventh-day Adventist Ch 7700 Carroll Ave Takoma Park MD 20912 *When difficult times come your way, you have a choice. You can become bitter or you can let God use the situation to make you better. Bitter of Better. Choose Better.*

KNOX, ANN LOUISE, minister, educator; b. Memphis, Dec. 2, 1935; d. Henry Berton Moody, Gladys Louise (Elford) Robbins; m. Wendell James Knox; children: James David, Jonathan Mark, Sarah Jo. BS, U. Houston, 1964; MA, Grace Christian Coll., 1985. Ordained minister Women's Minister's Forum; cert. tchr. Tex. Editor Tarpon News U. Corpus Christi, Tex., 1955-56; tchr. art and English Deepwater Jr. High Sch., Pasadena, Tex., 1964-66; pub. speaker women's groups and chs. various cities, U.S. and other countries, 1966-83; asst. minister Deepwater Ch.; prof., founder Deepwater Bible Sch.; founder, tchr. adult art Deer Park Art League, 1976-78; cons. Laporte (Tex.) Worship Ctr., 1988; pres. Broken Bread Ministries, Deer Park, 1980—; bd. dirs. Jack Wood Ministries, Dallas. Painter, scultpor; author: Glorifying God in Art, 1983, Wrestling with Angels, 1984, Baptism of Suffering, 1985. Mem. Internat. Ministers Forum, Women's Minister Forum, AGLOW (chmn. prayer 1976-77). Republican. Office: Broken Bread Ministries 302 E Oak Deer Park TX 77536

KNOX, CAROL RUTH, clergywoman, writer; b. Somerville, Mass., Dec. 16, 1938; d. Harold Lester and Gladys Ann (Laye) K. B.A., Tufts U., 1960; M.A., Brown U., 1964; Ph.D., Calif. Inst. Integral Studies, 1983. Ordained to ministry Unity Ch., 1970; tchr. Norton High Sch. (Mass.), 1960-62; dir. Mass. Assn. Adult Blind, Scituate, Mass., summers 1962-64; dir. music Ledyard High Sch., (Conn.), 1963-68; exec. dir., minister Unity Ctr., Walnut Creek, Calif., 1970—; speaker before civic groups; lectr. Diablo Valley Coll., John F. Kennedy U., 1971-84. Author: You've Got A Friend, 1974, Manna from Stones, 1978; Prayer of the Heart, 1983; Incredible Journey, 1984; also articles. Pres. bd. dirs. Synergy Sch., Martinez, Calif., 1978-79 (recipient award 1978); bd. dirs. Contra Costa County Mental Health Assn., 1979-81, Calif. Inst. Integral Studies, San Francisco, 1983—; mem. staff, bd. dirs. Rosebridge Inst., Walnut Creek, 1981—. Mem. Assn. Unity Chs. (v.p., dir. 1970—), Spiritual Realization Fellowship, Am. Bus. Women's Assn., AAUW. Republican. Home: 214 W 9th St Antioch CA 94509 Office: Unity Ctr Walnut Creek 1871 Geary Rd Walnut Creek CA 94596

KNOX, JAMES LLOYD, bishop; b. Tampa, Fla., Jan. 16, 1929; s. Carlos Stephen and Jessie (Hardee) K.; m. Edith Laney Strawn, June 2, 1951; children: Richard Michael, Carol Anne. AB, Fla. So. Coll., 1951; BD, Emory U., 1954; Cert., Presbyn. Lang. Sch., San Jose, Costa Rica, 1959. On trial Fla. Conf., 1952; ordained deacon, 1953; full connection, elder, 1954. Pastor United Meth. Ch., Williamson, Ga., 1952-54, Tampa, Fla., 1954-58; pastor Santiago de la Vegas Meth. Ch., Cuba, 1959-60; chaplain Wesley Sch., Cuba, 1959-60; pastor First Ch., Lomas de Zamora, Buenos Aires, Argentina, 1961-64; assoc. pastor First Meth. Ch., West Palm Beach, Fla., 1964—; now bishop N. Ala. Conf. First Meth. Ch., Birmingham, Ala. Editor: Land of Decision, 1961-64; contbr. articles to Together, World Outlook, others. Supt. Buenos Aires S. Dist., 1963-64; news corr. Argentina Bd. Missions; trustee Ward Coll., Barker Coll., Buenos Aires, 1961-64; mem. Gen. Bd. Meth. Ch. in Argentina, 1963-64. Office: United Meth Ch 898 Arkadelphia Rd Birmingham AL 35204

KNOX, RICHARD EVERT, clergyman; b. Quinlan, Tex., Aug. 17, 1917; s. Thomas Booth and Zana (Neighbors) K.; m. Mildred Pigg, June 7, 1939 (dec. Feb. 1975); children: Norma Sandra Peters, Matilda Ann Edens; m. Martha Pearl Hayden, Dec. 10, 1978. AA, Wesley Coll., Greenville, Tex., 1938; BA, East Tex. State, 1942, MA, 1956. Lic. radio operator. Supt. intermidates Sunday sch. First Bapt., New Boston, Tex., 1947-73, deacon, 1956—; pres. Bowie County Broadcasting Co. Inc., New Boston, 1974—, FGBMFI, New Boston, 1974—; operator Sta. KNBO Christian Radio, New Boston, 1977—; field rep. Full Gospel Bus. Men, northeast Tex., 1989—; disc jockey Sta. KNBO Radio Christian, New Boston, 1977—, daily techr., 1977—, pres., 1972—; internat. advisor Flame Fellowship Internat., 1984—; area advisor N.E. Tex. Area Womens Aglow Fellowship, 1976-85. With U.S. Army, 1945-46. Mem. New Boston C. of C., Lions (held all offices), Masons (master), Order of Ea. Star (worthy advisor). Home: 111 Hall St New Boston TX 75570 Office: Sta KNBO Radio PO Box 848 New Boston TX 75570

KNOX, ROBERT BURNS, religion organization administrator; b. Concord, N.H., Feb. 26, 1917; s. Ralph Burns Knox and Ruby Aileen (Gillette) Dixon; m. Barbara Macauley Lovejoy, July 4, 1941; children: Robert B. Jr., Karen Lovejoy Knox Campbell. BA, U. N.H., 1941; MA, George Washington U., 1956; Ministry Program, U. of the South, 1981. Lic. lay min. Episcopal Ch. Cadet USAF, 1940, Col., 1970; chief of Order Dept. RCA Distrib. Corp., San Antonio, Texas, 1972-76; ch. adminstr. St. George Episcopal Ch., San Antonio, 1977—; bd. dirs. Order of St. Luke the Physician (treas.); corp. mem. Sch. of Pastoral Care (treas.). Mem. interparish com. for Evangelism, San Antonio, 1987-89, compensation com. for Episcopal Diocese of West Tex., 1990—. Recipient several mil. awards including Legion of Merit with second award and cluster USAF, 1940-70. Episcopalian. Avocations: spectator sports, Hi-Fi Jazz recordings, stamps. Home: 10614 Mt Ida San Antonio TX 78213 Office: St George Episcopal Ch 6904 W Ave San Antonio TX 78213 *Joy and sadness are constants in our lives on earth. Throughout childhood and our adult lives we face ups and downs, never having been promised, and not experiencing, only the good life. But through it all, faith and trust in our Lord God brings us through those cycles and prepares us for the unknown life hereafter.*

KNUDSEN, RAYMOND BARNETT, clergyman, association executive, author; b. Denver, Nov. 11, 1919; s. Franklin Ole and Julia (Nielsen) K.; m. Edna Mae Nielsen, Jan. 26, 1940; children: Raymond Barnett, Silas John, Mark Allen, Ann DeLight (Mrs. Arthur James Semotan III). Student, Coll. Emporia, 1937-38, Wheaton Coll., 1938-39; B.A., U. Denver, 1941; Th.M., McCormick Theol. Sem., 1948; postgrad., U. Chgo., 1948; D.D., Burton Coll., 1955, LL.D., 1964; ThD, Miami Bible Inst., 1987. Pastor 1st Presbyn. Ch., Akron, Colo., 1937-39; Pastor 8th Ave. Presbyn. Ch., Denver, 1939-40; dir. Martin M. Post Larger Parish, Logansport, Ind., 1941-44; asst. Faith Presbyn. Ch., Chgo., 1945; pastor 1st Presbyn. Ch., Warsaw, Ill., 1946-52, 5th Presbyn. Ch., Springfield, Ill., 1952-63; sr. pastor Webb Horton Meml. Presbyn. Ch., Middletown, N.Y., 1963-70; exec. dir. for donor support Nat. Council Chs. of Christ in U.S.A., 1970-71, asst. gen. sec., 1971-77; pres. Nat. Consultation on Fin. Devel., 1977-85, chmn., 1985-88, chmn. emeritus, 1988—; lectr. philosophy Orange County (N.Y.) Community Coll., 1964-70; instr. Drew U. Sch. Theology, 1978-86, Perkins Sch. Theology So. Meth. U., 1986—; chmn. broadcasting press Synod of Ill., Presbyn. Ch., 1954-60, mem. gen. council, 1954-62; chmn. founding com. Ill. Presbyn. Home, Springfield, 1954; pres. Middletown Council Chs., 1967-69; chmn. Fifty Million Dollar Fund, Hudson River Presbytery, 1964-70; pres. Webb Horton Presbyn. Assocs.; v.p. Inst. Activation Research.; cons. Episc. Diocese of Pitts., 1977-85, Orthodox Ch. in Am., 1978-88, Christian Meth. Episc. Ch., 1983-88, Hawaii conf. United Ch. of Christ, 1983-86, Asbury Hills Camp, 1983-86; cons. Fla. Council of Chs., 1986—, Pitts. Experiment, 1987-88, Jesus Fellowship, Inc., 1987—, 1st Bapt. Ch., Washington, 1987-90, Cornstone Consultation, 1990—, Higher Dimensions, Tulsa, 1990, David M. Wright M.D. Found., Richmond, Va., 1991, Alfalit, Inc., Miami, Fla., 1991, Abundant Life, Richmond, 1991. Author: The Trinity, 1936, New Models for Financing the Local Church, 1974, 2d edit., 1985, New Models for Creative Giving, 1976, 2d edit., 1985, Models for Ministry, 1976, Developing Dynamic Stewardship, 1977, The Workbook, 1977, New Models for Church Administration, 1979, Christian Stewardship in a Period of Fiscal Change, 1984, Stewardship Enlistment and Commitment, 1986, Let Your Money Do the Talking, 1987, From "Commitment?" to "Commitment!", 1987, Wiltshire Village Cookbook, 1991; mem. rev. bd. Antenna, 1963-90; contbr. religious columns to publs.; syndicated newspaper column The Counselor. Mem. Middletown Narcotics Guidance Council, 1969-70; pres. bd. dirs. Occupations, Inc., 1964-69, treas., 1969-71, pres. emeritus, 1976—; bd. dirs. Aid to Retarded Children N.Y., 1963-66, United Presbyn. Student Found., 1962-70, Presbyn. Sr. Services, N.Y.C., 1981-85, Presbyn. Panel, 1981-87, Christian Collegiate Schs., Richmond, 1991; exec. bd. Orange County chpt. Aid Retarded Children; trustee Orange County Workshop for Disabled, 1963, Homemaker Service Orange County; pres. bd. trustees Camp Townsend, 1964-70. Recipient Author citation N.J. Inst. Tech., 1980, Cert. for Outstanding Ministry, Wheaton Coll., 1991. Mem. Nat. Temperance League (hon. v.p., chmn. nominating com. 1961-62), Alcohol Edn. Found. (dir.), Counselor Assn. Inc. (pres. 1954-82, chmn. bd. Ill. soc. 1955-88, chmn. emeritus 1988—), Greenview Shores Civic Assn. (founder, pres. 1989-90), Counselor Assn., Inc. (founder, pres. Fla. soc. 1990—). Clubs: Masons, Rotary (chmn. internat. contacts). Established Dr. Raymond B. and Edna M. Knudsen Library, 1st Presbyn. Ch., West Palm Beach, Fla., 1990. Home and Office: 1457 Brampton Cove Wellington West Palm Beach FL 33414 *We live in a global village in the shadow of a friendly, fatherly God. Through the structures of time and circumstances we move into the future and instead of closed doors we discover new directions, alternate routes, and challenging frontiers to bring us into each tomorrow. We discover the significance of selves as we lose ourselves in service to others. Through the interweaving of lives through the warp of generations and the woof of others we become a part of the fabric of time upon which the future stands with hope and promise.*

KNUDSEN, RAYMOND BARNETT, II, religious organization administrator; b. Denver, Sept. 25, 1941; s. Raymond Barnett I and Edna Mae (Nielsen) K.; m. Jane Ann Harsch, Jan. 17, 1970; children: Heidi Lynn, Heather Ann. BA, Ill. Coll., 1963; MDiv, McCormick Theol. Sem., Chgo., 1966. Ordained to ministry Presbyn. Ch., 1966. Asst. pastor 1st Presbyn. Ch., Wheaton, Ill., 1966-68; assoc. pastor 1st Presbyn. Ch., Wheaton, 1968-75, minister for corp. life and mission, 1975-77; dir. devel. Tarkio (Mo.) Coll., 1977-78, v.p., 1978-79; exec. v.p. Nat. Consultation on Fin. Devel., Hillsdale, N.J., 1979-82; pres. Nat. Consultation on Fin. Devel., Hillsdale, 1982-90; assoc. pastor for congl. care Kirk in the Hill Presbyn. Ch., Bloomfield Hills, Mich., 1990—; mem. candidates com. Presbytery of Chgo., 1972-77, chmn., 1973-77; mem. Detroit Presbytery; cons. Orthodox Ch. in Am. and Pitts. Expt.; founder AUTOGIVE. Author: Gift Annuity Workbook, 1983; author, editor: (newsletter) Stewardship U.S.A.; book reviewer Wheaton Pub. Library, 1968-71. Founding mem. Wheaton Youth Commn., 1968-69; mem. Higgins Scholarship Com., Chgo., 1972-77, chmn., 1975-77. Mem. The Counselor Assn., Inc. (trustee 1977—, pres. 1982—), Alpha Phi Omega (Disting. Svc. award 1963). Avocations: woodworking, computers, reading. Home: 4818 Quarton Rd Bloomfield Hills MI 48302 Office: Kirk in the Hills Presbyn Ch 1340 W Long Lake Rd Bloomfield Hills MI 48302

KNULL, ERHARD, minister; b. Radomsko, Poland, June 25, 1929; came to U.S., 1952.; s. Richard and Martha (Kamchen) K.; m. LydiaPenno, July 21, 1956; children: Carmen Ruth Knull Bloomster, Ralph Erhard Carl. BA, Sioux Falls Coll., 1960; BD, No. Am. Bapt. Seminary, 1961; post grad., U. Tuebingen, Fed. Republic Germany, 1961-62; MA, Kent state U., 1973; MDiv, North Am. Bapt. Seminary, 1984; postgrad., V.A. Chaplain Tng. Sch., St. Louis, 1974, Samaritan Counseling Ctr., Lakewood, Ohio, 1982-83. Ordained to ministry Bapt. Ch, 1963; cert. VA chaplain, Washington. Min. Rosenfeld Bapt. Ch., Drake, N.D., 1962-65, Missionary Bapt. Ch., Parma, Ohio, 1965-69; lectr. Kent (Ohio) State U., 1969; staff chaplain Cleve. Med. Ctr., Brecksville, 1970—; chaplain, counselor VA Community Outreach program, Cleve., 1978—. Contbr. articles to profl. jours. Active Parma Heights Bapt. Ch., also tchr., advisor men's fellowship. Mem. North Am. Bapt. Conf. (endorsed chaplain), North Am. Bapt. Sem. Alumni Assn. Baptist. Avocations: reading, bicycling, traveling, walking, gardening. Office: VA Med Ctr 10000 Brecksville Rd Brecksville OH 44141

KNUTSON, GERHARD I., bishop. Bishop Evang. Luth. Ch. in Am., Rice Lake, Wis. Office: Evang Luth Ch Am 12 W Marshall St Box 30 Rice Lake WI 54968*

KNUTSON, LANNY DEAN, minister; b. Canby, Minn., July 6, 1943; s. Lloyd Cecil and Mabel Marie (Peterson) K.; m. Anna Lee Lucas, July 10, 1972; children: Robert Aaron, Mandy Elizabeth, Signe Kathryn. BA, Augustana Coll., 1965; MDiv, Luther Theol. Sem., St. Paul, 1969. Ordained to ministry Am. Luth. Ch., 1969. Intern pastor 1st Luth. Ch., Onalaska, Wis., 1967-68; assoc. pastor 1st Luth. Ch., Bottineau, N.D., 1969-71; mission pastor Glasgow Air Base Ministry, Mont., 1971-72; asst. pastor Christ Luth. Ch., Regina, Sask., Can., 1973-77; pastor Christ Luth. Ch., Calgary, Alta., Can., 1978—; sec., v.p. Regina conf. Evang. Luth. Ch. Can., 1974-77, vice chmn. bd. communication, Saskatoon, Sask., 1976-80, chmn. bd., 1980-84; sec., pres. Regina Ministerial Assn., 1974-77; chmn., advisor Concord Can. Bookstore Com., Calgary, 1982-88; mem. Luth. Merger Task Force on Communication, Winnipeg, Man., Can., 1984-85; chairperson Office for Communication Mgmt. Com., Winnipeg, 1986-91. Editor Alta. Synod News, 1986—; contbr. articles to religious jours. Chmn. Ten Days for World Devel., Calgary, 1980-83. Mem. Alta. Pioneer Auto Club, Plymouth Owners Club (editor Plymouth Bull. 1987—). Home: 4407 Richmond Rd SW, Calgary, AB Canada T3E 4P5 Office: Christ Luth Ch, 4211 Richmond Rd SW, Calgary, AB Canada T3E 4P4

KOCH, DIETRICH-ALEX GERHARD, theology educator; b. Königsberg, Ostpreussen, Germany, Oct. 22, 1942. Student, U. Göttingen Heidelberg, Fed. Republic of Germany, 1963-71; habilitation, 1983. Ordained to ministry, 1974. Parish vicar Luth. Ch., Scheden, Fed. Republic of Germany, 1974-77; tchr. U. Mainz, Fed. Republic of Germany, 1977-84, prof., 1984-85; prof. U. Münster, Fed. Republic of Germany, 1985—. Author: Wundererzählungen des Markusevangeliums, 1975, Die Schrift als Zeuge des Evangeliums, 1986; editor: Festschrift W. Marxsen, 1989. Mem. N.T. Studies Soc., Sci. Soc. for Theology, Franz-Delitzsch Soc. Home: Universitätsstr 13-17, D-4400 Münster Federal Republic of Germany Office: Universitätsstr 13-17, D-4400 Münster Federal Republic of Germany

KOCH, GLENN A., minister; b. Eustis, Nebr., May 5, 1929; s. Arthur Otto Henry and Viola Belle (Lehmann) K.; m. Martina Marie Hanson, June 7, 1953; children: Vickie, Sandra, Donna, David, Ruth. BA, Christ Christian Coll., 1963; MA, U. No. Colo., 1974; MDiv, Concordia Sem., 1975; PhD, Christ Evang. Coll., 1975. Ordained to ministry Luth. Ch., 1962. Pastor, counselor Zion Luth. Ch., Burley, Idaho, 1962-68; chaplain USAF, Richards Gebarur, Mo., 1968-70, Bein Hoa, Vietnam, 1970-71, Davis Monthan, Ariz., 1971-75, Elmendorf, Alaska, 1976-79, Hill, Utah, 1979-83, Minot, N.D., 1983-85, Kaiserslautern, Germany, 1985-88, Layton, Utah, 1989—; pres. Cassia County Mental Health Group, Burley, 1963-67; pastoral advisor in field. Author (poetry): Tribut to Rain, 1957, The Counselor, 1960, The Losing Battle, The Aging Snowman, Speed, 1969, Thank You, 1975, Answer to a Mystery, 1976, Life's Changing Scenes, 1976, The Freeway, 1974. Dir. Subs for Santa, Hill AFB, Utah, 1982, Baskets for the Needy, Minot AFB, 1984. Cpl. USMC, 1946-53. Recipient Victor Medal, 1946-48, Bronze Star, 1971, Outstanding Svc. Medal, 1975, Meritorious Svc. Medal, 1979, 83, 85. Mem. Am. Bd. Christian Psychology (clin.). Home and Office: 5274 S 3100 W Roy UT 84067

KOCH, GLENN ALAN, seminary educator, administrator; b. Quinton, N.J., Feb. 23, 1932; s. Garth Colet and Pearl Louise (Storm) K.; m.Peggy Ann Barber, June 5,1954; children: Cheryl Ann, David Alan, Julie Alyson. BA, Marshall U., 1953; BD, Ea. Bapt. Theol. Sem., 1956, ThM, 1959; MA, U. Pa., 1962, PhD, 1976. Ordained to ministry Am. Bapt. Chs. U.S.A., 1957. Pastor 1st Community Bapt. Ch., West collingswood Heights, N.J., 1956-59; interim pastor Kings Community Bapt. Ch., Cherry Hill, N.J., 1959, Bapt. chs., Camden, N.J., Phila., Dividing Creek, N.J., Kennett Sq., Pa., 1956-84; prof. N.T. Studies Ea. Bapt. Theol. Sem., Phila., 1957-61, assoc. prof., 1969-76, prof., 1976—, assoc. dean, 1984-90, acting dean, 1980-83; dir. evening courses for Christian workers, 1960-63; asst. prof. Greek and religion, Ea. Coll., St. Davids, Pa., 1961-69; mem. Phila. Seminar on Christian Origins; instr. N.T. and religion courses adult evening schs., Phila., 1960-63; sponsor Holy Land tours, 1973—; ednl. cons. for colls. Collaborator with Centre d'Analyse et de Documentation Patristiques, 1972-75; co-author: Learning to Read New Testament Greek, 1983; contbr. articles to United Presbyn. and Am. Bapt. publs., Uniform lecture series The Bapt. Leader, book revs. to Christianity Today and Mission mags. Mem. Soc. Bibl. Lit. Home: 1401 Fairview Ave Havertown PA 19083 Office: Ea Bapt Theol Sem 6 Lancaster Ave Wynnewood PA 19096 *As a professor, I have kept on my desk a maxim of ancient wisdom which I look at from time to time: "Therefore, as one who teaches another, do you not teach yourself?".*

KOCH, SISTER IMELDA, nun; b. Petersburg, Nebr., July 26, 1927; d. Frank Joseph and Elizabeth Mary (Brachle) K. BS in Edn., Creighton U., 1955, MA, 1959; MA in Sacred Studies, St. Johns U., Collegeville, Minn., 1965; postgrad. clin. pastoral edn., St. Marys Hosp., Kansas City, Mo., 1978. Joined Benedictine Sisters, Roman Cath. Ch., 1946. Formation coord. Missionary Benedictine Sisters, Norfolk, Nebr., 1960-72, prioress, 1972-77; formation coord. Benedictine Sisters, Liberty, Mo., 1978—; prioress Queen of Angels Monastery, Liberty, 1989—; chaplain St. Joseph Hosp., Kansas City, Mo., 1978-80, St. Mary's Hosp., Kansas City, 1980-83; exec. dir. Immacolata Manor, Liberty, 1983—; elem. tchr. St. John Berchmans Sch., Raeville, Nebr., 1947-48, 50-51; jr. high tchr. St. Leonard Sch., Madison, 1951-60, prin., 1951-60. Mem. Leadership Conf. Women Religious, Conf. Am. Benedictine Prioresses, Nat. Religious Vocat. Conf., Monastic Liturgy Forum, Am. Benedictine Formation Conf. Home and Office: 2101 Hughes Rd Liberty MO 64068 *Life is the greatest gift we could receive, but also a great responsibility. We were created for happiness, here and hereafter. We have dignity and a purpose for our life, and a task that only we can do. In order to achieve our goals in life and have our lives make a difference in our world, we each have been gifted with gifts of grace and nature—personality, spirituality and great potential to strive for.*

KOCH, KARL WILLIAM, management analyst, minister; b. Seattle, May 21, 1933; s. William Henry and Dora Martha (Vorwerk) K.; m. Dorothea Ruth Bellmann, Aug. 23, 1958; children: Kristen Martha, Douglas William. BA, Concordia Sem., St. Louis, 1956, MDiv, 1959, MST, 1960; MA in Sociology, U. Cin., 1974. Ordained to ministry Luth. Ch.—Mo. Synod, 1960. Pastor Trinity Luth. Ch., Coal Valley, Ill., 1960-63, Concordia Luth. Ch., Pullman, Wash., 1963-69; Luth. campus pastor U. Cin., 1969-74; mgmt. analyst, dir. tng. programs State of Ohio, 1976-83; co-founder The Mentor Group Inc., Columbus, Ohio, 1985—; adj. faculty Franklin U., Columbus, 1980—; assigned vacancy pastor various chs. Ohio dist. Luth. Ch.—Mo. Synod, 1976—. Co-author: (with Donn Abdon) Leading and Managing for Excellence; (with Vicki C. McConnell) Computerizing the Corporation: The Intimate Link Between People and Machines; editor, mgr. police tng. Systems Series, 1974-79; author devotional writings. First v.p. Mental Health Assn., Rock Island, Ill., 1963; mem. Human Rels. Commn., Pullman, 1969; bd. dirs., treas. Mt. Airy Community Coun., Cin., 1974. Recipient award Home Energy Assistance Program of HHS, 1982. Home: 5445 Aqua St Columbus OH 43229 Office: The Mentor Group PO Box 14482 Columbus OH 43214 *Whatever we do, whether in religion or technology, it must benefit people, particularly those who are its immediate recipients.*

KOCH, KEVIN A., priest, teacher; b. Lincoln, Nebr., Sept. 23, 1958; s. Cornelius Michael and Ida Jane (Wirges) K. BA in Social Sci., Conception Sem. Coll., 1977-81; M of Divinity, St. Thomas Theol. Sem., 1981-85. Assoc. pastor St. Mathew's Ch., Gillette, Wyo., 1985-86, St. Mary's Cathedral, Cheyenne, Wyo., 1986—; instr. religion and morality Seton Cath. High Sch., Cheyenne, Wyo., 1986—; assc. pastor Cathedral of St. Mary, Cheyenne, 1986—, child care worker St. Joseph's Children's Home, Torrington, Wyo., 1981-82, chaplain asst. Fed. Correction Instn., Englewood, Colo., 1982-83, hosp. chaplain trainee W. Nebr. Gen. Hosp., Scottsbluff, 1984. Mem. Nat. Cath. Edn. Assn. Home: 100 W 21st Cheyenne WY 82003-1268 Office: St Mary's Cathedral PO Box 1268 Cheyenne WY 82003-1268

KOCH, ROBERT F., minister; b. Red Bud, Ill., June 27, 1956; s. Delbert F. and Alvira L. (Mehrtens) K.; m. Catherine L. Cummins, Aug. 12, 1978; children: William, Elizabeth. BA, McKendree Coll., Lebanon, Ill., 1978; MA, Northwestern U., 1982, PhD, 1988; MST, Garrett Sem., Evanston, Ill., 1984. Ordained to ministry United Ch. of Christ, 1983. Pastor St. John and Zion United Ch. of Christ Chs., Waterloo, Ill., 1983-89, St John United Ch. of Christ, New Athens, Ill., 1989—; mem. audio-visual com. Ill. South Conf., United Ch. of Christ, 1983—, chmn., 1987—, in-care student advisor, 1984—, mem. farm crisis and rural life ministry, 1985-88, mem. assoc. conf. min. search com., 1986, mem. ch. and ministry com., 1989—, chmn. in-care com., 1989—, del. Gen. Synod, 1991—. Bd. dirs. New Athens Home for Aged, 1989—; chmn. Toys for Tots Campaign, New Athens. Mem. Rotary. Home: 506 Mill New Athens IL 62264 Office: 301 S Market New Athens IL 62264

KOCH, THERESE, nun, eucharistic minister, administrator healthcare facility; b. Petersburg, Nebr., Oct. 28, 1924; d. Frank Joseph and Elizabeth 9Brachle) K. Student, Chadron State Tchrs. Coll., 1942, Creighton U., 1944, St. Mary's Coll., 1944-45, St. Louis U., 1957, Columbia U., 1960-61. Joined Religious Fedn. St. Scholastica, Roman Cath. Ch., 1977. Mem. Missionary Benedictine Sisters, Norfolk, Nebr., 1944-77; sec.-treas. Benedictine Sisters, Liberty, Mo., 1977—; transferred vows Fedn. St. Scholastica Priory, Tulsa, 1980-89, Queen of Angels Monastery, Liberty, 1989—; adminstr. Immacolata Manor, Liberty, 1981—, pres. bd., 1981-84, treas., 1981—, spiritual leader aux., 1982—; editor Immacolata newsletter. Recipient Charles Pfizer Co. award U.S. Civil Def., 1970; award of Merit Mid-Am. Coun. Boy Scouts Am., 1975; Soroptimist Internat. of Am. Women Helping Women award, 1984; Outstanding Liberty Citizens award, 1987. Home and Office: 2101 Hughes Rd Liberty MO 64068

KOCHAKIAN, GARABED DANIEL, priest, educator; b. Salem, Mass., Apr. 24, 1945; s. Roopen and Mary Elizabeth (Najarian) K.; m. Roberta Flora Carman, May 30, 1976. BA, Iona Col., New Rochelle, N.Y., 1966-70; MDiv, St. Vladimir's Orthodox Sem., Crestwood, N.Y., 1966-73. Ordained deacon Armenian Orthodox Ch., 1974, priest, 1976. Pastor Armenian Ch. of Our Saviour, Worcester, Mass., 1974-82, St. Mesrob Armenian Ch., Racine, Wis., 1982—; instr. Ednl. Inst., Nicosia, Cyprus, 1974; tchr. Worcester Pub. Schs., 1978-80; lectr. St. Nersess Armenian Sem., New Rochelle, N.Y.; on-call chaplain St. Luke's Hosp., Racine, Wis., 1988. Author: Armenian Portraits of Faith, 1989, Art in the Armenian Church, A Sacred Tradition, 1991, (student and tchr. texts) Come Let Us Worship, Living in God's World, Time With God, 1972, Sacraments, Symbols of Our Faith, 1983, We Believe, 1987, Bless O Lord, 1989, other ch. publs.; editor: St. Nersess Armenian Sem. Newsletter, 1987-89. Mem. Nat. Coun. Chs. (gov. bd. mem. 1982), Oriental Orthodox Chs. Coun., Acad. N.Am. Ecumenists, Nat. Assn. Armenian Studies and Research. Fluent in 3 languages. Avocations: art, music, icon painting. Office: St Mesrob Armenian Orth Ch 4605 Erie St Racine WI 53402

KOCHER, RONALD PAUL, minister; b. Omak, Wash., Mar. 27, 1952; s. Harvey Harold Kocher and Ena Mae (Yoder) Barnes; m. Claudia Margene Griffith, Aug. 19, 1972; children: Allison Nicolle, Lindsey Marie, Thomas Christian. AA, Cen. Coll., 1973; MA, George Fox Coll., 1979; MDiv, Western Evang. Sem., 1984. Ordained to ministry Free Meth. Ch. as deacon, 1985, as elder, 1987. Min. West Bethany Free Meth. Ch., Leoti, Kans., 1984-88, Crestway Free Meth. Ch., Wichita, Kans., 1988—; trustee Cen. Coll., McPherson, Kans., 1990—. Mem. Cen. Coll. Alumni Assn. (v.p. 1986-87, pres. 1988-89), Lions (pres. elect Leoti, Kans. 1988), Kiwanis (v.p. S.E. Wichita, Kans. 1990, pres. 1991). Home: 556 S Belmont St Wichita KS 67218-2202 Office: Crestway Free Meth Ch 601 S Crestway St Wichita KS 67218-2211

KOCHSMEIER, BRUCE STANLEY, minister; b. San Diego, Jan. 11, 1954; s. Stanley Wilfrid and Alberta Agnes (Ow) K.; m. Nancy Ruth Johnson, May 29, 1976; children: Kate Elizabeth, Harley Davidson. AB, San Diego State U., 1975; MDiv, Princeton Theol. Sem., 1985. Ordained to ministry Presbyn. Ch., 1985. Pastor First Presbyn. Ch., Hereford, Tex., 1985-88; assoc. pastor La Jolla (Calif.) Presbyn. Ch., 1988—; mem. youth and young adult ministry Presbytery of San Diego, 1988—; camps and leadership devel. subcom. Synod of So. Calif. and Hawaii, L.A., 1991—. Author: Guidelines to Getaways--A Handbook for the Motorcycle Adventurer, 1982. Mem. Am. Motorcycle Assn. Democrat. Home: 9075 Danube Ln San Diego CA 92126 Office: La Jolla Presbyn Ch 7715 Draper Ave La Jolla CA 92126 *How hopeful is life because Christ came for all. To remember that I am part of the all, is joy.*

KOCHTITZKY, LYNNE DAWSON, priest; b. Yonkers, N.Y., July 25, 1941; d. Alan Russell and Margaret Victoria (Black) Dawson; m. Rodney Morse Kochtitzky, May 23, 1981. RN, St. Luke's Sch. Nursing, 1962; BA, Marymount Manhattan, 1973; MPH, Columbia U., 1974; MDiv, Gen. Theol. Sem., 1982. RN; ordained to ministry Episcopal Ch. Staff nurse St. Luke's Hosp., N.Y.C., 1962-63; head nurse Roosevelt Hosp., N.Y.C., 1965-66; staff nurse Albert Einstein Med. Ctr., N.Y.C., 1966-68; instr. nursing Misericordia Sch. Nursing, N.Y.C., 1968-71, St. Luke's Sch. Nursing, N.Y.C., 1971-73; asst. prof. N.Y. Hosp. Cornell U., N.Y.C., 1974-79; chaplain St. Barnabas Nursing Home, Chattanooga, Tenn., 1982-83; asst. rector St. Paul's Episc. Ch., Franklin, Tenn., 1983-86; curate Christ Ch., Bronxville, N.Y., 1986—; mem. Episc. women's caucus Diocese of N.Y., chair ad hoc com. to study abortion, 1986-87; bd. dirs. Floating Hosp., N.Y.C., 1976-79, Jansen Meml. Hospice, Tuckahoe, N.Y., 1987—; cons. Concern for Dying, N.Y.C., 1979-82; lab trainer Lead Cons., Inc., Reynoldsburg, Ohio, 1986—. Mem. St. Luke's Sch. Nursing Alumnae (pres. 1979-81). Avocation: cooking. Home and Office: Christ Ch 17 Sagamore Rd Bronxville NY 10708

KOCISKO, STEPHEN JOHN, clergyman; b. Mpls., June 11, 1915; s. John Z. and Anna (Somosz) K. Ph.B., Propaganda Fide U., 1937, S.T.L., 1941. Ordained priest Roman Catholic Ch., 1941, consecrated bishop, 1956; chancellor Byzantine Cath. Diocese of Pitts., 1956; rector Byzantine Cath. Sem., Pitts., 1958-63; 1st bishop Byzantine Eparchy (diocese) of Passaic, 1963-69; met. archbishop of Pitts., 1969—. Address: 50 Riverview Ave Pittsburgh PA 15214

KOEDEL, ROBERT CRAIG, minister, historian, educator; b. Tarentum, Pa., July 1, 1927; s. Theodore and Evelyn (Dagan) K.; m. Barbara Ellen Wood, Jan. 6, 1962. B.A., Wheaton Coll., Ill., 1949; M.Div., Pitts. Theol Sem., 1953; M.A., U. Pitts., 1964; postgrad., Temple U., 1964-70. Ordained to ministry United Presbyterian Ch. U.S.A., 1953. Pastor Monaghan Presbyn. Ch., Dillsburg, Pa., 1956-59; asst. pastor Mt. Calvary Presbyn. Ch., Corapolis, Pa., 1959-60; assoc. pastor Dormont Presbyn. Ch., Pitts., 1960-64; mem. faculty Atlantic Community Coll., Mays Landing, N.J., 1966—, prof. social sci., history, religion, 1978—, chmn. dept. history, 1969-70, 78-79, asst. dean instrn., 1970-72; lectr. in history Stockton State Coll., 1985—; clergyman West Jersey Presbytery; lectr. local history and religion. Author: South Jersey Heritage: A Social, Economic and Cultural History, 1977, God's Vine in This Wilderness: Religion in South Jersey to 1800, 1980, Following the Water: The Shellfish Industry in South Jersey, 1983, Ships and the Sea Down Jersey, 1989; contbr. articles to profl. jours., articles to newspapers. Mem. Atlantic County Cultural and Heritage Adv. Bd., 1991—. Served as chaplain USAF, 1953-56. N.J. Hist. Commn. research grantee, 1974, 84. Mem. United Teaching Professions, Presbyn. Hist. Soc., N.J. Hist. Soc. (trustee 1985-88), Atlantic County Hist. Soc. (editor jour.), Gloucester County Hist. Soc., West Jersey Presbytery, Hist. Soc. Pa., Phila. Maritime Mus. Home: PO Box 64 Oceanville NJ 08231 Office: Atlantic Community Coll Mays Landing NJ 08330

KOEHLER-SAPP, JANICE MANCINELLI, deacon, communications executive; b. Colorado Springs, Colo., Jan. 2, 1948; d. Albert Daniel and Yolanda (Conte) Mancinelli; m. Edward Frank Koehler, Nov. 23, 1968 (div. 1981); 1 child, Jordan Conte; m. David Brewer Sapp, May 7, 1983; stepchildren: Lara Elizabeth, Catherine Leigh. BA, U. Md., 1971; MA, George Mason U., 1982; MDiv Wesley Theol. Sem., Am. U., Washington, 1988. Ordained deacon United Meth. Ch., 1986. Tchr. Pub. Sch. Bds., Montgomery County, Md., 1971-76, Stafford County, Va., 1976-78; instr. Quantico (Va.) Marine Base, 1978-79; editor CACI, Arlington, Va., 1979-81; proposal mgr. ORI, Arlington, 1982-83; pres., owner Janus Communications, Burke, Va., 1980-89; proposal mgr. No. Va. Office Magnavox, Falls Church, 1983-88; asst. pastor Mt. Vernon United Meth. Ch., Alexandria, Va., 1985-86; pastor Providence United Meth. Ch., Towson, Md., 1989-90. Author, coord. promotional mats, 1982; contbr. articles to children's publs. (award Va. Edn. Assn. 1978). Founder, Mothers without Custody, Offspring, Washington, 1980—; cons. Potency Restored, Silver Spring, Md., 1981—, Women's Kaleidoscope, Alexandria, Va., 1982—; ch. educator United Meth. Ch., Fairfax, Va., 1983-84, researcher women's issues, 1983. Recipient letter of commendation. PRI, Inc., Alexandria, 1979-80. Mem. Conf. Com. of Communications (Balt. ann. conf.), Rotary. Democrat. Home: 4015 Carriage Dr PO Box 1019 Skippack PA 19474

KOEHNLEIN, JOHN MARTIN, SR., minister, consultant; b. Phillipsburg, N.J., Mar. 27, 1951; s. C. Edgar and Hilda Katherine (Martin) K.; m. Suzanne Gaye Sproull, Aug. 23, 1980; children: Bennett, Shawn, Paula, Jay, John Jr. BA, Gettysburg Coll., 1973; MDiv, Luth. Theol. Sem., 1977, STM, 1989; postgrad., U. Iowa, 1991—. Ordained to ministry Evang. Luth. Ch. in Am., 1977. Pastor Faith Luth. Ch., Oklahoma, Pa., 1977-79, Orkney Springs (Va.) Luth. Parish, 1983-91; sem. cons., 1989—; dean Cen. Valley Luth. Conf., Shenandoah, Va., 1988-91; chmn. leadership support Luth. Ch., Salem, Va., 1984-89, mem. commn. on ministry, Salem, 1985-89, mem. continuing edn. com., Atlanta, 1988-89; chaplain Basye (Va.)/Bryce Mountain Lions, 1984-91, West Shenandoah Ruritan Club, Orkney Springs, 1984-91. Dir. Response, Woodstock, Va., 1984-86, Luth. Family Svcs. Va., Salem, 1985-88. Mem. Am. Soc. Ch. History, Soc. for Sci. Study of Religion, Am. Hist. Assn., Religious Rsch. Assn. Home and Office: 210 6th St # A-2 Coralville IA 52241

KOEKKOEK, JOHN WALLACE, minister; b. Long Beach, Calif., Mar. 25, 1935; s. John Herman and Jane (Wallace) K.; m. Laura Jeannette Sunkler, Aug. 20, 1954; children: Laura Koekkoek Wright, John Bradley, Julie Jane Koekkoek Lipp, Douglas Alan. BA in Christian Ministry, Minn. Bible Coll., 1955; BA in Psychology, Pepperdine Coll., 1958, MA in Edn. Psychology, 1960; postgrad., U. So. Calif., 1962-66. Lic. marriage and family counselor, Calif.; ordained to ministry Ch. of Christ, 1955. From assoc. min. to min. South Broadway Ch. of Christ, L.A., 1955-59; min. Del Amo Ch. of Christ, Torrance, Calif., 1959-60; prof. psychology Pacific Christian Coll., Long Beach and Fullerton, Calif., 1959-73; min. Norkenzie Christian Ch., Eugene, Oreg., 1973—. Bd. dirs. Christian Family Svcs., Eugene, 1975-77, San Jose (Calif.) Bible Coll., 1977-79. Mem. Lane Assn. Evangelicals (chmn. 1989—). Republican. Home: 1725 Adkins Eugene OR 97401 Office: Norkenzie Christian Ch 2530 Crescent Ave Eugene OR 97401

KOELEMAY, RALPH LAWRENCE, retired minister, marriage and family consultant; b. Port Neches, Tex., Feb. 10, 1926; s. Martin and Anna (Westerterp) K.; m. Ann Watkins, Sept. 12, 1951; children: LuAnn Koelemay Bearman, Ralph Larry II, Mary Lynne Koelemay Strickland, Donna Koelemay Berg. AA, Lon Morris Coll., 1948; BA, Vanderbilt U., 1951, BD, 1954, MDiv, 1973; MA in Teaching Social Sci., U. Wis., 1972. Ordained to ministry United Meth. Ch., 1951. Assoc. pastor United Meth. Ch., Nashville, 1951-52; pastor United Meth. Ch., Bell Springs and Nolensville, Tenn., 1952-55, Osceola, Spencer, Black River Falls and Plover, Wis., 1958-63, 68-71; pastor United Protestant Ch., New Richmond, Wis., 1963-68; human rels. and family rels. cons. Plover, Wis., 1971—; co-dir. Wis. Conf. Marriage and Family; condr. courses and seminars on faith, human rels., sexuality, and ethics; counselor, dir. youth camps. Chaplain, lt. col., USAF, 1955-58, mem. Res. 1958-86, ret. Mem. VFW, Acad. for Parish Clergy, Wis. Retired Mil. Officers, Retired Officer's Assn., Am. Legion. Avocations: reading, writing, traveling, gardening. Home and Office: 702 Opportunity Ln Plover WI 54467 *If one is to "think God's thoughts after Him," one must constantly explore the limits of life as we presently know it, turn the facets of Truth around and examine them from a new direction and/or in a different light.*

KOENIG, FRANZ CARDINAL, archbishop; b. Rabenstein, Austria, Aug. 3, 1905; D.D.; Ph.D.; hon. degrees univs. Vienna, Innsbruck, Salzburg, Zagreb, Am. univs. Ordained priest Roman Catholic Ch., 1933; prof. high sch.; lectr. U. Vienna, 1946-48, extraordinary prof., from 1948; bishop coadjutor, St. Poelten, 1952; archbishop of Vienna, 1956-85; cardinal, 1958; pres. Secretariat for Non-Believers, 1965-80, Pax Christi Internat., 1985-90. Mem. Am. Acad. Arts and Scis. Author: Christus und die Religionen der Erde, 1951, Religionswissenschaftliches Woerterbuch, 1956, Zarathustras Jenseitsvorstellungen und das Alte Testament, 1964, Die Stunde der Welt 1971, Der Aufbruch zum Geist, 1972, Das Zeichen Gottes, 1973, Der Mensch ist fuer die Zukunft angelegt, 1975, Kirche und Welt, 1978, Glaube ist Freiheit, 1981, Der Glaube der Menschen, 1985, Der Weg der Kirche, 1986, Lexikon der Religionen, 1987, König/Ehrlich, Juden und Christen haben eine Zukunft, 1988. Address: Wollzeile 2, 1010 Vienna Austria

KOENIG, ROBERT AUGUST, clergyman, educator; b. Red Wing, Minn., July 14, 1933; s. William C. and Florence E. (Tebbe) K.; BS cum laude, U. Wis., Superior, 1955; MA in Ednl. Adminstrn., U. Minn., 1965, PhD, 1973; MDiv magna cum laude, San Francisco Theol. Sem., 1969; postgrad. (John Hay fellow) Bennington Coll., summer, 1965; m. Pauline Louise Olson, June 21, 1962. Supr. music Florence (Wis.) High Sch., 1955-56; dir. instrumental music Chetek (Wis.), public schs., 1958-62; tchr. instrumental music and humanities Palo Alto (Calif.) Sr. High Sch., 1962-65; asst. to minister St. John's Presbyn. Ch., San Francisco, 1964-65; ordained to ministry Presbyn. Ch., 1970; minister Sawyer County (Wis.) larger parish, 1969-74; tchr. gen. music Jordan Jr. High Sch., Palo Alto, 1966-69; instr., Coll. Edn., U. Minn., 1969-71; adminstrv. asst. to pres. Lakewood State Community Coll., White Bear Lake, Minn., 1971-72; asst. to exec. dir. Minn. Higher Edn. Coordinating Bd., St. Paul, 1972, coordinator commn. and personnel services, 1972-74; instr. Inver Hills Community Coll., Inver Grove Heights, Minn., 1974; minister First Presbyn. Ch. of Chippewa Falls (Wis.), 1974-85; sr. pastor Grove Presbyn. Ch., Danville, Pa., 1985-88, First Presbyn. Ch., South St. Paul, Minn., 1988—; mem. study com. Presbytery of Chippewa, 1973-74, mem. ministerial relations com., 1974-77; adj. asst. prof. dept. ednl. adminstrn. U. Minn., Mpls., 1976-77; mem. faculty U. Wis. Extension, Eau Claire, 1977, chmn. 3d Ann. Bibl. Seminar, 1977, mem. faculty Communiversity, 1977-85; mem. internat. coordinating com. of ch. mission Synod of Lakes and Prairies, 1978-79; mem. ministerial relations com. Presbytery of No. Waters, 1977-82, chmn. ministerial relations com., 1981-82, moderator, 1983; chmn. Synod Designation Pastor Plan Cabinet 1982-84; chmn. Presbytery Council, 1982-84; chairperson Christian edn. com. Presbytery of Northumberland, 1987-88, mem. Presbytery council, 1987-88; mem. Christian edn. com. Synod of the Trinity, 1987-88, Danville-Riverside Area Ministerial Assn., 1985-88, pres., 1987-88; mem. South St. Paul Ministerial Assn., 1988—, pres., 1989-90. Bd. dirs. North Central Career Devel. Center, Mpls., 1978-84, chmn. fin. com., 1979-84, bd. dirs. devel. found., 1983-85; pres. Chippewa Valley Ecumenical Housing Assn., 1984-85. Served with U.S. Army, 1956-58; Korea. Lodges: Danville Elks; Wis. Masons (grand chaplain Wis. 1977-80, 83-85). Contbr. articles to profl. jours. Home: 6045 Bowman Ave E Inver Grove Heights MN 55076 Office: 535 20th Ave N South Saint Paul MN 55075

KOENIG, STEPHEN EDWARD, minister; b. Palm Beach County, Fla., June 29, 1945; s. Edward Albert and Florose Edyth (Gantt) K.; m. Patricia Louise Richter, June 1, 1968; children: Elizabeth, Jill, Alexander. AA, Concordia Luth. Jr. Coll., Ann Arbor, Mich., 1965; BA, Concordia Sr. Coll., Ft. Wayne, Ind., 1967; MDiv, Concordia Sem., St. Louis, 1971. Ordained to ministry Luth. Ch.-Mo. Synod., 1971. Vicar (intern) Bethany Luth. Ch., Parma, Ohio, 1969-70; from asst. to assoc. pastor Trinity Luth. Ch., Merrill, Wis., 1971-76; pastor Christ Luth. Ch., Anderson, Ind., 1976-86, St. James Luth. Ch., Reynolds, Ind., 1986—; zone pastoral advisor Luth. Women's Missionary League, Logansport, Ind., 1986-89, Internat. Luth. Laymens League, Wabash Valley, Ind., 1989—. V.p. Kiwanis, Merrill, 1972-76, County Housing Authority, Lincoln County, Wis., 1974-76, Am. Cancer Soc. Bd., Anderson, 1978-86. Mem. Ministerial Assn. Home: PO Box 315 Reynolds IN 47980 Office: St James Luth Ch PO Box 327 Reynolds IN 47980

KOENIGSBERG, SOL, retired association executive; b. Detroit, Dec. 11, 1924; s. Charles Phillip and Pearl (Fine) K.; m. Rosette Ostrowiecki; children: Michael, Beth. BA, Wayne State U., 1949; MSW, U. Pa., 1952. Caseworker Resettlement Svc., Detroit, 1950; med. social worker VA Hosp., Wilmington, Del., 1950-52; supr. Jewish Social Svc. Bur., Detroit, from 1952; exec. staff mem. Jewish Fedn. Detroit, to 1962; asst. dir. Milw. Jewish Fedn., 1962-68; exec. dir. Jewish Fedn. Greater Kansas City, Mo., 1968-89; ret., 1989; ind. cons. Kansas City, 1989—. Mem. editorial com. Jour. Jewish Communal Svc.; contbr. articles to profl. jours. Mem. Youth Guidance Bd., Oak Park, Mich., 1966; bd. dirs. Temple Emanuel, Milw., 1970. With USNR, 1943-46, PTO. Mem. NASW (chmn. Detroit chpt. 1960-61), Assn. Jewish Orgn. Pers. (pres. 1979-81), World Conf. Jewish Community Svc. (bd. dirs. 1985-89). Home: 640 W 69th Terr Kansas City MO 64113

KOESTER, CHARLES R., bishop; b. Jefferson City, Mo., Sept. 16, 1915. Student, Conception Acad., St. Louis, Prep. Sem. and Kenrick Sem., St. Louis, N.Am. Coll., Rome. Ordained priest Roman Catholic Ch. 1941. Ordained titular bishop Suacia and aux. bishop St. Louis, 1971—. Office: Chancery Office 4445 Lindell Blvd Saint Louis MO 63108

KOESTER, CRAIG RICHARD, religious educator; b. Northfield, Minn., Aug. 25, 1953; s. Richard Gill and Gloria Ann (Fossum) K.; m. Nancy Keysor; children: Matthew, Emily. BA, St. Olaf Coll., Northfield, 1976; MDiv, Luther Seminary, St. Paul, 1980; PhD with distinction, Union Seminary, N.Y.C., 1987. Pastor Immanuel Luth. Ch., Princeton, Minn., 1980-83; prof. Luther Northwestern Seminary, St. Paul, 1986—. Author: The Dwelling of God, 1989; contbr. articles to profl. jours. Mem. Soc. Bibl. Lit. (regional sec. 1990—), Cath. Bibl. Assn. Office: Luther Northwestern Sem 2481 Como Ave Saint Paul MN 55108

KOESTER, HELMUT HEINRICH, theologian, educator; b. Hamburg, Germany, Dec. 18, 1926; came to U.S., 1958; s. Karl and Marie-Luise (Eitz) K.; m. Gisela G. Harrassowitz, July 8, 1953; children: Reinhild, Almut, Ulrich, Heiko. Dr. theol., U. Marburg, Germany, 1954; Privatdozent, U. Heidelberg, Germany, 1956; Dr. theol. (hon.), U. Geneva. Ordained to ministry Luth. Ch., 1956; asst. pastor Hannover, Germany, 1951-54; teaching asst., then asst. prof. U. Heidelberg, 1954-56, 56-58, 59; mem. faculty Harvard U. Div. Sch., 1958—, John H. Morison prof. N.T. studies, 1964—, Winn prof. ecclesiastical history, 1968—; vis. prof. U. Heidelberg, 1963, Drew U., 1966, U. Minn., 1990. Author: Synoptische Ueberlieferung bei den Apostolischen Vaetern, in Texte und Untersuchungen, 1957, Trajectories through Early Christianity, (with James M. Robinson), 1971, Einfuehrung in das Neue Testament, 1979, Introduction to the New Testament, 1982, Ancient Christian Gospels, 1990, (with Francois Bovon) Genèse de l'écriture chrétienne, 1991; editor Harvard Theol. Rev., Hermeneia, Archaeological Resources for New Testament Studies, Encyclopedia of New Testament Archaeology. Assoc. trustee Am. Schs. Oriental Research, 1974-75; trustee William F. Albright Inst. Archaeol. Research, 1974-80. Served with German Navy, 1944-45. Guggenheim fellow, 1964-65; Am. Council Learned Socs. fellow, 1971-72, 78-79. Fellow Am. Acad. Arts and Scis.; mem. Soc. Bibl. Lit. (pres. 1990-91), Soc. Novi Testamenti Studiorum. Home: 12 Flintlock Rd Lexington MA 02173 Office: 45 Francis Ave Cambridge MA 02138

KOFINK, WAYNE ALAN, minister; b. Chgo., Apr. 21, 1949; s. Lawrence Howard and Catherine Elizabeth (Szlavik) K. MusB, Roosevelt U., 1971; MDiv, Luth. Sch. Theology, Chgo., 1976; BA in Philosophy, Fla. Internat. U., 1981, MS Adult Edn., 1985, EdD, 1991; postgrad., Westminster Choir Coll., 1982, St. Thomas U., 1984-85. Ordained to ministry Evang. Luth. Ch. in Am., 1977. Choir dir. Ascension Luth. Ch., Chgo., 1971-73; pastor Messiah Evang. Luth. Ch., Miami, Fla., 1977—; lectr. religious studies Fla. Internat. U., Miami, 1986—; sec., v.p. Luth. Campus Ministry of Dade County, Miami, 1979-85; mem. Fla. Synod Worship Consultation, Tampa, 1988—; trustee Guardian Shepherd Luth. Sch., Coral Gables, Fla., 1990—. Editor (newsletter) Doxology, 1986-87; contbr. articles to profl. jours. Mem. Miami-Coral Pk. Adult Edn. Ctr. Adv. Com., 1988—. Mem. Am. Acad. Religion, Soc. for Sci. Study Religion, Soc. Bibl. Lit., Liturgical Conf., Hymn Soc. Am. Home: 3840 SW 102 Ave D216 Miami FL 33165 Office: Messiah Evang Luth Ch 9850 Coral Way Miami FL 33165 *God gives every person the ability to make a positive contribution to life. The difference our particular gifts and opportunities allow us to make may seem insignificant in a world needing radical transformation, but we must do what is in our power. Success isn't determined by the size of the results, but by loving faithfulness.*

KOGER, ALFRED DENNIS, JR., minister; b. Paris, Tex., May 2, 1946; s. Alfred Dennis and Jean Elizabeth (Dunagan) K.; m. Joan Moseley, June 27, 1966 (div. Mar. 1973); 1 child, Matt; m. Beverly Janett Williams, June 7, 1975; children: Mandy, Michael, Melody. BA, East Tex. State U., 1968; MDiv, Southwestern Bapt. Theol. Sem., 1974; PhD, Baylor U., 1988. Ordained to ministry So. Bapt. Ch. Pastor Shady Grove Bapt. Ch., Greenville, Tex., 1970-73; min. outreach and single adults Shiloh Terr. Bapt. Ch., Dallas, 1974-78; pastor Shiloh Bapt. Ch., Crawford, Tex., 1978-83; chaplain, bible tchr. San Marcos (Tex.) Bapt. Acad., 1983—; conf. leader Sunday sch. bd. Shiloh Bapt. Ch., Nashville, 1975-78, San Francisco, 1976-77; pres. GTF, mem. spiritual life Baylor U., Waco, Tex., 1980. Contbr. articles to profl. jours. little league coach, San Marcos, Tex., 1989-90, player agt. challenger div., 1991. Mem. San Marcos Ministerial Assn., Soc. Biblical Lit.

KOHL, BARUCH FRYDMAN, rabbi; b. Milw., Feb. 7, 1951; s. Jack Kohl and Rachel Horowitz; m. Josette C. Frydman, May 24, 1970; children: Yakov, Moshe, Amir. BS in Edn., Northwestern U., 1972; MA, Jewish Theol. Sem., 1976. Ordained rabbi, 1977. Rabbi Congregation Ohav Shalom, Albany, N.Y., 1977—; Mem. rabbinic cabinet United Jewish Appeal, N.Y.C., 1981—; pres. Capital Dist. Bd. Rabbis, Albany, 1982-85, Empire Region-Rabbinical Assembly, Albany, 1985-88; mem. exec. com. Rabbinical Assembly, N.Y.C., 1985-91; chmn. Community Rels. Com. of Jewish Fedn., 1984-85, 90-91; trustee Hebrew Acad. of Capital Dist., 1983—. Mem. editorial bd. Conservative Judaism mag., 1983-90. Bd. dirs. Capital Dist. Coun. for Human Sexuality, Albany, 1979-83, Urban League Albany, 1987—; mem. exec. com. United Jewish Fedn., Albany, 1982-85, 90-91, chair com. for Judaic studies, 1990—; mem. com. Albany Tricentennial Commn., Albany, 1987; mem. pastoral care adv. com. Albany Med. Ctr. Hosp., 1985-89. Mem. Assn. for Jewish Studies, Rabbinical Assembly, Union for Traditional Judaism, Coalition for Alternatives in Jewish Edn., Jewish Law Assn. Avocation: reading. Office: Congregation Ohav Shalom New Krumkill Rd Albany NY 12208

KOHL, HAROLD, missionary educator; b. Linden, N.J., Dec. 13, 1923; s. Herman and Martha (Sperber) K.; m. Beatrice Minniebelle Wells, Mar. 21, 1946; children: Loren, Loretta, Lyndon. BA, Monmouth Coll., 1962; MA in Edn., NYU, 1968, postgrad., 1974; ThD in English Bible, Internat. Bible Inst., 1980. Ordained to ministry Assemblies of God Ch., 1948. Pastor, evangelist Assemblies of God Ch., W.Va., Md., 1944-50; pres. youth ministries Potomac Dist. Coun. Assemblies of God Ch., 1947-48; fgn. missionary Assemblies of God Ch., Colombo, Sri Lanka, 1950-56; pastor Assemblies of God Chs., N.J., 1956-61; missionary, tchr., educator Assemblies of God Ch., Far East, Pacific, Europe, 1961—; ednl. cons. Assemblies of God Ch., Far East, Pacific, 1980-83; pres. Bethel Bible Coll., Manila, 1963-68; pres., founder Far East Advanced Sch. Theology (now Asia Pacific Theol. Sem.), Manila, 1964-73, adj. prof., Baguio City, The Philippines, 1991—; dean Coll. div. Internat. Corr. Inst., Brussels, 1973-78, Belgium, 83-88, Rhode St. Genese, Belgium, 1988—, mem. external faculty, Brussels, 1988—. Mem. Soc. Pentecostal Studies, Religious Edn. Assn., Phi Delta Kappa, Phi Theta Kappa. Republican. Avocations: photography, reading, walking. Home: 429 Superior St Winchester VA 22601 *In a truly successful and satisfying life, the will of God is always paramount. At the heart of every personal decision there must be unreserved cooperation with the holy and wise will of God.*

KOHLER, RUSSELL EDWARD, chaplain, priest; b. Monroe, Mich., Nov. 12, 1943; s. Vernon A. "Barney" and Mary Elizabeth (Kellison) K. AB, Sacred Heart Sem., Detroit, 1968; grad., U. Detroit; grad. in theology, St. John's Provincial Sem. Ordained priest Roman Catholic Ch., Apr. 1973. Pastor St. Aloysius Ch., Detroit, 1974-80; chaplain Sinai Hosp., Harper-Grace Hosp., Detroit, 1982-91; pres. Mich. Pediatric Hospice Found., Irish Hills, 1985—; chaplain to Hispanic community Most Holy Trinity Ch., Detroit, 1989-91, pastor, 1991—; Exec. dir. Pope John XXIII Hospice, Detroit, 1975—; dir. St. Patrick's Pediatric Retreat, Irish Hills, Mich., 1979—. Founder The XXIII Club, First Sunday, 1975; bd dirs. Endurance Pediatric Pilgrimages, Discovery: Arts with Youth in Therapy; fleet chaplain Detroit Yacht Club, 1990. Mem. Internat. Pediatric Hospice Found. (pres. 1985—), Lions, KC, Order of Hibernians (appt. Mich. state chaplain 1988). Home: 11528 Killarney Hwy Irish Hills MI 48265

KOHLI, KAWAD, correspondent, religious organization representative. Corr. Sikh Found., Toronto, Ont., Can. Office: Sikh Found, 1 Younge St Ste 1801, Toronto, ON Canada M5E 5E1*

KOHN, WANDA JOY, social services administrator; b. Dunedin, Fla., Nov. 19, 1959; d. Ronald Gilbert and Joyce (Harding) Krippendorf; m. John Szakonyi, July 16, 1982 (div. June 1984); m. Robert Clayton Kohn, Aug. 9, 1986; stepchildren: Christa, Holly. AA, St. Petersburg Jr. Coll., Clearwater, Fla., 1981. Pres., co-founder Habitat for Humanity of Lake County, Fla., Inc., Fruitland Park, 1989—; youth advisor New Life Presbyn. Ch., Fruitland Park, 1986-91, work camp leader, 1988-90; counselor Pregnancy Care Ctr., Leesburg, Fla., 1988—. Member Concerned Women for Am., Clearwater, 1987. Home: 04317 Emmaus Rd Fruitland Park FL 34731

KOHN, WILLIAM HENRY, minister; b. Winnipeg, Man., Can., Sept. 27, 1915; s. William Lewis and Christine (Obermowe) K.; m. Marian Ruth Luenser, June 1, 1941; children: Kathy, Carol, Marian. Student, Concordia Coll., Milw., 1935, Concordia Theol. Sem., St Louis, 1939; D.D., Concordia Theol. Sem., St Louis, 1964; postgrad., Johns Hopkins. Ordained to ministry Lutheran Ch., 1940; pastor in Wis. and Md., 1939-56, Redeemer Luth. Ch., Hyattsville, Md., 1956-63; sec. Luth. Mission Soc. Md., 1946-48, pres., 1948-50; chmn. mission bd. Southeastern dist. Luth. Ch. Mo. Synod, 1951-54, pres., 1954-59; bd. dirs. Luth. Ch. Mo. Synod, 1959-63; pres. Southeastern dist., 1963-67, exec. sec. missions, 1967-74; sr. pastor Capitol Drive Luth. Ch., Milw., 1974-82, visitation pastor; ret., 1991; chmn. Luth. Immigration Service Com., 1960-67; bd. dirs. Luth. World Relief, 1967-74, Good Samaritan Med. Center, Milw., 1980-89; pres. Assn. Evang. Luth. Chs., 1976-84; bd. dirs. Luth. Council in U.S.A., 1978-84; mem., pres. Luth. World Ministries Commn., 1978-84; mem. Com. on Luth. Unity, 1978-82, Commn. for a New Luth. Ch., 1982-86. Served as chaplain AUS, 1943-46. Decorated Bronze Star. Home: 9507 Veirs Dr # 1 Rockville MD 20850

KOLB, ERWIN JOHN, church executive; b. Bay City, Mich., Aug. 6, 1924; s. John Frederick and Lydia (Lutz) K.; m. A. Bernice Homm, Aug. 29, 1948; children: Kathryn, Peter, David. BS, Concordia Sem., 1945, BD, 1948, MST, 1953; MS in Edn., So. Ill. U., 1953; PhD, Concordia Sem., 1968. Pastor Concordia Luth. Ch., Cottage Hills, Ill., 1949-51, Hope Luth. Ch., Highland, Ill., 1951-53, Zion Luth. Ch., Bethalto, Ill., 1953-61, Trinity Luth. Ch., Centralia, Ill., 1961-63; chaplain, prof. Concordia Tchrs. Coll., Seward, Nebr., 1963-72; exec. dir. evangelism Mo. Synod Luth. Ch., St. Louis, Mo., 1972-89; pastoral advisor Nat. Luth. Parent Tchr. League; chmn. bd. Parish Edn. Luth. Ch.So. Ill. Dist., Mo.; dean ACW Bible Inst , Collinsville, Ill. Author: (books) Christian Conversation About Sex, 1962, Prayer Primer, 1983, Witness Primer, 1986, (booklet) Christian Discipline, 1952, Judaism; mng. editor Christian Parent Mag., 1951-53; editor Nurture, Concordia Pulpit Resources, 1972—. Chaplain USAR, 1950-76. Mem. Luth. Edn. Assn., Luth. Human Relations Assn., Luth. Acad. for Scholarship, Mil. Chaplains Assn. Home: 12429 Matthew Ln Sunset Hills MO 63127 Office: Convcordia Pub House 3558 S Jefferson Ave Saint Louis MO 63118

KOLB, JOHN CARL, family therapist, minister; b. Bay City, Mich., Apr. 6, 1943; s. Carl Henry Edwin and Renate Marie (Krieger) K.; m. Malinda Marie Hartman, June 5, 1966; children: Rebecca Marie, Debra Renee, Charles Walter. BA, Concordia Sr. Coll., 1964; MDiv, Concordia Sem., St. Louis, 1968; MST, Christian Theol. Sem., Indpls., 1972; student McCormick Theol. Sem., 1975-76. Ordained to ministry Luth. Ch., 1968. Pastor Emanuel Luth. Ch., Arcadia, Ind., 1968-72; pres. Hamilton County (Ind.) Mental Health Assn., 1971-72; pastoral resident Luth. Gen. Hosp., Park Ridge, Ill., 1972-73; mental health therapist Northwestern Meml. Hosp. and Northwestern Inst. Psychiatry, Chgo., 1973-76; pastoral care fellow, chaplain Evanston (Ill.) Hosp., 1974-75, social worker, group therapist, asst. team leader Refocus Program, 1976-78; family therapist Luth. Child and Family Services, Indpls., 1978—; bd. dirs. Indy Force Soccer Club, 1989—; pastor Hosanna Luth. Ch., Oaklandon, Ind., 1980-88; vis. prof. Concordia Theol. Sem., Ft. Wayne, 1984-86; pastoral advisor Ind., Ky Dist. Luth. Laymen's League; chmn. Ind. Dist. of LCMS Pastors and Wives Retreat Com.; pres. Trinity Luth. Parent Tchr. League, 1982-84. Contbr. articles to religious publs. Garret Theol. Sem. fellow, 1974-75. Mem. Am. Assn. Pastoral Counselors (pastoral affiliate). Home: 2613 Sheffield Dr Indianapolis IN 46229 Office: Luth Family Counseling 1525 N Ritter St Indianapolis IN 46219 *Life is magnificently more than we experience. My struggle is to remain humble, patient, forgiving and appreciative in my experiences while trusting God rather than pushing myself and others farther and faster than humanly possible.*

KOLB, ROBERT ALLAN, religion educator; b. Fort Dodge, Iowa, June 17, 1941; s. Ralph Orrin and Eva Ann (Holm) K.; m. Pauline Joanne Ansorge, Aug. 14, 1965. B.A., Concordia Coll., 1963; M. Divinity, Concordia Sem., 1967; S.T.M., 1968; Ph.D., U. Wis., Madison, 1973. Ordained to ministry Lutheran Ch., 1972. Exec. dir. Ctr. for Reformation Research, St. Louis, Mo., 1972-77; mem. faculty Concordia Coll., St. Paul, Minn., 1977—, assoc. prof., 1981-86, full prof., 1986—, chmn. Div. Religion, 1982-87. Mem. Commn. Theology and Ch. Rels., Luth. Ch.-Mo. Synod, 1984—, chmn. 1990—, acting pres., 1990-91. Author: Andreae and the Formula of Concord, 1977; Nikolaus von Amsdorf, 1978; Speaking the Gospel Today, 1984, For All the Saints, 1987, Confessing the Faith, 1991; assoc. editor The Sixteenth Century Jour., 1977—; mem. editorial bd. The Lutheran Quarterly, 1986—; contbr. numerous articles to various periodicals. Mem. bd. Lexington-Hamline Community Coun.l, St. Paul, 1980-90. Mem. 16th Century Studies Conf. (pres. 1980-81), Am. Soc. Ch. History (mem. coun. 1978-81; mem. membership com. 1984-89), Am. Soc. Reformation Rsch. Republican. Home: 1292 Marshall Ave Saint Paul MN 55104 Office: Concordia Coll Hamline & Marshall Ave Saint Paul MN 55104

KOLCH, VICTOR FREDERICK, hospital chaplain; b. Stillwater, Okla., May 5, 1951; s. Frederick Luther and Anne Louise (Meisner) K.; m. Diane Virginia Laux, Aug. 25, 1973; children: Peter Matthew, Amy Lauren. AA, St. John's Coll., 1972; BS, Concordia Sr. Coll., 1973; MDiv, Concordia Sem. in Exile, 1977. Ordained to ministry Evang. Luth. Ch. in Am., 1977. Shared pastor Bristol (Conn.) Area Luth. Chs., 1977-79; chaplain Luth. Hosp., Ft. Wayne, Ind., 1979—. Bd. dirs. Washington House Treatment Ctr., 1980—. Republican. Office: Luth Hosp 3024 Fairfield Ave Fort Wayne IN 46807

KOLLAR, NATHAN R., religion educator; b. Braddock, Pa.; m. Judith Ann Gennusa; children: David J., Sharon A. BA in Philosophy and Edn., St. Bonaventure U., 1960; STB in Hist. Theology, San Alberto (Lateran) Coll., Rome, 1962; Licentiate in Sacred Theology, Cath. U. Am., 1964, STD in Systematic Theology, 1967; MA in Liturgy, U. Notre Dame, 1968; postdoctoral studies, Am. U., 1969, Syracuse U., 1979. Instr. theology Whitefriar's Hall, Washington, 1964-67; tchr. Salpointe High Sch., Tucson, 1967-68; asst. prof. Washington Theol. Coalition, 1968-71, U. St. Thomas, Fredericton, N.B., Can., 1971-74; asst. prof. St. John Fisher Coll., Rochester, N.Y., 1974-77, assoc. prof., 1977-82, prof., 1982—, chair dept. religious studies, 1979-82; adj. prof. U. Rochester, 1976-78, St. Bernard's Inst., Rochester, 1986-89; sr. lectr. U. Rochester, 1989—; cons. div. adult edn. U.S. Cath. Conf., 1970-73, Coun. Ind. Colls, 1987—. Author: Anointing of the Sick in the Anglican Church, 1967, Death and Other Living Things, 1973, Rochester Religions, 1976, Mapping the Occult: An Exercise in Religious Understanding, 1979, Songs of Suffering, 1982; (with others) That They May Live, 1972, Selected Proceedings of the National Conference, 1979, New Directions in Death Education and Counseling, 1981, Priorities in Death Education andCounseling, 1982, Creativity in Death Education and Counseling, 1983, Rising From History: U.S. Catholic Theology Looks to the Future, 1987, Disenfranchised Grief, 1989; editor, author: (with others) Options in Roman Catholicism, 1983; assoc. editor, mem. editorial bd. Explorations: Jour. for Adventurous Thought, 1984—; contbr. articles to religious jours. Assoc. dir. adult edn. Roman Cath. Diocese of Tucson-Phoenix, 1967-68; chair exec. bd. Urban Tng. Program, 1969-71, chair, 1970-72; chair coun. of conciliation Diocese of Rochester, 1984-86, mem. theol. commn., 1986—; bd. dirs. Nazareth Acad., 1985-88; chair evaluation sub-com., mem. exec. com. Adv. Com., Monroe County Office for Aging, 1989—; mem. adv. com. Genesee Region Home Care Assn. Hospice, 1989—; bd. dirs., mem. exec. com. Concern for Dying, 1983-86, mem. adv. bd., 1989—; mem. hospice care bd. Caritas, 1990—. Recipient Oustanding Svc. award Forum for Death Edn. and Counseling, 1983, Outstanding Vol. award Diocese of Rochester, 1988, Best Paper award So. Humanities Coun., 1990, Trustees' award St. John Fisher Coll., 1991; grantee St. John Fisher Coll., 1975, 82, 83, 87, Govt. of Can., 1988, Province of Que., 1990. Mem. Am. Acad. Religion (v.p., program dir. ea. internat. region 1977-78, internat. exec. com. 1978-80, pres. ea. internat. region 1978-79), Religious Edn. Assn., Coll. Theology Soc. (chmn. publ. awards com. 1978-82), Forum for Death Edn. and Counseling (fin. com. 1978-80, chair com. on religion and death 1986—), Can. Soc. for Study of Religion, Assn. for Can. Studies in U.S., Mid-Atlantic Assn. for Can. Studies, N.Y. State Assn. Gerontol. Educators, Assn. for Gerontology in Higher Edn., Am. Assn. for Higher Edn., Grief Resource Info. Edn. Forum (bd. dirs. 1984-89, chair edn. com. 1987-89). Home: 4224 West Lake Rd Canandaigua NY 14424-8314

KOLLIN, JONATHAN E., executive director; b. N.Y.C., Jan. 3, 1950; s. Jacob L. and Hermine S. (Rubinstein) K.; m. Shirley L. Kaftan, Nov. 10, 1973; children: Joshua, Michael. BA, Herbert H. Lehman Coll., 1973. Asst. adminstr. Congregation Emanu-El, N.Y.C., 1976-81; exec. dir. Jacksonville (Fla.) Jewish Ctr., 1978-79, Temple B'Nai Abraham, Livingston, N.J., 1981-83; dir. ops. Enterprise Mfg. Co., Phila., 1983-85; exec. dir. Beth Shalom Congregation, Elkins Park, Pa., 1985—. Mem. Nat. Assn. Synagogue Adminstrs., Nat. Assn. Temple Adminstrs., Del Valley Assn. Synagogue Adminstrs. (pres. 1988—). Democrat. Jewish. Avocations: computers, racquetball. Office: Beth Shalom Congregation Old York and Foxcroft Rds Elkins Park PA 19117

KOLLMANN, ALVIN VICTOR, minister; b. Royal, Ill., Nov. 7, 1929; s. Victor J. and Elda M. (Schneider) K.; m. Jacquelin Dee Briggenhorst, Aug. 29, 1953; children: Victor J., Sue C., Kenneth S., Richard A., David E. AA, Concordia Coll., 1949; BA, Concordia Theol. Sem., 1951, BDiv, 1954, MST, 1958; LLD, Concordia Coll., 1981. Ordained to ministry Luth. Ch., 1954. Pastor St. Paul Luth. Ch., West Frankfort, Ill., 1954-59, Good Shepherd Luth. Ch., Collinsville, Ill., 1959-78; prs. So. Ill. dist. Luth. Ch.-Mo. Synod, Belleville, Ill., 1976—. Pres. Collinsville Ministerial Assn., 1971-72. Mem. So. Ill. Dist. Luth. Ch.-Mo. Synod. (chmn. 1968-70, 2d v.p. Belleville chpt. 1970-74, 1st v.p. 1974-76), Lions (bd. dirs. Collinsville chpt. 1971-73). Home: 100 Windridge Collinsville IL 62234 Office: So Ill Dist Luth Ch Mo Synod 2408 Lebanon Ave Belleville IL 62221

KOLLMANN, VICTOR JOHN, minister; b. Christopher, Ill., Dec. 19, 1954; s. Alvin Victor and Jacquelin (Briggenhorst) K.; m. Angela Kay Bentley, July 29, 1978; children: Jonathan, Kristen, Jaclyn. AA, St. Paul's Coll., 1975; BA, Concordia Tchr.'s Coll., 1977; MDiv, Concordia Sem., 1981; D Ministry, Fuller Sem., 1991. Minister Our Shepherd Luth. Ch., Searcy, Ark., 1981-87; assoc. minister Concordia Luth. Ch., San Antonio, 1987—; seminar leader LC-MS Commn. Convocation, St. Louis, 1988; pastoral counselor Luth. Women's Missionary League, Little Rock, 1987. mem. youth bd. LC-MS South Dist., Memphis, 1983-87. Mem. San Antonio Pastoral Cir., Tex. Dist. Church Growth Com., 1990—. Home: 14003 Cedar Canyon San Antonio TX 78231 Office: Concordia Luth Ch 1826 Basse Rd San Antonio TX 78213

KOLLMEYER, JUSTIN PAUL, minister; b. Odessa, Tex., Mar. 1, 1950; s. Glen C. and Doris Lee (Meier) K.; m. Elaine Vernette Hinz, June 1, 1975; children: Jessica Elaine, Andrew Justin, Rebecca Elaine. BA, Valparaiso U., 1972; MDiv, Christ Sem.-Seminex, St. Louis, 1976; DMin, Columbia Theol. Sem., 1985. Ordained to ministry Evang. Luth. Ch. Am., 1976. Assoc. pastor Christ the King Luth. Ch., Miami, Fla., 1976-79; pastor Christ the King Luth. Ch., Tampa, Fla., 1979-84, Christ Our Redeemer Luth. Ch., Temple Terrace, Fla., 1984-86, Prince of Peace Luth. Ch., Fayetteville, Ga., 1986—; del. Evang. Luth. Ch. Am. Organizing Conv., Louisville, 1982; participant Nat. Inst. for Ch. Planning and Consultation, LaGrange, Ga., 1990. Officer Temple Terrace Ministerial Assn., 1979-86. Mem. The Alban Inst., Southeastern Synod Evang. Luth. Ch. in Am., Fayette County Ministerial Assn. (pres. 1987-88). Home: 155 Hanover Circle Fayetteville GA 30214 Office: Prince of Peace Luth Ch 257 Hwy 314 PO Box 1030 Fayetteville GA 30214 *The "successful" parish pastor is one whose life and ministry have touched people's hearts with this simple truth: "God loves you!, And so do I".*

KOLOWA, SEBASTIAN, bishop. Presiding bishop Evang. Luth. Ch. in Tanzania, Arusha. Office: Evang Luth Ch, POB 3033, Arusha Tanzania*

KOLP, ALAN LEE, educator; b. Winchester, Ind., Sept. 10, 1944; s. Richard Lee and Mildred Ann (Talley) K.; m. Letitia Ann Milner, Jan. 23, 1966; children: Felicity, Christina. BA, Guilford Coll., 1967; BD, Harvard Div. Sch., 1970; PhD, Harvard U., 1976. Asst. prof. religion Earlham Sch. Religion, Richmond, Ind., 1974-78, dean, 1978-84, assoc. prof., 1978—. Author: Participation Is Not a Spectator Sprot, 1976, Fresh Winds of the Spirit, 1991; contbr. articles to profl. jours. Mem. Am. Acad. Religion, Soc. Bibl. Lit., N.Am. Patristic Soc. Home: 234 College Ave Richmond IN 47374 Office: Earlham Sch Religion National Rd W Richmond IN 47374

KOLVENBACH, PETER HANS, priest, religious order superior; b. Druten, The Netherlands, 1928. Student U. Nijmegen (Netherlands), theology St. Joseph U., Beirut, linguistics, Paris, 1963-64, 66-67. Joined Jesuit Order Netherlands; ordained priest Roman Cath. Ch., 1961; prof. linguistics St. Joseph U., Beirut, 1968-81; provincial superior Beirut, 1974-81; rector Pontifical Oriental Inst., Rome, 1981-83; superior-gen. Soc. of Jesus, 1983—. mem. secretariat for promoting Christian Unity. Author: In Cammino Verso La Pasqua, 1988, Fedeli a Dio e all'uomo, 1990; also various articles and revs. in field of linguistics and spiritual theology; mem. of commns. Cath. Orthodox dialogue books. Address: Borgo Santo Spirito 4, 00193 Rome Italy

KOMINSKY, NEIL EDWARD, rabbi; b. Bklyn., May 18, 1944; s. Marvin and Phyllis June (Sampson) K.; m. Susan Fox Schiro, June 18, 1967 (div. 1984); children: David Thomas, Daniel Schiro; m. Deborah Alice Frank, June 22, 1986; 1 child, Jonathan Frank. BA magna cum laude, Harvard U., 1966; B in Hebrew Letters, Hebrew Union Coll.-Jewish Inst. Religion, Cin., 1968, MA in Hebrew Lit., 1970. Ordained rabbi, 1970. Asst. rabbi Leo Baeck Temple, L.A., 1970-72; rabbi Temple Beth Hillel, South Windsor, Conn., 1973-82; reform rabbinic advisor Harvard U.-Radcliffe Hillel, Cambridge, Mass., 1982-88, pres. United Ministry, mem. bd. of ministry, 1985-86; assoc. rabbi Temple Ohabei Shalom, Brookline, Mass., 1988-91; rabbi Temple Beth David of the South Shore, Canton, Mass., 1991—; dir. social action N.E. Coun./Union Am. Hebrew Congregations, Brookline, 1988-89. Contbr. numerous articles to profl. jours. Co-chair schs. and scholarships com. Harvard-Radcliffe Club of No. Conn., South Windsor, 1980-82; mem. Life Support Network, Harvard U., 1984-88, human studies com. Lesley Coll., Cambridge, 1990—. Mem. Cen. Conf. Am. Rabbis (mem. task force on women in the rabbinate 1976-91, chair 1978-84, pres. N.E. region 1989-91), Mass. Bd. Rabbis. Home: 134 Fuller St # 2 Brookline MA 02146 Office: Temple Beth David of South Shore 256 Randolph St Canton MA 02021

KOMITO, DAVID ROSS, educator; b. L.A., July 30, 1946; s. Sanford Arthur and Ruth (Ross) K.; m. Kay Hollingshead, May 1, 1988. BA, UCLA, 1967; MS, Ind. U., 1973, MA, 1974, PhD, 1979. Asst. to dean of studies Mt. Holyoke Coll., South Hadley, Mass., 1979-81; staff assoc. for acad. projects Amherst (Mass.) Coll., 1981-84; vis. asst. prof. U. Mass., Amherst, 1980-84, Wesleyan U., Middletown, Conn., 1984-85; asst. dir. Ctr. for Teaching and Learning, Stanford (Calif.) U., 1985-86; assoc. prof. John F. Kennedy U., Orinda, Calif., 1986—, dean, 1986-90. Author: Nagarjuna's "Seventy Stanzas:" A Buddhist Psychology of Emptiness, 1987. Grantee NEH, 1983. Office: John F Kennedy U 12 Altarinda Rd Orinda CA 94563

KOMP, DIANE MARILYN, pediatric oncologist, hematologist, former deacon; b. Bklyn., Aug. 6, 1940; d. Richard Rankin Carrier and Anna Florence (Daly) K. B.S. in Chemistry, Houghton (N.Y.) Coll., 1961; M.D., SUNY Downstate Med. Center, Bklyn., 1965; M.A. (hon.), Yale U., 1978. Intern Kings County Hosp., Bklyn., 1965-66; resident in pediatrics Kings County Hosp., 1965-67; fellow in pediatric hematology and oncology U. Va., 1967-69, asst. prof. pediatrics, 1969-73, asso. prof., 1973-76, prof., 1976-78; prof. pediatrics Yale U., 1978—, chief dept. pediatric hematology and oncology, 1978-85; cons. Nat. Cancer Inst. Author: Fenster in Den Himmel, 1990; also essays. Deacon 1st Congl. Ch., Guilford, Conn., 1983-90, chair bd. deacons, 1989. Recipient cert. of appreciation Va. div. Am. Cancer Soc.; Nat. Cancer Inst. grantee. Mem. Am. Soc. Hematology, Soc. Pediatric Research, Internat. Soc. Hematology, Am. Soc. Clin. Oncology, Am. Pediatric Soc., Alpha Omega Alpha. Office: 333 Cedar St LMP 4083 New Haven CT 06510

KONG, CHHON PHAN, minister; b. Pongro, Cambodia, May 4, 1952; s. Phan and Heng (Miev) K.; m. Sou Yam, Jan. 20, 1973 (div. Sept. 1979); 1 child, Socheat Phan; m. Arun Eng, Dec. 30, 1979; children: Jabez, Magdalene. B in Bibl. Studies, CUNY, 1989. Ordained to ministry Congregational Ch., 1991. V.p. Cambodian Ministries for Christ, Fairfield, Conn., 1984-86, pres., 1986—; pastor Cambodian Fellowship Black Rock Congl. Ch., Conn., 1982—; bd. dirs. Cambodia Christian Svcs., Conn., 1990—. Republican. Office: Cambodian Ministries for Christ 3685 Black Rock Turnpike Fairfield CT 06604

KONICKI, WILLIAM CHARLES, priest; b. Webster, Mass., July 22, 1952; s. Alice Roseanna (Champagne) K. BA in Philosophy, St. John's Sem. Coll., Brighton, Mass., 1974, MDiv in Theology, 1978; cert. advanced studies in youth ministry, Loyola U., Chgo., 1991. Ordained priest Roman Cath. Ch., 1978. Assoc. pastor St. Joan of Arc Parish, Worcester, Mass., 1978-81; dir. youth min. Diocese of Worcester, 1981—; adminstr. Cath. Youth Retreat Ctr., Worcester, 1983—; dir. Hatian Ministry Project, Worcester, 1988—; regional coord. New Eng. Diocese Dir. of Youth Ministry, Worcester, 1986—; chair person Youth Outreach and Evangelization Com., Washington, 1989—. Active Worcester Fights Back; mem. Diocesan Bd. Edn., 1983—; chair Adolescent Catechesis Team, 1985-87, Global Horizons Team, 1985-87. Named Boy of Yr. Boys' Club Am., 1969. Mem. Nat. Fedn. Cath. Youth Ministry. Office: Office for Youth Ministry 781 Grove St Worcester MA 01605

KONTOGIORGIS, MICHAEL THEODORE, minister; b. Boston, May 15, 1948; s. Theodore Michael and Panagiota (Andriopoulos) K.; m. Vicki Betty George, Aug. 27, 1972; children—Kristen, Patricia, Megan. B.A., Hellenic Coll., 1970; M.Div., Holy Cross Greek Orthodox Sch. Theology, 1973, S.T.M., 1974. Ordained deacon Greek Orthodox Ch., 1972, priest, 1973; driving instr. Cleve. Circle Auto Sch., Brookline, Mass., 1969-71; coordinator United Shoppers Assn., Randolph, Mass., 1971-73; asst. to dean Annunciation Greek Orthodox Cathedral of New Eng., Boston, 1973-75; parish priest Holy Trinity Greek Orthodox Ch., Orlando, Fla., 1975—; dir. Greek Orthodox Youth Actionline, Orlando, 1981, Greek Orthodox Altar Boys Workshop, Brooksville, Fla., 1981-83; chmn. Youth Commn., Greek Orthodox Diocese Atlanta, 1981-83; mem. Presbyters Council, Greek Orthodox Archdiocese North and South Am., N.Y.C., 1983—; co-producer, dir. Grecian Echoes radio program, Orlando, 1978; chaplain Orlando Police Dept., 1978-79; bd. dirs. Olympic Village, 1977-84, 1st v.p., 1979-83, pres., 1983-84. Author: The Altar Boy's Guidebook, 1981; editor weekly ch. newsletter Harbinger, 1975—. Named Sakellarios, Greek Orthodox Archdiocese North and S.Am., 1980; recipient Pectoral Cross and plaque for 10th anniversary of ordination Holy Trinity Greek Orthodox Ch., 1983. Mem. Greek Orthdox Clergy Assn. (sec. Atlanta Diocese 1981-83, pres. 1983—), Orthodox Clergy Fellowship North and Central Fla. (sec. 1982—), Holy Cross Greek Orthodox Sch. Theology Alumni Assn. Home: 106 Valencia Loop Altamonte Springs FL 32714 Office: Holy Trinity Greek Orthodox Ch 1217 Trinity Woods Ln Maitland FL 32751

KOOISTRA, PAUL DAVID, seminary administrator; b. Duluth, Minn., Oct. 11, 1942; s. David and Laura (Bowman) K.; m. Janet Carlson, June 27, 1964; children: Paul Jr., Shary, Jennifer. BA, U. Minn., 1964; MDiv, Columbia Sem., Decatur, Ga., 1967; PhD, U. Ala., 1980. Ordained to ministry Presbyn. Ch., 1967. Minister of edn. Pinelands Presbyn. Ch., Miami, 1967-69, Seminole Presbyn. Ch., Tampa, Fla., 1969-73; prof. christian edn. Belhaven Coll., Jackson, Miss., 1973-75; prof. edn. Reformed Theol. Sem., Jackson, 1975-85; pres. Covenant Theol. Sem., St. Louis, 1985—. Mem. Assn. Profs. and Researchers in Religious Edn., Kappa Delta

Pi, Phi Delta Kappa. Republican. Home and Office: Covenant Theol Sem 12330 Conway Rd Saint Louis MO 63141

KOOL, CORNELIUS ORVILLE, minister; b. Sioux County, Iowa, June 30, 1927; s. John and Anna Marie (Born) K.; m. Joyce Ann Woodward, June 12, 1950; children: Keith John, Kendra Joanne Kool Gruska, Kurt Orville, Karla Marie. BA, Westmar Coll., 1953; BD, No. Baptist Theol. Sem., Chgo., 1956, MDiv, 1972; D Ministry, No. Baptist Theol. Sem., Louisville, 1974. Ordained to ministry Am. Bapt. Assn., 1956, So. Bapt. Conv., 1961; clin. pastoral educator, Iowa. Asst. pastor First Baptist Ch., Bloomington, Ill., 1956-58; pastor Marion Ave. Baptist Ch., Aurora, Ill., 1958-61, Crawford Ave. Baptist Ch., Skokie, Ill., 1961-67; pastor First Baptist Ch., St. Charles, Ill., 1967-73, Bethalto, Ill., 1973-78; pastor Temple Baptist Ch., Sioux City, Iowa, 1978-85, College Ave. Baptist Ch., Normal, Ill., 1985-90, Marion Ave. Bapt. Ch., Aurora, Ill., 1990—; curator The Redford Sch. Theology and Church Vocations, Southwest Baptist U., 1984-85. TV speaker: (sign-off devotionals) Channel 9, Sioux City, 1980-81; columnist: Speaking Out, Ill. Baptist mag., 1976-77. Cpl. U.S. Army, 1945-46. Pres. of graduating class, No. Baptist Theol. Seminary, Chgo., 1956. Mem. Hosp. Clergy Staff/Ministerial Assn. (treas. 1986-88), Evang. Mins. Fellowship. Republican. Avocations: hunting, walking, cycling, piloting, traveling. Home: 610 Lebanon St Aurora IL 60505 Office: Marion Ave Bapt Ch 361 Marion Ave Aurora IL 60505 *The greatest joy of my life continues to be the personal knowledge of Jesus Christ, my Lord and Savior. Knowing God through Christ, has been the major factor in the formation of my life and ministry.*

KOON, DELORES K., minister, choir director; b. Ridgeland, S.C., Nov. 11; d. William E. and Jennie P. (Munch) Kelly; m. Louis L. Koon; children: Louis Lee Jr., Karen Lynne Koon Tabb. MusB, Stetson U., 1952. Min. music Southside Bapt. Ch., Lakeland, Fla., 1960-90; choir dir. Shepherd Rd. Presbytery, Lakeland, 1990—; tchr. voice Southside Acad. Music, 1985-90; condr. Rejoice Singers, 1989-91, owner, mgr. Delores Koon Ministries, Lakeland, 1989-91. Recipient Most Outstanding Musician on Mission award So. Bapt. Conv., 1988, Fla. Bapt. Conv., 1990. Democrat. Home: 3108 Cleveland Heights Rd Lakeland FL 33803

KOON, FRANK DAVID, broadcasting executive, layworker; b. Macon, Ga., Sept. 13, 1958; s. Frank Tallmadge and Mary (Montgomery) K.; m. Patti Denise Jones, Aug. 8, 1980; children: Lyla Adair, Kara Ranae, Jon David. Student, Centenary Coll., 1977-80. Gen. sales mgr. Sta. WHLO Radio, Akron, Ohio, 1988—. Republican. Mem. Assemblies of God. Office: Sta WHLO Radio 3535 S Smith Rd Akron OH 44313

KOONTZ, CHRISTIAN, English educator, nun; b. Juniata, Pa., June 22, 1930; d. Elmer Guy and Loretta Bridget (Gray) K. AA, Mt. Aloysius Jr. Coll., Cresson, Pa.; BA in English, Mercyhurst Coll., Erie, Pa., 1963; MA in English, Cath. U., 1967, PhD in English, 1971. Joined Sisters of Mercy, Roman Cath. Ch., 1958. Instr. in phys. edn. Mt. Aloysius Jr. Coll. and Acad., 1954-58; instr. in English, French, Math. various schs., 1958-65; teaching fellow in English Cath. U. Am., 1965-70; assoc. prof. English Mercyhurst Coll., 1970-74; dir. tutorial svcs., adj. prof. English Gannon U., Erie, Pa., 1975-79; assoc. prof. English Mercy Coll. Detroit, 1980-87, prof., 1987—; prof. English U. Detroit Mercy (merger of Mercy Coll. and U. Detroit), 1991—; lectr. in field. Author: Thea Bowman: Handing on Her Legacy, 1991, The Living Journal: A Way Toward Freedom in the Service of Life, 1991, Evoked By the Scriptures, 1990, Connecting: Creativity and Spirituality, 1986; editor: Ministry of Catechesis for Children: Guidelines for Elementary CCD, 1980, (with others) Life-Style Index, 1975. Trustee Mt. Aloysius Jr. Coll., 1970-75, exec. coun. Rsch. grantee Am. Assn. Colls. for Tchr. Edn., 1972. Mem. Coll. Conf. Composition and Communication, Nat. Coun. Tchrs. English, MLA, AAUP. *Life calls each of us beyond survival to well-being, and the essence of well-being is creativity.*

KOOSHIAN, PERCY VICTOR, minister; b. Pasadena, Calif., Nov. 5, 1933; s. George Byron and Suzanne Anik (Derghazarian) K.; m. Carolyn Ruth Howie, Dec. 28, 1962; children: Suzanne Elaine, Catherine May Love, Mark Allan. BA, Westmont Coll., 1955; MDiv, Fuller Theol. Sem., 1961, MRE, 1962. Ordained to ministry Bapt. Ch., 1968. Youth pastor Immanuel Bapt. Ch., Pasadena, 1961-62; min. of Christian edn. 1st Bapt. Ch., La Mesa, Calif., 1963-67; dir. of Christian edn. Calvary Bapt. Ch., The Dalles, Oreg., 1967-70; pastor Conservative Bapt. Ch., Cottage Grove, Oreg., 1970-85, Victory Bapt. Ch., Oregon City, Oreg., 1985—; bd. dirs. Conservative Bapt. Assn. of Oreg., Portland, Conservative Bapt. Fgn. Mission Soc., Wheaton, 1985-91; trustee Judson Bapt. Coll., Portland, 1977-83. Author: Ask, 1971; contbr. articles to profl. jours. Chmn., mem. Ch. and Sch. Coun., Cottage Grove, 1974-85, Ministerial Assn., Cottage Grove, 1974-85. With U.S. Army, 1956-62. Office: Victory Bapt Ch Meyers Rd and Gaffney Ln PO Box 5237 Oregon City OR 97045-9237

KOPER, FRANCIS BERNARD, priest; b. Wilmington, Del., Feb. 10, 1944; s. Frank L. and Mary A. (Grott) K. BA in Philosophy, St. Mary's Coll., Orchard Lake, Mich., 1967; STB, St. Mary's Sem., Balt., 1969, STM, 1971, D of Ministry, 1991; MA in Religious Edn., Seattle U., 1974. Ordained priest Roman Cath. Ch., 1971. Assoc. pastor St. Hedwig Parish, Wilmington, 1971-74; dir. field edn. Sts. Cyril & Methodius Sem., Orchard Lake, 1974-76, dean of students, 1975-77, rector, 1974—; youth moderator St. Hedwig's CYO, Wilmington, 1971-74; chaplain Polish Roman Cath. Union of Am. Soc. 1437, Wilmington, 1972-74. Mem. West Bloomfield (Mich.) Clergy Assn., 1974—. Mem. Midwest Assn. Theol. Schs.(exec. bd.), Nat. Cath. Ednl. Assn., Religious Edn. Assn., Priests' Conf. for Polish Affairs, Polish Libr. Assn., Cath. Theol. Soc. Am. Democrat. Avocations: camping, boating, skiing, gardening, model railroading. Home: 3555 Indian Trail Orchard Lake MI 48324 Office: Sts Cyril & Methodius Sem 3555 Indian Trail Orchard Lake MI 48324

KOPLITZ, RONALD GENE, minister; b. Oshkosh, Wis., Mar. 8, 1943; s. Norman Albert and Ruth Leonora (Abraham) K.; m. Mary Ellen Norma Garbisch, Aug. 6, 1966. BA, Wartburg Coll., 1965; MDiv, Wartburg Theol. Sem., 1969. Ordained to ministry Am. Luth. Ch., 1969. Pastor Otter Creek Luth. Ch., Highland, Wis., 1969-73, Fairview Luth. Ch., Avoca, Wis., 1969-73, Trinity and Immanuel Luth. Ch., Cashton, Wis., 1973-78, Bethany Luth. Ch., LaFarge, Wis., 1973-78; instl. chaplain Ariz. Dept. Corrections, Florence, 1981-83, Maricopa County Jail System, Phoenix, 1983—; mem. clergy roster Grand Canyon Synod, Evang. Luth. Ch. in Am., mem. Task Force on Death Penalty. Mem. Ariz. Justice Fellowship Task Force, Ariz. Correctional Chaplain's Assn. Home: 907 E Broadmor Dr Tempe AZ 85282 Office: Madison St Jail Office Sr Chaplain 225 W Madison St Phoenix AZ 85003 *Even the worst criminal can experience God's love and forgiveness if it is demonstrated in others.*

KOPMAR, JEROME BENJAMIN, cantor; b. Hartford, Conn., Sept. 21, 1936; s. Irving and Sophie (Scoler) K.; m. Goldye Abby Naftulin, Mar. 26, 1961; children: Bracha, Yosepha, Ari, Ilana. Student, Hartt Coll. Music; degree of cantor, Jewish Theol. Sem., 1961. Cantor Temple Israel, Albany, N.Y., 1961-63, Beth El Synagogue, Akron, Ohio, 1963-69, Beth Abraham Congregation, Dayton, Ohio, 1969—; vocal instr. Dayton Pub. Sch. for Arts, 1988—. Composer, recording artist many works of Jewish music. Recipient Solomon Schechter award. Home: 5100 Pebble Brook Dr Englewood OH 45322 Office: Beth Abraham Synagogue 1306 Salem Ave Dayton OH 45406

KOPP, CLARENCE ADAM, JR., clergyman; b. Huntington, Ind., May 25, 1927; s. Clarence Adam and Laverne Rose (Shull) K.; m. Virginia Margaret Willis, June 7, 1948; children: Debra, Denise, Daniel, Dale. BA, Huntington Coll., Ind., 1948; MDiv, Huntington Theol. Sem., 1950; DMin, Trinity Evan. Div. Sem., 1990. Ordained to ministry United Brethren Ch., 1950. V.p. Ind. Christian Endeavor, 1946-47; pastor Calvary United Brethren Ch., Rockford, Ohio, 1948-50; asst. pastor King St. United Brethren Ch., Chambersburg, Pa., 1950-53; pastor Prescott United Brethren Ch., Dayton, Ohio, 1953-68, N. Linden Ch. of United Brethren, Columbus, 1968-75; pastor, supt. Redeemer United Brethren Ch., Columbus, 1975-81; bishop Ch. of United Brethren in Christ, Huntington, Ind., 1981—; pres. Ohio Christian Endeavor, 1958-60; conf. supt. Ch. United Brethren in Christ-Ohio, 1962-71. Recipient Internat. Christian Endeavor Citizenship award, Internat. Soc. Christian Endeavor, 1952. Mem. Nat. Assn. Evangelicals, Alban Inst., N. Am. Soc. Ch. Growth, Internat. Soc. Christian Endeavor-Columbus (pres. 1987-91). Mem. Ch. of the United Brethren in Christ. Avocations: water skiing, boating, travel. Home: 2038 College Ave Huntington IN 46750 Office: Church of United Brethren 302 Lake St Huntington IN 46750 *My dream for the church of 2000 A.D. is a relevant, growing, serving organism which reveals a vibrant living God.*

KOPP, DAVID ANDREW, editor; b. Mutanda, Zambia, Aug. 28, 1949; s. Charles Joseph and Mary Lenore (Canfield) K.; m. Debra Layne Stevert, July 31, 1971 (div. Aug. 1990); children: Neil David, Taylor Philip, Jana Layne. BA, U. Wash., 1971; MA, U. Tex., 1976. Mag. editor Good Family mags., Sisters, Oreg., 1988—; editor, writer Inside View column Christian Parenting Today mag., 1988—; instr. at Christian writers' confs. Recipient Instr. of Yr. award Cen. Oreg. Community Coll., 1990. Mem. Evang. Press Assn. Office: Good Family Mags PO Box 850 Sisters OR 97759

KOPP, GEORGE PHILIP, JR., minister; b. Cin., July 17, 1927; s. George Philip and Ann Elizabeth (Suffield) K.; m. Janet Marie Thompson Schultz, Oct. 13, 1956. BA, Heidelberg Coll., 1950; BD, Eden Sem., 1955, MDiv, 1969. Ordained to ministry United Ch. of Christ, 1955. Pastor St. John Ch., Middlebrook, Va., 1955-60; pastor St. John's Ch., Middlebrook, Va., ret.; commd. ensign USN, 1954, advanced through grades to lt. comdr., 1976, served as chaplain; ret., 1976, ret., 1976; dir. Ctr. Atlantic Conf. United Ch. Christ, 1983-88. With USN, 1945-51, USNR, 1952. Home and Office: 308 Valley View Dr Staunton VA 24401

KOPPELL, BONNIE JANE, rabbi; b. Bklyn., Mar. 1, 1956; d. Leo Saul and A. Sandra (Raphan) K.; m. David Rubenstein, July 4, 1985; children: Jessie, Sarah. BA, Brandeis U., 1976; MA, Temple U., 1979. Ordained rabbi, 1981. Rabbi Jewish Fellowship of Davis (Calif.), 1983-85, Congregation Bayt Shalom, Greenville, N.C., 1985-87, Temple Beth Sholom, Mesa, Ariz., 1987—; mem. Am. Jewish Com., Jewish Family and Children's Svc., Jewish Peace Lobby. Capt./chaplain USAR. Mem. Mesa Ecumenical Clergy Assn. (pres. 1988—), Bd. Rabbis of Greater Phoenix (sec.-treas. 1990—, pres. 1991—), Reconstructionist Rabbinical Assn. (chmn. membership 1986—), Anti Defamation League, Hadassah. Democrat. Was first female rabbi in U.S. military. Office: Temple Beth Sholom 316 S LeSueur Mesa AZ 85204

KOPTAK, PAUL EDWARD, religion educator; b. Denville, N.J., Apr. 1, 1955; s. Edward John and Shirley Mae (Ewton) K.; m. Linda Joan Parker, June 11, 1983. AB, Rutgers U., 1977; MDiv, North Park Theol. Sem., 1986; PhD, Northwestern U., 1990. Campus staff Inter-Varsity Christian Fellowship, 1977-82; pastor Evang. Covenant Ch., 1984-85; instr. bibl. studies North Park Coll. and Theol. Sem., Chgo., 1988—; vis. lectr. Caribbean Grad. Sch. Theology, Kingston, Jamaica, 1989—. Contbr. articles to profl. jours. Mem. Bread for the World. Mem. Soc. Bibl. Lit., Inst. for Bibl. Rsch., Speech Communication Assn., Religious Speech Communication Assn., Kenneth Burke Soc. Office: North Park Coll and Theol Sem 3225 W Foster Ave Chicago IL 60625-4987

KORANGTENG, DANIEL AGYEI, minister; b. Pepeasee, Kwahu, Ghana, Mar. 27, 1927; s. Emmanuel Akwasi Bour and Martha Amma (Boadiwaa) K.; m. Mary Obiriwa; children: Agyei, Gladys Opoku Boahene, Christiana Asirifi, Dolores Amaning, Mary. Tchr.'s cert., Presbyn. Tng. Coll., 1948; cert., Trinity coll., Kumasi, Ghana, 1957; BD, U. Hamburg, Fed. Republic Germany, 1965; cert. in edn., Cape Coast U., Ghana, 1973. Cert. tch., catechist, Ghana; ordained to ministry Presbyn. Ch. Tchr. Presbyn. Middle Sch., Koforidua, Boso, Ghana, 1950-52, 54; dist. pastor Presbyn. Ch., Kumasi, Boso, Ghana, 1958-59, 60; chaplain Presbyn. Tng. Coll., Akropong-Akwapim, Ghana, 1966-76; vice prin. St. Andrews Coll., Mampong-Ashanti, Ghana, 1977-79; moderator Presbyn. Ch. Ghana, Accra, 1987—; bd. dirs. Union Trading Co., Ghana br. Author: Two Wives or One, 1972, Bible Concordance in Twi Lang. Chmn. bd. govs. Trinity Coll., Accra, 1989—. Office: Presbyn Ch Office, PO Box 1800, Accra Ghana

KORANTENG-PIPIM, SAMUEL, religion educator; b. Nkonya, Volta, Ghana, Dec. 10, 1957; s. Isaac and Pipim and Ellen Korantemah; m. Rebecca Abraham. BS in Engring., U. Sci. and Tech., Kumasi, Ghana, 1981; MDiv, Andrews U., 1987, postgrad. Coord. campus ministries Seventh-say Adventist Ch., Kumasi, 1982-84, sec. lay adv. coun. Cen. Ghana Conf., 1986-90; cons. Acad. Skills Ctr. Andrews U., Berrien Springs, Mich., 1987-91. Recipient Dehaan Work Excellence award, 1990; Andrews Sch. Grad. Studies fellow, 1988-89. Mem. Am. Acad. Religion, Adventist Theol. Soc., Soc. for Bibl. Lit., African Profl. Assn., Pan-African Club (v.p. 1985-86), Evang. Theol. Soc., Andrews Soc. Religious Studies, Sem. Doctoral Club (v.p., then pres. 1989-91). *I have discovered two important mileposts in my journey through life. First, God is able to transform our mishaps into Blessings. Second, the little things of life hold the keys to success. May these mileposts also serve as signposts during the remainder of our pilgrimage.*

KORBMAN, MEYER HYMAN, rabbi, public school administrator; b. Newark, Oct. 30, 1925; s. Abraham and Celia Korbman; m. Mildred Penn, Dec. 17, 1950; children: Marc, Riva, David. BA, Yeshiva U., 1949; MA, Seton Hall U., 1954. Ordained rabbi. Rabbi Congregation Beth El, Hightstown, N.J., 1951-70, Temple Israel, Union, N.J., 1970—; v.p. pub. schs. Newark, 1974—; mem. Coun. Congregations and Chs., Union, 1970—. Trustee Rabbinical Coll., N.J., 1952-54, Jewish Fedn., Union, 1970—; trustee, exec. bd. Grad. Inst. Talmudical Studies, 1954; apptd. mem. Sr. Citizens Adv. Commn., Union, 1976—. With U.S. Army, 1944-46. Recipient cert. of merit Newark Bd. Edn., 1978, Citizen of Yr. award B'nai Brith, 1986, award Union County Bd. of Chosen Freeholders, 1986, citation Union Twp., 1986, Gen. Assembly citation State of N.J., 1986, Notable Am. award of merit, 1987, cert. recognition Union Twp. Bd. Edn., 1987, Golden Circle award Israel Histadrut Found., 1988. Mem. NEA, Union County Bd. Rabbis, Essex County Bd. Rabbis, Newark Reading Resource Assn. (pres. 1969-72), City Adminstrs. and Suprs. Assn., Right to Read (N.J. bldg. dir. 1970-72), Internat. Reading Assn. Home: 2454 Ogden Rd Union NJ 07083 Office: Temple Israel of Union 2372 Morris Ave Union NJ 07083 *Life is so tenuous that it would be most prudent to live it in such a way as to leave good memories to those who come after us.*

KOREC, JAN CHRYZOSTOM CARDINAL, cardinal; b. Bosany, Slovakia, Czechoslovakia, Jan. 22, 1924. Bishop of Nitra, elevated to the Sacred Coll. of Cardinals, 1991, with titular ch. of Sts. Fabian and Venanzian. Office: Biskupsky Urad, Post Schranka 46A, 950 50 Nitra-Hrad Czechoslovakia*

KORINOW, IRA LEE, rabbi; b. Newton, Mass., Feb. 14, 1951; s. Maurice and Freida (Pecker) K.; m. Gail Lynne Jaffe, Feb. 20, 1977; children: Morry Lev, Doron Ephraim, Raanan Meir. BA in Religion, Boston U., 1973; MA in Hebrew Lit., Hebrew Union Coll., 1976, cert. crisis counseling, 1989. Ordained rabbi, 1978. Prin. Rodeph Sholom Religious Sch., N.Y.C., 1975-77; rabbi Temple B'nai Israel, Laconia, N.H., 1977-78, North Shore Congregation Israel, Glencoe, Ill., 1978-81, Temple Emanu-El, Haverhill, Mass., 1981—. Bd. dirs. Union Coun. for Soviet Jews, Washington, 1984-87, Action for Soviet Jewry, Waltham, Mass., 1983-88. Mem. Cen. Conf. Am. Rabbis (Soviet Jewry conf. 1981-87, Gerut com. 1991—), Rabbinical Assembly (corr. 1991—), Mass. Bd. Rabbis (sec. 1985-87, treas. 1987-89, v.p. 1989—), Greater Haverhill Clergy Assn. (pres. 1989—), Coalition for the Advancement Jewish Edn., Nat. Conf. for Soviet Jewry (bd. dirs. 1985—), Rotary. Home: 23 Singingwood Dr Haverhill MA 01830 Office: Temple Emanu-El 514 Main St Haverhill MA 01830

KORITANSKY, GREGORY EMIL, lay church worker; b. Cleve., June 30, 1949; s. Emil Jerry and Anna Lorraine (Prentis) K.; m. Gloria Ann Paschali, Dec. 5, 1970; children: Michael, Lorrie, Daniel. AAS in Electronics, Lakeland Community Coll., Mentor, Ohio, 1969. Deacon Hambden Congl. Ch., Chardon, Ohio, 1984-87, 90—, trustee, 1988-89; electronic technician ARGO-TECH, Cleve., 1979—. Staff sgt. USAF, 1970-77. Home: 9330 Bascom Rd Chardon OH 44024-9404

KORMELINK, SISTER HELEN JEAN, religious education administrator. Exec. dir. Cath. edn. Diocese of Peoria, Ill. Office: Cath Schs Supt 412 NE Madison Ave Peoria IL 61603*

KORNEGAY, ROY AUBRY, JR., minister; b. Shreveport, La., Aug. 15, 1937; s. Roy A. and Clara Agnes (Gray) K.; m. Janette Sewell, Feb. 6, 1937; children: Kari McClure, Karla Weatherly, Kathy Brooks. BA, Howard Payne U., 1959; M Religious Edn., Southwestern Bapt. Theol. Sem., Ft. Worth, 1961; MA, Southwestern Bapt. Theol. Sem., 1989. Ordained to ministry, Baptist Church. Minister of edn. 1st Bapt. Ch., Dumas, Tex., 1961-64, Texas City, Tex., 1964-67, Pampa, Tex., 1967-70; minister of edn. North Phoenix Bapt. Ch., Phoenix, 1970-71, 1st Bapt. Ch., Amarillo, Tex., 1971-86; dir. missions Amarillo (Tex.) Bapt. Assn., 1987—. Author ednl. materials; contbr. articles to mags. Mem. Metro Religious Edn. Assn. (pres. 1984), Southwestern Religious Edn. Assn. (Outstanding Minister of Edn. award 1985). Avocations: Biblical archaeology, stamp collecting, fishing, reading. Home: Rte 8 Box 32-4 Amarillo TX 79118 Office: Amarillo Bapt Assn 1800 S Western Amarillo TX 79106

KORNIS, FREDERICK VANCE, JR., evangelist; b. Kansas City, Mo., Mar. 8, 1950; s. Frederick Kornis and Mary Ellen (Bass) Porter; m. Barbara Lee Mendelsohn, Feb. 22, 1969; children: Summer, Jeremy, Faith, Vanessa. Theology diploma, Trinity Coll., Dunedin, Fla., 1975, BA in Religious Edn., 1976; MA in Religious Ministry, Faith Evang. Schs., Morgantown, Ky., 1986. Ordained to ministry So. Bapt. Conv., 1976. Evangelist Ambs. for Christ Internat., Open Air Campaigners, Kansas City, 1976—; dir. Open Air Campaigners, Balt.-Washington, 1981-84; missionary Open Air Campaigners, The Philippines, 1984-86, India, Fiji, Mex., Can. and U.S.A.; tchr. seminars Moody Bible Inst., Tenn. Temple U., Washington Bible Coll., Balt. Sch. of the Bible, 1977-84; area adviser Child Evangelism Fellowship, 1988—. Chaplain Balt. City Jail, 1976-84. Sgt. U.S. Army, 1968-71, Vietnam. Recipient svc. awards Washington D.C. Chaplains, 1978-83, Award of Honor Balt. Rescue Mission, 1980. Mem. Internat. St. and Evangelism Ministries Assn. Republican. Office: Ambs for Christ Internat 5945 King # 5 Shawnee KS 66203

KORSTJENS, KEITH ALLEN, minister; b. L.A., Apr. 19, 1929; s. John Edward and Roberta (Crabb) K.; m. Mary Jeanette Calvin, June 10, 1951; children: Kenneth, Karen. AB, Calif. Bapt. Theol. Coll., 1951; MA, Claremont Grad. Sch., 1968; PhD, Calif. Sch. Theology, 1977. Ordained to ministry Am. Bapt. Chs. in U.S.A., 1954. Dir. christian edn. First Bapt. Ch., West Los Angeles, Calif., 1949-50; dir. christian edn. and youth Fountain Ave. Bapt. Ch., Hollywood, Calif., 1951-53; min. christian edn. Calvary Bapt. Ch., Sacramento, 1953-54; min. christian edn. First Bapt. Ch., San Bernardino, Calif., 1955-57, Modesto, Calif., 1957-59; min. pastoral care and family life First Bapt. Ch., Pomona, Calif., 1959—. Author: Not A Sometimes Love, 1981. Mem. Christian Camping Assn., Christian Assn. Psychol. Studies, Pomona Valley Ministerial Assn. (pres. 1973), Phi Delta Kappa. Home: 721 Ridgefield Dr Claremont CA 91711 Office: First Bapt Ch 586 N Main St Pomona CA 91767 *Probably most of us are handicapped in life in one way or another. Some handicaps just show more than others. Thus, success and fulfillment in life have much to do with learning how to live above and beyond our handicap...indeed, even to capitalize on it!.*

KORTH, JAMES SCOTT, minister; b. Camden, N.J., Feb. 13, 1963; s. Clifford Lawrence Sr. and Norma Mary (Fults) K.; m. Margaret Alexandria Jones, June 9, 1984; 1 child, Joshua Scott. AA in Communications, Camden County Coll., 1986; BA in Bible, Phila. Coll. of Bible, 1988. Ordained to ministry Fellowship of Fundamental Bible Chs., 1988. Youth pastor Moorestown (N.J.) Bible Ch., 1985-88, sr. pastor, 1988—; pres. Bible Protestant Press, Glassboro, N.J., 1988—; trustee Fellowship of Fundamental Bible Chs. Bd. Trustees, Glassboro, 1990—; trustee, sec. South Jersey Student Prison Ministry, Moorestown, 1988—. Mem. Delta Epsilon Chi. Office: Moorestown Bible Ch 237 W Main St Moorestown NJ 08057

KORTHUIS, ROBERT CECIL, missionary, religious organization administrator; b. Denver, Mar. 31, 1934; s. Bennet Cecil and Phulamina Wahl (Smith) K.; m. Ellen Caroline Nelson, June 18, 1955; children: Robert Bennett, Daniel Jon, Carolyn Jean, Patricia Jan. ThB, Calvary Bible Coll., 1957. Missionary Am. Sunday Sch. Union, Cortez, Colo. and Denver, 1957-74; camp dir. Camp Id-Ra-Ha-Je, Bailey, Colo., 1974-85; missionary Am. Missionary Fellowship, North East, Colo., 1985—; missionary dir. Homestead Bible Camp, Roggen, Colo., 1986—; registrar Mountain Area Sunday Sch. Conv., Denver, 1986—; treas. Mountain Area Christian Educators, Denver, 1976-82; pres. Rocky Mountain Sectional Christian Camping Inst., Wheaton, Ill. 1970-81. Recipient Disting. Svc. award Colo. Jaycees, 1968, Rocky Mountain Camping award Christian Camping Inst., 1982, Disting. Leadership award Platte Canyon Sch. Dist., 1983. Mem. Christian Camping Internat. Republican. Home: 3501 Rd 75 Roggen CO 80652 Office: Homestead Bible Camp Rte 1 Roggen CO 80652

KORTZ, EDWIN WUNDERLY, clergyman, theology educator; b. Easton, Pa., Nov. 6, 1910; s. William Henry and Ada Julia (Wunderly) K.; m. Margaret E. Schwarze, July 30, 1937. B.A., Moravian Coll., 1931; B.D., Moravian Theol. Sem., 1934; S.T.M., Luth. Sem. of Phila., 1944; postgrad., Yale Sch. Alcohol Studies, summer 1945, Inst. Pastoral Care, Boston, summer 1948; S.T.D., Temple U., 1955; D.D. (hon.), Moravian Theol. Sem., 1960. Ordained to ministry Moravian Ch. in Am., 1935, consecrated bishop, 1966; pastor parishes in Va., Ohio and Pa., 1934-49; prof. practical theology Moravian Theol. Sem., 1949-56, 74-88, dir. profl. studies, 1979-84; exec. dir. Bd. Fgn. Missions, Moravian Ch., 1956-74, dir. career devel. for deacons, 1974-76; Denominational rep. Nat. Council Chs. Gen. Assemblies; mem. directing bd. Overseas Ministries div. Nat. Council Chs.; dir. bd. for Christian Work in Santo Domingo.; Chmn. publ. com. for Moravian Hymnal, 1969. Author: My Bible Tells Me What To Believe, 1947, What It Means To Be A Christian: Studies in the Beatitudes, 1988, A Manual For the American Provinces of the Moravian Church, 1988. Trustee Moravian Music Found., 1981-86; bd. dirs. Share-A-Home of Lehigh Valley, 1979-85; chaplain Moravian Hall Sq. Retirement Community, 1988—. Home: Moravian Hall Sq # 426A 175 W North St Nazareth PA 18064

KORZELIUS, LINDA DIANE, church lay worker, financial specialist; b. Teaneck, N.J., June 8, 1955; d. Joseph Robertson and Beatrice (Hoyt) K. BFA, Ramapo Coll. N.J., 1977. Mem., pastor's adv. coun. St. Joseph's Ch., Oradell, New Milford, N.J., 1985—; eucharistic min., catechist, mem. various coms. St. Joseph's Ch., Oradell and New Milford, N.J., 1985—; catechist St. Theresa Ch., Cresskill, N.J., 1985—; chairperson spiritual life com. St. Joseph Ch., Oradell, New Milford, 1991—; loan payoff specialist Alliance Funding Co., Montvale, N.J., 1990-91; asst. to treas. Yeben Assocs., 1991—. Mem. Ladies of Knights Bowling League (pres. Northvale, N.J. club 1990—). Avocation: painting. Home: 153 River Rd New Milford NJ 07646 *Life can present us all with every kind of challenge to shake our resolve and faith. Our consolation is in the many loving people we are blessed to walk the way with.*

KOS, RUDOLPH EDWARD, priest; b. Louisville, Apr. 29, 1945; s. Rudolph S. and Barbara Kos. AAS, El Centro Coll., 1970; BS, U. Tex., Dallas, 1977; MDiv, U. Dallas, 1981. Ordained priest Roman Cath. Ch., 1981; RN, Tex. Parochial vicar All Sts. Cath. Ch., Dallas, 1981-85, St. Lukes Cath. Ch., Irving, Tex., 1985-88; pastor St. John's Cath. Ch., Ennis, Tex., 1988—. Staff sgt. USAF, 1964-68. Mem. Ennis Min. Alliance (past pres. 1990), Mensa. Home and Office: St John's Cath Ch 401 E Lampasas St Ennis TX 75119 *Our call in life is not so much for self-perfection as it is to bring to perfection God's creation. Our faith enlivens our hope that this world, with the help of God, will live the peace, love and joy of the Kingdom now.*

KOSCHITZKY, MIRA, religious organization administrator. Pres. Can. Found. Jewish Culture, Willowdale, Ont. Office: Can Found Jewish Culture, 4600 Bathurst St, Willowdale, ON Canada M2R 3V2*

KOSKINAS, SILAS (HIS EXCELLENCY METROPOLITAN SILAS), metropolitan; b. Corfu, Greece, Dec. 27, 1919; came to U.S., 1946; Grad., U. Athens Theol. Sch., 1943; M.S.T., Boston U., 1957. Ordained deacon Greek Orthodox Ch., 1941, ordained priest, 1943; pastor Greek Orthodox Ch., Albuquerque, 1946; parishes in Greek Orthodox Ch., New London Conn., Boston, Pitts.; dean of St. Nicholas Cathedral, Pitts.; elevated to bishop, 1960; bishop of 8th archdiocesan dist. New Orleans, 1960-65; bishop of 1st archdiocesan dist. N.Y.C., 1965—; bishop new diocese of N.J., 1979—, mem. spl. del. to Rumania, 1970; v.p. Religion in Am. Life, 1972—,

Archdiocesan Coun. of Greek Orthodox Archidiocese, 1972—; chmn. Office of Fgn. Missions, Greek Orthodox Ch.; pres. Hellenic Coll./Holy Cross Sch. Theology, 1987-89. Contbr. numerous articles on Greek Orthodox faith to religious publs. Mem. bd. Appeal of Conscience Found. Recipient Gold Medallion award NCCJ. Office: Greek Orthodox Archdiocese 10 E 79th St New York NY 10021

KOST, ARTHUR DANIEL, pastor; b. Anoka, Minn., May 25, 1943; s. Arthur Jacob and Evelyn (Eden) K.; m. Jane Marie Cole, May 14, 1966; children: Chris Shaun, Dana Danielle, Brandon Jacob. BA in Bible and Theology, North Cen. Bible Sch., Mpls., 1966. Ordained to ministry Assembly of God, 1968. Pastor various chs., Minn., Iowa, Nebr., and Ill., 1966-85, Calvary Assembly of God, Stillwater, Minn., 1985—; bd. dirs., founding mem. KJLY Radio, Blue Earth, Minn.; coord. Jr. Bible Quiz, Mpls. metro area. Mem. Stillwater Ministerial. Home: 1412 Lookout St Stillwater MN 55082 Office: Assembly of God Ch 5805 Osgood Ave N Stillwater MN 55082

KOSTIZEN, ERWIN, minister; b. Lithuania, July 28, 1938; came to U.S., 1953; s. Leo and Sina (Zachris) L.; m. Carolyn Sue Archer, July 13, 1963; children: Pamela Sue Brackrog, Rebecca Lyn, Debra Kay, Joshua Erwin. AA, Concordia Coll., Milw., 1959; BA, Concordia Coll., Ft. Wayne, Ind., 1961; BD, MDiv, Concordia Sem., St. Louis, 1965. Pastor Messiah Luth. Ch., Clio, Mich., 1965—; 3d v.p. Mich. Dist. Luth. Ch.-Mo. Synod, 199—; Synod Conv. del. Mem. Albin Inst., Acad. Parish Clergy, Parish Leadership Seminars, Crossways Internat. Office: Messiah Luth Ch 520 Butler St Clio MI 48420

KOTOK, LAURENCE ALLAN, rabbi; b. Bayonne, N.J., Mar. 31, 1946; m. Merrill Beth Seltzer; children: David Maxwell, Rachel Elizabeth. BA, Rutgers Coll., 1967; B in Hebrew Letters, MA in Hebrew Lit., Hebrew Union Coll., 1972; postgrad., SUNY, 1985—. Ordained rabbi, 1972. Student rabbi Temple Beth Tefilloh, Brunswick, Ga., 1969-70, Sinai Temple, Marion, Ind., 1970-72; asst. rabbi Temple Sinai, Roslyn, N.Y., 1972-74; rabbi North Country Reform Temple Ner Tamid, Glen Cove, N.Y., 1974—; mem. U.A.H.C. Bio-Ethics Com., 1988—; prof. history N.Y. Inst. Tech., 1990, prof. religion Hofstra U., 1975; guest lectr. Hebrew Union Coll., others. Contbr. articles to profl. publs. Mem. numerous civic orgns. including Congrl. Commn. on Drugs and Drug Edn., 1990, Glen Cove Mayor's Steering Com., 1990, Interfaith Nutrition Network, 1989—; med. ethics bd. Glen Cove Community Hosp., 1987—, others. Recipient Civic Commitment award Anti-Defamation League, 1990; honoree/spl. participant various events including North Shore Community/United Jewish Appeal Event, 1975, 85, Israeli Independence Day/U.S. Congress, others. Mem. Jewish Child Care Assn. of N.Y. (trustee 1986—, pub. affairs com. 1988—, group homes and youth residences com. 1988—, nominating com. 1990), N.Y. Fedn. Jewish Philanthropies (various offices includeing pres. Commn. on Synagogue Rels. 1990), Nat. United Jewish Appeal (exec. com. 1982—, nat. campaign planning bd. 1986—), Nat. Rabbinic Cabinet (dir. rsch. planning and evaluation 1987—), Glen Cove Jewish Pres.'s Coun. (chmn. 1974—), others. Office: North Country Reform Temple Ner Tamid Crescent Beach Rd Glen Cove NY 11542

KOURY, ALEAH GEORGE, church executive, minister; b. Toronto, Ont., Can., Sept. 26, 1925; came to U.S. 1952, naturalized, 1960; s. Aleah George and Alice Maude (Jackson) K.; m. Patricia Lee Reynolds, July 11, 1950; children: Patricia Koury Garrison, Aleah George Wayne, Gregory Scott, Rebecca Koury, Cynthia Koury Canaday. BA, U. Toronto, 1948; postgrad., Fresno Coll., 1956, U. Mo., Kansas City, 1971; M Divinity, Midwestern Bapt. Theol. Sem., Kansas City, 1983. Ordained to ministry Reorganized Ch. of Jesus Christ of Latter-day Saints, 1946; ordained Apostle, 1966. Editor Consol. Press, Toronto, 1948-49; minister Independence, Mo., 1949, B.C., Alta., Can., 1950-52, B.C. and Seattle, 1952-56, Cen. Calif. dist., 1956-60; pastor, dist. pres. Utah and S.E. Idaho, 1960-62; asst. to Council of Twelve, 1962; field dir. Europe and Africa, 1966-68, Europe, N. Atlantic States Region and Latin Am., 1973-80; chaplain dir. Independence Regional Health Ctr., 1985-89. Author: Truth and Evidence, 1965, Appointee Handbook, 1966. Facilitator Bi-County Spl. Kids Project, Yuba and Sutter Counties, Calif., 1989. With Can. Army, 1944-46. Fellow Coll. of Chaplains (cert. chaplain); mem. Order of Evangelists (sec. 1980). Home: 2309 Pepperwood Dr Yuba City CA 95993 Office: 1103 Butte House Rd Yuba City CA 95991 *I find, and I believe it to be true, that I am at my best when I am learning, understanding, and applying new information.*

KOUSE, PHILIP CHARLES, clergyman; b. Delaware, Ohio, Apr. 19, 1952; s. Carl F. and Lillian M. (Cunningham) K.; m. Christine S. Paternoster, Dec. 17, 1976; 1 child, Jason. BA, Wright State U., 1975; MDiv, United Teol. Sem., 1978. Ordained to ministry United Meth. Ch. as deacon , 1977, elder, 1980. Reporter The Sun, Springfield, Ohio, 1970-75; local pastor Pacific N.W. Conf. of United Meth. Ch., Seattle, 1978-87; ch. planter Evang. Meth. Ch., Issaquah, Wash., 1987-88; coord. children's, youth and family ministries St. Luke's Episcopal Ch., Seattle, 1989-90; crisis intervention specialist Northwest Mental Health Svcs., Seattle, 1991—; mem. bd. advisors N.W. Prayer Ministry, Seattle, 1986-87, Wind of the Spirit Ministries, Silverdale, Wash., 1986-90. Mem. clergy adv. group South End Seattle Community Orgn., 1984-87. Mem. Wash. Karate Assn., San Juan 21 Fleet 1. Avocation: sailing. Home: 2511 NE 145th St Seattle WA 98155 Office: Northwest Mental Health Svcs 10900 SE 176th St Renton WA 98055

KOVACEVICH, CHRISTOPHER, bishop; b. Galveston, Tex., Dec. 25, 1928; s. Petar B. and Rista (Vujacic) K.; children: Petar V., Paul V., Valerie Kovacevich Backo, Velimir V. BD, St. Sava Sem., 1949; BA, U. Pitts., 1954, MLitt, 1957; M Divinity, Holy Sch. Theology, 1978; postgrad., Chgo. Theol. Sem., 1974-78. Ordained deacon/priest, 1951; consecrated bishop, 1978. Pastor St. Nicholas Serbian Orthodox Ch., Johnstown, Pa., 1951-54, St. Sava Serbian Orthodox Ch., Pitts., 1954-62, St. Archangel Michael Serbian Orthodox Ch., Chgo., 1962-78; bishop Serbian Orthodox Diocese Eastern Am. and Can. (now 2 separate dioceses), Edgeworth-Sewickley, Pa., 1978-85, bishop Am. diocese, 1985—; various positions Dept. Edn., Eccles. Ct., Diocesan Council, pastorates; Orthodox chaplain four univs., Pitts., Va Hosps., Pitts.; mem. governing bd. Nat. Council Chs. of Christ in USA; mem. Dialogue Commn. Orthodox/Roman Cath. Bishops in USA. Author manual for Serbian Orthodox Ch. Camps, 1960; co-author 50th anniversary history St. Archangel Michael Ch., 1976; co-editor Diocesan Jour. U.S.A., Can., chronical Shadeland Monastery history. Mem. Pitts. Bicentennial Com. Mem. World Council Chs. Avocation: golf. Home and Office: Serbian Orthdox Diocese of Ea Am Way Hollow Rd Box 368 Sewickley PA 15143

KOVACS, DIANNE ROHRER, minister; b. Oklahoma City, Jan. 29, 1958; d. Charles Larry Rohrer and Ann Harvey Whitten Coley; m. Brian Watson Kovacs, Dec. 18, 1981; 1 child, Amanda Lynn. BA, Centenary Coll., Shreveport, 1980; MDiv, Phillips Grad. Sem., Enid, Okla., 1984; postgrad.,)Perkins Sch. Theology, Dallas, 1980-81. Ordained to ministry United Meth. Ch.as deacon, 1982, as elder, 1986. Asst. pastor Federated Ch., Kingfisher, Okla., 1981-82; dir. N.W. Okla. Pastoral Counseling Ctr., Enid, Okla., 1982-84; assoc. pastor First United Meth. Ch., Yukon, Okla., 1984-87; pastor First United Meth. Ch., Hinton, Okla., 1987-91, St. Paul's United Meth. Ch., Lawton, Okla., 1991—; chmn. Conf. Worship Commn., Okla., 1988-92; vice chmn. Courtesies & Resolutions Com., Okla., 1988-91, Okla. Conf. (structure com. 1991-92. Dean's scholar, Phillips Grad. Sem., 1981-84; recipient Brown Leadership award, Centenary Coll., 1980. Mem. Okla. Women in Ministry, Hinton Ministerial Alliance (sec. 1988-91), Fellowship of United Meth. in Worship, Music and Other Arts, Order of St. Luke, Nat. Acd. for Preaching, 1990-91, Kiwanis. Democrat. Home: 212 E Parkland Dr Yukon OK 73099

KOVALCHUK, FEODOR SAWA, priest; b. Wakaw, Sask., Can., Mar. 5, 1924; came to U.S., 1926; s. Sawa John and Rose M. (Boryk) K.; m. Anna Ivanovna Korewik, May 23, 1948; children: Sergius, Basilissa, Natalia (dec.). AB, Columbia U., 1945; diploma, St. Vladimir's Sem., 1946; MA, Western Res. U., 1967, postgrad., 1970—. Ordained deacon, priest Russian Orthodox Cath. Ch., 1948, mitered archpriest. Asst. pastor St. Nicholas Cathedral, N.Y.C., 1948; pastor St. George Serbian Ch., Pitts., 1948-49, Holy Trinity Ch., Balt., 1949-52, Nativity of Christ, Youngstown, Ohio, 1952—; pastor of missions St. Seraphim's Ch., Cambridge, Mass., 1949, St. Mary's Ch., Holdinsford, Minn., 1949; dean Cen. States Deanery Russian Orthodox Cath. Ch., Youngstown, Ohio, 1983—, exec. sec. patriarchal parishes, 1971—. Translator, compiler: Abridged Typicon, 1974; editor, compiler: Holy Liturgy and Other Prayers, 1965, 7th edit., 1990, Wonder-Working Icons of Theotokos, 1985; editor One Church, 1977—; author pamphlets, booklets. Mem. Eastern Orthodox Clergy Assn. Office: Nativity of Christ Ch 727 Miller Ave Youngstown OH 44502-2326

KOWALEWSKI, FRANCIS PHILIP, JR., priest; b. Buffalo, June 17, 1922; s. Francis P. Sr. and Wanda M. (Kazmierczak) K. Student, Fredonia State Teaching Coll., 1940-43; BA, U. Mich., 1946; MA in Math., U. Buffalo, 1948; postgrad., Our Lady of Angels Sem., Niagara University, N.Y., 1954-56; —, Canisianum, Innsbruck, Austria, 1956-60. Ordained priest Roman Cath. Ch., 1959. Chaplain Alfred (N.Y.) U. and Alfred Agrl. Tech., 1960-61; prof. math., guidance dir. Notre Dame High Sch., Batavia, N.Y., 1961-81; parochial assoc. St. Mary of Angels, Olean, N.Y., 1981-84; pastor St. Patrick's Ch., Fillmore, N.Y., 1984—; pres. Cath. Guidance Assn., Buffalo, 1978-80. Chmn. Batavia (N.Y.) chpt. ARC, 1970-80, Rochester (N.Y.) Div. ARC, 1979-81. With U.S. Army, 1942-45. Mem. Fillmore Ministerial Assn., Am. Legion. Home and Office: 109 W Main St P O Box 198 Fillmore NY 14735-0198

KOWALSKI, PAUL RANDOLPH, minister; b. Anderson, S.C., June 20, 1934; s. Paul William and Margaret Katharine (Mitchell) K.; m. Mary Frances Bagwell, Aug. 2, 1958; children: Kelly Bagwell, Robin Marie. BS, Clemson U., 1956; MDiv, Columbia Theol. Sem., 1960; DD (hon.), Presbyn. Coll., 1976. Ordained to ministry Presbyn. Ch. (U.S.A.), 1960. Min. Pendleton (S.C.) Presbyn. Ch., 1960-62, Abbeville (S.C.) Presbyn. Ch., 1962-67; sr. min. Reid Meml. Presbyn. Ch., Augusta, Ga., 1967-74, First Presbyn. Ch., Greenville, S.C., 1974—; trustee outreach found. Presbyn. Ch. (USA), Charlotte, N.C., 1980—, vice chmn. 1990—, mem. coun. Synod of South Atlantic, 1985—. Bd. dirs. Columbia Theol. Sem., Decatur, Ga., 1976-85, Rabun Gap (Ga.) Nacoochee Sch., 1973-81, YMCA, Greenville; bd. visitors Presbyn. Coll., 1983-85. Named Young Man of Yr. Abbeville Jaycees, 1965; recipient Disting. Grad. award Clemson U., 1988. Mem. Rotary (pres. Augusta club 1970-71, Greenville club 1987-88, Paul Harris fellow 1988). Office: First Presbyn Ch 200 W Washington St Greenville SC 29601 *I have found Jesus' words in John 10:10 to be my personal philosophy and challenging goal of life—"I am come that you might have life and have it in all abundance."*

KOWNACKI, MARY LOU, association administrator; b. Erie, Pa., Nov. 29, 1941; d. Edward and Mary (Krzyzan) K. MA in Peace Studies, Antioch U., 1979. Joined Order St. Benedict, Roman Cath. Ch. Tchr. various schs., Pa., 1961-79; reporter Erie (Pa.) Daily Times, 1971-72; dir. Pax Ctr., Edie, Pa., 1972-85; nat. coord. Benedictines for Peace, Edie, 1980—; dir. formation Benedictine Sisters Erie, 1984—; nat. coord. Pax Christi USA, Erie, 1985—; lectr. Villa Marie Coll., Erie, 1981-83. Author: Let Peace Begin With Me, 1983, Peace Is Our Calling, 1981; contbr. articles to profl. jours.; contbg. editor Sojourners Mag., 1988—; mem. editorial bd. Spirituality Today, 1990—. Recipient Pacem Terris award Georgetown U., Washington, 1985; named Peace Pilgrim of Yr. Nazareth Bethlehem Pilgrimage, 1984. Home: 345 E 9th St Erie PA 16503 Office: Pax Christi USA 348 E 10th St Erie PA 16503

KOYAMA, KOSUKE, theological educator; b. Tokyo, Dec. 10, 1929; s. Zentaro and Tama (Uma) K.; m. Lois Eleanor Koyama, 1958; children: James, Elizabeth, Mark. BDiv, Drew U., 1954; MTh, Princeton U. Theol. Sem., 1955, PhDTh, 1959. Lectr. in theology Thailand Theol. Sem., Chiengmai, Thailand, 1960-68; dean S.E. Asia Grad. Sch. of Theol., Singapore, 1968-74; sr. lectr. U. Otago, Dunedin, New Zealand, 1974-80; prof. Union Theol. Sem., N.Y.C., 1980-82, prof. John D. Rockefeller Jr., 1982—. Author: Waterbuffalo Theology, 1974, No Handle on The Cross, 1977, Three Mile An Hour God, 1979, Mt. Fuji and Mt. Sinai, 1984. Fellow The Soc. for Arts, Religion and Contemporary Culture; mem. Am. Acad. Religion, Am. Theol. Soc. Office: Union Theol Sem Broadway at 120th St New York NY 10027

KRAABEL, ALF THOMAS, college dean, minister; b. Portland, Oreg., Nov. 4, 1934; s. Alf Mekinley and Marie Christine (Swensen) K.; m. Janice M. Hanson, Aug. 19, 1956; children: Allen, Thomas, Sarah. BA in Classics, Luther Coll., Decorah, Iowa, 1956; MA in Classics, U. Iowa, 1958; BD in N.T., Luther Theol. Sem., St. Paul, 1961; ThD, Harvard U., 1968. Asst. pastor Our Saviour's Luth. Ch., Mpls., 1961-63; faculty in religious studies and classics U. Minn., 1967-82; dean Luther Coll., Decorah, 1983—. Co-author: Khirbet Shema', 1976; editor: Goodenough on the Beginnings on Christianity, 1990; co-editor: The Future of Early Christianity, 1991. Fellow Oxford (Eng.) U., 1977-78, 81, 90, Am. Coun. Learned Socs., 1977-78, 81. Life mem. Classical Assn. Mid. West and South; mem. Am. Soc. for Study of Religion, Cath. Bibl. Assn., Studiorum Novi Testamenti Societas, Soc. Bibl. Lit. Home: 708 Ridge Rd Decorah IA 52101 Office: Luther Coll Dept Religion & Philosophy Decorah IA 52101

KRABBE, ALAN ROBERT, minister; b. Appleton, Wis., Mar. 2, 1945; s. Alvin Arthur and Florence Esther (Roate) K.; m. Susan Fowler, Dec. 27, 1987; children: Jill Marie, Jennifer Ann, Kelly Michelle, Joseph Michael Malsey. BS, Carthage Coll., Kenosha, Wis., 1967; MDiv, Northwestern Luth. Sem., St. Paul, 1971. Ordained to ministry Evang. Luth. Ch. in Am., 1971. Pastor St. Mark Luth. Ch., Batesville, Ind., 1971-74, Bethel Luth. Ch., Great Falls, Mont., 1974-78; assoc. pastor Cen. Luth. Ch., Yakima, Wash., 1978-81; pastor Bethany Luth. Ch., Spanaway, Wash., 1981-86; assoc. pastor St. Paul Luth. Ch., Neenah, Wis., 1989—; mem. synod exec. com. Ind.-Ky. Synod, 1973-74; chmn. Parish Life Commn., Great Falls, Mont., 1979-81; chaplain Neenah Police Dept., 1989—. Mem. bd. dirs. Reg. Coun. on Domestic Abuse, Neenah, 1990—, Youth-Go, Neenah, 1991!. Recipient Svc. award, Pierce County Fire Dept., 1986. Mem. Neenah Optimist (Law Enforcement award 1981). Office: St Paul Luth Ch 200 N Commercial Neenah WI 54956

KRABBE, DONALD LOUIS, military chaplain; b. Harvey, Ill., June 10, 1934; s. Arthur Lewis and Nancy Laverne (Jones) K.; m. Doris Gertie Langhout, June 4, 1957; children: Diana, David, Danica. BA, Concordia Sem., St. Louis, 1957; BA, MA, Concordia Sem., Springfield, Ill., 1961; MA, Claremont Grad. Sch., 1971. Ordained to ministry Luth Ch., 1961. Pastor Holy Trinity Luth. Ch., Covington, La., 1961-65; commd. ensign USN, USMC, 1965, advanced through grades to capt., 1980; navy chaplain USN, 1965—, USMC, 1989—. Avocation: sailing. Home: 5816 Stone Creek Dr Centreville VA 22020 Office: HQ USMC Code Rel Washington DC 20380-0001

KRABILL, ANTHONY LYNN, radio station manager; b. Washington, July 28, 1967; s. Joseph Lloyd and Betty Jean (Roth) K. BA in English, Ea. Mennonite Coll., 1989. Office: Sta WEMC 1200 Park Rd Harrisonburg VA 22801

KRAFT, CAROL JOYCE, deacon, German language educator; b. Jackson, Mich., Dec. 8, 1935; d. Lester Christian and Grace Florence (Amstutz) K. BA, Wheaton (Ill.) Coll., 1957; MA, Columbia U., 1958, U. Mich., 1960; postgrad., Middlebury Coll., 1963, 64, 72, Goethe Inst., Munich, 1976, 77. Ordained deacon Episcopal Ch., 1989. Assoc. prof. German Wheaton Coll., 1960—. Treas. St. Barnabas Episcopal Ch., Glen Ellyn, Ill., 1982—. Mem. Am. Assn. Tchrs. German, Am. Coun. on Teaching of Fgn. Langs., Delta Kappa Gamma. Home: 124 W Prairie St Wheaton IL 60187 Office: Wheaton Coll Dept Fgn Langs Wheaton IL 60187

KRAFT, ROBERT ALAN, history of religion educator; b. Waterbury, Conn., Mar. 18, 1934; s. Howard Russell and Marian Augusta (Northrop) K.; m. Carol Lois Wallace, June 11, 1955; children: Cindy Lee Shapiro, Scott Wallace, Todd Alan, Randall Jay. B.A. summa cum laude, Wheaton Coll., 1955, M.A., 1957; Ph.D., Harvard U., 1961. Teaching fellow Harvard U., 1959-61; asst. lectr. U. Manchester, Eng., 1961-63; asst. prof. religious studies U. Pa., 1963-68, assoc. prof., 1968-76, prof., 1976—, acting chmn. dept. religious studies, 1972-73, chmn., 1977-84, chmn. grad. program in religious studies, 1973-75, 76-84; vis. lectr. Lutheran Theol. Sem., 1965-66; coordinator Phila. Seminar on Christian Origins, 1963—; mem. Rev. Standard Version Bible Com., 1972—; bd. advs. Ancient Bibl. Manuscript Center for Preservation and Research, Claremont, Calif., 1978—; mem. series adv. bd. Berlin Akademie, 1971—. Contbr. articles and revs. to profl. publs. U. Pa. faculty fellow, summers 1965, 67, 73; Guggenheim fellow, 1969-70; Am. Council Learned Socs. fellow, 1975-76; Am. Council Learned Socs. travel grantee, 1970; Nat. Endowment for Humanities project grantee, 1978-79, 80-81, 82—. Mem. Soc. Bibl. Lit. (sec. Mid-Atlantic sect. 1965-69, pro-tem N.T. book editor Jour. Bibl. Lit. 1965-66, 70, editor Monograph series 1967-72, editor Pseudepigrapha series 1973-78), Studiorum Novi Testamenti Societas (editorial bd. 1973-76), Internat. Orgn. Septuagint and Cognate Studies (exec. com. 1969—), N.Am. Patristics Soc., Am. Soc. Papyrology, Assn. for Computers and Humanities, Assn. for Lit. and Linguistic Computing. Office: U Pa College Hall Box 36 Philadelphia PA 19104-6303 *To be critical in evaluating the work of others is not very difficult; the ability to evaluate one's own work critically is something to be cultivated.*

KRAFT, WILLIAM ARMSTRONG, retired priest; b. Rochester, N.Y., Apr. 13, 1926; s. William Andrew and Elizabeth Ruth (Armstrong) K. BA, St. Bernard Coll., 1947; ThM, Immaculate Heart Theol. Coll., 1951; D of Ministry, Claremont Sch. of Theology, 1981. Dir. and founder of Newman Apostolate Diocese of San Diego, Calif., 1951-63; dir. of pub. rels. Diocese of San Diego, 1956-63, dir. of cemeteries, 1964-70, exec. dir. of devel., 1979-91; founding pastor St. Therese of Child Jesus Parish, San Diego, 1956-70, Good Shepherd Parish, San Diego, 1970-77; pastor St. Charles Borromeo Parish, San Diego, 1977-79; bd. dirs. Cath. Charities, San Diego; bd. of consultors Diocese of San Diego, 1985-91, mem. Presbyteral Coun., 1985-91, mem. bldg. commn., 1977-91. Bd. dirs. Am. Nat. Red Cross, San Diego, 1956-63, Legal Aid Soc., San Diego, 1956-65, Travelers' Aid Soc., San Diego, 1956-65; mem. Presdl. Task Force, Washington, 1984—. Named Prelate of Honor to Pope, Pope John Paul II, Vatican City, 1985, Knight Comdr. of Equestrian, Pope John Paul II, Vatican City, 1984, Order of Holy Sepulchre, Knights of Columbus 4th degree. Mem. Benevolent and Protective Order of Elks, Univ. Club Atop Symphony Towers, Nat. Cath. Conf. for Total Stewardship (bd. dirs.), Nat. Cath. Devel. Conf., Nat. Soc. Fund Raising Execs. (cert.). Republican. Avocations: music appreciation, swimming. Home: 6910 Cibola Rd San Diego CA 92120

KRAMER, LAURIE MALOFF, religious organization administration; b. N.Y.C., June 4, 1948; d. Aaron N. and Muriel F. (Roden) Maloff; m. Joel R. Kramer, Sept. 6, 1969; children: Matthew, Elias, Adam. AB, Smith Coll., 1969, postgrad. in mgmt., 1990-91; MA in Teaching, George Washington U., 1971. Buffalo svcs. supr. Jewish Ctr. of Greater Buffalo, 1981-83; Jewish cultural arts dir. Jewish Community Ctr. of Greater St. Paul Area, 1984-86, group work supr., 1986-87, program dir., 1987-90, asst. dir., 1990—. Bush Found. leadership fellow, 1990; Jill Ker Conway Fund grantee, 1990; Brandeis U. fellow, 1989. Mem. Assn. of Jewish Communal Profls. Office: Jewish Community Ctr 1375 St Paul Ave Saint Paul MN 55116

KRANTZ, DOUGLAS EDWARD, rabbi; b. Los Angeles, May 10, 1948; s. Marvin and Natalie (Marschack) K.; m. Joan Rappaport, June 21, 1980; children: Jonathan B. Isacoff, Jennifer G. Isacoff, Benjamin A. BA, U. Calif., 1970; M in Hebrew Letters, Hebrew Union Coll., 1972. Ordained rabbi, 1975. Asst. rabbi Temple Israel, N.Y.C., 1975-78; rabbi Congregation B'nai Yisrael, Armonk, N.Y., 1979—. Mem. B'Reira (bd. dirs. 1975-78), Cen. Conf. Am. Rabbis (chair justice and peace com., vice chair social action commn.), Jewish Peace Fellowhip (bd. dirs. 1985—). Home: 19 Thornewood Rd Armonk NY 10504 Office: Congregation B'nai Yisrael 485 Bedford Rd Armonk NY 10504

KRANZ, PHILIP NEIL, rabbi, educator; b. Cleve., Apr. 8, 1943; s. Benjamin Robert and Alyce (Bogen) K.; m. Nancy Jean Weston, June 26, 1971; children: Rebecca Lyn, Abigail Dena. BA, Ohio State U., 1965; BHL, Hebrew Union Coll., Cin., 1968; MHL, Hebrew Union Coll., 1971. Ordained rabbi, 1971. Asst. rabbi Chgo. Sinai Congregation, 1971-74, assoc. rabbi, 1974-75, sr. rabbi, 1975-80; sr. rabbi Temple Sinai, Atlanta, 1980—; instr. Ga. State U., Atlanta, 1985—, Agnes Scott Coll., Decatur, Ga., 1988-90; mem. Rabbinic Bd. of Alumni Overseers Hebrew Union Coll., 1977-87. Mem. Class of 1985 Leadership Atlanta, 1984-85; pres. Planned Parenthood, Atlanta, 1985-87; mem. Atlanta Jewish Fedn., 1989; mem. Cen. Conf. of Am. Rabbis, 1990—. Home: 55 Brandon Ridge Dr Atlanta GA 30328 Office: Temple Sinai 5645 Dupree Dr NW Atlanta GA 30327

KRASOVEC, JOZE, theology educator; b. Sodna vas, Yugoslavia, Apr. 20, 1944; s. Jozef and Marija (Flis) K. D of Bibl. Studies, Pontifical Bibl. Inst., Rome, 1976; PhD, Hebrew U., Jerusalem, 1982; ThD in History of Religion, Religious Anthropology Inst. Cath. and Sorbonne, Paris, 1986. Prof. O.T. Theol. Faculty, Ljubljana, Yugoslavia, 1976—; researcher, pres. com. for New Slovenian Bible, 1985—. Author: Der Merismus, 1977, Antithetic Structure, 1984, Lexicon of Biblical Names in Slovene, 1984, La Justice (sdq) de Dieu, 1988; contbr. articles to profl. publs. Roman Catholic. Home: Dolnicarjeva 1, 61000 Ljubljana Yugoslavia Office: Theol Faculty, Poljanska 4, 61000 Ljubljana Yugoslavia

KRATZ, RUSSELL JOSEPH, deacon; b. N.Y.C., May 16, 1946; s. Joseph Francis and Sally (Kaplan) K.; m. Joan Alice Moehringer, June 25, 1971; children: Matthew, Timothy, Emily. BA, St. John's U., 1967; MA, Queens Coll., 1972; EdD, SUNY, Albany, 1978. Cert. sch. dist. adminstr., N.Y. Coord. continuing dioconate edn. Diocese Albany, 1979-87, mem. Jewish-Cath. Com., 1982-84, mem. staff formation for ministry program, 1987—; bur. chief Office Continuing Edn., N.Y. State Edn. Dept., Albany, 1983—; mem. Nat. Adv. Com. External Diploma Program, 1991—. Mem. adv. bd. Salvation Army, Albany Corps, 1987—. Recipient Jean L. Coon Meml. award N.Y. State Edn. Dept., Albany, 1989. Mem. Assn. Vocat. Edn. Adminstrs., N.Y. Assn. Community and Continuing Edn. (N.Y. State Edn. Dept. liaison 1984—, Profl. Svc. award 1989). Roman Catholic. Office: NY State Edn Dept 5045 Cultural Edn Ctr Albany NY 12230

KRAUS, DAVID, rabbi; b. Halifax, N.S., Can., Feb. 3, 1930; s. Martin and Sari (Heimlich) K.; m. Sonya Witten, Dec. 23, 1956; children: Benjamin W., Eva Leah. AB, Ind. State U., 1951; MEd, U. N.C., 1955. Rabbi 1979. Ednl. dir. Temple Israel, Charlotte, N.C., 1954-57; pres. Benco Steel, Inc., Hickory, N.C., 1960-65, Witten & Co., Inc., Hickory, 1958-73; account exec. Paine Webber, Charlotte, 1968-71; pres. Kraus & Son, Inc., Charlotte, 1971-74; circuit rabbi N.E. N.C. Circuit Rabbi, Rocky Mount, 1979-81; rabbi Temple Israel, Spartanburg, S.C., 1981-83, Temple Bethel, Fort Pierce, Fla., 1983-85, Beth Israel Congregation, Beaufort, S.C., 1986—. Bd. dirs. Caroline Hospice, Beaufort, S.C., 1989—, Beaufort Heart Assn., 1989—. Mem. So. United Synagogue Rabbis, Greater Carolinas Assn. Rabbis (sec. 1980-82), Am. Assn. Rabbis, Inst. Scrap Iron and Steel (dir. 1960-63), Ministerial Assn. (pres. Rocky Mount chpt. 1981, pres. Beaufort 1988), Hickory Jaycees (pres. 1965), Metrolina Trade Club (pres. Charlotte 1976), Hickory Optimists (v.p. 1967), Catawba Valley Hosiery Club (dir. 1967), Rotary, B'nai Brith, Jewish War Vets (chaplain 1983-85). Democrat. Jewish. Home: 306 East St Box 1493 Beaufort SC 29901

KRAUS, HANS-JOACHIM, retired theology educator, writer; b. Essen-Schonnebeck, Germany, Dec. 17, 1918; s. Ernst and Hedwig (Leveringhaus) K.; m. Ingrid Kossmann (dec.); children: Dagmar, Dorothea, Christiane, Adelheid; m. Brigitte Hoyer. ThD, U. Heidelberg, 1944; ThD R.C., U. Bonn, 1952; DD, U. Aberdeen, Scotland, 1975. Ordained to ministry. Pastor Rhein Kirche, Germany, 1944-48; mem. faculty U. Bonn, Fed. Republic Germany, 1948-54; prof. theology U. Hamburg, Fed. Republic Germany, 1954-68, U. Göttingen, Fed. Republic Germany, 1968-83; ret., 1983. Author: Psalmen I & II, 6 edits., Geschichte der Hist Krit Erforschung des Alten Testaments, 3 edits., Die Biblische Theologie, Worship in Israel, 1966, Systematische Theologie, 1983, Theology of the Psalms, 1986. Home: Zur Gloria 25, D-5600 Wuppertal 23, Federal Republic of Germany

KRAUS, HENRY EMERY, rabbi; b. Papa, Hungary, Aug. 27, 1914; came to U.S., 1957; s. Emil and Janka (Revesz) K.; m. Clara Pasternak, Sept. 17, 1946; 1 child, Marianne Janoff. PhD, U. Budapest (Hungary), 1938. Ordained rabbi, 1940. Rabbi Jewish Community, Siklos, Hungary, 1939-44, Kaposuar, Hungary, 1946-56; rabbi Temple Beth Torah, Gardena, Calif., 1957-69, Tempel Beth Ami, West Covina, Calif., 1969-85; chaplain City of Hope, Duarte, Calif., 1985—; chaplain sheriff dept. L.A. County, L.A., 1982—, Police Dept. L.A., 1987—, UCLA Med. Ctr., 1989—. Mem. Rabbinical Assembly Am. Home: 50 Camden Ave Los Angeles CA 90025

KRAUS, MICHAEL, minister. Pres. New Apostolic Ch. N.Am., Waterloo, Ont., Can. Office: New Apostolic Ch NAm, 267 Lincoln Rd, Waterloo, ON Canada N2J 2N8*

KRAUS, WILLIAM HENRY, rabbi; b. Phila., May 21, 1953; m. Ellen J. Lewis, June 18, 1978; children: Gideon, Micah. BA, Middlebury (Vt.) Coll., 1975; MAHL, Hebrew Union Coll., Cin., 1978. Ordained rabbi, 1980. Rabbi, dir. Jewish Scouting Programs, Boy Scouts Am., 1980-85; rabbi Temple Beth-El, Somerville, N.J., 1985-91; founder, dir. treatment ctr. for Jewish youth The Sancturary, 1991—; chmn. Somerset County Rabbinical Coun., 1990-91. Treas. Somerville Sr. Citizens Housing Corp., 1987—. Mem. Somerville Area Ministerial Assn. (pres. 1989-90), Cen. Conf. Am. Rabbis, Hebrew Union Coll. Alumni Assn., Optimist.

KRAUSE, HARRY ARTHUR, music minister, entertainer; b. Mt. Clemens, Mich., Sept. 7, 1951; s. Vern Karl and Shirley (Gleason) K. MusB, U. Mich., Ann Arbor, 1972. Music min. Immanuel Luth. Ch., St. Clair, Mich., 1968—; pianist St. Clair Inn, St. Clair, Mich., 1981—; dir. Handbell and Vocal Adult and Children's Choir, St. Clair, 1981—. Composer Mass of St. Peter, 1969. Dir. Richmond Community Theatre, 1969-73, cons. St. Clair Music/Study Club, 1982—. Mem. Port Huron Civic Theatre. Missouri Synod Lutheran. Home: 1715 N River Saint Clair MI 78079

KRAUSE, PAUL EDWARD, clergyman; b. Jersey City, May 13, 1956; s. Paul Edward and Helen (Daab) K.; m. Deborah Lyn Bone, June 10, 1978; children: Joshua Michael, Alexander Paul. BS, King's Coll., Briarcliff Manor, N.Y., 1978; MDiv, Denver Conservative Bapt. Sem., 1981. Ordained to ministry Evang. Free Ch. Am., 1991; cert. tchr. Evang. Tchr. Tng. Assn. Ch. planter, pastor Valley Evang. Free Ch., Kemmerer, Wyo., 1981-82, Trinity Evang. Free Ch., Port Jervis, N.Y., 1982-83; relief supr. Internat. Svc. Systems, Jersey City, 1982-84; mgr. Friendly Ice Cream Corp., Scotch Plains, N.J., 1984-86; devel. officer Christian Homes for Children, Hackensack, N.J., 1986-89; interim pastor Hoboken (N.J.) Evang. Free Ch., 1988-89, pastor, 1989—. Class bd. govs. King's Coll., 1987—. Democrat. Avocations: photography, baseball, cooking. Home: 209 Zabriskie St Jersey City NJ 07307 Office: Hoboken Evang Free Ch 833 Clinton St Hoboken NJ 07030 *It is often much better to be seen as a foolish man living for God, than a wise man without hope for tomorrow.*

KRAUSE, P(HILIP) ALLEN, rabbi; b. San Antonio, Sept. 7, 1939; s. Mortimer William and Marian (Monovitz) K.; m. Sharon Ruth Hofmann, Aug. 18, 1963; children: Stephen J., Gavriella E. BA, UCLA, 1961; BHL, Hebrew Union Coll., L.A., 1963; MAHL, Hebrew Union Coll., Cin., 1967. Rabbi Temple Beth Torah, Fremont, Calif., 1971-79, Temple Beth El, Salinas, Calif., 1979-83, Congregaton Beth Am, Los Altos Hills, Calif., 1983-84, Temple Beth El, Mission Viejo, Calif., 1984—; lectr. Calif. State U., Fullerton, 1988—; pres. Orange County Bd. Rabbis, 1988-90; chmn. Ad Hoc Rabbinic Com. To Save Ethiopian Jews, San Jose, 1979-84. Contbr. articles to profl. jours. Bd. dirs. Nat. Conf. Christians & Jews, 1990—. Mem. Pacific Assn. Reform Rabbis (exec. bd. 1989—), Am. Assn. Ethiopian Jews. Democrat. Home: 24612 Dardania Mission Viejo CA 92691 Office: Temple Beth El 28892 Marquerite Pkwy #210 Mission Viejo CA 92692

KRAUSS, HARRY EDWARD, minister; b. Phila., Aug. 3, 1945; s. Harry Edward and Josephine (Atkinson) K. A.B., William and Mary Coll., 1967; M.Div., Va. Theol. Sem., 1977. Ordained deacon Episcopal Ch., 1977, priest, 1978. Curate All Saints' Ch., Wynnewood, Pa., 1977-79, assoc. rector, 1979-80, rector, 1980—. Trustee Yarnall Library, U. Pa., Phila., 1979—; bd. dirs. Evangelical/Cath. Mission, Chgo., 1980—, Fellowship Witness, Alexandria, Va., 1984—; Soc. of Mary, Washington, 1983—; chaplain Soc. of Sons of St. George, Phila., 1979—, Mil. Order of Fgn. Wars, Phila., 1980—. Served to capt. U.S. Army, 1968-72. Decorated Bronze Star, Meritorious Service medal. Mem. Fellowship of Witness, Cath. Clerical Union, Soc. of Mary. Clubs: Rittenhouse, Union League (Phila.); Merion Cricket (Haverford, Pa.). Office: All Saints Ch Manor Rd Wynnewood PA 19096

KRAUSS, HERBERT MAX, retirement village administrator; b. Chgo., Mar. 28, 1915; s. Willy Arno and Elizabeth Minna (Winkler) K.; m. Ethelyn Mary Rasmussen, July 5, 1948; children: Stephen Herbert, Kirsten Elizabeth, Keary Richard, Herbert Andrew. BA with honors, Beloit Coll., 1937; MA, Oberlin Coll., 1941; MBA, U. Chgo., 1948. Adminstr. Burlington (Iowa) Hosp., 1948-54, Latrobe (Pa.) Hosp., 1954-63; assoc. dir. Genesee Hosp., Rochester, N.Y., 1963-67, dir., 1967-72; exec. dir. The Presbyn. Home, Evanston, Ill., 1973-82; ret., 1982. Contbr. articles to profl. jours. Bd. dirs. Genesee Valley Planning Coun., 1971-73. With U.S. Army, 1942-46. Decorated Silver Star, Purple Heart. Fellow Am. Coll. Hosp. Adminstrs.; mem. Am. Hosp. Assn., U. Chgo. Hosp. Adminstrs. Alumni Assn. (pres. 1960-61). Home: 95 Lazy Trail Penfield NY 14526

KRAVITZ, YAACOV JEFFREY, pastoral counselor, psychologist; b. Mt. Vernon, N.Y., Dec. 9, 1950; m. Terry E. Sutton. BA, Brandeis U., 1972; MEd, Temple U., 1975, EdD, 1983. Ordained rabbi, 1979; lic. psychologist Pa.; cert. pastoral counselor. Ednl. dir. Lehigh Valley Inst. for Judaic & Hebraic Studies, Allentown, Pa., 1979-80; edn. dir., asst. rabbi Congregation Bros. of Israel, Trenton, N.J., 1981-83; campus rabbi Jewish Community Ctr. of Balt., Johns Hopkins Univ., Balt., 1983-86; psychotherapist Pastoral Counseling and Edn. Ctr., Dallas, 1987-89; chaplain, coord. pastoral psychology svcs. Northwestern Inst. of Psychiatry, Fort Washington, Pa., 1990—; instr. Reconstructionist Rabbinical Coll., Wyncot, Pa., 1990—; dir., psychologist Inst. for Psychotherapy and Recovery, Elkins Park, Pa., 1989—. Mem. Am. Psychol. Assn., Am. Assn. Pastoral Counselors, Phila. Soc. Clin. Psychologists, Recontructionist Rabbinical Assn. Office: Inst Psychotherapy Recovery 8033 Old York Rd Ste 100 Elkins Park PA 19117

KRAWCZAK, ARTHUR HENRY, bishop; b. Detroit, Feb. 2, 1913; s. Joseph Casimer and Pauline (Kniga) K. B.A., Sacred Heart Sem., 1936; M.S.W., Catholic U. Am., 1951. Ordained priest Roman Cath. Ch., 1940. Assoc. St. Vincent Parish, Detroit, 1940-45, St. Stanislaus Parish, Detroit, 1945-49; youth dir. Archdiocese of Detroit, 1956-62; founder, pastor St. Martin de Porres Parish, Warren, Mich., 1962-71; pastor Ascension Paris, Warren, Mich., 1971—; aux. bishop Archdiocese of Detroit, 1973—; bishop N.E. region, 1977—. Mem. Detroit Youth Commn., 1958-62; chmn. Macomb div. United Community Services, 1977—; chmn. New Detroit Inc., 1977—. Home: St Elizabeth Briarbank 1315 N Woodward Bloomfield Hills MI 48304 Office: 1234 Washington Blvd Detroit MI 48226

KRAYBILL, PAUL NISSLEY, religious official; b. Bainbridge, Pa., June 7, 1925; s. John Rutt and Esther (Nissley) K.; m. Jean Kulp Metz, Dec. 22, 1951; children: Mary Jean, Dale Edward, Linda Sue, Carol Ann, Karen Louise. BA, Eastern Mennonite Coll., 1955. Asst. sec. Eastern Mennonite Bd. Missions and Charities, Salunga, Pa., 1953-58; overseas sec., gen. sec. Eastern Mennonite Bd. Missions and Charities, 1958-70, exec. sec., study commn. on ch. orgn., 1970-71; gen. sec. Mennonite Ch. Gen. Bd., Rosemont, Ill., 1971-77; exec. sec. Mennonite World Conf., 1973-90; pres. Mennonite Health Assn., 1990—; sec. Mennonite Christian Leadership, Landisville, Pa., 1969-80, Council Mission Bd. Secs., Rosemont, Ill., 1962-74; mem. Presidium Mennonite World Conf., 1967-73; pres. Mennonite Housing Aid, Inc., Lombard, Ill., 1975-81; ordained to ministry, 1981; Mem. exec. com., vice chmn. and trustee Am. Leprosy Missions, Bloomfield, N.J., 1967-80; pres. Tamarack Retirement Residences, Inc., 1985-91. Author: Change and the Church, 1970; Editor: Called to be Sent, 1964, Mennonite World Handbook, 1978. Named Alumnus of the Yr. Eastern Mennonite Coll., 1971. Mem. Am. Soc. Missiology. Home: 1320 Windsted Dr Goshen IN 46526 Office: Mennonite Health Assn 202 S 5th St Ste 100 PO Box 818 Goshen IN 46526

KREIDER, GLENN RICHARD, pastor; b. Danville, Pa., Apr. 19, 1956; s. Elvin L. and Thelma R. (Hershey) K.; m. Janice L. Kreider, June 25, 1977; 1 child, Jeneec N. BS in Bible Studies, Lancaster (Pa.) Bible Coll., 1986; ThM, Dallas Theol. Sem., 1990, postgrad., 1990—. Ordained to ministry Brethren in Christ Ch., 1990. Dir. Christian edn. Fellowship Ch., Cedar Hill, Tex., 1987-90, pastor, 1990—. Republican. Home: 306 Breseman St Cedar Hill TX 75104 Office: Fellowship Ch of Cedar Hill 1400 Kari Ann Dr Cedar Hill TX 75104

KREIMES, PAUL ALLEN, biblical studies educator; b. Lackawanna, N.Y., July 31, 1945; s. Harvey James and Margaret Genevieve (Erdmann) K. BA, Sacred Heart Sem., Detroit, 1968; MA, U. Detroit, 1973; MDiv, St. John's Sem., Plymouth, Mich., 1975; SSL, Pontifical Bibl. Inst., Rome, 1986. Acad. dean S.S. Cyri and Methodius Sem., Orchard Lake, Mich., 1986-88; dean students, asst. prof. O.T. Sacred Heart Major Sem., Detroit, 1988—. Mem. Cath. Bibl. Assn. Am., Soc. Bibl. Lit., Nat. Assn. Profs. Hebrew. Roman Catholic. Avocations: music, reading, tennis, traveling. Home: 2701 Chicago Blvd Detroit MI 48206 Office: Sacred Heart Major Sem 2701 Chicago Blvd Detroit MI 48206

KREITMAN, BENJAMIN ZVI, rabbi, Judaic studies educator; b. Warsaw, Poland, Dec. 25, 1920; came to U.S., 1925, naturalized, 1926; s. Jacob and Anna (Grabower) K.; m. Joyce Beth Krimsky, Aug. 7, 1956; children—Jamie, Jill. BA, Yeshiva U., 1939; MHL, Jewish Theol. Sem., 1942; MA, Vale U., 1951; DHL, Jewish Theol. Sem., 1952, DD (hon.), 1970. Ordained rabbi, 1943; rabbi Temple Israel, Wilkes-Barre, Pa., 1947; asst. rabbi Kehillat Israel, Brookline, Mass., 1947-48; rabbi Congregation Beth El, New London, Conn., 1948-52, Bklyn. Jewish Center, 1952-68, Congregation Shaare Torah, Bklyn., 1968-76; exec. v.p. United Synagogue Am., N.Y.C., 1976-89, exec. v.p. emeritus, 1989—; vis. prof. Judaic studies Bklyn. Coll., 1974-75, Jewish Theol. Sem., 1974-75. Cons. editor: (with others) Illustrated History of the Jews, 1962. Pres. Bklyn. Jewish Community Coun., 1973-76; mem. N.Y.C. Bd. Health, 1972-79; chmn. Bklyn. Borough Pres.'s Commn. Human Rels., 1963-70, Small Bus. Opportunities Corp. Bklyn., 1964-67; exec. vice chmn. World Coun. Synagogues, 1989—. Chaplain USNR, 1943-46. Mem. MERCAZ (exec. v.p. 1989—), Rabbinical Assembly, World Coun. Synagogues (exec. vice-chmn. 1989—), Am. Acad. Jewish Research, Assn. Coll. Profs. Home: 1612 Ditmas Ave Brooklyn NY 11226 Office: 155 Fifth Ave New York NY 10010

KRESS, RICKY ALLEN, minister; b. Nürenberg, Fed. Republic Germany, Sept. 1, 1959; s. Bobby Glenn and Elizabeth Ann (Bishop) K.; m. Beth Emily Slayton, Dec. 29, 1979; children: Michael Charles, Stephen Andrew. BA with honors, Anderson U., 1981; postgrad., Ashland Theol. Sem., 1984-85, John Carroll U., 1985-86. Ordained reverend Ch. of God, 1985. Sr. pastor 1st Ch. of God, Meadville, Pa., 1981-83, Greensburg (Ohio) Ch. of God, 1983-86; interim pastor Bethany Ch. of God, Sterling Heights, Mich., 1987-88; evangelist Ch. of God in Mich., Westland, 1987—; interim, assoc. pastor Riverside Park Ch. of God, Livonia, Mich., 1988-90; interim pastor Farmington Ch. of God, Farmington Hills, Mich., 1988-89; cons. Cath. hosps. fund raising, 1991—. Author, editor Illuminator Newsletter, 1983-86; contbr. articles to various newletters. Bd. dirs. Boys and Girls Clubs S.E. Mich., Detroit, 1986-89; adminstr. Community Food Bank, Green Twp., Ohio, 1983-86. Mem. Am. Mgmt. Assn., Nat. Assn. Hosp. Devel., Nat. Soc. Fund Raising Execs., Am. Prospect Rsch. Assn. (Mich. chpt.). Democrat. Home: 31705 Fairchild Westland MI 48185 Office: Mercy Health Found 34605 Twelve Mile Rd Farmington Hills MI 48331

KRESS, ROBERT, theological and religious studies educator. BA in Philosophy, St. Meinrad Coll., 1954; STB, U. Innsbruck, Austria, 1956, grad. in philosophy, 1965, Licentiate in Sacred Theology, 1958; postgrad., L'Eau Vive, Le Saulchoir, Paris, 1956; MA in Edn., U. Notre Dame, 1964; postgrad., Gregorian U., Rome, 1965-68; STD summa cum laude, U. St. Thomas, Rome, 1968. Ordained priest Roman Cath. Ch., 1958. Asst. prof. dept. systematic and dogmatic theology St. Louis U., 1971-73; assoc. prof., then prof. dept. philosophy and religion U. Evansville, Ind., 1973-79; assoc. prof. dept. theology Sch. Religious Studies, Cath. U. Am., 1979-84; vis. assoc. prof. religious studies U. Ill., Urbana, 1984-86; assoc. prof. dept. theol. and religious studies U. San Diego, 1986—, co-chmn. dept., 1986-89; vis. fellow Princeton U., 1970-71, Brown U., 1977; assoc. Danforth Found., 1976-82. Author: Whither Womankind? The Humanity of Woman, 1975 (Outstanding Book of Yr. award Coll. Theology Soc.), Christian Roots: No Alien God, 1978, The Difference That Jesus Makes: The Sacrament of the Forgiving God, 1981, A Rahner Handbook, 1982, The Church: Communion, Sacrament, Communication, 1985, The People's Church, 1986; cons. editor Theology Digest, 1971-75; editorial referee Horizons, 1974—; book reviewer Theol. Studies, N.C. News Svc., Thomist, Rev. of Politics, Living Light, others; contbr. numerous articles to profl. jours. Recipient Outstanding Faculty Achievement award Evansville U., 1978, Outstanding Tchr. of Yr. award, 1979; named Sigma Pi Outstanding Faculty Mem., U. San Diego, 1991; Henry J. Grimmelsman fellow, 1965-68; Habig Found. grantee, 1979, Kimball Found. rsch. grantee, 1986; NEH fellow, 1977, 91, Ludwig von Mises fellow Ctr. for Libertarian Studies, 1982-83. Mem. Am. Acad. Religion, Cath. Theol. Soc. Am. (chair continuing seminar 1986-89), Coll. Theology Soc. (chair sect. sacramental theology 1977-79, bd. dirs. 1980-83, chair sect. fashioning ch. for 21st century 1987-91), Soc. for Sci. Study Religion, Religious Educators Assn., others. Office: U San Diego Dept Theol and Religious Studies San Diego CA 92110

KRETZMANN, ADALBERT RAPHAEL ALEXANDER, clergyman; b. Stamford, Conn., Apr. 15, 1903; s. Karl and Thekla (Hueschen) K.; m. Josephine Heidelberg, Oct. 1, 1927 (dec. June 1982); children: Norman, Joan (Mrs. Gerhard Krodel). Grad., Concordia Coll., Bronxville, N.Y., 1923; B.D., Concordia Sem., St. Louis, 1927, D.D. (hon.), 1967; Litt.D. (hon.), Concordia Coll., Seward, Nebr., 1953; LL.D., Valparaiso U., 1959; D.D. (hon.), Wartburg Coll., Waverly, Iowa, 1966. Ordained to ministry Evang. Luth. Ch., 1927; asst. pastor Jersey City, 1924; prof. German Concordia Coll., Ft. Wayne, Ind., 1925-26; vacancy pastor Phila., 1926; supply pastor St. Louis, 1926-27; pastor St. Luke's Ch., Chgo., 1927-82; Chmn. Synodical Young People's Bd.; pres. Ill. dist. Walther League, 1930-32; sec. Luth. Hosp. Assn., 1929-31, Chgo. Luth. Pastoral Conf., 1929-33; bd. dirs. Luther Inst., Chgo., 1931-33; pastoral adviser Internat. Luth. Walther League, 1929-54; chmn. North Side Forum Christian Edn.; bd. dirs. Lakeview Community Council; lectr. on ch. art and liturgy Concordia Coll., River Forest, Ill., Concordia, St. Louis Corr. Sch. Staff; lectr. on youth work Concordia Sem., St. Louis, Concordia Tchrs. Coll., Seward, Nebr., Dr. Martin Luther Coll., New Ulm, Minn., Pacific Luth. U., Pacific Luth. Sem.; chmn. commn. worship, also commn. ch. architecture Luth. Ch.-Mo. Synod; art editor The Cresset; asso. editor Ch. Music, Luth. Witness; lectr. Luther Laymen's League Seminars. Author: Liturgical Renaissance in the Lutheran Church, 1968; contbg. author: Christmas Annual; also; the author of: prayers The Pastor at Work, 1960, The Pastor at Prayer, 1959; Summer speaker: prayers Internat. Luth. Hour, 1944, Liturgy and Church Art; others and also numerous religious writings.; Designer: also church seals Coll. Synodical; cons. in liturgical arts and design.; Chmn.: Chgo. Luth. Pastors Inst; radio speaker: WGN Mid-day Devotions; Sec.: radio devotions Family Worship Hour. Bd. dirs. Concordia Coll., River Forest, Ill., Ministers Life and Casualty Co., Mpls., Luth. Sr. Citizens Found., Luth. Brotherhood (chmn. fine arts), Augustana Hosp., Luth. Gen. Hosp., Luth. Deaconess Hosp.; pres. Chgo. Bible Soc.; dir., v.p. Wheatridge Found., also chmn. social service; bd. dirs. Tb Inst. (Lung Soc.) Chgo. and Cook County, Chgo. Lung Assn. Recipient Gutenberg award, 1963, Servant of Christ medal Concordia Coll., 1983, Religious Heritage of Am. Gold Medal, 1985. Mem. Am. Fedn. Art, Chgo. Art Inst. (life mem.), Concordia Hist. Inst., Am. Inst. Graphic Arts (adv. council religious teaching pictures), Met. Mus. (N.Y.), Walker Art Mus. (Minn.), Ch. Archtl. Guild Am., Guild for Religious Architecture, Am. Soc. Religious Architecture (dir.). Home: 1501 W Melrose St Chicago IL 60657

KRETZMANN, JUSTUS PAUL, minister; b. N.Y.C., Feb. 27, 1913; s. Karl and Thekla (Hueschen) K.; m. Norma Martha Kroehnke, Feb. 15, 1939; children—Karla (Mrs. Stanley Woell), Walter John. Student, Concordia Coll., Bronxville, N.Y., 1933; B.D., Concordia Sem., St. Louis, 1938, D.D. (hon.), 1965. Ordained to ministry Luth. Ch., 1939; asst. pastor in Buffalo, 1935-37, Bklyn., 1938-39; missionary Nigeria, W. Africa, 1939-51; pastor Luth. Ch. Atonement, Florissant, Mo., 1952—; world survey of missions, 1960, 61; chmn. bd. parish edn. Luth. Ch. Mo. Synod, 1959-73; chmn. Luth. Publicity Orgn., St. Louis, 1957-69, Luth. Assn. Larger Chs., 1970-73; mem. Luth. Med. Mission Council, 1959-69; pastoral adviser Luth. Med. Mission Assn.; guest lectr. Lindenwood Coll., St. Charles, Mo. Co-author: In Time...For Eternity, 1963; contbg. editor: Am. Luth; mem. editorial com.: St. Louis Luth; contbr. to religious publs. Bd. dirs. Care and Counseling, St. Louis.; mem. Florissant Hist. Soc., St. Charles County Hist. Soc. Home: 14 Arrowhead Circle St Charles MO 63301 Office: 1285 N Florissant Rd Florissant MO 63031

KRETZSCHMAR, ROBERT JAMES, pastor, counselor; b. Monroe, Mich., July 30, 1943; s. Carl R. Kretzschmar; m. Diane E. Hoopert; children: Ian, Tracey, James, Brendan, Matthew. BA, Concordia Coll., 1965; MDiv, Concordia Sem., 1969; MS in Counseling Psychology, Loyola Coll., Balt., 1984. Cert. counselor Nat. Bd. Cert. Counselors. Asst. pastor of youth ministry Trinity Luth. Ch., Roselle, Ill., 1969-71; pastor 1st Luth. Ch. of Towson, Md., 1971-75; dir. pastoral svc., chaplain The Union Meml. Hosp., Balt., 1975-77; pastor Bethany Luth. Ch. of Violetville, Balt., 1979-88; counselor, ctr. coord. Pastoral Counseling and Consultation Ctr. of Greater Balt., 1977—; pastor Calvary Luth. Ch. of Hamilton, Balt., 1990—. Mem. Am. Assn. Pastoral Counselors (regional profl. concerns com. 1982-88). Home: 9701 Red Clover Ct Baltimore MD 21234

KREUTZER, FRANKLIN DAVID, lawyer; b. Miami, Fla., June 5, 1940; s. Ernst and Elsa (Meitner) K.; m. Judith Sue Jacobs, June 16, 1963; children: Renee Charlotte, Jay Ernst. BBA, U. Miami, 1960, JD, 1964. Bar: Fla. 1964, U.S. Dist. Ct. (so. dist.) Fla. 1965, U.S. Ct. Appeals (5th cir.) 1971, U.S. Ct. Appeals (11th cir.) 1982, U.S. Supreme Ct. 1971. Assoc., Shevin, Goodman & Holtzman, 1964-65; ptnr. Wallace & Kreutzer, P.A., 1966-74; pvt. practice, Miami, 1974—; participant White House Seminar on Legal Interns, 1963; spl. asst. atty. gen. State of Fla., 1975-78; spl. counsel to comptroller State of Fla., 1975-78; gen. counsel Democratic Exec. Com. Dade County, 1968-70. Mem. City of Miami Pension & Retirement Bd., 1966-68; chmn. Miami Charter Rev. Bd., 1967-81; mem. Dade County Charter Rev. Commn., 1981-82; spl. master, guardian and atty. ad litem, Cir. Ct., Dade county, 1980—; gen. counsel, clk. of cir. and county cts. Dade County, Fla., 1990—; gen. counsel, clk. of Dade County Met. Commn., 1990—; pres. Greater Miami Hebrew Fla. Loan Assn., 1974-77; pres. Temple Zion, 1977-79; regional pres. S.E. region United Synagogue Am., 1980-84, v.p., 1983-85, chmn. council regional presidents, 1983-85; internat. pres. United Synagogue Am. Conservative Movement, 1985—; internat. v.p. World Coun. of Synagogues, 1985—; internat. v.p., exec. com., bd. dirs. Mercaz Conservative Zionism, 1984—; bd. dirs. Jewish Theol. Sem. of Am., 1985—; exec. com. Synagogue Council of Am., 1985—; mem. exec. com. Am. Israel Pub. Affairs, 1985—; mem. Nat. Jewish Community Rels. Adv. Coun.; mem. Conf. of Pres. of Major Am. Jewish Orgns., 1985—; bd. dirs. Gen. Coun. World Zionist Orgn., 1985—; hon. chmn. bd. dirs. Jewish Nat. Fund, 1989—; pres. South Fla. chpt. Cystic Fibrosis Found., 1970-74; endowment com. U. Miami, 1974—. Recipient cert. of appreciation City of Miami, 1968; named to Order Golden Donkey, Dem. Exec. Com. Dade County, 1970. Mem. ABA, Fla. Bar Assn., Fla. Trial Lawyers Assn., Dade County Trial Lawyers Assn., Dade County Bar Assn., Acad. Trial Lawyers Am., Omicron Delta Kappa, Phi Delta Phi. Democrat. Home: 8615 SW 48th St Miami FL 33155 Office: 3041 NW 7th St Ste 100 Miami FL 33125 also: United Synagogue Am 155 Fifth Ave New York NY 10010

KREY, ANDREW EMIL VICTOR, minister; b. Bklyn., Nov. 2, 1948; s. Rudolf E.M. and Gertrude Emily (Berhrens) K.; m. Sally June Olson, Nov. 24, 1973; children: Heather, Benjamin. BA, Northeastern U., 1972; MDiv, Luth. Theol. Sem., 1976. Ordained to ministry Luth. Ch., 1976. Pastor Zion Luth. Ch., Bristol, Conn., 1976-90; chaplain New Eng. Seamen's Mission, Providence, 1990—; chair 5 yr. plan for evangelism and stewardship Luth. Ch. Am., 1981-86; Luth. rep. Billy Graham So. New Eng. Crusade, Hartford, Conn., 1985. officer-in-charge indoctrination course for Navy chaplains USCG, Governors' Island, N.Y.C., 1985-87. Chair Greater Bristol Social Concerns Com., 1985-90; coord. various youth programs, Bristol, 1979-90; founder Cen. Conn. Soup Kitchen, Bristol, 1981—. Lt. comdr. USNR, 1978—. Named to Outstanding Young Men Am., Conn. Jaycees, 1983; recipient Disting. Svc. award WFSB-TV3, 1984. Mem. Internat. Christian Maritime Assn., N.Am. Maritime Ministry Assn. (bd. dirs. 1991—), Luth. Assn. for Maritime Ministry (pres. 1991—). Republican. Congregation resettled many refugees, 1976-90. Home: 140 Country Club Rd Waterbury CT 06708 Office: Seafarers' Ctr Mcpl Wharf PO Box 40335 Providence RI 02940-0335 *The primary task of Christ's church is to proclaim Jesus as Saviour and Lord through evangelism, service and advocacy. Individual committed Christians allow the church to reach this goal.*

KRIEG, ROBERT ANTHONY, religion educator, priest; b. Hackensack, N.J., Feb. 8, 1946; s. Anthony Benedict and Helen Adele (Battista) K. BA, Stonehill Coll., 1969; PhD, U. Notre Dame, 1976. Ordained priest Roman Cath. Ch., 1973. Asst. prof. in theology King's Coll., Wilkes Barre, Pa., 1975-77; asst. prof., dir. field edn. U. Notre Dame (Ind.), 1977-85, assoc. prof., dir. MDiv Program, 1985-91. Author: Story-Shaped Christology, 1988; contbr. articles to profl. publs. Trustee Stonehill Coll., North Easton, Mass., 1989—. Mem. Am. Acad. Religion, Cath. Theol. Soc. Am. (seminar moderator 1989-91). Home: Moreau Sem Notre Dame IN 46556 Office: U Notre Dame Dept Theology Notre Dame IN 46556

KRIEGBAUM, RICHARD ARNOLD, academic administrator; b. Long Beach, Calif., Mar. 26, 1941; s. Arnold Richard and Laura Elizabeth (Miller) K.; m. Elona Alice McKee, Aug. 25, 1962; children: Arnold Richard, Sonya Christina. BA, Wheaton (Ill.) Coll., 1963; MA, Ball State U., 1966; PhD, SUNY, Buffalo, 1976. Tchr. Warsaw (Ind.) Christian Sch., 1964-65, Warsaw Community High Sch., 1965-66; instr. Grace Coll., Winona Lake, Ind., 1966-67; assoc. prof. Wheaton Coll., 1967-76, dir. data processing, planning and mktg., 1976-83; v.p. adminstrn. Fresno (Calif.) Pacific Coll., 1984-85, pres., 1985—; bd. dirs. Scripture Press, Wheaton; resource scholar Christianity Today Mag., Carol Stream, Ill., 1985. Author: (with others) A Marketing Approach to Program Development, 1979. Mem. Christian Coll. Coalition (bd. dirs. 1988-91), Ind. Colls. No. Calif. (bd. dirs. 1985—), Rotary. Mennonite. Office: Fresno Pacific Coll 1717 S Chestnut Ave Fresno CA 93702

KRIEGER, BARRY ISRAEL, rabbi; b. Providence, Apr. 19, 1956; s. Seymour and Celia Krieger; m. Lorenne Shubart; children: Sarra, Kyam, Zivi. BS, cert. tchr., U. Mass., 1979; MA in Hebrew Letters, Reconstructionist Rabbinical, 1985; MEd, Temple U., 1985. Ordained rabbi, 1985. Rabbi B'nai Jacob, Phoenixville, Pa., 1984-85, Temple Israel, Athol, Mass., 1985-88, Ahavas Achim, Keene, N.H., 1988—. Mem. Reconstructionist Rabbinical Assn. Office: Congregation Ahavas Achim 84 Hastings Ave Keene NH 03431

KRING, STEPHEN, religious organization administrator. Pres. Assn. Regular Bapt. Chs., Delhi, Ont., Can. Office: Assn Regular Bapt Chs, 25 Sovereen St, Delhi, ON Canada N4B 1L6*

KRING, WALTER DONALD, minister; b. Lakewood, Ohio, Mar. 10, 1916; s. Walter DeVaine and Rebecca Olive (Shumaker) K. Exchange student, U. Hawaii, 1935-36; A.B., Occidental Coll., 1937, L.H.D., 1965; S.T.B., Harvard, 1940; LL.D., Emerson Coll., 1961; D.D., St. Lawrence U., 1968. Asst. Harvard Meml. Ch., 1939-41; asst. minister First Ch., Boston, 1939-41; asst. dept. history Harvard, 1939-41; minister First Presbyn. Ch., Hoosick Falls, N.Y., 1941-43, First Unitarian Ch., Worcester, Mass., 1946-55, Unitarian Ch. of All Souls, N.Y.C., 1955-78; emeritus Unitarian Ch. of All Souls, 1978—; pres. Beacon Press, Inc., 1955-59. Author: Religion is the Search for Meaning, 1955, Across the Abyss to God, 1966, Liberals Among the Orthodox: Unitarian Beginnings in New York City, 1819-1839, 1974, Henry Whitney Bellows, 1979, The Fruits of Our Labors: The Bicentennial History of the Second Parish in the Town of Worcester, Massachusetts, First Unitarian Church, 1985, Safely Onward: Vol. 3: History of the Unitarian Church of All Souls, New York City (1882-1978), 1991; exhibitor ceramics, Worlds Fair, Brussels, 1958. Dir. Worcester Craft Center; dir., pres. Spence Chapin Adoption Agency, 1970-71; pres. Artist-Craftsmen, N.Y., 1960-63, 70-72; Vis. com. Harvard Div. Sch., 1963-69; corporator Emerson Coll., 1960-82, Worcester Art Mus., 1950-55. Served with Chaplains Corps USNR, 1943-46. Recipient 1st prize high temperature stoneware Nat. Ceramic Show, 1954. Hon. life mem. Am. Mus. Natural History.; Mem. Worcester Ministers Assn. (pres. 1954-55), East Midtown Ministers Assn. (pres. 1959-62, 68-69), Am. Unitarian Assn. (sec. 1953-61), Harvard Divinity Sch. Alumni Assn. (past pres.; mem. council), Melville Soc. Am. (pres. 1979), Unitarian-Universalist Hist. Soc. (pres. 1982-86). Club: Worcester Econ. (pres. 1954-55). Address: Box 216 Brookfield MA 01506

KRIPKE, MYER SAMUEL, rabbi; b. Toledo, Ohio, Jan. 21, 1914; s. Jacob Michael and Nettie (Goldman) K.; m. Dorothy E. Karp, June 13, 1937; children: Saul A., Madeline F., Netta E. BA, NYU, 1933; MA, Columbia U., 1937; MHL, Jewish Theol. Sem. of Am., N.Y.C., 1937, DD, 1970.

Ordained rabbi 1937. Rabbi Beth El-Sinai Congregation, Racine, Wis., 1937-39, Patchogue (N.Y.) Jewish Ctr., 1939-41, Congregation Beth El, New London, Conn., 1941-46; Rabbi Beth El Synagogue, Omaha, 1946-75, rabbi emeritus, 1975—; adj. assoc. prof. theology Creighton U., Omaha, 1976—. Author: Insight and Interpretation, 1988; co-author: Let's Talk About Loving, 1980; religious columnist Omaha Jewish Press, 1984—; contbr. articles to profl. jours. Mem. Citizen's Assembly, United Way, 1982—. Mem. Nebr. Rabbinical Assn. (pres. 1972-73), Rabbinical Assy., B'nai B'rith, Zionist Orgn. Am., Rotary. Home: 11611 Burt St Omaha NE 68154 Office: Creighton Univ Theology Dep 24th & California Sts Omaha NE 68178 also: Beth El Synagogue 14506 California St Omaha NE 68154 *The pressing question of life's meaning is relieved by giving love and service to family, friends, and mankind, and by clinging to values and causes greater than ourselves.*

KRISCHE, VINCENT EDWARD, religious organization administrator, priest; b. Topeka, May 24, 1938; s. Frank Anthony and Pauline Marie (Melchior) K. BA, St. Thomas Coll., Denver, 1960; BTh, Cath. U. Am., 1964; MEd, St. Thomas Sem., 1964. Ordained priest Roman Cath. Ch., 1964. Assoc. pastor St. Agnes Parish, Roeland Park, Kans., 1964-67, Queen of the Holy Rosary, Overland Park, Kans., 1967-69; founder, dir. Washburn Cath. Campus Ctr., Topeka, 1969-77; dir. St. Lawrence Cath. Campus Ctr., Lawrence, Kans., 1977—; bd. dirs. Frank J. Lewis Inst., Lawrence, 1991; bd. govs. Kans. Sch. Religion, Lawrence, 1987—. Commr. Kans. Commn. on Govtl. Standards and Conduct, Topeka, 1990—; bd. dirs. United Way Douglas County, Lawrence, 1990—. Mem. Cath. Campus Ministry Assn. (Archbishop Hallinan award 1987), Nat. Assn. Diocesan Dirs. Campus Ministry, Kans. Univ. Religious Advisors (pres. 1990—), KC. Democrat. Home and office: St Lawrence Cath Campus Ctr 1631 Crescent Rd Lawrence KS 66044-3122

KRISS, M(ARY) ELISE, religious organization administrator, educator; b. LaPorte, Ind., June 8, 1947; d. Joseph Henry and Marcella Mae (Sramek) K. BS in Edn., St. Francis Coll., Ft. Wayne, Ind., 1973, MS in Edn., 1978; PhD, St. Louis U., 1984. Cert. tchr., Ind. Tchr. various elem. schs., 1969-77; prin. St. Mary Sch., Griffith, 1977-81; v.p. acad. affairs St. Francis Coll., Ft. Wayne, 1983-91, v.p. adminstrn., 1991—; mem. provincial coun. Sisters of St. Francis of Perpetual Adoration, Mishawaka, Ind., 1990—. Sec. St. Francis Coll. Bd. of Trustees, 1984-91, St. Francis Coll. Found. Bd., 1984-91, trustee, 1991—; bd. dirs. Stop Child Abuse & Neglect, 1988—, Sisters of St. Francis Health Svcs., Inc., 1990—; bd. dirs. Greater Fort Wayne Consensus Com., Inc., 1991—. Avocations: reading, guitar, ham radio, travel. Office: St Francis Coll 2701 Spring St Fort Wayne IN 46808

KROEHLER, ARMIN HERBERT, minister; b. Hardin, Mont., Apr. 20, 1922; s. Arthur Carl and Clara Marie (Baur) K.; m. Evelyn Mae Schroer, July 29, 1950; children: Kenneth, Kaye, Iris, Margaret, Christopher. BS, Colo. State U., 1943; BD, Eden Theol. Sem., 1949; STM, Lancaster Theol. Sem., 1968; DD, Eden Theol. Sem., 1978. Ordained to ministry United Ch. of Christ, 1949. Missionary, United Ch. Bd. for World Ministries, N.Y.C., 1950—; dir. Aizu Christian Rural Life Ctr., Aizu-Takada, Japan, 1979—. Author: Forth To Sow, 1961; The Renewal of the Church in Aizu, 1970; editor newspaper Aizu Shinsei, 1979—. Trustee Tsurukawa Rural Sem., Tokyo, 1978—. Lt. USN, 1943-46. Home and Office: 3651-1 Monju Higashi, Aizu Takada Machi, Fukushima Ken 969-62, Japan

KROHN, LARRY DALE, lay worker; b. Gary, Ind., Mar. 13, 1948; s. Kenneth Karl and Martha Jane (Way) K.; m. Martha Jo Prusz, Dec. 20, 1970; children: Sara Lynn, Brian Dale. BS, Ind. State U., 1970, MS, 1973. Cert. life tchr. gen. sci., phys. edn., health, Ind. Lay pulpit supply Ind.-Ky. Synod/Evangel. Luth. Ch. in America, Indpls., 1979—; chmn. ministry in daily life com. Ind.-Ky. Synod/Evangel. Luth. Ch. in America, 1985—; tchr. North Gibson Sch. Corp., Princeton, Ind., 1984—; sec. of coun. Our Saviour Luth. Ch., Princeton, 1980-84. Contbr. articles to newsletter. Pres. North Gibson Sch. Bd. Community Adv. Coun., 1983-84; chmn. March of Dimes Walk America, Princeton, 1988-90; bd. dirs., sec. Princeton Boys Club, 1983—. Mem. NEA, Ind. State Tchrs. Assn., Nat. Sci. Tchrs. Assn., Ind. Golf Coaches Assn., Nat. High Sch. Golf Coaches Assn., Optimist (pres. 1986-87). Home: 520 West Emerson Princeton IN 47670 Office: Princeton Community Mid Sch 410 E State St Princeton IN 47670

KROL, JOHN CARDINAL, retired archbishop; b. Cleve., Oct. 26, 1910; s. John and Anna (Pietruszka) K. Student, St. Mary's Sem., Cleve., 1937; J.C.B., Gregorian U., Rome, 1939, J.C.L., 1940; J.C.D., Cath. U. Am., 1942; Ph.D., La Salle Coll., 1961; LL.D., John Carroll U., 1955, St. Joseph U., 1961, St. John U., N.Y., 1964, Coll. Steubenville, 1967, Lycoming Meth. Coll., 1966, Temple U., 1964, Bellarmine-Ursuline Coll., 1968, Drexel U., 1970; D.S.T., Villanova U., 1961; L.H.D., Alliance Coll., 1967, Coll. Chestnut Hill (Pa.), 1975, Holy Family Coll., 1977; D.D., Susquehanna U., 1970; D.Theology, U. Lublin (Poland); HHD, Wheeling Coll., 1984. Priest Roman Catholic Ch., 1937, pvt. chamberlain, 1945, domestic prelate, 1951; parish asst., 1937-38; prof. Diocesan Sem.; also chaplain Jennings Home for Aged, 1942-43; vice chancellor Cleve. Diocese, 1943-51, chancellor of diocese, 1951-53, promoter of justice, 1951-53; consecrated bishop, 1953, auxiliary bishop to bishop of Cleve., also vicar gen. Diocese of Cleve., 1953-61; archbishop of Phila., 1961-88; apptd. chmn. bd. trustees The Papal Found., 1988—; elevated to Sacred Coll. of Cardinals, 1967; undersec. II Vatican Council, 1962-65; mem. Pontifical Commn. Communications Media, 1964-69; chmn. Nat. Cath. Office for Radio and TV, 1963-64, Nat. Cath. Office for Motion Pictures, Cath. Communications Found., 1965-70, Pa. Cath. Conf., 1961—; v.p. Nat. Conf. Cath. Bishops, 1966-71, pres., 1971-74; vice chmn. U.S. Cath. Conf., 1966-71, pres., 1971-74; mem. adminstrv. bd. and com. Nat. Conf. Cath. Bishops/U.S. Cath. Conf., 1983-86; mem. Pontifical Commn. for Mass Media Communications, 1964-69, Sacred Congregation for Evangelization of Nations, 1967-72, Sacred Congregation for Oriental Ch., 1967—, Sacred Congregation for Doctrine of Faith, 1973—; mem. 15 Mem. Council of Cardinals to study and counsel on Vatican finances, 1981; mem. Prefecture of Econ. Affairs of Holy See, 1982; pro.-pres. Extraordinary Synod of Bishops, Rome, 1985. Mem. Pres.'s Nat. Citizens Com. Community Relations; chmn. bd. govs., host 41st Internat. Eucharistic Congress, Phila., 1976; trustee Cath. U. Am., Washington, 1961-71, Nat. Shrine of Immaculate Conception, Cath. League for Religious Assistance to Poland; pres. Center for Applied Research in Apostolate, 1967-70; vice chmn. Com. for Yr. of Bible, 1983; mem. nat. adv. com. Deborah Hosp. Found., 1983; mem. President's Adv. Council for Pvt. Sector Initiatives, 1983-85; mem. council trustees Freedoms Found. at Valley Forge, 1985. Decorated comdr. of cross Order of Merit, Italy; Nat. Order Republic of Chad; recipient gold medal Paderewski Found., 1961; Nat. Human Relations award NCCJ, 1968; Father Sourin award Cath. Philopatrian Inst., 1967; John Wesley Ecumenical award Old St. George's Meth. Ch., 1967; Phila. Freedom medal, 1978; 1st ann. award Angelicum Soc. Am., 1985; Barry award Am. Cath. Hist. Soc., 1985; Copernicus award for advocation of peace throughout world, 1985; Legion of Honor gold medal Chapel of Four Chaplains, 1986; Person of Yr. award Congregation Beth Chaim, Feasterville, Pa., Person the Yr. award Congregation Beth Chaim, Feasterville, Pa., 1985, Shield of Blessed Gregory X Crusader, Nat. Assn. Holy Name Soc., 1986, Bob Hope 5-Star Civilian award Valley Forge Mil. Acad. and Jr. Coll., 1986, Immaculata award Immaculata Coll., 1987. Mem. Canon Law Soc. Am. (pres. 1948-49), Order Sons of Italy (hon.). Office: 222 N 17th St Philadelphia PA 19103

KROLL, C(HARLES) DOUGLAS, minister; b. Florence, S.C., June 19, 1949; s. Clifford Carl and Martha Kurtain (Gasque) K.; m. Lana Gale Gerling, May 1, 1976; children: Timothy, Matthew. BS, USCG Acad., 1971; MDiv, Luther Theol. Sem., 1980; MA, U. San Diego, 1985. Ordained to ministry Luth. Ch.-Mo. Synod, 1980. Assoc. pastor Faith Luth. Ch., Saginaw, Mich., 1980-81; instr. Luth. High Sch., San Diego, 1984-85; dean of chapel Luth. High Sch., LaVerne, Calif., 1985-86; pastor St. Paul's Luth. Ch., Pomona, Calif., 1986—; chaplain US Naval Reserve, various cities, 1981—, Old Baldy Coun. Boy Scouts Am., Ontario, Calif., 1986—; chmn. Nat. Luth. Com. on Civic Youth Agys., 1990—; dir. Scouting in the Luth. Ch. conf., 1991. Author: A History of Navy Chaplains Serving With the Coast Guard, 1982; contbr. articles to profl. jours. Mem. religious relationships com. Boy Scouts Am., 1991—. Lt. USNR, 1981-84. Recipient Lamb award Luth. Coun. USA, 1987, Silver Beaver award Boy Scouts Am., 1989. Mem. Am. Legion (chaplain 1990-91). Home: 524 Foxpark Dr Claremont CA 91711 Office: St Paul's Luth Ch 610 N San Antonio Ave Pomona CA 91767

KROLL, WOODROW MICHAEL, religious broadcaster; b. Ellwood City, Pa., Oct. 21, 1944; s. Frank Michael and Betty (Corbin) K.; m. Linda Kay Piper, June 26, 1965; children: Tracy, Timothy, Tina, Tiffany. BA, Barrington Coll., 1967; MDiv, Gordon-Conwell Theol. Sem., 1970; ThM, Geneva St. Alban' Sem., 1971, ThD, 1973. Pastor 1st Bapt. Ch., Middleboro, Mass., 1968-70; prof. Practical Bible Tng. Sch., Bible Sch. Park, N.Y., 1970-73, pres., 1980-90; assoc. dir. Christian Jew Found., San Antonio, 1973-75; chmn. div. religion Liberty U., Lynchburg, Va., 1975-80; pres. Practical Bible Tng. Sch., Bible School Park, N.Y., 1980-90; gen. dir. Back to the Bible, Lincoln, Nebr., 1990—. Author: (Homiletics textbook) Prescription for Preaching, 1978, Bible Country, 1982, Psalms: Poetry of Palestine, 1985, Early in the Morning I, 1986, Early in the Morning II, 1988, Tested by Fire, 1991, The Vanishing Ministry, 1991. Mem. Evang. Theol. Soc., Nat. Religious Broadcasters, Bibl. Archaeol. Soc. Republican. Baptist. Avocations: travel, writing. Office: Back To The Bible PO Box 82808 Lincoln NE 68501

KRONMANN, ROGER BATES, minister; b. Toledo, May 13, 1937; s. Thaeger Gilbert Kronmann and Cordelia Jane (Bates) Brodbeck; m. Rachel Louise Kloster, Jan. 23, 1965 (div.); children: Karl Christian, Paula Marie; m. Denise Lynn Sturm, June 14, 1985. BA, Capital U., 1959; BD, Trinity Sem., Columbus, Ohio, 1963; D Ministry, Eden Sem., 1973. Ordained to ministry Luth. Ch., 1963. Asst. pastor 1st Luth. Ch., Decorah, Iowa, 1963-65; pastor Bethany Luth. Ch., Webster Groves, Mo., 1965-70, Peace Luth. Ch., Glen Burnie, md., 1970-75, Univ. Luth. Ch., Gainesville, Fla., 1975-85, St. Timothy Luth. Ch., Crystal River, Fla., 1985—; sec. commn. for specialized ministries Fla. Synod, Luth. Ch. Am., Tampa, 1983-84. Author poems; composer hymn (1st place award 1969). Home: 8403 W Wings Ln Crystal River FL 32629 Office: St Timothy Luth Ch 1070 N Suncoast Blvd Crystal River FL 32629 *God is the source of my strength for today and my hope for the future.*

KROON, THOMAS JAY, minister, health care chaplain; b. Chilicothe, Ohio, Nov. 22, 1949; s. Thomas Jay and Mary Ann(Koch) K.; m. Marianne Marguerite Hruschka, Sept. 6, 1970; children: Joshua Thomas, Marie Katherine. BS in Sociology, Ill. State U., 1971; MDiv, Colgate Rochester Div Sch, 1975. Ordained to ministry Am. Bapt. Chs. in U.S.A., 1975. Pastor 1st Bapt. Ch., Fort Jefferson, L.I., N.Y., 1975-76; staff chaplain St. John's Home for Aged, Rochester, N.Y., 1977-85; dir. spiritual svcs. Wesley-on-East Nursing Home and Retirement Community, Rochester, 1985—. Bd. dirs. Conciliation Task Force, Rochester, 1990—. Fellow Coll. Chaplains; mem. Am. Soc. Aging. Democrat. Home: 101 Elmcroft Rd Rochester NY 14609 Office: Wesley-on-East Nursing Home and Retirement Community 630 East Ave Rochester NY 14607

KROUSE, STAN SAMUEL, pastor; b. Mena, Ark., Apr. 10, 1947; s. Samuel Krouse and Wanda Lee (Rhodes) Clark; m. Ann Caroline Bowden, June 20, 1965; children: Dena Annette, Jenica Rebecca. AA in Social Sci., Yuba Coll., 1967; BA in Philosophy, Calif. State U., Chico, 1969; MDiv., Golden Gate Bapt. Seminary, 1975; D of Ministry, Golden Gate Bapt. Sem., 1979. Ordained to ministry Bapt. Ch., 1974. Assoc. pastor 1st Bapt. Ch., Colusa, Calif., 1972-75; pastor 1st Bapt. Ch., Ripon, Calif., 1975-79, Calvary Bapt. Ch., Merced, Calif., 1980-81; founding pastor Grace Christian Fellowship, Lincoln, Calif., 1982-88; pastor Family Bible Ctr., Marysville, Calif., 1990—; bd. dirs. Solo Ministries, Campbell, Calif. Author: Discipleship/Evangelism in the Local Church, 1979. Mem. High Sch. Curriculum Com., Lincoln, 1984-87. Served with U.S. Army, 1969-71. Mem. Ripon Ministerial Assn. (pres. 1976-78), Cen. Valley Assn. (moderator 1978-79), Lincoln Ministerial Assn., Yuba-Sutter Ministerial Assn. Republican. Avocations: water and snow skiing, bicycling, swimming, volleyball, basketball. Home: PO Box 295 Meridian CA 95957-0295 Office: Family Bible Ctr 1608 Sampson St Marysville CA 95901

KRUEGER, DAVID KEITH, pastor, director; b. Chicago Heights, Ill., Jan. 3, 1936; s. Hubert Herbert and Irene (Mau) K.; m. Marian Friederika Voger, Aug. 31, 1958; children: Paul, Christine, Mark. AA, So. Suburban Coll., 1956; BTh, MDiv, Concordia Theol. Sem., 1971. Pastor Trinity St. Paul-St. John Luth. Ch., Neshkoro, Wis., 1962-67; youth chaplain Md. Correctional Inst., Hagerstown, 1968; pastor Bethesda Lord Jesus St. Paul Luth. Ch., Chgo., 1979-86; vacancy pastor Holy Trinity Luth. Ch., Chgo., 1986-87, Mt. Greenwood Luth. Ch., Chgo., 1987-89, Golgotha Luth. Ch., Chgo., 1989-90, St. Paul's Luth Ch., Beecher, Ill., 1990—; dir. spl. projects B.R.A.S.S. Found., Chgo. Author: Holy Land Travel Book, 1977, China-English Teaching Book, 1987. Founding mem. Habitat for Humanity, South Chicago, Ill., 1990—; state chaplain CAP, Iowa, Wis. and Ill., 1961—; bd. dirs. Nortown Community Coun., Chgo., 1974, Home Help for Srs., South Holland, Ill., 1985. Mem. Chgo. Coun. on Alcoholism (bd. dirs. 1972), South Suburban Coun. on Alcoholsim (bd. dirs. 1984), Problems of Alcoholism, Labor and Mgmt., Am. Parachute Assn., Luth. Laymen League (pastoral adviser Chgo. chpt. 1973—), Lions (chmn. Thornton, Ill. chpt. 1984—), Sertoma (bd. dirs. Chgo. chpt. 1973). Home: 3358 171st St Lansing IL 60438 Office: St Paul's Luth Ch Rte 1 Box 24 Beecher IL 60401

KRUEGER, DAVID MATTHEW, minister; b. St. Louis, Feb. 14, 1955; s. Donald Paul and Alice Margaret (Holden) K.; m. Linda Louise, Aug. 16, 1975. BA in Religion, S.W. Bapt. U., 1977; MA in Communication, Cen. Mo. State U., 1988. Pastor Coatsville (Mo.) Bapt. Ch., 1974-75, Flat Creek Bapt. Ch., Sedalia, Mo., 1977-82; pastor 1st Bapt. Ch., Adrian, Mo., 1982-88, Linn, 1988—. Author: Persuasive Techniques of the Unification Church, 1987; contbg. editor: Christian Computing Mag., 1988—. Pres. Adrian Community Svcs., 1980-82. Mem. Mo. Bapt. Computer Users Group (pres. 1989—). Republican. Office: 1st Bapt Ch Po Box 418 Linn MO 65051

KRUELLE, CARL HENRY, JR., pastor; b. Balt., Mar. 13, 1938; s. Carl Henry Sr. and Gertrude Louise (Evans) K.; m. Mary Anna Roemer, June 25, 1961; children: Carl III, John, Charles, Paul. B of Theol., Concordia Sem., Springfield, Ill., 1963. Ordained to Luth. Ch. Mo. Synod. 1963. Pastor Luth. Ch. of Our Redeemer, Foxboro, Mass., 1963-70, Holy Trinity Luth. Ch., Albion, Pa., 1970-79, Faith Luth. Ch., Girard, Pa., 1970-78, Our Redeemer Luth. Ch., Newark, Del., 1979—; dir. Bethesda Luth. Home, Watertown, Wis., 1982—, Martin Luther Found. Luth. Community Svcs., Wilmington, Del., 1980—. Contbr. articles to profl. jours. Mem. Newark Clergy, Train Collectors Assn., Toy Train Operators Soc. Office: Our Redeemer Luth Ch 10 Johnson Rd Newark DE 19713

KRUENER, HARRY HOWARD, clergyman; b. Bklyn., Nov. 6, 1915; s. Henry and Florence (Edwards) K.; m. Martha Easton, Oct. 5, 1941 (dec. July 1959); 1 son, John Francis; m. Cheryl Woddell, June 20, 1961 (div. Oct. 1981); 1 son, Philip C.; m. Nancy W., Mar. 20, 1982 (div. Oct. 1984). A.B., Haverford Coll., 1937; B.D., Andover Newton Theol. Sch., 1940; S.T.M., Boston U., 1954; D.D., Denison U., 1965. Ordained to ministry Bapt. Ch., 1940; minister Boston, 1940-48, Granville, Ohio, 1948-55; dean of chapel Denison U., 1955-60; minister Plymouth Ch. of Pilgrims, Bklyn., 1960-84, The Ridge Ch., Tenants Harbor, Maine, 1984-87; preacher Chautauqua, 1970, Am. Ch., Athens, Greece, 1971; Bd. mgrs. Am. Bapt. Fgn. Mission Socs.; exec. bd., membership sec. Nat. Assn. Coll. and Univ. Chaplains; del. Nat. Council Chs.; mem. United Ch. of Christ; pres. Bklyn. Council Chs., Bklyn. Clerical Union, Bklyn. Meml. Soc. Author: Specifically to Youth, 1959; Summer preacher, Nat. Radio Pulpit, 1954. Trustee Andover Newton Theol. Sch., Denison U. Mem. Nat. Assn. Bibl. Instrs., Masons (lodge chaplain), Phi Beta Kappa, Omicron Delta Kappa. Home: CR 35 Box 118 Thomaston ME 04861

KRUGLER, ARNOLD FRANK, minister; b. Chgo., Aug. 14, 1933; s. William and Florence Edna (Erber) D.; m. Margaret Edna Grewe, 1957; children: Kathryn Marta Krugler Gratz, Karl William (dec.). BA, Valparaiso U., 1955; B Ministry, Concordia Theol. Sem., Springfield, Ill., 1961; STM, Luth. Sch. Theology Chgo., 1968. Ordained to ministry Luth. Ch.-Mo. Synod, 1961. From instr. to assoc. prof. Concordia Tchrs. Coll., Seward, Nebr., 1961-77; pastor Salem Luth. Ch., Jacksonville, Ill., 1977-80, Mt. Olive Luth. Ch., Norfolk, Nebr., 1981-86, Zion Luth. Ch., Lincoln, Ill., 1986-88, Trinity Luth. Ch., Dwight, Ill., 1988—; mem. com. on family life and Bible study Luth. Ch.-Mo. Synod, St. Louis, 1984-87. Contbr. articles to profl. jours., chpt. to book. Bd. regents Concordia Coll., Seward, 1985-91; chmn. Seward County Rep. Party, 1966-69. Home: Rte 1 Box 132 Dwight IL 60420 *My life has been dominated by the incredible realization that God loves me, gave His Son for me, and on top of all that, gave me the privilege of serving humanity.*

KRUGLER, RICHARD ADOLPH, retired minister; b. Chgo., Sept. 15, 1925; s. William and Florence (Erber) K.; m. Edith Margaret Kleim, June 18, 1949 (dec. Oct. 1958); m. Mildred Eileen Worner Hilst, July 2, 1960 (dec. Dec. 1985); children: Jean E. Vahey, John R., Steven E., Ronald W., Barbara A. Muellenhagen, Shari L., Theodore J., Charles E., Thomas M.; m. Ruth Dorothy Schroeder Lail, Apr. 21, 1990. AA, Concordia Coll., 1945; BA, Concordia Sem., 1946. Ordained to ministry Luth. Ch.-Mo. Synod, 1949. Missionary Luth. Synodical Conf., Nigeria, West Africa, 1949-59; pastor Trinity Luth. Ch., Reed City, Mich., 1959-90, ret., 1990; cir. counselor Mich. Dist. Luth. Ch.-Mo. Synod, Big Rapids, 1960-70, mem. bd. evangelism, Ann Arbor, 1972-74, bd. dirs., 1974-82, mem. property and fin. com., 1976-82, chmn. commn. on adjudication, 1986-90; bd. dirs. Luth. Bible Translators, Aurora, Ill., 1966-61, 82-91, area rep., 1990—. Mem. Reed City Hosp. Bldg. Com., 1974. Mem. Rotary (sec. Reed City club 1983-89). Home and Office: 900 NW 95th St Vancouver WA 98665 *The meaning and purpose of life are defined by one's relationship and regard for Jesus Christ.*

KRUMM, JOHN MCGILL, bishop; b. South Bend, Ind., Mar. 15, 1913; s. William F. and Harriett Vincent (McGill) K. A.A., Pasadena Jr. Coll., 1933; A.B., U. Calif., 1935; B.D., Va. Theol. Sem., 1938, D.D. (hon.), 1974; Ph.D., Yale U., 1948; S.T.D. (hon.), Kenyon Coll., Gambier, Ohio, 1962; D.D. (hon.), Berkeley Div. Sch., Gen. Theol. Sem., 1975; L.H.D. (hon.), Hebrew Union Coll., Cin. Ordained to ministry Episcopal Ch., 1938; vicar Episc. chs., Compton, Lynwood and Hawthorne, Calif., 1938-41; asst. rector St. Paul's Ch., New Haven, 1941-43; rector Ch. of St. Matthew, San Mateo, Calif., 1943-48; dean St. Paul's Cathedral, Los Angeles, 1948-52; chaplain Columbia U., 1952-65; rector Ch. of Ascension, N.Y.C., 1965-71; bishop of So. Ohio, Episc. Ch., 1971-80; suffragan bishop in Europe Paris, 1980-83; assisting bishop Los Angeles, 1983—, St. Paul's Ch., Tustin, Calif., 1983—; vis. lectr. N.T., Berkeley Div. Sch., New Haven, 1942-53; vis. lectr. ch. history Va. Theol. Sem., Alexandria, 1942; instr. Prospect Hill Sch., New Haven, 1942-43; instr. religion U. So. Calif., 1950-52; chmn. clergy div. Univ. Religious Conf., L.A.; pres. San Mateo-Burlingame (Calif.) Coun. Chs., 1947-48, Ch. Fedn. L.A., 1951-52; chmn. nat. coun. Panel of Ams., 1952-61; interim pastor St. James' Ch., N.Y.C., 1990-91. Author: (with J.A. Pike) Roadblocks to Faith, 1953, Modern Heresies, 1961, The Art of Being a Sinner, 1967, Why Choose the Episcopal Church, 1974, (with others) Denver Crossroads, 1979, Letters from Lambeth, 1988, Flowing Like A River, 1989. Trustee Mt. Holyoke Coll., 1962-72, Bexley Hall of Colgate-Rochester, Kenyon Coll., Children's Hosp., Cin., 1971-80; chmn. Canterbury Irvine Found., U. Calif.-Irvine. Democrat. Clubs: Century Assn. (N.Y.C.); University (Cin.). Office: St Paul's Ch 1221 Wass Ave Tustin CA 92680

KRUMM, WILLIAM THOMAS, deacon; b. Steubenville, Ohio, Nov. 30, 1938; s. Thomas John and Mary Agnes (Berwanger) K.; m. Mary Ann Cheshier, June 9, 1962; children: Michael, Paul, James, Anne, Margaret, Anthony, Amy, Mark. BFA, U. Dayton, 1962, MA in Theology, 1985; diploma indsl. design, Sch. of Dayton Art Inst., 1963. Ordained deacon Roman Cath. Ch. Dir. religious edn. St. Patrick Parish, Troy, Ohio, 1976-80, St. Augustine Parish, Minster, Ohio, 1980-81; asst. dir. Office Religious Edn. Archdiocese Cin., Sidney, Ohio, 1981-83; dir. Archdiocese Cin., 1983-85, dir. diaconate office, 1985—; textbook com. Archdiocese Cin., Sidney, 1981-85, criminal justice task force, Dayton, 1977-81; adj. faculty Athenaeum of Ohio, Cin., 1986-89; bd. advisors Archdiocesan Cons. Svcs., Cin., 1988—. Writer, presentor ednl. videos Scripture and Christology, 1980; writer, presentor radio meditations WRBZ-FM, Cin., 1990; contbr. articles to profl. jours. Com. mem. Project 2001-Planning, Clermont County, Ohio, 1989-91. Mem. Nat. Assn. Permanent Deacon Dirs. Office: Archdiocese of Cin 100 E 8th St Cincinnati OH 45202 *One of the more noble human responses to what God does for us is prayer, and the most efficacious prayer is laughter. Laughter most clearly distinguishes us from all other life forms and so honors God's creation of human life.*

KRUPP, R(OBERT) A(LLEN), library administrator, author; b. Bronx, N.Y., May 16, 1951; s. Warren William and Sylvia Louise (Stone) K.; m. Collette Copeland, June 1, 1974. BA, Franklin and Marshall Coll., 1973; MA, U. Portland, 1977; MDiv, Western Bapt. Sem., 1977; PhD, Calif. Grad. Sch. Theology, 1977; MLS, U. Mich., 1981. Reference librarian Houston Pub. Library, 1981-83; assoc. librarian Western Bapt. Sem., Portland, 1983-84, library dir., 1984—, v.p. for adminstrn., 1988-91. Author: Saint John Chrysostom: A Scripture Index, 1984, A Primer on Theological Research Tools, 1990, Shepherding The Flock of God: The Pastoral Theology of John Chrysostom, 1991. Radcliffe-Ramsdel fellow U. Mich., 1981. Mem. Am. Theol. Library Assn., Evang. Theol. Soc., Assn. Coll. and Research Libraries, Conf. Faith and History, N. Am. Patristic Soc. Baptist. Home: 3394 NE 29th St Gresham OR 97030 Office: Western Bapt Sem 5511 SE Hawthorne Portland OR 97215

KRUSE, MARTIN, bishop, theologian; b. Lauenberg, Apr. 21, 1929; m. Marianne Kittel; children: Jan-Hinrich, Susanne, Bernhard, Bettina. Postgrad., univs. of Mainz, Heidelberg, Göttingen, Bethel, 1955-57; PhD, Loccum Luth. Sem., 1969. Curate Linz, Austria, 1953-55; pastor, lectr. Loccum Acad., 1965-70, sr. lectr., 1970-76; apptd. suffragan bishop Luth. Ch., Hanover, Fed. Republic Germany; apptd. mem. synod Evang. Ch. in Germany; bishop Evang. Ch. in Germany, Berlin and Brandenburg, Fed. Republic Germany, 1976—; mem. coun. Evang. Ch. in Germany, 1979, chmn. coun., 1985—; mem. cen. com. World Coun. Chs., 1983—. Author: Speners Kritik am landesherrlichen Kirchenregiment und ihre Vorgeschichte, 1971, Verführung zur Güte, other books. Address: Bachstrabe 1-2, D-1000 Berlin 21, Federal Republic of Germany

KRUZAN, TIMOTHY RAY, minister; b. Pekin, Ill., Oct. 17; s. Lawrence and Mary Ruth (Starrick) K.; m. Robin Reneé Kitchell, Aug. 4, 1979; children: Brian Matthew, Bethan Michelle (dec.), Erin Rebekah. Student, Cen. Bible Coll., 1979. Lic. to ministry Assemblies of God, 1988. Assoc. pastor Ellendale Assembly of God, Bartlett, Tenn., 1986-89, 1sst Assembly of God, Southhaven, Miss., 1989-91; pastor Victory Assembly of God, Adrian, Mo., 1991—; sectional youth rep. Miss. Dist. Assemblies of God, 1989—. Named Youth Rep. of Yr., Miss. Dist. Assembles of God, 1990. Republican. Home: 515 E 5th St Adrian MO 64720 Office: Victory Assembly of God 601 N Old 71 Hwy Adrian MO 64720

KUBIC, JOSEPH CRAIG, librarian; b. Alexandria, La., Sept. 29, 1956; s. Joseph Jr. and Mildred Catherine (Wade) K.; m. Donna Lynn Williams, Jan. 3, 1982; 1 child, Micah Wade. BA, N.W. La. Coll., 1977; MLS, La. State U., Baton Rouge, 1979; MDiv, Golden Gate Sem., 1983; postgrad., U. San Francisco, 1985-89. Mem. ALA, ATLA, SBLA, Czech and Slovak Club of Kansas City, Mo. (pres. 1990—), Kansas City Met. Libr. Network (coun. 1989—). Home: 17 NE Briarcliff Rd Kansas City MO 64116 Office: Midwestern Bapt Sem Libr 5001 N Oak Trafficway Kansas City MO 64118

KUCERA, DANIEL WILLIAM, college president, bishop; b. Chgo., May 7, 1923; s. Joseph F. and Lillian C. (Petrzelka) K. BA, St. Procopius Coll., 1945; MA, Catholic U. Am., 1950, PhD, 1954. Joined Order of St. Benedict, 1944, ordained priest Roman Cath. Ch., 1949. Registrar St. Procopius Coll. and Acad., Lisle, Ill., 1945-49, St. Procopius Coll., Lisle, 1954-56; acad. dean, head dept. edn. St. Procopius Coll., 1956-59, pres., 1959-65; abbot St. Procopius Abbey, Lisle, 1964-71; pres. Ill. Benedictine Coll. (formerly St. Procopius Coll.), Lisle, 1971-76; chmn. bd. trustees Ill. Benedictine Coll. (formerly St. Procopius Coll.), 1976-78; aux. bishop of Joliet, 1977-80; bishop of Salina Kans., 1980-83; archbishop of Dubuque Iowa, 1983—. Mem. KC (4 degree).

KUCHAREK, WILMA SAMUELLA, minister; b. Johnson City, N.Y., Sept. 19, 1954; d. Samuel and Wilma Kucharek; m. Thomas Drobena, Dec. 27, 1980; 1 child, Thomas Samuel. BA, Valparaiso U., 1976; MDiv, Luth. Theol. Sem., 1982, STM, 1985. Parish deaconess Trinity Luth. Ch., Merrillville, Ind., 1976-78; vice pastor Ascension Luth. Ch., Binghamton, N.Y., 1978-79; pastor Holy Emmanuel Luth. Ch., Mahanoy City, Pa., 1982-86; pastor St. John's Luth. Ch., St. Clair, Pa., 1982-86, Nanticoke, Pa., 1983-86;

pastor Holy Trinity Luth. Ch., Torrington, Conn., 1986—; chaplain CAP, 1983—; with learning ministry Slovak Zion synod Evang. Luth. Ch. in Am., 1985—, chairperson planning group region 7, 1986—. Co-author: Heritage of the Slavs, 1976. Mem. ARC (bd. dirs.), Slavic Heritage Inst. (pres.). Office: Slavic Heritage Inst PO Box 1882 Torrington CT 06790

KUCHARSKY, DAVID EUGENE, religious organization executive, editor; b. Pitts., Aug. 3, 1931; s. Leon and Marie (Dachko) K.; m. Patricia Eleanor Patterson, Aug. 31, 1957; children: Brenda Lee, Deborah Lynn, Sandra Lou, David John. B.A., Duquesne U., 1953; M.A., Am. U., 1961; postgrad., Catholic U., 1969-74; Litt.D. (hon.), Nyack Coll., 1978. Staff corr. UPI, Pitts., 1955-57; news editor Christianity Today, Washington, 1958-67, assoc. editor, 1967-71, mng. editor, 1971-76, sr. editor, 1976-77; editor, sr. v.p. Christian Herald Assn., Chappaqua, N.Y., 1977-85, pres., 1985—; dir. Christian Publs., Inc., Camp Hill, Pa. Author: The Man from Plains—The Mind and Spirit of Jimmy Carter, 1976. Trustee The King's Coll., Briarcliff Manor, N.Y., 1986—. Served to 1st lt. USAF, 1953-55. Mem. Authors Guild, Soc. Profl. Journalists. Club: Nat. Press. Avocations: running; tennis; radio-controlled model airplanes. Home: PO Box 254 Cross River NY 10518 Office: Christian Herald Assn 40 Overlook Dr Chappaqua NY 10514 *Meaningful life consists largely of responding to opportunities. We make the most of life's opportunities if first we respond to the one wherein God offers His redeeming love. That transaction enables us to recognize opportunities. That transcend the temporal without trivializing it.*

KUCHEMAN, CLARK ARTHUR, religion educator; b. Akron, Ohio, Feb. 7, 1931; s. Merlin Carlyle and Lucile (Clark) K.; m. Melody Elaine Frazer, Nov. 15, 1986. BA, U. Akron, 1952; BD, Meadville Theol. Sch., 1955; MA in Econs., U. Chgo., 1959, PhD, 1965. Instr., then asst. prof. U. Chgo., 1961-67; prof. Claremont (Calif.) McKenna Coll., 1967—, Claremont Grad. Sch., 1967—. Co-author: Belief and Ethics, 1978, Creative Interchange, 1982, Economic Life, 1988; contbg. editor: The Life of Choice, 1978; contbr. articles to profl. jours. 1st lt. USAF, 1955-57. Mem. Am. Acad. Religion, Soc. Christian Ethics, Hegel Soc. Am., N.Am. Soc. for Social Philosophy. Democrat. Mem. United Ch. of Christ. Home: 10160 60th St Riverside CA 92509 Office: Claremont McKenna Coll Dept Philosophy and Religion Pitzer Hall Claremont CA 91711 *Education and life itself have the same purpose, and, borrowing words from G. W. F. Hegel, "...the final purpose of education is liberation and the struggle for a higher liberation still."*

KUDAN, HAROLD LEWIS, rabbi; b. Glens Falls, N.Y., Mar. 12, 1932; s. Nathan Henry and Mary (Shelansky) K.; m. Phyllis Rosenberg, Sept. 12, 1954; children: David, Mark, Jonathan, Jeremy. BA, Skidmore Coll., 1954; MA in Hebrew Lit., Hebrew Union Coll., Cin., 1958, Rabbinical, 1959, DD (hon.), 1984. Ordained rabbi, 1959. Assoc. rabbi North Shore Congregation Israel, Glencoe, Ill., 1962-72; founding rabbi Am Shalom Congregation, Glencoe, 1972—; lectr. Barat Coll., Lake Forest, Ill., 1969-72. Mem. Ill. com. White Ho. Conf. on Children, Chgo., 1980-81; chmn. bd. dirs. Interfaith Housing Coun., Chgo. area; bd. dirs. Am. Jewish Com., Chgo., 1986-87, John Howard Assn., Chgo. Mem. Chgo. Bd. Rabbis (treas. 1969-71), Chgo. Assn. Reform Rabbis, Cen. Conf. Am. Rabbis, Standard Club. Home: 926 Sheridan Rd Glencoe IL 60022 Office: Am Shalom Congregation 840 Vernon Ave Glencoe IL 60022

KUDER, ALICE ANN, religious organization administrator; b. Chehalis, Washington, Dec. 13, 1957; d. Alphonse John and Mary Margaret (Sterns) K. AA, Centralia Community Coll., 1978; BA, Western Wash. U., 1980. Youth minister St. Nicholas Cath. Ch., Gig Harbor, Wash., 1980-84; dir. youth services Bergamo Conf. and Renewal Ctr., Dayton, Ohio, 1984—; cons. Archdiocese of Seattle, 1980-84, Archdiocese of Cin., 1984—. Author: Friends Forever, 1987. Big Sister United Way, Dayton, Ohio, 1985-86; mem. Pax Christi USA, Washington, 1982—, Bread for the World, Washington, 1979—; advocate Rape Relief, Tacoma, 1982-83. Mem. Nat. Assn. Female Execs. Democrat. Roman Catholic. Avocations: tennis, photography, sewing. Office: Bergamo Ctr 4400 Shakertown Rd Dayton OH 45430

KUDO, KENNETH MASAAKI, missionary; b. Miyazaki, Japan, Nov. 28, 1943; arrived in Brazil, 1976; s. Shisei and Miyako (Taniguchi) K.; m. Diane Leiko Suzuki, Oct. 15, 1947; children: Chery Ann Kimiko, Kevan Shisei. Student, Johns Hopkins U., 1962-65; BA, Univ. Hawaii, 1967; MDiv, Western Conservative Bapt. Sem, 1970. Pastoral staff Twin Lakes Bapt. Ch., Santa Cruz, Calif., 1970-74; missionary Overseas Crusades, Sao Paulo, Brazil, 1976—; affiliate staff Inter-varsity Christian Fellowship, Santa Cruz, 1970-74, Alianca Biblica Universitaria, Sao Paulo, 1977-80; field dir. Overseas Crusades, 1983-86, exec. dir. Avante, Brasilian Mission, Sao Paulo, 1987—; head pastor NewWave Ch., Sao Paulo, 1984—. Avocation: swimming. Office: Avante, Rua Barao do Triunfo 218, São Paulo Brazil *Crisis in the Japanese langaude means two things: danger and opportunity! In the world of crises, I found Jesus Christ to be the only stable source of peace and joy. He has become my master and friend over 28 years ago.*

KUENNETH, JOHN ROBERT, minister, religious organization administrator, liturgical artist, liturgical consultant; b. Litchfield, Ill., Feb. 6, 1932; s. Harold H. and Grace (Barrick) K.; m. Loralee Kay Raymond, Aug. 20, 1966; children: Christina Ann, Richard Raymond, Stephen John. BA, U. Denver, 1954; MDiv, Nashotah (Wis.) House, 1957. Ordained priest Episcopal Ch., 1958. Vicar Clear Creek Valley Missions, Georgetown, Colo., 1957-61; chaplain U. Denver, 1961-63; rector All Saints Ch., Sterling, Colo., 1963-67; rector St. James Ch., Wheat Ridge, Colo., 1967-71, Wichita, Kans., 1971-84; chaplain supr. Wesley Med. Ctr., Wichita, 1984-87; dir. instnl. ministries Episcopal Diocese Tenn., Nashville, 1987—; trustee, v.p. bd. trustees Diocese of Kans., 1971-75, chmn. Commn. on Ministry, 1979-84; cons. on ch. art and architecture, founder Domus Studio, Nashville, 1983—. Pres. Sterling Arts Coun., 1965-67; mem. Colo. Gov.'s Coun. on Arts and Humanities, 1966-67. Mem. Phi Beta Kappa. Home: 538 Hickory Trail Dr Nashville TN 37209 Office: Episcopal Diocese Tenn 42 Rutledge Hill Nashville TN 37210

KUEST, ROBERT DEAN, minister; b. Marysville, Calif., Nov. 28, 1944; s. Alvin Fox and Florence Anita (McDougald) K.; m. Peggy Lee Coffey, June 5, 1965; children: Robert Dean II, David Alvin, Sheila Renee, Scott Lee. BS, Pacific Christian Coll., 1966; MDiv, Lincoln Christian Seminary, Ill., 1970; postgrad., Fuller Theol. Seminary, Pasadena, Calif., 1988—. Minister Donovan (Ill.) Ch. of Christ, 1966-70, First Christian Ch., Greenville, Ill., 1970-72, Kingman (Ariz.) Christian Ch., 1972-75; sr. minister Glendale (Ariz.) Christian Ch., 1975—; bd. dirs., chmn. Harvest Herald (Ind.) Mission Bd., Nairobi, Kenya; pres. Ariz. Christian Conv., Phoenix, 1984, Ariz. Christian Minister's Fellowship, 1978-80, 87-88; exec. bd. United Christian Youth Camp, Prescott, Ariz., 1984-88. Contbr. articles to profl. jours. Scout master Boy Scouts Am., Glendale, 1983-88, com. chmn. 1983-84, 88-90, pack master, 1985. Named Outstanding Alumni Pacific Christian Coll., Fullerton, Calif., 1989; recipient Scouters Tng. award N.W. Dist. Theodore Roosevelt Coun., Phoenix, 1988. Mem. Alumni Assn. Pacific Christian Coll. Republican. Office: Glendale Christian Church 9661 N 59th Ave Glendale AZ 85302

KUFELDT, GEORGE, biblical educator; b. Chgo., Nov. 4, 1923; s. Henry and Lydia (Dorn) K.; m. Kathryn Rider, July 24, 1943 (dec. July 1956); children: Anita Kay Kufeldt Shelton, Kristina Sue Kufeldt Schmidt; m. Claudena Eller, June 21, 1957 (dec. Sept. 1978); m. Lydia Borgardt, Aug. 12, 1980. AB, Anderson Coll., Ind., 1945, ThB, 1946, MDiv, 1953; PhD, Dropsie U., 1974. Ordained to ministry Ch. of God, 1949. Pastor Ch. of God, Homestead, Fla., 1948-50, Ch. of God, Cassopolis, Mich., 1954-57, Ch. of God, Lansdale, Pa., 1957-61; prof. O.T. and Hebrew, Anderson U., 1961-90, prof. emeritus O.T., 1990—. Contbr. to Wesleyan Bible Commentary, vol. II, 1968, Nelson's Expository Dictionary of the Old Testament, 1980, Educating for Service, 1984, The Genesis Debate, 1986, Listening to the Word of God, 1990, Zondervan One-Vol. Bible Commentary, 1991. Dropsie U. fellow, 1961, 63; Land of the Bible Workshop grantee NYU, 1966. Mem. Soc. Bibl. Lit., Nat. Assn. Profs. of Hebrew, Am. Hellenic Ednl. Progressive Assn. (pres., Achievement award 1990) , Am. Hist. Soc. Germans from Russia (life, bd. dirs.). Home: 907 N Nursery Rd Anderson IN 46012

KUFTARO, AHMAD, religious leader. Grand mufti Islamic Faith, Damascus, Syria. Office: Office of Grand Mufti, Damascus Syrian Arab Republic*

KUHARIC, FRANJO CARDINAL, archbishop of Zagreb; b. Pribic, Yugoslavia, Apr. 15, 1919. Ordained priest Roman Cath. Ch., 1945; consecrated titular bishop of Meta and aux. bishop of Zagreb (Yugoslavia), from 1964; apostolic adminstr., 1969, archbishop, 1970, archdiocese of Zagreb, 1970; elevated to Sacred Coll. of Cardinals, 1983; pres. Yugoslav Bishops Conf., 1970; titular ch., St. Jerome of Croats. Mem. Council for Pub. Affairs of Ch., Congregation Clergy. Address: Kaptol 31, pp 553, 41000 Zagreb Yugoslavia

KUHLMANN, MARVIN EARL, minister; b. Chester, Nebr., Sept. 15, 1931; s. Walter Oscar and Hulda Katherine (Grabau) K.; m. Donna Mae Schneller, Oct. 17, 1954; children: Brent, Karen. AA, St. John's Coll., 1952; BA, Concordia Sem., 1954, BD, 1963, MDiv, 1972. Pastor St. Peter Luth. Ch., Westgage, Iowa, 1963-65, St. Stephen Luth. Ch., Liberty, Mo., 1965-71, St. Mark Luth. Ch., Flint, Mich., 1971-78, Holy Trinity Luth. Ch., Grandview, Mo., 1978—; mem. spiritual life com. Ozanam Home for Boys, Kansas City, Mo., 1978-87. Mem. Clay County Home Com., Liberty, 1967. Home: 204 Johnston Pkwy Raymore MO 64083 Office: Holy Trinity Luth Ch 5901 E 135th St Grandview MO 64030 *If you strive to serve and search to give life will never disappoint you.*

KUHN, PAUL, minister; b. Portland, Oreg., Oct. 13, 1935; s. Jacob, Jr. and Flora (Jacoby) K.; m. Denise Wolford, Apr. 7, 1978; 1 child, Angela D. McCall; m. Betty Christenson Meyer, March 16, 1956 (div. 1977); children: Timothy P., John Mark, Angela L. Fitzgerald, James A. BA, Cascade Coll., Portland, Oreg., 1956; BD, Western Evang. Sem., Gladstone, Oreg., 1959. Pastor Browns Pt. United Meth. Ch., Tacoma. Home: 5301 Browns Pt Blvd NE Tacoma WA 98422 Office: Browns Pt United Meth Ch 5339 Browns Pt Blvd NE Tacoma WA 98422

KUHNS, NANCY EVELYN, minister; b. Coaldale, Pa., June 5, 1947; d. Calvin Joseph and Helen Mary (Gerber) K.; m. Rodney W. Miller (div. 1975). BS in Bible, United Wesleyan Coll., 1969; MS in Early Childhood Edn., Marywood Coll., 1982; MDiv, Lancaster (Pa.) Theol. Sem., 1987. Ordained to ministry United Ch. of Christ, 1988. Organist, choir dir. Zion Stone Ch. of Snyder's, New Ringgold, Pa., 1976-86; pastor Rebersburg (Pa.) Charge United Ch. of Christ, 1987—; dir. day care ctr. Jim Thorpe and Lehighton, Pa., 1976-86. Fundraiser Am. Heart Fund, Lehighton, Pa., 1975-77, Am. Cancer Soc., Lehighton, 1975-77, ARC, Lehighton, 1975-77. Home: PO Box 156 Rebersburg PA 16872

KUJAWA, CLIFFORD JAMES, deacon; b. Toledo, Nov. 17, 1930. Ordained deacon Roman Cath. Ch., 1984. Permanent deacon Diocese of Toledo Roman Cath. Ch., 1984—. Home: 5338 Banbury Dr Toledo OH 43615-6808

KULAH, ARTHUR F., bishop. Resident bishop United Meth. Ch. in Liberia, Monrovia. Office: Liberia Cen Conf, PO Box 1010, Monrovia Liberia*

KULAT, TERRY L., lay worker; b. Westchester, Ill., Dec. 29, 1949; s. Elmer Gustaf and Elda Minnie (Pittelko) K.; m. Diane Lynn Diehl, July 29, 1972; 1 child, Cathryn Elayne. BA, Concordia U., 1971, MA, 1972. Cert. tchr. Dir. Trinity Luth. Presch. and Day Care, Lisle, Ill., 1974-86; dir. no. Ill. dist. Christian Single Helpmate Groups, Woodridge, Ill., 1986—; pres. no. Ill. dist. Dept. Early Childhood Edn., 1977-78; advisor grad. adv. com. Concordia U., River Forest, Ill, 1979-81. Contbr. articles to profl. jours. Home and Office: Christian Single Helpmate 6418 Bradley Woodridge IL 60517

KULI, VICKIE SUE, religion educator; b. Butler, Pa., Nov. 23, 1958; d. James Earl and Maxine Victoria (Kidd) Cary; m. John Charles Kuli Jr., May 27, 1978; children: Jamie Cathleen, John Charles III, James Curtis. AAS in Bus. Mgmt., Butler County Community Coll., Pa., 1978, AAS in Acctg., 1978. Cert. tax acct. Christian edn. dir., cons. First Presbyn. Ch., Perrysburg, Ohio, 1987—; self-employed seamstress, wallpaper hanger, Perrysburg, 1990—; various offices Presbyn. Ch. including tchr., elder, clk., various coms., choir mem., 1987—. Treas. Am. Red Cross, Massena, N.Y., 1984-86; pres. Welcome Wagon, Perrysburg, 1989-90; asst. den mother Boy Scouts of Am., Perrysburg, 1990-91. Mem. Phi Theta Kappa. Republican. Office: First Presbyn Church E 2nd and Elm Sts Perrysburg OH 43551

KULICK, FLORENCE OLIVIA POST, publisher; b. Bklyn., Sept. 17, 1923; d. Jacob Abraham and Emily (Mendis) Post; married Feb. 14, 1942; children: Spencer Lee, Fredda Pam, Matthew Post. BS, Stony Brook U., 1978. Pub. rels. officer U.S. Mcht. Marine Acad., N.Y.C., 1966-67; bd. dirs. East End Counseling Project, Southampton, N.Y., 1983—, adv. bd. East Hampton Town, 1983—. Editor: Danger, Insurance Fraud In Progress, 1987. Mem. Democratic Com., East Hampton, N.Y. Mem. AAUW (pres. 1987), Friends of Guild Hall (pres.), Hadassah (pres.). Avocations: swimming, tennis, golf, knitting, reading. Office: Carriage House Press Carriage Ln Barnes Landing East Hampton NY 11937

KULLMAN, WILLIAM FRANCIS, JR., religious studies educator; b. Bristol, Pa., Oct. 29, 1958; s. William Francis Sr. and Agnes Marie (Dranginnis) K.; m. Mary Elizabeth McKenna, Aug. 8, 1987; 1 child, Katherine McKenna Kullman. BA, U. Sranton, Pa., 1980; MA, Loyola U., 1983. Tchr. Loyola Acad., Wilmette, Ill., 1985—. NEH scholar, 1988. Mem. Am. Philos. Assn., Jesuit Philos. Assn., Inst. for Theologys Encounter with Sci. and Tech., Theta Alpha Kappa. Democrat. Roman Catholic. Home: 1155 Wesley Ave Evanston IL 60202 Office: Loyola Acad 1100 N Laramie Wilmette IL 60091

KUMMER, RUTH MARY ANN, therapist, consultant; b. Wyandotte, Mich., July 27, 1930; d. Archibald Jacob and Anna Lucille (Copp) Lambrix; m. Joseph Talbot Kummer, May 17, 1974; children: Frederic Joseph, Mariane, David T., Joseph T. B.S., Siena Heights Coll., 1960, M.A., 1969; student (NFS grantee) Wayne State U., 1965, postgrad in substance abuse. Tchr., Roman Catholic Diocese Chgo., 1948-52, Toledo, 1953-59, Detroit, 1959-67, tchr. jr. high sch. Diocese Lansing, Mich., 1967-68; prin. elem. sch. Archdiocese Detroit, Chelsea, Mich., 1968-69, dir. religious edn., 1970-74; clinic supr. edn. Breast Cancer Detection Ctr., U. Mich., Ann Arbor, 1975-79; chaplain, coord. lay ministers St. Joseph Hosp., Ann Arbor, 1980-84; pres. Roman Cath. Dominican Laity, Chgo., 1980-84, presentor Buffalo, 1983, del. Bologna, Italy, 1983; counselor Adult Edn., Ypsilanti Publ. Schs., 1986-89; cons., therapist The Knopf Co., Inc. 1989. Contbr. articles to profl. jours. Vol. Meals on Wheels, Ann Arbor, 1979. Mem. Chi Sigma Iota. Home: 3904 Golfside Rd Ypsilanti MI 48197

KUNATH, ANNE ROBINSON, clergywoman; b. Newberry, S.C., Jan. 21, 1932; d. Franklyn Tyler and Willie Doyle (Bostain) Robinson; m. Donald Walter Kunath, Apr. 27, 1961; children: Robin Anne, Bonnie Raye, Cindy Sue, John Walter, Stanley Tyler. BD, Brooks Divinity Coll., Denver, 1980. Ordained to ministry Divine Sci. Ch. of Today, 1975. Minister Divine Sci. Ch. of Today, San Antonio, 1975—. Author: Prayers and Inspirations for Senior Children of God, 1981, The Art of Making Things Happen, 1983, I'd be an Angel But...., 1985, Truthwalking, 1991, What Are You Giving Life To? 1991. Fellow Divine Sci. Fedn. Internat. (pres. 1984-85); mem. Internat. Platform Assn., South Cen. Tex. Internat. New Thought Alliance (dist. pres. 1979—), Am. Mensa Ltd. Home: 6020 Danny Kaye # 2201 San Antonio TX 78240 *Let no one condemn or criticize the beloved spark of the divine within you—not even yourself.*

KUNER, CHARLES MICHAEL, minister; b. San Diego, Nov. 28, 1951; s. Joe Frank and Verna Irene (Landis) K.; m. Judith Lyn Jenkinson, June 16, 1973 (div. June 1985); m. Jennifer Slemmons, May 11, 1986; children: Ellen Claire, Emma Catherine. AA, San Diego Mesa Coll., 1972; BA, San Diego State U., 1974; MDiv, Princeton Theol. Sem., 1977. Ordained to ministry Presbyn. Ch., 1977. Asst. pastor 1st Presbyn. Ch., Valparaiso, Ind., 1977-80; interim pastor Ogden Dune (Ind.) Community Ch., 1980-81, Kouts (Ind.) Presbyn. Ch., 1981-82; assoc. pastor 1st Presbyn. Ch., Topeka, 1982—; chaplain Kans. Ho. Reps., Topeka, 1988—. Bd. dirs. Topeka Youth Project, 1987-88, Topeka Housing and Info., 1985-88, Topeka Festival Singers, 1989—. Paul Harris fellow Rotary, 1991. Mem. Rotary (pres. Topeka chpt. 1989-90). Democrat. Home: 4100 SW Twilight Dr # 208 Topeka KS 66614 Office: First Presbyn Ch 817 Harrison St Topeka KS 66612 *The variety of ways in which the church must "be there" for persons in society today is vast. It is the task of the church to work out ways in which to minister to those who are broken by the challenges and frustrations of life.*

KÜNG, HANS, theologian, educator; b. Lucerne, Switzerland, Mar. 19, 1928; Licenciate philosophy Gregorian U., Rome, Italy, 1951; Licenciate theology, 1955; doctorate theology Inst. Catholique and Sorbonne, Paris, 1957; LL.D. (hon.), St. Louis U., U. Toronto; D.D. (hon.), Pacific Sch. Religion, Berkeley, Calif., U. Glasgow, U. Cambridge, Eng.; H.H.D. (hon.), Loyola U., Chgo.; L.H.D. (hon.), U. Mich. Ordained priest Roman Cath. Ch., 1954; mem. practical ministry Cathedral Lucerne, 1957-59; sci. asst. for dogmatic Cath. Theol. Faculty, U. Munster/Westfalen (Germany), 1959-60; prof. fundamental theology Cath.-Theologic Faculty, U. Tübingen (Germany), 1960-63, prof. dogmatic and ecumenical theology, 1963-80, prof. ecumenical theology, 1980—, dir. Inst. Ecumenical Research. 1963—; guest lectr. throughout U.S., Europe, Asia, Africa and Australia. Apptd. by Pope John XXIII as official theol. cons. to 2d Vatican Council, 1962-65. Recipient Oskar Pfister award Am. Psychiat. Assn., 1986. Mem. Am. and German PEN Club. Author: Justification: The Doctrine of Karl Barth and a Catholic Reflection, 1964, The Council, Reform and Reunion, 1961, That the World May Believe, 1963, Structures of the Church, 1964, The Council in Action, 1963, Freedom Today, 1966, The Church, 1967, Truthfulness, 1968, Menschwerdung Gottes, 1970, Infallible? -An Inquiry, 1971, Why Priests?, 1972, Fehlbar? Eine Bilanz, 1973, On Being a Christian, 1976, Signposts for the Future, 1978, Freud and the Problem of God, 1979, The Christian Challenge, 1979, The Church-Maintained in Truth, 1980, Does God Exist, 1980, Eternal Life?, 1984, Church and Change, 1986, Why I am Still a Christian, 1987, Theology for the Third Millennium: An Ecumenical View, 1988, (with Julia Ching) Christianity and Chinese Religions, 1989; (with others) Christianity and the World Religions: Paths to Dialogue with Islam, Hinduism, and Buddhism, 1986, Reforming the Church Today. Keeping Hope Alive, 1990, Global Responsibility. In Search of a New World Ethic, 1991; also numerous articles. Assoc. editor Jour. Ecumenical Studies, Revue Internationale de Theologie, Concilium; editor Theological Meditations, Ökumenische Forschungen, Ökumenische Theologie. Address: Waldhäuserstrasse 23, Tübingen Federal Republic of Germany Office: Eberhard-Karls-U Tübingen, Dept Cath Theology, D-7400 Tübingen Federal Republic of Germany

KUNG (GONG) PIN-MEI, IGNATIUS CARDINAL (IGNATIUS KUNG (GONG) CARDINAL PIN-MEI), cardinal; b. P'ou-tong, China, Aug. 2, 1901. Ordained priest Roman Cath. Ch., 1930; ordained bishop of Soochow, 1949; ordained bishop of Shanghai, 1950. Prisoner People's Republic of China, 1955-85; elevated to Sacred Coll. Cardinals, 1979; formally invested titular Ch. St. Sixtus, 1991—. *

KUNTIMA, DIANGIENDA, religious leader. Spiritual head Ch. of Jesus Christ for the Prophet Simon Kimbangu, Kinshasa, Zaire. Office: Eglise de Jesus Christ, BP 7069, Kinshasa Zaire*

KUNTZ, JOHN KENNETH, religion educator; b. St. Louis, Jan. 20, 1934; s. John Frederick and Zula Belle (Reed) K.; m. Ruth Marie Stanley, July 7, 1962; children: David Kenneth, Nancy Ruth. BA, Grinnell Coll., 1956; BD, Yale U., 1959; PhD, Union Theol. Sem., 1963. Ordained to ministry Meth. Ch., 1961. Tutor in O.T., Union Theol. Sem., N.Y.C., 1961-63; instr. Bibl. history Wellesley (Mass.) Coll., 1963-65, asst. prof., 1965-67; asst. prof. religion U. Iowa, Iowa City, 1967-70, assoc. prof., 1970-76, prof., 1976—, chmn. grad. studies Sch. Religion, 1980-83, 88—, chmn. lectures com., 1983-88, mem. jud. com., 1976-79, 1988-91, study abroad com., 1985-88, faculty senate, 1989—; min. South Bethel United Meth. Ch., Tipton, Iowa, 1974-79. Author: The Self-Revelation of God, 1967, The People of Ancient Israel, An Introduction to Old Testament Literature, History and Thought, 1974; contbr. articles to profl. jours. Bd. dirs. Wesley Found., Iowa City, 1986—. Recipient Huber Faculty Rsch. award Wellesley Coll., 1966, Old Gold Faculty Rsch. award U. Iowa, 1970, 79; Nat. Endowment Humanities grantee, 1971, 84; Alexander von Humboldt (Germany) fellow, 1971-72, 73, 79. Mem. Iowa Meth. Conf., Am. Acad. Religion, Soc. Bibl. Lit. (chmn. Bibl. Hebrew Poetry sect. 1989—), Am. Schs. Oriental Rsch., Cath. Bibl. Assn., Coun. Grad. Studies in Religion (sec.-treas. 1982-90), Coun. of Soc. for the Study of Religion (chmn. liaison com. 1984-90), Phi Beta Kappa (pres. 1978-79). Democrat. Home: 321 Koser Ave Iowa City IA 52246 Office: U Iowa 313 Gilmore Hall Iowa City IA 52242

KUNZ, JOHN MELVIN, minister; b. Boise, Idaho, Feb. 6, 1946; s. Reinhart and Emma Kunz; m. Susan Mary Barton, Aug. 25, 1967; children: Jennifer, Shaun, Sharla, Josh. AA, Boise Jr. Coll., 1966; BA, U. Idaho, 1968; ThM, Dallas Theol. Sem., 1972; DMin, Talbot Sem., 1980. Ordained to ministry Grace Bible Ch., 1972. Intern Calvary Bible Ch., Grass Valley, Calif., 1972-73; pastor Big Creek (Calif.) Community Ch., 1973—; bd. dir.s Sierra Meth. Chautauqua Bible Conf. Assn. (bd. dirs.). Contbr. columns to The Backwoods Badger, 1973-77. Pres., firefighter Big Creek Vol. Fire Dept., 1977-89; chmn. Early Childhood Edn., Sch. Site Coun., Sch. Improvement, Big Creek, 1976—; inspector Fresno County Election Dept., Big Creek, 1976—, registrar; mem. Nat. Republican Congl. Com., Calif. Republican Party. Recipient 20th Anniversary Leadership award Soc. Disting. Am. High Sch. Students, 1988. Mem. Concerned Women of Am., Bible-Sci. Assn., Heritage Found. Home: PO Box 1 Big Creek CA 93605 Office: Big Creek Community Ch PO Box 1 Big Creek CA 93605

KUPFERMAN, LAURIE A., religious organization administrator; b. Louisville, Oct. 2, 1966; d. Henry Morris and Barbara (Cassell) Altman; m. Steven Kupferman, Dec. 3, 1989. BA, Ind. U., 1988. Youth dir. asst. Jewish Community Ctr. of Louisville, 1988-89; youth dir. Jewish Community Ctr. of Birmingham (Ala.), 1989—. Home: 201 Bridle Ln Birmingham AL 35243 Office: Jewish Community Ctr 3960 Montclair Rd Birmingham AL 35213

KURASHIGE, WAYNE ITSUO, music minister; b. Honolulu, Apr. 7, 1955; s. Thomas Tamotsu and Mae Mutsuko (Fukuda) K. BBA, U. Hawaii, 1977; Grad. Cert. in Biblical Studies, Multnomah Sch. of Bible, 1984. CPA. Adminstr. Gateway Community Ch., Aiea, Hawaii, 1986—; youth minister Gateway Community Ch., Aiea, 1989-90, music minister, 1990-91; owner Yardkeepers, Alea, 1986—; dir. Gateway Community Ch., Aiea, 1986—. Precinct v.p. Rep. Party of Hawaii, Aiea, 1990-91, conv. del., 1988-91. Republican. Home: 99-012 B Kuahale St Aiea HI 96701 Office: Gateway Community Ch 98-211 # 616 Pali Momi St Aiea HI 96701 *In life I seek not a title but a testimony.*

KURFEES, MARSHALL THOMAS, minister; b. Mocksville, N.C., May 15, 1957; s. Jack Dempsey and Helen Louise (Alsobrooks) K.; m. Susan Kay Langley, July 19, 1986. BS in History & Social Sci., Campbell U., 1979; MA, MRE, Southwestern Bapt. Sem., 1982; postgrad., Southwestern Bapt. Theol. Sem., 1986—. Ordained to ministry Bapt. Ch., 1983. Discipleship and evangelism leader Southcliff Bapt. Ch., Ft. Worth, 1980-86; children's minister Mid-Cities Vineyard, Arlington, Tex., 1987-88; chaplain Autumn Years Lodge, Ft. Worth, 1988-90; pastor Alexandria Bay (N.Y.) Bapt. Ch., 1990—. Editor Salt Times mag., 1978-79. Mem. Nat. Hist. Soc., Chgo., 1975-91. Mem. Thousand Island Bapt. Assn. (interim dir. missions 1990—, discipleship tng. dir. 1990—, assn. moderator 1990—), Bapt. Conv. N.Y. (evangelism coun. 1990—, hist. com. 1990—). Democrat. Home: 92 Walton St Alexandria Bay NY 13607-1204 Office: Alexandria Bay Bapt Ch Bolton Ave Alexandria Bay NY 13607

KURIA, MANASSES, archbishop. Archbishop of Kenya and bishop of Nairobi The Anglican Communion, Nairobi. Office: POB 40502, Nairobi Kenya*

KURKO, GEORGIA ANNE, minister; b. Martins Ferry, Ohio, Feb. 26, 1962; d. George John and Margaret Ann (Horvath) K. BA, Wheeling Jesuit Coll., 1984; MRE, Cin. Bible Sem., 1986. Children's min. Community Christian Ch., Naperville, Ill., 1989—. Mem. Christian Ch. Office: Community Christian Ch 1163 E Ogden Ave Ste 705-105 Naperville IL 60563

KURONGKU, PETER, archbishop. Archbishop of Port Moresby The Roman Cath. Ch., Papua, New Guinea. Office: POB 1032, Port Moresby Papua New Guinea*

KURTH, KAREN KAY, lay worker; b. Lake City, Iowa, May 20, 1941; d. Walter and Mabel (Allen) Burk; m. William D. Kurth, Feb. 14, 1959; children: Jody E. Kurth Windschitl, Ronald R. LPN, St. Anthony's Sch. Practical Nursing, Carroll, Iowa, 1968. Owner Karen's Tole Rm., Lake View, Iowa, 1986—; sec. Iowa Bapts. for Life. Treas. Blackhawk Lake Sanitary Dist., Sac County, Iowa, 1988-91. Mem. Nat. Soc. Tole and Decorative Painters, Iowa Decorative Painters, Rep. Women Sac County (pres. 1988-90), Eagle Forum, Concerned Women for Am., Iowa Rutherford Inst. Home: RR1 Box 71 Lake View IA 51450

KURTH, ROBERT ALLEN, dean, chaplain; b. Milw., Dec. 27, 1949; s. Allen W. and Olga A. (Wenote) K.; m. July 7, 1973 (div. Oct. 1978); children: Kalleah R., Misty C.; m. Linda Sue Smith, June 2, 1990. AA, Concordia U., Milw., 1970; MS, Concordia U., Seward, Nebr., 1972; M in Christian Edn., Faith Sem., 1977; STD, Geneva Theol. Coll., 1989; MA, Liberty U., 1991. Cert. elem. tchr., Wis.; lic. alcohol and substance abuse counselor, Ill. Chaplain Luth. Hosp., Milw., 1973; adminstr. Martin Ctr., Milw., 1973-77; tchr. Milw. Pub. Schs., 1977-81; adminstr. St. Martin's Acad., 1981-83; chaplain Milw. Psychiatric Hosp., 1990—; dean St. Martin's Coll. and Sem., 1975—. Fellow Nat. Acad. Counselors and Family Therapists; mem. AACD, Nat. Assn. for Applied Arts and Scis. (pres. 1985—), Nat. Inst. Bus. and Indsl. Chaplains (chaplain 1984—), Am. Assn. on Mental Deficiency, Milw. Athletic Club. Anglican. Avocation: ministry. Home: 1718 W Congress St Milwaukee WI 53209 Office: St Martins Coll 3104 N Holton St Milwaukee WI 53212

KURTH, WOODROW WALTER, pastor, educator, mayor; b. Ford County, Kans., Jan. 7, 1914; s. Albert Carl and Maria Magdelena (Weiss) K.; m. Lucille Adelaide Tolleson, Jan. 28, 1940; children: Sondra Mae Kurth Brown, Richard Eric. BDiv, Concordia Sem., 1938; MS in History, Pitts. State U., 1958; MA in Sociology, Cen. Mo. State U., 1968. Ordained to ministry Luth. Ch.-Mo. Synod, 1940. Pastor St. John Luth. Ch., Palmer, Alaska, 1940-45, Anchorage Luth. Ch., 1940-45, Gloria Dei Luth. Ch., Huntington Park, Calif., 1945-48, Christ Luth. Ch., Rawlins, Wyo., 1948-53, Zion Luth. CH., Pittsburg, Kans., 1953-61, Christ Luth. Ch., Sweet Springs, Mo., 1980—; prof. St. Paul's Coll., Concordia, Mo., 1961-79. Mem. com. Freedom Twp., Lafayette County, Mo., 1978-82; chmn. Community Betterment Com., Concordia, 1967-71; mayor City of Concordia, 1974-78, 80-90. Mem. Lions (sec. Concordia chpt. 1967-87), Rotary (sec. Rawlins chpt. 1950-53). Republican. Home: 405 Lorien St Concordia MO 64020

KURTZ, VERNON HOWARD, rabbi; b. Toronto, Ont., Can., Jan. 8, 1951; came to U.S., 1972; s. Bernard and Dorothy (Gula) K.; m. Bryna Wise, June 17, 1973; children: Hadassa Michal, Shira Miriam. BA, York U., Toronto, 1971; MA, Jewish Theol. Sem., 1973; D in Ministry, Chgo. Theol. Sem., 1981. Ordained rabbi, 1976. Rabbi Congregation Rodfei Zedek, Chgo., 1976-88, North Suburban Synagogue Beth El, Highland Park, Ill., 1988—; pres. Chgo. region Rabbinical Assembly, 1988-90; v.p. Chgo. Bd. Rabbis, 1990—; vice chmn. rabbinic cabinet United Jewish Appeal, N.Y.C., 1991—. Editor: Orchard, 1984. Pres. Hyde Park-Kenwood Interfaith Coun., 1984-86. Recipient Rabbinic award Coun. Jewish Fedns., 1984, also Young Leadership award, 1985. Home: 1232 Sheridan Rd Highland Park IL 60035 Office: North Suburban Synagogue Beth El 1175 Sheridan Rd Highland Park IL 60035

KUSHNER, HAROLD SAMUEL, rabbi; b. N.Y.C., Apr. 3, 1935; s. Julius and Sarah (Hartman) K.; m. Suzette Estrada, Mar. 27, 1960; 1 child, Ariel. BA, Columbia U., 1955, MA, 1960; DHL, Jewish Theol. Sem., N.Y.C., 1972; DLH, U. Mass. Med. Ctr., 1987. Ordained rabbi 1960. Assoc. rabbi Temple Israel, Great Neck, N.Y., 1962-66; assoc. rabbi Temple Israel, Natick, Mass., 1966-90, rabbi laureate, 1991—. Author: When Bad Things Happen to Good People, 1981, When All You've Ever Wanted Isn't Enough, 1986, Who Needs God, 1990. 1st lt. U.S. Army, 1960-62. Home: 20 Robinhood Rd Natick MA 01760 Office: 145 Hartford St Natick MA 01760 also: care Summit Books 1230 Ave of the Americas New York NY 10020

KUZMA, PAUL DANIEL, youth pastor; b. Rapid City, S.D., Sept. 19, 1965; s. Paul Peter and Margo (Heine) K.; m. Deborah Colleen Flanagan, Mar. 15, 1986. Standard ministerial diploma, Life Bible Coll., L.A., 1983-87. Lic. min. Youth pastor Simi Valley (Calif.) Foursquare Ch., 1987—; youth rep. Calif. Dist. Foursquare Chs., 1991—. So. Calif. Dist. Foursquare Chs. (dist. youth coun. mem. 1989—). Office: Simi Valley Foursquare Ch 4200 Township Ave Simi Valley CA 93063

KVERNDAL, ROALD, maritime ministry consultant; b. Bromley, Kent, Eng., July 8, 1921; came to U.S., 1961; s. Olaf Gunvald and Valgjerd (Wroldsen) K.; m. Ruth Louise Ursin, June 27, 1953; children: Olaf, Evelyn, Jeanette, Marianne. Inter-BA, U. London, 1939; Marine Law Deg., Dept. Commerce Oslo, 1942; ThM, Ind. Theol. Sem., Oslo, 1953; ThD, Oslo U., 1984. Consular sec. Govt. Norway, Rouen, France, 1948-49; seafarers' chaplain Norwegian Seamen's Mission, 1954-69; theol. researcher Norwegian Rsch. Coun., Oslo, 1969-72; pastor Am. Luth. Ch., various locations U.S.A., 1972-83; exec. sec. Internat. Coun. Seamen's Agencies, Bellevue, Wash., 1979-91; maritime cons. Luth. World Fedn., Luth. Coun. in USA and Evan. Luth. Ch., 1984—. Author: Sjömannsetikk (Maritime Ethics), 1971, Seamen's Missions: Their Origin & Early Growth, 1986; editor Watermarks, 1979-91; contbr. articles to profl. jours. Lt. Norwegian Free Forces, 1943-45. Mem. Internat. Assn. for Mission Studies, Internat. Assn. for Study of Maritime Mission (internat. pres. 1990—), Soc. for Nautical Rsch., Luth. Assn. Maritime Ministry (hon. sec.). Lutheran. Avocations: swimming, travel. Home: 2513 162d Ave NE Bellevue WA 98008 Office: Lutheran Maritime Ministry 2513 162d Ave NE Bellevue WA 98008

KWOK, STEPHEN PIT-FUNG, minister; b. Hong Kong, Aug. 1, 1952; came to U.S., 1988; s. Wai Ying and Lai Wu (Ginan) K.; m. Pat Ling Yuen, Jan 8, 1977; 1 child, Jonathan Chun-Sin. BTh, Evangelical Theol. Coll., Hong Kong, 1976; MA, Trinity Evang. Div. Sch., 1989. Assoc. pastor Living Stones' Ch., Ch. of Christ, Hong Kong, 1976-77; pastor Wendell Meml. Ch. Evang. Free of Hong Kong, 1977-79; missionary Evang. Free of Hong Kong & Send Internat., Rep. of China, 1979—. Mem. China Evangelistic Comm. (founder, bd. dirs.), Pastors Prayer Fellowship of Chungli City (exec. com.), World Hakka Evangel. Assn. (bd. dirs.). Home: 2065 Half Day Rd Deerfield IL 60015

KWON, PETER HISANG, chaplain, marriage counselor; b. Seoul, Aug. 11, 1921; s. Tharm Kwon and Chong Ai Joe; 1 child, Peter H. Kwon Jr. BA, Yonsei U., Seoul, 1944; MDiv., San Francisco Theol. Sem., 1951; MA, Hartford S Minary Found., 1953. Lic. marriage, family and child counselor; cert. profl. mental health clergy. Sr. pastor Wahiawa (Oahu) Ch., Hawaii, 1953-59, Korean United Presbyn. Ch., Los Angeles, 1959-68; head chaplain John Wesley County Hosp., Los Angeles, 1968—; area chaplain Los Angeles County-U. So. Calif. Med. Ctr., Los Angeles, 1968—. Contbr. articles to profl. jours. Pres. Asian Pacific Counseling and Treatment Ctr., 1986—; pres. Asian Presbyn. Council, Los Angeles and Hawaii; vice chmn. Los Angeles County Com. on Aging. Recognized for Outstanding Services for Elderly Los Angeles City Mayor, Outstanding Block Club Mem. Los Angeles City Councilmen. Fellow: Coll. Chaplains; mem. Nat. Assn. Social Workers (cert.), State Assn. of the Counselor, Marriage, Family and Children, Nat. Council of Chs. (bd. dirs.). Democrat. Home: 1517 4th Ave Los Angeles CA 90019 Office: 1200 N State St Los Angeles CA 90033

KWONG, PETER KONG KIT, bishop; b. Hong Kong, Feb. 28, 1936; s. Kwok Kuen and Ching Lan (Chan) K.; Dip.Arts, Chung Chi Coll., 1962; B.D. Kenyon Coll., 1965, D.D., 1986; M.Theology, Colgate Rochester/Bexley Hall, 1971; m. Ha Wai Chung, July 31, 1965; children—Yim Ming, Veronica, Chun Ming, Ernest, Yan Ming, Grace. Ordained to ministry Anglican Ch., 1965; clergy-in-charge Crown of Thorns Ch., Tsuen Wan, Hong Kong, 1965-66; vicar St. James Ch., Wanchai, Hong Kong, 1967-70; curate St. Paul's Ch., Central, Hong Kong, 1971-72; warden Wen Lin Tang, Chinese U. of Hong Kong, 1972-79, asst. lectr., 1972-79; Diocesan sec. Diocese of Hong Kong and Macau of the Anglican Ch., 1979-80, bishop, 1981—. Chmn., Sheng Kung Hui Sec. and Primary schs., 1981—; hon. pres. Hong Kong Juvenile Care Centre, 1981—, Hong Kong Scout Assn., 1981—; hon. pres. Neighbourhood Advice Action Council, 1981-90, patron, 1990—; patron Comfort Care Concern; bd. dirs. Central Hosp., 1981-83, Chinese Christian Chs. Union, 1981—, United Christian Hosp., 1987—; mem. univ. ct. Hong Kong U., 1981—; exec. com. Hong Kong Christian Coun., 1980—, chmn., 1983-84; trustee Chung Chi Coll., Chinese U. Hong Kong, Alice Ho Mi u Ling Nethersole Hosp., 1983-85; hon. v.p. Hong Kong Girl Guides Assn., 1981—; pres. Hong Kong council Boys' Brigade, 1982—; mem. basic law drafting com. Hong Kong spl. adminstrv. region People's Republic of China, 1985-89, also mem. consultative com. Mem. Christian Assn. for Execs. (patron). Hong Kong Tchrs. Assn. (patron), Council of Chs. of East Asia (hon. treas. 1981-83). Address: 1 Lower Albert Rd, Hong Kong Hong Kong

KWONG, RAYMOND, minister; b. Hong Kong, May 11, 1954; came to U.S., 1969; s. Johnny C. and Kwan (Luke) K.; m. Anne W. Pang, Feb. 14, 1981; 1 child, Caleb. BS, U. Calif., Berkeley, 1976. Ordained to ministry Bapt. Ch., 1981. Min. outreach Bay Area Chinese Bible Ch., San Leandro, Calif., 1979-84; asst. pastor Holy Word Ch., San Francisco, 1984-86; founder, pastor Bible Bapt. Ch., San Francisco, 1986—; guest talk show Chinese Outreach, Millbrae, Calif., 1990—; host weekly radio broadcast Family Voice. Author newsletter Challenger, 1990—; mem. editorial staff newsletter Voice, 1990—. Com. mem. San Franciscans for Common Sense, 1989-90; founder, pres. Chinese Family Alliance, San Francisco, 1990—. Republican. Office: Chinese Family Alliance 450 Taraval St # 246 San Francisco CA 94116 *Stand for what is right, whether it is popular or unpopular, whether you might win or lose friends; but make sure you speak the truth in love.*

KYKER, CHARLES CLINTON, pastor; b. Greensboro, N.C., Dec. 23, 1962; s. Dennis Clinton and Roberta Jean (McKay) K.; m. Julie Mellisa White, Apr. 30, 1988; children: Mary Grace Caroline, Ashley Beth Mellisa. BA in Religion and Philosophy, Greensboro (N.C.) Coll., 1985; MDiv, Emory U., 1988; postgrad., Duke Div. Sch., 1991—. Youth min. Unity United Meth. Ch., Thomasville, N.C., 1982-83, Asbury United Meth. Ch., Greensboro, 1983-85; assoc. pastor First United Meth. Ch., Buford, Ga., 1985-87, Fayetteville, Ga., 1987-88, Waynesville, N.C., 1988-90; pastor Centenary United Meth. Ch., Clemmons, N.C., 1990—; del. World Meth. Regional Sem., Ghana, West Africa, 1986-87, World Meth. Internat. Seminar, Atlanta, 1987, 250th Celebration of Aldersgate, Eng., 1988; cert. new world missioner United Meth. Ch. Bd. of Discipline, Nashville, 1988. Student affiliate Atlanta Emergency Aid Ministry, 1986-87; bd. dirs. Haywood Christian Ministry, 1989-90. Sherman scholar Emory U., 1985-88. Mem. Clemmons Civic Club. Home: 319 B Frye Bridge Rd Clemmons NC 27012 Office: Centenary United Meth Ch 344B Hampton Rd Clemmons NC 27012

KYLE, JOHN EMERY, mission executive; b. San Diego, July 7, 1926; s. John E. and Agnes (McDaniel) K.; m. Lois Ellen Rowland, June 8, 1947; children: Arlette Marie, Jayson Duane, Marcus Justin, Darlene Patricia. BS in Agriculture, Oreg. State U., 1950; BDiv, Columbia Theol. Sem., 1961, MDiv, 1971. Ordained to ministry Presbyn. Ch. in U.S., 1961. Pastor Presbyn. Ch. in U.S., Hazard, Ky., 1961-63; adminstr. Wycliffe Bible Translators, Manila, Philippines, 1964-73; coord. Mission to the World, Presbyn. Ch. in Am., Decatur, Ga., 1974-77; exec. dir. Mission to the World Presbyn. Ch. in Am., Atlanta, 1988—; coord. Wycliffe Bible Translators, Washington, 1977-79; missions dir. Intervarsity Christian Fellowship, Madison, Wis., 1979-88; sr. buyer Easwest Produce Co.-Safeway Stores Inc., San Francisco, 1951-57; Trustee Evan. Fgn. Missions Assn., Washington, 1989—, Columbia Bible Coll. and Sem., 1982-86, Concerts of Prayer Internat., Mpls., 1988—, Overseas Missionary Fellowship, Robesonia, Pa., 1982-86, A.D. 2000 Movement, San Jose, Calif., 1989—. Author: Now This Generation, 1990; editor: The Unfinished Task, 1982, Finishing the Task, 1987, Urban Missions, 1988. Midshipman USNR, 1944-45. Recipient Presdl. Merit medal Pres. of Philippines. Mem. Evang. Fgn. Missions Assn., Nat. Assn. Evang., Assn. Ch. Missions Com., World Evang. Fellowship, AD 200 Movement. Home: 5747 Brooklyn Ln Norcross GA 30093 Office: Mission To the World PO Box 29765 Atlanta GA 30359-0765

KYLLO, DAVID OLE, minister; b. Colfax, Wash., Nov. 11, 1952; s. Ole Bernhardt and Barbara Ann (Eidem) K.; m. Rebecca Jean Lee, July 12, 1974 (div. July 1982); 1 child, Christina Marie; m. Charlotte June Runnels, July 5, 1986; stepchildren: Benjamin Pounds, Alicia Pounds. BA in Edn., Seattle Pacific, 1975; MDiv, Pacific Luth. Theol. Sem., Berkeley, Calif., 1979. Ordained to ministry Am. Luth. Ch., 1979. Intern Bethany Luth. Ch., Fredericksburg, Tex., 1979; pastor Zion Luth., Moulton, Tex., 1979-81; chaplain Austin (Tex.) State Hosp., 1981-82; chaplaincy dir. Warm Springs Rehab. Hosp., Gonzales, Tex., 1983-89; pastor Good Shepherd Luth. Ch., Bastrop, Tex., 1985-89; chaplaincy dir. Rehab. Inst. Chgo., 1989—; sec.-treas. Assn. of Chaplains of Tex., Houston, 1987-89; mem. Met. Chgo. synod com. on social ministry Evang. Luth. Ch. in Am., 1991—. Bd. dirs. C. of C. Med. Bd., Moulton, Tex., 1986-87; sec.-treas. Dirs. of Vols. in Agencies, Victoria, Tex., 1985-89. Mem. Mid Cen. Luth. Chaplains Assn. (treas. 1989—), Met. Ecumenical Chgo. Chaplains Assn. (sec.-treas. 1990—), Assn. Mental Health Clergy (cert.), Am. Congress Rehab. Medicine (religion and rehab. task force 1991—), North Shore Corvette Club (Highland Park, Ill., activity dir. 1989-91, v.p. 1991-92). Home: 441 E Erie St 4709 Chicago IL 60611 Office: Rehab Inst of Chgo 345 E Superior St Chicago IL 60611

KYRILL OF PITTSBURGH, BISHOP See YONCHEV, ELIA

KYSKA, MIROSLAV JAN, pastor; b. Staratura, Czechoslovakia, June 13, 1928; s. Gustav and Anna (Kostial) K.; m. Viera Uradnicek, July 4, 1953; children: Miroslava, Peter. Student, U. Marburg, 1969; ThD, Komensky's U., Czechoslovakia, 1986. Pastor Slovak Luth. Ch., Bratislava, until 1986; gen. sec. Slovak Luth. Ch., Czechoslovakia. Contbr. articles to profl. jours. Lutheran. Home: Palisady 48, 81106 Bratislava Czechoslovakia

LAARMAN, EDWARD JOHN, minister; b. Cadillac, Mich., Feb. 22, 1949; s. Jay Edward and Georgie Lucille (Sikkema) L.; m. Joan Rae DeJonge, June 18, 1971: children: Joel Edward, Benjamin John. BA, Calvin Coll., 1970; BD, Calvin Theol. Sem., 1978; PhD, U. Notre Dame, 1982. Ordained to ministry Christian Ref. Ch., 1986. Vis. asst. prof. Goshen (Ind.) Coll., 1982-83, U. Notre Dame, South Bend, Ind., 1983-84, U. Iowa, Iowa City, 1984-85; min. edn. and witnessing Calvin Christian Reformed Ch., Grand Rapids, Mich., 1985—; sec. Classical Home Missions Com., Grand Rapids, 1987-90. Author: Nuclear Pacifism, 1984; contbr. articles to profl. jours. Office: Calvin Christian Reformed Ch 700 Ethel Ave SE Grand Rapids MI 49506

LAASONEN, PENTTI, religion educator; b. Kitee, Finland, Dec. 24, 1928; s. Juho and Lilli (Inberg) L.; m. Aino Larikka, May 25, 1953; children: Leena, Helena, Marjatta, Jaana. ThD, U. Helsinki, 1967. Sr. tchr. Gymnasium of the State, Savonlinna, 1957-74; asst. prof. U. Helsinki, 1974-81, prof. ch. history, 1981—, dean faculty theology, 1987-90. Contbr. articles to profl. jours. Fellow Finnish Acad. Sci., Finnish Hist. Soc., Finnish Ch. Hist. Soc., Lions. Avocation: literature. Office: Univ of Helsinki, Fabianink 7, Helsinki Finland 00130

LABALA, JEFFERSON SEIZIEGBUOH, theology educator; b. Kpain, Liberia, Feb. 12, 1950; s. Saye Gongbe and Koh (Iron) L.; m. Hilderia La'Verne Brumskine, May 6, 1978; children: Wala-Loh, Wala-Neh, Wala-Zokeseh. BSc, U. Liberia, 1975; MTh, Southern Meth. U., 1981; postgrad., Wesley Sem., 1989—. Co-editor United Meth.-Luth. Curriculum Project, Monrovia, Liberia, 1977-78; asst. prof. Gbarnga (Liberia) Sch. of Theology, 1981-85, prof. of practical theology, 1987-89, acad. dean theology, 1987-89; missionary United Meth. Ch., Jos, Nigeria, 1985-87; pastor-in-charge East New Market (Md.)-Linkwood Charge, 1990—; sci. instr. Monrovia Coll., 1976-77; adminstrv. asst. Tubman Nat. Inst. Med. Arts, Liberia, 1976; coord. Lay Pastor Tng. Ctr., United Meth. Ch., Gbarnga, 1982-85; rep. Liberia Coun. Chs., Monrovia, 1983. Author: Food for Christian Growth, 1974, Leadership Manual, 1986, also others; editor Jour. Christian Ministry, 1988. Coord. Scripture Union, Gbarnga, 1984; bd. dirs. Campus Sch., Cuttington, Liberia, 1987, WVST-Gray High Sch., Gbarnga, 1987. Mem. West Africa Assn. Theol. Inst. (sec. Liberia zone 1988-89). Office: East New Market-Linkwood Charge 4111 East New Market-Rhodesdale Rd East New Market MD 21631 *Truth is a multifaceted phenomenon. People who become truly aware of this realization will become more tolerant of others in matters of religion.*

LABARGE, JOSEPH ALBERT, religious educator; b. St. Louis, Dec. 11, 1937; s. Joseph Albert and Bonita June (Tillison) LaB.; m. Maureen Murphy, May 30, 1970 (div. Oct. 1990); children: Joseph W., Michelle A., William M. PhB, Pontifical Gregorian U., Rome, 1959; STL, Pontifical Gregorian U., 1963; PhD, Cath. U. Am., 1971. Ordained priest Roman Cath. Ch., 1963, laicized, 1970. Assoc. pastor Christ the King Cath. Ch., Oklahoma City, 1963-66; assoc. prof. religion Bucknell U., Lewisburg, Pa., 1970—, chmn. dept. religion, 1985-89. Assoc editor: Horizons mag., 1977-82. Mem. Coll. Theology Soc., Am. Acad. Religion, Soc. Christian Ethics. Home: 708 St Paul St Lewisburg PA 17837-1351 Office: Bucknell U Dept Religion Coleman Hall A2D Lewisburg PA 17837

LABARRE, MARY CONNELLY, theology educator; b. Chgo., Apr. 21, 1945; d. Thomas John and Elizabeth 9Fromm) Connelly; m. Jerome Edward LaBarre, Feb. 17, 1968; children: Paul, Katherine, Sarah. BA in English, Trinity Coll., Washington, 1967; MA in Theology, U. Portland (Oreg.). USDA-FAS asst. editor Fgn. Agrl. Svc., Washington, 1967-69; publs. editor Good Samaritan Hosp., Portland, 1969-75; pastoral assoc. St. Andrew Cath. Ch., Portland, 1976-84; religion tchr. St. Mary's Acad., Portland, 1987—; adj. prof. religion and ministry dept. Marylhurst Coll., Portland, 1987—; adj. prof. theology U. Portland, 1990—; videotape lectr. DeSales Religious Edn. Program, 1987—. Co-founder, dir. Concerned Cath. Women, Portland, 1986—. Mem. Soc. Bibl. Lit., Am. Acad. Religion. Home: 2628 NE Stuart Dr Portland OR 97212

LABATE, FRANK RICHARD, minister; b. Phillipsburg, N.J., July 11, 1959; s. John Assunto and Constance (Cuva) L.; m. Ruth Anne Mayers, Aug. 22, 1982. BA in Theology, Columbia Union Coll., 1982; MDiv, Andrews U., 1987. Ordained to ministry Seventh-day Adventist Ch., 1989. Minister Seventh-day Adventist Ch., Yale, Va., 1983—; pres., owner Rick Labate Prodns., Yale, 1987—; bd. dirs. J&P Music Ministries, Marcellus, Mich., 1986—. Recording artist and orchestration arranger including (tape) Treasures of Yesteryear, 1988; author (sermon): The God Who Lets Us Begin Again, 1988. Named One of Top Ten Sermons for 1986 Andrews U., 1986. Home: PO Box 54 Yale VA 23897 *We must be careful not to equate life with living. Just like a doll which has life-like features but does not breathe or think, life can simulate living. My personal challenge each day is to transform the state of existence into the realm of quality living.*

LABIANCA, ØYSTEIN SAKALA, religion educator, archaeologist, anthropologist; b. Kristiansand, Norway, Sept. 10, 1949; came to U.S., 1962; s. Olav Michele and Kirsten (Olsen) LaB.; m. Asta Sakala, Sept. 3, 1972; children: Erik, Aren, Ivan. A in Religion and Behavioral Scis., Andrews U., Berrien Springs, Mich., 1971; MA in Anthropology, Loma Linda U., 1972; postgrad., Harvard U., 1972-73; PhD in Anthropology, Brandeis U., 1987. Chief anthropologist Heshbon Expdn., Andrews U.-Am. Sch. Oriental Rsch., Jordan, 1971-76, assoc. dir. Madaba Plains project, 1980—; chmn. dept. behavioral scis. Andrews U., 1983—; mem. core staff Wadi Tumilat project U. Toronto-Am. Schs. Oriental Rsch., Egypt, 1976—; guest lectr. on Bibl. archaeology, 1973—; vis. scholar dept. archaeology Cambridge U., Eng., 1991. Contbr. articles to profl. jours. Rsch. fellow Zion Rsch. Found., 1973, 76, NEH, 1978-79, 88-89. Mem. Am. Schs. Oriental Rsch. (organizer symposium on ancient Mediterranean food systems 1982-90, Albright fellow 1980-81), Am. Anthrop. Assn., Soc. for Am. Archaeology, Assn. Adventist Forums. Adventist. Home: PO Box 4075 Berrien Springs MI 49103 Office: Andrews U Inst Archaeology Berrien Springs MI 49104

LABRIE, JEAN-PAUL, bishop; b. Laurieville, Que., Nov. 4, 1922. Ordained priest Roman Catholic Ch., May 20, 1951; ordained titular bishop of Urci and aux. bishop of Que., May 14, 1977—. Office: 1073 Rue St Cyrille Quest, Quebec, PQ Canada G1S 4R5

LABROSSE, G., religious organization administrator. Pres. Glengarry-Prescott-Russell Christian Coun, Prescott, Ont., Can. Office: Glengarry-Prescott-Russell, Christian Coun/St-Eugene, Prescott, ON Canada K0P 1P0*

LACEY, MARTHA JANE, social worker; b. Clarkston, Mich., July 15, 1931; d. Hazen S. and Jeannette A. (Knox) Atkins; m. Thomas J. Lacey, Aug. 17, 1957; children: Eileen, Tod, Kathleen. BA, Mich. State U., 1952; MS Social Work, U. Wis., 1960. Cert. social worker, Ill., Acad. Cert. Social Workers, supervisory endorsement, Ill. Youth dir. YWCA, Aurora, Ill., 1956-58; social worker Community Consolidated Sch. Dist. 15, Palatine, Ill., 1973-88; ret. Vol. Campfire Girls, Cub Scouts, PTA, local Sunday sch., Arlington Heights, Ill., 1966-73; mem. adminstrv. bd. Los Ministerios Hispanos de los Suburbios Noroeste, Palatine, 1984—; mem. 1st United Meth. Ch. Arlington Heights. Mem. Campaign for Children Com. United Meth. Women (chairperson 1988—), Commn. for Ch. & Soc. (Social Concerns) (chairperson 1990—). Avocation: travel. Home: 4 Eton on Oxford Rolling Meadows IL 60008

LACHAT, MICHAEL RAY, Christian ethics educator; b. Chgo., Sept. 5, 1948; s. Nicholas John and Iva Louise (Petrey) LaC.; m. Marlene Kay. BA magna cum laude, Nebr. Wesleyan U., 1970; MDiv magna cum laude, Harvard U., 1973, PhD, 1980. Visiting asst. prof. Liberal Studies St. John's U., Collegeville, Minn., 1980-82; asst. prof. Christian ethics Meth. Theol. Sch. in Ohio, Delaware, 1982-86, assoc. prof., 1986-90, prof., 1990—; mem. Ethics and Econs. Coun., Columbus, Ohio, 1982—; del. Ohio State U. Commn. on Interprofl. Edn. and Practice, Columbus, 1983—; cons. bioethics com. Riverside Meth. Hosp., Columbus, 1985-88; philosopher in residence, keynote speaker Inst. for Artificial Intelligence Rsch., U. Ulm, Fed. Republic Germany, 1990. Editor Troeltsch and Modern Theology, 1986; contbr. articles to profl. jours. precinct committeeman, chmn. membership drive Delaware County Dem., 1982-85; bd. dirs. People In Need, Inc., Delaware, Ohio, 1982-84. Mem. Am. Acad. Religion, Soc. for Christian Ethics, Sierra Club, Phi Kappa Phi. Avocations: fishing, weight-lifting, folk music, camping. Home: 5850 Houseman Rd Ostrander OH 43061 Office: Meth Theol Sch in Ohio 3081 Columbus Pike Delaware OH 43015 *Self-sacrifice is not the goal of Christian ethics but merely an unfortunately often-needed means to an end. The end is friendship with God and a corresponding universal friendship among all creatures of the universe--a friendship involving reciprocity and equality. The task of all religionists today is to foster dialogue toward that end.*

LACHER, LAWRENCE ARTHUR, minister; b. Albuquerque, July 20, 1958; s. Lloyd Lewis and Betty Mae (Denman) L.; m. Lisa Jean Etzel, July 31, 1982; children: Cassandra Jean, Nathaniel James, Christian Lawrence. BA in Religion, Trevecca Nazarene Coll., 1980; MDiv, Nazarene Sem., 1984, postgrad. Ordained to ministry Ch. of the Nazarene, 1986. Pastor St. Paul United Ch. of Christ, Napoleon, Mo., 1983-84, Portland (Tex.) Ch. of the Nazarene, 1984-85, Moriarty (N.Mex.) Ch. of the Nazarene, 1985-88; prof. Nazarene Indian Bible Coll., Albuquerque, 1987-88; pastor First Ch. of the Nazarene, El Paso, Tex., 1988—; dir. N.Mex. Dist. Youth Camps Coun., 1990—, mem. dist. adv. bd., 1991—; dir. N.Mex. Dist. Adult Ministries, 1988-90; cons. on devel. of manual Church Planting Among Native Americans, 1989. Recipient Gt. Commn. Leaders awards San Antonio Dist. Ch. of the Nazarene, 1985, N.Mex. Dist. Ch. of the Nazarene, 1988; named one of Outstanding Young Men of Am., 1986. Office: First Ch of the Nazarene 2520 Silver El Paso TX 79930

LACHMAN, WADE RANDALL, clergyman; b. Ontario, Calif., Apr. 10, 1954; s. Richard George and Blanche (Bayless) L.; m. Mary Alice Harbour, Aug. 23, 1975; children: Crystal Kay, Miriam Joy. D in Christian Ministries, Melodyland Sch. Theology, 1977. Ordained to ministry Trinity Christian Ch., 1979. Youth pastor Trinity Christian Ctr., Riverside, Calif., 1974-76; pastor Agape Christian Fellowship, Lompoc, Calif., 1976-78; assoc. pastor Ch. of the Living Word, Corona, Calif., 1978-81; pastor Faith Fellowship, Soap Lake, Wash., 1983-89, Tonasket (Wash.) Foursquare Ch., 1989—; prin. Manzinita Christian Sch., Corona, 1979; drug counselor Teen Challenge, Corona, 1969-72; pres. Tonasket Ministerial Assn., 1990-91,

Colombia Basin Ministerial Assn., Ephrata, Wash., 1987-88. Del. nat. conv. Republican party, New Orleans, 1988. Office: Tonasket Foursquare Ch 415 S Whitcomb PO Box 1014 Tonasket WA 98855

LACHMANN, RAINER, theology educator; b. Marburg, Germany, Sept. 9, 1940; s. Otto and Helene (Viering) L.; m. Diethilde Harder, July 4, 1969; children—Mareike, Till, Lars. Dr. theology, U. Marburg; Habilitation, U. Erlangen-Nürnberg. Instr. U. Erlangen-Nürnberg, 1974-79; prof. U. Bamberg, Fed. Republic Germany, 1979—. Author: Der Religionsunterricht Chr. Gotthilf Salzmanns, 1974; Ethische Kriterien im Religionsunterricht, 1980. Editor: Religionsunterricht als religionspädagogische Herausforderung, 1982; Religionspädagogisches Kompendium, 1984, 3d edit., 1990; Gemeindepädagogisches Kompendium, 1987; Lebensweg und religiöse Erziehung 2 Bde., 1989. Home: Hetzerstrasse 3,, 8600 Bamberg Federal Republic of Germany Office: Univ Bamberg, H Markusplatz 3, PO Box 1549, 8600 Bamberg Federal Republic of Germany

LACKEY, DANIEL GRADY, minister; b. Winston-Salem, N.C., Aug. 23, 1958; s. Grady Wilford and Modest Lillian (Jennings) L.; m. Geneva McDaniel, Oct. 12, 1979; children: Seth Daniel, Jennifer Danielle. Student, Piedmont Bible Coll., Winston-Salem, 1977-79; B Ministry, Friendship Bible Inst., Ramseur, N.C., 1981; BRE, Covington Theol. Sem., Rossville, Ga., 1986, MRE, 1991. Ordained to ministry Bapt. Ch. Youth min. String Street Bapt. Ch., Martinsville, Va., 1976-78; pastor Grace Bapt. Ch., Brosville, Va., 1979-81, Faith Meml. Bapt. Ch., Danville, Va., 1982—. Coach Danville Soccer, 1987-90, Danville T-ball, 1990; com. mem. Citizens for Abstinence in Sex Edn., Danville, 1989-90. Recipient citizen's award Sta. WBTM, Danville, 1988. Republican. Home: 172 Laramie Circle Danville VA 24541 Office: Faith Meml Bapt Ch 135 Winstead Dr Danville VA 24541

LACKEY, E. K., archbishop. Archbishop Anglican Ch. Can., Ottawa, Ont. Office: Anglican Ch Can, 71 Bronson Ave, Ottawa, ON Canada K1K 6G6*

LA CORE, WALTER C., minister; b. Santa Monica, Calif., Feb. 27, 1930; s. Walter Ellsworth and Clara Mae (Casner) La C.; m. Eleanor Jeanne Hiatt, Feb. 10, 1950; children: Thomas Edward, Stanley Walter, Yvonne Marie La Core Thompson. Assoc. minister devel. First Bapt. Ch., Modesto, Calif., 1974—. Contbr. articles to profl. jours. Commr. Stanislaus County-Local Agy. Formation Commn., Modesto, 1960-74. Sgt. U.S. Army, 1948-54. Named Man of Yr., Am. Legion, Modesto, 1970. Fellow Nat. Assn. Ch. Bus. Adminstrn. (treas. 1987-89); mem. Christian Ministries Mgmt. Assn., Christian Legal Soc., Modesto Jr. C. of C. (pres. 1958, Young Many of Yr. award 1959), Lions (pres. 1972), Calif. State Tire Dealers Assn. (v.p. 1970). Republican. Office: First Baptist Church 808 Needham St PO Box 4309 Modesto CA 95352-4309

LACROIX, FERNAND, bishop; b. Quebec City, Que., Can., Oct. 16, 1919; s. Jean-Charles and Cecile (Dore) L. B.A., Sacred Heart Coll., Bathurst, N.B., 1937; licenciate in canon law, Angelicum U., Rome, 1949; Ph.D. (hon.), U. Moncton, 1971. Ordained priest Roman Catholic Ch., 1946; tchr. Holy Heart Sem., Halifax, N.S., Can., 1953-61; dir. Eudist students in Rome, 1950-53; superior Eudist Sem., Limbour, Que., 1961-66; superior gen. Eudist Fathers, Rome, 1966-70; bishop of Edmundston, N.B., Can., 1970-83. Address: 6125 lére Ave, Charlesbourg, PQ Canada G1H 2V9

LACY, CREIGHTON BOUTELLE, educator, minister; b. Kuling, Kiangsi, China, May 31, 1919; s. George Carleton and Harriet Lang (Boutelle) L.; m. Frances McGuire Thompson, June 20, 1944; 1 child, Linda Marie. AB, Swarthmore Coll., 1941; BD, Yale U., 1944, PhD, 1953. Ordained to ministry United Meth. Ch., 1948. Pastor various chs., New Haven, 1944-46, Waterbury, Conn., 1951-53; missionary to China United Meth. Bd. Missions, 1946-51; prof. Duke Div. Sch., Durham, N.C., 1953-88; assoc. dean Duke Div. Sch., Durham, 1975-80; Danforth vis. prof. philosophy Internat. Christian U., Tokyo, 1973-74; vis. prof. U. Zimbabwe, Harare, 1984; cons. Tainan Theol. Sem., Taiwan, 1987. Author: Is China a Democracy?, 1943, The Conscience of India, 1965, Frank Mason North, 1967, Indian Insights, 1972, The Word-Carrying Giant, 1977, Coming Home—to China, 1978. Fulbright grantee, 1966-67. Mem. Assn. Profs. Missions (pres. 1964-66), Am. Soc. Missiology, Soc. Values in Higher Edn., Phi Beta Kappa, Phi Tau Phi. Home: 2714 Dogwood Rd Durham NC 27705-5733 *In a life which has almost spanned the 20th century I find myself perplexed and frustrated by the irreconcilable contradictions and conflicts in fundamental values: liberty vs. equality, individual choice vs. general welfare, physical survival vs. quality of life, ecology vs. economy, justice vs. freedom, protection of minorities vs. collective good, profit as incentive or as greed, self-determination vs. unity, rights vs. responsibilities, power vs. exploitation, technological progress vs. negative side-effects, tolerance vs. conviction.*

LACY, JAMES HARGAN, minister; b. Pontiac, Mich., Oct. 25, 1951; s. Willian Jerold and Charlotte (Hargan) L.; m. Nancy Lynn Kleynenberg, Nov. 2, 1974; children: Andrew, Elizabeth, Sharon. BA, Bob Jones U., 1974; MA, N.W. Bapt. Sem., 1976; MRE, Grand Rapids Bapt. Sem., 1978; D of Ministry, Trinity Evang. Div. Sch., Deerfield, Ill., 1991. Ordained to ministry Bapt. Ch., 1974. Youth pastor New Hope United Brethren Ch., Camden, Mich., 1974-75; interim pastor McKenna (Wash.) Community Ch., 1976; sr. pastor Faith Bapt. Ch., Greenville, Mich., 1977-89, Fellowship Bapt. Ch., Racine, Wis., 1989—; founder Montcalm Area Ministerial Assn., 1982; chmn. Ken/Mont Assn. of Chs., 1983-84. State del. Montcalm County Reps., Stanton, Mich., 1986; pres. Flat River Right-To-Life Chpt., Greenville, 1987; big brother Racine Big Bros.-Big Sisters, 1989—. Recipient Brothers award Phi Kappa Soc., 1973. Mem. Gen. Assn. Regular Bapts. (del., pastor 1989—). *The greatest life ever lived, and the one most worthy of imitation, is that of Jesus Christ.*

LACY, KAREN BEVINS, pastoral counselor; b. Richmond, Va., July 14, 1946; d. Willard Ray and Helen Louise (Bevins) Thompson; m. Thomas G. Lacy II, Apr. 5, 1991. BA in Religious Studies, Va. Commonwealth U., Richmond, 1983; MRE, Presbyn. Sch. Christian Edn., Richmond, 1986; MDiv magna cum laude, U. Va., 1988; postgrad., Va. Union U., 1990—. Ordained to ministry, Christian Ch., 1988. Typist Bapt. Fgn. Mission Bd., Richmond, 1964-65; sec. Presbyn. Bd. Christian Edn., Richmond, 1965-67; breeder, trainer dogs and horses Richmond, 1967-79; pastor Liberty Christian Ch., Green Bay, Va., 1988-90; pastoral counselor in tng. Pastoral Counseling Ministries, Richmond, 1990—; preacher Antioch Christian Ch., Bowling Green, Va., 1990—, Bethpage Christian Ch., Frederick Hall, Va., 1990—; lectr. in field; conductor seminars in field. Editor Pastoral Counseling Ministries Newsletter. Republican. Christian Ch. Avocations: reading, jogging, fishing, horseback riding, hiking. Home: 109 N Lake Ave Richmond VA 23223 Office: Pastoral Counseling Minist 4200 Chamberlayne Ave Richmond VA 23227

LACY, PHILLIPS, church administrator; b. Waynesboro, Va., Feb. 11, 1945; s. Milo Glen and Mary-Paul (Phillips) L.; m. Melinda Jane Anderson, Dec. 27, 1972; children: Brian Phillips, Andrew Lloyd. BS in Polit. Sci., Lewis & Clark U., 1967; MA in Curriculum Devel., Calif. State U.-Dominguez, 1972; M in Internat. Mgmt., Am. Grad. Sch. Internat. Mgmt., 1975. Parish adminstr. Christ Ch. Cathedral, Houston, 1984—; ruling elder Claremont (Calif.) Presbyn. Ch., 1971-72, Presbyn. Ch., White Plains, N.Y., 1978-79, Grace Presbyn. Ch., Houston, 1991; bd. dirs., officer Houston Ch. Coop., 1988—. Bd. dirs. Brays Forest Improvement Corp., Houston, 1980. Mem. Nat. Assn. Ch. Bus. Adminstrn. (regional bd. dirs. 1990). Democrat. Office: Christ Ch Cathedral 1117 Texas Ave Houston TX 77002

LACY, RUSSELL GWINN, minister; b. Springboro, Ohio, Apr. 9, 1938; s. Van Russell and Leah Clina (Hartley) L.; m. Mildred Jean Kirk, Dec. 28, 1957; children: Patricia Lynn Harsh, Russell Brian Lacy. BA, Earlham Coll., 1968; MDiv, Wesley Theol. Sem., Washington, 1973; D of Ministry, United Theol. Sem., 1990. Ordained to ministry United Meth. Ch., 1975. Student pastor various Meth. Chs., Md., Ohio, 1963-73; pastor Liberty United Meth. Ch., Dayton, Ohio, 1973-75, Evang. United Meth. Ch., Union City, Ohio, 1975-80, Leipsic (Ohio) United Meth. Ch., 1980-83, Madisonville United Meth. Ch., Cin., 1983—; mem. adv. com. MA in Pastoral Ministry, Mt. St. Joseph-on-the-Ohio Coll., Cin., 1989—. Founding mem. Ednl. Recognition Assn., West Carrollton, Ohio, 1962; coun. mem. Village of Union City, Ohio, 1976; state clergy Marriage Encounter-United Meth., Ohio, 1983-86; bd. dirs. Madisonville Emergency Assistance Ctr., Cin., 1983—, Madison Villa Home for Elderly, Cin., 1983—, Samaritan Counseling Ctr., Cin., 1988—, pres. 1990, chmn. bd., 1991; sec. Urban Steering Com., 1990—. Recipient J.C. Penny Golden Rule cert. United Way, Cin., 1990. Office: Madisonville United Meth Ch 6130 Madison Rd Cincinnati OH 45227-1906

LADD, KENNETH PAUL, clergyman, counselor; b. Delphos, Ohio, Aug. 3, 1938; s. Lawrence Andrew and Velma (May) L.; m. Kay Elaine Saunders, July 15, 1961; children—Kristine Lynn (dec.), Kevin Lee, Kim Leann, Karin Lynette. B.A., Huntington Coll., 1962; M.Div., United Thwol. Sem., 1966; Ph.D., U. Beverly Hills, 1983. Cert. tchr., Ohio. Ordained to ministry United Methodist Ch., 1966; pastor Antioch Christian Ch., Ottoville, Ohio, 1958-59, Goblesville Cir. Evangel. United Brethren Ch., Huntington, Ind., 1960-62, Salem Evangel. United Brethren Ch., Bettsville, Ohio, 1962-65, First Evangel. United Brethren Ch., Wauseon, Ohio, 1965-67, St. Paul's United Meth. Ch., Bloomville, Ohio, 1967-68; chaplain Maumee Youth Camp, Liberty Ctr., Ohio, 1968-80; bd. dir. Counseling Ctr., Wauseon, 1980—; pastor Taylor United Meth. Ch., Delta, Ohio, 1980, Beulah United Meth. Ch., Winameg, Ohio, 1981—. Bd. dirs. Valley Oak Coun. Camp Fire Youth, 2d v.p.; chmn. Ohio Youth Commn. Chaplains; bd. dirs. Four County Mental Health Bd., vice chmn. Mem. Ohio State Chaplains Assn. (1st v.p.), Wauseon Ministerial Assn. (past pres.), Am. Assn. Counseling and Devel., Am. Mental Health Counselors Assn., Am. Assn. Profl. Hypnotherapists, Ohio Mental Health Counselors Assn., Ohio Assn. Counseling and Devel., Hope (bd. dirs.), Fellowship Christian Magicians (profl. magician), Internat. Brotherhood of Magicians, Soc. Am. Magicians. Contbr. articles to profl. jours. Home: 234 E Superior St Wauseon OH 43567 Office: 120 W Chestnut St Wauseon OH 43567

LADEHOFF, ROBERT LOUIS, bishop; b. Feb. 19, 1932; m. Jean Arthur Burcham; 1 child, Robert Louis Jr. Grad., Duke U., 1954, Gen. Theol. Sem., 1957, Va. Theol. Sem., 1980. Ordained deacon, priest The Episcopal Ch., 1957;. Priest in charge N.C. parishes, 1957-60; rector St. Christopher's Ch., Charlotte, N.C., 1960-74, St. John's Ch., Fayetteville, 1974-85; bishop, co-adjutor of Oreg., 1985, bishop, 1986—. Office: Diocese of Oreg PO Box 467 Lake Oswego OR 97034

LADRA, MICHAEL RALPH, minister; b. Glendale, Ariz., Oct. 14, 1946; s. Phil Harold and Dorothy (West) L.; m. Susie Elizabeth Ladra, June 21, 1969; children: Jonathan Clayton, Jennifer Michelle. BA in Philosophy and Humanities Honors, Stanford U., 1968; MDiv., Princeton Theol. Sem., 1971; D of Ministry, Fuller Theol. Sem., Pasadena, Calif., 1976. Ordained to ministry Presbyn. Ch., 1971. Assoc. pastor Park Blvd. Presbyn. Ch., Oakland, Calif., 1971-75; dir. of men's ministry Bible Study Fellowship, Oakland, Calif., 1975-77; sr. pastor Corona Presbyn. Ch., Denver, 1977-87, First Presbyn. Ch., Salinas, Calif., 1987—; pres. West Coast Presbyn. Pastors' Conf., 1981-88; mem. Presbyn. Com. on Candidates, Denver, 1984-87, Presbyn. USA Gen. Coun., 1989—. Bd. dirs. United Way, Salinas, Calif., 1987-89. Mem. Rotary Club (Bd. dirs. Salinas, Calif. chpt. 1987-89). Office: Salinas 1st Presbyn Ch 830 Padre Dr Salinas CA 93901

LAEUCHLI, SAMUEL, religion educator; b. Basel, Switzerland, Oct. 9, 1924; came to U.S., 1956; m. Evelyn Rothchild; children: Catherine, Samuel C. VDM, U. Basel, 1947; PhD, Union Theol. Sem., N.Y.C., 1950. Ordained to ministry Swiss Presbyn. Ch., 1967. Min. local ch. Dornach, Switzerland, 1950-56; prof. Garrett Theol. Sem., Evanston, Ill., 1956-67, Temple U., Phila., 1967—; exec. dir. Mimesis Inst., Yardley, Pa., 1980—; vis. prof. Barnard Coll., Hamburg U., Fed. Republic Germany, Princeton U.; guest lectr. McCormick Sem., Chgo., Union Theol. Sem., N.Y.C., univs. of Cologne, Darmstadt, U. Chgo. Div. Sch., Princeton Theol. Sem. Author: The Language of Faith: The Semantic Dilemma of the Early Church, 1962, The Serpent and the Dove: Five Essays on Early Christianity, 1966, Mithraism at Ostia: Mystery, Religion, and Christianity in the Ancient Port of Rome, 1967, Power and Sexuality: The Emergence of Canon Law at the Synod of Elvira, 1972, Religion and Art in Conflict: Introduction to a Cross-Disciplianry Task, 1980, Das Spiel vor dem dunklen Gott: Mimesis, ein Beitrag zur Entwicklung des Bibliodramas, 1987, Die Bühne des Unheils: das Menschheitsdrama als mythisches Spiel, 1988; (poetry) Between the Curtain and the Wind, 1963; (with Maurice Friedman and T. P. Burke) Searching in the Syntax of Things: Experiments in the Study of Religion; (with Evelyn Rothchild Laeuchli) Jesus und der Teufel—Begegnung in Der Wüste: Imagination, Spiel und Therapie in der Versuchungsgeschichte, 1991. Office: Temple U Dept Religion Philadelphia PA 19122

LAFEVER, ROBERT LYLE, minister; b. Chillicothe, Mo., Dec. 17, 1946; s. Robert Lyle Sr. and Mary Frances (Jacobs) LaF.; M. Connie Sue Garber, Dec. 2, 1978; 1 child, Sean. BA, Southwest Bapt. Sem., 1967. Ordained to ministry So. Bapt. Conv., 1968. Pastor 1st Bapt. Ch., Glasgow, Mo., 1969-71, Green Grove Bapt. Ch., Latham, Mo., 1971-76, Kidder (Mo.) Bapt. Ch., 1976-78, Newtown (Mo.) Bapt. Ch., 1978-81, Chula (Mo.) Bapt. Ch., 1981—; asst. moderator Mt. Zion Bapt. Assn., 1970-71. Contbr. articles to religious jours. Democrat. Home: 1705 Borden Chillicothe MO 64601 Office: Chula Bapt Ch Box 45 Chula MO 64635

LAFFEY, ALICE LEILA, theologian, educator; b. Pitts., Dec. 1, 1944; d. John Joseph and Marion (Caveney) Laffey. B.A., Carlow Coll., 1967; B. Sacred Scripture, Pontifical Bibl. Inst., Rome, 1974, Lic. in Sacred Scripture, 1976, D. Sacred Scripture, 1981. Instr. Carlow Coll., Pitts., summers 1974-84; adj. prof. Regina Mundi, Rome, 1978-80, Gregorian U., Rome, 1978-80; instr. St. Vincent Sem., Latrobe, Pa., 1980-81; assoc. prof. Old Testament, Coll. Holy Cross, Worcester, Mass., 1981—; vis. prof. U. San Francisco, summer, 1984, Assumption Coll. Worcester, 1982, 89; lectr. Seton Hill Coll., Greensburg, Pa., 1981. Author: Kings Chronicles, 1985, Introduction to the Old Testament, a Feminist Perspective, 1988; contbr. articles to profl. jours. Batchelor Ford fellow, 1985. Mem. Catholic Bibl. Assn., Soc. Bibl. Lit., Coll. Theology Soc., Catholic Theol. Soc. Am., Am. Acad. Religion, AAUP. Avocations: reading; crocheting. Office: Coll Holy Cross Coll Hill Worcester MA 01610

LAFFOON, LAURA ELIZABETH, youth minister; b. Atlanta, Dec. 3, 1962; d. Charles Gregory and Jayne Ann (Etchison) Bass; m. Jay William Laffoon, Dec. 8, 1984; 1 child, Torrey James. AS, Montreat (N.C.) Anderson Coll., 1982; BA in Christian Ministry, Belhaven Coll., Jackson, Miss., 1984. Youth minister Atlanta Youth for Christ, 1985-87, Cen. Mich. Youth for Christ, Alma, Mich., 1987—; nat. dir. jr. high ministry Youth for Christ USA, Denver, 1989—; bd. dirs. His Place Family Enrichment Ctr., Alma, 1989—. Contbg. editor Ministry Models Manual, 1991. Asst. cheerleading coach Gwinnett (Ga.) Schs., 1986, Alma (Mich.) pub. schs., 1987, head cheerleading coach, 1988—. Office: Cen Mich Youth for Christ PO Box 757 Alma MI 48801

LAFOLETTE, JAMES RICHARD, pastor; b. Escondido, Calif., Feb. 17, 1954; s. Doyle Ray Lafolette and Dorris Lori (Warren) Spearman; m. Rebecca Lou Kleinsasser, Aug. 2, 1975; children: Jeremy James, Timothy Jon. BA in Bibl. Lit., Simpson Coll., 1976. Ordained to ministry Christian Fellowship, 1979. Itinerant missionary David Barnard Evang. Assn., Australia, 1971-73; assoc. pastor Holy Spirit Ctr. Ch., San Francisco, 1974-79; assoc. youth pastor Christian Family Ctr., Azusa, Calif., 1979-80; pastor Christian Life Fellowship, San Francisco, 1981-88; exec. pastor Vineyard Christian Fellowship, San Francisco, 1988—; bd. dirs. Teen Challenge, San Francisco, 1983-88. Editor: Where You Belong, 1985. Home: 74 Lunado Way San Francisco CA 94127 Office: Vineyard Christian Fellowship 151 10th St San Francisco CA 94103 *Since life's changes are inevitable I've adopted my own beatitude of "Blesses sre the flexible for they shall not break."*

LAFOLLETTE, JOAN CHRISTINA, minister; b. Chgo., Apr. 23, 1959; d. Robert Louis and Anne (Downing) LaF.; m. David B. McCarthy, Oct. 12, 1986. AB, Oberlin Coll., 1981; MDiv with distinction, Harvard U., 1986. Ordained to ministry Presbyn. Ch. (U.S.A.), 1987. Interim pastor West Presbyn. Ch., Binghamton, N.Y., 1986-87, Union Presbyn. Ch., Endicott, N.Y., 1988-89; pastor Immanuel Presbyn. Ch., Binghamton, 1989—; interim Protestant chaplain SUNY, Binghamton, 1988; mem. com. on extended ministries Presbytery of Susquehanna Valley, N.Y., 1987-89, com. on ministry, 1989—; commr. Synod of N.E., 1991; mem. faculty Ghost Ranch Presbyn. Ctr., Abiquiu, N.Mex., 1991. Contbr. to: Peacemaking Through Worship, 1989, The Organizational Revolution, 1991. Bd. dirs. Good Shepherd-Fairview Home, Binghamton, 1989—. Mem. Nat. Assn. Presbyn. Clergy Women, Am. Guild Organists (chaplain Binghamton chpt. 1989-90), Am. Soc. Ch. History, Witherspoon Soc. Democrat. Office: Immanuel Presbyn Ch 549 Chenango St Binghamton NY 13901

LA FRAMBOISE, TERRY MICHAEL, educational administrator, minister; b. Williston, N.D., July 22, 1955; s. John Edward La Framboise and Susan Marie (Wilkie) Smith; m. Donna Faith Osborne, July 7, 1978; children: Michael, Nathanael, Jaylene. BA, Pacific Coast Bapt. Bible Coll., 1981. Ordained to ministry Bapt. Ch., 1987. Dir. bus ministry Bapt. Community Bible Ch., Norwalk, Calif., 1977-80, bd. dirs., 1980-86, asst. pastor, 1986-90; engr. Downey (Calif.) Community Hosp., 1981-86; prin. Bapt. Christian Schs., Norwalk, 1990—; engr. Downey (Calif.) Community Hosp., 1981-86. Vol. Norwalk Rep. Com., 1980, 84, 88. With USN, 1973-77. Mem. Internat. Fellowship Christian Sch. Adminstrs. Home: 14503 Maryton Norwalk CA 90650 Office: Bapt Christian Schs 12226 Alondra Blvd Norwalk CA 90650

LAGERQUIST, LYDIA DEANE, religion educator; b. Aberdeen, Md., Aug. 18, 1955; d. Clifford Deane and Lydia Mae (Bjorke) Lagerquist; m. Richard Dean Dunning, May 28, 1988. BA in History, Calif. Luth. Coll., 1976; MA in Ch. History, Luther Theol. Sem., 1980; PhD in History of Christianity, U. Chgo., 1986. Adj. instr. in religion Wittenberg U., 1984; instr. theology Valparaiso (Ind.) U., 1985-86, asst. prof. theology, 1986-88; asst. prof. religion, tutor in paracollege St. Olaf Coll., Northfield, Minn., 1988—; presenter in field. Author: (with others) Twentieth Century Shapers of American Popular Religion, 1989, Serving the Word: Lutheran Women Consider Their Calling, 1988, Encyclopedia Britannica Micropaedia, 16th edit., 1985; author: From Our Mothers' Arms: A History of Women in the American Lutheran Church, 1988; contbr. articles to Luth. Women Today and other religious jours. Mem. adv. b.d Minn. Hist. Soc. Women's History, St. Paul, 1990; participant, mem. adv. bd. Congregational History Project, U. Chgo., 1988-91; bd. dirs. Christian Community Action, Valparaiso, 1986-88; planning com. Women of the Evang. Luth. Ch. Am., Chgo., 1985-87; mem. Commn. for Publ., Luth. Hist. Conf., 1988—; exec. sec., bd. dirs. Luth. Women Caucus, Chgo., 1981-85; mem. women's studies com. St. Olaf Coll, Northfield, 1989-90, community activities com., 1989-91, campus ministry coun., 1989—. Recipient Award of Commendation, Concordia Hist. Inst., 1988. Mem. Am. Acad. Religion, Women Historians of the Midwest, Luth. Hist. Conf. Office: Saint Olaf Coll Northfield MN 55057

LAGHI, PIO CARDINAL, cardinal; b. Province Forli, Italy, May 21, 1922; s. Anthony and Laura (Conti) L. STD, Pontifical Lateran U., Rome, 1947, JCD, 1950. Ordained priest Roman Cath. Ch., 1946. Archbishop, 1969; entered diplomatic svc. Holy See, 1952; sec. Apostolic Nunciature, Nicaragua, 1952-54, India, 1961-64; sec. U.S. Apostolic Delegation, 1954-61; counselor Secretariate of State, Vatican City, Italy, 1964-69; apostolic del. to Jerusalem, 1969; apostolic pro-nuncio Cyprus, 1971; apostolic visitator Greece, 1972; apostolic nuncio Argentina, 1974-80; apostolic del. to U.S. Washington, 1980-84, apostolic pro-nuncio to U.S., 1984-90; permanent observer OAS, 1980-90; prefect Congregation for Cath. Edn., Vatican City, 1990—; elevated to cardinal Roman Cath. Ch., 1991.

LAGRONE, MARK M., education and youth minister; b. Memphis, Aug. 27, 1959; s. Billy Z. and Iris I. (Montgomery) LaG.; m. Janice Chipley, May 21, 1983. BA, Union U., 1982; MA of Religious Edn., Southwest Bapt. Theol., 1982. Summer missionary Germantown Bapt. Ch., Tn., 1980; dir. youth edn. P.T. Grace Presby. Ch., Jackson, Tn., 1981-82; ednl. intern Parkridge Bapt. Ch., Ft. Worth, 1985-86; min. edn., youth 2d Bapt. Ch., Arkadelphia, Ark., 1986—. Mem. organizational com. Christmas Store, Arkadelphia, 1988—, Boy Scout Coun., Arkadelphia, 1988—. Mem. Nat. Assn. Ch. Bus. Adminstrs. Republican. Home: 1214 Ctr St Arkadelphia AR 71923 Office: 2d Bapt Ch 810 S 12th Arkadelphia AR 71923

LAHA, ROBERT RANDALL, JR., minister; b. Elizabethtown, Ky., June 19, 1951; s. Robert Randall and Mary Elmina (Bates) L.; m. Sally Ann Schield, Nov. 4, 1972; children: Robert III, Jennifer Ann, Benjamin Ryan. BS, Milligan Coll., 1972; DMin, Union Theol. Sem., 1980, ThM, 1981. Ordained to ministry Presbyn. Ch., 1982. Assoc. pastor First Presbyn. Ch., Johnson City, Tenn., 1972-76; chaplain Richmond (Va.) Meml. Hosp., 1978-79; assoc. pastor First Presbyn. Ch., Richmond, 1980-89; pastor Campbell Meml. Presbyn. Ch., Weems, Va., 1989-91; sr. pastor Tuckahoe Presbyn. Ch., Richmond, Va., 1991—; instr. Union Theol. Sem., Richmond, 1983—; exec. coun. Presbytery of the James, Richmond, 1987-89, chair com. on ministry, 1987-88, mem. task force on urban ministry, 1985-89, mem. ch. devel., 1989—. Pres. Richmond First Club, 1987-88, bd. dirs. 1985-87; bd. dirs. Richmond Hill, 1985-87; scoutmaster Boy Scouts of Am., Johnson City, Tenn., 1972-76, commr., instr. Mem. Am. Assn. Pastoral Counselors. Democrat. Home: 9501 Oldhouse Dr Richmond VA 23233

LAHURD, CAROL JOAN, religion educator; b. Oak Ridge, Tenn., June 11, 1946; d. Clair Wilson and Marion (Mirfield) Schersten; m. Ryan Arthur LaHurd, Sept. 27, 1969; children: Jeremy, Kristin. BA summa cum laude, Augustana Coll., 1968; MA, U. Chgo., 1969; PhD, U. Pitts., 1987. Dir. parish edn. Holy Trinity Luth. Ch., Greenville, Pa., 1978-81; asst. prof. Coll. St. Thomas, St. Paul, Minn., 1988—. Active Other Faiths Working Group Luth. World Fedn., Adult Edn. Com. Holy Trinity Luth. Ch., Minn. Coun./Chs. Muslim-Christian Dialogue; v.p. Middle East Peace Now; water safety instr. ARC, St. Paul, 1985—. Rsch. Assistance grantee Coll. St. Thomas, 1989. Mem. Am. Acad. Religion, Soc. Bibl. Lit., Cath. Bibl. Assn. Democrat. Office: Coll St Thomas Mail # 4080 2115 Summit Ave Saint Paul MN 55105

LAI, JOHN CHRISTOPHER, minister; b. London, Ont., Can., May 25, 1953; s. Luigi Salvatore Lai and Betty Jean (Arthur) Norwich; m. Sandra Kay Huber, Mar. 14, 1981; 1 child, Christopher John. Cert. of completion, Calvary Pastor's Sch., Santa Ana, Calif., 1978; BA in Behavioral Sci. summa cum laude, Nat. U., San Diego, 1989; postgrad., Fielding Inst., Santa Barbara, Calif., 1990—. Ordained to ministry Calvary Chapel Ch., 1978. Sr. pastor Calvary Chapel, Escondido, Calif., 1978-82, Vineyard Christian Fellowship, San Marcos, Calif., 1982—; adj. instr. Horizon Sch. Evangelism, San Diego, 1979-81; adj. prof. Cathedral Bible Coll., Escondido, 1990. Composer/lyricist songs including All of Me, 1982, I Receive You, 1982; co-composer/lyricist Glorious, 1988. Mem. ASCAP, ASTD, Soc. for Applied Anthropology, Orgn. Devel. Inst., Am. Sociol. Assn., World Future Soc., Am. Mgmt. Assn., O.D. Network (San Diego).

LAI, WHALEN WAI-LUN, religion educator; b. Canton, People's Republic China, July 8, 1944. BA, Internat. Christian U., Tokyo, 1968; postgrad., U. Calif., Berkeley, 1968, Free U., Amsterdam, The Netherlands, 1969; PhD, Harvard U., 1975. Prof. religion U. Calif., Davis, 1977—. Editor: (with Lancaster) Early Ch'an in China and Tibet, 1983; contbr. articles to various jours. Fellow United Bd. Xian Higher Edn., 1964-68, Harvard U., Yenching, Kent fellow, 1969-74. Mem. Soc. for Study Chinese Religions, Harvard Ctr. for Study World Religions. Office: U Calif 922 Sproul Hall Davis CA 95616

LAIDLAW, COLLEEN L., religion educator; b. Elkhart, Ind., Oct. 23, 1948; d. Julian Pleasant and Letha (Jeffries) Gilliam; m. John Robert Laidlaw, June 14, 1969; children: Karen, Bryan, Kristine. Student, Carters Secretarial Sch., 1967-68. Coord. high sch. program, sacrament preparation St. Thomas the Apostle Parish, Elkhart, 1987—. Office: St Thomas Religious Edn 1405 N Main St Elkhart IN 46514

LAINE, JAMES ALAN, pastor; b. Newark, N.J., Feb. 22, 1947; s. Frank F. and Margareta A. (Romane) L.; children: Mauri A., Andrew M. BA, Grove City Coll., 1970; MDiv, Pitts. Theol. Sem., 1973; ThD, Internat. Sem., Orlando, Fla., 1981, postgrad.; PhD, Emmanuel Bapt. U., Shelby, N.C., 1990. Ordained to ministry, 1973; lic. pastoral counselor, temperament therapist. Pastor Morningside Presbyn. Ch., Pitts., 1970-71, Hebron United Presbyn. ch., Penn Hills, Pa., 1971-73, 1st Presbyn. Ch., Castle Shannon, Pa., 1973-77, Faith Community Ch., Bethel Park, Pa., 1977-88; organizer Morningside Area Community Council, Pitts., 1971-73; pastor. Desert Rock

Community Ch., Phoenix, 1989—; chaplain Penn Hills (Pa.) Police Dept., 1973-74; bd. dirs. Tri-Again Homes, 1975-76, WPCB-TV and WKBS-TV, Wall, Pa., 1987-89. Author: Biblical View of Demonology, 1981, Weapons of Our Warfare, 1983, Kingdom Living, 1987; co-author: Seduction? A Biblical Response, 1986. Posse mem. Mericopa County (Ariz.) Sheriff's Dept., 1990—. Mem. Nat. Christian Counselors Assn. (area rep.), Christian Assn. for Psychological Studies. Home: 4240 E Amberwood Dr Phoenix AZ 85044 Office: Desert Rock Community Ch 10827 S 51st St # 103 Phoenix AZ 85044

LAIR, ROBERT ED, JR., military officer; b. Anna, Tex., May 2, 1939; m. Judith Trevvett, Sept. 15, 1962; children: Marlene, Karen, Greg. BS in Edn., U. North Tex., 1960; BD, Southwestern Bapt. Theol. Sem., 1966, MDiv, 1973; BA, SUNY, 1976; D of Ministry, Emory U., 1977. Marine infantry officer 2d marine div. USMC, 1962-64, battalion staff officer, 1964, artillery officer, transp. officer 4th marine div., 1964-70; commd. USAR, advanced through grades to col., 1988, chaplain 108th div., 1970-85; budget officer, res. advisor to chief of chaplains U.S. Army, Washington, 1985—; adj. faculty U.S. Army Command and Gen. Staff Coll.; adj. faculty and part-time instr. several colls. and univs. in biblical studies, psychology, sociology and pub. speaking. Contbr. articles to profl. jours. Pastoral appointee for over 20 yrs. Western N.C. Ann. Conf. United Meth. Ch. Decorated Army Res. Components Achievement medal with two oak leaf clusters, Armed Forces Res. medal with Hourglass, Army Achievement medal wth oak leaf cluster, Nat. Def. Svc. medal with bronze svc. star, Armed Forces Expeditionary medal, Meritorious Svc. medal, Army Commendation medal, Army Gen. Staff badge; Merrill fellow Harvard U., 1974. Fellow Acad. Parish Clergy, Inc. (editor-in-chief Sharing the Practice jour., cert. 1982); Internat. Acad. Behavioral Medicine, Counseling and Psychotherapy (diplomate). Home: 5901 Mount Eagle Dr # 514 Alexandria VA 22303 Office: Hdqrs Dept of Army Office Chief of Chaplains (DACH-RA) Washington DC 20310-2700

LAIRD, DONALD RAY, minister; b. New Orleans, Oct. 29, 1950; s. Donald G. and Dorothy B. (Harris) L.; m. Paula J. Woods, Dec. 29, 1972; children: Tonya, Tamra. BS, Southwestern Assembly of God, 1973. Ordained to ministry Assemblies of God, 1977. Assoc. pastor First Assembly of God, Wichita Falls, Tex., 1973-78, Christian Ctr., Hobbs, N.Mex., 1978-82, Abundant Life Assembly of God, Lubbock, Tex., 1982-84; sr. pastor Andrews (Tex.) 1st Assembly of God, 1984-91, Caldwell (Tex.) 1st Assembly of God, 1991—; west plains sectional youth rep. Assembly of God, Lubbock, 1983-84. Charter pres. Optimist Club, Hobbs, 1980. Named Most Outstanding Pastor West Tex. Assemblies of God, West Tex. Dist., 1986-87, 90, Most Appreciated Pastor West Tex. Youth Dept., 1989-90. Office: 1st Assembly of God PO Box 744 Caldwell TX 77836

LAJARA, CECILIO NICOLAS, clergyman; b. Lares, P.R., Apr. 22, 1942; s. Eduardo Lajara and Camelia Rodriguez; m. Carmen Sanchez Lugo, Aug. 10, 1963; children: Iris, Mariselle, Juan Cecilio. BA, U. P.R., 1966; MDiv, Columbia Theol. Sem., Decatur, Ga., 1969; ThM, Columbia Theol. Sem., 1971; D Ministry, Luther Rice Sem., 1981. Ordained to ministry Presbyn. Ch. in Am., 1969. Pastor Atlanta Presbytery, 1969-74; missionary Mission to the World, Mex. and Guatemala, 1974-79; missionary to Latin Am. Mission to the World/Logoi, Miami, Fla., 1979-81; Latin Am. v.p. Evangelism Explosion Internat., Ft. Lauderdale, Fla., 1981-86; sr. v.p., internat. dir. Evangelism Explosion Internat., Ft. Lauderdale, 1986-88; internat. dir. Sola Fide Ministry, Decatur, Ga., 1989—; dir., organizer Sch. Theology, Mariano Guatemala U., Guatemala City, 1976-79, adviser to rector, 1977-79; mem. Guatemala Commn. on Higher Edn., 1978-79. Author: Community Action: A Christian Approach, 1972, Un Pueblo Con Mentalidad Teologica, 1975; translator: Mensaje desde la Cruz, 1974. Mem. North Ga. Presbytery. Republican. Avocations: fishing, reading, jogging, photography. Office: Presbyn Evangelist Fellow 42111 Flatshoals Rd Decatur GA 30031

LAKERS, ANNA MARIE, youth ministry director; b. Council Bluffs, Iowa, Aug. 5, 1961; d. Joseph Raymond and Ruth Eileen (Fettes) L. BA in Parish Ministry, Loras Coll., 1988. Liturgy commn. coord. St. Pius X Ch., Des Moines, 1983-85, Loras Coll., Dubuque, Iowa, 1987-88; dir. of youth ministry St. Mary Cath. Ch., Sterling, Ill., 1988-91, St. Walter Cath. Ch., Roselle, Ill., 1991—; asst. lay dir. St. Mary-Oregon (Ill.) Teens Encounter Christ Program, 1991, adult team mem., 1989—; rally asst. Diocese of Rockford, Ill., 1990—. Canvasser Whiteside County Dems., Sterling, 1990; singer Sterling Civic Choral; flutist Sterling Mcpl. Band, 1989-91. Fellow Nat. Fedn. Cath. Youth Ministry. Home: 260 Spring Hill Dr #302 Roselle IL 60172 Office: St Walter Parish 130 W Pine St Roselle IL 60172

LAKEY, OTHAL H., bishop. Bishop Christian Meth. Episcopal Ch., Cin. Office: Christian Meth Episcopal Ch 6322 Elwynne Dr Cincinnati OH 45236*

LAKRITZ, ISAAC, fundraising organization administrator; b. Milw., June 11, 1952; s. Jeffrey and Deborah (Margolis) L.; m. Lea Wininger, May 22, 1982; children: Eli, Jacob. BA, U. Wis., Milw., 1973, MA, 1974. Cert. secondary sch. tchr. Coordinator Jewish Student Services Hillel, Milw., 1972-74; analyst Israel Ministry Social Welfare, Jerusalem, 1975-76; exec. dir. Jewish Nat. Fund Wis., Milw., 1977; devel. dir. Milw. Jewish Home, 1977-78; asst. dir. N.Y. Assn. for New Americans, N.Y.C., 1978-81; nat. youth dir. Zionist Orgn. Am., N.Y.C., 1981-84; asst. dir. Jacksonville (Fla.) Jewish Fedn., 1984-87, exec. v.p., 1987-90; exec. dir. east cen. region Am. Soc. for Technion, Detroit, 1990—. Chmn. Israel Com. Conf. Jewish Communal Service, 1982—. Recipient Top Pub. Rels. award in N.Am. Coun. Jewish Fedn. Mem. Assn. Jewish Community Orgn. Personnel, Phi Kappa Phi. Avocations: opera, stamps. Office: Am Technion Soc 29645 W Fourteen Mile Rd Farmington Hills MI 48334 *Our task is to build a more just and compassionate world. With mankind's considerable technical expertise, we have shown that we can accomplish just about anything we really desire. Let us create an environment where that which is right and kind is desirable.*

LALLANCE, LEROY ODOM, music minister; b. Lakeland, Fla., June 7, 1954; s. Eugene Holtz Lallance and Rose (Barnes) Pace; m. Deborah Ann Carroll, Oct. 24, 1981. B of Music Edn., Fla. State U., 1980; MusM, Columbus Coll., 1983; postgrad., U. South Fla., 1990—. Ordained to ministry United Meth. Ch. as deacon, 1989. Assoc. min. of music First Bapt. Ch., Columbus, Ga., 1982-83; organist, assoc. min. music Bayshore Bapt. Ch., Tampa, Fla., 1983-84; diaconal min. music First United Meth., Ocala, Fla., 1984-89, Lake Magdalene United Meth. Ch., Tampa, 1989—; adjudicator Fla. Vocal Assn., 1974—; choral clinician, profl. concert artist throughout U.S. and Europe, 1974—. Mem. Am. Choral Dirs. Assn., Fla. Vocal Assn., Music Educators Nat. Conf. Home: PO Box 273601 Tampa FL 33688-3601 Office: Lake Magdalene United Meth 2902 Fletcher Ave W Tampa FL 33618

LAM, NORA, minister; b. Beijing, Sept. 4, 1932; d. H.T. and Evelyn Tak-Bun (Yip) Sung; m. S.K. Sung, Jan. 7, 1972; children: Paul, Ruth, Joseph, Gloria, Florence. LLB, Soochow U., 1953; DD (hon.), Melodyland Sch. Theology, 1982. Prof. law and history Soochow U., Shanghai, 1951-58; with dept. social welfare Hong Kong, 1959-61; with Bank of Las Vegas, Nev., 1967-68; evangelist, 1971—; founder Nora Lam Chinese Ministries Internat., 1974—, Asia Hope, 1982; evangelist, crusader TV and radio programs. Author: For Those Tears, 1973, China Cry, 1980, Bullet-Proof Believer, 1988, God's Never Too Late, 1988, Asians for Bush, 1988, China Cry (movie edit.), 1990. Recipient award Korean Assn. Social Work, 1977, Key to City Kaohsiung, Taiwan, 1977, Philanthropic award Sung Ro Won Babies Home Orphange, 1978, medal Pacific Cultural Found., 1978, award Overseas Chinese Affair's Commn., 1979, Key to City Oklahoma City, 1981, Internat. award Nat. Religious Broadcasters Assn., 1989, Key to City Shelby, N.C., 1990. Mem. Christian Legal Soc. Republican. Office: PO Box 24466 San Jose CA 95154

LAMAR, WILLIAM FRED, chaplain, educator; b. Birmingham, Ala., Jan. 4, 1934; s. William Fred Sr. and Everette (Kelley) L.; m. Roberta Anton, Sept. 17, 1955 (dec.); 1 child, Jonathan Frederick; m. Martha Anne Lee, June 7, 1986. BA, U. Ala., 1954; BD, Vanderbilt U., 1957; PhD, St. Louis U., 1972; D Min., Eden Theol. Sem., 1974. Minister United Meth. Ch., Bynum, Ala., 1959-61, Fultondale, Ala., 1961-65; campus minister U. Mo., Rolla, 1965-74; chaplain, prof., dir. overseas missions DePauw U., Greencastle, Ind., 1974—; ednl. cons. electric utilities, 1974—; advisor overseas vol. program UMC Ind., Indpls., 1980—. Author: (book) Role of the College Chaplain at the Church-Related College, 1984; designer electric utility computer programs, 1979-85. Vice chmn. County Welfare Bd., Rolla; bd. dirs. Sr. Vol. Program Action, Greencastle, 1977-80. Served to 1st lt. U.S. Army, 1957-59. Recipient Award of Honor, Ind. Gov's. Voluntary Action, 1976, Cross of Jerusalem, Episcopal Diocese of Guatemala, 1979; Danforth fellow, 1971-72. Mem. Nat. Campus Ministry Assn. (chmn. sci. and ethics network), Nat. Assn. Coll. Chaplains, Assn. Religion in Intellectual Life. Home and Office: 103 DePauw Ave Greencastle IN 46135

LAMASTER, FRANKLIN THOMAS, minister; b. Louisville, Jan. 30, 1955; s. Benjamin Turner and Shirley Lee (Suhr) LaM.; m. Cynthia Louise Treadwell, Dec. 28, 1977; children: Rebecca Turner, Ashley Treadwell, Erin Elizabeth Travis. BS in Sociology with honors, U. Louisville, 1979; MDiv in Religious Edn., So. Bapt. Theol. Sem., Louisville, 1982. Ordained to ministry So. Bapt. Conv. Min. edn. and youth Fredericksburg (Va.) Bapt. Ch., 1983-85; min. youth Temple Bapt. Ch., Newport News, Va., 1985-87; min. edn. Immanuel Bapt. Ch., Greenville, N.C., 1987—; youth cons. Bapt. Sunday Sch. Bd., Nashville, 1985, N.C. Bapt. State Conv., Cary, 1987; worship leader Va. Bapt. Religious Edn. Assn., 1986; youth ASSISTeam leader South Roanoke Bapt. Assn., Greenville, 1990. Vice chmn. Habitat for Humanity Greenville-Pitt County, 1990. Mem. So. Bapt. Alliance, N.C. Bapt. Religious Edn. Assn., Ea. Bapt. Religious Edn. Assn. Office: Immanuel Bapt Ch 1101 S Elm St Greenville NC 27858

LAMB, CHARLES F., minister; b. Maryville, Tenn., Dec. 18, 1934; s. C. Fred and Sadie Ellen (Tedder) L.; children: Elizabeth Susan, Linda Louise, Jennifer Janet; m. Betty Jane Zimmerman, Dec. 29, 1979. BA, Maryville Coll., 1956; MDiv, Grad. Sem. of Phillips U., 1961; D in Ministry, N.Y. Theol. Sem., 1990. Ordained to ministry Christian Ch., 1961. Pastor East Aurora Christian Ch., N.Y., 1961-71; assoc. regional min. Christian Ch., Disciples of Christ, Northeastern Region, Buffalo, N.Y., 1971-75; regional min. Christian Ch., Disciples of Christ, Northeastern Region, Buffalo, 1975—; mem. orgns. clergy and coun. of chs. Trustee Village of East Aurora, 1968-73; active environ. groups Conf. Mayors and Village Ofcls. N.Y., 1968-73. Mem. Conf. Regional Ministers and Moderators, Kiwanis. Democrat. Home: 1272 Delaware Ave Buffalo NY 14209

LAMB, MICHAEL K., pastor; b. Gassaway, W.Va., Nov. 28, 1958; s. Kenton Eugene and Edna Lavaun (Carte) L.; m. Diane Lynn Thomas, Dec. 27, 1980; children: Brittany, Ryan, Andrew. BS, Hyles Anderson Coll., 1982, MEd, 1984. Lic. to ministry, 1977; ordained to ministry Ind. Bapt. Ch., 1984. Asst. pastor Mt. Pisgah Bapt. Ch., Oliver Springs, Tenn., 1984-87; pastor Landmark Bapt. Ch., Parkersburg, W.Va., 1987—; bd. dirs. Mt. Salem Camp Grounds, West Union, W.Va., 1988—, Randy Taylor Revivals, Dallas, 1988—. Republican. Office: Landmark Bapt Ch 310 8th Ave Parkersburg WV 26101

LAMB, ROBERT LEE, religion educator; b. Nevada, Mo., Aug. 18, 1930; s. Lifus E. and Miriam (McConnell) Lamb; m. Rhealene Bryant, Aug. 5, 1961; children: Robert Earl, Mary Rebecca, Miriam Elizabeth. BA, Stephen F. Austin State U., 1951; postgrad., Westminster Choir Coll., 1951-52; MRE, Southwestern Bapt. Sem., 1955, 83, EdD, 1974. Ordained to the gospel ministry, 1966. Min. of music and religious edn. First Bapt. Ch., Richardson, Tex., 1953-54; dir. Christian edn., civilian Vogelweh Army Chapel, Kaiserslautern, Germany, 1954-56; prof. of religious edn. and religion Gardner-Webb Coll., Boiling Springs, N.C., 1962-76, 79—; chair, dept. religious studies and philosophy Gardner-Webb Coll., Boiling Springs, 1988-91; assoc. dir., home study sem. extension dept. So. Bapt. Sems., Nashville, Tenn., 1977-79; chair, bd. dirs. Christian Svc. Orgn., 1990-91; chair, pastoral ministries com. Kings Mountain Bapt. Assn., Shelby, N.C., 1990. Mem. Am. Acad. Religion, Soc. Bibl. Lit., Nat. Assn. Bapt. Profs. Religion, N.C. Bapt. Religious Edn. Assn. (chair crisis support group 1990—, past pres., v.p.), So. Bapt. Religious Edn. Assn. (v.p. 1990-91), Bapt. State Conv. of N.C. (chair min. support adv. com. 1990—), Lions Club (Boiling Springs, pres. 1984). Home: 122 Clinton St Boiling Springs NC 28017 Office: Gardner-Webb Coll Boiling Springs NC 28017

LAMB, TERA A., minister; b. St. Cloud, Minn., Aug. 27, 1943; d. Lloyd Clinton and Olga Ann (Pollock) Mallough; m. Sherman T. Lamb, Aug. 2, 1962 (div. 1975); 1 child, Shane Patrick. BA, U. Humanistic Studies, 1984. Staff cons. Infinite Winds Counseling Ctr., Encinitas, Calif., 1982—; staff minister Gateway Community Ch., Cardiff, Calif., 1986—, also bd. dirs. Mem. Assn. of TransPersonal Psychology. Avocations: hiking, dogs, painting. Office: 1667 San Elijo Ave Cardiff-by-the-Sea CA 92007

LAMBERT, JERRY D., academic administrator. Pres. Nazarene Bible Coll., Colorado Springs, Colo. Office: Nazarene Bible Coll Office of Pres 1111 Chapman Dr PO Box 15749 Colorado Springs CO 80935*

LAMBERT, JOHN PAUL, minister, evangelist; b. Chautauqua, Kans., Feb. 12, 1906; s. Homer George and May Lambert; m. Emily Ruth Kite, Apr. 3, 1925 (dec. Dec. 1980); children: John Patrick (dec.), Joan Lambert Quinlan, Judy May Lambert Adrain. Student, Calvary Bible Coll., Kansas City, Mo., 1935-37; DD, Fundamental Christian Coll., Kansas City, Mo., 1953. Ordained to ministry So. Bapt. Conv., 1937. Pastor So. Bapt. Ch., Bonner Springs, Mo., 1934-42; evangelist Bapt. Bible Fellowship, various cities, 1942-69; pastor Bible Bapt. Ch., Hutchinson, Kans., 1969-75; pastor, evangelist Bapt. chs., various cities, 1975-85; pastor Riverside Bapt. Ch., Hutchinson, 1985-91; pres., founder Am. Acad. Christian Counselors, 1975-91. Author: Mystery of the Ages, 1950, Indwelling Christ, 1969. Chaplain Hutchinson Police Dept, Reno County Sheriff's Dept., 1969-75. Recipient 50 Yrs. in Ministry award Bible Bapt. Fellowship Tribune, 1984, Christian Statesman award Westside Bapt. Ch., 1984, 50 Yrs. in Ministry Bible Bapt. Ch., 1984. Home: 316 W 11th St Hutchinson KS 67501 Office: Riverside Bapt Ch PO Box 2171 Hutchinson KS 67504-2171 *Why did God create the human race? I believe humanity was created for heaven. Each member of the race is offered a pardon from hell. If only the world would listen. P.S.—Persons were created to replace the angels who followed Lucifer, a false god in ruins.*

LAMBERT, LLOYD LAVERNE, minister; b. Agusta, Ill., June 5, 1925; s. Charles N. Sr. and Lena (Johnson) L.; m. Dorothy Mae Spaar, June 22, 1946; children: Rebecca, Toby, Michael, Carey. Student, Millikin U., Anderson (Ind.) Coll. Ordained to ministry Ch. of God (Anderson, Ind.), 1955. Founder, exec. dir. The Christian Ctr., Anderson, 1956—; chaplain Madison County Detention Ctr. Bd. dirs. Habitat for Humanity, Anderson, Recovery in Christ; past chmn. Nursing Home Ministries; past pres. Madison County Svcs. Coun.; past dep. sheriff Madison County Sheriff's Dept.; mem. adv. bd. for drug abuse St. John's Hosp.; chmn. Human Rels. Commn., City of Anderson, 1981-84; founder Home for Alcoholics, Anderson. With F.A., U.S. Army, 1943-46; PTO. Recipient spl. recognition Exchange Club Anderson, 1971, recognition Ind. Dept. Corrections, 1972, Liberty Bell award ABA, 1973, Outstanding Citizenship award Ind. Elks, 1973-74, Svc. to Mankind award Sertoma Club, 1980, Chief Anderson award, 1986, Elmo A. Funk Ideal of Svc. award, 1990. Mem. Anderson Ministerial Assn., Internat. Union Gospel Missions (past pres., sec.-treas. midwestern dist.), Rotary (past sargeant-at-arms and sec., pres. Anderson club 1975-76, Community Image award 1973, 80, Internat. Paul Harris fellow 1983). Home: 6914 Jackson St Anderson IN 46013 Office: The Christian Ctr 625 Main St PO Box 743 Anderson IN 46015

LAMBERT, PHILLIP J., minister; b. Chgo., Nov. 18, 1940; s. William Lee and Laney Arlia (Malone) L. Student, Gordon Coll., Mass., 1972-76. Ordained to ministry, Bapt. Ch. 1974. Assoc. minister Zion Bapt. Ch., Milw., 1971-72; asst. minister Ebenezer Bapt. Ch., Boston, 1973-76; asst. pastor Greater Mt. Hope Bapt. Ch., Chgo., 1976-78; asst. minister Met. Bapt. Ch., Chgo., 1978-84; assoc. minister Olivet Bapt. Ch., Chgo., 1984—; pub. aid income maint. specialist I, Ill. Dept. Pub. Aid, Chgo., 1978; Sun. sch. tchr. Olivet Bapt. Ch., 1990—, bible instr., 1989—; assoc chaplain Resthaven Nursing Home, Roxbury, Mass., 1973-76. Author: Black Theology, 1974. Vis. participant Norfolk Prison Fellowship, 1973-76. With U.S. Army, 1959-62. Recipient Disting. Life Time Citation in religious pub. svc., Cultural Citizens Found. for Performing Arts, 1990. Fellow Ministers Conf. Chgo. Vicinity, Chgo. Coun. Fgn. Rels.; mem. Masons. Home: 4701 N Beacon St Chicago IL 60640 Office: Olivet Bapt Ch 3101 S King Dr Chicago IL 60616

LAMBERT, ROBERT DANIEL, minister; b. Elkins, W.Va., Aug. 4, 1952; s. Fred Stanley and Ethel Virginia (Kisamore) L.; m. Jeann Ann Wolff, July 14, 1973; children: Tonya Dawn, Tamara Marie. Student, Zion Bible Inst., East Providence, R.I., 1970-72; Diploma, Free Gospel Bible Inst., Export, Pa., 1973. Pastor Ch. of God, Apollo, Pa., 1979, Leechburg, Pa., 1979-81; children ch. pastor First Assembly of God, Goshen, Ind., 1982-86; pastor Living Waters Tabernacle, Bristol, Ind., 1986—; pres. Cathedral of Faith Ministries, Leechburg, 1980-82; bd. dirs. Youngstown (Ohio) Rescue Mission. Composer gospel songs. Home: 415 S Wheatland Dr Goshen IN 46526-1656 Office: Living Waters Tabernacle East SR 120 16746 Bristol IN 46507

LAMBERTSON, MILTON DAVID, minister; b. Dry Creek, Mo., Dec. 26, 1940; s. Roy Franklin and Mary Irene (Terry) L.; m. Joyce Elizabeth Fillmore, June 2, 1961; children: Daniel Mark, Kimberly Lynn Lambertson Wandel. BA in Religious Edn., Trinity Coll. of Fla., Clearwater, 1964. Ordained to ministry Christian and Missionary Alliance, 1973. Tchr. Bible and history Macon (Ga.) Christian Acad., 1969-71; pastor Christian and Missionary Alliance chs., Fla., Ga., 1965-75; sr. pastor Bapt. chs., Can., 1975-82, Harmony Grove Community Ch., Dover, Pa., 1982-85, Dover Bible Ch., 1985—; pres. Jeff Davis County Evang. Ministerial Assn., Hazelhurst, Ga., 1968, Grand Manan (Can.) Evang. Ministerial, 1977; bd. dirs. Am. Tech. Outreach Ministeries, Inc., Hanover, Pa., 1990—; substitute tchr. Jeff Davis High Sch., Hazelhurst, 1966-69; chaplain prayer club Warner Robins High Sch., 1972-73; missionary trip to Africa, 1988, to India, 1990. Republican. Office: Dover Bible Ch 5005 Carlisle Rd Dover PA 17315

LAMB-HART, PAMELA NYLE, minister; b. Marion, Ohio, June 15, 1961; d. Richard Lee and Shirley Lee (Burton) Lamb; m. Gary Lee Lamb-Hart, Aug. 12, 1989. BA in Edn., Marshall U., 1983; MDiv, Meth. Theol. Sch., Delaware, Ohio, 1988. Ordained to ministry Meth. Ch. Dir. Christian edn. 1st United Meth. Ch., Huntington, W.Va., 1983-84; youth min. Maize Manor United Meth. Ch., Columbus, Ohio, 1984-86; pastor Peachblow United Meth. Ch., Delaware, 1985-88; lay min. to youth-young adults Epworth United Meth. Ch., Marion, 1988—; staff rep. Edn. Com., Marion, 1989—, Missions Beyond Marion Com., 1991—; Sunday sch. tchr., Marion, 1990—; dist. rep. Conf. Human Sexuality Com., Marion. Organizer Juvenile Detention Ctr. Com., Marion, 1990, Peace Rally for community, Marion, 1991. Mem. Susanna Wesley Circle. Republican. Office: Epworth United Meth Ch 249 E Center St Marion OH 43302

LAMBRO, EDWARD, priest, psychotherapist; b. N.Y.C.; s. George and Ann (Del Percio) L. BA, Immaculate Conception Coll., 1970; MDiv, St. Mary's U., 1974; MA, Seton Hall, 1988; PhD, Calif. Coast U., 1991. Ordained priest Roman Cath. Ch. Tchr., counselor De Paul High Sch., Wayne, N.J., 1974-77; chaplain, counselor Neumann Prep Sch., Wayne, N.J., 1977-81; pastor St. Casimir Ch., Paterson, N.J., 1981; pub. rels. dir., pres. Glennellyn Communications, Wayne, N.J., 1981—; psychotherapist Haelan Assocs., Wayne, N.J., 1986—, Chatham (N.J.) Psychiatric Group, 1988—; pub. rels. officer, dir. Eva's Shelter and Rehab. Programs, Paterson, 1989—; v.p. Richard J. Prodns., Inc., Wayne, 1977—; chmn. pastoral care Chilton Meml. Hosp., Pompton Plains, 1990—. Writer, dir.: (film) Cymbalist Search Saga, 1982 (Silver award 1982), (radio) The Lentan Series, 1984 (Gold Mic award 1984). Capt. USAF, 1987—. Mem. APA, UNICO Internat., Cath. Actors Guild. Avocations: photography, music. Home and Office: Box 3537 Wayne NJ 07474-3537

LAMM, NORMAN, university president, rabbi; b. Bklyn., Dec. 19, 1927; s. Samuel and Pearl (Baumol) L.; m. Mindella Mehler, Feb. 23, 1954; children: Chaye Lamm Warburg, Joshua B., Shalom E., Sara Rebecca Lamm Dratch. B.A. summa cum laude, Yeshiva Coll., 1949; Ph.D., Bernard Revel Grad. Sch., 1966; Dr. of Hebrew Letters (hon.), Hebrew Theol. Coll., 1977. Ordained rabbi, 1951; asst. rabbi Congregation Kehilath Jeshurun, N.Y.C., 1952-53; rabbi Congregation Kodimoh, Springfield, Mass., 1954-58, Jewish Center, N.Y.C., 1958-76; Erna and Jakob Michael prof. Jewish philosophy Yeshiva U., N.Y.C., 1966—; pres. Yeshiva U., 1976—, Rabbi Isaac Elchanan Theol. Sem., N.Y.C., 1976—; vis. prof. Judaic studies Bklyn. Coll., 1974-75; dir. Union Orthodox Jewish Congregations Am. Author: A Hedge of Roses, 1966, The Royal Reach, 1970, Faith and Doubt, 1971, Torah Lishmah, 1972 (rev. English edition 1989), The Good Society, 1974; editor: Library of Jewish Law and Ethics, 1975—; co-editor: The Leo Jung Jubilee Volume, 1962, A Treasury of Tradition, 1967, The Joseph B. Soloveitchik Jubilee Vol., 1984, Halakhot ve'Halikhot (Heb.): Essays on Jewish Law, 1990, Torah Umadda: The Encounter of Religious Learning and Worldly Knowledge in the Jewish Tradition, 1990. Trustee-at-large Fedn. Jewish Philanthropies, N.Y.; mem. exec. com. Assn. for a Better N.Y.; bd. dirs. Am. Friends-Alliance Israelite Universelle; mem. Pres.'s Commn. on the Holocaust, 1978-89; chmn. N.Y. Conf. on Soviet Jewry, 1970; mem. Halakhah Commn., Rabbinical Council Am. Recipient Abramowitz Zeitlin award, 1972. Mem. Assn. Orthodox Jewish Scientists (charter; bd. govs.). Office: Yeshiva U Office of Pres 500 W 185th St New York NY 10033 also: Rabbi Isaac Eichanan Theol Sem 2540 Amsterdam Ave New York NY 10033

LAMMERS, ANN CONRAD, counselor, ethics educator; b. Bryn Mawr, Pa., June 23, 1945; d. Howard Melvin Jr. Lammers and Louise Carey (Martien) Kelsey; m. Antone Gerhardt Singsen III, June 12, 1965 (div. Apr. 1977); children: Ann Hope Singsen, Molly McKee Singsen. Student, Brown U., 1963-65; BA, Barnard Coll., 1967; MDiv, Gen. Theol. Sem., N.Y.C., 1982; PhD, Yale U., 1987. German tchr. Valhalla (N.Y.) High Sch., 1967-69; textbook editor Harcourt Brace Jovanovich Inc., N.Y.C., 1974-79; counselor Episcopal Social Svc., Inc., Bridgeport, Conn., 1983-86; asst. prof. theology and ethics Church Divinity Sch. of the Pacific, Berkeley, Calif., 1986-90; teaching fellow Yale Divinity Sch., New Haven, 1983-86; vis. asst. prof. Christian ethics Santa Clara (Calif.), 1990-91. Editor: (textbook series) Unsere Freunde, Die Welt der Jugend, Civitas, 1986; translator: Rabbit Island, 1978. Grad. fellow Episcopal Ch. Found., N.Y.C., 1983, 84, 85, Yale U., 1982-86. Mem. Phi Beta Kappa. Democrat. Episcopalian. Avocations: swimming, hiking, writing poetry, singing. Home: 720 Evelyn Ave Albany CA 94706

LAMOIS, LOYD, religious education director. Dir. Cath. edn. Diocese of Arlington, Va. Office: Cath Edn 200 N Glebe Rd Ste 703 Arlington VA 22203*

LAMONT, JACK T., minister; b. Phila., June 1, 1957; s. Edward G. and Cecelia M. (Old) Lamont; m. Beverly J. Snead, Sept. 2, 1978; children: Jaime, Jake, Janelle. BS, Phila. Coll. Bible, 1990. Ordained to ministry, Regular Bapt. Ch., 1990. Assoc. pastor Bible Covenant Bapt. Ch., Media, Pa., 1990—; comdr. Awana Youth Ministry, Media, Pa., 1990—. Home: 542 S New Middletown Rd Media PA 19063 Office: Bible Covenant Bapt Ch 542 S New Middletown Rd Media PA 19065

LAMORE, GEORGE EDWARD, JR., clergyman, religion and philosophy educator; b. North Adams, Mass., June 17, 1930; s. George Edward and Victoria Mary (Bird) LaM.; m. Jane Esther Blackburn, June 27, 1953; children—Christian John, Wesley Paul. B.A., Williams Coll., 1953; M.Div. magna cum laude, Boston U., 1956, Th.D., 1959; honors citation, Iowa Wesleyan Coll., 1965. Ordained to ministry Methodist Ch., 1956; pastor Meth. Ch., Adams, Mass., 1951-58; dir. religious life, prof. religion and philosophy Iowa Wesleyan Coll., Mt. Pleasant, 1959-69; head dept. religion and philosophy Iowa Wesleyan Coll., 1969—, chmn. div. humanities, 1970—, chmn. div. human studies, 1983—; lectr. varied topics. Violinist, S.E. Iowa Symphony Orch., 1959—; Contbr. articles to profl. jours. and anthologies. Chmn. edn. com. Midwest Old Threshers Reunion, 1970—; founder, dir. The Minister and Mental Health. Roswell R. Robinson fellow Boston U., 1956-57. Mem. Am. Acad. Religion, Am. Philos. Assn. Home: 307 W Pearl St Mount Pleasant IA 52641 *The basic mandates of life to me are not ten but two in number-Relate and Grow! By relating to others and the world at large I outgrow myself-and that is the most basic urge within me.*

LANCASTER, JAMES WAYNE, JR., minister; b. Kalamazoo, Apr. 6, 1959; s. James Wayne Sr. and Irma (Sanabia) L.; m. Barbara Ann Fischer, Aug. 4, 1984; children: James Wayne III, Philip Andrew, Stephen Paul. BA magna cum laude, Trinity Coll., Dunedin, Fla., 1983; MDiv, New Orleans Bapt. Theol. Sem., 1986. Ordained to ministry So. Bapt. Conv., 1987. Assoc. evangelist His Glory Inc., Inverness, Fla., 1976-86, v.p., 1984—; pastor Forest Grove Bapt. Ch., Alachua, Fla., 1986-89, Blake Meml. Bapt. Ch., Lake Helen, Fla., 1989—. Author: Seven Guides to Biblical Understanding, 1988. Mem. Seminole Bapt. Assn. (track dir. Royal Ambs. 1990—). Republican. Home: 363 Baker Ave Lake Helen FL 32744

LANCASTER, MARK ALAN, minister; b. Cumberland, Md., Jan. 16, 1953; s. Melvin Eugene and Valarie Edna (Turner) L.; m. Marianne Kay Sickles, Nov. 21, 1981; 1 child, Joel Sickles. BS, Frostburg (Md.) State U., 1975; MDiv, Wesley Sem., Washington, 1983. Ordained to ministry United Meth. Ch., deacon, 1981, elder, 1985. Univ. chaplain The Am. U., Washington, 197983; pastor Aldergate United Meth. Ch., Balt., 1983-84, Westminster (Md.) United Meth. Ch., 1984-86, Emory United Meth. Ch., Upperco, Md., 1986—; regional mgr. Md. Food Com., Balt., 1991—; bd. dirs., vice-chmn. Interfaith Housing Devel. Corp., Williamsport, Md., 1990—; nat. bd. dirs. Heifer Project Internat., Little Rock, 1991—; bd. chmn. N.E. Social Action Prog., Hampstead, Md., 1988-90. Recipient Outstanding Svc. award on behalf of homeless Md. Gov.'s Task Force on Homelessness, 1989. Democrat. Home: 1035 Washington Rd Westminster MD 21157 Office: Md Food Com 204 E 25th St Baltimore MD 21218 *Human beings, no matter what their external differences, are so much more alike than they are different. The more vulnerable we allow ourselves to be with one another, the more we know this is true.*

LAND, RICHARD DALE, minister, religious organization administrator; b. Houston, Nov. 6, 1946; s. Leggette Sloan and Marilee (Welch) L.; m. Rebekah Ruth Van Hooser, May 29, 1971; children: Jennifer, Richard Jr., Rachel. BA, Princeton U., 1969; ThM, New Orleans Bapt. Theol. Sem., 1972; D.Phil., U. Oxford, Eng., 1980. Ordained to ministry So. Bapt. Conv. Pastor S. Oxford Bapt. Ch., Oxford, Eng., 1972-75; prof. theology and ch. history Criswell Coll., Dallas, 1975-76, acad. dean, 1976-80, v.p. for acad. affairs, 1980-88; exec. dir. Christian Life Commn. So. Bapt. Conv., Nashville, 1988—; mem. exec. com. Nat. Coalition against Pornography, Cin., 1989—; bd. dirs. Bapt. Joint Com. Pub. Affairs, Washington, 1987-90, Nat. Pro-Life Religious Coun., Washington. Cons. editor Criswell Study Bible, 1979. Mem. Gov.'s Task Force on Welfare Reform, Austin, Tex., 1988, Pres.'s Campaign for a Drug-Free Soc., Washington, 1991—; bd. drs. Nat. Law Ctr., Arlington, Va., 1991—. Mem. Nat. Assn. Evangs. (Wheaton, Ill., bd. dirs. 1991—), Conf. on Faith and History, Evang. Theol. Soc., So. Bapt. Hist. Soc., Rotary. Office: Christian Life Commn 901 Commerce Ste 550 Nashville TN 37202

LAND, STEVEN JACK, minister, theology educator; b. Jasper, Ala., Sept. 23, 1946; s. Dewey Jackson and Mary Lovinia (Anderson) L.; m. Peggy Goude, Dec. 25, 1969; children: Alanna, Laura, Jonathan. BA, Birmingham So. Coll., 1968; MDiv, Emory U., 1972, PhD in Theology, 1991. Ordained to ministry Ch. of God (Cleveland, Tenn.). Pastor Midtown Mission Ch. of God, Atlanta, 1976-91; assoc. prof. theology Ch. of God Sch. Theology, Cleve., 1979-91, assoc. dean, 1991—; founder, dir. Ataata's Mission Possible, Inc., 1970-81, pres., 1970-91; dean Pentecostal Inst., Inc., Atlanta, 1989-91; v.p. Evang. Ctr., Atlanta, 1990-91. Author: Do-Tell, 1974, A Passion for the Kingdom, 1991; author, editor: Church of God Heritage Papers, 1989; contbr. numerous articles to profl. jours., book chpts. Legis. aide Ga. Ho. of Reps., Atlanta, 1971; bd. dirs., mem. moral concerns com. Christian Coun. of Met. Atlanta, 1975-79; trustee Mission Acres Children's Home, Monroe, Ga., 1979-91. Mem. Am. Acad. Religion, Soc. for Pentecostal Studies, Evangelicals for Social Action. Republican. Home: 1563 Boxwood Trace Acworth GA 30101 Office: Ch of God Sch Theology 900 Walker St Cleveland TN 37320-3330 *One of the most powerful influences on my life (and that of countless others) has been the life and testimony of ordinary saints who, though weak and impoverished, gave themselves in prayer and service to others; we owe them a debt which we can only pay through imitation.*

LANDÁZURI RICKETTS, JUAN CARDINAL, former archbishop of Lima; b. Arequipa, Peru, Dec. 19, 1913. Ed. U. Arequipa and U. Antonianum, Rome. Ordained to priesthood, 1939; Franciscan Friar. Archbishop of Lima Peru, 1955-90; created Cardinal, 1962. Decorated Bailio Order of Malta, Primado del Presidente honorario vitalicio Conferencia, Episcopal Peruana; numerous other honors. Home: Luis Espejo 1064, Lima 13, Peru

LANDES, ALAN HALL, minister; b. Albuquerque, Oct. 16, 1951; s. Philip H. and Mary Louise (Norris) L; m. Carol J. Kloppel, Mar. 19, 1976; children: Stacey Michelle, Mark William. BA cum laude, Univ. Colo., 1976; MDiv, Princeton Theol. Seminary, N.J., 1979; D of Ministry, San Francisco Theol. Seminary, 1988. Ordained to ministry Presbyn. Ch., 1979. Assoc. pastor Cen. Presbyn. Ch., Longmont, Colo., 1979-88; sr. pastor Shepherd of the Hills Presbyn. Ch., Lakewood, Colo., 1988—; treas. Jeffco Self-Sufficiency Coun., Lakewood, 1990—; chmn. Jeffco Good News Coalition, 1991—. Bd. dirs. Jeffco YMCA, Lakewood, 1988—, Family Tree, Wheat Ridge, Colo., 1990-91; organizer Outreach United Resource Ctr., Longmont, 1986, Longmont Pub. Safety Chaplaincy, 1983. Named Outstanding Young Man of Am., 1982, 84; recipient Cooperative Svc. Delivery award Denver Regional Coun. Govts., Longmont, 1988, City Coun. Resolutions, Longmont City Coun., 1987, 88. Mem. Kiwanis, Lakewood Ministerial Assn. (pres. 1991). Republican. Office: Shepherd of the Hills Presbyn Church 11500 W 20th Ave Lakewood CO 80215

LANDES, GEORGE MILLER, biblical studies educator; b. Kansas City, Mo., Aug. 2, 1928; s. George Y. and Margaret B. (Fizzell) L.; m. Carol Marie Dee, Aug. 30, 1953; children: George Miller Jr., Margaret Dee, John Christopher. A.B., U. Mo., 1949; M.Div., McCormick Theol. Sem., 1952; Ph.D., Johns Hopkins U., 1956. Minister to youth Second Presbyn. Ch., Balt., 1952-53, Govans Presbyn. Ch., Balt., 1953-56; instr. Old Testament Union Theol. Sem., N.Y.C., 1956-58, asst. prof. Old Testament, 1958-62, assoc. prof., 1962-70, prof., 1970—; ann. prof. Am. Sch. Oriental Research, Jerusalem, Israel, 1967-68. Author: A Student's Vocabulary of Biblical Hebrew, 1961; editor, author: Report on Archaeological Work, 1975. Nettie F. McCormick fellow, 1952-54; Am. Council Learned Socs. fellow, 1967-68. Mem. Soc. Biblical Lit., Amman Ctr. Archaeol Research (v.p. 1969-79), Am. Schs. Oriental Research (sec.), Phi Beta Kappa. Home: 606 W 122d St New York NY 10027 Office: Union Theol Sem 3041 Broadway New York NY 10027

LANDES, LEO JULIUS, religious organization administrator; b. Revere, Mass., Feb. 19, 1924; s. Henry and Bessie (Nyman) L.; m. Nehama Rosenberg, April 3, 1948; children: Diana, Susan. BA, Yeshiva U., 1945; MA, Columbia U., 1948. CLU. Tchr., prin. Forest Hills (N.Y.) Jewish Ctr., 1948-53; adminstr. pension funds and welfare Joint N.Y. Retirement Bd., N.Y.C., 1959—; pvt. practice CLU Rockville Centre, N.Y., 1953—. Author, editor: Joint Retirement Bd. Newsletter, 1982—. Chmn. Ins. Div. United Jewish Appeal, Bklyn., 1963-65. Recipient Appreciation Cert. award United Synagogue Am., N.Y.C., 1975, Top of Table award Million Dollar Round Table, Chgo., 1977, Cert. Appreciation Jewish Theol. Sem., N.Y.C., 1980, Kavod award Cantors Assembly, N.Y.C., 1983. Mem. Church Alliance (steering com. 1978—), Ch. Pensions Conf. (pres. 1974—), Life Underwriters Assn., Chartered Life Underwriters. Jewish. Home: 16 Marlboro Ct Rockville Centre NY 11570 Office: Joint Retirement Bd 11 Penn Pla New York NY 10001

LANDES, MORRIS ALEX, rabbi; b. Vashiliskok, Vilna, USSR, Oct. 28, 1917; came to U.S., 1920; s. Henry A. and Henna Hiya (Nyman) L; m. Naomi Borkon, Mar. 4, 1945; children: Nina Ann, Sharon Fredelle, Marc Aaron. BA magna cum laude, Yeshiva U., 1939; PhD, U. Pitts., 1954. Ordained rabbi, 1941. Rabbi Cong. Ahavath Shalom, Lynn, Mass., 1941-43, Cong. Radef Shalom, Johnstown, Pa., 1943-45, Cong. Degel Israel, Lancaster, Pa., 1945-48, Cong. Adath Jeshurum, Pitts., 1948—, Cong. Cheseth Israel, Pitts., 1978—; chaplain Pa. State Correctional Instn., Pitts., 1971-88. Author: Trends in American Jewish Thought, 1954; book rev. editor: Horizon mag., 1950-52. Mem. nat. adminstrv. com. Am. Jewish Congress, N.Y.C., 1952, pres. Pitts. chpt. 1950-52; pres. Western Pa. Zionist Region, 1954-56, Pitts. Zionist Coun., 1955-66, Pitts. Zionist Dist., 1959-61, Tri-State Zionist Region, 1961-63, chmn. synogogue Coun. for Israel Bonds, 1965-80, founding pres. Pitts. Zionist Fedn., 1970-72. Named Man of Yr. Pitts, Zionist Dist., and Pitts. Israel Bond Orgn., 1961; recipient Leadership award Tri-State Zionist Region, 1963, Justice Brandeis award, 1971, Svc. award Israel Bond Orgn., 1973, Israel Svc. award Pitts. Zionist Dist., 1974, Svc. award United Bessarabians, 1974, Rabbi Ashinsky award, Hebrew Inst. Pitts., 1976; Nov. 13, 1988 was proclaimed Dr. Morris A. Landes day by mayor of Pitts. Mem. Zionist Orgn. Am. (nat. v.p. 1970-77, judge of ct. of honor 1980—, Herzl Anniversary award, 1954), Rabbinical Coun. Am. (v.p. 1956-58), Greater Pitts. Rabbinic Fellowship (pres. 1969-71, 1985-86), Rabbinical Alumni of Yeshiva U. (past v.p.), B'nai B'rith (chmn. adult edn. 1950-52). Home: 5520 Wellesley Ave Pittsburgh PA 15206 Office: Congregation Adath Jeshurum 5643 E Liberty Blvd Pittsburgh PA 15206

LANDGRAF, JOHN RALPH, seminary president; b. Detroit, Sept. 23, 1937; s. John and Emily (Majeske) L.; m. Lee Joslin, June 8, 1957 (div. 1973); 1 child, John Philip Landgraf; m. Anne Harroun, June 14, 1980. Dipl., Moody Bible Inst., Chgo., 1957; BMus, Wheaton (Ill.) Coll., 1959; MDiv, Am. Bapt. Sem. of the West, Berkeley, Calif., 1969; PhD, Claremont Sch. Theology, Calif., 1973. Diplomate Am. Assn. Pastoral Counselors; ordained to ministry, Am. Bapt. Chs. USA; lic. marriage, family and child counselor, Calif. Lectr. Ariz. Sate U., Tempe, 1972-75; dir. cons. and edn. Interfaith Counseling Svc., Scottsdale, Ariz., 1971-75; dir. The Ctr. for Ministry, Oakland, Calif., 1975-87; pres. Cen. Bapt. Theol. Sem., Kansas City, Kans., 1987—; adj. prof. Grad. Theol. Union, Berkeley, 1978-87, mem. profl. ethics group, 1984-90; adj. prof. U. Calif., Berkeley, 1976-87; mem. Nat. Commn. on Ministry, Valley Forge, Pa., 1988—. Author: Singling: A New Way to Live the Single Life, 1990, Creative Singlehood and Pastoral Care, 1982, How to Survive in the Ministry, 1982; contbr. articles to profl. jours. Mem. Am. Psychol. Assn., Assn. for Clin. Pastoral Edn., Am. Assn. Marriage and Family Therapy, Pastoral Care Network for Social Responsibility, Am. Assn. Counseling & Devel., Am. Bapt. Assn. of Sem. Adminstrs. Democrat. Am. Bapt. Chs. USA. Avocations: music performance, writing, reading, travel, hiking. Office: Cen Bapt Theol Sem Seminary Heights Kansas City KS 66102

LANDIS, HOMER WARREN, minister; b. New Hope, Va., Jan. 23, 1924; s. Henry Daniel and Elsie (Garber) L.; m. Wanda Francis Eavey, June 6, 1947; children: Katherine Elizabeth, Nancy Anne. BA, James Madison U., 1950; MDiv, Emory U., 1953; D of Ministry, Boston U., 1983. Ordained to ministry United Meth. Ch. as deacon, 1952, as elder, 1954; cert. clin. pastoral counselor. Pastor United Meth. Ch., Monterey, Va., 1952-54, Kilmarnock, Va., 1954-55; chaplain USAF, 1955-59; pastor United Meth. Ch., Newsoms, Va., 1959-61, Chuckatuck, Va., 1961-66; pastor Jolliff United Meth. Ch., Portsmouth, Va., 1966-69, United Meth. Ch., Marshall, Va., 1969-74, Phoebus United Meth. Ch., Hampton, Va., 1974-82; chaplain Dept. Vets. Affairs Med. Ctr., Hampton, Va., 1982—; pres. Va. United Meth. Chaplains Fellowship, Hampton, 1989—; work area leader Peninsula Dist. United Meth. Ch. Counsel on Ministries, 1975—. Author: A Descriptive Evaluative Study of Ministry in Hospice, 1983. Dir. Am. Ex-prisoner of War chpt., Hampton, 1990-91. Chaplain col., USAFR, 1943-83, ret. Decorated Purple Heart, Bronze Star, Prisoner of War medal, Meritorious Svc. medal, Air Force Commendation medal; Croix DeGuerre (France). Mem. Interfaith Ministerial Assn., Nat. Mil. Chaplains Assn., Nat. Assn. VA Chaplains, Assn. Pastoral Counselors, Lions. Home: 3 Hatteras Landing Hampton VA 23669

LANDIS, JAMES DAVID, publishing company executive, author; b. Springfield, Mass., June 30, 1942; s. Edward and Eve (Saltman) L.; m. Patricia Lawrence Straus, Aug. 15, 1964 (div.); children: Sara Cass; m. Denise Evelyn Tillar, July 20, 1983; children: Jacob Dean, Benjamin Nicholas. B.A. magna cum laude, Yale Coll., 1964. Asst. editor Abelard Schuman, N.Y.C., 1966-67; editor-sr. editor William Morrow & Co., N.Y.C., 1967-80, editorial dir., sr. v.p., pub. Quill trade paperbacks, 1980-85; sr. v.p. William Morrow & Co., 1985—, pub., editor-in-chief, 1988—; pub., editor-in-chief Beech Tree Books, 1985-87. Author: The Sisters Impossible, 1979, Daddy's Girl, 1984, Love's Detective, 1984, Joey and the Girls, 1987, The Band Never Dances, 1989, Looks Aren't Everything, 1990. Recipient Roger Klein award for editing, 1973; recipient Advocate Humanitarian, 1977. Mem. Phi Beta Kappa. Office: William Morrow & Co Inc 105 Madison Ave New York NY 10016

LANDIS, M. SCOTT, minister, administrative assistant; b. Sellersville, Pa., Oct. 13, 1955; s. Marvin Leatherman and Jacqueline C. (Derrick) L.; m. Janet Fay Hendricks, Aug. 13, 1977; children: Bryan, Derrick, Kara. BA in Religion, Temple U., 1977; MDiv., Ea. Bapt. Theol. Sem., 1980; MA in Pastoral Counseling, Moravian Theol. Sem., 1985. Ordained to ministry United Ch. of Christ, 1980; cert. pastoral counselor. Assoc. pastor New Goshenhoppen United Ch. of Christ, East Greenville, Pa., 1979-85; campus min. Ursinus Coll., Collegeville, Pa., 1985—; adminstrv. asst. to pres. Ursinus Coll., Collegeville, 1989—; del. Gen. Synod United Ch. of Christ, 1989-91; corp. dir. United Ch. Bd. for Homeland Ministries, 1990—. adv. Alpha Phi Omega, Collegeville, 1987; den leader Boy Scouts of Am., Trappe, 1990—, chaplain, 1990; del. County Commr. Study, Norristown, 1991; bd. dirs. Site Coun.-Perkiomen Valley Elem. Sch., Collegeville, 1991. Mem. Nat. Assn. Coll. and Univ. Chaplains, Ecology Com. (chair), Ursinus Ministerium, P.V. Watershed Assn. (Collegeville), Greenpeace, Nat. Wildlife Fedn., Sierra Club (Audubon chpt.). Democrat. Office: Ursinus College Box 1000 Main St Collegeville PA 19426

LANDIS, PAUL GROFF, bishop, mission executive; b. Lancaster, Pa., Jan. 31, 1932; s. Miles Bachman and Anna (Groff) L.; m. Anna Marie Hershey, Mar. 20, 1952; children: Daniel, Steven, Marie, Michael. Grad. high sch., Lancaster, 1950. Lic. to ministry Mennonite Ch., 1953, ordained as minister, 1958, as bishop, 1962. Camp chaplain Fla. Christian Ministry to Migrants, Homestead, 1952-54; dir. Mennonite Vol. Svc., Salunga, Pa., 1954-63; bishop Mellingers Mennonite Dist., Lancaster, 1962—; pres. Ea. Mennonite Bd. Missions, Salunga, 1980—; sec. Lancaster Mennonite Conf., Salunga, 1962-80; chmn. Mennonite Cen. Com.-U.S.A., Akron, Pa., 1979-84; assoc. dir. Mennonite Christian Leadership Found., Landisville, Pa., 1974-80; vice chmn. Mennonite Gen. Bd., Chgo., 1978-82. Mem. Nat. Migrant Com., N.Y.C., 1955-62, Commr. Com. for Child Welfare, Lancaster, 1958-62, Peace and Social Concern Com., Goshen, Ind., 1964-70. Home: 41 Brandt Blvd Salunga PA 17538 Office: Ea Mennonite Bd Missions Oak Ln and Brandt Blvd Box 628 Salunga PA 17538

LANDON, JOHN WILLIAM, minister, social worker, educator; b. Marlette, Mich., Mar. 24, 1937; s. Norman A. and Merle Irene (Lawrason) L. BA, Taylor U., 1959; MDiv, Northwestern U., Christian Theol. Sem., 1962; MSW, Ind. U., 1966; PhD in Social Sci., Ball State U., 1972. Regional supr. Iowa Dept. Social Welfare, Des Moines, 1965-67; acting chmn. dept. sociology Marion (Ind.) Coll., 1967-69; asst. prof. sociology and social work Ball State U., Muncie, Ind., 1969-71; asst. prof. social work, coord. base courses Coll. Social Professions U. Ky., Lexington, 1971-73, assoc. prof., coord. Undergrad. Program in Social Work Coll. of Social Work, 1974-85, prof., assoc. dean, 1985—; dir. social work edn. Taylor U., Upland, Ind., 1973-74. Author: From These Men, 1966; Jesse Crawford, Poet of the Organ, Wizard of the Mighty Wurlitzer, 1974; Behold the Mighty Wurlitzer, The History of the Theatre Pipe Organ, 1983; The Development of Social Welfare, 1986. Mem. AAUP, Coun. on Social Work Edn., Nat. Assn. Social Workers, Nat. Assn. Christians in Social Work, Am. Guild Organists. Home: 809 Celia Ln Lexington KY 40504 Office: U Ky Coll Social Work Lexington KY 40506-0027

LANDRIAULT, JACQUES EMILE, bishop emeritus; b. Alfred, Ont., Can., Sept. 23, 1921; s. Amedee and Marie-Louise (Brisebois) L. B.A., U. Ottawa; Licence in Theology, St. Paul U. Sem., Ottawa. Ordained priest Roman Cath. Ch., 1947; curate in Noranda Que.; chancellor Diocese Timmins, Ont., 1953; bishop of Cadi, titular bishop of Alexandria Ont., 1962-64, bishop of Hearst, 1964-71; bishop of Timmins, 1971-90, bishop emeritus, 1990—. Mem. Cath. Conf. Ont. Address: John Paul II Residence, 1243 Kilborn Pl Apt 201-206, Ottawa, ON Canada K1H 6K9

LANDRU, TRYGVE, minister; b. Orange, N.J., Oct. 9, 1928; s. Jakob Olsen and Nora Margit (Herdal) L.; m. Lillian Thelma Omley, June 28, 1952; children: Sandra Sue, Lois Joy, Andrea Lynne, Paul Trygve. BA, Bob Jones U., 1950; BD, Trinity Sem., 1953. Lic. to ministry Evang. Free Ch. Am., 1953, ordained, 1958. Pastor Evang. Free Ch., Canton, Ill., 1953-56, Winchester Community Ch., West Seneca, N.Y., 1956-65, Dix Hills Evang. Free Ch., Huntington Sta., N.Y., 1965-72, 1st Free Evang. Ch., Lakeland, Fla., 1972-78; dist. supt. New Eng. Dist. Assn., Trumbull, Conn., 1978-87; assoc. pastor, Kenosha Bible Ch., 1987—; exec. officer Free Ch. Youth Fellowship, Mpls., 1952-54; Hon. chaplain Winchester Hose Co. #1, West Seneca, 1956-64; chmn., Camp Spofford Bd. Govs., N.H., 1965-72; bd. dirs. Home Missions Bd., Mpls., 1976-78; mem. Minsterial Assn. Evang. Free Ch. Am. 1954—; chmn. bd. dirs. Southeastern Dist. Evang. Free Ch. Am., 1972-78; trustee Trinity Coll., Deerfield, Ill., 1989—. Home: 4770 84th St Kenosha WI 53142 Office: 5405 67th St Kenosha WI 53142

LANDRUM, MICHAEL ANTHONY, youth minister; b. Vidalia, Ga., Oct. 13, 1958; s. Clinton and Martha (McCranie) L.; m. Jackie Humphrey, Apr. 20, 1980; 1 child, Joshua Michael. BA, Gardner-Webb Coll., 1980; MDiv., S.W. Sem., 1984. Youth min. 1st Bapt. Ch., Cherryville, N.C., 1979-81, Cornerstone Bapt. Ch., Terrell, Tex., 1981-82, Meadlow Ln. Bapt. Ch., Arlington, Tex., 1982-84; min. to youth, assoc. pastor Kings Mountain (N.C.) 1st Bapt. Ch., 1984-87; min. to students 1st Bapt. Ch., Lake Wales, Fla., 1987—; mem. ministerial bd. advisors Gardner-Webb Coll., Boiling Springs, N.C., 1987-91; chmn. parent com. Dawson McAllister Student Conf., Lakeland, Fla., 1990. Mem. parent adv. com. Lake Wales High Sch., 1990-91; mem. Lake Wales Drug Awareness Coun., 1989. Mem. Ridge Bapt. Assn. (youth com. 1989—), Nat. Network Youth Ministries. Republican. Office: 1st Bapt Ch 338 E Central Ave Lake Wales FL 33853

LANDRY, GARY STEPHEN, priest; b. Maywood, Calif., Nov. 30, 1946; s. Steven Joseph and Lois Marie (Dufour) L. BA, St. Mary's Sem., Perryville, Mo., 1969; MDiv, DeAndreis Sem., 1984; MA, U. San Francisco, 1984. Ordained priest Congregation of the Mission, Province of the West, 1973. Asst. dean students St. Vincent's Sem., Lemont, Ill., 1973, tchr. sci. and math., 1973-76, dean students, 1973-75, vocation dir., 1976; asst. dean students St. Vincent's Sem., Montebello, Calif., 1976-77, tchr. sci. and math., 1976-85, dean students, 1977-80, rector, prin., 1980-86; cath mission vocation commn. Vincentian Community, Los Angeles, 1980-83, governing bd., 1980-82, corp. bd., 1983—. Recipient Good Sheperd award Friends of St. Vincent, 1984. Mem. Nat. Assn. Secondary Sch. Prins., Nat. Cath. Endl. Assn., Nat. Council Tchrs. Math., Nat. Sci. Tchrs. Assn., Calif. Assn. Chemistry Tchrs. Democrat. Avocations: art, woodworking, racquetball, volleyball. Home and Office: 1105 Bluff Rd Montebello CA 90640-6198

LANDRY, SISTER MARY LOUISE, nun; b. Old Town, Maine, Aug. 17, 1911; d. Herbert Albert and Caroline (Tardif) L. BS in Pharmacy, Fordham Coll., 1945; BA in French, St. Joseph's Coll., North Windham, Maine, 1951. Joined Sisters of Mercy, Roman Cath. Ch., 1929. Elem. tchr. parochial schs. Portland, Maine, 1929-42; chief pharmacist Mercy Hosp., Portland, 1945-68; instr. pharmacology Mercy Hosp. Sch. Nursing, Portland, 1950-68; asst. adminstr. Mercy Hosp., Portland, 1968-76; mem. gen. coun. Sisters of Mercy, Portland, 1968-74; rep. Sisters of Mercy, Portland West Ch. Alliance, 1965-76; mem. parish coun. St. Mary's Ch., Eagle Lake, Maine, 1976-91; chmn. worship and spiritual commn. St. Mary's Ch., Eagle Lake, 1976-91, lectr., eucharistic min., 1976-91; ret., 1987; chief pharmacist, mgr. Eagle Lake Pharmacy, Maine, 1976-87; instr. CCD program St. Mary's Parish. Author: Landry Family Tree, 1978. Trustee St. Joseph's Coll., North Windham, Maine, Blind Resource Children's Ctr. Bd., Healey Found. Fund; vol. corr. Consumer Adv. Bd. Mem. Maine Pharm. Assn. Democrat. Home: St Mary's Convent Church St Eagle Lake ME 04739 *When someone retires after a brilliant career, many avenues are still open to continue enrichment of one's life—volunteers are always in great demand.*

LANDRY, ROBERT MICHAEL, minister; b. Okinawa, June 28, 1954; came to U.S., 1954; s. Robert Lawes and Margaret Evelyn (McRea) L.; m. Cynthia Jo McAdory, Aug. 14, 1976; children: Jason, Beth, Michelle. BS in Indsl. Mgmt., Ga. Tech. U., 1976; MDiv, Southwestern Bapt. Theol. Sem., Ft. Worth, 1980; D of Ministry, Mid-Am. Bapt. Theol. Sem., Memphis, 1990—. Ordained to ministry Bapt. Ch., 1981. Coll. pastor 1st Bapt. Ch., Atlanta, 1975-77; min. evangelism and youth Britton Bapt. Ch., Oklahoma City, 1981-84; sr. pastor Univ. Bapt. Ch., Dayton, Ohio, 1984-87; assoc.dir. evangelism State Conv. Bapts. in Ohio, Columbus, 1987-89, dir. evangelism, 1989—; mem. faculty So. Bapt. Theol. Sem. Extension, Louisville, 1985-86; chmn. student ministry Greater Dayton Bapt. Assn., 1985-87. Mem. Southwestern Sem. Alumni Ohio (pres. 1988-89). Republican. Avocations: golf, basketball, computers, reading. Office: State Conv Baptists in Ohio 1680 E Broad St Columbus OH 43203

LANDSMAN, MICHAEL UDELL, minister; b. N.Y.C., July 22, 1949; s. George David and Ruth Naomi (Udell) L.; m. Martha Jean Larsen, Dec. 23, 1972; children: Michael Andrew, Linda Jeannette, Lawrence Wayne. BA in Bible, So. Calif. Coll., Costa Mesa, 1975; MBA, Golden State U., L.A., 1983; PhD, Golden State U., 1985; EdD, Honolulu U., 1987. Lic. min. Assemblies of God, 1973, ordained, 1975. Asst. pastor, then assoc. pastor Harbor Christian Ctr., 1972-77; police chaplain L.A. Police Dept., 1974-79; assoc. pastor Palos Verdes (Calif.) Faith Ctr., 1977-79; internat. dir. edn., assoc. pastor Faith Christian Fellowship, Tulsa, 1980-86; internat. Bible Sch. dir. Faith Fellowship Ministries, Edison, N.J., 1986-88; internat. admissions officer Honolulu U., 1989—; mem. Police Clergy Coun., L.A., 1974-79; founder World Outreach Bible Schs., 1979—; pres. Michael Landsman Ministries, Edison, 1986—; sec.-treas. Inspiration Ctr. Ch., Flemington, N.J., 1985—; founding trustee Covenant Ministries Internat., 1988. Author: Supportive Ministries, 1980, transl. in 4 langs., Doubling Your Ability, 1984, Attitude of A Servant, 1987, transl. in 2 langs. With U.S. Army, 1968-72, Korea. Recipient Commendation, L.A. Police Dept., 1977, Cert. of Svc., Faith Christian Fellowship, Tulsa, 1981. Fellow Internat. Acad. Edn.; mem. Nat. Geog. Soc., Smithsonian Inst., Sons of Norway. Republican. Avocations: gen. aviation, gun collecting, writing. Office: Faith Fellowship Ministries 2177 Oaktree Rd Edison NJ 08820 *In my life I have learned that wisdom and knowledge will be the elements that give stability to your life and strength to continue forward in any task.*

LANDWEHR, ARTHUR JOHN, minister; b. Northbrook, Ill., Mar. 8, 1934; s. Arthur John Sr. and Alice Eleanor (Borchardt) L.; m. Avonna Lee, Sept. 19, 1953; children: Arthur J. III, Andrea Lea Askow. BA, Drake U., 1956; BD, Garrett-Theol. Sem., 1959; DD (hon.), North Cen. Coll., 1980. Ordained minister in Meth. Ch. Pastor Lyndon (Ill.) United Meth. Ch., 1956-59, Marseilles (Ill.) United Meth. Ch., 1959-65, Faith United Meth. Ch., Lisle, Ill., 1965-69; sr. minister First United Meth. Ch., Elmhurst, Ill., 1969-75, Evanston, Ill., 1975-88; sr. minister Grace United Meth. Ch., Naperville, Ill., 1988—; trustee Garrett-Evang. Theol. Sem., Evanston, 1976—, 1st v.p. bd. trustees, 1977-86; del. to gen. conf. United Meth. Ch., 1976, 80, 84, 88, World Meth. Conf., Nairobi, Kenya, 1986; Wilson lectr., 1987; mem. com. on interprofl. cooperation Ill. Bar Assn.; preacher Adams Sermon, Bloomington, Ind., 1991, NMex. Ann. Conf., 1992, N.W. Tex. Conf., 1992. Author: In the Third Place, 1972; contbr. article to profl. jours. Recipient citation for human rels. City of Lisle, 1969; study grantee World Coun. Chs., Sri Lanka, 1983, Ecumenical Inst. for Advanced Studies, Tantur, Israel, 1977. Mem. AAAS, Am. Acad. Religion, Am. Theol. Soc., Ill. Bar Assn. (interprofl. cooperation com. 1991), Order of St. Luke, Univ. Club (pres. Evanston chpt. 1986-87), Rotary. Home: 520 E Highland Naperville IL 60540 Office: Grace United Meth Ch 300 E Gartner Naperville IL 60540 *It is evident to me that life is a gift surrounded in mystery. Like most mysteries, we wait for the moment of revelation in which there is aforementioned understanding. I've learned that without a radical lane life has no future.*

LANE, BELDEN CURNOW, religion educator, minister; b. Orlando, Fla., June 2, 1943; s. Edward H. and Jane E. (Jones) L.; m. Patricia Ann Lomas, July 1, 1967; children: Katrina, Jonathan. BA, Fla. State U., 1966; BD, Fuller Theol. Sem., 1969; PhD, Princeton Theol. Sem., 1976. Ordained to ministry Presbyn. Ch., 1972. Pastor First Presbyn. Ch., Ellicotville, N.Y., 1972-74, Jacksonville Presbyn. Ch., Bordentown, N.J., 1974-76; assoc. pastor First Presbyn. Ch., Phila., 1976-77; prof. Theology and Am. Studies St. Louis (Mo.) U., 1977—; mem. editorial bd. Spirituality Today, St. Louis, 1985—. Editor jour. The Christian Century, 1985—; Author: Landscapes of the Sacred, 1988 (Cath. Press Assn. award); contbr. articles to profl. jours. Recipient Burlington No. Outstanding Teaching award, 1988. Mem. Am.

Acad. Religion, Nat. Assn. for the Preservation of Storytelling, Phi Beta Kappa, Alpha Sigma Nu, Irving R. Feldman Writing Group. Democrat. Home: 7206 Shaftesbury Ave Saint Louis MO 63130 Office: Dept Theol Studies St Louis U 3634 Lindell Blvd Saint Louis MO 63108

LANE, DAVID EARLE, minister; b. Springfield, Ohio, Dec. 2, 1943; s. Albert Marian and Mary Kay (Hobbler) L.; m. Janis Ann Dowling, Oct. 11, 1967; children: David E. II, Derek E. BS in Bus., Miss. Coll., 1970; MDiv, Wesley Bibl. Sem., Jackson, Miss., 1984. Ordained to ministry Meth. Ch., 1982. V.p. bus. Wesley Bibl. Sem., Jackson, 1986-88; pastor 1st Wesleyan Meth. Ch., Anniston, Ala., 1988—; dir. Ala. Coalition for Life, Birmingham, 1989—. With U.S. Army, 1965-67. Home: 2501 Jefferson St Anniston AL 36201

LANE, GEORGE LINDSAY, retired minister; b. McKinney, Tex., Aug. 3, 1921; s. James Preston and Luvicy Elizabeth (Hamm) L.; m. Mary Ellen Hart, Nov. 4, 1940; 1 child, Frank P. Sr. BS, Wash. U., St. Louis, 1959, MA, 1971; MA in Mil. Sci. and Tactics, Army Command & Gen. Staff Coll, Ft. Leavenworth, Kans., 1969. Ordained to ministry Christian Ch. (Disciples of Christ), 1940. Pastor Sturgeon (Mo.) United Meth. Ch., 1970-75, Riggs (Mo.) United Meth. Ch., 1975-80, Hancock Christian Ch., Dixon, Mo., 1981-85, Mt. Carney Christian Ch., Lebanon, Mo., 1985-90. Lt. Col. U.S. Army, 1940-70. Mem. U.S. Officers Assn. (life), Ambassador's Club (life), VFW (life), DAV Retired (life). Republican. Home: RFD 1 Box 90C Climax Springs MO 65324 Office: HCR 71 Box 1985 Camdenton MO 65020

LANE, HAROLD ELBERT, minister, educator; b. Detroit, June 4, 1929; s. James Elbert and Dora Lucy (Chambers) L.; m. Dolores Lee Fuller, Dec. 21, 1951; children: James Edwin, Nancy Dawn. BA, Bob Jones U., Greenville, S.C., 1952; ThB, BD, No. Bapt. Sem., Chgo., 1958; D Ministry, U. Chgo., 1963; DD (hon.), Judson Coll., Elgin, Ill., 1971. Ordained to ministry Am. Bapt. Chs. in U.S.A., 1952. Sr. min. 1st Bapt. Ch., Jerseyville, Ill., 1960-65, Irving Park Bapt. Ch., Chgo., 1965-69; sr. min. 1st Bapt. Ch., Menlo Park, Calif., 1969-74, Indpls., 1974-78, Pasadena, Calif., 1978—; assoc. Golden Gate Coll., San Francisco, 1975—; prof. Canada Coll., Redwood City, Calif., 1976; adj. prof. Fuller Theol. Sem., Pasadena, 1980—; pres. Am. Bapt. Chs. in U.S.A., Covina, Calif., 1983, mem. exec. coun., 1984-88, program chmn. Pittsburg (Calif.) biennial, 19887-88; mem. Bd. Internat. Ministries, 1981-88. Author: (booklet) People with Purpose, 1975, dir. TV series, 1977. Trustee Judson Coll., Elgin, Ill., 1960-88; chaplain Y's Men Club, Pasadena, 1978—, pres., 1981-82; founder Prison Rehab. Program, San Francisco, 1976. Recipient John Mason Peck award Chgo. Bapt. Men, 1965; Joseph Dent award No. Bapt. Sem., 1987, Exceptional and Able Min. award, 1988. Mem. Exch. Club (bd. dirs. Pasadena 1990—), Rotary (com. chmn. Pasadena 1985-87). Republican. Home: 2076 Crescent Dr Pasadena CA 91001 Office: 1st Bapt Ch 75 N Marengo Ave Pasadena CA 91101

LANE, JEFFREY MARVIN, minister; b. Knoxville, Tenn., Apr. 4, 1960; s. Marvin Thomas and Betty Fay (Mouron) L.; m. Janice Ruth Peek, June 25, 1983. BA, Carson-Newman Coll., 1982; MDiv, Southeastern Bapt. Theol. Sem., 1986. Assoc. youth minister Durham (N.C.) Meml. Bapt. Ch., 1983-86; assoc. pastor Penelope Bapt. Ch., Hickory, N.C., 1986—; retreat leader So. Bapt. ch. various cities, 1983—. Author: Hickory Daily Record, 1987-88. Active Nat. Spinal Chord Injury Hotline, Balt., 1986—; vol. chaplain Frye Regional Med. Ctr., Hickory, 1986—; drama specialsit Yates Assn., Durham, 1987; mem. ASSIST team Theron-Rankin Assn., Hickory, 1988. Mem. Nat. Eagle Scout Assn., So. Bapt. Religious Educators, Coop. Christian Ministries, Southeastern Bapt. Theol. Sem. Assn. Clubs: Tennessee, Southeastern Sem. (pres. 1985-86). Avocations: golf, hiking, camping, drama. Home: 3507 Main Ave Dr NW Hickory NC 28601 Office: Penelope Bapt Church 3310 Main Ave NW Hickory NC 28601

LANE, JULIA A., nursing educator; b. Chgo., June 29, 1927; d. James and Julia (Ivins) L. BSN, DePaul U., 1956; MSN, Cath. U. Am., 1961; PhD, Loyola U., Chgo., 1974. Cert. nurse midwife. Staff nurse St. Joseph Hosp., 1954-55, Chgo. Bd. of Health, 1955-57; instr. South Chgo. Hosp. Sch. Nursing, 1957-58, dir. edn., 1960-63; assoc. prof. Loyola U. Sch. Nursing, 1963—, dean, 1974-91. Home: 300 N State # 4532 Chicago IL 60610 Office: Loyola U Marcella Neihoff Sch Nursing 6525 N Sheridan Rd Chicago IL 60626

LANE, KENNETH EDWARD, III, minister; b. St. Louis, Aug. 9, 1958; s. Kenneth Edward Jr. and Mary Ann (Meinecke) L.; m. Cynthia Kay Walker, Aug. 16, 1980; children: Kathryn Elizabeth, Spencer Christian. BA, Oral Roberts U., 1980; MDiv, Covenant Theol. Sem., 1983; ThM, Princeton Theol. Sem., 1989. Ordained to ministry Presbyn. Ch., 1984. Asst. pastor St. James Presbyn. Ch., Littleton, Colo., 1984-87; assoc. pastor First Presbyn. Ch., Graham, Tex., 1987-89; pastor First Presbyn. Ch., Neosho, Mo., 1989—. Mem. Presbyns. for Renewal (adv. 1990—), Neosho Ministerial Alliance (treas. 1990—). Home: 220 N High Neosho MO 64850 Office: 1st Presbyn Ch 215 N High Neosho MO 64850

LANE, PAUL ANDREW, minister; b. Raleigh, N.C., Aug. 22, 1961; s. William Earl and Mary Sue (Rankin) L.; m. Martha Darlene Martin, Aug. 3, 1986. BA in Philosophy, N.C. State U., 1984; MDiv, Southeastern Seminary, Wake Forest, N.C., 1987; D of Ministry, Drew Univ., Madison, N.J., 1990—. Ordained to ministry Southern Bapt. Ch., 1985. Counselor Camp Caraway, Asheboro, N.C., 1982; summer youth minister Calvary Bapt. Ch., Reidsville, N.C., 1983-84; minister Kittrell (N.C.) Bapt. Ch., 1985-87, First Bapt. Ch., Mayodan, N.C., 1987—; chmn. missions com. Dan Valley Bapt. Assn., Reidsville, N.C., 1989-91; com. on cooperative ministry Bapt. State Conv. of N.C., Cary, 1990-93. Bd. dirs. Scott Elem. Sch. PTA, Madison, N.C., 1989-91, United Way of West Rockingham County, Madison, 1991-94, Charter Hosp. Counseling Ctr., Madison, 1990—. Mem. So. Bapt. Alliance, Madison/Mayodan Ministerial Assn. (pres. 1990—), Kiwanis. Home: 700 West Main St Mayodan NC 27027 Office: First Bapt Church 101 South First Ave Mayodan NC 27027 *All persons are holy, for we are all created by God. This fact should guide us in all forms of relationships, both in the personal and corporate realms of life.*

LANE, WILLIAM LISTER, dean, religion educator; b. New Britain, Conn., Jan. 16, 1931; s. William John and Evelyn Lucinda (Moore) L.; m. Brenda Jean Whitaker, Aug. 7, 1974. BA, Wesleyan U., 1952; BD, Gordon Div. Sch., 1955; ThM, Westminster Theol. Sem., 1956; ThD, Harvard U., 1962. Prof. New Testament Gordon-Conwell Theol. Sem., South Hamilton, Mass., 1958-73; prof. religious studies Western Ky. U., Bowling Green, 1974-89; prof. Biblical studies, dean Sch. Religion Seattle Pacific U., 1989—; bd. dirs. Michael Care Creative Trust, Franklin, Tenn.; mem. acad. books com. Thomas Nelson Pubs., Nashville, 1985-88; mem. editorial bd. Abingdon Press, Nashville, 1990—. Author: The New International Commentary on the Gospel of Mark, 1974; co-author: The New Testament Speaker, 1969. Mem. Studiorum Novi Testamenti Soc., Soc. Biblical Lit., Cath. Biblical Soc., Phi Beta Kappa, Phi Alpha Chi, Phi Kappa Phi. Republican. Methodist. Office: Seattle Pacific U Sch Religion Seattle WA 98119

LANES, T. A., religious organization administrator. Exec. dir. Assemblies of God Internat. Fellowship, San Diego. Office: Assemblies God Internat Fellowship 8504 Commerce Ave San Diego CA 92121*

LANEY, HOWARD ELIMUEL, retired minister; b. Maiden, N.C., Sept. 8, 1925; s. Charlie Ivy and Lottie Mae (Huffman) L.; m. Margie Ree Abernathy, May 29, 1943; children: Carolyn (Mrs. Joe Wells), Ricky Allen, Debra Lynn. Student, Gardner-Webb Coll., 1949-51, Furman U., Lenoir-Rhyne Coll., 1955-56, Sch. Pastoral Care, Winston Salem, N.C., 1958. Ordained to ministry Bapt. Ch., 1949. Pastor Faith Bapt. Ch., Lincolnton, N.C., 1951-56, Liberty Grove, Roaring River Chs., North Wilkesboro, N.C., 1956-60, Starnes Cove Bapt. Ch., Asheville, N.C., 1960-67, Providence (N.C.) Bapt. Ch., 1967-69, Anderson Grove Bapt. Ch., Albemarle, N.C., 1969-77, Fairplains Bapt. Ch., North Wilkesboro, 1977-88; supply pastor Ctr. Bapt. Ch., North Wilkesboro, 1988—; chaplain Chevrolet Co., Asheville; coroner North Wilkesboro, 1990—. Mem. adv. bd. Campbell Coll., Buies Creek, N.C., 1981—; bd. dirs. Deafness Ctr, North Wilkesboro, 1956—, Rest Home, Crime Stoppers, Mulberry Fairplains Fire Dept., 1967— (Fireman of Yr. 1984), First Responders, 1986—. Mem. Stone Mountain Bapt. Assn. (moderator 1979), Wilkes Ministerial Assn. (treas. 1989—). Home: Rte 6 Box 54 North Wilkesboro NC 28659 *I have learned in life that to find myself and satisfaction is to lose myself in the life of others. This I have tried to do.*

LANEY, JAMES THOMAS, university president; b. Wilson, Ark., Dec. 24, 1927; s. Thomas Mann and Mary (Hughey) L.; m. Berta Joan Radford, Dec. 20, 1949; children: Berta Joan Vaughan, James T., Arthur Radford, Mary Ruth Laney Reilly, Susan Elizabeth Castle. BA, Yale U., 1950, BD, 1954, PhD, 1966; DD, Fla. So. Coll., 1977; LHD, Rhodes Coll., 1979; HHD, Mercer U., 1980; LLD, DePauw U., 1985; DD, Wofford Coll., 1986; LHD, Millsaps Coll., 1988, Austin Coll., 1990. Chaplain Choate Sch., Wallingford, Conn., 1953-55; ordained to ministry Meth. Ch., 1955; asst. lectr. Yale Div. Sch., 1954-55; pastor St. Paul Meth. Ch., Cin., 1955-58; sec. student Christian movement, prof. Yonsei U., Seoul, Korea, 1959-64; asst. prof. Christian ethics Vanderbilt U. Div. Sch., 1966-69; dean Candler Sch. Theology, Emory U., 1969-77, pres. univ., 1977—; vis. prof. Harvard Div. Sch., 1974; dir. Trust Co. of Ga., Coca-Cola Co. Author: (with J.M. Gustafson) On Being Responsible, 1968; also essays. Pres. Nashville Community Rels. Coun., 1968-69; mem. Yale Coun. Com., 1972-77; bd. dirs. Fund Theol. Edn.; chmn. United Bd. for Christian Higher Edn. in Asia, 1990—; bd. dirs. Atlanta Symphony, 1979—; chmn. overseers com. to visit Harvard Div. Sch., 1980-85; mem. Yale U. Coun., 1985—; chmn. so. dist. Rhodes Scholarship Com.; bd. dirs. Atlantic Coun., 1987—. With AUS, 1946-48. Selected for Leadership Atlanta, 1970-71; recipient Disting. Alumnus award Yale U. Div. Sch., 1979, Kellogg award for leadership in higher edn., 1983; D.C. Macintosh fellow Yale U., 1965-66. Mem. Am. Soc. Christian Ethics, Soc. for Values Higher Edn. (pres. 1987—), Council on Fgn. Relations, Atlanta C. of C., Commerce Club (bd. dirs.), Phi Beta Kappa, Omicron Delta Kappa. Home: 1463 Clifton Rd Atlanta GA 30329 Office: Emory U Office of President Atlanta GA 30322

LANG, BERNHARD, religion educator; b. Stuttgart, Fed. Republic Germany, July 12, 1946; s. Gert and Stefanie (Germautz) L. ThD, Tübingen U., Tübingen, Fed. Republic Germany, 1975; D. Habilitation, Freiburg U., Freiburg, Fed. Republic Germany, 1977. Prof. bibl. studies U. Tübingen, 1977-82; prof. Old Testament Gutenberg U., Mainz, Fed. Republic Germany, 1982-85; prof. religion U. Paderborn, Paderborn, Fed. Republic Germany, 1985—; vis. prof. Free U. Berlin, 1979, Temple U., Phila., 1982, Ecole d. Hautes Etudes en Sci. Sociales, 1991; acad. visitor London Sch. Econs., 1981-82. Co-author: (with Colleen McDannell) Heaven, a History, 1988 (many translations); author of several books; editor: Internationale Zeitschriftenschau für Bibelwissenschaft, 1980—. Mem. Soc. Bibl. Lit. Roman Catholic. Avocations: anthropology, history. Office: U Paderborn Fachbereich 1, Warburger Strasse 100, D 4790 Paderborn Federal Republic of Germany *Oddly enough, Christianity is the most neglected area of religious research. That research should be done (1) with sincere respect for religious people, (2) without compromising strict academic standards in the interest of (church) politics.*

LANG, CARROLL DENNIS, minister; b. Napoleon, N.D., Feb. 18, 1943; s. Lewie Carl and RoxAnne Gertrude (Koch) L.; m. Judith Louise Larson, Aug. 29, 1964; children: Nicole Marie, Inga Joy. BA, U. No. Iowa, 1965; MDiv, Wartburg Theol. Sem., Dubuque, 1969. Ordained to ministry Evang. Luth. Ch. in Am., 1969. Pastor 1st Luth. Ch., Galveston, Tex., 1969-71, Gilmore City, Iowa, 1971-76; pastor Silver Lake/Bristol Luth. Chs., rural Northwood, Iowa, 1976-82, Our Savior Luth. Ch., Stanhope, Iowa, 1982; interim pastor St. Mark's Luth. Ch., Storm Lake, Iowa, 1983, Zion Luth. Ch., Waterloo, Iowa, 1983; pastor Christ Luth. Ch., Ft. Dodge, Iowa, 1984—; spiritual dir. Nat. Luth. Secretariat, Mpls., 1986-89, newsletter editor, 1987—; chmn. Synod Assembly Worship Com., Western Iowa Synod, 1990—. Pres., clergy advisor Ft. Dodge Inter-Faith Forum, 1987-91; mem. planning com. Martin Luther King Day, Inc., Ft. Dodge, 1988—. Recipient Ecumenical award, Ft. Dodge Area Inter-Faith Forum, 1991. Mem. Ft. Dodge Ministerial Assn. (sec. 1986-88), NAACP (recorder 1989—), Civitan (chaplain 1986—). Home: 1052 N 23d Pl Fort Dodge IA 50501 Office: Christ Luth Ch 2220 10th Ave N Fort Dodge IA 50501

LANG, JOVIAN PETER, priest, religious educator; b. Sioux City, Iowa, June 2, 1919; s. Peter and Margaret (Horvath) L. AB, Our Lady of Angels Sem., Cleve., 1942; MLS, Case Western Res. U., 1950, MA, 1955. Joined Order of Franciscans, 1939, ordained priest Roman Cath. Ch., 1946. Libr., assoc. prof. Quincy (Ill.) Coll., 1947-55, 60-71; asst. prof. St. Joseph Sem., Westmont, Ill., 1955-57; archivist, asst. prof. Provicialate, St. Louis, 1957-60; asst. prof. U. South Fla., Tampa, 1971-74; mem. faculty St. Johns U., Jamaica, N.Y., 1974-89; assoc. prof. St. Vincent de Paul Regional Sem., Boynton Beach, Fla., 1989—; assoc. prof. libr. and info. sci., moderator conf. Libr.-Coll. Assocs, Jamaica, N.Y., 1976; presenter workshop Mary Coll., Bismarck, N.D., 1976, Libr.-Coll. Assocs., Caldwell, N.J., 1978; chmn. Panel on Handicapped, Met. Cath. Coll. Librs., Tarrytown, N.Y., 1980; dir workshop on handicapped Cath. Libr. Assn., N.Y.C., 1981; chaplain Teams of Our Lady, Massapequa, N.Y., 1978-89; adj. prof. libr. and info. sci., U. South Fla. east coast extension, 1989—. Author: Annual Guide for the Liturgy, 1958—, Catholic Library Association Profiles, 1967, Annual Ordo for the Celebration of Divine Office and the Mass, 1971—, Your Search Key to Library of Congress Classification, 1979; editor: Liturgy of Vatican, II (2 vols.), 1966, Pray Together (monthly), 1970—, St. Joseph Missal Guide, 1975—, St. Joseph Guide for the Liturgy of the Hours, 1974—, St. Joseph Guide for Christian Prayer, 1975—, Reference Sources: A Systematic Approach, 1976, Reference Sources for Small and Medium-Sized Libraries, 1984, Dictionary of the Liturgy, 1989, Reference Sources for Small and Medium-Sized Libraries , 5th edit., 1991; mem. editorial bd. Pierian Press, 1969—, Learning Today, 1981-87; contbr. articles to various publs. Chmn. Liturgical Commn. Sacred Heart Province, 1964-68; sec. Am. Franciscan Liturgical Commn., 1989—. Mem. American Franciscan Liturgical Commn. (sec. 1989—). Home and Office: St Vincent de Paul Regional Sem. 10701 S Military Trail Boynton Beach FL 33436-4811 *We are unique and have God-given gifts which we should use and develop. Critical thinking examines, takes possession of, and appreciates the best in any idea, making it one's own. Education creates motives to learn what is obligatory, beneficial, and significant so as to love God and neighbor.*

LANG, MARCUS TITUS, minister; b. Omaha, Oct. 1, 1920; s. Victor C. and Martha Mathilda (Kath) L.; children: Marcus P., Deborah L., Diana E., Cynthia A. BA, BDiv and MDiv, Concordia Theol. Sem., 1945; MA in Sociology, Washington U., St. Louis, 1945; postgrad., Universität Heidelberg, Fed. Republic of Germany, 1953-54. Pastor St. John Luth. Ch., Fayetteville, Ark., 1945-51, Grace Luth. Ch., Denison, Tex., 1954-60, Our Savior Luth. Ch., Abilene, Tex., 1954-60, St. James Luth. Ch., Lafayette, Ind., 1960-76, Messiah Luth. Ch./Prince of Peace Luth. Ch., Grand Junction, Colo., 1976-90; chmn., trustee Balance, Inc., Milw., 1960-90. Contbr. numerous articles to profl. jours. 1st lt. USAF, 1951-53. Home: 20352 Powderhorn Rd Hidden Valley Lake CA 95461 Mailing Address: Box 8857 HCR 82 Middletown CA 95461

LANG, MARTIN ANDREW, religion educator; b. Bklyn., May 2, 1930; s. Robert William and Ruth H. (Sweeting) L.; m. Carol Anne Johnson; children: Jay, Martin, Carol Anne. BA, Marist Coll., Poughkeepsie, N.Y., 1951; MA, Cath. U. Am., 1960, PhD, 1964. Co-founder, dir. Marist Inst. Theology, Poughkeepsie, 1964-68; founder, dir. St. Norbert Theol. Inst., Green Bay, Wis., 1968-70; dir. religious edn., founder patoral ministry program Fairfield (Conn.) U., 1970-88, prof. religious studies, 1988—; instr. pastoral ministry program Archdiocese of Hartford, Conn., 1984—; instr. edn. for parish svc. Trinity Coll., Washington, 1985—. Author: The Inheritance: What Catholics Believe, 1970, Acquiring Our Image of God, 1984; also numerous articles. Fellow Union Theol. Sem., 1966, Yale Div. Sch., 1967. Mem. AAUP, Am. Acad. Religion, Cath. Bibl. Assn. Democrat. Roman Catholic. Office: Fairfield U N Benson Rd Fairfield CT 06430

LANG, W. RICHARD, minister; b. Glendale, Calif., June 21, 1936; s. W. Richard and Elvira A. (Pearson) L.; m. Holly J. Mortensen, Aug. 12, 1967; children: Kristin M., John A. BA, Calif. Luth. U., 1964; ThM, Wartburg Theol. Sem., Dubuque, Iowa, 1969; cert. in insurance, Profl. Sch., Salem, Oreg., 1986, cert. in stock brokerage, 1988. Missionary Am. Luth. Ch. Japan Mission, Shizuoka, Japan, 1964-65; intern Am. Luth. Ch., Kasson, Minn., 1967-68; pastor Calvary Luth. Ch., Grants Pass, Oreg., 1969-75; healing evangelist So. Oreg. Renewal Ministry, Grants Pass, 1975-85, Assn. Evang. Cons., Salem, 1985—; stock broker, ins. agt. Securities Am., Salem, 1986—; tchr. Sch. Ministry, 1982-84. With. U.S. Army, 1960-62. Mem. Salem Evang. Pastors, Salem Life Underwriters, Full Gospel Businessmen, Salem. Republican. Home and Office: Lang & Assocs P O Box 7372 Salem OR 97303

LANGDON, HARRY NORMAN, deacon, humanities educator; b. Council Bluffs, Iowa, Mar. 24, 1929; s. Claude Haviland and Helen (Sweeney) L.; m. Jeanne Marie Sondag, Jan. 13, 1970; children: Mark, Laura. BA, U. Nebr., Omaha, 1951; MA, U. Nebr., Lincoln, 1955; PhD, U. Iowa, 1970; postgrad., Creighton U., 1972-74. Ordained deacon Roman Cath. Ch., 1972. Supr. adult Christian edn. Cath. Community, Council Bluffs, 1972-74; liturgy asst. St. Paul's Cath. Ch., Pensacola, Fla., 1974-76; diaconal community lectr. Diocese of Peoria, Ill., 1976-77; assoc. dir. diaconal community Diocese of Dodge City, Kans., 1977-82; dir. campus ministry Rockhurst Coll., Kansas City, Mo., 1982-86; dir. choir St. Agnes Ch., Fairway, Kans., 1983-84; prof. humanities Johnson County Community Coll., Overland Park, Kans., 1986—; dir. choirs Creighton U., Omaha, 1960-63, Rockhurst Coll., 1982-83. Author: Plays for Liturgy and Learning, 1988, Plays for Feast Days of the Church, 1991; also articles on religion and theatre. Singer Kansas City Symphony Chorus, 1988—; actor univ. and community prodns., Pensacola, Omaha, Kansas City, Dodge City; former dir. theatre U. West Fla., Pensacola, Creighton U. Recipient Excellence in Acting award Omaha Playhouse, 1966, Outstanding Writing award Am. Theatre Assn., 1968, Outstanding Tchr. award Burlington-No. Ry., 1989. Mem. Assn. Deacons Kansas City (pres. 1991-93), Waldo County Ministerial Assn. (pres. 1985-86), Phi Delta Kappa, Omicron Delta Kappa, Alpha Psi Omega. Home: 6146 Holmes Kansas City MO 64110

LANGE, CHARLOTTE, pastoral counselor; b. Phila., Mar. 19, 1931; d. Marion and Beatrice (Atkins) Roop; B.S. magna cum laude in Psychology, U. Md., 1979; M.S. in Pastoral Counseling, Loyola Coll., Balt., 1981, cert. advanced study in psychology, 1984. Lic. mental health counselor; cert. clin. mental health counselor; m. John E. Lange, Oct. 7, 1950; children—Ralph Ad, Helen Bratton Lange Dunn. Nurses aide Shriners Hosp. Crippled Children, Phila., 1948; pvt. duty practical nurse, 1949-50; civic worker, Bowie, Md., 1965-74; lay pastoral asst. St. James Episcopal Ch., Bowie, Md., 1976-80, pastoral counselor, 1980-87, St. Davids Episcopal Ch., Englewood, Fla., 1989—; supr. Acad. Cert. Clin. Mental Health Counselors, 1990; new ventures counselor, 1982-86. Speakers bur. Arthritis Found., award of appreciation, 1981; chmn. Arthritis Caring Together. Mem. Am. Assn. Pastoral Counselors (cert.), Alpha Sigma Lambda, Phi Kappa Phi, Alpha Sigma Nu. Democrat. Research on effect of arthritis on the family. *I believe in affirming the wholeness or holyness in people as they go through the process of emotional, spiritual and psychological exploration in their lives; thus giving them the courage to grow and change into the person that they want to be.*

LANGE, DIETZ CHRISTIAN, theologian, educator; b. Bremen, Fed. Republic Germany, Apr. 2, 1933; s. Louis P. A. and Amélie (Finke) L.; m. A.E. Ingeborg Berndt, June 1, 1963 (dec. 1976); children: Frank R., Judith. 1st Theol. Exam, U. Göttingen, Fed. Republic Germany, 1958; ThD, U. Zürich, 1962; 2nd Theol. Exam, Ev. Ch. Westphalia, Bielefeld, Fed. Republic Germany, 1963; Habilitation, U. Göttingen, 1973. Cert. Lang. Proficiency in English, U. Cambridge, Eng., 1987. Teaching asst. U. Göttingen, 1959-61, univ. asst., 1963-69, instr., 1971-77, prof., 1977—; asst. pastor Ev. Ch. Westphalia, Bochum and Witten, Fed. Republic Germany, 1961-63; mem. com. Evangelische Kirche in Deutschland, 1987-91. Co-editor: New Athenaeum-Neues Athenaeum, Madison, N.J., 1987—, Hermeneutische Untersuchungen fur Theologie, Tübingen, Fed. Republic Germany, 1990—; author: Christlicher Glaube und Soziale Probleme, 1964, others. Recipient scholarship Deutsche Forschungsgemeinschaft, 1969-71. Mem. Wissenschaftliche Gesellschaft für Theologie, Soc. Ethica. Avocations: modern languages, lit., hiking, cooking. Home: Insterburger Weg 1, D-3400 Göttingen Federal Republic of Germany Office: Vereinigte Theol Seminare, Platz der Göttinger Sieben2, D-3400 Göttingen Federal Republic of Germany

LANGER, ELIEZER, rabbi; b. San Francisco, Dec. 3, 1946; s. Moses I. and Zmira (Kasarnofsky) L.; m. Lucy Langenthal; children: Shoshana, Elisheva, Yaakov, Aryeh, Naftali. BA, Yeshiva U., 1968, MS, 1975. Ordained rabbi, 1975. Rabbi Beth Zion Congregation, Oshawa, Ont., Can., 1971-74, Beth Abraham-Jacob, Albany, N.Y., 1974-77, Beth Jacob Congregation, San Diego, 1977—; instr. City Coll. San Diego; mem. rabbinic cabinet United Jewish Appeal, Israel Bonds, Jewish Nat. Fund. Mem. Rabbinical Coun. Am. (regional v.p.), San Diego Vaad Horabonim (chmn.). Office: 4855 College Ave San Diego CA 92115

LANGEVIN, LOUIS-DE-GONZAGUE, bishop; b. Oka, Can, Oct. 31, 1921. BA, Seminaire de Philosophie de Montreal, 1944; postgrad. in theology, Scolasticat des Peres Blancs, Ottawa, 1946-50; Lic. in Theology, Gregorian U., Rome, 1957; Lic. in Holy Scripture, Sainte a l'Institut Biblique, Rome, 1957. Ordained priest Roman Catholic Ch. Provincial priest Blancs d'Afrique, Montreal, Que., Can; aux. bishop Diocese de St Hyacinthe, 1974-79, titular bishop, 1979; pres. Episcopal Commn. on Social Communications Conf. Cath. Bishops Can.; mem. Commn. for the Lay Apostate Conf. Bishops of Que. Decorated chevalier de l'Ordre du Saint-Sepulcre de Jerusalem lieutenance du Can., a Montreal, 1975, chevalier de Colomb du 4e Degre Assemblee Antoine Girouard de Saint-Hyacinthe Province de Que., Can. Home and Office: Eveche de Saint Hyacinthe, CO 190, 1900 rue Girouard ouest, Saint Hyacinthe, PQ Canada J2S 7B4

LANGFITT, JOHN NELSON, religious organization administrator; b. Chgo., Nov. 7, 1942; s. John Nelson Langfitt Sr. and Edith Frances (Reynolds) Greathead; m. Sandra Carol Brown, Dec. 27, 1964; children: Laurel Joanne, Merrill Elizabeth. BA, Stanford (Calif.) U., 1964; BDiv, San Francisco Theol. Sem., 1967; DTh, Grad. Theol. Union, 1973. Ordained to ministry Presbyn. Ch., 1971. Assoc. prof. religion, chaplain Ill. Coll., Jacksonville, 1971-81; exec. v.p., acad. dean, prof. religion Bethel Coll., McKenzie, Tenn., 1981-87; exec. presbyter John Knox Presbytery, Richland Center, Wis., 1987—; chair evaluation and goals com. Great Rivers Presbytery, Peoria, Ill., 1977-79; chair bills and overtures com. Memphis Presbytery, 1986; commr. gen. assembly United Presbyn. Ch., San Diego, 1978. Co-author: The College 1 Experience: Integrating Work, Leisure and Service, 1980; contbr. articles to profl. jours. Bd. dirs. Elm City Rehab. Ctr., Jacksonville, 1974-79. W.K. Kellogg Found. fellow, 1978. Mem. Am. Acad. Religion, Am. Assn. for Higher Edn., Soc. Bibl. Lit., Rotary (sec. McKenzie chpt. 1981-87), Richland County Rotary, Phi Delta Kappa. Democrat. Home: 591 N Central Ave Richland Center WI 53581 Office: John Knox Presbytery 1289 W Seminary St Richland Center WI 53581

LANGFORD, ROLAND EVANS, JR., clergyman; b. Balt., Sept. 13, 1936; s. Roland Evans and Florence (Cutty) L.; m. Hertha Jane Adler, July 13, 1963; children: Rosann Marie, Florence Elizabeth, Roland Evans III, H. Marie. BA, Johns Hopkins U., 1958; BD, Evang. Luth. Theol. Sem., Chgo., 1966; postgrad., Luth. Theol. Sem., 1989—. Ordained to ministry Evang. Luth. Ch. in Am. Pastor St. John's Evang. Luth. Ch., Perrysville, Ohio, 1966-70, Auburn Luth. Ch., Springfield, Ohio, 1970-75, St. Luke's Evang. Luth. Ch. Yondota, Curtice, Ohio, 1976-86, St. John's Evang. Luth. Ch., Hagerstown, Md., 1986-89, St. John Luth. Ch., Lancaster, Pa., 1990—; bd. dirs. constn. com. Ohio synod Luth. Ch. Am., Columbus, 1968-77. Columnist Sharing The Practice jour., 1990—. Bd. dirs. Good Shepherd Luth. Home, Ashland, Ohio, 1968-70; bd. dirs. Luth. Community Svcs., Springfield, 1973-75, v.p., then pres., 1974-75. Fellow Acad. Parish Clergy (bd. dirs. 1989-91, dean gen. studies pathway 1990—). Avocations: reading, gardening, fishing, bench-rest shooting. Office: St John Luth Ch 223 W Orange St Lancaster PA 17603-3747

LANGFORD, SIDNEY, minister; b. Phila., May 1, 1912; s. Chris and Alice Muriel (Burns) L.; m. Jennie Catherine Long, Jan. 22, 1938; children: Lois Langford Wing, Virginia Langford Stonehouse, David, Ronald. Diploma, Phila. Coll. Bible, 1933, Shelton Coll., 1934. Ordained to ministry Conservative Bapt. Assn. Am., 1934. Missionary Aba Sta., Zaire, 1935-38, supt., 1939-52; mem. Zaire Field Coun., 1946-52; field dir. Africa Inland Mission, so. Sudan, 1953-56, mem. internat. coun., 1955-77; U.S. dir. Africa Inland Mission, Pearl River, N.Y., 1956-77, mem. U.S. coun., 1956—, mem. urban outreach com., 1960-88, U.S. dir. emeritus, min.-at-large, 1977—; mem. ofcl.

bd., v.p. Interdenominational Fgn. Mission Assn. N.Am., 1964-72; chmn. U.S. coordinating com. African Com. for Rehab. So. Sudan, 1972-77. Editor Inland Africa, 1956-77. Mem. bd. reference Israel's Hope, 1965—, Missionary Retreat Fellowship, 1985—; mem. pres.'s coun. Phila. Coll. Bible, 1986—. Decorated Ordre of Cheval (Belgium); recipient Alumnus award Phila. Coll. Bible, 1970. Home: 21 Roxbury Pl Glen Rock NJ 07452 Office: PO Box 178 Pearl River NY 10965 *"For I am not ashamed of the gospel of Christ: for it is the power of God unto salvation to everyone that believeth." During 55 years of involvement in Africa I have seen the reality of this in thousands of transformed lives. My heart's desire is to show the compassion of Christ for the multitudes.*

LANGFORD, THOMAS A., elder; b. Alice, Tex., Oct. 20, 1930; s. Homer Thomas and Nettie Beatrice (Clemons) L.; m. Nellie Jo Cunningham, Aug. 23, 1953; children: David Ross, Curtis Paul. BA in English, U. Calif., 1956; MA in English, Tex. Tech. U., 1963; PhD in English, Tex. Christian U., 1967. Ordained to ministry Chs. of Christ, 1950. Elder Quaker Ave Ch. of Christ, Lubbock, Tex., 1976—; assoc. dean Tec. Tech. U., Lubbock, 1970—, prof. English dept., 1976—; lectr. chs. in various states, 1970—; leader seminars various chs., 1975—; chmn. vis. com. Abilene (Tex.) Christian U., 1983-87, Lubbock Christian U., 1988-90; bd. dirs. Smithlawn Maternity Home, Lubbock, 1988—, Misson Jour., Chapel Hill, N.C., 1975-85. Author numerous articles in religious/profl. jours., 1950—; editor proceedings Annual Conf. of So. Grad. Schs., 1986-91. Cabinet mem. United Way, Lubbock, 1978. Recipient Univ. fellowship Tex. Christian U., Ft. Worth, 1965, fellowship U.S. Office Edn., Washington, 1967, NEH, 1985. Mem. Assn. Tex. Grad. Schs. (pres. 1989-90), Modern Lang. Assn., Browning Inst., Tennyson Soc., Phi Kappa Phi (pres. 1989-90). Home: 3703 48th St Lubbock TX 79413 Office: Texas Tech U Lubbock TX 79409

LANGFORD, THOMAS ANDERSON, theology educator; b. Winston-Salem, N.C., Feb. 22, 1929; s. Thomas Anderson and Louie Mae (Hughes) L.; m. Ann Marie Daniel, Dec. 27, 1951; children: Thomas A. III, James Howard, Timothy Daniel, Stephen Hughes. A.B., Davidson Coll., 1951, D.D., 1975; B.D., Duke, 1954, Ph.D., 1958. Ordained to ministry Meth. Ch., 1952; from instr. to prof. religion Duke U., Durham, N.C., 1956—, prof. systematic theology, 1971—, William Kellon Quick Disting. prof. theology and Meth. studies, chmn. dept. religion, 1965-71, dean Div. Sch., 1971-81, vice provost for acad. affairs, 1984—, interim provost, 1990, provost, 1991—; vis. prof. U. N.C., 1962. Author: In Search of Foundations: English Theology 1900-1920, 1969, Introduction to Western Philosophy: Pre-Socratics to Mill, 1970; Editor: (with G.L. Abernathy) Philosophy of Religion, 1962, 2d edit., 1968, History of Philosophy, 1965, (with W.H. Poteat) Intellect and Hope, Essays in the Thought of Michael Polanyi, 1968, Christian Wholeness, 1979, The Harvest of the Spirit, 1981, Practical Divinity: Theology in the Wesleyan Tradition, 1983; Contbr. articles to profl. jours. World Meth. Council rep. in theol. discussions with Roman Catholic Ch. and Luth. World Fedn., 1975—, Reformed World Alliance, 1987; del. Gen. Conf. United Meth. Ch., 1976, 80, 84, 88; Southeastern Jurisdictional Conf., 1972, 76, 80, 84, 88; chmn. Duke self-study coordinating com. So. Assn. Colls. and Univs., 1975-76; trustee Bennett Coll., Greensboro; exec. com. World Meth. Council, 1976-81. Gurney Harris Kearns fellow, 1956-57; Dempster fellow, 1957; Am. Council Learned Socs. fellow, 1965-66; Soc. Religion in Higher Edn. fellow, 1969; named outstanding tchr. Duke, 1965; recipient E. Harris Harbison award Danforth Found., 1965-66. Mem. Am. Theol. Soc., Phi Beta Kappa. Office: Duke U Divinity Sch Durham NC 27706

LANGHINRICHS, RICHARD ALAN, minister; b. Moline, Ill., May 15, 1921; s. Albert William and Therese Irene (Etchingham) L.; m. Ruth Helen Imler, May 31, 1958; children: Julie, Jennifer. BS in Speech, Northwestern U., 1942; STB, Harvard U., 1965. Ordained minister, Unitarian Universalist Ch. Author N.Y.C., 1946-52; mgr. Edmond Martin Real Estate, N.Y.C., 1948-52; gen. mgr. Palace Quality Launderers, Detroit, 1952-62; minister to students First Parish, Cambridge, Mass., 1962-65; minister Unitarian Universalist Congregation, Ft. Wayne, Ind., 1965-89, minister emeritus, 1989—. Contbr. articles to profl. jours. Founder NE Ind. Meml. Soc., Ft. Wayne, 1965, Planned Parenthood NE Ind., 1978, ACLU of NE Ind., 1974; Ind. del. Citizens' Conf. To End War in Vietnam, Paris, 1971. Recipient Purple Heart, Bronze Star for Bravery USMCR, 1942-45; Distinguished Service award Ohio Valley UU Dist., 1986. Mem. Unitarian Universalist Ministers Assn. (trustee 1970-72), Ohio Valley Unitarian Universalist Dist. (pres. 1978-80), Fortnightly Club (pres. 1980-81), Rotary. Avocations: acting, theatre. Home: 459 Englewood Ct Fort Wayne IN 46807 Office: Unitarian Universalist Congregation 5310 Old Mill Rd Fort Wayne IN 46807

LANGLEY, MARK A., minister; b. Lubbock, Tex., May 23, 1946; s. Earl E. and Lois E. (Henson) L.; m. Virginia Lauretta Lacewell, Dec. 26, 1966; children: Greg, Jeremy, Aaron. BA, Wayland U., Plainview, Tex., 1969; MRE, Southwestern Bapt. Theol. Sem., Ft. Worth, 1974; M Music Edn., Cen. State U., Edmond, Okla., 1984. Ordained to ministry So. Bapt. Conv. Min. activities Normandale Bapt. Ch., Ft. Worth, 1970-75; min. music Mountain View Bapt. Ch., El Paso, Tex., 1975-76, Britton Bapt. Ch., Oklahoma City, 1980-84; min. music and edn. Trinity Bapt. Ch., Springfield, Oreg., 1976-80, Calvary Bapt. Ch., Idaho Falls, Idaho, 1984—; mem. exec. bd. Utah-Idaho So. Bapt. Conv., Salt Lake City, 1987-90. Mem. Religious Educators Am. Office: Calvary Bapt Ch 785 1st St Idaho Falls ID 83401

LANGLEY, TIMOTHY MICHAEL, minister; b. Shawnee, Okla., Mar. 11, 1954; s. R.V. and Alice Elizabeth (Alcorn) L.; children: Mary Elizabeth, Landon Grant. Student, Okla. U., 1967-71; AS, Acad. Health Scis., San Antonio, 1983; AA, Ft. Steilecuum County Coll., Tacoma, Wash., 1974; postgrad., E. Cen. U., 1976-78. Lic. to ministry S. Bapt. Ch., 1979, ordained, 1985. Min. music/youth Trinity Bapt. Ch., Ada, Okla., 1976-79, 1st Bapt. Ch., Idabel, Okla., 1979-81; min. music/edn. Henderson Hills Bapt. Ch., Edmond, Okla., 1982-83; music evangelist 1s So. Bapt. Ch., Del City, Okla., 1983-85; min. music Potee Park Bapt. Ch., St. Joseph, Mo., 1985-90; min. worship E. Metro Community Ch. So. Bapt. Conv., Aurora, Colo., 1990—; prin. Emanuel So. Christian Sch., Edmond, 1983-84; pres., clinician, composer Day Star Prodns., Aurora, 1985—; v.p. C Bar N Ministries, Gulf Shores, Ala., 1983—; pres. Lynnalynn Ministries Inc., St. Joseph, Mo., 1985-90; founder Mile High Music Conf., Aurora, 1991. Composer religious songs. Liaison sch. bd. Horizon Middle Sch., Aurora, 1990-91. With U.S. Army, 1973-76. Mem. Music Tex., Music Fla., Music Memphis, Mile High Music Conf., Idabel Rotary (music dir. 1979-80). Republican. Avocations: golf, fishing. Home: 17919 E Jarvis Pl Aurora CO 00130 Office: E Metro Community Ch So Bapt Conv 1730 S Abilene Ste 201 Aurora CO 80012

LANGLOIS, DONALD HAROLD, minister, librarian; b. Rochester, N.Y., Nov. 25, 1940; s. Harold Lionel and Eleanor Emma (Stout) L.; m. Ullrike Frances Baudisch, Aug. 28, 1965; children—Stephen, Eric. A.B., Kenyon Coll., 1962; M.Div., Gen. Theol. Sem., 1966; M.L.S., Queens Coll., 1973. Ordained priest Episcopal Ch., 1967. Asst. Christ Episcopal Ch., Hornell, N.Y., 1966-67; vicar Ch. of Redeemer, Addison, N.Y., 1967-72; librarian Martin Luther High Sch., Maspeth, N.Y., 1973-76; asst. St. George's Ch., Flushing, N.Y., 1973-76; dean Star Prairie Deanery, Rice Lake, Wis., 1981-84; rector Grace Episcopal Ch., Rice Lake, 1976-85; rector Holy Trinity Episc. Ch., Danville, Ill., 1985-87; reference libr. Glendale (Ariz.) Pub. Libr., 1987-89, Chandler (Ariz.) Pub. Libr., 1988-89, Phoenix Coll., 1989-90, Ariz. State Dept. Libr., Archives and Pub. Records, Phoenix, 1990—; asst. St. Augustine's Ch., Tempe, Ariz., 1991—; chmn. Diocesan Communications Dept., 1980-85; clerical del. Province V Synod, 1983-85. Editor The Herald, 1980-85. Contbr. articles to profl. jours. Bd. dirs. No. Pines Unified Services Ctr., Cumberland, Wis., 1980-85, Rice Lake Pub. Library, 1982-85; bd. dirs. Friends of Rice Lake Pub. Library, 1984-85, pres., 1979; gen. leader Knapp Street Hustlers 4-H, Rice Lake, 1982-85. Mem. Soc. of King Charles the Martyr, Sisterhood of Holy Nativity (priest assoc.), Beta Phi Mu. Avocations: archaeology, photography, sightseeing, reading. Home: 700 W Brown St # 5 Tempe AZ 85281-3566 Office: State Capitol Rsch Div 1700 W Washington St Phoenix AZ 85007

LANGSTAFF, ALAN MCGREGOR, minister; b. Sydney, N.S.W., Australia, Feb. 26, 1935; came to U.S., 1980; s. William and Catherine (McGregor) L.; m. Dorothy Mary Roan, Nov. 29, 1958; children: Beth Yvonne, Joy Heather Langstaff Plaisted. BArch, U. N.S.W., Sydney, 1959; MDiv, Melbourne (Australia) Coll. Divinity, 1975. Ordained to ministry Antioch Christian Fellowship, 1969. Pastor Meth. Ch. Australia, Sydney, 1963-73; dir. The Temple Trust, Sydney, 1973-81; pres. Vision Ministries, Mpls., 1981-84, Kairos Ministries, Mpls., 1984—; sr. pastor Antioch Christian Fellowship, Mpls., 1986—; sec.-treas. Twin City Christian TV, Mpls., 1984—. Author: The Antioch Church, 1991; editor Vision Mag., 1973-81; contbr. articles to jours. in field. Mem. Network Christian Mins., Ch. Growth Internat., Seoul, Korea (adv. bd. 1979—), Assn. Internat. Missions Soc. (adv. bd. 1989—). Home: 3703 Plymouth Rd S Minnetonka MN 55343 Office: Kairos Ministries Inc PO Box 27186 Golden Valley MN 55427-0186 *Your life is God's gift to you; what you do with it is your gift to Him. You only have one life to live, so live it to the full potential that He has given you.*

LANIER, JON ROBERT, minister; b. Columbus, Ohio, Feb. 2, 1963; s. Memphis Robert and Geraldine Magaline (Hunt) L.; m. Karen Elizabeth Williamson, Dec. 19, 1987. BS in Christian Ministry, Cin. Bible Coll., 1989. Ordained to ministry Ch. of Christ, 1991. Missionary Power Ministries, Edon, Ohio, 1983-85; camp youth dir. Lake James Christian Assembly, Angola, Ind., 1986; youth minister Oakley Ch. of Christ, Cin., 1986-88, Seerly Creek Christian Ch., Indpls., 1988-89; assoc. min. LaBelle View Ch. of Christ, Steubenville, Ohio, 1989-91; sr. min. McComb (Ohio) Ch. of Christ, 1991—; fine arts chmn. Ohio Teens for Christ, Columbus, 1990-93; preacher "Rejoice in the Lord" Sta. WSTV, Steubenville, 1990—. Editor: (newsletter) Oakley Tree, 1986-88. Counselor/youth Families of Mil. in Gulf War, Mingo, Ohio, 1990-91. Recipient 2d pl. award for photography City of Angola, Ind. Mem. Nat. Carver's Mus. Home: 224 E South St PO Box 36 McComb OH 45858 *The family is God's ordained method of transferring morals and values to the next generation. Youth need to be told and made to believe that they are significant and important, not because of what they have or don't have, but because they are made in the image of God.*

LANIGAN, SISTER KAREN MARIE, nun, religious order superior; b. Alexandria, Minn., Oct. 24, 1948; d. Thomas Walter and Bernadette Gladys (Cobert) L. BA, Coll. St. Francis, Joliet, Ill., 1973; MEd, Loyola U., Chgo., 1981; MA, Duquesne U., 1986. Joined Franciscan Sisters of the Sacred Heart, Roman Cath. Ch., 1966; cert. tchr., Ill.; cert sch. adminstr., Ill. Tchr. St. Mary's Sch., Avilla, Ind., 1969-72, tchr., prin., 1978-85; tchr. St. Mary's Sch., Park Forest, Ill., 1973-77, St. Charles' Sch., Ft. Wayne, Ind., 1977-78; formation directress novitiate Franciscan Sisters of the Sacred Heart, Mokena, Ill., 1987-89, gen. superior motherhouse, pres. assn., 1989—. Pres. bd. dirs. Queen of Angels Hosp. Inc., L.A., 1989—. Mem. Leadership Conf. Women Religious, Franciscan Fedn., Internat. Franciscan Conf., Internat. Union Superiors Gen. Home and Office: St Francis Woods RR 4 Mokena IL 60448

LANKFORD, S. A., religious organization administrator. Exec. dir. Ch. of God (Cleveland, Tenn.), Bramalea, Ont., Can. Office: Ch of God, PO Box 2036, Bramalea, ON Canada L6T 3S3*

LANNING, BILL LESTER, clergyman; b. Kansas City, Mo., Oct. 31, 1944; s. Lester Benjamin and Hazel Bernice (Perky) L.; m. Carmen Nadine Keeler, Sept. 4, 1966; children: Melanie, Mario. BA, SW Bapt. U., 1968; MA, Baylor U., 1971, PhD, 1976; postgrad., Wichita State U., 1989—. Pastor La Mission Bautista, Calvert, Tex., 1972-74; editorial asst. Jour. of Ch. and State, Waco, Tex., 1974-77; pastor Zion United Ch. of Christ, Kurten, Tex., 1977-88; instr. Blinn Coll., College Station, Tex., 1979-88; pastor First Congl. United Ch. of Christ, McPherson, Kans., 1988-91, Plymouth Congl. United Ch. of christ, Sedgwick, Kans., 1991—; presenter in field. Contbr. book revs. to JOur. of Ch. and State, Bryan Eagle. Mem. exec. coun. Boy Scouts Am., Bryan, 1977-81; del. Tex. Dem. Conv., Houston, 1980; judge 4-H Round-Up Family Life Edn., College Station, 1982, debate tournament, McPherson, Kans., 1988; bd. dirs. Tex. A&M Con. for Town and Country, College Station, 1981-86, Kid's Corner (Day Care), McPherson, 1988—; bd. dirs., v.p. Tex. Impact, Austin, Tex., 1983-88, Family Life Counseling Ctr., McPherson, 1988—. With USAF, 1962-65. Mem. Am. Acad. Religion, Am. Philos. Assn., Philosophy of Sci. Assn., North Am. Assn. for the Study of Religion, Conf. on Religion in South India, Kiwanis (chair spiritual aims McPherson club 1989—). Home: 1120 Central McPherson KS 67460 Office: Plymouth Congl Ch PO Box 138 Sedgwick KS 67135

LANOUE, JOHN LONG, religious organization administrator; b. Beaumont, Tex., Sept. 25, 1934; s. John Charles and Ruth Irene (Long) LaN.; m. Kaywin Joan Baldwin, Dec. 18, 1954; children—John Long, Lydia Kaywin. B.A., Stephen F. Austin U., 1957; M.Div., Southwestern Bapt. Theol. Sem., 1960; postgrad U. Houston, 1963, U. Tex.-Tyler, 1980-81. Cert. expedition leader Nat. Outdoor Leadership Sch. Ordained to ministry Baptist Ch., 1954; pastor churches, Tex., 1954-60, West Frankfort, Ill., 1960-62; campus minister U. Houston, 1962-69; state youth coordinator Bapt. Gen. Conv. Tex., Dallas, 1969-73; outdoor edn. cons. Bapt. Sunday Sch. Bd., Nashville, 1973-81; dir. Royal Ambassadors and Bapt. Young Men, Bapt. Gen. Conv. Tex., Dallas, 1981—. Dir. mobile unit disaster relief, Dallas, 1981—. Mem. Christian Camping Internat., Am. Camping Assn., NRA. Republican. Home: Rt 5 Box 221 Tyler TX 75706 Office: 511N Akard Suite 1129 Dallas TX 75201

LANPHER, BILL WESTON, college president, minister; b. Bernie, Mo., June 29, 1933; s. Weston and Norma Pearl (Bishop) L.; m. Janice Mae Thornhill, Aug. 28, 1954; children: David Geoffrey, James Eric. BS, Nyack Coll., 1955; BA, Wayne State U., 1956; MA, Mich. State U., 1958; D of Ministry, Drew U., 1984. Ordained to ministry Christian and Missionary Alliance, 1958. Min. various chs. Christian and Missionary Alliance, 1955-69; asst. v.p. Christian and Missionary Alliance, N.Y.C. and Nyack, N.Y., 1969-85; dean of students St. Paul Bible Coll., St. Bonifacius, Minn., 1985-87, pres., 1987—; trustee Beulah Beach Corp., 1966-68; treas. west cen. dist. Christian and Missionary Alliance, 1966-68, bd. mgrs., 1988—; mem. exec. com. Eccles. Endorsing Agts., 1978-79. Mem. Adminstrs. Higher Edn., Assn. Pres. Ind. Colls. and Univs., Nat. Assn. Evangs. (chmn. commn. on chaplains, bd. adminstrn. 1974-78, sec. commn. on chaplains 1978-80), Assn. Statisticians Am. Religious Bodies (pres. 1978-80), Nat. Conf. on Ministry to Armed Forces (chmn. com. on concerns 1983-85). Republican. Office: St Paul Bible Coll Saint Bonifacius MN 55375

LANPHER, DAVID GEOFFREY, minister; b. Lansing, Mich., Jan. 10, 1959; s. Bill W. and Janice M. (Thornhill) L.; m. Linda A. Thomas, July 3, 1982; children: Gordon W., Jonathon I. BA, Asbury Coll., 1981; MDiv, Alliance Theol. Sem., 1984. Ordained to ministry Christian and Missionary Alliance, 1986. Asst. pastor Upper St. Clair Christian and Missionary Alliance, Pitts., 1984-87; sr. pastor Washington Union Alliance Ch., New Castle, Pa., 1987-90; youth pastor Community Alliance Ch., Butler, Pa., 1990—; commn. chmn., Western Pa. Dist. Youth, 1987—; v.p., Greater Ne Castle Ministerium, 1988-90, sec., 1987-88. Office: Community Alliance Ch 800 Mercer Rd Butler PA 16001

LANSER, LESLIE JOHN, Christian radio broadcasting executive and owner; b. Sanborn, Iowa, Apr. 19, 1935; s. Brant P. and Johanna (VanderLugt) L.; m. Mildred Swank, Mar. 5, 1954 (div. Jan. 1978); m. Patricia L. Balk, June 14, 1986; children: Vaughn, Greg, Steve, Vicki, Rick, Curt, Brad, Heather, Kelly. Newspaper employee Pella (Iowa) Chronical, 1954-57; printer Hoekstra Printing, Grand Rapids, Mich., 1957-68; owner, gen. mgr. Lanser Broadcasting Corp., Holland, Mich., 1968—; deacon 1st Christian Ref. Ch., Grand Rapids, 1973-76; elder Christ Meml. Ch., Holland, 1991—. Pres. Holland Merchants Assn., 1981-82, Holland Chamber Orch., 1991—; v.p. Nat. Main St. Bd., Holland, 1984-85. With USNR, 1952-57. Mem. Holland C. of C. (chmn. 1990-91), Rotary (pres. Holland club 1989-90, Paul Harris award 1990). Mem. Ref. Ch. in Am. Home: 447 Brecado Ct Holland MI 49423 Office: Lanser Broadcasting Corp 5658 143d Ave Holland MI 49423

LANSFORD, THERON GEORGE, priest; b. Denton, Tex., June 13, 1931; s. Marcus L. and Lucile (Wallis) L.; m. Mary Cook, Sept. 1, 1959; children: Marcella, Thomas Leslie. BA, U. Tex., Austin, 1957, MA, 1959. Ordained priest Episcopal Ch., 1972. Asst. Holy Family Ch., Angola, Ind., 1971-74, priest-in-charge, 1974-80; diocesan missioner Diocese of No. Ind., South Bend, Ind., 1980—; dean students Tri-State U., Angola, 1965—; mem. com. on marriage and family Diocese No. Ind., 1983—; dep. to gen. conv. Episcopal Ch., 1970. Mem. APA, Nat. Assn. Coll. Pers. Adminstrs., Ind. Coll. Pers. Assn. (dir. 1970-72), U.S. Fencing Coaches Assn. (v.p.), Sigma Xi. Home: 403 Inglenook Pl Angola IN 46703 Office: Tri-State U Angola IN 46703

LANTZ, GEORGE BENJAMIN, JR., business executive, college president, consultant; b. Buckhannon, W.Va., Feb. 6, 1936; s. George Benjamin and Georgia Myrtle (Bodkin) L.; m. Mary Sue Powell, Feb. 25, 1957; children—Mary Lynne, Marsha, Kimberly, Rebecca, Todd. A.B. with honors, W.Va. Wesleyan Coll., 1960; S.T.B. with honors, Boston U., 1964, Ph.D., 1971. Minister United Meth. Pastorates, W.Va. and Mass., 1956-75; mem. faculty W.Va. Wesleyan Coll., Buckhannon, 1967-73, chmn. div. humanities, prof. humanities and religion, 1974-75; asst. to pres., ACE fellow Ohio Wesleyan U., Delaware, 1973-74; dean coll. Mount Union Coll., Alliance, Ohio, 1975-80, pres., 1980-85; v.p. adminstrn. and devel. Nesco, Inc., Hudson, Ohio, 1985-88; pres. U. Indpls., 1988—; cons. Coun. of Ind. Colls., Washington, 1982—; bd. dirs. The Fifth Third Bank. Trustee W.Va. Wesleyan Coll., 1986-88; bd. dirs. Associated Colls. of Ind., Community Hosps. Ind., Inc., Salvation Army Adv. Bd., Ind. Law Enforcement Tng. Bd., Greater Indpls. Progress Com., Arts Coun. Indpls., Ind. State chpt. Nat. Multiple Sclerosis Soc., World Trade Ctr. Indpls.; bd. govs. United Way Cen. Ind.; mem. Japan-Am. Soc. of Ind., Inc., Benjamin Harrison Meml. Commn., English Speaking Union., Ind. Soc. of Chgo.; mem. adv. group Midwest Partnership Ind. Colls.; mem. Blue Ridge panel Indpls. Bus. Jour. With U.S. Army, 1954-56. Recipient Cokesbury Grad. award Meth. Bd. Higher Edn. Fellow Am. Coun. Edn. (nat. adv. com., self-regulation initiatives), Coalition of Urban Colls.; mem. AAUP, Nat. Assn. Ind. Colls. and Univs. (commn. on financing higher edn.), Am. Assn. Higher Edn., bd. dirs. Nat. Assn. Schs. and Colls. of United Meth. Ch. (com. on internat. edn.), Internat. Assn. Univ. Pres., Soc. Bibl. Lit., North Central Assn. Colls. and Schs. (commr. 1978-85, cons., evaluator), Indpls. C. of C. (bd. dirs. 1990—), Columbia Club, Skyline Club, Kiwanis. Home: 4051 Otterbein Ave Indianapolis IN 46227 Office: U Indpls Office Pres 1400 E Hanna Ave Indianapolis IN 46227

LANTZ, W. FRANKLIN, religious executive; b. Chewsville, Md., June 29, 1930; s. Charles Reno and Mary Eva (Snyder) L.; m. June Ellen Lykens, Sept. 3, 1955; children: Annmarie, Timothy Paul. BA, Lebanon Valley Coll., Annville, Pa., 1957; MDiv, United Theol. Sem., Dayton, Ohio, 1960. Lic. nursing home adminstr., Pa. Pastor 1st Evang. United Brethren Ch., Mont Alto, Pa., 1960-63, St. Peter's United Ch. Christ, Frackville, Pa., 1963-67; occupancy dir., inspector Schuylkill County Housing Authority, Pottsville, Pa., 1968-69; asst. adminstr. Brethren Village, Inc., Lancaster, Pa., 1969-74; adminstr., chief exec. officer Brethren Village, Inc., 1974-80, v.p., pub. relations and devel., 1980-83; exec. dir. Homestead Village, Inc., 1983-85; interim pastor St. Paul's United Ch. of Christ, Red Run, Pa., 1985-86; exec. dir. Christian Concern Mgmt. & Devel., Inc., Norristown, Pa., 1986—; bd. dirs. Council for Health and Human Svc. Ministries, United Ch. of Christ, 1989—. Contbr. articles to profl. jours. Active Pa. Assn. Non-Profit Homes for Aging. Mem. Rotary. Republican. United Ch. of Christ. Avocations: reading, boating, swimming, tennis, travel. Home: 93 Peach Ln Lancaster PA 17601 Office: Christian Concern Inc 1514 W Marshall St Norristown PA 19403

LANZEN, GREGGORY EINAR, minister, religious educator; b. Moline, Ill., Dec. 15, 1951; s. Einar George and JoAn Aleen (Thurber) L.; m. Marcia Beth Thomson, Aug. 11, 1973; children: Scott, David, Nathan, Jeffery. BS, Faith Bapt. Bible Coll., Ankeny, Iowa, 1974. Youth minister Silvis (Ill.) Hts. Bapt. Ch., 1974-76, Oswego (Ill.) Bapt. Ch., 1976-78; assoc. pastor, dir. Christian Edn. First Bapt. Ch., Goshen, Ind., 1981—; coun. mem. Ill. Regular Bapt. Youth Coun., Oswego, 1976-78; assoc. rep. Word of Life Clubs, Goshen, Ind., 1984—, exec. assoc., Schroon Lake, N.Y., 1985—. Dir., editor youth tng. video The Good, Bad and Ugly, 1989, Jalopy Raid Round-up, 1990; contbr. articles to profl. jours. Firefighter, EMT Oswego Fire Dept., 1977-81, Elkhart Twp. Fire Dept., Goshen, 1982—, fire safety tchr., 1982—. Christian Edn. fellowship, Evang. Tchr. Tng. Assn., 1982, Honor Mem. Christian Edn. fellow, 1988. Republican. Home: 911 S Indiana Ave Goshen IN 46526 Office: First Bapt Ch 917 S Indiana Ave Goshen IN 46526 *I am constantly amazed at the fact that God can take a person with my inabilities and shortcomings, and make a success out of my life. If He can do it for me He will do it for anyone who will let Him.*

LAPOINTE, ROGER LUCIEN, religion educator; b. Kénogami, Que., Can., July 28, 1929; s. Pierre Antonio and Diana (Olsen) L. Licentiate in Philosophy and Theology, Rome, 1951; Angelicum, 1955; doctorate, Pontificum Inst. Biblicum, Rome, 1966. Assoc. prof. systematic theology St. Paul U., Ottawa, Ont., Can., 1970-75; assoc. prof. sociology of religion Ottawa U., 1976—. Author: Les Trois dimensions de l'herméeneutique, 1967, Consultation internationale sur le non-être, 1969, Dialogues bibliques et dialectique interpersonelle, 1971; Regard sur la société de consommation, 1973, Módèle dialectique du Christianisme, 1981, Socio-anthropologie due religieux: I. La regigion populaire au péril de la modernité, 1988, II. Le cercle enchanté de la croyance, 1989; editor SR (Studies in Religion/Sci. of religieuses), 1976-81; co-editor: Le divorce, 1973, Pluralism: Its Meaning Today, 1974; contbr. articles to profl. publs. Mem. Can. Soc. Theology (pres. 1971-74), Can. Soc. Study Religion (pres. 1984-86). Home: 285 Laurier St, Hull, PQ Canada J8X 3W9 Office: 177 Waller St, Ottawa, ON Canada K1N 6N5 *We must move beyond tolerance, even behond pluralism, toward an appreciation of humanity as definitively diverse.*

LAPORTE, JEAN-MARC, religious educator; b. Edmundston, N.B., Can., July 5, 1937; s. Jean-Murillo and Laurente (Levesque) L. BA, Loyola Coll., Montreal, Que., Can., 1957; MA, U. Montreal, 1958; STL, Regis Coll., 1968; Dr.es.Sc.Rel., Universite de Strasbourg, France, 1971. Ordained Jesuit priest Roman Cath. Ch., 1967. Prof. theology Regis Coll., Toronto, Ont., Can., 1971—, pres., 1975-82; mem. accrediting commn. Assn. Theol. Schs. of U.S. and Can., Dayton, Ohio, 1978-84, chmn. 1982-84. Author: Les Structures dynamiques de la grace, 1971, Patience and Power: Grace for the First World, 1988; editor: The Trinification of the World, 1978. Mem. Can. Theol. Soc., Cath. Theol. Soc. Office: Regis Coll, 15 Saint Mary St, Toronto, ON Canada M4Y 2R5

LAPP, JAMES MERRILL, clergyman, marriage and family therapist; b. Lansdale, Pa., July 20, 1937; s. John E. and Edith (Nice) L.; m. Nancy Sevartzentruber, Mar. 1, 1936; children: Cynthia Ann, J. Michael, Philip Alan. B.A., Eastern Mennonite Coll., 1960; B.D., Goshen Bibl. Sem., 1963; D.Min., Drew U., 1981. Ordained to ministry Mennonite Ch., 1963. Pastor Belmont Mennonite Ch., Elkhart, Ind., 1961-63; paster Perkasie Mennonite Ch., Pa., 1963-72, Albany Mennonite Ch., Oreg., 1972-81; dir. campus ministries Goshen Coll., Ind., 1981—; tchr. Christopher Dock Mennonite High Sch., Lansdale, Pa., 1963-70; moderator Pacific Coast Conf. of Mennonite Ch., Oreg., 1977-79, Mennonite Gen. Assembly, Lombard, Ill., 1985-87; exec. sec. gen. bd., 1988—. Contbr. articles to Mennonite Ch. publs. Mem. Am. Assn. Marriage and Family Therapy (cert.). Democrat. Avocation: gardening; baking. Home: 210 Oak Ln Goshen IN 46526 Office: Mennonite Church Gen Bd 528 E Madison St Lombard IL 60148

LAPP, JOHN ALLEN, religious organization administrator; b. Lansdale, Pa., Mar. 15, 1933; s. John E. and Edith Ruth (Nyce) L.; m. Alice Weber, Aug. 20, 1955; children: John Franklin, Jennifer Lapp Lerch, Jessica. BA, Ea. Mennonite Coll., 1954; MA, Case Western Res. U., 1958; PhD, U. Pa., 1968. From instr. to prof. history Ea. Mennonite Coll., Harrisonburg, Va., 1958-69; exec. sec. peace sect. Mennonite Cen. Com., Akron, Pa., 1969-72, exec. sec., 1985—; prof. history, dean Goshen (Ind.) Coll., 1972-79, prof. history, provost, 1979-84; rep. Ch. World Svc. and Witness, N.Y.C., 1985—; observer World Coun. Chs., Canberra, Australia, 1991. Author: Mennonite Church in India 1897-1962, 1972, The View from East Jerusalem, 1980; editor: Peacemaking in a Broken World, 1970; columnist Christian Living mag., 1963-80; mem. editorial bd. Mennonite Quar. Rev., 1972—; contbr. articles to profl. jours. Visitor N. Cen. Assn. Schs. and Colls., Chgo., 1976-84; pres. Rockingham Coun. on Human Rels, Harrisonburg, 1962-65; v.p. Va. Coun. on Human Rights, Richmond, 1965-69. Mem. Conf. on Faith and History, Mennonite Hist. Soc. (pres. 1972-84). Home: 13 Knollwood Akron PA 17501 Office: Mennonite Cen Com 21 S 12th St Akron PA 17501

LAPP, JOSEPH L., academic administrator, lawyer; b. Lansdale, Pa., Dec. 22, 1942; m. Hannah Mack, Aug. 29, 1964; 1 child, JoHanna Lynn. BA, Ea. Mennonite Coll., 1966; JD, Ill. Inst. Tech., 1972; Coll. Mgmt. Program, Carnegie Mellon U., 1987. Bar: Pa. 1972, U.S. Supreme Ct., 1982. Assoc. Clemens & Nulty, 510 E Board St, Souderton, Pa., 1972-73; ptnr. Tessler & Lapp, Franconia, Souderton, 1973-76; sole practice Souderton, 1976-79; ptnr. Souder, Rosenberger, Lapp & Bricker, Souderton, 1979-86; counsel Souder, Rosenberger & Bricker, Souderton, 1987; pres. Ea. Mennonite Coll. and Sem., Harrisonburg, Va., 1987—. Trustee Ea. Mennonite Coll. and Sem., 1973-86, chmn. acad. com., 1975-80, vice chmn. bd. trustee, 1975-80, chmn., 1980-86; Montgomery County Legal Aid Bd., 1973-86; pres. bd. dirs. Bethany Child Care Ctr., Phila., 1978-82, bd. dirs. 1974-86; mem. ch. coun. Plains Mennonite Ch., 1973-77, chmn. congregation and coun., 1981-83, com. ministerial retirement Franconia Mennonite Conf., 1976-87, mem. Park View Mennonite Ch., Harrisonburg, 1987—; mem. Rep. Nat. Com., 1983-86; v.p. Clayton-Kratz Fellowship, 1977-87; mem. com. health and welfare Mennonite Bd. Missions, Elkhart, Ind., 1979-82; bd. dirs., mem. fin. com. Indian Creek Found., Harleysville, Pa., 1983-87; bd. dirs. Ea. Pa. Mediation Svc., 1982-87. Mem. Pa. Bar Assn., Montgomery Bar Assn., Rotary. Home: 1280 Lincolnshire Dr Harrisonburg VA 22801 Office: Ea Mennonite Coll & Sem Office Pres Harrisonburg VA 22801

LAPSLEY, JAMES NORVELL, JR., minister, pastoral theology educator; b. Clarksville, Tenn., Mar. 16, 1930; s. James Norvell and Evangeline (Winn) L.; m. Brenda Ann Weakley, June 4, 1953 (dec. May 1989); children: Joseph William, Jacqueline Evangeline; m. Helen Joan Winter, Feb. 24, 1990. BA, Rhodes Coll., 1952; BD, Union Theol. Sem., 1955; PhD (Div. Sch. fellow, Rockefeller fellow), U. Chgo., 1961. Ordained to ministry Presbyn. Ch., 1955; asst. min. Gentilly Presbyn. Ch., New Orleans, 1955-57; instr. Princeton (N.J.) Theol. Sem., 1961-63, asst. prof., 1963-67, assoc. prof., 1967-76, prof. pastoral theology, 1976-80, Carl and Helen Egner prof. pastoral theology, 1980—, acad. dean, 1984-89. Editor: The Concept of Willing, 1967, Salvation and Health, 1972; chmn. editorial bd.: Pastoral Psychology Jour., 1975-84. Bd. dirs. Westminster Found., Princeton U., 1970-76. Danforth fellow Menninger Found., 1960-61. Mem. Am. Acad. Religion. Presbyterian. Home: 95 Mercer St Princeton NJ 08540 Office: Princeton Theol Sem CN 821 Princeton NJ 08540

LARDY, SISTER SUSAN MARIE, prioress; b. Sentinel Butte, N.D., Nov. 9, 1937; d. Peter Aloysius and Elizabeth Julia (Dietz) L. BS in Edn., U. Mary, Bismarck, N.D., 1965; MEd, U. N.D., 1972. Elem. tchr. Cathedral Grade Sch., Bismarck, 1958-67, Christ the King Sch., Mandan, N.D., 1967-68, 70-72, St. Joseph's Sch., Mandan, 1968-70; asst. prof. edn. U. Mary, Bismarck, 1972-80; adminstr., asst. prioress Annunciation Priory, Bismarck, 1980-84, prioress, major superior, 1984—; pres., bd. dirs. St. Alexius Med. Ctr., Bismarck, 1984—, Garrison (N.D.) Meml. Hosp., 1984—, U. Mary, Bismarck, 1984—. Chair Health Commn. of Diocese of Bismarck, 1991. Mem. Delta Kappa Gamma. Home: 7520 University Dr Bismarck ND 58504-9653

LARGE, TIMOTHY WALLACE, religious organization administrator; b. Palo Alto, Calif., Feb. 23, 1942; s. Charles Delano Henry and Jean Eleanor (Parker) L.; m. Vickie Lee Olson, Aug. 6, 1978; children: Jonathan Jeffrey, Sarah Jean. BSBA, Menlo Coll., 1964; MBA, U. Santa Clara, 1966; cert., Multnomah Sch. Bible, Portland, Oreg., 1973; M of Div., Talbot Theol. Sem., La Mirada, Calif., 1978. CPA, Calif. Acct. Bramer Accountancy Corp., Santa Fe Springs, Calif., 1974-76; instr. Biola Coll., La Mirada, Calif., 1978; acct. Conservative Bapt. Assn. So. Calif., Anaheim, 1978-83; CPA H. Canaday, P.A., Santa Fe Springs, 1983—; adminstr. Temple Baptist Ch., Perris, Calif., 1985-87; treas. Inst. Evangelico, La Puenta, Calif., 1987—; cons. Exec. Leasing, La Mirada, 1976—. Treas. Founders chpt. Kidney Found. So. Calif., Orange County, 1974-76; chaplain Christian Hosp. Med. Ctr., Perris, 1985—. Served with U.S. Army, 1965-69. Fellow Nat. Assn. Ch. Bus. Adminstrs.; mem. AICPA, Am. Mgt. Assn., Christian Ministries Mgt. Assn. Republican. Baptist. Avocations: bowling, ping pong, travel. Home: 26928 Potomac Dr Sun City CA 92381 Office: 14864 Valley Blvd La Puente CA 91744

LARGEN, FREDRICK JAMES, minister; b. Newark, Aug. 1, 1937; s. Frederick Jonathan and Wilma Inez (McElroy) L.; m. Donna Jean Schuetz, May 31, 1957 (div. Feb. 1978); children: Gail Jean Largen Weeks, Peter John, Sandra Ruth; m. Jennifer K. Caughey, May 20, 1978; children: Daniel Fredrick, Erica Jane. BA, Elmhurst Coll., 1959; BD, Lancaster Sem., 1962, ThM, 1962; postgrad., Union Theol. Sem., 1962-64. Ordained to ministry Bapt. Chs. in U.S.A., 1964. Youth pastor, asst. pastor, pastor Christ Ch., St. Marks, Wapwallopen Charge, Pa., 1959-63; tutorial asst. Greek and N.T. Lancaster (Pa.) Sem., 1961-62; rsch. asst. N.T. Union Theol. Sem., N.Y.C., 1962-64; pastor Foster Pk. Bapt. Ch., Chgo., 1964-66, Valley Community Ch., Burnsville, Minn., 1966—; bd. dirs. Mpls. Coun. Chs., 1968-69; owner, sec.-treas. The Kitchen Store Inc., Burnsville, 1979—; pres, FJL Assocs.; med. cons., Burnsville, 1975—; radio and TV appearances on behalf of Lyme disease, 1990. Author: Source of Gospel of Mark, 1962, The Christian Faith in the Modern World, 1981; inventor self-contained med. surg. units. Mem. Lebannon Twp. Planning Commn., Apple Valley, Minn., 1967-68; moderator Lebannon Twp., 1967-68; mayor City of Apple Valley, 1968-76; vice chmn., chmn. Dakota County Criminal Justice Coun., 1974-75. Recipient Minn. Valley Man of Yr. award Sun Newspapers, Mpls., 1970, Outstanding Community Svc. award City of Apple Valley, 1976; sr. scholar Lancaster Theol. Sem., 1962; Fred J. Largen Pk. named in his honor, City of Apple Valley, 1982. Republican. Home: 13140 Thomas Ave S Burnsville MN 55337 *There is but one choice in life. You must either side with God to end the chaos of an unfinished "creation" or continue to perpetuate it.*

LARKIN, WILLIAM THOMAS, bishop; b. Mount Morris, N.Y., Mar. 31, 1923; s. William Thomas and Julia A. (Beuerlein) L. S.T.D., Angelicum U., Rome, 1949. Ordained priest Roman Catholic Ch., 1947. Sec. to bishop Diocese of St. Augustine, Fla., 1949-51; assoc. pastor Holy Family Ch., North Miami, Fla., 1951-54; pastor Christ the King Ch., Jacksonville, Fla., 1954-67, St. Cecilia Ch., Clearwater, Fla., 1967-79; officialis, vicar gen. Diocese of St. Petersburg, Fla., 1967-79, bishop, 1979-88. Trustee St. Vincent de Paul Sem., Boynton Beach, Fla. Mem. Nat. Conf. Cath. Bishops (com. priestly life and ministry), Canon Law Soc. Office: Diocese of St Petersburg PO Box 40200 Saint Petersburg FL 33743

LA ROCQUE, EUGENE PHILIPPE, bishop; b. Windsor, Ont., Can., Mar. 27, 1927; s. Eugene Joseph and Angeline Marie (Monforton) LaR. B.A., U. Western Ont., 1948; M.A., Laval U., 1956. Ordained priest Roman Catholic Ch., 1952, consecrated bishop, 1974; asst. parish priest Ste. Therese Ch., Windsor, 1952-54; registrar, then dean men, lectr. Christ The King Coll., U. Western Ont., 1956-64; asst. spiritual dir. St. Peter's Sem., 1964-65; prin., dean King's Coll., 1965-68; pastor St. Joseph's Ch., Rivière-aux-Canards, Ont., 1968-70, Ste. Anne's Ch., Tecumseh, 1970-74; bishop of Alexandria-Cornwall, Ont., 1974—; dean Essex County, 1970-73; trustee Essex County Roman Cath. Separate Sch. Bd., 1972-74; 1st chmn. liaison com. between Can. Jewish Congress Can. Council Chs. and Can. Cath. Conf. Bishops, 1977-84; mem. Can. Cath. Conf. Bishops, pres. Senate Priests Can., 1973-74. Club: K.C. (3 deg., chaplain Ont. 1977-87). Address: 200 Montreal Rd, Box 1388, Cornwall, ON Canada K6H 5V4 *Belief in God, who creates my unique human life and has a loving plan and concern for each of his children, sustains me amidst the strains, challenges and turmoils of life.*

LARRISON, PEGGY JEANNE, lay worker; b. Cleve., Aug. 16, 1957; d. Edward Ray and Myrna Joanne (Masters) L. A.Child Devel., Muskingum Area Tech. Coll., Zanesville, Ohio, 1992. Sun. sch. tchr. Meth. Ch., Brunswick, Ohio, 1972-79, Luth. Ch., Medina, Ohio, 1982-85, Meth. Ch., Creston, Ohio, 1974-80; clown ministry Meth. Ch., Cresto, Ohio, 1979—; Sun. sch. supt. Wesleyan Ch., Cambridge, Ohio, 1987-89; Sun. sch. tchr. Meth. Ch., Ava, Ohio, 1990—.

LARRISON, ROGER A., clergyman; b. Akron, Ohio, Aug. 29, 1947; s. Warren W. and Josephine Larrison; m. Sharon Rae Larrison, July 3, 1971; children: Rene M., Jeremy J., Jennifer M., Jonathon D. AA, AAS in Commerce, Transp., Arts, Sales and Mdse., U. Akron, BS in Tech. Edn., BA in History, Sociology and Polit. Sci., MS in Edn., 1985. Ordained to ministry Assemblies of God Ch. Asst. pastor First Assembly of God, Akron, 1978-81; pastor First Assembly of God, Wadsworth, Ohio, 1981—. Home: 2828 Harpster Rd Rittman OH 44270 Office: First Assembly of God 951 High St Wadsworth OH 44281

LARSEN, DEAN LE ROY, church official; b. May 24, 1927; BA in English, Utah State U., 1950. Pres. 1st Quorums of Seventy, Mormon Ch., Salt Lake City, 1980—.

LARSEN, HARLAN WENDELL, minister; b. Tyler, Minn., July 3, 1928; s. Jacob and Vervella (Sharratt) L.; m. Betty Jane Anderson, Apr. 16, 1949; children: Deborah, Connie, Patricia, Judd, Judy. BA, Northwestern Coll., Mpls., 1952; MDiv, Cen. Sem., 1963; DD (hon.), Internat. Bapt. Coll., 1989. Ordained minister in Bapt. Ch., 1953. Pastor Minn., Wis., Mich., Colo., 1953-74; sr. pastor Pear Park Bapt. Ch., Grand Junction, Colo., 1974—; bd. dirs. Pear Park Bapt. Schs., Grand Junction, 1975—, Sta. KCIC-FM Christian Radio, Grand Junction, 1979—. Contbr. articles to religious publ. Mem. Soc. Broadcast Engrs. (past officer for all offices since 1981). Republican. Office: Pear Park Bapt Ch 3102 E Road Grand Junction CO 81504 *"For I am not ashamed of the gospel of Christ: for it is the power of God unto salvation to every one that believeth." Romans 1:16.*

LARSEN, JAMES RICHARD, minister; b. Ladysmith, Wis., Apr. 2, 1947; s. Norman H. and Gladys E. (McCracken) L.; m. Karen Rae Garrison, Sept. 16, 1967; children: Tiffany, Paul, Lori Jo. BA, Minn. Bible Coll., 1971; postgrad., Pepperdine U., 1967-70; MA, Pacific Christian Coll., 1979; DMin, Calif. Grad. Sch. Theology, Glendale, 1985. Ordained to ministry Christian Ch. Asst. min. Crenshaw Christian Ch., Inglewood, Calif., 1967-69; pastor Litchfield (Minn.) Ch. of Christ, 1969-73, Northside Christian Ch., Tucson, 1973-87, Rogue Valley Christian Ch., Medford, Oreg., 1987—; pres. Tucson Christian Ministers Fellowship, Tucson, 1977-80, Ariz. Christian Ministers Fellowship, Tucson, 1981-82, Ariz. Christian Conv., Phoenix, 1986; vice chmn. Oreg. Christian Evangelistic Fellowship, Portland, 1988—. Bd. dirs. Mayors Adv. Com., Litchfield, 1973, No. Cen. Accrediting Assn., Mpls., 1973. Mem. Kiwanis (pres. Medford, Oreg. chpt. 1989-90). Home: 820 S Oregon Jacksonville OR 97530 Office: Rogue Valley Christian Ch 1440 S Oakdale Ave Medford OR 97501

LARSEN, LLOYD ASHLEY, minister, youth ministry consultant; b. Evanston, Ill., July 4, 1936; s. Hans Kristian Larsen and Thora Benson; m. Janet Carolyn Baker, June 11, 1960; children: Amy Jo Larsen Hornsby, Sara Lynn Larsen Pozzi, Andrea Lee. AA, North Pk. Jr. Coll., 1956; BA, Augustana Coll., Rock Island, Ill., 1958; BD, North Pk. Theol. Sem., 1962; D of Ministry, Eden Theol. Sem., 1989. Pastor 1st Covenant Ch., Denver, 1960-61; assoc. pastor Salem Covenant Ch., Mpls., 1962-66, Salem United Ch. Christ, Tonawanda, N.Y., 1966-71; area dir. Young Life Campaign, Buffalo, 1971-78; sr. min. Univ. Congl. Ch., Orlando, Fla., 1978—; adj. faculty U. Cen. Fla., 1979—; chmn. dist. coun. United Ch. Christ, Cen. Fla. Author: The Invisible Generation, 1987, Do You Hear the Singing Beyond the Fire, 1988; contbr. to EOS Mag., 1988—. Pres. Tonawanda Kiwanis Club, 1970-71; adv. bd. Sta. WMFE-TV/FM. Recipient Disting. Svc. award Tonawanda Jr. C. of C., 1970, Meritorious Svc. award Fla. Conf. United Ch. Christ, 1988. Mem. Rotary (pres. U. Cen. Fla. club 1989—), Lambda Chi Alpha (Beta Eta chpt.). Avocations: woodworking, MG car restoration, travel, writing. Home: 8734 Pine Barrens Dr Orlando FL 32817 Office: Univ Congl Ch 9300 University Blvd Orlando FL 32817 *The challenge of the last decade of the Twentieth Century is for humanity to discover the Divine spark of love endowed within each one of us; to be bearers of peace and good will to all humanity by choosing to positively love and affirm the integrity of each of our fellow-travelers in life.*

LARSEN, PAUL EMANUEL, religious organization administrator; b. Mpls., Oct. 5, 1933; s. David Paul and Myrtle (Grunnet) L.; m. Elizabeth Helen Taylor, Mar. 19, 1966; children: Kristin, Kathleen. BA, Stanford U., 1955; MDiv, Fuller Theol. Sem., 1958; DSc Theology, San Francisco Theol. Sem., 1978. Ordained to ministry Evang. Ch., 1963. Asst. pastor Evang. Ch., Eagle Rock, Calif., 1958-59; pastor Pasadena, Calif., 1963-70, Peninsula Covenant Ch., Redwood City, Calif., 1971-86; pres. Evang. Covenant Chs., Chgo., 1986—. Author: Wise Up and Live, Mission of a Covenant. Home: 24 The Landmark Northfield IL 60093 Office: Evang Covenant Ch 5101 N Francisco Ave Chicago IL 60625

LARSON, ALLAN LOUIS, political scientist, educator, lay church worker; b. Chetek, Wis., Mar. 31, 1932; s. Leonard Andrew and Mabel (Marek) L. BA magna cum laude, U. Wis., Eau Claire, 1954; PhD, Northwestern U., 1964. Instr. Evanston Twp. (Ill.) High Sch., 1958-61; asst. prof. polit. sci. U. Wis., 1963-64; asst. prof. Loyola U., Chgo., 1964-68; assoc. prof. Loyola U., 1968-74, prof., 1974—. Author: Comparative Political Analysis, 1980, (essay) The Human Triad: An Introductory Essay on Politics, Society, and Culture, 1988; (with others) Progress and the Crisis of Man, 1976; contbr. articles to profl. jours. Assoc. mem. Paul Galvin Chapel, Evanston, Ill. Norman Wait Harris fellow in polit. sci. Northwestern U., 1954-56. Mem. AAAS, ASPCA, AAUP, Humane Soc. U.S., Northwestern U. Alumni Assn., Am. Polit. Sci. Assn., Am. Acad. Polit. and Social Sci., Acad. Polit. Sci., Midwest Polit. Sci. Assn., Spiritual Life Inst., Anti-Cruelty Soc., Nat. Wildlife Fedn., Noetic Scis. Inst., Humane Soc. U.S., Kappa Delta Pi, Pi Sigma Epsilon. Roman Catholic. Home: 2015 Orrington Ave Evanston IL 60201 Office: Loyola U 6525 N Sheridan Rd Damen Hall - Room 915 Chicago IL 60626 *We are each of us mysteries to ourselves. We are on a life-long search for meaning: questions about where we have come from, what we are doing and where we are going. The deepest desires of a person embody the spiritual quest. The Kingdom of God tells us where to place our priorities. Life is short. No one is untouched by tragedy. We are reminded every day of our finiteness. We care because it is our nature to care. Christianity teaches a reverence for life that urges us to transcend narcissism and selfishness.*

LARSON, ARTHUR CALVIN, minister; b. Shevlin, Minn., Feb. 17, 1938; s. Alfred Olaus and Pearl Agnes (Traaseth) L.; m. Sylvia Marlis Borud, Oct. 17, 1959; children: Calvin Anthony, Marcus Earl. BA, Concordia Coll., Moorhead, Minn., 1960; BTh, Luther Sem., St. Paul, 1965. Ordained to ministry Evang. Am. Luth. Ch., 1965. Min. Bagley (Minn.) Rural Luth. Parish, 1960-62, Our Redeemer and Faith Luth. Chs., Badger, Minn., 1965-69, Kindred (N.Dak.) Luth. Ch., 1970-79, Our Redeemer Luth Ch., Bryant, S.D., 1979-87, Nashwauk (Minn.) Luth. Ch., 1987—; puppeteer Am. Luth. Ch. and Evang. Luth. Ch. in Am., 1984—; dean Laurentian Conf., NE Minn. Synod, 1990—. Driver, attendant Kindred Ambulance Svc., 1974-79. Named Man of Yr., Kindred Jaycees, 1972. Home: 612 4th St Nashwauk MN 55769 Office: Nashwauk Luth Ch 302 3d St Nashwauk MN 55769

LARSON, BRIAN LOREN, minister; b. Joliet, Ill., Apr. 6, 1950; s. Bjorn and Violet (Nienaber) L.; m. Cheryl Lynn Carlson, Aug. 5, 1978; children: Rachel, Danny, Stephanie. Assoc. in LAS, Joliet Jr. Coll., 1972; BA in Bible, Theology, Moody Bible Inst., 1973; MDiv, Bethel Theol. Sem., 1976; D in Ministry in Pastoral Lead, Talbot Theol. Sem., 1984. Ordained to ministry Bapt. Ch. Youth pastor Elim Bapt. Ch., Chgo., 1969-73; sem. intern Wooddale Bapt. Ch., Richfield, Minn., 1973-76; assoc. pastor Whittier (Calif.) Area Bapt. Fellowsip, 1976-80; sr. pastor Walnut (Calif.) Valley Bapt. Fellowship, 1980—. Home: 405 Avenida Presidio Walnut CA 91789 Office: Walnut Valley Bapt Fellowship 20505 E Valley Blvd #105 Walnut CA 91789

LARSON, GERALD JAMES, religion educator; b. Chgo., Apr. 24, 1938; m. Claire I. Larson, 1960. AB, Blackburn Coll., 1960; MDiv, Union Theol. Sem., 1962; PhD, Columbia U., 1967; postgrad., Banaras Hindu U., Varanasi, India, 1969. Prof. religious studies/comparative religions U. Calif., Santa Barbara, 1970—; pres. United Ministries in Higher Edn. So. Calif. Religion, 1984-86. Author: Classical Sāmkhya, 1969, 2d edit., 1979, Myth in Indo-European Antiquity, 1975, Sāmkhya: A Dualist Tradition in Indian Philosophy, 1987, Interpreting Across Boundaries, 1989. Fellow Am. Soc. for Study of Religion, Soc. for Values in Higher Edn.; mem. Am. Acad. Religion, Am. Oriental Soc. (v.p. 1975), Soc. for Asian and CF. Philosophy (pres. 1984-86). Presbyterian. Office: U Calif Dept Religious Studies Santa Barbara CA 93106

LARSON, LAWRENCE RAYMOND, minister; b. Ft. Frances, Ont., Can., July 17, 1930; came to U.S., 1930; s. Clarence J. and Thilda (Jorve) L.; m. Elaine June McKenzie, Nov. 3, 1950; children: Janice, Mary Jane, Dorothy, Carol, Evangeline, Mark, Vicky. AA, Maunaolu Community Coll., Paia, Hawaii, 1959; BA in Theology, North Cen. Bible Coll., 1960; M. Bible Theology, Internat. Sem., 1980, D. Bible Theology, 1980. Ordained to ministry Assemblies of God, 1953. Evangelist Assemblies of God, Springfield, Mo., 1951-52; pastor Assemblies of God, Crookston, Minn., 1952-54; missionary Assemblies of God, Paia, Hilo, Hawaii, 1954-59; fgn. missionary Assemblies of God, Suva, Fiji Islands, Hawaii, 1960-75; pastor Assemblies of God, Hudson Falls, N.Y., 1975—; dist. youth dir. Hawaii Assemblies of God, 1956-58; founder-mgr. Assemblies of God Schs., Suva, 1961-72; field dir. All Assemblies of God Missions South Pacific, Suva, 1960-72; presbyter 37 chs. N.Y. Dist. Assemblies of God, Hudson Falls, 1978—. Editor Pentecostal ZEAL, 1968; editor: (sch. annuals) BEACON-Fiji Islands, 1964. Pres. Adirondack Clergy Assn., Hudson Falls, 1981-83; clergy rep. United Way Tri-County, Glens Falls, N.Y., 1990. Capt. Civil Air Patrol, 1957-59. Mem. Hudson Falls Clergy Assn. Home: 26 Lafayette St Hudson Falls NY 12839 Office: Gospel Lighthouse Ch 30 LaCrosse St Hudson Falls NY 12839

LARSON, RAYMOND EVERETT, pastor; b. Montebello, Calif., Aug. 19, 1954; s. Raymond Everett Sr. and Delores Jane (Lawrence) L.; m. Rebecca Lynn, June 18, 1977; children: Brandon Jeremy, Rhema Dawn. BA, So. Calif. Coll., 1976. Ordained to ministry, 1983. Youth pastor Orange (Calif.) Christian Assembly, 1976-78, Church of the Highlands, San Bruno, Calif., 1978-81; singles pastor Capital Christian Ctr., Sacramento, 1981-84; sr. pastor Bethel Ch., Redding, Calif., 1984—. Author: Season of Singleness, 1984, When the Womb is Empty, 1988, Personally God's, Personally Yours, 1991. Adv. bd. Chemical Peoples Abuse Plan, Redding, 1986, Crisis Pregnancy Ctr., Redding, 1985-88, Intervarsity Christian Fellowship, San Mateo, Calif., 1978-80. Mem. Shasta County Mins. Assn. (v.p. 1986-87). Republican. Office: Bethel Ch 2150 N Bechelli Ln Redding CA 96002

LARSON, ROBERT EDWARD, JR., pastor; b. Harrisburg, Pa., Sept. 23, 1939; s. Robert Edward and Fae Ann (Engle) L.; m. Dorothy Ellen Ray, Aug. 6, 1966; children: Kristin Ray, Andrea Nan, Gretchen Lyn, Brett Alan. BA, Wheaton (Ill.) Coll., 1961; BD (MDiv), Princeton Sem., 1965; STM, Luth. Sem., 1972; DMin, Lancaster Sem., 1986. Ordained to ministry Presbyn. Ch. (U.S.A.), 1965. Asst. pastor United Presbyn. Ch., Newton, Mass., 1965-67; assoc. pastor Pine St. Presbyn. Ch., Harrisburg, Pa., 1967-71; exec. dir. Contact Teleministries USA, Harrisburg, 1971-85; interim pastor Presbyn. Ch. of Old Greenwich (Conn.), 1985-87; sr. pastor Westminster Presbyn. C., Cedar Rapids, Iowa, 1987—; bd. dirs. Found. II, Cedar Rapids, 1988—; mem. coun. advisors U. Dubuque (Iowa) Theol. Sem., 1988—; sec. gen. Life Line Internat., Brisbane, Australia, 1982-87; mem. Presbytery of East Iowa Presbyn. Ch. (U.S.A.). Author: An Accreditation Manual for Telephone Ministries, 1986; editor: Preparing to Listen, 1981, Tele-Care: A Resource Manual for Caregivers, 1984. Mem. renew com. United Way of Ea. Iowa, Cedar Rapids, 1989, 90; bd. dirs. U. Dubuque, 1990—. Named Ark. Traveler, State of Ark., 1973; recipient honor cert. Freedoms Found., 1981. Mem. Linn County Assn. Evangelicals (pres. 1991—), Kiwanis. Home: 2301 Blake Blvd SE Cedar Rapids IA 52403 Office: Westminster Presbyn Ch 1285 3d Ave SE Cedar Rapids IA 52403

LARSON, RON LYNN, minister; b. Dekalb, Ill., May 7, 1957; s. Lawrence Albert and Florence Imogene (McRay) L.; m. Patricia Ann McCready, May 18, 1979; children: Joel Michael, Melanie Joy. BA in Religion, Carson-Newman Coll., 1979, BA in Sociology, 1979. Ordained to ministry Bapt. Ch., 1980. Youth min. Lake Hill Bapt. Ch., Orlando, Fla., 1978, sr. pastor, 1979-85; outreach min. First Bapt. Ch., Rogersville, Tenn., 1979; pastor Grace Bapt. Ch., Shenandoan Junction, W.Va., 1985-86; sr. pastor Covenant Bapt. Ch., Shepherdstown, W.Va., 1986—; v.p. So. Bapt. W.Va. Conv., 1989; moderator Tri-County Bapt. Assn., Shepherdstown, 1989; asst. budget dir. Shepherd Coll., 1991, student work dir., 1989—. Contbr. articles to religious mags. Recipient Fastest Growing Sunday Sch. award, Greater Orlando Bapt. Assn., 1984. Republican. Home: Rte 3 Box 94A Martinsburg WV 25401 Office: Covenant Bapt Ch P O Box 1674 Shepherdstown WV 25443

LARYEA, SETH ABANG, church administrator; b. Nungua, Ghana, Oct. 29, 1948; came to U.S., 1989; s. Stephen Odai and Rebecca (Mensah) L.; m. Uriel Koshie Lawson, Jan. 4, 1981; children: Shirley Naa Afoley, Eben Nii Afotey. BA, Andrews U., 1977; P.G.C.E., Cape Coast (Ghana) U., 1981; MA, Loma Linda U., 1990, edn. specialist, 1991. Tchr. Seventh-day Adventist Tchr. Tng. Coll., Ghana, 1977-80; edn. dir. South Ghana Conf. of Seventh-day Adventist, 1981-83; assoc. dir. Adventist Devel. and Relief Agy., Ghana, 1983-85; exec. sed. West African Hdqrs. of Seventh-day Adventist Ch., Ghana, 1986-89; grad. asst. Loma Linda U., Riverside, Calif., 1989-90, 91. Home: 4987 Sierra Vista # 2 Riverside CA 92505

LASATER, DAVID B., evangelist; b. Kansas City, Mo., Feb. 18, 1948; s. Fon and Sarah (Smith) L.; m. Susan Owen, May 16, 1970; children: Jennie Rebecca, Aaron David, Phillip Michael. AA, Casper (Wyo.) Jr. Coll., 1968; BA, Okla. Christian Coll., 1972; postgrad., Abilene (Tex.) Christian U. Evangelist Hoffman Heights Ch. of Christ, Aurora, Colo., 1974-77, College Street Ch. of Christ, Dinuba, Calif., 1977-80, Morrie Ave Ch. of Christ, Cheyenne, Wyo., 1980-81; evangelist Ch. of Christ, Lazbuddie, Tex., 1981-83, Naperville, Ill., 1984—; missionary Ch. of Christ, Logan, Utah, 1974-77. Editor religious jour., 1982. Named one of Outstanding Young Men Am., 1981, 83, 85. Mem. Naperville Police Chaplains Assn. (pres. 1988—, editor Assist monthly newsletter 1988—). Republican. Lodge: Rotary (sgt. at arms Dinuba 1978-80). Avocations: painting, sculpting, golf. Home: 1809 Lisson Rd Naperville IL 60565

LASHER, ESTHER LU, minister; b. Denver, June 1, 1923; d. Lindley Aubrey and Irma Jane (Rust) Pim; m. Donald T. Lasher, Apr. 9, 1950 (dec. Mar. 1982); children: Patricia Sue Becker, Donald T., Keith Alan, Jennifer Luanne Oliver; m. Avery W. Miley, May 1, 1989. Assoc. Fine Arts, Colo. Women's Coll., 1943; BA, Denver U., 1945; MA Religious Edn., Ea. Bapt. Sem., 1948; MA, Denver U., 1967. Ordained to ministry Bapt. Ch., 1988. Christian edn. dir. 1st Bapt., Evansville, Ind., 1948-52; minister Perrysburg Bapt. Ch., Macy, Ind., 1988—; libr. Peru (Ind.) Pub. Schs., 1990-91; sec. Ind. Ministerial Coun., Indpls., 1990-92; chairperson Women in Ministry, Indpls., 1988—; chmn. Fellowship Mission Circle, Rochester, Ind., 1988—; mem. Partnership in Ministry, Indpls., 1990—; bd. mgrs. Am. Bapts./Ind., 1991—. Pres. Toastmasters, Rochester, 1988; bd. dirs. Manitau Tng. Ctr., Rochester, 1988-90; v.p. Mental Health Assn., Rochester, 1987-90; founder Fulton County Literacy Coalition, Rochester, 1989-90. Named Outstanding Libr., Biog. Inst., 1989. Mem. Leadership Acad. (bd. dirs. 1988-90), Minister's Coun. Ind. (bd. dirs., sec.), Bus. and Profl. Women (pres. Greenwood, Ind. chpt. 1984-86), Rochester Women's Club (pres. 1989—), Rotary, Sigma Alpha Iota (advisor). Republican. Home: 1117 Rosewood Dr Peru IN 46970 Office: Perrysburg Bapt Ch PO Box 196 Macy IN 46951 *Wisdom is a powerful tool, without knowledge, it can entice or terrify an individual, all depending on how it is used with much forethought.*

LASNIER, FOREST WILFRED, retired lay minister; b. Newport, Vt., May 4, 1927; s. Arthur Joseph and Florence G. (Ellsworth) L.; m. Mary Evelyn Quimby, June 24, 1950; children: Mary Anne, Gary, Gregory. Diploma, trade sch., 1950; lay ministry student, 1965-68. Lic. lay min. McIndoes Falls. Congl., Vt., 1965-66, Brighton Congl., Island Pond, Vt., 1966-69, Plymouth Congl., East Charleston, Vt., 1969-80, 83-86, Ch. Messiah Universalist, St. Johnsbury, Vt., 1980-83, Granby Victory Congl., Vt., 1986-90, Guild Hall Community Ch., Vt., 1988-89; lic. lay min. Barnet Congregation, Vt., 1990, ret., 1990; moderator Northeast Assn., Vt., 1972-74. With USN, 1945-49, WWII. *In my life span I have encountered many failures. Yet these failures have proven to be only stepping stones to accomplishment instead of sheer defeat. Died Apr. 2, 1991.*

LASSEN-WILLEMS, JAMES RUTHERFORD, priest, poet; b. Coronado, Calif., Oct. 11, 1944; s. Everleigh Durward and Miriam May (Shepul) W.; m. Patricia Ann Crawford, July 3l, 1969 (div. June 197l); l child, Aaron Nikolai; m. Coryl Judith Lassen, Jan. 22, 1983. BA, San Diego State U., 1966; MDiv, Episcopal Div. Sch., Cambridge, Mass., 1984; MA, Boston Coll., 1989. Ordained deacon Episcopal Ch., 1984, priest, 1985, canon, 1986. Dir. exptl. coll. San Francisco State U., 1968-69; editor Isthmus, dir. Isthmus Found., San Francisco, 1973-78; grant writer Media Alliance, San Francisco, 1978; dir. outreach St. Mary Episcopal Ch., San Francisco, 1979-8l; asst. St. John's

Episcopal Ch., Westwood, Mass., 1983-85; dir. Abraham Accord, Episcopal Ch. U.S.A., Providence, 1985-88; canon to ordinary Bishop of R.I., Providence, 1986—. Author: (poetry) And She Finishes, 1973, Amidamerica, 1974, Opening the Cube, 1975, Harlequin Poems, 1976; contbr. poetry to revs. Nat. Endowment for Arts grantee, 1973-76; various scholarships, 1981-84, Boston Coll. fellow, 1984-86. Mem. PEN, Soc. St. John the Evangelist (assoc.). Democrat. Home and Office: 156 Broad St Pascoag RI 02859

LASSITER, VALENTINO, minister. Pres. Interchurch Coun. of Greater Cleve. Office: Interchurch Coun Greater Cleve 2230 Euclid Ave Cleveland OH 44115*

LATHAM, LYNDON CLINT, minister, investor; b. Breckenridge, Tex., Aug. 15, 1943; s. James Daniel Latham and Una Rosalie (Clark) Jones; m. Judy Ann Dunegan, June 6, 1964; children: Devonna Kris, Kendra Joy, Clint Rustin. Student, Ranger Coll., 1961-62, Amarillo Coll., 1961-63; BS, West Tex. State U., 1965, MA, 1973. Cert. tchr., Tex. Min. Fairlane Ch. of Christ, Amarillo, Tex., 1964-70, West Amarillo Ch. of Christ, Amarillo, 1970—. Contbr. articles to The Christian Appeal, The Gospel Tidings; editor and contbr. Truth for Youth, 1965-70; lead singer Psalms IV Quartet, Amarillo, 1971—. Youth program dir. Young Men's Hebrew Assn., Bklyn., 1939-41; founder East Northport Jewish Ctr., L.I., N.Y.; active Tifereth Israel Synagogue of San Diego, 1980-87, Tempe Beth Toran-Wellington, 1987—; pres., life mem. Horizon chpt. B'nai B'rith; founder, pres. A.R.M.D.I. Liksah chpt., 1982-87. Mem. Amarillo Ministerial Assn. (pres. 1981), Rotary (pres. Amarillo West Club 1977-78). Republican. Avocations: skiing, reading, singing, jogging, photography. Home: 6724 Arroyo Dr Amarillo TX 79108 Office: West Amarillo Ch of Christ 417 McMasters St Amarillo TX 79106 *As long as humanity is struggling to answer such basic questions as how did we come to exist, what is the meaning of life, why do the innocent suffer, and will life continue beyond death, there will be a demand for those who can help us grow in religious knowledge.*

LATHAM, MARY ELIZABETH, clergywoman; b. Cin.; d. Lawrence Lorenzo and Eugenia (Peters) Latham; B.A. cum laude, Asbury Coll., 1929. Tchr. math. and Latin, McAfee High Sch., Mercer County, Ky., 1929-32; entered ministry of evangelism Ch. of the Nazarene, 1933, ordained to ministry, 1937; traveled in work of evangelism and Christian edn., 1937-48; internat. dir. vacation Bible schs. Dept. Ch. Schs., Kansas City, Mo., 1948-67; dir. audiovisuals Ch. of the Nazarene, 1962-74; chmn. audiovisual com. Council of Chs. Greater Kansas City, 1955-58, chmn. com. on communications edn., 1966-67; chmn. Latham Communications, 1975—; also lectr. Recipient Albert F. Harper award Adult Ministries, Ch. of Nazarene, 1980. Author: Vacation Bible School, Why, What, and How, 1954, 9th rev. edit., 1968; Adventures with Jesus, 1948, rev. edits., 1951, 54, 57, 60, 63; Teacher, You Are an Evangelist, rev. edit., 1977; contbr. numerous covers and articles to periodicals; dir. prodn. films The Great Transition, motion picture of Nazarene Colls., 1964; Sing His Wonderful Name, 1965; Would You Believe It?, 1967; The Debtors and They Do Not Wait, 1968; The Way Out and God's Word for Today's World, 1969; Moving Ahead, 1970; Just for the Love of It, 1971; To Make a Miracle, 1972; To New Worlds, 1972; The Church of the Nazarene, 1974 (Disting. Svc. award 1990); The Alabaster Story, 1974; dir. filmstrips with cassettes How Young Is Our Welcome? and What Made the Orange Go Away?, 1976; producer videotape Roy T. Williams-The Man, The Leader, 1983. Address: 10268 Cedarbrooke Ln Kansas City MO 64131

LATHEM, R(AY) WARREN, JR., minister; b. Cumming, Ga., May 4, 1952; s. Ray Warren and Leila (Youngblood) L.; m. Jane Baird, Aug. 17, 1973; children: Ray Warren III, Jared Thomas. AA, Reinhardt Coll., Waleska, Ga., 1972; BA, Asbury Coll., Wilmore, Ky., 1974; MDiv, Emory U., Atlanta, Ga., 1977; Doctor of Ministry, McCormick Sem., Chgo., 1988. Ordained elder United Meth. Ch., 1978. Min. various chs., Ga., 1975-83; sr. min. Mt. Pisgah U Meth. Ch., Alpharetta, Ga., 1983-91; com. mem. Devel. Reinhardt Coll, Waleska, Ga., 1989-91; bd. mem. Drug Free North Fulton, Roswell, Ga., 1989-91, Covecrest Christian Retreat Ctr., Tiger, Ga., 1986-89. Author: Our Father...I Believe, 1983. Bd. mem. Heart Fund, Toccoa, Ga., 1978; chaplain Kiwanis Club, Toccoa, 1979, Greenville Lions Club, Ga., 1982. Recipient N. Ga. Conf. Evangelism award, 1985, 86, 87, 88, 90, Top Southeastern Juridictional award for Evangelism, 1986, 91; named to Honorable Order of Ky. Colonels. Mem. Masons. Office: Mt Pisgah United Meth Ch 9820 Nesbit Ferry Rd Alpharetta GA 30202

LATHROP, GORDON WENDEL, religion educator, minister; b. Glendale, Calif., Sept. 2, 1939; s. Robert Wendel and Maurita Wyliss (McComb) L.; m. Gail D. Ramshaw, June 20, 1987; children: Nathaniel, Anthony, Miriam, Monica. BA in Philosophy, Occidental Coll., 1961; BD cum laude, Luther Theol. Sem., St. Paul, 1966; ThDrs. cum laude, Cath. U. Nijmegen, The Netherlands, 1969. Ordained to ministry Evang. Luth. Ch. in Am. Assoc. youth dept. Nat. Coun. Chs., N.Y.C., 1962; campus min. U. Miami, Coral Gables, Fla., 1964-65; pastor Grace Luth. Ch., Darlington, Wis., 1969-71; univ. min. Pacific Luth. U., Tacoma, 1971-75; asst. prof. liturgy Wartburg Theol. Sem., Dubuque, Iowa, 1975-80, assoc. prof., 1980-84, chmn. div. ministry studies, 1981-84; prof. liturgy, chaplain Luth. Theol. Sem. at Phila., 1984—, Charles A. Schieren prof. theology, 1989—; internat. pres. Luther League, Am. Luth. Ch., 1960-61; lectr. Inst. Liturgical Studies, Valparaiso, Ind., 1973, 76, 78, 79, 82, 85, 90, St. John's U., Collegeville, Minn., 1978-79, Église Evangelique Lutherienne de Cameroun, Ngaondere, 1980, Martin Luther Jubilee, Washington, 1983, Festival Worship and Witness, Mpls., 1983, Seminario Evangelico de P.R., 1985, Union Theol. Sem., N.Y.C., 1986, Caribbean synod Luth. Ch. in Am., St. Croix, San Juan, P.R., 1987, Centennial of Common Svc., Phila., 1988, Pacific Luth. U., Tacoma, 1991. Author: The Joyful Fast: Lenten Meditations for Students, 1965, Lectionary Themes, 1976, Paschal Mission, 1983, Proclamation 4: Advent and Christmas B, 1990; also articles; (with Gabe Huck and Gail Ramshaw) An Easter Sourcebook: The Fifty Days, 1988; (with Gail Ramshaw) Lectionary for the Christian People, 3 vols., 1986, 87, 88; translator: Christian Worship in East and West: A Study Guide to Liturgical History (Herman Wegman), 1986; assoc. editor Worship, 1983—. Occidental Coll. Alumni scholar, 1957-59, Luth. World Fedn. scholar, 1966-69; Layne Found. fellow, 1959-66. Mem. N.Am. Acad. Liturgy (v.p. 1983, pres. 1984), Societas Liturgica, The Liturgical Conf. (bd. dirs. 1978-86), Phi Beta Kappa. Address: 7304 Boyer St Philadelphia PA 19119

LATRONICO, PHILIP FRANCIS ANTHONY, priest; b. Weehawken, N.J., Jan. 30, 1954; s. Francis Philip and Maria Louise (DiSavino) L. BS, Stevens Coll., 1976; MDiv, Seton Hall U., 1986, ThM, 1989. Ordained priest Roman Cath. Ch., 1986. Dir. His Place Coffeehouse, West New York, N.J., 1973-77; dir. religion dept. St. Joseph Grammer Sch., West New York, N.J., 1975-81; chaplain Community of God's Love, Rutherford, N.J., 1985—; dir. religious edn. St. Augustine Parish, Union City, N.J., 1985—; sec. Archdiocesan Commn. of Ecumenism and Interreligious Affairs, Newark, 1987—; cons. religion dept. Silver Burdett & Ginn, Morristown, N.J., 1987—. Chaplain Boy Scouts Am., Union, 1981-90, com. chmn., Rutherford, 1982-87. Home and Office: Community of Gods Love 70 W Passaic Ave Rutherford NJ 07070

LATTA, WILLIAM CHARLTON, retired clergyman; b. College Corner, Ohio, Mar. 30, 1902; s. Linton Thomas and Minnie Isadora (Rex) L.; m. Marjorie Faye Clippard, May 4, 1928; children—William Charlton, John Linton, Bruce. B.A., Miami (Ohio) U., 1924; Th.B., Xenia Theol. Sem., St. Louis, 1927, Th.M., 1928; D.D., Westminster Coll., 1951. Ordained to ministry United Presbyn. Ch., 1928; pastor Wellsville, Ohio, 1928-31, Oil City, Pa., 1932-45; pastor 1st United Presbyn. Ch., Oakmont, Pa., 1945-72; emeritus 1st United Presbyn. Ch., 1972—; assoc. pastor Bellefield Presbyn. Ch., Pitts., 1974-84; pastor emeritus Bellefield Presbyn. Ch., 1984—; Bd. dirs. Am. missions United Presbyn. Ch. N.Am., 1954-58, pres., 1956-58, chmn. gen. council Evangelism, 1951-58, co-chmn. commn. Evangelism, 1958-60, v.p. bd. nat. missions, 1958-62, pres., 1962-65, mem. gen. council, 1958-60, 62-64, chmn. exec. com. bd. nat. missions, 1962-65; vice moderator Pitts. Synod, 1956-57; mem. N.Am. council World's Presbyn. Alliance, 1966-68, del. meeting, Sao Paulo, Brazil, 1959; mem. gen. assembly Nat. Council Chs., 1963-66, mem. div. home missions, 1963-66, mem. joint com. Evangelism, 1951-65; mem. gen. council Pitts. Presbytery, 1962-74, chmn., 1962-63, chmn. nominating com., 1966-68, mem. evaluating com., 1969-74, trustee, 1976-82, mem. fin. com., 1976-82, trustee, mem. fin. com., 1976-82; mem. Oakmont Ministerial Assn., 1945-73, pres., 1970-73; chmn. com. to unite work bd. nat. missions Presbyn. Ch. U.S.A. and bd. Am. missions United Presbyn. Ch. N. Am., 1957-58; chmn. structure com. Bd. Nat. Missions, 1961-62; dir., tchr. at youth confs. Contbr. articles to religious publs. Bd. dirs. Pitts.-Xenia Theol. Sem., 1941-45, v.p., 1944-45; bd. dirs. Carnegie Library Oakmont, Pa., 1965-72; trustee Knoxville (Tenn.) Coll., 1954-75, v.p., 1970-72, chmn. com. personnel policies and salary adminstrn., mem. finance and bldg. and grounds coms., 1970-75. Home: 6675 Saltsburg Rd Pittsburgh PA 15235

LATTIMORE, VERGEL LYRONNE, minister, educator, counselor; b. Charlotte, N.C., Mar. 6, 1953; s. Vergel and Perlia Equilla (Gray) L.; m. Joy Renee Powell, Dec. 19, 1978; children: V. Alston, Adam Victor, Alia Joy. BA, Livingstone Coll., 1975; MDiv, Duke U. Div. Sch., 1977; PhD, Northwestern U., 1984. Ordained to ministry Meth. Ch., 1975. Campus min. Duke U. Chapel, Durham, N.C., 1976-77; asst. dean Duke U., Durham, N.C., 1977-79; dir. chaplain svcs. Community Hosp., Evanston, Ill., 1979-80; staff cpimse;pr Garrett Evang. Theol. Sem., Evanston, 1980-83; staff counselor Pastoral Psychotherapy Inst., Park Ridge, Ill., 1980-82; minority student advisor, resident dir. Kendall Coll., Evanston, 1980-83; pastoral counsel Onondaga Pastoral Counseling Ctr. Inc., Syracuse, N.Y., 1983-88; dir. counseling Syracuse Community Health Ctr. Inc., 1988-90; assoc. prof. Meth. Theol. Sch., Delaware, Ohio, 1990—; regional coord. Nat. Black Student Consultation Southwest U.S.A., 1978-80; rsch. cons. Nat. Acad. Peace and Conflict Resolution, Washington, 1979-80; chairperson Martin Luther King Community Celebration, Syracuse, 1985-90; pres. bd. dirs. PEACE Inc., Syracuse, 1989-90. Mem. Human Rights Commn., Syracuse, 1986-90, Social Svcs. Adv. Coun., Syracuse, 1988-90, City of Syracuse/Onondaga County Drug Abuse Commn., 1990, Ohio Coun. Chs. Criminal Justice Task Force, Columbus, 1991—. Named Mover and Shaker in Religion, Syracuse Herald Jour., 1988. Fellow Am. Assn. Pastoral Counselors (chmn. rsch. com. 1985-87); mem. AAUP, Ohio State U. Nat. Coun. on Alcoholism Summer Inst. on Addiction Studies, Alpha Phi Alpha. Avocations: biking, jogging, jazz, chess/. Home: 610 Olde North Church Dr Westerville OH 43081-3133 Office: Meth Theol Sch in Ohio PO Box 1204 3081 Columbus Pike Delaware OH 43015-0931

LATUS, TIMOTHY DEXTER, psychic consultant; b. Carlsbad, N.Mex., Nov. 18, 1946; m. Yolanda Torro, Dec. 14, 1981; children: Pluto, Patricia, Sally. BS in Mass Communications, N.Mex. State U., 1968; postgrad., U. of Metaphysics, 1986—, The Esoteric Inst., 1986—. Ordained Christian metaphysical minister. V.p. Soundville Records, Houston, 1969-72, Illuminati Video Prodn., Houston, 1972-75; pres. Haarick House Pub., St. Louis, 1975-79, Dallas, 1979-81; pres. Acad. Psychic Arts & Scis., N.Y.C., 1981, Albuquerque, 1982—, Dallas, 1985—; pres. Life Stage Publ. Corp., 1989—; gov. Ch. Creative Spirituality, Dallas, 1986—; minister, Universal Light of Cross Ch., Show Low, Ariz., 1984—. Author: Your Guardian Angel, 1987, Reach for Your Best Self, 1990; co-author, editor: Future Pathway Report, 1990, BYOP, 1991; author, editor: The Timothy Letter, 1990—; editor: Profile: Your 21st Century Child, 1987. Active Animal Legal Def. Fund. Named Outstanding Innovator Retail Week Mag., 1979, Mover and Shaker Video Rev. Mag., N.Y.C., 1980, Expert to address Worldwide Videogramme Expn., Cannes, France, 1972. Mem. ACLU, The Reincarnationists, N.Mex. Psychic Soc. (gov. emeritus 1985—), Am. Counselors Soc., Spiritual Adv. Coun., Free to Live, Sigma Delta Chi. Democrat. Office: 100 Turtle Creek Village Ste 363 PO Box 191129 Dallas TX 75219 *Acceptance of self-responsibility, I feel, is the key to personal growth. An Awakening of one's capacity for unconditional love and co-creativity with the Universe seems to inevitably follow.*

LAUBENTHAL, ALLAN R., academic administrator. Head St. Mary Sem., Cleve. Office: St Mary Sem 1227 Ansel Rd Cleveland OH 44108*

LAUBER, NANCY LEE AVERY, church administrator; b. Balt., Jan. 30, 1932; d. John Robert and Edith Irma Marguerite Avery; m. John Philip Lauber, June 17, 1950; children: Alison Ann Shrum, Melissa Littleton, John Avery. AA, Bard Avon, Balt., 1950; student, Emory U., 1986-87. Adminstrv. asst. St. Patrick's Episc. Ch., Atlanta, 1978-82, parish adminstr., 1982—. Fellow Nat. Assn. of Ch. Bus. Adminstrn. (sec. Peach State chpt. 1986-88, pres. 1988-90); mem. Atlanta Knitting Guild (v.p. 1990-91), Daughters of the King (bd. dirs. 1987-88). Home: 4762 Cambridge Dr Dunwoody GA 30338 Office: St. Patricks Episc Ch 5755 N Peachtree Rd Atlanta GA 30338

LAUER, BARBARA ESTELLE, church and community organization executive; b. Brinkley, Ark.; d. Richard and Cocab (Mahfouz) Ashy; m. John H. Lauer, Aug. 30, 1974. Student, Dominican Coll., 1953; cert. in religious edn. theology, Cath. U., 1960; cert. in Montessori edn., Springhill Coll., 1973; BA in Adminstrn. of Human Svcs., N.Y. State Coll., 1974. Creative-exec. dir. Tuscarawas County Coun. for Ch. and Community, New Philadelphia, Ohio, 1975—; cons. Sacred Heart Ch., New Philadelphia, 1983—, religious educator, 1976-80. Recipient Nat. Ecumenical award Nat. Coun. Chs., 1978; 10 yrs. Ecumenical recognition, 1984. Democrat. Home: 1055 Glen Dr N E New Philadelphia OH 44663 Office: Tuscarawas County Coun for Ch & Community 120 1st Dr S E New Philadelphia OH 44663 *The following has been my motivation for serving others-"The measure of love is to love without measure." One of my greatest joys in life is to help another achieve excellence and to strive and reach their potential.*

LAUGHERY, RONALD D., minister; b. Coal Run, Ohio, Aug. 17, 1940; s. James Leroy and Edith Marie (Coffman) L.; m. Martha Jane Toothman, Jan. 1, 1960; children: Jody Dean, Lucinda Jo Laughery Cowdery, Randal Shawn, Jamey Brian. Student, Mich. Christian Coll., 1960-61; BA in Bible with honorss, Ohio Valley Coll., 1984; postgrad., So. Christian U., 1991—. Pulpit min. Ch. of Christ, Louisville, 1961-66, Cuyahoga Falls, Ohio, 1966-73, Belpre, Ohio, 1973—; ednl. dir. Ohio Valley Christian Youth Camp, Waterford, Ohio, 1975-90. Editor: Equipping the Saints, 1989; contbr. to: What Does the Bible Teach, 1988. Mem. adv. bd. Ohio Valley Coll., Parkersburg, W.Va., 1980—; bd. dirs. Crisis Pregnancy Svcs., Parkersburg, W.Va., 1991—. Recipient PACE Svc. award Ohio Valley Coll., 1991. Home: Rte 2 Box 127 Little Hocking OH 45742 Office: Belpre Ch of Christ 2932 Washington Blvd Belpre OH 45714

LAUGHLIN, HUGH COLLINS, priest; b. Toledo, Ohio, Feb. 9, 1938; s. Hugh Clark and Isabel Virginia (Long) L.; m. Nancy Anne Crawford, Nov. 23, 1963; children: Hugh Crawford, Sarah Crawford. AB, Harvard U., 1960; MDiv, Ch. Div. Sch. of Pacific, 1963. Ordained priest Episcopal Ch., 1963. Curate Trinity Cathedral, Cleve., 1963-67; vicar St. Matthew's Episcopal Ch., Brecksville, Ohio, 1969-74; rector Trinity Episcopal Ch., Bloomington, Ind., 1974—; dean N.W. deanery Diocese of Ind., Indpls., 1974—, chmn. examining chaplains, 1979—, pres. standing com., 1985-88, dep. gen. convention, 1982—. Bd. dirs. Amethyst house, Bloomington, 1981—; mem. exec. com. Ctr. for Study of Religion and Am. Culture, Indpls., 1988—. Recipient Quality of Life award Bloomington Hosp., 1987. Home: 2147 Meadow Bluff Ct Bloomington IN 47401 Office: Trinity Ch PO Box 336 Bloomington IN 47402

LAUGHLIN, JOHN CHARLES HUGH, religion and archaeology educator; b. Asheboro, N.C., Sept. 5, 1942; s. Charles Franklin and Alice Loraine (Beggs) L.; m. Janet Lee Trogdon, Oct. 16, 1965; 1 child, John Joshua. BA cum laude, Wake Forest U., 1967; MDiv, So. Bapt. Theol. Sem., 1971, PhD, 1975. Pastor Coll. Ave. Bapt. Ch., Bluefield, W.Va., 1975-76; asst. prof. religion Hardin-Simmons U., Abilene, Tex., 1976-77, Palm Beach Atlantic Coll., West Palm Beach, Fla., 1977-79; assoc. prof. religion Averett Coll., Danville, Va., 1979-87, prof. religion, 1987—; area supr. Capernaum (Israel) excavation, 1981-87, Banias (Israel) excavation, 1989—. Author: (with others) Capernaum: Vol. 1, 1989. Guest speaker various schs., clubs and chs., Danville, 1979—. Served as sgt. U.S. Army, 1961-64. Garrett Teaching Fellow, So. Bapt. Theol. Sem., 1972. Mem. Nat. Assn. Bapt. Profs. of Religion, Am. Schs. Oriental Research, Soc. Bibl. Lit. Democrat. So. Baptist. Avocations: jogging, furniture refinishing, photography. Office: Averett Coll 420 W Main St Danville VA 24541 *After all is said and done, it seems to me that the greatest challenge of life is still to know, and be true to, oneself.*

LAUGHLIN, THOMAS BERNARD, priest; b. Omaha, July 26, 1925; s. David Edward and Marie (Killila) L. AB magna cum laude, Loras Coll., 1945; Licentiate in Sacred Theology, St. Mary's Sem., 1948; postgrad., U. Portland, 1949-50, Cath. U. Am., 1950-51; MA, Creighton U., 1955; postgrad., Inst. Theol. Continuing Edn., Rome, 1973. Ordained priest Roman Cath. Ch., 1948. Tchr. Cen. Cath. High Sch., Portland, Oreg., 1948-65, chmn. dept. fgn. langs., 1952-65, asst. prin., 1955-65; lectr. theology, prof. Latin Maryhurst (Oreg.) Coll., 1962-64; pastor St. Frederick's Ch., St. Helens, Oreg., 1965-66, St. Mary's Ch., Corvallis, Oreg., 1966-72, All Sts. Ch., Portland, 1973-83; social activities dir. Found. House, Jemez Springs, N.Mex., 1983-87; marriage counselor Albuquerque, 1987—; head chaplain Newman Ctr., Oreg. State U., 1966-72; pres. Corvallis Ministerial Assn., Religious Dirs. Assn. Oreg. State U.; v.p., then pres., mem. bd. edn. Priests Senate Archdiocese of Portland, 1967—; mem. adv. bd. Cath. Charities, 1975—. Founder Spectrum jour. Mem. Classical Assn. Oreg. (co-founder). Home and Office: 6303 Indian School Rd NE Albuquerque NM 87110

LAUNDERVILLE, DALE, academic administrator. Acting head St. John's U., Sch. of theology, Collegeville, Minn. Office: St John's U Sch Theol Collegeville MN 56321*

LAURSEN, ELMER, pastoral counselor; b. Tacoma, Wash., Dec. 31, 1916; s. Marinus and Anna Christine (Nielsen) L.; m. Beulah Fritch, Aug. 29, 1939; children: Carol Ann, John Perrin, Dana Elmer, Scott Raymond. BA, Concodia Coll., Moorhead, Minn., 1949; MDiv in Theology, Luther Theol. Sem., St. Paul, 1952; STM in Psychology of Religion, Andover Newton Theol. Sch., Newton Centre, Mass., 1953, D Ministry in Psychology of Religion, 1974. Ordained to ministry Evang. Luth Ch., 1952; cert. chaplain. Dir. chaplaincy Fairview Hosp., Mpls., 1953-57; pastor Luth. Ch. of Hope, Phoenix, 1957-60; dir. chaplaincy and CPE U. Calif. Med. Ctr., San Francisco, 1960-76; pastoral counselor Luth. Counseling Svc., Arcata, Calif., 1976—. Mem., chair County Mental Health Adv. Bd., Humboldt County, Calif., 1976-88; chair, mem. Humboldt Lit. Project, Humboldt County, 1985—; mem. Bio-Ethics Com., Humboldt County, 1989—; founding mem., chair Hospice of Humboldt County, 1976-83. Sgt. U.S. Army, 1945-46. Mem. Asns. Clin. Pastoral Edn. (supr. 1963-76, supr. emeritus 1976—, dir. Pacific region 1971-75). Home: 2750 Hilltop Ct Arcata CA 95521

LAURUS, ARCHBISHOP (LAURUS SKURLA), archbishop; b. Ladomirova, Czechoslovakia, Jan. 1, 1928; s. Michael Ivan and Helen Michael (Martinik) Skurla. BTh, Holy Trinity Sem., 1954. joined Holy Trinity Monastery, 1946; ordained deacon Russian Orthodox Ch. Abroad, 1950, ordained priest, 1957, consecrated bishop, 1967, elevated to archbishop, 1981. Instr. Old Testament Holy Trinity Sem., Jordanville, N.Y., 1960-65, instr. patristics, 1959—, instr. moral theology, 1973-76, insp., 1958-67, dean, 1973-76, abbot, 1976—, rector, chmn. bd., 1976—; bishop Diocese of Manhattan, 1967-76; bishop, then archbishop Diocese of Syracuse, 1976—; sec. Synod of Bishops, 1967-77, 1986—; pres. St. John of Kronstadt Meml. Fund, 1976—. Editor: Calendar, 1976—; contbr. articles to ch. publs. and periodicals. Mem. Orthodox Palestine Soc., 1986—. Home: Holy Trinity Monastery Jordanville NY 13361 Office: Synod of Bishops 75 E 93d St New York NY 10128

LAUSHWAY, FRANCIS AARON, priest; b. Providence, Mar. 31, 1952; s. Francis Clifford and Patricia Florence (Cady) L. BA, Providence Coll., 1974; STB, Dominican House of Studies, Washington, 1979, STL, 1981; MEd, U. Va., 1984, PhD, 1987. Ordained priest Roman Cath. Ch., 1980. Cath. chaplain U. Va., Charlottesville, 1981-84, grad. instr., 1984-87; asst. prof. Dominican House of Studies, Washington, 1987-90; vis. spl. lectr. Providence Coll., summers 1987-89; prior St. Mary's Priory, New Haven, 1989—; pastor St. Mary's Ch., New Haven, 1989—. Yale Religious Ministry, Cath. Campus Ministry Assn., Cath. Assn. for Theol. Edn. (ea. regional rep. 1989), Assn. for Theol. Field Edn., Order of Preachers. Address: 5 Hillhouse Ave New Haven CT 06505

LAUVER, ROBERT A., clergyman; b. Mt. Pleasant Mills, Pa., Apr. 26, 1943; s. Palmer A. and Mary Jane (Ebright) L.; m. Sandra Ann Womer, Sept. 5, 1964; children: Tamela, Tina, Timothy. ThB, Internat. Bible Coll., San Antonio, 1968; ThM, Christian Internat. U., Panama City, Fla., 1976. Ordained to ministry Pentecostal Ch. Youth leader Apostolic Faith Ch., Mt. Pleasant, Pa., 1960-64; asst. pastor Revival Temple, San Antonio, 1964-68; tchr. Internat. Bible Coll., San Antonio, 1968-72; pres., tchr. Susquehanna Bible Inst., Muncy, Pa., 1972-77; pastor New Life Temple, Muncy, 1977—; trustee GAP Youth Ministry, Hughesville, Pa., 1990; pres. Muncy Ministeries, 1988; pastor Revival Temple Fellowship. Sch. dir. Muncy Sch. Dist., 1983-90. Democrat. Home: 200 S Market St Muncy PA 17756 Office: New Life Temple Ch 206 S Market St Muncy PA 17756

LAUZON, ROBERT MAURICE, minister, accountant; b. Williams, Ariz., June 2, 1948; s. Loren Hampton and Harriet Julia (Silverstein) L.; m. Deborah Ann Bayley, Oct. 21, 1978; children: Michael, Sarah, Rebekah, Leah. BS, No. Ariz. U., 1971. Ordained to ministry Christian Fellowship Ch., 1983; CPA, Ariz. Min. Four Sq. Gospel Ch., Phoenix, 1983-84; min. Christian Fellowship Ch., Phoenix, 1984-88, Bridgeport, Conn., 1988-90, Bridgeport, 1990—; treas. Grace Fellowship Full Gospel Ch., Flagstaff, Ariz, 1990—, Nevville Found.World Missions Internat., Bridgeport, 1991—; bd. dirs. Compassion for Children.. Mem. AICPA, Christian Ministry Resources (instr. 1991). Home: 540 Westfield Ave Bridgeport CT 06606

LAVAN, SPENCER, academic administrator. Head Meadville/Lombard Theol. Sch., Chgo. Office: Meadville/Lombard Theol Sch Office of the Dean 5701 Woodlawn Ave Chicago IL 60637*

LAVDAS, LEONIDAS G., religion educator, meteorologist; b. Phila., Oct. 22, 1947; s. George L. and Jean E. (Barnett) L. BS in Meteorology, NYU, 1969; MS in Meteorology, Fla. State U., 1971. Rsch. meteorologist USDA-Forest Svc., Macon, Ga., 1972—; chmn. parish edn. dept. Faith Luth. Ch., Warner-Robins, Ga., 1986-90, mem. ch. coun., 1987-90, adult Sun. sch. tchr., 1986—. Author, actor: Pontius Pilate Solioquy, 1990, others; actor Macon Area Community Theater, 1977-79, Warner Robins Little Theater, 1985. Mem. AAAS, Am. Meteorol. Soc., Air and Waste Mgmt. Assn., Nat. Weather Assn., U.S. Chess Fedn., Religious Book Club. Home: 215 Sun Valley Dr Warner Robins GA 31093-1058 *It helps me to think of God as One who delegates much of His work on behalf of humanity to humans. He became human for our salvation, but left it for us to pass that message on by word and especially by examples of unselfish love. To do so, it seems wiser to me to try to follow His example of trust than resort to manipulative presumption.*

LAVELLE, DONALD EUGENE, pastor; b. New Haven, Apr. 29, 1933; s. Eugene Edward and Mildred Irene (Johnson) L.; m. Janet Elizabeth Ankersen, July 4, 1959; children: Stephen, Katherine, John. BA, Upsala Coll., 1955; MDiv, Augustana Sem., Rock Island, Ill., 1959. Pastor Zion Luth. Ch., Oil City, Pa., 1959-64, St. Andrew Luth. Ch., Coraopolis, Pa., 1964-68, St. Luke's Luth. Ch., Park Ridge, Ill., 1968-73, Salem Luth. Ch., Rockford, Ill., 1973—. Home: 4405 Pinecrest Rd Rockford IL 61107 Office: Salem Luth Ch 1629 S 6th St Rockford IL 61104

LAVELLI, EVELYN ELAINE, minister; b. Ware, Mass., June 28, 1955; d. Everett Dale and Clarinda Joanne (Archibald) Cox; m. Gary Lavelli, June 30, 1974; children: Daniel August, Angela Dorene. BS, Springfield (Mass.) Coll., 1986; MDiv, Andover Newton Theol. Sch., 1990. Ordained to ministry United Ch. of Christ, 1990. Asst. min. Mittineague Congl. Ch., West Springfield, Mass., 1989-90, assoc. min., 1990—; coord. Ecumenical Vacation Bible Sch., West Springfield, 1991. Mem. West Springfield Parish Assn. Home: 43 Warren St West Springfield MA 01089 Office: Mittineague Congl Ch 1840 Westfield St West Springfield MA 01089

LAVENDER, AARON EDWARD, minister; b. Cleve., Aug. 12, 1951; s. James Edward and Bernice (Thompson) L.; m. Ledora Lavender, July 7, 1973; children: Dwight, Brian, Jessica. B Religious Edn., Carver Bible Coll., Atlanta, 1980; M Ministry, Covington Theol. Sem., 1982, D Ministry, 1984. Ordained to ministry Bapt. Ch., 1981. Deacon, assoc. min. Community Bapt. Ch., East Cleveland, Ohio, 1975-77; youth min. Atlanta Bible Bapt. Ch., 1978-80; pastor Grace Bible Ch., Charleston, W.Va., 1981-86; sr. pastor

Grace Bapt. Ch., Kansas City, Mo., 1986—; v.p. Carver Bapt. Bible Inst., Kansas City, Mo., 1988—; pres. Fundamental Bapt. Fellowship Assn., Ft. Wayne, Ind., 1990—. Author: The Epistle of Hebrews, 1989, Lessons on the Prophet Elijah, 1989. Cpl. USMC, 1971-73. Named Young Man of Yr., East Cleveland Rozelle Civic Assn., 1969. Mem. Ministers Alliance Assn. (vice chmn. 1990—). Home: 6203 E 109th Terr Kansas City MO 64134 Office: Grace Bapt Ch 7203 Paseo Kansas City MO 64132 *Perhaps the greatest challenge facing churches today is to see to it that God's word is adequately and correctly read, taught, studied, and applied. I have chosen to commit myself to these in my personal life and in my pastoral ministry.*

LAVER, ROBERT CARL, minister; b. San Francisco, Aug. 30, 1957; s. Alexander Carl and Doris (Renzema) L.; m. Joni Lee Winchell, June 14, 1980; children: Randall James, Thomas Jon. BA, Puget Sound Christian Coll., 1980; MDiv., Emmanuel Sch. of Religion, 1987. Intern U. Christian Ch., Moscow, Idaho, summer 1979; interim min. Edmonds (Wash.) Ch. of Christ, summer 1980; assoc. min. Eastside Christian Ch., Albany, Oreg., 1980-84; sr. min. Cen. Christian Ch., Jonesborough, Tenn., 1984-87, 1st Christian Ch., Myrtle Point, Oreg., 1987—; bd. dir. Crisis Pregnancy Ctr., Coos Bay, Oreg., 1990—, Oreg. Christian Endeavor, Eugene, Oreg., 1980—. Contbr. articles to profl. jours. Vol. Oreg. Right to Life PAC, Coos Bay, 1990. Recipient Preaching award Internat. Christian Endeavor, Columbus, Ohio, 1983. Mem. Joneborough Ministerial Assn., Myrtle Point Ministerial Assn. (sec.-treas 1987—), Rotary (youth exchange 1990). Home: 1231 Doborout Myrtle Point OR 97458 Office: 1st Christian Ch PO Box 545 511 6th St Myrtle Point OR 97458

LAVERGNE, COLIN ROBERT, church administrator; b. Seattle, Aug. 27, 1949; s. Vernon Charles and Mildred Julie (Lokken) LaV.; m. Barbara Jean Linscott, June 12, 1976; children: Caleb, Luke, Anna, Benjamin, Daniel, Catherine, Gregory. BA in Theology, Seattle U., 1977. Adminstr. Resurrection Community, Seattle, 1972-77; mgr. Shepherd's Gate Christian Bookstore, Mpls., 1977-81; adminstr. Servants of the Lord, Inc., Mpls., 1981-85; owner Resurrection Books, Inc., Mpls., 1982—; dir. Charismatic Renewal Office, Mpls., 1986—; archdiocesan liaison Charismatic Renewal Office, 1991—; nat. adv. com. Cath. Charismatic Renewal, 1975-77, 87—. Mem. Christian Bookseller Assn., Religious Conf. Mgmt. Assn. Office: Charismatic Renewal Office 1203 E Lake Minneapolis MN 55407

LAVERMAN, BRUCE GLEN, minister; b. Chgo., May 9, 1940; s. John Bert and Henrietta (Vandenhandel) L.; m. Mary Ann Folkert, June 16, 1964; children: Mark, Susan, Julie, Tamara. BA, Hope Coll., 1962; MDiv, Western Sem., 1965. Ordained to ministry Ref. Ch. in Am. Pastor Bethany Ref. Ch., Sheboygam, Wis., 1965-69, Ref. Ch. of Palos Heights (Ill.), 1969-80; sr. pastor Westwood Community Ch., Omaha, 1980-85, Christ's Community Ch., Glendale, Ariz., 1985—; pres. Classis of Chgo., 1976-78, Classis of S.W., Phoenix, 1988-90. Contbr. articles to profl. publs. Pres. Moraine Valley Clergy Assn., Palos Park, 1975. Preaching scholar Western Theol. Sem., 1989. Home: 4602 W Redfield Glendale AZ 85306 Office: Christ's Community Ch 4530 W Thunderbird Glendale AZ 85306

LAVIN, PAUL EDWARD, priest; b. Pittston, Pa., Mar. 3, 1944; s. Paul James Lavin and Elizabeth (McGovern) Devlin. BA, King's Coll., Wilkes-Barre, Pa., 1965; MA, Niagra U., N.Y., 1968; cert. in theology, Katholieke U. Leuven, Belgium, 1971. Ordained priest Roman Cath. Ch., 1969. Assoc. pastor Mt. Calvary Cath. Ch., Forestville, Md., 1969-74; asst. dir. Cath. Youth Orgn., Archdiocese of Washington, 1974-78; Cath. chaplain Am. U., Washington, 1978-87; pastor Mother Seton Cath. Ch., Germantown, Md., 1987-91, St. Joseph's on Capitol Hill, Washington, 1991; nat. chaplain Jr. Cath. Daughters of Am., N.Y.C., 1974-82. Founder youth retreat ECHO, Washington, 1970, C.Y.O. Retreat Ctr., 1975. Home and Office: St. Joseph's on Capitol Hll 313 Second St NE Washington DC 20002

LAVINE, THELMA ZENO, philosophy educator; b. Boston; d. Samuel Alexander and Augusta Ann (Pearlman) L.; m. Jerome J. Sachs, Mar. 31, 1944; 1 child, Margaret Vera. A.B., Radcliffe Coll., 1936; A.M., Harvard U., 1937, Ph.D., 1939. Instr. Wells Coll., 1941-43, asst. prof., 1945-46; asst. prof. philosophy Bklyn. Coll., 1946-51; asst. prof. U. Md., 1955-57, assoc. prof., 1957-62, prof., 1962-65; Elton prof. George Washington U., 1965-85, chmn. dept., 1969-77; Clarence J.Robinson Univ. prof. George Mason U., Fairfax, Va., 1985—; lectr., seminar cons. Inter-Am. Def. Coll., 1975—. Author: TV course From Plato to Sartre, 1980, From Socrates to Sartre: The Philosophic Quest, 1984; co-author: History and Anti-History Philosophy, 1989, introduction to Collected Works of John Dewey, Vol. 16, 1990; contbr. articles to profl. jouurs., chpts. to books. Recipient Outstanding Faculty award U. Md., 1965, Outstanding Faculty award George Washington U., 1968, Alumnae Achievement award Radcliffe Coll., 1991; NEH sr. research fellow, 1980; Am. Enterprise Inst. Public Policy Research fellow, 1980-81, Va. Found. Humanities fellow, 1990. Mem. Am. Philos. Assn. (5th Ann. Romanell lectr. 1991), Soc. Advancement Am. Philosophy (exec. com. 1979—), Internat. Soc. Sociology Knowledge (pres. elect 1992—), Internat. Soc. Ednl., Cultural and Sci. Interchanges, Internat. Soc. Polit. Psychology, Metaphys. Soc. Am., Washington Philosophy Club (pres. 1967-68), Washington Sch. Psychiatry, Forum Psychiatry and Humanities, Cosmos Club, Radcliffe Club, Harvard Club, Phi Beta Kappa (pres. chpt. 1978-80). Home: 1625 35th St NW Washington DC 20007 Office: George Mason U Robinsons Profs E 207 Fairfax VA 22030

LAW, BERNARD FRANCIS CARDINAL, archbishop; b. Torreon, Mex., Nov. 4, 1931; s. Bernard A. and Helen A. (Stubblefield) L. B.A., Harvard U., 1953; postgrad., St. Joseph Sem., St. Benedict, La., 1953, Pontifical Coll. Josephinum, Worthington, Ohio, 1955. Ordained priest Roman Catholic Ch., 1961, consecrated bishop, 1973; editor Natchez-Jackson diocesan paper, Jackson, 1963-68; exec. dir. U.S. Bishops Com. for Ecumenical and Interreligious Affairs, 1968-71, chmn., from 1975; vicar gen. Diocese of Natchez-Jackson, 1971-73; bishop Diocese of Springfield-Cape Girardeau, Mo., 1973-84; archbishop Archdiocese of Boston Brighton, MA, 1984—; created cardinal, 1985; mem. adminstrv. com. Nat. Conf. Cath. Bishops, from 1975; mem. communication com. U.S. Cath. Conf., 1974, mem. adminstrv. bd., from 1975; mem. Vatican Secretariat for Promoting Christian Unity, from 1976; consultor Vatican Commn. Religious Relations with the Jews, from 1976; chmn. bd. Pope John XXIII Med.-Moral Research and Edn. Ctr., St. Louis, 1980-82; ecclesiastical del. of Pope John Paul II for matters pertaining to former Episcopal priests, 1981. Trustee Pontifical Coll. Josephinum, 1974-85, Nat. Shrine of Immaculate Conception, from 1975; bd. regents Conception (Mo.) Sem. Coll., from 1975. Office: Cardinal's Residence 2121 Commonwealth Ave Boston MA 02135

LAWLER, CHENEY PAUL, lay worker; b. Birmingham, Ala., Jan. 4, 1961; s. Cheney Jasper L. and Patricia (Bramlett) Hammonds; m. Melissa Jane Pope, Aug. 13, 1983; children: Cheney Luke, Mark Wesley. BA, Asbury Coll., 1984; MDiv, Asbury Sem., 1988. Ordained elder United Meth. Ch., 1990. Min. youth First United Meth. Ch., Cynthiana, Ky., 1985-87; assoc. pastor, youth dir. First United Meth. Ch., Tuscumbia, Ala., 1987—; dir. Behold Ministries, Tuscumbia, 1990—; cons., originator VisionQuest. Speaker tng. events, youth retreats, spl. gatherings including Aldersgate 250, WW Jam II, Rise of Fall Youth Conference. Named one of Outstanding Young Men in Am., 1989. Office: The Hammonds Lawler Corp 201 North St Albertville AL 35950 *I acn't remember who first said it but i love the saying "attempt something so big that unless God intervenes it is bound to fail". I want to live life as few regrets as possible. I want to try to live life day by day as if it were my last, gripped by a sense of destiny and passion.*

LAWLER, MICHAEL GERARD, theology educator, university dean; b. Saltcoats, Scotland, Jan. 7, 1933; came to U.S. 1970; s. Michael J. and Margaret (Cairns) L.; m. Susan R. Hoffman, Dec. 23, 1970; children—Michael, Anya, David. B.S. in Math., Nat. U., Dublin, Ireland, 1955, higher diploma, 1957; B.D. in Theology, Gregorian U., Rome, 1961, S.T.L., 1963; Ph.D. in Theology, Aquinas Inst., St. Louis, 1975. Instr. St. Joseph Coll., Nairobi, Kenya, 1963-67; asst. prof. Holy Ghost Coll., Dublin, 1968-69; asst. prof. theology Creighton U., Omaha, 1970-77, assoc. prof., 1977-81, prof., 1981—, dean Grad. Sch., 1985—; cons. Religious Edn. Office, Omaha. Author: Raid on the Inarticulate, 1980, Secular Marriage-Christian Sacrament, 1985, Sacrament of Service, 1985, From Tee to Green: A Book of Uncommon Prayers for Golfers, 1987, Symbol and Sacrament: Contemporary Sacramental Theology, 1987, Faith Trails, 1989, Theology of Ministry, 1990, Ecumenical Marriage and Remarriage, 1990, 1990; also articles. Profl. theologian Permanent Diaconate Program, Omaha, 1972-85. Fellow Danforth Found.; mem. Am. Acad. Religion, Religious Edn. Assn., Coll. Theology Soc., Cath. Theol. Soc. Am. Avocations: writing; cultural anthropology; golf. Office: Creighton U Grad Sch 25th and California Omaha NE 68178

LAWRENCE, CALEB JAMES, bishop; b. Lattie's Brook, N.S., Can., May 26, 1941; s. James Otis and Mildred Viola (Burton) L.; m. Maureen Patricia Cuddy, July 18, 1966; children: Fiona, Karen, Sean. B.A., Dalhousie U., Halifax, N.S., 1962; B.S.T., U. of King's Coll., Halifax, 1964, D.Div. (hon.), 1980. Ordained priest Anglican Ch. of Canada, 1965. Missionary priest St. Edmund's Anglican Parish, Gt. Whale River, Que., Can., 1965-74, rector, 1974-79; canon St. Jude's Cathedral, Frobisher Bay, N.W.T., Can., 1974-75; archdeacon of Arctic Que. Diocese of the Arctic, Toronto, Ont., Can., 1975-79; bishop Diocese of Moosonee, Schumacher, Ont., 1980—; mem. coun. of north Anglican Ch. Can., 1979—, mem. gen. synod, 1980—; mem. Anglican Coun. N.Am. and Caribbean, 1983-86. Translator liturgical services, hymns into Cree, 1970-80. Canon W.H. Morris travelling scholar U. of King's Coll., 1964. Home: PO Box 830, Schumacher, ON Canada P0N 1G0 Office: Anglican Ch of Can, Diocese of Moosonee, PO Box 841, Schumacher, ON Canada P0N 1GO

LAWRENCE, DAVID NORMAN, broadcasting executive, consultant; b. Kalispell, Mont., June 19, 1941; s. James Lynn and Lola Alameda (Greenfield) L.; m. Judy Arlene Burke, Aug. 22, 1965; children: Wendy Kay, Robert Lynn, Cary Lee. Student, John Brown U., 1959-62, N.W. Nazarene Coll., 1963-68; BA, Golden State U., 1987. Mgr. Sta. KHAP, Aztec, N.Mex., 1962-65; mgr. sales, program dir. Sta. KCVR, Lodi, Calif., 1968-73; dir. devel. Far East Broadcasting Co., Manila, 1977-78; dir. of media Far East Broadcasting Co., La Mirada, Calif., 1978-84; dir. internat. programming High Adventure, Simi Valley, Calif., 1984—; media cons. various orgns., L.A.; bd. dirs. Trans World Missions, Glendale, Calif., 1989—. Bd. dirs. Lodi Lions Profl. Baseball, 1971-76; pres. Kiwanis Club Greater Lodi, 1975; mem. pers. bd. City of Buena Park, Calif., 1989—, chmn., 1990. Recipient Outstanding Svc. award City of Buena Park, 1991; named Outstanding Club Pres., Kiwanis, 1975. Mem. Nat. Religious Broadcasters (various awards). Mem. Evang. Free Ch. Am. Home: 8180 Gordon Green Buena Park CA 90621 Office: High Adventure PO Box 7466 Van Nuys CA 91409 *Twentieth Century technology has radically changed the methods of world evangelization with most of our known world closed to the traditional methods. I have dedicated my life to cross political, religious and geographical barriers to meet the world's people on a personal level, allowing them to experience God in their own privacy.*

LAWRENCE, GENE GRANT, minister; b. Cin., Oct. 15, 1942; s. Raymond Floyd and Mary Alice (Skillman) L.; m. B. Faye Withrow, Dec. 24, 1959; children: Steven Grant, Ronald Lenn, John William. BS, Bapt. Bible Coll., 1970; MS, U. So. Miss., 1990. Ordained to ministry Bapt. Ch., 1971. Asst. pastor Landmark Bapt., Cin., 1970-71, Calvary Bapt., Ypsilanti, Mich., 1971-72; pastor Taylor (Mich.) Ctr. Bapt., 1972-79, Withamsville (Ohio) Ch., 1979-81, Bible Bapt. Ch., Petal, Miss., 1981-91; dean academics, field rep. Atlantic Bapt. Bible Coll., Chester, Va., 1991—; chaplain Taylor Police Dept., 1977-79, Community Hosp., Taylor, 1977-79. Bd. dirs. Bapt. Bible Coll. East, Peakskill, N.Y., 1976-82. Office: Atlantic Bapt Bible Coll 500 Baptist Dr PO Box 823 Chester VA 23831-9985

LAWRENCE, MICHAEL EDWARD, religious publishing executive; b. Maysville, Ky., Feb. 28, 1955; s. Riley Edward and Lillian Jean (O'Daire) L.; BA, Lambuth Coll., 1977; Cert. in Book Publishing, NYU, 1977; MBA, Middle Tenn. State U., 1982. Mgmt. trainee Abingdon Press/The United Methodist Pub. House, Nashville, 1977-78, asst. to multi-media resources mgr., 1978-79, product devel. supr., 1979-81, supplies and product devel. mgr., 1981-82, planning and devel. mgr., 1982-83, asst. mgr. ops. dept., 1983-84, dir. fin. and ops., 1983-85, sr. editor trade books, 1985-88, asst. dir. mktg., 1988, dir. mktg., 1989, mng. editor, adminstrv. dir., 1989-91, mng. editor, asst. editor in chief, 1991—. Office: 201 8th Ave S Nashville TN 37203

LAWRENCE, PHIL DEAN, lay minister, sales executive; b. Brady, Tex., Dec. 16, 1957; s. William Thruston and Anna Mae (Blackstock) L.; m. Peggy Ann Kinney, Aug. 1, 1981; 1 child, Nathaniel Thruston Lyle. BFA, Tex. Christian U., Ft. Worth, 1981. Pres. Chi Alpha Campus Ministries/Tex. Christian U., Ft. Worth, 1979-81; asst. lay pastor 1st United Meth. Ch., Bedford, Tex., 1987—; sales mgr. KNRB Radio, Ft. Worth, 1989—. Mem. Optimist Internat. (Ft. Worth). Home: 4820 Cable Dr Fort Worth TX 76137 Office: Sta KNRB Radio/Marsh Broadcast 121 NE Loop 820 Fort Worth TX 76053

LAWRENCE, RALPH ALAN, minister; b. Wendell, Idaho, Apr. 18, 1931; s. Wayne Harold and Evelyn Frances (McConnell) L.; m. Beverley Jean Miller, June 9, 1957 (div. 1974); children: Alan, Douglas, Kerry Philpot; m. Audrey Stall Sheldon, Dec. 28, 1975; children: Wayne Shelden, Mark Shelden, Sharon Glover, Laurel Bishop, Scott Shelden. BA in Bus. Adminstrn., Coll. of Idaho, 1953; MDiv, Boston U., 1956; DD (hon.), Coll. of Idaho, 1986. Ordained to ministry Meth. Ch., 1956. Min. youth Christ Ch., Kennebunk, Maine, 1954-56, Shoshone-Richfield (Idaho) Parish, 1956-60, St. Paul's Ch., Idaho Falls, Idaho, 1960-64, Nyssa (Oreg.) Meth. Ch., 1964-68, Pioneer United Meth. Ch., Portland, Oreg., 1968-74, 1st United Meth. Ch., Payette, Idaho, 1974-81; dist. supt. Ea. Dist., Oreg.-Idaho Conf., 1981-87; pastor Meridian (Idaho) United Meth. Ch., 1987—; del. World Meth. Conf., 1986, 91, Jurisdictional Conf., 1984; chmn. Oreg.-Idaho Conf. Bd. Discipleship, 1980-81; pres. Classic Journeys Internat., 1979—. Editor Idaho Conf. Jour., 1963-67. Pres. Peninsula-Portland (Oreg.) Optimist Club, 1972-73. Mem. Acad. Parish Clergy, Meridian C. of C., Kiwanis. Home: 4192 Tattenham Way Boise ID 83704 Office: PO Box 266 240 E Idaho St Meridian ID 83642 *Evidence of God's action in a person's life is best illustrated by caring, beyond conventional expectations, for one's fellow human beings.*

LAWRENCE, RAYMOND EUGENE, minister, academic administrator; b. Elliston, Ky., Nov. 14, 1921; s. Ray and Mary (Sams) L.; m. Eula Whiteker, Sept. 8, 1948; children: Deborah, Dora. BA, Georgetown Coll., 1949; MDiv, So. Bapt. Sem., 1973. Ordained to ministry, 1947. Pastor 1st Bapt. Ch., Mt. Vernon, Ky., 1953-57, Shelbyville, Ky., 1957-62; pastor Cen. Bapt. Ch., Corbin, Ky., 1962-72; asst. to pres. Cumberland Coll., Williamsburg, Ky., 1972-80; pres. Mid-Continent Bapt. Coll., Mayfield, Ky., 1981-87; dir. Kelley Univ. Coll. S.W. Bapt. U., Joplin, Mo., 1987—. Author: History of Ten Mile Association, 1948, Don't Give Up the Ship, 1972, Whiteker Dunn, 1976. Trustee Southeastern Bapt. Hosp., 1962-82, Cumberland Coll., 1970-72; bd. dirs. Western Recorder, 1965-70. With AUS, 1943-45. Home: 2010 Country Club Dr Joplin MO 64804 Office: SW Bapt U Kelley Univ Coll PO Box 2182 Joplin MO 64803

LAWS-BROWN, DIANE ELAINE, church administrator; b. San Diego, Calif., Jan. 26, 1946; d. John Robert and Willa Mae (Burch) Brokenbough, m. Phillip A. Laws, Feb. 26, 1966 (div. Jan. 1971); 1 child Shawn Vanessa; m. Geroge Bernard Brown, July 25, 1981; 1 child, Linda Yvonne. Sec. Eternal Promise Bapt. Ch., L.A., 1987-90; adminstr. Friendship Bapt. Ch., Yorba Linda, Calif., 1990—; treas., trustee Eternal Promise Bapt. Ch., L.A., 1987—. Office: Friendship Bapt Ch 17145 Bastanchury Rd Yorba Linda CA 92686

LAWSON, CAROLE JEAN, educator, author; b. San Antonio, June 18, 1944; d. Albert Joseph and Pearl Nettie (Garner) Fuller; m. James Ray Lawson, Sept. 7, 1962; children: Regina Anne Kacho, Clinton Ray. Founder Love Makes the World Go Around in Peace, Ft. Worth, Tex., 1988—; founder, dir. Healing Thru Love Seminars, Ft. Worth, Tex., 1988—; founder Sunshine 'n Rainbows Stress Overcomers, Ft. Worth, 1985-87; founder, head Omni-Vision Pub. and Prodns., Ft. Worth, 1990—. Pub. editor Omni Vision newsletter, 1985—; author: To God Be the Glory, poetry collection, 1988-90, The Reflection of God's Smile, 1991; sec. Lightly Speaking Forum, Ft. Worth, 1987-89. Author: My Rocky Mountain High, 1989; author poetry. Supporter of publicity Campaign for the Earth, 1990-91. Mem. NAFE. Home and Office: 1112 Edney St Fort Worth TX 76115 *With the energy shifting at excelerated speed to usher in the new, we must also excelerate our consciousness into the reality of Divine Love with inward harmony and peace. Without this individually expressed by each of us, there will be deterioration and insanity upon the earth resulting in loss of all life as we know it to be as never before experienced. Unconditional love is a must. God is Love!.*

LAWSON, DAVID JERALD, bishop; b. Princeton, Ind., Mar. 26, 1930; s. David Jonathon and Bonnetta A. (White) L.; m. Martha Ellen Pegram, July 16, 1950; children—John Mark, Karen Sue Lawson Strang. A.B., U. Evansville, 1955; M.Div., Garrett Theol. Sem., 1959; D.D., U. Evansville, 1977. Ordained to ministry United Methodist Ch. Pastor, Tell City United Meth. Ch., Ind., 1956-67, Beach Grove United Meth. Ch., Indpls., 1967-72; dist. supt. So. Ind. Conf., 1972-76, conf. council dir., 1976-82; pastor Carmel United Meth. Ch., Ind., 1982-84; bishop United Meth. Ch., Sun Prairie, Wis., 1984—; trustee North Central Coll., Naperville, Ill., 1984—, Meth. Health Service, 1984—, Cedar Crest Home, Janesville, Wis., 1984—, Christian Community Home, Hudson, Wis., 1984—. Author monograph: Administrative Spirituality. Contbr. articles to profl. jours. Mem. Wis. Coordinating Com., Nicaraqua, 1984, Community Dept. of Instnl. Chaplains of State, City Traffic Commn., Ind., Marion County Bd. Zoning Appeals, Ind. Democrat. Lodge: Lions (membership sec. Indpls. 1967-72). Home: 5113 Comanche Way Madison WI 53704 Office: United Meth Ch 750 Windsor St Ste 303 PO Box 220 Sun Prairie WI 53590

LAWSON, E. THOMAS, religion educator; b. Capetown, Republic of South Africa, Nov. 27, 1931; s. Robert Edward and Emily Gertrude (Swart) L.; m. Ruth Ann Jones, July 30, 1966; children: Sonya, Jennifer. B.D., U. Chgo., 1958, MA, 1961, PhD, 1963. Instr. religion Western Mich. U., Kalamazoo, 1961-63, asst., 1963-65, assoc., 1965-67, prof., 1967—. Author: Religions of Africa: Traditions in Transformation, 1984, Rethinking Religion: Connecting Cognition and Culture, 1990; editor Numen: International Review For The History of Religions; contbr. articles to profl. jours. Postdoctoral fellow Soc. for Values in Higher Edn., Council for Philos. Studies. Mem. Am. Acad. Religion, Soc. for Philosophy and Psychology, N.Am. Assn. for Study of Religion, (v.p. 1987), Am. Soc. for Study of Religion, Philosophy of Sci. Assn. Democrat. Avocations: painting; piano; computing. Home: 121 Monroe St Kalamazoo MI 49001 Office: Western Mich U Dept Religion Kalamazoo MI 49008

LAWSON, EVERETT LEROY, academic administrator, minister; b. Tillamook, Oreg., May 17, 1938; s. Elmer LaVerne Lawson and Margery Evelyn (Foltz) Alcott; m. Joy Annette Whitney, June 11, 1960; children: Kimberly Joy Denton, Candace Annette, Lane Whitney. BA, N.W. Christian Coll., 1960; AB, Cascade Coll., 1962; MA in Teaching, Reed Coll., 1965; PhD, Vanderbilt U., 1970. Ordained to ministry Christian Chs. and Chs. of Christ, 1959. Pastor, founder Tigard (Oreg.) Christian Ch., 1959-65; tchr. Tigard Union High Sch., 1962-64; candidate sec. Christian Missionary Fellowship, 1964-68; asst. prof. Milligan (Tenn.) Coll., 1965-73, v.p., 1970-73; sr. pastor East 38th St. Christian Ch., Indpls., 1973-79, Cen. Christian Ch., Mesa, Ariz., 1979—; pres. Pacific Christian Coll., Fullerton, Calif., 1990—; cons. Standard Pub. Co., 1977-90; adj. prof. Ky. Christian Coll., 1984-90; speaker nat. radio broadcast The Christian's Hour, 1987—; dir. Christian Missionary Fellowship, Indpls., 1968-90. Author: Very Sure of God, 1974; co-author: (with Tetsunao Yamamori) Introducing Church Growth, 1975, Church Growth: Everybody's Business, 1976; also 20 other books, commentaries, study books; contbr. articles to profl. jours. Mem. N.Am. Christian Conv. U.S.A. (pres. 1982), Brit.-Am. Fellowship Com. (bd. dirs. 1979—). Office: Cen Christian Ch 933 N Lindsay Rd Mesa AZ 85213 also: Pacific Christian Coll 2500 E Nutwood Ave Fullerton CA 92631

LAWSON, F. D., bishop. Bishop Ch. of God in Christ, Stillwater, Okla. Office: Ch of God in Christ PO Box 581 Stillwater OK 74076*

LAWSON, WILLIAM BURTON, clergyman; b. Mpls., Oct. 14, 1930; s. Lawrence Burton and Mabel Lucille (Lund) L.; m. Grace Elizabeth Dickson, July 30, 1955; children: William Lawrence, Thomas Baxter. BA, U. Minn., 1952; MDiv cum laude, Berkeley Div. Sch., New Haven, 1955, DD (hon.), 1979. Ordained priest Episcopal Ch., 1955. Vicar St. Edward's Episcopal Ch., Duluth, Minn., 1955-59; rector St. Stephen's Episcopal Ch., Bloomfield, Conn., 1959-65, St. Paul's Episcopal Ch., Natick, Mass., 1965-75, St. Stephen's Meml. Ch., Lynn, Mass., 1975—; presiding minister United Parish Natick, 1971-75; ecumenical officer Episcopal Diocese Mass., 1972—, mem. coun., 1972-76, 79-83; mem. exec. com. Episcopal Diocesan Ecumenical Officers, 1973-83, pres., 1978-82; mem. planning com. Nat. Workshop on Christian Unity, 1978-83, chmn., 1982-83; mem. Standing Commn. on Ecumenical Rels., 1978—; mem. governing bd. Nat. Coun. Chs. U.S.A., 1981—; mem. Anglican-Roman Cath. Dialogue, U.S.A., 1984-87; also numerous other career related offices. Author: A New Concept of Ordained Ministry, 1970; contbr. articles to religious publs. Trustee John Walcott Fund, Natick, 1970-75, Lynn Pub. Library, 1975-86, Union Hosp. Mental Health Ctr., 1977-81; mem. Natick Urban Redevel. Authority, 1973-75, Lynn Shelter Assn., 1984-87; pres. St. Stephen's Housing Corp., Lynn, 1975—. Diocese of Mass. Norman Nash fellow, 1984. Mem. N.Am. Acad. Ecuminists, Anglican Ctr. Com. in Rome, Rotary, Delta Tau Delta. Avocations: swimming, furniture restoration, reading. Home: 35 Grant Rd Lynn MA 01904 Office: St Stephen's Meml Ch 74 S Common St Lynn MA 01902

LAWTON, KIM AUDREY, religious journalist; b. Springville, N.Y., July 21, 1963; d. David Edwin and Judith Anne (Churchill) L. BA in Communication, Messiah Coll., Grantham, Pa., 1985. Washington editor Christianity Today Mag., 1987—. Writer book chpt., Elizabeth Dole, 1991; interviewer Pres. George Bush on religion, 1991. Mem. House and Senate Periodical Press Gallery, Nat. Press Club. Office: Christianity Today Mag 529 14th St NW Washington DC 20045

LAWTON, LEON REDFORD, religious organization executive; b. Battle Creek, Mich., May 21, 1924; s. Stephen Redford Lawton and Ethel Rosamond (Chapin) Lawton Scanlan; m. Dorothy Glee Brannon, Sept. 1, 1946; children: Duane E., Gordon P., Patricia G., Jeffrey G. AB, Salem Coll., 1948; BD, Calif. Bapt. Sem., 1951; MDiv, Am. Bapt. Sem. of West, Berkeley, Calif., 1951. Ordained to ministry Bapt. Ch., 1951. Pastor Seventh Day Bapt. Ch., L.A., 1950-56; missionary, pastor in Jamaica, W.I. Seventh Day Bapt. Missionary Soc., Westerly, R.I., 1956-64; dir. evangelism Seventh Day Bapt. Missionary Soc., Westerly, 1964-68; pastor Seventh Day Bapt. Ch., Lakewood, Colo., 1969; exec. v.p. Seventh Day Bapt. Missionary Soc., Westerly, 1970—. 1st sgt. U.S. Army, 1942-46, ETO. Recipient Gold Medal of Honor, Govt. of Netherlands, 1945. Avocation: stamp collecting. Home: 73 Granite St Westerly RI 02891 Office: Seventh Day Bapt Missionary Soc 119 Main St Westerly RI 02891

LAYCOCK, HAROLD DOUGLAS, law educator, religious writer; b. Alton, Ill., Apr. 15, 1948; s. Harold Francis and Claudia Anita (Garrette) L.; m. Teresa A. Sullivan, June 14, 1971; children: Joseph Peter, John Patrick. BA, Mich. State U., 1970; JD, U. Chgo., 1973. Bar: Ill. 1973, U.S. Dist. Ct. (no. dist.) Ill. 1973, Tex. 1974, U.S. Ct. Appeals (7th cir.) 1973, U.S. Dist. Ct. (we. dist.) Tex. 1975, U.S. Ct. Appeals (5th and 11th cirs.) 1975, U.S. Ct. Appeals (6th cir.) 1987, U.S. Supreme Ct. 1976. Law clk. to judge U.S. Ct. Appeals (7th cir.), Chgo., 1973-74; sole practice Austin, Tex., 1974-76; from asst. prof. to prof. law U. Chgo., 1976-81; prof. law U. Tex., Austin, 1981—, endowed professorships, 1983-88, assoc. dean for acad. affairs, 1985-86, endowed chair, 1988—, assoc. dean for rsch., 1991—; vis. prof. law U. Mich., 1990; reporter com. on motion practice Ill. Jud. Conf., 1977-78; atty. in religious liberty litigation. Author: Modern American Remedies, 1985, The Death of the Irreparable Injury Rule, 1991; mem. bd. advisors Religious Freedom Reporter, 1989—; mem. editorial bd. Jour. Ch. and State, 1990—; contbr. articles to law revs. Adv. bd. Consumer Services Orgn., Chgo., 1979-80; mem. exec. bd. Ctr. for Ch./State Studies, Depaul U., 1982-87, adv. com. on religious liberty Presbyn. Ch. USA, N.Y.C., 1983-88, advisor restatement of restitution, 1984-85; v.p. St. Francis Sch., 1990—; mem. bd. advisors L.M. Dawson Inst. for Ch./State Studies, Baylor U., 1990—. Fellow Internat. Acad. for Freedom of Religion and Belief; mem. Am. Law Inst., Chgo. Council of Lawyers (v.p. 1977-78), Assn. Am. Law Schs. (chmn., sec. on remedies 1983), AAUP (com. on Status of Women in Academic Profession 1982-85). Home: 4203 Woodway Austin TX 78731 Office: U Tex Law Sch 727 E 26th St Austin TX 78705

LAYMAN, FRED DALE, biblical literature educator; b. Marshfield, Mo., Sept. 27, 1931; s. Lee R. and Winnie A. (Thomas) L.; m. Donna J. Roberts, Aug. 2, 1952; 1 child, Steven. AB, Asbury Coll., 1954; BD, Asbury Theol. Sem., 1956; ThM, Princeton Theol. Sem., 1957; PhD, U. Iowa, 1972. Prof. bibl. lit. Friends U., Wichita, Kans., 1957-64, Asbury Coll., Wilmore, Ky., 1967-68, Asbury Theol. Sem., Wilmore, 1968—. Contbr. articles to profl. jours. Vice chmn. Planning and Zoning Commn., Nicholasville, Ky., 1977-85. Mem. Soc. Bibl. Lit. United Methodist. Avocations: music, sports. Office: Asbury Theol Sem Wilmore KY 40390

LAZAR, JEFFREY BENNETT, rabbi, educator; b. Chgo., Oct. 30, 1944; s. Buryl Jay and Zelda Rose (Sampson) L.; m. Barbara Ellen Bornstein, Sept. 3, 1967; children: Peter Philip, David Jonathan. BA in Fine Arts, Syracuse U., 1966; B. Hebrew Letters, Hebrew Union Coll., 1969, MA in Hebrew Letters, 1971. Ordained rabbi, 1971. Rabbi, educator Temple DeHirsch-Sinai, Seattle, 1971-72; rabbi, educator Temple Beth El, Steubenville, Ohio, 1972-74, Birmingham, Mich., 1974-78; educator Main Line Reform Temple, Wynnewood, Pa., 1978-82; rabbi, educator Temple Sinai, Atlanta, 1982—. Contbr. articles to profl. publs. Mem. Nat. Assn. Temple Educators (trustee 1978-84, 89—, editor newsletter 1979-84, Reform Jewish Educator 1988), Ednl. Dirs.' Coun., Cen. Conf. Am. Rabbis, Coalition for Advancement of Jewish Edn., Inst. for Creative Judaism. Home: 7592 Van Eyck Way Atlanta GA 30350 Office: Temple Sinai 5645 Dupree Dr NW Atlanta GA 30327 *I find that being able to see good in most people that I meet makes the work that I do both fulfilling and enjoyable. This enables me to transmit values I cherish and know that I have made a small difference in people's lives.*

LAZARETH, WILLIAM HENRY, bishop; b. N.Y.C., Mar. 10, 1928; s. Otto William and Marie (Mueller) L.; m. Jacqueline Howell, Jan. 29, 1955; children: Karen, Victoria, Paul. BA, Princeton U., 1948; MDiv, Luth. Sem., Phila., 1953; PhD, Columbia U.-Union Sem., 1958; DD (hon.), Muhlenberg Coll., 1966; LHD (hon.), Hamilton Coll., 1971; DD (hon.), Assumption Coll., 1983, Gen. Theol. Sem., 1991. Ordained to ministry Evang. Luth. Ch. in Am. as minister, 1956, as bishop, 1988. Dean, prof. theology Phila. Luth. Sem., 1956-76; dir. ch. and society dept. Luth. Ch. in Am., N.Y.C., 1976-80; dir. faith and order secretariat World Coun. Chs., Geneva, 1980-83; pastor Holy Trinity Luth Ch., N.Y.C., 1983-87; bishop Met. N.Y. Synod, N.Y.C., 1988—; del. assembly World Coun. Chs., 1975, 83, Luth. World Fedn., 1977. Author 15 books, latest being Growing Together in Baptism, Eucharist and Ministry, 1982, Two Forms of Ordained Ministry, 1991. Grantee World Coun. Chs., U. Tuebingen, Fed. Republic Germany, 1950; Samuel Trexler scholar U. Lund, Sweden, 1955, Franklin Clark Fry scholar U. Pa., 1973. Mem. Am. Theol. Soc., Am. Soc. Christian Ethics, Princeton U. Club. Office: Met NY Synod 390 Park Ave S New York NY 10016-8803

LAZOR, THEODOSIUS (HIS BEATITUDE METROPOLITAN THEODOSIUS), archbishop; b. Canonsburg, Pa., Oct. 27, 1933; s. John and Mary (Kirr) L. AB, Washington and Jefferson Coll., 1957, DD (hon.), 1973; BD, St. Vladimir's Orthodox Theol. Sem., 1960; postgrad., Ecumenical Inst., Bossey, Switzerland, 1961; DD (hon.), St. Vladimir's Orthodox Theol. Sem., 1986; DHL (hon.), Georgetown U., 1988. Tonsured monk Orthodox Ch. in Am., 1961, ordained priest, 1961; priest Nativity of Holy Virgin Mary Ch., Madison, Ill., 1961-66; elected bishop of Washington, 1967, Sitka and, Alaska, 1967, Pitts. and, W.Va., 1972; elected primate of Orthodox Ch. in Am., Met. All Am. and Can.; archbishop of N.Y., 1977, archbishop of Washington, 1981—. Address: Orthodox Ch Am PO Box 675 Rte 25A Syosset NY 11791

LAZOVSKY, LOUIS ARYEH, budget and planning executive; b. Chgo., Mar. 20, 1956; s. Sam and Florence (Kagan) L.; m. Saretta Lee Allswang, Aug. 31, 1981; children: Ben Zion Moshe, Eliyahu Dov, Tehilla Leah. BA in History with honors, Roosevelt U., 1976; Rabbinic ordination, Brisk Rabbinical Coll., 1977; MA in Pub. Policy Studies, U. Chgo., 1985. Cert. secondary tchr., Ill.; lic. real estate agt., Ill. Faculty mem. Ida Crown Jewish Acad., Chgo., 1976-78; dir. student housing, guidance counselor Brisk Rabbinical Coll., Chgo., 1977-79; dir. spl. student program for Soviet immigrants Harry S. Truman Coll., Chgo., 1979-85; exec. dir. Ark, Inc., Chgo., 1985-87; asst. dir. budget, planning Jewish Fdn. Met. Chgo., 1987—; spiritual leader, Rabbi Congregation B.H.H. Kesser Maariv Anshe Luknik, Chgo., 1984—; w.p. Chgo. Rabbinical Coun., 1979—; bd. dirs. Chgo. Bd. Rabbis, Merkaz Harabbanim, Chgo., Congregation B.H.H. Kesser Maariv Anshe Luknik, Assn. Jewish Communal Orgn., Personnel, Alumni Assn. Harris Sch. Pub. Policy Studies U. Chgo. Author: Highlights of the Weekly Torah Portions, 1991, In Search of Freedom, 1985; contbr. articles to mags. and newsletters. Bd. dirs. Harris Grad. Sch. Pub. Policy Studies, 1991—. Named Sherman scholar Brandeis U., 1989. Mem. Orthodox Union, Assn. Torah Advancement. Avocations: racquetball, golf, reading, writing. Home: 6434 N Trumbull Lincolnwood IL 60645 Office: Jewish Fedn Met Chgo 1 S Franklin Ben Gurian Way Rm 607 Chicago IL 60606 *Every commodity that we purchase comes with instructions and a limited warranty in order for us to understand how to use the product and be assured of its performance. The Almighty also provided mankind with an instruction manual and a guarantee—His Holy Bible. We must study and practice its precepts diligently in order to get the most out of our most valuable product—the gift of life itself.*

LEA, JAMES ALTON, minister; b. Russell, Ark., Feb. 7, 1950; s. Ralph Hamilton and Nellie Marie (Boswell); m. Claudia Jean Hall, Sept. 4, 1970; children: Ross Hamilton, Ginger Denise. BS, Ark. State U., 1973; MDiv, Bapt. Missionary Assn. Sem., Jacksonville, Tex., 1982; ThD, Trinity Theol. Sem., Newburgh, Ind., 1988. Ordained to ministry Bapt. Missionary Assn. Am., 1976. Pastor Twin Oaks Bapt. Ch., Kennett, Mo., 1976-79, Blackjack Bapt. Ch., Troop, Tex., 1979-82, Missionary Gulf Coast Bapt. Assn., Port Arthur, Tex., 1982-84, Russell (Ark.) Bapt. Ch., 1984-86, Breton Creek Bapt. Ch., Potosi, Mo., 1986-90, Mt. Zion Bapt. Ch., Poplar Bluff, Mo., 1990—. Contbr. articles to jours. in field. Mem. Gov.'s Youth Coun., Ark., 1967-68; scoutmaster Troop 480, Boy Scouts Am., Potosi, 1986-90, asst. scoutmaster Troop 166, Poplar Bluff, 1990—; instr. Prison Fellowship Mo., Jefferson City, 1991—. 1st lt. U.S. Army, 1973. Mem. Cane Creek Bapt. Assn. (moderator 1990-91), Bapt. Missionary Assn. Mo. (pres. 1988-90), Bapt. Missionary Assn. Ark. (nominating com. 1991—), Nat. Right to Life Com., Am. Family Assn. Office: Mt Zion Bapt Ch 1600 S Eleventh St Poplar Bluff MO 63901 *An individual's greatest need is to overcome the power of sin in one's life. A family's greatest need is to avoid divorce. Our schools' greatest need is to allow for the free discussion of God. America's greatest need is to outlaw unrestricted abortions. The churches' greatest need is to evangelize.*

LEACH, NORMAN EDWARD, minister; b. Farmingdale, N.Y., May 17, 1940; s. George Alexander and Irene Alice (Bowen) L. AB, U. Mo., 1962; postgrad., Mo. U. Sch. Social Work, 1962-63; MDiv, San Francisco Theol. Sem., 1970, D in Ministry, 1973. Ordained to ministry Presbyn. Ch., 1971. Mgr. Third Rail Coffee House First Presbyn Ch., San Anselmo, Calif., 1968-70; adj. staff cons. Golden Gate Mission Area Ch. and World Com. United Presbyn. Ch. USA, San Francisco, 1970-72; dir. San Francisco Bay Area Healing Community Program, 1975-89; program adminstr. San Fransisco Council Chs., 1976-82, interim acting exec. dir., 1982-84, acting exec. dir., 1984; exec. dir. San Fransisco Coun. Chs., 1984-89; with Lincoln Interfaith Coun., Lincoln, Nebr., 1989—; chmn. Presbytery Program Coordinating Council; mem. Presbytery Gen. Council, Presbytery Long-Range Planning Com., Presbytery Nominations Com., Presbytery Permanent Jud. Commn., Interfaith BiCentennial Com., San Francisco, 1975-76, No. Calif. Ecumenical Council, 1975-78, World Council Chs., Vancouver, B.C., Can., 1983; founding mem., pres. Presbyn. Disabilities Concerns Caucus 1981; bd. dirs. World Conf. on Religion and Peace West, 1975-77; founding mem., task force on disabilities Archdiocese of San Francisco, 1975-80. Editor, pub.: Heritage and Hope, 1978, (newspaper) To Free Mankind; mem. editorial bd. Caring Congregation Mag.; contbr. columns to mags., chpts. to books. Mem. Congress on Racial Equality, U. Mo., Columbia, 1958-63, Coalition on Nat. Priorities and Mil. Policy, Washington, 1967-71; bd. dirs. Cambodian-Am. Benevolent Assn., 1975-78, Ind. Living Expn., San Francisco, 1983-87, Am.-Israel Friendship League 1984-89, assoc. United Way Execs., San Francisco, 1982-89; founding mem. San Francisco Intergroup Clearinghouse, 1982-89; founder, pres. emeritus San Francisco Mayor's Council on Disabilities Concerns, 1982—. Recipient God and Country award Boy Scouts Am., 1955, Vigil Honor award, 1974, CORLE/ Nat. Council Chs. award, 1977, cert. of merit Mayor Dianne Feinstein, 1985, Freedom award No. Calif. Bd. Rabbis, 1987; named to Gov.'s Hall of Fame for Persons with Disabilities, 1988. Mem. Am. Acad. Polit. and Social Scis., Alpha Sigma Phi, Alpha Phi Omega, Pi Omicron Sigma. Home: 1459 46th Ave San Francisco CA 94122 Office: Lincoln Interfaith Coun 215 Centennial Mall S Rm 411 Lincoln NE 68508 Office: Lincoln Interfaith Coun Ste 402 Lincoln NE

LEADER, LOIS ANNE, parochial school educator; b. Chgo., June 24, 1953; d. Alan Hughes and Vera Jean (Newcomb) Welch; m. Eric Craig Leader, June 2, 1973; children: Aaron Seth, Arwen Evenstar. B in Adult Edn., Ariz. State U., 1979. Cert. spl. edn. tchr., Ariz. Tchr. Covenant Christian Sch., Phoenix, 1981—. Contbg. author The Duck Who Had Goosebumps, 1987; contbr. articles to various publs. Mem. Nat. Right to Life, Christians for Bibl. Equality. Republican. Reformed Presbyterian. Home: 2415 E Hatcher Rd Phoenix AZ 85028 Office: Covenant Christian Sch 1117 E Devonshire Phoenix AZ 85014 *Introduce a child to the love of reading and you give that child the gift of not just one lifetime, but of a multitude of lifetimes.*

LEAF, GLENN, minister, ecumenical agency administrator. Pres. Twin Cities Met. Ch. Commn., Mpls. Office: Twin Cities Meth Ch Commn 122 W Franklin Rm 218 Minneapolis MN 55404*

LEAHY, JOHN AUSTIN, pastor; b. Cleve., May 27, 1931; s. Joseph F. and Helen F. (Roberts) L. MA in History, John Caroll U., 1960, MEd, 1961; PhD in History, Case Western Res. U., 1988. Prof. Borromeo Coll., Wickliffe, Ohio, 1960-64; prin., dir. St. Vincent High Sch., Akron, Ohio, 1964-65; supt. elem. schs. Diocese of Cleve., 1965-73, ednl. cons., 1973-83; dir. Parmadale, Parma, Ohio, 1970-83; pastor St. Bartholomew Ch., Middleburg Heights, Ohio, 1983—. TV commn. Middleburg Heights, 1986—; bd. dirs. Cath. Counseling Ctr., Cleve., 1969—, trustee, 1973—. Mem. Nat. Cath. Edn. Assn. Home and Office: St Bartholomew Ch 14865 Bagley Rd Middleburg Heights OH 44130

LEAKE, KERRY ALEXANDER, music minister; b. Dyersburg, Tenn., July 30, 1966; s. Kerry Alexander Sr. and Joan Elizabeth (Stem) L. BM in Vocal Performance, Union U., 1989. Min. of music Pilot Oak (Ky.) Bapt. Ch., 1985; min. of music 1st Bapt. Ch., Newbern, Tenn., 1986, Bruceton, Tenn., 1987; min. of music, youth 1st Bapt. Ch., Dickson, Tenn., 1988—.

LEALMAN, BRENDA, religion educator; b. Yorkshire, U.K., June 12, 1939; d. John and Annie Elsie (Beard) L. BA with honors, U. Birmingham, U.K., 1961; postgrad. in edn., U. London, 1962. Religious edn. tchr. Sch. Staffordshire, U.K., 1963-69; head religious edn. dept. Sch. Leicester, U.K., 1970-79; nat. religious edn. adviser Christian Edn. Movement, London, 1979—; mem. com. Schs. Council, Curriculum Devel. Body, U.K., 1978-83; cons. for Dictionary of Religious Edn., CEM.SCM Press, London, 1982-83; co-dir. internat project on religion and values, CEM/Religious Experience Research Unit, Oxford, Eng., 1982-86; guest lectr. Acadia U., N.S., Can., 1986, Theol. Coll. Pangnirtung, Baffin Island, NWT, Can., 1986. Author: (with others) The Image of Life, 1980, Knowing and Unknowing, 1981, The Mystery of Creation, 1982, Christ-Who's That?, 1983, editor: Questions About Religion, series, 1982—, Questions About Religious Education, series, 1984; contbr. articles to profl. publs., poetry; 2 exhbns. photography. Recipient Walter Pothecary award Ct. Clothworkers, 1962; Goldsmiths Co. travel scholar, 1978; St. Luke's Found. grantee, 1982-85; Christian Edn. Movement/Westhill fellow, 1989—. Mem. Assn. Profs. and Researchs in Religious Edn., Profl. Council Religious Edn., Internat. Seminar on Religious Edn. and Values (lectr. 1982, 84, 86, 88, 90). Anglican. Avocations: arts, travel. Home: Flat 5 158 London Rd, Leicester LE2 1ND, England Office: Westhill Coll, Birmingham B29 6LL, England *I find that I am a compulsive traveller and this extends into my inner life. I move on by finding "hints" and "guesses" at "more than" in art, poetry, nature, the creative process itself. We must keep on travelling and exploring, discerning new images, renewing our models of the world and of God.*

LEAMAN, PAUL CALVIN, minister; b. New Lexington, Ohio, Feb. 10, 1929; s. Glen and Anna C. (Rickets) L.; m. Alice Marie Anderson, Sept. 25, 1948; children: Linda, Keith, Bruce, Neil, Kevin. Student, Apostolic Bible Inst., 1946-48. Pastor The Apostolic Ch., New Straitsville, Ohio, 1948-53; state youth pres. Ohio dist. United Pentecostal Ch., 1950-54; founder, pastor The Apostolic Ch., Jackson, Ohio, 1953-60; pastor The Apostolic Ch., Detroit, 1960-75, 1st United Pentecostal Ch., Saginaw, Mich., 1984—; Mich. dist. presbyter United Pentecostal Ch. Internat., 1961-75, 85-87, mem. fgn. missionary bd., United Pentecostal Ch. Internat., Hazelwood, Mo., 1970-75, regional field supr. fgn. missions, Latin Am./Caribbbean Region, 1975-84, Mich. dist. supt., 1987—. Home: 2740 Gabel Rd Saginaw MI 48601 Office: United Pentecostal Ch Mich Dist 2305 Williamson Saginaw MI 48601

LEANDER, DANIEL VANCE, retired minister, small business owner; b. Salina, Kans., May 30, 1925; s. Carl George and Lela Lena (Brewer) L.; m. Marlene Dorreice King, June 6, 1953; children: Don Carlton, Dale Wesley. BA, U. Kans., 1949; ThM, So. Meth. U., 1952; MEd, U. North Tex., 1969. Ordained to ministry United Meth. Ch. as deacon, 1954, as elder, 1956; cert. counselor, Tex. Pastor United Meth. Ch., numerous cities, Tex., 1954-71; pastoral counselor North Tex. conf. United Meth. Ch., Tex., 1971-74; pvt. practice Denton, Tex., 1974—; prin. D.L. Advt. and Pub. Rels., Denton, 1980—. Ch. editor, columnist Denton County Enterprise, 1978-88; writer Insights column, various newspapers, 1978—. With USN, 1943-46, ATO, PTO. Republican. Home: 1007 Windsor Dr Denton TX 76201 Office: DL Advt and Pub Rels 210 S Elm Ste G Denton TX 76201 *Life is a spiritual journey. Christians believe that the Bible provides a map, and God through Jesus and the Holy Spirit gives us directions. One of these directions tells us to live our lives for others. That is what love is all about. In fact, that is a secret of happiness.*

LEARY, CHARLES RANDOLPH, retired minister; b. Mingo, W.Va., Jan. 21, 1930; s. William Jennings Bryan and Mary Eva (Vandevander) L.; m. Juanita M. Lindsay, Dec. 27, 1950; children: David, Alvin, Sharon, Theresa. BA, Davis & Elkins, 1953; MDiv, Temple U., 1957. Ordained to ministry Episcopal Ch. as priest, 1959. Student worker Meth. Conf., Md., Del., 1952-57; asst. All Sts. Episcopal Ch., Wynnewood, Pa., 1957-59, St. Paul's Episcopal Ch., Dayton, Ohio, 1959-61; rector St. Christopher's Episc. Ch., Fairborn, Ohio, 1961-85. Author: Mission Ready!, Missionary Year B, 1st Half Pentecost, 1990. Bd. dirs. Fairborn Neighborhood Ctr., 1964—. Mem. Ministerial Assn., Rotary. Home: 133 Croskey Blvd Medway OH 45341

LEARY, NORMA JEAN EHRHART, organist, choir director, photographer, piano teacher; b. Pitts., Mar. 12, 1926; d. Wilbur Wenke and Laura Isabelle (Bailey) Ehrhart; m. James William Leary, Feb. 7, 1948; children: Timothy James, Matthew William, Nathan Ehrhart. Student, Flora Stone Mather Coll., Cleve., 1944-45, Grove City (Pa.) Coll., 1945-46, Pitts. Mus. Inst., 1946-47. Asst. organist Jamestown (Pa.) United Presbyn. Ch., 1940-50; organist, dir. choir United Meth. Ch., Jamestown, 1953—; radio newscaster, 1965-74, newspaper reporter, 1966—; owner, operator Miniatures Shop, Jamestown, 1988—; free-lance writer, contbr. Miniatures Dealer mag., Jamestown, 1991—; chmn. music com. U. Meth. Ch., Jamestown, 1954—, bd. dirs., 1970-90, dir. jr. choir, 1991—, also program dir. spl. events; tchr. Sharon Valley (Pa.) Writer's Guild, 1988, Thiel Coll., Greenville, Pa., 1989-91. Co-author: Greeting Card Handbook, 1981; composer high sch. musicals and choir anthems; contbr. articles to mags. Mem. Jamestown Study Class, 1950—, Jamestown Rep. Women, 1950-66, Mcpl. Authority Borough Coun., Jamestown, 1986—. Recipient 1st prize songwriters' contest Youngstown, Ohio, 1970, design prize Bicentennial Com., Jamestown, 1976, 1st photography prize Triangle Assn., 1981. Mem. VFW Aux. (pres. Jamestown chpt. 1949), Jamestown Hist. Soc. (pres. 1980-82), Lions (newsletter writer 1967-70). Home: 517 Liberty St Box 156 Jamestown PA 16134 *Training one's initial God-given abilities can give birth to additional, otherwise dormant, talents. Anything less than being persistent and forgiving of failures is lazy and faithless. Also, energy begets energy, inspiration and blessings when one is determined to bloom where planted.*

LEASE, GARY LLOYD, religion educator, dean; b. Hollywood, Calif., Sept. 27, 1940; s. Rex Lloyd Lease and Isabelle (Riehle) Reynolds; m. Patricia Ann Metkovich, Sept. 10, 1966 (div. 1986); 1 child, Dylan; m. Dorothea Ann Ditchfield, Aug. 26, 1988. BA, Loyola U., L.A., 1962; ThD, U. Munich, 1968. Prof. history of consciousness U. Calif., Santa Cruz, 1973—, assoc. chancellor, 1989-90, dean of humanities, 1990—; investigator various archaeol. excavations, 1974, 76, 80, 81. Author: Witness to The Faith, 1971; contbr. articles to profl. jours. Instr. hunter safety Calif. Dept. Fish and Game, 1971—. Fellow Nat. Def. Found., 1962, Danforth Found., 1967, NEH, 1971-72, Fulbright Commn., 1984. Mem. Am. Acad. Religion, Am. Hist. Assn., Am. Schs. Oriental Rsch., Am. Rsch. Ctr. in Egypt, Am. Soc. for Study Religion. Democrat. Office: U Calif History of Consciousness Santa Cruz CA 95064

LEASOR, JANE, religion and philosophy educator, musician; b. Portsmouth, Ohio, Aug. 10, 1922; d. Paul Raymond Leasor and Rana Kathryn (Bayer) Leasor-McDonald. BA, Wheaton Coll., 1944; MRE, N.Y. Theol. Sem., 1952; PhD, NYU, 1969. Asst. prof. Belhaven Coll., Jackson, Miss., 1952-54; dept. chmn. Beirut Coll. for Women, 1954-59; asst. to pres. Wheaton (Ill.) Coll., 1961-63; dean of women N.Y. Theol. Sem., N.Y.C., 1964-67; counselor CUNY, Bklyn., 1967-74; assoc. prof. Beirut U. Coll., 1978-80; tchr. internat. sch., Les Cayes, Haiti, 1984-85; pvt. tutor, 1985—. Author religious text for use in Syria and Lebanon, 1960; editor books by V.R. Edman, 1961-63, Time and Life mags. Mem. Am. Assn. Counselors, Am. Guild Organists. Republican. Episcopalian. Avocations: reading, gardening, golf, travel, history Islam religion. Home: 4102 Fallam Dr Malden WV 25306 *John Cardinal Newman wrote, "I sought to hear the voice of God and climbed the highest steeple. But God declared: 'Go down again; I dwell among the people.'" Words to live by.*

LEATHERWOOD, BARBARA JEAN, lay worker; b. Detroit, Oct. 24, 1939; d. Horace Jackson and Willie Mae (Baker) Jackson Lewis; m. Matthew Leatherwood; children: Malcolm Anthony, Matthew Jr., Jason C. Student, Paine Coll., 1987—. Lic. practical nurse. Lay worker Bethany Apostolic Faith Ch., Wayne, Mich., 1952-64; lay worker U.S. Army religious activities, Ft. Lewis, Wash., 1964-65, Bangkok, Thailand, 1965-71, Denver, 1971-74, Presidio, Calif., 1974-78, Landstuhl, Fed. Republic Germany, 1978-82, Ft. Gordon, Ga., 1982—. Founder, pres. Pinnacle Pl. Neighborhood Assn., Hephzibah, Ga., 1985—; mem. fin. com. Blacks in Govt., Ft. Gordon; vol., sta. chmn. ARC, Ft. Gordon, 1990-91; vol. Vol. Resource Ctr., 1984— (Vol. of Yr. 1989), United Way of Cen. Savannah, 1985— (Alvin J. Vogtle award 1990); outreach coord. Army Community Svc., Ft. Gordon, 1987— (Clara Barton award 1990, Civilian of Yr. award 1990). Home: 4020 Pinnacle Way Hephzibah GA 30815 Office: USASC&FG Army Community Svc Bldg # 34502 Fort Gordon GA 30905-5000

LEATHERWOOD, THOMAS LEE, JR., minister; b. Akron, Ohio, July 24, 1929; s. Thomas Lee and Lola Mae (Palmer) L.; m. Joan Yvonne Ownbey, Mar. 6, 1952; children: LoriLynn McClure, Thomas Lee. B.Div., Arlington Bapt. Coll., Tex., 1950; postgrad., Ashland Coll., Ohio, 1954-62; DDiv (hon.), Bible Bapt. Sem., 1974. Ordained to ministry Bapt. Ch., 1950; cert. pers. cons. Pastor Grace Bapt. Ch., Ft. Scott, Kans., 1950-52, Mansfield (Ohio) Bapt. Temple, 1952-77; cons. Bell Oaks Co., Atlanta, 1977-86; pastor Johnson Dr. Bapt. Ch., Athens, Ga., 1983-86, Suwanee First Bapt. Ch., Ga., 1986-89, Lower Hightower Bapt. Ch., Hiawassee, Ga., 1989—; com. mem. World Bapt. Fellowship missions com., Arlington, Tex., 1957-74. Mem. Gwinnett Bapt. Assn. (exec. bd. 1987-89). Republican. Baptist. Avocations: flying, fishing. Home: PO Box 638 Murphy NC 28906 Office: Lower Hightower Bapt Ch PO Box 1123 Hiawassee GA 30546

LEAVELL, LANDRUM PINSON, II, seminary president, clergyman, educator; b. Ripley, Tenn., Nov. 26, 1926; s. Leonard O. and Annie Glenn (Elias) L.; m. Jo Ann Paris, July 28, 1953; children—Landrum Pinson III, Ann Paris, Roland Q. II, David E. A.B., Mercer U., 1948; B.D., New Orleans Bapt. Theol. Sem., 1951, Th.D., 1954, D.D. Miss. Coll., 1981, Campbell U., 1989. Pastor Union Bapt. Ch., Magnolia, Miss., Crosby Bapt. Ch. (Miss.), First Bapt. Ch., Charleston, Miss., First Bapt. Ch., Gulfport, Miss., First Bapt. Ch., Wichita Falls, Tex., 1963-75; pres. New Orleans Bapt. Theol. Sem., 1975—. Mem. Bapt. Joint Com. Pub. Affairs, 1986-91; bd. dirs. So. Bapt. Hosp., New Orleans, 1985—. Recipient George Washington Honor medal Freedoms Found., Valley Forge, Pa., 1968. Mem. New Orleans C. of C. Lodge: Rotary. Author: Angels, Angels, Angels, 1973; Sermons for Celebrating, 1978; Twelve Who Followed Jesus, 1975; The Devil and His Domain, 1973; For Prodigals and Other Sinners, 1973; God's Spirit in You, 1974; The Harvest of the Spirit, 1976; John's Letters: Light for Living, 1970; Evangelism: Christ's Imperative Commission, 1979; The Doctrine of the Holy Spirit, 1983. Home: 4111 Seminary Pl New Orleans LA 70126 Office: 3939 Gentilly Blvd New Orleans LA 70126

LEAVER, VINCENT WAYNE, minister; b. Birmingham, Ala., Aug. 21, 1947; s. Vincent Hill and Doris (Eddins) L.; children: Meredith, Moriah, Michelle. BA in Religion, Birmingham-So. U., 1969; MDiv, Wesley Theol. Sem., Washington, 1973, D Ministry, 1974; PhD in Polit. Sci., Union for Experimenting Colls. and Univs. (now Union Inst.), Cin., 1979. Ordained to ministry United Meth. Ch., 1974. Assoc. pastor St. Paul's United Meth. Ch., Melbourne, Fla., 1974-75; pastor Sellers Meml. United Meth. Ch., Miami, Fla., 1975-80; urban min. Miami Urban Ministries, 1980-83; pastor Coral Way S.W. United Meth. Ch., Miami, 1983-90, North Ft. Myers (Fla.) United Meth. Ch., 1990; mem. core faculty Inst. Advanced Studies, Walden U., Mpls., 1990—; assoc. dean, dean Union for Experimenting Colls. and Univs., Miami, 1984-89; treas. Charlee of Dade County, Miami, 1980-83; bd. dirs. Epworth Village and Susannah Wesley Retirement Ctr., Miami. Author: Profile of Senior Citizen Programs, 1980, At All Times and in All Places, 1989, Clergy and Victims of Violent Crime, 1990; contbr. articles to profl. jours. Chairperson U.S.-Peoples Republic of China Peoples Friendship Assn., Miami, 1976-80, Criminal Justice Dade County Dem. Exec. Com., 1975-76, Brevard County Ams. for Dem. Action, Melbourne, Fla., 1973-74 (bd. dirs.); co-coord. Nat. Religious Leaders Task Force on Colls. and Sems., Washington, 1972; attended opening of U.S. embassy in Beijing, 1987. Fellow Parents of Murdered Children (min., Bill Bosler award 1988); mem. Am. Acad. Polit. and Social Sci., Assn. for Death Edn. and Counseling, Fla. Meth. Hist. Soc. Home: 5644 Lochness Ct North Fort Myers FL 33903 Office: North Fort Myers United Meth Ch 81 Pondella Rd North Fort Myers FL 33903

LEAVITT, ROBERT F., academic administrator. Pres. St. Mary's Sem. and U., Balt. Office: St Mary's Sem & U Office of the President 5400 Roland Ave Baltimore MD 21210*

LEAZER, GARY HERBERT, religious agency executive; b. Keokuk, Iowa, Dec. 14, 1944; s. Herbert Horace and Delphia Mae (Rube) L.; m. Ruth Marie Bilbo, Aug. 23, 1969; children—David Bilbo, Sonya Lorraine. B.A., Miss. Coll., 1971; M.Div., Southwestern Bapt. Theol. Sem., 1974, Ph.D., 1981; grad. student U. Iowa, 1984. Ordained to ministry Bapt. Ch., 1979; asst. dir. for sects and new religious movements Interfaith Witness Dept., Home Mission Bd. of So. Bapt. Conv., Atlanta, 1979-87 ; dir. Interfaith Witness Dept., 1987— ; teaching fellow Southwestern Bapt. Theol. Sem., Fort Worth, Tex., 1976; adj. prof. Midwestern Bapt. Theol. Sem., Kansas City, Mo., 1979. Served with U.S. Navy, 1965-69. Mem. Am. Acad. Religion, Assn. Bapt. Profs. Religion. Baptist. Contbr. articles to various denominational mags. Office: 1350 Spring St NW Atlanta GA 30367

LEBACQZ, KAREN ANEDA, minister, Christian ethics educator, consultant; b. Boston, June 5, 1945; d. Jean Victor and Evelyn Cleone (Johnson) L.; m. Dale H. Rominger, June 26, 1982 (div. Jan. 1989). BA, Wellesley Coll., 1966; MA, Harvard U., 1972, PhD, 1974. Ordained to ministry United Ch. of Christ, 1990. Instr. Boston U. Ctr. Law & Health Sci., Boston, 1971-72; asst. prof. Pacific Sch. Religion, Berkeley, Calif., 1972-79, assoc. prof., 1977-82, prof. christian ethics, 1982—. Author: Professional Ethics, 1984, Six Theories Justice, 1987, Justice in Unjust World, 1988, Sex in Parish, 1991. Commr. Nat. Commn. Protection Human Rsch. Subjects, Washington, 1974-78; bd. dirs. U.C.C. AIDS Ministry, No. Calif., 1987—; chmn. bd. dirs. Park Ridge Ctr., Chgo., 1988-90. Named Outstanding Young Woman of Am., 1976; grantee Lilly Endowment, 1985-89, Assn. Theol. Schs., 1986, NIH, 1980. Fellow Hastings Ctr.; mem. Soc. Christian

Ethics (bd. dirs. 1981-86, pres. 1989-90). Democrat. Office: Pacific Sch Religion 1798 Scenic Ave Berkeley CA 94709

LEBEL, ROBERT, bishop; b. Trois Pistoles, Que., Can., Aug. 11, 1924; s. Wilfrid and Alexina (Belanger) L. L.Theol., St. Paul U., Ottawa, 1950; D.Theol., Athenee Angelicum, Rome, 1951. Ordained priest Roman Cath. Ch., 1950, consecrated bishop, 1974; tchr. theology Major Sem., Rimouski, Que., 1951-65; rector Major Sem., 1963-65, Minor Sem., 1965-68; tchr. dogmatic theology U. Rimouski, 1970-74; aux. bishop St. Jean, Que., 1974-76; bishop Valleyfield, Que., 1976—. Contbr. ch. publs. Mem. Roman Synod on the Christian Family, 1980. Mem. Assemblee des Eveques Que., Conf. Can. Cath. Bishops, Soc. Canadienne de Theologie. Club: K.C. Address: 11 de l'Eglise, Valleyfield, PQ Canada J6T1J5

LE BRUN, JACQUES, theologian, religious science educator; b. Paris, May 18, 1931; s. Jean and Marguerite (Delvaux) Le B.; children: Jean-Baptiste, Sophie, Mathilde. Agregation des Lettres, U. Paris Sorbonne, 1955, Dr es Lettres, 1971; dip., Ecole Pratique Hautes Etudes, Paris, 1956. Pensionnaire Fondation Thiers, Paris, 1956-59; asst. U. Poitiers (France), 1959-63; research asst. Nat. Ctr. for Sci. Research, Paris, 1963-64; prof. Ctr. Nat. de Télé-Enseignement, Paris, 1964-78; dir. studies Ecole Pratique Hautes Etudes Sorbonne, 1978—. Author: La Spiritualité de Bossuet, 1972, Oeuvres (Fenelon), 1983, Recherches (R. Simon), 1983, Correspondence (Fenelon), 1987. Home: 57 Rue de Paradis, 75010 Paris France Office: Sorbonne Ecole pratique, Hautes Etudes, 5th Sect 45 Rue des Ecoles, 75005 Paris France

LEBRUN MORATINOS, JOSE ALI CARDINAL, archbishop of Caracas; b. Puerto Cabello, Venezuela, Mar. 19, 1919. Ordained priest Roman Catholic Ch., 1943; consecrated bishop of Arado and aux. bishop of Maracaibo (Venezuela), 1956; 1st bishop of Maracay, 1958-62; bishop of Valencia, 1962-72; titular archbishop of Voncaria and coadjutor archbishop of Caracas (Venezuela), 1972; archbishop of Caracas, 1980; elevated to Sacred Coll. of Cardinals, 1983; v.p. Venezuelan Bishops Conf. Mem. Congregation for Cath. Edn. Address: Arzobispado, Apartado 954, Caracas 101-A, Venezuela

LECHELER, ROBERT JOSEPH, academic administrator; b. Plum City, Wis., July 7, 1955; s. Albert Anthony and Joan Carolyn (De Marce) L.; m. Sherie Isabel Lowe, Aug. 11, 1979; children: Matthew, Lucas, Sarah. BS, U. Wis., La Crosse, 1978; MA, St. John's U., 1991. Cert. advanced religious. Tchr., coach Stockbridge (Wis.) Pub. Schs., 1978-80, St. Martin's Acad., Rapid City, S.D., 1980-83; tchr., coach McDonell High Sch., Chippewa Falls, Wis., 1983-87, chair dept., 1987-89; prin., tchr. St. Joseph Grade Sch., Cadott, Wis., 1987-89; dicesan dir. Diocese La Crosse, 1989—; adj. prof. Viterbo Coll., La Crosse, 1990—. Catechist St. Pius X Ch., La Crosse, 1990—; mem. Amnesty Internat., 1990—. Recipient Excellence in Teaching award, Chippewa Falls C. of C., 1987. Mem. ASCD, Nat. Cath. Edn. Assn., Nat. Conf. Diocesan Dirs., Wis. Dirs. Religious Edn. Fedn. Democrat. Roman Catholic. Avocations: exercise, family time, boating. Office: Dept Cath Edn 3710 E Ave S Box 4004 La Crosse WI 54602

LEDER, ARIE CORNELIS, religion educator; b. Wassenaar, The Netherlands, Apr. 16, 1946; m. Olga H. Grim, May 30, 1972; children: Nathania R., Nathan M., Aaron M., Sarah E. BA, Calvin Coll., 1970; B.D., Calvin Theol. Sem., 1973, ThM, 1982; postgrad., Toronto (Can.) Sch. Theology, 1985-87. Pastor Ebenezer Christian Reformed Ch., Trenton, Ont., Can., 1973-77; missinary Christian Reformed World Missions, P.R., 1977-85; lectr. Old Testament Calvin Theol. Sem., Grand Rapids, Mich., 1987-89, asst. prof. Old Testament, 1990—. Mem. Soc. Bibl. Lit. Mem. Christian Reformed Ch. Home: 2065 Union Blvd SE Grand Rapids MI 49507 Office: Calvin Theol Sem 3233 Burton SE Grand Rapids MI 49506

LEDLOW, ROBERT LOUIS, minister; b. Ragland, Ala., Feb. 6, 1934; s. Russell P. and Addie Ree (Kitchens) L.; m. Mary Nan Ray, Aug. 28, 1955; children: Elizabeth, Robert Louis Jr., David. BS, Samford U., 1957; ThM, New Orleans Bapt. Theol. Sem., 1961; D Ministry, Internat. Bible Sem., 1985. Ordained to ministry So. Bapt. Conv., 1953. Pastor Lost Mountain Bapt. Ch., Powder Springs, Ga., 1969-72, Berea Bapt. Ch., Auburndale, Fla., 1972-76, Shelbyville (Tenn.) Mills Bapt. Ch., 1976-79, 1st Bapt. Ch., Mt. Olive, Ala., 1979-86, West End Bapt Ch., Clanton, Ala., 1986—; cons. Ala. Bapt. Sunday Sch. Growth, Ala. Bapt. Ch. Adminstrn.; mem. exec. bd. Ala. Bapt. Conf., 1980-86. Chmn. United Way Chilton County, Clanton, 1991; mem. Study Com. Chilton County Bd. Edn., 1988-90. Mem. North Jefferson Bapt. Assn. (moderator 1979-81, 83-85), Chilton Unity Bapt. Assn. (Sunday sch. dir. 1986—, vice moderator 1989—), Kiwanis (bd. dirs. 1988-90, chmn. Peach Run 1988-91). Home: 202 Martha St Clanton AL 35045 Office: West End Bapt Ch 2005 2d Ave N Clanton AL 35045

LEDNICKY, H. MAURICE, academic administrator. Pres. Cen. Bible Coll., Springfield, Mo. Office: Cen Bible Coll 3000 N Grant Springfield MO 65803*

LE DONNE, CARMELLA ELIZABETH, religious organization administrator; b. Ateleat, Aquilla, Italy, Sept. 29, 1926; came to U.S., 1929; d. Louis and Elisabeth (Scuitto) Le Donne; m. Harold Bowzer, Dec. 19, 1944 (div. Feb. 1971); 1 child, Jerry; m. William Gordon Stone, July 10, 1971; stepchildren: William, Danielle Woodward, Tamara Lipscomb, Greg, Randy, Larry. AAS, Corning (N.Y.) Community Coll., 1976; BS in Bus., Elmira (N.Y.) Coll., 1979, MS i Gen. Edn., 1981. Adminstrv. asst. Corning Glass Works, 1950-82; adminstr. United Community Ch., Sun City Center, Fla., 1982—; adj. tchr. bus. Corning Community Coll., 1980-82; visitation lay person for ch. Mem. Profl. Secs. (pres. 1964-66), AAUW (recording sec. Sun City Center chpt. 1985—) , Kappa Delta Pi (alumni sec. Sun City Ctr., Fla.). Avocations: China painting, shell crafts, jogging, swimming. Home: 1835 Pebble Beach Sun City Center FL 33573 Office: United Community Ch 1501 La Jolla Ave Sun City Center FL 33573

LEE, ALFRED HARRISON, III, clergyman; b. Estelline, Tex., Mar. 11, 1932; s. Alfred Harrison and Lillie Mae (Thompson) L. B.A., Tex. Christian U., 1954; M.A., U. Ala., 1955; M.Div., Episcopal Theol. Sch., 1959. Ordained to ministry Episcopal Ch., 1959. Instr., U. Ala., 1955-56; priest in charge Karkloof Parish, Natal, South Africa, 1959-61; met. sec. United Soc. Christian Lit., London, 1962-65; hon. chaplain St. Bride's, London, 1964—; rector St. Luke's, Denison, Tex., 1965-70, Christ Ch., Dallas, 1970—; dean No. Deanery, 1967-70, Dallas Deanery, 1971-74, 83-84; chmn. Commn. on Ministry, 1971-83. Trustee, Deaconess Crow Found., 1970—, Episcopal Sem., Austin, 1980-83; bd. dirs. ARC, Dallas, 1975—. Republican. Episcopalian. Club: Athenaeum (London). Author: Window on Asia, 1963; Agony of Africa, 1964. Office: 534 W 10th St Dallas TX 75208

LEE, ALLAN WREN, clergyman; b. Yakima, Wash., June 3, 1924; s. Percy Anson and Agnes May (Wren) L.; m. Mildred Elaine Ferguson, June 16, 1946; 1 dau., Cynthia Ann. B.A., Phillips U., Enid, Okla., 1949; M.A., Peabody Coll. Tchrs., 1953; B.D., Tex. Christian U., 1955, D.D. (hon.), 1968. Ordained minister Christian Ch. (Disciples of Christ), 1949; pastor chs. in Tex. and Wash., 1955-71; gen. sec. World Conv. Chs. of Christ, Dallas, 1971—; mem. gen. bd. Christian Ch., 1971-73; pres. Seattle Christian Ch. Missionary Union, 1964-66, Wash.-No. Idaho Conv. Christian Chs., 1966. Author: Bridges of Benevolence, 1962, Wit and Wisdom, 1963, The Burro and the Bibles, 1968, Under the Shadow of the Nine Dragons, 1969, Reflections Along the Reef, 1970, Disciple Down Under, 1971, Meet My Mexican Amigos, 1972, One Great Fellowship, 1974, Fifty Years of Faith and Fellowship, 1980, Recollections of a Dandy Little Up-to-Date Town, 1985, also articles. Trustee, N.W. Christian Coll., Eugene, Oreg., 1985—; exec. v.p. Plano Dance Theater Bd., 1987-90; mem. TV panel Am. Religious Town Hall, 1986—, Secs. of Christian World Communions, 1971—. Recipient Disting. Service citation Children's Home Soc. Wash., 1967, Disting. Service award Bremerton Jaycees, 1959; Jamaica Tourist Bd. citation, 1984. Mem. Disciples of Christ Hist. Soc. (founder, life mem.), Religious Conv. Mgrs. Assn. (v.p. 1980—), Am. Bible Soc. (nat. adv. council 1985—). Club: Seattle Civitan (pres. 1962-64, lt. gov. Orewa dist. 1965). Home: 2112 Stone Creek Dr Plano TX 75075 Office: World Conv Chs of Christ 100 N Central Expwy Ste 804 Richardson TX 75080 *I make every effort to live a life patterned after the life and teachings of the Man of Nazareth, Jesus Christ—that is, to be compassionate, understanding, peaceful and loving.*

LEE, ANTHONY ASA, religious organization officer, publisher; b. Tuskegee Institute, Ala., Aug. 5, 1947; s. Asa Penn and Manila Hudlin (Smith) L.; m. Flor Geola, Apr. 29, 1979; children: Faizi Geola Lee, Taraz Geola Lee, Corinne Geola Lee. BA, UCLA, 1968; postgrad., U. Mich., 1968-69; MA, UCLA, 1974, C. Phil. in African History, 1976. Adminstrv. asst. Baha'i Nat. Ctr., Wilmette, Ill., 1969-72; sec. or chair L.A. Baha'i Assembly, 1972-84; sec. Manhattan Beach (Calif.) Baha'i Assembly, 1985—; mng. editor, owner Kalimat Press, L.A., 1978—. Author: Circle of Unity, 1984, Circle of Peace, 1986, Waging Peace, 1984; gen. editor: Studies in the Babi and Baha'i Religions series, 7 vols., 1982-92. Mem. Am. Acad. Religion, Soc. for Sci. Study Religion, Soc. for Scholarly Pub., African Studies Assn. Home: 826 Dianthus St Manhattan Beach CA 90266 Office: Kalimat Press 1600 Sawtelle Blvd 34 Los Angeles CA 90025

LEE, ARLON WAYNE, minister; b. Benson, Minn., May 31, 1948; s. Chester Arlon and Audrey La Vonne (Beck) L.; m. Lena Kathleen Remsing, Oct. 16, 1971; children: Alan James, Machelle Rae, Timothy John, Amy Joy, Rachel Ann. BA in Pastoral Studies, N. Cen. Bible Coll., Mpls., 1970. Ordained to ministry Assemblies of God, 1974. Pastor Assembly of God Ch., Palisade, Minn., 1971-74; pastor Assembly of God, Cavalier, N.D., 1974-82, Cando, N.D., 1982-87; founding pastor Bethel Assembly of God, E. Grand Forks, Minn., 1988-91; pastor Calvary Assembly of God, Milbank, S.D., 1991—; owner Archie's Piano and Pump Organ Svc., Grand Forks, 1974—; presbyter State Bd. for N.D. Assemblies of God, Bismarck, 1977-81, 83-87, men's dept. dir., 1985-88, N.D. comdr. for Royal Rangers, 1986-88, 91—; Midwest regional prodn. coord., 1989—; lectr. in field; youth camp and men's retreat speaker. Team mem. Towner County Emergency Svcs. Ambulance, Cando, 1985-87; leader Boy Scouts Am., Palisade, 1972-74. Recipient Silver Eagle award, Nat. Assemblies of God Royal Rangers Leaders, 1987-88, Nat. Merit award, 1989. Mem. Kiwanis. Home: 522 South Dakota St Milbank SD 57252-2813 Office: Calvary Assembly of God PO Box 549 Milbank SD 57252-0549 *Life can be full of discovery and growth in so many ways. I want to keep a heart that is young and full of joy in living my life to the potential God has given me.*

LEE, CHARLES EDWARD, retired minister; b. Mobile, Ala., May 10, 1927; s. William Clarence and Mittie Bertha (Herron) L.; m. Gwenyth Arlene Wilson, June 11, 1948; children: Gayle E., Laury D., Ronald W. BA in Theology, Cen. Bible Coll., Springfield, Mo., 1950; BA in Philosophy, U. West Fla., 1968. Ordained to ministry Assemblies of God, 1953. Pastor Assemblies of God chs., Marion, Montgomery, Ala., 1950-54, Bagdad, Fla., Huntsville, Ala., 1965-75; missionary, Nigeria, 1954-65; founder, pastor Weatherly Road Christian Ch., Huntsville, 1975-89; ret., 1989; gen. presbyter Assemblies of God, 1971-91, hon. lifetime gen. presbyter, 1991—; v.p. Greater Huntsville Ministerial Assn., 1974, pres. 1975. With USNR, 1944-46, PTO. Home: 4103 Cherokee Dr Huntsville AL 35801-1004 *The brevity of our encounter with life leaves none of opportunity's choices unimportant. Like each droplet that eventually helps determine the character of a great river, each choice, while seemingly so insignificant perhaps, yet makes a difference in the final result. We are ever rushing toward the endless expanse of eternity. Our status there is determined entirely by the choices made here.*

LEE, CLEMENT WILLIAM KHAN, association administrator; b. N.Y.C., Feb. 7, 1938; s. William P. and Helen L. BTh, Concordia Coll., 1958; MDiv, Concordia Theol. Sem., 1962; MA, New Sch. for Social Research, 1976. Asst. exec. dir. Greater Detroit Luth. Ctr., 1962; editor Detroit and Suburban Luth. Newspaper, 1963; assoc. communications dir. Met. Detroit Council of Chs., 1964; dir. media ops. Am. Bible Soc., N.Y.C., 1967; dir. media relations Luth. Council U.S.A., N.Y.C., 1971-82, asst. exec. dir. communications and interpretation, 1977-82; dir. dept. telecommunications Luth. Ch. in Am., N.Y.C., 1983-87; dir. electronic media Episcopal Ch., N.Y.C., 1987—, program dep. for communication, 1989—; media cons. Luth. Ch.-Mo. Synod, Spaulding for Children, Metro News of Metro N.Y., Synod of Luth. Ch. Am., archtl. newsletter Window, Luth. Deaconess Assn., Concordia Coll., Bronxville, Physicians for Social Responsibility, Wheatridge Found., Luth. Sch. Theology, Chgo.; chmn. broadcast ops. com. Nat. Council Chs. of Christ U.S.A., 1976-80; vice chmn. bd. mgrs. Communications Commn., 1977-80; chmn. inter-faith Media Data System, 1981; mem. TV awards com. N.Y. Council Chs.; mgr. Lutherans-in-Media Conf. I and II, 1980, Luth. Audio-Visual Conf., 1981; project dir. Lambeth Conf. Inter-Anglican Telecommunication Network, 1988; internat. computer network resource leader Religious Communications Congress 90, 1990; bd. dirs. FACTA TV News, Inc.; pres. N.Y. chpt. Religious Pub. Rels. Coun.; telecommunication cons. World Coun. of Chs., Canberra Assembly, 1990-91. Editor: Media Alert newsletter, 1980-86, Luth. Communication newsletter, 1983-87, Episcopal Media Adv. newsletter, 1989—; creator children's TV series Storyline; producer multi-image sequences, Augustana Jubilee, 1980, multi-image program Proclaim, 1984, multi-image effects, Milw. Conv., 1986, (films) Mission on Six Continents, 1975, Room for a Stranger, 1978, Winter Wheat, 1982; exec. producer, One in Mission, 1985, Gathering of the Family, 1988, Doers of the Word, 1988, The Tully-Freeman Report, 1988, Outpourings of Love, 1989, Faith on a Tightrope, 1989, Fresh Winds Blowing, 1989, Prophecy Fulfilled in Me, 1990, President Carter Center Health Video, 1990, To Walk in Beauty, 1990, Pathways for Peace, 1990. Mem. Metro N.Y. Synod Evangelical Luth. Ch. in Am. Communication Commn., Religious Pub. Rels. Coun. Recipient award Detroit Press Club Found., 1963, silver medal Internat. Film and TV Festival, 1975, 79, Creative Excellence award U.S. Indsl. Film Festival, 1986, Brit. Telecommunications award, 1988, Polly Bond award, 1989, 90; N.Y. TV Festival finalist, 1990. Mem. Assn. Edn. Communication Tech., Internat. Radio and TV Soc., Internat. Assn. Bus. Communicators, Internat. TV Assn., NATAS, World Assn. Christian Communication (chmn. N.Am. broadcast sect. 1975), Nat. Interfaith Cable Coalition VISN (members' corp.), Satellite TV Network (bd. dirs.). Office: Episcopal Ch Nat Office 815 2nd Ave New York NY 10017

LEE, DARRYL AUBURN, minister; b. Birmingham, Ala., Nov. 5, 1959; s. Percy Auburn Lee and Robbie (Revis) Smith; m. Sheryl Files, Dec. 18, 1982; children: LaDara, Darnita, Shernita. B of Gen. Studies, Samford U., 1986; postgrad., Bethany Theol. Sem., Dothan, Ala., 1988; letter of law, Faith Coll., Birmingham, 1990. Sect. S.S, B.T.U. Bethel Ch., Birmingham, 1966-78; youth pastor New Pilgrim Bapt. Ch., Birmingham, 1981-86; pastor Mt. Moriah Bapt. Ch., Birmingham, 1986-89, Greater Guiding Light Bapt. Ch., Birmingham, 1989—; pres. P&S Specialities, Birmingham, 1982—. Named Outstanding Young Man of Am., Jaycees, 1984, 89. Fellow Iota Beta Epsilon; mem. Masons, Shriners. Home: 2017 48th Place W Birmingham AL 35208

LEE, EDWARD MING, minister; b. Chgo., May 9, 1959; s. Young Kane and Tsang Ping (Dong) L.; m. Alice Yee Siu, May 19, 1984; children: Melissa Elizabeth, Matthew Eric. BS, Biola U., 1981; ThM, Dallas Theol. Sem., 1990. Ordained to ministry Dallas Chinese Bible Ch., 1990. Summer missions coord. Biola U., LaMirada, Calif., 1980-81; Bible instr. East Bay Bible Inst., 1981; elem. sch. tchr. Am. Heritage Christian Sch., Hayward, Calif., 1981-83; Christian edn. dir. Chinese Ind. Bapt. Ch., Oakland, Calif., 1983-84; asst. pastor Dallas Chinese Bible Ch., 1984—, Christian edn. advisor, 1986—; bd. dirs. Dallas Chinese Christian Youth Camp; del. Evang. Alliance Greater Dallas, 1989—; pres. Chinese Seminarians Fellowship, Dallas Theol. Sem., 1985-87. Editor Chinese Update, 1988. Mem. Nat. Right to Life Com., 1984—, Chinese Program Com., Dallas Theol. Sem., 1987—, Rep. Presdl. Task Force, 1989, Rep. Nat. Com., 1990. Fellow Chinese Pastors Dallas Metroplex; mem. Am.-born Chinese Pastors Tex. (bd. dirs. 1988—). Home: 2318 Bent Bow Dr Garland TX 75044

LEE, FRED, minister; b. Norfolk, Va., May 8, 1955; s. Fred and Edith R. (Perry) L.; m. Kathleen M. Lee, Aug. 12, 1978; children: Tyland, Chasity. Student, U. Ark.; AA, Mason Bible Sch., 1979, East Ark. U., 1989. Ordained to ministry Ch. of God in Christ, 1978. Pastor Ch. of God in Christ, Shearerville, Ark., 1983—; youth leader, Ark., 1972—; info. officer Ark. Land and Farm, Brinkley, 1990—. Author numerous religious pamphlets. Mem. The Govs. Conf. Bd., Ark., 1987; bd. dirs. Ea. Ark. Spl. Enrollment, Forrest City, 1988. Mem. NAACP, The Delta, Cogic Club (pres. Pine Bluff, Ark. 1975-76; advisor Forrest City 1985—). Home: Box 772 Forrest City AR 72335

LEE, ISAAC, minister; b. O-Dam-Ri, Hwanghae Do, Korea, Mar. 29, 1945; came to U.S., 1967; s. Chan-Bom and Choon-Bong (Kang) L.; m. Susan Lim, Sept. 18, 1973; children: Christina, Caroline. MDiv, Reformed Presbyn. Sem., L.A., 1982. Assoc. pastor Korean Presbyn. Ch. Phila., L.A., 1979-85; dir., founder Cornerstone Ministries Internat., L.A., 1985-89, Seattle, 1989—. Editor: Love North Korea, 1989. With U.S. Army, 1969-71, Korea. Home: PO Box 868 Lynnwood WA 98046 Office: Cornerstone Ministries Internat 3810-196th St SE Ste # 2 Lynnwood WA 98036

LEE, J. E., bishop. Bishop Ch. of God in Christ, Dallas. Office: Ch of God in Christ 742 Calcutta Dr Dallas TX 75241*

LEE, JEROME ODELL, minister; b. Chgo., July 28, 1955; s. Myrtle Carllillian Lee; m. Andrea Yvette White, Apr. 27, 1991. Student, Loop Jr. Coll., Chgo., 1973-75; BA, Bishop Coll., 1978; MDiv, Va. Union U., 1982, postgrad. Ordained to ministry Nat. Bapt. Conv. U.S.A., 1979; lic. min. So. Bapt. Conv. Pastor Pleasant Plain Bapt. Ch., Drewryville, Va., 1979-84, Spring Creek Bapt. Ch., Midlothian, Va., 1985—; instr. Christian edn. leadership teaching team Bapt. Gen. Conv. of Va., Richmond, 1981-85, Evans-Smith Leadership Inst., Va. Union U., Richmond, 1983-85. Del. Dem. State Conv., Richmond, 1989. Mem. Richmond Bapt. Assn., Tuckahoe Bapt. Assn., Bapt. Gen. Conv. Va. (asst. sec. clergy div. 1990—), Bapt. Min. Conf. Richmond. Office: Spring Creek Bapt Ch 11900 Genito Rd Midlothian VA 23112 *We live in a fallen would where evil can be thrust upon us at anytime. Yet God has the power to bring good from what others intend for harm. I rejoice in knowing that the promise of Romans 8:28 is being fulfilled daily.*

LEE, M. RUSSELL, minister, ecumenical agency administrator. Pres. Coun. Chs. Chemung County Inc., Elmira, N.Y. Office: Coun Chs Chemung County Inc 330 W Church St Elmira NY 14901*

LEE, MARY GENE, religion educator; b. Atlanta, Dec. 19, 1939; d. Walter Eugene and Lillie May (Clower) Morris; m. James Henry Lee, Dec. 28, 1971; children: Jennifer Addie, Kevin James, Jeremy Patrick. BA, Ga. State U., 1971, MEd, 1975; postgrad., Candler/Emory U., 1981-83. Dir. children ministries Haygood United Meth. Ch., Atlanta, 1976-83; dir. Christian edn. St. Timothy U. Meth. Ch., Stone Mountain, Ga., 1983-87; minister of progs. Grace United Meth. Ch., Atlanta, 1987—; chmn. Conf. Planning and Rsch. Com., Atlanta, 1987—; del. The Internat. Gathering, Ft. Worth, 1990. Author: (curriculum) Sunday School and Vacation Bible School, 1985—. Mem. DeKalb Mental Health and Mental Retardation Citizen's Adv. Bd., Decatur, Ga., 1983-85; officer Briarlake PTA, Decatur, 1983-89. Mem. Nat. Christian Educators Fellowship, North Ga. Christian Educators Fellowship (treas. 1985-87, communications officer 1987-89). Democrat. Home: 1584 Country Squire Ct Decatur GA 30033 Office: Grace United Methodist Ch 458 Ponce de Leon Ave Atlanta GA 30308

LEE, (O.) MAX, minister; b. El Dorado, Ark., July 5, 1931; s. O. Roy and Mattie Lee (Giddens) L.; m. Martha Elizabeth Perritt, Aug. 16, 1957; children: Alvis Robert, Jeffrey Max. BA, La. Tech. U., d1955; BDiv, So. Bapt. Theol. Sem., 1959, ThM, 1963; D Ministry, New Orleans Bapt. Theol. Sem., 1976. Ordained to ministry So. Bapt. Conv., 1955. Assoc. pastor Emmanuel Bapt. Ch., Houston, 1960-63; pastor East Pineville (La.) Bapt. Ch., 1963-66; pastor 1st Bapt. Ch., Port Allen, La., 1966-71, Winnsboro, La., 1972—; trustee Bapt. Message, 1976-82; mem. exec. bd. La. Bapt. Conv., Alexandria, 1982-87. Pres. Ministerial Alliance, Winnsboro, 1980; mem. adv. bd. Northeastern La. Vocat. Sch., Winnsboro, 1981—; mem. exec. bd. Mental Health Assn., Columbia, La., 1981—; chmn. exec. bd. N.E. La. U. Bapt. Student Union, Monroe, 1982-83; trustee So. Bapt. Theol. Sem., 1984—, La. Coll., 1987—. Mem. Sigma Tau Delta, Omicron Delta Kappa. Democrat. Home: 804 Nell Winnsboro LA 71295 Office: 1st Bapt Ch 502 Highland Winnsboro LA 71295

LEE, MELVIN JOSEPH, minister; b. New Orleans, Dec. 25, 1929; s. John and Isabelle (Green) L.; m. Dorothy Peterson, June 5, 1971; children: Betty, Barbara, Joseph, Edward. BS in Chemistry, So. U., New Orleans, 1970; MDiv, Union Bapt. Theol. Sem., New Orleans, 1988, ThM, 1989. Ordained to ministry Bapt. Ch., 1984. Assoc. min. 3d Missionary Bapt. Ch., St. Bernard, La., 1984-87, pastor, 1987—, chair deacon bd., 1974-84; coroner's investigator Orleans Parish, New Orleans, 1982—; bd. dirs. So. Gen. Missionary Bapt. Assn., New Orleans, 1987—, chmn. bldg. com., 1988—. Author: What Baptists Should Know, 1991; contbr. articles to profl. jours. Chmn. St. Bernard Community Devel. Corp., 1988—. Sgt. USAF, 1947-52. Democrat. Home: 7514 Dwyer Rd New Orleans LA 70126 Office: 3d Missionary Bapt Ch 206 Armstrong Rd PO Box 1012 Saint Bernard LA 70085 *Man's action are controlled by his beliefs. Therefore, to change a man's actions—change his beliefs.*

LEE, MORDECAI, agency adminstrator, political scientist; b. Milw., Aug. 27, 1948; s. Jack Harold and Bernice (Kamesar) L.; 1 child, Ethan. BA, U. Wis., 1970, MPA, Syracuse U., 1972, PhD, 1975. Guest scholar Brookings Instn., Washington, 1972-74; legis. asst. to Congressman Henry Reuss, Washington, 1975; asst. prof. polit. sci. U. Wis.-Whitewater and Parkside, 1976; mem. Wis. Ho. Reps., 1977-82; mem. Wis. Senate, 1982-89; exec. dir. Milw. Jewish Coun., 1990—; adj. prof. govt. U. Wis.-Milw. Jewish.

LEE, NELSON EUGENE, minister; b. Paoli, Ind., June 6, 1941; s. Roy Gilbert and Elsie Mae (Wesner) L.; m. Nancy Marie Myers, June 3, 1967; children: Cynthia Beth, Myra Kay, James Nelson. BA, Louisville Bible Coll., 1967, M in Sacred Lit., 1991. Ordained to ministry Ind. Christian Ch., 1967. Minister Mt. Carmel & Bethel Christian Chs., Campbellsburg and Orleans, Ind., 1964-67, Surprise Christian Ch., Brownstown, Ind., 1967-71, Honeytown Christian Ch., Seymour, Ind., 1968-71, Corinth Christian Ch., Lawrenceburg, Ky., 1971-81, Orleans Christian Ch., 1981—. Address: PO Box 183 Orleans IN 47452 *Of all the pursuits of mankind, there is none greater or of more significance than the pursuit of eternal life through Jesus Christ our Lord. For He alone has the words of eternal life.*

LEE, PETER JAMES, bishop; b. Greenville, Miss., May 11, 1938; s. Erling Norman and Marion (O'Brien) L.; m. Kristina Knapp, Aug. 28, 1965; children: Stewart, Peter James Jr. AB, Washington and Lee U., 1960; MDiv, Va. Theol. Sem., 1967; postgrad, Duke U. Law Sch., 1963-64; DD (hon.), Va. Theol. Sem., 1984, St. Paul's Coll., Lawrenceville, Va., 1985. Ordained priest Episc. Ch., 1968, bishop, 1984. Newspaper reporter, editor Pensacola, Fla., Richmond, Memphis, 1960-63; deacon St. John's Cathedral, Jacksonville, Fla., 1967-68; asst. min. St. John's Ch. LaFayette Sq., Washington, 1968-71; rector Chapel of the Cross, Chapel Hill, N.C., 1971-84; bishop coadjutor Episcopal Diocese of Va., Richmond, 1984-85, bishop, 1985—; pres. trustees of the funds Diocese of Va., 1985—; dir. Presiding Bishop's Fund for World Relief, 1986—. Rector bd. trustees Episcopal High Sch., Alexandria, Va., 1985—; chmn. Meml. Trustees, Richmond; chmn. Am. Friends of the Episcopal Diocese of Jerusalem. 1st lt. U.S. Army, 1961-62. Mem. Phi Beta Kappa, Omicron Delta Kappa. Office: Diocese Va 110 W Franklin St Richmond VA 23220

LEE, R. H. See **FITZGERALD, TIKHON**

LEE, RALPH BARRETT, JR., minister, administrator; b. Houston, Feb. 20, 1945; s. Ralph Barret and Jeannette (Burress) L.; m. Susan Joye Biederstadt, June 11, 1966; children: Ryan B., Jennifer Joyce. BBA in Fin., Baylor U., 1968; MDiv, Southwestern Bapt. Theol. Sem., Ft. Worth, 1978. Ordained to ministry Bapt. Ch., 1975. Pastor First Bapt. Ch., Pewaukee, Wis., 1978-84; ch. adminstr. Westbury Bapt. Ch., Houston, 1985-86; minister of edn., adminstr. Harpeth Heights Bapt. Ch., Nashville, Tenn., 1987—. Mem. Nat. Assn. Ch. Bus. Adminstrn. (treas. 1989—,treas. 1989-90, v.p. 1991—), Nashville Bapt. Religious Educators (v.p. 1989-90, pres. 1990-91). Home: 105 Andover Green Franklin TN 37064 Office: Harpeth Heights Bapt Ch 8063 Hwy 100 Nashville TN 37221 *Recently, I was asked "What are three wishes you have for your life?". I answered: to know Christ, to serve Christ, to be in the dead center of His Will.*

LEE, RICHARD FRANCIS JAMES, evangelical clergyman, apologist, researcher; b. Yakima, Wash., Sept. 13, 1967; s. Richard Francis and Dorothy Aldean (Blackwell). Diploma, Berean Coll., Springfield, Mo., 1989;

BA, U. Wash., Seattle, 1990. Lic. clergyman Gen. Coun. of the Assemblies of God, Seattle, 1989—. Author: Tell Me the Story, 1982. Named Most Likely to be President, Franklin High Sch., Seattle, 1986. Pentecostal. Avocations: collector, writer, itinerant speaker. Home: E 2604 Boone Avenue Spokane WA 99202 Office: Evangel Outreach Ministries E 2604 Boone Avenue Spokane WA 99202

LEE, ROBERT, former theological educator, consultant, author; b. San Francisco, Apr. 28, 1929; s. Frank and Shee (Fong) L.; m. May Gong, Feb. 4, 1951; children: Mellanie Lynn, Marcus Arthur, Matthew John, Wendy Gale, Michele Miko. A.B., U. Calif.-Berkeley, 1951; M.A., Pacific Sch. Religion, 1953; B.D. magna cum laude, Union Theol. Sem., 1954; Ph.D., Columbia U., 1958. Ordained to ministry United Ch. Christ, 1954; transferred to U.P. Ch., 1961; Western regional exec. sec. Chinese Student Christian Assn., 1949-50; assoc. sec. Stiles Hall, Univ. YMCA, Berkeley, Calif., 1950-52; dir. rsch. Protestant Council N.Y., 1954; from instr. to asst. prof. ch. and community Union Theol. Sem., 1955-61; lectr. philosophy Mills Coll. Edn., 1956-57; Margaret Dollar prof. social ethics, dir. Inst. Ethics and Soc., San Francisco Theol. Sem., 1961-83; v.p. acad. affairs Alaska Pacific U., 1983-85; pres., dir. Enfield Resources, 1985-87; dean Internat. Student Studies Heald Coll. Inst. of Tech., San Francisco, 1987-88; rsch. cons. Ctr. for Pacific Rim, U. San Francisco, 1989—; asst. v.p., dir. Asian Am. Philanthropy, United Way of Bay Area, 1990—; prof., area chmn. Grad. Theol. Union, 1962-70; vis. prof. Union Theol. Sem., summer 1964, Internat. Christian U., Tokyo, Japan, 1964-65, Assn. S.E. Asian Sems., Hong Kong, 1966; vis. scholar Stanford Grad. Sch. Bus., 1971-72; co-optd staff World Council Chs. Conf. Ch. and Soc., Geneva, 1966; lectr., TV appearances, 1956—; cons. ISI Corp., 1971-72, World Coll. West, 1977-83, Coun. on Founds., 1989—; theologian-in-residence Windward Coalition, Kilua, Hawaii, 1980; moderator Inst. Religion and Social Studies, Jewish Theol. Sem., 1960; assoc. Columbia Seminar, 1961; sr. fellow East-West Center, Honolulu, 1972-73; bd. advisors Walden U.; nursing home care specialist Found. Health Corp., 1987; mem. exec. com. Calif. State Bar Ct., 1989—. Author: Social Sources of Church Unity (selected for Kennedy White House Library), 1960, Religion and Leisure in America, 1964, Dictionary of Centers for the Study of Society, 1965, Stranger in the Land, 1967, (with Russ Galloway) The Schizophrenic Church, 1969, The Promise of John C. Bennett, 1969, (with Marjorie Casebier) The Spouse Gap, 1971, Marriage Enrichment Sharing Sessions, 1979, China Journal, 1980, Faith and the Prospects of Economic Collapse, 1981, Guide to Chinese American Philanthropy and Charitable Giving Patterns, 1990; editor: Cities and Churches, 1962, (with Martin E. Marty) Religion and Social Conflict, 1964, The Church and The Exploding Metropolis, 1965, Action/Reaction; Pacific Theol. Rev., (book revs. edit.) East/West; contbr. to profl. jours., books. Mem. adv. com. problems met. soc. U.P. Ch., 1961—, Center Study Democratic Instns., Coll. Marin, 1965—; bd. sponsors Christianity and Crisis; bd. dirs. Chinese for Affirmative Action, Am. Soc. Christian Ethics, Ctr. for Family in Transition, Family Service Agy. of Marin, Festival Theatre Found., Pacific S.W. Student YMCA, ISI Trust Fund, ISI Growth Fund, ISI Income Fund, Found. for Theol. Edn. S.E. Asia.; asst. v.p., bd. dirs. Asian Am. and Internat. Philanthropy, United Way Bay Area; bd. dirs. Marin Chinese Culture Ctr.; coord. for community rels. Peace Corps., 1991. Mem. Religious Rsch. Assn. (book rev. editor jour. 1959-65), Am. Sociol. Assn., Soc. Religion Higher Edn., Soc. for Sci. Study Religion, Center for Ethics and Social Policy, United Presbyn. Found. (trustee), Asians and Pacific Islanders in Philanthropy, Nan Hai Art Ctr. (trustee). Home: 717 Montecillo Rd San Rafael CA 94903

LEE, RUSSELL CURTIS, minister; b. Fosston, Minn., Apr. 26, 1932; s. Elmer B. and Hilda (Fjerstad) L.; m. M. Elaine Kleveland, June 10, 1956 (dec. May 1990); children: Deborah, Valerie. BA, Augsburg Coll., 1956; MDiv, Luther Sem., St. Paul, 1960; D Ministry, McCormick Sem., 1978. Ordained to ministry Luth. Ch., 1960. Asst. pastor Luth. Meml. Ch., Pierre, S.D., 1960-64; sr. pastor Faith Luth. Ch., Albuquerque, 1964—. Author: Coming Home: Getting Started in the Christian Faith and Life, 1991. Office: Faith Luth Ch 10000 Spain St NE Albuquerque NM 87111

LEE, SARA NELL, lay worker, small business owner; b. Amarillo, Tex., Oct. 31, 1934; d. Oscar Rand and Lois Peninah (Verner) Jackson; m. William Franklin Lee, Aug. 24, 1956 (div. Jan. 1979); children: David William, Melinda Jean. Student, Hardin Simmons U., 1954, U. Tex., El Paso, 1955-56. Pres., owner Am. Ch. Lists Inc., Arlington, Tex., 1971—. Mem. devel. com. ARC, Ft. Worth, 1986—; co-chmn. adv. com. Welcome House Teen Crisis Ctr., Arlington, 1988—. Mem. Christian Mgmt. Assn., Direct Mktg. Assn. North Tex. (sec. 1981), Direct Mktg. List. Coun., Arlington Postal Customer Coun., Arlington C. of C., Soroptimists (pres. Arlington chpt. 1983-85). Baptist. Office: Am Ch List Inc 1981 Stadium Oaks Ct Ste 100 Arlington TX 76011 *Life is a gift from God. It is to be lived to the fullest, permeated with love for God, people and ourselves and used as a vehicle to glorify God.*

LEE, THOMAS GAYLE LYCONGTHUAN, minister, survey statistician; b. Soctrang, Vietnam, Aug. 27, 1939; came to U.S., 1975; s. Thanh Cong Ly and Thom Thi Ta; married; 1 child, Lycongthuan Eleazar. BA in Math., U. Saigon, Republic of Vietnam, 1968; MA in Math., U. Tex., 1972; MA in Stats., Tex. A&M U., 1978; postgrad., Capital Bible Sem., Lanham, Md., 1983—. Ordained to ministry So. Bapt. Conv., 1985. Pastor 1st Vietnamese Bapt. Ch., Lanham, 1985-90, Clifton Pk. Vietnam Bapt. Ch., Silver Spring, Md., 1985—; area mgr. U.S. Census Bur., Phila., 1989—; coord. external affairs com. Overseas Vietnam Ch. Conf., 1985—. Capt., math. instr. Vietnamese Nat. Mil. Acad., 1966-75. Home: 625 6th Ave Lindenwold NJ 08021 Office: Clifton Pk Vietnam Bapt Ch 8818 Piney Br Silver Spring MD 20903 *I wish every creature in this universe would do what it must do according to its Creator's design so that all would have wonderful, abundant, and eternal lives together with each other and with the Creator.*

LEE, VIRGINIA DIANE, lay worker; b. Hackensack, N.J., Sept. 3, 1939; d. Harold Ehler and Marion Estelle (Pierrez) True; m. Jerald Dana Lee, June 7, 1962; children: Diana, Tara, James. BS, Albright Coll., 1961; MS, Ohio U., 1963. Deacon Presbyn. Ch. of Kennett Square, Pa., 1981-84, elder, 1988-91, asst. clk. of session, 1989-91, co-chmn. personnel com., 1989-90, chmn. personnel com., 1990-91; v.p. Presbyn. Women's Assn., Kennett Square, 1983-85; dressmaker, Mendenhall, Pa., 1984—. Mem. Winterthur (Del.) Guild, 1990, 91; alumna rep. for student recruitment Albright Coll., Reading, Pa., 1990, 91. Mem. AAUW (mem. scholarship com. Wilmington, Del. chpt. 1980, 81), Phi Upsilon Omicron. Republican. Home: PO Box 4 Mendenhall PA 19357 *If everyone lived by the Ten Commandments the world would have fewer problems.*

LEE, WILLIAM JAMES, clergyman, seminary administrator; b. Wooster, Ohio, Apr. 14, 1922; s. Norbert Henry and Matilda Rose (Sohl) L. Grad., St. Charles Coll., Balt., 1941; B.A., St. Mary's Sem., Balt., 1943; M.A., Catholic U. Am., 1947, Ph.D., 1961. Ordained priest Roman Catholic Ch., 1946; tchr. St. Joseph's High Sch., Mountain View, Calif., 1946-48; mem. Priests of St. Sulpice, 1949—; instr., registrar St. Edward's Sem., Kenmore, Wash., 1949-55; prof. social scis. St. Mary's Sem. Coll., Balt., 1958-68; acad. dean St. Mary's Sem. Coll., 1961-66, rector, 1966-72, pres., 1972-80; Mem. Urban Commn., Archdiocese of Balt., 1964-68; chmn. Justice and Peace Commn., 1973-80; cons. U.S. province Priests of St. Sulpice, 1971-79, gen. treas., 1979—, sec., 1981—. Author: Economic and Ethical Aspects of Right to Work Laws, 1961, (with Howes and Wood) Baltimore Urban Parish Study, 1967. Bd. govs. Citizens Planning and Housing Assn., Balt., 1963-73, v.p., 1965-67; bd. dirs. Balt. Neighborhoods, 1970-73. Mem. Am. Econs. Assn., Nat. Catholic Ednl. Assn. (chmn. sem. dept. 1974-75). Democrat. Address: 5408 Roland Ave Baltimore MD 21210

LEENE, HENDRIK, theology educator; b. Baarland, Zeeland, The Netherlands, Feb. 19, 1937; s. Gijsbertus and Jacoba Wilhelmina (Veerman) L.; m. Johanna Colpa, Nov. 13, 1962; children: Jacoba Sophia, Saskia Christina, Merel, Johanna. ThD, Vrije U., Amsterdam, The Netherlands, 1968, Dr. in Theology, 1987. Minister Reformed Chs. in The Netherlands, Schagen, 1965-69; tchr. Vrije U., Amsterdam, 1969-78, lectr., 1978-80, prof., 1980—. Author: De Vroegere En Nieuwe Dingen Bij Deuterojesaja, 1987. Mem. Oudtestamentisch Werkgezelschap. Home: Polanenstraat 17, 1165 GX Halfweg The Netherlands Office: Vrije U, De Boelelaan 1105, 1081 HV Amsterdam The Netherlands

LEERTOUWER, LAMMERT, religious educator; b. Groningen, Netherlands, Jan. 12, 1932; s. Johannes and Harmina (Mekel) L.; m. Elisabeth Rahder, Nov. 21, 1958; children: Johannes, Jacob, Joost. Degree, Groningen U., 1958, Groningen U., 1979. Asst. theology faculty Stak U., Groningen, 1958-63, jr. lectr., 1963-70, sr. lectr., 1970-79; asst. prof. Stak U., Leiden, Netherlands, 1979-80, prof., 1980—. Author: Het Beeld van de Ziel, 1979, (with others) Doolhof der Goden, 1980; editor: Iconography of Religions, 1970; contbr. articles to profl. jours. Active Broadcasting Coun., The Hague, Netherlands, 1981-87, Netherlands Coun. for Libra. and Info. Services, 1988—. Mem. Internat. Assn. for History Religions, Dutch Assn. for History Religions (pres. 1986—). Mem. Dutch Reformed Ch. Avocation: playing viola. Home: Rijnsburgerweg 36, 2333AB Leiden The Netherlands Office: U Leiden, Stationsweg 46, 2300RA Leiden The Netherlands

LEESEBERG, MARTIN WALTER, religious educator; b. Milw., Sept. 7, 1915; s. Ralph William and Ella Margurite (Klein) L.; m. Irma Ruth Christophel, Dec. 1, 1945; children: Karen Christine Haack, Lynnette Ruth Stamler, Marilyn Joy. ThM, Princeton (N.J.) Seminary, 1950; MA, Yale U., 1952; ThD, Concordia Seminary, St. Louis, 1961; DD, Emmanuel & St. Chad, Saskatoon, Saskatchewan, 1980. Pastor Salem Luth. Parish, West Burlington, Iowa, 1947-48, Bethlehem Luth. Parish, Georgetown, Conn., 1949-52; prof. Old Testament Luth. Theol. Seminary, Saskatoon, 1952-80, prof. emeritus, 1980—. Author: The Ever Circling Year, 1970, The Word Breaks Forth, 1985. 1st lt. U.S. Army, 1941-46, ETO. Home: 605 2311 McEown Ave, Saskatoon, SK Canada S7J 2H3 *Life is what you make of it. Making a living is not life, but when one is taught to live, that's life. Since life is short, let's make it worthwhile.*

LEETY, WILLIAM ROSS, minister; b. Pitts., Aug. 17, 1945; s. Ross Edward Leety and Jane Clatty Sharpe; m. Christine Marshall, June 8, 1968; children: David Marshall, Jessica Kate, Seth Alderson. AB, Gettysburg (Pa.) Coll., 1967; BD, Yale Div. Sch., 1971. Ordained to ministry, Presbyn. Ch. (USA), 1971. Pastor First Presbyn. Ch., Wyoming, N.Y., 1971-75, Dansville (N.Y.) Presbyn. Ch., 1975-83, Covenant Presbyn. Ch., Scranton, Pa., 1983—; moderator work group Synod of Trinity Communication & Stewardship Unit, Camp Hill, Pa., 1990—; moderator/mem. Safety Net Ministry with poor, Scranton, 1989-91. Contbg. editor essays on lectionary and poems, Presbyn. Outlook, 1990—. Bd. dirs. United Way, Lackawanna County, 1988-91; bd. dirs., pres. Scranton Neighbors Housing Project, 1983-88; mem. Lay Task Force of Lackawanna County Med. Soc., Dunmore, Pa., 1990—. Mem. Cen. City Ministries (pres. 1991). Democrat. Home: 816 Olive St Scranton PA 18510 Office: Covenant Presbyn Ch 550 Madison Ave Scranton PA 18510

LEFEBURE, LEO DENNIS, priest; b. Chgo., Nov. 20, 1952; s. Richard and Evelyn Marjorie (Hextell) L. BA, Loyola U., Chgo., 1973; STL, MDiv, Mundelein (Ill.) Sem., 1978; PhD, U. Chgo., 1987. Ordained priest Roman Cath. Ch., 1978. Assoc. pastor St. Stephen Ch., Des Plaines, Ill., 1978-82, Our Lady Help of Christians Ch., Chgo., 1982-87; instr. Mundelein Sem., 1987-89, asst. prof., 1989-91, assoc. prof., 1991—, chair dept. systematic theology, 1989—. Author: Toward a Contemporary Wisdom Christology, 1988, Life Transformed, 1989. U. Chgo. fellow, 1986-87. Mem. Am. Acad. Religion, Cath. Theol. Soc. Am., Soc. Buddhist-Christian Studies, Am. Theol. Soc. Home and Office: Mundelein Sem Mundelein IL 60060

LEFEVRE, JEAN ADELE, minister; b. London, June 6, 1930; came to U.S., 1982; d. Cecil Redvers and Florence Daisy May (Morris) Hadingham; m. John Reginald LeFevre, Aug. 5, 1947; children: John Philip Redvers, Calvin Gregor, Malcolm James Trevor. Student, White Eagle Sem., Rake, Hants, Eng., 1963-68; DD (hon.). Ordained to ministry Christian Ch., 1982. V.p. Theosophical Soc., Dar-Es-Salaam, Tanzania, 1949-60; lay leader Ch. of the White Eagle, Montgomery, Tex., 1960; elder Ch. of the White Eagle, Montgomery, 1968; mem. Interfaith, The Woodlands, Tex., 1983-89; hon. chaplain The Woodlands Hosp., 1989—. Author: The Earth Shall Feed Us, 1975; contbr. articles to profl. jours. Divisional commr. Girl Guides, Eng., India, Tanzania, 1947-60; grade 1 officer Red Cross, India and Tanzania, 1947-60 (long svc. medal, cert. merit); chmn. Spl. Adv. Com., Eng., 1960-81; bd. dirs. Nat. Coun. Women Great Britain; pres., chmn. several charities. Recipient Cert. Tchr. award Seneca Hist. Soc., 1976. Mem. Tex. Wildlife Coalition, Humane Soc. Office: Ch of the White Eagle St John's 9 St Beulah Montgomery TX 77356

LEFEVRE, PERRY DEYO, minister, theology educator; b. Kingston, N.Y., July 12, 1921; s. Johannes and Faye (McFerran) LeF.; m. Carol Baumann, Sept. 14, 1946; children: Susan Faye, Judith Ann, Peter Gerret. A.B., Harvard U., 1943; B.D., Chgo. Theol. Sem., 1946; Ph.D., U. Chgo., 1951. Ordained to ministry Congl. Ch., 1946. Instr. religion Franklin and Marshall Coll., 1948-49; asst., then assoc. prof. religion Knox Coll., 1949-53, Fed. Theol. Sem., U. Chgo., 1953-61; prof. constructive theology Chgo. Theol. Sem., 1961—, dean of faculty, 1961-81, acting dean, 1990-91. Author: The Prayers of Kierkegaard, 1956, The Christian Teacher, 1958, Introduction to Religious Existentialism, 1963, Understandings of Man, 1966, Philosophical Resources for Christian Thought, 1968, Conflict in a Voluntary Association, 1975, Understandings of Prayer, 1981, Aging and the Human Spirit, 1981, Radical Prayer, 1982; editor: Paul Tillich: The Meaning of Health, 1984, Spiritual Nurture and Congregational Development, 1984, Daniel Day Williams Essays in Process Theology, 1985, Pastoral Care and Liberation Praxis, 1986, Bernard Meland Essays in Constructive Theology, 1988, Creative Ministries in Contemporary Christianity, 1991. Mem. Phi Beta Kappa. Address: 5757 University Ave Chicago IL 60637

LEFF, MARVIN, religious organization executive; b. Bklyn., July 4, 1940; s. Harry and Mary (Akin) L.; m. Judith Sandra Henzel, Dec. 22, 1963; children: Marcia Ellen, Michael Eric, Brian Scott. BA, CUNY, 1962, MA, 1966. Personnel cons.; 1962-63; social case worker, 1963-64; high sch. tchr., 1964-68;; asst. dir. N.Y. State Am. Jewish Com., 1969-71; dir. S. E. region, 1971-72; field dir. Am. ORT Fedn.,, 1972-78; exec. dir. Amit. Women, 1978—; Bd. Chmn. Young Israel of Far Rockaway, 1973-75, pres. 1975-77; nat. v.p. Nat. Coun. of Young Israel, 1977-78; pres. Jewish Action Coalition 1972-74; v.p. Jewish Community council of Rockaway, 1974-76. Editor: Jewish Community Council of Rockaway Bull., 1976. Mem.: Urban Task Force Human Relations Commn.; Nat. Jewish Communal Relations Workers, Harry Truman Dem. Club. Office: Amit Women 817 Broadway New York NY 10003*

LEFFELL, ABRAHAM BERNARD, rabbi; b. Montreal, June 12, 1926; s. Jack and Marion (Richer) L.; m. Freda Deckelbaum, Sept. 14, 1948; children: Jonathan, Daniel, David, Michael. BA, McGill U., Montreal, 1947; MHL, Jewish Theol. Sem., 1954, DD, 1980. Ordained rabbi, 1954. Rabbi Shaare Zedek Congregation, Montreal, 1954-91, rabbi emeritus, 1991—; hon. chaplain Dominion Command, Royal Can. Legion, Ottawa, 1978-91; chmn. Jewish Chaplaincy Bd., Montreal, 1979-90; mem. bd. mgmt. Montreal Holocaust Meml. Ctr., 1990—. Mem. Rabbinical Assembly (co-founder Can. div., exec. coun. 1975-78), Jewish Mins. of Greater Montreal (bd. dirs., pres. 1965-68, 85-87), Montifiore Club. Home: 5511 Robinson Ave, Montreal, PQ Canada HAV 2P4 Office: Shaare Zedek Cong, 5305 Rosedale Ave, Montreal, PQ Canada H4V 2H7

LEGARE, HENRI FRANCIS, archbishop; b. Willow-Bunch, Sask., Can., Feb. 20, 1918; s. Phillippe and Amanda (Douville) L. B.A., U. Ottawa, 1940; theol. student, Lebret, Sask., 1940-44; M.A., Laval U., 1946; Dr. Social Sci., Cath. U. Lille, France, 1950; LL.D. (hon.), Carleton U., Ottawa, 1959, Windsor (Ont.) U., 1960, Queens U., Kingston, Ont., 1961, U. Sask., 1963, Waterloo (Ont.) Luth. U., 1965, U. Ottawa, Can., 1984; Doctor of Univ., U. of Ottawa. Ordained priest Roman Cath. Ch., 1943; prof. sociology Laval U., 1947, U. Ottawa, 1951; exec. dir. Cath. Hosp. Assn. Can., 1952-57; dean faculty social scis. U. Ottawa, 1954-58, pres., 1958-64; provincial Oblate Fathers, Winnipeg, Man., 1966-67; bishop of Labrador, 1967-72; archbishop Grouard-McLennan, Alta., 1972—. Contbr. articles to profl. jours. Chmn. Canadian Univs. Found., 1960- 62. Decorated grand cross merit Order Malta, 1964; order merit French Lang. Assn. Ont., 1965. Mem. Assn. Canadian Univs. (pres. 1960-62), Can. Conf. Cath. Bishops (pres. 1981-83), Internat. Assn. Polit. Sci. Address: Archbishop's House, CP 388, McLennan, AB Canada T0H 2L0

LEGGE, RUSSEL DONALD, religion educator, university dean; b. Milton, N.S., Can., Jan. 31, 1935; s. James Farish and Shirley Evelyn (McNutt) L.; m. Elma Gertrude Dingwell, Aug. 20, 1960; children: Cheryl Lee, Scott Douglas, Suzanne Rae, James Earl. BA, Transylvania Coll., 1962; STB, Harvard U., 1965; PhD, McMaster U., 1972. Ordained to ministry Christian Ch. (Disciples of Christ), 1965. Pastor Guelph (Ont., Can.) Christian Ch., 1965-67, Winger Christian Ch., Wainfleet, Ont., 1967-70; lectr. religious studies U. Waterloo, Ont., 1970-72, asst. prof., 1972-82, assoc. prof., 1982—, dir. studies St. Paul's United Coll., 1978-85, dean, 1985—, dir. Ctr. for Society, Tech. and Values, 1986-89; pres. Can. Coun. Chs., 1982-85; moderator Christian Ch. (Disciples of Christ) inCan., 1980-82. Mem. Can. Soc. for Study Religion. Home: 259 Lourdes St, Waterloo, ON Canada N2L 1P2 Office: U Waterloo, St Paul's United Coll, Waterloo, ON Canada N2L 3G5

LEGGETT, PAUL ARTHUR, minister; b. Montclair, N.J., July 3, 1946; s. Joseph Hoyt and Jane (Stenstrom) L.; m. Beth Petrie, Nov. 28, 1981; children: Elisabeth, Gwendolyn, James.. BS in Edn., Speech and Drama, Syracuse U., 1968; MDiv, Princeton Theol. Sem., 1971, ThM, 1973; PhD, Union Theol. Sem., N.Y.C., 1982. Ordained to ministry Presbyn. Ch. (U.S.A.), 1971. Interim pastor Disston Meml. Presbyn. Ch., Phila., 1971-72; asst. pastor Huntington Valley (Pa.) Presbyn. Ch., 1972-73; prof. theology Latin Am. Bibl. Sem., San Jose, Costa Rica, 1974-80; pastor Grace Presbyn. Ch., Montclair, 1981—; vis. lectr. Vassar Coll., Poughkeepsie, N.Y., 1979-80, 82-83; spl. cons. Gen. Assembly Mission Coun., 1980-81; chmn. Hispanic com. Newark Presbytery, 1982, ch. and soc. com., 1983—; moderator Newark Presbytery, 1989; vice-moderator spl. com. of 15, Brief Statement of Faith, Presbyn. Ch. U.S.A., 1990-91. Co-editor: Lectura Teologica del Tiempo Latino Americano, 1979; contbr. articles to profl. jours. Recipient Margot M. Studer award Montclair State Coll., 1984. Home: 63 Tuxedo Rd Montclair NJ 07042 Office: Grace Presbyn Ch 153 Tuxedo Rd Montclair NJ 07042 *The grace and mercy of God surround us in more ways than we can imagine.*

LEGUERRIER, JULES, bishop; b. Clarence Creek, Ont., Can., Feb. 18, 1915. Ordained titular bishop of Bavagaliana, Can.; ordained vicar apostolic of James Bay, Can., 1964-67; first bishop of Moosonee Ont., 1967—; Ordained priest Roman Cath. Ch., 1943. Office: Chancery Office, PO Box 40, Moosonee, ON Canada P0L 1Y0

LEHMAN, BARRY ALAN, minister; b. Jersey Shore, Pa., Aug. 4, 1948; s. Harold Keller and Dora (Moldawsky) L.; m. Valerie Anne Nocek, Apr. 22, 1972; 1 child, Elizabeth Anne. BA in Govt., Lehigh U., 1970; MDiv., Moravian Sem., 1975; postgrad., Luth. Sch. Theology, Chgo., 1990—. Ordained to ministry Moravian Ch., 1974. Youth minister Rosemont Luth. Ch., Bethlehem, Pa., 1972-73; pastor Grace Moravian Ch., Center Valley, Pa., 1974-77, Covenant Moravian Ch., York, Pa., 1977-84, Watertown (Wis.) Moravian Ch., 1984—; adj. faculty mem. Liberation Theology Nashaotah House Sem., 1987-90; synod del. Moravian Ch. North, Bethlehem, 1974, 78, 86; chmn. broadcast commn. York County Council Chs., 1979-84; vice chmn. bd. Moravian Ch. Camp, Hope, N.J., 1982-84; mem. Mt. Morris Program Moravian Ch. West, Madison, Wis., 1984-86; mem. bd. Watertown Counseling Ctr., 1985-90, planning com. Moravian West Dist. Conf., 1988; Moravian rep. Bd. United Christian Resource Ctr., Sun Prairie, Wis., 1988-90; part-time alcohol and drug counselor, 1990—. Author: Moravian study guide on AIDS; contbr. articles to profl. jours.; producer (radio series) Waging Peace, 1983; (cable TV series) Faith Alive, 1983-84. Mem. Moravian Western Christian Edn. Commn., 1986—, AIDS Community Edn. project, Watertown, Jefferson County (Wis.) AIDS Task Force, 1988—; mem. AIDS task force Wis. Conf. Chs., 1987-90, chmn. AIDS pastoral care network com., 1987-90; chmn. Moravian Western Video and Media Commn., 1986-90; chair Alcohol and Drug Task Force, Moravian Ch. Western Dist., 1990—; mem. Alliance for a Drug Free Watertown, 1990—. Mem. Watertown Clergy Roundtable, Watertown Mcpl. Band, Wis. Conf. of Chs. Broadcast Commn. Democrat. Avocations: audio/visuals, video prodn., computers, music. Office: Watertown Moravian Ch 510 Cole St Watertown WI 53094

LEHMAN, CURT, minister, head of religious organization. Pres. Berean Fundamental Ch., Lincoln, Nebr. Office: Berean Fundamental Ch 6400 S 70th St Lincoln NE 68516*

LEHMAN, DWIGHT ALLEN, minister; b. Waterloo, Iowa, Dec. 29, 1947; s. Glen Alvin and Geraldine Myrtle (Moorhead) L.; m. Gloria Ruth Nickolaus, June 26, 1971; children: Matthew Jay, Benjamin Allen, Sara Nicole. BA, Calvary Bible Coll., Kansas City, Mo., 1971; MA, Southeastern Bible Coll., Birmingham, Ala., 1990. Ordained to ministry Ind. Fundamental Chs. Am., 1969, Bible Ch., 1972. Assoc. pastor Mesa Hills Bible Ch., Colorado Springs, Colo., 1972-75, York (Pa.) Gospel Ctr., 1976-82; pastor Fox Valley Community Ch., Salem, Wis., 1975-76, Grandview (Iowa) Community Bible Ch., 1982-84; dean students Appalachian Bible Coll., Bradley, W.Va., 1984-89; pastor Plano (Ill.) Bible Ch., 1989—; bd. dirs. Ill. Bible Ch. Mission, Glenwood. Author: (booklet) The Real Thing! Outline Studies on First John, 1983; composer: A Servant in Action, 1985. Office: Plano Bible Ch 1111 W South St Plano IL 60545

LEHMAN, EDWIN, minister, head of religious organization. Pres. Luth. Ch. Can., Winnipeg, Man. also: 59 Academy Rd, Winnipeg, MB Canada R3M 0E2*

LEHMAN, JAMES ORTEN, library director; b. Apple Creek, Ohio, Dec. 22, 1932; s. Willis Albert and Sarean Aldula (Amstutz) L.; m. Dorothy Anna Amstutz, Sept. 5, 1953; children: Lynn, Orval, Gerald, Beverly, Alan. BA, Ea. Mennonite Coll., Harrisonburg, Va., 1959, MLS, Kent State U., 1965, cert. advanced studies in libr. sci., 1969. Prin., tchr. Sonnenberg Mennonite Sch., Kidron, Ohio, 1955-57, 59-60; libr., tchr. Cen. Christian High Sch., Kidron, 1961-68; asst. libr. Ea. Mennonite Coll. and Sem., 1969-73, dir. librs., 1973—; mem. hist. com. Mennonite Ch., Goshen, Ind., 1973-77, 87—; chmn. hist. com. Va. Mennonite Conf., Harrisonburg, 1975—; chmn. Ea. Mennonite Assoc. Librs. and Archives, Lancaster, Pa., 1977-89; various positions Sonnenberg Mennonite Ch., Lindale Mennonite Ch., 1955—. Author congl. and community histories in Ohio, 1969, 74, 75, 78, 80, 86, 90; contbr. numerous articles to religious jours. Served alt. mil. duty Univ. Hosp., Cleve., 1953-55. Mem. ALA, Va. Libr. Assn., Am. Assn. for State and Local History, Ohio Hist. Soc., Mennonite Ch. Hist. Assn., Lancaster Mennonite Hist. Soc., Mennonite Historians Ea. Pa., Kidron Community Hist. Soc. Office: Ea Mennonite Coll Libr 1200 Park Rd Harrisonburg VA 22801-2462

LEHNINGER, ERNST FRANCIS, minister, social services administrator; b. Plymouth, Nebr., May 2, 1917; s. Max F. and Anna L. L.; m. Margaret M. Rottman, Aug. 12, 1944; children: Robert Paul. BA, Northwestern Coll., Watertown, Wis., 1939; M in Religion, Wis. Luth. Seminary, 1942. Ordained to ministry Luth. Ch., 1942. Coach, educator Winnebago (Wis.) High Sch., 1942-45; pastor Riverview Mission, Appleton, Wis., 1945-50, Grace Evan Luth. Ch., Oshkosh, Wis., 1950-55; pub. rels. dir., asst. dir. Luth. Children's Friends Soc., Milw., 1956-57, exec. dir., 1957-66; exec. dir. Wis. Luth. Child & Family Svc., Milw., 1967-91. Mem. Am. Coll. Nursing Home Adminstrs. (pres. Wis. chpt.), Am. Assn. Homes for the Aging, Wis. Assn. Homes for the Aging (award of merit 1984), Child Welfare League Am., Wis. Coun. on Human Concerns, Wis. Coun. of Voluntary Family and Children's Agencies, Milw. Fedn. of Wis. Evang. Luth. Chs. (mem. welfare and relief com.), Wis. Evang. Luth. Synod, Rotary Internat. Home: 9302 Ridge Blvd Wauwatosa WI 53226

LEHR, JOHN FREDERICK, hospital administrator, minister; b. York, Pa., Dec. 6, 1946; s. Stanford Isadore Meisenhelter and Naomi Jane (Huson) L.; m. Janet Irene Senft, Mar. 14, 1970; children: Jason F., Amy S. BA, Susquehanna U., 1968; MDiv, Luth. Theol. Sem., 1972; DMin, Drew U., 1982. Ordained to ministry Luth. Ch., 1972. Assoc. pastor Christ Luth. Ch., Lancaster, Pa., 1974-75, St. Mark Luth. Ch., Hanover, Pa., 1975-76; pastor Meml. Luth. Ch., Shippensburg, Pa., 1976-80, Ascension Luth. Ch., South Burlington, Vt., 1981-90; dir. Wholistic Health Care Svcs., Good Shepherd Hosp., Allentown, Pa., 1990—; v.p., trustee Vt. Ecumenical Coun., Burlington, 1981-90; chmn., bd. dirs. Ecumenical Campus Ministry, U. Vt., Burlington, 1983-87; cons. Vt. Dept. Health, Burlington, 1984-86, Regional Genetics Group, Burlington, 1986-90. Mem. editorial com. You Can Fly,

1973. Mem. health profl. adv. com. Vt. March of Dimes, Burlington, 1986-90; bd. dirs. Green Mountain Adirondack chpt. Muscular Dystrophy Assn., Burlington, 1984-89; mem. renal adv. com. Med. Ctr. Hosp. of Vt., Burlington, 1982-86. Grantee Wheat Ridge Found., 1991; named For Exceptional Commitment, Muscular Dystrophy Assn., Albany, N.Y., 1989. Mem. Alban Inst., Nat. Coun. on Family Rels. (cert. family life educator). Democrat. Office: Good Shepherd 6th and Saint John Sts Allentown PA 18103 *Being well is not just an enterprise of the body and the mind; it is also an adventure of the spirit. Body, mind and spirti work together to fully establish well-being.*

LEHRBERGER, JAMES JOSEPH, religion educator, priest; b. San Francisco, Dec. 8, 1943; s. Martin Robinson and Frances Louise (Vest) L. BA in Philosophy, U. San Francisco, 1966; MA in Theology, U. Dallas, 1979, PhD, 1983. Ordained priest Roman Cath. Ch., 1976. Cistercian monk Our Lady of Dallas Abbey, Irving, Tex., 1976—; chaplain U. Dallas, Rome, 1978-81, Dallas Naval Air Sta., 1984—; asst. prof. philosophy U. Dallas, Irving, Tex., 1978—; chaplain Mother and Unborn Baby Care, Ft. Worth, 1986—, Crusaders for Life, U. Dallas, 1988—; instr. Ft. Worth Deacon Formation Program, 1987; participant Second Century Christianity Seminar. Contbr. papers, articles to profl. publs. Bd. dirs. Raphael Project, Dallas, 1990—. Earhart fellow Relm Found., 1966-67, St. Thomas More Inst. fellow, 1986-89. Mem. Am. Cath. Philos. Assn., Am. Acad. Religion (chair arts, lit. and religion sect. S.W. region 1991-92). Home: Cistercian Abbey 1 Cistercian Rd Irving TX 75039 Office: U Dallas Irving TX 75061 *The reformer and the saint differ absolutely. The reformer demands the world to reshape itself in his own image; the saint prays that God will reshape the world in His Own Image.*

LEHRMAN, IRVING, rabbi; b. Tiktin, Poland, June 15, 1911; came to U.S. 1916; s. Abraham and Rachel Minnie (Dinowitz) L.; m. Bella Goldfarb, May 21, 1935; children: David Lehrman, Rosalind Lehrman Messer. DHL, Jewish Theol. Sem. of Am., N.Y.C., 1948, DD, 1969; DHL, St. Thomas U., Miami, Fla., 1989. Ordained rabbi, 1943. Student rabbi Temple Shomrei Emunah, Montclair, N.J., 1939-43; rabbi Temple Emanu-El of Greater Miami, Miami Beach, Fla., 1943—; vis. prof. Homiletics Jewish Theol. Sem. of Am.; nat. pres. Synagogue Coun. of Am.; chmn. United Jewish Appeal Nat. Rabbinic Cabinet; chmn. Greater Miami Combined Jewish Appeal; chmn. bd. govs. Greater Miami State of Israel Bonds, mem. nat. rabbinic cabinet; hon. pres. S.E. region of Rabbinical Assembly of Am. Author: In the Name of God, collection of sermons, articles, 1979, L'Chaim, thoughts for Jewish living, 1985, Portraits in Charcoal, 1980. Mem. White House Commn. on Obscenity and Pornography, Aging, and Food, Nutrition and Health (co-chmn. religious task force); bd. dirs. Miami Jewish Home and Hosp. for Aged, Internat. Synagogue at JFK Airport, N.Y.C.; nat. v.p. Zionist Orgn. Am.; adv. bd. St. Thomas U., Nat. Conf. Christians and Jews; former mem. exec. com. UNESCO, Greater Miami Community Rels. Bd. Recipient silver medal NCCJ, Prime Min.'s medal State of Israel, Albert Einstein Brotherhood award Technion U., Golda Meir Leadership award State of Israel Bonds, Louis D. Brandeis award Zionist Orgn. Am., also others. Mem. Rabbinical Assn. Greater Miami (past pres.). Office: Temple Emanu-El 1701 Washington Ave Miami Beach FL 33139

LEIBRECHT, JOHN JOSEPH, bishop; b. Overland, Mo., Aug. 8, 1930. PhD, Cath. U., Washington. Ordained priest, Roman Cath. Ch., 1956. Supt. schs. St. Louis Archdiocese, 1962-81; bishop Springfield-Cape Girardeau, Mo., 1984—. Address: 601 S Jefferson Ave Springfield MO 65806

LEIDEL, EDWIN M., JR., minister; b. Balt., Oct. 13, 1938; s. Edwin M. and Gertrude (Stablefeldt) L.; m. Ira Pauline Voigt, June 20, 1964; children: Andrew, James. BS, U. Wis., 1961; MDiv, Nashotah House Sem., 1964; D Ministry, U. of the South, 1990. Rector St. Stephen's Ch., Racine, Wis., 1965-70; assoc. rector Christ Ch., Milw., 1970-75; rector St. Timothy's Ch., Indpls., 1975-80, 82-86, Christ Ch. Cathedral, Darwin, Australia, 1981-82, St. Christopher's Ch., St. Paul, 1986—. Contbr. articles to profl. jours. Served to lt. USN, 1960-62. Episcopalian. Home: 715 Forest Dale Rd Saint Paul MN 55112 Office: St Christophers Episc Ch 2300 N Hameline Ave Saint Paul MN 55113

LEIES, JOHN GERARD, minister; b. Chgo., July 5, 1909; s. Alex and Caroline (Eckebrecht) L. BA, St. Mary's U., San Antonio, 1933; MA in History, U. Fribourg, Switzerland, 1938; MEd, U. Notre Dame, 1964. Headmaster Marynook Coll., Galesville, Wis., 1942-50; chmn. dept. theology St. Mary's U., 1960-70, campus min. sch. law, 1973—. Travel grantee Hebrew Union Coll., 1965. Mem. Southwest Tex. Archaeology Soc. (pres., sec. 1970-75), Soc. Bibl. Lit., Conf. Christian and Jews, Am. Inst. Archaeology. Home: 520 Fordham Ln San Antonio TX 78228 Office: Saint Marys U Sch Law One Camino Santa Maria San Antonio TX 78228-8603

LEIGHTON, CHRISTOPHER PAUL, priest; b. Boston, June 4, 1954; s. Paul Edward and Susan (Squires) L.; m. Janet Dorman, Oct. 13, 1973; children: Alexander, Susannah, Deborah, Katherine. BA cum laude, U. Mass., 1976; MDiv, Trinity Episcopal Sch., Ambridge, Pa., 1979. Rector All Saints Ch., Aliquippa, Pa., 1979-85, St. David's Ch., Venetia, Pa., 1985—; new ch. chmn. Diocese of Pitts., 1985—, Cursillo spiritual dir., 1985—; tchr. Trinity Sch. for Min., Ambridge, 1980-82; mem. Episcopalians United, Shaker Heights, Ohio, 1986—, Brotherhood of St. Andrew, Pitts., 1982—. Author: Withinsight, 1972; producer New Chs. in Pitts., 1987; contbr. articles to profl. jours. Coach Peters Twp. Soccer Assn., 1986—. Mem. U. Mass. Alumni Assn. Home and Office: St Davids Episcopal Ch 905 E McMurray Venetia PA 15367 *Life without God is not life at all. Serving God where He wants you is life abundantly lived. He has blessed me to be a blessing to others in serving them.*

LEIMAN, SID ZALMAN, Judaic studies educator; b. N.Y.C., Nov. 3, 1941; s. Harold Isaac and Harriet (Gross) L.; m. Rivkah Landesman, Nov. 25, 1969; children—Akiva, Rose Nechama, Yocheved, Naomi. B.A., Bklyn. Coll., 1964; Rabbi, Mirrer Yeshiva Central Inst., 1964; Ph.D., U. Pa., 1970. Lectr. in Jewish history and lit. Yale U., 1968-70, asst. prof., 1970-72, assoc. prof., 1972-78; vis. scholar in Jewish law and ethics Kennedy Inst. Ethics, Georgetown U., Washington, 1977-78; prof. Jewish history and lit., dean Bernard Revel Grad. Sch.; dir. grad. Jewish edn. Yeshiva U., N.Y.C., 1978-81; prof. Judaic studies Bklyn. Coll., 1981—, chmn. dept., 1981-87. Author: The Canonization of Hebrew Scripture: The Talmudic and Midrashic Evidence, 1976, 2d edit., 1991; editor: The Canon and Masorah of the Hebrew Bible: An Introductory Reader, 1974; contbr. to: Ency. Judaica, 1972, Ency. Brit, 1974, Ency. Biblica, 1981. Morse fellow, 1971-72; Nat. Endowment for Humanities grantee, 1974. Mem. Am. Acad. Religion, Am. Schs. Oriental Research, Assn. for Jewish Studies, Soc. Bibl. Lit. Home: 140-02 69th Ave Kew Gardens Hills NY 11367 Office: Bklyn Coll Judaic Studies Brooklyn NY 11210

LEIMKILLER, FLOYD NELSON, minister; b. Chamois, Mo., May 15, 1944; s. M. Earl and Anna Agnes (Reynolds) L.; m. Virginia Mae Beazley, Aug. 17, 1964; children: Lela, Marcella. Student, SW Bapt. U., Bolivar, Mo., 1963. Ordained to ministry So. Bapt. Conv. Pastor Wooldridge (Mo.) Bapt. Ch., 1974-78, New Salem Bapt. Ch., Ashland, Mo., 1978-80, College Hill Bapt. Ch., Belle, Mo., 1981-89, Pilot Grove Bapt. Ch., California, Mo., 1989—. Mem. Ashland City Coun., 1980. Home: 1400 Westview Dr Jefferson City MO 65109 Office: Pilot Grove Bapt Ch HCR 61 Box 83 California MO 65018

LEINER, CARL ELTON, minister, psychotherapist; b. East St. Louis, Ill., May 16, 1952; s. Carl Garnett and Doris LaVern (Schmidt) L.; m. Janet Louise Pybas, Aug. 11, 1973; children: Cassandra Noelle, Carl Nikolas. Student, SW Bapt. Coll., 1970-74; BA, U. Md., Berlin, Fed. Republic Germany, 1980; MDiv, New Orleans Bapt. Theol. Sem., 1982, postgrad., 1982-84. Ordained to ministry Bapt. Ch., 1982. Commd. 2d lt. U.S. Army, 1981, advanced through grades to capt., 1985; linguist Russian lang. Berlin; chaplain with Res., 1981-85; chaplain Ft. Hood, Tex., 1985-88; prof. Union Bapt. Theol. Sem., New Orleans, 1983; supr. basic counseling students New Orleans Bapt. Theol. Sem., 1983; pastor, counselor, music and youth dir. various Bapt. chs., La. and Okla., 1980-85; child care worker St. Bernard Group Homes, Mireaux, La., 1983; therapist Many (La.) Mental Health Clinic, 1984; orgnl. leadership trainer U.S. Army Chaplain Bd., 1986-88; psychotherapist Pastoral Counseling Ctr., Las Vegas, Nev., 1988-90; clin. dir. family svcs. Westcare, Las Vegas, 1990-91; parish asst. 1st Presbyn Ch., Las Vegas, 1990—. Democrat. Home: 3581 E Gallup Ct Las Vegas NV 89121 Office: Westcare 1515 W Charleston Las Vegas NV 89102 *In Christ there is no East or West, in Him no South or North; but to find and understand Him one must Search both East and West and South and North.*

LEITCH, JOEL STEVEN, health facilities administrator; b. West Union, Iowa, Aug. 28, 1952; s. Thomas Richard and Avis Irene (Hanson) L. BS in Psychology, U. Idaho, 1979; MS in Clin. Psychology, Cen. Mo. State U., 1981. Nat. cert. addictions counselor; ordained to ministry Full Gospel Assemblies Internat., 1985. Youth pastor 1st United Meth. Ch., Cushing, Okla., 1981-84, Agra and Coyle, Okla., 1984-86; clin. counselor Valley Hope Treatment Ctr., Cushing, Okla., 1981-86; program dir. St. Joseph Med. Ctr., Ponca City, Okla., 1986-88; youth pastor Calvary Assembly of Gold, Stillwater, Okla., 1986-88; youth leader Broken Arrow (Okla.) Assembly of God, 1988-91; program mgr. St. Francis Hosp., Tulsa, Okla., 1988-89; dir. juvenile svcs., family support specialist Mental Health Svcs. of Tulsa, 1990-91; missionary Assemblies of God, Puerto Rico, 1991—; cons. Ct. Related Svcs., Anadarko, Okla., 1987-91; pvt. practice, Tulsa, 1985-91. Author: Suicide Intervention, 1990. Pres., founder Spirit Ministries, Inc., Okla., 1984—, Christian counselor; adv. bd. Okla. Nursing Vocat. Tech. Schs., 1985-91. Recipient Nat. Citizenship award, 1978; named Family Support Specialist of Yr. Okla. Mental Health & Substance Abuse Svcs., 1990. Mem. Okla. Drug and Alcohol Profl. Counselors Assn. (cert.), Nat. Assn. Alcohol and Drug Abuse Counselors (cert.), Okla. Assn. Lic. Profl. Counselors (lic.), Nat. Bd. Cert. Counselors (cert.), Chem. Abuse Program Dirs. Assn., Nat. Cert. Addictions Counselor. Republican. Mem. Assembly of God Ch. Home: PO Box 33032 Tulsa OK 74153 *I have found that people will never truly be happy in life until they accept full responsibility for their own actions, attitudes, and motivation without blaming others. This is best accomplished by turning them all over to Jesus Christ.*

LEITER, DONALD EUGENE, religious organization executive; b. Ashland, Ohio, Feb. 5, 1932; s. Harold Lewis and Sadie Helena (Watson) L.; m. Crystal Dianne Berkey, June 15, 1957; children: David Alan, Donald Eugene Jr., Dianne Elizabeth, Daniel Scott. BA, Manchester Coll., 1954; M of Div., Bethany Theol. Seminary, 1958; postgrad., Garret Theol. Seminary and Northwestern U., 1972. Ordained to ministry Ch. of the Brethren, 1956. Min. West Side Christian Parish, Chgo., 1955-58; pastor Ch. of the Brethren, Everett, Pa., 1958-59, Germantown Ch. of the Brethren, Phila., 1959-61; pastor, organizer Immanuel Ch. of the Brethren, Paoli, Pa., 1959-66; assoc. pastor Washington City Ch. of the Brethren, 1966-72; coord. Capitol Hill Group Ministry, Washington, 1968-72; exec. dir. Delmarva Ecumenical Agy., Wilmington, Del., 1972-81; pastor, organizer Christ Ch. of the Brethren, Carol Stream, Ill., 1981-84; exec. dir. Ga. Christian Coun., Macon, Ga., 1984-90, Christian Assocs. Southwest Pa., Pitts., 1991—. Scoutmaster, agy. rep. Boy Scouts Am., 1963-72; co-chmn. Upper Main Line Com. Conscience, 1965-66; mem. Neighborhood Planning Council, Washington, 1967-72; mem. Leadership Pitts., Citizens League S.W. Pa., Interfaith/Impact for Justice and Peace, Pitts. Points of Light Leadership Coun. Mem. Nat. Assn. Ecumenical Staff. Office: Christian Assocs SW Pa 239 Fourth Ave Ste 1817 Pittsburgh PA 15222-1769 *To keep perspective in our contemporary periods of charismatic enthusiasm, fundamentalist challenges and liberal causes I rely upon the biblical foundation of my early study of each occurrence in the Bible of the word "Spirit" in the context of who made reference to the Spirit, why was the Spirit invoked and what was the immediate context as well as the overall context within biblical literature.*

LEITH, JOHN HADDON, clergyman, theology educator; b. Due West, S.C., Sept. 10, 1919; s. William H. and Lucy Ann (Haddon) L.; m. Ann Caroline White, Sept. 2, 1943; children—Henry White, Caroline Haddon. A.B., Erskine Coll., 1940, D.D. (hon.), 1972; B.D., Columbia Theol. Sem., 1943; M.A., Vanderbilt U., 1946; Ph.D., Yale U., 1949; D.D. (hon.), Davidson Coll., 1978; D.Litt. (hon.), Presbyn. Coll., 1990. Ordained to ministry Presbyterian Ch. 1943. Pastor chs. in Nashville and Auburn, Ala., 1944-59; Pemberton prof. theology Union Theol. Sem., Richmond, Va., 1959—; vis. prof. Columbia Theol. Sem., Eckerd Coll., New Coll. at U. Edinburgh; adj. prof. Va. Commonwealth U.; mem. ad interim com. to revise book of ch. order Presbyn. Ch. U.S., 1955-61, mem. com. to write brief statement of faith, 1960-62, mem. com. to prepare brief statement of reformed faith, 1984-89; chmn. com. revision of chpt. 3 of Confession of Faith, 1959-60mem. permanent nominating com. gen. assembly, 1972-75; chmn. bd. Presbyn. Survey, 1961-70; bd. dirs. Presbyn. Outlook Mag., 1962—; moderator Presbyn. Synod N.C., 1977-78; mem. Gov.'s Commn. on Seasonal and Migrant Farm Workers, 1982—; mem. adv. coun. Ctr. of Theol. Inquiry, Princeton, N.J., 1989—. Author: Creeds of the Churches, 1963, 3d. rev. edit., 1982, The Church, A Believing Fellowship, 1965, rev., 1980, Assembly at Westminster, 1973, Greenville Church, The Story of a People, 1973, The Reformed Tradition, A Way of Being the Christian Community, 2d edit., 1981, John Calvin, the Christian Life, 1984, The Reformed Imperative, 1988, John Calvin's Doctrine of the Christian Life, 1989; editor: Guides to Reformed Theology, The Reformed Imperative, 1988, From Generation to Generation, 1990. Trustee Erskine Coll.; bd. dirs. Inst. Religion and Democracy, 1985—; mem. Richmond City com. Dem. Party, 1973—. Kent fellow, 1946-48; Folger Library fellow, 1964; grantee Advanced Religious Studies Found., 1974. Mem. Calvin Studies Soc. (pres. 1980-83). Home: 3311 Suffolk Ave Richmond VA 23227

LEKGANYANE, BARNABAS, bishop. Leader, bishop Zion Christian Ch., Transvaal. Office: Zion Christian Ch, Zion City, Moria, Transvaal Republic of South Africa*

LELIAERT, RICHARD MAURICE, priest, hospital chaplain; b. Mishawaka, Ind., Nov. 30, 1940; s. Maurice August and Lucy Leona (Stevens) L. BA, St. Francis Coll., Ft. Wayne, Ind., 1965; S.T.B., Cath. U. Am., 1967; postgrad., St. John's U., 1968, 69; PhD, Grad. Theol. Union, 1974. Ordained priest Roman Cath. Ch., 1967; cert. chaplain. Tchr. Crosier Sem., Onamia, Minn., 1967-69; asst. prof. Cath. Theol. Union, Chgo., 1974-77; assoc. prof. Nazareth Coll., Kalamazoo, Mich., 1977-87; staff chaplain St. Joseph Mercy Hosp., Pontiac, Mich., 1988, 89—; priest presenter Worldwide Marriage Encounter, Chgo., 1976-81; bd. dirs., planner World Marriage Day, Kalamazoo, 1984-85. Author: (with others) Death: Completion and Discovery, 1987, Dictionary of Christianity in America, 1990; also articles; co-editor: Brownson-Hecker Letters, 1979. Spiritual advisor for Cranbrook Hospice Com. Grantee NEH, 1982-84; named Danforth Assoc., Danforth Found., 1979-83. Mem. Assn. for Death Edn. and Counseling (cert. profl. death educator, treas. Mich. chpt. 1990—), Am. Acad. Religion, Am. Soc. Ch. History. Democrat. Home: 13249 Pennsylvania Rd Riverview MI 48192 Office: St Joseph Mercy Hosp 900 Woodward Ave Pontiac MI 48341

LELYVELD, ARTHUR JOSEPH, rabbi; b. N.Y.C., Feb. 6, 1913; s. Edward Joseph and Dora (Cohen) L.; m. Toby Bookholtz, Dec. 26, 1933 (div.); children: Joseph Salem, David Simon, Michael Stephen; m. 2d, Teela Stovsky, Dec. 5, 1964; children: Benjamin (dec.), Robin Beth. AB, Columbia U., 1933; M Hebrew Letters, Hebrew Union Coll., Cin., 1939; DD honoris causa, Hebrew Union Coll.-Jewish Inst. Religion, 1955; LittD (hon.), Cleve. Coll. Jewish Studies, 1986. Rabbi Congregation B'nai Jeshurun, Hamilton, Ohio, 1939-41, Temple Israel, Omaha, 1941-44; pres. Jewish Peace Fellowship, 1941-43; exec. dir. Com. Unity for Palestine, 1944-46, nat. vice chmn., 1944-48; assoc. nat. dir. B'nai B'rith Hillel Founds., N.Y.C., 1946-47; nat. dir. B'nai B'rith Hillel Founds., 1948-56; exec. v.p. Am.-Israel Cultural Found., 1956-58; rabbi Fairmount Temple, Cleve., 1958-86, sr. rabbi emeritus, 1986—; founder, bd. dirs. Am. Jewish Soc. for Service, 1941; mem. adv. bd. Pastoral Psychology Inst., Case Western Res. U. Sch. Medicine; B.G. Rudolph lectr. in Judaic Studies, Syracuse U., 1984; lectr. So. African Union for Prog. Judaism, 1985; vis. scholar Oxford Ctr. for Postgrad. Hebrew Studies, Oxford, Eng.; adj. prof. religion Case Western Res. U., 1979-80; Bernard Rich Hollander lectr. in Jewish Thought, John Carroll U., 1980—; Walter and Mary Tuohy chair in Interreligious Studies, John Carroll U., 1989; sr. teaching fellow Cleve. Coll. Jewish Studies, 1986—; sec. Joint Rabbinical Com. Conscientious Objectors, 1941-46; Am. vice chmn. World U. Service, 1955-65; nat. pres. Am. Jewish Congress, 1966-72, hon. pres., 1972—; Goldenson lectr. Hebrew Union Coll.-Jewish Inst. Religion, 1973. Author: Atheism is Dead, 1968 (paperback edit. 1970, 2d edit. 1985); contbg. author: Religion in the State University, Jewish Heritage Reader; Censorship: For or Against; Punishment: For or Against; Population Control: For or Against; contbr. Universal Jewish Ency., periodicals; mem. publs. com. Jewish Publ. Soc. Am. chmn. Omaha Fair Employment Practice Council, 1942-44; pub. panel chmn. WLB 1944; exec. com. Nat. Hillel Commn.; gen. chmn. Cleve. Jewish Welfare Fund, 1963; trustee Martin Luther King Ctr. for Social Change. Edward L. Heinsheimer fellow, 1939-41; recipient Centennial medal John Carroll U., 1986. Mem. Commn. on Social Action of Reform Judaism (hon. life), NAACP (hon. exec. com. Cleve. br.), Cen. Conf. Am. Rabbis (exec. bd., nat. v.p. 1973-75, pres. 1975-77), Synagogue Council Am. (nat. v.p. 1975-79, nat. pres. 1979-81), Am. Jewish League Israel (nat. v.p. 1962-84, hon. pres. 1984—), Nacoms, Phi Beta Kappa, Beta Sigma Rho. Lodge: B'nai B'rith. Office: Fairmount Temple 23737 Fairmount Blvd Beachwood OH 44122 *In his late years, Teilhard de Chardin seemed obsessed with the goal of "ending well." What he meant is made clear in his life and work and in his letters. Ending well is actually the secure knowledge that one has made meaningful contributions to the welfare of humanity. Hence, "ending well" means "living well."*

LEMKE, MICHAEL ROBERT, minister; b. Sioux Falls, S.D., Sept. 11, 1958; s. Robert Earl and Mary Jean (Thornburg) L.; m. Barb Brunstein, Aug. 19, 1989. BA in Religious Studies, BA in English, U. Denver, 1980; MDiv, Wartburg Sem., 1984. Ordained to ministry Luth. Ch., 1985. Asst. pastor Joy Luth. Ch., Parker, Colo., 1985-88, sr. pastor, 1988—; Chaplain Agree to Stop Abuse, Denver, 1989—, Parker Fire Dept., 1991. Participant Parker Ecumenical Alliance, 1985—. Republican. Office: Joy Luth Church 7051 E Parker Hills Ct Parker CO 80134

LEMKE, STEVE WARNER, philosophy and religion educator; b. Waco, Tex., Aug. 31, 1951; s. Calvin Aubrey and Wanda (Wilkes) L.; m. Carol Clapp Lemke, July 3, 1978. BA, La. Tech. U., Ruston, 1972; MDiv, Southwestern Bapt. Theol. Sem., Ft. Worth, 1976, MA, 1978, PhD, 1985. Youth asst. minister Univ. Bapt. Ch., Ft. Worth, 1978-79; pastor First Bapt. Ch., Santo, Tex., 1979-84; chmn. dept. religion and philosophy Williams Bapt. Coll., Walnut Ridge, Ark., 1984-88; pastor Hillcrest Bapt. Ch., Bryan, Tex., 1988-90; asst. prof. philosophy of religion Southwestern Bapt. Theol. Sem., Ft. Worth, 1990—; moderator Palo Alto Bapt. Assn., Mineral Wells, Tex., 1982-84; bd. mem. Camp Copass, Denton, Tex., 1980-84. Author: The Christian Philosophy of Emile Cailliet, 1985, Living Hope: Studies in I Peter, 1982, Joy in Christ: Studies in Philippians, 1980. Vol. chaplain Humana Hosp., College Station, Tex., 1988-90; cons. Terminally Ill Support Group, College Station, 1989-90; mem. spiritual life com. HCA Grenleaf Hsop., College Station, 1990—; bd. mem. Randolph County chpt. Am. Cancer Soc., 1986-88. Mem. Bapt. Assn. Philosophy Tchrs., Am. Acad. Religion, Am. Philos. Assn., Ark. Philos. Assn. Republican. Office: Southwestern Bapt Theol Sem PO Box 22000 22000 W Seminary Dr Fort Worth TX 76122 *The beginning of wisdom is the realization that God is personal. We know this God most clearly and personally in Jesus Christ.*

LEMMENES, MARK GLEN, minister; b. Ripon, Wis., Oct. 31, 1943; s. John Alvin and Muriel Gysbers (Bossenbroek) L.; m. Mary Lenora Hesselink, Sept. 1, 1967; children: Dirk Jacob, Peter Nathan. BA, Hope Coll., 1966; MDiv, Western Theol. Sem., 1970. Pastor Glendale (N.Y.) Reformed Ch., 1970-77, The Community Reformed Ch., Manhasset, N.Y., 1977-84; sr. pastor El Dorado Pk. Community Ch., Long Beach, Calif., 1984—; mem. Commn. on Worship, Holland, Mich., 1986—; pulpit exchange Rutherglen Congl. Ch., Glasgow, Scotland, 1979; pres. Classis of Queens, R.C.A., N.Y., 1975; exec. com. Classis of Nassau-Suffolk, R.C.A., L.I., N.Y., 1980-83. Chaplain, dir. Glendale Vol. Ambulance Corp, 1974-77; chaplain Rotary, Manhasset, 1977-83. Mem. Phi Mu Alpha Sinfonia. Office: El Dorado Pk Community Ch 3655 Norwalk Blvd Long Beach CA 90808-3296

LEMMON, GEORGE COLBORNE, bishop; b. St. John, N.B., Can., Mar. 20, 1932; m. Lois Jean Foster, June 7, 1957; children: Paul, Marilu, Robert. BA, U. N.B., 1959; Licentiate in Theology, Wycliffe Coll., Toronto, Can., 1962, BD, 1964, DD (hon.), 1991; DD (hon.), King's Coll., Halifax, N.S., Can., 1990. Ordained priest Anglican Ch. Can. Bishop Diocese of Fredericton (Can.), Anglican Ch. Can.; mem. nat. exec. com., nat. stewardship com. Anglican Ch. Can. Columnist The Daily Gleaner, 1986—. Active Mayor's Adv. Com. on Econ. Devel., Fredericton, 1991; sec. Crake Found. Inc.; founding mem. Cons for Christ, Fredericton. Mem. Irenaeus Fellowship. Office: Diocese of Fredericton, 115 Church St, Fredericton, NB Canada E3B 4C8

LEMON, JERRY WAYNE, minister; b. Lorenzo, Tex., Apr. 25, 1935; s. Lawrence Oliver and Alta Bernice (Eaves) L.; m. Martha Mae Durr, Dec. 30, 1956; children: Jerry Wayne, Jr., Cheryl Rhae, David Brent. BA, Baylor U., 1956; BD, Southwestern Bapt. Theol. Sem., 1960, MDiv, 1969; PhD, Baylor U., 1975. Ordained to ministry Bapt. Ch., 1956. Minister of youth First Bapt. Ch., Woodway, Waco, Tex., 1954-55; minister of music Cen. Bapt. Ch., Thornton, Tex., 1955-56; truck driver Cen. Freight Lines, Ft. Worth, 1957-61; pastor Valley Creek Bapt. Ch., Leonard, Tex., 1957-61; pastor First Bapt. Ch., Ganado, Tex., 1961-66, Chilton, Tex., 1967-71, Groesbeck, Tex., 1971-76, Seymour, Tex., 1976-80; pastor Garden Oaks Bapt. Ch., Houston, 1980-91; editor Bapt. Sunday Sch. Bd., Nashville, 1991—; curriculum writer Bapt. Sun. Sch. Bd., Nashville, 1985—. Author: Sunday School Adult, 1987, 88, 90. Baptist. Avocation: travel. Home: 5242 Edmondson Pike Apt 417 Nashville TN 37211

LEMONS, JIMMIE WAYNE, minister; b. Pine Bluff, Ark., Sept. 6, 1958; s. Jim Don and Ava Nell (Shumate) L.; m. Cynthia Diane Wiggins, Apr. 12, 1985. BA in Bibl. Studies, Evang. Coll., Springfield, Mo., 1983; MA in Bibl. Lit., Assemblies of God Theol. Sem., Springfield, Mo., 1988. Ordained to ministry Assemblies of God Ch., 1987. Assoc. youth pastor First Assembly of God Ch., Hattiesburg, Miss., 1985-86; campus pastor USM Chi Alpha, Hattiesburg, 1985-86; assoc., youth pastor Swartz First Assembly Ch., Monroe, La., 1986-90; campus pastor NLU Chi Alpha, Monroe, La., 1988-90; fgn. missionary DFM Assemblies of God, Springfield, Mo., 1990—; ch. outreach coord. S.C.O.P.E., Springfield, 1981-82. Home: 118 Birchwood Dr Monroe LA 71203 Office: Div Fgn Missions 1445 Boonville Ave Springfield MO 65802 *The vanities of life are shattered by servanthood, and helping others to know Christ makes life worthwhile.*

LENGERICH, SISTER DOROTHY ANNE, religion educator; b. Decatur, Ind.; d. Clement A. and Catherine E. (Gase) L. BA in Philosophy, U. San Diego, 1969; MA in Religious Edn., Mundelein Coll., 1972; cert. in liturgical music, St. Joseph Coll., Rennsselaer, Ind., 1981. Joined Victory Noll Sisters, Roman Cath. Ch. Tchr. religion Victory Noll Sisters, Huntington, Ind., 1934—; min. music, tchr. religion Cheyenne, Wyo., 1953-87; tchr. religion Diocese of Fresno, Monterey, Calif., 1964-67; dir. religious edn. Diocese of Detroit, 1972-78; dir. religious edn. St. Lawrence Parish, New Bedford, Mass., 1978-91, lector, 1980-91, min. music, 1980-91, eucharistic min., 1983-91, min. liturgy and music, 1991—. Office: St Lawrence Parish 91 Summer St New Bedford MA 02740

LENNICK, ROBERT BRENT, rabbi; b. Boston, May 4, 1956; s. Gerald and Ellen (Wolf) L.; m. Heidi Lee Esner, June 17, 1990. BA in Philosophy with honors, Clark U., 1978; MA in Hebrew Letters, Hebrew Union Coll., Jewish Inst. Religion, 1981. Ordained rabbi, 1984. Lectr. religion Denison U., Granville, Ohio, 1983-84; asst. rabbi Temple Emanuel, Denver, 1984-87; sr. rabbi Greenwich (Conn.) Reform Synagogue, 1987—; mem. Rabbinic cabinet Nat. United Jewish Appeal, N.Y.C., 1989—' bd. dirs. Am. Jewish Con., Conn., 1990—, Jewish Community Svcs.; internat. pres. United Synagogue Youth, N.Y.C., 1974-75; trustee Coun. Chs. and Synagogues, Stamford, Conn., 1990—, chair interfaith com. Editor, author: (booklet) A Shabbat Manual, 1985, The Seasons of Life, 1986; contbr. articles to religious publs. V.p. Mead Counselling Ctr., Greenwich, 1989—; mem. Greenwich Community Rels. Coun., 1987—, Dem. Town Com., 1988—; bd. dirs. Greenwich Pastoral Adv. Bd., 1990—. Recipient Community Rels. award Hebrew Union Coll., 1984. Mem. Cen. Conf. Am. Rabbis, Greenwich Fellowship of Clergy (v.p. 1991—), Greenwich Jewish Fedn. (bd. dirs. 1987—), B'nai Brith, Phi Sigma Tau. Avocations: oil painting, backpacking, studying guitar, sailing, reading. Home: 1465 E Putnam Ave Old Greenwich CT 06870 Office: Greenwich Reform Synagogue 200 Riverside Ave Riverside CT 06878

LENNOX, DAVID PRESTON, minister; b. Beverly, Mass., June 20, 1952; s. Robert Edgar and Evelyn Florence (Gould) L.; m. Angela Jane Garrett, Aug. 9, 1975. BA in English, Southeastern Mass. U., 1976; MDiv, Andover-Newton Theol. Sch., 1982, postgrad., 1991—. Ordained to ministry United Ch. of Christ, 1982. Youth min. United Ch. of Canton, Mass., 1980-81; pastor Kensington (N.H.) Congl. Ch., 1982—; moderator Rockingham Assn., N.H. Conf., United Ch. of Christ, 1989-91, mem. exec. com., 1989—; chaplain Exeter (N.H.) Fire Dept., 1990—; counselor So. Maine Pastoral Counseling Ctr., 1991—. Mem. Am. Assn. Pastoral Counselors, Internat. Fellowship of Fire Chaplains, Kiwanis (dir. Exeter area 1985—).

LENOX, MARJORY ALLEN, lay church worker; b. Pitts., Sept. 3, 1944; d. Anson Williams and Rebecca Jean (Davis) A.; m. Frank B. Lenox, July 24, 1971; children: Daniel Allen, Nathan Scott. BA in English and Speech, Grove City (Pa.) Coll., 1966; MEd in English and Edn., U. Pitts., 1970. Cert. tchr. secondary edn., Pa. Dir. communications and ch. growth Christ United Meth. Ch., Bethel Park, Pa., 1980—, dir. evangelism, 1986—. Author, editor weekly page United Meth. Reporter newspaper, 1980—, author cover page Reporter advt. brochure, 1986; contbr. articles to numerous mags. and jours. Coach Keystone Oaks Synchronized Swimmers, Pitts., 1969-74; founder, leader new residents' support group New Horizons, Bethel Park, 1980-87; founder, liaison MOMs Support Group, Bethel Park, 1986—; founder, leader Phase II Moms Support Group, Bethel Park, 1987—. Finalist writing contest USA Today, 1990. Mem. Ridgeview Park Women's Assn. Democrat. Home: 1138 Tidewood Dr Bethel Park PA 15102 Office: Christ United Meth Ch 44 Highland Rd Bethel Park PA 15102

LENZ, KENNETH ROBERT, management consultant, accountant, lay worker; b. Detroit, Oct. 30, 1957; s. Robert A. and Erma E. (Shultz) L.; m. Carol E. Bronner, June 28, 1986; 1 child, Karl K. BA cum laude, Rutgers U., Newark, 1979; postgrad., U. N.Mex., 1982-83. CPA, N.Mex., Colo., N.J. Mgmt. cons. Hildebrandt, Inc., Somerville, N.J., 1987—; various ch. positions Luth. Ch.-Mo. Synod, N.J. and N.Mex., 1976—; co-founder Christian Crisis Hotline, Albuquerque, 1982—; co-founder, chmn. N.Mex. Luth. High Sch. Assn., 1982-84; founder N.Mex. Luth. Singles Ministry, 1980-85, Cristos Broadcasting Corp. (N.J. nonprofit TV)m 1988—, Rocky Mountain Singles com.; parish avangelist, 1989—; cons. in field, 1988—. Author: How To Cut Audit Costs, 1980; contbr. articles to profl. jours. Mem. AICPA (editorial adv. task force 1986-88, speaker nat. conf., 1991, regonition plaque 1988), N.J. Soc. CPAs (various offices), Accts. in the Pub. Interest (pro bono assistance to non profit orgns. 1988—), Luth. Social Ministries N.J. (bd. dirs. 1986—). Home: 6 Kent Ct Annandale NJ 08801 Office: Hildebrandt Inc 501 Post Office Pla 50 Division St Somerville NJ 08876

LENZ, WILLIAM C., clergyman; b. Appleton, Wis., 1958; s. David and Jan (Verhagen) L.; m. Janet Gregg; children—Benji, Nathanael. Grad. David Wilkeson Inst. Christian Tng., Lindale, Tex., 1980. Ordained to ministry Christian Ch., 1981; exec. dir. Solid Rock Ministries, Appleton, 1980—, counselor to drug addicts-abusers, alcoholics, suicidals, 1980—; pastor New Corinthian Chapel, Appleton, 1983—; speaker numerous youth and civic groups, 1980—. Served with USCG, 1976-80. Recipient Speaking award Appleton Kiwanis Club, 1983, Services award Appleton Salvation Army, 1983. Mem. World Challenge, United Evangel. Churches. Avocations: hunting, fishing, backpacking, swimming, skiing. Home: 927 Wilson St Little Chute WI 54140

LEONARD, GRAHAM DOUGLAS, retired bishop; b. Greenwich, Eng., May 8, 1921; s. Douglas and Emily Mabel (Cheshire) L.; student Balliol Coll., Oxford, 1940-41; MA, 1947; student Westcom House, 1946-47; DD, Episcopal Theol. Sem., 1974; D.Cn.L. (hon.) Nahotah House, 1983; STD (hon.), Siena Coll., 1984; LLD (hon.), Simon Greenleaf Sch. Law, 1987; DD (hon.) Westminster Coll., Fulton, 1987; DLitt (hon.), Com. for Nat. Acad. Awards, 1989; m. Vivien Priscilla Swann, Jan. 2, 1943; children: James Vivian, Mark Meredith. Curate, Ardleigh, 1947-52, vicar, 1952-55; dir. edn. Diocese of Albans, 1958-62; gen. sec. Nat. Soc. and Sec. Ch. of Eng. Schs. Council, 1958-62; archdeacon of Hampstead, rector St. Andrew Undershaft, 1962-64; bishop Willesden, 1964-73; bishop of Truro, 1973-81; bishop of London, 1981-91, ret., 1991; dean Her Majesty's Chapels Royal, 1981-91; prelate Most Excellent Order of Brit. Empire, 1981-91; chmn. Ch. of Eng. Bd. for Social Responsibility, 1976-83; chmn. Bd. Edn., 1983-89; mem. House of Lords, 1977-91; Hensley Henson lectr. U. Oxford, Eng., 1991-92. Served to capt., Royal Army, 1941-45. Decorated knight comdr. Royal Victorian Order, 1991. Co-author: Growing into Union, 1970; The Gospel is for Everyone, 1971; God Alive: Priorities in Pastoral Theology, 1981, Firmly I Believe and Truly, 1985, Life in Christ, 1986. Home: 25 Woodlands Rd Witney, Oxfordshire OX8 6DR, England

LEONARD, JUANITA LOUISE EVANS, theology educator; b. Louisville, May 9, 1939; d. Walter Perry and B. Gertrude (Collins) Evans; m. Lawrence Samuel Leonard, June 24, 1961. BA in Sociology, Anderson U., 1961; MA in Social Services, U. Ind., 1963; postgrad., U. Minn., 1969; MA in Cross Cultural Stud, Fuller Theo. Seminary, 1987. Marriage therapist Family Service Madison County, Anderson, Ind., 1963-65; instr. sociology Anderson U., 1965-68, assoc. prof., 1987--; chief marriage therapist Dept. of Psychiatry, Ind. U. Med. Sch., 1969-72; inservice dir. Pastoral Counseling Inst., Indpls., 1972-73; instrn. materials dir. family life Nat. Christian Council of Kenya, 1973-76; assoc. in marriage and family Inst. of Pastoral Counseling, Indpls., 1976-78; assoc. pastor family ministries Ch. of God, Indpls., 1978-85; founding dir. Counseling Ctr. Ch. at the Crossing, Indpls., 1978-85; assoc. cross cultural relations Women of the Ch. of God, Anderson, Ind., 1987--; cons. Women Network of La. II Internat. Congress on World Evangelization, Manila, Philippines, 1989, urban ministry cons. Nat. Assn. Ch. of God, West Middlesex, Pa., 1988--, bd. mem. Wesleyan Urban Coalition, Chgo., 1987--. Editor: Youth are Saying..., 1976, Called to Minister Empowered to Serve, 1989; contbr., editor to local mags. Mem. AAUW, Nat. Assn. Social Workers, Acad. Cert. Social Workers, Am. Assn. Marriage Family Therapist (pres. 1978-82),. Avocations: internat. travelling, music. Office: Anderson U Sch Theology Anderson IN 46012

LEONARD, SISTER REGINA MARY, nun; b. Balt., Nov. 6, 1926; d. Frank and Marie (Pinzer) L. BS in Edn., Mt. St. Mary's U.; MA in Religious Edn., LaSalle U. Cert. profl. catechist, Roman Cath. Ch. Tchr. music and art Immaculate Conception, Elkton, Md., 1981-84; dir. religious edn. St. Francis de Sales, Balt., 1986-88, Our Lady of Fatima, New Castle, Del., 1988-89; coord. youth ministry St. Leo the Great, Lincroft, N.J., 1989—. Mem. Nat. Fedn. Cath. Youth Mins. Home: 546 Newman Springs Rd Lincroft NJ 07738-1406 Office: St Leo's Parish Ctr 50 Hurley's Ln Lincroft NJ 07738-1406

LEONARDICH, AGNES M., school system administrator. Supt. schs. Diocese of Monterey, Calif. Office: Dept Cath Schs 500 Church St PO Box 350 Monterey CA 93942*

LEONE, BRYAN ANTHONY, minister; b. Hartford, Conn., Oct. 29, 1946; s. Alvin Carmen and Rosemary (Pallotti) L.; m. Katherine Ann Lathan, Nov. 20, 1971; children: Timothy Adam, Emily Katherine. BA in Modern Lang., Holy Cross Coll., 1968; MA in Edn., Trinity Coll., Hartford, 1973; MS in Acctg., U. Hartford, 1977; MDiv, Luth. Theol. So. Seminary, Columbia, S.C., 1988. Ordained to ministry Evang. Luth. Ch. Am., 1988. Assoc. pastor Messiah Luth. Ch., South Williamsport, Pa., 1988-91; pastor St. Paul Luth. Ch., Biglerville, Pa., 1991—; organist Luth. Ch. of St. Mark, Glastonbury, Conn., 1981-84; pastoral assoc. St. Andrew's Luth. Ch., Columbia, S.C., 1985-86. City councilman Town of East Hartford, Conn., 1971-73, justice of the peace, 1970-74. With U.S. Army, 1968, Conn. NG, 1968-74. Named to Outstanding Young Men of Am., 1977. Republican. Lutheran. Home: 70 S View Dr Biglerville PA 17307 Office: St Paul Luth Ch PO Box 325 Biglerville PA 17307

LEPINE, ROBERT NEIL, radio station manager; b. Mpls., Jan. 12, 1956; s. James R. and Eileen S. (Cross) L.; m. Mary Ann Alaback, May 19, 1979; children: Amy Paricia, Katherine Ann, James Lloyd. BS in Communications, U. Tulsa, 1979. Sales rep. Sta. KCFO Radio, Tulsa, 1979-84; sales mgr. Sta. KRDS Radio, Phoenix, 1984; gen. mgr. Sta. KFIA Radio, Sacramento, 1985, Sta. KSLR Radio, San Antonio, 1985—; elder Fellowship Bible Ch., San Antonio, 1986—; mem. steering com. Nat. Christian Radio Seminar, 1990. Assoc. editor Mgmt. Editor, 1989—. Recipient Cert. of Recognition, Gospel Music Assn., Nashville, 1990, Award of Merit, Nat. Conf. Christians and Jews, Tulsa, 1979. Mem. Nat. Religious Broadcasters (sec. so. chpt. 1988-90). Office: Sta KSLR Radio 9601 McAllister Frwy San Antonio TX 78216

LEPP, TARA MARIE, physical education educator; b. Corning, Calif., June 26, 1958; d. Heinrich and Ila Jeane (Meents) L. BA, Calif. State U., Chico, 1980; MS, U. Oreg., 1982. Cert. athletic trainer. Student athletic trainer Calif. State U., Chico, 1979-80, U. Oreg., Eugene, 1980-81; exercise dir. Serenity Lane Alcohol Rehab. Ctr., Eugene, 1981-82; asst. prof. Linfield Coll., McMinnville, Oreg., 1982—, head athletic trainer, 1982—; leader/facilitator Children of Alcoholics, Linfield Coll., 1990; faculty Children's Summer Sports Program, Eugene, 1981. Contbr. articles to profl. jours. Med. coord. Oreg. Spl. Olympics, Eugene, 1981-82; med. trainer Athletes in Action Internat. Team, Scandinavia, 1986-87. Grad. teaching fellow U. Oreg., 1981-82. Mem. Nat. Athletic Trainers' Assn. Inc. (certification examiner 1984—), N.W. Athletic Trainers' Assn., Nat. Assn. Intercollegiate Athletics, Oreg. Athletic Trainers' Soc. (v.p. 1987-89), Oreg. Alliance of Health, Phys. Edn., Recreation and Dance, Fellowship of Chrisitan Athletes (leader 1985—), Sigma Beta Phi, Phi Kappa Phi. Avocations: bible study, cycling, camping, Nordic skiing, stained glass. Office: Linfield Coll 900 S Baker McMinnville OR 97128

LEPPICH, G(UY) MICHAEL, minister; b. St. Louis, Sept. 26, 1948; s. Joseph Willis and Mildred LaVerne (Gilbert) L.; m. Kathy Jo Elling, July 8, 1971; children: Janet, Julie, Daniel, Paul, Katherine. BA, Concordia Sr. Coll., Ft. Wayne, Ind., 1970; M in Div., Luth. Sch. Theology, Chgo., 1974; MEd, U. Mo., 1975. Ordained minister; lic. profl. counselor; cert. family mediator. Campus chaplain Ea. Ill. U., Charleston, 1971-72, U. Mo., St. Louis, 1972-75; pastor St. Timothy Luth. Ch., New Orleans, 1975-78; sr. pastor Our Savior Luth. Ch., McAllen, Tex., 1978-85; pastor Love Luth. Ch., New Orleans, 1985—. Mem. La. Mental Health Adv. Bd., New Orleans, 1987—; bd. dirs. Luth. Social Services, New Orleans, 1985—; numerous other activities. Mem. Am. Assn. for Counseling and Devel., (cert.) Am. Assn. Family Counselor and Mediators, Chi Sigma Iota. Lodge: Kiwanis (New Orleans) (v.p. 1978). Office: Love Lutheran Church 3730 MacArthur Blvd New Orleans LA 70114

LEPPIN, DANA MARIE, layworker; b. Berlin, Wis., Jan. 26, 1966; d. Harve E. and Arlene (Schatzke) L. Student, Carthage Coll., 1984-86; BS, U. Wis., 1986-88. Clown, layworker Carthage Coll., Kenosha, Wis., 1984-86; youth vol. 1st English Luth. Ch., Wisconsin Rapids, 1988-90; youth intern, dir. Evang. Luth. Ch. Am., Chgo., 1990—, Luth. Ch. Messiah, Lewiston, N.Y., 1990—; lifeguard YMCA, Niagara Falls, N.Y., 1990—. Mem. membership com. Wis. Social Svcs. Assn., 1988-90, Wis. Rapids Community Theater, 1989-90. Mem. Niagara Falls Little Theater.

LERUD, DAVID GLEN, minister; b. Salem, Oreg., Aug. 9, 1955; s. Glen Vernon and Audrey Veva (Ayers) LeR.; m. Claudia Ann Vick, June 15, 1979; children: Nathaniel David, Elizabeth Joy. BA, George Fox Coll., 1977; MDiv, Western Evang. Sem., 1980. Ordained to ministry Evang. Ch., 1980. Jr. high sch. youth pastor Salem (Oreg.) First Evang. Ch., 1977-79; asst. pastor music and edn. Wichita Evang. Ch., Milw., Oreg., 1979-83; assoc. pastor music and edn. Sweet Home (Oreg.) Evang. Ch., 1983-87; assoc. pastor music and worship Oreg. City Evang. Ch., 1987—; exec. officer Sweet Home Ministerial Assn., 1984-87; bd. dirs. Evang. Lit. Svc., Milw., Oreg., 1983-90. Dir. Choir Festival, Mid-Valley Festival of Choirs, 1985-87. Mem. Portland Area Evang. Mins. Assn., Western Evang. Sem. Alumni Assn. (bd. dirs. 1982-83). Home: 5370 SW Grove St West Linn OR 97068 Office: Oreg City Evang Ch 1024 Linn Ave Oregon City OR 97045

LESHER, WILLIAM ELTON, academic administrator; b. Pitts., May 24, 1932; s. Royal Elton and Ruth Minerva (Wagaman) L.: m. A. Jean Olson, Aug. 31, 1957; children: David William, Gregory Mark. BS, Wittenberg U., 1954; MDiv, Chgo. Luth. Theol. Sem., 1958; DD (hon.), Calif. Luth. Coll., 1075, Pacific U., Tacoma, Wash., 1975, Wittenberg U., 1987. Ordained to ministry Luth. Ch., 1958. Pastor Reen Meml. Luth., St. Louis, 1958-63, St. Luke Luth., Chgo., 1963-70; prof. Luth. Sch. Theol. Chgo., 1970-73, 1978—; pres. Pacific Luth. Sem., Berkeley, 1973-78. Author: It Will Be Your Duty, 1973. Mem. Bd. Global Mission Evang. Luth. Ch., Chgo., 1988—. Mem. Assn Theol. Schs. (pres. task force globalization 1986—). Democrat. Office: Luth Sch Theology Office Pres 1100 E 55th St Chicago IL 60615

LESJAK, RON FRANCIS, special education educator, deacon; b. Milw., Mar. 9, 1943; s. Joseph and Catherine (Wozniak) L.; m. Gail J., Nov. 26, 1966; children: Renee L., Sheri, Deanna C. BS in Spl. Edn., U. Wis.-Oshkosh, 1968; MS in Exceptional Edn., U. Wis.-Milw., 1971. Spl. educator Milw. Pub. Schs., 1968-70, Kenosha (Wis.) Unified Sch. Dist., 1971—. Deacon St. Mary's Parish, Milw., 1979—; coord. Kenosha County SHARE Food Program, 1985—; chairperson Archdioces of Milw. Deacon Personnel Bd., Milw., 1987-89. Mem. Coun. for Exceptional Children (treas. 1986-88, past pres. 1991-92), Nat. Assn. Deacon Orgn. (rep. 1990-92, newsletter editor 1990-92). Democrat. Roman Catholic. Avocations: golf, woodworking. Home: 4410 89th St Kenosha WI 53142 Office: Bradford High Sch 3700 Washington Rd Kenosha WI 53144

LESKE, ADRIAN MAX, minister, religion educator; b. Gumeracha, Australia, Apr. 14, 1936; arrived in Can., 1971; s. Wilhelm Theodor and Leonora Viola (Zacker) L.; m. Patricia Claire Kowald, May 5, 1961; children: Kylie Anne, Jane Patricia, Andrew Christopher. MDiv, Concordia Sem., St. Louis, 1960, MST, 1967, ThD, 1971. Ordained to ministry Luth. Ch.-Can., 1960. Parish min. Wellington, New Zealand, 1960-65, Waikerie, South Australia, Australia, 1966-69; asst. prof. religion, dean of students Concordia Coll., Edmonton, Alta., Can., 1971-75, assoc. prof. religion, head dept. religion, acad. dean, 1976-80, prof., 1980—, chmn. dept., 1978-81; mem. div. theology Luth. Coun. Can., 1978-81. Contbr. articles to theol. jours. Mem. Can. Soc. Study Religion, Can. Soc. Bibl. Studies, Soc. Bibl. Lit. Home: 10323 134th St, Edmonton, AB Canada T5N 2A9 Office: Concordia Coll, 7128 Ada Blvd, Edmonton, AB Canada T5B 4E4 *Reflecting the gracious love of God to one another, regardless of race, creed or color, can bring a very special element to society which makes life worthwhile.*

LESLIE, MARVIN EARL, minister; b. Boonville, Ind., Aug. 22, 1938; s. Ora Thomas and Mary Lucille (Kapperman) L.; m. Jenann Demuth, July 3, 1962; children: Elizabeth, Brian. BA, Bethel Coll., 1964; MDIV, Memphis Theol. Sem., 1967; D of Ministry, Valderbilt U., 1977; postgrad., Memphis State & Murray State U. Lic. profl. counselor, child care. Pastor Cumberland Presby. Ch., Springfield, Mo., 1967-73, Mayfield, Ky., 1973-75; pastor, assoc. pastor Cumberland Presby. Ch., Marshall, Tex., 1975-89; campus dir. Cumberland Presby. Children's Home, Denton, Tex., 1989-91; exec. dir. Cumberland Presby. Children's Home, 1991—; sec. interch. rels. com., Cumberland Presby. Ch., 1969-75, moderator, Tex. Synod, 1982-83, staled clk., 1986-89, moderator Mission Synod, 1990-91. Contbr. articles to profl. jours. Organizing chmn. Vol. Chaplains Assn., Marshall, 1979; pres. United Chs. Care Bd., Marshall, 1980, 81; chmn. Christmas in April Housing Project, Marshall, 1985. Lt. chaplains corps, USNR, 1971-80. Mem. Southwest Assn. Child Care Adminstrs., Optimist (sec. Marshall chpt. 1977-78), Kiwanis.

LESLIE, REO NAPOLEON, JR., minister, naval officer; b. Chgo., May 8, 1953; s. Reo Napoleon and Ernestine (Brown) L.; children: Erica, Hatshepsut. AA with high honors, Malcolm X Coll., 1973; BS with honors, Elmhurst Coll., 1974; MDiv, Garrett Theol. Sem., 1977; D of Ministry, Chgo. Theol. Sem., 1979; MS in Theology, McCormick Sem., 1982; MA in Internat. Rels., U.S. Internat. U., 1989; MS in Mgmt., Salve Regina Coll., 1990; MA in Nat. Security and Strategic Studies with distinction, Naval War Coll., 1990. Ordained to ministry United Ch. of Christ 1977. Chaplain Way Out Drug Abuse Ctr., Evanston, Ill., 1975-76, Evanston Twp. High Sch., 1976, Met. Ctr. for Corrections, Chgo., 1976-77; student liason person Univ. Ch., United Ch. of Christ, Chgo., 1977-78; protestant chaplain Westside VA Hosp., Chgo., 1978; chaplaincy dir. Community Hosp., Evanston, 1978-79; chaplain, spiritual dir. Boysville of Mich., Detroit, 1980-81; assoc. pastor Shrine of Black Madonna United Ch. of Christ, Detroit, 1972-81; commd. officer USN, 1981; advanced through grades to lt. comdr. Chaplain Corps USN, San Diego, 1981-91; chaplain Arlington (Va.) Nat. Cemetery USN, 1990-91; pastor Heritage United Ch. of Christ, Denver, 1992—; grad. adj. prof. Salve Regina Coll., Newport, R.I., 1990; bd. dirs. Ctr. for Studies of Person, La Jolla, Calif., 1988—. Author: Sermons for Stormy Seas, 1984, Peace in Troubled Waters, 1987, The Sacred and the Sword: How Religions View War, 1990; contbr. articles to profl. jours. Bd. dirs. San Diego County Ecumenical Conf., 1981-83, Jackie Robinson YMCA, San Diego, 1987-88. Recipient certs. of appreciation Bethel Bapt. Ch., San Diego, 1988, Newport Kiwanis Club, 1990, NAACP Newport Chpt., 1988, United Negro Coll. Fund San Diego Chpt.; recipient Navy Achievement Medal, USS Ranger, 1986, Community Svc. award Community Bapt. Ch., 1990, Spl. Recognition award S.E. Ministerial Alliance, 1989. Mem. Southeast Ministerial Alliance (sec. San Diego), Point Loma Ministerial Assn., Nat. Naval Officers Assn. Address: 2650 Jamacha Rd # 147 Rancho San Diego CA 92019 *Life is God's gift to us. What we do with our life is our gift to God. In order to fully live we must learn growing and glowing in God's name. In order to fully live we must learn from the past, prepare for the future and experience the present.*

LESLIE, ROBERT CAMPBELL, clergyman, counseling educator, writer; b. Concord, Mass., Oct. 20, 1917; s. Elmer Archibald and Helen Fay (Noon) L.; m. Paula Frances Eddy, June 14, 1941; children—William, Heather. A.B., DePauw U., 1939; S.T.B., Boston U., 1942, Ph.D., 1948. Lic. psychologist, Calif. Ordained to ministry United Methodist Ch., 1941; pastor The Methodist Ch., Peabody, Mass., 1941-43; chaplain Boston State Hosp., 1948-56; clin. assoc. Sch. Theology Boston U., 1948-56; prof. pastoral psychology Pacific Sch. Religion, Berkeley, Calif., 1956-82, prof. emeritus, 1983—,dean, 1979-80. Author: Jesus and Logotherapy, 1965; Sharing Groups in the Church, 1971; Man's Search for a Meaningful Faith, 1968, Health, Healing and Holiness, 1971; (with Wilhelm Wuellner) The Surprising Gospel, 1984; (with Margaret Alter) Sustaining Intimacy, 1978; (with Chiu Siok Hui) Between Person and Person, 1981; mem. editorial bd. Jour. Pastoral Care, 1965-82, Pastoral Psychology, 1959-67, Internat. Forum for Logotherapy, 1978—. Bd. dirs. Fred Finch Youth Ctr., Oakland, Calif., 1955—, pres., 1969. Served to maj. U.S. Army, 1943-46. Am. Assn. Theol. Schs. fellow, 1960; NIMH fellow, 1968. Fellow Am. Psychol. Assn., Inst. Logotherapy; mem. Am. Assn. Pastoral Counselors (Diplomate, Disting. Contbr. award 1983). Democrat. Home: 646 Santa Rosa Ave Berkeley CA 94707 Office: Pacific Sch Religion 1798 Scenic Ave Berkeley CA 94709

LESLIE, WILLIAM H(OUGHTON), minister; b. Norwalk, Ohio, July 10, 1932; s. William Houghton and Mildred (Wilkinson) L.; m. Adrienne Andrews, July 21, 1956 (div. July 1990); children: Laurel, Lisa, Andrews, Mark. Student, Bob Jones U., 1950-53; BA with honors, Wheaton (Ill.) Coll., 1954, MDiv, 1961; MA, Northwestern U., 1965, PhD, 1976. Ordained to ministry Bapt. Ch., 1957. Sr. pastor 1st Bapt. Ch., Pekin, Ill., 1956-59; asst. pastor Moody Meml. Ch., Chgo., 1959-61; sr. pastor La Salle St. Ch., Chgo., 1961-90; sr. assoc. Mid Am. Leadership Found., Chgo., 1990—; mem. faculty North Pk. Theol. Sem., Chgo., 1990—; frequent retreat and forum speaker. Contbr. articles to profl. jours. Pres. Chgo. Orleans Housing, Inc., 1970-87; bd. dirs. Just Life, Washington, 1986-90, Cabrini-Green Neighborhood Devel. Ptnrs., Chgo., 1986-89, Community Renewal Soc., Chgo., 1987—, Kesho Maruno, Chgo., 1988—, Internat. Urban Assocs., Chgo., 1989—, Community Youth Creative Learning Experience, Chgo., 1990—; gov. Opportunities Internat., Chgo., 1986—. Mem. Inst. for Spiritual Companionship (bd. dirs. 1986—), Inst. for Justice Ministries (bd. dirs. 1990—), Am. Acad. Religion, Soc. Bibl. Lit., Sem. Consortium for Urban Pastoral Edn. Home: 1300 Astor St Chicago IL 60610 Office: Mid Am Leadership Found 122 S Michigan Ave # 1250 Chicago IL 60603

LESNIEWSKI, SISTER SUZANNE (SISTER), religious education director; b. Chgo., Feb. 15, 1938; d. Harry and Pearl (Januchowski) Lesniewski. BA in History, Coll. St. Francis, Joliet, Ill., 1969; MA in Religious Edn., Mundelein Coll., 1975. Cert. Level III. Tchr., 1958-72; coord. religious edn. St. Matthew's Parish, Chamapign, Ill., 1972-76, Notre Dame Parish, Clarendon Hills, Ill., 1976-78; dir. religious edn. St. Mary's Parish, West Chgo., 1978-81, St. John the Baptist, Winfield, Ill., 1981-89, St. Joan of Arc, Lisle, Ill., 1989—. Mem. Nat. Coords. and Dirs. Religious Edn., Ill. Coords. and Dirs. Religious Edn. (pres., rep. Joliet Diocese), St. John the Baptist Parish Coun. and Bd. of Edn. Office: 4913 Columbia Lisle IL 60532

LESOURD, LEONARD EARLE, religious publisher, writer; b. Columbus, Ohio, May 20, 1919; s. Howard Marion and Lucile (Leonard) LeS.; m. Evelyn Chester, Aug. 21, 1948 (div. Mar. 1959); m. Catherine Marshall, Nov. 14, 1959 (dec. Mar. 1983); m. Sandra Jean Simpson, June 22, 1985; children: Linda, Chester, Jeffrey. BA, Ohio Wesleyan U., 1941. Editor Guideposts mag., N.Y.C., 1946-74; pub. Chosen Books, Tarrytown, N.Y., 1974—; pres. Breakthrough, Inc., Lincoln, Va., 1980—; elder First Presbyn. Ch., Delray Beach, Fla., 1968-77, New Covenant Presbyn. Ch., Pompono Beach, Fla., 1977-81; v.p. Prebyn. Reformed and Renewal Ministries, Oklahoma City, 1977. Author: Skybent, 1944, Strong Men, Weak Men, 1990; (with Catherine Marshall) My Personal Prayer Diary, 1978; editor: Touching The Heart of God, 1990; contbr. articles to Guidepost mag. Pres. PTA, Carmel, N.Y., 1956. 1st lt. USSAC, 1942-45. Mem. Fellowship Christian Athletes (sec., bd. dirs. 1970-76). Republican. Home: Evergreen Farm Lincoln VA 22078 Office: Breakthrough Inc Catherine Marshall Ctr Lincoln VA 22078 *I have discovered the key to achieving fulfillment in life is to be a servant. The more I serve others, the more God has blessed me with health, leadership roles and abundance.*

LESSARD, RAYMOND W., bishop; b. Grafton, N.D., Dec. 21, 1930. Student, St. Paul Sem., Am. Coll., Rome. Ordained priest Roman Catholic Ch. Mem. staff Congregation for Bishops, Roman Curia, 1964-73; consecrated bishop, 1973; bishop Diocese of Savannah Ga., 1973—. Office: Chancery 601 E Liberty St Savannah GA 31401-5196

LESTER, ANDREW DOUGLAS, religion educator, minister; b. Coral Gables, Fla., Aug. 8, 1939; s. Andrew and Dorothy (Atkinson) L.; m. Judith Laesser, Sept. 8, 1960; children: Scott Wayne, Denise Leanne. BA, Miss. Coll., 1961; BD, So. Bapt. Theol. Sem., 1964, PhD, 1968. Ordained to ministry Bapt. Ch., 1961. Min. to youth 1st Bapt. Ch., Memphis, 1960, Washington (Miss.) Bapt. Ch., 1960-61, Broadmoor Bapt. Ch., Jackson, Miss., 1961-62; pastor Buena Vista Bapt. Ch., Bryantsville, Ky., 1962-66; pastoral counselor Personal Counseling Svc., Jeffersonville, Ind., 1965-69; min. to youth Immanuel Bapt. Ch., Louisville, 1966-67; spl. instr. psychology and religion So. Bapt. Theol. Sem., Louisville, 1967-69, prof. psychology religion, 1976-91; asst. dir. dept. pastoral care N.C. Bapt. Hosp., 1969-70; prof. psychology and religion So. Bapt. Theol. Sem., Louisville, 1976-91; prof. pastoral care and psychology Brite Div. Sch., Tex. Christian U., Fort Worth, 1991—; dir. counseling svcs. N.C. Bapt. Hosp., 1970-71; marriage and family therapist Personal Counseling Svc., Inc., Clarkesville, Ind., 1965-69, 77-84; vis. prof. pastoral care Southeastern Bapt. Theol. Sem., 1972-77; vis. lectr. religion Grad. Sch., Wake Forest U., 1972-77. Author: Sex Is More Than a Word, 1973, It Hurts So Bad, Lord, The Christian Encounters Crisis, 1976, (with Judith L. Lester) Understanding Aging Parents, 1980; Coping with Your Anger: A Christian Guide, 1983, Pastoral Care for Children in Crisis, 1985, others; contbr. articles to profl. jours. Fellow Coll. Chaplains of Am. Protestant Hosp. Assn.; mem. Am. Assn. Pastoral Counselors (diplomate), Am. Assn. Marriage and Family Therapists. Democrat. Home: 6600 Castle Creek Dr Fort Worth TX 76132 Office: Tex Christian U Brite Div Sch Fort Worth TX 76129

LESTER, ROBERT CARLTON, religious studies educator; b. Lead, S.D., Feb. 1, 1933; s. Odell and Mary Olivia (Martin) L.; m. Donna Helene Larson, Apr. 15, 1954; children: Paul E., Charles F., R. Timothy. BA, U. Mont., 1955; BD, Yale U., 1958, MA, 1959, PhD, 1963. From asst. prof. to assoc. prof. Am. U., 1962-70; mem. faculty U. Colo., Boulder, 1970—, prof. religious studies, 1972—; vis. prof. Cornell U., 1968-69; vis. lectr. Dept. State., monthly, 1963-70; mem. faculty Humanities Inst, NEH, 1979. Author: Theravada Buddhism in Southeast Asia, 1973, Ramanuja on the Yoga, 1975, Srivacana Bhushana of Pillai Lokacharya, 1979, Buddhism: The Path to Nirvana, 1987. Ford. Found. fellow, 1960-62, Fulbright Hays fellow, 1967, 74-75, faculty fellow U. Colo., 1974-75, Am. Inst. of Indian Studies fellow, 1982-83, 88. Mem. Am. Acad. Religion, Assn. Asian Studies, Soc. Values in Higher Edn., Phi Kappa Phi. Office: U Colo Dept Religious Studies Boulder CO 80309

LESTER, TERRY THOMAS, pastor; b. Harrodsburg, Ky., Mar. 19, 1953; s. Za Thomas and Vivian (Romine) L.; m. Janet Coshgan, Dec. 28, 1974; children: Clay, Clark, Cary. BA, Georgetown (Ky.) Coll., 1975; MDiv, So. Bapt. Theol. Sem., 1978; D in Ministry, Lexington (Ky.) Theol. Sem., 1985. Asst. youth pastor Buckton Bapt. Ch., Frankfort, Ky., 1974-79; youth Makaksio (Hawaii) Bapt. Ch., summer 1975; pastor Red House Bapt. Ch., Richmond, Ky., 1979-87, First Bapt. Ch., London, Ky., 1987—; mem. exec. bd. Ky. Bapt. Conv., Cooksville, 1988-90; dir. Come-Unity Coop. Care, London, 1987—, Ky. Bapt. Homes for Children, 1989—. Author: From Within These Walls, 1979. Democrat. Office: First Bapt Ch 217 S Main London KY 40741

LESWING, JAMES BARTHOLOMEW, priest; b. Phila., Aug. 24, 1948; s. Herbert and Gladys Irene (MacFarlane) L.; children: Philip Brayton, Elizabeth Amadon. BA, Dickinson Coll., 1970; MDiv, Yale U., 1973. Ordained priest and deacon Episcopal Ch., 1973. Asst. rector St. Paul's Ch., Chatham, N.J., 1973-75; canon precentor St. Paul's Cathedral, Burlington, Vt., 1975-79; rector St. Peter's Ch., Monroe, Conn., 1979-88, St. Andrew's Ch., Downers Grove, Ill., 1988—; master of ceremonies The Diocese of Chgo., 1988—; mem. Diocesan Liturgical Commn., Chgo., 1988—, Task Force on Higher Edn., Chgo., 1990—; v.p. Downers Grove (Ill.) Ministerium, 1990—. Author: (study guide) Psalmody in Liturgy, 1991. Mem. Assn. of Diocesan Liturgy and Music Commns. Home: 1108 Franklin St Downers Grove IL 60515 Office: Saint Andrews Church 1125 Franklin St Downers Grove IL 60515

LETTOFSKY, ALAN BERNARD, religious organization administrator; b. Cleve., June 10, 1937; s. Phillip and Rose (Apple) L.; m. Jean Ann Loeb, Aug. 16, 1964; children: Sharon Rose, Deborah Meira, Seth Loeb. BA, Brandeis U., 1959; M. Hebrew Letters, Jewish Theol. Sem., N.Y.C., 1961; postgrad., Yale U., 1963-67; DD (hon.), Jewish Theol. Sem., N.Y.C., 1989. Ordained rabbi, 1963. Vis. prof. Seminario Rabinico, Buenos Aires, 1967-69; acting asst. prof. U. Va., Charlottesville, 1969-72; dir. B'nai B'rith Hillel, Madison, Wis., 1972-82; exec. dir. Cleve. Hillel, 1982—; pres. Assn. of Hillel/Jewish Campus Profs., 1980-82. Louis D. Brandeis hon. scholar, 1959, Cyrus Adler scholar, 1962; fellow Lehman Inst., 1960-63, Nat. Def. for Lang. Mem. Cleve. Bd. Rabbis (pres. 1989-91), Assn. for Jewish Studies (assoc.), Rabbinical Assembly, Reconstructionist Rabbinical Assembly, B'nai Brith. Office: Cleve Hillel 11291 Euclid Ave Cleveland OH 44106

LEVADA, WILLIAM JOSEPH, archbishop; b. Long Beach, Calif., June 15, 1936; s. Joseph and Lorraine (Nunez) L. B.A., St. John's Coll., Camarillo, Calif., 1958; S.T.L., Gregorian U., Rome, 1962, S.T.D., 1971. Ordained priest Roman Cath. Ch., 1961, consecrated bishop, 1983. Assoc. pastor Archdiocese of L.A., 1962-67, aux. bishop, vicar for Santa Barbara County, 1983-86; prof. theology St. John's Sem., Camarillo, Calif., 1970-76; ofcl. Doctrinal Congregation, Vatican City, Italy, 1976-82; exec. dir. Calif. Cath. Conf., Sacramento, 1982-84; archbishop Archdiocese of Portland in Oreg., 1986—. Trustee Cath. U. Am.; chmn. bd. dirs. Pope John XXIII Med.-Moral Rsch. and Edn. Ctr. Mem. Nat. Conf. Cath. Bishops (com. on doctrine, com. for pastoral letter on women in ch. and soc.), U.S. Cath. Conf., Cath. Theol. Soc. Am., Canon Law Soc. Am. Office: Archdiocese of Portland 2838 E Burnside St Portland OR 97214

LEVANG, PATSY LEE, principal; b. Williston, N.D., Sept. 2, 1949; d. Harry O. and Signe (Melland) Bredwick; m. Gary Vincent Levang, Nov. 22, 1972; children: Chad, Rhaegn, Margo. BS, N.D. State U., 1971. First Grade Profl. Educators cert. Adminstr., tchr. Johnson Corners Christian Acad., Watford City, N.D., 1982—; vol. Badlands gymnastics Watford City, 1983—. Sunday sch. tchr. Johnson Corners Wesleyan, Watford City, 1973—, youth leader, 1977-79, lady orgn. pres., 1978, 83. Republican. Home: HC03 Box 56 Keene ND 58847 Office: HCO3 Box 22 Watford City ND 58854

LEVANON, YOSEF, religion educator; b. Diar Beker, Turkey, June 1, 1941; came to U.S., 1970; s. Eliezer and Rahel (Aikurt) Bayaz; divorced; 1 child, Zohar. BA, Hebrew U., Jerusalem, 1965, cert. high sch. tchr., 1966, MA, 1969; postgrad., McGill U.; PhD, Clayton U., 1976. Dean Madrasha Coll., United Hebrew Schs., Detroit, 1971-78; ednl. cons. Bd. Jewish Edn., Milw., 1980-82; prin. Winnipeg Hebrew High Sch., Can., 1978-80; prof. Jewish history Spertus Coll. of Judaica, Chgo., 1982—; dir. religious edn. Niles Twp. Jewish Congregation, Skokie, Ill., 1982—; prof. Hebrew lang. and lit. No. Ill. U., DeKalb, 1990—. Author: Jewish Travellers in 12th Century, 1980. Sgt. Israeli armed forces, 1960-62. Mem. Nat. Assn. Temple Educators, Jewish Educators Assembly, Am. Assn. Jewish Educators. Republican. Home: 5845 N Virginia Ave Chicago IL 60659

LEVEILLE, WALTER HENRY, JR., minister, church official; b. Mt. Holly, N.J., Dec. 24, 1945; s. Walter H. and Virginia c. (Schute) L.; m. Susanne L. Just, Aug. 6, 1971; children: Heather Lynn, Scott David, Carrie Anne. BA, Toccoa Falls Coll., 1967; postgrad., Wheaton Coll., 1969-71, Trinity Sem., Newburgh, Ind., 1986—. Ordained to ministry Ind. Fundamental Chs. Am., 1971. Asst. pastor Christian and Missionary Alliance, Raleigh, N.C., 1967-68, Pinewood Alliance Ch., Longview, Tex., 1968-69; music dir. Cen. Bible Ch., Aurora, Ill., 1969-71; assoc. pastor The Chapel, Buffalo, 1971-83; exec. dir., TV-radio exec. producer LaHaye Ministries, San Diego, 1983-85; bus. mgr., dir. Christian edn. Shades Mountain Ind. Ch., Birmingham, Ala., 1985—; TV host World Vision Internat., Pasadena, Calif., 1979-80; dir. Vacation Bible Sch., Buffalo, 1973-82; summer missionary World Reach/Honduras, 1987; pres. bd. Jim Club Am., Bemus Point, N.Y., 1975-83; short-term missionary Guatemala, 1987, Honduras, 1988—, Peru, 1991—; pres. Leveille Assocs., Birmingham, 1989—. Author: (manuals) Youth Ministry, 1981, Leadership, 1987, Short-Term Missions, 1990, (book) A Commentary on the Book of Daniel, 1989. Bd. dirs. Christian Cen. Acad., Buffalo, 1980-83; exec. dir. Am. Coalition for Traditional Values, San Diego, 1984-85. Mem. Christian Ministries Mgmt. Assn., Evang. Theol. Soc., Evang. Tchr. Trainer Assn. (approved tchr.), Nat. Assn. Ch. Bus. Adminstrs. (v.p. local chpt. 1990), Delta Epsilon Chi, Eta Beta Rho. Republican. Avocations: trumpet, soloist, racquetball, reading, writing. Home: 582 Turtle Creek Dr Birmingham AL 35226 Office: Shades Mountain Ind Ch 2281 Old Tyler Rd Birmingham AL 35226

LEVELL, DORSEY E., ecumenical agency administrator. Exec. dir. Coun. Chs. of the Ozarks, Springfield, Mo. Office: Coun Chs of the Ozarks Box 3947 Springfield MO 65808*

LEVERINGTON, JAMES PATRICK, minister; b. Longmont, Colo., Nov. 23, 1950; s. Leonard Burdette and Nora Belle (Sims) L.; m. Katrella Ann Griffiths, Aug. 15, 1975; children: Kaley Elizabeth, Jared Steven. BA, U. Cen. Fla., 1978; MDiv, Southwestern Bapt. Sem., Ft. Worth, 1981. Ordained to ministry So. Bapt. Conv. Assoc. pastor Eastside Bapt. Ch., Orlando, Fla., 1975-77, Amb. Bapt. Ch., Orlando, 1977-78; pastor Woodbine (Tex.) Bapt. Ch., 1978-81, Victory Bapt. Ch., Orlando, 1982—; area com. coord. Inst. in Basic Life Principles, Orlando, 1985—. Author: (workbook) Foundations for Faith, 1988. Mem. Concerned Citizens of Orange County, Orlando, 1985-86, So. Baptists for Life, Ft. Worth, 1985—. Sgt. U.S. Army, 1970-73. Mem. Conservative Fellowship, Greater Orlando Bapt. Assn. (nat. Bapt. com. 1988—). Republican. Office: Victory Bapt Ch PO Box 720038 Orlando FL 32872

LEVESQUE, GEORGES-HENRI, priest, sociologist; b. Roberval, Que., Can., Feb. 16, 1903; s. Georges and Laura (Richard) L. B.A., Sem. de Chicoutimi, Que., 1923; Lecteur in Theology, Ottawa, Ont., 1930; Ph.D. in Sociology, U. Catholique de Lille, France, 1933; hon. doctorate, U. Vancouver, 1948, U. Man., 1950, U. Toronto, 1952, Antigonish U., 1953, U. Western Ont., 1953, Moncton U., 1954, U. Sask., 1961, U. Ottawa, 1961, Laval U., Que., 1963, U. Sherbrooke, 1967, McGill U., 1974, U. Montreal, 1976, Rwanda U., 1977, U. Quebec, Chicoutimi, 1985. Ordained priest Roman Catholic Ch., 1928; prof. social scis. U. Montreal (Que.), 1935-38; prof. social philosophy Laval U. (Que.), 1936-62, founder, 1st dean social scis., 1938-55; founder, 1st pres. Que. Coop. Council, 1939-44; mem. Que. Labour Council, 1941-51; co-founder Societe d'Education des Adultes, Camp Laquemac, 1944; mem. Que. Econ. Council, 1943, Can. Youth Commn., 1943-46; mem. Can. del co-chmn. Inter-Am. Seminar Social Studies, Havana, 1941; Can. del UNESCO Conf. on Adult Edn., Elsinore, Denmark, 1949; hon. v.p. Can U. Service Overseas, 1961-62; founder, 1st rector U. Nationale du Rwanda, Butare, 1963-71. Author (memoirs) Souvenances, 3 vols., 1983-89; founder, 1st dir., Ensemble mag., 1939; contbr. articles to jours. and mags. Mem. World Brotherhood, Geneva; mem. Internat. Assn. Non-Govt. Orgns., Brussels; mem. Can del. Conf. World Tensions, Bahia, Brazil, 1962; mem. Royal Commn. Devel. of Arts, Letters and Scis. (Can.), 1949-51; v.p. Can. Council, 1957-62; mem. Association Canadienne Francaise Avancement des Sciences, 1960-61. Decorated chevalier Legion d'Honneur France, 1950; decorated Internat. Cooperation medal, 1964; recipient Molson prize Can. Council, 1966, medal of Service, order of Can., 1967; decorated officer, 1972, companion, 1979, medal Les Anciens de l'Universite Laval, 1973; cp,dr/ Ordre National des Milles Colines Rwanda, 1977; honored by Que. Assembly of Bishops, 1979; recipient Royal Bank award, 1982. Fellow Royal Soc. Can. (v.p. 1962); mem. Societe des Ecrivains, Can. Polit. Sci. Assn. (pres. 1952), Union Internationale d'Etudes Sociales, Polish Inst. Arts and Scis., Inst. Man and Sci. of NYU. Home: 2715 Cote Ste-Catherine Rd, Montreal, PQ Canada H3T 1B6

LEVESQUE, LOUIS, bishop; b. Amqui, Que., Can., May 27, 1908; s. Philippe and Catherine (Beaulieu) L. B.A., Laval U., 1928, Ph.L., 1930, Th.D., 1932; S.S.L., Bib. Inst., Rome and Jerusalem, 1935. Ordained priest Roman Cath. Ch., 1932; tchr. holy scripture Rimouski, Que., 1936-51; bishop of Hearst, Ont., 1952-64; archbishop of Rimouski, 1964-73; Chmn. Canadian Cath. Conf., 1965-67; mem. Congregation Bishops, Rome, 1968-73. Mem. Cath. Bibl. Assn. Am. Home: 300 Ave du Rosaire, Rimouski, PQ Canada G5L 3E3

LEVIN, TONI ISOLA, lay worker; b. Pitts., Feb. 21, 1954; d. Anthony Eugene Isola and Anna Mae (Sherrock) Mong; m. John Richard Levin, June 7, 1986; 1 child, Rebecca. MA, Archdiocesan Catechetical Inst., St. Joseph's Sem., Dunwoodie, N.Y., 1986. Cert. dir. of religious edn., Archdiocese of N.Y. Coord. religious edn. St. Columba's Ch., N.Y.C., 1980-86; dir. religious edn. St. Agnes Ch., Greenwich, Conn., 1986-90, St. Patrick's Ch., Armonk, N.Y., 1986—. Mem. Nat. Cath. Edn. Assn. Roman Catholic. Home: Rockwood Rd Carmel NY 10512 Office: St Patrick's Ch PO Box 6 Armonk NY 10504

LEVINE, ERIC MICHAEL, religious organization administrator; b. Bronx, N.Y., July 7, 1952; s. Theodore Allen and Gloria Sondra (Rakow) L.; m. Roxanne Huberman, June 30, 1977. BA, CCNY, 1974; MSW, Yeshiva U., 1979. Cert. social worker, N.Y. Assoc. dir. CLAL-Nat. Jewish Ctr. for Learning and Leadership, N.Y.C., 1986-90; dir. L.I. United Jewish Appeal-Fedn. Jewish Philanthropies, Syosset, N.Y., 1990—; adj. asst. prof. Sch. of Social Work, Yeshiva U., N.Y.C., 1989-90; lectr. Stern Coll. for Women, Yeshiva U., 1982; mem. editorial bd. Jewish Social Work Forum, N.Y.C., 1986—; speaker, presenter in field. Contbr. articles to profl. publs. Bd. dirs. Hebrew Inst. of White Plains (N.Y.), 1990—. Mem. Soc. for Sci. Study of Religion, Am. Sociol. Assn., Assn. for Jewish Studies, Conf. of Jewish Communal Svcs., Nat. Assn. Social Workers, Religious Zionists Am. Office: LI United Jewish Appeal 6900 Jericho Turnpike Syosset NY 11791

LEVINE, HILLEL, rabbi, educator; b. Flushing, N.Y., May 28, 1946; s. Harold and Shirley (Peretz) L.; m. Shulamith Nebenzahl, Feb. 3, 1977; children: Hephzibah, Tiferet, Haninah. MA in Hebrew Lit., Jewish Theol. Sem. Am., 1967; MA, New Sch. for Social Rsch., 1969, Harvard U., 1971; PhD, Harvard U., 1974. Ordained rabbi, 1969. Prof. Yale U., New Haven, 1974-81, Boston U., 1981—. Author: The Kronika, 1984, Economic Origins of Antisemitism, 1991, Death of an American Jewish Community, 1992. Kent fellow Danforth Found., 1969-74, Lady Davis fellow, 1976-77; NEH rsch. grantee, 1978-81; U.S. exch. scholar to China, 1989. Mem. Am. Sociol. Assn., Assn. for Judaic Studies, Elizabethan Club, Harvard Club. Office: Boston U Religion Dept 745 Commonwealth Ave Boston MA 02215

LEVINE, SAMUEL BRUCE, minister; b. Little Rock, Sept. 9, 1949; s. Sam L.; m. Marlene Hauser, Jan. 10, 1971; children: Amanda, Silas. BA, Southwestern U., Memphis, Tenn., 1971; MDiv, Pitts. Theol. Seminary, 1977, D of Ministry, 1986. Asst. pastor Bethany Presbyn. Ch., Bridgeville, 1977-79, Frist Presbyn. Ch., Vero Beach, Pa., 1979-83; pastor Pacific Presbyn., Ballwin, Mo., 1983-89, Faith Presbyn. Ch., Des Peres, Mo., 1989—; founder I-44 Coop. Parish, Mo., 1986-89; asst. chmn. outdoor ministry com., 1989, others. Pres. PTO, Pacific, 1988, v.p. sch. bd., 1985-88; v.p. Pacific Soccer Assn., 1987-88; pres. Pacific Food Pantry, 1985-89. Home: 583 Bridgebend Manchester MO 63021 Offide: Faith Presbyterian Church 823 N Ballas Des Peres MO 63021

LEVINESS, PETER OSMUND, religious counselor; b. N.Y.C., July 17, 1958; s. Osmund William and Claudia (Speicher) LeV.; m. Roberta Harrison, July 28, 1984. B.A., Brown U., 1980, MA Boston Coll., 1988. Asst. group supr. Kolbourne Sch., New Marlborough, Mass., summer 1980; mem. staff Campus Crusade for Christ, Springfield, Mass., 1982-86. Recipient Russell Callow Meml. award U.S. Rowing Assn., 1979. Home and Office: 90 South St Apt 1 Westborough MA 01581

LEVOVITZ, PESACH ZECHARIAH, rabbi; b. Poland, Sept. 15, 1922; came to U.S., 1923; s. Reuben and Leah Zlate (Kustanowitz) L.; m. Bluma D. Feder, Feb. 5, 1945 (dec. 1970); children: Sivya, Yaakov; m. Eleanore Herman Klugmann, 1972 (dec. Nov. 1980); children: Maurice, Danny, Renee, Jackie; m. Frayde Twersky Perlow, Dec. 18, 1989; stepchildren: Yitzchok, Faige, Joseph. B.A., Yeshivah U., 1942. Rabbi Mesivtha Tifereth Jerusalem Rabbinical Sem., 1943, Congregation Sons of Israel, Lakewood, N.J., 1944—; founder, 1945; since dean Bezalel Day Sch.; Pres. Rabbinical Council Am., 1966-68, chmn. commn. on internat. affairs, 1972; asso. chmn. Soviet Jewry commn., 1980; mem. exec. com. Synagogue Council Am., 1953—; standing com. Conf. European Rabbis and Asso. Rabbis, 1964—; steering com. World Conf. Ashkenazi and Sephardi Synagogues; Co chmn. rabbinic cabinet Bonds for Israel, 1972; chaplain Lakewood Police Dept., 1950—; vis. chaplain Naval Air Sta., Lakehurst, N.J., 1945—; nat. chmn. ann. conv. Rabbinical Council of Am., 1971; v.p. Religious Zionists Am., 1974; nat. chmn. Vaad Haroshi Religious Zionists Am., 1975; pres. Beth Din of Am., 1986. Mem. adv. bd. Lakewood Housing Council, Nat. Community Relations Adv. Council, United Jewish Appeal; chmn. bd. Sons of Israel Sr. Citizens Housing Inc., 1980; mem. N.J. Drug Utilization Council.; chmn. adv. council on protection kosher legislation to Atty. Gen., State of N.J.; mem. exec. Ocean County Jewish Fedn., 1988. Recipient Revel Meml. award in religion and religious edn. Yeshivah Coll. Alumni Assn., 1967; award for outstanding rabbinic leadership Union of Orthodox Jewish Congregations Am., 1969; Nat. Assn. Hebrew Day Schs., 1980; chief Rabbi Issas Halevi Herzog Torah Fellowship award Religious Zionists Am., 1972; chmn. nat. conv., 1974; named Rabbi of Yr., Israel Bond Orgn., 1991. Mem. Conf. Presidents Nat. Jewish Orgns., Am. Conf. Soviet Jewry. Home: 631 8th St Lakewood NJ 08701 Office: Congregation Sons of Israel Madison Ave at 6th St Lakewood NJ 08701

LEVY, GLORIANN, adult education director; b. Bklyn., Oct. 20, 1943; d. Henry H. and Cele (Ehrlich) Grayman; m. Mark Bert Levy, Aug. 19, 1973; children: Jonathan, Daniel. BA, Hebrew U., Jerusalem, 1968, cert. tchr., 1968; MA, NYU, 1973. Cert. tchr., N.Y. Regional dir. Manhattan Young Judaea, N.Y.C., 1971-76; dir. United Synagogue Youth, Birmingham, Ala., 1978-84; Hebrew tchr. Temple Beth El, Birmingham, 1978-84; field worker United Synagogue Am., Port Jefferson, N.Y., 1984-87; tchr. of Judaic studies Solomon Schechter Day Sch., Commack, N.Y., 1984-85; dir. adult edn. Greater Hartford Jewish Community Ctr., West Hartford, Conn., 1987—. Mem. Emanuel Sisterhood (edn. v.p. 1989—). Office: Greater Hartford Jewish Community Ctr 335 Bloomfield Ave West Hartford CT 06117

LEWALLEN, ELINOR GRACE KIRBY, organization executive, lay church worker; b. Miltonvale, Kans., May 17, 1919; d. Osbourn Eddy and Grace Dale (Gorrell) Kirby; m. Thomas Monroe Lewallen, Jr., Aug. 14, 1948; children: Janet, Dean, Gary, Kent. BA, Baker U., 1943; postgrad., U. Colo., 1969-70, Iliff Sch. Theology, Denver, 1986, 90. Youth pres. Kans. Conf. United Meth. Youth, Baldwin, Kans., 1940-41; program dir. for young adults YWCA, Rockford, Ill., Denver, 1943-48; nat. pres. Fedn. Parents and Friends of Lesbians and Gays, Denver, 1987-88, chmn. Fedn. Parents-FLAG Religious Issues Task Force, 1988—; rsch. sec. values study Iliff Sch. Theology, 1977-84; numerous leadership roles Park Hill United Meth. Ch., Denver, 1953—, del. to ann. conv., Colo., 1979-88; mem. conf. task force on AIDS, Rocky Mountain Conf., 1986—, mem. com. on sexuality ministries, 1981—; presenter United Meth. Gen. Conf. Com. To Study Homosexuality, St. Louis, 1991. Chmn. impact neighborhood task force Denver Anti-Crime Coun., 1972-80; election judge, Denver 1981—; mem. Colo. Gov.'s Adv. Coun. on AIDS, 1987-88. Recipient award of recognition Denver Anti-Crime Coun., 1980, Outstanding Leadership award Nat. Fedn. Parents and Friends Lesbians and Gays, 1988. Mem. LWV, Assn. Group Workers (charter Colo. chpt.). Democrat. Home: 2258 Krameria St Denver CO 80207 *The images I have gathered through many years of growing and sharing in the world of so many beautiful gay/lesbian people would by now create a rose window in a cathedral. I stand in awe that our children are finding their strength without role models, their direction without roadmaps for their remarkable journeys. They are discovering their power through the testing of their spirits. They are walking through deep waters as many with AIDS daily face their mortality. They are leaving legacies of creativity, courage, and caring. How can I as parent, a friend and a committed Christian do less?.*

LEWIS, ALBERT L., former religious organization administrator, rabbi. Former pres. Rabbinical Assembly, N.Y.C. Office: Rabbinical Assembly 3080 Broadway New York NY 10011*

LEWIS, SIR ALLEN, former governor-general of St. Lucia; b. Oct. 26, 1909; s. George Ferdinand Montgomery and Ida Louisa (Barton) L.; m. Edna Leofride Theobalds, 1936; 5 children. Ed., St. Mary's Coll., St. Lucia; LL.B. with honours, U. London, 1941; LLD (hon.) U. West Indies, 1974. Bar: St. Lucia 1931, England 1946. Pvt. practice law, Windward Islands, 1931-59; acting magistrate, St. Lucia, 1940-41; acting Puisne Judge, Windward and Leeward Islands, 1955-56; judge Fed. Supreme Ct., West Indies, 1959-62, British Caribbean Ct. of Appeal, 1962, Ct. of Appeal, Jamaica, 1962-67, acting pres. Ct. of Appeal, 1966, acting chief justice, Jamaica, 1966, Chief justice West Indies Associated States Supreme Ct., 1967-72; chmn. Nat. Devel. Corp., St. Lucia, 1972-74; chancellor U. West Indies, 1975-89; gov. St. Lucia, 1974-79, gov.-gen., 1979-80, 82-87. Author: Revised Edition of Laws of St. Lucia, 1957. Ch. warden Holy Trinity Ch., 1939-59, mem. parochial coun., 1935-59, Island Ch. coun., 1935-59, also sec.; tchr., supr. Sunday sch.; mgr. Island Ch. schs.; mem. legis. counc., St. Lucia, 1943-51, Castries Town Council, 1942-56; pres. West Indies Senate, 1958-59; bd. dirs. St. Lucia br. Brit. Red. Cross Soc., 1955-59; active numerous govt. and pub. coms. on edn. and govt.; patron St. Lucia Assn. for Retarded Children, 1975—, St. Lucia Branch, Brit. Commonwealth Ex-Services League, 1975-80, 1983-87. Decorated Coronation medal, 1953; knight bachelor, 1968, knight Order of St. John of Jerusalem, 1975; Queen's Jubilee medal, 1977; knight grand cross of St. Michael and St. George, 1979; knight grand Cross Royal Victorian Order, 1985; grand cross Order of Saint Lucia, 1986, Order of Andres Bello (Venezuela), 1986; knight comdr. Order of St. Gregory, 1991. Anglican. Clubs: Golf, Yacht (St. Lucia). Avocation: gardening. Address: Beaver Lodge, The Morne PO Box 1076, Castries Saint Lucia

LEWIS, ALVIN THOMAS, minister, missionary; b. Meeteetse, Wyo., Aug. 21, 1912; s. Fred Thomas and Earnie Earl (Knauss) L.; m. Minnie L. Wallace, Apr. 19, 1941; children: Anita, Ruth, Flora, Hilma. AB, Westmont Coll., 1946. Ordained to ministry Evang. Ch., 1942. Missionary The Orinoco River Mission, Venezuela, S.Am., 1939-80; missionary Evang. Alliance Mission (merged with Orinoco River Mission), Wheaton, Ill., 1980-82, ret., 1982. Mem. S.W. Info. Svcs. Home: 2404 Cactus St Silver City NM 88061 *Human history is God's manuscript. His fingerprints are everywhere. The thoughtful will discern them, the heedless will pass by.*

LEWIS, CECIL DWAIN, minister; b. Dayton, Ohio, June 30, 1929; s. Clyde Dexter and Ina Candice (Harmon) L.; m. Jacqueline Ann Jones, July 29, 1951; children: Cynthia Lewis Parker, Constance Lewis Bunker. BA, Bob Jones U., 1951; MDiv, Grace Theol. Sem., Winona Lake, Ind., 1957; MA, Chapman Coll., 1972; postgrad., U.S.A. Chaplain Sch., 1973; PhD, Calif. Grad. Sch. Theology, Rosemead, 1991. Ordained to ministry Bapt. Ch., 1950. Asst. pastor Riverside Bapt. Ch., Decatur, Ill., 1951-54; pastor 1st Bible Ch., New Castle, Ind., 1961-64, Flint, Mich., 1964-66; commd. 1st lt. U.S. Army, 1966, advanced through grades to lt. col., 1980; chaplain U.S. Army, various places in U.S. and Vietnam, 1966-86; ret. U.S. Army, 1986; pastor Harmony Bapt. Ch., Waynesville, Mo., 1988-89; adj. prof. Drury Coll., 1984-90. Author: Training for Lay Leaders, 1981; tech. advisor, writer: (film) In Beginning, 1980; developer tng. programs for U.S. Army chaplaincy, 1978-82; contbr. articles to profl. jours. Bd. regents Liberty U., Linchburg, Va. Decorated Bronze Star (2); recipient Army Commendation award for heroism (3). Mem. Am. Assn. Marriage and Family Therapists. Home: R2 Box 131A Lake Forrest Heights Siloam Springs AR 72761

LEWIS, DANIEL JOSEPH, pastor; b. Billings, Mont., Apr. 7, 1950; s. Clarence Willis and Elaine Mallory (Gripe) L.; m. Margaret Lee Lewis, July 24, 1970; children: James, Travis, Chadney. B in Religious Edn., William Tyndale Coll., Farmington Hills, Mich., 1984; MA, U. Detroit, 1986. Dean of men Cascade Bible Coll., Portland, Oreg., 1973-75; dean of students Jackson (Miss.) Coll. Ministries, 1976-81; sr. pastor Troy (Mich.) Christian Chapel, 1981-90; adj. faculty Robert H. Whitaker Sch. Theology, Detroit, 1986-89, William Tyndale Coll., 1986-89, alumni pres., 1986-90, dir., African Christian Ministries, Detroit; sec. Diakonos, Inc., Bloomfield Hills, Mich., 1986-90. Contbr. articles to profl. jours. Active Christian Emphasis Birmingham (Mich.) YMCA, 1987-90. Recipient Gary Sovereign Meml. award William Tyndale Coll., 1984, Viola Mayhew award in Bible and Theology, 1984. Mem. Soc. Bibl. Lit., Global Christian Ministries. Home: 390 E Long Lake Rd Troy MI 48098 Office: Troy Christian Chapel 400 E Long Lake Rd Troy MI 48098

LEWIS, DONNA RUTH, lay church worker; b. Auburn, N.Y., Feb. 19, 1953; d. Harry Freeman and Marjorie Ruth (Russell) Phillips; m. William Ansil Lewis, Aug. 29, 1971; children: Mark, Heather, Jason, Kimberly. Student, Auburn Community Coll., 1970, Nazarene Bible Coll., Colorado Springs, Colo., 1972-73. Missionary pres. Hurdsfield (N.D.) Nazarene Ch., 1974-75; dir. vacation Bible sch. Seneca Falls (N.Y.) Nazarene Ch., 1975, publicity sec., 1975-77; publicity sec., youth dir. Atlasburg (Pa.) Nazarene Ch., 1983-87; leader ladies Bible study St. Petersburg (Pa.) Nazarene Ch., 1979-83; youth dir. Claytonia Nazarene Ch., West Sunbury, Pa., 1987-89; mem. woman's ministry coun. Pitts. dist. Ch. of Nazarene, Butler, Pa., 1988—, sec. missionary publicity, 1989; dir. family camp craft Pitts. Dist. Ch. of the Nazarene, Butler, 1980-85. Recruiter Right to Life, Washington, Pa., 1983-87; counselor Slippery Rock (Pa.) Crisis Pregnancy Ctr., 1987—; adv. family svc. project Mental Health Assn., Butler, 1988-90; coun. mem., playgroup leader Schuyler County Family Resource Ctr., Montour Falls, N.Y., 1977-79; art instr. Burgettstown (Pa.) Pub. Libr., 1984-86; speaker LIFT Ladies Bible Study Group retreat, Emlenton, Pa., 1987. Mem. Sunbury Clergy Wives (leader, pres., founder 1989—). Home: RD 1 Box 1066 Halston Rd West Sunbury PA 16061 *I have come to realize that there is nothing I am doing in the world of work, no matter how high I go, that can't be done by somebody else. But nobody else can do for my children what I can do: be their mother.*

LEWIS, DOUGLAS, art historian; b. Centreville, Miss., Apr. 30, 1938; s. Charles Douglas and Beatrice Fenwick (Stewart) L. B.A. in History; B.A. in History of Art, Yale U., 1960, M.A., 1963, Ph.D., 1967; B.A. in Fine Arts, Clare Coll., Cambridge (Eng.) U., 1962, M.A., 1966. Asst. in instrn. Yale U., 1962-64; asst. prof. art Bryn Mawr Coll., 1967-68; vis. lectr. U. Calif., Berkeley, spring 1970, fall 1979; adj. prof. Johns Hopkins U., 1973-77; curator sculpture and decorative arts Nat. Gallery Art, Washington, 1968—; professorial lectr. Georgetown U., 1980—; adj. prof. U. Md., 1988—; mem. art adv. com. Mt. Holyoke Coll. Art Mus.; vis. com. Smith Coll. Mus. Art; vice-chmn. nat. citizens stamp adv. com. U.S. Postal Service; adv. bd. Centro Palladiano, Vicenza, Italy, Friends of Benaki Mus. in Am. Author: The Late Baroque Churches of Venice, 1979, The Drawings of Andrea Palladio, 1981, intro. to Renaissance Master Bronzes, 1986. Mem. Am. fellowship com., Belgian-Am. Ednl. Found.; bd. dirs. Bauman Found. Recipient Copley medal Nat. Portrait Gallery, 1981; Chester Dale fellow; David E. Finley fellow Nat. Gallery Art, 1964-67; Rome Prize fellow Am. Acad. Rome, 1964-66. Mem. Coll. Art Assn. Am., Soc. Archtl. Historians, Nat. Trust Historic Preservation, Washington Collegium for the Humanities (adv. bd.), Manuscript Soc. Episcopalian. Clubs: Yale (N.Y.C.); Falcons (Cambridge U.). Office: Nat Gallery Art Washington DC 20565

LEWIS, EDWARD ALAN, religious organization adminstrator; b. Brazil, Ind., July 22, 1946; s. Edward and Ruth Margaret (Eberwein) L. B in Music Edn., Grace Coll., 1969; M in Divinity, Grace Sem., 1973. Asst. to pastor, youth dir. Grace Brethren Ch., Winona Lake, Ind., 1969-73; nat. dir. youth ministries Grace Brethren Ch. Christian Edn., Winona Lake, 1973-85; dir. candidate personnel Grace Brethren Fgn. Missions, Winona Lake, 1982-88; exec. dir. Grace Brethren Ch. Christian Edn., Winona Lake, 1985—. Mem. Grace Brethren Ch., Winona Lake, 1969—, exec. mem. denominational youth com., 1984—. Mem. Grace Sem. Alumni Assn. (pres. 1984-85), Ind. Dist. Ministerium, Nat. Ministerium Assn. Avocations: music, piano, singing, jogging, travel. Home and Office: PO Box 365 Winona Lake IN 46590

LEWIS, G. DOUGLASS, seminary president; m. Shirley Savage; children: Laura, Douglass Jr. BA, U. Tenn., 1957; BD, Vanderbilt U., 1960; PhD, Duke U., 1966. Ordained to ministry United Meth. Ch., 1966. Tchr., chaplain Tenn. Wesleyan Coll., 1964-67; dir. nat. coop. enlistment project Nat. Coun. Chs., 1967-71; dir. leadership program Inst. for Ministry Devel., 1971-74, bd. dirs.; instr., dir. field and D of Ministry programs Hartford (Conn.) Sem., 1974-82; pres. Wesley Theol. Sem., Washington, 1982—; mem. commn. on theol. edn. Univ. Senate, United Meth. Ch., com. on global higher edn. Bd. Higher Edn. and Ministry. Author: Resolving Church Conflicts, 1981; also articles. Chmn. bd. Ctr. for Parish Devel.; bd. dirs. Plowshares Inst. Mem. Assn. United Meth. Theol. Sch. (chair com. on global theol. edn.), Assn. Theol. Schs. in U.S. and Can. (chair com. on theol. edn. mgmt.). Office: Wesley Theol Sem 4500 Massachusetts Ave NW Washington DC 20016

LEWIS, GILES FLOYD, JR., priest; b. Orlando, Fla., Sept. 22, 1927; s. Giles Floyd and Florence Meriam (Baldwin) L.; m. Dorothy Jane Tauber, Oct. 3, 1957; children: Henrietta, Giles, Celia, Nathaniel. BS, Clemson Coll., 1949; MDiv, U. of South, 1957. Ordained to ministry Episcopal Ch. as deacon, 1957, as priest, 1958. Min.-in-charge All Saints Ch., Clinton, S.C., 1957-60; min.-in-charge Epiphany Ch., Laurens, S.C., 1957-60, priest-in-charge, 1960-63; asst. Christ Ch., Greenville, S.C., 1964; assoc. rector Christ Ch., Lexington, Ky., 1965-67; rector Bartholomew's Ch., Nashville, 1967-71; assoc. rector Ch. of St. John the Divine, Houston, 1972—; chaplain Tex. chpt. Soc. Companions of Holy Cross. Bd. dirs. Epilepsy Assn. Houston and Gulf Coast. Home: 6127 Longmont St Houston TX 77057 Office: Ch of St John the Divine 2450 River Oaks Blvd Houston TX 77019

LEWIS, GLENN JOSEPH, pastor; b. Louisville, June 23, 1960; s. Leonard Kenneth and Beverly Hope (Taylor) L.; m. Dorothy Jean Hudson, Feb. 5, 1983; children: Tricia, Renee, Lewis. BA in Theology, Andrews U., 1987; Mdiv, Andrews Theol. Sem., 1990. Pastor Wis. Conf. 7th Day Adventists, Madison, 1990—. With U.S. Army, 1979-83. Home and Office: 5907 Rattman Rd Madison WI 53704

LEWIS, HARVEY DELLMOND, JR., clergyman, educator; b. Florence, Tex., Jan. 29, 1918; s. Harvey Dellmond and Rosell Hawkins (Whittenberg) L.; m. Marie Frances Fuscia, Feb. 19, 1945; children—Olan Harvey, Rosell Marie Lewis Carr, Frances Ann Lewis Smith. B.A., Baylor U., 1939; Th.M., Southwestern Bapt. Theol. Sem., 1942; D.D. (hon.), Univ. Mary Hardin Baylor, 1980. Ordained to ministry So. Bapt. Conv., 1937. Pastor Calvary Bapt. Ch., Port Acres, Tex., 1946-48, First Bapt. Ch., Cleveland, Tex., 1948-51, First Bapt. Ch., Kerrville, Tex., 1951-55, Harlandale Bapt. Ch., San Antonio, 1955-58, First Bapt. Ch., Mt. Pleasant, Tex., 1958-63, Central Bapt. Ch., Marshall, Tex., 1963-76; v.p. devel. East Tex. Bapt. U., Marshall, 1976-84, dir. planned giving, 1984-85, acting pres., 1985-86; moderator Tryon Evergreen Assn., Bapt. Gen. Conv., 1949-51; trustee San Marcos Bapt. Acad., Tex., 1955-60, East Tex. Bapt. U., 1959-68, 70-77, Mex. Bapt. Bible Inst., San Antonio, 1955-58. Served chaplain USAAF, 1942-46. Mem. Marshall C. of C. Lodge: Masons (32 degree). Home: 3401 Indian Springs Marshall TX 75670 Office: East Tex Bapt Univ 1209 N Grove Marshall TX 75670

LEWIS, JAMES FREDRICK, educator; b. Ottumwa, Iowa, June 21, 1937; s. Frederick Roscoe and Alma Marie (Lumsdon) L.; m. Marylan Lois Johnson, June 21, 1958; children: Daniel, Amy, Timothy. BA, Bethel Coll., 1960; MDiv, Bethel Theol. Sem., 1963; PhD, U. Iowa, 1976. Pastor Hartwick (Iowa) Congl. Ch. United Ch. Christ, 1973-76; asst. prof. world religion, chairperson theology/religion Union Bibl. Sem., Pune/Yavatmal, India, 1977-81; assoc. prof. bibl. studies and world religion St. Paul Bible Coll. (now Crown Coll.), St. Bonifacius, Minn., 1981—; chairperson bible and theology dept. St. Paul Bible Coll. (now Crown Coll.), St. Bonifacius, 1981—; cons., evaluator Commn. on Insts. of Higher Edn., North Cen. Assn. of Colls. and Schs., Chgo., 1986—. Author: (with William Travis) Religious Traditions: Historical and Evangelical Perspectives, 1991. Mem. City Planning Commn., Waco, Tex., 1965-66; cert. ESL tutor Minn. Literacy Coun., Mpls., 1985-86. Mem. Am. Acad. Religion, Assn. of Profs. of Mission, Assn. Evang. Profs. Mission, The Evang. Theol. Soc. Republican. Office: Crown Coll Hwy 92 Saint Bonifacius MN 55375

LEWIS, JAY ARLAN, lay worker; b. Harvey, N.D., Nov. 29, 1962; s. Alden Wallace and Dorothy Lillian (Sand) L.; m. Valerie Jean Cummings, June 22, 1985; children: Terra Winona, Christian Victor, Valerie Mikel. Grad. in elec. tech., N.D. State Sch. of Sci., Wahpeton, 1982. Youth leader LeKoop Ministries, Bird Island, Minn., 1982-85, Word of Faith Ch., Willmar, Minn., 1985-87, Youth Alive, Hastings, Minn., 1989—, Jubilee Christian Ch., Hastings, 1989—; dir. Youth Alive Summer Camp, Paynesville, Minn., 1990—; elec. contractor Metro-Wide Electric, Cottage Grove, Minn., 1991—. Home: 7575 80th St South Cottage Grove MN 55016 Office: Jubilee Christian Church Po Box 54 Hastings MN 55033-0054

LEWIS, JEANETTE (JAN LEWIS), lay worker; b. Waco, Tex., Aug. 7, 1941; d. Ennis E. and Violet Oma Lee (Lamb) Jarrard; divorced; children: Cheryl Lewis Hulon, Paul Ennis. Grad. in pers. adminstrn., Tulsa Jr. Coll., 1989; postgrad., Oklahoma City U., 1990—. Organist various chs. Tex., 1960-84; vol., youth worker New Haven United Meth. Ch., Tulsa, 1986-88; program coord. 1st United Meth. Ch., Pryor, Okla., 1989-90; dir. singles and youth Linwood United Meth. Ch., Oklahoma City, 1990—; coord. Okla. Conf. Youth Vols. in Mission, 1990—, Okla. Conf. Single Adult Vols. in Mission, 1991; dean Okla. Conf. Singles Retreat, 1991. Mem. Okla. Youth Ministries Network, Bus. and Profl. Women Club (program chair 1983-84), Nat. Singles Leader Assn., Optimist Club (charter). Democrat. Office: Linwood United Meth Ch 3034 NW 17th Oklahoma City OK 73107

LEWIS, JEROME WHITNEY, minister; b. Binghamton, N.Y., Oct. 29, 1951; s. John Gregory and Cora Belle (Whitney) L.; m. Brenda Nina Gordon, Aug. 18, 1973; children: Timothy, Amy, Daniel. BS, Nyack Coll., 1975. Ordained to ministry Christian and Missionary Alliance, 1986. Bible study leader Bklyn. Gospel Team, Nyack, N.Y., 1969-75; youth leader 1st Bapt. Ch., Concord, N.H., 1976-81; asst. pastor Bethany Alliance Ch., Stratford, Conn., 1981-83; pastor Valley Alliance Ch., Nelliston, N.Y., 1986-89, Hambden Alliance Ch., Chardon, Ohio, 1989—; v.p. Mid Mohawk Valley Ministerium, Nelliston, 1984-85, pres., 1985-86. Home and Office: 9892 Old State Rd Chardon OH 44024

LEWIS, KEVIN, religion educator; b. Asheville, N.C., July 13, 1943; s. Burdett Gibson and Phebe Ann (Clarke) L.; m. Harriet Kirby, Aug. 9, 1969 (div. 1976); m. Becky Wingard, Dec. 23, 1976; children: Jacob, Helen. BA, Harvard U., 1965, St. John's Coll., Cambridge, Eng., 1967; MA, St. John's Coll., 1971, U. Chgo., 1969; PhD, U. Chgo., 1980. Asst. prof. religious studies Univ. S.C., Columbia, 1973-87; assoc. prof., 1987—; vis. rsch. fellow Durham Univ., Eng., 1985-86; Fulbright sr. lectr. Jagiellonian Univ., Krakow, Poland, 1988-89. Contbr. articles, reviews, poetry to profl. publs. Presbyn. grad. fellow Presbyn. Ch., 1970-72; named Outstanding Educator Am., Univ. S.C., 1975. Mem. Am. Acad. Religion, Brit. Conf. on Lit. and Religion, MLA, S.C. Acad. Religion (pres. 1983-84), Harvard Club of S.C. (sec.-treas. 1979-83), Penn Club (London), Sport Lit. Assn. Home: 4109 Parkman Dr Columbia SC 29206 Office: U SC Dept Religious Studies Columbia SC 29208

LEWIS, LARRY GENE, SR., minister; b. Ft. Worth, Dec. 27, 1945; s. Roger Valentine L. and Bertha (McKay) Kujala; m. Mona Letteljohn, Jan. 15, 1975 (div. 1985). Evangelist New Testament Fellowship, Dallas, 1986-87; assoc. pastor Good Shepperd Ch., Ft. Worth, 1986, World of Life Tabernacle, Dallas, 1986-88, Harritage Hts. Ch., Ft. Worth, 1988-90; evangelist Gospel Mins. & Chs. Inst., Phoenix, 1990—; window cleaner Tex. Window Cleaning, Ft. Worth, 1970—. With U.S. Army, 1964-66. Republican. Home: 533 W Beddell St Fort Worth TX 76115

LEWIS, MARK EUGENE, clergyman; b. Danville, Ind., Dec. 9, 1962; s. Robert Eugene and Martha Louise (Hudson) L. BA in Ch. Music, Milligan Coll., 1986. Ordained to ministry Christian Chs., 1987. Organist First Christian Ch., Johnson City, Tenn., 1982-85; minister music First Christian Ch., Tarpon Springs, Fla., 1986—; dir. Alexander Christian Found. Fla., Kissimmee, 1989—. Mem. Am. Guild Organists (mem. exec. bd. Clearwater chpt. 1987-89), Am. Choral Dirs. Assn. Republican. Home: 8551 Pilgrim Ct New Port Richey FL 34653 Office: First Christian Ch 2795 Keystone Rd Tarpon Springs FL 34689

LEWIS, MICHAEL EUGENE, minister; b. Washington, June 7, 1958; s. Walter Eugene and Dell (Minor) L.; m. Karen Armstrong, Dec. 17, 1983; children: Carissa Kay, Andrew Michael. BA, David Lipscomb Coll., 1980. Apprentice minister Vultee Ch. of Christ, Nashville, 1976-78; youth minister Arrington Ch. of Christ, Nolensville, Tenn., 1977-80, Crieve Hall Ch. of Christ, Nashville, 1980-82, Main Street Ch. of Christ, Manchester, Tenn., 1982-86; youth and family minister West End Ch. of Christ, Knoxville, Tenn., 1986—; steering com. Opryland Youth Rally, Nashville, 1982-89, Smoky Mountain Youth Rally, Knoxville, 1985-88; steering com. Youth Workers Enrichment Conf., Nashville, 1981—. Staff writer: (teen Christian mag.) Love Notes, 1986-88. Bd. dirs. Foster Care Rev. Bd., Coffee County, 1985, Sonshine Camp, Birmingham, 1982. Office: West End Church of Christ 8301 E Walker Spr Ln Knoxville TN 37923

LEWIS, PAUL WESLEY, lay worker; b. Laconia, N.H., July 27, 1963; s. Terrance Ralph and Ruth Elaine (Aldridge) L. BA in History, Southwest Mo. State U., 1985; MDiv., Assemblies of God Theol. Sem., 1988; postgrad., Southwest Mo. State U., 1985-89, Baylor U., 1989—. Asst. pastor Family Worship Ctr., Baton Rouge, La., 1981-83; asst. campus min., intern Univ. Christian Fellowship, Springfield, Mo., 1985-87; singles coord. Cen. Assemblies of God, Springfield, 1987-89; chmn. internat. com. Wesleyan Found., Waco, Tex., 1990—; leader Internat. Student Fellowship Bible Study, Waco, 1990—; grad. asst. Baylor Univ., Waco, 1989—; del. Leighton Ford Crusade, Springfield, 1986; seminar instr. Dr. Terry Lewis Ch. Growth Seminars, Springfield, and Laconia, N.H., 1987-89; trustee Wesleyan Found., Waco, 1991—. Mem. Am. Acad. Religion, Soc. Bibl. Lit., Chinese Student Assn., Chi Alpha. Home: 2014 S 2nd St # 54 Waco TX 76706

LEWIS, PHILIP JONAH, youth pastor; b. Indpls., Aug. 14, 1962; s. Charles Elwood and Dorothy Carroll (Baker) L.; m. Melinda Sue Eastburn; children: Noelle Joy, Bethany Faith. BS, Ind. Wesleyan U., 1984; MA, Asbury Theol. Sem., 1986. Ordained elder. Vol. youth worker Hillside Wesleyan Ch., Marion, Ind., 1979-83; intern youth worker Coll. Wesleyan Ch., Marion, 1983-84; youth pastor Largo (Fla.) Wesleyan Ch., 1986—; dir. youth worker program Nashville 88 Conv., 1986-88; dir. jr. high programming IMPACT 90 Conv., Cin., 1988-90; dist. Fla. youth pres. Wesleyan Ch., Fla., 1988—; exec. dir. programming Gatlinburg (Tenn.) 92, 1990—. Youth motivator Largo (Fla.) High Sch., 1987-89, Largo (Fla.) Middle Sch., 1989-90; FCA sponsor Clearwater (Fla.) High Sch., 1987-89; tutor Clearwater (Fla.) and Largo (Fla.) High Sch., 1987-89. Republican. Office: Largo Wesleyan Ch 1301 8th Ave NW Largo FL 34640

LEWIS, ROBERT HENRY, lay worker; b. Chillicothe, Tex., Oct. 16, 1921; s. William Arnet and Minnie Easter (Stuckey) L.; m. Miriam Agnes Kothgassner, Mar. 10, 1946; children: Cindy Kaye Lewis Shaw, Pamela Jo Lewis Owens. BSin Elec. Engring., Tex. Tech U., 1952; postgrad., U. Ala., 1965-70. Registered elec. engr. Tex., Ala. Retired engr., 1981; treas. Willowbrook Bapt. Ch., Huntsville, Ala., 1981—; Deacon Willowbrook Bapt. Ch., 1981. Mem. Ala. Rep. Club, Rep. PReddl. Task Force. With U.S. Army, 1942-46. Mem. Inst. Elec. Electronic Engrs. Home: PO Box 220 Lacey's Spring AL 35754 Office: Willowbrook Bapt Ch 7625 Bailey Cove Rd Huntsville AL 35802

LEWIS, ROGER ALLEN, minister; b. Pauls Valley, Okla., Aug. 3, 1953; s. Otis Andirenne and Earnestine (Siner) L.; m. Debra Ruth Tucker, May 28, 1977; 1 child, Jeremy Allen. Student, Southwestern Assembly God Coll., Waxahachie, Tex., 1987—. Evangelist Assemblies of God, Gainesville, Tex., 1973-76, Denton, Tex., 1977-80; assoc. pastor 1st Assembly of God, Gainesville, Tex., 1976-77; sr. pastor Glad Tidings Assembly of God, Lufkin, Tex., 1980-88; dist. youth dir. North Tex. Dist. Coun. Assemblies of God, Ft. Worth, 1988—; dir. decade of harvest North Tex. Dist. Coun. Assemblies of God., Ft. Worth, 1988-91, asst. dist. youth dir., 1983-88. Bd. pres. Angelina House Found., Lufkin, 1987; pres. Angelina County Ministerial Alliance, Lufkin, 1981-82. Office: Assemblies of God 700 NE Loop 820 Hurst TX 76053

LEWIS, TERENCE R. (TERRY LEWIS), minister; b. Washington, Nov. 5, 1938; s. Phillip H. and Ruth L. (Burnett) L.; m. Jo Ann Shake, June 19, 1969; children, Janet, Julie, Justina, Joshua. BA, St. Louis Christian Coll., 1964. Ordained to ministry Christian Ch., 1961. Min. Odin (Ill.) Christian Ch., 1961-65; dir. United Cerebral Palsy, Galesburg, Ill., 1965-68; min. Buckhorn Christian Ch. Wayesville, Mo., 1979-84; dir. pres. IHS Ministries Inc., Rolla, Mo., 1986—; pres. San Fernanco Valley Christian Men's Fellowship, Glendale, Calif., 1970. Author: The Minister and His Taxes, 1989. Mem. Nat. Assn. Tax Practitioners. Home and Office: PO Box 1883 Rolla MO 65401

LEWIS, THOMAS WAYNE, minister; b. Ft. Riley, Kans., Aug. 5, 1961; s. Marvin Singleton and Lorena Mae (Hopkins) L.; m. Brenda Carol Cullins, May 29, 1981; children: T.J., Timothy, Joshua. BA, Cen. Bapt. Coll., 1983. Ordained in ministry Bapt. Ch., 1983. Music dir. Needseveek Bapt. Ch., Greenbrier, Ark., 1980-82; music/youth dir. Rose Hill Bapt. Ch., DeQueen, Ark., 1983-84; pastor First Missionary Bapt. Ch., Joplin, Mo., 1985-86; assoc. pastor Ridgecrest Bapt. Ch., Amarillo, Tex., 1986-89; pastor Morningside Bapt. Ch., Snyder, Tex., 1989—; camp dir. BApt. Missionary Assn. Cen. West Tex. Encampment, Floydadd, 1990—. Republican. Office: Morningside Bapt Ch PO Box 197 Snyder TX 79549

LEWIS, TIMOTHY MILLER, religious music director, educator; b. Mt. Kisco, N.Y., June 25, 1959; s. Hobart Durban and Edith (Miller) L. BA, Manhattanville Coll., 1982; MusM, Manhattan Sch. Music, N.Y.C., 1991. Dir. music St. Luke's Ch., Katonah, N.Y., 1980-82, Ch. St. Mary the Virgin, Chappaqua, N.Y., 1982-88, Grace Ch., White Plains, N.Y., 1988—; artistic dir. Downtown Music at Grace Inc., White Plains, 1988—; assoc. condr. Pleasantville (N.Y.) Cantata Singers, 1988—; mem. faculty Westchester Conservatory Music, White Plains, 1991—. Mem. am. Guild Organists (exec. bd. 1989-91, sub-dean 1991—). Episcopalian. Avocations: antique automobiles, clocks, architecture. Office: Grace Ch 33 Church St White Plains NY 10601

LEWY, LEONARD JACK, rabbi; b. San Francisco, May 27, 1951; s. John Kurt and Ilse (Feibusch) L.; m. Judith Kay Scharf, July 31, 1983. BA in Jewish Studies, UCLA, 1974; postgrad., U. Judaism, Jerusalem, 1974-76, Student Ctr. and Hebrew U., Jerusalem, 1979; B.L., M.A., Jewish Theol. Sem., 1980. Ordained rabbi, 1980. Tchr. of liturgy and ritual Solomon Schechter Sch. Westchester, White Plains, N.Y., 1980-81; nursing and adult homes chaplain N.Y. Bd. Rabbis, Westchester County, N.Y., 1980-81; rabbi, dir. edn. Congregation B'Nai Israel, Tustin, Calif., 1981-83; dir. Julius C. Livingston B'nai B'rith Hillel Found., U. Okla., Norman, 1983-85, B'nai B'rith Hillen Found., New Orleans, 1985-87; chaplain Eisenberg Village of Jewish Homes for Aging, Reseda, Calif., 1988—; mem. funeral practices com. Southern Calif. Bd. Rabbis; mem. adv. com. Life Plus Clergy Network; mem. biomed. ethics com. Jewish Homes for Aging; mem. protective svcs. com. Jewish Family Svc.; participant Religion on the Line radio program; presenter in field; scholar-in-residence Camp Ramah in Calif., 1989. Mem. editorial bd. Davka Mag., 1973; mem. editorial com. Group for Religious Practice, 1975; contbr. articles to profl. publs. Mem. Assn. for Clin. Pastoral Edn., Jewish Communal Profls. of Southern Calif., N.Y. Bd. Rabbis, Nat. Assn. Jewish Chaplains (presenter D'var Torah 1991), Rabbinical Assembly, Valley Interfaith Coun., Leo Baeck Inst.

LEXAU, HENRY, editor; b. St. Paul, Feb. 8, 1928; s. Ole Hendrijk and Anne (Haas) L.; m. Eileen O'Hara, Oct. 18, 1952; children—Catherine, Margaret, Daniel, John, Elizabeth, Benjamin. B.A., Coll. St. Thomas, 1949. Asst. editor Catholic Digest, St. Paul, 1949-72, mng. editor, 1972-75, editor, 1975—; editor Catholic Digest Book Club, 1978—, A Treasury of Catholic Digest, 1986. Served with U.S. Army, 1950-52. Decorated Bronze Star. Roman Catholic. Home: 1941 Selby Ave Saint Paul MN 55104 Office: Cath Digest PO Box 64090 Saint Paul MN 55164

LEYPOLDT, CHARLES WESLEY, pastor; b. Oakland, Nebr., July 16, 1947; s. Woodrow William and Dorothy Catherine (Hennings) L.; m. Christine Lu Landon, July 11, 1970; children: Seth Landon, Anastasia Grace. BS, Nebr. Wesleyan U., 1969; MDiv, St. Paul Sch. of Theology, Kansas City, Mo., 1972. Ordained to ministry United Meth. Ch. as elder, 1973. Pastor United Meth. Ch., Davenport, Nebr., 1971-74, Ceresco, Nebr., 1974-78, Hebron, Nebr., 1978-79, Eustis, Nebr., 1987—; mem. Conf. Coun. on Ministries, 1988—; chmn. S.W. Dist. Coun. on Ministries, 1988-90; mem. Conf. Commn. on Christian Unity and Interreligious Concerns; bd. dirs. Dawson County Family Preservation, Inc., Nebr., 1989—. Active Dist. 44 Bd. Edn., Douglas, Nebr., 1980-84; clk., treas. Village of Douglas, 1982-85. Recipient Outstanding Young Man award U.S. Jaycees, 1981. Mem. Eustis C. of C. (sec. 1988-89, dir. 1988—), Masons. Democrat. Office: United Meth Ch 208 N Morton Eustis NE 69028

L'HEUREUX, N. J., JR., minister. Exec. dir. Queens Fedn. Chs., Richmond Hill, N.Y. Office: Queens Fedn Chs 86-17 105th St Richmond Hill NY 11418*

L'HOUR, JEAN, writer, interpreter, Bible researcher, clergyman; b. Ploudaniel, Brittany, France, June 6, 1932; s. Jean Joseph and Louise (Salou) L'H. Baccalaureate in Philosophy, Fgn. Missions Sem., Paris, 1950; Licentiate in Theology, Gregorian U., Rome, 1958; Licentiate in Bible Studies, Biblical Inst., Rome, 1960; cert. Old Testament research Ecole Biblique et Archeologique Francaise, Jerusalem, 1961. Ordained priest, Roman Catholic Ch., 1957. Prof. Bible, Theol. Coll., Penang, Malaysia, 1961-73; freelance Biblique researcher, Toulouse, France, 1973—; free-lance interpeter, Toulouse, Des Moines, Iowa, 1973—; author: La Morale De l'Alliance, 1966; La Morale de l'Ancien Testament, 1977; Si Je Savais Comment l'Atteindre, 1978; research, publs. on O.T., 1963—; condr. seminars, lectr. French Assn. Bible Research, 1961—; lectr., speaker on U.S. agr., France, 1980—. Editor Expo Corn, 1979—. Served with French Nat. Service, 1951-53. Mem. Paris Fgn. Missions Soc. Home: 72, rue Achille Viadieu, Toulouse 31400, France Office: France Mais, 4, rue Paul Bernies, Toulouse 31075, France

L'HUILLIER, PETER (ARCHBISHOP PETER), bishop; b. Paris, Dec. 3, 1926; came to U.S., 1980; s. Eugene Henri and Emmilienne (Haslin) L'H. Licenciate in Theology, Inst. Theologique Saint-Denys-Paris, 1949. Ordained priest Orthodox Ch. in Am., 1954. Priest Russian Ch., Paris, 1954-68, bishop, 1968-79; bishop Orthodox Ch. in Am., N.Y.C., 1980—. Office: Orthodox Ch in Am 33 Hewitt Ave Bronxville NY 10708*

LI, JOHN C. P., minister, educator; b. Hankou, Republic of China, Oct. 20, 1925; came to U.S., 1977; married, Jan. 1, 1969; children: Joshua, Elias. Grad., Concordia Bible Inst., Hong Kong, 1953, Taiwan U. Law Sch., Taipei, 1958, Concordia Theol. Sem., Taiwan, 1964. Ordained to ministry Luth. Ch., 1964. Pastor Peace Luth. Ch., Taipei, 1964-77, Immanuel Luth. Ch., Bayside, N.Y., 1977—; sec. Concordia Mid. Sch. (bd. of control), Taiwan, 1967-73; pres. China Evang. Luth. Ch., Taipei, 1972-74; prof. China Christian Bible Inst., 1974-76. Home: 53-08 94th St Elmhurst NY 11373 Office: Immanuel Luth Ch 210-10 Horace Harding Expwy Bayside NY 11364

LI, PETER JOSEPH, publisher; b. Hong Kong, July 8, 1938; s. Norman C. and Hazel (Chow) L.; m. Anna Abmayr, May 22, 1965; children: Lisa, Susan. BA in Journalism, Duquesne U., 1961. Dir. pub. George A. Pflaum, Publisher, Inc., Dayton, Ohio, 1963-71; pub., chmn. bd. Peter Li, Inc., 1971—; exec. dir. Nat. Cath. Ednl. Exhbn., 1988—. Bd. dirs. U.S. China Cath. Bur., Seton Hall, N.J., 1990—. Recipient Outstanding Svc. to Cath. Edn. award Diocese of Bklyn., 1989. Mem. Cath. Press Assn. (pub. Catechist mag. 1967, Today's Cath. Tchr. 1967, Vision, Venture, Good News, Promise, Tech. and Learning mags. 1980, Pflaum Student Mags. 1985, Early Childhood News 1989), Nat. Cath. Edn. Assn., Religious Book Pub. Assn., Nat. Ch. Goods Assn., Christian Book Sellers Assn. Roman Catholic. Office: 2451 E River Rd Dayton OH 45439

LI, PING-KWONG, religious organization administrator, minister; b. Hong Kong, Aug. 24, 1938; s. Kan-chuen and Foon (Leung) L.; m. Angela Fungkiu Siu, Feb. 25, 1967; children: Christopher Tin-yan, Grace Wingyan. BTh, Trinity Theol. Sem., Singapore, 1962; diploma pastoral studies, Birmingham U., 1972; postgrad., Westhill Coll., 1982. Ordained to ministry Meth. Ch., 1966. With Meth. Ch. Hong Kong, 1963—, supt. Hong Kong cir., 1972-81, 82-84, sec., 1982-84, exec. sec. missions and pastoral care div., 1985-86, supt. Kowloon cir., 1985-88, exec. sec. sch. edn. div., 1986-89, pres., 1988—. Chmn. bd. trustees Chung Chi Coll., 1988—, Hong Kong Christian Coun., 1989—; dir. local YMCA, 1990; v.p. The Boy's Brigade, Hong Kong, 1990, pres., 1991—; sec. Hong Kong Chinese Christian Chs. Union, 1988-91. Recipient Outstanding Youth award Hong Kong Jaycees, 1977. Office: Meth Ch Hong Kong, 1/F Yen Men Bldg, 98-108 Jaffe Rd Wan Chai Hong Kong *It is not how long, but how well; it is not a matter of quantity, but quality.*

LIBACKYJ, ANFIR, religion educator; b. Mosurivci, Ukraine, USSR, Sept. 8, 1926; came to U.S., 1955; s. Serhij and Kateryna (Slowinskyj) L. MSc, Liege (Belgium) U., 1954; PhD, Poly. U., N.Y.C., 1965; MDiv, Union Theol. Sem., N.Y.C., 1977. Rsch. scientist E.I. du Pont de Nemours Co., Phila., 1963-67; adj. prof. N.Y. Inst. Tech., N.Y.C., 1968-70, asst. prof., 1970-73; prof. St. Sophia Sem., South Bound Brook, N.J., 1977—. Author: The Ancient Monasteries of Kiev Rus, 1978; contbr. articles to profl. jours. Mem. Am. Acad. Religion, AAUP, Am. Acad. Polit. and Social Sci., Acad. Polit. Sci., Soc. for Sci. Study of Religion. Home: 84-22 107th Ave Jamaica NY 11417

LIBBY, WAYNE G., church business administrator; b. Washington, Apr. 14, 1938. Student, Franklin U., 1956. Owner Leesburg Christian Sch., Leesburg, Va., 1982-86; bus. adminstr. Christian Fellowship Ch., Vienna, Va., 1987—. With U.S. Army, 1961-63. Office: Christian Fellowship Ch 10237 Leesburg Pike Vienna VA 22182

LIBOWITZ, RICHARD LAWRENCE, rabbi, educator; b. Stamford, Conn., Oct. 30, 1948; s. Milton and Matilda (Elovitz) L.; m. Allyn Sue Menko, May 20, 1973; children: Jordan Franklin, Alexander Amihai. BA, U. Notre Dame, 1970; Te'udah, Haim Greenberg Inst., Jerusalem, 1971; MA, Temple U., 1973, PhD, 1979; Rabbi, Reconstructionist Rabbinical Coll., Phila., 1976. Rabbi Bet Am Shalom Synagogue, White Plains, N.Y., 1976-79; asst. prof. religion Carleton Coll., Northfield, Minn., 1979-83; rabbi Congregation Ner Tamid Delaware County, Springfield, Pa., 1983—; edn. dir. Anne Frank Inst. Phila., 1984-90. Author: Mordecai M. Kaplan and the Development of Reconstructionism, 1983; author, editor: Faith and Freedom, 1987, Methodology in the Academic Study of the Holocaust, 1988; editor Ra'ayonot, 1985-86. Bd. govs. Reconstructionist Rabbinical Coll., Wyncote, Pa., 1985-88. Research fellow Meml. Found. for Jewish Culture, 1976. Mem. Am. Acad. Religion, Assn. for Jewish Studies, Reconstructionist Rabbinical Assn., Notre Dame Club (Phila.). Avocations: golf, reading, running. Office: Ner Tamid Delaware County PO Box 266 300 W Woodland Ave Springfield PA 19064

LIBRANDE, LEONARD THEODORE, religion educator; b. Rice Lake, Wis., Sept. 14, 1943; moved to Can., 1970; s. Sam Anthony and Alida (Wolffe) L.; m. Linda Ann Walker, Sept. 21, 1978; children—Arend, Timothy, Benjamin. B.A., St. Louis U., 1968; M.A., McGill U., Montreal, Que., Can., 1973, Ph.D., 1976. Asst. prof. Carleton U., Ottawa, Ont., Can., 1976-81, assoc. prof. religion, 1981—, assoc. dean arts, 1990—. Home: 471

Hilson Ave, Ottawa, ON Canada K1Z 6C6 Office: Carleton U, Ottawa, ON Canada K1S 5B6

LICHTENSTEIN, AARON, religion educator; b. Milan, Italy, July 11, 1933; s. Mordecai and Pessa Lea (Kinek) L. BA, Bklyn. Coll., 1958; MA, NYU, 1963, PhD, 1967. Ordained rabbi, 1961. Dir. Jewish Culture Found. of NYU, N.Y.C., 1967-68; field worker Children's Salvation, Inc., Europe, 1969-70; B.Z. Immanuel sr. lectr. Jews' Coll., London, 1971-74; assoc. prof. of Jwish religion U. Denver, 1976-79; prof. CUNY, N.Y.C., 1981—; book editor Assn. Orthodox Tchrs., N.Y.C., 1982—. Mem. editorial staff Ency. Judaica, 1972; author: The Un-Chosen People, 1939-1945, 1978, The Seven Laws of Noah, 1981 (R.J.J. Press award 1986); contbr. chpt. to book: The Bible as Text, 1990. Sch. evaluator State of N.Y. Regents, Albany, 1987. NEH fellow, 1976, 79, 85, 86, 89. Mem. Assn. for Jewish Studies, Jewish Acad. Arts and Scis., Nat. Assn. Profs. of Hebrew (bd. advisors 1987—), Assn. Orthodox Jewish Tchrs. (exec. bd. 1987—). Office: CUNY 199 Chambers St-English New York NY 10007

LICHTERMAN, IVOR YITZCHAK, cantor; b. Cape Town, Republic of South Africa, Aug. 27, 1953; came to U.S., 1976; s. Jakub Lichterman and Maria (Teitelbaum) L.; m. Jan Michal Lacker, Apr. 5, 1981; children: Mayron Zev, Ariel Shaun, Jaclyn Sarali. BA cum laude, U. Cape Town, 1974, BA with honors, 1975; postgrad., Yeshiva U., N.Y.C., 1976-79. Asst. cantor Sea Point Congregation, Cape Town, 1972-76; cantor Temple Shalom, Westbury, N.Y., 1976-78, Temple Beth Emeth, Hewlett, N.Y., 1978-79, Congregation Agudath Sholom, Stamford, Conn., 1979-91, Congregation Anshei Israel, Tucson, 1991—. Rec. artist, soloist. Mem. Cantorial Coun. Am. (bd. dirs. 1980—), Cantor's Assembly (pres. Conn. region 1986-89). Office: Congregation Anshei Israel 5550 E 5th St Tucson AZ 85711

LICHTY, ROBERT ELDON, JR., missionary, religion educator; b. Kaimosi, Kenya, Nov. 20, 1940; (parents Am. citizens); s. Robert Eldon Sr. and Faith Joy (Andrews) L.; m. Victoria Patricia Robinson, Aug. 11, 1962. BS, Evang. Coll., Springfield, Mo., 1964; MS, Iowa State U., 1969. Tchr. Des Plaines (Ill.) Elem. Schs., 1964-67; chmn. dept. Christian edn. Open Bible Coll., Des Moines, 1967-70, Des Moines Community Coll., 1970-71; dir. Youth With A Mission, Tangier, Morocco, 1971-75, Rota and Madrid, 1975-86; dir. Ctr. for Ednl. Resource Devel. Youth With A Mission/U. of the Nations, Kailua Kona, Hawaii, 1987—; mem. coun., chmn. bd. edn. Luth. Ch. of Holy Trinity, Kailua Kona, 1989—. Mem. pres.' cabinet Cook County Young Reps., Maine Township, Ill., 1964-67; precinct, v.p. Kona Reps., Kailua Kona, 1989-90. Home: 74-5046 Lapa Nui Kailua Kona HI 96740 Office: Youth With A Mission/U of the Nations 75-5851 Kuakini Hwy Kailua Kona HI 96740

LIDDELL, BOBBY, JR. (MCCOY), minister; b. Birmingham, Ala., Sept. 15, 1952; s. Bobby M. and Stella Earcell (Gant) L.; m. Cathy Joan Loe, Aug. 18, 1972; children—Anthony Allen, Nathan Gant, Keri Jayne. Cert. Memphis Sch. Preaching, 1979; B.A., Ala. Christian Sch. Religion, 1984, M.A., 1986. Ordained to ministry Ch. of Christ, 1979. Electrician, contractor Little, Moore and Walter Constrn., Birmingham, 1972-77; minister Central Ch. of Christ, Winfield, Ala., 1979-83, Parrish Ch. of Christ, Ala., 1983-88, Bellview Ch. of Christ, Pensacola, Fla., 1988—; instr. Sch. of World Evangelism, Guin, Ala., 1980; dir. Campaign for Christ, Winfield, Ala., 1981, Parrish, 1984; speaker Daily Radio Broadcast, Parrish, 1984—; dir. Ann. Bellview Lectures. Editor The Defender, The Beacon; assoc. editor: (monthly publ.) The Christian Sentinel, 1979-83; contbr. articles to religious publs.; staff writer The Firm Found. Active Walker County and Parrish PTAs; sec. bd. dirs. Indian Creek Youth Camp; missionary trips to Singapore, Manila and Hong Kong. Mem. Memphis Sch. Preaching Alumni Assn. (recruitment chmn.), Ala. Christian Sch. Religion Alumni Assn. (v.p.). Republican. Avocations: Woodworking; volunteer work; photography. Home: 6474 Grenewell St Pensacola FL 32526 Office: Bellview Ch of Christ 4852 Saufley Rd Pensacola FL 32526

LIEBER, CHARLES DONALD, publisher; b. Scheveningen, The Netherlands, Jan. 30, 1921; came to U.S., 1941, naturalized, 1944; s. Edmund Z. and Gabrielle (Lifczis) L.; m. Miriam Levin, July 17, 1960; children: John Nathan, James Edmund, George Theodore, Anne Gabrielle. Student, U. Brussels, 1938-40; B.A., New Sch. for Social Research, 1948. With H. Bittner & Co. (Pubs.), N.Y.C., 1947-49; with Alfred A. Knopf, Inc., 1949-52; dir. coll. dept. Random House, N.Y.C., 1952-64; pub. Atherton Press, N.Y.C., 1964-67; pres. Atherton Press, Inc., N.Y.C., 1967-70; v.p. Aldine-Atherton, Inc., N.Y.C., Chgo., 1971-72; pres. Lieber-Atherton, Inc., N.Y.C., 1972—; gen. mgr. Hebrew Pub. Co., 1980-85, pres., 1985—; pres. Lieber Publs., Inc., N.Y.C., 1981—. Author: (with A.D. Murphy) Great Events of World History, 1964; chmn. publ. com., mem. editorial bd. Reconstructionist mag., 1983—. Chmn. West Side Jewish Community Council, Manhattan, 1978-82, mem. at large, 1974—; exec. bd. Jewish Reconstrn. Found., 1978-83, vice chmn., 1979-80, chmn., 1980-83, nat. bd. dirs., 1983—; trustee St. Ann's Sch., 1983-89; trustee Soc. for the Advancement Judaism, 1974-90, treas., 1976-79, co-chmn., 1979-81; bd. dirs. Hebrew Arts Sch., 1974-82, Fedn. Reconstructionist Congregations, 1983-91. Lt. AUS, 1942-46, CBI. Recipient Mordecai M. Kaplan award Jewish Reconstructionist Found., 1988. Mem. Coll. Pubs. Group (chmn. 1965-66), Assn. Jewish Book Pubs. (pres. 1988-90). Home: 389 W End Ave New York NY 10024 Office: Hebrew Pub Co 100 Water St PO Box 222 Spencertown NY 12165-0222

LIEBER, DAVID LEO, university president; b. Stryj, Poland, Feb. 20, 1925; came to U.S., 1927, naturalized, 1936; s. Max and Gussie (Jarmush) L.; m. Esther Kobre, June 10, 1945; children—Michael, Daniel, Deborah, Susan. B.A., CCNY, 1944; B.Hebrew Lit., Jewish Theol. Sem. Am., 1944, M.Hebrew Lit., 1948, D. Hebrew Lit., 1951; M.A., Columbia, 1947; postgrad., U. Wash., 1954-55, UCLA, 1961-63; L.D.H. hon., Hebrew Union Coll., 1982—. Ordained rabbi, 1948. Rabbi, 1948, Sinai Temple, Los Angeles, 1950-54; dir. (B'nai B'rith Hillel), Seattle, Cambridge, 1954-56; dean students U. Judaism, Los Angeles, 1956-63; Samuel A. Fryer prof. Bible, pres. U. Judaism, 1963-90, Skovron Disting. Svc. prof. Bibl. lit., 1990—; lectr. Hebrew UCLA, 1957-90; vice chancellor Jewish Theol. Sem., 1972—; mem. exec. council Rabbinical Assembly, 1966-69; vice chmn. Am. Jewish Com., Los Angeles, 1972-75; bd. dirs. Jewish Fedn. Council, Los Angeles, 1980-86, bd. govs. , 1986—. Mem. editorial bd.: Conservative Judaism, 1968-70. Served as chaplain USAF, 1951-53. Mem. Assn. Profs. Jewish Studies (dir. 1970-71), Phi Beta Kappa. Office: U Judaism 15600 Mulholland Dr Los Angeles CA 90077

LIEBERMAN, ELISSABETH, lay worker; b. N.Y.C., Nov. 16, 1964; d. Marvin and Norma Jay (Rosler) L. BA, U. Miami, 1986; MSW, Yeshiva U., N.Y.C., 1988. Field cons. United Jewish Appeal, Deerfield Beach, Fla., 1986-90; dir. univ. programs United Jewish Appeal, N.Y.C., 1990—; tchr. Judaica High Sch., Coral Springs, Fla., 1989—. Mem. Assn. Jewish Communal Profls.

LIEBIG, NELDA FAYE, church official, publisher; b. Seminole, Okla., Aug. 29, 1930; d. Charles Emmett and Georgia Alice (Duncan) Johnson; m. Carl Eugene Liebig, Aug. 15, 1954; children: Harriet, Elizabeth, Jim, Steve. BS in Edn., Pittsburg (Kans.) State U., 1953; postgrad., U. Wis., 1961, 66-67, Moody Bible Inst., Chgo., 1989. Ch. office sec., editor 1st Am. Luth. Ch., Oconto, Wis., 1980-85, 89—; editor, pub. Luth. Lay Renewal Internat., Oconto, 1990—; state chmn. Luth. Lay Renewal Oconto, 1980-85, regional dir., 1985—; sec. edn. Women of Evang. Luth. Ch. Conf., 1974-77. Author children's stories, devotional material, inspirational articles; editor religious newsletters, 1980—. Leader Girl Scouts U.S.A., Okla., Kans., Alaska, Wis., Am. Samoa, 1949-77; vol. Riverside Nursing Home, Oconto, 1985, Luther Home, Marinette, Wis., 1985-86. Recipient Lamb award Luth. Ch. Am., 1976, Thanks Badge, Girl Scouts U.S.A., 1978. Mem. Luth. Assn. Missionaries and Pilots (publicity rep., speaker). Home: 1430 Main St Oconto WI 54153 Office: 1st Am Luth Ch 511 Madison Oconto WI 54153

LIEBLING, MORDECHAI ELIAHU, rabbi; b. Bklyn., Oct. 29, 1948; s. Joel and Zelda (Finkleman) L.; m. Devorah Joy Bartnoff, June 21, 1981; children: Reena Shoshanna, Jonathan Tzvi, Lior Michael. BA, Cornell U., 1969; MA, Brandeis U., 1972; MHL, Reconstructionist Rabbinical Coll., Wyncote, Pa., 1985. Ordained rabbi, 1985. Student rabbi Manhattan Reconstructionist Havurah, N.Y.C., 1982-85; exec. co-dir. Pnai Or Religious Fellowship, Phila., 1984-85; dir. spl. projects Fedn. Reconstructionist Congregations and Havurot, N.Y.C., 1985-86; exec. dir. Fedn. Reconstructionist Congregations, Wyncote, 1986—; dir. Pnai-Or Religious Fellowship, Phila., 1985-90, Shalom Ctr., Phila., 1990—; adv. bd. Nat. Havurah Com., Miami, 1987—; policy com. Jewish Peace Lobby, Washington, 1990—. Co-author: Haggadah: Seder of Children of Abraham, 1984, Tu B'shevat Haggadah, 1985; mem. editorial bd. Reconstructionist, New Menorah. Bd. dirs. Interreligious Com. for Peace in Middle East, Phila., 1989—; dir., founder Shomrei Adamah Jewish Environ. Ctr., Phila., 1988—; mem. Clergy and Laity Concerned, N.Y.C., 1987—. Mem. Reconstructionist Rabbinical Assn., Assn. Jewish Pubrs., Phila. Bd. Rabbis, N.Y. Bd. Rabbis, Assn. Non-Profit Mgrs. Office: Fedn Reconstructionist Congregations and Havurot Church Rd and Greenwood Ave Wyncote PA 19095 *Through compassionate dialogue and action rooted in the Oneness, Interconnectedness, of all existence, we can heal our souls, our society and our planet.*

LIECHTY, RONALD WAYNE, minister; b. South Bend, Ind., July 13, 1933; s. Clarence Edgar and Verna Esther (Welty) L.; m. Marilyn Jean Gray, Aug. 1, 1954 (div. 1979); children: Brian, Susan, Sheryl; m. Anna Lucille Bach, July 18, 1981; children: Bryan, Audrey. BA, DePauw U., Greencastle, Ind., 1955; MD, Garett-Evang. Theol. Sem., Naperville, Ill., 1960; D of Ministry, Christian Theol. Sem., Indpls., 1982. Pastor Salem Evang. United Brethren Ch., Granger, Ind., 1958-63; exec. dir. Elkhart County (Ind.) Council/Churches, 1963-65; pastor Calvary United Meth. Ch., North Manchester, Ind., 1965-68, Dunlap United Meth. Ch., Elkhart, Ind., 1968-76, St. Andrew's United Meth. Ch., West Lafayette, Ind., 1976-80, First United Ch. Christ, Plymouth, Ind., 1983—; bd. dirs. Ind. Council of Chs., Indpls. 1963-68, Ind. Ky. Conf. UCC, Indpls. 1987-89; dir. Children's Work Council, Ind., 1965-70; del. Gen. Synod, United Church of Christ, 1987. Pres. County Council on Aging Plymouth, 1985, United Religious Council, Plymouth, 1990-92; bd.dirs. Victim Abuse Assistance Agy., Plymouth 1986; pres., bd. dirs. Bowen Mental Health Ctr., Warsaw, 1990-92. With USN, 1955-57. Named to Pioneer Hall of Fame, Ch. World Service, Indpls., 1987. Mem. Assn. Council United Churc h of Christ (pres. 1986-87), Ministerial Assn. (pres. 1986-87). Avocations: table tennis, drummer, sports, computer. Home: 12488 Meadow Dr Plymouth IN 46563 Office: First United Ch Christ 321 N Center St Plymouth IN 46563

LIESKE, HENRY LOUIS, minister; b. Henderson, Minn., Oct. 21, 1911; s. Henry Friedrich and Clara Margaretha (Blaesing) L.; m. Marguerite Virginia Jones, June 7, 1939; children: Jeanne Lieske Kirkpatrick, Jay, Joy Lieske Skelton, Janice (dec.), Jacquelyn Lieske Copeland, Judy Lieske Wabrek. Student, Concordia Jr. Coll., St. Paul, 1925-31; BD, Concordia Sem., St. Louis, 1935, MDiv, 1971; postgrad., Grad. Sch. Theology, Oberlin Coll., 1950-53, Cleve. Coll., Western Res. U., 1947-49, Portland State Coll., 1956-61. Ordained to ministry Luth. Ch.-Mo. Synod, 1938; became mem. of Assn. Evang. Luth. Chs., 1976; merged with Evang. Luth. Ch. in Am., 1987. Sec., asst. to sec. Luth. Ch., Mo. Synod, Kendallville, Ind., 1935-38; pastor, mission developer new Luth. congregations Warsaw and Plymouth, Ind., 1938-43; pastor St. John's Luth. Ch., Elyria, Ohio, 1943-55; founder, pastor, mission developer St. Timothy Luth. Ch., Portland, Oreg., 1955-67; pastor Redeemer Luth. Ch., Burnsville, Minn., 1967-76, Prairie Luth. Ch., Eden Prairie, Minn., 1979; chmn. bd. regents Concordia Coll., Portland, 1958-67; chmn., co-founder All-Luth. Welfare Assn. Oreg. (now Luth. Family Svc.), Portland, 1957-61. Researcher, compiler, contbr. manuscript collection: The Moderate Movement in the Lutheran Church-Missouri Synod, Oberlin Coll. Archives, 1977-80, supplemental placement, 1980—; author articles, conf. presentations. Chmn. East Portland chpt. Am. Field Svc. student exch. program, E. Portland and Gresham, Oreg., 1959-62; mem., chmn. Elyria Community Welfare Coun., 1951-55, del. nat. conf., 1955. Mem. Am. Philatelic Soc. (life), Postal History Soc. Minn. (writer, distbr. postal history resource books). Home: 55 Idaho Ave N Golden Valley MN 55427 *At 79 I continue to thrill over what I think are some of the chief emphases of the Christian religion: (1) that God EXISTS and rewards those who search for Him, (2) that there are concepts of RIGHT and WRONG (sometimes I succeed in following them, sometimes I miss the mark by a mile), (3) that the matchless amazing grace of God in Christ is the fantastic dynamic of the Christian religion, (4) that in all ages the church's proclamation needs to be both Law and Gospel, the Law to sensitize consciences to ethical and moral dimensions of life, the Good News to offer acceptance, forgiveness, new beginnings, power for growth and life eternal, and (5) the Good News needs to be the predominant and final word.*

LIFSHITZ, HOWARD VICTOR, rabbi; b. Chgo., Feb. 15, 1945; s. Louis and Ruth (Sulak) L.; m. Gail Susan Greenbert, Nov. 23, 1975; children: Jennifer, Jessica. BA in Sociology, Brandeis U., 1967; MA in Hebrew Lit., Jewish Theol. Sem., 1971. Ordained rabbi, 1973. Asst. rabbi Shaarey Zedek Congregation, Southfield, Mich., 1973-76; rabbi Bustleton-Somerton Synagogue, Phila., 1976-81, Congregation Beth Judea, Long Grove, Ill., 1981—. Bd. dirs. Jewish Family & Community Svc., Chgo., JYC-Klein Br., Phila., 1979-81. Mem. Rabbinical Assembly Am. (treas. Chgo. region 1990—). Office: Congregation Beth Judea Box 5304 RFD Long Grove IL 60047

LIFTON, ROBERT KENNETH, diversified companies executive; b. N.Y.C., Jan. 9, 1928; s. Benjamin and Anna (Pike) L.; m. Loretta J. Silver, Sept. 5, 1954; children: Elizabeth Gail Lifton Hooper, Karen Grace Lifton Healy. BBA magna cum laude, CCNY, 1948; LLB, Yale U., 1951. Bar: N.Y. 1952. Assoc. Kaye, Scholer, Fierman, Hays & Handler, N.Y.C., 1955-56; asst. to pres. Glickman Corp., N.Y.C., 1956-57; pres. Robert K. Lifton, Inc., N.Y.C., 1957-61; chmn. bd. Terminal Tower Co., Inc., Cleve., 1959-63; pres. Transcontinental Investing Corp., N.Y.C., 1961-72, chmn. bd., 1969-72; ptnr. Venture Assocs., 1972-89; pres. Preferred Health Care Ltd., 1983-88; chmn. bd. dirs. Marcade Group, Inc., 1986-91; bd. dirs. Four Winds, Inc.; bd. dirs., treas. Consol. Accessories Corp., 1980-88, Caron's Connection, Inc., 1985-89; mem. faculty Columbia U. Law Sch., 1973-78, Yale U. Law Sch., 1973-75; guest lectr. Practicing Law Inst., Yale Law Sch., Pace Inst., NYU; founder Nat. Exec. Conf., Washington, Inc.; chmn. oversight com. for Masters Degree, NYU Real Estate Inst., 1987-88. Author: Practical Real Estate: Legal Tax and Business Strategies, 1978; contbr. articles to profl. jours. and handbooks. Mem. McGovern econ. adv. com. 1972-73; chmn. parents com. Barnard Coll., 1976-78; mem. com. of the collection Whitney Mus., 1976-79; trustee Yale Sch. Fund, 1974-77, NYU Real Estate Inst., 1983-89; chmn. bd. dirs. Fund for Religious Liberty, 1987-88; pres. Am. Jewish Congress, 1988—. Lt. (j.g.) USN, 1952-55. Recipient Achievement award Sch. Bus. Alumni Soc. of CCNY, James Madison award Fund for Religious Liberty, 1987. Mem. Order of Coif. Home: 983 Park Ave New York NY 10028 Office: The Marcade Group Inc 805 3d Ave 26th Fl New York NY 10022

LIGGETT, JAMES DAVID, minister; b. Decatur, Ind., June 4, 1946; s. James David and Almeda (Buuck) L.; m. Rosemary, Aug. 21, 1971; children: Elisabeth, Mike, Kathy, Marie, Becky, Daniel. BA, Northwestern U., 1968; MDiv, Wis. Luth. Sem., 1972. Minister St. Matthew's Luth. Ch., Stoddard, Wis., 1972-81, St. John's Luth. Ch., Sleepy Eye, Minn., 1981—; bd. chmn. Luther High Sch., Onalaska, Wis., 1973-81; dist. sec. Minn. Dist. of WELS, 1986—; pastoral advisor D.M.L.C. Aux., New Ulm, Minn., 1985-87, O.W.L.S., 1985-87. Bd. dirs. Housing and Redevel. Authority, Sleepy Eye, 1986—, chmn., 1988; bd. dirs. Minn. Valley Luth. Sch., New Ulm, 1988—; coach Little League Baseball Assn., Sleepy Eye, 1986-88; chmn. Community Edn. Com., Sleepy Eye, 1989—. Lodge: Lions (community rep. 1983—). Avocations: golf, racquetball. Home and Office: 217 Walnut St SE Sleepy Eye MN 56085

LIGHT, ARTHUR HEATH, bishop; s. Alexander Heath and Mary Watkins (Nelson) L.; m. Sarah Ann Jones, June 12, 1954; children: William Alexander, Philip Nelson, John Page, Sarah Heath. BA, Hampden-Sydney Coll., 1951, DD, 1987; M.Div., Va. Theol. Sem., 1954, DD, 1970; DD, St. Paul's Coll., 1979. Ordained priest Episcopal Ch., 1955. Rector West Mecklenburg Cure, Boydton, Va., 1954-58, Christ Ch., Elizabeth City, N.C., 1958-63, St. Marys Ch., Kinston, N.C., 1963-67, Christ and St. Luke's Ch., Norfolk, Va., 1967-79; bishop Diocese of Southwestern Va., Roanoke, 1979—; pres. Province III Episcopal Ch., 1984—, mem. Council Advice to Presiding Bishop, 1985—. Author: God, The Gift, the Giver. Bd. dirs. United Communities Fund, 1969-79, Norfolk Seamen's Friends Soc., 1969-79, Tidewater Assembly on Family Life, 1970-79, Friends of Juvenile Ct., 1975-79, Va. Inst. Pastoral Care, 1971-72; bd. dirs., mem. exec. com. Va. Council Chs., 1979—; bd. dirs. Roanoke Valley Council of Community Services, 1980-83, Virginians Organized for Informed Community Effort (VOICE), 1981—; bd. dirs. Appalachian People's Service Orgn., 1981—, pres., 1981-85, v.p., 1989-91; mem. bio-med. ethics com. Eastern Va. Med. Sch., 1973-79, Lewis Gale Hosp., Salem, 1988—, Community Hosp. Roanoke Valley, 1990—; trustee Va. Episcopal Sch., Lynchburg, 1979—, Episcopal High Sch., Alexandria, 1979—, Boys' Home, Covington, 1979—, Stuart Hall Sch., Staunton, 1979—, St. Paul's Coll., Lawrenceville, 1979-88; chmn. com. on continuing edn. Va. Theol. Sem., Alexandria, 1985—, v.p. bd. trustees, 1987—; bd. dirs., co-chair rural residency program Appalachian Ministries Ednl. Resource Ctr., Berea, Ky., 1985-87; mem. Am. com. Kiyosato Ednl. Experiment Project, 1990—, v.p., 1991—; mem. Gen. Conv. Standing Com. on World Mission, 1989—; trustee Kanuga Conf. Ctr., 1991—. Fellow St. George's Coll., Jerusalem, 1978, 89; fellow in biomed. ethics U. Va., 1989. Democrat. Office: 1000 1st St SW PO Box 2278 Roanoke VA 24009

LIGHTHALL, TIMOTHY DUANE, minister; b. Adrian, Mich., July 7, 1962; s. Kenneth Duane and Joan Charlene (Lemm) L.; m. Lisa Marie Murrell, Dec. 28, 1985; children: Charissa Marie, Justin Duane. BA, Huntington Coll., 1985; MDiv, Southwestern Bapt. Theol. Inst., 1989. Ordained to ministry So. Bapt. Conv., 1991. Min. youth Manhatten Ave. Bapt. Ch., Tampa, Fla., 1984; youth evangelist Huntington, Ind., 1984-85; min. youth Oakview Bapt. Ch., Ft. Worth, 1986-89; min. youth and edn. Chapin (S.C.) Bapt. Ch., 1989—. Mem. So. Bapt. Religious Edn. Assn., S.C. Bapt. Religious Edn. Assn., S.C. Bapt. Youth and Recreation Mins. Assn. Home: 145 Heber Shealy Circle Chapin SC 29036 Office: Chapin Bapt Ch 950 Old Lexington Hwy Chapin SC 29036 *The Christian life is one of celebration. The Christian celebrates the fact that the God of the universe desires to personally communicate and relate with him or her. There can be no greater thing worth celebrating!.*

LIGHTSEY, RALPH, minister; b. Bristol, Ga., Nov. 27, 1918; s. Willis and Mamie Leon (Bryson) L.; m. Velma Wavine Reeves, Feb. 25, 1945; children: June Elizabeth, Ralph Nelson. BA, Mercer U., 1945; BD, Emory U., 1951; ThM, Columbia Theol. Sem., 1955; EdD, U. Ga., 1965. Ordained to ministry Nat. Assn. Free Will Bapts., 1940. Pastor chs., Ga., 1941-59, St. Mary's Ch., New Bern, N.C., 1959-63, New Light Ch., Morgan, Ga., 1964—; dean Free Will Bapt. Bible Coll., 1951-53; moderator South Ga. Assn., 1947-51, Ga. Assn., 1957-59; pres. South Ga. Sunday Sch. Conv., 1954-57; chmn. ordaining bd. Midway Assn. Free Will Bapts., 1986—. Contbr. articles to ch. publs. Home: 119 Woodlawn Dr Statesboro GA 30458 Office: PO Box 731 Statesboro GA 30458 *I try to treat all my fellow human beings in such a way that I never have to dodge them or cross the street to keep from meeting them.*

LIGHTY, WILLIAM CURTIS, minister; b. Hampton, Va., Oct. 19, 1956; s. William O. and Alma Louise (Stockton) L.; m. Carol Ann Benton, Aug. 5, 1978; children: Trisha Elaine, Ashley Lauren. BS, U. Colo., 1978; MRE, Southwestern Bapt. Theol. Sem., Ft. Worth, 1980. Ordained to ministry So. Bapt. Conv., 1980. Min. students 1st Bapt. Ch., New Orleans, 1980-81, Denton, Tex., 1981-86; pastor Chapel Hills Bapt. Ch., Colorado Springs, 1986—. Home: 8530 Boxelder Dr Colorado Springs CO 80920 Office: Chapel Hills Bapt Ch 2025 Parliament Dr Colorado Springs CO 80920 *Don't ever "stick"- if you "stick" in any system you stop growth, thusly, stop learning.*

LIGUORI, BROTHER JAMES A., school system administrator. Supt. schs. Archdiocese of Newark. Office: Edn Dept 100 Linden Ave Irvington NJ 07111*

LIKNESS, LAWRENCE RICHARD, religious organization administrator; b. Consort, Alta., Can., Sept. 30, 1929; s. Oscar and Doris Rose (Gourlie) L.; m. Doreen Ellen Anderson, June 21, 1952; children: Mark Lawrence, Steven Richard. BA, U. Sask., 1951; BD, Luther Theol. Sem., Saskatoon, Sask., Can., 1952; MTh, Luther Theol. Sem., St. Paul, 1971. Ordained minister Evang. Lutheran Ch. in Can. Parish pastor Our Saviour's Luth. Ch., Thunder Bay, Ont., Can., 1952-57, Mt. Zion Luth. Ch., Edmonton, Alta., 1957-62, Sherwood Park Luth. Ch., Winnipeg, Man., Can., 1962-68, Zion Luth. Ch., Saskatoon, 1968-77, Christ Luth. Ch., Scarborough, Ont., 1979-86; chmn. bd. Div. Congl. Life, Evangel. Luth. Ch. of Can., 1967-77; interim exec. dir Div. Congl. Life, Evangel. Luth. Ch. of Can., Saskatoon, 1977-79; exec. dir. Luth. Coun. in Can., Toronto, Ont., 1986—; commr. Inter-Luth. Commn. on Worship, 1966-77, chmn. 2 yrs.; sec. Ea. Synod Evang. Luth. Ch. in Can., 1986-87; sec. Can. Liturgical Soc., 1981—. Author: With These Promises, Our Christian Faith; contbr. articles to religious pub. Mem. Ea. Metro Curling Club Toronto (pres. 1988-89), Rotary. Office: Luth Coun Can, 25 Old York Mills Rd, Toronto, ON Canada M2P 1B5

LILLEY, JIMMY DAN, minister; b. Mitchell, La., Apr. 4, 1938; s. Sidney Lee and Myrtice (Dans) L.; m. Bonnieveve Mae Miller, June 2, 1962; children: Mark Daniel, Jonathan Paul, Sarah Elizabeth, Caleb James. BA in Bible, LeTourneau Coll., Longview, Tex., 1963; MDiv, Temple Bapt. Sem., Chattanooga, 1968, MRE, 1968; DD, Okla. Bapt. Coll., 1987. Ordained to ministry Ind. Bapt. Ch. Pastor Barron Rd. Bapt. Ch., Keithville, La., 1970-79, Kings Row Bapt. Ch., Alvin, Tex., 1979-83, Calvary Bapt. Ch., Douglas, Wyo., 1983-86, North Woodlawn Bapt. Ch., Derby, Kans., 1986-88, Hinkle Bapt. Ch., Lookout Mountain, Ga., 1988-91; dir. devel. Tenn. Temple U., Chattanooga, 1991—; treas. Frontier Bapt. Missions, Harlingen, Tex., 1972—. Republican. Office: Tenn Temple U 1815 Union Ave Chattanooga TN 37004

LILLICROPP, ARTHUR R(EGINALD), III, health facility administrator, priest; b. Rockville Center, N.Y., June 7, 1947; s. Arthur Reginald Lillicropp and Irene Nora Yerger. BA, Lafayette Coll., 1969; MDiv, Gen. Theol. Sem., 1974; MS in Pastoral Counselling, Loyola U., Balt., 1985. Ordained priest Episcopal Ch., 1974; cert. additions counselor, Md. Curate Christ and St. Stephen's Ch., N.Y.C., 1974-76; asst. rector Trinity Ch., Towson, Md., 1976-79; rector St. John's Episcopal Ch., Balt., 1979-85; dir. pastoral care Howard County Gen. Hosp., Columbia, Md., 1986—; addictions counselor Orchard Hill Treatment Ctr., Columbia, 1989—, also trustee; counselor Wellspring Pastoral Counselling Ctr., Columbia, 1990. Contbr. articles to profl. jours. Fellow Coll. Chaplains; mem. Am. Assn Pastoral Counselors, Am. Coun. Transplantation, Am. Trauma Soc., Rotary (chaplain Columbia club 1991). Democrat. Office: Howard County Gen Hosp 5755 Cedar Ln Columbia MD 21044

LILLIE, BETTY JANE, nun, biblical studies educator; b. Cin., Apr. 11, 1926; d. Harrison Arvil and Hilda Rose (Sante) L. BSEd, Coll. Mt. St. Joseph, 1955, BA, 1961; MA in Theology with distinction, Providence Coll., 1967, MA in Bibl. Studies with distinction, 1975; PhD, Hebrew Union Coll., 1982. Joined Sisters of Charity of Cin., Roman Cath. Ch., 1944. Tchr. various elem. and jr. high schs. Cin., 1947-64; tchr. high schs. Cin., Dayton, Ohio, Lansing, Mich., 1965-74; prof. grad. program Bibl. studies Providence Coll., 1979-83; assoc. prof. Bibl. studies Athenaeum of Ohio/Mt. St. Mary's Sem., Cin., 1982—; adj. prof. United Theol. Sem., Dayton, 1983-84, U. Cin., 1984—; cons. Progoff Intensive Jour. Program, N.Y.C., 1985—; dir. Israel studies program in Israel, Athenaeum of Ohio, Cin., 1989-90. Author: History of the Scholarship on the Wisdom of Solomon, 1983; contbr. book revs., articles to various publs. Mem. Cath. Bibl. Assn. (gov. task force 1987-91), Soc. Bibl. Lit., Ea. Gt. Lakes Bible Soc. (gov. working group 1985-91), Bibl. Archaeology Soc., Coun. on Study Religion, Midwest Jewish Studies Assn. (charter). Home: 2704 Cypress Way Apt 3 Cincinnati OH 45212 Office: Athenaeum Ohio Mount St Mary's Sem 6616 Beechmont Ave Cincinnati OH 45230

LIM, SONIA YII, minister; b. China, Jan. 1, 1924; arrived in The Philippines; d. Edward C. C. and King Hua (Co) Yii; m. Teddy T. Lim, Jan. 3, 1943; children: Dorothy, DoraMay Cantada, Sally Jane, Teddy Jr., Nellie Ann L. Tan, Raymond, Roger. AB, Am. Bordner Sch., Manila, 1944; postgrad., St. Thomas U., Manila, 1948, Cornell U., 1972; DD (hon.), Am. Fellowship Ch., Monterey, Calif., 1982; D of Prayer Tech., World Inst., Manila, 1989. Ordained to ministry Full Gospel Ch., 1981. Min. Internat. Fellowship of Clergy, Alta Vista, Calif., 1980-84; founder, pres. Dove Found. Internat. Inc., 1982—; min. Gospel Crusade Ministerial Fellowship Inc., Bradenton, Fla., 1983—; underwriter Insular Life Ins., Pasay, The Philippines, 1991—. Bd. dirs. Consumers Union of The Philippines, 1971—; chaplain, chmn. internat. rels. Mother's Day and Father's Day Coun., Manila, 1988—. Recipient Angel award Religion in Media, 1984, Golden Leadership award Humanitarian Ctr. The Philippines, 1988, Appreciation award Armed Forces of The Philippines, 1988, award Internat. Cops for Christ Inc., 1990; named Mother of Yr., Gintong Ina Found., 1988. Mem. Philippine Bible Soc. (life), Info. and Referral Svcs. The Philippines (life), Makati C. of C. and Industry (bd. dirs. 1968-72), Manila Bay Breakfast Club (bd. dirs. 1976—), Makati Breakfast Club (chaplain 1988—), Manila Overseas Press Club (assoc.). Mem. Movers Party. Office: Dove Found Internat Sunset View Towers, 2230 Roxas Blvd, Ste 402, Pasay City Metro Manila, The Philippines

LIMA, DAN DENNIS, minister; b. Hamilton, Bermuda, Feb. 19, 1946; s. Angelina Pedro Lima; m. Debra Joyce Kneisler, Aug. 18, 1973; children: Daniel Wayne, Dawn Elizabeth, Diana Marie. A.Bibl. Studies, Nazarene Bible Coll., Colorado Springs, Colo., 1978, A.Religious Edn., 1979; BA, Mid-Am. Nazarene Coll., Olathe, Kans., 1981; M.Pastoral Counseling, Olivet Nazarene U., Kankakee, Ill., 1989. Ordained to ministry, Ch. of the Nazarene. Youth leader Young Life Orgn., Hamilton, 1971-75; mgr. Navigators, Colorado Springs, 1976-79; assoc. pastor Ch. of the Nazarene, Wichita, Kans., 1981-84; youth pastor Ch. of the Nazarene, Grand Rapids, Mich., 1984-86; assoc. pastor Ch. of the Nazarene, Lafayette, Ind., 1986—; dist. v.p. Nazarene Youth Internat., N.W. Ind., 1986-89, dist. teen cap dir., 1986-89, dist. adult dir. Sun. Sch. Ministries, 1989—. Mem. Christian Assn. for Psychol. Studies, Am. Assn. of Christian Counselors, Am. Assn. Family Counselors. Home: 3613 Platte Ct Lafayette IN 47905 Office: First Ch of the Nazarene 3650 E Greenbush St Lafayette IN 47905

LIMBAUGH, MARC WAYNE, pastor; b. Gasden, Ala., Dec. 6, 1953; s. James Curtis and Marcelene M. (Moore) L.; m. Janet Gayle Spratling, Aug. 9, 1973; children: Rachel, Bethany, Jonathan. BTh., Liberty Bible Coll., 1976. Ordained to ministry Liberty Fellowship of Churches and Ministers, 1976. Youth pastor Revival Tabernacle, Gadsden, 1973; assoc. pastor New Covenant Ch., Jackson, Miss., 1976-79; sr. pastor New Covenant Ch., Harrisville, Miss., 1979—; dist. overseer Miss. Dist. Liberty Fellows, 1983—; presbyter Liberty Fellowship Chs., Birmingham, Ala., 1983—. Contbr. articles to local newspaper. Aux. mem. Harrisville Vol. Fire Dept. Named One of Outstanding Young Men of Am., 1986. Republican. Avocations: trumpet playing, music, writing, nature. Home: PO Box 224 Harrisville MS 39082 Office: New Covenant Ch Hwy 469 Harrisville MS 39082

LIMBURG, JAMES WALLACE, religion educator; b. Redwood Falls, Minn., Mar. 2, 1935; s. Stanley Wallace and Ella (Groote) L.; m. Martha Ylvisaker, Aug. 3, 1957; children: Kristi, David, Mark, Paul. BA, Luther Coll., Decorah, Iowa, 1956; BD, Luther Theol. Sem., St. Paul, 1961; MTh, Union Sem., Richmond, Va., 1962, PhD, 1969. Prof. religion Augustana Coll., Sioux Falls, S.D., 1962-78; prof. Old Testament Luther Northwestern Theol. Sem., 1978—. Author: The Prophets and the Powerless, 1977, Psalms for Sojourners, 1986, Hosea-Micah: Interpretation. A Bible Commentary for Teaching and Preaching, 1988; translator, editor: Judaism: An Introduction for Christians, 1987. Mem. Soc. Bibl. Lit., Cath. Bibl. Assn. Am. Mem. Evang. Luth. Ch. in Am. Office: Luther Northwestern Theol Sem 2481 Como Ave Saint Paul MN 55108

LIN, TIAN-MIN, religion educator; b. Taiwan, Dec. 21, 1935; came to U.S., 1961; parents U-ta and Ni-shi (Hsu) L.; m. Hsueh-man Lee, July 28, 1967; children: Stephen, May, Tina. BA, Nat. Taiwan U., 1959; MDiv, Yale U., 1964, MST, 1965; PhD, Boston U., 1969. Asst. prof. Tougaloo (Miss.) Coll., 1969-72; prof. Indiana U. Pa., 1972—. Author: The Life and Thought of Kierkegaard, 1974, Christianity and the Modern World, 1988; editor: Readings in the World's Living Religions, 1974, Introduction to Religion, 1987. Recipient Disting. Faculty award Indiana U. Pa., 1975. Mem. Am. Acad. Religion. Methodist. Home: 205 Forest Ridge Rd Indiana PA 15701 Office: Indiana U Pa Dept Philosophy & Religious Studies Indiana PA 15705

LINCOLN, EUGENE, religious organization executive; b. Marion, Ind., Oct. 5, 1923; s. Albert and Glenora Agnes (Townsend) L.; m. Darlene Jacqueline Boatwright, July 4, 1947; children: David Lee, Michael Eugene, Angelita Karolene, Jonathan Wayne. BS, Marion Coll., 1948; MA, Andrews U., 1973. Credentialed missionary Seventh-day Adventists, 1979. Editor The Sabbath Sentinel, Fairview, Okla., 1960-85; copy editor Rev. and Herald Pub. Assn., Hagerstown, Md., 1974-89; 1st v.p. Bible Sabbath Assn., Fairview, 1976-88, pres., 1988—; bd. dirs., mem. adv. bd. Seventh-day Adventist Missionary Found., Phoenix, 1980—. Author: Right Face, 1976, The High Cost of Loving, 1979, Understanding the Power of Prayer, 1984; contbr. articles to various pbuls. Democrat. Home: 1228 Wayne Ave Hagerstown MD 21740 Office: Bible Sabbath Assn Rte 1 Box 222 Fairview OK 73737 *I hope that when I leave the world, it will be partly because of my life in better shape that it was when I arrived here.*

LINDAHL, ELDER M., philosophy and religion educator; b. Iron River, Mich., Apr. 5, 1926; s. Harold A. and Martha (Durow) L.; m. Muriel R. Johnson, Aug. 5, 1950; children: Kristine, Wesley, Paul, Renee. BA, Mich. State U., 1951; MA, U. Mich., 1952; MDiv, North Park Sem., 1960; PhD, Northwestern U., 1966. Ordained to ministry Evang. Covenant Ch., 1962. Prof. philosophy and religious studies North Park Coll., Chgo., 1952-90, prof. emeritus, 1991—. Tech sgt. U.S. Army, 1944-46, ETO. Mem. Am. Acad. Religion, Am. Philos. Assn., Phi Kappa Phi, Phi Sigma Tau.

LINDBERG, CARTER HARRY, religious studies educator; b. Berwyn, Ill., Nov. 23, 1937; s. Gustaf Harry and Esther (Bell) L.; m. Alice Knudsen, June 4, 1960; children: Anne, Erika, Matthew. BA, Augustana Coll., 1959; MDiv, Luth Sch. Theology, 1962; PhD, U. Iowa, 1965. Assoc. prof. ch. history and theology Boston U., 1972-85, prof., 1985—; rsch. prof. Inst. Ecumenical Rsch., Strasbourg, France, 1979-82; pres. 16th Century Studies Conf., 1978-79; mem. continuation com. Internat. Congress for Luther Rsch., 1983—. Author: The Third Reformation?, 1983, Charismatic Renewal and the Lutheran Tradition, 1985, Martin Luther: Justified by Grace, 1988; co-author: Okumene am Ort, 1983; editor: Piety, Politics and Ethics, 1984; (with others) Luther's Ecumenical Significance, 1984, Christianity: A Social and Cultural History, 1991; editor book rev. Luth. Quar.; contbr. articles to profl. jours. Mem. Am. Soc. Reformation Rsch., Am. Soc. Ch. History, 16th Century Studies Conf., Luther Gesellschaft. Home: 113 Whitney St Northboro MA 01532 Office: Boston U Sch Theology 745 Commonwealth Boston MA 02215

LINDBERG, DAVID HENDERSON, minister; b. Warren, Pa., Sept. 13, 1937; s. Carl Leander and Leah Lucile (Henderson) L.; m. Patricia Ann Tabor, Aug. 21, 1959 (wid. Apr. 1975); children: Peter Carl, Amy Ruth; m. Susan Lynn Giese, Mar. 6, 1976; 1 child, Heather Sue. BA, Albion Coll., 1959; MDiv, Wesley Theol. Seminary, Washington, 1963. Ordained to ministry Meth. Ch., 1963. Pastor Jerome-Somerset (Mich.) Ctr., 1958-59, Tex. Meth. Cir., Cockeysville, Md., 1959-63, Fairall United Meth. Cir., Waynesburg, Pa., 1963-68, Beulah Park United Meth. Ch., McKeesport, Pa., 1968-80, New Brighton (Pa.) Parish, 1980—; statistician Western Pa. Conf., Mars, 1966-88; chmn. Bd. Pensions, Mars, 1989—; del. Northeastern Jurisdictional Conf., 1980-92. Bd. dirs. ARC, Waynesburg, 1966-68; sec. Corp. for Owner-Operator Projects, Beaver, Pa., 1987—; treas. Mon-Valley Coun. on Alcoholism, McKeesport, Pa., 1971-80. Named Jr. Citizen of Yr., Jaycees, Warren, 1955. Mem. Nat. Eagle Scout Assn., Lions, AF&AFM, Omicron Delta Kappa, Phi Mu Alpha Sinfonia. Office: First United Meth Church 1033 Sixth Ave New Brighton PA 15066-2029

LINDBERG, DENNIS ANTON, minister; b. Edgewood, Md., Feb. 27, 1945; s. Harry Anton and LaVerne Katherine (Blaska) L.; m. Jane Burnet Ward, Aug. 14, 1971; children: Mark Anton, Laura Jane, Luke Ward, Jonathan Peter. Student, Mich. Tech. U., Houghton, 1963-64; BA, Drury Coll., Splringfield, Mo., 1969; MDiv, Eden Theol. Sem., Webster Groves, Mo., 1972, postgrad., 1985—. Ordained to ministry United Ch. of Christ, 1972. Assoc. pastor Hope United Ch. of Christ, St. Louis, 1972-76; pastor Ivy Chapel of the United Ch. of Christ, Chesterfield, Mo., 1976—; Pres. Jeffco Pastor's Circle, St. Louis, 1979, 89, 90; chmn. commn. on leadership and prog. Mo. Conf. United Ch. of Christ, 1978-80, chmn. ann. mtg., 1980, 86; chmn. St. Louis Assn. Ch. and Min. Commn., 1990; clown Christian Clown Ministry, 1980—. s. Webelos leaders local chpt. Boy Scouts Am., 1984, 89, 90, chmn. com., 1985-88; featured leader Camp Miniwanca, Am. Youth Found., Shelby, Mich., 1980, 82, 84. Named hon. chaplain Order of the Arrow, Boy Scouts Am., St. Louis, 1976. Mem. St. Louis Ministerium (pres. 1978, 82, 83), Chesterfield C. of C. Office: Ivy Chapel United Ch Christ 620 N Woods Mill Rd Chesterfield MO 63017

LINDBERG, DONNA JEANNE, minister; b. Pontiac, Mich., Oct. 15, 1944; d. Hugo W. and Ina A. (Ballard) L.; children: Richard Ronald, Christopher Charles. BA, Adrian Coll., 1966; ThM, So. Meth. U., 1969. Ordained to ministry Meth. Ch., as deacon, 1967, as elder, 1971.. Assoc. pastor Beverly Hills United Meth. Ch., Birmingham, Mich., 1970-72, Port Huron (Mich.) United Meth. Ch., 1972-73, Livonia (Mich.) Newburg United Meth. Ch., 1973-74; pastor Rice Meml. United Meth. Ch., Redford, Mich., 1974-79, Hazel Park (Mich.) United Meth. Ch., 1979-83, Gaylord (Mich.) United Meth. Ch., 1983-89, Ann Arbor (Mich.) Dist. United Meth. Ch., 1989—; del. World Meth. Coun., Honolulu, 1981; cons. Clergy Women, Clergy Couples, Ethnic Min. Clergy Women, Detroit, 1984-88; mem. Jurisdictional Ct. of Appeals United Meth. Ch., Chgo., 1988—; registrar Detroit Conf. Bd. of Ordained Ministry, 1972-84; counselor Mich. Assn. of Problem Pregnancy Counselors, Birmingham, 1970-75; pres. Clergy Assn., Gaylord, 1984-88. Bd. dirs. Hospice, Gaylord, 1986-88, Big Bros./Big Sisters, Gaylord, 1985-87; mem. Sch. Bd. Adv. Com., Gaylord, 1984-89. Recipient Clergy of Yr. award Kiwanis Internat., 1988. Mem. Order Eastern Star. Office: Ann Arbor Dist United Meth 900 S Seventh St Ste 1 Ann Arbor MI 48103 *In a world where war is still a reality, basic human needs are in many places unmet and environmental concerns are pressing, it behooves us to seek the guidance of the One who created and sustains us and to Whom we are accountable.*

LINDBERG, DUANE R., minister. Presiding pastor The Am. Assn. Luth. Chs., Waterloo, Iowa. Office: Luth Chs Am Assn PO Box 416 Waterloo IA 50701*

LINDBERG, THOMAS HAROLD, minister; b. Mpls., Nov. 10, 1952; s. Harold Brynolf and Edna Serene (Sundet) L.; m. Sandra Kay Speich, May 26, 1973; children: Christopher, Thomas, Jonathan Mark, Amy Alyssa. BA, North Cen. Bible Coll., 1974; M in Theol. Studies, Gordon-Conwell Theol. Sem., 1976. Ordained to ministry Assemblies of God Ch., 1979. Min. edn. Brookfield (Wis.) Assembly of God, 1976-81; pastor First Assembly of God, Stevens Point, Wis., 1981—. Contbr. articles to profl. jours. Ministerial chmn. United Way, Stevens Point, 1985. Home: 3272 Soo Marie Stevens Point WI 54481 Office: First Assembly of God 1101 Hoover Rd Stevens Point WI 54481

LINDBLADE, ERIC NORMAN, JR., minister; b. Cleve., Dec. 17, 1952; s. Eric Norman and Helen Clara (Belger) L.; m. Susan Lee Clayton, Mar. 10, 1979; 1 child, Eric Alexander. BA, Duke U., 1975, MDiv, 1978. Ordained elder United Meth. Ch., 1982. Pastor Garysburg (N.C.) United Meth. Ch., 1978-80; assoc. pastor Univ. United Meth. Ch., Chapel Hill, N.C., 1980-81; pastor South Camden (N.C.) United Meth. Ch., 1981-86, East Rockingham (N.C.) United Meth. Ch., 1986-90, 1st United Meth. Ch., Rockingham, 1990—; chmn. N.C. Conf. Commn. on Christian Unity, Raleigh, N.C., 1988—; sec. N.C. Con. Coun. on Ministries, Raleigh, 1988—; del. N.C. Coun. Chs., Raleigh, 1984—, Nat. Workshop on Christian Unity, St. Louis, 1986—. Mem. Richmond County Civic Index, Rockingham, 1990—; chmn. Richmond County CROP Walk, Rockingham; registrar Rockingham Election Bd., 1987-88; bd. dirs. Richmond County Habitat for Humanity, Rockingham, 1990—. Mem. Richmond County Ministerial Assn. (pres. 1987-90), Civitan (chaplain Rockingham chpt. 1986-90). Republican. Home: 512 Scotland Ave Rockingham NC 28379 Office: 1st United Meth Ch 410 E Washington St PO Box 637 Rockingham NC 28379

LINDE, RICHARD B. L., minister; b. Lima, Ohio, May 5, 1919; s. Elmer Calvin and Mary Mae (Lindamood) Lugabill; m. Laraine Ogden, June 29, 1949; children: Richard Edwards, Thomas Hooker, Robert Downing. MDiv, Drew U., 1945; MBA, Harvard U., 1949; D of Ministry, Christian Theol. Sem., 1972. Ordained to ministry Meth. Ch., 1945. Assoc. min. Epworth-Euclid Meth. Ch., Cleve., 1949-54; min. Edwards Congl. Ch., Northampton, Mass., 1954-60; sr. min. 1st Congl. Ch., Elyria, Ohio, 1960-73; sr. min. Countryside Community Ch., Omaha, 1973-90, min. emeritus, 1990—; chmn. bd. dirs. and exec. com. Bd. Homeland Ministries, United Ch. Christ; cons. United Ch. Bd. for Homeland Ministries, 1990—; chmn. bd. dirs. Nebr. Conf. United Ch. Christ; bd. dirs. Together, Inc. Producer film documentaries for nat. TV. Pres. Lorain County Family Svc. Assn. Chaplain USNR, 1945-46. Recipient Meritorious Svc. award Army-Navy Commn. on Chaplains, Disting. Svc. award U.S. Com. UN. Mem. Harvard Bus. Sch. Assn., Lorain County Family Svc. Assn. (pres.), Explorers Club of N.Y., Rotary. Home: 60 Stanwell St Colorado Springs CO 80906

LINDEN, MATTHEW MCKINLEY, lay worker; b. Glendale, Calif., May 5, 1970; s. Arthur Ralph Linden and Mary Ann (Vervalin) Shuker. Student, Glendale Coll., 1988-91, Point Loma Nazarene Coll., 1991—. Dir. jr. high program Glendale (Calif.) YMCA, 1989-91; tchr. sr. high Sunday Sch. 1st Ch. of the Nazarene, Pasadena, Calif., 1989-91, dir. youth program, 1991—; waiter Stouffer's Restaurants, Glendale, 1991—. Republican. Home: 3900 Lomaland Dr # K-132 San Diego CA 92106 Office: Glendale YMCA 140 N Louise Glendale CA 91101 *If you're not giving-then you're not living.*

LINDERMAN, JEANNE HERRON, priest; b. Erie, Pa., Nov. 14, 1931; d. Robert Leslie and Ella Marie (Stearns) Herron; m. James Stephens Linderman; children: Mary Susan, John Randolph, Richard Webster, Craig Stephens, Mark Herron, Elizabeth Stewart. BS in Indsl. and Labor Rels., Cornell U., 1953; MDiv magna cum laude, Lancaster Theol. Sem., 1981; postgrad., clin. pastoral edn., Del. State Hosp., New Castle, 1981. Ordained priest, Episcopal Ch. Mem. pers. staff Hengerer Co., Buffalo, 1953-55; chaplain Cathedral Ch. St. John, Wilmington, Del., 1981-82; priest-in-charge Christ Episcopal Ch., Delaware City, Del., 1982-87; vicar Christ Episcopal Ch., 1987-91; assoc. rector St. Andrew's Episcopal Ch., Wilmington, Del., 1991—; chair human sexuality task force, Diocese of Del., 1981-82, mem. clergy compensation com. and diocesan coun., 1982-86, pres. standing com., 1991—, com. on constitution and canons, 1989. Author, editor hist. study papers. Bd. dirs., St. Michael's Day Nursery, Wilmington, 1985-88; mem. Cornell Univ. Secondary Schs. Com.; chmn. bd. dirs. Geriatric Svcs. Del., 1989—. Mem. Episcopal Women's Caucus, Del. Episcopal Clergy Assn., Nat. Assn. Episcopal Clergy, DAR, Mayflower Soc., Dutch Colonial Soc. Del., Stoney Run Questers, Cornell Women's Club Del., Women of St. James the Less, Women's Witnessing Community at Lambeth. Republican. Avocations: history, genealogy, travel. Home: 307 Springhouse Ln Hockessin DE 19707 Office: St Andrews's Episcopal Ch Eighth and Shipley Sts Wilmington DE 19801

LINDGREN, DONALD, minister; b. Lynn, Mass., May 28, 1930; s. Raymond and Effie Marshal (MacLeod) L. B.A., Yankton Coll, 1953; B.Th., Yankton Coll. Theology, 1954; Th.M., Eden Theol. Sem., 1961; postgrad., Edinburgh U. (Scotland), 1962-64. Ordained to ministry United Church of Christ, 1954. Minister Congl. Ch., Genoa, Nebr., 1953-56, Sauk Centre, Minn., 1956-60; interim minister Colonial Ch. Edina, Minn., 1960-61; asst. minister Ch. Highlands, White Plains, N.Y., 1961-62; minister Musselburgh Congl., Scotland, 1968—; hon. minister Congl. Ch., Genoa, Nebr.; hon. chaplain 297 Musselburgh Squadron, Air Tng. Corps. Author: Designs for Christian Living, 1962, Musselburgh in Old Picture Postcards, 1987, vol. 2, 1989, The Fifth of Fourth in Old Picture Postcard, 1989; contbr. articles to newspapers. Lodges: Rotary, Masons. Home: 8 The Grove, Musselburgh, Midlothian EH21 7HD, Scotland

LINDHOLM, RONALD DALE, minister; b. Valentine, Nebr., Aug. 31, 1958; s. Dale David and Dolores Cecil (Hennings) L.; m. Neita Faye Wilson, June 13, 1980; 1 child, David Alton. Student, W.Va. U., 1976-78; BS, U. Scranton, Pa., 1980; M of Divinity, Bapt. Bible Theol. Sem., Clarks Summit, Pa., 1985, postgrad., 1985—. Ordained to ministry Bapt. ch., 1981. Minister of music Emmanuel Bapt. Ch., Morgantown, W.Va., 1980-82; commdr. Heritage Bapt. Ch., Clarks Summit, 1982-83, pastoral apprentice, 1983-85, dir. visitation/outreach, 1983-85; interim pastor Bible Bapt. Ch., Cairo, N.Y., 1983; pastor Faith Bapt. Ch., Altoona, Pa., 1987—; itinerant Bible tchr. various chs. northeastern U.S., 1982-87; assoc. Bible teacher Way of Truth Ministries, 1990—; bd. dirs. Way of Truth Ministries Inc., 1991—. Reginald L. Matthews scholar Bapt. Bible Theol. Sem., 1985, Robert J. Williams scholar Bapt. Bible Theol. Sem., 1985. Republican. Avocations: long distance running, basketball, gardening, reading. Home: Box 9 Willowbrook Village Duncansville PA 16635 Office: Faith Bapt Ch 315 40th St Altoona PA 16602

LINDHOLM, WILLIAM CHARLES, clergyman; b. Perry, Iowa, Mar. 20, 1932; s. Lester Leander and Elizabeth (Winegar) L.; m. Patricia Ann Schneider, Feb. 14, 1953; children: Jonell, Jana, William Jr. BA, Augustana Coll., 1954; MDiv, Luth. Sch. Theology, Chgo., 1958. Ordained to ministry Luth. Ch., 1958. Pastor Grace Luth. Ch., Oscoda, Mich., 1958-70, Hope Luth. Ch., East Tawas, Mich., 1958-70, Holy Cross Luth. Ch., Livonia, Mich., 1970—; chmn. Nat. Com. for Amish Religious Freedom, 1967—. Editor: Michigan Synod News, 1970—. Bd. dirs. Carthage Coll., Kenosha, Wis., 1985—. Lutheran. Home: 15343 Susanna Circle Livonia MI 48154 Office: Holy Cross Luth Ch 30650 Six Mile Rd Livonia MI 48152

LINDLEY, CHARLES ALLEN, minister; b. Eugene, Oreg., May 27, 1950; s. Earl Foreest and Elsie Mirie (Kelner) L.; m. Janis Joy Norman, Aug. 28, 1971; children: Christopher, Elisabeth, Heather, Brandon. Student, Whitman Coll., 1968-70; BS, U. Oreg., 1973; MA in Christian Edn., Western Conservative Bapt. Sem., 1982. Ordained to ministry Ind. Fundamental Chs. Am., 1989. Assoc. pastor Meml. Bapt. Ch., Gresham, Oreg., 1984-86; pastor Christ's Bible Ch., Hamilton, Mont., 1986—; v.p. Mont. region Ind. Fundamental Chs. Am., 1988—. Mem. Ravalli County Ministerial Assn. (v.p., sec. 1989-90). Home: 317 S 5th St Hamilton MT 59840 Office: Christ's Bible Ch PO Box 1403 Hamilton MT 59840

LINDO, EDWIN THESSALONIANS, minister; b. Turlock, Calif., June 25, 1953; s. William Edward and Josephine Mary (Mello) L.; m. Tonja Debralee Herr, Oct. 30, 1971; children: Phillip Paul, Shonna Desiri. Student, Bethany Bible Coll., 1971, Berean Coll., 1973, Intern. Bible Inst. and Sem., 1980, Modesto Jr. Coll., 1982-85. Ordained to ministry Assemblies of God, 1984. Youth and music min. Keyes (Calif.) Assembly of God, 1973-79; sr. pastor, sect. youth dir. Livingston (Calif.) Assembly of God, 1979-80; asst. pastor Northwest Assembly of God, Salida, Calif., 1981-85; warehouseman Gen. Foods Corp., Modesto, Calif., 1982—; sr. pastor Airport Assembly of God Ch., Modesto, 1986—; dist. Bible Quiz coord. Assemblies of God, Santa Cruz, Calif., 1979-80; dir. of meals to the poor, Airport Assembly of God Ch., 1985—. Mem. Stanislaus County Safety Coun., Modesto, 1974-77; representing majority whip 15th Congl. dist., Nat. Prayer Breakfast and Sem., Washington, 1986; bd. dirs. Credit Union for Organized Labor, Modesto, 1991—. Merrell fellow Harvard Theol. Sem., 1986. Democrat. Office: Airport Assembly of God 603 Benson Ave Modesto CA 95354 *If in passing through this life I cannot make a positive impact upon another person, my life was spent in vain and useless.*

LINDQUIST, RAYMOND IRVING, clergyman; b. Sumner, Nebr., Apr. 14, 1907; s. Rev. Elmer H. and Esther (Nyberg) L.; m. Ella Sofield, Sept. 16, 1930; children: Ray Irving, Ruth Elizabeth Lindquist McCalmont. Student, Kearney State Coll., 1925; A.B., Wheaton Coll., Ill., 1929; student, Columbia Law Sch., 1929-30; A.M., Princeton U., 1933; Th.B. (Hugh Davies prize homiletics; Erdman prize Bible; Zwemer fellow Comparative Religions), Princeton Sem., 1933; D.D., Cumberland U., 1939, Ursinus Coll., 1980; LL.D., Bloomfield Coll., N.J., 1957, Eastern Coll., 1977; L.H.D., Calif. Coll. Medicine, 1963. Ordained to ministry Presbyn. Ch., 1934; dir. religious edn. Third Presbyn. Ch., Newark, 1931-34; minister Old First Presbyn. Ch., Orange, N.J., 1934-53, Hollywood First Presbyn. Ch., 1953-71; vis. prof. homiletics Bloomfield Sem., N.J., 1945-53; lectr. Princeton Sem., Pittcairn-Crabbe, Pitts., USAF, Israel, Germany, Johnston Island; lectr. UCLA, U. So. Calif.; lectr. Pentagon, Northwestern U.; Pres. bd. nat. missions United Presbyn. Ch., 1955-62, gen. council, 1955-62; v.p. Templeton Found. Author: Notes for Living. Bd. dirs. Presbyn. Ministers Fund, Phila., chmn. bd., 1980—; bd. dirs. Presbyn. Med. Center, Hollywood, Calif., 1954—, Met. YMCA, Los Angeles; trustee Princeton Theol. Sem., So. Calif. Presbyn. Homes., Olmstead Trust, Hollywood, Calif., 1954—. Recipient Gold medal Religious Heritage Am., 1984. Mem. Phi Kappa Delta. Clubs: Rotary (Los Angeles) (bd. dirs.), Los Angeles Country (Los Angeles); Symposium (Princeton); Glen Lake (Sparta, N.J.), Sunset Rock (Sparta, N.J.); Shadow Mountain (Palm Desert, Calif.). Home: 568 B Ave Sevilla Laguna Hills CA 92653 also: 21 Afterglow Rd Sparta NJ 07871 also: 74237 Old Prospector Trail Palm Desert CA 92260 *Faith is not jumping to conclusions: it is concluding to jump...The thought of God swings the world like a rock on a rope.*

LINDSAY, EMERY, minister; b. Sparta, Wis., July 14, 1951; s. Vernon and Aretha (Thomas) L.; m. Pearl Hendricks, Aug. 17, 1975; children: Camile, Melanie, Rachel, Erica, Brittany, Vernan. BS, LeMoyne Coll., Memphis, 1976; MA, Trinity Evang. Div. Sch., Deerfield, Ill., 1988. Ordained to ministry Ch. of Christ (Holiness) U.S.A., 1974. Pastor Christ Temple Ch., Memphis, 1974-76, Kansas City, Kans., 1976-81, Chgo., 1981-91; bishop No. Diocese Ch. of Christ (Holiness) USA, Chgo., 1991—; exec. bd. Ch. of Christ Holiness USA, 1980-88, mem. nat. pub. bd., 1980-88; sec. North Cen. Diocese, 1978-81. Corres. sec. Black Coun. of Chs., Chgo., 1983-87. With U.S. Army, 1974-76. Home: 8321 S Calumet Chicago IL 60619 Office: 62 W 111th Pl Chicago IL 60619

LINDSAY, FREDA THERESA, clergywoman, editor; b. Burstall, Sask., Can., Apr. 18, 1914; d. Gottfred and Kaity (Saklofsky) Schimpf; m. Gordon Lindsay, Nov. 14, 1937 (dec. 1973); children—Carole Ann Sorko-Ram, Gilbert Livingston, Dennis Gordon. B.A., L.I.F.E., 1938, D.D. (hon), 1977; LittD Oral Roberts U., 1987. Co-pastor Ch. of Foursquare Gospel, Oreg., 1950; pres., editor Christ for the Nations, Dallas, 1973-85, chmn. bd., 1985—. Author: My Diary Secrets, 1976; Freda, 1984. Editor books. Named Christian Woman of Yr. Acts Ministry Am. Christian Voice Found., 1983. Mem. Full Gospel Fellowship of Chs. and Ministers Internat. (v.p. 1977-87, bd. dirs. 1976). Republican. Avocations: reading; swimming. Office: Christ for the Nations Inc 3404 Conway St Dallas TX 75224

LINDSELL, HAROLD, clergyman, educator, editor; b. N.Y.C., Dec. 22, 1913; s. Leonard Anthony and Ella Briggs (Harris) L.; B.S., Wheaton Coll., 1938; M.A., U. Calif., 1939, Ph.D., N.Y. U., 1942; D.D., Fuller Theol. Sem., 1964; m. Marion Joanne Bolinder, June 12, 1943; children—Judith Ann (Mrs. William C. Wood), Joanne (Mrs. Robert Webber), Nancy J. (Mrs. Daniel Sharp), John H. Prof. history, missions, registrar Columbia Bible Coll., 1942-44; ordained to ministry Baptist Ch., 1944; prof. missions, assoc. prof. ch. history No. Bapt. Theol. Sem., 1944-47, prof., 1947-51, registrar, 1947-50, dean, 1950-51; dean faculty, prof. missions Fuller Theol. Sem., 1951-61, v.p., prof. missions, 1961-64; assoc. editor Christianity Today, 1964-67, editor, pub., 1968-78; prof. Bible, Wheaton (Ill.) Coll., 1967-68; prof. apologetics Simon Greenleaf Sch. Law, 1983-89, dir. M.A. program, 1984-89. Mem. exec. com. Internat. Congress on World Evangelization. Trustee emeritus Westmont Coll., Wheaton Coll.; chmn. emeritus Gordon Conwell Theol. Sem., Outreach, Christianity Today. Mem. Tournament Roses, Nat. Assn. Bible Instrs., Am. Hist. Assn., Am. Soc. Ch. History, Nat., Greater Washington (pres. 1966-67) assns. evangelicals, NEA, Am. Acad. Polit. and Social Scis., Evang. Theol. Soc. (pres. 1970-71), Pi Gamma Mu, Pi Kappa Delta, Alpha Gamma Omega. Republican. Clubs: Nat. Press, Cosmos (Washington). Author: Abundantly Above, 1944; The Thing Appointed, 1949; A Christian Philosophy of Missions, 1949; Park Street Prophet, 1951; (with C.J. Woodbridge) Handbook of Christian Truth, 1953; Missionary Principles and Practice, 1955; The Morning Altar, 1956; Daily Bible Readings from the Revised Standard Version, 1957; Christianity and the Cults, 1963; Harper Study Bible (rev. standard version), 1964, 91; When You Pray, 1969; The World, The Flesh and The Devil, 1974; The Battle for the Bible, 1976; God's Incomparable Word, 1978; The Bible in the Balance, 1979; The Lindsell Study Bible in the Living Bible, 1980; The Gathering Storm, 1980; Free Enterprise: a Judeo-Christian Defense, 1982; The Holy Spirit in the Latter Days, 1983; Armageddon Spectre, 1984, The People's Study Bible in King James and Living Bible, 1986, The New Paganism, 1987; also articles; editor: The Church's Worldwide Mission, 1966, Harper Study Bible (New Am. Standard Version), 1985, The Everyday Pocket Bible, 1988, Tyndale Words of God for Every Day, 1989, New Harper Study Bible (New Rev. Standard Version), 1991. Home: 5395 A Paseo del Lago Laguna Hills CA 92653

LINDSEY, HAL, writer; m. Jan Lindsey; 3 children. ThM, Dallas Theol. Sem. Former missionary Campus Crusade for Christ. Author: There's a New World Coming: "A Prophetic Odyssey", 1973, The Liberation of Planet Earth, 1974, The Promise, 1974, When Is Jesus Coming Again?, 1974, Homo Sapiens: Extinction or Evacuation, 1976, The Events That Changed My Life, 1977, The 1980's: Countdown to Armageddon, 1980, The Rapture, 1983, A Prophetical Walk through the Holy Land, 1983, Combat Faith, 1986, Road to Holocaust, 1989; (with Carole C. Carlson) The Late Great Planet Earth, 1970, Sata Is Alive and Well on Planet Earth, 1972, The Terminal Generation, 1976. Office: care Hal Lindsey Ministries PO Box 4000 Palos Verdes CA 90274*

LINDSEY, RICHARD LEE, minister; b. Waxahachie, Tex., July 5, 1948; s. Middleton Lee Foy and Daisy May (Lynch) L.; m. Rebecca Ann Hart, May 31, 1975; children: Christina Michelle, Christopher Matthew. BS, Southwestern Assemblies of God, Waxahachie, 1970; MA, Assemblies of God Theol., Seminary, Springfield, Mo., 1977; postgrad., La. State U., 1986-88. Ordained to ministry Assemblies of God, 1973. Evangelist Assemblies of God, 1972-74; pastor First Assembly of God Ch., Cleveland, Tex., 1978-80, Evangel Temple, Valley, Ala., 1981-83; dir. student ministry, prof. Jimmy Swaggert Bible Coll., Baton Rouge, La., 1984-86, dir. of testing, prof., 1986-88; pastor First Assembly of God, Toms River, N.J., 1988—; sec./treas. east cen. sect. of N.J. Dist. Assemblies of God, 1990—, com. mem. continuing edn. com., 1988—; com. mem. Chi Alpha com. South Tex. Dist., Houston, 1979. Named to Outstanding Young Men of Am., 1977. Office: First Assembly of God Ch 800 Bay Ave Toms River NJ 08753

LINDSEY, WILLIAM DENNIS, religious studies educator; b. Little Rock, Mar. 30, 1950; s. Benjamin Dennis and Hattie Clotine (Simpson) L. BA, Loyola U., New Orleans, 1972; MA, Tulane U., 1988; PhD, St. Michael's U., Toronto, Ont., Can., 1987. Instr. Xavier U., New Orleans, 1984-86, asst. prof., 1986-91, chair theol. dept., 1990-91; chair theol. dept. Belmont Abbey Coll., Belmont, N.C., 1991—; educator in elder law Law Clinic, Loyola U., 1989-90. Author: Ethics and Morality, 1989. Singing in a Strange Land, 1991; contbr. articles to profl. publs. Mem. acad. adv. bd. Inst. for Ministry, Loyola U., 1988—. Ctr. for Humanities fellow, 1989; United Negro Coll. Fund grantee, 1986; C. Douglas Jay scholar, 1983. Mem. Am. Acad. Religion, Coll. Theol. Soc. (pres. New Orleans chpt. 1990—), Catholic Theology Soc. Am. Democrat. Home: 615 Ridgeway Dr Belmont NC 28012 Office: Belmont Abbey Coll Dept Theology Belmont NC 28012

LINDSLEY, DANA FREDERICK, pastor; b. Caracas, Venezuela, Feb. 18, 1949; s. Charles Frederick and Adora Lou (Snedecor) L.; m. Janet Leigh Holmberg, Sept. 2, 1972; children: Andrew Nelson, Bryan Frederick, Jonathan David. BA, Occidental Coll., 1971; MDiv, Princeton Sem., 1974. Ordained to ministry Presbyn. Ch., 1974. Pastor Trinity Presbyn. Ch., Scotia, N.Y., 1974-84, 1st Presbyn. Ch., Pottstown, Pa., 1984—; pres. Cluster of Religious Com., Pottstown, 1986-89; chmn. coms. Albany (N.Y.) Presbytery, 1974-84. Mem. human rights commn. Indian Creek Found., Souderton, Pa., 1989—; mem. Institutional Rev. of Hosp., Pottstown, 1985—; sec. Community Devel. Corp., Pottstown, 1985-89; coun. officer Boy Scouts Am., 1985—. Recipient Hugh Scott (Community Svc.) award U.S. Senate, 1989. Home: 1530 N Adams St Pottstown PA 19464 Office: First Presbyn Ch 750 N Evans St Pottstown PA 19464

LINDSTROM, DONALD FREDRICK, JR., marriage and family therapist, consultant, priest; b. Atlanta, July 18, 1943; s. Donald Fredrick Sr. and Elizabeth (Haynes) L.; m. Marcia Pace, Dec. 30, 1983; children: Christopher, Eric, Ashley, Ellison. ABJ, U. Ga., 1966; MDiv, Va. Theol. Sem., 1969; JD, Woodrow Wilson Coll. Law, 1977; postgrad., U. West Fla., 1984. Lic. marriage and family therapist, Fla. Broadcast journalist radio and TV Atlanta and N.Y.C., 1961-68; priest, pastoral counselor Episc. chs., 1969—; pvt. practice Pensacola, Fla., 1984-91; vicar Holy Spirit Episcopal Ch., Gulf Shores, Ala., 1988-91; rector Episcopal Ch. Mediator, Meridian, Miss., 1991—. Writer, producer The Cry for Help, The Autumn Years. Chaplain Atlanta Police Dept., 1975-78; pres. N.W. Fla. chpt. Nat. Kidney Found., 1987-88; mem. Leadership Atlanta, 1975; trustee Fla. Trust for Hist. Preservation. Mem. Am. Assn. for Marriage and Family Therapy (clin.), Am. Assn. for Psychol. Type, Mental Health Assn. (life, bd. dirs. Pensacola chpt. 1986-88), Navy League, Order of Holy Cross (assoc.), Alpha Tau Omega. Avocations: music, photography, art collector. Office: Episcopal Ch Mediator 3825 35th Ave Meridian MS 39305

LINDVALL, MICHAEL LLOYD, clergyman, writer; b. Mpls., June 24, 1947; s. Lloyd Calvin and Jean Elizabeth (Painter) L.; m. Terri V. Smith, Sept. 8, 1973; children: Madeline, Benjamin, Grace. BA, U. Wis., Oshkosh, 1970; MDiv, Princeton U., 1974. Ordained to ministry United Presbyn. Ch., 1974. Assoc. pastor Drayton Avenue Presbyn. Ch., Ferndale, Mich., 1974-79; pastor 1st Presbyn. Ch., Northport, N.Y., 1979—; vice moderator Presbytery of L.I. (N.Y.), 1987-88; bd. dirs. United Presbyn. Residence, Woodbury, N.Y., 1987—. Author: Collection of Short Stories, 1991; contbr. short stories and articles to popular mags. Chaplain Northport Vol. Fire Dept., 1988—. Mem. Enigma Club (N.Y.), Bass Lake Sailing Club (Mich.). Avocations: sailing, motorcycling, bagpipes. Home: 5 Woodhull Pl Northport NY 11768 Office: 1st Presbyn Ch Church and Main Sts Northport NY 11768

LINENTHAL, EDWARD TABOR, religion educator; b. Boston, Nov. 6, 1947; s. Arthur J. and Eleanor (Tabor) L.; m. Ulla Hannele, June 7, 1974; children: Aaron Johannes, Jacob Arthur. BA, Western Mich. U., 1969; MDiv, Pacific Sch. Religion, 1973; PhD, U. Calif., Santa Barbara, 1979. Prof. U. Wis., Oshkosh, 1979—, John McN. Rosebush univ. prof., 1989-90; exec. dir. Wis. Inst. A Consortium for the Study for the Study of War, Peace and Global Cooperation, 1989-91. Author: Symbolic Defense: The Cultural Significance of the Strategic Defense Initiative, 1989, Changing Images of the Warrior Hero in America, 1983; co-editor: A Shuddering Dawn: Religious Studies and the Nuclear Age, 1989, Sacred Ground: Americans and Their Battlefields, 1991; contbr. articles to profl. jours. Mem. Am. Acad. Religion, Am. Studies Assn. Home: 1325 Parkside Ct Oshkosh WI 54901 Office: U Wis Dept Religious Studies Oshkosh WI 54901

LINGENFELSER, ANGELUS JOSEPH, clergyman; b. Leavenworth, Kans., Aug. 30, 1909; s. Max and Josephine (Bonaly) L.; B.A., St. Benedict's Coll., 1933; postgrad. Kans. State U., summers 1934-36, Catholic U. Am., summer 1960. Ordained priest Roman Catholic Ch., 1936. Pastor St. Johns Ch., Doniphan, Kans., 1937, 63-67, St. James Ch., Wetmore, Kans., 1938-48, Olathe Naval Air Base, Kans., 1948-63; instr. math., assoc. prof., bus. mgr. St. Benedict's Coll., Atchison, Kans., 1948-73; pastor St. Louis Ch., Atchison, 1968—; pres., dir. Atchison Industries, Inc. Bd. dirs., trustee, mem. administrv. bd. St. Benedict's Coll.; bd. dirs. Kans. Hist. Soc., Drainage Dist. 15-45, Rural Water Dist. No. 1, Atchison, Benedictine Coll.; bd. dirs. Maur Hill Sch., trustee, 1979; mem. Kans. State Bd. Water Resources, 1977; bd. dirs., pres. Atchison County Hist. Soc.; mem. Gov.'s Com. Lewis and Clark Trail. Hon. dir. Atchison County Soil Conservation; hon. chpt. farmer Future Farmers Am., 1970; recipient Liberty Bell award, 1981; named Citizen of Yr. for Mo.-Kans. area, 1983. Office: Benedictine Coll Atchison KS 66002

LINGERFELT, B. EUGENE, JR., minister; b. Highland Park, Mich., Dec. 18, 1955; s. Beecher Eugene and Nellie Beatrice (Sampson) L.; m. Suzanne Marie Martin, Aug. 7, 1976; children: Austin Stuart, Krystina Marie. BA, Cen. Bible Coll., Springfield, Mo., 1976; MDiv, Tex. Christian Univ., 1980; D of Ministry, Southwestern Bapt. Theol., Seminary, Ft. Worth, 1984. Ordained to ministry Bapt. Ch., 1984. Assoc. pastor Bethel Temple, Ft. Worth, 1978-82; missionary, guest lectr. East Africa Sch. of Theology, Nairobi, Kenya, 1982-83; marriage enrichment seminar speaker, 1983; founder and sr. pastor Cathedral of Praise, Arlington, Tex., 1984—. Co-author: Money: A Spiritual Force, 1985; contbr. articles to religious jours. Named to Outstanding Young Men of Am., 1980. Republican. Office: Cathedral of Praise PO Box 121234 Arlington TX 76012

LINNEMANN, HANS-MARTIN, religious organization administrator. Head Protestant Ch. of Westfalen, Bielefeld, Fed. Republic Germany. Office: Altstadten Kirchplatz 5, 4800 Bielefeld 1, Federal Republic of Germany*

LINNENKUGEL, RITA CATHERINE, parochial school administrator; b. Monroe, Mich., Jan. 22, 1948; d. Charles Edward and Polene Magdalene (Spencer) L. BA, Western Mich. U., 1970, MA in Counseling, 1973, MA in Ednl. Leadership, 1977; EdS in Ednl. Leadership, 1979. Cert. tchr., Mich. Sch. adminstr. St. John the Bapt. Sch., Monroe, 1985—; mem. supt.'s adv. coun. Archdiocese of Detroit, Roman Cath. Ch., 1987—. Contbr. articles, poems to profl. publs. Mem. Mich. Assn. Non-Pub. Schs., Monroe Vicariate Prins. (chair 1989—), ASCD. Office: St John the Baptist Sch 521 S Monroe St Monroe MI 48161

LINSCOTT, SCOTT, minister; b. Portland, Maine, Mar. 20, 1963; s. Donald Wescott and Beulah Beatrice (Cochran) L.; m. Robin Anne Copeland, June 2, 1984; children: Joshua Abram, Sharaya Michelle, Donald Jacob. BA in Journalism, U. Maine, 1981-85. Dir. Teens Alive Ministries, Biddleford, Maine, 1986—; state coord. Nat. Network Youth Ministries, San Diego, 1987—; dir. youth ministries Ea. Regional Assn. Advent Christian Chs., Rochester, N.H., 1988—. Editor youth mag. Young Advent Christian, 1990—; contbr. articles to profl. jours. Mem. Nat. Bd. Youth Ministry for Advent Christian Denomination. Republican. Office: Teens Alive Ministries PO Box 5003 Biddeford ME 04007

LINSEY, NATHANIEL L., bishop; b. Atlanta, July 24, 1926; s. Samuel and L. E. (Forney) L.; m. Mae Cannon Mills, June 8, 1951; children: Nathaniel Jr., Ricarldo Mills, Julius Wayne, Angela Elise. BS, Paine Coll., 1948, LLD (hon.), 1990; BD, Howard U., 1951; MA in Evangelism, Scarritt Coll., 1974; DD (hon.), Miles Coll., 1975, Tex. Coll., 1985. Ordained to ministry M.E.Ch. Nat. dir. youth M.E.Ch., 1951-52; pastor Rock of Ages M.E.Ch., 1952-53; presiding elder Columbia (S.C.) dist. M.E.Ch., 1953-55; pastor Vanderhorst M.E.Ch., 1955-56, Mattie E. Coleman M.E.Ch., 1956-62, Thirgood M.E.Ch., 1962-66; gen. sec. evangelism M.E.Ch., 1966-74, chmn. bd. lay activities, 1974-82, bishop 10th dist., 1978—, founder Congress on Evangelism, chmn. dept. fin., 1982-86, chmn. bd. evangelism, missions and human concerns, chmn. Coll. of Bishops, 1984. Pres. local chpt. NAACP, Knoxville, Tenn., 1957; trustee Miles Coll., Birmingham, Ala. Recipient Disting. Alumni award Paine Coll., 1978, Presdl. citation Nat. Assn. for Equal Opportunities in Higher Edn., 1979, Disting. Svc. award Govt. D.C., 1984, Pub. Svc. award Tex. Coll., 1984, Disting. Missionary award Calif. conf. M.E.Ch., 1985. Mem. World Meth. Coun., So. Calif. Ecumenical Coun. Chs. (pres. L.A. chpt. 1984). Democrat. Home: 2059 W Cedar Ln SW Atlanta GA 30011 Office: PO Box 170127 Atlanta GA 30317

LINSS, WILHELM CAMILL, religious educator; b. Erlangen, Fed. Republic of Germany, Mar. 21, 1926; came to U.S., 1952; s. Hans and Ingeborg Ursula (Egloffstein) L.; m. Margaret A. Wood, Aug. 29, 1953; children: Camilla M., Jeannie D., Andrew H. BD, Erlangen U., 1950; ThD, Boston U., 1955. Asst. pastor Evang. Luth. Ch. in Bavaria, Passau, Fed. Republic of Germany, 1950-52; asst. prof. Gustavus Adolphus Coll., St. Peter, Minn., 1954-57; prof. Cen. Luth. Theol. Seminary, Fremont, Nebr., 1957-67, Luth. Sch. Theology, Chgo., 1967—. Translator: The Resurrection of Jesus by Pinchas Lapide, Matthew 1-7: A Commentary by Ulrich Luz; contbr. articles to profl. jours. World Coun. Chs. scholar, 1950-51. Mem. Soc. Bibl. Lit., Chgo. Soc. Bibl. Lit. (pres. 1987-88). Home: 10534 S Hamilton Ave Chicago IL 60643 Office: Luth Sch Theology Chgo 1100 E 55th St Chicago IL 60615

LIOLIN, ARTHUR E., religious organization administrator; Chancellor. Albanian Orthodox Archdiocese in Am., East Milton, Mass. Office: Albanian Orthodox Archdiocese Am 60 Antwerp St East Milton MA 02185*

LIPE, MICHAEL ALEXANDER, minister; b. Mooresville, N.C., Aug. 10, 1944; s. Harold Cloe and Lucille Eva (Beam) L.; m. Jeanette Ann Mitchell, June 10, 1967; children: Heather Michelle, Jeremy Aaron, Damon Chandler. BS, Appalachian State U., 1966; MDiv, Southeastern Bapt. Theol. Sem., 1981, MRE, 1981. Ordained to ministry Bapt. Ch., 1978. Min. edn. and adminstrn. Westside Bapt. Ch., Titusville, Fla., 1978, First United Bapt. Ch., Charlottetown, P.E.I., Can., 1981-85; chaplain Eric M. Found. Meml. Hosp., Charlottetown, 1983-85; chmn. Christian Tng. Commn., P.E.I., 1982—; mem. exec. coun. Atlantic Bapt. Conv., 1983—; chmn. bd. dirs. Christian Communications, Charlottetown, 1984; mem. coun. for ordination Atlantic Bapt. Conv., 1982—; pres. Ch. Leadership Unltd., 1987—; curriculum con. Scripture Press Publs., Ltd., 1988—; faculty Acadia U., 1988—; mem. communications com. Bapt. World Alliance. Editor: Atlantic Baptist, 1985—; mng. editor: Tidings Mag., 1986—. Mem. Can. Assn. Pastoral Edn., Associated Ch. Press (various journalism awards), Can. Ch. Press (various journalism awards), Religious Pub. Rels. Coun., Inst. Pastoral Tng. Office: PO Box 756, Kentville, NS Canada B4N 3X9

LIPKE, DENNIS CHARLES, minister; b. Durban, Republic of South Africa, Africa, Sept. 22, 1946; s. William Charles and Violet Anne (Russouw) L.; m. Dale Norma Usher, Jan. 17, 1970; children: Charmaine Dale, Caroline May, Andrew Dennis. Diploma in theology, Bible Inst. Republic of South Africa, 1971; BTh., Rhodes U., Grahamstown, Republic of South Africa, 1977, BTh. with honors, 1986; postgrad., Wesley Theol. Sem., 1990—. Ordained to ministry Meth. Ch. as deacon, 1972, as elder, 1977. Min. Namaqualand Meth. Mission, Republic of South Africa, 1972-73; intern assoc. min. Valley Meth. Ch., Pretoria, Republic of South Africa, 1977; min. Strand Meth. Ch., 1978-82, Sunnyside Meth. Ch., Pretoria, 1983-87, Cartersville (Va.) Charge, 1987-89, Epworth United Meth. Ch., Falls Church, Va., 1989, Sleepy Hollow Parish, Falls Church, 1990—; dist. coord. of evangelism, supervising pastor Arlington Dist. United Meth. Ch., Va., 1990—; treas. Pretoria Coun. Chs., 1986-87. Home: 3441 Sleepy Hollow Rd Falls Church VA 22044 Office: Sleepy Hollow Parish 3435 Sleepy Hollow Rd Falls Church VA 22044

LIPMAN, EUGENE JAY, rabbi; b. Pitts., Oct. 13, 1919; s. Joshua and Bessie (Neaman) L.; m. Esther Marcuson, July 4, 1943; children: Michael H. (dec.), Jonathan N., David E. AB, U. Cin., 1941; MHL, Hebrew Union Coll., 1943, DD (hon.), 1968. Ordained rabbi, 1943. Rabbi Temple Beth El, Ft. Worth, 1943-44; dir. B'nai B'rith Hillel Found. U. Wash., Seattle, 1949-50; dept. dir. Union of Am. Hebrew Congregations, N.Y., 1951-61; rabbi Temple Sinai, Washington, 1961-85, rabbi emeritus, 1985—; lectr. in religion Am. U., Washington, 1961-68; lectr. in theology Cath. U. Am., Washington, 1967-79. Author: Yamim Nora'im, 1988; (with A. Vorspan) A Tale of Ten Cities, 1962, Justice and Judaism, 1956; editor: (textbook) The Mishnah, 1970; contbr. numerous articles to profl. jours. and chpts. to books. Pres. Cen. Conf. Am. Rabbis, 1987-89, Interfaith Conf. Met. Washington, 1982-84, Washington Bd. Rabbis, 1971-2; mem. bd. dirs., past pres. Nat. Capitol Area ACLU, 1965-77. Chaplain with armed forces 1944-46, 50-51. Teaching fellow Hebrew Union Coll., 1948-49. Mem. Commn. on Social Action. Democrat. Avocations: vegetable growing, log-splitting. Home and Office: 3512 Woodbine St Chevy Chase MD 20815

LIPMAN, WILLIAM MCCULLEM, JR., education director; b. Chgo., May 15, 1954; s. William M. and Dorothy Mae (Doty) L.; m. LeAnn Carol Bitner, Oct. 8, 1977; children: Elizabeth Renee, Andrew William, Rebekah Mae. BS, Ill. State U., 1976; MA, Dallas Theol. Sem., 1989. Cert. secondary sch. tchr., Ill. Elder discipleship Pekin (Ill.) Bible Ch., 1983-86; dir. edn. Trinity Fellowship, Richardson, Tex., 1987—; field instr., interns Dallas Theol. Sem., 1989—. Publicist Richardson Terrace PTA, 1990-91. Mem. Profl. Assn. Christian Educators, Am. Ednl. Rsch. Assn. (student). Republican. Home: 6201 Galaxy Garland TX 75042 Office: Trinity Fellowship 932 S Greenville Ave Richardson TX 75081 *Childhood is no mere stepping stone to adult life, it is instead foundational. For it is as a child that one learns to respond positively to the circumstances of life.*

LIPNER, JULIUS JOSEPH, comparative religion educator; b. Patna, India, Aug. 11, 1946; arrived in Eng., 1971.; s. Vojtech and Sylvia Teresa (Coutts) L.; m. Anindita Neogy, Feb. 20, 1971; children: Tanya, Julius. BA and Lic. in Philosophy summa cum laude, Pontifical Athenaeum, Pune, India, 1969; PhD, Kings Coll. U. London, 1974. Lectr. dept. Theology U. Birmingham (Eng.), 1973-74; lectr. comparative study of religion U. Cambridge (Eng.), 1975—; fellow St. Edmund's Coll., 1976—; lectr. 1981. Author: The Face of Truth, 1986, A Net Cast Wide, 1987; Purity, Abortion and Euthanasia (with others), 1988; contbr. articles and revs. to learned jours. Mem. Brit. Assn. History of Religions, Catholic Theol. Assn. Gt. Britain (founding mem.), Soc. for Study of Theology, Cambridge Theol. Soc. Roman Catholic. Avocations: reading, classical music. Office: Divinity Sch U Cambridge, St Johns St, Cambridge CB2 1TW, England

LIPOFF, NORMAN HAROLD, lawyer; b. N.Y.C., Dec. 9, 1936; s. Benjamin and Anna (Lippow) L.; m. Nancy B. Bressler, June 12, 1960; children—Ann, Elise. B.S.B.A., U. Fla., 1958, J.D. with honors, 1961; LL.M. in Taxation, NYU, 1962. With Carlton, Fields, Ward, Emmanuel, Smith & Cutler, Tampa, Fla., 1962-70; ptnr. Greenberg, Traurig, Hoffman, Lipoff, Rosen & Quentel, Miami, Fla., 1970—. Pres., Greater Miami Jewish Fedn.; nat. vice chmn., trustee, exec. com. United Israel Appeal; nat. chmn. United Jewish Appeal, 1990—; nat. chmn. Endowment Fund Devel. of Council of Jewish Fedns.; bd. govs. Tel-Aviv U.; bd. govs., exec. com. Jewish Agy. for Israel; mem. citizens bd. U. Miami; bd. dirs. U. Fla. Found.; trustee Law Ctr. Assn., U. Fla. Coll. Law. Recipient Pres.'s Leadership award Greater Miami Jewish Fedn., 1972, Pres.'s award Tel Aviv U., 1982, Brotherhood award NCCJ, 1988. Mem. ABA (tax sect.), Fla. Bar Assn. (chmn. tax sect. 1972, Outstanding Tax Lawyer in Fla. award 1989). Democrat. Home: Three Grove Isle Dr 1009 Coconut Grove FL 33133 Office: Greenberg Traurig Hoffman Lipoff Rosen & Quentel PA 1221 Brickell Ave 21st Fl Miami FL 33131

LIPPART, THOMAS E., minister; b. Prospect Park, Pa., Feb. 21, 1937; s. John and Mary (Brunner) L.; m. Margaret Free Schaal, June 17, 1961; children: Christina, Rebecca. BS in Metall. Engring., Mich. Tech. U., 1959; MDiv, Nashotah House, 1965. Ordained minister Episcopal Ch. Asst. St. Asaph's Ch., Bala-Cynwyd, Pa., 1965-67; vicar St. Mark's Ch., Cyrstal Falls, Mich., 1967-71; rector St. Stephen's Ch., Escanaba, Mich., 1971—. Editor diocesan newspaper Ch. in Haiwathaland, 1970-90. Fellow Va. Theol. Sem., 1989. Mem. Rotary. Home: 322 S 5th St Escanaba MI 49829 *To participate rather than to be spectator, to enable others to participate - this is life.*

LIPPER, DAVID ALAN, rabbi; b. Houston, June 27, 1961; s. Joseph Cronbach and Myra Jean (Blum) L.; m. Dora Rose Aboulafia, Dec. 21, 1986; children: Benjamin Israel, Miryam Esther. BA, U. Tex., 1983; MA in Hebrew Lit., Hebrew Union Coll., 1987. Ordained rabbi, 1988. Student rabbi Temple B'nai Israel, Kalamazoo, Mich., 1984-87; rabbinic intern Temple Israel, Dayton, Ohio, 1987-88; rabbi Congregation Emanu-El B'ne Jeshurun, Milw., 1988—; chaplain Israel Def. Forces, Jerusalem, 1983, Tex. Med. Ctr., Houston, 1986; researcher Jewish Fedn., Houston, 1986; adj. prof. Jewish studies Sacred Health Sch. Theology, Milw., 1991—. Editor jour. Vessels, 1986-88. Mem. Wis. Religious Coalition for Abortion Rights, Milw., 1988—; mem. Interfaith Coalition for Peace, Milw., 1988—; mem. Jewish Peace Lobby Policy Coun., Washington, 1990—. Mem. Cen. Conf. Am. Rabbis (editor ref. book Social Justice 1990), Wis. Rabbinic Fellowship (pres. 1989—), Wis. Coun. Rabbis (sec. 1990—), Am. Rabbinic Network for Ethiopian Jewry, Milw. Jewish Coun. (bd. dirs. 1991—). Home: 519 W Fransee Ln Glendale WI 53217 Office: Cong Emanu-El B'ne Jeshurun 2419 E Kenwood Blvd Milwaukee WI 53211 *Each one finds the Eternal in his or her own fashion. Meditation is central, inward turning is essential, the deeper we travel, the more we can understand.*

LIPPMAN, CHARLES DAVID, rabbi; b. Buffalo, Oct. 22, 1944; s. Hyman and Elinor Yetta (Lapat) L. BA cum laude, U. Buffalo, 1965. Ordained rabbi, 1970. Asst. rabbi Congregation Mishron Israel, Hamden, Conn., 1970-73; rabbi Beth Am Temple, Pearl River, N.Y., 1973-80; nat. dir. New Jewish Agenda, N.Y.C., 1980-81; rabbi Temple B'Nai Chaim, Georgetown, Conn., 1981—; mem. UAAC/CCAr Nat. AIDS Com., 1989—. Contbr. articles to publs. Mem. ACLU, UN Com. on Disarmament, Fellowship of Reconciliation to the UN, N.Y.C., 1975-88; adv. bd. Upper Room AIDS Ministry, N.Y.C., 1990—. Mem. N.Y. Bd. Rabbis, Cen. Conf. Am. Rabbis, Jewish Peace Fellowship, Religious Coalition for Abortion Rights, Jewish Peace Fellowship. Home: 235 W 75th St Apt 4Q New York NY 10023 Office: Tempe Bnai Chaim 82 Portland Ave Georgetown CT 06829

LIPPY, CHARLES HOWARD, religion educator; b. Binghamton, N.Y., Dec. 2, 1943; s. Charles Augustus and Natalie Grace (Setzer) L. BA magna cum laude, Dickinson Coll., 1965; MDiv magna cum laude, Union Theol. Sem., 1968; MA, Princeton U., 1970, PhD, 1972. Ordained to ministry United Meth. Ch. as elder, 1968. Interim pastor Litchfield (Pa.) Meth. Ch., 1962, Hornbrook (Pa.) Meth. Ch., 1966; prof. religion Clemson (S.C.) U., 1985—; vis. prof. Emory U., 1990-91. Author: Seasonable Revolutionary, 1981, Bibliography of Religion in the South, 1985, The Christadelphians in North American, 1989; editor: Religious Periodicals of the U.S., 1986; co-editor: Encyclopedia of the American Religious Experience, 1988, Twentieth-Century Shapers of American Popular Religion, 1989; contbr. articles to religious pubs. Grantee NEH, 1975, 78, 83; vis. scholar U. N.C., 1984. Mem. Am. Acad. Religion, Orgn. Am. Historians, Am. Soc. Ch. History, S.C. Acad. Religion (pres. 1981-82), Popular Culture Assn., Clemson Bridge Club (pres. 1979). Democrat. Home: 3339 Centerville Rd Anderson SC 29625 Office: Clemson U Dept Philosopy and Religion Hardin Hall Clemson SC 29634-1508

LIPSCOMB, JOHN BAILEY, priest; b. Arlington, Va., July 25, 1950; s. Clyde Bailey and Rosella (Herman) L.; m. Marcia Hinton Mason, Dec. 28, 1968; children: Matthew Mason, Natalie Mason. BA in Philosophy, U. N.C., 1973; MDiv, U. of South, Sewanee, Tenn., 1974; DMin, Grad. Theo. Found., South Bend, Ind., 1986. Ordained deacon Episcopal Ch., 1974, priest, 1975. Vicar St. Pauls/St. Thomas, Diocese of Fla., Federal Point, 1974-76; asst. to rector St. James Ch., Greenville, S.C., 1976-78; rector Good Shepherd Diocese of Upper S.C., Greer, S.C., 1978-81; assoc. rector St. James Ch., Baton Rouge, 1981-86; rector Christ Ch., Diocese of Western La., Bastrop, 1986-89, Ch. of the Good Shepherd, Lake Charles, La., 1989—; spiritual dir. Cursillo, Diocese of Upper S.C., 1978-80; dean Baton Rouge Convocation, Diocese of La., 1983-86, Monroe Convocation, Diocese of Western La., Monroe, 1988-89, Lake Charles Convocation, 1990—; exec. bd. commn. on ministry, Diocese of Western La. Chmn. bd. Baton Rouge Women's Shelter Prog., 1983-86; treas. bd. Baton Rouge Urban Ministry Coalition, 1983-86; vol. ctr. bd. of Lake Charles, 1990—; bd. dirs. Calcasieu Women's Shelter, Lake Charles, 1990—; chaplain La. Army N.G., 1986—. Fellow Grad. Theol. Found. Republican. Avocations: computers, golf, backpacking, boating. Home: 4948 E Saint Charles Ave Lake Charles LA 70605 Office: Church of Good Shepherd 715 Kirkman St Lake Charles LA 70601

LIPSCOMB, OSCAR HUGH, archbishop; b. Mobile, Sept. 21, 1931; s. Oscar Hugh and Margaret (Saunders) L. S.T.L., Gregorian U., Rome, 1957; Ph.D., Cath. U. Am., 1963. Ordained priest Roman Cath. Ch., 1956; consecrated bishop Roman Cath. Ch., 1980. Asst. pastor Mobile, 1959-65; tchr. McGill Inst., Mobile, 1959-60, 61-62; vice chancellor Diocese of Mobile-Birmingham, 1963-66, chancellor, 1966-80; pastor St. Patrick Parish, Mobile, 1966-71; lectr. history Spring Hill Coll., Mobile, 1971-72; asst. pastor St. Matthew Parish, Mobile, 1971-79, Cathedral Immaculate Conception, Mobile, 1979-80; adminstr. sede vacante Diocese of Mobile, 1980, now archbishop; pres. Cath. Housing Mobile, Mobile Senate Priests, 1978-80; chmn. com. on doctrine Nat. Conf. Cath. Bishops, 1988-91. Author articles, papers in field. Pres. bd. dirs. Mobile Mus., 1966-76; trustee Ala. Dept. Archives and History, Cath. U. Am., Washington, 1983—; chmn. bd. govs. N.Am. Coll., Rome, 1982-85. Mem. Am. Cath. Hist. Assn., So. Hist. Assn., Ala. Hist. Assn. (pres. 1971-72, exec. com. 1981-88), Hist. Mobile Preservation Soc., Lions. Address: 400 Government St PO Box 1966 Mobile AL 36633

LIPSKI, ALEXANDER, deacon, retired educator; b. Berlin, July 29, 1919; came to U.S., 1947; s. Jack and Margaret (Gollust) L.; m. Ruth Maria Kunkel, Sept. 11, 1949; children: Beatrice, Irene, Sophia. BA in History, U. Calif., Berkeley, 1950, MA in History, 1951, PhD in History, 1953. Prof. religious studies Calif. State U., Long Beach, 1958-83; deacon St. Cornelius Ch., Long Beach, 1982—; master of formation Secular Order Discalced Carmelites, Long Beach, 1987—. Author: Life and Teaching of Sri Ananda Mayi Ma, 1977, Thomas Merton and Asia, 1983, Essays on Carmelite Saints, 1990. Roman Catholic. Republican. Home: 7127 Rosebay St Long Beach CA 90808 Office: St Cornelius Cath Ch 5500 E Wardlow Rd Long Beach CA 90808 *The secret of happiness for me is to become God-centered rather than self-centered. God-centeredness is proven by unselfish, loving service of* *our fellow human beings who are all made in the divine image, even though at times appearing in distressing disquise.*

LIPTOCK, EDWARD RICHARD, priest; b. Scranton, Pa., Nov. 15, 1929; s. Andrew Joseph and Mary Elizabeth (Palko) L. AB, Mount St. Mary's Coll. Sem., 1951. Ordained priest Roman Cath. Ch., 1955. Catechist Bishop O'Reilly High Sch., Kingston, Pa., 1963-67, Bishop O'Hara High Sch., Dunmore, Pa., 1967-68; pre cana dir. Mid-Valley Area, Dunmore, Pa., 1967-68; pastor All Saints Ch., Dunmore, Pa., 1985—; defender of the bond, pro-synodal judge marriage tribunal Diocese Scranton, 1967—; regional coord. religious edn. Susquehanna and Wyoming Counties, Pa., 1969-71; v.p. bd. pastors Bishop Neumann High Sch., Williamsport, Pa., 1980—. Contbg. editor: The Catholic Light, 1967-71. Mem. Canon Law Soc. Am. (sec.-treas. 1971-73), Diocesan Coun. Cath. Women (bd. dirs. 1990—). Home: 324 Ward St Dunmore PA 18512 Office: Chancery Bldg 300 Wyoming Ave Scranton PA 18503

LIRELY, STEPHEN W., minister; b. Champaign, Ill., Mar. 20, 1955; s. Ivan Lavelle Lirely and Barbara Marie (Miller) Swinburne; m. Joyce Ann Havel, Nov. 26, 1977 (div. Jan. 1986); m. Ann Elizabeth Watson Hood, July 11, 1987; 1 child, Lara Elizabeth; stepchildren: Jill Christine Baxter, Scott Robert Baxter. BA, Mackendree Coll., 1977; MDiv, Christ Seminary, St. Louis, 1984. Ordained elder Meth. Ch., 1986. Pastor Mulberry Grove (Ill.) United Meth. Ch., 1977-82; youth pastor St. Paul United Meth. Ch., Rosewood Hgts., Ill., 1982-84; pastor West Frankfort (Ill.) First United Meth. Ch., 1984-86; youth and Christian edn. pastor East Peoria (Ill.) First United Meth. Ch., 1986-90; youth and singles pastor Whitefish Bay (Wis.) United Meth. Ch., 1990—; bd. dirs. Wesley Found., Milw., co-chmn. Bridgepoint Prodns., Inc., O'Dell, Ill. Recording artist: (cassette) No Place Like Home, 1987. Mem. youth leadership com., Glendale, Wis., 1991. Named to Outstanding Young Men of Am., 1983. Office: Whitefish Bay United Meth 819 E Silverspring Dr Whitefish Bay WI 53217

LISCHER, RICHARD ALAN, minister, theology educator; b. St. Louis, Nov. 12, 1943; s. Herbert Friedrich and Edna (Alsbrook) L.; m. Tracy Ruth Kenyon, June 4, 1966; children: Richard Adam, Sarah Kenyon. BA with highest honors, Concordia Coll., Ft. Wayne, Ind., 1965; MA in English, Washington U., St. Louis, 1967; BD, Concordia Sem., 1969; PhD in theology, U. London, 1971. Ordained to ministry Luth. Ch. in Am., 1972. Pastor Emmanus Luth. Ch., Dorsey, Ill., 1972-74, Prince of Peace Luth. Ch., Virginia Beach, Va., 1974-79; asst. prof. homiletics, Div. Sch. Duke U., Durham, N.C., 1979-84, assoc. prof., 1984-89, prof., 1989—; bd. dirs. Contact telephone counseling, Virginia Beach, 1978-79; cons. Luth. World Ministries, N.Y.C., 1979. Author: Marx and Teilhard, 1979, A Theology of Preaching, 1981, Speaking of Jesus, 1982; editor: Theories of Preaching, 1987; Contbr. articles to religious jours. Recipient Younger Scholar's award Assn. Theol. Schs., 1983; scholar Aid Assn. for Luths., 1965-69. Leathersellers Guild, London, 1970-71; fellow Luth. World Fedn., 1969-71. Mem. Acad. Homiletics. Democrat. Home: 3932 Westchester Durham NC 27707 Office: Duke U Div Sch Durham NC 27706

LISMAN, MICHAEL RAY, government administrator, clergyman; b. Richlands, Va., Feb. 3, 1952; s. Daniel and Rosevet W. Lisman. m. Diedre Lynn Payne, Sept. 15, 1972; children—Mich'El, Alexandria. B.A. in Communications, Kent State U., 1977; M.R.E., Berean Bible Coll., 1980. Ordained to ministry Apostolic Faith, 1980. Acad. dean Berean Bible Coll., Akron, Ohio, 1981-83; adj. faculty Youngstown State U., Ohio, 1982-84; retng. mgr. Alt. EEO Office and SYEP Coordinator Pvt. Ind. Council, Akron, 1982—; youth motivator Youth Motivational Task Force, Akron, 1983—; chmn. bus devel. com. 4th Ward Council, Akron, 1984—; owner, mgr. Alexandria's Books & Christian Supply, Akron, 1983—. Founding minister Maranatha Apostolic Ministries. Mem. Christian Booksellers Assn. Office: Pvt Industry Coun 105 E Market St Akron OH 44320

LITCHFIELD, KENT, priest; b. N.Y.C., Sept. 20, 1938; s. Stanton Grover and Bertha Stone (Hebard) L.; m. Helen Katherine Stonier-Hamnett, May 25, 1972; 1 child, Katherine Lillianna. BA, San Diego State U., 1972; MDiv, Ch. Div. Sch. of Pacific, 1987. Ordained to ministry Episcopal Ch., 1987. Curate, asst. All Saint's Episcopal Ch., Vista, Calif., 1987-88; rector Christ Episcopal Ch., Elizabethtown, Ky., 1988—; mem. Ecclestical Ct., Diocese of Ky., 1990—; dir. All Saint's Camp, Leitchfield, 1990—. Mem. Foster Care Rev. Bd. of Hardin County, 1988—; pres. Save-A-Teen, Elizabethtown, 1989—; chaplain AIDS Support Group, Elizabethtown, 1989—; facilitator Saudi Support Group, 1990—. Recipient Meritorious Svc. Commendation USMC, 1984, Naval Achievement medal USMC, 1971. Mem. Ministerial Assn. (v.p. 1989), Kiwanis Club of Vista. Republican. Home: 237 Oakwood Dr Elizabethtown KY 42701 Office: Christ Episcopal Ch 122 N Mulberry Elizabethtown KY 42701

LITCHFIELD, LANDIS HUGH, religion educator; b. Norfolk, Va., July 12, 1940; s. Landis Hughes and Lucretia O'Brian L.; m. Sarah Jane Sherwood, Aug. 23, 1963; children: Christopher David, Laura Lynn, Timothy Hugh. BA, U. Richmond, 1961; BD, Southwestern Bapt. Theol. Sem., 1965, ThD, 1971. Ordained to ministry So. Bapt. Conv., 1964. Pastor Stanfield Bapt. Ch., Henrietta, Tex., 1964-65; assoc. pastor, youth min. Gambrell St. Bapt. Ch., Ft. Worth, 1966-68; interim pastor Southwestern Bapt. Ch., Johnson City, Tenn., 1969-70; pastor Azalea Bapt. Ch., Norfolk, Va., 1971-88; prof. homiletics N.Am. Bapt. Sem., Sioux Falls, S.D., 1988—; mem. gen. bd. Bapt. Gen. Assn., Richmond, Va., 1986-88. Author: Preaching the Christmas Story, 1984, Preaching the Easter Story, 1986, Sermons on Those Other Special Days, 1990. Named to Tidewater Hall of Fame, Am. Softball Assn., 1986. Mem. Acad. Homiletics, Acad. Preachers. Home: 4300 S Lewis Sioux Falls SD 57103 Office: NAm Bapt Sem 1321 W 22d St Sioux Falls SD 57105

LITES, LARRY TOMMIE, religious organization human resources manager; b. Lake City, Fla., Mar. 5, 1947; s. Tommie Jordan and Hennie Mae (Smith) L.; m. Buris Joan Adkinson, June 14, 1968; children: David Hamilton, Jonathan Andrew, Jason Alexander. AS in Turf Mgmt., Lake City Jr. Coll., 1968; Bible Tng. Cert., Internat. Sch. Theology, San Bernardino, Calif., 1972; BSBA, U. Phoenix So. Calif., Costa Mesa, Calif., 1985. Golf course mgr. The Deerwood Club, Jacksonville, Fla., 1969-72; conf. svcs. adminstr. Campus Crusade for Christ, San Bernardino, 1972-76; prayer/care counseling adminstr. Campus Crusade for Christ, 1976-80, human resources adminstr., 1980-84, human resources and staff benefits fund mgr., 1985—; recruiter Campus Crusade for Christ, San Bernardino, 1980—, seminar tchr., 1974—. Vol. chaplain Loma Linda (Calif.) Vets. Hosp., 1980-86; soccer coach Am. Youth Soccer Assn., San Bernardino, 1980-88, baseball coach Little League Baseball, San Bernardino, 1980-89; mission bd. chmn. Immanuel Baptist Ch., San Bernardino, 1978-85. Sgt. USNG, 1968-74. Mem. Christian Ministries Mgmt. Assn., Christian Businessmen's Com. Republican. Baptist. Avocations: writing, horseback riding, family activities. Home: 5654 Wadsworth Ave Highland CA 92346

LITTELL, FRANKLIN HAMLIN, theologian, educator; b. Syracuse, N.Y., June 20, 1917; s. Clair F. and Lena Augusta (Hamlin) L.; m. Harriet Davidson Lewis, June 15, 1939 (dec. 1978); children: Jennith, Karen, Miriam, Stephen; m. 2d Marcia S. Sachs, 1980. BA, Cornell Coll., 1937, DD, 1953; BD, Union Theol. Sem., 1940; PhD, Yale U., 1946; Dr. Theology (hon.), U. Marburg, 1957; ThD (hon.), Thiel Coll., 1968; other hon. degrees, Widener Coll., 1969, Hebrew Union Coll., 1975, Reconstructionist Rabbinical Coll., 1976, Gratz Coll., 1977, St. Joseph's U., 1988. Dir. Lane Hall, U. Mich., 1944-49; chief protestant adviser to U.S. High Commr., other service in Germany, 1949-51, 53-58; prof. Chgo. Theol. Sem., 1962-69; pres. Iowa Wesleyan Coll., 1966-69; prof. religion Temple U., 1969-86; adj. prof. Inst. Contemporary Jewry, Hebrew U., Israel, 1973—; Inaugural Ida E. King Disting. vis. prof. Holocaust studies Stockton (N.J.) State Coll., 1990-91; guest prof. numerous univs. Author numerous books including The Anabaptist View of the Church: an Introduction to Sectarian Protestantism (Brewer award Am. Soc. Ch. History), 1952, rev. edit., 1958, 64, From State Church to Pluralism, 1962, rev., 1970; (with Hubert Locke) The German Church Struggle and the Holocaust, 1974, 90; The Crucifixion of the Jews, 1975, 86, The Macmillan Atlas History of Christianity, 1976, German edit., 1976, 89 , (with Marcia Sachs Littell) A Pilgrim's Interfaith Guide to the Holy Land, 1981; A Half-Century of Religious Dialogue: Amsterdam 1939-1989; editor or assoc. editor numerous jours. including Jour. Ecumenical Studies, A Jour. of Ch. and State and Holocaust Genocide Studies; author weekly syndicated columns, also over 300 major articles or chpts. of books in field of modern religious history. cons. NCCJ, 1958-83; mem. exec. com. Notre Dame Colloqium, 1961-68; vice chmn. Ctr. for Reformation Research, 1964-77; nat. chmn. Inst. for Am. Democracy, 1966-69, sr. scholar, 1969-76; co-founder, officer Ann. Scholars' Conf. on Ch. Struggle and Holocaust, 1970—; pres. Christians Concerned for Israel, 1971-78, Nat. Leadership Conf. for Israel, 1978-84, pres. emeritus 1985—; founder, chmn. ecumenical com. Deutscher Evangelischer Kirchentag, 1953-58; co-founder, cons. Assn. Coordination Univ. Religious Affairs, 1959—; mem. U.S. Holocaust Meml. Council, 1979—; founder, pres. Nat. Inst. on Holocaust, Temple U., 1975-83, Anne Frank Inst., Phila., 1983-89; co-founder, pres. Phila. Ctr. on Holocaust, Genocide and Human Rights, 1989—; mem. exec. com. Remembering For The Future, Oxford and London, 1988—; named observer to Vatican II; mem. Internat. Bd. of Yad Vashem, Jerusalem, 1981—. Decorated Grosse Verdienstkreuz (Fed. Republic Germany); recipient Jabotinsky medal, Israel, Ladislaus Laszt Internat. Ecumenical award Ben Gurion U. of Negev, 1991. Mem. PEN, European Assn. Evang. Acads. (co-founder), Locust Club, Yale Club, George Town Club, Phi Beta Kappa, Phi Beta Kappa Assocs. Home: PO Box 172 Merion PA 19066

LITTLE, GEORGE DANIEL, clergyman; b. St. Louis, Dec. 18, 1929; s. Henry and Agathe Cox (Daniel) L.; m. Joan Philips McCafferty, Aug. 22, 1953; children—Deborah Philips, Cynthia McCafferty, Alice Annette, Daniel Ross, Benjamin Henry. A.B., Princeton U., 1951; M.Div., McCormick Theol. Sem., Chgo., 1954; LL.D. (hon.), Huron Coll., 1977. Ordained to ministry Presbyn. Ch., 1954; pastor East London Group Ministry, Presbyn. Ch. Eng., 1954-56, Friendship Presbyn. Ch., Pitts., 1956-62; asso. dir. dept. urban ch., planning assoc. Bd. Nat. Missions, United Presbyterian Ch. U.S.A., N.Y.C., 1962-72; assoc. for budgeting Gen. Assembly Mission Council, 1973-76, exec. dir. council, 1976-84; pastor First Presbyn. Ch., Ithaca, N.Y., 1984—. Home: 1315 Hanshaw Rd Ithaca NY 14850

LITTLE, GERALD BOB, minister; b. Lexington, Tex., Jan. 28, 1939; s. Earl H. and Agatha (Proske) L.; m. Claudine White, June 10, 1961; 1 child, Blake Little. BA, Howard Payne Coll., Brownwood, Tex., 1962; BD, Southwestern Bapt. Sem., Ft. Worth, 1965, MDiv, 1968; D Ministry, Luther Rice Sem., Jacksonville, Fla., 1980. Ordained to ministry Bapt. Ch., 1962. Pastor Hasse Bapt. Ch., 1962-65, First Bapt. Ch., Luling, Tex., 1965-69; First Bapt. Ch., LaGrange, Tex., 1969-72; pastor First Bapt. Ch., Taylor, Tex., 1972-76, Ashdown, Ark., 1976-82; pastor Oak Grove Bapt. Ch., Nacogdoches, Tex., 1984—; chmn. fin. com. Shelby-Dochyes Assn., Nacogdoches, 1985-90, vice-moderator, 1989-90; chmn. Bapt. Student Union Commn., Nacogdoches, 1990. pres. Treatment Ctr., Nacogdoches, 1990. Mem. Ministerial Alliance (pres. 1990). Home: 5021 Colonial Dr Nacogdoches TX 75961 Office: Oak Grove Bapt Ch 2603 SE Stallings Dr Nacogdoches TX 75961

LITTLE, JOHN TROY, music and youth minister; b. Marshall, Mo., Mar. 24, 1964; s. James Henry III and LaVerne Juliett (Epps) L.; m. Connie Sue Marshall, May 26, 1984; children: Jennifer Ann, Julianne Elizabeth. BS, Cen. Mo. State U., 1985; postgrad., Midwestern Bapt. Sem., 1988-89. Ordained to minitry So. Bapt. Conv., 1988. Min. music and youth First Bapt. Ch., Odessa, Mo., 1984-86; min. music Tryst Falls Bapt. Ch., Kearney, Mo., 1987-88; min. music, youth and edn. Kensington Ave Bapt. Ch., Kansas City, Mo., 1988-89; min. music and youth 1st Bapt. Ch., Chester, Ill., 1989-91, Aurora, Mo., 1991—; assoc. music dir. Nine Mile Bapt. Assn., Pinckneyville, Ill, 1990—; pres. Assn. Mins. Fellowship, Pinckneyville, 1991—. Office: 1st Bapt Ch Locust and Jefferson Aurora MO 65605

LITTLE, TIMOTHY ALAN, minister; b. Asheville, N.C., Feb. 9, 1963; s. Kenneth Ray and Gale (Coffey) L.; m. Robin Alexandria Daly, July 26, 1985; 1 child, Teague Alan. BA, N.C. Sch. of Arts, 1985; M of Ch. Music, New Orleans Bapt. Theol. Sem., 1988. Music dir. Abernathy Meml. Meth. Ch., Rutherford College, N.C., 1981-82; soloist & sect. leader Ardmore United Meth. Ch., Winston Salem, N.C., 1983-85; min. of music & youth Lee's Creek Bapt. Ch., Bogalusa, La., 1985-86; assoc. min. of music, youth & edn. First Bapt. Ch., Luling, La., 1986—. com. chair St. Charles Social Concerns, Luling, 1988—, pres. 1989-90. Home: 325 Woodland Dr Boutte LA 70039 Office: First Bapt Ch PO Box 155 Luling LA 70070

LITTON, JAMES HOWARD, organist, conductor; b. Charleston, W.Va., Dec. 31, 1934; s. James Howard and Bessie Blue (Binford) L.; m. Lou Ann Hall, Dec. 27, 1957; children: Bruce Edward, Deborah Ann, David Allan, James Richard. MusB, Westminster Choir Coll., 1956, MusM, 1958. Organist St. Paul's Luth. Ch., Charleston, 1950-52; organist, dir. 1st Meth. Ch., Plainfield, NJ., 1954-58; organist, choirmaster Trinity Ch., Southport, Conn., 1958-64, Christ Ch. Cathedral, Indpls., 1964-68; organist, dir. music Trinity Ch., Princeton, N.J., 1968-82, St. Bartholomew's Ch., N.Y.C., 1982—; dir. music, condr. The Am. Boychoir, The Am. Boychoir Sch., Princeton, 1985—; mem. standing cmmn. on ch. music, Nat. Episcopal Ch., 1970-85, chm. svc. mus. com., 1976-85; mem. nat. coun. Assoc. Parishes, Alexandria, Va., 1980-86; mem. exec. edn. com. The Hymnal, 1982. Editor canticle series: Hinshaw Music, 1978-85, The Plainsong Psalter, 1988; Am. editor Duty and Delight, 1983-85; co-editor Albemarle Choral Series, 1988—; recs. for Philips, Music Masters, Mus. Heritage, Ocaso, Reunion, Sony Classics. Trustee Princeton U. Concerts, 1970-74, Am. Boychoir Sch., Princeton, 1974-78. Recipient Alumni award Westminster Choir Coll., 1981. Fellow Royal Sch. Ch. Music; mem. Assn. Anglican Musicians (nat. pres. 1966-67), Am. Guild Organists, Royal Coll. Organists, Am. Choral Dirs. Assn. Democrat. Home: 8 Carnation Pl Lawrenceville NJ 08648 Office: St Bartholomew's Ch 109 E 50th St New York NY 10022 also: 19 Lambert Dr Princeton NJ 08540

LITTON, TERRY EDMUND, clergyman; b. Hagerstown, Md., Nov. 23, 1941; s. Isaac B. and Margaret (Metz) L.; m. Wandalee Hofsteter, Aug. 18, 1962; children: Michelle Ann, Beth Ann, Amy Lee. BA, Ashland Coll., 1963; MDiv, Evang. Theol. Sem., Naperville, Ill., 1967; DMin, Boston Theol. Sem., 1984. Ordained to ministry United Meth. Ch., 1967. Pastor Evang. United Brethren Ch., McZena, Ohio, 1962-65, Ch. at Lake, Chippewa Lake, Ohio, 1967-70, Emmanuel United Meth. Ch., Ashland, Ohio, 1970-76, Trinity United Meth. Ch., Orrville, Ohio, 1976-84, lst United Meth. Ch., Cambridge, Ohio, 1984—. Mem. Masons, Kiwanis, Shriners. Republican. Home: 1206 Greenacre Dr Cambridge OH 43725 Office: lst United Meth Ch 641 Steubenville Ave 267 Cambridge OH 43725

LIVENGOOD, MICHAEL GENE, minister; b. Danville, Ill., Aug. 12, 1953; s. H. B. and Anita Marie (Potts) L.; m. Linda Sue Gordon, Feb. 19, 1974; children: Timothy Wayne, Scott Allen. BA in Bible and Pastoral Studies, N. Cen. Bible Coll., Mpls., 1972-74. Ordained to ministry Assemblies of God Ch., 1977. Pastor Cuba (Ill.) Assembly of God Ch., 1974-77, 1st Assembly of God Ch., Paris, Ill., 1977-84; evangelist Assemblies of God Itinerant Ministry, 1984—; dean Ill. Assemblies of God Youth Camps, Carlinville, Ill, 1977—; pres. Paris Ministerial Fellowship, 1982-84; mem. Nat. Evangelist Com. Gen. Coun. Assemblies of God, Springfield, Mo., 1990—; serve various state and sectional offices Assemblies of God. newspaper columnist The Cuba Journal, 1974-77; Contbr. articles to religious publs. Mem. Civic Fund Raising Com., City of Paris, 1982. Named Teen of Month, Kiwanee's Club, Robinson, Ill., 1972. Home and Office: Mike Livengood Ministries P O Box 1455 Danville IL 61834-1455

LIVERMORE, DAVID ANDREW, minister; b. Rochester, N.Y., July 18, 1967; s. Richard Harvey and Marjorie Evangeline (Hall) L. BA in Speech, Grand Rapids Bapt. Coll., 1989; BS in Edn., Calvin Coll., 1989; postgrad., SUNY, Brockport, 1989—. Lic. to ministry Bapt. Ch., 1989. Youth min. Grace Bapt. Ch., Brockport, 1989—; subs. tchr. Brockport High Sch., 1990—. Home: 6090 Brockport/Spencerport Rd # 5 Brockport NY 14420 Office: Grace Bapt Ch 5220 Lake Rd S Brockport NY 14420

LIVERMORE, PAUL WEBSTER, theologian, educator; b. Kansas City, Mo., Feb. 26, 1944; s. Harry Edmond and Sarah Elizabeth (Walker) L.; m. Alice Viola Hoke, June 2, 1964; children: Geoffrey Lucas, Alicia Christine. AB, Greenville Coll., 1966; MDiv, Asbury Sem., Wilmore, Ky., 1969; ThM, Princeton Sem., 1972, PhD, 1978. Ordained to ministry Free Meth. Ch. N.Am., 1970. Asst. prof., then assoc. prof. religion Roberts Wesleyan Coll., Rochester, N.Y., 1976-81, George L. Skinner prof., 1985—; pastor Ransomville (N.Y.) Free Meth. Ch., 1981-85; mem. Study Commn. on Doctrine, Free Meth. Ch. N.Am., 1979—, del. Gen. Conf., 1985, 89. Contbr. articles to religious and theol. jours. NEH fellow, 1988. Mem. Wesleyan Theol. Soc., Am. Acad. Religion, Soc. Bibl. Lit. Home: 29 College Dr North Chili NY 14514 Office: Roberts Wesleyan Coll 2301 Westside Dr Rochester NY 14624

LIVINGSTON, GEORGE HERBERT, clergyman, Old Testament educator; b. Russell, Iowa, July 27, 1916; s. George Wendell and Clara Lutheria (Baker) L.; m. Maria Gertruida Saarloos, Aug. 12, 1937; children—Burton George, Nellie Maria, David Herbert. B.A. in Religion, Wessington Springs Coll., 1937; A.B., Kletzing Coll., 1945; B.D., Asbury Theol. Sem., 1948; Ph.D., Drew U., 1955. Ordained to ministry Free Meth. Ch. Pastor, Free Meth. Ch., Beaver Dam and Birchwood, Wis., 1937-39, Free Meth. Ch., Marion, Cedar Rapids and Oskaloosa, Iowa, 1939-45, United Meth. Ch., Lynchburg, Ohio, 1947-48, United Meth. Ch., Callicon, N.Y., 1948-51; dean Wessington Springs Coll., S.D., 1951-53; prof. O.T., Asbury Theol. Sem., Wilmore, Ky., 1953-87; dir. Inst. Holy Land Studies, Jerusalem, 1959, chmn. assoc. schs., 1964-74; field supr. Archeol. Expedition to Ai, Deir Diwan, Israel, 1966, 68. Author: Genesis, Aldersgate Bibl. Series, 1961, Jeremiah, Aldersgate Bibl. Series, 1963; the Pentateuch in its Cultural Environment, 1974. Contbr. articles to profl. publs. Recipient Higher Edn. award Free Meth. Ch., 1979. Mem. Am. Schs. Oriental Research, Evang. Theol. Soc., Wesleyan Theol. Soc., Nat. Assn. Profs. of Hebrew, Theta Phi. Republican.

LIVINGSTON, JAMES CRAIG, religion educator; b. Grand Rapids, Mich., July 12, 1930; s. Leo A. and Olive (Osterhaven) L.; m. Jacqueline Ouellette, Sept. 4, 1954; children—Sarah Elizabeth, Susannah Craig. B.A., Kenyon Coll., 1952; M.Div., Union Theol. Sem., 1956; Ph.D., Columbia U., 1965. Tutor Union Theol. Sem., N.Y.C., 1960-63; asst. prof. religion So. Methodist U., Dallas, 1963-68; assoc. prof., founding chmn. dept. religion Coll. of William and Mary, Williamsburg, Va., 1968-72, prof. religion, 1973—, now Walter G. Mason prof. religion, dean undergrad. program, 1973-78, chmn. dept. religion, 1980-84, 90-91; vis. fellow Clare Hall Cambridge U., Eng., 1967-68. Author: Modern Christian Thought, 1971, The Ethics of Belief, 1974, Religion and Government in other Countries, 1985, Matthew Arnold and Christianity, 1986, Anatomy of the Sacred, 1988; editor: Literature and Dogma, Matthew Arnold, 1970, Tradition and the Critical Spirit: Catholic Modernist Writings of George Tyrrell, 1991. Recipient Decennial Bross prize, 1980; Outstanding Faculty award Commonwealth of Va., 1989; Am. Council Learned Socs. fellow, 1972-73; Nat. Endowment for Humanities fellow, 1979-80, 89-90; Woodrow Wilson Internat. Ctr. for Scholars fellow, 1989-90. Mem. Am. Acad. Religion, Nineteenth Century Theology Group, Soc. for Values in Higher Edn., Phi Beta Kappa (hon.). Democrat. Episcopalian. Home: 105 Cove Rd Williamsburg VA 23185

LI YUHANG, religious organization administrator. Chmn. China Daoist Assn., Beijing. Office: Temple White Cloud, Xi Bian Men 100045, Beijing People's Republic of China*

LJUNGBERG, BETTY MARION, librarian; b. Worcester, Mass.; d. Hugo Waldemar and Eva (Sahlin) L. BS, Columbia U., N.Y.C., 1956, MS, 1982. Librarian Interch. Ctr., N.Y.C., 1982—. Home: 417 Riverside Dr New York NY 10025 Office: Interchurch Ctr Rm 900 475 Riverside Dr New York NY 10115

LLOYD, JAMES MELWOOD, II, music minister; b. Martinsburg, W.Va., July 1, 1955; s. James Melwood and Anna Florence (Pittman) L.; m. Diane Marie Hafner, May 14, 1977; 1 child, Jessica Marie. BS in Ministerial Biblical Studies, Valley Forge Christian Coll., 1977. Ordained to ministry Assemblies of God, 1980. Assoc. pastor music and youth Pennsville (N.J.) Assembly of God, 1977-78; asst. pastor, music minister Trinity Assembly of God, Lanham, Md., 1978-80; assoc. pastor youth and music Pleasant Valley Assembly of God, Altoona, Pa., 1980-88; minister music & Christian edn. First Assembly of God, Wilmington, Del., 1988-89; assoc. pastor, music minister Shrewsbury (Pa.) Assembly of God, 1989—; music dir. N.J. sect. N.J. Dist. Coun., Trenton, 1977-78; hosp. chaplain Salem (N.J.) County Hosp., 1977-78; youth dir. South Cen. West sect. Pa.-Del. Dist. Coun., Camp Hill, Pa., 1983-88. Recipient Voice of Democracy award DAR, 1972. Republican. Home: 106 Covington Dr Shrewsbury PA 17361 Office: Shrewsbury Assembly of God 234 N Main St Box 164 Shrewsbury PA 17361

LLOYD, JIMMIE MITCHELL, lay worker; b. Darlington, S.C., Mar. 27, 1948; s. Maxie Eston and Gladys (Walters) L.; m. Marilyn Atkinson, Dec. 20, 1952 (div. Nov. 1987); children: Lisa Michele, Michael Daniel; m. Ann C. Lloyd, June 9, 1990. A in Bus., Florence-Darlington Tech. Coll., 1977; cert. Bible tchr. Community Free Will Bapt. Ch., Florence, S.C., 1972-85, 86—, also chmn. bd. dirs.; terr. mgr. Kraft Gen. Food Dairy, Richmond, Va., 1970—; Bible tchr, dir. Caring Christian Singles, Florence, 1988-90. Mem. Palmetto Christian Sch. Bd., Florence, 1974-80. With U.S. Army, 1966-69. Home: Rte 4 Box 335 Timmonsville SC 29161

LLOYD, JOSEPH WILSEY, minister, chaplain; b. Oconomowoc, Wis., Jan. 24, 1940; s. John George and Sevilla Mary (Wilsey) L.; m. Hope Marie Willie, Aug. 25, 1962; children: John David, Judith Lynn, Christine Marie Lloyd-Cagle, Elizabeth Sevilla. Student, Cedarville (Ohio) Coll., 1961-64; BA, Bishop Coll., Dallas, 1973; postgrad., Wheaton (Ill.) Coll., 1974-75; MDiv, No. Bapt. Theol. Sem., Lombard, Ill., 1976. Ordained to ministry Am. Bapt. Chs. in U.S.A., 1977. Min. Christian edn. Morgan Park Bapt. Ch., Chgo., 1973-76; pastor E.C.H.O. Bapt. Parish, Humeston, Iowa, 1976-80, 1st Bapt. Ch., Alliance, Nebr., 1980-84, Mt. Olive Bapt. Ch., Cherokee, Iowa, 1984-88, 1st Bapt. Ch., Ft. Madison, Iowa, 1988—; chaplain dist. 13, Iowa State Patrol, Des Moines, 1985—; mem. region pers. com. and area program bd. Mid-Am. Bapt. Chs., Des Moines, 1988—. Columnist Pastor's Paragraphs, New Era, Humeston, 1976-80. Jackson del. Iowa Dem. Conv., 1988; religious counselor The Crossing Point, Ft. Madison. Recipient cert. of commendation Iowa State Patrol, 1986, Law Enforcement award Optimist Internat., 1988. Mem. Internat. Conf. Police Chaplains, Mid-Am. Bapt. Mins. Coun., Am. Bapt. Mins. Coun., Tri State Gun Club (Montrose, Iowa). Home: 29 29th Pl Fort Madison IA 52627 Office: 1st Bapt Ch 301 24th St Fort Madison IA 52627

LOBENSTINE, CLARK, minister, ecumenical agency administrator. Exec. dir. Interfaith Conf. Met. Washington. Office: Interfaith Conf Met 1419 V St NW Washington DC 20009*

LOCASIO, ANN LEE, clergywoman; b. Gary, Ind., Aug. 11, 1959; d. Victor J. and Elizabeth (Parker) L. BA summa cum laude, Cleve. State U., 1981; MDiv cum laude, So. Meth. U., 1986. Ordained to ministry United Meth. Ch., 1986. Pastor Medina and Center Point (Tex.) United Meth. Chs., 1986-88, Medina United Meth. Ch., 1988-89; assoc. pastor, campus minister 1st United Meth. Ch., San Marcos, Tex., 1989—; leader seminars on calling and caring ministries United Meth. Ch., Austin, Tex., 1989—. Named One of Outstanding Young Women of Am., 1991. Mem. Order of St. Luke (assoc.). Democrat. Office: First United Meth Ch 129 W Hutchison St San Marcos TX 78666

LOCHER, GOTTFRIED WILHELM, theology educator; b. Wuppertal-Elberfeld, Germany, Apr. 29, 1911; arrived in Switzerland, 1932, naturalized Swiss citizen; s. Gottfried Wilhelm and Egberdina Margarete (Oberman) L.; m. Irene Agnes Schöffner, Nov. 8, 1936 (dec. Mar. 1982); children: Johannes Theophil, Gottfried Wilhelm, Huldrych Caspar, Regula Wya. Student, U. Königsberg, Germany, 1930-32, U. Zürich, Switzerland, 1932-33, 35-36, U. Bonn, Germany, 1934-35; ThD honoris causa, U. Basel, Switzerland, 1982, U. Debrecen, Hungary, 1988. Ordained to ministry Swiss Reformed Ch., 1936. Min. Reformed Ch., Binningen, Switzerland, 1936-41, Feuerthalen, Switzerland, 1941-54, Riehen, Switzerland, 1954-58; Dr. theology U. Zürich, 1950, lectr. systematic theology, 1954-58; prof. systematic theology and history dogma U. Bern, Switzerland, 1958-79; dean theol. faculty U. Bern, 1964-66, rector, 1968-69; mem., pres. Theol. coun. Swiss Protestant Ch., Switzerland, 1960-75; mem. presidium Internat. Congress on Calvin Rsch., 1960-84; mem. dialog-com. Reformed and Roman Catholic Chs., Rome, 1960-80. Author: Die Theologie Huldrych Zwinglis Bd. I, 1952, Der Eigentumsbegriff als Problem evangelischer Theologie, 1954, 2nd edit. 1962, Huldrych Zwingli in neuer Sicht, 1969, Die Zwinglische Reformation im Rahmen Europas, 1978, Zwingli's Thought--New Perspectives, 1981, Zwingli und die schweizerische Reformation, 1982, Der Berner Synodus von 1532, Bd. I., 1984, Bd. II, 1988, Losend dem Gotteswort!, 1985, Zwingli en de Nederlanden, 1990, Festschrift G. W. Locher, 1991. Home: Jennershausweg 21 2, CH 3098 Köniz BE, Switzerland

LOCK, JAMES SIDNEY, minister; b. Starkeville, Miss., Aug. 25, 1927; s. James and Sidney (Chambers) L.; m. Jo Thornton, June 6, 1951; children: Sidney L. Caldwell, James Stephen. BS, Auburn U., 1949; MDiv, Duke Divinity Sch., 1952; DMin, Drew Theol. Sch., 1984. Ordained to ministry Meth. Ch., 1954. Pastor White Meml./Wesley Charge, Henderson, N.C., 1951-52, Ashford Charge, Ala. West Fla. Conf., Ashford, Ala., 1952-57, Hartford (Ala.) First Meth. Ala. West Fla. Conf., 1957-61, Kingswood Meth. Ch. Ala. West Fla. Conf., Mobile, Ala., 1961-66; assoc. dir. Ala.-West Fla. Conf. Coun., Andalusia, Ala., 1966-71; pastor First United Meth. Ch., Atmore, Ala., 1971-76, Dalraida United Meth. Ch., Montgomery, Ala., 1976-84, First United Meth. Ch., Ft. Walton Beach, Fla., 1984—; mem. bd. edn. Ala. West Fla. Conf., 1956-64, 71-72, bd. evangelism, 1964-66, Blue Lake commn., 1964-70, coun. on finance and adminstrn., 1972-80; chairperson bd. missions Ala. West Fla. Conf., 1984-88, resource person task force on prison ministries and prison reform, 1975-76; ministerial adv. bd. to Birmingham So. Coll. Ala. West Ala. Conf., 1975—, chairperson, 1975-81. Mem. Loop Lions Club, 1963-66; pres. Atmore Rotary Club, 1972-73; bd. dirs. Deep South coun. Girl Scouts Am., 1972-76; bd. dirs. Atmore United Fund, 1974-76, pres., 1976; v.p. NW Fla. Health Coun., 1990-91; bd. dirs. Cath. Social Svcs., Okaloosa County, 1989—. Mem. Kiwanis (Ft. Walton Beach club, bd. dirs. 1990-91, chairperson spiritual aims com. 1990-91). Office: First United Meth Ch 103 1st St SE Fort Walton Beach FL 32548-5893

LOCKE, KEVIN, flutist, lecturer, consultant; b. June 23, 1954; s. Charles and Patricia (McGillis) L.; m. Dorothy Stickwan, Nov. 24, 1975; children: Kimimila, Ohiyes'a, Waniya. BS, U. N.D., 1976; MA, U. S.D., 1977. Mem. aux. bd. Bahá'í Faith, 1986-88; mem. Nat. Spiritual Assembly of Bahá'ís, 1988—; lectr., cons. on Am. Indian values, belief systems, social structures and edn., Can., People's Republic of China, Spain, Australia, Africa. Nat. Heritage fellow Nat. Endowment for Arts. Address: Box 241 Mobridge SD 57601

LOCKERBIE, ANDREW NORVILLE, minister; b. Summers Point, N.J., Sept. 28, 1961; s. Andrew Norville Jr. and Gloria Anne (Dooley) L.; m. Leigh Anne Hough, July 31, 1982; children: Andrew Norville IV, Ashleigh. BA in Youth, Pacific Coast Bapt. Bible Sch., San Dimas, Calif., 1984. Ordained to ministry Bapt. Ch., 1984. Bus. mgr. Cen. Bapt. Ch., Huntington Beach, Calif., 1984—. Home: 7261 La Mancha Apt A Huntington Beach CA 92647 Office: Cen Bapt Ch 7661 Warner Ave Huntington Beach CA 92647

LOCKHART, GEORGE RICHARD, minister; b. Backhannon, W.Va., July 28, 1953; s. Richard Leslie and Neva Frye (Jordan) L.; m. Beverly Lynn Bird, Aug. 16, 1975; children: James Richard, Rachel Marie. BS in Bus. Mgmt., W.Va. Inst. Tech., 1976; MDiv, Sortheastern Theol. Sem., 1979; DD, New World Bible Inst., 1985. Ordained to ministry Am. Bapt. Chs., 1979. Pastor Dorcas-Maysville Bapt. Parish, Arthur, W.Va., 1978-81, Albright (W.Va.) Bapt. Parish, 1981-85, First Bapt. Ch., Oil City, Pa., 1985-88, 1st Bapt. Ch., Mannington, W.Va., 1988-90, Cen. Fellowship Bapt. Ch., 1991—; instr. Gulf Shore Christian Coll., 1991—. Mem. Goshen Bapt. Assn. (mem. ordination com. Morgantown W.Va. chpt. 1984-85), W.Va. Bapt. Assn. (area v.p. 1984-85), Goshen Bapt. Mins. Assn. (pres. 1984), Oil City Ministerial Assn. (pres. 1987), Mannington Ministerial Assn. (pres. 1989), North Cen. W.Va. Christian Edn. Assn. (chmn. 1989), Preston County Mins. Assn. (pres. 1984). Address: 1831 18th Ave NE Naples FL 33964 *No where in society is the love of God realized than in the local church. While every church faces the problems of the modern age, it is the working together of the members of the church that makes a difference in the world around us.*

LOCKHART, NELL HENDERSON, religious association executive, consultant; b. Birmingham, Ala., Jan. 3, 1936; d. Homer DuBose and Myrtle Nell (Isbell) Henderson; m. James Edward Lockhart, Aug. 25, 1956; children—Jonathan Mark, Leigh Anne. B.A., Howard Coll. (now Samford U.), 1956; postgrad. Meramec Community Coll., 1976-77. Tchr. pub. schs., Birmingham, 1956-57, Louisville, 1957-60, Atlanta, 1960-61; research librarian Christian Civic Found. St. Louis, 1972-76; dir. communications, program and spl. events Religious Heritage of Am., St. Louis, 1978-81, chief adminstrv. officer, 1981-82, exec. v.p., 1982-85, editor Newsbriefs newsletter, 1982-85; account exec. St. Louis Scene, Inc., 1985—. State officer Mo. Hosp. Assn. Aux. and Vol. Services, Jefferson City, 1967-72; pres. Mo. Baptist Hosp. Aux., St. Louis, 1968—. Mem. Meeting Planners Internat. (pres. St. Louis chpt. 1983-84), Religious Pub. Relations Council (v.p. 1980), Nat. Assn. Female Execs., St. Louis Soc. Assn. Execs., Kirkwood Hist. Soc. Republican. Baptist. Club: Woodgate Women's (pres. 1965-66) St. Louis. Home: 1238 Woodgate Dr Kirkwood MO 63122 Office: St Louis Scene 8600 Delmar Penthouse Suite 1 Saint Louis MO 63124

LOCKHART, WILLIAM HOWARD, minister; b. Schenectady, June 26, 1957; s. Robert William and Chiquita (Schilling) L.; m. Susan Finck, Aug. 3, 1985; children: Lydia Clare Finck, Karl McCabe Finck. BS in Urban Studies, U. Calif., Riverside, 1979; MDiv magna cum laude, Gordon-Conwell Theol. Sem., 1984. Ordained to ministry Presbyn. Ch. (U.S.A.), 1985. Deacon Calvin Presbyn. Ch., San Jose, 1979-80, youth dir., 1980; student pastor Hyde Park-Mattapan Presbyn. Ch., Boston, 1981-85; pastor Third Presbyn. Ch., Wheeling, W.Va., 1985-91; dir. Laughlin Meml. Chapel, Wheeling, W.Va., 1985—; clk. Congl. Devel. Com. Upper Ohio Valley Presbytery, 1989-90, chmn. task force on hearing impaired, 1990—. Bd. dirs. E. Wheeling Civics, 1987—; co-founder Greater Wheeling Coalition for Homeless, 1987, pres., 1987-90, treas., 1990—. Recipient Community Svc. award, E. Wheeling Civics, 1989. Mem. Presbyn. Health Edn. and Welfare Assn.. of Presbyn. Ch. USA, Phi Beta Kappa, Phi Alpha Chi. Office: Laughlin Meml Chapel 129 1/2 18th St Box 6195 Wheeling WV 26003

LOCKWOOD, DANIEL RALPH, religion educator; b. Portland, Oreg., Sept. 29, 1948; s. Milton Cutts and Esther (Williams) L.; m. Janet Yuko Iguchi, Dec. 30, 1972; 1 child, Elise Nicole. AB cum laude, Westmont Coll., 1970; ThM with high honor, Dallas Theol. Sem., 1976, ThD, 1982. Ordained to ministry Cen. Bible Ch., 1980. Instr. in Christian Edn. Dallas Theol. Sem., 1977-79; interim pastor Lewisville (Tex.) Congl. Ch., 1978-79; assoc. pastor adult edn. Mountain Park Ch., Lake Oswego, Oreg., 1988-91; prof. theology Multnomah Sch. of Bible, Portland, 1979—, v.p., 1990—; dean grad. sch. Multnomah Grad. Sch. Ministry, Portland, 1990—. Elder Mountain Park Ch. Mem. Evang. Theol. Soc. (vice chmn. N.W. regional chpt. 1986-87, chmn. 1987-88), Portland Soc. Magicians (v.p. 1983-84). Home: 9834 SW Quail Post Rd Portland OR 97219 Office: Multnomah Grad Sch 8435 NE Glisan Portland OR 97220

LOCKWOOD, ROBERT PHILIP, publishing executive; b. Yonkers, N.Y., Dec. 21, 1949; s. Albert Francis and Evelyn (Toburn) L.; m. Christiana Lynn Nowels, July 21, 1973; children—Ryan Robert, Theresa Lynn. B.A. in History, Fairfield U. Assoc. editor Our Sunday Visitor, Huntington, Ind., 1971-77, dir. books, 1982—, editor, 1977-85, dir., editor in chief, 1985-87, pub., 1987-90, pres., chief exec. officer, 1990—. Author: 70 Years of Our Sunday Visitor, 1982; contbr. articles to profl. jours., numerous periodicals. Chmn. St. Mary's Sch. Bd., Huntington, 1984-85; coach Huntington Catholic High Sch. Tennis, 1983-85. Mem. Cath. Press Assn. (editorial com. 1983—), Fort Wayne Press Assn. Avocations: writing; tennis. Home: 921 West Sherwood Terr Fort Wayne IN 46807

LODAHL, MICHAEL EUGENE, religion educator; b. Soap Lake, Wash., July 19, 1955; s. Kenneth Eugene and Virginia Maybelle (Liner) L.; m. Janice Elaine Watson, June 12, 1980; children: Sonya, Heather, Bryan. BA, NW Nazarene Coll., 1977; MDiv, Nazarene Theol. Sem., 1981; PhD, Emory U., 1988. Ordained minister in Ch. of the Nazarene, 1983. Pastor La Puente (Calif.) Ch. of the Nazarene, 1981-84, Crest Ch. of the Nazarene, Thomaston, Ga., 1986-87; interim pastor Overland Ch. of the Nazarene, Boise, Idaho, 1988-89; prof. theology NW Nazarene Coll., Nampa, Idaho, 1988—. Contbr. articles to profl. jours. Fellow Ctr. for Ethics and Religious Pluralism Shalom Hartman Inst.; mem. Am. Acad. Religion, Wesleyan Theol. Soc. Office: NW Nazarene Coll 623 Holly St Nampa ID 83686 *To affirm the reality of God is full of risk. And the only God worth affirming is One who also is at risk in the very act of creating.*

LODDING, MARY ENID, director religious education; b. Chgo., Mar. 14; d. Edward Henry and Lillian (Lencik) L. BA, Seattle U., 1958, MA in Religious Studies, 1971. Joined Sisters of Charity, Roman Cath. Ch. Tchr. various Cath. Schs., 1947-68; pastoral assoc. Cath. Newman Ctr., Iowa City, Iowa, 1968-78; dir. religious edn. Our Lady of the Wayside, Arlington Heights, Ill., 1978-88, St. Philip the Apostle, Addison, Ill., 1988—; mem. Sisters Coun., Davenport, Iowa, 1975-78; first Eucharistic min., first pastoral assoc. Diocese of Davenport, Iowa City, 1975; chaplain Christian Family Movement, Arlington Heights, 1978-88. Mem. Ill. Parish Coords. and Dirs. Religious Edn. Roman Catholic. Office: St Philip the Apostle 1233 W Holtz Addison IL 60101

LOE, DANIEL ROBERT, lay worker; b. Birmingham, Ala., June 3, 1956; s. Armon D. and Ann E. (Honeycutt) L.; m. Cheryll Lynn Abbott, Mar. 19, 1977; children: Jennifer B., Jonathan D., Jamie L., Jessica N. Sunday sch. tchr. Parkway Village Bapt. Ch., Memphis, 1981-90, deacon, 1982—; mng. rep. Covenant Life Ins. Co., Memphis, 1984—; bd. dirs. Parkway Village Bapt. Ch., 1989—, chmn. deacons, 1989-90; participant Amerasian Mentor Project, Memphis, 1991. Named Deacon of Yr., Parkway Bapt. Ch., 1989, 90. Mem. Memphis Life Underwriters Assn., Gen. Agts. and Mgrs. Conf. Office: Covenant Life Ins Co 2730 Colony Park Dr Ste 7 Memphis TN 38118

LOE, ROLAND WESLAY, minister; b. Camden, Ark., Dec. 22, 1955; s. Harold Gradon and Ruby Nell (Nichols) L.; m. Isabel Billarreal, Jan. 9, 1976; children: Samantha I., Toni E. BA with honors, East Tex. Bapt. Coll., 1978; MDiv, Southwestern Bapt. Theol. Sem., 1982. Ordained to ministry So. Bapt. Conv., 1982. Pastor Faith Temple Bapt. Ch., Terrell, Tex., 1982-84; missionary Home Mission Bd., So. Bapt. Conv., Uintah/Ouray Reservation, Utah, 1984; pastor Piney Grove Bapt. Ch., Lewisville, Ark., 1984-85, 1st Bapt. Ch., Ector, Tex., 1985-88, Cornerstone Bapt. Ch., Texarkana, Ark., 1988—; chaplain Terrell Police Dept., 1982-84; ch. extension cons. Ark. Bapt. State Conv., Little Rock, 1984-85; host, producer TV talk show Common Ground, 1990-91; mem. spiritual adv. bd. East Tex. Bapt. U., Marshall, 1990—; bd. dirs. Bapt. Student Union So. Ark. U., Magnolia, 1991; mem. exec. bd. Ark. Bapt. State Conv., 1991—. Chmn. Mayor's Coun. for Improved Racial Rels., Terrell, 1983. Recipient Nat. Appreciation award Soc. of Disting. Am. High Sch. Students, 1987. Mem. S.W. Ark. Bapt. Assn. (dir. mission devel. 1988—). Office: Cornerstone Bapt Ch 2101 Hays Texarkana AR 75502

LOEFFLER, HENRY KENNETH, clergyman, counselor; b. San Antonio, Nov. 9, 1938; s. Henry William and Marie Bertha (Schroeder) L.; m. Judith Rae Kohlmann, Aug. 4, 1962; 1 child, Michael Matthew. B.A., Tex. Luth. Coll., 1959; B.D., M.Min., Trinity Sem., Columbus, Ohio, 1963; M.S.T., Andover Newton Theol. Sch., 1970; D.Min., 1982; Ph.D., Boston Coll., 1981. Ordained to ministry, Am. Luth. Ch., 1963; lic. psychologist, Mass., R.I., Tex. Pastor Am. Luth. Parish Eastern Colo., 1963-65; exec. dir. Pastoral Counseling Clinic, Inc., Newport, R.I., 1970-74; dir. The Counseling Clinic, Inc., Middletown, R.I., 1974—. Bd. dirs. ARC, Newport, R.I.; judo coach; counseling service to mil. personnel. Served as chaplain, USN, 1965-69. A.E. Darby fellow, 1980-81. Mem. Am. Acad. Counselors and Family Therapists (nat. treas.), Am. Assn. Counseling and Devel., Am. Assn. Pastoral Counselors (diplomate), Am. Orthopsychiat. Assn., Am. Psychol. Assn., Assn. Mil. Surgeons U.S., Nat Bd. Cert. Counselors, Nat. Council Family Relations, Psychiat. Out-patient Clinics Am., R.I. Personnel and Guidance Assn., R.I. Psychol. Assn. (sec. clin. steering com.), U.S. Judo Assn., Quahog Judo Club, Aquidneck Island Judo Club. Home: 99 Emmanuel Dr Portsmouth RI 02871 Office: 82 E Main Rd Middletown RI 02840

LOEHR, SISTER MARLA, college president; b. Cleve., Oct. 7, 1937; d. Joseph Richard and Eleanore Edith (Rothschuh) L. BS, Notre Dame Coll., South Euclid, Ohio, 1960; MAT, Ind. U., 1969; PhD, Boston Coll., 1988. Joined Sisters of Notre Dame, Roman Cath. Ch., 1956; cert. high sch. tchr., counselor, Ohio. Mem. faculty Notre Dame Acad., Cleve., 1960-64, John F. Kennedy High Sch., Warren, Ohio, 1964-66; adminstrn. asst., dir. residence halls Notre Dame Acad., Chardon, Ohio, 1966-72; dean students Notre Dame Coll., South Euclid, 1972-85, acting acad. dean, 1988, pres., 1989—; cons. Nat. Cons. Network, Washington, 1978-85; facilitator Coun. for Ind. Colls., Washington, 1980-84. Author: Mentor Handbook, 1985; co-author: Notre Dame College Model for Student Development, 1980. Hon. mem. Segund Montes Solidarity City Campaign. Grantee Cleve. Found., 1980, Title VIII - Office Edn., Washington, 1981-83. Mem. Am. Assn. Higher Edn., Assn. Governing Bds., Pax Christi, Alpha Sigma Nu. Avocations: photography, hiking, reading, sports. Office: Notre Dame Coll Ohio 4545 College Rd South Euclid OH 44121

LOESCH, ROBERT KENDRICK, minister; b. West Palm Beach, Fla., Nov. 20, 1941; s. Russell T. and Polly (Francis) L.; m. Bonnie Frazier, June 15, 1963 (div. 1976); children—Shelley Lynn, Donald Russell; m. 2d, Patricia Fanjoy, Aug. 6, 1976 (div. 1987); children—Jason Robert (dec.), Christine Kimberly, Sandra Jean. B.A., Oberlin Coll., 1963; B.D., Yale Divinity Sch., 1966; M.A., Hartford Sem., 1971, Dr. Ministry, 1987. Ordained minister United Ch. Christ, 1966. Asst. pastor First Congregational Ch., West Haven, Conn., 1964-66; pastor North Canaan Congl. Parish, Canaan, Conn., 1966-73; pastor First Congl. Ch., Madison, Conn., 1973-75; pastor United Ch. Christ, Oakdale, Conn., 1976-78; pastor Taftville (Conn.), 1978-83; program dir. Norwich (Conn.) Sr. Citizens Ctr., 1981-82; assoc. pastor First Ch. Christ, Congl., Springfield, Mass., 1983-87; program dir. Palmer (Mass.) Assocs., 1987—. Author: James F. English, 1975; contbr. articles to profl. jours. and newspapers; lectr., participant religious confs. Class agt. Oberlin Coll. Alumni Fund, 1978-87, Yale Alumni Fund, 1979-87; mem. Friends of the Quadrangle, Springfield, Mass., 1983—, World Affairs Council, 1983—, East Forest Park Civic Assn., 1983—, Downtown Ministry Task Force, 1983-87; chmn. Springfield UN Day, 1984-86; v.p., chmn. pub. relations Council of Chs. of Greater Springfield; coordinator pub. info. Al-Anon Family Groups Greater Springfield. Mem. Hampden Assn. United Ch. Christ (scribe), Found. Christian Living, Am. Assn. Ret. Persons, Assn. Yale Alumni, Alumni Assn. Oberlin Coll., Nat. Women's Hall of Fame, UN Assn., Albert Schweitzer Ctr., Acad. of Parish Clergy, Graymoor Ecumenical Inst. (assoc.). Democrat. Clubs: Conn. Valley Yale, Conn. Valley Congregational (pres. 1985-87). Home: 19 Virginia St Springfield MA 01108 Office: First Ch Christ Court Sq Springfield MA 01103

LOEW, RALPH WILLIAM, clergyman, columnist; b. Columbus, Ohio, Dec. 29, 1907; s. William Louis and Wilhelmina (Bauer) L.; m. Genevra Maxine Uhl, June 8, 1939; children—Carolyn Maxine, Janet Elaine. A.B., Capital U., 1928; M.Divinity, Hamma Div. Sch., Springfield, Ohio, 1931; D.D., Wittenberg U., 1947; L.H.D., Susquehanna U., 1972, Wagner Coll., 1974; LL.D., Hartwick Coll., 1979. Ordained to ministry Luth. Ch., 1931. Pastor Millerburg (Ohio) Luth. Parish, 1931-37; asso. pastor Luth. Ch. Reformation, Washington, 1937-44; pastor Holy Trinity Luth. Ch., Buffalo, 1944-75; Del. Luth. World Fedn., Lund, Sweden, 1947, Helsinki, Finland, 1968; Knubel-Miller lectr. United Luth. Ch., 1955; lectr. Retreat for Chaplains, Nat. Luth. Council, Berchtesgaden, Germany, 1956; Brit-Am. exchange preacher, 1966, 72; participant Long Range Planning Conf., India, 1968; pres. bd. fgn. missions United Luth Ch. Am., 1956-60, mem. exec. council, 1962-66, pres. bd. world missions, 1970-72, chmn. div. world missions and ecumenism, 1972-76; dir. dept. religion Chautauqua Instn., 1973-84; pres. ct. adjudication Luth. Ch. Am. Author: The Hinges of Destiny, 1955, The Church and the Amateur Adult, 1955, Confronted by Jesus, 1957, Lutheran Way of Life, 1966, Christmas in the Shadows, 1968, He is Coming Soon, 1972; Contbr.: weekly column From My Window, Buffalo Courier-Express, 1952-82; syndicated column Finding The Way, 1960-67. Pres. Buffalo and Erie County council Chs., 1950-51, Community Action Orgn., Buffalo and Erie County; pres. bd. trustees Margaret L. Wendt Found.; trustee Chautauqua Instn., 1988—; pres. WNY Grantmakers, 1988-90. Home: 342 Depew Ave Buffalo NY 14214

LOEWENSTEIN, EGON ISRAEL, rabbi; b. Berlin, Oct. 2, 1912; s. Ernst and Jenny (Levy) L.; m. Kaethe Brauer, June 7, 1939. PhD, Jewish Theol. Sem., Breslau (now Wroclaw, Poland), Germany, 1939. Ordained rabbi, 1939. Rabbi Jewish Community, Gleiwitz, Germany, 1938-39, Santiago, Chile, 1939-70; rabbi Congregation Emet V-Emuna, Jerusalem, 1970—; mem. directory Zionist Fedn. of Chile. Home and Office: Rehov Paran 10, PO Box 18331, 91181 Ramot Eshkol Israel

LOFF, BETTY GARLAND, religious administrator, educator; b. L.A., Aug. 18, 1932; d. Lewis Michael and Bernice (Siberz) Hohenthaner; m. Daniel David Loff, May 1, 1951; children: Dana Elizabeth, Tamra Marie. Grad., Lamson Dental Coll., L.A., 1950-51; M in Catechist, Diocese Phoenix, 1971; M in Pastoral Ministry, U. San Francisco, 1986, postgrad., 1986—. Dental asst. various offices L.A., 1952-53; office mgr. Supply Co, Phoenix, 1968-71; adminstrv. asst. Diocese Phoenix Religious Edn., 1971-75; adminstrv. aast., intern religious edn. St. Theresa Ch., Phoenix, 1975-79; dir. religious edn. St. Paul Ch., Phoenix, 1979—; chmn. Catechetical Congress Diocese, 1971-89, Diocesan Religious Edn. Adv. Bd., Phoenix, 1983-86; mem. steering & formation com., co-chmn., spirituality com. CADRE-Profl. Orgn. for Dirs. & Coords. Religious Edn., Phoenix, 1986—; insvc. facillitator Retreat Team. Author-editor Catechetical Congress Job Description booklet, 1974; contbr. articles to profl. jours. Mem. Ariz. Masterworks Chorale (affiliate Phoenix Symphony Orch., 1989—). Recipient Concern for Kids in the Community award Gen. Fedn. Women's Clubs, 1985. Mem. Nat. Cath. Edn. Assn., Religious Edn. Assn. Phoenix (sec. 1972-83). Avocations: sailing, singing, instr. of retreat team, facillitator of inservice. Office: St Paul Cath Ch 330 W Coral Gables Dr Phoenix AZ 85023

LOFFREDO, EUGENE EDWARD, deacon; b. Paterson, N.J., Apr. 24, 1932; s. Thomas Gaetano and Ida (Amatuzzi) L.; m. Pearl Theresa Chidiac, Nov. 27, 1954; children: Mary Claire Loffredo Hanson, Margaret Loffredo Murphy, Jeanne Loffredo Cutrona, Eileen Loffredo Smith, Cathleen, Donna. BS in Religious Studies, Sacred Heart U., 1989. Deacon St. Gabriel Roman Cath. Ch., Milford, Conn., 1980-90; pastoral assoc. Blessed Sacrament Roman Cath. Ch., Bridgeport, Conn., 1990—. Home: 562 Milford Point Rd Milford CT 06460 Office: Blessed Sacrament Ch 275 Union Ave Bridgeport CT 06607

LOFTON, JAMES THOMAS, minister; b. Natchez, Miss., Dec. 21, 1938; s. Thomas Hilton and Anne Taylor (Burns) L.; m. Janis Pauline Roberts, Aug. 3, 1959; children: James Thomas II, Gregory Kyle, Mark Hilton. Student, SW Assemblies of God Coll., Waxahachie, Tex., 1957-58. Ordained to ministry Assemblies of God, 1962. Sr. pastor Assemblies of God Ch., Jal, N.Mex., 1960-65, Biloxi, Miss., 1965-70, Flagstaff, Ariz., 1970-75, Phoenix, 1975-80; sr. pastor Music City Assembly of God Ch., Nashville, 1980—; mem. fgn. missions bd. Assemblies of God, Springfield, Mo., 1975-78, gen. presbyter, 1978-80, 89—; exec. presbyter Ariz. Assemblies of God, Phoenix, 1978-80; exec. presbyter Tenn. Dist., Assemblies of God, Nashville, 1988—, bd. dirs., 1988—; bd. dirs. Am. Indian Bible Inst., 1975-80, Western Bible Inst., 1975-80, Bethany Bible Coll., 1978; pres. Flagstaff Ministerial Alliance, 1973-75. Contbg. author: Higher Goals, 1978, Holy Spirit Digest, 1983. Chaplain, Keesler AFB, Miss., 1965-70, Tenn. Senate, Nashville, 1989—. Named Man of Yr., Sta. KOAI-TV, NBC, Flagstaff, 1975. Republican. Office: Music City Assembly of God 5240 Edmondson Pk PO Box 110356 Nashville TN 37211 *Spiritual values must be the core of life, if we are to live with meaning. Within the home of every Christian family spiritual values should be taught and caught by its members. Our churches are only as strong as the families who comprise them. If Christianity is to take root in society, it must be done so at the point where our families live, work and play.*

LOFTON, OLLIE RAE, lay worker; b. Dixie, Ark., Aug. 27, 1926; d. Rayfield and Cleo (Woods) Bush; m. Emmanuel Lofton, June 23, 1969. BS, Tenn. State U., 1961; MS, Ark. State U., 1966. Cert. elem. tchr., spl. edn. tchr., adminstr. and supr., Ark. Youth dir. St. Paul Missionary Bapt. Ch., Blytheville, Ark., 1960-69; Sunday sch. tchr. St. Paul Missionary Bapt. Ch., Wardell, Mo., 1972—, pres. WMU, 1990—; adminstr. Blytheville Pub. Sch., 1969-90, retired, 1990. Pres. Miss. County Spl. Workshop Bd., Blytheville, 1987-89. Recipient Community Svc. award Talents Unltd. Music Program, 1985, Miss. County EOC Head Start, 1989, Alpha Phi Alpha, 1990, Svc. to Edn. award Ark. Sch. Adminstrv. Assn., 1990. Mem. Pemiscot-Dunkin Dist. Assn. (2d v.p. 1990—, pres. Ministers' Wives 1990—, co-chair state convention 1990—), Miss. County Black Cultural Assn. (co-chmn. 1990—, Community Svc. award 1986), Ark. Assn. Women's Clubs, Inc. (state treas. 1985—), Order of Eastern Star (sec. to matron 1987-89). Home: 812 S Franklin Blytheville AR 72315

LOGAN, CYNTHIA WEEKS, minister; b. Newark, Nov. 18, 1950; d. Vernon Adams and Ruth Mary (Kreidler) Weeks; m. John Caldwell, Sept. 30, 1983; stepchildren: Kevin Caldwell, Colby Adger. BA, Sam Houston State U., 1972; MA, Presbyn. Sch. Christian Edn., 1976; MDiv, Austin Presbyn. Theol. Sem., 1979. Ordained to ministry Presbyn. Ch., 1979; cert. Christian edn. tchr. Dir. edn. Spring Br. Presbyn. Ch., Houston, 1976; assoc. pastor Oak Cliff Presbyn. Ch., Dallas, 1979-84, Preston Hollow Presbyn. Ch., Dallas, 1984—; dir. S.W. Career Devel. Ctr., Arlington, Tex., 1988—, pres. bd., 1991—; trustee Austin (Tex.) Presbyn. Theol. Sem., 1989—; dir. Austin Sem. Assn. Bd., 1989—; moderator Grace Presbytery, Tex., 1984. Mem. Clergywomen Community Dallas (convenor 1989, 90), Alban Inst., Amnesty Internat., Habitat for Humanity. Office: Preston Hollow Presbyn Ch 9800 Preston Rd Dallas TX 75230

LOGAN, DAYTON NORRIS, minister; b. Athens, Ga., Sept. 6, 1927; s. Mahlon Benjamin and Alma (Della) L.; m. Doris Pauline Shepherd, Aug. 7, 1948. Cert., Mercer U., 1957. Ordained to ministry So. Bapt. Conv., 1949. Pastor Shiloh Bapt. Ch., Danielsville, Ga., 1949-56, High Shoals (Ga.) Bapt. Ch., 1950-53, Friendship Bapt. Ch., Danielsville, 1950—; pres. Logan Paving Co., Athens, Ga., 1963—; moderator Sarepta Bapt. Assn., Athens, 1977; trustee Penfield (Ga.) Christian Home, 1986—, chmn., 1990. Mem. Civitans (pres. Whitehead-Athens 1966-67, former chaplain). Home: 125 Jefferson River Rd Athens GA 30607 Office: 1000 Winterville Rd Athens GA 30608 *There are many steps carefully climbed in going right, but it only takes one short one down to go wrong, so watch where you step.*

LOGAN, LANGSTON DUVALL, minister; b. Sandylevel, Va., Mar. 13, 1951; s. Obie Lorenzo and Lucy Mae (Musgrove) L.; m. Sharon Ann Clark, July 3, 1971; children: Langston, Brittney LaShar, Jessie Langston. AB, Va. Sem. & Coll., Lynchburg, 1982; MDiv, Va. Sem. & Coll., 1984; postgrad., Va. Episcopal Sem., 1986. Ordained to ministry, Bapt. Ch., 1978. Pastor Sunflower Bapt. Ch., Nathalie, Va., 1979-88, Lawson Chapel Bapt. Ch., Roxboro, N.C., 1988—; homiletics instr. Va. Sem. & Coll., 1984-87, Shaw U. Div. Sch., Raleigh, 1990—; cons. in field. Steering com. Person County Sch. Bd., Roxboro, 1989; treas. Northend Sch. PTA, Roxboro, 1989—. Mem. Banister Bapt. Assn. (adv. bd. 1985), E. Cedar Grove Assn. (ordaining coun. 1989), NAACP, Roxboro Ministerial Assn., Roxboro Ministerial Alliance (pres. 1989—), Sertoma (exec. bd. 1989), Masons. Democrat. Baptist. Avocations: swimming, jogging, reading, writing, travel. Address: Rte 2 Box 148 Roxboro NC 27573

LOGAN, ROBERT M., minister. Pres. United Chs. Williamsport (Pa.) and Lycoming County. Office: United Chs Williamsport & Lycoming County 202 E Third St Williamsport PA 17701*

LOGAN, STEWART JAY, clergyman; b. Denver, June 24, 1958; s. Straud W. and Willa L. (Wallace) L.; m. Andrea Therese Lapinsky, July 14, 1990. BA, Bob Jones U., 1981. Tchr., coach Grace Bapt. Ch., Farmington, N.Mex., 1981-84, dir. youth and music, 1981-88; pastor singles The Exciting Tabernacle Bapt. Ch., Farmington, 1989—; maintenance auditor Mesa Airlines, Farmington, 1989; co-dir. Rocky Mountain Christian Singles Network, Farmington, 1990. Referee N.Mex. Activities Assn., Farmington, 1982-91. Home: 905 N Tucker Apt 3 Farmington NM 87401

LOGAN, THOMAS WILSON STEARLY, SR., priest; b. Phila., Mar. 19, 1912; s. John Richard and Mary (Harbison) L.; m. Hermoine Hill, Sept. 3, 1938; 1 son, Thomas Wilson Stearly. AB, Lincoln U., 1935, LLH (hon.), 1985; cert., Gen. Theol. Sem., 1938; STM, Phila. Divinity Sch., 1941; DD,

Va. Sem., 1988; LLH (hon.), St. Augustine Coll., 1984. Ordained priest Episcopal Ch., 1938. Vicar St. Philip Ch., N.Y.C., 1938-40, St. Michael's and All Angels Chs., Phila., 1940-45; rector Calvary Ch., Phila., 1945-84, rector emeritus, 1984—; pres. worker's conf. Episcopal Ch., 1951-61; canon St. Mary's Cathedral, Phila.; dean Schykill (Pa.) Deanery; former pres. Hampton (Va.) Mins. Conf., 1960-61; mem. diocesan coun.; police chaplain; chaplain Phila. Gen. Hosp. Bd. dirs. YMCA, Black Mus., Phila.; trustee Haverford State Hosp.; pres. Downington (Pa.) Sch.; life mem. Lincoln (Pa.) U. Mem. NAACP (life), Alpha Phi Alpha (life), Masons (33 degree, past grand master Pa.), Shriner (imperial chaplain). Home: 46 Lincoln Ave Yeadon PA 19050

LOGAN, WILLIAM STEVENSON, archdeacon, religious organization administrator; b. Detroit, Mar. 10, 1920; s. William Stevenson and Evelyn Lucille (Castle) L.; m. Mary Adelaide Siddall, Dec. 1, 1951; children: Mary Shore, Margaret Elizabeth, William Stevenson. BSChemE, U. PA., 1941; M in Automotive Engring., Chrysler Inst. Engring., 1943; MDiv, Episcopal Theol. Sch., 1951; MA, U. Mich., 1980. Ordained priest Episcopal Ch., 1951. Vicar Our Savior Ch., Saugus, Mass., 1949-51; curate Christ Ch., Detroit, 1951-52; rector St. Martin's Ch., Detroit, 1952-63; program dir. Diocese of Mich., Detroit, 1963-73, archdeacon, 1973-85; archdeacon; ret., 1985; Hon. canon Cathedral Ch. St. Paul, Detroit, 1968; v.p. Mich. Coun. Chs., Lansing, 1968-70; nat. chmn. Conf. Diocesan Execs., 1980-81. Contbr. articles to profl. jours. Chmn. Gov.'s Fair Campaign Practices com., Detroit, 1977—; subcom. chmn. Mayor's Com. on Human Resources Devel., Detroit, 1964-73. Lt. (j.g.), USNR, 1945-46. Mem. Engring. Soc. Detroit, United Ministries in Higher Edn. (pres. 1971-73, 80-82), Detroit Boat, Prismatic Club, Wranglers Club. Home: 1514 Chateaufort Pl Detroit MI 48207 Office: Cathedral Ch of St Paul 4800 Woodward Ave Detroit MI 48201

LOGIE, DENNIS WAYNE, minister; b. Longmont, Colo., Mar. 18, 1940; s. Wayne Edward and Fern Maxine (Jacobson) L.; m. Burgl Dagmar Kaiser, Jan. 15, 1961; children: Hans Dennis, Heidi Elisabeth. Student, Stanford U., 1958-60, Fuller Sem., 1978. Ordained to ministry Christian Ch., 1977. Systems officer Crocker Nat. Bank, San Francisco, 1964-76, dir. data processing edn., 1976-78; minister 1st Christian Ch., Redwood City, Calif., 1978-81, sr. minister, 1981—; del. Heavenly Hills Christian Camp, Twain-Harte, Calif., 1978--; founder, bd. dirs. No. Calif. Ministers Retreat, San Rafael, Calif., 1983--. Contbr. articles and essays to various publs. Mem. parents adv. group Selby Lane Sch., Atherton, Calif., 1974-76; treas. Band-Aids, Woodside (Calif.) High Sch., 1976-79; co-founder, bd. dirs. Lay Inst. for Tng., Redwood City, 1976-81; bd. dirs. San Jose (Calif.) Christian Coll., 1976-82, 88--. Mem. No. Calif. Evangelistic Assn. (bd. dirs. 1987--), Redwood City Clergy Assn. (pres. 1979-85, 88--), Calif. PTA (life). Republican. Avocations: tennis, softball. Home: 164 Oakfield Ave Redwood City CA 94061 Office: 1st Christian Ch 233 Topaz St Redwood City CA 94062

LOHMEYER, JAMES ARTHUR, family therapist, clergyman; b. Clay Center, Kans., Feb. 7, 1947; s. Arthur Henryand Mildred Elizabeth (Loges) L.; m. Elizabeth Ann Segerhammar, June 20, 1970; children: Joseph James, Scott Arthur. BA, Bethany Coll., Lindsborg, Kans., 1969; MDiv, Luth. Sch. Theology, Chgo., 1973. Ordained to ministry Luth. Ch., 1974; cert. alcohol/drug addictions counselor. Pastor Scherer Meml. Luth. Ch., Chapman, Kans., 1974-82, Faith Luth. Ch., Junction City, Kans., 1974-82; chaplain, chem. dependency counselor Hoisington (Kans.) Luth. Hosp. (now Clara Barton Hosp.), 1982—, family therapist, 1986—; pastor Garfield (Kans.) Luth. Ch., 1987—. Bd. dirs. Luth. Social Svc. Kans. and Okla., Wichita, 1986—, sec., 1989—. Mem. Kans. Alcoholism and Drug Abuse Counselors Assn. Democrat. Lutheran. Office: Family Recovery Ctr Clara Barton Hosp 250 W 9th St Hoisington KS 67544

LOHMULLER, MARTIN NICHOLAS, bishop; b. Phila., Aug. 21, 1919; s. Martin Nicholas and Mary Frances (Doser) L. B.A., St. Charles Borromeo Sem., Phila., 1942; D.Canon Law, Catholic U. Am., 1947. Ordained priest Roman Catholic Ch., 1944; officialis Diocese Harrisburg, Pa., 1948-63; vicar for religious Diocese of Harrisburg, 1958-70; pastor Our Lady of Good Counsel parish, Marysville, Pa., 1954-64, St. Catherine Labouree Parish, Harrisburg, 1964-68; consecrated bishop, 1970; vicar gen. Archdiocese Phila., 1970—; aux. bishop of Phila., 1970—; pastor Old St. Mary's Parish, Phila., 1976-89, Holy Trinity Parish, Phila., 1976-89.

LOHR, HAROLD RUSSELL, bishop; b. Gary, S.D., Aug. 31, 1922; s. Lester ALbert and Nora Helena (Fossum) L.; m. Theola Marie Kottke, June 21, 1947 (div. Dec. 1973); children: Philip Kyle, David Scott, Michael John; m. Edith Mary Morgan, Dec. 31, 1973. BS summa cum laude, S.D. State U., 1947; PhD, U. Calif.-Berkeley, 1950; MDiv summa cum laude, Augustana Theol. Sem., Rock Island, Ill., 1958. Ordained to ministry Augustana Luth. Ch., 1958; installed as bishop, 1980. Research chemist Argonne Nat. lab., Lemont, Ill., 1950-54; pastor Luth. Ch. of Ascension, Northfield, Ill., 1958-70; assoc. exec. Bd. Coll. Edn., N.Y.C., 1970-73; dir. research Div. Profl. Leadership, Phila., 1973-77, assoc. exec., 1977-80; synodical bishop Luth. Ch. in Am., Fargo, N.D., 1980-87; synodical bishop Evang. Luth. Ch. in Am., Moorhead, Minn., 1988-91, ret., 1991; mem. exec. council Luth. Ch. in Am., N.Y.C., 1982-87; mem. commn. of peace and war, 1983-85. Contbg. author: Growth in Ministry, 1980; also articles to sci. jours. Bd. dirs. Gustavus Adolphus Coll., 1980-87, Luther Northwestern Sem., St. Paul, 1980-87, Concordia Coll., Moorhead, Minn., 1988-91; mem. ch. coun. Evang. Luth. Ch. in Am., Chgo., 1990-91; mem. bd. govs. Chgo. Ctr. for Religion and Sci., 1987—. Served as 1st lt. inf. U.S. Army, 1943-46, ETO. Recipient Suomi award Suomi Coll., 1983. Mem. Phi Kappa Phi. Democrat. Home: 1210 49th Ave S Fargo ND 58104

LOHSE, BERNHARD, minister, educator; b. Hamburg, Fed. Republic of Germany, May 24, 1928; s. Walter and Wilhelmine (Barrelet) L.; m. Annelotte Lohse, Aug. 27, 1955; children: Reinhard, Joachim, Andreas. Abitur, Gelehrtenschule, Hamburg, 1947; ThD, U. GÖttingen, Lower Saxony, Fed. Republic of Germany, 1952. Ordained minister Luth. Ch., Feb., 1954. Privatdozent U. Hamburg, Fed. Republic of Germany, 1957-63; vis. prof. Claremont Coll., Calif., U.S., 1961; prof. ch. history U. Hamburg, Fed. Republic of Germany, 1964—; vis. prof. Yale U., New Haven, Conn., U.S., 1967. Home: Wittenbergener Weg 40, D-2000 Hamburg 56 Federal Republic of Germany Office: Fachbereich Evang Theologie, Sedanstrasse 19, 2000 Hamburg Federal Republic of Germany

LOHSE, EDWARD E., minister, international religious organization head. Pres. United bible Socs., Reading, Eng. Office: United Bible Socs, 7th Fl, Reading Bridge House, Reading RG1 8PJ, England*

LOKKEN, JAMES ARNOLD, minister, data processing company executive; b. Pasadena, Calif., Apr. 15, 1933; s. Martin O. and Agnes (Trano) L. BA, Pacific Luth. Coll., Tacoma, Wash., 1955; MDiv, Luth. Sem., St. Paul, 1959. Ordained to ministry Evang. Luth. Ch., 1959. Youth pastor 1st Luth. Ch., Brookings, S.D., 1964-66; prodn. dir. Liturgical Conf., Washington, 1968-78; asst. pastor St. Francis Luth. Ch., San Francisco, 1982—; data processing mgr. Electrographic Corp., San Francisco, 1979—. Author, editor: Now the Silence Breaks, 1980; asst. editor Luth. Forum, 1966-68; editor Luth. New Yorker, 1975-76. Office: St Francis Luth Ch 152 Church St San Francisco CA 94114

LOLLA, JOHN JOSEPH, minister; b. Norwalk, Ohio, June 16, 1953; s. John J. Sr. and Mildred Jane (Hoyt) L.; m. Julie Ann Else, May 7, 1977; children: Meredith Ann, Carolyn Elizabeth. BA, Coll. Wooster, 1976; MDiv, Princton Theol. Sem., 1980. Asst. minister Southminster Presbyterian Ch., Pitts., 1980-83; minister Presbyterian Ch. Plum Creek, Pitts., 1983—; chair peacemaking task force Pitts. Presbytery, 1984-86, chair Middle East youth tour, 1986-1991, mem. gen. coun., 1989-91, evaluation and budgeting, 1988-90, chmn., 1990, planning and fin., 1991—, chmn. 1991—; chairperson Shalom I, II, III, IV confs., 1984-89, interim com., 1990; mem. Anne Frank Exhibit Clergy Adv. Com., 1989-90. Mem. Jewish-Christian Dialogue, Pitts., 1988-89, Reformed-Cath. Dialogue, Pitts., 1989-89; mem. clergy adv. com. Forbes Regional Hosps., 1989-91. Recipient John Alan Swink prize in preaching, 1980, Synod Peacemaking award Synod of the Trinity, Elkins, W.Va., 1989, spl. recognition award St. Francis Hosp. Chem. Dependency Unit, Pitts., 1986, Presbytery Peacemaking award Pitts. Presbytery, 1989, Communications award Am. Lebanese Congress, 1990. Mem. Pitts. Presbytery, The Pitts. Cleric. Republican.

LOLLEY, WILLIAM RANDALL, minister; b. Troy, Ala., June 2, 1931; s. Roscoe Lee and Mary Sara (Nunnelee) L.; m. Clara Lou Jacobs, Aug. 28, 1952; children: Charlotte, Pam. AB, Samford U., 1952, DD (hon.), 1980; BD, Southeastern Sem., 1957, ThM, 1958; ThD, Southwestern Sem., 1962; DD (hon.), Wake Forest U., 1971, U. Richmond, 1984; LLD (hon.), Campbell U., 1986; LittD (hon.), Mercer U., 1988. Ordained to ministry So. Bapt. Conv., 1951; pastor First Bapt. Ch., Winston-Salem, N.C., 1962-74; pres. Southeastern Bapt. Theol. Sem., Wake Forest, N.C., 1974-88; pastor First Bapt. Ch., Raleigh, N.C., 1988-90, Greensboro, N.C., 1990—. Author: Crises in Morality, 1963, Bold Preaching of Christ, 1979. Democrat. Club: Rotary. Home: 3200 W Market St Greensboro NC 27403 Office: First Bapt Ch Greensboro NC 27403

LOMRANTZ, MERLE ROBIN, Jewish school educator; b. N.Y.C., Mar. 28, 1954; d. Herbert A. and Doris (Sapinkopf) Cohen; m. Larry Lomrantz, Nov. 27, 1976; children: Jamie, Tracey. BS in Human Devel., Syracuse U., 1975. Tchr. jr. dept. YM-YWHA of North Jersey, Wayne, N.J., 1977—, unit supr., 1986-87, CIT supr., 1989-90, special camp coord., 1990—; advisor Jewish Students Assn., William Paterson Coll., Wayne; v.p. bd. edn., membership com. Temple Adath Shalom, Dover, N.J., 1990—, chair membership com., 1988-90, chair bd. edn., 1986-88. Mem. Nat. Coun. Jewish Women (mem. fundraising com., Jewish holiday programming, 1978-88). Home: 23 Clifford Dr Towaco NJ 07082-2000 Office: YM-YWHA of North Jersey 1 Pike Dr Wayne NJ 07470

LONA REYES, ARTURO, bishop; b. Aguascalientes, Mex., Nov. 1, 1925. Ordained priest Roman Cath. Ch., 1952; elevated to bishop of Tehuantepec, Mex., 1971—; consecrated, 1971. Address: Iglesia Catedral, Apartado Postal 93, CP 71760 Tehuantepec Oa, Mexico

LONG, BURKE O'CONNOR, religion educator. BA, Randolph-Macon Coll., 1961; BD, Yale U., 1964, MA, 1966, PhD, 1967. Asst. prof. Wellesley Coll., 1967-68; asst. prof., then assoc. prof. Bowdoin Coll., 1968-78, prof. religion, 1979—, chmn. dept. religion, 1972, 78-81, 85-90, chair Spindel lectures in Judaic studies, 1982-88; acad. visitor London Sch. Econs., 1974-75; vis. prof. Sch. Theology Claremont, 1978, Emory U., 1982, 88, Hebrew U. Jerusalem, 1983-84; sr. Fulbright lectr. for Israel, 1983-84; dir. regional project NEH, 1984; guest lectr. at colls., univs., internat. congresses. Author: The Problem of Etiological Narrative in the Old Testament, 1968, I Kings with an Introduction to Historical Literature, 1984, 2 Kings, 1991; also articles; series editor: Sources for the Study of Greek Religion, 1979, A Handbook of Ancient Hebrew Letters, 1982, Prophecy in Cross-Cultural Perspective, 1986, Letters From Ancient Egypt, 1990, Hittite Myths, 1991; editor, author (with others): Canon and Authority: Essays in Old Testament Religion and Theology, 1977, Images of God and Man: Old Testament Short Stories in Literary Focus, 1981, Rethinking the Place of Biblical Studies in the Academy, 1990; editor Sources for Bibl. Study, 1977-85, Writings From the Ancient World, 1988—; editorial cons. Scholars Press, Fortress Press, Univ. Press Am.; mem. editorial bd. Jour. for Study of Old Testament, Jour. Bibl. Lit., Semeia. Pres. Holocaust Human Rights Ctr. Maine. Rockefeller fellow, 1966-67, Yale U. fellow, 1981, Am. Jewish Archives fellow, 1991, Am. Philos. Soc. Mellon fellow, 1991. Mem. Soc. Bibl. Lit. (rsch. and publ. com. 1984, program com. 1985-89, fellow 1979), World Union Jewish Studies, Internat. Orgn. for Study of Old Testament, Inst. for Antiquity and Christianity, Phi Beta Kappa. Address: 16 McLellan St Brunswick ME 04011

LONG, CHARLES HENRY, JR., clergyman, publisher; b. Phila., Feb. 13, 1923; s. Charles Henry and Evelyn Agnes (Boyd) L.; m. Nancy Ingham, Feb. 14, 1946; children—Christine, Charles H. III, Robert, Jeremy. B.A. Yale U., 1944; D.MDiv, Va. Sem., 1946, D.Div., 1976; S.T.M., Phila. Luth. Sem., 1966; S.T.D. Episcopal Sem. Ky., 1983; L.H.D. Episcopal Sem. Southwest, 1984. Ordained priest Episcopal Ch., 1947. Missionary, Episcopal Ch., Nanking, China, 1946-49; far east rep. Yale-China Assn., Hong Kong, 1954-58; study sec. World Student Christian Fedn., Geneva, Switzerland, 1958-60; rector St. Peter's Ch., Glenside, Pa., 1960-73; exec. dir. World Council of Chs., N.Y.C., 1974-78; pub., editor Forward Movement Publs., Cin., 1978—. Author: Vancouver Voices, 1983, Who Are the Anglicans?, 1988; editor: The Compulsion of the Spirit, 1983; various religious guides; asst. editor: Anglican Theol. Rev. V.p. Greater Phila. Coun. Chs., 1963-66. Fellow Coll. of Preachers; mem. Evang. Edn. Soc. (bd. mgrs. 1963—, v.p. 1969-78), Soc. Promotion Christian Knowledge (trustee 1984-89), Yale-China Assn. (trustee 1961-73). Clubs: University (Cin.), Literary. Avocations: music, golf. Office: Forward Movement Pubs 412 Sycamore St Cincinnati OH 45202

LONG, CHARLES HOUSTON, history of religion educator; b. Little Rock, Aug. 23, 1926; s. Samuel Preston and Diamond Geneva (Thompson) L.; m. Alice Freeman, June 21, 1953; children—John, Carolyn, Christopher, David. Diploma, Dunbar Jr. Coll., 1946; B.D., U. Chgo., 1953, Ph.D., 1962; L.H.D., Dickinson Coll., 1971. Mem. faculty U. Chgo., 1956-74, prof. history of religions, 1971-74; mem. faculty U. Chgo. Div. Sch., 1956-74, prof., 1971-74, dean students, 1956-60; William Rand Kenan, Jr. prof. history of religions U. N.C., Chapel Hill, 1974—; also bd. govs. U. N.C. (U. N.C. Press); prof. history of religions Duke U., 1974-88; Jeannette K. Watson prof. history of religions Syracuse U., 1988—, dir. humanities doctoral program, 1988-91; prof. dept. religious studies, dir. Rsch. Ctr. in Black Studies U. Calif., Santa Barbara, 1991—; dir. seminar Nat. Endowment Humanities, summers 1977, 78, yr. 1979-80; bd. commrs. Assn. Am. Colls. ; bd. govs. U. N.C. Press, 1975-87. Author: Alpha: The Myths of Creation, 1963; founding editor (with others): History of Religions jour., 1961-74; editor (with Joseph Kitagawa and Mircea Eliade) History of Religions: Essays in Understanding, 1959, Myths and Symbols: Essays in Honor of Mircea Eliade, 1969, Significations, 1986; gen. editor series Studies in Religion, 1978—; editorial bd. cons. Ency. Britannica; founding editor, editorial advisor jour. History of Religions, 1990—; contbr. articles to hist.-religious jours., Ency. Britannica., Ency. Religion. Mem. N.C. Humanities Council; bd. dirs. Fund for Theol. Edn. Served with USAAF, 1944-46. Recipient Alumnus of Yr. award Div. Sch., U. Chgo., 1987, profl. achievement citation U. Chgo. Alumni Assn., 1991; Guggenheim fellow, 1971-72. Mem. Am. Acad. Religion (pres. 1973-74), Internat. Assn. Historians Religion, Am. Soc. Study Religion (founder), Soc. Study Black Religion (founder). Office: U Calif 4607 South Hall Santa Barbara CA 93106

LONG, CONNIE SUE, church youth worker; b. Warrensburg, Mo., Sept. 4, 1954; d. Raymond Barnes and Charlene (Frampton) L. MusB, Cen. Mo. State U., Warrensburg, 1976, MS, 1982. Choir dir. Slater (Mo.) Christian Ch., 1983-87; youth worker, choir dir. United Meth. Ch., Ft. Morgan, Colo., 1987—; guidance counselor Ft. Morgan KE-3 Schs., 1986-91; guidance and placement specialist Morgan Community Coll., Ft. Morgan, Colo., 1991—; counselor Up With Youth, Estes Park, Colo., 1988, 90. Contbr. articles to newspapers. Bd. dirs. United Way, Ft. Morgan, 1990-93. Mem. United Meth. Women, Clarinet Soc., Music Educators N.C., P.E.O. (treas.). Home: 716 E 9th St Fort Morgan CO 80701 Office: Morgan Community Coll 17800 Rd 20 Fort Morgan CO 80701

LONG, GARDA THERESA, lay worker; b. Cleve., Aug. 11, 1925; d. Francis Ralph and Suzanne Margaret (Smithson) Delaney; m. William Harley Long, Sept. 27, 1948; children: Margaret, Deborah, William P., Sharon. Prin. CCD, Andover, Ohio, 1970-89, coord. confirmation, 1968-89, coord. re-new program, 1987-89, tchr. 8th grad., 1990—; sec. Altar Rosary Soc., Andover, 1989—; sec. Mission Soc., Andover, 1987—; spl. min., canton, Andover; chmn. Christian formation Parish Coun.; mem. Diocesan Pastoral Coun., 1987-91, mem. friendly visitors com., 1990, outreach com., 1980, co-chmn., coord. ann. dinner. Presiding judge Election Poll Booth, Andover. Mem. VFW Aux. Democrat. Home: 443 S Main St Andover OH 44003

LONG, JAMES DEWITT, church organist, German language educator; b. Dayton, Ohio, Jan. 27, 1948; s. DeWitt Apple and Mildred Luetta (Forrest) L.; m. Valerie Jean Browne, July 15, 1972; children: Martha Jean, Jamie Ann. BEd, Wright State U., 1970. Cert. secondary sch. tchr., Ohio. Asst. organist Zion Luth. Ch., Dayton, 1964-68; organist 1st Christian Ch. (Disciples of Christ), Kettering, Ohio, 1967-72, organist, dir., 1971-72; organist Englewood (Ohio) United Meth. Ch., 1972—, organist, dir., 1986-89; tchr. German Northmont City Schs., Clayton, Ohio, 1970—. Accompanist Dayton's Boys' Choir, 1969-84; organist Cin. May Festival, 1974. Named Outstanding Young Educator of Yr., Jaycees, Englewood, 1978; Nat. Fed. Students German scholar, 1974. Mem. NEA, Am. Assn. Tchrs. German, Ohio Modern Lang. Tchrs. Assn., Northmont Dist. Edn. Assn., Ohio Edn. Assn., Am. Guild Organists. Republican. Home: 441 Nies Ave Englewood OH 45322-2009 Office: Northmont Sr High Sch 4916 National Rd Clayton OH 45315 also: Englewood United Meth Ch 107 N Walnut St Englewood OH 45322

LONG, JAMES STANLEY, minister; b. Milan, Tenn., May 9, 1952; s. James Jeff and Nancy Jean (Cloyd) L.; m. Martha Jean Overton, Nov. 27, 1974; children: Laura Blair, Lindsay Erin. BA, Bethel Coll., McKenzie, Tenn., 1974; ThM, Liberty Bible Coll., Pensacola, Fla., 1978. Dist. overseer Liberty Fellowship Pastors and Chs., Birmingham, Ala., 1981—; pres. Arab (Ala.) Ministerial Assn., 1982-83. Bd. dirs. Liberty Christian Coll., Pensacola, 1988—, Shin's Martial Arts, Winchester, Tenn.; counselor Critical Incident Stress Debriefing, Columbia, Tenn., 1989—; mem. So. Cen. Tenn. Coun. on Youth, Columbia; vol. fireman Huntland (Tenn.) Fire Dept.; vice chmn. Franklin County Rep. Party, Winchester, 1990—. Recipient cert. of appreciation Cub Scouts, Huntland, 1988. Mem. Franklin County Ministerial Assn. Home: Rte 1 Box 167 Huntland TN 37345 Office: Abundant Life Ch Rte 2 Box 2117 Winchester TN 37398

LONG, JAY EDWARDS, educator, minister; b. Sweet Valley, Pa., June 18, 1938; s. McKinley and Sarah Hazel (Edwards) L.; m. Mary Ruth Shoop, Aug. 15, 1959; children: Brent, Brenda. BS, Bloomsburg U., 1959, MEd, 1964; postgrad., U. Scranton, Bapt. Bible Coll., 1971-72; EdD, Temple U., 1989. Ordained to ministry, 1974. Tchr. pub. schs., Pa., 1959-70; instr. religious studies Bapt. Bible Coll., Clarks Summit, Pa., 1970-73, assoc. prof., 1982—; pastor Mehoopany (Pa.) Bapt. Ch., 1972-82. Author: Personal Bible Study, 1983, The Bible's Answers to Teen's Dilemmas, 1984; contbr. articles to profl. jours. Pres. Mehoopany PTA, 1976, sec. Endless Mt. Pastors Fellowship, 1975-81. Mem. ASCD, Nat. Coun. Tchrs. English, Nat. Bus. Edn. Assn., Assn. Bus. Communication, Eastern Bus. Edn. Assn., Pa. Bus. Edn. Assn., Delta Pi Epsilon. Republican. Home: 17 Hunts Ct Clarks Summit PA 18411 Office: Bapt Bible Coll 538 Venard Rd Clarks Summit PA 18411

LONG, JOHN VERNON, clergyman; b. Texhoma, Okla., May 13, 1946; s. Floyd Alva and Verna Blanche (Gaddy) L.; m. Diana Lee Burton, June 7, 1969; children—Anne Melinda, Nathaniel Lawrence, Jennifer Lee. Student Panhandle State Coll., 1964-65; B.Sacred Lit., Th.B., Ozark Bible Coll., 1971; M. in Ministry, Ky Christian Coll., 1986. Ordained to ministry Christian Ch., 1969. Pastor, Alba (Mo.) Christian Ch., 1970-73, Humboldt (Kans.) Christian Ch., 1973; asst. pastor Shelbina (Mo.) Christian Ch., 1974-76; minister Youth Brownsburg (Ind.) Christian Ch., 1976-78; pastor Brook (Ind.) Christian Ch., 1978-80, First Christian Ch., Villa Grove, Ill., 1980-87, Antioch Christian Ch., Odessa, Tex., 1987— ; bd. advs. Milligan Coll., 1978-80, Christian Campus House, U. Ill., 1981-82. Mem. physician selection com., Newton City, Ind., 1979-80; pres. George Ade Hosp. Chaplain Assn., 1979-80; asst. mgr. Villa Grove Little League, 1980. Named Outstanding Young Religious Leader, Villa Grove Jaycees, 1982; recipient Cert. of Appreciation, S. Newton High Sch., 1979. Mem. Nat. Assn. Nouthetic Counselors, Villa Grove Ministerial Alliance (pres.), Newton City Assn. Chs. (pres.), Villa Grove C. of C., Alumni Assn. Ozark Bible Coll. Club: Rotary (pres., dist. area coordinator youth exchange) (Villa Grove). Home: 4649 Lamont Odessa TX 79762 Office: Antioch Christian Ch 4040 Maple Odessa TX 79762

LONG, JOSH GETZEN, minister, retired educator; b. Newberry, Fla., July 28, 1923; s. Levy Nathan and Della Dicey (Sapp) L.; m. June Joyce Meilstrup, Sept. 1, 1950; children: Sylvia June Long Gray, Merrie Carol Long Shoemaker, Daniel Leroy, Bryan Alan, Cynthia Long Lasher. BA, Stetson U., 1965; ThM, So. Bapt. Coll., Jacksonville, Fla., 1987. Ordained to ministry So. Bapt. Conv., 1947; cert. tchr., Fla. Coord. Stetson Bapt. Nursing Home, DeLand, Fla., 1978-84; tchr. Enterprise Elem. Sch., Valusia County, Fla., 1965-85; pastor Calvary Bapt. Ch., DeLand, 1984—; ret. tchr. pub. schs.; mem. mission devel. com. Seminole Bapt. Assn., Orange City, Fla., 1988—. Democrat. Home: 1141 Glenwood Trails De Land FL 32720 Office: Calvary Bapt Ch 650 E Michigan Ave DeLand FL 32724

LONG, LEM, JR., publishing house director. Gen. mgr. pub. house African Meth. Episcopal Zion Ch., Charlotte, N.C. Office: African Meth Episcopal Zion Ch PO Box 30714 Charlotte NC 28230*

LONG, NORRIS FRANKLIN, JR., minister; b. Atlanta, Oct. 29, 1958; s. Norris Franklin Sr. and Margolese Laura (Jones) L.; m. Mary Kay Hollingsworth, June 8, 1980; children: Laura Jean, Hannah Leigh. BA in History, Berry Coll., Rome, Ga., 1980; MDiv, Emory U., 1984. Ordained elder Meth. Ch., 1986. Tchr. Jackson County Schs., Jefferson, Ga., 1980-81; pastor in charge Bethlehem United Meth. Ch., Bremen, Ga., 1981-84, Cave Spring (Ga.) United Meth. Ch., 1984-87, Vinings United Meth. Ch., Atlanta, 1987-88; minister, program and adminstrn. Decatur (Ga.) 1st United Meth. Ch., 1988—. Avocations: travel, cooking, reading, aviation, photography. Office: Decatur 1st United Meth Ch 300 E Ponce de Leon Decatur GA 30030

LONG, PHILIP LOWELL, SR., minister, investment advisor, securities broker, former air force officer; b. Lincoln, Nebr., July 15, 1921; s. Charles Warren Long and Lorene Dickerson; m. Ethel Lucile Clark, Aug. 8, 1959 (div. Feb. 1980); children: Philip L. Jr., James W.; m. Lucretia Faye Shaw, May 1, 1982. B in Music Edn., Phillips U., 1953. Commd. USAF, 1942, advanced through grades to lt. col., ret., 1964; dir. choir Christian chs. La. and Ariz., 1937-39, 43-44; min. music 1st Christian Ch., Mc Allen, Tex., 1942-43; dir. choir Protestant chapels C.Z., 1948-51; dir. choir Community Ch., Valparaiso, Fla., 1951-56, 1st Christian Ch., Falls Church, Va., 1956-59, Protestant Chapel, Ramstein, Fed. Republic Germany, 1960-63, Park Hill Christian Ch., North Little Rock, Ariz., 1966-77; min. music Camelback Christian Ch., Scottsdale, Ariz., 1988—; sales rep. U.S. Life Equity Sales Corp., Tempe, Ariz., 1990—; exec. dir. Martha Louise Lincoln Charities Trust, Tempe, 1972—, Ministry Through Music Edn., Tempe, 1977—. Home: 3921 S Kenneth Pl Tempe AZ 85282 Office: PMI Advisors Inc PO Box 23836 Tempe AZ 85285

LONG, STEVEN ALAN, minister; b. Dayton, Ohio, July 26, 1959; s. Robert H. and Patricia A. (Bingoff) L.; m. Kathryn L. Emmert, Dec. 19, 1981; children: Justin, Zachary, Kelsey. BA, Fla. Christian Coll., 1983; MA, Trinity Evang. Div. Sch., 1986; postgrad., Marquette U., 1986—. Ordained to ministry Christian Ch., 1984. Min. Cen. Christian Ch., Waukegan, Ill., 1984-88; min. Community Christian Ch., Moline, Ill., 1988—. Recipient Preaching award, 1983, Greek award, 1982 Fla. Christian Coll. Office: Community Christian Ch 4330 12th Ave Moline IL 61265

LONG, THOMAS LAWRENCE, pastor; b. Washington, Jan. 29, 1953; s. Thomas Lawrence and Lucy Ann (McVey) L. BA in English, Cath. U. Am., 1975, MA in Theology, 1981; MA in English, U. Ill., 1977. English instr. U. Ill., Urbana, 1975-77; pastoral assoc. St. Nicholas Ch., Virginia Beach, Va., 1977-78, Our Lady of Nazarene Ch., Roanoke, Va., 1978-81; instr. Montgomery Community Coll., Rockville, Md., 1979; assoc. pastor St. Joseph's Ch., Petersburg, Va., 1981-84; assoc. pastor Christ the King Ch., Norfolk, Va., 1984-86, pastor, 1986—; chmn. Diocesan Communications Commn., Richmond, Va., 1981-85; pub. relations officer Petersburg Downtown Chs. United, 1982-85; diocesan dir. Cath. Communications Campaign, Richmond, 1986—; guest lectr. William and Mary Coll., 1982—, Old Dominian U., 1982—, Norfolk State U. Author: Let the Children Come to Me, 1988; contbr. articles to pubs. Adv. bd. AIDS Housing and Edn. Fund, Norfolk, 1986—. Mem. Eastside Ministerial Assn. (v.p. 1985-86), Amnesty Internat., Phi Kappa Phi. Avocations: swimming, snorkeling, cooking, photography, music. Home: 3341 Tidewater Dr Norfolk VA 23509 Office: Christ the King Ch 1803 Columbia Ave Norfolk VA 23509

LONG, WILLIAM LESLIE, minister, educator; b. Meridian, Miss., Dec. 24, 1958; s. James DeWitt and Mary Grace (Johnson) L.; m. Sheila Jean Clifton, Feb. 24, 1984; 1 child, LaVonda Kay Byrum Ward. MusB, William Carey Coll., Hattiesburg, Miss., 1980; M Ch. Music, So. Bapt. Theol. Sem., Louisville, 1982; MDiv, Bethany Theol. Sem., Oak Brook, Ill., 1989.

Ordained to ministry So. Bapt. Conv., 1981, Ch. of Brethren, 1989. Min. music and edn. lst Bapt. Ch., Rainsville, Ala., 1982-84; staff min. Arlington (Va.) Bapt. Ch., 1984-87; pastor Dundalk C. of Brethren, Balt., 1989—; adj. instr. Dundalk (Md.) Community Coll., 1990—; dist. coord. Mid-Atlantic dist. Ch. of Brethren, Ellicott City, Md., with People of Covenant, Ch. of Brethren, Elgin, Ill., 1990—. Mem. Md. Interfaith Coalition against Domestic Violence. Mem. Md. Religion and Labor Inst. (assoc.). Home: 113 Kentway Dundalk MD 21222-4410 Office: Dundalk Ch of Brethren 2660 Yorkway Baltimore MD 21222-4432

LONNING, INGE JOHAN, theologian, educator, rector; b. Bergen, Norway, Feb. 20, 1938; d. Per and Anna (Strømø) L.; m. Kari Andersen, June 23, 1962; children: Hans Petter, Ingeborg, Karle Jussie, Lars Inge. Student, U. Oslo, Norway, 1962, D of Theology, 1977; D of Div., Luther Coll., 1986. Ordained to ministry Luth. Ch., 1963. Asst. prof. theology U. Oslo, Norway, 1966-70, prof., 1971—, rector, 1985—; chmn. bd. dirs. Pastoral Seminary Ch. Norway, 1977-89, Ecumenical Commn., 1982-90, Norwegian Research Council for Sci. and the Humanities, 1980-84, Norsk Korrespondanseskole, Oslo, 1986—, Universitetsforlaget, 1988—. Editor: Selected Works of Martin Luther, 6 Volumes, 1977-83, jour. Kirke og Kultur, 1968—. Mem. Oslo City Council, 1971-75, Sch. Bd. City Oslo, 1971-79, Nordic Council Research Policy, 1983-88; leader several gov. commns. on health policy, 1984-89; pres. Nat. Coun. Univs., 1989—. Served as lt. with Royal Norwegian Navy, 1964-65. Named to Royal Norwegian St. Olavs Order, 1986; recipient Star of Order of Merit Fed. Republic Germany, 1986. Mem. Det Norske Videnskapsakademi, Det Kongelige Norske Videnskabers Selskab, Scandinavian-German Soc. Philos. Religion. Conservative. Home: Skullerudstubben 22, 1188 Oslo 11, Norway Office: Universitetet I Oslo, POB 1072, Blindern, 0316 Oslo 3, Norway

LØNNING, PER, bishop; b. Bergen, Norway, Feb. 24, 1928; s. Per and Anna (Strømø) L.; m. Ingunn b.Bartz-Johannessen, Aug. 5, 1929; children: Per Eystein, Jan Tore, Ingunn Margrete, Dag Audun. Candidate theology, Free Theol. Faculty, Oslo, 1949; ThD, U. Oslo, Norway, 1955, PhD, 1959; LittD (hon.), St. Olaf Coll., Northfield, Minn., 1986. Asst. pastor Lilleborg Luth. Ch., Oslo, 1951-53; lectr. Oslo Tchr.'s Tng. Coll., 1954-64; dean Bergen Cathedral, Norway, 1964-69; bishop of Borg Fredikstad, Norway, 1969-75, resigned as bishop, 1975; prof. history Christian Thought U. Oslo, Denmark, 1976; research prof. Inst. Ecumenical Research, Strasbourg, France, 1981-87; bishop of Bergen Norway, 1987—; chmn. Norwegian Pastors' Assn., 1962-64; vis. prof. U. Aarhus, Denmark, 1976. Author: The Dilemma of Contemporary Theology, Off the Beaten Path, Pathways of the Passion, Creation: An Ecumenical Challenge?, 30 other books on theology, philosophy, and religious devotion, 1954—. Active Norwegian Parliament, Oslo, 1957-65; mem. Sch. Bd. Oslo, 1960-64; mem. Nat. Broadcasting Council, 1968-77. Recipient Pax Christi award St. John's U., Collegeville, Minn., 1975. Mem. Royal Norwegian Soc. Scis., Norwegian Acad. Scis. and Humanities. Avocations: skiing, swimming, outdoors. Home: Landaaslien 78, N-5030 Bergen Norway

LONT, WALLACE EUGENE, dean, education educator; b. Cato, N.Y., Dec. 21, 1940; s. Wallace M. and Lillian M. (Forbes) L.; m. Nancy Jean Lont, Apr. 4, 1963; children: Rebecca Lynn, Beth Ann. BTh, Bapt. Bible Coll., 1963; MA, Bob Jones U., 1971, PhD, 1975. Pastor Pines Brook Bapt. Ch., Walton, N.Y., 1963-65, Calvary Bapt. Ch., Greenville, Mich., 1966-69; prof. Bob Jones U., Greenville, S.C., 1972-76; pastor Calvary Bapt. Ch., Sault Ste Marie, Mich., 1976-86; acad. dean Spurgeon Bapt. Bible Coll., Mulberry, Fla., 1988—; prin. Sault Christian Acad., Sault Ste. Marie, 1979-85; coord. Fundamental Preaching Fellowship, Sault Ste. Marie, 1982-86; acad. dean Immanuel Bapt. Coll. of Can., Sault Ste. Marie, Ont., Can., 1981-86; chmn. Awana Adv. Bd. of No. Mich., Cadillac, 1979-86. Mem. Faith Bapt. Ch., tchr., 1987—, Awana comdr., 1989—. Home: 104 Stevenson Rd Winter Haven FL 33884 Office: Spurgeon Bapt Bible Coll 4440 Spurgeon Dr Mulberg FL 33860

LOOKSTEIN, HASKEL, rabbi; b. N.Y.C., Mar. 21, 1932; s. Joseph H. and Gertrude S. (Schlang) L.; m. Audrey Katz, June 21, 1959; children: Mindy Cinnamon, Debbie Senders, Shira Baruch, Joshua. BA, Columbia U., 1953; MA, Yeshiva U., 1963, PhD, 1979. Ordained rabbi, 1958. Rabbi Congregation Kehilath Jeshurun, N.Y.C., 1958—; prin. Ramaz Sch., N.Y.C., 1966—; pres. N.Y. Bd. Rabbis, N.Y.C., 1986-88; chmn. rabbinic cabinet United Jewish Appeal, N.Y.C., 1985-87. Author: Were We Our Brothers' Keepers? The Public Response of American Jews to the Holocaust, 1938-44, 1985. Chmn. N.Y. Coalition for Soviet Jewry, N.Y.C., 1989—; v.p. United Jewish Appeal-Fedn., N.Y.C., 1988—. Mem. Rabbinical Coun. Am. (v.p. 1990—). Office: Congregation Kehilath Jeshurun 125 E 85 St New York NY 10028

LOOMAN, GARY JOHN, minister; b. Zeeland, Mich., Feb. 27, 1938; s. Abraham and Jeanette (Lievense) L.; m. Roberta O. Brookmann, June 7, 1963; children: Sue Kristen, Karen Beth, Ann Michelle. BA, Hope Coll., 1960; BDiv, Western Sem., Holland, Mich., 1963; ThM, Princeton Sem., 1965; D Ministry, Ea. Bapt. Sem., Phila., 1985. Ordained to ministry Ref Ch. in Am., 1963. Asst. pastor Ref. Ch. Metuchen, N.J., 1963-66; assoc. pastor Immanuel Presbyn. Ch., Albuquerque, 1966-69; pastor La Mesa Presbyn. Ch., Albuquerque, 1969-78; sr. pastor Apostle United Presbyn. Ch., West Allis, Wis., 1978-91, 1st United Presbyn. Ch., Belleville, Ill., 1991—; trustee Presbytery of Milw., 1989-91. Founder, pres. West Allis Community Communications Corp., 1982-88. Fellow Acad. Parish Clergy; mem. Rotary (chaplain West Alis club 1982-91). Office: 1st United Presbyn Ch 1303 Royal Heights Rd Belleville IL 62223 *When profound religious faith is the foundation of a family, each member moves society toward wholeness.*

LOONEY, RICHARD CARL, bishop; b. Hillsville, Va., Feb. 14, 1934; s. Carl and Ruth (Bourne) L.; m. Carolyn Adele McKeithen, Sept. 3, 1957; children: Teresa, David, Jonathan. BA, Emory and Henry Coll., 1954; postgrad., Edinburg (Scotland U.), 1956; BD, Emory U., 1957; postgrad., Union Theol. Sem., Richmond, Va. Ordained to ministry United Meth. Ch. as deacon, 1955, as elder, 1959. Pastor Rising Faawn (Ga.) Cir., 1957-61, Pleasant View-Wyndale Charge, Abington, Va., 1961-65, Pleasant View, Abington, Va., 1965-67, White Oak United Meth. Ch., Chattanooga, 1968-71, Broad St. United Meth. Ch., Cleveland, Tenn., 1972-75; dist. supt. Chattanooga Dist., 1976-78; pastor Munsey Meml. United Meth. Ch., Johnson City, Tenn., 1979-86, Church St. United Meth. Ch., Knoxville, Tenn., 1987-88; elected bishop Southeastern Jurisdiction, United Meth. Ch., Macon, Ga., 1988—. Office: The United Meth Ctr PO Box 13616 Macon GA 31208-3616

LOOSEN, SISTER ANN MARITA, nun, health care executive; b. Kansas City, Mo., May 1, 1923; d. Irving R. and Mary Louise (Meaney) L. BS in Nursing, St. Mary Coll., Leavenworth, Kans., 1965; MHA, U. Minn., 1967. Joined Sisters of Charity, Roman Cath. Ch. Adminstr. Kennedy Child Study Ctr., Santa Monica, Calif., 1968-75; assoc. adminstr. St. John Hosp. and Health Ctr., Santa Monica, 1971-75; asst. dir. hosps. Sisters of Charity of Leavenworth (Kans.) Health Svcs. Corp., 1975-78; adminstr. St. John Hosp., Leavenworth, 1978-80; pres. St. Francis Hosp. and Med. Ctr., Topeka, 1980-91; pres., chief exec. officer Providence-St. Margaret Hosp. and Health Ctr., Kansas City, Kans., 1991—; bd. dirs. Cath. Health Affairs Kans., St. John's Hosp. and Health Ctr., Santa Monica, Calif., Providence-St. Margaret Health Ctr., Kansas City, Kans., Commerce Bank, Topeka. Bd. dirs. ARC, Santa Monica, in 1970s. Fellow Am. Coll. Health Care Execs.; mem. Kans. Hosp. Assn. (bd. dirs. 1986—), Topeka C. of C. (bd. dirs. 1984-86). Avocations: music, reading, cooking, hiking. Office: Providence-St Margaret Hosp and Health Ctr 8929 Parallel Kansas City KS 66112

LOPEZ, ABEL, minister; b. Guasave, Sinaloa, Mexico, Dec. 3, 1950; came to U.S. 1963; s. Juan and Teodora (Ramirez) L.; m. Aug. 4, 1974; children: Juan Carlos, Abel Jr., David Fernando. ThB, Montemaselog, Mexico, 1973; MDiv, Andrews U., Berrien Springs, Mich., 1979; DMin, Fuller Sem., Pasadena, 1991. Ordained to ministry Seventh Day Adventist Ch. Pastor Seventh-Day Adventist Ch., Huntington Park, Calif., 1974-76; student pastor Seventh-Day Adventist Ch., Berrien Springs, Mich., 1977-79, La Puente, Calif., 1979-80; pastor Seventh-Day Adventist Ch., Oxnard, Calif., 1981-85, Carson, Calif., 1985-89, San Gabriel, Calif., 1989—. Author: Watchtower Society and Spiritism, 1990. Home: 5124 N Acacia St San Gabriel CA 91776 Office: Seventh-Day Adventist Ch 5124 Acacia St San Gabriel CA 91776-2105

LOPEZ, CHARLES JOSEPH, JR., minister, counselor; b. Chgo., Oct. 17, 1948; s. Charles Joseph and Wilma Pauline (Steinhauer) L. AA, Concordia Coll., St. Paul, 1968; BA in Psychology, U. Ill., Chgo., 1971; MDiv, Luth. Sch. Theology, Chgo., 1975, STM, 1978; PhD, Columbia Pacific U., 1986. Ordained to ministry Evang. Luth. Ch. in Am., 1975. Asst. pastor Iglesia de el Redentor, Bogota, Colombia, 1973-74; asst. chaplain St. Louis State Sch., 1974-76; dir. Spanish ministries Luth. Family & Children's Svcs., St. Louis, 1975-76; pastor Holy Trinity Luth. Ch., Rockaway, N.J., 1978-86, Grace Luth. Ch., Coraopolis, Pa., 1986—; pastoral counselor Clergy Cons., Summit, N.J., 1976-86, Luth. Social Svcs., Pitts., 1986-89; mem. dist. faculty Search Bible Studies, Rockaway, 1983-86. Author: Pastoral Care and Counseling Abstracts, 1977, Pittsburgh Book of Daily Prayer, 1990; also revs. in religious jours. Mem. softball team Holy Trinity Luth. Ch., Rockaway, 1978-86, Grace Luth. Ch., Coraopolis, 1986—, volleyball team, 1990—; trustee Eger Home, S.I., N.Y., 1984-86; bd. dirs. Luther Northwestern Sem., St. Paul, 1984—; mem. clergy bd. Robert Morris Coll., Coraopolis, 1991—. Scholar Luth. World Fedn., Colombia, 1973-74, Aid Assn. for Luths., 1973-74. Mem. Am. Assn. Pastoral Counselors, Assn. of Mental Health Clergy, Acad. Parish Clergy, Guild of Clergy Counselors. Avocations: hiking, travel, symphony, theatre, yachting. Office: Grace Luth Ch 1796 Brodhead Rd Coraopolis PA 15108

LOPEZ, RICHARD, priest; b. El Paso, Tex., Aug. 23, 1962; s. Luis and Helen (Guerra) L. BA, Pontifical Coll. Josephinum, 1984; postgrad., U. Notre Dame, 1984-86; MDiv., St. Patrick's Sem., 1988. Ordained priest Roman Cath. Ch., 1989. Deacon St. Stephens, El Paso, 1988-89; priest St. Pius X, El Paso, 1989—; chaplain Cath. Daughters of Am., El Paso, 1989—; dir. Rite of Christian Initiation of Adults, El Paso, 1989—; tchr. Tepeyac Inst. for Formation of Lay Mins., El Paso, 1989—. Chaplain Enrique H. Pena Juvenile Detention Facility, Project Challenge, Crossroads, El Paso, 1989—; coord. Ministry to Persons with AIDS at St. Pius X, El Paso, 1990—. Democrat. Home: 1050 N Clark Dr El Paso TX 79905

LOPEZ AVINA, ANTONIO, archbishop; b. Chalchihuites, Mex., Aug. 20, 1915. Ordained priest Roman Cath. Ch., 1939. Bishop of Zacatecas, Mex., 1955-61; archbishop of Durango, Mex., 1961—. Office: Arzobispado Apartado Postal 116, Durango Mexico

LÓPEZ DE VICTORIA, JUAN DE DIÓS, bishop. Ordained priest Roman Cath. Ch., 1927; titular bishop of Metropolis in Asia; aux. bishop San Juan, P.R., 1963—. Address: PO Box S 1967 San Juan PR 00903

LOPEZ RODRIGUEZ, NICOLAS DE JESUS CARDINAL, archbishop, cardinal; b. Barranca, La Vega, Dominican Republic, Oct. 31, 1936; s. Perfecto Ramón López Salcedo and Delia Ramona (Rodríguez) de López. BST, Santo Tomás de Aquino Seminario Pontificio; Licenciatura en Ciencias Sociales, St. Thomas in Urbe Pontifical U., Rome; PhD (honoris causa), Cath. U. Santo Domingo, 1991, Cath. Pontifical U., 1991. Ordained priest Roman Cath. Ch., 1961. Vicario cooperador de la Catedral Diocese of La Vega, 1961-63, canciller, sec. Curia Diocesana, 1966, párroco de la Catedral, 1969, vicario de pastoral, pro-vicario gen., 1970, vicario gen., 1976; bishop Diocese of San Francisco de Macorís, 1978; met. archbishop of Santo Domingo Dominican Republic, 1981; cardinal Roman Cath. Ch., 1991; rector Univ. Nordestana de San Francisco de Macorís, 1979-84. Decorated Orden del Mérito de Duarte, Sánchez y Mella; de la Gran Cruz de Isabel La Católica (Spain). Office: Archbishopric of Santo Domingo, Isabel La Católica # 55, PO Box 186 Santo Domingo Dominican Republic

LOPEZ TRUJILLO, ALFONSO CARDINAL, archbishop of Medellin; b. Villahermosa, Colombia, Nov. 8, 1935. Ordained priest Roman Catholic Ch., 1960. Instr. maj. sem., Colombia; pastoral coordinator Internat. Eucharistic Congress, Bogota, Colombia, 1968; vicar gen. of Bogota, 1970-72; consecrated bishop of Boseta, 1971; aux. bishop of Bogota, 1971-72; sec.-gen. CELAM, 1972-78, pres., 1979-83; organizer 1979 Puebla Conf.; apptd. coadjutor archbishop of Medellin (Colombia), from 1978; archbishop of Medellin, 1979; elevated to Sacred Coll. of Cardinals, 1983; pres. Bishop's Conf. Mem. Social Communications Commn. Latin Am. Address: Arzobispado, Calle 57, 48-28, Medellin Colombia

LOPPNOW, MILO ALVIN, clergyman, former church official; b. St. Charles, Minn., Jan. 13, 1914; s. William and Doretta (Penz) L.; m. Gertrude Stoltz, Feb. 6, 1942; children—Donald, Bruce, David. B.A., Moravian Coll., 1937; M.Div., Moravian Theol. Sem., 1940, D.D., 1970. Ordained to ministry Moravian Ch. in Am., 1940; pastor congregations nr. Wisconsin Rapids, Wis., 1940-41, Waconia, Minn., 1941-53; pastor congregations nr. Lakeview Ch., Madison, Wis., 1953-64; dist. pres. Western Dist. Moravian Ch., Madison, 1965-78; elected bishop, 1970. Chmn. Youth Commn., Madison, 1957-63; Trustee Moravian Coll., 1954-78, Moravian Theol. Sem., Bethlehem, Pa.; former chaplain, dir. devel. Marquardt Meml. Manor, Watertown, Wis.

LORD, CHARLES ROBERT, retired missionary, minister, theology educator; b. Grinnell, Iowa, Jan. 5, 1920; s. Jesse Cornelius and Elizabeth Lord; m. Josephine Swift, June 2, 1945; children: Beth, Donna, Ronald. BA, Berea Coll., 1942; cert. in profl. teaching, Grinnell Coll., 1954; MA, U. Iowa, 1961; MDiv, Moravian Theol. Sem., Bethlehem, Pa., 1975. Ordained to ministry United Ch. of Christ, 1975. Ednl. missionary United Ch. of Christ, Chikore Mission, Rhodesia, 1954-66; lic. min. Cove Springs United Ch. of Christ, Troy, Ohio, 1968-69; min. Christian edn. New Goshenhoppen United Ch. of Christ, East Greenville, Pa., 1970-75; tchr. Moravian Theol. Coll., Mbeya, Tanzania, 1976-82; pastor Immanuel United Ch. of Christ, Woodman, Wis., 1983-86, Carrier (Okla.) Congl. United Ch. of Christ, 1986-89; ret., 1989. Vol. chaplain Hospice of North Va., Arlington, 1990, Common Cause, Washington, 1990. Mem. Vienna Camera Club. Democrat. Home: 7301 Hughes Ct Falls Church VA 22046

LORD, WARREN JOHN, lay minister; b. Lowell, Mass, Jan. 27, 1948; s. John W. and Doris Rita (Burke) L.; m. Diane Doris St. Louis, Oct. 9, 1969 (div. 1975). BS, N.D. State U., 1969; MHS, Dartmouth Coll., 1972. Cert. physician's asst. Pres. Dioces Phoenix Divorced and Separated Coun., 1988-89; counselor to divorced and separated Franciscan Renewal Ctr., Scottsdale, Ariz., 1981-88, leader singles group, 1987-90; leader divorced and separated St. Andrew's Cath. Ch., Chandler, Ariz., 1989—; psychiat. physician's asst. CODAMA, Phoenix, 1990—; del. Divorced and Separated Coun., Phoenix, 1987-91. Sgt. USAF, 1965-68. Mem. Ariz. State Assn. Physician's Assts., Vietnam Vets. of Am. Democrat. Home: 2220 W Palomino Dr Chandler AZ 85224 Office: CODAMA 1424 S 7th Ave Ste D Phoenix AZ 85007

LORENZ, FELIX ALFRED, JR., minister; b. Topeka, Apr. 5, 1922; s. Felix A. and Amanda Olga (Jensen) L.; m. Fern McGee, Sept. 5, 1943 (div. 1953); m. Lucille Dahltorp, June 26, 1955; children: Barbara, Ellen, Felix III, David, Christian, Rosalie. B of Music Edn., U. Minn., 1948; postgrad., Am. U., 1950-52; MA in Religion, Andrews U., 1952; postgrad., Peabody Coll., 1956-59, Vanderbilt U., 1958-60, Inst. for Advanced Pastoral Studies, 1978-82. Ordained to ministry United Ch. of Christ, 1984; accredited pub. rels. counselor Pub. Rels. Soc. Am. Assoc. pastor Cass Meth. Ch., Detroit, 1963-78, St. John's—St. Luke United Ch. of Christ, Detroit, 1982-88; interim pastor Greerfield Congl. Ch., Dearborn, Mich., 1989; pastor St. Paul's United Ch. of Christ, Dearborn Christian Ch. (Disciples of Christ), Dearborn Heights, Mich., 1990—; chmn. Detroit Met. Assn. Outreach, 1990—; chaplain Office Wayne County Sherrif. Contbr. articles to religious jours. Recipient Alumnus of Achievement award Andrews U., 1977. Mem. Internat. Conf. Police Chaplains, Conf. on Liberal Religion, Fellowship Christian Magicians (pres. Mich. chpt. 1970-75), Lions (v.p. Detroit chpt. 1961-62), Detroit Athletic Club, Detroit Press Club, Mensa, Intertel. Home: 46640 W 7 Mile Rd Northville MI 48167-1777 Office: Dearborn Christian Ch 922 Beech Daly Dearborn Heights MI 48127 *Only by living genuine altruism can one find self-fulfillment. I live a rich, full life because there were those before me who strove to leave the world better than they found it. That is the crux of ethics and morality.*

LORIMER, THOMAS HAROLD, minister; b. Elmhurst, Ill., Dec. 5, 1955; s. Dr. Frank Martin and Linda Leone (Lautzenhiser) L.; m. Rebekah Ann Mathes, Aug. 13, 1976; children: Amy Beth, Stephen Andrew, David Wesley, Daniel Paul. BA summa cum laude, Olivet Nazarene U., Kankakee, Ill., 1977, MA, 1981, M in Ch. Mgmt., 1988. Assoc. pastor First Ch. Nazarene, Ottawa, Ill., 1977-79; pastor Kempton (Ill.) Ch. Nazarene, 1979-83, First CH. Nazarene, Waukesha, Wis., 1983-84, Clarion (Iowa) Ch. Nazarene, 1984-90, First Ch. Nazarene, Fort Madison, Iowa, 1990—; abstractor Religous and Theol. Abstracts, Myerstown, Pa., 1983—; dir. lay training Iowa Dist. Sunday Sch. Ministries Bd., 1989—; sec. treas. Clarion (Iowa) Ministerial Assn., 1988-90; treas. Iowa Dist. Nazarene World Missionary Soc., 1991—. Author: Why Not? Why is Premarital Sex Wrong?, 1989, An Index to Money, 1987. Dir. Wright County Right to Life, Iowa, 1985-90; active mem. North Lee County Right to Life, 1990—. Benner Scholar Olivet Nazarene U., 1978-79. Mem. Am. Mensa, Ltd., Tri-State Homeschool Assn. (newsletter editor 1990—). Home: 511 22nd St Ft Madison IA 52627 Office: Church of the Nazarene 503 22nd St Fort Madison IA 52627 *All around are open doors of opportunites and relationships. Walking through one open door does not mean I must close the others. I chose to leave open all the doors I can. Someday, I may need to walk through the others.*

LORING, RICHARD TUTTLE, priest; b. Boston, Oct. 23, 1929; s. Richard Tittle and Helen (Dexter) L. BA cum laude, Harvard U., 1951; STB, Gen. Theol. Sem., N.Y.C., 1957, DTh, 1968. Ordained priest Episcopal Ch., 1958. Jr. curate All Saints Episcopal Ch., Dorchester, Mass., 1957-59; fellow, tutor Gen. Theol. Sem., 1959-63; assoc. priest St. John's Lattingtown Ch., Locust Valley, N.Y., 1959-63; asst. Grace Episcopal Ch., Elmira, N.Y., 1963-67; rector St. Luke's Episcopal Ch., Chelsea, Mass., 1968—; exec. sec. gen. bd. examining chaplains Episcopal Ch., Boston, 1983-90; mem. Chelsea Ecumenical Coun., 1968—, treas. 1981-82, 88—, chmn., 1973-78, 82-83. Nash fellow, 1977. Mem. Margaret Coffin Prayer Book Soc., Clerical Club (sec.-treas.), Parsons Club. Home and Office: St Luke's Ch 201 Washington Ave Chelsea MA 02150

LORNTZ, JOYCE HANSCOM, chaplain, family and marriage counselor; b. Astoria, Oreg., Aug. 9, 1945; d. Russell Loring and Ouida Eloise (Sprague) Hanscom; m. E. John Lonrtz, Sept. 14, 1969; children: Breyette, Tarina. BS in Edn., Atlantic Union Coll., South Lancaster, Mass., 1968, AS in Nursing, 1969, MPH, 1987, MA, 1990. Nat. cert. counselor. Chaplain Loma Linda (Calif.) U. Med. Ctr., 1990-91; assoc. pastor Fletcher (N.C.) SOA Ch., 1991—; speaker family life workshops in east and west coastal regions; pres. Women in Ministry, SE Calif. Conf. Seventh-day Adventists; co-chmn. Chaplains for Women in Ministry, Adventist Chaplains Ministry. Mem. AACD, Am. Mental Health Counselors Assn. Avocation: gardening. Home: PO Box 324 Loma Linda CA 92354 Office: PO Box 429 Fletcher NC 28732

LORSCHEIDER, ALOISIO CARDINAL, archbishop of Fortaleza; b. Linha Geraldo, Brazil, Oct. 8, 1924. Joined Franciscan Order, Roman Cath. Ch., 1942; ordained priest, 1948; prof. theology The Antonianum, Rome; dir. Franciscan Internat. House of Studies; consecrated bishop of Santo Angelo (Brazil), 1962; archbishop of Fortaleza (Brazil), 1973—; elevated to Sacred Coll. of Cardinals, 1976; pres. Latin Am. Bishops Conf., 1975; gen. sec. Brazilian Bishops Conf., 1968-71, pres., 1971-79. Address: Cardinal's Residence, CP 81, 60 001 Fortaleza Est do Ceará, Brazil

LOSHUERTOS, ROBERT HERMAN, clergyman; b. San Francisco, Apr. 28, 1937; s. Joseph Guillermo and Ruth Margarethe (Erdmann) L.; m. Carolyn Angela Reinartz, Aug. 6, 1960; children: William Frederick, John Martin. AA, San Francisco City Coll., 1957; BA, Wittenburg U., 1959; MDiv, Luth. Theol. So. Sem., Columbia, S.C., 1963. Ordained to ministry Evang. Luth. Ch. in Am., 1963. Asst. pastor Meml. Evang. Luth. Ch., 1963-64, Trinity Luth. Ch., Riverside, Calif., 1964-66; pastor Our Saviours Luth. Ch., Oxnard, Calif., 1966-71; assoc. pastor Luth. Ch. of Good Shepherd, Buena Park, Calif., 1971-73; pastor St. Mark's Luth. Ch., Huntsviile, Ala., 1973-80; exec. min. Interfaith Mission Svc., Huntsviile, 1980—; chmn. personnel/mutual ministry com. Southeastern synod Evang. Luth. Ch. in Am., Atlanta, 1988—. Active Humanitarian Svcs. Com., Huntsville, 1985—, Leadership 2000, Huntsville, 1988-89; chmn. adminstrn. com., bd. dirs. Williams-Henson Luth. Home, Knoxville, Tenn., 1986—; pres. Target Success task force Dept. Human Resources, City of Huntsville, 1988—, chmn. Mayor's Homeless Adv. Com., 1989—. Recipient Brotherhood award NCCJ, 1989, Martin Luther King Jr. Unity award Alpha Phi Alpha, 1990. Mem. Nat. Assn. Ecumenical Staff. Office: Interfaith Mission Svc 411-B Holmes Ave Huntsville AL 35801

LOSTEN, BASIL HARRY, bishop; b. Chesapeake City, Md., May 11, 1930; s. John and Julia (Petryshyn) L. BA, St. Basil's Coll., 1953; STL, Cath. U., Washington, 1957. Ordained priest Ukranian Cath. Ch., 1957. Personal sec. to archbishop, 1962-66; contr. Archdiocese, 1966-75; apptd. monsignor, 1968; apptd. titular bishop of Arcadiopolis and aux. bishop Ukrainian Cath. Archeparchy of Phila., 1971-77; vicar gen., 1971, apostolic adminstr., 1976-77; bishop of Stamford, Conn., 1977—. Pres. Ascension Manor. Club: Union League (Phila.).

LOTOCKY, INNOCENT H., bishop; b. Petlykivci Stari, Buchach, Ukraine, Nov. 3, 1915; came to U.S., 1946; s. Stefan and Maria (Tytyn) L. Student at various religious insts., Ukraine, Czechoslovakia; Ph.D. in Sacred Theology, U. Vienna, Austria. Ordained priest Ukrainian Catholic Ch., consecrated bishop, 1981; cert. tchr., Mich. Superior-novice master Order St. Basil, Dawson, Pa., 1946-51; provincial superior U.S. province Order St. Basil, N.Y., 1951-53; novice master Order St. Basil, Glen Cove, N.Y., 1958-60; pastor-superior St. George Ch., N.Y.C., 1953-58; pastor St. Nicholas Ch., Chgo., 1960-62; pastor-superior Immaculate Conception Ch., Hamtramck, Mich., 1962-81, also tchr., 1962-81; bishop Diocese St. Nicholas, Chgo., 1981—; provincial counselor U.S. province Order St. Basil, 1962-80, del. to gen. chpt. Rome, 1963. Active numerous civic orgns. Mem. Nat. Council Cath. Bishops. Home and Office: Diocese St Nicholas in Chgo 2245 W Rice St Chicago IL 60622

LOTTES, JOHN DOUGLAS, minister; b. Lafayette, Ind., Sept. 18, 1946; s. John Clarence and Mary Louise (Schnaible) L.; m. Victoria Elizabeth Baker, June 6, 1970; children: David, Joel. BS, Ind. U., 1968; MDiv, Concordia Sem., St. Louis, 1973; ThM, Harvard U., 1977. Ordained to ministry Luth. Ch., 1974. Pastor Zion Luth. Ch., Oxford, Mass., 1974-80; asst. pastor Good Shepherd Luth. Ch., Westboro, Mass., 1980-81, Bethel Luth. Ch., St. Louis, 1982-89; dir. ongoing rels. Stephen Ministries, St. Louis, 1982-87; campus pastor Luth. Campus Ministry, St. Louis, 1989—; Evang. Luth. Ch. Am. rep. New Eng. Luth. Fedn., Boston, 1979-81. Mem. Soc. Bibl. Lit., St. Louis Met. Campus Ministries. Office: Luth Campus Ministry 7001 Forsyth Saint Louis MO 63105

LOTTINVILLE, MARY-MARGARET, religious educator; b. Evanston, Ill., Apr. 20, 1949; d. Gerald Joseph and Margaret Rita (O'Brien) L. BA in Art Edn., Mt. St. Joseph Coll., Ohio, 1972; MA in Edn., Xavier U., Cin., 1978. Tchr. St. Williams Elem. Sch., Cin., 1972-76, Our Lady of Rosary Sch., Cin., 1979-80; asst. dir. religious edn. Guardian Angel Parish, Cin., 1981-83, dir. religious edn., 1983—. Mem. Cin. Summer Fair, 1988—. Mem. Nat. Cath. Edn. Assn., Cin. Religious Edn. Assn. Office: Guardian Angel Parish 6539 Beechmont Ave Cincinnati OH 45230

LOTZ, DENTON, minister, church official; b. Flushing, N.Y., Jan. 18, 1939; s. John Milton and Adeline Helen (Kettell) L.; m. Janice Robinson, Mar. 15, 1970; children: John-Paul, Alena, Carsten. BA, U. N.C., 1961; STB, Harvard Div. Sch., 1966; ThD, U. Hamburg, Fed. Republic Germany, 1970; DD (hon.), Campbell U., 1982, Ea. Bapt. Sem., 1991. Ordained to ministry Bapt. Ch., 1966. Prof. mission Bapt. Sem., Ruschlikon, Switzerland, 1972-80; dir. evangelism Bapt. World Alliance, McLean, Va., 1980-88, gen. sec., 1988—; fraternal rep. Am. Bapt. Internat. Ministries To Ea. Europe, Valley Forge, Pa., 1970-80. Author, editor: Baptists in the USSR, 1987; editor: Spring Has Returned to China, 1987. V.p. CARE, N.Y.C., 1981. 1st lt. USMC, 1961-63. Mem. Internat. Religious Liberty Assn. (pres. 1990-91). Office: Bapt World Alliance 6733 Curran St McLean VA 22101

LOUCKY-RAMSEY, JOANNA RUTH, clergyperson; b. Syracuse, N.Y., Oct. 13, 1954; d. Lubomir George and Mildred Mary (Droppa) Loucky; m. William John Ramsey, Aug. 9, 1980. BA in English, Stephens Coll., 1976, BFA in Creative Writing, 1976; MA in Religious Studies, N.Am. Bapt. Sem., 1983; cert. in urban ministry, Sem. Consortium Urban Pastoral Edn., 1982; MDiv., N.Am. Bapt. Sem., 1981. Ordained to ministry Am. Bapt. Ch., 1985. Minister music and youth Emerson Ave. Bapt. Ch., Indpls., 1983-87; chaplain Marion County Children's Guardian Home, Indpls., 1983-86; assoc. pastor First Bapt. Ch., Portland, Oreg., 1987—. Mem. Dept. World Mission Support, gen. mgr. Am. Bapt. Chs. Oreg. Mem. Fellowship Am. Bapt. Musicians, Am. Guild English Handbell Ringers, Am. Choral Dirs. Assn., Am. Bapt. Ch.'s (ministers coun.), Assn. Downtown Chs. (social action com.). Office: First Bapt Ch 909 SW 11th Ave Portland OR 97205

LOUDERMILK, GARY WAYNE, minister; b. Temple, Tex., Apr. 27, 1947; s. Curtis Wayne and Juanele (Coffey) L.; m. Mary Malinics, Aug. 30, 1968; children: Kevin, Jennifer. BA, Baylor U., 1969; MDiv, Southwestern Bapt. Theol. Sem., 1972, DMin, 1983. Ordained to ministry Bapt. Ch., 1970. Pastor Mildred Bapt. Ch., Corsicana, Tex., 1970-73, Hillcrest Bapt. Ch., San Angelo, Tex., 1973-78, Harvey Bapt. Ch., Stephenville, Tex., 1979-80, First Bapt. Ch., Flower Mound, Tex., 1980—; vice moderator Denton (Tex.) Bapt. Assn., 1990—, prayer coord., 1989—. Author: On Going Prospect Discovery and Personal Evangelism, 1983; contbr. articles to profl. pubs. Trustee Lewisville (Tex.) Ind. Sch. Dist., 1985-91. Office: First Bapt Ch 1901 Timbercreek Rd Flower Mound TX 75028

LOUGHRAN, JAMES NEWMAN, philosophy educator, former university president; b. Bklyn., Mar. 22, 1940; s. John Farley and Ethel Margaret (Newman) L. A.B., Fordham U., 1964, M.A., 1965, Ph.D. in Philosophy, 1975; Ph.D. (hon.), Loyola Coll., Balt., 1985. Joined S.J., 1958; ordained priest Roman Catholic Ch., 1970. Instr. philosophy St. Peter's Coll., Jersey City, 1965-67; asst. dean Fordham U., Bronx, N.Y., 1970-73; tchr. philosophy Fordham U., Bronx, 1974-79, 82-84, dean, 1979-82; pres. Loyola Marymount U., L.A., 1984-91. Contbr. numerous articles and revs. to popular and scholarly jours. Trustee St. Peter's Coll., Jersey City, 1972-78, Xavier U., Cin., 1981-84. Mem. Am. Philos. Assn. Avocation: tennis.

LOUK, SISTER ROSE AGNES, motivational seminars lecturer; b. LaCrosse, Wis., Aug. 17, 1920; d. William Joseph and Mary Agnes (McNamara) L. B.S., Coll. St. Scholastica, 1954; M.S., SUNY, Buffalo, 1973. Joined Franciscan Sisters of Perpetual Adoration, Roman Cath. Ch., 1949; registered record adminstr. Med. record adminstr. St. Anthony Hosp., Carroll, Iowa, 1954-56, 58-62, St. Francis Hosp., LaCrosse, 1962-63, Sacred Heart Hosp., Idaho Falls, Idaho, 1963-69; instr. Viterbo Coll., La Crosse, 1962-63; med. record educator Intermountain RMP, Salt Lake City, 1969-72; assoc. prof. Carroll Coll., Helena, 1973-88. Contbr. articles to profl. jours. Mem. Am. Med. Record Assn. (bd. dirs. 1965-68, exec. bd.). Home: 205 S Grant # 205 Denver CO 80209 *The fullness we achieve as human beings is enhanced by the value and dignity of the human work we perform. In his encyclical letter on human labor, Pope John Paul II stated, "Work serves to add to the heritage of the whole human family, of all people living in the world." It is important to bring joy to our workplace.*

LOURANCE, ROBERT L., clergyman; b. Mountain View, Mo., July 10, 1949; s. William Vernon and Dorothy Mae (Christy) L.; m. Darlene J. Smith, Apr. 11, 1972; children: Eric G. Young, Angelia Annette, Robert Dwight. Tchr. cert., Berean Sch., 1983; grad. theology, Trinity Theol. Sch., 1991. Ordained to ministry Assemblies of God Ch., 1977. Pastor First Assembly of God Ch., Imboden, Ark., 1974-75, Bernie, Mo., 1975-77, Augusta, Kans., 1979-86, Duncan, Okla., 1986—; police chaplain Augusta (Kans.) Police Dept., 1982-86; sec. Ministerial Alliance, Augusta, 1982-86; pres. Pentecostal Alliance, Duncan, 1987-89; hosp. chaplain Duncan Regional Hosp., 1987—. With USN, 1968-72. Home: 805 N 5th St Duncan OK 73533 Office: First Assembly of God Ch 801 N 5th St Duncan OK 73533

LOURDUSAMY, SIMON CARDINAL, former archbishop; b. Kalleri, Pondicherry, India, Feb. 5, 1924. ordained Roman Cath. Ch., 1951. Consecrated bishop Titular Ch. Sozusa, Libya, 1962; titular archbishop Philippi, 1964; archbishop Bangalore, 1968-71; proclaimed cardinal, 1985; sec. Congregation for the Evangelization of Peoples, 1973-85; pres. Pontifical Missionary Work. Home: Palazzo dei Convertendi, 64 Via dei Corridori, 00193 Rome Italy Office: Congregation for Ea Chs, Plazzo dei Convertendi, Via della Conciliazione 34, 00193 Rome Italy

LOUTH, ANDREW, clergyman, theologian; b. Louth, Lincolnshire, Eng., Nov. 11, 1944; s. Cecil George and Mary (Coptcoat) L.; m. Janet Worlock Sisson, July 30, 1966; children—Charles, Mary, Sarah. B.A., U. Cambridge, Eng., 1965; M.Th., Edinburgh U., Scotland, 1968; M.A., U. Oxford, Eng., 1970. Ordained priest Anglican Ch., 1969. Curate, St. Stephen's Ch., Bristol, Eng., 1968-70; fellow Worcester Coll., U. Oxford, 1970-85, lectr. in theology U. Oxford, 1971-85; head dept. religion Goldsmiths' Coll., London, 1985—. Author: Origins of the Christian Mystical Tradition, 1981; Discerning the Mystery, 1983; also articles. Office: Goldsmiths College, London SE14 6NW, England

LOUTH, REXFORD L., minister; b. Ft. Rucker, Ala., Apr. 3, 1962; s. Donald L. and Sharon (Hammons) L.; m. Janet S. Crouse, Sept. 29, 1979; children: Crystalyn S., Stephanie K. Cert., Bible Inst. Ch. of God, Cleveland, Tenn., 1984. Ordained to ministry, Ch. of God. Dist. youth dir. Ch. of God, Huntington, Ind., 1980-91, youth pastor, 1981; pastor Ch. of God, Bluffton, Ind., 1981-89, Colorado Springs, Colo., 1989—; reg. youth bd. mem. Ch. of God, 1990—. Named Dist. Dir. of the Yr., Ch. of God, State of Ind., 1980-81. Office: Ch of God 401 W Bijou St Colorado Springs CO 80909

LOUX, GORDON DALE, organization executive; b. Souderton, Pa., June 21, 1938; s. Curtis L. and Ruth (Derstine) L.; m. Elizabeth Ann Nordland, June 18, 1960; children: Mark, Alan, Jonathan. Diploma, Moody Bible Inst., Chgo., 1960; BA, Gordon Coll., Wenham, Mass., 1962; BD, No. Bapt. Sem., Oak Brook, Ill., 1965, MDiv, 1971; MS, Nat. Coll. Edn., Evanston,Ill., 1984; LHD (hon.), Sioux Falls Coll., 1985. Ordained to ministry, Bapt. Ch., 1965. Assoc. pastor Forest Park (Ill.) Bapt. Ch., 1962-65; alumni field dir. Moody Bible Inst., Chgo., 1965-66, dir. pub. rels., 1972-76; dir. devel. Phila. Coll. Bible, 1966-69; pres. Stewardship Svcs., Wheaton, Ill., 1969-72; exec. v.p. Prison Fellowship Ministries, Washington, 1976-84, pres., chief exec. officer, 1984-88; pres., chief exec. officer Prison Fellowship Internat., Washington, 1979-87, Internat. Students, Inc., Colorado Springs, Colo., 1988—. Author: Uncommon Courage, 1987, You Can Be a Point of Light, 1991; contbg. author: Money for Ministries, 1989, Dictionary of Christianity in America, 1989. Bd. dirs. Evang. Coun. for Fin. Accountability, Washington, 1979—, vice chmn., 1981-84, 86-87, chmn., 1987-89; vice chmn. Billy Graham Greater Washington Crusade, 1985-86. Named Alumnus of Yr., Gordon Coll., 1986. Republican. Home: 740 Bear Paw Ln Colorado Springs CO 80906 Office: Internat Students Inc Box C Colorado Springs CO 80901

LOUX, JOSEPH ANTHONY, JR., clergyman; b. Albany, N.Y., Oct. 2, 1945; s. Joseph Anthony and Claire (Finkle) L.; m. Marjorie Anne Bronk, May 5, 1973; 1 child, Joseph Anthony III. AA cum laude, Jr. Coll. of Albany, 1965; BA in History and English, SUNY-Albany, 1967; MDiv cum laude in Counseling, New Brunswick Theol. Sem., 1970; Doctorandus in de Godgeleerdheid in Ch. History, U. Leyden, Netherlands, 1972; PhD, Roosevelt U., Brussels, Leyden (The Netherlands) U., 1985. Pastor, tchr. Helderberg Ref. Ch., Guilderland Ctr., N.Y., 1973-86, 2d Ref. Ch., Coxsackie, N.Y., 1986—; internat. lectr. and Bible tchr., conf. leader; pres. Loux Music Pub. Co., 1984—, Dovehouse Editions, Ottawa, Ont., Can., 1988—; organized Guilderland Interfaith Coun., 1973; retreat dir. Capital Dist. Ch. Women United, 1973; dir. Capital Area Coun. Chs., 1975-76, Catskill Mountain Housing Devel. Corp., 1988—; organizer, chmn. 350th Ann. Com. Synod of Albany, Ref. Ch. in Am., 1977-78, sec. Commn. on History, 1979-82, pres. Reverend Classis of Schenectady, 1982-83. Author: The Boels of Hilversum, 1970; Moderation vs. Dogma, 1972, Boels Complaint against Frelinghuisen, 1980; also contbr. articles in profl. jours. Organizer, chmn. Town of Guilderland Bicentennial com., 1975-76; founder, organizer Capital Dist. chpt. Am. Recorder Soc., 1976; founder mem. adj. faculty Schenectady County Community Coll., 1982-83, SUNY, Albany, 1973. Pilgrim fellow Hervormde Kerk, Dordrecht, Netherlands, 1971-73. Mem. Ref. Ch. Am. Hist. Soc. (organizer, founder Rensselaerswyck chpt. No. 1). Home: 2 Hawley Ln Hannacroix NY 12087-0034 Office: 2d Reformed Ch 16 Washington Ave Coxsackie NY 12087

LOVE, BRUCE BLACKBURN, religious organization administrator; b. Gobles, Mich., Apr. 5, 1929; s. William W. and Myrtle May (Ramey) L.; m. Verla Nan Lindstrom, Aug. 1, 1953; children: Robert Bruce, Janice Love Speakman. AA, Moody Bible Inst., Chgo., 1952; postgrad., Ind. U., 1957-59, Kennedy Sinclaire, 1975, Calif. Coast U., Santa Anna, 1987. Ordained to ministry Evangelical Free Ch. Exec. dir. Lake County Youth For Christ, Gary, Ind., 1953-59; v.p. Youth For Christ Internat., Wheaton, Ill., 1959-70; exec. dir. Metro Chgo. Youth For Christ, Wheaton, 1970-84; assoc. pastor Wheaton Free Ch., Wheaton, 1984—; pres. Moody Alumni Assn., Chgo., 1978-80; trustee Slavic Gospel Assn., Wheaton, 1979-87; cons. Ch. Growth Services, South Bend, Ind., 1986-87. Author: International Camping, 1959, Escape From Truth, 1969; classroom curricula Management and Fund Raising, 1979-85; contbr. articles to mags. Mem. exec. bd. YMCA, Glen Ellyn, 1970; mem. Govs. Youth Council, Gary, 1969-72, Presdl. Task Force, Wheaton, 1980-87, Rep. Party Official Task Force, 1983-87. Recipient TV Special of Yr. award Johnny Cash, 1979, citation for Youth Work Pres. Reagan, 1985, citation Govs. Hatfield, Walsh, Thompson, Brown and Clemant, 1970-75; Nat. Camp Dir. of Yr., Ind., 1970;. Mem. Free Ch. Am. Republican. Avocations: gardening, sports, antiques. Home: 22 W 155 Buena Vista Glen Ellyn IL 60137 Office: Wheaton Free Ch 520 E Roosevelt Rd Wheaton IL 60187

LOVE, HARRY WILLARD, minister; b. Athens, Ohio, Feb. 1, 1949; s. harry Franklin and Mertie Kathleen (Simonton) L.; m. Phyllis Elnora Summers, June 6, 1970; children: Elnora Kathleen, Harry Samuel. BA, Ky. Christian Coll., 1971; MA, Ohio U., 1973. Ordained to ministry in Ch. of Christ, 1971. Acad. dean Ohio Bible Inst., Beverly, 1973-75; sr. minister East Athens Ch. of Christ, Athens, Ohio, 1975—; adv. bd. mem. Reach Out on Campus Ministry, Athens, 1976—; program dir. Ohio Valley Christian Assembly, Pomeroy, 1980-89. Sch. bd. mem. Alexander Local Schs., Albany, Ohio, 1985—; bd. dirs., chmn. Athens County United Way, 1980-84; bd. dirs. Am. Cancer Soc., Athens, 1983-89; bd. dirs., chmn. Vis. Nurses Assn. Athens County, Athens, 1984-86. Mem. Athens County Ministerial Assn. (chmn. 1983, 89), Ky. Christian Alumni Assn., Spartan Boosters (v.p. 1990—). Home: 5232 Baker Rd New Marshfield OH 45766 Office: East Athens Ch of Christ 1 Townsend Pl Athens OH 45701

LOVE, JANICE, lay worker, educator; b. Montgomery, Ala., Oct. 11, 1952; d. James Neal and Bennie Jean (Burnham) L.; m. Peter Carl Sederberg, Dec. 28, 1984; 1 child, Rachel Elin. BA, Eckerd Coll., St. Petersburg, Fla., 1975; MA, Ohio State U., 1977, PhD, 1983. Pres. Ala.-West Fla. conf. coun. on youth ministry Meth. Ch., 1969-71, mem. S.C. Conf. Bd. Missions and Commn. on Christian Unity, 1988—, mem. bd. mgrs. bd. of missions, 1970-72; mem. gen. bd. of global ministries United Meth. Ch., 1972-76, del. to World Coun. of Chs. 5th, 6th and 7th assemblies, 1975, 83, 91; mem. cen. com. World Coun. of Chs., 1975—, mem. exec. com. and moderator of justice and svc. unit II, moderator, 1983-91; asst. prof. dept. govt. and internat. studies U. S.C., Columbia, 1982-91, assoc. prof., 1991—. Author: U.S. Anti-Apartheid Movement, 1985; contbr. articles to polit. sci. jours. and religious publs. Mem. Internat. Studies Assn., African Studies Assn., Nat. Women's Studies Assn. Office: U SC Govt and Internat Studies Columbia SC 29208

LOVE, JIMMY CARSON, minister; b. Dayton, Ohio, June 26, 1962; s. John F. and Mary M. (Wilson) L.; m. Anna Jo Davis, May 11, 1985. BA in Bible and Missions, Harding U., Searcy, Ark., 1984; postgrad., Harding Grad. Sch., Memphis, 1985—; MS in Community Agy. counseling, Henderson U., 1991. Ordained to ministry Ch. of Christ, 1985. Minister Ch. of Christ, Shirley, Ark., 1985-86, Clinton, Ark., 1986-90; youth minister Ch. of Christ, Hot Springs, Ark., 1990—. Mem. Am. Assn. Christian Counselors. Office: 700 Richard St Hot Springs AR 71913

LOVELACE, DAVID WAYNE, priest; b. Richmond, Va., Oct. 21, 1948; s. Ray Lancaster and Charlotte Page (Seal) L.; m. Bonnie Lynn McCreary, Feb. 13, 1971 (div. 1983); children: Meredith, Adrian; m. Elaine Alvina Henley, July 8, 1989; 1 child, Caroline. AA, Ferrum Coll., 1968; BA, Emory and Henry Coll., 1970; MDiv, Va. Theol. Sem., 1976; ThM, Columbia Theol. Sem., 1990. Ordained as priest Episcopal Ch. Priest-in-charge St. James Episcopal Ch., Belhaven, N.C., 1976-79; asst. to rector Good Shepherd Episcopal Ch., Rocky Mount, N.C., 1979-82; rector St. Paul's Episcopal Ch., Newnan, Ga., 1982—; dean S.W. Atlanta Convocation, Newnan, 1989—; organizer Good Shepherd Soup Kitchen and Shelter, Rocky Mount, 1979-82; mem. exec. bd. Diocese of Atlanta, 1989-90.—. Chmn. ARC, Newnan, 1990—; bd. dirs. Community Action for Improvement, Newnan, 1986—; chmn. Coweta Community Food Pantry, Newnan, 1985—; counselor Mainstay Counseling and Psychol. Svc., Newnan, 1988—. Recipient Cert. of Merit, City of Rocky Mount, 1981, Coweta Community Pantry, 1989. Mem. Newnan Ministerial Assn. (pres. 1984-86), Clergy Ordn. of Diocese of Atlanta. Home: 10 Woodland Trail Newnan GA 30263 Office: St Paul's Episc Ch 576 Roscoe Rd Newnan GA 30264 *The challenge of the church and its clergy is to be on the cutting edge of society. We need not be ahead of the times, rather prepared to assist in transformation and growth.*

LOVELACE, SUSAN MARIE FITE, lay worker; b. Shelby, N.C., Dec. 16, 1952; d. Henry Julian and Doris Jean (Melton) Fite; m. Jerry Eugene Lovelace, Aug. 25, 1973; 1 child, Jonathan David. Grad. high sch., Kings Mountain, N.C., 1971. Cert. audiometric technician, S.C. Co-dir. youth, tchr. David Bapt. Ch., Kings Mountain, 1973-77, single adult leader, tchr., 1978-83, 88-90; chairperson single adult coun. Kings Mountain Bapt. Assn., Shelby, N.C., 1989-91. Chmn. staff appreciation com. PTO, Kings Mountain, 1988-91. Recipient 3d pl. painting awards N.C. State, 1985-86. Democrat. Home: 2334 David Baptist Church Rd Kings Mountain NC 28086 *As Satan steals away our time, he eliminates time for the priorities in our lives—family, friends, Bible study, and prayer. It is only when we discipline ourselves and face this bully on the battlefield of prayer that the problems Satan causes return to their normal size and become less urgent—and to "sit at Jesus' feet" becomes the priority it was meant to be.*

LOVELESS, ALTON E., church administrator; b. Greenbrier, Ark., Aug. 10, 1937; s. William Daniel and Mildred Lucille (Blair) L.; m. Ellen Delois Draby, Aug. 18, 1958; children: Randall Scott, Steven Lynn. BA in Theology, Hillsdale Coll., Moore, Okla., 1980; BA in Religious Edn., Covington Theol. Sem., Rossville, Ga., 1980, MA in Religious Edn., 1981; PhD in Bus. Adminstrn., Columbia Pacific U., San Rafael, Calif., 1985; DD (hon.), Bethany Theol. Sem., Dothan, Ala., 1988. Pastor Free Will Bapt. Chs., Ark., 1955-66, First Free Will Bapt. Ch., Joplin, Mo., 1966-70; cons. Christian edn. Scripture Press Pubs., Wheaton, Ill., 1970-74; exec. sec. Ohio State Assn. Free Will Bapts., Columbus, 1974—; chmn. curriculum com. Nat. Sunday Sch. Bd., Nashville, 1974-84; pres. Free Will Bapt. Book Dealers, Nashville, 1974—; cons. fgn. mission dept. Nat. Free Will Bapt. Ch., 1982—, mem. fgn. mission bd., 1989—. Editor: The Ambassador mag., 1974—, The Gem, 1969-70; contbr. short stories to pubs. Chmn. Nat. Hist. Commn., Nashville, 1974-85. Avocation: photography. Home: 4970 Botsford Dr Columbus OH 43232 Office: Free Will Bapt State Office 2777 S High St PO Box 17401 Columbus OH 43207

LOVERING, EUGENE HARRISON, JR., religion educator; b. Englewood, N.J., June 11, 1952; s. Eugene Harrison and Annelle (Rodecape) L. BA, So. Meth. U., Dallas, 1973, MTh, 1977, PhD, 1988. Ordained to ministry as deacon Meth. Ch., 1974, as elder, 1978. Asst. pastor Tyler St. United Meth. Ch., Dallas, 1975-76; assoc. pastor First United Meth. Ch., Lake Jackson, Tex., 1977-79; asst. to dir. Ctr. for Study of Religion in the Greco-Roman World, Dallas, 1984-87; vis. instr. So. Meth. U., Dallas, 1987-88; asst. exec. dir. Soc. Bibl. Lit., Atlanta, 1990—; mem. steering com. Grad. Program in Religious Studies, So. Meth. U., Dallas, 1981-83. Author: The Collection, Reduction and Early Circulation of the Corpus Paulinum, 1988; translator various German essays. Mem. Soc. Bibl. Lit., Am. Soc. Ch. History. Home: 5088 Patriot Dr Stone Mountain GA 30087-1416 Office: Soc Bibl Lit 1549 Clairmont Rd Ste 204 Decatur GA 30033-4635

LOVETTE, LAWRENCE ROGER, minister; b. Columbus, Ga., Oct. 15, 1935; s. John W. and Ruth (Kelley) L.; m. Gayle Mills, Jan. 28, 1961; children: Leslie Susan Lovette Jennette, Jon Matthew. AB, Samford U., 1957; BD, So. Bapt. Theol. Sem., Louisville, 1961; M Ministry, Lexington Theol. Sem., 1974. Ordained to ministry So. Bapt. Conv., 1961. Min. Dawson Bapt. Ch., Philpot, Ky., 1961-64, Blairs (Va.) Bapt. Ch., 1964-69, Faith Bapt. Ch., Georgetown, Ky., 1969-75; sr. min. lst Bapt. Ch., Clemson, S.C., 1975-88, 2d Bapt. Ch., Memphis, 1988—. Author: For the Dispossessed, 1973, A Faith of Our Own, 1976, Journey toward Joy, 1977, Questions Jesus Raised, 1986, Come to Worship, 1990. Home: 1460 Eastridge Dr Memphis TN 38120 Office: 2d Bapt Ch 4680 Walnut Grove Rd Memphis TN 38120

LOVIN, ROBIN WARREN, minister, university dean, educator; b. Peoria, Ill., Mar. 22, 1946; s. Harvey Gifford and Irene (Warren) L. BA, Northwestern U., 1968; BDiv, Harvard U., 1971, PhD, 1978. Pastor United Meth. Ch., Freeport, Ill., 1971-72, Fenton, Ill., 1972-74; assoc. prof. U. Chgo., 1978-91; dean Theol. Sch. Drew U., 1991—; bd. visitors Duke Divinity Sch., Durham, N.C., 1984-90. Author: Christian Faith & Public Choices, 1984; editor: Religion and American Public Life, 1986, (with others) Cosmogony and Ethical Order, 1985; editor: Jour. of Religion, 1985-91; mem. editorial bd. Jour. of Religious Ethics, 1982—, Jour. of Law & Religion, 1983—. Guggenheim Found. fellow, 1987-88. Mem. Am. Acad. Religion (sect. chair 1987-90), Soc. Christian Ethics (bd. dirs. 1986-90). Democrat. Home: 12 Loantaka Way Madison NJ 07940 Office: Drew U Theological Sch Madison NJ 07940

LOVORN, THOMAS EUGENE, minister, educator; b. Grenada, Miss., Mar. 24, 1938; s. Cell Roane and Myrtle Iris (Parker) L.; m. Janie Johnson, Dec. 24, 1967; 1 child, Nancy Christine. BA, Miss. Coll., 1960; BDiv, MDiv, New Orleans Bapt. Theol. Sem., 1964; ThD, Luther Rice Sem., 1973. Cert. in pastoral care; cert. Billy Graham Sch. Evangelism, 1974; lic. to ministry So. Bapt. Conv., 1955; ordained 1957. Pastor Bethany Bapt. Ch., Slate Spring, Miss., 1956-57, Ellard Bapt. Ch., Bruce, Miss., 1957-61; assoc. pastor 1st Bapt. ch., Poplarville, Miss., 1961-64, Suffolk, Va., 1964-68; sr. pastor 1st Bapt. ch., Cheraw, S.C., 1968-79; radio evangelist, Bible tchr., author Chesterfield Community Coll., Cheraw, 1969-84; sr. pastor East Ridge Bapt. Ch., Chattanoogo, 1979-84; Bible tchr. Chattanooga Bible Inst., 1983-85; sr. pastor Monumental Bapt. Ch., Petersburg, Va., 1985—; writer, preacher Morning Worship Hour WAVY-TV, Portsmouth, Va., 1965-67; tchr. So. Bapt. Conv. Sem. Extension, 1969—; host Luther Rice Video Bible Class, Jacksonville, Fla., 1975; S.C. Gov.'s Goodwill Amb. to Jamaica, W.I., 1970, Tenn. Gov.'s Goodwill Amb. to Jamaica, 1981. Co-author: (with Janie Lovorn) Building a Caring Church, 1986, How to Grow A Caring Church, 1991, We Care, 1991, Growing a House of Prayer, 1992, How to Have a Praying Church, 1992. Bd. dirs. Caribbean Christian Ctr. for the Deaf, Knockpatrick, Jamaica, 1970—; mem. Pastoral Adv. Bd. Bapt. Coll. Charleston, S.C., 1975-79. Recipient Hamilton County, Tenn. Good Citizenship award, commendation from Mayor of Chattanooga and Pres. Reagan. Office: Monumental Bapt Ch PO Box 1551 2925 S Crater Rd Petersburg VA 23805

LOWDEN, JANICE MARIE ELY, minister; b. Waynesboro, Va., Oct. 11, 1956; d. Wesley Richard and MaryE (Marks) Ely; m. Robert William Lowden, Apr. 16, 1983. BS in Spl. Edn., James Madison U., 1978; MDiv, Luth. Theol. Sem., Gettysburg, Pa., 1986. Ordained to ministry Evang. Luth Ch. in Am., 1988. Pastor Luth. Ch. of Living World, Columbia, Md., 1988—; sec., bd. dirs., Luth. Social Svcs. Md., Balt., 1989-91; mem., del., Columbia Coop. Ministry, Columbia, 1988—; mem. Howard County Clergy Social Justice, Columbia, 1988—; dean Balt.-West Conf., Del.-Md. Synod Evang. Luth. Ch. in Am., 1991—. Vol. Community Integration Assn. Retarded Citizens, Columbia, 1990—; dir. Am.-Soviet Peace Walk, Columbia, 1988. Mem. Inst. Christian Jewish Studies. Democrat. Office: Luth Ch of Living World 5885 Robert Oliver Pl Columbia MD 21045

LOWDERMILK, ROBERT ELBERT, III, minister, religious educator; b. Greensboro, N.C., July 9, 1951; s. Robert Elbert Jr. and Virginia (Overby) L.; m. Ellen Currie Sapp, July 14, 1973. A.B., Guilford Coll., 1973; M.Div., Duke U., 1976; D. Ministry, Southeastern Bapt. Theol. Sem., 1981. Ordained to ministry United Methodist Ch. College chaplain High Point Coll., N.C., 1976-79, dean of students, 1979-82; campus minister, dean of student devel. Catawba Coll., Salisbury, N.C., 1983-84, campus minister, asst. prof. religion, 1984—; dir. freshman orientation and advising, 1984—; chmn. div. campus ministry Bd. of Higher Edn. and Campus Ministry, Western N.C. Conf. United Meth. Ch., 1984—. Contbr. materials to The Upper Room, Ch. Sch. Today. Recipient L. E. Moody award High Point Coll., 1978, Algernon Sydney Sullivan award Catawba Coll., 1985. Mem. Am. Coll. Personnel Assn., Inst. Soc., Ethics, and Life Scis., Assn. for Counseling and Devel., U.S. Field Hockey Assn. (SE sect. umpiring chmn. 1983-86, nat. umpire's rating 1987). Avocations: field hockey officiating; piano; organ; calligraphy. Home: 707 Wiltshire Village Salisbury NC 28144 Office: Catawba Coll Campus Minister's Office 2300 W Innes St Salisbury NC 28144

LOWE, ALAN DENNIS, minister; b. Atlanta, May 24, 1953; s. Linzsey and Naomi Jane (White) L.; m. Melonye Dawn Bartlett, June 9, 1979; 1 child, Jonathan Daniel. Student Ga. Inst. Tech., 1971-72; B.S. in Bible Education, Columbia Bible Coll., 1975; postgrad. Southwestern Bapt. Theol. Sem., 1976-77; BS in Architecture, Ga. Inst. Tech., 1980; MDiv, New Orleans Bapt. Theol. Sem., 1987. Ordained minister, Dunwoody (Ga.) Bapt. Ch., 1986. Interim ministerial asst. College Park Second Bapt. Ch., Ga., 1976; constrn. supt. Woodland Homes, Inc., Jonesboro, Ga., 1977; archtl. draftsman Tipton Masterson Assocs., Atlanta, 1978-80; archtl. apprentice John J. Harte Assocs., Inc., Atlanta, 1981; design/devel. cons. Continental Fin. Corp., Marietta, Ga., 1981-83; cons., mgr. computer drafting, archtl. apprentice Zachary W. Henderson, AIA, Inc., Roswell, Ga., 1983-85; archtl./design cons. Clinton M. Day Cos., Inc., Norcross, Ga., 1984-85, C.P. Day Devel. Co., Norcross, 1985; photographer Zachary W. Henderson, AIA, Inc., Roswell, Ga., 1983-85; minister of youth, assoc. pastor Norwood (La.) Bapt. Ch., 1986-87. Deacon Dunwoody Bapt. Ch., 1984-85; singer Messengers Quartet, 1981-83; vice-chmn. deacons, dir. Single Adults, College Park Second Bapt. Ch., 1970-83; chmn. zoning com., v.p. Terramont Homeowners Assn., Inc., Roswell, Ga., 1984-85. Recipient Design and Detailing Excellence award Zachary W. Henderson, AIA, Inc., Atlanta, 1983. Republican. Avocations: music; antique car restoration; reading; photography.

LOWE, BILLY TROY, minister; b. Anderson, S.C., Dec. 2, 1949; s. Cecil Troy and Doris (Rogers) L.; m. Brenda Alice Madden, Jan. 1, 1982; children: Joe Sanford Rosser Jr., Laura Kate Rosser. BA, Newberry Coll., 1977; MDiv, Columbia Sem., 1980; DMin, McCormick Sem., 1991. Ordained to ministry Presbyn. Ch., 1980. Pastor Calvary Presbyn. Ch., Elberton, Ga., 1980—; dir. Constructores Para Cristo, Piedras Negras, Mex., 1989; counselor Desert Storm Support Group, Elberton, 1991; commr. Presbyn. Gen. Assembly, Salt Lake City, 1990; rep. Ga. Christian Coun., Macon, 1988—; exec. com. Athens (Ga.) Regional Hosp., 1983-85. Officer Ga. Easter Seals, Elberton, 1982; clergy sponsor Fellowship of Christian Athletes, Elberton, 1982; mem. Acad. Boosters, Elberton, 1984—, PTA, Elberton, 1985-86. Sgt. USAF, 1969-73, Vietnam. Mem. Rotary, Optimists. Home: Rt 1 Box 202 Elberton GA 30635 Office: Calvary Presbyn Ch 118 Carey St Elberton GA 30635

LOWE, GARY ALLEN, minister; b. El Campo, Tex., Dec. 11, 1951; s. William Edwin and Joan Alice (Reynolds) L.; m. Sandra Lynn Brown, May 30, 1975; children: Matthew, Abby. BA in Bible, Abilene Christian U., 1974, MS in Ministry, 1976. Bible chair dir. Western Tex. Coll., Snyder, 1977-79; preacher Broadway Ch. of Christ, Eden, Tex., 1979-82, Arlington Heights Ch. of Christ, Corpus Christi, Tex., 1983—. Cubmaster Boy Scouts Am., Corpus Christi, 1988; vol. hospice, 1989—. Office: Arlington Heights Ch of Christ 2722 Rand Morgan Corpus Christi TX 78410 *I've found comfort in this quote: "None of us have the power or the responsibility to make things turn out right for anybody else."*

LOWE, JEANNE CATHERINE, lay worker; b. Jersey City, Apr. 12, 1942; d. James Carl and Florence Christine (Nier) L. BA, Montclair (N.J.) State Coll., 1963; SMM, Union Theol. Sem., 1970, MDiv, 1987; MA, U. Notre Dame, 1989. Choir dir. Grace Luth. Ch., Jersey City, 1958-60; parish deaconess Immanuel Luth. Ch., Terre Haute, Ind., 1965-66; deaconess dept.

chaplaincy Atlantic dist. Luth. Ch.-Mo. Synod, N.Y.C., 1966-68; instr. to asst. prof. Concordia Coll., Bronxville, N.Y., 1970-75; exec. sec. Lawson-Gould Music Pubrs., N.Y.C., 1975-76; music dir. Norwegian div. Trinity Luth. Ch., Bklyn., 1976-77; religious counselor Luth. Ministry at MIT, 1978; mentor theol. edn. ministry Trinity Ch., N.Y.C., 1979-81; music dir. organ and choirs Old First Ref. Ch., Bklyn., 1986-87; organist St. Michael & All Angels Ch., South Bend, Ind., 1988-90; organist and choir dir. St. Anne's Episcopal Ch., Warsaw, Ind., 1990-91; pvt. instr. music, 1961—; free lance musician organ, violin, viola, 1961—; chorister Harvard U. Choir, 1977-78; piano instr. Prep. div. Bklyn. Coll., 1978-81; dir. Sunset Pk. Sch. Music, Bklyn., 1980-84; exec. dir. The Roosa Sch. Music, Bklyn., 1981-86; teaching asst. summer session U. Notre Dame, 1988, teaching asst. theology, 1988-89, piano instr., 1988—, adj. asst. prof. Freshman writing program, 1989—; instr. world religions Sch. Faith and Ministry, Diocese of No. Ind., 1990-91. Author: Meditations on the Stations of the Cross, 1991. Community bd. dirs. Sta. WNIT-TV, Elkhart, 1989-90. Mem. Am. acad. Religion, Soc. Bibl. Lit., Cath. Bibl. Assn., Am. Cath. Philos. Soc., Sigma Alpha Iota. Mem. Evang. Luth. Ch. Am. Home: 1237 Blaine Ave South Bend IN 46616 Office: U Notre Dame 344 O'Shaughnessy Hall Notre Dame IN 46556

LOWE, JOE ALLEN, minister; b. Midland, Tex., Dec. 20, 1945; s. Homer Allen and Theresa (Lowry) L.; m. Shirley Christy, Apr. 9, 1965; children: Robert Allen, John David, Steven Scott. BS, Howard Payne Coll., 1968; MDiv, Tex. Christian U., 1976; postgrad, Princeton Theol., 1990. Cert. secondary tchr.; ordained to the ministry Christian Ch. Tchr. Bible history Midland (Tex.) Ind. Sch. Dist., 1968-73; assoc. min. First Christian Ch., Denison, Tex., 1974-76; campus min. United Campus Ministries, Warrensburg, Mo., 1976-78; nurture min. Meml. Christian Ch., Midland, Tex., 1978-84; assoc. min. 1st Christian Ch., Corpus Christi, Tex., 1984-91; sr. min. South Shore Christian Ch., Corpus Christi, 1991—; chmn. Cen. Area Youth Coun., Tex., 1980-84; moderator Youth Ministry Coun. S.W., 1984-87, Bluebonnet Area Youth Coun., 1988-92; advisor Gen. Youth Coun., U.S. and Can., 1985-87. Mem. IMPACT, 1974-82, Nat. Peace Acad., 1973-78; coach YMCA basketball, 1980-81, Little League, Youth Flag Football teams, Denison and Midland, 1967-68, 70, 74. Recipient Friend of Youth City award, 1989; O.H. Karr Ministerial scholar Tex. Christian U., 1975-76. Mem. Youth Ministry Coun. (moderator 1989-93), Ministerial Alliance. Home: 7042 Monarch Corpus Christi TX 78413 Office: South Shore Christian Ch 4710 S Alameda Corpus Christi TX 78412 *My guiding principle is that Christianity is a relationship. Therefore, it must be lived as a relationship-we experience the love of God only in relationship to another (others) and thus only in relationship can we teach Christianity. In short, the slogan "They may not always remember what you said but they will never forget how you made them feel".*

LOWE, JOHN FLETCHER, JR., priest; b. Greenville, S.C., Mar. 11, 1932; s. John Fletcher and Mary Oliver (Conyers) L.; m. Mary Frances Adamson, June 27, 1959; children: John, Elizabeth, Suzanne. AB in Econs., Washington and Lee U., 1954; MDiv, Gen. Theol. Sem., 1959. Ordained to ministry Episcopal Ch. as priest, 1960. Vicar Ch. of the Ascension, Seneca, S.C., 1959-63, St. Barnabas' Episc. Ch., Lynchburg, Va., 1963-67; exec. sec. Christian Social Rels., Richmond, Va., 1967-70; rector Ch. of the Holy Comforter, Richmond, 1970-85, Immanuel Episc. Ch., Wilmington, Del., 1985—; mem. Presiding Bishop's Fund World Relief Bd., N.Y.C., 1988-92; hon. canon St. Peter's Cathedral, Diocese of Bukedi, Uganda, 1983—; chairperson nat. hunger com. Episc. Ch., N.Y.C., 1977-82; mem. standing com. Diocese of Va., 1982-85. Contbr. articles and sermons to publs. Mem. governing bd. Va. Interfaith Ctr. for Pub. Policy, Richmond, 1981-85; mem. ciitzen's adv. bd. Richmond Juvenile & Domestic Rels. Ct., 1981-85; mem. human values com. St. Mary's Hosp., Richmond, 1981-85; mem. rsch. and community planning com. United Way of Greater Richmond, 1982-84; mem. VA. State Crime Commn. Task Force on Prevention/Diversion Youth, Richmond, 1967-77. Mem. Interfaith Ministers Action Coun., Del. Episc. Clergy Assn., Episcopal Peace Fellowship, Endowed Episcopal Parishes. Home: 112 Dickinson Ln Wilmington DE 19807

LOWEN, ALLEN WAYNE, educational administrator, clergyman; b. Covington, Va., Nov. 8, 1946; s. James Ervin and Florence Maude (Taylor) L.; m. Sharon Kay Tyler, Aug. 29, 1969; children: Kristen Dawn, Kimberly Danielle, Gabrielle Brooke. BA, Cin. Bible Coll., 1969; MA, Cin. Christian Sem., 1971, MDiv, 1972; PhD U. Mo., 1986. Ordained to ministry Christian Ch., 1969. Min. Mt. Olivet Ch. of Christ, Williamstown, Ky., 1968-70, Ch. of Christ-Delhi, Cin., 1970-73; prof. Central Christian Coll., Moberly, Mo., 1973-87, acad. dean, 1976-87; pres. Fla. Christian Coll., Kissimmee, 1987—. Editor Adam Newsletter, 1980-84. Contbr. articles to profl. jours.; editor Adam Newsletter, 1981-86. Committeman Charitan Coun. Boy Scouts Am., Moberly, 1974; pres. Regal Oak Shores Homeowners' Assn., Kissimmee, 1988-91. Mem. Am. Assn. Higher Edn., Mo. Assn. Collegiate Registrars and Admission Officers, Am. Assn. Bible Colls. (chmn. commn. on computers 1985-86), Biblical Numismatic Assn., Internat. Tae Kwon Do Assn. (3d degree black belt), Kappa Delta Pi. Republican. Mem. Christian Ch. Home: 1801 Cheryl Ln Kissimmee FL 34744 Office: Fla Christian Coll 1011 Osceola Blvd Kissimmee FL 34744

LOWENTROUT, PETER MURRAY, religious studies educator; b. Salinas, Calif., Mar. 14, 1948; m. Christine Ione, Sept. 30, 1980; 1 child, Mary. AB, U. Calif., Riverside, 1973; PhD, U. So. Calif., L.A., 1983. Assoc. prof. religious studies Calif. State U., Long Beach, 1981—. Contbr. articles to profl. jours. Capt. Orange County Fire Dept., Orange, Calif., 1977—. Mem. Am. Acad. Religion (regional pres. 1989-90), Ctr. for Theology and Lit. U. Durham (Eng.). Office: Calif State U Dept Religious Studies 1250 Bellflower Blvd Long Beach CA 90840 *Though it is the hatred in life that seems most quickly to catch our attention, there is far more love in the world. Learning to see that love and helping others to do so is life's best work.*

LOWERS, HARRY DEAN, minister; b. Clarion, Pa., Nov. 30, 1960; s. Harry O. and Esther M. (Seybert) L.; m. Gail L. Campbell, June 30, 1984; 1 child, Martha Jane. BS in Earth Sci., Clarion U. Pa., 1981; cert. pastoral ministry, Warner So. Coll., 1985. Ordained to ministry United Meth. Ch., 1988. Pastor youth 1st United Meth. Ch., Sligo, Pa., 1979-83, 1st Presbyn. Ch., Haines City, Fla., 1984-85; pastor 1st Ch. of God of Reformation, Florence, S.C., 1985-86, The Ch. of God, Clarksburg, W.Va., 1986-89, 1st Ch. of God, Kane, Pa., 1989—. Office: 1st Ch of God 204 N Fraley St Kane PA 16735

LOWERY, JAMES LINCOLN, JR., minister; b. Utica, N.Y., July 28, 1932; s. James Lincoln and Mary (Rhodes) L.; m. Anita Wu, June 20, 1959; children: Monique Lowery Foster. AB, Harvard Coll., 1954; MDiv, Va. Theol. Sem., 1959. Ordained to ministry Episcopal Ch. as deacon, 1959, as priest 1960. Asst. Grace Episcopal Ch., Elmira, N.Y., 1959-62; rector St. Pauls Episcopal Ch., Greenwich, N.Y., 1962-68; field rep. Assn. of Episcopal Clergy, Boston, 1969-71; exec. dir. Enablement Inc., Boston, 1971—; mem. bd. for ch. deployment Episcopal Ch., N.Y.C., 1976-82; mem. outplacement Working Party Profl. Ch.; leadership com. Nat. Coun. of Chs., N.Y.C., 1985-87. Author: Peers Tents and Owls, Case Histories of Tentmakers; contbr. articles to profl. jours. Pres. Neighborhood Ten Assn., Cambridge, Mass., 1976-80; moderator Eastman Village Dist., Grantham, N.H., 1981-84. 1st lt. AUS, 1954-58. Harvard Prize scholar Harvard Coll., 1950; Procter fellowship Episcopal Div. Sch., 1968-69. Mem. Gen. Theol. Libr. (pres.), Religions Rsch. Assn., World Future Soc., Assn. for Creative Change in Religions and Vol. Systems, Harvard Club (Boston, N.Y.). Office: Enablement Inc 14 Beacon St # 707 Boston MA 02108

LOWERY, JOHN CLAYTON, JR., minister; b. Verda, Ky., Apr. 19, 1940; s. John Clayton and Christine (Coffer) L.; m. Janet Bauer, Dec. 25, 1958; children: Stephanie Lynne, John Clayton III, Jim Dwayne. Grad. high sch., Dayton, Ohio. Lic. to ministry Ch. of God (Cleveland, Tenn.), 1984, ordained, 1989. Asst. Pub. Fin. Co., Dayton, 1968; with Declo Products div. GM, Kettering, Ohio, 1969-88; asst. pastor Eastview Ch. of God, Dayton, 1985-87; pastor Parkridge Ch. of God, Springfield, Ohio, 1987—. Staff sgt. USMC, 1958-68. Home: 355 Canova Ln Dayton OH 45431 Office: Parkridge Ch of God 3321 Dayton Rd Springfield OH 45506

LOWERY, JOSEPH E., clergyman; m. Evelyn Gibson; 3 daus. Student, Knoxville Coll., Ala. A&M Coll., Payne Coll., Wayne U., Payne Theol. Sem., Garrett Theol. Sem., Chgo. Ecumenical Inst.; AB, BD, LLD, Clark Coll., 1975; DD (hon.), Morehouse Coll.; DLitt (hon.), Dillard U.; LLD (hon.), Atlanta U. Ordained to ministry United Methodist Ch.; pastor Warren St. United Meth. Ch., Mobile, Ala., 1952-61; adminstrv. asst. to Bishop Golden, Nashville, 1961-64; pastor St. Paul United Meth. Ch., Birmingham, Ala., 1964-68, Central United Meth. Ch., Atlanta, 1968-86, Cascade United Meth. Ch., 1986—; co-founder SCLC, v.p., until 1967, chmn. bd., 1967-77, pres., 1977—; mem. Commn. on Religion and Race, chmn. merger rev. com. United Meth. Ch., 1968-76; del. World Meth. Council, London, Gen. Confs. United Meth. Ch.; instr. Candler Sch. Theology and Nursing Sch., Emory U., 1970-71. Chmn. Coordinating Com. on Civil Rights in Nashville, 1963-64; pres. Ministerial Alliance, Birmingham, Birmingham OEO Community Action Agy., Enterprises Now, Inc.; bd. dirs. Meth. Pub. House, 1960-72, Met. Atlanta Rapid Transit Authority, 1975—, Martin Luther King, Jr. Ctr. for Social Change; co-chair 20th anniversary March on Washington, 1983. Recipient Equal Opportunity award Atlanta Urban League, 1975, awards Nat. Conf. Black Mayors, Martin Luther King Jr. Peace prize, Martin Luther King, Jr. Ctr. for Non-Violent Social Change, 1990, Martin Luther King Jr. Human Rights award George Washington U., 1990, also awards Ebony mag., others; named one of 15 Greatest Black Preachers Ebony mag. Office: So Christian Leadership Conf 334 Auburn Ave NE Atlanta GA 30303

LOWERY, KEM GERALD, minister, office worker; b. Atlanta, Apr. 7, 1965; s. Kenneth Gerald and Donna LEe (Eller) L.; m. Paula Denise Walker, Apr. 8, 1989. B in Religious Edn., Tenn. Temple U., 1990. Ordained min. Bapt. Ch. Youth pastor East Hiram (Ga.) Bapt. Ch., 1980-82; evangelist Neighborhood Bible Time, Boulder, Colo., 1985-89; pastor youth Victory Bapt. Ch., Loganville, Ga., 1989-90, Corinth Bapt. Ch., Stone Mountain, Ga., 1991—; mail clk. Milco, Duluth, Ga., 1989—; jail preacher Highland Park Bapt. Ch., Chattanooga, Tenn., 1983-88, visitation, 1983-89, pre-sch. class, 1989. Mem. Future Farmers of Am. (Paulding County, Dallas, Ga., chaplain 1982). Republican. Home: 301 D Wiloaks Dr Snellville GA 30278 Office: Corinth Bapt Ch 1836 Rockbridge Rd Stone Mountain GA 30087

LOWERY, MARK DAVID, theology educator; b. Culver City, Calif., Aug. 24, 1955; m. Madeleine M. Murphy, Nov. 24, 1979; children: David, Daniel, Benjamin, Elizabeth, Nathan, Rebecca. BA, Marquette U., 1977, MA, 1980, PhD, 1989. Tchr. Cath. Meml. High Sch., Waukesha, Wis., 1980-88; prof. U. Dallas, Irving, Tex., 1988—. Author: Ecumenism: Seeking Unity Amidst Diversity, 1984; contbr. articles to profl. jours. Summer grantee NEH, 1986. Mem. Am. Acad. Religion (sect. organizer 1990-91). Roman Catholic. Home: 1016 Grosse Point Irving TX 75061 Office: U Dallas 1845 Northgate Ave Irving TX 75062

LOWERY, WILLIAM THEOPHILUS, JR., minister; b. Cuba, N.Y., Apr. 16, 1957; s. William T. and Violet M. (Marville) L.; m. Linda Ann Stahl, July 19, 1980; children: William T. III, Havalah, Joshua, Patrick, Tela, David. BA in Religion and Philosophy, Roberts Wesleyan Coll., 1979; MDiv., Asbury Theol. Sem., 1986. Club dir. Youth for Christ, Avon, N.Y., 1975-77; asst. pastor Albion (N.Y.) Free Meth., 1977-79; pastor Free Meth. Ch., Belfast, N.Y., 1979-80; itinerant pastor Free Meth. Ch., Versailles, Ky., 1983-86; sr. pastor Jamestown (N.Y.) Free Meth., 1986—; chmn. com. ch. planting Genesee Annual Conf., West Seneca, N.Y., 1987—, bd. adminstrv. members, 1989—; rep. N.E. Ch. Planting and Evangelism Steering Com., Indpls., 1991. Bd. dirs. Meals on Wheels, Jamestown, 1991. Named Outstanding Young Men of Am., 1986. Mem. Jamestown Area Ministerial Assn. (treas. 1990—), Jamestown Area Holiness Assn. (pres. 1990—), Rotary Internat. (Jamestown). Republican. Home: 197 Thayer St Jamestown NY 14701

LOWRY, BARRY KEITH, minister; b. Baton Rouge, July 30, 1957; s. Charles M. and Carolyn (Dodd) L.; m. Kaye Matney, May 9, 1980; children: Erin Kaye, Daniel Keith, John Mark. BA in Communication, La. Coll., 1982; MRE, Southwestern Bapt. Theol. Sem., Ft. Worth, 1988. Ordained to gospel ministry Bapt. Ch., 1986. Min. music New Prospect Bapt. Ch., Dry Prong, La., 1980-83; prodn. dir. media svcs. dept. La. Bapt. Conv., Alexandria, 1981-84; ops. engr. ACTS Network, Radio and TV Commn. SBC, Ft. Worth, 1984-85; min. youth and edn. 1st Bapt. Ch., Eastland, Tex., 1986-87, Bethany Bapt. Ch., Breckenridge, Tex., 1987-89; min. edn. 1st Bapt. Ch., Dickson, Tenn., 1989—. Recipient Advanced Christian Devel. Diploma, Bapt. Sunday Sch. Bd., 1989. Mem. Southwestern Bapt. Religious Edn. Assn., So. Bapt. Religious Edn. Assn., Nashville Bapt. Religious Edn. Assn. (dir. teaching improvement ASSIST team 1989—). Office: 1st Bapt Ch PO Box 519 Hwy 70 Bypass Dickson TN 37055

LOWRY, CHARLES WESLEY, clergyman, lecturer; b. Checotah, Okla., Mar. 31, 1905; s. Charles Wesley and Sue (Price) L.; m. Edith Clark, June 14, 1930; children: Harriet Richards Lowry King, Charles Wesley, Atherton Clark, James Meredith Price; m. Kate Rowe Holland, Jan. 11, 1960. BA, Washington and Lee U., 1926, DD, 1959; MA, Harvard U., 1927; BD, Episcopal Theol. Sch., 1930; DPhil, Oxford (Eng.) U., 1933. Ordain deacon Episcopal Ch., 1930. Priest Episcopal Ch., 1931; traveling fellow Episc. Theol. Sch., 1930-32; Episc. chaplain U. Calif., 1933-34; prof. systematic theology Va. Theol. Sem., 1934-43; rector All Saints' Ch., Chevy Chase, Md., 1943-53; lectr. theology Seabury Western Theol. Sem., 1947, Phila. Div. Sch. (Bohlen lectr.), 1947, 49-50, Gen. Theol. Sem., 1951-52; chmn. Bd. Examining Chaplains, Diocese of Washington, 1945-53, sec., standing com., 1945-51; ofcl. del. from U.S. Internat. Conv. on Peace and Christian Civilization, Florence, Italy, 1952; chmn., exec. dir. Found. for Religious Action in Social and Civil Order, 1953-59, pres., 1960—, project research dir. on morals revolution, 1973-75; cons. FCDA, 1953-55; cons. Air War Coll., 1953, lectr., 1953-54; lectr. Naval War Coll., 1955, Nat. War Coll., 1957, 59-61, Command and Staff Coll., 1961-62, Indsl. Coll. Armed Forces, 1963, Inst. Lifetime Learning, 1964-66, Campbell Coll. Sch. Law, 1979, 80; also lectr. various seminars; lectr. philosophy and polit. sci. Sandhills Community Coll., 1967-69, 71, 89; spl. lectr. Oxford (Eng.) Poly. Coll., 1974; spl. lectr. Washington and Lee U., 1977, baccalaureate preacher, 1984; dir. Nat. Conf. on Spiritual Founds. Am. Democracy, Washington, 1954-55, 57, 59; minister The Village Chapel, Pinehurst, N.C., 1966-73; mem. faculty Wallace O'Neal Day Sch., Southern Pines, N.C., 1976—; columnist Pinehurst Outlook, 1977-78, Moore County News, 1978-79, The Pilot, 1979—; priest assoc. Emmanuel Epis. Ch., Southern Pines, 1981—. Author: The Trinity and Christian Devotion, 1946, Christianity and Materialism (Hale Sermon), 1948, Communism and Christ, rev. edit, 1962 (Brit. edit. 1954), Conflicting Faiths, 1953, The Ideology of Freedom vs. The Ideology of Communism, 1958, To Pray or Not to Pray, rev. edit, 1968, The Kingdom of Influence, 1969, William Temple: An Archbishop for All Seasons, 1982, The First Theologians, 1986, Constitution Commentary, 1989; (with others) Anglican Evangelicalism, 1943, Encyclopaedia of Religion, 1945, The Anglican Pulpit To-Day, 1953; editor: Blessings of Liberty, 1956-90; contbr. articles to profl. publs. Chmn. Nat. Jefferson Davis Hall of Fame Co., 1960, 64-65; candidate for U.S. Congress 10th Dist. Va., 1962; mem. N.C. Bicentennial Constn. Conv., 1985-89. Recipient George Washington medal Freedoms Found., 1955, 59, 61, 68, other award, 1953, 81. Mem. Am. Peace Soc. (past pres.), Am. Polit. Sci. Assn., Internat. Platform Assn., Am. Theol. Soc. (treas. 1955-70, 72, past v.p.), Cum Laude Soc. (pres. O'Neal chpt.), World Conf. Faith and Order, Phi Beta Kappa, Omicron Delta Kappa, Delta Sigma Rho, Sigma Upsilon. Clubs: Achilles (Oxford and Cambridge); Rotary (dist. gov. 1970-71), Chevy Chase, Pinehurst Country, Nat. Press. Address: Box 1829 Pinehurst NC 28374 *A religious view of life is not an easy optimism. The serious person knows the force of moral evil or sin. But when in the great religions we meet a Power that transforms, we see with new eyes. We are saved by hope and by faith and love.*

LOWRY, EUGENE LAVERNE, educator, minister; b. Meade, Kans., Sept. 6, 1933; s. Austin Lynn and Myrtle Louise (Jordan) L.; m. Sarah Cheatum, Oct. 3, 1976; children: Mark, Diane, Jill. BA, Southwestern Coll., 1955; BD, Drew Theol. Sem., 1958; MA, Columbia U., 1958; EdD, U. Kans., 1972. Ordained to ministry United Meth. Ch., 1956. Pastor St. Paul Meth. Ch., West New York, N.J., 1955-59; assoc. pastor 1st Meth. Ch., Wichita, Kans., 1959-62, Country Club United Meth. Ch., Kansas City, Mo., 1962-64; pastor Coll. Heights United Meth. Ch., Kansas City, Mo., 1964-68; lectr. St. Paul Sch. Theology, Kansas City, 1962-68, asst. prof., 1968-73, assoc. prof., 1973-79, prof. preaching and communication, 1979—, dir. doctoral studies, 1974-81, interim acad. dean, 1984-85. Author: How to Preach a Parable, 1989, Doing Time in the Pulpit, 1985, The Homiletical Plot: The Sermon as Narrative Art Form, 1980; contbr. articles to profl. jours. Recipient Masterbuilder award Southwestern Coll., 1955. Mem. Am. Acad. Homiletics, Am. Fedn. Musicians, Kansas City Theol. Studies, Am. Acad. Religion. Office: St Paul Sch Theology 5123 Truman Rd Kansas City MO 64127

LOWRY, FREDERICK SHERWOOD, minister, association director; b. Providence, May 12, 1935; s. David Sherwood and Lucy Cecile (Casey) L.; m. Leuntje Alida Schipper, Apr. 25, 1967; children: David Sherwood, Jan Willem Schipper. AB, Dartmouth Coll., 1956; M of Div., Yale U., 1959; cert., Ecumenical Inst., Geneva, 1963. Ordained to ministry, United Ch. of Christ, 1960. Pastor Orient Congrl. Ch., L.I., N.Y., 1960-64; adminstrv. asst. Miss. Delta Ministry Nat. Council Chs., Greenville, 1964-67; dir. Migrant Ministry Washington State Council Chs., Seattle, 1967-69; child care worker Kitsap Youth Homes, Bremerton, Wash., 1969-70; dir. Woburn (Mass.) Council Social Concern, 1970-73; pastor Plymouth Congrl. Ch., Syracuse, N.Y., 1974-80; exec. dir. Community Ministry Fairfax County, Reston, Va., 1980—. Mem. sch. adv. com.-Human Life Curriculum, 1982—, Planned Parenthood Adv. Com., Fairfax, 1982—, Fairfax Com. 100, 1983—, Emergency Shelter Study Com., Fairfax County, 1986, Fairfax County Social Services Appeal Bd., 1987—; mem. adv. bd. North Va. Youth Service Coalition, Fairfax, 1985—. Mem. Nat. Assn. Ecumenical Staff, Washington Area Community Ministries, Interfaith Conf. Washington. Democrat. Home: 1579 Inlet Ct Reston VA 22090 Office: Community Ministry Fairfax 1920 Association Dr Rm 507 Reston VA 22091

LOWRY, TERRY BRYSON, minister; b. Cartersville, Ga., Aug. 13, 1951; s. Albert J. and Cornelia B. Lowry; m. Beatrice Jane Shellhorse, June 2, 1971; children: Terry B. Jr., Carolyn Jane, Paul Joseph. Student, Jacksonville State U., 1969-71; MusB, U. Ala., 1973. Ordained to ministry So. Bapt. Conv., 1981. Min. music Raleigh White Bapt. Ch., Albany, 1973-74, Southside Bapt. Ch., Griffin, Ga., 1974-75, First Bapt. Ch., Adel, Ga., 1975-87, Bowdon (Ga.) Bapt. Ch., 1987—; accompanist Sons of Jubal, Atlanta, 1982-84. Concert artist; composer, arranger several musical pieces. Officer Bowdon Band Boosters, 1988-90; vol. Am. Cancer Soc., Cystic Fibrosis Found. Winner Gt. Talent Search Sta. WSB-TV, 1969; recipient Meritorious Svc. award Ga. Bapt. Conv., 1985. Mem. Music Educators Nat. Conf., Ga. Music Tchrs. Assn., Nat. Music Educators Assn., Ga. Music Educators Assn. Home: PO Box 66 Bowdon GA 30108 Office: Bowdon Bapt Ch PO Box 250 Bowdon GA 30108

LOWRY, WAYNE MITCHELL, minister; b. Princeton, Ky., Nov. 28, 1934; s. Mitchell J. and Lula Ethlyn (Small) L.; m. Annette Freeman, July 7, 1956; children: Mark Freeman, Mitchell Elvin. BS, Bethel (Tenn.) Coll., 1956; postgrad., Scarritt Coll., 1958-59, U. Dubuque, 1963-65. Ordained to ministry United Presbyn. Ch. (U.S.A.), 1956. Pastor chs., Ind., Tenn., Okla., Ohio, 1956-70; sr. pastor Harvard U., Cambridge, Mass., 1970-71, 2d Presbyn. Ch., Portsmouth, Ohio, from 1971; mem. mission coun. Synod of Covenant, 1973—, Presbytery of Scioto Valley, 1973—; trustee Nat. Ch. Residences, Waverly, Ohio. Merrill fellow Harvard U. Div. Sch., 1970-71. Home: PO Box 1282 Portsmouth OH 45662

LOY, SAMUEL WHITE, minister; b. Burlington, N.C., June 16, 1949; s. William Thomas Loy and Mary Ruth (Hoyle) Qualls; m. Wanda Kay Murphy, June 25, 1967; children: Andrew, Kathryn. BA, Elon Coll., 1982; MDiv, Duke U., 1986. Ordained to ministry United Meth. Ch. as deacon, 1986, as elder, 1988. Mgr. maintenance dept. textile plant, Burlington, 1976-81; min. Walnut Grove United Meth. Ch., Hurdle Mills, N.C., 1981-84, Phillips Chapel United Meth. Ch., Graham, N.C., 1984-86; assoc. min. St. James United Meth. Ch., Greenville, N.C., 1986—. Founder, pres. Greenville Community Shelter, 1987-90. Staff sgt. N.C. NG, 1968-75. Mem. Kiwanis (Spiritual Aims award Carolinas dist. 1991). Home: 102 Dellwood Dr Greenville NC 27858 Office: St James United Meth Ch 2000 E 6th St Greenville NC 27858

LOZANO, JOHN MANUEL, priest; b. Lora del Rio, Spain, June 18, 1930; came to U.S., 1976; s. Antonio and Rosario (Nieto) L. BA, Licentia in Theology, U. Catholique, Angers, France, 1956; Licentia in Bibl. Scis., Bibl. Inst., Rome, 1958; ThD, Angelicum U., Rome, 1959. Joined Clarentians Soc., 1948; ordained priest Roman Cath. Ch., 1956. Prof. spirituality Claretianum, Rome, 1962-67, dir. studium, 1961-68; prof. theology and history of spirituality Inst. della Vita Religiosa, Lateran U., Rome, 1971—; prof. spirituality Cath. Theol. Union, Chgo., 1979—; consultor Roman Congregation for Causes of the Saints, 1970—. Author: Mystic and Man of Action, 1977, Discipleship, 1981, 2d edit., 1983, Life as a Parable, 1985; contbg. author: I Mondi dell'Uomo, 1977, Together Before the Lord, 1983, Ency. of Religion, 1985. Mem. Cath. Theol. Soc. Am., Soc. for Sci. Study Religion. Address: 5540 S Everett Ave Chicago IL 60637

LU, MATTHIAS, priest, educator; b. Lu Kia-tun, Pao-ting, China, June 2, 1919; came to U.S.; naturalized; s. Paul and Rose (Yang) L. Student, St. Vincent's Maj. Sem., China, 1937-38; PhB, Pontifical Urbaniana U., Rome, 1939, BTh., 1941, Licentiate in Philosophy, 1942, Licentiate in Sacred Theology, 1944, PhD, 1946; postgrad., U. Toronto, Can., 1948-56, Pontifical Inst. Mediaeval Studies, 1948-59, St. Francis Xavier U., Antigonish, Can., 1949-51; PhD (hon.), Scicluna Internat. U., 1987. Ordained priest Roman Cath. Ch., 1942. Lectr. in philosophy Fujen U., Peiping, China, 1946-48; asst. pastor, chmn. ednl. com. for parish co-ops Thorold, Ont., Can., 1951-56; instr. U. Notre Dame, Ind., 1956-58; asst. prof. St. John's U., Collegeville, Minn., 1959-62; asst. prof. St. Mary's Coll., Moraga, Calif., 1962-72, scholar in residence, 1973—, dir. St. Thomas Aquinas Internat. Ctr. for Everyone, 1974—; prof. U. Ottawa, Can., 1957-59; vis. lectr. St. Bonaventure U., N.Y., 1958-59, Cath. U. Paris, 1960; rsch. assoc. U. Calif., Berkeley, 1962—; chaplain Christian Bros. St. La Salle Schs., 1963—, local br. 11, Italian Cath. Fedn., Oakland, Calif., 1983—, Oakland coun. KC, 1978—; instr. Holy Names Coll., Calif., 1965-69; assoc. prof. John F. Kennedy U., Calif., 1966; vicar for Chinese and East Asian peoples Roman Cath. Ch., 1969-86; mem. Oakland Priests' Senate, 1972-75; vis. prof. Ignatius Inst., U. San Francisco, 1981-82; dir. Chinese transls. Lublin U. Internat. Transl. Ctr., 1984-86. Author, translator in field; also articles; producer program Stas. KUSF-FM, KSMC-FM, 1972—. Recipient Pro Ecclesia et Pontefice medal Pope Pius XII, 1939, Gold medal Pope John Paul II and Bishop of Oakland, 1985, Einstein medal Internat. Albert Einstein Acad. Found., 1988. Hon. mem. Mexican Cath. Philos. Soc.; mem. AAAS, Am. Philos. Assn., Am. Cath. Philos. Assn., Am. Oriental Soc., Am. Acad. Polit. and Social Sci., Cath. Theol. Soc. Am., Soc. Internat. pour l'Etude de la Philosophie Médiévale, Chinese Hist. Soc. Am., Internat. Soc. St. Thomas Aquinas, Internat. Jacques Maritain Soc., Internat. Soc. Metaphysics, Internat. Assn. Symbolic Logic, Internat. Soc. Chinese Philosophy, Internat. Assn. for Christian Thought, World Congregation of Bros. Christian Schs., (affiliated bro. 1988—). Office: St Thomas Aquinas Internat Ctr St Mary's Coll Box 3014 Moraga CA 94575 *Independence with Interdependence; Solidarity and Reciprocity; Compassion and Mercy; Truth, Justice, Friendship and Liberty are the principles directing the advancement of peace and happiness, if understood under the light of the harmony between the wisdom of God in the Bible and the logic of Human reason in all achievements. The key is the harmony between Faith and Reason.*

LUBACHIVSKY, MYROSLAV IVAN CARDINAL, archbishop; b. Dolyna, West Ukraine, June 24, 1914; came to U.S., 1947, naturalized, 1952; s. Eustahi and Anna (Oliynik) L. Student, Theol. Acad. Lviv; Grad., Faculty of Theology, U. Innsbruk, 1939, S.T.D., 1942; M. in Biblical Studies, Papal Biblical Inst., 1943; M.Phil., Gregorian U., Rome, 1945; student in medicine U. Rome, before 1947. Ordained priest Cath. Ch. of the Ukranian Rite, 1938. Began pastoral career in U.S., 1947, apptd. archbishop of Ukranian-rite archeparchy of Phila., 1979; coadjutor archbishop of Lviv of the Ukranians, 1980; archbishop of Lviv and major archbishop of Ukranians, 1984, created cardinal, 1985; titular ch., St. Sofia. Office: Piazza Madonna, dei Monti 3, 00184 Rome Italy

LUBBEN, HENRY CLAUS, minister; b. Teaneck, N.J., Sept. 20, 1938; s. Henry C. Jr. and Ida Gertrude (Templin) L.; m. Sally Jean Brown, May 31, 1964; children: Suzanne E. Spurgetis, Steven M. BTh., Concordia Theol. Sem., Springfield, Ill., 1964. Ordained to ministry Luth. Ch.-Mo. Synod, 1964. Pastor Messiah Luth. Ch., Grand Rapids, Mich., 1964-67; pastor True Light Luth. Ch., N.Y.C., 1967-68, Mt. Calvary Luth. Ch., Greenville, Mich., 1968-70; dir. pub. rels. Bethesda Luth. Home, Watertown, Wis., 1970-72;

exec. dir. Cedar Lake Lodge, LaGrange, Ky., 1972-76; pastor Trinity Luth. Ch., Taylorville, Ill., 1976-81, Immanuel Luth. Ch., Rock Island, Ill., 1981—; chmn. editorial commn. ofcl. periodicals Luth. Ch.-Mo. Synod, 1977-81, chmn. bd. dirs. communications svcs., 1981-83, chmn. communication svcs. com. Cen. Ill. Dist.; exec. editor The C.I.D. Rudder, 1977-91. Author: (study guide) Are You Joking, Jeremiah?, 1979, Portals of Prayer, 1986, 2d edit., 1989. Mem. Christian County Mental Health Bd., Taylorville, 1977-81. Recipient Jericho Friend award Cedar Lake Lodge, 1981, Servus Ecclesiae Christi award Concordia Theol. Sem., Ft. Wayne, Ind., 1982. Mem. Rotary (v.p. Rock Island club 1985—). Office: Immanuel Luth Ch 1923 5th Ave Rock Island IL 61201 *In my life I have discovered God never fails to answer prayer-"Yes", "No", "Wait", or "You should have known better than to ask for that."*

LUBOW, AKIBA, rabbi; b. Los Angeles, Calif., May 10, 1949; s. William and Marian (Spector) L. BA, Ind. U., 1972; BHP, U. Judaism, Los Angeles, 1980; MA, Jewish Theological Seminary, N.Y., 1984. Special asst to gov. State Calif., Sacramento, 1975-78; rabbi Bellmore (N.Y.) Jewish Ctr., 1986-87, congregation Shaare Zedek, N.Y., 1985-86; assoc. rabbi Birth Sholom Kneseth Israel Congregation, St. Louis; bd. mem. Cen. Agy. Jewish Edn., St. Louis, 1987--, St. Louis Schechter Day Sch., 1987--. Mem. Rabbinical Assembly, St. Louis Rabbincial Assn., St. Louis Rabbinical Assembly. Democrat. Home: 815 Westwood Dr Apt 2N Saint Louis MO 63205 Office: Birth Shalon Kneseth Israel 1107 Linden Ave Saint Louis MO 62117

LUCADO, MAX LEE, minister; b. San Angelo, Tex., Jan. 11, 1955; s. Jack Derrell and Thelma Esther (Kincaide) L.; m. Denalyn Lucado, Aug. 8, 1981; children: Jenna, Andrea, Sara. BS, Abiliene Christian U., 1977, MA, 1981. Ordained to ministry Ch. of Christ. Assoc. min. Cen. Ch. of Christ, Miami, Fla., 1979-82; missionary Tijunca-lareja de Cristo, Rio de Janeiro, 1983-88; pulpit min. Oak Hills Ch. of Christ, San Antonio, 1988—. Author: On the Anvil, 1985, No Wonder They Call Him Savior, 1986, God Came Near, 1987, Six Hours One Friday, 1989 (Gold medallion 1990), Applause in Heaven, 1990. Office: Oak Hills Ch of Christ 8308 Fredericksburg Rd San Antonio TX 78229

LUCAS, ARTHUR MONROE, clergy member; b. Alexandria, Va., Aug. 24, 1947; s. Talbot Paul Lucas and Jean Perry (Giles) Lucas Jenkins; m. Lou Matthews, Aug. 9, 1969; children: Katherine Elizabeth, Martin Brandon. BA, U. Va., 1969; MDiv, Duke U., 1973. Ordained to ministry United. Meth. Ch., 1976. Resident in clin. pastoral edn. Meml. Hosp. System, Houston, 1973-76; dir. pastoral care Meth. Med. Ctr., St. Joseph, Mo., 1976-84; dir. pastoral care and counseling Heartland Health System, St. Joseph, 1984-85, exec. dir. Heartland Health Ministries, 1985-86, adminstr. Heartland Samaritan Ctr., 1986-90; dir. pastoral care Barnes Healthcare System, St. Louis, 1990—; rsch. asst. urban policy study NIMH, Durham, N.C., 1971-72; presenter pastoral care workshops and profl. confs.; coord. program for pastoral care bd. ordained ministry Mo. West Ann. Conf., United Meth. Ch., 1983-90, chmn. NW dist. com. on superintendency, 1985-90, mem. NW dist. coun. on ministries, 1977-90, rep. to regional prison chaplaincy screening com. United Meth. div. chaplains and related ministries, 1980—. Contbr. articles to various publs. Corr. sec. bd. dirs. Robidoux Resident Theatre, 1988-90. Fellow Coll. Chaplains of Am. Protestant Health Assn.; mem. Assn. Clin. Pastoral Edn. (cert. supr.). Avocations: reading, travel. Office: Barnes Hosp at Washington U Med Ctr 1 Barnes Hosp Pla Saint Louis MO 63110

LUCAS, BERT ALBERT, pastor, social services administrator, consultant; b. Hammond, Ind., Mar. 26, 1933; s. John William and Norma (Gladys) Graham; m. Nanci Dai Hindman, Sept. 10, 1960; children: Bradley Scott, Traci Dai. BA, Wheaton Coll., 1956; BD, No. Bapt. Theol. Sem., 1960, ThM, 1965; MSW, U. Mich., 1971; D in Marriage and Family, Ea. Bapt. Theol. Sem., 1988. Lic. social worker, Ohio; ordained clergyman Am. Baptist Conv.; cert. family life educator. Chaplain Miami Children's Ctr., Maumee, Ohio, 1967-83; assoc. pastor First Bapt. Ch., La Porte, Ind., 1959-62; pastor Maumee Bapt. Ch., 1963-67; adminstrv. social work supr. Lucas County (Ohio) Children Svcs., 1967—; pastor Holland (Ohio) United Meth. Ch., 1979-90; adj. prof. Bowling Green (Ohio) State U., 1972-79; family life cons. New Horizon's Acad., Holland, 1984-86, co-dir. family svcs. 1985-86; cons. parenting, marriage enrichment, Toledo, 1986—. Rep. precinct capt., Toledo, 1984. Bert A. Lucas Day proclaimed City of Holland, 1984. Mem. AACD, Am. Assn. Marriage and Family Therapy (assoc.), Assn. for Couples in Marriage Enrichment, Hist. Preservations of Am. (Community Leader and Noteworthy Ams. award 1976-77), Council Family Rels.

LUCAS, CALVIN GLENN, minister; b. Carp, Ont., Can., May 24, 1929; s. Robert and Jessie Verna (Ireland) L.; m. Phyllis Barbara Napier, Oct. 12, 1968; 1 child, Robert Shaun. BA, Queen's U., Kingston, Ont., 1950; postgrad., Queen's Theol. Coll., 1954; MA, Carleton U., Ottawa, Ont., 1973; DD, Victoria U., Toronto, Ont., 1986. Ordained to ministry United Ch. of Can., 1954. Parish min. Bethune, Sask., Can., 1954-55, Fitzroy Harbour, Ont., 1956-59, Montreal, Que., Can., 1959-63; collection historian Fortress of Louisborg Restoration Project, 1963-66; archivist-historian United Ch. of Can., Victoria U., Toronto, $, 1966-86. Mem. World Meth. Hist. Soc. (pres. 1981-86). Home: 29 Toronto St S, Markdale, ON Canada N0C 1H0

LUCAS, ROY EDWARD, JR., minister; b. Shawnee, Okla., Dec. 19, 1955; s. Roy Edward Sr. and Shirley Ann (Padgett) L.; m. Roberta Lee Duncan, Feb. 28, 1975; children: Jonathon Edward, Jerebeth Glenae. BA, Okla. Bapt. U., 1978, BA in Edn., 1979; MDiv, Southwestern Bapt. Theol. Sem., Ft. Worth, 1984, MRE, 1985, postgrad., 1989—. Ordained to ministry So. Bapt. Conv., 1978; cert. elem. tchr., Okla. Assoc. pastor Temple Bapt. Ch., Shawnee, 1975, Calvary Bapt. Ch., Shawnee, 1975-79; pastor Brandon (Tex.) Bapt. Ch., 1982-85, Fox (Okla.) Bapt. Ch., 1985-90, Union Hill Bapt. Ch., Purcell, Okla., 1990—; instr. Sem. Ext.-Enon Associated, Ardmore, Okla., 1986-89; teaching fellow Southwestern Bapt. Sem., 1989. Home: 612 N 6th Purcell OK 73080 Office: Union Hill Bapt Ch Rte 2 Box 80 Purcell OK 73080

LUCAS, STEPHEN LEE, pastor; b. Muncie, Ind., Mar. 26, 1948; s. Carlos and Irene (Estep) L.; m. Barbara J. Taylor, Dec. 26, 1969; children: Candi, Jennifer, Sarah, Rachel, Tiffani, Stepheni. BA in Bible and Theology, Appalachian Bible Coll., 1977. Ordained to ministry Bible Ch., 1977. Asst. pastor Piney View (W.Va.) Bible Ch., 1974-77; pastor Mt. Hope (W.Va.) Bible Ch., 1975-79, Community Bible Ch., Paris, Ill., 1979-82, Maroa (Ill.) Bible Ch., 1982—. Served with U.S. Army, 1968-71, Korea. Mem. Ind. Fundamental Chs. of Am. Avocations: writing songs, singing, playing guitar. Home: PO Box 357 Maroa IL 61756 Office: Maroa Bible Ch 312 W Jackson Maroa IL 61756

LUCAS, VALERIE PATRICIA, minister, writer; b. Bridgeport, Conn., Apr. 1, 1951; d. Alexander and Kathleen Pearl (Golding) L. Student, Cen. Conn. State U., 1969-71, Sancta Sophia Sem., 1985-89. Mgr., account rep. News Publ. Co., Statford, Conn., 1971-77; ins. sales person Mutual of Omaha, Westport, Conn., 1978-80, ins. sales mgr., 1980-82; mktg. assoc. Mutual of Omaha, Omaha, 1982-83, advt. copywriter, 1983-85; dir. Indwelling Christ Ctr., Omaha, 1986—, Rev., 1989—; field rep. Light of Christ Ch., Tahlequah, Okla., 1989-91. Mystical Christian. Home and Office: 12107 Arbor St Apt 7 Omaha NE 68144 *All the exquisite beauty that surrounds us in the external world is merely an amateur painting—a rough copy—of the glorious original that lies within.*

LUCE, DENNIS CHARLES, minister; b. Fort Dix, N.J., Oct. 4, 1962; s. Robert Emmett and Janice Laree (Robertson) L.; m. Shelly Rene Sobczak, Aug. 20, 1988. BA in Religion, So. Calif. Coll., Costa Mesa, 1985. Ordained to ministry Assemblies of God, 1991. Youth pastor Bonita (Calif.) Valley Christian Ctr., 1985-90, Life Ctr. Assembly, Lakewood, Calif., 1990—. Mem. So. Calif. Dist. Coun. Assemblies of God Youth Ministries (sect. rep. San Diego, 1987-90, sect. rep. Orange County, 1990—). Office: Life Ctr Assembly 6022 E Candlewood St Lakewood CA 90713 *The Christian life is like walking up a down esculator. Effort must be expended to gain ground. If one stands still, then he is inevitably carried downward. We must make a conscious effort to better our Christian walk for growth is not natural.*

LUCHIES, JOHN ELMER, religion educator; b. Fremont, Mich., May 19, 1912; s. John J. and Minnie (Van Hemert) L.; m. Marian Elizabeth Stehouwer, Sept. 1, 1938. AB in Philosophy, Calvin Coll., 1935; ThB, Calvin Sem., 1938; ThM in Ethics, Princeton Theol. Sem., 1939, PhD in Philosophy of Religion magna cum laude, 1947; postgrad., U. Chgo., 1951, Ohio State U., 1957-58. Ordained to ministry Christian Ref. Ch., 1942; Presbyn. Ch. (USA), 1967. Pastor various chs. Lansing, Mich., Muskegon, Mich., Wheaton, Ill. and Holland, Mich., 1942—; prof. religion, philosophy Wheaton Coll., Ohio State U., Ind. U., Defiance (Ohio) Coll. and Hope Coll., Mich., 1942—; pastor Presbyn. Ch. (USA), 1965-78; chmn. religion and philosophy dept. Defiance Coll., 1970-88, head humanities div., 1972-78; dir. Wheaton Philos. Conf., 1951-60; lectr. in field. Contbr. articles to profl. jours. Teaching fellow Princeton Theol. Sem., 1940-42. Home: 797 Brook Village Dr Holland MI 49423 Office: Pillar Christian Reformed Ch 57 E 10th St Holland MI 49423

LUCHS, FRED EMIL, clergyman, lecturer; b. Ridgeway, Pa., Apr. 2, 1904; s. Simon and Margaretha (Ruef) L.; m. Evelyn Mae Coulter, Aug. 8, 1933; children: Lewis Richard, Mark William, Michael Charles, Margaret Jane. BD, U. Chgo., 1931; DD, Franklin and Marshall Coll., 1952. Served as pastor throughout the U.S. 1931-73; assoc. editor 20th Century Quarterly, 1945-55; established 1st co-ed youth camp in U.S., 1932; exchange preacher to Eng. and Am. Chs. in Berlin and Paris, 1939; interim pastor St. John's Evang. Protestant Ch., Columbus, Ohio, 1973; chaplain aboard 14 trips worldwide; mem. Gen. Motors speakers, 1960-72; spl. lectr. Ohio U.; participant lect. tours in Europe. Author: Lenten Tryst, 1947, If I Had Never Been Born, 1987, Christmas Letters: 1945-87, 1987; writer weekly prayers Christian Century; works trans. into several langs. Nat. Sermon contest winner, 1949; named One of Ten Best Speakers in Am. Internat. Speakers Network, One of Ten Outstanding Presbyn. Preachers in U.S., 1952; Honorary Alumnus award Ohio U., 1985. Home: 93 Wonder Hills Dr Athens OH 45701

LUCIDO, FRANK A., school system administrator; b. Mexico City, Mex., Apr. 2, 1945; s. Ruben De La Rosa (stepfathather) and Mary Alice (Aguilar) De la Rosa; m. Ramona G. Lucido, Nov. 22, 1975; children: Gabriel, Monica. BA, Tex. A&I U., 1967, MS, 1973; MS, Corpus Christi State U., 1978; MA, Incarnate Word, San Antonio, 1989. Tchr., coach S.S. Cyril and Methodious Sch., Corpus Christi, 1981-91; tchr., coach, dept. chairperson Foy H. Moody High Sch., Corpus Christi, 1973-77, adminstrv. asst., 1980-83; asst. registrar Del Mar Jr. Coll., Corpus Christi, 1977-80; prin. St. Pius X Sch., Corpus Christi, 1983-88; dir. religious edn., assoc. supt. Diocese of Corpus Christi, 1988-91; adj. prof. Tex. A&I U., Kingsville, 1978-79, 86-87, Incarnate Word Pastoral Inst., Corpus Christi, 1988-91, Corpus Christi State U., Tex., 1981-91; asst. camp dir. Camp Stewart, Hunt, Tex., 1966-80; mem. Nat. Conf. of Diocesean Dirs. m. Nat. Cath. Edn. Assn., Corpus Christi Area Bilingual Edn. Assn. (pres. 1989-91), Phi Delta Kappa (rsch. rep. 1981-82). Roman Catholic. Office: Diocese of Corpus Christi 1200 Lantana St Corpus Christi TX 78407

LUCKENBAUGH, CARROLL CHARLES, minister; b. York County, Pa., Aug. 25, 1935; s. Charles and Cora Ellen (Myers) L.; m. Phyllis Pauline, Aug. 29, 1959; children: Bryan Scott, Julia Ann, Charles David. BA, Franklin and Marshall Coll., 1957; BD, Lancaster Theol. Sem., 1960; postgrad., Yale U., 1970-72; MDiv, Lancaster Theol. Sem., 1973; postgrad., Johns Hopkins U., 1975-90. Ordained to ministry United Ch. of Christ, 1960. Assoc. pastor Zion United Ch. Christ, North Canton, Ohio, 1960-63; assoc. pastor Trinity United Ch. Christ, Hanover, Pa., 1963-66, sr. pastor, 1967—; moderator, chmn. bd. dirs. Pa. Cen. Conf., Harrisburg, 1975-77; pres. Hanover Area Coun. Chs., 1975-76. Chmn. York County Bd. Pks. and Recreation, 1969-89 (Recognition award 1989); chaplain Hanover Fire Dept; pres. adv. bd. The Brethren Home, New Oxford, Pa., 1980-84 (Founders Club award 1989); bd. dirs. YMCA. 1976, York County Wildlife Protection and Preservation, 1990-91. Mem. Vis. Nurse Assn. (adv. bd., pres. 1976), Franklin and Marshall Coll. Alumni Assn., Lancaster Theol. Sem. Alumni Assn., Lake Club, Masons, Knights Templar (chaplain 1984). Home: 28 Lee St Hanover PA 17331 Office: Trinity United Ch Christ 116 York St Hanover PA 17331-3126 *In my vocation, there is a feeling of serenity at the end of a day when you have endeavored to minister in God's name and someone said: "Thanks for being there when we needed you".*

LUCKER, RAYMOND ALPHONSE, bishop; b. St. Paul, Feb. 24, 1927; s. Alphonse and Josephine (Schiltgen) L. B.A., St. Paul Sem., 1948, M.A., 1952; S.T.L., U. St. Thomas, Rome, 1965, S.T.D., 1966; Ph.D., U. Minn., 1969. Ordained priest Roman Cath. Ch., 1952, bishop, 1971. Asst. dir. Confrat. of Christian Doctrine, Archdiocese of St. Paul, 1952-58, dir., 1958-68; prof. catechetics St. Paul Sem., 1957-68; dir. dept. edn. U.S. Cath. Conf., Washington, 1969-71; consecrated bishop, 1971; aux. bishop of St. Paul and Mpls., 1971-76; bishop of New Ulm, Minn., 1976—. Author: Aims of Religious Education, 1966, Some Presuppositions on Released Time, 1969, My Experience: Reflections on Pastoring, 1988; contbg. author: Catholic Social Thought, 1990, The Universal Catechism Reader, 1990. Recipient Nat. Catechetical award, 1991. Home: 1400 6th N St New Ulm MN 56073 Office: Catholic Pastoral Ctr 1400 6th N St New Ulm MN 56073

LUDLOW, ANNE, ecumenical agency director. Adminstrv. coord. Wyo. Ch. Coalition, Laramie. Office: Wyo Ch Coalition 1215 Gibbon Laramie WY 82070*

LUDLOW, MARK ANTHONY (TONY), minister; b. Ft. Smith, Ark., July 25, 1957; s. Albert Jack Ludlow and Patricia Ruth Abernathy; m. Cynthia Kay Goad, Apr. 22, 1978; children: Matthew Clayton, Melissa Jean, Nathan Wells. BA, Memphis State U., 1983; M of Div., Mid Am. Bapt. Theol. Sem., 1986. Ordained to ministry Bapt. Ch., 1985. Assoc. minister Leawood Bapt. Ch., Memphis, 1981-85; pastor Hickory Grove Bapt. Ch., Coldwater, Miss., 1985—; counselor Suicide and Crisis Intervention Ctr., Memphis, 1982-84; chaplain VA Hosp., Memphis, 1985. Instr. ARC, Ft. Smith, 1970-72; vol. St. Jude's Children's Research Hosp., Memphis, 1980; chaplain Memphis Fire Dept., 1983-84. Served to sgt. USMC, 1975-81. Recipient Letter of Appreciation Suicide and Crisis Intervention Ctr., 1984; named one of Outstanding Young Men of Am., 1985. Avocation: endurance athletics. Home and Office: Rt 4 Box 475 Coldwater MS 38618

LUDOLF, MARILYN MARIE KEATON, lay worker; b. Morganton, N.C., July 19, 1932; d. Charles Jefferson and Dora Esther (Whitener) Keaton; m. Edwin Forrest Ludolf, Dec. 22, 1957; children: David Forrest, Jonathan Charles. BA, Lenoir Rhyne, 1954. Youth worker Cen. Bapt. Ch., Greenville, S.C., 1964-71, Park Bapt. Ch., Rock Hill, S.C., 1958-64; with coll. students Becks Bapt. Ch., Winston Salem, N.C., 1971-89; lay worker singles Calvary Bapt. Ch., Winston Salem, 1989—; tchr. Winston-Salem/Forsyth County Sch. System, 1972—; youth seminar leader youth activities Park Bapt., Rock Hill, S.C.; youth-Sunday sch. Tng. Union-All areas of Ch. Work, Greenville, S.C.; pub. speaker, sem. leader. Contbr. to Guideposts and Bapt. publs. Pres. Old Town Woman's Club, Winston-Salem, 1975-77. Mem. Nat. Edn Assn., N.C. Edn. Assn., ASCD, Pub, Sch. Tchrs., Old Town Woman's Club (pres. 1975-77, Woman of Yr. 1977). Republican. Home: 3745 Whitehaven Rd Winston Salem NC 27106 Office: Old Richmond Sch 6315 Tobaccoville Rd Tobaccoville NC 27050 *Enjoy life. This is Not a Dress Rehearsal. It is a temporary assignment. We each choose our behavior daily. Choose life! The greatest decision I ever made was to let go and let God lead in my life!.*

LUDWIG, GLENN EDWARD, minister; b. Lancaster, Pa., Aug. 19, 1946; s. George Earl and Betty Jane (Rapp) L.; m. Beth Runk, Aug. 26, 1968 (div. Dec. 1982); children: Matthew Scott, Melissa Meredith; m. K. Estella Weiser, Aug. 19, 1983. BA, Susquehanna U., 1969; MDiv, Lancaster Theol. Sem., 1973. Ordained to ministry Luth. Ch. in Am., 1973. Pastor Washingtonville (Pa.) Luth. Parish, 1973-75; assoc. pastor St. Paul Luth. Ch., Hanover, Pa., 1975-80; chaplain Susquehanna U., Selinsgrove, Pa., 1980-85; sr. pastor 1st Luth. Ch., Elliott City, Mo., 1985—; chmn., bd. dirs., Luth. Youth Encounter, Mpls., 1978-88. Author: Building an Effective Youth Ministry, 1979, Keys to Building Youth Ministry, 1988, You Have Been Bought, 1988, (with others) Surviving in Ministry, 1990. Democrat. Home and office: 1st Luth Ch 3604 Chatham Rd Elliott City MO 21042

LUDWIG, JOHN, JR., elder. Moderator United Christian Ch., Cleona, Pa. Office: United Christian Ch 528 W Walnut St Cleona PA 17042*

LUDWIG, THEODORE MARK, religious studies educator; b. Oxford, Nebr., Sept. 28, 1936; s. Paul W. and Thekla (Friedrich) L.; m. Kathleen Plackemeier, June 26, 1960; children: Kevin, James, Gregory, Keith. BA, Concordia Sem., St. Louis, 1958, MDiv, 1961, ThD, 1963; PhD, U. Chgo., 1975. Ordained to ministry Luth. Ch., 1963. Missionary Japan Luth. Ch., 1963-67; prof. theology Valparaiso (Ind.) U., 1968—, chair dept. theology, 1988—. Author: The Sacred Paths: Understanding the Religions of the World, 1989; co-editor: Transitions and Transformations in the History of Religions, 1980; contbr. articles to profl. publs. Danforth Found. assoc., 1977—; NEH fellow, 1981-82; recipient Disting. Teaching award Valparaiso U. Alumni Assn., 1979. Mem. Am. Acad. Religion, Soc. Biblical Lit., Soc. Study Japanese Religion, Am. Schs. Oriental Rsch. Home: 506 Lafayette Valparaiso IN 46383 Office: Valparaiso U Dept Theology Valparaiso IN 46383

LUEBBERS, RITA MARY, religious education director; b. Burlington, Iowa, Jan. 11, 1956; d. Hans Dietrich and Maria Elizabeth (Rastetter) L. AA, Black Hawk Jr. Coll., 1976; BA, St. Ambrose Coll., 1978; M of Pastoral Studies, Loyola U., 1987. Cert. tchr., Ill. Vol. tchr. Sacred Heart Religious Edn., Moline, Ill., 1972-79, dir. religious edn., 1990—; religion tchr. Alleman High Sch., Rock Island, Ill., 1979-85, Notre Dame High Sch., Peoria, Ill., 1986-90; mem., speaker Teens Encounter Christ Program, Rock Island and Peoria, 1975—. Dist. outreach com. woman Anchor & Compass Clubs, 1990-91. Mem. Nat. Assn. Parish Coords. & Dirs. of Religious Edn., Ill. Parish Coords. & Dirs. of Religious Edn. Home: 1625 14th St Moline IL 61265 Office: Sacred Heart Ch 1608 13th St Moline IL 61265 *While many people doubt the existence of God, all I need to do is to look at events and circumstances occurring in my life to see God's hand at work guiding my life's journey.*

LUEBKE, MARTIN FREDERICK, retired curator; b. Concord, Wis., Oct. 2, 1917; s. Frederick John and Martha (Kretzmann) L.; m. Dorothy Lorraine Kutschinski, July 5, 1947; children: Judith, Charles. BS, Concordia Coll., 1941; MA, U. Mich., 1952; PhD, U. Ill., 1966; postdoctoral Cambridge U., 1974. Tchr. Our Savior Luth. Sch., Chgo., 1938-45; prin. Immanuel Luth. Sch., Grand Rapids, Mich., 1945-58; prof., dean. Concordia Theol. Sem., Springfield, Ill., 1958-76, Ft. Wayne, Ind., 1976-80; curator Saxon Luth. Meml., Frohna, Mo., 1980-86; asst. to pastor Chapel of the Cross-Luth., St. Louis, 1987—. Editor: Curriculum in Process, 1963; contbr. articles to profl. jours. Bd. dirs. Mich. Dist. Luth. Ch., Mo. Synod, 1957-58; mem. bd. parish edn. Luth. Ch., Mo. Synod, 1962-75; commr., sec. Perry County Tourism Commn., Perryville, Mo., 1983-86; bd. dirs. River Heritage Assn., Cape Girardeau, Mo., 1984-86. Faculty fellow Aid Assn. Luths., 1963, 73; recipient Outstanding Educators Am. award, 1972. Avocations: music, tour hosting. Home: 6507 Dolphin Circle Florissant MO 63033 *Success for me has meant that I be a visionary, a doer, an organizer and one who prays and has a passion for people and the faith that goals will be accomplished.*

LUECK, DWAYNE MARTIN, stewardship counselor; b. Shelbyville, Ill., May 23, 1953; s. Gilmore Arthur and Viola E. (Meyer) L.; m. Cheryl Lynn, Aug. 5, 1983; children: Alison Lynn, Benjamin Issac, Kimberly Anne. Grad., Concordia Coll., Milw., 1973; BA, Concordia Theol. Sem., 1975; MDiv, Concordia Sem., 1979. Pastor Trinity Luth. Ch., Martinsburg, Nebr., 1979-84, St. John Luth. Ch., Newcastle, Nebr., 1979-84; vacancy pastor St. Paul Luth Ch., Concord, Nebr., 1980-83; asst. pastor Redeemer Luth. Ch., Bartlesville, Okla., 1984-86, pastor, 1986-87; stewardship counselor North Wis. Dist. Luth. Ch., Wausau, 1987—. Co-author: (stewardship program) Back to Basics in Giving, 1989. Fireman Martinsburg Fire Dept., 1981-84. Office: North Wis Dist 3101 Seymour Ln Wausau WI 54401

LUEDDE, CHRISTOPHER SHRYOCK, Episcopal priest; b. St. Louis, May 25, 1951; s. Fullerton Woods Luedde and Jeanne Louise (Herring) Horner; m. Susan Marie Knowlton, Jan. 6, 1973; children: Carrie Marie, Shawn Fullerton. BA in Philosophy, Kans. U., 1973; MDiv, Pitts. Theol. Sem., 1976. Ordained diaconate Episcopal Ch., 1977, priest, 1977. Asst. rector North Lackawanna Parish, Carbondale, Pa., 1976-78; vicar St. Mark Ch., Bridgeport, Mich., 1978-85; assoc. rector Trinity Ch., Toledo, 1985-86, interim rector, 1986-87; rector St. Paul Episcopal Ch., Maumee, Ohio, 1987—; trustee Pitts. Theol. Sem., 1976-78; mem. coun. Diocese of Bethlehem (Pa.), 1976-78, Diocese of Ohio, Cleve., 1987-90. Trustee YMCA, Carbondale, 1977-78, Planned Parenthood of N.W. Ohio, Toledo, 1988-90; pres. bd. trustees East Side Soup Kitchen, Saginaw, Mich., 1984; mem. Sch. Improvement Coun., Maumee Sch. Dist., 1990—, Citizen's Adv. Bd. Toledo Mental Health Ctr., 1991—. Office: St Paul Episcopal Ch 310 Elizabeth St Maumee OH 43537

LUEHRMAN, KATHLEEN SUZANNE, church organist, sales representative; b. Lexington, Mo., Oct. 9, 1956; d. Vincent Francis and Laura Elizabeth (Snodgrass) Rosewell; m. Robert Kenneth Luehrman, Feb. 17, 1979; 1 child, Kristin Elizabeth. B in Music Edn., Cen. Mo. State U., 1979, cert. in vocal, 1990. Cert. instrumental and vocal tchr., Mo. Organist 1st Christian Ch., Lexington, 1973-84; tchr. Immaculate Conception Cath. Sch., Lexington, 1980-83; organist 1st Christian Ch., Odessa, Mo., 1984—; deacon 1st Christian Ch., Odessa, Mo., ž, 1988—; treas. 1st Christian Ch., Odessa, Mo., 1990—, dir. men's choir, 1987—; ind. sales agt. Mary Kay Cosmetics, Odessa, 1989—; counselor S.W. Area Ch. Camps, Branson, Mo., 1985-86. Mem. Lexington Bus. and Profl. Women, 1980-83; mem., v.p. Odessa Bus. and Profl. Women, 1983-88. Recipient Young Careerist award Odessa Bus. and Profl. Women, 1985, Area Young Careerist 2d pl. award Area Bus. and Profl. Women, 1985. Office: 1st Christian Ch 224 W Dryden Odessa MO 64076

LUEKING, FREDERICK DEAN, pastor; b. Kansas City, Mo., June 21, 1928; s. Fred C. and Tyra L. (Lloyd) L.; m. Beverly Ann Frano, Aug. 16, 1958; children: Ann Anderson, Christopher, Sarah, Joel. AA, St. John's Coll., 1947; MDiv, Concordia Sem., St. Louis, 1954; PhD, U. Chgo., 1960. Ordained to ministry Luth. Ch., 1954. Asst. pastor Grace Luth. Ch., River Forest, Ill., 1954-62, pastor, 1962—; bd. dirs. Christian Century Found., Chgo., Oak Park/River Forest Family Svc.; pres. Acad. Parish Clergy, Cleve., 1977-79. Author: Mission in the Making, 1968, Grace Under Pressure, 1979, Preaching: The Art of Connecting God & People, 1985, From Ashes to Holy Wind, 1989. Named Alumnus of Yr. U. Chgo., 1979. Mem. Acad. Parish Clergy (Disting. Svc. 1984), Optimist Club. Home and Office: 7300 W Division River Forest IL 60305

LUETCHENS, MELVIN HARVEY, minister, religious organization administrator; b. Murdock, Nebr., July 5, 1939; s. Herold Alvin and Ruth Lydia (Schroeder) L.; m. Jolane Jeanne Bakley, June 24, 1962; children: Brenton Todd, Shawn Curtis, Lara Sue. BA, Westmar Coll., 1961; MDiv, Garrett Evang. Sem., Evanston, Ill., 1964; MA in Counseling, U. Nebr., 1971, PhD, 1981. Ordained to ministry United Meth. Ch., 1964. Pastor Mira Valley United Meth. Ch., Ord, Nebr., 1964-67; assoc. minister, dir. Cornerstone Campus Ministries, Lincoln, Nebr., 1967-71, minister, dir., 1971-82; exec. sec. Interchurch Ministries of Nebr., Lincoln, 1982—; bd. ordained ministry Nebr. Conf. United Meth. Ch., 1975—. Mem. gov.'s task force on violence against women and children State of Nebr., 1984, gov.'s health promotion coordinating council State of Nebr., 1985—, mayor's long term care com. City of Lincoln, 1985-86, elderly housing options project state of Nebr., 1985, Nebr. Pantry Network, 1986; trustee Westmar Coll., LeMars, Iowa, 1978-82; bd. dirs. Child Guidance Ctr., Lincoln, 1983—. Mem. Nat. Assn. Ecumenical Staff. Republican. Lodge: Kiwanis. Avocations: gardening, racquetball, home and car repair. Home: 6311 Adams St Lincoln NE 68507 Office: Interchurch Ministeries 215 Centennial Mall S Rm 411 Lincoln NE 68508

LUFFMAN, DALE EDWARD, minister; b. Salem, Oreg., Mar. 8, 1947; s. Gordon Henry and Frances Edna (Claiborne) L.; m. Judith Kay Wirrick, Aug. 22, 1970; children: Aaron Edward, Micah David, Paul Richard. BA, Mt. Angel Coll., 1970; MEd, Lewis and Clark Coll., 1977; MA in Theol. Studies, Princeton Theol. Sem., 1986; postgrad., Pittsburgh Theol. Sem., 1989—. Ordained to ministry Reorganized LDS Ch., 1968. Pastor Reorganized LDS Ch., Woodburn, Oreg., 1970-72, Portland, Oreg., 1972-77; mem. regional staff N. Atlantic states Reorganized LDS Ch., Mt. Laurel,

N.J., 1979-85; judicatory exec. Reorganized LDS Ch., Kirtland, Ohio, 1986—; vice chair edn. com. Ecumenical Ministries Oreg., Portland, 1975-79; mem. adj. faculty Temple Sch., Independence, Mo., 1985—. Contbr. articles to religious jours.; book reviewer Saints Herald, 1991. Bd. dirs. Temple Grove Campgrounds Assn., Transfer, Pa., 1986—, Kirtland Pub. Libr., 1988—, Kirtland Area Svc. Coun., 1986—, Lake County Community Svc. Coun., Willoughby, 1989—; chair budget adv. com. human resources City of Portland, 1977-78; pres. Rose City Park Neighborhood Assn., Portland, 1976-77. Mem. Kirtland Clergy Assn., Kiwanis (dir. Kirtland club 1990—). Democrat. Home: 7809 Joseph St Kirtland OH 44094 Office: Reorganized LDS Ch 9017 Chillicothe Rd Kirtland OH 44094

LUGO, LUIS ROBERT, minister; b. Charlotte Amalie, Virgin Islands, Oct. 25, 1946; s. Philip and Carmen (Delilea) L.; m. Andrea Charlotte Grace, Jan. 28, 1966; children: Luis J.R., Kyle, Stephen, Robin, Michael, Mark. Student, Ala. Sch. of Religion, Sunset Sch. Preaching, 1968-71; BTh, Internat. Bible Sem., MTh, 1983. Instr. Bible Caribbean Christian Coll., Rio Piedras, P.R., 1971; minister Ch. of Christ, St. Croix, 1971-76, Chattanooga, Tenn., 1976-78, Valdosta, Ga., 1978-81, Tampa, Fla., 1981-89, Kansas City, Kans., 1980—; com. mem. Nat. Leadership Com., Kansas City, 1986—. Author: Pattern of New Testament Christianity, 1977, Homosexuality and Youth, 1979, Chronological Books of the Bible, 1980. Com. mem. Mayors Task Force on Police and Community, Tampa, 1985; exec. dir. Sickle Cell Found., St. Croix, 1972; pres. Toastmasters Assn., 1984. Named Outstanding Young Men Am., 1981. Republican. Office: Roswell Ch of Christ 2900 Roswell Ave Kansas City KS 66104-4075

LUHN, ROBERT DANIEL, pastor; b. Baker, Oreg., Oct. 25, 1948; s. Robert R. and Coralyn E. (Cook) L.; m. Kathleen L., Aug. 23, 1969; children: Jennifer, Elizabeth, Christina. BA, Northwest Nazarene Coll., 1970; Mdiv, Nazarene Theol. Sem., 1973. Ordained to ministry Nazarene Ch., 1980. Pastor Ch. of Nazarene, Yankton, S.D., 1973-75; asst. pastor Spokane (Wash.) Valley Nazarene, 1975-80; pastor Ch. of Nazarene, Othello, Wash., 1980—. Home: 825 Oak Othello WA 99344 Office: Ch of Nazarene 825 Ash Othello WA 99344

LUITHLY, DOUGLAS ERIC, lay worker; b. Burlington, Iowa, July 9, 1953; s. Lisle Lewis and Jeanette Eilene (Thornton) L. Student, Coe Coll., 1971-73, Iowa Wesleyan Coll., 1980-81, Aims Community Coll., 1983; AS, Colo. State U., 1983; postgrad., St. Thomas Sem., Denver, 1987-89; AA (hon.), Northland Pioneer Coll., Holbrook, Ariz., 1979. Electronic technician, customer svc. Colo. Memory Systems, Loveland, 1985—; mem. St. John's Religious Edn. Com., Loveland, 1987-89. Precinct capt., com. person Larimer County Dem. Party, Loveland, 1980—; mem. City of Loveland Constrn. Adv. Bd., 1986-91; chairperson City of Loveland Cable TB Adv. bd., 1988-91; stakeholder Agenda for the 90s, Loveland, 1991—; mem. Leadership Loveland, St. Elizabeth Ann Seton Social Concerns Com., Ft. Collins, Colo., 1990—, City-Wide Peace and Social Justice Coalition, Ft. Collins, 1990—. Mem. AFICCSE/Christian Singles in Action, Loveland (founding mem., pres. 1986-89). Home: 2527 SW 10th St Loveland CO 80537

LUJAN, PAUL HAROLD, clergyman; b. Las Vegas, N.Mex., Nov. 7, 1964; s. Frank Jr. and Virginia Esperanza (DeAragon) L. BA, N.Mex. Highlands U., 1987. Religion educator Our Lady of Sorrows Ch., Las Vegas, N.Mex., 1985-88; seminarian Mt. Angel (Oreg.) Sem., 1988-89; pastoral asst. Our Lady of Guadalupe Ch., Santa Fe, 1989—; dir. Religious Catechetical Instrn. of Adults Program, Santa Fe, 1989—; youth leader, Santa Fe, 1989—. Named Master Catechist Archdiocese of Santa Fe, 1988. Mem. Archdiocesan Religious Catechetical Instrn. of Adults Com., Pastoral Coun. Democrat. Office: Our Lady of Guadalupe Ch 417 Agua Fria St Santa Fe NM 87501

LUKE, CHARLES STANLEY, minister; b. Hahira, Ga., Dec. 10, 1952; s. Charles Vernon and Alma Ruth (Hughes) L.; m. Martha Dollar, Mar. 11, 1972; children: Kimberle, Kyle. BA, Luther Rice Sem., 1983, postgrad., 1984. Ordained to ministry So. Bapt. Conv., 1973. Minister Corinth Bapt. Ch., Lake Park, Ga., 1972-76, 81-90, Pleasant Way Bapt. Ch., Valdosta, Ga., 1976-77, Aenon Bapt. Ch., Tallahassee, 1977-81, Northside Bapt. Ch., Brunswick, Ga., 1990—; vol. chaplain South Ga. Med. Ctr., Valdosta, Ga., 1984-90; mem. Korean-Am. Crusade, Seoul, 1988. Mem. Valdosta Bapt. Assn. (chmn. evangelism com. 1985-88, moderator 1988-90). Democrat. Home: 22 Apache Rd Brunswick GA 31520 Office: Northside Bapt Ch 180 Chapel Crossing Rd Brunswick GA 31520

LUKER, MAURICE SYLVESTER, JR., religion educator; b. Louisville, June 4, 1934; s. Maurice Sylvester L. and Beatrice (Edlin) Hartley; m. Ann Johnson, Mar. 15, 1956 (dec. 1973); children: Maurice S. III, Amy Luker Cloud; m. Jean Knarr, Mar. 1, 1976; 1 child, Marc Anton. BA, So. Meth. U., Dallas, 1956; BD, Drew U., 1959; postgrad., U. Basle, Switzerland, 1960-61; PhD, Drew U., Madison, N.J., 1968. Assoc. min. Lakeside United Meth. Ch., Richmond, Va., 1961-62; min. Union City (N.J.) United Meth. Ch., 1962-64; instr. Upsala Coll., East Orange, N.J., 1963, Ohio Wesleyan U., Delaware, 1964-65; prof. religion Emory (Va.) & Henry Coll., 1965—; min. 7-Mile Ford/Mountain View United Meth. Chs., Chilhowee, Va., 1988-89, Charles Wesley United Meth. Ch., Abingdon, Va., 1990—; asst. field supr. Drew-McCormick Archaeol. Expedition to Shechem, Jordan, 1960; staff mem. Hebrew Union Coll. Archaeol. Expedition to Gezer, Israel, 1968; area supr. Joint Archaeol. Expedition to Tell El-Hesi, Israel, 1971, 73, 75, 77, Joint Archaeol. Expedition to Caesarea Maritima, Israel, 1984, 87. Author: The Figure of Moses in the Plague Traditions, 1968; contbr. articles and revs. to profl. jours. Mellon grantee, Mednick grantee. Mem. Am. Acad. Religion, Am. Schs. Oriental Rsch., Cath. Bibl. Soc., Soc. Bibl. Lit., Va. Conf. United Meth. Ch. Democrat. Avocations: archaeology, reading, tennis. Home: 216 Stonewall Heights Abingdon VA 24210 Office: Emory & Henry Coll Emory VA 24327

LULL, DAVID JOHN, association administrator; b. Mt. Kisco, N.Y., Oct. 14, 1944; s. John Vernon and Viola Dell (Hersey) L.; m. Karen Lee Cloyed, June 4, 1966. BA, Iowa Wesleyan Coll., 1966; BD with honors, So. Meth. U., 1969; PhD, Claremont Grad. Sch., 1978. Ordained to ministry United Meth. Ch., 1970. Min. Port Ewen (N.Y.) United Meth. Ch., 1969-71; lectr. Sch. Theology at Claremont, Calif., 1978-81; asst. prof. Yale Div. Sch., New Haven, 1981-84, assoc. prof., 1984-87; exec. dir. Soc. Bibl. Lit., Decatur, Ga., 1987—; trustee Scholars Press, Atlanta, 1987—. Author: Spirit in Galatia, 1980; (with others) Biblical Preaching on the Death of Jesus, 1980; contbr. articles to religious jours. Nat. Meth. Tuition scholar Iowa Wesleyan Coll., 1963; John Monroe Moore fellow Bd. Edn., United Meth. Ch., 1971, Dempster fellow, 1972; Conant Fund grantee Bd. Theol. Edn., Episcopal Ch., 1983, 86. Mem. Am. Acad. Religion, Am. Coun. Learned Socs. (del. 1987—), Nat. Humanities Alliance (del. 1987—), Soc. Bibl. Lit. Office: Soc Bibl Lit 1549 Clairmont Rd Ste 204 Decatur GA 30033-4635

LULL, TIMOTHY FRANK, theology educator; b. Fremont, Ohio, Apr. 8, 1943; s. Raymond Robert and Ruth Jane (Cole) L.; m. Mary-Carlton O'Neal, Aug. 23, 1969; children: Christopher R.C., Peter M.C. BA, Williams Coll., 1965; BD, Yale U., 1968, M in Philosophy, 1971, PhD, 1977. Teaching fellow Yale Div. Sch., New Haven, 1968-70, instr. pastoral theology, 1970-71; pastor Grace Luth. Ch., Needham, Mass., 1972-77; asst. prof. systematic theology Luth. Theol. Sem., Phila., 1977-83, assoc. prof., 1983-86, prof., 1986-89; acad. dean, prof. systematic theology Pacific Luth. Theol. Sem., Berkeley, Calif., 1989—; teaching pastor Harvard Divinity Sch., Cambridge, Mass., 1973-77; cons. Nat. Humanities Faculty, Concord, Mass., 1974-79; vis. lectr. Stonehill Coll., North Easton, Mass., 1976; vis. scholar St. Edmund's Coll., Cambridge, Eng., 1983-84, 87; core doctoral faculty Grad. Theol. Union, Berkeley, 1990—, chairperson Coun. of Deans. Author: Called to Confess Christ, 1980, (with others) Views from the Pews, 1983, Lutherans in Ecumenical Dialogue, 1990; editor: Martin Luther's Basic Theological Writings, 1989 (Religious Book Club award, 1990). Mem. Am. Acad. Religion, Anglican Luth. Soc., Soc. Christian Ethics, Soc. Values in Higher Edn., Williams Club, N.Y.C. Democrat. Avocations: Brit. and Am. fiction, hiking. Home: 905 Creston Rd Berkeley CA 94708 Office: Pacific Luth Theol Sem 2770 Marin Ave Berkeley CA 94708

LUMENTA, D. J., religious organization administrator. Chmn. Protestant Ch. in Indonesia, Jakarta. Office: Protestant Ch, Jalan Medan, Merdeka Timur 10, Jakarta-Pusat Indonesia*

LUN, SEAHAWK, minister; b. Hong Kong, Mar. 27, 1956; came to U.S., 1974; s. Tin-On and Anna Y. (Lai) L.; m. Betty Pui-chun Hui, Dec. 29, 1979; children: Lydia, Joshua. BSME, U. Houston, 1978; M. Theology, Dallas Theol. Sem., 1982. Ordained to ministry Christian and Missionary Alliance Ch., 1985. Interim pastor Dallas Chinese Bible Ch., 1981-82, asst. pastor, 1982-83; pastor Grace Chinese Alliance Ch., Walnut Creek, Calif., 1983-87; asst. pastor L.A. Chinese Alliance Ch., 1987—; pres. Southwestern State Chinese Christian Student Assn., Denton, Tex., 1981. Contbr. articles to Christian mags., 1982—. Mem. Evang. Tchr. Assn. (Tchrs. Diploma 1982). Office: LACAC 2828 Glendale Blvd Los Angeles CA 90039 *Christianity is not for fence-sitters. Once rescued from sin's penalty by faith in Christ, the believer enters an engaging, transforming relationship with God that should be marked with unparalleled intensity and zeal. God gave His all to save us. In return, without coercion, He asks us to love Him with all of our heart, soul and mind, to serve Him cheerfully and wholeheartedly, to worship Him with grateful fervor.*

LUNCEFORD, JOE ELBERT, religion educator; b. Slate Springs, Miss., Jan. 20, 1937; s. Elbert Elmore and Clara Emma (West) L.; m. Ora Lea McLeod, May 27, 1960; children: William Taylor, James Kenneth. BA, Miss. Coll., 1962; BD, New Orleans Bapt. Theol. Sem., 1966; PhD in N.T., Baylor U., 1979. Ordained to ministry So. Bapt. Conv., 1960. Commd. 1st lt. USAF, 1966, advanced through grades to capt., 1968; separated, 1975; pastor Pleasant Grove Bapt. Ch., Rosebud, Tex., 1975-81; asst., assoc. prof. Georgetown (Ky.) Coll., 1981—; res. chaplain USAFR, 1975—. Contbr. articles to profl. jours. Col. USAFR, 1990—. Mem. Soc. Bibl. Lit., Nat. Assn. Bapt. Prof. Religion, Res. Officers Assn. Home: 1088 Graves Pike Stamping Ground KY 40379 Office: Georgetown Coll Box 77 Georgetown KY 40324

LUND, ERIC, religion educator; b. New Haven, Sept. 6, 1948; s. Gunnar and Kathryn Marie (Ibsen) L.; m. Cynthia Wales, Aug. 24, 1974; children: Karsten, Hannah. BA, Brown U., 1970; MDiv, Yale U., 1974, MA, MPhil, 1977, PhD, 1979. Asst. prof. dept. religion St. Olaf Coll., Northfield, Minn., 1979-85, assoc. prof., 1986—. Contbr. articles to profl. publs. Mem. Am. Acad. Religion, Am. Soc. Ch. History, 16th Century Studies Assn., Medieval Acad. Am., Phi Beta Kappa (officer local Minn. chpt. 1979—). Home: 202 S Lincoln St Northfield MN 55057 Office: St Olaf Coll Northfield MN 55057

LUNDBOM, JACK RUSSELL, religion educator; b. Chgo., July 10, 1939; s. C. Russell and Dorothy (Ohlson) L.; m. Linda Larson, Aug. 15, 1964; children: David, Jean. BA, Mich. State U., East Lansing, 1961; postgrad., Am. U. Beirut, Lebanon, 1964-65; BD, North Park Theol. Sem., Chgo., 1967; PhD, Grad. Theol. Union, Berkeley, 1973. Ordained to ministry Evang. Covenant Ch., 1979. Pastor Thomaston (Conn.) Covenant Ch., 1982-88; prof. Old Testament Yale Div. Sch., New Haven, 1983; sr. Fulbright prof. U. Marburg, Fed. Republic Germany, 1989-90; vis. prof. Old Testament Uppsala (Sweden) U., 1990-91; mem. Boston Marathon Clergy Com., Hopkington, Mass., 1981-82; Fulbright lectr. Leeds U., Sheffield U., Manchester U., Durham U., Uppsala U., 1989; asst. prof. U. Calif., Berkeley; vis. prof. Andover Newton Theol. Sch., Newton Centre, Mass.; vis. scholar Harvard Div. Sch. Author: Jeremiah: A Study in Ancient Hebrew Rhetoric, 1975; contbr. articles to Theol. Dictionary of the Old Testament, Anchor Bible Dictionary, also to profl. jours. Mem. bd. Emanuel Hosp., Turlock, Calif., 1979-80. Am.-Scandinavian Found. fellow, Uppsala U., 1990-91; NEH grantee Cambridge U., Eng., 1991-92. Mem. Soc. Bibl. Lit., Cath. Bibl. Assn. Mem. Evang. Covenant Ch. Home: 5254 N Spaulding Ave Chicago IL 60625

LUNDGREN, LAWRENCE ELMER, pastor; b. Coudersport, Pa., Jan. 2, 1952; s. LeRoy Laurence and Dorothy Elaine (McLaughlin) L.; m. Deborah Louise Mott, June 15, 1974; children: Lara, Lorelle. BA magna cum laude, Houghton Coll., 1973; MDiv, Asbury Theol. Sem., 1976; DMin, Drew U., 1984. Assoc. pastor Kidder Meml. United Meth. Ch., Jamestown, N.Y., 1976-78; sr. pastor Alexander/Darien United Meth. Ch., Alexander, N.Y., 1979—; dir., mentor program Bd. of Ordained Ministry, WNY Conf., 1989. Pres., dir. Regional Action Phone, Batavia, N.Y., 1986-89; pres. Alexander Cen. Sch. Bd. Edn., 1987—. Mem. Western Genesee Ministerial Assn., Theta Phi. Democrat. Methodist. Avocations: camping, computers, watching birds of prey. Home and Office: Alexander/Darien United 10540 Main St Alexander NY 14005-0235

LUNDGREN, MARK DAVID, church music director, educator; b. Saginaw, Mich., Nov. 22, 1958; s. Albert L. and Ruth Ann (Haist) L.; m. Rita L. Haubner, June 26, 1982; 1 child, Sarah K. BA, Albion Coll., 1979; MusM, Ea. Ky. U., 1981; postgrad., U. Ga., 1985-87. Cert. tchr., Mich. Dir. music Trinity United Presbyn. Ch., Paramus, N.J., 1982-83; organist, dir. Christian edn. 1st Christian Ch., Athens, Ga., 1985-87; dir. music 1st Bapt. Ch., Saginaw, 1989—; tchr. Saginaw Sch. Dist., 1987—; reviewer Choral Jour., Am. Music Tchr. Mem. Fellowship Am. Bapt. Musicians, Am. Choral Dirs. Assn., Am. Guild Organists, Music Educators Nat. Conf., Fellowship Christian Athletes, Phi Mu Alpha Sinfonia. Republican. Baptist. Office: 1st Bapt Ch Saginaw 322 N Jefferson Ave Saginaw MI 48607 *When we spend time praising the Lord, He will bring us into a closer relation with His love.*

LUNDGREN, ROBERT ALLEN, clergyman; b. Pitts., May 19, 1957; s. George Allen and Leona Mae (Dorcon) L.; m. Dolores Barbara Cosenza, Mar. 9, 1957; children: John Michael, Jessica Lee, Rachel Joy. BS in Chem. Engring., U. Pitts., 1979; ThM, Dallas Theol. Sem., 1986. Ordained to ministry Evang. Free Ch., 1986. Pastor, ch. planter, counselor East Suburban Evang. Free Ch., Penn Hills, Pa., 1988—; club dir. high sch. youth Christian Youth Crusade, Pitts., 1978-79; Bible tchr. Boys Brigade, Brainard Ave. Bapt. Ch., Chgo., 1979-81; Sunday sch. tchr. coll. age Moss Bluff (La.) Bible Ch., 1981-83; summer missionary to El Salvador, Iglesia Nazareth, San Salvador, 1983. Telephone crisis counselor Dallas Crisis Counseling Ctr., Dallas, 1988. Mem. Nat. Right to Life. Republican. Home: 169 Everglade Dr Pittsburgh PA 15235 *My motivation for ministry is that "God is able to manifest His glory and might through my manifold imperfections." (2 Corinthians 4:7).*

LUNDSTROM, LOWELL, academic administrator. Pres. Trinity Bible Coll., Ellendale, N.D. Office: Trinity Bible Coll 50 6th Ave S Ellendale ND 58436*

LUNSFORD, DONALD WAYNE, clergyman; b. Boss, Mo., Apr. 26, 1938; s. Donald Arthur and Aileen (Nelson) L.; m. Beverly Ann Stratemeyer, July 31, 1960; children—Mark Dwayne, Angela Dawn. Student Southwestern U., 1955-58, Pioneer Theol. Sem., 1958-60. Ordained to ministry Ill. Dist. Assemblies of God Ch., 1957, Gen. Council of Assemblies of God, 1961. Founding pastor Assemblies of God Ch., Evansville, Ind., 1960-63, 1st Assembly of God Ch., Colorado Springs, 1971-80, Clearwater, Fla., 1980—; evangelist Assemblies of God, Springfield, Mo., 1963-71; asst. dist. supt. Rocky Mountain dist. Assemblies of God., 1978-80; gen. presbyter Gen. Council Assemblies of God, 1978-80, 88—; asst. dist. supt. Peninsular Fla. Dist., Lakeland, 1988—, exec. presbyter, 1983-88. Contbr. articles to religious jours. Home: 1739 S Greenwood Ave Clearwater FL 34616

LUNZ, ELISABETH, minister; b. Charleston, S.C., Apr. 16, 1939; d. George Robert and Elsie (Melchers) L.; m. Manfred Eugen Hoffmann, Jan. 6, 1983; stepchildren: Christopher Andrew, Joanne Marie. BA, Agnes Scott Coll., 1960; MA, Duke U., 1961; PhD, Tulane U., 1969; MDiv, Interdenominational Theol. Ctr., Atlanta, 1980. Ordained to ministry Presbyn. Ch. (U.S.A.), 1980. Staff assoc. women's office Presbyn. Ch. (U.S.A.), Atlanta, 1980-83, assoc. women's ministry unit, 1988—; stated clk., assoc. exec. Synod of South, Atlanta, 1983-87; interim pastor 1st Presbyn. Ch., Cohutta, Ga., 1987-88; mem. coun. Greater Atlanta Presbytery, 1988—; program coord. Joint Commn. for Women's Concerns, Atlanta, 1990-91; scholar in residence Candler Sch. Theology, Emory U., 1977-78. Co-editor: Voices of Experience, 1991. Woodrow Wilson fellow, 1960; NEH summer scholar, 1976. Mem. Am. Acad. Religion, Nat. Assn. Parliamentarians, Huntington's Disease Soc. Am. (bd. dirs. Ga. chpt. 1991—), Phi Beta Kappa. Office: Presbyn Ch USA SE Regional Office 159 Ralph McGill Blvd Rm 411 Atlanta GA 30308 *Power, love and wisdom are qualities which patriarchal culture denies to women. Power, love and wisdom are vital aspects of the feminist experience of God to be reclaimed and shared with the global community.*

LUONUANSUU, JAMES GREGORY, telecommunications administrator, youth minister; b. Warren, Ohio, June 6, 1966; s. Louis Henry Luonuansuu and Lauralee (Villers) Baughman. Student, U. Bibl. Studies, 1990—. Youth min. Ch. of Christ, Windham, Ohio, 1987-90; office mgr. Valley Telecom Inc., Warren, 1988—. Democrat. Home: 722 Laird Ave SE Warren OH 44484 Office: Valley Telecom Inc 1227 Youngstown Rd SE Warren OH 44484

LURIE, SUSAN SHEILA GALITZER, religious organization administrator; b. N.Y.C., May 9, 1948; d. Louis and Estelle (Kellerman) Galitzer; m. Michael Lurie, June 21, 1969; children: Jacqueline K., Erica I. BA, Lehman Coll., 1969; MA, Hunter Coll., 1973. Cert. primary sch. educator, N.Y. Tchr., head program for 4 yr. olds. Larchmont (N.Y.) Temple Nursery Sch., 1978-87; Sunday sch. tchr. Larchmont Temple, 1982-87; dir.nursery sch. Bronx House (N.Y.) Jewish Community Ctr., 1987-89; agy. program dir. Bronx (N.Y.) House, Jewish Community Ctr., 1989—. Bd. dirs. Larchmont Temple Youth, 1984-87, Performing Arts Curriculum Experience Parents Com., Mamaroneck (N.Y.) High Sch., 1987—; mem. Early Childhood Com., Larchmont Temple, 1990—. Mem. United Jewish Appeal/Fedn. Jewish Philanthrophies (subcom. on early childhood 1988—), Early Childhood Dirs. Group (chairperson 1988—), Assn. Jewish Ctr. Profls. (exec. com. 1990—, Excellence in Svc. award 1989, 91), Jewish Early Childhood Assn., Early Childhood Edn. Coun. Home: 5 Leafy Ln Larchmont NY 10538 Office: Bronx House Jewish Community Ctr 990 Pelham Pkwy S Bronx NY 10461

LUSTIGER, JEAN-MARIE CARDINAL, archbishop of Paris; b. Paris, Sept. 17, 1926; s. Charles and Gisèle Lustiger. Ed. U. Paris, Sorbonne and Carmelite Sem., Inst. Catholique de Paris. Ordained priest Roman Catholic Ch., 1954. Chaplain to students Sorbonne, 1954-69; dir. Centre Richelieu, 1959-69; pastor Sainte-Jeanne-de-Chantal parish, Paris, 1969-79; consecrated bishop, 1979; bishop of Orléans, 1979-81; archbishop of Paris, 1981—; elevated to cardinal, 1983. Author: Sermons d'un curé de Paris, 1978; Pain de vie, Peuple de Dieu, 1981; Osez croire/Osez vivre, 1985; Premiers pas dans la prière, 1986, Six sermons aux élus de la Nation, 1987, Le Choix de Dieu, 1987, La Messe, 1988, Le sacrement de l'Onction des malades, 1990, Dieu merci, les droits de l'homme, 1990, Nous avons rendez-vous avec l'Europe, 1991. Address: Maison diocésaine, 8, rue de la Ville-l'Evêque, 75384 Paris France

LUTER, ASA BOYD, JR., educator; b. Dallas, July 10, 1949; s. Asa Boyd Sr. and Ann (Williams) L.; m. Catherine Lichtenwalter, June 12, 1977; children: Joanna, Natalie, Timothy. BS, Miss. State U., 1971; ThM, Dallas Theol. Sem., 1976; ThD, Dallas Sem. Grad. Sch., 1985. Dean of students, instr. in bible and history Crichton Coll., Memphis, 1976-77; sr. pastor Ch. in the Valley, Canyon Lake, Tex., 1977-83; asst. prof. bible and theology Le Tourneau Coll., Longview, Tex., 1983-84; sr. pastor Christ Presbyn. Ch., San Antonio, 1984-87; assoc. prof. of bible Talbot Sch. Theology, Biola U., La Mirada, Calif., 1988—; adj. prof. N.T., Golden Gate Bapt. Sem., So. Calif. Campus, Brea, 1992. Contbr. articles to profl. jours., bible dictionaries, commentaries, study bibles. 1st lt. U.S. Army, 1971-76. Named Outstanding Young Men of Am., U.S. Jaycees, 1985; rsch. grantee Biola U., 1988-89, 91. Fellow Inst. Bibl. Rsch.; mem. Evang. Theol. Soc. (regional office 1983-88, nat. com. 1983), Soc. Bibl. Lit. Republican. Home: 28672 Tomelloso Mission Viejo CA 92692 Office: Biola U Talbot Sch Theology 13800 Biola Ave La Mirada CA 90639 *As faith walks through the stretching circumstances of life, there is daily a full measure of the amazing and the amusing, if you will simply open your eyes.*

LUTHER, DALE EUGENE, minister; b. Millington, Ill., Jan. 3, 1932; s. Harry Eugene and Mary (Eichelberger) L.; m. Catherine Bruce, Sept. 5, 1954 (div. Aug. 1977); children: Bruce, Flora, Terry, Perry, Scott, Glen; m. Diane Penelope Dueball, Dec. 30, 1977. AA, Kendall Coll., 1951; BA, Nebr. Wesleyan U., 1953; ThM, Iliff Sch. Theology, Denver, 1956. Ordained to ministry Meth. Ch. as elder, 1958. Pastor Willard United Meth. Ch., Oak Park, Ill., 1981-84, United Meth. Ch., Seneca, Ill., 1984-89, Franklin Grove (Ill.) United Meth. Ch., 1989-90, Harmon (Ill.) United Meth. Ch., 1990—; chaplain Katherine Shaw Bethea Hosp., Dixon, Ill., 1990—; dir. United Protestant Youth, Lockport, Ill., 1964-66; condr. mission tour United Meth. Ch., Ottawa, Ill., 1985-87, ch. builder, Seneca, 1985-89. Contbr. articles to Vantage Point, 1982-88; composer cantata Come, Rejoice With Us. Organizer Chem. People, Seneca, 1985, Survivors of Suicide, Dixon, 1991; bd. mem. Ill. Drug Ednl. Alliance, 1984-89; chmn. Am. Cancer Soc., Jo Daviess County, Ill., 1979-81. Recipient Alumni Svc. award Kendall Coll., 1964. Fellow Nat. Assn. Ch. Bus. Adminstrs.; mem. Coll. Chaplains. Home: 1038 S Peoria Ave Dixon IL 61021 *In a world where the spirit of the mysterious realm seems to be so powerful, there is that Creator who has given all life, that is still in charge and wherein victory and fulfillment is found. If not, wherein lies life and that grace that is so basic for the ones called Christians?.*

LUTHER, JAMES BORDEN, priest, counselor; b. Terre Haute, Ind., Sept. 20, 1960; s. Stephen Grinnell and Marjorie (Schwarz) L. BA in Psychology, Purdue U., 1981, MS in Counseling, 1983; MDiv, U. Notre Dame, 1985; postgrad. in counseling psychology, Indiana U., 1990—. Ordained priest Roman Catholic Ch., 1986; cert. counselor. Counselor St. Mary's Coll., South Bend, Ind., 1982-84; pre-marital counselor U. Notre Dame, South Bend, Ind., 1984-85; assoc. pastor Blessed Sacrament Ch., W. Lafayette, Ind., 1985-89. Contbr. articles to profl. jours. Mem. Am. Assn. for Counseling and Devel. (software reviewer 1987-89)., Am. Psychol. Assn. (student mem.). Avocations: motorcycling, running. Home: 718 Woodbridge Dr Bloomington IN 47408 Office: Bishop's Office PO Box 260 Lafayette IN 47902

LUTHY, DAVID, religious organization contact. Corr. Old Order Amish Ch., Aylmer, Ont., Can. Office: Old Order Amish Ch, Pathaway Pub/Rte 4, Aylmer, ON Canada N5H 2R3*

LUTTON, JOHN V., minister; b. Muncie, Ind., July 13, 1939; s. Oliver M. and Doris Rosemary (Chancellor) L.; m. Johnetta Adams, Aug. 6, 1962; children: Rebecca Kay Lutton Stout, John V. Jr. Student, Olivet Nazarene Coll. Ordained to ministry Ch. of the Nazarene, 1974. Pastor Ch. of the Nazarene, Cowan, Ind., 1966-69, Anderson, Ind., 1969-73, Ligonier, Ind., 1973—. Mem. Ligonier City Coun., 1988—; pres. Ligonier Bd. Works and Pub. Safety, 1989—; dep. Noble County Sheriff's Dept., Albion, Ind., 1984—. With USN, 1957-61. Mem. N. Am. Assn. Ventriloquists. Republican. Home: 100 W Miller St Ligonier IN 46767 Office: Ch of the Nazarene 100 W Miller St Ligonier IN 46767

LUTTRELL, RUTH, religious organization executive; b. Lakewood, Ohio, Aug. 22, 1926; d. John Martin and Ann (Milan) Tidik; m. Donald D. Luttrell, Feb. 24, 1946 (dec. May 1987); children: Janet L., David John, Donna Jean. Student, Bapt. Bible Inst., Cleve., 1944-46, Lakewood Bus. Sch., 1944-46, Bob Jones U., 1946. Co-founder Calvary Evang. Mission, Inc./Sta. WIVV, San Juan, P.R., 1952—, Calvary Evang. Mission, Inc./Sta. WBMJ, San Juan, 1985—; sec.-treas. Calvary Evang. Mission, Inc., 1957-86, pres., 1987—; rep. Child Evangelism Fellowship Internat., Vieques Island, P.R., 1952-56; bd. dirs. Palmas Community Ch., Humacao, P.R., 1980. Mem. editorial staff: New Life Bible Correspondence School, 1960, God's Great Commission and You, 1971. Recipient Outstanding Civic award Mcpl. Govt. Vieques Island and Santurce, 1956, 70, 73, 89, Hurrican Hugo Svc. award Govt. of P.R., 1990. Mem. Nat. Religious Broadcasters (bd. dirs. N.J. chpt. 1987—, English coord. Caribbean chpt. 1987—, Pioneer Broadcaster in Caribbean award 1988,, Missionary Leadership in Caribbean Communications award 1989, Pioneer Broadcaster in Caribbean award U.S. Hispanic div. 1988), Nat. Assn. Evangelicals, Evang. Assn. of Missions Agys., Radio Broadcasters Assn. P.R., Disusiones Inter-Americanas, Navy League, Christian Women's Club, Christian and Profl. Women's Club (area rep. 1991—). Home and Office: Calvary Evang Mission Inc 1409 Ponce de Leon 4th Fl San Juan PR 00907

LUTZ, ANNA DEPPEN, minister; b. Dalmatia, Pa., Mar. 19, 1929; d. Raymond and Helen (Hepner) Deppen; m. Earlin Harold Lutz, June 11, 1950; children: Rebecca Ann, Earlin David. BA, Cedar Crest Coll., 1950; MDiv, Moravian Sem., 1970. Ordained to ministry United Ch. of Christ, 1970. Dir. Christian edn. 1st United Ch. of Christ, Quakertown, Pa., 1964-70, min. Christian edn., 1970-91, co-pastor, 1991—; mem. Quakertown Ministerium, 1970—, pres., 1975-87; chmn. Christian edn. Pa. W/e. Conf. United Ch. of Christ, 1968-76, vice moderator, 1976-78, moderator, 1978-80, chmn. Div. Ch. and Ministry, 1988-91; instr. Christian Edn. Moravian Sem., 1971-74. Contbr. articles, poems, sermons, devotional materials to mags. in field. Trustee Cedar Crest Coll., 1980-83, Lancaster Sem., 1979-91. Mem. United Ch. Bd. for World Ministries (staff and salary com. 1978-81, chmn. world svc. strategy com., 1978-91), Alumni Assn. Moravian Sem. (organizing bd. 1971-71, 1980-83, pres. 1982-83), Quakertown Women's Club (sec. 1966-68), Order of Eastern Star. Home: 332 Park Ave PO Box 437 Quakertown PA 18951-0437 Office: 4th and Park Ave PO Box 437 Quakertown PA 18951-0437

LUTZ, EARLIN HAROLD, minister; b. Snyders, Pa., Aug. 1, 1928; s. Norman Charles and Evelyn (Kistler) L.; m. Anna Lucinda Deppen, June 11, 1950; children: Rebecca Ann, Earlin David. BA, Muhlenberg Coll., 1949; BDiv, Lancaster Sem., 1951; MST, Temple U., 1953, DST, 1958. Ordained to ministry United Ch. of Christ, 1951. Pastor Tremont (Pa.) Charge United Ch. of Christ, 1950-55, Trinity United Ch. of Christ, Norristown, Pa., 1955-61, First United Ch. of Christ, Quakertown, Pa., 1961—; bd. dirs. Pa. S.E. conf. United Ch. of Christ, Collegeville, chmn. div. ch. and ministry, chmn. budget and fin., chmn. conf. ctr. bldg. com. Chmn. Bucks County Redevel. Auth., Doylestown, Pa., Bucks County Housing Authority; pres. Quakertown Community Sch. Bd.; mem., pres. Quakertown Community Hosp.; bd. dirs. LifeQuest Health Care System, Quakertown. Fulbright scholar U. Tuebingen, 1953-54. Mem. Rotary (chaplain), Masons (32d degree). Republican. Home: 332 Park Ave PO Box 437 Quakertown PA 18951-0437

LUTZ, LOMA LEE, minister; b. Downy, Calif., Feb. 11, 1946; d. Edward Hughston and Lucille (Kirk) Castine; m. Samuel Lee Sullivan, Jan. 27, 1968 (div. June 1983); children: Denni Jo, Lee Eric.; m. Johnnie Paul Lutz, Aug. 15, 1984. BA in Religion and Religious Edn., Phillips U., Enid, Okla., 1968; postgrad., Houston Grad. Sch. Theology, Houston, 1988-91. Ordained to ministry Christian Ch. (Disciples of Christ), 1991. Youth dir., Christian edn. dir. First Christian Ch., Edmond, Okla., 1968-71; ch. sec., children's worker First Christian Ch., Huntsville, Tex., 1972-75; program coordinator Grandperson's Ctr., Huntsville, 1977-79; program dir. ARC, Huntsville, 1982-84, Jefferson St. United Meth. Ch., Natchez, Miss., 1986-88; assoc. min., dir. urban ministries program Iglesia Cristiana El Redentor, Houston, 1989—; asst. min. 1st Christian Ch., Katy, Tex., 1990-91; youth coord. Natchez Cluster United Meth. Ch., 1987-88. Editor: (newsletters) Good News, 1989-90, Connections, 1989-90. Mem. Christian Educators Fellowship of United Meth. Ch., Assn. Christian Ch. Educators. Republican. Lodge: Order Ea. Star. Avocations: music, sewing, clowning. Home: 10910 Gulf Frwy # 287 Houston TX 77034 Office: Iglesia Cristiana El Redentor 8811 Frey Rd Houston TX 77034 also: 1st Christian Ch 22101 Morton Ranch Rd PO Box 5328 Katy TX 77449 *How one interprets lifes ups and down depends largely upon ones concept of and relationship with God. I work at keeping a personal and constant relationship with a loving and gracious God.*

LUXA, MARCEY, ecumenical agency administrator. Adminstrv. sec. Chs. United Inc., Cedar Rapids, Iowa. Office: Chs United Inc 222 29th St SE Cedar Rapids IA 52403*

LUXEMBURG, JACK ALAN, rabbi; b. Feb. 16, 1949; s. Milton Irwin and Bernice Esther (Adler) L.; m. Barbara Elaine Etkind, June 15, 1975; children: Daniel, Michael. BA, Trinity Coll., 1970; MA in Hebrew Letters, Hebrew Union Coll., 1973; D of Ministry, Wesley Theol. Sem., 1987. Ordained rabbi, 1976. Rabbi intern B'nai B'rith Hillel at Ohio State U., Columbus, Ohio, 1973-74; regional dir. Hashachar/Young Judaea, Cin., 1972-75; student rabbi Temple Ahavat Shalom, Coriopolis, Pa., 1975-76; assoc. rabbi Main Line Reform Temple, Wynnewood, Pa., 1976-81; rabbi Temple Beth Ami, Rockville, Md., 1981—; bd. dirs. Jewish Social Svc. Agy., Rockville, United Jewish Appeal Fedn., Greater Washington Charles E. Smith Jewish Day Sch., Rockville; exec. com. mem. Jewish Community Council of Greater Washington, 1985-87. Mem. Montgomery County (Md.) Civil Rights Minority Group, 1988, Inter-Religious Com. on Drug Abuse, Montgomery County, 1989; bd. dirs. Washington Area Community Investment Fund, Washington, 1988-89; mem. Citizens Adv. Council Montgomery County (Md.) Sch. Bd., 1981-83. Recipient leadership award Am. Jewish Congress, 1988; Rabbinic Honoree, Coun. of Jewish Fedn., 1991. Mem. Nat. Rabbinical Cabinet of United Jewish Appeal (exec. com. 1986—), Am. Jewish Congress (regional pres. 1987—, nat. governing coun. 1987—), Cen. Conf. Am. Rabbis (regional pres. 1990—, nat. exec. com. 1990—), Washington Bd. Rabbis (v.p. 1989—). Office: Temple Beth Ami 800 Hurley Ave Rockville MD 20850 *Few things are complete in themselves. Words require deeds; action requires purpose. Knowledge requires understanding; intellect requires soul. Individuality requires community; life requires love. Only in the service of the sacred do all things find Shalom—wholeness and peace.*

LYDEN, JOHN C., educator; b. Seattle, Jan. 13, 1959; s. Waldo B. and Corinne B. (Jarandson) L.; m. Elizabeth I. Ruby, Aug. 4, 1985. BA, Wesleyan U., 1981; MA, Yale U., 1983; PhD, U. Chgo., 1989. Vis. asst. prof. Albion (Mich.) Coll., 1989-91; asst. prof. Dana Coll., Blair, Nebr., 1991—. Leo Baeck Inst. fellow, 1989. Mem. Am. Acad. Religion. Office: Dana Coll Blair NE 68008

LYDOLPH, DONALD JOSEPH, deacon; b. Fairfield, Iowa, July 9, 1945; s. Paul Edward and Martha Lee (Newcomb) L.; m. Jane Selovich, July 5, 1969; children: Amy Sue, Wendy Marie, Martha Jean. Ordained deacon Roman Cath. Ch., 1981. Religion educator St. Dominic, Sheboygan, Wis., 1968—, religious edn. coord., 1976-79, high sch. coord., 1981-82; permanent deacon Archdiocese Milw., 1981—; supr. Kohler (Wis.) Co., 1968—; night chaplain St. Nicholas Hosp., Sheboygan, 1981-91. Sgt. USMC, 1963-68, Vietnam. Mem. Cath. Knights Club. Democrat. Home: 2317 Knoos Ct Sheboygan WI 53083

LYKE, JAMES PATTERSON, bishop; b. Chgo., Feb. 18, 1939. A.B. in Philosophy, Quincy (Ill.) Coll., 1963; M.Div. in Theology, St. Joseph Sem., Teutopolis, Ill., 1967; Th.D., Union Grad. Sch., Cin., 1981. Joined Order Friars Minor, Roman Cath. Ch., 1959, ordained priest, 1966, consecrated bishop, 1979. Tchr. religion Padua Franciscan High Sch., Parma, Ohio, 1966-67; adminstr. Father Bertrand Elem. Sch., Memphis, 1968-69; pastor St. Thomas Ch., Memphis, 1969-77, Ch. of St. Benedict the Black, 1977-79; also dir. Newman Center, Grambling (La.) State U., 1977-79; aux. bishop Diocese of Cleve., 1979-90, also Episcopal vicar for urban region; apostolic adminstr. Archdiocese Atlanta, 1990—; Mem. denominational execs. Interch. Council Greater Cleve., race relations com. Greater Cleve. Roundtable. Coord. Black Cath. Hymnal; contbr. articles to religious jours., book chpts. Recipient Martin Luther King Jr. awar St. Benedict the Black Sch., 1980, Ann. Gold Medallion award Black Cath. Ministries and Laymen Coun., Diocese of Pitts., 1980, Man of Yr. award Nat. Assn. Negro Bus. and Profl. Women's Club, 1981, Martin Luther King Jr. award Diocese of Newark, 1986, others. Mem. NAACP, Nat. Conf. Cath. Bishops (migration com., black liturgy subcom. of bishops com. on liturgy), U.S. Cath. Conf., Nat. Black Cath. Clergy Conf., Ohio Cath. Conf., Urban League, So. Poverty Law Center, Bread for the World, Nat. Black Evangelist Assn., Pax Christi U.S.A., Nat. Black Cath. Clergy Caucus (pres. 1977-79), Pontifical Coun. COR UNUM. Lodges: Knights St. Peter Claver, K.C. (4th deg.). Address: 680 W Peachtree St NW Atlanta GA 30308

LYLE, W. W., bishop. Bishop, pres. The Reformed Episcopal Ch., Coquitlam, B.C., Can. Office: Reformed Episcopal Ch, 1544 Broadview Ct, Coquitlam, BC Canada V3J 5X9*

LYLES, RONNY CARTER, minister; b. Decatur, Tex., June 26, 1950; s. Charlie Carter and Doris Nell (Martin) L.; m. Brenda Maxine Kabler, Aug. 2, 1970; children: Timothy, Ronda, Philip, Clifton. BA in Religion, Dallas Bapt. U., 1972; MDiv, Southwestern Bapt. Seminary, Ft. Worth, 1974, PhD in Old Testament, 1980. Pastor Brookston (Tex.) Bapt. Ch., 1971-74; pastor 1st Bapt. Ch., Rio Vista, Tex., 1974-77, Grandview, Tex., 1977-81; pastor South Main Bapt. Ch., Pasadena, Tex., 1981—; trustee Bapt. Mission Ctr., Houston, 1989—, Houston Bapt. U., 1984—; mem. State Missions Commn., Dallas, 1989—. Contbr. articles to profl. jours and lessons to Bible sch. series. Key communicator Ind. Sch. Dist., Pasadena, 1986-88. Mem. Soc. Bibl. Lit., Rotary (sgt. at arms Pasadena chpt. 1982—). Republican. Office: South Main Bapt Ch PO Box 1072 Pasadena TX 77501

LYNCH, DERRICK CHARLES, youth minister; b. Aurora, Mo., May 13, 1966; s. Billy Ralph and Evelyn Louise (McGinnis) L.; m. Julie Denise Jenkins, Jan. 6, 1990. BA, Okla. Bapt. U., 1988; postgrad., New Orleans Bapt. Sem., 1988, S.W. Bapt. Sem., 1990-91. Ordained to ministry So. Bapt. Conv., 1989. Youth min. Ea. Heights Bapt. Ch., Bartlesville, Okla., 1986-87; interim youth min. Immanuel Bapt. Ch., Shawnee, Okla., 1987-88; assoc. youth min. Henderson Hills Bapt. Ch., Edmond, Okla., 1989; youth min. 1st Bapt. Ch., Mustang, Okla., 1989-91; min. youth/ch. growth 1st Bapt. Ch., Shelbyville, Tenn., 1991—; messenger So. Bapt. Conv., Dallas, 1985; co-chmn. youth com. Bill Glass Crusade for Christ, Mustang, 1990. Mem. Okla. Youth Mins. Assn., New Duck River Bapt. Assn. (associational youth min. 1991). Republican. Home: 112 Lantern Ln Shelbyville TN 37160 *Youth are not the church of tomorrow; they are the church of today. The biggest service we can provide youth today is to show them who they are and what they can do in Christ.*

LYNCH, SISTER FRANCIS XAVIER, nun, development director; b. Watertown, N.Y., Oct. 21, 1918; d. George Francis and Sarah Emma (Nicholson) L. BS in Nursing, Cath. U. Am., 1944, MS in Adminstrn., 1948, postgrad. in chemistry, 1949-51; Dr. Humane Letters (hon.), Long Island U., 1967. Tchr. St. Leo Sch., N.Y.C., 1939-40, Holy Angels Sch., Buffalo, N.Y., 1940-41; operating room supr. Champlain Valley Hosp., Plattsburgh, N.Y., 1941-42; instr. Biology & Biol. Scis. D'Youville Coll., Buffalo, N.Y., 1944-48; head dept. Biology D'Youville Coll., Buffalo, 1948-51, dean Sch. of Nursing, 1951-62, pres., 1962-68; initiator expansion program Grey Nuns Motherhouse, Yardley, Pa., 1969-71; dir. devel. Grey Nuns of the Sacred Heart, Yardley, Pa., 1971—; cons. to Hosps. operated by Grey Nuns and their schs. of Nursing, 1955-62; mem. N.Y. State Bd. Nurse Examiners (Regents), 1952-64. Bd. dirs. A. Barton Hepburn Hosp., Ogdensburg, N.Y., 1976—. Mem. AAUW, Nat. Cath. Dev. Conf. (charter, v.p., bd. dirs., Disting. Svc. award), Am. Biographical Inst. (bd. advisors), Ctr. for the Study of the Presidency, World Affairs Coun., Am. Acad. Polit. Sci., Nat. Soc. of Fund Raising Execs., Lower Bucks County C. of C., Phila. Mus. Art. Democrat. Avocations: reading, travel, nature study. Home and Office: Grey Nuns of Sacred Heart 1750 Quarry Rd Yardley PA 19067

LYNCH, GEORGE EDWARD, retired bishop; b. N.Y.C., Mar. 4, 1917; s. Timothy John and Margaret Mary (O'Donnell) L. A.B., Fordham U., 1938; S.T.L., Catholic U., 1943, J.C.D., 1946; LL.D. (hon.), Mount St. Mary's Coll., Emmitsburg, Md., 1979. Parish priest Diocese of Raleigh, N.C., 1943—; diocesan chancellor Diocese of Raleigh, 1953-62, aux. bishop, 1970-85, officialis (in charge of diocesan tribunal), 1951-81. Author: Auxiliary Bishops, 1946. Roman Catholic. Home: PO Box 274 East Station Yonkers NY 10704

LYNCH, JOHN E., history educator; b. N.Y.C., Oct. 21, 1924; s. John E. and Julia (Glennon) L. AB, St. Paul's Coll., 1947; MA, U. Toronto (Can.), 1956; M.S.L., Medieval Inst., Toronto, 1959; PhD, U. Toronto, 1965. Prof. St. Paul's Coll., Washington, 1959-72; prof. Cath. U. Am., Washington, 1968—, assoc. acad. v.p. for grad. studies, 1991—. Author: Theory of Knowledge of Vital du Four, 1972; editor: Guide to the Fathers, 1965-68; book rev. editor The Jurist, 1973-80. Mem. Am. Hist. Assn., Canon Law Soc. Am. (consultor 1972-74, v.p. 1974-75, Role of Law award 1984), Am. Cath. Hist. Assn. (exec. coun. 1984-87), Am. Soc. Church History, AAUP. Democrat. Roman Catholic. Home: 3015 4th St NE Washington DC 20017 Office: Cath U Am Washington DC 20064

LYNDAKER, BRUCE WAYNE, minister, teacher; b. Lowville, N.Y., July 24, 1952; s. Ralph Michael and Margie Ann (Lehman) L.; m. Pamela Jane Combs, July 29, 1972; children: Rebekah, Jessica, Erica, Anika. BS in Bible Studies, Secondary Edn., Eastern Mennonite Sem., Harrisonburg, Va., 1975; MDiv, Goshen (Ind.) Bibl. Sem., 1983; D of Ministry, Ashland (Ohio) Theol. Sem., 1990. Ordained to ministry Mennonite Ch., 1973. Pastor Mennonite Ch., Petaskey, Mich., 1976-81, Forks Mennonite Ch., Middlebury, Ind., 1983-84, Pleasant Hill Mennonite Ch., Burton, Ohio, 1984-89; pastor, tchr. Burton (Ohio) Assembly of God Sch., 1989-90; tchr. Geauga Christian Sch., Burton, 1989-90; tchr., admnstr. River Valley Mennonite Sch., Castorland, N.Y., 1990—. Home: RD # 1 Box 221A Castorland NY 13627

LYNE, TIMOTHY J., bishop; b. Chgo., Mar. 21, 1919. Grad., St. Mary of the Lake Sem., Mundelein, Ill. Ordained priest to Roman Cath. Ch., 1943; ordained titular bishop of Vamalla and aux. bishop of Chgo., 1983. Address: 730 N Wabash Chicago IL 60611

LYNN, EDWIN CHARLES, minister, architect; b. Harford, Conn., Nov. 12, 1935; s. Charles Knox and Edna (Crowther) Lynn; m. Marjorie Ann Grimm, Sept. 20, 1958; children: Bruce Charles, Sharyl Spring. BArch cum laude, Syracuse U., 1958; ThM, Thomas Starr King Sch. for the Ministry, Berkeley, Calif., 1967. Registered architect, Colo. Architect Jerome Nagel, Architect, Denver, 1959-61; dir. midwest area Great Books Found., Chgo., 1961-64; minister First Unitarian Soc., Milford, N.H., 1967-72, Northshore Unitarian Universalist Ch., Danvers, Mass., 1972—; archtl. cons. to chs., 1967—; staff E. Coast Great Books Inst., Colby Coll. Waterville, Maine, 1970-76; chairor Unitarian Universalist Assn. Pamphlet Commn., Boston, 1983; denomination counselor Unitarian Universalist, Harvard U., Cambridge, Mass., 1986. Author: Tired Dragons: Adapting Church Architecture to Changing Needs, 1972; pamphleteer. Bd. dirs. Monadnock Concerts, Peterborough, N.H., 1971-72, N. Shore Friends, Danvers, 1972-78, Hospice of N. Shore, Beverly, Mass., 1980— (pres. 1985), Isaac Munroe Found., Peabody, 1985—. Served with U.S. Army, 1958-59. Recipient Disting. Citizen award Jr. C. of C., 1970, Nat. Sermon award Soc. for Alcohol Edn., 1984. Fellow Harvard U.; mem. Unitarian Universalist Minister Assn. Democrat. Home: 30 Newbury Rd Ipswich MS 01938

LYNN, ROBERT WOOD, theologian, educator, dean; b. Wheatland, Wyo., Apr. 3, 1925; s. William McGregor and Janet (Reid) L.; m. Katharine Mitchell Wuerth, Mar. 8, 1952; children—Thomas Taylor, Janet MacGregor, Elizabeth Mitchell, Sarah McKee. A.B., Princeton U., 1948; B.D., Yale U., 1952; Th.D., Union Theol. Sem., N.Y.C., 1962. Ordained to ministry Presbyn. Ch., 1952; asst. minister Montview Presbyn. Ch., Denver, 1952-59; mem. faculty Union Theol. Sem., N.Y.C., 1959-75, dean Auburn program, 1960—, prof., 1965-75; v.p. Lilly Endowment, Inc., 1976-84, sr. v.p., 1985-89; vis. prof. Drew U., Andover Newton Theol. Sch., Fordham U., Tchrs. Coll., Columbia U.; scholar in residence Bangor Theol. Sem., 1989—. Author: Protestant Strategies in Education; co-author: The Big Little School; also articles. Trustee Louisville Sem., 1990—, Yale U., 1991—. Served with AUS, 1943-44. Woodrow Wilson fellow, 1948-49; Presbyn. Grad. fellow, 1959-60. Home: Box 3290 Leeds ME 04263

LYNN, WILLIAM DORY, priest, religion educator, academic dean; b. Rocky Mount, N.C., Dec. 25, 1922; s. William Daub and Annie (Quigley) L. BA, Georgetown U., 1947, MA in Edn., 1951; Licentiate in Sacred Theology, Woodstock Coll., 1955; postgrad., Fordham U., 1956-57; STD, Gregorian U., Rome, 1962. Joined S.J., Roman Cath. Ch., 1941, ordained priest, 1954. Asst. prof. theology Loyola Coll., Balt., 1959-60; asst. prof. dogmatic theology Cath. Maj. Sem., Rangoon, Burma, 1960-66; adj. prof. Woodstock (Md.) Coll., 1966-68; asst. prof. Daegun Coll., Kwangju, Republic of Korea, 1970-71; assoc. prof. St. Joseph's Coll., Phila., 1971-73; asst. prof. St. Vincent de Paul Sem., Boynton Beach, Fla., 1973-74; prof. St. Francis Sem., Loretto, Pa., 1974-79; prof. systematic dogma Pontifical Coll. Josephinum, Columbus, Ohio, 1979—, acad. dean Sch. Theology, 1983—. Author: Redemptive Merit of Christ: The Nature of Its Causality According to St. Thomas Aquinas, 1962; also articles. Office: Pontifical Coll Josephinum Sch Theology 7625 N High St Columbus OH 43235

LYNN, WILLIAM MAX, financial administrator; b. Fox, Okla., July 20, 1927; s. Warren A. and Mary (Johnston) L. BS, UCLA, 1952; m. Elinor Jane Treiber, Feb. 28, 1953; children: Kevin Edward-Holmes, Daniel Warren, Nancy Edith, Colleen Erin. With publicity dept. Metro-Goldwyn-Mayer Studios, Culver City, Calif., 1952-53; dir. bus. and fin. United Ch. of Religious Sci., L.A., 1953-82, asst. chief exec. officer, 1982-85, dir. devel., 1985-87; exec. dir. Sci. of Mind Found., 1987-89; lectr., cons. fin. adminstrn. and devel. With AUS, 1945-48. Mem. Am. Mgmt. Assn., Am. Soc. for Tng. and Devel., Conf. Bd., Nat. Assn. Ch. Bus. Adminstrs., Town Hall, Newcomen Soc. Am., Acacia, City Club (San Marino), Rotary. Republican. Home: 2100 El Molino Ave San Marino CA 91108 also: 125 Michele Ln Santa Fe NM 87501

LYNNE, ROBERT D., bishop; b. Turtle Lake, N.D.; m. JoAnn Keister, 1954; children: Mark, Janna Lynne Viseth, Jane. Grad., Wartburg Coll., Waverly, Iowa, PhD (hon.), 1987; grad., Wartburg Theol. Sem., Dubuque, Iowa. Ordained to ministry Evang. Luth. Ch. in Am., 1957. Pastor local ch. Mott, N.D.; pastor Good Shepherd Luth. Ch., Bismarck, N.D.; bishop Western N.D. synod, Evang. Luth. Ch. in Am., 1987—; chaplain Heartview Addiction Treatment Ctr., Mandan, N.D., 1967—; mem. Luth. Conf. Bishops, region III coun. N.D. Conf. Chs.; chairperson office communication and mission support Am. Luth. Ch., 1980-85, western N.D. dist. coun., 1981-86. mem. lay adv. bd., former chairperson bd. St. Alexius Med. Ctr., Bismarck; mem. steering com. Commitment to Mission. Robert D. Lynne scholarship fund established in his name, Wartburg Sem. Mem. Mental Health Assn. N.D. (children and youth com.). Office: Evang Luth Ch in Am 721 Memorial Way Bismarck ND 58502*

LYONS, CHARLES DAVID, minister; b. Olive Hill, Ky., June 12, 1932; s. Mike A. and Maudie Lee (Campbell) L.; m. Sue K. Hanna, Aug. 1, 1951 (dec. Mar. 1989); children: Michael David, Norman Dean (dec. 1987); m. Patricia W. Durham, Mar. 31, 1990; stepchildren: Beverly Phillips, Rebecca Smith, David, Danny Ray.. Diploma, Clear Creek Bapt. Sch., 1956; student, So. Sem., 1974, Samford U., 1982. Ordained to ministry So. Bapt. Conv., 1955. Pastor various chs. Ky., 1955—; pastor Macedonia Bapt. Ch., Burning Springs, 1962-67, First Bapt. Ch., East Bernstadt, 1967-72, Fleming Bapt. Ch., 1972—; moderator Boonville Bapt. Assn., 1965-66, Pine Mountain Assn., 1973-74; mem. bd. counsellors Calvary Coll.; assoc. home mission bd. So. Bapt. Conv., 1975—; chaplain Neon Fire and Rescue Orgn., 1976—; dir. missions Lynn Camp and North Concord Bapt. Assns., 1985—. Named to Hon. Order of Ky. Cols. Home and Office: PO Box 1027 Barbourville KY 40906

LYONS, EARLE VAUGHAN, JR., minister; b. Phila., Oct. 18, 1917; s. Earle Vaughan and Marie Meta (Anderson) L.; m. Eleanor Jean Morris, Sept. 6, 1946; children: Earle Vaughan III, William Morris, Jean Eleanor. BA, Maryville Coll., 1940; ThM, Princeton Theol. Sem., 1942; MA, U. Pa., 1952, Chapman Coll., 1977. Ordained to ministry Presbyn. Ch. (U.S.A.), 1943. Asst. pastor West Presbyn. Ch., Wilmington, Del., 1943-44; commd. lt. (j.g.) USN, 1944, chaplain WWII, Korea, Vietnam, ret., 1974; assoc. pastor Mission Hills Ch., San Diego, 1974-78, sr. pastor, 1978-85; officer in charge Chaplain Corps rsch. team, Washington, 1963-64, USN Chaplains Sch., Newport, R.I., 1967-71; chmn. planned giving So. Calif. conf. United Ch. of Christ, 1982-84, bd. dirs. San Diego county Ecumenical Conf., 1975—; team mem. Focus Five Daily TV program, 1976—; mem. ch. and ministry com. San Diego Assn. United Cch. of Christ, 1984—; mem. honor roll NCCJ, 1982-83; exec. dir. San Diego County Ecumenical Conf., 1987—. Contbr. articles to USN Chaplains Bull. Chmn. Vet's Conf. San Diego, 1975-76; bd. dirs. St. Paul's Manor, Green Manor, 1st Congl. Tower, San Diego, 1979-84. Decorated Legion of Merit with combat V, Commendation medal, Honor medal 1st class Govt. of Vietnam; recipient Honor medal Freedoms Found. at Valley Forge, 1974, Cath. Bishops Christian Unity award, 1985, Peacemaker award, 1990. Mem. Calif. Coun. Chs. (bd. dirs.), Rotary. Home: 2727 Azalea Dr San Diego CA 92106

LYONS, GEORGE, religion educator; b. Richmond, Ind., Dec. 9, 1947; s. Galen H. and Georgia M. (Sebby) L.; m. Terre Lynn Hickok, May 24, 1969; children: Kara Joy, Nathanael David. BA, Olivet Nazarene U., 1970; MDiv, Nazarene Theol. Sem., 1973; PhD, Emory U., 1982. Prof. bibl. lit. Olivet Nazarene U., Kankakee, Ill., 1977-91, coord. grad. religion lit. program, 1986-90, chmn. dept. bibl. lit., 1989-91; prof. bibl. lit. N.W. Nazarene Coll., Nampa, Idaho, 1991—; guest lectr. Nazarene Theol. Sem., Kansas City, Mo., 1982, 86, 89, Nazarene Bible Coll., Brisbane, Australia, 1989-91. Author: Pauline Autobiography, 1985, Holiness in Everyday Life, 1992; co-author: A Dictionary of the Bible, 1984; contbr. articles to profl. publs. Mem. doctrine of ch. commn. Ch. of Nazarene, Kansas City, 1985-89, mem. curriculum com., 1990—; coord. Kankakee County Hunger Walk, 1985-90. Mem. Soc. Bibl. Lit., Wesleyan Theol. Soc. (sec. membership com. 1986, 2d v.p. 1992). Home: 4012 Ivy Dr Nampa ID 83686 Office: NW Nazarene Coll Holly and Dewey Sts Nampa ID 83686 *Contentment is a state of mind, not a place on the map. It is found in taking life as it is and making the most of it. Since some situations and people will never change, we must abandon childish fantasies of Utopia and adapt to life in the real world.*

LYONS, RICHARD W., school system administrator. Supt. schs. Diocese of Superior, Wis. Home: 706 7th Ave E Superior WI 54880 Office: Office of Schs Supt 1201 Hughitt Ave Box 969 Superior WI 54880*

LYRA, SYNESIO, JR., minister, theology educator; b. Recife, Brazil, Aug. 24, 1938; s. Synesio and Nisia (Gueiros) L.; m. Louise Kline, Sept. 21, 1968; children: Hans Eric, Christina Marie. MDiv, Faith Theol. Sem., 1961; D of Theology, Free U., Amsterdam, The Netherlands, 1964; D of Religion, Newport U., 1981. Ordained to ministry Presbyn. Ch. Asst. prof. Shelton Coll., Cape May, N.J., 1965-69; prof. theology grad. sch. Columbia (S.C.) Grad. Sch., 1969-71; asst. prof. Covenant Theol. Sem., St. Louis, 1971-76; minister of edn. The Crystal Cathedral, Garden Grove, Calif., 1976-79, dean lay ministers tng. ctr., 1976-79; assoc. prof. theology Internat. Sch. Theology, San Bernardino, Calif., 1979-88; minister pastoral care Coral Ridge Presbyn. Ch., Ft. Lauderdale, Fla., 1988—; pres., bd. dirs. Crystal Garden Cath. Acad., Garden Grove, 1977-78; minister Mayflower Ch., Laguna Hills, Calif., 1982-88; lectr. in field. Contbr. articles to profl. jours., columnist; author (study manual and audio cassettes) A New Laity. Lodge: Rotary (past bd. dirs., Paul Harris Fellow 1985). Avocations: reading, piano playing, travelling, gardening. Office: Coral Ridge Presbyn Ch 5555 N Federal Hwy Fort Lauderdale FL 33308

LYSLE, YOLONDA SHEA, religious organization administrator; b. Louisville, Oct. 5, 1959; d. Elmer Pleas and Sarah Maxine (Britt) L. BS in Recreation, Ea. Ky. U., 1982; MDiv in Christian Edn., So. Bapt. Theol. Sem., Louisville, 1987. Coord. congress and nominating com. Progressive Nat. Bapt. Conv., Washington, 1988—; instr. Progressive Nat. Bapt. Conv., Congress Edn., Washington, 1988-93, Ea. Bapt. Sch. Religion, Bklyn., 1989-94; mem. United Bapt. Fellowship, Louisville, 1983-87, Women in Ministry, Louisville, 1985-87. Mem. Alpha Kappa Alpha. Office: Bethany Bapt Ch 460 Marcus Garvey Blvd Brooklyn NY 11216-2529 *The harmony of our races and cultures depends upon the transformation of our minds, spirit and soul which creates a level of sacrifice, cooperation and charity that through this life can be experienced to its fullest.*

LYSON, VALERIE MARIE, minister; b. Spokane, Wash., Nov. 24, 1962; d. Allen Carl and Nellie Anne (Albinati) L. BA, U. Wash., 1985; MDiv, Pacific Sch. of Religion, 1988. Ordained to ministry Christian Ch. (Disciples of Christ), 1989. Chaplain intern Austin Coll., Sherman, Tex., 1988-89; resident chaplain St. Luke's Episcopal Hosp., Houston, 1989-90; staff chaplain Hermann Hosp., Houston, 1991—; chair worship com., elder 1st Christian Ch., Houston, 1991—. Home: 7100 Almeda Rd # 1301 Houston TX 77054-2132 *In my life, God comes alive through the people that I meet and come to know. God's incarnation is complete in my relationships with others.*

MAAHS, CHARLES H., bishop. Bishop Mo.-Kans. Evang. Luth. Ch. in Am., Shawnee Mission, Kans. Office: Evang Ch in Am 6400 Glenwood Ste 210 Shawnee Mission KS 66202*

MAAHS, KENNETH HENRY, SR., religion educator; b. Peoria, Ill., June 19, 1940; s. Silas Henry Maahs and Lydia Nettie (Heinold) Blessman; m. Vivian Louise Dawn Englert, Sept. 1, 1962; children: Kirsten Allison Dawn, Kenneth Henry Jr. BA in Philosophy/Theology magna cum laude, Simpson Coll., 1962; MDiv, Fuller Theol. Sem., Pasadena, Calif., 1965; ThM in N.T. Studies, Princeton Theol. Sem., 1966; PhD in Old Testament Studies, So. Bapt. Theol. Sem., Louisville, 1972. Ordained to ministry Missionary Ch./Am. Bapt. Conv., 1968. Instr. Nyack (N.Y.) Coll., 1966-67, Bethel Coll., Mishawaka, Ind., 1968; prof. Bibl. studies Ea. Coll., St. Davids, Pa., 1972—, Abram Clemens chair, 1986—, chmn. dept. religion-philosophy, 1985-88, chmn. humanities div., 1988—; interim pastor Columbus (N.J.) Bapt. Ch., 1975-76, Roxborough Bapt. Ch., Phila., 1980-81, Bapt. Temple, Blue Bell, Pa., 1981-83, Willowgrove (Pa.) Bapt. Ch., 1988, Belmont Bapt. Ch., Broomall, Pa., 1989, Lower Merion Bapt. Ch., Bryn Mawr, Pa., 1989-90, 2d Bapt. Ch. Germantown, Pa., 1990—; adj. prof. Ea. Bapt. Theol. Sem., 1980, 83, 85, 89, Lay Acad. of Phila. Bapt. Assn., 1984-86, 88, 90, Fuller Theol. Sem./Young Life's Inst. Youth Ministries, 1986-87, 89.; keynote speaker Am. Bapt. Women's Regional Conf., 1983; feature lectr. Am. Bapt. Commn. on Continuing Edn., 1985. Recipient Legion of Honor award Chapel of Four Chaplains, 1983, Lindback award Ea. Coll., 1984; named Prof. of Yr. Ea. Coll., 1983-84. Mem. Soc. Bibl. Lit., Delta Epsilon Chi. Republican. Home: 346 E Valley Forge Rd King of Prussia PA 19406 Office: Ea Coll Saint Davids PA 19087

MABEY, JOELLE LYNN, religious educator; b. Allentown, Pa., Apr. 23, 1967; d. Robert Louis and Ginger Elaine (Fenstermaker) Johnson; m. Matthew Edward Mabel, Nov. 3, 1990. AA, Pinebrook Jr. Coll., Coopersburg, Pa., 1987; ASB, Allentown (Pa.) Bus. Sch., 1989; postgrad., United Wesleyan Coll., Allentown, 1990. Camp counselor Penn-Jersey Wesleyan Ch., Bethlehem, Pa., summer 1985; youth cabinet del. Penn-Jersey Dist., Bethlehem, Pa., 1987—, seminar leader, summer 1990; asst. dir., tchr. Gingerbread House, Bethlehem, Pa., 1988—; mem. nominating com. Penn-Jersey Dist. Wesleyan, 1990-91; sponsor youth Calvary Wesleyan Ch., Bethlehem, 1987-89, Emmanuel Ch., 1989—. Republican. Home: 809 Center St Bethlehem PA 18018 Office: Gingerbread House 1414 Pennsylvania Ave Bethlehem PA 18018

MABSON, ROBERT LANGLEY, clergyman; b. New Orleans, Apr. 17, 1931; s. Eugene Beall and Eva Louise (Lea) M.; m. Minnie Augusta Lewis, Dec. 22, 1953; children: Lewis, Susan Jane, Laura Lea. BA, Tulane U., 1952; postgrad., Union Theol. Sem., 1952-55; M. of Religious Edn., Pres. Sch. Christian Edn., 1955; MS, La. State U., 1964. Ordained to ministry Presbyn. Ch., 1955. Pastor Mt. Pleasant Presbyn. Ch., Sinks Grove, W.Va., 1955-57; dir. Christian edn. Barbee Larger Parish, Perry, Mo., 1957-59; pastor 1st Presbyn. Ch., Talihina, Okla., 1959-63; chaplain USPHS Hosp., 1959-63; head librarian, prof. Meth. Coll., Fayetteville, N.C., 1964-66; pastor Eastland Presbyn. Ch., Memphis, 1966-78, asst. libr. Memphis Theol. Sem., 1967-74; chaplain Calvary Colony Alcoholic Rehab. Ctr., also Kings Daus. and Sons Home, Memphis, 1979-83; pastor Ebenezer Presbyn. Ch., Strong, Ark., 1983-84, Sulphur Springs Cumberland Presbyn. Ch., Louann, Ark., 1984-88; mem. Presbyn. Council Evangelism, 1959-63; mem. Covenant Presbytery, 1973-84, stated clk., 1973-75 moderator, 1976; mem. Mound Prairie Presbytery, 1984-88, Ark. Presbytery, 1989. Author: Presbyterian Missionary Labors in Kiamichi Valley, Oklahoma, 1850-1960. Recipient Congl. Community Service award, 1978. Address: PO Box 92 Mount Holly AR 71758 *My purpose has been to help others, and to encourage all to be good listeners—there is too much talking by too many ministers.*

MACBURNEY, EDWARD HARDING, bishop; b. Albany, N.Y., Oct. 30, 1927; s. Alfred Cadwell and F. Marion (McDowell) MacB.; m. Anne Farnsworth, Feb. 20, 1965; W. Norton Grubb, Page F. Grubb, James S. Grubb. AB, Darmouth Coll., 1949; STB, Berkeley Divinity Sch., 1952; HHD (hon.), St. Ambrose U., 1987; DD (hon.), Nashotah House, 1988. Ordained to ministry Episcopal Ch. as deacon, 1952, as priest, 1952, as bishop, 1988. Asst. St. Thomas' Ch., Hanover, N.H., 1953-63, rector, 1963-73; dean Trinity Cathedral, Davenport, Iowa, 1973-87; bishop Diocese of Quincy, Peoria, Ill., 1988—. Trustee Berkeley Divinity Sch., New Haven, 1964-70, St. Luke's Hosp., Davenport, 1973-87, Nat. Orgn. Episcopalians for Life, Fairfax, 1991—, Naskotah House, 1991—; v.p. Episcopal Synod Am., Ft. Worth, 1988—; mem. panel White House Fellowships, St. Louis, 1976-84; bd. dirs. Noel, 1991—. Democrat. Address: Diocese of Quincy 3601 N North St Peoria IL 61604

MACCHIA, FRANK DOMONICK, minister; b. Gary, Ind., July 15, 1952; s. Mike Domonick and Elizabeth (Pilla) M.; m. Verena Knecht, Feb. 18, 1978. BA, So. Calif. Coll., 1974; MA, Wheaton (Ill.) Coll., 1976; MDiv, Union Theol. Sem., N.Y.C., 1980; ThD insigni cum laude, U. Basel, Switzerland, 1989. Ordained to ministry Assemblies of God, 1978. Pastor Trinity Gospel Ch., Itasca, Ill., 1974-78, 80-84; instr. Chgo. Bible Coll., 1977-78, Valley Forge Christian Coll. Extension, N.Y.C., 1978-80; pastor Christian Assembly Ch., Hobart, Ind., 1989—. Author: Spirituality and Social Liberation: The Message of the Blumhardts in the Light of Wuerttemberg Pietism, 1991. Recipient Jacob Burckhardt prize Johann von Goethe Found., U. Basel, 1988. Mem. Am. Acad. Religion, Soc. Pentecostal Studies. Home: 785 Heritage Rd Apt 111 Valparaiso IN 46383 Office: Christian Assembly Ch 7498 Grand Blvd Hobart IN 46342 *In all that we think, do, or say, we seek to express the inexpressible, namely, the divine Word. All of our language, customs, and accomplishments fall under the judgment and promise of this Word as we are called to new forms of obedience and utter silence. This is life.*

MACCHIA, STEPHEN ANTHONY, minister; b. Winchester, Mass., Aug. 22, 1956; s. Italo and Ruth Naomi (Humbert) M.; m. Ruth Lynn Broek, July 20, 1979; children: Nathan Stephen, Rebekah Ruth. BA, Northwestern Coll., Orange City, Iowa, 1978; MDiv, Gordon-Conwell Theol., Seminary, South Hamilton, Mass., 1983. Ordained to ministry Evang. Ch., 1983. Dir. jr. high ministries Grace Chapel, Lexington, Mass., 1978-80, minister to children, 1980-83, assoc. minister, 1984-89; pres. Evangelistic Assn. of New Eng., Burlington, Mass., 1989—; seminar leader Internat. Bible Soc., Colorado Springs, 1989—, Internat. Ctr. for Learning, Indpls., 1986-88; cons. Gospel Light Publs., Ventura, Calif., 1983-88; chmn. New Eng. Assn. for Christian Edn., Boston, 1983-85; bd. dirs. Nat. Assn. Dirs. of Christian Edn., Oklahoma City, 1987-89. Author, pub.: (monthly newspaper) The New England Christian, 1989—. Com. mem. Lexington (Mass.) Hist. Soc., 1988—. Recipient Martin Luther King, Jr. scholarship Stoneham (Mass.) High Sch., 1974, Faculty Hons. award Northwestern Coll., Orange City, 1978. Mem. Nat. Assn. Evangelicals (bd. dirs. 1989—), Christian Mgmt. Assn. (chpt. pres. 1990—). Home: 12 Brookside Ave Lexington MA 02173 Office: Evangelistic Assn New Eng 279 Cambridge St Burlington MA 01803

MACCOLLAM, JOEL ALLAN, clergyman, consultant; b. Albany, N.Y., Dec. 19, 1946; s. Allan and Edith MacCollam; m. Jann M. Scherer, May 3, 1975. BA, Hamilton Coll., 1968; MDiv, Gen. Theol. Sem., 1972; LLD, Calif. Grad. Sch. Theology, 1987. Ordained in Episc. Ch. Assoc. rector St. James' Ch., Oneonta, N.Y., 1973-74; rector St. Stephen's Ch., Schuylerville, N.Y., 1974-78; assoc. rector St. Mark's Ch., Glendale, Calif., 1978-79; dir. devel. Door of Hope Internat., Glendale, 1981-82, cons., 1982-90; v.p. Voice of Americanism, Glendale, 1982-85; pres. World Emergency Relief, Glendale, 1985—; ind. radio producer Glendale, 1986—; pres. Acclaimed Communications, 1986—. Author: The Way Doctrine, 1977, Carnival of Souls, 1978. Cons. various Rep. and conservative causes; bd. dirs. Santa Fe Christian Schs., Solana Beach, Calif. Mem. Nat. Soc. Fund Raising Execs., Christian Mgmt. Assn. Office: World Emergency Relief PO Box 1518 Carlsbad CA 92008

MACCULLEY, ROBERT JOHN, deacon; b. Buffalo, Nov. 18, 1918; s. Robert M. and Blanche (Roche) MacC.; m. Rita T. Schroeder, Apr. 13, 1944; children: Robert, Mary Rita, Kathleen, Kevin, Margaret, Christine. Student, Canisius Coll., 1937-39, Niagara U., 1946-49; ThB, Sacred Heart Sem., 1973; ThM, U. Detroit, 1977. Deacon St. Mary Redford Parish, Detroit, 1972-81; acad. dir. Diaconal Studies, Sacred Heart Sem., Detroit, 1977-81; chmn. deacons assembly Archdiocese of Detroit, 1972-76; deacon St. Aidan's Parish, Livonia, Mich., 1982—; pres. Livonia Ministerial Assn., 1985—; adj. instr. Madonna U., Livonia, 1981—; com. Detroit Christian Communication Coun., 1982; personnel com. Mich. Ecumenical Commn., 1984-89; Christian-Muslim commn. mem., Dearborn, Mich., 1986—; rep. Ecumenical Inst., Southfield, Mich., 1989. Author: By These Holy Oils, 1976. Maj. Infantry, 1940-49. Recipient Silver Star, Bronze Star, Purple Heart, Combat Infantry Badge, Belgian Croix de Guerre. Mem. KC, Sigma Alpha Sigma. Home: 25043 Woodridge Triangle Farmington Hills MI 48335 Office: Saint Aidan's Parish 17500 Farmington Rd Livonia MI 48152

MACDONALD, CHARLES RAY, minister; b. Spartanburg, S.C., Apr. 28, 1929; s. James and Ethyl (Ray) MacD.; m. Jeanne Harrison, Oct. 23, 1954; children: Joan Harrison MacDonald, Robert Charles, Susan MacDonald Roddey. SB, MIT, 1951, SM, 1952; MDiv, Union Sem., Va., 1958, ThM, 1966; D Ministry, Princeton Sem., 1983. Ordained to ministry Presbyn. Ch., 1958. Estimator J. A. Jones Constrn. Co., Charlotte, N.C., 1952-54; chief estimator W. H. Weaver Constrn. Co., Greensboro, N.C., 1954-55; pastor Fairfield (Va.) & McCutchen Presbyn. Chs., 1958-62, Woodlawn Presbyn. Ch., Hopewell, Va., 1962-65, Green Hill Presbyn. Ch., Wilmington, Del., 1966-87; clk., bus. mgr. Presbytery of Detroit, 1987-89; assoc. pastor Kirk in the Hills Presbyn. Ch., Bloomfield Hills, Mich., 1989—; stated clk. Lexington Presbytery, Staunton, Va., 1960-62, New Castle Presbytery, Wilmington, 1973-80. Vice pres. Limen House, Wilmington, 1986; pres. Citizens Housing Alliance of Del., Wilmington, 1973, Wawaset Park, Wilmington, 1982. Home: 44614 Charnwood Ct Plymouth MI 48170 Office: Kirk in the Hills Presbyn Ch 1340 W Long Lake Rd Bloomfield Hills MI 48302

MACDONALD, CLAUDIA L., ecumenical agency administrator. Exec. dir. The Niagara Coun. of Chs. Inc., Niagara Falls, N.Y. Office: Niagara Coun Chs 229 2nd St Niagara Falls NY 14303*

MACDONALD, DAVID ROY, minister, educator; b. Highland Park, Mich., Mar. 17, 1940; s. Roy Kenneth and Mary (Halley) MacD.; m. Rose Mary Revoir, June 12, 1965; children: Mary Ellen, Rebecca Anne, Deborah Jean, Sarah Charis. Diploma, Grand Rapids (Mich.) Sch. of Bible, 1968; BA in Christian Edn., Freedom U., 1977, MA in Christian Edn., 1979; ThM, Living Light Sem., Roseville, Ill., 1988, ThD, 1988. Ordained to ministry Bapt. Ch., 1976. Pastor, dir. Hampton (Fla.) Bapt. Ch. and Sch., 1981-83, Heritage Hills Ch. and Sch., Bellevue, Mich., 1984—; photographer Bellevue, 1987-90. With U.S. Army, 1960-63. Home: 13101 M-66 Bellevue MI 49021 Office: Heritage Hills Bible Ch RR 03 Box 13015 M66 Bellevue MI 49021

MACDONALD, DENNIS RONALD, theology educator; b. Chgo., July 1, 1946; s. James Ronald and Mildred (Friend) MacD.; m. Diane Louise Prosser, June 9, 1973; children: Katya Louise, Julian Peter. AB, Bob Jones U., 1968; MDiv McCormick Theol. Sem., Chgo., 1974; PhD, Harvard U., 1978. Asst. prof. Goshen Coll. (Ind.), 1977-80; asst. prof. N.T., Iliff Sch. Theology, Denver, 1980-83, assoc. prof., 1983-90, prof., 1990—; vis. prof. Harvard Div. Sch., 1985-86, Union Theol. Sem., 1991. Author: The Legend and The Apostle, 1983, Apocryphal Acts of Apostles, 1986, There Is No Male and Female, 1986, The Acts of Andrew and The Acts of Andrew and Matthias, 1990; also articles in religious jours. Clarence G. Campbell fellow Harvard U., 1975-76; grantee Ind. Council on Humanities, 1978; Young scholar Assn. Theol. Schs., 1983; recipient summer stipend NEH, 1983. Mem. Soc. Bibl. Lit. (v.p. Rocky Mountain region 1983-84, pres. 1984-85). Democrat. Congregationalist. Office: Iliff Sch of Theology 2201 S University Blvd Denver CO 80210

MAC DONALD, JAMES HECTOR, bishop; b. Whycocomagha, N.S., Can., Apr. 28, 1925; s. Alexander and Mary (MacEachern) Mac D. Student, Holy Cross Novitiate, North Dartmouth (Mass.), 1945-46, Notre Dame U., 1946-49, St. Joseph's U., N.B., 1949-50, Scholasticat Notre Dame de Ste. Croix, Ste. Genevieve (Que.), 1950-54, Divine Word Inst., London (Ont. Can.), 1977. Ordained priest Roman Catholic Ch., 1953; mem. Holy Cross Mission Band, Montreal, Que., Can., 1954-56; dir. Holy Cross Minor Sem., St. Joseph, N.B., Can., 1956-62; sec. provincial council Holy Cross Fathers, 1956-63; dir. vocations Torryburn, N.B., 1962-63; superior Holy Cross House of Studies, Fredericton, N.B., 1964-69; asst. provincial Holy Cross Fathers, 1966-72, bursar, 1969-72, dir. personnel, 1969-75; pastor St. Michael's Parish, Waterloo, Ont., 1969-77; aux. bishop Waterloo, 1978-82; bishop Charlottetown, P.E.I., Can., 1982—. Office: PO Box 907, 350 N River Rd, Charlottetown, PE Canada CIA 7L9

MACDONALD, JOEL BRIAN, minister; b. Redmond, Oreg., Mar. 26, 1946; s. Fred E. and Sheila (Bowman) MacD.; m. Dorothy Eileen Carlson, Dec. 2, 1972; children: Kristen, Kara, Brian, Bethany. BS in Math., Oreg. State U., 1968; MDiv, Western CB Sem., Portland, Oreg., 1976. Ordained to ministry Conservative Bapt. Assn. Am., 1977. Minister of evangelism and discipleship Hanson Meml. Bapt. Ch., Portland, Oreg., 1976-87; sr. pastor Southwood Bapt. Ch., Woodbury, N.J., 1987—; adj. prof. Multnomah Sch. Bible Grad. Sch., Portland, 1986. Sec. Mcpl. Alliance and Youth Comm., Gloucester County, N.J., 1990—. Lt. USN, 1968-72. Office: Southwood Bapt Ch 11 Griscom Ln Woodbury NJ 08096

MACDONALD, JOHN ALEXANDER, minister; b. Pitts., Nov. 19, 1956; s. Somerled Donald St. Maur and Myrta Gardner (Robertson) M.; m. Gail Taylor Hastings, July 24, 1982; children: John Alexander Jr., Anne Parry. Student, Univ. de Rennes, France, 1977-78; BA with honors, Dickinson Coll., 1979; postgrad. in Theology, Trinity Coll., Bristol, Eng., 1979-80; MDiv, Trinity Episcopal Sch., Ambridge, Pa., 1986. Asst. dir. pers. South Am. Missionary Soc., Union Mills, N.C., 1980-81, missionary, 1981-83; assoc. to the dean Trinity Cathedral, Pitts., 1986-88; assoc. rector St. Andrew's Episcopal Ch., Longmeadow, Mass., 1988-91; v.p. Bethlehem Haven Shelter for Women, Pitts., 1986-88; del. Diocese of Pitts. Convs., 1983-88. Author: Blind Man, 1980, Terminus, 1981, Pachunga, 1986; editor: (mag.) SAMS News, 1981. Mem. Episcopal Ch. Missionary Community, Fellowship of Witness, Episcopalians United, South Am. Missionary Soc. (bd. dirs. 1990—). Home: 186 Longmeadow St Longmeadow MA 01106 Office: St Andrews Episcopal Ch 335 Longmeadow St Longmeadow MA 01106

MACDONALD, JOSEPH FABER, bishop; b. Little Pond, P.E.I., Can., Jan. 20, 1932. Ordained priest Roman Cath. Ch., 1963; ordained bishop Diocese of Grand Falls, Nfld., Can., 1980—. Office: PO Box 771, Grand Falls, NF Canada A2A 2M4

MACDONALD, JOSEPH NEIL, minister; b. Goderich Province, Ont., Can., Oct. 8, 1950; came to U.S., 1974; s. Joseph Neil and Mary Irene Margaret (Bagnell) MacD.; m. Carolyn Elizabeth Garbutt, Sept. 11, 1971; children: Scott, Andrew, Stephen, Jesse. Student, Emmanuel Bible Coll., 1969-71; BA, Heritage Bapt. U., 1991. Ordained to ministry Bapt. Ch., 1974. Sr. pastor Evang. Bapt. Ch., Amerstburg, Ont., 1972-74; asst. pastor Marietta (Ga.) Bapt. Tabernacle, 1974-75; sr. pastor Faith Bapt. Ch., Port Hope, Ont., 1975-80, Turbotville (Pa.) Bapt. Ch., 1980-88, North Woodlawn Bapt. Ch., Derby, Kans., 1989—; pres. MacDonald Ministries, Inc., Derby, 1989—; adminstr. Derby Christian Sch., 1989—, Derby Christian Day Care, 1989—. Home: 1503 Baltimore Pl Derby KS 67037 Office: PO Box 100 Derby KS 67037

MAC DONALD, SISTER MATTHEW ANITA, college president; b. N.Y.C., June 15, 1938; d. Matthew John and Jean (Ottobre) MacDonald. A.B., Chestnut Hill Coll., Phila., 1960; M.A., U. Pa., 1970, Ph.D., 1973. Cert. tchr. in English and social studies, Pa. Joined Sisters of St. Joseph of Chestnut Hill, Roman Catholic Ch., 1962; fellow in acad. adminstrn. Bryn Mawr Coll., 1974-75; assoc. prof. Chestnut Hill Coll., Phila., 1974—, dir. continuing edn., 1975-80, pres., 1980—; cons.; mem. Phila. Archdiocesan Speakers Bur., 1977—; evaluator Middle States Assn.; chairperson exec. com. Sisters of St. Joseph Coll. Consortium, 1986-88. Bd. dirs. Chestnut Hill Community Assn., 1980—; mem. Mayor's Commn. on Women, Phila., 1981-83; dir. NCCJ, 1980-82; nat. adv. bd. commn. social justice Order Sons of Italy; vice chair Pa. Commn. for Women, 1987—; trustee U. Scranton, 1989—. Fellow Philosophy of Edn. Soc., Am. Council Edn.; mem. Am. Inst. Italian Culture, Commn. Ind. Colls. and Univs. (pres.), Nat. Cath. Edn. Soc., Teilhard de Chardin Soc., Assn. Continuing Higher Edn., Found. for Ind. Colls. (exec. com. 1986-90). Democrat. Home and Office: Chestnut Hill Coll Philadelphia PA 19118-2695

MACDOUGALL, MARY KATHERINE, minister, counselor, author; b. Mt. Auburn, Ill., May 30; d. Fay Dudley and Kittie Mae (Alexander) Slate; m. Wayne Fox McMeans, Apr. 6, 1929 (dec. May 1938); children: David Fox, Nancy McMeans Richey; m. Harold Alexander MacDougall, Aug. 31, 1940 (dec. July 1949); children: Alexander, Kent, Alan; m. Lynn Gregory Schneider, Aug. 17, 1989. BA, U. Mich., 1930; postgrad., U. Tex., Austin, U. Tex. Ordained to ministry Unity Ch., 1978. Tchr. Sandusky (Mich.) High Sch., 1939-42; editor Abilene (Tex.) Reporter News, 1950-54, Tex. Mut. Ins. Assn. Mag., Austin, 1956-57; tchr. William B. Travis High Sch., Austin, 1957-58; editor Austin Am. Statesman, 1958-59; tchr. S.F. Austin High Sch., 1959-70; adj. prof. U.Tex., Austin, 1972-74; minister Unity Ctr. Positive Prayer, Austin, 1975-90. Author: (children's) Black Jupiter, 1960; What Treasure Mapping Can Do For You, 1968; Prosperity Now, 1969; Healing Now,. 1970; Making Love Happen, 1970; Happiness Now, 1971; Dear Friend, I Love You, 1980; Sē Prospero...Ahora, 1982, Sē Sano... Ahora, 1983; Dear Me, I Love You, 1986, others. Del., State Dem Conv., Austin, 1990. Recipient minor journalistic awards. Mem. Women in Communication Inc., Delta Kappa Gamma. Avocations: distance bicycling, jazz, reading, travel. Home: 2511 Hartford Rd Austin TX 78703 *One of the most helpful understandings we can have is to realize that God's love and wisdom are always available and will, when we call for God's help, bring good no matter what is going on in our lives. This is saying, "God's will be done, not mine."*

MACE, ALAN ARTHUR, minister; b. St. Francis, Kans., Sept. 17, 1946; s. Roby Clyde and Lillus Ruth (Poulignot) M.; m. Janice Marie Drake, June 2, 1968; children: Anne-Marie, Christina Ann. BA, Phillips U., Enid, Okla., 1968; MDiv, Tex. Christian U., 1971; EdD, Vanderbilt U., 1983. Ordained to ministry Christian Ch. (Disciples of Christ, 1971. Min. Ill. St. Christian Ch., Lewistown, Ill., 1971-72; assoc. min. Riverside Ave. Christian Ch., Jacksonville, Fla., 1972-75, Hillside Christian Ch., Wichita, Kans, 1975-78, Vine St. Christian Ch., Nashville, 1978-81; sr. min. 1st Christian Ch., Tullahoma, Tenn., 1981—; moderator Christian Ch. in Tenn., Nashville, 1990—, middle area moderator, 1983-86. Author: Curriculum Development in Christian Education, 1983; contbr. articles to religious mags. Religious award chair Boy Scouts Am. Elk River Dist., Tullahoma, 1985—. George Peabody Disting. scholar Vanderbilt U., 1978, 79, 80. Mem. Tullahoma Ministerial Assn. (pres. 1982-83, v.p. 1987-88), Contact Lifeline of the Highland Rim (pres. 1983, 85, 87, Lifetime Achievement award 1991), Tenn. Assn. Chs. (bd. mem. 1990—), Rotary. Democrat.

MACE, EUGENE WILLIAM, chaplain; b. Greensburg, Kans., Aug. 14, 1933; s. Lloyd Valentine and Violet Sophia (Wibbeler) M.; m. Sally Ann Barstow, Feb. 3, 1961; children: Eric Charles, Michelle Louise, Bruce Alan. BA, Sterling (Kans.) Coll., 1955; MTh, So. Meth. U., 1958. Ordained elder, United Meth. Ch., 1960; cert. supr. clin. pastoral edn.; cert. chaplain. Pastor Little River (Kans.) and Mitchell Meth., 1958-61, Beverly (Kans.) and Tescott Meth. Chs., 1961-64, Trousdale (Kans.) Meth. Ch., 1964-65; chaplain intern Larned (Kans.) State Hosp., 1964-65; chaplain resident Hartford (Conn.) Hosp., 1965-67, staff chaplain, 1967-68; dir. pastoral care Hamot Hosp., Erie, Pa., 1968-74; assoc. chaplain, dir. clin. pastoral edn. Meth. Med. Ctr., Peoria, Ill., 1974-88, dir. pastoral care, 1988—. Bd. dirs. Planned Parenthood Assn., Erie County, pres.; by-laws com. West Peoria Residents Assn.; commr. Joint Commn. for Accrediation of Pastoral Svcs. Mem. Assn. for Clin. Pastoral Edn. (mem. standards com. Eastern region, chairperson North region accreditation com., rep. nat. accreditation commn.). Avocation: rebuilding automobiles. Home: 2011 W Callender Peoria IL 60604 Office: Meth Med Ctr Ill 221 NE Glen Oak Peoria IL 66636

MACGILLIVRAY, LOIS ANN, academic administrator; b. Phila., July 8, 1937; d. Alexander and Mary Ethel (Crosby) MacG. BA in History, Holy Names Coll., 1966; MA in Sociology, U. N.C., 1971, PhD in Sociology, 1973. Joined Sisters of Holy Names of Jesus and Mary, 1955. Research asst. U. N.C., Chapel Hill, 1969-70, 71-72, instr. sociology, 1970-71; sociologist Rsch. Triangle Inst., Durham, N.C., 1973-75, sr. sociologist, 1975-81; dir. Ctr. for Population and Urban-Rural Studies, Research Triangle Inst., Durham, N.C., 1976-81; pres. Holy Names Coll., Oakland, Calif., 1982—; mem. steering com. Symposium for Bus. Leaders Holy Names Col., 1982—; mem. policy bd. Univ. Oakland Met. Forum, co-convenor panel on edn. and youth. Bd. dirs. Oakland Coun. Econ. Devel., 1984-86. Mem. Am. Sociol. Assn., Assn. Ind. Calif. Colls. and Univs. (exec. com. 1985—, vice chmn. 1989—), Regional Assn. East Bay Colls. and Univs. (past pres., bd. dirs. 1982—). Avocation: birding. Home: 3500 Mountain Blvd Oakland CA 94619-9989 Office: Holy Names Coll 3500 Mountain Blvd Oakland CA 94619-9989

MACGREGOR, GEDDES, author, emeritus philosophy educator; b. Glasgow, Scotland, Nov. 13, 1909; came to U.S., 1949, naturalized, 1957; s. Thomas and Blanche (Geddes) MacG.; m. Elizabeth Sutherland McAllister, Aug. 14, 1941; children: Marie, Martin. B.D., U. Edinburgh, 1939, LL.B., 1943; D. Phil., U. Oxford (Queen's Coll.), 1945, D.D., 1959; D. ès L. summa cum laude, U. Paris, 1951; L.H.D. (hon.), Hebrew Union Coll., 1978. Ordained priest Episcopal Ch., 1968. Sr. asst. chaplain to dean of Chapel Royal, St. Giles' Cathedral, Edinburgh, 1939-41; minister Trinity Ch., Pollokshields, Glasgow, 1941-49; asst. to prof. logic U. Edinburgh, 1947-49; Rufus Jones assoc. prof. philosophy and religion Bryn Mawr Coll., 1949-55, prof., 1955-60; examiner Swarthmore Coll., Hebrew Union Coll.; dean grad. sch. religion, prof. philos. religion U. So. Calif., 1960-66, Disting. prof. philosophy, 1966-75, Disting. prof. philosophy emeritus, 1975—; vis. prof. U. B.C., 1963, 66, 73, Hebrew Union Coll., 1964-65, World Campus Afloat, Orient, 1974, Mediterranean, 1975, McGill U., 1976, Inst. Shipboard Edn. Round-the-World Voyage, 1977, U. Iowa, 1979, U. Sask., 1979; life fellow Coll. Preachers Wash. Nat. Cathedral; vis. fellow Ezra Stiles Coll., dept. religious studies Yale, 1967-68, Coll. Preachers, Washington Nat. Cathedral, 1991; canon theologian St. Paul's Cathedral, Los Angeles, 1968-74; honorary canon St. Paul's Cathedral, San Diego, 1987—; spl. preacher St. Paul's Cathedral, London, 1969; spl. preacher Westminster Abbey, 1970; Birks lectr. McGill U., 1976; Warren lectr. U. Dubuque, 1979; guest lectr. Am. Scottish Found., 1981, Rikkyo U., Tokyo, 1981; lectured widely on four continents, since 1981. Author: Aesthetic Experience in Religion, 1947, Christian Doubt, 1951, Les Frontières de la morale et de la religion, 1952, From a Christian Ghetto, 1954, The Vatican Revolution, 1957, The Thundering Scot, 1957, The Tichborne Impostor, 1957, Corpus Christi, 1959, Introduction to Religious Philosophy, 1959, The Bible in the Making, 1959, The Coming Reformation, 1960, The Hemlock and the Cross, 1963 (Gold medal, Calif. Lit. award 1964), God Beyond Doubt, 1966, The Sense of Absence, 1968, A Literary History of the Bible, 1968, So Help Me God, 1970, Philosophical Issues in Religious Thought, 1973, The Rhythm of God, 1974, He Who Lets Us Be, 1975, 87, Reincarnation in Christianity, 1978, German transl. 1985, Portuguese transl., 1991, Gnosis, 1979, Scotland Forever Home, 1980, 84, 88, reissued as Scotland: An Intimate Portrait, 1990, The Nicene Creed Illumined by Modern Thought, 1980, Reincarnation as a Christian Hope, 1981, The Gospels as a Mandala of Wisdom, 1982, The Christening of Karma, 1984 (German transl. 1986), Apostles Extraordinary, 1986, Angels, 1988, Dictionary of Religion and Philosophy, 1989, Images of Afterlife: Beliefs from Antiquity to Modern Times, 1992; editor: Immortality and Human Destiny: A Variety of Views, 1986; contbr. to encys. and periodicals. Regent Am-Scottish Found., N.Y.C., 1968—. Served with Brit. civil def.; Chaplain Red Cross World War II. Recipient medal nat. soc. SAR, 1989. Fellow Royal Soc. Lit. (life); mem. Am. Philos. Assn., Am. Acad. Religion, Speculative Soc. (extraordinary life mem.), Edinburgh U. Dialectic Soc. (hon. life, past pres.), Internat. Soc. for Philos. Enquiry (diplomate, highest hon. award 1991), Am. Mensa, English-Speaking Union, St. Andrew's Soc. Los Angeles (hon. chaplain, historian, pres. 1987-88), The Athenaeum, Commonwealth Trust (London), Union Soc. (Oxford), Phi Kappa Phi (Disting. award 1982). Home: 876 Victoria Ave Los Angeles CA 90005-3751 *Ever since I was old enough to handle money I abhorred debt as slavery and I have since grown to account political forms of debt an even more unendurable yoke.*

MACGREGOR, MALCOLM DOUGLAS, minister; b. Oakland, Calif., Feb. 21, 1945; s. Gregor Donal and Bernice Madeline (Chadbourne) MacG.; m. Mary Margaret "Meg" Little, Feb. 8, 1964; children: Gregor D., George D., Margaret Mary, Gordon D. BS, Portland State U., 1967. Ordained to ministry Internat. Ch. Foursquare Gospel, 1977; CPA, Oreg. Lectr. in field. Author: Your Money Matters, 1977, Financial Planning Guide for Your Money Matters, 1978, Money Matters for Kids, 1980. Bd. dirs. North Clackamas Sch. Dist., Milwaukie, Oreg., 1970-72; treas., mem. bd. regents Life Bible Coll., L.A., 1978-83; mem. Health Facilities Cost Control Commn., 1973-76. Mem. NAE. Home: 4618 SW Pacific Coast Hwy

Waldport OR 97394 Office: Reality Ministries PO Box 5926 San Jose CA 95150

MACGREGOR, STEPHEN MAYO, clergyman; b. Balt., Mar. 17, 1957; s. George Irving and Rose Hilda (Dahlke) MacG.; m. Cindy Kay Maddox, June 4, 1983; children: Bethany, Berea, Jordan. Diploma, Berean Coll., 1984; BA, Southwestern Assemblies of God, 1990. Ordained to ministry Assemblies of God Ch., 1987. Nat. outreach team worker World Challenge, Teen Challenge, Dallas, 1981-82; pastor Damascus Rd. Assemblies of God Ch., 1983-85; asst. pastor Bethesda (Md.) Assemblies of God Ch., 1986-87; missions pastor First Assembly of God Ch., Marlinton, W.Va., 1988-90; pastor youth evangelism Highway Assembly of God Ch., Fredericksburg, Va., 1990—; mem. Com. on Home Missions and Small Ch. Devel.; mem. Spl. Conf. White House, Coaliton Religious Leaders, Washington. Recipient Christian Leadership award Leadership Coun. Mem. Nat. Religious Broadcasters, Am. Coalition Traditional Values, Moral Majority. Republican. Home: 10819 Leavells Rd Fredericksburg VA 22405 Office: Highway Assemblies God Ch 2221 Jefferson Davis Fredericksburg VA 22401

MACHADO, JOÃO SOMANE, bishop; b. Morrumbene, Mozambique, May 16, 1946; s. Somane Machado and Uassitissa Fafetine; m. Nocia Madonela, Nov. 11, 1975; children: Thyreza Loyde, Jorge Floyd, Sergio Abraão, Francina Beth. BA in Theology, U. Sao Paulo, 1978; MA in Theology, U. Zaire, 1984. Youth leader United Meth. Ch., Inhambane, Mozambique, 1968-69; choir dir. Free Meth. Ch., Inharrime, Mozambique, 1969-71, dir. Christian edn., tchr., 1974-75; tchr., dir. Theol. Sch., Cambine, Mozambique, 1979-82; pastor, tchr., asst. to bishop Cambine, Mozambique, 1984-88; bishop United Meth. Ch., Maputo, Mozambique, 1988—. Home: Ave Kwame Krumah #931, Maputo Mozambique Office: Igreja Metodista Unida, Caixa Postal 2640, Maputo Mozambique

MACHARG, KENNETH DAVID RILEY, missionary, broadcaster; b. Detroit, Dec. 4, 1942; s. Alfred Moss and Virginia Ruth (Riley) MacH.; m. Alice Mathilde Ballantine, Sept. 10, 1965; children: Beth MacHarg Brown, Brian. BA, Maryville Coll., Tenn., 1965; MDiv, Louisville Presbyn. Theol. Sem., 1968; postgrad., U. Louisville, 1972-73, U. Dubuque Theol. Sem., 1975-76. Ordained to ministry United Ch. of Christ, 1968. Pastor West Louisville United Ch. of Christ, 1969-74, Margarita (Republic of Panama) Union Ch., 1974-77, St. Luke's United Ch. of Christ, Jeffersonville, Ind., 1977-79; exec. dir. Kentuckiana Interfaith Community, Louisville, 1979-90; missionary broadcaster HCJB, Quito, Ecuador, 1990—; guest lectr. Louisville Presbyn. Sem., Spalding U., Bellarmine Coll., U. W.I., Jamaica; cons. Henson Broadcasting Co., Louisville, 1984—, Louisville United Against Hunger; spl. rep. World Radio Missionary Fellowship, Ky. and Ind. Author: Tune In The World, The Listener's Guide to International Shortwave Radio, 1983; also articles; former co-editor Internat. Radio mag.; editor The Mission Herald, 1991—. Advisor Hispanic ministry, chair missions com. St. Matthew's Bapt. Ch.; mem. bd. advisors Habitat for Humanity, 1989—. Recipient cert. of appreciation City of Louisville, Disting. Citizen award City of Louisville, Outstanding Young Religious Leader award Jeffersonville Jaycees, Disting Svc. awards City of Louisville, Dare to Care, Bd. Aldermen of Louisville; named to Hon. Order of Ky. Cols. Mem. Louisville Assn. Community Ministries (chair 1986-90). Democrat. Address: care Sta HCJB, Casilla 691, Quito Ecuador also: care Sta HCJB Box 553000 Opa Locka FL 33055-0401

MACHARSKI, FRANCISZEK CARDINAL, archbishop of Krakow; b. Cracow, Poland, May 20, 1927. D.Theology. Ordained priest Roman Cath. Ch., 1950; engaged in pastoral work, 1950-56; theol. studies, Fribourg, Switzerland, 1956-60; tchr. pastoral theology Faculty Theology, Krakow, 1963; rector Archdiocesan Sem., Krakow, 1970; archbishop of Krakow, 1979—; elevated to Sacred Coll. of Cardinals , 1979; titular ch., St. John at the Latin Gate; mem. Congregation of Clergy, 1979, Congregation of Cath. Edn., 1981, Congregation for Bishops, 1983, coun. for pub. affairs, 1984; mem. Congregation for Insts. of Consecrated Life and for Socs. of Apostolic Life, 1989; v.p. Polish Bishops Conf., 1979; vice chair Sci. Coun. Polish Episcopate, 1981, Episcopate Com. for Gen. Ministry, 1979; chair Episcopate Com. for Cath. Sci., 1983; mem. Episcopate Com. for Emigration Ministry, 1988. Address: ul Franciszkanska 3, 31-004 Krakow Poland

MACHLE, EDWARD JOHNSTONE, emeritus educator; b. Canton, China, Sept. 29, 1918; s. Edward Charles and Jean (Mawson) M.; m. Neva Hull, Aug. 29, 1942; children—Stewart, Douglas, Kathi; m. Mary Lou Reynolds, Dec. 15, 1970; 1 child, Michelle; stepchildren—Rebecca, Richard, Harvey, Robin. Student, Pacific Lutheran Jr. Coll., 1937; B.A., Whitworth Coll., 1939; B.D., San Francisco Theol. Sem., 1942, M.A., 1944; Ph.D., Columbia U., 1952. Ordained to ministry Presbyn. Ch., 1942; minister in Concrete, Wash., 1942-43; asst. minister San Francisco, 1943-44, Mineola, N.Y., 1944-46; instr. Columbia, 1946-47; asst. prof. U. Colo., 1947-53, asso. prof., 1953-63, prof., 1963-80, emeritus, 1981—, chmn. dept., 1951-52, 56-58, 66-69; vis. lectr. U. Alta., summer 1960, Iliff Sch. Theology, 1962, Evergreen State, 1981, Peninsula Coll., 1986—; in-parish research dir. San Francisco Theol. Sem.; dir. music St. Andrew Presbyn. Ch., Boulder, Colo., 1961-70; guest lectr. ch. music U. Colo. Sch. Music, 1950-65; disting. faculty fellow Sheldon Jackson Coll., 1986-88. Mem. Am. Phil. Assn., Soc. Asian and Comparative Philosophy, Acad. Religion. Presbyterian. Home: 515 Simmons St Port Angeles WA 98362 *Faith is largely willingness to learn of what can destroy us. Idolatry feeds on our fear of having faith. Research methods spring from the soil of our cultured idolatries. Thus, to learn, faith must at times be a traitor to "learning."*

MACINTOSH, MICHAEL KIRK, minister; b. Portland, Oreg., Mar. 26, 1944; s. Wilbur MacIntosh and Ruth (Lane) Osborn; m. Sandra Crill Riddet, Apr. 3, 1971 (div. 1968), remarried Apr. 1971; children: Melinda, David, Megan, Jonathan, Phillip. M of Ministry, Azusa Pacific U., Calif., 1988, MDiv, 1989. Ordained to ministry Calvary Chapel, 1972. Asst. pastor Calvary Chapel, Santa Ana, Calif., 1971-72; dir. Maranatha Music, Santa Ana, Calif., 1972-74; pastor Horizon Christian Fellowship, San Diego, 1975—; pres. Youth Devel. Inc., San Diego, 1988—, Horizon Internat. Ministries, San Diego, 1980—; guest speaker Billy Graham Evang. Crusade, Anaheim, Calif., 1985. Author: Attributes of a Christian Woman, 1979, Finding God, 1989; creator, host TV program Wake Up America, 1977 (Emmy award); speaker various radio programs. Police chaplain San Diego Police Dept., 1988—, reserve officer, 1983-89; commr. San Diego Crime Commn., 1988-89; assisted in release of 7 Siberians from U.S. Embassy in Moscow, 1982. With USNG, 1962-65. Mem. San Diego Evang. Assn., Internat. Assn. Police Chaplains. Avocations: swimming, jogging, flying, hiking, golf. Office: Horizon Internat 4575 Ruffner St San Diego CA 92111

MACK, FRANK J., minister; b. Lueders, Tex., May 14, 1922; s. Frank W. and Malinda Elizabeth (George) M.; m. A. Inez Pearson, June 10, 1944; 1 child, Ranelda Inez (Mrs. Donald Hunsicker). Student, S.W. Assemblies God Bible Sch., Ft. Worth, 1942-43, Cen. Bible Inst., Springfield, Mo., 1944-46; DD (hon.), Belin Meml. U., Chillicothe, Mo., 1959; ThD, Trinity So. Bible Sem., Mullins, S.C., 1963, DD (hon.), 1963; D Counseling (hon.), Mid-States Bible Coll., Des Moines, 1974. Ordained to ministry Assemblies of God, 1944, Ind. Assemblies of God, 1951; Full Gospel Fellowship, 1972. Evangelist, 1941-47; pres. Christ's Ambs. West Tex. Dist. Assembly of God, 1944-47; pastor Cen. Assembly of God, Lubbock, Tex., 1946-47, First Assembly of God, Yuma, Ariz., 1947-48; evangelist Nat. Interdenom. Healing, 1948-73; pastor Christian Ctr., Ft. Worth, 1966-67; dir. Pastoral Counseling Ctr., Ft. Worth and Gadsden, Ala., 1973-80; min. Bethel Revival Tabernacle, Gadsden, Ala., 1974-79; tchr. Ch. and Family Inst. of Bibl. Studies, Gadsden, 1977-79; min., counselor, tchr. The Lord's Ch., Bellflower, Calif., 1980—; radio and TV ministry, including Keys for Charismatic Living, Ft. Worth, 1973-74, Counseling Corner, PTL TV Network, 1974-79; founder, pres. Upper-Room Christian Fellowship, Inc., 1961—. Author: Doom's Day Weapon, 1964, Eleventh Hour Reapers, 1970, The Pentecostals' Ten Commandments, 1972, The Holy Spirit in the Life and Ministry of Jesus, 1973. Mem. Internat. Assn. Christian Clin. Counselors, Internat. Assn. Christian Pastoral Counselors (cert. diplomat), Christian Assn. Psychol. Studies. Home: 13443 Mulberry Dr Whittier CA 90605 Office: The Lord's Ch 9740 Flower St Bellflower CA 90706 *God's Spirit at work through us heals the sick, mends broken hearts, and restores relationships. The Holy Spirit is not a cultural homogenizer; He is the maximizer of human diversity and potential—the source of abundant life.*

MACK, MICHAEL LAVOY, youth leader, engineer; b. Owosso, Mich., Mar. 28, 1959; s. L.C. Charles and Janet Thelma (Greene) M.; m. Mary Lynn Clark, July 26, 1980. BS in Mech. Engring., Mich. State U., 1981. Hunger corps vol. Food for the Hungry, Potosi, Bolivia, 1986-88; youth leader Niles (Mich.) Evangelical Free Ch., 1989—; sr. engr. Bendix Automotive Brakes, South Bend, Ind., 1988—. Mem. So. Automotive Engrs. Evangelical Free. Home: 52423 Portage Rd South Bend IN 46628 *God created man to have fellowship with Him. It doesn't take an engineer to recognize the fact that things generally work best when they are used as the inventor intended.*

MACK, THOMAS RUSSELL, religious organization administrator, management consultant; b. Independence, Iowa, May 22, 1955; s. Russell John and Anna (Catherin) M.; children: Christopher E., Stephen A. BA, Morningside Coll., 1978; MBA, U. S.D., 1988. V.p. fin. Shepherd Ministries, Inc., Milo, Iowa, 1981—, also bd. dirs.; mem. counseling ministry, bd. dirs. Zadok, Inc., Des Moines, 1981-84; dir. rsch. Urim Rsch., Inc., Independence, 1988—.

MACKAY, FAYE L., ecumenical agency administrator. Head Moncton Area Coun. Chs., Hillsborough, N.B., Can. Office: Moncton Area Coun Chs, Site 9/Comp 7/RR #1, Hillsborough, NB Canada E0A 1X0*

MACKELLAR, JAMES MARSH, minister; b. Wilkes-Barre, Pa., June 23, 1931; s. Gordon and Anita Ferous (Cornelius) MacK.; m. A. Eugenia Orthey, Aug. 20, 1955; children: Ian James, Margaret Alice, Bruce William. BA, Cornell U., 1952; MDiv, Princeton Theol Sem., 1955. Ordained to ministry Presbyn. Ch. in U.S.A., 1955. Pastor 1st Presbyn. Ch., Dryden, N.Y., 1955-59, Waverly, N.Y., 1959-65, Stirling, N.J., 1965-76; pastor Forest Presbyn. Ch., Lyons Falls, N.Y., 1976-85; stated clk. Presbytery, Newton, N.J., 1970-75, Presbytery of No. New Eng., 1987—; stated clk. Synod of the N.E., 1975—, Presbytery of No. New Eng., 1987—. Capt. Twp. Passaic, N.J., First Aid Squad, 1974-76. Mem. Nat. Assn. Parliamentarians (registered parliamentarian), Vt. Ecumenical Coun. and Bible Soc. (v.p. 1990-91, pres. 1991—). Home: RD 1 Box 229 Newport Center VT 05857 Office: 3049 E Genesee St Syracuse NY 13224

MACKENZIE, DONALD MATTHEW, JR., minister; b. Chgo., Mar. 25, 1944; s. Donald Matthew Sr. and Ruth Vicory (Yoakum) M.; m. Judith Joy Petterson, May 31, 1966; children: Mary Hye Won, Alice Eun Ah. AB, Macalester Coll., 1966; MDiv, Princeton (N.J.) Sem., 1970, ThM, 1971; PhD, NYU, 1978. Assoc. dir. field edn. Princeton Sem., 1971-80; assoc. pastor Nassau Presbyn. Ch., Princeton, 1980-83; pastor The Ch. of Christ at Dartmouth Coll., Hanover, N.H., 1983—; examiner D in Ministry program Princeton Sem., 1980—; adj. prof. practical theology Bangor (Maine) Theol. Sem., 1991—. Contbr. articles to profl. jours. Bd. dirs. Trenton (N.J.) Ecumenical Area Ministry, 1977-83, Wesley-Westminster Found., Princeton U., 1981-83. Mem. Assn. Profs. and Researchers in Religious Edn., Grafton Orange Assn. United Ch. of Christ, N.H. Conf. United Ch. of Christ (trustee 1990—), Phi Delta Kappa. Democrat. Home: 16 Conant Rd Hanover NH 03755 Office: Ch of Christ Dartmouth Coll 40 College St Hanover NH 03755 *I think the biggest challenge facing us in the near future is to accept the essential uncertainty of human experience and to look for guidance to the Gospel, which I believe is a guide to living with uncertainty.*

MAC KENZIE, JAMES DONALD, clergyman; b. Detroit, Nov. 17, 1924; s. James and Ida Catherine (Conklin) M.; student Moody Bible Inst., 1946-49, Union Theol. Sem., 1952; m. Elsie Joan Kerr, May 7, 1960; children—Janet Eileen, Kayly Kathleen, Christy Carol, Kenneth Kerr. Ordained to ministry Presbyn. Ch., 1953; pastor Calvary Ch., Swan Quarter, N.C., Edenton (N.C.) Presbyn. Ch., 1952-60, Kirkwood Ch., Kannapolis, N.C., 1960-64, Barbecue and Olivia Ch., Olivia, N.C., 1964-71, Elise Ch., Robbins, N.C., 1971-87, Horseshoe Presbyn. Ch., Carbonton, N.C., 1971—. Historian, Fayetteville Presbytery, 1975—, chmn. hist. com., 1983—, moderator, 1978. Founder, Conf. on Celtic Studies, Campbell Coll., Buies Creek, N.C., 1972—; councillor Conf. on Scottish Studies (Can.), 1968-75. With AUS, 1943-45, ETO. Decorated Purple Heart, Bronze Star; recipient Disting. Citizen award, Robbins, 1983. Fellow Soc. Antiquaries Scotland; mem. N.C. Presbyn. Hist. Soc. (pres. 1972-74, Author's award 1970, 75, Cert. Merit 1975), Harnett Hist. Soc. (pres. 1968-71, Distinguished Service award 1970), Irish Uilleann Pipers Soc., Gaelic Soc. of Inverness, An Comunn Gaidhelach (life). Author: Colorful Heritage, 1970; editor: The Uilleann Piper, 1974—; contbr. articles to profl. jours. Home: PO Box 867 Robbins NC 27325 *I would be like Jesus.*

MACKENZIE, JOHN ANDERSON ROSS, educator, minister; b. Edinburgh, Scotland, Aug. 26, 1927; came to U.S., 1959; s. Donald Ross and Edith Agnes (Anderson) M.; m. Flora Margaret Duncan, July 14, 1951; children: Sheena, Donald, Alasdair. MA with honors, Edinburgh U., 1949, BD with Distinction, 1952, PhD, 1962; Teol. Lic., U. Lund, Sweden, 1964. Ordained to ministry Ch. of Scotland, 1953. Min. St. Andrew's Clermiston, Edinburgh, 1954-59, Westminster Presbyn. Ch., Richmond, Va., 1959-64; prof. ch. history Union Theol. Sem., Va., 1964-81; sr. min. 1st Presbyn. Ch., Gainesville, Fla., 1981-89; dir. dept. religion Chautauqua (N.Y.) Instn., 1989—; adj. prof. Cath. U., Washington, 1965-71; vis. prof. Orthodox Theol. Sem., Kottayam, India, 1972-73. Author: Trying New Sandals, 3d edit., 1977, Christian Passages, 1986, (with Elaine Kaye) William Edwin Orchard: A Study in Christian Exploration, 1990. Mem. Downtown Redevel. Agy., Gainesville, 1983-89; bd. dirs. North Fla. Retirement Village, Gainesville, 1984-89, chmn. 1987-89; bd. dirs. Samaritan Ctr., Gainesville, 1987-89. Recipient Patronal medal Cath. U. Am., Washington, 1977. Democrat. Home: 65 W Summit Ave Lakewood NY 14750 Office: Chautauqua Instn Dept Religion Chautauqua NY 14722

MACKEY, JEFFREY ALLEN, minister; b. Kingston, N.Y., July 12, 1952; s. Allen William and Vivian Mathilda (Hornbeck) M.; m. Martha LaVonne Webster, Dec. 18, 1971; children: Guy Linwood, Kenyon Paul, Geoffrey Joel. BS, Nyack Coll., 1974; D of Sacred Lit., Ridgedale Theol. Sem., 1975; M Ministry, Trinity Coll., Andover, N.Y., 1976; D Ministry, Mansfield Sch. Div., 1985, Grad. Theol. Found., 1990. Ordained to ministry Congl. Christian Ch., 1974. Min. music Neversink Valley Bapt. Ch., Huguenot, N.Y., 1969-70; pastor Ponckhockie Congl. Ch., Kingston, 1971-74, The Alliance Ch., Andover, 1974-76; acad. dean Macon (Ga.) Bible Inst., 1976-78; min. Oak Grove Gospel Tabernacle, Williamsport, Pa., 1977-80, 69th St. Alliance Ch., Phila., 1980-83; sr. min. Vestavia Alliance Ch., Birmingham, Ala., 1983-87, Hope Alliance Ch., New Hartford, N.Y., 1987-91; pastoral assoc. Grace Ch., Utica, N.Y, 1991—. Author: A Worship Manifesto, 1986, Indicatives and Imperatives, 1987, Christ's Centripetal Cross, 1990; contbr. numerous articles to profl. jours. Mem. Nat. Fedn. for Decency, Birmingham, Alcohol and Drug Abuse Prevention Treatment Program, Birmingham, 1987-88. Mem. Am. Assn. Christian Schs., Fellowship Christian Sch. Adminstrs., Evang. Theol. Soc., Am. Assn. Sch. Adminstrs., Am. Guild Organists. Republican. Avocations: organ and piano playing, collecting art and statues, hymn writing, walking, restoring antique automobiles. Home: Rt 1 Box 246B New Hartford NY 13413 Office: Grace Ch Episcopal 6 Elizabeth St Utica NY 13501

MACKEY, SALLY, retired religious organization administrator; b. Seattle, Feb. 17, 1930; d. Rillmond Weible and Helen Annajane (Bovee) Schear; m. Hallie Willis Mackey, May 22, 1953; children: Melinda Kay, John Mark, Heather Lynn. BA, U. Wash., 1951; postgrad., San Francisco Theol. Sem., 1951-53. Teenage program dir., camp dir. YWCA, Seattle, 1953-55; sponsor, devel. Wash. Assn. Chs. Immigration and Refugee Program (affiliate Ch. World Svc.), Seattle, 1979-85, dir., 1985-90; bd. dirs., v.p. Ch. Coun. Greater Seattle, 1974-84 ; bd. dirs. Wash. Assn. Chs., 1976-79; mem. Gen. Assembly Mission Coun. Presbyn. Ch., N.Y.C., 1979-83, adv. com. on ecumenical rels., Presbyn. Ch. (U.S.A.), Louisville, 1989—; Presbyn. Ch. (U.S.A.) del. to Caribbean Area Coun. World Alliance Reformed Chs., 1987—. Home: 2127 SW 162d St Seattle WA 98166

MACKEY, SHELDON ELIAS, minister; b. Bethlehem, Pa., Nov. 20, 1913; s. Elias and Pearl Elizabeth (Cunningham) M.; m. Marie Louise Dillinger, Sept. 20, 1939; children—Peter David, John Harry, Mary Susan, Timothy Andrew, Philip James. A.B., Moravian Coll., 1936; B.D., Lancaster Theol. Sem., 1939; D.D., Franklin and Marshall Coll., 1954; LL.D., Ursinus Coll., 1958. Ordained to ministry Evang. and Reformed Ch., 1939; pastor Pa. congregations, 1939-54; adminstrv. asst. to pres. Evang. and Reformed Ch., 1954-57, sec., 1957-78; also editor Yearbook, dir. correlation and sec. gen. council Gen. Synod; co-sec. United Ch. of Christ, also sec. exec. coun., adminstrv. com., 1957-61, mem. fin. and budget com., exec. sec. stewardship coun., 1961-79, bd. dirs. Pa. S.E. Conf. United Ch. of Christ. Contbr. articles to religious publs. Bd. dirs. Ursinus Coll.; trustee Lancaster Theol. Sem. Mem. Nat. Council Chs. in U.S.A. (chmn. sect. stewardship and benevolence, mem. exec. com.). Club: Phi Alpha Clergy. Home: 10 Arianna Ln Exton PA 19341 *Life has a dimension which lies beyond the visible or physical. I believe that this dimension which lies at the heart of my faith is also revealed in art, music and literature. We need to reach out into this dimension which makes life most real.*

MACKEY, STANLEY D., religious organization administrator. Pres. Can. Tract Soc., Mississauga, Ont. Office: Can Tract Soc, Box 203/Port Credit PO, Mississauga, ON Canada L5G 4L7*

MACKIN, THEODORE JAMES, priest, theology educator; b. West Hollywood, Calif., Oct. 23, 1922; s. Thomas Sinclair and Marie Theresa (Zinsley) M. A.B., Gonzaga U., Spokane, Wash., 1946, M.A., 1948; S.T.D., Gregorian U., Rome, 1958. Joined S.J., Roman Catholic Ch., 1940, ordained priest, 1953. Asst. prof. theology Santa Clara U., Calif., 1958-64, assoc. prof., 1964-72, prof., 1972—, John Nobili prof., 1980—. Author: Marriage in the Catholic Church: What is Marriage?, 1982, Marriage in the Catholic Chruch: Divorce and Remarriage, 1984. Mem. Cath. Theol. Soc. Am., Am. Acad. Religion. Democrat. Home and Office: Santa Clara U Religious Studies Dept Santa Clara CA 95053

MAC KINNON, GREGORY ALOYSIUS, religion educator, former university president; b. Antigonish, N.S., Can., June 16, 1925; s. William Francis and Mary Patricia (Chisholm) MacK. BA, St. Francis Xavier U., 1946; STL, Ottawa U., 1961, STD, PhD, 1964. Ordained priest Roman Cath. Ch., 1950. Assoc. pastor Mt. Carmel Parish, New Waterford, N.S., 1950-54; mem. faculty St. Francis Xavier U., Antigonish, 1954-60, 63-90, assoc. dean arts, dir. summer sch., 1970-78, pres., 1978-90, vice chancellor, 1978-90; mem. acad. council Atlantic Inst. Edn., 1975-78; pres. Atlantic Ecumenical Commn., 1974-76; mem. adv. com. Internat. Devel. Office, Can.; chmn. Council N.S. Univ. Presidents, 1985—. Chmn. Nova Scotia Home Care Adv. Com., 1987—. Commr. N.S. Royal Commn. on Forestry, 1982-84. Mem. Assn. Atlantic Univs. (exec. council), Assn. Univs. and Colls. Can. (exec. heads), Soc. for Sci. Study Religion, Coll. Theology Soc. Office: St Francis Xavier U, PO Box 116, Antigonish, NS Canada B2G 1C0

MACKLIN, F. DOUGLAS, bishop. Bishop Ch. of God in Christ, Memphis. Office: Ch of God in Christ 1230 Tipton Memphis TN 38071*

MAC KNIGHT, JAMES, minister. Gen. supt. The Pentecostal Assemblied Can., Mississauga, Ont. Office: Pentecostal Assemblies Can, 3081 Ness Ave, Winnipeg, MB Canada R2Y 2G3*

MACKY, PETER WALLACE, religion educator, minister; b. Auckland, New Zealand, July 22, 1937; came to U.S., 1939; s. Wallace Armstrong and Mary MacLean (Whitfield) M.; m. Nancy Ann Space, Sept. 9, 1961; children: Cameron, Christopher. AB in Engring., Harvard U., 1957; BA in Theology, Oxford (Eng.) U., 1962, MA, 1966, PhD in N.T., 1967; BD, Princeton Theol. Sem., 1963, ThD, 1970; postdoctoral studies, Fuller Sem., 1981. Ordained to ministry United Presbyn. Ch. (U.S.A.), 1967. Flight test engr. Lockheed Aircraft, 1957-59; instr. Princeton Theol. Sem., 1964-65, 67; asst. pastor Pacific Palisades (Calif.) Presbyn. Ch., 1967-70; asst. prof. religion Westminster Coll., New Wilmington, Pa., 1970-74, assoc. prof., 1974-83, prof., 1983—, chair dept. religion and philosophy, 1983-88; mem. task force on women Shenango Presbytery, Presbyn. Ch. (U.S.A.), 1974-76, chair task force, 1974-76; interim preacher San Marino (Calif.) Community Ch., 1981; instr. New Orleans Bapt. Theol. Sem., 1982; lectr. Chautauqua Instn., 1984, 86, Pitts. Theol. Sem., 1986, Princeton Theol. Sem., 1986, Writing Acad. Ann. Conf., Madison, Wis., 1986. Author: The Bible in Dialogue with Modern Man, 1970, Violence: Right or Wrong?, 1973, The Pursuit of the Divine Snowman, 1977, Candles in the Dark: Modern Parables, 1986, The Centrality of Metaphors in Biblical Thought: A Theory of Interpretation, 1990; also articles; (with others) A Guide to Contemporary Hermeneutics: Major Trends in Biblical Interpretation, 1986. Tchr. adult class New Wilmington United Presbyn. Ch., 1971—, dir. jr. ch., 1972-82. Rhodes scholar, 1960; Rockefeller fellow, 1965-66; NEH grantee, 1975, 79. Mem. Soc. Bibl. Lit. Home: RD 1 Susan Trace New Wilmington PA 16142 Office: Westminster Coll New Wilmington PA 16172

MACLEAN, IAIN STEWART, minister, educator; b. Bellville, South Africa, Jan. 6, 1956; came to U.S., 1984; s. William Mathie and Elizabeth (Symes) M. BA, U. Cape Town, South Africa, 1976, U. South Africa, Pretoria, 1982; BD, Rhodes U., Grahamstown, South Africa, 1980; ThM, Princeton Theol. Sem., 1985; postgrad. studies in theology, Harvard Divinity Sch., 1991—. Ordained to ministry Presbyn. Ch., 1979. Min. Presbyn. Ch. (So. Africa), Grootfontein, Namibia, 1979-81, Heidelburg, South Africa, 1981-84; dir. edn. First Parish, United Congl. Ch., Lincoln, Mass., 1985-87; min. edn. First Congl. Ch., West Boylston, Mass., 1987-90; teaching fellow Harvard U., Cambridge, Mass., 1987—; pulpit supply Presbytery of Boston, 1985—. Danforth fellow, 1991. Mem. Am. Acad. Religion, Soc. Bibl. Lit., Royal Philatelic Soc. (Bronze medal 1973). Office: 45 Francis Ave Cambridge MA 02138 *Human beings are called to responsible living and (re) creating of life. This will involve struggle and conflict, but its reward will be in a life well lived for others.*

MACLEAN, PETER DUNCAN, minister; b. N.Y.C., Sept. 6, 1930; s. Charles Waldo and Grace Elizabeth (Mentzer) MacL.; m. Barbara Crockett, June 7, 1952 (div. 1969); children: Elizabeth, Andrea, Timothy, Margaret; m. Margaret Ellen Mayer, Oct. 3, 1970; 1 child, Matthew. BA, Trinity Coll., Hartford, Conn., 1952; MDiv, Gen. Theol. Sem., N.Y.C., 1955. Ordained Presbyter, Episcopal Ch., 1955. Rector St. James Episcopal Ch., St. James, N.Y., 1967-70; dir. personnel Pratt Inst., Bklyn., 1970-74; indsl. counselor MacField Texturing, Mayodan, N.C., 1974-76; rector St. Mary's Episcopal Ch., Shelter Island, N.Y., 1976—; chaplain Shelter Island Fire Dept., 1976—; pres. The Anglican Found., Inc., Mineola, N.Y., 1985—; cons. The Parish Resource Ctr., Rocky Point, N.Y., 1988—. Author/editor newsletter, The Inside Tract, 1980-84, The Outside Tract, 1990—. Pres. Ea. Long Island Hosp., Greenport, N.Y., 1986-89; convener Shelter Island Sr Citizens, 1986-90; adult leader Boy Scouts Am., Shelter Island, 1976—. Lt. comdr., USNR, 1964-67. Mem. Lions (pres. 1978-79). Democrat. Office: Saint Marys Episcopal Ch PO Box 1660 Shelter Island NY 11964-1660

MACLEOD, DONALD, clergyman, educator; b. Broughton, N.S., Can., Dec. 31, 1913; s. Donald Archibald and Anne (MacKenzie) M.; m. Norma Eliner Harper, Jan. 5, 1948 (dec. Mar. 1972); children: John Fraser, David Ainslie, Anne, Leslie. A.B., Dalhousie U., Halifax, N.S., 1934, M.A., 1935, LL.D., 1978; B.D. (E.F. Grant scholar), Pine Hill Div. Hall, Halifax, 1938, D.D., 1970; Th.D., U. Toronto, 1947. Teaching fellow dept. English Dalhousie U., 1935-38; ordained to ministry Presbyn. Ch., 1938; minister First Ch., Louisburg, N.S., 1938-41; assoc. minister Bloor St. Ch., Toronto, 1941-45; sr. tutor Men's Residences Victoria Coll., Toronto, 1943-45; teaching fellow dept. homiletics Princeton Theol. Sem., 1946-47; asst. prof., 1947-53, assoc. prof., 1953-61, prof., 1961—, Francis L. Patton prof., 1982—; lectr. Princeton Summer Inst. Theology, 1948—; vis. lectr. Westminster Choir Coll., 1952, 55-58; lectr. Gettysburg Sem., 1952, Jr. Pastors Sch., Reading, Pa., 1954, Conf. on Evangelism, Whitby, Ont., 1957, Hampton (Va.) Inst., 1957, Union Sem., Richmond, Va., 1958, Crozier Sem., Chester, Pa., 1961, Ann. Pastors Conf. Am. Luth. Ch., Green Lake, Wis., 1966, Coll. Preachers, Nat. Cathedral Washington, 1967; lectr. continuing edn. Presbyn. Coll., Montreal, 1972-75; Mullins lectr. So. Baptist Theol. Sem., 1970; Kyes' lectr. Kirk in the Hills, Detroit, 1973; Oliver lectr. Nazarene Theol. Sem., 1985; Jameson Jones lectr. Duke U. Sch. Div., 1987; chmn. Synod Com. on Capital Ch., Trenton, N.J.; mem. coms. Christian edn., candidates and credentials, social edn. and action Presbytery New Brunswick; commr. Gen. Assembly United Presbyn. Ch., Oklahoma City, 1965; spl. preacher Princeton, Lehigh, Muhlenberg, Mt. Allison U., Duke U. and Rutgers U. Chapels, Chgo. Sunday Evening Club, Am. Preacher Series Eaton Meml. Ch., Toronto, Chatauqua Evangelist, Riverside Ch., N.Y.C., Fifth Ave. Presbyn Ch., N.Y.C., Nat. Presbyn. Ch., Washington, Preaching

Mission McGuire AFB, Chaplains Seminars, USAF, 1967-68; adv. bd. Chapel of Princeton U. Author: Word and Sacrament, 1960, Presbyterian Worship, 1965, 2d edit., 1981, Higher Reaches, 1971, Proclamation, 1975; editor: Here Is My Method, 1952, Princeton Pulpit Prayers, 1987, Know the Way, Keep the Truth, Win the Life, 1987, The Problem of Preaching, 1987, Palms and Thorns, 1990; editor: Princeton Sem. Bull., 1956-82, Translator Dynamics of Worship, 1967; mem. editorial bd. Theology Today, 1948-61, Pulpit Preaching, 1970—, Pulpit Digest, 1980—; Am. corr.: The United Church Observer, 1947-56; N.J. corr.: The Christian Century, 1957-65; ecumenical editor Good News, Sunday Pubis. Inc., 1983—; contbr. Vols. I and IV of Great Sermons and articles profl. publs. Established biennial series: Donald Macleod Lectureship on Preaching, Congl. Ch., Short Hills, N.J., 1989. Fellow Am. Assn. Theol. Schs.; mem. Am. Assn. Theol. Profs. in Practical Fields (exec. com.), Ch. Service Soc. (past v.p.), Clan Macleod Soc. Am. (chaplain), Am. Acad. Homiletics (founder, pres.). Address: PO Box 101 Princeton NJ 08542 *Too often we interpret the Boy Scouts' slogan "Be Prepared" as a caution against danger or disaster, but its thrust is largely positive. It implies being prepared for every opportunity. Never did I have any particular position in mind, but every door which has opened to me found me ready and equipped for it.*

MACLEOD, JOHN DANIEL, JR., religious organization administrator; b. Robbins, N.C., Mar. 16, 1922; s. John Daniel Sr. and Sarah Cranor (McKay) MacL.; m. Helen Frances Boggs, Sept. 18, 1945 (dec. Aug. 1990); children: Sarah MacLeod Owens, Mary Marget, John Daniel III, William Boggs. AB, Davidson (N.C.) Coll., 1942; M in Div., Union Theol. Sem., Richmond, Va., 1945, ThM, 1949, ThD, 1952. Ordained to ministry Presbyn. Ch., 1945. Pastor Carolina Beach (N.C.) Presbyn. Ch., 1945-48, Brett-Reed Presbyn. Ch., Sweet Hall, Va., 1949-53, Keyser (W.Va.) Presbyn. Ch., 1953-63; exec. Appomattox Presbytery, Lynchburg, Va., 1963-67, Norfolk (Va.) Presbytery, 1967-76, Westminster Presbytery, St. Petersburg, Fla., 1976-81; exec. Synod of N.C., Raleigh, 1981-88, ret., 1988; interim exec. Coastal Carolina Presbytery, Fayetteville, 1991—; moderator Presbyn. Synod of Va., 1969, Synod of Mid-Atlantic, 1990; mem., chmn. various local and nat. Presbyn. Ch. coms. Trustee Warren Wilson Coll., 1985-89, N.C. Presbyn. Hist. Soc., 1981—, Mary Baldwin Coll., 1960-68, Davis and Elkins Coll., 1955-61, Massanetta Springs Conf. Ctr., 1956-62; active Mineral County Redevel. Commn., Keyser, 1960-63; mem. N.C. Gov's. Adv. com. on Citizen Affairs, Raleigh, 1983-84; bd. advisors Wake Forest U. Div. Sch., 1991—. Nominee Moderator Presbyn. Ch. USA Gen. Assembly, 1987. Mem. St. Andrews Soc. (Southern Pines, N.C.) (bd. dirs. Tampa, Fla. chpt. 1976-81). Democrat. Avocations: genealogy, history, travel. Home: 809 Winston Ave Fayetteville NC 28303

MACLIN, HARRY TRACY, JR., minister; b. Oklahoma City, Nov. 27, 1925; s. Harry Tracy and Winnie Grace (Nelson) M.; m. Alice Marie Nystrom, Aug. 30, 1947; children: Susan Carol, Catherine Marie, Gregory Paul, Ruth Ellen. BA, So. Meth. U., 1949, ThM, 1952; certificat de L'Enseignement, Ecole Colonial, Brussels, 1954; DD, Asbury Coll., 1987. Ordained to ministry United Meth. Ch., 1953. Assoc. pastor, youth dir. Lakewood Meth. Ch., Dallas, 1950-52; dir. tchr. tng. inst. Cen. Zaire Ann. Conf., Lodja, 1954-59; founder, dir. Cen. Zaire Ann. Conf. Sch. for Christian Lay Workers, Lodja, 1955-59; dist. missionary, dir. rural schs. Lodja/Lomela dists. Cen. Zaire Ann. Conf., Lodja, 1957-59; assoc. prof. Kayeka-Kimbulu Sch. Theol. So. Zaire Ann. Conf., Mulungwishi, 1959-60; dir. broadcasting and audio visual svcs. All Africa Conf. Chs., Nairobi, Kenya, 1962-71; founder, dir. All Africa Christian Communications Inst., Nairobi, 1964-70; liason officer Radio Voice of the Gospel, Addis Ababa, Ethiopia, 1962-71; program counselor Southeastern Jurisdictional Coun. on Ministries, United Meth. Chs., Atlanta, 1972-74; dir. joint communications com. United Meth. Chs., Atlanta, 1972-74, field rep. for cultivation, div. edn. and cultivation Bd. Global Ministries, Southeastern jurisdiction, 1974-84; pres. Mission Soc. for United Meths., Atlanta, 1984-91, cons., 1991—; vis. lectr. Internat. Inst. Christian Communication, Salisbury, Rhodesia, 1971, Chandler Sch. Theology, Emory U., 1974-75. Contbr. articles to religious jours. Mem. Dept. ch.-related communications World Assn. for Christian Communication, mem. cen. com., 1968-71. Recipient Knight Grand Comdr. of the Humane Order of African Redemption, Republic Liberia, 1964. Home: 1723 E Clifton Rd N E Atlanta GA 30307 Office: PO Box 1103 Decatur GA 30031-1103

MACMANAMY, GARY ALLAN, minister; b. Pontiac, Mich., Apr. 17, 1946; s. Allan Alden and Sue Ann (Carlton) MacM.; m. Janine McKinley, June 18, 1971; children: Sarah Gayle, James Colin. BBA, East Tex. State U., 1970; MDiv, Southwestern Bapt. Theol. Sem., 1980. Youth min. Evang. Meth. Ch., Duncanville, Tex., 1976-78; chaplain Police Dept., Duncanville, 1979-80; pastor First Bapt. Ch., Bloomington, Tex., 1981-85, Calvary Bapt. Ch., Lawton, Okla., 1986-91, Country Estates Bapt. Ch., Midwest City, Okla., 1991—; trustee Bapt. Sunday Sch. Bd., Nashville, 1989—, So. Bapt. Found., Nashville, 1990—. Steering com. Task Force for A Drug Free Community, Lawton, Okla., 1990—. Mem. Commanche Cotton Bapt. Assn. (moderator 1989-91), Am. Bus. Club. Republican. Home: 521 S Davidson Midwest City OK 73110 Office: Country Estates Bapt Ch 1000 S Midwest Blvd Midwest City OK 73110 *I am discovering the path to the abundant life is to take myself less seriously and God most seriously.*

MACNAMARA, LAURIE JO, lay worker, economist; b. Abington, Pa., Nov. 1, 1963; d. Robert John and Linda Lois (Fox) MacN. AB, Muhlenberg Coll., 1985; MA in Law and Diplomacy, Tufts U., 1987. Mem. choir Abiding Presence Luth. Ch., Ewing, N.J., 1976-85, sec. youth group, 1978-80; mem. choir Luther Place Ch., Washington, 1987—, trustee, mem. ch. coun., 1988-89, coord. C.Am. com., 1988-90; mem. task force Metro D.C. Synod, Evang. Luth. Ch. Am., Washington, 1988—; group leader El Salvador del. Evang. Luth. Ch. Am., San Salvador, 1990; internat. economist U.S. Dept. Commerce, Washington, 1987—. Author: Latin American Trade Review, 1988, 3d edit., 1990. Mem. Bread for World, Witness for Peace. Recipient award N.J. Luth. Brotherhood Fellowship, 1981. Mem. Women in Internat. Trade, Amnesty Internat. (bd. dirs. 1984-85), Phi Beta Kappa. Democrat. Home: 19-A Auburn Ct Alexandria VA 22305 Office: US Dept Commerce 14th and Constitution Ave Rm 3025 Washington DC 20230 *We must endeavor to introduce the non-poor to the poor. It is only by sharing their stories, by breaking bread with them, that we gain the strength to take on the joyful burden of servanthood.*

MAC NEIL, JOSEPH NEIL, archbishop; b. Sydney, N.S., Can., Apr. 15, 1924; s. John Martin and Kate (Mac Lean) Mac N. BA, St. Francis Xavier U., Antigonish, N.S., 1944; postgrad., Holy Heart Sem., Halifax, N.S., 1944-48, U. Perugia, 1956, U. Chgo., 1964; JCD, U. St. Thomas, Rome, 1958. Ordained priest Roman Cath. Ch., 1948. Pastor parishes in N.S., 1948-55; officialis Chancery Office, Antigonish, 1958-59; adminstrn. Diocese of Antigonish, 1959-60; rector Cathedral Antigonish, 1961; dir. extension dept. St. Francis Xavier U., Antigonish, 1961-69, v.p., 1962-69; bishop St. John, N.B., Can., 1969-73; chancellor U. St. Thomas, Fredericton, N.B., 1969-73; archbishop of Edmonton, Alta., 1973—; chmn. Alta. Bishops' Conf., 1973—; chmn. bd. Newman Theol. Coll., Edmonton, 1973—, St. Joseph's Coll. U. Alta., Edmonton, 1973—. Vice chmn. N.S. Voluntary Econ. Planning Bd., 1965-69; bd. dirs. Program and Planning Agy., Govt. of N.S., 1969; exec. Atlantic Provinces Econ. Coun., 1968-73, Can. Coun. Rural Devel., 1965-75; bd. dirs. Futures Secretariat, 1981, Ctr. for Human Devel., Toronto, Ont., Can., 1985—; mem. bd. mgmt. Edmonton Gen. Hosp., 1983; mem. Nat. Com. for Participation in Can. Habitat, 1976. Mem. Canadian Assn. Adult Edn. (past pres. N.S.), Canadian Assn. Dirs. Univ. Extension and Summer Schs. (past pres.), Inst. Research on Public Policy (founding mem.), Can. Conf. Cath. Bishops (pres. 1979-81, mem. com. on ecumenism 1985-91, com. on missions 1991—). Address: Archbishop of Edmonton, 8421 101st Ave, Edmonton, AB Canada T6A 0L1

MACQUADE, ROBERT, religious organization administrator. Pres. Can. Bapt. Fedn., Moncton, N.B. Office: Can Bapt Fed, 54 Bessborough Ave, Moncton, NB Canada E1E 4A2*

MACQUARRIE, JOHN, divinity educator; b. Renfrew, Scotland, June 27, 1919; s. John and Robina (McInnes) M.; m. Jenny Fallow Welsh, Jan. 17, 1949; children—John Michael, Catherine Elizabeth, Alan Denis. M.A., U. Glasgow, 1940, Ph.D., 1954, D.Litt., 1964; D.D., U. Oxford, Eng., 1981; S.T.D. (hon.), U. of South, Tenn., 1967, Gen. Theol. Sem., N.Y., 1968; D.D. (hon.), U. Glasgow, 1969. Ordained priest, 1965. Lectr., U. Glasgow, Scotland, 1953-62; prof. systematic theology Union Theol. Sem., N.Y.C., 1962-70; Lady Margaret prof. div. U. Oxford, Eng., 1970-84; pres. Inst. Religion and Theology of Gt. Britain and Ireland, 1982-85. Author: Principles of Christian Theology, 1966, Existentialism, 1972, In Search of Humanity, 1982, In Search of Deity, 1984, Jesus Christ in Modern Thought, 1990. Capt. Brit. Army, 1945-48. Territorial Decoration, Brit. Army, 1962. Fellow Brit. Acad. Address: 206 Headley Way, Oxford, Oxford OX3 7TA, England

MACQUEEN, ANGUS JAMES, retired minister; b. Port Morien, N.S., Can., July 3, 1912; s. Duncan Archibald and Lillian Jane (Wadden) MacQ.; m. Netta May MacFadyen, Oct. 28, 1936; children: Marian Janet (Mrs. Colin H.H. McNairn), Joan Elizabeth (Mrs. John F.T. Warren), Barbara Jane, Heather Margaret (Mrs. Nicholas Pittas). B.A. with honors, Mt. Allison U., Sackville, N.B., 1933, LL.D., 1959; B.D., Pine Hill Div. Hall, Halifax, N.S., 1938, D.D., 1958; LL.D., U. Western Ont., 1959; D.D., Victoria U., Toronto, Canada, 1959. Ordained to ministry United Ch. of Can., 1935; pastor Port Hawkesbury, N.S., 1936-39, Antigonish, N.S., 1939-42, St. John, N.B., 1942-46; pastor Robertson United, Edmonton, Alta., 1946-51, First-St. Andrew's United Ch., London, Can., 1951-64, St. George's United Ch., Toronto, 1964-80; ret. St. George's United Ch., 1980; chmn. bd. evangelism and social service United Ch. of Can., 1954-58, moderator gen. council, 1958-60; also mem. various coms.; chancellor Mt. Allison U., 1977-85; Ecumenical rep. to chs., U.S., Europe, Africa.; Chmn. bd. dirs. United Ch. Observer, 1973-80. Author: Superman is An Idiot, The Ten Commandments, (autobiography) Memory Is My Diary, Vols. 1-2; contbg. author: 7 books others; contbr. articles to religious jours., Can., Britain, U.S. Home: 326 Douglas Ave, Toronto, ON Canada M5M 1H1

MADDELA, ORLANDO, religious organization administrator. Chmn. Nat. Spiritual Assembly, Baha'i Faith, Manila, 1991—. Office: Nat Spiritual Assembly, POB 5681, Manila Metro Manila, The Philippines*

MADDEN, SISTER LORETTO ANNE, nun, administrator; b. Denver, Aug. 21, 1922; d. Edward Joseph and Mary Agnes (Kelly) M. AB, Loretto Heights Coll., 1943; MA, Cath. U. Am., 1955, PhD, 1960. Joined Sisters of Loretto, Roman Cath. Ch., 1946. Tchr. Immaculate Conception High Sch., Las Vegas, N.Mex., 1946-54; from instr. to prof. Loretto Heights Coll., Denver, 1954-73; exec. dir. Colo. Cath. Conf., Denver, 1974—. Chmn. Colo. Social Legis. Com., Denver, 1974-80, legis. liaison, 1984—; chair Caring Connection/Providers' Adv. Com., 1983—; chair Colo. Health Care Campaign, 1989-90, vice chair, 1990-91. Recipient St. Vincent de Paul award St. Thomas Theol. Sem., 1982, Martin Luther King, Jr. Humanitarian award, 1986, Child Health and Welfare award Colo. chpt. Am. Acad. Pediatrics, 1986, Good Citizenship award Colo. Common Cause, 1986, Disting. Svc. award Colo. Civil Rights Commn., 1987, Tribute for Caring award Hospice of Peace, 1988, Florence Sabin award Colo. Pub. Health Assn., 1989; Bonfils scholar Denver Post, 1939, J.K. Mullen scholar, 1955. Home: 1075 Corona St #311 Denver CO 80218 Office: Colo Cath Conf 200 Josephine St Denver CO 80206 *Today is given to me as a precious gift from God. May I live it to the fullest in service of God and people.*

MADDOX, GREGGORY ROY, minister; b. Pontiac, Mich., Oct. 16, 1957; s. Roy Lee and Zeolar (Mack) M.; divorced; 1 child, Brice Greggory. BA, VA. Union U., 1985, MDiv, 1987. Ordained to ministry Bapt. Ch., 1982. Asst. to the pastor Friendship Missionary Bapt. Ch., Pontiac, Mich., 1978-80; minister of youth and children 1st Bapt. Ch. South Richmond (Va.), 1981-83; pastoral asst. St. James Bapt. Ch., Varina, Va., 1985; pastor Mars Hill Bapt. Ch., Southampton County, Va., 1985-88, Guildfield Missionary Bapt. Ch., Danville, Va., 1989—; chaplain United Meth. Family Svcs. Va., Richmond, 1986-88, Sch. of Theology Va. Union U., Richmond, 1984-85; pres. J.E. Jones Minister's Lyceum Va. Union U., Richmond, 1983-84; mem. personnel com. United Meth. Family Svcs., 1986. Bd. dirs. Alliance for Excellence, Danville, 1991—, Youth Alive Crusade Inc., Danville, Pittsylvania County, Va., 1991—; v.p. Am. Heart Assn. Pittsylvania County, 1990—; mem. Crop Walk for Hunger, organizer, 1984; mem. Forster Brother/Sister Program 1st Bapt. Ch. South Richmond, Va., 1985-87. C.H. Marshall Meml. scholar Va. Union U., 1985; named Outstanding Young Man of Am., Nat. Jaycees, 1984. Mem. Cherrystone Bapt. Assn. (v.p. div. clergy 1990—), Mich. Assn. for Leadership Devel. (v.p. 1982-83), Alpha Phi Alpha. Home: 224 Parker Rd Apt 24 Danville VA 24540 Office: Guildfield Missionary Bapt Ch Rte 2 Box 97A Dry Fork VA 24549

MADDOX, JAMES KELLY, JR., clergyman; b. Dublin, Ga., Apr. 25, 1946; s. James Kelly Jr. and Joyce (Marchman) M.; m. Melbe Dianna Hodge, Mar. 19, 1972 (div. Feb. 1980); children: Ramona, Brandon; m. Janice Elizabeth Powell, July 26, 1986; stepchildren: Mandy, Misty, Marybeth. BA, Carson-Newman Coll., 1976; tchr. cert., Ga. Coll., 1979. Ordained to ministry Bapt. Ch., 1975. Pastor Montrose (Ga.) Bapt. Ch., 1975-76, Harrison (Ga.) Bapt. Ch., 1976-77, Pleasant Springs Bapt. Ch., Dublin, Ga., 1977-79; interim pastor White Springs Bapt. Ch., Dublin, 1985-86; pastor Brewton Bapt. Ch., Dublin, 1986—. With USAF, 1968-72. Mem. Laurens County Bapt. Assn. (chmn. coop. program com. 1987—, chmn. discipleship tng. com. 1989—), East Dublin Lions (chaplain 1989—). Home: Rte 9 Box 159 Dublin GA 31021 Office: Brewton Bapt Ch Rt 2 Box 398 Dublin GA 31021

MADDOX, JOHN EARL, minister, educator; b. Clayton, Ala., Sept. 14, 1935; s. John and Eddie Mae (Jarrett) M.; m. Bennie Lee Farrior, Mar. 12, 1955; children: Dondee Earl, John S., Tammie Gail. ThB, St. Stevens Bible Coll., 1971; MRE, Washington Saturday Coll., Howard U. Campus, 1982, D Ministry, 1985. Ordained to ministry Bapt. Ch., 1981. Lay minister Mt. Zion Bapt. Ch., Havre D'Grace, Md., 1955-56; Sunday sch. tchr. Post Chapel, Ft. George G. Meade, Md., 1959-60; deacon 1st Bapt. Ch., Landover, Md., 1973-80, assoc. minister, 1980-81; pastor Gethsemane Bapt. Ch., Mitchellville, Md., 1981—; co-host Holy Land Tour, Jerusalem, 1983; instr. Washington Saturday Coll., Sch. Religious Edn., Howard U. Campus, Washington. Editor-in-chief GBC Herald, 1989—. Commr. Marlton Control Commn., Upper Marlboro, Md., 1976-79; mem. project evaluation group on elderly abuse Prince Georges County, Upper Marlboro, 1985-90. Warrant officer U.S. Army, 1953-73. Decorated Bronze Star, Commendation medal, others. Recipient cert. of appreciation Pres. Richard M. Nixon, 1973, others. Mem. Bapt. Ministers Conf. of Washington D.C. and Vicinity, Bapt. Assn. and Auxiliaries of So. md. and Vicinity. Democrat. Home: 12603 Northton Ct Upper Marlboro MD 20772

MADDOX, ODINGA LAWRENCE, minister; b. Akron, Ohio, Mar. 6, 1939; s. Stephen Henderson and Exia Pearl (Jefferies) M.; children: Sharon Lynette, Lawrence Jr., Stephen Henderson III. BS, Livingstone Coll., 1974; M in Divinity, Hood Theol. Sem., 1977; postgrad., Trinity Luth. Sem., 1986—. Minister Pleasant Ridge A.M.E. Zion Ch., Gastonia, N.C., 1971-78, St. Peter's A.M.E. Zion Ch., Cleve., 1978-85, First A.M.E. Zion Ch., Columbus, Ohio, 1985—; bd. dirs. M.J. Simms and Assocs., Inc.; educator Bd. of Edn., Cleve., 1978-85. Mem. staff, writer A.M.E. Zion Ch. Sch. Lit., 1979-83; dir. evangelism Ohio Ann. Conf., bd. evangelism, A.M.E. Zion Ch., Charlotte, N.C., 1983-85; del. A.M.E. Zion Ch. Gen. Conf., St. Louis, 1984, 88; trustee Coalition of Concern Clergy, Inc., Columbus, 1985. Mem. Ohio Council Chs., Interdenominational Ministerial Alliance (pres. 1986—), Alpha Phi Alpha. Home: 1295 E Gates St Columbus OH 43216 Office: First AEM Zion Ch 873 Bryden Rd Columbus OH 43205

MADDOX, RANDY LYNN, religion educator; b. Jerome, Idaho, Sept. 3, 1953; s. Thane Eugene and Velma Lou (Lewis) M.; m. Aileen Francis Chadwick, May 24, 1975; children: Erin, Jared. BA in Religion, N.W. Nazarene Coll., 1975; MDiv, Nazarene Theol. Sem., 1978; PhD, Emory U., 1982. Lic. to ministry Ch. of Nazarene, 1975, ordained 1982;, ordained United Meth. Ch., 1989. Lectr. in Bible Nazarene Sem., Kansas City, Mo., 1976-79; asst. prof. religion, assoc. prof. Sioux Falls (S.D.) Coll., 1982—; adj. faculty Luther-Northwestern Sem., St. Paul, 1983; lectr. Shalom Ctr., 1983—. Author: Toward an Ecumenical Fundamental Theology, 1984; editor: Aldersgate Reconsidered, 1990; also articles. Mem. Wesley Theology Soc., Am. Acad. Religion, Am. Theol. Soc. Home: 3105 S 9th Ave Sioux Falls SD 57105 Office: Sioux Falls Coll 1501 S Prairie Sioux Falls SD 57105

MADDOX, ROGER WAYNE, minister; b. Sayre, Okla., Apr. 22, 1950; s. Earnest Clifford and Wilma Nell (Walkup) M.; m. Judith Ellen Mann, Aug. 23, 1968; 1 child, Deidra. AA in Gen. Edn., Sayre Jr. Coll., 1970; BA in Comml. Art, Southwestern Okla. State U., 1972, MEd in Art Edn., 1982; MDiv, Southwestern Bapt. Theol. Sem., 1989. Ordained to ministry So. Bapt. Ch., 1989. Cert. tchr. Okla., 1979, Tex., 1987. Evangelist Wedgwood Bapt. Ch., Ft. Worth, 1984-86; Mardi Gras evangelist New Orleans, 1985-86; physical plant journeyman Southwestern Bapt. Theol. Sem., Ft. Worth, 1984-87; mission pastor Wedgwood Bapt. Ch. to Oak Park Chapel, Ft. Worth, 1985-86; pastor First Bapt. Ch., Arnett, Okla., 1989—. Exhibited in jurored shows, 1982; represented in Shorney Art Gallery, 1981—. Recipient Excellence in Teaching award Ft. Worth Ind. Sch. Dist., 1987-88; featured artist Art Gallery Mag., 1982. Republican. Home: 204 Washington PO Box 243 Arnett OK 73832 Office: First Bapt Ch 224 N Main PO Box 243 Arnett OK 73832 *It is one thing to accept Jesus Christ as the Son of God; however, it is another matter to receive Him as the redeeming Son of God.*

MADDOX, RONALD C., religious organization administrator. Gen. sec. The Buddhist Soc., London. Office: Buddhist Soc, 58 Eccleston Sq, London SW1V 1PH, England*

MADERA, JOSEPH J., bishop; b. San Francisco, Nov. 27, 1927. Ed., Domus Studiorum of the Missionaries of the Holy Spirit, Coyoacan, D.F., Mexico. Ordained priest Roman Cath. Ch., 1957, coadjutor, 1980. Bishop of Fresno, 1980-91; aux. bishop Archdiocese for Mil. Svcs., Silver Springs, Md., 1991—.

MADGES, WILLIAM, religion educator; b. Detroit, Dec. 9, 1952; s. Michael Joseph and Mary Regina (Plevyak) M.; m. Marsha Lynn Erickson, Sept. 15, 1984, children: Katherine, Sarah. AB with honors, Xavier U., Cin., 1974; MA in Div., U. Chgo., 1976, PhD, 1986. From instr. to asst. prof. Xavier U., Cin., 1983-89, assoc. prof., 1989—. Author: The Core of Christian Faith, 1987; co-author: Faith, Religion and Theology, 1990; contbr. articles to profl. jours. ITT Internat. Fellow Inst. Internat. Edn., N.Y.C., 1974-75, Div. Sch. Fellow U. Chgo., 1980-81, Deutscher Akademischer Austauschdienst fellow German Acad. Exch. Svc., 1981-82; recipient Univ. Fellowship U. Chgo., 1982-83. Mem. AAUP (chpt. pres. 1990—), Am. Acad. Religion, Cath. Theol. Soc. Am. (chair and convener Hist. Theology Seminar 1986-89), Coll. Theol. Soc. Democrat. Roman Catholic. Office: Xavier U 3800 Victory Pkwy Cincinnati OH 45207 *One of our greatest challenges today is whether we can formulate a vision of reality that is inclusive, holistic, relational and respectful of diversity and whether we can live out that vision in morally and ecologically appropriate ways.*

MADINGER, CHARLES BRENT, minister; b. Indpls., Aug. 6, 1952; s. Charles Emmanuel and Winifred Louise (Amick) M.; m. Barcy Ellen Craig, May 15, 1976; children: Bethany Leigh, Brittany Hope. BS, Cin. Bible Seminary, 1976; MDiv, Cin. Christian Seminary, 1980; D of Ministry, Fuller Theol. Seminary, Pasadena, Calif., 1989. Ordained to ministry Christian Ch., 1976. Assoc. pastor E. 38th St Christian Ch., Indpls., 1980-89; ihstr. Atlanta Christian Coll., East Point, Ga., 1989-90; sr. pastor Peachcrest Christian Ch., Lithonia, Ga., 1989-90, Brighton (Mich.) Christian Ch., 1990—. Softball coach, mgr. Warren Little League, Indpls., 1987-88, Cen. Dekalb Youth Athletic Assn., Stone Mountain, Ga., 1989-90, Brighton Community Edn. Softball, 1991. Mem. Rotary (chaplain 1987-89). Republican. Office: Brighton Christian Church 4309 Buno Rd Brighton MI 48116

MADORE, SISTER BERNADETTE, college president; b. Barnston, Que., Can., Jan. 24, 1918; came to U.S., 1920, naturalized; d. Joseph George and Mina Marie (Fontaine) M.; A.B., U. Montreal, 1942, B.Ed., 1943; M.S., Cath. U. Am., 1949, Ph.D., 1951. Joined Sisters of St. Anne, Roman Cath. Ch., 1935. Instr. math. and English, Marie Anne Coll., Montreal, Que., 1943-44; prof. biology, dean of coll. Anna Maria Coll., Paxton, Mass., 1952-76, v.p., 1975-77, pres., 1977—; fund-raising cons.; corporator YWCA. Past bd. dirs. Central Mass. chpt. ARC; bd. dirs. Worcester Coll. Consortium; former trustee Worcester Boys Club. Mem. AAAS, Am. Soc. Microbiology, Nat. Assn. Biology Tchrs., Am. Assn. Higher Edn., Worcester C. of C. Home and Office: Anna Maria Coll Sunset Ln Paxton MA 01612-1198

MADSEN, DAVID BURTON, clergyman; b. Waterloo, Iowa, Dec. 20, 1946; s. Robert Lawrence and Claudia Dade (McFarland) M.; m. Marcia Marie McCann, June 1, 1969; children: Jared Timothy David, Sarah Koren Elizabeth. BA, U. No. Iowa, 1969; M.Div., San Francisco Theol. Sem., 1972, M Theology, 1974, D.Min., 1987. Ordained to ministry, Presbyn. Ch., 1972. Asst. pastor Community Ch. of Mill Valley, Calif., 1971-74; assoc. pastor First Congl. Ch., Portland, Oreg., 1974-81; sr. pastor Cottage Grove Ave. Presbyn. Ch., Des Moines, 1981—; pres. Iowa Commn. United Ministries in Higher Edn., des Moines, 1986-90; dir. Racial/Ethnic Ministry Gen. Assy., Presbyn. Chn., Louisville, 1987—; coordinating coun. Korean-Am. Ministries, Presbyn. Ch. (U.S.A.). Contbr. sermons to profl. jours. Mem. Drake Devel. Com., Des Moines, 1985-86, Mayor's Budget Task Force, Portland, 1977-80; treas. Downtown Community Orgn., Portland, 1975-81; bd. dirs. Help All Children Be Proud. Recipient award for meritorious performance Council on Ch. and Race, N.Y.C., 1987. Mem. Self-Devel. of People (chmn. 1985—). Democrat. Avocations: tennis, biking, photography. Office: Cottage Grove Presbyn Ch 1050 24th St Des Moines IA 50311

MADUAKOR, OBIAJURU, educator; b. Isulo, Anambra, Nigeria, July 5, 1942; s. Albert Enemo Maduakor and Angelina Afubekwe Okeke; m. Chijioke Obiageli Nwankwo, July 12, 1969; children: Ifeanyi, Chukwuka, Chinedu. BA with honors in English, U. Ibadan (Nigeria), 1965; MA in English, U. Leeds (England), 1972; PhD in English, U. Ottawa (Canada), 1977. Lectr. U. Gabon, Libreville, 1971-72; instr. U. Ottawa, 1972-77; asst. prof. U. Ife (Nigeria), 1978-81; assoc. prof. U. Nigeria, Nsukka, 1984-86, prof., 1987—; chief moderator prose fiction Joint Admissions and Matriculation Bd., Lagos, Nigeria, 1982—. Author: Wole Soyinka: An Introduction to His Writing, 1987; contbr. articles to profl. jours. Mem. African Lit. Assn., Literary Soc. Nigeria. Avocations: lawn tennis, table tennis. Home: Godway House, Isulo Orumba LGA, Anambra State Nigeria Office: Univ Nigeria Dept English, Nsukka Anambra State, Nigeria

MADURI, BRUCE CARL, broadcasting executive; b. Bedford, Ohio, Sept. 20, 1956; s. Carl Anthony and Lucianna (Trassare) M.; m. Laura Jean Mercek, Sept. 27, 1979; children: Sarah, Gina, Leah, Daniel, Vince. Student, Kent State U., 1974-77. Pres., chief operating officer Genesis Communications, Inc., Atlanta, 1988—. Republican. Presbyterian. Office: Genesis Communications Inc 805 Peachtree St NE 6th Floor Atlanta GA 30308

MADURO, ÓTTO, philosophy and sociology of religion educator; b. Caracas, Venezuela, Apr. 14, 1945; s. Josè Manuel and Celia (Lang) M.; m. Nancy Noguera. Grad. in Philosophy, U. Central de Venezuela, 1968; Cath. U. Louvain (Belgium), 1973, Ph.D. magna cum laude in Philosophy of Religion, 1977, M.A. magna cum laude in Sociology of Religion, 1978. Instr. U. de los Andes, Estado Mèrida, Venezuela, 1969-71, asst., 1971-75, aggregate, 1975-81, assoc. prof. philosophy and sociology of religion, 1981-86; invited lectr. U. Notre Dame, Ind., 1982; vis. prof. Maryknoll Sch. Theology, 1982, 85, 86, 87—; cons. for various Cath. religious orders including Jesuits, Maryknoll, Dominicans. Author: Marxismo Religion, 1977; Revelación y Revolución, 1970; Religion y Lucha de Clases, 1979, English edit., German edit., Portugese edit. Sec. edn. Christian Dem. Youth, Venezuela, 1965-67; mem. nat. council Christian Left Party, Venezuela, 1967-69. Recipient essay prize Nat. Council on Cultural Affairs, Venezuela, 1977-78. Mem. Internat. Sociol. Assn. (research com. on sociology of religion), Internat. Conf. on Sociology of Religion, Internat. Cath. Movement of Intellectuals-Pax Romana, Association Française de Sociologie Religieuse (Paris), Soc. for Sci. Study Religion (U.S.), Assn. for Sociology of Religion (U.S.). Roman Catholic. Office: Maryknoll Sch Theology Maryknoll NY 10545

MAEL, BARRY SHELDON, religious organization administrator; b. Boston, Feb. 8, 1958; s. Seymour and Freda (Oppenheim) M.; m. Diane Jade Flecker, Nov. 11, 1990. BA, Yeshiva U., N.Y.C., 1979, MSW, 1982. Sr. adult worker JCC, 1982-86; children's camping dir. St. Paul Jewish Community Ctr., 1986-89; program dir. Riverdale YM-YWHA, Bronx, 1989—. Sherman scholar, Brandeis U., 1989. Mewm. Assn. Jewish Ctr. Profls., Nat.

Assn. Social Workers. Republican. Home: 31 S 4th St Highland Park NJ 08904 Office: YM-YWHA of Riverdale 5625 Arlington Ave Riverdale NY 10471

MAEROV, SHELLY, religious organization head. Pres. Jewish Fedn. Edmonton, Alta., Can. Office: Jewish Fedn, 7200-156th St, Edmonton, AB Canada T5R 1X3*

MAES, JOHN LEOPOLD, theologian, psychologist, educator; b. Watertown, Mich., Aug. 6, 1923; s. John and Mary (Cornwell) M; m. Mary M. Johnson, Aug. 28, 1942; 1 child, John David. BTh, Owosso Coll., 1948; AB, Mich. State U., 1954, MA, 1957, PhD, 1963. Ordained to ministry United Meth. Ch., 1963, United Ch. Christ, 1976; lic. health care provider in psychology, Mass. Pastor Houghton Lake, Mich., 1948-52, Francestown, N.H., 1977-80; assoc. prof. Sch. Theology Boston U., 1963-72, adj. prof., exec. dir. Danielsen Inst., 1982-89, bd. govs., 1967-82, prof. emeritus, cons., 1989—; prof., acad. dean Franklin Pierce Coll., Rindge, N.H., 1972-75; cons., pvt. practice, 1975-82; bd. govs. Danielsen Inst., 1967-82. Author: Suffering: A Caregiver's Guide, 1990; (with others) Fathering: Fact or Fable, 1977, Maturity and the Quest for Spiritual Meaning, 1988; contbr. articles to profl. jours. Mem. Am. Assn. Pastoral Counselors (diplomate, bd. govs. 1966-71, chmn. ctrs.and tng. com. 1967-71), Am. Psychol. Assn. Democrat. Home: PO Box 25 Islesboro ME 04848 also: 4419 56th St W Bradenton FL 34210 *In the long run it doesn't matter what the causes of suffering are; the unavoidable personal task is to put life back together, making meaning of the environment in which it is lived, and to go on from there.*

MAGANA GARCIA, SABAS, bishop; b. Morelia, Mexico, Jan. 24, 1921. Ordained priest Roman Cath. Ch., 1944; bishop of Matamoros Mexico, 1969—. Office: Diocese of Matamoros, Apartado 70, Tamaulipas CP 87300, Mexico

MAGARY, DENNIS ROBERT, religious educator, minister; b. Peoria, Ill., June 19, 1951; s. Geroge Robert and Marian Louise (Anderson) M.; m. Pamela Kay Miller, Aug. 25, 1973; children: Adam James, Brooke Elizabeth, Chelsea Joy. BA cum laude, Ft. Wayne Bible Coll., 1973; MDiv magna cum laude, Trinity Evang. Div. Sch., 1977, postgrad., 1977—; MA, U. Wis., 1983, postgrad., 1983—. Ordained to ministry Missionary Ch., 1988. Asst. pastor Indian Lakes Community Ch., Bloomingdale, Ill., 1975-77; instr. Bible Trinity Coll., Deerfield, Ill., 1978-84; asst. prof. Old Testament and Semitic langs. Trinity Evang. Div. Sch., Deerfield, 1984—, chmn. dept. Old Testament and Semitic langs., 1990—; teaching asst. Bibl. Hebrew U. Wis., Madison, 1981-84; instr. Old Testament Inst. Christian Studies, Madison, 1983-84. Mem. Evang. Theol. Soc., Soc. Bibl. Lit., Nat. Assn. Profs. Hebrew in Insts. of Higher Learning, Evang. Tchr. Tng. Assn., Delta Epsilon Chi. Home: 405 Westmoreland Dr Vernon Hills IL 60061 Office: Trinity Evang Div Sch 2065 Half Day Rd Deerfield IL 60015

MAGAW, JAMES ELLSWORTH, religious denomination administrator; b. Stockdale, Ohio, Dec. 2, 1932; s. Clarence W. and Edith V. (Horton) M.; m. Bonnie Lee Thompson, Nov. 26, 1953; children: Krista D., James Ellsworth II. BA cum laude, Rio Grande (Ohio) Coll., 1954; MDiv, Oberlin (Ohio) Coll., 1958. Min. North Fairfield (Ohio) Meth. Ch., 1954-60, Trinity Meth. Ch., McConnelsville, Ohio, 1960-66, St. Mark United Meth. Ch., Galion, Ohio, 1966-71, Trinity United Meth. Ch., Shelby, Ohio, 1971-79; sr. min. Gay St. United Meth. Ch., Mt. Vernon, Ohio, 1979-84; dist. supt. Cambridge (Ohio) dist. United Meth. Ch., 1984—; dean of cabinet East Ohio Conf., United Meth. Ch., North Canton, 1988—; bd. dirs. United Meth. Communications, Nashville, 1988—; del gen. conf. United Meth. Ch., St. Louis, 1988, del. jurisdictional conf., 1984, 88. Author: When Round Pegs Won't Stay Round, 1982, Exodus Into 20th Century, 1984; contbr. articles to Alive Now. Chmn. Family Svcs. Orgn., Galion, Ohio, 1969-70; bd. mem. Moundbuilders Guidance Ctr., Mt. Vernon, 1980-84; trustee Meth. Theol. Sch. in Ohio, Delaware, 1984—. Mem. Rotary (pres. 1970, 77). Avocations: writing, conducting workshops.

MAGEE, BRUCE ROBERT, minister; b. Brookhaven, Miss., Apr. 24, 1958; s. Robert Solomon and Vivian Eve (Spell) M.; m. Brenda Kay Berry, Aug. 7, 1982. BA, La. Tech. U., 1980; M in Div., New Orleans Bapt. Theol. Sem., 1983, postgrad., 1987. Pastor Vernon (La.) Bapt. Ch., 1977-80; fellow New Orleans Bapt. Theol. Sem., 1983-86; pastor Tangipahoa (La.) Bapt. Ch., 1983—; asst. minister Temple Bapt. Ch., Ruston, La., 1979-80. Named One of Outstanding Young Men of Am., 1985. Home and Office: Tangipahoa Bapt Ch PO Box 166 Tangipahoa LA 70465

MAGEE, GORDON LLOYD, minister; b. Waterloo, Iowa, May 5, 1951; s. Lloyd Earl and Marion Ollie (Slee) M.; m. Denna Diane Tisue, Mar. 11, 1972; children: Carey Beth, Courtney Renee, Cassie Danielle. Student, U. No. Iowa, 1969-70; AA with highest honors, Northwestern Coll., Roseville, Minn., 1981, BA in Ministries with highest honors, 1982. Min. Christian edn. Emmanuel Evangel. Free Ch., Steinbach, Manitoba, Can., 1982-86; sr. pastor Mission Evangel. Free Ch., Mission, B.C., Can., 1986-87, Faith Evangel. Free Ch., Minocqua, Wis., 1989—. Office: Faith Evangelical Free Ch PO Box 985 Minocqua WI 54548

MAGEE, LESLIE JAE, minister; b. Lincoln, Nebr., Sept. 24, 1933; s. Jae Evans and Margaret Louise (Pape) M.; m. Beulah Jeanne Folkerts, June 13, 1955; children: Pennie, Judith, Virginia. BA, Northwestern Coll., Mpls., 1955; MDiv, Denver Sem., 1958. Ordained to ministry Conservative Bapt. Ch., 1959. Missionary Conservative Bapt. Fgn. Mission Soc., Wheaton, Ill., 1958-83; pastor Washington Heights Bapt. Ch., Ogden, Utah, 1983—; state moderator Utah Conservative Bapt. Ch., 1985-89; bd. dirs. Conservative Bapt. Home Mission Soc., Wheaton, 1990—, field chmn., Brazil, 1962-64, Portugal, 1975-82. Office: Washington Heights Bapt Ch 1770 E 6200 S Ogden UT 84405 *One of the greatest thrills in my life has been to see how the gospel message is able to cross all social and cultural barriers and transform lives.*

MAGEE, THOMAS ESTON, JR., minister; b. DeRidder, La., Aug. 9, 1947; s. Thomas Eston and Doris Maxine (Gallion) M.; m. Linda Ruth Lewis, Nov. 9, 1967. Student, McNeese State U., 1966-69; BTh, Tex. Bible Coll., 1972. Ordained to ministry United Pentecostal Ch., 1973. Asst. pastor United Pentecostal Ch., Pasadena, Tex., 1969-72; instr. Tex. Bible Coll., Houston, 1970-72, dean of women, 1970-71; evangelist United Pentecostal Ch., various locations, U.S., 1972-77; pastor 1st United Pentecostal Ch., Ragley, La., 1977—; sect. youth dir. La. Dist. United Pentecostal Ch., Ragley, 1979-83; sect. Sunday Sch. dir., 1984-86; sect. sec.-treas., 1989—. Named col., La. Gov., 1975. Democrat. Home: Rte 1 Box 90-A Longville LA 70652 Office: 1st United Pentecostal Ch PO Box 44 Ragley LA 70657 *As a minister, I am looked upon as the one who has all the "right" answers to life's problems. I have discovered that life is not always fair but God is always just.*

MAGGAL, MOSHE MORRIS, rabbi; b. Nagyecsed, Hungary, Mar. 16, 1908; came to U.S., 1950, naturalized, 1960; s. David and Ester (Fulop) Gelberman; m. Rachel Delia Diamond, July 8, 1951; children: Davida Elizabeth DeMonte, Michelle Judith Weinstein, Elana Ilene. BA, Nat. Rabbinical Sem., Budapest, Hungary, 1933, Rabbinical degree, 1934; postgrad., U. Zurich, Switzerland, 1935, Hebrew U., Jerusalem, 1936; PhD (hon.), Ben Franklin Acad., Washington, 1979; DDW (hon.), The New Sem., N.Y.C., 1988. Rabbi Temple Meyer-David, Claremont, N.H., 1951-52, Temple Beth Aaron, Billings, Mont., 1952-54, Alhambra (Calif.) Jewish Center, 1955-57, Temple Beth Kodesh, Canoga Park, Calif., 1959-61, Congregation Ahavath Israel, Hollywood, Calif., 1966-70, Temple Emanu-El, Las Vegas, Nev., 1988—; civilian chaplain USAAF Base, Great Falls, Mont., 1952-54; Editor Hebrew weekly Iton Meyuhad, Tel Aviv, 1940-47; asso. editor Heritage newspaper, Los Angeles, 1958-60; lectr. Free Enterprise Speakers Bur., Coast Fed. Savs. & Loan Assn., 1971-76; instr. adult edn. class Temple Beth Sholom, Las Vegas, 1990—; mem. U.S. Congl. Adv. Bd. Author: Acres of Happiness, 1968, The Secret of Israel's Victories: Past, Present and Future, 1983; editor Voice of Judaism, 1960—. Pres. Beverly Hills Zionist Orgn., 1973-77; exec. v.p. So. Pacific Region, 1973—; mem. Los Angeles-Eilat Sister City Com.; Mem. Speakers Bur. of Com. for Re-election of Pres., 1972; hon. lt. col. New Spirit of 76 Found.; mem. nat. adv. bd. Ben Franklin Acad., Inst. Advanced Studies.; Calif. chmn. Spirit of '76 Found. Served with Israel Def. Army, 1948-49. Recipient Nat. Sermon Contest award Spiritual Moblzn., 1952, citation Crusade for Freedom, 1952, Am. Patriot award Ben Franklin Soc., 1981; named to Los Angeles Bicentennial Com. Speakers Bur. for Am. Revolution Bicentennial Adminstrn., 1975; Hon. sheriff Yellowstone County Mont., 1954; hon. adviser to Cecil B. DeMille for film The Ten Commandments, 1954. Mem. Nat. Jewish Info. Service (founder, pres. 1960—), Town Hall of Calif., World Affairs Council, Internat. Visitors Program. Democrat. Club: Greater Los Angeles Press. Home: 3761 Decade St Las Vegas NV 89121

MAGIDA, ARTHUR JAY, newspaper editor, writer; b. N.Y.C., Aug. 24, 1945; s. Paul and Florence (Krell) M.; m. Helen Margaret Zeidler; children: Sarah, Amy, Molly. BA, Marlboro Coll., 1967; MA, Georgetown U., 1972, Calif. Sch. Profl. Psychology, 1979. Gen. reporter Harrisburg (Pa.) Patriot, 1967-68, York (Pa.) Gazette and Daily, 1968-69; writer, editor Ralph Nader's Congress Project, Washington, 1972-74; environ. reporter Nat. Jour., Washington, 1974-76; dir. publs. energy conservation project Nat. Assn. Pks. and Recreation, Washington, 1979-83; freelance writer, editor Washington, 1979-83; asst. editor Balt. Jewish Times, 1983-89, sr. writer, 1990—. Author: The Environment Committees, 1975; contbr. articles to Conde Nast Traveler, Washington Post, Balt. Sun., Christian Sci. Monitor, Boston Globe, mag. and op-ed page, numerous others, also widely reprinted; editor: Foster Care and Families, 1980. Recipient Simon Rockower awards for excellence in Jewish journalism, 1984-86, 89-90, Smolar award for excellence in N.Am. Jewish journalism Coun. Jewish Fedns., 1988, 90, A.D. Emmart award A.D. Emmart Fedn., Balt., 1988-90, Nat. Mass Media awards NCCJ, 1989-90, Excellence in Journalism award Soc. Prof. Journalists Md. chpt., 1990. Mem. Soc. Profl. Journalists (Excellence in Journalism award Md. chpt. 1991). Democrat. Home: 1919 Fairbank Rd Baltimore MD 21209 Office: Baltimore Jewish Times 2104 N Charles St Baltimore MD 21218

MAGIN, DOUGLAS RICHARD, minister; b. Rochester, N.Y., Oct. 6, 1947; s. Jerome August and Marjorie B. (Merzke) M.; m. Carol Elaine Gares, June 12, 1971; children: Jonathan Mark, Sharon Lynne, Susan Carol, Jennifer Joy. BS, Houghton Coll., 1969; MDiv., Bethel Theol. Sem., 1972. Ordained to ministry Am. Bapt. Chs.in U.S.A., 1973. Dir. of staff Ontario Bible Conf., Oswego, N.Y., 1970; dir. of youth Univ. Ave. Congl. Ch., St. Paul, 1971; min. of Christian edn. and youth First Bapt. Ch., Troy, Ohio, 1972—; camp dir. Camp Chaffee, Troy, 1972-76, Kirkwood Camp and Conf. Ctr., Wilmington, Ohio, 1977—; youth dir. Ohio Bapt. Bible and Missions Conf., Wilmington, 1977—. Mem. Nat. Assn. Evangelicals Christian Edn. Assn. (rep. for conservative congl. christian conf. 1991). Home: 1255 Skylark Dr Troy OH 45373 Office: First Bapt Ch 53 S Norwich Rd Troy OH 45373 *The purpose in my life is not my job or vocation but the message I develop in my walk with God. My responsibility is to deepen my message. God's responsibility is to broaden my ministry.*

MAGNESS, MILTON S., minister; b. Ft. Worth, Dec. 30, 1952; s. Bonner Clinton and Elizabeth Marie (Harris) M.; m. Brenda Kay Harman, Apr. 10, 1949; children: Melodi Shea, Marci Suzanne. BA cum laude, Sam Houston State U., Huntsville, Tex., 1978; MRE, Southwestern Theol. Sem., Ft. Worth, 1980; DMin, Luther Rice Sem., Jacksonville, Fla., 1986. Minister of youth Bapt. Temple, Baytown, Tex., 1975-76; pastor Magnolia Bapt. Ch., Cleveland, Tex., 1976-78; pastor First Bapt. Ch., Melissa, Tex., 1978-80, Farmersville, Tex., 1980-83, Bowie, Tex., 1983-86; pastor Colonial Hills Bapt. Ch., Cedar Hill, Tex., 1986—; state leader C.W.T. Seminars, Bapt. Gen. Conv. Tex., state leader W.I.N.H. schs. Pubr./author sermon research svc.: Magness Notes, 1989; contbr. articles to profl. jours. Career advisor Vocation Adv. Council, Farmersville, 1982-83. Mem. Dallas Bapt. Assn. (chmn. budget and fin. com. 1988—). Avocations: running, guitar, ham radio operator. Home: 317 Meadowglen Cedar Hill TX 75104 Office: Colonial Hills Bapt Ch 820 E Wintergreen Rd Cedar Hill TX 75104

MAGNUS, MARTIN, religious organization head. Conf. supt. United Brethren in christ, Ont. Conf., Guelph. Office: United Brethren Christ, 118 Ross Ave, Kitchener, ON Canada N2A 1V4*

MAGNUSON, WARREN ROGER, church official; b. Mpls., Dec. 5, 1921; s. Edwin John and Hulda (Smith) M.; m. Margaret Linnea Johnson, June 9, 1944. A.A., Bethel Coll., 1942; B.A., U. Minn., 1946; B.D., Bethel Theol. Sem., 1946; hon. degree, Judson Coll., Elgin, Ill., 1973. Ordained to ministry Bapt. Ch., 1946. Pastor Immanuel Bapt. Ch., St. Paul, 1943-46, Washington Ave. Bapt. Ch., Ludington, Mich., 1947-50, 1st Bapt. Ch., Willmar, Minn., 1950-54, Cen. Bapt. Ch., St. Paul, 1954-69; gen. sec. Bapt. Gen. Conf., Arlington Heights, Ill., 1969—. Moderator Minn. Bapt. Conf., 1959, trustee, 1965-69; moderator Bapt. Gen. Conf., 1965, mem. bd. missions, 1965—; Mem. exec. com. Bapt. Joint Com. on Pub. Affairs, 1970—, chmn., 1970-72; mem. exec. com. Gen. Commn. on Chaplains and Armed Forces Personnel, 1969—, Bapt. World Alliance, 1970—; chmn. Bapt. World Congress, 1980—, Bapt. World Aid Div., 1982—; Bd. regents Bethel Coll.; chmn. steering com. U.S. Ch. Leaders, 1985—. Mem. Nat. Assn. Evangelicals (adminstrv. council 1970—), Am. Bible Soc. (adv. council 1969—). Home: Nordhaven Rt 1 Box 350D Aitkin MN 56431 Office: Bapt Gen Conf 2002 Arlington Heights Rd Arlington Heights IL 60005

MAGOULIAS, NICHOLAS JOHN, priest; b. Cin., Oct. 11, 1931; s. John Efstratios and Constantina (Dounias) M.; m. Marilyn Contas, Jan. 16, 1960; children: Jonathan, Carolyn. BD, Holy Cross Sem., Brookline, Mass., 1957. Ordained to ministry Greek Orthodox Ch. as deacon, 1960, as priest, 1960. Rector St. Paul's Greek Orthodox Ch., Hempstead, N.Y., 1960-88; dean St. Paul's Greek Orthodox Cathedral, Hempstead, N.Y., 1988—; pres. Nassau-Sufolk Greek Orthodox Clergy Fedn., 1981-85, Dion Found., Inc., Hempstead, 1981—; trustee Hellenic Coll., Holy Cross Greek Orthodox Theol. Sch., John F. Kennedy Libr. Minorities; mem. 1st Diocesan Bd., Astoria, N.Y., 1982—, spiritual ct. Greek Orthodox Archdiocese-Diocese N.Y., Astoria, 1977-80, 82-83; project and rsch. dir. installation of extensive 13th Century Byzantine mosaics. Editor The Epistle, 1963—. Recipient Heritage award J.F.K. Libr. Minorities, N.Y.C., 1972, St. Paul's Golden Leaves and Golden Medallion award, 1975, 85, Medallion of St. Barnabas Archbishop Athenagoras Gt. Britain, 1974, Community Svc. award Nassau County, 1990; named Oikonomos, Greek Orthodox Ch., 1967, Protopresbyter, 1971. Office: St Paul's Greek Orthodox Cathedral 110 Cathedral Ave Hempstead NY 11550 *Life's complications can bear ease with the love and acceptance of God's eternal wisdom. Place life's direction in His hands so that you might surmount the tragedies of world offerings through His loving kindness and tender mercies.*

MAGRILL, JOE RICHARD, JR., minister; b. Marshall, Tex., Aug. 7, 1946; s. Joe Richard Sr. and Mary Belle (Chadwick) M. BA summa cum laude, E. Tex. State U., 1967; MDiv, Princeton Theol. Sem., 1970, ThM, 1972; MLS, Rutgers, 1971. Ordained to ministry Cumberland Presbyn. Ch., 1970. Order libr. Princeton (N.J.) Theol. Sem., 1969-72; libr., prof. Memphis Theol. Sem., 1972-79; asst to stated clk. office Gen. Assembly Cumberland Presbyn. Ch., Memphis, 1979-84, exec. dir. bd. fin., 1989—; editor The Cumberland Presbyterian, Memphis, 1984-87; sec.-treas. Hist. Found. of Cumberland Presbyn. Ch., 1980—. Editor: In the Valley of the Cauca, 1981, One Family Under God, 1982. Office: Cumberland Presbyn Ch Fin Bd 1978 Union Ave Memphis TN 38104

MAGRUDER, ROBERT A., youth pastor; b. Vicksburg, Miss., July 12, 1958; s. Edward Henry and Betty Jane (Blind) M.; m. Vicki Dianne Biship, Dec. 19, 1981; children: Matthew A., Micha W. AD in Religious Edn., New Orleans Bapt. Sem., 1987, AD in Pastoral Ministry, 1989. Youth pastor Woodlawn Bapt. Ch., Vicksburg, 1983-84; min. music and youth 1st Bapt. Ch., Foxworth, Miss., 1985-86, Grammery, La., 1986-87; youth pastor 1st Bapt. Ch., Covington, La., 1987-89, Dunedin, Fla., 1989—. Mem. Bapt. Assn. Suncoast. Office: 1st Bapt Ch 500 Wood St Dunedin FL 34698

MAGUIRE, JOSEPH F., bishop; b. Boston, Sept. 4, 1919. Ed., Boston Coll.; St. John's Sem., Boston. Ordained priest Roman Catholic Ch., 1945, named monsignor, 1964; successively asst. pastor St. Joseph Ch., Lynn, Mass., St. Anne Ch., Readville, Mass., Blessed Sacrament Ch., Jamaica Plain, Mass., St. Mary Ch., Milton, Mass.; sec. to Cardinal Cushing Boston, 1962-70; sec. to Archbishop Medeiros, 1970-71, consecrated titular bishop of Macteris and aux. bishop of Boston, 1972-76; apptd. coadjutor bishop of Springfield, Mass., 1976-77; succeeded as bishop of Springfield, 1977—; archdiocesan cons., from 1968. Office: Chancery Office 76 Elliot St PO Box 1730 Springfield MA 01105

MAGUIRE, MAX RAYMOND, clergyman; b. Dwight, Kans., June 12, 1928; s. Ray Thomas and Helen Olive (Paulson) M.; m. Martha Ellen Berndt, Dec. 27, 1958; children: Kimberly, Kenton. BA, Wichita State U., 1955; MDiv, San Francisco Theol. Sem., 1958. Ordained to ministry United Presbyn. Ch. in U.S.A., 1958; lic. marriage and family therapist, Minn. Pastor various chs. Lawrence, Kans., 1958-61; chaplain Big Spring (Tex.) State Hosp., 1961-65, Presbyn. Hosp. Ministry, Rochester, Minn., 1965-71; chaplain, dir. chaplaincy svcs. Abbott-Northwestern Hosp., Mpls., 1971—; moderator Presbytery of Sheldon Jackson, 1970-71; clin. supr. Assn. for Clin. Pastoral Edn. (past pres., chmn. N. Cen. region 1975—). Contbr. articles on clin. pastoral psychology to religious jours. Recipient Disting. Svc. award Va. Commonwealth U. Med. Coll. Va., 1984. Fellow Am. Assn. Pastoral Counselors; mem. Coll. Chaplains (past pres.), Am. Assn. Marriage and Family Therapists (clin.). Home: 8412 115th St S Cottage Grove MN 55016 Office: 800 E 28th St Minneapolis MN 55407

MAHADY, SISTER CATHERINE MARY, nun, religious organization administrator, consultant; b. Bklyn., Jan. 3, 1936; d. Daniel James and Margaret Mary (McMurray) M. BA in History, Regis Coll., 1965; MA in Social Scis., Bklyn. Coll., 1972; MBA, Bellarmine Coll., 1987. Joined Ky. Dominicans, Roman Cath. Ch., 1955. Tchr. Dominican Acad., Plainville, Mass., 1957-67; prin. St. Simon Jude Acad., Bklyn., 1967-73; asst. to supt. schs. Diocese of Bklyn. and Queens, 1973-75; pres. St. Catharine Coll., Springfield, Ky., 1975-83; v.p. adminstrn. and bus. Pikeville Coll., Ky., 1983-86; dean admissions and fin. aid Spalding U., 1986-88; v.p. for stewardship, mem. governing bd. Ky. Dominican Sisters, St. Catharine, 1988-92. Mem. Council Ind. Ky. Colls. and Univs. (pres. 1981-83, sec./treas. 1977-79, v.p. 1979-81), Leadership Conf. Religious Women (nat. fin. com. 1990-92, nat. treas. 1991-92), Coll. and Univ. Bus. Officers, Phi Theta Kappa (hon. fellow). Democrat. Avocations: reading, travel. Address: Dominican Congl Offices Saint Catharine KY 40061

MAHAR, PATRICK LARRY, minister; b. London, Aug. 12, 1963; came to U.S., 1964; s. Larry Francis and Iolanda (Olivia) M.; m. Brenda Louise Vespa, Aug. 3, 1985; 1 child, Marissa Adriana. Diploma, Southeastern Coll., 1986, BA, 1987. Ordained to ministry Assemblies of God Ch., 1990. Assoc. pastor 1st Assembly of God Ch., Pine Bluff, Ark, 1988-89, Calvary Assembly of God Ch., Beckley, W.Va., 1989-91; pastor Gardner Chapel Assembly of God Ch., New Castle, Pa., 1991—; dist. youth rep. Appalachian dist. Assemblies of God, Beckley, 1989-91. Office: Gardner Chapel Assembly of God New Castle PA 16101

MAHATHERO, VISUDDHANANDA, monk; b. Hoarapara, Raozan, Bangladesh, Feb. 23, 1909; s. Karmadhan and Cintabati Barva. Ed., Bidyalanker Pariven, Sri Lanka, 1934, Sudharshan Pali Coll., Chittagong, Bangledesh, 1939-42. Pres. Buddhist Monastery, Kamalapur Dhaka, Bangladesh, 1950—; vice chmn. Buddhist Religious Welfare Trust, Bangladesh, 1984—; sec. Pali Sanskrit Bd., Bangladesh, 1968—; exec. dir. Asian Conf. Religion and Peace, Singapore, 1983—; mem. internat. coun. World Conf. Religion and Peace, N.Y.C., 1984—; pres. Asian Buddhist Conf. on Peace, Mongolian People's Republic, 1986—. Author: Buddhism in Bangladesh, 1983, Raktajhara Din, 1983, Sinhal Braman, 1989. Recipient awards Govt. of Pakistan, 1962, 65, Atish Gold medal Atish Dipankar Birth Anniversary Com., 1986. Mem. World Fellowship Buddhists (pres. Bangladesh chpt. 1950—). Avocations: reading, songs, nursing children. Home: Atish Dipankar Sarak, Dhaka Bangladesh Office: World Fedn Buddhists Ctr, Buddhist Monastery, Kamalapur Dhaka 14, Bangladesh

MAHER, JOHN FRANCIS, chemical engineer, deacon; b. Bklyn., May 14, 1938; s. James Edward abd Alice Rita (O'Brien) M.; m. Marilyn Louise Young, Aug. 20, 1960; children: John Francis II, Gregory, Michael, Mary-Alice. BChE, Villanova (Pa.) U., 1960; MBA, W. Va. U., 1969, MA, 1989. Ordained deacon Roman Cath. Ch., 1983. State chaplain Boy Scouts Am., Wheeling, W.Va., 1980-88; deacon Roman Cath. Ch., Wheeling, W.Va., 1983—; sr. engr. Ormet Corp., Hannibal, Ohio, 1978—; litury chmn. St. Johns Men's Club, St. Marys, W.Va., 1969-83, Christ our Hope Parish, Harrisville, 1983—. Author manual: Plant Operations, 1986. NSF grantee, 1959. Mem. Am. Inst. Chem. Engrs. (vice chmn. 1971-73), K.C., Jaycees, Kiwanis, Beta Gamma Sigma. Home: 1008 Oakwood Ter Saint Marys WV 26170 Office: Ormet Corp PO Box 176 Hannibal OH 43931

MAHER, JOSEPH ANTHONY, priest; b. Phila., Mar. 13, 1929; s. Patrick and Margaret (Doolan) M.; m. Catherine Mary Mae Namee, July 1, 1978; 1 child, James. BA, Villanova U., 1952; MA, Cath. U., 1956; PhD, NYU, 1971. Ordained priest Roman Cath. Ch., 1955; became Episcopal priest, 1981. Prin. Augustinian Acad., S.I., N.Y., 1966-71; assoc. prof. Villanova (Pa.) U., 1971-75; pastor St. Thomas of Villanova Ch., Rosemont, Pa., 1975-78; curate Grace Episcopal Ch., Ocala, Fla., 1981-83; vicar Holy Child Episcopal Ch., Ormand Beach, Fla., 1983—; dir. elections and nominations annual convention Diocese of Cen. Fla., Orlando, 1988—, mem. commn. on ministry, 1988—; trustee U. of the South, Sewanee, Tenn., 1990. Contbr. articles to religious publs.; author pamphlet Stations of Cross for Elderly, 1978. Bd. dirs. Halifax Home Health Assn., Daytona Beach, Fla., 1985—. Named Man of Yr. Sanford Srs., 1981. Mem. Alban Inst. (mem. continuing edn. program), Daytona Deanery (dean 1985-88).

MAHER, PAUL REGIS, archabbot, academic administrator; b. Latrobe, Pa., Nov. 30, 1925; s. William Andrew and Edna (Hunt) M. Ph.D., Pontifical Atheneum of St. Anselm, Rome, 1957. Ordained priest Roman Catholic Ch. Joined Benedictine Order; archabbot St. Vincent Archabbey, Latrobe; also chancellor St. Vincent Coll. Office: St Vincent Archabbey Latrobe PA 15650

MAHER, TERRY MARINA, religious organization administrator; b. Phila., Oct. 13, 1955; d. Thomas Michael and Marion Teresa (Corbett) M. BA in History and Religious Studies, U. San Diego, 1977; M in Theol. Studies, Cath. Theol. U., Chgo., 1989. Dir. religious edn. Diocese of San Diego, 1977-80; dir. religious edn. Archdiocese of Cin., 1982-84, assoc. dir. youth ministry, 1984-87; pastoral assoc. Diocese of Toledo, 1989—. Sec. social concerns bd. Met. Chs. United, Dayton; Justice com. Sisters of The Precious Blood; active Tour to Explore conditions in Nicaragua, New Orleans, 1983; founder Care and Share Ctr. City of Sandusky; Ohio state chancellor Internat. educators for World Peace. Mem. Sanctuary, Pledge of Resistance, Internat. Assn. Educators for Peace (state chancellor). Democrat. Avocations: racquetball, biking, non-violent sports. Home: 1219 E Perkins Ave Apt J5 Sandusky OH 44870 Office: Saints Peter & Paul Ch 510 Columbus St Sandusky OH 44870

MAHIN, JAMES RICHARD, minister; b. Santa Monica, Calif., Aug. 31, 1948; s. Charles Melvin and Lucille Lillian (Johnson) M.; m. Christina Chen, June 30, 1972; children: Michael, Mark, Michelle. BA, UCLA, 1969; ThD, Claremont McKenna Coll., 1973. Ordained to ministry United Meth. Ch. Assoc. min. Orangethorpe United Meth. Ch., Fullerton, Calif., 1973-75; sr. min. Palisades United Meth. Ch., Capistrano Beach, Calif., 1975-86; sr. min. Foothills United Meth. Ch., La Mesa, Calif., 1986—. Recipient Bishop's Growth award Calif.-Pacific Ann. Conf., Pasadena, 1986-89. Republican. Office: Foothills United Meth Ch 4031 Avocado Blvd La Mesa CA 92041

MAHLE, PATSY BEGHTEL, clergywoman, pastoral counselor; b. Huntington, Ind., Jan. 9, 1942; d. Fred Andress and Lila Margaret (Bradford) Beghtel; m. Ralph Jerry Mahle, Feb. 24, 1961; children—Christine, Jerry Bradford. Student, Carnegie Coll., 1959-61, Perkins Sch. Theology, 1982—. Med. technologist Middletown Hosp. (Ohio), 1962-67, Physician and Surgeon Clinic, Dallas, 1972-77; advanced resident for chaplaincy in emergency area Parkland Meml. Hosp., Dallas, 1978-79, mem. pastoral care dept., 1979-83, staff chaplain emergency area, 1980—. Mem. Am. Assn. Clin. Pastoral Educators, Assn. Pastoral Counselors. Methodist. Home: 3810 Old Faithful Irving TX 75062 Office: 5201 Harry Hines Blvd Dallas TX 75235

MAHNER, JERRY WAYNE, minister; b. Topeka, Feb. 16, 1964; s. Robert Eugene Mahner and Shirley Ann (Shimeall) Jackson; m. Sandra Ann Hope,

Nov. 29, 1986. BA in Music, Bapt. Bible Coll., Springfield, Mo., 1986. Ordained to ministry Bapt. Ch. Min. music and youth Grace Bapt. Temple, San Antonio, 1986-87; min. music and young marrieds Ramseur Bapt. Ch., Paris, Tenn., 1987-89; min. music and youth Capitol City Bapt. Ch., Des Moines, 1989—. Home: 4101 Amherst St Des Moines IA 50313 Office: Capitol City Bapt Ch 4112 Amherst St Des Moines IA 50313

MAHONEY, JAMES P., bishop; b. Saskatoon, Sask., Can., Dec. 7, 1927. Ordained priest Roman Cath. Ch., 1952; bishop Saskatoon, 1967—. Office: Chancery Office, 106 5th Ave N, Saskatoon, SK Canada S7K 2N7

MAHONEY, JAMES PATRICK, bishop; b. Kingston, N.Y., Aug. 16, 1925. Grad., St. Joseph's Sem., 1951. Ordained priest Roman Cath. Ch., 1951, consecrated bishop, 1972. Pastor various chs., to 1972; titular bishop of Ipagro and aux. bishop of N.Y. Mahopac, N.Y., 1972—; Episcopal vicar North Westchester, N.Y., from 1978. Office: 235 Msgr O'Brien Blvd Mahopac NY 10541

MAHONY, ROGER MICHAEL, archbishop; b. Hollywood, Calif., Feb. 27, 1936; s. Victor James and Loretta Marie (Baron) M. A.A., Our Lady Queen of Angels Sem., 1956; B.A., St. John's Sem. Coll., 1958, B.S.T., 1962; M.S.W., Catholic U. Am., 1964. Ordained priest Roman Cath. Ch., 1962, ordained bishop, 1975, created cardinal priest, 1991. Asst. pastor St. John's Cathedral, Fresno, Calif., 1962, 68-73, rector, 1973-80; residence St. Genevieve's Parish, Fresno, Calif., 1964—, adminstr., 1964-67, pastor, 1967-68; titular bishop of Tamascani, aux. bishop of Fresno, 1975-80; chancellor Diocese of Fresno, 1970-77, vicar gen., 1975-80; bishop Diocese of Stockton (Calif.), 1980-85; archbishop Archdiocese of L.A., 1985-91, cardinal priest, 1991—; diocesan dir. Cath. Charities and Social Svc. Fresno, 1964-70, exec. dir. Cath. Welfare Bur., 1964-70; exec. dir. Cath. Welfare Bur. Infant of Prague Adoption Service, 1964-70; chaplain St. Vincent de Paul Soc., Fresno, 1964-70; named chaplain to Pope Paul VI, 1967; mem. faculty extension div. Fresno State U., 1965-67; sec. U.S. Cath. bishops ad hoc com. on farm labor Nat. Conf. Bishops, 1970-75; chmn. com. on pub. welfare and income maintenance Nat. Conf. Cath. Charities, 1969-70; bd. dirs. West Coast Regional Office Bishops Com. for Spanish-Speaking, 1967-70; chmn. Calif. Assn. Cath. Charities Dirs., 1965-69; trustee St. Patrick's Sem., Archdiocese of San Francisco, 1974-75; mem. adminstrv. com. Nat. conf. Cath. Bishops, 1976-79, 82-85, 87-90, com. migration and refugees, 1976—, chmn. com. farm labor, 1981—, com. moral evaluation of deterrence, 1986-88; cons. com. for ProLife Activities, 1990—; mem. com. social devel. and world peace U.S. Cath. Conf., 1985, chmn. internat. policy sect., 1987-90; com. justice and peace, Pontifical Couns., 1984-89, 90—, pastoral care of migrants and itinerant people, 1986—, social communications, 1989—. Mem. Urban Coalition of Fresno, 1968-72, Fresno County Econ. Opportunities Commn., 1964-65, Fresno County Alcoholic Rehab. Com., 1966-67, Fresno City Charter Rev. Com., 1968-70, Mexican-Am. Council for Better Housing, 1968-72, Fresno Redevel. Agy., 1970-75, L.A. 2000 Com., 1985-88, Fed. Commn. Agrl. Workers, 1987—, Blue Ribbon Com. Affordable Housing City of L.A., 1988; mem. commn. to Draft an Ethics Code for L.A. City Govt., 1989-90; bd. dirs. Fresno Community Workshop, 1965-67; trustee St. Agnes Hosp., Fresno. Named Young Man of Yr. Fresno Jr. C. of C., 1967. Mem. Canon Law Soc. Am., Nat. Assn. Social Workers. Home: 114 E 2d St Los Angeles CA 90012 Office: Archdiocese of LA 1531 W 9th St Los Angeles CA 90015

MAIDA, ADAM J., bishop; b. East Vandergrift, Pa., Mar. 18, 1930. Student, St. Vincent Coll., Latrobe, Pa., St. Mary's U., Balt., Lateran U., Rome, Duquesne U. Ordained priest Roman Cath. Ch., 1956, as bishop, 1984. Bishop of Green Bay Wis., 1984—. Office: 1910 S Webster PO Box 66 Green Bay WI 54305

MAIER, FRANCIS XAVIER, newspaper editor; b. N.Y.C., Oct. 12, 1948; s. Edwin Albert and Sarah Claire (Degnan) M.; m. Suann Therese Malone, Dec. 26, 1970; children: Jude Matthew, John Luke, Mary Margaret Ann. B.A. in Communication Arts, U. Notre Dame, 1970; M.F.A. in Film and TV Prodn, N.Y. U., 1972; postgrad. screenwriting fellow, Am. Film Inst., 1973-74. Cameraman, film editor Don Connors Prodns., N.Y.C., 1970-71; staff writer Communications Distbn. Inc., N.Y.C., 1972-73; freelance screenwriter L.A., 1973-78; mem. editorial staff Nat. Cath. Register, L.A., 1978—, editor, 1979—; adv. bd. Inst. Religion and Democracy; cons. in field. Author articles in field. Roman Catholic. Home: 2171 Belhaven Ave Simi Valley CA 93063 Office: Nat Cath Register 6404 Wilshire Blvd Ste 900 Los Angeles CA 90048

MAIER, PAUL LUTHER, author, educator, minister; b. St. Louis, May 31, 1930; s. Walter A. and Hulda (Eickhoff) M.; m. Joan M. Ludtke, June 17, 1967; children: Laura Ann, Julie Joan, Krista Lynn, Katherine Marie. A.B., Concordia Sem., St. Louis, 1952, B.D., 1955; M.A., Harvard U., 1954; postgrad., Heidelberg (W. Ger.) U., 1955; Ph.D. summa cum laude, U. Basel, Switzerland, 1957. Ordained to ministry Lutheran Ch., 1958; Luth. campus chaplain Western Mich. U., Kalamazoo, 1958—; prof. history Western Mich. U., 1959—. Author: Caspar Schwenckfeld, 1959, A Man Spoke, A World Listened, The Story of Walter A. Maier,, 1963, Pontius Pilate, 1968, First Christmas, The True and Unfamiliar Story, 1971, First Easter, The True and Unfamiliar Story, 1973, First Christians, Pentecost and the Spread of Christianity, 1976, The Flames of Rome, 1981, In the Fullness of Time, 1991; also articles; editor: The Improvement of College and University Courses in the History of Civilization, 1965, The Best of Walter A. Maier, 1980; assoc. editor: Josephus-The Jewish War, 1982; editor, translator: Josephus-The Essential Writings, 1988 (Gold medallion book award Evangelical Christian Pubs. Assn., 1989). Recipient Detur award Harvard U., 1950; Alumni award teaching excellence Western Mich. U., 1974; Disting. Faculty Scholar award, 1981; Prof. of Yr. citation Council for Advancement and Support of Edn., 1984; Acad. citation Mich. Acad. Sci., Arts and Letters, 1985. Mem. Am. Hist. Assn., Bach Soc. Kalamazoo, Phi Kappa Phi. Address: 8383 W Main St Kalamazoo MI 49009

MAIHACK, SAMUEL PAUL, minister; b. Moline, Ill., July 21, 1955; s. Frederick Edward and Helen Louise Maihack; m. Barbara Lynne Hardy, May 21, 1977; children: Michael, Jill, Kimberly. BA in History, U. Iowa, 1977; MDiv with honors, Denver Theol. Sem., 1980. Ordained to ministry Conservative Congl. Christian Conf., 1982. Assoc. pastor Community Ch. Portage Lakes, Akron, Ohio, 1980-86; assoc. pastor Browncroft Community Ch., Rochester, N.Y., 1986-89, sr. pastor, 1989-90; staff rep. The Navigators Ch. Discipleship Ministry, Rochester, 1991—; assoc. staff The Navigators, Rochester, 1989—; duty chaplain Rochester Gen. Hosp., 1990—. Youth coach Kenmore Soccer Assn., Akron, 1984-85, Bayview YMCA, Rochester, 1989—. Mem. Conservative Congl. Christian Conf. Home and Office: 501 Hollywood Blvd Webster NY 14580

MAIKOWSKI, FATHER THOMAS ROBERT, priest, educational director; b. Milw., Oct. 20, 1947; s. Thomas Robert and Eugenia A. (Rogowski) M. BA, St. Francis Coll., Milw., 1970, MS in Edn., 1972; MA, Cardinal Stritch Coll., 1974; MDiv, Kenrick Sem., St. Louis, 1976; BA, Notre Dame Coll., St. Louis, 1976; MEd, Marquette U., 1977; PhD, St. Louis U., 1980; postgrad., U. San Francisco. Ordained priest Roman Cath. Ch., 1976; cert. secondary sch. tchr. and adminstr., Ariz., N.Mex.; cert. elem. tchr., N.Mex. Tchr., adminstr. Cathedral High Sch., Gallup, N.Mex., 1976-78; supt. of schs. Diocese of Gallup, 1978-90, dir. edn., 1990—; prin., tchr. The Cath. Acad., Farmington, N.Mex., 1980-90. Contbr. articles to religious jours. Capt. USAFR. Mem. Nat. Cath. Ednl. Assn. (exec. com. 1978-81, 87-90), Religious Edn. Assn., Am. Assn. on Mental Retardation, Assn. for Supervision and Curriculum Devel., N.Mex. Assn. Non-pub. Schs. (bd. dirs. 1981-84), Phi Delta Kappa. Address: PO Box 1028 Gallup NM 87305

MAIN, A. DONALD, bishop. Bishop Upper Susquehanna region Evang. Luth. Ch. in Am., Lewisburg, Pa. Office: Evang Luth Ch in Am 241 Fairgrown Rd Box 36 Lewisburg PA 17837*

MAIN, DOUGLAS MARTIN, Christian education minister; b. Oskaloosa, Iowa, Aug. 20, 1959; s. James Noble and Elaine Kay (Medrud) M.; m. Teresa Faye Kroeker, Dec. 20, 1980; 1 child, Lauren Alyssa. BA in Psychology, Mid-Am. Nazarene Coll., 1981; MRE, Nazarene Theol. Sem., 1984; postgrad., Ft. Hays State U., 1987—. Campus min. Nazarene Student Ctr., Stillwater, Okla., 1984-86; youth min. Maryvale Ch., Phoenix, 1986; assoc., Christian edn. Great Bend (Kans.) Nazarene Ch., 1986—. Mem. Am. Assn. Counseling and Devel., Nazarene Multiple-Staff Mins. Assn. Avocations: athletics, livestock.

MAIN, N. JAMES, educator, administrator; b. Moravia, Iowa, Dec. 27, 1929; s. R. Forrest and Doris Thelma (Darby) M.; m. Elaine K. Medrud, Jan. 26, 1951; children: Jolaine Kay, James Daniel, Douglas Martin. BA, Cen. Coll., Pella, Iowa, 1952; MA, No. Iowa U., 1959; DEd, U. Okla., 1969. Music supr. Iowa Pub. Schs., 1952-63; assoc. prof. Bethany Nazarene Coll., Okla., 1963-68; prof. Mid Am. Nazarene Coll., Olathe, Kans., 1968—; acad. dean European Nazarene Bible Coll., 1985-89; asst. acad. dean, internat. student advisor Mid Am. Nazarene Coll., 1989—; min. of music Marshalltown Ch. of Nazarene, Iowa, 1954-58, First Ch. of Nazarene, Oskaloosa, Iowa, 1959-63, First Ch. of Nazarene, Oklahoma City, 1963-65; presenter music workshops, 1969—. Arranger choral anthems and hymns. Mem. Music Educators Nat. Conf., Phi Delta Kappa, Phi Delta Lambda (pres. 1983-84). Office: Mid Am Nazarene Coll Box 1776 Olathe KS 66061 *In a dynamic world of increasingly rapid change each person must determine goals for a meaningful existence and find methods to implement them. The opportunities for personal growth, fulfillment and service have never been greater; the demand for individuals to utilize these opportunities more universal.*

MAINELLI, HELEN KENIK, religion educator, library director; b. Cleve., Aug. 6, 1935; d. Joseph and Mary (Urbancic) Kenik; m. Eugene Francis Mainelli, Aug. 16, 1980. BA, Siena Heights Coll., Adrian, Mich., 1959; MS, Barry U., Miami, Fla., 1970; PhD, St. Louis U., 1978; M in Libr. and Info. Studies, U. Calif., Berkeley, 1987. Asst. prof. bibl. theology Jesuit Sch. Theology, Chgo., 1976-81; asst. prof. Old Testament Interdenominational Theol. Sem., Atlanta, 1982-83; assoc. prof. Old Testament Columbia Theol. Sem., Decatur, Ga., 1983-84; assoc. prof. spirituality Holy Names Coll., Oakland, Calif., 1984-89; assoc. prof. theol. bibliography No. Bapt. Theol. Sem., Lombard, Ill., 1989—; libr. dir. Sem. Libr. Bethany & No. Bapt., Oak Brook, Ill., 1989—. Author: Design for Kingship: The Deuteronomistic Narrative Technique in 1 Kings 3:4-15, 1983, Numbers. Collegeville Bible Commentary, 1985; contbr. articles to religious publs. Mem. Am. Theol. Libr. Assn., Cath. Bibl. Assn. (exec. bd. 1979-81, 85-87), ALA, Soc. Bibl. Lit., Cath. Theol. Soc. Am., Coll. Theology Soc., Art Inst. Chgo. Roman Catholic. Office: Bethany & No Bapt Libr Butterfield and Meyers Rds Oak Brook IL 60521 *As awareness of the passage of years gives way to the passage of days, I grow more aware that the purpose of life is the use of my gifts for others.*

MAINOR, THOMAS FOY, minister, educator; b. Eufaula, Ala., Sept. 2, 1934; s. Walter Foy and Susie Virginia (Matteson) M.; m. Elizabeth Raye Cox, June 11, 1961; children: Karen Elizabeth Mainor Perry, Thomas Matteson. Student, U. Miami, 1957, U. Va., 1960; AB in History, Davidson Coll., 1961; MDiv, Union Theol. Sem., Richmond, Va., 1964. Ordained to ministry Presbyn. Ch. (U.S.A.), 1964. Pastor Falling Spring Presbyn. Ch., Glasgow, Va., 1964-67; campus min., campus urban pastor Synod of Va., Norfolk and Wiliamsburg, 1967-80; mem. faculty, chaplain Ea. Va. Med. Sch.-Med. Ctr. Hosps., Norfolk, 1980-85; staff dir. health costs policies task force Presbyn. Ch. (U.S.A.), Phila., 1985-88; interim pastor New Life Presbyn. Ch., Albuquerque, 1989; dir. Med. Ctr. Ministry, Presbytery of Chgo. and No. Ill. Conf. United Meth. Ch., 1990—; mem. adj. faculty McCormick Theol. Sem., Chgo., 1990—, Rush U., Chgo., 1990—, U. Ill., Chgo., 1990—. Contbr., assoc. editor: Health Care and Its Costs: A Challenge to the Church. 1988; editor: Prayers for Healing and Wholeness, 1983. Chaplain N.Mex. Hosp. for Severely and Profundly Retarded, Los Lunas, 1989. Sgt. USMC, 1953-57. Mem. Coll. Chaplains, Soc. for Health and Human Values, Presbyn. Health Network, Health and Medicine Policy Rsch. Group. Democrat. Office: Med Ctr Ministry 606 S Ashland Ave Chicago IL 60607

MAITLAND, DAVID JOHNSTON, chaplain, educator; b. Medford, Mass., May 11, 1922; s. John Todd and Jane (Campbell) M.; m. Elizabeth Burton Green, Sept. 1, 1945; children: Margaret Todd, James Campbell. BA, Amherst Coll., 1943; MDiv, Union Theol. Sem., 1946; MS, U. Wis., 1953; PhD, Columbia U., 1959; DD, Northland Coll., 1983. Campus min. Wis. United Ch. of Christ, Madison, 1946-52; chaplain Beloit (Wis.) Coll., 1952-54; stated supply Good Shepherd Presbyn. Ch., 1954-56; chaplain, prof. Carleton Coll., Northfield, Minn., 1956-86; prof. emeritus Carleton Coll., Northfield, 1986—. Author: Against the Grain, 1981, Looking Both Ways, 1984, Aging: A Time for New Learning, 1987, Aging as Counterculture, 1991. Active First Congregational Ch., Northfield, 1956—, Minn. U.C.C. Conf., Mpls., 1956—. Fellow Soc. for Values Higher Edn. (steering com., bd. dirs. 1970-80), Nat. Assn. Coll. Univ. Chaplains (v.p., pres., historian 1970—). Democrat. Mem. United Ch. of Christ. Avocations: tennis, jogging, gardening, cross-country skiing. Home: 600 E 1st St Northfield MN 55057 Office: Carleton Coll Northfield MN 55057

MAJERNIK, BARBARA ELLEN, principal; b. Kankakee, Ill., May 9, 1942; d. Harold F. and Dorothy May (Bruner) Larkin; m. John Andrew Majernik, Aug. 13, 1966; children: Joanne, Paula, Carol. BS in Edn., Ill. State U., 1964; MS in Edn., No. Ill., 1989. Cert. tchr., Ill. Religious edn. tchr. St. Mary's Ch., Dixon, Ill., 1964-66, St. James Ch., Belvidere, Ill., 1968-69; prin. St. James Sch., Belvidere, 1985—. Mem. Nat. Cath. Edn. Assn., Zonta Internat. (bd. dirs. 1988—), Belvidere C. of C. (exec. dir. 1982-85).

MAJESKE, DANIEL LEE, lay church worker, educator; b. Saginaw, Mich., June 24, 1947; s. Fred F. and Doris A. (Fredrickson) M.; m. Roberta K. Brawner, July 20, 1974; children: Rebekah K., Rachel K. BA, Oakland U., 1969; MA, Saginaw Valley U., 1979. Cert. tchr., adminstr., Mich. Tchr. Holly (Mich.) Area Schs., 1985—; prin. Cen. Christian Acad., Muskegon, Mich., 1981-84; worship leader Cen. Assembly of God, Muskegon, 1981-84, First Assembly of God, Bay City, Mich., 1984-85, Riverside Tabernacle, Flint, Mich., 1985-88; treas. Riverside Tabernacle, Flint, 1986-90; mem. choir and worship team Mt. Zion Temple, Clarkston, Mich., 1991—. Mem. NEA, Mich. Edn. Assn., Repub. Nat. Com., Nat. Right to Life Assn. Home: 4941 Harbor Pointe Dr Waterford MI 48329

MAJETTE, L. DEAN, minister; b. Hampton, Va., Dec. 5, 1947; s. Walter F. and Daisy M. (Woodard) M.; m. Tate Bradley, Aug. 4, 1972; children: Bradley Lynn, Helen Claire, John Fox. BS in History, Campbell U., 1970; MDiv, So. Bapt. Theol. Sem., 1973, DMin, 1984. Ordained to ministry Bapt. Ch., 1973. Assoc. pastor Hampton Heights Bapt. Ch., Greenville, S.C., 1973-76; pastor Green Hill Bapt. Ch., Rutherfordton, N.C., 1976-84, Ox Hill Bapt. Ch., Fairfax, Va., 1984—; mem. religious liberty coun. Bapt. Joint Com. on Pub. Affairs, Washington, 1990—; trustee chmn. Thermal Belt Bapt. Youth Shelter, Forest City, N.C., 1982-84; moderator Green River Bapt. Assn., Rutherfordton, 1983; mem. Bapt. Gen. Bd. N.C., 1983-84. Bd. dirs. Campbell U., Buie's Creek, N.C., 1983—. Mem. Rotary (bd. dirs. Dulles, Va. chpt. 1991—, chmn. shcolarship com. 1990—). Home: 3453 Briar Gate Ct Fairfax VA 22033 Office: Ox Hill Bapt Ch 4101 Elmwood St Chantilly VA 22021

MAJIED-MUHAMMAD, ARTHUR, religious education educator, writer; b. Norfolk, Va., Feb. 1, 1921; s. Walter Herbert and Pearleaner (Washington) McIver; m. Catherine Delphia Edwards, Mar. 14, 1943; children: Wynona, Sandra, Arthur Jr., Conrad, Michelle. BS in Math., Morgan State U., 1954; MS in Math., Howard U., 1957. Software specialist Defense Industry, Calif., 1952-85; educator pub./pvt. schs., Md./Calif.; pvt. bus., Muslims., Calif. With U.S. Army, 1943-45, ETO. Fellow United Islamic Ctrs. (treas. 1984—). Democrat. Muslim. Avocations: chess, jogging, writing novels.

MAJOR, GERALD HILSON, JR., religious organization administrator; b. Scranton, Pa., Aug. 23, 1931; s. Gerald Hilson Sr. and Ruth (Ivey) M.; m. Janice Lyn Bittle; children: Gerald Hilson III, Sandra Jean. BA, Bob Jones U., 1955, MA, 1957. Ordained to ministry Bapt. Ch., 1956. Exec. dir. Youth for Christ, Scranton, 1957-74; regional dir. Youth for Christ N.E. U.S., 1963-74; pastor Faith Community Ch., Glenburn, Pa., 1977-85; exec. dir. Internat. Needs, Inc., Scranton, 1985-91; world exec. Internat. Needs, Inc., New Zealand, 1988-91; v.p. Internat. Needs, Inc., Scranton, 1991—; bd. dirs. Youth for Christ Internat., Wheaton, Ill., 1969-71, Missionary Retreat Fellowship, Lake Ariel, Pa., 1985-90. With U.S. Army, 1949-52. Republican. Office: 111 Wyoming Ave Box 889 Scranton PA 18501

MAKARI, VICTOR EMMANUEL, minister; b. Assiût, Egypt, Apr. 9, 1941; s. Emmanuel Makari and Amina-Victoria (Hanna) Shaheed; m. Jane Lee Dill, Aug. 7, 1965; children: Peter, John. Diplome, Assiût Am. Coll., 1956; BTh, Cairo Theol. Sem., 1959; MDiv, Princeton Theol. Sem., 1964; ThM, Columbia Theol. Sem., Decatur, Ga., 1965; PhD, Temple U., 1976. Assoc. pastor Wayne (Pa.) Presbyn. Ch., 1967-72; minister of edn. Overbrook Presbyn. Ch., Columbus, Ohio, 1973-79; sr. pastor Indianola Presbyn. Ch., Columbus, 1980—; vis. prof. Islamic studies Ohio Wesleyan U., Delaware, 1985, 87; cons. World Alliance of Reformed Chs., Geneva, The Presbyn. Ch., N.Y.C., 1986—. Author: The Social Factor In Ibn Taymiyyah's Ethics, 1983. Bd. dirs. The Program Agy., Presbyn. Ch. (U.S.A.), N.Y.C., 1974-83, pres., 1979-82; del. Gen. Council of World Alliance Reformed Chs., Ottawa, Ont., Can., 1982; mem. Presbyn. Gen. Assembly Council, N.Y.C., 1979-82. Mem. Am. Acad. Religion, Presbytery of Scioto Valley. Avocations: travel, photography, Arabic literature and poetry, classical music.

MAKHULU, WALTER PAUL KHOTSO, archbishop; b. Johannesburg, Republic of South Africa, July 2, 1935; s. Paul M.; m. Rosemary Makhulu, 1966; 1 child. Student, Coll. of the Resurrection, Birmingham, Republic of South Africa, St. Andrews Coll., Birmingham, Republic of South Africa. Area sec. Ea. Africa and African refugees Commn. on Inter-Ch. Aid Refugee and World Service, World Council of Chs., 1975-79; bishop Botswana, 1979—; archbishop Cen. Africa, 1980—; pres. All Africa Conf. of Chs., 1981-86, World Council of Chs., 1983; hon. curate Holy Trinity, Geneva. Named Officier l'Ordre des Palmes Academiques, 1981. Avocations: music, internat. affairs. Home: PO Box 769, Gaborone Botswana Office: World Coun Chs, 150 rte de Ferney, POB 66, 1211 Geneva 20, Switzerland

MALATESTA, BROTHER EDWARD JOSEPH, JR., priest, educator; b. Paterson, N.J., May 31, 1932; s. Edward Joseph Sr. and Concetta (Caratozzolo) M. BA, Santa Clara (Calif.) U., 1953; MA, Gonzaga U., 1955; STL, Les Fontaines, Chantilly, France, 1962; SSL, Pontifical Bibl. Inst., Rome, 1965; SSD, Pontifical Bibl. Inst., 1975. Joined S.J., Roman Cath. Ch., ordained priest, 1961. Priest Calif. Province of Soc. of Jesus, 1948—; dir. Inst. Chinese-Western Cultural History U. San Francisco, 1984—. Mem. Am. Cath. Hist. Assn., Assn. for Asian Studies, Cath. Bibl. Assn. Am., Soc. for Bibl. Lit. Office: U San Francisco Inst Chinese-Western Cultural History 2130 Fulton St San Francisco CA 94117 *I find myself more and more looking back to discover new riches in the Traditions I belong to, looking around to find God, hidden and manifest, in every person and each event, looking ahead to a world united in the manifold beauty of its diversity, looking towards the Love that draws all things.*

MALCHOW, BRUCE VIRGIL, religion educator; b. Chgo., Jan. 7, 1940; s. Virgil George and Ruth Dorothy (Sylvester) M.; m. Roberta Jeannine Hawkins June 22, 1963; children: Timothy Bruce, Laura Jeannine. BA, Concordia Coll., Fort Wayne, Ind., 1961; MDiv, Concordia Seminary, St. Louis, 1965, STM, 1966; PhD, Marquette U., 1972. Mission developer Lamb of God Luth. Ch., Balt., 1966-68; asst. prof. religion Concordia Coll., Milw., 1968-74; assoc. pastor Lake Park Luth. Ch., Milw., 1974-76; prof. Old Testament Sacred Heart Sch. Theology, Hales Corners, Wis., 1976—; coord. Luth.-Cath. dialogue Wis.-Upper Mich. Synod Luth. Ch. Am., 1979-80; co-chairperson Luth.-Cath. dialogue, Milw., 1979-80, mem. 1979-82; mem. Milw. Assn. for Interfaith Rels., 1983—; mem. ecumenical rels. com. Wis.-Upper Mich. Synod, 1980-85. Author: Because He First Loved Us, 1982; contbr. articles and revs. to profl. jours. Mem. Soc. Bibl. Lit. Office: Sacred Heart Sch Theology PO Box 429 Hales Corners WI 53130

MALCOLM, ROBERT CALVIN, evangelist; b. Mpls., Aug. 1, 1928; s. Elvin Joseph and Irene Mavorning (Hulting) M.; m. Kari Marie Torjesen, Aug. 28, 1954; children: Kirsten Elisabeth, Lois Ellen. BS in Agr., U. Minn., 1952; BTh., Fuller Sem., 1955; postgrad., Union Theol. Sem., 1957, McCormick Theol. Sem., 1987—. Mem. staff Navigators, L.A., Chgo., 1954-56; pastor United Presbyn. Ch., Hinkley, Minn., 1956-, Orangeburg, N.Y., -1959; fraternal evangelist United Presbyn. Ch., The Philippines, 1959-74; staff evangelist Twin Cities Area Presbyn. Ch., Mpls., 1974-80; mission pastor Hope Presbyn. Ch., Richfield, Minn., 1980-90; ret. Hope Presbyn. Ch., Richfield, 1990; working with Lao, Korean congregations, Twin City area, 1990—; cons. United Ch. Chirst in The Philippines, 1965-74. Home: 3175 105th St Inver Grove Heights MN 55077

MALCOM, HARRIS RAY, minister; b. Monroe, Ga., July 12, 1953; s. William and Eleanor (Harris) M.; m. Phyllis Elaine Rainwater, Aug. 19, 1973; children: Shauna, Natalie, Katie. Student, Truett McConnell Jr. Coll., 1973; BS, Mercer U., 1976; MRE, Bapt. Theol. Sem., Ft. Worth, 1978. Ordained to ministry So. Bapt. Conv., 1978. Min. to youth 1st Bapt. Ch., Alpharetta, Ga., 1974-75; min. youth and edn. Immanuel Bapt. Ch., Mineral Wells, Tex., 1977-78; assoc. pastor for edn. 1st Bapt. Ch., Canton, Ga., 1978-81; pastor Byron (Ga.) Bapt. Ch., 1981-87, 1st Bapt. Ch., Camilla, Ga., 1987—; dir. pastoral ministries Tucker Bapt. Assn., Camilla, 1988—, moderator, chmn. exec. com., 1990—; mem. exec. com. Ga. Bapt. Conv. Home: Rte 4 Box 79 Camilla GA 31730 Office: 1st Bapt Ch 27 E Broad St Camilla GA 31730

MALE, (ERNEST) WILLIAM, religious educator; b. Streator, Ill., Nov. 7, 1927; s. (Ernest) Gordon and Mary Leta (Morrell) M.; m. Ella Beth Kauffman, Sept. 3, 1950; children: Martha, Mary, Ruth, Rebecca. AB, Western Mich. U., 1952; BD, Grace Theol. Sem., 1955; EdM, Temple U., 1959; PhD, Ind. U., 1968. Ordained to ministry Grace Brethren Ch., 1955. Pastor 1st Brethren Ch., Phila., 1955-59; prof. Grace Coll. and Sem., Winona Lake, Ind., 1959—; acad. dean Grace Coll., Winona Lake, Ind., 1962-74; dean Grace Theol. Sem., Winona Lake, Ind., 1976-87; asst. to pres. Grace Coll. and Sem., Winona Lake, Ind., 1987-89, planned giving officer, 1989—. Mem. Nat. Fellowship of Brethren Ministers, Warsaw Kiwanis Club, Phi Delta Kappa. Republican. Avocations: bird watching, flying. Home: 1615 S Cherry Creek Ln Warsaw IN 46580 Office: Grace Coll Theol Sem 200 Seminary Dr Winona Lake IN 46590

MALHERBE, ABRAHAM JOHANNES, VI, religion educator, writer; b. Pretoria, South Africa, May 15, 1930; came to U.S., 1951; s. Abraham Johannes V and Cornelia Aletta (Meyer) M.; m. Phyllis Melton, May 28, 1953; children: Selina, Cornelia, Abraham Johannes VII. BA, Abilene Christian U., 1954; STB, Harvard U., 1957; student, U. Utrecht, The Netherlands, 1960-61; ThD, Harvard U., 1963; LLD (hon.), Pepperdine U., 1981; LHD (hon.), Centre Coll., 1990. Minister Ch. of Christ, Lexington, Mass., 1956-63; asst. and assoc. prof. Abilene (Tex.) Christian U., 1963-67; vis. scholar Harvard Divinity Sch., Cambridge, Mass., 1967-68; assoc. prof. Abilene Christian U., 1968-69, Dartmouth Coll., Hanover, N.H., 1969-70; assoc. prof. Yale Divinity Sch., New Haven, Conn., 1970-77, prof., 1977-81, Buckingham prof., 1981—, assoc. dean acad. affairs, 1987-89. Author: Social Aspects of Early Christianity, 1983, Moral Exhortation, 1986, Paul and the Thessalonians, 1987, Ancient Epistolary Theorists, 1988, Paul and the Popular Philosophers, 1989; contbr. articles to profl. jours.; inspiration for book: Greeks, Romans and Christians: Essays in Honor of Abraham J. Malherbe, 1990. Recipient teaching award Abilene Christian U., 1965, 67; NEH fellow, 1973. Mem. Soc. Biblical Lit., North Am. Patristic Soc., Studiorum Novi Testamenti Societas, South African New Testament Soc. (hon.), Religious Studies Rev. (editoral bd. 1980—), The Second Century, Novum Testamentum (editorial bd. 1991—). Mem. Ch. of Christ. Home: 71 Spring Garden St Hamden CT 06517 Office: Yale Divinity Sch 409 Prospect St New Haven CT 06510

MALICK, JOAN BRADNER, clergywoman; b. Cleve., Aug. 11, 1943; d. John Alexander and Leah Lucille (Coleman) Bradner; m. Clarence Malick, June 15, 1965 (div. Dec. 1975); 1 child, Rebecca Leigh. BFA, Boston U., 1965, MEd, 1970; MDiv, McCormick Theol. Sem., 1978; cert. sex edn., counseling, tng., Karl Menninger Sch. Psychiatry, 1987. Ordained to ministry Presbyn. Ch. Asst. prof. Winnetka (Ill.) Presbyn. Ch., 1978-81; dir. field based programs McCormick Sem., Chgo., 1981-82; interim assoc. pastor Palatine (Ill.) Presbyn. Ch., 1982-83; assoc. prof. First Presbyn. Ch., McAlester, Okla., 1983-88, Second Presbyn. Ch., Indpls., 1988—. Illustrator: What's Good About Divorce?, 1977. Recipient Outstanding Community Svc. award McAlester Ministerial Alliance, 1988. Mem. Am. Assn. Sex Educators, Counselors, Therapists, The Menninger Found. Home: 1402 Misty Ln Indianapolis IN 46260 Office: Second Presbyn Ch 7700 N Meridian St Indianapolis IN 46260

MALIN, DAVID ALAN, broadcasting executive; b. Flint, Mich., Oct. 1, 1951; s. Otis E. and Grace A. (Dahlstrom) M.; m. Ilene J. Bursick, May 19, 1973; children: Christy, David A., Jeremy, Zachary. BS, Cen. Mich. U., Mt. Pleasant, 1973. Mgr. Sta. WUGN-FM, Midland, Mich., 1976-79; program mgr. Family Life Radio, Tucson, Ariz., 1979-84; gen. mgr. No. Christian Radio, Gaylord, Mich., 1984-89, chief exec. adminstr., 1989—; dir. Moody Broadcasting Affiliate Adv. Bd., Chgo., 1986. Coach Youth Soccer and Little League, Gaylord, 1986—. Named Affiliate Mgr. of Yr., Moody Broadcasting Network, 1988. Mem. Christian Mgmt. Assn. Office: No Christian Radio Inc Box 695 Gaylord MI 49735-0695

MALINO, JEROME R., rabbi; b. N.Y.C., June 7, 1911; s. Wolf and Henrietta (Rosenbaum) M.; m. Rhoda Simon, June 9, 1936; children: Frances, Jonathan. B.A., CCNY, 1931; M.H.L., Jewish Inst. Religion, 1935; L.H.D. (hon.), Alfred (N.Y.) U., 1958; D.D. (hon.), Hebrew Union Coll., 1960. Rabbi Baldwin (N.Y.) Jewish Center, 1934-35, United Jewish Center, Danbury, Conn., 1935-81; rabbi emeritus United Jewish Center, 1981—; chaplain Fed. Corrections Inst., Danbury, 1940-83; lectr. Western Conn. State U., 1983-84; adj. lectr. Hebrew Union Coll.-Jewish Inst. Religion, 1983—. Mem. Danbury Bd. Edn., 1949-69; bd. dirs. Danbury Community Action Com.; mem. Danbury Charter Revision Com., 1976, Mayor of Danbury Ad Hoc Com. Racism, 1976. Mem. Central Conf. Am. Rabbis (pres. 1979-81), Assn. Religious Communities (pres. 1982-84), Jewish Peace Fellowship, Inst. Religion in Age of Sci., Danbury Music Center, Danbury Concert Assn. Home: 77 Garfield Ave Danbury CT 06810 Office: 141 Deer Hill Ave Danbury CT 06810 *The best way to enhance the meaning of one's own life is to place human values everywhere before all other considerations.*

MALLER, ALLEN STEPHEN, rabbi, sociologist; b. N.Y.C., June 11, 1938; s. Isaac Harry and Gloria (Sonnenblum) M.; m. Judith Lynn Coopersmith; children: Ariyeh Herzl, Aviva Miriam. BA, UCLA; BHL, Hebrew Union Coll., L.A.; MA, Hebrew Union Coll., Cin. Ordained rabbi, 1964. Rabbi Temple Akiba, Culver City, Calif., 1967—; pres. Nat. Jewish Hospitality com., L.A., 1975—. Author: God, Sex and Kabbalah, 1989, (children's book) The Rubic's Cube, 1964; editor: (high holy day prayer book) Tikkun Nefashot. Office: Temple Akiba 5249 S Sepulveda Blvd Culver City CA 90230

MALLORY, CHARLES SHANNON, bishop; b. Dallas, Sept. 9, 1936; s. William Lee and Hazelle (Wisdom) M.; children: Karin, Teresa, James, Mary, Patrick. BA, UCLA, 1958; MDiv, Gen. Sem., N.Y.C., 1961; MA, Rhodes U., Republic South Africa, 1970; ordained to ministry. Rector Parish Districts of Namibia, Africa, 1961-62; mission dir. Diocese of Damaraland, Africa, 1962-69, archdeacon, 1964-69; coll. chaplain U. Rhodes, 1970-71; lectr. Makerere (Uganda) U., 1971-72; diocesan bishop Diocese of Botswana, 1972-78; asst. bishop Diocese of L.I., N.Y., 1978-80; diocesan bishop Diocese of El Camino (Calif.) Real, 1980—. Office: Diocese El Camino Real PO Box 1903 Monterey CA 93942

MALLORY, MARILYN MAY, lay worker; b. Tulsa; d. John Scott and Mildred (Dennis) M.; m. Louis Goosen, 1970 (div. 1983). BA, Stanford U., 1965; BD, Cath. U., Nijmegen, The Netherlands, 1970, licentiate in theology, 1972, PhD, 1977. Lay worker The Netherlands, 1970—; dir. YWCA, San Francisco, 1990-91; exec. dir. No. Calif. Caths. for Free Choice, 1991—; rep. Caths. For a Free Choice, Washington, 1989-90. Author: Christian Mysticism, 1977 (Dutch award 1977); contbr. articles to Revista de Espiritualidad. Canfield Found. scholar, 1961; Nijmegen U. Student Fund rsch. grantee, 1973. Mem. Cath. Theol. Soc. Am., Am. Acad. Religion, NOW (chair polit. action com. East Bay chpt. 1989-90). Democrat. Roman Catholic. Home: 3375 Alma St # 165 Palo Alto CA 94306 *I am coming to see increasingly that giving tithes to any church that does not ordain women is like taxation without representation. Women should vote with their wallets and refuse to give any tithes to such churches.*

MALLORY-YOUNG, SHIRLEY, religion educator; b. Bronwood, Ga., July 15, 1942; d. Clarence and Lula (Perry) Mallory; m. Howard Smith, June 1, 1966 (div. June 1967); m. Nathaniel Young, Aug. 20, 1988. BA, Bethune Cookman Coll., 1964; MEd, Stetson U., 1981; PhD, Fla. State U., 1985. Pres., prin. Christian Dynamics, Ft. Lauderdale, Fla., 1986—; instr. Jesus Ministries-Bible Coll., Miami, Fla., 1989-90; dir. Christian edn. H.O.P.E. Ministries, Lauderhill, Fla.; founder, pres. Christian Dynamics Bible Coll. and Grad. Sch. Author religious ednl. materials: Lord, Teach Us Me to Pray, 1986, Putting on the Whole Armour of God, 1990, Family Altar Prayer Guide, 1991; seminar: Management of Today's Church, 1989. Mem. Delta Sigma Theta, Inc., Phi Delta Kappa, Inc., Kappa Delta Pi. Democrat. Home: 4330 NW 11th St Lauderhill FL 33313 Office: PO Box 491224 Fort Lauderdale FL 33349

MALLOY, EDWARD ALOYSIUS, priest, university administrator, educator; b. Washington, May 3, 1941; s. Edward Aloysius and Elizabeth (Clark) M. BA, U. Notre Dame, 1963, MA, 1967, ThM, 1969; PhD, Vanderbilt U., 1975. Ordained priest Roman Cath. Ch., 1970. Instr. U. Notre Dame, Ind., 1974-75, asst. prof., 1975-81, assoc. prof., 1981-88, prof. theology, 1988—, assoc. provost, 1982-86, pres. elect, 1986, pres., 1987—; bd. regents U. Portland, Oreg., 1985—; cons. Cath. Bishops of Ind. Author: Homosexuality and the Christian Way of Life, 1981, The Ethics of Law Enforcement and Criminal Punishment, 1982; contbr. articles to profl. jours. Mem. steering com. Gov. Evan Bayh's Commn. for a Drug-Free Ind., 1989—; spl. commn. World Congress of Cath. Educators; bd. nominators Am. Inst. Pub. Svc., 1989—; bd. dirs. Sister Thea Bowman Black Cath. Edn. Found., 1989—, Nat. Collegiate Athletic Assn. Found., 1989—; trustee Nat. Citizens Commn. on Alcoholism, 1989—; mem. Bishops and Pres.'s Com., Assn. Cath. Colls. and Univs., 1988—; gen. coun. Internat. Fedn. Cath. Univs., 1988—; mem. Pres.'s Adv. Coun. on Drugs, 1989—; bd. dirs. Points of Light. Mem. Cath. Theol. Soc. Am., Am. Soc. Christian Ethics, Bus.-Higher Edn. Forum, The Conf. Bd. Address: U Notre Dame 141 Sorin Hall Notre Dame IN 46556 Office: U Notre Dame Office of President Notre Dame IN 46556

MALONE, JAMES WILLIAM, bishop; b. Youngstown, Ohio, Mar. 8, 1920; s. James Patrick and Katherine V. (McGuire) M. A.B., St. Mary Sem., Cleve., 1945; M.A., Cath. U. Am., 1952, Ph.D., 1957. Ordained priest Roman Catholic Ch., 1945; asst. pastor Youngstown, 1945-50; supt. schs. Diocese of Youngstown, 1952-65; instr. ednl. adminstrn. St. John's Coll., Cleve., 1953; aux. bishop of Youngstown, 1960-68; bishop, 1968—; apostolic adminstr. Diocese Youngstown, 1966-68; adv. Bishops' Com. Ecumenical and Interreligious Affairs, Nat. Conf. Cath. Bishops, v.p., 1980-83, pres., 1983-86; mem. adminstrv. com., mem. nat. adv. coun., co-chmn. Cath./United Meth. Nat. Dialogue; mem. Episcopal Bd., consultor bishops' com. liturgy; bd. dirs. Cath. Conf. Ohio; mem. gen. bd. Ohio Coun. Chs.; chmn. Commn. on Social Devel. & World Peace. Trustee Cath. U. Am.

MALONE, RICHARD, theology educator; b. Phila., Mar. 31, 1937; s. John and Anne (McDermott) M. STD, Pontifical Lateran U., Rome, 1965; JCL, Pontifical Lateran U., 1971. Ordained priest, 1962. Official Congregation Doctrine of the Faith, Vatican City, Italy, 1966-76; exec. dir. NCCB Com. on Doctrine and Com. for Pastoral Research, Washington, 1976-86; prof. theology Pope John XXIII Nat. Sem., Weston, Mass., 1986—; fellow Cambridge Ctr. Study of Faith and Culture, Cambridge, Mass., 1986—. Editorial bd. Am. Edit. of Communio, 1985; editor: Theology of Priesthood, 1985, The Kung Dialogue, 1980; co-editor: Contemporary Perspectives on Christian Marriage, 1984. Prelate of Honor, Secretariate of State, Vatican City, 1982. Mem. Cath. Theol. Soc. Am., Cath. Bible Soc. Am., Cath. Commn. on Intellectual and Cultural Affairs. Democrat. Roman Catholic. Avocations: tennis, biking, hiking. Home and Office: St Charles Seminary Overbrook PA 19096

MALONE, ROBERT WINSTON, JR., music minister; b. Florence, Ala., July 23, 1951; s. Robert Winston and Geraldine (Austell) M.; m. Debra Blackwelder, Aug. 11, 1973; children: Heather, Adam, Robby. BS in Music Edn., U. North Ala., 1973; M of Ch. Music, Southwestern Bapt. Sem., Ft. Worth, 1977; postgrad., Auburn U. Ordained to ministry So. Bapt. Conv., 1981. Min. music, youth Lindale (Ga.) Bapt. Ch., 1977-79, 1st Bapt. Ch., Manchester, Tenn., 1979-81; music missionary Fgn. Mission Bd., So. Bapt. Conv., 1981-88; min. adult music dept. M. Calvary Bapt. Ch., Albertville, Ala., 1989—; cons. Ala. Sr. Adult Ministry Conv., 1991. Mem. Marshall Bapt. Assn. (associational music dir., asst. team mem.), Am. Guild English Handbell Ringers, Lions. Republican. Home: 401 Sims Ave Albertville AL 35950 Office: Mt Calvary Bapt Ch 201 Rose Rd Albertville AL 35950

MALONEY, DANIEL LEO, priest; b. Devils Lake, N.D., Nov. 24, 1941; s. Leo Edward and Eileen Gertrude (Kain) M. BA, St. John's U., 1964; MA, Fordham U., 1970. Ordained priest Roman Cath. Ch., 1968. Philosophy educator U. of Mary, Bismarck, N.D., 1973-75, 80—; monastic adminstr. Assumption Abbey, Richardton, N.D., 1975-79; hosp. chaplain Mercy Hosp., Devils Lake, N.D., 1979-80; chaplain Annunciation Priory, Bismarck, 1983—; co-dir. for religious Diocese of Bismarck, 1984—. Mem. Bismarck Ministerial Association, Diocesan Ecumenical Commn. Avocations: walking, bridge. Office: Univ of Mary 7500 University Dr Bismarck ND 58504-9652

MALONEY, J. PATRICK, minister, educator, seminary administrator; b. Pitts., Feb. 19, 1929; s. James Deasy and Helen (Crouse) M.; m. Bettie Jean Silvus, Dec. 1, 1953; children: Sharon Shakespeare, Lori Spencer, Mitzi Kelley. BA, Jacksonville U., 1961; BD, New Orleans Bapt. Theol. Sem., 1964; PhD, St. Marys Sem. and U., Balt., 1973. Ordained to ministry So. Bapt. Conv., 1960. Pastor Fairfield Bapt. Chapel, Jacksonville, Fla., 1958-61, 1st Bapt. Ch., Thomas, La., 1963-64, Hayne Boulevard Bapt. Ch., New Orleans, 1964-67, Kent Bapt. Ch., Landover, Md., 1969-77, Fisher Rd. Bapt. Ch., 1977-83, Mission Oaks Bapt. Ch., East Ridge, Tenn., 1983—; prof. Sem. Extension So. Bapt. Conv., Nashville, 1973—; acad. v.p. Oxford Grad. Sch., Dayton, Tenn., 1982-86; dir. Mission Oaks Sem. Extension Ctr., East Ridge, 1990—; corr. sec. Bapt. Mins. Conf. Chattanooga, 1991—. Mem. Soc. Bibl. Lit., Cath. Theol. Soc. Am., Evang. Theol. Soc., Near East Archaeol. Soc., Oxford Soc. Scholars. Home: 1210 John Ross Rd East Ridge TN 37412 *The "real" change of direction for my life came when in 1957 (Dec.) I became a Christian.*

MALONEY, LINDA MITCHELL, religion educator; b. Houston, Apr. 10, 1939; d. David Bruce and Alta Marguerite (Chevrier) Mitchell. AB, St. Louis U., 1965, PhD, 1968, MA, 1983; M.I.B.S., U. S.C., 1981; ThD, U. Tübingen, Fed. Republic Germany, 1990. Asst. prof. New Testament Franciscan Sch. Theology, Berkeley, Calif., 1989—. Author: The Captain from Connecticut, 1986, All That God Had Done with Them, 1991. Mem. Sierra Club, Calif. Postdoctoral fellow Smithsonian Inst., 1969-70. Mem. Soc. Bibl. Lit., Cath. Bibl. Assn., Cath. Theol. Soc. Am., Am. Hist. Assn., Coordinating Com. on Women in the Hist. Profession, Am. Acad. Religion, Appalachian Mountain Club (Boston). Roman Catholic. Office: Franciscan Sch Theology 1712 Euclid Ave Berkeley CA 94709

MALONY, HENRY NEWTON, JR., psychologist; b. Birmingham, Ala., May 17, 1931; s. Henry N. and Amie (Milligan) M.; m. Suzanna Davis, Nov. 23, 1953; children—Laurence E., Allen D., Michael N. B.A., Birmingham-So. Coll., 1952; M.Div., Yale U., 1955; M.A., Peabody Coll., Vanderbilt U., 1961, Ph.D., 1964. Lic. psychologist, Calif. Ordained to ministry Methodist Ch., 1953; pastor chs., 1955-59; chaplain Davidson County Hosp., Nashville, 1959-61; psychologist Frankfort (Ky.) State Hosp., 1964-65; prof. psychology Tenn. Wesleyan Coll., 1965-69; prof., dir. program in integration of psychology and theology Grad. Sch. Psychology, Fuller Theol. Sem., Pasadena, 1969—. Served with Army N.G., 1957-64. Mem. Am. Psychol. Assn., Western Psychol. Assn., Calif. Psychol. Assn., Christian Assn. for Psychol. Studies, Am. Assn. Pastoral Counselors. Democrat. Author: Current Perspectives in the Psychology of Religion, 1978, Understanding Your Faith, 1979, Wholeness and Holiness, 1983, Living The Answers, 1981, Christian Conversion, 1982; others.

MALPICA-PADILLA, RAFAEL, bishop. Bishop of Caribbean region Evang. Luth. Ch. in Am., Santurce, P.R. Office: Evang Luth Ch in Am Bo-Obrero St PO Box 14426 Santurce PR 00916*

MALSON, CHARLES FRANCIS, JR., pastor; b. Hume, N.Y., Apr. 2, 1951; s. Charles Francis and Doris Muriel (Crowl) M.; m. Kathy Jean Miracle, Oct. 6, 1971; children: April Lyn, Audrey Jean, Owen Charles. BA in Christian Edn., Huntington (Ind.) Coll., 1977, M Christian Ministries, 1979. Ordained to ministry Ch. United Brethren in Christ, 1977. Pastor McCallum United Brethren Ch., Delton, Mich., 1977-81, Brown Corners United Brethren Ch., Clare, Mich., 1981—; mem. Conf. Coun. Adminstrn., Mich., 1986—, Commn. on Ministry, Ch. United Brethren in Christ, Ind., 1989—. Contbr. articles to denominational mag. Republican. Home: 5040 S Cornwell Ave Clare MI 48617 Office: Brown Corners United Brethren Ch 5540 S Clare Ave Clare MI 48617

MALTSBERGER, DAVID CHARLES, minister; b. Fayetteville, N.C., Feb. 19, 1960; s. Hassell J. and Royce J. (Adam) M.; m. Elaine Tucker, June 2, 1980; children: Connor, Reuben, Martin. BA, East Tex. Bapt. U., 1981; MDiv, Southwestern Bapt. Theol. Sem., 1987, postgrad. in Religious Studies, 1987—. Ordained to ministry So. Bapt. Conv., 1978. Missionary Fgn. Mission Bd. So. Bapt. Ch., Arequipa, Peru, 1982-84; pastor Iglesia Bautista Nueva Vida, Alvaredo, Tex., 1984-85; with merchandising dept. Premier Pubs., Ft. Worth, 1985—; lay worker South Hills Bapt. Ch., Ft. Worth, 1988—. Mem. Israel Exploration Soc., Soc. Bibl. Lit., Am. Schs. of Oriental Rsch. Home: 4720 McCart Fort Worth TX 76115

MALUGA, THOMAS MICHAEL, minister; b. Hammond, Ind., Oct. 11, 1937; s. Steve and Mary A. (Minchuk) M.; m. Carol Sue Smith, Mar. 2, 1985; children: Angela Renee, Thomas Solomon. BS, Ind. State U., 1979, MS, 1981; ThM, Dallas Theol. Sem., 1985. Ordained to ministry So. Bapt. Conv., 1986. Asst. pastor Sugar Creek Bapt. Ch., West Terre Haute, Ind., 1979-81; ministry leader Strategies to Elevate People Found., Dallas, 1981-85; sr. pastor Vickery Bapt. Ch., Dallas, 1986—. Editor Vickery Together Newsletter. Community leader Vickery Together Crime Watch, Dallas, 1990-91. Named one of Outstanding Young Men. Am., U.S. Jaycees, 1980. Republican. Home: 7018 Winchester St Dallas TX 75231 Office: Vickery Bapt Ch 5814 Ridgecrest Dallas TX 75231 *Experiencing (not just knowing about) God's love for me is essential to my growth as a person, and, thus, to my growth in making a Christ-like impact on the world. What keeps God's love for me fresh (and not taken for granted) is to "consider the kindness and sternness of God." (Romans 11:22).*

MAMIE, PIERRE, bishop. Bishop of Lausanne, Geneva and Fribourg Roman Cath. Ch., Switzerland. Office: 86 rue de Lausanne, BP 271, 1700 Fribourg Switzerland*

MAMO, GEORGE WILLIAM, foundation executive; b. Phila., May 22, 1955; s. Bartholomew George and Beatrice Mary (Hills) M.; m. Kay Lynn Herrlein, July 11, 1981; 1 child, George Wesley. BA, Rutgers U., Camden, N.J., 1976; postgrad., Am. U., 1976-78, U. Md., 1977. Lic. in ministry Baptist Ch., 1985. Asst. to pres. Greater Laurel (Md.) Area C. of C., 1976-77; asst. to dir. pub. works City of Bowie, Md., 1977-78; asst. exec. dir. Tau Epsilon Phi Fraternity, Atlanta, 1978-79, exec. dir., 1979-82; exec. dir. The TEP Found., Atlanta, 1978-82; dir. Samaritan House, Atlanta, 1982-83; exec. dir. Cen. Atlanta Churches, Inc., 1983-85; v.p., adminstr. Feed The Children, Oklahoma City, 1985—. Co-author: Travel Patterns in the Baltimore Washington Corridor, 1976. Mem. Atlanta Mayor's Task Force on Homeless, 1983-85; deacon 1st Bapt. Ch. Atlanta, 1984-85, Putnam City Bapt. Ch., Oklahoma City, 1986—. Recipient faculty award Rutgers U., 1976. Mem. Christian Ministries Mgmt. Assn. Republican. Office: Feed The Children 333 N Meridian Oklahoma City OK 73107-6507

MANDELBAUM, BERNARD, rabbi, homiletics educator; b. N.Y.C., Jan. 12, 1922; s. Jacob and Ida (Cohen) M.; m. Judith Werber, May 27, 1945 (dec. Apr. 1980); children: Joel, Dasi, David, Debra, Naomi; m. Marcelle Rettner, June 24, 1985. B.A., Columbia U., 1942; M.H.L., Jewish Theol. Sem. Am., 1946, D.H.L., 1951. Ordained rabbi, 1946. With Jewish Theol. Sem. Am., 1946—, prof. homiletics, prof. Midrash rabbinical dept., 1963-71; dir. Religious Psychiat. Center, 1960-71, pres., 1966-71, emeritus, 1971—; program editor Eternal Light, 1955-61. Author: Pesikta de Rab Kahana, 1962, The Wisdom of Solomon Schechter, 1963, The Maturing of the Conservative Movement, 1967, Choose Life, 1968, Add Life to Your Years, 1973, (with Yaacov Agam) Art and Judaism, 1981; editor: From the Sermons of Milton Steinberg, 1954, Assignment in Israel, 1960, Only Human: The Eternal Alibi, 1963, You Are Not Alone: The Conquest of Loneliness, 1988, Tales of the Fathers of the Conservative Movement, 1989. Mem. exec. com. Histadruth Invt., 1955-65; pres. Am.-Israel Cultural Found., 1973-77; exec. v.p., dir. research Synagogue Council Am., 1979-82; pres. Found. for Future Generations, 1985—. Recipient Sylvania TV award, 1959. Mem. Internat. Conf. Jewish Scholarship; mem. Am. Acad. Jewish Research, Phi Beta Kappa. Home: 55 Bonita Vista Rd Mount Vernon NY 10552

MANDL, HERBERT JAY, rabbi; b. Balt., Jan. 9, 1945; s. Sigmund and Ruth (Lefkowitz) M.; m. Barbara Sue Toltzis, Aug. 18, 1968; children: Aron M., Seth S., Debra A., Miriam D. AB, Johns Hopkins U., 1965; MHL, Jewish Theol. Sem., 1967; PhD, U. Montreal, 1981. Ordained rabbi, 1969. Lectr. U. Alta., Edmonton, 1969-71; sr. rabbi Beth Shalom Synagoge, Edmonton, Alta., Can., 1970-71; asst. rabbi Congregation Shaar Hashomayim, Montreal, Que., Can., 1971-77; sr. rabbi Kehilath Israel Synagogue, Kansas City, Kans., 1977—; vis. lectr. U. Mo., Kansas City, 1987—, Rockhurst Coll., adj. prof., 1989—; chaplain Kansas City Police Dept., 1988—. Bd. dirs. Shalom Geriatric Group, Kansas City, 1985—, Jewish Fedn., Kansas City, 1977—; chmn. State Mo. Health Facilities Rev. Commn., Jefferson City, 1980-86; chmn. Kansas State Holocaust Commn., Topeka, 1987—; mem. Kansas City Sister City Commn., 1980—, Kans. Pub. Disclosure Commn., 1991—. Mem. Rabbinical Assembly (com. Jewish law and standards 1989—), Internat. Order Police Chaplains, Rabbinical Assn. Kansas City (pres. 1980-81), Union for Traditional Judaism (panelist on Jewish law 1985—), B'nai Brith. Office: Kebilath Israel Synagogue 10501 Conser Overland Park KS 66212

MANDLI, JEAN, religious organization administrator. Exec. dir. Ctr. for Community Concerns, Racine, Wis. Office: Ctr Community Concerns 1501 Villa St Racine WI 53403*

MANERS, WENDELL R., music minister; b. Clanton, Ala., Sept. 24, 1955; s. R.P. and Alice (Cleckler) M.; m. Nancy Lynne DeVaughn, Nov. 1, 1974; children: Jared Wendell, Jenna Lynne. B in Music Edn., Troy State U., 1981; MRE, Southwestern Bapt. Theol. Sem., 1984. Lic. to Gospel ministry, 1981. Minister music Shiloh Bapt. Ch., Clanton, Ala., 1975-76; minister music and youth Collins Chapel Bapt. Ch., Jemison, Ala., 1976-78, Southside Bapt. Ch., Greenville, Ala., 1978-82, First Bapt. Ch., Oxford, Ala., 1984-87; minister music and activities Hepzibah Bapt. Ch., Talladega, Ala., 1987—. Recipient Ministerial scholarship Chilton Ministerial Assn., Clanton, Ala., 1976. Mem. Jaycees, Ala. Singing Men. Avocations: golf, fishing, oil painting, hunting. Office: Hepzibah Bapt Ch Rte 5 Box 163 Talladega AL 35160

MANFRED, CARL LAWRENCE, clergyman; b. St. Peter, Minn., May 10, 1918; s. Conrad A. and Eda (Anderson) Peterson; m. Miriam Hildegard Peterson, Dec. 27, 1942; children: Peter Timothy, Mark Thomas, Carol Miriam, David John. B.A., Gustavus Adolphus Coll., 1939; grad., Augustana Theol. Sem., Rock Island, Ill., 1943; D.D., Northwestern Luth. Sem., 1975. Ordained to ministry Luth. Ch., 1943. Pastor in Cedar Rapids, Iowa, 1943-46, Duluth, Minn., 1946-52; assoc. youth dir. Augustana Luth Ch., 1952-62; youth dir. Luth. Ch. Am., Phila., 1963-64; asst. to pres. Minn. Synod, Luth. Ch. Am., 1965-76; sr. pastor Normandale Luth. Ch., Edina, Minn., 1976-82; visitation minister Christ Presbyn. Ch., Edina, 1982-90. Author: Living Our Faith, 1970, Facing Forward, 1987; Co-author: Adventuring with Christ in the Church Staff Vocations, 1955; Editor: Youth's Favorite Songs, 1955, The Uniting Word, annual devotional guides, 1954-62, Jr. High Programs, vol. 2, 1963. Home: 5227 Oaklawn Ave Edina MN 55424

MANGRUM, JOHN FULLER, priest; b. Grand Rapids, Mich., May 22, 1922; s. Melvin Fuller and Mary Dennison (Gailey) M.; m. Shirley Renton Stahelin, May 26, 1956. AB cum laude, Western Mich. U., 1943; MDiv, Berkeley Div. Sch., 1949; LHD (hon.), U. Tampa, 1974; DST (hon.), Geneva Theol. Coll., 1979. Ordained deacon Episcopal Ch., 1949; priest, 1950. Rector Ch. of Redeemer and Wingman Camp, Avon Park, Fla., 1961-64, St. Mary's Episcopal Ch., Tampa, Fla., 1964-74; dean St. John's Cathedral, Jacksonville, Fla., 1974-77; rector St. Martin's Episcopal Ch., Clewiston, Fla., 1977-79, St. David's in the Pines Episcopal Ch., Wellington, Fla., 1979-90; columnist Wellington (Fla.) Town Crier, 1990—; dean, Episcopal Diocese, Wellington, 1984-87; prof., theol., Sch. Ministry, Ft. lauderdale, Fla., 1980-91; mem. exec. bd., Diocese Southeast Fla., Miami, 1978-89. Pres., supr. Acme Improvement Dist., Wellington, 1980-91; viola sect. Fla. West Coast Symphony, Sarasota, 1961-74, Jacksonville Symphony, 1974-77; commdr. VFW, Wellington, 1989-90; bd. dirs. Boys and Girls Clubs, 1965-91. Capt. USAF, 1942-1946. Named Leadership in Community, KC, Wellington, 1989. Mem. Fla. Children's Home Soc. (bd. dirs. 1986-91), Fellowship Christian Athletes (chaplain 1986-91), Seagull Ministries for Retarded (bd. dirs. 1987-91), Rotary (pres. 1981-82, Gladney award 1990). Republican. Home: 12181 Sycamore Ln Wellington FL 33414 *In over 40 years of ordained life, the greatest privilege has been to know the lay persons in the church—the Holy Family of God.*

MANGUM, PETER GORDON, minister; b. Eureka, Calif., Mar. 21, 1957; s. Paul Daniel and Geraldine Edna (Webb) M.; m. Sally Jean Leep, May 22, 1982; children: Amanda Rae, Daniel Ray, Joshua Peter. Student, Point Loma Coll., 1975-77; BA in Religion, N.W. Nazarene Coll., 1979. Ordained to ministry Ch. of Nazarene, 1978, as elder, 1990. Youth pastor Biltmore Ch. of Nazarene, Phoenix, 1976; jr. high pastor Coll. Ch. of Nazarene, Nampa, Idaho, 1977-78; assoc. pastor North Nampa Ch. of Nazarene, Nampa, 1978-79; minister youth and Christian edn. Omaha Cen. Ch. of Nazarene, 1983-84; minister youth and Christian edn. Seattle First Ch. of Nazarene, 1984—, assoc. youth and Christian edn., 1984-87; assoc. youth and Christian edn. Dayton Beavercreek Ch. of Nazarene, 1987-88, Howell (Mich.) Ch. of Nazarene, 1988—; dir. coll. career ministries Wash. Pacific Dist. Nazarene Youth Internat., 1984—; chmn. bd. Christian life Chattanooga Ch. of Nazarene, 1982-83; del. internat. inst. Phila. Dist. Ch. of Nazarene, 1974. Named one of Outstanding Young Men of Am., 1982. Mem. Nazarene Multiple Staff Assn., Point Loma Coll. Alumni Assn., N.W. Nazarene Coll. Alumni Assn., Nat. Network Youth Workers. Republican. Avocations: organized and leisure sports, table games. Home: 2160 Brewer Rd Howell MI 48843

MANGUM, WILLIAM DAVID, clergyman; b. New Orleans, July 22, 1953; s. Billy Andrew and Rena Celestia (Dunlap) M.; m. Billy Andrew and Rena Celestia (Dunlap) M.; m. Elizabeth Lynette Fuller, Sept. 18, 1971; children: Jonathan David, Sarah Lynette. BA, Harding U., 1975; MA, Wichita State U., 1982; postgrad., La. State U., 1983-88. Ordained to ministry Ch. of Christ. Minister North Heights Ch. of Christ, Batesville, Ark., 1974-78, Poplar Ave Ch. of Christ, Wichita, Kans., 1978-83, Belle Chasse (La.) Ch. of Christ, 1983-88; pulpit minister North Cen. Ch. of Christ, Indpls., 1988—; chmn. Indpls. Ch. of Christ Minister's Assn., 1989—; dir. Mid-Am. Evangelism Seminar, Ch. of Christ Regional Conf., Indpls., 1991; grad. asst. La. State U., Baton Rouge, 1983-88. Vol. police chaplain Wichita Police Dept., 1979-83. Recipient Community Svc. award Wichita Police Dept., 1982. Office: North Cen Ch of Christ 9015 Westfield Blvd Indianapolis IN 46240

MANION, SYNDE, pastor; b. San Fernando, Calif., Dec. 23, 1956; s. Thomas Francis and Frances Henerreta (Mecham) M. BA in Religion and Social Welfare with honors, Pacific Luth. U., Tacoma, Wash., 1978; MDiv in Pastoral Care, Pacific Luth Theol. Sem., Berkeley, Calif., 1982; MA in Clin. Psychology with honors, Calif. State U., Dominguez Hills, Carson, 1991. Ordained to ministry Luth. Ch., 1984. Dir. Turning Point Women's Ctr., Luth. Social Svcs., San Jose, Calif., 1986-87; pastor Trinity Luth. Ch., Hemet, Calif., 1984-86, Resurrection Luth. Ch., Redondo Beach, Calif., 1987—; clergy panel Betty Ford Ctr., Rancho Mirage, Calif., 1984-86; marriage, family and child counselor, Calif., 1991—; ministry coord. South Bay Conf. Evang. Luth. Ch. Am., So. Calif. West Synod, 1989-91, discipline com., 1991-97; bd. dirs. campus ministry No. Calif. Am. Luth. Ch., 1986-87. Author: Funeral Sermon, 1991. Vol. counselor Battered Women Shelter,

Denver, 1980-81; counselor, community educator Denver Gen. Hosp. Rape Crisis Ctr., 1981, San Pablo (Calif.) County Rape Crisis Ctr., 1981-84; co-founder, pres. bd. dirs. Hement-San Jacinto Ctr. Against Sexual Assault, 1984-86; bd. dirs., chair com. Mt. San Jacinto (Calif.) Alliance for the Mentally Ill., 1986-88. Mem. Psi Chi. Democrat. Office: Resurrection Luth Ch 330 Palos Verdes Blvd Redondo Beach CA 90277

MANISCALCO, JAMES WILLIAM, youth pastor, organist; b. Detroit, Aug. 1, 1953; s. Joseph Maniscalco and Ann Lynn (Laurence) Kennedy; m. Margaret Ruddy, Sept. 13, 1975; children: Dominic, Julia. BA, Wayne State U., 1977; MA, Ashland Theol. Sem., 1991. Registered music therapist. Youth pastor Christ Gospel Tabernacle, St. Clair Shores, Mich., 1982-90, Calvin East Presbyn., Detroit, 1990—; social worker Bon Secours Hosp., Grosse Point, Mich., 1988—. Office: Calvin East Presbyn 6125 Cadieux Detroit MI 48224

MANKEL, FRANCIS XAVIER, priest, school system superintendent; b. Knoxville, Tenn., Nov. 8, 1935; s. George Whitehead Sr. and Willia Frances (Duncan) M. BA, St. Ambrose U., 1957; STB, St. Mary's Coll., Balt., 1959, STL, 1961; MEd, Loyola Coll., Balt., 1965. Ordained priest Roman Cath. Ch. Assoc. pastor Holy Ghost Ch., Knoxville, 1962-67; prin. Knoxville Cath. High Sch., 1967-79; pastor Sacred Heart Ch., Lawrenceburg, Tenn., 1979-84, St. John Neumann Ch., Knoxville, 1984-87, Sacred Heart Cathedral, Knoxville, 1987—; vicar gen., chancellor Cath. Diocese Knoxville, 1988—. Bd. dirs. Knoxville area chpt. ARC, 1986—. Mem. Am. Guild Organists, Knoxville Ministerial Assn. Home: 711 Northshore Dr Knoxville TN 37919

MANLEY, JOHN STEVAN, religious organization official; b. Quincy, Ill., Oct. 11, 1949; s. Harry Russell and Mary Ella (Balzer) M.; m. Helen Jean Denniston, June 7, 1969; children: Brenda Jean, John Russell, Andrew Jay. BA, Kansas City Coll. and Bible Sch., 1971, B in Missions, 1975. Ordained to ministry Wesleyan Holiness Assn. Chs., 1973. Pastor Wesleyan Holiness Ch., Peoria, Ill., 1971-75, Ann Arbor, Mich., 1975-78, Portage, Pa., 1981-85; gen. supt. Wesleyan Holiness Assn., Dayton, Ohio, 1985—; prin. Holiness Christian Sch., Petersburg, Mich., 1976-78; sec. Evangelistic Faith Missions, Bedford, Ind., 1984—, All Tribes Indian Schs., Bernalillo, N.Mex., 1991—; bd. dirs. Inter-Ch. Holiness Conv., Salem, Ohio. Republican. Office: Wesleyan Holiness Assoc Chs 108 Carter Ave Dayton OH 45405

MANLEY, ROBERT MERRILL, JR., minister; b. Bryan, Tex., Nov. 20, 1947; s. Robert Merrill and Bessie Pearl (Barnett) M.; m. Dorothy Lee Taylor, Sept. 1, 1969; children: Robert Merrill III, Dawn Renee. BA, U. Tex., San Antonio, 1980; MDiv, Trinity Theol. Sem., Newburg, Ind., 1989; ThD, Trinity Theol. Sem., 1991. Ordained to ministry So. Bapt. Conv., 1972. Assoc. pastor Dellview Bapt. Ch., San Antonio, 1978-80; tchr. Tex. Bible Coll., San Antonio, 1985-88; pastor Marshall Bapt. Ch., San Antonio, 1980-88, Cen. Gardens Bapt. Ch., Nederland, Tex., 1988—; dir. United Bd. Missions, Port Author, Tex., 1988—; pres. New Life Ctr., Beaumont, Tex., 1988—. Author: How Sunday Schools Grow, 1980. Chaplain Jefferson Juvenile Detention Ctr., Beaumont, 1990—. Mem. Golden Triangle Bapt. Assn. (exec. mem.), Internat. Platform Soc., Tex. Bapt. Hist. Soc., S.W. Theol. Soc. Baptist. Home: 107 4th Ave Nederland TX 77627 Office: Cen Gardens Bapt Ch 112 4th Ave Nederland TX 77627 *The quality of life we live is determined by the choices we make. Since we never know when we are making life-changing choices, we must make each choice express love.*

MANN, ANDREW HUDSON, JR., minister; b. Phila., July 7, 1947; s. Andrew Hudson and Evelyn Virginia (Chambers) M.; m. Margaret Ames, Aug. 30, 1970; 1 child, Ryan Elizabeth. BA, Bucknell U., 1969; MDiv, Pitts. Theol. Sem., 1972; DMin, McCormick Theol. Sem., Chgo., 1981. Ordained to ministry Presbyn. Ch., 1972. Assoc. pastor 1st Presbyn. Ch., Endicott, N.Y., 1972-81; pastor 1st Presbyn. Ch., Flourtown, Pa., 1981-91, Little Falls Presbyn. Ch., AArlington, Va., 1991—; dir. camps Susquehanna Valley Presbytry, Bainbridge, N.Y., 1974-81, mem. camps bd. Phila. Presbytery, 1982-87, vice moderator, 1983-84, mem. task force on new ch. devel., 1988-91. Author: A Shelter for Battered Women, 1981. Founder, pres. S.O.S. Shelter, Inc., Endicott, 1976-81; mem. N.Y. Gov.'s Task Force on Domestic Violence, Albany, 1979-81; mem. animal welfare com. Hahnemann U. Hosp., Phila., 1985-91. N.Y. State Dept. Social Svc. grantee, 1977. Avocations: reading, gourmet cooking, racquetball. Home: 5614 N 22d St Arlington VA 22205 Office: Little Falls Presbyn Ch 6025 Little Falls Rd Arlington VA 22207

MANN, DAVID WILLIAM, minister; b. Elkhart, Ind., Apr. 17, 1947; s. Herbert Richard and Kathryn (Bontrager) M.; m. Brenda Marie Frantz, June 7, 1969; children: Troy, Todd, Erika. BA, Bethel Coll., 1969; MS, Nat. Coll., 1986. Ordained to ministry Missionary Ch., 1978. Campus life dir. Youth for Christ, Elkhart, 1969-77; denominational youth dir. Missionary Ch., Ft. Wayne, Ind., 1977-81, Christian edn. dir., 1981-88, U.S. dir. missions, 1990—; assoc. dir. World Ptnrs., Ft. Wayne, 1988-90; dir. Missionary Ch. Vol. Svc., Ft. Wayne, 1983—. Author: (with others) Youth Leaders Source Book, 1985; contbr. articles to prof. jour. Mgr. Little League, Ft. Wayne, 1981-89, bd. dirs. 1986. Mem. Nat. Assn. Evangelicals, Evangelical Fgn. Mission Assn., Denominational Execs. in Christian Edn. (chmn. 1988), Aldersgate Pub. Assn. (bd. dirs. 1985, 87), Nat. Christian Edn. Assn. (exec. com. 1987-89). Avocations: baseball, skiing, fishing, woodworking. Home: 10025 Crown Point Dr Fort Wayne IN 46804 Office: Missionary Ch 3901 S Wayne Fort Wayne IN 46807

MANN, FRED RYCHEN, minister; b. Lebanon, Tenn., Apr. 7, 1937; s. Herbert Berry and Alice Pearl (Webber) M.; m. Alvonia Joyce Miller, July 7, 1956; children: Stephen Lee, Jeffry Mark, Scott Andrew. BA, Tenn. Temple U., 1961; MRE, Temple Bapt. Sem., 1963. Lic. to ministry So. Bapt. Conv., 1954, ordained, 1958. Founder, pastor Cottageville (W.Va.)-Evans Bapt. Ch., 1963-66; pastor Fundamental Bapt. Ch., Prosperity, W.Va., 1966-73, Berean Bapt. Ch., Portsmouth, Ohio, 1973-85, West Huntsville Bapt. Ch., Huntsville, Ala., 1985-87, Breezy Hill Bapt. Ch., Graniteville, S.C., 1987—. Mem. Bapt. Internat. Missions Inc. (action com. 1975—), Assn. Bapts. for World Evangelism (adv. bd. 1989—). Republican. Home: 622 Ascauga Lake Rd Graniteville SC 29829 Office: Breezy Hill Bapt Ch PO Box 235 Graniteville SC 29829

MANN, GARY ALLEN, religious educator; b. Burlington, Wis, Apr. 2, 1954; s. George Kendig and Pauline Delores (Lenox) M; m. Valerie Nudd, Jan 11, 1975; 1 child, Michelle Marie. BA in Theology and Theater, Luther Coll., 1976; MDiv, Wartburg Theol. Sem., 1980; MPhil, Drew U., 1983, PhD in Theol. and Religious Studies, 1988. Ordained to ministry Luth. Ch. Am., 1981. Minister Vicar Zion Luth. Ch., West Union, Iowa, 1978-79; assoc. pastor Good Shepherd Luth. Ch., Somerville, N.J., 1981-82; pastor Holy Trinity Luth. Ch., Wildwood, N.J., 1982-90; asst. prof. of religion Augustana Coll., Rock Island, Ill., 1990—; pastoral rep. Synodical Evangelism Task Force, Trenton, N.J., 1981—; del. Cape May County Child Abuse and Neglect Study Team, N.J., 1982—. Recipient Grad. Acad. grant Drew U. Grad. Sch., 1980-84. Mem. Wildwood Pastoral Assn. (v.p. 1983-84, pres. 1984—), Am. Acad. Religion, Soc. Bibl. Lit., Ctr. for Religion and Sci. Democrat. Home: 2555 Lindenwood Dr Bettendorf IA 52722 Office: Augustana Coll Rock Island IL 61201

MANN, GORDON HOSSLEY, clergyman; b. Charleston, S.C., May 28, 1928; s. Henry Jonathan and Florence Groome (Hossley) M.; m. Caroline Hampton Mullally Ladue, Sept. 29, 1953; children: Caroline Mann McMillan, Sarah Spencer, Susan Mann Levy. BS, Coll. Charleston, S.C., 1950; MDiv, Va. Theol. Sem., 1953; PhD, Pacific Western U., 1986. V.p., chaplain Voorhees Coll., Denmark, S.C., 1953-55; assoc. rector Ch. of the Good Shepherd, Lookout Mountain, Tenn., 1956-60; chaplain, rector Emory-at-Oxford/Good Shepherd, Covington, Ga., 1960-64; asst. to the Ex-Bishop Diocese of Atlanta, 1969-75; rector All Saints Episcopal Ch., Mobile, Ala., 1975-83, Trinity-by-the Cove Episcopal Ch., Naples, Fla., 1983-87; vicar All Saints Ch., Hilton Head Island, S.C., 1987—; pvt. cons. Orgn. Devel., Southeast U.S., 1971—. Author: Behavior Science, Management & Ministry, 1986; contbr. articles to The Winston Press, Va. Sem. Jour. Mem. standing com. Diocese of Cen. Gulf Coast, 1976-79; pres. Mobile Social Svcs., Archdiocese of Mobile, 1980-83; bd. dirs. Community Chest and Council, Mobile, 1982, Naples Found., 1983-85. O.S., ATS, 1945. Recipient citation for excellence Am. Cancer Soc., Atlanta, 1962, pub. svc. award Area Interfaith Disaster Svc., Mobile, 1981. Mem. Port Royal Club (Naples), Carolina yacht Club (Charleston). Democrat. Home: 5 Anna Ct Hilton Head Island SC 29926 Office: All Saints Episcopal Ch PO Box 22884 Hilton Head Island SC 29925

MANN, JOHN MARTIN, minister; b. McKeesport, Pa., Nov. 18, 1946; s. Glenn Grant and Mary Dorothy (Flaherty) M. BA, Clarion State Coll., 1967; MDiv, Duke U., 1970, ThM, 1972; D Ministry, Wittenberg U., 1976. Ordained to ministry Luth. Ch. in Am., 1972. Pastor 1st Luth. Ch., Edinboro, Pa., 1971-82; sr. pastor St. John's Luth. Ch., Erie, Pa., 1982—; instr. Edinboro State Coll., 1971-82; adj. prof. religion Thiel Coll. Greenville, Pa., 1980-82, baccalaureate preacher, 1980-84, trustee, 1974-80, 82—; chmn. synod vocations examining com. N.W. Pa.-W.Va. Synod, 1984-88; chmn. intersynodical candidacy com. N.W. Pa.-Allegheny Synods, 1988-90; chmn. ch. vocations examining com. N.W. Pa. Synod, 1990—; chmn. Luth. Coalition of Erie, 1990-91; dean Cond. I, Northwestern Pa. Synod, 1991—. Contbr. articles to profl. jours. Bd. dirs. Luth. Home, Erie, 1976-79, 82—, Inter-Ch. Ministries N.W. Pa., 1979-84, South Erie Hillside Community Orgn., 1982—, Holy Trinity Community Ctr., Erie, 1984-88, Nesting Inn, 1988—, Hospice Met. Erie, 1988—; chmn. Erie City Strategy for Luths., 1989—. Recipient Outstanding Young Man of Am. award Jaycees, 1982. Mem. Luth. Assn. Larger Chs., Am. Assn. Pastoral Counselors, Luth. Campus Ministry Assn. Home: 3910 Trask Ave Erie PA 16508 Offie: St Johns Luth Ch Peach at 23d Erie PA 16502 *In a word where materialism, hedonism and the selfish concerns of humanity have threatened the survival of nations and the planet, on the eve of the third millenium, we need now as never before to be convinced of the Gospel and to proclaim it in life.*

MANN, KENNETH WALKER, minister, psychologist; b. Nyack, N.Y., Aug. 22, 1914; s. Arthur Hungerford and Ethel Livingston (Walker) M. AB, Princeton U., 1937; STB, Gen. Theol. Sem., N.Y.C., 1942; MS, U. Mich., 1950, PhD, 1956. Ordained priest Episcopal Ch., 1941. Diplomate Am. Assn. Pastoral Counselors; lic. clin. psychologist, Calif., Conn.; lic. marriage, family and child counselor, Calif. Vicar in Valley Cottage, Pearl River, N.Y., 1941-43; priest in charge Yonkers, N.Y., 1943-45; dir. youth work and Christian edn. Diocese L.A., 1945-47; curate in Beverly Hills, Calif., 1947-49; counselor Bur. Psychol. Svcs., U. Mich., 1951-52; chaplain, clin. psychologist dept. psychiatry St. Luke's Hosp., N.Y.C., also priest-psychotherapist Cathedral St. John Divine, N.Y.C., psychol. examiner ministerial candidates Diocese N.Y., 1952-58; assoc. chaplain Hosp. Good Samaritan, L.A., 1958-65; exec. pastoral svcs., exec. coun. Episc. Ch. N.Y.C., 1965-70; program officer Acad. Religion and Mental Health, N.Y.C., 1970-72; sr. adviser profl. affairs Inst. Religion and Health, 1972-79; sr. psychol. staff Silver Hill Found., New Canaan, Conn., 1974-84; pres. Rockland County (N.Y.) Mins. Assn., 1942-43; exec. sec. social svc. commn. Diocese N.Y., 1943-45; chmn. div. pastoral svcs. Diocese L.A., 1958-65; field dir. Western region Acad. Religion and Mental Health, 1958-61; assoc. nat. chaplain U.S. Power Squadrons, 1956-57. Author: On Pills and Needles, 1969, Deadline for Survival—A Survey of Moral Issues in Science and Medicine, 1970; contbr. articles to profl. jours. Pres. Adoption Inst. L.A., 1964; mem. edn. com. Calif. Heart Assn., 1962-64; trustee, treas. Acad. Religion and Mental Health, 1954-59, mem. profl. bd., 1960-70; trustee Vis. Nurse Assn. L.A., 1963-65, Children's Home Soc. Calif. in L.A., 1964-65, North Conway Inst., 1966-80. USPHS grantee, 1950-51. Fellow AAAS; mem. APA (chmn. com. rels. between psychology and religion 1956-58), Western Psychol. Assn., Calif. Psychol. Assn., L.A. County Psychol. Assn., N.Y. Acad. Scis., Planetary Soc., Assembly Episc. Hosps. and Chaplains, Upper Nyack Tennis Club, The Club (Diocese N.Y.), Princeton Club N.Y. Republican. Home: 32 Tallman Ave Nyack NY 10960 *I have strongly held to the principle that the total "health" of mankind cannot be considered apart from the values and aspirations by which people live, and by which they may even be prepared to die. Amidst the confusions that exist today over loyalties, traditions, and ideals, many are asking: What is the right way to behave? How should I think? What kind of person am I supposed to be? To help such people in quandary to live responsibly, and still be true to their individuality, is a large task, but it is one that is central to a religious ministry. It has always been my chief concern.*

MANN, LOUIE LYNN, church administrator; b. Hinton, Okla., Sept. 21, 1940; s. Leon and Clarabel (Garrett) M.; m. Jane Elizabeth May, Feb. 12, 1946; 1 child, Eric Tyson. BS, Okla. State U., 1962. Asst. dir. aux. enterprise Okla. State U., Stillwater, 1963-65, mgr. food services, 1965-69, adminstrv. asst. to athletic dir., 1969-73; asst. athletic dir. So. Meth. U., Dallas, 1973-77, dir. properties, 1977-81; dir. properties First Bapt. Ch., Dallas, 1981—. Deacon First Bapt. Ch., Dallas. Mem. Nat. Assn. Coll. Bus. Adminstrs. Republican. Home: 6245 Town Hill Dallas TX 75214 Office: First Bapt Ch 1707 San Jacinto Dallas TX 75201

MANN, NATHANIEL EDWARD, minister, pilot; b. Atlanta, Sept. 11, 1953; s. Eben Corey and Vivian (Vaughan) M.; m. Gail Dixon, Dec. 29, 1974; children: Melissa, Marlene, Melody. BA, Mercer U., 1975; MDiv, Southwestern Bapt. Theol. Sem., 1978, DMin, 1986. Ordained to ministry So. Bapt. Conv., 1972; cert. flight instr. Pastor Friendship Bapt. Ch., Hiawassee, Ga., 1971; youth evangelist southeastern U.S., 1972; assoc. pastor Rowland Hills Bapt. Ch., Stone Mountain, Ga., 1972-74; pastor Rock Creek Bapt. Ch., Mineral Wells, Tex., 1975-78; missionary So. Bapt. Fgn. Mission Bd., Brazil, 1978-91; pastor Trinity Bapt. Ch., Keystone Heights, Fla., 1991—; chaplain CAP, Shelby, N.C., 1991—. Author: (books) The Holy Spirit and His Gifts, 1975, Witnessing to Jehovah Witnesses, 1978; (newsletter) The Holy Spirit and His Gifts, 1975; contbr. articles to profl. jours. Active ARC. Israel Study grantee KT,1990; Scholars in Ministry scholar Southwestern Bapt. Theol. Sem., 1987. Republican. Office: Trinity Bapt Ch PO Box 1099 Keystone Heights FL 32656

MANN, TIMOTHY CHUN-CHOCK, minister; b. New Orleans, May 29, 1961; s. James W. L. and Diana (Tung) M.; m. Ann Carol McGaha, Feb. 20, 1988. BS, Baylor U., 1983; MusM, Southwestern Bapt. Theol. Sem., Ft. Worth, 1987. Ordained to ministry Bapt. Ch., 1988. Youth intern Oak Park Bapt. Ch., New Orleans, 1981; min. music and youth First Bapt. Ch., Eagle Lake, Tex., 1982; centrifuge staff mem. Bapt. Sunday Sch. Bd., Nashville, 1984-87; min. youth and coll. Brookwood Bapt. Ch., Birmingham, Ala., 1988—; pres. Baylor U. Assn. Ch. Musicians, Waco, Tex., 1981-82; pres. music sch. Southwestern Bapt. Theol. Sem., Ft. Worth, 1986; pres. Over-the-Mountain Youth Ministeries Assn., Birmingham, 1989-90. Republican. Office: Brookwood Bapt Ch 3449 Overton Rd Birmingham AL 35223

MANNEY, RUSSELL FIELD, JR., clergyman; b. Detroit, Oct. 11, 1933; s. Russell Field and Mildred Allison (Lamb) M.; m. Mary Janet Fairbanks, June 9, 1955; children—Russell III, Timothy, Thomas. B.B.A., U. Detroit, 1959; student Trinity Coll., 1950-51; postgrad. Mich. Sch. Theology, 1963-68, Seabury Western Theol. Sem., 1981-82. Ordained priest Episcopal Ch., 1983. Controller, City of Troy, Mich., 1959-61, City of Grosse Pointe Woods, Mich., 1961-64; city mgr. Harper Woods, Mich., 1964-68; pres. Prescot Press Inc., East Detroit, Mich., 1968-81; acct., 1959-81; treas., dir. Metamora Hills Inc., Metamora, Mich., 1965-81; vicar St. Matthew's Episcopal Ch., Flat Rock, Mich., 1982-84; treas. chpt. Cathedral Ch. St. Paul, Detroit, 1978-83, provost, 1984—; bd. dirs. Cathedral Found., 1981—, Cathedral Bookstore, 1981—; instr. Wayne State U., 1971-72. Leader, Boy Scouts Am., Harper Woods, 1973-76; bd dirs. Harper Woods Citizens for Good Govt., 1969-70, Scanyu Youth Aid Internat., 1986—; trustee, alumni dir. Whitaker Sch. Theology, 1983-85. Mem. Roseville C. of C. (sec., bd. dirs. 1973-78). Home: 18987 Huntington St Harper Woods MI 48225 Office: Cathedral Ch St Paul 4800 Woodward Ave Detroit MI 48201

MANNING, GARY LON, theology educator, minister; b. San Antonio, Sept. 28, 1947; s. Burl William and Leona Jo (McCugh) M.; m. Paulette Cunningham, Aug. 22, 1968; children—Troy, Tami. B.S., Howard Payne U., 1969; M.R.E., Southwestern Bapt. Theol. Sem., 1972, Ed.D., 1982. Ordained to ministry Baptist Ch. Minister music, youth and edn. Emmanuel Bapt. Ch., Waco, Tex., 1972-75; minister edn. Emmanuel Bapt. Ch., Temple, Tex., 1975-76; pastor Acad. Bapt. Ch., Little River, Tex., 1976-82; prof. Wayland Bapt. U., Plainview, Tex., 1982—. Rec. artist: Part the Waters, 1976. Mem. Am. Assn. Marriage and Family Therapy (assoc.), Assn. Couples for Marriage Enrichment (retreat leader). Democrat. Avocations: golf; camping. Home: 1110 Borger St Plainview TX 79072 Office: Wayland Bapt Univ 1900 W 7th St Plainview TX 79072

MANNING, WILLIAM C., minister; b. Hollywood, Fla., Feb. 13, 1945; s. John C. and Jewell L. Manning; m. Donna Lynn Craig, June 12, 1971; 1 child, Jonathan Craig. AB in Religion, So. Nazarene U., 1967; MDiv, Nazarene Theol. Sem., 1976; D Ministry, Midwestern Bapt. Theol Sem., 1978. Ordained to ministry Ch. of the Nazarene, 1979. Assoc. minister First Ch. of the Nazarene, Tulsa, 1967-68, Southgate Ch. of the Nazarene, Colorado Springs, Colo., 1968-71, First Ch. of the Nazarene, Kansas City, Mo., 1974-84; pastor First Ch. of the Nazarene, Charlotte, N.C., 1984—. Author: The Promise of the Spirit, 1987; columnist Slices of Life, Bread mag., 1983-85; curriculum writer: Nazarene Word Action Series, 1981-82, New Life Primer, 1987; contbr. articles to Christian mags. and periodicals. Home: 6415 Rollingridge Dr Charlotte NC 28211 Office: Charlotte First Ch Nazarene 701 Scaleybark Rd Charlotte NC 28209 *Happiness was never meant to be the goal of life, but rather the by-product of a life well lived. It is determined not so much by where you live, but by how you live.*

MANOR, ROBERT MICHAEL, evangelist; b. Portland, Ind., July 4, 1953; s. Robert Jesse and Margaret Joan (Shultz) M.; m. Shawn Beatty, June 28, 1975; children: N. Parker, Micah R., Kylie N. BA in Bible Study, Bob Jones U., 1984. Ordained minister Bapt. Ch., 1988. Pastor Fellowship Bapt. Ch., Portland, 1985-90; mem. program staff Wilds Christian Camp, Brevard, N.C., 1980-85; staff evangelist Colonial Hills Bapt. Ch., Indpls., 1990—; minister Jay County Jail, Portland, 1989-90; chaplain Jay County Hosp., Portland, 1985-90; prog. dir. Harvest Youth Rally, Connersville, Ind., 1987—. Asst. sec. bd. dirs., chaplain Jay CountyBoys Club, Portland, 1988-90. Home: 6402 Bayside South Dr Indianapolis IN 46240 Office: Colonial Hills Bapt Church 8140 Union Chapel Rd Indianapolis IN 46240

MANOR, VRANNA LEE, church librarian; b. St. Paul, Wis., Dec. 15, 1946; d. Philip Oliver and Doris Pamela (Bowman) Selander; m. Perry John Manor, June 7, 1969; children: Rebecca Ann, Betsy Lynne, Philip Andrew. BS, U. Wis., 1968, MLS, 1982. Libr. High Pt. Ch. (formerly Middleton Bapt. Ch.), Madison, Wis., 1975—, High Pt. Christian Sch. (formerly Middleton Christian Sch.). Mem. Evangel. Ch. Libr. Assn., South Cen. Libr. System, Friends of the Cooperative Children's Book Ctr. Office: High Point Church/High Pt Christian Sch 7702 Old Sauk Rd Madison WI 53717

MANSBRIDGE, MICHAEL, archdeacon. Archdeacon in the Gulf The Anglican Communion, Abu Dhabi, United Arab Emirates. Office: St Andrew's Ch, POB 262, Abu Dhabi United Arab Emirates*

MANSFIELD, GREGORY JAMES EDWARD, priest; b. Martinsville, Ind., Nov. 8, 1957; s. J. George and Marcia Lee (Meyers) M.; m. Mary Ann Owens, Nov. 2, 1990. BA, Huntington Coll., 1980; MDiv, Harvard U., 1986, MEd, 1986; D of Ministry, Grad. Theol. Found., 1990. Ordained priest Episcopal Ch., 1986. Chaplain Ball State U., Muncie, Ind., 1986-88; curate Grace Episcopal Ch., Muncie, 1986-88; assoc. rector St. Paul's, Kansas City, Mo., 1988—; ch. and coll. commn. Diocese of Indpls., 1986-88; bd. dirs. WBST Pub. Radio, Muncie, 1986-88; chair Christian Social Ministries, Kansas City, 1989-90. Co-author: Let's Go: Greece, 1984, Let's Go: Italy, 1984. Recipient Pfeiffer prize Am. Sch. Oriental Rsch., 1986. Mem. Coll. Preachers, Phi Delta Kappa, Woodside Raquet Club, Harvard Club. Republican. Home: 4029 Warwick Blvd Kansas City MO 64111 Office: St Paul's Episcopal Ch 11 E 40th St Kansas City MO 64111

MANSKE, BRIAN EDWARD, minister; b. Swift Current, Sask., Can., Dec. 11, 1949; came to U.S., 1979; s. Edward and Edna Florence (Croissant) M.; m. Caroline Ruth Ehney, May 30, 1970; 1 child, Donnie James Michael. DD (hon.), Stanton U., 1986. Ordained to ministry Christ the Great Shepherd Fellowship, 1979. Evangelist various chs., Can., U.S., Mex., 1968-76, Pentecostal Assemblies Can., Can., 1977-79, Assemblies of God, Dallas, 1979-81; pstor First Southern Assembly of God, Norman, Okla., 1981-84; pastor, founder Shiloh Christian Ctr., Norman, 1984-89; evangelist, founder Spirit of Life World Outreach Ministries, Inc., DeSoto, Tex., 1989—.

MANSON, JOYCE LAVERNE, minister. Staff, pub. edn. task force Ch. Coun. Greater Seattle, Wash., 1987; sr. substitute tchr. Seattle (Wash.) Pub. Schs., 1989-90, 90-91; convener Synod of Alaska/N.W. Assn. Presbyn. Tentmakers, 1987; ch. coun. rep. Interfaith Coun. Wash., Seattle, 1990; mem. Sister Ch. with Leningrad Program, Ch. Coun. Greater Seattle, 1991. Author: Voices of Experience: Lifestories of Clergywomen in the Presbyterian Church (U.S.A.), 1991. Home: 611 32nd Ave Seattle WA 98122

MANSON, MICHAEL ASHER, rabbi, lawyer; b. Tel Aviv, Oct. 29, 1931; s. Jan and Rosa (Rubinstein) M.; m. Shoshana Haller; children: Sapir, Daniel Maxim. JD, Hebrew U., Jerusalem, 1959; BA in Hebrew Lang., Hebrew Unio Coll., L.A., 1967; MA in Hebrew Lang., Hebrew Unio Coll., Cin., 1959. Bar: Israel. Asst. atty. Rotenstreich Law Offices, Tel Aviv, 1957-59; pvt. practice law Manson Law Offices, Tel Aviv, 1959-63; legal advisor Indsl. and Comml. Bank, Tel Aviv, 1960-63; clergyman Temple Emanuel, McAllen, Tex., 1969-74, Ahavas Chessed Congregation, Mobile, Ala., 1974-78, Beth Israel Congregation, Wallingford, Conn., 1978-86, B'nai Jacob Congregation, Bakersfield, Calif., 1986-88, Beth Tefilah Synagogue, San Diego, 1988—; chaplain Naval Hosp., San Diego, 1990—; speaker Cult Awareness Network, Wallingford, 1979-85. Pres. 21st region Coun. on Alcoholism, McAllen, Tex., 1973, v.p. ARC, Wallingford, 1984, chmn. Ethics Com., Wallingford, 1985, Housing Authority, 1984-86; religious leader, cons. Russian Refugee Programs, San Diego, 1988—; mem. Gov.'s Com. on Elderly, Gov.'s Com. on Health. Recipient Masada award State of Israel, 1975, Cert. of Merit S.W. Ala. Coun. on Alcoholism, 1976, Youth award Am. B'nai B'rith, 1985, Cert. of Appreciation ARC, 1986. Mem. Rabbinical Assembly, Cen. Conf. Am. Rabbis (nat. com. on Russian Jewry, nat. com. on youth and drugs), Masons (master). Republican. Avocations: music, theatre, pub. speaking, langs. Office: Congregation Beth Tefilah 4967 69th St San Diego CA 92115

MANTON, KARIS BREWSTER, missionary, educator; b. Putian, Fujian, Republic of China, Apr. 12, 1903; d. William Nesbitt and Elizabeth (Fisher) Brewster; m. Frank Ernest Manton, Mar. 29, 1930 (dec. 1987); children: Karis Taylor, Thomas, David, William. BA, Ohio Wesleyan U., 1926; postgrad., Drew U., 1931, Rutgers U., 1934. Tchr. English and phys. edn. Hamilton High Sch., Putian, 1926-28; tchr. English HwaNan Women's Coll., Fuzhou, Republic of China, 1928-30; social worker, asst. supr. Emergency Relief Admin., Bergen County, N.J., 1932-36; missionary Meth. Mission Bd., Rangoon, Burma, 1937-66; speaker in field, 1966—. Bd. dirs., adviser YWCA HwaNan Coll. China, 1928-30; lay del. Meth. Ch. S.E. Asia, Singapore, 1956, Gen. Conf. Meth. Ch. Chgo., 1966, Nat. YWCA, acting pres.; pres. Nat. Coun. Women Burma; missionary Taipei, Taiwan, 1967-72; mem nominating com. Cen. Ill. Conf. United Meth. Women, 1980-83, chmn. 1983, dist. pres. 1976-79; bd. dirs. Cunningham Children's Home, Urbana, Ill., 1976-79, chmn. nominating com. 1984-87; guest First Sec. of Fujian Province to celebrate 85th birthday, China, 1988; bd. dirs. Champaign County Assn. for Mental Health, 1983—, exec. sec., 1976-82. Mem. AAUW, Internat. Rels. (chmn), Am. Womens Assn. (pres., bd. dirs. Burma chpt.), Am. Assn. Retired Persons (chmn. health care com. 1987-89). Avocations: oil and Chinese brush painting, Japanese flower arranging, chinese scroll mounting. Home: 707 E Florida Ave Urbana IL 61801

MANUEL, DAN DOUGLAS, minister; b. Marshall, Tex., Mar. 24, 1947; s. John Douglas and Gladys (Phillips) M.; m. Audrey R. Manuel, Mar. 16, 1968; children: Danna Ruth, Amanda Kay. AS, Tyler Jr. Coll., 1974; AA, Trinity Valley Community Coll., 1975. Min. Ch. of Christ, Dallas, 1968, Buna, Tex., 1969-71, Natchitoches, La., 1971-72, Palestine, Tex., 1972—; bd. mem. City Cemetery Bd., Palestine, 1990-91; TV personality Give Me the Bible, Jacksonville, Tex., 1990-91. Contbr. weekly articles Palestine Herald Press, 1973-91; staff writer Pulpit Digest. Home: 102 Crescent Dr Palestine TX 75801 Office: Crockett Rd Ch of Christ 1717 Crockett Rd Palestine TX 75801

MANUEL, KEITH HARLEY, minister; b. Hartland, N.B., Can., Aug. 5, 1947; s. Garnet Murray and Eleanor Lucy (Costigan) M.; m. Judy Lillian Hurlbut, May 9, 1970; children: Shawn, Brent. BS, McGill U., Montreal, Que., Can., 1969, MS, 1971; MRE, Liberty Bapt. Theol. Sem., Lynchburg, Va., 1983. Lic. to ministry Bapt. Ch., 1985. Owner, operator crop farm N.B., 1971-81; adminstrv. pastor Wesleyan Ch., Woodstock, N.B., Can.,

1981, Heritage Bapt. Ch., Lynchburg, 1986—. Office: Heritage Bapt Ch 219 Breezewood Dr Lynchburg VA 24502

MANUEL, KENNETH R., minister; b. Indpls., June 29, 1961; s. Leonard A. and Leatha P. (Wells) M. BA, Bishop Coll., 1983; MDiv, Butler U., 1990. Ordained to ministry Am. Bapt. Ch. Youth dir. Mt. Tabor Bapt. Ch., Dallas, 1981-85; youth pastor St. John Bapt. Ch., Indpls., 1986-88, pastor youth, 1986-88; pastor youth Oasis of Hope Bapt. Ch., Indpls., 1988—; cons. Youth Ministry U., Congress of Black Chs., Washington, 1986—; trustee advisor Midwest Youth Conf., Indpls., 1988—. Sec. Martin Ctr. Coll., Indpls., 1986—; mem. Big Bros. Indpls., 1983-91. Named Big Brother of Yr. Big Bros. Am., 1984, 90, Youth Min. of Yr. Group mag., 1990. Office: Oasis of Hope Bapt Ch 1701 E 25th St Indianapolis IN 46218

MANUEL, ORION WENDELL, minister; b. Reidsville, N.C., Dec. 16, 1939; s. James Orion and Edna Erle (McCollum) M.; m. Marg Scott Blackwell, Sept. 6, 1964 (dec. Apr. 1976); children: James William, Patrick Yancey; m. Quinn Dalton Wilson, Dec. 12, 1976; stepchildren: Erich, Phillip. BA, U. N.C., 1963; MDiv, Union Theol. Sem., Richmond, Va., 1965; DMin, McCormick Theol. Sem., 1977. Ordained to ministry Presbyn. Ch. Asst. minister Parish of Kilmallie, Corpach, Scotland, 1965-66, 1st Presbyn. Ch., Danville, Va., 1967-70; chaplain United Campus Chapel, Redford, Va., 1970-79; minister Trinity Presbyn. Ch., Starkville, Miss., 1979—; moderator St. Andrew Presbytery, Miss., 1990. Convener Nat. Issue Forum, Starkville, 1987—; chmn. Oktibbeha Emergency Food and Shelter Bd., Starkville, 1985—. Mem. Univ. Common Ministry (pres. 1985-86), Starkville Ministerial Assn. (pres. 1986-87), Rotary. Office: Trinity Presbyn Ch PO Box 794 Starkville MS 39759

MANUEL, RON ERVIL, minister, secondary school educator; b. Banner Elk, N.C., June 14, 1951; s. Joe Ervil and Mae (Miller) M.; m. Paula Forrester; children: David, Marlana. BS, Milligan Coll., 1973; MS, East Tenn. State U., 1987. Ordained to ministry Christian Ch., 1973; cert. tchr., Tenn. Min. 1st Christian Ch. of Spruce Pine, N.C., 1980-83, Cen. Ch. of Christ, Lenoir, N.C., 1983-89, 1st Christian Ch. of Boone, N.C., 1990—; high sch. tchr. Johnson County Bd. Edn., Mountain City, Tenn., 1979—; singer N.C. Mountain Christian Chs. Conv., 1988, speaker, 1989-90. Composer religious songs. Home: Rte 3 Box 48 Mountain City TN 37683 Office: 1st Christian Ch of Boone PO Box 384 Hwy 421 Boone NC 28607

MAPES, GORDON BIDWELL, minister; b. L.A., Jan. 18, 1961; s. Gordon Bidwell and Carolyn Ann (McClaskey) M. BA, U. Calif., San Diego, 1983; MDiv, Princeton Theol. Sem., 1987—. Ordained to ministry Presbyn. Ch. (U.S.A.), 1987. Chaplain Bklyn. Meth. Hosp., 1985; intern assoc. Front Royal (Va.) Presbyn. Ch., 1985-86; pastor Massies Mill and Harmony Presbyn. Chs., Nelson County, Va., 1987—; commr. Synod Mid Atlantic, Winston-Salem, N.C., 1990; substitute tchr. Nelson County Schs., 1988—; mem. new ch. devel. com.; bd. dirs. Va. Coun. Chs., Presbtery Div. of Mission. Contbr. articles to Nelson County newspaper, 1989-91. Bd. dirs. Literacy Vols., Nelson County, 1989—, Nelson County Child Care Ctr.; commr. Gov.'s Migrant and Seasonal Farmworkers Bd., Richmond, 1990—. Mem. Nelson County Hist. Soc. Democrat.

MAPES, RICHARD MATHER, SR., minister; b. New Haven, Sept. 7, 1925; s. Milton Crawford and Gladys Merwin (Blakeslee) M.; m. Marianne Fenner, June 16, 1951; children: Cynthia, Richard Mather Jr., Catherine, Carolyn. AB, Yale U., 1949; BDiv, Yale Divinity Sch., 1952; DD, Tougaloo (Miss.) Coll., 1982. Sr. minister Olmsted Community Ch., Olmsted Falls, Ohio, 1952-61; asst. conf. minister Ohio Congl. Chs., Cleve., 1961-63; dir. field edn. Oberlin & Vanderbilt Divinity Sch., Nashville, 1963-67; minister Trinity Congl. Ch., Pepper Pike, Ohio, 1967-71; sr. minister First Ch. Congl., Painesville, Ohio, 1971-76, Naples (Fla.) United Ch. of Christ, 1976-91, 1st Congl. Ch., Branford, Conn., 1991—; bd. dirs. Uplands Retirement Village, Pleasant Hills, Tenn. Bd. dirs. Collier County Sch. Bd., Naples, 1982-84, Alcohol, Drug and Mental Health Bd. Dist. 8, Ft. Myers, Fla., 1988-91, United Way of Collier County, Naples, 1988-90. Staff sgt. inf. U.S. Army, 1943-46, ETO/PTO. Mem. Naples Ministerial Assn. (pres. 1980-81), Kiwanis (pres. Naples chpt. 1982-83). Democrat. Home: 32 Turtle Bay Dr Branford CT 06405

MAPLE, GILBERT ROY, minister; b. Fairborn, Ohio, Sept. 23, 1945; s. Gilbert Roy and Katherine (Matteef) M.; m. Mary Ann McDowell, June 14, 1969; children: Gregory John, Jeffrey Allen. BS, Western Ill. U., 1967; MS, No. Ill. U., 1972. Asst. prof. Trinity Coll., Deerfield, Ill., 1967-75; pastor Reeve Evangel. Free Ch., Clear Lake, Wis., 1975-81; sr. pastor Brooklyn Park (Minn.) Evangel. Free Ch., 1981-87, Felton (Calif.) Evangel. Free Ch., 1987—; trustee Trinity Coll., 1988-91. Vice-pres. Gold Standard Barbershop Chorus, Scotts Valley, Calif., 1991. Mem. Evangel. Free Ch. of Am. Ministerial Assn. Home: 195 Webster Drive Ben Lomond CA 95005 Office: Felton Evangel Free Church PO Drawer E-1 Felton CA 95018

MAPLES, DONNA ELAINE, religious educator; b. Bay City, Tex., May 20, 1953; d. John Cecil and Clara Ann (Moore) M. BA in English and Math., Baylor U., 1974; MA in English, Vanderbilt U., 1978; postgrad. U. Mo.-Columbia, 1981—. Assoc., Woman's Missionary Union, Mo. Bapt. Conv., Jefferson City, 1976-80, tng. design group mgr. Woman's Missionary Union, Birmingham, Ala., 1984—. Author: Friends Are For Helping, 1982. Mem. Am. Soc. for Tng. and Devel., Mo. Folklore Soc. Baptist. Office: Woman's Missionary Union PO Box C-10 Birmingham AL 35283

MAPLES, WILLIAM BRUCE, JR., minister; b. Nashville, Feb. 25, 1953; s. William Bruce Sr. and Joyce (Allen) M.; m. Nina Lee Griffin, Sept. 1, 1973; children: William Griffin, Benjamin Thomas. BS in Music Edn., Tenn. Tech. U., 1975; MS in Music Edn., Western Ky. U., 1977; MA in Christian Edn., So. Sem., 1985. Ordained to ministry So. Bapt. Conv., 1985. Min. music, youth Lincoln Heights Bapt. Ch., Tullahoma, Tenn., 1980-81, Calvary Bapt. Ch., Glasgow, Ky., 1982-85; min. music and edn. Ridgeview Bapt. Ch., Chattanooga, 1985-90, Signal Mountain (Tenn.) Bapt. Ch., 1991—. Contbr. articles to ch. jours. Mem. Tenn. Ch. Music Conf., Christian Educators Network, Bapts. Committed, Hamilton County Religious Educators Assn., Hamilton County Bapt. Assn. (adult and instrumental music div. 1988—). Home: 315 Arrow Dr Signal Mountain TN 37377-3010 Office: Signal Mountain Bapt Ch 939 Ridgeway Ave Signal Mountain TN 37377-3720

MARCH, PHILIP KAPPES, lay worker, sales executive; b. Canton, Ohio, Mar. 22, 1929; s. Thorald Truxton and Ruth Whitmore (Kappes) M.; m. Elizabeth Randolph Farrar, Dec. 28, 1955 (div. Nov. 1985); children: Duncan Maxwell, Erica Randolph, Victoria Hughes. Student, Colby Coll., Waterville, Maine, 1947-50; BS, Ohio State U., 1951. Mktg. dir. Life-Study Fellowship, Noroton, Conn., 1974-77; mgr. east coast Russ Reid Advt., Pasadena, Calif., 1978; freelance editor Chosen Books, Chappaqua, N.Y., 1979; v.p. advt./mktg. Christian Herald Assn., Chappaqua, 1979-85; v.p. sales List Svcs. Corp., Bethel, Conn., 1986—; vestryman, lay reader Christ's Ch., Easton, Conn., 1990—; lay reader St. Paul's Ch., Darien, Conn., 1973-84; vestryman St. Stephen's Ch., Ridgefield, Conn., 1970-73; founder TGIF Christian Men's Fellowship, N.Y.C., 1968-72. Contbr. articles to mags. Mem. Evang. Christian Pub. Assn., Evang. Press Assn., Direct Mktg. Assn. (mem. non-profit coun.). Republican. Home: 395 Purdy Hill Rd Monroe CT 06468 Office: List Svcs Corp 6 Trowbridge Dr Bethel CT 06801

MARC'HADOUR, GERMAIN PIERRE, priest, retired English educator; b. Langonnet, Morbihan, France, Apr. 16, 1921; s. Yves and Marie Marc'hadour. Licentiate, Cath. U., Angers, France, 1945; Dr, Sorbonne U., 1969. Ordained priest Roman Cath. Ch., 1944. Tchr. Diocesan High Sch., Pontivy, France, 1945-52; asst. prof. English, Cath. U., 1952-60, assoc. prof., 1961-70, titular prof., 1970-89, emeritus prof., 1989—; rsch. asst. Yale U., New Haven, 1960-61, editor Thomas More's works, 1959-90; fellow Folger, Huntington and Newberry librs. Author: L'Univers de Thomas More, 1963, Thomas More et la Bible, 1969, The Bible in the Works of Thomas More, 5 vols., 1969-72.; editor 2 books of Thomas More, 1981, 90; translator: Erasme et More: Correspondence, 1985; adv. editor W. Tyndale's works. Recipient Chancellor's medal Rockhurst Coll., Kans., 1978, Palmes Académiques, Govt. of France, 1988; Festschrift Miscellanea Moreana dedicated to him, 1989. Mem. MLA, Renaissance Soc. Am., Amis J.H. Newman, Assn. Guillaume Budé, Amici Thomas Mori (internat. sec. 1963—). Avocation: playing with words and languages. Home: 29 rue Volney, 49005 Angers France Office: Moreanum, BP 808, 49008 Angers Cedex 01, France

MARCHANT, DAVID ISAAC, SR., pastor, Christian counselor; b. Savannah, Ga., May 1, 1947; s. James Price Sr. and Jewel Rebecca (Stevens) M.; m. Cherry Lucille Sanders, May 21, 1970; children: Rebecca Lucille, David Isaac Jr. Gen. edn. diploma, Ga. Lic. temperament therapist/pastoral counselor. Ordained deacon Evangel Temple Ch., Savannah, 1976-78, ordained elder, 1978-80, ordained pastor, 1980—; dir. Career Tng. Inst., Savannah, 1972-73; resident counselor/house parent Parent & Child Youth Devel. Svcs. Inc., Savannah, 1974-80. With U.S. Army, 1966-68. Mem. Nat. Assn. Christian Counselors (lic. counselor), Savannah Protestant Ministerial Assn. (del. 1982—). Republican. Office: Evangel Temple Church 5704 Jasmine Ave Savannah GA 31406

MARCHMAN, VICTOR YATER, lay worker; b. Cleburne, Tex., Nov. 17, 1927; s. George S. Marchman and Bertha Pollack Marchman; m. Anna Marie Kosanke, Feb. 28, 1953; children: Van, Cheryl Marchman Moseley, Monte. BBA, Baylor U., 1951. owner-mgr. John's Drygoods, Henrietta, Tex., 1953—; Sunday sch. tchr. 1st Bapt. Ch., Henrietta, 1954-85, Sunday sch. dir., 1986—, trustee, 1960—; deacon, chmn. several pulpit com., Henrietta. Pres., state dir. U.S. Jaycees, 1960-62; councilman Clay County, Henrietta; scoutmaster Boy Scouts Am., 1965-85; mem. sch. bd. Henrietta Ind. Sch., 1979-81. With U.S. Army, 1945-47. Named Outstanding Citizen, Henrietta C. of C. Mem. Kiwanis (Henrietta club, pres., bd. dirs.). Home: 301 E Crafton Henrietta TX 76365

MARCHO, ROBERT KENT, college program director; b. Santa Monica, Calif., Apr. 16, 1943; s. Marvin Leroy and Anita Pearl (Irby) M.; m. Alvadean Mashburn, Jan. 5, 1969; children: Christopher, Craig, Carrie, Amy. BTh, Calif. Grad. Sch. Theology, Glendale, 1983; MDiv, Abilene (Tex.) Christian U., 1987; postgrad., Fuller Sem., Pasadena, Calif., 1987—. Pulpit min. South 11th and Willis Ch. of Christ, Abilene, 1983-87, Sunset Ch. of Christ, Carlsbad, N.Mex., 1987-90; dir. recruiting, grad. advisor Abilene Christian U., 1990—; mem. Soc. Bibl. Lit., 1983-87. Contbr. articles to mags. Mem. Baytown Women's Shelter, 1979-83; trustee Ouachita Christian Schs., Monroe, La., 1976-79. Home: 725 Gary Ln Abilene TX 79601 Office: Abilene Christian U ACU Sta Box 8430 Abilene TX 79699

MARCIAL, MINETTE, broadcasting executive; b. Miami, Fla., Oct. 7, 1963; s. Micheal A. Marcial and Sauri (Proenza) Harris. BS, Ga. Coll., Milledgeville, 1985. Copywriter, producer WDJC-FM 93.7, Birmingham, Ala., 1987-88, prodn. mgr., co-mgr., 1988—. Freelance talent Sav-A-Life, Birmingham, 1988-89; concert organizer Kinas Ranch, Birmingham, 1989; mistress of ceremonies Cystic Fibrosis, Birmingham, 1988. Mem. NAFE, Gospel Music Assn., Birmingham Advt. Club, C. of C.

MARCIL, SISTER MARY KAREN, sister; b. Troy, N.Y., July 13, 1938; d. George and Mary (Cunningham) M. AA, Maria Coll., 1961; BA, Coll. of St. Rose, 1964; MS, SUNY, 1974. Joined Sisters of Mercy, Roman Cath. Ch., 1958; cert. secondary tchr. English, supr.-adminstr., N.Y. Vice prin. Mercy High, Albany, N.Y., 1968-70, prin., 1970-76; pers. coun. Sisters of Mercy, Albany, 1976-83, pres., 1986—; edn. coord. Com. Maternity Ctr., Albany, 1983-86; mem. Fedn. of Sisters of Mercy, Silver Spring, Md., 1986—; pres. St. Peter's Hosp. Bd., Albany, 1986—; chmn. Ea. Mercy Health System Mems., Radnor, Pa., 1989—; bd. dirs. Maria Coll., 1981—. Office: Sisters of Mercy 634 New Scotland Ave Albany NY 51848-9834

MARCINKUS, PAUL C., archbishop; b. Cicero, Ill., Jan. 15, 1922. Ordained priest Roman Catholic Ch., 1947; served in Vatican secretariat Rome, from 1952; ordained titular bishop of Orta, 1969, ordained titular archbishop of Orta, 1981; sec. Inst. for Religious Works (Vatican Bank), 1968-71, pres., 1971—; named pro-pres. Pontifical Commn. for Vatican City State, 1981—. Office: Inst for Religious Work, Vatican City Vatican City

MARCONI, DOMINIC ANTHONY, clergyman; b. Newark, Mar. 13, 1927; s. Sabato Joseph and Antoinette (Ricciardi) M. B.A., Seton Hall U., 1949; postgrad., Immaculat Conception Sem., Mahwah, N.J., 1952; S.T.L., Catholic U., Washington, 1953. Ordained priest Roman Cath. Ch., 1953; asso. pastor St. Anthony's Ch., Union City, N.J., 1953-66; asso. dir. family life apostolate Archdiocese of Newark, 1966-70, dir., 1970-75; co-dir. div. for services to elderly Associated Cath. Charities, 1975-76; aux. and regional bishop Union County, 1976—. Club: K.C. Address: 238 E Blancke St PO Box 534 Linden NJ 07036

MARCOS, M. A., religious organization leader. Archpriest The Coptic Ch. in Can., Agincourt, Ont. Office: Coptic Ch Can, 40 Glendinning Ave, Agincourt, ON Canada M1W 3E2*

MARE, WILLIAM HAROLD, Bible educator, talk show host; b. Portland, Oreg., July 23, 1918; s. Scott Creighton and Sallie Gertrude (Knight) Brown, m. Clara Elizabeth Potter, Mar. 23, 1945; children: Myra Ann, Sally Elizabeth, Nancy Lee, William Harold, Jr., Judith Eileen. B.A. (hon. soc.), Wheaton Coll., 1941; B.D., Faith Theol. Sem., 1945; M.A., Wheaton Coll., 1946; Ph.D., U. Penn., 1961. Ordained to ministry Presbyterian Ch., 1945. Grad. fellow, tchr. Wheaton Coll., Ill., 1941-42; tchr. Faith Theol. Sem., Wilmington, Del., 1946-53, pastor Presbyn. Chs., Denver, Charlotte, N.C., 1953-63, prof. classics Covenant Coll. St. Louis, 1963-64; prof. N.T., Covenant Theol. Sem., St. Louis, 1963—; dir. Near East Sch. of Archaeology, Jerusalem, 1962, 64; archaeologist Jerusalem, Raddana, Heshbon, Moab, summers 1970, 72, 74, 76, 79; dir. Abila of Decapolis Excavation, No. Jordan, 1980—. Contbr. articles to profl. jours. Author: First Corinthians Expositors Bible Commentary, 1976; Mastering New Testament Greek, 1977; Archaeology of the Jerusalem Area, 1987; translator Bible 1st Corinthias Notes, 1991. Treas. Mo. Roundtable, St. Louis, 1981—. Mem. Archeol. Inst. Am. (pres. St. Louis chpt. 1978-80), Nr. East Archeol. Soc. (pres. 1971—), Evang. Theol. Soc., Am. Schs. Oriental Research, Soc. Bibl. Lit. Republican. Club: Classical (St. Louis) (pres. 1977-79, 1987-89). Avocation: photography. Home: 978 Orchard Lakes Dr Saint Louis MO 63146 Office: Covenant Theol Sem 12330 Conway Rd Saint Louis MO 63141

MARGALIT, SHLOMO, educator; b. Tiberias, Israel, Apr. 30, 1914; s. Nehemiah and Bath-Sheva (Kuperman) M.; m. Dina Rivlin, Feb. 8, 1938; children: Nehemiah, Yael Margalit Moses. DHL (hon.), Gratz Coll., 1985. Ordained rabbi, 1933. Rabbi Kefar Vitkin, Israel, 1934; religion instr. Haifa, Israel, 1937; assoc. rabbi Congregation Rodeph Shalom, Atlantic City, 1955; prof. Hebrew, Bible, Rabbinics Gratz Coll., Phila., 1959-85; Contbr. articles to profl. jours. With Israel Def. Forces. Mem. Am. Assn. of Jewish Edn., Nat. Coun. of Jewish Edn., Hebrew Tchrs. and Prins. of Am. (chtp. past pres.), Histadruth Ivrith of Am., Master Har-Zion Lodge-Jerusalem. Avocations: poetry, singing. Home: 1448 Devereaux Ave Philadelphia PA 19149-2701 Office: Gratz Coll 10 St and Tabor Rd Philadelphia PA 19149-2701

MARGÉOT, JEAN CARDINAL, bishop; b. Quatre-Bornes, Mauritius, Feb. 3, 1916. Student, Royal Coll. Curepipe, Mauritius, Licentiate in Philosophy, 1934; Licentiate in Theology, Gregorian U., Rome, 1938. Ordained, 1938, vicar gen., 1956, bishop, 1969, nominated cardinal, 1988; pres. Bishop's Conf. of Indian Ocean Islands, 1985; mem. Pontifical Coun. for the Family, Rome, 1988—, Pontifical Coun. for Tourism and Emigration, Rome, 1988—, Sacred Congregation for Evangelisation of People. Contbr. numerous letters and articles to jours. Decorated Chevalier de l'Ordre Nat. de la Légion d'Honneur, 1988; named Hon. Citizen Town of Quatre-Bornes, 1986, Hon. Citzen Town of Beau-Bassin/Rose-Hill, 1986, Hon. Citizen Dist. of Grand Port/Savanne, 1989. Home and Office: Evêché, 13 Mgr Gonin St, Port Louis Mauritius

MARILUPE, SISTER See MIER-Y-TERÁN, MARIA GUADALUPE

MARINELLO, THOMAS J., pilot; b. Troy, N.Y., Jan. 30, 1955; s. Andrew and Helen (Laurenzo) M.; m. Patricia K. Bridges, Aug. 18, 1984; 1 child, Laura C. BS in Internat. Affairs, USAF Acad., 1977; ThM, Dallas Theol. Sem., 1988. Deacon, pastoral worker Grace Bible Ch., North Little Rock, Ark., 1979-83; tchr., pastoral worker Garland (Tex.) Bible Chapel, 1984-90; pilot So. Air Transport, Miami, 1989-90, Tepper Aviation, 1990—; commended worker, missionary Christian Missions in Many Lands, Coleraine, No. Ireland, 1987. Capt. USAF, 1977-84. Mem. Soc. Bibl. Lit., Evang. Theol. Soc. Republican. Home: 1029 Troon Dr E Niceville FL 32578-4062

MARING, NORMAN H., retired religious educator; b. Chester, Pa., Dec. 1, 1914; s. Waldo Earle and Emily (Hill) M.; m. Sara Amelia Johnson, Apr. 21, 1935; children: Donald, Helen, Ruth. BA, Eastern Coll., 1939; BTh., Ea. Bapt. Theol. Sem., 1941; MA, U. Md., 1941, PhD, 1948. Asst. prof. history Eastern Coll., Phila., 1948-52; prof. ch. history Ea. Bapt. Theol. Sem., Phila., 1952-84, dean of faculty, 1972-78, emeritus prof. ch. history, 1984—; vis. prof. history Hardin-Simmons U., Abilene, Tex., 1950; vis. prof. Am. Christianity Temple U., Phila., 1963-64; pres. Am. Bapt. Hist. Soc., Valley Forge, Pa., 1965-69; mem. editorial bd. Foundations: a Baptist Journal of History and Theology, Rochester, N.Y., 1958-69; mem. Coun. on Theol. Edn. Am. Bapt. Chs./USA, Valley Forge, 1970-75; mem. Commn. on Denominational Identity Am. Bapt. Chs./USA, Valley Forge, 1985-88. Author: Baptist Manual of Polity and Practice, 1963, rev. edit., 1991, Baptists in New Jersey, 1964, American Baptists: Whence and Whither, 1968, The Christian Calendar in the Free Churches, 1968. Faculty fellowship grantee Assn. Theol. Schs. (sabbatical in Europe), 1965; recipient Outstanding Ministry award Alumni Assn. Ea. Bapt. Theol. Sem., 1984. Mem. Am. Soc. Ch. History, Conf. on Faith and History. Democrat. Home: 1784 C Ebenezer Rd Rock Hill SC 29732

MARIOTTINI, CLAUDE FRANCISCO, religion educator; b. Rio de Janeiro, Dec. 24, 1942; came to U.S., 1963; s. Waldemiro and Palmyra (Bastos) M.; m. Donna Sue Anderson, Oct. 27, 1967; children: Claude Jr., Chris, James. BA, Calif. Bapt. Coll., 1968; MDiv, Golden Gate Bapt. Sem., 1971; PhD, So. Bapt. Sem., 1983; postgrad., Grad. Theol. Union, 1971-73. Instr. So. Bapt. Theol. Sem., Louisville, 1982; assoc. prof. of Old Testament S.W. Bapt. U., Bolivar, Mo., 1983-88, No. Bapt. Theol. Sem., Lombard, Ill., 1988—; pastor Meml. Bapt. Ch., San Jose, Calif., 1973-78, Radcliff (Ky.) Spanish Bapt. Ch., 1979-83. Contbr. articles to profl. publs. Mem. Soc. Biblical Lit., Cath. Biblical Assn. Am., Am. Sch. Oriental Rsch. (pres. Cen. States chpt. 1987-88), Nat. Assn. Bapt. Profs. Religion, Biblical Archeol. Soc. Republican. Home: 6425 Clark Dr Woodridge IL 60517 Office: No Bapt Theol Sem 660 E Butterfield Rd Lombard IL 60148

MARJANCZYK, JOSEPH ANICETUS, priest; b. Elizabeth, N.J., Apr. 17, 1921; s. Joseph John and Catherine Frances (Cwik) M. BA, Seton Hall U., 1941; MDiv, Darlington Sem., 1975. Ordained priest Roman Cath. Ch., 1945; named monsignor, 1979. Asst. pastor St. Valentine's Ch., Bloomfield, N.J., 1945-72; pastor St. Adalbert's Ch., Elizabeth, 1972-83, Our Lady of Mt. Carmel Ch., Bayonne, N.J., 1983—; named protonotary apostolic, 1988; vicar Episcopal South Hudson Vicariate, 1991; prof. Polish Master Sch. Fgn. Langs., Seton Hall U., 1948-60; chmn. pers. bd. Archdiocese of Newark, 1972-74, mem. pastoral coun., 1972-83, trustee 1975-86; chmn. adminstrv. com., mem. exec. bd. Archdiocesan Pastoral Coun., 1972-84; dean Union County East Deanery, 1975-83; Polish Apostolate rep. Nat. Conf. Cath. Bishops Com. on Migration, 1989—, chmn. Polish adv. bd. to conf. office for pastoral care of migrants and refugees, 1989—. Chmn. bd. dirs. Polish Cultural Found., 1974-90; trustee Seton Hall U., 1978—, Immaculate Conception Sem., South Orange, N.J., 1979-86; commr. bd. edn. City of Elizabeth, 1979-83; nat. chaplain Polish Army Vets. Assn. Am., 1980—; founder, pres. N.J. chpt. John Paul II Found., 1986—; chmn. exec. bd. Polish chapel renovation and redication Nat. Shrine of Immaculate Conception, Washington, 1986-89. Decorated Gold Order of Merit (Republic of Poland). Mem. Archdiocesan Polish Clergy Soc. (hon. pres. 1979—), Polish Am. Priests Assn. (mem. exec. com. 1991—), Polish Am. Congress, Polish Am. Hist. Assn., N.J. Hist. Soc., Polish Am. Numis. Assn., Polonians Club, KC. Home: PO Box 456 Point Pleasant NJ 08742 Office: 39 E 22d St Bayonne NJ 07002

MARKAVITCH, STANLEY G., school administrator; b. Muskegon, Mich., June 1, 1943; s. Peter J. and May B. M.; m. Vickie L. Cech, Mar. 19, 1966; children: Julianne, Jennifer. BA, Mich. State U., 1965, EdS; MA, Ea. Mich. U., 1967. Speech therapist Pontiac (Mich.) pub. schs., 1965-66, Northville (Mich.) pub. schs., 1967-68; speech therapist St. Joseph (Mich.) pub. schs., 1968-70, social sci. tchr., 1970-74; community edn. dir. Bridgman (Mich.) pub. schs., 1974-80, asst. prin./athletic dir., 1980—. Trustee, Wildwood Homeowners Assn., Bridgeman; bd. dirs. Berrien County chpt. ARC, Benton Harbor. Mem. Mich. Intersch. Athletic Adminstrs. Assn., Nat. Intersch. Athletic Adminstrs. Assn., Nat. Assn. Sec. Sch. Prins., Mich. Assn. Sec. Sch. Prins., Elks. Home: PO Box 441A Wildwood Est Bridgman MI 49106 Office: Bridgman High School 9964 S Gast Rd Bridgman MI 49106

MARKER, JUDITH, ecumenical agency administrator. Exec. dir. East End Coop. Ministry, Pitts. Office: E End Coop Ministry 250 N Highland Ave Pittsburgh PA 15206*

MARKHAM, ROBERT WILSON, III, minister; b. Providence, Dec. 4, 1943; s. Robert Wilson Jr. and Virginia (Dyer) M.; m. Roberta Marilyn Joyal, Aug. 22, 1964; children: Brenda Gail, Todd Andrew. BA, Ottawa (Kans.) U., 1966; MDiv, Crozer Theol. Sem., Chester, Pa., 1969. Ordained to ministry Am. Bapt. Chs. in U.S.A., 1969. Assoc. pastor 1st Bapt. Ch., Elmira, N.Y., 1969-73; pastor 1st Bapt. Ch., Rockport, Mass., 1973—; asst. spiritual dir. Mass. Episcopal Cursillo, 1990—. Bd. dirs. Mass. Dept. Mental Retardation, 1983; pres. Greater Cape Ann Human Svcs. Inc., Gloucester, Mass., 1982-90; mem. sch. improvement coun. Rockport High Sch., 1987-89; chmn. local coun. Boy Scouts Am., 1990; chmn. sex edn. curriculum com. Rockport Sch. System, 1991—. Named to Legion of Honor, Order of DeMolay, 1980. Mem. Adoniram Judson Bapt. Assn. (moderator 1989-91), Am. Bapt. Chs. Mass. (mem. dept. spl. needs 1985—, bd. dirs. 1989-91, chmn. planning team 1989-91), Cape Ann Interfaith Commn. (pres. 1977-80), Mass. Bapt. Found. for Campus Ministry (pres. 1980-86). Office: 1st Bapt Ch 2 High St Rockport MA 01966 *Christ came not only to secure for us a glorious future but make us secure enough to live in the present.*

MARKIEWICZ, ALFRED JOHN, bishop; b. Bklyn., May 17, 1928. Student, St. Francis Coll., Bklyn., Immaculate Conception Sem., Huntington, N.Y. Ordained priest Roman Cath. Ch., 1953, ordained titular bishop of Afufenia and aux. bishop of Rockville Centre, N.Y., 1986. Vicar for Nassau Diocese of Rockville Centre. Office: Diocese of Rockville Centre 50 N Park Ave Rockville Centre NY 11570*

MARKLEY, WILLIAM AMBROSE, minister; b. Lynchburg, Va., Mar. 30, 1932; s. Raymond Law and Mary Lydia (Thrush) M.; m. Shelbia Jean Bixler, Aug. 5, 1961; 1 child, Marlinda Kay Markley Smith. BA, Gettysburg (Pa.) Coll., 1955; BS, Gettysburg Sem., 1960, STM, 1966. Ordained to ministry United Luth. Ch. in Am., 1960. Pastor UCLA Luth. Ch. Am., 1960-80; pastor Zion Meth. Ch., North East, Md., 1988—; chaplain Indsl. and Comml. Ministry, Harford Meml. Hosp., 1988. With U.S. Army, 1955-56. Mem. Lions. Office: West Cecil United Parish 94 Old Zion Rd North East MD 21901 *Thirty-some years in His Service has taught me the absolute validity of His Teaching and the Word of God. There is no firmer foundation than His Will.*

MARK OF FORT LAUDERDALE, BISHOP See FORSBERG, MARK

MARKOVICH, ERIC, minister; b. Lake City, Pa., May 24, 1964; s. William and Ruth (Duran) M.; m. Theresa Dawn Masonbrink, Feb. 2, 1991. BA in Philosophy and Econs., Ind. U. of Pa., 1986; MDiv, Trinity Luth. Sem., 1990. Ordained to ministry Luth. Ch. Min. Bethlehem Luth. Ch., Toledo, 1990—. Office: Bethlehem Luth Ch 114 W Plumer St Toledo OH 43605-3328

MARKS, CHARLES HERBERT, minister; b. Mount Vision, N.Y., Feb. 13, 1930; s. William Herbert and Mabel (Gray) M.; m. Marilyn Cone, June 13, 1954; children: Valerie Lyn, Michelle Eileen, Drew Charles, Robert Stuart. BA, Utica Coll., 1953; MDiv, Drew Theol. Sem., 1956; MA, Syracuse U., 1966; hon. alumnus, Eisenhower Coll., 1973. Ordained to ministry United Meth. Ch., 1957. Pastor United Meth. chs. in No. and Cen.

N.Y. Confs., 1950—; sr. pastor St. Paul's United Meth. Ch., Ithaca, N.Y., 1987—. Author: Letters to a Modern Parent, 1976; contbr. poetry to jours. in field. Mem. town bd. Minetto, N.Y., 1966-68. Mem. Masons. Democrat. Home: 208 E Court St Ithaca NY 14850 Office: 402 N Aurora St Ithaca NY 14850 *I want to be a part of something vital that began before me and lasts after me. And I want to be part of something noble that begins with me and endures beyond me.*

MARKS, JUSTIN DAVIS, JR., minister, guidance counselor; b. Cynthiana, Ky., Oct. 17, 1940; s. Justin Davis Sr. and Mary Preston (Butler) M.; m. Lois Johnson, Sept. 9, 1965; children—Justine Lovell, Justin Davis III. BA in Bible and Christian Edn., Am. Bapt. Coll. Bible, Nashville, 1965; Diploma, Sch. Bible Prophecy, Atlanta, 1966; MDiv, Lexington Theol. Sem., 1977; ThD, Bernadean U. , 1979. Ordained to ministry Nat. Bapt. Conv. U.S.A., 1967. Pastor, Cadiz 2d Bapt. Ch., Ky., 1967-72, 1st Bapt. Ch., Nicholasville, Ky., 1973-77, Fellowship Bapt. Ch., Evansville, Ind., 1978—; guidance counselor Earle C. Clements Jr. Community Coll., Morganfield, Ky., 1978—; dean, tchr. Cen. Am. U. Extension, Kansas City, Mo., 1985—; dean Marks/Caldwell Bible Inst., Evansville, 1985—; dean Christian Leadership Conf., 1974-75; instr. barbering West Ky. Area Vocat. Tech. Sch., 1966-72; mission State Bapt. Conv., 1963. Sr. patrol leader Blue Grass coun. Boy Scouts Am., Lexington, Ky. Mem. Jessamine County Ministers Assn., Masons. Democrat. Home: 421 S Evans St Evansville IN 47713 Office: Earle C Clements Job Corps Ctr Morganfield KY 42437

MARKS, RICHARD DICKINSON, religion educator; b. Boston, Apr. 13, 1942; s. Charles Dickinson and Cecelia (Elliott) M.; m. Sandra Lee Gardner, Oct. 29, 1966 (dec. June 1986); children: Scott, Christopher, Lee, Todd, Heidi; m. Penny Lou Eckstine, June 13, 1987. BSBA, Northeastern U., Boston, 1966; MS in Mgmt., Frostburg State, 1979. Youth min. Cen. Bapt. Ch., Westfield, Mass., 1973-74; leader Young Life, Westfield, 1973-75; exec. dir. YMCA, Waynesboro, Pa., 1975—; elder, coun. head Presbyn. Ch., Waynesboro, 1980-82. Contbr. articles to profl. jours. Sunday sch. tchr. Presbyn. and Brethren in Christ, Waynesboro, 1977—. Capt. USAF, 1966-70. Mem. Assn. Profl. Dirs. (pres. 1980-82, Adminstrv. Excellance award 1984, 86), Rotary (pres.). Republican. Office: YMCA 810 E Main St Waynesboro PA 17268

MARKSTROM, PAUL RAGNVALD, clergyman; b. Skanninge, Sweden, May 30, 1921; came to U.S., 1922; s. Gustaf Eric and Elsa Marie (Markstrom) Karlson; m. Berniece Elva Hoehn, June 1, 1944; children: Paul Eugene, Sondra Kay Markstrom Todd. Student Zion Bible Inst., 1940-41, Central Bible Coll. and Sem., Springfield, Mo., 1941-44, So. Methodist U., 1948, Southwestern State Coll., 1961-62, Am. Clin. Pastoral Assn., 1962-63.Ordained to ministry Assemblies of God Ch., 1947; Pastor Assembly of God Ch., Ely, Nev., 1944-46, Newburgh, N.Y., 1946-49, Bucklin, Kans., 1950-57, Coldwater, Kans., 1958-63; instr. Cen. Bible Coll. and Sem., 1966-72; dir. Instl. Chaplaincies of Assemblies of God, Springfield, Mo., 1963-86, dir. spl. ministries, 1974-80; dir. Am. Indian Bible Coll., Phoenix, 1974-80. Mem. Nat. Assn. Evangelicals (chmn. spl. ministries com. 1967-80), Am. Protestant Correctional Chaplains Assn. (dir. 1963, pres. central region 1974, sec. 1983-86), Ministerial Assn. (pres. 1953-60). Republican. Lodge: Lions. Author: Bible Basics, 1964; The Book of Acts, 1965; The Five Books of Moses, 1965; The Four Gospels, 1966; Outstanding Bible Profiles, 1967; Summary of The Old Testament, 1966. Volunteers in Corrections, 1977; Chaplains Manual, 1973. Contbr. articles to profl. jours. Home: 1520 Devon St Springfield MO 65804 Office: 1445 Boonville St Springfield MO 65802

MARKUM, JOSEPH LEE, minister; b. Monterey Park, Calif., Sept. 4, 1964; s. Arvel Dean and Patricia Ann (Cikovich) M.; m. Lynne Diane Thomass, May 29, 1987; 1 child, Matthew Dean. BA, Pacific Christian Coll., 1988. Ordained to ministry non-denominational Christian ch. Youth minister Community Christian Ch., San Juan Capistrano, Calif., 1987—; camp dean, dir. conventions Angeles Crest Christian Camp, Fullerton, Calif., 1988—. Vol. Capistrano Unified Sch. Dist., San Juan Capistrano, 1989—, Rep. Party, Orange County, Calif., 1988. Mem. Concerned Women of Am. Office: Community Christian Ch 31612 El Camino Real San Juan Capistrano CA 92675

MARKUM, RICHARD ALAN, minister; b. Chattanooga, Dec. 13, 1959; s. Wiley Robert and Peggy Marie (Von Shaaf) M.; m. Pamela Denise Lane, Oct. 10, 1981; children: Kristen Michele, Timothy Robert. Student, U. Tenn., 1980-82; B in Ministry, Covington Theol. Sem., 1989, M in Ministry, 1990. Minister Kings Point Bapt. Ch., Chattanooga, 1979-81, Ridge View Bapt. Ch., Chattanooga, 1983-84, Cen. Bapt. Ch. of Hixson, Chattanooga, 1984-85, East Chattanooga Bapt. Ch., Chattanooga, 1985-86; minister First Bapt. Ch., Whitwell, Tenn., 1986-89, Dayton, Tenn., 1989—; el. So. Bapt. Conv., Whitwell, 1989, Tenn. Bapt. Conv., Dayton, 1989-90; youth evangelism specialist Sequatchie Valley Bapt. Assn., Whitwell, 1988-90. Fellow Tenn. Valley Lay-Ministerial Assn., Marion County Lay-Ministerial Assn. Republican. Office: First Bapt Ch E 3d and Cedar Sts Dayton TN 37321

MARKWOOD, LEWIS ARDRA, minister; b. Denver, Aug. 21, 1932; s. Calvin Horace and Lillias (Williams) M.; m. P. Janel Hacker, June 20, 1954; children: Cherie Lynn, Christopher Lewis, Catherine Leigh. MusB, Hardin-Simmons U., 1957; MDiv, Southwestern Bapt. Theol. Sem., Ft. Worth, 1962. Ordained to ministry So. Bapt. Conv. Pastor 1st Bapt. Ch., Lueders, Tex., 1961-64, Roscoe, Tex., 1964-69; pastor Southtown Bapt. Ch., Bloomington, Minn., 1969-72, Trinity Bapt. Ch., Des Moines, 1972-85, Cambrian Heights Bapt. Ch., Calgary, Alta., Can., 1985—; pres., mem. exec. bd. Can. conv. So. Bapt. Conv., Calgary, 1989—. Pres. Can. conv. So. Bapt. Found., Cochrane, Alta., 1987-89. Staff sgt. USAF, 1951-53. Mem. Calgary Evang. Ministerial Assn. (v.p. 1986-90), Midwest Bapt. Assn. (bd. dirs., moderator 1986-89). Republican. Home: 156 Edgemont Estates Dr NW, Calgary, AB Canada T3A 2M3 Office: Cambrian Heights Bapt Ch, 240 Cardiff Dr NW, Calgary, AB Canada T2K 1S2

MARLOWE, TOMMY HEROLD, minister; b. Shreveport, La., Mar. 21, 1939; s. Arthur and Vera Lucille (Norwood) M.; m. Charlotte Oveta Flanagan, Aug. 7, 1959; children: Tamara, Sharon, Sheila, Tommy Jr. BS, E. Tex. Bapt. U., 1969; ThM, New Orleans Bapt. Sem., 1971; D of Ministry, Drew U., 1984. Ordained to ministry So. Bapt. Conv., 1961; lic. clin. pastoral educator. Pastor So. Bapt. Chs., La., Tex., Miss., 1961-73; missionary So. Bapt. Chs., Togo, West Africa, 1973-76; chaplain U.S. Army, 1976—; chaplain 1st Brigade 1st Inf. U.S. Army, Ft. Riley, Kans., 11989—. Served to lt. col. U.S. Army, 1976-91. Decorated Bronze Star. Democrat. Office: HHC 1st Brigade 1st Inf Div US Army Fort Riley KS 66442

MAR MARKUS (MARK I. MILLER), patriarch, primate; b. Kansas City, Mo., Aug. 18, 1927; s. Oliver Newton and Lena Mintern Skelton (foster parents); m. Phyllis Kathryn M. Parsons, Aug. 25, 1962; children: Wayne Mark, Mark Christopher Charles. DD (hon.), St. Paul's Sem., Toronto, Can., 1968; JCD (hon.), St. John's Sem., Louisville, 1970. Ordained priest Am. Orthodox Cath. Ch., 1964, consecrated to bishop, 1965. Priest Am. Orthodox Cath. Ch., Louisville, 1964-65; bishop N.Am. Orthodox Cath. Ch., L.A., 1965-75; archbishop Byzantine Cath. Ch., L.A., 1975-88, met. gen., 1988-91, patriarch/primate, 1991, primate of the chs., met. of Lagos, patriarch of West Africa, 1991—. Author: Disciplinary Canon Laws, 1968, Clergy Guide Book, 1970. Democrat. Avocations: walking, hiking, photography. Home: 1401 El Centro Ave Los Angeles CA 90028 Office: Byzantine Cath Ch The Primatial See PO Box 3682 Los Angeles CA 90078-3682

MARMION, WILLIAM HENRY, clergyman; b. Houston, Oct. 8, 1907; s. Charles Gresham and Katherine (Rankin) M.; m. Mabel Dougherty Nall, Dec. 28, 1935; children: William Henry, Roger Mills Nall. B.A., Rice U., 1929; M.Div., Va. Theol. Sem., 1932, D.D. (hon.), 1954. Ordained deacon Episcopal Ch., 1932, priest, 1933; priest in charge St. James, Taylor, Tex., and Grace Ch., Georgetown, Tex., 1932-35; asso. rector St. Mark's Ch., San Antonio, 1935-38; rector St. Mary's-on-the-Highland, Birmingham, Ala., 1938-50, St. Andrew's Ch., Wilmington, Del., 1950-54; bishop Episcopal Diocese of Southwestern Va., Roanoke, 1954-79; ret., 1979; Former dir. diocesan camps for young people in, Tex. and Ala., headed diocesan youth work, several yrs; dep. to Gen. Conv. Episcopal Ch., 1943, 46, alternate dep., 1949, 52; del. to Provincial Synod; mem. exec. council Episcopal Ch., 1963-69; chmn. Ala. Com. on Interracial Cooperation, 4 yrs. Trustee Va. Theol. Sem., Va. Episcopal Sch., St. Paul's Coll.; pres. Appalachian Peoples Service Orgn.; interim warden Coll. of Preachers, 1981-82. Home: 2730 Avenham Ave SW Roanoke VA 24014

MAROVITCH, ANTOINE, bishop. Vivcar apostolic, monsignor, titular bishop of Igilgili Latin Rite, roman Cath. Ch., Istanbvul. Office: Olcek Sok 83, 30230 Harbiye, Istanbul Turkey*

MARPLE, DOROTHY JANE, retired church executive; b. Abington, Pa., Nov. 24, 1926; d. John Stanley and Jennie (Stetler) M. A.B., Ursinus Coll., 1948; M.A., Syracuse U., 1950; Ed.D., Columbia U. Tchrs. Coll., 1969; L.H.D., Thiel Coll., 1965, Gettysburg Coll., 1979, Ursinus Coll., 1981; D. Humanitarian Services, Newberry Coll., 1977; DD, Trinity Luth. Sem., 1987. Counselor, asst., office dean undergrad. women Women's Coll., Duke, 1950-53; dean women, fgn. student adv. Thiel Coll., 1953-61; asst. social dir. Whittier Hall, Columbia Tchrs. Coll., 1961-62; exec. dir. Luth. Ch. Women, Luth. Ch. Am., Phila., 1962-75; asst. to bishop Luth. Ch. Am., 1975-85; coord. Transition Office New Luth. Ch. in U.S.A., 1986-87; asst. gen. sec. ops. Nat. Coun. Chs. of Christ in U.S., N.Y.C., 1987-89; coordinator Luth. Ch. in Am. commn. on function and structure, 1970-72. Mem. Pi Lambda Theta. Home: 8018 Anderson St Philadelphia PA 19118

MARQUES, JOAO REIS, religious organization administrator. Pres. Rio Buddhist Vihara, Rio de Janeiro. Office: Sociedade Budista-St Teresa, Dom Joaquim Mamede 45,, Rio de Janeiro RJ 20.241, Brazil*

MARQUETTE, GAYLE DEAN, music minister; b. Red Wing, Minn., Jan. 22, 1932; s. Fauntleroy Edward and Marie Belle (Wholenhaus) M.; m. Janice Erdin, Jan. 6, 1960; children: Dayle, Tonya. Student, U. Alaska, 1953, U. Ill., 1954-56. Music dir. S.S. Super Chaplewood EFC, Rockford, Ill., 1954-56, First Bapt. Ch., Jasper, Ind., 1960-71, Evang. Free, Sarasota, Fla., 1971-79; minister of music First Brethren, Sarasota, 1987-89, Faith Bapt., Nokomis, Fla., 1989—; TV producer Marquette Video Prodn., Nokomis, 1990—; dir. Free Folk Gospel Singers, Sarasota, 1970-80, The Proclamations, Sarasota, 1990—; music dir. OMS Winter Conv., Lake Yale, Fla., 1981—. Composer various hymns. Candidate Sarasota Airport Authority, 1983, Sarasota County Commn., 1985. Staff sgt. USAF, 1950-54. Republican. Home: 150 Laurel Oaks Rd Nokomis FL 34275 Office: PO Box 1528 Nokomis FL 34274

MARQUEZ, EMILIO EUSTAQUIO, clergyman, educator; b. Vinales, Pinar Del Rio, Cuba, Nov. 2, 1938; came to U.S., 1969; s. Emiliano Marquez and Berta Maria (Suarez) Izquierdo. Grad., Calif. Coll. Commerce, 1972; ministerial studies, Sch. Ministry of United Ch. Religious Sci., L.A., 1980; DD, PhD, Ind. Ch. Religious Sci., Long Beach, Calif., 1981, MDiv, 1991; PhD (hon.), Religious Sci. Theol. Sem., Ramona, Calif., 1989. Lic. to ministry United Ch. Religious Sci., 1980. Acct. Wilmington, Calif., 1972-74; agt. real estate Cerritos, Calif., 1974-78; practitioner licensee United Ch. Religious Sci., L.A., 1979-80; licentiate min. United Ch. Religious Sci., El Paso, Tex., 1980; pastor, dean Ind. Ch. Religious Sci., Long Beach, 1981-85; founder, pastor, dean Ind. Ch. Religious Sci., Ramona and Escondido (Calif.), 1988—; dean Religious Sci. Theol. Sem., Escondido, 1988—; ind. reporter, writer on various religions. Area liaison AIDS Wholistic Response, Ramona, 1991—. With Cuban Army, 1956-59. Mem. Religious Sci. Ecumenical Coun. (head 1990—). Democrat. Originator, promoter Religion's Day observance. Avocation: ecumenicism work. Office: Ind Ch Religious Sci Theol Sem 716 E Valley Pkwy # 121 Escondido CA 92025

MARRAPESE, CASTO, priest; b. Calvi, Caserta, Italy, Nov. 26, 1918; came to U.S. 1949; s. Lorenzo and Margherita (Mandara) M. Student, Angelicum U., Rome, 1943. Ordained priest, Roman Cath. Ch. Philosophy prof. PIME Sem., Aversa, Italy, 1944-46; theology prof. PIME Sem., Naples, Italy, 1946-49; procurator PIME Sem., Oakland, N.J., 1956-67; pastor St. John Bapt. Ch./Diocese of Columbus (Ohio), 1974—. Author: Water From the Old Fountain, 1989, Sale & Pepe, 1990. Home: 720 Hamlet St Columbus OH 43215 Office: St John Bapt Ch 720 Hamlet St Columbus OH 43215

MARRS, RICK ROY, religion educator; b. Tucson, Ariz., May 28, 1952; s. Roscoe R. and Jennie Vivian (Young) M.; m. Paula Hagler, Aug. 26, 1972; children: Staci Ann, Jeremy Randall. BA, Abilene Christian U., 1973, MDiv, 1976; PhD, Johns Hopkins U., 1982. Assoc. prof. Pepperdine U., Malibu, Calif., 1987—; deacon Conejo Valley Ch. of Christ, Thousand Oaks, Calif., 1988—. Contbr. articles to profl. jours. Mem. Soc. Bibl. Lit., Cath. Bibl. Soc. Mem. Christian Ch. Office: Pepperdine U Malibu CA 90265

MARRUS, ELIOT, rabbi. Pres. Buffalo Area Met. Ministries Inc. Office: Buffalo Area Met Ministries 775 Main St Ste 405 Buffalo NY 14203*

MARS, ALVIN, religion educator; b. Phila., Mar. 13, 1943; s. Jacob Samuel and Mary (Chipperstein) M.; m. Marilyn Barbara Gross, June 26, 1966; children: Gordon Israel, Jonathan Judah, Hadassah. BA, Temple U., 1964; B. Hebrew Letters, Gratz Coll., 1964; PhD, Dropsie Coll., 1970; D. Pedagogy (hon.), Jewish Theol. Sem. Am., N.Y.C., 1989. Dir. edn. and youth Beth Sholom Congregation, Elkins Park, Pa., 1965-72; headmaster Solomon Schechter Day Schs., Phila., 1972-77; dir. Camp Ramah in Calif., L.A., 1977-84; v.p. acad. affairs U. Judaism, L.A., 1984-89; exec. v.p. Brandeis-Bardin Inst., Calif., 1989—; bd. dirs. L.A. Hebrew High Sch., 1990—. Contbr. articles to profl. publs. Mem. Religious Edn. Assn., Jewish Educators Assembly Am. (v.p. 1975-77), Coun. for Jewish Edn. (bd. dirs.), Assn. for Jewish Studies. Office: Brandeis-Bardin Inst 1101 Peppertree Ln Brandeis CA 93064

MARSCH, MITCH, minister; b. Bushnell, Fla., Mar. 13, 1953; s. W.M. and Grace (Connell) M.; m. Judy Outlaw, July 30 1971; children: Jeremy, Jennifer, Alizia. Student, Luther Rice Sem., 1973, Fla. Bapt. Theol. Coll., 1977. Ordained to ministry Bapt. Ch. Music/youth minister New Hope Bapt. Ch., Wauchule, Fla., 1977-79, 1st Bapt. Ch., Williston, Fla., 1979-81; music evangelist Daystar Ministries, Dothan, Ala., 1981-85; music/youth minister Mt. Calvary Bapt. Ch., Albertville, Ala., 1985-89; minister music Behtlehem Bapt. Ch., Roebuck, S.C., 1989—. Office: Bethlehem Bapt Ch PO Box 223 Roebuck SC 29376

MARSHALL, ARTHUR, JR., bishop; b. High Point, N.C., Mar. 2, 1914; s. Arthur and Nellie (Kindle) M.; m. Mary Ann Stotts, May 3, 1952; 1 son, Arthur Clifford. A.B., Livingstone Coll., 1937, D.D., 1962; S.T.B., Boston U., 1951. Ordained deacon A.M.E. Zion Ch., 1934, elder, 1936, consecrated bishop, 1972; now bishop 7th Episcopal area, Atlanta; Mem. council Meth. World Conf.; chmn. bd. publs. A.M.E. Zion Ch.; pres. Kansas City (Mo.) Ministerial Alliance, 1956; mem. exec. com. Mo. Council Chs., 1961; mem. gen. bd. Nat. Council Chs., 1963; mem. exec. council St. Louis Interfaith Council, 1966. Chmn. bd. trustees Clinton Coll.; trustee Livingstone Coll.; mem. nat. council Minority Bus. Enterprise; v.p. bd. dirs. NAACP. Recipient Meritorious Service award Kansas City Coll., St. Louis Citizens award St. Louis Argus. Mem. Alpha Phi Alpha. Home: 3141 Pyrite Circle Atlanta GA 30331 Office: PO Box 41138 Ben Hill Station Atlanta GA 30331

MARSHALL, BRUCE THOMAS, minister; b. Quincy, Ill., Aug. 5, 1947; s. Floyd William and Frieda Vera (Dege) M.; m. Patricia Jeanne Creatura, Sept. 6, 1975; 1 child, Katherine. AB, Earlham Coll., Richmond, Ind., 1969; MA, Meadville Theol. Sch., Chgo., 1972; D of Ministry, Chgo. Theol. Sem., 1974. Ordained to ministry Unitarian Ch., 1975. Min. Unitarian Ch. of Flint, Mich., 1974-81, Unitarian Universalist Fellowship of Huntington, N.Y., 1981—; mem. Greenfield Group, 1982—. Author: A Holy Curiosity, 1990. Exec. com. Planned Parenthood, Suffolk County, N.Y., 1985-87, v.p., Flint, 1977-81; founding mem. Hospice of Flint, 1977-79, Meml. Soc. of Flint, 1977-81. Mem. Unitarian Universalist Mins. Assn. Democrat. Home: 53 Pilgrim Path Huntington NY 11743 Office: Unitarian Universalist Fellowship 109 Browns Rd Huntington NY 11743

MARSHALL, CAROLYN ANN M., church official, consultant; b. Springfield, Ill., July 18, 1935; d. Hayward Thomas and Isabelle Bernice (Hayer) McMurray; m. John Alan Marshall, July 14, 1956 (dec. Sept. 1990); children: Margaret Marshall Bushman, Cynthia Marshall Kyrouac, Clinton, Carol. Student, De Pauw U., 1952-54; BSBA, Drake U., 1956; D of Pub. Svc. (hon.), De Pauw U., 1983; LHD (hon.), U. Indpls., 1990. Corp. sec. Marshall Studios, Inc., Veedersburg, Ind., 1956-89, exec. cons., 1989—; sec. Gen. Conf., lay leader South Ind. conf. United Meth. Ch., 1988—; Carolyn M. Marshall chair in women's studies, women's div. Gen. Bd. Global Ministries United Meth. Ch., Bennett Coll., Greensboro, 1988; cons. Lucille Raines Residence, Indpls., 1977—. Pres. Fountain Cen. Band Boosters, Veedersburg, 1975-77; del. Gen. Conf., United Meth. Ch., 1980, 84, 88, pres. women's div. Gen. Bd. Global Ministries, 1984-88; bd. dirs. Franklin (Ind.) United Meth. Home, 1988—. Carolyn McMurray Marshall chair in women's studies established in her honor at Bennett Coll. by women's div. of Gen. Bd. Global Ministries, United Meth. Ch., 1988. Home: 204 N Newlin St Veedersburg IN 47987-1358

MARSHALL, CODY, bishop. Bishop No. Ill. Ch. of God in Christ, Chgo. Office: Ch of God in Christ 8836 Blackstone Chicago IL 60637*

MARSHALL, GEORGE NICHOLS, minister, author; b. Bozeman, Mont., July 4, 1920; s. James Wallace and Grace (Nichols) M.; m. Barbara Ambrose, June 14, 1946 (div. 1966); 1 child, Charles Hopkinson. AB, Tufts U., 1940, STB, 1941, AM, 1943; MA, Columbia U., 1942; ThM, Harvard U., 1946; PhD, Walden U., 1976; DD, Meadville/Lombard Theol. Sch., 1976. Ordained to ministry Unitarian Ch., 1941. Pastor, Natick, Mass., 1941-43, Plymouth, Mass., 1946-52, Niagara Falls, N.Y., 1952-60; pastor Ch. of Larger Fellowship, Boston, 1960-85, minister emeritus, 1985—. Author: Church of the Pilgrim Fathers, 1950, Unitarian Universalism as a Way of Life, 1966 (revised as Challenge of A Liberal Faith, 1979, 3d edit., 1988), An Understanding of Albert Schweitzer, 1966, (with David Poling) Schweitzer, A Biography, 1970, new edit., 1989, Facing Death and Grief, 1981, (biography) Buddha, His Quest for Serenity, 1978, 2d edit., 1990; co-author: Encounters with Eternity, 1986, rev. edit. under title How Different Religions View Death and Afterlife, 1991, Introduction to Hibakusha, 1986, A. Powell Davies and His Times, 1990. Recipient Gustavus Myers Ctr. award U. Ark., 1991. Assoc. dir. dept. extension Unitarian-Universalist Assn., 1960-70; treas. Unitarian Ministers Assn., 1954-56; chmn. Unitarian Commn. Ch. and Returning Servicemen, 1944-46; sec. Commn. Unitarian Universalist Union, 1949-53, Council Liberal Chs., 1953-55; pres. Niagara Falls Religious Fellowship, 1950-52. Bd. dirs. N.Y. chpt. Americans for Democratic Action, 1955-56; pres. Niagara County Planned Parenthood Assn., 1953-59, mem. N.Y. State bd., 1955-59; chmn. Unitarian Universalist Commn. Scouting; mem. Boy Scouts Am., 1960-70; del. White House Conf. Against Discrimination, 1958; program chmn. Albert Schweitzer Fellowship, N.Y.C., 1972—. Capt. USAAF, 1943-46. Recipient Freedom House award of merit, 1949. Mem. Albert Schweitzer World Confedn. (sec.), Am. Friends of Albert Schweitzer. Home: 233 Summerwalk Cir Chapel Hill NC 27514

MARSHALL, JEFFREY ALLAN, minister, principal; b. Wilkensburg, Pa., Sept. 25, 1959; s. Edward Harry and Clara May (Bichsel) M.; m. Cathy Diane Alston, July 1, 1983; children: Katie-Sarai, J. Micah. BA in Social Work, Asbury Coll., Wilmore, Ky., 1982. Licensed to ministry Assembly of God, 1985. Asst. pastor Full Gospel Ch. of Carnegie, Pa., 1984-89; pastor singles South Hills Assembly of God, Bethel Park, Pa., 1989—; prin. Hillcrest Christian Sch., Bethel Park, 1989—; worship leader South Hills Assembly of God; guest preacher Pa.-Del. Dist. Assembly of God. Rep. Ky. Intercollegiate State Legis., 1980-82. Mem. HIS Schs. Republican. Home: 211 Adeline Ave Pittsburgh PA 15228 Office: Hillcrest Christian Sch 2500 Bethel Church Rd Bethel Park PA 15102

MARSHALL, JOHN ALOYSIUS, bishop; b. Worcester, Mass., Apr. 26, 1928; s. John A. and Katherine T. (Redican) M. A.B. cum laude, Holy Cross Coll., Worcester, 1949; postgrad., Sem. de Philosophie, Montreal, Can., 1949-50; S.T.L., Pontifical Gregorian U., Rome, 1954; M.A. in Guidance and Psychology, Assumption Coll., Worcester, 1964. Ordained priest Roman Catholic Ch., 1953, consecrated bishop, 1972; parish priest in Mass., 1954-57; asst. vice rector Pontifical N. Am. Coll., 1957-61; instr. Acad. Sacred Heart, Worcester, 1961-62, St. Vincent Hosp. Sch. Nursing, Worcester, 1961-62; headmaster St. Stephen Cath. High Sch., Worcester, 1962-68; spiritual dir. Pontifical N. Am. Coll., 1968-71, bus. mgr., 1969-71; bishop of Burlington Vt., 1972—; chmn. com. priestly formation Nat. Conf. Cath. Bishops, 1975-78. Bd. dirs. Champlain Coll., Burlington, from 1974, Wadhams Hall, Ogdensburg, N.Y., from 1974. Address: Chancery Office 351 North Ave Burlington VT 05401

MARSHALL, JUDY K., lay worker; b. L.A., Apr. 19, 1958; d. Gregory and Mary Cal-Ida (Linn) M. Student, Concordia Luth. Coll., 1976, 77, Moorpark Coll., 1977-79, St. Louis U., 1979, 80. Tchr. Sunday sch. Luth. Ch., Thousand Oaks, Calif., 1986-90; co-leader Conejo Valley Luth. Singles, Thousand Oaks, 1987-89; leader Conejo Valley Luth. Singles, Thousand Oaks, Calif., 1989-90; sec. Luth. Ch.-Mo. Synod Singles Ministry, 1989-90; cons. Pacific S.W. Dist. Luth. Ch.-Mo. Synod, Irvine, Calif., 1990—; owner Wine & Roses Catering, Newbury Park, Calif., 1985—; co-dir. Single Retreat, Luth. Ch.-Mo. Synod, Thousand Oaks, 1985-90; sec. ch. coun. Redeemer Luth., Thousand Oaks, 1986-89. Vol. Hospice of Conejo, Thousand Oaks, 1982-83, Big Bros./Big Sisters, Thousand Oaks, 1985, Luth. Social Svcs., Thousand Oaks, 1988-90, Zoe Christian Ctr. for Homeless, 1990. Democrat. Home: 4265 Greenwood St Newbury Park CA 91320 Office: Wine & Roses Catering 4265 Greenwood St Newbury Park CA 91320

MARSHALL, MURRAY MARK, JR., minister; b. Denison, Tex., Dec. 26, 1918; s. Murray Mark and Alta Pearl (Cagle) M.; m. Reccie Geraldine Taylor, Aug. 31, 1945; children: Murray Malcolm, Marilyn. BA, Abilene Christian U., 1940; MA, Ea. N.Mex. U., 1950. Ordained to ministry Ch. of Christ, 1936. Min. Marlin (Tex.) Ch. of Christ, 1941-43; min. Groom (Tex.) Ch. of Christ, 1944-46, Overton Rd. Ch. of Christ, Dallas, 1955-62, Union City (Ga.) Ch. of Christ, 1962-65, Southside Ch. of Christ, Ennis, Tex., 1976—; devotional speaker Ennis Odd Fellows, 1980—. Author: Our New Testament: An Appreciation, 1972, Reasons to Believe, 1977; contbr. articles to religious periodicals. Republican. Home: 2700 Linda Dr Ennis TX 75119 Office: Southside Ch of Christ 2700 Linda Dr Ennis TX 75119-7618

MARSHALL, RICH JAMES, minister; b. Wymore, Nebr., May 2, 1944; s. Virgil Ralph and Laverne D. (Vrodman) M.; m. Wilma Dea Coop, June 18, 1965; children: Rich II, Valerie. BA, Nebr. Christian Coll., 1966. Pastor Wildewood Christian Ch., Ralson, Nebr., 1965-67, West Hill Christian Ch., Portland, Oreg., 1967-69, Knoot Ave. Christian Ch., Anaheim, Calif., 1969-77; assoc. pastor Los Gatos (Calif.) Christian Ch., 1977-79; pastor Crossroads Bible Ch., San Jose, Calif., 1979—; bd. dirs. OC Internat., Milpitas, Calif., Harvest Evangelism, San Jose; bd. dirs., chmn. Pacific Christian Coll., Fullerton, Calif. Speaker tape series, How to Pray, 1989, Giving God's Way, 1989, Reaching Silicon Sam, 1990, Victory of Christ, 1990. Recipient Disting. Alumni award Nebr. Christian Coll., Norfolk. Republican. Office: Crossroads Bible Ch 1670 Moor Park San Jose CA 95128

MARSHALL, ROBERT JAMES, church executive; b. Burlington, Iowa, Aug. 26, 1918; s. Robert McCray and Margaret Emma (Gysin) M.; m. Alice Johanna Hepner, Feb. 6, 1943; children: Robert Edward, Margaret Alice Niederer. A.B., Wittenberg U., 1941; B.D., Chgo. Luth. Theol. Sem., 1944; postgrad., U. Chgo., 1949-52; D.D., Carthage Coll., 1961, Wittenberg U., 1963, Northwestern Luth. Sem., 1969, Waterloo U., 1970; L.H.D., Gettysburg Coll., 1965; LL.D., Augustana Coll., 1968, Wagner Coll., 1968, Muhlenberg Coll., 1969, Upsala Coll., 1969, Wittenberg U., 1969; S.T.D., Thiel Coll., 1971; J.C.D., Susquehanna U., 1969; Litt.D., Roanoke Coll., 1970; Lit.D., Newberry Coll., 1972; D. Theol., St. Olaf Coll., 1974. Ordained to ministry Lutheran Ch., 1944; pastor Grace Luth. Ch., Alhambra, Calif., 1944-47; instr. religion Muhlenberg (Pa.) Coll., 1947-49, head dept. religion, 1952-53; prof. O.T. interpretation Chgo. Luth. Theol. Sem., Maywood, Ill., 1953-62; pres. Ill. Synod Luth. Ch. in Am., 1962-68, Luth. Ch. in Am., N.Y.C., 1968-78; dir. mission, service and devel. Luth. World Ministries, 1978-80; prof. O.T., Luth. Theol. So. Sem., Columbia, S.C., 1981—; Mem. exec. com. Luth. World Fedn., 1968-78; mem. central com., exec. com. World Council Chs., 1968-80, commn. on inter-ch. aid, refugees and world service, 1980—; mem. governing bd. Nat. Council Chs. of Christ in U.S.A., 1968-78, 85-87; mem. Commn. for a New Luth. Ch., 1982-86; mem. exec. com. Luth. Council in U.S.A., 1968-78; bd. dirs. Luth. World Relief, 1968—, pres., 1980—, mem. exec. council, 1964-68; chmn. on Evang. Luth. Ch. Am., 1963-64, mem. ch. council, standing com. on ecumenical affairs, 1987—; mem. ch. world service com. Nat. Council Chs., 1978—, chmn., 1985-87; mem. adv. com. vol. fgn. aid AID, 1979—, vice chmn.,

1981—; ann. prof. Am. Sch. Oriental Research, Jerusalem, 1958-59; exec. bd. Chgo. Conf. on Religion and Race, 1964-68. Author: The Mighty Acts of God. Bd. dirs. Grand View Coll., 1966-68, Augustana Coll., 1963-68, Luth. Sch. Theology, 1963-68, Augustana Hosp., Chgo., 1963-68, Luth. Hosp., Moline, Ill., 1963-68, Wheat Ridge Found., 1984—. Mem. Chgo. Soc. Bibl. Research (sec. 1962-68), Nat. Assn. Profs. Hebrew, Soc. Bibl. Lit. and Exegesis, Am. Bible Soc. (bd. mgrs. 1968-80). Office: 4201 N Main St Columbia SC 29203 *Travel lightly through this world. Stay free for each new calling, determined according to the need defined by others and life's purpose defined by yourself. Live gratefully and work faithfully with those committed to a common good.*

MARTENS, LARRY D., academic administrator. Pres. Mennonite Brethren Biblical Sem., Fresno, Calif. Office: Mennonite Brethren Biblical Sem 4824 E Butler at Chestnut Ave Fresno CA 93727*

MARTENSEN, HANS LUDVIG, bishop. Bishop of Copenhagen, Roman Cath. Ch. Office: Katolsk Bispekontor, Bredgade 69a, 1260 Copenhagen Denmark*

MAR THOMA, ALEXANDER, head of religious order. Met. Mar Thoma Syrian Ch. of Malabar, Kerala, India. Office: Mar Thoma Sabba Office, Tiruvalla 689-101, Poolatheen Kerala India*

MARTIAN, DAN LEONARD, minister; b. Yakima, Wash., Mar. 10, 1959; s. Leonard and Marie Ann (Odle) M. AA, Northwest Coll., 1980; BA in Communication, Wash. State U., 1983; MDiv., Louisville Presbyn. Sem., 1989. Ordained min. Presbyn. Ch. Youth coord. Mt. Baker Pk. Presbyn. Ch., Seattle, 1984-85; chaplain Humana Univ. Hosp., Louisville, 1986; intern pastor Terrace Heights Presbyn., Yakima, 1987-88; student pastor Sharon Presbyn. Ch., Augusta, Ky., 1988-89; pastor Rennerdale Presbyn. Ch., Carnegie, Pa., 1989—. Tv camera operator Ednl. TV, Yakima, 1978; crisis line counselor Crisis Line, Yakima, 1988. Republican.

MARTIN, ANGELIQUE MARIE, evangelist; b. Glendale, Ariz., Jan. 11, 1954; d. Clifford Leonard Scott and Quint Etta (Roberson) Willis; m. Robert Joseph Martin, Sept. 29, 1973 (div. 1977); 1 child, Lavena Jaime. Grad. high sch., San Francisco, 1972. Customer support rep. IBM Corp., San Francisco, 1973—. Democrat. Home: 4429 San Carlos Ave Oakland CA 94601

MARTIN, CATHERINE, religious educator; b. Phila., Oct. 24, 1948; d. Andreas Harold and Catherine Josephine (Wawrzyniak) Dambach; m. Robert Edgar Martin, Oct. 24, 1981. BS in Biology magna cum laude, Alvernia Coll., Reading, Pa., 1971; MA in Adminstrn., Supervision, Seton Hall U., South Orange, N.J., 1984; MPhil in Sociology of Religion, Drew U., Madison, N.J., 1989, PhD in Sociology of Religion. Tchr. Allentown (Pa.) Cen. Cath. High Sch., 1971-73, Little Flower High Sch., Phila., 1973-75; prin. St. Cecilia High Sch., Kearny, N.J., 1976-78; co-dir. Nat. Renew Office, Archdiocese of Newark, 1978-81; dir. religious formation St. Raphael Parish, Livingston, N.J., 1982—. Author: Renew Leadership Book, 1982; contbr. articles to profl. jours. Mem. Am. Acad. Religion, N.J. Dirs. of Religion Edn. Assn. Home: 62 Hemlock Rd Little Falls NJ 07424 Office: St Raphael Parish 346 E Mt Pleasant Ave Livingston NJ 07039

MARTIN, CHARLES WADE, pastor; b. Athens, Ga., June 7, 1952; s. William Edward and Winifred (Maxwell) M.; m. Rebecca Hankins, May 26, 1973; children: John Wade, Elizabeth Lynn. BA, Asbury Coll., 1974; MDiv, Asbury Theol. Sem., 1977, MA in Religion, 1977; postgrad. in hist. geography of Palestine, Inst. Holy Land Studies, 1977; postgrad. in audience psychology and behavior, Wheaton Grad. Sch., 1981, postgrad. in principles of rsch., 1982-83; DMin in Preaching and Worship, Fuller Theol. Sem., 1982; postgrad. in missiology and cultural anthropology, Trinity Evangelical Div. Sch., 1986-87, D in Missiology, 1989; postgrad. in missiology and cultural anthropology, Ft. Wayne Bible Coll., 1987. Lic. to preach by United Meth. Ch., 1972; ordained deacon United Meth. Ch., 1975; ordained elder United Meth. Ch., 1978; ordained to ministry First Bapt. Ch., 1983. Pulpit supply preacher Statesboro Dist. United Meth. Ch., 1970-72, pulpit supply preacher Ky. Annual Conf., 1972-77; pastor Mt. Moriah United Meth. Ch., Matthews, Ga., 1977-80; staff min. in youth work and leadership devel. First United Meth. Ch., Sylvania, Ga., 1981-83; co-pastor Black Creek United Meth. Ch., Newington, Ga., 1982-87; interim pastor Little Horse Creek Bapt. Ch., Woodcliff, Ga., 1986-87, pastor, 1987—; exec. dir. Evan. Ministries of Sylvania, Inc., 1978—; tour escort to Israel, 1979, Israel and Egypt, 1981, Greece, 1982; interim Bible tchr., First Bapt. Ch., Sylvania, 1983-84. Contbr. articles to profl. jours. Avocations: archaeology, linguistics, social psychology, human development, educational psychology. Home: 206 Pinecrest Dr Sylvania GA 30467 Office: Evang Ministries Sylvania PO Box 1664 Sylvania GA 30467 *True life is measured by quality, not by quantity. The Christian should ask, "How much can I be like Christ?" not "How little can I be like Christ and still make it?" The answer to the first question is found in Christian holiness. The answer to the second question is found in the carnal Christian.*

MARTIN, DALE ROSS, clergyman; b. Johnson City, Tenn., Sept. 16, 1935; s. Horace Oval and Golda P. (Hicks) M.; m. Daris B. Martin, June 7, 1959; 1 child, Darlene Martin Lane. BA, Carson Newman Coll., 1959; MDiv, Southeastern Bapt. Theol. Sem., 1964. Ordained to ministry Bapt. Ch., 1956. Minister chs. in N.C. and Tenn., 1956-80, Calvary Bapt. Ch., Reidsville, N.C., 1980—; Chaplain Vets. Hosp.; mem. gen. bd. N.C. Bapt. State Conv.; mem. exec. com. Tenn. Bapt. Conv. Home and Office: Calvary Bapt Ch Rt 8 Box 341 Reidsville NC 27320-8841 *When we think of all the great philosophies in the world, perhaps the most profound is, "Jesus loves me, this I know."*

MARTIN, DANNY DAVID, religious organization administrator; b. Spokane, Wash., Mar. 24, 1946; s. David John Camac and Leona Bessie (Newman) M.; m. Joan Eleanor Kimball, Aug. 23, 1968; children: Scott Camac, Andrew Glenn, Amy Kathleen. BA, Simpson Bible Coll., 1968; MDiv, Trinity Evang. Div. Sch., 1971; PhD, Somerset (Eng.) U., 1990. Exec. dir. Job Therapy, Seattle, 1973-78; dir. internat. pers. World Concern, Seattle, 1978-81; Asia coord. World Relief Corp., Wheaton, Ill., 1981-82; pres. Mission to Unreached Peoples, Kent, WA, 1982—; bd. ref. Issachar, Lynnwood, Wash., 1984—; assoc. dir. Tentmaker Internat. Exch., 1991; bd. dirs. United Mission to Nepal, 1990—. Author: Career Planning Kit, 1984, The Gift of Work, 1990. Named Citizen of the Day, KIXI Radio, Seattle, 1979. Mem. World Evang. Fellowship, Evang. Fgn. Missions Assn., Assn. Internat. Mission Svcs. Office: Mission to Unreached Peoples 19309 West Valley Hwy #R-102 Kent WA 98020 *There is no cause to which one can commit one's life that can compare with communicating the good news of Christ through world and deed to those without knowledge of the Savior.*

MARTIN, DAVIS CARNEY, religion educator; b. Elizabeth City, N.C., Feb. 6, 1923; s. D.C. Sr. and Ida (Roughton) M.; m. Carolyn Galloway M., May 17, 1946; Jonny, Greg, Carol Janeen. BA, Wake Forest U., 1943; ThM, Southwestern Sem., 1946, MRE, 1953; ThD, New Orleans Sem., 1967. Prof. Grand Canyon U., Phoenix, 1952-60; dean st. affairs William Carey Coll., Hattiesburg, Miss., 1966-71; prof., chmn. dept. Christian studies Grand Canyon U., Phoenix, 1971—. Author (Bible commentaries) Joshua, Judges, & Ruth, 1980, Habakkuk, Jeremiah, Lamentations, 1985, I Kings, 1987. Republican. Baptist. Avocation: woodworking. Office: Grand Canyon U PO Box 11097 Phoenix AZ 85061-1097

MARTIN, DEAN MONROE, religion and philosophy educator; b. Lebanon, Mo., Aug. 4, 1942; s. Francis V. and Monta V. (Butcher) M.; m. Delores Ann Burson, Mar. 27, 1965; children: William Todd, Aron Monroe. BA, William Jewell Coll., 1964; BD, Yale U., 1967; PhD, Baylor U., 1972; postgrad. Duke U., summer 1976, Univ. Coll. Swansea (Wales), summer, 1981, Yale U., fall 1985. Instr. U.S. Internat. U., San Diego, 1971-72, asst. prof., 1972-74; asst. prof. religion and philosophy Campbell U., Buies Creek, N.C., 1974-78, assoc. prof., 1978—, chmn. humanities div., 1982-86; interim pastor various Baptist Chs.; deacon Buies Creek 1st Bapt. Ch. Contbr. articles in profl. jours. Past pres. PTA; coach Little League Baseball. Mem. Am. Acad. Religion, Soc. Christian Philosophers, Assn. Bapt. Profs. of Religion, Soc. for Philosophy Religion, Bapt. Assn. Philosophy Tchrs., Lambda Chi Alpha, Omicron Delta Kappa. Republican.

MARTIN, DEMAS BUNYAN, minister; b. Maverick, Tex., Apr. 6, 1934; s. Samuel Jack and Queenie (Stinebagh) M.; m. Margaret Josephine Thornton, June 6, 1957; children: Samuel T., Timothy A., David E. BA, Baylor U., 1956; BD, Southwestern Bapt. Theol. Sem., Ft. Worth, 1963, MDiv, 1973; D Ministry, Luther Rice Sem., Jacksonville, Fla., 1981. Ordained to ministry So. Bapt. Conv., 1958; cert. hosp. chaplain. Pastor youth Trinity Bapt. Ch., Ft. Worth, 1957-58; pastor Indian Creek Bapt. Ch., Mineral Wells, Tex., 1958-63, 1st Bapt. Ch., Huron, Ohio, 1963-66, Lakeside Bapt. Ch., McMurray, Pa., 1966-71, Southside Bapt. Ch., Mt. Holly, N.J., 1971-74, Calvary Bapt. Ch., Ft. Wayne, Ind., 1974-79, Marion Avenue Bapt. Ch., Aurora, Ill., 1980-90, Natural Bridge (Va.) Bapt. Ch., 1990—; home missionary home mission bd. So. Bapt. Conv., Mt. Holly, 1971-74. Author: Forgiving Others, 1981. Recipient award for fast ch. growth So. Bapt. Conv., 1977. Mem. Southwestern Bapt. Theol. Sem. Alumni Assn. (pres. Ind. 1976). Home: Rte 2 Box 504D Natural Bridge VA 24578 Office: Natural Bridge Bapt Ch PO Box 35 Natural Bridge VA 24578 *The most exciting thing about life I know is that it doesn't have to end. Jesus solved the guilt and fear of death problems through His cross and resurrection. By personal faith in Jesus we have the hope of eternal life.*

MARTIN, DENNIS MICHAEL, Bible studies educator; b. Dallas, Apr. 8, 1952; s. D.I. and Virginia Ruth (Sanders) M.; m. Beth Markham, June, 1975; children: Philip Michael, Garrett Emerson. BA, Dallas Baptist Coll., 1974; M Div., Southwestern Sem., 1977, PhD, 1980; postgrad. Yeshiva U., N.Y., U. Pa., U. Tübingen, Fed. Republic Germany. Adj. prof. Southwestern Sem., Ft. Worth, 1977-80; instr. Golden Gate Sem., Mill Valley, Calif., 1980-81, asst. prof., 1984-89. assoc. prof., 1989—; assoc. prof. Calif. Baptist Coll., Riverside, 1981-84. Mem. Soc. Bibl. Lit., Nat. Assn. Bapt. Profs. Religion, Inst. for Bibl. Rsch. Office: Golden Gate Sem Strawberry Point Mill Valley CA 94941

MARTIN, DOUGLAS, broadcast executive; b. Owatonnc, Minn., Mar. 25, 1955; s. Howard Edward Martin and Lavon Eloise (Keck) Bonham; m. Mary Ruth Martin, Aug. 22, 1981; children: Joshua, Kristen, Rebeccah, Peter. BA in Mgmt., U. Phoenix, 1987. Disc jockey Sta. KKTY, Albuquerque, 1979-80, account exec., 1980-81, 1981-82, gen. mgr., 1982-85; pres. Good News Communications, Tucson, 1985—. V.p., music min. Calvary Chapel, Tucson, 1986—; bd. dirs. Youth for Christ, Tucson, 1986-87, Fellowship Christian Athletes, Tucson, 1988-89; pres. Lightline. With USN, 1974-75. Recipient Cert. of Appreciation, State of N.Mex., Alburquerque, 1983, 84. Mem. Christian Broadcasters Assn. (pres. 1988—), Media Fellowships of Tucson (pres.), Tucson Broadcasters Assn., Tucson Advt. Club. Republican. Avocations: windsurfing, skiing, mountain biking, basketball, music. Office: Good News Communications 3222 S Richie Tucson AZ 85713

MARTIN, ERNEST LEE, academic administrator; b. Meeker, Okla., Apr. 20, 1932; s. Joel Chester and Lula Mae (Quinn) M.; m. Helen Rose Smith, Aug. 26, 1957 (div. 1980); children: Kathryn, Phylliss, Samuel; m. Ramona Jean Kensey, June 27, 1987. BA, Ambassador Coll., 1958, MA, 1960, PhD, 1966. Dean faculty Ambassador Coll., St. Albans, Eng., 1960-72; chmn. dept. theology Ambassador Coll., Pasadena, Calif., 1972-74; dir. Found. for Bibl. Rsch., Pasadena, 1974-84, Acad. for Scriptural Knowledge, Portland, 1985—. Author: Birth of Christ Recalculated, 1980, The Original Bible Restored, 1984, Secrets of Golgotha, 1987, The Star That Astonished the World, 1991. Tech. sgt. USAF, 1950-54. Mem. SBL, Palestine Exploration Assn. Home: PO Box 25000 Portland OR 97225 Office: Acad for Scriptural Knowledge 4804 SW Scholls Ferry Rd Portland OR 97225 *Christianity is the teaching that all humanity is destined to be reconciled to God, and that is my prime philosophical belief.*

MARTIN, GARY DEWAYNE, clergyman; b. Hemet, Calif., Jan. 16, 1954; s. James Robert and Jewell Ilene (Rogers) M.; m. Nancy Elizabeth Young, Aug. 11, 1973; children: Anna Louise, Erin Elizabeth. BA, Calif. Bapt. Coll., 1976; M. Religious Edn., Golden Gate Sem., 1982; postgrad., Luther Rice Sem., 1989—. Ordained minister in Bapt. Ch., 1976. Assoc. pastor Valle Vista Bapt. Ch., Hemet, 1972-76; pastor First Bapt. Ch., Gustine, Calif., 1976-77; assoc. pastor Calvary Bapt. Ch., Modesto, Calif., 1977-80; pastor Santa Cruz Ave. Bapt. Ch., Modesto, Calif., 1981-86, First Bapt. Ch., Winton, Calif., 1986—; instr. Calvary Bible Inst., Modesto, 1984-86, Cen. Valley Sem. Extension, Turlock, Calif., 1987—, dir. 1988—. Vice-moderator Cen. Valley Bapt. Assn., Turlock, 1986-87; asst. dir. Bapt. Dist. Children's Camps, Jenness Park, Sonora, Calif., 1986—. Named Outstanding Young man in Am., U.S. Jaycees, Montgomery, Ala., 1986. Democrat. Avocations: reading, woodworking, basketball, long distance running. Home: 7289 N Anne Circle Winton CA 95388 Office: First Southern Baptist Ch 7264 W Myrtle Ave Winton CA 95388

MARTIN, JACK ELMO, minister; b. Yellow Springs, Ohio, Oct. 20, 1936; s. Albert E. and Minnie J. (Peterson) M.; m. Zemeta Ruth Robbins, Apr. 9, 1961; children: John A., Deborah G. B Sacred Lit., AB, Cin. Bible Sem., 1958, BTh., 1959. Ordained to ministry Christian Ch., 1959. Pastor Christian Ch., Miami, Okla., 1959-61, Springfield, Mo., 1961-63, Bethel, Ohio, 1963-71, Orlando, Fla., 1971-79, Broken Arrow, Okla., 1979-88, Apache Junction, Ariz., 1988—; dir. N.Am. Christian Conv., 1974-84, Christ In Youth, Joplin, Mo., 1965—; pres. Fla. State Conv., 1978, Okla. State Conv., 1987. Contbr. articles to profl. jours. Home: 6128 E Boston Mesa AZ 85205 Office: Community Christian Church 1150 W Superstition Apache Junction AZ 85220

MARTIN, JACQUES CARDINAL, archbishop; b. Amiens, France, Aug. 26, 1908. Ordained priest Roman Cath. Ch., 1934. Elected bishop of Nablus Palestine, 1964; elevated to archbishop, 1986, created cardinal,, 1988. Address: 00120 Vatican City Vatican City

MARTIN, JAMES ALFRED, JR., religious studies educator; b. Lumberton, N.C., Mar. 18, 1917; s. James Alfred and Mary (Jones) M.; m. Ann Bradsher, June 1, 1936 (dec. 1982); m. Nell Gifford, Jan. 6, 1984. A.B., Wake Forest Coll., 1937, Litt.D. (hon.), 1965; M.A., Duke U., 1938; Ph.D., Columbia U., 1944; student, Union Theol. Sem., 1940-43; M.A. (hon.), Amherst Coll., 1950. Ordained to ministry Bapt. Ch., 1944; asst. pastor Roxboro (N.C.) Ch., 1937-38; instr. philosophy and psychology Wake Forest Coll., 1938-40; asst. philosophy religion Union Theol. Sem., N.Y.C., 1941-44; Danforth prof. religion in higher edn. Union Theol. Sem., 1960-67, adj. prof. philosophy religion, 1967-82; prof. religion Columbia U., 1967-82, prof. emeritus, 1982—, chmn. dept., 1968-77; asst. prof. religion Amherst Coll., 1946-47, asso. prof., 1947-50, prof., 1950-54, Marquand and Stone prof., 1954-57, Crosby prof. religion, 1957-60; ordained deacon P.E. Ch., 1953; vis. prof. Cornell U., summer 1948, Mt. Holyoke Coll., 1949-50, 52-53, 59-60, State U. Iowa, summer 1959, U. N.C., summer 1964; Univ. prof. Wake Forest U., 1984—; vis. prof. religious studies U. Va., 1984; asso. mem. East-West Philosophers Conf., U. Hawaii, 1949. Author: Empirical Philosophies of Religion, 1944, (with J.A. Hutchison) Ways of Faith, 1953, rev., 1960, Fact, Fiction, and Faith, 1960, The New Dialogue between Philosophy and Theology, 1966, Beauty and Holiness, 1990; contbr. articles to profl. jours. and encys., chpts. to books. Chmn. bd. visitors Wake Forest Coll., 1981-83. Served as lt. chaplain USNR, 1944-46, PTO. Recipient Disting. Alumnus award Wake Forest U., 1971. Mem. Soc. Values in Higher Edn. (Kent fellow, pres. 1964-69), Am. Theol. Soc. (v.p. 1981-82, pres. 1982), Soc. Theol. Discussion, Soc. Philosophy of Religion, Phi Beta Kappa, Omicron Delta Kappa, Pi Kappa Alpha. Home: PO Box 6746 Winston-Salem NC 27109-6746 *My experience of life has increasingly underscored the central importance of honesty-in understanding of oneself, and in perceptions of and relations to others. The quest for honesty entails a relentless and often painful search for truth. Acceptance of truth, and of others as they truly are, requires grace. The goal is to speak the truth in love.*

MARTIN, JAMES LUTHER, JR., clergyman, former educator; b. Lone Wolf, Okla., July 22, 1917; s. James Luther and Nora Belle (Williams) M. A.B., Oklahoma City U., 1938; B.D., Yale U., 1941, Ph.D., 1951; fellow, Fund Advancement Edn., Cambridge U., 1954-55. Ordained to ministry Meth. Ch., 1944; asst. pastor St. John's Meth. Ch., New Rochelle, N.Y., 1941-43; pastor Port Jefferson (N.Y.) Meth. Ch., 1943-46; asso. prof. dept. philosophy and religion Coll. Idaho, 1946-55, prof., 1955-57, chmn. dept., 1951-57; prof. religion Denison U., 1957-85, chmn., 1957-63, 67-73, coordinator non-Western studies, 1965-75, chmn. senate, 1972-73; mem. Consultation on Religion in S. India. Contbr. to scholarly publs. Asso. dir. leadership tng. sch., nat. student YM and YWCA, Berkeley, Calif., 1953; nat. adv. bd. student YMCA, 1956-57; chmn. Northwest Conf. Religion in Higher Edn., 1956. Am. Inst. Indian Studies fellow Poona, Madras, India, 1963-64. Mem. Assn. for Asian Studies, Am. Acad. Religion, AAUP, ACLU, Internat. Assn. for Tamil Research, Internat. Assn. Buddhist Studies. Democrat. Home: 20 Samson Pl Granville OH 43023

MARTIN, J(AMES) PHILLIP, church official; b. Huntsville, Ala., Mar. 4, 1952; s. John Paul and Marguerite (James) M.; m. Gloria L. Little, June 23, 1973; children: Lauren, Andrea. B in Mus. Edn., Samford U., 1974; MA in Religious Edn., Southwestern Bapt. Theol. Sem., 1976, MA, 1983. Ordained to ministry So. Bapt. Conv.; cert. ch. bus. adminstr. Minister edn. and music 1st Bapt. Ch., Richmond, Tex., 1976-78; minister edn. South Avondale Bapt. Ch., Birmingham, Ala., 1978-82; ministry edn. adminstrn. 1st Bapt. Ch. Chamblee, Atlanta, 1982-86; sr. educator, adminstr. South Main Bapt. Ch., Houston, 1986—. Named Outstanding Young Man of Am., Jaycees, 1975. Fellow Nat. Assn. Ch. Bus. Adminstrn. (pres. So. Bapt. Ch. div.); mem. Ea. Bapt. Religion Edn. Assn., So. Bapt. Religious Educators. Office: South Main Bapt Ch 4100 Main St Houston TX 77002

MARTIN, JAMES TURNER, JR., minister; b. Little Rock, July 20, 1953; s. James T. and Polly (Burks) M.; m. Charlotte Maye Coil, Aug. 11, 1978; children: Christine, Jamie. BA in Bus., U. North Tex., 1976; BA in Bible, Internat. Bible Coll., Florence, Ala., 1978; MDiv, Abilene Christian U., 1982; DMin, Harding Grad. Sch. Religion, Memphis, 1985. Min. Coll. Ch. of Christ, Florence, 1982-90, Gladstone Ch. of Christ, Kansas City, Mo., 1990—. Office: Gladstone Ch of Christ 5703 N Flora Kansas City MO 64118

MARTIN, JERRY, clergyman; b. Canton, Ohio, Jan. 28, 1941; s. G.G. and Junita (Lawhorn) M.; m. Norma L. Howerton, 1965; children: Bruce, Eric, Melissa. BS, Evangel Coll., Springfield, Mo., 1967; MA in Christian Edn., Talbot Theol. Sem./Biola Coll., 1975. Ordained minister Bapt. Ch., 1974. Minister Christian edn., minister of youth Harbor Trinity Bapt. Ch., Costa Mesa, Calif., 1972-79; minister Christian edn. Bible Fellowship Ch., Ventura, Calif., 1979-85; minister high sch. students Grace Community Ch., Tempe, Ariz., 1985-86; minister Christian edn. Reinhardt Bible Ch., Dallas, 1986-91, 1st Bapt. Ch., Oxnard, Calif., 1991—; curriculum cons. Gospel Light Publs., 1974—; mem. faculty Congress on Christian Edn., Mexico City, summer 1991. Contbr. articles to profl. jours. Water safety instr. ARC, 1968—; bd. dirs. Tex. Sunday Sch. Assn., 1986—. Mem. So. Calif. Dirs. Christian Edn., Nat. Assn. Disr. Christian Edn. (bd. dirs.), Nat. Assn. Single Adult Leaders, Internat. Bible Soc. (seminar leader), Children's Christian Ministries Assn., Phi Mu Alpha Sinfonia. Avocations: photography, water sports, music, backpacking. Home: 936 W 5th St Oxnard CA 93030

MARTIN, JERRY D., minister; b. Tom Bean, Tex., July 20, 1935; s. Carl Haizlip and Una B. (Pruitt) M.; m. Donna Kay Heath, June 26, 1965; children: Chad Heath, Jordan Leighann. BA, Harding Coll., 1957; BD, Crozer Theol. Sem., 1966, ThM, 1970; D of Ministry, McCormick Theol. Sem., 1981. Ordained minister, 1970. Pastor Chicago Ave. Christian Ch., Columbus, Ohio, 1968-73, Boardman Christian Ch., Youngstown, Ohio, 1973-83, Cen. Christian Ch., Danville, Ill., 1983—. Mem. Am. Assn. Pastoral Counselors. Democrat. Avocations: tennis, reading, travel. Home: 503 Dennis Dr Danville IL 61832 Office: Cen Christian Ch 1101 N Vermilion Danville IL 61832

MARTIN, JOHN EDWARD, minister, retired educator; b. Niagara Falls, N.Y., May 22, 1930; s. Paul Preston and Dorothy Amelia (Wolcott) M.; m. Mary Louise Becker, Aug. 25, 1956 (dec. Apr. 1983); children: Alice Gretchen Martin Houseworth, Bonnie Beth Martin Padlo; m. Audrey Elizabeth Finley Foster, Dec. 30, 1984. BS, SUNY, Buffalo, 1957; MS, SUNY, 1962; cert., Wesley Theol. Sem., 1986. Ordained to ministry United Meth. Ch. as deacon, 1989. Pastor Owens Mills United Meth. Ch., Chemung, N.Y., 1977-79, Epworth United Meth. Ch., Elmira, N.Y., 1979-81, Erin and Sullivanville United Meth. Chs., Horseheads, N.Y., 1983-87, Pennellville (N.Y.) United Meth. Ch., 1987—; coord. communications Ont. dist. United Meth. Ch., Mexico, N.Y., 1988—. Editor ch. newsletters The Parish Paper, 1982-87, The Tie That Binds, 1987—. Staff sgt. USMC, 1950-52. Home and Office: County Rte 54 Pennellville NY 13132-0205

MARTIN, JOHN EMMETT, minister; b. Syracuse, N.Y., July 3, 1951; s. Emmett John and Judy (Knowles) M.; m. Nora Jean Marshall, July 24, 1991; children: Erin McKenna, Joshua Emmett, Christian Thomas. AAS, Alfred Ag. & Tech. Coll., Alfred, N.Y., 1971; BS in Biochemistry, Coll. Environ. Sci., Syracuse, N.Y., 1973; MDiv, Princeton Theol. Sem., 1979; postgrad., Wayne State U., Detroit, 1973-74, Coll. Environ. Sci. and Forestry, Syracuse, N.Y., 1974-76. Ordained to ministry Presbyn. Ch. (U.S.A.), 1979. Assoc. pastor Northminster Presbyn. Ch., Endwell, N.Y., 1979-83; pastor First Presbyn. Ch., Lowville, N.Y., 1983-90; organizing pastor W. Valley Presbyn. New Ch. Devel., Phoenix, 1990—; bd. dirs. VanderKamp Camp and Conf. Ctr., Cleveland, N.Y., 1983-86; spiritual care coord. Lewis County Hospice, Lowville, 1989-90; pres. Lewis County Ministerium, Lowville, 1988-90; del. to gen. assy. Presbyn. Ch. (USA), Salt Lake City, 1990; cons. conflict mgmt. Utica (N.Y.) Presbytery, 1986-90. Chmn. bd. Lewis County Head Start, Lowville, 1986-90; organizing com. Lewis County Friends of Hospice, 1988-89; mem. Crisis Task Force, Lowvill Acad., 1989-90; mem. Community Svcs. Bd., Lowville, 1983-90. Mem. Alban Inst., Bread for the World. Democrat. Office: W Valley Presbyn NCD 2707 N 115th Ave Phoenix AZ 85039 *As long as one neighbor cares about another neighbor, there is hope for this world.*

MARTIN, JOHN GOVERNOR, minister; b. Aiken, S.C., Jan. 4, 1929; s. Booker T. and Essie (Thompson) M.; m. Ruth Collins, Feb. 1965; children: Walter John, Devadia M.; m. Annette Martin. BS, S.C. State Coll., 1950; MS, Howard U., 1956, MDiv, 1972; postgrad., Christian Theol. Sem., 1965. Ordained to ministry So. Bapt. Conv., 1966. Chief chemist Children's Hosp., Washington, 1958-60; enzyme researcher Dr. Jacob J. Weinstein's Lab. Washington Hosp. Ctr., Washington, 1959-60; statistician Bapt. Ministers Conf., Washington, 1968—; pastor Holy Comforter Bapt. Ch., Washington, 1972—; host, moderator WYCB-AM radio, Washington, 1981—; mem. debit mgmt. staff Supreme Life Ins., Washington, 1978—. Author: Nature and Chemical Changes in the Human Body of Vital Importance in Health and Disease, 1960, The Christian Concept in Crisis, 1965, Redirecting Health Care Scientists to Evolutionary Chemistry and Biological Synthese, 1981, Cosmic Science, 1985, Health and Cosmology, 1985; (case study) Robert L. Lindsay October 1980 through October 1986; over 700 written sermons; contbr. med. articles to profl. jours. Candidate for councilman-at- large Washington, 1976, for chairmanship city coun., 1978; chmn. religious com. of D.C. Host Com., U.S. Presdl. Inaugural, 1977; founder, exec. dir. Third World Assembly and Polit. Party, Washington, 1979—, candidate for pres. of U.S., 1980, 84, 88; mem. Washington Mayors Budget Adv. Com., 1982— (econ. adv. com. 1985-87). Staff sgt. USAF, 1950-54. Decorated Grand Coun. Confed. Chivalry, Knight of Humanity Order of the White Cross, chevalier grand cross Order Militaire de la Milice du Saint Sepulchre, missionary patron Missionaries of the White Cross, chevalier grand comdr. Order St. Sampson, knight grand cross Order St. John the Baptist Am., chevalier comdr. Urkunde Order Signum Fidei, chevalier grand croix avec grand cordon Order International des Chevaliers de Letoile de la Paix, noble Royal Coll. Heraldry; recipient Statesman award; named Staff Mgr. of Yr., Nat. Ins. Assn., 1968;. Fellow Internat. United Writers Assn.; mem. D.C. Bapt. Conv. (bd. dirs. 1972—), Am. Bapt. Conv., So. Bapt. Conv., Nat. Bapt. Conv. U.S.A., Internat. Platform Assn., Am. Biog. Inst. (dep. gov., life fellow, hon. rsch. bd. advisors), World Inst. Achievement (life), Confedn. Chivalry, Am. Legion, Smithsonian Instn., Grand Coun. and World Parliament Chivalry (amb. to 3d World Parliament), High Chamber Internat. Parliament (Italy, sen. mem.), Nat. Trust for Hist. Preservation, Alpha Theta Nu Omega (nat. pres. 1971—). Office: Holy Comforter Bapt Ch PO Box 29101 Washington DC 20017 *The command of the 21st century is to restructure our religious, scientific, economic and technological knowledge. Cosmic science and cosmology will take preeminence as guidelines for the New Age.*

MARTIN, JOHN GREGORY, minister; b. Chattanooga, July 31, 1963; m. Laura Wilson; children: Benjamin, Austin. BA, Bryan Coll., 1985; MDiv, Bapt. Theol. Sem., New Orleans, 1987. Lic. to ministry Bapt. Ch., 1981, ordained to ministry, 1983. Summer youth pastor 1st Bapt. Ch., Swartz Creek, Mich., 1982; pastor 1st Bapt. Ch., Richard City, Tenn., 1983-86; interim min. music and youth Big Level Bapt. Ch., Wiggins, Miss., 1986; pastor Commn. Rd. Bapt. Ch., Long Beach, Miss., 1986—; bd. dirs. home mission bd. So. Bapt. Conv., 1989—; mem. tellers com. Miss. Bapt. Conv., 1988, resource person Here's Hope 1990, Simultaneous Revival, 1988-90; presenter devotionals WLOX TV, Biloxi, Miss., 1988—. Mem. Gulf Coast Bapt. Assn. (pres. min.'s conf. 1990-91, mem. credentials com. 1989-91, chmn. evangelism com. 1987-92). Home: 701 Rita Ln Long Beach MS 39560 Office: Commn Rd Bapt Ch 19148 Commission Rd Long Beach MS 39560-2311

MARTIN, JOHN VICTOR, minister; b. Winfield, Kans., Feb. 18, 1948; s. James Victor and Mary Ellen (Longmate) M.; m. Charlotte Yianakopulos, June 1970 (div. 1975); m. Sharon Kay Rogers, Mar. 12, 1977; children: Anne Elizabeth, Alex James. BA, Southwestern Coll., Winfield, Kans., 1970; MDiv, Asbury Theol. Sem., Wilmore, Ky., 1974; MEd, Wichita (Kans.) State U., 1983. Ordained to ministry United Meth. Ch., 1980. Min. Free Meth. Ch., Killarney, Man., Can., 1974-75; assoc. min. 1st United Meth. Ch., Scott City, Kans., 1977-79; min. United Meth. Ch., Douglass, Kans., 1979-83, 1st United Meth. Ch., Sterling, Kans., 1983-88, Trinity United Meth. Ch., Salina, Kans., 1988—. Mem. Am. Assn. Marriage and Family Therapy. Office: Trinity United Meth Ch 901 E Neal Salina KS 67401

MARTIN, LAURA ANN, pastor; b. Balt., July 8, 1953; d. Nancy Ann (Kirby) Hesterberg. BS in Edn. cum laude, Rider Coll., 1978; MDiv with highest honors, Wesley Sem., Washington, 1982, D Ministry, 1987. Ordained to ministry United Meth. Ch. as deacon, 1981, as elder, 1984. Pastor Blades (Del.) and Asbury United Meth. Chs., 1981-83; assoc. pastor Bethesda United Meth. Ch., Salisbury, Md., 1983-88; pastor Calvary United Meth. Ch., Milford, Del., 1988—; chmn. Commn. on Equitable Salaries, Peninsula Ann. Conf., Dover, 1987%, bd. dirzs. Peninsula United Meth. Found., 1990—. Bd. dirs., treas. Milford Sr. Ctr., Inc., 1988—; EMT, Carlisle Fire Co., Milford, 1989—, chaplain, 1991—. Mem. Ruritan Club (sec. Milford 1990), Pi Omega Pi. Office: Calvary United Meth Ch 301 SE Front St Milford DE 19963 *The best and most wonderful thing that can happen to you in this life is that you should be silent and let God work and speak. Let me read with open eyes the book my days are writing, and learn.*

MARTIN, LYNN GARY, minister; b. Roswell, N.Mex., Dec. 1, 1936; s. Hubert C. and Vera Edith (Jordon) M.; m. Betty Jewell Russell, May 16, 1953; children: Steven Lynn, David Alan. Grad. high sch., Modesto, Calif. Ordained to ministry Pentecostal Ch. of God, 1956. Tchr. high sch. Pentecostal Ch. of God, Ukiah, Calif., 1960-70; pastor Pentecostal Ch. of God, Sebastopol, Calif., 1970-71; tchr. religion Piner High Sch., Santa Rosa, Calif., 1971; pastor Pentecostal Ch. of God, Modesto, Calif., 1971-73, Visalia, Calif., 1973-81; tchr. religion Coll. of Sequoias, Visalia, Calif., 1979-80; evangelist Pentecostal Ch. of God, Fresno, Calif., 1989—; dist. dir. home missions, chmn. bd. Pentecostal Ch. of God, Roseville, Calif., 1962-69. Author: Beware Your Facade Is Showing, 1990. Home and Office: 1624 Myrtlewood Dr Ceres CA 95307 *I feel one of the greatest needs in the world today is to apply the word of God to the inner man or spiritual man instead of the man of the flesh. The real person is the person of the spirit, which is created eternal.*

MARTIN, MALCOLM CHESTER, priest, ecumenical officer, consultant; b. Presque Isle, Maine, May 7, 1926; came to Brazil, 1963; s. Levi Martin and Clara (Sirois) M. Grad. Aroostook Sch. Commerce, 1948; BA, St. John's Sem., 1955; MA, St. Paul's U., Can., 1972. Joined Atonement Friars, ordained priest Roman Cath. Ch., 1962. Pastor, Our Lady Sorrows Parish, Rio Verde, Goias, Brazil, 1965-71; monastery coord. Atonement Friars, Graymoor, Garrison, N.Y., 1973-77; ecumenical officer Archdiocese São Paulo, Brazil, 1977; ecumenical officer, cons. Nat. Conf. Bishops, Brasilia, Fed. Dist., 1980—; coord. Atonement Friars, São Paulo, 1977-85; prof. ecumenics Intercultural Formation Ctr., Archdiocesan Missionary Commn., Health Ministry, Sems. in Archdiocese of São Paulo, Curitiba, Marilia & Aparecida, Brazil, 1977—. Author: Unity and Fraternity, 1982, Pastoral Ecumenism, 1987; contbr. religios articles to various pubs. Editor Boletim, Reconcilliation, 1985—. With U.S. Army, 1944-46. Mem. Roman Cath.-Anglican Dialogue Commn., Roman Cath.-Jewish Dialogue Commn., Conf. of Bishops' Commn. for Study of New Religious Movements. Avocations: tennis, swimming. Office: Atonement Friars, R Afonso de Freitas 704, 04006 São Paulo Brazil

MARTIN, MARK STEVEN, pianist, music consultant; b. East St. Louis, Ill., Aug. 28, 1963; s. Robert Edward Martin and Willie Mae (Gillispie) Taylor; m. Donalle Renee Thomas, Mar. 19, 1988; children: Jennifer L. Jefferson, Antoinette R., Mark S. II. BA in Music cum laude, Lane Coll., Jackson, Tenn., 1986. Pianist Sunday sch. New Jerusalem Ch., East St. Louis, 1976-79; pianist Mt. Zion Bapt. Ch. Boys Choir, East St. Louis, 1981-82; dir. youth music Mt. Zion Bapt. Ch. Children's Choir, East St. Louis, 1988-90; min. music Brown's Community A.M.E. Zion Ch., East St. Louis, 1987-88; pianist, accompanist Newstead Ave. Bapt. Ch., St. Louis, 1990—; del. Ill. State Congress Christian Edn., 1976-86, Dist. Congress Christian Edn., 1976-86. Mem. Nat. Assn. Negro Musicians, Chorister's Guild, Police Marksman Assn. Ill. Sheriff Assn., Nat. Rifle Assn., Southern Cross Club Lodge 112 (jr. warden 1991—), Queen Elizabeth Club (chpt. 16 patron 1990-91), Kappa Kappa Psi. Democrat. Baptist. Avocations: bowling, shooting, playing clarinet, traveling. Home: 207 Kathryn St East Saint Louis IL 62203-2422

MARTIN, MICHAEL JOHN, priest; b. Chgo., June 7, 1950; s. John M. and Margie (Kotowski) M. BA, Knox Coll., 1972; MA, Cath. U. of Am., 1976; M of Christian Spirituality, Creighton U., 1986. Joined Paulist Fathers, Roman Cath. Ch.; ordained priest, 1977. Assoc. pastor St. John's U. Parish, W. Va. U., Morgantown, 1977-82, St. Thomas Aquinas U. Parish, U. Colo., Boulder, 1982-87; pastor St. Nicholas Ch., North Pole, Alaska, 1987—; mem. continuing edn. faculty Alaska Pacific U., Anchorage, 1991—; cons. Diocese of Fairbanks, Alaska, 1987—, dir. Urban Deacon Program, 1988—; del. Ordained Ministry Formation Com., Fairbanks, 1989—; bd. dirs. Love, Inc., Fairbanks, 1990—. Home and Office: St Nicholas Ch 707 St Nicholas Dr North Pole AK 99705

MARTIN, MITCH WAYNE, minister; b. Stillwater, Okla., Sept. 15, 1957; s. Lloyd Wayne and Sharon Louise (Wessel) M.; m. Myra Jane Tripp, May 31, 1980; children: Dustin Wayne, Kristin Jane. BA, Okla. Bapt. U., 1980; MDiv, Golden Gate Bapt. Theol., Seminary, Mill Valley, Calif., 1983. Ordained to ministry Bapt. Ch., 1983. Bus minister Calvary Bapt. Ch., Shawnee, Okla., 1978-80; assoc. pastor North Hills Bapt. Ch., Vallejo, Calif., 1980-83; pastor Emmanuel Bapt. Ch., The Dalles, Oreg., 1983-86, First Bapt. Ch., Orofino, Idaho, 1987-88, Quinault Bapt. Ch., Kennewick, Wash., 1988—; exec. bd. Northwest Bapt. Conv., Portland, Oreg., 1989-93, 1st v.p. Pastor's-Layman's Conf., 1991, pres. 1992; dir. assn. Sunday Sch. improvement support team in Mid-Columbia Zone, Interstate Bapt. Assn., Portland, 1986; chmn. counseling com. Luis Palau Evangelistic Crusade, Tri-Cities, Washington, 1990-91; chmn. student work com. Interstate Bapt. Assn., 1983-86, other. Recipient Prichard scholarship Okla. Bapt. U., Shawnee, 1978-80; Singleton Presdl. scholar Golden Gate Bapt. Theol. Seminary, 1980-81. Home: 2207 Concord Richland WA 99352 Office: Quinault Baptist Church 5400 W Canal Dr Kennewick WA 99336-1319 *Humble yourself in the sight of the Lord and He will lift you up. (James 4:10).*

MARTIN, OSMOND PETER, bishop. Bishop of Belize City-Belmopan, Roman Cath. Ch., Belize. Office: Bishop's House, 144 N Front St, POB 717, Belize City Belize*

MARTIN, PAUL, charitable organization executive. Comdr.-in-chief, pres. of corp. Am. Rescue Workers, Phila. Office: Am Rescue Workers 2827 Frankford Ave Philadelphia PA 19134*

MARTIN, RAY ELWOOD, minister; b. Tulsa, Mar. 27, 1942; s. John Elwood and Grace Mae (Swearingin) M.; m. Judith Gail Harrison, Jan. 19, 1960; children: Raylene, Annette, Tamara, Sheryl, Kimberly. DDiv, New World Bible Inst., 1986; postgrad., Fuller Sem., Pasadena, 1986. Ordained to ministry, So. Bapt. Conv. Minister Mingo Bapt. Ch., Tulsa, 1980—; cert. cons. Performax Systems Internat. and Carlson Co., 1980—; lectr. in field; v.p. Bapt. Gen. Conv., 1982-83; vice moderator Tulsa Bapt. Assn., 1983-84, chmn. life com., 1983-84; founder Mingo Bible Coll., 1987. Author: Powers of Heaven Shaken, 1979, Hell, 1979; contbr. articles to profl. jours. Chmn. Mayor's Task Force Transitional Housing, Tulsa, 1987, Transitional Housing for Homeless, HUD, 1990. With USAR, 1960-66. Recipient Ch. and Community Ministry award, Excellence in Community Ministries, Tulsa Bapt. Assn., 1990, Award for Leadership in Baptisms for state of Okla., 1981, others. Mem. Masons. Home: 7319 E King St Tulsa OK 74115 Office: Mingo Bapt Ch 4319 N Mingo Rd Tulsa OK 74116

MARTIN, RAY IVAN, family counselor, minister; b. Rock Port, Mo., Aug. 28, 1930; s. Charles Beck and Ivan Leah (Baker) M.; m. Mary Ann Wisecup, June 19, 1955; children: Craig Thomas, Cynthia Rae, Ivan Arthur, Clinton John. BA, Simpson Coll., 1955; STB, ThM, Boston U., 1957, ThD, 1968. Profl. hypnotherapist; cert. cons.; ordained to ministry United Meth. Ch. Pastor 1st Meth. Ch., North Attleboro, Mass., 1960-67; minister of counseling 1st Meth. Ch., Des Moines, 1967-72; dir., founder Des Moines Pastoral Counseling Ctr., 1972-76; owner, dir. Care & Counseling, Des Moines, 1976—; fellow, cons. New Eng. Acad. Hypnosis, Beverly, 1981—. Pres. Highland Park-Des Moines Bus. Club, 1985-86. Danielson Pastoral Counseling Ctr. fellow Boston U., 1958-59; recipient Award of Honor, Clarinda Mental Health Clinic, Des Moines, 1969-72. Mem. Am. Acad. Family Mediators, Am. Assn. Profl. Hypnotherapists (profl.). Democrat. Avocations: smallcraft woodworking, reading, sailing, motorcycling, trailoring. Home: 2523 Sherwood Dr Des Moines IA 50310 Office: Care and Counseling 700 W Euclid Ave Des Moines IA 50313

MARTIN, RAYMOND ALBERT, theology educator; b. Mt. Carroll, Ill., Nov. 3, 1925; m. Alice Bast, May 29, 1949; children: Bill, Barbara, Mary, Tim. BA, Wartburg Coll., 1947; BD, Wartburg Theol. Sem., 1951; ThM, Princeton Theol. Sem., 1952, PhD, 1957; postdoctoral studies, Harvard Div. Sch., 1963-64. Instr. Greek Wartburg Coll., Waverly, Iowa, 1952-54; reference librarian Princeton (N.J.) Theol. Sem., 1957; missionary to India Luth. Ch., 1957-69; prof. Old Testament and N.T. Gurukul Luth. Theol. Coll., India, 1957-69; treas. Gurukul Sem., 1958-69, librarian, 1962-63; prof. bibl. and intertestmamental studies Wartburg Theol. Sem., Dubuque, 1969—; vis. prof. bibl. studies United Theol. Coll., Bangalore, India, 1981, Santal Theol. Sem. in Benagaria, Santal Parganas, Bihar, India, 1985, Austin Presbyn. Theology Sem., 1989; co-founder, sec. Soc. Bibl. Studies in India, 1965-69. Author: The Syntax of the Greek of Jeremiah, 1957, India List of Theological Periodicals, 1967, Syntactical Evidence of Semitic Sources in Greek Documents, 1974, Syntactical and Critical Concordance to the Greek Text of Baruch and the Epistle of Jeremiah, Vol. XII of the Computer Bible, 1977, An Introduction to New Testament Greek, 1976, James in Augsburg Commentary on the New Testament, 1982, An Introduction to Biblical Hebrew, 1987, Syntax Criticism of the Synoptic Gospels, 1987, Syntactical Concordance to the Correlated Greek and Hebrew Texts of Ruth, Vol XXX of the Computer Bible, 1988, 89, Syntax Criticism of Johannine Literature, The Catholic Epistles and The Gospel Passion Accounts, 1989; contbr. articles and papers to profl. publs. Home: 1810 Lombard St Dubuque IA 52001 Office: Wartburg Theol Sem 333 Wartburg Pl Dubuque IA 52001 *I am sure that neither death nor life, nor angels, nor principalities, nor things present, nor things to come, nor powers, nor height, nor depth, nor anything else in all creation, will be able to separate us from the love of God in Christ Jesus our Lord. (Romans 8:38, 39).*

MARTIN, ROBERT EUGENE, JR., minister; b. West Chester, Pa., Apr. 24, 1948; s. Robert Eugene Sr. and Marion (Miller) M.; m. Kathryn Gail Howell, July 5, 1969; children: Joy Noelle, Melody Anne. BA, Shelton Coll., 1971; postgrad., Temple U., 1972; M in Divinity, New Covenant Bible Coll., Charlotte, N.C., 1985. Ordained to ministry Bapt. Ch., 1982. Sales rep. CCEC/McCullagh Leasing Co., Inc., West Chester, 1973-77; fin. lease mgr. Penske Leasing, Inc., Reading, Pa., 1977-78; v.p., gen. mgr. Marcus David Leasing Co., Charlotte, 1978-80; pres. Martin Automotive Co., Monroe, N.C., 1980-82; sr. minister Waxhaw (1982—) Bapt. Ch., 1982—; lectr. Charlotte Speakers' Bur., 1982—. Author: Is Marriage a Life Sentence?, 1984. Candidate for N.C. Ho. of Reps., Raleigh, 1982; mem. sch. bd. Calvary Christian Sch., Coatesville, Pa., 1975-78. Mem. Nat. Assn. Fleet Adminstrs., Union Bapt. Ministerial Assn. Democrat. Avocations: backpacking, jogging, sailing, biking. Office: Waxhaw Bapt Ch 8213 Old Waxhaw-Monroe Rd Waxhaw NC 28173

MARTIN, ROGER JOHN, minister; b. N.Y.C., Mar. 19, 1951; s. John Victor Martin and Ethel Lillian (Beyl) Hook; m. Jane Elisabeth Sterling, JUne 16, 1973; children: Jody Lynn, Joshua Edward. BA, Bloomfield Coll., 1973; MDiv, Louisville Presbyn. Theol. Sem, 1976. Pastor First Presbyn. Ch., Littlefield, Tex., 1976-77, Follansbee, W. Va., 1978-83, Hudson Falls, N.Y., 1983—. Bd. dirs. Washington County Cancer Soc., Cambridge, N.Y., 1983-89, Washington County Child Care Coun., Fort Edward, N.Y., 1988—; bd. dirs., pres. Men's Opportunity Project, 1989—; adjunct chaplain, Glens Falls (N.Y.) Hosp., 1987—. Mem. Albany Prebytery (chmn. PS & S com. 1987-89). Office: First Presbyn Ch 9 River St Hudson Falls NY 12839

MARTIN, RONALD DEWITT, college president, minister; b. Charlotte, N.C., May 4, 1946; s. Samuel Dewitt and Nellie Grace (Edwards) M.; m. Lynda Carolyn Craven, Aug. 20, 1967; 1 child, Jonathan Arnold. Diploma, Charlotte Bus. Coll., 1965; BA in Christian Edn., Lee Coll., 1970; LittD (hon.), West Coast Christian Coll., 1987. Pastor Ch. of God, N.C., 1968-80, 84-86; state dir. youth and Christian edn. depts. Ch. of God, Charlotte, 1980-84; pres. East Coast Bible Coll., Charlotte, 1986—; mem. state youth bd. Ch. of God, Charlotte, 1972-78, state coun., 1984-86; mem. gen. bd. edn. Ch. of God., Cleveland, Tenn. Contbr. articles to profl. jours. Named State Alumni Chpts.' Pres. of Yr., Lee Coll. Alumni Assn., Alumnus of Yr., Tenn. chpt. Lee Coll. Alumni Assn., 1985. Mem. Lee Coll. Alumni Assn. (Alumnus of Yr. 1984). Avocation: golf.

MARTIN, RONALD KEITH, minister; b. Cin., Dec. 6, 1956; s. William D. and Doris R. (Doxsey) M.; m. Roshelle June Wilson, Sept. 21, 1977; children: Kimberly Elizabeth, Melissa Ruth. BS, Lee Coll., 1984. Lic. to ministry Ch. of God, 1977, ordained, 1988. Youth pastor Ch. of God Worship Ctr., Balt., 1984-87; evangelist Ch. of God, Cleveland, Tenn., 1986-88; pastor Sweetwater Valley Ch. of God, Philadelphia, Tenn., 1988—; charter mem. Fellowship Christian Police Officers, Cleveland, 1978-80; dist. youth dir. Gh. of God, Balt., 1984-87, Philadelphia, 1989—; youth camp, retreat speaker, Cleveland, 1989—. Producer, host video series: The Occult and Its Effect on Our Families, 1990. Anti-drug speaker, Cleveland Police Dept., 1979-88. Recipient Disting. Svc. to Mankind award U.S. Jaycees, 1983; named Officer of Yr., Cleveland Police Dept., 1980. Mem. Nat. Youth Leaders Assn., Fraternal Order Police (treas. 1980-83), Rotary (Loudon chpt.). Home and Office: PO Box 137 Philadelphia TN 37846

MARTIN, RUSSELL, priest; b. Atlanta, June 21, 1958; s. Hayes Blair Fleming and Marilyn Peoples (Martin) Stein; m. Lynn Marie Kuhlman, July 10, 1982; 1 child, Blair Kathryn. BA, Western Wash. U., 1981; MDiv, Nashotah House, Wis., 1988. Ordained to ministry Episc. Ch. as deacon, 1988, as priest, 1988. Youth chaplain St. Luke's, Racine, Wis., 1986-88; curate Holy Apostle's, Ft. Worth, 1988-89, St. Dunstan's, San Diego, 1989—; chaplain Daus. of the Kng., Diocese of San Diego, 1990—; coun. mem. diocesan coun. Diocese of San Diego, 1991—, bd. dirs. com. on youth and camping, 1989—, bd. dirs. com. on scouting, 1989—. Office: St Dunstan's Episcopal Ch 6556 Park Ridge Blvd San Diego CA 92120

MARTIN, STEELE WADE, minister; b. Chgo., Aug. 31, 1926; s. Leon Wade and Eleanor Marie (Pickel) M.; m. Priscilla Fallis Clark, May 28, 1953; 1 child, Candace Clark Martin Mittman. BA, Northwestern U., 1947; MDiv, Gen. Theol. Sem., 1951, MST, 1956. Ordained to ministry Episcopal Ch., 1951. Fellow and tutor Gen. Theol. Sem., N.Y.C., 1951-53; assoc. St. Margaret's Ch., South Bronx, N.Y., 1953-54; rector St. Mary's Ch., East Providence, R.I., 1954-59; teaching missionary Brazil, 1959-62; rector St. Michael's Ch., Brattleboro, Vt., 1962-74, Christ Ch., Quincy, Mass., 1974-88; interim rector St. Stephen's Ch., Providence, R.I., 1988—; fellow Coll. Preachers, Washington; dir. Gen. Theol. Libr., Boston, 1970—; trustee Mass. Bible Soc., Boston, 1979-85; dir. Enablement, Inc., Boston, 1984—; dep., mem. staff Gen. Conv. of Episcopal Ch., 1969-76. Author: Blue Collar Ministry, 1989. Protestant chaplain Quincy Fire Dept., 1978-88. Mem. Interim Ministry Network, Boston Mins. Club, Providence Art Club. Office: St Stephens Ch 114 George St Providence RI 02906

MARTIN, TARA KATHLEEN, church secretary; b. St. Paul, Aug. 21, 1956; d. Harold John and Catherine (Capaul) Holly; m. Glen David Martin, Apr. 11, 1987; children: Holly Catherine, G. Reid. BA, Coll. of St. Teresa, Winona, Minn., 1978. Sec. First Presbyn. Ch., Denton, Tex., 1987—; pres. Ch. Secs. Assn. of Denton County, 1990—. Home: 1309 Greenbriar Denton TX 76201 Office: 1st Presbyn Ch 1114 W University Dr Denton TX 76201-1850

MARTIN, THOMAS MICHAEL, religion educator; b. Bklyn., Aug. 2, 1940; s. George Edward and Agnes Regina Martin; m. Mary Ann Langenhorst, Aug. 5, 1967; children: Brian, Shawn. BS, Spring Hill Coll., 1962; MA, Fordham U., 1965; PhD, Syracuse U., 1972. Grad. asst. Syracuse (N.Y.) U., 1968-70; asst. prof. dept. religious studies U. Dayton, Ohio, 1970-75, assoc. prof., 1975-81, prof., 1981—, chair dept. religious studies, 1989—. Author: Christian Family Values, 1984, What Should I Teach?, 1988, The Challenge of Christian Marriage, 1990, Images of the Imageless, 1991. Mem. Coll. Theology Soc., Assn. Grad. Programs in Ministry (assoc. coord. 1991—). Roman Catholic. Office: U Dayton Dept Religious Studies Dayton OH 45469

MARTIN, TROY WAYNE, religion educator; b. Seminole, Tex., Mar. 15, 1953; s. Troy Sibbley and Lavalta Ruth (Floyd) M.; m. Sheryl Mae Couch, June 23, 1974; children: Andrea Valen, Amie Danae. BA, So. Nazarene U., 1974, MA, 1978; MDiv, Nazarene Theol. Sem., 1980; PhD, U. Chgo., 1990. Pastor First Ch. of the Nazarene, Atchison, Kans., 1979-81; assoc. pastor Ch. of the Nazarene, Lemont, Ill., 1982-88; asst. prof. Olivet Nazarene U., Kankakee, Ill., 1988-91, Saint Xavier Coll., Chgo., 1991—. Mem. Soc. Bibl. Lit., Am. Acad. Religion, Wesleyan Theol. Soc., Chgo. Soc. Bibl. Rsch. Home: 513 S Cleveland Bourbonnais IL 60914 Office: Saint Xavier Coll Chicago IL 60655 *The best I can do is the least I can do for God.*

MARTIN, WARHAM LANCE, minister; b. Denver, May 14, 1937; s. Faybert and Mary Elizabeth (Carper) M.; m. Carol Beth Conder, Jan. 31, 1959; children: Carla, Mary, Lance Jr., Sarah. BA, DePauw U., 1959; BD, Union Theol. Seminary, N.Y.C., 1962; PhD, U. St. Andrews, Scotland, 1968. Ordained deacon, 1968, elder, 1970. Min. of youth 1st United Meth. Ch., Pasadena, Calif., 1967-68, min. of edn., 1968-85, assoc. pastor, 1986—; vis. prof. Christian edn. sch. theology Claremont, Calif.; shepherd alumni Western U.S. St. Mary's Coll., U. St. Andrews, 1989—. Pub. numerous pastoral prayers in profl. jours. Active Camp Sky Meadows, Vocal Choir Rainbow, 1969—, Annual Youth Choir Tour, 1971—, Summer Drama Program, 1973—, Old Fashioned Family Christmas, 1976—, Carpenter's Children Vacation Bible Sch., 1979—, Epworth Weekday Christian Preschool, 1979—, Handbell Choir Rainbow, 1979—, Wesley Conservatory of Music, 1985—. Mem. Christian Educator's Fellowship, Pasadena Dist. Bd. Ministries, DePauw U. Alumni Assn. (pres. L.A. area 1979—). Office: First United Meth Ch 500 E Colorado Blvd Pasadena CA 91101

MARTIN, WARREN GREGORY, pastor; b. Charlottesville, Va., May 24, 1948; s. Frank Warren and Charlotte Anne (Kennedy) M.; m. Vanita DeNice Loftin, Aug. 7, 1971; children: Kristina Dawn, Melanie Alyce, Benjamin Gregory. BA, Lenoir Rhyne Coll., 1971; MDiv, Hamma Div., 1975. Ordained to ministry Evangelical Luth. Ch. Asst. pastor First Evang. Luth. Ch., Ellicott City, Md., 1975-82; pastor Zion Evang. Luth. Ch., Williamsport, Md., 1982—; sec. Howard County Ministerial Assn., Ellicott City, 1978-81, Williaimsport Area Ministerium, Williamsport, 1983-88, pres., 1989-90; v.p. Washington County Coun. Chs., Md., 1990-91. Mem. Citizen's Adv. Com., Williamsport, 1990-91; Substance Abuse Study Task Force, Howard County, Md. Mem. Rotary Internat. (v.p. Williamsport chpt. 1990-91). Democrat. Home: 6 N Clifton Dr Wiliamsport MD 21795 Office: Zion Evang Luth Ch 35 W Potomac St Williamsport MD 21795

MARTIN, WAYNE, academic administrator. Pres. Arlington (Tex.) Bapt. Coll. Office: Arlington Bapt Coll Office of the President 3001 W Division Arlington TX 76012*

MARTIN, WAYNE WILLARD, minister; b. Seattle, Sept. 13, 1943; s. Frank Lionel and Catherine Van Lieu (Mattoon) M.; m. Nancy Leslie Garnett, Dec. 28, 1967; children: Leslee, Erin, Jacob, Joby, Jaymee, Skyler. BS, Wheaton (Ill.) Coll., 1966; M Divinity, Boston U., 1979, D Ministry, 1983. Ordained to ministry United Ch. Christ, 1980. Tchr. N.H. Pub. Schs., Rochester, 1971-75; assoc. pastor Westwood (Mass.) 1st Parish, 1977-79, Pioneer Congl. Ch., Sacramento, 1979-81; pastor Westview Congl. Ch., Spokane, Wash., 1981-84; pastor St. Luke's United Ch. Christ, Phila., 1984-91, Trappe, Pa., 1991—; chaplain Eastern Wash. State Hosp., 1983-84; nat. mem. United Ch. Christ Devel. Com.; bd. dirs. Clergy for Soc. Responsibility, Spokane, 1981-84, Christians for Urban Justice, Boston, 1975-79. Author-translator: The Gospel of Mark: A New Translation for Children, 1984; contbr. articles to various mags. Mem. founding bd. Peace and Justice League Spokane, 1982-84. With USN, 1967-71, Vietnam. Mem. Sierra Club, Union Concerned Scientists, Greenpeace USA, Handgun Control, Bread for the World, Amnesty Internat. Democrat. Avocations: writing, teaching, backpacking, jazz. Home: 349 Trinity Ave Ambler PA 19002 Office: St Luke's United Ch Christ 200 Main St Trappe PA 19426

MARTIN, WILLIAM CONWAY, minister; b. Clarksville, Tenn., Sept. 13, 1956; s. Maurice Milton and Julia Lee (Graden) M.; m. Gloria Jean Young, Nov. 26, 1986; children: Christopher Shaun, Andrew Graden, Ouida Ann. BS, U. Ala., Tuscaloosa, 1977; MA, U. Ala., Birmingham, 1979; MDiv, Mid-Am. Bapt. Theol. Sem., 1984; postgrad., So. Bapt. Theol. Sem., 1985—. Ordained to ministry So. Bapt. Conv., 1984, Am. Bapt. Chs. U.S.A., 1990. Min. of music and youth Curve (Tenn.) Bapt. Ch., 1982-83; youth min. 1st Bapt. Ch., Stuttgart, Ark., 1983-84; asst. pastor Redeemer Bapt. and 1st Presbyn. Chs., Louisville, 1985-86; pastor 1st Bapt. Ch., Huntingburg, Ind., 1986-89; assoc. pastor 1st Bapt. Ch., Peoria, Ill., 1989—; mem. Area III Christian Edn. Com., Bloomington, Ill., 1989—, The Mins. Coun., 1989—; bd. dirs. Friendship House of Christian Svc., Peoria, 1990—. Named Outstanding Young Religious Leader, Hungtingburg Jaycees, 1988. Mem. SAR. Republican. Home: 141 E Southgate Rd Peoria IL 61614 Office: 1st Bapt Ch of Peoria 411 W Lake Ave Peoria IL 61614

MARTINELLI, GIOVANNI INNOCENZO, religious leader. Apostolic vicariate of Tripoli, titular bishop of Tabuda, aspostolic administr. of Benghazi RomanCath. Ch., Libya. Office: Apostolic Vicariate, POB 365, Tripoli Libya*

MARTINEZ, ANTHONY LEONARD, priest; b. Albuquerque, Mar. 26, 1961; s. Benny Chavez and Berna (Saiz) M. BS, Coll. Santa Fe (N.Mex.), 1985; MDiv, Pontifical Coll. Josephina, Columbus, Ohio, 1989. Ordained priest, Roman Cath. Ch., 1989. Parochial vicar Our Lady of the Annunciation, Albuquerque, 1989—; commn. mem. Archdiocese of Santa Fe AIDS Commn., 1990—; chmn. force N.Mex. Conf. Chs. AIDS Task Force, 1990—; chaplain K.C., 1989-91. U. N.Mex. acad. scholar, achieved award, 1983-84, Cert. of Achievement K.C., 1990. Mem. Nat. Assn. Pastoral Musicians, Assn. for Religious and Value Issues in Counseling, Am. Assn. Counseling and Devel. Office: Our Lady of Sorrow 403 Valencia St Las Vegas NM 87101

MARTINEZ SOMALO, EDUARDO CARDINAL, archbishop; b. Banos de Rios Tobia, Spain, Mar. 31, 1927. Ordained priest Roman Cath. Ch., 1950. Elected bishop of Tagara, later archbishop, 1975, created cardinal,, 1988, under sec. of state to Vatican. Office: 00120 Vatican City Vatican City

MARTINI, CARLO MARIA CARDINAL, archbishop of Milan; b. Turin, Italy, Feb. 15, 1927. Joined Soc. of Jesus, Roman Cath. Ch., 1944, ordained priest, 1952; biblical scholar; sem. prof., Chieri, Italy, 1958-61; prof., rector Pontifical Biblical Inst., 1969-78; rector Pontifical Gregorian U., 1978-79; archbishop of Milan, 1980; elevated to Sacred Coll. of Cardinals, 1983. Author: theological, biblical and spiritual works. Mem. Council for Pub.

Affairs of the Ch. Address: Palazzo Arcivescovile, Piazza Fontana 2, 20122 Milan Italy

MARTINO, DAVID, clergyman; b. Sharon, Pa., Dec. 23, 1958; s. Jerry and Julia Ann (Kulka) M.; m. Susan Oldsey, Mar. 14, 1981; children: Jeremy David, Jonathan James, Nicholas Michael. BS in Religion, Valley Forge Christian Coll., 1980; MDiv, Ashland Theol. Sem., 1986; postgrad., Ea. Bapt. Theol. Sem., 1990—. Ordained to ministry Assemblies of God Ch., 1990. Asst. pastor Farrell (Pa.) Christian Assembly, 1980-86; assoc. pastor Assembly of God, Pennsburg, Pa., 1986—; zone ministries dir. Christian Ch. N.Am., Farrell, 1982-85; mem. adv. com. Life Mgmt. Cons., Sharon, Pa., 1982-85; dir. Pa. State U. Campus Fellowship, Sharon, 1982-85; missionary sec. East Cen. Assemblies of God, Pennsburg, 1989-90. Family therapist Cath. Social Agy., Allentown, Pa., 1990-91. Mem. Soc. Pentecostal Studies. Home: RD 1 Pennsburg PA 16148

MARTOIA, RONALD STEVEN, minister, biblical studies educator; b. Ypsilanti, Mich., May 19, 1962; s. Ronald James and Patricia Ann (Skinner) M.; m. Valerie Jo Russell, Mar. 22, 1986; children: Ronald James II., Skyler Steven. BA, Oral Roberts U., 1984; MDiv, Trinity Evangel. Div. Sch., Deerfield, Ill., 1987; postgrad. studies, Fuller Theol. Sem., 1988—. Assoc. pastor Calvary Way Ch., Deerfield, Ill., 1985-86; sr. pastor Charis Christian Ctr., Jackson, Mich., 1987—; adjunct prof. Spring Arbor Coll., Jackson, 1987—. Mem. Evangel. Theol. Soc., Soc. Bibl. Lit., Soc. Pentecostal Studies, Evangel. Philos. Soc., Soc. of Christian Philosophers. Office: Charis Christian Ctr Box 6225 Jackson MI 49204 *The role of scholarship is to serve the church in appropriately contextualized ways. The role of the church is to make known the meaning and purpose of life, and how a Christian Worldview is both practical and relevant.*

MARTS, ALBERT LEE, choirmaster, rehabilitation counselor; b. Wichita, Kans., Oct. 23, 1950; s. Albert L. and Thalia Nian (Filby) M.; m. Pamella Ann McFarland, Nov. 20, 1971 (div. Jan. 1990); children: Damien, Dominique; m. Barbara Lea Jackson, July 7, 1990; stepchildren: Benjamin, Matthew. BS in Bible and Psychology, Manahttan Christian Coll., 1973; MA in Psychology, Eastern N.Mex. U., 1976; D Christian Counseling, Bethany Theol. Sem., 1974. Ordained to ministry Christian Ch., 1987. Minister Latham (Kans.) Christian Ch., 1970-71, Farmington (Kans.) Christian Ch., 1972-73; youth minister Southside Christian Ch., Kansas City, Mo., 1971-72; choirmaster Cannon AFB (N.Mex.) Chapel, 1983-89, St. James Episcopal Ch., Clovis, N.Mex., 1990—; vocat. rehab. counselor div. Vocat. Rehab., Clovis, 1989—. Mem. Assn. Applied Psychophysiology and Biofeedback, Rotary (pres. Clovis chpt. 1987-88). Home: 1434 Axtell Clovis NM 88101

MARTY, FRANCOIS CARDINAL, former archbishop of Paris; b. Pachins, France, May 18, 1904. s. Francois and Zoé Gineste. Ordained priest Roman Cath. Ch., 1930; bishop of St.-Flour, 1952; titular archbishop of Emesa, also coadjutor archbishop of Rheims, 1959; archbishop of Rheims, 1960-68, of Paris, 1968-81; elevated to Sacred Coll. of Cardinals, 1969; titular ch. St. Louis of France; ret. as archbishop, 1981; ordinary for Eastern Rite Catholics in France without ordinaries of their own rites; mem. Congregation Oriental Chs., Congreagtion Clergy, Sacraments and Divine Worship, Commn. Revision of Code of Canon Law. Address: Monastère des, dominicaines de Monteils, 12200 Villefranche-de-Rouergue France

MARTY, MARTIN EMIL, religion educator, editor; b. West Point, Nebr., Feb. 5, 1928; s. Emil A. and Anne Louise (Wuerdemann) M.; m. Elsa Schumacher, 1952 (dec. 1981); children: Frances, Joel, John, Peter, James, Micah, Ursula; m. Harriet Lindemann, 1982. MDiv, Concordia Sem., 1952; STM, Luth. Sch. Theology, Chgo., 1954; PhD in Am. Religion and Intellectual History, U. Chgo., 1956; LittD (hon.), Thiel Coll., 1964; LHD (hon.), W.Va. Wesleyan Coll., 1967, Marian Coll., 1967; HHD (hon.), Providence Coll., 1967; DD (hon.), Muhlenberg Coll., 1967; LittD (hon.), Thomas More Coll., 1968; DD (hon.), Bethany Sem., 1969; LLD (hon.), Keuka Coll., 1972; HHD (hon.), Willamette U., 1974; DD (hon.), Wabash Coll., 1977; LLD (hon.), U. So. Calif., 1977, Valparaiso U., 1978; LHD (hon.), St. Olaf Coll., 1978, De Paul U., 1979; DD (hon.), Christ Seminex, 1979, Capital U., 1980; LHD (hon.), Colo. Coll., 1980; DD (hon.), Maryville Coll., 1980, North Park Coll. Sem., 1982; LittD (hon.), Wittenberg U., 1983; LHD, Rosary Coll., 1984; LHD (hon.), Rockford Coll., 1984; DD (hon.), Va. Theol. Sem., 1984; LHD (hon.), Hamilton Coll., 1985, Loyola U., 1986; LLD (hon.), U. Notre Dame, 1987; LHD (hon.), Roanoke Coll., 1987, Mercer U., 1987, Ill. Wesleyan Coll., 1987, Roosevelt U., 1988, Aquinas Coll., 1988; LittD (hon.), Franklin Coll., 1988; HHD (hon.), No. Mich. U., 1989; LHD (hon.), Muskingum Coll., Coe Coll., Lehigh U., 1989, Hebrew Union Coll. and Governors State U., 1990, Whittier Coll., 1991; DD (hon.), St. Xavier Coll. and Colgate U., 1990, Mt. Union Coll., 1991, Tex. Luth. Coll., 1991, Aurora U., 1991. Ordained to ministry Luth. Ch., 1952. Pastor Washington, 1950-51; asst. pastor River Forest, Ill., 1952-56; pastor Elk Grove Village, Ill., 1956-63; prof. history of modern Christianity Div. Sch. U. Chgo., 1963—, Fairfax M. Cone Disting. Service prof., 1978—; assoc. editor Christian Century mag., Chgo., 1956-85, sr. editor, 1985—; co-editor Ch. History mag., 1963—; pres. Park Ridge (Ill.) Ctr.: An Inst. for Study of Health, Faith and Ethics, 1985-89. Author: A Short History of Christianity, 1959, The New Shape of American Religion, 1959, The Improper Opinion, 1961, The Infidel, 1961, Baptism, 1962, The Hidden Discipline, 1963, Second Chance for American Protestants, 1963, Church Unity and Church Mission, 1964, Varieties of Unbelief, 1964, The Search for a Usable Future, 1969, The Modern Schism, 1969, Righteous Empire, 1970 (Nat. Book award 1971), Protestantism, 1972, You Are Promise, 1973, The Fire We Can Light, 1973, The Pro and Con Book of Religious America, 1975, A Nation of Behavers, 1976, Religion, Awakening and Revolution, 1978, Friendship, 1980, By Way of Response, 1981, The Public Church, 1981, A Cry of Absence, 1983, Health and Medicine in the Lutheran Tradition, 1983, Pilgrims in Their Own Land, 1984, Protestantism in the United States, 1985, Modern American Religion. The Irony of It All, Vol. 1, 1986, An Invitation to American Catholic History, 1986, Religion and Republic, 1987, Modern American Religion. The Noise of Conflict, Vol. 2, 1991; contbr. articles to religious publs.; editor: Context, 1969—. Second Opinion, 1990; sr. editor: The Christian Century, 1956—. Sr. scholar-in-residence The Park Ridge Ctr., 1989—. Fellow Am. Acad. Arts and Scis., Soc. Am. Historians; mem. Am. Soc. Ch. History (pres. 1971), Am. Cath. Hist. Assn. (pres. 1981), Am. Acad. Religion (pres. 1987-88), Am. Antiquarian Soc. Home: 239 Scottswood Rd Riverside IL 60546 Office: U Chgo Div Sch 1025 E 58th St Chicago IL 60637

MARTYN, JAMES LOUIS, religion educator emeritus; b. Dallas, Oct. 11, 1925; s. William Pitt and Ruby (Bettis) M.; m. Dorothy Lee Watkins, June 10, 1950; children: Timothy, Peter C., David P. B.S. in Elec. Engring, Tex A. and M. Coll., 1946; B.D., Andover Newton Theol. Sch., 1953; M.A., Yale U., 1956, Ph.D., 1957. Instr. Wellesley Coll., 1958-59; mem. faculty Union Theol. Sem., N.Y.C., 1959—; Edward Robinson prof. Bibl. theology Union Theol. Sem., 1967-87, Edward Robinson prof. emeritus, 1987—, adj. prof. religion, 1973-87; Chmn. N.T. seminar Columbia U., 1965-67, 75—; seminar dir. Ecumenical Inst. for Advanced Theol. Studies, Jerusalem, 1974-75; vis. prof. Yale U., 1982, 88, 91-92. Author: History and Theology in the Fourth Gospel, 1968, rev. and enlarged edit., 1979, (with Charles Rice) Proclamation of Easter, 1975, The Gospel of John in Christian History: Essays for Interpreters, 1979; also articles.; Editor: (with L.E. Keck) Studies in Luke-Acts, 1966, 2d edit., 1980. Fulbright scholar Germany, 1957; Guggenheim fellow, 1963. Mem. Soc. Bibl. Lit. (past pres. Mid-Atlantic sect.), Studiorum Novi Testamenti Societas. Home: 124 Downs Rd Bethany CT 06524

MARUYAMA, ALLEN, minister; b. Las Animas, Colo., Nov. 6, 1926; s. Masakuni and Umeyo (Amino) M.; m. Rose Edna Jarboe, May 10, 1954; children: Sarah Rose, John Allen. BS, U. Colo., 1950; BD and MA, McCormick Sem., 1953; STM, U. Dubuque Sem., 1966; lPhD, Aquinas Sch. Theology, 1972. Ordained to ministry Presbyn Ch. (U.S.A.), 1953. Pastor Gleason and Hogarty (Wis.) Presbyn. Chs, 1953-57, Prairie du Sac and Mazomanie (Wis.) Presbyn. Chs., 1957-62; assoc. pastor Westminister Presbyn. Ch., Dubuque, Iowa, 1962-72, Montview Blvd. Presbyn. Ch., Denver, 1972-75; moderator Adv. Com. on Profl. Devel., Louisville, 1985-91; mem. Gen. Assembly Nominating Com., Presbyn. Ch. (U.S.A.), Louisville, 1989— (commr. 1962, 71, 80, 90); v.p. Denver Area Interfaith Conf., 1990—. Contbr. articles to profl. jours. Chmn. Mayor's Youth Coun. and Citizens Adv. Com., Dubuque, 1965-72; mem. Govs.'s Com. for Prayer Breakfast, Denver, 1975—; v.p. Pluralism in Am. Life, Denver, 1985—. Sgt. U.S. Army, 1945-46. Recipient Recognition award McCormick Theol. Sem., 1985, Scroll of Appreciation Vocation Agy., Presbyn. Ch., Louisville, 1987, Faith and Freedom award Religious Coalition on Abortion Rights, Denver, 1987. Mem. Adv. Commn. on Profl. Devel. (chair 1987-91), Presbytery of Denver (moderator 1979, permanent jud. commn. 1990), Am. Legion. Home: 380 Ursula St Aurora CO 80011 Office: Montview Presbyn Ch 1980 Dahlia St Denver CO 80220

MARVIN, JOHN GEORGE, clergyman, church organization executive; b. Summit, N.J., May 8, 1912; s. George and Caroline (Whitman) M.; B.S., Davidson Coll., 1933; Th.B., Princeton Theol. Sem., 1936; D.D., Coll. of Emporia, 1964; LL.D., Tarkio Coll., 1964; m. Elizabeth Anne Wheater, June 30, 1944; children—Caroline Wheater Dorney, Elizabeth Anne West, Martha Jane Hobbs, Frances Alice Heidel. Ordained to ministry Presbyterian Ch., 1936; pastor, Windsor, N.Y., 1936-37, Montrose, Pa., 1937-44, Lewistown, Pa., 1944-52, Denton, Tex., 1952-61; presbytery exec. Greater Kansas City, Mo., 1961-65; pastor 1st Presbyn. Ch., Bartlesville, Okla., 1965-69; sr. minister Chevy Chase Presbyn. Ch., Washington, 1969-77, pastor emeritus, 1978—; interim sr. minister Catonsville Ch., Balt., 1978, 3d Ch., Rochester, N.Y., 1978-79, 1st Ch., Ft. Worth, 1979-80, Gaithersburg, Md., 1980-81, Westfield, N.J., 1981-82, Ch. of Palms, Sarasota, Fla., 1982-83, Bethel Ch., Balt., 1983-84, Pine Shores Ch., Sarasota, Fla., 1984, Interfaith Chapel, Silver Spring, Md., 1984-87; mem. exec. com. Pa. Council Chs., 1949-52, Tex. Council Chs., 1953-61; mem. exec. com., long range chmn. Greater Kansas City Council Chs., 1962-65; chmn. campus Christian Life Tex. Synod, 1958-61; chmn. nat. mission Pa. Synod, 1949-52; sec. nomination com. Gen. Assembly U.P. Ch., 1955-58, chmn. com. on baptized children, 1969-70, mem. com. of nine on synod bounderies, 1970-72; bd. dirs. Midwest Christian Counseling Ctr., Kansas City, Mo., 1963-69, Presbyn. Homes of Okla., Inc., 1966-69; mem. jud. commn. Synod of Okla.-Ark., 1966-69; mem. strategy com. Bd. Nat. Missions, 1968-70, British-Am. Preaching Exchange, preaching missions to Alaska and Mexico; leader and lectr. on religious heritage tours in Europe, Mid. East, Egypt, Caribbean and Orient, 1972-84. Bd. dirs. Tarkio Coll., 1961-67, Westminster Found., Pa. State U., 1945-52, North Tex. State U., 1952-61; mem. ministerial relations com. Nat. Capital Union Presbytery, 1973-78; bd. visitors Warren Wilson Coll. Mem. Beta Theta Pi. Republican. Club: Rotary. Contbr. articles to religious publs. Home: 14500 Elmhan Ct Silver Spring MD 20906

MARX, ROBERT JOSEPH, rabbi; b. Cleve., Aug. 17, 1927; s. Sylvester and Lucile (Kline) M.; m. Marjorie Plant, Dec. 21, 1948; m. K. Ruth Marx, Aug. 16, 1981; 1 child, Richard. BA, U. Cin., 1948; MHL, Hebrew Union Coll., Cin., 1951; PhD, Yale U., 1958; DHL, Hebrew Union Coll., Cin., 1976. Ordained rabbi, 1951. Asst. rabbi Temple Beth Zion, Buffalo, 1951-54; rabbi Temple Sinai, Stamford, Conn., 1954-58; dir. Union of Am. Hebrew Congregations, Chgo. and N.Y.C., 1958-73; rabbi Congregation Solel, Highland Park, Ill., 1973-83, Congregation Hakafa, Glencoe, Ill., 1983—; founder Jewish Coun. on Urban Affairs, 1964—; sec. Cen. Conf. Am. Rabbis, 1976. Bd. dirs. Leadership Coun. Met. Chgo., 1969—; pres. Clergy and Laity Concerned, Chgo., 1964-69, 86-89 (King-Heschel award 1990). Recipient Christopher House award, 1991. Home: 27 Crescent Dr Glencoe IL 60022 Office: Congregation Hakafa Box 409 Glencoe IL 60022

MARXHAUSEN, VICTOR HERSCHEL, minister; b. Waltham, Minn., May 27, 1926; s. Ernst John August and Aurelia Marie (Schaefer) M.; m. Evelyn Bertha Rengstorf, June 18, 1950; children: Timothy John, Mary Beth, Martha Jane, Jonathan James. BTh, Concordia Theol. Sem., Springfield, Ill., 1949. Ordained to ministry Luth. Ch.-Mo. Synod, 1949. Pastor Immanuel Luth. Ch., Roseau, Minn., 1949-53, Bethlehem Luth. Ch., Morristown, Minn., 1953-58, Our Savior Luth. Ch., Hutchinson, Minn., 1958-67; pastor Trinity Luth. Ch., White Bear Lake, Minn., 1967-89, ret., 1989; bd. dirs. Minn. dist. Mo. Synod, 1969-82, dist. sec., exec. com., 1969-74, chmn. dist. fin. com., 1974-80, dist. v.p., 1974-78, mem. synod bd. pub. rels., 1981-85; mem. commn. on ch. lit. Mo. Synod, 1972-78, bd. dirs., 1983—; chmn. Ch. Extension Fund, 1974; counselor Minn. South dist. Luth. Women's Missionary League, 1966-72; toured Seven Chs. of Asia Minor, 1972. Recipient Servus Ecclesiae Christi award, 1978. Home: 4154 Hillaire Rd White Bear Lake MN 55110

MARXSEN, WILLI, theologian, educator; b. Kiel, Fed. Republic Germany, Sept. 1, 1919; s. Carl and Sophie M. (Appel) M.; m. Dora Clausen; children: Charlotte, Hartmut, Dorothea. ThD, U. Kiel, 1948; ThD (hon.), Theol. Fak. Kiel, 1961; DD (hon.), U. Dubuque, Iowa, U.S., 1988. Pastor Evangelical Kirche Lübeck, Lübeck, Fed. Republic Germany, 1949-53; studieninspektor Predigerseminar, Preetz, 1953-56; prof. New Testament Kirchliche Hochschule, Bethel, 1956-61; prof. New Testament U. Münster, 1961-84, emeritus, 1984—. Author: Einleitung in das Neue Testament, 1963, Die Auterstehung Jesu von Nazareth, 1968, Ethik im Neuen Testament, 1989, Jesus and Easter, 1990. Home: Von-Stauffenberg Str 40, D-4400 Münster Federal Republic of Germany

MASER, FREDERICK ERNEST, clergyman; b. Rochester, N.Y., Feb. 26, 1908; s. Herman A. and Clara (Krumm) M.; m. Anne S. Spangeberg, Aug. 3, 1933; m. Mary L. Jarden, Dec. 25, 1959. AB, Union Coll., Schenectady, N.Y., 1930; MA, Princeton U., 1933; MDiv, Princeton Theol. Sem., 1933; DD, Dickinson Coll., 1957; LL.D. (hon.), McKendree Coll., 1964. Ordained to ministry Methodist Ch., 1933. Pastor Alice Focht Meml. Ch., Birdsboro, Pa., 1933-38; pastor Central Ch., Frankford, Phila., 1938-45, St. James Ch., Olney, Phila., 1945-53; dist. supt. Northwest dist. Phila. Meth. Ann. Conf., 1953-58; pastor Old St. George's Ch., Phila., 1958-67; on sabbatical leave Europe, 1967-68; acting dean students Conwell Sch. Theology, 1968-69; dir. pub. relations Eastern Pa. Conf. United Meth. Ch., 1969-72; exec. sec. World Meth. Hist. Soc., 1971-74; cons. commn. on archives and history United Meth. Ch., 1974—; Tipple lectr. Drew U., Madison, N.J., 1977; spl. lectr. N.Am. sect. World Meth. Hist. Soc., Ashbury Sem., Wilmore, Ky., 1984—; rep. from Northeast Jurisdiction to TV Radio and Film Commn. Meth. Ch., 1952-60; exec. com. Am. Hist. Socs. of Meth. Ch., 1952-68; vice chmn. N.E. Jurisdictional Hist. Socs., 1948; chmn. div. evangelism Pa. Council Chs., 1953-58; mem.-at-large TV, Radio and Film Commn. Meth. Ch., 1960-64; del. Phila. Ann. Conf. to Jurisdictional Conf. of Meth. Ch., 1952; leader ministerial del. to Gen. Conf. Meth. Ch., Mpls., 1956; del. 9th World Conf. of Methodism, Lake Junaluska, 1956, 10th Conf., Oslo, 1961, 12th Conf., Denver, 1971, 13th Conf., Dublin, 1976, 14th Conf., Hawaii, 1981; dir. pub. relations Phila. Meth. ann. conf., 1961-68; exec. sec. World Meth. Hist. Soc., 1971-74. Author: The Dramatic Story of Early American Methodism, 1965, The History of Methodism in Central Pennsylvania, 1971, Challenge of Change-The Story of a City's Central Church, 1982, Robert Strawbridge, First American Methodist Circuit Rider, 1983, The Story of John Wesley's Sisters or Seven Sisters In Search of Love, 1988; co-author: Proclaiming Grace and Freedom, 198, Christina Rossetti, 19914; mem. editorial bd. Meth. History, 1971-75; editor in chief Jour. Joseph Pilmore, 1968; mem. editorial bd., author History American Methodism, 1964, Ency. World Methodism, 1974, Second Thoughts on John Wesley, 1977; contbr. articles to religious jours. Trustee George Ruck Trust, 1958-82; mem. adv. council Wesley Theol. Sem., Washington, 1960-72. Recipient St. George's Gold medal award for disting. service to Meth. Ch., 1967, Citation Temple U., 1971, (with Mary L. Maser) Phyllis Goodhart award Bryn Mawr Coll. Libr., 1988, cert. appreciation for disting. svc. in field of hisory to United Meth. Ch. Commn. on Archives and History. Mem. Pa. Acad. Fine Arts, Colonial Phila. Hist. Soc. (dir. 1956-64), Ch. History Soc., Union League, Philobiblon Club, Princeton Club (Phila.), Dickens Fellowship Club (N.Y.C.), Phi Beta, Phi Alpha. Home: 705 Benson Manor Jenkintown PA 19046 *Life offers many honors but the older I grow, the more I realize that the highest honor is to have one's name written in the Lamb's Book of Life.*

MASK, LARRY W., minister; b. San Antonio, June 23, 1949; s. Earlie Stephen and Sarah Lynn (Wood) M.; m. Irene O. Nichols, Aug. 9, 1969; children: Tamara L., Tara L., Tandra L. BA in Christian Adminstrn., San Antonio Theol. Sem., 1988, MS in Counseling, 1990, D in Min., 1991. Ordained to ministry Assembly of God Ch. Pastor First Assembly of God, Devine, Tex., 1977-79, New Life Assembly of God, San Antonio, 1981-84; pastor counseling Faith Assembly of God, San Antonio, 1984-90; pastor Southside Assembly of God, San Antonio, 1990—; bd. dirs. Radical Christian Tng., San Antonio, 1989—, Inst. Ch. Planting, San Antonio, 1990—. Author: Devotions For The Camp, 1988. With U.S. Air Force, 1969-80. Republican. Home: 122 Langford San Antonio TX 78221 Office: Southside Assembly of God 503 Moursund San Antonio TX 78221

MASLIN, SIMEON JOSEPH, rabbi; b. Boston, Mar. 18, 1931; s. H. Leon and Frances Ruth (Savitz) Masovetsky; m. Judith Marian Blumberg, Aug. 22, 1954; children: Naomi Beth Godel, David Maslin, Eve Lisa Goldberg. BA, Harvard U., 1952; MA, U. Pa., 1954; BHL, Hebrew Union Coll., Cin., 1956; DMin, Chgo. Theol. Sem., 1979. Ordained rabbi, 1957. Rabbi Monroe Temple of Liberal Judaism, Monroe, N.Y., 1957-62; rabbi Congregation Mikve Israel-Emanuel, Curacao, The Netherlands Antilles, 1962-67, Kehillath Anshe Maariv, Chgo., 1967-71, K.A.M. Isaiah Israel, Chgo., 1971-80, Congregation Keneseth Israel, Elkins Park, Pa., 1980—; pres. Bd. Rabbis of Greater Phila., 1989-91; treas., exec. bd. Mazon: A Jewish Response to Hunger, L.A., 1985—. Author: Gates of Mitzvah, 1979, Sabbath Eve Seder, 1971, One God, Sixteen Houses, 1990; contbr. articles to profl. jours. Pres. Hyde Park-Kenwood Coun. of Chs. and Synagogues, Chgo., 1972-74; exec. bd. Jewish Fedn. Greater Phila., 1987—. Mem. Hebrew Union Coll. Alumni Assn. (pres. 1984-86), N.Am. Rabbinical Coun. of World Union for Progressive Judaism (pres. 1986-90), Cen. Conf. Am. Rabbis (bd. dirs. 1975-77), Jewish Publ. Soc. (bd. dirs. 1991—). Office: Congregation Keneseth Israel York Rd & Township Line Elkins Park PA 19117

MASON, DAVID RAYMOND, theologian, educator; b. Hagerstown, Md., Nov. 6, 1936; s. Edwin L'Huillier and Camilla Schindel (Roulette) M.; m. Margaret Grace Curtis, June 29, 1963; children: Katharine Elizabeth, Charles Quin, Thomas Edwin. AB, W.Va. U., 1959; STB, Gen. Theol. Sem., N.Y.C., 1962; MA, U. Chgo., 1969, PhD, 1973. Ordained priest Episcopal Ch., 1962. Vicar All Sts. Episcopal Ch., South Charleston, W.Va., 1962-66; instr. YMCA Community Coll., Chgo., 1968-72; asst. prof. religious studies John Carroll U., University Heights, Ohio, 1972-77, assoc. prof., 1977-82, prof., 1982—. Author: Time and Providence, 1982; editor: Talking About God, 1983; contbr. articles to religion jours. Pres. Kanawha Valley Coun. on Human Rels., Charleston, W.Va., 1966. Episcopal Ch. Found. fellow, 1970-71, Grauel fellow John Carroll U., 1979, 86. Mem. Am. Acad. Religion, Metaphysical Soc. Am., Soc. for Study of Process Philosophies, Conf. Anglican Theologians, Rowfant Club. Democrat. Home: 2277 N St James Pkwy Cleveland Heights OH 44106 Office: John Carroll U Dept Religious Studies University Heights OH 44118

MASON, HAROLD LEE, minister; b. South Bend, Ind., Dec. 11, 1944; s. Harold J. and Naomi Maybelle (Kline) M.; m. Karen Sue Maxwell, Apr. 8, 1966; children: Kristina, Jennifer, Flora, Joshua. BA, Cin. Bible Coll., 1967, BTh., 1968; PhD, Calif. Grad. Sch. Theology, 1975. Ordained to ministry Christian Ch., 1967. Min. Felicity (Ohio) Ch. of Christ, 1965-68, Twin Cities Christian Ch., Oceanside, Calif., 1968-71, 1st Christian Ch., Downey, Calif., 1971-77, Madeira Ch. of Christ, Cin., 1977—; insstr. pub. speaking Cin. Bible Coll., 1984—; trustee Woodland Lakes Christian Camp, Cin., 1979-89; pres. Ohio Christian Conv., 1990. Author: Evangelistic Sermons, 1981. Mem. Christian Restoration Assn. (trustee, v.p. 1980—), Christian Benevolent Assn. (trustee 1991), Alumni Assn. Cin. Bible Coll. (pres. 1989-90). Home: 9867 Belleford Ct Cincinnati OH 45242 Office: Madeira Ch of Christ 7421 E Galbraith Rd Cincinnati OH 45243

MASON, HERBERT WARREN, JR., author, religion educator; b. Wilmington, Del., Apr. 20, 1932; s. Herbert Warren and Mildred Jane (Noyes) M.; m. Jeanine Young, June 25, 1982; children from previous marriage: Cathleen, Paul, Sarah. AB, Harvard U., 1955, AM, 1965, PhD, 1969. English tchr. Am. Sch. Paris, 1959-60; asst. prof. St. Joseph's Coll., Gorham, Maine, 1960-62; vis. lectr. Simmons Coll., Boston, 1962-63; vis. lectr. in Islamic Hist. Tufts U., Medford, Mass., 1965-66; teaching fellow in English Harvard U., Cambridge, Mass., 1962-66, teaching fellow in Islamic Hist., 1966-67; translator Bollingen Found., N.Y.C., 1968-72; prof. History and Religion Boston U., 1972—. Author: Reflections on the Middle East Crisis, 1970, Two Statesmen of Medieval Islam, 1971, Gilgamesh, 1971 (Nat. Book award nomination), The Death of al-Hallaj, 1979, Moments in Passage, 1979, (novel) Summer Light, 1980; translator: La Passion d'al-Hallaj, 4 vols., Bollingen Series (Louis Massignon), 1983, A Legend of Alexander, 1986, Memoir of a Friend: Louis Massignon, 1988, Testimonies and Reflections, 1989; co-editor Humaniora Islamica; contbr. articles, essays, reviews, fiction, reviews and poetry to popular fiction mags. Sec. Inter-racial Riverside Assn., Cambridge, Mass., 1965-67; trustee Bd. Charity of Edward Hopkins, Boston Athenaeum. Fellow Soc. for Values in Higher Edn.; mem. PEN (bd. dirs. Delos chpt.), Medieval Acad. Am., Am. Oriental Soc., Am. Acad. Religion, Mark Twain Soc., Inst. Internat. des Recherches Louis Massignon in Paris (dir. edn.). Home: The Common Phillipston MA 01331 Office: Boston U 745 Commonwealth Ave Boston MA 02215

MASON, JAMES DONALD, minister; b. Florence, Ala., Oct. 5, 1937; s. George and Addie Lee (Rice) M.; m. Cassandra June Wornal, Feb. 25, 1961; children: Arthur Burns, Jay Donald, Allan Dale, Melita Lee. BA, Samford U., Birmingham, Ala., 1959; MDiv, So. Bapt. Theol. Sem., 1962; MA, U. Ala., 1963; DMin, Columbia Theol. Sem., 1980. Ordained to ministry So. Bapt. Conv., 1963. Asst. prof. of history William Jewell Coll., Liberty, Mo., 1965-67; missionary to Zambia Fgn. Mission Bd., Richmond, Va., 1967-77; pastor Park Ave Bapt. Ch., Atlanta, 1976-80, Coosada (Ala.) Bapt. Ch., 1980-87, Sandy Plains Bapt. Ch., Marietta, Ga., 1988—; cons. home mission bd. Project Assistance to Churches in Transitional Communities. Pres. PTA Millbrook (Ala.) Middle and Jr. High Schs., 1981-82; bd. govs. West El Med. Ctr., Millbrook, 1983-86; trustee Millbrook Jr. High Sch., 1983-86; textbook selection com. Elmore County Bd. Edn., Wetumpka, Ala., 1983-85; community adv. com. Mabry Middle Sch., Marietta, Ga., 1989—. Mem. Noonday Bapt. assn. (chmn. friendship internat. house com. 1988—), Phi Alpha Theta, Omicron Delta Kappa. Home: 2751 Zachary Lake Dr Marietta GA 30064 Office: Sandy Plains Bapt Ch 2825 Sandy Plains Rd Marietta GA 30066 *In the struggle between the positive and the negative influences of life, a person, through his past experiences and relationships, largely makes the choices which affect the direction of his life.*

MASON, JAMES LESTER, retired religion educator, minister; b. Alma, Nebr., Dec. 8, 1923; s. Albert Joshua and Estella Mae (Shaw) M.; m. Norma Nadine Shearer, Mar. 7, 1942; Gail Mason Brilling, Rodney, Nadine Mason Walsworth, Albert. BA, Gustavus Adolphus Coll., 1950; BDiv, Bethel Sem., 1953; MA, Colo. State Coll. Edn., 1955; PhD, U. So. Calif., 1969. Ordained to ministry Bapt. Gen. Conf., 1948/. Parish min. Bapt. Gen. Conf., Arlington Heights, Ill., 1952-68, 79-85; prof. Bethel Coll. and Sem., St. Paul, 1968-79; parish min. Oakmont Community Ch., Santa Rosa, Calif., 1985—; chmn. speech and drama dept. Bethel Coll., St. Paul; trustee Bethel Coll. and Sem., St. Paul, 1957-62, regent, 1980-85; moderator 2 dist. confs., Nebr., Wyo., Colo. and Calif., 1950's, 60's. Contbr. articles to various publs.; speaker, guest radio and TV programs. Cpl. USAAC, 1943-45, MTO. Decorated unit Croix De Guerre avec palm (France). Republican. Home: 6687 Oakmont Dr Santa Rosa CA 95409

MASON, JOE BEN, prison mission executive; b. Texhoma, Tex., Oct. 24, 1910; s. Lloyd Elliot and Lillie Mae Mason; m. Helen Sutton, May 1936 (dec. 1971); 1 child, Joe Lawrence; m. Ada Giebelhaus, Mar. 25, 1972. 2-yr. cert., Amarillo Coll., 1932; student, U. Tex., 1933, Biola U., L.A., 1954; ThD (hon.), Faith Bible Coll. and Sem., Lagos, Nigeria, 1988. Ins. adjuster Md. Casualty Co., El Paso, Tex., 1935-36, FCAB Co., El Paso and Lubbock, Tex., 1937-41; owner, mgr. Mason Claim Svc., Phoenix, 1945-54; founder, dir. Prison Mission Assn., Inc., Weatherford, Tex., 1955-90. With USN, 1943-45. Mem. Marketplace Ministries. Republican. Avocations: reading, travel. Home: 3993 10th St Apt 513 Riverside CA 92501

MASON, MICHAEL DUANE, minister; b. Grand Rapids, Mich., Apr. 27, 1950; s. Howard Edward and Eathel May (Pilant) M.; m. Donna L. Hatfield, July 9, 1972; children: Roberta Lynne, Christopher Michael. B Sacred Lit., Gt. Lakes Bible Coll., Lansing, Mich., 1972; MA, Mich. State U., 1980. Ordained to ministry Chs. of Christ, 1972. Assoc. libr. Mich. Dept. Edn., Lansing, 1968-73; assoc. min. 1st Ch. of Christ, Angola, Ind., 1970-73; assoc. min. youth and edn. 1st Ch. of Christ, Jackson, Mich., 1973-79; sr. min. 1st Ch. of Christ, Jackson, 1979—; chmn. Mich. Bible Bowl, 1976-86; mem. continuation com. Mich. Christian Conv., Lansing, 1990—, pres., 1991-92. Author: Going for the Gold, 1984; contbr. articles to profl. jours. Pres. bd.

dirs. Community Pantry Serving Jackson County, Jackson, 1982-88; mem. dirs. Emergency Needs Coalition, Jackson, 1984-89; mem. adv. bd. Jackson Pub. Schs., 1986-90. Named Honored Min. Grand Commandery KT, 1987, Assoc. of Yr., Am. Bus. Women's Assn., Jackson, 1990. Mem. Evang. Tchr. Tng. Assn. Office: 1st Ch of Christ 2395 W High Dr Jackson MI 49203

MASON, WILLIAM ARTHUR, priest; b. Buffalo, N.Y., Oct. 22, 1945; s. James William and Elizabeth (Germony) M. AA, Oblate Coll., 1965; PhB, Gregorian U., Rome, 1968, Sacred Theology Licentiate, 1972; postgrad., Xavier U., 1981-87. Ordained priest Roman Cath. Ch., 1971. Assoc. pastor St. Michael's Ch., Brattleboro, Vt., 1972-75; facilitator Oblates of Mary Immaculate, Newburgh, N.Y., 1975-79; pastor St. Francis Xavier, Miami, Fla., 1979-87; sabbatical St. Mary's Ch., Oakland, Calif., 1987-88; pastor St. Joseph's Ch., St. Petersburg, Fla., 1988—; facilitator Oblates of Mary Immaculate, U.S., 1980—; nat. chmn. Oblate Region of U.S., 1981—; area v.p. People United to Lead Struggle for Equality, Miami, 1983-87. Co-author: Parish Food Co-op, 1984. Bd. dirs. Comunity Action Agy., Dade County, Fla., 1982-87; bd. dirs. Campaign for Human Devel., 1988—, Black Family Svc. Ctr., 1990—. Recipient Disting. Svc. award People United to Lead Struggle for Equality, 1986, Offl. Proclamation Dade County Govt., 1987, recognition award Diocese of St. Petersburg, 1990. Mem. NAACP. Democrat. Home and Office: St Joseph Ch 2624 Union St S Saint Petersburg FL 33712 *Belief in a God becoming human deepens our self-esteem. It is in the dignity of our God dwelling within that we can relate to each other in a just and loving way.*

MASSANARI, RONALD LEE, religion educator; b. Champaign, Ill., June 4, 1941; s. Karl Louis and Christine (Yoder) M.; m. Rhoda May Nyce, June 9, 1963; children: Nicole, Danielle. BA, Goshen Coll., 1963; MA, U. Wis., 1965; BD, Garrett Theol. Sem., 1966; PhD, Duke U., 1969. Vis. instr. U. N.C., Chapel Hill, 1968-69; vis. asst. prof. Duke U., Durham, N.C., 1969-70; prof. religious studies Alma (Mich.) Coll., 1970—, Charles A. Dana prof., 1985—; adj. prof. San Francisco Theol. Sem., San Anselmo, Calif., 1975—. Contbr. articles to profl. publs. Bd. dirs. Mich. Coun. Humanities, Lansing, 1978-82. Danforth fellow, 1967-69, Danforth assoc., 1979—; NEH grantee, 1972. Mem. Am. Acad. Religion. Democrat. Mennonite. Office: Alma Coll Alma MI 48801

MASSAR, MICHAEL MAURICE, minister; b. Big Spring, Tex., May 8, 1949; s. Milan M. and Merle (Clark) M.; m. Lisa Luckett, May 13, 1972; children: Matthew Dann, Patrick Clark, Meredith Leigh. BA, Baylor U., 1974; MRE, Sothwestern Bapt. Theol. Sem., Ft. Worth; D of Ministry, Grad. Theol. Found., South Bend, Ind., 1988. Ordained to ministry So. Bapt. Conv. Min. to youth 1st Bapt. Ch., Waco, Tex., 1973-74; assoc. pastor 7th and James Bapt. Ch., Waco, 1974-82; sr. pastor Wildewood Bapt. Ch., Spring, Tex., 1982-89; sr. min. 1st Bapt. Ch., Clemson, S.C., 1989—; pres. N.W. Assistance Ministry, Houston. Author: Before You Marry; columnist The Messenger; contbr. articles to religious jours. Pres. Clemson Community Care, 1990-91, Clemson Congregations in Touch, 1991—; active Leadership Clemson, 1991. Fellow Grad. Theol. Found., S.E. Homiletics Assn.; mem. Rotary. Office: First Bapt Ch 397 College Ave Clemson SC 29631

MASSEY, DEOBRAH PRESCOTT, religious organization administrator; b. Covington, Ga., Jan. 14, 1956; d. Johnny Sparks and Velma Pauline (Lassiter) P.; m. Gary K. Massey, July 26, 1975. BA in Early Childhood Edn., DeKalb Tech. U., Decatur, Ga., 1974. Banking official 1st Nat. Bank, Covington, 1974-78, Birmingham (Ala.) Trust Nat. Bank, 1978-79, 1st Tenn. Bank, Memphis, 1979-80, C/S Nat. Bank, Atlanta, 1980-81; adminstrv. asst. Presbyt. Ch. USA, Covington, 1981—. Active Nat. Rep. Cen. Com., Chronic Fatigue Syndrome Soc., Habitat for Humanity Found., Nat. Clean and Beautiful Commn., Friends of the Earth Found., MADD, Atlanta Olympic Com., Covington Community Food Pantry. Mem. Presbyn. Women (chmn. 1986-88), Satsuki Garden Club (yearbook editor 1988—), Amateur Photographers Internat., Garden Clubs Ga., Nat. Coun. State Garden Clubs, Greenpeace Internat., Ga. Fedn. Women's Clubs, Atlanta Lawn Tennis Assn., Main St., U.S.A., Atlanta Braves Diamond Club, Jr. Women's Club (1st v.p. 1986-87), Ch. Secs. Am., Jaycees, Bulldog Club. Avocations: photography, travel, reading. Home: 6171 Farmington Ln Covington GA 30209 Office: Presbyn Ch USA 1169 Clark St Covington GA 30209

MASSEY, JAMES EARL, clergyman, educator; b. Ferndale, Mich., Jan. 4, 1930; s. George Wilson and Elizabeth (Shelton) M.; m. Gwendolyn Inez Kilpatrick, Aug. 4, 1951. Student U. Detroit, 1949-50, 55-57; B.Th., B.R.E., Detroit Bible Coll., 1961; A.M., Oberlin Grad. Sch. Theology, 1964; postgrad. U. Mich., 1967-69; D.D., Asbury Theol. Sem., 1972; postgrad. Pacific Sch. Religion, 1972, Boston Coll., 1982-83. Ordained to ministry Church of God, 1951. Assoc. minister Ch. of God, Detroit, 1951-53; sr. pastor Met. Church of God, Detroit, 1954-76, pastor-at-large, 1976; speaker Christian Brotherhood Hour, 1977-82; prin. Jamaica Sch. Theology, Kingston, 1963-66; campus minister Anderson Coll., Ind., 1969-77, asst. prof. religious studies, 1969-75, assoc. prof., 1975-80, prof. N.T. and homiletics, 1981-84; dean of chapel and univ., prof. religion and society Tuskegee U., Ala., 1984—; chmn. Commn. on Higher Edn. in the Ch. of God, 1968-71; vice chmn. bd. publs. Ch. of God, 1968-78; dir. Warner Press, Inc. Author: When Thou Prayest, 1960; The Worshipping Church, 1961; Raymond S. Jackson, A Portrait, 1967; The Soul Under Siege, 1970; The Church of God and the Negro, 1971; The Hidden Disciplines, 1972; The Responsible Pulpit, 1973; Temples of the Spirit, 1974; The Sermon in Perspective, 1976; Concerning Christian Unity, 1979; gen. editor: Christian Brotherhood Hour Study Bible, 1979; Designing the Sermon, 1980; co-editor Interpreting God's Word for Today, 1982; editor Educating for Service, 1984; The Spiritual Disciplines, 1985, The Bridge Between, 1988; mem. editorial bd. The Christian Scholar's Rev. Leadership mag.; contbg. editor Preaching mag. Mem. Corp. Inter-Varsity Christian Fellowship; bd. dirs. World Vision. Served with AUS, 1951-53. Recipient research scholarship Christianity Today Inst. Mem. Nat. Assn. Coll. and Univ. Chaplains, Nat. Com. Black Churchmen, Nat. Negro Evang. Assn. (bd. dirs. 1969—). Office: Tuskegee U Office Dean of Chapel Tuskegee AL 36088

MASSEY, JOAN LESLIE, lay worker; b. Beaufort, S.C., Apr. 17, 1966; d. Syd Douglas and Jeane (Barnes) M. Cert. in acctg., Pickens Tech. Sch., Jasper, Ga., 1986. Fin. sec. Bapt. Ch. of Beaufort, 1989—. Vol. March of Dimes, 1987—, United Way, 1990—, Cystic Fibrosis Found., Ellijay, Ga., 1989—; youth leader Young Life, 1989—. Mem. Bapt. Young Women. Home: 125 Elliott St Beaufort SC 29902 Office: Bapt Ch of Beaufort 600 Charles St Beaufort SC 29902

MAST, GREGG ALAN, clergyman; b. Grand Rapids, Mich., Feb. 7, 1952; s. Corneal and Stella (DeVries) M.; m. Vicki Kopf, May 19, 1973; children: Andrew, Katherine, David. BA, Hope Coll., Holland, Mich., 1974; MDiv, New Brunswick (N.J.) Sem., 1976; MPhil, Drew U., Madison, N.J., 1981, PhD, 1985. Ordained to ministry Reformed Ch., 1976. Pastor Second Reformed Ch., Irvington, N.J., 1978-85; minister social witness and worship Reformed Ch. Am., N.Y.C., 1985-88; sr. minister The First Ch. in Albany (N.J.), 1988—; lectr. New Brunswick Sem. and Westminster Choir Coll., 1980-85; travel seminar leader Cen. Am., Soviet Union, Middle East, 1985-90. Author: Living Free - Ten Guides to Service, 1989; contbr. articles to profl. jours. Bd. mem. The Whitny Young Health Clinic, Albany, 1989—. Mem. N.Am. Acad. Liturgy. Home: PO Box 613 Guilderland NY 12084 Office: The First Ch in Albany 110 N Pearl St Albany NY 12207

MASTERMAN, PATRICIA DINAN, deacon, editor; b. Amarillo, Tex., Nov. 4, 1927; d. Wilfrid Irvin and Catherine Frances (Gavin) Dinan; m. John Shelby Masterman, July 9, 1955 (div. 1969); children: David Dinan, Thomas Gavin. BA summa cum laude, Colo. Coll., 1949. Ordained to ministry Episcopal Ch. as deacon, 1985. Editor Episcopal Diocese of N.W. Tex., Lubbock, 1972-88, Episcopal Diocese of Ft. Worth, 1988-89, All Sts. Episcopal Cathedral, Ft. Worth, 1989-90, All Saints' Episcopal Parish, Ft. Worth, 1991—; mem. staff Presbyn. Night Shelter, 1989-90. Editor, reporter parish newsletter Pro Omnibus Sanctis, 1988—. Bd. dirs. Westaid, Ft. Worth, 1989-91. Mem. Episcopal Communicators, North Am. Assn. for Diaconate, Phi Beta Kappa. Office: All Saints Episcopal Ch 5001 Crestline Rd Fort Worth TX 76107

MATAGA, PETERO, archbishop. Archbishop of Suva, Roman Cath. Ch., Fiji. Office: Archdiocesan Office, Nicholas, House, Pratt St, POB 109, Suva Fiji*

MATE, MARTIN, bishop; b. Port Rexton, Nfld., Can., Nov. 12, 1929; s. John and Hilda (Toope) M.; m. Florence Mabel Hooper, Nov. 12, 1962; children: Carolyn, Elizabeth, Phyllis, John, Carl. L.Th., Queens Coll., St. John's Nfld., 1953; B.A. with honors, Bishop's U., Que., 1966, M.A. with honors, 1967. Ordained deacon Anglican Ch. of Can., 1952, priest, 1953, elected bishop, 1980, consecrated, 1980. Curate Anglican Cathedral, St. John's, 1952-53; rector Pushthrough Parish, Nfld., 1953-58; incumbent St. Anthony Mission, Nfld., 1958-64; rector Cookshire Parish, Que., 1964-67, Catalina Parish, Nfld., 1967-72, Pouch Cove Parish, Nfld., 1972-76; treas. Diocese of Eastern Nfld. and Labardor, St. John's, 1976-80; bishop Diocese of Eastern Nfld. and Labrador, St. John's, 1980—; mem. liturgical, programme, exec. and fin. coms. Anglican Diocese of Nfld. and Diocese of Eastern Nfld. and Labrador, 1972—; mem. provincial synod and provincial council Anglican Province of Can., 1975—; mem. gen. synod, nat. exec and adminstrn. and fin. com. Anglican Ch. of Can., 1975—. Home: 25 E Meadows Ave, Saint John's, NF Canada A1A 3M6 Office: Diocese of Eastern Nfld, & Labrador Anglican Ch, 19 Kings Bridge Rd, Saint John's, NF Canada A1C 3K4

MATERA, RICHARD ERNEST, minister; b. Hartford, Conn., July 13, 1925; s. Charles Carlo and Philomena Antoinette Cecile (Liberatore) M.; m. Marylynn Olga Beuth, Sept. 3, 1949; children: Thomas Charles, Nancy Jean Matera Dye. Student, Trinity Coll., Hartford, 1943, Biarritz Am. U., France, 1945; BA magna cum laude, Colgate U., 1949; MDiv, Andover Newton Theol. Sch., 1953; DD, Calif. Christian U., 1981. Ordained to ministry Bapt. Ch., 1952. Dir. youth work Quincy Point (Mass.) Congl. Ch., 1949-50; pastor, dir. vacation ch. sch. Panton and Addison (Vt.) chs., 1950; min. Thompson (Conn.) Hill Ch., 1950-51, Waldo Congl. Ch., Brockton, Mass., 1951-54, Cen. Congl. Ch., Orange, Mass., 1954-59; sr. min. 1st Congl. United Ch. of Christ, Berea, Ohio, 1959-71, St. Paul Community Ch., Homewood, Ill., 1971-76; min. Mont Clare Congl. United Ch. of Christ, Chgo., 1980—; pres. Millers River Coun. Chs., 1957-58; mem. dept. ch. world responsibility Mass. Coun. Chs., 1957-59; chmn. internat. affairs com. of state social action com. United Ch. of Christ, 1962-63, del. Gen. Synod, Chgo., mem. peace priority task force Western Res. Assn., 1967-70, mem. commn. on ch. and ministry Ohio conf., 1968-71, chmn. dept. ch. and community Western Res. Assn. Coun., Cleve., 1969-70, mem. peace and internat. rels. com., 1973; mem. ad hoc com. on Vietnam Greater Cleve. Coun. of Chs. of Christ, 1966-68; probation officer DuPage County Probation Dept., Wheaton, Ill., 1985-86. Capt. Cleve. United Fund, 1961-63, Colgate Fund Dr., 1963; trustee Cleve. Union, 1961-63, Berea United Fund, 1963-69; mem. Berea Coun. on Human Rels., 1965-71, U.S. com. Christian Peace Conf., Prague, Czechoslovakia, 1967—; del Action Conf. on Nat. Priorities, Washington, 1969; bd. dirs., mem. ecumenical mission com. Community Renewal Soc., Chgo., 1972-76; bd. dirs. Respond Now, Chicago Heights, Ill., 1972—; mem. Pres.'s Coun., Chgo. Theol. Sem., 1973—; pres. Mended Hearts Inc., Downers Grove, Ill., 1989-90. With U.S. Army, 1943-46, ETO. Austen Colgate scholar, 1946-49. Fellow Profl. Assn. Clergy; mem. Planetary Soc., Jacques Cousteau Soc., Antique Automobile Club, Hupmobile Club, Cadillac Club, Phi Beta Kappa. Democrat. Home and Office: 5 E Memorial Dr Bensenville IL 60106-2541

MATESICH, SISTER MARY ANDREW, college president; b. Zanesville, Ohio, May 5, 1939. BA, Ohio Dominican Coll., 1962; MS, U. Calif., Berkeley, 1963, PhD in Chemistry, 1966. Asst. prof. chemistry Ohio Dominican Coll., Columbus, 1965-70, assoc. prof., from 1970, chmn. dept., 1965-73, acad. dean, 1973-78, pres., 1978—. Petroleum Research Fund grantee Ohio Dominican Coll., 1965-68; NSF grantee Case Western Res. U. and Ohio Dominican Coll., 1969-72. Mem. Council Ind. Colls. (bd. dirs. 1985—), Nat. Assn. Ind. Colls. and Univs. (bd. dirs. 1986—), Assn. Ind. Colls. and Univs. Ohio (chmn. 1984-86). Office: Ohio Dominican Coll 1216 Sunbury Rd Columbus OH 43219

MATHENEY, MATTHEW PIERCE, religion educator; b. El Dorado, Ark., Sept. 24, 1930; s. M. Pierce and Harriett (Waters) M.; m. Katherine Elizabeth Clippard, July 29, 1952; children: Susan Veronica, Matthew Pierce IV, Kendall Clippard. BA, Baylor U., 1952; MA, Brown U., 1958; BD, So. Bapt. Seminary, Louisville, 1957, ThD, 1965. Instr. So. Bapt. Seminary, 1958-60; asst. prof. Midwestern Bapt. Seminary, Kans. City, Mo., 1960-65, assoc. prof., 1965-72, prof. Old Testament and Hebrew, 1972—; pastor Satin (Tex.) Bapt. Ch., 1951-52, Highland Park 2d Bapt. Ch., Louisville, 1953-58, Sardinia Bapt. Ch., Westport, Ind., 1958-60. Author: (study guides) Hosea: God's Wounded Love, 1975, Studies in Psalms, 1984. Pres. Northland Mayors and Citizens Human Rels. Coun., Kans. City, Mo., 1976. Edgar Lee Marston scholar Brown U., 1952-53; AATS faculty fellow Harvard Div. Sch., 1968-69, Albright Inst. Archaeol. Rsch. sr. fellow, 1987-88. Mem. Am. Schs. Oriental Rsch., Soc. Bibl. Lit., Bibl. Archaeology Soc., Lahav Rsch. Project (area supr. 1986—), Kans. City Soc. Theol. Studies (pres. 1971-72). Home: 5221 N Garfield Kansas City MO 64118 Office: Midwestern Bapt Sem 5001 N Oak St Trafficway Kansas City MO 64118

MATHENY, PAUL EDWARD, JR., religious organization administrator and educator; b. Orangeburg, S.C., Mar. 25, 1947; s. Paul Edward Sr. and Charsey (Moreau) M.; m. Betsey Cox, Aug. 9, 1969; children: Paul Edward III, Marianne. AA, Anderson (S.C.) Coll., 1967; BA, Mars Hill Coll., 1969; MA, Southwestern Bapt. Theol. Sem., 1972. Minister of music and edn. First Bapt. Ch., Thomasville, N.C., 1972-76, Oakview Bapt. Ch., High Point, N.C., 1976-77; minister of edn. and adminstrn. Blvd. Bapt. Ch., Anderson, 1977—; A.S.S.I.S.T. Saluda Bapt. Assn., 1985-88; state worker S.C. Bapt. Conv., Columbia, 1980-89; met. dir. Bapt. Sunday Sch. Bd., Nashville. Recipient Good Citizenship award Lions, Bamberg, S.C., 1965. Mem. Nat. Assn. Ch. Bus. Adminstrs. Republican. Avocations: landscape, new home constrn. Office: Boulevard Bapt Ch 700 Boulevard Anderson SC 29621

MATHENY, ROBERT DUANE, clergyman; b. Long Beach, Calif., Nov. 17, 1924; s. Harry and Ethel Mae (Brothers) M.; m. Norma Elizabeth Cheverton, June 22, 1949; children: Sarah Elizabeth, Paul Duane. BA, Tex. Christian U., Ft. Worth, 1945; MDiv, Tex. Christian U., 1949; postgrad., Princeton Theol. Sem., 1960, U. Chgo., 1952, Pacific Sch. Religion, 1955. Ordained to ministry Christian Ch. (Disciples of Christ), 1950; cert. grief counselor. Minister 1st Christian Ch., Conroe, Tex., 1948-50; minister First Christian Ch., Center, Tex., 1950-53, Jacksonville, Tex., 1953-63; sr. minister First Christian Ch., Richardson, Tex., 1963-68, Covenant Christian Ch., Tucker, Ga., 1968-70, Winter Park Christian Ch., Winter Park, Fla., 1970-76, First Christian Ch., Bay City, Tex., 1976-80, Oaks Christian Ch., Houston, 1980-83; sr. minister, pastor St. Charles Ave. Christian Ch., New Orleans, 1983-89; outreach grief cons. Lake Lawn Metairie Funeral Home, New Orleans, 1986—, St. Bernard Meml. Funeral Home, Chalmette, La., 1988—. Contbr. articles to profl. jours. Pres. Civic Music Assn., Jacksonville, Tex., 1958-63. Mem. AACD, Tex. Conf. Chs. (pres. 1965), Greater New Orleans Fedn. Chs. (exec. bd. 1987—), La. Interchurch Conf. (v.p. 1987-90), Assn. for Death Edn. and Counseling, Masons, Rotary, Alpha Psi Omega. Democrat. Avocations: opera, drama, walking, history. Home: 3721 Nashville Ave New Orleans LA 70125 Office: LL Metairie Funeral Home 5100 Pontchartrain Blvd New Orleans LA 70124

MATHENY, RUTH ANN, editor; b. Fargo, N.D., Jan. 17, 1918; d. Jasper Gordon and Mary Elizabeth (Carey) Wheelock; m. Charles Edward Matheny, Oct. 24, 1960. B.E., Mankato State Coll., 1938; M.A., U. Minn., 1955; postgrad., Universidad Autonoma de Guadalajara, Mex., summer 1956, Georgetown U., summer, 1960. Tchr. in U.S. and S.Am., 1939-61; asso. editor Charles E. Merrill Pub. Co., Columbus, Ohio, 1963-66; tchr. Confraternity Christian Doctrine, Washington Court House, Ohio, 1969-70; assoc. editor Jr. Cath. Messenger, Dayton, Ohio, 1966-68; editor Witness Intermediate, Dayton, 1968-70; editor in chief, assoc. pub. Today's Cath. Tchr., Dayton, 1970—; editor in chief Catechist, Dayton, 1976-89, Ednl. Dealer, Dayton, 1976-80; v.p. Peter Li, Inc., Dayton, 1980—. Editorial collaborator: Dimensions of Personality series, 1969—; co-author: At Ease in the Classroom; author: Why a Catholic School?, Scripture Stories for Today: Why Religious Education?. Mem. Bd. Friends Ormond Beach Library. Mem. EDPRESS, Nat. League Am. Pen Women, Nat. Coun. Cath. Women, Cath. Press Assn., Nat. Cath. Ednl. Assn., 3d Order St. Francis (eucharistic minister 1990—). Home: 26 Reynolds Ave Ormond Beach FL 32174 Office: Peter Li Inc 2451 E River Rd Dayton OH 45439 *In a world that is constantly changing, a strong religious faith is a dependable compass through which we are able to stay on a positive, forward course.*

MATHENY, TIMOTHY EARL, religious consultant; b. Huntington, W.Va., Oct. 17, 1952; s. Carl Paul and Betty Lou (Gordon) M.; children: Sara Beth, Philip Earl. BA, Harding U., 1974; M in Theology, Harding Grad. Sch. Religion, 1977; D Ministry, Fuller Theol. Sem., 1987. Lic. securities broker. Minister Madison (Tenn.) Ch. of Christ, 1977-81; exec. dir. Ctr. for Ch. Growth, Houston, 1981-87; dist. rep. A.M.I. Securities, Amarillo, Tex., 1987-89; investment banker Commonwealth Ch. Fin., 1989—; cons. in field. Mem. N. Am. Soc. for Ch. Growth. Mem. Ch. of Christ. Avocations: model R.R., photography, snow skiing. Office: PO Box 300113 Houston TX 77230

MATHER, HERBERT, minister; b. Madelia, Minn., Sept. 30, 1934; s. Earl E. and Essie (Archerd) M.; m. Lillian Richter, June 9, 1957; children: Michael, Peter, Alan, Linda. BA, Hamline U., 1957; BD, Drew U., 1960. Ordained to ministry Meth. Ch., 1960. Pastor Springs Valley Larger Parish, French Lick, Ind., 1960-66, Whiteland (Ind.) United Meth. Ch., 1966-74, Huntingburg (Ind.) United Meth. Ch., 1974-79; assoc. dir. Conf. Coun. on Ministries, Bloomington, Ind., 1979-86; asst. gen. sec. Gen. Bd. Discipleship, Nashville, 1986—; bd. dirs. Ecumenical Ctr. for Stewardship Studies, Indpls., 1986—. Author: Planning a Shepherding Program for Your Congregation, 1985, Becoming a Giving Church, 1986, Gifts Discovery Workshop, 1986, Celebrate Giving, 1988, Letters for All Seasons, 1991. Avocations: carpentry, photography. Office: Gen Bd Discipleship 1908 Grand Ave PO Box 840 Nashville TN 37202

MATHER, JOHN CARL, minister; b. L.A., Oct. 19, 1938; s. Carl N. and Dorothy (Williams) M.; m. Peggy Jo Frutschy, Feb. 20, 1972; children: Cynthia, Thomas. BA, Stanford U., 1960; MDiv, Princeton Theol. Sem., 1963. Ordained to ministry Presbyn. Ch. (U.S.A.), 1963. Pastor 1st Presbyn. Ch., Hamburg, N.J., 1963-65; assoc. pastor Pleasant Hills Larger Parish, West Leisenring, Pa., 1965-68; asst. pastor Fremont Ave. United Presbyn. Ch., Bellevue, Pa., 1968-69; pastor Carroll United Presbyn. Parish, Carrollton, Ohio, 1969-77, 1st Presbyn. Ch. (U.S.A.), South Lyon, Mich., 1977-91; commr. Gen. Assembly, Presbyn. Ch. (U.S.A.), 1986. Chmn. bd. Tri-County Community Action Agy., Ulrichsville, Ohio, 1974-77; bd. dirs. A-Jay Svcs. Inc, Ann Arbor, Mich, 1991—; mem. sch. dist. adv. coms. on substance abuse and on the reproductive system, South Lyon, Mich, 1991—.'

MATHER, SHIRLEY BROWN, lay worker; b. Evansville, Ind., June 27, 1948; d. Arthur L. and Inez (Hall) Brown; m. Clement M. Mather, Jr., Jan. 30, 1976. BS, Murray State U., 1971. Ch. clk. Liberty Bapt. Ch., Madisonville, Ky., 1983-84, Sunday sch. tchr., study course leader, 1980—, ch. treas., 1985—, ch./pastor sec., 1988—; media ctr. dir. Little Bethel Bapt. Assn., Madisonville, 1986—, hist. com. chmn., 1990—; sec.-treas. Gideons Internat. Aux.-Hopkins County West Camp, Madisonville, 1990—. Author: A History of Liberty Baptist Church, 1983, The Sesquicentennial History of Little Bethel Baptist Association, 1986. Recipient Sunday Sch. Leadership diploma So. Bapt. Conv./Sunday Sch. Bd., 1991. Home: 1925 Manitou Rd Manitou KY 42436 Office: Liberty Bapt Ch 100 Liberty Ch Dr Madisonville KY 42431

MATHER-HEMPLER, PORTIA ANN, minister; b. Port Townsend, Wash., June 10, 1949; d. Howard Lester and Portia Davis (Bentley) Mather. BA, U. Oreg., 1972; postgrad., Ripon Coll. Cuddesdon, Oxford, Eng., 1982-83; MDiv., Ch. Div. Sch. of Pacific, 1984. Ordained to ministry Episcopal Ch. as deacon, 1984, as priest, 1985. Dir. religious edn. St. Thomas Episcopal Ch., Eugene, Oreg., 1975-78; adminstrv. sec. Campus Interfaith Ministry U. Oreg., Eugene, 1978-79; sec. Christian edn. Diocese of Oreg., Portland, 1979-80; curate All Saints Episcopal Ch., Palo Alto, Calif., 1984-87; asst. rector St. John's Episcopal Ch., Olympia, Wash., 1987-90; interim asst. rector St. Andrew's Episcopal Ch., Saratoga, Calif., 1991—; mem. Santa Clara Deanery Christian Educators, Diocese of El Camino Real, Calif., 1985-86. Avocations: cooking, fishing, travelling, needlepoint, reading. Office: St Andrew's Episcopal Ch PO Box 2789 Saratoga CA 95070

MATHEWS, JAMES HAROLD, minister; b. Longview, Tex., Nov. 28, 1946; s. James Harold Sr. and Ruth Mildred (Gaines) M.; m. Carol Elaine Hartin, Aug. 2, 1969; children: Katherine Elizabeth, Patrick Alan, Suzanne Elaine. Student, Howard Payne U., 1965-73, Southwestern Bapt. Theol. Sem., 1984-87. Minister youth and music First Bapt. Ch., Goldthwaite, Tex., 1973-75, Freeman Heights Bapt. Ch., Garland, Tex., 1975-78; minister youth and music N.W. Bapt. Ch., Austin, Tex., 1978-81, Marshall, Tex., 1981-84; minister music and adminstrn. N.W. Bapt. Ch., West Columbia, Tex., 1984—; min. First Bapt. Ch., West Columbia, Tex.; pres. bd. Tex. Bapt. Encampment, Palacios, 1989-90. Bd. dirs. Cen. Emergency Med. Svcs., West Columbia, Tex., 1986-91, v.p., 1989-90. Mem. Soda Lake Assn. (assist team Marshall chpt. 1983-86), Mills Assn. (assoc. music dir. Goldthwaite chpt. 1969-73), Austin Assn. (assoc. music dir. Austin chpt. 1978-80), Rotary (bd. dirs. West Columbia chpt. 1987-90, sec. 1990-91). Home: 341 Freeman West Columbia TX 77486 Office: First Bapt Ch 226 S Broad PO Box 326 West Columbia TX 77486

MATHEWS, JOHN, bishop. Bishop Apostolic Overcoming Holy Ch. of God Inc., Dayton, Ohio. Office: Apostolic Overcoming Holy Ch of God Inc 12 College St Dayton OH 45407*

MATHEWSON, PETER SCOTT, minister; b. Rockville, Conn., Jan. 17, 1947; s. Daniel A. and Emma Isabel (Shipman) M.; m. Sandra Lea Yoak, Aug. 27, 1971; children: Amy Renee, Stacy Elizabeth. Dipl. in Bible, Lancaster (Pa.) Bible Coll., 1968; AB, Malone Coll., Canton, Ohio, 1970; MDiv, Ashland (Ohio) Theol. Sem., 1975. Ordained to ministry, Am. Bapt. Chs. USA. Youth dir. Calvary United Meth. Ch., Canton, 1968-71; pastor Stanwood Community Ch., Navarre, Ohio, 1972-76, Westville Congl. Ch., Beloit, Ohio, 1976-84, Community Christian Ch., Columbus, Ohio, 1984-91; chmn. bd. dirs. Child Evangelism Fellowship, Columbus, 1985-91; cons. Youth for Christ, Columbus, 1984-89; chmn. pastoral care Alliance (Ohio) Community Hosp., 1977-84; treas. Community Action of Mahoning County, Sebring, 1978-84; chaplain Copeland Oaks, Sebring, 1979-84. Bd. trustees Community Mediation Svcs., Columbus, 1988. Mem. Ruritan. Home: 655 Rosehill Rd Reynoldsburg OH 43068 Office: East Livingston Bapt Ch 6500 E Livingston Ave Reynoldsburg OH 43068 *Of all the things helpful in life, a good attitude about the past, present and future is imperative. The attitude give roots and wings to life.*

MATHIA, MARY LOYOLA, nun, educator; b. Hempstead, N.Y., Sept. 14, 1921; d. Paul John and Laura Marie (Linck) Mathia. B.A., Coll. Mt. St. Joseph, 1953; M. Pastoral Studies, Loyola U.-Chgo., 1980. Joined Sisters of Charity of Cin., Roman Cath. Ch., 1941. Tchr. various schs. Ohio and Mich., 1943-62, St. John Bapt. Sch., Chillum, Md., 1962-63; social studies tchr. and dept. chmn. Holy Name High Sch., Cleve., 1963-69; ednl. cons. Diocese of Cleve., 1970-78; dir. edn. St. Benedict Ch., Crystal River, Fla., 1979—; founding prin. Cen. Cath. Sch. of Citrus County, Lecanto, Fla., 1985-90, v.p. devel. and pub. rels., 1990-91; parish cons., 1986—. Republican. Office: Cen Cath Sch Citrus County 4340 W Homosassa Trail Lecanto FL 32661 *Society today is crying out for stability and a purpose for life. Only a God-centered education can fill the void created by the noise of external forces and the deadening of creative ideas stemming from a computer, media—saturated environment. As ministers of the Gospel our "quiet whispers" must penetrate the minds of a weary people, inspire them and bring them safely to the harbor of salvation in Christ Jesus Our Lord.*

MATHIEU, DANIEL ROBERT, pastor; b. Lewiston, Maine, Sept. 7, 1950; s. Robert L. and Rita C. (Champagne) M.; m. Theresa C. Lebrun, May 17, 1969; children: Yvonne T., Rita D. BA in Theology, Trinity Bible Inst., 1982; postgrad., Barstown Jr. Coll., 1987. Lic. min., 1982; ordained to ministry Assemblies of God, 1985. Tchr. Sunday sch. Calvary Community Ch., Norwalk, Calif., 1978, min. of pastoral care, 1984-86; pastor of youth Trinity Assembly of God, Gray, Maine, 1982-84; pastor Trinity Assembly of God, Daggette, Calif., 1986-89, Calvary Chapel Assembley of God, Sawyer, N.D., 1989—; chaplain Daggette Fire Dept., 1986-89, Sawyer Fire Dept.,

1989—, Velva (N.D.) Ambulance Svc., 1989—, Mouse River Fire Assn., Sawyer, 1991—. Vol. fire figter, EMT Sawyer Fire Dept., Daggette Fire Dept.; EMT Velva Ambulance Svc.; asst. chmn. Dagette Jr. High Sch. PTA, 1987. *Life is a race run all too often from the one who gives life, Jesus Christ. If men would run to God instead of from Him, life would be better for all mankind.*

MATHIEU, ROBERT EDWARD, minister; b. Altoona, Pa., Nov. 25, 1941; s. Robert Melvin and Betty Ruth (Mehaffie) M.; m. Sharon Patricia Hunter, Aug. 14, 1965; children—Robert Renton, Shari Lynn. Diploma Faith Sch. Theology, 1965; diploma in urban studies Westminster Sem., 1975, Covenant Sem., 1976. Asst. pastor Bethel Pentecostal Tabernacle, Washington, 1966-73; youth dir. Capitol Sect. A/G, Washington, 1967-74; missionary Am. Missionary Fellowship, Washington, 1970—; pastor Anacostia Gospel Chapel, Washington, 1977—; founder, dir. D.C. Christian Ministries, Washington, 1978—; bd. dirs. Staddard Bapt. Home, Washington, 1980—; sec. Intercollegiate Pentecostal Conf., 1980-82. Pres. Malcolm X Elem. Sch. PTA, Washington, 1978; officer Congress Heights Community Assn., Washington, 1981-83; bd. dirs. Anacostia Econ. Devel. Corp., Washington, 1984—. Recipient Humanitarian award Howard U., 1980; Citywide Father of Yr. award D.C. Fedn. Civic Assn., 1982; Outstanding Community Service award Congress Heights Community Assn., 1985. Mem. Nat. Black Evangelical Assn., Washington City Bible Soc. (bd. dirs. 1975—). Home: 1100 Savannah St SE Washington DC 20032 Office: DC Christian Ministries 1100 Savannah St SE Washington DC 20032

MATHIEU, ROBERT ERNEST, priest; b. Winchendon, Mass., May 6, 1947; s. Robert Joseph and Lenore Marie (Bernard) M. BA, Holy Apostles Sem., 1970; MDiv, Christ the King Sem., 1976. Ordained priest Roman Cath. Ch., 1976. Pastor Santo Nino Ch., Aragon, N.Mex., 1980-82, Immaculate Heart of Mary Ch., Page, Ariz., 1982-86, Sacred Heart Ch., Waterflow, N.Mex., 1986-88, San Rafael (N.Mex.) Ch., 1989—; youth dir. Diocese of Gallup (N.Mex.), 1988-89. Home and Office: PO Box 145 San Rafael NM 87051

MATHIS, ROBERT LLOYD, pastor; b. Detroit, Oct. 18, 1942; s. William Hardy and Barbara Jane (Roark) M.; m. Catherine Anne Hayes, Aug. 21, 1965; children: Virginia, Elizabeth, Andrew. BA, Western Mich. U., 1965; MDiv, Colgate Rochester Div. Sch., 1969. Pastor First Bapt. Ch., Indiana, Pa., 1973-79, Moshanticut Park Bapt. Ch., Cranston, R.I., 1979-89, Bristol (Conn.) Bapt. Ch., 1989—. Graduate Leadership R.I., 1987. Mem. Mins. Coun. of Conn., Roger Williams Fellowship of Am. Bapt. (pres. 1991—), Bristol Area Assn. for Ministry (pres.). Home: 79 Woodhaven Rd Bristol CT 06010 Office: Bristol Bapt Ch 43 School St Bristol CT 06010-6085

MATHIS, ROBERT REX, church administrator, educator; b. Harrison, Ark., Dec. 27, 1947; s. Rex Clayton and Jannie Fay (Garner) M.; m. Maryln Odene Floyd, Aug. 23, 1968; 1 child, Karissa Odalyn. BA, Wayland Bapt. Coll., 1969; MEd, U. Tex., El Paso, 1976; MRE, Southwestern Theol. Sem., 1979; EdD, Southwestern Bapt. Theol. Sem., 1984. Min. edn. Mountain View Bapt. Ch., El Paso, Tex., 1974-77, Ridglea Bapt. Ch., Ft. Worth, 1977-81; assoc. pastor 1st Bapt. Ch., Santa Fe, N.Mex., 1981-86; assoc. prof. ednl. founds., chmn. div. Christian edn. New Orleans Bapt. Theol. Sem., 1986—. Contbr. articles to profl. jours. Sgt. U.S. Army, 1971-74. Recipient Albert Marsh award, Southwestern Bapt. Theol. Sem., 1981. Mem. Nat. Assn. Ch. Bus. Adminstrs., Southwestern Bapt. Religious Edn. Assn., Southern Bapt. Religious Edn. Assn. Office: New Orleans Bapt Theol Sem 3939 Gentilly Blvd New Orleans LA 70126

MATHIS, WILLIAM HENRY, III, minister; b. San Francisco, Dec. 23, 1963; s. William Henry II and Wandarae (Toliver) M.; m. Vickie Bonita Gee, June 20, 1984. BA in Religion and Philosophy, Bishop Coll., Dallas, 1984; postgrad., Colgate Rochester (N.Y.) Div. Sch., 1984. Ordained to ministry Bapt. Ch., 1986. Asst. pastor Providence Bapt. Ch., Richmond, Calif., 1980-84; asst. pastor children's ch. Concord Bapt. Ch., Dallas, 1981-83; dir. evangelism Friendship-West Bapt. Ch., Dallas, 1983-87; asst. pastor Resurrection Bapt. Ch., Dallas, 1987—; detention officer Dallas County Sheriff Dept., 1987—; advisor Providence Bapt. Ch., 1981—; mem. nominating com. Outstanding Young Men of Am., Birmingham, Ala., 1985-87. Author: (bible study) Quality Time with the Savior, 1984, (evangelism) Effective Witnessing in the 20th Century, 1985 (Book of Promise award 1984). Chaplin Bishop Coll. Ministers Lyceum, 1983-84; liaison Dallas Ind. Sch. Dist., 1985—. Recipient Congeniality award Tex. Assn. Developing Coll., Marshall, 1984; named one of Outstanding Young Men of Am., 1985. Mem. NAACP (pres. Bishop Coll. chpt. 1983-84), Bishop Coll. Alumni Assn., Colgate Rochester Alumni Assn., Dallas Bapt. Assn. (dir. evangelism 1986—), Dallas Tchrs. Credit Union, Dallas Sheriff Assn. Democrat. Avocations: chess, basketball. Home: 1550 Sunset Village Dr Duncanville TX 75137 Office: Union Missionary Bapt Ch 910 E Liedbetter Dallas TX 75216

MATHISON, JOHN ED, minister; b. Florala, Ala., Mar. 19, 1938; s. Marion Clyde and Mary Margaret (Speer) M.; m. Joan Walters, June 8, 1963; children: Vicki, Si. BA, Huntingdon Coll., 1960; BD, Candler Sch. of Theology, Atlanta, 1963; MTh., Princeton Seminary, 1964; D of Ministry, Candler Sch. of Theology, Atlanta, 1978. Asst. minister Capitol Heights Meth. Ch., Montgomery, Ala., 1964-66; minister South Brookley Meth., Mobile, Ala., 1966-70, Trinity Meth., Phenix County, Ala., 1970-72, Frazer Meml. United Meth. Ch., Montgomery, Ala., 1972—; chmn. evangelism Bd. of Discipleship, Nashville. Author: Fishing For Birds, 1985, Every Member in Ministry, 1989. Trustee Huntingdon Coll., Montgomery, 1980-88; del. Gen. Conf. United Meth. Ch., 1984, 88. Named Man of Yr., YMCA, Montgomery, 1978; recipient Disting. Svc. award Jaycees, Montgomery, 1980. Home: 6472 Wynwood Place Montgomery AL 36117 Office: Frazer Meml United Meth Ch 6000 Atlanta Hwy Montgomery AL 36117

MATHISON-BOWIE, STEPHEN LOCH, minister; b. Leonia, N.J., Dec. 31, 1955; s. Glenn Edward and Doreen Maye (Lindo) B.; m. Tiare Louise Mathison, Sept. 11, 1982. BA, U. Wash., 1977; MDiv, Fuller Theol. Sem., 1987. Ordained to ministry Presbyn. Ch. Assoc. pastor Cen. Presbyn. Ch., Eugene, Oreg., 1988-91. Mem. Cascades Presbytery, U.S.G.A., Eugene Ministerial Alliance (N.W. regional steering com.), Witness for Peace. Democrat. Presbyterian. Avocations: song writing, clowning, golf, comedy. Home: 460 E 31st Ave Eugene OR 97405-3745 Office: Cen Presbyn Church 1475 Ferry St Eugene OR 97401

MATHISON-BOWIE, TIARE LOUISE, minister; b. Seattle, Apr. 17, 1953; d. Maynard John and Elain Marie (Anderson) M.; m. Stephen Loch Bowie, Sept. 11, 1982. BA, Evergreen St. Coll.; MDiv, Fuller Theol. Sem., Pasadena, Calif., 1987. Ordained to ministry Presbyn. Ch. Program officer Flintridge Found., Pasadena, Calif., 1984-87; devel. dir. Connelly Sch. for Girls, Anaheim, Calif., 1987-88; assoc. pastor Cen. Presbyn. Ch., Eugene, Oreg., 1988—. Mem. Am. Acad. of Religion, Cascades Presbytery, Eugene Ministerial Alliance. Democrat. Presbyterian. Avocations: writing, research on women's issues, politics. Home: 460 E 31st Ave Eugene OR 97405-3745 Office: Cen Presbyn Church 1475 Ferry St Eugene OR 97401

MATHRE, LAWRENCE GERHARD, minister, federal agency administrator; b. Vancouver, B.C., Can., Mar. 24, 1925; s. Lawrence Alfred and Nellie Josephine (Thompson) M.; m. Blanche Kathleen Brudevold, Aug. 2, 1951; children: James Lawrence, Jerome Keigh, John Mark, Joel David. BA, St. Olaf Coll., 1948; MDiv., Luther Sem., 1952; MA, Phillips U., 1962. Ordained to ministry Evang. Luth. Ch. in Am., 1952. Pastor First Luth. Ch., Fargo, N.D., 1952-54, Bethlehem Luth. Ch., Buffalo Center, Iowa, 1952-57; founder, pastor Prince of Peace Luth. Ch., Oklahoma City, 1957-63; chaplain fed. prison system U.S. Dept. Justice, Okla., Wash., Ill. and Calif., 1963-73; chaplain dir. Western and N.C. regions U.S. Dept. Justice, 1973-83; pastor Hope Luth Ch., San Mateo, Calif., 1984-87, Zion Luth. Ch., Stockton, Calif., 1987—; assoc. prof. part time Pacific Luth. U., Parkland, Wash., 1970-72. With AUS, 1943-45, ETO. Decorated Bronze Star. Mem. Am. Protestant Correctional Chaplains Assn. (nat. pres. 1974), Am. Correctional Chaplains Assn. (nat. pres. 1977), Assn. Clin. Pastoral Edn. (regional chmn. 1979-83, v.p. 1977-79, treas. 1984-89), Lions (chaplain San Mateo club 1985-87). Republican. Home: 2228 Meadow Lake Dr Stockton CA 95207 Office: Zion Luth Ch 808 W Porter Stockton CA 95207 *It is not nearly as important what happens to you as it is what you do about what happens to you. A life lived for oneself is empty; a life lived with and for others is full. You truly find yourself when you are well related—to God and to others.*

MATNEY, DONALD RAY, clergyman; b. Neodesha, Kans., Sept. 23, 1946; s. Marlin E. and Julia C. (Meadows) M.; m. Dolores G. Matney; children: Patricia C., Brian L. BA in Bus. and Pub. Adminstrn., George Mason Coll., 1972; MDiv, Wesley Sem., 1975; D in Ministry, Drew U., 1985. Ordained to ministry Meth. Ch. as deacon, 1973, as elder, 1976. Pastor N.Y. Hill-Sandy Hook Charge United Meth. Ch., Brunswick, Md., 1973-77; assoc. pastor Hughes United Meth. Ch., Wheaton, Md., 1977-82; pastor Cape St. Claire United Meth. Ch., Annapolis, Md., 1982-90, Trinity United Meth. Ch., Annapolis, Md., 1990—; chmn., bd. dirs. Annapolis Pastoral Counseling, 1983-88; mem. bd. advisors Compassionate Friends, Annapolis, 1988—; mem. coun. on fin. Balt. Conf., 1984—, co-chmn., steering com. for capital funds, 1989—. Chaplain Co. 19, Rescue Squad, Brunswick, 1974-77. With U.S. Army, 1966-68, Vietnam. Recipient Cert. for Svc. Compassionate Friends, 1987. Mem. Jaycees (sec. Brunswick chpt. 1976-77, Outstanding Jaycee award 1977), Kiwanis (bd. dirs. Wheaton chpt. 1980-82, Life mem. award 1981). Home: 1318 West St Annapolis MD 21401 Office: Trinity United Meth Ch 1300 West St Annapolis MN 21401

MATOS, JOSEPH FEDERICO, minister; b. Wilmington, Del., Nov. 28, 1966; s. Federico Matos and Joyce Elaine (Purcell) Aker. BA in Religious studies, Southwest Bapt. U., 1988. Lic. to ministry So. Bapt. Conv., 1984. Pastor Plad (Mo.) Bapt. Ch., 1989—; mgr. Action TV and Appliance Rentals, Bolivar, Mo., 1990—.

MATSUNAGA, KIKUO, religion educator; b. Nagoya, Japan, May 11, 1933; s. Tokujiro and Yoshie Matsunaga; m. Junko Kanno, June 4, 1966; children: Tomoo, Nobutsugu, Yuhko. BA, Internat. Christian U., Tokyo, 1957; M.Th., Tokyo Union Theol. Sem., 1960; S.T.M., Union Theol. Sem., N.Y.C., 1965; PhD, McGill U., Montreal, Can., 1970. Minister United Ch. Christ, Fugimigaoka Kyokai, Tokyo, 1960-64; minister United Ch. Christ, Ushigomeharaikatamachi Kyokai, Tokyo, 1970-84; lectr. Tokyo Union Theol. Sem., 1970-72, instr., 1972-74, asst. prof., 1974-79, prof., 1979—, pres., 1983-87, 90—; bd. counsellors Joshi Gakuin, Tokyo, 1988—, Tokyo Union Theol. Sem., 1987-89, 90—, Ferris Jogakuin, 1988—, Internat. Christian U., Tokyo, 1984-88, 90—. Author: What is the Church, 1976, The God, the Only Son Jesus, 1988, Jesus in History, 1989, Commentary on John's Gospel, 1991, Commentary on Johannine Letters, 1991. Trustee Fellis Women's Sch., Yokohama, Japan, 1989—, Joshi Gakuin, Tokyo, 1991—. Mem. Japan Assn. of New Testament Studies (bd. trustees 1970—), Japan Assn. of Christian Studies (trustee 1991—), Japan Bibl. Inst., Societas Nev Testamenti Studieum. Office: Tokyo Union Theol Sem, Osawa 3 10 30, Mitaka Tokyo, Japan 181

MATTER, EDITH ANN, religion educator; b. Ft. Smith, Ark., Dec. 29, 1949; d. Robert Allen and Faye Bert (Overton) M. AB, Oberlin Coll., 1971; MA in Religious Studies, Yale U., 1975, PhD, 1976. Prof. religious studies U. Pa., Phila., 1976—. Author: The Voice of My Beloved: The Song of Songs in Western and Medieval Christianity, 1990; editor: De Partu Virginis, 1985. Tchr., lectr. Pa. Humanities Coun., 1984. Faculty fellow Van Pelt Coll. House, 1981-86, summer rsch. fellow ACLS, 1978, rsch. fellow NEH, 1979, 88; grantee Am. Philos. Soc., 1977, 81, 84. Mem. Medieval Acad. Am., Am. Acad. Religion, Delaware Valley Medieval Assn. Democrat. Home: 941 Annin St Philadelphia PA 19147 Office: U Pa Dept Religious Studies Box 36CH Philadelphia PA 19104-6303

MATTERN, ALEXANDER WATSON, retired minister; b. Lindenwold, N.J., Aug. 8, 1916; s. Joseph and Mae (Watson) M.; m. Bernice Hannah Huntington, June 15, 1946; children: Alexander, William. Student, Moody Bible Inst., 1942; Evang. Tchr. Tng. Assn. cert., Phila. Coll. of Bible, 1956; ThB, Clarksville Sch. Theology, 1976, ThM, 1977, ThD, 1978. Ordained to ministry Ind. Fundamental Chs. in Am., 1958. Founder, pastor East Berlin (N.J.) Community Ch., 1958-84, pastor emeritus, 1984—; instr. Grace Bible Inst.; pres. Lower Camden County Fellowship Fundamental Chs.; mem. adv. bd. on child evangelism Camden County, 1982—; past sec. Christian Tng. Missionary Fellowship; former chmn. Protestant sector chaplain ministry ea. div. West Jersey Hosp.; participant Sermon of Week, Courier Post newspaper. Author: (booklet) Search for Truth. Mem. Evang. Mins. Conf., Ind. Fundamental Chs. Am. Home: 316 S Berlin Rd Lindenwold NJ 08021 *If we do not stand on our principles, one may doubt our having any. Knowing what we believe is no more important than knowing why we believe.*

MATTERN, JACK ROGER, religious organization director; b. Taipei, Taiwan, Apr. 25, 1960; came to U.S., 1962; s. James Philip and Nancy Margaret (Jack) M. BS, Pa. State U., 1982. New staff Campus Crusade for Christ, Mpls., 1982-83; sr. staff Campus Crusade for Christ, Ithaca, N.Y., 1983-85; dir. Campus Crusade for Christ, Phila., 1985—; mem. sr. staff Campus Crusade for Christ, Bangkok, Thailand, 1984. Mem. Alpha Epsilon Delta. Republican. Presbyterian. Avocations: music, volleyball. Home and Office: 4418 Pine St Philadelphia PA 19104

MATTERN, PERRY CHALMERS, pastor, music educator; b. Wauseon, Ohio, Feb. 20, 1950; s. Chalmers Asa and Laura Louise (Warwick) M.; m. Maureen Elise Early, June 19, 1971; children: Rachel Joanne, Sarah Renée. BA in Religion, U. Tenn., 1972; MDiv., Christian Theol. Sem., Indpls., 1976. Ordained to ministry Disciples of Christ Ch., 1976. Intern minister E. Main St. Christian Ch., Elwood, Ind., 1972-75; pastor First Christian Ch., Fostoria, Ohio, 1976-78, Dawson Springs, Ky., 1978-80; minister of youth and edn. Washington Ave. Christian Ch., Elyria, Ohio, 1980-84; assoc. pastor First Christian Ch., Salem, Ohio, 1984-85; pastor Cen. Christian Ch., Marion, Ohio, 1985—. Active Salem Peace Fellowship, 1984-85; supporter Salem Community Theatre, 1985; singer and guitarist Salem Madrigal Singers, 1984; coach Olympics of Mind; treas., bd. dirs. Marion Employment Resource Ctr., Marion Adolescent Pregnancy Program; v.p. Marion County Ministerial Assn.; exec. advisor local Boy Scout troop.; bd. dirs. ARC. Mem. Christian Ch. in Ohio, Marion County Minister's Assn., Disciples of Christ Hist. Soc. Democrat. Avocations: computer programming, auto mechanics, music. Office: Cen Christian Ch 421 Mount Vernon Ave Marion OH 43302

MATTHEWS, ALDEN EWART, missionary; b. Chgo., Sept. 10, 1921; s. Harold Shepard and Grace Hazel (Waters) M.; m. Derrith Jane Lovell, June 15, 1944; children—Cynthia Ann Lasater, Jacqueline, Ellen Rosamond Alger. B.A., Grinnell Coll., 1943; B.D., Chgo. Theol. Sem., 1946, D.Min., 1976; M.S.T., Union Theol. Sem., 1952. Ordained to ministry United Ch. of Christ, 1946. Missionary United Ch. Bd. World Ministries, N.Y.C., 1946—; exec. sec. United Ch. Christ in Japan, Tokyo, 1975—; trustee, councillor Tsurukawa Rural Inst., Tokyo, 1957—, Japan Internat. Christian U., Tokyo, 1965—, Kobe Coll., Nishinomiya, 1965-73, 1975— ; trustee Keiwa High Sch., Niigata, 1968—, Obirin Gakuen, Tokyo, 1972—, Matsuyama Jonan High Sch., Matsuyama, Japan, 1972—, Asia Rural Inst, 1977—, Audio Visual Aid Commn. Nat. Christian Council, Tokyo, 1963—, Christian Lit. Soc., Tokyo, 1964—; councillor Japan Ch. World Service, 1984—. Editor: (with others) Japan Christian Yearbook, 1956. Contbr. articles to profl. jours. Pres. Nojiri Lake Assn., Nagano Prefecture, Japan, 1978, Nojiri Lake Assn. Holding Body, 1979—. Recipient Alumni Grinnell Coll., award 1958. Mem. Fellowship Christian Missionaries Japan, Am. Soc. Missiology, Asiatic Soc. Japan, Internat. House Japan, Democrat. Club: Tokyo Lawn Tennis. Home: 3-25 Hachiyama-cho, Shibuya-ku, Tokyo 150, Japan Office: United Ch of Christ in Japan, 2-3-18 Nishi Waseda/Shinjuku-ku, Tokyo 160, Japan

MATTHEWS, CHRISTIAN WILLIAM, JR., minister; b. Jersey City, Oct. 12, 1934; s. Christian William and Lydia Louise (Weller) M.; m. Elaine Louise Ochs, June 18, 1955; children: Christian William III, Patricia Louise, Judith Ann, Barbara Jean. BA, King's Coll., 1956; MRE, Ea. Theol. Sem., 1960, MDiv, 1962; MEd, U. Del., 1961; ThM, Princeton Theol. Sem., 1965; DD, Grove City Coll., 1988. Ordained to ministry Presbyn. Ch. (U.S.A.), 1962. Dir. Christian edn. United Presbyn. Ch., Manoa and Havertown, Pa., 1959-62; asst. min. 1st Presbyn. Ch., Norristown, Pa., 1962-65; assoc. min. Marble Collegiate Ch., N.Y.C., 1965-68; sr. min. Fox Chapel Presbyn. Ch., Pitts., 1968-79, Christ Presbyn. Ch., Toledo, 1979—; mem. The Fellowship, Washington, Synod Gen. Coun. Presbyn. Ch. U.S.A.; chmn. Synod Evangelism; leader marriage and family seminars; mem. alumni fund bd. Princeton Theol. Sem.; mem. Kirk coun., Alma Coll.; cons. Presbyn. Ch. in U.S.A., Nat. Com. for Prison Reform, County Human Svc. Commn. Author: Lingering with Luke—A Study of the Life of Christ, 1976, Marriage and Family Study Course, 1983; developer (nat. program for Presbyn. chs.) Risk Evangelism; signer Lausanne Covenant of Internat. Congress on World Evangelization. Chmn. Com. for Ecol. Instrn.; founding pres. Samaritan Counseling Ctr.; sec. The Ability Ctr.; bd. dirs. area coun. Boy Scouts Am., Met. Toledo Chs. United, North Toledo Community Ctr., AASK-Mid Am., Toledo Leadership Found.; mem. Coun. for Religion and Psychiatry. Office: 4835 Turnbridge Rd Toledo OH 43623 *As I reflect upon life, I believe that God is at work in our world bringing together people of faith to meet the complex challenges confronting us at this time of history. Working together, we are able to encourage, strengthen, and support one another in meeting the needs of our world.*

MATTHEWS, DAVID, clergyman; b. Indianola, Miss., Jan. 29, 1920; s. Albert and Bertha (Henderson) M.; m. Lillian Pearl Banks, Aug. 28, 1951; 1 dau., Denise. A.B., Morehouse Coll., Atlanta, 1950; student, Atlanta U., 1950, Memphis Theol. Sem., 1965, Delta State U., Cleveland, Miss., 1969, 71, 72; D.D. (hon.), Natchez (Miss.) Jr. Coll., 1973, Morris Booker Meml. Coll., 1988. Ordained minister Nat. Baptist Conv. U.S.A., 1946; pastor chs. in Miss., 1951—, Bell Grove Baptist Ch., Indianola, 1951—, Strangers Home, Greenwood, 1958—; tchr., chmn. dept. social sci. Gentry High Sch., Indianola, 1958-83; moderator Sunflower Baptist Assn., 1957—; pres. Gen. Baptist Conv. Miss., 1958—, former lectr., conv. congress religious edn.; v.p. Nat. Baptist Conv. U.S.A., 1971—; del. to Nat. Council Chs., 1960, supr. oratorial contest, 1976; pres. Gen. Missionary Bapt. State Conv. Miss., 1974—. Mem. Sunflower County Anti-Poverty Bd., 1965-71, Indianola Bi-Racial Com., 1965—; mem. Gov.'s Advisory Com.; col. on staff Gov. Finch, 1976-80; mem. budget com. Indianola United Fund, 1971—; chmn. bd. Indianola FHA, 1971—; trustee Natchez Jr. Coll.; mem. Miss. Gov.'s Research and Devel. Council, 1984—; apptd. mem. So. Govs. Ecumenical Coun. Infant Mortality, 1987. Served with U.S. Army, 1942-45, PTO. Recipient citation Morehouse Coll., 1950, citation Miss. Valley State Coll., 1956; J.H. Jackson Preaching award Midwestern Baptist Laymen Fellowship, 1974; Gov.'s Merit award, 1975. Mem. NEA, Miss., Indianola tchrs. assns. Democrat. Home: PO Box 627 Indianola MS 38751 *I have learned not to seek honors and success but to become so involved in worthwhile works that I lose myself and by such actions success and honors have come.*

MATTHEWS, RICHARD DAVID, minister, religious association executive; b. Van Wert, Ohio, May 16, 1933; s. Dale T. and Evelyn (Riley) Matthews Kear; m. Marie Elvira Manera, Feb. 13, 1954; children—Evi Marie, David Salvator, Thomas Joe, John Wesley. B.D., Luther Rice Sem., Fla., 1980; Th.D., Clarksville Sch. Theology, Tenn., 1976. Ordained to ministry Ind. Baptist Ch., 1962. Pastor Chs. in Wis., 1959-65; missionary evangelist Overseas Crusades, Inc., Santa Barbara, Calif., 1965-70, Gospel Missionary Union, Kansas City, Mo., 1970-76; gen. dir. Mission Outreach Soc., Oregon, Wis., 1970—; exec. dir. Assn. N.Am. Missions, Madison, Wis., 1982-86; broadcaster UPI religious network, 1987—; bd. dirs. Franklin Ministries Inc.; coun. reference various mission agys. Author: From Whence Cometh My Help, 1976; also articles. Editor Roundtable mag., 1982-86. Served with USAF, 1951-56; Korea. Republican. Mem. Assn. Attending Clergy (chmn. 1988—), Assn. Family and Conciliation Cts., Am. Assn. Christian Counselors, Optimists Club. Avocations: amateur radio, gardening, clock repair, camping, hunting. Office: PO Box 227 Madison WI 53715

MATTHEWS, SAMPSON, minister; b. Meridian, Miss., July 30, 1933; s. Sandy Joseph and Carrie Matthews; m. Joanne Ewing; children: Joyce, Dorothy, Mark, Terrence, Sharon, Tammy, Samuel Justin. Student, Jackson State U., 1953-54, Detroit Bible Coll., 1968; BA in Religion, Seattle Pacific U., 1970; DD (hon.), Urban Bible Inst., 1984. Ordained to ministry Baptist Ch. , 1967. Ins. agt. Wright Mut. Ins. Co., 1960-63; with Chrysler Corp., 1964-75; pastor Mt. Hebron Bapt. Ch., Ferndale, Mich., 1974—; tchr. Bapt. Missionary and Edn. Conv. Mich., State Sunday Sch. Congress of Christian Edn., Nat. Bapt. Conv., U.S.A. Inc. Vol. various coms. Dem. Party; appointee by Gov. Mich. to Mich. Employment Security Commn., 1990—. With U.S. Army, 1954-56. Recipient appreciation award Wayne County Sheriff Dept., award Detroit Bus. Inst., Coun. of Bapt. award So. Bapt. Sem. Adminstrn. Mem. Coun. Bapt. Pastors of Detroit and Vicinity (pres. Detroit chpt. 1989—, Outstanding Plant Devel. in Religion award 1989), Fellowship Dist. Assn. (1st vice moderator). Home: 19441 Archer Detroit MI 48219 Office: Mt Hebron Bapt Ch 20740 Reimanville Ave Ferndale MI 48220

MATTHEWS, W. W., bishop. Bishop emeritus Ch. of God by Faith Inc., Ozark, Ala. Office: Ch God by Faith Inc PO Box 907 Ozark AL 36360*

MATTHEWS, WALTER CHARLES JOHN, religion educator; b. Rockville Centre, N.Y., Dec. 22, 1950; s. Henry Robert and Rita Margaret (Perkins) M.; m. Claire Catherine Casey, Aug. 12, 1978; children: Christian Sean, John Patrick, Catherine Claire. BA in Art, U. Tex., 1971; MA in Religious Edn., Fordham U., 1976. With Cath. Charismatic Renewal, N.Y.C., 1976-78; asst. dir. religious edn. St. Pius X Sch., Rochester, Minn., 1978-79, dir., 1979-80; adminstr. Regional Svc. Com. Cath. Charismatic Renewal, Mpls., 1980-84; assoc. dir. Nat. Svc. Com. Cath. Charismatic Renewal, South Bend, Ind., 1984-91, Locust Grove, Va., 1991—; mem. Pontifical Coun. for the Laity, Vatican City, 1990—, Leadership Coun. Cath. Laity, Silver Spring, Md., 1990—. Contbr. articles to religious jours. Office: Chariscenter USA PO Box 628 Locust Grove VA 22508-0628

MATTHIESEN, LEROY THEODORE, bishop; b. Olfen, Tex., June 11, 1921; s. Joseph A. and Rosa (Englert) M. BA, Josephinum Coll., Columbus, Ohio, 1942; MA, Cath. U., Washington, 1961; LittD, Register Sch. Journalism., Denver, 1962. Ordained priest Roman Cath. Ch., 1946. Editor West Tex. Cath., Amarillo diocese, from 1948; prin. Alamo Cath. High Sch, from 1969; pastor St. Francis parish, from 1972; ordained bishop of Amarillo, Tex., 1980—. Office: PO Box 5644 Amarillo TX 79117

MATTISON, CHARLES ALBERT, minister; b. Anderson, S.C., Dec. 30, 1939; s. Charles Henry and Alma (Watkins) M.; m. Patricia Ann Rich, Nov. 11, 1980; children: Robyn, Charles, Chad, Cayce. BS, Johnson C. Smith U., 1962; DDS, Meharry Med. Coll., Nashville, 1968; MA, Fuller Theol. Sem., Pasadena, Calif., 1984; D of Ministry, Calif. Grad. Sch. Theology, Glendale, 1987. Pvt. practice dentistry L.A., 1970-83; assoc. pastor Pilgrim Congl. Ch., L.A., 1985-88; pastor Lincoln Meml. Congl. Ch., L.A., 1988—. With USN, 1968-70. Home and Office: 4573 Don Milagro Dr Los Angeles CA 90008

MATTISON, RONALD PAUL, SR., pastor; b. Corning, N.Y., Mar. 19, 1951; s. Paul Charles and Joyce Marie (Williams) M.; m. Natalie Catherine Newton, Sept. 18, 1971; children: Malinda Renee, Ronald Paul Jr., Kevin Derek. AS, Corning Community Coll., 1971; BS in Ceramic Engring. cum laude, Alfred U., 1978; BS in Engring., Bible, and Theology, United Wesleyan Coll., Allentown, Pa., 1988. Ordained elder, Wesleyan Ch., 1990. Pastor Gates Wesleyan Ch., Rochester, N.Y., 1988—; vice chmn. Cen. N.Y. Dist. Wesleyan Youth, 1990—; dist. youth pres., 1989-90; dist. coord. Wesleyan missions dept. youth Wesleyan Ch., Indpls., 1990—. Republican. Office: Gates Wesleyan Ch 2060 Long Pond Rd Rochester NY 14606

MATTIX-WAND, PAULA JANE, religious educator director; b. Vandalia, Ill., July 29, 1967; d. Edwin Leon and Mary Jane Frances (Niendiek) Mattix; m. Gerard August Wand, June 17, 1989. BS in Edn., Ill. State U., 1989; postgrad., St. Mary of the Woods (Ind.), 1990—. Dir. religious edn. St. Francis Newman Ctr., Muncie, Ind., 1989-90, Cath. Community of Carlinville (Ill.), 1990—. Mem. Ill. Parish Coords. and Dirs., Nat. Cath. Catechists Soc. Home: 1001 N Montgomery Litchfield IL 62056 Office: Holy Family Sch Religion 535 S West St Carlinville IL 62626

MATTO, KENNETH BRUCE, writer, religious organization administrator; b. Perth Amboy, N.J., May 1, 1953; s. Steve and Ethel Irene (Czok) M. B Ministry, Bethany Bible Coll., Dothan, Ala., 1988; M Ministry, Bethany Theol. Sem., Dothan, 1989, D Ministry, 1990. Ordained to ministry Christian Ch., 1990. Pres. The Bibl. Found., Edison, N.J., 1990—. Author: Gods Nobodies—A Misunderstanding, 1990, Focus on Issues, 1991. Mem. Writers Info. Network, Christian Writers Fellowship Internat. Home: 51 1st

St Edison NJ 08837-2628 *There is nothing too big for Christ, there is nothing too small for Christ. Somewhere in between I call home.*

MATTOX, EDWARD IRVIN, JR., minister; b. Memphis, Feb. 28, 1956; s. Edward I. Sr. and Virginia O. (Hall) M.; m. Carol D. Cummings, Dec. 10, 1983; 1 child, Alicia Nicole. BA, Union U., 1978; MDiv, Southwestern Bapt. Theol. Sem., 1981; D of Ministry, Midwestern Bapt. Theol. Sem., 1987. Minister of music, youth Hickory Grove Bapt. Ch., Trenton, Tenn., 1976-78, Friendship Bapt. Ch., Montalba, Tex., 1978-79, 1st Bapt. Ch., Strawn, Tex., 1979-81; chaplain Rsch. Med. Ctr., Kansas City, Mo., 1982; pastor 1st Bapt. Ch., Pattonsburg, Mo., 1982-88, Park Heights Bapt. Ch., Middleburg Heights, Ohio, 1988-90, Forest Park Bapt. Ch., Farmington Hills, MI, 1990—. Mem. Middleburg Heights C. of C., Greater Cleve. Bapt. Assn. (chmn. personnel com. 1988-89, communications com. 1988—), Harrison Bapt. Assn. (pianist 1983-85, music dir. 1985, 87). Baptist. Avocations: music, weightlifting (numerous awards), running. Home: 6471 Smith Rd Brook Park OH 44142 Office: Forest Park Bapt Ch 26805 Farmington Rd Farmington Hills MI 48334

MATTOX, JOSEPH EDWARD, pastor, missionary, educator; b. Nitro, W.Va., Dec. 24, 1950; s. Joseph Franklin and Pauline A. (Hudson) M.; m. Elva Colunga, Sept. 4, 1976; children: Joseph Christopher, Benjamin Noel. BA, Mid-Am. Bible Coll., 1972; MA in Christian Edn., Anderson U., 1974; MDiv, Anderson Sch. Theology, 1976; postgrad., Pan Am. U., 1982; EdD, U. San Diego, 1991. Assoc. min. Garfield Pk. Ch. of God, Indpls., 1976-78; prin. Turabo Gardens Christian Acad., Caguas, P.R., 1978-81; missionary Mission Bd. Ch. of God, Anderson, Ind., 1978-88; dir. Ctr. for Christian Studies in N.W. Mex., 1984-88; sr. pastor 1st Ch. of God, San Bernardino, Calif., 1988—; dist. circulation mgr. Anderson Newspapers Inc., Anderson, 1973-76; bd. dirs. Inter-Am. Publs. Com., 1986-88, Missionary Bd. Ch. of God, 1989—; chair bus. com. West Coast Ministerial Assembly, 1989-91; vice chair Commn. Higher Christian Edn., S. Calif. Ch. of God, 1991—. Author: (Spanish workbook) Handbook for Church Workers, 1984, An Evaluation of Theological Education by Extension in Northwest Mexico, 1991; contbr. articles to profl. jours. Organizational rep. Cub Scout, San Bernardino, 1991. Recipient Alumni Missionary of Yr. award Mid-Am. Coll., Oklahoma City, 1986. Home: 26284 23d St Highland CA 92346 Office: 1st Ch of God 2595 E Date St Highland CA 92346

MATTSON, ROBERT BERNARD, minister; b. Baumholder, Fed. Republic Germany, May 20, 1963; (parents Am. citizens); s. James Magnus and Maxine Shelton (Reed) M.; m. Sandra Elaine Sanders, June 2, 1990. Student, U. Mary Hardin-Baylor, 1981-88. Lic. to ministry So. Bapt. Conv., 1982. Min. music Willow Grove Bapt. Ch., Moody, Tex., 1982, East Side Bapt. Ch., Killeen, Tex., 1982-83, 84-88, Keys Valley Bapt. Ch., Belton, Tex., 1983-84, Meml. Bapt. Ch., Killeen, 1988—; mem. exec. bd. Bell Bapt. Assn., Belton, 1982—; messenger So. Bapt. Conv., 1985-90; mem. Killeen Bapt. Mins. Conf., So. Bapt. Ch. Music Conf. Author: Building on His Promises, 1982, Down by the Creek Bank, 1984. Chmn. Killeen High Sch. Centennial Com., 1982, Nolanville (Tex.) Sesquicentennial Com., 1985-86, Nolanville Arthritis Found., 1986. Mem. Full Gospel Businessmens Fellowship. Republican. Home: 208 Dahlia Ct Killeen TX 76542 Office: Meml Bapt Ch 200 S Gray St Killeen TX 76541

MATTSON, VERNON WILLIAMS, theology educator; b. Salt Lake City, Jan. 15, 1934; s. Vernon W. and Ellen (Williams) M.; m. Georgia M. Jensen, Dec. 19, 1958; children—Anna, Denise, Shane, David, Paul, Steven. B.S., Brigham Young U., 1960, M.R.E., 1969. Tchr., Ch. Jesus Christ of Latter-day Saints, Salt Lake City, 1960—, lectr., 1977—; pres. Buried Records Prodns., Salt Lake City, 1978—. Author: The Dead Sea Scrolls and Other Important Discoveries, 1979. Served with USN, 1952-54. Mem. Am. Schs. Oriental Research, Soc. Early Hist. Archeology, Found. Ancient Research and Mormon Studies. Republican. Home: 3439 W 7260 S West Jordan UT 84084

MATULA, DENNIS LEE, clergyman; b. Baldwin, Wis., July 1, 1949; s. Leslie Edward and Mary Ann (Meyer) M.; m. Julie A. Johnson, Aug. 20, 1971; children: Stacey, Nicole. BME, U. Minn., 1972. Ordained to ministry Assn. Faith Chs. and Ministries, 1980; registered profl. engr., Minn., Mo.; cert. profl. in packaging and material handling. Youth leader 1st Assembly of God, Nevada, Mo., 1972-76; young adult tchr. So. St. Paul Assembly of God, 1976-79; sr. pastor Jubilee Christian Ch., Hastings, Minn., 1979—; lectr. Hazelden Found., 1980; pres. Creative Media Svcs., 1984—; cons. Ch. Growth, 1989—. Bd. dirs. Men of the Word, Hastings, 1980-90; camp dir. Zoe Youth Camps, Paynesville, Minn., 1982-85; exec. dir. Youth Alive, Mpls., 1985-90. With USNG, 1969-75. Recipient J.F. Lincoln Found. award, 1972, Valley Forge Honor cert. Freedom Found., 1974. Mem. Gideons Internat. (pres. 1974-79), Charismatic Bible Ministries. Mem. Ind. Charismatic Ch. Office: Jubilee Christian Ch 11125 W Point Douglas Rd Hastings MN 55033

MATUREN, MICHAEL ANDREW, lay church worker, sales professional; b. Saginaw, Mich., Sept. 9, 1964; s. Howard Andrew Jr. and JoAnne Louise (Johnson) M.; m. Susan Mary Emerick, Aug. 8, 1987. BS, Cen. Mich. U., 1988. Dir. youth Lakeview Community Ch., Goodrich, Mich., 1989-91, with pulpit supply, 1990; del. cen. conf. Brethren in Christ, 1989-90; sales rep. Rich Plan Food Svc., Mt. Pleasant, Mich., 1982-89; pubs. cons. Herff Jones Yearbooks, Ortonville, Mich., 1987-90; sales rep. Am. Orthodontics, Sheboygan, Wis., 1990—; cons. Motivation Unltd., Ortonville, 1988—. Contbr. articles to profl. jours. Bd. dirs. Camp Lakewview, Goodrich, 1990. Mem. Soc. Profl. Journalists. Office: Upon This Rock Ministries 1 Southlawn Ct Saginaw MI 48602

MATUSSE, BENTO BARTOLOMEU, religious organization administrator. Pres. Bapt. Conv. of Mozambique, Maputo. Office: Bapt Conv, CP852, Avda Maguiguane 386, Maputo Mozambique*

MATUSZEWSKI, STANLEY, priest; b. Morris Run, Pa., May 4, 1915; s. Andrew and Mary (Czekalski) M.; grad. St. Andrew's Prep. Sem., Rochester, N.Y.; student La Salette Coll., Hartford, Conn., Scholastic Sem., Altamont, N.Y. Ordained priest Roman Catholic Ch., 1942; disciplinarian, prof. classics, La Salette Sem., Olivet, 1942-46, dir., 1948—; superior Midwest province LaSalette Fathers; founding editor Our Lady's Digest, 1946—; exec. bd. Nat. Catholic Decency in Reading Program; faculty adv. Midwest Conf. of Internat. Relations Clubs sponsored 1944 in Chgo. by Carnegie Endowment for Internat. Peace. Trustee Nat. Shrine of Immaculate Conception, Washington. Honored by Rochester, N.Y. Centennial Com. 1934 as Monroe County (N.Y.) orator. Mem. Mariological Soc. Am. (1954 award), Missionaries of Our Lady of La Salette, Catholic Press Assn., Canon Law Soc., Catholic Broadcasters' Assn., Religious Edn. Assn., Polish-Hungarian World Fedn. (trustee). K.C. Author: Rochester Centennial Oration; Youth Marches On. Home: Box 777 Twin Lakes WI 53181

MATZ, MARY DILL, religion educator; b. Delaware County, Pa., Aug. 10, 1931; d. Charles Morgan and Olive (Wise) Dill; m. William Wismer Matz, Jan. 8, 1955; children: William Wismer Jr., Randall Charles. BA, Grove City Coll., 1953; MDiv, Moravian Theol. Sem., 1975; D. Ministry, Drew U., 1982. Ordained to ministry Moravian Ch., 1975. Dir. Christian edn. 1st Presbyn. Ch., Athens, Ohio, 1953-54; asst. minister Cen. Moravian Ch., Bethlehem, Pa., 1975-77; dir. ednl. ministries Moravian Ch., No. Province, Bethlehem, 1975-77; mem. steering com. Ch. Urban Action Fund, Lehigh Valley, Pa., 1980—; bd. dirs. New Bethany Ministries, Bethlehem, 1985-87; chair edn. for Christian life and mission Nat. Coun. Chs., 1985-87, chair edn., communication and discipleship unit, 1990—, v.p. Nat. Coun. Chs., 1990—. Author: Ministry Together, 1982, Choices and Values in a Rapidly Changing World, 1990. Bd. dirs., mem. allocations com. United Way, Northampton County, Pa., and WarrenCounty, N.J., 1977-85; bd. dirs. YWCA, Bethlehem, 1982-88; pres., bd. dirs. Meals on Wheels, Northampton County, 1977-83; news broadcaster blind radio sta. RADPRIN, Northampton and Warren Counties, 1990—. Mem. Assn. Retarded Citizens, Citizens Outreach Visitors (bd. dirs. 1990—), Assn. Presbyn. Ch. Educators, Assn. Psychol. Type, Internat. Assn. Women Ministers, Nat. Coun. on Aging, Rotary. Home: 3138 Patterson Dr Bethlehem PA 18017 Office: Moravian Ch No Province 1021 Center St PO Box 1245 Bethlehem PA 18016 *Life involves balancing the paradoxes: of firmness and understanding, of empathy and challenge, of receiving and giving, of acceptance and confrontation, of the theoretical and the practical, of study and action, of learning and teaching.*

MATZ, MILTON, clinical psychologist, management relations consultant, rabbi; b. N.Y.C., June 30, 1927; s. Joshua E. and Sonja (Kviat) Matz; m. Anne L. Jaburg, June 20, 1952; children—Deborah, David. B.A., Yeshiva U., 1947; M.H.L., rabbinic ordination, Hebrew Union Coll., 1952, D.D. (hon.), 1977; Ph.D., U. Chgo., 1966. Cert. Ohio Psychol. Assn. Bd. Examiners Psychologists, 1966; lic. Ohio Bd. Psychology, 1973. First lt. USAF, 1952-54; asst. rabbi Kehilath Anshei Maariv Temple, Chgo., 1954-57; rabbi Congregation B'nai Jehoshua, Chgo., 1957-59; dir. pastoral psychology, asso. rabbi The Temple, Cleve., 1959-66; sr. staff psychologist Fairhill Psychiat. Hosp., Cleve., 1966-69; adj. prof. Cleve. State U., 1966-70; clin. instr. Case-Western Res. Sch. Medicine, 1966-73, asst. clin. prof., 1973—, dir. Pastoral Psychology Service Inst., 1973—, clin. dir. bereavement project, 1978—; pvt. practice clin. psychology, Beachwood, Ohio, 1966—; mng. ptnr. Matz Assocs., Beachwood, 1966—; cons. dir. Erie Pastoral Psychology Inst., 1977-89; mng. ptnr. Mgmt. Relations Cons. div. Matz Assocs., Beachwood, 1984—; cons. dir. pastoral tng. project Central Conf. Am. Rabbis, 1978-79; co-chair outreach com. to interfaith families Cleve. chpt. Am. Jewish Com., 1991—; lectr. mgmt. relations, negotiation and mediation skills. Sec., v.p. Greater Cleve. Bd. Rabbis, 1964-66; bd. mem. Jewish Children's Bur. and Bellefaire Jewish Community Ctr., Cleve., 1952-64; advisory bd. Div. Child Welfare, Cuyahoga County, Ohio, 1962-66; founding mem. Cuyahoga County Community Mental Health and Retardation Bd., Cleve., 1967-71, chmn., 1972-73; chmn. Central Conf. Am. Rabbis Com. on Judaism and Health, N.Y.C., 1975-79. Diplomate Am. Assn. Pastoral Counselors; mem. Am., Ohio psychol. assns., Soc. for Indsl. and Orgnl. Psychology, Am. Assn. Pastoral Counselors, Ohio Acad. Profl. Psychology (trustee 1984—). Author numerous papers and articles on interpersonal communication, dispute resolution, treatment of marital conflict and grief, primary prevention of mental illness, psychology and religion, and pastoral tng.; recipient commendation for outstanding leadership in mental health Bd. Commrs. of Cuyahoga County, 1973. Home: 3346 Stockholm Rd Shaker Heights OH 44120 Office: 3609 Park East Beachwood OH 44122

MAU, DWAYNE HOLGER, minister; b. Chgo., June 17, 1942; s. John Arthur and Leona An (Plummer) M.; m. Janice Barter, June 20, 1971; children: Joy Lyn, David John. AA, Concordia Coll., Milw., 1962; BA, Concordia Sr. Coll., Ft. Wayne, Ind., 1964; MDiv, Concordia Sem. Coll., St. Louis, 1968; M in Christian Edn., Presbyn. Sch. Christian Edn., 1969; LLD (hon.), Concordia Coll., Bronxville, N.Y., 1991. Ordained to ministry Luth. Ch.-Mo. Synod. Asst. pastor Good Shepherd Luth. Ch., Plainview, N.Y., 1969-74; pastor St. John Luth. Ch., Flushing, N.Y., 1974-80; staff exec. mission and edn., Atlantic Dist. The Luth. Ch.-Mo. Synod, 1980—; adminstr. Luth. Sch. of Flushing, 1975-80; chmn. Task Force-Urban Ministry, St. Louis, 1987—; bd. dirs. Wartburg Luth. Svcs.; v.p. Conf. of Edn. Exec., 1985-88. Contbr. articles to profl. jours. Mem. Plainview Against Drug Abuse, 1970-73; bd. dirs. adminstrv. com. Queens (N.Y.) Citizen Orgn., 1977-81, pres., 1979-81. Mem. Luth. Edn. Assn., Luth. Schs. Assn. (bd. dirs. 1978—, Educator of Yr. 1988), N.Am. Mission Enablers. Home: 47-42 157th St Flushing NY 11355 Office: The Luth Ch Mo Synod Atlanta Dist 171 White Plains Rd Bronxville NY 10708

MAULDIN, KENNETH LAURENCE, retired minister; b. Dalhart, Tex., Apr. 24, 1918; s. Charles Ross and Edna Lanora (Johnson) M.; m. Kathryn Rowell, 1942; children: Robert Laurence, Michael Douglas. BA, Trinity U., San Antonio, 1940, DD (hon.), 1950; MDiv, McCormick Theol. Sem., Chgo., 1943; ThM, Austin Presbyn. Sem., 1956. Ordained to ministry Presbyn. Ch. (U.S.A.), 1943. Pastor 1st Presbyn. Ch., Port Arthur, Tex., 1943-50; organizing pastor Univ. Presbyn. Ch., San Antonio, 1950-54; pastor, head staff St. Andrew's Presbyn. Ch., Dallas, 1954-62, Westminster Presbyn. Ch., Amarillo, Tex., 1962-67, 1st Presbyn. Ch., Topeka, 1967-83; ret., 1983; interim pastor 1st Presbyn. Ch., Huntsville and Midland, Tex., Trinity Presbyn. Ch., North Park Presbyn. Ch., Ridgeview Presbyn. Ch., Dallas. Author: Table Talk with Jesus, 1980. Home: 1212 Cedar Pine Ln Little Elm TX 75068

MAUPIN, VIRGINIA LEE, religious organization administrator; b. Los Angeles, Apr. 2, 1924; d. Sam Guy and Phyllis Evelyn (Ford) Snyder; m. Willis Preston (Jack) Maupin, July 23, 1944; children: Andrea, Thomas, Shirley. Student, San Diego State U., 1942-44. Sec. Comml. Refrigeration, San Diego, 1944-45; sec. fin. First Presbyn. Ch., Richardson, Tex., 1961-64, sec. fin., Pastor's, 1964-70; adminstr. First Presbyn. Ch., Richardson, 1970—. Mem. Nat. Assn. Ch. Bus. Adminstrs., Network (bd. dirs., sec., treas. 1985-86). Club: Richardson Woman's (pres. 1961-62). Avocations: bridge, needlework, walking, grandchildren, reading. Home: 404 Inglewood Dr Richardson TX 75080

MAURER, ARMAND AUGUSTINE, priest, former philosophy educator; b. Rochester, N.Y., Jan. 21, 1915; arrived in Can., 1957; s. Armand Augustine and Louise (Ribson) M. B.A., U. Toronto, Ont., Can., 1938, M.A., 1943, PH.D., 1947; M.S.L., Pontifical Inst. Mediaeval Studies, Toronto, 1945. Joined Congregation Priests of St. Basil, Roman Cath. Ch., 1940; ordained priest, 1945; lectr. in philosophy St. Michael's Coll., U. Toronto, 1946-55, asst. prof. philosophy, 1955-58, assoc. prof., 1948-62, prof., from 1962; asst. prof. philosophy Pontifical Inst. Mediaeval Studies, 1949-53, prof., 1953-84; ret., 1984. Author: Medieval Philosophy, 1962, 2d rev. edit., 1982, (with others) Recent Philosophy: Hegel to the Present, 1966, St. Thomas and Historicity, 1979, About Beauty, 1983; editor: Siger of Brabant. Quaestiones in Metaphysicam, 1983, Being and Knowing. Studies in Thomas Aquinas and Later Medieval Philosophers, 1990; contbr. numerous articles to philos. Jours. Guggenheim fellow, 1954-55. Mem. Royal Soc. Can., Am. Cath. Philos. Assn. (pres. 1979), Metaphys. Soc., Soc. Internat. pour l'Étude de la Philosophie Médiévale. Home and Office: 59 Queens Park Crescent, Toronto, ON Canada M5S 2C4

MAURER, JOSE CLEMENTE CARDINAL, German ecclesiastic; b. Puttlingen, Trier, Mar. 13, 1900. Ordained priest Roman Cath. Ch., 1925. Titular Bishop of Cea, 1950-51; Archbishop of Sucre, Bolivia, 1951-83; elevated to Sacred Coll. of Cardinals, 1967; entitled SS. Redentore e S. Alfonso in via Merulana. Address: Arzobispado, Casilla 205, Sucre Bolivia

MAURER, TERRY SCOTT, youth and music minister; b. Canton, Ohio, Aug. 30, 1953; s. Gene Scott and Miriam Elizabeth (Colledge) M.; m. Deborah Frances Monroe, Mar. 9, 1974; children: Sarah Marie, Benjamin John. BS in Ch. Music, Cin. Bible Sem., 1975; postgrad., Lincoln Christian Coll., 1989. Minister of music Bright (Ind.) Christian Ch., 1973-74; team mem. Christ in Youth, Cin., 1974-75; min. of youth First Christian Ch., Moweaqua, Ill., 1975-91, min. of music and worship, 1991—. Pres. Ill. Christian Teen Conv., 1980-81, publicity and program chmn.; exec. bd. mem. Little Galilee Christian assembly, 1978-83, sec. bd., 1981, pres. bd., 1990, dean and faculty, 1976—; pres. Moweaqua Ministerial Alliance, 1989-91, v.p., 1991—; mem. Moweaqua Drug, Alcohol Action Group, 1989—. Mem. Moweaqua Lions. Avocations: hunting, fishing, trapping, singing, music. Home: 317 E South St Moweaqua IL 62550 Office: First Christian Ch 220 S Macon St Moweaqua IL 62550 *The greatest task of the Christian today is to be Christlike in a world that largely doesn't seem to care who Christ was or what He did for them.*

MAVRODES, GEORGE ION, philosophy educator; b. Albuquerque, Nov. 23, 1926; s. Tasso and Kathryne (Dardis) M. B.S., Oreg. State Coll., 1945; B.D., Western Baptist Theol. Sem., 1953; Ph.D., U. Mich., 1961. Instr. Princeton U., N.J., 1961-62; asst. prof. philosophy U. Mich., Ann Arbor, 1962-67, assoc. prof. philosophy, 1967-73, prof. philosophy, 1973—. Author: Belief in God, 1970; editor: Problems and Perspectivies in the Philosophy of Religion, 1967, The Rationality of Belief in God, 1970; contbr. articles to profl. jours. Served with USN, 1945-46. Mem. Am. Philos. Assn., Soc. Philosophy in Religion, Soc. Christian Philosophers. Republican. Mem. Christian Reformed Ch. Avocations: camping; hiking; photography. Home: 3371 Burbank St Ann Arbor MI 48105

MAXFIELD, DALE ALLEN, pastoral associate; b. Breese, Ill., Aug. 4, 1952. BA in Theology, Quincy Coll., 1976; MA in Religious Studies, St Louis U., 1981. Lic. radio broadcaster. Tchr. religion Order of Friars Minor, Quincy, Ill., 1972-75, Quincy Notre Dame High Sch., 1976-78; diocesan dir. of adult edn. Diocese of Belleville, Ill., 1978-82; diocesan dir. of religious edn. Diocese of Evansville, Ind., 1982-83; dir. religious edn. various parishes So. Ill., 1983-85; dir. religious edn. St. Paul Parish, Highland, Ill., 1985-90, St. Albert Parish, Fairview Hts., Ill., 1990-91; pastoral assoc. St. George Parish, New Baden, Ill., 1991—; adj. prof. Aquinas Inst., St. Louis, 1983-84; religious edn. cons. Tabor Pub., Allen, Tex., 1989—. Contbr. articles to profl. jours. Mem. Nat. Cath. Edn. Assn., Nat. Assn. Parish Coords./Dirs., Ill. Assn. Parish Coords./Dirs. Office: St George Parish 200 N 3d St New Baden IL 62265 *The language of the kingdom is laughter, and music is its vocabulary.*

MAXIMOS, BISHOP (MAXIMOS DEMETRIOS AGHIORGOUSSIS), bishop; b. Callimassia, Chios, Greece, Mar. 5, 1935; s. Evanghelos G. and Lemonia G. (Rythianou) A. Licentiate, Patriarchal Sch. Theology, Halki, 1957; Baccalaureate, U. Louvain, Belgium, 1964, Th.D., 1964. Ordained to ministry Greek Orthodox Ch., 1957; chaplain U. Louvain, 1957-64; pastor chs. Brussels, Rome, Brookline, Mass., Manchester and Newport, N.H., 1960-78; observer-del. II Vatican Council, 1964-65; chaplain Holy Cross Sem., Brookline, 1967-76; prof. systematic theology Holy Cross Sch. Theology, Brookline, 1967-79, Christ Savior Sem., Johnstown, Pa., from 1979; bishop Greek Orthodox Diocese Pitts., 1979—; mem. Orthodox-Roman Cath. Consultation, from 1967; v.p. Nat. Council Chs. Christ U.S., 1979-81; ecumenical officer Greek Orthodox Archdiocese N. and S. Am., 1978-79, chmn. synodal coms. ecumenical affairs, spiritual renewal and youth, from 1979. Author articles in field. Mem. Orthodox Theol. Soc. Am., AAUP, Christian Assos. Pitts., Pa. Council Chs., W.Va. Council Chs., Helicon Cultural Soc. Office: Greek Orthodox Diocese Pittsburgh 5201 Ellsworth Ave Pittsburgh PA 15232 *My ministry is such that it requires a total commitment to its goals, but first of all a total commitment to Christ. In my childhood, I was fortunate to be guided by excellent parents and grandparents, who gave me not only the necessary security and stability, but also the inspiration to imitate their personal commitment to the Lord. I fully trust in the grace of the Lord, but I also have always accepted my responsibility for everything I have done.*

MAXWELL, ARTHUR GRAHAM, religion educator emeritus; b. Watford, Eng., July 18, 1921; came to U.S., 1936; s. Arthur Stanley and Rachel (Joyce) M.; m. Rosalyn Gildersleeve, Sept. 9, 1943; children—Lorna (Mrs. George Andersson), Audrey (Mrs. David Zinke), Alice (Mrs. Don Lucas). B.A., Pacific Union Coll., 1943, M.A., 1944; Ph.D., U. Chgo. Div. Sch., 1959. Asst. prof. bibl. langs. Pacific Union Coll., Angwin, Calif., 1944-52; asso. prof., head dept. bibl. langs. Pacific Union Coll., 1952-59, prof., chmn. div. religion, 1959-61; dir. div. religion, prof. N.T., Loma Linda (Calif.) U., 1961-76; prof. N.T., 1976-88, emeritus prof., 1988—. Author: You Can Trust the Bible, 1967, I Want to be Free, 1970, Can God Be Trusted?, 1977; contbr.: Seventh-day Adventist Bible Commentary, 1957. Mem. Soc. Bibl. Lit., Am. Acad. Religion, Soc. for Sci. Study Religion, Cath. Bibl. Assn. Am., Internat. Soc. Bible Collectors. Home: 25047 Crestview Dr Loma Linda CA 92354

MAXWELL, DAVID RANDAL, minister; b. Paragould, Ark., June 26, 1949; s. Wylie Wilson and Juanita May (Nesler) M.; m. Nan Elizabeth Morris; 1 child, Scott Randal. BA, Ouachita Bapt. U., 1971; MDiv, Southwestern Bapt. Sem., Ft. Worth, 1974. Pastor First Bapt. Ch., DeValls Bluff, Ark., 1969-71; minister of music & youth Calvary Bapt. Ch., DeSoto, Tex., 1971-74; pastor Hillside Bapt. Ch., Camden, Ark., 1975-79, West Bapt. Ch., Batesville, Ark., 1979—; summer youth dir. East Main Bapt. Ch., El Dorado, Ark.; day camp unit leader Ridgecrest Bapt. Conf. Ctr., Ridgecrest, N.C.; incorporator Batesville Internat. Ctr., Batesville, Ark.; 2d v.p. Ark. Bapt. State Pastor's Conf., 1986, 1st v.p., 1987; trustee Williams Bapt. Coll., Walnut Ridge, Ark.; mem. adv. com. Sta. KAAB, 1987—, Ark. Bapt. State Bapt. Student Union Adv. Com., 1987—. Contbr to profl. mags. Adv. com. Indepedence County Extension Home Life, Batesville, 1987—; hon. chaplain, adv. com. Inter-med Nursing Home, Batesville, 1983—; mem. Am. Heart Assn.; bd. dirs. Independence Co., 1989—, Help and Hope, 1990—. Named one of Outstanding Young men of Am., 1985. Mem. Liberty Bapt. Assn. (moderator), Independence Bapt. Assn. (moderator), Ark. Christian Civic Found. (bd. dirs. 1986—), Independence County Christian Civic Found. (bd. dirs. 1986—, pres. 1986, 1st v.p. 1987), Batesville Area Minister's Fellowship (pres. 1983). Lodges: Kiwanis (bd. dirs. Camden club), Rotary (bd. dirs. Batesville club). Home: 960 Hill St Batesville AR 72501 Office: West Bapt Ch 1100 North Central Ave Batesville AR 72501

MAXWELL, NEAL A., church official; m. Colleen Hinckley; four children. B in Polit. Sci., M in Polit. Sci., U. Utah, LLD (hon.); LLD (hon.), Brigham Young U.; LittD (hon.), Westminster Coll.; HHD (hon.), Utah State U. Legis. asst. U.S. sen. Wallace F. Bennett, Utah; exec. v.p. U. Utah, Salt Lake City; various secular positions including bishop Salt Lake City's Univ. Sixth Ward, mem. gen. bd. youth orgn., adult correlation com. and one of first Regional Reps. of the Twelve; elder Ch. Jesus Christ Latter Day Sts., Asst. to the Council of Twelve, 1974-76, mem. of Presidency of First Quorum of the Seventy, 1976-81, mem. of Council of Twelve Apostles, 1981—; bd. dirs. Quester Corp., Deseret News Pub. Co. Mem. Quorum of the Twelve Ch. of Jesus Christ of Latter-Day Saints, Salt Lake City. Recipient Liberty Bell award Utah State Bar, 1967; named Pub. Adminstr. of Yr. Inst. Govt. Service Brigham Young U., 1973. Office: LDS Church Quorum of the Twelve 47 E S Temple St Salt Lake City UT 84150

MAXWELL-DOHERTY, MELISSA MARGARET, minister; b. Long Beach, Calif., Oct. 10, 1955; d. Robert Daniel and Maxine Lois (Cotton) Maxwell; m. Scott Joseph Maxwell-Doherty, July 11, 1981; children: Kyle Joseph, Nathan Elias. BS in Psychology, Calif. Luth. U., 1977; MDiv, Pacific Luth. Theol. Sem., 1981. Assoc. pastor Salem Luth. Ch., 1981-84; pastor Prince of Peace Luth. Ch., Phoenix, 1984-91, Calvary Luth. Ch., Grand Forks, N.D., 1991—. Mem. mass gathering team E.L.C.A. Youth Gathering, 1987-88, 90-91; conf. rep. Grand Canyon Synod Coun., Phoenix, 1987—; chaplain A.L.C. Gen. Conv., San Diego, 1982; planning team Clergy Women on the West Conf., San Diego, 1982-83; sec. Nat. Bd. of Luther League, Mpls., 1973-76; mem. United Blood Svcs. Ethics Adv. Bd., Scottsdale, Airz., 1987-89; del. UN Conf. on Human Settlement, Vancouver, B.C., Can., 1976. Leo Laine grant Calif. Luth. U., 1975-77. Mem. Sertoma. Office: Calvary Luth Ch 1405 S Ninth St Grand Forks ND 58201

MAY, C(ALVIN) WALTER, JR., minister, electrical engineer; b. San Antonio, June 25, 1938; s. Calvin Walter and Katherine Hester (Carter) M.; m. Virginia Anne Rowland, Dec. 20, 1975. BSEE, U. Tex., 1964; MA in Religious Edn., Southwestern Bapt. Theol. Sem., Ft. Worth, 1988, postgrad., 1988—. Ordained to ministry So. Bapt. Conv., 1984; registered profl. engr., Tex. Mgr. tech. svcs. Lower Colorado River Authority, Austin, Tex., 1964-84; assoc. pastor adminstrn. Bannockburn Bapt. Ch., Austin, Tex., 1984—. Mem. adv. com. Tex. Energy and Natural Resources Commn., 1973-77. Mem. Nat. Assn. Ch. Bus. Adminstrs. (pres. local chpt. 1984-85), Christian Ministries Mgmt. Assn., Austin Bapt. Assn. (fin. com. 1987—), Tex. Safety Assn., Austin Pers. Assn. Home: 10605 Ames Ln Austin TX 78739-1532 Office: Bannockburn Bapt Ch 7100 Brodie Ln Austin TX 78745-5012

MAY, CECIL, JR., academic administrator. Pres. Magnolia Bible Coll., Kosciusko, Miss. Office: Magnolia Bible Coll Office of the Presidnet PO Box 1109 Kosciusko MS 39090*

MAY, DAVID JOE, pastor; b. Marion, Ohio, Dec. 14, 1951; s. Joe C. May and Eleanor (Howard) Weaver; m. Rhonda Jean Boggs, July 26, 1969; children: Jason, Nichole, Soni. Grad. high sch., Xenia, Ohio, 1969. Pres. David May Ministries, Inc., Xenia, 1984—; pastor Harvest Fellowship Ch., Xenia, 1985—; prin. Harvest Fellowship Sch., Xenia, 1987-89; chaplain Greene County Jail, Xenia, 1987—. Trustee Greene County Youth Activity Fund, Xenia, 1989—; gov. Internat. Congress Local Chs., Washington, 1989—. Mem. Full Gospel Businessmen Internat. Office: Harvest Fellowship Ch 42 W 2d St Xenia OH 45385

MAY, EDWARD JAMES, minister, religious affiliation administrator; b. Houston, Dec. 1, 1929; s. Levi John and Edith Mary (Pynn) M.; m. Shirley Estelle Horn, June 15, 1956; 1 child, Allen Kyle. BA, Baylor U., 1961; diploma, Southwestern Bapt. Theol. Sem., 1963. Ordained to ministry So. Bapt. Conv., 1949. Dir. Christian Outreach Ministries, Montgomery County, Tex., 1972—. Mem. Montgomery County Ministerial Assn. (past pres.), Tex. Hosp. Auxs. Home: 99 Yupon Circle PO Box 677 Montgomery TX 77356 *Perhaps the greatest need in our world today is for all of us once again to learn to wait upon the Lord. We must learn that waiting time is never wasted time. If we wait with Him, we will be ready to go when the time to go comes.*

MAY, ERNEST MAX, religious organization administrator; b. Newark, July 24, 1913; s. Otto Bernard and Eugenie (Morgenstern) M.; m. Harriet Elizabeth Dewey, Oct. 12, 1940; children: Ernest Dewey, James Northrup, Susan Elizabeth. BA, Princeton, 1934, MA, 1935; PhD in Organic Chemistry, U. Chgo., 1938; LittD (hon.), Montclair State Coll., 1989. With Otto B. May, Inc., Newark, 1938-73; successively chemist, gen. mgr. Otto B. May, Inc., 1938-52, pres., 1952-73; trustee Youth Consultation Service Diocese of Newark, 1952-59, 61-66, 68—, pres. Youth Consultation Service, 1971-75, hon. dir., 1975—; dir. Cone Mills Corp., 1971-75, mem. exec. com., 1968-71; Tech. adviser to spl. rep. trade negotiations, 1964-67. Councilman, Summit, N.J., 1963-70; Mem. Summit Environ. Com., 1971-75, chmn., 1974—; pres. Family Svc. Assn. Summit, 1959-61, Mental Health Assn. Summit, 1954, Summit Coun. Chs. Christ, 1962-63; mem. exec. com. Christ Hosp., Jersey City, 1971—, v.p., chmn., 1974—; chmn. Summit Hwy. Adv. Com., 1976—; trustee, organizer Summer Organic Chemistry Inst., Choate Sch., Wallingford, Conn.; mem. Union County Mental Health Bd., 1973-76; bd. dirs. N.J. Mental Health Assn., 1974-81; trustee Montclair (N.J.) State Coll., 1975-85, vice-chmn., 1976-80, chmn., 1980-83; adviser applied prof. psychology Rutgers U., 1976—; mem. Nat. Commn. on Nursing, 1980-83; adviser dept. music Princeton U.; trustee Assn. for Children in N.J., 1975—, Citizen's Com. on Biomed. Ethics in N.J., 1984—. Fellow Am. Inst. Chemists; mem. Am., Swiss, German chem. socs., Synthetic Organic Chem. Mfrs. Assn. (bd. govs. 1952-54, 63-70, v.p. 1966-68, chmn. internat. comml. rels. com. 1968-73, hon. mem.), Vol. Trustees Not-For-Profit Hosps. (trustee 1986-88), N.J. Hosp. Assn. (coun. on edn. 1990-91), Sigma Xi. Republican. Episcopalian (vestry 1950-60). Clubs: Metropolitan Opera (N.Y.), Chemists (N.Y.); Beacon Hill (Summit, N.J.); Essex (Newark); Nassau (Princeton). Home: 57 Colt Rd Summit NJ 07901 also: State Rd Chilmark MA 02535 *To live right and help others live right too, each in his own way.*

MAY, FELTON EDWIN, bishop; b. Chgo., Apr. 23, 1935; s. James Albert May and Florine C. (Felton) May Caruthers; m. Phyllis Elizabeth Henry, June 22, 1963; children: Daphne Endrea, Felton Edwin II. B.A., Judson Coll., 1962; M.Div., Crozer Theol. Sem., 1970; DD, Lycoming Coll., 1989, Lebanon Valley Coll., 1989, Wesley Coll., Dover, Del., 1990. Ordained deacon United Meth. Ch., 1962, elder, 1970. Asst. pastor St. James Meth. Ch., Chgo., 1961-63; pastor Maple Park United Meth. Ch., Chgo., 1963-68; assoc. exec. dir. Meth. Action Program, Wilmington, Del., 1968-70, Ezion-Mt. Carmel United Meth. Ch., Wilmington, 1970-75; dist. supt. Peninsula Conf., United Meth. Ch., Easton, Md., 1975-81; coun. dir. Peninsula Conf., United Meth. Ch., Dover, 1981-84; bishop United Meth. Ch., Harrisburg, Pa., 1984-90; spl. assignment Cou. of Bishops, Washington, 1990-91. Author: Developmental Evangelism (workbook), 1979; co-contbr. articles to mags.; co-author church sch. curriculum. Mem. Atty.'s Grievance Com., Annapolis, 1979-81; bd. govs. Wesley Sem., Washington, 1975—; bd. dirs. Boy Scouts Am., Dover, 1981-83, Wesley Coll., 1972-83, Wilmington Parking Authority, 1974, Del. Health and Social Svc. Commn., Dover, 1972; mem. Del. Civil Rights Com., Wilmington, 1970; trustee Lycoming Coll., Lebanon Valley Colls. With U.S. Army, 1957-59. Avocations: oil painting; tennis; plants; travel. Home: PO Box 239 Hummelstown PA 17109 Office: United Meth Ch Harrisburg Area 900 S Arlington Ave Harrisburg PA 17109

MAY, JOHN LAWRENCE, archbishop; b. Evanston, Ill., Mar. 31, 1922; s. Peter Michael and Catherine (Allare) M. M.A., St. Mary of Lake Sem., Mundelein, Ill., 1945, S.T.L., 1947. Ordained priest Roman Catholic Ch., 1947; asst. pastor St. Gregory Ch., Chgo., 1947-56; chaplain Mercy Hosp., Chgo., 1956-59; v.p., gen. sec. Cath. Ch. Extension Soc. U.S., 1959-67, pres., from 1967; ord. titular bishop of Tagarbala and aux. bishop, Chgo., 1967-69; pastor Christ The King Parish, Chgo., 1968-69; bishop of Mobile, Ala., 1969-80, archbishop of St. Louis, 1980—. Mem. Nat. Conf. Cath. Bishops (pres. 1986—, past v.p.). Office: care Chancery Office 4445 Lindell Blvd Saint Louis MO 63108

MAY, LOUIS PHILIP, III, church organization official; b. Lawton, Okla., Apr. 5, 1958; s. Louis Philip Jr. and Erma Dean (Burkhead) M.; m. Adrienne Marie Direen, Dec. 15, 1990. BA, Miss. Coll., 1980; postgrad., Southwestern Bapt. Theol. Sem., Ft. Worth, 1980-81, 83-87. Video prodn. asst. Bapt. Sunday Sch. Bd., Nashville, 1983; staff writer Restoration mag. James Robison Evangelism Assocs., Ft. Worth, 1984-85; coord. worship media Southcliff Bapt. Ch., Ft. Worth, 1984-87; sound and lighting specialist So. Bapt. Sunday Sch. Bd., Glorieta, N.Mex., 1987—; deacon 1st Bapt. Ch. Santa Fe, 1989—, speech coach, 1990—; media cons. May Prodns., Ft. Worth, 1984-87; dir. media libr. Santa Fe Bapt. Assn., 1987—, mem. exec. coun., 1987—, sound and lighting cons., 1988—. Contbr. articles to profl. jours. Republican. Home: PO Box 269 Glorieta NM 87535 Office: So Bapt Sunday Sch Bd Glorieta Bapt Conf Ctr PO Box 8 Glorieta NM 87535 *Growth is when the valleys' depths become higher than the old mountain tops.*

MAY, MELANIE ANN, theologian; b. Wash., Jan. 6, 1955; d. Russell Junior and Arlene Virginia (Ringgold) May. AB, Manchester Coll, 1976; MDiv., Harvard Div. Sch., 1979; AM, Harvard U., 1982, PhD, 1986. Teaching fellow Harvard Univ., Div. Sch., Cambridge, Mass., 1981-83; asst. head tutor Harvard Univ., Cambridge, 1983-84; staff (program for women) Ch. Brethren Gen. Bd., Elgin, Ill., 1985-87; ecumenical officer Ch. Brethren Gen. Bd., Elgin, 1985-91; adj. faculty Bethany Theol. Sem., Oak Brook, Ill., 1986—; assoc. gen. sec. human resources Ch. Brethren Gen. Bd., Elgin, 1987-91; vis. prof. Harvard Divinity Sch., Spring, 1991; adj. faculty Garrett-Evamg. Theol. Sem., Evanston, Ill., 1991-92. Author: Bonds of Unity, Women, Theology and Worldwide Church, 1989, For All the Saints: the Practice of Ministry in the Church, 1990, Women and Church: the Challenge of Solidarity in an Age of Alienation, 1991; assoc. edito Jour. Ecumenical Studies. Quality Ministerial candidates, 1987—, chmn. commn. Faith and Order, Nat. Council, N.Y., 1988; mem. standing commn. Faith and Order, World Coun. Chs., 1991—. Mem. N.Am. Acad. Economists, Am. Acad. Religion. Avocations: reading, gardening, swimming. Home: 18 W 711 22nd St Lombard IL 60148 Office: Ch Brethren Offices 1451 Duncee Ave Elgin IL 60120

MAY, WILLIAM EUGENE, theology educator; b. St. Louis, May 27, 1928; s. Robert W. and Katherine Ann (Armstrong) M.; m. Patricia Ann Keck, Oct. 4, 1958; children: Michael, Mary, Thomas, Timothy, Patrick, Susan, Kathleen. BA, Cath. U., 1950, MA, 1951; PhD, Marquette U., 1968. Assoc. editor Newman Press, Westminster, Md., 1954-55; editor Bruce Pub. Co., Milw., 1955-68, Corpus Books, Washington and N.Y.C., 1969-70; prof. theology Cath. U., Washington, 1971-91, Pope John Paul II Inst., Washington, 1991—. Author: Christ in Contemporary Thought, 1971 (Best Book award Coll. Theology Soc.), Becoming Human, 1974, Human Existence, Medicine and Ethics, 1977, Sex, Marriage and Chastity, 1981, Sex and Sanctity of Life, 1984, Catholic Sexual Ethics, 1985, Moral Absolutes, 1989, Introduction to Moral Theology, 1991. Recipient Thomas Linacre award Nat. Fedn. Cath. Physicians Guilds, 1983. Mem. Fellowship Cath. Scholars (Cardinal Wright award 1980), Theol. Soc. Am., Am. Cath. Philos. Assn. Home: 4412 Saul Rd Kensington MD 20895 Office: Pope John Paul II Inst 487 Michigan Ave NE Washington DC 20017

MAYE, RICHARD BOYKIN, clergyman; b. Uniontown, Ala., Oct. 25, 1933; s. Johnny and Frances (May) Boykin; B.A., Sangamon State U., Springfield, Ill., 1972, M.A., 1972, PhD, Internat. Theol. Sem., Van Nuys, Calif.; m. Rose Owens, June 24, 1978; children—Darryl Kermit, Byron Keith, Larry Lewis-Maye. Juvenile parole agt. Ill. Dept. Corrections, Chgo., 1967-70, adminstrv. asst., Springfield, 1970-72; lectr. polit. sci. Ill. State U., Normal, 1973-77; ordained to ministry Baptist Ch., 1960; pastor Pleasant Grove Bapt. Ch., Springfield, 1970—; mem. faculty Chgo. Bapt. Inst., 1968-70. Mem. Springfield Civil Service Comn., 1979—; mem. sch. integration commn., Springfield, 1977-79; bd. dirs. Morgan-Washington Home Girls, Springfield, 1977, Lincoln Library, Springfield, 1975-76, Springfield Area Arts Council; mem. grad. council So. Ill. U., 1975-76; mem. citizen's adv. com. Ill. Dept. Children and Family Services, Springfield, 1980-81, now chairperson com.; chmn. bd. dirs. Access to Housing, Springfield, 1981-83; sec., bd. dirs One Ch., One Child; bd. dirs. United Way, Sangamon County, Ill. Served with AUS, 1954-56. Grad. fellow U. Iowa, 1977-78, 79-80; grad. dean fellow So. Ill. U., 1975-76; recipient Citizen of Year award Springfield NAACP, 1976, Public Service award U.S. Dist. Ct., Springfield, 1978. Mem. Nat. Polit. Sci. Assn., Greater Springfield Interfaith Assn. (v.p.).

MAYER, HAROLD ALBERT, III, religion educator; b. Pitts., May 31, 1954; s. Harold Albert Jr. and Dolores Barbara (Anderson) M.; m. Sandra Kay Littlefield, Dec. 23, 1978; children: Harold A. IV, Ashley Kay. BSE, Memphis State U., 1977; MA in Religious Edn., Southwestern Bapt. Theol. Sem., 1984. Tchr., coach Rossville (Tenn.) Acad., 1977-79, Glenmore Acad., Memphis, 1979-80, Gleason (Tenn.) High Sch., 1980-82; youth min. Live Oak Bapt. Ch., Jacksboro, Tex., 1982-84; vol. coord. World Relief, Ft. Worth, 1982-85; dir. edn. ministry Mandarin Bapt. Ch., Jacksonville, Fla., 1985-88; min. of edn. Sheridan Hills Bapt. Ch., Hollywood, Fla., 1988—; spl. worker Fla. Bapt. Conv., 1987—. Named Coach of Yr., MCAA, 1979, one of Outstanding Young Men Am., 1985. Mem. Fla. Bapt. Religious Edn. Assn., So. Bapt. Religious Edn. Assn., Jacksonville Bapt. Assn. (mem. Assist Team 1985—), Fla. Round Table (pres. 1991). Republican. Avocations: running, basketball. Home: 307 N 31st Rd Hollywood FL 33021 Office: Sheridan Hills Bapt Ch 3751 Sheridan St Hollywood FL 33021

MAYER, PAUL AUGUSTIN CARDINAL, archbishop; b. May 23, 1911. ordained Roman Cath. Ch., 1935. Consecrated bishop Titular See Satrianum; then archbishop, 1972, proclaimed cardinal, 1985; pres. Pontifical Commn. Ecclesia Dei. Address: Via Rusticucci 13, 00193 Rome Italy

MAYER, ROBERT JAMES, religion editor; b. San Francisco, May 4, 1952; s. William Alex and Nova Marie (Harrison) M.; m. Renee Laverne Ehrhart, Dec. 2, 1978. BS, U. San Francisco, 1974; MA, Fuller Theol. Sem., 1977; grad. tchr. diploma, Evang. Tchr. Tng. Assn. Assoc. pastor Valley Advent Christian Ch., L.A., 1980-82; dir. publs. Advent Christian Gen. Conf., Charlotte, N.C., 1982—; mem. exec. com. Mid-Atlantic Sunday Sch. Assn., Charlotte, 1983-86; chmn. ministerial com. Piedmont Advent Christian Conf., Charlotte, 1987-91, conv. com. 1992 Evang. Press Assn. Conv., Overland Park, Kans., 1990—. Mem. Evang. Theol. Soc. (assoc.). Republican. Office: Advent Christian Gen Conf 14601 Albemarle Rd Charlotte NC 28227

MAYERON, CAROL ANN, cantorial soloist; b. Mpls., Jan. 14, 1951; d. Phillip Jerome and Shirley (Shapiro) Richter; m. Robert Charles Mayeron, May 27, 1973; children: Jennifer Lynn, Molli Beth. BS summa cum laude, U. Minn., 1973. Mem. choir Adath Jeshurun Synagogue, Mpls., 1967-74; cantorial soloist, dir. music Bet Shalom Congregation, Hopkins, Minn., 1981—; del. Joint Commn. on Synagogue Music, Paramus, N.J., 1987—; tutor B'nai Mitzvah Temple Israel, Mpls., 1988-90. Active Mpls. Children's Health Ctr. Aux., 1977—; coach Golden Valley (Minn.) Girls Jr. Softball, 1987-88, 90-91; co-chair Meadowbrook Parent Coun., Golden Valley, 1988. Mem. Am. Conf. Cantors (bd. dirs. 1989—), Hadassah (life mem., various offices), Nat. Coun. Jewish Women, Guild Temple Musicians (sec. 1987-89, pres. 1989—). Office: Bet Shalom Congregation 201 Ninth Ave N Hopkins MN 55343

MAYERS, RONALD BURTON, philosophy and religion educator; b. Greensburg, Pa., July 26, 1940; s. James Lansen and Rachel Marie (Ludwick) M.; m. Charlotte Ann Cassell, Aug. 24, 1963; children: Stephen, Charissa. BTh, Bapt. Bible Sem., 1964; BA, SUNY, Binghamton, 1965; MA, Syracuse U., 1967, PhD, 1972; M of Theology, Western Theol. Sem., Holland, Mich., 1973. Pastor Upper Lisle Bapt. Ch., Whitney Point, N.Y., 1964-69; prof. Grand Rapids (Mich.) Bapt. Coll. and Sem., 1969—; commr. Ottawa County, Mich., 1979-80, 83-90; trustee Bapts. for Life, 1986-91; trustee Grand Rapids Right-To-Life, 1976-80. Author: Both/And: A Balanced Apologetic, 1984, Evangelica Perspectives, 1987, Religious Ministry In A Trancindentless Culture, 1980; editor: Christian Theology, 1976, Elementary Theology, 1977; contbr. articles to profl. jours. Mem. Am. Philos. Assn., Am. Acad. Religion, Evang. Theol. Soc., Evang. Philos. Soc., Mich. Acad. Arts, Letters and Scis. Republican. Office: Grand Rapids Coll Sem 1001 E Beltline Grand Rapids MI 49505

MAYES, ILA LAVERNE, minister; b. Eldorado, Okla., Dec. 23, 1934; d. Thomas Floyd and Irene Elizabeth (Buchanan) Jordan; m. Forrest Clay Mayes, July 2, 1954; children: Barbara, Marian, Cynthia, Janice. BA, U. Tex., 1973; MSW, U. Mich., 1976; MDiv, Austin Presbyn. Sem., 1986. Ordained to ministry Presbyn. Ch. (U.S.A.), 1986; cert. social worker. Pastor First Presbyn. Ch., Childress and Memphis, Tex., 1986—; mem. Austin Sem. Alumni Bd., 1991—, Synod of the Sun Evangelism Com., Denton, 1990—, Presbytery Commn. on Ministry, Lubbock, 1986-90. Chmn. ARC, Childress, 1990; bd. dirs. Am. Cancer Soc., Childress, 1988-89. Mem. AAUW, Atalantlean Club, Mortarboard, Alpha Chi, Alpha Lambda Delta. Home: 309 Ave B SE Childress TX 79201 Office: First Presbyn Ch 311 Commerce Childress TX 79201 *You and I live in a wonderful tension between the past and the future. As our Faith in God helps us to reinterpret the past and reshapes our future, we grow and change. I like that.*

MAYFIELD, MICHAEL DOUGLAS, minister; b. Springfield, Ill., June 5, 1951; s. Thomas Richard and Barbara Jean (Raisch) M.; m. Vickie Sue Lusch, June 10, 1974; children: Adam Douglas, Sarah Beth, Leah Michelle. BA, So. Ill. U., 1974; MDiv, So. Bapt. Theol. Sem., 1990. Ordained to ministry United Meth. Ch., 1989. Pastor Mt. Etna United Meth. Ch., Thompsonville, Ill., 1984-85, Energy and Colp (Ill.) United Meth. Ch., 1985-90, Creal Springs (Ill.)-New Burnside United Meth. Ch., 1990—. Home: PO Box 376 Creal Springs IL 62922 *God's plan for our lives is the only one that gives meaning and enrichment to this earthly existence. Life lived in personal relationship with God through Christ, filled with the Holy Spirit, is every individual's privilege.*

MAYO, JAMES H., bishop. Bishop 4th dist. African Meth. Episcopal Ch., Chgo. Office: African Meth Episcopal Ch 400 E 41st St Ste 114 PO Box 53539 Chicago IL 60653*

MAYS, CHARLES WILLIAM, minister; b. Colfax, Wash., Apr. 7, 1940; s. William Charles and Thelma Irene (Myklebust) M.; m. Sandra Jean Erickson, Aug. 25, 1962; children: Marsha Jeanne, Steven Paul, Mary Beth. BA, Pacific Luth. U., 1962; BD, Luther Theol. Sem., St. Paul, 1966; D Ministry, Pacific Luth. Theol. Sem., Berkeley, Calif., 1981. Ordained to ministry Evang. Luth. Ch. in Am., 1966. Pastor Bethlehem Luth. Ch., Fairfax, Va., 1966-74, Lord of Life Luth. Ch., Renton, Wash., 1974-83; sr. pastor Univ. Luth. Ch. of Hope, Mpls., 1984-87; lead pastor Holy Trinity Luth. Ch., Port Angeles, Wash., 1988—; pres. Evang. Luth. Ch. in Am. Regional Pastoral Conf., 1979-80, 88-91; v.p. Wash. Assn. Chs., Seattle, 1987-88, North Pacific dist. Am. Luth. Ch., Seattle, 1987-88; sec. task force on study theol. edn. Evang. Luth. Ch., Chgo., 1989—. Contbr. articles to profl. jours. Chairperson Fairfax Activity Ctr. for Ret. Adults, 1970-74; mem. Wash. State White House Conf. on Family, 1981. Recipient Centennial Hon. award Pacific Luth. U., 1990. Mem. Mpls. Ministerial Assn. (sec. 1986-87). Democrat. Home: 720 N Lincoln Ave Port Angeles WA 98362 Office: Holy Trinity Luth Ch 301 E Lopez St Port Angeles WA 98362 *Far more important than what I think about God is what God thinks of me and of the whole creation. Even when we cannot hold God, God holds us in the firm grasp of His love.*

MAYS, GEORGE FRANCIS, minister; b. Springfield, Ohio, Feb. 17, 1956; s. Sylvester Francis Mays and Dorothy (Hirsch) Mays Oppie; m. Becky Lou Rollins, Aug. 2, 1979; 1 child, Joseph David. BS, Campbellsville Coll., 1982; MDiv, Ashland (Ohio) Theol. Sem., 1989. Ordained to ministry United Ch. Christ, 1990. Pastor Emmanuel Chapel, Wellington, Ohio, 1984-88, First Congl. Chs., Florence-South Amherst, Ohio, 1988-90, First Congl. Ch., Lodi, Ohio, 1990—; mem. United Ch. Christ coms., Canton, Ohio, 1990—. Mem. Rotary. Republican. Home: 36 E Main St Greenwich OH 44837 Office: First Congl Ch 114 Church St Lodi OH 44254 *I believe today's church, which seems to be bent on conforming to the world, would be farther ahead if it looked backward, back to the scriptures, the gospel and the Christ who inspired its creation.*

MAYS, JACK EDWIN, music minister; b. Lynchburg, Va., Feb. 2, 1948; s. Olen Leonard and Tessie (Havery) M.; m. Linda Ann Parsons, July 31, 1971; children: Carmen Celena, Devin O'Neil. BA in Music Edn., U. Richmond, 1970; MM, Hardin Simmons U., 1974. Ordained to ministry Bapt. Ch., 1978. Min. of youth Cen. Bapt. Ch., Richmond, Va., 1968-70, min. music and youth, 1974-87; tchr. Hampton (Va.) City Schs., 1970-71; min. music and youth Youth 1st Bapt. ch., Petersburg, Va., 1987-88, Berea Bapt. Ch., Rockville, Va., 1988—. Pianist Va. Bapt. Male Chorale, sec., 1989-90. Sgt. USAF, 1971-74. Named Outstanding Young Religious Leader Chesterfield (Va.) Jaycees, 1976. Home: 525 Watch Hill Rd Midlothian VA 23113 Office: Berea Bapt Ch PO Box 280 Rockville VA 23146

MAYSE, MARILYN ANN, minister, hospital chaplain; b. St. Joseph, Mo., Apr. 4, 1941; d. Warren Clyde and Katherine Ann (Frasier) M. BM, Okla. Bapt. U., 1963; MusM, North Tex. State U., 1965, Ea. Ky. U., 1977; MDiv, Southeastern Bapt. Theol. Sem., 1983. Instr. music Hardin-Simmons U., Abilene, Tex., 1964-66; missionary journeyman So. Bapt. Fgn. Mission Bd., Nigeria, 1968-70; preparatory piano tchr. Samford U., Birmingham, Ala., 1970-72; music tchr. John Carroll High Sch., Birmingham, 1971-72; asst. prof. music Campbellsville (Ky.) Coll., 1972-79; chaplain resident Bapt. Med. Ctrs., Birmingham, 1979-82; chaplain, clin. pastoral edn. supr. Bapt. Med. Ctr.-Montclair, Birmingham, 1983—; chmn. faculty Campbellsville Coll., 1977-78. Soprano soloist Episc. Cathedral of the Advent, Birmingham, 1986—. Fellow Coll. of Chaplains; mem. Assn. Clin. Pastoral Edn. (cert. supr.), Am. Assn. Pastoral Counselors, Women in Ministry So. Bapt. (bd. dirs. 1983-86). Office: Bapt Med Ctr Montclair 800 Montclair Rd Birmingham AL 35213

MAZAK, RICHARD ALLAN, clergyman, physicist, educator, consultant; b. Milw., Aug. 30, 1932; s. Stephan G. and Anne Olga (Rybarik) M.; m. Sandra G. Kropf, June 11, 1960; children—Lynn, Pamela, Scott. B.A., Concordia Sem., St. Louis, 1954, diploma in theology, 1958; M.A., U. Tex.-Austin, 1964, Ph.D., 1968. Ordained minister Lutheran Ch. Mo. Synod, 1960. Asst. prof. physics Concordia Coll., Milw., 1958-65; assoc. prof. Concordia Coll., River Forest, Ill., 1965-73; pastor Trinity Luth. Ch., San Angelo, Tex., 1973-79; pastor Mt. Olive Luth. Ch., Newton, N.C., 1979—; v.p. Austin Sci. Assocs. (Tex.), 1969-73; tchr. Catawba Valley Tech. Coll., Hickory, N.C., 1979-83; cons. in field. Bd. dirs. Am. Cancer Soc., San Angelo; mem. Spl. Task Force on Edn. Catawba County. NSF fellow, 1960, 61, 62, 63, 64, 66-68. Mem. Am. Phys. Soc., Am. Inst. Physics, Am. Assn. Physics Tchrs. Lodge: Lions. Contbr. articles to profl. jours. Home: 1010 E 23d St Newton NC 28658 Office: 7 Mount Olive Rd Newton NC 28658

MAZIARZ, EDWARD ANTHONY, philosophy educator; b. Milw., Mar. 6, 1915; s. John and Mary (Matusiak) M. BS, St. Joseph's Coll., Rensselaer, Ind., 1944; MA, Cath. U. Am., 1941; MS, U. Mich., 1945; PhD, U. Ottawa, Can., 1949; summer student, U. Va., 1944, U. Laval, 1947. Ordained priest Roman Cath. Ch., 1940; instr. philosophy Marian Coll., Fond du Lac, Wis., 1941-42; faculty St. Joseph's Coll., 1943-66, prof. philosophy and math., 1958-66, acad. dean, 1955-63; prof. philosophy Loyola U., Chgo., 1966-84, prof. emeritus, 1984—. Author: The Philosophy of Mathematics, 1950, You: Become a Full Person, 1983; Translator: A Short History of Philosophy, 1955, Redemption Through the Blood of Jesus, 1960, A Short History of Philosophy, 2d edit, 1960; co-author: Greek Mathematical Philosophy, 1967, Human Being and Being Human, 1969; editor: Value and Values in Evolution: A Symposium, 1979. Mem. AAAS, Am. Acad. Religion, Am. Math. Soc., Am. Cath. Philos. Assn., Am. Philos. Assn., Assn. Symbolic Logic, History of Sci. Soc., Philos. Sci. Assn., Soc. for Sci. Study Religion, Delta Epsilon Sigma (nat. pres. 1951-53). Home: 1033 W Loyola #1007 Chicago IL 60626 Office: Loyola U Dept Philosophy 6525 N Sheridan Rd Chicago IL 60626

MAZZOCCOLI, SYLVESTER ANTHONY, deacon, secretary; b. Morristown, N.J., June 11, 1939; s. Rockey Philip and Elizabeth Ann (Bolcar) M.; m. Maryjoan T. Rodeawald, Sept. 2, 1961; children: Anthony William, Laura Theresa. BS in Commerce, Rider Coll., 1963. Cert. deacon chaplain in gen. health care. Mem. parish staff St. Virgil's Ch., Morris Plains, N.J., 1976—; chaplain's asst. Morristown Rehab. Ctr., 1976-85; counselor, instr. work and sch., West Orange and Paramus, N.J., 1976—. With USNR, 1956-62. Mem. IBM Club (pres. 1966—), KC (4th degree). Roman Catholic. Home: 12 Glenbrook Rd Morris Plains NJ 07950 Office: IBM Corp PO PM3 140 E Ridgewood Ave Paramus NJ 07653 *It's nice to be important but it's even more important to be nice.*

MBANG, SUNDAY COFFIE, minister; b. Eket, Akwa Ibom, Nigeria, Aug. 26, 1936; s. Coffie Eka and Judith (Ukpong) M.; m. Enobong Esukuku, Dec. 16, 1978; children: Ini-Abasi Abisoye, Idorenyin, Nyakno Samuel. Diploma, Trinity Coll., Umuahia, Nigeria, 1964; BA, U. Ibadan, Nigeria, 1971; M of Theol., Harvard U., 1977. Cir. min. Meth. Ch., Ikot Abasi, Nigeria, 1965-66, N000, Ikot Ekpene, Nigeria, 1967-68; chaplain Meth. Boys' High Sch., Oron, Nigeria, 1971-72; bishop Meth. Ch., Lagos, Nigeria, 1980-84; patriarch, prelate Meth. Ch., 1985—; $D $D, $D; lectr., U. Ibadan, 1978-79; mem. Presidium, World Meth. Coun. Patron Idua Youth Assn., Lagos, Nigeria, 1985-90, Widows Assn. Nigeria, 1985-90, Meth. Youth Assn., 1985-90; trustee Meth. Ch. Nigeria, YMCA of Nigeria. Mem. Christian Coun. Nigeria (chmn. 1988—), Christian Assn. Nigeria, World Meth. Coun. Office: Meth Ch Nigeria, 21/22 Marina, Lagos Nigeria

MCAFEE, (HUBERT) WAYNE, minister; b. Ft. Worth, Feb. 4, 1951; s. Hubert Cassell and Anna Mae (Cummins) McA.; m. Margaret Anne Gibson, Nov. 27, 1975; children: Heather Anne, Bethany Michelle. AA, Tarrant County Jr. Coll., 1970; student, Tex. Christian U., 1970-72; BS in Religious Edn., Howard Payne U., 1974; MRE, Southwestern Bapt. Theol. Sem., 1975. Min. of students First Bapt. Ch., Palestine, Tex., 1975-77, South Main Bapt., Pasadena, Tex., 1977-83, First Bapt. Ch., Hurst, Tex., 1983-87, First Bapt. Oak Cliff, Dallas, 1987—; seminar leader Tex. Bapt. Gen. Conv., Dallas, 1978-91; chmn. youth com. Greater Dallas Ministerial Alliance, 1989-91; bd. trustees Heart of Tex. Bapt. Encampment, Brownwood, Tex., 1989-91. Contbr. articles to profl. jours. Chaplain asst. Brownwood State Sch., 1972-74; chaplain Pasadena (Tex.) Police Dept., 1979-83; Rudolph, Flying Santa U.S.A., Bedford, Tex., 1983-91. Mem. Nat. Met. Youth Mins. Assn., Alpha Phi Omega. Home: 2800 Greg Dr Bedford TX 76021 Office: First Bapt Ch Oak Cliff 7710 S Westmoreland Dallas TX 75237

MCALACK, MATTHEW MARK, minister; b. Camden, N.J., Mar. 27, 1961; s. John and Charlotte Ann (Frett) McA.; m. Michele Bardeer, June 7, 1986; children: Zachary, Jeremy. BS in Bible, Phila. Coll. of Bible, 1983; ThM, Dallas Theol. Sem., 1987. Pastor English ministry Chinese Christian Testimony, Wyckoff, N.J., 1987-90; youth pastor Manahawkin (N.J.) Bapt. Ch., 1990—. Office: Manahawkin Bapt Ch 400 Beach Ave Manahawkin NJ 08050

MC ALLISTER, GERALD NICHOLAS, retired bishop, clergyman; b. San Antonio, Feb. 23, 1923; s. Walter Williams and Leonora Elizabeth (Alexander) McA.; m. Helen Earle Black, Oct. 2, 1953; children—Michael Lee, David Alexander, Stephen Williams, Elizabeth. Student, U. Tex., 1939-42, Va. Theol. Sem., 1948-51; D.D. (hon.), Va. Theol. Sem., 1977. Rancher, 1946-48; ordained deacon Episcopal Ch., 1953, priest, 1954; deacon, priest Ch. of Epiphany, Raymondville, Ch. of Incarnation, Corpus Christi, St. Francis Ch., Victoria, all Tex., 1951-63; 1st canon Diocese of W. Tex., 1963-70; rector St. David's Ch., San Antonio, 1970-76; consecrated Episcopal bishop of Okla., Oklahoma City, 1977-89, ret., 1989; bishop-in-residence Episcopal Theol. Sem., Austin, Tex., 1990—; trustee Episcopal Theol. Sem. of S.W., 1961—, adv. bd., 1974—; mem. Case Commn. Bd. for Theol. Edn., 1981-82; pres. Tex. Council Chs., 1966-68, Okla. Conf. Chs., 1980-83; bd. dirs. Presiding Bishop's Fund for World Relief, 1972-77, Ch. Hist. Soc., 1976—; chmn. Nat. and World Mission Program Group, 1973-76; mem. Structure of Ch. Standing Commn., 1979, mem. standing com. on Stewardship/Devel., 1979-85; founder Chaplaincy Program, Bexar County Jail, 1968; mem. governing bd. nat. council Ch. of Christ, 1982-85; chmn. standing commn. on stewardship Episcopal Ch., 1983-85; v.p., trustee The Episc. Episc. Theol. Sem. of Soutwest, 1987—. Author: What We Learned from What You Said, 1973, This Fragile Earth Our Island Home, 1980. Bd. dirs. Econ. Opportunity Devel. Corp., San Antonio, 1968-69; mem. exec. com. United Way, 1968-70, vice-chmn., 1970. Served with U.S. Mcht. Marines,

1942; to 1st lt. USAAF, 1942-45. Recipient Agudas Achim Brotherhood award, 1968. Address: 507 Bluff Estates San Antonio TX 78216

MCALLISTER, ROBERT JOSEPH, priest, publisher; b. Balt., Aug. 29, 1918; s. Robert Emory and Ann Gertrude (Doran) McA. BA, Loyola Coll., Balt., 1940; PhL, Gregorian U., Rome, 1945; STL, Gregorian U., 1952. Joined Soc. of Jesus, Roman Cath. Ch., 1940, ordained priest, 1951. From asst. pastor to pastor St. Ignatius Ch., Hill Top, Md., 1954-58; student counselor Gonzaga High Sch., Washington, 1958-64; asst. to nat. dir. Apostleship of Prayer, N.Y.C., 1964-70, nat. dir., 1970—; mem. adv. coun. Internat. Inst. of Heart of Jesus, 1972—, Apostolate for Family Consecration, 1975—, bd. sponsors Priestly Heart Program, 1976—. Home: 3 Stephen Ave New Hyde Park NY 11040 Office: Apostleship of Prayer Inc 3 Stephens Ave New Hyde Park NY 11040

MCANINCH, ARTHUR NEAL, JR., pastor; b. Little Rock, Ark., Nov. 9, 1935; s. Arthur Neal and Virginia (Shephard) McA.; m. Sonja Kay Jackson, Aug. 11, 1959; children: Virginia Kay Tuley, Elizabeth Anne Wilson, Sabrina Catherine. B of Career Arts, Dallas Bapt. Coll., 1977; MDiv, Southwestern Bapt. Theol. Sem., 1979. Ordained to ministry Bapt. Ch., 1978. Pastoral asst. Lakeview So. Bapt. Ch., Fairview Hts., Ill., 1975, Hillcrest Park Bapt. Ch., Arlington, Tex., 1975-80; pastor Emmanuel Bapt. Ch., Carlinville, Ill., 1980-85, First Bapt. Ch., Glen Rose, Tex., 1985-88, Fairlanes Bapt. Ch., Borger, Tex., 1988—; commd. lt. USAF, 1955, advanced through grades to maj., ret., 1975; pres. Clergy Fellowship, Carlinville, 1982-84; vice moderator Paluxy Bapt. Assn., Cleburne, Tex., 1986-88; ch. devel. dir. Palo Duro Bapt. Assn., Pampa, Tex., 1988—. Contbr. articles to profl. jours. Decorated D.F.C., Bronze Star, air medal with eight oak leaf clusters. Mem. Retired Officers Assn. Republican. Home: 122 Pecan Borger TX 79007 Office: Fairlanes Bapt Ch 3000 Fairlanes Blvd Borger TX 79007

MCARTHUR, JOHN DICKSON, JR., minister; b. Dayton, Ohio, June 2, 1955; s. John Dickson Sr. and Barbara Eve (Hartsock) McA.; m. Holly Grace Brooks, Aug. 14, 1976; children: Gypsy Ann, Candace Sue, Cathy Lou, Erika Kay, John Dickson III. AB in Christian Ministries, Cin. Bible Coll., 1977; postgrad., Lincoln Christian Sem., 1988-89. Ordained to ministry, 1977. Min. Pomeroy (Ohio) Ch. of Christ, 1977-79, Chestnut St. Ch. of Christ, Hoopeston, Ill., 1979-84; assoc. min. Windsor Rd. Christian Ch., Champaign, Ill., 1984-90; min. Erlanger (Ky.) Ch. of Christ, 1990—. Workshop leader Seminar Sun. Sch. Day, 1988-89, Radio program Christians Only, 1983-84, Youth Rally, 1990. Pres. Vermillion County Soc. Churches of Christ, 1983, Area Christian Ch. Mins. Assn., Champaign, 1988-89; publicity vice-chair Ill. Teen Conv., Springfield, Ill., 1989-90; sec., v.p. Campus Christian Fellowship Dir., Urbana, Ill., 1987-90. Mem. Camp Northward (bd. dirs.), Erlanger/Elsmere United Ministry. Office: Erlanger Ch of Christ 458 Graves Ave Erlanger KY 41018

MCAULIFFE, SISTER ELIZABETH ANN, nun, education educator; b. Providence, May 3, 1945; d. David George and Grace Gertrude (Sunderland) McA. BA in Chemistry, Biology, Salve Regina Coll., 1968; MS in Chemistry, U. N.H., 1975; EdD in Curriculum and Instrn., Pa. State U., 1985. Joined Sisters of Mercy, Roman Cath. Ch., 1963. Tchr. Tyler Sch., Providence, 1968-71; tchr. chemistry, biology Bishop Feehan High Sch., Attleboro, Mass., 1971-75; prin. Bishop Gerrard High Sch., Fall River, Mass., 1975-80; from instr. to assoc. prof. dept. edn. Salve Regina U., Newport, R.I., 1980—, dir. secondary edn. program, 1990; mem. Adv. Bd. for Edn. and Spl. Edn., Newport, 1985—, apptd. dir. secondary edn. program, 1990; presenter papers at profl. confs.; leader workshops. Contbr. articles to edn. publs. Chair, Province Steering Com., Cumberland, R.I., 1986-89; sec. Newport County Cath. Regional Sch. Bd., Middletown, R.I., 1987—; mem. Inst. Chpt. Steering Com., Washington, 1988-91. Mem. Assn. Curriculum and Devel, Am. Edni. Rsch. Assn., Assn. Tchr. Educators, Nat. Assn. Tchr. Educators, Mercy Higher Edn. Colloquium, New Eng. Assn. Tchrs. of Math. Avocations: tennis, dancing, walking, reading. Office: Salve Regina U Ochre Point Ave Newport RI 02840

MCAULIFFE, JOSEPH ROBERT, minister, publisher; b. Syracuse, N.Y., June 9, 1950; s. John E. and Millie (Lonergon) McA.; m. Kay Ellen Eberle, Apr. 29, 1972; children: Shannon, Laura, Marisa, Scott. B in Liberal Studies, Bowling Green State U., 1975, MA, 1979. Ordained to ministry Christian Ch., 1973. Pastor Bowling Green (Ohio) Covenant Ch., 1971-85, San Jose Covenant Ch., 1979-80, Tampa (Fla.) Covenant Ch., 1985—; staff writer Chalcedon Found., Vallecito, Calif., 1985—; current affairs editor Sta. WCIE, Lakeland, Fla., 1987—; bd. dirs. Internat. Ch. Relief Fund, Santa Rosa, Calif. Editor (newsletter) Bus. Gram, 1983 (Merit award 1985). Recipient Merit award Evang. Press Assn., 1985. Mem. Assn. Reformed and Charismatic Chs. Chmn. Fla. dist. VI, Alcohol-Drug Abuse-Mental Health Planning Coun.; vice chmn. Hillsborough County Children Svcs. Bd.; exec. com. Rep. Party, 1985—. Office: Tampa Covenant Ch 13320 Lake Magdalene Blvd Tampa FL 33618

MC AULIFFE, MICHAEL F., bishop; b. Kansas City, Mo., Nov. 22, 1920. Student, St. Louis Prep. Sem., Cath. U. Ordained priest Roman Cath. Ch., 1945; consecrated bishop, 1969; bishop diocese of Jefferson City Jefferson City, Mo., 1969—. Office: Chancery Office 605 Clark Ave PO Box 417 Jefferson City MO 65102

MC BAIN, LEROY DOWARD, minister, retired seminary president; b. Bottineau, N.D., July 18, 1917; s. Isaiah Daniel and Ada (Wassen) McB.; m. Olive Ann Fountain, May 30, 1940; children: Ada Marianne (Mrs. Gary Barrett), Loren Doward, Robert Mark, Margaret Melissa, Joy (Mrs. William Nolte). A.B., Eastern Baptist Theol. Sem., Phila., 1943, Th.B., 1943, D.D., 1959; spl. student, Columbia, also Union Theol. Sem., N.Y.C., 1946-49, Mansfield Coll., Oxford, Eng., 1971, Harvard Div. Sch., 1973, Princeton Theol. Sem., 1980. Ordained to ministry Bapt. Ch., 1943. Minister Bapt. Chs., Allentown, N.J., 1941-43; minister Clifton, N.J., 1943-52, Bklyn., 1952-54, Covina, Calif., 1954-62; minister 1st Bapt. Ch., Phoenix, 1962-77; pres. Am. Bapt. Sem. of the West, Berkeley, Calif., 1977-84; vis. prof. Calif. Bapt. Theol. Sem., Covina, 1956-86; Pres. Am. Bapt. Conv., 1967-68, Valley of Sun Council Chs., Phoenix, 1965-66; mem. gen. bd., also dept. internat. affairs Nat. Council Chs., 1959-68; del. World Council Chs., New Delhi, India, 1961; chmn. bd. Am. Bapt. Sem. West, 1970-71; nat. pres. evangelistic life style com. Am. Bapt. Conv. Author: Up Your Ante; Co-author: Born Again and Living Up To It. Merrill fellow Harvard Divinity Sch., 1972. Mem. Am. Acad. Homiletics.

MCBEAN, SHARON ELIZABETH, church administrator; b. Chgo., July 15, 1937; d. Archibald Lewis Jr. and Mary Elizabeth (Rees) McBean; m. Harold D. Sanders, Oct. 27, 1956 (div. Nov. 1976); children: Debra Sue Sanders, Catherine Leigh Sanders Ferguson. BA cum laude, La Roche Coll., 1977; MS in Edn., Duquesne U., 1978. Adminstrv. asst. 1st Presbyn. Ch., Santa Barbara, Calif., 1988-89, bus. mgr., 1989—; deacon 1st Presbyn. Ch., Santa Barbara, 1987-89. Mem. Ch. Bus. Adminstrn. Assn. (pres.), Nat. Assn. Ch. Bus. Adminstrs. Presbyterian.

MCBEE, RICHARD HARDING, microbiologist; b. Eugene, Oreg., May 15, 1916; s. Elmer Francis and Cora Cochrane (Clow) McB.; m. Virginia Helen Brown, June 15, 1940; children: Gail Elizabeth, Richard Harding Jr., Christopher Alan, Anne Katherine. Student, U. Oreg., 1934-36; BS in Chemistry, Oreg. State U., 1938, MS, 1940; postgrad., U. Md., 1939-41; PhD in Bacteriology, Wash. State U., 1948. Diplomate Am. Bd. Med. Microbiology. Bacteriologist Md. State Dept. Health, 1941-43; asst. prof. microbiology Mont. State U., Bozeman, 1949-51, assoc. prof., 1951-55, prof., 1955-76, prof. emeritus, 1976—, head dept. botany and microbiology, 1964-68, dean Coll. Letters and Sci., 1968-74; vestry and sr. warden St. James Ch., Bozeman, Mont., 1950-78; mem. commn. on ministry Diocese of Mont., Helena, 1970-76, mem. commn. on evangelism, 1979-82; mem. diocesan council Diocese of Mont., 1979-81; mem. commn. on lay ministry Diocese of Eastern Oreg., The Dalles, 1982-87, mem. commn. on ministry, 1984—, mem. standing com., 1984-90, pres., 1986-90; bd. dirs. McBee Lab., Oreg., High Desert Sch. Theology and Ministry, 1989-91; rsch. assoc. Rowett Rsch. Inst., Bucksburn, Aberdeenshire, Scotland, 1960; cons. in microbiology Anaconda Copper Mining, Inc., Frito-Lay, Inc., Midwest Rsch. Inst., NSF, Antarctica Office Naval Rsch., 1956-57; reader gen. ordination exams., 1986-91; vis. scientist Smithsonian Tropical Rsch. Inst., Balboa, Republic Panama. Co-author: General Bacteriology, 1955, 2d ed. 1962, Introductory Microbiology, 1973; contbr. numerous articles to sci. and religious jours.; patentee anaerobic tube roller. Mem. Hood River (Oreg.) Sch. Bd., 1985—. Served to capt. U.S. Army, 1943-46. Fellow NRC, 1948-49; research grantee NSF, 1951-74, NIH, 1953-57. Fellow AAAS, Am. Acad. Microbiology; mem. Am. Soc. Microbiology (pres. N.W. br. 1960, councilor 1962), Rotary (Paul Harris fellow 1991). Republican. Home: 3599 Belmont Rd Hood River OR 97031

MCBIRNIE, WILLIAM STEUART, academic administrator; b. Toronto, Ont., Can., Feb. 8, 1920; came to U.S., 1920; s. William Stuart and Betty Ethel (Potter) McB.; m. June Paulsen Thompson. BA, Kletzing Coll., 1944; BD, Bethel Sem., 1945; MRE, Southwestern Bapt. Theol. Sem., 1948, DRE, 1953; DD, Trinity Bible Coll., 1958; PhD, Calif. Grad. Sch. Theol., 1973, ThD, 1976; PhD (hon.), Daegu U., Republic of Korea, 1982. Ordained to ministry So. Bapt. Conv., 1939. Pastor Trinity Bapt. Ch., San Antonio, Tex., 1949-59, United Community Ch., Glendale, Calif., 1961-89; pres. Calif. Grad. Sch. Theology, Glendale, Calif., 1989—; co-founder Calif. Grad. Sch. Theology, 1969. Author: Search for the Twelve Apostles, 1973, Search for the Tomb of Christ, 1981, Search for the Early Church, 1982, numerous others. Recipient Angel awards (3) Religion in Media; Pilgrims medal State of Israel, 1967, George Washington Honor Gold medal Freedoms Found., 1978; named one of Five Outstanding Young Texans Tex. Jaycees, 1956. Republican. Home: 1923 Baycrest Santa Ana CA 92704 Office: 400 Freedman Way Anaheim CA 92816-0600

MCBRIDE, RALPH HAROLD, broadcasting executive; b. Beaumont, Tex., Nov. 17, 1932; s. Van Harold and Vivian (Walker) McB.; m. Cynthia Lynn Liming, Dec. 26, 1976; children: Carissa Renee, Kyle Harold. Student, Tex. A&M U., Bryan, Tex., 1975; Mech. Engr., Lamar U., Beaumont, 1977. Gen. mgr. Voice in the Wilderness Broadcasting, Inc., Bridge City, Tex., 1983—; ednl. tutor Boy's Haven, Beaumont, 1983—; pres. Voice in the Wilderness Broadcasting, Bridge City, 1978—; v.p. The King's Musician, Beaumont, 1984-89, sec., 1989—. County del. Rep. party, 1988-90, state del., 1990; mem. Am. Family Assn., Tupelo, Miss.; mem. adv. bd. Women's Aglow Fellowship Internat., Orange, Tex., 1990—; mem. Tex. Bandwagon, Beaumont, 1990—. Recipient Life-Time Achievement award Nat. Right to Life, 1991. Office: KTFA 92 FM 2000 Roundbunch Bridge City TX 77611 *Men grope blindly in the dark seeking success in life until they reach for God and His ways; only then is true fulfillment found.*

MCBRIEN, RICHARD PETER, theologian; b. Hartford, Conn., Aug. 19, 1936; s. Thomas Henry and Catherine Ann (Botticelli) McB. AA, St. Thomas Sem., 1956; BA, St. John Sem., 1958, MA, 1962; D in Sci. of Theology, Gregorian U., 1967. Assoc. pastor Our Lady of Victory Ch., West Haven, Conn., 1962-63; prof., dean of studies Pope John XXIII Nat. Sem., Weston, Mass., 1965-70; prof. theology Boston Coll., Newton, Mass., 1970-80, dir. inst. of religious edn. and pastoral ministry,, 1975-80; prof., chmn. dept. theology U. Notre Dame, 1980-91; cons. various dioceses and religious communities in the U.S. and Can., 1965—; vis. fellow John F. Kennedy Sch. Govt. Harvard U., Cambridge, 1976-77; mem. Council on Theol. Scholarship and Research Assn. of Theol. Schs., 1987-91. Author: Do We Need Church?, 1969, Catholicism, 1980 (Christopher award 1981), 2 vols., Caesar's Coin: Religion and Politics in America, 1987; editor: Encyclopedia of Religion, 1987. Recipient Best Syndicated Weekly Column award Cath. Press Assn. of U.S. and Can., 1975, 77, 78, 84. Mem. Cath. Theol. Soc. of Am. (pres. 1973-74, John Courtney Murray award 1976), Coll. Theology Soc., Am. Acad. Religion. Office: Univ of Notre Dame Dept of Theology Notre Dame IN 46556

MCCABE, SISTER DANIEL MARIE, nun, religious organization executive; b. Ansonia, Conn., Sept. 30, 1924; d. Daniel J. and Delia Theresa McCabe. RN, St. Mary's Hosp., Waterbury, Conn., 1945; BS, Coll. of Mary Immaculate, Hartford, Conn., 1954; MHA, St. Louis U., 1957; LHD (hon.), Sacred Heart U., Bridgeport, Conn., 1981. Joined Sisters of St. Joseph of Chambery, Roman Cath. Ch., 1946. Asst. administr. St. Francis Hosp., Hartford, 1957-63; administr. St. Joseph Med. Ctr., Stamford, Conn., 1963-85, pres., chief exec. officer, 1985—; trustee St. Camillus Health Ctr., Conn. Cath. Hosp. Coun.; mem. adv. bd. Inst. for Religious Edn. and Pastoral Studies Sacred Heart U.; mem. New Eng. Healthcare Assembly, New Eng. Conf. Cath. Hosps. Recipient Ella T. Grasso Community Svc. award Judeo-Christian Women Fairfield County, Conn., 1984, Outstanding Woman of Yr. award Soroptimist Internat., 1984, Spl. Svc. award Fairfield Found., Inc., 1986. Fellow Am. Coll. Healthcare Execs.; mem. Conn. Hosp. Assn. (mem. com. on govt.), Alliance for Health (trustee), Northeast Hosp. Network (trustee). Home and Office: St Joseph Med Ctr 128 Strawberry Hill Ave Stamford CT 06904-1222

MCCABE, JOSEPH E., religion educator; b. Bridgeville, Pa., Apr. 23, 1912; s. John S. and Rebecca (Fife) McC.; m. Margaret W. McCabe, Apr. 1, 1944; children: Jonathan Brandt, Alice Elizabeth. AB, Muskingum Coll., 1937, DD (hon.), 1957; MA, Ohio State U., 1940; BTh, Princeton Theol. Sem., 1943, MTh, 1947; PhD, U. Edinburgh, Scotland, 1951; LLD (hon.), Monmouth Coll., 1960; LHD (hon.), Waynesburg Coll., 1964; LittD, St. Thomas Coll., St. Paul, 1067. With First Presbyn. Ch., Lambertville, N.J., 1946-53, Presbyn. Ch. of Chestnut Hill, Phila., 1953-58; pres. Coe Coll., Cedar Rapids, Iowa, 1958-70, chancellor, 1970-77, pres. emeritus, 1977—; moderator Presbytery of New Brunswick, N.J., 1958; chmn. bd. trustes Beirut U. Coll., 1967-72. Author: Power of God in Parish Program, 1958 (Religious Book Club award), Ministers Service Book, 1962 (Religious Book Club award), Challenging Careers in the Church, 1960, Handel's Messiah, 1977. Acad. counsel Hoover Presdl. Libr., West Branch, Iowa, 1970-90, trustee; mem. bd. advisors Beirut U. Coll. Lt. USN, 1943-46, PTO. Mem. C. of C. (trustees Cedar Rapids chpt. 1958—), Cedar Rapids Country Club. Republican. Home: 1300 13th St NW Apt 401-A Cedar Rapids IA 52405 Office: Coe Coll 1220 First Ave NE Cedar Rapids IA 52402

MCCABE, RICHARD EDMUND, priest; b. Milw., Sept. 15, 1929; s. John and Margaret Mary (Burke) McC. BS, Regis Coll., 1951; postgrad., St. Mary's Theol. Sch., Houston, 1954-58; MSW, Worden Sch., San Antonio, 1962. Ordained priest Roman Cath. Ch., 1958. Parish priest St. Louis, Austin (Tex.), 1958-62; chaplain Seton Hosp., Austin, 1962-64, Adoration Convent, Austin, 1964—; founder, pastor Lakeway Ch., Austin, 1966—; founder, bd. dirs. Cath. Charities, Diocese of Austin, 1962—, cons. nat. disasters, 1965—; founder, bd. dirs. St. Vincent de Paul Soc., Austin, Waco, Tex., Temple, Tex., cons. nat. disasters, 1965—; founder, bd. dirs. Christ Child Soc. Ladies of Charity; pres. Austin Conf. Chs., 1970-71; founder St. Vincent de Paul Stores, Austin, Waco, Temple, Rosebud, Tex., Round Rock, Tex., Taylor, Tex., Lockhart, Tex. Chmn., mem. profl. adv. com. Austin Mental Health and Mental Retardation Ctr., 1971—; founder, bd. dirs. Caritas of Austin, Waco and Temple, Big Bros. of Austin, Gov.'s Retirement Residence, Austin; founder, v.p. Capitol Kidney Found.; pres. Internat. Coops., Austin Rehab. Ctr., Inc., Austin Coun. on Alcoholism; bd. dirs. Project Adopt, Campaign for Human Devel. Recipient Svc. to Juvenile Ct. award, 1962, Svc. to Mankind award, 1972. Mem. Acad. Cert. Social Workers, Nat. Assn. Social Workers, Town and Gown Club, Headliners Club. Home: 1004 W 32d St Austin TX 78705 Office: Cath Charities 901 W Martin Luther King Austin TX 78701

MCCACHERN, CYNTHIA CORNWELL, minister, primary school educator; b. Urbana, Ill., Feb. 28, 1964; d. Ronald Eugene and Joyce Anne (Wilhoit) Cornwell; m. John Carey McCachern, Dec. 29, 1990. BA in Bible and Elem. Edn., Milligan Coll., Tenn., 1985; MDiv with honors, Emmanuel Sch. Religion, Johnson City, Tenn., 1988. Ordained to ministry Christian Ch., 1988; cert. elem. tchr., Okla., Ill., Tenn. Assoc. min. Hopwood Meml. Christian Ch., Milligan College, 1985-89; min. youth and young adults 1st Christian Ch., Chgo., 1989-90; tchr. kindergarten Oakhurst Acad. for the Gifted and Talented, Oklahoma City, 1990-91; tchr. elem. grades gifted and talented students Western Heights (Okla.) Sch. Dist., 1991—. Author: Beside the Waters of the Buffalo: A History of Milligan College to 1941, 1989; contbg. author to devotional bible; contbr. articles to mags. Vol. coord. Edmond (Okla.) Habitat for Humanity, 1991—. Named Outstanding Young Min., Standard Pub. Co., 1989. Mem. Chgo. Area Youth Mins. Assn. (treas. 1989-90). Republican. Home: 2712 NW 159th Edmond OK 73013

MCCAFFREY, LEIGH GRAFFAM, pastor; b. Burlington, Vt., May 21, 1958; d. Leslie Howard and Lois May (Currie) Graffam; m. Matthew James McCaffrey, May 30, 1980; 1 child, Hannah Christine. BA magna cum laude, St. Michael's Coll., 1980; MDiv cum laude, Andover Newton (Mass.) Theol. Sch., 1988. Dir. christian edn. First Ch. of Christ, Groton, Conn., 1980-85; cons. in christian edn. First Congl. Ch., Lynn, Mass., 1988; co-pastor First Congl. Ch., Haverhill, N.H., 1988—. Author: (chpt. in book) YETS: Youth Experience in Travel & Service, 1990. Mem. improvement program Woodsville High Sch., N.H., 1989—. Office: First Congl Ch Parsonage on the Common Haverhill NH 03765-0102

MCCAGNEY, NANCY, religion educator; b. N.Y., June 10; d. John Warren and Marjorie McCagney. BA in Philosophy, U. Wis., 1965, MA in Philosophy, 1971; MA in Religious Studies, U. Calif., Santa Barbara, 1984, PhD in Religious Studies, 1991. Asst. prof. Calif. State U., Chico, 1988—. Mem. approximately 40 environ. orgns. Mem. Am. Acad. Religion, Internat. Assn. Buddhist Studies, Soc. of Asian & Comparative Philosophy. Home: 3051 Sunnyside Ln Paradise CA 95969 Office: Calif State U Dept Religious Studies Chico CA 95929-0740

MCCAHILL, PATRICK PHILIP, priest; b. Bronx, N.Y., Jan. 20, 1943; s. Patrick and Bridget (Reilly) McC. BA, St. Joseph's Sem. & Coll., Yonkers, N.Y., 1964, MDiv, 1968; MA, NYU, 1970; MS, St. John's U., 1974. Ordained priest Roman Cath. Ch., 1968. Assoc. pastor various chs. N.Y.C., 1968-80; assoc. moderator N.Y. Cath. Deaf Ctr., N.Y.C., 1969-83; dir. St. Elizabeth's Ch., N.Y.C., 1983—, adminstr., 19806. Home and Office: St Elizabeths Ch 211 E 83d St New York NY 10028

MCCAIN, MARTIN GEORGE, pastor; b. Phila., July 14, 1951; s. Alphonso J. and Josephine (Simmons) McC.; m. Terri Lynn Kendrick, Apr. 21, 1979; children: Martin, Mia. BA, Va. Union U., 1974; MDiv, Gammon Interdenominational Theol. Ctr., Atlanta, 1976. Ordained to ministry United Meth. Ch., 1974. Pastor Alexander United Meth. Ch., 1974-77, Jackson Street United Meth. Ch., Richmond, Va., 1978-79; assoc. pastor St. Mark United Meth. Ch., Chgo., 1979-81; pastor Barnes United Meth. Ch., Indpls., 1981—; mem. com. Va. Conf., United Meth. Ch., Richmond, 1977-78; bd. dirs. Black Meths. for Ch. Renewal, Atlanta, 1979-81; supr. field edn. Christian Theol. Sem., Indpls., 1986—; sec. Indpls. Chs. Ednl. Excellence, 1988—. State rep. Atlanta Young Reps., 1976; bd. dirs. Urban League, Richmond, 1978; mem. Efficiency Commn., Indpls. Pub. Schs., 1990-91; bd. dirs., v.p. Martin U., Indpls., 1989—. Crusade scholar United Meth. Ch., 1976. Fellow Acad. Parish Clergy; mem. Indpls. Ministerial Alliance (treas. 1984-86), Naval Res. Assn., Masons, Alpha Phi Alpha. Home: 3715 Watson Rd Indianapolis IN 46205 Office: Barnes United Meth Ch 900 W 30th St Indianapolis IN 46208

MCCALL, CHARLES ANTHONY, minister, special education educator; b. San Francisco, Sept. 20, 1965; s. Samuel Leon and Marva (Johnson) M. BS, U. Nev., Las Vegas, 1989. Lic. to ministry So. Bapt. Conv., 1985, ordained, 1991. Youth choir pres. Second Bapt. Ch., Las Vegas, 1985-87, youth min., 1985—, Sunday sch. tchr., 1985—, youth Sunday sch. supt., 1986—; spl. edn. tchr., Clark County Sch. Dist. Walter Braken Elem. Sch., Las Vegas, 1989—; first v.p. Nev. and Calif. Youth and Young Adults Bapt. Conv., Las Vegas, 1987. Fellow NAACP, Clark County Tchr. Assn. Democrat. Home: 1208 Leonard Ave Las Vegas NV 89106 Office: Second Bapt Ch 500 W Madison Ave Las Vegas NV 89106

MCCALL, DUKE KIMBROUGH, clergyman; b. Meridian, Miss., Sept. 1, 1914; s. John William and Lizette (Kimbrough) McC.; m. Marguerite Mullinnix, Sept. 1, 1936 (dec. 1983); children—Duke, Douglas H., John Richard, Michael W.; m. Winona Gatton McCandless, Feb. 2, 1984. B.A., Furman U., Greenville, S.C., 1936; M.Div., So. Bapt. Sem., Louisville, 1938; Ph.D., So. Bapt. Sem., 1943; LL.D. (hon.), Baylor U.; D.D. (hon.), Furman U., U. Richmond, Stetson U.; Litt.D., Georgetown Coll. Ordained to ministry, Bapt. Ch., 1937. Pastor Broadway Bapt. Ch., Louisville; pres. New Orleans Bapt. Theol. Sem., 1943-46; exec. sec. So. Bapt. Exec. Com., Nashville, 1946-51; pres. So. Bapt. Theol. Sem., Louisville, 1951-82; chancellor So. Bapt. Theol. Sem., 1982—; pres. Bapt. World Alliance, Washington, 1980-85; chmn. bd. dirs. Covenant Life Ins. Co., 1989-90. Author: God's Hurry, 1948, Passport to the World, 1951, Broadman Comments, 1957, 2d edit. 1958; editor: What is the Church. Recipient E. Y. Mullins Denominational Service award. Democrat. Avocations: golf; boating. Home: Southporte One PH-3 3322 Casseekey Island Rd Jupiter FL 33477 Office: So Bapt Theol Sem 2825 Lexington Rd Louisville KY 40280

MCCALL, EMMANUEL LEMUEL, minister; b. Sharon, Pa., Feb. 4, 1936; s. George and Myra Mae (Preston) McC.; m. Emma Marie Johnson, Aug. 23, 1958; children: Emmanuel L., Evalya Lynette. BA, U. Louisville, 1958; MDiv, So. Bapt. Sem., Louisville, 1962; MRE, So. Bapt. Sem., 1963; D in Ministry, Emory U., 1976. Ordained to ministry Bapt. Ch., 1959. Assoc. pastor Joshua Tabernacle Bapt. Ch., Louisville, 1954-60; pastor 28th St. Bapt. Ch., Louisville, 1960-68; assoc. dir. Home Mission Bd. So. Bapt. Conv., Atlanta, 1968-74, dept. dir., 1975-87, div. dir., 1988-91; pastor Christian Fellowship Bapt. Ch., Atlanta, 1991—; co-chmn. bd. trustees Interdenominational Theol. Ctr., Atlanta, 1990—. Author of 3 books; contbr. chpts. to 13 books. Recipient E.Y. Mullins Humanitarian award Am. Bapt. Coll., 1990, E.Y. Mullins Disting. Denominational Svc. award So. Bapt. Theol. Sem., 1990. Mem. Nat. Alumni Assn. So. Bapt. Theol. Sem. (pres.-elect 1990, pres. 1991—). Office: 3280 Hazelwood Dr SW Atlanta GA 30311

MCCALL, G. DANIEL, minister; b. Marion, N.C., May 14, 1932; s. George Samuel and Elizabeth Mae (Daniel) McC.; m. Linda Bradley Todd, Sept. 7, 1957; children: G. Daniel Jr., Bradley T., George S. II, Mary Linda. BS in Econs., Davidson Coll., 1954; D Min. M., Columbia Theol. Sem., Decatur, Ga., 1960, D Ministry, 1987; ThM, Princeton Theol. Sem., 1961; DD (hon.), Presbyn. Coll., Clinton, S.C., 1987. Ordained to ministry Presbyn. Ch. (U.S.A.). Pastor 1st Presbyn. Ch., Highlands, N.C., 1961-65, Brevard (N.C.)-Davidson River Presbyn. Ch., 1965-71, Starmount Presbyn. Ch., Greensboro, N.C., 1971-75, Reid Meml. Presbyn. Ch., Augusta, Ga., 1975—. 1st lt. inf. U.S. Army, 1954-56; capt. USAR. Princeton Theol. Sem. fellow, 1960-61. Mem. Columbia Theol. Sem. Alumni Assn. (pres. in 1980s), Univ. Hosp. Clergy Assn. (pres. in 1980s), Kiwanis (pres. 1987-88, past bd. dirs.), Rotary (pres. 1962-63). Republican. Home: 435 Scotts Way Augusta GA 30909 Office: Reid Meml Presbyn Ch 2261 Walton Way Augusta GA 30904

MCCALL, ROBERT DONNELL, missionary; b. San Saba, Tex., Feb. 11, 1927; s. Roy King and Nell Eugenia (Donnell) McC.; m. Virginia Lancaster Montgomery, Apr. 7, 1953 (dec.); children: Robert D. Jr., Roy King, Frances Nell McCall Rosenbluth; m. Jessie McElroy Junkin, Dec. 29, 1990. Student, Austin Coll., 1944-45, 46-47; BA in Humanities, Bob Jones U., 1949; BD, Columbia Theol. Sem., 1952, STD, 1975; ThM, Austin Presbyn. Sem., 1960. Ordained to ministry Presbyn. Ch. (USA), 1952. Missionary to Japan, 1952-63, pastor evangelist to Taiwan aboriginal tribes, 1963-86; assoc. gen. sec. Presbyn Ch. in Taiwan, 1986-89; missionary coworker Ami (tribal) Presbytery, Taitung, Republic of China, 1991—. Trustee Taiwan Theol. Coll., Taipei, 1980-91. With USN, 1945-46, PTO. Named Disting. Alumnus Columbia Theol. Sem., 1991. Democrat. Office: Presbyn Ch (USA) Global Mission Unit 100 Witherspoon St Louisville KY 40202-1396 *During 39 years of service as a missionary of the Presbyterian Church I have been impressed with the depth of God's grace and mercy, and his faithfulness in using all of us—his people—to share the gospel and minister to the world.*

MCCALLISTER, GARY DEAN, lay worker; b. Mountain Grove, Mo., Nov. 21, 1947; s. Willard and Kalah (Saladin) M.; m. Sherrie Glass, Sept. 26, 1970; children: Kalah Elaine, Gary Shane. Student, Clark County Community Coll., Las Vegas, N.V., 1991, UNLU, Las Vegas, N.V., 1991. Cert. christian edn., United Meth., youth ministry, Annual Conf. Ch., 1992., lay speaker. Deli mgr. Lucky's, Las Vegas, N.V., 1983—; chairperson Trinity United, 1991—; youth cons. Meth. Ch., 1991—. Home: 6005 Carpenteria Way Las Vegas NV 89108

MCCALLUM, MICHAEL DEAN, minister; b. Council Bluff, Iowa, Sept. 12, 1953; s. Everett Leslie and Mary Lavern (Fries) McC.; m. Shirley Joann Kennett, Jan. 17, 1976; children: Matthew, Christopher, Kevin. BS in

Acctg., Dana Coll., 1975; MDiv, U. Dubuque, 1981. Ordained to ministry Presbyn. Ch. (U.S.A.), 1983. With sem. U. Dubuque (Iowa), 1977-81; pastor United Presbyn. Ch., Hanover, Ill., 1981-89, First Presbyn. Ch., Millier, S.D., 1989—. Capt. USAR, 1972—. Mem. Hand County Ministerial Assn. (treas.-sec. 1989—), Kiwanis (treas. Miller chpt. 1989—). Republican. Home: 317 W First Ave Miller SD 57362-1306 Office: First Presbyn Ch 321 W 1st Ave Miller SD 57362-1306

MCCANDLESS, J(ANE) BARDARAH, religion educator; b. Dayton, Ohio, Apr. 16, 1925; d. J(ohn) Bard and Sarah Catharine (Shuey) McC. BA, Oberlin Coll., 1951; MRE, Bibl. Sem., N.Y.C., 1953; PhD, U. Pitts., 1968. Dir. Christian edn. Wallace Meml. United Presbyn. Ch., Pitts., 1953-54, Beverly Heights United Presbyn. Ch., Mt. Lebanon, Pa., 1956-61; instr. religion Westminster Coll., New Wilmington, Pa., 1961-65, asst. prof., 1965-71, assoc. prof., 1971-83, prof. religion, 1983—, chair dept. religion and philosophy, 1988—; leader Christian edn. workshops Presbytery of Shenango, Presbyn. Ch. (U.S.A.), 1961—, Synod of Trinity, 1972, 76. Author: An Untainted Saint...Ain't, 1978; contbr. articles to profl. jours., Harper's Ency. Religious Edn. Mem. session New Wilmington Presbyn. Ch., 1977-79. Mack grantee Westminster Coll., 1962-63, Faculty rsch. grantee, 1972, 78, 90. Mem. Religious Edn. Assn., Assn. Profs. and Researchers in Religious Edn. (mem. exec. com. 1978-80), Soc. for Sci. Study Religion, Phi Beta Kappa, Pi Lambda Theta. Office: Westminster Coll Dept Religion and Philosophy New Wilmington PA 16172 *I have found that following Jesus Christ as Savior and Lord makes life, in light or shadow, a great adventure.*

MCCANN, JERRY CLINTON, JR., religion educator; b. Richmond, Va., Aug. 10, 1951; s. Jerry Clinton and Nan Coker (Carter) McC.; m. Nancy Lee Rowland, Aug. 13, 1977; children: Jennifer Grace, Sarah Carter. BA, Davidson (N.C.) Coll., 1973; DMin, Union Seminary, Richmond, 1977, ThM, 1978; PhD, Duke U., 1985. Co-pastor Warrenton, Littleton and Stanley White Presbyn. Chs., Roanoke Rapids, N.C., 1978-87; grad. teaching asst. Duke U., Durham, N.C., 1978-81; asst. prof. Old Testament Eden Theol. Seminary, St. Louis, 1987—; vis. asst. prof. religion Davidson Coll., 1985-86; del. Gen. Assembly Presbyn. Ch. USA, Indpls., 1985; chmn. Presbyn. Latchkey Program, Roanoke Rapids, 1984-87. Contbr. articles to profl. jours. Active Gov.'s Com. on Hazardous Waste, Raleigh, N.C., 1983-84. A.G. Kearns fellow Duke U., 1979-81. Mem. Soc. Bibl. Lit. (chair psalms consultation 1988—), Cath. Bibl. Assn., Calvin Studies Soc. (adv. coun. Interpretation 1991—), Phi Beta Kappa. Democrat. Office: Eden Theol Seminary 475 E Lockwood Ave Saint Louis MO 63119

MCCANN, OWEN CARDINAL, archbishop emeritus; b. Woodstock, South Africa, June 26, 1907; s. Edward and Susan Mary (Plint) McC. PhD, Urbanianum; BCom, Cape Town, DLitt (hon.); DHL (hon.) Portland, Maine. Ordained priest Roman Cath. Ch., 1935, titular bishop of Stettorio and vicar apostolic of Cape Town (South Africa), 1950; 1st archbishop of Cape Town, 1951-84, ret., 1984; created cardinal, 1965; titular ch. St. Praxedes. Editor (weekly Cath. newspaper) So. Cross, 1986—. Office: Cathedral Pl, 12 Bouquet St, Cape Town 8001, Republic of South Africa

MCCANN, THOMAS RYLAND, JR., minister; b. Columbus, Miss., May 28, 1944; s. Thomas Ryland and Shirley Elizabeth (Jones) McC.; m. Beverly Jane Marshall, Nov. 26, 1966; children: Jane, Thomas Scott, Stephen. Student, U. Hawaii, 1962-64; BA in Polit. Sci., U. Richmond, 1966; MPA, U. N.C., Chapel Hill, 1971; MDiv, Southeastern Sem., 1985, DMin, 1990. Ordained to ministry So. Bapt. Conv., 1983. Pastor Wakefield Cen. Bapt. Ch., Zebulon, N.C., 1983-86; pastor 1st Bapt. Ch., Dunn, N.C., 1986-91, Martinsville, Va., 1991—; mem. gen. bd. Bapt. State Conv., Cary, N.C., 1990, mem. coun. on Christian life and pub. affairs, 1990, svcs.-rendered com., 1990; sec. Dunn Ministerial Assn., 1989—; v.p. Mcpl. Advisors, Inc., Virginia Beach., Va., 1975-82; county adminstr. James City County, Va., 1973-75; budget dir. Alexandria, Va., 1970-73; dep. dir. Model Cities, Winston-Salem, N.C., 1967-70. Mem. City Planning Bd., Dunn, 1989—; chmn. Dunn Drug Abuse Task Force, Dunn, 1989—; co-chmn. Evening in the Park Com., Dunn, 1987—. Mem. Pi Sigma Alpha. Office: 1st Bapt Ch 23 Starling Ave Martinsville VA 24112 *My goal today is not to get ready for tomorrow but to prepare for eternity. Tomorrow won't last, but eternity is forever.*

MCCANTS, CLYDE TAFT, minister; b. Anderson, S.C., Jan. 9, 1933; s. Edwin Clyde and Mary Rachel (Taft) McC. AB, Erskine Coll., 1954; MA, Duke U., 1956; M of Div., Erskine Theol. Sem., 1970; D of Ministry Columbia Theol. Sem., 1987. Ordained to ministry, 1970. English faculty Elon Coll., N.C., 1955-60, Erskine Coll., Due West, S.C., 1960-65; faculty English and dept. chmn. Gaston Coll., Gastonia, N.C., 1965-67; pastor Lauderdale Ch., Lexington, Va., 1970-73; dir. ch. extension Gen. Synod, Assoc. Ref. Presbyn. Ch., 1973-77; pastor First A.R. Presbyn. Ch., Burlington, N.C., 1977-78; asst. and assoc. prof. ministry Erskine Theol. Sem., 1978-82; pastor Greenville A.R.P. Ch., Greenville, S.C., 1982—; trustee Erskine Coll., 1973-78; moderator Gen. Synod of Assoc. Ref. Presbyn. Ch., 1978-79; chmn. Presbyn. Council on Chaplains and Mil. Personnel, Washington, 1983-84. Author: The God Who Makes History, 1976, David, King of Israel, 1978; contbr. articles to profl. jours. Democrat. Lodge: Kiwanis. Avocations: classical vocal recordings. Home: 151 Century Dr Apt 138 Greenville SC 29607 Office: 741 Cleveland St Greenville SC 29601

MCCARNEY, HOWARD JOHN, clergyman; b. Spiesville, Pa., Apr. 11, 1921; s. Guy Emory and Ethel (Hamlen) McC.; m. Ruth Naomi Sowers, Apr. 7, 1945; children—Kathryn McCarney Foster, Christine McCarney Gotwalt, Elizabeth. A.B., Gettysburg Coll., 1942, D.D., 1962; B.D., Luth. Theol. Sem., Gettysburg, 1945. Ordained to ministry Lutheran Ch. in Am., 1945. Field sec. Luth. Theol. Sem., 1945-46; chaplain Gettysburg Coll., 1946-50, now trustee; pastor Zion Luth. Ch., Middletown, Md., 1950-56, St. Matthew Luth. Ch., Hanover, Pa., 1957-66; bishop Central Pa. Synod Luth. Ch. Am. Office: Room 208 Central Pa Synod Luth Ch Am 900 S Arlington Ave Harrisburg PA 17109

MC CARRICK, THEODORE EDGAR, archbishop; b. N.Y.C., July 7, 1930; s. Theodore Egan and Margaret (McLaughlin) McC. Student, Fordham U., 1950-52; AB, St. Joseph's Sem., 1954, AM, 1958; MA, Cath. U., 1960, PhD, 1963; LLD, Mt. St. Vincent Coll., 1967; STD, Inter-Am. U., 1969; STD (hon.), Niagara U., 1982; LHD (hon.), St. John's U., 1974, St. Peter's Coll., 1987. Ordained priest Roman Cath. Ch., 1958. Asst. chaplain Cath. U. Am., Washington, 1959-61, dean students, 1961-63, asst. to rector, dir. univ. devel., 1963-65, instr. dept. sociology, 1961-65; domestic prelate, 1965; pres. Cath. U. P.R., 1965-69; assoc. dir. edn. Archdiocese of N.Y., 1969-71; sec. to Cardinal-Archbishop N.Y., 1971-77; titular bishop of Rusubisir, aux. bishop N.Y., 1977-81; 1st bishop Diocese of Metuchen, N.J., 1981-86; 4th archbishop Newark, 1986—; mem. policy bd. Washington Consortium, Peace Corps, 1962-63, Pontificial Commn. for Migrants and Refugees, 1987; chmn. U.S. Bishops Com. on Migration, 1986-89 ; pres. Nat. Coun. for Spanish-Speaking People, 1961-65; chmn. Gov.'s Commn. for Higher Edn. in P.R., 1968, P.R. Adv. Coun. on Tech. and Vocat. Edn., 1968-69. Mem. Fed. Commn. for Study of Migration and Econ. Devel., 1989—; Episcopal promoter, Apostleship of the Sea, 1989—. Named knight grand cross Holy Sepulchre. Clubs: K.C, Am. Assn. Knights Malta (chaplain 1978-82). Office: 31 Mulberry St Newark NJ 07102

MCCARTER, NEELY D., seminary president emeritus; s. Robert William and Nell (Dixon) McC.; m. Jean Maxwell, May 28, 1954; children: Robert Sidney, Robin Jeanette, Shirley Jean. AB, Presbyn. Coll., 1950, LittD, 1983; BD, Columbia Theol. Sem., 1953; postgrad., Columbia U., 1968; ThM, Union Theol. Sem., 1958; MA, Yale U., 1959, PhD, 1961. Ordained to ministry Presbyn. Ch. U.S., 1953. Pastor U. Fla., Gainesville, 1953-58; prof. Christian edn. Columbia Theol. Sem., Decatur, Ga., 1961-66; Robert and Lucy Reynolds Critz prof. Christian edn. Union Theol. Sem., Va., 1966-73, dean, 1973-79; pres. Pacific Sch. Religion, 1979-91; pres. emeritus Pacific Sch. Religion, Berkeley, Calif., 1991—, 1991—. Author: Hear the Word of the Lord, 1964; co-author: The Gospel on Campus, 1959, Help Me Understand, Lord, 1978; co-editor: Preaching In and Out of Season, 1990. Address: PO Box 153 Dillon Beach CA 94929

MCCARTHY, CATHERINE THERESA, lay worker; b. Lewiston, Maine, June 1, 1957; d. Joseph Francis and Eleanor Marie (Rock) McC. BA, No. Calif. Bible Coll., 1987. Home fellowship leader Evang. Christian Fellowship, San Jose, Calif., 1983-85; deaconess single adult ministries Christian Community Ch., San Jose, 1987—; mem. bd. edn. Christian Community Acad., 1991—; prodn. mgr. Orbit Semiconductor, Inc., Sunnyvale, Calif., 1990—.

MCCARTHY, DAVID BRUCE, minister; b. Owatonna, Minn., Mar. 8, 1955; s. Harold Charles and Barbara Susan (Kaercher) McC.; m. Joan Christina LaFollette, Oct. 12, 1986. BA cum laude, Carleton Coll., 1977; AM, Duke U., 1979; MDiv with distinction, Harvard U., 1985. Ordained to ministry Presbyn. Ch. (U.S.A.), 1986. Pastor John Hus Presbyn. Ch., Binghamton, N.Y., 1986—; mem. 1st Ward Clergy, Binghamton, 1986—, convener, 1987-89; dir. Metro Interfaith, 1988—; moderator Broad Ave.-North Presbyn. Ch., Binghamton, 1989—; moderator Permanent Jud. Commn., Presbytery of Susquehanna Valley, 1986—, mem. com. on preparation for ministry, 1986—, bills and overtures com., 1988-91, presbytery coun., 1990-91; mem. ecumenical and worship com. Broome County Coun. Chs., N.Y., 1989—; mem. planning, evaluation and rev. com. Synod of N.E., 1990-91, presbytery rep. synod mission coun., 1990-91, commr., 1990; mem. faculty Ghost Ranch, Abiquiu, N.Mex., 1991. Editor Report from Susquehanna Valley, 1989-90; contbr. author: The Organizational Revolution, 1991. Capt. United Way Appeal, Broome County, 1990-91. Mem. Am. Soc. Ch. History, Witherspoon Soc. (editorial asst. 1989—). Home: 22 Seymour St Binghamton NY 13905 Office: John Hus Presbyn Ch 47 Glenwood Ave Binghamton NY 13905

MCCARTHY, EDWARD ANTHONY, archbishop; b. Cin., Apr. 10, 1918; s. Edward E. and Catherine (Otte) McC. M.A., Mt. St. Mary Sem., Norwood, Ohio, 1944; Licentiate Canon Law, Cath. U. Am., 1946; D. Canon Law, Lateran U., Rome, 1947; S.T.D., Angelicum, Rome, 1948. Ordained priest Roman Catholic Ch., 1943; sec. to archbishop of Cin., 1944-65, ord. titular bishop of Tamascani and aux. bishop of Cin., 1965-69, bishop of Phoenix, 1969-76, coadjutor archbishop of Miami, 1976-77, archbishop of Miami, 1977—. Office: Pastoral Ctr 6301 Biscayne Blvd Miami Shores FL 33138

MC CARTHY, JOHN EDWARD, bishop; b. Houston, June 21, 1930; s. George Gaskell and Grace Veronica (O'Brien) McC. Student, St. Mary's Sem., Houston, 1949-56; M.A., St. Thomas U., Houston, 1979. Ordained priest Roman Catholic Ch., 1956; served various Houston Cath. parishes; exec. dir. Nat. Bishops Com. for Spanish speaking, 1966-68; asst. dir. Social Action Office, U.S. Cath. Conf., 1967-69; exec. dir. Tex. Cath. Conf., Houston, 1973-79; ordained titular bishop of Pedena and aux. bishop Diocese of Galveston-Houston, 1979-86; installed third bishop of Austin, 1986—; Bd. dirs. Nat. Center for Urban Ethnic Affairs, Mexican-Am. Cultural Center, Sisters of Charity of the Incarnate Word, Houston, from 1981, St. Thomas U., Houston, from 1980. Mem. Cath. Conf. for Urban Ministry. Democrat. Office: N Congress and 16th PO Box 13327 Austin TX 78711

MCCARTHY, JOHN PAUL, educator; b. Oil City, Pa., Oct. 21, 1948; s. William Henry and Evelyn Dorothy (Siembida) McC.; m. Mary Theresa Schlow, June 23, 1973; 1 child, Sean. BA, STM, St. Mary's U., Balt., 1974; PhD, U. Chgo., 1986. Asst. prof. Loyola U., Chgo., 1985—. Contbr. articles to profl. jours. Woodrow Wilson Found. fellow, 1984. Mem. Am. Acad. Religion, Coll. Theology Soc. (bd. dirs., chair rsch. com. 1987—). Home: 1122 W Morse Ave Unit E Chicago IL 60626 Office: Loyola U 6525 N Sheridan Ave Chicago IL 60626

MCCARTHY, SCOTT (CORNELIUS MCCARTHY), priest; b. London, Aug. 23, 1947; came to U.S., 1963; s. John and Margaret (McMahon) McC.; 1 adopted child, Brian. BA, St. Patrick's Coll., Mountain View, Calif., 1970; MDiv, St. Patrick's Sem., Menlo Park, Calif., 1973, cert. in specialized pastoral edn., 1974, MA in Liturgy, 1978; D of Ministry, Jesuit Sch. Theology, 1979; cert. in Hispanic ministry, Loyola Marymount U., 1981. Ordained priest Roman Cath. Ch., 1974. Assoc. pastor St. Joseph's Ch., Capitola, Calif., 1974-78, Holy Cross Ch., Santa Cruz, Calif., 1978-81, Old Mission San Luis Obispo (Calif.) Ch., 1981-83; pastor Our Lady of Refuge Ch., Castroville, Calif., 1983—; mem. presbyteral coun. Diocese of Monterey, 1981—, dean San Luis Obispo Deanery, 1981-82, dean Monterey Deanery, 1987—; dir. clergy ongoing edn. Divine Worship Commn., 1988—; sabbatical at Crow Indian Reservation, Mont., 1991. Author: Handbook for Ecumenical Services, 1978, Creation Liturgy, 1987, Celebrating the Earth, 1991. Home and Office: Our Lady of Refuge Ch PO Box 1147 Castroville CA 95012

MCCARTHY, (ROBERT) TIMOTHY, religious organization executive, lawyer; b. Milw., June 16, 1929; s. Frank Joseph and Amy Martha (Knospe) M.; m. Geraldine Edith Wilson, Dec. 27, 1951 (wid. June 1990); children: Denise M., Patricia J., Kathleen A., Timothy F. BS, Marquette U., 1951; JD, U. Iowa, 1954. Bar: Iowa, 1954. Solicitor gen. State of Iowa, Des Moines, 1965-66; exec. dir. Iowa Cath. Conf., Des Moines. Office: Iowa Cath Conf 818 Ins Exch Bldg Des Moines IA 50309

MCCARTHY, WILLIAM JOHN, priest; b. Hartford, Conn., May 19, 1934; s. William J. and Alice Elise (Cote) McC. AA, St. Thomas Sem., 1954; BA, St. Mary's Sem., 1956; STB, North Am. Coll., 1958; ThM, Holy Apostles Coll., 1982. Ordained priest Roman Cath. Ch., 1959. Co-pastor St. Anthony Ch., Bristol, Conn., 1978-80; founder, co-dir. My Father's House Retreat Ctr., Moodus, Conn., 1982—; bd. dirs. YMCA, Torrington, Conn., dir. svcs. to elderly, 1965-68. Author: Listening to Father, Loving with the Son, Living in the Spirit, The Spirit in St. Paul, 1989. Inst. rep. Boy Scouts Am., Club Scouts Am., Girl Scouts U.S.; mem. Right to Life. Maj. USAF Aux., 1985—. Mem. Missionaries of Holy Apostles, Assn. Christian Therapists, U.S. Mil. Chaplains. Address: My Father's House PO Box 22 Moodus CT 06469-0022

MCCARTHY, WILLIAM ROBERT, minister; b. Tacoma, Wash., Nov. 17, 1941; s. Denward Sylvester and Florence Elizabeth (Lohan) McC.; m. Bernice Bigler, Apr. 22, 1962; children: Brian Edward Earl, Sean David. BS, Oreg. State U., 1966; MDiv, Nashotah House, 1975. Ordained deacon Episcopal Ch., 1975, priest, 1975. Curate St. Michael's Ch., Barrington, Ill., 1975-77; vicar St. Anselm's Ch., Park Ridge, Ill., 1977-81; rector Christ Ch. Parish, Waukegan, Ill., 1981-89, Ch. of Good Samaritan, Corvallis, Oreg., 1989—; diocesan cursillo officer Diocese Chgo., 1977-85; spiritual dir. Ecumenical Cursillo Community, Chgo., 1977-83; mem. steering com. Happenings in Christianity, Chgo., 1978-80; chmn. Bishop's Adv. Commn. on Renewal and Evangelism, Chgo., 1983-85; mem. diocesan coun. Diocese of Oreg., 1991—; bd. dirs. Oreg. Episcopal clergy Assn., 1990—, sec., 19991—. Contbr. articles to profl. jours. Bd. mem. Waukegan Area Crime Stoppers, 1982-85; founder, chmn. FOCUS 90 Com. for Downtown Devel., 1988-89; charter bd. dirs. Waukegan Downtown Assn., 1983-89, v.p., 1986-87, pres., 1987-88; founder, exec. dir. Share/Food Waukegan Area, 1985—; bd. dirs. YMCA of Lake County, 1985—; trustee Good Samaritan Hosp., Corvallis, 1989—. With USNR, 1962-65. Mem. Assn. for Psychol. Type, Internat. Platform Assn., Exchange Club, Rotary, Masons, Phi Sigma Kappa. Office: Ch of the Good Samaritan 333 NW 35th St Corvallis OR 97330

MCCARTY, CHARLES BARRY, academic administrator; b. Atlanta, May 7, 1953; s. LeRoy Thomas and Lorraine (Presley) McC.; m. Patricia Boyd Powell, Aug. 23, 1975; children: Ryan, Noah, Ian. BS, Roanoke Bible Coll., 1975; MA, Abilene Christain U., 1977; PhD, U. Pitts., 1980. Prof. Roanoke Bible Coll., Elizabeth City, N.C., 1980-88; pres. Cin. Bible Coll. & Sem., 1989—; parliamentarian Southern Bapt. Conv., 1986-91. Author: A Parliamentary Guide for Church Leaders, 1987, Well Said and Worth Saying: A Public Speaking Guide for Church Leaders, 1991. Chmn. N.C. Social Svcs. Commn., Raleigh, N.C., 1985-88, N.C. State Rep. Conv., 1984; delegate Rep. Nat. Conv., Dallas, 1984, New Orleans, 1988. Office: Cin Bible Coll & Sem 2700 Glenway Ave Cincinnati OH 45204

MCCARTY, DORAN CHESTER, religion educator; b. Bolivar, Mo., Feb. 3, 1931; s. Bartie Lee and Donta Marian (Russell) McC.; m. Gloria Jean Laffoon, June 14, 1952; children: Gaye, Risë, Marletta, Leslie. AA, Southwest Bapt. Coll., 1950; AB, William Jewell Coll., 1952; BD, So. Bapt. Theol. Sem, 1956, PhD, 1963. Pastor 1st Bapt. Ch., Switz City, Ind., 1956-62, Pleasant Hill, Mo., 1962-65; pastor Susquehanna Bapt. Ch., Independence, Mo., 1965-67; prof. Midwestern Bapt. Theol. Sem., Kansas City, Mo., 1967-81, Golden Gate Bapt. Theol. Sem., Mill Valley, Calif., 1981-87; coordinator Northeastern Bapt Sch Ministry, N.Y.C., 1987—; exec. dir. Sem. External Edn. Div., Nashville, 1988—; cons. Bapt. Home Mission Bd., 1981—; assoc. dean So. Bapt. Theol. Sem., Louisville, 1989. Author: Rightly Dividing the Word, 1973, Teilhard de Chardin, 1976, The Supervision of Ministry Students, 1978, The Supervision of Mission Personnel, 1983, The Inner Heart of Ministry, 1985, Working With People, 1987, Leading the Small Church, 1991; editor: Key Resources, 5 vols., Broadman Leadership Series, 16 vols. Recipient Life Service award Southwest Bapt. U., Bolivar, 1973, William Jewell Coll. Achievement citation, 1987. Mem. Assn. for Theol. Field Edn. (chairperson 1979-81), Inst. Theol. Reflection (exec. dir. 1978-86), Fellowship In Service Guidance Dirs. (pres. 1986-87, Lewis Newman award 1988). Home: 1600 Roundhill Dr Nashville TN 37211 Office: Northeastern Bapt Sch Ministry 236 W 72d St New York NY 10023 *As I have experienced life, grace affords priviledge, priviledge calls forth duty, duty depends on transcendence and transcendence provides enrichment.*

MCCARTY, HARVEY DWIGHT, minister; b. Oklahoma City, Nov. 4, 1932; s. Johnny Wendell and Vera Aloma (Whitley) McC.; m. Shirley Ann DeBerry, Oct. 5, 1957; children: Karen Diana, Kevin Dwight. BA, So. Meth. U., 1955; MDiv, Southwestern Bapt. Theol. Sem., 1964, postgrad., 1964-65; postgrad., Mid-Am. Bapt. Sem., 1974; DMin, Calif. Grad. Sch. Theology, 1983; DD, Hindustan Bible Coll., Madras, India, 1981. Ordained to ministry So. Bapt. Conv., 1963. Min. youth Trinity Bapt. Ch., Lake Charles, La., 1958-60; assoc. pastor Univ. Bapt. Ch., Ft. Worth, 1960-65; sr. pastor Univ. Bapt. Ch., Fayetteville, Ark., 1965—; mem. exec. bd. Ark. Bapt. Conv., Little Rock, 1971—; pres. Ventures for Christ, Inc.; tour host to Holy Land, 1971, 72, 73, 77; guest instr. N.T., John Brown U., 1968-69; guest instr. evangelism Southwestern Bapt. Sem., 1972; speaker weekly TV program statewide. Author weekly newspaper column Live It Up, 1974—. Chmn. bd. Ark. Inst. Theology; bd. dirs., state chaplain Fellowship Christian Athletes; mem. bd. reference Mid-Am. Bapt. Theol. Sem.; chaplain U. Ark. Razorbacks, Ark. Air N.G.; asst. to chief of chaplains, Brig. Gen., Ret.; bd. govs. Washington Regional Med. Ctr., Fayetteville, 1973-76. Served with USAF, 1955-63, Res. and Air Guard, 1964-88. Mem. Fayetteville C. of C. (bd. dirs. 1970-73), Kiwanis (past pres. Fayetteville club). Home: 1932 Wheeler St Fayetteville AR 72701 Office: 315 W Maple St Fayetteville AR 72701

MCCARTY, STEPHEN ROBERT, minister; b. Tulsa, Okla., Sept. 18, 1948; s. Clyde Nelson and Emma Nadine (Morgan) McC.; m. Marilyn Marie Sawyer, Dec. 27, 1969; children: Amy, Aaron. BS, Lewis and Clark Coll., 1970; MCM, Western Cons. Bapt. Seminary, Portland, Oreg., 1985, MA, 1985. Lay worship leader, choir dir. Bethany Bapt. Ch., Billings, Mont., 1975-81, Calvary Bapt. Ch., The Dalles, Oreg., 1981-85; minister of worship, bus. mgr. Village Bapt. Ch., Beaverton, Oreg., 1985—; steering com. Portland Worship Network, 1987—; chmn. Bapt. Worship Festival, Portland, 1988, 90. Recipient Acad. Merit award Western Cons. Bapt. Seminary, 1985. Mem. Christian Mgmt. Assn. Republican. Home: 18770 NW Ukiah Portland OR 97229 Office: Village Baptist Church 330 SW Murray Blvd Beaverton OR 97005

MCCASKILL, RICHARD SHERWIN, minister; b. Michigan City, Ind., Apr. 11, 1961; s. James Howard and Sherry Lee (Sellers) McC.; m. Lorie Marie Crocker, July 30, 1982; children: Brett, Blake. BA, Freed-Hardeman U., 1983; postgrad. for MDiv, Harding Grad. Sch. of Religion. Ordained to ministry Ch. of Ch., 1981. Youth min. Bemis Ch. of Christ, Jackson, Tenn., 1982-84; assoc. min. Campbell St. Ch. of Christ, Jackson, 1984-85; min. Maury City (Tenn.) Ch. of Christ, 1985-87; assoc. min. Main St. Ch. of Christ, Milan, Tenn., 1987—; instr. Freed-Hardeman Future Ch. Leaders, Henderson, Tenn., 1981—, mem. preachers club, 1981-83, mem. Evang. Forum, 1981-83; mem. chaplain assn. City of Milan Hosp., 1987—; counselor Prepare/Enrich, Mpls., 1988—. Mem. Roritan Club (sec. 1987), Freed-Hardeman Nat. Alumni Assn. (pres.-elect 1992, v.p. 1991). Home: 4045 N Main St Milan TN 38358 Office: Main St Ch of Christ 2026 S Main St Milan TN 38358

MCCAULEY, KEVIN BRUCE, minister; b. San Jose, Calif., May 19, 1954; s. Bruce and Marie (Gallaway) McC.; m. Georga Ann Fonner, June 25, 1977; children: Jennifer, Ryan, Kyle, Sean. AA, West Valley Community Coll., 1974; BA, San Diego State U., 1976; MA, U. San Francisco, 1980. Ordained to ministry Ind. Bible Ch., 1986. Tchr., vice prin. Los Gatos (Calif.) Christian Sch., 1977-84; pastor Christian edn. Crossroads Bible Ch., San Jose, 1982—; chmn. Christian Leaders and Sunday Sch., San Jose, 1989—. Author: (curriculum) Christian Influences on American History, 1980; chair editorial com. West mag., 1990. Active Coalition of Christians in Govt., San Jose; mem. Citizens for Excellence in Edn., Costa Mesa, Calif., 1991. Mem. Nat. Assn. Evangs., Greater San Jose Assn. Evangs. (exec. com. 1990—), Child Evangelism Fellowship (adv. com. 1989—), Profl. Assn. Christian Educators, Nat. Assn. Christian Educators, Awana (dir. San Jose chpt.). Democrat. Home: 4062 San Ramon Way San Jose CA 95111 Office: Crossroads Bible Ch 600 Meridian Ave Ste 202 San Jose CA 95126 *Many opportunities to do good present themselves to us in the course of our daily lives. To choose to involve our lives with those that are of eternal value and consequence is the greater good. To impact this world beyond the scope of one lifetime is an awesome and humbling thing.*

MCCAULEY, RAYNOR, pastor; b. Johannesburg, Republic of South Africa, Oct. 1, 1949; s. James and Doreen Priscilla (Miller) McC.; m. Lyndie Trehair, Mar. 13, 1976; 1 child, Joshua. Student, Rhema Bible Tng. Centre, Tulsa, 1978. Profl. body-builder, owner health studios Republic of South Africa, 1958-76; pastor, evangelist Rhema Ministries of South Africa, Randburg, 1979—. Author: Our God Reigns, 1985. Avocation: football. Office: Rhema Ministries of South Africa, Hans Schoeman Dr, 2125 Randburg Republic of South Africa

MCCAW, LYLE STEVEN, minister; b. Toledo, Oreg., Apr. 4, 1960; s. Darrell Chester and Blanche Ione (Faxon) McC.; m. Lori Janet Malott, Dec. 7, 1985; 1 child, Rebekah Jane. BA, Puget Sound Christian Sem., 1983. Ordained to ministry Christian Ch., 1984. Youth minister Liberty Christian Ch., Salem, Oreg., 1983-84, Rogue Valley Christian Ch., Medford, Oreg., 1985-88; preaching minister White City (Oreg.) Christian Ch., 1988—; sec. Jackvon County Bd. Christian Edn., Medford, Oreg., 1986-87, v.p., 1987-88, pres., 1988-90; sec. So. Oreg. Christian Camp, Klamath Falls, Oreg., 1986—; pres. Huckleberry Hunter Camp, 1990—. Mem. Neighborhood Watch, White City, 1990. Recipient Aardvark award LaGreeno Exec. Coun., 1982. Office: White City Christian Ch 3100 Antelope Rd White City OR 97503

MCCLAFFERTY, JOHN JOSEPH, clergyman; b. N.Y.C., Apr. 9, 1906; s. John and Margaret (Moran) McC. AB, Cathedral Coll., 1927; grad., St. Joseph's Sem., 1930; AM, Cath. U. Am., 1932; diploma, N.Y. Sch. Social Work, 1936; LLD, Loyola U., L.A., 1947. Cert. social worker, N.Y. State. Ordained priest Roman Catholic Ch., 1930, apptd. papal chamberlain, 1943; apptd. Domestic Prelate, 1953, Protonotary Apostolic, 1965; asst. dir. div. social action Catholic Charities, N.Y.C., 1936-41; dir. div. social research Catholic Charities, 1941-47; Dean Nat. Cath. Sch. of Social Service, Catholic U. Am., 1947-55, asst. to rector for univ. devel., 1955-63; pastor St. Peter's Ch., S.I., 1963-66, St. Francis de Sales Ch., N.Y.C., 1966-81; pastor emeritus St. Francis de Sales Ch., 1981—; chaplain Carmel Richmond Nursing Home, S.I., N.Y., 1982—; Exec. sec. Nat. Legion Decency, 1936-47; mem. bd. consultors Ch. of the Air CBS, 1940-47; bd. advisors Radio Chapel MBS, 1941-47; bd. dirs. Casita Maria Settlement, 1941-47; com. discrimination N.Y. State War Council, 1942-44; Am. del. to Pan-Am. Congress, Caracas, Venezuela, 1948; del. 3d Congress of Inter-Am. Cath. Social Action Confederation, Rio de Janeiro, Brazil, 1948; Mem. Point Four Mission to Colombia, S.A., 1951. Editor: Cath. U. of Am. Bull, 1956-63. Mem. nat. exec. fact-finding coms. Mid-Century White House Conf. on Children and Youth, 1950; Del. White House Conf. Children and Youth, 1960. Served as capt. (chaplain) 5th regiment of N.Y. Guard, 1941-43; col. (chaplain) Hdqrs. N.Y. Guard, 1943-49. Recipient Univ. Pres.'s medal Cath. U. Am., 1988. Fellow Royal Soc. Health; mem. Nat. Assn. Social Workers, Acad. Cert. Social Workers. Home: 88 Old Town Rd Staten Island NY 10304

MCCLAIN, GREGORY DAVID, minister; b. Anderson, S.C., June 6, 1957; s. Lemuel David and Mary Josephine (Hawkins) McC.; m. Anne Leigh Blackwell, May 21, 1983; 1 child, Jonathan David. AS, Anderson Coll., 1977; BA, Erskine Coll., 1979; MDiv, Southeastern Bapt. Theol., Seminary, Wake Forrest, N.C., 1982. Ordained Boulevard Bapt. Ch., 1983. Youth pastor First Bapt. Ch., Woodruff, S.C., 1980, Walterboro, S.C., 1981; chaplain extern Bapt. Med. Ctr., Columbia, S.C., 1982; assoc. pastor First Bapt. Ch., South Boston, Va., 1983-86; minister Corrottoman Bapt. Ch., Lancaster, Va., 1986—; pres. Dan River Bapt. Pastors, Halifax, Va., 1984-85; preacher-jr. high weekend, Va. Bapt. Gen. Assn., 1986, faculty youth week, 1984-88; v.p. Lancaster Ministerial Assn., 1987-88. Active CROP walk, South Boston, Va., 1984-85; coach YMCA youth soccer, South Boston, 1985; merit badge counselor Boy Scouts Am., Lancaster, 1990—; mem. Lancaster Ednl. Task Force, 1988. Mem. Ruritan Club (chaplain 1990—). Office: Corrottoman Baptist Church Rte 2 PO Box 1355 Lancaster VA 22503 *The Kingdom of God exists wherever God is king.*

MCCLAIN, RICHARD ALLEN, minister; b. Tipton, Ind., Apr. 17, 1960; s. Kennith D. and Wilma (Ensey) McC.; m. Wava Brown, June 7, 1982. BA, Gulf-Coast Bible Coll., Houston, 1983; MDiv, Anderson Univ. Sch. Theology, 1986. Ordained to ministry Ch. of God, 1986. Minister of youth First Nazarene Ch., Houston, 1981-83; minister Pikes Peak Christian Ch., Daleville, Ind., 1984-86; assoc. minister First Ch. of God, Charleston, W.Va., 1986—; chmn. W.Va. State Bd. Christian Edn. of Ch. of God, Charleston, 1989-91, vice-chmn. 1988-89; mem. Coordinating Coun. of Ch. of God in W.Va., 1987-91. Author sr. high sch. curriculum, 1990-91. Mem. Glenwood Elem. Sch. Improvement Com., Charleston, 1991. Office: First Church of God 915 Main St Charleston WV 25302

MCCLAIN, TOMEY VAN, minister; b. Dallas, June 10, 1952; s. George Tomey McClain and Charlcie Van (Allen) Perry; m. Nancy Ruth Parsons, Aug. 13, 1977; children: Amber Rachel, Vanessa Ruth. BA, Dallas Bapt. U., 1974; MDiv, Southwestern Bapt. Theol. Sem., 1977, PhD, 1985. Minister music, youth Cen. Bapt. Ch., Weatherford, Tex., 1979-81; asst. pastor LaPrada Bapt. Ch., Garland, Tex., 1981-83; interim pastor Chapel of the Lake, Wills Point, Tex., 1983-85; pastor First Bapt. Ch., Quinlan, Tex., 1985-89, Calvary Bapt. Ch., Kemp, Tex., 1989; interim pastor Floyd (N.Y.) Bapt. Ch., 1989-90; pastor Long Falls Bapt. Ch., Carthage, N.Y., 1991—; asst. prof. O.T. and Hebrew Mid-Am. Bapt. Theol. Sem., N.E. br., Schenectady, 1989—. Author: Tawakoni News, 1987. Mem. Hunt Bapt. Assn. So. Bapts. for Life (founder 1987), Tawakoni Ministerial Assn. (pres. 1987-89), Hunt Bapt. Assn. (chmn. Christian Life 1987-89), Kiwanis (dir. 1987). Home: 9 Fawn Dr Scotia NY 12302 Office: Mid-American Bapt Theol Sem 2810 Curry Rd Schenectady NY 12303 *The greatest decision I ever made was to receive Jesus Christ as my personal Lord and Savior. Another great decision was to believe in the absolute infallibility and inerrancy of the Holy Scriptures, the Bible.*

MCCLAIN, WILLIAM B., religion educator; b. Gadsden, Ala., May 19, 1938; s. Frank Bural and Malinda Virginia (Williams) McC.; m. Jo Ann Mattos; children: William Bobby Jr., David Wilson. AB summa cum laude, Clark Atlanta U., DD, 1991. Pastor Union United Meth. Ch., Boston, 1968-78; exec. dir. Multi-Ethnic Ctr. for Ministry NE Jurisdiction United Meth. Ch., Drew U., Madison, N.J.; prof. homiletics and worship Wesley Theol. Sem., Washington, 1980—; speaker in field; lectr. theology Boston Coll., 1973-78. Author: Travelling Light: Christian Perspectives on Pilgrimage and Pluralism, 1981, Black People in the Methodist Church: Whither Thou Goest?, 1984, Strangers at Home, 1980, The Soul of Black Worship, 1980, Songs of Zion, 1981, Come Sunday: The Liturgy of Zion, 1990, Heritage and Hope: African American Presence in Methodism, 1991; contbr. articles to publs. Mem. NAACP. Rockefeller fellow, 1960-62, Walker fellow, 1960; Crusade scholar, 1961-63; Lilly grantee, 1987—. Fellow Soc. for Study Black Religion, Acad. of Homiletics; mem. Black Methodists for Ch. Renewal (one of founders), Am. Acad. Religion, N.Am. Acad. Liturgy, Alpha Phi Alpha. Democrat. Home: 500 Round Table Dr Fort Washington MD 20744 Office: Wesley Theol Sem 4500 Massachusetts Ave NW Washington DC 20016

MCCLARAN, RAY E., bishop. Presiding bishop Reorganized Ch. of Jesus Christ of Latter Day Saints, Independence, Mo. Office: Reorganized Ch of Jesus Christ of Later Day Sts PO Box 1059 Independence MO 64051*

MCCLARY, DAVID LYNN, minister; b. Indpls., July 21, 1950; s. Frank William and Mary Lou (May) McC.; m. Thelma Louise Cleveland, Jan. 2, 1971; children: Benjamin David, Abigail Louise, Aaron Frank, Andrew William. ThB, Ozark Christian Coll., 1973. Ordained to ministry Christian Ch., 1973. Assoc. min. East Tulsa Christian Ch., Tulsa, 1970-81; min. Alta Loma Christian Ch., Rancho Cucamonga, Calif., 1981—. Mem. Inland Empire Mins. Fellowship (pres. San Bernardino, Calif. 1983-84), Rancho Cucamonga Ministerial Alliance (pres. 1984-85). Office: Alta Loma Christian Ch 6386 Sapphire St Rancho Cucamonga CA 91701-3115

MCCLEAN, L. ROBERT, religious organization administrator. Chairperson Nat. Interreligious Svc. Bd. for Coinscientious Objectors, N.Y.C. Office: Nat Interreligious Svc Bd Conscientious Objectors 750 Connecticut Ave NW Washington DC 20009*

MCCLELLAN, CRAIG THOMAS, minister; b. Cin., Oct. 3, 1948; s. Marvin R. and Jeannette (Kimball) McC.; m. Patti Elaine Seeley, June 21, 1985; children: Heather, Scott. BSEd, Miami U., Oxford, Ohio, 1970; MDiv, Harvard U., 1976. Ordained to ministry United Ch. of Christ, 1976. Assoc. pastor King's Chapel, Boston, 1976-77; pastor Channing Ch., Rockland, Mass., 1977-78, 1st Ch., Barre, Vt., 1978-82, Congl. Ch., East Weymouth, Mass., 1982-84, St. John-St. Matthew United Ch. of Christ, Cin., 1985—; mem. cons. United Ch. of Christ, Mass. and Ohio, 1983—; refugee resettlement worker Ch. World Svc., Vt. and Ohio, 1981, 86, 89; instr. Cen. Vt. Community Coll., Barre, 1981-82; chmn. Cin. Assembly, United Ch. of Christ Mission Priority Bd., 1991. Mgmt. analyst City of Cin., 1970-72; founding bd. dirs. Cen. Vt. Hospice, Barre, 1981-82; chmn. bd. dirs. Project Ind. Elderly and Handicapped, Barre, 1979-80; chair CROP Walk, Barre, 1980, 81, Cin., 1988, 89. Named Outstanding Young Man Vt., Jaycees, 1981; John Haynes Holmes fellow, 1975-76. Mem. Am. Acad. Religion, Acad. Preachers, Acacia Fraternity, Omicron Delta Kappa. Office: St John-St Matthew UCC 691 Fleming Rd Cincinnati OH 45231 *Deep at the core of the universe, hidden but ever-present, waiting to be discovered, is the Eternal Light of Jesus Christ. The Human and Holy One enkindles the divine spark in our souls and behold we are aflame with the way, the truth, and the life!.*

MCCLELLAN, KARI LEE, minister; b. Wheeling, W.Va., Apr. 17, 1951; d. William John and Flora Bella (McQuiston) Turner; m. Ralph L. McClellan Jr., Apr. 1988; 1 child, Mardi Lyn. BA in Religion and Philosophy, Westminster Coll., 1973; MDiv, Princeton Theol. Sem., 1976. Ordained to ministry Presbyn. Ch. (U.S.A.), 1976. Asst. to pastor Lenape Valley Ch., New Britain, Pa., 1973-74, St. Mark's Luth. Ch., Trenton, N.J., 1974-76; chaplain Yardville (N.J.) Prison, 1974-76; asst. pastor, then assoc. pastor 1st Presbyn. Ch., Levittown, Pa., 1976-79, sr. pastor, 1979—. Pres. Local Ministerium, Levittown/Fairless Hills, 1980-81; trustee Princeton Theol. Sem., 1983—. Named Citizen of Yr. Levittown/Fairless Hills, 1982. Mem. Princeton Regional Alumni Assn. (v.p. Pa. and Del. chpts. 1979—). Home: 28 Fruitree Rd Levittown PA 19056 Office: 1st Presbyn Ch 5918 Emilie Rd Levittown PA 19057

MCCLELLAN, LARRY ALLEN, minister; b. Buffalo, Nov. 3, 1944; s. Edward Lurelle McClellan and Helen (Denison) Erland; m. Diane Eunice Bonfoey, Aug. 19, 1973; children: Kara E., Seth C. Student, U. Ghana, 1964-65; BA in Psychology, Occidental Coll., 1966; MTh, U. Chgo., 1969, D Ministry, 1970. Ordained to ministry Presbyn. Ch. (U.S.A.), 1970. Prof. of sociology and community studies Govs. State U., University Park, Ill., 1970-86; interim pastor Presbyn. Ch. (U.S.A.), Chgo. area, 1980-86; sr. pastor St. Paul Community Ch., Homewood, Ill., 1986—; adj. prof. Govs. State U., University Park, Ill., 1987—; trustee Internat. Coun. Community Chs., 1989-91, pres. 1991—. Author: Local History South of Chicago, 1988; developer social simulation games; contbr. articles to profl. publs. Mayor Village of Park Forest South (name now University Park), Ill., 1975-79; co-organizer S. Region Habitat for Humanity, Chgo. area, 1989; pres. S. Suburban Heritage Assn., Chgo. area, 1988-91. Fellow Layne Found., 1966-70, NEH, 1979. Mem. Am. Acad. Religion, Assn. for Sociology of Religion, Am. Assn. State and Local History, Ill. State Hist. Soc. (Spl. Achievement award 1989), Chgo. Hist. Soc., S. Suburban Ministerial Assn. (pres. 1989-91). Office: St Paul Community Ch 18200 Dixie Hwy Homewood IL 60430

MCCLELLAN, THOMAS LEE, priest; b. Wilmington, Del., Feb. 9, 1942; s. William and Mary McC. B.A., Muhlenberg Coll., 1965; M.Div., Episcopal Div. Sch., 1970; postgrad. Cambridge U., 1972-74, St. George Coll., Jerusalem, 1976. Ordained deacon and priest Episcopal Ch., 1971. Master, tchr. Chestnut Hill Acad., Phila., 1970-72; pastoral asst. Ch. of Advent, Kennett Square, Pa., 1971-72; assoc. rector St. David's Ch., Wayne, Pa., 1974-76; assoc. chaplain St. Andrew's Sch., Middletown, Del., 1976-78; rector St. Mary's at the Cathedral, Phila., 1978—; cathedral canon Cathedral Ch. of Christ, Phila., 1978—; chmn. Diocesan Youth Com., Diocese Pa., 1981—; elected dean, 1987—; mem. Episcopal-Jewish Dialogue, Diocese Pa., 1981—; mem. Diocesan Council, Phila., 1985; cons. Ptnrs. in Mission, Bujumbura, Burundi, East Africa, 1978; bishop's rep. Interfaith Witness for Peace, Quaker Hdqrs., Phila., 1984—; chaplain to srs. Cathedral Village, Bishop White Lodge, Phila., 1979; Episcopal rep. March 27 March to Independence Hall, Phila., 1982, Com. to Remember Hiroshima after 40 Years, Phila., 1985; bd. mem. Diocesan News, The Episcopalian, 1981—; liturgical officer Wissahickon Deanery, 1981—. Bd. dirs. Higher Edn., 1985—; appointed mem. Standing Mission Strategy Commn., 1988—. Served with U.S. Army, 1965-67. Grantee Episcopal Ch. for Overseas Mission. Mem. 21st Ward Ministerium (pres. 1984—). Club: The Racquet (Phila). Avocations: architecture: tennis. Home: Harts Ln Miquon PA 19452 Office: St Mary's at the Cathedral 630 E Cathedral Rd Philadelphia PA 19128

MCCLELLAND, PATRICIA G., minister; b. Warsaw, Mo., July 12, 1944; d. Gail Raymond and Martha Carolyn (Lewis) Easton; m. Lester E. McClelland, Aug. 18, 1974; 1 child, Melody. BS, U. Mo., 1968; MA, Drury Coll., 1972. Cert. tchr., Mo., Kans.; lic. counselor; ordained to ministry Unity Ch., 1986. Instr. U. Mo., Kansas City, 1968, 71-74, Park Coll., Parkville, Mo., 1968-70; spl. cons. Kansas City Pub. Schs., 1970-71; author edn. materials, 1975-78; inst. U. Wis., 1978-79; min. Milw., 1979-81; instr. Sem. Unity Sch. Christianity, 1983-85; co-min. Unity Ch. Pitts., 1985-86; sr. min. Unity Ch., Anderson, Ind., 1986-87; sr. minister Unity Ch., Warren, Ohio, 1987-88, Massillon, Ohio, 1988-90; dir. housing Southwestern Coll., Winfield, Kans., 1989-91; founding min. Council Bluffs Unity Ch., Iowa. Methodist. Mem. NAFE, Nat. Assn. of Self-Employed, Internat. New Though Alliance, Internat. Platform Assn. Home: 7932 E Avon Ln Lincoln NE 68505 Office: Southwestern Coll 100 College St Winfield KS 67156 *Our inheritance as Children of God is a world where everything necessary is available for every human being to live a happy, healthy, peaceful, abundant life. The choice to do so, as well as the work to fulfill that choice, is up to us both individually and collectively.*

MCCLESKEY, DALE WADE, minister; b. Tezuitlan, Puebla, Mex., Mar. 16, 1952; (parents Am. citizens); s. Melbourne Walker and Loyce Marie (Hammonds) McC.; m. Cheryl Elizabeth Kaltwasser, June 2, 1972; children: Jason Corey, Jodi Elizabeth. BA cum laude, Wayland Bapt. Coll., Plainview, Tex., 1973; MDiv, Southwestern Bapt. Theol. Sem., Ft. Worth, 1977, D Ministry, 1986. Ordained to ministry So. Bapt. Conv., 1977. Chaplain Boy Scouts Am., Camp Tres Ritos, N.Mex., 1971; assoc. pastor 1st Bapt. Ch., Dimmitt, Tex., 1973; pastor 1st Bapt. Ch., Ruidoso Downs, N.Mex., 1977-86, Bethel Bapt. Ch., Roswell, N.Mex., 1986—; mem. exec. bd. Bapt. Conv. N.Mex., 1982-85, Internat. Bapt. Bible Inst., El Paso, Tex., 1984-89; moderator Pecos Valley Bapt. Assn., Artesia, N.Mex., 1988—. Contbr. articles to newspapers. Bd. dirs. Lincoln County Alcoholism Assn., Ruidoso Downs, 1983-84, N.Mex. Substance Abuse Inst., Albuquerque, 1989—; counselor Lincoln County Mental Health Assn., Ruidoso Downs, 1985; bell ringer Salvation Army, Roswell, 1989-90. Mem. Roswell Ministerial Alliance. Office: Bethel Bapt Ch 2420 N Garden Roswell NM 88201

MCCLINTON, DANNY GARDNER, music minister; b. Springfield, Mo., July 9, 1944; s. Ronald Ellis and Eloise (Gardner) McC.; m. Myla Baker, Aug. 21, 1965; children: Darin Scott, Travis Alan. BEd, S.W. Tex. U., 1971, MEd, 1977; postgrad., S.W. Theol. Sem., 1980; diploma, USN Sch. Music. Ordained to ministry So. Bapt. Conv., 1974. Min. of music Hot Wells Bapt. Ch., San Antonio, 1969-70, Northside Bapt. Ch., San Antonio, 1970-71, Bapt. Temple, Big Spring, Tex., 1971-74, Windsor Park Bapt. Ch., Austin, Tex., 1974-78, Village Bapt. Ch., Oklahoma City, 1978-79, 1st Bapt. Oak Cliff Ch., Dallas, 1979—; adj. prof. Dallas Bapt. U., 1990—; music dir. Big Spring Bapt. Assn., 1973-74, Austin Bapt. Assn., 1977-78, Dallas Bapt. Assn., 1990—; band dir. Christway Acad., Dallas, 1981-84. Election judge Dallas Dem. Party, 1982; v.p. Alumni Parents Assn. S.W. Tex. U., 1986. With U.S. Army, 1962-65, Korea. Mem. So. Bapt. Ch. Mus. Conf., Nat. Assn. Tchrs. Singing, Am. Guild English Handbell Ringers, Christian Inst. Dirs. Assn., Singing Men of Tex. Avocations: ranching, golf. Office: 1st Bapt Oak Cliff Ch 7710 Westmoreland Dallas TX 75237

MCCLOSKEY, GARY NEIL, priest, religious educator; b. S.I., N.Y., Feb. 24, 1951; s. William Bannon and Julia Margaret (Dempsey) McC. B.A., Villanova U., 1973; M.A., Catholic U. Am., 1976, postgrad., 1976-77; Ph.D., U. Miami, 1984. Ordained priest Roman Catholic Ch., 1977. Dir. student activities Biscayne Coll., Miami, 1977-79, instr. religious studies, 1977-80, coordinator Title III, asst. to pres., 1979-81, asst. prof. religious studies, 1980-81; dir. religious edn., sch. minister St. John Neumann High Sch., Golden Gate, Fla., 1981-84; asst. to acad. v.p. St. Thomas U., 1984-85, asst. acad. v.p., 1985—; grant writing cons. Biscayne Coll., 1981-84; instr. pastoral ministry program Diocese of Orlando, Fla., 1982—. Mem. state coordinating com. Pax Christi Fla., 1983—; mem. Network, Catholic Social Justice Lobby, 1981. Title III grantee, 1980-83. Mem. Am. Ednl. Research Assn., Assn. Profs. and Researchers in Religious Edn., Religious Edn. Assn., Religious Research Assn., Assocs. for Research in Pvt. Edn., Assn. Supervision and Curriculum Devel., Phi Delta Kappa. Republican. Lodge: K.C. (state chaplain Columbian Squires 1981-85). Office: 16400 NW 32nd Ave Miami FL 33054

MCCLUN, MAURICE CRAIG, minister; b. Alhambra, Calif., Apr. 11, 1954; s. Maurice L. and Lola A. (Williams) McC.; m. Donna K. Howe, July 26, 1975. BA, St. Paul Bible Coll., St. Bonifacius, Minn., 1976; MDiv, Bethel Theol. Sem., St. Paul, 1979. Ordained to ministry Christian Ch., 1981. Pastor Lone Jack (Mo.) Christian Ch., 1981-87; assoc. pastor First Christian Ch., Bonner Springs, Kans., 1987—; co-chair. Habitat for Humanity, Bonner Springs, 1990—. Western Dist. Christian and Missionary Alliance and Omaha Gospel Tabernacle scholar, 1974. Home: 14416 W 69th Shawnee KS 66216 *A sign in a hospital room reads in part, "prevent cross contamination." As a Christian, that is the direct opposite of what I want to do with my life.*

MCCLUNG, RONALD ALLEN, minister; b. Richwood, W.Va., Mar. 29, 1958; s. Harold and Paula Yvonne (Coleman) McC.; m. Sharon Ann Hoppe; children: Patrick Neil, Coleman Allen. Student, Marshall U., 1983; MDiv., Southwestern Theol. Sem., 1985. Youth pastor Birchill Bapt. Ch., Ft. Worth, 1985; assoc. pastor Emmanuel Bapt. Ch., Charleston, W.Va., 1986-89; pastor Kanawha City Bapt. Ch., Charleston, 1989—; youth leader Youth Leader Core, Charleston, 1987-89; mem. Bapt. Campus Ministries W.Va., 1991—. Mem. Am. Bapt. Ministerial Coun., Lions. Republican. Home: 3313 Staunton Ave Charleston WV 25304 Office: Kanawha City Bapt Ch 4500 Venable Ave SE Charleston WV 25304

MCCLURE, BRUCE EDWARD, clergyman; b. West Memphis, Ark., July 26, 1954; s. Edmond and Nicie (Sturghill) McC.; m. Bernice Strong; children: Marcus, Edwin, Brian, Bryon. BS in Bible, Okla. Christian Coll., Oklahoma City, 1980; MS in Counseling, Troy (Ala.) State U., 1988. Ordained to ministry Ch. of Christ. Salesman Manning Lumber, West Memphis, Ark., 1972-73; acctg. clk. W.R. Grace & Co., Memphis, 1973-78; minister Ch. of Christ, Okla., 1978-87, Opelika, Ala., 1987—. Pres. Parents Adv. Com., Opelika, 1987; bd. dirs. Lee County Youth Devel., Opelika, 1988—, Lee County Shelter Battered Women, Opelika, 1989—, Opelika Boys Club, Opelika, 1989—. Mem. Am. Assn. Counseling Devel. Democrat. Avocations: bowling, writing, fishing, cooking.

MCCLURE, MICHAEL LAWRENCE, minister; b. Chattanooga, Apr. 27, 1952; s. Robert Franklin and Eddie Mae (Carden) McC.; m. Catherine Leora Kellogg, Jan. 15, 1983; children: Amanda Rose, Sean Robert, Michael Edward. Student, Tenn. Temple U., 1970-76; Grad. of Theology, Pensacola Christian Coll., 1981. Lic. to ministry Bapt. Ch., 1973, ordained, 1984. Bus pastor Highland Park Bapt. Ch., Chattanooga, 1971-73; camp counselor Fort Bluff Camp, Dayton, Tenn., 1975-76; summer pastoral staff Faith Bapt. Ch., Margate, Fla., 1972, bus dir., 1973; dean of students, youth dir. Heritage Christian Sch./Calvary Bapt. Ch., Pompano Beach, Fla., 1977-80; evangelist Men of Valour Ministries, Pompano Beach, 1980-82; youth pastor Congress Ave. Bapt. Ch., Delray Beach, Fla., 1982; youth pastor West Park Bapt. Ch., Delray Beach, Fla., 1982-83, interim pastor, 1983-84, sr. pastor, 1984—; founder, dir. West Park Bapt. Summer Day Camp, 1984—; bd. dirs. Operation Concern, Inc., Boynton Beach, Fla.; cert. instr. Gospel Martial Arts Union, Sioux Falls, S.D., 1989—. Republican. Office: West Park Baptist Church 4004 W Lake Ida Rd Delray Beach FL 33445

MCCLURE, MITCHELL LEE, pastor; b. Cleveland, Tenn., July 14, 1957; s. Joe M. and Freida (Jones) McC.; m. Sherri L. Parson, Jan. 25, 1980; children: Sara E., Jonathan A. AS, Cleveland State Community Coll., 1976; BS, East Tenn. State U., 1979. Ordained to ministry Ch. of God (Cleve.), 1990. Minister youth and Christian Edn. Johnson City (Tenn.) Ch. of God, 1977-79; assoc. pastor Gray (Tenn.) Ch. of God, 1979-80, pastor, 1980-89; pastor Lake Hills Ch. of God, Chattanooga, 1989-91, Clinton (Tenn.) Ch. of God, 1991—; chaplain North Park Hosp. Mem. Hixson Ministerial Assn. Home: 401 Scruggs Ave Clinton TN 37716 Office: 729 S Main Clinton TN 37716

MCCLURE, STEVAN TERRANCE, minister; b. Joplin, Mo., Aug. 1, 1962; s. William Terrance and Martha Lorene (Risner) McC.; m. Ginger Sue Gruenwald, June 14, 1983; children: Ethan Daniel, Lydia Anna. AB in Ministry, El Paso Sch. Missions, 1983, AB in Missions, 1983. Commd. to ministry, Christian Ch., 1982. Minister Westside Christian Ch., El Paso, Tex., 1982-84, Cane Valley & Greensburg (Ky.) Christian Chs., 1984-87, Smoky Mt. Christian Ch., Sevierville, Tenn., 1987—; bd. dirs. Mission Svcs., Inc., Knoxville, 1990—; mem. adv. com. Mountainbrook Found., 1991. Contbr. articles to profl. jours. Pres. Sevierville Assn. Chs., 1989-90. Recipient Ch. Growth award, Nat. Ch. Growth Ctr., Washington, 1982. Mem. Fellowship of Christian Ministers, Ind. Order Foresters. Republican. Home and Office: Smoky Mt Christian Ch 125 S Boulevard Way Sevierville TN 37862

MCCLURG, PATRICIA A., minister; b. Bay City, Tex., Mar. 14, 1939; d. T.H. and Margaret (Smith) McC. BA, Austin Coll., 1961; M in Christian Edn., Presbyn. Sch. of Christian Edn., 1963; BD, Austin Presbyn. Theol. Sem., 1967; postgrad., So. Meth. U., 1971-73; DD (hon.), Austin Coll., 1978. Dir. Christian edn. 2d Presbyn. Ch., Newport News, Va., 1963-65; asst. pastor Westminster Presbyn. Ch., Beaumont, Tex., 1967-71; assoc. pastor 1st Presbyn. Ch., Pasadena, Tex., 1969-71; assoc. exec. Synod of Red River, Denton, Tex., 1973-75; dir. gen. assembly mission bd. Presbyn. Ch., Atlanta, 1975-86; assoc. exec. for mission The Presbytery of Elizabeth, Plainfield, N.J., 1986-91; exec. Presbytery of New Castle, Newark, 1992—; pres. Nat. Coun. Chs. of Christ in the U.S.A., N.Y.C., 1988-89, v.p., 1985-87; del., budget com. chmn. World Coun. Chs. Assembly, Vancouver, Can., 1985; sect. leader World Coun. Chs. Mission and Evang. Confs., Melbourne, Australia, 1980. Contbr. articles to prof. jours. Mem. chs. spl. commn. on South Africa, N.Y.C., 1985—, Anti-Pollution Campaign, Pasadena, 1970. Recipient Disting. Alumni award Austin Coll., 1979. Democrat. Presbyterian. Lodge: Rotary. Avocations: shell collecting, reading, minor house repairs.

MCCOID, DONALD J., bishop; b. Wheeling, W.Va., Dec. 31, 1943; s. Roy Conrad adn Alberta Virginia (Sturm) McC.; m. Saundra Ernette Piisila, Oct. 20, 1973; children: Kimberly, Elizabeth. AB, West Liberty (W.Va.) State Coll., 1965; MDiv, Luth. Theol. Sem., Phila., 1968; DD (hon.), Thiel Coll., 1983. Ordained to ministry Evang. Luth. Ch. in Am. Pastor St. Luke's Luth. Ch., Monessen, Pa., 1968-72; assoc. pastor St. John's Luth. Ch. Highland, Pitts., 1972-74; area Luth. coord. Western Pa.—W.Va. synod, Luth. Ch. Am., Clarksburg, W.Va., 1974-77; sr. pastor Trinity Luth. Ch., Latrobe, Pa., 1977-87; bishop Southwestern Pa. synod, Evang. Luth. Ch. in Am., Pitts., 1987—; bd. dirs. Pa. Coun. Chs., Harrisburg. Bd. dirs. Religious Leadership Forum, Pitts., 1988—; mem. exec. com. Christian Assocs. S.W. Pa., Pitts., 1988—; active Citizens League S.W. Pa., Pitts., 1990—. Office: Evang Luth Ch in Am SW Pa Synod 9625 Perry Hwy Pittsburgh PA 15237

MCCOLLUM, ODELL, minister; b. Reidsville, N.C., Feb. 16, 1926; s. Roy Sr. and Carrie Lee (Hodge) McC.; m. Margaret May Adkins, Aug. 7, 1948; children: Larry Odell and Tresa Lynette. DD (hon.), United Christian Coll., N.C., 1974; D of Sacred Letters (hon.), United Christian Coll., N.Y., 1979. Ordained to ministry United Holy Ch. Am., Inc., 1958. Pastor House of Prayer, Warren, Ohio, 1957-65, Gospel Tabernacle, Columbus, Ohio, 1964—; bishop United Holy Ch. of Am., 1972; Pres. N.W. Dist. United Holy Ch.; 2nd v.p. United Holy Ch. of Am.; bd. dirs. One Church, One Child, Columbus. Program chmn. 100th Anniversary Jour., United Holy Ch. of Am., Inc., 1986. With U.S. Army, 1944-46. Democrat. Home: 3206 Blue Ridge Rd Columbus OH 43219 Office: Gospel Tabernacle 1205 Hildreth Ave Columbus OH 43203 *It is not what you receive that is most important, but what you give. Christ gave his life for mankind. Love gives.*

MCCOLLUM, RICHARD ALTON, II, music and youth minister; b. Bamberg, S.C., July 5, 1959; s. Richar Alton and Rose Marie (Grooms) McC.; m. Christi Lanier Wiggins, Apr. 9, 1988; 1 child, Richard Alton III. BA in Journalism, U. S.C., 1981; MA in Religious Edn., Southwestern Bapt. Theol. Sem., 1985. Lic. to ministry So. Bapt. Conv., 1985. Min. of music 1st Bapt. Ch., Gaston, S.C., 1977-81, Bamberg, S.C., 1981-84; min. music and youth 1st Bapt. Ch., Bridgeport, Tex., 1984-86; min. music and edn. Flint Groves Bapt. Ch., Gastonia, N.C., 1986-90; min. music and youth 1st Bapt. Ch., Mullins, S.C., 1990—. Recs. include Tell Me the Story, 1987. Mem. S.C. Ch. Music Orgn. Office: 1st Bapt Ch 305 N Main St Mullins SC 29574

MCCOMB, JACKIE ROY, minister; b. Columbia, Miss., Feb. 6, 1940; s. William Odell and Willie Nola (Reed) McC.; m. Donna Martin, Aug. 15, 1965; children: Cynthia, Donovan, David. BA, Miss. Coll., 1967; ThM, New Orleans Bapt. Theol. Sem., 1969, DD, 1974. Ordained to ministry Bapt. Ch., 1964. Pastor Mt. Zion Bapt. Ch., Brookhaven, Miss., 1968-71; pastor First Bapt. Ch., Sardis, Miss., 1971-74, Pearl, Miss., 1974-76, Columbia, Miss., 1976—; trustee New Orleans Bapt. Sem., 1986—. Contbr. articles to profl. jours. Curriculum com. Columbia Sch. Bd. Mem. Rotary Club. Office: 1st Bapt Ch 900 High Sch Ave Columbia MS 39429

MCCOMISKEY, THOMAS EDWARD, religion educator; b. Paterson, N.J., Aug. 22, 1928; s. Samuel Thomas and Christine (Hawthorne) McC.; m. Eleanor Mary Carp, June 22, 1957; children: Karen Christine, Douglas Samuel, Bruce Thomas. BA, The King's Coll., Briarcliff Manor, N.Y., 1953; MDiv., Faith Theol. Sem., 1956; ThM, Westminster Theol. Sem., 1975; MA, PhD, Brandeis U., 1963, 65. Ordained to ministry Bapt. Ch., 1956. Pastor Community Ch. of Folsom, Pa., 1956-59, Bible Bapt. Ch., Trenton, N.J., 1959-61; prof., chmn. dept. biblical studies The King's Coll., 1964-69; prof. Old Testament and semitic langs. Trinity Evang. Div. Sch., Deerfield, Ill., 1969-90, prof. Old Testament exegesis and Biblical theology, 1990—, chmn. dept., acting dir. PhD program, 1990-91. Author: The Covenants of Promise, 1985, Reading Scripture in Public: A Guide for Preachers and Lay Readers, 1991, commentaries in field; editor, translator: The Holy Bible: The New International Version, 1969-77; co-editor: (with John Woodbridge) Doing Theology in Today's World, 1991. NDEA fellow, 1961-64. Fellow Am. Coll. Bibl. Theologians (presider 1987—), Soc. Bibl. Lit., Evang. Theol. Soc. Republican. Home: 2 Hawthorn Dr Hawthorn Woods IL 60047 Office: Trinity Evang Div Sch 2065 Half Day Rd Deerfield IL 60015

MCCONACHIE, MICHAEL PAUL, minister; b. Dallas, Jan. 4, 1956; s. Paul Jacob and May Elizabeth (Rice) McC.; m. Cynthia Anne Chase, Dec. 29, 1984; children: Amy Elizabeth, David Michael. BA, U. Tex., 1978; MA, U. Mo., 1979, PhD, 1985; MDiv, Brite Divinity Sch., Ft. Worth, 1989. Ordained to ministry Christian Ch. (Disciples of Christ), 1989. Pastor Harrisburg (Mo.) Christian Ch., 1981-83; assoc. pastor First Christian Ch., Corsicana, Tex., 1986-87; pastor Stevens Park Christian Ch., Dallas, 1987-89, First Christian Ch., Paris, Mo., 1989—; prof. U. Mo., Columbia, 1990-91;

sec. Coop. Camping Com., Columbia, 1989—; bd. dirs. NE Area Christian Ch., Columbia, 1991-92. Mem. Rotary (sec. Paris chpt. 1991-92). Office: First Christian Ch Box 223 Paris MO 65275 *In Jesus Christ, God has extended to humanity an invitation to life—abundant and eternal, now and to come. How we respond to the invitation determines our life now and our destiny in eternity.*

MCCONKEY, DAVID DALE, minister; b. Chillicothe, Ohio, Sept. 13, 1949; s. Marvin E. and Ruth P. (Rice) McC.; m. Karla Jo Jones, July 12, 1973; children: Bradley E., Clayton C., Joshua D., Alyson E. BA in Religion, Ea. N.Mex. U., 1979; MDiv, Southwestern Bapt. Theol. Sem., Ft. Worth, 1982. Ordained to ministry So. Bapt. Conv., 1982. Pastor First Bapt. Ch., Santa Rosa, N.Mex., 1982-83, Rio Rancho, N.Mex., 1983—; 1st v.p. Bapt. Conv. of N.Mex., 1989-90. With USAF, 1969-77. Mem. Cen. Assn. Ministerial Fellowship (pres. 1985-87), Cen. Bapt. Assn. (moderator 1987-89). Home: 1905 Grande Blvd Rio Rancho NM 87124 Office: First Bapt Ch 3805 19th Ave Rio Rancho NM 87124

MCCONNEL, GEORGE HUNT, minister; b. Pitts., Feb. 16, 1947; s. William Bruce and Grace (Hunt) McC.; m. Jill Palmer, June 14, 1969; children: James Stewart, Erin Phillips. BS, Lehigh U., 1969; MDiv, Princeton Theol. Sem., 1978; postgrad., Emory U., 1987—. Ordained to ministry Presbyn. Ch. (U.S.A.), 1978. Assoc. min. for Edn. Shadyside Presbyn. Ch., Pitts., 1978-82; sr. min. 1st Presbyn. Ch., Jamestown, N.Y., 1983—; bd. dirs., com. chmn. Presbyn. Homes of Western N.Y., Buffalo, 1985-90; mem. Presbytery Western N.Y. (chmn. stewardship com. 1983-85, candidates com. 1984-85, chmn. pers. com. 1989—); mem. Jamestown Ecumenical Ministries, 1985-87. Mem. Chautauqua Area Regional Found. (chmn. com. 1987—), Jamestown Area Ministerial Assn. (sec., treas. 1984-87), Moonbrook County Club (com. mem. 1982—). Named one of Outstanding Young Men in Am., Am. Jaycees, 1981. Home: 2 Spruce St Jamestown NY 14701 Office: 1st Presbyn Ch 509 Prendergast Ave Jamestown NY 14701

MCCONNELL, CALVIN DALE, clergyman; b. Monte Vista, Colo., Dec. 3, 1928; s. Roy and Leota Fern (Taylor) McC.; m. Mary Caroline Bamberg, Sept. 2, 1952 (dec. Apr. 1986); children: David William, Mark Andrew; m. Velma Duell, Dec. 17, 1988. B.A., U. Denver, 1951; M.Div., Iliff Sch. Theology, 1954; S.T.M., Andover Newton Theol. Sem., 1967. Ordained to ministry United Meth. Ch.; pastor Meth. Ch., Williams, Calif., 1955-58, 1st United Meth. Ch., Palo Alto, Calif. and Stanford U. Wesley Found., 1958-61; chaplain and asst. prof. religion Willamette U., Salem, Oreg., 1961-67; pastor Christ United Meth. Ch., Denver, 1968-72; pastor 1st United Meth. Ch., Boulder, Colo., 1972-79, Colorado Springs, Colo., 1979-80; bishop United Meth. Ch., Portland Area, 1980-88, Seattle Area, 1988—. Trustee U. Puget Sound, Iliff Sch. Theology. Office: 2112 3d Ave Ste 301 Seattle WA 98121

MCCONNELL, DALE ALAN, minister; b. Okemah, Okla., Nov. 6, 1952; s. Wayne Ray McConnell and Dolley Lee (Nichols) Phillips; m. C. Diane Littleton, Aug. 5, 1978; children: Melissa, Michelle, Megan. BA, Okla. Bapt. U., 1975; MDiv, Southwestern Bapt. Theol. Sem., Ft. Worth, 1979, PhD, 1981. Ordained to ministry So. Bapt. Conv., 1981. Teaching fellow in systematic theology Southwestern Bapt. Theol. Sem., 1981; pastor 1st Bapt. Ch., Kahoka, Mo., 1981-84, Excelsior Springs, Mo., 1984-91; pastor 1st Calvary Bapt. Ch., Kansas City, Mo., 1991—; adj. prof. evangelism Midwestern Bapt. Sem., Kansas City, 1987-88; adj. prof. preaching William Jewell Coll., Liberty, Mo., 1991—; trustee SW Bapt. U., Bolivar, Mo., 1990—. Contbr. numerous articles to religious publs. Democrat. Home: 16200 W 79th Terr Lenexa KS 66219 Office: 1st Calvary Bapt Ch 3921 Baltimore Kansas City MO 64111

MCCONNELL, JOHNNY DUFF, minister; b. Anderson, S.C., June 24, 1961; s. Johnnie Calvin and Edna Jean (Timmerman) McC. BA in Psychology, Clemson U., 1983, postgrad., 1989—. Minister of youth and children Bethel Bapt. Ch., Seneca, S.C., 1982-85, Return Bapt. Ch., Seneca, 1988—; personnel adminstr. K-Mac Svcs., Inc., Seneca, 1979—. Mem. Personnel Assn. of Oconee and Pickens Counties. Home: Rte 6 PO Box 468 Seneca SC 29678 Office: K-Mac Svcs Inc 108 K-Mac Drive Seneca SC 29678 *Along with others, I believe our world is being destroyed thorugh the destruction of the "family." Is it not time for this group to return to the stand our Lord had in store?.*

MCCONNELL, WILLIAM THOMAS, III, minister; b. Louisville, Sept. 20, 1946; s. William Thomas Jr. and June (Redding) McC.; m. Patricia Burrus, Sept. 7, 1968; children: William, Margaret, David, Robin; m. Nancy Cothern, July 23, 1988. AB, Ea. Ky. U., 1970; MDiv, Asbury Theol. Sem., 1971; D Ministry, Kingsway Theol. Sem., 1976. Ordained to ministry Christian Ch. (Disciples of Christ), 1972. Pastor 1st Christian Ch., Mitchellville, Iowa, 1974-78, Stanford, Ill., 1978-82; pastor La Grange (Ky.) Christian Ch., 1982-85, Falmouth (Ky.) Christian Ch., 1986—; owner, chief Pendleton County Emergency Med. Svcs., Falmouth, 1989—; pres. McLeanCounty Ministerial Assn., Bloomington, Ill., 1980-82, Oldham county Ministerial Assn., La Grange, 1983-83, Dist. Six Christian Chs., Lexington, Ky., 1988-89. Author column Falmouth Outlook, 1988—; contbr. articles to religious jours. Advisor Bd. Edn. Allin Twp., 1979-82; chmn. Adult Edn. Adv. Bd., Falmouth, 1989—; adult leader Boy Scouts Am., 1970— (Dist. award of merit 1983, Outstanding Dist. Scouter 1984). Mem. Pastoral Counselors Assn. Am., Pendleton County Ministerial Alliance, Pendleton County Coop. Chs., Rotary, Sigma Nu. Democrat. Office: Falmouth Christian Ch 303 W Shelby St Falmouth KY 41040 *We live our lives following the path of our decisions. Some decisions have little impact on our lives. Some decisions alter the entire course of our lives. The problem is, we usually can't tell one from the other. Decide to live each day well.*

MCCORKLE, EDDIE DALE, youth minister; b. Stamford, Tex., June 20, 1963; s. Eddie Robert and Phyllis Regina (Ake) McC.; m. Beverly Anne Bergschicker, May 14, 1988. BA in Bible, Harding U., 1990. Pulpit preacher Ch. of Christ, Miles, Tex., 1980-84; youth min. Ch. of Christ, Carlsbad, Tex., 1985-87, Searcy, Ark., 1988-90, Raleigh, N.C., 1990—; athletic dir. Heart of Tex. Bible Camp, Brady, Tex., 1981-90. Republican. Office: Ch of Christ 700 Brooks Ave Raleigh NC 27607

MCCORMICK, CURTISS DEAN, clergyman; b. Oklahoma City, June 16, 1938; s. Hershal Fallis and Florence Odema (Vaught) McC.; m. Edith Ann Toon, June 1, 1959; 1 child, Rebecca Ann McCormick Dorsey. Student, Cen. Bible Coll., Springfield, Mo., 1957, Oklahoma City U., 1959; BA in Religion and Philosophy, So. Nazarene U., Bethany, Okla., 1964; MA in Bibl. Lit., Assemblies of God Theol. Sem., 1988. Ordained to ministry Assemblies of God, 1961. Youth pastor Grace Assembly of God Ch., Oklahoma City, 1959-64, Trinity Meml. Assembly of God Ch., Dallas, 1964-65; evangelist, Okla., 1965-66; pastor Crescent Park Assembly of God Ch., Gt. Bend, Kans., 1966-69, lst Assembly of God Ch., Haysville, Kans., 1969-72; dir. Kans. youth and edn. Assemblies of God, Wichita, 1972-78; sr. pastor lst Assembly of God Ch., Wichita, 1978—; presbyter Kans. Assemblies of God, Wichita, 1972—, sec.-treas., 1978-79, asst. supt., 1979—; gen. presbyter Assemblies of God, Springfield, 1978—; sec. Kans. Assemblies of God Missions, 1978—. Contbr. articles to Advance mag. Democrat. Office: lst Assembly of God Ch 1144 S Main St Wichita KS 67213

MCCORMICK, GINGER G., church treasurer, auditor; b. Carrollton, Ga., June 26, 1962; d. J. Donald and Jean (Hall) McC. BBA in Acctg., West Ga. Coll., 1983. Youth coord. Bowdon (Ga.) First United Meth. Ch., 1984-88; youth coord. Shiloh United Meth. Ch., Carrollton, Ga., 1990—, treas., 1991—; internal auditor LaMar Mfg. Co., Bowdon, 1988—. Named Outstanding Young Careerist Carrollton Bus. and Profl. Women, 1990. Home: 583 Dixson Rd Bowdon GA 30108 Office: LaMar Mfg Co 152 City Hall Ave Bowdon GA 30108

MCCORMICK, LARRY DAVID, minister, theology educator; b. St. Louis, Nov. 29, 1950; s. James Albert and Eunice Lydia (Arbeiter) McC.; m. Ruth Alice Shaw, June 8, 1974. BS, Valparaiso U., 1972; MDiv, Christ Sem., St. Louis, 1976; MA, St. John's U., N.Y.C., 1986; PhD, Fordham U., 1990. Ordained priest Evang. Luth. Ch. Am., 1976. Asst. pastor Emmanuel Luth. Ch., Phila., 1976-79; prof. N.T. Fordham U., N.Y.C., 1986—; asst. pastor Grace Luth. Ch., Teaneck, N.J., 1979-82; pastor Holy Trinity Luth. Ch., North Bergen, N.J., 1987—. Mem. Soc. Bibl. Lit., Am. Schs. Oriental Rsch. Office: Fordham U Fordham Rd New York NY 10458

MCCORMICK, RICHARD ARTHUR, priest, religion educator, writer; b. Toledo, Oct. 3, 1922; s. Edward J. McCormick. BA, Loyola U., Chgo., 1945, MA, 1950, hon. degree, 1989; STD, Gregorian U., Rome, 1957; hon. degree, U. Scranton, 1975, Wheeling Coll., W.Va., 1976, Jesuit Sch. Theology, Berkeley, Calif., 1982, Siena Coll., 1985, U. Louvain, 1986, Coll. Holy Cross, 1986, Seattle U., 1987, Fordham U., 1988, Xavier U., 1988, U. San Francisco, 1989, Georgetown U., 1990, Cath. Theol. Union, 1991. Joined S.J., Roman Cath. Ch., 1940, ordained priest, 1953. Prof. moral theology Jesuit Sch. Theology, Chgo., 1957-73; Rose F. Kennedy prof. Christian ethics Georgetown U., Washington, 1974-86; John A. O'Brien prof. U. Notre Dame, Ind., 1986—; rsch. assoc. Woodstock Theol. Ctr., Washington, 1974-86; past mem. Ethics Adv. Bd., HEW; mem. Cath. Commn. on Intellectual and Cultural Affairs; lectr. in field. Author: Ambiguity in Moral Choice, 1973, Notes on Moral Theology, 1965 through 1980, 1980, Notes on Moral Theology 1981-1984, 1984, Health and Medicine in the Catholic Tradition, 1984, The Critical Calling: Moral Dilemmas Since Vatican II, 1989; co-author: (with Paul Ramsey) Doing Evil to Achieve Good, 1978; contbr. to numerous books, articles to Christianity and Crisis, New Cath. World, other religious jours.; co-editor: (with Charles E. Curran) Readings in Moral Theology I: Moral Norms and Catholic Tradition, 1979, Readings in Moral Theology II: The Distinctiveness of Christian Ethics, 1980, Readings in Moral Theology III: Morality and Authority, 1981, Readings in Moral Theology IV: The Use of Scripture in Moral Theology, 1982, Readings in Moral Theology V: Official Catholic Social Teaching, 1986, Readings in Moral Theology VI: Dissent in the Church, 1988, Readings in Moral Theology VII: The Natural Law, 1990; former assoc. editor Am. mag.; editorial advisor Theology Digest, Hosp. Progress jours.; mem. editorial bd. Jour. Religious Ethics, Fetal Medicine, Jour. Contemporary Health Law and Policy. Former trustee U. Detroit, Fairfield U. Recipient Henry Knowles Beecher award Hastings Ctr., 1988; Inst. Soc., Ethics and Life Scis. fellow. Mem. Am. Acad. Arts and Scis., Cath. Theol. Soc. Am. (past pres., Cardinal Spellman award 1969), Am. Soc. Christian Ethics (past bd. dirs.), Am. Hosp. Am. (spl. bioethics com.), Nat. Hospice Orgn. (bioethcis com.), Cath. Health Assn. (bioethics com.), Am. Fertility Soc. (ethics com.). Office: U Notre Dame Dept Theology Notre Dame IN 46556

MCCOSH, EARL CURTIS, minister; b. Loudon County, Tenn., Feb. 27, 1933; s. Phillip J. and N. Ruth (Jenkins) McC.; m. Jane Caroline May, Aug. 22, 1952; children: Kendall Curtis, Devon Chaney, Rodney Vonoie. BA, Carson Newman Coll., Jefferson City, Tenn., 1965; MDiv, So. Bapt. Theol. Sem., Louisville, 1970, DMin, 1980. Ordained to ministry So. Bapt. Conv., 1965. Pastor Mitchell Springs Bapt. Ch., Rutledge, Tenn., 1965-67, Whites Run Bapt. Ch., Carrollton, Ky., 1967-70; Pastor Mars Hill Bapt. Ch., Knoxville, 1970-74, Emmanuel Bapt. Ch., Jefferson City, Tenn., 1974-78, Grace Bapt. Ch., Morristown, Tenn., 1978-82, Cen. Hts. Bapt. Ch., Dandridge, Tenn., 1982-89, Cherokee Hills Bapt. Ch., Morristown, Tenn., 1989—; exec. bd. Tenn. Bapt. Conv., Brentwood, 1976-91; moderator Jefferson County Assn. Bapts., 1976-77, Nolachucky Assn. Bapts., 1981-82. Author: Establishing Communication Between Church and Pastor, 1980. Support coord. Coalition for Support of Mil. Families, Morristown, 1990—. Sgt. U.S. Army, 1953-56, 1st lt., 1956-59; capt. USNG, 1960-72; chaplain col. Tenn. Air N.G., 1972-82; with USAFR, 1985-88. Decorated Legion of Merit. Mem. Odd Fellows. Home: 1028 Iroquois Ave Box 461 Morristown TN 37815 Office: Cherokee Hills Bapt Ch 1025 Peck Ave Box 506 Morristown TN 37815

MCCOURT, ROBERT REILLY, priest; b. Bklyn., Feb. 15, 1935; s. Robert A. and Ann T. (Reilly) McC. BA, Cathedral Coll., 1957; STB, Cath. U., 1961; MDiv, Cathedral Coll., 1980. Ordained priest Roman Cath. Ch., 1961. Asst. pastor St. Frances De Chantal Ch., Bklyn., 1961, Holy Rosary Ch., Bklyn., 1961-70; pastor St. Clement Pope Ch., South Ozone Park, N.Y., 1970-82, St. Pascal Baylon Ch., St. Albans, N.Y., 1982—; elevated to reverend monsignor, 1988. Bd. dirs. Mary Immaculate Hosp, Jamaica, N.Y., Hollis Local Devel. Corp., St. Albans, Priest's Senate, Bklyn., 1972-81, Immaculate Conception Sem. Alumni, Huntington, N.Y., 1977-80, Office of Black Ministry, Bklyn., 1984-89. Home: 112-43 198th St Saint Albans NY 11412

MCCOWN, LOWRIE BRUCE, religious organization administrator; b. New Castle, Pa., Nov. 3, 1952; s. John Edgar and Mary Irene (Taylor) McC.; m. Randi Jane West, May 28, 1976; children: Taylor, Nathan, Hannah. BA in History, Gordon Coll., 1974; postgrad., Gordon Conwell Theol. Sem., 1976, 77. Youth min. Pioneer Meml. Ch., Solon, Ohio, 1974-75; campus assoc. Coalition for Christian Outreach, Pitts., 1977-80; area rep. Fellowship of Christian Athletes, Pitts., 1980-83; nat. dir. of programs Fellowship of Christian Athletes, Kansas City, Mo., 1984-90; v.p. of programs, corp. officer Fellowship of Christian Athletes, Kansas City, 1990—; elder Gashland Presbyn. Ch., Kansas City, 1990—, com. chairperson Christian edn., 1990—. Mem. Nat. Network Youth Ministry, Am. Soc. Assn. Execs., Christian Camping Internat., Meeting Planners Internat. Home: 319 N Ridge Liberty MO 64068 Office: Fellowship Christian Athletes 8701 Leeds Rd Kansas City MO 64129

MCCOWN, WAYNE GORDON, religion educator; b. Compton, Calif., Mar. 9, 1942; s. George Arnold and Lewise Daisy (Nasby) McC.; m. Darlene Elizabeth McCown, June 14, 1962; children: Mark Wayne, Peter Lewis. BA, Seattle Pacific U., 1963; BD, Asbury Theol. Sem., Wilmore, Ky., 1966; MA, U. Wash., 1967; ThM, Union Theol. Sem., Richmond, Va., 1968, PhD, 1970. Ordained elder Free Meth. Ch., 1964. Asst. prof. Seattle Pacific U., 1970-73; prof., dean Western Evang. Sem., Portland, Oreg., 1973-85; supt. So. Calif.—Ariz. conf. Free Meth. Ch. N.Am., L.A., 1985-88; sr. v.p., provost Roberts Wesleyan Coll., Rochester, N.Y., 1988—; supt. So. Calif.-Ann. Conf. Free Meth. Ch., 1985-88; sec. study commn. on doctrine Free Meth. Ch., Indpls., 1985—. Editor: God's Word Interpreted for Today's World, 1979; contbr. articles to religious jours. Supt. So. Calif.-Ariz. Conf. Free Meth. Ch., 1985-88; asst. pastor North City Free Meth. Ch., 1963-64, 66-67, 70-72; coord. Faith and Life Free Meth. Ch., 1976-77; interim pastor Lebanon Free Meth. Ch., 1977; asst. dir. John Wesley Sem. Found., 1972-85; ptnr. Western Evang. Sem., 1973—; mem. study commn. on doctrine Free Meth. Ch., 1978-85. Recipient Alumni Medallion award Seattle Pacific U., 1981; fellow Roberts Wesleyan Coll., Seattle Pacific U. Mem. Soc. Bibl. Lit., Wesleyan Theol. Soc. (pres. 1980-81), Alpha Kappa Sigma, Theta Phi. Office: Roberts Wesleyan Coll 2301 Westside Dr Rochester NY 14624-1991

MCCOY, BERTIE ELIZABETH, pastor; b. Jones, Okla., Apr. 9, 1922; d. Bert Earl and Lizzie Nellie (Wood) DeGroot; m. Frank LCarence McCoy, Aug. 3, 1948. Student, Hills Bus. coll., 1941. Founder, pastor Assemblies of God, Luther, Okla., 1945-55; evangelist Assemblies of God, Jones, Okla., 1956-58, 62-65; founder, pastor Assemblies of God, Arvin, Calif., 1958-61, Echoes of Faithod, Las Vegas, 1966—; check writer Fed. Reserve Bank, Oklahoma City, Okla., 1941-46; pres., Youth Rallies Okla. County, Jones, 1945-55. Founded, built 7 Assemblies of Gof Chs., Oklahome City area, 1945-58, 1 Ch., Arvin, Calif., Orgn. Chs. Echoes of Faith, Las. Vegas, 1962—, 3 Chs., Las Vegas, 1 Ch. Flint, Mich.; missionary worker, Israel, China. Republican. Home: 601 Tiffany Ln Las Vegas NV 89101 Office: Echoes of Faith 1401 E Washington Las Vegas NV 89101

MCCOY, CARROLL PIERCE, retired minister; b. Hennessey, Okla., Sept. 14, 1920; s. Victor Pierce and Mary Ruth (Meyer) McC.; m. Florence Louise Hogle, July 31, 1964. BS, Okla. State U., 1947; BD, S.W. Bapt. Theol. Sem., 1952, MRE, 1953. Min. Christian Ch., Mutual, Okla., 1955-59, 81-89; ret., Buffalo, Okla., 1959-64, Gage, Okla., 1964-71, Arnett, Okla., 1971-80. With USN, 1942-46. Mem. Rotary (past pres. Gage Club), Kiwanis (past sec.-treas. Arnett club). Democrat. Home: Rt 2 Box 26 Vici OK 73859

MCCOY, GLENN WESLEY, religion educator; b. Hatfield, Ark., July 4, 1933; s. Raymond Wesley and Elizabeth Irene (McDonald) McC.; m. Dorla Deane Medford, Aug. 29, 1957; children: Annette Kathleen, John Wesley, Stanley Glenn. BA, Ouachita Bapt., 1956; MDiv, Southwestern Sem., 1958, ThM, 1961, D Ministry, 1980; MA, Ea. N.Mex. U., 1970. Pastor First Bapt. Ch., Ruidoso Downs, N.Mex., 1959-61, Mt. View Bapt. Ch., Roswell, N.Mex., 1961-63; campus minister, tchr. N.Mex. Highlands U., Las Vegas, Nev., 1963-71; prof. religion Ea. N.Mex. U., Portales, 1971—. Pres. Am. Heart Assn., Portales, 1986-88. Mem. Soc. Bibl. Lit., So. Bapt. Campus Ministers, Am. Sch. Oriental Rsch., Kiwanis (treas. Portales club 1979—). Office: Eastern NMex U Box 2005 Portales NM 88130

MCCOY, HOWARD BRUCE, minister; b. St. Louis, Feb. 16, 1956; s. James Wilbert and Marjorie Jean (Bartram) McC.; m. Cynthia Kay, May 20, 1978; children: Katie Jean, Zachary Sloan. Student, Liberty U., 1976-77, 80; B of Ministry, Covington Theol. Sem., 1989, M of Ministry, 1991, postgrad., 1991—. Ordained to ministry Bapt. Ch., 1981. Music dir. Thomas Rd. Bapt. Ch., Lynchburg, Va., 1978-80; music evangelist self-employed, Clearwater, Fla., 1981-83; music dir., theory instr. Trinity Coll., Dunedin, Fla., 1982-83; assoc. pastor music First Bapt. Ch. of Indian Rocks, Largo, Fla., 1983-90; sr. pastor Davis Islands Community Ch., Tampa, Fla., 1990—; music dir. Life Action Crusade Ministries, Buchanan, Mich., 1974-75; high tenor, soloist Dick Anthony's 16 Swinging Men, Mpls., 1981—; guest soloist Christian TV Network, Clearwater, 1980—. Campaign speaker Bob Dole for Pres., Clearwater, 1988; debate cons. ANAMUS, Mt. Prospect, Ill., 1989—. Recipient Music scholarship Gen. Assn. Regular Bapt., 1973; named to Outstanding Young Men Am., 1988. Mem. ANAMUS (cons., fellow 1989—), Suncoast Bapt. Assn. Republican. Home: 1135 Candler Rd Clearwater FL 34625 Office: Davis Island Community Ch 97 Biscayne Blvd Tampa FL 33606 *When Peter got out of the boat to walk to his Lord he began to sink but he walked on water! We may slip along the way but fulfillment comes to those who set their goals and dare to get out of the boat and attempt greatness!.*

MCCOY, JERRY DAN, religion educator; b. Muskogee, Okla., Aug. 31, 1941; s. Jerome Eric and Mary Elizabeth (Smith) McC.; m. Virginia Ruth Cox, June 29, 1963; children: Robert Brian, John Stewart, Daniel Kirk. AB, Depauw U., 1963; MA, Northwestern U., 1966; MDiv, Christian Theol. Sem., 1969; PhD, Columbia U., N.Y.C., 1973. Ordained to ministry Christian Ch., 1969. Pastor First Christian Ch., Youngstown, Ohio, 1973-77; prof. of religion Eureka (Ill.) Coll., 1977-78, dean of coll., 1978-83, prof. religion, 1983—; cons., evaluator North Cen. Assn. of Colls. and Schs., Chgo., 1981—. Contbr. articles to profl. jours. Pres. Eureka Christian Ch., 1989-91, elder, 1979—. Mem. Am. Acad. Religion, Assn. Disciples Theol. Discussion, Ctr. for Process Studies. Avocations: gardening, fishing. Office: Eureka Coll 300 E College Ave Eureka IL 61530

MCCOY, JOE AARON, lay worker; b. Bartley, W.Va., Dec. 19, 1927; s. Stewart Goerge and Mary Margaret (Runion) McC.; m. Hazel Lamb, 1952 (div. 1959); m. Norma Jene Beck, Apr. 13, 1988. Student, Tech. Sch. Cleve., 1956, Tech. Sch. Cleve., 1960. Writer religious tracts, 1950. With U.S. Army, 1948-50. Home: 5107 Boca Chica Blvd # 30 Brownsville TX 78521

MCCOY, MICHAEL RYAN, educator; b. Miami, Sept. 5, 1950; s. Harold Joseph and Naomi (Hensley) McC.; m. Daisy Anne Cox, June 9, 1973; 1 child, Christopher Ryan. BA, Emory & Henry Coll., 1972; MDiv, Princeton Sem., 1975; PhD, Emory U., 1986. Ordained to ministry United Meth. Ch. as deacon, 1973, as elder, 1976. Pastor Vance Cir., Henderson, N.C., 1975-78, LaFayette (Ga.) Cir., 1978-80; prof. Ferrum (Va.) Coll., 1980-86; prof. religion, head dept. Union Coll., Barbourville, Ky., 1986-91; bd. dirs. Ky. Inst. for European Studies. Author: Spirit of These Days, 1990; author: (with others) Twentieth Century Shapers of American Religion, 1989; contbr. articles to profl. jours. Dir. Rainbow Coalition, Ky. 5th Dist., 1989—; commr. Franklin County Recreation Com., Va., 1984-86; treas. Ky. Coun. for Internat. Edn., 1989—. Mem. Am. Acad. Religion, Am. Soc. Ch. History. Democrat. Home: 23 Perkins St Saint Johnsbury VT 05819

MCCOY, STEVEN WAYNE, minister; b. Portland, Oreg., Feb. 2, 1953; s. James Lester and Irene (Shonk) McC.; m. Andrea Morene, June 12, 1976; children: Natalie, Jennifer, Olivia, Andrew. B in Bible Studies, Prairie Bible Inst., Three Hills, Alta., 1973; BA, Southeastern Bible Coll., Birmingham, Ala., 1975; ThM, Dallas Theol. Sem., 1979. Min. Grace Community Ch., Santa Fe, 1979-84, Redwood Valley (Calif.) Community Ch., 1984—. Mem. Christian Action Coun., Ukiah, Calif., 1989—. Republican. Mem. Ind. Fundamentasl Chs. Am. Office: Redwood Valley Community Ch PO Box 183 Redwood Valley CA 95470

MCCRABB, DONALD R., religious ministry director; m. Catherine Olds; 1 child, Andrew Thomas. BA in Religion, BA in Polit. Sci., Wright State U., 1975; MA in Theology, U. Dayton, 1978; grad. program, Jesuit Renewal Ctr., Milford, Ohio, 1984. Cert. catechetical leader, Roman Cath. Ch. Campus min. Newman Ctr., Wright State U., Dayton, Ohio, 1975-76; grad. asst. U. Dayton, 1976-78; pastoral assoc. St. Raphael Cath. Ch., Springfield, Ohio, 1978-82; Cath. campus min. Cen. State U., Wilberforce U., 1982-85; exec. dir. Cath. Campus Ministry Assn., 1985—; mem. planning com. Cath. Edn. Futures Project, 1985-88; bd. dirs., site visitor Commn. on Cert. and Accreditation, U.S. Cath. Conf., 1986—. Home: 265 Illinois Ave Dayton OH 45410 Office: Cath Campus Ministry Assn 3000 College Pk Ave Dayton OH 45469

MCCRACKEN, SHIRLEY ANN ROSS, educational consultant; b. Rochester, N.Y., Aug. 15, 1937; d. Bernard Anthony Ross and Marian Elizabeth (Taliento) Heimann; m. Paul Arthur McCracken, June 25, 1971; children: Donna Ann, Glenn Allan. BA in Math., Nazareth Coll., 1959; MS in Math., Marquette U., Milw., 1968; PhD in Human Behavior, LaJolla U., 1980. Cert. math., Eng. tchr., Calif. Tchr., dept. chair Mount Carmel High Sch., Auburn, N.Y., 1959-68; asst. workshop supr. Jewish Vocat. Svc., Milw., 1968; rehab. counselor Curative Workshop, Milw., 1968-69; tchr. Anaheim (Calif.) Union High Sch. Dist., 1969-72; cons. Anaheim Hills, Calif., 1980-87; dir. religious edn. San Antonio Ch., Anaheim Hills, 1987-90; instr. Orange (Calif.) Catechetical Inst., 1989—; cons. Cath. parishes, Orange County, 1990. Author: Take Off to a New You, 1979, Creative Leadership; poem: The Creative Women, 1977 (award winner 1977); editor: Planning Model for Leadership, Decision Making, Management Training; staff handbook com. Orange Catechetical Inst., 1989—. Treas. Broadmoor Northridge Community Assn., Anaheim Hills, 1976; corr. sec. Anaheim Hills Friends of Libr., 1980; bd. dirs. Friends of Libr. Found., Orange County; mem. Anaheim Mus. 1985-91; mem. elem./jr. high religious edn. adv. bd. Diocese of Orange, Calif., 1990-92; commr. Budget Adv. Commn., City of Anaheim, Calif., 1991—. Mem. AAUW (officer Anaheim br., Calif. State div., Anaheim Hills br.), Nat. Coun. Tchrs. Math., Ebell Club (sec. 1977-78, 91-92, 4th v.p. 1978-79). Avocations: crafts, needlework, travel. Home: 6553 Calle del Norte Anaheim CA 92807

MCCRAW, JAMES ALVIN, minister; b. Collins, Miss., Sept. 23, 1929; s. John Alvin and Alice Maynorine (Keys) McC.; m. Laverne Smith, Dec. 7, 1950; children: Jerry Wayne, Tina Maria McCraw Matune, James Tracy. BS in Math., U. So. Miss., 1955; MA in Indsl. Engring. Edn., U. Ala., Tuscaloosa, 1967. Ordained to ministry So. Bapt. Conv., 1986. Min. edn. Flint River Bapt. Ch., Huntsville, Ala., 1975-77; min. edn. Hillsboro Heights Bapt. Ch., Huntsville,, 1977-81, min. single adults, 1981—; cons. on single adult Ala. Bapt. State Conv. Montgomery, 1981—; mem. nominating com. Madison Bapt. Assn., Huntsville, 1985, chmn., 1986, advisor on single adults, 1986—, chmn. pub. affairs com., 1987, chmn. ombro a ombro com., Huntsville and Sao Paulo, Brazil, 1987-89; ret. civilian employee U.S. Army, Redstone Arsenal, Ala., 1984. Mem. citizens adv. com. Huntsville City Coun., 1985—, mem. nominating com., 1989, chmn., 1990. Staff sgt. USAF, 1949-52. Recipient various certs. of appreciation ch. orgns., Ala., Richmond, Va.; Outstanding Performance award U.S. Army Missile Command, 1965, 69, 75, Career Edn. award, 1966, Mr. Depot award USMC, 1984. Mem. Greater Huntsville Ministerial Assn. Republican. Home and Office: 3302 Fairacres Rd Huntsville AL 35805

MCCREARY, DAVID NEAL, clergyman; b. L.A., Feb. 14, 1945; s. Raymond Arthur and Carrie Roxanne (Fitze) McC.; m. Karen Norris Harrington, Mar. 19, 1978; 1 child, Mary. BA, Occidental Coll., L.A., 1966; postgrad., Grad. Sch. Ecumenical Studies, Bossey, Switzerland, 1969-70; D Ministry, Claremont Coll., L.A., 1974, PhD, 1985. Ordained to ministry Meth. Ch., 1975. Pastor Elgin (Nebr.) United Meth. Ch./Park United Ch. Christ, 1974-76; asst. prof. Nebr. Wesleyan U., Lincoln, 1977, 78-79, 81; pastor Alliance (Nebr.)/Lakeside United Meth. Ch., 1983-86, Aurora (Nebr.)/Marquette United Meth. Ch., 1986-89, Syracuse (Nebr.)/Unadilla United Meth. Ch., 1989—; outreach worker Lincoln Commn. on Aging, 1977-78; fraternal worker Gossner Indsl. Mission, Mainz, West Germany,

1970-72. Occidental fellow U. Mainz, 1965, ecumenical fellow Evang. Ch. Germany, 1970, 71, Dempster fellow United Meth. Ch., 1981, Oxford Inst. scholar United Meth. Ch., 1982. Mem. Am. Acad. Religion., Syracuse C. of C., Lions. Democrat. Home and Office: PO Box 250 Syracuse NE 68446

MCCREESH, DONALD S., religious organization administrator. Chmn. YMCA in Can. Toronto. Office: Young Mens Christian Assoc, Can/2150 Yonge St, Toronto, ON Canada M4S 2A9*

MCCRORY, SARAH GRAYDON, church lay leader, retired lawyer; b. Columbia, S.C., Sept. 30, 1921; d. Clinton Tompkins and Raven (Simkins) Graydon; m. Marvin Lowery McCrory, Dec. 15, 1944; children: Clinton, Raven McCrory Wallace, Margie McCrory Hicks, Alice McCrory Felts, Elliott. AB, Hollins Coll., 1942; LLB, U. S.C., 1944. Bar: S.C. Vestrywoman, jr. warden, sr. warden St. Martin's Parish, Columbia, 1972-75, tchr. adult edn., chmn. long range planning, 1975-88, coord. adult ministries, 1988—; past mem. Episcopal Radio and TV Bd., Atlanta; past chmn. Total Ministry Conf., dep. Diocesan Conv., mem. constn. and canons com. Episcopal Diocese of Upper S.C.; dep. Gen. Conv., Nat. Episcopal Ch., 1973, 79—, past mem. constn. and canons com., chmn. Gen. Conv. Consecration of Bishops, 1988, mem. Nat. Commn. on Racism, 1989—; bd. dirs. Kanuga Confs., N.C., 1983-88, mem. program com., 1986-91, archivist, 1989—, also mem. minorities com. Past chmn. bd. dirs. Speech and Hearing Clinic, Columbia, Sci. Mus., Columbia; past mem. bd. dirs. Columbia Mus. Art; former precinct officer Columbia Dem. Com.; former mem. Habitat for Humanity, Columbia; former mem. bd. dirs. Columbia Day Care. Named Vol. of Yr., Woodman of World, 1973. Mem. Fortnightly Book Club (past pres.), Phi Beta Kappa. Home: 5036 Wittering Dr Columbia SC 29206

MCCUAIG, MALCOLM ADAMS, minister; b. Montreal, Que., Can., May 5, 1936; came to U.S., 1985; s. Lorne Anderson and Dorothy (Adams) McC.; m. Brenda Lang, June 16, 1962 (div. 1984); children: Donna, Karen, Ian; m. Marion Campbell, May 24, 1985. BA, Sir George Williams U., 1958; BD, Presbyn. Coll., 1961; D. Ministry, Christian Theol. Sem., 1971. Ordained to ministry Presbyn. Ch. in Can., 1961. Minister St. Andrew's Presbyn. Ch., Thompson, Man., Can., 1961-63, Knox Presbyn. Ch., Carberry, Man., 1963-65, Kirk of St. James, Charlottetown, P.E.I., Can., 1965-72, Knox Presbyn. Ch., Ottawa, Ont., Can., 1972-85; sr. pastor Old Stone Ch., Cleve., 1985—; chmn. bd. congl. life Presbyn. Ch. in Can., Toronto, Ont., 1978-84. Trustee Greater Cleve. Roundtable, 1987—; mem. Leadership Cleve., 1990; chmn. P.E.I. Labor-Mgmt. Coun., Charlottetown, 1967-72; chaplain, hon. capt. Cleve. City Police, 1986—. Mem. Rotary, Mayfield Golf Club. Home: 12 Pond Dr Rocky River OH 44116 Office: Old Stone Ch 91 Public Sq Cleveland OH 44113 *Gratitude is a practised art, not a gift we are given. If we are not intentional about it, we soon take blessings for granted and end up cynical enough to believe that we deserve our affluence.*

MCCUEN, R. DAVID, priest; b. Phila., Aug. 31, 1953; s. David Harold McCuen and Margorie Vivian (Lobb) Rist; m. Michele Mary Hesselbarth, Dec. 30, 1972; 1 child, Kristina Faith. BSin Zoology, U. Md., 1977; MS in Environ. Studies, So. Ill. U., 1979; MDiv, Va. Theol. Sem., 1990. Ordained priest Episcopal Ch., 1990. Coord. ministry program Episcopal Ch. of St. John the Baptist, Phoenix, 1985-87; seminarian assoc. St. Paul's Episcopal Ch., Washington, 1988-90; curate St. Paul's Episcopal Ch., Bakersfield, Calif., 1990—. Office: St Paul's Episcopal Parish 2216 17th St Bakersfield CA 93301 *Life is the opportunity to learn of the wondrous person of God, and the glorious gift of his love. With each day, as we learn of God, we also receive the opportunity to express our love for him by loving and caring for each other (rightly) in the name of Jesus Christ.*

MCCUISTION, ROBERT WILEY, hospital administrator, management consultant; b. Wilson, Ark., June 15, 1927; s. Ed Talmadge and Ruth Wiley (Bassett) McC.; m. Martha Virginia Golden, June 11, 1949; children: Beth, Dan, Jed. A.B. in History and Polit. Sci, Hendrix Coll., Conway, Ark., 1949; J.D., U. Ark., 1952. Bar: Ark. 1952. Practice in Dermott, Ark., 1952-57; dep. pros. atty. 10th Jud. Dist. Ark., 1953-57; bus. mgr. St. Mary's Hosp., Dermott, 1953-56, asst. administr., 1956-57; administr. Stuttgart (Ark.) Meml. Hosp., 1957-60, Forrest Meml. Hosp., Forrest City, Ark., 1960-68; assoc. administr. St. Edward Mercy Hosp., Ft. Smith, Ark., 1968-70; pres. Meml. Med Center, Corpus Christi, Tex., 1970-79; administr. Methodist Hosp., Mitchell, S.D., 1979-85, cons., 1985-86; mgmt. cons., owner Creative Leadership Concepts, Fayetteville, Ark., 1985—; administr. Cen. United Meth. Ch., Fayetteville, 1986-91; sec. Ark. Hosp. Adminstrs. Forum, 1958-59, pres., 1959-60; pres. Ark. Hosp. Assn., 1964-65, Areawide Health Planning, 1970; v.p. Ark. Conf. Cath. Hosps., 1970; chmn. Twin City Hosp. Council, 1968; v.p. Ark. Assn. Mental Health, 1966-70. Div. chmn. Forrest City United Community Svcs., 1971, Corpus Christi United Way Community Svcs., 1972, DeSoto coun. Boy Scouts Am., Explorer adviser, 1954-57. With USAAF, World War II. Recipient Eminent Leadership award DeSoto Area council Boy Scouts Am., 1956. Mem. Am. Assn. Hosp. Accountants (pres. Ark. chpt. 1957), S.D. Hosp. Assn. (dist. chmn. 1980-81), Mid-West Hosp. Assn. (trustee 1963-65), Am. Coll. Health Execs. (life). Methodist (vice chmn., sec. ofcl. bd. 1957, lay del. S.D. ann. conf. 1980-85). Lodge: Rotary (pres. Forrest City 1964-65). Home and Office: 2545 Ridgely Dr Fayetteville AR 72701

MCCULLOH, GERALD WILLIAM, religion educator,; b. St. Paul, May 3, 1941; s. Gerald Otho and Evelyn (Butler) McC.; m. Karen Jane Smith, June 10, 1967; children: Gerald Jonathan, Heather Emily. BA magna cum laude, Vanderbilt U., Nashville, 1962; MDiv, Harvard U., 1965; MA, U. Chgo., 1968, PhD, 1973. Meth. vicar Campus Ministry Harvard, Cambridge, Mass., 1964; assoc. prof. theology Loyola U. Chgo., 1968—, assoc. Protestant chaplain univ. ministry, 1974-90, assoc. dir. Univ. Rsch. Svc., 1990—. Author: Christ's Person & Life Work in the Theology of Albrecht Ritschl, 1990; contbr. articles and revs. to religious publs. Chmn. coun. Kilmer Sch., Chgo., 1976-78; bd. dirs. Rogers Park Community Coun., Chgo., 1980-84; v.p. bd. trustees United Ch. Rogers Park, 1977-82; elder Tenn. Conf. United Meth. Ch., 1969—. Alfred P. Sloan Found. scholar Vanderbilt U., 1958-62; English Speaking Union fellow Cambridge U., 1970-71, NEH fellow Jewish Theol. Sem., 1978-79. Mem. Am. Acad. Religion (treas. 19th century theology group, sect. chmn. theology and philosophy of religion Midwest region 1987—), Am. Soc. Ch. History. Home: 5432 Warren St Morton Grove IL 60053-3639 Office: Loyola U Chgo 6525 N Sheridan Rd Chicago IL 60626 *The service of God in the task of civilization begins anew each day. Religion sustains the call to participate, offers a means to respond and provides a consolation for those so engaged.*

MCCULLOUGH, CHARLES FRANKLIN, minister; b. Roswell, N.Mex., Sept. 9, 1952; s. Lloyd Franklin and Susan Lavern (Hatenborg) McC.; m. Karen Berea Irwin, Dec. 20, 1975; children: Sarah, Joy, Grace. BA, John Brown U., 1975; MDiv, Southwestern Bapt. Theol., Seminary, Ft. Worth, 1981, PhD, 1987. Minister to youth Handley Bapt. Ch., Ft. Worth, 1978-81; teaching fellow Southwestern Bapt. Theol. Seminary, Ft. Worth, 1982-85; instr. Tarrant County Jr. Coll., Ft. Worth, 1983-84; pastor White Rock Bapt. Ch., Los Alamos, N.Mex., 1986—. Bd. dirs. YMCA, Los Alamos, 1989—; pres. Los Alamos Minsterial Alliance, 1988, 1992. Office: White Rock Bapt Church 80 La Paloma Los Alamos NM 87544

MCCULLOUGH, DAVID JAMES, music minister; b. Caviti City, Philippines, Oct. 28, 1962; s. James Irving McCullough and Nina Charlene (Reed) Russell; m. Megan Lynn Spruill, Nov. 30, 1985; 1 child, Elizabeth Claire. BS in Ch. Music, Trevecca Nazarene Coll., 1986, postgrad., 1987-89. Pub. rels. rep. Trevecca Nazarene Coll., Nashville, 1983-85; minister of music Agape Fellowship Ch., Nashville, 1985-86, 87—, assoc. pastor, young adult coord., adminstr. help for needy, 1987—; gospel singer "Spirit" Williams & Assocs., Nashville, 1986-87; worship leader Ashland City Wide Revival, 1985-86. Vol. pilot ARC, Nashville, 1989—. Mem. Aircraft Owners and Pilots Assn., Phi Mu Alpha. Republican. Home: 4539 Sears Rd Pegram TN 37143 Office: Agape Fellowship Ch 645 Old Hickory Blvd Nashville TN 37209

MCCULLOUGH, DONALD WAYNE, minister; b. Ellensburg, Wash., May 10, 1949; s. John Howard and Ione Dorthea (Isaak) McC.; m. Karen Lee Jensen, June 19, 1970; children: Jennifer Lee, Joy Marie. BA, Seattle Pacific U., 1971; MDiv, Fuller Theol. Sem., Pasadena, Calif., 1974; PhD, Edinburgh U., Scotland, 1980. Ordained to ministry Presbyn. Ch. U.S.A. 1974. Pastor

Rainier Beach Presbyn. Ch., Seattle, 1974-78, Solana Beach (Calif.) Presbyn. Ch., 1980—. Author: Waking from the American Dream, 1988, Finding Happiness in the Most Unlikely Places, 1990; contbr. articles to profl. jours. Mem. Presbytery San Diego. Democrat. Home: 606 S Nardo Solana Beach CA 92075 Office: Solana Beach Presbyn Ch 120 Stevens Ave Solana Beach CA 92075

MCCULLOUGH, LELAND GRAVES, III, minister; b. McAllen, Tex., May 7, 1954; s. Leland Graves Jr. and Mary Elizabeth (White) McC.; m. Emily Ann Fulgham, Dec. 21, 1977; children: Elizabeth Brown Dossett, Leland Graves IV. BA, Washington & Lee U., 1976; DMin, Union Theol. Sem., Richmond, Va., 1983. Ordained to ministry Presbyn. Ch., 1982. Pastor 1st Presbyn. Ch., Spearman, Tex., 1982-87, Winnfield, La., 1987—. Republican. *God is love and in Him is no darkness at all. And this is eternal life, even now, that we know God and Jesus Christ whom He has sent. To know God is to love Him first and wholly and to love neighbor as self second.*

MCCULLOUGH, MICHAEL WILLIAM, JR., minister, educator; b. Chgo., May 5, 1950; s. Albert Charles and Magnolia Salome Jane (Ingraham) Henry; m. Denise Sharon Desvignes, July 23, 1977. AA in Speech and Broadcast Communications, Kennedy-King Coll., 1970; BA in Interpersonal Communications, Trinity Coll., Deerfield, Ill., 1988; MA in Religion cum laude, Trinity Evang. Div. Sch., Deerfield, Ill., 1988; MDiv in Urban Ministry, No. Bapt. Theol. Sem., 1990. Ordained to ministry Christian Ch., 1971; cert. urban pastoral educator; cert. tchr., Ill. Exec. dir. Gospel Crusader Revivals Inc., Chgo., 1971-79; assoc. pastor, youth pastor Southside Tabernacle, Chgo., 1977-78; assoc. min. Hyde Park Fellowship, Chgo., 1978-79; sr. pastor Gospel Crusader Revival Tabernacle, Chgo., 1979-88, Metro-Outreach Fellowship Ch., Chgo., 1988—; substitute tchr. South Suburban Sch. Dists. 133, 147, 149, 167, 171, 172, Chgo., 1989—; mem., counselor Ministerial Adv. Coun. Chgo. Voc. High Schs., 1986—; exec. dir. Metro Evang. Svc. Sems. and Global Endeavors, Inc., Chgo., 1988; urban ch. cons. M.E.S.S.A.G.E., Inc., 1988—; v.p., acad. dean, prof. Bible, theology, Christian edn. Urban Inst. in Christian Studies, 1988—; instr. religion and humanities Prairie State Coll., Chicago Heights, Ill, 1991—; co-founder, dir. Washington-Westgate Scholastic Fund, 1991—. Urban scholar Trinity Coll., 1987-88; Urban scholar Sem. Consortium for Urban Pastoral Edn., 1988-89; Faculty scholar No. Bapt. Theol. Sem., 1988-90. Mem. Roseland Clergy Assn., Nat. Assn. Black Seminarians, Nat. Black Evang. Assn., Am. Acad. Religion, N.Am. Soc. for Ch. Growth, Soc. for Bibl. Lit., Soc. for Pentecostal Studies, Trinity Evang. Div. Sch. Alumni Assn., No. Bapt. Theol. Sem. Alumni Assn., Sem. Consortium for Urban Pastoral Edn. Alumni Assn. Office: MESSAGE Inc PO Box 289050 Chicago IL 60628-9050

MCCULLOUGH, MURRAY LESTER, minister, church music director; b. Miami Beach, Fla., Mar. 29, 1943; s. Murray Jefferson and Jessie Elmira (Powers) McC.; m. Jo Ann Rush, Feb. 25, 1966; 1 child, Melody Ann McCullough Revell. BA, Fla. State U., 1965; M in Ch. Music, Southwestern Bapt. Theol. Sem., 1976; postgrad., Westminster Choir Coll., 1982. Ordained to ministry So. Bapt. Conv., 1974. Min. music Parkway Bapt. Ch., Tallahassee, Fla., 1963-65; interim min. music Allapattah Bapt. Ch., Miami, Fla., 1965-66; min. music and youth Midland Park Bapt. Ch., North Charleston, S.C., 1966-67; min. music El Camino Bapt. Ch., Sacramento, 1968-69, Trinity Bapt. Ch., Ft. Worth, 1970-72, Murray Hill Bapt. Ch., Jacksonville, Fla., 1972-83; assoc. dir. dept. ch. music Fla. Bapt. Conv., Jacksonville, 1983-88; dir. dept. ch. music Ark. Bapt. State Conv., Little Rock, 1988—; conf. leader Fla. Bapt. Conv., 1975-88, Bapt. Sunday Sch. Bd., Nashville, 1983—; choral condr. Christian Arts, Inc, New Hyde Park, N.Y., 1982; dir. Fla. Bapt. Singing Men, Jacksonville, 1976=88, Master' Singers, Little Rock, 1988—. Contbr. articles to profl. jours.; composer, arranger sacred music. Bd. dirs. ARC, Charleston, 1966, Air Force Aid Soc., Sacramento, 1968-69. Capt. USAF, 1966-70. Mem. ASCAP, Am. Choral Dirs. Assn., Am. Guild of English Handbell Ringers, Fla. Bapt. Ch. Music Conf. (sec. 1981-83), So. Bapt. Conv. Music Conf. (denominational rep. 1988—), So. Bapt. Conv. State Music Dirs.' Fellowship (pres. 1991-92). Avocations: golf, composing, racquet ball. Home: 8804 Old Spanish Trail Little Rock AR 72207 Office: Ark Bapt State Conv 525 W Capitol Little Rock AR 72201

MCCULLY, JOHN RAYMOND, JR., deacon, biblical literature educator; b. Louisville, Miss., Mar. 14, 1935; s. John Raymond and Hazel Gertrude (Warner) McC.; m. Ruth Barlow, June 2, 1957; children: Joy Lyn, Suzanne Cheryl, John David. Ba, Miss. Coll., 1957; MA, U. Miss., 1960; PhD, Rice U., 1976. Ordained deacon Roman Cath. Ch., 1979. Deacon Archdiocese Dubuque, Ames, Iowa, 1979—; asst. prof. Bibl. lit. Iowa State U., Ames, 1968—; tchr. First Bapt. Ch., Oxford, Miss., 1957-60, tchr., deacon, Starkville, Miss., 1960-64; tchr., deacon Willow Meadows Bapt. Ch., Houston, 1964-68, First Bapt. Ch., Ames, 1968-76, St. Cecilia Cath. Ch., Ames, 1979—; bd. mem. Cath. Charities Archdiocese Dubuque, 1987—; regional rep. Diaconal Bd. Deacons, Dubuque, 1989—. Mem. Cath. Bibl. Assn., Medieval Assn. Midwest (pres. 1988-89, v.p. 1989-90), KC. Democrat. Home: 1214 Wilson Ames IA 50010

MCCUMONS, BRENDA K., youth pastor; b. Brown City, Mich., Aug. 13, 1951; d. Orville B. and Leta Jane (Hollenbeck) McAllister; m. John D. McCumons, Sept. 5, 1970. ASN, Lansing (Mich.) Community Coll, 1972. Sun. sch. tchr. United Missionary Ch., Brown City, Mich., 1965-69; youth pastor Christian Ch., Lapeer, Mich., 1984—; staff nurse emergency dept. Lapeer Reg. Hosp., 1979—; owner Nutrition Plus Co., Lapeer, 1982—. Home and Office: 91 Hartley Lapeer MI 48446

MCCUNE, BARRY LYNN, minister; b. Bluffton, Ind., Feb. 23, 1952; s. Harold Kenneth McCune and Jeanette Allebelle (Lantz) Johnson; m. Andrea Lee Sprunger, June 13, 1975; children: Holly Marie, Shauna Leigh, Carmen Joy. Student, Ind. U.-Purdue U., Ft. Wayne, Ind., 1971-72; BA, Summit Christian Coll., Ft. Wayne, 1978; postgrad., Grace Theol. Sem., Winona Lake, Ind., 1981-82, Huntington (Ind.) Coll., 1985—. Lic. to ministry Missionary Ch. Inc., 1987, ordained 1989. Pastor Petroleum (Ind.) United Meth. Ch., 1984-87, Trinity Missionary Ch., Burton, Mich., 1987—; dir. Wells County Migrant Ministry, Bluffton, Ind., 1985-87. With USAF, 1970-76. Republican. Home: 4447 Killarney Park Dr Burton MI 48529 Office: Trinity Missionary Ch 2077 E Bristol Rd Burton MI 48529 *One of the greatest challenges the Christian faces today is to stand on the solid ground of God's Holy Word, the Bible, against all evil and the evil powers of darkness, so that people will see the truth about the Lord Jesus Christ - that He is their only hope.*

MCCUNE, GEORGE WASHINGTON, JR., minister; b. Spring Valley, N.Y., Dec. 7, 1921; s. George Washington and Sadie A. (Shadboldt) McC.; m. Margaret Virginia Graves, Aug. 1, 1947; children: Sharon Lynn, Scott Leigh, Stephen George. Student, Bob Jones Coll., 1941-45; AB, Ea. Bapt. Sem., Phila., 1946; ThM, Bibl. Sem. N.Y.C., 1950. Ordained to ministry So. Bapt. Conv., 1945. Min., pastor First Congl. Ch., Spring Valley, N.Y., 1947-49; pastor Tallman (N.Y.) Congl. Ch., 1947-50; missionary Conservative Bapt. Fgn. Mission Soc., Wheaton, Ill., 1950-81; assoc. pastor Wieuca Rd. Bapt. Ch., Atlanta, 1981—; missionary Japan Conservative Bapt. Fgn. Missionary Soc., Wheaton, 1950-54, mid-west and so. rep., 1956-81. Republican. Home: 1200 Ridgefield Dr Roswell GA 30075 Office: Wieuca Rd Bapt Ch 3626 Peachtree Rd NE Atlanta GA 30326 *The Bible had a life changing influence in my life style, directing me in a positive way to share its contents with others nationally as well as overseas.*

MCCURDY, KAREN REA, minister, religion educator; b. Mo., Aug. 25, 1938; d. Guy Tricillian and Phyllis Maxine (Muckenheiter) Shiverdecker; m. Terrell Eugene McCurdy; children: Terra Jean, Karen Rae, Victoria Lynn, Michael Lee, Lorelie Marie. Co-pastor Calvary Grace Church of Faith, Joplin, Mo., 1987—, tchr. Sch. Evangelism, 1990—; secy./treas. Terry McCurdy Ministries, Joplin, Mo. Author 16 numerous religious texts. Nondenom./Full Gospel-Calvary Grace Ch. of Faith. Home: 2101 N Brownell Joplin MO 64801-1228 Office: Terry McCurdy Ministries 2101 N Brownell Joplin MO 64801-1228 *In this pressurized decade there is truly a place of refuge and peace! Whether a person is well educated and seemingly secure...or not, this place is no respecter of persons. It is the Word of the Living God of the Universes, the Bible!.*

MCCURLEY, TOM, minister; b. Gloster, Miss., Mar. 13, 1941; s. Clinton Eugene and Willie Virginia (Freeman) McC.; m. Donna Mae Shill, May 12, 1963; children: Stephen Todd, Clinton Jai, Brent Wesley. BA, Miss. Coll., 1970; MDiv, New Orleans Bapt. Theol. Sem., 1975. Ordained to ministry So. Bapt. Conv., 1963. Min. 1st Bapt. Ch., Jeanerette, La., 1972-73, Soc. Hill Bapt. Ch., Oakvale, Miss., 1974-77, West Ellisville (Miss.) Bapt. Ch., 1977-81, Calvary Bapt. Ch., West Point, Miss., 1981-85, Williamsville Bapt. Ch., Kosciusko, Miss., 1986-91, 1st Bapt. Ch., Oakdale, La., 1991—; moderator Clay County Bapt. Assn., West Point, 1983-85; mem. exec. com. Miss. Bapt. Conv. Bd., Jackson, 1984-85. Mem. Attala Bapt. Assn. (moderator 1987-89, dir. pastoral ministry 1989). Democrat. Home: 515 Azalea Pl Oakdale LA 71463 Office: 1st Bapt Ch 117 S 12th St Oakdale LA 71463

MCCUTCHEON, ELWYN DONOVAN, minister; b. Paden, Miss., Sept. 14, 1912; s. Samuel Powell and Callie Americus (Gipson) McC.; m. Hattye Gertrude White, July 21, 1940; 1 child, Martha Sue McCutcheon Perry. Grad. high sch., Tishomingo, Miss. Ordained to ministry Primitive Bapt. Ch., 1948. Pastor Bethel Primitive Bapt. Ch., Bruce, Miss., 1948-49, Laodicea Primitive Bapt. Ch., Springs (Thaxton), Miss., 1949—; dir. Harmony Valley Singing Schs., Pontotoc, Miss., 1970-90. Author: (booklets) Doctrine of Grace, 1965, This We Believe, 1982, From Sonship to Discipleship, 1990; contbr. articles to profl. publs. Home: County Rd 209 PO Box 35 Thaxton MS 38871-0035

MCCUTCHEON, JAMES NORTON, minister; b. N.Y.C., Mar. 10, 1929; s. Chester Sample and Sarah Anne (McCartney) McC.; m. Janet Marie Emery, Jan. 12, 1963; children: James Norton, Janet Marie, George Chester. BS in Indsl. Adminstrn., Yale U., 1950; MDiv, Union Theol. Seminary, 1956; ThM, Harvard U., 1960. Assoc. min. South Congl. Ch., Pittsfield, Mass., 1956-60; sr. min. Cen. Ch., Worcester, Mass., 1960-70, 1st Congl. Ch., Kalamazoo, 1970-78, Wayzata (Minn.) Community Ch., 1978—. Author: The Pastoral Ministry, 1978. Mem. Soc. Bibl. Lit. Mem. Christian Ch. Home: 2148 Sheridan Hills Rd Wayzata MN 55391

MCDADE, ROBERT GARY, minister; b. Pine Bluff, Ark., Sept. 2, 1951; s. Robert Ed McDade; m. Sheila Lynn Walker, Dec. 25, 1970; children: Jason, Jared. BA in Bible Studies, Freed-Hardeman U., Henderson, Tenn., 1979; MA, Ala. Christian Sch. Religion, 1985. Minister Hillsboro Ch. of Christ, Hillsboro, Tenn., 1979-82, Gragg Ave. Ch. of Christ, Memphis, 1982—. Served with USN, 1970-76. Home: 3610 Kipling Memphis TN 38128 Office: Gragg Ave Ch of Christ 3802 Gragg Ave Memphis TN 38108

MCDANIEL, ANTHONY LAMAR, music and youth minister; b. Balt., Mar. 7, 1965; s. Elmond Lamar and Ardys Clarene (Becker) McD.; m. Kendra De Ann Houck, June 23, 1989; 1 child, Alivia De Ann. BME, Lee Coll., 1987. Lic. to ministry Ch. of God, 1988. Min. of music and youth East Calhoun (Ga.) Ch. of God, 1986-88, Univ. Ch. of God, Tampa, Fla., 1988-89, Pleasantdale Ch. of God, Atlanta, 1989-91, Evang. Temple Ch. of God, Balt., 1991—. Named Nat. Teen Talent Choir Winner Internat. Youth and Christian Edn. Dept., 1988. Mem. Mins. of Music Assn., Nat. Youth Leaders Assn. (del. 1986—). Republican. Home: 4404 Pintail Ct Baltimore MD 21237 Office: Evang Temple Ch of God 7000 Rossville Blvd Baltimore MD 21237 *All I can be, all the time, everywhere, for the benefit of others and myself and for the promotion of the principles Jesus Christ so well exemplified when He walked this earth.*

MCDANIEL, ARLIE LEO, clergyman; b. Lonoke, Ark., Oct. 7, 1915; s. Maud L. and Louverna (Stringer) McD.; m. Ella Mae Owens, Dec. 25, 1939; children: Arlie Leo, Alana McDaniel Combs, Angela McDaniel Cyr, Alice Ruth, Adrian Owen, Arden Allen, Anson Mark. AB, Baylor U., 1942; postgrad., Golden Gate Bapt. Sem., 1955-57; DD (hon.), Calif. Bapt. Coll., 1969. Ordained to ministry Bapt. Ch. Pastor Harvard-Terrace Ch., Fresno, Calif., 1952-57, First Ch., Barstow, Calif., 1957-60; exec. sec.-treas. Calif. Bapt. Found., Fresno, 1960-62; pastor Bethel Ch., Escondido, Calif., 1962-67, 1st So. Bapt. Ch., Ventura, Calif., 1967—; mem. exec. bd. Ark. Bapt. Conv., 1950-52; pres. So. Bapt. Gen. Conv. Calif., 1957-58, pres. bd. dirs. 1957-58; pres. Calif. Child care and family svcs. So. Bapts. Calif. 1967-68; pres. bd. dirs. Calif. Bapt. Found., 1958-60, bd. dirs., 1962—. With U.S. Army, 1931-34, 42-46. Mem. Masons, Kiwanis (bd. dirs.). Republican. Home: 298 N Aliso St Ventura CA 93001 Office: 65 S MacMillan St Ventura CA 93003

MCDANIEL, CHARLES EDWIN, minister; b. Martinsville, Va., Nov. 1, 1937; s. Charlie J. and Dorothy (Vaughan) McD.; m. Illa Faye Hildebrand, Nov. 14, 1939; children: Michael David, Michelle Diedre. BA, Washington Bible Coll., 1964; ThM, Capital Bible Seminary, Lanham, Md., 1979; PhD, Internat. Seminary, Plymouth, Fla., 1991. Ordained to ministry So. Bapt. Conv., 1967. Pastor Union Community Ch., North Beach, Md., 1964-77, Hollies Bapt. Ch., Keller, Va., 1971-74, Fairport Bapt. Ch., Reedville, Va., 1974-84, Friendship Bapt. Ch., Drakes Branch, Va., 1984—; leader Summer Missionary Inst., Vancouver Island, Can., 1960; counselor Pastoral Counseling and Care Sch., Lynchburg, Va., 1985-90. Vol. fireman Reedville (Va.) Fire Dept., 1974-76; active Boy Scouts Am., Reedville, 1974-76; vol. tchr. Literacy Vols. of Am., Keysville Southside, Va., 1988-91; counselor Counseling Support Group, Va. Bapt. Hosp., Lynchburg, 1985. Republican. Home: Rte 1 PO Box 196A Drakes Branch VA 23927 Office: Friendship Bapt Ch Rte 1 PO Box 196A Drakes Branch VA 23937 *Life seems like a beach at times; the sands keep changing and shifting, the tide comes and goes on a constant pattern, harder at times, gentle at others. But the shore is always there. Life may change, get rough and unbearable at times, but life goes on and God, who never changes, is always there.*

MCDANIEL, GEORGE WILLIAM, priest; b. Washington, Iowa, May 4, 1942; s. Merritt Eugene and Dolores Marie (Keifer) McD. BA, St. Ambrose U., Davenport, Iowa, 1966; MA, Aquinas Inst. Theology, Dubuque, Iowa, 1974, U. Iowa, 1977; PhD, U. Iowa, 1985. Ordained priest Roman Cath. Ch., 1970. Assoc. pastor St. Peter's Cath. Ch., Keokuk, Iowa, 1970-73, St. Patrick's Cath. Ch., Ottumwa, Iowa, 1973-74; dean students St. Ambrose U., Davenport, 1974-76, assoc. dir. devel, 1976-77, instr. history, 1977-82, asst. prof. history, 1982-89, assoc. prof. history, 1989—; rector St. Ambrose Sem. Davenport, 1989—; mem. Nat. Com. Rituals & Emblems, 1982-84, Lambda Chi Alpha. Pres. alumni bd. Lambda Chi Alpha U. Iowa, 1983-86. Hoover scholar, 1982, 85. Mem. Orgn. Am. Historians, Am. Hist. Assn., State Hist. Soc. Iowa (pres. 1984-86, trustee 1981-86, 88-91), U.S. Capitol Hist. Assn., Victorian Soc. Iowa, Lambda Chi Alpha. Home: 518 W Locust St Davenport IA 52803 Office: St Ambrose U 518 W Locust Davenport IA 52803

MCDANIEL, JUNE E., religious studies educator; b. N.Y.C., June 26, 1952; d. Murray Van and Sylvia Harriet (Feintuck) Steckman; m. Robert McDaniel (div); m. James M. Denosky, Mar. 26, 1987. BA, SUNY, Albany, 1974; MTS, Emory U., Atlanta, 1980; PhD, U. Chgo., 1986. Lectr. U. Chgo., 1986-87; rsch. assoc. U. Ill. Med. Ctr., Chgo., 1987-88; lectr. DePaul U., Chgo., 1987-88; asst. prof. religious studies Coll. Charleston (S.C.), 1988—; steering com. Ritual Studies Group, AAR, 1987-89, chmn., 1989—. Author: Madness of the Saints, 1989; contbr. articles to profl. jours. Coll. Charleston grantee, 1990, 89; U. Chgo. S. Asian Studies grantee, 1984; Am. Inst. Indian Studies grantee, 1983. Mem. Am. Acad. Religion, Assn. Asian Studies, Soc. for Tantric Studies. Avocations: painting, writing, piano, white-water rafting. Office: Dept Philosophy/Religion 16 Glebe St Charleston SC 29424

MCDANIEL, MICHAEL CONWAY DIXON, bishop, theologian; b. Mt. Pleasant, N.C., Apr. 8, 1929; s. John Henry and Mildred Juanita (Barrier) McD.; m. Marjorie Ruth Schneiter, Nov. 26, 1953; 1 son, John Robert Michael. B.A., U. N.C., 1951; B.D., Wittenberg U., 1954; M.A., U. Chgo., 1969, Ph.D., 1978; D.D. (hon.), Lenoir-Rhyne Coll., 1983; LL.D., Belmont Abbey Coll., 1984. Ordained to ministry United Lutheran Ch. in America, 1954. Pastor Faith Luth. Ch., Faith, N.C., 1954-58, Ch. of the Ascension, Savannah, Ga., 1958-60; assoc. dir. evangelism United Luth. Ch. in Am., N.Y.C., 1960-62; sr. pastor Edgebrook Luth. Ch., Chgo., 1962-67; prof. Lenoir-Rhyne Coll., Hickory, N.C., 1971-82; pastor, guest lectr. Wittenberg U., Springfield, Ohio, 1970-71; Raymond Morris Bost disting. prof. Lenoir-Rhyne Coll., Hickory, N.C., 1982, dir. Ctr. for Theology, prof., 1991—; bishop N.C. Luth. Ch. in Am., Salisbury, 1982-87; bishop N.C. Evang. Luth. Ch. Am., Salisbury, 1988-91, chmn. cons. bishops governing council, 1987-

89; chmn. humanities div. Lenoir-Rhyne Coll., 1973-82; cons., grant coord. NEH, 1977-79; master tchr. Hickory Humanities Forum, 1981—; chmn. humanities div. Lenoir-Rhyne Coll., 1973-82; chmn. task force on ecumenical and interfaith relationships Commn. Forming a New Luth. Ch., 1983-87; rep. Luth. Orthodox Dialogue In U.S.A., 1983—; chmn., cons. bishops governing coun. Evang. Luth Ch. Am., 1987-89. d. Author: Welcome to the Lord's Table, 1972. Mem. Englewood Human Relations Council, N.J., 1959-60; pres., bd. trustees Edgebrook Symphony, Chgo., 1965-67; sec. Chgo. Astron. Soc., 1966-67; pres. Community Concerts Assn., Hickory, N.C., 1977-80. Served to sgt. U.S. Army, 1946-48, Korea. Luth. World Fedn. fellow, 1967-69, Mansfield Coll. fellow U. Oxford, 1989; named Vol. of the Yr., Western Piedmont Symphony, 1982; recipient Disting. Alumnus award Trinity Luth. Sem., 1990. Home: 125 42d Ave Cir NE Hickory NC 28601 Office: Lenoir-Rhyne Coll Hickory NC 28603 *Since Christian faith is a joyous relationship with God, Christian hope is courageously counting on God's promises, and Christian love a daily adventure. The Christian approaches each aspect of life as An Adventure in Courageous Joy.*

MCDANIEL, NEIL BLAKE, lay minister; b. Norman, Okla., Oct. 30, 1954; s. Neil Owen and Nina Faye (Liddeke) McD.; m. Kathleen Garza, Dec. 10, 1983. BS in Edn., U. Tex., 1976; MA in Bibl. Studies, Dallas Theol. Sem., 1984; postgrad., U. Tex., 1977-78. Campus intern staff The Navigators, Austin, Tex., 1979-80; coll. minister Grace Covenant Ch., Austin, Tex., 1982-86; founder, sr. pastor Univ. Bible Ch., Austin, Tex., 1989—; sponsor Malaysian/Singaporean Christian Fellowship, Austin, 1984-86; founder, sponsor Campus Vision, Austin, 1986—; deacon, vice chmn. First Evang. Free Ch., Austin, 1987, elder, vice chmn., 1988. Liaison Tex. Union Adv. Coun., Austin, 1991. Houston Endowment scholar, 1972-74. Home: 12420 Thompkins Austin TX 78753 Office: Univ Bible Ch 4015 Guadalupe Austin TX 78751 *The church in the United States at the close of the twentieth century is on the verge of impotence. We desperately need an infusion of virility from men and women with Biblical vision, wholehearted commitment and personal holiness.*

MCDANIELS, B. T., bishop. Bishop Northeastern Nebr. region Ch. of God in Christ, Omaha. Office: Ch of God in Christ 1106 N 31st St Omaha NE 68103

MC DAVID, JOEL DUNCAN, retired bishop, clergyman; b. Georgetown, Ala., June 10, 1916; s. Harry and Ola Elizabeth (McCaskill) McD.; m. Milah Dodd Gibson, Aug. 29, 1942; children—Ben A., Joel G., Karen Anne. B.A., Millsaps Coll., 1941; B.D., Emory U., 1944; D.D. (hon.), Birmingham So. U., 1959, Fla. So. Coll., 1973, Bethune Cookman Coll., 1973, Millsaps Coll., 1976, Emory U., 1981. Ordained to ministry Methodist Ch., 1944. Pastor in Grand Bay, Ala., 1944-46; pastor in Toulminville, Ala., 1946-50, Auburn, Ala., 1950-58, Montgomery, Ala., 1958-66; pastor in Dauphin Way Ch., Mobile, Ala., 1966-72; bishop United Meth. Ch., Lakeland, Fla., 1972-80, Atlanta Area, 1980-84; churchman in residence Candler Sch. Theology, Emory U., 1984—; instr. Auburn U., Ala., 1950-58; mem. Ala. Ethics Commn., 1966-67. Author: Waiting, 1969. Bd. dirs. YMCA, 1959-72, ARC, 1955-58, Family Guidance, 1961-65; trustee Huntingdon Coll., 1951-72, Fla. So. Coll., 1972—, Bethune Cookman Coll., 1972—, Emory U., 1972—, Mobile Gen. Hosp. Sch. Nursing, 1968-72. Named Man of Yr., Montgomery Ala., 1965. Mem. United Meth. Southeastern Jurisdiction Council (v.p. 1968-72, mem. higher edn. commn. 1956-60, structure commn. 1968-72, gen. conf. del. 1960, 64, 66, 68, 70, 72, gen. bd. discipleship 1972-80, gen. council ministries 1980). Home: 1425 Council Bluff NE Atlanta GA 30345

MCDERMOTT, ELAINE MARY, seniors facility administrator; b. Bklyn., July 30, 1937; d. Alfred Alexander and Mary Cecilia (Jamate) Mashnouk; m. James Thomas McDermott, Aug. 24, 1957; children: John, Joan, William, Mary, Thomas (dec.), Paul. Student, Madonna Coll., 1983. Adminstr. Marian Oakland-West, Farmington Hills, Mich., 1984—; chair St. Michael Visitors to Sick, Southfield, 1985—, eucharistic minister, 1981—. Patient adv. Citizens for Better Care, Detroit, 1975-81, mem. community care com., 1986-88; sec. Sr. Adult Adv. Coun., Southfield, 1985-91; mem. Commn. on Sr. Adults; mem. Farmington Hills Commn. on Aging, 1991. Mem. Mich. Soc. Gerontology. Home: 27745 Cordoba Dr Farmington Hills MI 48334 Office: Marian Oakland-West 29250 W 10 Mile Rd Farmington Hills MI 48336

MCDILL, THOMAS ALLISON, minister; b. Cicero, Ill., June 4, 1926; s. Samuel and Agnes (Lindsay) McD.; m. Ruth Catherine Starr, June 4, 1949; children: Karen Joyce, Jane Alison, Steven Thomas. Th.B., No. Baptist Sem., Oakbrook, Ill., 1951; B.A., Trinity Coll., 1954; M.Div., Trinity Evang. Div. Sch., 1955, DD, 1989; D.Ministries, Bethel Theol. Sem., 1975. Ordained to ministry Evang. Free Ch. Am., 1949. Pastor Community Bible Ch., Berwyn, Ill., 1947-51, Grace Evang. Free Ch., Chgo., 1951-58, Liberty Bible Ch., Valparaiso, Ind., 1959-67, Crystal Evang. Free Ch., Mpls., 1967-76; v.p., moderator Evang. Free Ch. of Am., 1973-74, chmn. home missions bd., 1968-72, chmn. exec. bd., 1973-90, pres., 1976-90, ret., 1990; min. at large Evang. Free Ch. Am., 1991—. Contbr. articles to publs. Chmn. bd. Trinity Coll., Deerfield, Ill., 1974-76; bd. govs. Trinity Western Coll.; bd. dirs. Trinity Evang. Divinity Sch. Mem. Evang. Free Ch. Ministerial Assn., Evang. Ministers Assn., Nat. Assn. Evangelicals (bd. adminstrn. 1976—, mem. exec. com. 1981-88), Greater Mpls. Assn. Evangelicals (bd. dirs., sec. bd. 1969-73). Home: 4246 Goldenrod Ln Plymouth MN 55442 Office: 6421 45th Ave N Minneapolis MN 55428

MCDONALD, ALONZO LOWRY, JR., business executive; b. Atlanta, Aug. 5, 1928; s. Alonzo Lowry Sr. and Lois (Burrell) McD.; m. Suzanne Moffitt, May 9, 1959; four children. AB in Journalism, Emory U., 1948; MBA with distinction, Harvard U., 1956. Asst. to sales mgr. air conditioning div. Westinghouse Electric Corp., Staunton, Va., 1956-57; Western zone mgr. Westinghouse Electric Corp., St. Louis, 1957-60; assoc. N.Y. office McKinsey & Co., Inc., 1960-64, prin. London office, 1964-66, mng. prin. Zurich Office, 1966-68, mng. dir. Paris Office, 1968-73; mng. dir., chief exec. officer of firm worldwide, 1973-76; dir. N.Y. Office, 1976-77; dep. spl. trade rep., also ambassador in charge U.S. del. Tokyo round of Multilateral Trade Negotiations, 1977-79; acting spl. trade rep. Washington, 1979; asst. to Pres. U.S., White House staff dir., 1979-81; mem. faculty Harvard U. Grad. Sch. Bus. Adminstrn., Boston, 1981; pres. The Bendix Corp., Southfield, Mich., 1981-83; chmn., chief exec. officer Avenir Group, Inc., Bloomfield Hills, Mich., 1983—. Vestry Am. Cathedral in Paris, 1970-73; vestry, warden St. Joseph of Arimathea Episcopal Ch., Elmsford, N.Y., 1974-77; trustee CED, 1975—; chmn. Williamsburg Charter Found., Washington, 1986-90, Second Watch Found., Burke, Va., 1990—; mem. dean's adv. coun. Harvard U. Div. Sch., Boston, 1989—; internat. bd. dirs. United Way, 1990—. Served with USMCR, 1950-52. Mem. Coun. Fgn. Rels., Trinity Forum (chmn. steering com. 1990—). Office: 5505 Corporate Dr Suite 400 Troy MI 48098

MC DONALD, ANDREW J., bishop; b. Savannah, Ga., Oct. 24, 1923; s. James Bernard and Theresa (McGrael) McD. AB, St. Mary's Sem., Balt., 1945, STL, 1948; JCB, Cath. U. Am., 1949; JCD, Lateran U., Rome, 1951. Ordained priest Roman Cath. Ch., 1948. Consecrated bishop, 1972; curate Port Wentworth, Ga., 1952-57; chancellor Diocese of Savannah, 1952-68; vicar gen., from 1968, vice oficialis, 1952-57, oficialis, 1957; pastor Blessed Sacrament Ch., 1963; named papal chamberlain, 1956, domestic prelate, 1959; bishop Diocese of Little Rock, 1972—. Office: Diocese of Little Rock 2415 N Tyler St PO Box 7239 Little Rock AR 72217

MCDONALD, CHARLES MORRIS, minister; b. Little Rock, Aug. 30, 1948; s. Brooks Henry Morris and Mary Jo (Pruitt) Lanham; m. Anita Raye Gortney, Dec. 12, 1970; 1 child, Lyndsay Ellen. BA in Bible, Mt. Vernon (Ohio) Bible Coll., 1975. Ordained to ministry Internat. Ch. Foursquare Gospel, 1978. Asst. pastor Foursquare Gospel Ch., Little Rock, 1975-77, New Castle, Ind., 1978-79; pastor Foursquare Gospel Ch., Terre Haute, Ind., 1979-82, New Castle, 1982—; divisional supt. Gt. Lakes dist. Indpls. div. Internat. Ch. Foursquare Gospel, New Castle, 1983—; bd. dirs. Mt. Vernon Bible Coll., 1984-87. With USN, 1966-69. Mem. New Castle Ministerial Assn. (treas. 1979, sec. 1983, pres. 1986). Home: 1044 Woodcrest Dr New Castle IN 47362 Office: Foursquare Gospel Ch 3200 S 14th St New Castle IN 47362

MCDONALD, CRAYDON DEAN, pastoral psychologist; b. Denver, Dec. 22, 1946; s. Donald D. and Irene (Dunlavy) McD.; m. Laurie Weston, Dec. 4, 1982; children: Ian, Brendan, Tavis. BFA, Parsons Sch. Design, N.Y.C., 1970; MDiv cum laude, St. Paul Sch. Theology, Kansas City, Mo., 1979; D Ministry, Wesley Theol. Sem., Washington, 1982; PhD, Boston U., 1987. Lic. psychologist, Mass., Wis., Ill.; ordained to ministry United Meth. Ch., 1982. Youth minister United Meth. Ch., 1974-76, minister, 1976-82; pastoral psychologist Worcester (Mass.) Counseling Ctr., 1982-87, Lake Geneva, Wis., 1987—; cons. psychologist Walworth County Human Svcs., Elkhorn, Wis., 1989—; cons. pastoral psychologist Luth. Social Svcs., Elkhorn, 1990—; cons. psychologist Delaven Davian Schs., 1989—, Ecumenical Pastors Assn., Elkhorn, 1989—. Author: Personality and Cognitive Theology, 1982, Type A Coronary Prone Behavior and Narcisism, 1987. Mem. Am. Assn. Pastoral Counselors, Am. Psychol. Assn. (program com. div. 42). Democrat. Home: 1830 Sycamore Twin Lakes WI 53181 Office: 905 Marshall Lake Geneva WI 53147 *I have seldom found what a person does to be as significant as the motivation for doing it.*

MCDONALD, DONALD MICHAEL, minister, consultant; b. Birmingham, Ala., Oct. 4, 1947; s. John Wesley and Lulu (Teague) M.; m. Judith Brown, Aug. 23, 1969; children: Barbara Ann, Amy Lynn, Carol Elizabeth. BA in Indsl. Design, Auburn U., 1971; MBA in Mgmt., Calif. State U., San Bernadino, 1985; MA in Biblical Studies, Internat. Sch. Theology, 1985; postgrad., Tex. A&M U., 1989—. Ordained to Bapt. ministry, 1976. Dir. internat. summer projects Campus Crusade for Christ, San Bernardino, 1972-79; founder, dir. mgmt. discipling Crusade for Christ, San Bernardino, 1980-89; with Texas A&M U., College Station, Tex., 1989; founder, dir. Inter-Dynamics, 1988—. Author: (with others) Magnetic Fellowship, 1988; contbr. articles to profl. jours. Mem. Am. Soc. for Tng. and Devel., Acad. of Mgmt., Am. Mgmt. Assn. Avocations: history, hiking. Office: Tex A&M U Inter-Dynamics care Dept Mgmt College Station TX 77843-4221

MCDONALD, GARY EUGENE, lay missionary; b. Spokane, Sept. 25, 1943; s. Raymond Eugene and Florence Evelyn (Eneroth) McD.; m. Claire Lillette Lucas, Nov. 1969; children: Lisa Sherry, Ryan Gary, Kim Kristine. BA, Eastern Wash. U., 1970; MA, Webster U., 1991. Missionary Seventy Reorganized Ch., Independence, Mo., 1986—; purchasing agt. Allied-Signal Inc., Kansas City, Mo., 1982—. Contbr. articles to profl. jours. Mem. ACLU, Kansas City, 1991. With USNR, 1966-72. Mem. Nat. Assn. Purchasing Mgmt. Democrat. Home: 1701 N Emery Independence MO 64050

MCDONALD, JAMES, minister. Gen. min. Va. Coun. Chs. Inc., Richmond. Office: Va Coun Chs Inc 2321 Westwood Ave Richmond VA 23230*

MCDONALD, JEANNE STANA, lay worker; b. N.Y.C., June 7, 1942; d. Paul and Gertrude Louise (Klein) S.; m. Wallace Hector McDonald, June 29, 1969. Grad. high sch., Wantagh, N.Y. Fleet mgr. Atlantic Fleet Group, West Islip, N.Y., 1986—; treas. Ch. of St. Jude, Wantagh, 1985—, chair Episcopal Charities Appeal, 1987—, vestryman, 1985-90, bldg. com., 1987—, lector, 1988—; del. Diocesean Conv., Garden City, N.Y., 1990. Mem. Nat. Vehicle Leasing Assn., Nat. Assn. Fleet Adminstrs.

MCDONALD, KENNETH MALCOLM, lay worker; b. Abilene, Tex., July 7, 1954; s. Kenneth Lincoln and Mary Annabel (Evans) McD.; m. Rana Kay Parrish, June 23, 1979; children: Kellie Suzanne, Koury Shea. BME, McMurry Coll., Abilene, Tex., 1977; MM, U. Tex., 1978. Music dir Grace United Meth. Ch., El Paso, Tex., 1979-81, St. Paul United Meth. Ch., Abilene, 1981-83, First United Meth. Ch., Pampa, Tex., 1983-88, Polk St. United Meth. Ch., Amarillo, Tex., 1988—; ch. clinician Tex. Choral Dirs. Conv., San Antonio, 1991—; music coord. N.W. Tex. Ann. Conf., Amarillo, 1991. Mem. Fellowship of United Meth. Musicians, Tex. Choral Dirs. Assn., Choristers Guild, Alpha Chi. Home: 6805 Old Kent Rd Amarillo TX 79109 Office: Polk St United Meth Ch 1401 S Polk St Amarillo TX 79109

MCDONALD, LARRY STEVEN, minister; b. Jackson, Miss., Aug. 31, 1956; s. Grady Leo and Elizabeth Eudean (Sullivan) McD.; m. Tina Christine Stewart, May 18, 1985; children: Benjamin, Rebecca. BA, Miss. Coll., 1979; MDiv, Internat. Sch. Theology, San Bernardino, Calif., 1982; DMin, Ref. Theol. Sem., Jackson, Miss., 1987—. Ordained to ministry, So. Bapt. Conv., 1984. Tchr. Jackson (Miss.) Pub. Schs., 1982-84; minister edn. Paul Truitt Bapt. Ch., Pearl, Miss., 1984-85; pastor Cruger (Miss.) Bapt. Ch., 1986-87, County Line Bapt. Ch., Puckett, Miss., 1987-90, Castlewoods Bapt. Ch., Brandon, Miss., 1990—; bd. dirs. Lamb of God Ministries, Jackson, 1982—, Practical Evangelism, Jackson, 1986—; exec. com. Family Life Conf., Jackson, Little Rock, 1991—. Mem. Evang. Theol. Soc., Rankin Bapt. Pastors Assn. (pres. 1991—, exec. com. 1986—, mem. order of bus. com. 1991—, chmn. deacon com. 1989-91), N.W. Rankin Pastors Assn. (treas. 1990-91, pres. 1991—). Office: Castlewoods Bapt Ch 175 Stonecastle Dr Brandon MS 39042

MCDONALD, LEWIS NEWTON, minister; b. Waco, Tex., Mar. 30, 1937; s. Lewis Stephens and Lucy Parks (Moncrief) McD.; m. Patsy Lee Akridge; children: Steven Wayne, David Lewis, John Mark. BA, Baylor U., 1960; BD, Southwestern Bapt. Theol. Sem., 1963, MDiv, 1973. Pastor Reliance Bapt. Ch., Bryan, Tex., 1963-65, South Ave. Bapt. Ch., Pasadena, Tex., 1965-71; sr. min. Oak Grove Bapt. Ch., Bel Air, Md., 1971-90; min. Meml. United Meth. Ch., Poolesville, Md., 1991—; pres. Bapt. Conv. Md., 1980-82. Contbr. articles to profl. jours. Trustee Southwestern Bapt. Theol. Sem., Ft. Worth, 1979-89; fellow Rotary Internat., Pasadena, 1968-71. Recipient Key to the City, City of Pasadena, 1971. Mem. So. Bapt. Conv. (com. on coms. 1974), Bapt. Conv. Md. (preacher ann. sermon. 1976). Avocations: slow-pitch softball, racquetball. Home and Office: PO Box 358 Poolesville MD 20837 *The best word I know to define life is the word "gift." When we finally come to the moment in life's journey when we discover that life is a gift, we stop holding on to life so tightly. We let go enough to learn how to thank God for the gift.*

MCDONALD, PHILLIP WAYNE, minister; b. Bedford, Ind., June 15, 1951; s. Melvin Phillip and Bonetta (Nickell) McD.; m. Thelma Ruth Lee, Oct. 25, 1975; children: April Dawn, Dusty Dawn, Joshua Phillip, Wendy Dawn. Student, Oakland City Coll., 1969; BSL, Ozark Christian Coll., 1973; postgrad., Ind. U., New Albany, 1974-75. Ordained to ministry Ind. Christian Ch., 1974. Youth min. Paoli (Ind.) Christian Ch., 1973-76, Shelby Christian Ch., Shelbyville, Ky., 1976-83, Hillcrest Christian Ch., Bedford, 1983—; dean camp weeks Wonder Valley Ch. Camp, Salem, Ind., 1973-91, dir., 1989-91; coord. tchr. tng. seminar, Shelbyville, 1977; preacher boy chmn. various men's meetings., 1977-91; instr. ARC 1st aide Bedford schs., 1989-91. Author: (booklet) Children's Worship, 1984-91; (manual) The Dating Game, 1987-89; editor Youth News, 1983-91; creator simulation game Journey To Hell, 1985. Chmn. missions Ind. Teen Conv., 1990; treas. So. Ind. Men's Retreat, 1988-91; chmn. Kiamichi Men's Clinic, 1982-85. Recipient several svc. plaques various orgns., Cert. for Svc. Ind. Teen Conv., Indpls., 1987. Mem. So. Ind. Youth Mins.

MCDONALD, RANDY, minister; b. McAllen, Tex., Nov. 3, 1947; s. T.M. and Dorothy (Vaughn) McD.; m. Eva Jacqueline Jordan, Aug. 23, 1978; children: Shea Jordan, Ty Judson. BA, Hardin-Simmons U., 1969; MDiv, Southwestern Bapt. Theol. Sem., Ft. Worth, 1973. Ordained to ministry So. Bapt. Conv., 1972. Evangelist So. Bapt. Conv., 1968-82; min. evangelism 1st Bapt. Ch. Oak Cliff, Dallas, 1982; assoc. pastor Calvary Bapt. Ch., McAllen, 1982-85; pastor Bapt. Temple, McAllen, 1985—; trustee Zephyr Bapt. Encampment, Mathis, Tex., 1989—. Mem. Citizen's Com. on Sexual Edn., McAllen, 1990, 91. Republican. Home: 3208 Goldcrest McAllen TX 78504 Office: Bapt Temple 2001 Trenton Rd McAllen TX 78504

MCDONALD, S(TEPHEN) MATT(HEW), church administrator; b. Evansville, Ind., Mar. 5, 1969; s. David Louis and Donna Sue (Gray) McD. Student, Cen. Bible Coll., Springfield, Mo., 1989—. Music dir., bd. dirs. Youth Encounter the Savior, Ky., 1985—; summer youth pastor, worship leader Chapel Hill United Meth. Ch., Henderson, Ky., 1990—; pianist Yellowcreek Bapt. Ch., Owensboro, Ky., 1987-88; summer youth intern Belleview United Meth. Ch., Smith Mills, Ky., 1988, 89; worship leader St. Pius X, Owensboro, 1987-88; vol. youth sponsor King's Chapel Christian Ctr., 1990—. Home: 826 Lamont Ln Henderson KY 42420 Office: Chapel Hill United Meth Ch 985 Bend Gate Rd Henderson KY 42420

MCDONALD, THERESA BEATRICE (PIERCE) (MRS. OLLIE MCDONALD), church official; b. Vicksburg, Miss., Apr. 11, 1929; d. Leonard C. Pierce and Ernestine Morris Templeton; m. Ollie McDonald, Apr. 23, 1966. Student, Tougaloo Coll., 1946-47, Roosevelt U., 1954-56, 59-62, 64, U. Chgo. Indsl. Rels. Ctr., 1963-64. Vol. rep. Liberty Bapt. Ch., Am. Legion Aux., VA West Side Hosp., Chgo., 1971-73; nat. instr. ushers dept. Prog. Nat. Bapt. Conv. Inc., Washington, 1973-75, nat. sec. ushers dept., 1975-76, v.p. at large, 1980-82, chmn. pers. com., 1982-84; mem. faculty Congress of Christian Edn., 1978-85; mem. pub. rels. staff Liberty Bapt. Ch., Chgo., 1973-79, trustee, 1987—; cons., lectr. in field; guest speaker TV and radio programs. Participant White House Regional Confs., 1961. Recipient Christian Svc. award Prog. Nat. Bapt. Conv. Inc., 1986. Mem. Bethlehem Bapt. Dist. Assn. Chgo. (asst. sec. 1982-84), Ch. Women United in Greater Chgo. (Ecumenical Actions com. 1981-83), Am. Legion (Outstanding Svc. award 1972, 73), Order Ea. Star. Address: 9810 S Calumet Ave Chicago IL 60628

MCDONALD, WILLIAM H., bishop. Bishop Ea. Kansas region Kansas City. Office: Ch of God in Christ 1627 N 78th St Kansas City KS 66112*

MCDONNELL, JOHN MICHAEL, minister; b. Wenatchee, Wash., Aug. 15, 1954; s. William Joseph Sr. and Esther Allene (Walker) McD. BS, U. North Ala., 1985; MDiv in Christian Edn., So. Bapt. Theol. Sem., 1990. Assoc. pastor for edn. and youth 1st Bapt. Ch., Nashville, Ga., 1991—; summer recreation coord. William T. Walker, Louisville, 1987-91. Newspaper columnist, Nashville, 1991. With U.S. Army, 1980-84. Avocation: golf. Home: 106 W Marion Ave Apt A Nashville GA 31639 Office: 1st Bapt Ch 301 W Washington Ave Nashville GA 31639

MCDONOUGH, REGINALD MILTON, religious organization executive; b. Mt. Vernon, Tex., Aug. 16, 1936; s. J.C. McDonough and Gladys (White) Branch; m. Joan Bird, Aug. 28, 1956; children: Michael Keith, Teri Royce. BS, East Tex. Bapt. U., 1957; MRE, New Orleans Bapt. Theol. Sem., 1960, DEd, 1967; DD, U. Richmond, 1988. Ordained to ministry Bapt. Ch. Minister Bapt. Ch., Arcadia, La., 1959-60; instr. East Tex. Bapt. U., Marshall, 1960-61; minister edn. North End Bapt. Ch., Beaumont, Tex., 1961-64; cons. ch. adminstrn. Bapt. Sun. Sch. Bd., Nashville, 1964-65, supr. ch. adminstrn., 1965-78, dept. dir., 1978-80; exec. v.p. exec. com. So. Bapt. Conv., Nashville, 1981-86; exec. dir. Bapt. Gen. Assn. Va., Richmond, 1987—. Author: Working with Volunteer Leaders in the Church, 1976, Keys to Effective Motivation, 1979, A Church on Mission, 1980; editor monthly mag. Bapt. Program, 1981-86. Recipient Eagle Scout award Boy Scouts Am., 1951, Disting. Alumnus award, New Orleans Bapt. Theol. Sem., 1979, Disting. Achievement award East Tex. Bapt. U. Alumni Assn., 1984. Mem. Soc. Religious Orgns. Mgrs. Avocations: flying, skiing, golfing. Home: 12800 Knight Cross Rd Midlothian VA 23113 Office: Va Bapt Gen Bd PO Box 8568 Richmond VA 23226

MCDONOUGH, SHEILA DOREEN, religion educator; b. Calgary, Alta., Can., Dec. 13, 1928; d. Bartly Thomas and Marjore (Simmons) McD.; m. Michel Despland, Sept. 13, 1979; (div. 1986); children—Emma, Alexis. B.A., M.A., Ph.D., McGill U., Montreal, Que., Can. Lectr. Kinnard Coll., Lahore, Pakistan, 1957-60, Selly Oak Coll., Birmingham, Eng., 1963-64; prof. religion Sir George Williams Coll., Concordia U. Montreal, 1964—. Author: Pakistan and the West, 1963; The Authority of the Past, 1970; Muslim Ethics Modernity, 1984. Mem. Am. Acad. Religion, Can. Soc. Study of Religion. Office: Concordia Univ, 1455 W Maisonneuve, Montreal, PQ Canada H3G 1M5

MC DOW, MALCOLM RAY, minister; b. Honey Grove, Tex., Jan. 28, 1936; s. James Luther and Josephine Ivodell (Webb) Mc D.; m. Melba Lee Justice, Dec. 22, 1962; children: Melissa Lee, Melody Lyn. BA, Baylor U., 1958; BD, Southwestern Bapt. Sem., 1962; ThD, New Orleans Bapt. Sem., 1968; postgrad., U. Edinburgh, Scotland, 1966, Oxford U., 1988-89. Ordained to ministry So. Bapt. Conv., 1958. Pastor various chs. Tex., La., 1957-61; youth min. 1st Bapt. Ch., Houston, 1962-63; pastor Cherry Rd. Bapt. Ch., Memphis, 1969-77; dir. evangelism Tenn. Bapt. Conv., 1977-82; prof. evangelism Southwestern Bapt. Theol. Sem., Ft. Worth, 1982—; supr. doctoral students New Orleans Bapt. Sem., 1975-76; speaker So. Bapt. Conv. Trustee, mem. religious adv. bd. Union U., Jackson, Tenn.; pastor advisor Tenn. Brotherhood Dept. Mem. Shelby Bapt. Assn. (chmn. fin. com., chmn. evangelism com.). Home: 7208 Lake Mead Arlington TX 76016 Office: Box 22478 Fort Worth TX 76122

MCDOWELL, DANIEL E., minister; b. Buffalo, N.Y., Nov. 27, 1959; s. Walter Earl McDowell and Mary Freda (Howard) Griffith; m. Terri Lynn Island, May 29, 1981; children: Laura Danielle, Deborah Lynn, Sarah Margaret. BA, Sioux Falls Coll., 1981; MDiv, Eastern Bapt. Seminary, Phila., 1987. Ordained to gospel ministry, Am. Bapt. Ch., 1988. Asst. pastor First Bapt. Ch., North Platte, Nebr., 1981-84; pastoral intern Woodland Presbyn. Ch., Phila., 1985-87; pastor Lincolnville Bapt. Ch., Centerville, Pa., 1987—; pres. Union City (Pa.) Area Ministerium, 1988-91. Bd. dirs. Nebr. Fellowship Christian Athletes, Lincoln, 1983-84; sec./treas. North Platte Ministerial Assn., 1982-84; pres. Eastern Seminary Student Body, 1985-86. Named to Outstanding Young Men of Am., 1983. Mem. Am. Bapt. Minister's Coun. Republican. Home and Office: Rte 2 PO Box 103 Centerville PA 16404

MC DOWELL, JOHN B., bishop; b. New Castle, Pa., July 17, 1921; s. Bernard A. and Louise M. (Hannon) McD. B.A., St. Vincent Coll., 1942, M.A., 1944; M.A., Catholic U. Am., 1950, Ph.D., 1952; Litt.D. (hon.), Duquesne U., 1962; grad., St. Vincent Sem., Latrobe, Pa. Ordained priest Roman Catholic Ch., 1945, consecrated as titular bishop of Tamazuca and aux. bishop of Pitts., 1966—; asst. pastor St. Irenaeus Ch., Oakmont, 1945-49; asst. supt. schs. Diocese of Pitts., 1952-55, supt. schs., 1955-70, vicar for edn., from 1970; now vicar gen.; pastor Epiphany Parish, Pitts., 1969—; papal chamberlain to Pope Pius XII, 1956, to Pope John XXIII, 1958; domestic prelate to Pope Paul VI, 1964; chmn. ad hoc com. on moral values in our soc. Nat. Conf. Cath. Bishops, from 1973, Bishops Com. for Pastoral on Moral Values, from 1976; mem. Internat. Council for Catechesis, from 1975. Co-author elem. sch. religions series, jr. high sch. lit. series, elem. sci. series and elem. reading series; contbr. ednl. articles to various publs.; former editor: Cath. Educator Mag. Bd. dirs. Allegheny County Community Coll.; bd. dirs. Western Pa. Safety Council, Duquesne U. Named Man of Yr. in Religion Pitts., 1970, Educator of Yr., United Pvt. Acad. Schs. Assn., 1978, Man of Yr., Pitts. chpt. KC, 1989. Mem. Nat. Cath. Ednl. Assn., Cath. Ednl. Assn. Pa., Omicron Delta Kappa Gamma Circle (hon.). Office: Epiphany Ch 1018 Centre Ave Pittsburgh PA 15219 also: Chancery Office 111 Blvd of Allies Pittsburgh PA 15222

MCDOWNEY, SHERYL BLOWE, religion educator; b. Petersburg, Va., Nov. 27, 1955; d. Learne Crawford and Grace (Massenburg) Blowe; m. Preston Amos McDowney, Dec. 23, 1989; stepchildren: Romona, Andre. Bs in Criminal Justice, Va. Commonwealth U., 1978; MA in Christian Edn., Presbyn. Christian Edn. Coll., 1985. Dir. Christian Edn. Zion Bapt. Ch., Richmond, Va., 1983-85, Bethany Bapt. Ch., Bklyn., 1985-87, Bapt. Gen. Conv. Va., Richmond, 1987—; bd. dirs. Ecumenical Resource Ctr., Richmond, 1988—; lectr. Staley Found., Larchmont, N.Y., 1991—. Instr. in First Aid ARC, Richmond, 1980-83; trainer, tchr. Literacy Vols. Am., Richmond, 1980-85; leader Girl Scout Coun. Bklyn., 1986-87. Mem. Black Educator's Fellowship (coord. 1989—), Va. Coun. Chs. (chairperson program com. 1990—). Home: Rte 1 Box 23 Colonial Beach VA 22443 Office: Bapt Gen Conv Va 1500 N Lombardy St Richmond VA 23220-1711

MCELFRESH, PAUL KEITH, minister; b. El Paso, Tex., Aug. 3, 1956; s. Lewis Frederick and Ethel Pauline (Cox) McE.; m. Debra Ann Woodley, Dec. 19, 1978; children: Paul Keith II, Alyssa Denae. B Ministry, Calif. Grad. Sch. Theology, 1985. Ordained to ministry So. Bapt. Conv., 1983; cert. Critical Incident Stress Debriefing Team, Am. Critical Incident Stress Found. Music dir. Calvary Bapt. Ch., Riverside, Calif., 1974-75; min. music and youth 1st Bapt. Ch., Moreno Valley, Calif., 1976-78; youth dir. Immanuel Bapt. Ch., San Bernardino, Calif., 1978-79; pastor Eagle Mountain

Bapt. Ch., Desert Center, Calif., 1983-85; min. edn. and youth Cooper Avenue Bapt. Ch., Yuba City, Calif., 1985-91; min. youth Longview Heights Bapt. Ch., Olive Branch, Miss., 1991—; youth cons. Calif. So. Bapt. Conv., Fresno, 1979—, Sunday sch. cons., 1988-89, cert. masterlife discipleship program, 1985, basic marriage enrichment retreat, 1985; dir. youth camp Shasta/Sierra Butte Assns., Mt. Hope and Forresttown, Calif., 1986—; moderator Sierra Butte Assn., Chico, Calif., 1989-89. Mem. sch. bd. Desert Center Unified Sch. Dist., 1985; chaplain Yuba City Fire Dept., 1989—, Sutter County Fire Dept., Yuba City, 1989—. Mem. Sutter-Yuba Chaplains Assn. Republican. Home: 1208 N Parkway Rd Memphis TN 38104 Office: Longview Heights Bapt Ch 4501 Goodman Rd Olive Branch MS 38659

MCELHANNON, CHARLES EDWARD, minister; b. Ft. Lewis, Wash., Feb. 12, 1956; s. James Everett McElhannon and Yasuko (Tanaka) Anderson; m. Marie Elizabeth Morton, June 22, 1979; children: Jessica Lauren, Rebekah Marie. BA, Union U., Jackson, Tenn., 1978; MDiv, So. Bapt. Theol. Sem., Louisville, 1983. Ordained to ministry Bapt. Ch., 1984. Pastor Meml. Bapt. Ch., Laconia, Ind., 1982-84, Gibson (Tenn.) Bapt. Ch., 1984-88, Valley View Bapt. Ch., Nashville, 1988—; pres. Gibson County Pastor's Conf., Trenton, Tenn., 1987-88; com. on resolutions Tenn. Bapt. Conv., Brentwood, 1987-88. Contbr. articles to mags. Mem.-parent Girl Scouts U.S. Brownie troop 651, Nashville, 1989-91. Judson/Rice scholar So. Bapt. Theol. Sem., 1980. Mem. Nashville Bapt. Pastor's Conf., Assn. Religious Educators. Home: 1518 Harwood Dr Nashville TN 37206 Office: Valley View Bapt Ch 2442 Eastland Ave Nashville TN 37206-1134 *I want to be able to look back on my life and know that I have honored God and that I have drawn others to Him.*

MCELHANNON, JAMES R., minister, sales executive; b. Henryetta, Okla., July 19, 1944; s. Marvin K. and Rosetta (Been) McE.; m. Gwendolyne K. Hill, Feb. 21, 1964; children: T. Michele, Shawn R. Student, Northeastern State U., 1965-66, El Reno (Okla.) Jr. Coll., 1974, U. Ark., Little Rock, 198-81. Ordained to ministry Assemblies of God, 1966. Pastor chs. Ark., La., Okla., 1966-85; dir. children 1st Assembly of God, Jonesboro, Ark., 1985—; regional sales mgr. R.L. Polk & Co., Memphis, 1985—. Sgt. USAR, 1963-69. Named Pastor of Yr. La. Assemblies of God, 1977. Mem. Lions. Democrat. Home and Office: 3517 Sunwood Jonesboro AR 72401

MCELRATH, CHARLES THOMAS, minister; b. Dec. 2, 1946; s. Clayton Ellsworth and Jane Elizebeth (Shoop) McE.; m. Deanna Gail Morgan, Dec. 1, 1973; children: Tammy Jo, Thomas James. Student, Liberty U., Lynchburg, Va.; Corrs. Sch. Cert., Moody Bible Inst., Chgo., 1986. Lay worker Ch. of the Brethren-Lost Creek, McAllisterville, Pa., 1979-82; pastor Valley Alliance Ch., Wellsboro, Pa., 1982—. With U.S. Army, 1966-69, Fed. Republic Germany. Republican. Christian Missionary Alliance. Home and Office: Rte 4 Box 182 Wellsboro PA 16901 *To stop within an inch of a goal will eventually cost that goal to be lost! The only safe place to stop is with the inward testimony, beyond all doubt that the work is done.*

MCELVEEN, GAIL MARIE, educator; b. Houston, May 16, 1954; d. William Conlee and Evelyne Lily (Brautigam) McE. BS in Biology, Sam Houston State U., Huntsville, Tex., 1977, cert. in teaching, 1982; ThM, Logos Bible Coll., 1991. Cert. biology and English tchr., Tex. Tchr. biology Harlandale Ind. Sch. Dist., San Antonio, 1984-91, tchr. comparative religions, 1989-90; sponsor, tchr. El Shaddai Bibl. Studies Club, San Antonio, 1990-91, writer life sci. curriculum, 1989-91, mem. prin.'s adv. com., 1985-90. Mem. Christ for the Nations, Dallas, Ctr. for Ministry to Muslims, Mpls., 1989—, The Stronghold Found., San Antonio, 1989—. Recipient Outstanding Sci. Educator award Sigma Xi, 1991. Mem. Acad. Freedom Legal Def. Fund, Rutherford Inst., Friends of Zion, Maoz. Republican. Charismatic Christian. Home: 4858 Castle Lance San Antonio TX 78218 *We were chosen to live in this prophetic dispensation because God deemed our talents necessary to act upon this move with power and authority.*

MCELWAIN, DAVID BRUCE, minister; b. National City, Calif., Jan. 6, 1947; s. Bruce Degeer and Marjorie Porter (Buswell) McE.; m. Patricia Ann Dismuke, June 4, 1971; children: Julia Ann, Meredith Ann, Alan David. BS, Harding U., Searcy, Ark., 1974; MA in Religion, Harding Grad. Sch., Memphis, 1976. Ordained to ministry Ch. of Christ. Min. Univ. Pkwy. Ch. of Christ, Balt., 1976-79, Sparta (Ill.) Ch. of Christ, 1979-82, Ann Arbor (Mich.) Ch. of Christ, 1982-87, Godfrey (Ill.) Ch. of Christ, 1987—; vol. chaplain Menard (Ill.) Correctional Inst., 1979-82. Democrat. Home: 6416 Humbert Rd Godfrey IL 62035 Office: Godfrey Ch of Christ 6412 Humbert Rd Godfrey IL 62035

MCELWAIN, TIMMIE MCKINNON, minister; b. Uniontown, Pa., Nov. 30, 1939; s. Clarence Wardell and Emma Kate (Sennet) McE.; m. Judith Irene Silva, Sept. 10, 1960; children: Deneen Marie, Dean Paul. AA, Johnson Wales U., 1980. Ordained to ministry Ind. Pentecostal Ch., 1984. Youth worker Zion Gospel Temple, East Providence, R.I., 1971-75; youth worker Apponaug Pentecostal Ch., Warwick, R.I., 1975-78, Sun. sch. tchr., 1976-78, lay minister, 1978-84; pastor Swansea (Mass.) Word of God Ch., 1985—; tng. supr. Providence Gas Co., 1966-91; lectr. in field. With USN, 1957-66. Mem. Full Gospel Businessmen's Fellowship Internat. Home: 22 Griffith Dr Riverside RI 02915 Office: Providence Gas Co 477 Dexter St Providence RI 02907

MC ENROE, JAMES JOSEPH, priest, religion educator, seminary administrator; b. St. Louis, May 12, 1946; s. James Joseph and Irene Catherine (Lehr) Mc E. BA, Cardinal Glennon Coll., 1969; MA, St. Louis U., 1981; ThD, U. Toronto, Ont., Can., 1986. Ordained priest Roman Cath. Ch., 1973. Tchr. religion Rosati Kain and Duchesne High Sch., St. Louis, 1972-81; assoc. pastor St. Mary Magdalene Parish, Brentwood, Mo., 1986-87; prof. theology, dir. field edn. Kenrick-Glennon Sem., St. Louis, 1987—; mem. formation team Office of Ministry, St. Louis, 1986—; guest lectr. Toronto Sch. Theology. Mem. Am. Acad. Religion, Cath. Assn. Theol. Field Educators, Assn. Theol. Field Educators, Cath. Theol. Soc. Am. Home: St Cecelia Rectory 5418 Louisiana Saint Louis MO 63111 Office: Kenrick-Glennon Sem 5200 Glennon Dr Saint Louis MO 63119

MCENTIRE, BILLY RAY, minister; b. Rutherfordton, N.C., Feb. 14, 1960; s. Kenneth Wray and Sara Dwain (Griffin) McE.; m. Wanda Lynn Powell, Dec. 13, 1986. BA in Religion, Gardner-Webb Coll., 1983; MDiv, Southeastern Seminary, Wake Forest, N.C., 1987. Ordained to ministry Fellowship Bapt. Ch., 1987; lic. minister 1979. With South Mountain Bapt. Camp, Conelly Springs, N.C., 1982; youth minister Casar (N.C.) Bapt. Ch., 1982-84; minister Home Mission Bd. of So. Bapt. Conv., Atlanta, 1986, Pleasant Grove Bapt. Ch., Aulander, N.C., 1987—; messenger So. Bapt. Conv., 1980—, N.C. Bapt. State Conv., Raleigh, 1987—; Royal Ambassador leader, choir mem., tchr. Pleasant Grove Bapt. Ch. Named to Outstanding Young Men of Am., 1988, 89. Mem. West Chowan Bapt. Assn. (outreach dir. 1987-90, chmn. resolution com. 1988-91). Home: Rte 1 PO Box 39 Aulander NC 27805 Office: Pleasant Grove Church Rte 1 PO Box 39 Aulander NC 27805

MCFALL, KAY LYNN, lay worker; b. Odessa, Tex., May 1, 1966; d. Bedford Keith and Margaret Ann (Hills) McF.; m. David Elliott Cobb, Aug. 26, 1989. BA, Tex Christian U., 1988; MA, U. Chgo., 1989. Coord. Victim Defender Reconciliation Program, Bloomington, Ill., 1990—. Coord. Tex. Christian U. chpt. Amnesty Internat., Ft. Worth, 1987-88; mem. Students for A Dem. S. Africa, Tex. Christian U., Ft. Worth, 1986-88. Recipient Disciples Div. House Scholarship, Disciples Div. House Found., Chgo., 1988-90. Mem. Soc. Bibl. Lit., Am. Acad. Religion. Democrat. Home: 104 N Center Box 32 Colfax IL 61728 Office: VORP of McLean County PO Box 972 Bloomington IL 61701

MCFARLAND, BARBARA GRAVES, Christian education director; b. Balt., Mar. 29, 1949; d. Roosevelt and Emma (Jackson) Graves; m. Dennis Carol McFarland, July 18, 1970. BS, Morgan State U., 1977; MA, St. Mary's Sem. and Univ., 1984; MDiv, Noward Sch. Divinity, 1990. Youth minister Mt. Zion Bapt. Ch., Balt., 1981-86, Mt. Lebanon Bapt. Ch., Balt., 1986-87; dir. Christian edn. Enon Bapt. Ch., Balt., 1988—; 1st. v.p. Spiritual Life Commn. of Clergywomen of Md. and Vicinity, Balt., 1990—. Mem. Biblical Inst. for Social Change, Washington, 1990-91; planner Assoc. Black Charities, Balt., 1991; participant BUILD (Baltimoreans United in Leadership Devel.), 1991. Recipient Mgr. award, 1986, Best Mgr. award, 1987, Recognition award Howard U. Sch. Divinity, 1991. Mem. Interdenominational Ministerial Alliance, NAACP. Home: 7603 Perring Terr Baltimore MD 21234 Office: Enon Bapt Ch 601 N Schroeder St Baltimore MD 21217

MC FARLAND, NORMAN FRANCIS, bishop; b. Martinez, Calif., Feb. 21, 1922; student St. Patrick's Sem., Menlo Park, Calif.; J.C.D., Cath. U. Am. Ordained priest Roman Catholic Ch., 1946, consecrated bishop, 1970; titular bishop of Bida and aux. bishop of San Francisco, 1970-74; apostolic adminstr. Diocese of Reno, 1974-76; bishop Diocese of Reno-Las Vegas, 1976-87, Diocese of Orange, Calif., 1987—. Office: Marywood Ctr 2811 E Villa Real Dr Orange CA 92667

MCFARLANE, ADRIAN ANTHONY, minister; b. Annotto Bay, Caribbean, Jamaica, Mar. 15, 1946; came to U.S., 1981; s. Samuel Augustus and Alice (Henry) McF.; m. Glady Primrose Manasseh, Jan. 16, 1966; children: Adrianne Antonette, Dietrich Alister. BA cum laude, Milliken U., 1971; MDiv, Princeton Theol. Sem., 1974; PhD, Drew U., 1985. Chaplain Knox Coll., Spalding, Jamaica, 1974-77; pastor St. Paul's Kirk, Kingston, Jamaica, 1977-81; stated supply Tremont Prebyn. Ch., Bronx, N.Y., 1982-85; pastor Witherspoon St. Presbyterian Ch., Princeton, N.J., 1985—; adjunct asst. prof. Rider Coll., Lawrenceville, N.J., 1990—. Justice of the Peace Govt. of Jamaica, Kingston, 1978. Mem. Am. Philos. Assn., Am. Acad. Religion, Soc. for Christian Philosophers. Home: 453 Walnut Ln Princeton NJ 08540 Office: Presbyn Ch 124 Witherspoon St Princeton NJ 08540

MCGANN, JOHN RAYMOND, bishop; b. Bklyn., Dec. 2, 1924; s. Thomas Joseph and Mary (Ryan) McG. Student, Cathedral Coll. Immaculate Conception, 1944, Sem. Immaculate Conception, Huntington, 1950; LL.D., St. Johns U., 1971; L.H.D., Molloy Coll., 1977, Niagara U., 1983, St. Joseph's Coll., 1983, Adelphi U., 1985. Ordained priest Roman Catholic Ch., 1950, Episcopal ordination, 1971; asst. priest St. Anne's, Brentwood, 1950-57; asst. chaplain St. Joseph Convent, Brentwood, 1950-54; tchr. religion St. Joseph Acad., 1950-54; asso. Cath. chaplain Pilgrim State Hosp., 1950-57; asst. chancellor Diocese of Rockville Centre, 1957-67, vice chancellor, 1967-71; sec. to Bishop Kellenberg, 1957-59; elevated to papal chamberlain, 1959; sec. to Bishop Kellenberg, 1959-70; apptd. titular bishop of Morosbisdus and aux. bishop of Rockville Centre, 1970-76, bishop, 1976—; Del. Sacred Congregation for Religious to Marianists, 1973-76; theol. cons. Nat. Conf. Cath. Bishops, Rome, 1974, treas. 1984-87; mem. adminstrv. com., 1977-79; Anglican/Roman Cath. task force on pastoral ministry of bishops, 1978-81, nat. adv. coun. U.S. Cath. Conf., 1969-70, 81-83, treas. 1984-87; mem. health affairs com., 1972-75, adminstrv. bd., 1976-79, sem. admissions bd. Diocese Rockville Centre, 1971-76, diocesan boundary commn., 1971-76, Tri-Conf. Religious Retirement Project, 1985-88; mem. Papal visit, 1986-87. Bd. Diocesan Services, Inc., 1971-76; com. that established Consultation Services for Religious, 1972-74; vicar gen. Diocese Rockville Centre, 1971-76, episcopal vicar, Suffolk County, 1971-76; mem. N.Y. State Cath. Conf. Com. on Prison Apostolate, 1971-74, U.S. Bishops' Com. for Apostolate to Laity, 1972-76, Rockville Centre Diocesan Bd. Consultors, 1969-76; episcopal mem. N.Y. State Cath. Com., 1974-78; chmn. N.Y. State Bishops' Com. on Elective Process, 1974—, Com. Religious Studies in Pub. Edn., 1975-79; mem. com. on ednl. concerns, com. on priests senates and couns. N.Y. State Cath. Conf.; Bd. dirs. Good Samaritan Hosp., West Islip, N.Y., 1972-76, chmn., 1976—; trustee Cath. Charities Diocese of Rockville Centre, 1971-76; trustee St. Charles Hosp., Port Jefferson, N.Y., 1972-76, chmn., 1976—; pres. Mercy Hosp., St. Francis Hosp., Diocesan Commodities, Inc., 1976—; chmn. Consolation Residence, 1976—; bd. advisers Sem. Immaculate Conception, 1975—; treas. Nat. Conf. Cath. Bishops U.S. Cath. Conf., 1984-87, ad hoc com. on stewardship, 1988—, tri-conf. commn. on religious life and ministry, 1988—; mem. Papal Visit, 1986-87, Tri-conf. Religious Retirement Project., 1985-88; chmn. Nat. Conf. Cath. Bishops/U.S. Cath. Conf. Telecommunications Network Am., 1990. Office: 50 N Park Ave Rockville Centre NY 11570

MCGARVEY, DONALD LEROY, minister; b. Alton, Ill., July 25, 1953; s. David L. and Mary B. (Thompson) McG.; m. Kristine G. McCullough. BA, North Cen. Bible Coll., Mpls., 1975. Ordained to ministry Assemblies of God, 1978. Evangelist, tchr. Champaign, Ill., 1975-83; elem. cons. Denominational Sunday Sch. Dept., Springfield, Mo., 1984-85; pastor Christian edn. 1st Assembly of God, Rockford, Ill., 1986-89, Cedar Rapids, Iowa, 1990—. Contbr. articles to religious jours. Mem. Linn Christian Edn. Assn. (bd. dirs. 1990—), Ea. Iowa Sunday Sch. Assn. (bd. dirs. 1991—). Office: 1st Assembly of God 3233 Blairs Ferry Rd NE Cedar Rapids IA 52402

MCGARY, BETTY WINSTEAD, minister, counselor, group therapist; b. Louisville, June 21, 1936; d. Philip Miller and Mary Jo (Winstead) McG.; married, 1960 (div. 1979); children: Thomas Edward, Mary Alyson, Andrew Philip Pearce. BS, Samford U., 1958; MA in Christian Edn., So. Bapt. Theol. Sem., 1961; EdD, U. Louisville, 1988. Ordained to ministry Bapt. Ch., 1986; cert. secondary tchr., Ky., Ga. Min. to youth Broadway Bapt. Ch., Louisville, 1958-60; learning disability and behavior disorders specialist Jefferson County Schs., Muscogee Schs., Cobb County Schs., Louisville, Columbus, Ga., Atlanta, 1964-88; min. to adults South Main Bapt. Ch., Houston, 1986-90; assoc. pastor Calder Bapt. Ch., Beaumont, Tex., 1991—; marriage enrichment cons. Pastoral Inst., Columbus, 1973-76; co-founder and coord. Ctr. for Women in Ministry, Louisville, 1983-86, exec. bd. dirs. 1983—; cons. Tex. Christian Life Commn., Ft. Worth, 1989—; co-therapist pvt. practice of Elizabeth Brodie, M.D., Houston, 1989—. Author: (with others) The New Has Come, 1988; co-editor nat. newsletter Folio: A Newsletter for Southern Bapt. Women in Ministry, 1983-86. Vice-chairperson exec. bd. dirs. handicapped Boy Scouts Am., Houston, 1986—. Recipient citation for Disting. Svc. So. Bapt. Theol. Sem., 1984, Dean's citation Outstanding Achievement U. Louisville, 1988. Mem. So. Bapt. Alliance (exec. bd. dirs. 1988—, v.p. 1990—), So. Bapt. Women in Ministry (pres. 1988-90). Democrat. Avocations: gardening, interior design, travel. Home: 2107 Bartlett Houston TX 77098 Office: Calder Bapt Ch 1005 N 11th St Beaumont TX 77702 *All around us there are new opportunities for creating, ordering, liberating and healing our world. It is our calling and our challenge to be God's partners in these holy purposes.*

MCGAUGHEY, DOUGLAS R., religion educator; b. Hoosick Falls, N.Y., June 11, 1947; s. Melvin R. and Grace (Taylor) McG.; m. Elizabeth Ayers, Nov. 25, 1966 (div. 1981); 1 child, Sarah; m. Margit Martha Mayr, Mar. 25, 1982; children: Hanna, Kerstin. BA, Boston U., 1969; MDiv, Chgo. Theol. Sem., 1973; PhD, U. Chgo., 1983. Ordained elder United Meth. Ch. Minister United Meth. Ch., Brownsville & S. Reading, Vt., 1971-72, Monroe Center, Ill., 1976-77, Berlin and Grafton, N.Y., 1977-79; asst. prof. Greensboro (N.C.) Coll., 1983-87, Willamette U., Salem, Oreg., 1988—. Contbr. articles to profl. publs. Mem. Am. Acad. Religion, Amnesty Internat. (group coord. Salem chpt. 1988—). Office: Wilamette U 900 State St Salem OR 97301

MCGAUGHY, LANE CLIFFORD, minister, religion educator; b. Washburn, Maine, July 24, 1940; s. Clifford Joseph and Irene Mae (Knowles) McG.; divorced; children: Lane Jr., Charis. BA, Ohio Wesleyan U., 1962; BD, Drew Theol. Sem., 1965; postgrad., U. Tübingen, Fed. Republic Germany, 1965-66; MA, Vanderbilt U., 1969, PhD, 1970. Ordained to ministry United Meth. Ch. Asst. min. Meth. Ch., Morristown, N.J., 1963-65; asst. and assoc. prof. U. Mont., Missoula, 1969-81; prof. Willamette U., Salem, Oreg., 1981—; vis. prof. U. Nebr., Lincoln, 1977; bd. dirs. Alton L. Collins Retreat Ctr., Eagle Creek, Oregon, 1985—; mem. Bd. Ordained Ministry United Meth. Ch., Oreg., Idaho, 1986—. Author: Einai as a Linking Verb, 1972, Workbook for Greek Grammar, 1976; editor Willamette Jour., 1985-88; contbr. articles to jours. in field. Mem. Soc. Bibl. Lit. (pres. Pacific N.W. 1984-85), Am. Acad. Religion. Home: 32640 N Fork Rd Lyons OR 97358 Office: Williamette U Dept Religion 900 State St Salem OR 97301

MCGEACHY, DANIEL PATRICK, III, minister; b. Atlanta, Nov. 19, 1929; s. Daniel Patrick Jr. and Beth (McClure) McG.; m. Alice Neely, Aug. 28, 1952; children: Daniel Patrick IV, Lois Elizabeth, Martin Neely. BD, Union Theol. Sem., Richmond, Va., 1954, ThM, 1955; STM, San Francisco Theol. Sem., San Anselmo, Calif., 1970, STD, 1982. Ordained to ministry Presbyn. Ch., 1954. Pastor 1st Presbyn. Ch., Sylva, N.C., 1955-59, Gainesville, Ga., 1959-66; pastor Westminster Presbyn. Ch., Nashville, 1966-73, Rockvale (Tenn.) Cumberland Presbyn. Ch., 1975-81; assoc. pastor Downtown Presbyn. Ch., Nashville, 1976—; writer, Nashville, 1973—; chair div. internat. mission Presbyn. Ch. U.S., 1972-73; mem. joint com. on worship PCUS-USA, 1973-76; mem. Commn. on the Liturgy, Consultation on Ch. Union, 1977-83. Author: A Matter of Life and Death, 1966, Common Sense & the Gospel, 1969, The Gospel According to Andy Capp, 1973, Traveling Light, 1975, Help, Lord!, 1978. Pres. Jr. C. of C., Sylva, 1957, Project Return, Inc., Nashville, 1977, 87. Recipient Disting. Svc. award Jr. C. of C., Sylva, 1959, Gainesville, 1965. Democrat. Home: PO Box 3151 Nashville TN 37219 Office: Downtown Presbyn Ch 154 5th Ave N Nashville TN 37219

MCGEE, THOMAS W., academic administrator. Pres. St. Louis Christian Coll., Florissant, Mo. Office: St Louis Christian Coll 1360 Grandview Dr Florissant MO 63033*

MC GEHEE, H. COLEMAN, JR., bishop; b. Richmond, Va., July 7, 1923; s. Harry Coleman and Ann Lee (Cheatwood) McG.; m. June Stewart, Feb. 1, 1946; children: Lesley, Alexander, Coleman III, Donald, Cary. BS, Va. Poly. Inst., 1944; JD, U. Richmond, 1949; MDiv, Va. Theol. Sem., 1957, DD, 1973. Bar: Va. 1949, U.S. Supreme Ct. 1954; ordained to ministry Episcopal Ch., 1957. Spl. counsel dept. hwys. State of Va., 1949-51, gen. counsel employment svc., 1951, asst. atty. gen., 1951-54; rector Immanuel Ch.-on-the-Hill, Va. Sem., 1960-71; bishop Diocese of Mich., Detroit, 1971-90; mem. adv. bd. Nicaraguan Network, Ctr. for Peace and Conflict Studies, Wayne State U.; bd. dirs. Mich. Religious Coalition for Abortion Rights, 1976—; trustee Va. Theol. Seminary, 1978—; pres. Episc. Ch. Pub. Co., 1978-85. Columnist: Detroit News, 1979-85; weekly commentator pub. radio sta. WDET-AM, Detroit, 1984-90. Mem. Gov.'s Commn. on Status of Women, 1965-66, Mayor's Civic Com., Alexandria, 1967-68; sponsor Nat. Assn. for ERA, 1977-85; pres. Alexandria Legal Aid Soc., 1969-71; bd. dirs. No. Va. Fairhousing Corp., 1963-67; pres. Mich. Coalition for Human Righs, 1980-89; chmn. Citizens' Com. for Justice in Mich., 1983-84; sponsor Farm Labor Orgn. for Children, 1983-85; bd. dirs. Pub. Benefit Corp., Detroit, 1988-90, Mich. Citizens for Personal Freedom, 1989—, Poverty and Social Reform Inst., Detroit, 1989—, Bread for the World, 1990—, Ams. United for Separation of Ch. and State, 1990, ACLU Oakland County, Mich., 1991—; co-chair Lesbian-Gay Found. Mich., 1991—. 1st lt. C.E., U.S. Army, 1943-46. Named Feminist of Yr., Detroit NOW, 1978; recipient Humanitarian award Detroit ACLU, 1984, Phillip Hart medal Mich. Women's Studies Assn., 1984, Sayre award for justice and peace Episc. Peace Fellowship, 1988, Spirit of Detroit award, 1989, Archbishop Romero award Mich. Labor Com., 1990. Mem. Detroit Econ. Club (bd. dirs.). Home: 1496 Ashover Dr Bloomfield Hills MI 48304 Office: Diocese of Mich 4800 Woodward Ave Detroit MI 48201

MCGEHEE, MICHAEL DAVID, religious educator; b. Montgomery, Ala., June 1, 1952; s. Henry Vester and Anna (Sharp) McG.; m. Jerilyn Ree Wise, Apr. 24, 1974. BA, U. Tex., El Paso, 1974; MDiv, Colgate Rochester Divinity Sch, 1981; PhD, Brown U., 1985. Prof. theology Coll. St. Benedict, St. Joseph, Minn., 1985—. Author: God's Word Expressed in Human Words: The Bible's Literary Forms, 1991; columnist St. Cloud (Minn.) Times, 1986—, Mpls. Star Tribune, St. Paul Pioneer Press; contbr. articles to profl. jours. With USN, 1970-71. Mem. Soc. Bibl. Lit., AAUP. Baptist. Office: Coll Saint Benedict Dept Theology Saint Joseph MN 56374

MCGEHEE, RANDY GENE, minister; b. Stillwater, Okla., Nov. 20, 1952; s. Donald L. and Stella I. (Mayfield) McG.; m. Diane M. King, Aug. 22, 1975; children: Erin K., Calley A., Patrick O. Student, Kans. State Tchrs. Coll., 1971-75; degree in ministerial studies, Berean Sch. Bible, 1985; student, Sch. of Ministry-Dist. Ill., 1986, 88. Ordained to ministry Assemblies of God, 1988. Min. of music Clinton Parkway Assembly of God, Lawrence, Kans., 1980-85; asst. pastor First Assembly of God, Springfield, Ill., 1985-87; sr. pastor First Assembly of God, Paris, Ill., 1987—; pres. Paris Ministerial Fellowship, 1989-90, sec., 1988-89; v.p. Chaplain's Program-Paris Hosp., 1990-91. Republican. Office: First Assembly of God 213 W Blackburn Paris IL 61944

MCGILL, KENNETH ALAN, minister; b. Jefferson City, Mo., Oct. 15, 1955; s. J.H. McGill and Carolyn (Butts) Laughlin; m. Laura Ladd, Sept. 28, 1984; children: Deborah, Jami, Travis, Kristopher, Megan. BS in Psychology, Southwest Mo. State U., 1977; MDiv, St. Paul Sch. Theology, Kansas City, Mo., 1981; postgrad., So. Meth. U. Ordained to ministry United Meth. Ch., 1979. Min. Fordland and Pleasant Hill United Meth. Chs., 1977-78, Centerview (Mo.) United Meth. Ch., 1978-79, Trenton (Mo.) area chs., 1979-82, Ozark (Mo.) United Meth. Ch., 1982-85, Kings Way United Meth. Ch., Springfield, Mo., 1985-87, Ava (Mo.) United Meth. Ch., 1987—; adj. instr. Drury Coll., Springfield; site chmn. Camp Galilee, El Dorado Springs, Md., 1984—; trustee United Meth. Camps, Mo. West Annual Conf., 1984—. Pres. Ava Area Ministerial Alliance, 1988-91; mem. community svc. com. Douglas County Youth and Family orgn. Recipient Disting. Svc. award, Jaycees, Trenton, 1980, Outstanding Young Religious Leader award, 1980. Mem. Avea Area C. of C., Lions, Kiwanis. Office: PO Box 356 900 SW 4th Ave Ava MO 65608

MCGILLEY, SISTER MARY JANET, nun, educator, writer, academic administrator; b. Kansas City, Mo., Dec. 4, 1924; d. James P. and Peg (Ryan) McG. B.A., St. Mary Coll., 1945; M.A., Boston Coll., 1951; Ph.D., Fordham U., 1956; postgrad., U. Notre Dame, 1960, Columbia U., 1964. Social worker Kansas City, 1945-46; joined Sisters of Charity of Leavenworth, 1946; tchr. English Hayden High Sch., Topeka, 1948-50, Billings (Mont.) Central High Sch., 1951-53; faculty dept. English St. Mary Coll., Leavenworth, Kans., 1956-64; pres. St. Mary Coll., 1964-89, Disting. prof. English and Liberal Studies, 1990—. Contbr. articles, fiction and poetry to various jours. Bd. dirs. United Way of Leavenworth, 1966-85; mem. Mayor's Adv. Coun., 1967-72, Leavenworth Planning Coun., 1977-78; bd. dirs.Kans. Ind. Coll. Fund, 1964-89, exec. com., 1985-86, vice chmn., 1984-85, chmn., 1985-86. Recipient Alumnae award St. Mary Coll., 1969; Disting. Service award Baker U., 1981, Leavenworth Bus. Woman of Yr. Athena award, 1986. Mem. Nat. Coun. Tchrs. of English, Nat. Assn. Ind. Colls. and Univs. (bd. dirs. 1982-85), Kans. Ind. Coll. Assn. (bd. dirs. 1964-89, treas. 1982-84, v.p. 1984-85, chmn. exec. com. 1985-86), Am. Coun. Edn. (com. on women in higher edn. 1980-85), Am. Assn. Higher Edn., Kansas City Regional Coun. for Higher Edn. (bd. dirs. 1965-89, treas. 1984-85, v.p. 1986-88), Ind. Coll. Funds Am. (exec. com. 1974-77, trustee-at-large 1975-76), North Cen. Assn. Colls. and Schs. (exec. commr. Com. on Insts. Higher Edn. 1980-88, vice chair 1985-86, chair 1987-88), Leavenworth C. of C. (bd. dirs. 1964-89), Assn. Am. Colls. (commn. liberal learning 1970-73, com. on curriculum and faculty devel. 1979-82) St. Mary Alumni Assn. (hon. pres. 1964-89), Delta Epsilon Sigma. Democrat. Office: St Mary Coll 4100 S 4th St Trafficway Leavenworth KS 66048-5082

MCGILVRAY, ANDREW ROBERT, educator, minister; b. N.Y.C., Aug. 2, 1933; s. Andrew Murray and Agnes Cecilia (Barrett) McG.; B.A., U. Niagara, 1959; Licentiate in Theology, U. Fribourg, 1963; M.A., Villanova U., 1969; Ed.D., Cath. U. Am., 1980. With DuPont Co., Wilmington, Del., 1953; entered Oblates of St. Francis de Sales, Roman Cath. Ch., 1953—; tchr. Northeast Cath. High Sch., Phila., 1955-57; dept. head, tchr. Salesianum Sch., Wilmington, 1963-72; prin. Bishop Ireton High Sch., Alexandria, Va., 1972-75; dir. Salesian Studies Inst., 1975-86 ; assoc. prof. Allentown Coll. of St. Francis de Sales, Center Valley, Pa., 1980—, chmn. dept. edn., 1980-88, 90—; mem. sch. bd. Diocese of Allentown (Pa.), 1984-90. Fulbright grantee, Germany, summer 1970. Mem. Assn. Tchr. Educators, Pa. Assn. Tchr. Educators, Pa. Assn. Colls. and Tchr. Educators, Assn. Supervision and Curriculum Devel., Pa. Assn. Supervision and Curriculum Devel., Am. Assn. Tchrs. German, Nat. Cath. Edn. Assn., Phi Delta Kappa. Roman Catholic. Author: Handbook of the Salesian Studies Program of Small Group Discussion, 1978; The Effects of Two Instructional Strategies Upon the Increase of Selected Discussion Behaviors of Groups of Religious Identifying and Applying Their Charism as a Congregation, 1980; Multimedia Approaches to Salesian Studies, 1985; Using the Computer to Prepare Future Teachers, 1986. Home: Wills Hall Center Valley PA 18034 Office: Allentown Coll St Francis de Sales Center Valley PA 18034

MCGINN, BERNARD JOHN, religious educator; b. Yonkers, N.Y., Aug. 19, 1937; s. Bernard John and Catherine Ann (Faulds) McG.; m. Patricia

Ann Ferris, July 10, 1971; children: Daniel, John. BA, St. Joseph's Sem., Yonkers, N.Y., 1959; Licentiate in Sacred Theology, Gregorian U., Rome, 1963; PhD, Brandeis U., 1970. Diocesan priest Archdiocese N.Y., N.Y.C., 1963-71; prof. U. Chgo., 1969—; program coord. Inst. for Advanced Study of Religion, Divinity Sch., U. Chgo., 1980—. Author: The Calabrian Abbott, 1985, Meister Eckhart, 1986; editor: (series) Classics of Western Spirituality, 1978, (book) God and Creation, 1990. Home: 5701 S Kenwood Chicago IL 60637 Office: U Chgo Divinity Sch 1025 E 58th St Chicago IL 60637

MCGINNIS, SHEILA, nun, religious order superior; b. Troy, N.Y., Sept. 29, 1938; d. Frank J. and Catherine J. (Bond) McG. Cert. RN, Miserica, Phila., 1963; cert. midwife, CMI, 1964; BSN, Cath. U. Am., 1972. Joined Med. Mission Sisters, Roman Cath. Ch., 1956. Assembly mem. Med. Mission Sisters, Washington, S.E. Asia; asst. sector superior, then sector superior Med. Mission Sisters, Phila. Mem. CODEL (pres. bd. dirs.), NCCCC/USA (unit com.). Home and Office: 8400 Pine Rd Philadelphia PA 19111

MCGLADE, ANNE MARY, youth ministry administrator; b. St. Paul, Jan. 30, 1960; d. William E. and Marianne Dorothy Reynolds; m. Neil B. McGlade (div. June 1990). BA in Youth Ministry, St. Scholastica Coll., 1982; MA in Religious Edn., Loyola Coll., New Orleans, 1987. Dir. youth ministry St. Margaret Mary Cath. Ch., Winter Park, Fla., 1982-87; profl. youth ministry coord. Diocese of Cen. Fla., Orlando, 1987—; pastoral care cons. Laurel Oaks Psychol. Hosp., Orlando, 1988—; sr. leader Young Life Cen. Fla., Winter Park, 1982-87. Office: Diocese of Cen Fla 1019 E Robinson St Orlando FL 32801

MCGLOIN, FATHER JOSEPH THADDEUS, priest, writer; b. Council Bluffs, Iowa, Dec. 2, 1917; s. Dennis J. and Clara (Finn) McG. BA, St. Louis U., 1941, MA, 1943, PhL, 1943; S.T.L., St. Mary's (Kans.) Coll., 1950. Joined S.J., 1936, ordained priest Roman Cath. Ch., 1949. Tchr., counselor, dir. youth groups Regis High Sch., Denver, 1951-61; founder Sodality Coun. Denver; tchr., counselor St. Margaret's Acad., Mpls., 1962-65; writer-in-residence Santa Barbara, Calif., 1967-70; writer, tchr., counselor Marymount Mil. Acad., Tacoma, Wash., 1970-74; pastor Sacred Heart Ch., Alturas, Calif., 1974-75; chaplain, counselor Villa Nazareth, Fargo, N.D., 1975-79; dir. retreats Good Counsel Retreat Ho., Waverly, Nebr., 1979-81; author-in-residence Creighton U., Omaha, 1981—. Authorof over 50 books including I'll Die Laughing!, 1984, Living to Beat Hell, 1982, The Way I See Him: A Writer's Look at Jesus, 1986, Listen, Lord (Prayer for Plodders), 1987, Graduating into Life, 1988, How to Get More Out of the Mass, 1989, Graduating into Happiness, 1989, Vale La Pena, It's Worth the Price, 1991. Home and Office: Creighton U Omaha NE 68178-0522

MCGLOTHLIN, JAMES IRA, pastor; b. Dublin, Tex., July 21, 1947; s. George Ira and Ina Jo (Pittman) McG.; m. Patricia Yvonne De Hart, Aug. 21, 1970; children: Samuel Andrew, Anna Elizabeth. BA, Howard Payne U., 1969; MDiv, Southwestern Bapt. Theol. Sem., 1972, DMin, 1976. Ordained to ministry Bapt. Ch., 1969. Pastor Morgan Mill (Tex.) Bapt. Ch., 1971-73, 1st Bapt. Ch., Rosebud, Tex., 1973-76; sr. pastor 1st Bapt. Ch., Galena Park, Tex., 1976-82, Galveston, Tex., 1982-85; sr. pastor Lakeside Bapt. Ch., Dallas, 1986—; trustee Bockner Bapt. Benovelences, Dallas, 1989—; bd. dirs. human welfare coordinating bd. Bapt. Gen. Conv. Tex., Dallas, 1982-88, exec. bd., 1984-86. Trustee Howard Payne U., Brownwood, Tex., 1979-88. Mem. Eastern Hills Country Club. Office: Lakeside Bapt Ch 9150 Garland Rd Dallas TX 25218

MCGOLDRICK, RUTH FRANCES, religious organization administator; b. Quincy, Mass., Oct. 13, 1934; d. Orrin Francis and Florence Elizabeth (Taylor) McG. BS in Bus. Edn., Boston Coll., 1959; M in Religious Edn., St. Mary's Sch. Theology, 1965. Instr. theology and spirituality New England area, 1959-73; formation coord. Sisters of Providence, Holyoke, Mass., 1969-73, 89-91; exec. dir. Religious Formation Conf., Washington, 1973-76; program dir. Genesis Spiritual Life Ctr., Westfield, Mass., 1976-91; workshop and retreat dir. Genesis Spiritual Life Ctr., U.S.A., Can., Eng. and Ireland; mem. exec. council Sisters of Providence, 1977-85; writer, speaker Women of Providence in Collaboration, 1980-86, 91; active numerous religious orgns. Co-editor, author: Facets of Future: Religious Life, 1976; editor (newsletter) In-Formation, 1974-76; founding editor (newsletter) In-Formation; contbr. numerous articles to profl. jours. and private pubs. Mem. nat. adv. com. Internat. Women's Yr., Washington, 1976; liaison, participant nat. bicentennial projects, Washington, 1976; mem. bd. sponsors Nat. Intensive Jour. Program, N.Y.C., 1977—; founding mem. Diocesan support groups for separated and divorced people, 1981-83; exec. adv. bd. The Neurofibromatosis Assn. Inc., Granby, Mass., 1986-90. Recipient Women's award Springfield (Mass.) Dailey News, 1967, Inst. Women Today award, 1976, White House invitation Gerald Ford, 1976. Mem. Inst. for Research in Spirituality (v.p. 1976—), Retreats Internat. Democrat. Roman Catholic. Avocations: Irish studies, journal writing, travel, art, cultural events. Home: Manna House 53 Mill St Westfield MA 01085 Office: Genesis Spiritual Life Ctr 53 Mill St Westfield MA 01085 *I see the Providence of God at work in our lives wherever creative and healing energies are manifested in or through us or others.*

MCGOVERN, SEANN EUGENE, church musician; b. Duluth, Minn., Aug. 15, 1963; s. Eugene George and Dolores Isabel (Quick) McG. AA, Crosier Sem. Jr. Coll., 1984; BA in Philosophy, St. Mary's Coll., Winona, Minn., 1986. Activity asst. Nopeming Nursing Home, Duluth, 1987-88; ednl. asst. Ind. Sch. Dist. 709, Duluth, 1988-89; program implementer Duluth Regional Care Ctr., 1989-90; tax preparer H&R Block, Duluth, 1990-91; musician St. Lawrence Cath. Ch., 1990—; vocalist for svcs. various area funeral homes, 1986—. Roman Catholic. Avocation: music.

MCGOWIN, (WILLIAM) DAVID, JR., minister, religion educator; b. Ft. Myers, Fla., Nov. 22, 1942; s. William David and Ruby Jane (Oneil) McG.; m. Judith Carolyn McGriff, Sept. 10, 1965; 1 child, David Harris. BA, Samford U., 1966; ThM, New Orleans Bapt. Theol. Sem., 1971; D Ministries, Luther Rice Sem., Jacksonville, Fla., 1981. Lic. to ministry So. Bapt. Conv., 1964; ordained, 1966. Min. Canseyville Bapt. Ch., Meridian, Miss., 1971-73, Brent (Ala.) Bapt. Ch., 1973-76, New Prospect Bapt. Ch., Prattville, Ala., 1976-77; pastor 1st Bapt. Ch., Warrior, Ala., 1976-84, Berney Points Bapt. Ch., Birmingham, Ala., 1984-85, 1st Bapt. Ch., Conway, Ark., 1985-87, Woodland Heights Bapt. Ch., Conway, 1987-88, 1st Bapt. Ch., Hanceville, Ala., 1988—; prof. religion Howard Coll. Extension, Warrior, 1978-83, So. Sem. Extension, Warrior, 1983-85, Wallace Community Coll., Hanceville, 1988—. Author: Pastoral Guidebook to Outreach Ministry, 1981, Wherever the Spirit Moves, 1985. Chaplain Ala. N.G. Home: PO Box 646 Hanceville AL 35077

MCGRADY, SANDRA JEAN, minister; b. Tuxedo, N.Y., Aug. 12, 1958; d. William David and Joan Beverly (Kincaid) McG. Cert., Orange County Community Coll., Middletown, N.Y., 1978; BS, SUNY, New Paltz, 1980; MDiv, United Theol. Sem., 1984. Ordained to ministry United Meth. Ch. as deacon, 1986, as elder 1990. Student assoc. pastor Oakwood United Meth. Ch., Dayton, Ohio, 1982-84; youth min. Cornwall (N.Y.) United Meth. Ch., 1984-85; assoc. pastor St. Paul's United Meth. Ch., Syracuse, N.Y., 1985-88; pastor Onondaga (N.Y.) Mission, 1985-88, Truxton-East Homer (N.Y.) United Meth., 1988—; dist. youth coord. Seven Valleys Dist., Homer, N.Y., 1988—, Onondaga Dist., Syracuse, 1986-88; sec. Native Am. Devel. Com., Syracuse, 1986-88. Active Older Native Am. Outreach Program, Syracuse, 1985-88, Cortland Nutrition Program, 1988-90; chaplain Corland Meml. Hosp., 1990—. Home: Box 17 2662 Rte 13 East Homer NY 13056

MCGRANAHAN, LARRY CLAYTON, JR., minister; b. Wichita Falls, Tex., Sept. 7, 1971; s. Larry Clayton and Terry Jewell (Ellis) McG.; m. Jamie Gayle Stewart, Jan. 12, 1991. Ed. high sch., Neosho, Mo., 1989. Lic. to ministry So. Bapt. Conv., 1989. Lay youth worker Calvary Bapt. Ch., Neosho, 1989-90; min., dir. youth 1st Bapt. Ch., Neosho, 1990—; owner Lawn Svc., Neosho, 1986—. Mem. Youth Min. Alliance, Aite Imasu Do Fedn. Republican. Home: 1413 Ozark Dr Neosho MO 64850 Office: 1st Bapt Ch Main and Jefferson Neosho MO 64850 *God knows no defeat!.*

MCGRATH, JOHN ANTHONY, priest; b. Bklyn., Jan. 17, 1935; s. Francis Patrick and Theresa Helen (Wilson) McG. BA, U. Dayton, 1957; MA, Ohio State U., 1962; STL, Fribourg (Switzerland) U., 1966; Drs.Theol., Nijmegen (Netherlands) U., 1968. Religious bro. Soc. of Marianists, Dayton, Ohio, 1953—; religious priest Soc. of Marianists, Fribourg, 1966—; order adminstr. Soc. of Marianists, Balt., 1969-77, order provincial, 1977-85; community chaplain Soc. of Marianists, Dayton, 1987—; asst. prof. religious studies U. Dayton, 1987—; trustee U. Dayton, 1980-86; bd. dirs. Bishops' Nat. Adv. Bd., Washington, 1983-87; exec. com. Cath. Religious of Balt., 1983-85. Mem. Coll. Theology Soc., Cath. Theol. Soc. Am., Cath. Hist. Assn., Am. Acad. Religion, Soc. for the Scientific Study of Religion, U.S. Cath. Hist. Soc. Office: U Dayton 300 College Park Ave Dayton OH 45469

MCGRATH, MARCOS GREGORIO, archbishop. Archbishop of Panama Roman Cath. Ch.; pres. Cath. Bishops' Conf. in Sri Lanka Roman Cath. Ch., Colombo. Office: Arzobispado, Apdo 6386, Panama City 5, Republic of Panama*

MCGRATH, THOMAS AUGUSTINE, priest, psychologist, educator; b. Quincy, Mass., May 4, 1919; s. Thomas Martin and Anna (Cronin) McG.; BA, Boston Coll., 1943, MA, 1944; MA, Cath. U. Am., 1948; Ph.D., Fordham U., 1960. Lic. psychologist, Conn. Joined Soc. of Jesus, 1937; ordained priest Roman Cath. Ch., 1950; dir. psychol. services Fairfield (Conn.) U., 1957-68, chmn. dept., 1962-70, 73-76; prof. psychology, 1969—; cons. to industry. Mem. Am. Psychol. Assn., Am. Mgmt. Assn. Office: Fairfield U Psychology Dept Fairfield CT 06430

MCGRAW, BURL DAVID, III, minister; b. Eastland, Tex., June 15, 1947; s. Burl David Jr. and Bettye (Yielding) McG.; m. Freida Ann Lewis, June 8, 1967; children: Shelley, Sherrey. BS, Okla. Bapt. Coll., 1981. Ordained to ministry Bapt. Ch., 1981. Assoc. pastor Socorro (N.Mex.) Bapt. Temple, 1979-80; pastor Victory Bapt. Ch., Stephenville, Tex., 1982-83, Bapt. Temple Ch., Kermit, Tex., 1983-87, Victory Bapt. Ch., Paris, Tex., 1987-88, Bible Bapt. Ch., San Angelo, Tex., 1988—; family, marriage and dependency counselor Bible Bapt. Ch., San Angelo, 1988—; min. Tom Green County Jail, San Angelo, 198—, Eden (Tex.) Detention Ctr., 1990—. Author: Present Prejudice from the Pulpit to the Pew, 1991. With USN, 1965-68, Vietnam. Decorated Nat. Def. medal, Vietnam Campaign medal. Republican. Home: 2767 Catalina Dr San Angelo TX 76901 Office: Bible Bapt Ch 409 Paint Rock Rd San Angelo TX 76903

MCGRAW, GERALD EARL, minister, educator; b. Oil City, Pa., May 26, 1932; s. Caudy Earl and Gladys Lavina (Snyder) McG.; m. Martha Swauger, Aug. 7, 1956; children: Philip Earl, David Keith. Diploma in theology, Nyack Coll., 1953; BA, Houghton Coll., 1954; MA in Theol., Wheaton Coll., 1958; M of Div., Chgo. Grad. Sch. Theol., 1970; D of Ministry, Southeastern Bapt. Theol. Seminary, 1975; PhD, NYU, 1986. Ordained to ministry Christian and Missionary Alliance, 1958. Pastor Christian and Missionary Alliance Chs., Butler, Hollidaysburg, Meadville, Pa., 1956-68; prof. in Bible, Greek Manahath Ednl. Ctr., Altoona, Pa., 1961-63; prof. in Bible, theol. Toccoa Falls (Ga.) Coll., 1968—, dir. Sch. of Bible, Theol., 1968—, Fuller E. Callaway prof. of Bibl. studies, 1970—; adj. instr. Alliance Theol. Sem., Nyack, N.Y., 1989—. Contbr. articles to theol. jours., books. Trustee Manahath Ednl. Ctr., Hollidaysburg, 1968-73; pres. Cleve. Community Club, Madison, S.C., 1977-79; dir. Freedom Team Bible Conf. Ministries, 1972—, Shamaim Ministries, Westminster, S.C., 1977—; bd. dirs. Internat. Ctr. for Bibl. Counseling, Sioux City, Iowa, 1988—. Mem. Evang. Theol. Soc. (regional sec., treas. 1974-77, v.p. 1977-78, pres. 1978-79), Am. Acad. Religion, Religious Edn. Assn., Welseyan Theol. Soc. Republican. Avocations: gardening, reading, philately. Home: Rt 4 Box 264 Westminster SC 29693 Office: Toccoa Falls Coll PO Box 800725 Toccoa Falls GA 30598-0725 *Despite the grim realities of human need, we can offer immeasurable possibilities for progress if a person chooses the humble route of full submission to the kingdom of God and radical dependence on divine resources. Commitment to God logically involves a commitment to excellence.*

MCGREW, MICHAEL BRUCE, music minister; b. N.Y.C., Nov. 11, 1950; s. Palmer Whittemore and Dorothy Jean (Thorsen) McG.; m. Peggy Joan McGuffie, Nov. 21, 1970; children: Jennifer Dawn, Jeremy Michael. B in Music Edn., Stetson U., 1979; M of Ch. Music, Southwestern Bapt. Theol. Sem., Ft. Worth, 1981. Ordained to ministry So. Bapt. Conv., 1981. Min. youth 5th Ave. Bapt. Ch., St. Petersburg, Fla., 1983-87; min. music Pinecrest Bapt. Ch., Sanford, Fla., 1976-79, Univ. Bapt. Ch., Arlington, Tex., 1979-81, Main St. Bapt. Ch., Leesburg, Fla., 1981-83, Palma Sola Bay Bapt. Ch., Bradenton, Fla., 1987—; music chmn. Outreach Manatee, Bradenton, 1990—; mem. Dominica mission team Fgn. Mission Bd., So. Bapt. Conv., 1985. James Parrish scholar Stetson U., 1978-79. Mem. Choristers Guild, Am. Choral Dirs. Assn., So. Bapt. Ch. Conf., Fla. Bapt. Ch. Conf., Fla. Bapt. Singing Men. Home: 1518 67th St W Bradenton FL 34209 Office: Palma Sola Bay Bapt Ch 4000 75th St W Bradenton FL 34209 *Church musicians must constantly continue to learn. We have found a gift so rich that we've given our lives to studying, using and sharing it. Life is far more than merely a rehearsal for heaven. It is to be enjoyed to the fullest every moment.*

MCGROGAN, JAMES P., school system administrator. Supt. schs. Diocese of Gary, Ind. Office: Office Schs Supt 9292 Broadway Merrillville IN 46410*

MCGUIRE, ANNE MARIE, religion educator; b. New Haven, Oct. 5, 1951; d. John Patrick and Marie Anna (Laughlin) Mc G.; m. William Joseph Werpehowski, June 14, 1980; 1 child, Stephen John. BA, Barnard Coll., 1973; MA, Columbia U., 1975, Yale U., 1976; MPhil, Yale U., 1979, PhD, 1983. Instr. religious studies Villanova (Pa.) U., 1980-82; asst. prof. Haverford (Pa.) Coll., 1982-89, assoc. prof., chairperson dept., 1989—. Contbr. articles to religious jours. Whitehead fellow Haverford Coll., 1985-86. Mem. Soc. Bibl. Lit. (rep.-at-large to coun.), Coll. Theology Soc. Roman Catholic. Office: Haverford Coll Dept Religion Haverford PA 19041

MCGUIRE, DENNIS LEE, minister; b. Guam, Apr. 17, 1957; came to U.S., 1960; s. Stuart James and Minnie Joyce (Miller) McG.; m. Linda Louise Avrit, July 25, 1981. BS in Bible and Theology, San Jose Bible Coll., 1981. Ordained to ministry Oasis Fellowship Chs., 1983. Asst. pastor South Valley Chapel, San Jose, Calif., 1980-82; co-pastor Oasis Christian Fellowship, Grand Terrace, Calif., 1983-84; pastor, founder Oasis Christian Fellowship of Woodcrest, Riverside, Calif., 1984—, bd. dirs., 1985—; dir. Oasis Music Resource Ctr., Riverside, 1985—; exec. producer tapes Spirit Song, 1982, Branches, 1988; chaplain Riverside Fire Dept., 1991—. Mem. Riverside C. of C. Office: Oasis Christian Fellowship 17940 Van Buren Blvd Ste D Riverside CA 92508

MCGUIRE, SHIRLEY ELIZABETH, religious education director; b. Spangler, Pa., Oct. 13, 1944; d. Marinus Henry and Aurelia (Chiappelli) Dumm; m. Harry Paul McGuire, July 30, 1966; children: Scott, Timothy. Diploma, Mercy Hosp., 1965. RN, Pa. Catechist St. Nicholas Parish, Nicktown, Pa., 1976—; dir. religious edn. St. Nicholas Parish, Nicktown, 1989—, dir. Rite of Christian Initiation of Adults, 1989—. Mem. Parish Pastoral Coun., Nicktown, 1990-91, chmn. edn. commn., 1990-91. Democrat. Home: PO Box 61 Nicktown PA 15762

MC HALE, JOHN JOSEPH, baseball club executive; b. Detroit, Sept. 21, 1921; s. John Michael and Catherine M. (Kelly) McH.; m. Patricia Ann Cameron, Feb. 15, 1947; children—Patricia Cameron II, John Joseph, Kevin F., Anne F., Brian F., Mary M. A.B. cum laude, U. Notre Dame, 1947. Profl. baseball player, 1941-42, 45-47; asst. dir. minor league clubs Detroit Tigers Baseball Club, 1948, asst. farm dir., 1948-53, dir. minor league clubs, 1954-55, dir. player personnel, 1956-57, gen. mgr., 1957-58; v.p., gen. mgr. Milw. Braves Baseball Club (became Atlanta Braves Baseball Club 1961), 1957-61, pres., gen. mgr., 1961-67; adminstrv. asst. to commr. baseball N.Y.C., 1967-68; pres. Montreal Expos Baseball Club, 1968-87, dep. chmn., chief exec. officer, 1987—; dir. Perini Corp., Monenco Ltd., Montreal. Board dirs. St. Mary's Hosp., West Palm Beach, Fla., 1986—; trustee Jacksonville U., 1991. Club: Nat. Monogram (U. Notre Dame). Address: Harbor Ridge 2014 Royal Fern Ct 2014 Royal Fern Ct Palm City FL 34990

MCHALE, SISTER M. PERPETUA, nun; b. Rochester, N.Y., Jan. 4, 1920; d. William J. and Isabelle (Brown) McH. Teaching cert., Nazareth Normal, 1941; BA in English, Nazareth Coll., 1970, MA in Edn., 1975. Joined Roman Cath. Ch. Tchr., elem. St. John's Evang., Rochester, 1941-55; dir. of novices Sister of Mercy, Rochester, 1955-61; tchr. Our Lady of Mercy, Victor, N.Y., 1961-72; dir. religious edn. St. Patricks, Victor, 1973-90, parish visitor, 1990—. Home: 1437 Blossom Rd Rochester NY 14610 Office: St Patricks 115 Maple Ave Rochester NY 14564

MCHANN, JAMES CLARK, JR., college president; b. Vicksburg, Miss., July 19, 1950; s. James Clark and Alma Faye (Fletcher) McH.; m. Rebecca Tope, Jan. 30, 1978; children: James David, Jessica Heather. BA in Philosophy, Miss. Coll., Clinton, 1972; ThM in N.T., Dallas Theol. Sem., 1977; PhD in Hermeneutics, U. Aberdeen (Scotland), 1987. Assoc. pastor Hope United Meth. Ch., Akron, Ohio, 1977-78; mem. faculty Internat. Sch. Theology, San Bernardino, Calif., 1978-87; pres. Internat. Sch. Theology, San Bernardino, 1987-90, William Tyndale Coll., Farmington Hills, Mich., 1990—. Author: The Three Horizons, 1991; contbr. articles to profl. jours. Sunday sch. tchr., speaker, preacher various chs. Mem. Am. Acad. Religion, Soc. Bibl. Lit., Christian Mgmt. Assn., Fellowship Evang. Sem. Pres. Office: William Tyndale Coll 35700 W 12 Mile Rd Farmington Hills MI 48331

MCHATTEN, MARY TIMOTHY, religious educator; b. Castle Hill, Maine, Oct. 20, 1931; d. Herman Mayhew and Verna Mae (Sharp) McH. MEd, Boston Coll., 1963; MA, Providence (R.I.) Coll., 1971; PhD, U. Ottawa, 1979; eleve titulaire, Ecole Biblique, Jerusalem, 1984. Prof. sci. St. Joseph's Coll., North Windham, Maine, 1964-65; prof. Scripture Kino Inst., Phoenix, 1973-89, Mount Angel Seminary, St. Benedict, Oreg., 1989—. Mem. Soc. Bibl. Lit., Cath. Bibl. Assn., Bibl. Archaeology Soc. Home: 840 S Main St Mount Angel OR 97362 Office: Mount Angel Seminary Saint Benedict OR 97373 *Although we all have our meadow of life—the outcome depends on the flowers we pick.*

MCHUGH, BRIAN JOSEPH, priest; b. Lowell, Mass., Aug. 22, 1959; s. Robert Joseph and Jane Marie (Golen) McH. BA cum laude, U. Lowell, 1981; MDiv, St. John's Sem., Brighton, Mass., 1988. Ordained priest Roman Cath. Ch., 1988; cert. secondary history tchr., Mass. Jr. high sch. tchr. St. Charles Parish, Woburn, Mass., 1981-83; deacon Immaculate Conception Ch., Salem, Mass., 1987-88; priest St. Francis Xavier Ch., South Weymouth, Mass., 1988—. Mem. U. Lowell Honor Soc. in Edn., K.C. Democrat. Avocations: tennis, reading. Home and Office: 261 Pleasant St South Weymouth MA 02190

MCILHONE, JAMES PATRICK, religion educator; b. Chgo., July 14, 1948; s. John Vincent and Sheila (Scully) McI. MDiv, St. Mary of Lake Sem., 1974, STL, 1975; PhD, Marquette U., 1987. Ordained priest Roman Cath. Ch., 1974. Assoc. pastor Our Lady of the Wayside Ch., Arlington Heights, Ill., 1974-80, Santa Maria del Popolo Ch., Mundelein, Ill., 1980-87; assoc. prof. Mundelein Sem., 1987—; Author: The Word Make Clear, 1989; contbr. articles to profl. publs. Mem. Cath. Bibl. Assn., Am. Acad. Religion, Soc. Bibl. Lit., Chgo. Soc. Bibl. Rsch., Bibl. Archeol. Soc. Home: 189-5 Howard Ct Fox Lake IL 60020 Office: Mundelein Sem U St Mary of Lake Mundelein IL 60060

MCILVEENE, CHARLES STEELE, minister; b. McNeil, Ark., Feb. 11, 1928; s. Bonnie Leonard and Lillian Irene (Owen) McI.; m. Betty Marie Fahlberg, Aug. 12, 1952; children: Carol Ann, Mary Elizabeth, Charles Scott. BA, Hardin-Simmons U., 1949; BD, Southwestern Bapt. Theol. Sem., 1953, MRE, 1954, D Ministry, 1980. Ordained to ministry So. Bapt. Conv. 1948. Asst. pastor Broadmoor Bapt. Ch., Shreveport, La., 1954-57; pastor Lakeshore Bapt. Ch., Shreveport, 1957-61, Trinity Bapt. Ch., Lake Charles, La., 1961-71, 1st Bapt. Ch., Lufkin, Tex., 1971—; mem. exec. bd. La. Bapt. Conv., 1961-67, 70-71, 1st v.p., 1964; evangelist, S.Am., 1960, The Philippines, 1968, Republic of Korea, 1970, Australia, 1985, Republic South Africa, 1989; pres. Shreveport Ministerial Assn., 1959, Calcasieu Parish Ministerial Assn., 1961-63, Angelina County Ministerial Assn., 1982-83; moderator Carey Bapt. Assn., 1963-65; bd. dirs. Bapt. Gen. Conv. Tex. 1971-84, 1st v.p., 1984, mem. human welfare coordinating bd., 1984-90; mem. com. on bds. So. Bapt. Conv., 1967. Contbr. articles to religious jours. Trustee La. Coll., 1965-71, East Tex. Bapt. Coll., 1971-90; bd. dirs. local chpts. Am. Cancer Soc., Am. Heart Assn., Angelina County United Way. Home: 1305 Woodland St Lufkin TX 75901 Office: PO Box 1448 Lufkin TX 75901

MCINNES, VAL AMBROSE GORDON, priest; b. London, Ont., Can., Apr. 21, 1929; came to U.S., 1954; s. Angus and Genevieve (Rodgers) McI. BA, U. Western Ont., 1952; postgrad., U. Leyden, 1953; diploma in law, Internat. Ct., The Hague, The Netherlands, 1953; MA, U. Windsor, 1954; PhB, Aquinas Inst., 1957, PhL, 1958, PhD, 1966. Joined Order of Preachers, Roman Cath. Ch., 1954, ordained priest, 1961. Instr. moral theology St. Thomas Coll., St. Paul, 1962-65; head dept. philosophy and theology King's Coll., U. Western Ont., 1965-66; dir. Cath. Ctr., Tulane U., New Orleans, 1967-70, pastor univ. community of St. Thomas More, 1970-79, founder, dir., exec. sec. chair for Judeo-Christian studies, 1979—; del. 1st World Conf. on Religion and Peace, Kyoto, Japan, 1970, 2d Conf., Louvain, Belgium, 1974; prior St. Anthony of Padua Priory, 1976-83; sr. chaplain Knights of St. Lazarus, 1978—; knight comdr., chaplain Order of Holy Sepulcher, 1991; bd. dirs. Am. Assn. of St. Lazarus, 1979—; dir. Vatican Pavilion, La. World Expn., 1984; mem. Concilium Vaticum Mus. Adv. Bd., 1985—; bd. dirs. Religious Ecumenical Access Channel (REACH), 1989—; adj. prof. Sch. of Medicine, Tulane U., 1969-80, Univ. Coll., 1970-79; cons. Republic of China, 1991. Producer TV series Faith to Faith, 1987—. Bd. dirs. La. Coun. for Music and Performing Arts, 1967—, chmn. fine arts, 1969-78, pres., 1978-87; founding mem., v.p. La. Renaissance, Religion and Arts, 1976-82, pres., 1977-78; founder, pres. Patrons of The Vatican Mus. in the South, Inc., 1988-90; bd. dirs. So. Dominican Found., 1986—, Fra Angelico Bd., 1991—, Aquinas Ctr. Theology Bd., Emory U., 1991—. Recipient LCMPA medal, 1977, Canova medal, Vat. Mus., 1985; UNESCO scholar, 1963; grantee Can. Coun., 1966. Mem. Omicron Delta Kappa. Home: 775 Harrison Ave New Orleans LA 70184 Office: Tulane U Univ Chapel Sophie Newcomb Coll 1229 Broadway New Orleans LA 70118

MCINTEER, JIM BILL, minister, publishing executive, farmer; b. Franklin, Ky., June 16, 1921; s. William Thomas and Mary Edna (Rutherford) McI.; m. Betty Bergner, July 20, 1943; children: MariLynn McInteer Canterbury, Mark Martin. Cert., David Lipscomb Coll., Nashville, 1940; BA, Harding U., 1942; LLD (hon.), Pepperdine U., 1980, Harding U., 1991. Ordained to ministry Ch. of Christ. Minister Ch. of Christ, Sheridan, Ark., 1942-46, Isabel, Kans., 1947, Locust Grove, Ky., 1948-52, Grace Ave. Ch., Nashville, 1952-56, West End Ch., Nashville, 1956-86; nat. evangelist, 1986—; bus. mgr., pres., pub. 20th Century Christian, Nashville, 1947—; farmer, Franklin,, 1948—. Author: Tiny Tot's Bible Reader, 1956, Great Preachers of Today, 1966. Bd. dirs. Harding U., Searcy, Ark., 1950—, Potter Children's Home, Bowling Green, Ky., 1960—, Fanning Found., Nashville, 1975—, Campbell Trust Fund, Nashville, 1978—. Recipient Alumnus of Yr. award David Lipscomb Coll., 1985, Diakonia award David Lipscomb U., 1990, Disting. Christian Svc. award Pepperdine U., 1991. Mem. SAR. Lodge: Civitan Internat. (dist. chaplain 1975). Avocations: photography, woodcutting, vegetable gardening. Home: 1100 Belvidere Dr Nashville TN 37204 Office: 20th Century Christian Inc 2809 Granny White Pike Nashville TN 37204 *That glorious truth about all of Jesus' words: "They found it exactly as He said." Then why not preach it exactly as He said it—surely there is no safer way.*

MCINTOSH, JAY RICHARD, minister; b. Paducah, Ky., Sept. 1, 1968; s. Tommy Cook and Madeline Sue (Holt) McI. BA, Union U., Jackson, Tenn., 1991. Lic. to ministry So. Bapt. Conv. Recreation asst. First Bapt. Ch., Paducah, Ky., 1986-87; youth minister Gates (Tenn.) Bapt. Ch., 1988-90, First Bapt. Ch., Rutherford, Tenn., 1990—; co-program dir. Youth Leadership Seminar, Jackson, 1990—. New Orleans Bapt. Theol. Sem. scholar, 1991. Mem. Ministerial Assn. of Union U. (pres. 1989-90), West Tenn. Youth Ministers, Bapt. Student Union (pres. student govt.), Lambda Chi Alpha, Pi Gamma Mu. Home: 231 Canterbury Cove Paducah KY 42001 Office: First Bapt Ch PO Box 277 Rutherford TN 38369

MCINTYRE, RALPH JACKSON, minister; b. Double-Branch, Ga., Aug. 18, 1923; s. Summie Jackson and Dessie Bell (Towery) McI.; m. Frances Bonnie Houston, May 22, 1946; children: Terry Blaine, Karen Elaine McIntyre Cole. BA, Elysion Coll., 1977, Coll. Pentecost, 1979; D of Ministry, Drew U., 1981. Ordained to ministry United Pentecostal Ch. Internat., 1963. Pastor First United Pentecostal Ch., Glen Burnie, Md., 1957-65; pastor Apostolic Life Ctr. United Pentecostal Ch. Internat., Essex, Md., 1965—; pastor and sectional presbyter United Pentecostal Ch. Internat., W.Va., Md., 1966-73, pastor and sec., treas. E. cen. dist., 1973-74; pastor and dist. supr. Md. and D.C. dists. United Pentecostal Ch. Internat., Md., 1974-88; prin. Christian Sch., 1976-86; bd. dirs. Kent Christian Coll., Dover, Del., 1980-82; hon. bd. dirs. Md. D.C. dist. United Pentecostal Ch. Internat., Md., 1988—, Hazelwood, Mo., 1988—. With USN, 1943-45. Home: 4 Right Wing Dr Baltimore MD 21220 *My wisdom would be that if the desire is strong enough most any realistic goal can be attained regardless of how great the challenge.*

MC INTYRE, ROBERT WALTER, church official; b. Bethlehem, Pa., June 20, 1922; s. Simon Jesse and Ruth (Young) McI.; m. Edith Jones, Sept. 1, 1944 (dec. Jan. 1953); m. Elizabeth Norman, Nov. 6, 1953; children: Judith McIntyre Keilholtz, Joy McIntyre McCallum, John, James, June McIntyre Brannon. Student, Miltonvale Wesleyan Coll., 1939-43; B.Religion, Marion Coll., 1944, B.A., 1959; postgrad., Ball State U., 1960-61. Ordained to ministry The Wesleyan Ch., 1945. Pastor Marengo, Ohio, 1944-47, Columbus, Ohio, 1947-52, Coshocton, Ohio, 1952-55; exec. sec. dept. youth The Wesleyan Ch., Marion, Ind., 1955-68; editor The Wesleyan Youth, Marion, 1955-68; gen. editor The Wesleyan Ch., editor The Wesleyan Adv., Marion, 1968-73; assoc. editor The Preacher's Mag., Marion, 1973-88; gen. supt. The Wesleyan Ch., Marion, 1973-88; mem. gen. bd. adminstrn. The Wesleyan Ch., 1955-88, mem. Commn. Christian Edn., 1959-73, 76-80, chmn. Commn. Christian Edn., 1976-80, mem. exec. bd., 1968-88; chmn. Commn. on World Missions, 1973-76, Commn. on Publs., 1980-84, Commn. on Extension and Evangelism, 1984-88; spl. asst. to the pres. Ind. Wesleyan U., Marion, 1988—; denominational rep., bd. adminstrn. Nat. Assn. Evangelicals, 1973-83, exec. com., 1978-80, 81-87, 2d v.p., 1981-82, 1st v.p., 1982-84, pres., 1984-86, mem., 1973—; denominational rep. The Lord's Day Alliance, 1973-76; trustee Marion Coll., Asbury Theol. Sem., 1976—. Author: Ten Commandments for Teen-Agers, 1965; editor: Program Pathways for Young Adults, 1964, Mandate for Mission, 1970; contbr. articles to religious jours. Mem. Christian Holiness Assn. (chmn. social action commn. 1971-73, sec. 1973-76), Wesleyan Theol. Soc., Best Years Fellowship (gen. dir. 1990—). Home: 4613 S Star Dr Marion IN 46953 Office: Ind Wesleyan Univ 4201 S Washington St Marion IN 46952

MCIVER, DAVID WILLIAM, broadcasting executive; b. Glenwood, Minn., May 15, 1960; s. Daniel N. and Geri (Armerding) McI.; m. Sherrie L. Kuehne, July 14, 1984; children: Jordan, Kyle. BA in Bibl. Studies, Bethel Coll., 1982. Gen. mgr. Sta. KBHL Radio, Osakis, Minn., 1987—. Office: Sta KBHL Radio Box 247 Osakis MN 56360

MCIVER, GUY HARDING, minister; b. Columbus, Ohio, Nov. 20, 1939; s. Addie Harding and Martha Viola (Glass) McI.; m. Jeanne Elizabeth Payne, June 10, 1961; children: Molly, Guy Jr., William, Kathryn. BS in Edn., Ohio State U., 1961; MDiv, Pitts. Sem., 1966. Ordained to ministry, Presbyn. Ch. (U.S.A.), 1966. Pastor First Presbyn. Ch., Crestline, Ohio, 1966-68; assoc. pastor First Presbyn. Ch., Chillicothe, Ohio, 1968-72; pastor First Presbyn. Ch., Sidney, Ohio, 1972-90; campus pastor Sinclair Community Coll., Dayton, Ohio, 1990—; instr., lectr. Sinclair Community Coll., Dayton, 1990—; coun. mem. Ohio Presbyn. Homes, Sidney, Ohio, 1972-88; unit presbytery dir. Synod of the Covenant, Columbus, 1985—. Home: 1915 Benson Dr Dayton OH 45406 Office: Sinclair Community Coll 444 W Third St #10-317 Dayton OH 45402

MCKAY, CHARLES DOUGLAS, youth and music director; b. Moberly, Mo., July 24, 1957; s. Charles Edward McKay and Hazel Mae (Barnes) Gladney; m. Barbara Lois Gibson, June 12, 1982; children: William Edward, Andrea Pauline, Robert Douglas. MusB, S.E. Mo. State U., 1979. Music/youth dir. Bethany Bapt. Ch., Cape Girardeau, Mo., 1977; music dir. Charleston (Mo.) First Bapt. Ch., 1979; music/youth dir. Southside Bapt. Ch., Cape Girardeau, 1981; youth dir. New Salem Bapt. Ch., Lutesville, Mo., 1982; music dir. Third St. Bapt. Ch., Kennett, Mo., 1983-85; music/youth dir. First Bapt. Ch., Winfield, Mo., 1989—; vocal music tchr. Francis Howell Sch. Dist., St. Charles, Mo., 1989—; music dir. Cuirre Assn. Missions, Troy, Mo., 1987-89; v.p. Vocal Chairperson for All-Dist. Choir S.E. Mo. Music Educators, Cape Girardeau, 1982-84, Div. 5 S.E. Mo. Band Assn., 1982. Recipient John Philip Sousu Band award Elsberry High Sch., 1975; named Mem. Mo. All-State Choir, 1975. Mem. Phi Mu Alpha Sinfonia Iota Psi Chpt. (historian 1976, pledge instr. 1979, best pledge 1975, best active mem. 1979). Republican. Home: 503 N 4th St Elsberry MO 63343 Office: First Bapt Ch Second & Cherry PO Box 105 Winfield MO 63389

MCKAY, JAMES A., ecumenical agency director. Head Oshawa Ecumenical Group, Ont., Can. Office: Oshawa Ecumenical Group, 333 Rossland Rd N, Oshawa, ON Canada L1J 3G4*

MC KAY, SAMUEL LEROY, clergyman; b. Charlotte, N.C., Oct. 15, 1913; s. Elmer Ranson and Arlena (Benfield) McK.; A.B. cum laude, Erskine Coll., 1937; B.D. cum laude, Erskine Theol. Sem., 1939; postgrad. U. Ga., 1941-42, Union Theol. Sem., 1957; m. Martha Elizabeth Caldwell, Apr. 29, 1939; children—Samuel LeRoy, Mary Louise, William Ranson. Ordained to ministry of Presbyn. Ch., 1940; pastor Prosperity Assoc. Ref. Ch., Fayetteville, Tenn., 1942-46, Bethel Assoc. Ref. Ch., Oak Hill, Ala., 1946-50, 1st Asso. Ref. Ch., Salisbury, N.C., 1950-53, 1st Ch. U.S., Dallas, N.C., 1953-60, First Ch., Kernersville, N.C., 1960-66, Cooleemee (N.C.) Presbyn. Ch., 1966-69, Broadway (N.C.) Presbyn. Ch., 1969-80, Cape Fear Presbyn. Ch., 1983-91, Sardis Presbyn. Ch., 1984-86; stated clk. Gen. Synod Assoc. Ref. Presbyn. Ch., 1950-53; commr. Gen. Assembly Presbyn. Ch. U.S., 1960, 69; permanent clk. Winston-Salem Presbytery, 1961-69, chmn. leadership edn. com., 1962-66, chmn. Christian edn. com., 1967-68; chmn. nominations com. Fayetteville Presbytery, 1977-79; mem. hunger task force Fayetteville Presbytery, 1984-88, chmn. com. on Bangladesh, 1985-87; supr. chaplaincy program Davie County Hosp., 1968-69. Pres. Dallas PTA, 1955-56; bd. mgrs. Kernersville YMCA, 1962-66, chmn. membership com., 1963, treas., 1964, pres., 1965-66; bd. dirs. Winston-Salem-Forsyth County YMCA, 1965-66. Mem. Kernersville Area Ministers Assn. (pres. 1963-64), N.C. Poetry Soc. (dir. 1971—, chmn. poetry contests 1970-72, 83-88, editor ann. book Award-Winning Poems 1972-90; pres. 1971-74), Clan MacKay Soc. N.Am. (pres. 1971-75, chaplain 1976-90—, coun. 1983-90, honored guest, prin. speaker 1985 internat. gathering Glasgow, Scotland 1985, speaker at Clan Mackay Soc. Centenary Celebration, Edinburgh, Scotland, 1988, elected hon. mem. 1988). Lodge: Lions. Author: (poems) Harbinger; contbr. articles and sermons to periodicals and publs. *Perhaps the first thing to mark one's breeding is respect for the person of others and courtesy in matters of disagreement.*

MCKEEVER, JAMES M., economist; b. Dallas, June 8, 1929; s. John Reavis and Athalea May (Smith) McK.; m. Jean I Patterson, Apr. 11, 1976. BS in Math., So. Meth. U., 1954; MS in Econ., Columbia Pacific U., PhD in Econ., 1985; ThD, New Covenant Internat. Bible Coll., Auckland, New Zealand, 1986. Economist James A. Lewis Petroleum, Dallas, 1954-58; economist, sr. applied scientist IBM, Dallas, L.A., 1958-68; pres. Triversal Industries, L.A., 1968-73, Jalco, Vancouver, BC, Canada, 1974-76, Omega Ministries, Medford, Oreg., 1976—; speaker in field. Author: Financial Guidance, The AIDS Plague, Be Prepared, Close Encounters of the Highest Kind, The Future Revealed, You Can Overcome, Become Like Jesus, The Rapture Book, Supernatural Power, Believe It or Not... It's in the Bible, Claim Your Birthright, Why Were You Created, Jesus For the Rest of Your Life, The Knowledge of Good and Evil, How You Can Know the Will of God, Only One Word, Is There Really Going To Be an Antichrist?, Whatever Happened to Hope?, How to Avoid the Mark of the Beast, Where Will You Be 300 Years From Now?, Christians Will Go Through the Tribulation and How to Prepare for It; editor: McKeever Money Strategy Newsletter, End-Times Digest. Recipient Key Man award, IBM, Gold Angel award, Excellence in Media. Mem. Rep. Presidential Task Force, Presidential Inner Circle, Rep. Senatorial Inner Circle. Avocations: tennis, skiing, badminton, volleyball, rafting. Office: McKeever Mutual Funds 132 W Main Medford OR 97501

MCKELVEY, JOSEPH HAROLD, JR., minister; b. Roswell, N. Mex., Nov. 30, 1952; s. Joseph Harold and Lorraine (Stuart) McKelvey; m. Terri Lynn Morrison, Nov. 10, 1973; children: Kathryn Dianne, Michael Joseph. BA, Honolulu U., 1987, MBA, 1989. Youth pastor Cambridge (Md.) Christian Fellowship, 1981-82; pastor Christian Faith Fellowship, Middletown, N.Y., 1982—; pres. Christian Faith Fellowship, Inc., Middletown, 1982—. With USAF, 1971-75. Mem. Covenant Ministries Internat., (trustee Edison, N.J. 1988—), LeSea End Times Joseph Program, South Bend, Ind. (internat. dir. 1988-90). Home: 10 Monica Ct Middletown NY 10940 Office: Christian Faith Fellowship 10 E Main St Middletown NY 10940

MCKEMY, DAVID SCOTT, evangelist; b. Melbourne, Fla., May 11, 1962; s. Robert L. and Noreda (McCarty) McK.; m. Shannon M. Manning; 1 child, Andrew James. BTh, Jackson Coll. of Ministry, Miss., 1983. Evangelist United Pentecostal Ch., Melbourne, Fla., 1983—; gospel musician The McGruders, 1987—. Musician: (tapes) David McKemy and His Harmonica, 1986, Straight From the Harp, 1990 (Four Star Rating). Republican. Home: 728 Peregrine Dr Indialantic FL 32903-4721

MC KENNA, DAVID LOREN, seminary president, clergyman; b. Detroit, May 5, 1929; s. William Loren and Ilmi E. (Matson) McK.; m. Janet Voorheis, June 9, 1950; children: David Douglas, Debra Lynn, Suzanne Marie, Robert Bruce. AA, Spring Arbor Jr. Coll., 1949; BA magna cum laude in History, Western Mich. U., 1951; MDiv, Asbury Theol. Sem., 1953; MA, U. Mich., 1955, PhD (Clifford Woody scholar), 1958; LLD, Houghton Coll., 1974, Spring Arbor Coll., 1976, Lewis and Clark Coll., 1978, Seattle U., 1982, Marion Coll., 1983; LHD, Roberts Wesleyan Coll., 1986. Ordained to ministry Free Methodist Ch. N.Am., 1950; dean of men Spring Arbor Jr. Coll., 1953-55, instr. psychology, 1955-60, acad. dean, 1955-57, v.p., 1958-60, pres., 1961-68; lectr. higher edn. U. Mich., 1958-60; asst. prof., coord. Ctr. for the Study of Higher Edn., Ohio State U., Columbus, 1960-61; pres. Seattle Pacific U., 1968-82, Asbury Theol. Sem., 1982—; del. World Meth. Coun., London, 1966, Nairobi, Kenya, 1987, Singapore, 1991, v.p. N.Am. sect., 1987—; chmn. Mich. Commn. Coll. Accrediting, 1966-68; bd. dirs. Council Advancement Small Colls., 1964-67; pres. Assn. Free Meth. Colls., 1968-70; chmn. Christian Coll. Consortium, 1970-74; participant Internat. Congress World Evangelization, 1974, Consultation on World Evangelization, Pattaya, Thailand, 1980, Lausanne II, Manila, 1989; mem. bd. adminstrn., exec. com. Nat. Assn. Evangelicals, 2d v.p., 1975-81; bd. reference Black Evangelistic Enterprise, Evangelicals for Social Action, Ugandan Relief, Youth for Christ Internat. Author: The Jesus Model, 1976, Awake, My Conscience!, 1977, The Communicator's Commentary: Mark, 1982, The Communicator's Commentary: Job, 1986, Renewing Our Ministry, 1986, Mega Truth, 1986, The Whisper of His Grace, 1987, Discovering Job, 1988, Power to Follow, Grace to Lead, 1989, Love Your Work, 1990, The Coming Great Awakening, 1990; exec. editor: The Urban Crisis, 1969, Minister's Personal Library, 1987-89, Religious Book Club, 1989—; nat. radio commentator: This is Our World, 1983—; contbr. articles to profl. jours. Pres. United Community Services, Jackson, Mich., 1968, Wash. Coll. Assn., 1970, 76; trustee United Way, Pacific Sci. Ctr., Seattle Found., Spring Arbor Coll., 1983—; bd. dirs. Bread for the World, 1980-86, Jr. Achievement, 1966-68, Land O'Lakes council Boy Scouts Am., 1965-68; mem. Wash. State Council Postsecondary Edn., 1969-74, Pacific Sci. Ctr., 1969-82, Seattle Found., 1975-82; v.p. Bluegrass Tomorrow, 1989—; chmn. R & D com. United Way Bluegrass, 1984-89, bd. dirs., 1987—. Named One of Outstanding Young Men of Year Jr. C. of C., 1965, Seattle and Puget Sound Outstanding Citizen of Yr., 1976. Mem. Assn. Am. Colls. (dir. 1974-77), Ind. Colls. Wash. (pres. 1969-71, co-chmn. 1968-70, 79-80), Wash. State Council Econ. Edn. (dir. 1980), Am. Council Edn. (interassn. pres.'s com. on accreditation 1979-80), N.W. Assn. Schs. and Colls. (commr. 1975-79), N. Central Assn. Colls. and Schs. (chmn., dir. 1966-68), Nat. Assn. Ind. Colls. and Univs. (dir. 1976-80, sec. 1978), Council Postsecondary Accreditation (dir. 1979—), Seattle C. of C., Wash. Friends of Higher Edn., Wash. Athletic Club (bd. govs.), Rainier Club (Seattle), The Diet Club, Lafayette (Ky.) Club, Lexington Tennis Club, Rotary (pres. Jackson chpt. 1966-67, Paul Harris fellow 1982), Phi Kappa Phi. Office: Asbury Theol Sem Office of Pres Wilmore KY 40390

MCKENNA, JOHN EMORY, religion teacher; b. Cleve., Oct. 30, 1935; s. Charles Emory and Margaret Elizabeth (Hyde) McK.; m. Nancy Ann McVicker, Oct. 3, 1972; 1 child, Paul Drew. AB in Phys. Chemistry, Princeton U., 1957; MDiv in Theology, Fuller Theol. Sem., 1979, PhD in Hist. Theology summa cum laude, 1987; student, San Francisco State Coll., 1967-71. Intern to Centrum of Hollywood Hollywood, Calif., 1976-79; tchr. of Christian edn. various chs., Calif., 1979—; teaching fellow in Hebrew Fuller Theol. Sem., Pasadena, Calif., 1979-87; adj. prof. in sci. and religion Fuller Theol. Sem., Pasadena, 1986, adj. prof. in Hebrew and Old Testament, 1987—; adj. prof. of Hebrew and Old Testament Internat. Theol. Sem., L.A., 1983-85; v.p. Flight to Freedom, San Juan Capistrano, Calif., 1976—. Contbr. book reviews, poetry and articles to profl. jours.; patentee in field. With U.S. Army, 1958-61. Recipient scholarship, Princeton U., 1953-57, William Sanford LaSor award, Fuller Theol. Sem., 1979. Mem. Am. Sci. Affiliation, The Nat. Assn. Profs. Hebrew, Soc. for Pentacostal Studies, John Witherspoon Inst. Republican. Avocations: reading, writing. Office: Fuller Theol Seminary Pasadena CA 91182

MCKENNA, JOHN HOLCOMB, priest, theology educator; b. Bklyn., May 25, 1936. Student, Marquette U., St. Joseph's Coll., Princeton, N.J.; BA in Philosophy summa cum laude, Mary Immaculate Sem. & Coll., 1960, MDiv in Theology magna cum laude, 1964; Licentiate in Sacred Theology cum laude, Trierer Theol. Fakultat, Fed. Republic Germany, 1968, STD summa cum laude, 1971. Joined Congregation of the Mission, Roman Cath. Ch., 1956, ordained priest, 1964. Instr. theology St. Joseph's Coll., Emmitsburg, Md.; instr., spiritual dir. St. Vincent dePaul Sem., Boynton Beach, Fla., 1970-71, Sem. Our Lady of Angels, Albany, N.Y., 1971-72; prof. theology St. John's U., Jamaica, N.Y., 1972—, John A. Flynn chair, 1991—, chairperson dept. theology, 1981-87, spl. asst. to v.p. in charge campus ministry; chaplain cen. house Daus. of Charity, Emmitsburg; advisor com. on liturgy Nat. Conf. Cath. Bishops; vis. scholar Yale U., 1988. Author: Eucharist and Holy Spirit, 1975; (with others) New Eucharistic Prayers: An Ecumenical Study of their Development and Structure, 1987; contbr. to: The New Dictionary of Theology, 1987, New Catholic Encyclopedia, 1973-74, The New Dictionary of Sacramental Worship, 1990; contbr. articles to profl. jours. Bd. dirs. Pastoral Inst., Diocese of Bklyn., 1975—. Recipient Bene award Modern Liturgy jour., medal St. John's U., 1986. Mem. Soc. for Sci. Study of Religion, Cath. Theol. Soc. Am., Coll. Tchrs. Soc. Am., Nat. Liturgical Conf., N.Am. Acad. Liturgy (v.p. 1981, pres. 1982), Skull and Circle Soc. (hon.).

MCKENZIE, ELIJAH GEORGE, minister; b. Birmingham, Eng., June 28, 1964; came to U.S., 1981; s. Israel Woodrow and Adina (Morgan) McK.; m. Marion Fox, Apr. 1, 1991. BA, Atlantic Union Coll., 1983; MDiv, Andrews U., 1985. Ordained to ministry Bapt. Ch., 1982. Asst. pastor Ellenville (N.Y.) Bapt. Ch., 1984-86; pastor Riverhead Bapt. Ch., L.I., N.Y., 1988-91. Author: Dead Sea Scrolls, 1987. Mem. Rosicrucians. Democrat.

MCKEVITT, GERALD LAWRENCE, priest, historian; b. Longview, Wash., July 3, 1939; s. Edward Henry and Evelyn (Acock) McK. BA, U. San Francisco, 1961; MA, U. So. Calif., L.A., 1964; PhD, UCLA, 1972; BST, Gregorian U., Rome, 1975. Ordained priest Roman Cath. Ch., 1975. Univ. archivist Santa Clara (Calif.) U., 1975-85, chmn. history dept., 1984-88, prof. history, 1975—, univ. historian, 1985—. Author: Univ. of Santa Clara, A History, 1851-1977; contbr. articles to profl. jours. Trustee Gonzaga U., Spokane, 1988—. Fellow NSF, 1985-87, U.S. Dept. Health, Edn. and Welfare, 1961-63. Mem. Am. Hist. Assn., Am. Cath. Hist. Assn., Am. Italian Hist. Assn., Am. Soc. Ch. History, Western History Assn., Calif. Hist. Soc. Roman Catholic. Home: Univ Santa Clara Nobili Hall Santa Clara CA 95053 Office: Santa Clara Univ History Dept Santa Clara CA 95053

MCKILLOP, SISTER M. LUCILLE, academic administrator. Pres. Salve Regina-The Newport Coll., R.I. Office: Salve Regina-The Newport Coll Newport RI 02840*

MCKIM, DONALD KEITH, minister; b. New Castle, Pa., Feb. 25, 1950; s. Keith Beatty and Mary Alisan (Leslie) McK.; m. LindaJo Horton, Feb. 28, 1976; children: Stephen, Karl. BA cum laude with honors in Religion, Westminster Coll., New Wilmington, Pa., 1971; MDiv magna cum laude, Pitts. Theol. Sem., 1974; PhD, U. Pitts., 1980. Ordained to ministry Presbyn. Ch. (U.S.A.), 1975. Stated supply pastor Friendship Parish, Slippery Rock, Pa., 1970-81; prof. theology U. Dubuque (Iowa) Theol. Sem., 1981-88; interim pastor Trinity Presbyn. Ch., Berwyn, Pa., 1988-91; mem. Theology Task Group Presbyteries' Coop. Com., Presbyn. Ch. (U.S.A.), 1983-91, group chmn., 1987-91. Author: (with Jack B. Rogers) The Authority and Interpretation of the Bible: An Historical Approach, 1979 (Book of Yr. award Eternity mag. 1980); What Christians Believe about the Bible, 1985, Ramism in William Perkins' Theology, 1987, Theological Turning Points, 1988; editor: The Authoritative Word: Essays on the Nature of Scripture, 1983, Readings in Calvin's Theology, 1984, How Karl Barth Changed My Mind, 1986, A Guide to Contemporary Hermeneutics, 1986, Major Themes in the Reformed Tradition, 1991, Encyclopedia of the Reformed Faith, 1992. Mem. Calvin Studies Soc. (v.p. 1987-89, pres. 1989-91), Am. Soc. Ch. History, Am. Acad. Religion, Presbyn. Hist. Soc., 16th Century Studies Soc. Home: 60 Dayleview Rd Berwyn PA 19312

MCKINLEY, ELLEN BACON, priest; b. Milw., June 9, 1929; d. Edward Alsted and Lorraine Goodrich (Graham) Bacon; m. Richard Smallbrook McKinley, III, June 16, 1951 (div. Oct. 1977); children: Richard IV, Ellen Graham, David Todd, Edward Bacon. BA cum laude, Bryn Mawr Coll., 1951; MDiv Yale U., 1976; STM, Gen. Theol. Sem., N.Y.C., 1979; PhD, Union Theol. Sem., N.Y.C., 1988. Ordained to ministry Episcopal Ch. as deacon, 1980, as priest, 1981. Intern St. Francis Ch., Stamford, Conn., 1976-77; pastoral asst. St. Paul's Ch., Riverside, Conn., 1979-80, curate, 1980-81; priest assoc. St. Saviour's Ch., Old Greenwich, Conn., 1982-90; asst. St. Christopher's Ch., Chatham, Mass., 1987-88, interim asst., Trinity Ch., Princeton, N.J., 1990-91. Mem. Episcpal Election Com., Diocese of Conn., 1986-87, Com. on Human Sexuality, 1987-90; Com. on Donations and Bequests Diocese of Conn., 1987-90; sec., Greewich Com. on Drugs, 1970-71; bd. dirs. Greenwich YWCA, 1971-72. Mem. Episcopal Women's Caucus, New Eng. Women Ministers Assn., Colonial Dames Am., Jr. League. Clubs: Sulgrave, Rocky Point. Avocations: theatre, concerts, swimming, sailing, reading, architecture, building and remodeling houses. *God has a sense of humor and is unwilling for me to take myself too seriously or think I am in charge of my life. Whenver I have had my life organized, something unexpected rearranged it. I have come to chuckle at myself with God while following unexpected paths.*

MCKINLEY, ERNEST COLEMAN, minister, accountant; b. Evansville, Ind., July 5, 1955; s. James Thomas and Geneva (Shields) McK.; m. Debra Jean Lindsey, Mar. 5, 1977; children: Shuan David, Lindsay Brooke. AS, Ind. State U., 1986; BTh, Internat. Sem., Plymouth, Fla., 1989. Ordained to ministry Pentecostal Ch. Pastor Ch. of God of Prophecy, Vincennes, Ind., 1983-87, Kingsport, Tenn., 1987-89, Columbia, Tenn., 1989—; bd. dirs. Good Samaritan of Columbia, 1989—; mem. Ministerial Rev. Bd., Hendersonville, Tenn., 1989—, Maury County Ministerial Assn., Columbia, 1989; instr. Sharing Eternal Life Ministry, Cleve., 1989—; radio min., 1986—. Contbr. articles to profl. publs. Chaplain Civil Air Patrol, Maury County, Tenn., 1989—. With U.S. Army, 1974-79. Republican. Home: 1420 Perkins Ln Columbia TN 38401 Office: Ch of God of Prophecy 1423 Williamsport Pike Columbia TN 38401

MCKINNELL, JAMES CHARLES, minister, county official; b. Zenda, Wis., Mar. 22, 1933; s. James Charles and Margaret Joyce (Wiedenhoft) McK.; m. Letha Miriam Miller, Mar. 22, 1959; children: James Charles, Andrew Craig. BA, Grinnell Coll., 1957; BD, Bethany Bibl. Sem., Chgo., 1961; D Ministry, Bethany Theol. Sem., Oak Brook, Ill., 1978. Ordained to ministry Ch. of the Brethren, 1960. Assoc. pastor Hagerstown (Md.) Ch., 1959-60; pastor Worthington (Minn.) Ch., 1961-67, Bethany Ch., New Paris, Ind., 1967-74, Rockford (Ill.) Ch., 1974-83, Sun Valley Ch., Birmingham, Ala., 1983-86, Chesterfield Ch., Richmond, Va., 1986—; adminstrv. asst. Chesterfield Human Svcs. Adminstrn., 1987—; pres. Nobles County Coun. Chs., Worthington, 1966-67; dir. Elkhurst/Kosciusko Migrant Ministry, New Paris, 1968-70; mem. workshop com. Ch. of the Brethren Ann. Conf., Elgin, Ill., 1974-75, timekeeper , 1989. Author: Church Growth and the Brethren, 1979; contbr. articles to Brethren Life and Thought mag. Vol. chaplain Johnson Willis Hosp., Richmond, 1988—, Lucy Corr Co. Nursing Home, Chesterfield, 1988—. Mem. Tidewater Pastors Assn., Phi Beta Kappa. Home: 1530 Wagon Wheel Rd Midlothian VA 23113 *The discovery of hope in the Scriptures leads me to the decision of faith in Jesus Christ, who helps me develop love for God and love for others.*

MCKINNELL, LETHA MIRIAM, minister, elementary school educator; b. Troy, Kans., May 21, 1929; d. Edgar Jay and Mary Fern (Eby) Miller; m. James Charles McKinnell, Mar. 22, 1959; children: James Charles, Andrew Craig. BA, McPherson Coll., 1951; MRE, Bethany Bible Sem., 1959; MEd, St. Francis Coll., Ft. Wayne, Ind., 1971. Lic. to ministry Ch. of the Brethren, 1983; cert. elem. tchr. Ill., Iowa, Va. Asst. pastor Sun Valley Ch. of the Brethren, Birmingham, Ala., 1983-86, Chesterfield Ch. of the Brethren, Richmond, Va., 1986—; vol. chaplain Johnson Willis Hosp., Richmond, 1988—; chaplain Lucy Corr County Nursing Home, Chesterfield, 1988—; chaplain in tng. Bapt. Montclair, Birmingham, 1985-86; tutor One to One Sch., Richmond, 1987—. Den mother Cub Scouts Boy Scouts Am., New Paris, Ind., 1970-72. Mem. NEA (life), Tidewater Pastors Assn. (exec. com. 1990—), New Covenant Ch. Fellowship (steering com. Hopwell, Va. chpt. 1990—). Avocation: acrylic landscape painting. Home: 1530 Wagon Wheel Rd Midlothian VA 23113

MCKINNEY, B., bishop. Pres., bishop Holiness Ch. of God Inc., Graham, N.C. Office: Holiness Ch of God Inc 602 E Elm St Winston-Salem NC 27253*

MCKINNEY, BOB WAYNE, minister, evangelist; b. Wichita, Kans., Apr. 30, 1939; s. Edward S. and Marie E. (Peppers) McK.; m. Janice Lorraine McKinney, May 4, 1964; children: Rebecca L. McKinney Womack, Edward M. BA, Berean Christian Coll., Ridgedale Theol. Sem., 1965. Minister Rock (Kans.) Christian Ch., 1974; minister and founder Orchard Valley Christian Ch., Wichita, 1975-90; evangelist and founder Deeper Faith Message Evangelistic Inc., Wichita, 1978—, Deep Faith Ch., Porcupine, S.D., 1982-90; pres. Deeper Faith Message Assn., Wichita, 1985—; pres., founder Deeper Faith Ch., Ghana, West Africa, 1980—; evangelist, founder Sioux Indian Mission Work, Porcupine, S.D., 1982—. Author: Prayer Healing, 1980, 216 Promises of God, 1988. Recipient Cert. of Award, Dr. Allen Fitzner, Chiropractor, 1978. Republican. Home and Office: Deeper Faith Message Evang 4926 Newell Wichita KS 67212

MCKINNEY, DOUGLAS WARD, religious organization administrator, minister; b. Wichita, Dec. 16, 1953; s. Wesley Eugene and Glenna (Phillips) McK.; m. Carol Lynette Sapp, June 12, 1982; children: Andrew, Christopher. BA, Baker U., 1976; cert. teaching, U. Ark., 1978; MS in Adult Edn., U. Okla., 1982; postgrad., Kans. State U., 1990—. Ordained to ministry United Meth. Ch., 1980. Dir. nurture ministry Cen. United Meth. Ch., Rogers, Ark., 1976-78; min. youth St. Luke's United Meth. Ch., Oklahoma City, 1978-82; dir. youth and young adults East Heights United Meth. Ch., Wichita, 1982-88, dir. adult ministry, 1988—; founder adult edn. program East Heights Acad., 1984—; founding leader, trustee East Side Shepherds Ctr., Wichita, 1989—; founder peer counselling devel. program, 1986; pres. Kans. West Conf. Christian Educators, 1986-88. Rep. coun. City of Wichita, 1985; mediator Wichita Bar Assn. and Neighborhood Justice Ctr., 1988—; pres., founder Benton County Suspected Child Abuse and Neglect, 1977. Mem. Christian Educators Fellowship, Religious Edn. Assn., Heartland Mediators Assn., Zeta Chi, Beta Theta Pi. Democrat. Home: 3015 Oakland Wichita KS 67211 Office: East Heights United Meth Ch 4407 E Douglas Wichita KS 67218

MCKINNEY, EDGAR DEAN, minister; b. Columbus, Ind., Sept. 22, 1952; s. Harvey E. and Letha D. (Scott) McK.; Brenda E. Richwine, Feb. 4, 1972;

1 child, Michael. B Ministry in Ch. Music, Fla. Bapt. Theol. Coll., Graceville, 1985. Ordained to ministry So. Bapt. Conv. as deacon, 1976, as priest, 1991. Deacon Eastside Bapt. Ch., Dover, Fla., 1976; min. music Hopewell Bapt. Ch., Plant City, Fla., 1980-81, Hillcrest Bapt. Ch., Ozark, Ala., 1981-85; assoc. pastor, min. praise Westside Bapt. Ch., Ashburn, Ga., 1985—; associational dir. music Turner Bapt. Assn., Ashburn, 1985-88, vice moderator, 1986-88, moderator, 1988-90. Hon. chaplain Ala. N.G., Ozark, 1984-85; coach, chaplain Tiftarea Acad. Football Team, Tifton, Ga., 1989-90. Recipient Outstanding Young Man of Am. award U.S. Jaycees, 1982. Mem. Turner County Ministerial Assn. (sec.-treas. 1985—). Republican. Home: Rte 2 Box 875 Ashburn GA 31714 Office: Westside Bapt Ch 316 W Madison Ave Ashburn GA 31714

MC KINNEY, JAMES CARROLL, baritone, educator; b. Minden, La., Jan. 11, 1921; s. William C. and Carolyn (Hilman) McK.; m. Elizabeth Richmond, Aug. 28, 1949; children: James Carroll, Timothy Richmond, John Kevin. Student, La. Poly. Inst., 1938-41; student, Stanford U., 1943-44; MusB, La. State U., 1949, MusM, 1950; D.Mus. Arts, U. So. Calif., 1969; student in, London, 1979-80, 86. Grad. asst. La. State U., 1949-50; asst. prof. music theory Southwestern Baptist Theol. Sem., Ft. Worth, 1950-54; chmn. dept. music theory, composition Southwestern Baptist Theol. Sem., 1954-56, dean Sch. Ch. Music, 1956—; baritone soloist First Presbyn. Ch., Hollywood, Calif., 1957-58, First Methodist Ch., Ft. Worth, 1963-67; guest tchr. U. So. Calif., 1958; vis. evaluator Nat. Assn. Schs. Music; vis. lectr. Hong Kong Bapt. Coll., Hong Kong Bapt. Theol. Sem., 1971-72; participant Internat. Congress Voice Tchrs., Strasbourg, France, 1987; faculty mem. Symposium on Care of the Profl. Voice, N.Y.C., 1988, Phila., 1989, 90, 91. Presented solo recitals; appeared TV and choral prodns., Bangkok, Thailand, Hong Kong, Israel, Jordan, 1971-72; Author: The Beginning Music Reader, 1958, The Progressing Music Reader, 1959, You Can Read Music, 1960, The Advanced Music Reader, 1961, Mastering Music Reading, 1964, Study Guide for Fundamentals of Music, 1964, Vocal Fundamentals Kit, 1976, Vocal Development Kit, 1977, The Diagnosis and Correction of Vocal Faults, 1982, Five Practical Lessons in Singing, 1982 (trans. into Korean, Portuguese, and Spanish). Bd. dirs. Ft. Worth Symphony Orch. Assn., Ft. Worth Civic Music Assn., Van Cliburn Internat. Piano Competition, Ft. Worth Opera, 1987—; bd. dirs., pres. So. Bapt. Ch. Music Conf. Served AUS, 1941-45. Mem. Music Tchrs. Nat. Assn. (pres. Ft. Worth chpt.), Music Educators Nat. Conf., Nat. Assn. Tchrs. Singing (lt. gov., editor jour. 1987—), Am. Choral Dirs. Assn., Tex. Assn. Music Schs. (pres.), Ft. Worth Voice Tchrs. Forum (pres.), Phi Mu Alpha Sinfonia, Omicron Delta Kappa, Phi Kappa Phi, Pi Kappa Lambda. Baptist. Office: Southwestern Bapt Theol Sem 1809 W Broadus PO Box 22000 Fort Worth TX 76122 *The longer I live, the more certain I become that the basic value systems passed on to me by my parents are valid. Inherent in all their systems were personal integrity and abiding respect for the rights of others. My chief hope is that I may be as effective as they in transmitting these values to my own children and to the students with whom I come in contact.*

MCKINNEY, JEAN, minister; b. Des Moines, Oct. 25, 1935; d. Fred F. and Emily Estella (Anderson) Anderson; m. John F. McKinney, Aug. 20, 1960; children: Karin Lynn, Kristin Louise, Robert Huston, John F. BS, St. Francis Coll., Joliet, Ill.; RN, Iowa Luth. Sch. Nursing, Des Moines. Cert. min. of health. Min. of health, parish nurse St. John's Luth. Ch., Des Moines, 1986—. Home: 3802 Forest Ave Des Moines IA 50311-2623 Office: St John's Luth Ch 601 Keoway Des Moines IA 50309

MCKINNEY, JOHNNY FRANK, minister, educator; b. Johnson City, Tenn., Apr. 29, 1952; s. James L. and Peggy (Holt) McK.; m. Sandra Kay Tipton, Apr. 2, 1971; children: Amy Michele, Mark Allen. BA, Milligan (Tenn.) Coll., 1974; MDiv, So. Bapt. Theol. Sem., Louisville, 1977, D Ministry, 1984. Ordained to ministry So. Bapt. Conv., 1971. Pastor Forks of Elkhorn Bapt. Ch., Frankfort, Ky., 1976-78, Southside Bapt. Ch., Johnson City, 1978-81, Litz Manor Bapt. Ch., Kingsport, Tenn., 1981-86, 1st Bapt. Ch., Gaffney, S.C., 1986—; adj. prof. Gardner-Webb Coll., Boiling Springs, N.C., 1987—, mem. ministerial bd. assocs., 1988-91; pres. Cherokee Pastoral Counseling Ctr., Gaffney, 1988—; mem. gen. bd. S.C. Bapt. Conv., Columbia, 1991—. Support counselor Contact Teleministries, Johnson City, 1979-81; vol. Kingsport Recreation Dept., 1981-86, Cherokee Recreation Dist., Gaffney, 1990. Office: 1st Bapt Ch 200 N Limestone St Gaffney SC 29342

MC KINNEY, JOSEPH CRESCENT, bishop; b. Grand Rapids, Mich., Sept. 10, 1928; s. Joseph Crescent and Antoinette (Theisen) McK. Student, Seminaire de Philosophie, Montreal, Can., 1948-50; S.T.L., Collegio di Propaganda Fide, Rome, Italy, 1954. Ordained priest Roman Cath. Ch., 1953. High sch. prof. St. Joseph Sem., Grand Rapids, 1954-62; asst. pastor Sacred Heart Parish, Mt. Pleasant, Mich., 1962-65; pastor St. Francis Parish, Conklin, Mich., 1965-68; asst. chancellor Diocese of Grand Rapids, 1965-68; pastor St. Andrew Cathedral, Grand Rapids, 1968-69; ordained titular bishop of Lentini and aux. bishop Grand Rapids, 1968-85; vicar gen. Diocese of Grand Rapids, 1968-85; pastor Our Lady Of Consolation, Rockford, Mich., 1985—; adminstr. Sede Vacante, 1969; pastor St. Stephen's Ch., Grand Rapids, 1971-77, Sacred Heart Parish, Muskegon Hts., Mich., from 1977.

MCKINNEY, LARRY EMMETT, religious educator; b. Tulsa, July 19, 1949; s. Emmett Albert and Lillian Warren (Seyle) McK.; m. Janet Kay Freeman, July 11, 1981. BFA, Tex. Tech. U., 1972; MDiv, Midwestern Bapt. Seminary, Kans. City, Mo., 1981; MA in Religious Studies, Cen. Bapt. Seminary, Kans. City, Kans., 1985. Reader svcs. libr. Midwestern Bapt. Seminary, 1981-85, instr. Bibl. studies, 1985-90, asst. prof. archaeology, 1990—; curator Morton Mus. Archaeology, Kans. City, Mo., 1990—. Contbr. articles to profl. jours.; contbr: Layman's Bible Dictionary, 1990. Archaeology travel grantee Endowment for Bibl. Rsch., 1987. Mem. Am. Numismatic Soc. (assoc.), Soc. Bibl. Lit., Am. Schs. Oriental Rsch. Home: 6002 NE Bircain Pl Kansas City MO 64118 Office: Midwestern Bapt Seminary 5001 N Oak St Trafficway Kansas City MO 64118

MCKINNEY, MICHAEL LEROY, minister; b. Charleston, S.C., Jan. 8, 1946; s. E. A. and Lillian (Seyle) McK.; m. Brenda June Davis, Jan. 28, 1972; children: Marcie, Marla. BSIE, Tex. Tech. U., 1969; MDiv., Midwestern Bapt. Theol. Sem., 1974, DMin., 1980. Ordained to ministry So. Bapt. Ch., 1972. Assoc. pastor Gashland Bapt. Ch., Kansas City, Mo., 1971-73; pastor Selma Bapt. Ch., Festus, Mo., 1973-77, Ashworth Rd. Bapt. Ch., Des Moines, 1977-88, Leawood (Kans.) Bapt. Ch., 1988—; adj. prof. Midwestern Bapt. Theol. Sem., Kansas City, 1989—. Author: (book) Equipping Deacons to Confront Conflict, 1988, (booklet) Why Women Deacons?, 1990. Named Alumnus of Yr., Midwestern Bapt. Theol. Sem., 1988. Mem. Rotary Club (Shawnee Mission, Kans.). Home: 6118 W 90 Terr Overland Park KS 66207 Office: Leawood Bapt Ch 8200 State Line Rd Leawood KS 66206

MCKINNEY, WILLIAM, academic administrator, sociologist; b. Salem, Mass., Mar. 14, 1946; s. William J. and Mary A. (O'Leary) McK.; m. Linda Roberts, Sept. 7, 1968. BA, Colby Coll., 1968; MA, Hartford (Conn.) Sem., 1970, MDiv, 1971; PhD, Pa. State U., 1979. Ordained to ministry United Ch. of Christ, 1971. Rsch. dir. United Ch. Bd. for Homeland Ministries, N.Y.C., 1974-85; dean, prof. Hartford Sem., 1985—; pres. Religious Rsch. Assn., N.Y.C., 1983-84; mem. Project Team for Congl. Studies, 1980—. Co-author: Religion's Public Presence, 1982, Varieties of Religious Presence, 1984, Handbook for Congregational Studies, 1986, American Mainline Religion, 1987. Fellow Hartford Sem., 1972, Colby Coll., 1974. Office: Hartford Sem 77 Sherman St Hartford CT 06105

MCKINNON, EDWARD KURT, minister; b. Athens, Ga., May 2, 1956; s. Walter Edward and Edna Jean (McLeroy) McK.; m. Madelyn Carol Johnson, July 29, 1978; children: Jessica Lynn, Christopher Alan. B.Music Edn., U. Ga., 1978; M.Ch. Music, New Orleans Bapt. Theol. Sem., 1980. Ordained to ministry, So. Bapt. Conv., 1978. Minister music and youth New Hebron (Miss.) Bapt. Ch., 1979-80, Gonzalez (Fla.) Bapt. Ch., 1980-84, First Bapt. Ch., Ashland, Ala., 1984-85, Second Bapt. Ch., Griffin, Ga., 1985-88; minister music Capitol Height Bapt. Ch., Montgomery, Ala., 1988-91, Trinity Bapt. Ch., Ocala, Fla., 1991—; pres. Montgomery Singing Men, 1990—; faculty Shocco Springs State Wide Music Wk., 1985, 89, 90, faculty discipleship tng., 1990; exec. bd. Montgomery Bapt. Assn.; choir dir. Super Summer W.O.W., 1986; others in past. Mem. Ala. Singing Men. Democrat. Office: Trinity Bapt Ch 1600 SE 58th Ave Ocala FL 32671

MC KINSTRY, JOHN ROTHROCK, academic dean; b. Magnolia, Miss., Sept. 21, 1914; s. John Logan and Margaret Gordon (Rothrock) McK.; B.S., Memphis State U., 1935; postgrad. U. Louisville, 1967, Dartmouth Coll., 1968, U. Cin., 1969; M.A., Samford U., 1974; m. Charlotte Fisher, Sept. 14, 1941; children—Charlotte, Suzanne, John, Margaret, Lynn. With So. Bell Telephone Co., various locations, 1941-78, div. traffic mgr., Louisville, 1956-68, gen. traffic mgr., gen. mktg. mgr., Birmingham, Ala., 1969-78; exec. asst. to minister of communications State of Bahrain, 1978-80; adminstr. Birmingham Theol. Sem., 1980-88, dean, 1988—. Pres. Birmingham Crisis Center, 1975; pres. bd. trustees Briarwood Presbyn. Ch., 1986—. Mem. Birmingham C. of C., Ala. C. of C., Am. Hist. Assn., SCV, Order Stars and Bars, Soc. of Cincinnati, Presbyn. Hist. Soc. Ala. (sec.). Republican. Presbyterian. Clubs: Downtown, The Club, Relay House, Vestavia Country, Kiwanis. Author: History of the Telephone in Birmingham, 1975; editor, pub. The Rothrock Family of Brick Church, Tenn., 1965; The Herron Family of Gibson County, Tenn., 1975; co-pub., co-editor: The Presbyterian Church in Alabama, 1977. Home: 4710 Shady Waters Ln Birmingham AL 35243 Office: 2200 Briarwood Way Birmingham AL 35243

MCKINSTRY, ROBERT, minister; b. Aliceville, Ala., Apr. 25, 1944; s. Temp and Maggie (Rice) McK.; m. Frankie Lee Sealey, Feb. 13, 1965; children: Jocelyn Ferna, Chanda Denise. Journeyman cert., Internat. Corr. Schs., 1979; student, Mid-West Apostolic Bible Coll., Chgo., 1980-81, Ivy Tech. Coll., Gary, Ind., 1988-89, Emmaus Bible Coll., 1990-91. Ordained to ministry Pentecostal Chs. of thr Apostolic Faith Assn., 1988; cert. indsl. wireman. Deacon Victory Apostolic Faith Ch. Inc., Chgo., 1977-80, asst. supt., 1976-77, treas., 1978—, pres. minister's alliance, 1979—; asst. pastor, v.p. Victory Ch. Inc., Chgo., 1979—; indsl. electrician Republic Engineered Steels, Gary, 1975—. Mem. United Steelworkers Am. (treas. lcoal 3069 1991, bd. dirs. 1991, leadership cert. 1987). Home: 600 Johnson St Gary IN 46402 Office: Victory Apostolic Faith Ch 8053 S May St Chicago IL 60620 *In my life, I have discovered that the impossible can be dissolved. With God, it is not possible for anything to be impossible. Put your intellect to work.*

MCKNIGHT, BILLY EDWARD, minister; b. Norfolk, Nebr., Dec. 6, 1956; s. Robert Earl and Laura Ellen (Johnson) McK.; m. Kimberly Sue Reams, June 14, 1980; 1 child, Tana Leigh. AS, Cin. Bible Coll., 1981, BA, 1986. Ordained to ministry Christian Ch., 1980. Gospel singer Gospelites, Dobbins, Calif., 1975-79; store detective J.C. Penney, Marysville, Calif., 1978; security officer Golden Bear Security, Marysville, 1977-79; log cabin assembler Beetle Log, Inc., Okmulgee, Okla., 1979; police chaplain Covington Police Dept., 1980-84; minister of youth Latonia Christian Ch., Covington, Ky., 1979-83, sr. minister, 1983—; pres. North Am. Christian Conv., 1984. Contbr. articles to profl. jours. Coach Softball Ladies Team Latonia Christian Ch., Covington, 1986; sponsor Soc. Disting. Am. High Sch. Students, 1980-86. Named one of Outstanding Young Men Am., 1985; recipient Cert. of Appreciation award City of Covington, 1981. Mem. North Ky. Minister Assn. (pres. 1984—), Cin. Bible Sem. Alumni Assn. Republican. Avocation: hunting, fishing, basketball, softball. Office: Latonia Christian Ch 39th & Decoursey Ave Covington KY 41015

MCKNIGHT, JAMES E., bishop. Bishop Ch. of God by Faith Inc., Gainesville, Fla. Office: Ch God by Faith Inc PO Box 121 Gainesville FL 32601*

MCKNIGHT, WILLIAM EDWIN, minister; b. Grenada, Miss., Mar. 21, 1938; s. Leslie Spurgeon and Lucy Jennings (Sistrunk) McK.; m Sue Belle Roberts, Aug. 5, 1960; children: Susan Michele, William Roberts. BA, Millsaps Coll., 1960; BD, Lexington (Ky.) Theol. Sem., 1963. Ordained to ministry, 1964. Chaplain intern Grady Hosp., Atlanta, 1963-64; pastor First Christian Ch., Cleveland, Miss., 1964-67, Inverness, Miss., 1964-67; assoc. pastor First Christian Ch., Jackson, Miss., 1967-70; regional minister Christian Ch. (Disciples of Christ) in Miss., Jackson, 1971—; Bd. dirs. Nat. City Christian Ch., Washington; mem. Gen. Bd. of the Christian Ch., Indpls., 1969—; bd. mem. Christian Ch. Fin. Council, Indpls., 1979-82, So. Christian Services, Macon, Ga., 1986—; mem. bd. higher edn., St. Louis, 1979-80. Named one of Outstanding Young Men Am. U.S. Jaycees, 1976. Mem. Miss. Religious Leadership Conf. (pres. 1984-85), Conf. Regional Ministers and Moderators (pres. 1985-86). Office: Christian Ch in Miss 1619 N West St Jackson MS 39202

MCKOWN, STEVE, minister; b. Ft. Smith, Ark., Jan. 6, 1948; s. Everette E. and Anita Barnes (Wise) McK.; m. Sue Ballard; children: Scott, Stuart, Stephen. BA, La. Coll., 1970; MDiv, Southwestern Bapt. Theol. Sem., 1973; DMin, Midwestern Bapt. Theol. Sem., 1992. Ordained to ministry, So. Bapt. Conv., 1970. Pastor First Bapt. Ch., Haslet, Tex., 1971-73, Davis Blvd. Bapt. Ch., Ft. Worth, Tex., 1973-76; assoc. pastor Immanuel Bapt. Ch., El Paso, Tex., 1976-82; pastor Portland Ave. Bapt. Ch., Oklahoma City, 1982—; Christian life com. chmn. Bapt. Gen. Conv. of Okla., Oklahoma City, 1988-90. Capital Bapt. Assn. (pres. pastor's conf. 1991, 1st vice moderator 1990-91). Office: Portland Ave Bapt Ch 1301 N Portland Oklahoma City OK 73107

MCLAIN, ERIC ROBBINS, missionary; b. Long Beach, Calif., Apr. 11, 1943; s. Ramon Louis and Nellie Louise (Robbins) McL.; m. Lana Gayle Hunt, June 25, 1966; 1 child, Erica Michelle. BS, Western Bapt. Coll., 1965; postgrad., San Francisco Bapt. Sem., 1966-67. Missionary Bapt. Mid-Missions of Brazil, Cleve., 1968—, bush pilot, mechanic, 1976—; chmn. bd. Belem Bapt. Sem., Brazil, 1983—. Mem. Mid-Brazil Field Coun. (sec. 1987, pres. 1988—), Amazon Region Coun. of Bapt. Mid Missions (pres. Manus, Brazil chpt. 1987—), Aircraft Owners and Pilots Assn., Rotary. Republican. Avocations: sports aviation, amateur radio, linguistics, banjo, trombone. Office: Mid Brazil Aviation, Caixa Postal 638, 66.000 Belem Brazil

MCLARRY, NEWMAN RAY, minister, consultant; b. Sulphur Springs, Tex., July 23, 1923; s. Clarence Burt and Jessie (Carpenter) McL.; m. Mary Sue Freeman, Aug. 17, 1947; children: Sharon McLarry Simmons, Deena McLarry McKindles. BA, Tex. A&M U., 1944; BDiv., Southwestern Bapt. Theol. Sem., 1955. Ordained to ministry So. Bapt. Conv., 1947. Pastor Curtis Bapt. Ch., Augusta, Ga., 1954-58, First Bapt. Ch., Ft. Smith, Ark., 1958-61; assoc. dir. div. evangelism Home Mission Bd. So. Bapt. Conv., Atlanta, 1961-64; pastor N.W. Bapt. Ch., Oklahoma City, 1965-75; v.p. World Evangelism Found., Dallas, 1975-84; pastor Lake Highlands Bapt. Ch., Dallas, 1985—; pres. McLarry & Assocs., Inc., Dallas, 1977—. Author: When Shadows Fall, 1960, His Good and Perfect Will, 1965, Why We Believe, 1968; editor: Handbook on Evangelism, 1965; contbg. author 4 books. Trustee Okla. Bapt. U., Shawnee, 1971-74, Ark. Bapt. Hosp., Little Rock, 1958-59; mem. state bd. Okla. State Dept. Mental Health, Oklahoma City, 1972-74. Capt. U.S. Army, 1943-46, ETO. Decorated Silver Star, Purple Heart with oak leaf cluster; Merit award (France). Mem. VFW (life, charter pres. 1 chpt. 1946-49). Office: McLarry & Assocs PO Drawer 823213 Dallas TX 75382 *Attitudes are oftentimes more important than aptitudes.*

MCLAUGHLIN, BERNARD J., bishop; b. Buffalo, Nov. 19, 1912. Ed., Urban U., Rome. Ordained priest Roman Catholic Ch., Dec. 21, 1935; ordained titular bishop of Mottola and aux. bishop of Buffalo, 1969—. Address: 1085 Englewood Ave Kenmore NY 14223

MCLAUGHLIN, JOSEPH MICHAEL, religious order administrator; b. Boston, Aug. 16, 1943; s. Joseph M. and Mary E. (O'Hare) McL. AB, St. Michael's Coll., 1966; MDiv., U. St. Michael's, 1969; AM, St. Michael's Coll. U. Toronto, 1972. Ordained May 16, 1970. Gen. councilor Soc. St. Edmund, Burlington, Vt., 1976-82, treas. gen., 1982-86, superior gen., 1986—; dir. sem. St. Basil's Coll., Toronto, 1972-76; asst. prof. St. Michael's Coll., Winooski, 1978—; v.p. Edmundite So. Missions, Inc., Selma, Ala., 1986—. Author: From Pontigny, 1978. Chmn. Prudential Com., Town of Colchester, Vt., 1982-87; clk. Prudential Com., Colchester, 1979-85; mem. Burlington Community Land Trust, 1983—; trustee, sec. St. Michael's Coll., Winooski, 1979—, chmn. bd. trustees, 1986—. Mem. Assn. Gov. Bds., Conf. Major Superiors of Men, Union Superiors Gen. Roman Catholic. Avocations: reading, running. Home and Office: Soc St Edmund Fairholt S Prospect St Burlington VT 05401

MCLAUGHLIN, LINDEN DALE, minister; b. Kansas City, Kans., Jan. 26, 1956; s. Euell Linden and Dorothy Niell (Francis) McL.; m. Marcia Elizabeth Randall, July 12, 1980; children: Kathleen Faith, Patrick Linden, Bonnie Francis. BA in Sociology, Austin Coll., 1978; MA in Christian Edn., Dallas Theol. Sem., 1985. Ordained to ministry Christian Chs., 1985. Staff min. Inter-Varsity Christian Fellowship, Austin, Tex., 1979-80, Wichita, Kans., 1980-81; dir. christian edn. Sherman (Tex.) Bible Ch., 1981-85; pastor christian edn. Plano (Tex.) Bible Ch., 1985—. Mem. Profl. Assn. Christian Educators (seminar coord. 1988-90, conv. dir. 1991—), Tex. Sunday Sch. Assn. (v.p. 1989-90). Home: 3600 18th St Plano TX 75074 Office: Plano Bible Chapel 1900 Shiloh Rd Plano TX 75074

MCLAUGHLIN, MICHAEL JAMES, minister; b. Seattle, Mar. 30, 1952; s. James Albert and Grace Elenor (Jay) McL.; m. Linda Sue Faulkenberry, June 16, 1974; children: Andrew, Amy. BA in Christian Edn., Biola U., 1975; MDiv, Western Sem., 1979. Regional dir. N.W. Rocky Mt. region N.W./Rocky Mt. Region Christian Med. & Dental Soc., Portland, Oreg., 1984—. Mem. com. Grace Community Ch., Gresham, Oreg., 1981, Concerned Parents of Parkrose Teens, Portland, 1989. Mem. Am. Acad. Med. Ethics, Christian Med. and Dental Soc. (chmn. nat. student com. 1988—). Republican. Avocations: snow skiing, tennis, cycling, woodworking, guitar. Office: Christian Med & Dental Soc 306 SW First Ste 110 Portland OR 97204

MCLAUGHLIN, NINIAN, principal; b. Glasgow, Scotland, May 28, 1948. BS in Edn., Digby Stuart Coll., London, 1971; MA, London (Eng.) U., 1972; PhD, Pa. State U., 1983; ALCM, London Coll. Music, 1970. Tchr. Strathclyde Edn. Dept., Glasgow; prin. Altoona Johnstown Diocese, Hollidaysburg, Pa. Mem. Prins. Acad., NCEA, ASCD, Nat. Cath. Educator's Assn.

MCLAUGHLIN, RUSSELL LYNN, minister; b. Abilene, Tex., Apr. 6, 1963; s. James Ralph and Connie L. (Miller) McL.; m. Karen Denice Raygor, Aug. 15, 1987. Mission degree, Sunset Sch. Preaching, 1982; BA in Bible, Lubbock Christian U., 1986; MA in Bible Related Studies, Abilene Christian U., 1990. Coll. min. Sunset Ch. of Christ, Lubbock, Tex., 1987-88; min. youth Huntsville (Tex.) Ch. of Christ, 1988—; coord. Leadership Tng. for Christ. Chaplain Huntsville City Coun., 1988—; vol. chaplain Walker County Jail, Huntsville, 1988—, Tex. Dept. Corrections, Huntsville, 1988—. Mem. Soc. Bibl. Lit., Am. Acad. Religion.

MC LEAN, GEORGE FRANCIS, clergyman, philosophy of religion educator; b. Lowell, Mass., June 29, 1929; s. Arthur and Agnes (McHugh) McL. Ph.L., Gregorian U., Rome, 1952, S.T.L., 1956; Ph.D., Cath. U. Am., 1958. Joined Order Oblates of Mary Immaculate, 1949; ordained priest Roman Catholic Ch., 1955; prof. metaphysics, philosophy of religion Cath U. Am., Washington, 1958—; research scholar U. Madras, 1969, 77-78, 85, U. Paris, 1970, Ctr. for Oriental Rsch., Cairo, 1991. Author: Man's Knowledge of God According to Paul Tillich, 1958, Perspectives on Reality, 1966, An Annotated Bibliography of Philosophy in Catholic Thought, 1966, A Bibliography of Christian Philosophy and Contemporary Issues, 1966, Readings in Ancient Western Philosophy, 1970, Ancient Western Philosophy, 1971, Plenitude and Participation, 1978, Tradition and Contemporary Life: Hermeneutics of Perennial Wisdom and Social Change, 1986; editor: numerous books including Philosophy and the Integration of Contemporary Catholic Education, 1962, Philosophy in a Technological Culture, 1964, Christian Philosophy and Religions Renewal, 1966, Philosophy and Contemporary Man, 1968, Religion in Contemporary Thought, 1973, Traces of God in a Secular Culture, 1973, The Impact of Belief, 1974, The Role of Reason in Belief, 1974, New Dynamics in Ethical Thinking, 1974, Philosophy and Civil Law, 1975, Freedom, 1976, Inter University Cooperation in Research, 1976, Ethical Wisdom East and/or West, 1977, Man and Nature 1978, 2d edit., 1989, Act and Agent: Philosophical Foundations of Moral Education and Character Development, 1986, 92, Psychological Foundations of Moral Education and Character Development, 1986, 92, Character Development in Schools and Beyond, 1987, Place of the Person in Social Life, 1988, Person and God, 1988, The Nature of Metaphysical Knowledge, 1988, The Social Context and Values: Perspectives of the Americas, 1989, Culture Human Rights and Peace in Central America, 1989, On Reading the Philosophers for the 21st Century, 1989, Research on Culture and Values, 1989, Relations Between Cultures, 1991, Urbanization and Values, 1991, Person and Society, 1991, Moral Imagination and Character Development, 1992, The Humanization of Social Life: The Situation and Dilemmas of Change on Our Time, 1992, Ethics at the Crossroads, 1992, Foundations of Moral Education in the Chinese Tradition, 1991, The Human Person and Philosophy, 1991, Beyond the Limits of Privatism and Statism: Social Inventions in Poland and the U.S.A., 1991; area editor: New Cath. Ency. Mem. Am. Cath. Philos. Assn. (nat. sec. 1965-80), World Union Cath. Philos. Socs. (sec. gen. 1973—), InterUniv. Com. Research and Policy Studies (sec. 1975-77), Internat. Soc. Metaphysics (gen. sec. 1974—), Council Research in Values and Philosophy (sec. 1980—), Internat. Fedn. Philos. Socs. (dir. 1978-88), Cath. Learned Socs. and Scholars (sec. 1975-77). Home: 391 Michigan Ave NE Washington DC 20017 Office: Cath U Am Washington DC 20064

MCLEAN, JOHN ANDREW, religion educator; b. Detroit, June 6, 1951; s. Andrew McGowan and Betty Jane (Pollitt) McL.; m. Diane Elizabeth Edgar, June 5, 1976; children: Daniel, Kathryn, Joanna. BRE, Tyndale Coll., 1978; ThM, Dallas Sem., 1982; MA in Nr. Ea. Studies, U. Mich., 1987, PhD, 1990. Asst. prof. William Tyndale Coll., Farmington Hills, Mich., 1984-89; assoc. prof. Grand Rapids (Mich.) Bapt. Coll., 1990—. Mem. Soc. Bibl. Lit., Evang. Theol. Soc. Office: Grand Rapids Bapt Coll 1001 E Beltline NE Grand Rapids MI 49505

MCLEAN, M., minister, academic administrator. Pres. St. John's Coll., Winnipeg, M.B., Can. Office: St John's Coll, 400 Dysart Rd, Winnipeg, MB Canada R3T 2M5*

MCLEAN, MARK DAVID, clergyman; b. Cin., Sept. 26, 1947; s. Davis James and Katherine JoAnn McL.; m. Junko Elaine McLean, Sept. 20, 1969; children: Scott, Christina. BA summa cum laude, So. Calif. Coll., 1974; MST, Harvard U., 1976, PhD in Near Eastern Langs./Civilizations, 1982. Lic. to ministry Assemblies of God, 1974, ordained, 1982; cert. Master Chaplain, 1991. Keeper of the coins Harvard Semitic Mus., Cambridge, Mass., 1979-85; chaplain Saugus (Mass.) Police Dept., 1979-82, Community Chaplain Svc., Springfield, Mo., 1983—; assoc. prof. Bibl. studies and philosophy dept. Evangel Coll., Springfield, 1982—; adj. prof. Assemblies of God Theol. Sem., Springfield, 1987—; mem. com. on continuing edn. Internat. Conf. of Police Chaplains, 1986—, adv. bd. on Old Testament surveys Baker Book House, Grand Rapids, Mich., 1990; Midwest regional dir. Police Chaplains, 1991—. Author: (with others) Reaching Beyond: Chapters in the History of Perfectionism, 1986; contbr. articles to profl. jours. Bd. dirs. Westside Community Betterment Assn., 1983-84. With U.S. Army, 1968-71. Decorated Army Commendation medal; tuition grantee Layne Found., 1973-79, grad. seminar grantee Am. Numismatic Soc., 1979; grad. fellow Am. Numismatic Soc., 1980. Mem. Am. Acad. Religion, Community Chaplain Svc. (treas. 1984—, sec. 1984-85, v.p. 1986, pres. 1987-89), Internat. Conf. Police Chaplains, Soc. for Pentecostal Studies, Soc. Bibl. Lit. (convener for Old Testament sect. Midwest regional 1984), Am. Schs. Oriental Rsch., Mo. Police Chiefs Assn. (assoc.). Office: Evangel Coll 1111 N Glenstone Ave Springfield MO 65802-2191

MCLEAN, STUART DRUMMOND, clergyman, religion educator; b. Chgo., Dec. 13, 1929; s. Milton Duncan and Ruth (Shuman) McL.; m. Mary L. McLean, June 18, 1954; children: Calvin, David, Catherine. BA, Oberlin (Ohio) Coll., 1952; BD, Yale U., 1955; MA, U. Chgo., 1962, PhD, 1968. Assoc. pastor McKinley Found., Champaign, Ill., 1955-59; campus minister Stanford U., Palo Alto, Calif., 1964-69; asst. prof. U. Santa Clara (Calif.), 1969-75, Ariz. State U., Tempe, 1976-77; assoc. prof. Christian ethics and Christian edn. Phillips Grad. Sem., Enid, Okla., 1977—. Author: Humanity in the Thought of Karl Barth, 1981. Chairperson Save the Cimarron, Enid, Okla., 1989-90. Democrat. Presbyterian. Home: 2702 E Randolph Enid OK 73701 Office: Phillips Grad Sem PO Box 2335 Univ Sta Enid OK 73702

MCLEAN, TERENCE DANIEL, pastor; b. Toledo, Sept. 25, 1942; s. Daniel J. and Mary A. (Braden) McL.; m. Carol M. McLean, June 3, 1963; 1 child, Elizabeth J. Student, Bowling Green (Ohio) State U., 1960-62, U. Toledo, 1962-65. Pastor Sugarcreek Bapt., Belibrook, Ohio, 1987, Grace Bible Ch, Beavercreek, Ohio, 1987—; pres. Grace Sch. of the Bible, Beavercreek, 1991; owner Beavercreek Christian Bookstore, 1980—; bible tchr. Lebanon (Ohio) Correctional Inst., 1987-90; columnist Beavercreek Current Newspaper, 1987—; radio broadcaster several stas., 1984—; evangelist over 150 chs., 1984-87. Bd. dirs. Twp. Zoning Com., Sugarcreek, 1989—. Office: Grace Bible Ch PO Box 87 Alpha OH 54301-0087

MCLELLAN, DANIEL, academic administrator. Head Christ King Sem., East Aurora, N.Y. Office: Christ King Sem 711 Knox Rd PO Box 607 East Aurora NY 14052*

MCLEOD, THOMAS HENRY, minister; b. Leesburg, Fla., Feb. 26, 1949; s. J. Milburn and Alice Betty (Morgus) McL.; m. Deborah Avann Smith, Mar. 27, 1982; children: William Henry, John Edward. AB, Harvard U., 1971; MDiv, Duke U., 1985. Pastor Killian Pines United Meth. Ch., Miami, Fla., 1986-91, Riverview (Fla.) United Meth. Ch., 1991—; elder Fla. Ann. Conf. Democrat. Home: 10711 Riverview Dr Riverview FL 33569 Office: Riverview United Meth Ch 8002 US 301 S PO Box 518 Riverview FL 33569

MCLEROY, THOMAS STANDIFER, university dean, business educator; b. Freeport, Ill., Apr. 23, 1929; s. Mark Burton and Harriet Proctor (Clarke) McLeR.; m. Marion Joyce Busjahn, Aug. 9, 1957; children: Thomas Franklin, Laurie Jo, Jeffrey Mark. BS in Acctg., Bob Jones U., 1952; MS in Bus. Edn., No. Ill. U., 1955, EdD in Bus. Edn., 1968. Tchr. East Leyden High Sch., Franklin Park, Ill., 1955-66, chmn. bus. edn. dept., 1958-66; asst. prof. bus. edn. and office adminstrn. U. Wis., Whitewater, 1966-67, assoc. prof., 1967-69, prof. bus. edn. and office adminstrn., 1969—, dean continuing edn., summer session and extension, 1970—; mem. faculty senate U. Wis., Whitewater, 1970-76, sec. faculty senate, 1971-72, chairperson camp-conf. coord. com., 1970-86, chairperson adv. com. on outreach, 1970—, chairperson summer sch. adv. com., 1975—; mem. North Cen. Conf. on Summer Session, 1970—, sec./treas., 1978-87; advisor Pi Omega Pi, Whitewater, 1966-82. Bd. dirs. Fairhaven Corp. Retirement Home, Whitewater, 1979—, v.p., 1980-90, pres., 1990—; bd. dirs. Christian Home for Handicapped, Walworth, Wis., 1977—, pres., 1980-85, 89; mem. Whitewater City Coun., 1970-75, 78-82; pres., 1971-75. Cpl. U.S. Army, 1952-54. Adminstrv. fellow Am. Coun. on Edn., 1969-70; recipient Outstanding Alumnus Grad. Honors award Coll. Bus., No. Ill. U., 1973, 1st Ann. Lyle Maxwell award, 1974, Whitewater Rotary Club 25 Yr. Svc. award, 1989; named to Hall of Fame, Kettle Moraine Press Assn., 1989. Mem. N.Am. Assn. Summer Session (treas. 1987-89, pres.-elect 1989-90, pres. 1990-91), Nat. Univ. Continuing Edn. Assn., Kiwanis (charter, Whitewater Breakfast Club, v.p. 1978-79, pres. 1979-80). Avocations: reading, golf. Home: 1215 W Melrose St Whitewater WI 53190 Office: Univ Wis 800 W Main St Whitewater WI 53190

MCMAHAN, JOSEPH LOUIS, minister; b. Morton, Wash., July 4, 1958; s. Benjamin Franklin and Agnes Margaret (Dvoracek) McM.; m. Valerie Ann Adams, July 31, 1981; 1 child, Steven. Student, Inst. of Holy Land Studies, Jerusalem, Israel, 1978-79; BA, N.W. Nazarene Coll., 1980; MDiv, Nazarene Theol. Sem., 1984. Ordained to ministry Ch. of the Nazarene, 1986. Adult div. tchr. Shawee (Kans.) Ch. of the Nazarene, 1982-84, intern, 1983; pastor Lindsay (Calif.) Ch. of the Nazarene, 1984-91, Jerome (Idaho) Ch. of the Nazarene, 1991—; assoc. Ch. Growth, Inc., 1990. Chaplain freshman class N.W. Nazarene Coll., 1976; chmn. Fourth of July Com., Lindsay, 1988, Spiritual Aims Com., Lindsay, 1987; pres. Lindsay/Strathmore Ministerial Assn., 1986; bd. dirs. Calif. Coun. on Alcohol Problems, Sacramento, 1989-91. Mem. Kiwanis (bd. dirs. Lindsay 1988). Republican. Home: 725 16th Ave E Jerome ID 83338 Office: Ch of the Nazarene 100 E D Jerome Jerome ID 83338

MCMAHAND, WILLIE BEE, clergyman, construction company executive; b. Simpsonville, S.C., Mar. 11, 1932; s. Alvin and Ethel (Simpson) McM.; m. Queenell Wideman, Sept. 20, 1951 (dec. Apr. 1972); children: David Lewis, Donnie Lee, Arithe, Willie B. Jr., Samuel, Joseph Emanuel; m. Hilda Baldwin, June 30, 1973. Diploma, Emmaus Bible Inst., 1978; BTh, Morris Coll., Sumter, S.C., 1984, DD (hon.), 1983; MM, Bethany Theol. Sem., 1987. Ordained Bapt. min., 1961. Pastor Bapt. chs., Walhalla, S.C., Landrum, S.C., Travelers Rest, S.C., Iva, S.C., Fountain Inn, S.C., Enoree, S.C.; pastor Flat Rock Bapt. Ch., Piedmont, S.C., 1974—; pres., owner McMahand Constrn. Co., Greenville, S.C., 1969—; preacher throughout Africa; moderator Reedy River Bapt. Assn., Union No. 3, Seneca River Assn., Tyger River Union; fin. coord. O.R. Reuben Ch. Ctr., Morris Coll.; supr. S.C. Ushers' Aux. Trustee Morris Coll.; del. S.C. Dem. Conv., 1984, 88; coord. Jesse L. Jackson for Pres., Greenville, 1988; campaign mgr. for S.C. Cureton for Ho. of Reps., Greenville, 1988; pres. Greenville Dem. Precinct 24, 1988. Recipient A.T. Eaddy award Morris Coll., awards Reedy River Bapt. Assn., leadership appreciation award S.C. Ho. of Reps., 1989, Springfield Bapt. Ch. Black Heritage Leadership award, 1989, Mayoral Effective Leadership Appreciation award 1989, Black Elective Ofcl. Leadership Appreciation award, 1989, Greenville and Vicinity Fellowship Presdl. award, 1986, ann. appreciation award NAACP, 1989, Presdl. award S.C. Bapt. Edn. and Missionary Conv., 1989, also others. Mem. Greenville Bapt. Ministers Fellowship (pres. 1985). Home: 18 Dunlap Dr Greenville SC 29605 Office: Flat Rock Bapt Ch 250 Flat Rock Rd Piedmont SC 29673

MCMAHON, JOHN ROBERT, priest; b. Pitts., Dec. 5, 1940; s. John Robert McMahon and Alma Fuchs. BA, Pontifical Coll., 1966; MA in Sociology, U. Detroit, 1969. Ordained priest Roman Cath. Ch., 1966. Sec. to Archbishop Coleman Carroll Miami, Fla., 1966-67; sent to study, 1967-69; dir. Rural Life Archdiocese of Miami, Fla., 1969-82; dir. Pastoral Field & Edn. program Seminary, Fla., 1971-82; pastor St. John Fisher Parish, West Palm Beach, Fla., 1982-84, St. Joan of Arc Parish, Boca Raton, Fla., 1984—; Diocesan dir. Campaign for Human Devel., 1982; Episcopal Vicar Cath. Charities Diocese, Palm Beach, Fla., 1984—; cons. Diocese of Palm Beach, 1982; mem. Presbyn. Coun. Diocese of Palm Beach, 1982, Greater Boca Raton Ecumenical Assn. Bd. dirs. Boca Raton Affordable Housing Task Force, 1991; mem. Oversight Com. Child Svcs., Palm Beach County, Social Devel. Com. Fla. Cath. conf. Home: 370 S W 3rd St Boca Raton FL 33432

MCMAHON, MICHAEL DAVID (MICK MCMAHON), evangelist, minister; b. Newman, Calif., Feb. 2, 1958; s. James David and Marva Jean (Gary) McM; m. Helen Louise Chamberlain, July 9, 1988. AA, Modesto Jr. Coll., 1979; BA, Calif. State U., Turlock, 1983; lay cert., Nazarene Bible Coll., 1987. Ordained to ministry Ch. of the Nazarene, 1991. Lay evangelist Ch. of the Nazarene, Colorado Springs, Colo., 1985-87; pastor, evangelist Ch. of the Nazarene, Lakeville, Mass., 1988; sr. pastor Lakeville Ch. of the Nazarene, 1989-91; evangelist Evangelism Ministries, Kansas City, Mo., 1991—. Mem., champ golf team CSUS NCAA, 1980-81, PGA, 1981-83. Address: Evangelism Ministries 6401 The Pasco Kansas City MO 64131

MCMANAMAN, BROTHER RAYMOND, theology educator; b. Waukegan, Ill., July 14, 1929; s. Raymond John and Fraces (Tonigan) McM. M.A., St. Mary's Coll., Winona, Minn., 1956; M.A., Seattle U., 1972; D.Min., Aquinas Inst. Theology, 1977; S.T.D., San Francisco Theol. Sem., 1981. Joined Christian Bros., Roman Cath. Ch., 1947. Prin. St. Francis High Sch., Wheaton, Ill., 1963-66, La Salle High Sch., Cin., 1966-68, St. Paul High Sch., Chgo., 1968-70; dean students Lewis U., Romeoville, Ill., 1960-63, tchr., 1961-63, 72—, chmn. dept. religious studies, 1974-77, 79-91; bd. dirs. Commn. for Catholic Impact, Lockport, Ill., 1974-75; Ednl. Policies Com., Romeoville, 1974-76, profl. status com., 1977-84; dir. Inst. for Parish Ministry, Joliet, Ill., 1974-77. Author: The Seven Sacraments, 1981. Mem. Coll. Theology Soc., Nat. Catholic Evangelization Assn., Theta Alpha Kappa (treas. 1984-87). Avocations: hiking, swimming, reading. Home and Office: Lewis U Romeoville IL 60441

MCMANNERS, JOHN, ecclesiastical history educator, chaplain; b. Ferryhill, Durham, Eng., Dec. 25, 1916; s. Joseph and Ann McM.; m. Sarah Carruthers Errington; children—Hugh, Helen, Peter, Ann. B.A. with 1st class honors, Oxford U., 1939, LL.D., 1978; LL.D., Durham U., 1982. Fellow St. Edmund Hall, Oxford, Eng., 1948-56; prof. U. Tasmania, Australia, 1956-59, U. Sydney, Australia, 1959-66, U. Leicester, Eng., 1966-72; prof. eccles. history U. Oxford, Eng., 1972-84; fellow, chaplain All Souls Coll., Oxford U., 1984—; dir. studies Ecole Pratique des Hautes Etudes Sect. IV, Paris, 1980-81; mem. Doctrine Commn. of Ch. of Eng., 1978-83. Author: French Ecclesiastical Society under the Ancien Régime, 1960; Men, Machines and Freedom, 1966; The French Revolution and the Church, 1969; Death and the Enlightenment, 1981; Church and State in France 1870-1914, 1972; editor, contbr. Oxford Illustrated History of Christianity, 1990. Served to maj. Brit. Army, 1939-45, Middle East. Decorated officer Royal Order of King George I of the Hellenes; commandeur dans l'Ordre des Palmes Académiques, 1990; recipient Wolfson Lit. prize, 1982; hon. fellow St. Edmund Hall, 1983. Fellow Brit. Acad., Royal Hist. Soc., Australian Acad. Humanities; mem. Eccles. History Soc. Mem. Ch. of Eng. Avocation: tennis. Office: Oxford U, All Souls Coll, Oxford OX1 4AL, England

MCMANUS, CHARLES E., school system administrator. Supt. schs. Diocese of Worcester, Mass. Office: Sch Dept 49 Elm St Worcester MA 01609*

MCMANUS, FREDERICK RICHARD, priest, educator; b. Lynn, Mass., Feb. 8, 1923; s. Frederick Raymond and Mary Magdalene (Twomey) McM. AB, St. John's Sem., Brighton, Mass., 1947; JCD, Cath. U. Am., 1954; LLD (hon.), St. Anselm's Coll., Manchester, N.H., 1964; SJD (hon.), Coll. of Holy Cross, Worcester, Mass., 1989. Ordained priest Roman Cath. Ch., 1947. Assoc. pastor various chs., Mass., 1947-50; sec. to met. tribunal Archdiocese of Boston, 1950-51; prof. canon law and moral theology St. John's Sem., 1954-58; prof. canon law Cath. U. Am., Washington, 1958—, vice provost, dean grad. studies, 1974-83; acad. v.p. Cath. Univ. Am., Washington, 1983-85; O'Brien-O'Connor Disting. Prof. of canon law, 1990—; dir. secretariat Bishop's Com. on Liturgy, Nat. Conf. Cath. Bishops, Washington, 1965-75; pres. Liturgical Conf., 1959-62, 64-65; treas. Internat. Commn. English in Liturgy, 1964—; bd. dirs. Am. Coun. on Edn.; trustee Mt. St. Mary's Coll., Emmitsburg, Md. Author: Congregation of Sacred Rites, 1954, Rites of Holy Week, 1956, Revival of the Liturgy, 1963, Sacramental Liturgy, 1967, (with Ralph Keifer) The Rite of Penance, 1975, Thirty Years of Liturgical Renewal, 1987, Liturgical Participation: An Ongoing Assessment, 1988; editor: The Jurist, 1959—; contbr. articles to jours. Recipient Pax Christi award St. John's U., Collegeville, Minn., 1964, Michael Mathis award U. Notre Dame, 1978, Presdl. award Nat. Cath. Edn. Assn., 1983. Mem. AAUP, Canon Law Soc. Am. (Role of Law award 1973), Cath. Theol. Soc. Am. (John Courtney Murray award 1990), N.Am. Acad. Liturgy (Berakah award 1979), Cath. Commn. Cultural and Intellectual Affairs, Assn. Cath. Colls. and Univs. (bd. dirs. 1979-80, chmn. 1980-82), Joint Com. Cath. Learned Socs. and Scholars (chmn. 1981—). Office: Cath U Am Washington DC 20064

MCMANUS, HAROLD LYNN, clergyman, church history educator; b. Sanford, N.C., Sept. 27, 1919; s. James Burch and Mary Elizabeth (Glass) McM.; m. Louise Virginia Paschall, Dec. 28, 1946; children—Harold Lynn, Kermit Neal, Marcia Louise. A.B., Wake Forest Coll., 1941; Th.M., So. Bapt. Theol. Sem., 1944; S.T.M., Yale, 1948, Ph.D., 1953. Ordained to ministry Baptist Ch., 1944; pastor in Conn. and Ga., 1944-48; instr. Wake Forest Coll., summer 1948; assoc. prof. ch. history Roberts dept. Christianity Mercer U., 1949-53, Roberts prof. ch. history, 1953-85, chmn., 1963-83. Served as chaplain USNR, 1944-46; capt. Res. Mem. Am. Hist. Assn., AAUP, Am. Soc. Ch. History, Blue Key, Scabbard and Blade, Omicron Delta Kappa, Delta Kappa Alpha, Pi Kappa Alpha. Club: Palaver (Macon). Home: 346 Wesley Circle Macon GA 31204

MCMANUS, JAMES DONALD, minister; b. Lancaster, S.C., Feb. 20, 1942; s. James Hawley and Willie Mae McM.; m. Judie Beth Baskin, June 18, 1965; children: James Donald, William Lee. BA, Campbell U., Buies Creek, N.C., 1965; MDiv, Southeastern Bapt. Theol. Sem., Wake Forest, N.C., 1970; DMin, Union Theol. Sem., Richmond, Va., 1977. Ordained to ministry, So. Bapt. Conv., 1963. Student pastor Mt. Croghan (S.C.) Bapt. Ch., 1963-66, Mt. Olvie Bapt. Ch., 1963-66; pastor Kelford (N.C.) Bapt. Ch., 1969-77, Lawtonville Bapt. Ch., Estill, S.C., 1977-79, First Bapt. Ch., Kershaw, S.C., 1979-87, Cornerstone Bapt. Ch., Camden, S.C., 1988—; religion instr. U. S.C., Lancaster, 1983—; mem. com. on coms. of S.C. Bapt. Conv., 1984-85; pres. Moriah Assn. Pastor's Conf., Lancaster, 1981. Author: Martha Franks—One Link in God's Chain, 1990, Toodle-oo Taxahaw: 101 Tales or a Small History of the World, 1991; contbr. articles to profl. jours. Social worker Chgo. Boys Club, 1962-63. Home: Route 2 Box 361-1A Lancaster SC 29720

MCMANUS, MICHAEL JOHN, religion columnist; b. Springfield, Ohio, June 11, 1941; s. John Grever and Ruth (Fisher) McM.; m. Harriet Ecker, Oct. 16, 1965; children: Adam Joseph, John Ecker, Timothy Michael. AB, Duke U., 1963. Layman St. Paul's Episcopal Ch., Darien, Conn., 1971-87, Fourth Presbyn. Ch., Bethesda, Md., 1987—; radio commentator Dobson's Family News in Focus, 1990—; syndicated columnist Bethesda and Stamford, Conn., 1977—. Author 550 weekly columns, Ethics and Religion, 1981—, 40-page Introduction to Final Report of Atty. Gen.'s Commn. Pornography, 1986 (Media Awareness award Religious Alliance Against Pornography); syndicated columnist in 145 papers. Exec. dir. Choices for '76, Regional Plan Assn., N.Y.C., 1970-74; founder Northeast Gov.'s Coalition and Northeast-Midwest Congl. Coalition. Exec. dir. Choices for '76, Regional Plan Assn., N.Y.C., 1970-74; founder N.E. Gov.'s Coalition and N.E.-Midwest Congl. Coalition, 1976. Mem. Religion Newswriters Assn. Home and Office: 9500 Michaels Ct Bethesda MD 20817 *America is the world's most religious nation, with 4-10 times the church attendance of Europe. But is also the least ethical with rates of crime, illegitimacy, divorce, and abortion that are 2-100 times higher than Europe. The church is partly to blame, because it avoids ethics, rather than showing how right conduct grows our of right belief. I try to suggest practical ethical solutions any church or individuals can take.*

MCMANUS, RONALD FRANK, minister; b. New Orleans, Jan. 4, 1949; s. Selby Frank and Mary Pauline (Guiberteau) McM.; m. Joan Harriet Kennan, May 30, 1969; children: Gregory, Kevin. BA, Southeastern Coll., 1970; MA, Assemblies of God Theol. Sem., 1980. Dir. youth and Christian edn. Crichton Assembly of God, Mobile, Ala., 1969-72; youth dir., assoc. pastor Bethel Ch., San Jose, Calif., 1972-74; youth specialist, workers tng. Assembly of God Internat. Hdqrs., Springfield, Mo., 1974-81; sr. pastor First Assembly of God, Winston-Salem, N.C., 1981—; gen. presbyter Assemblies of God., Springfield, 1987—; exec. com. Forsyth County Ministers Coalition, Winston-Salem, 1990—; chmn. Christian edn. study com. Assembly of God., Springfield, 1989—. Author: Guiding Youth; contbr. articles to profl. mags. Mem. Leadership Winston-Salem; Forsyth County-SAFE Initiative, Drug and Alcohol Coalition, Winston-Salem; bd. dirs. Assemblies of God Theol. Sem., 1991—. Home: 4136 Rock Hill Rd Pfafftown NC 27040 Office: First Assembly of God 3730 University Pkwy Winston-Salem NC 27106 *Success is summed up in simply fulfilling God's will for your life rather than measuring your life by others. Faithfulness to the call will reap eternal fruit.*

MCMASTER, BELLE MILLER, religious organization administrator; b. Atlanta, May 24, 1932; d. Patrick Dwight and Lila (Bonner) Miller; m. George R. McMaster, June 19, 1953; children: Lisa McMaster Stork, George Neel, Patrick Miller. BA, Agnes Scott Coll., 1953; MA, U. Louisville, 1970, PhD, 1974. Assoc. corp. witness Presbyn. Ch. USA, Atlanta, 1974-77, dir. corp. witness, 1977-81, dir. div. corp. and social mission, 1981-87; dir. social justice and peacemaking unit Presbyn. Ch. USA, Louisville, Ky., 1987—; vice moderator chs. commn. internat. affairs, World Coun. Chs., 1984-91; chairperson commn. internat. affairs, Nat. Coun. Chs., N.Y.C., 1986-89, v.p., 1990—, chairperson ch. world svc. and witness unit com., 1990—. Author: Witnessing to the Kingdom, 1982; contbr. articles to profl. jours. Pres. League of Women Voters, Greenville, S.C., 1963-64; bd. dirs. Interfaith Housing, Atlanta, 1975-81. Danforth fellow, 1969-74. Mem. MLA, South Atlantic MLA, Soc. for Values in Higher Edn., Phi Beta Kappa. Office: Presbyn Ch USA and Social Justice Unit 100 Witherspoon St Louisville KY 40202

MCMASTERS, LARRY WAYNE, principal; b. Milford, Del., Sept. 22, 1950; s. Blair Sheridan and Joyce (McDorman) McM.; m. Becky Lewis, May 18, 1971; 1 child, Yolanda Michelle. BS in Christian Edn., Lee Coll., Cleveland, Tenn., 1973. Tchr. Azalea Garden Christian Sch., Norfolk, Va., 1973-85, adminstr., prin., 1986—, varsity volleyball and basketball coach, 1976-86; youth pastor South Richmond (Va.) Ch. of God, 1985-86, Azalea Garden Ch. of God, 1986—. Avocations: woodworking. Home: 3106 Beamon Ct Norfolk VA 23513 Office: Azalea Garden Christian Sch 5160 Beamon Rd Norfolk VA 23513

MCMICHAEL, HENRY GEORGE, educator; b. Orangeburg, S.C., June 7, 1950; s. Henry George and Mary Eloise (Salvo) McM.; m. Karen Louise Sowell, June 29, 1974; children: John Henry, Kathryn Anne. BBA, Bapt. Coll., Charleston, S.C., 1973; BRE, New Orleans Bapt. Theol. Sem., 1982, M in Pastorial Ministry, 1984. Pastor, tchr. Leefield Bapt. Ch., Brooklet, Ga., 1974-78; pastor, tchr., worship leader Bethlehem Bapt. Ch., Warthen, Ga., 1978-87; camp pastor Washington Bapt. Assn., Crawfordville, Ga., 1979-87; chaplain Leefield and Warthen Fire Depts., 1974-87; annointed pastor Bethlehem Bapt. Ch., Warthen, 1987-91; tchr. WACO Sch. Bd., Sandersville, Ga., 1991—; chaplain Washington Farm Bur., Warthen, 1979-83; v.p. Washington Bapt. Pastor's Fellowship, Sandersville, Ga., 1980-82, 86—; pres. Washington Pastor's Fellowship, Sandersville, 1982-83. Chaplain, treas. Washington County Ch. Bapt. Club, Sandersville, 1980-82; bd. dirs. Boy's Ranch, Davisboro, Ga., 1986-87. Mem. Washington Bapt. Assn. (moderator 1986, '87, speaker to assn. 1987), Washington County Minister's Assn. (radio devotion chmn. 1979-83, treas. 1984-87, good samaritan dir. 1984-87, Peace award 1986), Civitan (Wahington County pres. 1984-85, Voice award 1985, pres. Waco chpt. 1987—). Democrat. Avocations: deer hunting, life guard and swimming, fishing, gardening, chickens. Home: PO Box 5033 Sandersville GA 31082

MCMILLAN, LEONARD DAVID, family life specialist, consultant, lecturer; b. Harvard, Ill., Dec. 7, 1938; s. Pearly and Jean (Carter) McM.; m. Karen R. Meyer, Dec. 8, 1956; 1 child, Mitchel D. BA, Andrews U., Berrien Springs, Mich., 1972, MDiv, 1975; PhD, Ephraim-Moore U.-Theol. Sem., Holden, Mo., 1984. Dir. family life and youth Wis. Conf., 7th-day Adventist Ch., Madison, 1974-76; mem. Wash. Conf. 7th-day Adventist Ch., Bothell, 1976-83; mem. South African Union 7th-day Adventist Ch., Bloemfontein, 1983-84; pastor Upper Columbia Conf. 7th-day Adventist Ch., Spokane, Wash., 1984-86; dir. family life Potomac Conf. 7th-day Adventist Ch., Staunton, Va., 1986—. Author: Why Can't My Mate Be More Life Me?, 1986, An Owner's Guide to Male Midlife Crisis, 1986, Person to Person, 1987, The Family of God and How To Live with Them, 1988, Slaying Your Dragons, 1989. With USAF, 1956-60. Mem. Nat. Coun. on Aging, Am. Assn. Pastoral Counselors, Nat. Coun. on Family Rels. (cert. family life educator), Assn. Adventist Family Life Profls. (pres. 1991-93). Avocations: restoring classic automobiles, writing, remodeling, landscaping. Office: Potomac Conf PO Box 1208 Staunton VA 24401 *In my opinion, all of life now and hereafter can be summed up in a single word: Relationships!.*

MCMILLEN, FRANCINE ANNA, pastoral assistant; b. San Francisco, Jan. 18, 1943; d. Frank S. and Liberty D. (Vedovelli) Junta; m. Donald G. McMillen, June 19, 1965; children: Angela Marie, Anthony Frank, Maria Dominica. BA, Calif. State U., San Jose, 1964. Tchr. Fremont (Calif.) Unified Sch. Dist., 1964-66, Alaska-On-Base Schs., Fairbanks, 1967-68; saleswoman Weinstock's Dept. Store, Reno, 1974-76; pastoral asst. Holy Cross Ch., Sparks, Nev., 1979—; assoc. dir. religious edn. Diocese of Reno-Las Vegas, 1981-86; media cons. Office Religious Edn., Reno, 1986—. Mem. exec. bd. Warmline, Reno, 1982; pres., sec. Swope Mid. Sch. Parent Group, Reno, 1983-85; bd. dirs. Ronald McDonald House, Reno. Recipient commendation Washoe County Sch. Dist., Reno, 1985, Ronald McDonald House, 1989. Mem. Dirs. Religious Edn. Diocese of Reno-Las Vegas, AAUW (officer Reno 1979-81). Democrat. Home: 1080 Porter Circle Reno NV 89509

MCMILLON, LYNN A., religion educator, minister; b. Henryetta, Okla., Aug. 26, 1941; s. Roy W. McM.; m. Joy L. Cole, Sept. 1, 1962; children: Jeff, Greg. BA, Okla. Christian Coll., 1963; MA, ThM, Harding Grad. Sch. Religion, 1966; PhD, Baylor U., 1972. Ordained to ministry Ch. of Christ, 1972; lic. marital and family counselor. Prof. Bible Okla. Christian U., Oklahoma City, 1966—; min. Ch. of Christ, Oklahoma City, 1971-76; pvt. practice counseling Oklahoma City, 1973—. Author: Doctrines of Demons, 1975, Restoration Roots, 1985. Office: Okla Christian U Bible Div Box 11000 Oklahoma City OK 73136

MCMINN, RICHARD LYNN, chaplain; b. Abilene, Tex., Oct. 13, 1957; s. Milton and Margaret (Kennedy) McM.; m. Karen Lynn Knight; children: Nicolas, Shelby. BA in Psychology, Hardin-Simmons, 1981, MA in Psychology/Theology, 1983. Ordained to ministry So. Bapt. Ch., 1982. Pastor First Bapt. Ch., McCaulley, Tex., 1982-84; chaplain Hendrick Med. Ctr., Abilene, Tex., 1984-85; pastor First Bapt. Ch., Benjamin, Tex., 1985-86; pastoral counselor First Bapt. Ch., Abilene, 1986; staff chaplain St. Francis Med. Ctr., Monroe, La., 1986-87, Schumpert Med. Ctr., Shreveport, 1987—; facilitator Schumpert Guest Relations, Shreveport, 1988—; lay visitor tng. Bapt. Chs., Shreveport, 1987—, stress mgmt., 1987—. Fellow Coll. of Chaplains; mem. Am. Assn. for Counseling and Devel. Avocations: basketball, classic car restoration. Home: 885 Ed's Blvd Shreveport LA 71107 Office: Schumpert Med Ctr 915 Margaret Pl Shreveport LA 71101

MCMULLEN, HORACE MARTIN, minister; b. Montreal, Quebec, Can., Apr. 5, 1913; came to U.S., 1920; s. Horace Dwight and Bessie Carrie (Martin) McM.; m. Marie-Louise Strehlau, Jan. 12, 1941; children: Gary, Deedee, Laura, Daniel. PhB, U. Vt., 1935; MDiv, Andover Newton Theol., Seminary, Netwon Centre, Mass., 1938, STM cum laude, 1944. Lic. marriage and family therapist, Utah. Minister Woodbury Union Ch., Warwick, R.I., 1938-40, Edgewood Congregational Ch., Cranston, R.I., 1941-47; prin. Near East Sch. of Theology, Beirut, Lebanon, 1947-54; pres. Aleppo (Syria) Coll., 1954-58; minister First Parish Ch., Brunswick, Maine, 1959-62, Holladay United Ch. of Christ, Salt Lake City, 1962-78; various to minister Community of Christ Presbyn. Ch., 1982-84; pastor of counseling ministry Wasatch Presbyn. Ch., 1984—; interim minister First Bapt. Ch., Salt Lake City, 1986; lectr. Am. Univ., Beirut, 1966-67, Westminster Coll., 1967-68, 82-84; adj. prof. San Francisco Theol. Seminary, 1983-85; others; dir. DaySpring Prog., Westminster Coll., Salt Lake City, 1978-82. Contbr. articles to profl. jours. Active various civic orgns. including cons. bd. dirs. Olympus View Hosp., 1986—, Salt Lake County Mental Health Bd., chmn. 1968-71; others. Mem. Am. Assn. Marriage and Family Therapists (clin. mem.). Democrat. Home: 2546 Lincoln Lane Salt Lake City UT 84124 Office: Wasatch Presbyn Church 1626 South 1700 East Salt Lake City UT 84108

MCMULLIN, C. DAVID, minister; b. Sedalia, Mo., Aug. 13, 1955; s. Charles L. and Doris P. (Robertson) McM.; m. Connie Jo Bates, Aug. 21, 1976; children: Joshua D., Sarah A., Zachary D. BA, S.W. Bapt. U., 1977; M in Religious Edn., S.W. Bapt. Theol. Sem., 1980. With Wetterau Builders Inc., St. Louis, 1974-77; minister of edn. First Bapt. Channelveiw, Tex., 1980-81, First Bapt. Waynesville, Tex., 1982-83; pastor First Bapt. of Crocker, Mo., 1983-87, Cedar Pointe Bapt. Ch., Wichita, Kans., 1987—. Conf. leader Home Mission Bd. of So. Bapt. Conv., Atlanta, 1987—. Avocations: woodworking, reading, softball, family. Office: Cedar Pointe Bapt Ch 9221 E 31st South Wichita KS 67210

MCMUNN, RICHARD E, editor, writer; b. Peoria, Ill., Apr. 2, 1949; s. Earl A. and Doris L. (Vollmer) McM.; m. Diane Marie Corrigan, Dec. 16, 1972; children: Shannon Marie Margaret, Erin Maureen (dec.), Meaghan Bridget Colleen. BS, Bradley U., Peoria, 1971. Intern Peoria Jour. Star, Ill., 1969-70; news editor The Catholic Post, Peoria, Ill., 1970-74; asst. editor So. Cross, San Diego, 1974-77; editor Our Sunday Vis., Huntington, Ind., 1977-84; dir. publs. Cath. League for Religious and Civil Rights, Milw., 1985-88; editor Columbia Mag. of Knights of Columbus, New Haven, 1988—; print sales Con P. Curran, St. Louis, 1984. Editor: Quest for Religious Freedom, 1984, Quest for Religious Freedom II, 1986, Religion in Politics, 1985, Pius XII's Defense of Jews and Others, 1987. Bd. mem. Sacred Heart Sch., New Haven, 1989—. Mem. Knights of Columbus (grand knight 1990—), Sacred Heart Acad. Father's Club (treas. 1991—), Sigma Delta Chi (outstanding journalism graduate 1971). Roman Catholic. Home: 28 Canterbury Rd Hamden CT 06514 Office: Knights of Columbus 1 Columbus Pla New Haven CT 06507

MCNABB, EDWARD TIMBERLAKE, JR., minister; b. Chgo., Mar. 9, 1951; s. Edward Timberlake and Diane L. (DuPlantier) McN.; m. Cynthia Jo

Lyons, Sept. 17, 1978 (div. July 1980); m. Annetta Talbot Beauchamp, Nov. 20, 1982; children: Edward Tay, Elizabeth Talbot. BA in English, U. of the South, Sewanee, Tenn., 1973; MDiv, Va. Theol. Sem., Alexandria, 1978. Ordained to ministry Episcopal Ch. as deacon, 1978, as priest, 1979. Assoc. rector Grace-St. Luke's Episcopal Ch., Memphis, 1978-85; rector Episcopal Ch. of the Advent, Sumner, Miss., 1985-89, Trinity Episcopal Ch., Pinopolis, S.C., 1989—; bd. mem., grants chair Miss. Delta Habitat for Humanity, Sumner, Miss., 1985-89; co-dir. Community Ministries, Inc., Sumner, 1985-89; founding dir. Bread Box Emergency Food Program, Sumner, 1986-89; founding bd. mem. Habitat for Humanity, Moncks Corner, S.C., 1989—. Author: (sound recording) Walker of the Way, 1982, Take to the Wing, 1987; co-author: Book of Acts Study, 1985. Mem. Sumner Vol. Fire Dept., 1985-89. Mem. ASCAP, NATAS. Home: Box 4678 Pinopolis SC 29469 Office: Trinity Episcopal Ch Box 4678 Pinopolis SC 29469

MCNABB, ROBERT HENRY, minister; b. Charles City, Iowa, Jan. 28, 1917; s. John Henry and Gail (Gants) McNabb; m. Doris Jean Patrick, Oct. 25, 1947; children: Daniel, Allen, Roy, Gail, Marjori. BA, Cornell Coll., 1943; STB, Boston U., 1946, postgrad., 1946-47. Ordained to ministry Meth. Ch., 1945. Min. United Meth. Ch., Greeley, Iowa, 1947-49; missionary United Meth. Ch., Honolulu, 1949-55; min. Oreg.-Idaho conf. United Meth. Ch., 1955-74; missionary United Meth. Ch., Juneau, Alaska, 1974-80; min. United Meth. Ch., Ontario, Oreg., 1980-83, Palmerston-North, New Zealand, 1983-84; min. United Ch. of Christ, Olaa 1st Hawaiian Ch., Kurtistown, Hawaii, 1986—; senate chaplain Alaska State Senate, Juneau, 1976-78; chaplain Jr. CAP, Juneau, 1978-80. Mem. Rotary (pres.-elect Ontario 1983), Kiwanis, Lions. Democrat. Home: SR 11004 Keaau HI 96749 Office: Olaa 1st Hawaiian Ch Box CD Kurtistown HI 96760 *If we truly believe in and worship a God who created all things and people then we must believe that all people, regardless of color, culture, religion or economic status, are our brothers and sisters, children of the same God.*

MCNABB, TALMADGE FORD, religious organization administrator; b. Johnson City, Tenn., Mar. 22, 1924; s. Robert Pierce and Dora Isabelle (Bailey) McN.; m. Nesbia Orlene Boswell, Dec. 3, 1950 (dec.); children: Darlene Roberta, Marla Dawn; m. Pirkko Marjotta, Nov. 1962; children: Valerie Ann, Lisa Rhea, Marcus Duane. Student, East Tenn. State U., 1941-43, 46; BA, S.W. Coll. Assemblies of God, Waxahachie, Tex., 1947, BTh, 1949; BS, Birmingham Southern Coll., 1952; MA, U. Ala., 1952; HHD (hon.), S.E. Univ., Greenville, S.C., 1978. Evangelist Assemblies of God, 1948-49; pastor 1st Assembly of God, Warrior, Ala., 1949-53; commd. 1st lt. U.S. Army, 1955, advanced through grades to lt. col., 1966; chaplain U.S. Army, Ft. Rucker, Ala., 1953-54, Korea, 1954-55, 66-67, Ft. Benning, Ga., 1957-59, France, 1959-61, Ft. Knox, Ky., 1961-66, Ft. Dix, N.J., 1967-69; chaplain William Beaumont Hosp. U.S. Army, El Paso, Tex., 1971-72; ret. U.S. Army, 1972; writer, evangelist, speaker, 1973—; pres., founder Worldwide Christian Ministries, Browns Mills, N.J., 1981—; writer, evangelist, speaker, 1973—. Contbr. articles on religious and ethnic topics to newspapers and mags. Mem. DAV (life), Mil. Ret. Officers Assn. (life), Mil. Chaplains Assn. (life, del.). Republican. Home and Office: Worldwide Christian Ministries 1 Springfield Rd Browns Mills NJ 08015 *I believe every person born into this world is gifted by God the Creator with special talents and gifts, and has a niche to fill no other person can fill; to fulfill God's purpose for us is our greatest accomplishment.*

MCNALLY, JEANNE MARGARET, nun; b. N.Y.C., Nov. 22, 1931; d. Edward J. and Margert E. (Weyland) McN. Diploma, Mercy Sch. Nursing, 1956; AD, Sacred Heart Coll., 1956, LHD (hon.), 1981; BS, Cath. U. Am., 1958, MS, 1963, PhD, 1969, JCL, 1990. Joined Sisters of Mercy, Roman Cath. Ch., 1949. Tchr. elem schs. N.C., 1949-53; instr. med.-surg. nursing Mercy Sch. Nursing, Charlotte, N.C., 1958-61, med. supr., 1958-61, dir. nursing edn., 1963-71; assoc. prof. psychology Belmont (N.C.) Abbey Coll., 1970; assoc. prof. psychology Sacred Heart Coll., Belmont, 1969-71, assoc. prof. ednl. psychology, 1972-74; vis. lectr. Fordham U., N.Y.C., 1972; dir. formation and continuing edn. Sisters of Mercy, N.C., 1972-74, asst. superior gen., 1972-76; gen. councillor Sisters of Mercy, 1969-72, dir. formation, 1972-74, dir. ministry, 1976-80, superior gen., 1980-88; judge Tribunal Diocese of Charlotte, 1988—; vis. prof. N.C. Cen. U., 1978-79; adj. prof. nursing Sch. Nursing U. N.C., Chapel Hill, 1974-78, assoc. v.p. acad. affairs gen. adminstrn., 1978-80, rsch. assoc. Health Svcs. Rsch. Ctr., 1979-84, cons. 1980-84; cons. in field. Author monographs; contbr. numerous articles to profl. jours., chpts. to books. Mem. Task Force on the Role of Nursing in High Blood Pressure Control Nat. Heart, Lung and Blood Inst.; mem. Gov.'s Task Force on Maldistribution and Supply of Health Care Pers.; bd. dirs. Mercy Hosp., 1980-88, St. Joseph Hosp., 1980-88, Holy Angels, Belmont, 1981-88; trustee Sacred Heart Coll., 1969-88; mem. com. on social devel. and internat. peace Nat. Conf. Cath. Bishops; mem. adv. bd. St. Louis U. Med. Ctr.; liaison Leadership Conf. on Women Religious to nat. treas. Religious Inst. Nurse scientist fellow Yale U., 1967, 80, fellow Harvard U., 1977. Fellow Am. Acad. Nursing; mem. Fedn. Sisters of Mercy of the Ams. (chmn. med.-surg. div. practice, Congress on nursing practice, paper clin clin. nurse specialist, ad hoc com. cert. of advanced practitioners, vice chmn. med.-surg. div. practice, N.C. Med. Soc. (ad hoc com. on entry into profl. nursing practice, chmn. nominating com., baccalureate and higher degree forum), Pi Gamma Mu, Sigma Theta Tau. Republican. Home: Sacred Heart Convent Belmont NC 28012

MCNALLY, SISTER MARY SARAH (JOAN T. M. MCNALLY), nun, educator; b. Phila., Feb. 8, 1937; d. Hugh Patrick Michael and Sarah Isabella Rita (McCrea) McN. BA in Humanities, Gwynedd Mercy Coll., 1965; MA in Religious Studies, St. Charles Sem., 1977; cert., Sacred Congregation, Rome, 1977. Joined Cath. Sisters of Mercy, 1960; lic. tchr., Pa. Tchr. religion Prendergrast High Sch., Drexel Hill, Pa., 1972-76, Gwynedd Mercy Acad., Gwynedd Valley, Pa., 1976-78, Merion Mercy Acad., Merion Station, Pa., 1978-87; with Office of Religious Edn. Svcs. Sisters of Mercy, Merion Station, 1987—; pastoral asst. St. Justin Martyr Ch., Penn Valley, Pa., 1991—; lectr. Gwynedd-Mercy Coll., Gwynedd Valley, Pa., 1976-78, St. Charles Sem., Overbrook, Pa., 1977—; tchr. elem. religion tchrs. Archdiocese of Phila., 1985—; asst. pastor St. Mary's of the Assumption, Manayunk, Pa., 1989—; with Prison Ministry, 1983; alt. del. gen. chpt. Sisters of Mercy, 1980, 85, del. 1988; tchr. religion Mater Misericordia Acad., also chmn. dept.; tchr. elem. religion Diocese of Del., 1991—; tchr. scripture in ch. ministry program St. Charles Sem., 1991—; tutor math. and reading. Moderator Community Svc. Corps; active Helping Other People Eat. Home and Office: 515 Montgomery Ave Merion Station PA 19066

MCNALLY, RICHARD PATRICK, priest; b. Fall River, MA, Mar. 2, 1950; s. Michael Jerome and Anna Catherine (Wall) McN. BA, St. Mary's Coll., Winona, Minn., 1972; MA, Washington Theol. Union, Silver Spring, Md., 1978; Licentiate in Sacred Theology, Gregorian U., Rome, 1982. Joined Congregation Sacred Hearts, Roman Cath. Ch., ordained priest. Assoc. pastor St. Mary's and St. Francis chs., Fairhaven, Mass., 1975-80; retreat dir. Sacred Hearts Retreat House, Wareham, Mass., 1982-83; pastor Sts. Peter and Paul's Ch., Rochester, N.Y., 1983-86; dir. initial formation Congregation of Sacred Hearts, Cheverly, Md., 1986-88; provincial superior Congregation of Sacred Hearts, Fairhaven, 1988-91, provincial councillor, 1982-88; assoc. pastor St. Ann's Ch., Kaneohe, Hawaii, 1991—; chpt. del. Congregation of Sacred Hearts, El Escorial, Spain, 1988. Trustee Washington Theol. Union, 1988-91. Home: 46-129 Haiku Rd Kaneohe HI 96744

MCNAMARA, JULIA M(ARY), academic administrator, foreign language educator; b. N.Y.C., Dec. 13, 1941; d. John P. and Julia (Dowd) McN. BA in History and French, Ohio Dominican Coll., 1965; MA in French, Middlebury Coll., Paris, 1972; PhD in French Lang. and Lit., Yale U., 1980; DHL (hon.), Sacred Heart U., Hamden, Conn., 1984. Mem. faculty St. William Sch., Pitts., 1963-64, Holy Spirit Sch., Columbus, Ohio, 1964-65, Newark (Ohio) Cath. High Sch., 1965-66, Northwest Cath. High Sch., West Hartford, Conn., 1966-69, St. Vincent Ferrer High Sch., N.Y.C., 1969-70, St. Mary's High Sch., New Haven, 1971-74; lectr. french Albertus Magnus Coll., New Haven, 1976-80, dean of students, 1980-82, acting pres., 1982-83, pres., 1983—; prof. French Albertus Magnus Coll., 1981—; mem. Conn. Health and Edn. Facilities Authority, Hartford, 1983—; chair Conn. Conf. Ind. Colls., Hartford, 1990-92, sec.-treas. 1986—, chmn., 1990-92; lectr. in field; assoc. fellow Yale U., Morse Coll.; bd. dirs. New Haven Savs. Bank. Chairperson United Way Greater New Haven, 1987; bd. dirs. St. Mary's High Sch., New Haven, 1982-91, ARC, New Haven Savs. Bank, 1990—; trustee Yale/New Haven Hosp., 1984—, mem. bioethics com., mem. investment com., chmn. investor responsibility com., vice chair bd., 1991—, chair med. com., 1989-91; adv. bd. Bank of Boston-Conn., 1983-87; adv. com. Jr. League Greater New Haven, 1985; trustee Hartford Sem., 1985-91. Fulbright fellow, Paris, 1977-78; Yale U. fellow, 1974-78, Am. Council on Edn. fellow, 1981; recipient Disting. Woman in Leadership award New Haven YWCA, 1984, Veritas award Providence Coll., 1987, Greater New Haven Jr. Achievement Ann. award, 1990. Mem. Fulbright Alumni Assn., New Haven C. of C. (bd. dirs. 1984-90), New England Assn. Schs. and Colls. (appeals bd. 1986-88). Roman Catholic. Office: Albertus Magnus Coll 700 Prospect St New Haven CT 06511-1189

MC NAMARA, LAWRENCE J., bishop; b. Chgo., Aug. 5, 1928; s. Lawrence and Margaret (Knusman) McN. B.A., St. Paul Sem., 1949; S.T.L., Catholic U. Am., 1953. Ordained priest Roman Catholic Ch., 1953; parish priest, tchr. Kansas City-St. Joseph Diocese, 1953-57; dir. diocesan Refugee Resettlement, 1957-60; chaplain Jackson County Jail, 1957-64; exec. dir. Campaign for Human Devel., 1973-77; bishop of Grand Island Nebr., 1978—. Recipient award Cath. Relief Services. Office: Chancery Office 311 W 17th St PO Box 996 Grand Island NE 68802 also: PO Box 1531 Grand Island NE 68802

MCNAMEE, SISTER CATHERINE, educational association executive; b. Troy, N.Y., Nov. 13, 1931; d. Thomas Ignatius McNamee and Kathryn McNamee Marois. B.A., Coll. of St. Rose, 1953, D.H.L. (hon.), 1975; M.Ed., Boston Coll., 1955, M.A., 1958; Ph.D., U. Madrid, 1967. Grad. asst. Boston Coll., 1954-55; asst. registrar Boston Coll. (Grad. Sch.), 1955-57; acad. v.p. Coll. St. Rose, Albany, N.Y., 1968-75; dir. liberal arts Thomas Edison Coll., Trenton, 1975-76; pres. Trinity Coll., Burlington, Vt., 1976-79, Coll. St. Catherine, St. Paul, 1979-84; dean Dexter Hanley Coll., U. Scranton, Pa., 1984-86; pres. Nat. Cath. Ednl. Assn., Washington, 1986—. Bd. dirs. Am. Forum, Kotz Grad. Sch. Mgmt., Minn., Boston Coll. Spanish Govt. grantee, 1965-67; OAS grantee, 1967-68; Fulbright grantee, 1972-73. Mem. Am. Assn. Execs., Assn. Cath. Colls. and Univs., Internat. Fedn. Cath. Univs., Delta Epsilon Sigma, Delta Kappa Gamma. Roman Catholic. Club: Zonta. Office: Nat Cath Ednl Assn 1077 30th St NW Ste 100 Washington DC 20007

MCNAMER, ELIZABETH FORSTER, philosophy educator; b. Tipperary, Ireland, Dec. 21, 1936; came to U.S., 1958; m. William R. McNamer, May 13, 1961; children: Bruce, Sarah, Bridget, Amy, Deirdre. BA, Gonzaga State U., 1976, MA, 1978; EdD, Mont. State U., 1990. Instr. Ea. Mont. Coll., Billings, 1985—; co-founder Scripture from Scratch Workshop, 1984—; reader radio program Tea and Poetry. Author: Manual for Scripture from Scratch, 1991, Christian Family Life: The Education of Heloise, 1992; contbr. articles to profl. jours. Named one of Outstanding Young Women Am., 1972; recipient Salute Women award, 1988. Mem. Soc. Bibl. Lit., Am. Acad. Religion. Office: Eastern Mont Coll Billings MT 59101

MCNAUGHTON, ROBERT DOUGLAS, minister; b. Lansing, Mich., Mar. 10, 1936; s. Basil Robert and Helen (Hubbard) McN.; m. Carol Lou Conklin, Aug. 16, 1958; children: Timothy, Brian, Susan, Ann. BA, Mich. State U., 1958; MDiv, North Park Theol. Sem., Chgo., 1962; D Ministry, McCormick Theol. Sem., Chgo., 1976. Ordained to ministry Evang. Covenant Ch. Am., 1962. Pastor chs., Minn.-Ind., 1959-62; pastor Covenant Ch., Orange, Mass., 1962-66, South Plainfield, N.J., 1966-73; sr. pastor Covenant Congl. Ch., Cromwell, Conn., 1973—; protestant chaplain Minimum Security Prison, Warwick, Mass., 1965-66; mem. Inter-Ch. Rels. Commn., Chgo., 1986—; vice chmn. East Coast Conf., Cromwell, 1989—; observer 7th assembly World Coun. Chs., Canberra, Australia, 1991; sec. East Coast Conf. Ministerium, 1966-69, chmn., 1980-83; vice sec. Covenant Ministerium, 1983-86. Author: (devotionals) Home Altar, 1983. Chmn. Juvenile Offenders Bd., South Plainfield, 1971-73; mem., developer community rose garden U.S. Constn. Bicentennial Celebration, Cromwell, 1989; chmn. bd. dirs. Children's Home Cromwell, 1991—. Grantee Greater Hartford Jaycees, State of Conn., Evang. Covenant Ch., A.N. Pierson Florists, 1988-90. Mem. Cromwell Clergy Assn. (chmn. 1980—). Democrat. Office: Covenant Congl Ch 82 Hicksville Rd Cromwell CT 06416

MCNEELY, RICHARD IRVING, clergyman, educator, retired military officer; b. Goodland, Kans., Nov. 24, 1928; s. Henry Irving and Emma Madeline (Dendurent) McN.; m. Jean Paton Graham, June 17, 1950 (div. Nov. 1981); children: Dennis Dean, Kathleen Jean McNeely Comer, Michael Craig; m. Alma Gretchen Orman, Dec. 18, 1981. BA, Westmont Coll., 1950; ThM, Dallas Theol. Sem., 1954, ThD, 1963; PhD, U. So. Calif., L.A., 1986. Ordained to ministry Presbyn. Ch. Dir. choral edn. Royal Ln. Bapt. Ch., Dallas, 1952-54; asst. pastor 1st Brethren Ch., Long Beach, Calif., 1954-58; min. of music Scofield Meml. Ch., Dallas, 1958-59; prof. Midwest Bible Coll., St. Louis, 1959-60; prof. Biola Coll., La Mirada, Calif., 1960-66, 69-80, assoc. dean, 1980-81; commd. USNR, 1962, advanced through grades to capt., 1988; chaplain USN Desron 21, San Diego, 1966-68; ret. USNR, 1988; pastor 1st Presbyn. Ch., Libby, Mont., 1989-90, Blackfoot Parish, Seeley Lake, Mont., 1990-91; campus pastor Mont. State U., Bozeman, 1991—. Author: I and II Kings, 1979; contbr. articles to profl. jours. Mem. Evang. Theol. Soc. (chpt. pres. 1979), Am. Sic. Affiliates, Kiwanis (spiritual aims dir., bd. dirs. 1985-90). Republican. Avocation: aviation. Home: 2960 Spring Meadows Dr Bozeman MT 59715

MCNEIL, DENNIS MICHAEL, priest; b. Cleve., Oct. 6, 1949; s. Bernard L. McNeil and Theresa (Busher) Stone. BA, Borromeo Coll., 1971; MDiv, St. Mary Sem., Cleve., 1975. Ordained priest Roman Cath. Ch., 1975. Assoc. pastor Assumption of Mary Parish, Brook Park, Ohio, 1975-79, St. Charles Parish, Parma, Ohio, 1979-81, St. Matthew Parish, Akron, Ohio, 1981-87, St. Mary Parish, Painesville, Ohio, 1987-91, St. Joseph Parish, Cuyahoga Falls, Ohio, 1991—; founder, spiritual dir. Soc. St. Monica, 1986—. Editor, author The Monican newsletter, 1988—. Mem. KC. Republican. Avocations: reading science fiction, photography, travel. Office: St Joseph Parish 215 Falls Ave Cuyahoga Falls OH 44221

MCNEIL, MARK FRASHER, broadcast executive; b. Fresno, Calif., Aug. 19, 1954; s. Dale E. and Dona Dean (Frasher) McN.; m. JoAnn Patrice Koltiska, Feb. 2, 1985; children: Michael, Mitchell, Michelle. BS, Calif. State U., Long Beach, 1981. CPA, Calif. Chief fin. officer Am. Sunrise Communications, Huntington Beach, Calif., 1984-90; pres. Guardian Communications, Inc., Cin., 1990—. Mem. AICPA, Calif. Soc. CPAs. Republican. Mem. Internat. Ch. of Foursquare Gospel. Office: Guardian Communications Inc PO Box 31440 Cincinnati OH 45231 *Our family motto is: Press On!.*

MCNEILL, DOUGLAS ARTHUR, priest; b. Bklyn., Mar. 6, 1942; s. Daniel Patrick and Elizabeth (Gallagher) McN. Student, Sacred Heart Sem., 1965, MTh, 1968; MS in Edn., Fordham U., 1973. Chief exec. officer St. Bonaventure Indian Missions, Thoreau, N.Mex., 1974—; chmn. Diocesan Pers. Bd., Gallup, N.Mex., 1975-81, Greater Thoreau (N.Mex.) Found., 1986—; founder Blessed Kateri Tekakwitha Acad., Thoreau, 1980; Episcopal vicar McKinley Vicariate, Gallup, 1985—. Candidate N.Y. State Assembly, Bklyn., 1972, Gallup-McKinley Sch. Bd., Gallup, 1976; mem. N.W. N.Mex. Drug Coun., Gallup, 1990—; exec. bd. dirs. S.W. Indian Found., Gallup, 1976-82; mem. Thoreau Water & Sanitation Bd., 1976-86. Mem. Diocesan Pastoral Coun., Diocesan Presbyteral Coun., Nat. Cath. Devel. Conf., Diocesan Religious Edn. (bd. dirs. Gallup chpt. 1973-86), Propagation of the Faith Soc. (bd. dirs. Gallup chpt. 1980—), K.C. (chaplain 1987—). Republican. Roman Catholic. Avocations: physical fitness, exercise, travel. Home: First & Olive PO Box 1120 Thoreau NM 87323 Office: St Bonaventure Indian Missions 200 Lenore Thoreau NM 87323 *Life can be an exciting, productive enterprise or we can simply choose to tear down those who believe so. I have chosen to believe and to live.*

MCNEILL, ODESSA M., evangelist, educator; b. Greensboro, N.C., Sept. 26, 1945; d. Elliot and Annie Lucenda (Cathey) Lilly; m. Reynold A. Jude, Sr., June 1, 1963 (div.); 1 child, Reynold A. Jude, Jr.; m. William A. McNeill, Jr., July 6, 1974. Gen. Bible cert., Manhattan Bible Inst., 1980; BRE, Am. Bible Inst., 1982; MRE, United Bible Coll. and Sem., 1990. Instr. Ea. Bible Inst., Irvington, N.J., 1980—; evangelist Mt. Zion Pentecostal Ch., Elizabeth, N.J., 1983—; clk., demurrage dept. Sealand Svc. Inc., Elizabeth, N.J., 1970—; coord. religious edn. Mt. Zion Pentecostal Chs. Inc., Elizabeth, 1985—, retreats and seminars for chs., 1985—; cert. behavior cons., lectr., counsellor. Democrat. Home: 26 Warren St Carteret NJ 07008 Office: Sealand Svc Inc McLester St Elizabeth NJ 07207

MCNICOL, BRUCE R., religious organization administrator. Pres. Christian Brethren, Wheaton, Ill. Office: Christian Brethren 218 W Willow Wheaton IL 60187*

MCNULTY, FRANK JOHN, priest; b. Bayonne, N.J., Sept. 27, 1926; s. Frank G. and Elizabeth (McDermott) McN. BA, Seton Hall U., 1948; STL, Cath. U., 1952, STD, 1963. Ordained priest Roman Cath. Ch., 1952. Parish priest St. Aloysius, Jersey City, 1952-61; sem. prof. Immaculate Conception, South Orange, N.J., 1961-80; vicar for priests Archdiocese of Newark, 1980-86; pastor Blessed Sacrament, Roseland, N.J., 1986—; v.p. Senate of Priests, Newark, 1970-75; retreat dir.; lectr. theology. Author: Invitation to Greatness, 1970, Should You Ever Feel Guilty, 1975, Preaching Better, 1986. Named to address Pope John Paul II on behalf of US priests, 1987; named Person of the Week, ABC News, 1987. Mem. Cath. Theol. Soc. Am. Home and Office: 28 Livingston Ave Roseland NJ 07068

MCNUTT, CHARLIE FULLER, JR., bishop; b. Charleston, W.Va., Feb. 27, 1931; s. Charlie Fuller and Mary (Ford) McN.; m. Alice Turnbull, Mar. 3, 1962; children: Thomas Ford, Charlie Fuller III, Alison Turnbull. AB, Washington and Lee U., 1953; MDiv, Va. Theol. Sem., 1956, DD (hon.), 1981; MS, Fla. State U., 1970. Ordained to ministry Episcopal Ch., 1956. Vicar, Christ Ch., Williamston, W.Va., 1956-60; asst. rector St. John's Episc. Ch., Tallahassee, Fla., 1960-62; rector St. Luke's Episc. Ch., Jacksonville, Fla., 1962-68; planning dir. Diocese of Fla., 1968-74; archdeacon of Jacksonville Diocese of Fla., 1970-74; rector Trinity Episc. Ch., Martinsburg, W.Va., 1974-80; consecrated bishop Episc. Diocese Cen. Pa., Harrisburg, 1980—; bd. dirs. Pa. Coun. Chs., Harrisburg, chmn. dept. social ministry, 1982-86, pres., 1991—. Bd. dirs. Appalachian People's Svc. Orgn., pres., 1985-87; bd. dirs. Boy Scouts Am., Harrisburg, 1981-86; mem. exec. coun. Nat. Ch., 1988—; mem. standing com. on program, budget and fin. Nat. Episcopal Ch., 1983-90; co-chmn. Pa. Conf. Interch. Cooperation. Mem. Phi Beta Kappa. Democrat. Home: 2428 Lincoln St Camp Hill PA 17011 Office: Episcopal Diocese Cen Pa 221 N Front St Ste 201 Harrisburg PA 17101

MCPHEE, SISTER GLENN ANNE, school system administrator. Supt. Cath. schs. Archdiocese of San Francisco. Office: Office of Supt Cath Schs 443 Church St San Francisco CA 94114*

MCPHERSON, RICHARD WILLIS, minister; b. Toronto, Ont., Can., June 4, 1948; came to U.S., 1970; s. Willis Grant and Vera Frances (Coulter) McP.; m. Charlote A. Shotwell, July 3, 1971; 1 child, Dayna Patrice. Grad., Ea. Pentecostal Bible Coll., Peterboro, Ont., 1970; BA, Cen. Bible Coll., Springfield, Mo., 1971. Ordained to ministry Assemblies of God, 1974. Min. youth First Assembly of God, Portland, Oreg., 1971-76; assoc. pastor Trinity Ch., San Antonio, 1976-84; sr. pastor Faith Temple, Corpus Christi, Tex., 1984—; co-sponsor Corpus Christi Bay Area Pastors Fellowship, 1984—; sec. Decade of Harvest sect. Assemblies of God, Corpus Christi, 1989—, sectional mem., 1990—; mem. ministerial rels. com. South Tex. dist. Assemblies of God, 1991—. Contbr. articles to profl. jours. Republican. Home: 6205 Bourbonais Dr Corpus Christi TX 78414 Office: Faith Temple 4425 S Staples St Corpus Christi TX 78411

MC PHERSON, ROLF KENNEDY, clergyman, church official; b. Providence, Mar. 23, 1913; s. Harold S. and Aimee (Semple) McP.; m. Lorna De Smith, July 21, 1931; children—Marlene (dec.), Kay. Grad., So. Cal. Radio Inst., 1933; D.D. (hon.), L.I.F.E. Bible Coll., 1944; LLD (hon.), L.I.F.E. Bible Coll., Los Angeles, 1988. Ordained to ministry Internat. Ch. Foursquare Gospel, 1940. Pres. Internat. Ch. Foursquare Gospel, L.A., 1944-88, dir., 1944—; pres., dir. L.I.F.E. Bible Coll., Inc., L.A., 1944-88. Mem. Echo Park Evangelistic Assn. (pres. 1944—). Office: 1910 W Sunset Blvd Ste 600 Los Angeles CA 90026

MCQUEEN, DOUGLAS VAN, minister; b. Hammond, Ind., Mar. 24, 1958; s. H. Van and Dorothy May (Tabb) McQ.; m. Deborah Lynn Hoffman, Aug. 9, 1980; children: Randall Van, Natalie Lynn. MusB, Howard Payne U., 1981; M in Religious Edn., Southwestern Bapt. Theol. Sem., 1987. Ordained to ministry So. Bapt. Conv., 1986. Min. Elmwood Bapt. Ch., Abilene, Tex., 1980-81, 1st Bapt. Ch., Stamford, Tex., 1981-83, Kingsland Bapt. Ch., Katy, Tex., 1983-87, Richland Bapt. Ch., Richardson, Tex., 1987-89, 1st Bapt. Ch., Greenville, Tex., 1989—; asst. team leader Double Mountain County Assn., Stamford, 1981-82; super summer staff Bapt. Gen. Conv. of Tex., Dallas, 1982-91; regional vacation bible sch. clinician Bapt. Gen. Conv. of Tex., Union Assn., Houston, 1986; sr. adult com. Hunt Bapt. Assn., Greenville, 1990-91. Bd. Drug Free Greenville, Tex., 1991. Named Disting. Person, Outstanding Young Men of Am., 1983. Office: 1st Bapt Ch 2703 Wesley Greenville TX 75401

MCQUEEN, PAUL DENNIS, minister; b. Oakland, Ill., Sept. 15, 1945; s. Hubert Franklin and Glenna (Senter) McQ.; m. Robert Rose Mourant, June 29, 1968; children: Alison Marie, Regina Rose, John Paul. BBA, Fla. State U., 1968; MDiv, Nashatah House, 1981. Ordained to ministry Episcopal Ch., 1981. Asst. rector Trinity Episcopal Ch., Vero Beach, Fla., 1981-82; rector Golria Dei Episcopal Ch., Cocoa, Fla., 1982-90; exec. dir. Canterbury Retreat and Conf. Ctr., Oviedo, Fla., 1990—, also bd. dirs., 1984-89; bd. dirs. Profl. Youth Ministry Inst., Orlando, Fla., 1990, Hospice, Vero Beach, 1981-82. Democrat. Office: Canterbury Retreat/Conf Ctr 1601 Alafaya Trail Oviedo FL 32705

MCQUILKIN, JOHN ROBERTSON, college administrator; b. Columbia, S.C., Sept. 7, 1927; s. Robert C. and Marguerite (Lambie) McQ.; m. Muriel Elaine Webendorfer, Aug. 24, 1948; children: Helen Marguerite, Robert Paul (dec.), David John, Virginia Anne, Amy Lambie, Douglas Kent. B.A., Columbia Bible Coll., 1947; M.Div., Fuller Theol. Sem., 1950; postgrad., No. Bapt. Theol. Sem., 1947-48. Prof. Greek, religious edn. and theology Columbia (S.C.) Bible Coll. and Sem., 1950-52, pres., 1968-90, chancellor, 1990—; headmaster Ben Lippen Sch., Asheville, N.C., 1952-55; missionary The Evang. Alliance Mission, Japan, 1956-68; acting pres. Tokyo Christian Coll., 1963-65. Author: Measuring the Church Growth Movement, 1974, Understanding and Applying the Bible, 1983, The Great Omission, 1984, An Introduction to Biblical Ethics, 1988; contbr. articles to religious jours.

MCRAE, CORNELIUS, academic administrator. Pres. Pope John XXIII Sem., Weston, Mass. Office: Pope John XXIII Nat Sem Office of the Rector 558 South Ave Weston MA 02193*

MCRAITH, JOHN JEREMIAH, bishop; b. Hutchinson, Minn., Dec. 6, 1934; s. Arthur Luke and Marie (Hanley) McR. B.A., Loras Coll., Dubuque, Iowa, 1956. Ordained priest, Roman Cath. Ch., 1960. Assoc. pastor St. Mary's Ch., Sleepy Eye, Minn., 1960-64, assoc. pastor, 1968-71; pastor St. Michael's Ch., Mickoy, Minn., 1964-67, St. Leo's Ch., St. Leo, Minn., 1967-68; dir. Nat. Cath. Rural Life, Des Moines, 1971-78; vicar gen. Diocese of New Ulm, Minn., 1978-82; bishop Owensboro, Ky., 1982—. Home: 501 W 5th St Owensboro KY 42301-2130 Office: 600 Locust St Owensboro KY 42301-2130

MCRAY, JOHN ROBERT, religion educator; b. Holdenville, Okla., Dec. 17, 1931; s. Marvin Eugene and Opal (Roberts) McR.; m. Naomi Annette Jackson, Oct. 24, 1937; children: John Jr., David, Barrett. BA, David Lipscomb U., Nashville, 1954; MA, Harding U., Searcy, Ark., 1956; PhD, U. Chgo., 1967. Asst. prof. Bible, Greek, ch. history Harding U., 1958-66; assoc. prof. Bible, Greek, ch. history David Lipscomb U., 1966-71; prof. religious studies Middle Tenn. State U., Murfreesboro, 1973-79; prof. New Testament and archaeology Wheaton (Ill.) Coll., 1980—; lectr. in archaeology Vanderbilt U., Nashville, 1978, Moscow State U., 1991; archaeology cons. Nat. Geographic Mag., Washington, 1988—; lectr. State of Israel, 1984. Author: New Testament Introduction and Survey, 1961, Archaeology and the New Testament, 1991; editor: The Eternal Kingdom, 1961, Index to the Biblical Archaeologist, 1970, Cumulative Index to the BASOR, 1972. Recipient J.W. McGarvey award Restoration Quarterly, 1960, award Christian Rsch. Found., 1962. Mem. Soc. Bibl. Lit. (pres. 1978), Near East Archael. Soc. (bd. dirs. 1985—), Inst. for Bibl. Rsch., Am.

Schs. Oriental Rsch. (bd. dirs. 1972—), Chgo. Soc. for Bibl. Rsch., Civitan (pres. Murfreesboro chpt. 1975-76). Mem. Ch. of Christ. Office: Wheaton Coll Grad Sch 501 E Seminary Ave Wheaton IL 60187

MCREYNOLDS, PAUL ROBERT, biblical studies educator; b. Kansas City, Mo., Oct. 17, 1936; s. Edgar Bert and Rose Beatrice (Justice) McR.; m. Madeline G. Hart., Apr. 13, 1957; children: Mark Stephen, Jeffrey Paul. BA in Religion, Pacific Christian Coll., 1958; BA, Calif. State U., Long Beach, 1959; MA in Religion, Butler U., 1961; PhD in Religion, Claremont (Calif.) Grad. Sch., 1969; MBA, Pepperdine U., 1980. Enrolled Agt. IRS. Asst. pastor Compton (Calif.) First Christian Ch., 1957-59, '65-68; pastor Monrovia (Ind.) Christian Ch., 1959-61, First Christian Ch., Flagstaff, Ariz., 1961-65; prof. New Testament & Greek Pacific Christian Coll., Fullerton, Calif., 1967—; owner Personal Fin. Planning, Claremont, Calif., 1986—. Author: (book) Commentary on Mark, 1989; contbr. articles to profl. jours. Chm. Nat. Commn. For Am. Assn. of Bible Colls., Fayetteville, Ark., 1976-82. Mem. Internat. Greek New Testament Com., 1969—, Clinebell Inst. (treas. 1989—), Western Assn. of Schs. and Colls., N.W. Assn. of Schs. and Colls., Soc. Bibl. Lit., Inst. Bibl. Rsch., Assn. Enrolled Agts. Republican. Home: 1916 N Mills Ave Claremont CA 91711 Office: Pacific Christian Coll 2500 E Nutwood Fullerton CA 92631

MCRIGHT, PAIGE MAXWELL, minister; b. Ft. Bragg, N.C., July 29, 1946; d. William Pollock and Muriel (Owen) Maxwell; m. Dan A. McRight, July 15, 1972; children: William Austin, Robert Adam Owen. BA, Agnes Scott Coll., Decatur, Ga., 1968; MDiv, Princeton Theol. Sem., 1971. Ordained to ministry Presbyn. Ch. (U.S.A.), 1971. Chaplain Presbyn. U. of Pa. Med. Ctr., Phila., 1971-72; chaplain, addiction counselor Clayton Mental Health Ctr., Riverdale, Ga., 1972-78; assoc. presbyter Atlanta Presbytery, 1980-89; staff assoc. Gen. Assembly Mission Bd., Atlanta, 1984-86; assoc. pastor First Presbyn. Ch., St. Petersburg, Fla., 1989—; chmn. bills and overtures com. Presbytery of Tampa Bay, St. Petersburg, 1989, mem. com. on preparation for ministry; mem. theol and ch. vocations Synod S. Atlantic, Jacksonville, Fla., mem. task force on candidates Gen. Assy. Presbyn. Ch. (USA), 1981-85. Bd. dirs. Career Counseling Ctr., St. Petersburg, 1989—, Pinellas Habitat for Humanity, St. Petersburg. Mem. Alban Inst., Assn. for Clin. Pastoral Edn., Assn. Profl. Christian Educators, Kiwanis. Democrat. Home: 501 66th Ave S Saint Petersburg FL 33705 Office: First Presbyn Ch 701 Beech Dr Saint Petersburg FL 33705

MCSWAIN, LARRY LEE, academic administrator, religion educator; b. Pond Creek, Okla., Nov. 10, 1940; s. Joseph Kelly McSwain and Glorene May Brown Kirk; m. Rebecca Sue Stidham, Aug. 26, 1963; children: Laura Suzanne, Michael Lee. BA, Okla. State U., 1963; BD, Southwestern Bapt. Theol. Sem., 1966; STD, So. Bapt. Theol. Sem., 1970. Ordained to ministry So. Bapt. Conv. Pastor Morrison (Okla.) Bapt. Ch., 1961-63, Vernon (Ind.) Bapt. Ch., 1967-69; sr. rsch. asst. urban studies ctr. U. Louisville, 1968-70; asst. then assoc. prof. ch. and community So. Bapt. Theol. Sem., Louisville, 1970-88, dean sch. theology, 1988-91, provost, 1991—; bd. dirs. Acts, Nashville, 1988-91. Co-author: Conflict Ministry in Church, 1981, Church Organization Alive, 1987; contbg. author numerous books; contbr. articles, book reviews to religious jours. Curriculum grantee Assn. Theol. Schs., 1976-77; named Cons. of Yr. So. Bapt. Conv., 1987, also Recognition award, 1988. Mem. Soc. for Scientific Study of Religion, Religious Rsch. Assn., Assn. for Study of Religion, So. Bapt. Rsch. Fellowship. Democrat. Office: So Bapt Theol Sem 2825 Lexington Rd Louisville KY 40280

MCSWEEN, ALLEN CREWS, JR., minister; b. Clinton, S.C., Sept. 24, 1943; s. Allen Crews and Irene (Dillard) McS.; m. Susan Doris Higgins, Aug. 14, 1965; children: Jean Louise, Michael Allen. BA, Davidson Coll., 1965; BD, Union Theol. Seminary, 1968, D in Ministry, 1978; M in Sacred Theology, Yale U., 1969. Pastor Meadowthorpe Presbyn. Ch., Lexington, Ky., 1969-74, Trinity Presbyn. Ch., Laurinburg, N.C., 1974-82, The Presbyn. Ch., Bowling Green, Ky., 1982-91, Fourth Presbyn. Ch., Greenville, S.C., 1991—; bd. advisors Mountain Retreat Assn., Montreat, N.C., 1987—. Assoc. editor Jour. for Preachers, 1981-88; editor at large The Presbyn. Outlook, 1989; contbr. articles to profl. jours. Drum fellow, 1968. Democrat. Lodge: Rotary. Home: 15 Craigwood Rd Greenville SC 29607 Office: Fourth Presbyn Ch 703 E Washington St Greenville SC 29607

MCVANN, MARK E., religion educator; b. Washington, Aug. 28, 1950; s. Paul Edward and Ruth Marie (Harris) McV. BS, Moorhead State U., 1972; MA, Loyola U., Chgo., 1979; PhD, Emory U., 1984. Assoc. prof. Lewis U., Romeoville, Ill., 1979—. Exec. editor Listening/Jour. Religion and Culture. Young scholars fellow Cath. Bibl. Assn. Mem. Cath. Bibl. Assn., Soc. Bibl. Lit., Am. Acad. Religion, Coll. Theology Soc. Roman Catholic. Office: Lewis U Rte 53 Romeoville IL 60441

MCVEY, VERNIE LUTHER, minister; b. Stafford, Kans., Jan. 24, 1917; s. Joe and Nellie Jane (La Master) McV.; m. Estella Ruth Stowe, July 19, 1945; children: Margaret, David, John (dec.), Mary Ellen. BA, Olivet Nazarene U., 1944, ThB, 1948; postgrad., Hamline U., 1956-57, Garrett Theol. Sem., 1958, Mich. State U., 1963, No. Mich. Community Coll., Petoskey, 1964, Kirtland Community Coll., Roscommon, Mich., 1978. Pastor Ch. of the Nazarene, Waukesha, Wis., 1943-44, 45-47, Ft. Clark, N.D., 1947-48, Hecla, S.D., 1948-52; supply pastor The Meth. Ch., Onida and Blunt, S.D., 1952-55, Corona, Summit and Peever, S.D., 1955-58; pastor Ch. of the Nazarene, Gaylord, Mich., 1961-65; pastor Ch. of the Nazarene, Merritt, Mich., 1965-72, evangelist, 1972-73; pastor Ch. of the Nazarene, West Branch, Mich., 1973-79, LeRoy, Mich., 1979-83, Fond du Lac, Wis., 1988—; pres., editor The Challenge Pub. Concern, Inc., Fond du Lac, 1954—. Apptd. mem. Fond du Lac City Ethics Bd., 1989—; apptd. mem. hosp. ethics com. St. Agnes Hosp., Fond du Lac, 1989—. Mem. Fond du Lac Ministerial Assn. Home and Office: 173 E Second St Fond du Lac WI 54935-4463

MCWHIRTER, DAVID IAN, librarian; b. Tonawanda, N.Y., June 5, 1937; s. William Bole and Ruth Lena (Schultz) McW.; m. Donna Jean Hoyt, Sept. 9, 1961; children: Heather Linette McWhirter Yeik, Leslie Fiona. BLS, SUNY, Geneseo, 1959; BDiv, Lexington (Ky.) Theol. Sem., 1962; MLS, Syracuse U., 1967. Asst. libr. Christian Theol. Sem., Indpls., 1962-76; dir. libr. and archives Disciple of Christ Hist. Soc., Nashville, 1976—. Hon. mem. Gordon Pipers, Indpls., 1976. Mem. Am. Theol. Libr. Assn., Tenn. Theol. Libr. Assn., Tenn. Archivists (treas. 1977—). Democrat. Home: 2606 Oakland Ave Nashville TN 37212 Office: Disciples of Christ Hist Soc 1101 19th Ave S Nashville TN 37212

MCWILLIAM, JOANNE ELIZABETH, religion educator; b. Toronto, Ont., Can., Dec. 10, 1928; d. Cecil Edward and Edna Viola (Archer) McW.; m. Leslie S. Dewart, Aug. 26, 1954 (div. Nov. 1975); children, Leslie Mary Dewart Giroday, Elizabeth Dewart McEwen, Sean, Colin; m. C. Peter Slater, June 6, 1987. BA, U. Toronto, 1951, MA, 1953; MA, U. St. Michael's, Toronto, 1966, PhD, 1968. Asst. prof. religious studies U. Toronto, 1968-74, assoc. prof., 1974-87, prof., 1987, chairperson dept. religious studies, 1990—. Author: The Theology of Grace of Theodore of Mopsuestia, 1971, Death and Resurrection in the Fathers, 1986; editor: Augustine: Rhetor to Theologian, 1991, Toronto Jour. Theology. Mem. Can. Soc. for Patristic Studies (pres. 1987—), Conf. Anglican Theologians (pres. 1990—), Can. Soc. for the Study of Religion, Can. Theol. Soc., Am. Theol. Soc., Am. Acad. Religion. Anglican. Office: U Toronto Trinity Coll, 6 Hoskin Ave, Toronto, ON Canada M5S 1H8

MCWILLIAMS, WARREN LEIGH, religion educator; b. Fort Smith, Ark., Dec. 12, 1946; s. George Leslie and Werdna Jane (Johnson) McW.; m. Patricia Kay Long, May 31, 1968; children: Amy Elizabeth, Karen Annette. BA, Okla. Bapt. U., 1968; MDiv, So. Bapt. Theol. Sem., 1971; MA, Vanderbilt U., 1974, PhD, 1974. Asst. prof. religion Stetson U., Deland, Fla., 1974-76; vis. prof. So. Bapt. Theol. Sem., Louisville, 1976; asst. prof. religion Okla. Bapt. U., Shawnee, 1976-82, Auguie Henry assoc. prof. Bible, 1982-88, prof., 1988—. Author: Free in Christ, 1984, The Passion of God, 1985, When You Walk Through the Fire, 1986; also articles. Mem. Am. Acad. Religion, Nat. Assn. Bapt. Profs. Religion, AAUP, Okla. Bapt. Hist. Soc. Democrat. Office: Okla Bapt U Shawnee OK 74801

MEAD, JUDE, clergyman, educator; b. Waltham, Mass., May 26, 1919; s. J. Edward and Teresa Florence (Lawless) M.; student Holy Cross Coll., 1936-38, St. Paul Monastery, 1938-39; BA, Passionist Monastic Sem., 1946; MA, St. Michael Monastery, 1962; LLD (hon.), Mt. St. Joseph Coll., 1966; S.T.D., Teresianum U., Rome, 1975. Ordained priest Roman Catholic Ch., 1946, joined Passionist Order, 1938; spiritual dir. St. Michael Monastery and Sem., 1947-51; asso. editor SIGN, 1951-52; mem. Passionist Mission Band, 1952-58; dir. St. Gabriel Retreat House, Boston, 1958-64; internat. preacher of retreats for clergy, religious and laity groups for Passionist Order, 1964—; prof. spiritual theology Immaculata Coll., 1976-87; prof. good counsel summer sch. formative theology and spirituality Inst. on Religious Life, Chgo., 1988—; lectr. in field; panelist Internat. Congress on Wisdom of Cross, Rome, 1975; mem. provincial adv. bd., Eastern Province Passionists; apptd. postulator by Holy See for the beatification cause of Mother Angeline Teresa, 1990. Recipient Papal Cross of Jerusalem (D'argent) (Vatican), Soteriological award Confraternity of the Passion, 1985. Mem. Cath. Bib. Assn. Gt. Britain, Inst. on Religious Life (adv. bd. 1987). Author books, including: Priestly Spirituality, 1975; St. Paul of the Cross: A Source/Work Book For Paulacrucian Studies, 1983; St. Gabriel, Passionist, Youthful Gospel Portrait, 1986, Mother M. Angeline Teresa, O. Carm.: Daughter of Carmel-Mother to the Aged, 1990; contbr. articles to profl. publs. Home and Office: Passionist Monastery 86-45 178th St Jamaica NY 11432 *In an egocentric society the memory of the Passion and Death of Jesus is the best proof of God's love for us and the best motivation for love of one another.*

MEAD, JUDITH LEE, minister; b. Aurora, Ill., Mar. 27, 1933; d. Harry Judson and Grace Irene (Johannsen) M. BA, U. Redlands, 1956; BD, San Francisco Theol. Sem., 1959; STM, Iliff Sch. Theol., 1969; PhD, U. Denver, 1979. Ordained to ministry Presbyn. Ch. (U.S.A.), 1959. Student asst. pastor Vallejo (Calif.) Community Presbyn. Ch., 1958-59; asst. pastor First Presbyn. Ch., Carlsbad, N.Mex., 1959-60; assoc. pastor First Presbyn. Ch., Lakewood, Colo., 1961-65; pastor South Park Presbyn. Ch., Fairplay, Colo., 1966-68, First Meth. Ch., Pierce, Colo., 1971-78, First Presbyn. Ch., Nunn, Colo., 1971-78; assoc. for women's program United Presbyn. Ch. (U.S.A.), 1979-87; assoc. for women's ministry Presbyn. Ch. (U.S.A.), Kansas City, Mo., 1987-89; pres. Highland Ministerial Alliance, Weld County, Colo., 1975-79. Mem. bd. govs. Aims Community Coll., Greeley, Colo., 1976-78. Mem. Presbytery of Boulder. Republican. Avocations: reading, writing, travel.

MEAD, LOREN BENJAMIN, religious institute administrator; b. Florence, S.C., Feb. 17, 1930; s. Walter Russell and Dorothy (Nauss) M.; m. Polly A. Mellette, Aug. 25, 1951; children: Walter Russell, Christopher Allen, Barbara Holladay Mead Wise, Philip Sidney. BA, U. of the South, 1951, DD (hon.), 1982; MA, U. S.C., 1951; MDiv, Va. Sem., Alexandria, 1955, DD (hon.), 1984; DD (hon.), Berkeley Div. Sch., New Haven, 1986. Ordained priest Episcopal Ch., 1956. Rector Trinity Episcopal Ch., Pinopolis, S.C., 1955-57, Ch. of the Holy Family, Chapel Hill, N.C., 1957-69; exec. dir. Project Test Pattern, Washington, 1969-74; founder, pres. Alban Inst., Washington, 1974—. Author: New Hope for Congregations, 1972, Critical Moment, 1988, The Once and Future Church, 1991. Recipient Spl. Achievement award Interim Pastor Network, 1990. Mem. Acad. Parish Clergy (bd. dirs. 1973-75), Soc. for Advancement of Continuing Edn. for Ministry. Democrat. Office: Alban Inst 4125 Nebraska Ave NW 2nd Fl Washington DC 20016

MEAD, MILLARD WILMER, minister; b. Cherry Valley, Ohio, May 27, 1930; s. Myrlen Lomas and Winifred Irene (Mills) M.; m. Janet Wilma Hummell, Aug. 7, 1948; children: Jacqueline Mead Doyle, David, Susan Mead Dyer. BS, Kent State U., 1970; MDiv, Meth. Sch. Theology, 1973. Ordained to ministry United Meth. Ch., 1974. Pastor Johnston Federated United Meth. Ch., Cortland, Ohio, 1963-75, Grace United Meth. Ch., Bucyrus, Ohio, 1975-84, St. Mark Ch., Galion, Ohio, 1984—; dist. sec. United Meth. Ch., 1974-75, mem. conf. coun. on ministry, 1973-76, 80-84, dist. coun. ministry, 1974; mem. East Ohio Conf. Archives and History, 1976—, sec. commn., 1976-84; mem. East Ohio Conf. Historian, 1984-88; East Ohio Conf. del. United Meth. Conf., Hawaii, 1981, World Meth. Camp Meeting, Ocean Grove, N.J., 1984; pres. North Cen. Jurisdiction Archives and History, 1984-88. Mem. adv. coun. agr. Trumbull County, Ohio, 1968-75, Commn. on Aging, 1973-75; chmn. svc. unit Salvation Army, Cortland, 1973-75; trustee Flat Rock Children's Home, 1975—, pres. bd. trustees, 1989—. Recipient Young Farmers award Dairyman's Coop. Sales Assn., 1962, Nat. Hwy. Safety award, 1975. Mem. Coun. on Ministries, Gen. Conf. Archives and History, East Ohio Conf. Town and Country Fellowship, United Meth. Hist. Soc. (charter), United Meth. Hist. Soc. Ohio (past v.p., pres., now treas.-sec.), Grange Club (master 1955-65), Masons (coun.). Address: 950 N Market St Galion OH 44833

MEAD, PATRICK ALLEN, clergyman; b. Lawrenceville, Ill., Dec. 16, 1956; s. Bill and Catherine (Kee) M.; m. Kami Lynn Taylor, June 28, 1979; chidren: Kara Kaleen, Duncan Taylor McKay. BS in Psychology, Columbia Pacific U., San Rafael, Calif., 1984, MS in Psychology, 1986; PhD in Therapy, Internat. Coll., London, 1987. Ordained to ministry Ch. of Christ. Minister Ch. of Christ, Norfolk, Va., 1980-82; missionary Ch. of Christ, Glasgow, Scotland, 1983, Irvine, Scotland, 1984-85; minister Ch. of Christ, Lancaster, Ohio, 1985—; psychotherapist, dir. Christian Therapy Ctr., Lancaster, 1985—. Author: Becoming a Christian Counselor, 1986, Freedom and Unity in Religion, 1990. Lt. col. gov.'s staff State of Ala., 1975; col. State of Ky., 1988. Mem. Am. Assn. Profl. Hypnotherapists (assoc.), United Assn. Christian Counselors, Mensa. Office: Lancaster Ch of Christ 1779 Granville Pike Lancaster OH 43130

MEADE, DAVID GLENN, minister; b. Oil City, Pa., Mar. 28, 1950; s. Robert Glenn and Avonell Marie (Weaver) M.; m. Elizabeth Louise Mesh, Sept. 7, 1974; children: Kara Leanne, Andrew Robert, Nathan Edward. BA, Houghton (N.Y.) Coll., 1972; MDiv, Gordon Conwell Theol. Sem., South Hamilton, Mass., 1975; ThM, Princeton (N.J.) Theol. Sem., 1980; PhD, U. Nottingham, Eng., 1984. Ordained to ministry United Meth. Ch., 1973. Pastor Westmont United Meth. Ch., Johnstown, 1975-79; lectr. in N.T. St. Johns Theol. Coll., Bramcote, Eng., 1982-83; asst. prof. of N.T. Houghton Coll., 1984-90; pastor St. Pauls United Meth. Ch., Niagara Falls, N.Y., 1990—. Author: Pseudonymity and Canon, 1985. Mem. Found. for Theol. Edn. (fellowship 1980-84), Soc. Bibl. Lit. Home: 748 4th St Niagara Falls NY 14301 Office: St Pauls United Meth Ch 723 7th St Niagara Falls NY 14301

MEADE, KENNETH ALBERT, minister; b. Sweet Valley, Pa., June 14, 1935; s. Delbert H. and Dorothea I. (Myers) M.; m. Jeanette H. Quigley, Dec. 18, 1954 ; children: Jane M. Meade Ulm, Mark K. Ministerial cert., Ea. Christian Inst., East Orange, N.J., 1955; DD (hon.), Milligan Coll., Tenn., 1986, Ea. Christian Coll., Bel Air, Md., 1986. Ordained to ministry Ch. of Christ, 1955. Student min. Ch. of Christ, Bklyn. and Greenpoint, N.Y., 1952-53; mem. Meade-Bennett Evangelistic Team, East Orange, 1953-55; sr. min. Ch. of Christ at Manor Woods, Rockville, Md., 1956—; pres. N.Am. Christian Conv., Cin., 1986, Ea. Christian Conv., Rockville, 1969, 74, 82. Contbr. numerous articles to religion mags. Trustee Milligan Coll. Recipient Award of Honor, Am. Legion, 1952, Highest Comml. award Lehman High Sch. Alumni Assn., 1952. Office: Ch of Christ at Manor Woods 5300 Norbeck Rd Rockville MD 20853-2399

MEADE, WILLIAM WAYNE, lay worker; b. Richmond, Va., Oct. 4, 1965; s. Ronald Charles and Linda (Keeton) M.; m. Lethia Michaux, Jan. 21, 1989. BA in Religion/Philosophy, Atlantic Christian Coll., 1988; postgrad., Lexington, Theol. Sem., 1988-89. Youth min. Rocky Fork Christian Ch., Sandford, N.C., 1984-85, Battery Park Christian Ch., Richmond, Va., 1987-88; youth counselor Christian Ch. of Va., Lynchburg, Va., summer 1988, Christian Ch. of N.C., Wilson, summer 1988; dir. Understanding Needs In Today's Youth (Unity), Richmond, 1988—; youth counselor St. Joseph Villa, Richmond, 1989; missionary to Europe, Sports Outreach Interaction, Minatowka, Minn., 1990; missionary to Guatemala, Mechanicville (Va.) Christian Ctr., 1991. Office: UNITY 613 D Ellerson Mill Dr Mechanicsville VA 23111

MEADOR, JOSEPH DOUGLAS, minister; b. Lubbock, Tex., Nov. 17, 1958; s. Joe Berry and Norma Jean (Moore) M.; m. Karen Adele Moore, Jan. 4, 1980; children: Rachel, Esther, Hannah, Sarah, Lydia. AAS, South Plains Coll., 1979; BA with distinction, U. Tex., Odessa, 1980; diploma in Bible, Memphis Sch. of Preaching, 1983; MTh with highest honors, Bethany Theol. Sem., 1985, STD with highest honors, 1990. Ordained to ministry Ch. of Christ, 1983. Assoc. minister Getwell Ch. of Christ, Memphis, 1981-83; minister Ch. of Christ, Poole, Ky., 1983-86, Madisonville (Ky.) Ch. of Christ, 1987-90, Blvd. Ch. of Christ, Las Vegas, Nev., 1990—. acad. dir. Coll. of the Bible, Madisonville, 1987-90; faculty Southwestern Sch. of Religion, Las Vegas, 1990—. Author: (with others) The Book of Philippians, 1987, The Book of John, 1988, The Bible: None Like It, 1988, The Providence of God, 1989, The Minor Prophets, 1990; founding editor In Word & Doctrine Jour., 1986-90; editor Homiletica Sacra, 1991—. Mem. Am. Acad. Religion, Acad. of Homiletics, Religious Speech Communication Soc., Medieval Acad. Am., Soc. Philosophers in Am. (Yale). Home: 5817 Granada Ave Las Vegas NV 89107 Office: Blvd Ch of Christ 4000 W Oakey Blvd Las Vegas NV 89102

MEADOR, PRENTICE AVERY, JR., minister; b. Portland, Tenn., Feb. 8, 1938; s. Prentice Avery Sr. and Margaret (Staggs) M.; m. Barbara J. Morrell, July 1, 1960; children: Lori Ann, Mark, Kimberly. BA, David Lipscomb Coll., 1960; MA, U. Ill., 1961, PhD, 1964. Ordained to ministry Ch. of Christ, 1956. Min. Ch. of Christ, San Fernando, Calif., 1966-71, Springfield, Mo., 1974-88; min. Prestoncrest Ch. of Christ, Dallas, 1988—; asst. prof. U. Wash., Seattle, 1971-74; lectr. S.W. Mo. State U., Springfield, 1974-85; adj. prof. Abilene (Tex.) Christian U., 1988—; news journalist Channel 8, Dallas. Author: Preaching to Modern Man, 1969, Who Rules Your Life?, 1979, Sermons for Today, 1981, Walk With Me, 1990; asst. editor: Power for Today mag., 1989—. Del. White House Conf. of Family, Mpls., 1980; chmn. Gov.'s Com. on Youth and Children, Jefferson City, Mo., 1981; mem. chancellor's coun. Pepperdine U., Malibu, Calif., 1989—; nat. spokesperson Child Care Agencies; trustee Abilene Christian U., 1989—. Winner Framed George Washington medal of honor Freedom Found. of Valley Forge, 1985. Avocations: running, golf, tennis, hunting. Office: Prestoncrest Ch of Christ 6022 Prestoncrest Ln Dallas TX 75230

MEADORS, MARSHALL LEROY, JR., minister; b. Kingstree, S.C., Jan. 1, 1933; s. Marshall LeRoy and Sarah (Lucius) M.; m. Hannah Campbell; children: Mary Jane, Marshall Leroy III, James Campbell, John Paschal. AB, Wofford Coll., 1955; MDiv, Emory U., 1958; DD (hon.), Wofford Coll., 1979. Min. McBee United Meth. Ch., 1958-61, Trinity United Meth. Ch., Crescent Beach, S.C., 1961-66, Berea Friendship United Meth. Ch., Greenville, S.C., 1966-68, 1st United Meth. Ch., Marion, S.C., 1968-72; sr. min. St. John's United Meth. Ch., Anderson, S.C., 1972-81; dist. supt. Columbia (S.C.) Dist., 1981-87; sr. min. Buncombe St. United Meth. Ch., Greenville, S.C., 1987—; del. S.E.J. and Gen. Conf., Balt., 1984, St. Louis, 1988, Louisville, 1992, World Meth. Conf., Honolulu, Nairobi, 1981-86, Singapore, 1991; pres. Conf. Coun. on Fin. and Adminstrn., 1987—; dir. Gen. Bd. Higher Edn. and Ministry, Nashville, 1988—. Trustee Spartanburg Meth. Coll., S.C., 1975-87, Anderson County Sch. Dist. 5, S.C., 1975-81; gov. appointee S.C. Joint Legis. Study Commn. on Aging, Columbia, 1979-83, S.C. Commn. on Aging, Columbia, 1981-87. Named to Order of Palmetto, 1987. Mem. Phi Beta Kappa. Office: Buncombe St United Meth Ch 200 Buncombe St Greenville SC 29601

MEADOWS, KEVIN BLANE, youth minister; b. Goldsboro, N.C., Aug. 7, 1965; s. Donald Earl and Susie Aster (Elmore) M.; m. Cynthia Ann Railey, May 16, 1987; 1 child, Kendall Blake. BA in Philosophy, N.C. State U., 1987; MDiv, So. Bapt. Theol. Sem., Louisville, 1991. Licensed to the Gospel Ministry, 1985. Min. youth Oakdale Bapt. Ch., Statesville, N.C., summers 1984-85, First Bapt. Ch., Yadkinville, N.C., summer 1986; min. jr. high youth Middletown (Ky.) United Meth. Ch., 1988-90; min. youth family life activities Vinton (Va.) Bapt. Ch., 1991—; messenger So. Bapt. Conv., New Orleans, 1990; asst. lay dir. Chrysalis Community Louisville, 1990; intern Bread for the World, Louisville, 1990-91. Contbr. cartoons to profl. jours. Mem. Seminarians United Against Hunger, So. Bapt. Theol. Sem., 1990-91. Democrat. Address: 218 Jackson Ave Vinton VA 24179 *Perhaps the greatest evil that permeates our world today is that of hunger. Solving this disastrous human crisis will depend on our love of justice and hatred of apathy.*

MEADOWS-ROGERS, ARABELLA THOMAS, minister; b. Frankfurt, Ger., July 15, 1949; d. Jordan Thomas and Sarah (Flinn) Rogers; m. Robert Denton Meadows-Rogers, Aug. 12, 1972; children: Matthew, Sarah. BA, Duke U., 1974; MDiv, Union Theol. Sem., N.Y.C., 1974. Ordained to ministry Presbyn. Ch., 1975. Assoc. pastor West Park Presbyn. Ch., N.Y.C., 1975-78; pastor Univ. Hts. Presbyn. Ch., Bronx, 1978-82, West Delhi (N.Y.) Presbyn. Ch., 1983-85; assoc. pastor First Presbyn. Ch., Durham, N.C., 1985—; pres. Genesis Home, Inc., Durham, 1989—; del. Nat. Gen. Assy., Phila., 1978. Named YWCA Woman of the Yr. in Religion, 1990. Home: 305 E Main Durham NC 27713 Office: First Presbyn Ch 305 E Main Durham NC 27701

MEAN, JOHN D., minister. Dist. supt. Nova Scotia-N.F. dist. United Pentecostal Ch. in Can., Dartmouth, N.S. Office: United Pentacostal Ch, PO Box 2183 DEPS, Dartmouth, NS Canada B2W 3Y2*

MEANY, NEILL RICHARD, priest, educator; b. Milbank, S.D., July 27, 1923; s. Richard William and Corinne Lemina (Plouf) M. BA in Liberal Arts, Gonzaga U., 1946, MA in Eng., 1959; STB, Alma Coll., Los Gatos, Calif., 1955. Joined S.J., Roman Cath. Ch., 1941, ordained priest, 1954. Tchr. Bellarmine High Sch., Tacoma, 1948-51; tchr./counselor Marquette High Sch., Yakima, Wash., 1956-60, Gonzaga Prep. Sch., Spokane, 1960-65; mgr., undersec. Jesuit Provincial Adminstrn., Portland, Oreg., 1965-71; asst. pastor St. Joseph Ch., Yakima, 1971-79; adminstr. St. Patrick Parish, Granger, Wash., 1979-81; dir. publs. Jesuit Provincial Adminstrn., Portland, 1981-84; province archivist Gonzaga U., Spokane, 1984—; formation advisor Bishop White Sem., Spokane, 1986—; chaplain Sisters of Good Shepherd, Spokane, 1986—. Mem. Soc. Am. Archivists. Avocations: arts and crafts, photography, heraldry. Home: 502 E Boone Ave Spokane WA 99258 Office: Oregon Province Archives Gonzaga U Spokane WA 99258

MEASE, RONALD FRANKLIN, retired minister; b. Williamstown, Pa., Jan. 29, 1929; s. Harold Franklin and Helen Mae (Yeager) M.; m. Jean Elizabeth Starner, June 12, 1953; children: Eric Franklin, Alice Ann. BA, Muhlenberg Coll., Allentown, Pa., 1951; BD, Phila. Sem., 1954. Pastor Friedens Luth. Ch., Friedensville, Pa., 1954-57; assoc. pastor Zion Luth. Ch., Wilmington, Del., 1957-64; pastor Trinity Luth. Ch., Balt., 1964-67; dir. urban/migrant ministries Md. State Council Chs., Balt., 1967-69; coordinator Greater Indpls. Luth. Parish, 1969-72; pastor-campus pastor First Luth. Ch., Ind. U./Purdue U., Indpls., 1972-73; pastor Ch. of the Savior, Williamsport, Pa., 1973-90; bd. dirs. Luth. Found. North Cen. Pa., Williamsport, 1980-90, United Chs. of Lycoming County, 1975-78; chmn. Com. on Budget and Prog., Upper Susquehanna Synod., Williamsport, 1986-87; mem. Com. on Fiscal Mgmt., Upper Susquehanna Synod, Lewisburg, 1988—. Bd. dirs. Latchkey of Williamsport, Inc., 1988-90. Democrat. Evangelical Lutheran. Avocations: cooking, chess, reading, electronics, camping, wine making. Home: 2371 Hillside Ave Williamsport PA 17701-4268

MECK, LYNETTE, religious organization administrator. Exec. sec. The Mennonite Cen. Com., Akron, Pa. Office: Mennonite Cen Comm 21 S 12th St Akron PA 17501*

MEDARIS, EDWARD GENE, religious organization administrator; b. Kenefic, Okla., Sept. 22, 1929; s. Thomas Edward and Ida Alyce (Airington) M.; m. Martha Jane Medaris, Aug. 6, 1960; children: Gina Lian Medaris Murrow, Timothy Edward. BA, Baylor U., 1953; BD, Southwestern Bapt. Theol. Sem., 1962; MDiv, Southwestern Bapt. Theol. Sem., 1973, 1973; BA in Journalism, U. Alaska, 1976. Ordained to ministry, Bapt. Ch. Minister Univ. Bapt. Ch., Fairbanks; religion columnist Fairbanks Daily News-Miner; dir. communication and pub. rels. State Conv. Bapts.-Ind., Indpls.; exec. dir. Presbyn. Hospitality House, Fairbanks. Author: Ted McRoberts: North Country Marshall, 1986. Capt. USAF, 1953-63. Alaska Press Club scholar. Mem. Tanana Valley Bapt. Assn., Bapt. Press Assn., Bapt. Pub. Rels., Nat. Child Welfare League, Alaska Assn. of Homes for Children. Home: 220 Steelhead Rd Fairbanks AK 99709

MEDARIS, JOHN BRUCE, clergyman, retired army officer; b. Milford, Ohio, May 12, 1902; s. William Roudebusch and Jessie (LeSourd) M.; m.

Gwendolyn Hunter, May 19, 1920 (div. 1930); 1 dau., Marilyn C. (Mrs. Eugene Stillings); m. Virginia Rose Smith, Aug. 29, 1931 (dec. 1984); children: Marta Virginia (Mrs. Charles G. Smith, Jr.), John Bruce, Jr.; m. Frances Faye Farmer McNally, 1989. Student, Ohio State U., 1919-21; Sc.D., Rollins Coll., 1958, U. Ala., 1958, N.Mex. State U.; LL.D., Pa. Mil. Coll., 1958, U. Chattanooga, 1958; D.Space Sc., Fla. Inst. Tech., 1963. Rated army aviator, 1956. Began career as enlisted man USMC, 1918-19; commd. lt. inf. U.S. Army, 1921, advanced through grades to maj. gen., 1955; attached 29th and 33d Inf. Regts., 1921-26, Ordnance Corps, 1926-27; res. officer, 1927-39; exec. officer Cin. Ordnance Dist.; then asst. dist. control officer Office (Chief of Ordnance); exec. contract distbn. sect. Office Under Sec. War, 1938-42; bn. comdr., ordnance officer II Corps, Tunisia, Sicily; ordnance officer 1st Army, Eng.; also organized, operated Field Army Ordnance Service, 1st U.S. Army in Europe; ordnance officer 5th Service Command, also Army Ground Forces; chief U.S. Army Mission to Argentina, 1949-52; exec., asst. chief ammunition br., indsl. div. Office Chief Ordnance, 1953, asst. chief ordnance, chief indsl. div., 1953-55; comdg. gen. Army Ballistic Missile Agy., Huntsville, Ala., 1955-58, U.S. Army Ordnance Missile Command, 1958-60; ret.; pres., chief exec. officer Lionel Corp., 1960-62, vice chmn. bd., 1962-63; chmn. bd. Electronic Teaching Labs. Washington, 1960-61; mem. bd., chmn. exec. com. All-State Devel. Corp., Miami, 1962-63; pres. Medaris, Cruger & Patterson (co. name changed to Medaris Mgmt., Inc. 1966), 1963-70, chmn. bd., 1970-78; Ordained deacon Episcopal Ch., 1969, priest, 1970; assoc. rector Episcopal Ch. of Good Shepherd, Maitland, Fla., 1973-79; priest Anglican Ch., 1979-89; rector Anglican Ch. of Incarnation, Orlando, Fla., 1979-81; rector emeritus Anglican Ch. of Incarnation, 1981-89; canon missioner Dio. South, Anglican Cath. Ch., 1981-83, canon theologian, 1984, archdeacon, 1984-86, archdeacon emeritus, 1986; exec. officer to Bishop Ordinary, 1987; chaplain, missioner Internat. Order St. Luke, 1972—; vicar Anglican Mission Holy Cross, 1987-89; pres., chief minister Mountain Ctr. for Renewal, 1987-89; bd. pres. Pershing Commn. for Tacna-Arica Plebiscite, 1925. Author: Countdown for Decision, 1960. Mem. Planning Commn. Diocese Central Fla., 1973-76; Fla. chmn. Radio Free Europe, 1963-64; v.p., dir. Pan Am. Funds, 1965-73; pres., dir. Chapel of Astronauts, Inc., 1969-72, dir., mem. exec. com., 1972-73; dir. World Center for Liturgical Studies, 1972-73, chmn. bd., 1973-74; mem. sci. adv. com. state Ala., Councilman, Maitland, 1965-68. Decorated D.S.M. with oak leaf cluster; Order de Coronne de Chene Luxembourg; Legion of Merit with 2 oak leaf clusters; Soldiers Medal; Bronze Star; Legion of Honor France; recipient Freedoms Found. awards, 1959, 60, John Young award, 1977; named to Ordnance Hall of Fame, 1973; Disting. fellow Am. Soc. Nuclear Medicine, 1981. Fellow AIAA; mem. IEEE (sr.), Explorers Club, Am. Ordnance Assn. (life), Am. Legion (life), Mil. Chaplains Assn. (life), Assn. Ordnance-Industry Physicians, Scabbard and Blade, Sigma Tau. Clubs: Wildcat Cliffs Country (Highlands, N.C.) (hon.). Home (summer): Rte 2 Box 23E Highlands NC 28741 Address: Granada Apt 503 525 E Semoran Blvd PO Box 415 Fern Park FL 32730

MEDICI, STELIOS PRINCE CASTANOS DE', church dignitary, diplomat, educator; b. Athens, Greece, Apr. 18, 1927; s. Anthony and Mary (Vrachnos) de'M.; m. Hebe Mary Deirmendjoglou, Aug. 15, 1956. Grad., Athens Coll., 1945; Cert. in Adminstrv. Law, U. Lausanne, 1948, Lic. in Polit. Sci., 1949, Dr. in Polit. Sci., 1953. Counsellor, Greek Del. to Gen. Assembly UN, 1951-52; counsellor, then charge de mission Internat. Burs. Intellectual Property, Geneva and Bern, Switzerland, 1953-59; prof. U. Strasbourg (France), 1956-66; grand referendary Holy Apostolic and Ecumenical See, Paris, 1967—; staff Syntheses mag., Brussels, 1964-66; mem. Ministry of Fgn. Affairs, Paris, 1964—. Author: Reponse a Heidegger sur L'Humanisme, 1966; Athenagoras Ier, 1968; Introduction to Holocracy, 1977; Note sur Odysseus Elytis, 1979. Served with inf. Greek Army, 1949-51. Decorated comdr. Order of St. Mark (Greece); grand cross Order of St. Stephen; bailiff grand cross Sovereign Order of St. John of Jerusalem, Knights of Malta. Mem. Internat. Union of Christian Knighthood (honors com.), Internat. Acad. Lutece (hon.), Am. Acad. Polit. and Social Sci., Soc. for Comparative Legislation, Hellenic Inst. of Internat. and Fgn. Law (corr.). Home: 6 Ave du Premier Mai, CH 1020 Renens Vaud, Switzerland

MEECE, BERNARD CLAYTON, clergyman, church administrator; b. Somerset, Ky., Mar. 7, 1927; s. Bernard and Myrtle (Sweeney) M.; m. Georgia Ann Curry, Sept. 2, 1950; children—Judith, Jeannine, Jacquelyn. A.B., Transylvania U., 1949, D.D., 1980; B.D., Lexington Theol. Sem., 1952; D.Min., Drew U., 1981. Ordained to ministry Christian Ch. (Disciples of Christ), 1952. Pastor, 1st Christian Ch., Cadillac, Mich., 1952-57; assoc. minister N.C. Christian Soc., Wilson, 1957-62; pastor 1st Christian Ch., DeLand, Fla., 1962-69, Sarasota, Fla., 1969-81; regional minister Christian Ch. in N.C., Wilson, 1981—; dir. Ch. Fin. Council, Indpls., 1983-87. Mem. screening com. Sarasota Sch. Bd., 1975-81; trustee Atlantic Christian Coll., Wilson, 1981—. Lodge: Kiwanis (pres. Sarasota club 1976-77). Home: 805 Trinity Dr Wilson NC 27893 Office: Christian Ch in NC 509 NE Lee St PO Box 1568 Wilson NC 27893

MEEGAN, SISTER ELIZABETH, school system administrator. Supt. Cath. schs. Diocese of Phoenix. Office: Office of Schs Supt 400 E Monroe Phoenix AZ 85004*

MEEK, PETER HUNT, minister; b. Bangor, Maine, Apr. 23, 1943; s. Frederick Mayer and Amy (Hunt) M.; m. Barbara Anne Beach, Apr. 19, 1969; 1 child, Amy Esther Beach. BA, Amherst (Mass.) Coll., 1965; MDiv, Union Theol. Sem., 1968; D in Ministry, Hartford (Conn.) Sem., 1984. Assoc. minister First Ch. of Christ, Woodbridge, Conn., 1968-72; sr. minister Berlin (Conn.) Congl. Ch., 1972-80, Hancock United Ch. of Christ, Lexington, Mass., 1980—. Mem. guidance adv. com. Lexington Pub. Schs., 1987—; v.p. trustees Cary Meml. Libr., Lexington, 1988—. Mem. Mass. Congl. Charitable Soc., Boston City Mission Soc. (corp. 1982—), Lexington Clergy Assn. (pres. Lexington chpt. 1985), Arundel Yacht Club, Masons (grand chaplain 1986-90). Home: 23 Hancock St Lexington MA 02173 Office: Hancock United Ch of Christ 1912 Massachusetts Ave Lexington MA 02173 *At no time since the end or WWII have traditional religious communities had such a crucial role on the world stage. A rediscovery of religious values and practice will decisively shape the first years of the new millenium...*

MEEK, SUSAN JANE, lay worker; b. Peoria, Ill., Mar. 23, 1944; d. Harold Chester and Lura Louise (Pollock) Weaver; m. Jimmy Mitchel, Dec. 22, 1965; children: Keith, Lora, Mitch. Grad. high sch., Chillicothe, Ill., 1962. Sec. First Bapt. Ch., Adamsville, Tenn., 1970—; sec.-treas. Women's Missionary Union, First Bapt. Ch., 1990-91. Mem. Tenn. Bapt. Conv. Ch. Secs. Orgn. Office: First Bapt Ch 222 W Main PO Box 216 Adamsville TN 38310

MEEKS, MARK ANTHONY, minister; b. Dallas, Sept. 24, 1946; s. Frederick Earl and Lillie Mae (Chaddick) M.; m. Debra Ann Yeager, Oct. 30, 1985; children: Jessica, Lillian, Sonya. AA, Dallas Bapt. Coll., 1967; BA, U. Tex. at Arlington, 1969; postgrad., Southwestern Bapt. Sem., 1969-72; MDiv, So. Bapt. Sem., 1973. Ordained to ministry Bapt. Ch., 1973. Pastor Grace Bapt. Ch., Heidelberg, Fed. Republic Germany, 1973-76; co-dir. Karis Community, Denver, 1978-80; spiritual leader Capitol Heights Presbyn. Ch., Denver, 1979—; mem. ecumenical ministry team Capitol Heights Presbyn and Ten-Thirty Cath. Community, Denver, 1982—. Regional coord. Amnesty Internat., Denver; bd. dirs. Cornerstone Peace and Justice Ctr., Support Systems Consol., Karis Community. Mem. Capitol Hill United Ministries (pres. 1986—, chaplain 1991—). Home: 500 St Paul Denver CO 80206 Office: Capitol Heights Presbyn Ch 1100 Fillmore Denver CO 80206 *The primary sacrament is the sacrament of presence. God's first and most enduring question is "Where are you?" Our life long task is to become present to God in and through all the stuff of our existence.*

MEEKS, M(ERRILL) DOUGLAS, II, dean, researcher, theology educator, author; b. Memphis, Apr. 24, 1941; s. Merrill Douglas and Evelyn (Yost) M.; m. Helen Blair Gilmer, June 5, 1963; children: Merrill Douglas III, John William. Student, Vanderbilt U., 1959-60; BA, Rhodes Coll., 1963; BDiv, Duke Div. Sch., 1966; PhD, Duke U., 1971. Ordained to ministry, United Meth. Ch., United Ch. of Christ. Instr. in theology Duke Div. Sch., Durham, N.C., 1967-68; Wissenschaftliche asst. Protestant theol. faculty Tubingen (Fed. Republic of Germany) U., 1968-70; asst. prof. religion Huntingdon Coll., Montgomery, Ala., 1970-71; asst. prof. theology and ethics Eden Theol. Sem., St. Louis, 1971-74, assoc. prof. theology and ethics, 1974-78, prof. systematic theology and philosophy, 1978-90; dean, prof. systematic theology Wesley Theol. Sem., Washington, 1990—; chairperson sect. on liberation theology Am. Acad. of Religion, 1979-89; co-chairperson Oxford (Eng.) Inst. Meth. Theol. Studies, 1981—. Author: Origins of the Theology of Hope, 1974, God the Economist, 1989; editor: Future of Methodist Theological Traditions, 1986, What Should Methodists Teach, 1990. Fulbright Commn. fellow Tubingen U., 1968-70, Inst. for Ecumenical and Culture Rsch. fellow, 1983. Fellow Am. Acad. Religion, Soc. Christian Ethics, Soc. for Values in Higher Edn., Gesellschaft für Theologie. Home: 1608 Ingram Terr Silver Spring MD 20906 Office: Wesley Theol Sem 4500 Massachusetts Ave NW Washington DC 20016

MEEKS, WAYNE A., religious studies educator; b. Aliceville, Ala., Jan. 8, 1932; s. Benjamin L. and Winnie (Gavin) M.; m. Martha Evelina Fowler, June 10, 1954; children—Suzanne, Edith, Ellen. BS, U. Ala.-Tuscaloosa, 1953; BD, Austin Presbyn. Theol. Sem., 1956; MA, Yale U., 1964, PhD, 1965; Doctor Theologiae honoris causa, U. Uppsala, Sweden, 1990. Instr. religion Dartmouth Coll., Hanover, N.H., 1964-65; asst. prof. religious studies Ind. U., Bloomington, 1966-68, assoc. prof., 1968-69; assoc. prof. religious studies Yale U., New Haven, 1969-73, prof. religious studies, 1973-84, Woolsey prof. Bibl. studies, 1984—. Author: Go From Your Father's House, 1964; The Prophet-King, 1967; First Urban Christians, 1983; Moral World of the First Christians, 1986. Contbr. articles to profl. jours. Fulbright fellow, 1956-57; Kent fellow, 1962-64; NEH fellow, 1975-76; Guggenheim fellow, 1979-80. Mem. Soc. Bibl. Lit. (pres. 1985), Am. Acad. Religion (bd. dirs. 1974-77), Studiorum Novi Testamenti Societas (editorial bd. 1979-82), Bibl. Theologians. Democrat. Presbyterian. Avocations: cabinet-making; hiking. Office: Yale U Dept Religious Studies PO Box 2160 Yale Station New Haven CT 06520

MEENAN, ALAN JOHN, clergyman, theological educator; b. Belfast, No. Ireland, Feb. 7, 1946; came to U.S., 1970; s. John and Elizabeth (Holland) M.; m. Vicky Lee Woodall, May 6, 1974; children: Kelly Elizabeth, Katie Michelle, Kimberly Brooke. BA, Queen's U., Belfast, 1970; MDiv, Asbury Theol. Sem., Wilmore, Ky., 1972, ThM, 1975; PhD, Edinburgh U., 1981. Ordained to ministry Presbyn. Ch., 1973. Pastor Wilmore Presbyn. Ch., 1972-74; asst. pastor St. Giles' Cathedral, Edinburgh, Scotland, 1974-77; head staff 3d Presbyn. Ch., Richmond, Va., 1977-84, Canoga Park (Calif.) Presbyn. Ch., 1984-89, First Presbyn. Ch., Amarillo, Tex., 1989—; vis. lectr. Nairobi (Kenya) Grad. Sch. Theology, 1983, 89. Contbr. revs. to religious publs., including Asbury Bible Commentary. Tchr. Chogoria High Sch., Meru, Keyna, 1965-66. Yale U. rsch. fellow, 1976-77. Mem. Tyndale Fellowship for Bibl. Rsch., Theta Phi. Avocations: travel, photography, reading, swimming. Office: First Presbyn Ch 1100 Harrison St Amarillo TX 79101

MEETER, DEAN RAY, minister; b. Parkston, S.D., June 20, 1947; s. Raymond L. and Evelyn (Plooster) M.; m. Gwendolyn Joy Noteboom, June 5, 1969; children: Rachel, Nathan, Jodie, Jonathan. BA, Northwestern, Orange City, Iowa, 1969; MA in Divinity, Western Sem., Holland, Mich., 1973. Ordained to ministry Reformed Ch. Pastor Bethel Reformed Ch., Leafa, Minn., 1973-77, Hope Reformed Ch., Montevideo, Minn., 1977-87; assoc. pastor Community Reformed, Sioux Falls, S.D., 1987-90, congregational pastor, 1990—; pres. Dakato Classis, Reformed Ch. in Am., 1991, mem. com. for addictions and abuse, 1991. Republican. Cub master Boy Scouts Am., Montevideo, 1983-87; pres. Montevideo-Ministerial Assn., Montevideo, 1985-86; participant Al Anon, Sioux Falls, 1990-91. Home: 800 Annway Dr Sioux Falls SD 57103 Office: Community Reformed Ch 3800 E 15th St Sioux Falls SD 57103 *Jesus's supreme example to me in my life has not been just the fact that He brought grace, but that He lived out grace throughout His ministry.*

MEGGS, MARGARET L., religious educator; b. Springfield, Tenn., Aug. 30, 1953; d. Emerson Alford and Margaret Wilkerson (Fort) M. AA with honors, Martin Meth. Coll., 1973; BA magna cum laude, Lambuth Coll., 1975; MA with highest honors, Scarritt Grad. Sch., 1986. Abstractor Vanderbilt TV News Archive, Nashville, 1976-79; coord. spl. projects Am. Cancer Soc., Nashville, 1979; coord. membership Nebr. Ednl. TV, Lincoln, 1979-81; assoc. dir. devel. Children's Hosp. Vanderbilt U., Nashville, 1981-82; devel. asst. Scarritt Grad. Sch., Nashville, 1983-84; religious edn. cons., writer United Meth. Ch. Ministry of Laity, Nashville, 1984-85; adminstrv. asst. Opportunity Devel. Ctr., Nashville, 1986-89; adminstrv. asst. Women's Studies Program Vanderbilt U., Nashville, 1989—; dir., co-founder Womanflight Ctr. for Women's Spirituality, Nashville, 1986—; cons., ritualist Unitarian Universalist Women's Fedn., Nashville, 1986-89; workshop leader Women-Ch. Conf., Cin., 1987; workshops leader Woman Quest Convocation, Lake Geneva, Wis., 1990, Woman Spirit Inst., Highlands, N.C., 1991. Contbr. articles to jours. and newsletters; editor newsletters; editing team Meth. Ch. guide, 1985. Vol. domestic violence shelter YWCA, Nashville, 1986, 89; steering com. Take Back the Night March/Rally, Nashville, 1988; co-sec. Tenn. Alliance for Choice, Nashville, 1989-90. Named Vol. of Yr., Sta. WDCN-TV, 1978, Outstanding Young Woman Am., 1983, 86, Young Career Woman Yr., Music City B&PW, 1984. Mem. AAUW (life, br. pres. 1984-86, chmn. br. nominating com., div. pub. info. chair 1985-87, asst. editor bulletin 1987-89, program v.p. 1988-90), Mid. Tenn. Women's Studies Assn. (charter, newsletter editor 1986-88, treas. 1988-89, convenor 1990-91), NOW (cons., ritualist 1988—). Unitarian Universalist. Avocations: circle dancing, reading, travel. Office: Vanderbilt U PO Box 86 Station B Nashville TN 37235

MEHL, JOHN EDWARDS, minister, educator; b. Wilkes-Barre, Pa., June 18, 1936; s. Daniel Retheiser and Eunice M. (Edwards) M.; m. Janet Cathern Wood, Oct. 12, 1963; children: Christopher W., Bradley Matthew. BA, Dartmouth Coll., 1958; MDiv, Pitts. Theol. Sem., 1962; ThM, Union Theol. Sem., 1967; PhD, U. Pitts., 1976. Ordained to ministry Presbyn. Ch. (U.S.A.), 1962. Assoc. min. Wallace Meml. Presbyn. Ch., Greentree, Pa., 1962-66; assoc. dean students, instr. religion Washington and Lee U., Lexington, Va., 1968-70; editor Thesis Theol. Cassettes, Pitts., 1970-79; mng. editor Kerygma Program of Bible Study, Pitts., 1980-85; dir. D of min. program Pitts. Theol. Sem., 1985—; bd. dirs. Desert Ministries, Pitts.; cons. Kerygma Program, Pitts., 1985—. Editor: (study program) The Bible in Depth, 1984, Shalom, 1985, Interpretation, 1986, Discovering the Bible, 1989. Committeeman Dem. Party, 1977-79. James A. Jones scholar Union Sem., Va., 1967. Mem. Assn. Prof. and Researchers in Religious Edn., Assn. for Doctor Min. Edn., Phi Beta Kappa. Democrat. Office: Pitts Theol Seminary 616 N Highland Ave Pittsburgh PA 15206

MEHLHAFF, HARVEY, clergyman. Moderator North American Bapt. Conf., Oak Brook, Ill.; sr. pastor Faith Bapt. Ch., Mpls. Office: N Am Bapt Conf 1 S 210 Summit Ave Oakbrook Terrace IL 60181

MEHLIS, DAVID LEE, publishing executive; m. Marjie Bauman; children: Michelle, Stephen. BA in Arts and History, Wheaton Coll., 1965; postgrad., Trinity Evang. Sem., 1965-67. Various positions in mktg., then v.p. and gen. mgr. David C. Cook Pub. Co., Elgin, Ill., 1967—, now pres., chief exec. officer; trustee Judson Coll., Elgin, 1991. Mem. Christian Booksellers Assn. (bd. dirs.), Evang. Christian Pub. Assn. (bd. dirs.). Office: David C Cook Pub Co 850 N Grove Ave Elgin IL 60120

MEHR, VERN CONRAD, minister, educator; b. San Francisco, Oct. 23, 1949; m. Vina D. Tull, Oct. 12, 1968; children: Christopher, Jonathan, Vern Adrian, Benjamin. BA, Union U., Jackson, Tenn., 1975; grad., Lambuth Coll., 1983; MEd, Memphis State U., 1984, postgrad., 1984-88; postgrad., Trevecca Nazarene Coll., 1987-89. Lic. to ministry So. Bapt. Conv., 1967, ordained, 1983. Youth dir. Mt. Zion Bapt. Ch., McNairy, Tenn., 1968-75; Sunday sch. tchr. Piney Grove Bapt. Ch., Silerton, Tenn., 1975-82; pastor Forty forty Bapt. Ch., Bethel Springs, Tenn., 1983—; tchr. Whiteville (Tenn.) Elem. Sch., 1981—, Jackson State Community Coll., 1987—. Contbr. articles to profl. jours. Chaplain, capt. CAP, Savannah, Tenn., 1989—; cubmaster, asst. scoutmaster, asst. dist. chmn., trainer Boy Scouts Am., 1977-83, 91; mem. aux. Tenn. Performing Arts Coun. Adv. Com. Mem. Tenn. Bapt. Chaplains Assn., Shiloh Bapt. Assn (mem. exec. com. 1983—), Tchr. Study Coun., Aviation's Creative Educators Sci., Kappa Delta Pi. Home: Rte 2 Box 210-A Bethel Springs TN 38315 *A little knowledge is dangerous; a little faith is disastrous. Our society's ideal mores can be kept high only as long as faith remains high.*

MEIER, JOHN PAUL, priest, educator; b. N.Y.C., Aug. 8, 1942; s. Paul Ulrich and Elizabeth (O'Reilly) M. BA, St. Joseph's Coll., Yonkers, N.Y., 1964; STL, Gregorian U., Rome, 1968; SSD, Bibl. Inst., Rome, 1976. Ordained priest Roman Cath. Ch., 1967. Prof. N.T. St. Joseph Sem., Yonkers, 1972-84, Cath. U. Am., Washington, 1984—; mem. Internat. Dialogue between Roman Caths. and Disciples of Christ, 1983—; Scripture cons. Com. on Doctrine of the Nat. Conf. Cath. Bishops, 1987—. Author: The Vision of Matthew, 1979, Matthew Commentary, 1980, Antioch and Rome, 1983, A Marginal Jew, Vol. 1, 1991; gen. editor Cath. Bibl. Quar., 1985-88. Recipient papal gold medal Gregorian U., Rome, 1968, papal gold medal Bibl. Inst., 1976. Home and Office: Cath U Am Sch Religious Studies Curley Hall Washington DC 20064

MEIKLE, SUSAN ELIZABETH, minister; b. Japan, July 16, 1956; came to U.S., 1956; d. William Anthony and Mary Jane (Stephens) M.; m. D. Bruce Long, June 3, 1978 (div. Dec. 1983); m. Stephen Keith Black, Aug. 10, 1985. BA, U. Calif., Santa Barbara, 1977; MDiv, San Francisco Theol. Sem., 1987. Ordained to ministry United Meth. Ch. as deacon, 1987, as elder, 1989. Pastor Trinity United Meth. Ch., Colusa, Calif., 1987-89; assoc. pastor Willow Glen United Meth. Ch., San Jose, Calif., 1989-90; pastor 1st United Meth. Ch., Red Bluff, Calif., 1990-91, Woodside Rd. United Meth. Ch., Redwood City, Calif., 1991—; chairperson new ch. devel. standing com. Calif.-Nev. Annual Conf., San Francisco, 1991—. Mem. Alban Inst., Process & Faith Program of the Ctr. for Process Studies.

MEINHOLD, ARNDT, theology educator, clergyman; b. Scheibenberg, Germany, Nov. 24, 1941; s. Harry Albert and Margarethe (Grützmacher) M.; m. Dorothea Christel Georgi, Aug. 9, 1966; children—Chajim, Hauke, Wiebke. Dr. theology, Ernst-Moritz-Arndt-Universität, 1971; Dr. theol. habil., U. Leipzig, 1990. Ordained to ministry Meth. Ch., 1972. Pastor, United Methodist Ch. in German Dem. Republic, Stralsund, 1970-71, Dessau, 1971-77; prof. Old Testament, Katechetisches Oberseminar/Kirchliche Hochschule, Naumburg/Saale, German Dem. Republic (now Fed. Republic Germany), 1977—. Author: Das Buch Esther, 1983, Die Sprüche, 1991; contbr. articles to religious publs. Served as Bausoldat German armed forces, 1966-67. Home: August-Bebel-Strasse 1, 4800 Naumburg an der Saale Federal Republic of Germany Office: Kirchliche Hochschule, Domplatz 8, 4800 Naumburg an der Saale Federal Republic of Germany

MEISNER, JOACHIM CARDINAL, archibishop of Cologne; b. Breslau, Germany, Dec. 25, 1933; s. Walter and Hedwig Meisner. Ed. U. Erfurt, Pastoral Sem. at Neuzelle. Ordained priest Roman Cath. Ch., 1962. Chaplain St. Agidien, Heiligenstadt, 1963-66, St. Crucis, Erfurt, 1966; rector Diozesencaritas of Erfurt, 1966-76, suffragan bishop, 1975-80; bishop of Berlin, 1980-89; pres. Berliner Bischofskonferenz, 1982-89; elevated to cardinal, 1983; archibishop of Cologne, 1989—. Author: Das Auditorium Coelicum am Dom zu Erfurt, 1960; Nachreformatorische katholische Frommigkeitsformen in Erfurt, 1971; Sein, wie Gott uns gemeint hat-Betrachtungen zu Maria, 1988; contbr. articles to mags. Address: Kardinal-Frings-Str 10, D-5000 Cologne 1, Federal Republic of Germany

MEITZEN, MANFRED OTTO, religious studies educator; b. Houston, Dec. 12, 1930; s. Otto Hugo and Laura Emma (Munsch) M.; m. Fredrica Haden Kilmer, May 16, 1970. BA, Rice U., 1952; MDiv, Wartburg Sem., 1956; PhD, Harvard U., 1961. Assoc. prof. religious studies Rocky Mountain Coll., Billings, Mont., 1961-65; assoc. prof. religious studies, chmn. dept. W.Va. U., Morgantown, 1965-70, prof., chmn. religious studies, 1970—, chmn. program humanities Coll. Arts and Scis., 1972-77, mem. senate, 1968-82, 84—, clin. prof. psychiatry, Sch. Medicine, 1991—; vis. scholar Christ Ch. Coll., Oxford (Eng.) U., 1973; columnist Morgantown Dominion-Post, 1975-76, 80-89. Contbr. articles to profl. jours. and chpts. to books. Harvard Div. Sch. scholar, 1957; fellow, 1958; Rockefeller fellow, 1959-60; Sheldon Traveling fellow, 1961; W.Va. U. Study grantee, 1970; recipient Outstanding Tchr. award W.Va. U., 1971-72, Coll. Arts & Scis., 1979-80, 87-88, Outstanding Educator Am. award, 1974-75, W.Va. Assocs. award, 1974-75. Mem. Am. Guild Organists, Am. Acad. Religion, W.Va. Assn. for Humanities (pres. 1976-77), Harvard Alumni Assn., Univ. Profs. for Acad. Order (nat. 1st v.p. 1977-79, nat. pres. 1979, dir. 1974—, nat. sec.-treas. 1986-91), Am. Rifle Assn., Rice U. Alumni Assn., Harvard Found. for Advanced Study and Research, Delta Phi Alpha. Lutheran. Home: 119 Forest Dr Morgantown WV 26505 *It is very important, particularly in our times, not to sell one's own ideas and convictions short in face of the increasing pressure in academe and throughout society to comply with standardized opinion on moral, political and social issues.*

MEJIA, SISTER FELICIANA, nun; b. Ft. Stockton, Tex., Dec. 11, 1943; d. Crespin Romero and Petra (Ramirez) M. BA, Incarnate Word Coll., 1975; MA, St. Mary's U., San Antonio, 1988; cert. spirituality and worship, Jesuit Sch. Theology, Berkeley, Calif., 1976. Pastoral assoc. Santa Lucia Cath. Ch., El Paso, 1981-86; asst. dir. Religous Studies/Religious Formation, San Antonio, 1976-81; houseparent St. Joseph's Ctr., Dallas, 1970-72, St. Margaret's Ch., El Paso, 1969-70; dir. RENEW, Lubbock, Tex., 1988-91; pres. Nat. Sisters Vocations Conf. for Ariz., N.Mex., Tex., 1983-84; mem. Com. Religious to Hispanic Ministry, Orange, Calif., 1980. Editor: Empowerment by the Holy Spirit, 1990. Sec. West Tex. Community Devel., Lubbock, 1990—; mem. Hispanic Women Assn. Mem. Las Hemanas. Office: Diocese of Lubbock PO Box 98700 Lubbock TX 79499-8700

MELAND, BERNARD EUGENE, theologian, educator; b. Chgo., June 28, 1899; s. Erick Bernhard and Elizabeth (Hansen) M.; m. Margaret Evans McClusky, Aug. 6, 1926 (dec.); children: Bernard Eugene (dec.), Richard Dennis. A.B., Park Coll., 1923, D.D., 1956; student, U. Ill., 1918, 23-24, McCormick Theol. Sem., 1924-25; B.D., U. Chgo., 1928; Ph.D., 1929; postgrad., U. Marburg, Germany, 1928-29. Ordained to ministry Presbyn. Ch., 1928; prof. religion and philosophy Central Coll., Fayette, Mo., 1929-36; asso. prof. religion, head dept. Pomona Coll., Claremont, Calif., 1936-43; prof. religion Pomona Coll., 1943-45, Clark lectr., 1947; prof. constructive theology U. Chgo., 1945-64; prof. emeritus U. Chgo. (Div. Sch.), 1964, vis. prof. theology, 1965-68, pastors inst. lectr., 1945; vis. prof. philosophy of religion Union Theol. Sem., N.Y.C., 1968-69; Hewitt vis. prof. humanities Ottawa U., Kans., 1971; Barrows lectr., Calcutta and Bangalore, India, Rangoon, Burma; vis. lectr. Serampore Coll., India, 1957-58; Burrows lectr. U. Calcutta, Poona, 1964-65. Author: Modern Man's Worship, 1934, (with H.N. Wieman) American Philosophies of Religion, 1936, Write Your Own Ten Commandments, 1938, The Church and Adult Education, 1939, Seeds of Redemption, 1947, America's Spiritual Culture, 1948, The Reawakening of Christian Faith, 1949, Higher Education and the Human Spirit, 1953, Faith and Culture, 1953, The Realities of Faith: The Revolution in Cultural Forms, 1962, The Secularization of Modern Cultures, 1966, Fallible Forms and Symbols, 1976; editor, contbr.: The Future of Empirical Theology, 1969; co-editor: Jour. Religion, 1946-64. Served with U.S. Army, 1918. Mem. Am. Theol. Soc. (v.p. 1951-52, pres. Midwest div. 1960-61). Home: 5842 Stony Island Ave Chicago IL 60637

MELASHENKO, E. LONNIE, minister; b. Regina, Sask., Can., Feb. 14, 1947; came to U.S., 1957; s. Joseph and Anne (Koleada) M.; m. Jeannie Jones, Aug. 27, 1967. BA, Loma Linda U., 1968; MDiv, Andrew U., 1970. Ordained to ministry Seventh-day Adventists, 1974. Summer minister Pomona (Calif.) Seventh-day Adventist Ch., 1968; assoc. pastor Vallejo Dr. Seventh-day Adventist Ch., Glendale, Calif., 1970-72; sr. pastor Camarillo (Calif.) Seventh-day Adventist Ch., 1972-77; assoc. dir./speaker It Is Written Telecast, Thousand Oaks, Calif., 1977-81; sr. pastor Paradise (Calif.) Seventh-day Adventist Ch., 1981-91; radio announcer Voice of Prophecy, L.A., 1988-91, speaker elect, 1991—; announcer It Is Written telecast, Thousand Oaks, 1977-91. Author: So-o, You're Going To Have a Seminar, 1980. Bd. dirs. Exch. Club Ctr. for Prevention of Child Abuse, Chico, Calif., 1989-91, Feather River Hosp., Paradise, 1984-91. Office: Voice of Prophecy Box 2525 Newbury Park CA 91319

MELCHIOR, BENT, rabbi; b. Beuthen, Germany, June 24, 1929; s. Marcus and Meta (Schornstein) M.; m. Lilian Weisdorff; 4 children. Rabbinical diploma, Jews' Coll., London, 1963. Ordained rabbi, 1963. Vol. Haganah and Israel Defence Forces, 1948-49; tchr. Jewish Day Sch., Talmud Torah, Copenhagen, 1949-58; rabbi of Jewish community Copenhagen, 1963-70; chief rabbi of Denmark, 1970—; co-founder Danish Zionist Fedn., 1946; chmn. Jewish Youth Organisation, 1954-55; pres. Keren Hayesod, Denmark,

1968-70; v.p. World Coun. Synagogues, 1970-79; mem. Presidium World Conf. for Soviet Jewry, 1971—; lectr. on Jewish lit. Copenhagen U., 1971-84. Editor Israel mag., 1949-54; author version of history of 1st part of the Bible in Danish lang., textbook on Judaism; transl. The Pentateuch, Pesach Hagaddah; contbr. numerous articles to mags. and profl. jours. Chmn. Denmark Com. for Soviet Jewry, 1970—; bd. dirs. Danish Refugee Coun.; active coordination com. on human rights Danish Fgn. Ministry, other social, cultural and human rights groups. Decorated Order of Knighthood (Denmark); Fighters' Order (Israel); recipient various awards. Mem. B'nai B'rith (pres. Denmark lodge 1979-81, 83-84, pres. coun. Scandinavian lodges 1984-88, v.p. cen. com. dist. 19 1985-87). Address: 27, Frederiksborggade, DK-1360 Copenhagen K, Denmark Office: The Synagogue, Krystalgade 12, Copenhagen Denmark

MELCZEK, DALE J., bishop; b. Nov. 9, 1938. A.B., St. Mary Coll., Orchard Lake, Mich.; M.Div., St. John Sem., Plymouth, Mich.; M.A. in Edn., U. Detroit; postgrad., U. Notre Dame. Ordained priest, Roman Catholic Ch., 1964, appointed aux. bishop, 1982, regional bishop, 1983. Assoc. pastor St. Sylvester Ch., Warren, Mich., 1964-70, co-pastor, 1970-72; pastor St. Christine Ch., Detroit, 1972-75; vicar West Detroit Vicariate, 1973-75; asst. vicar for parishes Archdiocese of Detroit, 1975-77, sec. to archbishop and vicar gen., 1977-82, archdiocesan consultor, 1972-83, aux. bishop, titular bishop of Trau, 1982—; regional bishop Detroit N.W. Region, 1983—.

MELENDEZ, MICHAEL SEAN, priest; b. Bklyn., July 13, 1962; s. Ramon and Anne (Dowding) M. BA in English, Cathedral Coll., Douglaston, N.Y., 1984; MDiv, Seminary of the Immaculate, Conception, Huntington, N.Y., 1989. Ordained priest Roman Cath. Ch., 1989. Parochial vicar St. Brigid's Ch., Bklyn., 1989—. Mem. KC (chaplain 1990—). Democrat. Home: 409 Linden St Brooklyn NY 11237 Office: St Bridgid S Church 409 Linden St Brooklyn NY 11237-5820

MELFORD, JOEL EUGENE, religion educator; b. N.Y.C., May 15, 1951; s. Joseph and Lynne (Malfetano) M.; m. Leann Schiavello, Dec. 28, 1986. BA magna cum laude, Iona Coll., 1985; MA, St. Joseph Seminary, Yonkers, N.Y., 1987; postgrad., Fordham U., 1990—. Chmn. religious studies dept. Acad. of Our Lady of Good Counsel, White Plains, N.Y., 1988—. Recipient Philosophy medal Iona Coll., New Rochelle, N.Y., 1985. Mem. Nat. Cath. Ednl. Assn. (assoc.), Delta Epsilon Sigma, Psi Chi, Theta Alpha Kappa, Phi Sigma Tau. Office: Good Counsel Academy 52 North Broadway White Plains NY 10603 *We who are ministers of education have a moral obligation to God, ourselves, and our students to constantly strive and present the truth as purely, charitably, and compassionately as we can.*

MELGOZA OSORIO, JOSE, bishop; b. Coalcoman, Mexico, Feb. 17, 1912. Ordained priest Roman Cath. Ch., 1938; bishop of Cuidad Valles, 1970-79, Netzahual Coyotl, Mexico, 1979—. Office: Apartado 89, Col Evolucion, Netzahualcoyotl Mexico 57000 CD

MELLISH, JOHN MARK, minister; b. Owosso, Mich., Feb. 5, 1952; s. John William and Joyce Beatrice (Belleville) M.; m. Beverly Dale Mitchell, Mar. 3, 1973; children: Steven, John, Shane. AS in Bibl. Studies, Nazarene Bible Coll., Colorado Springs, Colo., 1978. Ordained to ministry Nazarene Ch., 1980. Min. Ch. of the Nazarene, S.C., 1978-81, Fla., 1981-86; min. Merritt Rd. Ch. of the Nazarene, Ypsilanti, Mich., 1986—; dir. youth camp So. Fla. Dist., Boca Raton, 1982-86; mem. dist. ctr. bd. Ea. Mich. Dist., Howell, 1987-90. Mem. Citizens for Quality Edn., Ypsilanti, 1990; pres. Ypsilanti Community Athletic Assn., 1988-90. With USN, 1970-74. Recipient Pres.'s award So. Fla. Dist.-Youth, 1983, 86, Citation of Merit award Nazarene Bible Coll., 1985. Republican. Home: 6560 Merritt Rd Ypsilanti MI 48197 Office: Merritt Rd Ch of Nazarene 6560 Merritt Rd Ypsilanti MI 48197

MELLNIK, DAVID CARL, music minister; b. High Point, N.C., May 29, 1955; s. Alexander and Roella (Marr) M.; m. Elizabeth Weddington, Oct. 12, 1979; children: Margaret E., Sarah R. MusB, U. N.C., Greensboro, 1982; postgrad., Manhatten Sch. Music, N.Y.C., 1983; M Ch. Music, So. Sem., Louisville, 1986. Min. music McLean (Va.) Bapt. Ch., 1987—; sec. Va. Bapt. Male Chorale, 1991—. Mem. Nat. Choral Dirs. Assn., Am. Guild Eng. Handbell Ringers, Hymn Soc. Am., Choirsters Guild, Presbyn. Assn. Musicians, So. Bapt. Alliance. Home: 107 James Dr S W Vienna VA 22182 Office: McLean Bapt Ch 1367 Chain Bridge Rd McLean VA 22101

MELLON, BRADLEY FLOYD, pastor, religion educator; b. Suffern, N.Y., Sept. 20, 1949; s. Floyd and Ethel Dorothea (Hastings) M.; m. Marilyn Estelle Rapp, Aug. 7, 1976; children: Melissa Joy, Kimberly Hope. BA, Houghton Coll., 1971; MDiv with high honors, Bibl. Sem., Hatfield, Pa., 1980, MST, 1985; postgrad., Dropsie Coll., 1986—, Westminster Sem., 1986—. Ordained to ministry Ind. Bapt. Ch., 1980. Youth min. High Sch. Evangelism, Tenafly, N.J., 1971-75; assoc. pastor Trinity Ch., Clifton, N.J., 1975-77; sr. pastor Grace Ind. Ch., Molino Village, Pa., 1981-88, Kimmels Ch. of God, Orwigsburg, Pa., 1988-91; lectr. New Testament Westminster Sem., Phila., 1988—. Mem. adv. bd. Salvation Army, Montclair, N.J., 1977; chaplain svcs. Town Coun., Hatfield, Pa., 1979-80. Mem. Am. Acad. Religion (assoc.), Soc. Bibl. Lit. (assoc.), Interdisciplinary Bibl. Rsch. Inst. (assoc.), Bibl. Sem. Student Assn. (pres. 1979-80), Bibl. Sem. Alumni Assn. (v.p. 1989-90, pres. 1990-91). Home: 8 Valley Dr Telford PA 18969 Office: Westminster Sem PO Box 27009 Philadelphia PA 19118

MELLON, DAVID DUANE, church organization executive, clergyman; b. Duquesne, Pa., Dec. 14, 1931; s. David Duane and Mary Jane (Bennett) M.; m. Nancy Orahood, June 11, 1955; children: Jeffrey David, Janet Marie. BA, Coll. of Wooster, 1953; MDiv, Pitts. Theol. Sem., 1956; MEd, U. Pitts., 1960; DD (hon.), Union Bapt. Sem., Birmingham, Ala., 1972. Ordained to ministry Presbyn. Ch. (USA), 1956. Pastor 1st Presbyn. Ch., Brilliant, Ohio, 1956-60; asst. pastor, 1st Presbyn. Ch., Akron, Ohio, 1960-63; assoc. pastor West Side Presbyn. Ch., Ridgewood, N.J., 1963-67; exec. dir. Coun. Chs. Greater Trenton, N.J., 1967-72, Capitol Regional Conf. Chs., Hartford, Conn., 1972-81; rep. Presbyn. Mins. Fund, 1981-84; exec. min. New Britain (Conn.) Area Conf. Chs., 1984—; mem. governing bd. Nat. Coun. Chs., 1975-81; pres. Consumer Credit Counseling Svc. Conn., 1978-81; founding mem., later treas. North Cen. Conn. HMO, 1973-81; co-chmn. Greater Hartford Interfaith Com. for Soviet Jewry; mem. Presbytern So. New Eng. and Cen. Assn., United Ch. of Christ; exec. producer, host Celebrate, Sta. WVIT-TV. Author: Christian Education in the Church School, 1968. Mem. Conn. Gov.'s Energy Task Force, 1979-81; mem. program adv. com. Sta. WFSB-TV, 1977-81; bd. dirs. Human Rels. Agy. New Britain, 1985-87; chmn. policy com. Friendship Ctr.; corporator, mem. YMCA, New Britain and Berlin, 1985—, Community Mental Health Affiliates, Hartford Sem., New Britain Meml. Hosp., Conn. Coalition of Homeless, Conn. Anti-Hunger Coalition; mem. institutional ethics com. New Britain Gen. Hosp., co-chair chaplains' adminstrv. com.; chmn. hazardous waste com. City of New Britain; pres. Sheldon Child Guidance Clinic, past pres., mem. campus ministry bd. Cen. Conn. State U.; mem. Task Force on Elderly Day Care Svcs. for New Britain Area; coord. area food banks, food drives; co-chmn. WINFEST; mem. Food For All, fin. distbn. com., moderator; active numerous other civic activities. Recipient nat. merit award in religion Pi Lambda Sigma, 1972, citation Hartford Common Coun., 1975, Community Svc. Programming award WVIT-TV, Channel 30, 1985, Cert. Recognition New Britain Pub. Sch., 1986, Vol. Svc. award United Way, 1988, Outstanding Svc. award Salvation Army, 1990. Office: New Britain Area Conf Chs 19 Chestnut St New Britain CT 06051 *It is important that we deal honestly with life and carpe diem.*

MELSON, RICHARD DAVID, evangelist, data analyst, computer specialist, meeting facilitator; b. Buffalo, Dec. 15, 1957; s. David Jr. and Ruthie Mae (Jones) M.; m. Valerie Gail Miller, Aug. 25, 1979; children: Victoria Grace, Rachel Denise, Ashley Marie. Student, SUNY, Fredonia, 1975-77; diploma of completion, So. Calif. Sch. Evangelism, 1984; BA in Religion, Summit Theol. Sem., Ft. Wayne, Ind., 1987, postgrad., 1988—. Tchr. Bible Ch. of Christ, Pacoima, Calif., 1980-82; tchr. Bible, preacher Ch. of Christ, Buena Park, Lancaster, Beaumont, Calif., 1982-84; evangelist Ch. of Christ, Chgo., 1984-85, Dayton, Ohio, 1985—; evangelist Webster St. Ch. of Christ, Dayton, 1985—; facilitator, data analyst Antioch Pub. Co., Yellow Springs, Ohio, 1988—. Editor: The Book of Ephesians, 1985; contbr. tracts, articles to profl. jours. Pres. Fairview Elem. Sch. Community Edn. Coun., Dayton, 1990-91. Republican. Home: 164 W Fairview Ave Dayton OH 45405 Office: Webster St Ch of Christ 4917 Webster St Dayton OH 45414-4830

MELTON, JOHNNY, minister; b. Nashville, Apr. 7, 1952; s. Jesse Ruel and Mary Alice (Jenkins) M.; m. Karen Darlene Horton, Aug. 28, 1975; children: James Patrick, Jonathan Ruel, Carrie Anne. AA, Freed-Hardeman U., Henderson, Tenn., 1972; BA, So. Christian U., Montgomery, 1988; MA, So. Christian U., 1990; postgrad., Erskine Theol. Sem., Due West, S.C., 1990—. Minister Fairfield Ch. of Christ, N.C., 1973-74, Union Ch. of Christ, S.C., 1974-77, Plaza Ch. of Christ., Charlotte, 1978-79; assoc. minister Providence Rd. Ch. of Christ, Charlotte, 1979-80; minister Abilene Ch. of Christ., Statesville, N.C., 1980-88, Hickory (N.C.) Ch. of Christ, 1988—; bd. dirs. Carolina Bible Camp, Carolina Christian Pub. Inc. Mng. editor Carolina Christian mag., 1987—; contbg. writer, author, editor profl. jours. Republican. Mem. Ch. of Christ. Avocations: coaching recreation league soccer and baseball, tennis. Home: Rt 2 Box 137 Conover NC 28613 Office: PO Box 397 Hickory NC 28601

MELTON, WADE ANTHONY, religion educator; b. Lima, Ohio, May 6, 1957; s. Andrew Floranoid and Delores Ruth (Parlette) M.; m. Lesa Ann Bolen, June 29, 1991; 1 child, Derrick. BS, Summit Christian Coll., Ft. Wayne, Ind., 1988; postgrad., Winebrenner Seminary, Findlay, Ohio, 1990—. Ordained to ministry Ch. of God, 1988. Assoc. pastor Thornville (Ohio) United Meth. Ch., 1978-79; ministry dir. Power and Light Ministries, Inc., Lima, 1983-85; v.p. TCA Artist Representation, Columbus, Ohio, 1985-87; minister of youth and Christian edn. First Ch. of God, Lima, 1980-90; ministry dir. Tumbling Walls Ministries, Inc., Mt. Cory, Ohio, 1990—; dir. Profl. Youth Workers Fellowship, Lima, 1989-91; cons. Ohio State Youth Bd., Marengo, Ohio, 1990—; chmn. Ohio State Youth Bd., Marengo, 1984-90; NAC Satellite Affiliate Host, Youth Ministry TV Network, Shreveport, La., 1989-91; adv. bd. Summit Christian Coll., 1989—. Named to Outstanding Young Man of Am., 1987, 90. Mem. Evangel. Tchr. Tng. Assn., Religious Conf. Mgmt. Assn.. Office: Tumbling Walls Ministries 307 W Washington St Mount Cory OH 45868 *The Christian education ministry in the local church must enable parents to equip their children to think Christianly and critically.*

MELVIN, BILLY ALFRED, clergyman; b. Macon, Ga., Nov. 25, 1929; s. Daniel Henry and Leola Dale (Seidell) M.; m. Marcia Darlene Eby, Oct. 26, 1952; children: Deborah Ruth, Daniel Henry II. Student, Free Will Baptist Bible Coll., Nashville, 1947-49; B.A., Taylor U., Upland, Ind., 1951; postgrad., Asbury Theol. Sem., Wilmore, Ky., 1951-53; B.D., Union Theol. Sem., Richmond, Va., 1956; D.D., Azusa (Calif.) Coll., 1968; LL.D. (hon.), Taylor U., 1984. Ordained to ministry Free Will Baptist Ch., 1951; pastor First Free Will Baptist Chs., Newport, Tenn., 1951-53, Richmond, 1953-57; pastor Bethany Ch., Norfolk, Va., 1957-59; exec. sec. Nat. Assn. Free Will Baptists, 1959-67; exec. dir. Nat. Assn. Evangelicals, 1967—. Office: Nat Assn Evangs PO Box 28 Wheaton IL 60189

MELVIN, BOB RAYMOND, minister; b. Portsmouth, Va., June 4, 1934; s. Flavell Bryan and Georgia Mae (Parker) M.; m. Carol Evelyn Bainter, Oct. 8, 1954; children: Robin Dawn Osbourne, Bob Raymond Jr. BA, U. Richmond, 1969; MDiv, So. Bapt. Theol. Seminary, Louisville, 1972. Minister Spotswood Bapt. Ch., Fredericksburg, Va.; pres. Va. Bapt. Bible Conf., 1990-91. Home: 3 Myrtle Ct Fredericksburg VA 22408 Office: Spotswood Bapt Church 4009 Lafayette Blvd Fredericksburg VA 22408

MELZONI, THOMAS, JR., minister; b. Harlan, Ky., Nov. 24, 1952; s. Thomas M.; m. E. Trina Martin. BS, Wright State U., 1974; MS, PhD, Columbia Pacific U., 1984, 86; MA, So. Bapt. Theol. Sem., 1991. Ordained to ministry So. Bapt. Conv., 1974. Minister of edn. Far Hills Bapt. Ch., Dayton, Ohio, 1975-78, Dauphin Way Bapt. Ch., Mobile, Ala., 1978-80, First Bapt. Ch., Wichita Falls, Tex., 198-82; exec. dir. ministries First Bapt. Ch., Dallas, 1982-85; sr. pastor Cen. Bapt. Ch., Oak Ridge, Tenn., 1985-89, 9th and O Streets Bapt. Ch., Louisville, 1989-91, 1st Bapt. Ch., Hickory, N.C., 1991—; com. on coms. Ky. Bapt. Conv., 1991; chmn. So. Bapt. Com. on Resolutions, 1986; advisor Criswell Coll., Dallas, 1991. Mem. So. Bapt. Metro Religious Edn. Assn. (pres. 1985). Office: 1st Bapt Ch Hickory 150 Fourth St NW Hickory NC 28601

MENARD, SISTER ELIZABETH DELIA, religious order prioress; b. Mooers, N.Y., Oct. 28, 1940; d. Bernard Joseph and Marie Adele (Arcouette) M. BA in English, So. Conn. State Coll., 1970, MS in Edn., 1975; MA in Religious Studies, Providence Coll., 1982. Cert. elem. and jr. high sch. tchr. Tchr. St. Bernadette Sch., New Haven, Conn., 1961-70, St. Peter Sch., Plattsburgh, N.Y., 1970-74; formation/vocation dir. Dominican Sisters Novitiate, North Dartmouth, Mass., 1974-82; adult educator Salem (N.H.) Deanery Christian Life Ctr., 1982-86; prioress gen. Dominican Sisters St. Catherine of Siena, Fall River, Mass., 1986—; vice prin. St. Peter Sch., Plattsburgh, 1970-74; del. gen. chpts. Dominican Sisters, Fall River, 1974, 78, 82, 86, mem. gen. coun., 1982—; adv. coun. Parable Conf. for Dominican Life and Mission, River Forest, Ill., 1986—, exec. com., 1990—. Mem. Pax Christi, Leadership Conf. Women Religious, Dominican Leadership Conf., LCWR/CMSM Collaborative Investment for Housing (sec.-treas. 1989—). Office: Dominican Sisters St Catherine of Siena 37 Park St Fall River MA 02721

MENDELSOHN, JACK, clergyman, author; b. Cambridge, Mass., July 22, 1918; m. Ruth P. Mendelsohn, Dec. 26, 1949 (div. 1969); children: Channing T., Deborah T., Kurt A.; m. Joan Silverstone Hall, Aug. 3, 1969; 1 stepdau., Lisabeth Hall. BA, Boston U., 1939; STB, Harvard U., 1945; DD (hon.), Meadville Theol. Sch., 1962. Ordained to ministry Unitarian Universalist Ch., 1945. Min. in Rockford, Ill., 1947-54, Indpls., 1954-59; min. in Arlington St. Ch., Boston, 1959-69; sr. min. 1st Unitarian Ch., Chgo., 1969-79; min. 1st Parish, Bedford, Mass., 1979-88; emeritus min., 1988—; ptnr. Halcyon House, 1979-85; mem. adj. faculty Meadville Theol. Sch, U. Chgo., 1969-79; officer to the univ. Harvard U., 1981—. Author: Why I Am a Unitarian, 1960, God, Allah and Ju Ju, 1962, The Forest Calls Back, 1965, The Martyrs, 1966, Channing, The Reluctant Radical, 1971, Alone Together, 1979, The Freeze Movement as an Ethical Achievement, 1983, Being Liberal in an Illiberal Age, 1985. V.p. Unitarian Svc. Com., 1963-67; pres. Urban League Greater Boston, 1966-68; bd. dirs. World Affairs Coun. Boston, 1962-66; chmn. Alliance to End Repression, Chgo., 1970-76; mem. adv. coun. Comprehensive Health Planning, Chgo., 1969-79; pres. Hyde Park-Kenwood Coun. Chs. and Synagogues, Chgo., 1974-76; chmn. William Ellery Channing Bicentennial Celebration Com. 1979-80; pres. Abraham Lincoln Centre, Chgo., 1977-79, Binder Schweitzer Hosp. Found., N.Y.C., 1965-73, Chgo. Meml. Assn., 1969-79, Civil Rights Project, Inc., sponsors TV series Eyes on the Prize, 1987—; sr. adviser to Jesse Jackson, 1984—, trips to Syria, Cen. Am., Cuba; pres. continental Unitarian Universalist Mins. Assn., 1987-89. Named Collegium Disting. Alumni Boston U., 1988. Mem. NAACP, ACLU, Internat. Inst. Boston (bd. dirs. 1962-68), Harvard Club (Boston), Harvard Faculty Club (Cambridge). Address: 33 Halifax St Boston MA 02130

MENDENHALL, GEORGE EMERY, educator; b. Muscatine, Iowa, Aug. 13, 1916; s. George Newton and Mary Christine (Johnson) M.; m. Eathel Louise Tidrick, Dec. 6, 1943; children—George David, Lauri Philip, Stanley Theodore, Gordon Louis, Stephen Robert. B.A., Midland Coll., Fremont, Nebr., 1936, Litt.D., 1959; B.D., Gettysburg Sem., 1938; Ph.D., Johns Hopkins, 1947. Ordained to ministry Luth. Ch., 1942. Pastor in Laramie, Wyo., 1942-43; asst. prof. Hamma Div. Sch., 1947-50, assoc. prof., 1950-52; assoc. prof. U. Mich., 1952-58, prof., 1958-86, prof. emeritus, 1986—; chmn. com. studies religion U. Mich. (Coll. Lit. Sci. and Arts), 1957-67, chmn. council grad. studies religion, 1964-66; dir. Euphrates archaeol. expdn. to Syria, 1971; ann. prof. Am. Sch. Oriental Research, Jerusalem, Jordan, 1955-56, dir., 1965-66; dir. Am. Center Oriental Research, Amman, Jordan, 1975; vis. prof. Pontifical Bibl. Inst., Rome, 1985; field supr. Brit. Sch. of Archaeology in Jerusalem in excavation Jericho, 1956; part time vis. prof. Inst. Archaeology and Anthropology, Yarmouk U., Irbid, Jordan, 1987—. Author: Law and Covenant in Israel and the Ancient Near East, 1955, The Tenth Generation: The Origins of the Biblical Tradition, 1973, The Syllabic Inscriptions from Byblos, 1985, Cons. editor, contbr.: Interpreters Dictionary of the Bible, 1962, Anchor Dictionary of the Bible; contbr.: profl. jours. Ency. Brit. Pres. Lutheran Student Found., U. Mich., 1962-65; Trustee Chgo. Luth. Theol. Sem., 1956-69. Served to lt. (j.g.) USNR, 1943-46, PTO. Sr. fellow Nat. Endowment for Humanities, 1971. Mem. Am. Oriental Soc. (pres. Middle West br. 1950-51, asso. editor jour. 1954-59), Soc. Bibl. Lit. (pres. Midwest sect. 1960), Archaeol. Inst. Am., Am. Schs. Oriental Research, Bibl. Colloquium (pres. 1963-65), Phi Beta Kappa. Home: 1510 Cedar Bend Dr Ann Arbor MI 48105 Office: U Mich Ann Arbor MI 48109

MENDENHALL, LAURA SHELTON, minister; b. Tyler, Tex., Oct. 4, 1946; d. Robert Lewis and Grace (Doss) S.; m. Charles M. Mendenhall III, June 7, 1970; children: Maury Lynne, Matthew Lewis. BA, Austin Coll., 1969; MA, Presbyn. Sch. Christian Edn., Richmond, Va., 1971; MDiv, San Francisco Theol. Seminary, 1980. Cert. secondary tchr. Staff educator San Gabriel Presbytery, 1977-80; assoc. pastor First Presbyn. Ch., Orlando, Fla., 1980-83, Cen. Presbyn. Ch., Austin, Tex., 1983-87; co-pastor First Presbyn. Ch., Victoria, Tex., 1987-91; sr. pastor Westminster Presbyn. Ch., Austin, 1991—; keynote speaker, preacher Mo. Ranch Presbyn. Conf. Ctr., Kerrville, tex., 1983-91, Montreat (N.C.) Presbyn. Conf. Ctr., 1985-92; workshop leader/preacher Theology and Worship Unit/Gen. Assembly Presbyn. Ch., Louisville, 1990-91; moderator Mission Presbytery, 1990-91; del. gen. assembly Presbyn. Ch., 1992. Contbr. articles to profl. jours; author: Holy Baptism and Services for the Renewal of Baptism, 1988. Named Disting. Alumni, Austin Coll., 1990. Office: Westminster Presbyn Church PO Box 5488 Austin TX 78763

MENDENHALL, N. DALE, minister; b. Kokomo, Ind., Aug. 26, 1951; s. Norman Lee and Joyce Ann (Hosier) M.; m. Joan Patricia Scott, Aug. 15, 1976 (wid. June 1982); m. Catherine Irene Guard, Nov. 21, 1982; children: Kristen, Kathryn, Jerry, Matthew. BA, Ind. U., Kokomo, 1973; MDiv, Wesley Theol. Sem., Washington, 1976; postgrad., McCormmick Theol. Sem., Chgo., 1989—. Ordained to ministry United Meth. Ch., 1977. Pastor Zion United Meth. Ch., Lucerne, Ind., 1976-78, Leesburg (Ind.) United Meth. Ch., 1982-87; assoc. pastor 1st United Meth. Ch., Logansport, Ind., 1976-78, High Street United Meth. Ch., Muncie, Ind., 1978-82; pastor Garrett (Ind.) United Meth. Ch., 1987—; sec. global ministries Ft. Wayne (Ind.) Dist. United Meth. Ch., 1988—, mem. dist. bd. global ministries, 1988—, mem. dist. coun. on ministries, 1988—, clergy mem. North Ind. conf. bd. global ministries, 1988—. Democrat. Office: Garrett United Meth Ch 110 W Houston St Garrett IN 46738

MENDENHALL, ROBERT ALAN, missionary, military professional; b. Oakland, Calif., Dec. 10, 1952; s. Max Kebert and Rita Marjorie (Smith) M. BA, Incarnate Word Coll., 1975; AA in Health Care Mgmt., Community Coll. Air Force, 1990. Enlisted USAF, 1977; non-commd. officer in charge personnel and adminstrn. sect. 36 TFW (Geilenkirchen) Clinic, Fed. Republic Germany, 1990—; sec./treas. missions dept. Tree of Life Ch., San Angelo, Tex., 1988-90, missionary, Fed. Republic Germany, 1990—. Mem. Non-Commd. Officers Assn. Republican. Home: PSC Box 1526 APO New York NY 09104

MENDEZ, THOMAS, minister; b. Pocatello, Idaho, June 5, 1952; s. Magdaleno Silvas and Alvina (Fred) M.; m. Teresa Ann Kling, Sept. 1, 1976; children: T. Markus, Michelle L., Michael M. BA in Sociology, Idaho State U., 1990. Lic. to ministry, Bapt. Ch., 1981, ordained 1982. Youth dir. First So. Bapt. Ch., Pocatello, Idaho, 1978-81; minister Mountain View Bapt. Ch., Fort Hall, Idaho, 1981-90; equipper First Indian Bapt. Ch., Dallas, 1991—; vice-moderator Eastern Idaho So. Bapt. Assn., Idaho Falls, 1982-83, assoc. Sunday Sch. dir., 1981-87, assoc. youth dir./Vacation Bible Sch., 1982-86, seminary extension dir., Blackfoot, Idaho, 1983-87; ch. devel. leader Bapt. Sunday Sch. Bd., 1989—. Author: (Bible study quarterly) American Indian Version/Adult Bible Study, 1987-91, (teacher's quarterly) American Indian Version/Adult Bible Study, 1990. Mem. Blackfoot Ministerial Assn., 1981-90, Native Am. So. Bapt. Fellowship, Dallas, 1985-91, Nev. Ind. Fellowship, Austin, 1987-90. Named to Outstanding Young Men of Am., 1984, 85. Democrat. Home: Rte 6 PO Box 510 Pocatello ID 83202 Office: Southwestern Bapt Theol Seminary 4708 Merida Ave Fort Worth TX 76115

MENDHAM, PETER MILLER, priest, college dean; b. Sydney, Australia, Mar. 22, 1944; s. Paul Miller and Sally (Gerrett) M.; m. Gillian Joan Varcoe; children: Lindy, Rachel. BA with honors, Macguarie U., Sydney, 1971; BDiv, Melbourne (Australia) Coll. Div., 1978; diploma in edn., Canberra (Australia) U., 1982. Ordained priest Anglican Ch. Australia, 1978. Parish min. Anglican Ch. Australia, Canberra, 1979-80; religion educator Canberra Girls' Grammar Sch., 1981-84; parish priest Anglican Ch. Australia, Bungendore, NSW, 1985-87; coll. dean, priest St. Mark's Nat. Theol. Ctr., Canberra, 1988—; founder Middle Earth Christian Resource Ctr., Sydney. Australia, 1975-79. Editor St. Mark's Rev., 1984-88. Office: St Mark's Theol Ctr, 15 Blackall St, Barton 2600, Australia *Given the many troubles of life, for most people ambition is limited to what is possible or to what is just beyond the possible: food, shelter, health and maybe happiness for themselves and their children. I will be satisfied with my life to the extent that I enable that to happen in the lives of those around me.*

MENDRINAS, KONSTANTINE, priest; b. Newark, Jan. 23, 1943; s. George Konstantine and Esther Mary (Laskaris) M.; m. Roxanne Baxter, Aug. 20, 1967; children: Alexandra, George. BA, Fairleigh Dickinson U., 1967; MDiv, Holy Cross Seminary, Brookline, Mass., 1981. Ordained, 1981. Music tchr. Woodside Elem. Sch., River Vale, N.J., 1967-72, West Ridge Elem. Sch., Park Ridge, N.J., 1972-73; owner, operator Woodside Music Edn. Ctr., Park Ridge, 1973-78; asst. pastor St. Demetrios Greek Orthodox Ch., Jamaica, N.Y., 1981-82, Weston, Mass., 1985—; pastor, instr. Ch. of Virgin Mary, Cohasset, Brookline, Mass., 1982-85; music educator, cons. North Attleboro (Mass.) Jr. High Sch., 1987—; composer dept. religious edn. North and South Am. Greek Orthodox Archdiocese, Brookline, 1987—; founder Olive Tree Press, Medfield, Mass., 1988—. Author, composer: Divine Liturgy Hymnal, 1989, Me and My World, 1989. Avocations: carpentry, reading, hiking, computer technology, fishing. Home: 5855 Pilar Ct San Jose CA 95120 Office: Saint Demetrios Ch 57 Brown St Weston MA 02193

MENKE, GARELD GLENN, minister; b. Barberton, Ohio, Aug. 6, 1958; s. Donald Ray and Barbara (Liddle) M.; m. Sheryl Lynn Augustynovich, June 19, 1982; children: Abigail Marie, Mary Elizabeth. Grad., Genesis Bible Sch., 1978; BA in Bibl. Theol., Berean Coll., 1991. Ordained to ministry Assemblies of God, 1985. Youth pastor Wadsowrth (Ohio) 1st Assembly, 1978-79, asst. pastor, 1981-86; lay missionary Youth With A Mission, Saipan, 1979-80; assoc. pastor Grace Assembly, Spring City, Pa., 1987—; chaplain Montgomery County Geriatric Ctr., Royersford, Pa., 1988—; chaplain Phoenixville Hosp., 1989—; rep. east cen. sect. missionary Assemblies of God, Spring City, 1990—, mem. gen. coun., 1983—, mem. Pa.-Del. dist. coun., 1987—. Mem. Springford Mins. Assn.

MENNICKE, VICTOR OTTOMAR, minister, fundraiser, retired military officer; b. Reeseville, Wis., Mar. 1, 1927; s. Victor August Walter and Elsie Louise (Reutlinger) M.; m. Geraldine Ellen Patrick, Aug. 23, 1947; children: Ellen Suzanne Mennicke Barnes, Victoria Marie Mennicke Merwin, Patricia Lynn Mennicke Levine. MDiv, Christ Sem., St. Louis, 1974. Ordained to ministry Luth. Ch.-Mo. Synod, 1974. Commd. 2d lt. U.S. Army, 1945, advanced through grades to lt. col., 1967, ret., 1969; exec. dir. Luth. Ch.-Mo. Synod, St. Louis, 1969-74; dir. plans and programs Concordia Coll., Austin, Tex., 1974-75; dir. Luth. Ch. Am. Found., N.Y.C., 1978-82; pastor Good Shepherd Luth. Ch., Sarasota, Fla., 1982—; cons. in devel., 1975-77; bd. dirs. Luth. Music Prog., Lincoln, Nebr., 1983—; chmn. chaplaincy prog. Sarasota Ministerial Assn., 1989—; pres. Bach Found. Holy Trinity Luth. Ch., N.Y.C., 1979-82. Author manuals, booklet. Decorated Legion of Merit, Bronze Star. Recipient Bronze medal Concordia Hist. Inst., 1971. Mem. U.S. Army Ret. Officers Assn. (chaplain Sarasota chpt. 1983—), Cruisemaster Club, Sunrise Country Club. Home: 6325 Approach Rd Sarasota FL 34238 Office: Good Shepherd Luth Ch 5659 Honore Ave Sarasota FL 34233

MENO, JOHN PETER, chorepiscopus; b. Carlinville, Ill., Aug. 22, 1942; s. John Victor and Margaret Mary (Cena) M.; m. Rolanda A. Abyad, Sept. 14, 1968; 1 child, Peter James. MA, Am. U. Beirut, 1969; STM, Union Theol. Sem., 1972. Ordained priest Syrian Orthodox Ch. of Antioch, 1972, elevated to chorepiscopus, 1983. Gen. sec. Archdiocese of Syrian Orthodox Ch. in

U.S. and Can., Lodi, N.J., 1972—; cathedral rector St. Mark's Syrian Orthodox Cathedral, Hackensack, N.J., 1975—; co-sec. Standing Conf. of Oriental Orthodox Chs. in Am., N.Y.C., 1973—. Editor: Hymns of the Syrian Orthodox Church of Antioch, 1976. Home: 45 Fairmount Ave Hackensack NJ 07601 Office: Syrian Orthodox Archdiocese 49 Kipp Ave Lodi NJ 07644

MENSENDIEK, CHARLES WILLIAM, missionary educator; b. Ft. Madison, Iowa, July 2, 1925; s. Richard August and Anna Marie (Kruckemeyer) M.; m. Barbara Kathryn Dunn, June 27, 1959; children—Jeffrey, Martha, Kathryn. B.A., Elmhurst Coll., 1945; B.D., Eden Theol. Sem., 1948; Ph.D., Columbia Joint Union, 1957; D.D. (hon.), Eden Sem., 1975. Ordained to ministry Evang. and Reformed Ch., 1948. Missionary, Evang. and Reformed Ch., Sendai, Japan, 1948-51; pastor Salem Evang. and Reformed Ch., Rochester, N.Y., 1955-60, Plymouth Congregation, Buffalo, 1960-63; missionary tchr., prof., United Ch. Christ Christian Studies, Tohoku Gakuin U., Sendai, 1963-91; prof. Tohoku Gakun U.,1991—; asst. Shiogama United Ch., Japan, 1976—. Author: A Man For His Times, 1972, Not Without A Struggle, 1985, With Uncommon Kindness, 1990, To Japan with Love, 1991. Trustee Tohoku Gakuin U., Sendai, 1977-91. Mem. Theol. Assn. Japan. Democrat. Home: Komegafukuro 2-1-44, Sendai Japan 980 Office: United Ch Bd World Ministries UCBWM, 475 Riverside Dr, New York NY 10115

MENSHOUSE, ALYSSA TEFS, minister; b. Springfield, Mass., Nov. 28, 1947; d. Edwin Otto and Audrey Belle (McClure) Tefs; m. Leslie William Menshouse, Mar. 9, 1968; children: Bryan, Aaron. BA, Ashland U., 1986; MDiv, Pitts. Theol. Sem., 1989, doctoral studies, 1991—. Ordained to ministry Presbyn. Ch. (U.S.A.), 1989. Lay leader East Hills Presbyn. Ch., Mansfield, Ohio, 1981-87; intern Christ Presbyn. Ch., Canton, Ohio, 1987-89; minister United Presbyn. Ch., Cin., 1989—; elder in Christian edn. East Hills Presbyn. Ch., Mansfield, Ohio, 1984-87; chair Com. on Preparation for Ministry, Bainbridge, N.Y., 1989—; mem. gen. coun. Susquehanna Valley Presbytery. Contbr. meditations Cortland (N.Y.) Standard, 1989—. Mem. troop com. Boy Scouts Am., Cincinnatus, N.Y., 1989—; mem. adv. bd. Girl Scouts U.S.A., Cincinnatus, 1989—; affiliate Citizens Against Radioactive Dumping, Cortland, 1989—; mem. com. on alcohol and substance abuse Cincinnatus Cen. Sch. 1990; bd. dirs., mem. exec. bd. Seven Valleys Coun. on Alcohol and Substance Abuse, 1989-91; bd. dirs. Cortland-Chenango Rural Svcs., 1989—. Mem. Otselic Valley Ministerial Assn., Cortland County Coun. Chs., Ch. Women United, Presbyn. Women's Assn. Home: 5750 Colonial Arc PO Box 16 Cincinnatus NY 13040 Office: United Presbyn Ch Birchwood Acres PO Box 149 Cincinnatus NY 13040 *It seems to me that in this world so full of violence, suspicion, fear, and envy we need to remember to look for the presence of Christ in each person rather than for what makes them different, unattractive or unappealing.*

MENSING, STEPHEN GUSTAV, bishop; b. Phila., Aug. 6, 1946; s. William Lipshutz and Dorthey (Maurer) M.; m. Molly Northouse, Oct. 17, 1986. BA in Human Svcs., Antioch U., Yellow Springs, Ohio, 1977; MEd in Counseling, Antioch U., Phila., 1979; ThM, Body of Christ Sem., Nashville, 1983; ThD, Body of Christ Sem., Texarkana, Tex., 1990. Ordained to ministry Congregation of Christ Ch., 1979. Dir. religious edn. Body of Christ Ministries, 1st Ch. Body of Christ, Phila., 1979-82, pastor, 1983-89; asst. dir. West African missions Congregation of Christ Ch., Ghana and Nigeria, 1988-89; bishop Congregation of Christ Ch., Phila., 1989—, dir. global missions, 1990—; dir. Ctr. for Multi-Perspective's Counseling, Phila., 1986—. Author: Gold in the Black Hills, 1981, Star Gazing Through Binoculars, 1986, Become Your Own Counselor, 1988, Breathwerk, 1991, Life-Skills Self-Helpapedia, 1991. Pres. I Act Internat., Phila., 1984; v.p. Phila. Interfaith Coun., 1984; bd. dirs. Soc. for Emotional Edn., Phila., 1986. Mem. Penn-Jersey Assn. Pastoral Counselors (pres. 1988-89), West african Missionary Soc., AACD, Christian Ethicist Soc., Am. Pastoral Counselors Soc. Democrat. Home: 2123 S 22d St Philadelphia PA 19145 Office: Congregation of Christ 2123 S 22d St Philadelphia PA 19145 *The spiritual life calls on us to live fully, reasonably, and with an open-mind. The spiritual life draws on experience rather than words. The spiritual life brings our focus to others.*

MENTER, WILLIAM GEORGE, minister; b. Pemberville, Ohio, Mar. 1, 1934; s. Irvin Henry and Vondale Caroline (Kohring) M.; m. Carol Louise Reitzel, Aug. 11, 1957 (div. 1988); children: Deborah Razor, Daniel Menter, David. BSBA, Bowling Green State U., 1956; MDiv, Evangelical Luth. Theol. Sem., Columbus, Ohio, 1960; DMin, Trinity Luth. Sem., Columbus, Ohio, 1983. Ordained minister, Luth. Ch., 1960. Pastor Christ Luth. Ch., Agincourt, Ont., Can., 1960-65, St. Paul Luth. Ch., Imlay City, Mich., 1965-82, Faith Luth. Ch., Saginaw, Mich., 1985—; interim pastor Univ. Luth. Ch., East Lansing, Mich., 1982; v.p. Image Prodns., Port Huron, Mich., 1983-85. Mem. Writing Acad. (pres. 1985-86), Rotary (pres. Imlay City chpt. 1979-80). Office: Faith Luth Ch 2405 Bay St Saginaw MI 48602 *I know of no greater gift that forgiveness of one soul of another.*

MENTZE, ROBERT WILLIAM, minister; b. San Diego, Calif., Sept. 29, 1952; s. Walter William and Margaret Jane (Troxel) M. BA summa cum laude, San Diego State U., 1974; MDiv, San Francisco Theol. Seminary, San Anselmo, Calif., 1977; postgrad., Westminster Theol. Sem., Escondido, Calif., 1990—. Writer, announcer Family Radio Network, El Cajon, Calif., 1970-74; youth dir. intern First Presbyn. Ch., San Diego, 1973; youth dir. Marin Covenant Ch., San Rafael, Calif., 1974-77; assoc. pastor Westminster Presbyn. Ch., Escondido, Calif., 1977-84; pastor Community Presbyn. Ch., Lakeside, Calif., 1984—; chmn. worship com. Presbytery of San Diego, 1988, evangelism com., 1992; adv. bd., treas. Lakeside (Calif.) Christian Helps Ctr., 1988—. Composer numerous songs, hymns, anthems and keyboard works. Founder Lakeside Ministerial Assn., 1985, pres., 1986, 90-91. Gov.'s scholar State of Calif., 1970; recipient Community Svc. award Kiwanis Internat., Escondido, 1982. Fellow Phi Kappa Phi (life, grad. fellow 1974); mem. Phi Beta Kappa, Phi Eta Sigma (sr. advisor 1973-74). Office: Community Presbyn Church 9908 Channel Rd Lakeside CA 92040

MENUEZ, D. BARRY, religious organization administrator; b. Benton, Ohio, Feb. 28, 1933; s. Kyle LeRoy and Roxie Beulah (Rottman) M.; m. Mary Jane Sidley, Aug. 30, 1956 (div. 1974); children: Douglas, Stephanie, Jane, Ross; m. Jean Venable, June 30, 1989; 1 stepchild, Alan. BD, Kenyon Coll., 1955; MDiv, U. Chgo., 1971; LHD, Berkeley-Yale Div. Sch., 1990. Dir. office of ministries Episcopal Ch. Ctr., N.Y.C., dir. coun. for devel. of ministry, exec. edn. for mission and ministry, sr. exec. for missions ops., 1986—; v.p. Indsl. Areas Found., Garden City, N.Y., 1974—. 1st lt. USAF, 1955-57. Recipient Disting. Christian Svc. award Seabury-Western Theol. Sem., 1988. Home: 345 E 81st St # 10B New York NY 10028 Office: Episcopal Ch Ctr 815 2d Ave New York NY 10017

MERCADANTE, LINDA ANGELA, theologian, minister; b. Newark; d. Gene and Gertrude (Schacht) M.; 1 child, David. BA, Am. U., 1968; MCS, Regent Coll., 1978; PhD, Princeton (N.J.) Theol. Sem., 1986. Ordained to ministry Presbyn. Ch., 1987. Journalist, columnist The Beacon, Pequannock, N.J., 1970-71, The Daily Record, Morristown, N.J., 1971-74; reference libr. Speer Libr. Princeton Theol. Sem., 1985-86; assoc. prof. theology Meth. Theol. Sch., Delaware, Ohio, 1987—; adj. prof. religion Trenton (N.J.) State Coll., 1987; ofcl. reader scholarship com. Presbyn. Ch. of U.S.A.; mem. staff Ctr. for Women & Religion, Berkeley, Calif., 1980, Presbytery Scioto Valley, 1987—. Author: From Hierarchy to Equality, 1978, Gender, Doctrine and God: The Shakers & Contemporary Theology, 1990; contbr. articles to profl. jours. Bd. dirs. interfaith task force NOW, N.J., 1983-84. Recipient Younger Scholar award Assn. Theol. Schs., 1991; fellow Inst. for Ecumenical and Cultural Rsch., Collegeville, Minn., 1992. Mem. Am. Acad. of Religion (speaker, chair mktg. com.), Am. Soc. of Ch. History (speaker). Office: Meth Theol Sch 3081 Columbus Pike Delaware OH 43015

MERCADO, LUIS FIDEL, academic administrator; b. Barranquitas, P.R., Apr. 24, 1925; s. Marcelino and Juana (Marrero) M.; m. Clara Sherman; children: Samuel, Sara, Lydia, Carlos, Ruth, Victor. BA in History, Goshen Coll., 1949; BD, Ea. Bapt. Theol. Sem., 1952; MA Latin Am. History, U. Pa., 1952; ThD, Harvard Div. Sch., 1967. Pastor Bapt. Chs., Barranquitas, 1952-53, Cagua, P.R., 1954-61; exec. min. Bapt. Chs., P.R., 1972-76; vis. prof. Evang. Sem. P.R., 1956-58, prof., 1966-70, pres., 1976—. Office: Evang Sem PR 776 Ponce de Leon Ave Hato Rey PR 00918

MERCALDO, DANIEL, clergyman; b. Bklyn., Aug. 9, 1939; s. Isaac M. and Rose (Giangola) M.; m. Evangeline Ruth Spencer, Aug. 16, 1958; children: Timothy James, Deborah Rose. BA in Religious Edn., Central Bible Coll., 1961. Ordained minister interdenominational ch., 1963. Founder, pastor Gateway Cathedral, S.I., N.Y., 1965—. Contbr. articles to mags. Founding com. Crisis Pregnancy Ctr., State Island, 1984. Recipient Bldg. award Staten Island C. of C., 1974, 78. Mem. Nat. Assn. Evangelicals (exec. com., bd. adminstrn. 1975—), Romanian Missionary Soc. (bd. dirs. 1981—), Correll Missionary Ministries (v.p. 1979—), Ministerios Missionarios Correll (Lisbon, Portugal, pres. 1986—). Avocations: photography, sports, travel, music. Office: Gateway Cathedral 200 Clarke Ave Staten Island NY 10306

MERCER, CALVIN RICHARD, religion educator; b. Kinston, N.C., Aug. 27, 1953; s. Calvin R. and Edna Ruth (Kennedy) M.; m. Marilyn Michele Miller, Aug. 18, 1975. BA in Journalism and Psychology, U. N.C., 1975; MDiv cum laude, Southeastern Bapt. Theol. Sem., Wake Forest, N.C., 1977, ThM, 1979; PhD, Fla. State U., 1983. Assoc. prof. of religious studies East Carolina U., Greenville, 1985—. Author: Norman Perrin's Interpretation of the New Testament: From "Exegetical Method" to "Hermeneutical Process," Vol. 2 Studies in American Biblical Hermeneutics, 1986; contbr. articles and book revs. to religious jours. Pres. Contact Teleministries Helpline, Smithfield, N.C., 1984-86; founding bd. dirs. Harbor Rape and Spouse Abuse Network, Smithfield, 1984-90. Recipient Summer Seminar award NEH, 1984, award N.C. Humanities Coun., 1986; So. Regional Edn. Bd. grantee, 1986, East Carolina U. grantee, 1986, 90, Ford Curriculum Devel. grantee Duke/U.N.C. Ctr. for Rsch. on Women, 1987. Mem. Am. Acad. Religion (grantee 1990), Soc. Bibl. Lit., Authors Guild, Coll. Theology Soc., Nat. Women's Studies Assn., Studiorum Novi Testamenti Societas. Democrat. Avocations: backpacking, canoeing, camping, racquetball, skiing. : Office: East Carolina U Dept Philosophy Greenville NC 27858-4353

MERCER, MARGARET FRANCIS, theologian; b. Orange, N.J., Aug. 6, 1936; d. Courteneay and Margaret (French) Overman; m. Douglas Mercer, Aug. 3, 1957 (div. Apr. 1989); children: Derek, Gray, Courtney, Ashley, Kristen, Nicholas. BA, Columbia U., 1981; MDiv., Union Sem., 1984, STM, 1990; postgrad., Union Theol. Sem., 1990—. Ordained to ministry Am. Bapt. Ch., 1987. Chaplain Riker's Island Correctional Facility, N.Y.C., 1983-87; ct. advocate N.Y.C. Criminal Justice System, 1985-87; pastoral counselor Union Sem., N.Y.C., 1989—; trustee Hosp. Chaplaincy, N.Y.C., 1986-90. Bd. dirs. U.S. Commn. for Refugee Relocation, N.Y.C., 1989—, United Bd. for Higher Edn. in Asia, N.Y.C. 1990—. Mem. AAPC, Soc. Christian Ethics (del. 1985—), Amnesty Internat. (del. 1984—), Phi Beta Kappa. Baptist. Home: 60 E 92d St New York NY 10128 Office: Union Theol Sem 3041 Broadway New York NY 10027

MERCER, MARK KENT, religion educator; b. Gladewater, Tex., Aug. 7, 1953; s. Neal Wilbur and Ophelia (Smith) M.; m. Susan Dean Mercer, June 18, 1975; children: Meredith, Valerie, Preston. BA, Tex. Tech. U., Lubbock, 1975; ThM, Dallas Theol. Sem., 1979, ThD, 1987. Instr. religion Christ for the Nations Inst., Dallas, 1988—. Mem. Soc. Bibl. Lit. Home: 2729 Wesleyan St Irving TX 75062 Office: Christ for the Nations Inst 3404 Conway Dallas TX 75224

MERCIECA, JOSEPH, archbishop; b. Victoria, Gozo, Malta, Nov. 12, 1928; s. Saverio and Giovanna (Vassallo) M. BA, London U., 1950; DST, Gregorian U., Rome, 1953; JUD, Lateran U., Rome, 1957. Ordained priest Roman Cath. Ch., 1952. Rector Gozo Sem., 1958-69; judge Roman Rota, Rome, 1969-74; aux. bishop of Malta, 1974-76, archbishop of Malta, 1976—; consultor Congregation of Sacraments, Vatican City State, 1976, Congregation for Doctrine of Faith, 1976; mem. Apostolic Segnatura, Rome, 1991—. Home: Archbishop's Palace, Mdina Malta Office: Archbishop's Curia, PO Box 29, Valletta Malta

MEREDITH, DONALD LLOYD, librarian; b. Batesville, Miss., Sept. 11, 1941; s. Duward Lee and Julia Mae (Ferguson) M.; m. Evelyn Charlene Rickett, Aug. 15, 1964; Christopher Todd, Tracey Hope. BA, Harding U., 1964; MTh, Harding Grad. Sch., 1967; MS in Libr. Sci., U. N.C., 1968. Asst. libr. Harding Grad. Sch. Religion, Memphis, 1968-70, assoc. libr., 1970-83, libr., 1983—. Mem. Am. Theol. Libr. Assn., Tenn. Theol. Libr. Assn. (pres. 1981-82), Memphis Libr. Coun. (chmn. 1982-83). Home: 4897 Welchshire Memphis TN 38117 Office: Harding Grad Sch Libr 1000 Cherry Rd Memphis TN 38117

MEREDITH, FRANK HOMER, music director; b. Washington, Dec. 3, 1953; s. Robert J. and Rosemary G. (Neal) M.; m. Elizabeth C. Hurd, June 30, 1979; children: Christopher H., Jonathan J., Nathan M. BS in Music Edn., The King's Coll., Briarcliff Manor, N.Y., 1976; M.Mus. in Brass Performance, Ithaca Coll., N.Y., 1978; postgrad., Northwestern U., Evanston, Ill., 1985. Cert. water specialist I. Music dir. Van Riper Ellis Meml. Ch., Fairlawn, N.Y., 1975-76, Pineview Community Ch., Albany, N.Y., 1988—; owner Schoharie Valley Water Sys., Schoharie, N.Y., 1988—; soloist (euphonium, trumpet, trombone, vocal) in numerous chs. throughout N.E. U.S.; bass trombone GlimmerGlass Opera, Utica Symphony, Catskill Symphony, 1978—. Conductor Schoharie Valley Concert Band, 1979-87; exec. coun. N.Y. State Sch. Music Assn., 1985-87. Mem. N.Y. State Water Quality Assn., Am. Fedn. Musicians, Tubists Universal Brotherhood Assn., Pi Kappa Lambda. Home: PO Box 57 Schoharie NY 12157 Office: Pineview Community Ch 251 Washington Ave Ext Albany NY 12205-5504

MERKLEIN, HELMUT MARTIN, theology educator; b. Aub, Fed. Republic of Germany, Sept. 17, 1940; s. Martin and Anna Maria (Beck) M. Diploma in theology, U. Bamberg, Bamberg, Federal Republic of Germany, 1964; ThD, U. Würzburg, Federal Republic of Germany, 1972, Habilitation, 1976. Chaplain Diocese of Bamberg, Rehau, 1965-68, Würzburg, 1968-72; asst. in theology U. Würzburg, 1972-77; prof. U. Wuppertal, Federal Republic of Germany, 1977-80, U. Bonn, Federal Republic of Germany, 1980—; dir. New Testament Sem., Cath.-Theol. Fac., U. Bonn, 1980—. Author: Kirchliches Amt im Epheserbrief, 1973, Gottesherrschaft als Handlungsprinzip, 3d edit., 1984, Jesu Botschaft von der Gottesherrschaft, 3d rev. edit., 1989, Studien zu Jesus und Paulus, 1987. Home: Toepferstr 6, Wachtberg Federal Republic of Germany D-5307 Office: Univ Bonn, Regina-Pacis-Weg 1a, Bonn Federal Republic of Germany D-5300

MERKOREWOS, ABUNE, head of religious order. Patriarchate archbishop Ethiopian Orthodox Ch., Addis Ababa. Office: POB 1283, Addis Ababa Ethiopia*

MERRELL, JAMES LEE, editor, clergyman; b. Indpls., Oct. 24, 1930; s. Mark W. and Pauline F. (Tucker) M.; m. Barbara Jean Burch, Dec. 23, 1951; children: Deborah Lea Merrell Griffin, Cynthia Lynn, Stuart Allen. A.B., Ind. U., 1952; M.Div., Christian Theol. Sem., 1956; Litt.D., Culver-Stockton Coll., 1972. Ordained to ministry Christian Ch., 1955; asso. editor World Call, Indpls., 1956-66; editor World Call, 1971-73; pastor Crestview Christian Ch., Indpls., 1966-71; editor The Disciple, St. Louis, 1974-89; sr. v.p. Christian Bd. Publ., 1976-89; sr. minister Affton Christian Ch., St. Louis, 1989—. Author: They Live Their Faith, 1965, The Power of One, 1976, Discover the Word in Print, 1979, Finding Faith in the Headlines, 1985. Chmn. bd. Kennedy Meml. Christian Home, Martinsville, Ind., 1971-73; trustee Christian Theol. Sem., 1978-81. Recipient Faith and Freedom award Religious Heritage of Am., 1983. Mem. Associated Ch. Press (award 1973, 79, 80, 81, 82, dir. 1974-75, 78-81, 1st v.p. 1983-85), Christian Theol. Sem. Alumni Assn. (pres. 1966-68), Religious Pub. Rels. Coun. (awards 1979, 80, 84, 87, 90, pres. St. Louis chpt. 1985-86), Sigma Delta Chi (award 1952), Theta Phi. Home: 5347 Warmwinds Ct Saint Louis MO 63129 Office: Disciples 9625 Tesson Ferry Rd Saint Louis MO 63123 *As a religious communicator and as a pastor, I have always believed in applying the same standards in the sacred realm as in the secular. I have tried to pursue the truth, to keep my constituency informed, to celebrate the noble in life, to fight against those who would lie, distort and hide God's truth in the name of some supposed good.*

MERRIFIELD, CARLDEAN, minister; b. LaGrange, Ind., Feb. 24, 1924; s. Sidney Sanger and Iva Elizabeth (Choler) M.; m. Patsy Lou Minnick, Nov. 3, 1946; children: Linda, Barbara, Carldean, Jr., Diane, Jacki, David. GI Agrl. Farming, LaGrange High, LaGrange, Ind., 1947-51; Local Pastor's Study, Garrett-Evang. Theol. Seminary, Evanston, Ill., 1978-85. Ordained minister Meth. Ch., 1985. Farmer Wolcottville, Ind., 1943-46; minister East Springfield United Meth. Ch., nr. LaGrange, Ind., 1972—, Mongo (Ind.) United Meth. Ch., 1972—, Plato United Meth. Ch., nr. LaGrange, 1972—; postmaster U.S. Postal Svc., Wolcottville, 1963-88; postal svc. cons. People to People Citizen Ambassador Program, Beijing, Nanaging, Shanghia, Fughow, and Yangzhou, China, Hong Kong, 1987. Bd. dirs. LaGrange County Hosp. 1962-69, bd. pres. 1969-73; bd. mem. U.S. Draft Bd. LaGrange 1955-70, bd. pres. 1970-75. With USN, 1943-46, PTO. Recipient Excellent Merit Award, U.S. Postal Svc. Wolcottville 1986,'87,'88; named LaGrange County Citizen of the Year, LaGrange County Jaycees 1972. Mem. Nat. Assn. of Postmasters, LaGrange County Ministerial Assn., Wolcottville Ministerial Assn. (sec.-treas. 1989), Local Pastors Assn. of Am., The Gideons Internat., Am. Legion (Chaplain 1955, 1975), Masons. Democrat. Avocations: fishing, stamp collecting, rare coin collecting. Home: PO Box 398 Wolcottville IN 46795

MERRILL, ARTHUR LEWIS, theology educator; b. Tura, Assam, India, Sept. 14, 1930; s. Alfred Francis and Ida (Walker) M.; m. Barbara Jean Mayer, Aug. 18, 1951 (dec. June 1978); children: Margaret Jean, Katherine Merrill Nelson, Robert L.; m. Margaret Z. Morris, Sept. 11, 1985. BA, Coll. of Wooster, 1951; BD with distinction, Berkeley Bapt. Div. Sch., 1954; PhD, U. Chgo., 1962. Ordained to ministry United Ch. of Christ, 1954. Asst. prof. Bapt. Missionary Tng. Sch., Chgo., 1957-58; assoc. prof. Mission House Theol. Sem., Plymouth, Wis., 1958-62; assoc. prof. United Theol. Sem. of Twin Cities, New Brighton, Minn., 1962-67, prof., 1967—, dir. libr. svcs., 1983—. Co-author: Biblical Witness and the World, 1967; co-editor: Scripture in History and Theology, 1977; contbr. articles to profl. publs. ATS-Lilly postdoctoral fellow, 1966-67. Mem. Soc. Biblical Lit., Am. Schs. Oriental Rsch., Israel Exploration Soc., Minn. Theol. Libr. Assn. (pres. 1988-89). Home: 214 Windsor Ct New Brighton MN 55112 Office: United Theol Sem 3000 5th St NW New Brighton MN 55112

MERRILL, EUGENE HAINES, religion educator; b. Anson, Maine, Sept. 12, 1934; s. Orrin Hastings and Ruby Miriam (Haines) M.; m. Janet Louise Hippensteel, Dec. 18, 1960; 1 child, Sonya Leigh. BA, Bob Jones U., 1957, MA, 1960, PhD, 1963; MA, NYU, 1970; MPhil, Columbia U., 1976, PhD, 1985. Prof. Bob Jones U., 1963-66, Berkshire Christian Coll., Lenox, Mass., 1968-75; prof. Old Testament studies Dallas Theol. Sem., 1975—; bd. dirs. Chaplain Ministries, Inc., Dallas. Author: (book) An Historical Survey of the Old Testament, 1966, Qumran and Predestination, 1975, Kingdom of Priests, 1987, 1,2 Chronicles, 1988; contbg. author five books; contbr. articles to profl. jours. Mem. Am. Oriental Soc., Am. Schs. Oriental Rsch., Evang. Theol. Soc., Near East Archaeol. Soc., Am. Coun. Asian Christian Acad. (bd. dirs. 1979—), Soc. Bibl. Lit. Republican. Home: 9314 Westview Rd Dallas TX 75218 Office: Dallas Theol Sem 3909 Swiss Ave Dallas TX 75204 *Birth provides potentiality, life demands responsibility, death will judge according to opportunity.*

MERRILL, JOSEPH HARTWELL, association executive; b. Norway, Maine, Jan. 16, 1903; s. Wiggin L. and Ella M. (Porter) M. Grad. high sch. Head retouching dept. Bachrach, Inc. (photographers), Newton, Mass., 1937-61; sec. Mass. Assn. Spiritualists, 1953-61; exec. sec. Nat. Spiritualist Assn. Chs., Milw., 1961-71; v.p. Nat. Spiritualist Assn. Chs., 1971-73, pres., 1973—; v.p. Internat. Spiritualist Fedn. Spiritualists, London, 1975-81; lectr. social legislation for oldsters Townsend Orgn. Served with AUS, 1942-43. Address: 13 Cleveland Ave Lily Dale NY 14752

MERRILL, MICHAEL BRADLEY, minister; b. Bethesda, Md., Sept. 18, 1953; s. Robert and Joan (Schwab) M.; m. Pamela Joy Staines, Apr. 5, 1975; children: Matthew, Timothy, Kathryn, Joshua. BS, Roberts Wesleyan Coll., 1975; MDiv, Asbury Theol. Sem., 1978. Ordained to ministry Free Meth. Ch. of N.Am. as deacon, 1979, as elder, 1981. Pastor youth Yorkshire (N.Y.) Free Meth. Ch., 1978-80; pastor Parma Free Meth. Ch., Hilton, N.Y., 1980—; prof. Greek and Bible Robert Wesleyan Coll., North Chili, N.Y., 1981-89; dir. youth ministries Free Meth. Ch. of N.Am., Indpls., 1989—; elder Genesee Conf. of the Free Meth. Ch. Mem. Alpha Kappa Sigma, Theta Phi. Home: 1021 Parma-Hilton Rd Hilton NY 14468 Office: Free Meth Ch 1021 Parma-Hilton Rd Hilton NY 14468 *The greatest gift a parent can give his or her child is not an inheritance, education, security or experience. It is self-esteem. If a child grows up with a sense of eternal value, all other things can come.*

MERRIMAN, WILLIS J., minister. Exec. dir. Inter-Ch. Ministries Northwestern Pa., Erie. Office: Inter-Ch Ministries Northwestern Pa 252 W 7th St Erie PA 16501*

MERRITT, JAMES GREGORY, SR., minister; b. Gainesville, Ga., Dec. 22, 1952; s. Glenn Monroe and Miriam Estelle (House) M.; m. Teresa Ovalene York, Mar. 13, 1991; children from previous marriage: James Jr., Jonathan, Joshua. BBA cum laude, Stetson U., 1974; MDiv, So. Bapt. Theol. Sem., Louisville, 1979, PhD, 1982. Ordained to ministry So. Bapt. Conv., 1976. Pastor Buck Grove Bapt. Ch., Brandenburg, Ky., 1979-83, Highland Bapt. Ch., Laurel, Miss., 1983-85, 1st Bapt. Ch., Snellville, Ga., 1985—; mem. exec. com. So. Bapt. Conv., Nashville, 1991—. Author: God's Prescription for a Healthy Christian, 1990. Recipient Outstanding Young Man of Am. award Snellville Jaycess, 1986. Office: 1st Bapt Ch 2400 Main St E Snellville GA 30278

MERRITT, MICHAEL GRADY, minister; b. Lincoln, Nebr., Aug. 28, 1962; s. William Edward and Shirley Ann (Johnson) M.; m. Marcee Yvonne Lotts, Nov. 4, 1984. Student, New Life Bible Coll., Cleveland, Tenn., 1983. Ordained to ministry, Evang. Ch. Mgr. The Lightclub Concert Ministries,, Warner Robins, Ga., 1980-82; music minister Evang. Ch. of Grace, Knoxville, 1985—. Songwriter, artist River Records/Purefire Pub., Nashville, 1990—; composer, singer recording: Mercy River, 1990; author: How to Love Your Wife and Play the Tunes, 1991. Mem. ASCAP.

MERTENS, GLENN CHARLES, minister; b. Milw., Sept. 2, 1957; s. Paul Carl and Dorothy (Bieber) M.; m. Doris Jane Huffman, Jan. 1, 1977; children: Nathan, Nicholas, Joshua, Janelle. BS, Liberty Bapt. Coll., 1979; MDiv, Trinity Evang. Divinity Sch., 1982. Ordained to ministry Evang. Free Ch. of Am., 1990. Ch. planter Evang. Free Ch. Bartlesville, Okla., 1983-84; assoc. pastor Kettle Moraine Evang. Free Ch., Delafield, Wis., 1987—; mem. Milw. metro adv. com. Evang. Free Ch., 1988—, mem. dist. youth commn., Madison, 1990—. Author: Growing in Your Relations with Christ, 1990. Mem. human growth and devel. com. Nashotah (Wis.)/Bark River Sch. Dist., 1990—. Office: Kettle Moraine Evang Free Ch N6 W31449 Alberta Dr Delafield WI 53018 *The Spiritual future of our generation lies in our hands. Seize the Day and make a difference for Jesus Christ that will matter for eternity!.*

MERTENS, SISTER MARY SUE, religious organization administrator; b. Jefferson City, Mo., June 27, 1944; d. Edward Theodore and Dorothy Catherine (Rackers) M. BS in Edn., U. Mo., 1972; MS in Ednl. Adminstrn., U. Dayton, Ohio, 1980. Cert. elem. tchr., elem. sch. adminstr. Tchr. St. John Sch., Imperial, Mo., 1964-65, St. Elizabeth Sch., Granite City, Ill., 1965-68, St. Andrew Sch., Tipton, Mo., 1968-69, Ascension Sch., Normandy, Mo., 1969-80; prin. Ascension Sch., 1980-85; provincial, pres. Sisters of Divine Providence, Normandy, 1986—; bd. dirs. St. Elizabeth Med. Ctr., Granite City. Mem. Leadership Conf. Religious Women, Nat. Assn. Ch. Personnel Adminstrs. Roman Catholic. Avocations: biking, sailing, camping. Home: 12685 Parktrails Florissant MO 63033 Office: Sisters Divine Providence 8351 Florissant Rd Saint Louis MO 63121

MERWIN, DAVID, minister; b. Des Moines, Iowa, May 15, 1932; s. Chauncey and Alice (Eyestone) M.; m. Judy Anne Sherman, Mar. 23, 1952; children: Stephanie Anne, Sarah Alice. BTh, Internat. Bible Coll., 1960; cert. in Korean language, Yonsei U., Seoul, 1965. Pastor Community Ch., San Antonio, 1958-60; missionary Far East Apostolic Mission, San Antonio, 1961-80; missions pastor Bethel Temple, Evansville, Ind., 1980-85; sr. pastor, chmn. bd. Temple of Praise, Evansville, Ind., 1985-91; asst. to sr. pastor Living Hope Fellowship, Aloha, Oreg., 1991—; trustee Temple of Praise, Evansville; bd. dirs. Bethel Fgn. Mission Found., Evansville; mission chmn. Far East Apostolic, Taejon, Korea, 1965-80. With U.S. Army, 1954-56,

Korea. Recipient Key to City, Mayor of Seoul, Korea, 1964. Mem. Bethel Ministerial Assn. (bd. dirs.). Republican. Office: Living Hope Fellowship PO Box 6522 Aloha OR 97007-0522 *I owe so much to my parents who were great examples and lived their lives totally surrendered to God.*

MESCHELOFF, MOSES, rabbi; b. N.Y.C., June 12, 1909; s. Mayer and Bessie (Kroll) M.; m. Magda Schonfeld, Mar. 10, 1935; children: Renah Rahelle, Efraim Zev, David Joseph. BA, CCNY, 1932; DHL, Hebrew Theol. Coll., 1980. Ordained rabbi, 1932. Rabbi Congregation Machzike Hadas, Scranton, Pa., 1932-36, Congregation United Sons of Israel, North Adams, Mass., 1936-37, Congregation Beth Jacob, Miami Beach, Fla., 1937-55, Congregation K.I.N.S. of West Rogers Park, Chgo., 1955—. Author: In the Priest's Office, Covenant of Abraham, Right Before the King, The Parting of Ways. Mem. exec. com. Northtown Rogers Park Mental Health Coun., Coun. for Jewish Elderly; mem. Mayor's Commn. of Dept. Human Svcs., Chgo. Named to Hall of Fame, City of Chgo., 1986. Mem. Chgo. Bd. Rabbis (exec. com.), Chgo. Rabbinical Coun. (exec. com.), Chgo. Zionist Orgn. (exec. com.), North Town Community Coun. (exec. com.), Associated Talmud Torahs (bd. dirs.), Religious Zionist Coun. (bd. dirs.). Home: 6644 N Fairfield Ave Chicago IL 60645 Office: Congregation KINS 2800 W North Shore Ave Chicago IL 60645

MESSENGER, RICHARD BRYAN, pastor; b. Akron, Ohio, Dec. 20, 1953; s. Amos Hayes and Mary Rosa (DeLuca) M.; m. Margaret Elaine Griffiths, June 11, 1977; children: Rachel, Renee. BA in Theology, Cen. Bible Coll., Springfield, Mo., 1978. Ordained to ministry Assemblies of God, 1978. Assoc. pastor Lighthouse Tabernacle, Indpls., 1978-80; pastor East Liberty Assembly of God Ch., Akron, 1980—; chaplain Am. Guild Organists, Akron, 1985. Editor: Permanent Waves Made Easy, 1982. Office: East Liberty Assembly of God Ch 772 E Turkeyfoot Lake Rd Akron OH 44319

MESSER, DONALD EDWARD, theological school president; b. Kimball, S.D., Mar. 5, 1941; s. George Marcus and Grace E. (Foltz) M.; m. Bonnie Jeanne Nagel, Aug. 30, 1964; children: Christine Marie, Kent Donald. BA cum laude, Dakota Wesleyan U., 1963; M. Divinity magna cum laude, Boston U., 1966, PhD, 1969; LHD (hon.), Dakota Wesleyan U., 1977. Asst. to commr. Mass. Commn. Against Discrimination, Boston, 1968-69; asst. prof. Augustana Coll., Sioux Falls, S.D., 1969-71; assoc. pastor 1st United Meth. Ch., Sioux Falls, 1969-71; pres. Dakota Wesleyan U., Mitchell, S.D., 1971-81, Iliff Sch. Theology, Denver, 1981—. Author: Christian Ethics and Political Action, 1984, Contemporary Images of Christian Ministry, 1989, Send Me? The Itinerary In Crisis, 1991, The Conspiracy of Goodness, 1992; contbr. articles to Face To Face, The Christian Century, The Christian Ministry. Active Edn. Commn. of U.S., 1973-79; co-chmn. Citizens Commn. Corrections, 1975-76; vice chmn. S.D. Commn. on Humanities, 1979-81. Dempster fellow, 1967-68; Rockefeller fellow, 1968-69. Mem. Soc. Christian Ethics, Am. Acad. Religion, Assn. United Methodist Theol. Schs. (v.p. 1986-91, pres. 1991—). Democrat. Office: Iliff Sch Theology Office Pres 2201 S University Blvd Denver CO 80210

MESSER, JOHN ROBERT, deacon; b. Mankato, Minn., June 19, 1938; s. Robert J. and Phyllis Ann (Creedon) M.; m. Pamela Leona, June 21, 1963; children: Thang Lai, Debra, Jeffery, Noel. Student, John Marshall Law Sch., 1953-57. Ordained deacon Roman Cath. Ch., 1977. Deacon Archdiocese L.A., 1977—; parish adminstr. St. Anthony's Ch., San Gabriel, Calif., 1981—; Co-owner Pamela's, Azusa, Ontario, Calif., 1963—; chaplain Christian Svcs. Program, San Gabriel, 1976—; San Gabriel diaconate regional chairperson Ministry Com., Archdiocese L.A., clergy deanery mem., workshop presenter; hon. chaplain USN, USS Mobil, 1986. Mem. East Valleys Orgn., San Gabriel Valley, 1989—. Mem. San Gabriel Valley Parish Adminstrs. Republican. Office: St Anthonys Cath Ch 1901 S San Gabriel Blvd San Gabriel CA 91776

MESTICE, ANTHONY F., bishop; b. N.Y.C., Dec. 6, 1923. Grad., St. Joseph Sem., N.Y. Ordained priest Roman Catholic Ch., 1949. Ordained titular bishop of Villa Nova and aux. bishop Diocese of N.Y., Poughkeepsie, 1973—. Office: Chancery Office 1011 1st Ave New York NY 10022

METHODIOS OF BOSTON, BISHOP See TOURNAS, METHODIOS

METRICK, RICHARD LEE, JR., minister, counselor; b. Beckley, W.Va., Aug. 29, 1958; s. Richard Lee and Betty Sue (Raines) L.; m. Starr Lynn Bright, Aug 2, 1980; children: Heather, Hollie, Hanna. BA in Pastoral Theology, Appalachin Bible Coll., Bradley, W. Va., 1980; MA in Counseling, Liberty U.; PhD in Counseling Psychology, Emmanuel Bapt. U., 1990. Lic. poastoral counselor, temperament therapist. Tchr., music minister Bible Bapt. Ch., Clinton (Md.) Christian Sch., 1980-83; pastor Walnut Hills Bapt. Ch., Huntington, W. Va., 1983-86, Eckhart Bapt. Ch., Frostburg, Md., 1986—; founder, counselor Christian Counseling Svcs., Frostburg, 1989—. Contbr. articles to religious jours.; host weekly radio show The Pastor's Study, 1985-86; dir., founder, Youth Quiz Teams, Youth in Fellowship, 1985-86. Mem. Nat. Christian Counselors Assn., Am. Assn. for Counseling and Devel., United Assn. for Christian Counselors, Ind. Fundamental Chs. of Am. Home: RFD #3 Box 75 Frostburg MD 21532 Office: Eckhart Bapt Ch RR 3 Box 75 Frostburg MD 21532 *One of the greatest fabrications bewildering and deceiving believers is façade-christianity. May we never masquerade Christianity by surrendering to the impositions of those regarding superficial pretense superior to Divine revolution of the inner self which, thereby, transforms character and conversation.*

METTLER, KEN G(LEN), minister; b. Amery, Wis., Nov. 27, 1948; s. Glen Joseph and Ruth Magdalene (Eliason) M.; m. Barbara Jean Litzkow, June 16, 1972; children: David Allen, Laura Ruth, Stephanie Joy. BA, St. Paul Bible Coll., 1971; MDiv, So. Sem., 1976, DDiv, 1977. Ordained to ministry Evang. Free Ch. Am., 1976. Pastor Calvary Bible Ch., Viper, Ky., 1971-85; dist. supt. East Cen. Dist., Hazard, Ky., 1975-85; pastor Fern Cliff Free Ch., Wayland, Iowa, 1985-88, Evang. Free Ch., Cooperstown, N.D., 1988—; chmn. Twin Rocks Bible Camp, Viper, 1975-85; dist. bd. dirs. No. Plains Dist., Evang. Free Ch. Am., 1991—. Dist. editor Evang. Beacon, 1971-85. Named to Ky. Cols., 1980. Mem. Evang. Free Ch. Ministerial, Ky. Dist. Assn., Perry County Ministerial (pres. 1982-85), Waco Ministerial, Cooperstown Ministerial, Town and Country Garden Club (pres. 1989—). Republican. Home: Rte 2 Box 41 Cooperstown ND 58425 Office: Evang Free Ch Rte 2 Box 41 Cooperstown ND 58425

METTS, WALLIS C., minister, broadcasting company executive; b. Elko, S.C., May 8, 1932; s. Joel Allen and Lillian T. (Hair) M.; m. Jo Ann Prince, Sept. 30, 1951; children: Wallis C. Jr., Roselyn Toy Metts Coxey, Juliann Joy Metts Clark. Bachelor's degree, Tenn. Temple U., 1961; DD (hon.), Fla. Bible Coll., 1985. Ordained to ministry Bapt. Ch. Pastor Russell Park Bapt. Ch., Ft. Myers, Fla., 1961-64, Southside Bapt. Ch., Ft. Myers, 1964-69, Berean Bapt. Ch., Hixson, Tenn., 1969-79; editor, info. dir. Christian Law Assn., Cleve., 1979-80; pastor Calvary Bapt. Ch., Englewood, Fla., 1981—; pres. Heritage Christian Acad., Englewood, 1981—, Sta. WSEB, Englewood, 1989—; bd. reference Tenn. Temple U., Chattanooga, 1985—; nat. field dir. Christian Legal Def., Leesburg, Fla., 1980-81; chaplain Tenn. Assembly, Nashville, 1975. Author: (book) Brighter Side, 1976, Deep River, 1977, Your Faith On Trial, 1978. Named Hon. Dep. Sarasota County Sheriff Dept., 1990. Mem. Nat. Assn. Religious Broadcasters, Fla. Assn. Christian Schs., Colls., Tenn. Assn. Christian Schs. Republican. Home: 20 Harbour Ln Englewood FL 34223 Office: Calvary Bapt Ch 75 N Pine St Englewood FL 34223

METZ, DONALD S., religion educator; b. Buena Vista, Pa., Mar. 17, 1916; s. Leon and Ida (Myrtle) M.; m. Eva Irene Moran, Oct. 25, 1939. BA, Ea. Nazarene Coll., 1939; BD, Lancaster Theol. Sem., 1946; MA, U. Md., 1951; DRE, Southwestern Bapt. Theol. Sem., 1955; PhD, Okla. U., 1961. Ordained to ministry Ch. of the Nazarene, 1939. Pastor Ch. of the Nazarene, N.Y., Pa., Md., 1939-51; prof. theology So. Nazarene U., Bethany, Okla., 1951-67; acad. dean Mid-Am. Nazarene Coll., Olathe, Kans., 1967-74, 75-83, prof. philosophy and religion, 1983-85. Author: Speaking in Tongues, 1969, Biblical Studies in Holiness, 1971, Commentary-1 Corinthians, 1972, History of Mid-America Nazarene College, 1991; editor: Dept. of Ch. Schs., 1974-76. Bd. dirs. Bethany (Okla.) Pub. Sch. System, 1962. Republican. Home: 1533 Sunvale Dr Olathe KS 66062

METZ, RONALD IRWIN, retired priest, addictions counselor; b. Walthill, Nebr., Aug. 11, 1921; s. Harry Elmer and Emma Rilla (Howe) M.; m. Helen Chapin, July 14, 1951; children: Mary Selden Metz Evans, Helen Winchester Metz Ketchum, Grace Chapin. BA in Chinese and Far Ea. Studies, U. Calif., Berkeley, 1945; MA in Mid. Ea. Studies, Am. U., Beirut, 1954; M Div., Yale U., 1969, STD, 1975. Ordained priest Episcopal Ch., 1969. Intelligence officer various govtl. intelligence agys., Far East and Washington, 1944-52; exec. Arabian/Am. Oil Co., Dhahran and Riyadh, Saudi Arabia, 1954-66; deacon, priest Grace Cathedral, San Francisco; priest St. George's Cathedral, Jerusalem, 1969; exec. asst. to archbishop Jerusalem and Med. East Archbishopric, 1969-75; rector Ch. of the Holy Spirit, Erie, Pa., 1976-81; chaplain Brent Sch., Baguio, Philippines, 1981-82; counselor of chemically dependent Washington, 1982—; addictionologist, vol. New Beginnings Treatment Ctr., P.I.W. Hosp., Washington, 1989-90, Found. Next Step Outpatient Treatment Ctr., Washington, 1991—; adj. clergy St. Margaret's Ch., Washington; mem. D.C. Diocesan Commn. on Alcohol and Drug Abuse, Washington, 1982-89. Bd. dirs. Mid. East Inst., Washington, 1959-60, Pub. Broadcasting Sta., n.w. Pa., 1976-81; mem. adv. bd. Children's Aid Internat., 1988-89. Served to col. U.S. Army, 1942-45, CBI, OSS. Decorated Bronze Star. Mem. Iran Diocesan Assn. U.S.A, Phi Beta Kappa, Sigma Chi (chaplain D.C. alumni assn. 1982—). Democrat. Avocations: home movies, double crostics. Home: 3001 Veazey Terr NW #334 Washington DC 20008

METZENBACHER, GARY WILLIAM, library administrator; b. Erie, Pa., May 30, 1953; s. William Wallace and Joyce Ann (Kestel) M. B.A. in Bibl. Lit., Taylor U., 1975; N.H.A. diploma, Ind. U.-Indpls., 1976; M.A. in Theology, Western Evang. Sem., 1979; M.L.S., Ind. U., Bloomington, 1983. Ordained to ministry Evangelical Ch., 1976. Nursing home adminstr. Community Care Ctr., Decatur, Ind., 1976; pastor Arcadia Bible Ch., Ind., 1976, Washington Valley, Cambridge Springs, Pa., 1977; assoc. pastor Collins View Ch., Portland, Oreg., 1978-82; singles pastor Valley View Ch., Portland, 1982—; library dir. Western Evang. Sem., Portland, 1982—; library cons. Azuza Pacific U., Calif., 1983, Warner Pacific Coll., Portland, 1984-87. Author: Church Growth Through TEE, 1979; contbr. articles to profl. jours. Mem. ALA, Am. Theol. Library Assn., Assn. Christian Librarians (reviewer chpt. 1985—), N.W. Assn. Christian Libraries (pres. 1985-90), Wesleyan Theol. Soc., Assn. for Profl Edn. for Ministry, Assn. Coll. and Research Libraries. Republican. Home: 4407 SE Roethe #16 Milwaukie OR 97267 Office: Christian Ch of Clackamas PO Box 926 Oregon City OR 97045 *Life is hard enough without adding problems to it. Friends help each other.*

METZGER, BRUCE MANNING, clergyman, educator; b. Middletown, Pa., Feb. 9, 1914; s. Maurice Rutt and Anna Mary (Manning) M.; m. Isobel E. Mackay, July 7, 1944; children—John Mackay, James Bruce. A.B., Lebanon Valley Coll., 1935, D.D., 1951; Th.B., Princeton Theol. Sem., 1938, Th.M., 1939; A.M., Princeton U., 1940, Ph.D., 1942; L.H.D., Findlay U., 1962; D.D., St. Andrews U., Scotland, 1964; D.Theol., Münster U., Fed. Republic Germany, 1970; D.Litt., Potchefstroom U., South Africa, 1985. Ordained to ministry Presbyn. Ch., 1939. Teaching fellow N.T. Princeton Theol. Sem., 1938-40, mem. faculty, 1940—, prof. N.T. lang. and lit., 1954-64, George L. Collord prof. N.T. lang. and lit., 1964-84, emeritus, 1984—; vis. lectr. Presbyn. Theol. Sem. South, Campinas, Brazil, 1952, Presbyn. Theol. Sem. North, Recife, Brazil, 1952; mem. Inst. Advanced Study, Princeton, 1964-65, 73-74; scholar-in-residence Tyndale House, Cambridge, 1969; vis. fellow Clare Hall, Cambridge, 1974, Wolfson Coll., Oxford U., 1979, Macquarie U., Sydney, Australia, 1982, Caribbean Grad. Sch. of Theology, Jamaica, 1990, Seminario Internacional Teológico Bautista, Buenos Aires, 1991; mem. mng. com. Am. Sch. Classical Studies, Athens, Greece.; mem. Standard Bible com. Nat. Coun. Chs., 1952—, chmn., 1975—; mem. seminar N.T. studies Columbia U., 1959-80; mem. Kuratorium of Vetus-Latina Inst., Beuron, Germany, 1959—; adv. com. Inst. N.T. Text Rsch., U. Münster, 1961—, Thesaurus Linguae Graecae, 1972-80; Collected Works of Erasmus, 1977—; chmn. Am. com. versions Internat. Greek N.T., 1950-88; participant internat. congresses scholars, Aarhus, Aberdeen, Bangor, Basel, Bonn, Brussels, Cairo, Cambridge, Dublin, Exeter, Heidelberg, Frankfurt, London, Louvain, Manchester, Milan, Munich, Münster, Newcastle, Nottingham, Oxford, Rome, St. Andrews, Stockholm, Strasbourg, Toronto, Trondheim, Tübingen; mem. Presbytery, N.B. Author: The Saturday and Sunday Lessons from Luke in the Greek Gospel Lectionary, 1944, Lexical Aids for Students of New Testament Greek, 1946, enlarged edit., 1955, A Guide to the Preparation of a Thesis, 1950, An Introduction to the Apocrypha, 1957, Chapters in the History of New Testament Textual Criticism, 1963, The Text of the New Testament, Its Transmission, Corruption, and Restoration, 1964, (with H.G. May) The Oxford Annotated Bible with the Apocrypha, 1965, The New Testament, Its Background, Growth, and Content, 1965, Index to Periodical Literature on Christ and the Gospels, 1966, Historical and Literary Studies, Pagan, Jewish, and Christian, 1968, Index to Periodical Literature on the Apostle Paul, 1970, 2nd edit., A Textual Commentary on the Greek New Testament, 1971, The Early Versions of the New Testament, 1977, New Testament Studies, 1980, Manuscripts of the Greek Bible, 1981, The Canon of the New Testament, 1987, (with Roland Murphy) The New Oxford Annotated Bible with the Apocrypha, 1991; mem. editorial com.: Critical Greek New Testament, 1956-84; chmn. Am. com., Internat. Greek New Testament Project, 1970-88; sec. com. translators: Apocrypha (rev. standard version); editor: New Testament Tools and Studies, 14 vols, 1960-91, Oxford Annotated Apocrypha, 1965, enlarged edit., 1977; Reader's Digest Condensed Bible, 1982; co-editor: United Bible Societies Greek New Testament, 1966, 3d edit., 1975; compiler: Index of Articles on the New Testament and the Early Church Published in Festschriften, 1951, supplement, 1955, Lists of Words Occurring Frequently in the Coptic New Testament (Sahidic Dialect), 1961, Annotated Bibliography of the Textual Criticism of the New Testament, 1955, (with Isobel M. Metzger) Oxford Concise Concordance to the Holy Bible, 1962; contbr. articles to jours. Chmn. standard bible com. Nat. Coun. Chs., 1977—. Recipient cert. Disting. Svc. Nat. Coun. Chs., 1957, Disting. Alumnus award Lebanon Valley Coll. Alumni Assn., 1961, citation of appreciation Laymen's Nat. Bible Assn., 1986, Disting. Alumnus award Princeton Theol. Sem., 1989, lit. competition prize Christian Rsch. Found., 1955, 62, 63, E.T. Thompson award, 1991. Mem. Am. Philos. Soc., Soc. Bibl. Lit. (pres. 1970-71, past del. Am. coun. learned socs.), Am. Bible Soc. (bd. mgrs. 1948—, chmn. com. transls. 1964-70), Am. Philol. Assn., Studiorum Novi Testamenti Societas (pres. 1971-72), Cath. Bibl. Assn., N.Am. Patristic Soc. (past pres.), Am. Soc. Papyrologists; hon. fellow, corr. mem. Higher Inst. Coptic Studies, Cairo; corr. fellow Brit. Acad. Republican. Home: 20 Cleveland Ln Princeton NJ 08540 Office: Princeton Theol Sem Mercer St Princeton NJ 08542

METZLER, GLENN ELAM, minister; b. Lititz, Pa., Nov. 22, 1945; s. Elam B. and Anna Mary (Martin) M.; m. Esther G. Stoltzfus, July 1, 1967; children: Gwenda L., Millie E., Danita K., Laurel M. BA in Family Counseling, U. Maine, Augusta and Farmington, 1981. Ordained to ministry Mennonite Ch., 1985. Dir. voluntary svc. Mennonite Ch., Hallowell, Maine, 1972-74; pastor Mennonite Ch., Augusta, 1975—; chmn. New Eng. Fellowship of Mennonite Chs., 1986—; carpenter, Augusta, 1979—. Bd. mem. Maine Interfaith Flood Recovery Inc., Waterville, Maine, 1987-88. Mem. Augusta Clergy Assn. Home: R 1 Box 338 Readfield ME 04355

MEULEMAN, GEZINUS EVERT, philosophy of religion educator; b. Smilde, The Netherlands, July 8, 1925; s. Johan Hendrik and Anna A. (Kampherbeek) M.; m. Anna C. Mak, Oct. 23, 1951; children: Johan H., Catharina, Geert J., Evert A. Grad., Theol. U., Kampen, 1947; D in Theology, Free U., Amsterdam, 1951. Min. Reformed Ch., 1951—; sr. lectr. systematic theology Prot. Theol. Faculty, Aix-en-Provence, France, 1954-59; prof. theology Free U., Amsterdam, 1959-90, prof. emeritus, 1990—, dean, faculty of theology, 1966-67, 74-76, 86, vice-rector, 1967-76; pres. standing com. on external ecumenical rels. Reformed Ch. in The Netherlands, 1968-88; pres. European area World Alliance of Reformed Chs., 1973-80, mem. exec. com., 1978-89. Contbr. articles to profl. jours. Recipient Knight in the Order of the Dutch Lion, The Netherlands, 1977. Mem. Reformed Ch. Home: Michelangelostraat 65, 1077 BV Amsterdam The Netherlands Office: Free U, Dept Theology, De Boelelaan 1105, 1081 HV Amsterdam The Netherlands

MEUSCHKE, PAUL JOHN, minister; b. Castle Shannon, Pa., Dec. 11, 1927; s. John and Flora Ann (Voigtmann) M.; m. I. Lucille Lewis, May 17, 1956; children: David Paul, Eric Lewis. BA, U. Pitts., 1950; BDiv, Drew U., 1953, STM, 1954; DD (hon.), Ohio No. U., 1973. Ordained to ministry United Meth. Ch., 1953. Pastor Creighton Center (Pa.) United Meth. Ch., 1954-59, Dormont (Pa.) United Meth. Ch., 1959-64; sr. pastor Franklin Street United Meth. Ch., Johnstown, Pa., 1964-70, Baldwin Community United Meth. Ch., Pitts., 1972-78; supt. dist. Western Pa. Conf. United Meth. Ch., Pitts., 1970-72, Butler, 1978-84; sr. pastor South Ave. United Meth. Ch., Wilkinsburg, Pa., 1984—; del. NE Jurisdiction Conf., 1968, 72, 76, 80, 84, 88, 92, Gen. Conf., 1972, 80, 84, 92. Trustee Albright Coll., 1974-84; incorporator Johnstown Day Ctr., 1968; bd. incorporators Lee Hosp., Johnstown, 1968-70; pres. Zoar Home for Mothers and Children, Allison Park, Pa., 1976-78; bd. dirs. United Way, Johnstown, 1967-70. With U.S. Army, 1946-47. Mem. Lions (bd. dirs. 1966-68), Kiwanis, Rotary. Home: 1074 Old Gate Rd Pittsburgh PA 15235 Office: South Ave United Meth Ch 733 South Ave Pittsburgh PA 15221

MEWS, KURT FREDERICK, religion educator, youth minister; b. Euclid, Ohio, Aug. 1, 1962; s. Werner Kurt Frederick and Barbara Lee (Koester) M.; m. Lisa LeAnn Nicely, May 28, 1988. AA, Concordia Coll., Ann Arbor, Mich., 1982; BA magna cum laude, Concordia Coll., River Forest, Ill., 1984; postgrad., U. Mo., 1989—. Cert. Luth. tchr., dir. Christian edn. Intern dir. Christian edn. Faith Luth. Ch., Vista, Calif., 1984-85; tchr., youth min. St. John Luth. Ch., Defiance, Ohio, 1985-88; min. youth and edn. Immanuel Luth. Ch., Boonville, Mo., 1988—; group leader Luth. Ch.-Mo. Synod, St. Louis, 1988; group speaker Nat. Youth Gathering, Denver, 1989; dir. Boonslick Ch. league softball, Boonville, 1989-90; com. del. Mo. dist., St. Louis, 1990—; retreat leader Mo. dist. Youth Retreat, Concordia, Mo., 1990—. Mem. com. Boonslick area Vo-Tech. Sch., Boonville, 1989-90; speaker Parents as First Tchrs., Boonville, 1991. Mem. Luth. Edn. Assn. (pres. 1985—), Theol. Educators in Associative Ministries (pres. 1985—), Lions (sec. 1989-90). Home: 315 Walnut St Boonville MO 65233 Office: Immanuel Luth Ch RR #2 Box 179A Boonville MO 65233

MEYER, BRUCE KARL, minister; b. Coldwater, Mich., July 31, 1962; s. Robert Bruce and Beth Marie (McCracken) M.; m. Kathryn Jamie Slonaker, June 20, 1987; children: Ryan, Stephen. BA, Bob Jones U., 1984, MA, 1985; MDiv, Calvary Bapt. Theol. Sem., 1989. Ordained to ministry Bapt. Ch., 1989. Pastor Fellowship Bapt. Ch., Huffman, Tex., 1990—. Evangelism Found. Bob Jones U. grantee, 1984; named one of Outstanding Young Men of Am., 1985. Office: Fellowship Bapt Ch 24210 E Lake Houston Pkwy Huffman TX 77336-4442

MEYER, DOUGLAS LEROY, minister; b. Albert Lea, Minn., July 13, 1951; s. Donald LeRoy and Ona (Kuntson) M.; m. Christine Ann Nelson, June 22, 1975; children: Andrew Martin, Timothy Paul, Jonathan Christopher. BA in English and Philosophy, Augustana Coll., Rock Island, Ill., 1973; MDiv, Luther Theol. Seminary, St. Paul, 1977. Ordained to ministry Luth. Ch. Pastor Trinity Luth. Ch., Chgo., 1977-82, Cross of Glory Luth. Ch., Lockport, Ill., 1982—; chairperson Luth. Rsch. and Planning Coun., Chgo., 1987—, new and existing ministries subcom. No. Ill. synod Evang. Luth. Ch. Am., 1987—. Bd. dirs. Disabled Americans Rally for Equality, Chgo., 1981—; exec. bd. Rainbow coun. Boy Scouts Am., Joliet, Ill., 1988—, Trailways Girl Scout Coun., Joliet, 1988-90. Mem. Am. Acad. Religion, Soc. Bibl. Lit., Rotary. Home: 15550 Badger Ln Lockport IL 60441 Office: Cross of Glory Luth Ch 15625 Bell Rd Lockport IL 60441 *My constant struggle is to find the balance in life between that which the Gospel reveals as possible and that which humanity makes probable.*

MEYER, GREGORY JAMES, college chaplain; b. Milw., Aug. 23, 1949; s. Gordon Baird and Barbra Mary (Karnes) M.; m. Karen Lee Bravick, Aug. 7, 1971; children: Joshua Aaron, Zachary Micah Baird. BA, Carroll Coll., Waukesha, Wis., 1971; MDiv, Louisville Presbyn. Theol. Sem, Louisville, 1974; DMin, Louisville Presbyn. Theol. Sem, 1984. Chaplain/faculty Blackburn Coll., Carlinville, Ill. Home: 1006 N Charles St Carlinville IL 62626 Office: Blackburn College 700 College Ave Carlinville IL 62626

MEYER, JACOB OWEN, minister; b. Myerstown, Pa., Nov. 11, 1934; s. Jacob John and Mary May (Bross) M.; m. Velma Ruth Foreman, June 28, 1935; children—Mary E., Joseph G., Jacob C., Daniel K., Jonathan S., Rachel A., Micah D., Nathaniel A., Solomon E., Sarah A. Student Thomas A. Edison Coll., 1972-73, Evang. Sch. Theology, Myerstown, Pa., 1974-82, Inst. Holy Land Studies, Jerusalem, Israel, 1983, Dropsie Coll., 1984. Founder, pres. Assemblies of Yahweh, Bethel, Pa., 1966—, Obadiah Sch. of the Bible, Bethel, 1974—; ptnr., gen. mgr. Shalom Farm, Bethel, 1976—; editor Sacred Name Broadcaster mag., 1968—, Narrow Way mag., 1969—. Author: Commentary on Galatians, 1983, Memorial Name—Yahweh, 1987; editor Bible transl. The Sacred Scriptures-Bethel edit., 1981. Pres. Tulpehocken PTA, 1975. Office: Assemblies of Yahweh Route 1 78 E PO Drawer C Bethel PA 19507

MEYER, KENNETH MARVEN, academic administrator; b. Chgo., Nov. 27, 1932; s. Kenneth M. and Lorraine B. (Reiff) M.; m. Carol Jean Ebner, June 12, 1953; children: Keith, Kevin, Caryn. BD, Trinity Coll., 1954, MDiv, 1956; DMin., Luther Rice, 1978. Pastor Crystal Evang. Free Ch. in Am., Mpls., 1959-66, also bd. dirs.; pastor 1st Free Ch., Rockford, Ill., 1969-74; pres. Trinity Evangel Div. and Coll., Deerfield, Ill., 1974—; bd. dirs. Deerfield State Bank; chancellor Miami christian Coll.; chief exec. officer Radio WMCU, Miami, Fla. Author: Guide to Financial Planning, 1987, (monograph) Turning Point Psalms, 1981. Mem. Nat. Assn. Evangelicals. Mem. Evangelical Free Ch. Avocations: money mgmt., reading. Office: Trinity Evang Divinity Sch Office of the Pres 2065 Half Day Rd Deerfield IL 60015

MEYER, KENT ALAN, clergyman; b. Elgin, Ill., Jan. 11, 1955; s. Walter Edward Meyer and Janice (Longbrake) Vorbeck; m. Debra Ann Rosa, Dec. 18, 1981; 1 child, Mark John. BA, Macalester Coll., St. Paul, 1977; MA, U. Chgo., 1978; MDiv, Chgo. Theol. Sem., 1982; PhD, U. Chgo., 1989. Ordained to ministry United Ch. of Christ, 1984. Co-pastor Zion United Ch. Christ & Royalton Congl. United Ch. Christ, Dale, Wis., 1984-91; pastor Fed. Ch. of Green Lake (Wis.), 1991—; mem. at large exec. com. N.E. Wis. Assn., United Ch. Christ, Appleton, 1987—. Albert Palmer fellow Chgo. Theol. Sem., 1981. Mem. Am. Acad. Religion, Phi Beta Kappa. Democrat. Home: 393 Scott St Green Lake WI 54941 Office: PO Box 471 Green Lake WI 54941 *We know too much. We need to unlearn ourselves, the world, and God, and seek again to sink our roots in awe. "...for God is in heaven, and you upon earth; therefore, let your words be few." (Eccl. 5:2b).*

MEYER, LAURENCE LOUIS, clergyman; b. Rockford, Ill., Jan. 26, 1940; d. Louis John and Leona Anna (Lorenz) M.; m. Ona Ruth Klema, July 13, 1941; children—Michael Laurence, David John, Jonathan Louis Rudolph. A.A., Concordia Coll., St. Paul, 1960; B.A., Concordia Sr. Coll., 1962; M.Div., Concordia Sem., St. Louis, 1966. Ordained to ministry Lutheran Ch. Mo. Synod. 1966. Pastor, St. Peter-Bethlehem Luth. Chs., Waterville-Elysian, Minn., 1966-70, Emanuel Luth. Ch., Hamburg, Minn., 1970-82, Redeemer Lutheran Ch., Richland, Wash., 1982—; editor Minn. South Luth. Dist., Mpls., 1974-82, chmn. pub. relations, 1978-82; pastoral advisor Minn. South Luth. Laymen League, 1979-82; mem. stewardship com. N.W. Dist. Luth. Ch., Portland, Oreg, 1984-86, mem. communications com., 1984—, 5th v.p. N.W. dist., 1985—, chmn. property mgmt. com., 1986—. Contbr. articles to Luth. Witness mag., 1974-83, Northwest Passage mag. Home: 518 Thayer Dr Richland WA 99352

MEYER, LESTER ALLEN, minister; b. Beaver, Okla., Apr. 26, 1923; s. James Lester and Leah Rachel (Fox) M.; m. Mattie Ada Cozart; children: Carol, Richard, Annette. BA, Phillips U., 1948; ThM, So. Meth. U., 1950; DD (hon.), Okla. City U., 1970. Ordained to ministry Meth. Ch., 1950. Minister Trinity Meth. Ch., Enid, Okla., 1950-56; minister Meth. Ch., Comanche, Okla., 1956-59, Broken Arrow, Okla., 1959-62; minister Edmond (Okla.) Meth. Ch., 1962-65, Linwood Meth. ch., Oklahoma City, 1965-70; dir. Conf. Coun. on Ministries, Okla., 1970-73; dist. supt. Stillwater (Okla.) Dist., 1973-76, Tulsa Dist., 1976-79; sr. minister United Meth. Ch. of Nicols Hills, Oklahoma City, 1979-85; dist. supt. Okla. City North Dist., 1985—.

With USN, 1942-45. Democrat. Avocations: drama, sailing, travel. Home and Office: 1231 Kenilworth Oklahoma City OK 73114

MEYER, MARSHALL THEODORE, rabbi; b. N.Y.C., Mar. 25, 1930; s. Isaac and Anita Sarah (Silberstein) M.; m. Naomi Friedman, June 19, 1955; children: Anita Sara, Dodi Daniela, Gabriel Isaac. AB, Dartmouth Coll., 1952, LHD (honoris causa), 1982; M of Hebrew Lit., Jewish Theol. Sem., 1958; postgrad., Hebrew U., Jerusalem, 1955-56, Columbia U., 1957-59, Union Theol. Sem., 1957-59; DST (honoris causa), Jewish Theol Sem. Am., 1981; DD (honoris causa), Kalamazoo Coll., 1985; DHL honoris causa, Hebrew Union Coll., 1990. Ordained rabbi, 1958. Founder, rector Sem. Rabinico Latinoamericano, Buenos Aires, 1962; founder, sr. rabbi Community Bet El, Buenos Aires, 1963; sr. rabbi Congregation B'Nai Jeshurun, N.Y.C.; spl. counsel to chancellor Jewish Theol. Sem. Am., N.Y.C.; Latin Am. dir. World Coun. Synagogues, 1961; founder, dir. Camp Ramah, Cordoba, Argentina, 1964; cons. Secretariat Human Devel. and Family, Dept. Health, Govt. of Argentina; mem. exec. theol. cons. com. Argentine Nat. Inst. Mental Health; mem. internat. editorial adv. com. population reports George Washington U. Med. Ctr.; mem. bd. govs. N.Y. Bd. Rabbis. Editor: Jewish Liturgy, 1968, Social and Religious History of the Jews (Salo W. Baron), 1969, 8 vols.; mem. editorial bd. Cuadernos, 1970—; founder, editor Ediciones Seminario Rabinico Latinoamericano, Maj'shavot; founder, editor: Library of Science and History of Religions, Editorial Paidos. Apptd. to Nat. Commn. for Disappeared Persons, Buenos Aires; founding co-pres. Jewish Movement for Human Rights, Buenos Aires; bd. dirs. Joint Distbn. Com., Am. Com. for Israel Peace Ctr., Am.'s Watch, U.S. Interreligious Com. for Peace in Mid. East, Homes for the Homeless, West Side Community Coun., Witness for Peace, Ctr. on Violence and Human Survival at John Jay Coll. Criminal Justice, Christianity and Crisis, Jewish Fund for Justice, Mazon, Partnership of Faith in N.Y.C., Tucker Found.; other orgns.; bd. visitors Dartmouth Coll.; mem. presdl. commn. Argentine Permanent Assembly for Human Rights; founding mem. higher Inst. Religious Studies in Ecumenical Affairs, Buenos Aires. Decorated Order of Liberator San Martin (Argentina); recipient L'Dor award Internat. B'nai Brith, 1984, Human Rights award New Jewish Agenda, 1985, Maimonides prize Instituto Superior de Estudio Religiosos, 1987, Louis D. Brandeis award Am.-Israeli Civil Liberties Coalition, 1990; sr. fellow Dartmouth Coll., 1951-52, Reynolds fellow, 1955-56, Montgomery fellow, 1991; Merrill fellow, Harvard Sch. Div., 1992. Mem. Rabbinical Assembly, Argentine Inst. Higher Religious Studies (founder). Office: Congregation B'Nai Jeshurun 270 W 89th St New York NY 10024

MEYER, MARVIN WAYNE, academic administrator, religion educator; b. Grand Rapids, Mich., Apr. 16, 1948; s. Martin and June (Van Ostenburg) M.; m. Bonita Kay Bratt, Dec. 30, 1969; children: Stephen Frederick, Jonathan James, Elisabeth Anne. AB, Calvin Coll., 1970; MDiv, Calvin Theol. Sem., 1974; PhD, Claremont (Calif.) Grad. Sch., 1979. Griset chair dept. religion, assoc. prof. religion Chapman Coll., Orange, Calif., 1985—. Author: The Letter of Peter to Philip, 1981, The Secret Teachings of Jesus, 1984, (with others) Q-Thomas Reader, 1990; editor: The Ancient Mysteries, 1987; contbr. articles to profl. jours. Mem. Am. Acad. Religion, Am. Rsch. Ctr. in Egypt, Coptic Magical Texts Project Inst. for Antiquity and Christianity, Jesus Seminar, Internat. Assn. for Coptic Studies, Soc. Bibl. Lit. Home: 2544 E Jackson Orange CA 92667 Office: Chapman Coll Dept Religion 333 N Glassell Orange CA 92666

MEYER, MICHAEL ALBERT, historian, educator; b. Berlin, Nov. 15, 1937; came to U.S., 1941; s. Charles Matthaeus and Susanne Paula (Frey) M.; m. Margaret Jane Mayer, June 25, 1961; children: Daniel Alexander, Jonathan Eugene, Rebecca Ellen. BA, UCLA, 1959; BHL, Hebrew Union Coll., 1960, PhD, 1964. Asst. prof. Hebrew Union Coll., L.A., 1964-67; assoc. prof. Hebrew Union Coll., Cin., 1968-72, prof. Jewish history, 1972—; vis. asst. prof. UCLA, 1965-67; vis. sr. lectr. Haifa (Israel) U., 1970-71, Ben Gurion U., Beersheba, Israel, 1971-72; vis. prof. Hebrew U., Jerusalem, 1977-78. Author: Origins of the Modern Jew, 1967, Ideas of Jewish History, 1974, Response to Modernity, 1988, Jewish Identity in the Modern World, 1990. Am. Coun. Learned Socs. fellow, 1982. Fellow Am. Acad. Jewish Rsch.; mem. Leo Baeck Inst. (exec. com. 1985—, internat. pres. 1991—). Democrat. Jewish. Avocation: tennis. Home: 1031 Avondale Ave Cincinnati OH 45229 Office: Hebrew Union Coll 3101 Clifton Ave Cincinnati OH 45220

MEYER, MICHAEL MARTIN, religion educator; b. Cleve., Dec. 19, 1945; s. Joseph Henry and Constance (Atkinson) M.; m. Margaret Mary Leaver, June 22, 1974; 1 child, Joseph Ivo. BA, St. Charles Borromeo, Wickliffe, Ohio, 1967; MA, U. Detroit, 1970; D Ministry, Ecumenical Theol. Ctr., Detroit, 1987. Ordained deacon Roman Cath. Ch., 1970, cert. pastoral min., 1983. Dir. religious edn. Archdiocese of Detroit, 1971-73, 75—; tchr. religion Gilmour Acad., Gates Mills, Ohio, 1973-75; moderator Archdiocesan Pastoral Coun., Detroit, 1985-87. Trustee Novi Community Sch. Dist. Bd., 1983—. Paul Harris fellow, Rotary Internat., Novi, 1988. Mem. Am. Fed. Musicians, Singing Artist (local 5), Nat. Sch. Bd. Assn., Nat. Cath. Edn. Assn. Home: 41088 Malott Novi MI 48375 Office: Our Lady Good Counsel 1151 William St Plymouth MI 48170

MEYER, PAUL WILLIAM, biblical literature educator emeritus; b. Raipur, India, May 31, 1924; s. Armin Frederick and Hulda Dorothea (Klein) M.; m. Mary Louise Yonker, Sept. 3, 1948; children—Katherine Priode, Elizabeth Cooper. B.A., Elmhurst Coll., 1945; B.D., Union Theol. Sem., 1949, Th.D., 1955. Instr. Union Theol. Sem., N.Y.C., 1952-54; asst. prof. Div. Sch., Yale U., New Haven, 1954-62; assoc. prof. Div. Sch., Yale U., 1962-64; prof. N.T. interpretation Colgate Rochester (N.Y.) Div. Sch., 1964-70; prof. N.T. Div. Sch., Vanderbilt U., Nashville, 1970-78; Helen H.P. Manson prof. N.T. lit. Princeton (N.J.) Theol. Sem., 1978-89, prof. emeritus, 1989—; adj. prof. dept. religious studies Univ. N.C., Chapel Hill, 1989—. Served with U.S. Army, 1943-45. Morse fellow Yale U., 1961-62; Fulbright research grantee U. Gottingen, W. Ger., 1961-62. Mem. Soc. Bibl. Lit. and Exegesis, Studiorum Novi Testamenti Societas, Am. Theol. Soc., AAUP. Presbyterian.

MEYER, RICHARD CHRISTOPHER, clergyman; b. Hilo, Hawaii, July 1, 1948; s. Christopher Edward Meyer and Betty Ann (Brandt) Cardona; m. Trudy Castleman Meyer, Sept. 25, 1970; children: Joshua James, Jennifer Joy. BA, UCLA, 1970; MDiv, Fuller Theol. Sem., 1975. Ordained to ministry Presbyn. Ch., 1975. Assoc. pastor West Hills Presbyn. Ch., Omaha, 1975-81; pastor Brookings (Oreg.) Presbyn. Ch., 1981-83, West Hills Presbyn. Ch., Omaha, 1983—; conf. speaker Faith at Work, Columbia, Md., 1986—; small group cons., 1984—. Author: One Anothering, 1990; author Faith at Work mag. column, 1982—. Office: West Hills Presbyn Ch 3015 82d Ave Omaha NE 68124

MEYER, SISTER ROBERTA, school system administrator. Supt. schs. Diocese of Lubbock, Tex. Office: Office of Schs Supt PO Box 98700 Lubbock TX 79499*

MEYERS, ALAN GORDON, religion educator, minister; b. St. Louis, Dec. 1, 1947; s. Ellis Leonard and Melba Belle (Sharp) M.; m. Rosemary Casey, June 14, 1969. BA, Princeton U., 1969; MDiv, Princeton Sem., 1972; PhD, Union Theol. Sem. Va., 1987. Ordained to ministry Presbyn. Ch. (U.S.A.), 1972. Stated supply minister Westminster Presbyn. Ch., Troy, N.Y., 1972-75; pastor United Presbyn. Ch., Lawrence, Mass., 1975-81; parish assoc. Oak Hill Presbyn. Ch., St. Louis, 1990—; asst. prof. Lindenwood Coll., St. Charles, Mo., 1989—. Mem. Celestial Intervention Agy., St. Louis. Mem. AAUP, Am. Acad. Religion. Home: 1108 Des Peres Ave Saint Louis MO 63119 Office: Lindenwood Coll 209 S Kings Hwy Saint Charles MO 63301 *Prayer plus sensible action is a better policy than either prayer alone or action alone.*

MEYERS, CAROL LYONS, theology educator; b. Wilkes Barre, Pa., Nov. 26, 1942; d. Harry J. and Irene R. (Winkler) Lyons; m. Eric Mark Meyers, June 25, 1964; children: Julie Kaete, Dina Elisa. AB with honors, Wellesley Coll., 1964; MA in Near Ea. and Judaic Studies, Brandeis U., 1966, PhD, 1975. Area supr. Joint Expdn. to Tell Gezer, Israel, 1964-67; editorial asst., asst. to registrar Ashdod Excavation Project, Israel, 1963, 64-65; quadrangle dir. Brandeis U., Waltham, Mass., 1965-67; teaching asst. Boston Area Seminar Internat. Students, 1965; area supr., lect. Joint Expdn. to Khirbet Shema, Israel, 1970-71, area supr., 1971, field supr., 1972; assoc. dir. Joint Expdn. to Meiron, Israel, 1978; co-dir. Joint Sepphoris Project, Israel, 1985—; instr. Bible Acad. Jewish Studies without Walls, N.Y.C., 1974-78; instr. Ctr. Continuing Edn., Duke U., Durham., N.C., 1978-79; asst. prof. religion Duke U., Durham., N.C., 1977-84, assoc. prof., 1984-90, assoc. dir. women's studies, 1985-90, prof., 1990—, acting dir. women's studies, 1992. Author: The Tabernacle Menorah, 1976, Excavations at Ancient Meiron, Upper Galilee, Israel, 1971-72, 74-75, 77, The Word of the Lord Shall Go Forth, 1983, Haggai, Zechariah 1-8, 1987, Discovering Eve: Ancient Israelite Women in Context, 1988, Sepphoris, 1991; contbr. articles to profl. jours. Bd. dirs. Bethel Community, Durham, 1980. Wellesley Coll. scholar, 1962-64, Brandeis U. fellow, 1967-69, Thayer fellow Albright Inst. Archaeol. Rsch., Jerusalem, 1975-76, NEH Fellow 1982-83, 90-91, Oxford Ctr. for Postgrad. Hebrew Studies fellow, 1982-83, Queen Elizabeth House fellow, U. Oxford, 1982-83, Howard Found. fellow, 1984-85, Ctr. Theol. Inquiry fellow, 1990-91, Dduke Rsch. Coun. 1988, 90; grantee Ednl. Found. Girls, 1963, 64, Brandeis U., 1966, Undergrad. Teaching Coun. Duke U., 1978-79, Coop. Program In Judaic Studies, 1981. Mem. Jewish Fedn., Am. Acad. Religion, Am. Sch. Oriental Rsch. (fellowship com. 1979-82, editorial com. 1978—), Archaeol. Inst. Am. (v.p. 1976, sec. treas. 1984—), Assn. Jewish Studies, Brit. Sch. Archaeology Jerusalem, Cath. Bibl. Assn., Albright Inst. Archaeol. Rsch. (v.p. 1972—), Israel Exploration Soc., Soc. Bibl. Lit. (steering com. seminar on monarchy 1982), chmn. seminar 1981), Nat. Women's Studies Assn., Soc. for Values Higher Edn., Hadassah (edn. chmn. 1970-71). Mem. Jewish Reconstructionist Ch. Home: 3202 Waterbury Dr Durham NC 27707 Office: Duke U Dept Religion PO Box 4735 Durham NC 27706

MEYERS, OUIDGA LORIS MOORE, church administrator; b. Kingsville, Tex., Aug. 21, 1944; d. Edward McCutcheon Jr. and Georgia Graves (Martin) Moore; m. Charles Jack Meyers, June 27, 1968; children: Christy Julianne, Misty Kethleen, Charles Andrew. Student, Arlington State Coll., 1963-65. Cert. lay speaker, 1985. Sec. Ch. of Good Shepherd, Arlington, Tex., 1962-64, Arlington State Coll., Wesley Found., 1964-65, Epworth Meth. Ch., Arlington, 1965-66, Met. Bd. Missions, Ft. Worth, 1966-67, W.F. Dist. United Meth. Ch., Wichita Falls, Tex., 1987-90; adminstrv. asst. to min. 1st United Meth. Ch., Wichita Falls, 1990—; sec. to bd. dirs., Mid. State U., Wesley Found., 1990—; dir. worship, Bd. Discipleship, North Tex. Conf., United Meth. Ch., 1990—. Writer of musical plays. Mem. Mins. Wives (v.p. 1984-85). Democrat. Home: 2309 Hayes Wichita Falls TX 76309 Office: 1st United Meth Ch 909 10th St Wichita Falls TX 76307

MEYERS, RAYMOND FRANCIS, JR., youth minister, safety engineer; b. Pitts., Aug. 20, 1960; s. Raymond F. and Janet A. (Baltos) M. Student, U. Pitts., 1978-79, 82-83; BSChemE, Grove City Coll., 1982. Tchr. religious edn. St. Patrick's Ch., Dallas, 1985-89, leader jr. youth group, 1988-90; tchr. religious edn. St. John Neumann Ch., Charlotte, N.C., 1987-88, Good Shepherd Ch., Cin., 1990—; loss prevention engr. Quantum Chem. Corp., Cin., 1990—. Mem. Soc. Fire Protection Engrs., Am. Inst. Chem. Engrs., Nat. Fire Protection Assn. Home: 8347 Rollinghitch Ct Maineville OH 45039

MEYERS, RONALD ROY, educator; b. New Castle, Ind., July 25, 1944; s. Harold Lloyd and Lucile Gertrude (Good) M.; m. Charlotte Alice Holmes, Oct. 28, 1945; children: Daniel Paul, Aaron Joel. BTh, Mt. Vernon Bible Coll., 1966; MA, Fuller Theol. Sem., 1983; MDiv, Asian Ctr. Theol. Studies, 1986; PhD in Intercultural Studies, Fuller Theol. Sem., 1989. Ordained to ministry Internat. Ch. Foursquare Gospel, 1969. Asst. pastor Foursquare Gospel Ch., Gettysburg, Pa., 1966-68; pastor Foursquare Gospel Ch., Durham, Ontario, Can., 1968-73; prof. Foursquare Gospel Mission, Taejon, Korea, 1973-78; adminstr. Foursquare Gospel Mission, Seoul, Korea, 1979-86; founding pastor Foursquare Gospel Ch., Doylestown, Pa., 1986-89; prof., adminstr. N.Y. Worl Mission Theol. Coll., N.Y.C., 1989-91; prof. intercultural studies Beijing, 1991—; sec., Eastern Coun. Foursquare Chs., Seoul, 1984-86. Republican. Address: PO Box 4296 Lincoln NE 68504

MHELAN, SIR MUHAMMAD, religious organization executive. Chief justice, pres. Supreme Muslim Secular Coun., Amman, Jordan. Office: Chief Justice & Pres Suppreme, Muslim Secular Coun, Amman Jordan*

MICALLEF, FRANCIS, bishop. Vicar apostolic, titular bishop of Tinia in Proconsulari Roman Cath. Ch., Kuwait City. Office: Bishop's House, POB 255, 13003 Safat Kuwait City Kuwait*

MICELI, MOTHER IGNATIUS, missionary sister; b. N.Y.C., Mar. 14, 1918; d. Joseph and Cecelia (Torre) M. BS, Regis Coll.; MEd, Loyola U., New Orleans; M Religious Edn., Seattle U.; postgrad., U. Denver, 1968-69. Coordinator religious programs All Souls Ch., Englewood, Colo., 1968-71, dir. home instr. for adults, 1971-72, dir. adult edn., 1972—; dir. religious edn. Assumption, Welby, Colo., 1973-77, Holy Cross, Thornton, Colo., 1971-73; instr. religion various missions, 1968—. Author: (poems) Leaves Of Thought, 1980, Random Thoughts and Meditations, 1968, Colorado and St. Francis Xavier Cabrini, M.S.C., poetry and photography book Life's Seasons; VCR The Life of Mother Cabrini, The History and Meditations on the Rosary. Mem. Internat. Bibl. Assn., Religious Edn. Assn. U.S., Religious Edn. Assn. Can., Kappa Delta Pi. Avocations: photography, camping, hiking, fishing, jeeping. Home: Cabrini Shrine Golden CO 80401 Office: All Souls Ch Religious Edn Office 435 Pennwood Circle Englewood CO 80110

MICHAEL, CHARLES RICHARD, minister; b. Ardmore, Ala., Sept. 19, 1955; s. Charles Billy and Dorthea (Fogg) M.; m. Deborah Lynn Ruf, Aug. 22, 1975; children: Erin Paige, Chad Bryant. BS in Religion, Athens State Coll., 1979; MRE, So. Bapt. Theol. Sem., 1981. Ordained to ministry So. Bapt. Conv., 1979. Pastor English Bapt. Ch., Hardinsburg, Ky., 1979-81, Bethel Bapt. Ch., Anderson, Ala., 1981-90; assoc. pastor First Bapt. Ch., Athens, Ala., 1990—. Home: PO Box 1378 Athens AL 35611 Office: First Bapt Ch PO Box 529 201 E Hobbs Athens AL 35611

MICHAEL, R(ANDALL) BLAKE, religion educator, writer, minister; b. Lexington, N.C., Aug. 17, 1948; s. Flynn Leonard and Dorothy Lee (Koontz) M.; m. Marlyn Compton Albright, July 25, 1970; 1 child, Meredith Cameron. BA in Sociology with highest honor, U. N.C., 1970; MDiv magna cum laude, Harvard U., 1972, AM in Comparative Religion, 1975, PhD in Comparative Religion, 1979; student Mysore U., India, 1975-76. Teaching fellow in history of religion Harvard U., Cambridge, Mass., 1974-76; teaching asst. in religious studies Brown U., Providence, 1976-78; instr. religion Ohio Wesleyan U., Delaware, 1978-79, asst. prof., 79-84, assoc. prof., 1984-91, Swan-Collins-Allen prof., 1991—, chmn. dept. religion, 1981-86, dir. off-campus programs, 1984-87, 89—; adj. asst. prof. Meth. Theol. Sch., Delaware, 1983-88. Author: The Origins of Virasaiva Sects, 1991; contbr. articles to profl. jours. Rotary Internat. Travelling fellow, Mysore, 1976; research grantee NEH, 1982, faculty devel. grantee Ohio Wesleyan U., 1983, 88. Mem. Am. Acad. Religion, Assn. Asian Studies, Ohio Acad. Religion, Kiwanis, Phi Beta Kappa. United Methodist. Avocations: camera and car collection, soccer, swimming. Office: Ohio Wesleyan Univ Dept Religion 50 S Henry St Delaware OH 43015

MICHAEL, STANLEY REGINALD, minister; b. St. John's, Antiqua, Apr. 14, 1944; came to U.S., 1970; s. Maurice E. and Lillian (Davis) M.; m. Annette Maerie Walwyn, Dec. 20, 1970; children: Sharon, June, Marlene. AA, Caribbean Union Coll., Trinidad and Tobago, 1969; BA, Oakwood Coll., Huntsville, Ala., 1977; MA, Andrews U., 1978; PhD, Boston U., 1985. Ordained to ministry Seventh-day Adventists, 1973. Pastor Seventh-day Adventist Ch., V.I., 1969-77, 85-86; tchr. Seventh-day Adventist High Sch., V.I., 1981-83; sem. prof. U. East Africa, Kenya, 1988; pastor Flatbush Seventh-day Adventist Ch., Bklyn., 1989—. Mem. Assn. for Sociology of Religion, Soc. for Sci. Study Religion. Home: 118 Patterson Ave Hempstead NY 11550 Office: Flatbush Seventh-day Adventist Ch 261 E 21st St Brooklyn NY 11226 *Among life's greatest gifts is time. Use it wisely.*

MICHAEL, STANLEY VERMONT, religious organization administrator; b. Berkeley Springs, W.Va., June 29, 1928; s. Oakley Alston and Lola Emma (Widmeyer) M.; m. Ruth Uldene Kerr, Sept. 1, 1951; children: Starla Renee' Michael Blair, LaVonne Janee' Michael McDaniel. Ministerial cert., Cen. Bible Coll., 1950. Co-pastor Assembly of God, Hartville, Mo., 1950; pianist/quartet Assemblies of God Youth Dept., Springfield, Mo., 1950-51; assoc. pastor Lindale Assembly of God, Houston, 1951-53; pastor Donna (Tex.) Assembly of God, 1953-54; organist, clerk Sun. Sch. dept. Gen. Coun. Assemblies of God, Springfield, 1954-55, promotions coord. radio dept., 1955-65, nat. sec. benevolence/stewardship, 1966-69, nat. sec. benevolences dept., 1969—; v.p., sec. Bethany Retirement Home, Lakeland, Fla., 1966-85, Hillcrest Children's Home, Hot Springs, Ark., 1966—, Highlands Child Placement Svcs., Kans. City, Mo., 1966—; exec. com., bd. dirs. Nat. Interfaith Coalition on Aging, Athens, Ga., 1973—. Editor: Caring, 1966—; contbr. articles to profl. jours. Chaplain Ozark Squadron Confederate Air Force, Springfield, 1989—. Republican. Avocations: Lincoln momentos, small glass items, coins. Home: 3030 E Rocklyn Springfield MO 65804 Office: Assemblies of God 1445 Boonville Springfield MO 65802

MICHAELS, GENEVA LANE, lay worker, retired elementary school administrator; b. Dayton, Ohio, June 27, 1929; d. William Bert and Ethel Lee (Jackson) O'Neal; m. James Edward Michaels, Oct. 6, 1951 (dec. Mar. 1989); children: Ethel Adeline, Geneva Lee, Jamie Bert. Student, Cedarville Coll., 1952-54, Liberty Bible Home Inst., Lynchburg, Va., 1991, Zola Levitt Jewish Christian Inst., Dallas, 1991. Dir. youth, tchr. Bible, musician Ft. McKinley (Ohio) Bapt. Ch., 1952-56; dir. youth, musician Sidney (Ohio) Bapt. Ch., 1957-59; tchr. Bible, musician Hope Bapt. Ch., Kettering, Ohio, 1959-64; dir. youth Liberty Bapt. Ch., Xenia, Ohio, 1978-82, tchr. Bible, head of music, Gospel soloist, musician, 1978—; sec. Huffman Elem. Sch., Dayton, 1964-65, pres., 1965-70. Recipient cert. and blue ribbon Ohio State PTA, 1964-65, 67. Mem. Smithsonian Instn. Republican. Home: 417 Huffman Ave Dayton OH 45403 Office: Liberty Bapt Ch 44 Kinsey Rd Xenia OH 45385 *As a teenager, I was presented with the statement, "In later life, I'll win or lose, depending on how, now I choose." I believe life is a trust from Almighty God, and my life is either a stepping stone or a stumbling block, thereby touching lives along the way. I have chosen to be a stepping stone as I pass through life, and hope others can say they are blessed for having known me.*

MICHAELS, JAMES E., bishop. Office: St Francis De Sales Parish 614 S Oakwood Ave Beckley WV 25801

MICHAELSEN, APRIL LYNN, minister; b. Sept. 19, 1957; d. Herman Frederick Michaelsen and Florence Virginia (Rapp) Gattanella. BA, Fairleigh Dickinson U., 1979, MA, 1983; MDiv, Luth. Theol. Sem., 1987. Ordained to ministry Evang. Luth. Ch. in Am., 1987. Asst. pastor Nativity Luth. Ch., Reading, Pa., 1987-88; pastor Sons of Zebedee Luth. Ch., Saltsburg, Pa., 1988—. Office: Sons of Zebedee Luth Ch 422 Salt St Saltsburg PA 15681

MICHALKO, JÁN, bishop; b. Važec, East Slovakia, Oct. 16, 1912; s. Ján Michalko and Anna (Duranová) Michalková; m. Alžbeta Škovranová, Apr. 6, 1946; children: Alžbeta Darina, Viera, Ján Vladimír, Ludmila. BA in Theology, Slovak Luth. Sem., Czechoslovakia, 1937, ThD, 1946, ThD (honoris causa), 1989; ThD (honoris causa), Friedrich Schiller U., Fed. Republic Germany, 1963; PhD (honoris causa), Christian Theol. Acad., Poland, 1974, Evang. Theol. Acad., Hungary, 1978, Muhlenberg Coll., 1988, Orthodox Theol. Sem., Czechoslovakia, 1988. Ordained to ministry Slovak Evang. Luth. Ch. Czechoslovakia. Clergyman Slovak Evang. Luth. Ch. Czechoslovakia, Važec, 1937; clergyman parish office Slovak Evang. Luth. Ch. Czechoslovakia, Bratislava, 1937-38; clergyman Slovak Evang. Luth. Ch. Czechoslovakia, Spišská Nová Ves, 1938-42, Pozdišovce, 1942-47, Myslenice, 1947-54, Rača, 1954-59; clergyman Slovak Evang. Luth. Ch. Czechoslovakia, Bratislava, 1959-70, gen. bishop, 1970-90; prof. systematic and practical theology Slovak Luth. Sem., Bratislava, 1953; chmn. com. of liturgy and spiritual life Luth. World Fedn., Geneva, 1965-77, mem. exec. com., 1970-76; chmn. liturgical com. Slovak Evang. Luth. Ch. Czechoslovakia, Bratislava, 1970-90, mem. com. for preparation of 1st Slovak lang. hymnal; chmn. com. mgmt. Tranoscius pub. house, LiptovskY Mikulás, Czechoslovakia, 1970-90; mem. com. of world's mission and evangelization World Coun. Chs., 1957-90; mem. com. Leuenberg Dialogues. Author: Kázňové smery v evanjelickej cirkvi, 1955; also articles; editor: Evanjelická Postila, Cirkevné listy jour., 1952-64; editor in chief Služba slova, 1952-90; prime leader, mem. com. of 1st transl. of Bible into modern Slovak lang., 1977. Mem. com. Found. Dr. Martin Niemüller, Wiesbaden, Fed. Republic Germany, Theol. Sem. Mem. Societas Ethica, Conf. European Chs. Address: For estate of Ján Michalko, Vlčkova 1, 811 06 Bratislava Czechoslovakia *Died Dec. 10, 1990.*

MICHALKO, RUTH GRUPE, music minister; b. Park Ridge, Ill., Aug. 2, 1927. Student, Liberty U., Concordia U. Organist Barrington (Ill.) Bible, 1941—; pianist Chippewa Falls (Wis.) Bible Ch., 1949-51; music tchr. Studio, High Sch. Edn., Chgo., 1956-73; pianist VFW 3579, Park Ridge, 1960—; dir. music, sec. St. Stephen Luth. Ch., Shelby, Mich., 1989—. Editor: (newsletter) Ch. News, 1989; (tract) Fishy, 1991. Mem. Assn. Luth. Ch. Musicians (liturgical organist), VFW Aux. (v.p., chmn. North Port, Fla. chpt. 1977-81), Am. Legion Aux. (pres. 9th dist. 1975). Home: 317 N Michigan Ave Shelby MI 49455 Office: St Stephens Luth Church 7400 W Johnson Rd Shelby MI 49455

MICHAUD, HILDA JEAN, religious education director; b. Sheridan, Maine, Aug. 21, 1937; d. Eugene Fred and Eva May (Prue) Damboise; m. Ralph J. Michaud, Aug. 10, 1957 (dec. July 1985); children: Laura Doherty, Ralph J. Jr., Elizabeth A. BS, U. Maine, Presque Isle, 1967. Cert. elem. edn. Cath. Youth Orgn. moderator St. Denis Cath. Youth Orgn. Youth Group, Ft. Fairfield, Maine, 1974-84; twilight encounter leader Christian Life Ctr., Caribou, Maine, 1975-79; Eucharistic min. St. Denis Parish, Ft. Fairfield, 1981—, lector of the word, 1982—, parish coun. pres., 1988—, dir. religious edn., 1988—, dir., tchr. in home pre-sch., 1988—, lay pres. for communion svcs., 1991—, mem. leadership tng.-core team for renewal program, 1991—; Ultreya leader for Cursillo Group; mem. healing team Holy Rosary Ch., Sacred Heart Ch. Bd. mem. Am. Heart Assn., Cary Med. Ctr., Caribou, 1986—. Mem. NEA, Maine Tchrs. Assn., Region I Catechetical Leaders, Am. Assn. Ret. Persons, Jr. C. of C. Wives (Ft. Fairfield v.p. 1965-66), Ft. Fairfield (Maine) Tchrs. Club (v.p. 1982-83). Office: St Denis Parish 43 Main St Fort Fairfield ME 04742 *Where would we be in this world if it were not for the love of friends? You can not put a price tag on a valuable friendship, only treasure it always.*

MICHEL, THOMAS FRANCIS, religion educator; b. St. Louis, Feb. 5, 1941; s. Victor James and Bernadette Bridget (Fox) M. BA, Cardinal Glennon Coll., 1963; M Religious Edn., Kenrick Sem., 1967; PhD, U. Chgo., 1978. Mem. Soc. of Jesus (Jesuits). Lectr. Northwestern U., Evanston, Ill., 1974-75; asst. prof. Columbia U., N.Y.C., 1977-78; prof. Inst. Filsafat Teologi, Yogyakarta, Indonesia, 1978-85, Gregorian U., Rome, 1986-88; ofcl. Pontifical Coun. Interreligious Dialogue, Vatican City, 1981-89; vis. prof. St. Paul Sem., Davao, Philippines, 1982-83, Dansalan Coll., Marawi City, Philippines, 1983; counsellor for Islamic affairs, Soc. Jesus, Rome, 1984-88. Author: A Muslim Theologian's Response to Christianity, 1985, Analytical Index of Bulletin, 1987; editor: Islam: Continuity and Change, 1987; author 65 articles in field. Fulbright Hays rsch./Am. Rsch. Ctr. grantee, Egypt, 1976; Fulbright teaching fellow Ankara U., Dokuz Eylul U. and Selçuk U., Turkey, 1986-89. Democrat. Roman Catholic. Home: Borgo S Spirito 5, 00193 Rome Italy Office: Pontifical Council, Interreligious Dialogue, 00120 Vatican City Vatican City

MICHELMAN, HENRY D., rabbi. Exec. v.p. Synagogue Coun. Am., N.Y.C. Office: Synagogue Coun Am 237 Lexington Ave New York NY 10016*

MICHELSEN, CLIFFORD STANLEY, clergyman, former missionary; b. Mpls., June 14, 1913; s. Marcus and Marie Johanna (Ophus) M.; m. Lillian Augusta Shervey, Nov. 26, 1949; children—Craig Sheldon, Cheryl Susan; 1 child by previous marriage—Gerald Everett. C.Th., Luther Sem.-St. Paul, 1949; M.A., Sch. World Mission, 1969. Ordained to ministry Am. Lutheran Ch., 1962. Missionary, The Sudan Mission, Am. Luth. Ch., Cameroon, 1951-75, supt. mission, 1969-75; founder Evang. Luth. Ch. of Senegal, 1975-80; dir. l'Eglise Evangelique Lutherienne du Senegal, Dakar, Senegal, 1983-84; ret., 1985; now vis. pastor Living Word Luth. Ch., Mpls. Republican. Home: 5209 36 Ave S Minneapolis MN 55417

MICHENER, DAVID LAWRENCE, JR., minister; b. Willoughby, Ohio, July 12, 1962; s. David Lawrence and Freda Marie (Short) M.; m. Donna Ann Loveless, June 2, 1984; children: David Lawrence III, Dustin Jeremiah. BS in Bible, Bapt. Bible Coll., Clarks Summit, Pa., 1984. Ordained to ministry Gen. Assn. Regular Bapt. Chs., 1986. Assoc. pastor 1st Bapt. Ch., Johnson City, N.Y., 1984—; youth speaker, mem. youth adv. bd. Gen. Assn. Regular Bapt. Chs., Schaumburg, Ill., 1990—; curriculum cons. to Bapt. press, 1989—. Contbr. articles to denominational publs. Bd. dirs. Vision for Youth, 1985—; soccer coach Johnson City High Sch., 1987-89. Mem. Rutherford Inst., Wildcat Friends and Alumni Assn. Office: 1st Bapt Ch 12 Baldwin St Johnson City NY 13790

MICHON, HUBERT, archbishop. Archbishop of Rabat Roman Cath. Ch., Morocco. Office: Archeveche, 1 reu Abou Inane, BP 258, Rabat Morocco*

MICKELSEN, SISTER COLLEEN, religion educator, nun; b. Kenmare, N.D., Aug. 23, 1949; d. Lawrence Harvey and Colleen Unice (Johnson) M. AA, Assumption Coll., Richardton, N.D., 1971; BS in Elem. Edn., English, U. Mary, Bismarck, N.D., 1975; MA in Edn., Coll. St. Thomas, St. Paul, 1987. Joined Benedictine Sisters, Roman Cath. Ch., 1968. 3d and 4th grade tchr. St. Nicholas Sch., Garrison, N.D., 1971-73; 3d grade tchr. St. Leo Sch., Minot, N.D., 1973-74; 1st and 2nd grade tchr., prin. St. Nicholas Sch., 1975-81; 4th grade tchr. St. Patrick's Sch., Dickinson, N.D., 1981-86; 7th, 8th grade tchr. St. Mary's Sch., Malta, Mont., 1986-91; master tchr. St. Patrick Sch., 1984-86; trustee, chmn. Marillac Bd. Dirs., Bismark, N.D., 1981-86; trustee, sec. Sacred Heart Priory Bd., Richardton, 1981-86. Contbr. articles on edn. to home newspapers, poetry to jours. Home: 9516th St W Dickinson ND 58601

MICKELSON, ARNOLD RUST, church commission executive, consultant; b. Finley, N.D., Jan. 8, 1922; s. Alfred B. and Clara (Rust) M.; m. Marjorie Arveson, June 8, 1944; 1 son, Richard. BA, Concordia Coll., Moorhead, Minn., 1943, LLD (hon.), 1972; LLD (hon.), Calif. Luth. U., 1983, Luther Coll., 1987. Owner, mgr. Luther Book Store, Decorah, Iowa, 1946-48; credit supr. Gen. Motors Acceptance Corp., Fargo, N.D., 1948-53; mgr. Epko Film Service, Fargo, 1953-58; asst. to pres. No. Minn. dist. Evang. Luth. Ch., 1958-61, No. Minn. dist. Am. Luth. Ch., 1961-66; gen. sec. The Am. Luth. Ch., Mpls., 1967-82; coordinator Commn. for a New Luth. Ch., Mpls., 1982-87; pres. A.M. Cons., Amery, Wis., 1987—; councilor Luth. Council in U.S.A., 1966-82, sec., 1969-72, pres., 72-75; mem. U.S.A. Nat. Com. Luth. World Fedn., 1966-82, sec., 1966-69, 72-75, v.p., 1979-81, pres., 1981-82; mem. Consultation on Luth. Unity, 1970-76, sec., 1970-73, chmn., 1974-76; mem. Com. on Luth. Unity, 1976-82; del. 4th Assembly World Council Chs., Uppsala, Sweden, 1968, 5th Assembly, Nairobi, Kenya, 1975; chmn. Faith-in-Life Dialogue, Fargo-Moorhead, 1964, observor-trainer, Duluth, 1965; gen. sec. emeritus Am. Luth. Ch., 1982—; pres. Cen. Luth. Ch., Mpls., 1992—. Mem. Conf. on Inflation, 1974, Mpls.-St. Paul Town Meeting Council, 1968-76; bd. govs. Midwest League, 1979—; bd. mgrs. Am. Bible Soc., 1979—; trustee Suomi Coll., 1981—. Served with AUS, 1943-46. Recipient Civic Service award Eagles, 1965, Ch. award Suomi Coll., 1987, Judge Graven Lay Leadership award Wartburg Coll., 1990. Mem. Ch. Staff Workers Assn. (past pres.), Concordia Coll. Alumni Assn. (past pres.), Alpha Phi Gamma, Zeta Sigma Pi. Club: Mpls. Athletic. Home: 1235 Yale Pl Apt 409 Minneapolis MN 55403 Office: AM Cons Rte 3 Box 204-A Amery WI 54001

MICKEY, PAUL ALBERT, former minister, educator; b. Amanda, Ohio, May 13, 1937; s. Martin Ephraim and Ellen (Koons) M.; m. Jane Eleanor Becker, Oct. 12, 1962; children: Bruce Jon (dec.), Sandra Lee. BA, Harvard U., 1963; MDiv, Princeton Theol. Sem., 1966, PhD, 1970. Ordained to ministry United Meth. Ch., 1966, laicized, 1991. Pastor Hope United Meth. Ch., Cleve., 1966-67, St. Paul's United Meth. Ch., Bay Head, N.J., 1969-70; prof. Div. Sch., Duke U., Durham, N.C., 1970—; rep. Assn. for Clin. Pastoral Edn., Atlanta, 1972-91; nat. bd. CONTACT Teleministries, Harrisburg, Pa., 1985-88; nat. chmn. Good News, Wilmore, Ky., 1978-80. Author: Pastoral Assertiveness, 1978, Essentials of Wesleyan Theology, 1980, Tough Marriage, 1986, Sex with Confidence, 1988, Breaking Free from Wedlock Deadlock, 1989, 12 Keys To A Better Marriage, 1990, Of Sacred Worth?, 1991; co-author: Conflict and Resolution, 1973, What New Creation, 1974, Clergy Families: Is Normal Life Possible?, 1991. With USAF, 1955-59. Procter & Gamble fellow, 1961-63; Princeton Theol. Sem. pastoral theology fellow, 1967-70. Republican. Avocation: aviation. Office: Duke U Div Sch Durham NC 27706

MICKLER, RANDELL ROBERT, JR., minister; b. Madison, Fla., Dec. 2, 1948; s. Randell Robert and Teddy (Reese) M.; m. Diane Drake, July 29, 1972; children: Rob, Ashley. BA, U. Ga., 1971; MDiv, Emory U., 1973; D of Ministry, McCormick Seminary, Chgo., 1991. Ordained to ministry United Meth. Ch. as elder, 1975. Assoc. minister First United Meth. Ch., Dalton, Ga., 1974-76; minister Newborn (Ga.) - Starrsville, 1976-78; sr. minister First United Meth. Ch., Bowdon, Ga., 1978-83, Calhoun, Ga., 1983-88; sr. minister Mt. Bethel United Meth. Ch., Marietta, Ga., 1988—; mem. bd. ordained ministry North Ga. Conf., 1979-85; pres. ministerial assn. Gordon County, Calhoun, Ga., 1986-87; trustee Wesley Ctr., Athens, Ga., 1988-91; guest minister Fla. United Meth. Men, Leesburg, Fla., 1991: mem. dist. com. on ministry. Named to Outstanding Young Men of Am., 1981, 82; recipient Best Sermon Giver award Best of Cobb: Inside Cobb mag., 1989, Revivalist award St. Paul United Meth. Ch., Cobb County, 1990, others. Mem. Rotary. Home: 5112 Hampton Lake Dr Marietta GA 30068 Office: Mt Bethel United Methodist 4385 Lower Roswell Rd Marietta GA 30068

MICKLEY, RICHARD STROUD, lawyer; b. Marion, Ohio, Apr. 21, 1939; s. Henry Arthur and Miriam Laura (Stroud) M.; m. Carolyn Latham, Sept. 6, 1964; children: Bruce Latham, Andrew Kenneth. BA, Coll. Wooster, 1961; JD, Ohio State U., 1970. Bar: Ohio 1971, U.S. Dist. Ct. (so. dist.) Ohio 1973, U.S. Dist. Ct. (no. dist.) Ohio 1980, U.S. Tax Ct. 1975. Assoc., Grigsby & Allen, Marysville, Ohio, 1971-73; pvt. practice, Marysville, 1973-77, 79, 90—; asst. county prosecutor Union County (Ohio), 1973-75, 78; ptnr. Mckinley & Mickley, 1978, Mickley & McNemar, Marysville, 1980-85; estate adminstr. U.S. Bankruptcy Ct., 1986-89; city law dir. City of Marysville, 1982-85. Pres. Serve Inc., 1981, 84. Served to capt. USAF, 1962-68. Mem. Union County Bar Assn. (pres. 1973), Ohio State Bar Assn. Republican. Presbyterian (mem. jud. commn. Presbytery Scioto 1981-87, coun. 1987-91, vice moderator 1991—). Lodges: Lions (pres. 1979), Masons (master 1977). Avocations: church committee work; woodworking; gardening. Home: 891 Catalpa Pl Marysville OH 43040 *God doesn't require us to be perfect. Through Christ our faults are forgiven, for which we are forever in debt. We show our love for God by loving our neighbors.*

MIDDENDORF, MICHAEL PAUL, clergyman; b. St. Paul, Apr. 27, 1959; s. Marvin Luther and Melba Catherine (Eckert) M.; m. Lana Lee Kinunen, July 20, 1985. BA, Concordia Coll., St. Paul, 1981; MDiv, Concordia Sem., St. Louis, 1987, STM, 1989, ThD, 1990. Admissions counselor Concordia Coll., St. Paul, 1980-83, guest instr., 1982-83; guest instr. Concordia Coll., River Forest, Ill., 1989, Concordia Sem., St. Louis, 1990; vicar Bethlehem Luth. Ch., Lakewood, Colo., 1985-86. Walther faculty devel. fellow Concordia Sem., St. Louis, 1988-90. Mem. Soc. Bibl. Lit. Lutheran. Home: 810 14th St NE Jamestown ND 58401 Office: Concordia Luth Ch 502 1st Ave N Jamestown ND 58401

MIDDLETON, JOAN KIRKLAND, lay worker; b. Joaquin, Tex., Apr. 9, 1936; d. Hubert Hulon and Florence Alice (Adams) Kirkland; m. Charles Edward Middleton, Dec. 1, 1955; children: Debra Joan Beasley, Charles Kirkland. Grad. high sch., West Monroe, La. Tchr. Landmark Missionary Bapt. Ch., West Monroe, 1954—, ch. clk., 1965-68, children ch. dir., 1988—; ret. Manville Forest Products, West Monroe, 1963-88. Co-pres. N.E. La. Alzheimers Assn., Monroe, 1991. Democrat. Baptist. Home: 101 Dianne St West Monroe LA 71292 *Each generation needs religious men and women with zeal and leadership to guide our youth in becoming productive and responsible citizens.*

MIDDLETON, JOHN FRANCIS MARCHMENT, anthropology educator; b. London, May 22, 1921; married; 2 children. BA, U. London, 1941; BSc, U. Oxford, Eng., 1949; DPhil in Anthropology, U. Oxford, 1953. Lectr. anthropology U. London, Eng., 1953-54, 56-63; sr. lectr. U. Cape Town, Republic of South Africa, 1954-56; prof. Northwestern U., Evanston, Ill., 1963-66; prof. anthropology NYU, 1966—, Yale U., New Haven, 1966-72; prof. African anthropology Sch. of Oriental & African Studies London U., 1972-81, Yale U., 1981—; dir. Internat. African Inst., 1973-74, 80-81; rsch. in anthropology Uganda, 1949-53, Zanzibar, 1958, Nigeria, 1963-64, Ghana, 1976-77, Kenya, 1986; vis. prof. U. Va., Oreg., Lagos, Nigeria, Ecole Pratique des Hautestudes, Paris. Author: Kikuyu of Kenya, 1953, Lugbara Religion, 1960, Land Tenure in Zanzibar, 1961, The Lugbara of Uganda, 1965, others. Mem. Royal Anthrop. Inst. Gt. Brit. and Ireland. Avocations: social anthropology of Africa, religion, politics. Office: Yale Univ Dept History New Haven CT 06520

MIDDLETON, LUCY LAURA, educational administrator; b. Ft. Worth, Aug. 27, 1941; d. Melvin B. and Lucy L. (Gerloff) M. BA, Marillac Coll., 1965; MA, St. Louis U., 1972. Cert. tchr., Mo., La., Calif. Tchr. St. Ann's Sch., Normandy, Mo., 1980-83, St. Francis Xavier Sch., St. Louis, 1983-86; dir. religion edn. Our Lady of the Angels Sch., Kinloch, Mo., 1986-87; prin. Our Lady of Mt. Carmel Sch., St. Louis, 1987-90, Linda Vista Cath. Sch., Chesterfield, Mo., 1990—; bd. dirs. Hosea House, St. Louis. Mem. Network, Washington, 1980—; bd. mem. Mt. Vernon Condominiums, Glendale, Mo., 1991—. Mem. NCEA, ASCD. Office: Linda Vista Cath Sch 1633 Kehrs Mill Rd Chesterfield MO 63005

MIDGETT, VANCE LLEWELLYN, pastor; b. New London, Conn., Feb. 10, 1959; s. Llewellyn Daniels and Addie Houston (Wilkens) M. BA in Religion, Gardner-Webb Coll., 1983; MDiv, Southeastern Bapt. Sem., 1986. Ordained to ministry Bapt. Ch., 1986. Youth dir. Freedom Bapt. Ch., Wilmington, N.C., 1980-85; assoc. pastor Plainview Bapt. Ch., Durham, N.C., 1986-87; assoc. pastor youth and coll. students Calvary Bapt. Ch., Wilmington, N.C., 1987—. Supporter Life Line Crisis Pregnancy Ctr., Wilmington, 1988—. Mem. Wilmington Bapt. Assn. (assoc. youth dir. 1988—, resort coun. 1987—), Fellowship Christian Athletes, N.C. Religious Edn. Assn., Bapt. Youth Mins. Assn. Home: 6612 Sunwood Circle Wilmington NC 28405 Office: Calvary Bapt Ch 423 N 23rd St Wilmington NC 28405

MIDTEIDE, PER J., religious organization administrator. Gen. sec. Norwegian Bapt. Union, Stabekk, Norway. Office: Norwegian Bapt Union, Micheletsvei 62, 1320 Stabekk Norway*

MIER-Y-TERÁN, MARIA GUADALUPE (SISTER MARILUPE), nun; b. Mexico City, June 7, 1950; came to U.S., 1973; d. Jesus and Josefina (Suárez) M. BA in Edn., Inst. Femenino Mex., Mexico City, 1969, Corpus Christi State U., 1982; MS in Mid-Mgmt. Adminstrn., Corpus Christi State U., 1983; lic. en teologia, U. LaSalle, Mexico City, 1990. Joined Sisters of Mercy of the Blessed Sacrament, Roman Cath. Ch., 1970. Elem. tchr., dir. religious edn. Holy Family Sch., Corpus Christi, Tex., 1976-83, prin., 3d grade tchr., 1985-86; jr. high sch. tchr. St. Joseph's Sch., Barstow, Calif., 1983-85, prin., 1990—; jr. high sch. tchr. St. John of the Cross Sch., Lemon Grove, Calif., 1986-90; 2d grade tchr. Simon Bolivar Cath. Sch., Mexico City; adult edn. and Bible educator St. John of The Cross Sch., 1987-90, R.C.I.A. instr., 1988-90; cathechist St. Joseph's Sch., 1990—. Home: 555 E Mountain View Ave Barstow CA 92311 Office: St Joseph's Sch 555 E Mountain View Ave Barstow CA 92311

MIHELICH, JEFFERY C., minister; b. Indio, Calif., Dec. 14, 1954; s. Albert M. and Wanda C. (Crabtree) M.; m. Cindy S. Stearns, June 9, 1972; children: Misty, Joshua, Crystal. ABS, Nazarene Bible Coll., 1981; BTh, Trinity Coll. of Bible, 1985; M Ministry, Trinity Sem., 1988. Ordained to ministry Ch. of the Nazarene, 1983. Owner Four Seasons Heating and Air Conditioning, Herrin, Ill., 1977-79; pastor Ch. of the Nazarene, Uvalde, Tex., 1981-84, New Braunfels, Tex., 1984—; chmn. Bd. Ministerial Studies, San Antonio, 1988-90; dir. adult ministries San Antonio Dist. Ch. of the Nazarene. 1987-89; founder, chmn., tchr. Sch. Ministry, 1988. Host radio program New Directions, 1990—; inventor computer bull. bd. Mararatha, 1990—. Bd. dirs. Crisis Ctr., 1985-87. Mem. Nazarene Youth Internat. Home and Office: 1465 IH 35 e New Braunfels TX 78130

MIKOLAIZYK, MARIAN, school system administrator. Supt. schs. Diocese of Saginaw, Mich. Office: Office Edn-Formation Supt 5800 Weiss St Saginaw MI 48603*

MIKULANIS, DENNIS L., minister. Pres. San Diego Country Ecumenical Conf. Office: Ecumenical Conf 4075 Park Blvd PO Box 3628 San Diego CA 92103*

MILAM, CHRISTINE MARIE, minister; b. Cavite, The Philippines, Aug. 15, 1956; (parents Am. citizens); came to U.S., 1958; d. Robert Howard and Christina (McNeill) M. BA, U. Md., 1979; MDiv in Pastoral Counseling, Southeastern Bapt. Theol. Sem., Wake Forest, N.C., 1983. Ordained to ministry So. Bapt. Conv., 1984. Chaplain N.C. Meml. Hosp., Chapel Hill, 1983; assoc. pastor Wakeminster Bapt. Ch., Raleigh, N.C., 1985-87; chaplain Grossmont Hosp., La Mesa, Calif., 1990—; asst. activities Point Loma (Calif.) Convalescent Hosp., 1990-91. Vol. Big Sisters, San Diego, 1988—; vol. chaplain Brighton Pl. East, San Diego, 1989—. Lt. USNR, 1981—. Mem. Naval Res. Assn., Women Officers Assn., Mil. Chaplains Assn., San Diego Navy Waves, Stars and Stripes (chaplain San Diego chpt. 1989—), Navy League (chaplain San Diego chpt. 1989—), Md. Alumni Internat., Alumni Assn. Southeastern Bapt. Sem., Internat. Tng. in Communication Club (toastmistress 1988-90, sec. 1989-90). Home: 4930 Del Mar # 103 San Diego CA 92107 *At a women's retreat in Rota, Spain, a question was asked to me, "Chaplain, what is your favorite hymn?" I responded, "Jesus loves me."*

MILES, DOUGLAS IRVING, clergyman, pastor; b. Balt., Apr. 10, 1949; s. Walter Arthur Harris and Odessa Roberta (Southers) Miles; m. Rosanna White, Nov. 14, 1971; children: Harvey Eugene, Dante Kwiyisi. BA, Johns Hopkins U., 1970; MA in Theology, St. Mary's Sem., Balt., 1981; DD, Va. Coll. and Sem., 1980. Ordained minister. Community organizer Neighborhood Action Group, Balt., 1968-70; asst. pastor St. Mark's United Meth. Ch., Balt., 1970-71; dir. consultation and edn. Provident Community Mental Health Ctr., Balt., 1971-72; co-dir. Inst. Constrn., Balt., 1972-74; branch mgr. First Nat. Bank Md., Balt., 1974-75; dir. United Way Cen. md., Balt., 1975-76; community relations officer Mass Transit Adminstrn., Balt., 1976-78; pub. relations dir. Project P.L.A.S.E., Balt., 1978-80; pastor Calvary C.M.E. Ch., Pasadena, Calif., 1988-89; pastor Greenwood C.M.E. Ch., Memphis, Calif., 1989—, Memphis, 1989—. Pres. Interdenominational Ministerial Alliance, Balt., 1985-87; exec. com. mem. Baltimoreans United in Leadership Devel., 1982-88; 2nd. v.p. Balt. NAACP, 1983-84; sec. Interdenominational Ministerial Alliance, Pasadena, Calif., 1988—. Recipient PLAQUE Pub. Spirit award People Not Politics, 1982, Outstanding Leadership award Baptist Ministers Conf., 1985, Outstanding Service award Park Heights Community Corp., 1987, Outstanding Leadership award Ainsworth Paint & Chem. Corp., 1986. Mem. Progressive Nat. Bapt. Collentica (instr. 1983-88), Hampton Inst. Minister's Conf. (bd. dirs. 1988—), NAACP (2nd v.p., 1983-84), So. Calif. Annual Conf. CMB (dir. evangelism 1988—), Interdenominational Ministerial Alliance (sec. 1988—), Fulton Heights Club (pres. 1973, 80). Democrat. Baptist. Avocations: creative writing, photography, reading, sports.

MILES, JOHN P., minister; b. Crowley, La., Nov. 11, 1929; m. JoAnn Ridgway; children: Deborah Ann, John II, Rebeka Lynn. BD, Southern Meth. U., 1954; LLD, Shorter Coll., 1970; DD, Hendrix Coll., 1983; LLD (hon.), Africal Episcopal Ch. Ordained to ministry United Meth. Ch. Pastor various United Meth. Chs., Ark., St. James United Meth. Ch., Little Rock; chmn. Hilmar and Caroline Fick Ednl. Found.; founder, coord. officer Little Rock Religious Forum; mem. Little Rock annual conf. United Meth. Ch., 1952—, vice chmn. social concerns, chmn. evangelism, vice chmn. fin. and adminstrn., mem. Episcopal com., conf. del.; mem. World Meth. Coun.; speaker in field. Past bd. dirs. Ouachita Regional Mental Health Ctr.; organizer Little Rock Task Force on Racism; producer video tapes Ark. State Health Dept. Mem. Ams. for Separation of Ch. and State. Office: St James United Meth Ch 321 Pleasant Valley Dr Little Rock AR 72212

MILES, MARGARET RUTH, theology educator; b. Lancaster, Pa., May 18, 1937; d. Kenneth Leroy and Mary Lillian (Brown) M.; m. Owen C. Thomas, June 6, 1981; children: Susan Katherine Burris, Richard David Burris. BA, San Francisco State U., 1969, MA, 1971; PhD, Grad. Theol. Union, Berkeley, Calif., 1977; MA (hon.), Harvard U., 1985. Instr. Modesto (Calif.) Jr. Coll., 1971-76, Columbia (Calif.) Jr. Coll., 1973-76; asst. prof. Harvard Divinity Sch., Cambridge, Mass., 1978-81, assoc. prof., 1981-85, prof., 1985-87, Bussey prof. hist. theology, 1987—. Author: Augustine on the Body, 1979, Fullness of Life, 1981, Image as Insight, 1985, Practicing Christianity, 1988, Carnal Knowing, 1989, Desire and Delight, 1991; editor 2 books; contbr. numerous articles to profl. jours. Recipient Pres.'s award Harvard U., 1983; Guggenheim fellow, 1981-82,Rockefeller fellow, Bellagio, Italy, 1982; grantee NEH, 1981. Mem. Am. Assn. Religion, Am. Hist. Soc., Am. Theol. Soc., Am. Soc. Ch. History. Democrat. Episcopalian. Club: Am. Lute Seminars (v.p. 1976—). Avocation: lute. Office: Harvard Divinity Sch 45 Francis Ave Cambridge MA 02138

MILES, PATRICIA LOUISE, lay worker; b. L.A., Dec. 26, 1947; d. Chester John and Mildred (Singleton) Comeaux; m. Berkley Logan, Mar. 15, 1969 (div. July 1974); m. Phillip Miles, July 11, 1987. Student, El Camino, 1970-75. Cert. cosmetologist. Adminstrv. asst. L.A., 1987—, evangelist, 1989—; pub. rels. Ch. of God, L.A., 1990—; dir. Creative NAS House, L.A., 1990—; pub. rels. dir. Second Jurisdiction C.O.G.Y.C., 1990—. Editor: Spirit World, 1988; author, editor: Getting Acquainted With Yourself, 1974. Community activist, L.A., 1980—. Recipient Appreciation award Sch. Bd. Calif., 1985, Appreciation award State of Calif., 1990, Commendation award City of L.A., 1989, Humanitarian award, 1990. Mem. Bus. & Profl. Women, Cen. City Assn. (pres. 1973-75), Pub. Rels. Soc. Am. Democrat. Home: 17048 Wedgeworth Dr Hacienda Heights CA 91745 Office: Creative NAS House 8224 S Broadway Los Angeles CA 90003

MILESI, LUCA, religious organization administrator. Apostolic adminstr. of Asmara, Latin Rite, Roman Cath. Ch., Ethiopia. Office: 107 National Ave, POB 224, Asmara Ethiopia*

MILEWSKI, STANLEY E., academic administrator. Pres. Saints Cyril and Methodius Sem., Orchard Lake, Mich. Office: SS Cyril & Methodius Sem Orchard Lake MI 48033*

MILHAVEN, JOHN GILES, religious studies educator; b. N.Y.C., Sept. 1, 1927; s. John Michael and Rose (Burns) M.; m. Anne Teresa Lally, May 21, 1970; 1 child, Shelly. B.A., Woodstock Coll., 1949, M.A. in Teaching, Licentiate in Philosophy, 1950; Licentiate in Theology, Facultés Théologiques de la Compagnie de Jésus d'Enghien, Belgium, 1957; Ph.D. in Philosophy, U. Munich, Germany, 1962. Instr. philosophy Canisius Coll., Buffalo, 1951-53; asst. prof. philosophy Fordham U., N.Y.C., 1961-66; assoc. prof. moral theology Woodstock Coll., Md., 1966-70; assoc. prof. religious studies Brown U., Providence, 1970-76; prof. religious studies Brown U., 1976—; lectr. med. ethics Georgetown U. Med. Sch., Washington, 1966-68. Author: Towards a New Catholic Morality, 1970, Good Anger, 1989; contbr. articles to various publs. Mem. Am. Acad. Religion, Soc. Christian Ethics, Cath. Theol. Soc. Am. Roman Catholic. Home: 20 Penrose Providence RI 02906 Office: Brown U Dept of Religious Studies Providence RI 02912 *I believe I succeeded when I effectively shared with others something of my evasive but persistent experience of human life as important.*

MILHOUSE, PAUL WILLIAM, bishop; b. St. Francisville, Ill., Aug. 31, 1910; s. Willis Cleveland and Carrie (Pence) M.; m. Mary Frances Noblitt, June 29, 1932; children: Mary Catherine Milhouse Hauswald, Pauline Joyce Milhouse Vermillion, Paul David. A.B., U. Ind. (formerly Ind. Cen. U.), 1932, D.D., 1950; B.D., Am. Theol. Sem., 1937, Th.D., 1946; L.H.D., Westmar Coll., 1965; S.T.D., Oklahoma City U., 1969; D.D., So. Meth. U., 1969. Ordained to ministry United Brethren Ch., 1931; pastor Birds, Ill., 1928-29, Elliott, Ill., 1932-37, Olney, Ill., 1937-41; pastor 1st Ch., Decatur, Ill., 1941-51; asso. editor Telescope-Messenger, 1951-58; exec. sec. gen. council Evang. United Brethren Ch., 1959-60, bishop, 1960-68; bishop United Meth. Ch., 1968—; pres. Council United Meth. Bishops, 1977-78; bishop-in-residence Oklahoma City U., 1980-91. Author: Enlisting and Developing Church Leaders, 1946, Come Unto Me, 1946, Lift Up Your Eyes, 1955, Doorways to Spritual Living, 1950, Except the Lord Build the House, 1949, Christian Worship in Symbol and Ritual, 1953, Laymen in the Church, 1957, At Life's Crossroads, 1959, Phillip William Otterbein, 1968, Nineteen Bishops of the Evangelical United Brethren Church, 1974, Organizing for Effective Ministry, 1980, Theological and Historical Roots of United Methodists, 1980, Detour Into Yesterday, 1984, Okla. City U., Miracle at 23d and Blackwelder, 1984, Transforming Dollars into Service, A History of Methodist Manor, 1987, St. Lukes of Oklahoma City, 1988; also articles; editor: Facing Frontiers, 1960. Trustee So. Meth. U., 1968-80; trustee Oklahoma City U., 1968-80, hon. life trustee, 1980—, Meth. Home, 1968-80, Francis E. Willard Home, 1968-80, Meth. Manor, 1968-80, Boys Ranch, 1968-80, Last Frontier council Boy Scouts Am., 1968-80; hon. life trustee United Theol. Sem. Recipient Disting. Alumnus award Ind. Central U. now U. Ind., 1978; Disting. Friend award Oklahoma City U., 1979; Disting. Service award Oklahoma City U., 1980; Top Hand award Oklahoma City C. of C., 1980; Bishop Paul W. Milhouse award, 1990. Mem. Mark Twain Writers Guild, Epsilon Sigma Alpha, now Alpha Chi. *Life is a gift to be lived in harmony with the purpose of God, who holds us accountable.*

MILI, JUDE JOSEPH, priest, religious organization administrator; b. Somerville, Mass., Dec. 27, 1931; s. Spiridione and Gelsomina (Scipione) M. BA, Immaculate Conception Coll., Troy, N.Y., 1955; MA in Theology, Antonianum, Rome, 1961, STD, 1964; MA in Counselling, W.Va. U., 1972. Joined Order of Friars Minor, 1950, ordained priest Roman Cath. Ch., 1959. Dir. Christian Reneval Ctr., Morgantown, W.Va., 1972—; provincial councilor Franciscan Province of Immaculate Conception-U.S.A., 1980-83; mem. Nat. Marriage Encounter Bd., 1969-74, Nat. Program Com. for Christian Family Movement in U.S.A., 1973-75, Ea. Regional Bd. of Charismatic Reneval in Cath. Ch.-Ea. U.S.A., 1974-77. Pres. Citizens Concerned for Community Values, Morgantown, 1986—. Home and Office: Good Counsel Friary Rte 7 Box 183 Tyrone Rd Morgantown WV 26505-9199

MILLAR, BRAD STEWART, minister; b. Berkeley, Calif., Apr. 21, 1961; s. Russell Ward Millar and Loel (Marston) Buckley; m. Mary Elizabeth Scofield, July 25, 1981; children: Bethany Joy, Nathanael Stewart. BA with honors, Calif. State U., Fullerton, 1985. Youth camp staff Sonshine Co., Bell Gardens, Calif., 1980, 83-84; youth pastor Community Bible Ch., Fountain Valley, Calif., 1985-87; min. Hollywood (Calif.) Christian Life Ctr., 1987—; home missionary Gen. Coun. Assemblies of God, Springfield, Mo., 1989—; worship dir. Community Bible Ch., Fountain Valley, 1986-87, Hollywood Christian Life Ctr., 1987—, So. Calif. Assemblies of God Youth Camp, Twin Peaks, Calif., 1986-90. Composer songs; contbr. articles to profl. jours. Mem. Gold Key Nat. Honor Soc. Republican. Office: Hollywood Christian Life 5057 Sunset Blvd Hollywood CA 90027

MILLARD, GEORGE RICHARD, bishop; b. Dunsmuir, Calif., Oct. 2, 1914; s. George Ellis and Constance (Rainsberry) M.; m. Mary Louise Gessling, June 29, 1939; children: George, Martha, Joseph. A.B., U. Calif.-Berkeley, 1936; B.D., Episcopal Theol. Sch., Cambridge, Mass., 1938; S.T.M., Pacific Sch. Religion, 1958; D.D., Ch. Div. Sch. Pacific, 1960; M.A., U. Santa Clara, 1983. Ordained to ministry Episcopal Ch. as priest 1938. Asst. in Episc. Ch., N.Y.C., 1938-39, Waterbury, Conn., 1930-40; rector in Episc. Ch., Danbury, Conn., 1940-50, Alameda, Calif., 1951-59; suffragan bishop Episc. Diocese Calif., 1960-76; bishop of San Jose, 1969-76; exec., venture in mission program, exec. council Episc. Ch., 1977-78; bishop in charge Am. Chs. in Europe, 1978-80, bishop in charge ch. divinity sch. pacific exec. office for alumni/ae affairs, 1978-80; dean Convocation of Oakland, Calif., 1957-60; chmn. dept. missions Diocese Calif., 1958-60; mem. Joint Commn. on Structure, Episc. Ch., 1967-76. Chmn. Maria Kip Orphange; chmn. devel. program U. Calif. at Berkeley Student Coop. Assn., 1966; coord. Ch. Div. Sch. Pacific Alumni Affairs, 1986-88. Mem. The Club of Rome.

MILLEN, JOHN CLYDE, minister; b. Landour, U.P., India, Sept. 9, 1941; came to U.S., 1946; s. Theodore Wier and Charis (Murley) M.; m. Priscilla Anne Sherwin, June 8, 1967; children: Scot Andrew, Laura Anne, Chad William, Katharine Irene. AA, Monmouth Coll., 1963; BS, U.S. Naval

Acad., 1967; MDiv, Va. Sem., 1974. Ordained to ministry Episcopal Ch. as priest, 1976. Asst. chaplain Episcopal High Sch., Alexandria, Va., 1974-78; assoc. rector St. John's Episcopal Ch., McLean, Va., 1978-80; rector St. Francis Episcopal Ch., Great Falls, Va., 1979-85, St. Mark's Episcopal Ch., Columbus, Ohio, 1985-89, Ch. of the Holy Nativity and Sch., Honolulu, 1989—; sec. standing com. Diocese of Hawaii, 1990—; chair commn. on ministry Diocese of So. Ohio, 1987-89; dean region 5 No. Fairfax County, Diocese of Va., 1981-85; pres. United Coll. Ministries in No. Va., 1981-83; mem. Commn. on Ministry, Hawaii, 1990—; mem. program com. Camp Mokuleia, Hawaii, 1990—; mem. Fuller Sem., Hawaii, 1989—. Bd. dirs. Community Mental Health, Alexandria, 1972-74; bd. dirs. PTA, Cooper Intermediate Sch., McLean, 1980-82. Capt. USMC, 1967-71. Mem. Hawaii Episcopal Clergy Assn., East Oahu Clergy Fellowship. Home: 144 Nenue St Honolulu HI 96821 Office: Ch of Holy Nativity and Sch 5286 Kalanianaole Hwy Honolulu HI 96821

MILLER, AMOS W., rabbi; b. N.Y.C., Apr. 9, 1927; s. Joseph and Frances (Hershberg) M.; m. Hannah B. Wiedman, Jan. 25, 1953; children: Seth, Fredric, Felicia. BA, Bklyn. Coll., 1947; MA, Columbia U., 1953; MHL, Jewish Theol. Sem., 1951, DHL, 1961. Ordained rabbi 1951. Rabbi Cong. Beth Sholom, Long Beach, N.Y., 1953—; mem. N.Y. Bd. Rabbis, N.Y.C., 1954—; del. World Zionist Congress, Jerusalem, 1988; chmn. membership com. Rabbinical Assembly, 1980-84, chmn. Israel com., 1984-88; bd. dirs. Hillel Sch. for Conversion, 1968—. Author: Understanding the Midvach, 1965, Abraham: Friend of God, 1973. 1st lt. U.S. Army, 1951-53. Recipient Disting. Svc. award Jewish War Vets., 1961. Mem. Rabbinical Assembly of Nassau-Suffolk (pres. 1978-80). Home: 210 Greenway Rd Lido Beach NY 11561 Office: Cong Beth Sholom 700 E Park Ave Long Beach NY 11561

MILLER, ARCHIE RANDOLPH, church official; b. Monroe, La., July 22, 1955; s. Archie Preston and Willie Von (Jennings) M.; m. Cynthia Rene Thornhill, Nov. 27, 1982. BA, Fla. State U., 1977; M.Ch. Music, New Orleans Bapt. Theol. Sem., 1981. Youth minister First Bapt. Ch., McComb, Miss., 1978-79; minister music and youth Woodlawn Bapt. Ch., Rayville, La., 1979-80; minister music Red Bluff Bapt. Ch., Greensburg, La., 1980-81; minister mus. and youth First Bapt. Ch., Jonesboro, La., 1981-83; asst. dir. Continental Singers, Thousand Oaks, Calif., 1981; minister mus., youth First Bapt. Ch., Cape Coral, Fla., 1983—; instrumental music cons. Royal Palm Assn. Fla. Bapt. Conv., 1985-86; adminstr. Cape Coral Christian Sch., 1986. Bd. dirs. Nehemiah Prodns., Fort Myers, Fla., 1984—, S.W. Fla. Handbell Festival, 1985—; assn. youth dir. Royal Palm Bapt. Assn., 1984—. Mem. Am. Guild English Handbell Ringers, S.W. Fla. Bapt. Singing Men. Republican. Avocations: sport fishing, hunting, scuba diving. Home: 2544 SE 21 Pl Cape Coral FL 33904 Office: First Bapt Ch 4117 Coronado Pkwy Cape Coral FL 33904

MILLER, BENCE C., academic administrator. Pres. God's Bible Sch. and Coll., Cin. Office: God's Bible Sch & Coll 1810 Young St Cincinnati OH 45210*

MILLER, BENNETT F., rabbi; b. Rochester, N.Y., June 19, 1948; s. Eli and Helen (Brenner) M.; m. Joan Goldberg, July 4, 1971; children: Ellie, Carrie. BA, U. Cin., 1970; MA in Hebrew Lit., Hebrew Union Coll.-Jewish Inst. Religion, Cin., 1974; DMin, Princeton Theol. Sem., 1988. Ordained rabbi Union Am. Hebrew Congregations (Ref.), 1974. Instr. liturgy Hebrew Union Coll., Jerusalem, 1971-72; asst. rabbi Anshe Emeth Meml. Temple, New Brunswick, N.J., 1974-77, sr. rabbi, 1977—; pres. N.J. Coalition of Religious, 1987—; mem. Cen. Conf. Am. Rabbis; exec. rabbinic cabinet United Jewish Appeal, 1981—; chmn. pastoral care dept. Robert Wood Johnson Univ. Hosp., New Brunswick, 1985—. Author: Synagogue Music for Today, 1974, Why Pray, 1979, Developing a Program for New Members Leading towards Covenant, 1988. Mem. exec. com. New Brunswick Tercentennial Com., 1980; mem. N.J. Adv. Coun. on Holocaust, Trenton, 1982-85. Recipient Heritage award State of Israel Bonds, 1985. Mem. N.J. Assn. Reform Rabbis (pres. 1986-88). Democrat. Office: Anshe Emeth Meml Temple 222 Livingston Ave New Brunswick NJ 08901

MILLER, BERNARD KEITH, religious organization administrator, civil engineer; b. St. Joseph, Mo., Mar. 21, 1953; s. Lewis Author and Helen Lucile (Hunziger) M., m. Mary Kay Allen, Aug. 28, 1983; children: Paul Ryan, Jessica Kathryn, Bethany Marissa. BSCE, U. Wyo., 1975; MSCE, U. Minn., 1977; MDiv, Western Conservative Baptist Sem., 1987, ThM, 1988. Registered profl. engr., Colo.; ordained to ministry Conservative Bapt. Ch., 1988. Commd. 2d lt. USAF, 1975, advanced through grades to capt., 1980, resigned, transferred to res., 1983; maj. USAFR, 1987—; project design engr. USAF, Ellsworth AFB, S.D., 1977-79; engring. staff officer USAF, Ramstein Air Base, Germany, 1979-81; civil engring. instr. USAF Acad., Colorado Springs, Colo., 1981-83; assoc. dep. chief ops. 62nd civil engring. squadron USAF Res., Mc Chord AFB, Wash., 1987-90, assoc. base civil engr. 62nd civil engring. squadron, 1990—; missionary ch. planter Greater Europe Mission, Gothenburg, Sweden, 1988—. Deacon Lents Conservative Baptist Ch., Portland, 1985-87. Named one of Outstanding Young Men of Am., 1987, 88. Mem. ASCE. Republican. Avocations: camping, reading, photography, wood working, tennis.

MILLER, BERTIN, priest, social administrator; b. Joliet, Ill., May 15, 1936; s. William Sumner Ellsworth and Mary Marguerite (Hanrahan) M. BA, Quincy Coll., 1960; STB, Antonianum, Rome, 1964. Ordained priest Roman Cath. Ch., 1964. Chaplain Mo. State Correction Farmington/Pacific, Hillsboro, Mo., 1988—; exec. dir. Evergreen Hills Homes, Dittmer, Mo., 1973-88; dir. Il Ritiro, Dittmer, 1977—; spiritual dir. St. Michael's Inst., Sunset Hills, Mo., 1986-90; lectr. Marsh, Curtis, McCall, St. Lousi, 1986—. Chaplain Cedar Hill (Mo.) Fire Dept., 1989—; assoc. mem. Nat. Coun. on Sexual Addiction, Inc. Mem. Lions, Elks, KC (4th deg.). Home and Office: Il Ritiro Little Retreat Eime Rd PO Box 38 Dittmer MO 63023

MILLER, BEVERLY JEAN, minister, educator, lay worker; b. Sparta, Wis., Aug. 20, 1955; d. James Arthur and Fay Ann (Karis) M. BS in Edn., U. Wis., 1978, MS in Edn. Adminstrn., 1991. Tchr. St. Joseph's Sch., Boyd, Wis., 1979-91; adminstr. St. Joseph's Sch., Boyd, 1988-91; mem. adv. coun. Diocese of LaCrosse, Wis., 1989-91; eucharistic minister, alto singer Holy Ghost Choir, Chippewa Falls, Wis., 1989—; elem. prin. Eau Claire (Wis.) Coordinated Cath. Sch. System. Mem. ASCD, Wis. Reading Assn., Wis. Math. Coun., Indianhead Math. Coun., Eau Claire Area Reading Coun., Chippewa Valley Astron. Soc. (sec. 1986—), Chippewa Valley Community Chorus. Office: Eau Claire Coordinated Cath Sch System Eau Claire WI 54703

MILLER, BONNIE L., elementary school prinicpal; b. Buffalo, June 21, 1942; d. Dan and Roberta H. (Merlau) LaQuay; m. Donald P. Miller, Aug. 3, 1963; children: Shelley Ann, Mark Perry. BS, SUNY, Buffalo, 1963; MS, Nova U., Ft. Lauderdale, Fla., 1987. Tchr. Iroquois Cen. Sch., East Aurora, N.Y., Starpoint Cen. Sch., Pendleton, N.Y., St. Raphaels Sch., St. Petersburg, Fla.; tchr. grade 4 and 6, lang. arts, curriculum chmn. Shorecrest Prep. Sch., St. Petersburg, prin. Mem. Nat. Coun. Tchrs. English, Assn. for Supervision and Curriculum Devel. Home: 8801 15th Ln N Saint Petersburg FL 33702

MILLER, BRUCE BARNETT, II, religion educator; b. Dallas, June 26, 1961; s. Bruce Barnett and Jody (Scurry) M.; m. Tamara Neal, July 2, 1983; children: Bart, Jimmy, David, Melanie, Ben. BA, U. Tex., 1982; ThM, Dallas Theol. Sem., 1986. Ordained to ministry Ind. Bible Ch., 1986. Intern Ctr. for Ch. Renewal, Dallas, 1982-86; coll. dir. Fellowship Bible Ch. N., Plano, Tex., 1986-89; pastor Community Bible Fellowship, Van Alstyne, Tex., 1986-88; instr. Dallas Theol. Sem., 1989-90; dir. Bibl. Inst. for Leadership Devel. Ctr. for Ch. Renewal, Dallas, 1990; dir. tutoring Profl. Tutoring, Dallas, 1983-90; dir. leadership tng. Fellowship Bible Ch. North. Mem. Am. Acad. Religion, Evang. Theol. Soc., Evang. Philos. Soc., Soc. Christian Philosophers, Phi Beta Kappa. Home: 4004 Overdowns Plano TX 75023 Office: Dallas Theol Sem 3909 Swiss Ave Dallas TX 75204 also: 200 Chisholm Pl Ste 234 Plano TX 75075

MILLER, C. RAY, religious organization administrator. Chmn. United Brethren in Christ, Huntington, Ind. Office: United Brethren Christ 302 Lake St Huntington IN 46750*

MILLER, CHARLES HENRY, JR., university dean; b. Parsons, Kans., Oct. 23, 1933; s. Charles Henry and Mary Alice (O'Connor) M. BA in English, St. Mary's U., San Antonio, 1955; STL, U. Fribourg, Switzerland, 1964; SSL, Pontifical Bibl. Inst., Rome, 1969; STD, San Anselmo Coll., Rome, 1973. Ordained priest Roman Catholic Ch., 1964. Tchr. Institut Collegial Provencher, St. Boniface, Man., Can., 1955-57, Eugene Coyle High Sch., Kirkwood, Mo., 1957-59; tchr., chaplain Villa St-Jean Internat. Sch., Fribourg, Switzerland, 1965-67; teaching asst. U. Fribourg, Switzerland, 1966-67; lectr. to assoc. prof. St. Louis U., 1970-79; assoc. prof. to prof. St. Mary's U., San Antonio, 1979—; dean humanities and social sci. St. Mary's U., 1987—; mem. Soc. of Mary, St. Louis, 1952—. Author: As It Is Written, 1973; contbr. articles to profl. jours. Mem. Tex. Com. for the Humanities, 1990—; trustee Am. Ctr. Oriental Rsch., Amman, Jordan, 1989—. Fulbright fellow, Israel, 1978-79. Mem. Soc. Bibl. Lit., Am. Schs. Oriental Rsch., Cath. Bibl. Assn., Am. Acad. Religion, Am. Assn. Higher Edn., Archaeol. Inst. Am., Phi Sigma Iota. Roman Catholic. Avocations: hiking, fishing, hunting, camping. Office: St Marys' U One Camino Santa Maria San Antonio TX 78228

MILLER, CHRISTOPHER CHARLES, clergyman; b. Allentown, Pa., Apr. 21, 1956; s. Warren Allen Miller and Marilyn Luanna (Andrews) Klibbe; m. Jeanne Marie Barela, Dec. 29, 1979; children: Scott Christopher, Erin Elizabeth. BA, U. Colo., 1978, MA, 1979; MDiv with honors, Denver Sem., 1985. Ordained to ministry Evang. Presbyn. Ch., 1985. Tchr. sci. Denver Pub. Schs., 1979-80; salesman Alcan Aluminum Corp., Denver, 1980-82; pastor Family of Faith Ch., Denver, 1985-86, So. Gables Ch., Denver, 1987—. Author, editor: (divorce recovery workshop) Beginning Again, 1988-90. Mem. Nat. Assn. Singles Leaders. Avocations: running, building model airplanes, indoor plants. Home: 12137 W Aquaduct Dr Littleton CO 80127 Office: So Gables Ch 7700 W Woodard Dr Denver CO 80227

MILLER, CLARK LLOYD, minister; b. Bethesda, Md., Nov. 3, 1954; s. Robert J. and Lois (Larsen) M.; m. Kimberly R. Miller, Dec. 20, 1975; children: Benjamin C., Heidi M., Lars A. BA, Ashland U., 1976; MDiv, Ashland Theol. Sem., 1980, postgrad., 1991—. Ordained to ministry Brethren in Christ Ch., 1990. Assoc. pastor Fairview Ave. Brethren in Christ Ch., Waynesboro, Pa., 1980-81; pastor Uniontown (Pa.) Brethren in Christ Ch., 1981-85; assoc. pastor Cumberland Valley Brethren in Christ Ch., Dillsburg, Pa., 1985-89; pastor Highland Brethren in Christ Ch., West Milton, Ohio, 1989—; bd. dirs. Bd. for Media Ministry Brethren in Christ Ch., Nappanee, Ind., 1986—. Office: Highland Brethren In Christ Ch 7210 S Jay Rd West Milton OH 45383

MILLER, CLIFF D., religious organization administrator; b. Detroit, Aug. 20, 1944; s. Clifford Andrew and Marion (Uzon) M.; m. Bonita Jean Fincher, June 26, 1971; children: Zachary, Jacob, Brianna. BA, Azusa Pacific U., 1971, MA, 1972; postgrad., Clairmont Grad. Sch., 1974-75. Cert. marriage counselor. Asst. dean of students Azusa (Calif.) Pacific U., 1970-75; dean of student svcs. Seattle (Wash.) Pacific U., 1975-78; exec. dir. Sammamish Bible Camp, Bellevue, Wash., 1980-84, Black Lake Bible Camp, Olympia, Wash., 1984-89; chief exec. officer Michindoh Ministries, Hillsdale, Mich., 1990—; trustee Pemberton Found., San Diego, 1974-77; bd. dirs. Pacific N.W. Covenant Bd. of Camping, Bellevue, 1982-84. Precient chmn. Rep. Party, Olympia, 1988-90, precinct chmn., 1988-90; search and rescue mem. 4 Wheel Search and Rescue, Olympia, 1988-90; instr. ARC, Covina, Calif., 1968-74. With USMC, 1964-67, Vietnam. Mem. Christian Camping Internat. (pres. N.W. sect., 1987-89), Am. Camping Assn., Kiwanis. United Brethren in Christ. Home: 1191 S Lake Pleasant Hillsdale MI 49242 Office: Michindoh Ministries 4545 E Bacon Rd Hillsdale MI 49242

MILLER, CURTIS HERMAN, bishop; b. LeMars, Iowa, May 3, 1947; s. Herman Andrew and Verna Marion (Lund) M.; m. Sharyl Susan Vander-Tuig, June 2, 1969; children: Eric, Nathan, Paul. BA, Wartburg Coll., 1969; MDiv., Wartburg Sem., 1973; DD (hon.), Wartburg Coll., 1987. Assoc. pastor Holy Trinity Luth. Ch., Dubuque, Iowa, 1973-75; pastor St. Paul Luth. Ch., Tama, Iowa, 1975-82; coord. for congl. life Am. Luth. Ch. Iowa dist., Storm Lake, 1982-87; bishop Western Iowa Synod Evang. Luth. Ch. in Am., Storm Lake, 1987—. Bd. regents Waldorf Coll., Forest City, Iowa, 1987—; bd. dirs. Luth. Social Svcs. of Iowa, Des Moines, 1987. Office: Evang Luth Ch Am Western Iowa Synod 318 E 5th St Storm Lake IA 50588

MILLER, DALE MAURICE, minister; b. Bloomington, Ind., Feb. 27, 1948; s. Daryl Maurice and Anne Margaret (Walker) M.; m. Susan Elaine Anderson, Sept. 18, 1971; children: Andrew Walker, Katherine Kristine, Sarah Rebecca, Samuel Dale. MusB in Piano Performance, Ill. Wesleyan U., 1970; MDiv, Garrett Theol. Sem., Evanston, Ill., 1974; cert. in ch. bus. adminstrn., Candler Sch. of Theology, Atlanta, 1985; D of Ministry, United Theol. Sem., Dayton, Ohio, 1991. Ordained to ministry United Meth. Ch. as elder, 1975. Assoc. min. 1st United Meth. Ch., Plymouth, Mich., 1974-76; min. Stony Creek United Meth. Ch., Ypsilanti, Mich., 1976-81, Meml. United Meth. Ch., Gadstone, Mich., 1981-87; sr. min. Cen. United Meth. Ch., Flint, Mich., 1988—; sec. exec. com. Detroit Conf. United Meth. Ch. Coun. on Fin. and Adminstrn., Southfield, Mich., 1988—; mem. ethics com., instl. rev. bd. McLaren Hosp., Flint, 1990—. Reviewer brass compositions News Notes, 1988-90. Announcer Flint Southwestern Acad. Boys' Swim Team, 1990-91. Mem. United Meth. Assn. of Ch. Bus. Adminstrs. Home: 1721 Lynbrook Dr Flint MI 48507 Office: Cen United Meth Ch 1309 N Ballenger Hwy Flint MI 48504 *God offers us a vital life, but we must be willing to accept the risks that accompany such a journey.*

MILLER, DARRYL RAY, production company executive, church music director; b. Xenia, Ohio, May 15, 1949; s. Delbert Russell and Hazel (Jenkins) M.; m. Susan Denice Johnson, Dec. 22, 1976; 1 child, Susan Anne Johnson. BA, Cedarville Coll., 1971; postgrad., U. Cin., 1971-76; M in Ch. Music, Scarritt Coll., 1982; fellow (hon.), Wessex Theol. Coll., Eng., 1989. Music dir. Xenia City Schs., 1971-78; dir. music Lake View Park Ch., Oklahoma City, 1978-80; adminstrv. asst. Scarritt Coll., Nashville, 1982-83; dir. music Andrew Price United Meth. Ch., Nashville, 1982-85; instr. Middle Tenn. State U., Murfreesboro, 1983-85; assoc. dir. of music Coral Ridge Presbyn. Ch., Fort Lauderdale, Fla., 1985-90; pres. Triangle Prodns., Nashville, 1990—; mem. guest faculty Baylor U. Sch. Music, Waco, Tex., 1987, 88, Skills for Success Workshops, Orlando, Fla., 1991. Mem. Am. Guild Organists (dean 1987-89, exec. dir. 1991—), Am. Choral Dirs. Assn., Am. Guild English Handbell Ringers. Republican. Mem. United Meth. Ch. Avocations: travel, cooking, computers. Home: 2811 Paden Dr Nashville TN 37206 Office: Triangle Prodns PO Box 68173 Nashville TN 37206

MILLER, DAVID LEROY, religion educator; b. Cleve., Feb. 25, 1936; s. DeWitt L. and Mary (Hartsough) M.; m. Donna Zirkle, June 28, 1958 (div. 1981); children: Dianna, John; m. Patricia Cox, Aug. 11, 1984. BA, Bridgewater Coll., 1957; BD, Bethany Sem., Chgo., 1960; PhD, Drew U., 1963. Prof. religion Drew U., Madison, N.J., 1963-67; prof. religion Syracuse (N.Y.) U., 1967—, Watson-Ledden prof. Author: The New Polytheism, 1974, Christs, 1981, Three Faces of God, 1986, Hells and Holy Ghosts, 1989. Named Outstanding Tchr. of Yr., Univ. Coll., Syracuse U., 1979-80, Univ. Scholar-Tchr. of Yr., Syracuse U., 1980-81. Fellow Soc. for Arts, Religion, and Culture (pres. 1991—); mem. Am. Acad. Religion, Internat. Soc. for Neoplatonic Studies. Mem. Ch. of the Brethren. Office: Syracuse U Dept Religion 501 Hall of Languages Syracuse NY 13244-1170

MILLER, DAVID TEEKELL, minister; b. Shreveport, La., May 29, 1956; s. John Smith and Shirley Ann (Teekell) M.; m. Margaret Blackmore, June 27, 1981; children: Cameron, Lauren, John Scott. BA, Hardin-Simmons U., 1978; MDiv, Southwestern Bapt. Theol. Sem., Ft. Worth, 1981; D of Ministry, Southwestern Bapt. Theol. Sem., 1989. Assoc. youth min. 1st Bapt. Ch., Edinburg, Tex., 1975; summer missionary to Alaska Home Missionary Bd., 1977; coll. min. Pioneer Dr. Bapt. Ch., Abilene, Tex., 1977-78; assoc. pastor 1st Bapt. Ch., Andrews, Tex., 1981-85; pastor Sunray (Tex.) Bapt. Ch., 1986—; exec. bd. mem. Bapt. Gen. Conv., Dallas, 1987—; bd. young assocs. Hardin-Simmons U., Abilene, 1987—. Author: The Establishment of a Suicide Prevention Ministry Team, 1989 (M.E. & Mrytle Williamson Meml. award 1990). Mem. Trans-Can. Assn. (evangelism chmn. 1987—, moderator 1991—). Office: Sunray Bapt Ch PO Box 383 Sunray TX 79086

MILLER, DAVID WAYNE, minister; b. Greenfield, Ind., Jan. 18, 1961; s. Joseph Wayne Miller and Mable (Lavonne) Wells; m. Brenda Mea Smith, Apr. 13, 1982 (div. Aug. 1988); children: Angel Lynn, Joseph Wayne, Christine Ann; m. Donella Loraine Mumpower, June 27, 1989; stepchildren, Fred James Mumpower, Matthew Jon Mumpower, Heather Ann Mumpower. D. Bible Knowledge, United Christian Bible Inst., 1987; cert. in sestematic theology, Am. Bible Acad.; diploma in Bible law, Christian Com. to Teach Bible, 1989. Ordained to ministry United Christian Ch. Minister United Christian Ch. and Ministerial Assn., Cleve., 1988—; Bd. dirs. Least of These Ministries, Muncie, Ind., 1985—. Fellow Convicts for Christ; mem. ACLU. Democrat. Home: Po Box 2081 Muncie IN 47307 Office: Least of These Ministries PO Box 2081 Muncie IN 47307 *Jesus said "that what you did to the least of these my brother's you did also unto me". (Matthew 24). This is a command to help those "least" around us. In doing so, we minister to Jesus and make life better for someone else.*

MILLER, DEAN ARTHUR, history and comparative religion educator; b. Chgo., July 29, 1931; s. Donald Braud and Bessie Edith (Garrison) M.; m. Elizabeth Walter Nov. 1955; m. Mona McGurk, June 1966; children—Douglas, Kenneth, Scott, Eric; m. Martha Herriott Swift, Oct. 13, 1980. B.S., Northwestern U., 1953; M.A., Columbia U., 1958; Ph.D., Rutgers U., 1963. Adj. asst. prof. St. Peter's Coll., Jersey City, 1962-63; asst. prof. U. Rochester, N.Y., 1963-68, assoc. prof., 1968-71, prof., 1971—, prof. history and comparative religion, 1975—. Author: The Byzantine Tradition, 1966, Imperial Constantinople, 1969; co-editor: Incognita; contbr. articles to profl. jours. Served with U.S. Army, 1956-59. Mem. Am. Acad. of Religion. Democrat. Presbyterian. Avocations: reading detective fiction; travel; canoeing. Home: 10848 S Hoyne Ave Chicago IL 60643

MILLER, DENZIL RAY, clergyman; b. Shamrock, Tex., Jan. 17, 1946; s. Joe Earl and Melba Nell (Franks) M.; m. Sandra Jane Easter; children: Linda, Karen, Robert. BS, Southwestern Assemblies of God, 1969; MA, Stephen F. Austin State U., 1984. Ordained to ministry Assemblies of God Ch., 1988. Pastor Assembly of God Ch., Fowler, Colo., 1969-75, First Assembly of God Ch., Nacogdoches, Tex., 1975—; youth dir. Rocky Mountain dist. Assemblies of God, Littleton, Colo., 1974-75, Christian edn. rep. North Tex. dist., Ft. Worth, 1979-88, Christian edn. asst. dir., 1988—; sect. dir. Decade of Harvent, Lufkin, Tex., 1990—; committeeman Lufkin sect. Assemblies of God, 1984—. Mem. Nacogdoches County Ministerial Alliance (pres. 1990). Home: 1116 Spring Valley Nacogdoches TX 75961 Office: First Assembly of God 1610 SW Stallings Dr Nacogdoches TX 75961

MILLER, DEVIN LEE, minister; b. Milw., Oct. 2, 1965; s. LeeRoy and Marilyn (Reynolds) M.; m. Denise Rochelle Fair, Aug. 11, 1990. BS, U. Minn., 1990. Choir dir. Mt. Zion Bapt. Ch., Milw., 1986-88; asst. chir dir. Pilgrim Bapt. Ch., St. Paul, 1988—, youth pastor, music staff leader, 1990—; state asst. music dir. Minn. State Bapt. Conv., Mpls., St. Paul, 1989—. Tri-chair Collaborative Movement for Improvement, St. Paul, 1990; mem. com. Twin Cities Against Drugs and Violence, Mpls., 1990. Mem. Phi Beta Sigma (pres. 1985-87). Democrat. Home: 7350 Bristol Village Dr #234 Bloomington MN 55438 Office: Pilgrim Bapt Ch 732 W Central Ave Saint Paul MN 55104 *We who are in the ministry are not the only persons chosen to live the life of Christ. All must strive to lead those we know and don't know to the life of Christ.*

MILLER, DIANE MARIE WYNNE, minister; b. Rochester, Minn., Nov. 27, 1948; d. Ervin William and D. Marie (Wynne) M.; m. Michael D. Durall, May 13, 1979; children: Graham Wynne Durall, Drew McCallum. BA, Macalester Coll., 1972; MDiv, Harvard Div. Sch., 1976. Interim minister Follen Ch., Lexington, Mass., 1975-76; from asst. minister to interim sr. minister The First Unitarian Soc. of San Francisco, 1976-81; sr. minister The First Ch. in Belmont, Mass., 1981—; del. on ch. staff Fin. Coun., Boston, 1982-85; mem. Melcher Book Award Com., Boston, 1985-87. Co-author: Coming Out of Marriage, 1974; bd. govs. Kairos Jour., 1977-80. Mem. Unitarian Universalist Ministers Assn., Ministerial Sisterhood. Office: First Ch in Belmont 404 Concord Ave PO Box 113 Belmont MA 02178

MILLER, DONALD EUGENE, minister, educator; b. Dayton, Ohio, Dec. 2, 1929; m. Phyllis Gibbel, Aug. 19, 1956; children: Bryan Daniel, Lisa Kathleen, Bruce David. Student, Manchester Coll., 1947-49; MA, U. Chgo., 1952; postgrad., United Theol. Sem., 1955-56; BD, Bethany Theol. Sem., 1958; PhD, Harvard U., 1962; postgrad., Yale U., 1968-69, Cambridge (Eng.) U., 1975-76. Ordained minister Ch. of the Brethern, 1957. Dir. material aid Brethren Svc. Commn. in Europe, 1952-54; tchr. Madison Twp. High Sch., Trotwood, Ohio, 1954-55; social worker Dayton, 1954-56; tchr. Gregory Sch., Chgo., 1957-58; interim pastor Salem Ch. of the Brethern, Dayton, 1959; assoc. prof. Christian Edn. and Ethics Bethany Theol. Sem., Oak Brook, Ill., 1961-70, prof., 1970-82, dir. grad. studies, 1973-86, Brightbill prof. ministry studies, 1982-86; gen. sec. Ch. of the Brethern Gen. Bd., Elgin, Ill., 1986—; lectr. Pastoral Psychotherapy Inst., Park Ridge, Ill., U. Chgo., Princeton Theol. Seminary, Princeton, N.J.; guest tchr. Theol. Coll. No. Nigeria, 1983. Author: A Self Instruction Guide Through Brethren History, 1976, The Wingfooted Wanderer: Conscience and Transcendence, 1977, The Self Study of the Chicago Cluster of Chicago Schools, 1981, Story and Context: An Introduction to Christian Education, 1986, The Gospel and Mother Goose, 1987; (with Warren F. Groff) The Shaping of Modern Christian Thought, 1968; (with Jack L. Seymour) Marking Choices, 1981, Contemporary Approaches to Christian Education, 1982, Theological Approaches to Christian Education, 1990; (with Robert W. Neff and Graydon F. Snyder) Using Biblical Stimulations, vol. 1, 1973, vol. 2, 1975; (with James N. Poling) Foundation for a Practical Theology of Ministry, 1985; designer programs include Edn. for A Shared Ministry, 1976-86, Tng. in a Ministry, 1984; TV host Christianity and the Arts, 1963. Mem. faith and order commn. Nat. Counc. Chs., 1976-81; del. to Russian Orth. Chs., 1967. Fellow Case Study Inst., 1972; rsch. fellow U. Chgo., 1951-52; teaching fellow Harvard U., 1960-61; faculty fellow Am. Assn. Theol. Schs. Faculty, 1968-69. Mem. Assn. for Profl. Edn. for Ministry (editor yearbook 1972, pres. 1976), Assn. Profs. and Researchers in Religious Edn. (pres. 1968), Am. Theol. Soc., Am. Soc. Christian Ethics., Religious Edn. Assn. Office: Ch of the Brethren 1451 Dundee Ave Elgin IL 60120

MILLER, DONALD KENNETH, JR., religious organization administrator; b. Winter Park, Fla., July 12, 1966; s. Donald Kenneth Sr. and Margaret Sue (Horton) M.; m. Regina Lilla Barker, Dec. 9, 1989. BS in Edn., Ga. So. U., 1989. Youth dir. Garden City (Ga.) United Meth., 1985, Metter (Ga.) United Meth. Ch., 1986, Pittman Pk. United Meth. Ch., Statesboro, Ga., 1987-88; dir. youth, children, young adults Avalon United Meth. Ch., Albany, Ga., 1989—, dist. del., 1989—; equipment, transportation dir. Lifeguard Summer Ministry, Statesboro, Youth Advance Team, Statesboro, 1988-89; sec. Albany Network Youth Mins., 1989—. Mem. Fellowship of Youth Workers, Profl. Christian Educators, Albany Network Youth Mins. Republican. Office: Avalon United Meth Ch 3018 Gillionville Rd Albany GA 31707

MILLER, EDDIE LEROY, philosophy and religious studies educator, author; b. L.A., Apr. 6, 1937; s. William Don Miller and Georgia Leota (Davidson) Barrington; m. Yvonne Marie Farrar, July 6, 1956 (div. June 1975); children: Terryl Eddie, Timothy Allen, Tad Stephen; m. Cynthia Lou Carter, Mar. 3, 1979; 1 child, Sean Davidson Miller. BA in Philosophy, U. So. Calif., 1959, MA in Philosophy, 1960, PhD in Philosophy, 1965; ThD, U. Basel (Switzerland), 1981. Jr. mathematician Bendix Computer Co., L.A., 1961-62; inst. philosophy Calif. Luth. Coll., Thousand Oaks, 1962-64; asst. prof. philosophy St. Olaf Coll., Northfield, Minn., 1964-66; asst. prof. philosophy U. Colo., Boulder, 1966-70, dir. theology forum, 1968—, assoc. prof. philosophy/religious studies, 1970-76, prof. philosophy/religious studies, 1976—; book rev. editor Theol. Students Fellowship Bull., Chgo., 1986-87. Author: Salvation-History in the Prologue of John, 1989 (CUSP award 1989), Questions That Matter, 3rd edit., 1992, God and Reason, 1972; editor: (anthologies) Classical Statements of Faith and Reason, 1970, Philosophical and Religious Issues, 1971. Mem. Studiorum Novi Testamentum Societas, Am. Acad. Religion, Soc. Christian Philosophers, Soren Kierkegaard Soc. Democrat. Lutheran. Avocations: violin, Plains Indians, skiing, tennis. Home: 4220 Corriente Pl Boulder CO 80301 Office: U Colo Philosophy Dept Campus Box 232 Boulder CO 80309

MILLER, EDWIN WALTER, minister; b. Benton Harbor, Mich., July 3, 1922; s. August F. and Clara (Zoschke) M.; m. Mary Weir, June 8, 1945; children: Jonathan, James, Elizabeth, Deborah. BA in Lit., Wheaton Coll., 1945, MA in Bibl. Lit., 1947; MDiv, Ea. Bapt. Theol. Sem., 1966. Ordained to ministry Bapt. Ch., 1948. Pastor Elim Chapel, Racine, Wis., 1945, Cass Ch., Downers Grove, Ill., 1946-48, Parma Heights (Ohio) Bapt. Ch., 1948-58, Immanuel Bapt. Ch., Wilmington, Del., 1959-89; visitation pastor 1st Presbyn. Ch., Springfield, Pa., 1990-91; bd. dirs. Sunday Breakfast Mission, Wilmington, Del. Family Found., Wilmington. Bd. dirs. Del. Geriatrics Svcs., Wilmington, 1970-80, Prison Fellowship, Wilmington, 1978-86. Mem. Nat. Assn. Evangelicals (bd. dirs. 1960-91), Del. Assn. Evangelicals (pres. 1966-91). Republican. Home: 1210 Bruce Rd Wilmington DE 19803

MILLER, ELDON H., minister; b. Hutchinson, Kans., Aug. 20, 1937; s. Henry A. and Mary (Yoder) M.; m,. Ella June Gingerich, May 22, 1958; children: Elaine Rose, Evelyn Joyce, Elwood Dean. Student, Berlin Bible Sch., 1955-57. Ordained to ministry Mennonite Ch., 1960. Vol. svc. worker Conservative Mennonite Conf., Irwin, Ohio, 1958-59; missionary, pastor Buckhorn Creek Mennonite Ch., Rowdy, Ky., 1960—; youth camp adminstr. Bethel Mennonite Camp, Rowdy, 1960-80; land agt. Ky. May Coal Co., Jackson, 1979—; bd. dirs. Bethel Mennonite Camp, Rowdy, 1962-85, 90—, maintenance coord., 1961-78; chmn. Breathitt County Evang. Crusade, Jackson, Ky., 1990-91; chmn. Ea. Ky. Coun., Rowdy, 1984-91. Bd. dirs. Breathitt County Soil Conservation Svc., Jackson, 1975—. Home and Office: 3020 Bethel Church Rd Rowdy KY 41367

MILLER, EMMETT GENE, religious organization administrator; b. Knoxville, Tenn., June 17, 1929; s. Norman Emmett and Ruth Naomi (Bible) M.; m. Doris Mae Romero, Nov. 11, 1950 (div. Feb. 1982); children: Charlotte Ann, Barbara Jean, Michael Shawn; m. Georgette, Mar. 26, 1982. Grad. high sch., Madisonville, Ky., 1948. Bd. dirs. United Meth. Ch., Laurel, Miss., 1960-62; bd. dirs., worship chmn. United Meth. Ch., Merced, Calif., 1968-70; deacon Cen. Presbyn. Ch., Merced, 1984, elder, commn. chmn., 1985-88, ch. bus. adminstr., 1989—. Pres. ARC, Merced, Am. Cancer Soc., Merced, United Way, Merced. With USAF, 1948-68. Mem. Merced C. of C. (v.p.), Rotary (Paul Harris fellow, bd. dirs., master lodge 99 1970), Shriners (pres. local chpt. 1971), Yosemite Lodge (master 1970). Democrat. Home: 3903 Annapolis Ct Merced CA 95348 Office: Cen Presbyn Ch 520 W 20th St Merced CA 95340

MILLER, ERNEST ARTHUR, religious organization officer; b. Burlington, Iowa, May 29, 1925; s. John Arthur and Frieda (Maurer) M.; m. Mary June Klaas, June 13, 1949. MusB, Northwestern U., 1949. Music sec. cen. region Salvation Army, Chgo., 1963-70, pub. rels. sec., 1970-74; dir. nat. pub. affairs Salvation Army, Washington, 1974—, dir. World Svc. Office, 1977-81, cons., 1981—. Office: Salvation Army 1025 Vermont Ave NW Ste 350 Washington DC 20005

MILLER, EVERETT GEORGE, SR., minister, labor studies educator; b. Pumphrey, Md., June 27, 1921; s. Everett Caldwell and Anna (Frderick) M.; m. Ruth Elizabeth Dressel, Feb. 21, 1938 (dec. 1947); m. Eleanor Mae Schaeffer, Aug. 26, 1950 (div. Aug. 1975); children: Everett, Charles F., Marc A., Paul J.; 1 foster child, Heidi; m. Mary Estelle Landry, June 27, 1981. AA, Towson State U., 1950; BA, Western Md. Coll., 1952; STB, Westminster Sem., 1955; MA, U. Md., 1968; MDiv, Wesley Sem., 1971; DD (hon.), Dundalk Sch. Religion, 1968. Ordained to ministry Meth. Ch., 1955; lic. psychologist, Md. Various appointments Balt. Ann. Conf., Washington, 1948-63; pastor Dundalk (Md.) United Meth. Ch., 1963-73, Orangeville Meth. Ch., Balt., 1981-84, Rohrersville (Md.) Charge, 1984-85; conf. sec. Christian Social Concerns, Balt., 1955-59; pres. Dundalk Sch. Religion, 1966-78; prof. labor studies, lobbying Dundalk Community Coll., 1973-91; project dir. various rsch. grants, 1976-80; pastor Arlington United Meth. Ch., Balt., 1985—; pres. McKendree Sch. Religion, Balt., 1991—. Author: Freeborn, A Life, 1955 (Earp award). Del. Met. Balt. coun. AFL-CIO, 1973—; lobbyist Am. Fedn. Tchrs., Baltimore County, 1981-83. Recipient citation VFW, 1977, community svc. citation Oper. Engrs., 1981; Community Svc. award Balt. United Way, 1978, 79. Mem. Univ. and Coll. Labor Edn. Assn., Md. Labor Edn. Assn. (pres. 1973—), Labor Edn. Alumni Assn. (sec. 1976-91), Md. Religion and Labor Inst. (pres. 1980—), Indsl. Rels. Rsch. Assn., Inst. Inddsl. Engrs. (sr.). Home: 301 W Cold Spring Ln Baltimore MD 21210 Office: 5268 Reisterstown Rd Baltimore MD 21215 *A religious faith must be reasonable if it is to be effective. A true Christian is simply a person who can love and forgive as Jesus did.*

MILLER, F(REDERICK) RICHARD, JR. (MUHAMMAD ABDUR-RAZZAQ), religious order executive; b. Pitts., Sept. 18, 1940; s. F. Richard Sr. and Orbie Pauline (Johnson) M.; m. Myrna Elaine Jerome, Apr. 6, 1966. AB in Sociology, Dartmouth Coll., 1962. Exec. treas. Bawa Muhaiyaddeen Fellowship, Phila., 1972—, trustee, 1973—; head Imam Mosque of Shaikh M.R. Bawa Muhaiyaddeen, Phila., 1984—; trustee Mosque of Shaikh Bawa Muhaiyaddeen, Phila., 1985—; mem. Interfaith Support Group Phila. Commn. Human Rels., 1989—; del. Majlis Ash-Shura, mem. econ. devel. com., Phila., 1991. With U.S. Army, 1963-65. Office: Mosque of M R Bawa Muhaiyaddeen 5820 Overbrook Ave Philadelphia PA 19131 *This world may be a university, a stage, or a prayer mat. If we deem it a stage and we great actors, it is not truly Life: it is a brief dream. When death's curtain falls, the light is turned up and we see reality. Such drama seems beautiful only in the absence of light. If we deem it a university, in pursuit of knowledge we learn how little we know, leading us to humility, awe of God, surrender to God, knowledge of right and wrong, loving God, wanting only Him, to purification and longing to act with divine qualities of the Messenger of God, to understanding and wisdom, glorifying and praising God, becoming the love and mercy of God; becoming trustworthy. We can then join the gentle folk who deem the entire earth a prayer mat, remembering God and bowing humbly before God with each breath. In their mouths are God's words, through their hands God gives, and in their hearts God embraces all mankind with loving-kindness. They are "Who's Who" in Allah's book.*

MILLER, GARETH B., religious organization administrator, minister; b. Harrisonburg, Va., Apr. 12, 1928; s. Joseph Wampler and Waltine (Brower) M.; m. Gunhild Tonnessen, Mar. 3, 1956; 1 child, Grace Virginia. BS in Agr., Va. Polytech. Inst. & State U., 1949; BDiv, So. Bapt. Theol. Sem., 1952. Ordained to ministry Bapt. Ch., 1948. Pastor So. Bapt. Conv., Remington & Jeffersonton, Va., 1956-61; founder, pres. FARMS Internat., Inc., N.Y.C., 1961—. Lt. (s.g.) USN, 1953-55. Mem. Coun. for Community Consciousness (pres. N.Y.C. chpt. 1976—), Morality in Media (bd. dirs. N.Y.C. chpt. 1975—), RCDA (v.p. N.Y.C. chpt. 1980—), Rotary (chmn. devotional com. N.Y.C. chpt. 1983-84). Home: 614 Albert Pl Ridgewood NJ 07450 Office: FARMS Internat Inc 123 W 57th St Ste 808 New York NY 10019

MILLER, GARY ROBERT, college chaplain; b. Syracuse, N.Y., Dec. 15, 1944; s. s. Glenn John and Winafred (Scammell) M.; m. Marilyn Barnes, June 1, 1968; children: Jon, Cynthia, Amy. AB, Dartmouth Coll., 1966; MDiv, Yale U., 1970; D Ministry, Princeton Theol. Sem., 1983. Ordained to ministry Presbyn. Ch. (U.S.A.), 1970. Asst. pastor Union Presbyn. Ch., Schenectady, 1970-73; chaplain Lafayette Coll., Easton, Pa., 1973—; commr. Gen. Assembly, Presbyn. Ch. (U.S.A.), Mpls., 1986. Bd. dirs. Safe Harbor, Easton, 1989—, Lehigh Valley Coalition for Affordable Housing, Bethlehem, Pa., 1990—. Grantee Pa. Campus Compact, 1990. Mem. Nat. Assn. Coll. and Univ. Chaplains (v.p. 1990-91, pres. 1991-92), Presbyn. Coll. Chaplains Assn. (editor newsletter 1986-88, 90—, pres. 1988-90). Democrat. Office: Lafayette Coll Office of the Chaplain Easton PA 18042-1769

MILLER, GENE EDWARD, minister; b. Estherville, Iowa, Mar. 22, 1954; s. Bernard Dean and JoElla Helen (Culbertson) M.; m. Elaine Lore Bauer, Mar. 15, 1975; children: Karl, Karyn. BA, Buena Vista Coll., 1976; MDiv, United Theol. Sem., New Brighton, Minn., 1983; D Ministry, Pitts. Theol. Sem., 1988. Ordained to ministry United Ch. of Christ, 1983. Pastor Trinity United Ch. of Christ, Lewisville, Ohio, 1983-86, St. Peter's United Ch. of Christ, Geneva, Iowa, 1986—; sec., bd. dirs. Iowa Conf., United Ch. of Christ, Des Moines, 1986—; treas. N.E. Assn. of Iowa Conf., 1989—; rural mins. contact United Ch. Bd. for Homeland Mins., N.Y.C., 1987—. Author: A Believer Speaks, 1979, For the Family, 1984, A Christian Response to the Family Farm Crisis, 1988; contbr. numerous articles to profl. jours. Bd. dirs. Rural Answers Inst., Geneva, 1986—; mediator Iowa Farmer/Creditor Mediation Svc., Des Moines, 1986-88; cons. Hospice of North Iowa, 1988—; mem. Ackley (Iowa) Econ. Devel. Commn., 1989—. Recipient Local Community Mission award United Ch. Bd. for Homeland Mins., 1989. Mem. Ackley Ministerial Assn. (pres. 1986-88), Franklin County Ministerial Assn. Republican. Home and Office: St Peter's United Church of Christ RR 1 Box 78 Geneva IA 50633

MILLER, GERALD E., bishop. Bishop Allegheny dist. Evang. Luth. Ch. in Am., Altoona, Pa. Office: Evang Luth Ch in Am 701 Quil Ave Altoona PA 16602*

MILLER, HAROLD RICHARD, minister; b. Muscatine, Iowa, Apr. 5, 1930; s. John Thomas Miller and Veda (Maples) Holgate; m. Patricia Ann Honts, Sept. 7, 1951; children: Denise D., Thomas M., Julie A., Kathryn L., Steven B. ThB, Bapt. Bible Sem., Johnson City, N.Y., 1959; postgrad., Bapt. Bible Sem.; DD (hon.), Bapt. Bible Sem., Clarks Summit, Pa.; postgrad., Grace Sem. Ordained to ministry Gen. Assn. of Regular Bapt. Chs., 1961. Pastor Bevier Regular Bapt. Ch., Binghamton, N.Y., 1955-61, Bethel Bapt. Ch., Iowa Falls, Iowa, 1961-66; campus missionary Bapt. Mid-Missions, Iowa Falls & Cedar Falls, Iowa, 1967-82; missionary, pastor Bapt. Mid-Missions, Coralville, Iowa, 1982-87, Bapt. Mid-Missions, Berean Bapt. Ch., Boulder, Colo., 1987—; chmn. N.Am. campus Bapt. Mid-Missions, 1966-76, mem. exec. field com., 1969—; bd. dirs. Grand Rapids (Mich.) Bapt. Coll. and Sem., 1978—, others; trustee Iowa Regular Bapt. Camp, 1964-66; chmn. Coun. of Six, Rocky Mountain Assn. Regular Bapt. Ch., 1990—; mem. exec. com. Coun. of Ten, Iowa Regular Bapt. Chs., 1985-87; del. to S.Am. and Cen. Am. to help establish campus ministries. Author manual: Campus Bible Fellowship, 1977. With USN, 49-50, 51-53. Republican. Home: 5122 Williams Fork Trail # 105 Boulder CO 80301 Office: Berean Bapt Ch 5475 S Boulder Rd Boulder CO 80307 *Both evidence and experience are essential for the understanding of life and its meaning. So the Bible has become my evidence, and Jesus Christ my experience.*

MILLER, HAYWARD LAYWON, clergyman; b. Panama City, Fla., May 15, 1954; s. William Leslie and Ouida (Mason) M.; m. Dianne Lynn Gunnell, May 24, 1974; children: Joshua Hayward, Kristen Nicole. AA, Gulf Coast Community Coll., 1974; BA, Fla. State U., 1977. Youth dir. St. Andrew Assembly of God, Panama City, 1974-75; orch. dir. Evang. Assembly of God, Tallahassee, 1976-77; assoc. pastor Christian Ctr., Panama City, 1977-82, Living Word Fellowship, Panama City, 1982—. Vol., dir. div. youth svcs. Juvenile Detention Ctr., Panama City, 1977-82. Mem. Fellowship Contemporary Christian Ministries, Bay County Ministerial Assn. (sec. Panama City club 1980-81). Home: 904 N Bay Dr Panama City FL 32444 Office: Living Word Fellowship 1815 Wilson Ave Panama City FL 32405

MILLER, ISRAEL, rabbi, university administrator; b. Balt., Apr. 6, 1918; s. Tobias and Bluma (Bunchez) M.; m. Ruth Joan Goldman, Oct. 16, 1945; children: David, Michael, Deborah, Judith. B.A. magna cum laude, Yeshiva Coll., 1938, D.D., 1967; M.A., Columbia U., 1949. Ordained rabbi, 1941. Rabbi Kingsbridge Heights Jewish Center, Bronx, 1941-68; rabbi emeritus Kingsbridge Heights Jewish Center, 1968—; asst. to pres. Yeshiva U., N.Y.C., 1968-70; v.p. Yeshiva U., 1970-80, sr. v.p., 1980—; counselor B'nai B'rith Hillel Found., Hunter Coll., Bronx, 1951-60; lectr. homiletics Yeshiva U., 1954-55; prof. applied rabbinics Rabbi Isaac Elchanan Theol. Sem., 1968—. Editor: Sermon Manual, 1951. V.p. Bronx Coun. Am. Jewish Congress, 1954-60, Bronx Coun. Jewish Edn., 1964-68; pres. Rabbinical Coun. Am., 1964-66, hon. pres., 1966-68; mem. exec. com. World Zionist Orgn., 1971-76; chmn. Am. Jewish Conf. on Soviet Jewry, 1965-67, Am. Zionist Council, 1967-70; pres. Am. Zionist Fedn., 1970-74, hon. pres., 1974—; v.p. Religious Zionists Am., 1966-68; religious cons., retreat master Dept. Def. in, Europe, 1954, 63-64, Alaska, 1958, Japan, 1960; Vice chmn. Conf. Pres.'s Am. Jewish Orgns., 1969-74; chmn. Conf. Pres.'s Major Am. Jewish Orgns., 1974-76; vice chmn. N.Y. Jewish Community Rels. Coun., 1976—; exec. com. Bronx coun. Boy Scouts Am., 1951-58; mem. Nat. Citizens Com. Community Rels., 1946—; bd. dirs. Nat. Jewish Welfare Bd., v.p., 1969—; chmn. Commn. Jewish Chaplaincy, 1962-65; bd. dirs. Bd. Jewish Edn. N.Y.C., Nat. Jewish Community Relations, United Israel Appeal, 1968—; bd. dirs., acting pres. Conf. on Jewish Material Claims Against Germany, 1983, pres., 1984; pres. Conf. on Jewish Material Claims Against Austria, 1984; sec. Meml. Found. for Jewish Culture, 1973—; bd. govs. Jewish Agy. for Israel, 1971-76; vice chmn. Am. Israel Pub. Affairs Com., 1983; mem. Jerusalem Com., 1990—. Served as chaplain USAAF, 1945-46. Recipient Bernard Revel award Yeshiva Coll. Alumni Assn., 1961, Nat. Rabbinic Leadership award Union of Orthodox Jewish Congregations, 1966, 81, Shofor award Boy Scouts Am., 1965, Frank L. Weill award Nat. Jewish Welfare Bd., 1972; Man of Year award Nat. Council Young Israel, 1976; Dr. Harris J. Levine award B'nai Zion, 1979; others. Mem. Jewish War Vets. (nat. chaplain 1962-63), Assn. Jewish Chaplains Armed Forces (pres. 1955-56), Rabbinic Alumni Yeshiva U. (pres. 1960-62). Home: 2619 Davidson Ave Bronx NY 10468 Office: Yeshiva U 2540 Amsterdam Ave New York NY 10033 *In life I have found the verbs more important than the nouns and adjectives. We show who we are by how we act, respond, love or hate.*

MILLER, JAMES ALVIN, minister; b. Ft. Worth, Tex., Oct. 20, 1944; s. J. Hershel and Marzelle (Burdine) M.; m. Linda S. McNeal, May 31, 1964; children: Doug, Todd. BA, U. Tex., 1968; MDiv, Southwestern Bapt. Theol. Sem., 1978, DMin, 1984. Ordained to ministry So. Bapt. Conv., 1972. Pastor Inspiration Point Bapt. Ch., Ft. Worth, 1972-74, Ridglea W. Bapt. Ch., Ft. Worth, 1974-80, Park Hts. Bapt. Ch., San Angelo, Tex., 1981—. Named Disting. Alumnus, Castleberry High Sch., Booster of the Yr., Lake View High Sch., 1988. Office: Park Hts Bapt Ch 810 Austin San Angelo TX 76903

MILLER, JAY ANTHONY, minister; b. Baldwin Park, Calif., Dec. 15, 1959; s. Allen Roger and Barbara Anne (Offinga) M.; m. Gayle Jean Taylor, July 16, 1983; children: Abram Anthony, Kaleb Nathanael. BA, So. Calif. Coll., 1981; MA, Azusa Pacific U., 1982; postgrad., Westminster Sem., Escondido, Calif., 1983; ThD, Bethany Theol. Sem., Dothan, Ala., 1986. Lic. to ministry Friends Ch., 1982, ordained, 1986; ordained by Am. Bapt. Chs. in U.S.A., 1988. Youth pastor Glendora (Calif.) Friends Ch., 1980-81; sr. pastor Santee (Calif.) Friends Ch., 1982-84, Alhambra (Calif.) Friends Ch., 1987-88; asst. pastor Garden Grove (Calif.) Friends Ch., 1985-87; sr. pastor 1st Bapt. Ch., Monrovia, Calif., 1989—; Christian edn. cons. Friends Chs., Whittier, Calif., 1985-88; regional chmn. evangelism Am. Bapt. Chs., Covina, Calif., 1990—. Chaplain Tustin (Calif.) Community Hosp., 1981, Alhambra Police Dept., 1987-91, Monrovia Police Dept., 1991; pres. Monrovia Police Chaplains. Recipient commmendation City of MOnrovia, 1990. Mem. Am. Bapt. Chs. MMins. Coun., Monrovia Mins. Assn. Office: 1st Bapt Ch Monrovia- Arcadia 223 S Encinitas Ave Monrovia CA 91016 *In this ever changing, fast lane, hurried society that we all live in, I have found it necessary to slow down and "know that He is God" and to remain firm on the foundation of the Word of God.*

MILLER, JOAN MARIE NONNENMOCHER, church secretary; b. Lancaster, Pa., Apr. 20, 1935; d. Jason Kurtz and Lillie Serena (Fisher) Nonnenmocher; m. Richard Horace Miller, July 21, 1956; children: Carol L. Hendershot, Ann M. Wolf, Susan D. Fegley. AA, Harrisburg Inst. Med. Arts, 1955. Med. asst. E.M. Solomon, M.D., Lancaster, 1955-56; sec. G.W. Davis Oil Co., Lancaster, 1956-59; office mgr. Progressive Design and Machine Co., Lancaster, 1973-81; sec., office mgr. Covenant United Meth. Ch., Lancaster, 1981—. Mem. Profl. Assn. of United Meth. Ch. Secs. (cert. sec. 1988). Republican. Avocations: counted cross stitch, knitting, crocheting, tole painting. Home: 20 Strasburg Pike Lancaster PA 17602-4120 *Each day is a gift to us from God and is filled with many blessings. How we use this gift of God is our gift to Him. This thought about each day helps us to fill our time with worthwhile and meaningful acts of love and kindness to others.*

MILLER, SISTER JOELLA, school system administrator. Supt. schs. Diocese of Rockford, Ill. Office: Office Schs Supt 1260 N Church St Rockford IL 61103*

MILLER, JOHN ANTONIO, nun; b. St. Louis, Sept. 23, 1942; s. Kenneth Joseph and Leona Jane (Berni) M. BA in Math., Fontbonne Coll., 1973; MA in Gerontology-Health Svcs. Mgmt., Webster U., 1986. Joined Sisters of Most Precious Blood, Roman Cath. Ch., 1960; lic. nursing home adminstr., Mo. Mem. staff Ecclesiastical Art Dept., O'Fallon, Mo., 1965-75, Ctr. Planned Change, St. Louis, 1975-76; adminstr. St. Joseph Retirement Ctr., O'Fallon, 1976-81, St. Elizabeth Adult Day Care Ctr., St. Louis, 1981—; profl. advisor Barnes Home Health Agy., St. Louis, 1988—; mem. adv. bd. St. Louis U. Geriatric and Rsch. Adv. Bd., 1990—; region VII rep. Nat. Coun. on Aging, Nat. Inst. Adult Day Care, 1989—. Named Woman of Achievement, St. Louis Suburban Jours.-KMOX, 1988; recipient Take Time to Care award Masonic Home, St. Louis, 1989. Mem. Mo. Adult Day Care Assn. (treas. 1989—). Home and Office: St Elizabeth Adult Day Care Ctr 3401 Arsenal Saint Louis MO 63118

MILLER, JOHN HAROLD, priest, journal editor; b. New Orleans, Dec. 29, 1925; s. Joseph Thomas and Mary Rose (Unland) M. PhB, Angelicum, Rome, 1948, STB, 1950, STL, 1952; STD, Theol. Faculty, Trier, Fed. Republic Germany, 1955. Joined Order of Holy Cross, 1943; ordained priest Roman Cath. Ch., 1951. Lectr. theology Cath. U. Am., Washington, 1958-60, staff editor New Cath. Ency., 1963-65; asst. prof. U. Notre Dame, South Bend, Ind., 1960-63, assoc. prof., 1963-67; assoc. prof. Loyola U., New Orleans, 1965-74; dir. office religious edn. Archdiocese New Orleans, 1975-76; provincial superior So. Province Holy Cross, New Orleans, 1976-80; editor Social Justice Rev., St. Louis, 1986—. Author: Fundamentals of Liturgy, 1960, Signs of Transformation in Christ, 1963, Called by Love, Love Responds, 1990. Home and Office: Cath Ctr Union Am 3835 Westminster Pl Saint Louis MO 63108

MILLER, JOHN HENRY, clergyman; b. Ridgeway, S.C., Dec. 3, 1917; s. Fletcher and Frances Helo (Turner) M.; BA, Livingstone Coll., 1941; M. Div., Hood Theol. Sem., 1945; postgrad. Hartford Theol. Sem. Found., 1954; m. Bernice Frances Dillard, June 27, 1945; children: George Frederick, John Henry. Ordained to ministry, AME Zion Ch., 1939-40; ordained bishop, 1972. Bishop, 10th Dist., 1972-80, 8th Dist., Dallas, 1980-84, 7th Dist., 1984-88, 5th Dist, 1988—; mem. Gov.'s Advocacy Com. on Children and Youth, 1985—; chmn. bd. AME Zion Ch. Trustee Livingstone Coll.; former chmn. bd. Lomax-Hannon Jr. Coll.; chmn. bd. Black Reps. N.C., 1985—; chmn. hon. degrees com. L.C. Mem. NAACP, World Meth. Council, Alpha Phi Alpha. Republican. Clubs: Masons, Elks. Office: African Meth Episcopal Zion Ch 8605 Caswell Ct Raleigh NC 27613

MILLER, JOHN RONALD, minister; b. L.A., Jan. 4, 1938; s. Clarence Raymond and Yolanda Sarah (Capenaro) M.; m. Madelon Louise Tetaz, Mar. 26, 1966; children: Sarah Louise, John Ronald. BA, Southwestern Coll., 1960; MDiv, Drew U., 1963; MA, Rutgers U., 1966. Ordained to ministry United Meth. Ch., 1965, United Ch. Christ, 1966. Pastor Burden (Kans.) Meth. Ch., 1958-60; min. Wilson Meml. Union Ch., Watchung, N.J., 1961—; mem. Consultation on Ch. Union, Princeton, N.J., 1982—, com. on disabled United Ch. of Christ, Montclair, N.J., 1982—. Chmn. Dorthea Dix Chapel Bldg. Program; pres. Trenton Psychiat. Hosp.-State of N.J., 1985. Southwestern Coll. scholar, 1960, Tipple scholar, 1960. Mem. Nat. Coun. Chs. of Jesus Christ (governing bd. 1985—), Internat. Coun. Community Chs. (moderator ecumenical commmn. 1984—, regional trustee, exec. bd. 1987, v.p. exec. bd. 1991), Optimists. Home: 9 Stony Brook Dr Warren NJ 07060 Office: Mary E Wilson Meml Union Ch 7 Valley Rd Watchung NJ 07060 *Once a person accepts that life is difficult one is free to meet its challenges.*

MILLER, JOHN STEWART ABERCROMBY SMITH, minister; b. Gibraltar, May 3, 1928; s. James Jarvie and Mary Stewart (Whyte) M.; m. Lorna Vivien Fraser, Sept. 11, 1956; children: Vivien Mary Louise, Kenneth John Stewart. STM, Union Theol. Sem., N.Y., 1953; BD, Edinburgh U., Scotland, 1952, MA, 1949. Ordained to ministry Ch. of Scotland, 1954. Asst. min. St. Giles' Cathedral, Edinburgh, Scotland, 1953-54; min. St. Andrew's Ch., Hawick, Scotland, 1954-59, Sandyhills Ch., Glasgow, Scotland, 1959-67, Mortlach & Cabrach Ch., Banffshire, Scotland, 1967-75, Morningside United (Ch. of Scotland and Congl. Union of Scotland), Edinburgh, 1975—; vis. instr. Columbia Theol. Sem., Decatur, 1986; hon. assoc. min. Peachtree Presbyn. Ch., Atlanta, 1986; chaplain Sea Cadet Corps. Contbr. articles to profl. publs. Mem. Scottish Ch. History Soc., Scottish Ch. Svc. Soc. Democrat. Avocations: reading, music, exploring Britain. Home: 1 Midmar Ave, Edinburgh EH10 6BS, Scotland

MILLER, JOHN ULMAN, minister, author; b. N.Y.C., Dec. 9, 1914; s. Clarence James and Edythe Gladys (Shaffer) M.; m. Marcella E. Hubner, June 12, 1937; children: John U., Mark C. (dec.), Mary Kay (Mrs. Charles Bolin, dec.), Gretchen (Mrs. Ernest Micka). BA cum laude, Taylor U., 1937; MA, Butler U., 1942; DD, Geneva (Wis.) Theol. Coll., 1968. Ordained to ministry Bapt. Ch., 1937; pastor First Bapt. Ch., Bluffton, Ind., 1946-49, Boston, 1949-56; pastor Tabernacle Ch., Utica, N.Y., 1956-63, United Ch. of Christ, Hagerstown, Ind., 1963-66, St. John's Evang. Ch., Louisville, 1967-77; Participant Churchmen Weigh News, WNAC, Boston, 1953-56; preacher Meml. Chapel; instr. religion N.Y. Masonic Home, Utica, 1957-62; broadcast weekly services WKBV, Richmond, Ind., 1965-66; preacher Fellowship Chapel WHAS, Louisville, 1967-77; maintains 24 hour Dial-A-Prayer, Louisville, 1968-77; minister Royal Poinciana Chapel, Palm Beach, Fla., 1978-84; ret., 1984. Author: Only to the Curious, The Voice of St. John, Providence on Pilgrimage, Two Wonders I Confess, Stop! Look! Listen!, He Opened the Book, Christian Ethic in the Sermon on the Mount, Windows on the Agony, Prayers Under Pressure, 1989. Chmn. Campaigns Crippled Children, Tb, U.S.O., 1946-49. Capt. USAAF, 1942-45, PTO. Named Community Leader Am. News Pub. Co., 1969. Mem. Ind.-Ky. Conf. United Ch. of Christ, Bach Soc. Louisville. Home: 4409 Green Pine Dr Louisville KY 40220 *Reverence is my name—the unwritten law of the universe, the invisible order of time, the cardinal virtue of life. Call me sovereign, for so I am, the gift of God to the world of man. Follow me, if you will, and I will disclose to you the life of God in the affairs of man. Charity is my attitude—the most pure of all gifts in the world, the ever redemptive spirit of time, the reconciling power of life. Call me sovereign, for so I am, the gift of God to the world of man. Seek me, if you will, and I will disclose to you the blessings of the eternal in the world of the temporal. Justice is my goal—the incredible design of the universe, the rightness of all things, the inescapable oughtness of life. Call me sovereign, for so I am, the gift of God to the world of man. Pursue me if you will and I will disclose to you the triumph of right amid the shadows of wrong.*

MILLER, JUDEA BENNETT, rabbi; b. N.Y.C., Dec. 10, 1930; s. David and Yetta (Holzberg) M.; m. Anita C. Kaufman, Nov. 11, 1932; children: Jonathan A., Rebecca E. Gottesman. BA, NYU, 1952; B in Hebrew Lit., Jewish Inst. Religion, 1954; MA in Hebrew Lit., Hebrew Union Coll., 1957, DD (hon.), 1982. Ordained rabbi, 1957. Rabbi Temple Emanu-El, Wichita, Kans., 1959-65, Temple Tifereth Israel, Malden, Mass., 1965-73; sr. rabbi Temple B'rith Kodesh, Rochester, N.Y., 1973—; chaplain VA Hosp., Bedford, Mass., 1965-73, Canandaigua, N.Y., 1973—; mem. faculty Tufts U., Medford, Mass., 1966-73; chmn. for World Jewry Affairs of Rabbinic Cabinet, U.S.A. Editor Orchard (publ. Nat. Rabbinic Cabinet of United Jewish Appeal). Served to capt. U.S. Army, 1957-59. Mem. Assn. Mental Health Chaplains, Cen. Conf. Am. Rabbis. Home: 240 Hibiscus Dr Rochester NY 14618 Office: Temple B'rith Kodesh 2131 Elmwood Ave Rochester NY 14618

MILLER, JUDITH ANN, financial executive; b. Chgo., Sept. 8, 1941; d. Frank G. and Kathryn M. (Stocklin) Bell; m. William J. Shrum, Aug. 3, 1958 (div. 1976); children: Steven W., Vickie L. White, Lisa A. Rhodes, Mark A., Brian D.; m. William L. Miller Jr., Nov. 28, 1976. Student, Ind. Cen. Coll., 1959-60, DePauw U., 1964-65. Office cashier, mgr. G.C. Murphy Co., Indpls., 1967-70; asst. treas., office mgr. Missions Blvd. Fed. Credit Union, Indpls., 1970-72; treas., office mgr. Bd. Higher Edn., Christian Ch. (Disciples of Christ), Indpls. and St. Louis, 1972-77; dir. fin. Mt. Olive United Meth. Ch., Arlington, Va., 1978-79; exec. dir. Interfaith Forum on Religion, Art and Architecture, Washington, 1979-82; devel. assoc. Nat. Benevolent Assn., Des Moines, Iowa, 1982-85; adminstrv. asst. Davis, Hockenberg, Wine, Brown, Koehn & Shors, Des Moines, 1985-88; fin. officer Episcopal Diocese of Iowa, Des Moines, 1988—. Mem. citizen adv. coun. Parkway Schs., St. Louis, 1976-77; county rep., mem. Fairfax County Sch. Bd. adv. coun., Springfield, Va., 1979-81; treas. congl. campaign Des Moines, 1983-85; mem. exec. St. Louis Children's Home, 1976-78; v.p., treas. Emmaus Fellowship Project on Aging, Washington, 1980-82; bd. dirs. Urban

Mission Coun., Des Moines, 1983-86, Pre-Trial Release Prog., Des Moines, 1984-87; mem. steering com. Iowa Interfaith Network on AIDS, Des Moines, 1989—. Named Vol. of Yr., Iowa Victorian Soc., 1985, Our Community Kitchen, 1986. Mem. Nat. Soc. Fund Raising Execs. (chpt. sec. 1985-87), Nat. Assn. Ch. Bus. Adminstrs., NAFE. Democrat. Mem. Christian Ch. (Disciples of Christ). Avocations: camping, sewing, knitting, reading, cooking. Home: 1207 21st St West Des Moines IA 50265 Office: Episcopal Diocese of Iowa 225 37th St Des Moines IA 50312

MILLER, JUDITH ANN, religion educator; b. Toledo, Feb. 21, 1952; d. Jack J. Mehlman and Patricia Ann McStay; children: Jason, Jaclyn. BA, Mary Manse Coll., 1974; MA in Edn., U. Toledo, 1991. Sunday sch. tchr. Cathedral of Praise, Sylvania, Ohio, 1985—; classroom tchr., art tchr. Cathedral Christian Sch., Sylvania, 1987—. Home: 6003 Durbin Sylvania OH 43560 Office: Cathedral Christian Sch 5242 McGregor Ln Sylvania OH 43560

MILLER, KEN LEROY, religious studies educator, consultant, writer; b. San Antonio, July 29, 1933; s. Eldridge and Paskel Dovie (Vick) M.; m. Eddie Juanell Crawford, June 14, 1952 (dec. Apr. 1981); children: Kimberly Miller Stern, Kerry, Karen Miller Davis; m. Carolyn Gayle Jackson, May 4, 1982; children: Sheila Stanley, Keith Conatser. BA, Abilene Christian U., 1956; MEd, Trinity U., 1965; EdD, Ariz. State U., 1975. Cert. tchr., Tex. Tchr. SAn Antonio Ind. Sch. Dist., 1957-58; tchr., adminstr. N.E. Ind. Sch. Dist., San Antonio, 1958-69; prin. Ralls (Tex.) Ind. Sch. Dist., 1969-70; minister of edn. S.W. Ch. of Christ, Phoenix, 1970-74; adminstr., tchr. Lubbock (Tex.) Christian Sch./U., 1974-77; minister of edn. Sunset Ch. of Christ, Lubbock, 1977-87; prof. religious edn. Harding U., Searcy, Ark., 1987—; curriculum cons. Sweet Pub. Co., Dallas., 1988-91; leader workshops and seminars in chs. and Christian schs., Tex., Ark., Okla., Ariz., Calif., Tenn., N.Mex., London, La., Nev., Nassau, Bahamas, 1955—. Author: Moral/Religious Stages of Development, 1975, (curriculum) Old Testament Personalities, 1980; editor: Recipes for Living/Teaching, 1982, (curriculum) Growing in Knowledge, 1977-90, the MINNITH series, 1991; guest editor, contbr. Christian Family, 1984. With U.S. Army, 1954-56. Mem. Christian Edn. Assn., Religious Edn. Assn., Assn. Secondary Schs. and Colls., Alpha Psi Omega, Sigma Tau Delta. Republican. Mem. Ch. of Christ. Avocations: fishing, hunting, reading, travel, writing, poetry readings. Home: 5 Robinwood Searcy AR 72143 Office: Harding U 500 E Center St Searcy AR 72143

MILLER, LAIRD O'NEIL, JR., pastoral counselor, educator; b. Pitts., June 12, 1915; s. Laird O'Neil Sr. and Hettie Evelyn (Shouse) M.; m. Ursula Elizabeth Sprau; children: William C., Ann Kline, Mary M. Croxton, Sarah K. Bomholt. AB, Washington & Jefferson Coll., 1937, DD, 1972; MDiv, Western Theol. Sem., 1952; MST, N.Y. Theol. Sem., 1967. Mem. corp. trust office Allegheny Trust Co., Pitts., 1937-39; city planner Allegheny County, Pa., 1939; time and load study engr. Pitts. Rwys. Co., 1939-42; prof. speech and drama Washington & Jefferson Coll., Washington, 1947-52; pastor Lebanon Presbyn. Ch., West Mifflin, Pa., 1952-53, 1st Presbyn. Ch., Mars, Pa., 1953-60; assoc. pastor 1st Presbyn. Ch., Cranford, N.J., 1960-62, Noroton Presbyn. Ch., Darien, Conn., 1962-74; chaplain Greenwich (Conn.) Nursing Home, 1976-81, ret. Bd. dirs. Mayor's Task Force on Drugs, Stamford, Conn., 1966-69, YMCA, Darien, 1964-72, Family Counseling Svc., Darien, 1964-72, Hospice, Frederick, Md., 1981. Staff sgt. U.S. Army, 1942-47. Mem. Presbytery of So. New Eng. (stated clk. 1968-73, moderator 1967), Synod of New Eng. (moderator 1972-73). Democrat. Avocations: writer, public speaking. Home: 12 Morgan Circle Swarthmore PA 19081

MILLER, LARRY JOE, evangelist; b. Huntingburg, Ind., Mar. 17, 1954; s. Gordon Russel and Nona Maxine (Winienger) M.; m. Jolene Kay Daniel, May 17, 1974; children: Benjamin Daniel, Joshua Joe. BS, Ky. Christian Coll., 1981. Ordained to ministry Christian Ch., 1981. Chaplain asst. Ky. Christian Coll., Grayson, 1977-78; youth min. Beech Street Christian Ch., Ashland, Ky., 1979-80; facilities mgr., dir. sch. shop Ind. Children's Christian Home, Ladoga, 1981-86; elder, evangelist New Market (Ind.) Christian Ch., 1982; min. Waveland (Ind.) Christian Ch., 1987-89; elder, evangelist Brady Lane Christian Ch., Lafayette, Ind., 1990—; owner, operator Miller Constrn., Grayson, 1979-81; human resources rep. Subaru-Isuzu Automotive, Lafayette, 1989—. Democrat. Home: 3419 Coventry Ln Lafayette IN 47905 Office: Subaru-Isuzu Automotive Hwy 38 E Lafayette IN 47905 *Life is short, and must be used to its fullest potential for His glory.*

MILLER, LISA LYNN MORRIS, religion educator; b. Abilene, Tex., Jan. 31, 1962; d. William Earl and Helen Lucille (Coston) Morris; m. Jeffrey Richard Miller, July 21, 1984; children: Sierra Elizabeth, Kirk Evan. BA, Carroll Coll., 1984. Dir. Christian edn., youth worker 1st United Meth. Ch., Marinette, Wis., 1985—; mem. dist. com. on edn. Wis. Conf., 1990, dist. coun. on youth ministries, 1991. Recipient Zac Davies award Carroll Coll., Waukesha, Wis., 1984. Mem. Am. Bible Soc., Peo-CX, Delta Zeta, Theta Alpha Kappa. Office: First United Meth Church 3230 Schooldale Dr Marinette WI 54143 *As the sun sets at the end of each day I pray that thru my life the Son shines in the heart of another. For happiness is found in unselfish service to others, in service to our Lord.*

MILLER, LLOYD LAWRENCE, clergyman; b. Melvina, Wis., Aug. 13, 1938; s. Lawrence Lloyd Miller and Irene Marie (Ornes) Miller-Mitchell; m. Janet Joanne Winterfield, Aug. 20, 1960; children: Dion Daniel, Dana Deann Miller Neuharth, Aaron Andrew. BA, Luther Coll., 1961; BD, Wartburg Sem., 1965, MDiv, 1976. Ordained pastor Luth. Ch., 1965. Pastor Salem-Emmanuel Luth. Ch., Long Lake, S.D., 1965-69, Emmanuel Luth. Ch., Gackle, N.D., 1969-75, Zion Luth. Ch., Eureka, S.D., 1975-86; sr. pastor Our Savior's Luth. Ch., Flandreau, S.D., 1986—; internship supr. Wartburg Sem., Dubuque, Iowa, 1976-84. Organizing pres. Long Lake PTA, 1967; charter mem. Gackle Lions Club, 1972; organizing pres., Eureka Lions Club, 1981; Lions zone chmn. S.D. Lions 5SE, Flandreau, 1988-89. Melvin Jones fellow Lions Internat., 1988. Mem. Moody County Ministerial Assn. (sec. 1987-90), Lions (Flandreau club, sec. 1988-90, pres. 1986-88). Republican. Avocation: gardening. Home: 419 S Wind St Flandreau SD 57028-1739 Office: Our Saviors Luth Ch 505 S Wind St Flandreau SD 57028-1741

MILLER, LYLE G., bishop. Bishop Sierra Pacific dist. Evang. Luth. Ch. in Am., Oakland, Calif. Office: Evang Luth Ch in Am 401 Roland Way #240 Oakland CA 94641*

MILLER, MARK ANDREW, priest, educator; b. Rochester, N.Y., June 19, 1943; s. William John and Katherine Josephine (Le Fevre) M. BA, St. Bernard's Sem., Rochester, 1965, MDiv, 1969; MA, Cath. U. Am., 1979; ThD, U. St. Michael's Coll., Toronto, Ont., Can., 1990. Ordained priest Roman Cath. Ch., 1969. Assoc. pastor Diocese of Rochester, 1969-78, 82-90, sabbatical asst., 1990—; vis. asst. prof. St. Bernard's Inst., Rochester, 1983—; mem. Diocesan Theol. Commn., Rochester, 1985-90, Diocesan Archives Com., 1987—. Pres. N.E. Ecumenical Cluster, Rochester, 1988-91. Mem. Am. Cath. Hist. Assn., Am. Soc. Ch. History, U.S. Cath. Hist. Soc. Office: St Bernard's Inst 1100 S Goodman St Rochester NY 14620

MILLER, MARK I. See MAR MARKUS

MILLER, MARLIN EUGENE, seminary administrator; b. Iowa City, Nov. 29, 1938; s. Marner and Lala (Hochstettler) M.; m. Ruthann Gardner, June 12, 1960; children: Rachel, M. Eric, Lynelle. BA in English, Goshen Coll., 1960; D. Theology, U. Heidelberg, Fed. Republic Germany, 1968. Ordained minister in Mennonite Ch., 1971. Assoc. prof. theology Goshen Bibl. Sem., Elkhart, Ind., 1975-78, prof. theology, 1978—, pres., 1975-90; pres. Goshen Bibl. Sem./Mennonite Bibl. Sem., Elkhart, 1990—; co-chair Inter-Mennonite Confession of Faith Com., Elkhart, 1986—, Apostolic Peace Witness Dialogue Nat. Faith and Order, N.Y.C., 1989-91. Author: Der Uebergang, Schleiermachers Theologie Des Reiches Gottes Im Zusammenhang Seines Gesamtdenkens, 1970, Chistology, Mennonite Encyclopedia V, 1990, Baptism in the Mennonite Tadition, 1990. Fellow Ctr. for Theol. Inquiry, Princeton, 1987. Mem. Am. Acad. Religion, Karl Barth Soc. North Am., Soc. for Christian Ethics, Rotary. Office: Mennonite Bibl Sems 3003 Benham Ave Elkhart IN 46517-1999

MILLER, MARTIN EUGENE, school system administrator, negotiator; b. Decatur, Ill., May 14, 1945; s. Floyd Homer and Vivian LaVerne (Gould) M.; m. Sherry Kay Bandy, May 25, 1968; children: Liane, Laura. BS, U. Ill., 1968; MEd, U. North Fla., 1974. Cert. math. tchr.; cert. ednl. adminstrn. and supervision. Tchr. Decatur (Ill.) Pub. Schs., 1968, Clay County Sch. Bd., Orange Park, Fla., 1970-74; coordinator cert. personnel Clay County Sch. Bd., Green Cove Springs, Fla., 1974-77, dir. instructional personnel, 1977-78, dir. personnel services, 1978-81, asst. supt. for human resources and labor rels., 1981—; mem. Edn. Standards Commn., Tallahassee, 1985—, vice chmn., 1988—; past mem. Blue Cross-Blue Shield Adv. Coun., Jacksonville, Fla.; past mem. Fla. Ednl. Leaders Forum. Served as staff sgt. USAF, 1968-70. Mem. Am. Assn. Sch. Personnel Adminstrs. (chmn. constn. and bylaws com. 1984-85), Fla. Assn. Sch. Personnel Adminstrs. (v.p. 1980-83, pres. 1983-85, bd. dirs. 1989—), Am. Assn. Sch. Adminstrs., Fla. Assn. Sch. Adminstrs., Fla. Pub. Employer Labor Rels. Assn., Phi Delta Kappa. Democrat. Presbyterian. Avocations: home computers, music, swimming. Home: 1612 Bay Circle W Orange Park FL 32073 Office: Clay County Sch Bd 900 Walnut St Green Cove Springs FL 32043

MILLER, MARY HOTCHKISS, lay worker; b. Washington, Dec. 4, 1936; d. Neil and Esther LeMoyne (Helfer) H.; m. Ronald Homer Miller, May 20, 1961; 1 child, Timothy Ronald. BA, Western Md. Coll., 1958; MRE, Union Theol. Sem., 1960; Cert., Windham House, N.Y.C., 1960. Dir. Christian Edn. Bruton Parish ch., Williamsburg, Va., 1960-61; dir. Christian Edn. (part-time) All Saints Episcopal Ch., Bklyn., 1961-62; adminstrv. and program asst., Christian Social Rels. Dept., Exec. Coun. Episcopal Ch. U.S.A. Episcopal Ch. Ctr., N.Y.C., 1967-72; nat. treas., chmn. Episcopal Peace Fellowship, Washington, N.Y.C., 1972-85; exec. sec. Episcopal Peace Fellowship, Washington, 1989—; bd. dirs., exec. com. Nat. Campaign for Peace Tax Fund, Washington, 1989—; bd. dirs., consultative coun. Nat. Interreligious Svc. Bd. for COs, Washington, 1989—. Contbr. articles to Witness mag. and jours., newsletters in field; book reviewer for The Living Ch., 1978—; designer ch. vestments and banners. Democrat. Office: Episcopal Peace Fellowship PO Box 28156 Washington DC 20038

MILLER, SISTER MARY STEPHANIE, nun, health care administrator; b. Morrilton, Ark., Aug. 27, 1940; d. Simon John and Elizabeth Josephine (Pfeifer) M. BS, St. Louis U., 1964, Maryville Coll., St. Louis, 1973. Fiscal svcs. dir. St. Edward Mercy Hosp., Ft. Smith, Ark., 1964-68, asst. adminstr., 1969-71; asst. treas. Sisters of Mercy-Province St. Louis, 1973-74, treas., 1974-80; adminstrv. asst. St. John's Regional Health Ctr., Springfield, Mo., 1981-82, v.p., 1982—, also chair bd. dirs.; treas. St. Joseph's Regional Health Ctr., Hot Springs, Ark., 1982—; chair bd. dirs. Mercy Hosp., Mansfield, Mo. Home: 1260 E Sunshine Springfield MO 65804 Office: St John's Regional Health Ctr 1235 E Cherokee Springfield MO 65804 *It is difficult to maintain a sense of priority when surrounded by so many areas of concern each day. A question which has helped me in setting priorities is, "In the light of all eternity, of what consequence will it be?".*

MILLER, MOSES WILLIAM, JR., minister, school system administrator; b. Cokesbury, S.C., Aug. 13, 1950; s. Moses William Sr. and Annie Mae (Goggins) M.; m. Geraldine Morton, Apr. 27, 1974. BS, Lander Coll., 1982; MDiv, Erskine Theol. Sem., 1986. Pastor African Meth. Episcopal Ch., Clinton, S.C., 1979-84, United Meth. Ch., Orangeburg, S.C., 1985-88, African Meth. Episcopal Ch., Greenwood, S.C., 1989—; environ. coord. Greenwood Sch. Dist. 50, 1989—; com. chairperson Greenwood Ministerial Alliance, 1990—. With USN, 1969-70. Named Outstanding Young Man in Am., Outstanding Young Men of Am., 1984. Home: 202 Sycamore Dr Greenwood SC 29646 Office: Mt Pisgah Afrcn Mth Epsc Ch 501 Hackett St Greenwood SC 29646

MILLER, PATRICK DWIGHT, JR., religion educator, minister; b. Atlanta, Oct. 24, 1935; s. Patrick Dwight and Lila Morse (Bonner) M.; m. Mary Ann Sudduth, Dec. 27, 1958; children: Jonathan Sudduth, Patrick James. AB, Davidson Coll., 1956; BD, Union Theol. Sem., Va., 1959; PhD, Harvard U., 1964. Ordained to ministry Presbyn. Ch., 1963. Pastor, minister Trinity Presbyn. Ch., Traveler's Rest, S.C., 1963-65; asst. prof. Bibl. studies Union Theol. Sem., Richmond, Va., 1966-68, assoc. prof., 1968-73, prof., 1973-84, dean of faculty, 1979-83; prof. of Old Testament Theology Princeton (N.J.) Theol. Sem., 1984—. Author: The Divine Warrior in Early Israel, 1973, The Hand of the Lord, 1977, Sin and Judgment in the Prophets, 1982, Interpreting the Psalms, 1986, Deuteronomy, 1989; editor: Theology Today, 1990—. Mem. Soc. of Bibl. Lit. (sec.-treas. 1987-88), Colloquium for Bibl. Rsch. (rev. standard version translation com. 1974—). Democrat. Presbyterian. Home: 89 Mercer St Princeton NJ 08540 Office: Princeton Theol Sem CN821 Princeton NJ 08542

MILLER, PAUL ALLEN, religion educator; b. Ft. Wayne, Ind., Oct. 20, 1955; s. Basil A. and Gloria J. (Witmer) M.; m. Anna E. DeWilligen, 1981; 1 child, Nathan J. AB in Religious and Classical Studies, Ind. U., 1978, MS in Computer Sci., 1982; postgrad., Trinity Evang. Div. Sch., 1979-80. Instr. Indiana U., Bloomington, 1979-82; prof. Aurora (Ill.) U., 1982-84, Trinity Coll., Deerfield, Ill., 1984-89; exec. dir. The Gramcord Inst, Vancouver, Wash., 1984—; rsch. prof. computer-assisted Bibl. studies Multnomah Grad. Sch. Ministry, Vancouver, 1991—. Author (software) Gramcord, 1978. Named Metz Disting. Scholar Ind. U., 1974, Curry Disting. Classics Scholar, 1977, Beinecke Disting. Scholar Sperry & Hutchison Found., 1978. Mem. Soc. of Bibl. Lit. Republican. Office: The Gramcord Inst 2218 NE Brokview Dr Vancouver WA 98686

MILLER, PAUL HENDERSON, clergyman, educational administrator; b. Charlotte, N.C., Nov. 17, 1928; m. Eveline Ruth Farmer, Oct. 19, 1954; children: Catherine Elizabeth, Philip Edward, Steven Paul, Judith Karol. BA, Emory U., 1950; MDiv, So. Bapt. Theol. Sem., Louisville, 1952, MA, 1958, grad. specialist in religious edn., 1961, EdD, 1969; postgrad. Furman U., Greenville, S.C., 1977. Ordained to ministry Bapt. Ch., 1953. Minister to students, Berkeley, Calif., 1952; minister Central Bapt. Ch., Atlanta, 1952-53, Second Bapt. Ch., Augusta, Ga., 1953-56, First Bapt. Ch., Americus, Ga., 1956-58, Farmdale Bapt. Ch., Louisville, 1958-62, Immanuel Bapt. Ch., Louisville, 1962-64; prof. religious edn. Nigerian Bapt. Theol. Sem., Ogbomosho, 1964—, registrar, 1970-80, dir. acad. affairs, 1979—, dep. prin., 1982-84; co-dir. First Consultation of Profls. in Religious Edn., Nigeria, 1967; mem. exec. com. Kwara Bapt. Conv., Nigeria, 1969-76, 81—, treas., 1969-71; adminstrv. cons. Kwara Bapt. Assns. (Nigeria), 1969-76; dir. First Nigerian Nationwide Music Conf., 1970; mem. Nigerian Bapt. Adult Edn. Exec. Com., 1973—; bd. dirs. Nigerian Bapt. Book Stores, Ltd., 1974—; mem. adv. bd. and mgmt. com. Joint Bapt. Pastors Sch., Nigeria, 1975-85; dir. Continuing Edn. Inst. for Denominational Religious Ednl. Workers in Nigeria, 1967, 80, 82; teaching fellow So. Bapt. Theol. Sem., 1959-63, vis. scholar, 1981; scholar-in-residence Southwestern Bapt. Theol. Sem., 1985, 90; chmn. theol. edn. council Nigerian Bapt. Conv., 1982—; mem. Nigerian Bapt. Staff Reorgn. Com., 1983—; mem. Nigerian Bapt. Stewardship Commn., 1968-71, chmn., 1970-71; chmn. Nigerian Bapt. Conv. Com. on Evaluation of Conv. Orgn., 1974-81. Basketball coach YMCA, Augusta, 1954-56; mem. Atlanta Opera Co., 1947-48; bd. dirs. Nigeria Tng. Center for the Blind, 1966—; mem. exec. com. Nigerian Red Cross, 1981—; mem. extension adv. bd. Fuller Theol. Sem., Nigeria, 1987—. Mem. Am. Acad. Religion, Am. Assn. Adult and Continuing Edn., Assn. Supervision and Curriculum Devel., Am. Soc. Missiology, Religious Edn. Assn. (U.S. and Can.), So. Bapt. Religious Edn. Assn., Nigerian Nat. Council on Adult Edn., Assn. Profs. and Researchers in Religious Edn., West African Assn. Theol. Instns. (chief examiner in Christian edn. 1974—, bd. examiners 1974—, chmn. Christian Edn. Sect. 1978—, nat. adminstrv. sec. for Nigeria 1979), Nigerian Assn. Theol. Instns. (exec. com. 1984—), Assn. Christian Higher Edn. in Nigeria (v.p. 1975—), Accrediting Council Theol. Edn. in Africa (exec. com., 1977-78), West Africa Regional Commn. on Accreditation (chmn. 1979-82, chmn. various coms.). Author: The Direction and Progress of Nigerian Baptist Sunday School Work, 1850-1965, 1968; editorial bd. Literacy Voices, 1986—, Ogbomoso Jour. Theology, 1985—; contbr. articles to publs. in field. Office: Nigerian Bapt Theol Sem, Box 30, Ogbomosho Nigeria

MILLER, PAUL MARTIN, education supervisor; b. Bainbridge, Pa., Apr. 2, 1914; s. Martin Z. and Rosa (Good) M.; m. Bertha Mumma, May 14, 1938; children: Rebecca, John James, Rosemary. AB, Goshen Coll., 1949; ThB, Goshen Bibl. Sem., 1950, BD, 1952; ThM, Southern Bapt. Theol. Sem., 1954, ThD, 1956. Ordained to ministry Mennonite Ch., 1947, as bishop, 1952. Supr. clin. pastoral edn. Philhaven Hosp., Mt. Gretna, Pa., 1986—; min., Mennonite Ch., Lancaster County, Pa. Author: Equipping for Ministry in East Africa, 1969, Group Dynamics in Evangelism, 1977, The Devil Did Not Make Me Do It, 1982, Leading The Family of God, 1983. Mem. Assn. Clin. Pastoral Edn. Home: 1001 E Oregon Rd Litiz PA 17543 Office: Philhaven Hosp 283 S Butter Rd Mount Gretna PA 17064

MILLER, PHILIP VERNON, minister; b. Albuquerque, Nov. 16, 1948; s. Urban James and Dorothy Lucille (Bash) M.; m. Paula Colker, May 29, 1971; children: Hope Elizabeth, Emily Victoria. BA, Tex. Christian U., 1970; ThM, So. Meth. U., 1973, DMin, 1974. Ordained to ministry Christian Ch. (Disciples of Christ), 1973. Assoc. min. First Christian Ch., Abilene, Tex., 1974-78; sr. min. Madison Ave. Christian Ch., Covington, Ky., 1978-85, 1st Christian Ch., Paducah, Ky., 1985-91, South Hills Christian Ch., Ft. Worth, 1992—; pres. western Ky. area Christian Ch., 1988-90, chair ecumenical concerns, 1989-91; chair pub. affairs Paducah Coop. Ministry, 1989-91. Contbr. articles to religious jours. Liaison officer USAF Acad., 1986-91; chaplain/capt. USAFR, 1985—. Named Outstanding Chaplain Air Res. Pers. Ctr., Denver, 1989. Mem. Paducah Area Mins. Fellowship (pres. 1990-91), Disciples Pastors for Theol. Discussion, Air Force Assn., Res. Officers Assn., Coun. on Christian Unity (assoc.), Rotary (bd. dirs. Paducah club 1989-91). Democrat. Office: South Hills Christian Ch 3200 Bilglade Rd Fort Worth TX 76133 *We can hide many kinds of ugliness behind the pretty mask of religion. God cares less about the external things, "the forms of outward rite," than about our inner thoughts and attitudes that result in our actions.*

MILLER, PHILLIP ALLEN, minister; b. Palestine, Tex., Oct. 7, 1954; s. J.B. and Jessie Mae (Richardson) M.; m. Janice Kay Sullivan, Aug. 15, 1975; children: Jay Brian, Jana Kay. B Gen. Studies, U. Tex., Tyler, 1978; MRE, Southwestrn Bapt. Theol. Sem., Ft. Worth, 1983. Lic. to ministry So. Bapt. Conv., 1972. Min. music and youth Trinity Bapt. Ch., Corsicana, Tex., 1975-80; min. music and edn. 2d Bapt. Ch., Huntsville, Tex., 1981-84; min. edn. and music 1st Bapt. Ch., Denison, Tex., 1984—. Mem. Southwestern Bapt. Religious Edn. Assn. (v.p. 1989, pres. support coun. 1990-91), Tex. Bapt. Mins. Edn. Assn. (v.p. 1990-91, pres. 1991-92), Lions. Office: 1st Bapt Ch 601 Woodard St Denison TX 75020

MILLER, RALPH MENNO, minister, religious organization administrator; b. Hubbard, Oreg., Mar. 22, 1925; s. Samuel S. and Catherine (Hooley) M.; m. Evelyn Irene Whitfield, Feb. 23, 1947; children: Judith Karen, Donna Joyce. D of Ministry, Internat. Bible Inst. and Sem., 1985. Owner, operator M & M Logging, Sweet Home, Oreg., 1952-56; support person Children's Farm Home, Palmer, Alaska, 1956-58; pastor North Pole (Alaska) Assembly of God, 1959-68, Sitka (Alaska) Assembly of God, 1968-78; pioneer pastor Sand Lake Assembly of God, Anchorage, 1978-84; sec., treas. Alaska Dist. Assemblies of God, Anchorage, 1978—, presbyter, 1964—; gen. presbyter Gen. Council Assemblies of God, Springfield, Mo.; exec. presbyter Alaska Assemblies of God, Anchorage, 1978—; exec. dir. Alaska Ch. Builders, 1984—, Revolving Loan Fund, Anchorage, 1984—, Little Beaver Camp, Big Lake, Alaska, 1984-90. Pres. PTA, North Pole, 1964-66. Republican. Avocations: flying, sports, woodworking, gardening. Home: 2111 Tasha Dr Anchorage AK 99502-5466 Office: Alaska Dist Assemblies of God 1048 W Internat Airport Rd # 101 Anchorage AK 99518

MILLER, RANDOLPH CRUMP, clergyman, emeritus religion educator; b. Fresno, Calif., Oct. 1, 1910; s. Ray Oakley and Laura Belle (Crump) M.; m. Muriel Phyllis Hallett, June 9, 1938 (dec. May 1948); children: Barbara Hallett, Phyllis Muriel (Mrs. Victor A.B. Symonds), Carol Christine (Mrs. Laurance Blanchard Rand III), Muriel Randolph (Mrs. Richard Frank Merenda); m. Elizabeth Rives Williams Fowlkes, June 16, 1950; children: Frank Vaughan Fowlkes, Elizabeth Rives Fowlkes (Mrs. Richard Cushman Carroll, Jr.). Student, Harvard Sch., Los Angeles, 1921-27; A.B., Pomona Coll., 1931; postgrad., Episcopal Theol. Sch., 1935-36, D.D. (hon.), 1961; Ph.D., Yale, 1936; S.T.D. (hon.), Ch. Div. Sch. of Pacific, 1952; D.D. (hon.), Pacific Sch. Religion, 1952, Berkeley Div. Sch., Yale U., 1981. Ordained to ministry Episcopal Ch., 1935; instr. philosophy religion and Christian edn. Ch. Div. Sch. Pacific, 1936-40, asst. prof., 1940-45, assoc. prof., 1945-50, prof., 1950-52; prof. Christian edn., div. sch. Yale, New Haven, 1952-63; Horace Bushnell prof. Christian nurture Yale, 1963-81, Bushnell prof. emeritus, 1981—; exec. sec. Religious Edn. of U.S. and Can., 1982-85; vis. prof. Div. Sch. Harvard and Episcopal Theol. Sch., spring 1954, Union Theol. Sem., spring 1957, Andover Newton Theol. Sem., spring 1963, Berkeley Div. Sch., 1964, Theol. Coll., Serampore, West Bengal, India, 1966, Drew U. Div. Sch., 1968, Sch. Theology, Claremont, Calif., 1976, Presbyn. Sch. Christian Edn., Richmond, Va., spring 1982; Episc. chaplain U. Calif., 1937-40; vicar St. Alban's Ch., Albany, Calif., 1940-51, rector, 1952. Author: What We Can Believe, 1941, A Guide for Church School Teachers, 1943, rev. edit., 1947, Challenge of the Church, 1945, Religion Makes Sense, 1950, The Clue to Christian Education, 1950, A Symphony of the Christian Year, 1954, Education for Christian Living, 1956, rev. edit., 1963, Biblical Theology and Christian Education, 1956, Be Not Anxious, 1957, I Remember Jesus, 1958, Christian Nurture and the Church, 1961, Your Child's Religion, 1962, 75, Youth Considers Parents as People, 1965, The Language Gap and God, 1970, Living with Anxiety, 1971, Live Until You Die, 1973, The American Spirit in Theology, 1974, This We Can Believe, 1976, The Theory of Christian Education Practice, 1980; editor: (with Henry H. Shires) Christianity and the Contemporary Scene, 1943, Church and Organized Movements, 1946; editor Religious Education (jour.), 1958-78, mng. editor, 1982—; contbr. articles to profl. publs. Chmn. dept. Christian edn. Diocese of Calif., 1944-47, 49-50; dir. ch. edn. Trinity Ch., N.H., 1961-71; founder Highlands Inst. Mem. Religious Edn. Assn. (chmn. bd. 1957-60, William Rainey Harper award 1978), Assn. Profs. and Researchers in Religious Edn., Nat. Council P.E. Ch. (curriculum div. 1947-52, writer, cons. 1952-56), Hazen Pacific Coast Theology Group (chmn. 1945-52). Home: 21 Autumn St New Haven CT 06511-2220 Office: Yale U 409 Prospect St New Haven CT 06511-2177 *Just as Thomas Aquinas christianized Aristotle, so modern theologians must come to terms with Alfred North Whitehead. This perhaps is the great metaphysical task of modern theology.*

MILLER, RICHARD A., minister; b. Bronx, N.Y., July 11, 1940; s. George J. and Christine (Fahrbach) M.; m. Rosemary Fry, June 5, 1962; children: Mary Lynn Mentink Miller, David Christian, Richard Andrew. BA, Cen. Coll., 1962; MDiv, New Brunswick Sem., 1965; ThM, N.Y. Theol. Sem., 1975; cert. pastoral counselor, Postgrad. Ctr. Mental Health, 1975. Ordained to ministry Reformed Ch. Am. Pastor Stanton (N.J.) Reformed Ch., 1965—; chmn. evangelism Classis of Raritan, N.J., 1968-69. Chaplain Hunterdon County Jail, Flemington, N.J., 1976—, Readington Twp. Police, Whitehouse Station, N.J., 1978—, Hunterdon County Sheriffs' Dept., Flemington, 1989—; chmn. N.J. dist. Hunterdon Dems., 1988—. Named Outstanding Citizen of Community, Stangon Grange, 1978. Mem. Am. Protestant Correctional Chaplain's Assn. Home: PO Box 114 Stanton NJ 08885

MILLER, RICK DEAN, minister; b. Canton, Ohio, Nov. 10, 1954; s. Robert Clyde and Shirley Iona (Morris) M.; m. Pamela Ann Smith, June 5, 1976; children: Jeremy David, Joshua Eric. AB, Ky. Christian Coll., 1976, ThB, 1977, MMin, 1985. Ordained to ministry Ind. Christian Chs., 1980. Min. youth 1st Christian Ch., Martins Ferry, Ohio, 1977-85, Russell, Ky., 1985-91; min. Mt. Pleasant Christian Ch., Bedford, Ind., 1991—; dir. Mission Evangelism, Bklyn., 1985—, Teen Mission USA, 1987—. Named Outstanding Young Minister, N. Am. Christian Conv., 1989. Home: Rte 17 Box 519 Bedford IN 47421

MILLER, RICK LARRY, pastor; b. Yreka, Calif., Aug. 19, 1961; s. Robert and Irma Ilse (Siedler) M. BA in Religion, Biblical Langs., Christ Coll., Irvine, Calif., 1983; MDiv, Concordia Theol. Sem., Ft. Wayne, Ind., 1987. Ordained to ministry Luth. Ch., 1987. Vacancy pastor Cross of Christ Luth. Ch., Bountiful, Utah, 1989-90; pastor 1st Luth. Ch., Tooele, Utah, 1987-91, Trinity Luth. Ch., Rangely, Colo., 1991—; sec., treas. Utah Circuit Pastor's Conf. Luth. Ch. Mo. Synod, 1988-91; mem. Dist. Campus Ministries Com., Denver, 1989-91, Utahns for Doctrinal Awareness, Salt Lake City, 1990-91. Author: Evangelism Resource Book, 1983, Congregation Evangelism Manual, 1987. Mem. Tooele Ministerial Alliance, 1987-91; friend Tooele Narcotics Anonymous, 1989-91. 1st lt. USAR, 1984—. Republican. Home: 218 S White # 2 Rangely CO 81648 Office: Trinity Luth Ch 736 E Main

Rangely CO 81648 *This thing called life is a very strange and complicated animal. I can thank no one but The Lamb of God for revealing the rhyme and reason of it all. Jesus, thank You.*

MILLER, ROBERT ALLAN, minister; b. Johnstown, Pa., Apr. 11, 1944; s. Charles Daniel and Jane (Kinkead) M. BA, Westminster Coll., 1966; BD, Princeton Sem., 1970, ThM, 1971; D of Ministry, Pitts. Sem., 1987. Ordained to ministry Presbyn. Ch. Asst. pastor N.E. Presbyn. Ch., North East, Pa., 1973-76; assoc. pastor Cross Roads Presbyn. Ch., Monroeville, Pa., 1977-81; resident supr. United Cerebral Palsy, Pitts., 1981—. Fund-raising chmn. YMCA, Wilmerding, Pa., 1985-88. Democrat. *Albert Einstein once remarked that the most important question to ask in life is: "Is the Universe a friendly place in which to live?" Faith answers yes to this question. In faith, I can live with a little more abandon, spontaneity, and "devil-may-care."*

MILLER, ROBERT LINDSEY, bishop; b. Eagle Grove, Iowa, June 24, 1933; m. Doris Mandsager; children: Tedd, Darrell, Diane. BA, St. Olaf Coll., 1966. Pastor Luth. congregations, St. Louis Park, Minn., Riverside and Santa Barbara, Calif., First Luth. Ch., Fullerton, Calif.; bishop Pacifica Synod, Evang. Luth. Ch. in Am., Yorba Linda, Calif., 1988—. Office: Evang Luth Ch in Am 23655 Via Del Rio Ste B Yorba Linda CA 92686

MILLER, ROBERT ORAN, bishop. Bishop Episcopal Ch., Birmingham, Ala., 1988—. Office: Episcopal Ch 2104 Vestavia Lake Dr Birmingham AL 35216*

MILLER, ROBERT RAY, minister; b. Chandler, Okla., Oct. 26, 1954; s. George Albert and Frances Helen (Baker) M.; m. Anne Marie Matekerl, Jan. 15, 1981; children: Ray Philip, Tori Anne. BA in Religion, Okla. Bapt. U., 1976; MDiv, Southwestern Bapt. Sem., 1980; D of Ministry, Midwestern Bapt. Sem., 1991. Ordained to ministry So. Bapt. Conv., 1975. Min. 1st Bapt. Ch., Wellston, Okla., 1975-77; chaplain Bapt. Med. Ctr., Oklahoma City, 1980-81; min. Witcher Bapt. ch., Oklahoma City, 1981, 1st Bapt. Ch., Raymore, Okla., 1981—; prof. Sem. Extension So. Bapts., Oklahoma City, 1982-84; head vol. chaplains Belton (Mo.) Rsch. Hosp., 1988—. Pres. Jaycees, Wellston, Okla., 1976; founder Citizens for a Better Cass County, Raymore, 1988. Recipient Outstanding Citizen award Witcher Community, Oklahoma City, 1987. Mem. Assn. Clin. Pastoral Edn., Blue River Bapt. Assn. (exec. com. 1987-90). Home: 108 W Maple Raymore MO 64083 Office: 1st Bapt Ch 116 S Washington Raymore MO 64083

MILLER, ROBERT ROYCE, priest; b. Chgo., Jan. 5, 1944; s. George James and Genevieve Mary (Royce) M. BA, Loras Coll., 1965; MDiv, St. Paul Sem., 1975. Ordained priest Roman Cath. Ch., 1969. Assoc. pastor Good Counsel Ch., Aurora, Ill., 1969-71, St. Patrick Ch., St. Charles, Ill., 1971-79; pastor St. James Cath. Ch., Belvidere, Ill., 1979-91, St. Thomas More Ch., Elgin, Ill., 1991—; mem. faculty, asst. prin. St. Edward High Sch., Elgin, Ill., 1971-76; v.p. Priests Senate, Rockford, Ill., 1982-84; chmn. Rockford Diocese Presbyteral Coun., 1985-88. Author: That All May Be One, 1976. Defender of bond Rockford Diocesan Tribunal, 1982—. Mem. Canon Law Soc. Am., Boone County Ministerial Assn. (pres. 1982-84), Clergy Relief Soc. (v.p. Rockford Diocese chpt. 1990—). Home and Office: St Thomas More Ch 215 Thomas More Dr Elgin IL 60123

MILLER, RODERICK JOSEPH, minister; b. Abington, Pa., Oct. 13, 1953; s. Robert Leroy and Alice Matilda (Bogdanoff) M.; m. Janet Elizabeth Powers, Oct. 3, 1981; 1 child, Jordan. BA, Allegheny Coll., 1976; MDiv, Wesley Sem., 1982. Ordained to ministry United Meth. Ch., 1985. Asst. campus minister Allegheny Coll., Meadville, Pa., 1974-76; US-2 missionary United Meth. Ch., Camden, N.J., 1976-78; ednl. asst. St. Thomas Ch., Manassas, Va., 1979-81; assoc. minister 1st United Meth. Ch., Laurel, Md., 1982-84; minister Union Chapel Ch., Joppa, Md., 1984—; disaster response coord. Balt. Conf. United Meth. Ch., 1989—, mem. dist. superintendency com., Joppa, Md. 1988—, Balt. Conf. Global Ministries, 1990—; treas. Wesley Sem. Community Coun., Washington, 1980, chairperson, 1981. Asst. Juvenile Ct., Camden, 1978. Seminarians scholar Wesley Sem. Faculty, 1980. Democrat. Home: 1412 Stockton Rd Joppa MD 21085 Office: Union Chapel Ch 1012 Old Joppa Rd Joppa MD 21085

MILLER, ROGER FREDERICK, minister; b. Galesburg, Ill., Nov. 24, 1950; s. Robert Karl and Naomi (Bulmer) M.; m. Evie May Caskey, Aug. 12, 1971; children: Sarah Evie, Seth Robert. Student, Grandview Coll., 1971-73; BA, Drake U., 1974; MDiv, Lexington Theol. Sem., 1977. Ordained to ministry Christian Ch., 1977. Student pastor New Liberty (Ky.) Christian Ch., 1974-77; pastor 1st Christian Ch., Falls City, Nebr., 1977-80, Cen. Christian Ch., Jefferson, Iowa, 1981-87, 1st Christian Ch., Muscatine, Iowa, 1987—; ch. camp dir. Christian Ch. in Upper Midwest, Des Moines, 1983—, mem. Task Force on Mens' Ministry, 1988-90, mem. Regional Bd., 1988—; walk coord. Iowa Ch. World Svc.-CROP, Jefferson, 1981-85, Muscatine, 1990—; mem. adv. bd. Iowa CROP, 1985-88. Author: What Can I Say, 1987; co-author: When My Grandma Died, 1986; contbr. articles, poems to mags. Mem. Family Resources Bd., Muscatine, 1989—; bd. dirs. Great River Mental Health Ctr., 1988-91. Named to Outstanding Men Am., U.S. Jaycees, 1980. Mem. Masons. Democrat. Avocations: golf, photography, reading, films, camping. Office: 1st Christian Ch 700 Kindler Ave Muscatine IA 52761

MILLER, RUSSELL EDMUND, lay worker, energy investment banker; b. Schenectady, N.Y., Mar. 23, 1942; s. L. Russell and Arline (Wooden) M.; m. Nancy Steeble, June 6, 1964; children: Laura, Ted, Sarah, Andrew. AB, Bowdoin Coll., 1964; MBA, Columbia U., 1966. Met. chmn. Christian Bus. Men's Com., Balt., 1976-84; deacon Timonium Presbyn Ch., Balt., 1978-83; dir. Balt. Billy Graham Crusade, 1982; trustee Washington Bible Coll., Lanham, Md., 1982-90, chmn., 1987-90; trustee Arlington Bapt. Ch., Balt., 1985-89; dir. Balt. Logos Com. of Operation Mobilization, 1987, Ch. Disciples Ministry Coun. Navigators, Colorado Springs, Colo., 1989—; v.p. Alex Brown & Sons Inc., Balt., 1981-90; pres. Miller & Co., Balt., 1991—. Chmn. Energy Conservation Com., Balt., 1983-85. 1st lt. U.S. Army, 1967-74. Republican. Home and Office: 315 Broxton Rd Baltimore MD 21212

MILLER, SARAH PEARL, librarian; b. Wilkensburg, Pa., Aug. 31, 1938; d. Samuel Henry and Anna Deborah (Shirley) Lyons; m. Paul Victor Miller, Apr. 15, 1989; children: Cheryl, Michael, Daniel, Lorel. BS, Indiana U. of Pa., 1960; MREM, Denver Conservative Bapt. Sem., 1965; MA, U. Denver, 1966. Libr. Denver Conservative Bapt. Sem., 1966—. Mem. Am. Theol. Libr. Assn. (bd. dirs. 1978-81, 90—, index bd. 1983-90). Home: 15707 E Grand Ave Aurora CO 80015 Office: Denver Sem PO Box 10000 Denver CO 80210

MILLER, STEPHEN DUANE, minister; b. Ionia, Mich., July 2, 1952; s. David E. and V. Marie (Barry) M.; m. Pamela J. Rider, Aug. 25, 1974; children: Kristine N., Stephen C. BA, Anderson (Ind.) Coll., 1974. Ordained to ministry Ch. of God, 1982. Assoc. pastor Broadview Park Ch. of God, Greeley, Colo., 1975-77, Highview Rd. Ch. of God, Washington, Ill., 1977-80, 1st Ch. of God, Effingham, Ill., 1980-88, K-Springs Ch. of God, Chelsea, Ala., 1988—; leader youth workshops, convs., camp and conf. music programs; mem. camp meeting program, Chelsea, 1991. Home and Office: Rd 39 Chelsea AL 35043-1600

MILLER, TERRY KEITH, minister; b. Fayette, Ala., May 9, 1959; s. Frederick Norman and Sarah Avis (House) M.; m. Teresa Stamps, Oct. 6, 1990. MusB, Samford U., 1984, M in Music Edn., 1989. Ordained to ministry So. Bapt. Conv., 1991. Min. music, youth and edn. Northridge Bapt. Ch., Northport, Ala., 1989-91; min. music and sr. adults Greenwood Bapt. Ch., Valdosta, Ga., 1991—; data processor AmSouth Bank, Birmingham, Ala., 1984-85; coord. computer help ctr. Samford U., Birmingham, 1986-88; bd. dirs. Tuscoba Camp, Tuscaloosa, Ala., 1990-91. Composer sacred music. Mem. Rotary (editor newsletter Tuscaloosa club 1990-91), Pi Kappa Alpha (sec. 1985-87, advisor 1987-88, Alumnus award 1988), Phi Mu Alpha Sinfonia (bd. dirs. 1984). Office: Greenwood Bapt Ch 1645 E Park Ave Valdosta GA 31601

MILLER, THEODORE CURTIS, radio station engineer; b. Washington, June 22, 1953; s. Arthur Alvin and Ellen Jane (Van Der Molen) M.; m. Jean Laura Pennington, June 4, 1977; children: Nathaniel, Carolee. BS in Radio Tech., Moody Bible Inst., 1977. 1st class lic., FCC. Audio visual technician Moody Bible Inst., Chgo., 1974-75; studio engr. Sta. WMBI, Chgo., 1974-76; rec. technician Webb Rec. Co., Chgo., 1975-77; chief engr. Sta. KNWC, Sioux Falls, S.D., 1977—. Republican. Baptist. Avocations: woodworking, photography, amateur radio. Office: Sta KNWC Rural Rt #3 Box 23 Sioux Falls SD 57106 *That I may glorify Christ in all that I do.*

MILLER, THOMAS EARL, JR., church pension fund director; b. Nashville, Apr. 30, 1936; s. Thomas Earl and Mattie Virginia (Parker) M.; m. Cecile Zania Tyler, June 21, 1958; children: Thomas Earl, Marianne Miller Ringlesbach. BA, Carson-Newman Coll., Jefferson City, Tenn., 1958; BDiv, Southeastern Bapt. Theol. Sem., Wake Forest, N.C., 1963; MS, Va. Commonwealth U., 1985; DHL (hon.), Bluefield (Va.) Coll., 1987. Ordained to ministry, So. Bapt. Conv., 1963. Minister of edn. Bayside Bapt. Ch., Virginia Beach, Va., 1963-65; dir. pub. rels. and personnel Va. Bapt. Hosp., Lynchburg, 1965-68; asst. pastor First Bapt. Ch. of Clarendon, Arlington, Va., 1968-70; assoc. editor Religious Herald, Richmond, 1970-86; dir. pub. rels. and sr. v.p. Annuity Bd. of So. Bapt. Conv., Dallas, 1986—. Recipient George Washington medal and Cash award, Freedoms Found. at Valley Forge, 1962. Office: Annuity Bd of So Bapt Conv PO Box 2190 Dallas TX 75221-2190

MILLER, THOMAS MARSHALL, SR., minister; b. Franklin, Pa., July 17, 1948; s. Lawrence Frederick Jr. and Elnora Mary (Marshall) M.; m. Patricia Ann Reiley, Aug. 13, 1983; children: Thomas Marshall Jr., Rachel Ana, James Isaac. BS, Phila. Coll. of Bible, 1970; MDiv, Reformed Episcopal Sem., 1974. Ordained to ministry Ref. Episcopal Ch., 1975, 76, to Anglican Ch. N.Am., 1988. Pastor St. Paul's Reformed Episcopal Ch., St. Petersburg, Fla., 1975-88; chaplain Pinellas County Jail, Clearwater, Fla., 1985-88; prof. St. Petersburg Theol. Sem., 1985-88; pastor St. Michael's Ind. Anglican Ch., Fort Erie, Ont., Can., 1988-89, Buttzville (N.J.) and Free Union United Meth. Chs., 1989—; mem. Bd. Fgn. Missions Reformed Episcopal Ch., Phila., 1978-88; pres. bd. dirs. Internat. House, St. Petersburg, 1980-86; co-founder Evang. Pastors, 1980-88. Contbr. articles to jours. in field. Block capt. Neighborhood Watch, St. Petersburg, 1985-88; precinct clk. local and county elections, St. Petersburg, 1985-88; rep. County Office on Aging, Belvidere, N.J., 1991; adv. com. County Human Svcs., 1991—. Capt., chaplain CAP, 1982-86. Recipient Svc., Guidance award Fraternal Order Police Lodge 48, 1987. Mem. Order of St. Luke, Buttzville Ministerium (pres. 1989-91, named Clergyman of Yr. 1991), Acad. Parish Clergy. Home and Office: Buttzville United Meth ch Box 54 Green Pond Rd Buttzville NJ 07829 *My goal in life is to serve, teach and live in such a way that I will always bring glory to my Lord and Savior Jesus Christ.*

MILLER, TIMOTHY ALAN, religion educator; b. Wichita, Kans., Aug. 23, 1944; s. Paul Alfred and Margaret Jean (Thompson) M.; m. Tamara Lea Dutton, Aug. 11, 1982; children: Jesse Dutton Miller, Abraham Dutton Miller. BA, U. Kans., 1966; MDiv, Crozer Theol. Sem., 1968; MA, U. Kans., 1969, PhD, 1973. Ordained to ministry Congl. Ch., 1968. Minister Bethany Park Christian Ch., Lawrence, Kans., 1968-71; lectr. religious studies U. Kans., Lawrence, 1969-88, asst. prof. religious studies, 1988—; chair Lawrence Unitarian Fellowship, 1989-90. Author: Following in His Steps, 1987, American Communes 1860-1960, 1990, The Hippies and American Values, 1991; co-author: The Sauna Book, 1977; editor: When Prophets Die, 1991; co-editor Am. Studies, 1982-86; contbr. articles to profl. jours.; editor Plumber's Friend, 1981-89. Mem. Mid-Am. Am. Studies Assn., Communal Studies Assn. (bd. dirs. 1989—), Am. Acad. Religion (chair new religious movements group 1983—). Office: U Kans Dept Religious Studies 103 Smith Hall Lawrence KS 66045

MILLER, TIMOTHY CURTIS, minister; b. Sandusky, Ohio, May 24, 1954; s. Curtis D. and Dorothy H. (Gysan) M.; m. Barbara Miller, June 19, 1976; children: Jason, Andrew, Letha. AA, Waldorf Jr. Coll., Forest City, Iowa, 1974; BA, Capital U., Columbus, Ohio, 1976; DD, Trinity Sem., Columbus, Ohio, 1980. Ordained to ministry Evang. Luth. Ch. Am., 1980. Pastor Plummer (Minn.) Luth. Parish, 1980-84, Pontoppidan Luth. Ch., Elliott, Ill., 1984-86, St. John's Luth. Ch., Loogootee, Ind., 1986-91, Newport (Ky.) Luth. Ch., 1991—; bd. mem. Luth. Community Action, Evansville, Ind., 1990-93. Bd. mem. Hoosier Uplands, Mitchell, Ind., 1987—; bd. mem., sec. Martin County Community Corrections, Shoals, Ind.; v.p. Am. Cancer Soc., Loogootee, 1986. Mem. Lion's Club (v.p. 1983). Home: 720 Overton St Newport KY 41071 Office: Newport Luth Ch 8th and Saratoga Box 1636 Newport KY 41072

MILLER, TIMOTHY WAYNE, minister, evangelist; b. Anchorage, Sept. 5, 1962; s. Dorothy Loeta (Davis) M. BA, Okla. Bapt. U., 1987. Ordained to ministry So. Bapt. Conv., 1983. Youth min. 1st Bapt. Ch., Cromwell, Okla., 1982-83, Wanette, Okla., 1985-87; missionary Home Mission Bd., So. Bapt. Conv., Billings, Mont., 1987-88; youth min. 1st Bapt. Ch., Farwell, Tex., 1988-90; youth min., staff evangelist 1st Bapt. Ch., Stigler, Okla., 1990—; bd. dirs., staff evangelist Tim Miller Ministries. Democrat. Home: Box 214 Stigler OK 74462 Office: 1st Bapt Ch 209 N Broadway Box 33 Stigler OK 74462

MILLER, VERNON DALLACE, minister; b. McClure, Ill., Sept. 27, 1932; s. Homer Lee and Marie Kathleen (White) M.; m. Alice Elizabeth Wright, July 25, 1954; children: Ronald, Philip, Elizabeth, Annette, Douglas. Student, Moody Bible Inst., 1950-53, S.E. Mo. State, 1954, So. Ill. U., 1956-57; BA, Cedarville Coll., 1963, LittD, 1988. Ordained to min. Bapt. Ch., McClure, 1953. Pastor Camp Creek Bapt. Ch., Murphysboro, Ill., 1953-54, Bible Fellowship Bapt. Ch., Carterville, Ill., 1954-57, Faith Bapt. Ch., Mattoon, Ill., 1957-60, Immanuel Bapt. Ch., Arcanum, Ohio, 1961-63; editor, bus. mgr. Regular Bapt. Press, Chgo., 1963-70; pres. Ch. Bldg. Cons., Chgo., 1971-87; exec. editor, treas. Gen. Assn. of Regular Bapt. Chs., Schaumburg, Ill., 1987—; trustee Awana Youth Assn., Streamwood, Ill., 1965-83, Grand Rapids (Mich.) Bapt. Coll. and Sem., 1981-91, Shepherds Bapt. Ministries, Union Grove, Wis., 1965—. Editor: (mag.) The Baptist Bulletin, 1987—. Del. Ill. Small Bus. Com., Springfield, Ill., 1984. Mem. Christian Ministries Mgmt. Assn. Republican. Office: Regular Bapt Press 1300 N Meacham Rd Schaumburg IL 60173-4888

MILLER, WARREN, bishop. Bishop Ch. of God in Christ, Cleve. Office: Ch of God in Christ 3618 Beacon Dr Cleveland OH 44122*

MILLER, WARREN WILLIAM, minister; b. Lexington, N.C., June 14, 1954; s. William Briggs and Mary Ruth (Greer) M.; m. LuAnn Southern, Aug. 19, 1978 (div. Oct. 1989); m. Scheryl Ann Cannon, May 4, 1991; children: Jeremy, Michelle, Joshua, Joseph. BA in Religion, Elon Coll., 1976; MDiv, Southeastern Bapt. Theol., Seminary, Wake Forest, N.C., 1979; postgrad., Lenior Rhyne Coll., 1988-89. Summer youth dir. Lakeview Bapt. Ch., Hickory, N.C., 1977, Cen. Bapt. Ch., Hickory, 1979; minister of edn. and youth First Bapt. Ch., King, N.C., 1980-82, Yaldese, N.C., 1982-89; minister of edn. and youth First United Meth. Ch., North Wilkesboro, N.C., 1990—; pres., founder Net Ministries, Valdese, 1985—; campus minister Bapt. Student Union, Western Piedmont Coll., Morganton, N.C., 1986-89; bd. dirs. Ministerial Bd. Assocs., Gardner Webb Coll., Boiling Springs, N.C.; youth and children cons. Assist Teams/Catawba River Assn., Morganton, 1983-89, Habitat for Humanity, Homeless Shelter. Contbr. articles to profl. jours.; editor: (youth newsletter) Powerline, 1979—. Vol. Meals on Wheels Project, Valdese, 1985-88; pres. King Recreation Com., 1980-81. Recipient B.S. Basknight award Religion Dept. Elon Coll., N.C., 1974, Outstanding Young Am. award So. Bapt. Conv., Nashville, 1987. Mem. N.C. Profl. Youth Ministers (regional coord. 1988), N.C. Religious Educators Assn., Southeast Religious Educators Assn., Christian Puppeteers, Wilkes Ministerial Assn., Leadership Soc. of Elon Coll. Republican. Home: Rte 4 PO Box 923 Wilkesboro NC 28697 Office: First United Methodist Ch 6th and E PO Box 1145 North Wilkesboro NC 28659 *I may not be able to change the world—however, I can change the world for one individual!.*

MILLER, WILLIAM CHARLES, theological librarian, educator; b. Mpls., Oct. 26, 1947; s. Robert Charles and Cleithra Mae (Johnson) M.; m. Brenda Kathleen Barnes, July 24, 1969; children—Amy Renee, Jared Charles. BA, Ind. Wesleyan U. (formerly Marion Coll., Ind.), 1968, MLS, Kent State U. (Ohio), 1974, PhD, 1983, postgrad. U. Kans., 1984-84, MA in Religious Studies, Cen. Bapt. Theol. Sem., 1988. Ordained to ministry Ch. of Nazarene, 1986. Libr. technician Kent State U., 1972-74; catalog libr. Mt. Vernon Nazarene Coll. (Ohio), 1974-76; catalog and acquisitions libr., 1976-78; dir. libr. svcs., prof. theol. bibliography Nazarene Theol. Sem., Kansas City, Mo., 1978—; adj. rsch. assoc. U. Kans., 1984-85; cons. Mid-Am. Nazarene Coll., Olathe, Kans., 1983; bd. dirs. Small Libr. Computing Inc. Author: Holiness Works: A Bibliography, 1986; editor TUG Newsletter, 1984-87 (bd. dirs. 1985-88), Jour. Religious and Theol. Info., 1990—. Served with U.S. Army, 1968-72. Mem. Assn. Study of Higher Edn., Kansas City Met. Libr. Network (coun. mem. 1987-89), Am. Theol. Libr. Assn. (bd. dirs. 1985-88), Kansas City Theol. Libr. Assn. (pres. 1985-89), Wesleyan Theol. Soc., Beta Phi Mu. Home: 1441 E Meadow Ln Olathe KS 66062 Office: Nazarene Theol Sem 1700 E Meyer Blvd Kansas City MO 64131

MILLER, WILLIAM LEE, JR., minister; b. Mammoth Spring, Ark., Dec. 27, 1926; s. William L. and Janie Katherine (Murrell) M.; m. Marion Evelyn O'Neal, Mar. 23, 1947 (div. 1976); children: Georgia Katherine Miller Beach, William Lee III; m. Judith Ann Bell, Nov. 28, 1977. AB, Phillips U., 1950, LittD, 1968; postgrad., U. Ark., 1951-52, Tex. Christian U., 1958, U. Ky., 1961; BD, Lexington Theol. Sem., 1961. Ordained to ministry Christian Ch. (Disciples of Christ), 1950. Pastor 1st Christian Ch., Rogers, Ark., 1952-59; v.p. Bd. Higher Edn., Indpls., 1962-68; pres. Bd. Higher Edn. Christian Ch. (Disciples of Christ), 1968-77; v.p. devel. Nat. City Christian Ch. Corp., Washington, 1977-82; upper Midwest regional min., pres. Christian Ch. (Disciples of Christ), Des Moines, 1982—; dir. Christian Ch. Found., Indpls., 1968-77, 84—; trustee Bethany Coll., W.Va., 1972-85, Culver Stockton Coll., 1970-77, 82—, Tougaloo Coll., Jackson, Miss., 1970-76. Precinct committeeman Dem. Party, Indpls., 1968-72; bd. dirs. St. Louis Christian Home, 1956-59; chmn. Coop. Coll. Registry, Washington, 1963-70. Served with USCG, 1945-47. Mem. Disciples of Christ Hist. Soc., Coun. Christian Unity (exec. com. 1968-77), Nat. Evangelitic Assn. (bd. dirs. 1983-86), Am. Assn. Higher Edn., Masons, KT, Sigma Chi. Home: 1207 21st St W Des Moines IA 50265 Office: Christian Ch (Disciples of Christ) PO Box 1024 Des Moines IA 50311

MILLER, WILLIAM SHANNON, deacon; b. Kansas City, Mo., Dec. 3, 1926; s. John Shannon and Eunice Millicent (Barrington) M.; m. Clara Anne D'Orazio, Nov. 21, 1945; children: Cynthia Jeanne, Cheryl Anne, Carolyn Sue, Christine Marie. Student, Ashland Coll., 1975-76, St. Paul Sch. Theology, 1976-77, Rockhurst Coll., 1977-79. Ordained deacon Episcopal Ch., 1979. Assisting deacon St. Michael's Ch., Independence, Mo., 1979-83; bishop's deacon Diocese of Western Mo., Kansas City, 1979-83; assisting deacon All Saints Ch., Kansas City, 1984—; del. Diocese of Huron, London, Ont., Can., 1962-66, Diocese of Ohio, Cleve., 1969-75, Diocese of Western Mo., 1976-78; chmn. Venture in Mission, Metro Deanery, 1978-80, coord., 1978-84. Editor, founder Deacons Doin's newsletter, 1983—; contbr. articles to profl. jours. Vol., mem. speakers bur. Hospice Care, Inc., Pinellas Park, Fla., 1983-84. With USCG, 1944-46. Recipient Export Mktg. award US CSC, 1973, Meritorious Svc. award Warren Rupp Co., 1976, Yr.'s Spl. Commendation award Hospice Care, Inc., 1984, also others. Fellow Harry S. Truman Libr. Inst. (hon.); mem. Am. Mental Health Fund. Home: 402 Point Dr Lee's Summit MO 64064 Office: All Saints Episcopal Ch 9201 Wornall Rd Kansas City MO 64114 *The best example of really loving yourself comes through the self-respect created by loving and helping others. True love of self is a direct result of loving others—and loving God.*

MILLEY, DAVID CLARK, pastor, management consultant; b. Everett, Mass., Mar. 14, 1941; s. Norman and Rowena (Noftle) M.; m. Carol Jean Kuykendoll, Aug. 19, 1961; children: David Lee, Rhonda Lyn. Student, Northeastern Bible Coll.; ThD, Gulf Coast Sem., 1985. Ordained to ministry, Evangelical Ch., 1985. Asst. pastor First Assembly of God, Hamilton, Ohio, 1961-62, Calvary Temple, Columbus, Ohio, 1962-63; founder, dir. Teen Challenge/Boston Drug Rehab., 1963-65; sr. pastor Hamburg (N.J.) Assembly of God, 1966-77, Walpole (Mass.) Assembly of God Ch., Inc., 1978—; exec. v.p. Caribbean Basin Internat., Inc., Calif., 1980—; cons. N.E. area bd. Women's Aglow, Walpole, 1974-84, World Harvest for Christ, Miami, Fla., 1980—; coord., bd. dirs. Third World Missions/Constrn. Work, Port-au-Prince, Haiti, 1980—. Mem. N.J. Planning Bd., 1970-75; pub. rels. dir. Emerge Ministries, Akron, Ohio, 1984-85. Republican. Avocations: racquetball, softball leagues, collector of old and small bibles. Office: Christian Life Ctr PO Box 415 Elm St Walpole MA 02081

MILLGRAM, ABRAHAM EZRA, retired rabbi; b. Kamenietz, Russia, Feb. 1, 1901; came to U.S., 1912; s. Israel M. Milgram and Mollie Kries; widowed; 1 child, Hillel I. BS, CCNY, 1924; MA, Columbia U., 1926; PhD, Dropsic U., 1945; D in Hebrew Lit. (hon.), Jewish Theol. Sem., 1956. Ordained rabbi, 1927. Rabbi Congregation Beth Shalom, Wilmington, Del., 1927-30, Congregation Beth Israel, Phila., 1930-40; mem. Hillel found. U. Minn., Mpls., 1940-45; dir. edn. United Synagogue Am., N.Y.C., 1945-61, ret., 1961. Author: Jewish Worship, 1971 (Best Book of Yr. on a Jewish theme), Jerusalem Curiosities, 1991; editor: Medieval Hebrew Literature, 1938, Sabbath: The Day of Delight, 1945, Great Jewish Ideas, B'nai Brith, 1962. Home: 12 Ben Maimon, Jerusalem 92261, Israel

MILLIGAN, CHARLES STUART, theology educator, minister; b. Sterling, Colo., Jan. 30, 1918; s. Martin Gatewood and Jonnie Carlyle (McCown) M.; m. Phyllis Ann Krider, Aug. 22, 1942 (div. June 1964); children—Kathleen, Stacia Ann, Deborah, Stuart; m. Nancy Swan Whitnell, July 9, 1965. A.B., U. Denver, 1939; Th.M., Iliff Sch. Theology, Denver, 1942, Th.D., 1952; S.T.M., Harvard U., 1948, Ph.D., 1951. Ordained to ministry United Ch. of Christ, 1942. Instr. U. Denver, 1939-42; min. Federated Ch., Paonia, Colo., 1943-46, 1st Ch. (Congregational), East Derry, N.H., 1947-50, West Somerville Congl. Ch., Mass., 1950-57; instr., assoc. prof. Tufts U., Medford, Mass., 1951-57; assoc. prof. Iliff Sch. Theology, Denver, 1957-61, prof., 1961-88, prof. emeritus, 1988—; theologian-in-residence Windward Coalition of Chs., Kailua, Hawaii, 1989; vis. prof. Colo. Women's Coll., Denver, 1966-68, U. Denver, 1958-62, Colo. Coll., Colorado Springs, 1972-84, 89; cons. U.S. Nat. U., San Diego, 1983. Author: Guide to Contemporary Philosophy of Religion, 1971; co-editor: Bernhardt's Functional Philosophy of Religion, 1989; editor The Iliff Rev., 1958-88. Chmn. Colo. br. ACLU, Denver, 1960-62; chmn. Colo. Com. To Abolish Capital Punishment, Denver, 1966-69; commr. Denver Mayor's Commn. on Community Relations, 1973-74. Recipient Community Service award Am. Jewish Com., 1982; E.I. Warren fellow, 1942, 46-47; Lilly Found. fellow, 1965, Am. Theol. Schs. faculty fellow, 1969-70. Mem. Am. Acad. Religion, Union Concerned Scientists, Religious Coalition for Abortion Rights, Am. Profs. for Peace in Middle East. Democrat. Home: 2266 S Columbine St Denver CO 80210 Office: Iliff Sch Theology Denver CO 80210 *The great choice is between viewing faith as a journey together or faith as a fortress. We have come to the time when we must outgrow the fortress mentality and learn to live with the spirit of adventure and cooperation.*

MILLIKAN, KIM YAEGER, communications director; b. St. Louis, Nov. 23, 1954; d. Gerald A. and Mary Nell (Black) Yaeger; m. David McCombs Millikan, July 2, 1978; children: Carissa Leigh, Lindsey Claire, Joel Yaeger. BA, U. Ariz., 1976, MA, 1979. Acct. exec. The Competitive Edge, Albuquerque, 1979; computing ctr. communications staff U. N.Mex., Albuquerque, 1980-82; newsletter editor Northwoods Presbyn. Ch., Houston, 1987—, dir. communications, 1991. Office: Northwoods Presbyn Church 3320 FM 1960 W Houston TX 77068

MILLINER, EDWARD LEE, JR., navy chaplain; b. Ft. Bragg, N.C., Sept. 28, 1951; s. Edward Lee and Peggy Joe (Cotton) M.; m. Donna Lee Bell, Oct. 30, 1971; children: April, Jonathan, James. BS, Lee Coll., 1974; MDiv, Southeastern Bapt. Theol. Sem., 1978, ThM, 1980; D Ministry, Luther Rice Sem., 1991. Ordained to ministry Bapt. Ch., 1977. Pastor Rock Spring Bapt. Ch., Townsville, N.C., 1978-82; commd. lt. (j.g.) USN, 1982, advanced through grades to lt. comdr., 1988, chaplain, 1982—. Mem. Evang. Theol. Soc., Mil. Chaplains Assn. U.S.A. Republican. Home: 60 Cavalla Ct Groton CT 06340 Office: USN Navy Submarine Base NL0N Groton CT 06340 *The pace and challenges of modern life require the expenditure of much personal energy. In my life I have discovered the renewal of spirit through moments of solitude, stillness and silence.*

MILLS, DENISE, lay worker; b. Newberry, S.C., Apr. 8, 1965; d. Wyman Harman and Evangeline (Berry) M. Grad., Newberry High Sch., 1983.

Tchr. Vacation Bible Sch., Newberry, 1984—, Sun. Sch., Newberry, 1988—; dir. Bapt. Young Women, Newberry, 1989—; tchr. mission trips, various locations, 1987-89; tchr. Mission Friends, Newberry, 1987—, mem. choir, 1986—, leader Weekday Bible Club, 1990—. Active March of Dimes Walk Am., Am. Diabetes Assn. Bike-a-Thon. Mem. Gospel Music Assn. (assoc.). Home: 2218 Adelaide St Newberry SC 29108-4529 *We are to be an encourager to share Christ love with all we meet. There is no task we can not handle. What ever God calls us to do, He has already equipped us to handle—standing faithful and firm in Christ to be a light in this world.*

MILLS, HUEY ALLEN, minister, religious school administrator; b. Grimesland, N.C., June 20, 1946; s. Charlie Samuel and Eula Mae (Elks) M.; m. Pamela Lavon Cox, Aug. 28, 1966. B in Sacred Lit., Holmes Theol. Sem., 1968; BA, Central (S.C.) Wesleyan Coll., 1970; MRE, Heritage Bible Grad. Sch., Dunn, N.C., 1974. Lic. counselor. Pastor Cordover (N.C.) Pentecostal Holiness Ch., 1970-71; registrar Heritage Bible Coll., Dunn, 1971-74; prof. Founds. Bible Coll., Benson, N.C., 1974-76; adminstr. Faith Christian Sch., Lancaster, S.C., 1984—; del. youth conv. Pentecostal Holiness Ch., 1976, gen. conv., 1977, 81; trustee and pastor Fellowship Bible Ch., Lancaster, 1982—. Author: Manual of C.E. for Ch., 1976; pub. The Trinity Trumpet mag., 1979, editor, 1980. Poll worker Rep. Party, Lancaster, 1986—, del. state conv., Columbia, S.C., 1989, precinct pres. Lancaster County, 1989—. Mem. ASCD, Am. Assn. Christian Schs., S.C. Assn. Christian Schs. Home: 602 Davis St Lancaster SC 29720 Office: Faith Christian Ch Rte 7 Box 269-A Lancaster SC 29720 *"What doth the Lord require of thee but to do justly and to love mercy and to walk humbly with thy God." (Micah 6:8).*

MILLS, KENNETH EUGENE, minister; b. Houston, Apr. 24, 1946; s. James Walter Jr. and Jimmie Lee (Layton) M.; m. Kay Marie Word, Sept. 27, 1980; children: Rebecca, Jennifer. Student, Harding U., 1963-65, 70, SUNY, Albany, 1985. Ordained to ministry Ch. of Christ, 1980. Minister Ch. of Christ, Bellevue, Ohio, 1968-70; assoc. minister Ch. of Christ, Okmulgee, Okla., 1980-81; minister SW Ch. of Christ, Little Rock, 1982-85; assoc minister West Ark. Ch. of Christ, Ft. Smith, 1986-89; minister Chastain Ch. of Christ, Mulberry, Ark., 1990—. Contbr. articles to mags. Mem. Southeastern Profl. Photographers Assn., Atlanta, 1976-79, Profl. Photographers Am., 1976-79, Memphis Conv. & Visitors Bur., 1979, Ft. Smith C. of C., 1985. Home: Rte 1 Box 273 Rudy AR 72952 Office: PO Box 1629 Van Buren AR 72956 *Becoming a person of completeness is a God-given possibility which encompasses a life-long process and provides a continual sense of fulfillment.*

MILLS, LAWRENCE DONALD, JR., minister; b. Amarillo, Tex., Aug. 9, 1946; s. Lawrence Donald and Ruth (Harris) M.; m. Rita LaVelle Harper, Aug. 9, 1968; children: Rebecca Lynn, Timothy Alan. BS in Agrl. Bus., W. Tex. State U., 1970; MRE, Southwestern Bapt. Theol. Sem., 1983. Ordained to ministry So. Bapt. Conv., 1985. Edn. and youth dir. Bluff Dale (Tex.) Bapt. Ch., 1980-83; pastor Duffau (Tex.) Bapt. Ch., 1983-87, Riverside Bapt. Ch., Stephenville, Tex., 1987-89; interim pastor Lingleville (Tex.) Bapt. Ch., 1990-91; pastor Round Grove Bapt. Ch., Dublin, Tex., 1991—; discipleship tng. dir. 1st Bapt. Ch., Stephenville, Tex., 1990—; owner L & M Ind. Claims Svc., Stephenville, Tex., 1990—; moderator Erath Bapt. Assn., Stephenville, 1990-91, chmn. calendar com., 1987-90, chmn. missions com., 1988-91. Corres. Hico News Rev., 1984-88. Mem. Long Range Planning Com. for Water/Waste Water, City of Stpehenville, 1990; pres. Hochheim Prairie County Farm Mutual, 1986-88. Home and Office: 253 Davis Ave Stephenville TX 76401 *When the rest of the world fails and walks out on us, Jesus is there to walk into our life and be our friend.*

MILLS, LESLIE LEE, minister; b. Dallas, Nov. 18, 1943; s. Albert Lee and Virdia Inez (Avery) M.; m. Virginia Ann Darden, Mar. 5, 1966; 1 child, LeeAnn. BA, East Tex. Bapt. U., 1966; MDiv, Southwestern Bapt. Theol Sem., Ft. Worth, 1969; D Ministry, Luther Rice Sem., Jacksonville, Fla., 1980. Ordained to ministry So. Bapt. Conv., 1965. Pastor 1st Bapt Ch., Groveton, Tex., 1975-81, Bethel Bapt. Ch., New Caney, Tex., 1981-82; min. missions Cen. Bapt. Ch., Baytown, Tex., 1982-84; pastor Hibbard Meml. Bapt. Ch., Houston, Tex., 1984-87, 1st Bapt. Ch., Weslaco, Tex., 1987—. Trustee Valley Bapt. Acad., Harlingen, Tex., 1980-87. Mem. Weslaco C. of C., Lions. Home: 706 S Ohio Weslaco TX 78596 Office: 1st Bapt Ch 600 S Kansas Weslaco TX 78596 *At this point in life it is far more important to know God than anything else or any other person. Times change. People change. God is the one constant to anchor to in life. Therefore, I must seek to know Him.*

MILLS, LISTON OURY, theology educator; b. Wilmington, N.C., Aug. 7, 1928; s. Leonard Liston and Ruby Preston (Oury) M.; m. Jennie Ellen Windsor, Dec. 28, 1962; 1 child, Sarah Elizabeth. BA, Davidson Coll., 1950; BD, So. Bapt. Theol. Sem., 1953, ThM, 1957, ThD, 1964. Ordained to ministry So. Bapt. Conv., 1953. Asst. pastor 5th Ave. Bapt. Ch., Huntington, W.Va., 1957-58; pastor Kent (Ind.) Bapt. Ch., 1960-62; successively instr, asst. prof., assoc. prof. Vanderbilt U. Div. Sch., Nashville, Oberlin Alumni prof. pastoral theology and counseling, 1962—, Alexander Heard Disting. Svc. prof., 1991—, acting dean, 1989; vis. prof. Earlham Grad. Sch. Theology, Richmond, Ind., 1965, St. Luke's Sch. Theology, Sewanee, Tenn., 1972, 73, 74, 85, So. Bapt. Theol. Sem., 1980, Lexington (Ky.) Theol. Sem., 1981; vis. lectr. Yale U. Div. Sch., New Haven, 1969; cons. Tenn. Dept. Mental Health, Nashville, 1964-65, Tenn. Personnel Dept., Nashville, 1967-68, VA Med. Ctr., Nashville, 1972—, Chief of VA Chaplains, Washington, 1975, 78; Ingersoll lectr. Harvard U., Cambridge, Mass., 1971; Upperman lectr. Tenn. Technol. U., Cookeville, 1973; Stringfellow lectr. Drake U., Des Moines, 1974. Editor: Perspectives on Death, 1969; assoc. editor: Dictionary of Pastoral Care and Counseling, 1990; editor Pastoral Psychology, 1974-82; contbr. articles to jours. Bd. dirs. Family & Children's Svc., Nashville, 1978-81, Tenn. Pastoral Counseling Ctrs., Nashville, 1984—, St. Thomas Home Health Care, Nashville, 1986—. 1st lt. U.S. Army, 1953-55. Named Alumni Educator of Yr, Vanderbilt U., 1984; fellow So. Bapt. Theol. Sem., 1959-62, Assn. Theol. Schs., 1968-69. Mem. Soc. for Sci. Study of Religion, Assn. for Profl. Edn. for Ministry (pres. 1972-74), Assn. for Clin. Pastoral Edn., Soc. for Pastoral Theology, Omicron Delta Kappa. Office: Vanderbilt U Div Sch Nashville TN 37240

MILLS, PHYLLIS JOY, missionary; b. Independence, Mo., Apr. 13, 1930; d. Edgar and Mabel Irene (Melotz) Nichols; m. Robert Stanhope Mills, June 3, 1950; children: Kathryn Bright, Ruth Engelbreght, Donna Harkness, Rebecca Cloete. BA, Lincoln Christian Coll., Lincoln, Ill., 1973. Missionary Ch. of Christ, Gospel Tract Ctr., S. Africa, 1953—. Author: Some of God's Children, 1971; editor 4 booklets: Women of the Bible, transl. into Zulu, Xhosa, 1980-86; contbr. articles to profl. jours. Office: Gospel Tract Centre, PO Box 1347, Alberton 1450, Republic of South Africa

MILLS, ROBERT PAUL, minister; b. Wilmington, Del., Aug. 21, 1956; s. Dorson Speary and Margaret Jean (Bodine) M.; m. Marjorie Dale Platts, June 28, 1980; 1 child, Timothy. MusB, Houghton Coll., 1978; MusM, Hartt Sch. of Music, West Hartford, Conn., 1983; MDiv, Princeton Theol. Seminary, N.J., 1988. Ordained to ministry Presbyn. Ch., 1988. Pastor Big Creek Presbyn. Ch., Rensselaer, Mo., 1988—; summer chaplain Del. State Hosp., New Castle, 1987; corrs., editorial advisor The Presbyn. Layman, Springfield, Pa., 1989—; moderator, nominating com. Mo. Union Presbytery, 1991. Author: (sermon) Come and See . . . Be Still and Know, 1991 (1st place Faith, Science and Technology sermon contest 1991). Editor: (newsletter) Salem County Habitat for Humanity, N.J., 1984-88; bd. dirs., pres. Battered Women's Shelter/Avenues, Hannibal, Mo., 1989—. Named to Outstanding Young Men of Am., 1981. Mem. Pi Kappa Lambda. Republican. Home: Rte 1 PO Box 196 Hannibal MO 63401 Office: Big Creek Presbyterian Ch Rte 1 Box 196 Hannibal MO 63401 *As we approach the 21st century and life becomes increasingly complex, the eternal wisdom found within the Bible equally increases in its value.*

MILLS, ROSALIE JANE GREGORY, clergyperson; b. Ottumwa, Iowa, Aug. 24, 1947; d. Robert Todd and Margaret Kathryn (Bentzinger) Gregory; m. Larry Eugene Mills, Mar. 30, 1973; 1 child, Jason Novell. BS, U. Tex., Austin, 1970; MS Edn., So. Ill. U., 1974; student, Fuller Theol. Sem., Pasadena, 1985-87. Ordained elder, A.M.E. Zion Ch., 1986; notary pub., Calif. Adminstrv. sec. Coldwell Banker, L.A., 1978-84; office mgr. Lincoln Property Co., L.A., 1984-89, Glendale, Calif., 1989—; assoc. pastor 1st A.M.E. Zion Ch., Pasadena, Calif., 1983-90; also dir. Christian edn. 1st A.M.E. Zion Ch.; sec. L.A. dist. Ministerial Alliance, A.M.E. Zion Ch., 1986-89, pres. 1989-90. Mem. NAFE, Nat. Notary Assn. Democrat. Avocations: crafts, reading, music. Home: 628 Alexander Apt 6 Glendale CA 91203 Office: Lincoln Property Co 800 N Brand Blvd Ste 360 Glendale CA 91203

MILLS, STEVEN REYNARD, minister; b. Gillette, Wyo., Oct. 2, 1957; s. Ralph Reynard and Alice Louise (Garman) M. BA in Bibl. Lit., N.W. Coll. Assemblies of God, Kirkland, Wash., 1980. Ordained to ministry Assembly of God Ch., 1982. Intern Shoreline Community Ch., Seattle, 1979-80; assoc. pastor Camas (Wash.) Assembly of God Ch., 1981-86; pastor Faith Assembly of God Ch., Greybull, Wyo., 1986-89; cons. ch. growth evangelism Gen. Coun. Assemblies of God, Springfield, Mo., 1989—; youth rep. N.W. Dist. Assembly of God, Kirkland, 1984-86, mem. ch. growth commn., 1985-86; sec.-treas. men's dept. Wyo. Dist. Assembly of God, Casper, 1987-89, asst. dist. youth dir., 1988-89. Author-editor: Branch Sunday School Manual, 1990; contbr. articles to various publs. Chmn. Food Basket drive, Christmas Carol com., Greybull, 1987-89. Mem. Nat. Assn. Evangs. (chmn. 1987-89), S. Big Horn County Assn. Republican. Office: Gen Coun Assemblies of God 1445 Boonvalle Ave Springfield MO 65802

MILLS, WILLIAM DOUGLAS, minister; b. Hobbs, N.Mex., Aug. 4, 1959; s. Merle Milton and Dorothy June (Hammick) M. BA, N.Mex. State U., 1981; MDiv, Duke Divinity Sch., 1984, ThM, 1985. Ordained to ministry United Meth. Ch. as elder, 1987. Pastor Townsville (N.C.) United Meth. Ch., 1985-86, El Pueblito United Meth. Ch., Taos, N.Mex., 1986-88, New Covenant United Meth. Ch., Farmington, N.Mex., 1988—; chair Tres Rios Habitat for Humanity, Farmington, 1991; staff coord. World Meth. Conf., Nairobi, Kenya, 1986; lectr. San Juan Coll., Farmington, 1989. Author: A Daily Lectionary, 1986; contbr. articles to profl. jours. Mem. Order of St. Luke, Soc. St. John the Evangelist. Home: 17 Rd 6050 NBU 1001 Farmington NM 87401 Office: New Covenant United Meth Ch 4600 College Blvd Farmington NM 87402

MILNE, DALE STEWART, minister, educator; b. Berkeley, Calif., Sept. 9, 1945; s. Curtis LeRoy and Edna Rose (LeDuc) Mills; m. Leslie J. Carey; 1 child, Andrew. BA, San Jose (Calif.) State U., 1979; DMeta, Universal Life Ch., 1988. Pres. Restored Chs. of Jesus Christ Assn., 1987-88; editor Colo. Interdenominational Conf. for Clergy Newsletter, 1987-88; apostle, ch. historian Ch. of Christ with the Elijah Message, 1989-90; amb. Universal Life Ch., 1990—; elder Unification Ch.; bd. dirs. New Am.'s Mt. Zion. Contbr. articles to profl. jours. Del. Colo. Model Constn. Conv., Denver, 1987; mem. The Persecuted Ch. Commn., 1985-88, 90—, The Internat. Fedn. for World Peace, 1990—; mem. constl. revision com. SJSU, 1979-80, improvement of instrn. com., 1979-80; mem. Philatelic Music Cir., 1984-85, Lenni Lenape Hist. Soc., 1985-86, Mormon History Assn., 1985-87, Citizens for Decency Through Law, 1986-87, Am. Acad. of Religion, 1985-87, Soc. of Bibl. Lit., 1986-87. With Signal Corps, U.S. Army, 1967-70. Avocations; languages, linguistics, world religions, history, hiking. Home: 1118-13th St # A37 Boulder CO 80302

MILONE, ANTHONY M., bishop; b. Omaha, Sept. 24, 1932. Grad., North American Coll. (Rome). Ordained priest Roman Catholic Ch., 1957. Ordained titular bishop of Plestia and aux. bishop Diocese of Omaha, 1982; apptd. bishop Mont. Diocese, Great Falls-Billings, 1987. Office: 3208 2nd Ave S Great Falls MT 59405

MILTON, HOWARD WILLIAM, JR., minister; b. Phila., Nov. 8, 1946; s. Howard William Sr. and Matilda Ida (Mackley) M.; m. Joyce Ann Wolff, Aug. 15, 1970; children: Hope Noelle, H. William III, G. Brian. BA in Counseling Psychology, Widener U., 1975; MDiv, Wesley Theol. Sem., 1982; postgrad., Millersville U., 1980-82; cert., Chestnut Hill Coll., 1991. Ordained to ministry Meth. Ch., 1984; cert. secondary tchr., Pa. Crisis tchr. Phila. Sch. Dist., 1970-72; pastor Charlestown United Meth. Ch., Paoli, Pa., 1972-77, First United Meth. Ch., Columbia, Pa., 1977-82, Trinity-Grace United Meth. Ch., Reading, Pa., 1982-85, First United Meth. Ch., Perkasie, Pa., 1985—; dir. Innabah United Meth. Ch. Program Ctr., Spring City, Pa.; bd. sec. Day One Ministries, Allentown, Pa., 1989—; N.E. coord. Transforming Congregations, Bakersfield, Calif., 1989—; founder, bd. dirs. Reading Pastoral Counseling Ctr., Reading, 1983-85. Mem. Commn. on Recreation, Columbia, 1978-82. Home: 404 Race St Perkasie PA 18944 Office: First United Meth Ch 501 Market St Perkasie PA 18944

MILTON, J. MARGARET, religious consultant; b. Gorham, Maine, Nov. 19, 1934; d. George Milton and Margaret (Ross) Chesley; m. Gordon Gerald Schaeffer, June 10, 1977. BA, UCLA, 1959; MDiv, San Francisco Theol. Sem., 1977. Exec. dir., founder Ecumenical Convalescent Hosp. Ministry, San Rafael, Calif., 1977-90, cons. for tng. and resource devel., 1990—. Author: Let Us Worship God Together: A Liturgy for the Nursing Home Congregation; Leader's Guide, 1988. Mem. Am. Soc. on Aging, Forum on Religion and Aging. Presbyterian. Office: Ecumenical Convalescent Hosp Ministry Marin PO Box 2447 San Rafael CA 94912

MILTON, NATHAN MONROE, minister, evangelist; b. Greensboro, N.C., July 16, 1961; s. Winfield Jr. and Agnes (Womack) M.; m. Laura Ann Payne, Dec. 19, 1987; 1 child, Mikalah Milan. Student, N.C. Agrl. and Tech. State U., 1979-81. Ordained to ministry Ch. of Apostolic Faith, 1979. Lay speaker to minister Ch. of the Apostolic Faith, Greensboro, 1975—; evangelist Power House of Deliverance/Ch. of the Apostolic Faith, 1979—, religion instr., 1987—; mem. nat. youth bd. 2nd Adminstrv. Asst. Minister's Staff, Greensboro; shipping/receiving clk. Potpourri Press, Greensboro, 1979-86; active Shirley Caesar Evangelistic Crusade, 1975—, Back to the Bible Retreat, 1986—. Author: (lesson plan) Salvation/Gifts of the Spirit, 1988, Ministry of God's Word, 1990, National Youth Guide Book/Church of the Apostolic Faith, 1978; contbr. articles to profl. jours. Mem. NAACP. Democrat. Home: 708 Woodlake Dr Greensboro NC 27406

MIMS, BILLY BURNS, JR., minister; b. Greensboro, N.C., June 18, 1946; s. Billy Burns Mims and Virginia Lucille (Umbaugh) Calhoun; m. Sherry Lynne Foust, Dec. 21, 1968; children: John Thomas, Stephen Frederick. BA, U. N.C., 1968; MDiv, Luth. Theol. So. Sem., 1972; D in Ministry, Union Theol. Sem., Richmond, Va., 1983. Ordained to ministry Luth. Ch., 1972. Vicar Trinity Luth. Ch., Jacksonville, Fla., 1970-71; pastor Wittenberg Luth. Ch., Granite Quarry, N.C., 1972-74, Incarnation Luth. Ch., Columbia, S.C., 1974-79, Orangeburg (S.C.) Luth. Ch., 1979-87, Beth Eden Luth. Ch., Newton, N.C., 1987—; trustee Lutheridge, Arden, N.C., 1980—, chmn. bd. Lutheridge-Lutherock Ministries, 1991—; dean Amelia dist. S.C. Synod, Luth. Ch. in Am., 1983-87; chmn. profl. leadership svc. com. S.C. Synod, 1982-84, mem. worship com., 1989—, sec. Western Piedmont Conf., 1991—. Contbr. articles to religious jour. Mem. Catawba Meml. Hosp., chaplain adv. com. and biomed. ethics bd., 1991—. Recipient award cert. Am. Assn. Blood Banks, 1983. Mem. Orangeburg Regional Hosp. Vol. Chaplains Assn. (pres. 1981-83). Office: Beth Eden Luth Ch 400 N Main Ave Newton NC 28658

MINDACH, REX ALLEN, religion educator; b. Indpls, Dec. 24, 1957; s. Fred Carl and Jane L. (Crosby) M.; m. Julie Rénee Wadsworth, June 1, 1985; children: Sophie Mae, Adrian Crosby. BS, Concordia Coll., St. Paul, 1985. Cert. tchr., MN. Tchr. King of Kings Luth. Sch., Roseville, Minn., 1985, Zion Luth. Sch., Fallbrook, Calif., 1985-86; tchr., head master Faith Acad. Christian Sch., Wadena, Minn., 1986—; youth advisor, Sunday sch. tchr. St. Paul Luth. Ch., Spearfish, S.D., 1978-81; Sunday sch. tchr. Leaf River Christian Ch., Wadena, 1986-87. Mem. Assn. Christian Schs. Internat. (cert.). Republican. Home: 2524 Latdka Dr Alexandria MN 56308 Office: Faith Acad Christian Sch Rt 3 Box 152A Wadena MN 56482

MINEAR, JUDITH, school system administrator. Supt. schs. Diocese of Wheeling-Charleston, W.Va. Office: Office Schs Supt 11-13th St PO Box 230 Wheeling WV 26003*

MINEAR, PAUL SEVIER, minister, religion educator; b. Mt. Pleasant, Iowa, Feb. 17, 1906; s. George L. and Nellie (Sevier) M.; m. Gladys O. Hoffman, June 14, 1929; children: Paul Lawrence, Richard Hoffman, Anita Sue Minear Fahrni. A.B., Iowa Wesleyan U., 1927, LL.D., 1942; B.D., Garrett Bibl. Inst., 1930, D.D., 1981; A.M., Northwestern U., 1930; Ph.D., Yale U., 1932; Th.D., U. Utrecht, 1962; LL.D., U. Notre Dame, 1966; D.D., Aberdeen U., 1974. Asst. prof. Hawaii Sch. Religion, Honolulu, 1933-34; prof. N.T., Garrett Bibl. Inst., 1934-44; ordained to ministry Meth. Ch., 1938, Congl. Christian Ch., 1944; Norris prof. N.T., Andover Newton Theol. Sch., 1944-56; prof. N.T., Yale U. Div. Sch., 1956-71, Winkley prof. Bibl. theology, 1958-71, dir. grad. studies in religion, 1959-61; vice rector Ecumenical Inst. for Advanced Theol. Study, Jerusalem, 1970-72; dir. faith and order World Council Chs., 1961-63; vis. prof. Episcopal Theol. Sch., 1953, Cath. U., 1975, United Theol. Coll., Vancouver, 1976, Princeton Theol. Sem., 1977, Brite Div. Sch., 1979, Emory U. Sch. Theology, 1980, Phillips U., 1986; Hoover lectr. U. Chgo., 1957; Dudleian lectr. Harvard U., 1954; Fulbright lectr. U. Utrecht, 1958-59; Stone lectr. Princeton Theol. Sem., 1967; Shaffer lectr. Yale U., 1974; Gheens lectr. Louisville Bapt. Sem., 1980; Kantonen lectr. Trinity Luth. Theol. Sem., 1982; mem. Faith and Order Commn., 1952-74, chmn., 1963-67; mem. Standard Bible Translation Com., 1960-89. Author: An Introduction to Paul, 1936, And Great Shall Be Your Reward, 1941, Eyes of Faith, 1946, The Choice, 1948, The Kingdom and the Power, 1950, Christian Hope and the Second Coming, 1954, Jesus and His People, 1956, Horizons of Christian Community, 1959, Images of the Church in the New Testament, 1960, The Gospel of Mark, 1962, I Saw a New Earth, 1969, The Obedience of Faith, 1971, Commands of Christ, 1972, I Pledge Allegiance, 1975, To Heal and To Reveal, 1976, To Die and To Live, 1977, New Testament Apocalyptic, 1981, Matthew: The Teacher's Gospel, 1982, John: The Martyr's Gospel, 1984, Death Set to Music, 1987, The God of the Gospels, 1988; co-author: Kierkegaard and the Bible, 1953, Pentecost 2, 1981; editor: Nature of the Unity We Seek, 1957, Faith and Order Findings, 1963.

MINER, JAMES EDWARD, youth minister; b. Columbus, Ohio, Oct. 16, 1953; s. Charles Patrick and Norma Jean (Hosey) M.; m. Kathi Ann Murphy, May 7, 1983; children: Jodi, Cori, James. AS, Coll. of DuPage, 1973; BS, No. Ill. U., 1975; postgrad., Loyola U., 1991—. Tchr. religious edn. St. Mary's Parish, West Chicago, Ill., 1989—, youth min., 1990—; youth min. adv. staff Diocese of Joliet (Ill.), 1990—; parish dir. Early Adolescent Ministry Program, 1989—; owner, founder Advanced Systems & Assocs., West Chicago, 1986—. Author, editor newsletter Youth Quar.; contbr. editorials, poems to profl. jours. Mem. Thorium Action Group, West Chicago, 1988—. Recipient Sales Performance of Yr. award Robinson Nugent, Inc., New Albany, Ind., 1985. Mem. Jr. High Min.'s Assn. Roman Catholic. Home: 423 E National St West Chicago IL 60185 Office: St Mary's Parish 140 N Oakwood West Chicago IL 60185 *Still the greatest challenge that faces humanity remains the task of eliminating prejudice in all forms—always the hopes for a new generation and dreams of the older one.*

MINER, LENWORTH ROBERT, JR., minister; b. Portland, Oreg., Mar. 30, 1946; s. Lenworth Robert and Ida Mae (Green) M. BS, Wayne State U., 1972; cert., Cleve. Inst. Electronics, 1976; MDiv, Howard U., 1983. Ordained to ministry Bapt. Ch., 1985. Asst. min. Christian edn. Gethsemane Bapt. Ch., Washington, 1981-83; grad. asst. to dean of chapel Howard U., Washington, 1982-83; assoc. min. Second Bapt. Ch., Ypsilanti, Mich., 1984-88; pastor St. Stephen Bapt. Ch., Pontiac, Mich., 1988-91. With USN, 1966-69. Mem. Oakland County Ministerial Fellowship, Greater Pontiac Dist. Assn., Huron Valley Dist. Assn., Wolverine Bapt. State Conv., Nat. Bapt. Conv. U.S.A. Inc., NAACP, Urban League, Alpha Phi Alpha. Home: 20522 Plymouth A-4 Detroit MI 48228

MINICUCCI, DARYL SHARP, consultant; b. Camden, N.J., July 31, 1954; d. Charles Bird and Ida Shirley (Frampton) Sharp; m. Thomas Donald Minicucci, May 4, 1985; children: Laura Sharp, Christopher James. BSN, U. Del., 1976; MSN in Psychiat. Nursing, U. Pa., 1980. RN, N.Y.; cert. clin. specialist psychiat. nursing. Chairperson christian edn. Christ Ch., Manlius, N.Y., 1989—; cons. Episcopal Diocese of Cen. N.Y., Syracuse, 1989—, Manlius, 1990—; mem. Cons. Commn., Syracuse, 1989—, Commn. on Lay Ministry, Syracuse, 1989-90. Facilitator coord. for parent programs Fayetteville-Manlius Chem. People, 1990—. Grantee NIMH, 1979-80, NIH, 1978. Mem. ANA (Coun. of Specialists in Pscyhiat./Mental Health Nurses 1983—), N.Y. State Nurses Assn., Assn. for Creative Change, Alban Inst. Democrat. Home and Office: 8036 Merrimac Dr Manlius NY 13104

MINNEY, BRUCE KEVIN, evangelist, refrigeration executive; b. Cleve., Dec. 22, 1958; s. Leonard Clavel Minney and Wilma Catherine (Elliott) Sage; m. Penelope Sue Pertuset, May 20, 1983; 1 child, Joshua Kevin. Student, Cin. Bible Coll., 1977-84. Religious educator Andover (Ohio) Ch. of Christ, 1978, youth worker, 1978; evangelist N. E. Crusaders for Christ, Cin., 1979; emergency med. tech. Milford-Miami (Ohio) Twp. Med. Svcs., 1980-83; youth leader Milford (Ohio) Ch. of Christ, 1984-86, deacon, drama ministry, 1986—; parts dept. mgr. Otis Refrigeration Svc., Inc., Cin., 1984—. Avocations: disc golf, dulcimer, theater. Home: 1192 Emily Dr Milford OH 45150 Office: Otis Refrigeration Svc Inc 4224 Airport Rd Cincinnati OH 45226 *I believe the success of our race depends on our focus. Self-centered goals may only be reached at the expense of others. Eventually, individual gain can only lead to the success of one greater.*

MINNICH, MARTHA JEAN, minister; b. Thayer, Kans., June 4, 1921; d. Harrison Melborn and Ola Edith (Breuer) M. Student, jr. coll., Chanute, Kans., 1944-45, Nat. Bible Coll., Wichita, Kans., 1947. Ordained to ministry Christian Ch., 1950. Min. various chs., Helper, Kans., 1950-56, Savonburg, Kans., 1951-55, Moran, Kans., 1955-85; counselor Hidden Haven Christian Camp, 1950-74, mem. bd. dirs.; producer, speaker weekly radio program Moments with the Master, 1960—. Bd. dirs. Marmaton Housing Inc., Moran; mem. adv. bd. Moran Manor Nursing Home, 1972-75. Mem. Bus. Profl. Womens Club (pres. 1964-65, Woman of Yr., 1966). Home: Box 95 Moran KS 66755 *"What I do today is important because I'm exchanging a day of my life for it," was a statement I read several years ago. I believe that most of us would make wiser use of our time if we would keep this in mind. I know that this has been a challenge to me.*

MINNICK, CARLTON PRINTESS, JR., bishop; b. Greensboro, N.C., Sept. 8, 1927; s. Carlton Printess and Catherine (Johnson) M.; m. Mary Ann Adams, Sept. 5, 1946; children: Mary Ann, Gregory Carlton, Patte Carroll, Jonathan Allan. Student. U. Va., 1944-45; BA, Lynchburg Coll., 1954; BD, Union Theol Sem. in Va., 1957, MTh, 1958. On trial Va. Conf., 1954, ordained deacon United Meth. Ch., 1955, full connection, 1956, elder, 1957. Pastor Mt. Airy charge United Meth. Ch., 1951-54, pastor Goochland charge, 1954-58; pastor St. James Meth. Ch. United Meth. Ch., Ferrum, 1958-1963; pastor Westhampton Meth. Ch. United Meth. Ch., Richmond, 1963-67; pastor Mt. Olivet United Meth. Ch. Arlington, 1973-78; supt. Alexandria Dist. United Meth. Ch., 1978-80, bishop, 1980—, resident bishop Jackson, Miss. area, 1980-84; bishop United Meth. Ch., Raleigh, N.C., 1984&. Named Rural Minister of Yr., Va. Conf., 1958. Mem. Gen. Bd. Global Ministries (pres. United Meth. Com. on Relief 1988-93). Office: United Meth Ch PO Box 10955 Raleigh NC 27605

MINNICK, DONALD EDWARD, minister; b. St. Joseph, Mo., Feb. 22, 1935; s. Donald Clyde and Thelma Mae (Turner) M.; m. Susann Sonner, June 23, 1957; children: Michael, Cynthia, Anna, Linda. BA, Grinnell (Iowa) Coll., 1957; MDiv, Chgo. Theol. Sem., 1961, DD, 1990. Assoc. minister First Congl. Ch., Wisconsin Rapids, Wis., 1961-64; minister First Congl. Ch., Mukwonago, Wis., 1964-68, Council Bluffs, Iowa, 1968-73; sr. minister Northfield (Ill.) Community Ch., 1973—; vice chair, bd. trustees Chgo. Theol. Sem., 1981-89; bd. dirs. Chgo. Elder United Ch. Mem. Lions (pres. Northfield chpt. 1990—).

MINOR, JOHN THOMAS, minister, librarian; b. Winston-Salem, N.C., Sept. 30, 1939; s. Roy Hunter and Nellie (Johnson) M.; m. Barbara Joyce Cuthbert, June 6, 1965; 1 child, David Hunter. BA in Polit. Sci., Moravian Coll., 1963; postgrad., Moravian Theol. Sem., 1963-65; MDiv, Christian Theol. Sem., 1966; MSLS, U. N.C., 1971; cert. in adminstrn., Nat. Archives/Am. U. Ordained to ministry Moravian Ch., 1966. Parish min. Bd. World Mission Moravian Ch., St. Kitts, Trinidad and Tobago, 1966-68; libr. dir. Moravian Coll. and Theol. Sem., Bethlehem, Pa., 1984—. Book rev. editor James Burnside Bull. Rsch., 1989—; Am. bibliographer Unitas Fratrum, 1989—. Mem. Am. Theol. Libr. Assn., Southeastern Pa. Theol. Libr. Assn. (editor Teamwork newsletter 1986—), Theta Phi. Democrat. Home: 2436

Langhorne Dr Bethlehem PA 18017 Office: Moravian Coll & Theol Sem 1200 Main St Bethlehem PA 18018

MINOR, ROBERT NEIL, religious studies educator; b. Milw., Oct. 2, 1945; s. Carl Frederick and Alice Charlotte (Bates) M.; m. Kris Ann Boyenga, Aug. 8, 1970 (div. July 1985); 1 child, Matthew Robert. BA in Biblical Studies, Trinity Coll., Deerfield, Ill., 1967; MA in Biblical Studies, Trinity Evang. Div. Sch., Deerfield, Ill., 1969; PhD in History of Religions, U. Iowa, 1975. Asst. prof. in history of religions Allegheny Coll., Meadville, Pa., 1975-77; prof., chair dept. religious studies U. Kans., Lawrence, 1977—. Author: Sri Aurobindo: The Perfect and the Good, 1978, Bhagavadgita: An Exegetical Commentary, 1982, Modern Indian Interpreters of the Bhagavadgita, 1986, Radhakrishnan: A Religious Biography, 1987; contbr. articles to profl. publs., chpts. to books. Grantee Am. Inst. for Indian Studies, 1981, NEH, 1983-84. Mem. Am. Acad. Religion, Assn. for Asian Studies, N.Am. Assn. for Study of Relision. Home: 3709 W 24th St Lawrence KS 66047 Office: U Kans Smith Hall Lawrence KS 66045 *Recognizing that people have real differences on religious matters is not the cause of intolerance, and denying that these are real differences is not the basis for tolerance. There is no virtue in tolerating someone who agrees with you. Tolerance requires the recognition of real disagreement by real and significant others. Then we can learn to live with significant others.*

MINOR, RONALD RAY, minister; b. Aliceville, Ala., Nov. 3, 1944; s. Hershel Ray and Minnie Ozell (Goodson) M.; m. Gwendolyn Otella Newsome, July 25, 1970; 1 child, Rhonda Rene. BA in Ministerial, Southeastern Bible Coll., 1971, BA in Secondary Edn., 1973; DDiv, Southern Bible Coll., 1984. Ordained to ministry Penecostal Ch. of God, 1968. Gen. sec., treas. Pentecostal Ch. of God, Joplin, Mo., 1979—; dist. supt. Pentecostal Ch. of God, Philadelphia, Miss., 1975-79; pastor Pentecostal Ch. of God, Bartow, Fla., Orient Park Tabernacle, Tampa, Fla.; pres. Pentecostal Young People's Assn., Fla. and Miss.; sec. Gen. Bd. Pentecosatal Ch. of God, Joplin, 1979; bd. dirs. Nat. assn. Evangs., Wheaton, Ill., 1981—; adv. coun. Am. Bible Soc., N.Y.C., 1979—; sec. Commn. Chaplains, Washington, 1991—. Home: 2625 E 13th St Joplin MO 64801 Office: Pentecostal Ch of God 4901 Pa Joplin MO 64802

MINOR, RUDIGER RAINER, bishop; b. Leipzig, Germany, Feb. 22, 1939; s. Ludwig and Lina (Minnert) M.; m. Gerlinde Johanna Mueller, Oct. 24, 1964; children: Mechthild, Bertram, Friedrun. Diploma in Theology, Karl Marx U., Leipzig, 1962, ThD, 1968; postgrad, United Meth. Theol. Sem., Bad Klosterlausnitz, German Dem. Republic, 1965-66. Rsch. asst. Karl Marx U., Leipzig, 1962-64; pastor United Meth. Ch., various cities, 1964-76; lctr. United Meth. Theol. Sem., Bad Klosterlausnitz, 1969-76, prof. ch. history, 1976-86, pres., 1984-86; bishop United Meth. Ch., Dresden, Germany, 1986—; v.p. World Meth. Hist. Soc., 1986-91; bd. dirs. United Meth. Bd. Ch. and Soc. Author: Methodism in Saxony, 1968; contbr. articles to profl. jours. Home and Office: United Meth Ch, Wiener Str 56, 0-8020 Dresden Federal Republic of Germany

MINSHALL, BRINTON PAYNTER, pastor; b. Chester, Pa., Feb. 14, 1943; s. Melvin and Frances (Paynter) M.; m. Grace Ambron, Jan. 16, 1975 (div. Sept. 1987); m. Kathy Robertson, May 12, 1988; children: Tim, Chrissy, Art, Chris, Joe, Lee. A in Div., Southeastern U., Wake Forest, N.C., 1980; BA, Thomas Edison State, 1981; MDiv, Emory U., 1985; postgrad., Boston U., 1985-90. Ordained to ministry United Ch. of Christ. Chief exec. officer GASA Security Corp., Cape May, N.J., 1965-78; pastor Middleburg United Meth. Ch., Middleburg, Fla., 1985-87, Family of God United Ch. Christ, Middleburg, Fla., 1987-89; sr. pastor First United Ch. of Christ, Hollywood, Fla., 1989—. Author newspaper articles, 1985--. Mem. Inter-Faith Council, 1986-88. Mem. Jacksonville Ministry Assn. (v.p. 1986-88). Democrat. Avocation: oil painting. Home and Office: 200 N 46th Ave Hollywood FL 33021

MINTON, JOSEPH KELLY, SR., minister; b. Little Rock, Nov. 27, 1943; s. Thomas Edward and Theda Rieff (Jamison) M.; m. Ruth Elizabeth Elliott, Oct. 21, 1967; children: Joseph Kelly Jr., Virginia, Christopher, John. BS, U.S. Naval Acad., 1966; MDiv, Southwestern Bapt. Theol. Sem., 1977, DMin, 1986. Ordained to ministry Bapt. Ch., 1978. Pastor Lazybrook Bapt. Ch., Houston, 1978—; mem. exec. com. Bapt. Gen. Conv. of Tex., Dallas, 1988-93; pres. Union Bapt. Assn. Minister's Conf., 1990-91. Author: Equipping Deacons in Times of Death and Dying, 1986. Bd. dirs. Hospitality House, Huntsville, Tex., 1990—. Comdr. USNR, 1986-89, ret. Home: 1835 Millwood Houston TX 77008 Office: Lazybrook Bapt Ch 1822 W 18th St Houston TX 77008

MINTS, PAUL STEPHEN, minister; b. Abilene, Tex., Apr. 16, 1966; s. Jackie Ray and Carolyn June (Gee) M.; m. Shannon Elizabeth Sims, June 14, 1991. BBA, Hardin Simmons U., 1989; postgrad., Southwestern Bapt. Theol. Sem., Ft. Worth, 1988—. Ordained to ministry So. Bapt. Conv., 1984. Intern Pineer Drive Bapt. Ch., Abilene, 1985-87; summer youth min. 1st Bapt. Ch., Pecos, Tex., 1986, Idalou, Tex., 1988, 89; interim min. youth Grand Avenue Bapt. Ch., Ft. Smith, Ark., 1987; dir. student ministries Grace Temple Bapt. Ch., Dallas, 1989—; mem. metro youth coun. Dallas Evang. Alliance, 1990—; region rep. Cen. Dallas Network Youth Ministries, Oak Cliff, Tex., 1990—. Composer religious songs. Scholar Order Ea. Star, 1990, 91, Douglas Laird scholar Grace Temple Bapt. Ch., 1990, 91. Office: Grace Temple Bapt Ch 831 W 10th St Dallas TX 75208

MIRACLE, BIANCA JUTTA, lay worker, public relations coordinator; b. Nürnberg, Fed. Republic Germany, Feb. 6, 1965; came to U.S., 1970; d. Heinz Shirmer and Barbara (Kröber) deMik. BA in Communications, Biola U., 1990. Officer women's guild and auxiliary St. Albans Ch., Irvine, Calif., 1988—; critical path analyst McDonnell Douglas, Long Beach, Calif., 1989-90. Vol. Hotline Crisis Ctr., Anaheim, Calif., 1989. Mem. Women in Communications, Pub. Rels. Soc. Am. Home: 1427 E 23d St Long Beach CA 90806

MIRKOVICH, JOSEPH ALLEN, minister, church administrator; b. Mineola, N.Y., Oct. 31, 1954; s. Joseph and Dorcas (Pinder) M.; m. Betty Jean Mudd, July 27, 1974; children: Jason Scott, Beverly Jean. Student, Lee Coll., 1971-74. Ordained to ministry Ch. of God, 1974. Metro evangelist Ch. of God, Norfolk, Va., 1975-76; pastor Ch. of God, Peterstown, W.Va., 1976-77, Tampa, Fla., 1977-80; sr. pastor Pathway Christian Ctr., Ch. of God, Longwood, Fla., 1980-90; evangelism and home missions dir. Ch. of God State of N.Y., Farmingdale, 1990—; lectr., dir. Ch. of God Christian Schs., Longwood, 1982-84; bd. dirs. Ch. of God Assn. Christian Schs., Fla., 1986-88, prison commn. Ch. of God, N.Y., 1990—, spiritual commn. Ch. of God, Cleveland, Tenn., 1990—. Sec.-treas. Optimist Club, Longwood, 1984; v.p. Lee Alumni Assn., 1982-86; advisor Feed the Hunger-Sharing Ctr., Longwood, 1989; organizer Neighborhood Crime Watch, Longwood, 1987-89. Home: 14 9th Ave Farmingdale NY 11735 Office: Ch of God Exec Offices 1 Hemlock Dr Farmingdale NY 11735

MIRSKY, NORMAN BARRY, rabbi, Jewish studies educator; b. Toledo, Jan. 5, 1937; s. Joseph and Florence (Ponemen) M.; m. Elaine Torf, June 1, 1958; children: Rebekah Florence, Aaron Ephraim. Student, U. Mich., 1955-56; BA, U. Cin., 1959; MA, Hebrew Union Coll., 1963; PhD, Brandeis U., 1971. Ordained Rabbi, 1963. Instr. contemporary Jewish studies and sociology Hebrew Union Coll., Cin., 1967-68, asst. prof., 1969-72, assoc. prof., 1973-76; assoc. prof. Hebrew Union Coll., Los Angeles, 1976-80, prof., 1980—; cons. research task force Future Reform Judaism, N.Y.C., 1983—; vis. rabbi Temple Isaiah, Los Angeles, 1984—. Author: Unorthodox Judaism, 1978; contbr. articles to profl. jours. V.p. Labor Zionist Alliance, Los Angeles, 1980-82; bd. dirs. Jewish Fedn. Council, West Los Angeles, 1981-83; pres. Santa Monica (Calif.) Reform Rabbinic Community, 1986—. Jacob Zishv traveling fellow Hebrew Union Coll., 1964-67, Merrill fellow Brandeis U., 1964-67. Mem. Cen. Conf. Am. Rabbis, Assn. Sci. Study Religion, Assn. Jewish Studies, Los Angeles Bd. Rabbis, Pacific Assn. Reform Rabbis. Democrat. Avocations: tennis, writing. Office: Hebrew Union Coll-Jewish Inst of Religion Dept Contemporary Jewish Studies 3077 University Mall Los Angeles CA 90007-3796

MIRVIS, EPHRAIM YITZCHAK, rabbi; b. Johannesburg, Republic of South Africa, July 9, 1956; arrived in Ireland, 1982; s. Lionel and Freida (Katz) M.; m. Valerie Lynn Kaplan, May 7, 1979; children: Liora, Hillel, Daniel, Noam, Eitan. Rabbinic ordination, Harry Fishel Inst., Jerusalem, 1980; BA, U. South Africa, 1984. Lectr. Machon Meir, Jerusalem, 1980-82; rabbi Dublin (Ireland) Hebrew Congregation, 1982-85; chief rabbi Irish Jewish Community, 1985—. Chmn. bd. mgmt. Stratford Jewish Schs., 1985—; chmn. Joint Israel Appeal, 1985—. Mem. Conf. European Rabbis (exec. mem. 1985—), Mizrachi Orgn. (chmn. 1985—), Irish Coun. for Oppressed Jews (chmn. 1985—). Office: Office of Chief Rabbi, 1 Zion Rd, Rathgar, Dublin 6, Ireland

MISCHELL, PATRICIA LUCILLE, author, minister; b. Hurricane, W.Va., July 5, 1936; d. William and Gladys Lou (Tabor) Chapman; children—Rene Victoria, Cynthia Ann, Steven Joseph Zang. Student pub. schs., Blue Ash, Ohio. Founder, Hope Ministries and Positive Living Ctr.; pres. World of ESP; cons. Sci. Bur. of Investigation in N.Y.; affiliated with Tour Crafters of Cin.; lectr. in field; parapsychologist. Author: Beyond Positive Thinking, 1985. Mem. PSI Center, Positive Living Found., Assn. for Spiritual Devel. and Research, Spiritual Frontiers Fellowship, The Rosicrucian Order, Assn. for Research and Enlightenment, Internat. Enterpreneurs Assn., Nat. Fedn. Ind. Bus., Noohra Found. Office: Positive Living Center-Hope Ministry 8425 Vine St Cincinnati OH 45216

MISCHKE, CARL HERBERT, religious association executive; b. Hazel, S.D., Oct. 27, 1922; s. Emil Gustav and Pauline Alvina (Polzin) M.; m. Gladys Lindloff, July 6, 1947; children: Joel, Susan Mischke Blahnik, Philip, Steven. B.A., Northwestern Coll., Watertown, Wis., 1944; M.Div., Wis. Luth. Sem., Mequon, 1947. Ordained to ministry Evang. Lutheran Ch. Parish pastor Wis. Synod, 1947-79; pres. Western Wis. Dist. Evang. Luth. Ch., Juneau, 1964-79; v.p. Wis. Luth. Synod, Milw., 1966-79, pres., 1979—. Office: Wis Evang Luth Synod 2929 N Mayfair Rd Milwaukee WI 53222

MISENHEIMER, PATRICIA MOBLEY (TRISH MISENHEIMER), lay church worker, church secretary; b. Barstow, Calif., Apr. 22, 1943; d. Jesse Ralph and Elizabeth (Gard) Mobley; divorced; children: Paul David Smith, Susanne Rachelle Smith; m. Robert Joseph Misenheimer, Mar. 22, 1985 (div. Nov. 1985). Student, Life Bible Coll., L.A., 1960-62. Pianist, leader high sch. youth group Foursquare Ch., Barstow, 1959-61; pianist, coord. jr. ch., Foursquare Ch., Arlington, Calif., 1964-66; pianist, tchr. Grace Bapt. Ch., Newhall, Calif., 1971-75; pianist, jr. high dir. choir 1st Bapt. Ch., Lake Arrowhead, Calif., 1975-78; pianist, mem. cabinet, visitation team, tchr. 1st Bapt. Ch. Singles Ministry, Pomona, Calif., 1978-85, pianist, mem. Regional Single Adult Task Force, leader, 1988-90; pianist, tchr., mem. bd. curriculum devel. 1st Evang. Free Ch., Single Parent Fellowship, Fullerton, Calif., 1985-88; sec. Todd Meml. Chapel, Pomona, 1984—. Mem. Com. to Re-call Clay Bryant, Pomona, 1989; treas. Com. to Elect Bob Jackson, Pomona, 1991. Barstow Bus. and Profl. Women's scholar, 1961. Mem. Nat. Notary Assn. (cert.). Republican.

MISLIN, KIM MARIE, religion educator; b. Buffalo, May 17, 1959; d. William H. and Verna M. (Rockelman) M.; m. William D. Milroy, July 1980 (div. 1984); 1 child, W. David. BA, SUNY Empire, Buffalo, 1985; MDiv, Gen. Theol. Sem., N.Y.C., 1988; postgrad., Denver U., 1990—. Chaplain AMI Hosps., Denver, 1988-89; dir. religious edn. St. Timothy's Episcopal Ch., Littleton, Colo., 1989-90, Lakewood (Colo.) United Ch. Christ, 1990-91, 1st Congl. Ch., Prescott, Ariz., 1991—; cons. presiding bishop's task force on religious edn. in parishes, N.Y.C., 1987. Editor: (jour.) Teaching Resource, 1991—. Mem. Nature Conservancy, Sierra Club; cubmaster Boy Scouts Am., 1990—. Recipient Seymour Preaching Prize Gen. Theol. Sem., N.Y.C., 1987. Mem. Assn. Profs. and Researchers in Religious Edn. Democrat. Home: 333 W Leroux St # D1 Prescott AZ 86303 Office: 1st Congl Ch 216 E Gurley St Prescott AZ 86301

MISNER, PAUL, theology educator; b. Akron, Ohio, Feb. 14, 1936; s. Francis De Sales and Madge (Mee) M.; m. Barbara Ruybal, Aug. 19, 1972. BA, St. Charles Borromeo Sem., Phila., 1958; postgrad., Gregorian U., Rome, 1962; ThD, U. Munich, 1969. Assoc. pastor St. Basil Parish, Pitts., 1962-65; asst. prof. theol. Boston Coll., 1969-75; dir. devel. Am. Sch. Oriental Research, Cambridge, Mass., 1977-79; asst. prof. theol. Marquette U., Milw., 1979-83, assoc. prof. theol., 1983—; cons. Nat. Assn. Diocesan Ecumenical Officers, 1985, 87; vis. prof. U. Cologne, Fed. Republic Germany, 1991. Author: Papacy and Development, 1976, Social Catholicism in Europe, 1991; editor N. Söderblom's Briefwechsel 1909-1931, 1981; assoc. editor Jour. Ecumenical Studies, 1986-90; contbr. articles to profl. jours. Fellow Bradley Inst. Dem., 1988. Fulbright fellow West German Commn., 1975-76, 1985-86. Mem. N.Am. Acad Ecumenists (bd. dirs., pres. 1984-85), Am. Acad. Religion, Coll. Theology Soc. (publs. chmn. 1982-83), Am. Cath. Hist. Assn., Am. Hist. Assn. Democrat. Roman Catholic. Home: 3292 N 47th St Milwaukee WI 53216 Office: Theology Dept Marquette U Milwaukee WI 53233

MISSELBECK, THEODORE ALBERT, religious organization administrator; b. Paterson, N.J., Jan. 20, 1950; s. William Edward and Lillian (Zimmerman) M.; m. Vi Misselbeck; children: Timothy, Matthew. BA, Montclair State Coll., 1975. Cert. tchr. health edn., K-12. Adminstr. Christians United for Jesus, Waco, Tex., 1984—, New Life World Outreach Ministries, Millville, N.J., 1986—; founder/dir. Career Movement Ctr., Millville, 1988—. Editor: (Christian clip-art) Vision Graphics, 1984-90; creative dir. quarterly in field. Sgt. USAF, 1969-72. Home: 210 Mulberry St Millville NJ 08332 Office: New Life World Outreach Ministries 1 Bluebird Lane PO Box 5500 Millville NJ 08332 *In my endeavours I have found that wars are won in the planning room, rarely on the battlefield, and I always precede my planning with prayer.*

MITCHELL, ALBERT WILLIAM, minister; b. Camden, N.J., Oct. 30, 1944; s. Albert William and Margaret Elizabeth (Goode) M.; m. Alice Denise Currey, Nov. 20,1976 (dec. Mar. 1983); children: Melissa, Mark, Mary Alice; m. Elizabeth Anne Stone, Sept. 10, 1983. BS, Phila. Coll. Bible, 1966; ThM, Dallas Theol. Sem., 1970. Ordained to ministry Conservative Bapt. Assn. Am. Pastor Bellmawr (N.J.) Bapt. Ch., 1974-81, Warminster (Pa.) Bapt. Ch., 1981—. Mem. Hudson-Essex Terraplane Club (registrar 1990—). Republican. Office: Warminster Bapt Ch 709 Morristown Rd Warminster PA 18979

MITCHELL, CARL GENE, religion and psychology educator; b. Santa Paula, Calif., July 29, 1926; s. Hubert R. and Isophine (McCalister) M.; m. Frances C. Rotramel, Feb. 8, 1953; children: Mickey S., Cary L., Michelle Mitchell Glover. BS in Ednl. Psychology, Pepperdine U., 1949, MA in Religion, 1966; diploma in Italian, U. Florence, Italy, 1960; PhD in Ednl. Psychology, U. So. Calif., 1967. Ordained to ministry Ch. of Christ, 1949; lic. marriage, family and child therapist, Calif. Minister Ch. of Christ, various locations, Calif., Ark., Italy, 1949—; prof. religion and psychology Pepperdine U., Malibu, Calif., 1955-80, chmn. dept. religion, 1976-80, also dean student affairs, 1984-87; prof., asst. dir. Italy program Harding U., Searcy, Ark., 1980-84; dir. Florence, Italy programs Pepperdine U., 1987—; lectr., U.S., Europe, Cen. Am., South Am. Author: Christian Evidence, 1958, Christian Psychology, 1958; (monograph) Vocational Evangelism, 1982. Bd. dirs. African Christian Hosp. Found., Searcy, 1978—, Calif. Christian Sch., Sepulveda, 1965—, Christian Childrens Services, Santa Fe Springs, Calif., 1985—. Mem. Am. Psychol. Assn., Am. Assn. Marriage and Family Therapists, World Mental Health Assn. Republican. Avocations: tennis, golfing, travelling. Home: 24327 Baxter Dr Malibu CA 90265 Office: Pepperdine U Pacific Coast Hwy Malibu CA 90265

MITCHELL, CHRISTOPHER WRIGHT, religious publisher; b. Palo Alto, Calif., Nov. 4, 1957; s. John Wright and Carol Ann (Clifford) M.; m. Carol Kristine Prentice, Aug. 6, 1977; children: David, Noah. BS, U. Wis., 1978, MA, 1980, PhD, 1983; MDiv, Concordia Seminary, St. Louis, 1987. Ordained to ministry Luth. Ch., 1987. Pastor South Shore Trinity Luth. Ch., White Bear Lake, Minn., 1987-89; theol. editor Concordia Pub. House, St. Louis, 1989—; summer guest prof. Concordia Seminary, 1987-92. Author: The Meaning of BRK "To Bless" in the Old Testament, 1987; contbr. articles to profl. jours. Henry Vilas fellow, 1978, 79. Mem. Soc. Bibl. Lit., Nat. Assn. Profs. Hebrew, Phi Kappa Phi. Office: Concordia Pub House 3558 S Jefferson Ave Saint Louis MO 63118

MITCHELL, DANIEL ROY, religious educator; b. Somerville, Mass., July 23, 1942; s. Burton Clements and Dorothy Ruth (Hersom) M.; m. Nancy Lee Bowers, July 23, 1966; children:L Marianne Grace, Martha Ruth, Melanie Joy, Daniel Roy. BA, Washington Bible Coll., Washington, 1964; BD, Capital Bible Sem., 1969; STM, Dallas Theol. Sem., 1972, ThD, 1981. Chmn. dept. theol. studies and ch. history Liberty U., Lynchburg, Va., 1976—; bd. referee Evang. Ent., Topeka, 1987—; mem. adj. faculty ABECAR, Sao Paulo, Brazil, 1985—; bd. advisors Word Alive Ministries, Toms River, N.J., 1985—. Gen. editor: The Annotated Study Bible, 1988; contbg. author bible commentary: The Liberty Bible Commentary, 1986; assoc. editor mag. The Fundamentalist Jour., 1985—. Mem. Evang. Theol. Soc., Soc. Christian Philosophers. Republican. Baptist. Avocations: art, creative writing. Home: 102 Wooldridge Cir Lynchburg VA 24502 Office: Liberty U PO Box 20000 Lynchburg VA 24502

MITCHELL, DOUG, ecumenical agency administrator. Exec. dir. Greater Birmingham (Ala.) Ministries. Office: Greater Birmingham Ministries 1205 N 25th St Birmingham AL 35234*

MITCHELL, DOUGLAS CHANNING, minister; b. West Palm Beach, Fla., Dec. 16, 1964; s. Jerry Ronald and Shirley Ann (Roberts) M.; m. Christine Kelly Lawrence, June 2, 1990. BA, Oral Roberts U., 1986. Licensed to ministry Ch. of God (Cleveland, Tenn.), 1985. Youth pastor Maranatha Ch., Palm Beach Gardens, Fla., 1986—; wing chaplain Oral Robert U., Tulsa, 1985-86; children's camp dir. Maranatha Ch., Palm Beach Gardens, 1985; youth camp asst. dir. Summer Retreat Youth Pastor Assn., Tampa, Fla., 1989-90. Dorm chmn. Oral Roberts U., 1984-85. Mem. Fla. Youth Leaders Assn. (bd. dirs. 1988-90, sec. 1990-91), Fellowship of Christian Athletes (asst. huddle leader 1987—). Home: 2017 North Palm Circle Juno Beach FL 33408 Office: Maranatha Ch PO Box 31149 Palm Beach Gardens FL 33410 *I have found that my destiny in life, does not rest in my sole committment to the future, but in my day to day committment to God. Actions of the present lead to our destiny in the future.*

MITCHELL, HENRY HEYWOOD, clergyman; b. Columbus, Ohio, Sept. 10, 1919; s. Orlando Washington and Bertha (Estis) M.; m. Ella Muriel Pearson, Aug. 12, 1944; children—Henry Heywood IV (dec. Apr. 1972), Muriel M., Elizabeth Ann, Kenneth R. B.A. cum laude, Lincoln U., 1941; B.D., Union Theol. Sem., 1944; M.A., Calif. State U.-Fresno, 1966; Th.D., Sch. Theology at Claremont, 1973. Ordained to ministry Baptist Ch., 1944. Asst. minister Concord Ch., Bklyn., 1942-44; dir. religions activities, instr. English, N.C. Central U., Durham, 1944-45; exec. staff No. Calif. Bapt. Conv., Oakland, 1945-59; pastor Second Ch., Fresno, 1959-66, Calvary Bapt. Ch., Santa Monica, Calif., 1966-69; Martin Luther King Meml. prof. black ch. studies Colgate Rochester Div. Sch., N.Y., 1969-74; dir. Ecumenical Ctr. for Black Ch. Studies, Los Angeles, 1974-82; adj. prof. Sch. Theology at Claremont, Calif., 1974-82, Fuller Theol. Sem., Pasadena, Calif., 1974-82; adj. prof. Am. Bapt. Sem. of West, Berkeley, Calif., 1974-82, U. LaVerne, Calif., 1974-82; prof. religion and pan-African studies Calif. State U.-Northridge, 1981-82; mem. spl. pastoral ministries staff 2d Bapt. Ch., Los Angeles, 1978-82; dean, prof. history and homiletics Sch. Theology, Va. Union U., 1982—; Lyman Beecher lectr. Div. Sch., Yale U., New Haven, 1974; cons. to World Council Chs., London, 1969; ind. cons. on human relations and theol. edn. for blacks, 1968—. Author: Black Preaching, 1970, 2d edit., 1979; Black Belief, 1975; The Recovery of Preaching, 1977. Contbr. articles to profl. jours. Trustee U. Redlands. Mem. Soc. for Study Black Religion, Nat. Com. for Black Churchmen, Martin Luther King Fellows, Inc., Phi Kappa Epsilon, Phi Kappa Phi. Office: Sch Theology Va Union U 1601 W Leigh St Richmond VA 23220

MITCHELL, IRVIN SHARP, priest; b. West Chester, Pa., Apr. 15, 1934; s. Walter Sharp and Carol Mae (Reagan) M.; m. Loretta Margaret Starr, May 9, 1953; children: Irvin Reagan, Mark Alan. BA, Indiana U. Pa., 1966; MDiv, Va. Theol. Sem., 1969; DMin, Tex. Christian U., 1984. Ordained priest Episcopal Ch. Asst. rector St. Barnabas on the Desert Ch., Scottsdale, Ariz., 1969-72, St. Andrew's Episcopal Ch., Ft. Worth, 1972-78; rector, headmaster St. Alban's Parish and Day Sch., Arlington, Tex., 1978-82; rector St. Paul's Episcopal Ch., Gainesville, Tex., 1982-86, All Sts. of the Desert Ch., Sun City, Ariz., 1986—; mem. standing com. Episcopal Diocese of Ariz., Phoenix, 1990—, chmn. investment com., 1987—; sec. com. to form Dioceses of Dallas and Ft. Worth, 1982, 83; 1st pres. standing com. Episcopal Diocese of Ft. Worth, 1983-84. Author: Ministry to Transients, 1979, Using the New Book of Common Prayer, 1984. Pres., bd. dirs. Tarrant County Assn. for the Blind, Ft. Worth, 1972-82; bd. dirs. Union Gospel Mission, Ft. Worth, 1975-80; chaplain Sun City Fire Dept., 1986—. Recipient Svc. award The Salvation Army, Armstrong County, Pa., 1966. Mem. Order of St. Luke (missioner, chaplain 1970—), Ridgelea Country Club, Shady Valley Country Club, Kittanning Country Club. Home: 16818 Burns Dr Sun City AZ 85351 Office: All Sts of the Desert Ch 9502 Hutton Dr Sun City AZ 85351

MITCHELL, KENNETH REECE, theologian, family therapist; b. Cin., June 7, 1930; s. Ernest Reece and Louise Gibson (Phillips) M.; m. Judith Bard, July 11, 1953; children: David, Susan, Catherine. AB, Princeton U., 1952, BD, 1955; PhD, U. Chgo., 1965. Ordained to ministry Presbyn. Ch., 1955. Pastor Calvary Presbyn. Ch., St. Louis, 1956-58; asst. prof. Vanderbilt U., Nashville, 1962-65; dir. religion and psychiatry Menninger Found., Topeka, 1965-76; dean U. Dubuque (Iowa), 1976-80; Schultz prof. pastoral theology Eden. Sem., Webster Grove, Mo., 1980-85; chmn. N.W. Coun. for Theol. Studies, Seattle, 1985-89; Fulbright prof., Nijmegen, Netherlands, 1972. Author: Psychological and Theological Relationships in Multiple Staff Ministry, 1964, Hospital Chaplain, 1967, Multiple Ministries, 1988; co-author: All Our Losses, All Our Griefs, 1985. Mem. Am. Assn. Pastoral Counselors (diplomate), Soc. for Pastoral Theology.

MITCHELL, LEONEL LAKE, religion educator; b. N.Y.C., July 23, 1930; s. Leonel E.W. and Doris (Lake) M.; m. Beverly Ann Mills, Dec. 19, 1953; children: Anne, David. BA, Trinity Coll., Hartford, Conn., 1951; STB, Berkeley Divinity Sch., New Haven, 1954, DD (hon.), 1991; STM, Gen. Theol. Seminary, N.Y.C., 1956, ThD, 1964. Lectr., ch. history Berkeley Divinity Sch.; asst. prof., liturgy U. Notre Dame, Ind., 1971-78; prof. of liturgy Seabury-Western Theol. Seminary, Evanston, Ill., 1978—; hon. canon St. James Cathedral, South Bend, Ind., 1972—. Author: Baptismal Anointing, 1966, Meaning of Ritual, 1977, Praying Shapes Believing, 1987; asst. editor: Anglical Theol. Rev., 1978—. Recipient ADLMC award Assn. Diocesan Liturgy and Music Commns., 1989. Mem. Associated Parishers for Liturgy and Mission (coun.), N.Am. Acad. Liturgy Soc. Episcopalian. Home: 644 Haven St Evanston IL 60201 Office: Seabury-Western Theol Sem 2122 Sheridan Rd Evanston IL 60201

MITCHELL, MOZELLA GORDON, educator, minister; b. Starkville, Miss., Aug. 14, 1936; d. John Thomas and Odena Mae (Graham) Gordon; m. Edrick R. Woodson, Mar. 20, 1951 (div. 1974); children: Cynthia LaVern, Marcia Delores Woodson Miller. AB, LeMoyne Coll., 1959; MA in English, U. Mich., 1963; MA in Religious Studies, Colgate-Rochester Divinity Sch., 1973; PhD, Emory U., 1980. Instr. in English and Speech Alcorn A&M Coll., Lorman, Miss., 1960-61; instr. English, chmn. dept. Owen Jr. Coll., Memphis, 1961-65; asst. prof. English and religion Norfolk State Coll., U. Norfolk, Va., 1965-81; asst., then assoc. prof. U. South Fla., Tampa, 1981—; pastor Mount Sinai AME Zion Ch., Tampa, 1982-89; presiding elder Tampa dist. AME Zion Ch., 1988—; co-dir. Ghent VISTA Project, Norfolk, 1969-71; vis. asst. lectr. U. Rochester, N.Y., 1972-73; vis. assoc. prof. Hood Theol. Sem., Salisbury, N.C., 1979-80; cons. Black Women and Ministry, Interdenominational Theol. Ctr. Author: Spiritual Dynamics of Howard Thurman's Theology, 1985, Howard Thurman and the Quest for Freedom, Proc. 2d Ann. Howard Thurman Convocation (Peter Lang), 1992; staff writer AMEZION Sunday sch. lit. 1981—; editlr Martin Luther King Meml. Series in Religion, Culture and Social Devel., 1987—; contbr. articles to profl. jours., essays to books; mem. editorial bd. Cornucopia Reprint Series, Syndham Hall Press. Bd. dirs. Nat. Farmworkers Ministry, Tampa, 1987—, AME Zion Ch. Connectional Coun., Charlotte, 1984—; mem. Tampa-Hillsborough County Human Rels. Coun., 1987—; pres. Fla. Coun. Chs., Orlando, 1988-90; del. 7th Assembly World Coun. Chs., Canberra, Australia, 1991. Recipient ecumenical leadership citation Fla. Coun. Chs., 1990; fellow Nat. Doctoral Fund, 1978-80; grantee NEH, 1981, Fla. Endowment for Humanities, 1990—, U. South Fla. Rsch. Coun., 1990—.

Mem. Coll. Theology Soc., Am. Acad. Religion, Soc. for the Study of Black Religion, Joint Ctr. for Polit. Studies, Black Women in Ch. and Soc., Alpha Kappa Alpha. Phi Kappa Phi. Democrat. Methodist. Avocations: piano, poetry, tennis, bicycling, Scrabble. Office: U South Fla 310 CPR 4202 Fowler Ave Tampa FL 33620 *In my estimation, people are people, whatever the race, class or status. Between the front yard and the back porch of each individual dwells the real person, to whom I like to direct my approach.*

MITCHELL, MYRTLE L., ecumenical agency administrator. Exec. dir. Inner City Renewal Soc., Cleve. Office: Inner City Renewal Soc 2230 Euclid Ave Cleveland OH 44115*

MITCHELL, ORLAN E., clergyman, former college president; b. Eldora, Iowa, Mar. 13, 1933; s. Frank E. and Alice G. (Brown) M.; m. Verlene J. Huehn, June 10, 1952; children: Jolene R., Stephen M., Nadene A., Timothy M., Mark E. B.A., Grinnell Coll., 1955; B.D., Yale U., 1959, M.Div., 1965; D.Min., San Francisco Theol. Sem., 1976. Ordained to ministry United Ch. of Christ, 1959; pastor chs. Sheridan Twp., Iowa, 1954-55, New Preston, Conn., 1956-59, Clarion, Iowa, 1959-69, Yankton, S.D., 1969-77; pres. Yankton (S.D.) Coll., from 1977; now conf. minister Iowa Conf. United Ch. Christ. Mem. Sch. Bd., Clarion, Iowa, 1965-69, mem., Yankton, S.D., 1973-77, pres., 1976; bd. dirs. Lewis and Clark Mental Health Center. Mem. S.D. Found. Pvt. Colls., S.D. Assn. Pvt. Colls., Colls. of Mid-Am. Democrat. Lodges: Kiwanis; Masons. Office: 600 42d St Des Moines IA 50312

MITCHELL, PATSY MALIER, religion educator; b. Greenwood, Miss., Aug. 28, 1948; d. William Lonal and Lillian (Walker) Malier; m. Charles E. Mitchell, Apr. 20, 1970; children: Christopher, Kara, Angela. BS in Edn., Delta State U., 1970, MEd, 1974, Edn. Specialist, 1979; MA in Ch. Ministries, Ch. of God Sch. Theology, 1990; postgrad., Tenn. Temple U., 1990—. Cert. sch. adminstr. Youth, Christian edn. dir. Ch. of God, Minter City, Miss., 1975—; teen talent dir. Ch. of God, Minter City, 1983—, missions rep., 1975—; dist. Christian edn. dir. Ch. of God, Cleveland, Miss., 1983-85; sch. adminstr. Ch. of God, Cleveland, 1985—; del. Ch. of God Edn. Leadership, Cleveland, Tenn., 1990; del., speaker Christian Schs. Internat., Chattanooga, Tenn., 1991. Contbr. articles to profl. jours. Dir. St. Jude Children's Hosp., Memphis, 1991; vol. 4-H Club, Greenwood, Miss., 1985-91. Named to Outstanding Young Women of Am., 1983; recipient Community Pride award Chevron, 1988. Mem. Christian Sch. Adminstrs., Christian Schs. Internat., Ch. of God Edn. Assn., Delta State Alumni Assn., Ch. of God Sch. of Theology Alumni Assn. Democrat. Home: Rte 1 Box 72A Minter City MS 38944 *The greatest gift that God has given mankind is the capacity to love and encourage others. It is God's gift to us and our gift to others.*

MITCHELL, RALPH DAVID, minister; b. Detroit, Sept. 28, 1934; s. Vincent and Alice Louise (Smith) M.; m. Ileen Marie Beilby, June 22, 1957; children: Timothy Mark, David Allen, Deborah Corrine. BA in English, U. Mich., 1956; BD, McCormich Theol. Sem., 1961; ThM, San Francisco Sem., 1971, ThD, 1981. Ordained to ministry, Presbyn. Ch., 1961. Pastor 1st Presbyn. Ch., Neodesha, Kans., 1961-65, Belleville, Kans., 1965-68, Fredonia, Kans., 1968-78; pastor Avery United Presbyn. Ch., Bellevue, Nebr., 1978-82, Trinity Presbyn. Ch., Independence, Mo., 1982—; stated clk. Presbytery of So. Kans., Wichita, 1975-78, chmn. gen. coun., 1974-75; moderator bicentennial Heartland Presbytery, Kansas City, Mo., 1978-89; mem. spl. governance com. Presbyn. Ch. (U.S.A.); stated clk. Synod of Mid-Am., Overland Park, Kans., 1982—. Scoutmaster Boy Scouts Am., Fredonia, 1970-76, dist. commr. Quivara coun., Wichita, 1976-77, asst. coun. commr., 1977-78. Recipient merit award Boy Scouts Am., 1973, Silver Beaver award Boy Scouts Am., 1976; Paul Harris fellow Rotary Internat., 1988. Mem. Nat. Assn. Parliamentrians (reg. mem., treas. 1989—), Indpendence MinisterialASsn. (sec. 1986-87), Rotary (pres. Independence-West chpt. 1989-90). Avocations: racquetball, woodworking, running. Home: 2604 S Evanston Independence MO 64052

MITCHELL, ROBERTA KING, minister; b. Abington, Pa., June 21, 1951; d. Paul Sargent and Louise (King) Mitchell; m. Peter William Calvert, July 28, 1984. AB, Brandeis U., Waltham, Mass., 1973; MDiv, Harvard U., 1976, ThM, 1989; JD, Am. U., Washington, 1979. Ordained to ministry, Unitarian Universalist Assn., 1976; bar: Mass. 1986. Extension minister Unitarian Fellowship of London, Ont., 1982-85; interim minister Unitarian Ch. S. Australia, Adelaide, 1985; assoc. minister at large Benevolent Fraternity, Boston, 1985-88; assoc. dean, asst. prof. ministry Meadville Lombard Theol. Sch., Chgo., 1989—; dist. trustee Mass. Bay Dist., Unitarian Universalist Assn., Boston, 1984-85. Mem. ABA, Unitarian Universalists for Jewish Awareness (pubs. officer 1990—), Unitarian Universalist Ministers Assn., Soc. of Profls. in Dispute Resolution. Office: Meadville Lombard Theol Sch 5701 S Woodlawn Ave Chicago IL 60637

MITCHELL, SADIE STRIDIRON, minister; b. Phila., Jan. 4, 1922; d. Joseph Alphonso and Lucinda Gertrude (Clifton) Stridiron; m. Charles Thomas Mitchell Jr., Aug. 19, 1946; children: Sadye Mitchell Lawson, Charlene Mitchell Wiltshire, Charles Thomas III. BS in Edn., Temple U., Phila., 1942; MS in Ednl. Adminstrn., U. Pa., 1968; EdD, Nova U., 1978; MDiv, Luth. Theol. Sem., Phila., 1990. Ordained deacon Episcopal Ch., 1987; priest, 1988. Educator, 1942-81, Diocese of Pa., Phila., 1987-88; priest intern Diocese of Pa. (St. Mark's), Phila., 1988-89; priest Christ Ch., Upper Merion, Pa., 1989-90; priest asst. St. Luke's Ch., Phila., 1990—; chmn. Clergy Adv. Com. of Episcopal Community Svcs., Phila., 1990—; mem. Bd. Coun., Episcopal Community Svcs., 1990—; coordinator youth ministries St. Luke's Ch.; assoc. chaplain Hosp. of U. Pa., Phila., 1987—. Sec. Bethesda Ct. Personal Care Instn., Phila., 1988—; mem. Family Svcs. Bd., Phila., 1991—. Recipient Award of Merit, Phila. Assn. Sch. Adminstrs., 1982. Mem. Am. Acad. Religion, Soc. Bibl. Lit., Phila. Theol. Inst., NAACP, Delta Sigma Theta (chaplain 1988—). Democrat. Home: 2431 N 50th St Philadelphia PA 19131 Office: St Luke's Episcopal Ch 5421 Germantown Ave Philadelphia PA 19144 *In forging my way through the vicissitudes of life, I have found it most helpful to be at first contemplative, prayerful, and reflective. In the depths of inner-consciousness my humanness is then open to growth and transformation.*

MITCHELL, SANFORD CARVETH, minister; b. Columbus, Ohio, Feb. 28, 1942; s. Carveth P. and Kathryn Ann (Rogers) M.; m. Judith Ann Weber, Aug. 14, 1965; children: Jeffrey Carveth, Rodney Lewis. BA, Wittenberg U., 1964; MDiv, Hamma Sch. Theology, 1967; MA, Bowling Green (Ohio) State U., 1971; DD (hon.), Ashland (Ohio) Theol. Sem., 1990. Ordained to ministry Evang. Luth. Ch. in Am., 1967. Assoc. pastor First Luth. Ch., Findlay, Ohio, 1967-71; pastor Zion's Defiance, Ohio, 1971-79; sr. pastor Trinity Luth. Ch., Ashland, Ohio, 1979—; pastor, evangelist Evang. Luth. Ch. in Am., 1977—. Editor Homiletics Jour., 1988-90. Office: Trinity Luth Ch 508 Center St Ashland OH 44805

MITCHELL, SCOTT EUGENE, minister; b. Lawrence, Kans., Feb. 12, 1936; s. William Owen and Maude (Myers) M.; m. Mary Elizabeth Mason, June 22, 1956; children: Deborah, Kathy, Keith, Gary. AA, Cen. Christian, 1956; BS, Abilene Christian U., 1959, MS, 1967. Minister Ch. of Christ, Everett, Wash., 1960-64, 68-76, Rotan, Tex., 1964-68, Milwaukie, Oreg., 1976—; bd. dirs. Yamhill (Oreg.) Christian Camp, 1975—; steering com. Area Ch. of Christ Meeting, Portland, 1984—; ministers consortium Columbia Christian Coll., Portland, 1980—. Mem. Lions Club. Home: 3502 SE Pinehurst Milwaukie OR 97222 Office: Linwood Ch of Christ 10110 SE Linwood Ave Milwaukie OR 97222

MITCHELL, TIMOTHY CHARLES, minister; b. Baton Rouge, Jan. 25, 1950; s. Charles Preston and Gertrude (Artigue) M.; m. Shirley Ann Herrington, Dec. 18, 1971; children: Joel Lynn, Marchele Renee, Sharla Ann. BTh with honors, Tex. Bible Coll., 1972. Ordained to ministry United Pentecostal Ch. Internat., 1973. Pastor 1st Pentecostal Ch., Donaldsville, La., 1972-75; evangelist various pastorates United Pentecostal Ch. Internat., 1975-80; founder, pastor N.T. Christian Ctr., Montgomery, Ala., 1981—; harvestime dir. Ala. dist. United Pentecostal Ch., 1986—, youth leader sect. 6, 1984-86; writer for adult Sunday sch. lessons United Pentecostal Ch. Internat., 1991—. Contbr. articles to profl. jours. Recipient Pres. Club Membership award Ind. Life Ins., Jacksonville, Fla., 1982. Republican. Home: 6804 Inverness Rd Montgomery AL 36116 Office: NT Christian Ctr 4560 Narrow Line Rd Montgomery AL 36116 *"Then Peter said unto them, Repent, and be baptized every one of you in the name of Jesus Christ for the remission of sins, and ye shall receive the gift of the Holy Ghost (KJV)." Acts 2:38.*

MITCHUM, VIRGIL ALLEN, clergyman; b. Six Mile, S.C., Apr. 21, 1914; s. E.A. and Mozelle (Davis) M.; m. Mary Parks, Mar. 24, 1937; children—Walter Allen, Marilyn (Mrs. Alton C. Hollingsworth), Martha Theresa (Mrs. James Funnell). Th.B., Central (S.C.) Wesleyan Coll., 1943; postgrad., High Point (N.C.) Coll., 1946; D.D., Houghton Coll., 1964. Ordained to ministry Wesleyan Methodist Ch., 1939; pastor in Walhalla, S.C., 1937-39, Westminster, S.C., 1937- 40, Oakway, S.C., 1939-40, Cateeche and Central, S.C., 1940-46, Glenwood, S.C., 1946-49; tchr. Bible Central Wesleyan Meth. Coll., 1943-44, 46-48; pres. S.C. conf. Wesleyan Meth. Ch., 1949-57; nat. asst. sec. home missions and ch. extension and evangelism Wesleyan Meth. Ch., 1957-59, nat. sec. ch. extension and evangelism, 1959-63; gen. supt. Wesleyan Meth. Ch. Am., 1963-68; gen. supt. Wesleyan Ch. (merger Wesleyan Methodist and Pilgrim Holiness Chs.), 1968-84, gen. supr., emeritus, bd. pension, 1984—; Ofcl. visitor 9th World Meth. Conf., 1956; mem. S.C. Bd. Christian Action, 1949-57; pres. S.C. Wesleyan Youth Soc., 1943-45, 47-49; pres. So. Area Youth, 1945-47; mem. World Meth. Council, 1968-84; ofcl. visitor 13th Meth. Conf., Dublin, Ireland, 1976. Bd. dirs. Central Wesleyan Coll., 1950-57, 84—, vice chmn., 1954-57; vice chmn. bd. trustees Hephzibah Children's Home, Macon, Ga., 1984—, chmn., 1988—. Mem. Nat. Assn. Evangelicals, Nat. Holiness Assn. (bd. dirs.). Home: 2301 Norris Hwy Central SC 29630

MITTEN, DAVID GORDON, classical archaeologist; b. Youngstown, Ohio, Oct. 26, 1935; s. Joe Atlee and Helen Louise (Boyd) M.; children: Claudia Antonia Sabina, Eleanor Elizabeth. BA, Oberlin Coll., 1957; MA in Classical Archaeology, Harvard U., 1958, PhD in Classical Archaeology, 1962. Instr. dept. fine arts Harvard U., Cambridge, Mass., 1962-64, Francis Jones asst. prof. classics, 1964-68, assoc. prof., 1968-69, James Loeb prof. classical art and archaeology, 1970—, curator ancient art Harvard U. Art Mus., 1976—; assoc. dir. Harvard-Cornell Sardis Expdn., 1976; Whitehead vis. prof. archaeology Am. Study of Classical Studies, Athens, Greece, 1990-91. Author: (with S.F. Doeringer) Master Bronzes from the Classical World, 1967, Classical Bronzes: Mus. Art, R.I. School of Design, 1975, (with Arielle P. Kozloff) The Gods Delight: The Human Figure in Classical Bronze, Cleve. Mus. Art, 1988. Woodrow Wilson fellow Harvard U., 1958; Fulbright fellow Am. Sch. Classical Studies at Athens, 1959-60; Archaeol. Inst. Am. Olivia James fellow, 1969-70; John Simon Guggenheim Found. fellow, 1976-77. Mem. Archaeol. Inst. Am., Assn. Field Archaeology (co-founder), Am. Schs. Oriental Rsch., Brit. Sch. Archaeology (Athens, Greece), Am. Numismatic Soc. Office: Harvard U Sackler Museum 316 Cambridge MA 02138

MITTERLING, RICHARD ALAN, minister; b. Warsaw, Ind., Feb. 11, 1961; s. James Albert and Patricia Louise (Henley) M.; m. Laura Ann Jerrils, May 26, 1984; children: James Richard, Jennifer Lynn. BA, Anderson Coll., 1986; MDiv, Anderson (Ind.) Sch. Theology, 1987. Youth pastor North Ave. Ch. of God, Battle Creek, Mich., summer 1982, Akron (Ind.) Ch. of God, 1983; pastor Elwood (Ind.) Ch. of God, 1986-87, LaPaz (Ind.) Ch. of God, 1987—; distributor Amway Corp., LaPaz, 1989—; sec. Yellow Creek Lake Camp Bd. Trustees, Claypool, Ind., 1990—, vice chmn., 1990, treas., 1991; mem. Yellow Creek Lake Youth Camp Com., Claypool, Ind. Chmn. Operation Andrew, Clyde Dupin Crusade, Plymouth, Ind., 1991. Home: 203 Walnut St PO Box 65 LaPaz IN 46537 Office: Lapaz Ch of God 601 S Michigan St PO Box 65 Lapaz IN 46537

MIXER, DENNIS LYNN, minister; b. Good Hope, Ill., Aug. 15, 1952; s. Arlie Andrew and Bertha Minnie (Hohner) M.; m. Cheryl Anne Kuespert, July 12, 1975; children: Elisabeth Anne, Rebecca Lynn. BA, U. Md., Yokoa, Japan, 1981; MDiv, Southwestern Bapt. Theol. Sem., Ft. Worth, 1984; DMin, Golden Gate Bapt. Theol. Sem., Mill Valley, Calif., 1991. Ordained to ministry, So. Bapt. Conv. Youth minister Cen. Bapt. Ch., Urasoe City, Japan, 1977-80; counselor N. Richland Hills Bapt. Ch., Ft. Worth, 1981-83; assoc. pastor Willow Springs Bapt. Ch., Alvorado, Tex., 1983-84; pastor Lindell Ave. Bapt. Ch., San Angelo, Tex., 1984-87, Calvary Bapt. Ch., Tucson, 1987—; chaplain Suncrest Cae Home/Cascados Retirement Community, Tucson, 1988—, Tom Green County Juvenile Detention Facility, San Angelo, 1985-87, Tom Green County Sheriff's Office, 1984-87; pastoral adv. bd. Tucson Psychiatric Inst., 1989—. Author various planning guides, tng. guides. Bd. dirs. Crime Stoppers, San Angelo, 1985-87; mem. Foster Care Rev. bd., Ariz. Supreme Ct., 1990—; advisor Desert Storm Troop Support Coalition, Tucson, 1991. Recipient Meritorious Svc. Award, Am. Heart Assn., 1977, Achievement Svc. medal, 1977; recipient Meritorious Svc. award, Tom Green County Sheriff, 1987. Office: Calvary Bapt Ch 758 S Columbus Blvd Tucson AZ 85711

MIXER, RONALD WAYNE, minister; b. Mpls., Jan. 22, 1954; s. Joseph William and Faith Amour (Minor) M.; m. Glenda Renae Fjordbak, June 22, 1974; children: Rachelle Renae, Danielle Kaye. BA, North Cen. Bible Coll., 1977; M in Ministry, Internat. Bible Sem., 1983. Ordained to ministry. Dir. ch. ministry Rock River Christian Ctr., Rock Falls, Ill., 1977-79; dir. christian edn. Cen. Assembly of God, Tulsa, 1979-80; sr. pastor Manchester (Iowa) Assembly of God, 1980-83, Richmond (Mo.) Assembly of God, 1983-84, Odessa (Mo.) First Assembly of God, 1984-87; field rep. Am. Bible Soc., N.Y.C., 1988—. Commr. Olathe (Kans.) Human Rels. Commn., 1990—. Named one of Outstanding Young Men in Am., U.S. Jaycees, 1986. Mem. Kansas City chpt. Mo. Assemblies of God Minsters. Republican. Avocation: racquetball. Office: Am Bible Soc 15720 W 150th Terr Olathe KS 66062 *If, at the end of my life, those who have known me can say, "we could see the Fruit of the Spirit in his living", then I shall have lived well.*

MIXON, ROY DARVIN, religious organization executive; b. Metter, Ga., Apr. 6, 1922; s. Charles Fairey and Dorothea (Mincey) M. Student, Bible Inst., Cleveland, Tenn. Ga. state sec. Ch. of God of Prophecy, 1949-63, Del. and N.J. state overseer, 1963-68, Nebr. state overseer, 1968-70; nat. overseer Ch. of God of Prophecy, Eng., 1970-74; Australia, Asia and Pacific mission rep. Ch. of God of Prophecy, 1974-77, European, African and Middle East mission rep., 1977-80; ministerial dir. gen. hdqrs. Ch. of God of Prophecy, Cleveland, 1980—; v.p. Bible Tng. Inst., London, Bristol, Birmingham, Manchester, Sheffield, Eng. Author 7 books. With AUS, 1942-45, ETO. Recipient Disting. Svc. award Ch. of God of Prophecy. Republican. Home: 3ll3 Woodmore Ln PO Box 4ll4 Cleveland TN 37311 Office: Ch of God of Prophecy Bible Pl Cleveland TN 37311

MIYATA, GEN, history of religion educator; b. Kyoto, Japan, Feb. 11, 1933; s. Zenichiro and Ine (Yoshida) M.; m. Hiroko Fujiwara, Feb. 3, 1968; children: Kenichi, Mamoru, Teizo. BA, Tokyo U., 1956, MA, 1958. Lectr. Tenri U., Tenri, Japan, 1964-70; assoc. prof. Tenri U., 1970-79, prof., 1979—; vis. prof. Ind. U., Bloomington, 1980-81; chairperson dept. religious studies Tenri U., 1981-87, 89-91, dean faculty letters, 1987-89, 91—. Mem. Japanese Assn. for Am. Studies (councilor 1972—), Japanese Assn. for Religious Studies (dir. 1989—). Tenrikyo. Office: Tenri U, 1050 Somanouchi cho, Tenri Nara, Japan 632

MIZE, ROBERT HERBERT, JR., bishop; b. Emporia, Kans., Feb. 4, 1907; s. Robert Herbert and Margaret Talman (Moore) M. B.A., U. Kans., 1928 grad. Gen. Theol. Sem., N.Y.C., 1932, S.T.D., 1960. Vicar ch. missions Episcopal Ch., Hays Kans., 1932-41, Wakeeney, Kans., 1941-45; founder, dir. St. Francis Boys' Homes, Ellsworth and Salina, Kans., 1945-60; bishop of Damaraland Anglican Ch., Windhoek, Southwest Africa, 1960-68, asst. bishop, Gaberone, Botswana, 1968-70, 73-76; vicar Trinity Episcopal Ch., Marshall, Mo., 1970-73; assisting bishop Episcopal Ch. Diocese of San Joaquin, Fresno, Calif., 1978-88; dir. Gen. Theol. Seminary's Assoc. Mission, Hays, 1933-41; vicar St. Raphael's Episcopal Ch., Oakhurst, Calif., 1977-81. Mem. Phi Beta Kappa, Sigma Delta Chi, Phi Delta Theta. Office: Episcopal Diocese of San Joaquin 4159 E Dakota Ave Fresno CA 93726

MIZZELL, MARY ELIZABETH, religious research assistant; b. Opelika, Ala., Apr. 23, 1952; d. Vancy Harding and Zara (Beckett) Mizzell; m. Hooshmand N. Rouhani, Sept. 25, 1946 (div. 1984); children: Lili Rouhani, James. BS in Early Childhood Edn., U. So. Ala., Mobile, 1976; MDiv, Emory U., Atlanta, 1989. Ordained to ministry, Internat. Ministerial Fellowship, 1990. Tchr. Mobile County pub. schs., 1981-84; lead tchr. 3rd grade St. Mark United Meth. Day Sch., Mobile, 1984-86; acting asst. dir. World Meth. Evangelism Inst. World Meth. Coun., Atlanta, 1988; rsch. asst. Mt. Paran Ch. of God, Atlanta, 1988—; resource coordinator Mt. Paran Ch. of God, 1989-90, prayer assistance minister, 1989-90; founder Abundant Living Fellowship, Atlanta, 1988; del. vol. World Meth. Evangelism Inst., 3rd Internat. Seminar, 1987. Editor: Manual of Administrative Procedures, 1989, Abundant Living Fellowships, 1988; contbr. articles to profl. jours. Sherman scholar, Candler Sch. Theology, Emory U., 1986-89. Mem. Internat. Ministerial Fellowship, Christians for Bibl. Equality, U. So. Ala. Alumni Assn., Emory U. Alumni Assn. Avocations: painting, piano, reading, camping. Office: Paran Church of God 2055 Mount Paran Rd NW Atlanta GA 30327

MOBERG, DAVID OSCAR, sociology educator; b. Montevideo, Minn., Feb. 13, 1922; s. Fred Ludwig and Anna E. (Sundberg) M.; m. Helen H. Heitzman, Mar. 16, 1946; children: David Paul, Lynette, Jonathan, Philip. AA, Bethel Jr. Coll., 1942; AB, Seattle Pacific Coll., 1947; MA, U. Wash., 1949; PhD, U. Minn., 1952. Assoc. instr. U. Wash., Seattle, 1948-49; faculty Bethel Coll., St. Paul, 1949-68, prof. sociology, 1959-68, chmn. dept. social scis., 1952-68; prof. sociology Marquette U., Milw., 1968-91, prof. emeritus, 1991—, chmn. dept. sociology and anthropology, 1968-77; cons. Nat. Liberty Found., 1970-71, Nat. Interfaith Coalition on Aging, 1973-75, nat. adv. bd., 1980-89; guest researcher Sociology of Religion Inst., Stockholm, summer 1978; adj. prof. San Francisco Theol. Sem., 1964-73, McCormick Theol. Sem., 1975-78, 81-82; vis. prof. U. So. Calif., 1979, Princeton Theol. Sem., 1979, So. Bapt. Theol. Sem., 1982; mem. adv. bd. Ecumenical Ministry with Mature Adults, 1983—; resource scholar Christianity Today Inst., 1985—. Author: The Church as A Social Institution, 1962, 2d edit. 1984, (with Robert M. Gray) The Church and the Older Person, 1962, 2d edit., 1977, Inasmuch: Christian Social Responsibility in the 20th Century, 1965, White House Conference on Aging: Spiritual Well-Being Background and Issues, 1971, The Great Reversal: Evangelism and Social Concern, 1972, 2d edit, 1977, Wholistic Christianity, 1985; also articles, chpts. in symposia.; editor: International Directory of Religious Information Systems, 1971, Spiritual Well-Being: Sociological Perspectives, 1979, Rev. Religious Research, 1968-72, Jour. Am. Sci. Affiliation, 1962-64, Adris Newsletter, 1971-76; co-editor Research in the Social Scientific Study of Religion, 1986—; mem. editorial bd. Christian Univ. Press, 1979-84. Fulbright lectr. U. Groningen, Netherlands, 1957-58, Fulbright lectr. Muenster U., West Germany, 1964-65. Fellow Am. Sci. Affiliation (editor jour. 1962-64, publs. com. 1984—, social Ethics com. 1985-88), Gerontol. Soc. Am.; mem. Am. Sociol. Assn., Internat. Sociol. Assn. (sociology of religion research com. 1972—), Wis. Sociol. Assn. (pres. 1969-71), Midwest Sociol. Assn. (Wis. bd. dirs. 1971-73), Assn. Devel. Religious Information Systems (coordinator ADRIS 1971—, editor ADRIS newsletter 1971-76), Religious Research Assn. (editor Rev. Religious Research 1968-72, contbg. editor 1973-77, assoc. editor 1983—, bd. dirs. 1959-61, 68-72, pres. 1981-82, H. Paul Douglass lectr. 1986), Assn. for Sociology of Religion (exec. coun. 1971-73, pres. 1976-77), Soc. for Sci. Study Religion (exec. council 1971-74), Evangelicals for Social Action (planning com. 1973-75), Christian Sociol. Soc. (steering com. 1973-81, newsletter lit. reviewer 1981—), Family Research Coun. (assoc. 1985-88, rsch. network 1989—), Psychologists Interested in Religious Issues (profl. affiliate, 1984—), Midwest Coun. for Social Research on Aging (fellow 1961-64, 87—), Am. Soc. on Aging, Forum on Religion and Aging. Home: 2619 E Newberry Blvd Milwaukee WI 53211 Office: Dept Social and Cultural Sci Marquette U Milwaukee WI 53233 *As I try to live with eternity's values in view, my entire lifetime seems to grow ever briefer instead of lengthier.*

MOBERLY, MERVYN EUGENE, minister; b. Webster City, Iowa, Nov. 21, 1936; s. Maurice Merle and J. Eunice (Karr) M.; m. Margaret Eloise Hiebert, Dec. 21, 1955; children: Mary Moberly Morris, Mark, Miriam Moberly McBride, Malcam. BA, Ozark Bible Coll., 1958; postgrad., St. Louis Christian Coll., 1962; DD (hon.), Oak Forest U., 1976; postgrad., Cin. Christian Sem., 1986, Thiel Coll., 1987. Ordained to ministry Ch. of Christ, 1958. Min. Lawrence Heights Christian Ch., 1970-72, Sunset Park Ch. of Christ, Pueblo, Colo., 1972-74, North Grand Ch. of Christ, Ames, Iowa, 1964-70, 74-83, Fort Madison (Iowa) Christian Ch., 1983-86; evangelist Christian Evang. Mission, Des Moines, 1983-86; min. Andover (Ohio) Ch. of Christ, 1986-87, Iowa City Ch. of Christ, 1987—; evangelist Christian Evangelist Mission, Des Moines, 1987—; archeology dig mem. Joint Expdn. to Ai, Ramallah, Israel, 1972; instr. Woodland Hills Christian Coll., Des Moines, 1969-70, Iowa Christian Inst., Ames, 1967-69. Author: Corinth and You, 1958; contbr. articles to profl. publs. Committeeman Rep. Orgn. Johnson County, Iowa City, 1990-91. Recipient Past Pres. award Iowa Christian Conv., Des Moines, 1987. Republican. Home and Office: 4643 American Legion Rd SE Iowa City IA 52240 Office: Iowa City Ch of Christ 4643 American Legion Rd SE Iowa City IA 52240 *My whole philosophy of life and service is different because of my belief in God as Creator, who revelead His covenant offers to mankind in the Bible.*

MOBLEY, FORREST CAUSEY, JR., priest; b. Atlanta, Aug. 2, 1941; s. Forrest Causey and Jeannette Bertha (Apffel) M.; m. Nancy Joyce Mister, Sept. 1, 1961; children: Alison Leigh Mobley Gorrie, Mark Forrest, Andrew Stephen. BBA, U. Miami, 1961; MDiv, Gen. Theol. Seminary, N.Y.C., 1966; DMin, Fuller Theol. Seminary, Pasadena, Calif., 1989. V.p. Cullen & Mobley, Inc., Delray Beach, Fla., 1959-63; curate St. Andrew's Episc. Ch., Ft. Pierce, Fla., 1966-69; rector St. Andrew's By-the-Sea Episc. Ch., Destin, Fla., 1969-76; canon evangelist Cath. of St. Philip, Atlanta, 1976-80; dean St. Matthew's Cath., Laramie, Wyo., 1980-85; dir. Lake Martin Episc. Retreat, Tallassee, Ala., 1985—; pres. Mobley Mgmt. Inc., Tallassee, 1987—; tchr.-counselor, marriage counselor Lake Martin Episc. Retreat, 1985—. Mem. Am. Assn. Sex Counselors, Therapists and Educators, Christian Asns. Psychol. Svcs., Nat. Coun. on Family Rels., Family Life Educators (life, clin.), Rotary. Avocations: scuba, needlepoint. Home: Lake Martin Episc Retreat Rte I Box 169-M Tallassee AL 36078

MOCH, MARY INEZ, nun, teacher, librarian; b. Chgo., Aug. 13, 1943; d. Charles Michael and Mary Anna (Howanic) M. AA, Felician Coll., Chgo., 1964; BA, Mundelein Coll., 1968; MA, No. Ill. U., 1976. Joined Felician Sisters, Roman Catholic Ch., 1961. Tchr. St. Turibius Sch., Chgo., 1964-65, St. Damian Sch., Oak Forest, Ill., 1966-67, 75-80; tchr., librarian St. Florian Sch., Hatley, Wis., 1968-72, Christ the King Sch., Lombard, Ill., 1972-75; librarian Providence High Sch., New Lenox, Ill., 1980-82; dir. libr. svcs. Montay Coll., Chgo., 1982—. Mem. ALA, Cath. Libr. Assn., Pvt. Acad. Librs. Ill. (sec.-treas. 1987-90), Felician Libr. Svc. (co-author audio visual processing manual 1980, sec. 1979-80). Office: Montay Coll 3750 W Peterson Ave Chicago IL 60659

MOCK, LEILANI ANN, religious education administrator, consultant; b. Boston, July 18, 1944; d. Raymond Clayton and Audrey Mary (MacDonald) Lunde; children—Dean, Cheryl, Vicki, Jennifer. Dir. religious edn. St. Jerome Cath. Ch., Houston, 1974-78, Christ the Good Shepherd, Spring, Tex., 1978-84, St. Pius Cath. Ch., Pasadena, Tex., 1984—; ptnr. South West Ctr. for Ministry, Houston, 1985—. Contbr. articles to profl. jours. Mem. edn. com. Conf. of Catholic Women, Houston, 1984—; vice chmn., organizer Girl Scouts U.S.A., Houston, 1974-78. Mem. Am. Soc. Tng. and Devel., Nat. Assn. Lay Ministry, Religious Edn. Assn., Nat. Assn. Dir. Religious Edn. (rep. 1981—, pres. 1982-86), Diocesan Assn. of Dir. Religious Edn. (pres. Houston 1979-82). Roman Catholic. Avocations: travel; reading; art; music. Home: 601 Cypress Station Dr #1302 Houston TX 77090 Office: St Pius Cath Ch 824 S Main Pasadena TX 77506

MOCKO, GEORGE PAUL, minister; b. Little Falls, N.Y., Feb. 15, 1934; s. George and Anna (Swancara) M.; m. Elizabeth Carol Davidson, Sept. 2, 1956; children: David, Paul, Kristopher, Elissa. BA, Hartwick Coll., 1956; BD, Phila. Sem., 1959, STM, 1972; DD (hon.), Gettysburg Coll., 1978. Ordained to ministry Evang. Luth. Ch. in Am., 1959. Pastor Jacob's and Outwood Chs., Pine Grove, Pa., 1959-62; assoc. pastor St Mark's Ch., Wilmington, Del., 1962-65, sr. pastor, 1965-78; sr. pastor Ascension Evang. Luth. Ch., Towson, Md., 1978-91; bishop Del.-Md. Synod Evang. Luth Ch. in Am., Towson, 1991—. Author books; contbr. articles to profl. jours. Home: 501 Sussex Rd Baltimore MD 21204 Office: Evang Luth Ch in Am 7604 York Rd Towson MD 01204 *Colossians speaks of Christ as the one in whom "all things hold together". I know that Christ is the one who holds me together. Proclaiming and living his life, the church holds our society together.*

MODICA, MICHAEL ANGELO, minister; b. Trenton, N.J., Aug. 29, 1952; s. Michael A. and Josephine (Zapula) M.; m. Renee Verzi, Oct. 28, 1978; children: Michelle Renee, Michael A., Sara Joy, Samuel Joseph. Diploma, U.S. Army Sch. Transp., Ft. Eustus, Va., 1971; student, Mercer County Community Coll., Trenton, 1971-72; diploma in ministerial studies, Berean Coll., 1983. Ordained to ministry Assembly of God Ch., 1986. Lay youth dir. First Assembly of God Ch., Pennington, N.J., 1978-81; youth and outreach pastor Trinity Assembly of God Ch., Deltona, Fla., 1981-83, assoc. pastor, 1981—; prodn. planner, TransAmerica-Delaval, Trenton, 1979-81, also vol. counselor to troubled pers.; inner-city outreach servant, Trenton, 1979-81; coord. Inst. in Basic Youth Conflicts, (hdqrs.) Oakbrook, Ill., 1980-90; bd. dirs. Youth Alive Ministries, 1981—, Singles Alive Ministries, 1986—; advisor Womens Aglow, Deland, 1991—; co-founder, counselor Trinity Christian Acad., Deltona. Author: (manual) Procedure for Combining Advance Loans, 1975; reviewer: Ministries Today mag. Supporter Young Reps., 1973. With U.S. Army, 1970-71. Mem. Am. Inst. Banking, Sigma Pi (v.p. 1972-73). Home: 914 Sylvia Dr Deltona FL 32725 Office: Trinity Assembly of God Ch and Acad 875 Elkcam Blvd Deltona FL 32725 *If we were worth the death of the Lord Jesus Christ, He is worth living for.*

MOERMOND, CURTIS ROGHAIR, minister; b. O'Brien County, Iowa, July 5, 1941; s. Earl C. and Evelyn (Roghair) M.; m. Pauline Watkins, June 12, 1971; children: Christian, Elizabeth, Rebecca, Kathrine. BS in Edn., Concordia Coll., 1965; BD, Concordia Theol. Sem., 1969, MDiv., 1974, M Ministry, 1988. Ordained to ministry Luth. Ch.-Mo. Synod, 1969. Pastor Evangelical Luth. Ch. of England, London, 1969-72; pastor Luth. Ch.-Mo. Synod, Potter, Nebr., 1972-77, Wilton, Iowa, 1977—; internat. counselor Luth. Women's Missionary League, St. Louis, 1985-89; del. synodical convs. Luth. Ch.-Mo. Synod, 1977, 83, 89, workshop presenter Gt. Commn. Convocation, St. Louis, 1988, 2d v.p. Iowa Dist. East, Cedar Rapids, 1983-91, 1st v.p., 1991—. Doctrinal editor: (periodical) Luth. Women's Quarterly, 1985-89; author: (book) Announcing the Advent, 1991; contbr. to book Concordia Pulpit, 1984, 85, 90. Mem. Wilton C. of C. (bd. dirs. 1978). Republican. Office: Zion Luth Ch 1000 Maurer St Wilton IA 52778

MOFFETT, SAMUEL HUGH, retired educator, minister; b. Pyongyang, Korea, Apr. 7, 1916; (parents Am. citizens); s. Samuel Austin and Lucia Hester (Fish) M.; m. Elizabeth Barnwell Tarrant, June 30, 1942 (dec. Jan. 1955); m. Eileen Flower, Sept. 15, 1956. AB in Classics summa cum laude, Wheaton (Ill.) Coll., 1938; ThB, Princeton Theol. Sem., 1942; PhD in Religion, Ch. History, Yale U., 1945; postgrad., Coll. Chinese Studies, Peking, 1947-48; LittD (hon.), Yonsei U., Seoul, Republic of Korea, 1981; DD (hon.), King Coll., Bristol, Tenn., 1985. Ordained to ministry Presbyn. Ch. (USA), 1943. Asst. pastor 1st Presbyn. Ch., Bridgeport, Conn., 1943-44; interim pastor 1st Presbyn. Ch., New Haven, 1944-45; dir. youth work Presbyn. Bd. Fgn. Missions, 1945-46; mem. faculty Yenching U., Peking, 1948-49, Nanking (China) Theol. Sem., 1949-50; vis. lectr. Princeton (N.J.) Theol. Sem., 1953-55, Henry W. Luce prof. ecumenics and mission, 1981-86, chmn. ch. history dept., 1983-86, guest prof., 1986-87, prof. emeritus, 1986—; prin. Kyongan Higher Bible Sch., Andong, Korea, 1957-59; assoc. pres. Presbyn. Theol. Sem. Korea, Seoul, 1970-81, prof. ch. history, 1960-81, dean grad. sch., 1966-70, hon. pres., 1981—; dir. Asian Ctr. for Theol. Studies and Missions, Seoul, 1974-81, hon. pres., 1981—; bd. dirs. Yonsei U., 1957-81, Soongsil U., 1969-81, Korean Bible Soc., Christian Lit. Soc. Korea, Whitworth Coll., Spokane, Wash., 1973-79; commn. rep. in Korea Presbyn. Ch. (USA), 1960-64; mem. U.S. Edn. Commn. in Korea, 1966-67; chmn. theol. consultation World Alliance Reformed Chs., Nairobi, 1971; trustee Princeton-in-Asia, 1984—. Author: Wher'er The Sun, 1953, The Christians of Korea, 1962; (with others) Joy for an Anxious Age, 1968, First Encounters: Korea 1880-1910; contbr. articles, book revs. to various publs. Pres. Royal Asiatic Soc., Korea, 1968, councillor, 1963-81. Decorated Order of Civil Merit Peony medal Republic of Korea, Medal of Aaron and Hur U.S. Army Chaplains. Vis. scholar Cambridge U., 1970-71, 76-77; fellow Ctr. for Theol. Inquiry, Princeton, 1986-90. Mem. Am. Soc. Ch. History, Am. Soc. Missiology (pres. 1986-87), Am. Assn. Profs. of Missions (pres. 1985-86), Overseas Ministries Study Ctr. (dir. 1986—), Nassau Club. Republican. *It is worthy of our consideration that most important function in life is to know the truth and act with love.*

MOFFITT, TERRY ERVIN, academic dean; married; 1 child. AB in Secondary Social Studies Edn., U. N.C., 1981, postgrad. Tchr., coach, bus. dir. High Point, N.C., 1981-84; tng. mgr., sales engr. Kay Chem. Co., Greensboro, N.C., 1984-87; acad. dean Wesleyan Christian Acad., High Point, 1987—; presenter papers at N.C. State conv. Assn. Christian Schs. Internat., 1989-90. Mem. High Point City Citizens Adv. Coun., 1988-89, High Point City Coun., 1989, County Commn. on the Needs of Children, 1990; chmn. social action com., 1st Wesleyan Ch., High Point, Sunday sch. tchr.; soccer, basketball coach U. N.C.; mem. Rep.'s. exec. com. Guilford County, precinct chmn., del. to dist. and state Rep. convs. from Guilford County, del. to So. Rep. Leadership Conf. Named Conf. Soccer Coach of Yr., 1983, Region 6 Soccer Coach of Yr., 1983; Found. for Econ. Edn. fellow, FEE Theol. Conf. on Econs. fellow. Mem. ASCD, Internat. Fellowship Christian Sch. Adminstrs., Nat. Orgn. on Legal Problems in Edn., Guilford County Conservative Caucus, Nat. Assn. Secondary Sch. Prins., Conservatives for Freedom. Address: 3102 Woodview St High Point NC 27260

MOGYORDY, LAURA JANE, religious organization director; b. Cleve., June 18, 1960; d. Steven Zoltan and Margaret (Volchko) M. BS in Mktg., Miami U., Oxford, Ohio, 1982. Credit analyst asst., credit statement processor The Standard Oil Co. Ohio, Cleve., 1980-81; agt. asst., receptionist Stone & Youngberg investment Securities, La Jolla, Calif., 1982; optometrist asst. Assocs. in Vision Care, Inc., Cleve., 1983; telemarketing rep. Ohio Bell Telephone Co., Cleve., 1983; pub. relations writer, asst. Josh McDowell Ministryof Campus Crusade for Christ, Richardson, Tex., 1983-84; advt., promotions mgr. Josh McDowell Ministry of Campus Crusade for Christ, Richardson, Tex., 1985-88; dir. mktg. Christian Leadership Ministries of Campus Crusade for Christ, Dallas, 1988—. Vol. phone counselor Richardson Crisis Ctr., Richardson, 1986. Mem. Am. Mktg. Assn. (Outstanding mem. 1981-82, copy editor, ad salesman Scope mag., nat. publ. award 1982) , Quill and Scroll, Mu Kappa Tau, Pi Sigma Epsilon. Avocations: aerobics, running, tennis, traveling, French. Office: Christian Leadership Ministries 14679 Midway Rd Ste 100 Dallas TX 75244

MOHLER, JAMES AYLWARD, religious studies educator; b. Toledo, July 22, 1923; s. Edward Francis Sr. and Gertrude Dorothy (Aylward) M. Litt.B., Xavier U., 1946; PhL, Loyola U., 1949, STL, 1956, M of Social and Indsl. Rels., 1959; PhD, U. Ottawa (Can.), 1964; STD, U. St. Paul, Can., 1966. Ordained to ministry Roman Cath. Ch., 1955. Tchr. religion, algebra, latin, econs. St. Ignatius High Sch., Chgo., 1949-52; catechetics Indian Missions, Saulte St. Marie, Mich., 1954-56; instr. theology John Carrol U., Cleve., 1960-65, asst. prof., 1965-69, assoc. prof., 1969-74, prof., 1974—. Author: Man Needs God, An Interpretation of Biblical Faith, 1967, The Beginning Eternal Life, The Dynamic Faith of Thomas Aquinas, 1968, Dimensions of Faith, Yeterday and Today, 1969, Origin and Evolution of the Priesthood, A Return to the Sources, 1970, Heresy of Monasticism, 1971, The School of Jesus, 1973, Cosmos, Man, God, Messiah, An Introduction to Religion, 1973, Sexual Sublimation and the Sacred, 1978, Love, Marriage and the Family, Yesterday and Today, 1982, Late Have I Loved You, 1991. Fellow Union Theol. Sem., 1966, Ecumenical Inst. World Coun. Chs., Celigny, Switzerland, 1966, Inst. St. Serge, Paris, 1968, Gregorian U., Rome, 1968, Israel, 1968, Campion Hall, Oxford, Eng., 1968, Jochi Daigaku, Tokyo, 1972, Tien Ednl. Inst., Taipei, Repbulic of China, 1972, St. Joseph's Coll., Darjeeling, India, 1974, St. Xavier Coll., Bombay, India, 1974, Yale U., New Conn., 1978. Mem. Assn. Asian Studies, Am. Acad. Religion, Cath. Theol. Soc., Soc. Jesus. Avocations: writing, photography, horticulture, viticulture, fishing. Home and Office: John Carroll U Rodman Hall Cleveland OH 44118

MOHLER, JAMES WILLIAM, minister; b. Lynwood, Calif., Nov. 8, 1955; s. Lionel Louis and Shelia (Howard) M.; m. Miriam Ruth Moses, Aug. 23, 1980. MusB cum laude, Biola U., 1979, postgrad., 1990; MA in Christian Edn., Talbot Sem., 1984. Ordained to ministry Am. Bapt. Ch., 1986. Min. to jrs., middlers 1st Bapt. Ch., Downey, Calif., 1977-86; min. children and youth 1st Bapt. Ch., Scottsdale, Ariz., 1986—; adj. prof. Biola U., La Mirada, Calif., 1985-86; leader Tonto Rim Am. Bapt. Camp, Payson, Ariz., 1986—. Mem. project area com. City of Downey, 1985-86. Recipient Scholastic REcognition award, nat. Assn. Profs. of Christian Edn. Avocations: camping, racquetball, music, puppetry. Office: 1st Bapt Ch 7025 E Osborn Road Scottsdale AZ 85251 *By helping young people recognize their value to God, I have found young people eager to serve and grow in Christ. It is important to teach self-esteem based on God's love before they get caught up in adolescent issues.*

MOHLER, RICHARD ALBERT, JR., minister, editor; b. Lakeland, Fla., Oct. 19, 1959; s. Richard Albert Sr. and Janet Rae (Johnson) M.; m. Mary Ann Kahler, July 16, 1983; 1 child, Mary Katherine. BA with honors, Samford U., 1980; MDiv, So. Bapt. Theol. Sem., 1983, PhD, 1989. Lic. to ministry So. Bapt. Conv., 1978; ordained, 1983. Pastor Union Grove Bapt. Ch., Bedford, Ky., 1982-87; Garrett teaching fellow So. Bapt. Theol. Sem., Louisville, 1983-86, coord. found. support, asst. to pres., 1983-87, asst. to pres., dir. capital funding, 1987-89; editor The Christian Index, Atlanta, 1989—; mem. pub. rels. adv. com. So. Bapt. Conv., 1990—, tellers com., 1990, com. on resolutions, 1991. Author: Evangelical Theology and Karl Barth, 1991; author, editor: The Changing of the Evangelical Mind, 1991; assoc. editor Preaching mag., 1985—; contbr. numerous essays, book chpts., articles to profl. jours. Bd. dirs. Ga. Coun. for Civic and Moral Concerns, Atlanta, 1989—. Mem. Am. Acad. Religion, Soc. Bibl. Lit., Evang. Theol. Soc., Nat. Assn. Bapt. Profs. Religion, So. Bapt. Press Assn., So. Bapt. Hist. Soc. Home: 1111 Crabapple Cove Lawrenceville GA 30245 Office: The Christian Index 2930 Flowers Rd S Atlanta GA 30341

MOHNEY, NELL W., educator; b. Shelby, N.C., Oct. 31, 1921; d. John Wonnie and Maude (Ferree) Webb; m. Ralph Wilson Mohney, Dec. 31, 1948; children: Richard Bentley, Ralph Wilson Jr. BA, Greensboro Coll., 1943; LHD (hon.), Tenn. Wesleyan Coll., 1982. Dir. youth work Western N.C. Conf., Salisbury, 1945-48; dir. Christian edn. 1st United Meth. Ch., Lenoir, N.C., 1943-45, Washington Pike Meth. Ch., Knoxville, Tenn., 1952-56; dir. adult ministries 1st Centenary United Meth. Ch., Chattanooga, 1967-73, dir. membership devel., 1973-81; dir. membership devel. 1st Broad St. United Meth. Ch., Kingsport, Tenn., 1981-87; speaker, seminar leader for bus., profl., religious orgns. S.E. U.S., 1960—; adj. staff Bd. Discipleship Sect. on Evangelism, Nashville, 1987—. Author: Inside Story, 1979; co-author: Parable Churches, 1989, Churches of Vision, 1990; contbr. weekly article Chattanooga News, 1977—, Kingsport Times, 1981—. Recipient Freedom Founds. award for writing, Valley Forge, Pa., 1973, for speaking, 1974, Key to City of Chattanooga, 1979; named disting. Alumnae Greensboro Coll., 1988. Mem. World Meth. Coun., United Meth. Women. Republican. Home: 1004 Northbridge Ln Chattanooga TN 37405

MOHNEY, RALPH WILSON, minister; b. Paris, Ky., May 20, 1918; s. Silas Phillip and Clarine (Wilson) M.; m. Nell Marie Webb, Dec. 31, 1948; children—Richard Bentley, Ralph Wilson. B.A., Transylvania Coll., 1940; B.D., Vanderbilt U., 1943; S.T.M., Boston U., 1945; postgrad., Harvard, Garrett Bibl. Inst.; D.D., Emory and Henry Coll., 1959. Ordained elder Meth. Ch., 1944; pastor Winter Street Congl. Ch., Bath, Me., 1943-45, Manker Meml. Meth. Ch., Chattannoga, 1945-50, Washington Pike Meth. Ch., Knoxville, 1950-56; supt. Kingsport dist. Holston Conf. Meth. Ch., 1956- 59; pres. Tenn. Wesleyan Coll., 1959-65; sr. minister Centenary Meth. Ch., 1965-66, First Centenary United Meth. Ch., Chattanooga, 1967-81, First Broad St. United Meth. Ch., Kingsport, Tenn., 1981-87; asst. dir. Growth Plus Ministries Gen. Bd. Discipleship, Chattanooga, 1988—, Disting. evangelist in residence, 1991—; staff mem. Large Ch. Initiative, 1988-89; Staley Disting. lectr. Columbia Coll., 1973, Emory and Henry Coll., 1975, Pfeiffer Coll., 1976, Union Coll., 1977; del. World Conf. Christian Youth, Oslo, Norway, 1947; adult counselor Meth. Youth Caravan to Poland., 1947; chmn. Holston Conf. Commn. on World Peace, 1952-56; leader Annual Lenten Pilgrimage to Holy Land, 1973-80; pres. Holston Council on Finance and Administrn., 1968-76, mem., 1976-84; mem. Gen. Council Finance and Adminstrn., 1976-84, mem. exec. com., 1976-80; chmn. Commn. on Christian Higher Edn., 1956-59; res. del. Gen. Conf. Meth. Ch., del. jurisdictional conf. Meth. Ch., 1960, 68; del. Meth. Ch. (Gen. Conf.), 1976; mem. Gen. Bd. Christian Social Concerns, 1960-72, World Council Meth. Ch., 1966-70; mem. steering com. United Meth. TV Presence and Ministry, 1979-81; mem. S.E. radio and film commn. Meth. Ch., 1968-76; dir. Holston Conf. Found., 1984—; exchange minister Eng., 1984, New Zealand, 1987. Bd. dirs. E. Tenn. State Coll. Wesley Found., 1955-59, U. Tenn. Wesley Found., 1956-62; pres. Athens United Fund, 1965, Affiliated Ind. Colls. Tenn., 1963-65, Chattanooga Meth. Ministers Assn., 1966-67, Chattanooga Clergyman's Assn., 1968. Mem. Pi Kappa Alpha, Pi Kappa Delta. Club: Kiwanis. Home: 1004 Northbridge Ln Chattanooga TN 37405

MOHOLY, NOEL FRANCIS, clergyman; b. San Francisco, May 26, 1916; s. John Joseph and Eva Gertrude (Cippa) M.; grad. St. Anthony's Sem., Santa Barbara; S.T.D., Faculte de Theologie, Universite Laval, Quebec, Que., Can., 1948. Joined Franciscan Friars, 1935; ordained priest Roman Catholic Ch., 1941; tchr. fundamental theology Old Mission Santa Barbara, 1942-43, sacred theology, 1947-58; tchr. langs. St. Anthony's Sem., 1943-44; Am. adminstr. (handling affairs of the cause in U.S.) Cause of Padre Junipero Serra, 1950-55, vice postulator, 1958—; retreat master San Damiano Retreat, Danville, Calif., 1964-67. Mem. Ann. Assay Commn. U.S. Mint, 1964. Occupied numerous pulpits, assisted in several Franciscan Retreat Houses; condr. series illustrated lectrs. on cause of canonization of Padre Junipero Serra to students of all Franciscan study houses in U.S., summer 1952, also speaker in field at various clubs of Serra Internat. in U.S., Europe and Far East, on NBC in documentary with Edwin Newman, Padre Serra, Founding Father, 1985, PBS on Firing Line with William F. Buckley: Junipero Serra—Saint or Sinner, 1989, CBS, ABC broadcasts and conducted own local TV series. Mem. Bldg. Com. for Restoration Hist. Towers and Facade of Old Mission Santa Barbara, 1950-53; exec. dir., treas. Old Mission Restoration Project, 1954-58; mem. Calif. Hist. Landmarks Adv. Com., 1962-71, Calif. Hist. Resources Commn., 1971-76, Calif. Bicentennial Celebration Commn., 1967-70; pres. Serra Bicentennial commn., 1983-86, dir. Old Spanish Days in Santa Barbara, Inc., 1950-58, Nat. and internat. authority on Saint Irenaeus, mariology, Calif. history (particularly history of Father Serra). Decorated Knight comdr. Order of Isabella la Catolica, 1965. Pres. Father Junipero Serra 250th Anniversary Assn., Inc., 1964—. Named hon. citizen Petra de Mallorca, 1969, Palma de Mallorca, 1976; recipient Cross of Merit Sovereign Mil. Order of Knights Malta, 1989. Mem. Mariol. Soc. Am., Native Sons Golden West, Associacion de los Amigos de Padre Serra, K.C., Calif. Missions Study Assn. Author: Our Last Chance, 1931; Saint Irenaeus; the Father of Mariology, 1952; The California Mission Story, 1975; The First Californian, 1976; co-author (with Don DeNevi) Junipero Serra, 1985; producer phonograph records Songs of the California Missions, 1951, Christmas at Mission Santa Barbara, 1953, St. Francis Peace Record, 1957; producer The Founding Father of the West, 1976. Home: St Boniface Friary 133 Golden Gate Ave San Francisco CA 94102-3899 Office: Serra Cause Old Mission Santa Barbara CA 93105-3697 *Religion is the intellect's acknowledgement of the truth and the will's acceptance of the fact that God is our Creator and Father and the consequent realistic living demanded by such radical dependence upon the Supreme Being.*

MOHR, DAVID ALLEN, minister; b. Dubuque, Iowa, May 11, 1950; s. John and Gertrude Kathleen (Tweetmeier) M.; m. Diane (div. Jan. 1983); 1 child, Joshua; m. Sarah Smith, Jan. 3, 1986; 1 child, Jessica. BA, Augusta Coll., 1972; MDiv, Luther Northwestern, 1976. Ordained to ministry Luth. Ch., 1976. Pastor Ascension Luth., Ranch Palos Verdes, 1975-80, Prince of Peace Luth., Phoenix, 1980-84, Our Savior's, Lafayette, Calif., 1985—. Author: The Covenant of the Cross, 1987; co-author: Creative Worship, From Birth to Death: A Lenten Journey; recordings: Lift Up Your Hands, 1986, A New Life Begins, 1989. Home: 994 Carol Ln Lafayette CA 94549 Office: Our Saviors Luth Ch 1035 Carol Ln Lafayette CA 94549

MOHR, JEFFREY JON, minister; b. Palo Alto, Calif., June 2, 1947; s. Harold Alfred and Louise Pennock (Hobbs) M.; m. Paticia Jo Smith, June 23, 1985; children: Kevin Alexander Edwards, Kelly Marie Edwards, Alexander Timothy. BS, Humboldt State U., Arcata, Calif., 1969; MDiv, Princeton Theol. Sem., 1973; D of Ministry, United Theol. Sem., Dayton, Ohio, 1990. Pastor Anderson Valley United Meth. Ch., Boonville, Calif., 1973-78, Biggs/Princeton United Meth. Ch., Biggs, Calif., 1978-84; dir. Colusa County United Meth. Chs., Colusa, Calif., 1983-84; pastor New Jasper United Meth. Ch., Xenia, Ohio, 1984-90; dir. Outreach Miami Valley Christian TV, Dayton, Ohio, 1985-90; pastor Pioneer United Meth. Ch., Auburn, Calif., 1990—. Sec. Anderson Valley Lions Club, Boonville, Calif., 1976-78; pres. Biggs (Calif.) Lions Club, 1983-84; chaplain Lions Dist. 13-J, Jamestown, Ohio, 1986-87, pres. Jamestown Lions Club, 1987-88. Mem. Christian Ministries Mgmt. Assn. (v.p. 1988-90). Office: Pioneer United Meth Ch 1338 Lincoln Way Auburn CA 95603

MOHR, STEVEN AUGUST, minister; b. L.A., Apr. 19, 1955; s. Emil August and Juliette Mazine (Nelson) M.; m. Linda Margaret Martin, Apr. 2, 1978; children: Christina, Matthew, Joshua, David. BS, Luth. Bible Inst., 1981; MDiv, Fuller Sem., 1987. Youth dir. Redeemer Luth. Ch., Fridley, Minn., 1979-81, Abiding Savior Luth. Ch., Mounds View, Minn., 1981-83, Trinity Luth. Ch., San Gabriel, Calif., 1983-86, Grace Luth. Chs., Covina and Glendora, Calif., 1986-87; lay min. Good Shepherd Luth. Ch., Torrance, Calif., 1987-91; min. Beautiful Savior Luth. ch., Milwaukie, Oreg., 1991—; chmn. Evang. Luth. Ch. in Am., Region II Synod B Youth Commn., L.A., 1989-90, adult rep., 1988-89. Chaplain Santa Monica Hosp., 1991—. Republican. Home: 10115 SE Stanley Milwaukie OR 97222 Office: Good Shepherd Luth Ch 21100 Victor St Torrance CA 90503

MOISE, LESLIE, minister; b. Mole St. Nicolas, Haiti, July 13, 1959; came to U.S., 1984; s. Nicolas C. and Julienne (Nemorin) M.; m. Josette H. Bedminster, Aug. 16, 1985; 1 child, Audrey L. BA, Seventh-day Adventist Franco Haiti Inst., Port-au-Prince, 1984; MDiv, Seventh-day Adventist Theol. Sem., 1991. Crusade coord. Hebron Seventh-day Adventist Ch., Bklyn., 1984, Horeb Seventh-day Adventist Ch., Bklyn., 1984; pastor Allegheny East Conf., Phila., 1985-88, Annapolis, Md., 1990—; dir. Campus Ministry, Port-au-Prince, 1982-83. Mem. Soc. Bibl. Lit., Adventist Theol. Soc. Office: Beacon Light Seventh-day Adventist Ch 1943 Drew St Annapolis MD 21401

MOKROSCH, REINHOLD ERICH, theology educator; b. Hamburg, Fed. Republic of Germany, Feb. 22, 1940; s. Erich Georg and Christa (Greve) M.; Viola Held, Aug. 25, 1967; children: Verena, Pascal. Staatsexamen, U. Tübingen, Federal Republic of Germany, 1965, Phd, 1971; Staatsexamen, U. Darmstadt, Federal Republic of Germany, 1975. Asst. prof. theology U. Tübingen, 1969-74; clergyman Mössingen Protestant Ch., Federal Republic of Germany, 1973-75; prof. U. Darmstadt, 1975-83; prof., dir. U. Osnabrück, Federal Republic of Germany, 1984—; mem. Senate, U. Osnabrück, 1989—. Author: Religious Philosophy of Freedom, 1976, The Religious Conscience, 1979, Religious Education and Peace, 1980, Middle Ages, 1981, Christian Value Education, 1987, Moral Development and Education, 1989, Sermon on the Mount and Daily Life, 1991. Mem. Internat. Soc. Religious Edn. and Values, Internat. Soc. for Promotion of Christian Higher Edn., Soc. for Value Rsch. (chmn. 1987), Soc. Religious Paedagogics of Univs. in Germany (chmn. 1983-86), Soc. Protestant Educators in Germany (bd. dirs. 1984-87). Lutheran. Avocations: violin, tennis, Greek literature. Home: Felix-Nussbaumstr 20, Osnabrück Federal Republic of Germany D4500 Office: Univ Osnabrück, PO Box 4469, Osnabrück Federal Republic of Germany D4500

MOKUKU, PHILIP STANLEY, bishop. Bishop of Lesotho The Anglican Communion, Maseru. Office: Bishop's House, POB 87, Maseru Lesotho*

MOLAN, JOHN EDWARD, clergyman; b. Manchester, N.H., Apr. 24, 1927; s. John E. and Katherine (Maher) M.; student St. Anselm's Coll., 1944-45, 47; A.B., St. Mary's Sem., 1949, S.T.B., 1951; M.S.W., Boston Coll., 1962. Ordained priest Roman Cath. Ch.; asst. pastor St. Joseph Cathedral, Manchester, 1953-60; asst. dir. N.H. Cath. Charities, Manchester, 1958-63, dir., 1963-75; diocesan coordinator health affairs, 1963-80; pastor Immaculate Conception Ch., Portsmouth, N.H., 1975-83; pastor Our Lady of Perpetual Help, Manchester, N.H., 1983-84; dean Dover Deanery, 1979-83; papal chamberlain monsignor, 1965, prelate of honor, 1970. Protonotary Apostolic, Knight of the Holy Sepulchre, 1987; chmn. bldg. and real estate bd., coordinator legal affairs Diocese of Manchester, 1984—, vicar gen., 1985—, co-sec. for temporalities, 1986—. Served with AUS, 1945-46. Mem. Acad. Cert. Social Workers. Home: 2345 Candia Rd Auburn NH 03032-1132

MOLINE, JACK LOUIS, rabbi, author; b. Chgo., Aug. 10, 1952; s. Herbert Allan and Cyrena Dolly (Goodman) M.; m. Ann-Elizabeth Davidson, June 19, 1977; children: Jennie Pearl, Julia Nessa, Maxwell Herbert. BS in Speech, Northwestern U., Evanston, Ill., 1974; BHL, U. Judaism, L.A., 1979; MA, Jewish Theol. Sem., 1982. Dir. youth activities Seaboard Region United Synagogue, Silver Spring, Md., 1974-76; interim dir. B'nai B'rith Hillel Found., Charlottesville, Va., 1976-77; winter dir. Camp Ramah, Ojai, Calif., 1977-78; tour guide Universal Studios Tour, Universal City, Calif., 1977-79; rabbinic intern Temple Ramat Zion, Northridge, Calif., 1978-79; rabbi B'nai Israel Congregation, Danbury, Conn., 1980-87; Jewish chaplain Fed. Correctional Inst., Danbury, 1982-86; rabbi Agudas Achim Congregation, Alexandria, Va., 1987—. Author: Growing Up Jewish, 1987, Jewish Leadership & Heroism, 1987. Mem. Rabbinical Assembly (chair resolutions com. 1984-86, conv. co-chair 1989, exec. coun. 1990—). Avocations: humor, photography, racquetball. Office: Agudas Achim Congregation 2908 Valley Dr Alexandria VA 22302

MOLITOR, SISTER MARGARET ANNE, nun, former college president; b. Milford, Ohio, Sept. 19, 1920; d. George Jacob and Mary Amelia (Lockwood) M. B.A., Our Lady of Cin. Coll., 1942; M.Ed., Xavier U., 1950; LL.D.; M.A., Catholic U. Am., 1963, Ph.D., 1967. Joined Sisters of Mercy, 1943; tchr. elementary schs. Cin., 1946-50, secondary schs., Cin. and Piqua, Ohio, 1951-60; faculty Edgecliff Coll., Cin., 1962-73; pres. Edgecliff Coll., 1973-80; archivist Cin. Province Sisters of Mercy; research cons. various religious communities. Bd. dirs. Citizens Com. on Youth; trustee Chatfield Coll., Clermont Mercy Hosp.; mem. Area Coun. Planning Task Force, Cin. Community Devel. Adv. Coun.; pres. Better Housing League of Greater Cin. Recipient Woman of Year award Cin. Enquirer, 1977, 200 Greater Cincinnatians Bicentennial award, 1988. Mem. Greater Cin. Consortium Colls. and Univs. (pres. 1980). Address: 2335 Grandview Ave Cincinnati OH 45206

MOLLDREM, MARK JEROME, minister; b. Chgo., July 22, 1947; s. Ariel Robert and Esther Luella (Grindland) M.; m. Shirley Jean Bennett, Aug. 29, 1969; children: Jeffrey Hanson, Jennifer Lynn. AA, Luther Bible Inst., Mpls., 1967; BA, Concordia Coll., Moorhead, Minn., 1971; MDiv, Luther Theol. Sem., St. Paul, 1975; D of Ministry with distinction, Luther Northwestern Theol. Sem., St. Paul, 1989. Ordained to ministry Evang. Luth. Ch. in Am., 1975. Pastor Peace-Bethlehem Luth. Ch., Cobb-Edmund, Wis., 1975-80; assoc. pastor lst Evang. Luth. Ch., Beaver Dam, Wis., 1981—; mem. Beaver Dam Conf. Clergy, Evang. Ch. Am., 1988—; group leader ENCORE: Marriage Enrichment, 1982-90; leader spiritual life group chmn. dependency unit Unified Svcs., Juneau, 1983-90; coord. Coalition Luth. Chs. in Dodge County, 1986-89. Author: Lutheran Adult Instruction Manual, 1979; contbr. articles to religious and martial arts publs. Actor Tell-A-Tale Theater, Beaver Dam, 1982-85; coord. Singles United, Dodge County, 1982—; advisor Community Supportive Care, Chronic Mentally Ill, Juneau, 1983-86; treas. Childbirth-Parenting Edn. Assn., Dodge County, 1984; coord. Jr. Players, Community Theater, Beaver Dam, 1984-85; pastoral advisor Resettlement Com. for Romanian Refugees, 1985-86; cert. instr. Tac Kwon Do, 1988—; chmn. Dodge County Bd. Fed. Emergency Mgmt. Agy., 1990—. Recipient Outstanding Support award People Against A Violent Environment, Dodge County, 1983, cert. of appreciation Beaver Dam Martial Arts Ctr., 1983. Mem. Beaver Dam Ministerium. Home: 805 Fairfield Dr Beaver Dam WI 53916 Office: lst Evang Luth Ch 311 W Mackie St Beaver Dam WI 53916 *The purpose of ministry is to proclaim the gospel of Jesus Christ. This occurs not only from the pulpit but also in the public square. I want my whole life to reflect the love of God in all I say and do.*

MOLUF, ROBERT TIMOTHY, editor; b. Midland, Mich., July 16, 1955; s. Peder Edward and Oriole Helga (Gidlof) M.; m. Miriam Ann Arntson, Aug. 14, 1976 (div. 1985); m. Lynn Edith Dahlquist, Nov. 2, 1985; children: Stefan Dahlquist, Elsa Dahlquist. BA, Pacific Luth. U., 1976; MDiv, Luther Northwestern Theol. Sem., St. Paul, 1983. Editorial asst. Augsburg Pub. House, Mpls., 1976-78, asst. editor, 1978-80, assoc. editor, 1981-83, editor gen. books, 1983-87; sr. editor Augsburg Books/Augsburg Fortress, Pubs., Mpls., 1988-89; editorial dir. Augsburg Books/Augsburg Fortress, Pubs.,

1989—. Lutheran. Office: Augsburg Fortress Pubs Box 1209 Minneapolis MN 55440

MON, J(OSEPH) J(OHN) GERARD, deacon, educator; b. Jamaica, N.Y., Dec. 26, 1930; s. Joseph John and Eleanor Margaret (MacDonald) M. Counselor Braid Inst., Pitts., 1958-63; coord. adult edn. Diocesan Union, Pitts., 1963-68; dir. religious edn. St. Bernard Parish, Pitts., 1965-68; dir. continuing edn. for deacons Archdiocese of Hartford, Conn., 1981-89; coord. family life program Enfield Deanery, 1988—; lay min. St. Bernard/St. Martha Parish, Pitts. and Enfield, Conn.; mem. deacons' coun. Archdiocese of Hartford, 1981-89; coord. pastoral care St. Bernard Parish, Enfield, 1987-88. Chair Safety Coun., Enfield, 1969-79; active N. Cen. Conn. Bd. REALTORS, Conn. Assn. REALTORS, Nat. Assn. REALTORS, Hartford, 1970-89; mem. pastoral care com. Johnson Meml. Hosp., Stafford, Conn., 1980—. With USN, 1950-58. Named Man of Yr., Conn. Realtors, 1979. Mem. Coun. of Chs. (ecumenical ministry Bible study group 1981—), Toastmasters (numerous offices and awards, Man of Yr. 1970). Home: 8 Debbie Ln Enfield CT 06082 Office: St Bernard Parish 426 Hazard Ave Enfield CT 06082

MONAGHAN, PATRICIA (MARY), administrator; b. Bklyn., Feb. 15, 1946; d. Edward Joseph and Mary Margaret (Gordon) M.; m. Roland E. Wulbert, July 26, 1985. BA, U. Minn., 1967, MA, 1971; MFA, U. Alaska, 1980. Mem. English faculty Tanana Valley Community Coll., 1977-87, dept. head., 1985-87; dir. Continuing Edn. St. Xavier, Chgo., 1990—; founding editor Friendly Women, 1976; bd. dirs. Women of Power, Boston, 1986—. Author: Book of Goddesses and Heroines, 1981, rev. edit., 1990; author of poems; contbr. articles to profl. jours. Mem. Nat. Women's Studies Assn., Modern Lang. Assn. (mem. exec. com. 1988-90). Democrat. Home: 1625 W 101st St Chicago IL 60643 *Women, who fill the churches each week, are awakening to the fact that we do not also lead the services. What will religion be like when we do?.*

MONDAY, DERRELL WAYNE, minister; b. Lubbock, Tex., Dec. 15, 1948; m. Janna Gayle Bertrand, Aug. 20, 1971; children: Amy Lychelle, D'Lynn Kathleen, Emily Kay. BS, Hardin-Simmons U., 1971; MDiv, Southwestern Bapt. Theol., Seminary, Ft. Worth, Tex., 1977, D of Ministry, 1984. Ordained to ministry So. Bapt. Conv., 1972. Assoc. pastor First Bapt. Ch., Hillsboro, Tex., 1975-77; pastor Bethel Bapt. Ch., Eastland, Tex., 1977-82, Rotan, Tex., 1982-85; enlistment coord. Internat. Crusades, Dallas, 1985-87; pastor First Bapt. Ch., Iowa Park, Tex., 1987—; pres. Wichita-Archer-Clay Assn. Minister's Conf., Wichita Falls, Tex., 1989-90, moderator, 1991—, Big Country Bapt. Assembly Exec. Bd., Leuder, Tex., 1980-82; moderator Cisco Assn., Eastland, 1979-81; Christian life dir. Wichita Archer Clay Assn., 1988-91, moderator, 1991—. Named to Outstanding Young Men of Am., Community Leaders of Am. Mem. Iowa Park C. of C. (bd. dirs. 1989—), Lions (pres. 1990-91). Office: First Baptist Church 300 N Yosemite PO Box 847 Iowa Park TX 76367 *No greater gift exists than the gift of God's eternal forgiveness through Jesus Christ. I am constantly amazed and overwhelmed that God has given the privilege of dispersing this great treasure to someone such as I.*

MONDEN, VINCE LAMONTE, minister; b. Chgo., Feb. 21, 1961; s. Eddie and Barbara Jean (Wilson) M.; m. Marnita Patrice West, Aug. 1, 1981; children: Quentin Arness, Cory Trammell. BTh, Internat. Sem., Plymouth, Fla., 1990. Ordained to ministry Assembly of God Ch. Evangelist Bethesda Gospel Tabernacle, Chgo., 1980-88; evangelist, tchr. Hope Tabernacle Assembly, Chgo., 1989-90; pastor Life Ctr. Assembly of God, Detroit, 1990—. Office: Life Ctr Assembly of God 19305 Cameron Detroit MI 48203-1304

MONET, JACQUES, priest, historian, educator; b. St. Jean, Que., Can., Jan. 26, 1930. B.A., U. Montreal, 1955; Ph.L., U. Immaculee-Conception, 1956, Th.L., 1957; M.A., U. Toronto, 1961, Ph.D., 1964. Joined S.J., Roman Cath. Ch., 1949, ordained priest, 1966. Tchr. history St. Mary's U. High Sch., Halifax, N.S., Can., 1956-58; sessional lectr. Loyola Coll., Montreal, Que., 1964-67; asst. prof. history U. Ottawa, Ont., Can., 1968-69, assoc. prof., 1969-81, prof., 1981-82, adj. prof., 1982—, chmn. dept. history, 1972-77; pres. Regis Coll., U. Toronto, 1982-88, dir. Can. inst. of jesuit studies, 1988—; research officer to gov. gen. of Can., 1976-78; mem. selection com. Killam Research Fellowships, Can. Council, 1982-86; lectr. in field; chmn. acad. council Jesuit Fathers of Upper Can., 1973-79. Author: The Last Cannon Shot: A Study of French Canadian Nationalism, 1838-51, 1969, Dictionary of Canadian Biography, Vol. I, 1966, Vol. X, 1972, Vol. IX, 1977, Vol. VII, 1988, Vol. XII, 1990, La Monarchie au Canada, 1979, The Canadian Crown, 1979, La première révolution tranquille, 1981; editor Historical Papers, 1969-72; asst. editor Social History/Histoire Sociale, 1969-72; mem. editorial bd. Jour. Can. Studies, 1970—; contbr. chpts. to books, articles and revs. to profl. jours. Mem. Huronia Hist. Devel. Council, 1971-76, 81-85 ; chmn. admissions com. Sch. Grad. Studies, U. Ottawa, 1971-72; bd. mgmt. St. Paul's Coll., U. Man., 1973-82, bd. govs., 1982-85; mem. stamp adv. council Can. Post, 1978-87. Recipient Jubilee medal, 1977; Gov. Gen. Gold medal, 1978. Mem. Can. Hist. Assn. (council 1969-72, French lang. sec. 1969-74, pres. 1975-76), Social Scis. Fedn. Can., Can. Cath. Hist. Assn., Royal Soc. Can. (chmn. centenary com. 1979-82, Centenary medal 1982). Office: Regis Coll, Toronto, ON Canada M4Y 2R5

MONETTE, BROTHER PAUL RAOUL, retired parochial educator; b. Montreal, Que., Can., June 10, 1910; s. Raoul and Olivine (Filion) M. BA, U. Montreal, 1935, BA in Edn., 1940; MA in Edn., St. Michaels Coll., Winooski, Vt., 1944. Tchr. Mt. Assumption Sch., Plattsburgh, N.Y., 1933-36, 44-46, Prevost High Sch., Fall River, Mass., 1936-38, Notre Dame Inst., Alfred, Maine, 1939-44; missionary tchr. Uganda, 1946-61, Tanzania, 1961-76; ret. Seton Cath. Cen. Sch., Plattsburgh, N.Y., 1976. Home: 25 N Catherine St Plattsburgh NY 12901-2899 *Beyond the mineral, plant and animal kingdoms, there is the human kingdom and penetrating them all, there is the Divine Kingdom, the Kingdom of God which is the Divine creative Energy of Wisdom and Love that, by giving humans their reason, enables them to co-create with or impede the Divine Loving and Wise Energy.*

MONEY, HENRY THOMAS, minister; b. Louisville, Ky., Apr. 13, 1933; s. Milton Thomas and Ethel Mae (Heft) M.; m. Suzanne Lewis Silverman, June 15, 1960 (div. Aug. 1975); children: Terri, Tom Jr.; m. Sarah Cromartie, Jan. 15, 1977; children: Caroline and Christine (twins). AB, Transylvania U., 1955; MDiv, Lexington Theol. Seminary, Ky., 1958; MA, East Carolina U., 1960. Sr. minister Hooker Meml. Christian Ch., Greenville, N.C., 1958-64, Peachtree Christian Ch., Atlanta, 1964-85, The Kirk of the Corners Christian Ch., Norcross, Ga., 1985—; Active various religious activities including trustee Lexington Theol. Sem., 1975—, pres. Lex. Theol. Seminary Alumni, 1973-74; v.p. Christian Coun. of Metro Atlanta, 1976-85; chmn. Christian Pastors of Atlanta, 1970-72, Christian Coll. of Ga., 1970-74; chmn. bd. Campbell-Stone, 1990—, Atlanta InterFaith Broadcasters TV Sta., 1990—; others. Mem. Rotary, Optimist, Phi Delta Theta. Democrat. Home: 335 Hepplewhite Dr Alpharetta GA 30202 Office: The Kirk of the Corners Christian Church 6060 Spalding Drive Norcross GA 30092

MONJAR, HARVEY, religious organization administrator. Gen. overseer Christian Nation Ch. U.S.A., Lebanon, Ohio. Office: Chirstian Nation Ch USA Box 513 Lebanon OH 45036*

MONK, ROBERT CLARENCE, clergyman, educator; b. Holly Grove, Ark., July 7, 1930; s. Olin C. and Mary (Clay) M.; m. Carolyn Parker, Aug. 31, 1952; children: Robbi L. Monk Harms, Ellen Monk Winstanley. BA in Sociology, Tex. Tech. U., 1951; BD in Theology, So. Methodist U., 1954; MA in Religion, Princeton U., 1963, PhD in Religion, 1963. Ordained to ministry, United Meth. Ch., 1954. Dir. Wesley Found. Tex. A&M U., College Station, 1954-58; assoc. dir. Meth. Student Movement Tex., Austin, 1961-64; prof. religion McMurry U., Abilene, Tex., 1964—; cons., Jour. Am. Acad. Religion, 1972-76, Archives and History Commn., Northwest Tex. conf. Meth. Ch.; bd. dirs. Jour. of Second Century, Abilene, 1982—. Author: John Wesley: His Puritan Heritage, 1966; author (with others): Exploring Religious Meaning, 1972, 3d edit., 1986, Exploring Christianity, 1984, 2d edit., 1990, Methodist Excitement in Texas, 1984. Fellow Lilly Found., 1959, Sam Taylor Found., 1988, Danforth Found. fellow. Mem. Am. Acad. Religion (regional sec. 1989, bd. dirs. 1989—), Am. Soc. Ch. History. Democrat. Avocations: fishing, painting. Home: 1609 Vegas St Abilene TX 79605 Office: McMurry U Abilene TX 79697

MONK, WILLIAM HOOVER, clergyman; b. Washington, May 17, 1930; s. Jeemes Henry and Jannie (Allen) M.; m. Shirley Louise Smith, June 1954 (div. 1968); children—Wayne William, Daryl Louis, Karen Renay, Owen Lamont; m. Sarah Irving, June 13, 1976; children—Tiara Charrise, Jairon Paul. Student Fordham U., 1975-76; B.A., Oakwood Coll., 1985; postgrad. Lincoln Meml. U., 1986. Ordained to ministry Seventh-day Adventist Ch., 1983. Lit. evangelist Ch. Conf., N.Y.C., 1956-59; fund raiser Oakwood Coll., Huntsville, Ala., 1978-79; minister Seventh-day Adventist Ch., Nashville, 1979—. Composer, Be My Wife (song), 1958. Served with U.S. Army, 1954-55. Mem. Morristown Ministerial Assn., Morristown C. of C. Democrat.

MONROE, JOHN ROGER, minister; b. Johnson City, Tenn., Feb. 15, 1949; s. John Roberts and Helen (Kirkpatrick) M.; m. Susan Kilgore, June 15, 1974; children: Sarah Roberts, Miles Kirkpatrick. BA in History, Hampden-Sydney Coll., 1971; DMin, Union Theol. Sem., 1976. Ordained to ministry Presbyn. Ch., 1977. Assoc. minister 1st Presbyn. Ch., Fayetteville, Ark., 1976-81; minister Forest Hills Presbyn. Ch., Martinsville, Va., 1981—; commr. 196th Gen. Assembly Blue Ridge Presbytery, 1984, chmn. candidates com., 1982—; chmn. youthwork com. Ark. Presbytery, 1977-81. Chmn. Citizens for Peace, Martinsville, 1984; bd. dirs. Mental Health Assn., Martinsville, 1984, W.C. Ham Ctr., Martinsville, 1984. Mem. Rotary. Democrat. Office: Forest Hills Presbyn Ch 725 Beechnut Ln Martinsville VA 24112

MONROE, MICHAEL BLANE, education minister; b. Seattle, May 22, 1954; s. Tommy Lee and Glenda Carol (Duncan) M.; m. Janet Lynae Bryan, Apr. 14, 1979; children: Bryan Daniel, Brooke Erin, Brandon Michael. BA, Lubbock Christian U., 1976; MRE, Abilene Christian U., 1991. Min. edn. East Side Ch. of Christ, Snyder, Tex., 1980-91, Pleasant Ridge Ch. of Christ, Arlington, Tex., 1991—; bd. dirs. Christian Edn. Assn., Indpls., 1991—. Asst. Weblos den leader Boy Scouts Am., 1991. Home: 5610 Ridge Dr Arlington TX 76016 Office: Pleasant Ridge Ch of Christ 6102 W Pleasant Ridge Rd Arlington TX 76016 *The only sure path to true and lasting success is that great paradox taught and lived by Jesus of Nazareth: "If anyone wants to be first, he must be the very last, and the servant of all."*

MONROE, STACEY WELLER, religion educator; b. Plattsburg, N.Y., Jan. 21, 1962; d. Lee Weller and Barbara Dean (Viets) Gregory; m. Marshall Blake Monroe, Aug. 20, 1988. BS, Houghton Coll., 1983; postgrad., Perkins Sch. Theology, Dallas. Dir. Christian edn. Friendswood (Tex.) United Meth. Ch., 1987-89; youth ministries assoc. St. Luke's United Meth. Ch., Houston, 1989-90; dir. Christian edn. Coker United Meth. Ch., San Antonio, 1990—. Mem. Christian Educators Fellowship (exec. com. 1985-90). Office: Coker United Methodist Ch 231 E North Loop Rd San Antonio TX 78216

MONSEN, DAVID ELMER, minister; b. Oak Park, Ill., Apr. 9, 1946; s. Elmer Sonne and Olga (Solheim) M.; m. Linda J. Osmundson, June 8, 1968; children: Michael J., Andrew D. BA in Communications, Pacific Luth. U., 1968; MDiv, Pacific Luth. Theol. Sem., Berkeley, Calif., 1979. Ordained to ministry Luth. Ch., 1980. Pastor Emmanuel Luth. Ch., Yelm, Wash., 1980-84; pastor, developer Luth. Ch. Am., Helena, Mont., 1984-86; pastor New Life Luth. Ch., Helena, 1986—; producer, dir. KHQ-TV, Spokane, Wash., 1970-76; mem. Synod Coun., Great Falls, Mt., 1988-89; chaplain, St. Peter's Community Hosp., Helena, 1990—. Sgt. USAFR, 1971-76. Office: St Peter's Community Hosp 2475 Broadway Helena MT 59601 *Too often I confuse joy and happiness. Joy is a gift of perception which guides one to thanksgiving. Happiness is the emotional response of living joyfully.*

MONSON, THOMAS SPENCER, church official, publishing company executive; b. Salt Lake City, Aug. 21, 1927; s. George Spencer and Gladys (Condie) M.; m. Frances Beverly Johnson, Oct. 7, 1948; children—Thomas L., Ann Frances, Clark Spencer. B.S. with honors in mktg, U. Utah, 1948; M.B.A., Brigham Young U., 1974, LL.D. (hon.), 1981. With Deseret News Press, Salt Lake City, 1948-64; mgr. Deseret News Press, 1962-64; mem. Council Twelve Apostles, Ch. of Jesus Christ of Latter Day Saints, 1963-85, mem. first presidency, 1985—, bishop, 1950-55; pres. Canadian Mission, 1959-62; chmn. bd. Deseret News Pub. Co., 1977—; dir. Beneficial Life Ins. Co., Key Bank of Utah, Deseret Mgmt. Corp., Continental Western Life Ins. Co., Western Am. Life Ins. Co.; pres. Printing Industry Utah, 1958; bd. dirs. Printing Industry Am., 1958-64; mem. Utah exec. bd. U.S. West Communications. Mem. Utah State Bd. Regents; nat. exec. bd. Boy Scouts Am.; Trustee Brigham Young U.; mem. 1st Presidency The Ch. of Jesus Christ of the Latter Day Saints, 1985—, council Twelve Apostles, 1963-85. Served with USNR, 1945-46. Recipient Recognition award, 1964, Disting. Alumnus award U. Utah, 1966; Silver Beaver award Boy Scouts Am., 1971; Silver Buffalo award, 1978. Mem. Utah Assn. Sales Execs., U. Utah Alumni Assn. (dir.), Salt Lake Advt. Club, Alpha Kappa Psi. Club: Exchange (Salt Lake City). Office: SDS Ch 47 E South Temple St Salt Lake City UT 84150 also: Deseret News Pub Co 30 E First St PO Box 1257 Salt Lake City UT 84110

MONTAZERI, HOSSEIN ALI, religious leader. Ayatollah of Teheran Islamic Faith, Qom, Iran. Office: Madresseh Faizieh, Qom Iran*

MONTEVILLA, JULIO VARGAS, minister; b. La Paz, Bolivia, May 20, 1943; came to U.S., 1972; m. Lydia Maldonado, June 24, 1973; children: Amy, Keren, Lilybeth. BA, River Plate Coll., Argentina, 1965; MDiv, Theol. Sem., Puerto Rico, 1984. Ordained to ministry Seventh-day Adventists, 1976. Pastor Mision Boliviana Adventista, La Paz, Bolivia, 1966-70, Assn. Puerto Rico Este, San Juan, 1971-86, Tex. Conf. Seventh-day Adventist Ch., Alvarado, 1986—; del. World Wide Coun. Seventh Day Adventist Ch., 1975, 80, 85, 91. Radio, TV speaker in Latin Am. countries, 1970-72. Home and Office: 9834 Mango St Houston TX 77075

MONTGOMERY, CARL HALLOWAY, JR., minister; b. Phila., May 6, 1952; s. Carl H. and Geneva (Bruce) M.; m. Sheila Showell, May 4, 1974; 1 child, Yeve Gennele. ThB, Loyola Coll., Balt., 1986; MEd in Vocat. Rehab. Counseling, Coppin State Coll., 1988. Ordained to ministry Bible Way Chs. World Wide, 1981; cert. profl. counselor, rehab. counselor, pastoral counselor, Md. V.p. Internat. Young People's Union Bible Way World Wide Chs., Washington, 1985; adj. gen. to presiding bishop, mem. constn. revision com., 1991; exec. sec., dist. elder 5th jurisdictional dist., Mid-Atlantic Diocese Bible Way World Wide Chs., Balt., 1991; asst. sec. gen. World Fellowship Black Pentecostal Chs., 1987—; rehab. specialist Md. State Dept. Edn., Balt., 1988—; assoc. pastor 1st Apostolic Faith Ch., Balt., 1989-91; pastor Grace Ch. Christ, Balt., 1992—; founder, pres. Grace of God Ministries, Balt., 1989—, "Grace for Living" Media Ministry. Author: Worship Is Not An Option, 1991. Mem. Am. Assn. for Counseling, Nat. Rehab. Assn., Nat. Christian Counselors Assn. Democrat. Office: Div Vocat Rehab 1515 W Mount Royal Ave Baltimore MD 21217 *In a complex world with competitive societies, ambition can rapidly evolve into a green-eyed monster consuming everything in its path, including oneself. But in subtle splendor it becomes purified when immersed in Divine purpose.*

MONTGOMERY, DARLENE THELMA, religious organization administrator; b. Valley Falls, Kans., Oct. 27, 1929; d. Edgar and Arlouine (Collins) Moore; m. Sterling Montgomery, July 1, 1950 (dec. July 1976); children: Sterling Jr., Terri Lynne, Phillip, Michelle. BA, Washburn U., 1964; MSW, Kans. U., 1972. Lic. social worker, Kans. Social worker County Welfare Dept., Topeka, 1957-68, social work supr., 1968-73; instr. social work, dir. staff devel. State Dept. Social and Rehab. Services, Topeka, 1973-77, social services adminstr., 1977-86; adminstrv. asst. Susanna Wesley United Meth. Ch., Topeka, 1986—. Pres. County Community Resources Council, Topeka, 1983-84. Mem. Kans. Conf. Social Welfare (sec. fin. 1976-80, v.p. 1984-85), Mid Am. Congress on Aging, Delta Sigma Theta (pres. 1985-87), Kappa Mu Epsilon. Democrat. Methodist. Home: 5442 SW 12th Terr Topeka KS 66604 Office: Susanna Wesley United Meth Ch 7220 Asbury Dr Topeka KS 66614

MONTGOMERY, JAMES ERVIN, minister; b. Cherryville, N.C., May 2, 1951; s. John Frank and Johnida (Patterson) M.; m. Velrry Jean Sweezy, July 15, 1971; children: James E. Jr., Scottie Austin. AA in Pastoral Ministries, Fruitland Bapt. Bible Inst., 1984; BA, Mid-Atlantic Bible Sem., 1986, MDiv, 1987, D Ministry, 1987, D Ministry (hon.), Gardner-Webb Coll., 1981. Ordained to ministry Nat. Bapt. Conv. U.S.A. Pastor Macedonia Missionary Bapt. Ch., Waco, N.C., 1978—; exec. bd. chmn. Ebenezer Bapt. Assn., Shelby, N.C., 1982—, evangelism chmn., 1985—, 3d vice moderator, 1988—; pres. Shelby Ministerial Conf., 1986. Author: Ethics and Decalogue, 1986, Black Churches: Their Problems, 1987. Bd. dirs. Cleve. Community Coll., Shelby, 1988—. Mem. Ruritan Club (bd. dirs. Ulysses chpt. 1988—), Hopewell Lodge. Democrat. Home: Rte 2 Box 74M 186 Mill Rd Cherryville NC 28021 Office: Macedonia Missionary Bapt Ch PO Box 280 Waco NC 28169

MONTGOMERY, JAMES WINCHESTER, retired bishop; b. Chgo., May 29, 1921; s. James Edward and Evelyn Lee (Winchester) M. BA, Northwestern U., 1943; STB, Gen. Theol. Sem., N.Y.C., 1949, STD (hon.), 1963; DD (hon.), Nashotah House, 1963, Seabury-Western Theol. Sem., 1969; LLD (hon.), Shimer Coll., 1969; LHD, Iowa Wesleyan Coll., 1974. Ordained deacon and priest Episcopal Ch. Curate St. Luke's Ch., Evanston, Ill., 1949-51; rector St. John Evangelist Ch., Flossmoor, Ill., 1951-62; suffragan bishop Episcopal Diocese Chgo., 1962-65, bishop coadjutor, 1965-71, bishop, 1971-87, ret. Mem. Phi Beta Kappa, Delta Upsilon. Office: Episcopal Ch Diocese of Chgo 65 E Huron St Chicago IL 60611

MONTGOMERY, MICHAEL HENRY, minister; b. Decorah, Iowa, Apr. 12, 1955; s. Henry Irving and Barbara Louise (Hook) M.; m. Peggy S. McClanahan, Oct. 27, 1984; children: David Henry McClanahan, Daniel Edward McClanahan. BA, Coe Coll., 1977; MBA, U. Chgo., 1980; MDiv, Chgo. Theol. Sem., 1983. Ordained to ministry United Ch. of Christ, 1983. Intern various chs. and ministries Iowa, Ill., Mass., 1978-83; intern treasury dept. United Ch. Bd. World Ministries, N.Y.C., 1981-82; pastor Peace United Ch. of Christ, Tilden, Nebr., 1983-89; co-minister United Ch. of Christ, Congregational, Ames, Iowa, 1989—; registrar Northeastern Assn., Nebr., 1986-89; mem. exec. com. Coordinating Ctr. for Women in Ch. and Soc. of United Ch. of Christ, 1987-89. Organizer Tilden Food Pantry, 1986; bd. dirs. United Way, Ames, 1991. Mem. Ames Ministerial Assn. (pres. 1991-92). Democrat. Home: 112 Sandburg Ct Ames IA 50010 Office: United Ch of Christ Congregational 6th & Kellogg PO Box 603 Ames IA 50010

MONTROSE, DONALD W., bishop; b. Denver, May 13, 1923. Student, St. John's Sem., Calif. Ordained priest Roman Cath. Ch., 1949. Aux. bishop Roman Cath. Ch., Los Angeles, 1983; bishop Diocese of Stockton, Calif., 1985—. Office: Diocese of Stockton 1105 N Lincoln St PO Box 4237 Stockton CA 95204

MONTZ, FLORENCE STOLTE, church official; b. Lowden, Iowa, June 7, 1924; d. Emil L. and Emma Marie (Meier) Stolte; m. C. R. Montz, June 15, 1947; children: Jennifer Montz Rechlin, Fredrick John. BS, RN, U. Iowa, 1947; LLD (hon.), Concordia Coll., Bronxville, N.Y., 1984; LHD (hon.), Concordia Coll., St. Paul, 1988. RN, Iowa. V.p., then pres. N.D. dist. Luth. Women's Missionary, Luth. Ch.-Mo. Synod, Bismarck, 1960-68, 1st v.p. internat., 1967-71, pres., 1971-75; editor Better Health mag. Luth. Ch.-Mo. Synod, Bismarck, 1983—, also bd. dirs. Mem. Sigma Theta Tau. Home: Box 1293 Bismarck ND 58502

MOODEY, JAMES R., bishop; b. Bklyn., Dec. 9, 1932. BA, Hamilton Coll., Clinton, N.Y., 1954; grad., Episcopal Theol. Sch., 1957. Ordained priest Episcopal Ch., 1957. Asst. to rector Christ Ch., Cin., 1957-60; vicar Ch. of the Nativity, Newcastle, Del., 1960-65; rector St. Luke's Ch., Scranton, Pa., 1965-76, St. Paul's Ch., Phila., 1977-83; bishop coadjutor Trinity Cathedral, Cleve., from 1983; bishop Diocese of Ohio, Cleve., 1984—. Office: Diocese of Ohio 2230 Euclid Ave Cleveland OH 44115

MOODY, GREGORY, minister; b. East Orange, N.J., Aug. 8, 1966; s. Floyde Bennett and Thelma (White) M.; m. Kessey Lauanda Hill, Aug. 6, 1988; 1 child, Gregory Marcel. BS, Bowles Bible Inst., Roselle, N.J., 1990, MS, 1991; Cert., Inst. Motivational Living, Pa., 1990. Lay worker Mason Temple, Conway, S.C., 1985-88, pres. ushers bd., 1988-89; Bible and Religion educator United Deliverance Tabernacle, Newark, 1990—, minister music, 1989—, asst. to pastor, 1990—; dir., recreation therapist Delaire Nursing Home, Linden, N.J.; bus. cons. United Deliverance Tabernacle, 1989-90, adminstr., 1991—. Author/editor Reaching Out For Someone Jour., 1989—. Named Outstanding Youth Worker, Way of the Cross Ch., 1988, Appreciation Cert., Mason Temple Ch. of God in Christ, 1988-89, United Deliverance Tabernacle, 1989-91. Home: 1037 Main St Rahway NJ 07065 Office: United Deliverance Tabernac 628 Chestnut St Elizabeth NJ 07203-1946

MOODY, JAY L., youth director; b. Canton, Ohio, Jan. 6, 1961; s. Donald Moody and Alyce (Deckerd) Beck; m. Jolene S. Moody, Jan. 23, 1980; children: Stefanie M., Nicole S. Student, Walsh Coll., North Canton, Ohio, 1988—. Owner Moody Concessions, East Canton, Ohio, 1979—; youth dir. Martin Luther Luth. Ch., Canton, 1989—. Councilman East Canton Village Coun., 1988—; mem. East Canton Festival Com. Mem. Jr. Order United Am. Mechanics. Republican. Lutheran. Avocation: swimming. Home: 311 Center St East Canton OH 44730

MOODY, JOHN HENRY, minister; b. Seattle, Aug. 10, 1945; s. Henry Thornton Jr. and Ruby Fern (Johnson) M.; m. Melody Ann Hentiksen, Aug. 5, 1967; children: Eric John, Anna Marlene. BA in Psychology, Pacific Luth. U., 1967; MDiv, Luther Theol. Sem., 1971; D of Ministry, San Francisco Theol. Sem., 1977. Ordained to ministry Luth. Ch., 1972. Exec. dir. Tri-Cities Chaplaincy, Kennewick, Wash., 1971-86, Interfaith Ministries Hawaii, Honolulu, 1987—; exec. bd. Widowed Persons Wash., Seattle, 1973-78, Hospice Hawaii, Honolulu, 1988—; chmn. Pacific Region ACPE, L.A., 1991—; cons. Episc. Ministries & Alaska PAcific U., Salt Lake City, 1987-91, Alaska Pacific U., Anchorage, 1986-90. Contbr. articles to profl. jours. Chaplain Civil Air Patrol, Honolulu, 1989—. Fellow Coll. Chaplains (cert. chmn. Hawaii 1989—); mem. Assn. Mental Health Clergy, Assn. Clin. Pastoral Edn. (cert. supr. health clergy 1981). Avocations: hiking, golf, travel, jogging. Home: 1382 A Kamahele St Kailua HI 96734 Office: Interfaith Ministries 1660 S Beretania St Honolulu HI 96826

MOODY, LARRY ALAN, theologian, educator, therapist; b. Junction City, Kans., Aug. 5, 1945; s. Dwight Lyman and Addie Ione (Spaulding) M.; m. Sharon Lea Heft, May 31, 1964; children: Michael Dwight, Paul Alan. BA, Baker U., 1968; MDiv, United Theol. Sem., 1972; PhD, Aquinas Inst. Theol., Dubuque, Iowa, 1980. Ordained to ministry United Meth. Ch., 1973. Pastor Gilboa-Pleasant Grove United Meth. Ch., Gilboa, Ohio, 1969-72; asst. pastor 1st United Meth. Ch., Whitewater, Wis., 1972-73; pastor Ash Creek-Boaz United Meth. Ch., Richland Center, Wis., 1973-79, Trinity United Meth. Ch., Madison, Wis., 1979-88, Wesley United Meth. Ch., Marshfield, Wis., 1988—; prof. Mt. Senario Coll., Ladysmith, Wis., 1986—. Contbr. articles, commentaries for profl. jours. Coord. Viet Namese Resettlement Program, Richland County, Wis., 1975-76; chair Assn. of Clergy and Health Profls. Wis., Madison, 1982-86; mem. Genetic Counseling Task Force for State of Wis., 1982-88; bd. dirs. John Wesley Theol. Inst., Chgo., 1984-88; chair United Meths. of Greater Madison, Inc., 1984-86, Bd. Higher Edn., Wis. Conf., 1984-88, Madison Hosps. Chaplaincy Com., 1984-88, North Cen. Leadership Devel. Com., 1990—. Recipient Someone Spl. award Sta. WIBA, Madison, 1983; A.D. Jellison fellow Baker U., 1965-68, Dean Elbright scholar, 1967-68. Mem. Nat. Acad Counselors and Family Therapists (cert.), Am. Assn. Marriage and Family Therapy. Home: 1601 S Erickson Ave Marshfield WI 54449-5127 Office: Wesley United Meth Ch 205 E Third St Marshfield WI 54449-3799

MOODY, LINDA ANN, college chaplain; b. Garden City, Mich., Oct. 19, 1954; d. Dean A. Moody and Barbara (E.) Caton. BA, U. Mich., 1975, MA, 1976; MDiv, So. Seminary, Louisville, 1980; postgrad., Grad. Theol. Union, Berkeley, Calif. Instr. Mich. Lang. Sch., Anaco, Venezuela, 1975, Escuela Anaco, Anaco, Venezuela, 1976, English Lang. Inst. U. Mich., Ann Arbor, 1976; tchr. Concord (Mich.) High Sch., 1976-78; chaplain Brookville Lake Ministry, Ind., 1979-80; min. Beechmont United Meth. Ch., Louisville, 1979-80; assoc. dir., instr. English Ctr. for Internat. Women Mills Coll., Oakland, Calif., 1981-89, chaplain, 1985—, internat. student advisor, 1990—; coord. UN Decade Women Regional Meeting, 1985, Nat. Steering Com.,

Women Ministry Conf. Am. Bap. Ch., 1986-88, Com. Ministry Am. Bapt. Ch. West, 1987-89, adv. bd. Refugee Project, Am. Bapt. Ch. of West, 1985—. Editor: Journal of Women and Religion, 1976; contbr. articles to profl. jours. Bd. dirs. Lakeshore Ave Bapt. Ch., 1985-88; chmn. Women in Theology Task Force, 1979-80, Am. Bapt. Campus Found., 1975-76. Stephen Bufton scholar, 1987, Margaret Frost trust scholar, 1979, project renew grant, AAUW, 1987. Mem. Am. Acad. Religion, Nat. Assn. Coll. U. Chaplains, Nat. Campus Ministry Assn. Office: Mills Coll Office Chaplain 5000 MacArthur Blvd Oakland CA 94613 *In the midst of injustice we light candles, beat drums, ring bells, because we hope.*

MOODY, RANDALL DOUGLAS, minister; b. Phoenix, Mar. 26, 1962; s. Don Arthur and Lora Faye (Cozort) M.; m. Lara Lee Williams, Dec. 13, 1986; children: Caleb Andrew, Cailee Jordan. BA in Communications, Abilene Christian U., 1985, BS in Ministry, 1985, MA in Communications, 1987. Ordained to ministry Chs. of Christ, 1978. Min. of youth Ch. of Christ, Farmington, N.Mex., 1987-89; involvement min. Ch. of Christ, Pasadena, Tex., 1989—; chmn. bd. Four Corners Youth Encampement, Farmington, 1988-89, bd. dirs. 87-88; bd. dirs. Houston Summer Youth Series, Pasadena, 1989—, Leadership Tng. for Christ, Dallas; speaker youth seminars. Author: One Another: The Allelon Deluge, 1991; contbr. articles to jours. in field. Mem. Pi Kappa Delta. Home: 4810 Gardenia Trail Pasadena TX 77505 Office: Watters Rd Ch Christ 3616 Watters Rd Pasadena TX 77504 *Stop. Take a moment to hug your children. Show affection to your husband. Embrace your wife. Family love is still the essential ingredient for life.*

MOODY, ROBERT ARTHUR, pastor; b. Alexandria, La., Sept. 23, 1956; s. Melvin Manuel and Arlene Lois (Basch) M.; m. Shirley Jean Quick, June 14, 1980; children: Katie Ruth, Tabitha Ann, David Benjamin, Hannah Marie, Rebekah Ena, Sandy Kay. Ch. planter, pastor New Life Assemblies of God, Chesaning, Mich., 1982-85, Faith Fellowship Assemblies of God, Kincheloe, Mich., 1984-89, St. Ignace (Mich.) Assemblies of God, 1987-89, Joy Fellowship, Indian River, 1988—, New Beginnings Assemblies of God, Boyne City, 1989—, Open Door Assemblies of God, Lewiston, 1990—; dir. Light for the Lost Assemblies of God, Mich., 1982-84, Minute Men Assemblies of God, Mich., 1988—. Home: PO Box 339 Wolverine MI 49799 Office: Joy Fellowship Assemblies of God 8600 Straits Hwy Indian River MI 49749

MOODY, WILLIAM RALPH, lay worker; b. Columbus, Ga., Dec. 27, 1919; s. Bert Squares and Savannah Ostella (Dorough) M.; m. Ruth Addaleene Barker, Mar. 3, 1946; children: Margaret Ruth, William Ralph. BBA, Emory U., 1947. Dir. music Woodlawn Bapt. Ch., Decatur, Ga., 1956-62, Cresthill Bapt. Ch., Decatur, 1962-64, Clairmont Bapt. Ch., Atlanta, 1964-85; acct. Grady Meml. Hosp., Atlanta, 1969-84; treas. Hosp. Authority Employees Credit Union, Atlanta, 1976-84. Elder, vol. adults and children's music program 1st Presbyn. Ch., Johnson City, Tenn. Mem. Sons of Jubal. Home: 1602 Fairway Dr Johnson City TN 37601

MOOERS, MALCOLM MINTER, retired minister; b. Pleasantville, N.J., Apr. 9, 1924; s. Hadley Victor and Grace Madeline (Price) M.; m. Marjorie Tose, Sept. 13, 1947; children: Richard, Marilyn, John, Deborah. BS in Edn, Boston U., 1945; MDiv, Andover Newton Theol. Sch., 1948. Ordained to ministry United Ch. of Christ, 1948. Pastor Mt. Sinai (N.Y.) Congl. Ch., 1948-52, The Community Ch., Huntington, N.Y., 1952-59; pastor The Congl. Ch. of Huntington, 1959-89, ret., 1989; dep. chief chaplain Centerport (N.Y.) Fire Dept., 1960-90; moderator Suffolk Assn. N.Y. Conf., 1975-76, N.Y. Conf. United Ch. Christ, 1976-79; del. The Congl. Christian Ch, 1952-56, United Ch. Christ, 1985-87. Bd. dirs. Freedom Ctr., Huntington Station, N.Y., 1961-68, Planned Parenthood, Huntington, 1963-73, Sr. Citizens Housing Com., Huntington, 1981-89; mem. com. Martin L. King Jr. Remembrance, Huntington. Recipient plaques Town of Huntington, 1989, Centerpoint Fire Dept. 1990. Mem. Clergy Assn. Huntington (pres. 1980-85, scroll 1985, treas. 1985-90, citation 1989), Huntington Men's Chorus Club (pres. 1977-79), Kiwanis, Masons. Home: 135 Sims Creek Ln Jupiter FL 33458

MOON, JOHN SCAFA, religious organization executive, evangelist; b. Kennewick, Wash., June 8, 1960; s. Lantha Scafa and Terry (Lee) Moon; m. Shari Lynn Schoessler, Aug. 18, 1984; children: Jonathan Christopher, Stephanie Grace. BA in Econs., Wash. State U., 1984. Sales assoc. Kinney's Stores, Moscow, Idaho, 1984-85, Coldwell Banker Beasley Realty, Pullman, Wash., 1985-87; campus evangelist Maranatha Campus Ministries, Pullman, 1987-90; pres., evangelist Lord of All Ministries, Woodinville, Wash., 1990—; Apostolic cons. Vashon (Wash.) Christian Fellowship, 1990. Missionary evangelist Maranatha Campus Ministries, N.Z., 1989, Lord of All Ministries, Poland, 1990, Scotland, 1990. Mem. Ministerial Fellowship of U.S.A. Republican. Avocation: watersking. Office: Lord of All Ministries PO Box 3003 Woodinville WA 98072

MOON, ROBERT PRESTON, minister; b. Columbus, Ga., Jan. 15, 1958; s. Joseph Calvin and Helen (McElveen) M.; m. Vicky Jean Davis, Jan. 24, 1981; children: Mary Helen, Joseph, Michael. B in Gen. Studies, Samford U., 1983. Lic. to ministry Bapt. Ch., 1983, ordained, 1988. Min. music 1st Bapt. Columbiana (Ala.) Ch., 1982-83; min. youth and music Cedar Grove Bapt. Ch., Leeds, Ala., 1979-82, Helena (Ala.) Bapt. Ch., 1983-87; assoc. pastor West End Bapt. Ch., Clanton, Ala., 1987—; v.p. Chilton-Unity Pastor's Conf., Clanton, 1990-91. Editor Parent Line mag. Facilitator for foster high sch. students Dept. Human Resources, Clanton, 1991; advisor Future Homemakers of Am. Chilton County High Sch., Clanton, 1991. Named Outstanding Young Religious Leader, Clanton Jaycees, 1991. Mem. Chilton-Unity Bapt Assn. (exec. com. 1989-91), Network Youth Mins. Home: 205 Hoyt Brownie Rd Clanton AL 35045 Office: West End Bapt Ch 2005 2d Ave N Clanton AL 35045

MOONEY, MARY MARGARET, nurse, educator; b. Halstad, Minn., Mar. 10, 1939; d. John Leo and Mary Frances (O'Gorman) M. BS, St. Scholastica Coll., Duluth, Minn., 1964; MS, Case Western Res. U., 1972; DNSc, Catholic U., 1980. RN, N.D. Tchr. St. Anthony's Sch., Fargo, N.D., 1957-60; nursing supr. St. Ansgar's Hosp., Park River, N.D., 1964-68; adminstr. City Hosp., New Rockford, N.D., 1968-70; sch. nurse Case Western Res. U., Cleve., 1970-72; prof. nursing Univ. of Mary, Bismarck, N.D., 1972-74, 79-83, 89—; mem. coun. Presentation Sisters, Fargo, 1974-77, 80-89, pres., 1983-89; clin. nurse Providence Hosp., Washington, 1977-79. Author: Centennial History, 1982, Reminiscence on Path Taken, 1990; contbr. articles, columns to profl. publs., chpt. to book. Bd. dirs. Shanley High Sch., Fargo, 1983-89, Cath. Health Corp., Omaha, 1979-83, Cath. Family Svc., Fargo, 1983—, Villa Maria, Fargo, 1988-89, Leadership Conf. of Women's Religious, 1987-89. Named Woman of Yr., Fargo YMCA, 1988. Mem. NLN, N.D. State Nurses Assn. (v.p. 1981-83, writing award 1983. Democrat. Roman Catholic. Office: Univ of Mary 7500 University Dr Bismarck ND 58504

MOOR, JAMES TALLEY, minister; b. Atlanta, Feb. 3, 1948; s. W. Talley and Mina M. (Underwood) M.; m. Julie Marie Nohlgren, May. 29, 1972; children: Allyson M., Joshua T. BA, Emory U., 1970, MDiv, 1977; MA, U. N.C., 1973. Ordained to ministry United Meth. Ch. as deacon, 1975, as elder, 1978. Youth min. Commerce (Ga.) United Meth. Ch., 1973-77; assoc. pastor Gainesville (Ga.) 1st United Meth. Ch., 1977-79; pastor Trinity-Bethel United Meth. Ch., Clermont, Ga., 1979-83, Blairsville (Ga.) United Meth. Ch., 1983-85; staff assoc. North Ga. Conf. Coun. Ministries, Dahlonega, Ga., 1985-91; pastor North Decatur (Ga.) United Meth. Ch., 1991—; supervising pastor Gainesville dist. United Meth. Ch., 1984-89.. Sec. Gainesville Dist. Commn. on Ordained Ministry, 1982-90; bd. dirs. Ga. Tech Wesley Found., Atlanta, 1986—, North Ga. Coll. Wesley Found., Dahlonega, 1985—. Home: 650 N Superior Ave Decatur GA 30033 Office: 1523 Church St Decatur GA 30030

MOORE, SISTER ANNE, school system administrator. Supt. secondary schs. Diocese of Fall River, Mass. Office: Diocesan Dept Edn Supt Secondary Schs 423 Highland Ave Fall River MA 02720*

MOORE, BENITA ANN, religious studies and English educator; b. Mt. Etna, Iowa, Mar. 25, 1931; d. John Linus and Teresa Ellen (Keefe) M. AA, Ottumwa Heights Coll., Ottumwa, Iowa, 1950; BA, Marycrest Coll., Davenport, Iowa, 1952; MA, U. Iowa, 1959, PhD, 1976. Tchr. music, English Williams (Iowa) Ind. Pub. Sch., 1952-54, Ottumwa Heights Coll. and Acad., 1954-58, St. Mary's-Lenihan High Sch., Marshalltown, Iowa, 1958-66, St. Austin's Sch., Mpls., 1966-67; instr. music and English Marycrest Coll., Davenport, Iowa, 1967-69, asst. prof., 1974-77, assoc. prof., 1977-86, prof. religious studies and English, 1986—. Author: Escape Into a Labyrinth: F. Scott Fitzgerald, 1988. Precinct chairperson, conv. del. Dem. Party, Scott County, Iowa, 1972-88. NEH summer fellow, U. N.C., 1979, U. N.Mex., 1984, U. Ariz., 1988, Univ. House fellow Mellon U. Mem. Am. Acad. Religion, Modern Lang. Assn. Roman Catholic. Office: Teikyo Marycrest U 1607 W 12th St Davenport IA 52804

MOORE, C. THOMAS, clergyman; b. Cin., Sept. 16, 1930; s. Clark Ralph and Mary Ellen (Bidwill) M. MA in Philosophy, Aquinas Inst., 1954; S.T.L., S.T.Lr., U. de Fribourg (Switzerland), 1958, S.T.D., 1961; S.S.L., Pontifical Bibl. Commn., 1966. Agrégé de l'Ecole Biblique, Jerusalem; joined Order of Friars Preachers, Roman Cath. Ch. Prof. New Testament Aquinas Inst., Dubuque, Iowa, 1966-76; pastor St. Pius V Ch., Chgo., 1976-80; Newman chaplain U. Ariz., Tucson, 1980-85; assoc. pastor St. Pius X Ch., Tucson, 1985-88; dir.-pastor Aquinas Newman Ctr., U. N.Mex., Albuquerque, 1988—; pres. Peace Info. Com., Dubuque, 1970-76; mem. priests senate Archdiocese of Dubuque, 1970-76. Bood rev. editor Cross & Crown, 1966-76. Bd. dirs. Pilson Neighbors Community Coun., Chgo., 1977-80; mem. quality of life com. St. Joseph-St. Mary's Hosps., 1985-88; mem. Iowa Dem. Caucus, Dubuque, 1975. Mem. Soc. Bibl. Lit., Cath. Bibl. Assn. Am. Home and office: 1815 Las Lomas NE Albuquerque NM 87106

MOORE, CLARK, ecumenical agency administrator. Exec. dir. United Bd. of Missions, Port Arthur, Tex. Office: United Bd Missions 1701 Bluebonnet Ave PO Box 3867 Port Arthur TX 77643*

MOORE, DANIEL THOMAS, clergyman; b. Rochester, N.Y., Feb. 8, 1953; s. Harry Winthrop Jr. and Kathleen Patricia (Smith) M.; m. Diana Lynn Moore, June 4, 1977; children: Christopher Matthew, Jason David. BS in Engring., Cornell U., 1975; MDiv, Boston U., 1979; MS in TV, Radio and Film, Syracuse U., 1990. Ordained elder in United Meth. Ch. Computer programmer Cornell Campus Store, Ithaca, N.Y., 1972-74; TV engr. Cornell. Coll. Engring., Ithaca, 1974-75; nigh-time dir. Cable Channel 2 Ceracci Cable, Ithaca, 1975; pastor Port Byron United Methodist Ch., Port Byron, N.Y., 1979-82, Dundee & Starkey United Meth. Ch., Dundee, N.Y., 1982-85; writer United Meth. Communications, Nashville, 1984-88; dir. N.Y. West Area Radio Ministry, Syracuse, 1985—; editorial supr. United Meth. Communications, Nashville, 1986-88; dir. communications N. Cen. N.Y. Annual Conf. of United Meth. Ch., Syracuse, 1987-88; with GN TV Ministry, Macon, Ga.; pres., founder Pilgrimage Prodns., Inc., N. Syracuse, N.Y., 1984—; dir. radio news Gen. Conf.-United Meth. Ch., St. Louis, 1988; radio news correspondent World Meth. Conf. for Ecumedia News, Nairobi, Kenya, 1986; short term missionary United Meth. Com. on Relief, Burundi, 1987. Author: Faith Break, a radio script service for United Methodist Ch., 1991. Mem. Port Byron Coun. Chs., 1979, Dundee Meals on Wheels, 1984; pres. Dundee Coun. Chs., 1984; chmn. Boy Scout Troop Com., Port Byron, 1981. Oxnam-Leibman fellow Boston U. Sch. Theology, 1979; recipient 2d Place award Christopher's Nat. Video Contest for Coll. Students, 1989. Mem. United Meth. Assn. Communicators, Eta Kappa Nu. Avocations: guitar playing, composing, singing, camping, computer programming, carpentry. Home: 1361 Greentree Pkwy Macon GA 31210 Office: GN TV Ministry 2525 Beech Ave Macon GA 31204

MOORE, DEBORAH DASH, religion educator; b. N.Y.C., Aug. 6, 1946; d. Martin and Irene (Golden) Dash; m. MacDonald Smith Moore, June 15, 1967; children: Mordecai, Mikhael. BA, Brandeis U., 1967; MA, Columbia U., 1968, PhD, 1975. Asst. prof. Vassar Coll., Poughkeepsie, N.Y., 1976-84, assoc. prof., 1984-88, profl., 1988—. Author: At Home in America, 1981, B'Nai Brith and the Challenge of Ethnic Leadership, 1981; editor Yivo Annual, 1990, 91. NEH fellow, 1979, 89, Meml. Found. fellow, 1983, Fulbright Found. fellow, 1984; Littauer Found. grantee, 1990. Mem. Nat. Found. for Jewish Culture (acad. adv. panel), Immigration History Soc. (bd. dirs. 1983-86), Assn. for Jewish Studies (bd. dirs. 1981-85), Am. Jewish Hist. Soc. (acad. coun. 1977—). Democrat. Home: 620 Fort Washington Ave New York NY 10040 Office: Vassar Coll Dept Religion Poughkeepsie NY 12601

MOORE, DONALD BRUCE, minister; b. Tyler, Tex., Apr. 14, 1941; s. Bruce H. and Evelyn F. (Brown) M.; m. Janice Monk, Aug. 13, 1966; children: Melanie, Matthew, Jonathan. BA in Chemistry, Baylor U., 1963; MDiv, Southwestern Bapt. Theol. Sem., Ft. Worth, 1967, D Ministry, 1977. Ordained to ministry So. Bapt. Conv., 1966. Pastor Elwood (Tex.) Bapt. Ch., 1965-66, 1st Bapt. Ch., Hanover, Pa., 1967-71; dir. child evangelism Birchman Ave. Bapt. Ch., Phila., 1971-74; asst. pastor Birchman Ave. Bapt. Ch., Ft. Worth, 1975-77; pastor Monroeville (Pa.) Bapt. Ch., 1978—; asst. dir. Basic Youth Conflicts, Pitts., 1983-85; mem. Pa.-South Jersey Exec. Bd., Harrisburg, Pa., 1983-86; moderator Pitts. Bapt. Assn., 1985. Mem. Kiwanis. Home: 403 Gingerbread Ln Waxahachie TX 75165 Office: Monroeville Bapt Ch 2456 Tillbrook Rd Monroeville PA 15146

MOORE, DONALD L., pastor; b. Galenn, Kans., Apr. 20, 1933; s. John W. and Edith (King) M.; married, July 9, 1961; children: Ronald, Dawn, Marion. Student, Pitts Teaching Coll. Pastor Greater Home Ch., Chgo., 1967-79, Greater Mt. Hermon Bapt. Ch., Benton Harbor, Mich., 1982—. Home: 153 Parkwood Ln South Bend IN 46619 Office: Mt Harmon Bapt Ch PO Box 9074 Benton Harbor MI 49023

MOORE, E. HARRIS, bishop. Bishop Western Mo. Ch. of God in Christ, Kansas City. Office: Ch of God in Christ 405 E 64th Terr Kansas City MO 64131*

MOORE, EMERSON JOHN, bishop; b. N.Y.C., May 16, 1938. Student, Cathedral Coll., N.Y.C., St. Joseph's Sem., N.Y., NYU, Columbia U. Sch. Social Work. Ordained priest Roman Cath. Ch. 1964. Ordained aux. bishop of Curubi and aux. bishop Diocese of N.Y., N.Y.C., 1982—. Office: Chancery Office 1011 1st Ave New York NY 10022

MOORE, FRANK TIMOTHY, minister; b. Georgetown, S.C., Oct. 20, 1951; s. Frank Spivey and Harriett Virginia (Avant) M.; m. Peggy Elaine McGrew, Apr. 19, 1975; children: Wesley, Kyla, Samuel, Lauren. BSBA, Pembroke State U., 1973; MDiv, New Orleans Bapt. Theol. Sem., 1983. Ordained to ministry Bapt. Ch., 1984. Pastor Porter Swamp Bapt. Ch., Cerro Gorde, N.C., 1983—. Mgr. Dixie Youth Baseball, Cerro Gorde, 1986—. Mem. Columbus Bapt. Assn. (chmn. ordination com. 1990-91, pres. pastor's conf. 1986-87, v.p. pastor's conf. 1985-86). Republican. Home: PO Box 98 Hwy 76 Cerro Gordo NC 28430

MOORE, GEORGE EAGLETON, history educator; b. Osaka, Japan, Mar. 25, 1927; s. Lardner Wilson and Grace (Eagleton) M.; m. Velora Ruth Hieb, Aug. 22, 1953; children: Robert Wallace, Martha Ann, James Kennon. BA, U. Calif., Berkeley, 1951, MA, 1959; PhD, U. Calif., 1966. Tchr. Salinas (Calif.) Elem. Sch. Dist., 1954-56, Piedmont (Calif.) Unified Sch. Dist., 1956-62; prof. dept. history San Jose (Calif.) State U., 1964—, chair dept., 1986-90, chair dept. humanities, 1991—, chair acad. senate, 1973-74, 86-87. 1st lt. M.I. Corps, U.S. Army, 1945-48, col. USAR, 1948-76. Mem. Assn. for Asian Studies, Asian Studies on the Pacific Coast., Piedmont Tchrs. Assn. (pres. 1960-61), Sigma Nu. Democrat. Presbyterian. Avocations: hiking, gardening. Home: 35 Rincon Rd Kensington CA 94707 Office: San Jose State U 1 Washington Sq San Jose CA 95192

MOORE, HELEN MILLER, religious educator; b. Chattanooga, Oct. 3, 1942; d. Frank Lubbock and Jane Anne (Saunders) Miller III; m. Fredrick Sebert Brewer Jr., Dec. 28, 1962 (div. 1973); children: Hadley, Courtney, Kendall, Frederick; m. Tom Moore III, Nov. 3, 1973; 1 child, Grayson. BA in Social Wk., Regis Coll., Weston, Mass., 1982; MEd in Counseling Psych., Harvard U., 1984; MDiv, Harvard Div. Sch., 1987; PhD in Pastoral Psychology, Boston U., 1987—. Dir. Edn. for Ministry Trinity Ch., Boston, 1990—; pastoral psychotherapist Boston, 1987—. Fellow Coll. of Chaplains; mem. Am. Assn. Pastoral Counselors, Mass. Psychoanalytic Soc., N.E. Soc. Group Psychotherapists, Assn. for Clin. Pastoral Edn., Harvard Club. Home: 95 Suffolk Rd Chestnut Hill MA 02167 Office: Trinity Ch in Boston Copley Sq Boston MA 02116

MOORE, JACK LYNNE, clergyman; b. DeKalb, Miss., July 9, 1920; s. Lynne McNary and Lilla Troy (Bishop) M.; m. June 21, 1941 (dec. Apr. 1989); children: Peggy Ann, Michael L., Judy B., William S., James L., Suzi M. BS, Miss. State Coll., 1941; MA, U. So. Miss., 1950; MDiv, Austin Presbyn. Theol. Sem., 1960. Ordained to ministry Presbyn. Ch., 1960. Pastor Alpine Presbyn. Ch., Longview, Tex., 1960-62; evangelist Presbytery NE Tex., Dallas, 1962-66; assoc. pastor 1st Presbyn. Ch., Dallas, 1966-73, 74-76, sr. pastor, head staff, 1973-74, founder, dir. stewpot ministry, 1974-76; pastor Community Presbyn. Ch., Port Aransas, Tex., 1976-86; interim pastor, head staff San Pedro Presbyn. Ch., San Antonio, 1987-89; interim pastor West Isle Presbyn. Ch., Galveston, Tex., 1989-90; interim pastor, head staff Hope Presbyn. Ch., Austin, Tex., 1990—; moderator Presbytery NE Tex., 1964-65; chaplain Dallas County Jail, 1968-76; creator, dir. Joint Effort Leisure Ministry, Port Aransas, 1978-86; dean Synod Sch., Trinity U., San Antonio, 1973-76. Author: From a Listening Heart, 1975, Christmas Presence, 1987; writer feature page In A Mirror Dimly, 1972-86; newspaper columnist Scattershooting, 1977-89. 1st lt. USMCR, 1942-46, PTO. Mem. Christian Writers Assn., Wilson Ctr. (assoc.), Smithsonian Assocs., Sierra Club. Democrat. Avocations: white water rafting, tennis. Office: Hope Presbyn Ch 11512 Olson Dr Austin TX 78750

MOORE, JAMES ALFRED, minister; b. Union, S.C., Oct. 19, 1957; s. James Alfred and Joyce (Tankersley) M.; m. Karen Elizabeth Holcombe, Feb. 11, 1979; children: Stephanie Leigh, Amie Marie. BA, Gardner-Webb Coll., Boiling Springs, N.C., 1979; MDiv, New Orelans Sem., 1982; DMin, Columbia Sem., Decatur, Ga., 1987. Ordained to ministry, So. Bapt. Conv. Pastor Bethel Bapt. Ch., Fairfax, S.C., 1982-84, Pine Forest Bapt., Langley, S.C., 1984-88, First Bapt. Ch., Enoree, S.C., 1988—; vol. chaplain St. Joseph Hosp. Augusta, Ga., 1986; CPE, Univ. Hosp., Augusta, 1987-88; exec. com. Bapt. Committeed of S.C., 1989—; nominating com. S.C. Bapt. Conv., 1990—. Editor S.C. Moderate Bapt. Newsletter, 1990—. Mem. com. Allendale Alcohol and Drug Commn., 1983-84, Sex edn. Study Com., Spartanburg Dist. 4 Schs., 1990—. Democrat. Home: PO Box 288 Enoree SC 29335 Office: First Bapt Ch PO Box 216 Enoree SC 29335

MOORE, JAMES FRASER, theology educator; b. Kansas City, Mo., Aug. 10, 1946; s. Ben Hawkins and Alice Winifred (Bassett) M.; m. Elaine Marie Osborn, June 8, 1968; children: Dana Beth, Michael James. BA, Park Coll., Kansas City, Mo., 1968; MDiv, Luther Theol. Sem., 1972; PhD, U. Chgo, 1982. Cer. Ordained to Ministry Luth. Ch., 1972. Pastor Rock Creek Luth. Ch., Rock Falls, Wis., 1972-77, Bethany Luth. Ch., Chgo., 1977-80; instr. theology Valparaiso (Ind.) U., 1980-82, asst. prof., 1982—, assoc. prof., 1989—; coord. edn. North Wis. Dist.-ALC, Wausau, 1973-77; dir. study program Valparaiso U., Cambridge, Eng. 1987-89. Author: Sexuality and Marriage, 1987; contbr. articles to profl jours. Fellow Am. Luth. Ch. U. Chgo., 1977-80, rsch. fellow Valparaiso U., 1985. Mem. Am. Acad. Religion (coord. conv. 1980—), Soc. Bibl. Lit., Cambridge U. Theol. Soc. Democrat. Avocation: performing and composing music. Home: 253 S Mich Ave Valparaiso IN 46383 Office: Valparaiso U Dept Theology Valparaiso IN 46383

MOORE, JAMES RUSSELL, minister; b. Traverse City, Mich., Nov. 19, 1962; s. Allen and Doris Ann (Lather) M.; m. Kimberly Joy McCann, June 7, 1986. BA, Ind. Wesleyan U., Marion, 1985, MA, 1986. Ordained to ministry Wesleyan Ch., 1991. Asst. pastor Oak Park (Ill.) Wesleyan Ch., 1986-87, Moeller Rd. Wesleyan Ch., Ft. Wayne, Ind., 1987—; sec. treas. Three Rivers Sun. Sch. Assn., Ft. Wayne, 1990—; sec. Ind. N. Wesleyan Men, Marion, 1989-91. Mem. Wesleyan Theol. Soc., Profl. Assn. Christian Educators. Home: 4822 Hessen Cassel Rd Fort Wayne IN 46806 Office: Moeller Rd Wesleyan Ch 7722 Moeller Rd Fort Wayne IN 46806 *Service with the strength God provides is the key to Christian leadership. God desires we follow the humble example of His son Jesus.*

MOORE, JERRY LEE, minister; b. St. Louis, May 5, 1945; s. Stella Mae Barr; m. Linda Louise Rhymer, Aug. 27, 1966; children: Jason Scott, Sarah Lynn. BA in Psychology, Semo State U., 1972. Part time asst. pastor Assembly of God, Cahokia, Ill., 1972-73; part time asst. pastor, youth pastor Assembly of God, Poplar Bluff, Mo., 1973-78; asst. pastor, youth pastor Assembly of God, Poplar Bluff, 1978-80; asst. pastor Assembly of God, Mesa, Ariz., 1980-81; pastor New Covenant Fellowship, Poplar Bluff, 1981—; self employed contractor Scottcity, Mo., 1973-78. Del. Republican Party, St. Louis, 1988. With USAF, 1966-70. Home: 1932 Meadows Rd Poplar Bluff MO 63901 Office: New Covenant Fellowship 3191 Oak Grove Rd Poplar Bluff MO 63901 *If we are to be all we can be, then let us remove the blinders from our eyes, the limitations from our thoughts and eliminate the impossibilities by believing "we can do all things through Christ who is our strength!".*

MOORE, JOHN STERLING, JR., minister; b. Memphis, Aug. 25, 1918; s. John Sterling and Lorena (Bounds) M.; m. Martha Louise Paulette, July 6, 1944; children: Sterling Hale, John Marshall, Carolyn Paulette. Student, Auburn U., 1936-37; AB, Samford U., 1940; ThM, So. Bapt. Theol. Sem., 1944. Ordained to ministry So. Bapt. Conv., 1942. Pastor chs. Pamplin, Va., 1944-48, Amherst, Va., 1949-57; pastor Manly Meml. Bapt. Ch., Lexington, Va., 1957-84, pastor emeritus, 1984—; mem. Hist. Commn., So. Bapt. Conv., 1968-75; pres. Va. Bapt. Pastor's Conf., 1963. Author: History of Broad Run Baptist Church, 1762-1987, 1987; co-author: Meaningful Moments in Virginia Baptist Life, 1715-1972, 1973; editor Va. Bapt. Register, 1972—; contbr. articles to profl. jours. Chmn. Lexington Mayor's Com. on Race Rels., 1962-65; bd. dirs. Stonewall Jackson Hosp., 1967-72, pres., 1969-71; treas. Rockbridge Mental Health Clinic, 1971-84. Recipient Disting. Svc. award Hist. Commn., So. Bapt. Conv., 1988. Mem. Am. Soc. Ch. History, So. Bapt. Hist. Soc. (bd. dirs. 1972-91, pres. 1975-76, sec. 1977-85), Va. Bapt. Hist. Soc. (exec. com. 1963—, pres. 1984-85), Va. Hist. Soc., Masons. Home: 8709 Gayton Rd Richmond VA 23229

MOORE, JOSEPH KENDALL, minister; b. Spartanburg, S.C., Nov. 4, 1957; s. Hezzie Harvey Jr. and Nancy (Seay) M.; m. Shelby Jean Sullivan, Mar. 26, 1976; 1 child, Dana Nicole. AS, North Greenville Coll., 1991. Youth and children pastor Peace Free Will Bapt. Ch., Spartanburg, 1980-86; youth pastor Enoree (S.C.) 1st Bapt. Ch., 1986-88; pastor West End Bapt. Ch., Woodruff, S.C., 1988—; chaplain Lower Piedmont Rescue, Woodruff, 1988—. Mem., past capt. Enoree Fire and Rescue, 1974-88. Recipient Svc. to Youth award. Peace Free Will Bapt. Youth, Spartanburg, 1987, Vol. Citizen award Inman Mills, Enoree, 1986. Mem. Internat. Brotherhood Magicians. Home: 115 Bridwell Rd Woodruff SC 29388-9300 Office: W End Bapt Ch PO Box 205 Woodruff SC 29388

MOORE, KEITH ALBERT, lay minister; b. Corinth, Miss., Aug. 12, 1947; s. Joseph Otis and Doris Marie (Gurley) M.; m. Jan Avi Ballard, Sept. 18, 1971 (div. Sept. 1979); children: Danielle Nicole Phebus, Courtney Jo-Ella Phebus; m. Jeanette Litchfield, Feb. 5, 1988; stepchildren: James Andrew Madison, Arthur Hayden Litchfield, Angel Marie Litchfield. Diploma, Apostolic Missionary Inst., 1968. Pastoral intern Calvary United Pentecostal Ch., Ottawa, Ont., Can., 1968-69; evangelist United Pentecostal Ch., 1969-71; pastor 1st United Pentecostal Ch., London, Ont., Can., 1972-75; lay min. 1st United Pentecostal Ch., 1975-88; lay min. children's ministries East Nashville United Pentecostal Ch., 1989—. Office: East Nashville United Pentecostal Ch 3514 Broadway Dr Nashville TN 37207-1776

MOORE, KENNETH WAYNE, minister; b. Montpelier, Miss., Dec. 31, 1950; s. E.W. and Allene (Holliday) M.; m. Janice Marie Martin, July 19, 1969; children: Kellie Renee, Joseph Wayne, Christopher Levi. AA, Clarke Coll., Newton, Miss., 1972; BS, Miss. Coll., Clinton, Miss., 1974; MDiv, New Orleans Bapt. Theol. Sem., 1988, DMin, 1990. Ordained to ministry, So. Bapt. Conv., 1970. Interim pastor Woodland Bapt. Ch., 1970; pastor Wahalak Bapt. Ch., Kemper County, Miss., 1971; interim pastor West End Bapt. Ch., West Point, Miss., 1972; Interim pastor Freeny Bapt. Ch., Carthage, Miss., 1972; pastor Corinth Bapt. Ch., Carthage, Miss., 1973-76, Sallis (Miss.) Bapt. Ch., 1976-83, Enon Bapt. Ch., Jayess, Miss., 1983-91, 1st Bapt. Ch., Walnut Ridge, Ark., 1991—; moderator Walthall Bapt. Assn., Tylertown, Miss., 1991, dir. evangelism, 1984-90, pres. pastor's conf., 1984-

86. Author: Family Ministry, 1990. Pres. Tylertown Band Boosters, 1989—; mem. Children's Rev. Bd., Walthall County Welfare Dept., 1988-91. Home: 204 Montgomery Walnut Ridge AR 72476 Office: 1st Bapt Ch PO Box 547 Walnut Ridge AR 72476 *Someone once said, "As the home goes so goes the nation." I would like to add, "As the home goes, so goes the nation and the church." Home is the training ground for life, and parents need to be careful how they prepare the troops.*

MOORE, LANCE WAYNE, minister; b. Pensacola, Fla., June 1, 1957; s. Robert Alfred and Vivian May (Jensen) M.; m. Diana May Teem, June 9, 1984; 1 child, Melissa. BA in English with honors, Auburn U., 1985; MDiv cum laude, Emory U., Atlanta, 1987. Ordained to ministry Meth. Ch. as elder. Pastor Cokesbury United Meth. Ch., Pensacola, Fla., 1988-91, Loxley (Ala.) United Meth. Ch., 1991—. Named one of Outstanding Young Men Am., 1985. Avocations: writing, music, water sports. Address: PO Box 56 Loxley AL 36651

MOORE, LANE REYNOLDS, minister; b. Shreveport, La., Mar. 26, 1958; s. Robert Lane and Melba (Reynolds) M.; m. Rebecca Lynn Wood, Aug. 11, 1984; children; Tyler Lane, Ashlen Rebecca. BS, NE La. U., 1980. Dir. TV ministry Willow Point Bapt. Ch., Shreveport, 1982-85; min. evangelism Summer Grove Bapt. Ch., Shreveport, 1988—, min. coll. students, 1989—. Mem. Coll. Met. Ministers Assn. Republican. Home: 8044 Cardigan Way Shreveport LA 71129 Office: Summer Grove Bapt Ch 9215 Mansfield Rd Shreveport LA 77118

MOORE, M. JOANNE, parochial school educational administrator; b. Phila., July 31, 1945; d. William Carl and Mary Josephine (Fuss) Mostertz; m. Earle M. Moore, Jr., June 15, 1974; children: Jennifer Lynne, Jessica Lee. Student, U. Heidelberg, Fed. Republic Germany, 1965-66; BA, Westminster Coll., Pa., 1967; MS in Edn., U. Pa., 1985. Cert. tchr., Pa. Adminstr. St. Barnabas Episcopal Ch., Phila., 1974-78, prin., 1978-91; del. to Diocesan Conv., Phila., 1974—; mem. coun. Episcopal Diocese of Pa., Phila., 1976-82, mem. strategy com., 1976-82, chmn. conv. planning com., 1984-87, mem. standing com., 1987—. Bd. dirs. Germantown YMCA, Phila., 1984-86. Mem. Nat. Assn. Episcopal Schs. (nat. governing bd. 1987-91), Pa. Assn. Pvt. Acad. Schs. (bd. dirs. 1978-81), Coun. for Religion in Ind. Schs., Elem. Sch. Heads Assn. (bd. dirs. 1986-90, nat. pres. 1988-89). Home: 627 Glen Echo Rd Philadelphia PA 19119 Office: St Barnabas Episcopal Sch 5421 Germantown Ave Philadelphia PA 19144

MOORE, SISTER MARIE, nun, hospital executive; b. Nashville, Feb. 21, 1933; d. Edgar James and Rose Elizabeth (Edwards) M. Grad., Mercy Sch. Nursing, 1957; B.S.N., Edgecliff Coll., 1957; M.S.N., Boston Coll., 1963; postgrad., U. Ala., 1972-73, Yale U., 1990-91. Joined Sisters of Mercy, Roman Catholic Ch., 1951; supr. St. Mary's Meml. Hosp., Knoxville, Tenn., 1957-61; instr. St. Mary's Meml. Hosp. Sch. Nursing, 1963-65; dir. St. Mary's Meml. Hosp. (Sch. Nursing), 1965-67; asst. adminstr. nursing St. Rita's Hosp., Lima, Ohio, 1967-71; pres. St. Mary's Med. Center, Knoxville, 1971-83; regional councilor Sisters of Mercy, Cin., 1983-90; pres., chief exec. officer Mercy Hosp. and Med. Ctr., Chgo., 1991—; dir. 1st Tenn. Bank, 1981-86; Mem. Tenn. Bd. Nursing, 1976-82; mem. Knox County Health Planning Council; sec.-treas. Coordinated Hosp. Services, 1973-83; pres. Knox Area Hosp. Council, 1976. Bd. dirs. Greater Knoxville Area C. of C., 1980-82. Recipient Brotherhood award NCCJ, 1979, Samaritan award, 1983. Mem. Tenn. Hosp. Assn. (past dir.), Ohio Nurses Assn. (past dir.); fellow Am. Coll. Hosp. Adminstrs. Democrat. Office: Mercy Hosp and Med Ctr Stevenson Expwy at King Dr Chicago IL 60616

MOORE, PAUL, JR., bishop; b. Morristown, N.J., Nov. 15, 1919; s. Paul and Fanny Weber (Hanna) M.; m. Jenny McKean, Nov. 26, 1944 (dec.); children: Honor, Paul III, Adelia, Rosemary, George Mead, Marian Shaw, Daniel Sargent, Susanna McKean, Patience; m. Brenda Hughes Eagle, May 16, 1975. Grad., St. Paul's Sch., Concord, N.H., 1937; B.A., Yale U., 1941; S.T.B., Gen. Theol. Sem., N.Y.C., 1949, S.T.D. (hon.), 1960; D.D. (hon.), Va. Theol. Sem., 1964, Berkeley Divinity Sch., 1971; PhD (hon.), City Coll. N.Y. Ordained to ministry Protestant Episcopal Ch., 1949; mem. team ministry Grace Ch., Jersey City, 1949-57; dean Christ Ch. Cathedral, Indpls., 1957-64; suffragan bishop Washington, 1964-70; bishop coadjutor Diocese, N.Y., 1970-72; bishop Diocese, 1972-89; lectr. St. Augustine's Coll., Canterbury, Eng., 1960; chmn. commn. Delta ministry Nat. Coun. Chs., 1964-67; mem. urban div., nat. exec. coun. Episcopal Ch., 1952-68; dep. to Gen. Conv., 1961, Anglican Congress, 1963; chmn. com. 100; legal def. fund NAACP; chmn. East Timor Project. Author: The Church Reclaims the City, 2d edit, 1970, Take A Bishop Like Me, 1979. Former trustee Bard Coll.; trustee Gen. Theol. Sem., Trinity Sch., Berkeley Div. Sch. at Yale U., N.Y.C.; mem. Fund for Free Expression; mem. advt. coun. Gov.'s Com. on AIDS, 1983-87. Served to capt. USMCR, 1941-45, PTO. Decorated Navy Cross, Silver Star, Purple Heart.; recipient Margaret Sanger award Planned Parenthood, 1984, Frederick Douglas award North Star Fund, 1989, Freedom of Worship medal Franklin and Eleanor Roosevelt Inst., 1991; Yale Corp. sr. fellow, 1987-90. Club: Century (N.Y.C.). Home and Office: 55 Bank St New York NY 10014

MOORE, RALPH O., minister; b. Fulton, Ky., June 18, 1941; m. Nancy Lee Dame, May 14, 1961; children: Yvonne Michelle Gray, Brent Moore, Melissa Lee Moore. Cert., Sunset Sch. Preaching, 1971; BA, Lubbock Christian Coll., 1979; MEd, Tex. Tech. U., 1981; postgrad., Austin Presbyn. Theol. Sem., 1991—. Ordained to ministry Ch. of Christ. Min. Ch. of Christ, Meadow, Tex., 1974-75, Kailua, Hawaii, 1975-78, Lorenzo, Tex., 1978-83, Ozona, Tex., 1985—; pulpit min. Sherwood Ch. of Christ, Odessa, Tex., 1983-85; instr., dean Honolulu Sch. Biblical Studies, 1977-78. Contbr. articles to local newspaper. Active Hospice, Odessa, 1984-85. With USN, 1959-68. Mem. Lions Club. Republican. Home and Office: Church of Christ PO Box 982 Ozona TX 76943

MOORE, RANDALL KEITH, minister; b. Burlington, N.C., Mar. 21, 1958; s. Billy Ray and Gwendolyn (Bryant) M.; m. Pamela Blalock; children: Jessica, Brittany, Caroline. BA in Pub. Speaking, Tenn. Temple U., 1981; ThM, Dallas Theol. Sem., 1985; postgrad., Fuller Theol. Sem., 1990—. Ordained to ministry Bapt. Ch., 1987. Pastoral intern Cedar Heights Bapt. Ch., Cedar Falls, Iowa, 1983; assoc. pastor Bapt. Temple, Burlington, 1985—; counselor Camp Joy for Youth, Chattanooga, 1977; chaplain Alamance Christian Sch., Graham, N.C., 1975-76; singer, counselor Life Action Singers, Buchanan, Mich., 1978; interim pastor Faith Community Ch., South Boston, Va., summer 1987. Author: What Jesus Said, 1992; contbr. articles to religious jours.; host inspirational talk show Sta. WHPE. Leader, singer Tenn. Temple U. Quartet, Chattanooga, 1977. Named to Ky. Cols., 1990. Mem. Evang. Theol. Soc., Internat. Platform Assn. Home and Office: 1500 Otway St Burlington NC 27215

MOORE, ROBERT GEORGE, minister; b. Plainview, Tex., Sept. 26, 1949; s. Abb Thomas and Mary Jeanne (Miller) M.; m. Kathryn A. Wattenburger, Aug. 13, 1974. BBA, Tex. Tech. U., 1973; MDiv, Midwestern Bapt. Theol. Sem., Kansas City, Mo., 1976; MA, Rice U., 1982, PhD in Religious Studies, 1991—. Ordained to ministry Bapt. Ch., 1977. Music and edn. minister Englewood Bapt. Ch., Kansas City, Mo., 1974-77; minister to students South Main Bapt. Ch., Houston, Tex., 1977-80; pastoral staff Second Bapt. Ch., Lubbock, Tex., 1985-89; chaplain resident Hermann Hosp., Houston, 1990-91, St. Luke's Episcopal Hosp., Tex. Med. Ctr., Houston, 1991—. Minister leader United Way, Lubbock, Tex., 1988. Recipient travel and study grant Rice U., Houston, 1981-82. Mem. Soc. Bibl. Lit. Home: 2476 Bolsover # 268 Houston TX 77005 Office: St Lukes Episcopal Hosp PO Box 20269 Houston TX 77225

MOORE, ROBERT HENRY, retired minister, counselor; b. Hector, N.Y., 1906; m. Pauline E. Moore. Student, Meekers Bus. Coll., Elmira, N.Y., 1925-29; BA, Nat. Coll. Law, Washington, 1933; BD, Delancey Div. Sem., N.Y., 1933. Cert. in family counseling and religious psychology. Min. Protestant Episcopal Ch., 1931-49, United Meth. Ch., 1950-68; pvt. practice counseling and supply work, 1968-86, ret., 1991. Author: The Holy Hobo, 1990; (study courses) Theology for Layman, Learning to Affirm the Power of God. Home and Office: Colonial Hills # 3 5849 Thrush Dr New Port Richey FL 34652 *A wise man seeks Godly wisdom before wealth, holy happiness before health and praises God and fellow humans before praying for self.*

MOORE, ROBERT ROOD, minister, educator; b. Kittanning, Pa., Apr. 6, 1937; s. Howard Mason and Tirza (Rood) M.; m. Dora Lucille Dunmire, Aug. 6, 1956; children: Robert Rodney, Tania Lynn. BA, Emory and Henry Coll., 1969; MDiv, Asbury Theol. Sem., 1972; PhD, Emory U., 1982. Ordained to ministry United Meth. Ch., 1976. Pastor local chs. Tenn., Ky. and Ga., 1965-75; asst. prof. religion Asbury Coll., Willmore, Ky., 1978-82, assoc. prof., 1982-86, prof. religion, 1986—; v.p. Disciplined Order of Christ, Nashville, 1979—; mem. Holston Conf. Bd. Ministry United Meth. Ch., Knoxville, Tenn., 1984—. With USAF, 1955-69. Mem. Soc. Bibl. Lit., Evang. Theol. Soc., Nat. Assn. Evangs., Wesley Theol. Soc., Sigma Mu, Theta Phi. Home: 223 Kimberly Nicholasville KY 40356 Office: Asbury Coll Lexington Ave Wilmore KY 40390

MOORE, RONALD, deacon; b. Chgo., Sept. 19, 1939; s. Alva Edison and Dorothy Laverne (Stucker) M.; m. Alice Marie Mincel, Oct. 3, 1959; children: Ronald, Maria, Michael, William, Karyn, Dusty, Kimberly. BA cum laude in Humanities, Christian Bros. U., Memphis, 1987; MA cum laude in Theology, Memphis Theol. Sem., 1990; postgrad. in Philosophy, U. Tenn., 1990—. Deacon St. Mary's Ch., Bolivar, Tenn., 1985—; parish coun. pres. St. Mary's Ch., 1980-82, religious edn. tchr., 1978-89; vol. chaplain Western Mental Health Hosp., Bolivar, 1983-90. Pres. bd. Loaves & Fishes, Inc., Hardeman County, Tenn., 1983-90. With USAR, 1956-60. Recipient Spl. Achievement award Christian Bros. U., 1987, Excellence in N.T. award Memphis Theol. Sem., 1990; Field Trial Mus. fellow, 1990-91. Mem. Alpha Chi. Home: PO Box 362 Lenoir City TN 37771

MOORE, RONALD QUENTIN, minister; b. Langley, S.C., Aug. 12, 1939; s. George Quentin and Jennie Evelyn (Workman) M.; m. Doris Lorene Jones, July 5, 1959; children: David Quentin, Timothy Ray, Phillip Edward. BTh, Holmes Theol. Sem., Greenville, S.C., 1960; BA, Central (S.C.) Wesleyan Coll., 1969; MEd, Clemson U., 1975; postgrad., Columbia (S.C.) Bible Sem., Fuller Theol. Sem.; DD (hon.), Holmes Coll. of the Bible, Greenville, S.C., 1991. Ordained to ministry Pentecostal Holiness Ch. Founder, pastor Pentecostal Holiness Ch., Belvedere, S.C., 1961-64; pastor Pentecostal Holiness Ch., Easley, S.C., 1965-70, Taylor Meml. Pentecostal Holiness Ch., Anderson, S.C.; asst. dir. world missions dept. Pentecostal Holiness Ch., Okla., 1975-90; pres. Southwestern Coll. Christian Ministries, Oklahoma City, 1990—; chmn. Pastoral Care Dept. Internat. Pentecostal Holiness Ch., Oklahoma City, 1989—. Assoc. editor: (mag.) Worldorama; exec. editor: INSIGHT, Southwestern Alumni Assn., 1990—; contbr. articles to Advocate Pentecostal Holiness Church. Office: Southwestern Coll Christian Ministries 7210 N W 39th Expwy Bethany OK 73008

MOORE, STEVEN CARROLL, priest; b. Redmond, Oreg., May 16, 1949; s. George William and Adele (Lafoon) M. BA in English Lit., St. Thomas Coll., Seattle, 1972; MA in Systematic Theology, St. Thomas Sem., Seattle, 1976. Tchr. St. Mary's (Alaska) High Sch., 1970-71, Monroe Cath. High Sch., Fairbanks, Alaska, 1976-79; assoc. pastor St. Elizabeth Ann Seton Ch., Anchorage, 1979-82; staff asst. Chancery Archdiocese of Anchorage, 1982-85, vicar gen., 1985—; bd. dirs., treas. Alaska Housing Ministry Inc., Anchorage, 1983-87; treas. Fed. Diocesan Liturgical Commn., Washington, 1985-87. Bd. dirs., pres. Alaska AIDS Assistance, Anchorage, 1984—. Roman Catholic. Avocations: music, art. Home: PO Box 14-0347 Anchorage AK 99514-0347 Office: Archdiocese of Anchorage 225 Cordova Anchorage AK 99501

MOORE, THOMAS EDWARD, minister; b. Rockford, Ill., June 26, 1942; s. John Edward and Mary Virginia (Leary) M.; m. Judith Joye Lantz, Apr. 21, 1962; children: Treche Michelle, Trent Michael, Toby Matthew. Student, No. Ill.U., 1961-62; student Rock Valley Coll., 1968-69; student, Christian Life Bible Coll., 1978-86. Ordained to ministry Assemblies of God, 1989. Pastor Christian Deaf Ctr., Rockford, 1985-87, Galva (Ill.) Assembly of God, 1987—; sectional rep. Men's Ministry, Ill., 1990—; mem. Gen. Coun. Assemblies of God. EMT, fireman Stillman Valley (Ill.) Fire Protection Dist., 1962-76. Office: Assembly of God 302 SE 2d St Galva IL 61434 *God has placed us here to carry out His purposes. I think Romans 1: 6 states it very clearly, "And you also are among those who are called to belong to Jesus Christ." Belonging to Christ, I must exemplify Him.*

MOORE, TOM D., clergyman; b. Broken Bow, Nebr., May 10, 1928; s. William Hudson and Ruth Hope (Holden) M.; m. Ardel Marie Curry, Aug. 12, 1948; children: Judy Fay, Jean Kay, Sheryl Maria, Thomas Darrell, Laura Ardel. BA, Bapt. Bible Coll., Denver, 1956, MA, 1966; D in Psychology, Nectarian Coll. of Philosophy, Kansas City, Mo., 1970. Ordained to ministry, 1953. Founder, pastor Messiah Bapt. Ch., Denver, 1955—; founder, adminstr. Lakewood Christian Schs., Denver, 1960—; founder, pres. Messiahville Bapt. Bible Coll., Denver, 1970—, Save a Child, Inc., Denver, 1980—. Republican. Baptist. Avocations: antique collecting, travel, music. Office: Christian Schs Lakewood 3241 W 44th Ave Denver CO 80211

MOORE, WILFRED EUGENE, minister, educator; b. Great Lakes, Ill., Aug. 2, 1954; s. Abraham Jesse and Ruth Hazeline (Burnett) M. BA in English, Northeastern U., Chgo., 1977. Cert. tchr., 6-12, Ill. Youth leader, dir. New Birth Ch. of God in Christ, Chgo., 1974-82; youth leader St. Mark Ch. of God in Christ, Chgo., 1982-88; mgr. Corinthian Temple Ch. of God in Christ, Chgo., 1988-90; minister of music Christ Bible Ctr., Chgo., 1991—; tchr. Rosa Parks Mid. Sch., Chgo., 1987—; pres., chief exec. officer Celebrity Cons. and Mgmt., Chgo., 1988—; exec. dir. Cabrini Youth Enrichment, Chgo., 1990-91; founder, dir. The Pentecostal Sounds, Chgo., 1977-88; founder, exec. dir. Gospel's 1st Celebrity Roast and Toast, 1991—; dir. promotions and mktg. Estarion Records, 1991—. Composer (recorded albums) A New Beginning, 1985; choral conductor in competition, City of Chgo., Simple Medley, 1982, Top Ladies of Distinction award 1984. Recipient Alumni award Northeastern U., 1985, Tchr. of Yr. award ISA Sch., Chgo., 1986. Mem. NARAS, Nat. Coun. Tchrs. of English. Democrat. Home: 6700 South Crandon # 11-B Chicago IL 60649 Office: Celebrity Cons and Mgmt PO Box 438819 Chicago IL 60643 *True Brotherly Love is when one allows himself to share in the process of creating the minds and images that add substance to one's life. Spreading knowledge and awareness topped with understanding, giving life to one even when that brother may turn it away.*

MOORE, WILLIAM DAVID, minister; b. Andalusia, Ala., June 2, 1949; s. Manning Lamar and Jeanette (Floyd) M.; m. Rebecca Ann Harper, Jan. 1, 1972; children: Holly, Joy. BA, Samford U., 1970; MDiv, Southwestern Bapt. Theol. Sem., Ft. Worth, 1972; PhD, Baylor U., 1978. Ordained to ministry So. Bapt. Conv., 1969. Assoc. pastor 1st Bapt. Ch., Hillsboro, Tex., 1973-75; pastor Deer Park Bapt. Ch., Newport News, Va., 1975-81, Southside Bapt. Ch., Dothan, Ala., 1981-87, Immanuel Bapt. Ch., Pine Bluff, Ark., 1987—; pres. Sta. ACTS-TV 65, Pine Bluff, 1987—; mem. exec. bd. Ark. Bapt. Conv., Little Rock, 1987—. Bd. dirs. Sav-A-Life Wiregrass, Dothan, 1982-87, Charter Woods Psychiat. Hosp., Dothan, 1985-87; tech. dir. All-Civic Night, Pine Bluff, 1989-90; grad. Leadership Pine Bluff, 1989; div. chmn. United Way, Pine Bluff, 1990. Home: 1704 W 34th St Pine Bluff AR 71603 Office: Immanuel Bapt Ch 1801 W 17th St Pine Bluff AR 71603

MOORER, WILLIAM BOWLING, minister, religious organization administrator; b. Muskogee, Okla., Aug. 29, 1935; s. Charles Allen and Margaret Lorraine (Bowling) M.; m. Helen Irene Ludwig, Aug. 28, 1960; children: David Edward, Anne Elizabeth. Student, Northeastern Okla. State U., 1953-56; BA in English, U. Tex., El Paso, 1957; ThM, So. Meth. U., 1961; MS, Okla. State U., 1972, EdD, 1976. Ordained to ministry United Meth. Ch., 1959. Pastor Christ United Meth. Ch., Enid, Okla., 1974-80; sr. pastor Wickline United Meth. Ch., Midwest City, Okla., 1980-85; sr. pastor 1st United Meth. Ch., Duncan, Okla., 1985-88, Clinton, Okla., 1988-90; exec. dir. Okla. Conf. of Chs., Oklahoma City, 1990—. Mem. Okla. Acad. for State Goals, 1990—; chair Regional AIDS Interfaith Network Bd., Okla., 1991. Named Humanitarian of Yr. Clinton Assn. for Rights and Equality, 1990. Mem. Nat. Acad. Counselors and Family Therapists (clin.). Democrat. Office: Okla Conf Chs 2901 Classen PO Box 60288 Oklahoma City OK 73146

MOOSE, ELTON LEROY, minister, counselor, senior center executive; b. New Castle, Pa., Dec. 4, 1935; s. Lloyd David and Alma Ruth (Barner) M.; m. Kathleen Faye Brock, Aug. 10, 1957; children: Rebecca Ruth Moose Oyler, Paula Kaye Moose Dunn. BTh, God's Bible Sch. and Coll., 1957, BA, 1959; MS in Counseling and Psychology, Carolina Christian U., 1990. Ordained to ministry as elder Free Meth. Ch. N.Am., 1959; lic., cert. pastoral counselor. Min. Free Meth. Ch. N.Am., Ohio Conf., 1959—; exec. dir. Fairborn (Ohio) Multipurpose Sr. Ctr., 1984—; mem. conf. evangelism Free Meth. Ch., Ohio, 1976-83; chaplain Mercy Meml. Hosp., Urbana, Ohio, 1976-83; chaplain Champaign County Jail, Urbana, 1980-83. Sec.-treas. Greene County Coun. on Aging, Xenia, Ohio, 1985-87; chmn. Greene County Mental Health Task Force, Xenia, 1989-91, Greene County Mental Health Coalition, 1991—; mem. adv. coun., coord. support group Med. Sch., Wright State U., Fairborn, 1991—. Mem. Nat. Christian Counselors Assn., Nat. Coun. on Aging, Greene County Coun. on Aging, Miami Valley Gerontology Coun., Am. Assn. Ret. Persons (Community award 1990), Eagles Club. Home: 1542 Marinette Dr Springfield OH 45503 Office: Fairborn Multipurpose Sr Ctr 325 N 3d St Fairborn OH 45324 *"A turn in the road is not a dead end." We often believe we've hit a dead end on life's road when we discover it's only turn in life's road. Life's purpose may have twists and turns. It's never a freeway without curves and turns.*

MOOSE, SISTER MARY IMMACULETTE, nun, elementary educator; b. Canton, Ohio, June 22, 1921; d. Irvin Louis and Eva Catherine (Strain) M. BA in Social Sci., Mt. St. Mary's Coll., 1953; MA in Edn. Psychology, Loyola U., 1966. Joined Sisters of Notre Dame, 1939. Elem. sch. tchr. Cath. schs. ., Cleve., 1941-47; tchr. Sisters of Notre Dame, L.A., 1947-65; prin. Cath. schs. L.A. and Oakland, Calif., 1965-81; elem. supr. Notre Dame schs. L.A., 1981—; chairperson Conf. of Religious Directions in Edn., Calif., 1990-91; supr. U. San Francisco Credential Tchrs., Calif., 1991—. Contbr. aritcles to profl. jours. Grantee Archdiocese of L.A., 1978. Mem. Notre Dame Ednl. Assn. (regional chairperson, steering com.), Nat. Coun. Math Tchrs., Western Assn. Schs. and Colls. (chairperson evaluation com.). Republican.

MORALES REYES, LUIS, bishop; b. Churumuco, Mexico, July 5, 1936. Ordained priest Roman Cath. Ch., 1962. Named titular bishop Burca, 1976; bishop Diocese of Tacambaro, Mex., 1979—; coadjutor bishop Diocese of Torreón, 1985—; bishop of Torreón, 1990—. Office: Obispado Apartado 430, 27000 Torreón, Coah Mexico

MORAN, JOHN, religious organization administrator. Pres. The Missionary Ch., Fort Wayne, Ind. Office: Missionary Ch 3901 S Wayne Ave Fort Wayne IN 46807*

MORAND, BLAISE E., bishop; b. Tecumseh, Ont., Can., Sept. 12, 1932. Ordained priest Roman Cath. Ch., 1958. Ordained coadjutor bishop Diocese of Prince Albert, Sask., Can., 1981, bishop, 1983—. Office: Diocese of Prince Albert, 1415 4th Ave W, Prince Albert, SK Canada S6V 5H1

MORDEN, JOHN GRANT, priest; b. London, Eng., Aug. 17, 1925; s. Walter Grant and Doris (Henshaw) M; m. Elizabeth Grace Tannahill, Sept. 7, 1949; children: Ann, Margaret, James (dec.), Peter, Mary. BA, U. Toronto, 1949, LTh, 1952, BD, 1953; DD, Wycliffe Coll., Toronto, 1963; STM, Union Theol. Sem., N.Y.C., 1954; DTh, Gen. Episc. Sem., N.Y.C., 1961; DD, Huron Coll., London, 1985, Trinity Coll., Toronto, Can., 1986, St. John's Coll., Winnipeg, Can., 1988. Ordained deacon, 1951, priest Anglican Ch. Can., 1952. Asst. curate Toronto, Ont. Can. and White Plains, N.Y. chs., 1951-56; rector St. Matthews Ch., Toronto, 1956-57; rector of the Chapel Huron Coll., London, Ont., Can., 1957-90, prof. theology and religious studies, 1962-90, prin., 1962-84, prin. emeritus, 1984—; archdeacon Diocese of Huron, 1967-90, archdeacon emeritus, 1990—; mem. Gen. Synod of Anglican Ch. of Can., 1961-86, nat. exec. com. Gen. Synod, 1973-76; mem. Provincial Synod of Province of Ont., 1961-85; chmn. Bd. Examiners of Anglican Ch. of Can., 1969-74. Mem. senate U. Western Ont., 1959-84. Home: 286 Steele St, London, ON Canada N6A 2L1 *While God, as revealed in the life and teaching of Jesus Christ, gives meaning to my life, I have learnt that the same God has acted and spoken through all the great religious traditions of makind. I have to search out his truth in love with my neighbors of all faiths and cultures.*

MORE, SISTER MARY THOMAS (SISTER), health care administrator; b. Scotland, Aug. 26, 1916; came to U.S., 1961; d. Ninian and Mary Campbell (Grant) Morton. Grad. RN, St. Anne Hosp., Fall River, Mass., 1964; BS, Boston Coll., 1966, MS, 1968. Joined Dominican Sisters, Roman Cath. Ch.; cert. nursing home adminstr. Instr. psychiat. nursing Taunton State Hosp., Fall River Schs. Nursing, 1968-72; adminstr. Madonna Manor Nursing Home, North Attleboro, Mass., 1972-79; asst. adminstr. St. Anne's Hosp., Fall River, Mass., 1979-81; adminstr. Madonna Manor Nursing Home, North Attleboro, 1981-86; exec. dir. Hospice Care of Greater Taunton, Taunton, Mass., 1986—. Bd. dirs. New. Eng. Conf. Cath. Health Assn., Paul Dever State Sch.; coord. Mayor's AIDS Task Force. Mem. Nat. Hospice Orgn., Mass. Hospice Fedn., Kiwanis (chaplain Taunton club), Sigma Theta Tau. Roman Catholic. Avocations: music, swimming. Office: Hospice Care Greater Taunton 88 Washington St Taunton MA 02780

MOREIRA NEVES, LUCAS CARDINAL, archbishop; b. Sã João del Rei, Brazil, Sept. 16, 1925. Ordained priest Roman Cath. Ch., 1950. Elected to titular Ch. of Feradi Maggiore, 1967; consecrated bishop, 1967, archbishop, 1979; transferred to titular Ch. of Vescovio,, 1987; then São Salvador da Bahia,, 1987; created cardinal, 1988. Address: Paláacio de Sé, Praca da Sé 1, 40 000 Salvador BA, Brazil

MORELAND, RAYMOND THEODORE, JR., minister; b. Balt., Mar. 12, 1944; s. Raymond Theodore and Mary Elaine (Leiman) M.; m. Sandra Kay Levering, Aug. 3, 1980. BA, Randolph Macon Coll., 1966; MDiv, Wesley Theol. Sem., Washington, 1970, D of Ministry, 1973; MA in Religious Edn., Ecum. Inst. St. Mary's Sem., Balt., 1989—. Assoc. pastor Essex United Meth. Ch., Balt., 1969-70; pastor Carrols-Gills-Stevenson United Meth. Ch., Luthervilee, Md., 1970-71; assoc. Eastport United Meth. Ch., Annapolis, Md., 1971-73; pastor Mt. Carmel-New Market United Meth. Ch., Frederick, Md., 1973-80, Graceland United Meth. Ch., Balt., 1980-83, Trinity United Meth. Ch., Martinsburg, W.Va., 1983-91, John Wesley United Meth. Ch., Hagerstown, Md., 1991—; v.p., bd. dirs. Epworth Fed. Credit Union, Balt.; mem., past chmn. Balt. Conf. Com. on Edn.; ch. rep. Am. Bible Soc. Writer, producer, dir., host weekly radio religious program Sta. WEPM, Martinsburg, 1982—. Mem. Eastern Panhandle AIDS Task Force, Martinsburg, W. Va.; past pres., v.p. Martinsburg-Berkeley County Ministerial Assn., 1987-88. Recipient Nat. Preaching Fellowship, Bd. of Higher Edn., United Meth. Ch., 1971. Mem. Am. Assn. Clin. Pastoral Edn., Christian Educators Fellowship, Am. Acad. of Religion, Acad. Parish Clergy, Nat. Tchr. Edn. Project, Fellowship of United Meth. Ch. for Music, Worship and the Arts, Mason, Knight Templar. Democrat. Home: 1408 Hamilton Blvd Hagerstown MD 21742 Office: John Wesley United Meth Ch 129 N Potomac St Hagerstown MD 21740 *Life lived at the level of deepest intentionality allows one to celebrate and to suffer with meaning and with hope. Life then becomes the gift of God's intentional love enabling us to live beyond our human means by grace.*

MOREMEN, WILLIAM MERRILL, minister; b. Long Beach, Calif., Dec. 22, 1927; s. Raymond and Alice (Northrup) M.; m. Grace Ellen Partin, Sept. 5, 1953; children: Margaret, John, Katherine. BA, Pomona Coll., 1949; MDiv, U. Chgo., 1953; postgrad., Mansfield Coll., Oxford, Eng., 1955-56, Claremont Sch. Theol., 1972, Pacific Sch. Religion, 1980. Ordained to ministry United Ch. of Christ, 1956. Min. Tehachapi (Calif.) United Ch. of Christ, 1957-60; min. Christian edn. San Bernardino (Calif.) United Ch. of Christ, 1960-64; min. Western Knoll United Ch. of Christ, L.A., 1964-72; sr. min. 1st Congl. United Ch. of Christ, Washington, 1972-83, Eden United Ch. of Christ, Hayward, Calif., 1983—; adj. faculty Pacific Sch. of Religion, Berkeley, Calif., 1989—, Intermet Sem., Washington, 1973-77, Lancaster (Pa.) Theol. Sem., spring 1979; mem. staff, bd. dirs. Pacific Ctr. for Spiritual Formation, San Francisco Bay Area; adv. bd. dirs. Shalem Inst. for Spiritual Formation, Washington. Author: Developing Spiritually and Professionally, 1984, Watch and Pray, 1987, (with others) Spirit Awakening, 1988. Home: 23051 Avis Ln Hayward CA 94541 Office: Eden United Ch of Christ 21455 Birch St Hayward CA 94541

MORENO, GUILLERMO FERNANDEZ, minister; b. San Antonio, Aug. 28, 1948; s. Willie Luna and Frances (Fernandez) M.; m. Delia Guerra, June 6, 1971; 1 child, Guillermo. BA, U. Calif., L.A., 1976, MA, 1978; MA, Bob Jones U., 1981, PhD, 1988. Ordained to ministry Christian Ch. Min. Latin Am. Coun. of Christian Chs., Brownsville, Tex., 1967—; pastor Latin Am. Coun. of Christian Chs., Brownsville, 1969—, Latin Am. Coun. of Christian Chs. Galilea, L.A., 1988—; instr. Cladic Sem., L.A., 1969—; choir dir. Cladic Sem., L.A., 1967-79; evangelist Latin Am. Coun. Christian Chs., U.S.A., summers 1968—; visiting instr. Clases Biblicas, Monterrey, Mex., summers 1975—; mgr. Cladic Bible Book Store, L.A., 1984-86. Author Bible Doctrine seminar; contbr. articles to profl. jours. Mem. Sigma Delta Pi Spanish Honor Soc. (lifetime), Bob Jones U. Alumni Assn. Republican. Home: 1311 E Mauretania St Wilmington CA 90744 *The Christian life is a rewarding process by which we learn daily to depend more on God and less on ourselves.*

MORENO, LYDIA HOLGUIN, minister; b. Tucson; d. Vicente Franco and Julia Holguin Moreno. BA, U. Ariz., 1973; MDiv, Sch. Theology at Claremont, 1986. Ordained to ministry United Meth. Ch., 1985. Min. Wesley United Meth. Ch., North Las Vegas, Nev., 1986-91, Hope United Meth. Ch., Tucson, 1991—. Mem. Assn. Meths. for Action and Renewal (pres. Desert Southwest Ann. Conf. 1990—). Office: Hope United Meth Ch 6740 S Santa Clara Ave Tucson AZ 85706

MORENO, MANUEL D., bishop; Educator U. of Calif., L.A., St. John's Sem., Camarillo, Calif. Ordained priest Roman Cath. church, 1961. Ordained aux. bishop of Los Angeles, titular bishop of Tanagra, 1977; installed as bishop of Tucson, 1982—. Office: 192 S Stone Ave PO Box 31 Tucson AZ 85702

MORETON, THOMAS HUGH, minister; b. Shanghai, China, Dec. 2, 1917; came to U.S., 1946; s. Hugh and Tsuru M; m. Olive Mae Rives, Apr. 1, 1947 (dec. Apr. 1986); children: Ann Rives Moreton Smith, Andrew Hugh, Margaret Evelyn Moreton Hamar; m. Selma Littig, June 7, 1986. LLB, 1939, BD, 1942, PhD, 1946; ThD, Trinity Sem., 1948; LittD, 1949. Ordained to ministry Brit. Bapt. Ch., 1942. Min. various chs., also tchr. Seaford Coll. Eng., 1945-46; tchr. coll. and sem. level. div. courses various schs., Atlanta, Oklahoma City, 1946-51; founder Tokyo Gospel Mission, Inc., House of Hope, Inc., Tokyo, 1951—; also World Gospel Fellowship, Inc., Norman, Okla., 1967—; pastor chs., Moore, Okla., Shawnee, Okla., Ada, Okla., Del City, Okla., Tahlequah, Okla. and Oklahoma City, 1968—; preacher numerous fgn. countries; internat. tour dir. Contbr. articles to religious jours. Charter mem. Am.-Japan Com. for Assisting Japanese-Am. Orphans. Chaplain AUS, 1952-63. Recipient various awards Japanese govt. Fellow Royal Geog. Soc., Philos. Soc.; mem. Royal Soc. Lit., Am.-Japan Soc., Israel-Japan Soc.

MOREY, ANN-JANINE, English educator; b. Atlanta, Oct. 31, 1951; d. Donald Franklin and Martha Ann (Ballew) M.; m. Todd Hedinger, July 19, 1986; 1 child, Lucia Rose Hamilton Morey. BA, Grinnell Coll., 1973; MA, U. So. Calif., L.A., 1977, PhD, 1979. Assoc. prof. So. Ill. U., Carbondale, 1979—; mem., bd. dirs. Univ. Christian Ministries, Carbondale, 1981-82. Author: Apples and Ashes, 1982, Religion and Sexuality in American Literature, 1992; contbr. articles to profl. jours. Vol. Synergy: Crisis Intervention Ctr., Carbondale, 1984-86, bd. dirs., 1985-86; sustaining mem. So. Poverty Law Ctr., Birmingham, Ala., 1986—. Dissertation fellow Soroptimist Found., L.A., 1978-79. Mem. Am. Acad. Religion (panel judge awards for excellence 1989-91), MLA, Soc. for Values in Higher Edn., Am. Studies Assn. Office: So Ill U Dept of English Carbondale IL 62901

MOREY, GEORGE L., minister; b. St. Joseph, Mo., Dec. 12, 1954; s. George LeRoy and Shirley Jean (Miller) M.; m. Norma June Colwell, May 6, 1978; children: George Matthew, Mark Aaron. BA, Vennard Coll., University Park, Iowa, 1987; MA, Olivet Nazarene U., Bourbonnais, Ill., 1990. Ordained to ministry Evang. Ch. N.Am. Pastor Hemple (Mo.) Community Ch., 1982-83, Coleridge Community Ch., Knoxville, Iowa, 1984-85, Grace Evang. Ch., Hinton, Iowa, 1987—. Twp. del. Plymouth County Rep. Com., Hinton, 1988. Mem. LeMars Area Ministerial Assn. (del. 1990—), Hinton Ministerial Assn. (pres. 1990—). Home: 305 W Main St Hinton IA 51024 Office: Grace Evang Ch 109 N Prospect Hinton IA 51024

MORGAN, BRYAN MCLAURY, minister; b. Borger, Tex., Mar. 12, 1955; s. Walter Eugene and Audry Dolores (Fagan) M.; m. Melissa Kay Ward, Feb. 16, 1980; children: Christopher Charles, Andrew William. BA, Hardin-Simmons U., 1978; MDiv, Southwestern Bapt. Theol. Sem., 1982. Ordained to ministry So. Bapt. Conv., 1984. Pastor Willis Bapt. Ch., Kingston, Okla., 1982-85, Emmanuel So. Bapt. Ch., Coweta, Okla., 1985—; mission pastor First Bapt. Ch., Coweta, 1985-86; moderator Johnston-Marshall Bapt. Assn., Madill, Okla., 1984-86. Bd. dirs. Children's Adv. Bd., Wagoner County, Okla., 1990. Mem. Tulsa Bapt. Assn. Republican. Home: 13621 S 285th East Ave Coweta OK 74429-7016 Office: Emmanuel So Bapt Ch 28110 E 127 St South Coweta OK 74429-7016

MORGAN, DAVID FORBES, minister; b. Toronto, Ont., Can., Aug. 3, 1930; came to U.S., 1954; s. Forbes Alexander and Ruth (Bamford) M.; m. Delores Mae Storhaug, Sept. 7, 1956; children—Roxanne Ruth, David Forbes II. BA, Rocky Mt. Coll.; ThB, Coll. of the Rockies, M.Div.; postgrad. Bishop's Sch. Theology; LittD (hon.), Temple Coll., 1956, D.C. Nat. Coll. Ordained priest. Pres., Coll. of the Rockies, Denver, 1960-73; prior Order of Christ Centered Ministries, Denver, 1973—; canon pastor St. John's Cathedral, Denver, 1982—; bd. dir. Alpha Inc., Denver, 1981—. Author: Christ Centered Ministries, A Response to God's Call, 1973; Songs with A Message, 1956. Clubs: Oxford, Denver Botanic Garden. Home: 740 Clarkson Denver CO 80218 Office: St Johns Cathedral 1313 Clarkson Denver CO 80218

MORGAN, DENNIS BRENT, minister, psychologist; b. Kansas City, Mo., Dec. 28, 1949; s. Ira Pershing and Josephine (Langworthy) M. BA, Pittsburg (Kans) State U., 1971, MS, 1976; postgrad., U. Kans., 1976; PsyD in Psychology, Western Colo. U., 1978. Diplomate Am. Bd. Psychotherapy (bd. dirs. 1982—). Chief psychologist Sierra Vista Psychol. Hosp., Highland, Calif., 1980; psychol. asst. Ctr. for Active Psychology, Riverside, Calif., 1981—; chief psychologist HSA Heartland Hosp., Nevada, Mo., 1983-84, Profl. Psychol. Svc., Kansas City, Mo., 1976—; sr. pastor Heartland Ch., Kansas City, 1989—; v.p. psychol. svcs. Group Dynamics, Dallas, 1978—; mem. staff Kellogg Psychiat. Hosp., Corona, Calif., Long Beach Neuropsychiat. Inst., Charter Baywood Hosp., Coll. Hosp., Cerritos, Calif., 1983—; mem. faculty Crystal Cathedral Lay Mins. Tng. Ctr., mini-seminary, San Juan Capistrano Community Ch. Author: Manage Your Stress Before It Manages You, 1983. Maj. U.S. Army, 1971-89. Mem. Nat. Psychiat. Assn. (life), Am. Assn. Christian Counselors, Nat. Assn. Disability Examiners, Mo. Assn. Disability Examiners, Mo. State Psychol. Assn., Ret. Officers Assn. U.S.A., U.S. Navy League, Kansas City Club, Univ. Club of Kansas City, Psi Chi, Lambda Chi Alpha (pres. Kansas City alumni chpt., adv. bd. Pittsburg). Office: 4537 Broadway Ste 1-South Kansas City MO 64111-3366

MORGAN, DENNIS LEE, minister; b. Liberty, Ky., Oct. 16, 1947; s. Brooklyn Dennis and Hazel Jeanette (Maupin) M.; m. Donna Kay May, June 27, 1970; children: Melissia, Rebecca, Dennis Jr. B in Ministry, Clear Creek Bapt. Bible Coll., Pineville, Ky., 1988. Pastor Fairland Bapt. Ch., Albany, Ky., 1985-87, Thomas Bapt. Ch., Irvine, Ky., 1988—; prin. operator Morgan's Heating 4 Air, Irvine, Ky., 1988-91; RA dir., SS Dir., trustee, youth dir., Ellisburg Bapt. Ch., Hustonville, Ky., 1981-84. with U.S. Army, 1967-69. Decorated Bronze Star, Comanation, 1969. Republican. Home: 5460 Dug Hill Rd Irvine KY 40336 Office: Thomas Baptist Church 5460 Dug Hill Rd Irvine KY 40336

MORGAN, DONN FARLEY, Old Testament educator; b. Syracuse, N.Y., Sept. 12, 1943; s. Robert Earle and Eloise (Farley) M.; m. Harriet Kemp, June 3, 1967 (div. 1975); children: Curtis Matthew, Lauren Michelle; m. Alda Marsh, Dec. 27, 1975. AB, Oberlin (Ohio) Coll., 1965; BD, Yale U., 1968; MA, Claremont (Calif.) Grad. Sch., 1972, PhD, 1974. Prof. of Old Testament, ch. div. Sch. of Pacific, Berkeley, Calif., 1972—, acad. dean, 1985—, acting dean, pres., 1988-90. Author: Wisdom in Old Testament Traditions, 1981, Between Text and Community, 1990; editor: Ras Shamra Parallels, 1972. Assn. Theol. Schs. rsch. grantee, 1978, Episcopal Ch. grantee, 1984, Nat. Conf. Christians and Jews fellow, 1986. Mem. Soc. Bibl. Lit. Office: Ch Div Sch Pacific 2451 Ridge Rd Berkeley CA 94705

MORGAN, GEORGE WESLEY, minister; b. Hagerstown, Md., Mar. 6, 1941; s. George Willis and Bessie Mildred (Valentine) M.; m. Peggy Kathryne Lumm, Sept. 1, 1963; children: Lizanne Noelle, David Edwin. AA, Hagerstown (Md.) Jr. Coll., 1963; AB, Bethany Coll., 1971; D of Ministry, Lexington (Ky.) Theol., Seminary, 1976. Ordained to ministry Christian Ch. (Disciples of Christ), 1972. Minister First Christian Ch., Pineville, Ky., 1973-78; exec. assoc., regional minister Christian Ch. in N.C., Wilson, 1978-83; dir. Christian Ch. Div. Homeland Ministries, Indpls., 1983-85; minister First Christian Ch., Texas City, Tex., 1985—; mem. com. on ministry Christian Ch. in Southwest, Ft. Worth, 1986—, chair, 1990—; mem. So. Acad. of Teaching, Indpls., 1966—, chair, 1981-84; chair Leader Devel. Dept., Coastal Plains Area, Houston, 1990—, Dept. of Ministry, 1986-90. Author: Teacher As Learner As Teacher, 1976, Christian Stress Management, 1984; editor: Design Manual, 1983, Trainer Development, 1984. Chmn. Pineville Community Ctr., 1975-78, Pineville InterFaith Housing Assn., 1977-78, Texas City New Focus, 1990—, steering com. CASA of Galveston County, Texas City, 1990—. Recipient Leadership award Hagerstown Jr. Coll., 1963; named Minister of Yr. Conservation Club of W.Va., 1969, Community Leaders and Noteworthy Ams., 1978. Mem. Cameron Ministers Assn. (pres. 1966-69), Ohio Valley Ministers Assn. (pres. 1968-69), Pineville Ministers Assn. (pres. 1974-77), Texas City Ministers Fellowship (pres. 1986—), Kiwanis (bd. dirs. Pineville chpt. 1976-78, bd. dirs. Texas City chpt. 1990-91). Home: 2803 20th Ave N Texas City TX 77590 Office: First Christian Church PO Drawer B Texas City TX 77592 *I believe that everything is curriculum! We can learn from every experience. I also believe that life is a choice. God has given us the ability and the freedom to choose our response to every event in life.*

MORGAN, JOHN PIERPONT, deacon; b. Logansport, Ind., Apr. 2, 1948; s. Robert and DeLoris Jean (Reed) M.; m. Cheryl Ann Raney, March 21, 1970; children: Jenelle, Jaydine. Student, St. Paul Bible Coll., 1966-69. Jr. high leader Hazel Park Alliance Ch., St. Paul, 1966-67; from retirement home leader to half-way house leader St. Paul Bible Coll., 1967-69; jr. high leader Medinah (Ill.) Bapt. Ch., 1970-78, 86—; sales rep. Fuji Am., Inc., Gurnee, Ill., 1986—; deacon, mem. missions com. Medinah Bapt. Ch., Ill. Home: 440 Sycamore Ave Roselle IL 60172 Office: Fuji America 1840 Northwestern Ave Gurnee IL 60031

MORGAN, KAREN D., organist, choirmaster; b. Atlanta, Ga., Feb. 12, 1953; d. Lyman Wallace and Evelyn Louise (Garrison) M.; m. Dick Allen Chapman, Jul. 1974 (div. Dec. 1976). MusB, Fla. St. U., 1975; MusM, Westminster Choir Coll., 1981. Organist/choirmaster Grace Episc. Ch., Lockport, N.Y., 1981-86, Christ Episc. Ch., Mobile, Ala., 1986--. Composer religious music. Mem. Assc. Anglican Musicians, Am. Guild Organists. Episcopal. Office: Christ Episcopal Church 115 S Conception St Mobile AL 36602 *It is amazing how often one can get what one needs just by asking for it in a straightforward manner. James 4:26: "You do not have because you do not ask." So ask!.*

MORGAN, KENNETH WILBUR, minister; b. Wheeling, W.Va., May 27, 1944; s. Wilbur Wallace and Ella Jesse (Cline) M.; m. Cynthia Shearer, June 1, 1968; 1 child, Shannon Michelle. BA, Ky. Wesleyan Coll., 1983; MDiv, Theol. Sem., Louisville, 1986; postgrad., So. Bapt. Sem., Louisville. Ordained to ministry So. Bapt. Conv., 1984. Evangelist So. Bapt. Conv., Owensboro, Ky., 1981-84; min. pastoral care Walnut St. Bapt. Ch., Owensboro, 1983-84; pastor Sorgho (Ky.) Bapt. Ch., 1984-87, Coll. Heights Bapt. Ch., Elyria, Ohio, 1987—; messenger So. Bapt. Conv., Nashville, 1984—, State Conv. Bapts. in Ohio, Columbus, 1987—. Initiator, mem. Citizens for Lorain, Ohio, 1990; founder Prime Timers, Elyria, 1989; mem. Roundtable Ohio, Solon, 1990, Ohio Legis. Watch, Mt. Vernon, 1990; bd. dirs. Love Inc., Elyria. Recipient Outstanding Retailer award assorted venders, Ky., 1981; Harrodsburg Found. scholar, 1985. Republican. Home: 133 Notre Dame Circle Elyria OH 44035-1638 Office: College Heights Bapt Ch 980 Abbe Rd Elyria OH 44035

MORGAN, LARRY RONALD, minister; b. Springhill, La., Mar. 12, 1936; s. Woodrow Wilson Morgan and Alma Elizabeth (Dunn) Burch; m. Elizabeth Dianne Baker, May 24, 1958; children: Elizabeth Denise Morgan Davis, Dennis Kevin. ADiv, Bapt. Missionary Assn. Theol. Sem., Jacksonville, Tex., 1990. Ordained to ministry Bapt. Ch., 1971. Clk., carrier U.S. P.O., Springhill, La., 1956-71; assoc. pastor Webb Chapel Bapt. Ch., Dallas, 1971-72, pastor, 1972—; clk., trustee Bapt. Missionary Assn. Sem., Jacksonville, 1983-86; chmn. bd. trustees Bapt. Progress, Dallas, 1984-87. Pres. PTA Browning Elem. Sch., Springhill, 1969-70. With USAR, 1959-66. Mem. Bapt. Missionary Assn. Am. (v.p. hdqrs. Little Rock 1985-86, pres. 1986-88), Dallas County Bapt. Assn. (moderator 1982-84). Home: 14517 Heartside Pl Dallas TX 75234 Office: Webb Chapel Bapt Ch 13565 Webb Chapel Rd Dallas TX 75234

MORGAN, MARK BRYAN, evangelist, business and communications translator; b. Sinton, Tex., June 8, 1957; arrived in Chile, 1977; s. Phillip Roy and Betty Jean (Barnes) M.; m. Ximena del Carmen Fernandez, Dec. 27, 1980; children: Lindsay Star, Kristopher Mark, Kaylee Rianne, Ana Paulina (foster dau.). Student, Fla. Coll., 1975-76, Centro Estudios y Servicios Internat., Vina del Mar, Chile, 1979, Ariz. Inst. Banking, 1982, Phoenix Coll., 1982, Baxter Inst., Tegucigalpa, Honduras, 1985, U. Austral, Valdivia, Chile, 1986, 89, U. Catolica de Santiago, 1989—. Evangelist Ch. of Christ, Phoenix, 1975-76, Chile and Argentina, 1977-78, Chile and Colombia, Valparaiso-Quillota, Chile, 1979-80, Valdivia, 1983—; translator TV sta., Cath. U., Valparaiso, 1980; translator legal dept. Cemento Melon/Blue Circle Corp., La Calera, Chile, 1981; with pub. relations dept., TV commentator Municipality of Vina del Mar, Chile, 1981; researcher Valley Nat. Bank, Phoenix, 1982; pres. Morgan Enterprises, 1983—. Translator, editor: Fellowship, To Teach a Teacher, Training for Service, Bible Authority, The Finger of God, Basic Principles of Christ I and II, Hebrews, 1988, Now That I'm a Christian, 1987. Democrat. Avocations: sports, movies, international relations, reading, researching political economy. Home: Geromino Urmeneta, 202 Valdivia Chile Office: Church of Christ, Casilla 37, 202 Geronimo Urmeneta Chile also: Morgan Enterprises, Beauchef 610 #6, Valdivia Chile

MORGAN, ROBERT CRAWLEY, bishop; b. Birmingham, Ala., Sept. 15, 1933; s. Robert Bailey and Irene (Myers) M.; m. Martha Virginia Storey, Dec. 27, 1958; children: Lesli Leigh, Carol Irene, Robert Crawley. AB, Birmingham-So. Coll., 1955; BD, Emory U., 1958. On trial N. Ala. Conf., ordained deacon United Meth. Ch., 1957, full connection, elder, 1959. Pastor Wesley Chapel Meth. Ch., Sylacauga, Ala., 1957-62, Epworth Meth. Ch., Huntsville, Ala., from 1962; created bishop, assigned Miss. Conf. United Meth. Ch., Jackson, 1984—. Mem. Conf. Bd. Edn., 1959—; chmn. Conf. family com., 1964—. Office: United Meth Ch PO Box 1147 Jackson MS 39205 Other: PO Drawer U Grenada MS 38901

MORGAN, RONALD KEITH, chaplain; b. Johnstown, Pa., Apr. 27, 1934; s. Clinton E. and Vada A. (Hoffman) M.; m. Dorla Dean Kinsey, Mar. 31, 1954 (div. 1974); children: Gail Habecker, Gwen Carpenter, Glee Doody, Gay Mercer; m. Jane Lawry Malone, Sept. 24, 1983. BA, Juniata Coll., 1956; MDiv, Bethany Theol. Sem., 1960; M of Sacred Theology, United Theol. Sem., 1971. Ordained to ministry Ch. of the Brethren, 1957, Luth. Ch., 1987. Pastor Community Ch. of the Brethren, Hutchinson, Kans., 1960-66, Mack Meml. Ch. of the Brethren, Dayton, Ohio, 1966-72; chaplain Fallsview Psychiat. Hosp., Cuyahoga Falls, Ohio, 1972-74, dir. pastoral care, 1974-80; chaplain, clin. pastoral educator Fairview Gen. Hosp., Cleve., 1980-86; dir. pastoral care Cleve. Clinic Found., 1986—; pastoral counselor St. Paul's Episcopal Ch., Akron, Ohio, 1974-76; instr. EMERGE Ashland Theol. Sem., Akron, 1976-80; clin. asst. prof. pastoral psychology Coll. Medicine N.E. Ohio U., 1978-80; cons. for chaplaincy Allen Meml. Hosp., Oberlin, Ohio, 1982-86. Mem. Clergy and Laity Concerned About Vietnam, 1967-72, coord. 1969-70; mem. adv. bd. dirs. United Mins. in Higher Edn., Dayton, 1967-69, chmn. 1969. Rockefeller scholar, 1959-60. Fellow Coll. Chaplains (cert. chaplain, Ohio cert. com.); mem. Assn. Clin. Pastoral Edn. (cert. supr., chmn. standards com. 1986-88), Audobon Soc. (pres. Akron chpt. 1974-75). Republican. Avocations: birdwatching, golf, classical music, travel, photography. Home: 7200 Timber Ln Olmsted Falls OH 44138-1174 Office: Cleve Clinic Found Pastoral Care Dept 9500 Euclid Ave Cleveland OH 44195

MORGAN, SHERLI JO, religious association educator; b. Guymon, Okla., Mar. 13, 1953; d. James Leslie and Zola Loyce (Fike) M.; student Panhandle State U., 1971, Amarillo Coll., 1972; B.S., Southwestern Assemblies of God Coll., 1977; M.B.A., Belmont Coll., 1979. Dir. computer data J.C. Penney Co., Dallas, 1975-77; dir. pub. relations Your Place Inc., Nashville, 1978-79; asst. dir. artists relations and sales IBC Records Inc., Nashville, 1979-80; dir. music and Christian edn. First Assembly of God Ch., Lakewood, Calif., 1980—; pvt. instr. voice and piano. Pres., Young Republicans, 1972, 73; vol., Rep. campaigns, 1980. Mem. Country Music Assn., Gospel Music Assn., Female Execs. Club, Ch. Music Dirs. Assn., Women So. Calif. Coll. Mem. Assembly of God. Club: Hope of our Heritage. Office: First Assembly of God Ch 6022 E Candlewood St Lakewood CA 90713

MORGAN, THOMAS OLIVER, bishop; b. Jan. 20, 1944; s. Charles Edwin and Amy Amelia (Hoyes) M.; m. Lillian Marie Textor, 1963; three children. BA, U. Sask., Can., 1962; BD, King's Coll., London, Ont., 1965; DD (hon.), Coll. of Emmanuel and St. Chad, Sask., 1986. Curate Ch. of the Saviour, Blackburn, Lancashire, Can., 1966-69; rector Ch. of the Saviour, Porcupine Plain, Sask., 1969-73, Kinistino, 1973-77, Shellbrook, 1977-83; archdeacon Indian Missions Sask., 1983-85; bishop Diocese of Sask., Prince Albert, 1985—. Office: Diocese of Sask, Box 1088, Prince Albert, SK Canada S6V 5S6

MORGAN, TIMOTHY GALE, minister; b. Clinton, Ky., Apr. 8, 1959; s. Charles Thomas and Lottie Mae (King) M.; m. Janet Darlene Dement, Nov. 27, 1987. Assoc. pastor 2d Bapt. Ch., Clinton, Ky., 1983-86, New Life Ch., Mayfield, Ky., 1986-88; youth pastor Farmington (Mo.) Ch. of Nazarine, 1989—; asst. mgr. Shoe-Me-Rent-to-Own, Festus, Mo., 1989-91. Home: Rte 3 Box 3445 Farmington MO 63640

MORGAN-LEE, VERONICA, religious organization adminstrator; b. New Orleans, Apr. 14, 1948; d. Lloyd Paul and Juanita (Welton) Morgan; m. George D. Lee, Aug. 12, 1978; 1 child, Ayisha Amata. BA, Mt. St. Scholastica Coll., 1969; MSW, St. Louis U., 1973; PhD, U. Pitts., 1986. Asst. prof. soc. work Ottawa (Kans.) U., 1973-80; mgr. internal control Xerox Corp., Pitts., 1981-83; dir. Office Black Cath. Ministries Black Cath. Ministries, Pitts., 1986—; owner, cons. Soc. and Behavioral Assocs., Kansas City, Mo., and Pitts., 1979—. Mem. Nat. Assn. Social Workers, Nat. Cath. Ednl. Assn., Black Assn. South Hills (pres. 1986-88). Democrat. Avocations: reading, collecting black arts and cen. artifacts, civic work. Office: Black Cath Ministries 111 Blvd of Allies Pittsburgh PA 15222

MORGANTE, JOHN-PAUL, religious organization administrator, minister; b. Yonkers, N.Y., June 26, 1962; s. Enzo and Teresa (DellaToffola) M.; m. Ellen Rothberger, May 26, 1984; children: Camden Anne, Bethany Nicole. BA, U. So. Calif., L.A., 1984. Ordained to ministry Christian Ch., 1987. Adminstrv. dir. Victory Ministries Internat., Lomita, Calif., 1984—. Mem. cen. com. Orange County (Calif.) Reps., 1988-89; intern U.S. Rep. Robert Badham, Washington, 1983, campaign worker, 1984, Assemblyman Curt Pringle, 1988, Garden Grove, Calif., 1988; campaign worker U.S. Senator Chic Hech, 1982, U.S. Rep. Robert Dornan, 1984, Reagan/Bush, 1984. Avocations: golf, travel. Office: Victory Ministries Internat 1825 W Lomita Blvd Ste 400 Lomita CA 90717

MORHAIM, ABRAHAM, rabbi; b. Bklyn., June 19, 1932; s. Haim and Calie (Cohen) M.; m. Victoria Yousha, Aug. 30, 1952; children: Hyman, Calie, Jeffrey, Esther, David. Diploma in teaching, Yeshiva U., 1953, BA, 1954; M. Hebrew Letters, Jewish Theol. Sem., 1958, DD, 1984. Ordained rabbi, 1958. Rabbi United Sephardim of Bklyn., 1958-64, Congregation Bet El De Mex., Mexico City, 1964-65, Temple Ner Tamod, Peabody, Mass., 1965—; chaplain Boston Children's Hosp., 1971—. Mem. Rabbinical Assembly, Mass. Bd. Rabbis, New Eng. Rabbinical Assn. (pres. 1972-74), N. Shore Rabbinic Assn. (pres. 1982-84), Peabody Clergy Assn. (pres. 1976-78). Home: 3 Apple Hill Rd Peabody MA 01960 Office: Temple Ner Tamid 368 Lowell St Peabody MA 01960

MORIARTY, MICHAEL GERALD, clergyman; b. New Bedford, Mass., Aug. 2, 1960; s. Edward Francis and Simonne Claudette (Carrier) M. BS in Mgmt. Sci., SUNY, Geneseo, 1983; AA in Practical Theology, Christ For The Nations Bible Inst., 1985; MTh, Wesley Bibl. Sem., 1988. Ordained to ministry Immanuel Bible Ch., 1988. Singles and coll. pastor Immanuel Bible Ch., Springfield, Va., 1988—; mem. adv. bd. Fellowship Christian Athletes, No. Va. area, 1990—. Counselor No. Va. Mental Health Clinic, Fairfax, 1991—. Mem. Evang. Theol. Soc., Nat. Assn. Single Adult Leaders. Office: Immanuel Bible Ch 5211 Backlick Rd Springfield VA 22151

MORIE, SCOTT, pastor; b. Knoxville, Tenn., Nov. 4, 1956; s. Don E. and Helen (Insco) M.; m. Sharon Evans, Dec. 20, 1980; children: Murry, Heather, Paige, Melissa. BS in Bus. Mgmt., Okla. State U., 1984; M in Divinity, Mid-Am. Bapt. Theol. Sem., Memphis, 1987. Youth dir. Gracemont Bapt. Ch., Tulsa, 1978-81; minister youth Arrow Heights Bapt. Ch., Broken Arrow, Okla., 1981-83; pastor Gladden Bapt. Ch., Parkin, Ark., 1985—. Home: 30950 Center Ridge Westlake OH 44145

MORIN, LAMAR HOWARD, minister, music educator; b. Houston, Nov. 30, 1962; s. Richard Emile and Lois Mae (Legate) M.; m. Lynn Kieffer, Dec. 28, 1982; children: Matthew, Michael, Marcus. B in Music Edn., Ea. N.Mex. U., 1984; MA in Religious Edn., Southwestern Bapt. Theol. Sem., 1987. Min. music 1st Bapt. Ch., Dora, N.Mex., 1982-84; min. music and youth Cen. Bapt. Ch., Stamford, Tex., 1985-87, Bethel Bapt. Ch., Roswell, N.Mex., 1987—; tchr. music, choral dir. Carlsbad (N.Mex.) Jr. High Sch., 1984; pres. N.Mex. Singing Churchmen, Albuquerque, 1990—. Mem. Roswell Youth Min. Assn. (charter). Avocations: music composing, sports. Home: 601 E Mescalero Roswell NM 88201 Office: Bethel Bapt Ch 2420 N Garden Roswell NM 88201

MORNEAU, ROBERT FEALEY, bishop; b. New London, Wis., Sept. 10, 1938; s. Leroy Frederick and Catherine (Fealey) M. M.A., Catholic U., 1962; D.Div.(hon.), 1979. Ordained priest Roman Catholic Ch., 1966, consecrated bishop, 1979. Instr. philosophy Silver Lake Coll., Manitowoc, Wis., 1966-78; dir. ministry to priests program Green Bay, Wis., 1979-85; aux. bishop Diocese of Green Bay, 1979—. Author: Our Father Revisited, 1978, Trinity Sunday Revisited, 1980, Discovering God's Presence, 1980, Mantras for the Morning, 1981, Mantras for the Evening, 1982, Principles of Preaching, 1982, Seasonal Themes, 1984, Mantras for Midnight, 1985; contbr. articles to profl. jours. Bd. trustees St. Norbert Coll. Mem. Nat. Conf. Catholic Bishops, Bishops Com. on Priestly Formation, Com. on Edn. U.S. Catholic Conf. Home: St Margaret Mary Parish 666 Division St Neenah WI 54495-6000 Office: PO Box 66 Green Bay WI 54305

MORRA, JOYCE ANN, pastor, ministry administrator; b. Steubenville, Ohio, Oct. 2, 1941; d. Emmett Alfred Bailie and Maxine Virginia (Maley) Porreca; m. Edward Daniel Morra, Mar. 17, 1961; children: Edward D. Jr., Michael T., Tracey Jo. BA, Southeastern Coll., 1990. Office mgr. M & M Equipment Sales Co., Burgettstown, 1985—; tchr. spiritual gifts North Way Christian Community, Wexford, Pa., 1987—; leader Women's Home Group North Way Christian Community, Wexford, 1990—; pastor, founder Living Water Ministries, Burgettstown, Pa., 1991—; adv. bd. Vineyard Christian Fellowship, Burgettstown, 1984-87; leader Women's Home Group Destiny Christian Fellowship, Coraopolis, Pa., 1991—. Editor: Citizen's Prints Newspaper, Burgettstown, 1969. Auditor Hanover Twp. Mcpl. Bd., Burgettstown, 1972. Mem. Women's Aglow Fellowship (pub. rels. 1983-84, corr. sec. 1984-85, v.p. 1985-87). Home: RD 1 Box 81-E Burgettstown PA 15021 Office: Living Water Ministries RD 1 Box 81-F Burgettstown PA 15021

MORRELL, ROBERT ELLIS, language educator; b. Johnstown, Pa., Jan. 19, 1930; s. Ellis Hiram and Helen Barbara (Rohrig) M.; m. Sachiko Kaneko, Nov. 7, 1954; 1 child, Audrey. BS in Music, Duquesne U., Pitts., 1952; MA in Philosophy, U. Chgo., 1959; PhD in Japanese Lang. and Lit., Stanford U., 1969. Prof. dept. Asian and Near Eastern langs. and lit.

Washington U., St. Louis, 1965—. Author: Sand and Pebbles (Shasekishu), 1985, Early Kamakura Buddhism: A Minority Report, 1987; co-author: The Princeton Companion to Classical Japanese Literature, 1985; contbr. articles to profl. jours. Mem. Winston-Salem Bd. Aldermen, 1981-89. Lt. (j.g.) USN, 1952-55. Recipient Fulbright-Hays faculty rsch. award, Kyoto, Japan, 1971; Nat. Def. Fgn. Lang. fellow, Stanford U., 1959-64. Mem Assn. Asian Studies, Internat. Assn. Buddhist Studies. Democrat. Home: 7637 Carswold Dr Clayton MO 63105 Office: Washington U Dept Asian and Nr Ea Langs and Lit Saint Louis MO 63130

MORRETTE, THOMAS JOHN, deacon; b. Schenectady, N.Y., May 29, 1950; s. Anthony Francis and Susan (De Angelis) M. BA magna cum laude, Siena Coll., 1972; MDiv, St. Joseph's Sem., Yonkers, N.Y., 1975; MS in Counseling and Psychology, SUNY, Albany, 1985, postgrad., 1991—. Ordained deacon Roman Cath. Ch., 1988; cert. tchr., N.Y. Dir. religious edn. Sts. John and Mary's Ch., Chappagua, N.Y., 1979—; coord. Permanent Diaconate Formation Program-Archdiocese of N.Y. St. Joseph's Sem., 1988—. Mem. Psychol. Assn. Northeastern N.Y., Assn. of Mary Immaculate (past pres. male br. Palm Coast, Fla.). Home: 11 N Jay St Schenectady NY 12305 Office: Sts John & Mary's Ch 30 Poillon Dr Chappaqua NY 10514 *Ours is a God of mercy...mercy unto mercy unto mercy.*

MORRILL, MICHAEL DEAN, religious organization administrator; b. Boston, Feb. 23, 1955; s. Robert Benjamin and Dorothy Jean (Farley) M.; m. Elizabeth Meta Dean, Aug. 6, 1977; children: Danielle, Matthew. AA, BA, Thomas Edison State U., 1990; MDiv, Southern Bapt. Theol. Sem., 1990. Ordained to ministry Am. Bapt. Chs. in USA, 1985. Youth dir. Centre United Meth. Ch., Malden, Mass., 1978-80; pastor Enon Bapt. Ch., Salem, Ind., 1985-86, 1st Bapt. Ch., Crothersville, Ind., 1987-90; exec. dir. Christian Chs. United, Harrisburg, Pa., 1990—; co-chair Christian-Jewish Dialogue, Harrisburg, 1991; mem. steering com. Interreligious Forum Greater Harrisburg, 1990—. Author play: The Bridge, 1989 (award Nat. Religious Playwriting Contest). Sec. People Organized and Working to Eliminate Racism, Harrisburg, 1990—. Recipient Middle East award Patillo Found., 1988, Jefferson Cup, Jefferson County, 1988; named Ky. Col., Commonwealth of Ky., 1988; Michael Morrill Appreciation Day in his honor, Gov. of R.I., 1985; Endowment for Biblican Rsch., Am. Schs. for Oriental Rsch., 1989. Mem. Nat. Assn. Evangelicals, Am. Schs. Oriental Rsch., Am. Bapt. Ministers Coun. Home: 2542 N 2d St Harrisburg PA 17110 Office: Christian Chs United 900 S Arlington Ave #128 Harrisburg PA 17109

MORRIS, CHARLES DENNISON, minister; b. Wallkill, N.Y., Oct. 11, 1948; s. Joseph Wilson and Lois (Morehouse) M.; m. Deborah Den Ouden, June 20, 1970; children: Jamie Caryn, Rachel Jo. BA in History, Central Coll., 1970; MDiv, New Brunswick Theol. Sem., 1973, Western Theol. Sem., 1973. Ordained to ministry Reformed Ch. Minister Brookdale Reformed Ch., Bloomfield, N.J., 1974-77; assoc. minister Reformed Ch., Colts Neck, N.J., 1977-85, sr. minister, 1985—; mem. bd. theol. edn. Reformed Ch. in Am., 1986—; mem. exec. com. New Brunswick Theol Sem., 1986—; chair (clergy) Putting People in Mission, Particular Synod of Mid-Atlantics, 1988-89. Capt. Fire Co. Number 1, Colts Neck, 1990-91; mem. Community Sch. Alliance, Colts Neck, 1989—. Office: Colts Neck Reformed Ch Rte 537W Box 57 Colts Neck NJ 07722

MORRIS, DEWITT TALMAGE, clergyman; b. Memphis, Mar. 27, 1962; s. DeWitt Talmage Morris and Diana (Barber) O'Neil; m. Rachel Smith, July 30, 1988. BS, Crichton Coll, Memphis, 1988. Ordained to ministry Assemblies of God Ch., 1987. Mem. Teen Challenge, Cape Giradeu, Mo., 1980-84; gym dir. Park Commn., Memphis, 1985-86; children's pastor Raleigh Assemblies of God, Memphis, 1984-85, gym dir., 1984-88; psychiat. technician Park Gen. Hosp., Springfield, Mo., 1988—; counselor Mid-Am. Teen Challenge, Cape Girardeau, 1989—. Mem. CAP, Memphis, 1979. Mem. MAC Computers. Republican. Avocations: photography, computers, lifting weights. Home: 350B N Clifton Springfield MO 65802 Office: Mid Am Teen Challenge Rte 1 PO Box 1089 Cape Girardeau MO 03701

MORRIS, FRED, minister; b. Sartinville, Miss., Oct. 24, 1934; s. Haley Edgar and Ruby (Boyd) M.; m. E. Marilyn Hill, Dec. 21, 1957; children: Fred Jr., Kerry D., Kenneth W., Sandra M. Diploma Leadership/Mgmt./Security Schs., USAF, Little Rock, 1957. Ordained to ministry Bapt. Ch., 1970. Minister New Hope Bapt. Ch., Meadville, Miss., 1970-73, Wellman Bapt. Ch., Brookhaven, Miss., 1973-78, Cloverdale Bapt. Ch., Natchez, Miss., 1978-80, Wanilla Bapt. Ch., Monticello, Miss., 1980-83, Lone Star Bapt. Ch., Collins, Miss., 1983-87, Ramah Bapt. Ch., McCall Creek, Miss., 1987—. Sgt. USAF, 1954-59, Alaska, Japan. Home and Office: Rte 2 PO Box 217 McCall Creek MS 39647

MORRIS, HENRY MADISON, JR., educator, college president; b. Dallas, Oct. 6, 1918; s. Henry Madison and Ida (Hunter) M.; m. Mary Louise Beach, Jan. 24, 1940; children: Henry Madison III, Kathleen Louise, John David, Andrew Hunter, Mary Ruth, Rebecca Jean. BS with distinction, Rice Inst., 1939; MS, U. Minn., 1948, PhD, 1950; LLD, Bob Jones U., 1966; LittD, Liberty U., 1989. Registered engr., Tex. Jr. engr. Tex. Hwy. Dept., 1938-39; from jr. engr. to asst. engr. Internat. Boundary Commn., El Paso, 1939-42; instr. civil engring. Rice Inst., 1942-46; from instr. to asst. prof. U. Minn., Mpls., also research project leader St. Anthony Falls Hydraulics Lab., 1946-51; prof., head dept. civil engring. Southwestern La. Inst., Lafayette, 1951-57, Va. Poly. Inst., Blacksburg, 1957-70; v.p. acad. affairs Christian Heritage Coll., San Diego, 1970-78, pres., 1978-80; dir. Inst. for Creation Research, 1970-80, pres., 1980—. Author: (with Richard Stephens) Report on Rio Grande Water Conservation Investigation, 1942, That You Might Believe, 1946, 2d edit., 1978, (with Curtis Larson) Hydraulics of Flow in Culverts, 1948, The Bible and Modern Science, 1951, rev. edit., 1968, (with John C. Whitcomb) The Genesis Flood, 1961, Applied Hydraulics in Engineering, 1963, The Twilight of Evolution, 1964, Science, Scripture and Salvation, 1965, 2d edit., 1971, Studies in the Bible and Science, 1966, Evolution and the Modern Christian, 1967, Biblical Cosmology and Modern Science, 1970, The Bible has the Answer, 1971, Science and Creation: A Handbook for Teachers, 1971, (with J.M. Wiggert) Applied Hydraulics, 1972, A Biblical Manual on Science and Creation, 1972, The Remarkable Birth of Planet Earth, 1973, Many Infallible Proofs, 1974, Scientific Creationism, 1974, 2d edit., 1985, Troubled Waters of Evolution, 1975, The Genesis Record, 1976, Education for the Real World, 1977, 3d edit., 1991, The Scientific Case for Creation, 1977, The Beginning of the World, 1977, 2d edit., 1991, Sampling the Psalms, 1978, 2d edit., 1991, King of Creation, 1980, Men of Science, Men of God, 1982, Evolution in Turmoil, 1982, The Revelation Record, 1983, History of Modern Creationism, 1984, The Biblical Basis for Modern Science, 1984, Creation and the Modern Christian, 1985, Science and The Bible, 1986, Days of Praise, 1986, The God Who is Real, 1988, The Remarkable Record of Job, 1988; (with Martin Clark) The Bible Has The Answer, 2d edit., 1987; (with Gary E. Parker) What is Creation Science, 1982, 2d edit., 1988, The Long War Against God, 1989, (with John D. Morris) Science, Scripture and the Young Earth, 1989; Creation and the Second Coming, 1991; research bulls., tech. articles, reports and booklets. Fellow AAAS, ASCE, Am. Sci. Affiliation; mem. Am. Soc. Engring. Edn. (sec.-editor civil engring. div. 1967-70), Trans-Nat. Assn. Christian Schs. (pres. 1983—), Creation Research Soc. (pres. 1967-73), Am. Geophys. Union, Geol. Soc. Am., Am. Assn. Petroleum Geologists, Geochem. Soc., Gideons (pres. La. 1954-56), Phi Beta Kappa, Sigma Xi, Chi Epsilon, Tau Beta Pi. Baptist. Home: 6733 El Banquero San Diego CA 92116 *The Bible is the inerrant word of God and thus should be believed and obeyed in all things.*

MORRIS, HUNTER MASON, minister; b. San Angelo, Tex., Apr. 23, 1933; s. Gilbert Marvin and Doris Elizabeth (Mason) Morris; m. Janet Louise Pettis, June 12, 1959; children: Wade, Lee. BA, U. Tex., 1955; postgrad., Episcopal Theol. Sem., Austin, Tex., 1960. Ordained to ministry Episcopal Ch., 1960. Rector All Sts. Ch., Crockett, Tex., 1960-64; exec. dir. St. Vincent's House, Galveston, Tex., 1964-68, Episcopal Pastoral Ctr., Houston; assoc. rector St. John the Divine, Houston, 1964-68; exec. dir. Houston Met. Ministries, 1968-71, Episc. Mission Soc. N.Y., N.Y.C., 1971-72; exec. officer Diocese of Ariz., Phoenix, 1972-77; rector Emmanuel Episcopal Ch., Lockhart, Tex., 1977-84; diocesan missioner Diocese of West Tex., Holy Spirit Ch., Dripping Springs, 1984—; chief exec. officer H.J.M. Properties, Austin, 1981—; treas. Episcopal Urban Caucus, Boston, 1983—; pres. Conf. Jubilee Officers, N.Y.C., 1988—; grants chmn. Jubilee Ministry, N.Y.C., 1988—. Mem. Coalition for Human Needs, N.Y.C., 1989—; pres. Austin Regional Matrix against Drug Abuse, 1984—; v.p. Capitol Area coun. Boy Scouts Am., 1980-85; regional dir. NCCJ, Austin, 1986-88; chmn. Austin-Travis County Jail Coordinating Com., 1989—; mem. City of Austin Mayor's Liason-Police Dept., Fire Dept. Social Svcs., 1991—. Capt. USMC, 1955-57; chaplain USNR, 1964—. Home: 8707 Crystal Creek Cir Austin TX 78746 Office: Holy Spirit Episcopal Ch Box 521 Dripping Springs TX 78620

MORRIS, JERALD VINSON, minister; b. Cotter, Ark., July 31, 1931; s. James Hubert and Esther Marie (Thrasher) M.; m. Estel Myree Glover, Jan. 10, 1953; children: Jerald Vinson Jr., Denise Myree. Student, So. Calif. Bible Coll., 1959-60, 61-62, Orange Coast Coll., 1960-61; BTh, Internat. Bible Inst. and Sem., 1983, ThM, 1984. Ordained to ministry Assemblies of God, 1969. Pastor Assemblies of God, McDermitt and Yerington, 1963-67; pastor Assembly of God, MacDoel, Calif., 1967-69, Buena Vista, Colo., 1969-73, Bisbee, Ariz., 1973-77, Tolleson, Ariz., 1977-81; pastor North Loma Linda Assembly of God, San Bernardino, Calif., 1982-85; evangelist Assemblies of God, 1985-86; pastor River Chapel Assembly of God, Riviera, Ariz., 1986—; active ministerial alliance various communities, 1963—; dir. Colo. River Christian Ministerial, 1986-89. Chmn. Are You Interested Drug Prevention Program, Buena Vista, 1970-73; v.p. Ariz. State Teen Challenge Bd. Dirs., Phoenix, 1977-81; vice chmn. Bullhead Against Drugs, Bullhead City, Ariz., 1987-90. With U.S. Army, 1948-52. Mem. Alliance (treas. 1989-90), Ariz. Dist. Coun. Assemblies of God (dist. presbyter 1988—). Republican. Home: 899 San Juan Dr Bullhead City AZ 86442 Office: River Chapel Assembly of God 805 Marina Blvd Riviera AZ 86442

MORRIS, JOHN BURNETT, clergyman; b. Brunswick, Ga., Feb. 10, 1930; s. Hervey Clark and Anne (Burnett) M.; m. Harriet Barnes Pratt, Aug. 25, 1952; children—Anne, Christopher, John Burnett, Ellen. B.A., Columbia U., 1951; B.D., Va. Theol. Sem., 1954. Ordained priest, Episcopal Ch., 1955. Vicar St. Barnabas' Ch., Dillon, S.C., 1954-58; founder, exec. dir. Episcopal Soc. for Cultural and Racial Unity, Atlanta, 1958-67; spl. asst. So. Regional Council, Atlanta, 1968-71, U.S. Office for Civil Rights, 1971-80; proprietor Julian Burnett, Books, Atlanta, 1980—. Del. Democratic Nat. Conv., 1968. Recipient Bishop Lichtenberger Human Rights award Episcopal Diocese of Chgo., 1968. Editor: South Carolinians Speak, 1957; contbr. articles to periodicals. Address: 4655 Jett Rd NW Atlanta GA 30327

MORRIS, JOSEPH ANTHONY, priest; b. Phila., June 3, 1953; s. Joseph Albert and Lois (Riley) M. BA, Niagara U., 1976; MDiv, Mary Immaculate Sem., 1979; postgrad., Grad. Theol. Union, Berkeley, Calif. Dir./tchr. St. Joseph's High Sch. Sem., Princeton, N.J., 1980-82; dir. Vincentian House Coll. Sem., Ozone Park, N.Y., 1987-89; prof. Christ the King Sem., East Aurora, N.Y., 1990—; campus minister Dominican Coll., San Rafael, Calif., 1983-85. Mem. Soc. Bibl. Lit., Am. Acad. Religion, Soc. New Testament Study, Westar Inst. Cath. Bibl. Assn. Home and Office: 711 Knox Rd East Aurora NY 14052-0607

MORRIS, MARY LOU A., religious organization administrator; b. Dayton, Ohio, May 15, 1941; d. O. Franklin and Frances Louise (Miller) Rosenberger; m. James Robert Morris, Apr. 9, 1965; children: Joe, Lisa, Angie. BS in Acctg., U. Dayton, 1963; MBA, Tex. Tech U., 1967. Fin. adminstr. 1st United Meth. Ch., Lubbock, Tex., 1979—. Mem. Nat. Assn. Ch. Bus. Adminstrs. (cert., v.p. elect). Office: 1st United Meth Ch 1411 Broadway Lubbock TX 79401-3207

MORRIS, MICHAEL THOMAS, priest, theology educator; b. Santa Monica, Calif., Oct. 19, 1949; s. Charles Martin and Elizabeth Ann (Kuykendall) M. BFA, U. So. Calif., L.A., 1971; MDiv, St. Albert's Coll., 1978; MA in Art History, U. Calif., Berkeley, 1979, PhD in Art History, 1986. Ordained priest Roman Cath. Ch., 1977. Prof. theology and arts Dominican Sch., Grad. Theol. Union, Berkeley, 1983—; lectr. art history St. Mary's Coll. of Calif., Moraga, 1988-90. Contbr. articles to profl. jours. Trustee Dominican Sch., Grad. Theol. Union, Berkeley, 1985-89. Robert Fowler scholar U. So. Calif., L.A., 1967-71; Jacques Maritain Soc. fellow Jacques Maritain Soc., 1981-82; recipient Young Scholars award Associated Theol. Scsh. of the U.S. and Can., 1990-91. Fellow Soc. for Art, Religion & Contemporary Culture; mem. Am. Acad. Religion, Coll. Art Assn. Republican. Home: PO Box 5185 Moraga CA 94575 Office: Dominican Sch Philosophy and Theology 2401 Ridge Rd Berkeley CA 94709

MORRIS, BROTHER PATRICK NICHOLAS, religious order superior; b. N.Y.C., July 22, 1939; s. Nicholas Joseph and Beatrice (Murphy) M. BS, Iona Coll., 1961; MA, U. Detroit, 1968. Joined Congregation Christian Bros., Roman Cath. Ch., 1965. Dir. religious edn. Our Lady Mt. Carmel Parish, Tenafly, N.J., 1969-71; tchr. religion Brother Rice High Sch., Birmingham, Mich., 1971-74; tchr., religious superior Leo High Sch., Chgo., 1974-80; tchr. Damien Meml. High Sch., Honolulu, 1980-81; provincial superior Congregation Christian Bros., Chgo., 1981—; pres. Brother Rice High Sch. Corp., St. Laurence High Sch. Corp., Chgo., 1984—, Christian Bros. Inst. Mich. Corp., Birmingham, 1984—, Christian Bros. Inst. Calif. Corp., Salinas, 1984—, Congregation Christian Bros. Hawaii Corp., Honolulu, 1984—. Recipient La Salle award Lewis U., 1987. Mem. Conf. Maj. Superiors Men, Nat. Assembly Religious Bros. (liaison 1987—), Cath. Conf. Ill. (adv. bd. dirs. 1987—). Address: Congregation Christian Bros Brother Rice Provincialate 9237 S Avalon Chicago IL 60619

MORRIS, PATRICK WAYNE, minister; b. Harrisonburg, Va., Aug. 16, 1955; s. Elzie Jarrels and Carrie May (Raines) M.; m. Sharon Ann Souder, Dec. 21, 1975; children: Jessica Leigh, Patrick Wayne Jr. Cert. bibl. studies, Ea. Mennonite Sem., 1987; B of Gen. Studies, James Madison U., 1990; postgrad., Lancaster Theol. Sem., 1990—. youth leader St. Paul's Youth Group, Amityville, 1990—. Lay leader Friedens United Ch. of Christ, Mt. Crawford, Va., 1975-87; pastor Mt. Olivet United Ch. of Christ, Dyke, Va., 1987-90; student pastor St. Paul's United Ch. of Christ, Ammityville, Pa., 1990—. Screening coord. Mercy House, Harrisonburg, 1988-90. Mem. Young Farmers (v.p. 1976-77).

MORRIS, ROBERT RENLY, minister, clinical pastoral education supervisor; b. Jacksonville, Fla., Feb. 15, 1938; s. Joseph Renly and Sybil (Stephens) M.; m. Lenda Smith, Dec. 7, 1963; children: Christopher Renly, Jennifer Kelly. BA, U. Fla., 1959; MDiv, Columbia Theol. Sem., Atlanta, 1962, ThM, 1967, D Ministry, 1990. Ordained to ministry Presbyn. Ch. (U.S.A.), 1962. Min. to students Ga. State Coll., Atlanta, 1959-60; asst. min. Trinity Presbyn. Ch., Atlanta, 1960-62; min. Clanton (Ala.) Presbyn. Ch., 1963-65, Kelly Presbyn. Ch., McDonough, Ga., 1965-67; pastoral counselor Ga. Assn. for Pastoral Care, Atlanta, 1966-68; coord. pastoral svcs. Winter Haven (Fla.) Hosp. and Community Health Ctr., 1969-79; min. Presbytery of Greater Atlanta, mem. div. pastoral care, 1984-86; dir. clin. pastoral edn. Emory U. Affiliated Hosps., Atlanta, 1979—. Contbr. book chpts., articles to profl. jours. Mem. steering com. for instl. ministry Martin Luther King Ctr. for Nonviolent Social Change, AIDS Task Force, Atlanta, 1988—, Task Force on Chem. Dependency, 1988. Mem. Am. Assn. Pastoral Counselors, Coll. Chaplains, Am. Assn. Marriage and Family Counselors (clin.), Assn. for Clin. Pastoral Edn. (cert. supr., gen. assembly nominating com. 1984, chmn. 1985, coord. ann. conf. 1986, long range planning com. of C com., standards com. S.E. region 1990—), Beta Theta Pi. Democrat. Avocations: antique collecting, canoeing, fishing, sailing. Home: 542 Cross Creek Point Stone Mountain GA 30087 Office: Emory U Hosp Dept Pastoral Svcs 1364 Clifton Rd NE Atlanta GA 30322

MORRIS, WILLIAM COLLINS, minister; b. Cleve., Apr. 27, 1936; s. William Collins and Mary Janet (Traill) M.; m. Sarah Payton Weaver, June 18, 1963; children: John David, Patrick Gabriel. BA, Duke U., 1958; MDiv, Episcopal Theol. Sem. S.W., 1961. Ordained priest Episcopal Ch., 1961. Vicar St. Albans Ch., Davidson, N.C., 1961-66; priest of the staff St. Peter's Ch., Oxford, Miss., 1966-68; assoc. chaplian St. Albans Ch., Baton Rouge, 1968-71; rector All Saints Ch., River Ridge, La., 1971—; chmn. Dept. Communications, Diocese of La., New Orleans, 1978—; dep. to gen. conv. Diocese of La., 1976-82, 85-88, 91. Contbr. articles to profl. jours. Pres. Family Svc. of Greater New Orleans, 1991. Mem. La. Episcopal Clergy Assn. (bd. dirs., editor), Rotary. Democrat. Office: All Saints Ch 100 Rex Dr River Ridge LA 70123

MORRISON, BARTON DOUGLAS, minister; b. Westminster, Calif., Dec. 3, 1965; s. Willis Carrol and Elva Adelee (Cashman) M.; m. Becky Lynn Goodin, June 3, 1988. B in Music Edn., Okla. Bapt. U., 1988; MusM, Southwestern Bapt. Theol. Sem., 1991. Cert. gen. and vocal music tchr., Okla. Organist, asst. Birchman Bapt. Ch., Ft. Worth, 1988-90, min. music, 1990—; ch. accompanist Trinity Bapt. Ch., Westminster, 1979-83, Southwestern Bapt. Theol. Sem., Ft. Worth, 1988-91; vocalist, pianist Continental Singers, Thousand Oaks, Calif., 1982-83; chapel pianist Okla. Bapt. U., Shawnee, 1983-88; music asst. 1st So. Bapt. Ch., Del City, 1984-85; organist, asst. Univ. Bapt. Ch., Shawnee, 1985-88; organist, pianist Falls Creek Bapt. Assembly, Davis, Okla., 1985-86, 88-89. Mem. Music Educators Nat. Conf., Am. Choral Dirs. Assn. (student adv. com. 1990-92), Phi Mu Alpha Sinfonia (sec. 1985-88), Zeta Pi Lambda (svc. com. 1985-88). Avocations: reading, golf. Office: Birchman Bapt Ch 9100 N Normandale Fort Worth TX 76116

MORRISON, GLENN LESLIE, minister; b. Cortez, Colo., Feb. 26, 1929; s. Ward Carl Morrison and Alma Irene (Butler) Anderson; m. Beverely Joanne Buck, Aug. 26, 1949; children: David Mark, Betty Jo Morrison Mullen, Gary Alan, Judith Lynn Morrison Oltmann, Stephen Scott. Student, San Diego State U., 1948-49, Chabot Coll., 1968-69. Ordained to ministry Evang. Ch. Alliance, 1961. Dir. counseling and follow-up Oakland (Calif.) Youth for Christ, 1954-56; pres. Follow Up Ministries, Inc., Castro Valley, Calif., 1956—; assoc. pastor 1st Covenant Ch., Oakland, 1956-58; exec. dir. East Bay Youth for Christ, Oakland, 1960-66; supervising chaplain Alameda County (Calif.) Probation Dept., 1971-90; vol. chaplain Alameda County Sheriff's Dept., 1971—; seminar leader Calif. Dept. Corrections, Sacramento, 1978—, mem. chaplains coordinating com., 1988—; founder, dir. God Squad Vol. Program for Prison Workers, 1972—. Author: Scripture Investigation Course, 1956. Mem. Am. Correctional Assn., Am. Protestant Correctional Chaplains Assn. (regional pres., sec. 1980-86, nat. sec. 1986-88). Office: Follow Up Ministries Inc PO Box 2514 Castro Valley CA 94546

MORRISON, HOWARD B., rabbi; b. Boston, May 9, 1960; s. Ruben and Helen F. (Scott) M.; m. Joanna Sasson, Nov. 4, 1990. BSBA, Boston U., 1982; cert., Jewish Theol. Sem., 1987. Ordained rabbi, 1987. Rabbi Congregation Beth Shalam, Union, N.J., 1987—; tchr. Solomon Schecter Day Sch., Cranford, N.J., 1987—. MemUnion Community Rels. Com., 1989—. Lt., chaplain USAF, 1987—. Mem. Rabbinical Assembly, Union County Bd. Rabbis, Union Glergy Assn., Union for Traditional Judaism, N.Y. Bd. Rabbis. Home: 2027 Vauxhall Rd Union NJ 07083

MORRISON, HOWARD CLARK, minister; b. Phoenix, Mar. 15, 1958; s. Marvin Richard and June (Neely) M.; m. Jana Frederick, June 2, 1984. BS in Agr. Bus., U. Ariz., 1981; ThM in Christian Edn., Dallas Theol. Sem., 1985. Ordained to ministry Ind. Bible Ch., 1985. Missions adminstr. Northwest Bible Ch., Dallas, 1983-85; singles pastor Grace Covenant Ch., Austin, Tex., 1985-87; pastor of adult ministries Grace Covenant Ch., Austin, 1987—. Mem. Young Men's Bus. League, Austin C. of C. Republican. Club: Toastmasters (Austin) (ednl. v.p. 1987). Avocations: basketball, choir, guitar.

MORRISON, JOHN ALAN, lay worker; b. Houston, Mar. 23, 1955; s. Ray Alan Morrison and Anita Jeraldyn (Houchin) May; m. Cynthia Lynn Blundell, May 14, 1978; 1 child, Paul Alan. Grad. high sch., Carrollton, Tex., 1973. owner Cornerstone Glassworks, Dallas, 1988—; mem. Creator's Craftsmen, Dallas, 1990—. Pres. Dallas Soc. Glass Artists, 1991, sec., 1990. Recipient Milkewon award. Office: Cornerstone Glassworks 2530 Joe Field Rd 11 Dallas TX 75229

MORRISON, JOHN EMERSON, III, English educator, minister; b. N.Y.C., Sept. 21, 1941; s. John Emerson Jr. and Constance Ruth (Holland) M.; m. Mary Susan Gray, June 5, 1965; children: John Emerson IV, Heather Jean. BA, Dartmouth Coll., 1963; M Sci. Edn., Hofstra U., 1968; MA in Liberal Studies, SUNY, Stony Brook, 1973. Cert. seconday sch. tchr., N.Y.; ordained to ministry Episcopal Ch. Tchr. English Bay Shore (N.Y.) High Sch., 1963—; asst. pastor Grace Episcopal Ch., Massapequa, N.Y., 1980—; instr. theology George Mercer Sch. Theology, Garden City, N.Y., 1982—; asst. spiritual dir., L.I. Cursillo, Garden City, 1982-86, 1988—. Contbr. articles to profl. jours. Bd. mgrs. Camp De Wolfe, Wading River, N.Y., 1983-85. C.S. Lewis summer sch. grantee Wales, 1984; C.S. Lewis Inst.: The Christian and the Contemporary U. grantee, Union Free Sch. Dist. Diocese L.I., St. Hilda's Coll., U. Oxford, Eng., 1988. Mem. Mythopoeic Soc., N.Y. C.S. Lewis Soc. (bd. dirs. 1982-84, 86-88). Republican. Home: 510 Manatuck Blvd Brightwaters NY 11718 Office: Bay Shore High Sch 155 Third Ave Bay Shore NY 11706

MORRISON, LARRY ELLIS, minister; b. Tuscaloosa, Ala., Apr. 26, 1955; s. Luther Ellis and Mattie Lou (Weeks) M.; m. Sallie Grace Beverage, Sept. 3, 1977; children: Lindsay Brooke, Katie Elizabeth. BA in Communication, U. Ala., Tuscaloosa, 1977; MRE, Southwestern Bapt. Theol. Sem., 1980. Lic. to ministry So. Bapt. Conv., 1982, ordained 1988. Minister of edn./youth 2d Bapt. Ch., West Helena, Ark., 1980-82, Calvary Bapt. Ch., West Memphis, Ark., 1982-84, Normandale Bapt. Ch., Montgomery, Ala., 1984-88; minister of edn. and bus. adminstrn. Five Points Bapt. Ch., Northport, Ala., 1988—; dir. Bapt. Student Union, Phillips County Community Coll., Helena, 1980-82; assoc. dir. Vacation Bible Sch., Montgomery Bapt. Assn., 1987. Mem. nominating com. Huntington Pl. Elem. Sch. PTA, Northport, Ala., 1991, 1st v.p., 1991-92. Circlewood Bapt. Found. religious edn. scholar, 1977-80. Mem. Tuscaloosa County Bapt. Assn. (asst. team dir. 1988-89, dir. teaching improvement 1990-91). Home: 124 Huntington Pl Northport AL 35476 Office: Five Points Bapt Ch 3718 36th St Northport AL 35476 *"...the greatest of these is love." (I Cor. 13:13) I have discovered life at it's best as I allow God's love to permeate my life. Love for God, my Family, and Friends make life great! Therefore, I am committed to sharing God's love.*

MORRISON, LLOYD RICHARD, minister; b. Oil City, Pa., Feb. 8, 1959; s. Richard Harold and Donna Marie (Schwab) M.; m. Susan Elaine Hall, May 30, 1981; children: Jeremy, Timothy, Kristy, Amy. BS, Houghton Coll., 1981; MDiv, Gordon-Cornwell Theol. Sem., 1986. Ordained to ministry Christian and Missionary Alliance, 1988. Pastor Trinity Alliance Ch., Fairfax, Va., 1986-91, 1st Alliance Ch., Hockessin, Del., 1991—; sec. Mid-Atlantic Dist., Rockville, Md., 1990—. Home: 8 Fieldstone Cir Hockessin DE 19707

MORRISON, LORENA ANN, Christian school administrator; b. Palatka, Fla., Oct. 28, 1943; d. John Chandler Presser and Clyde Samathia (Hicks) Weatherholtz; m. Junius Davis Morrison, June 15, 1968; children: Anna Elizabeth, Nathan Robert. BA, Miami Christian Coll., 1966, Southeastern Bible Coll., 1971; MA, U. Ala., 1973; EdS, Fla. Atlantic U., 1986, DEd, 1989. Cert. tchr., Fla. Mem. Phi Kappa Phi, Delta Epsilon Chi. Home: 2655 Collins Ave # 1011 Miami Beach FL 33140 Office: Miami Christian Sch 200 NW 109th Ave Miami FL 33172

MORRISON, RICHARD NEELY, lay worker; b. Mesa, Ariz., June 4, 1947; s. Marvin R. and June (Neely) R.; m. Elaine Grangaard, Dec. 8, 1973; children: Julie Catherine, Ellen Christine. BS, No. Ariz. U., 1970; JD, U. Houston, 1977; MAV, San Francisco Theol. Seminary, 1991. Bar: Ariz. 1978, U.S. Ct. Appeals (9th cir.) 1983, U.S. Supreme Ct., 1983. Trustee Sch. of Theology, Claremont, Calif., 1986—, v.p., 1989-90, vice-chmn. exec. com., 1989—; counsel Ryley, Carlock and Applewhite, Phoenix, 1990—; lay observor Bd. Ordained Ministry, Desert Southwest Conf., United Meth. Ch., Phoenix, 1987—; local preacher The Meth. Ch., Gilbert, Ariz., 1969-71; chmn. Religious Studies Assocs., Ariz. State U., 1988-89. Bd. dirs. Ariz. Partnership for Air Transp., Phoenix; advisor Morrison Inst. for Pub. Policy, Ariz. State U., Tempe; pres. Ariz. Rep. Caucus, 1984-85. Lt. USN, 1970-76. Recipient Disting. Achievement award Ariz. State U., 1989. Fellow Ariz. Bar Found.; mem. Maricopa County Bar Assn., Native Am. Rights Fund, F&AM, Rotary. Home: 12920 E Elliot Gilbert AZ 85234 Office: Ryley Carlock & Applewhite 101 N 1st Ave #2600 Phoenix AZ 85003-1973

MORRISON, STEVEN EUGENE, minister; b. Portland, Oreg., May 2, 1947; s. Robert E. and Helen L. (Masxcy) M.; m. Susan E. Zinck, Aug. 24,

1969; children: Ben, Daisy, Danielle, Robert. BA, Pacific Luth. U., 1969; MDiv, Luth. Sch. Theology, 1972; M Ministry, Fuller Theol. Sem., 1978. Ordained to ministry Luth. Ch. in Am., 1972. Pastor Christ Luth. Ch., Yakima, Wash., 1972-76; mission developer Family of God Luth. Ch., Bremerton, Wash., 1976-77, lead pastor, 1977-88; asst. to bishop S.W. Synod Evang. Luth. Ch. Am., Tacoma, 1988—; chmn. Luth. Pub. Policy Bd., Wash., 1990—, Synod Fin. Com., Wash., 1986-8; chmn. evangelism com. Luth Ch. in Am., Wash., 1984-86; del. PLU Corp., Tacoma, 1988—; mem. chaplaincy bd. Harrison Hosp., Yakima, 1974-76. Author: (dramas) Home Altar, 1980, View from the Cross, 1985, Way to the Cross, 1986. Chmn. Phase 3 Key 73, Yakima, 1973. Mem. Alban Inst., Amnesty Internat.

MORRISON, SUSAN M., bishop; d. D. David and Katherine Morrison. Student, Drew U., Boston U. Ordained to ministry United Meth. Ch., 1974. Short-term missionary to Brazil; assoc. pastor Silver Spring, Md.; pastor Greenbelt, Md.; former mem. nat. jud. coun., dist. supt. Balt. conf. United Meth. Ch., 1980-86, dir. Balt. conf. coun., 1986—; bishop Eastern Pa. and P.R. confs. United Meth. Ch., Valley Forge, Pa., 1988—. Office: United Meth Ch PO Box 820 Valley Forge PA 19482

MORRISON, TIMOTHY ARTHUR, minister; b. Greenville, Pa., July 18, 1949; s. Emery Lee and Helen Myra (MacDonald) M.; m. Cathryn Marta Kohari, July 14, 1990; children from previous marriage: Joel Emery, Sean Charles. BA with honors, Lehigh U., 1971; MDiv, United Theol. Sem. Twin Cities, 1974; D Ministry, Andover-Newton Theol. Sch., 1980. Ordained to ministry United Ch. of Christ, 1974. Assoc. pastor for Christian edn. and youth ministry United Ch. of Christ, Bethlehem, Pa., 1974-75, High St. United Ch. of Christ, Auburn, Maine, 1975-78; missionary United Ch. of Christ Bd. for World Ministries, specialist in Christian edn., prin. Evang. Presbyn. Ch. Sem., Peki, Ghana, 1978-81; organizing pastor United Ch. Fox Valley, Aurora, Ill., 1981-84; pastor Suffield (Ohio) United Ch. of Christ, 1984-90; interim assoc. pastor 1st Congl. United Ch. of Christ, Hudson, Ohio, 1991; pastor Pilgrimage U. Ch. of Christ, Marietta, Ga., 1991—; leader clown workshops for United Ch. of Christ. Contbr. articles to profl. jours. Vice chmn. Auburn Housing Authority, 1977-78; v.p. Western Regional Coun. on Alcohol Abuse and Alcoholism, Lewiston, Maine, 1976-78; mem. Aurora Revenue Sharing Com., 1982. Mem. Masons, Rotary (charter mem. local chpt.). Democrat. Home: 5083 Ravenwood Dr NE Marietta GA 30066 *I am continually amazed at our world's constant pursuit of the essence and intention of love. We need to know. We want to know. It seems to me St. Paul described love ultimately, completely when he wrote: "Love is patient and kind, not jealous or boastful, not arrogant or rude. Love does not insist on its own way. Love bears all things, believes all things, hopes all things, endures all things."*

MORROW, DANNY RAY, religious organization administrator; b. Cullman, Ala., Dec. 9, 1957; s. Harvey C. and Barbara Ann (Walker) M.; m. Paula Dale Hendrix, May 26, 1978; children: Zachary Daniel, Bethany Delano. Student, U. No. Ala., 1976-77, So. Benedict Coll., 1977-79, Birmingham South, 1979-80. Exec. dir. Shepherds Way Ministries, Cullman, Ala., 1987—; exec. adminstr. ABC Pregnancy Ctr., Cullman, 1987—; sales mgr. Harvey's Motors, Cullman, 1983—; media coord. Ala. Pro-Life Coalition, Montgomery, 1989—; cons. Area CPCs in Ala., North Ala., 1990—. Author: How to Start a CPC, 1990. Coord. Pro-Life Coalition, Cullman, 1989—. Recipient Citizenship award Cullman City Coun., 1989. Home: 1809 Northwest Ln Cullman AL 35055 Office: ABC Pregnancy Ctr PO Box 362 Cullman AL 35056

MORSE, TERRY WAYNE, clergyman; b. Grand Rapids, Mich., Aug. 6, 1946; s. Fred Myron and Elizabeth Ida (Cheney) M.; m. Martha Ellen Hale, Aug. 11, 1968; children: Charles Eric, Alyssa Marie. BA, Houghton Coll., 1968; MDiv, Union Theol. Sem., Richmond, Va., 1971, D Ministry, 1984. Ordained to ministry Presbyn. Ch. (U.S.A.), 1972. Student pastor Ellicottville (N.Y.) Community Ch., 1967-68; interim pastor El Portal (Calif.) Community Ch., 1971-72; pastor 1st Presbyn. Ch., English Town, N.J., 1972-83, Painted Post, N.Y., 1983—; chmn. com. on ministry Genneva Presbytery, 1989—, mem. mission coun., 1989—; commr. mission coun. Synod of N.E., 1989—, Glassboro, N.J., 1989—, commr. Synod, 1990, mem. nominating com., 1990-91; dir. Painted Post Ch. Facilities Corp., 1983—. Editor: (workbook) Custom Design Your Wedding, 1984. Chplain Vol. Fire Dept., English Town, 1980-83, Painted Post, 1985—; mem. chaplain adv. com. Corning (N.Y.) Hosp., 1987—. Recipient Community Svc. award Monmouth County Action Program, 1975. Home: 102 W Chemung St Painted Post NY 14870 Office: 1st Presbyn Ch 201 N Hamilton St Painted Post NY 14870

MORTON, CHARLES BRINKLEY, retired bishop, former state legislator; b. Meridian, Miss., Jan. 6, 1926; s. Albert Cole and Jean (Brinkley) M.; m. Virginia Roseborough, Aug. 26, 1948; children—Charles Brinkley, Mary Virginia. JD with distinction, U. Miss., 1949; MDiv optime merens, U. South, 1959, DD, 1982. Bar: Miss. 1949, Tenn.; ordained to ministry Protestant Episcopal Ch. as deacon and priest, 1959. Sole practice Senatobia, Miss., 1949-56; mem. Thomas & Morton, Senatobia, Miss., 1952-56, Miss. Ho. of Reps., 1948-52, Miss. Senate, 1952-56; priest-in-charge Ch. of Incarnation, West Point, Miss., 1959-62; rector Grace-St. Luke's Ch., Memphis, 1962-74; dean Cathedral of Advent, Birmingham, Ala., 1974-82; bishop Episcopal Diocese of San Diego, 1982-91; ret., 1992. Contbr. articles to law and hist. jours. Mem. Miss. Commn. Interstate Coop., 1952-56, Miss. State Hist. Commn., 1952-56; chmn. bd. Bishop's Sch., La Jolla, Calif., Episcopal Community Services, San Diego; trustee Berkeley Div. Sch., Yale U.; active numerous civic and cultural groups. Served with AUS, World War II, Korea; col., chaplain Res. ret. Decorated Silver Star, Bronze Star medal with cluster, Purple Heart, Combat Inf. Badge; recipient Freedoms Found. Honor medal, 1967, 68, 72. Mem. Mil. Order World Wars, Am. Legion (past post comdr.), Phi Delta Phi, Tau Kappa Alpha, Omicron Delta Kappa, Phi Delta Theta. Lodge: Rotary.

MORTON, DAVID, minister. Pres. ACCORD-Area Chs. Togethr Serving, Battle Creek, Mich. Office: ACCORD-Area Chs Together Serving 124 E Michigan Ave Battle Creek MI 49017*

MORTON, RUSSELL SCOTT, theological librarian; b. Portland, Oreg., Nov. 27, 1954; s. Eugene Randall and Kathryn Hazel (Myers) M. MA, U. Chgo., 1986; MDiv, Western Evang. Seminary, Portland, 1980; ThM, Luth. Sch. Theology, Chgo., 1983, ThD, 1985. Libr. tech. asst. Cath. Theol. Union, Chgo., 1980-85; cataloger Western Evang. Seminary, 1986-87, adj. prof., 1986-87; reference libr. Perkins Sch. Theology, Dallas, 1989-91, libr. cataloging/spl. collections, 1991—; adj. prof. Seattle Pacific U., 1988-89. Mem. Soc. Bibl. Lit., Cath. Bibl. Assn., Wesleyan Theol. Soc. Mem. Free Meth. Ch. Home: 5716 Caruth Haven # 224 Dallas TX 75206 Office: So Meth U Perkins Sch Theology Bridwell Libr Dallas TX 75275

MOSBY, RALPH JOSEPH, minister; b. Kansas City, Mo., Feb. 11, 1931; s. Ralph Mosby Sr. and Ruth (Robinson) Collier; m. Kathleen Theresa Johnson, May 29, 1971; children: Audwin Joaquin, Gregory Johnson. BA, Redlands U., 1962; MDiv, Am. Bapt. Sem., 1968; PhD, Calif. Grad. Sch. Theology, 1973. Ordained to ministry Bapt. Ch.; cert. adult edn. tchr. (life). Assoc. min. Trinity Bapt. Ch., L.A., 1965-71; sr. pastor Immanuel Bapt. Ch., L.A., 1971-73, St. John Bapt. Ch., Long Beach, Calif., 1974—; instr. Am. Bapt. Sem. of West, Covina, Calif., 1968-69, Angeles Bible Coll., Hawthorne, Calif., 1974-75, L.A. Trade Tech. Coll., 1974-80, Long Beach City Coll., 1974-90. Bd. dirs. Long Beach Area Citizenship Involved, 1975—, Cable Com. Adv. Commn., Long Beach, 1983—, African Am. Coordinating Coun., Long Beach, 1989—; pres. Long Beach Housing Action Assn., 1976-78. Recipient Commendation of Svc. award County of L.A., City of Long Beach, 1983-86. Mem. South Coast Ecumenical Coun. (pres. 1988-89 Pastor of Yr. 1984), Christian Fellowship Union of Chs. (pres. 1985-88), Black Am. Bapt. of Pacific S.W. (pres. 1985-88, Svc. award 1988), Theta Alpha Phi. Home: 4350 Cerritos Ave Long Beach CA 90807

MOSELEY, DORCAS JEAN, organist, college secretary; b. Blacklick, Pa., Sept. 8, 1939; d. Russell Bowman and Pearl (Flegal) Henry; m. William Lawrence Moseley, Dec. 29, 1962; children: Karen Gayle, Cynthia Diane. Secretarial diploma, Jones Bus. Coll., Orlando, Fla., 1958. Organist Univ. Congl. Ch., Orlando, 1968—; sec. Rollins Coll., Winter Park, Fla., 1980—. Mem. United Ch. of Christ. Home: 4600 N Goldenrod Rd Winter Park FL 32792

MOSELY, RALPH ELLINGTON, III, industrial and environmental safety executive, religious organization director; b. Chattanooga, Tenn., Aug. 2, 1944; s. Ralph Ellington Jr. and Sara Ester (Smith) M.; m. Karen Lee Whittemore, May 15, 1965; children: Sara Michelle, Jennie Lee. B.S., Tenn. Tech. U., 1967; M.B.A., U. Tenn., 1978. Cert. safety profl. Sr. loss prevention cons. Liberty Mut. Ins. Co., Atlanta, Birmingham, Ala. and Memphis, 1968-74; gen. mgr. Pacific Eastern Corp., Nashville, 1974-76; sr. cons., div. mgr. Resource Cons., Inc., Brentwood, Tenn., 1976-77; corp. dir. employee and environ. safety Genesco, Inc., Nashville, 1977-87; pres., chief exec. officer Mosely & Assocs., Inc., Nashville, 1987—; pres. Mosely/Cole Enterprises Inc., 1990—; assoc. prof. Tenn. State U., Nashville, 1977-85; cons. safety engring. Alley, Young & Baumgartner, Brentwood, Tenn., 1983—; cons. indsl. hygiene Barcon, Inc., LaVergne, Tenn., 1984—. Chmn. Metro. Nashville Safety Adv. Bd., 1981—; sec./treas., bd. dirs. Mary Frances Varallo Ministry, Nashville, 1988—; min. adminstrn. Victory Fellowship Ch., Nashville, 1987—; pres., exec. dir. World Missionary Support, Inc., Nashville, 1990—; bd. dirs. Tenn. Soc. Prevention Blindness, Nashville, 1990—. Editor: (book) Noise Control—A Guide for Workers and Employers, 1984; co-editor: (book) Refresher Guide for the Safety Professional, 1985, 88; cons. editor: (books) Readings in Noise Control, 1985, Ergonomics: A Practical Guide, 1989; author, pub.: (tng. manual) Awareness Training Series: Hazard Communications, 1986; editor: (manual) Ministry Manager, 1991; contbr. articles to profl. jours. Vice-chmn. Metro Nashville Safety Adv. Bd., 1981-85, chmn., 1985—; mem. ergonomics com. Meharry Med. Ctr., Nashville, 1984-85; vice chmn. safety and health environ. com. Tenn. Mfrs. Assn., Nashville, 1983—. Served to capt. U.S. Army, 1966-68. Recipient awards of appreciation Mayor of Nashville, 1981, 83, Gov. of Tenn., 1983, Resolution of Appreciation, Tenn. Ho. of Reps., 1983. Mem. Am. Soc. Safety Engrs. (chpt. pres. 1978-79, most outstanding mem. 1979, 88), Nat. Safety Coun. (gen. chmn. meat and leather sect. 1983-85, bd. dirs. 1987-89, exec. com. indsl. div. 1984-87, award of appreciation 1984-85), program chmn. ergonomics com. 1984-85), Am. Indsl. Hygiene Assn., Southeastern Occupational Health Conf., Inc. (bd. dirs. 1981-85), Tenn. Safety Congress (co-chmn. 1985-87, exec. com. 1980—, treas. 1980-87). Republican. Avocations: long distance running; tennis; golf; auto repair. Home: 4505 Harding Rd Apt 123 Nashville TN 37205 Home: World Missionary Support Inc 1415 Murfreesboro Rd Ste 232 Nashville TN 37217

MOSES, LIONEL ELLIOTT, rabbi; b. Toronto, Sept. 4, 1949; came to U.S., 1973; s. Joseph Phillip and Molly (Stone) M.; m. Joyce Rappaport, Dec. 20, 1981; children: Zev Gershon, Jeremy Samuel, Ezra Melekh. BS in Chemistry, U. Toronto, 1970, MA in Near East Lit., 1973; MA in Judaica, Jewish Theol. Seminary, N.Y.C., 1975. Ordained rabbi, 1977. Asst. rabbi Westchester Jewish Ctr., Mamaroneck, N.Y., 1977-81; rabbi Jewish Ctr. Jackson Heights, N.Y., 1981-87, Mosaic Law Congregation, Sacramento, Calif., 1987—; v.p. commn. synagogue rels. N.Y. Fedn., 1985-87; mem. Com. on Jewish Law and Standards, N.Y.C., 1984—; sec. Joint Bet Din Conservative Movement, N.Y.C., 1989—. Mem. Rabbinical Assembly, Soc. for Bibl. Lit., N.Y. Bd. Rabbis, Chevra Ctr. for Learning and Leadership, No. Calif. Bd. Rabbis, United Jewish Appeal Rabbinic Cabinet. Office: Mosaic Law Congregation 2300 Sierra Blvd Sacramento CA 95825

MOSIER, EDWARD BERT, minister; b. Clinton, Okla., July 25, 1947; s. Bert E. and Martha V. (Fike) M.; m. Martha Louise Blocker, Dec. 21, 1979; children: Bennett Ryan, Katie Elizabeth. BS, Abilene (Tex.) Christian U., 1969; MS, Sam Houston State U., 1975. Ordained to ministry Ch. of Christ, 1969. Singles minister Westbury Ch. of Christ, Houston, 1976-79; youth minister Edmond (Okla.) Ch. of Christ, 1979-81; minister of youth/family life Highland Oaks Ch. of Christ, Dallas, 1981-89; family minister Meadowlark Ch. of Christ, Ft. Collins, Colo., 1989-91; assoc. minister Park Pla. Ch. of Christ, Tulsa, 1991—; mem. adv. bd. York Coll., 1987—; bd. dirs. Inst. Adolescent Studies, Hendersonville, Tenn., 1986—; pres. Nurturing the Seed Family Seminars, Tulsa, 1990. Editor: Brick by Brick Teen Discipleship, 1987; author youth curriculum: Teen Study of James, 1988, Teen Study of 1, 2, 3 John, 1988. Mem. adv. bd. Tex. Distributive Edn. Clubs Am., Austin, 1976-78. Home: 1802 S Aster Ct Broken Arrow OK 74012 Office: Park Pla Ch of Christ 5925 E 51st Tulsa OK 74135 *The greatest challenge facing fathers today is that of nurturing the family. If I do not nurture my wife and children, lead them to serve God and serve other people, especially those in need, then I have failed. My success should be measured by the spiritual strength of my family.*

MOSKAL, ROBERT M., bishop; b. Carnegie, Pa., Oct. 24, 1937; s. William and Jean (Popivchak) M. BA, St. Basil Coll. Sem., Stamford, Conn., 1959; lic. sacred theology, Cath. U. Am., 1963; student, Phila. Mus. Acad. and Conservatory of Mus., 1963-66. Ordained priest Ukrainian Cath. Ch. 1963. Founder, pastor St. Anne's Ukrainian Cath. Ch., Warrington, Pa., 1963-72; sec. Archbishop's Chancery, Phila., 1963-67; apptd. vice-chancellor Archeparchy of Phila., 1967-74; pastor Annunciation Ukrainian Cath. Ch., Melrose Park, Phila., 1972-74; named monsignor, 1974; chancellor archdiocese, pastor Ukrainian Cath. Cathedral of the Immaculate Conception, Phila., 1974-84; apptd. bishop, 1981; Ordained titular bishop of Agathopolis and aux. bishop Ukrainian-Rite Archeparcy of Phila., 1981-83; first bishop Diocese of St. Josaphat, Parma, Ohio, 1983—; pro-synodal judge Archdiocesan Tribunal, Phila., 1965-67; founder Ukrainian Cath. Hour: God is with Us, Sta. WIBF-FM, Phila, 1972-77, Christ Among Us, Sat. WTEL, 1975—; mem. Ukrainian Cath. Ch. Liturgical Subcommn., 1980; host to His Holiness Pope John Paul II. Bd. dirs. Ascension Manor, Inc., Phila., 1964-84, sec.-treas., 1964-78, exec. v.p., 1977-84. Office: 5720 State Rd PO Box 347180 Parma OH 44134

MOSKOWITZ, SEYMOUR, rabbi; b. N.Y.C., Mar. 20, 1930; s. Sol and Ida (Leve) M.; m. Selma G. Watenmaker, June 23, 1957; children: Tal J., Gil J.L., Jonina L. BA, Yeshiva U., 1954; MHL, Boston Hebrew Coll., 1960; THM, Duke U., Durham, N.C., 1970; DMin, N.Y. Theol. Sem., 1980. Ordained rabbi, 1957. Rabbi Congregation Agudath Achim, Shreveport, La., 1986—. Col. U.S. Army, 1957-86. Mem. Rabbinical Coun. Am., Vaad Horabonim of Mass., Assn. Tex. Rabbis. Office: Congregation Agudath Achim 9401 Village Green Dr Shreveport LA 71115

MOSLEY, GLENN RICHARD, religious organization administrator, minister; b. Akron, Ohio, May 23, 1935; s. James Garfield and Viola Mildred (Wiseman) M.; m. Martha Lorella Mitchell, July 17, 1952; children: Glenn R. Jr., Mark, Tracey, Susan, Kristin, Sean, Gregory, Debra, Robert. BA, Wayne State U., 1974, MA, 1974; PhD, Walden U., 1976; MS in Adminstrn., Cen. Mich. U., 1991; DD (hon.), Unity Sch. Christianity, Kansas City, Mo., 1976. Ordained to ministry Unity Ch., 1961. Letter writer, student min. Silent Unity Prayer Soc., Kansas City, Mo., 1957-59; min. Unity Ch., Flushing, N.Y., 1959-64, Des Moines, 1964-65; co-min. Unity Ch., N.Y.C., 1965-68; min. Unity Temple, Detroit, 1968-75, Unity Ch., Akron, 1975-85; exec. dir. Assn. Unity Chs., Lee's Summit, Mo., 1985—. Author: Learning to Live with People, 1972, Unity Methods of Self-Exploration, 1975, Secular Religious Simulations Compared, 1980; pub. numerous cassettes, articles, poems and pamphlets; mem. editorial staff Jour. Thanatology, 1966-76. Mem. John Templeton Found. (Sewanee, Tenn., judge for Templeton prize for progress in religion), Rep. Presdl. Coun. Office: Assn Unity Chs 401 SW Oldham Rd Lee's Summit MO 64081 *The Religious Truth message we teach is eternal, and the techniques for teaching it work best for me when I am eternally evolving new ways to teach which meet a great diversity of learning styles. There are less than 3000 days left in the 1990s; what an exciting decade in which to live and teach.*

MOSLEY, GODFREY THOMAS, priest; b. Washington DC, Aug. 8, 1953; s. Hermitt and Thelma (Gaskins) M. BA, U. Scranton, 1975; ThM, Mt. St. Mary's Sem., 1979; D of Canon Law, U. St. Thomas, Rome, 1987. Assc. pastor Ch. of St. Margaret, Seat Pleasant, Md., 1979-80; asst. to dir. Office of Worship, Wash. D.C., 1980-81; assoc. pastor Holy Spirit Ch., 1980-81; secy. to archbishop archdiocese of Washington, 1981-84, vice chancellor, 1987-90; secy. Parish Life and Worship, 1990-; trustee Assc. Cath. Charities Wash. D.C., St. Ann's Infant Home Hyattsville, Md., John Carroll H.S. Wash. D.C. Mem. Canon Law Soc. Am., Eastern Region-Canon Law Soc. Roman Catholic. Home: 5212 First St NW Washington DC 20011 Office: Archdiocese of Washington PO Box 29260 Washington DC 20017

MOSLEY, ROY EDWARD, minister; b. Dearborn, Mich., Jan. 9, 1963; s. George Edward Jr. and Barbara (Tallman) M.; m. Lisa Dawn Burba, Aug. 13, 1988. BBA, Middle Tenn. State U., 1985; MDiv, So. Bapt. Theol. Sem., 1989. Ordained to ministry So. Bapt. Conv., 1989. Ministerial intern Belle Aire Bapt. Ch., Murfreesboro, Tenn., 1985; asst. min. Waverly (Tenn.) First Bapt. Ch., 1986; min. youth and edn. Auburndale Bapt. Ch., Louisville, 1986-89, Beacon Hill Bapt. Ch., Somerset, Ky., 1989—; advisor Somerset Community Coll., 1989-90. Vol. Fellowship Christian Athletes, Pulaski County, Ky., 1989-90. Named Vol. of Yr. Fellowship Christian Athletes of Pulaski County, 1990, 91. Mem. Religious Educators Assn., Pulaski Bapt. Assn. Office: Beacon Hill Bapt Ch 4510 Old Monticello Rd Somerset KY 42501

MOSS, LLOYD GLENN, minister; b. Burlington, Iowa, Apr. 8, 1947; m. Linda Bernice Wade, June 26, 1967; children: Tina Marie, Teresa Lynn. AS in Religious Edn., AA in Divinity, Midwestern Bapt. Theol. Sem., Kansas City, Mo., 1981; B Ministry, Covington Theol. Sem., Roseville, Ga., 1989, M Ministry, 1990, D Ministry, 1991. Ordained to ministry So. Bapt. Conv., 1977. Pastor Mid-Town Bapt. Ch., Milw., 1977-78, Cen. Bapt. Ch., Kansas City, 1979-81, Lake Park Bapt. Ch., Racine, Wis., 1981-82, Northside Bapt. Ch., Racine, 1982-87, Calvary Bapt. Ch., Antioch, Ill., 1987—. With USN, 1965-78. Office: Calvary Bapt Ch 554 Parkway Ave Antioch IL 60002

MOSS, OTIS, JR., minister; b. LaGrange, Ga.; s. Otis and Magnolia Moss; m. Edwina Hudson Smith; children: Kevin, Daphne, Otis III. BA, Morehouse Coll., 1956; MDiv, Morehouse Sch. Religion, 1959; postgrad., Inter-Denominational Theol. Ctr., 1960-61; D of Ministry, United Theol. Sem., Dayton, Ohio, 1990. Ordained to ministry Bapt. Ch. Pastor Mt. Olive Bapt. Ch., LaGrange, 1956-59, Providence Bapt. Ch., Atlanta, 1956-61, Mt. Zion Bapt. Ch., Lockland, 1961-75; co-pastor Ebenezer Bapt. Ch., Atlanta, 1971; pastor Olivet Inst. Bapt. Ch., Cleve., 1975—; del. World Bapt. Conf., Beirut, 1963; mem. rev. Com. Harvard Div. Sch., 1975-82; trustee Morehouse Coll., 1979—, Morehouse Sch. Religion, 1974—; lectr. in field; clergy mission to Republic of China, Tawain, 1984; cons. in field. Columnist Atlanta Inquirer, 1970-75; contbr. articles to profl. jours. Nat. bd., trustee, Martin Luther King Jr. Ctr. of Social Change, 1971—; bd. dirs. Operation PUSH, 1971—, acting nat. pres., 1971—. Recipient Human Rels. award Bethune Cookman Coll., 1976, Gov.'s award in Civil Rights, Ohio, 1983, Black Profl. of Yr., Black Profl. Assn., Cleve., 1983; named One of Am.'s 15 Greatest Black Preachers, Ebony Mag., 1984; spl. guest lectr./preacher for U.S. Army and Navy in Japan, 1985; guest min. Japan's Tokyo Bapt. Ch., 1985; guest of Taegu (South Korea) U., 1985; delivered Easter sermon on nationwide CBS-TV, 1986; invited to conduct Martin Luther King Jr. programs in Japan for U.S. Army and Navy, 1986; scholarship named in his honor Cen. State U., 1988. Mem. NAACP, Masons, Alpha Phi Alpha. Home: 22850 Shaker Blvd Shaker Heights OH 44122 Office: Olivet Instl Bapt Ch 8712 Quincy Ave Cleveland OH 44106

MOSS, ROBERT A., lay worker, educator; b. Phila., Sept. 9, 1915; s. Frank Hazlett and Rebecca Anna (Hunter) M.; m. Huldah Justice Bradley, June 26, 1941 (div. Oct. 1980); children: Heidi Ungermann, Robert A. Jr., Marty Moss-Coane; m. Maria G. Cattell, Apr. 23, 1983. AB, Princeton U., 1938. Tchr. of religion Groton Sch., Groton, Mass., 1938-51; head of religion dept. Groton Sch., Groton, 1951-58; head St. Andrew's Sch., Middletown, Del., 1958-76; tchr. of religion Westtown Sch., Westtown, Pa., 1977-87; dir. Coun. for Religion in Ind. Schs., Washington, 1978-84; adj. prof. ethics Lincoln U., Lincoln University, Pa., 1987-88; tchr. of ethics Episcopal Diocese of Pa. Tng. Sch., Phila., 1990—; mem. ethics com. So Chester County Med. Ctr., West Grove, Pa., 1988—; mem. Commn. on Human Sexuality Diocese of Pa., Phila., 1989-90. Researcher 100 yr. history of Coun. for Religion in Ind. Schs., 1990—. Mem. Coun. for Religion in Ind. Schs. (chmn. 1970-76); mem. Del. Valley Ethics Com. Democrat. Home: 543 Bayard Rd Kennett Square PA 19348

MOSSACK, ROBERT ALAN, minister, counselor; b. Nashville, Aug. 2, 1956; s. Frank Robert and Bettye Joyce (Luther) M.; m. Ellen Darlene Kindall, June 5, 1978; children: Allison, Eric. BA summa cum laude, David Lipscomb Coll., 1978; MA in Religion magna cum laude, Harding Grad. Sch., 1982. Cert. profl. counselor, Tenn.; ordained to ministry Ch. of Christ, 1978. Minister Flippin (Ky.) Ch. Christ, 1976-78; assoc. minister youth Westwood Ch. Christ, McMinnville, Tenn., 1978-80; assoc. minister youth and counseling Smyrna (Tenn.) Ch. Christ, 1982-83; dir. Middle Tenn. Christian Ctr., Murfeesboro, 1983-86; minister family life Hixson (Tenn.) Ch. Christ, 1986—. Contbr. articles to religious jours. Named one of Outstanding Young Men Am. Outstanding Young Men Am., 1979, 81, 85, Outstanding Young Religious Leader McMannville Jaycees, 1979. Mem. Am. Assn. Marital and Family Therapy (assoc.), Am. Assn. Christian Counselors, Psi Chi. Avocations: running, writing, computers, team sports, golf. Home: 3527 Valley Dr Chattanooga TN 37415 Office: Hixson Ch Christ 1505 Cloverdale Dr Hixson TN 37343

MOTE, DENNIS K., religious organization administrator; b. Troy, Ohio, June 1, 1952; s. Max D. and Flora E. (Sanders) M.; m. Rhonda Lou Perry, Aug. 17, 1974; children: Sarah Elizabeth, Susannah Joy. BA, Marion (Ind.) Coll., 1970; M in Divinity, Asbury Theol. Sem., 1980; postgrad., Fuller Theol. Sem., 1987—. Ordained to ministry. Interim pastor Russiaville (Ind.) Friends Ch. Western Yearly Meeting Friends, 1972-73; asst. pastor Little Ridge Friends Ch. Ind. Yearly Meeting Friends, Fairmount, Ind., 1973-74; pastor Hemlock (Ind.) Friends Ch., 1974-77; chaplain Ky. State Boys Sch., Danville, 1977; asst. pastor Danville (Ky.) Ch. Nazarene, 1978; youth pastor Cloverbottom Baptist Ch., Willmore, Ky., 1979; pastor Long Lake Friends Ch. Ind. Yearly Meeting Friends, Traverse City, Mich., 1980-83, Trinity Evangelical Friends Ch., Martinsville, Va., 1983-86; dir. ch. planting Evangelical Friends Ch. Greater Richmond, Va., 1987—; founding ch. planting pastor West End Friends Ch., Richmond, 1987; chaplain Traverse City Long Lake Vol. Fire Dept., 1980-83. Inventor green bean processing machine, 1986. Bldg. dir. Camp Hawthorneburg Family Ministry Ctr., Silar City, N.C., 1983-86; exec. sec. Clyde Dupin Evangelical Ministry, Martinsville, Va., 1985; vol. Richmond Friendly Day Care, 1986—. Named one of Outstanding Young Men Am., 1985. Mem. Wesleyan Theol. Soc. Avocations: wood working, furniture making, tennis, gardening. Home: Rt 10 Box 775 Mechanicsville VA 23111 Office: Rt 10 Box 774 Mechanicsville VA 23111

MOTTE, SISTER MARY MARGARET, missionary; b. Providence, Dec. 4, 1936; d. Edwin Gerard and Emma Veronica (O'Donnell) M. BA, St. Joseph's Coll., Bklyn., 1962; MA, Boston Coll., 1963, MEd, 1967, PhD, 1972. Mem. Mission Resource Office Franciscan Missionaries of Mary, Rome, 1974-81; dir. Nat. Mission Conf. U.S. Cath. Mission Assn., Washington, 1982-83; asst. provincial U.S. Province-Franciscan Missionaries of Mary, N.Y.C., 1984-87, 91—; coord. Nat. Ecumenical Mission Consulate U.S. Cath. Mission Assn., Nat. Cath. Consulate U.S.A., 1985-87; dir. Mission Resource Ctr. Franciscan Missionaries of Mary, North Providence, 1988—; also bd. dirs. U.S. Cath. Mission Assn., Washington; trustee Maryknoll Sch. of Theology, 1990—, Overseas Ministries Study Ctr., 1991—; exec. com., bd. dirs. Agrl. Missions/NCCC-USA, N.Y.C. Co-editor: Misson in Dialogue, 1982; contbg. editor Internat. Bull. of Missionary Rsch., New Haven, 1980—; contbr. articles to profl. jours. Doctoral fellowship Boston Coll., 1966; Walsh-Price fellowship Maryknoll Fathers & Bros., 1979. Mem. Am. Soc. Missiology (bd. dirs., v.p. 1991—), Am. Profs. of Mission (v.p. 1990-91). Home and Office: 399 Fruit Hill Ave North Providence RI 02911

MOTTRAM, RICHARD DONALD, JR., minister; b. San Francisco, July 1, 1943; s. Richard Donald and Virginia (Likins) M.; m. Charlotte Zink, Sept. 5, 1965. Student, N.W. Nazarene Coll., Nampa, Idaho, 1961-65, Nazarene Theol. Sem., Kansas City, Mo., 1979-80, Olivet Nazarene U., Kankakee, Ill., 1981-82. Ordained to ministry, Ch. of the Nazarene, 1988. With Nazarene Pub. House, Kansas City, Mo., 1972-81; pastor Ch. of the Nazarene, Caro, Mich., 1981-84, Tuttle, N.D., 1984-87, Seneca Falls, N.Y., 1987-89, Watertown, S.D., 1989—; sch. bus driver Watertown Sch. Dist. #144, 1990—; zone pres. Nazarene Youth Internat., Caro, 1981-84; zone chmn. Sun. Sch. Ministries, 1984-89; pres. Tuscola County Holiness Assn., Caro, 1982-84; Dakota dist. dir. Continuing Lay Tng., Watertown, 1990—. Chaplain Steele (N.D.) Nursing Home, 1985-87; bd. dirs. House of Concern, Seneca Falls, N.Y., 1988-89, treas., 1989; mem. Crisis Mgmt. Team,

Watertown, 1990—. Mem. Tuscola County Ministerial Assn. (v.p. 1982-83), Watertown Area Ministerial Assn. Office: Ch of the Nazarene 501 E Kemp Ave Watertown SD 57201 *I desire that my life be a demonstration of the love of compassion that Jesus shared.*

MOTZ, SIMION, minister; b. Rostoci, Romania, Aug. 4, 1926; came to U.S., 1978; s. George and Agrima (Tomsa) M.; m. Maria Ban, July 10, 1947; children: Dorin, Daniel, Nicoleta, Eugene. Grad., Normal Sch. for Tchrs., Arad, Romania, 1947; diploma, MIU, Saliste, Romania, 1952. Ordained to ministry Ind. Bapt. Ch., 1981. Lay preacher Bapt. chs. Romania; imprisoned for religious activity Gherla, Ostrov, Romania, 1958-62; lay preacher, Sunday sch. tchr. Bapt. chs. Romania, 1963-77; missionary, evangelist, acct. to various Communist countries Glendale, Calif., 1978-88; pres. The Suffering Ch. Ministries, Norcross, Ga., 1988—. Author: On The Way of the Cross In Kings Service, 1982, Clarifications About The Holy Spirit, 1984, Dew Drops: Sermons, Meditations, 1984, The Final Events of the Bible, 1987, The Complete Salvation of God, 1987. Home and Office: 1186 Creeldale Dr Norcross GA 30093 *I learned that the present conditions of life, good or bad, rich or poor are the best to serve God and to do something good. Use them to the full without dreaming for better, because you will not have them again. They are a blessing; you will see this later and will regret for complaining instead of thanking God and using them.*

MOTZEL, JACQUELINE MARY religious organization administrator; b. St. Louis, May 10, 1936; d. Edwin Francis and Frances Teresa (Grospoeler) M. BS in Radiol. Tech., St. Louis U., 1960; AB in Theo., St. Joseph's Coll., Rensselaer, Ind., 1969; MS in Counseling and Devel., U. Wis., 1971; cert. liturgical studies, U. Notre Dame, 1988; cert. ch. music ministry, Fontbonne Coll., 1988. Asst. radiol. technologist St. Mary's Health Ctr., St. Louis, 1960-62; sup. radiol. technologist St. Mary's Health Ctr., Jefferson City, Mo., 1962-63; tech. dir. of sch., dept. head Radiol. Tech. St. Mary's Hosp. Med. Ctr., Madison, Wis., 1963-70; with formation ministry Franciscan Sisters of Mary, St. Louis, 1969-78; with House of Prayer Franciscan Sisters of Mary, Pacific, Mo., 1978-81; asst. to congl. coun. Franciscan Sisters of Mary, St. Louis, 1981-86, coord. worship-heritage, 1986-87; dir. pilgrimages Commissariat of the Holy Land, St. Louis, 1988-90; rel. sec. ministry options Intercongl. Job Project, St. Louis, 1990; social ministry facilitator Cath. Social Svc., Belleville, Ill., 1991—; chairperson liturgy St. Louis Archdiocesan Commn. for Sacred Liturgy, Music and Art, 1987-91; chairperson centenary com. Franciscan Sisters of Mary, St. Louis, 1971-73; spiritual asst. Secular Franciscan Frat., Cuba, Mo., 1988—. Vol. ARC, 1991—. Recipient Vol. Svc. award Life Crises Svcs. Inc., 1970-81, Pastoral Ministry Vol. Merit award St. Mary's Health Ctr., 1984, Pilgrim Shell awrd Latin Patriarchate, 1989; invested in Equestrian Order of Holy Sepulchre of Jerusalem. Mem. Am. Assn. Counseling and Devel., Assn. Religious Value/Issues in Counseling, Nat. Pastoral Musicians, Nat. Pastoral Musicians (St. Louis chpt. 1986—). Roman Catholic. Office: Cath Social Svc 617 S Belt West Belleville IL 62220

MOTZER, PAUL D., clergyman, counselor; b. Dahlgren, Ill.; s. Narvel Darvin and Evelyn Louise (Jenner) M.; children: Timothy Paul, Julie Elizabeth Loftis, David Edwin; m. Frances Koteles, June 28, 1980. BA, McKendree Coll., 1957; student, Eden Theol. Sem., 1960; MDiv, Garrett Theol. Sem., 1962; postgrad., Fielding Inst., 1978-79; D of Ministry, Nat. Christian U. Mo., 1980; MS, U. San Francisco, 1989. Ordained to ministry United Meth. Ch., 1962; lic. profl. counselor; registered intern, Calif., Tex.; mem. S. Ill. Ann. Conf., U. Meth. Ch. Commd. capt. USAF, 1966, advanced through grades to lt. col., 1987; stationed at USAF, Hamilton AFB, Calif., 1966-69, Alaskan Air Command, Alaska, 1969-70, Tinker AFB, Okla., 1970-73, USAF Europe, Zweibrucken AFB, Fed. Republic of Germany; stationed at Randolph AFB, Tex., 1976-80, Kusan AFB, Republic of Korea, 1980-81, Vandenberg AFB, Calif.; ret., 1987; pastoral counselor Santa Maria, Calif., 1987—; conducts seminars and workshops; marriage and family course tchr. L.A. Met. Coll., Kunsan, Republic of Korea, 1980. Contbr. articles to profl. jours. Mem. Santa Barbara County Alcoholism Adv. Bd., 1988—. Mem. Internat. Transactional Analysis Assn., Ret. Officers Assn., Am. Assn. for Counseling and Devel., Calif. Assn. Marriage and Family Therapists, Assn. for Religious Values in Counseling, Ministerial Assn., Santa Maria Valley Ministerial Assn. (v.p. 1984-87), Masons, Lions (pres. 1962-64). Democrat. Avocations: licensed pilot, swimming. Home: 1114 River Birch Ct Santa Maria CA 93454

MOULDER, WILTON ARLYN, children's home development director; b. Atlanta, July 1, 1931; s. Ottis Arrell and Eula Mae (Whitlock) M.; m. Margie Nell Harrington, Mar. 12, 1955; children: W. Arlyn Jr., Carol Elaine. Student, Ga. Inst. Tech., Atlanta, 1949-50; BA, Emory U., Atlanta, 1953, MDiv, 1956, D Ministry, 1977. Ordained to ministry Meth. Ch. as deacon, 1954, as elder, 1956; cert. fin. planner, cert. fund raising exec. Pastor St. Luke Meth. Ch., Atlanta, 1956-57, St. Matthew Meth. Ch., East Point, Ga., 1957-62; assoc. pastor Druid Hills Meth. Ch., Atlanta, 1962-64; pastor Duluth (Ga.) United Meth. Ch., 1964-69; devel. dir. United Meth. Children's Home, Decatur, Ga., 1969—; self-employed cons.; trustee United Meth. Found., Atlanta, 1984—; del. Jurisdictional Conf., Lake Junaluska, N.C., 1984; mem. bd. pension North Ga. Conf., Atlanta, 1988—; sect. chmn. United Meth. Assn. Health and Welfare Ministries Pub. Rels. and Devel., 1978-80. Author: Financial Planning for Clergy Families, 1987. Judge Ga. Occupational Award of Leadership Program, Decatur, 1985—; bd. dirs. DeKalb Coll. Found., Decatur, 1990—. Mem. Inst. Cert. Fin. Planners, Nat. Soc. Fund Raising Execs., Internat. Assn. Fin. Planning, Rotary (bd. dirs. Decatur club 1988-90). Home: 4104 Warrior Trail Stone Mountain GA 30083 Office: United Meth Childrens Home 500 Columbia Dr Decatur GA 30030

MOULTON, PHILLIPS PRENTICE, religion and philosophy educator; b. Cleve., Dec. 24, 1909; s. E. Phillips and Myrtle (Skeel) M.; m. Mary Cochran, June 14, 1947; children: Katharine, Lawrence. A.B., Ohio Wesleyan U., 1931; postgrad., Marburg U., Germany, 1931-32, Princeton Theol. Sem., 1941-42, Boston U., summers 1941-42; B.D., Yale U., 1942, Ph.D., 1949. Research dir. Cleve. Guidance Service, 1936-37; religious work sec. Cleve. YMCA, 1937-40; nat. dir. univ. work Fed. Council Chs., 1944-47; coordinator religious activities Chgo. U., 1948-51; lectr. religion in higher edn. Union Theol. Sem., N.Y., 1951-54; chmn. dept. philosophy, coordinator gen. edn. program Simpson Coll., Iowa, 1954-58; pres. Wesley Coll., prof. religion U. N.D., 1958-65, chmn. dept., 1963-65; prof. philosophy Adrian (Mich.) Coll., 1965-76; lectr. and cons. on small coll. athletics. Leader World Student Christian Fedn. Conf., 1951; Danforth lectr. religion and higher edn. Boston U., Northwestern U., summers 1953, 54; dir. Nat. Meth. Gt. Books Project, 1957; T.W. Brown fellow postdoctoral research Haverford Coll., 1965, 67-68; vis. scholar Union Theol. Sem., N.Y.C., 1971-72, Center for Study Higher Edn., U. Mich., 1976-78. Author: (with W.E. Kerstetter) Experiment in General Education, 1957, Violence—Or Aggressive Nonviolent Resistance, 1971, The Living Witness of John Woolman, 1973, Enhancing the Values of Intercollegiate Athletics at Small Colleges, 1978; editor: Community Resources in Cleveland, Ohio, 1937, The Journal and Major Essays of John Woolman, 1971 (Am. Assn. State and Local History award of merit 1972), Ammunition for Peacemakers, 1986 (winner Pilgrim Press manuscript contest). Pres. Midwest Faculty Christian Fellowship, 1957-58; U.S. del. Ecumenical Youth and Internat. YMCA Conf., 1939; chmn. Nat. Danforth Campus Workshop, 1957; speaker 14th Internat. Philosophy Congress, Vienna, 1968. Am. Philos. Soc. research grantee, 1968; Inst. Internat. Edn. fellow, 1931-32; Hough fellow in sociology, 1936-37; Taylor Theol. fellow, 1931-32; Univ. scholar Yale, 1944-45. Mem. Am. Acad. Religion (past pres. Midwest region), Audubon Soc., Fellowship of Reconciliation, Phi Beta Kappa, Delta Sigma Rho, Omicron Delta Kappa, Beta Theta Pi. Methodist, Quaker. Home: 225 Brookside Dr Ann Arbor MI 48105 *At age 16 I discovered the most important thing in life - a strong Christian faith. This has given me motivation, stability, and direction. It has stimulated me to question generally-accepted values, to distinguish the significant from the trivial, the enduring from the temporal. I believe the Christian interpretation of life provides the perspective needed to make one's efforts worthwhile.*

MOULTON, RICHARD WAY, minister; b. Norfolk, Va., June 11, 1948; s. Robert Eugene and Betsy (Babcock) M.; m. Nancy Neal, Dec. 29, 1967; children: Richard Way, Angela, Paul, Mindy, Randall. BS in Math., Rose-Hulman Inst. Tech., Terre Haute, Ind., 1970; MS in Computer Sci., Northwestern U., Evanston, Ill., 1972; MDiv, Trinity Luth. Sem., Columbus, Ohio, 1977. Ordained to ministry Am. Luth. Ch., 1977. Mem. tech. staff Bell Telephone Labs., Naperville, Ill., 1970-72; staff engr. GTE Automatic Elec., Melrose Park, Ill., 1972-73; pastor Christ Luth. Ch., Harrisburg, Ill., 1977-78, Faith Luth. Ch., Orlando, Fla., 1979-81, Hosanna! Ch., Orlando, 1981-86; engring. mgr. Stromberg-Carlson Corp., Lake Mary, Fla., 1979-89; cons. Moulton Rsch. Inc., Altamonte Springs, Fla., 1989—; pastor Northland Community Ch., Longwood, Fla., 1990—; cons. Martin-Marietta Corp., Orlando, 1990—. Avocations: music composing, guitar, keyboards, basketball, reading. Office: 530 Dog Track Rd Longwood FL 32750

MOUNT, MARGARET ELIZABETH DOYLE, educator, clergywoman; b. Franklin, Pa., Sept. 1, 1926; d. James A. and Cynthia A. (Adams) Doyle; m. Lewis F. Mount, Sept. 1, 1948; children: Martin Fillmore, Arnold Adams, Cynthia Mary Mount Boffoli. BA in Bible, Fla. Beacon Coll., 1964; MA in Religious Edn., Trinity Coll. and Sem., 1970. Ordained to ministry Open Bible Standard Chs., Inc., 1969. Instr. Fla. Beacon Coll. and Sem., Largo, Fla., 1959-69; head secretarial sci. dept. Trinity Coll. and Sem., Dunedin, Fla., 1969-73; instr. ednl. svcs. St. Leo (Fla.) Coll., from 1973. Home: 4601 18th Ave Saint Petersburg FL 33713

MOUNTCASTLE, WILLIAM WALLACE, JR., philosophy and religion educator; b. Hanover, N.H., July 10, 1925; s. William Wallace and Grace Elizabeth (Zottarelli) M.; m. Barbara Kaye Griffin, Oct. 19, 1979; 1 child, Cathleena; stepdaughter, Dasha; children from earlier marriage: Christine, Susan, Gregory, Eric. BA, Whittier Coll., 1951; STB, Boston U., 1954, PhD, 1958. Ordained to ministry United Meth. Ch. Asst. prof. philosophy and religion High Point (N.C.) Coll., 1958-60; mem. So. Calif. Ann. Conf. United Meth. Ch., 1954-60; assoc. prof., head dept. philosophy Nebr. Wesleyan U., Lincoln, 1960-63; mem. Neb. Ann. Conf. United Meth. Ch., 1960—; prof. philosophy Fla. So. Coll., Lakeland, 1967-69; M.L. Tipton prof. philosophy and religious studies U. W. Fla., Pensacola, 1969—, assoc. prof. philosophy and religion, 1969-79, prof. philosophy and religion, 1979-84, M.L. Tipton prof. philosophy and religion, 1984—. Author: Religion in Planetary Perspective, 1979; contbr. articles to jours. in field. 1st lt. USAAF, 1942-49, PTO. Mem. NEA/United Faculty Fla., Am. Assn. Religion, Am. Philos. Assn.,. Democrat. Home: 4549 Sabine Dr Gulf Breeze FL 32561 Office: U West Fla Dept Philosophy & Religious Studies Pensacola FL 32561

MOURANY, HAMID ANTOINE, archbishop. Archbishop Diocese of Damascus Roman Cath. Ch., Syria. Office: Vicariat Patriarcal, Maronite, Bab Touma, Damascus Syrian Arab Republic*

MOWERY, NORMAN GLENN, minister; b. Chambersburg, Pa., Nov. 7, 1947; s. John and Pauline (Bert) M.; m. Linda Lee, Aug. 29, 1970; children: Nathan Lee, Lori Lee. BA, Messiah Coll., 1971; MDiv, Ashland Sem., 1975; DMin, San Francisco Theol. Sem., 1981. Ordained to ministry Meth. Ch. Pastor United Meth. Ch., Burlingame, Calif., 1975-79, Marysville, Calif., 1979-84, Clovis, Calif., 1984-88; pastor Epworth United Meth. Ch., Berkeley, Calif., 1988—; chairperson New Ch. Devel., San Francisco, 1984-89, Mission Strategy, San Francisco, 1988—. Author: The Church as Family, 1981. Pres. St. Louis team Rotary Club, Berkeley, 1990. Democrat. Home: 1036 Creston Rd Berkeley CA 94708 Office: United Meth Ch 1953 Hopkins St Berkeley CA 94707

MOWERY, ROBERT LONG, minister, librarian; b. Rochester, Pa., Mar. 22, 1934; s. Herman Victor and Mary Margaret (Long) M.; m. Janet Bartholomew, Dec. 27, 1958; children: Philip L., Patricia Anne. BS in Mech. Engring., Purdue U., 1956; MDiv, Garrett-Evang. Theol. Sem., Evanston, Ill., 1960; MA in Religion, Northwestern U., 1961, PhD in N.T., 1967; MLS, U. Ill., 1968. Ordained to ministry United Meth. Ch. as deacon, 1957, as elder, 1960. Pastor Odell (Ill.) Meth. Ch., 1963-66, Pesotum (Ill.) Meth. Ch., 1966-68; Humanities libr. Ill. Wesleyan U., Bloomington, 1968—; v.p. Corn Belt Libr. System, Normal, Ill., 1989—. Author: (with others) The Living Text, 1985, Soc. Bibl. Lit. Seminar Papers, 1989-91; contbr. artices to profl. jours. Trustee Ill. State U. Wesley Found., 1987—. Mem. AAUP, ALA, Soc. Bibl. Lit., Soc. Bibl. Lit. Cen. States Region (co-convenor N.T. sect. 1989—), Ill. Libr. Assn., Ill. Libr. Computer Systems Office (stats mgmt. subcom. 1989—). Office: Ill Wesleyan U Box 2899 Bloomington IL 61702

MOY, RUSSELL GLENN, minister; b. Detroit, Feb. 26, 1953; s. Harry and Dorothy (Jhung) M.; m. Victoria Eng Lee, Aug. 20, 1977; children: Aaron, Kevin. BA in Gen. Studies, U. Mich., 1975; MDiv, Calvin Theol. Sem., 1980; postgrad. in religious edn., Sch. Theology at Claremont, Calif., 1988—. Ordained to ministry Am. Bapt. Ch. Pastor 1st Chinese Bapt. Ch., Sacramento, 1981-87. Mem. Soc. Biblical Lit., Am. Acad. Religion, Religious Edn. Assn. Democrat. Home: 32 Blair Ln Dearborn MI 48120

MOYE, DONALD WAYNE, minister; b. Eldorado, Ill., May 24, 1950; s. Will J. and Eva (Miner) M.; m. Glenda Faye McKinney, May 25, 1974; children: Christopher, Timothy, Joshua, Andrew, Kathryn, Stephen, Suzanna. MusB, Okla. Bapt. U., 1973. Ordained to ministry So. Bapt. Conv., 1975; cert. nouthetic counselor. Min. music 1st Bapt. Ch., Vidalia, Ga., 1974—; bd. dirs. Reach Out Ministries, Atlanta, 1974-79; regional cons. youth ministries Ga. Bapt. Conv., Atlanta, 1975-78; dir. music Daniell Bapt. Assn., Ailey, Ga., 1975-79, 84-85, 89. Coord. music Christmas parade City of Vidalia, 1982, 84, mem. centennial com., 1990; dist. del. Toombs County (Ga.) Reps., 1989. Mem. Vidalia Ministerial Assn., Daniel Bapt. Ministerial Assn. (sec.-treas. 1980-82, v.p. 1982-84), Meadows Meml. Hosp. Chaplaincy Assn. (pres. 1983-84, 88, sec. 1985, v.p. 1988), Phi Mu Alpha (pres. 1972-73), Omicron Delta Kappa. Home: 1517 Ridgeway Dr Vidalia GA 30474 Office: 1st Bapt Ch 101 E 1st St PO Box 631 Vidalia GA 30474 *Life is a brief opportunity to develop character, invest in the lives of others and to glorify God our creator. Each of us will give an account for how we have done in bringing pleasure to our heavenly Father.*

MOYÉ, ULYSSES GRANT, II, music minister, composer; b. Kinston, N.C., Apr. 6, 1942; s. Ushry Walter And Agnes R. M.; m. Catherine Murphy,Feb. 17, 1963; children: Karen A., Donovan O., Andrea D.; foster children: Anthony, Aaron. B in Music Edn., Howard U., 1970, M in Music Edn., 1974; postgrad., Peabody Conservatory Music, Balt., 1973, 74, U. Md., 1978, Trinity Coll., 1979, U. Va., 1978-82, Loyola Coll., Bat., 1979, Johns Hopkins U., 1982, 89, 90, George Mason U., 1982, 86, 88, George Washing U., 1983, U. S.C., 1989, Washington Bible Coll. and Sem., 1990, 91; D Sacred Laws and Letters (hon.), N.C. Christian Bible Coll., 1991. Min. music, organist 1st Bapt. Ch., Kinston, 1955-60, Greater New Hope Bapt. Ch., Washington, 1961-83; dir., founder Moyé Ensemble, Washington, 1965—; adminstr. Fairfax County Va. Bd. Edn., Alexandria, 1979—; pres., coord. Dacumba Sacred Music Network, Washington, 1981—; clinician, cons. Washington, 1981—; dir. music ministries Mt. Pleasant Bapt. Ch., Balt., 1983—; asst. acad. dean Nat. Conv. Gospel Choirs and Choruses U.S.A. Inc., Cleve., Chgo., 1989—. Author: Dacumba Sacred Music Handbook; composer 40 sacred music compositions. Recipient Black History Music award McGuire AFB, 1979, Commendation Svc. award United Black Coll. Fund Inc., 1990. Mem. Nat. Assn. Secondary Sch. Prins., Va. Assn. Secondary Sch. Prins., Am. Soc. Composers and Publishers, Omega Psi Phi (music dir. 1962—), Phi Mu Alpha Sinfonia (v.p., 1961—), Phi Delta Kappa. Democrat. Home: 5243 Kenstan Dr Camp Springs MD 20748 Office: Fairfax County Va Bd Edn Burkeholder Adminstrn Ctr Fairfax VA 22030

MOYER, BRUCE EUGENE, minister; b. Lexington, Ky., Feb. 23, 1953; s. Harold Eugene and Clarice (Hire) M.; m. Ruth Alice Atherton, Aug. 3, 1973. BA, Vennard Coll., 1975; MDiv, Wesley Bibl. Sem., 1980; ThM, Trinity Evang. Div. Sch., Chgo., 1986; postgrad., Marquette U. Ordained to ministry Evang. Ch., 1980. Pastor Evang. Ch., Mpls., 1975-77, dir. missions, 1990—; pastor Evang. Ch., Jackson, Miss., 1977-80; missionary Evang. Ch., Bolivia, S.Am., 1980-85; prof. Vennard Coll., University Park, Iowa, 1988-90. Author: Christian Theology, 1985. Mem. Wesleyan Theol. Soc., Delta Epsilon Chi. *It will be impossible to keep God at the center of life unless we take time to keep Him at the center of each day.*

MOYER, CHARLES MILTON, minister; b. Sellersville, Pa., Nov. 3, 1937; s. Charles Wesley and Gladys Mae (Clymer) M.; m. Dorothy Anne Pepper, June 6, 1964; 1 child, Charles Michael. BA, Del. State Coll., Dover, 1964; MDiv, Wesley Theol. Sem., Washington, 1967; DMin, Ea. Bapt. Sem., Phila., 1976. ordained to ministry United Meth. Ch., 1967. Minister United Meth. Ch., Harbeson, Del., 1964-67, Felton, Del., 1967-71, Camden-Woodside, Del., 1971-85; minister Milford (Del.) Ave. Ch., 1985—. Home: 424 Kings Hwy Milford DE 19963-1768

MOYER, JAMES CARROLL, religion educator; b. Norristown, Pa., Nov. 30, 1941; s. Raymond Carroll and Mary Letitia (Bishop) M.; m. Roberta Helen Goff, Aug. 28, 1965; children: Brenda, Marsha, Rebecca. BA, Wheaton Coll., 1963; MDiv, Gordon Div. Sch., 1966; MA, Brandeis U., 1968, PhD, 1969. From asst. prof. history to assoc. prof. religious studies S.W. Mo. State U., Springfield, 1970-79, prof. religious studies, 1979-85, head dept. religious studies, 1985—; deacon U. Heights Bapt. Ch., Springfield, 1983-85. Co-editor: Scripture in Context, 1983. Elder 1st and Calvary Presbyn. Ch., Springfield, Mo., 1974-76. NEH grantee, 1980, 84, 86; named Burlington No. Tchr. of Yr. S.W. Mo. State U., 1984; Archeol. fellow Hebrew Union Coll., 1969-70. Mem. Soc. Bibl. Lit. (regional sec. 1983-89), Am. Schs. of Oriental Rsch. (assoc. trustee 1985-87, Bibl. archaeologist 1989—, mem. com. on publs. 1984-87, book rev. editor, mem. editorial bd. 1989—), Cath. Bibl. Assn., Nat. Assn. Bapt. Profs. Religion. Home: 634 E Cardinal Springfield MO 65810 Office: SW Mo State U Dept Religious Studies Springfield MO 65804

MOYER, MARGARET ELLEN DEMPSEY, Christian religion education director; b. Chgo., Feb. 19, 1938; d. Robert Casey and Jean Elizabeth (Weaver) Dempsey; m. Frederic Derr Moyer; children: Elisa Jean Moyer McDermott, Anne Rebecca, Cameron Derr, Emily Ruth. BS in Music Edn., U. So. Ill., 1960; M in Christian Edn., Garrett-Evangelical Theol. Sem, 1988. Dir. Christian religion edn. Glencoe (Ill.) Union Ch., 1986-89, Northbrook (Ill.) United Meth., 1989—; bookkeeper Moyer Assocs., Inc., Glencoe, 1982—; chair, various offices United Meth. Women Wesley Found., Urbana, Ill., 1970's; class agt. Garrett Evangelical Theol. Sem., Evanston, Ill., 1989—; women's aux. exec. bd. Salvation Army, Chgo., 1989—; treas. Glencoe (Ill.) Unio Ch. Women's Guild. Author: (column newletter) The Bellringer, 1986-89, The Messenger, 1989—, Women's Libr. Club Newsletter, 1990—. Dir. choral and music Tudor Ct. Community Theater, Glencoe, 1981-85, 90, 91, Tower Players Community Theater, Winnetka, 1982; music dir. Jr. High Project, Cen. Sch. Jr. High, Glencoe, 1985. Mem. Christian Educators Fellowship, Religious Educators Assn., PEO Sisterhood (Winnetka, Ill., various coms. 1976—), Woman's Libr. Club (Glencoe, pres. 1984-86, 90—), Sigma Alpha Iota (pres. 1958-59). Home: 534 Park Ave Glencoe IL 60022

MOYER, MARK HENRY, minister; b. Ashland, Ky., Aug. 28, 1955; s. Henry Proctor and Delores (Castle) M.; m. Joan McCormick, Aug. 13, 1977; children: Joshua, Erin. BA, Mars Hill Coll., 1977. Ordained to ministry Bapt. Ch., 1980. Minister of music and youth Fishersville (Va.) Bapt. Ch., 1980-87, Ridgewood Bapt. Ch., Roanoke, Va., 1987—; pvt. music instr., Roanoke, 1980—. Mem. Va. Bapt. Male Chorale, 1980—. Mem. Augusta Bapt. Assn. (music dir. 1982-85, youth com. chmn. 1984-87), Roanoke Valley Bapt. Assn. (youth com. mem. 1987-90, v.p. music dirs. 1988-90). Home: 877 Bolejack Blvd Roanoke VA 24019 Office: Ridgewood Baptist Church 703 Hemlock Rd Roanoke VA 24017 *There is a lot of "Doom and Gloom" in this world in which we live. We may either accept this fate or choose to live in the abundance of God's glorious grace under His "riches in glory through Christ Jesus."*

MROVKA, DAVID ANTHONY, association administrator; b. Springfield, Ill., May 7, 1949; s. Anthony John and Minnie Lee (Rawls) M.; m. Rita Ann Mueller, June 24, 1978; children: Eric David, John Anthony. BA in Psychology cum laude, Lewis U., 1971; MA in Morals and Theology, Mt. St. Mary's Coll., Emmitsburg, Md., 1976; MS in Clin. and Counseling Psychology, Augusta Coll., 1984; MS in Systems Mgmt., U. So. Calif., 1987; PhD in Adminstrn. and Mgmt., Walden U., 1991. Diplomate Am. Bd. Counselors. Pres. Internat. Assn. Ethicists, Inc., Chgo., 1985—, pres. Acad. Ethical Studies, 1985—. Exec. editor Jour. Ethical Studies, 1985—; contbr. articles, papers to profl. publs. Deacon Diocese of Arlington (Va.), Roman Cath. Ch., 1975-76. Fellow Acad. Ethical Studies (sr.) (Coll. Bioethical Ethics, Coll. Forensic Ethics, Coll. Normative Ethics, Coll. Orthobehavioral Ethics, Coll. Social Ethics), Internat. Assn. Ethicists, Inc. (sr., trustee 1985—); mem. Am. Acad. Religion, AAAS, Am. Philos. Assn., Am. Soc. Trial Cons. (profl. standards com. 1987-88, com. on disciplinary procedures (1989—), N.Y. Acad. Scis., Soc. Bus. Ethics, Human Factors Soc., Psi Chi, Phi Sigma Tau, Phi Mu Alpha Sinfonia. Office: Internat Assn Ethicists Inc 117 W Harrison Bldg 6th Floor Ste I-104 Chicago IL 60605 *Ethical development is most maturely expressed when one is more concerned with "doing right than being right."*

MUCK, DAVID WESLEY, church mission executive; b. Buffalo, Feb. 11, 1939; s. Kenneth Arlington and Lila Marie (Mojonnier) M.; m. Yvonne Carol Jurrens, Sept. 3, 1960; children: Bradley David, Michele Marie. AA, Rochester (Minn.) Jr. Coll., 1959; BS, Mankato State U., 1961. Bus. mgr. Fellowship of Bapts., Elyria, Ohio, 1964-69; credit supr. Johns Manville Co., Cleve., 1969-72; fin. dir. ch. bldg. com. Bapt. Mission N.Am., Elyria, 1972-90; acctg. mgr. Green Circle Growers, Oberlin, Ohio, 1990—; owner, operator D & B Reprodn. Svc., North Ridgeville, Ohio, 1972-87. With U.S. Army, 1961-63. Home: 38401 Sugar Ridge Rd North Ridgeville OH 44039 Office: Bapt Mission of N Am 137 Winckles St PO Box 455 Elyria OH 44036

MUCK, TERRY CHARLES, religious publisher; b. Batavia, N.Y., June 24, 1947; s. Webster Charles and Oaklie Mae (Floyd) M.; m. Judith Lee Keim, Sept. 15, 1970; children: David, Paul, Joseph. BA, Bethel Coll., St. Paul, 1969; MDiv, Bethel Theol. Seminary, St. Paul, 1973; PhD, Northwestern U., 1977. Editor Leadership Jour., Wheaton, Ill., 1980-85, Christianity Today Mag., Wheaton, 1985—; prof. religion Wheaton Coll., 1986—. Author: Liberating Leader's Prayer Life, 1984, When to Take A Risk, 1986, Alien Gods on American Turfs, 1990; author, editor: Sins of the Body, 1988. Fulbright Hayes rsch. grantee, 1976-77. Mem. Soc. for Buddhist-Christian Studies (bd. dirs. 1989—), Pali Text Soc., Am. Acad. Religion, Evang. Theol. Soc., Soc. for Scientific Study Religion. Home: 602 S Gables Blvd Wheaton IL 60187 Office: Christianity Today Mag 465 Gundersen Dr Carol Stream IL 60188

MUCKERMAN, SISTER ANN, school system administrator. Supr. dept. edn. Diocese of Bernardino, Calif. Office: Edn Dept 1739 N D St San Bernardino CA 92405*

MUCKERMAN, NORMAN JAMES, priest, writer; b. Webster Groves, Mo., Feb. 1, 1917; s. Oliver Christopher and Edna Gertrude (Hartman) M. B.A., Immaculate Conception Coll., 1940, M. in Religious Edn., 1942. Ordained priest Roman Catholic Ch., 1942. Missionary Redemptorist Missions, Amazonas, Para, Brazil, 1943-53; procurator missions Redemptorist Missions, St. Louis, 1953-58; pastor, adminstr. St. Alphonsus Ch., Chgo., 1958-67, St. Gerard, Kirkwood, Mo., 1967-71; mktg. mgr. circulation Liguori Pubs., Liguori, Mo., 1971-76; editor Liguorian Mag., Liguori, Mo., 1977-89. Author: How to Face Death Without Fear, 1976; Contbr. regular articles to mag. Recipient Nota Dez award Caixa Fed. Do Para, Brazil, 1958. Mem. Catholic Press Assn. (cons. 1971—, bd. dirs. 1976-85, pres. 1981-84, St. Francis De Sales award 1985), St. Louis Press Club, Crystal Hills Golf Club. Avocations: golf; travel; reading.

MUCOWSKI, RICHARD JOHN, priest, psychologist; b. Phila., Aug. 30, 1944; s. Raymond and Mary (Michaleczka) M. MS in Counseling, Niagara U., 1974; MA in Theology, Washington Theol. Union, 1971; MA in Sociology, U. Notre Dame, 1973; EdD in Counseling, SUNY, Albany, 1977; PhD in Clin. Psychology, The Fielding Inst., Santa Barbara, Calif. Lic. psychologist; diplomate Internat. Acad. Behavioral Medicine, Counseling and Psychotherapy; ordained to priesthood, Roman Cath. Ch., 1971. Instr. Bishop Timon High Sch., Buffalo, N.Y., 1971-73; instr. Siena Coll., Loudonville, N.Y., 1973-74, asst. prof., 1977-82, assoc. prof., 1982-85, prof., 1985-87; v.p. adminstrn. St. Bonaventure (N.Y.) U., 1987-88, exec. v.p., 1989—; fellow Harvard U. Inst. for Ednl. Mgmt., Cambridge, Mass., 1989;

postdoctoral fellow in neuropsychology Thomas Jefferson U., Phila., 1987, 91; cons. psychologist Roman Cath. Diocese of Albany, 1982-87, Serra Assocs., L.A., 1988—. Contbr. book revs. and articles to profl. jours., 1973—. Trustee St. Bonaventure U., 1986-87, Diocesan Counseling Ctr., Buffalo, 1989—. Mem. APA, AAUP, Assn. for Religious and Values Interest in Counseling (bd. dirs. 1981-85, 89—), Am. Assn. Counseling and Devel.(governing bd. 1991—, co-chair ethics com. 1991—), Am. Sociol. Assn., Am. Ednl. Rsch. Assn., Psi Chi. Avocations: racquetball, spectator sports, basketball. Home: Collins Hall Box CA Saint Bonaventure NY 14778 Office: St Bonaventure Univ Hopkins Hall Saint Bonaventure NY 14778

MUDGE, LEWIS SEYMOUR, theologian, educator, university dean; b. Phila., Oct. 22, 1929; s. Lewis Seymour and Anne Evelyn (Bolton) M.; m. Jean Bruce McClure, June 15, 1957; children: Robert Seymour, William McClure, Anne Evelyn. B.A., Princeton, 1951, M. Div., 1955, Ph.D. (Kent fellow), 1961; B.A. with honors in Theology, Oxford (Eng.) U., 1954, M.A. (Rhodes scholar), 1958. Ordained to ministry Presbyn. Ch., 1955. Presbyn. univ. pastor Princeton, 1955-56; sec. dept. theology World Alliance Ref. Chs., Geneva, 1957-62; minister to coll. Amherst Coll., 1962-68, asst. prof. philosophy and religion, 1962-64, assoc. prof., 1964-70, prof. philosophy and religion, 1970-76, chmn. dept. philosophy and religion, 1968-69, 75-76; dean faculty, prof. theology McCormick Theol. Sem., Chgo., 1976-87, San Francisco Theol. Sem., 1987—; prof. Grad. Theol. Union, Berkeley, Calif., 1987—; mem. commn. on faith and order Nat. Council Chs., 1965—; sec. spl. com. on confession faith United Presbyn Ch., 1965-67, chmn. spl. com. on theology of the call, 1968—; chmn. theol. commn. U.S. Consultation on Ch. Union, 1977—; co-chmn. Internat. Ref.-Roman Cath. Dialogue Commn., 1983—; observer Extraordinary Synod Bishops, 1985. Author: One Church: Catholic and Reformed, 1963, Is God Alive?, 1963, Why is the Church in the World?, 1967, The Crumbling Walls, 1970, The Sense of a People: Toward a Church for the Human Future, 1992; also numerous articles and revs.; editor: Essays on Biblical Interpretation (Paul Ricoeur), 1980, (with James Poling) Formation and Reflection: the Promise of Practical Theology, 1987. Pres. Westminster Found. in New Eng., 1963-67; chmn. bd. Nat. Vocation Agy., 1972—; mem. com. selection Rhodes Scholars, Wis., 1983-85, Iowa, 1986—. Mem. Phi Beta Kappa. Democrat. Home: 130 Bolinas Ave San Anselmo CA 94960 Office: San Francisco Theol Sem 2 Kensington Rd San Anselmo CA 94960

MUDGE, MICHAEL ALLEN, pastor; b. Cumberland, Md., Oct. 4, 1958; s. Thomas Edgar and Dollie Mae (Rice) M. AA, Allegany Com. Coll., Cumberland, Md., 1979; BA, Frostburg State, Md., 1980; MDiv, Asbury Theol. Sem., Wilmore, Ky., 1988. Cert. edn. for Ministry U. of the South, 1984. Pastor Crellin Underwood United Brethren Ch., Oakland, Md., 1988—; com. chmn. Pa. Conf. United Brethren Ch., Chambersburg, 1990—. Author: McKaig Jour., 1984. Sec. Mountain Top Crisis Pregnancy Ctr., Mountain Lake Park, Md., 1989—. Democrat. Home: Star Rte 2 Box 188 Oakland MD 21550

MUEHLENBERG, EKKEHARD FRIEDRICH WILHELM, church history educator; b. Friedrichshafen, Germany, July 29, 1938; s. Friedrich Wilhelm and Ursula (Parlow) M.; m. Marianne Langerbeck, Dec. 16, 1963; children: Christopher, Sibylle. Dr. Theol., U. Mainz, Fed. Republic Germany, 1963, Dr. Theol. Habilitation, 1968. Ordained to ministry Luth. Ch., 1985. Assoc. prof. Sch. Theology, Claremont, Calif., 1968-72, prof., 1972-78; prof. ch. history Georg August U., Göttingen, Fed. Republic Germany, 1978—. Co-editor: Patristische Texte und Studien, 1986—. Studienstiftung deutschen Volkes grantee, 1961-68. Mem. Patristische Kommission (dir. work dept. 1979—), Göttingen Acad. Sci. (dir. Kommission Erforschung altchristlichen Mönchtums 1985—). Home: Am Goldgraben 6, D-3400 Göttingen Federal Republic of Germany Office: U Göttingen Theol Fac, Platz Göttinger Sieben 2, D-3400 Göttingen Federal Republic of Germany

MUELLER, DAVID LIVINGSTONE, religion educator; b. Buffalo, Oct. 5, 1929; s. William Arthur and Mary Martha (Fink) M.; m. Marilyn T. Mueller, July 25, 1959; children: Charles David, Mary Elizabeth. Student, Colgate U., 1947-49, U. Heidelberg, Germany, 1949-50; BA, Baylor U., 1951; MDiv., So. Bapt. Theol. Sem., 1954; PhD, Duke U., 1957. Asst. then assoc. prof. religion Baylor U., Waco, Tex., 1957-61; assoc. prof. then prof. theology So. Bapt. Theol. Sem., Louisville, 1961—, Joseph Emerson Brown chair theology, 1991—. Author: An Intervention to the Theology of Alfred Ritschl, 1969, Karl Barth, 1972, Foundation Karl Barth's Doctrine and Reconciliation, 1991. Mem. Am. Acad. Religion (participant Euroam. studies seminar), Nat. Assn. Bapt. Profs. Religion. Office: So Bapt Theol Sem 2825 Lexington Rd Louisville KY 40280

MUELLER, FRANCIS E., ecumenical agency administrator. Pres. Alaska Christian Conf., Fairbanks. Office: Alaska Christian Conf 1316 Peger Rd Fairbanks AK 99709*

MUELLER, GENE LEON, minister; b. Norfolk, Nebr., July 29, 1950; s. Rudolph August and Verna Lois (Hays) M.; m. Carol Pauline Stolle, Sept. 1, 1979; children: Jenny Lynn, Julie Ann, James August. BA, Nebr. Christian Coll., 1989, BTh, 1989. Ordained to ministry, Christian Ch., 1990. Sr. minister Calhoun (Ky.) Christian Ch., 1989—. Mem. Lions. Republican. Office: Calhoun Christian Ch 385 Main St Calhoun KY 42327 *Life's purpose must be focused on fulfilling God's will for you. So much of our secular society only knows serving self, but the Christian must serve others.*

MUELLER, HERBERT ADOLPH, clergyman; b. Lone Elm, Mo., June 2, 1914; s. John H. and Anna (Vetter) M.; m. Elfrieda Rische, May 20, 1939; children: Susanne Mueller Engstrom, Thomas Mueller, Joanne Mueller Jeske. Grad., Concordia Coll., Milw., 1934, Concordia Sem., St. Louis, 1938; D.D., Concordia Sem., St. Louis, 1976; LL.D., Concordia Coll., Seward, Nebr., 1966. Ordained to ministry Luth. Ch., 1940. Pastor Lombard, Ill., 1938-43, Bethlehem Luth. Ch., Dundee, Ill., 1943-69; sec., bd. dirs. No. Ill. dist. Luth. Ch.-Mo. Synod, 1951-65; sec., bd. dirs. Luth Ch.-Mo. Synod, 1965-83, mem. bd. higher edn., 1960-65, mem. commn. constl. matters, 1965-83; chaplain Internat. Ctr., Luth. Ch.-Mo. Synod, 1983—. V.p. Luth. Council in U.S.A., 1973-76, sec., 1976-79, 82-84, pres., 1979-82. Address: 705 S Laclede Station Rd Apt 175 Webster Groves MO 63119

MUELLER, JOHN ALFRED, church executive; b. Milw., Apr. 19, 1906; s. Theodore J. and Catherine (Quehl) M.; m. Ruth M. Zehnder, Aug. 16, 1930; children—Annette (Mrs. Milford Brelje), John G. B.E., Concordia Tchrs. Coll., River Forest, Ill., 1927. Instr., minister of music Atonement Luth. Ch., Dearborn, Mich., 1927-42; minister music and edn. Jehovah Luth. Ch., Detroit, 1942-47; field rep. Luth. Laymens League, St. Louis, 1947-50; mem., field services dir. Luth. Laymens League, 1950—. Composer mus. compositions for choirs and quartettes, 1965. Bd. dirs. Luth. Ch.-Mo. Synod. Recipient Christus Vivit medallion Concordia Theol. Sem., 1974; Disting. Service award Bd. Dirs. Luth. Ch.-Mo. Synod, 1978. Home: 9907A Heritage Dr Saint Louis MO 63123 Office: 2185 Hampton Ave Saint Louis MO 63139 *I am of the considered opinion that life without Christ is dull, drab and has no real meaning. But life with Christ is a happy and joyful one, with a very real meaning.*

MUELLER, MARY KAY, church lay worker; b. Fargo, N.D., Feb. 2, 1953; d. John Allen Ressler and Beverly Ann (Jansen) Hammer; m. William Ludwig Mueller, Apr. 29, 1978; children: Katherine Anne, Michelle Beverly. BA in English and LS, Concordia Coll., Moorhead, Minn., 1975. Supt. Sunday sch. St. Matthew Luth. Ch., Moorestown, N.J., 1986-88, mem. ch. coun., 1988—, editor Pictorial Directory, 1989; freelance writer. Contbr. book revs. to Modern Liturgy, also contbr. to The Lutheran. Parent vol. Baker Sch., Moorestown, 1985—. Recipient award for book reviewing N.J. Press Women, 1983, playwriting award Atlantic Community Coll., 1984. Home: 516 Bartram Rd Moorestown NJ 08057

MUENICH, GEORGE RAYNOR, minister; b. Michigan City, Ind., Aug. 31, 1939; s. George Rudolph and Beatrice Edythe Ann (Dominick) M.; m. Erika Katharina Bieber, June 24, 1978; children: Renate Marie Louise, Margaret Elise Gabrielle. BS in Physics, Calif. Inst. Tech., 1961; D of Theology, Friedrich-Alexander Univ., Erlangen, Germany, 1975. Ordained to ministry Luth. Ch. in Am., 1976. Pastor Grace Luth. Ch., Gas City, Ind., 1976-78; interim pastor Wittenberg U., Springfield, Ohio, 1978-79; pastor St. Mark Luth.Ch., Grandview, Ind., 1980-81, Trinity Luth. Ch., Rockport, Ind., 1981, Redeemer Luth. Ch., Jasper, Ind., 1981-90, Zion German Luth. Ch., Brooklyn Heights, N.Y., 1990—; regional worship leader Ind.-Ky. Synod, Indpls., 1982-87, chmn. worship Music Task Force, 1984-87; mem. Dubois County Ministerial Assn., 1981-90, sec.-treas., 1982-83; mem. Jasper Deutscherverein, 1981-90, bd. dirs., 1982-88. Author: Der Hauptgottesdienst der Lutherischen Kirche Amerikas, 1973; The Victory of Restorationism, 1984. 1st lt., USAF, 1962-65. Recipient Gen. Motors Nat. Scholarship, Gen. Motors Found., 1957; Nat. Merit scholar, 1957; Humanities award State of Ind., 1984. Mem. Am. Acad. Religion, Hymn Soc. Am., N.Am. Acad. Liturgy, Societas Liturgica, Soc. Bibl. Lit., Liturgical Conf. Luth. Liturgical Renewal (bd. dirs. 1988—, pres. 1989—), Erlanger Wingolf Club. Republican. Home: 132 Henry St Brooklyn Heights NY 11201 Office: 125-131 Henry St Brooklyn Heights NY 11201

MUHAMMAD, WALLACE D., religious leader; b. Detroit, Oct. 30, 1933; s. Elijah and Clara M.; m. Shirley Allen, Apr. 28, 1959; children: Laila, Bakeerah, Ngina, Wallace, Sadrud-Din. Ed., Muhammad U. of Islam. Leader Am. Muslim Mission (formerly World Community of Al-Islam in the West), Chgo., 1975-85; U.S. rep. World Council of Masajid, Mecca, Saudi Arabia, 1986—, Forum of Spiritual Parliamentary Leaders for World Survival, Oxford, Eng., 1988. Author: The Book of Muslim Names, 1976, The Man and The Woman in Islam, 1976, As the Light Shineth from the East, 1980, Religion on the Line, 1983, African-American Genesis, 1986, Focus on Al-Islam, 1988. Recipient Walter Reuther Humanitarian award, Four Freedoms award, numerous others. Office: MACA Fund PO Box 1061 Calumet City IL 60409 also: The World Community of Islam in the West 7351 S Stony Island Ave Chicago IL 60649

MUHS, BETH ANN, minister; b. N.Y.C., Jan. 16, 1957; d. William Joseph and Patricia Lucille (Stephenson) Riley; m. Karl Frederick Muhs, June 22, 1985; children: Erik David, Jillian Noel. BA, Malone Coll., 1978. Ordained to ministry Salvation Army, 1981. Asst. officer Salvation Army, Middletown, Ohio, 1981-83; tchr. Salvation Army Tng. Sch., Suffern, N.Y., 1983-85; commanding officer Salvation Army, Marietta, Ohio, 1985-87; trainee Salvation Army Adult Rehab. Ctr., Bklyn., 1987-88; dir. spl. svcs. Salvation Army Adult Rehab. Ctr., Wilkes Barre, Pa., 1988—; choir and band leader Salvation Army, Wilkes-Barre, 1988—; counseling seminar Gordon Conwell Sem., Boston, 1982. Office: The Salvation Army 163 Hazel St Wilkes-Barre PA 18702 *Someone has once said to live your life by these five points: Develop your mind and talents; develop your physical being; keep your integrity; live in the world, not of the world, and finally, strengthen your faith. By this shall I live.*

MUIR, JOHN TODD, JR., minister; b. Ft. Worth, Tex., May 6, 1936; s. John Todd and Essie Oree (Daniel) M.; m. Judith Ann Moss, Aug. 23, 1958; children: Deborah, John Todd III, Angela. BA, Tex. Christian U., 1958, MDiv, 1962, MTh, 1969; DMin, So. Meth. U., Dallas, 1977. Ordained to ministry Christian Ch. (Disciples of Christ), 1962. Pastor River Oaks Christian Ch., Ft Worth, 1962-66, Cen. Christian Ch., Galveston, Tex., 1966-70, Casa View Christian Ch., Dallas, 1970-75, First Christian Ch., Wichita Falls, Tex., 1976—; chmn. bd. Pastoral Counseling Ctr., Wichita Falls, 1985—; mem. ethics com. Bethania Reg. Health Ctr., Wichita Falls, 1989—.

MULAC, PAMELA ANN, priest, pastoral counselor; b. Salem, Ohio, Dec. 6, 1944; d. Elmer John and Dorothy Adelaide (McGee) M.; m. George Robert Larsen, Aug. 8, 1987. Student, Bryn Mawr Coll., 1962-64; AB, U. Chgo., 1966; MDiv, Seabury-Western Theol. Sem., 1974; PhD, Garrett Evang. Theol. Sem., Northwestern U., 1988. Ordained to ministry Episcopal Ch. as priest, 1978. Asst. deacon, priest St. Luke's Ch., Evanston, Ill., 1974-84; asst. priest St. Mark's Ch., Upland, Calif., 1984-88; asst. priest St. Ambrose Ch., Claremont, Calif., 1988-90, assoc. priest for pastoral care, 1991—; pastoral counselor Swedish Covenant Hosp., Chgo., 1975-84; adj. lectr. Seabury-Western Theol. Sem., Evanston, 1981-82, trustee, 1981-84; pastoral counselor Walnut (Calif.) Valley Counseling Ctr., 1984-89; adj. lectr. marriage and family therapy program Azusa Pacific U., 1988-89, adj. lectr. operation impact, 1991—. Bd. dirs. Cathedral Shelter Chgo., 1980-84; co-chairperson Leader's Sch. Cursillo, Chgo., 1981-83; mem. Commn. on Alcoholism, Diocese of L.A., 1985-87. Episcopal Ch. Found. fellow, 1978-81. Mem. Am. Assn. Pastoral Counselors (sec. Pacific region 1984-85, treas. 1984—, fin. chair 1988—), Assn. Clin. Pastoral Edn. Home and Office: 2964 Gambrel Gate La Verne CA 91750

MULCAHEY, SISTER PATRICIA, school system administrator. Supt. schs. Archdiocese of Omaha. Office: Office Schs Supt 3212 N 60th St Omaha NE 68104*

MULCAHY, JOHN J., bishop; b. Dorchester, Mass., June 26, 1922. Student, St. John's Sem., Mass. Ordained priest, Roman Catholic Ch. 1947. Rector Pope John XXIII Sem. for Delayed Vocations, 1969-73; ordained titular bishop of Penafiel and aux. bishop Diocese of Boston, 1975—. Office: Archdiocese Boston 58 Blaney Swampscott MA 01907

MULCAHY, ROBERT CHARLES, deacon, school administrator; b. Woonsocket, R.I., May 23, 1940; s. James A. and Aurore V. (Dubois) M.; m. M. Anita Ouellette, Aug. 1, 1970; children: Maureen Elizabeth, Charlene Marie. AB cum laude, Providence Coll., 1961; MEd, R.I. Coll., 1966; MA, Clark U., 1968. Ordained deacon Roman Cath. Ch., 1976; cert. secondary sch. prin., supt. Asst. prin. Woonsocket Jr.-Sr. High Sch., 1972—; deacon asst. St. Joseph's Ch., Woonsocket, 1976—; lectr. Providence Coll., 1989—; del. Roman Cath.-Luth. Assemby, Holyoke, Mass., 1985; supr. Colllege Bd. Test Ctr., 1979—. Asst. editor, co-author: Woonsocket, Rhode Island: A Centennial History, 1988. Pres. Woonsocket Tchrs.' Guild, 1962; corporator Landmark Med. Ctr., Woonsocket, 1974-91; mem. Woonsocket Hist. Dists. Commn., 1979-90; founder, advisor SADD chpt., Woonsocket, 1982-88; mem. Youth Festival Com., Woonsocket, 1989-91, Heritage Corridor Commn., 1989-91. Recipient award Drug Dependency Inst., Yale U., 1990, Exemplary Contbn. to Edn. award Woonsocket Edn. Dept., 1991; Experienced Tchr. fellow Clark U., 1967-68, NSF fellow Bridgewater State Coll., 1971. Mem. Nat. Assn. Secondary sch. Prins., Delta Epsilon Sigma. Home: 153 Nancy Ct Woonsocket RI 02895

MULDER, DENNIS MARLIN, religious organization executive; b. Renville, Minn., Feb. 15, 1943; s. Lambert and Ruby (Gerdes) M.; m. Sharon Kaye Meyer, Aug. 16, 1963; children: Michael Glen, Kendall James, Eric Scott. BA, Calvin Coll., Grand Rapids, Mich., 1965; BDiv, Calvin Sem., 1969. Missionary Christian Ref. Bd. World Missions,, Republic of China, 1969-76; dir. Asian ministries The Bible League, South Holland, Ill., 1976-85, chief exec. officer, 1985—. Office: The Bible League 16801 Van Dam Rd South Holland IL 60473

MULDER, EDWIN GEORGE, minister, church official; b. Raymond, Minn., Mar. 25, 1929; s. Gerrit and Etta (Dresselhuis) M.; m. Luella Rozeboom, June 14, 1952; children: Timothy, Mary, Mark, Elizabeth. BA, Cen. Coll., Pella, Iowa, 1951, DD (hon.), 1979; BD, Western Theol. Sem., Holland, Mich., 1954. Ordained to ministry Ref. Ch. in Am., 1954. Pastor Reformed Ch. in Am., 1954-83, v.p. particular N.J. Synod, 1975-76, pres. particular N.J. Synod, 1976-77, v.p., then pres. Gen. Synod, 1978-80, gen. sec., 1983—; chair U.S. Ch. Leaders, 1989—; mem. exec. com. World Alliance Reformed Chs., 1990—, Nat. Coun. Chs., 1991; mem. cen. com. World Coun. Chs., 1991—. Trustee Cen. Coll., 1968—. Office: Ref Ch in Am 475 Riverside Dr New York NY 10115

MULDER, JOHN MARK, theology educator, clergyman; b. Chgo., Mar. 20, 1946; m. Mary Margaret Hakken, June 29, 1968; children: Aaron Martin, Anna Cornelia. AB, Hope Coll., 1967; MDiv, Princeton U., 1970, PhD in History, 1974; LLD, Centre Coll., 1984; DD, Southwestern at Memphis, 1984; DHL Bellarmine Coll., 1990. Ordained to ministry Presbyn. Ch., 1970. Instr. in Am. ch. history Princeton Theol. Sem., N.J., 1974-75, asst. prof., 1975-80, assoc. prof., 1980-81; pres., prof. theology Louisville Presbyn. Theol. Sem., Ky., 1981—; pastor Rensselaerville Presbyn. Ch., N.Y., 1977. Chmn. com. to develop seal for reunited Presbyn. Ch. (U.S.A.), 1983-85. Author: Woodrow Wilson: The Years of Preparation, 1978. Editor books, essay and paper collections. Contbr. articles and essays to profl. publs. Grantee Am. Philos. Soc., 1976, Nat. Hist. Publs. and Records Commn., 1978. Recipient Francis Makemie award, Hist. Found., 1978. Mem. Presbyn. Hist. Soc. (dir.), Am. Soc. Ch. History, Cath. Hist. Assn., Am. Acad. Religion, Orgn. Am. Historians, Am. Hist. Assn., Ky. Humanities Council, Acad. Parish Clergy. Office: Presbyn Theol Sem 1044 Alta Vista Rd Louisville KY 40205

MULDER, MARTIN JAN, theologian; b. Ter Aar, Netherlands, Dec. 25, 1923; s. Albertus and Johanna Hermina (Plettenburg) M.; m. Jitske Andringa, Dec. 9, 1949; children: Ab, Hermien, Sian, Rieta, Lydia, Regien, Jan, Heleen, Benny. D in Theology, Free U., Amsterdam, 1962; MA in Semitic Lit., State U., Leiden, Netherlands, 1969. Pastor Dutch Reformed Ch., various cities, 1949-64; asst. prof. Free U., 1964-70, prof., 1970-79; prof. theology State U. Leiden, The Netherlands, 1979-89, prof. emeritus, 1989—; pres. bd. dirs. Bible Mus., Amsterdam, 1975-82; bd. dirs. Dutch Bible Soc., Haarlem, 1972-81; adv. dep. gen. synod Dutch Reformed Ch.; dir. Peshitta Inst. State U., Leiden, 1981-89. Author many books and articles. Home: Amperestraat 48, 1171 BV Badhoevedorp The Netherlands

MULDOON, JANE KATHERINE, sister; b. Buffalo, Apr. 10, 1938; d. Hugh Joseph and Margaret (Maher) M. BA, Medaille Coll., 1964; M in Sacred Sci., St. Bonaventure U., 1975; MLS, SUNY, Geneseo, 1979. Elem. sch. tchr. Diocese of Buffalo, 1961-78; libr. Trocaire Coll., Buffalo, 1978-81, dir. libr. svcs., 1981—. Fellow Cath. Libr. Assn. (pres. Western N.Y. chpt. 1987-89). Home: 625 Abbott Rd Buffalo NY 14220 Office: Trocaire Coll 110 Red Jacket Pkwy Buffalo NY 14220 *Life is a gift from God to be used to the full.*

MULL, MARTIN, religious organization head. Former dist. supt. The Wesleyan Ch., Sussex, N.B., Can.; now gen. sec. evangelism and ch. growth The Wesleyan Ch., Indpls. Office: Wesleyan Ch PO Box 50434 Indianapolis IN 46206*

MULLEN, FRANK ALBERT, university official, clergyman; b. Lafayette, Ind., Apr. 7, 1931; s. Albert Edwin and Bernice Elizabeth (Weidlich) M.; m. Ruth Charlotte Ackerman, May 28, 1960 (dec. Oct. 1969). BA, Wabash Coll., Crawfordsville, Ind., 1953; MDiv, Yale U., 1956; DD (hon.), Berkeley Div. Sch., New Haven, 1988. Ordained to ministry Christian Ch. (Disciples of Christ), 1956. Exec. dir. YMCA of Wilmington, Del., 1956-60, YMCA of Greater N.Y., N.Y.C., 1960-74; dir. devel. Bapt. Med. Ctr., N.Y.C., 1980-83; assoc. dir. Campaign for Yale, Yale U., N.Y.C., 1974-79; dir. devel. Div. Sch. Yale U., New Haven, 1984—; dir. planned giving Guideposts, Inc., Carmel, N.Y., 1983-84. Trustee Park Avenue Christian Ch., N.Y.C., 1970—. Recipient Liberty Bell award Queens County Bar Assn., 1969, Alumni award of merit Wabash Coll., 1970; Wright fellow Yale U., 1955, fellow Trumbell Coll., 1985—. Mem. Assn. Theol. Schs., Coun. for Advancement Secondary Edn., Wellness Asssn. Home: 178-33 Croydon Rd Jamaica Estates NY 11432 Office: Yale U 409 Prospect St New Haven CT 06511 *Live for others. It is the only true way to find happiness.*

MULLENS, WILLIAM LEONARD, minister; b. Mart, Tex., Apr. 9, 1919; s. William James and Minnie Louise (Burney) M.; m. Frances Marcella Pye, July 7, 1939; children: Lynne, David, Denise, Stacy. Student, Tex. U., 1937-38, Baylor U., 1939-40, Del Mar Coll., 1955-56. Evangelist Chs. of Christ, 1938—, Edgefield Ch. of Christ, Dallas, 1949-55, Ayers St. Ch. of Christ, Corpus Christi, Tex., 1955-59, Kimball Sq. Ch. of Christ, Dallas, 1964-77, Salado (Tex.) Ch. of Christ, 1977—; lectr. colls., univs. including Abilene (Tex.) Christian U., Harding U., Searcy, Ark., others; established chs. in Tex. and Bermuda. Author: Unity in Christ-Teach Us To Pray, 1963; editor column Firm Found., 1954-85; author lessons World Bible Sch.; contbr. articles to profl. jours. Pres. bd. trustees Christian Acad., Dallas, 1972—. Mem. Christian Mins. Assn. (pres. 1978), Lions. Republican. Home and Office: 1012 Arrowhead Salado TX 76571 *It is better to build up than to tear down. You do more to promote the good than you can do in condemning the evil. Building up the good will do more to destroy the bad than anything else you may attempt.*

MULLER, EARL CANNON, priest; b. Columbia, S.C., Aug. 18, 1947; s. Philip H. and Catherine (Cannon) M. BS in Physics and Philosophy, Spring Hill Coll., Mobile, Ala., 1971; MDiv in Theology, Regis Coll., Toronto, 1977; PhD in Theology, Marquette U., 1987. Instr. in sci. and math. Jesuit High Sch., Tampa, Fla., 1971-74; instr. in theology Spring Hill Coll., 1984-87; asst. prof. theology Marquette U., 1987—. Author: Trinity and Marriage in Paul, 1989. Schmitt fellow Marquette U., 1979-81. Mem. Cath. Bibl. Assn., Soc. Bibl. Lit., N.Am. Patristics Soc., Cath. Theol. Soc. Am. Office: Marquette U Dept Theology Milwaukee WI 53233 *All for the greater glory of God.*

MÜLLER, EMILIO EDUARDO, minister; b. Cardenas, Matanzas, Cuba, July 16, 1945; came to U.S., 1973; s. Emilio Octavio and Celia Luisa (Arellano) M.; m. Gisela Villagarcia, Jun 3, 1966 (div. 1974); children: Lisel, Karell, Sheila; m. Juana Elina Bacallao, Mar. 7, 1976. BA, J.S. Commas Inst., Cardenas, 1963; MDiv, Emory U., 1979. Pastor Presbyn. Ch., Placetas, Cuba, 1963-64; sr. pastor United Meth. Ch., Tampa, Fla., 1979-82, Key West, Fla., 1982-85; field staff Bd. Global Ministries, N.Y.C., 1985—; cons. Hispanic ministries Bd. Global Ministries, N.Y.C., 1983-85, MARCHA, Perth Amboy, N.J., 1979—; active southeast urban ministries Southeastern Jurisdiction/del., 1979-81. Author: Cada Celebracion, 1990; columnist newspaper, 1990; contbr. articles to profl. jours. Sec./treas. Cuban Commn. of Tampa, Fla., 1980-81; sec. Hispanic Conf. Com., Fla., 1983. Mem. Hispanic Staff Forum (sec./treas. 1989). Democrat. Home: 904 W Alicia Ave B-1 Tampa FL 33604 Office: Bd of Global Ministries 475 Riverside Dr Rm 320 New York NY 10015

MULLER, LYLE DEAN, religious organization administrator; b. Owatonna, Minn., Mar. 9, 1935; s. Robert John and Esther Ida (Eaker) M.; m. Marlene K. Kliemek, Sept. 7, 1957; children: Mark, Susan. BA, Valparaiso U., 1956; MDiv, Concordia Sem., 1961. Ordained to ministry Luth. Ch.- Mo. Synod. Pastor Emmanuel Luth. Ch., Ft. Wayne, Ind., 1961-63, Trinity Luth. Ch., Danville, Ill., 1963-69, St. Luke Luth. Ch., Itasca, Ill., 1969-79; exec. evangelism and missions no. Ill. Dist. Luth. Ch.-Mo. Synod, Hillsdale, 1979-90; exec. dir. evangelism svcs. Luth. Ch.-Mo. Synod, St. Louis, 1990—. Author: (manuals) Good News Day, 1982, Witness Workshop, 1983, Ministry to Inactives, 1987, Assimilation, 1988. Office: Luth Ch Mo Synod 1333 S Kirkwood Rd Saint Louis MO 63122

MULLER-ORTEGA, PAUL EDUARDO, religion educator; b. Englewood, N.J., Dec. 4, 1949; s. Walter Boice and Maria Rosa (Ortega) M.; m. Virginia Elizabeth Lewis, Dec. 29, 1973 (div. Feb. 1990); m. Jane M. Linderman, Dec. 1, 1990. BA, Yale U., 1971; MA, U. Calif., Santa Barbara, 1979, PhD in Religious Studies, 1985. Assoc. prof. South Asian religions Mich. State U., East Lansing, 1985—, chairperson dept. religious studies, 1990—; editor Tantric studies series SUNY Press, Albany, 1988—. Author: The Triadic Heart of Shiva, 1988; editor Tantric Studies series, 1988—. Mem. Am. Acad. Religion, Am. Oriental Soc., Assn. Asian Studies, Soc. Asian and Comparative Philosophy, Soc. Tantric Studies. Democrat. Avocations: chess, mystery novels. Home: 2473 Graystone Dr Okemos MI 48864 Office: Mich State U Dept Religious Studies 114 Morrill Hall East Lansing MI 48824

MULLIGAN, ANNETTE MARIE, minister; b. Pomona, Calif., May 14, 1959; d. Anna Grace Dickson Mulligan. AA, Art Inst. Atlanta, 1979; BA, Azusa (Calif.) Pacific U., 1985. Coll. intern Grace Bapt. Ch., Glendora, Calif., 1983-84; early childhood intern Grace Bapt. Ch., 1984-85, children's minister, 1985—. Mem. Children's Christian Ministries Assn. (pres. 1991), Awana Clubs (comdr. 1986—). Republican. Baptist. Home: 158 W Juanita Ave Glendora CA 91740 Office: Grace Baptist Church 1515 S Glendora Ave Glendora CA 91740

MULLIGAN, MARTHA ELIZABETH, nun; b. Central Falls, R.I., Aug. 17, 1939; d. Walter Francis Xavier and Margaret E. (Riley) M. BA, Salve Regina Coll., 1961; MEd, Bridgewater State Coll., 1971. Cert. libr. sci., Mass.; joined Religious Sisters of Mercy. Tchr. St. Edward Sch., Pawtucket, R.I., 1962-64, Holy Name Sch., New Bedford, Mass., 1964-67, St. Mary

Sch., North Attleboro, Mass., 1967-76; assoc. vocation dir. Diocese of Providence, 1976-80; prin. St. John the Evangelist Sch., Attleboro, Mass., 1980—; vocation dir. Sisters of Mercy, Province Providence, 1971-78, mem. enrichment com., 1982-85. Liturgical and sacred dancer. Mem. Ambulance Task Force, Attleboro, 1983. Mem. ASCD, Nat. Cath. Edn. Assn., Mercy Elem. Edn. Network. Home: 103 Oakland Ave Pawtucket RI 02861 Office: St John the Evangelist Sch 13 Hodges St Attleboro MA 02703

MULLIN, RANDY GENE, youth and music minister; b. Plainview, Tex., Sept. 2, 1964; s. Earl Dean and Neva Jean (Barbee) M.; m. Valerie Kathleen Spears, Mar. 14, 1987; children: Lindsey Marie, Adam Bryant. BA in Theology and Religious Edn., Dallas Bapt. U., 1989. Part-time youth/music minister Trinity Heights Bapt. Ch., Carrollton, Tex., 1985-89; youth/music minister First Bapt. Ch., Clarendon, Tex., 1989—; youth dir. Panfork Bapt. Assn., Tex. Panhandle, 1990—. Named Outstanding Young Men Am., 1989. Home: 515 S Parks PO Box 1087 Clarendon TX 79226 Office: First Bapt Ch 301 S Bugbee PO Box 944 Clarendon TX 79226

MULLINS, EDWARD LEE, minister; b. Wheeling, W.Va., Aug. 11, 1944; s. Ezekiel and Mayme (Webb) M.; m. Diana Margaret Young, June 30, 1973; children: Jason Burle, Amanda Marie. BBA, Marshall U., 1966; MDiv, Va. Theol. Seminary, Alexandria, 1971. Vicar Saint Marks, Berkeley Spring, W.Va., 1971-74; assoc. rector Grace, Silver Spring, Md., 1974-78; rector Emmanuel, Cumberland, Md., 1978-85, St. Bartholomew's, Poway, Calif., 1985—; chmn. evangelism Diocese of San Diego, Calif., 1987—, vice-chmn. diocesan coun., 1987-90; mem. Episcopal Community Svcs., 1986-89, mem. budget and rev. bd., 1986—, mem. Commn. on Ministry, 1990—. Author: Survey Notes - Old Testament, 1988, Survey Notes - New Testament, 1988. Fellow Rotary. Office: Saint Barts 16275 Pomerado Rd Poway CA 92064 *Our task as ministers is to pray often and care deeply. For in our prayers, we draw closer to God. And in our caring, we draw closer to each other.*

MULLIS, M. JOYCE, missionary educator; b. Charlotte, N.C., Feb. 26, 1953; d. Floyd M. and Clara (Jordan) M. Theology degree, Tenn. Temple Bible Sch., 1974; BS, Tenn. Temple U., 1979. Cert. Edn., Tenn. Sch. and missionary tchr., office mgr. Internat. Bapt. Ch. and Christian Schs., Bklyn., 1979—; children's ch. dir. Internat. Bapt., Bklyn, 1979-83; bus captain Sunset Bus Route, 1981-91; sunday sch. asst., 1980-91. Home: 1942 Kimball St Brooklyn NY 11234 Office: International Baptist Ch 302 Vanderbilt St Brooklyn NY 11218

MULLIS, MADELINE GAIL HERMAN, choir director; b. Lenoir, N.C., Oct. 26, 1936; d. William Richard and Madeline Edythe (Harris) Herman; m. Thad McCoy Mullis Jr., Dec. 18, 1960 (div. Oct. 1978); children: Thad McCoy III, Myra Lynn, Martin Harper. MusB, U. N.C., Greensboro, 1958; MA, Appalachian State U., 1963. Cert. elem., secondary instrumental and choir music tchr. N.C. Jr. choir dir. St. Stephens Luth. Ch., Lenoir, 1968-80, sr. choir dir., 1960—, handbell choir dir., 1970—, deacon, 1980—, Sunday sch. tchr., 1983-86; music tchr. Caldwell County Schs., Lenoir, 1958-65, 77—; chairperson St. Stephens Worship and Music, Lenoir, 1988-91; del. N.C. Synod Conv., Hickory, N.C., 1990; pres. Agape Women's Circle, Lenoir, 1991—. Chairperson Sesquicentennial Children's Chorus, Caldwell County, 1991. Hon. mem. N.C. Ctr. for Advancement of Teaching; mem. NEA, Assn. Luth. Musicians, N.C. Assn. Educators, Music Educators Nat. Conf., N.C. Music Educators Assn., Am. Orff-Schulwerk Assn., Community Music Club (v.p.). Republican. Home: 119 Ellison Pl NE Lenoir NC 28645 Office: St Stephens Luth Ch 1406 Harper Ave NW Lenoir NC 28645 also: Happy Valley Sch PO Box 130 Patterson NC 28661

MULLNER, TIMOTHY PAUL, minister; b. Bismarck, N.D., Jan. 26, 1959; s. Mike J. and Cordella T. (Klein) M.; m. Margo Mae Dougherty, Aug. 22, 1990; children: Jordan Christopher, Eric Thomas, Sean Michael. BA in Youth Ministry, Coll. St. Scholastica, Duluth, Minn., 1981; MM in Spirituality, Seattle U., 1988. Pastoral assoc., youth minister Sacred Heart Ch., Glen Ullin, N.D., 1981-83; dir. youth ministry Diocese of Bismarck, 1983-86, mem. Diocesan Renew Team, 1986-91; youth ministry coord. St. Stephen's Ch., Anoka, Minn., 1991—; mem. Christian Formation Team, St. Stephen's Ch., 1991—, liaison Inst. for Polit. Life, Kansas City, Mo., 1989-90; singer A Change of Heart music group, Mandan, N.D., 1983—; workshop presenter Upper Midwest Youth Ministry Coun., Mpls., 1991. Named Bush Summer Fellow, Bush Found., Bismarck, 1986-88; recipient youth devel. grant, Anoka Dist. #11, 1991, multi-cultural youth ministry grant, K.C., Bismarck, 1985. Fellow Cath. Ext. Soc., Washington, 1986; mem. Youth Ministry Network, Prairie Pastoral Ministers Assn., Nat. Fedn. Cath. Youth Ministry, KC (officer). Office: Church of Saint Stephen 516 School St Anoka MN 55303

MULROY, BERTRAND CLAIR, deacon; b. New London, Wis., Jan. 11, 1913; s. Michael L. and Elizabeth (Cannon) M.; m. Irene H. Mulroy, Aug. 10, 1940; children: Michael J., Patrick D. BA, St. Norbert Coll., 1934. Ordained deacon Roman Cath. Ch. Staff asst. Mayor, Milw., 1962-84; permanent deacon Archdiocese Milw., 1975—, dir. ecumenism, 1984—. Mem. bd. ARC, Milw. chpt. 1972-81). Maj. U.S. Army, 1951-57. Recipient Alma Mater award St. Norbert Coll., De Pere, Wis., 1971. Mem. Pub. Rels. Soc. Am. (pres. Wis. chpt. 1969, Dorothy Thomas Black award 1990), St. Bernardine Communications Guild (past pres. 1971), Alexian Village Milw. (bd. mem. 1980-88), Milw. Press Club. Democrat. Home: 4848 N Lydell Ave Apt 331 Milwaukee WI 53217 Office: Archdiocese Milw 3501 S Lake Dr Milwaukee WI 53207

MULVEE, ROBERT EDWARD, bishop; b. Boston, Feb. 15, 1930; s. John F. and Jennie T. (Bath) M. B.A., U. Sem. Ottawa, 1953, Ph.B., 1953; M.R.E., Am. Coll., Louvain, Belgium, 1957; D. Canon Law, Lateran U., Rome, 1964; D.D. (hon.), Rivier Coll., Nashua, N.H., 1979. Ordained priest Roman Catholic Ch., 1957; asst. chancellor of diocese, 1964-72, named monsignor, 1966, elevated to domestic prelate, 1970, named chancellor, 1972; aux. bishop Roman Catholic Diocese of Manchester, N.H., 1977-85; bishop of Wilmington, 1985—. Trustee Nat. Shrine Imaculate Conception, Washington D.C, 1987. Mem. Nat. Conf. Cath. Bishops (campaign for human devel. com. 1985, joint com. Orthodox and Roman Cath. Bishops 1986, chmn. bd. bishops Am. Coll. of Louvain, Belgium, 1986, Cath. Relief Services bd., 1987); Nat. Conf. Cath. Bishops/ U.S. Cath. Conf. (adminstrv. com. and bd. dirs. 1986, com. on personnel and adminstrv. services 1987). Office: 1925 Delaware Ave Ste 1A Wilmington DE 19899

MULVIHILL, DAVID JAMES, priest; b. Chgo., Nov. 7, 1946; s. Harry Hamilton and Marie Sylvia (Ryska) M. BA, U. St. Mary of the Lake, Mundelein, Ill., 1968, MDiv, 1972; Diploma in Italic Antiquities, U. Stranieri, Italy, 1971; JCL, Gregorian U., Rome, 1987, JCD, 1990. Ordained priest Roman Cath. Ch., 1972. Deacon St. John Fischer Parish, Chgo., 1971-72; assoc. St. Benedict Parish, Chgo., 1972-77, St. Christina Parish, Chgo., 1977-82, St. Odilo Parish, Berwyn, Ill., 1982—; judge Met. Tribunal, Chgo., 1983—, Ct. of Appeal, Chgo., 1983—; chaplain Instituto di Merlo Bianco, Florence, Italy, 1985, Maddalena Island Naval Base, Sardinia, Italy, 1986, Gaeta Naval Base, Italy, 1987-89. Author: De Subdito Formae, 1990, Those Bound to Canonical Form, 1991. Decorated knight Equestrian Order of Holy Sepulchre. Mem. Canon Law Soc. Am., Cath. Lawyers' Guild Chgo., N.Am. Coll. Rome Alumni. Avocation: linguist. Home: St Odilo Parish 2244 S East Ave Berwyn IL 60402 Office: Met Tribunal PO Box 1979 Chicago IL 60690

MULVIHILL, JOHN EDWARD, priest; b. Chgo., Nov. 19, 1939; s. Harry Hamilton and Marie Sylvia (Ryska) M. MA, Lic. in Philology, Aquinas Inst., 1967; STD, Gregorian U., Rome, 1971; D Ministry, San Francisco Theol. Sem., 1990. Ordained priest in Roman Cath. Ch., 1964. Vicar for Men and Women Religious, Archdiocese of Chgo., 1971-83; judge Met. Tribunal, Chgo., 1980-89, Interdiocesan Appellate Tribunal, Chgo., 1983-90; curate St. John Bosco Parish, Chgo., 1965—; lectr. Inst. for Continuing Theol. Edn., Rome, 1970, Inst. of Spirituality, River Forest, Ill., 1976; lectr. clin. pastoral edn. St. Joseph Hosp., Chgo., 1989; exec. bd. Nat. Assn. Vicars for Religious, 1974-80. Author: Ministerial Priest, 1971, Second Nuptials, 1988, Pastoral Symposium, 1989. Decorated knight Equestrian Order of the Holy Sepulchre of Jerusalem; fellow Roman Acad., Rome, 1964; recipient Cross of the Holy Land, Papal Custos, Jerusalem, 1965. Mem. Canon Law Soc. Am., Am. Acad. Religion, Cath. Theol. Soc. Am., Internat. Soc. for Metaphysics, Am. Cath. Philos. Assn. (life). Home and Office: St John Bosco Rectory 2250 N McVicker Chicago IL 60639-2723

MUMBA, STEPHEN, bishop. Bishop of Lusaka The Anglican Communion, Zambia. Office: Bishop's Lodge, POB 30183, Lusaka Zambia*

MUMFORD, PATRICIA RAE, religious organization administrator; b. Oklahoma City, Feb. 25, 1932; d. Raymond William and Mildred Louise (Wisdom) Gallagher; m. Donald Earl Mumford, April 6, 1951; children: Raymond Scott, Kenneth Earl, Robert Paul. Columnist The Sapulpan, Sapulpa, Okla., 1949-51; continuity writer Sta. KRMG, Tulsa, 1951-52; with continuity and production TV stas., Phoenix, Las Vegas, Denver, 1953-57; continuity and traffic radio stas. KPOI and KKUA, Honolulu, 1965-71; part-time program asst. Hawaii Council of Chs., Honolulu, 1972-80, assoc. dir., acting dir., 1980-85, exec. coordinator, 1986-87; exec. dir. Hawaii Council of Chs., Kailua, Hawaii, 1987—. Contrib. articles to newspapers, newsletters and mags. Bd. dirs. UNA-Hawaii, Meml. Soc. of Hawaii, Vol. Leadership Devel. program, Hawaii Pub. Broadcasting Authority Adv. Bd., Honolulu, 1978-82; mem. Hawaii State Commn. on Martin Luther King Jr. Holiday, 1988—. Named Outstanding Woman of Yr., City and County of Honolulu, 1982. Mem. Nat. Assn. of Ecumenical Staff (service award 1987), Ch. Women United, Honolulu, (local and state pres., mem. Nat. Council 1965-72). Democrat. Mem. Christian Ch., United Presbyn. Ch.

MUMME, JAMES HORACE, minister, retired educator; b. Quincy, Ill., May 17, 1926; s. Horace Elijah and Minnie Eva (Wiederrecht) M.; m. Vida Faye Robinson, Dec. 6, 1947; children: Stephen, Lois, Deborah, Philip, Teri, Cheryl. Student, U. Ariz., 1947, Azusa Pacific U., 1950; BS, Ariz. State U., 1952, MS, 1976; postgrad., Phoenix Coll., 1955-56, Goshen Coll., 1957. Ordained to ministry Evang. Meth. Ch., 1951. Min. Evang. Meth. ch., Phoenix and Eloy, Ariz., 1951—; coord. Mexican missions Evang. Meth. ch., Eloy, 1961-64, dir. World missions, 1980-90; tchr. Berea Bible Inst., Bolivia, 1959-60, Phoenix Coll., 1962-63, Eloy Jr. High Sch., 1966-75, Santa Cruz Valley High Sch., 1975-85; bd. dirs. Nat. Inst. for Forgotten Individual, Mex., 1962-90, OMS Internat., Greenwood, Ind., 1968-76, World Gospel Mission, Marion, Ind., 1980-82, World Relief Corp., Wheaton, Ill., 1980-84. Author: (ann. vols.) Evangelical S.S. Comm., 1965-71; missions editor columns Viewpoint mag., 1962-90; newspaper columnist Words to Live By, 1975-91. Chmn. Pinal County (Ariz.) Rep. Com., 1970, 80; nominee to Ariz. State Senate, 1970, 86; bd. dirs. Ariz. State Health Planning Coun., 1972-75, Dept. Commerce Econ. Devel. Adv. Bd., 1986-88. With USN, 1944-46, PTO. Recipient 35-yr. award Evang. Meth. Ch., 1990. Mem. Wesleyan Theol. Soc. Home: 4125 N Catalina Dr Eloy AZ 85231 Office: Toltec Evang Meth Ch 4210 N Francisco Dr Eloy AZ 85231

MUNCY, BOBBY W., minister; b. Runnels County, Tex., June 23, 1931; s. Lonnie Theodore and Mittie (Harville) M.; m. Dorothy Ann Lennon, June 19, 1959; children: Stephen Wayne, Dottie Jean. BA, Howard Payne Coll., Brownwood, Tex., 1962, Southwestern Theol. Sem., Ft. Worth, Tex., 1966. Ordained to ministry, So. Bapt. Conv. Pastor Northside Bapt. Ch., Mason, Tex., 1959-62, Indian Gap Bapt. Ch., Hamilton, Tex., 1962-63, McGee Valley Bapt. Ch., Daisy, Okla., 1965—. With U.S. Army, 1948-59. Home: PO Box 30 Daisy OK 74540

MUNDADAN, ANTHONY MATHIAS, religion educator; b. Karingamthuruth, North Parur Taluk, India, Nov. 12, 1923; s. Varied Tharyaku and Teresa Varied (Manadan) M. MTh, De Nobili Coll., Pune, India, 1954; licentiate, Gregorian U., Rome, 1957, PhD, 1960. Tchr. religion Latin Grammar Sch., Alwaye, Kerala, India, 1954-55, Dharmaram Coll. Pont. Inst. (now Dharmaram Vidya Kshetram), Bangalore, India, 1960—; rector Dharmaram Coll. Pont. Inst., Bangalore, India, 1975-78; pres. Dharmaram Inst., Bangalore, India, 1976-80; provincial supr. Carmelites of Mary Immaculate Congregation, Cochin, India, 1975-78, 90—. Author: Arrival of the Portuguese, 1967, 16th Century Tradition of St. Thomas Christians, 1970, History of Christianity in India, 1984, Indian Christians Search for Identity and Struggle for Autonomy, 1984; assoc. editor: Indian Church History Rev., Bangalore, 1973—. Mem. St. Thomas Acad. Research (convenor 1980—), Ch. History Assn. India (chmn So. India Br. 1969-85, 89—, gen. editor 1984—), Indian Theol. Assn., Internat. Assn. Mission Studies. Home and Office: Dharmaram Coll, Bangalore Karnataka 560029, India

MUNDAY, ROBERT STEVENSON, priest, academic dean; b. Benton, Ill., Oct. 19, 1954; s. Robert Meade and Kathryn (McCollum) M.; m. Christina Ellen Karroll, July 31, 1976. BA, So. Ill. U., 1976; MDiv, Mid-Am. Bapt. Theol. Sem., Memphis, 1979, ThD, 1984; MLS, Vanderbilt U., 1986; postgrad., Duquesne U. Ordained priest Episcopal Ch., 1990. Chaplain St. Jude Children's Rsch. Hosp., Memphis, 1981-84; instr. Mid-Am. Bapt. Theol Sem., Memphis, 1984-86; libr. dir. Trinity Episcopal Sch. for Ministry, Ambridge, Pa., 1986—, assoc. prof. systematic theology, 1986—, assoc. dean for adminstrn., 1987—. Chmn. bd. dirs. Life Choices, Memphis, 1984-86; bd. dirs. Cen. Pitts. Crisis Pregnancy Ctr., 1989—, pres., 1990—. Mem. Nat. Orgn. Episcopalians for Life (bd. dirs., pres. 1991—), Fairfax Va., Theol. Edn. Commn., Episcopal Synod Am., Am. Acad. Religion, Am. Theol. Libr. Assn., Brotherhood St. Andrew (life), Fellowship of St. Alban and St. Sergius. Home: 235 Chestnut St Sewickley PA 15143 Office: Trinity Episcopal Sch for Ministry 311 Eleventh St Ambridge PA 15003 *Life is about possibility and transformation—the possibility of being lifted above mere human existence to be the creatures we are ideally in the mind of God. The possiblility of that transformation is the good news of our redemption in Jesus Christ.*

MUNDEY, PAUL ESTON RISSER, minister; b. Hagerstown, Md., Aug. 20, 1951; s. Eston George and Anna Rebecca (Harne) M.; m. Robin Ann Risser, June 29, 1980; children: Peter, Sarah. BS, Towson State Coll., 1973; MDiv., Fuller Theol. Sem., 1977; postgrad., Johns Hopkins U., 1982-83; cert. bus. adminstrn., U. Ill., Chgo., 1990. Pastor Fairview Ch. of Brethren, New Market, Va., 1974-76, Friendship Ch. of the Brethren, Linthicum Heights, Md., 1977-83; mem. staff for evangelism, gen. bd. People of the Covenant, Ch. of the Brethren, Elgin, Ill., 1983-86; staff for evangelism People of the Covenant, mem. gen. bd. Ch. of the Brethren, Elgin, Ill., 1983-86, mem. staff for evangelism Korean ministries, mem. gen. bd., 1986-90, dir. evangelism and congregational growth, mem. gen. bd., 1990—; cons. Conf. on World Mission and Evang. World Coun. Chs., San Antonio, 1989; mem. adv. bd. Religion in Am. Life, Princeton, N.J., 1990—, Nat. Leadership Inst., Lubbock, Tex., 1990—; accredited visitor World Coun. Chs. Assembly, Canberra, Australia, 1991; mem. Commn. on Worship and Evangelism Nat. Coun. Chs. Christ, 1989—. Co-author: New Life for All, 1987, Including and Involving New People, 1989; contbr. articles to profl. jours. Home: 1273 Blackhawk Dr Elgin IL 60120 Office: Ch of Brethren Gen Bd 1451 Dundee Ave Elgin IL 60120 *Traditionally the church has been overly cautious in navigating the tides of tomorrow. Resisting the currents we have tended to cling to the "river bank", to that which is safe, secure and predictable. In order for churches to develop and grow, however, we need to learn to "ride the river" to face the future, navigating the trends before us.*

MUNDSCHENK, PAUL ERNEST, religion educator; b. N.Y.C., Oct. 12, 1938; s. Fred Peter and Margaret Ingeborg (Bernson) M.; m. Nancy Ann Madsen, Mar. 4, 1978; 1 child, David Christopher. AB, Gettysburg Coll., 1962; postgrad., Princeton Theol. Sem., 1966-68; PhD, Claremont Grad. Sch., 1976. Instr. religion Marietta (Ohio) Coll., 1972-75; prof. religious studies Western Ill. U., Macomb, 1975—. Contbr. articles to profl. jours. Vol. U.S. Peace Corps, Colombia, 1963-65. Grantee NEH, 1976, 81, 85, 87, Am. Coun. Learned Socs., 1978. Mem. Am. Acad. Religion, Assn. for Asian Studies, Midwest Conf. on Asian Affairs. Democrat. Home: 700 Glenview Dr Carbondale IL 62901 Office: Western Ill U Dept Philosophy Religious Studies Macomb IL 61455 *With so many concerns battling for our attention and the world's fate hanging in the balance, I still find it most important to maintain perspective, to appreciate life and to be able to laugh.*

MUNGANDU, ADRIAN, archbishop. Archbishop of Lusaka Roman Cath. Ch., Zambia. Office: 41 Wamulwa Rd, POB 32752, Lusaka Zambia*

MUNIVE ESCOBAR, LUIS, bishop; b. Santa Ana Chiautempan, Mexico, June 21, 1920. Ordained priest Roman Cath. Ch., 1944; bishop of Tlaxcala Mexico, 1959—. Office: Apartado 84, Tlaxcala CP 90000, Mexico

MUNOZ, DOROTHY D., youth ministry coordinator; b. Marinette, Wis., Apr. 13, 1927; d. Andrew Richard and Barbara Dawn (Smith) Danielson; widowed; children: Debra, Frank, Dawn, Dale. Studen, Marinette County Coll., 1945. Catechist St. Gregory's, Phoenix, 1982-87, coord. widowed outreach, 1983-84, asst., 1984-87, asst. care program, 1984-86, coord. youth ministry, 1987—; eucharistic min. St. Gregory's, Phoenix, 1986—, liturgy com., 1987—, parish coun. mem., 1987—, lector, 1991. Office: St Gregorys Parish 3424 N 18th Ave Phoenix AZ 85015

MUNOZ NUNEZ, RAFAEL, bishop; b. Vista Hermosa, Mex., Jan. 14, 1925; s. Francisco and Sara Munoz Nunez. Student, Seminario Conciliar de Guadalajara, Mex., Seminario Interdiocesano de Montezuma, N.Mex. Ordained priest Roman Cath. Ch., 1951. Nat. asst. Accion Catolica Mexicana; sec. Apostolic Del. in Mex.; consecrated bishop of Zacatecas Mex., 1972; bishop Diocese of Aguascalientes, Mex., 1984—. Office: Galeana 105 Nte, Apartado Postal No 167, CP 20000 Aguascalientes Mexico

MUNRO, WINSOME, retired minister; b. Pilgrims Rest, Republic of South Africa, Oct. 23, 1925; d. Henry Charles and Maria M. (Borcherds) M. BA, Witwatersrand U., Johannesburg, Republic of South Africa, 1945; BD, Birmingham U., Eng., 1962; MST, Union Theol. Sem., 1967; EdD, Columbia U., 1974. Asst. prof. religion Siena Coll., Loudonville, N.Y., 1979-80; asst. prof. Christian edn. U. Dubuque (Iowa) Theol. Sem., 1980-82; pastor 1st Presby. Ch., Andrew & Emeline Presby. Chs., Iowa, 1982-84; asst. prof. religion Luther Coll., Decorah, Iowa, 1984-86; asst. prof. religion St. Olaf Coll., Northfield, Iowa, 1986-91, asst. prof. religion emerita, 1991—; organizing sec. Christian Edn. Movement South Africa, 1959-65. Author: Authority in Paul and Peter, 1983, Harpers Bible Dictionary, 1985; editor Christian Edn., 1959-65; contbr. articles to profl. jours. Com. mem. So. Africa Resource Ctr., Mpls., 1984-90; Minn. rep. Africa Network, Evanston, Ill., 1986-90. Mem. Soc. Bibl. Lit., Cath. Bibl. Assn., Inst. for Contextual Theology (Republic of South Africa. Home: 206 N Plum Northfield MN 55057

MUNSEY, FRANK TORRANCE, minister; b. Caldwell, Idaho, Oct. 29, 1922; s. Cassius Marcellus and Hazel Pearl (Torrance) M.; m. Deloris Mildred Beach, Sept. 8, 1943; children: Marilyn Lee Munsey Kreuder, Michael Frank. BTh, Walla Walla Coll., 1946; postgrad., U. Mont., 1956-59; postgrad. (summer), Seventh-day Adventist Sem., 1957. Ordained to ministry, 1950. Pastor Upper Columbia (Wash.) Conf., 1946-49, Fairbanks and Anchorage, 1950-53, Mont. Conf., 1953-62, Nev.-Utah Conf., 1962-65; pastor Reno Seventh-day Adventist Ch., Santa Cruz, Calif., 1965-74, Ceres, Calif., 1974-85; retired, 1985; mem. exec. com. Alaska Mission, 1952-53, exec. com. Nev.-Utah Conf., 1962-65, Cen. Calif. Conf., 1974—; chaplain Pacific Press Pub. Assn., 1988-90. Contbr. articles to religious jours. Home: 22517 Bauman Dr Wilder ID 83676

MUNSON, ROGER L., bishop. Bishop Northwestern Minn. Evang. Luth. Ch. in Am., Duluth, Minn. Office: Evang Ch in Am 3900 London Rd Duluth MN 55804*

MUNTEAN, GEORGE, music minister; b. Arad, Romania, Apr. 19, 1950; came to U.S., 1973; s. Nicolae Muntean and Letitia Pecican; m. Terezia Isfan, May 15, 1973; children: George Jr., David, Clara, Diana. Grad. music sch., Romania, 1968. Min. music Romania, 1973, U.S., 1973—; min. music Romanian Ch. of God, Sacramento, 1990—.

MURAKAMI, TOSHIO, bishop. Bishop Buddhists Chs. Can., Vancouver, B.C. Office: Buddhist Chs Can, 220 Jackson Ave, Vancouver, BC Canada V6A 3B3*

MURDOCK, DELMAR CURTIS, music minister; b. Atlanta, Sept. 3, 1952; s. Delmar Lazelle and Peggy Ann (Morgan) M.; m. Georganne Chatham, May 13, 1972; 1 child, Winston Curtis. MusB, U. Ala., 1974, BS in Edn., 1975, MA, 1977. Ordained to ministry Bapt. Ch., 1982. Minister of music/ youth Northwood Hills Bapt. Ch., Northport, Ala., 1973-77, First Bapt. Ch., Jackson, Ga., 1977-81; minister of music/adminstrn. Clarkston (Ga.) Bapt. Ch., 1981-88; minister of music Beech Haven Bapt. Ch., Athens, Ga., 1988—; handbell dir. The Sons of Jubal, Atlanta, 1982—; exec. com. Ga. Bapt. Conv., Atlanta, 1987-88; faculty mem. Youth Music Camp Ga. Bapt. Conv., 1981. Contbr. articles to profl. jours. Bd. dirs. United Way of Butts County, Jackson, Ga., 1979-81; chmn. Cystic Fibrosis Found., Jackson, 1978-81; mem. blood svcs. com. East Ga. Chpt. ARC, Athens, 1990—. Dean's Scholar, U. Ala. Grad. Sch., 1976. Mem. Am. Guild English Handbell Ringers, Chorister's Guild, Ga. Bapt. Ch. Music Conf. (v.p. 1990-92), So. Bat. Ch. Music Conf., Pi Kappa Lambda. Home: 1210 Old Farm Rd Watkinsville GA 30677 Office: Beech Haven Bapt Ch 2390 W Broad St Athens GA 30606

MURK, LYNDON KEITH, minister; b. Amor, Minn., June 12, 1926; s. Gilbert Gabriel and Mabel (Lien) M. BA, Augustana Coll., Rock Island, Ill., 1947; MA, Pacific Luth. U., 1971. Ordained to ministry Luth. Ch., 1951. Pastor Bethel Luth. Ch., Gt. Falls, Mont., 1951-64, Tacoma, 1964—; chaplain Boy Scouts Am., 1960, 73, 77, Am. Guild Organists, Tacoma, 1979—; pres., dir. Assoc. Ministries, Tacoma, 1974-78. Author: The Influence of Martin Bucer, 1971. Recipient Silver Beaver award Boy Scouts Am., 1960, Vigil Honor Order of Arrow Boy Scouts Am., 1960, Lamb award Luth. Coun. USA, 1975. Mem. Hymn Soc. Am., Soc. for Preservation and Encouragement of Barber Shop Quartet Singing in Am. (treas. Tacoma chpt. 1975—), Kiwanis (dir. Gt. Falls club 1957-61, pres. 1960, dir. Tacoma club 1984—), Order of Runeberg (pres. 1980-82). Home: 7240 S Bell St Tacoma WA 98408 Office: Bethel Luth Ch 905 S 54th St Tacoma WA 98408

MURPHREE, JON TAL, clergyman, philosophy and theology educator; b. Wedowee, Ala., Dec. 17, 1936; s. Hobart and Winnie Mae (Crumpton) M.; m. Sheila Marie Black, June 12, 1971; children: Marisa, Mark. BA, Asbury Coll., Wilmore, Ky., 1959; MDiv, Asbury Theol. Sem., 1964; MA, U. Ky., 1975. Ordained to ministry Meth. Ch., 1964. Pastor Meth. Ch., Wedowee, 1953-56, Crandall, Ind., 1956-59, Clarksville, Ind., 1959-60; gen. evangelist United Meth. Ch., 1965-80; adminstrv. dir. Servants in Faith and Tech., Lineville, Ala., 1980-81; prof. philosophy, theology and homiletics Toccoa Falls Coll., Toccoa, Ga., 1981—. Author: Adventure Not Alone, 1969, Giant of a Century Trail, 1969, The Incredible Discovery, 1972, When God Says You're Okay, 1975, A Loving God and a Suffering World, 1981, Made to Be Mastered, 1984, Serving in Faith, 1990, The Love Motive, 1990; editor Evangelade Echoes, 1965-80, The Provoker, 1980-81; contbr. articles to profl. jours. Avocations: sports, carpentry, reading. Home: 936 Green Valley Dr Toccoa GA 30577 Office: Toccoa Falls Coll PO Box 800307 Toccoa Falls GA 30598

MURPHY, CAROL ROZIER, librarian, writer, editor; b. Boston, Dec. 7, 1916; d. Charles Rozier and Mildred Johnston (Knight) M. AB, Swarthmore Coll., 1937; MA, Am. U., 1941. Assoc. editor Approach, Rosemont, Pa., 1948-67; mem. publs. com. Pendle Hill, Wallingford, Pa., 1949—; mem. worship and ministry com. Swarthmore (Pa.) Friends Meeting, 1976-82, Phila. Yearly Meeting, 1982-85; librarian Swarthmore Friends Meeting, 1983—; mem. book services com. Phila. Yearly Meeting, 1985—. Author 17 Pendle Hill Pamphlets, 1949-89; contbr. articles and essays to profl. jours. Mem. Ch. and Synagogue Library Assn. Democrat. Home: 201 S Swarthmore Ave Swarthmore PA 19081 *Religion derives its life from immediate apprehension of a reality more fundamental than the secular, a reality which manifests itself in Nature and at the same time judges it. Religion flowers in lives of loving communion.*

MURPHY, CLAUDE WAYNE, minister; b. Montpelier, Va., Dec. 1, 1946; s. Marshall and Viola Lucille (Lowry) M.; m. Diana Fay Lease, Aug. 18, 1967; children: Marianne Celeste, Rebecca Denise. BA in Bibl. Studies, Ea. Christian Coll., 1983; M in Ministry, Ky. Christian Coll., 1985; MA in Practical Ministries, Cin. Christian Sem., 1990. Ordained to ministry Chs. of Christ, 1967. Min. Ringgold Ch. of Christ, Hagerstown, Md., 1968-70, Grover (Pa.) Ch. of Christ, 1970-75, Blvd. Christian Ch., Balt., 1975-81; dean adminstrv. svcs. Ea. Christian Coll., Bel Air, Md., 1981-86, trustee, 1976-81, 88-91; min. Levittown (Pa.) Christian Ch., 1986—; dir. Mid-Atlantic Christian Ch. Evangelism, Balt., 1975—; asst. coord. Ea. Christian Conv., Joppatowne, Md., 1978—; mem. guidance com. Dept. of Missions,

Bel Air, 1979—. Mem. NRA (life). Home: 65 Deep Dale Dr E Levittown PA 19056 Office: Levittown Christian Ch 1481 Frosty Hollow Rd Levittown PA 19056 *You are not what you think you are, but what you think, you are.*

MURPHY, FREDERICK JAMES, religion educator; b. Worcester, Mass., Aug. 16, 1949; s. James Francis and Hazel Louise (Pettway) M.; m. Leslie Sue Trencher, July 19, 1980; children: Rebecca Miriam, Jeremy Trencher. AB, Harvard U., 1971, AM, 1981, PhD, 1984; BD, U. London, 1978. Assoc. prof., dept. chair Coll. of Holy Cross, Worcester, 1983—. Author: The Structure and Meaning and Second Baruch, 1985, The Religious World of Jesus, 1991; also articles. Mem. Am. Acad. Religion, Soc. Bibl. Lit., Cath. Bibl. Assn., Coll. Theology Soc. Roman Catholic. Home: 196 Beaconsfield Rd Worcester MA 01602 Office: Coll Holy Cross 1 College St Worcester MA 01610

MURPHY, IRENE HELEN, publishing executive; b. Boston; d. Charles Leo and Irene Muriel (Finney) M. BA, Regis Coll., 1958; MA, Boston Coll., 1963, Northeastern U., Boston, 1968, Manhattanville Coll., 1969. Tchr. elem. sch. Boston, high sch. dir. guidance, ednl. adminstr., prof. master tchr. program, 1969—; prof. N.Y.C.; dir. sch. svcs. Glencoe Pub. Co., Mission Hills, Calif., 1969—, v.p.; vis. lectr. univs., including Boston Coll., Sacred Heart U., St. John, Nfld., Regis Coll., Teachers Coll., Sidney, Australia, Teachers Coll., Melbourne, Australia, McGill U., Mont., Providence (R.I.) Coll. Author series ednl. games for children. Recipient Gold Seal Recognition award Today's Cath. Tchr., 1987. Mem. Nat. Cath. Edn. Assn., Nat. Assn. Female Execs., AAUW, Jordan Hosp. Club, St. Peter Cath. Women's Club, Adminstrs. Club, Passport Club. Roman Catholic. Avocations: sports, music, art work, poetry, literature. Home: 59 Summer St Plymouth MA 02360 also: 2677 SW Thunderbird Trail Stuart FL 34997 Office: Benziger Pub Co 15319 Chatsworth Mission Hills CA 91346-9609 *In our times perhaps the greatest need of all is to return to the meaning of the Sacred in life, the importance of Presence—God's presence and the presence of others in building a true community with global implication of respect for all.*

MURPHY, JAMES HENRY, priest, educator; b. Dublin, Ireland, May 15, 1959; s. Philip Patrick and Barbara Mary (O'Hare) M. BA, Nat. U. Ireland, 1980; BDiv, U. London, 1983; diploma in Pastoral Studies, All Hallows Coll., Dublin, 1984; higher diploma in Edn., Dublin U., 1987; PhD in English, Univ. Coll., Dublin, 1991. Joined Congregation of Mission, 1976, ordained priest Roman Cath. Ch., 1985. Dir. adult edn., mem. retreat team All Hallows Coll., 1984-85; tchr. English and Religious Studies, dir. liturgy Castleknock Coll., Dublin, 1985-89; researcher Univ. Coll., Dublin, 1989-91; lectr. in English, dir. M.A. programme All Hallows Coll., Dublin, 1991—. Author: No Bland Facility, 1991. Avocations: reading, walking. Home and Office: All Hallows Coll, Dromcondra, Dublin 9, Ireland

MURPHY, JOHN FRANCIS, clergyman; b. Lexington, Ky., Feb. 25, 1923; s. John Francis and Elizabeth (Geary) M. A.B., St. Meinrad's Sem. Coll., 1946; S.T.L., Cath. U. Am., 1947; hon. degrees, 1958, St. Thomas Inst., St. Ambrose Coll., Bellarmine Coll., Mt. St. Mary Coll., Barry Coll., Austin Coll., Thomas More Coll. Instr. Villa Madonna Coll. (named changed to Thomas More Coll. 1968), Covington, Ky., 1948-51, acad. dean, 1951-53, pres., 1953-71; apptd. v.p. for univ. rels. Cath. U. Am., Washington, 1971-74; exec. dir. Assn. Cath. Colls. and Univs., Washington, 1974-80; dir. pastoral planning and research Diocese of Covington, Ky., 1980-87; pastor St. Agnes Ch., Ft. Wright, Ky., 1982—. Charter mem. Covington-Kenton County Commn. on Human Rights. Named domestic prelate by Pope John XXIII, 1960. Address: 1680 Dixie Hwy Fort Wright KY 41011

MURPHY, BROTHER (PATRICK) MARK, religious order superior; b. San Francisco, Sept. 26, 1942; s. William and Florence (Coleman) M. AB, St. Mary's Coll., Moraga, Calif., 1965; MA, U. Detroit, 1971. Joined Bros. of the Christian Schs., Roman Cath. Ch.; ordained priest Roman Cath. Ch. Tchr. San Joaquin Meml. High Sch., Fresno, Calif., 1965-70; tchr., prin. St. Mary's Coll. High Sch., Berkeley, Calif., 1977-80; aux. visitor De La Salle Inst., Moraga, Calif., 1980-87, pres., visitor, provincial, 1987—; v.p. Regional Coun. Christian Bros., 1989—; bd. dirs. Camping Unltd., Berkeley, Calif. Chmn. bd. trustees St. Mary's Coll., Moraga, 1989—; bd. dirs. Queen of the Valley Hosp., Napa, Calif., 1989—. Office: De La Salle Inst 4401 Redwood Rd Napa CA 94558-9708

MURPHY, MICHAEL JOSEPH, retired bishop; b. Cleve., July 1, 1915; s. William and Mary Bridget (Patton) M. B.A. in Philosophy, Gregorian U., Rome, 1938; S.T.L., Catholic U. Am., 1942. Ordained priest Roman Catholic Ch., 1942; prof. pro-tem St. Mary Sem., Cleve., 1943-45, prof., 1947-48, vice-rector, 1948-63, rector, 1963-76; Episcopal vicar Chancery Office, Cleve., 1976-78; coadjutor bishop of Erie, Chancery office (Pa.), 1978-82, bishop of Erie, 1982-90; cons. com. on doctrine Nat. Conf. Cath. Bishops. Recipient first Ann. Sem. Dept. award Nat. Cath. Ednl. Assn. Home: 130 E 4th St Erie PA 16507 Office: St Mark Ctr PO Box 10397 Erie PA 16514-0397

MURPHY, SISTER MICHELLE, nun; b. N.Y.C., July 2, 1927; d. Michael A. and Elizabeth A. (Sweeney) M. BA, Marymount Coll., 1949; MA, Laval U., 1950; MBA with distinction, Pace U., 1980. Joined Religious Order of Sacred Heart of Mary, Roman Cath. Ch., 1945; CPA, N.Y.; cert. mgmt. acct. Provincial treas. Religious of Sacred Heart of Mary, N.Y.C. and Tarrytown, N.Y., 1964-76; audit staff Peat Marwick Mitchell, N.Y.C., 1980-81; asst. prof. Lubin Sch. Bus. Pace U., Pleasantville, N.Y., 1981-84; v.p. fin., treas. Marymount U., Arlington, Va., 1984—; trustee Marymount Sch. N.Y., N.Y.C., 1969—, Loyola Marymount U., L.A., 1989—; v.p. Sisters' Coun., Arlington, Va., 1984-90; regent Marymount Sch., Richmond, Va., 1985—; del. Internat. Plan Group, Religious of Sacred Heart of Mary, Rome, 1988, 89. Mem. AICPA, Nat. Assn. Accts., Inst. Cert. Mgmt. Accts., Nat. Assn. Col. and Univ. Bus. Officers, So. Assn. Coll. and Univ. Bus. Officers. Home and Office: 2807 N Glebe Rd Arlington VA 22207

MURPHY, NANCEY CLAIRE, Christian philosophy educator; b. Alliance, Nebr., June 12, 1951; d. Richard D. and Shirley Marie (Walker) M.; m. James William McClendon, Jr., July 30, 1983; 1 child, André G. Fedán. BA, Creighton U., 1973; PhD, U. Calif., Berkeley, 1980; ThD, Grad. Theol. Union, 1987. Vis. instr. philosophy Dominican Sch. Philosophy and Theology, Berkeley, 1987-88; vis. asst. prof. religion Whittier (Calif.) Coll., 1988-89; asst. prof. Christian philosophy Fuller Theol. Sem., Pasadena, Calif., 1989—. Author: Theology in the Age of Scientific Reasoning, 1990; contbr. articles to profl. jours. NSF fellow, 1973-76. Mem. Ctr. for Theology and the Natural Scis. (bd. dirs. 1984—), Am. Acad. Religion, Soc. Christian Philosophers. Baptist. Office: Fuller Theol Sem 135 N Oakland Ave Pasadena CA 91182

MURPHY, PHILIP FRANCIS, bishop; b. Cumberland, Md., Mar. 25, 1933; s. Philip A.M. and Kathleen (Huth) M. Ed. St. Mary Sem., Balt., N.Am. Coll., Rome. Ordained priest Roman Catholic Ch., 1958; asst. pastor St. Bernardine Ch., Balt., 1959-61; asst. vice rector N.Am. Coll., Rome, 1961-65; sec. to Cardinal Archbishop, Balt., 1965-74, chancellor, 1975; ordained titular bishop of Tacarata and aux. of Balt., 1976—. Office: Archdiocese of Balt 320 Cathedral St Baltimore MD 21201

MURPHY, REGINA, religious organization administrator; b. Buffalo, May 27, 1945; d. Walter Timothy and Mary Elizabeth (Strauss) M. BA, Cath. U. Am., 1967; MA, Marquette U., 1975. Tchr. Mt. St. Mary Acad., Kenmore, N.Y., 1967-69, St. Mary's Sem., Buffalo, 1969-71, St. Jude High Sch., Sumter, S.C., 1971-75; prin. St. Jude High Sch., 1975-79; tchr. Mt. St. Mary Acad., Kenmore, 1979-82; asst. prin. Mt. St. Mary Acad., 1982-86, contr., 1986-87, investment mgr., 1987-88; assoc. dir. Office Research & Planning, Cath. Diocese of Buffalo, 1988-91; dir. dept. rsch. and planning Cath. Diocese of Buffalo, Bufflao, 1991—; trustee Sisters of St. Mary of Namur Kenmore, 1984-88; ethics instr. Cath. Diocese of Buffalo, 1987—. Contbr. articles to profl. jours.; composer hymns. Mem. Hastings Ctr. Mem. Nat. Pastoral Life Ctr. Conf. for Pastoral Planning and Coun. Devel. Democrat. Roman Catholic. Avocations: sewing, reading, music, tennis. Office: The Cath Ctr 795 Main St Buffalo NY 14203

MURPHY, ROLAND EDMUND, retired religion educator, priest; b. Chgo., July 19, 1917; s. John and Marian (Haugh) M. MA in Philosophy, Cath. U. Am., 1943, STD, 1948, MA in Semitics, 1949; SSL, Rome Bibl. Inst., 1958. Joined Order of Carmelites, Roman Cath. Ch., 1935, ordained priest, 1942. Prof. O.T., Cath. U. Am., Washington, 1948-70; George Washington Ivey prof. O.T., Duke U. Div. Sch., Durham, N.C., 1971-86, prof. emeritus, 1986—. Author: Wisdom Literature, 1981, The Song of Songs, 1990; co-editor: The New Jerome Biblical Commentary, 1990; contbr. articles to profl. jours. Mem. Cath. Bibl. Assn., Soc. Bibl. Lit. Home: Whitefriars Hall 1600 Webster St NE Washington DC 20017

MURPHY, SHARON MARGARET, academic administrator, journalism educator; b. Milw., Aug. 2, 1940; d. Adolph Leonard and Margaret Ann (Hirtz) Feyen; m. James Emmett Murphy, June 28, 1969 (dec. May 1983); children: Shannon Lynn, Erin Ann. BA, Marquette U., 1965; MA, U. Iowa, 1970, PhD, 1973. Cert. K-14 tchr., Iowa. Tchr. elem. and secondary schs., Wis., 1959-69; dir. publs. Kirkwood Community Coll., Cedar Rapids, Iowa, 1969-71; instr. journalism U. Iowa, Iowa City, 1971-73; asst. prof. U. Wis., Milw., 1973-79; assoc. prof. So. Ill. U., Carbondale, 1979-84; dean/prof. Marquette U., Milw., 1984—; pub. relations dir. and editor Worldwide mag., Milw., 1965-68; reporter Milw. Sentinel, 1967; Fulbright sr. lectr. U. Nigeria, Nsukka, 1977-78. Author: Other Voices: Black, Chicano & American Indian Press, 1971; (with Wigal) Screen Experience: An Approach to Film, 1968, (with Murphy) Let My People Know: American Indian Journalism, 1981, (with Schilpp) Great Women of the Press, 1983; editor: (book, with others) International Perspectives on News, 1982. Bd. dirs. Youth Communication, Inc., Washington, 1986—, Dow Jones Newspaper Fund, N.Y., 1986—. Recipient Medal of Merit, Journalism Edn. Assn., 1976, Outstanding Achievement award Greater Milw. YWCA, 1989; named Knight of Golden Quill, Milw. Press Club, 1977; Nat. headliner Women in Communication, Inc., 1985. Mem. Assn. for Edn. in Journalism and Mass Communications (pres. 1986-87), Accrediting Council on Edn. Journalism and Mass Communications (v.p. 1983-86), Internat. Communication Assn., Tempo, Soc. Profl. Journalists. Democrat. Roman Catholic. Office: Marquette U Coll of Communication Journalism and Performing Arts Milwaukee WI 53233

MURPHY, TERRENCE JOHN, priest, college president; b. Watkins, Minn., Dec. 21, 1920; s. Frank and Mary (Lee) M. B.A., St. Paul Sem., 1946; M.A., U. Minn., 1956; Ph.D., Georgetown U., 1959. Ordained priest, Roman Catholic church, 1946, became monsignor, 1966. Asst. pastor various parishes, 1946-49; chaplain USAF, 1949-54; mem. faculty Coll. St. Thomas, St. Paul, 1954-61, dean of students, 1961-62, exec. v.p., 1962-66, pres., 1966—; del. Congress Cath. Edn., Rome, 1972; mem. Minn. Pvt. Coll. Council., Minn. Pvt. Coll. Fund.; bd. dirs. Am. Nat. Bank, St. Paul, Waldorf Corp., St. Paul. Author: Censorship: Government and Obscenity, 1963. Bd. dirs. Mt. St. Mary's Coll. of Md., Associated Colls. Twin Cities, Minn. Wellspring. Mem. Nat. Cath. Ednl. Assn., Assn. Post-Secondary Ednl. Instns. Minn., Assn. Am. Colls., Internat. Fedn. Cath. Univs. (dir.). Office: Coll St Thomas 2115 Summit Ave Saint Paul MN 55105

MURPHY, THOMAS AUSTIN, bishop; b. Balt., May 11, 1911; s. Thomas Andrew and Ella Cecilia (Brady) M. Student, St. Charles Coll., Balt., 1925-31; A.B., St. Mary Sem., Balt., 1935, S.T.B., 1937. Ordained priest Roman Cath. Ch., 1937; pastor Ch. St. Rose of Lima, Balt., 1961—; auxiliary to archbishop of Balt., 1962—, titular bishop of Appiaria. Office: 320 Cathedral St Baltimore MD 21201

MURPHY, THOMAS JOSEPH, archbishop; b. Chgo., Oct. 3, 1932; s. Barthomew Thomas and Nellie M. AB, St. Mary of the Lake Sem., 1954, STB, 1956, MA, 1957, STL, 1958, STD, 1960. Ordained priest Roman Cath. Ch., 1958. Various positions with Archdiocese of Chgo.; bishop of Great Falls-Billings Mont., 1978-87; coadjutor archbishop of Seattle, 1987-91, archbishop of Seattle, 1991—. Office: Archdiocese of Seattle 910 Marion St Seattle WA 98104

MURPHY, WILLIAM F., priest, monsignor, religion educator; b. Boston, May 14, 1940; s. Cornelius John and Norma (Duggan) M. AB, St. John Sem., Brighton, Mass., 1961; S.T. Lic., Pontifical Gregorian U., Rome, 1965, S.T.D., 1974. Ordained priest in Roman Cath. Ch. Asst. pastor Archdiocese of Boston, 1965-70; asst. prof. theology Emmanuel Coll., Boston, 1968-74, Pope John XXIII Sem., Weston, Mass., 1974; under-sec. Pontifical Coun., Justice and Peace, Rome, 1974-87; sec. for community rels. Archdiocese of Boston, Brighton, 1987—; lectr. social ethics St. John Sem., Brighton, 1987—. Author: Social Ethics, 1978, 80, International Politics, 1983, Theology, 1985. Mem. Tavern Club (Boston). Home: 1518 Beacon St Waban MA 02168 Office: Roman Cath Archdiocese of Boston 2101 Commonwealth Ave Brighton MA 02135

MURRAY, SISTER ANNE, nun, school principal; b. Mullingar, Ireland, July 8, 1934; d. Patrick and Mary Catherine (Browne) M. BA, U. San Diego, 1965; MA, U. San Francisco, 1975. Cert. tchr., Calif. Tchr. Holy Spirit Grade Sch., San Diego, 1960-67, tchr., prin., 1969-73; tchr. St. Anthony Grade Sch., San Bernardino, Calif., 1967-69, St. Columba Grade Sch., San Diego, 1973-74; prin. Our Lady of the Assumption, San Bernardino, 1975-83, Notre Dame High Sch., Riverside, Calif., 1983—; staff El Carmelo Retreat House, Redlands, 1983—. Office: Notre Dame High Sch 7085 Brockton Ave Riverside CA 92506

MURRAY, BARBARA ANN, lay minister; b. Ft. Knox, Ky., June 29, 1948; d. Leonard Orrie and Karen Lydia (Grabis) M. AA, Elizabethtown (Ky.) Community Coll., 1968; BA magna cum laude, Cardinal Stritch Coll., Milw., 1988. Min. youth Holy Family Ch., Ashland, Ky., 1988-90; coord. youth ministries Roman Cath. Diocese of Lexington, Ky., 1991. Corr. The Messenger jour., 1989, Cross Roads, 1990-91. Mem. Nat. Assn. Religious Women, Pax Christi U.S.A., Kappa Gamma Pi. Democrat. Home: 631 S Limestone Lexington KY 40508 Office: Cath Diocese of Lexington 1310 Leestown Rd Lexington KY 40508

MURRAY, BERNARD JOSEPH, former theology educator, former municipal government administrator; b. Syracuse, N.Y., Sept. 11, 1915; s. Robert Thomas and Elizabeth Amelia (Reagan) M.; m. Ann Teresa Hynes, June 7, 1975. BA in Liberal Arts, Georgetown U., 1939; Ph.L., Woodstock Coll., 1940, BS in Theology, 1945, Th.L., 1947. Joined S.J., Roman Cath. Ch., 1934, ordained priest Roman Cath. Ch., 1946, received papal dispensation from religious vows and clerical celibacy, 1974. Assoc. prof. theology LeMoyne Coll., Syracuse, 1948-53, 60-63, chmn. dept., 1952-53, 60-63; assoc. prof., chmn. dept. Canisius Coll., Buffalo, 1953-56; assoc. prof. Loyola Coll., Montreal, Que., Can., 1956-57; assoc. prof., asst. chmn. dept. Fordham U., N.Y.C., 1957-60; exam. mgr. N.Y.C. Transit Authority, 1980-90. Co-author: Christ in His Members, 1955; contbr. articles to Am. mag. Democrat. Home: 271 Ave C # MF New York NY 10009 *I sum up my life experience in the one word, trust—trust in the loving concern of God my Father, shown to me in the life, teaching and example of my Brother, the crucified and risen Jesus and in the abiding if mysterious guidance of my Friend, the indwelling Spirit. I look forward to death as the entrance into the Great Adventure.*

MURRAY, CHARLES B., minister; b. San Antonio, June 23, 1948; s. Don and Ellen Jean (Weldon) M.; m. Karon L. Black, Aug. 20, 1967; children: Angela, Nathan. BA, Hardin-Simmons U., 1970; MDiv, Southwestern Bapt. Theol. Sem., Ft. Worth, 1973, D Ministry, 1976. Ordained to ministry So. Bapt. Conv., 1967. Interim pastor Makakilo Bapt. Chapel, Makakilo City, Hawaii, 1968; pastor Drasco Bapt. Ch., Winters, Tex., 1968-71; assoc. pastor North Richland Hills (Tex.) Bapt. Ch., 1972-74; pastor Trinity Bapt. Ch., Loveland, Colo., 1974-80, 1st Bapt. Ch., Ellisville, Mo., 1980—; mem. exec. com. So. Bapt. Conv., Nashville, 1989—; vice chmn. exec. bd. Colo. Bapt. Gen. Conv., Denver, 1978. Author: Genesis: Book of Beginnings, 1988, You Are a Gifted Child, 1989, The Message from the Tabernacle for Today, 1990. Trustee S.W. Bapt. U., 1982-90. Charles Haddon Spurgeon fellow William Jewell Coll., 1986, Walter Pope Binns fellow, 1988. Mem. Alpha Mu Gamma. Office: 1st Bapt Ch 137 Clarkson Rd Ellisville MO 63011 *The joy of my life and ministry is to introduce people to the vital and valuable truth that a relationship with God is not just to get man to heaven but rather to get God out of heaven into man.*

MURRAY, DANIEL AUGUSTINE, rector, educator; b. Phila., Nov. 27, 1937; s. Daniel Joseph and Catherine Theresa (Hoban) M. BA, St. Charles Sem., 1961; STL, Gregorian U., 1965; SSL, Pontificial Bib. Inst., 1970. Ordained priest Roman Cath. Ch., 1964. Asst. pastor St. Richard Ch., Phila., 1965; prof. Cardinal O'Hara High Sch., Springfield, Pa., 1965-67; student priest Cath. U. of Am., Washington, 1967-68, Pontifical Bib. Inst., Rome, 1968-70; weekend asst. Nativity Ch., Media, Pa., 1970—; prof. sacred scripture St. Charles Sem., Overbrook, Pa., 1970—, rector, 1988—, bd. trustees, 1974—, sec. bd. trustees, 1983—, chairperson instl. planning com., 1984-88; auditor Synod of Bishops, Rome, 1990. Gen. editor: The Catholic Study Bible, 1985, The Living Word in the Living Church, 1986; author weekly column The Sunday Mass in Focus, 1980-88. Mem. Cath. Bibl. Assn., Fellowship of Cath. Scholars. Romam Catholic. Home and Office: 1000 E Wynnewood Rd Overbrook PA 19096

MURRAY, DAVID, pastor, social worker; b. Chgo., Mar. 4, 1953; s. Julius and Alberta (Tolbert) M. m. Debra McKnight, Oct. 7, 1989; 1 foster child, Maurice Ruffin. BS in Criminal Justice, Wayne State U., Detroit, 1982; DDiv, God's Divine Emancipation Tng., 1975; MA in Teaching, Wayne State U., 1989. Cert. K-8 tchr., Mich. Pastor First Holy Temple Ch., Detroit, 1975—; asst. payments worker Mich. Dept. of Social Svcs., Detroit, 1981-85, social svcs. specialist, 1985—. Inventor cardiovascular display system. Pres., bd. dirs. Project Care, Detroit, 1975; mem. Detroit Police Reserve, 1978-83, chaplains corps Southfield Police Dept., 1978-83; instr. CPR ARC, Detroit, 1979, advanced 1st aid, 1980—; chaplain Detroit Receiving Hosp., 1978—; religious worker Wayne County Youth Home, 1988—; instr., trainer Am. Heart Assn., Detroit, 1983—; active Big Bros./Big Sisters Am.; religious worker Wayne County Youth Home, 1988—. Recipient cert. Appreciation IRS, Acctg. Aid Soc., 1987, Mayor of Detroit Proclamation, 1987, Detroit City Clk. Disting. Citizen award, 1988, Wayne County Commrs. cert. Appreciation, Mich. Senate Spl. tribute, 1988, U.S. Senate proclamation, 1988, Spirit of Detroit award, 1988, TV 2 Jefferson award 1991 cert. nomination. Mem. NAACP, NASW, Internat. Conf. Police Chaplains, Am. Assn. Counseling Devel., Detroit Fedn. Tchrs., Mich. Police Chaplains Assn., Mich. Conf. Police Chaplains, Eighth Point Investigations, Detroit Police Chaplains Corps, Detroit Police Officers Assn., Masons, Golden Key (nat. honor soc.). Avocations: table tennis, music. Home: 18994 Oak Dr Detroit MI 48221

MURRAY, DAVID ALEXANDER, minister; b. Mobile, Ala., July 26, 1947; s. Henry Alexander and Peggy (Hoover) M.; m. Kathryn Hefner, May 31, 1970 (dec. May 1973); m. Deborah Lou Patronas, June 1, 1974; 1 child, Jonathan David . BS in Edn., Ark. State U., 1970; M of Div. with honors, Midwestern Bapt. Theol. Sem., 1973. Enlisted U.S. Army, 1970, advanced through grades to capt., resigned, 1978; tchr., coach Ind. Meth. Ch. Sch., Mobile, 1974-76, Chickasaw (Ala.) Acad., 1976-78; tchr. Williamson High Sch., Mobile, 1978-79; pastor Georgetown-Chuncula (Ala.) Meth. Ch., 1979-81, Ebenezer United Meth. Ch., Wagarville, Ala., 1981-85, Curtis Meml. United Meth., Dothan, Ala., 1985—; Deacon Meth. Ch., 1981, elder, 1983; mem. Bd. Ordained Dist. Ministry, Dothan, 1986-87. Mem. Bd. of Ch. and Soc. Avocations: music, sports. Home: Rte 2 Box 75 Deatsville AL 36022

MURRAY, DAVID MICHAEL, priest; b. Phila., Mar. 12, 1940; s. Noel Lewis Murray and Margaret Watson (Reid) Robinson; m. Kathleen Anne McBeth, June 10, 1979; children: Shane, Brady, Brian, Noel. Student, Ga. State U., 1971-73; MA, Pitts. State U., 1981, 82; MDiv, U. of the South, 1987. Profl. musician, Nashville, 1964-67; office mgr. AMSCO Union Oil Co., Atlanta, 1968-71; broadcast journalist Sta. WYZE, Atlanta, 1973-76, Horne Industries, Searcy, Ark. and El Dorado, Kans., Sta. KKOW Radio, Pittsburgh, Kans., 1979-84; lectr. speech U. of the South, Sewanee, Tenn., 1985-87; project officer Diocese Kans., Topeka, 1987-90; rector Grace Episcopal Ch., Ottawa, Kans., 1987-89; bus. mgr. Diocese of Kans., Topeka, 1989-90, canon adminstr., 1990—. Contbr. article to profl. jours. Mem. Crawford County Mental Health Bd., Pittsburgh, Kans., 1981-83. With U.S. Army, 1961-64. DuBose scholarship, 1985-87, Mercer scholarship Diocese of Long Island, Sewanee, 1985-87. Mem. Alban Inst. Washington, Associated Parishes Alexandria, Va., Coll. Preachers Washington, Kiwanis. Democrat. Avocations: photography, model railroading, guitar. Office: Diocese of Kans 835 SW Polk St Topeka KS 66612

MURRAY, FERNE HANNAH, minister; b. Lindsay, Calif., Feb. 21, 1918; d. Price Ervin and Hannah (Hylton) Robertson; m. Raymond P. Murray, July 23, 1938 (dec. Oct. 1987); children: Ronald Paul, William Raymond, Sharon Yvonne. Grad., Bethany Bible Coll., 1938, postgrad., 1955; cert. social work, U. Calif., Berkeley, 1957; cert. deferred gifts & trusts, G.M. Caswell Assoc., 1978. Co-pastor Tabernacle Assembly of God, Ukiah, Calif., 1941-45; dir. religious edn. 1st Assembly of God, Santa Cruz, Calif., 1945-61; exec. sec. Northern Calif. NEv. Women's Orgn., Santa Cruz, 1952-58; co-pastor Calvary Temple Assembly of God, Concord, Calif., 1962-69; aminstr., asst. dept. devel. World Evangelism, San Diego, 1977-79; cons., State Dept. Social Welfare, Sacramento, 1957-77; nat. chmn. girls orgn. Assemblies of God, Springfield, Mo., 1952-54, guest speaker N.J. dist. Author: Journey into His Presence, 1978, Triumphant Through Adversity, 1988, (manual) WMC Missionary Manual, 1953. Recipient Founders award, citation, Bethany Bible Coll., 1989. Republican. Home: 2 N Stone Edge Rd Bedminster NJ 07921 *My late minister husband suffered with Parkinson's disease and heart problems for 17 years. In caring for him, I found a strength and support in God that gave both of us a deep peace. I found that God's grace is sufficient.*

MURRAY, GEORGE WILLIAM, religious organization administrator; b. Wilmington, Del., Apr. 22, 1945; s. John Wier and Eleanor (Stephens) M.; m. Esther Annette Brice, June 14, 1969; children: Heather, Laura, Frank, Julie. BA, Columbia Bible Coll., 1967; MA, Columbia Bibl. Sem., 1981; postgrad., U. Perugia, Italy, 1971-73, Bibl. Theol. Sem., Hatfield, Pa., 1975, 76, Trinity Evang. Div. Sch., Deerfield, Ill., 1987—. Asst. to pres. Columbia (S.C.) Bible Coll., 1968, 69; missionary Bible Christian Union, Inc., Italy, 1971-83; dir. So. Europe Bible Christian Union, Inc., Italy, Spain, Portugal and Greece, 1980-83; exec. dir. Bible Christian Union, Inc., Europe, 1983—; trustee, exec. v.p. Bible Evangelism, Inc., Hatfield, 1972—; trustee, treas. Columbia Bible Coll. and Sem., 1985—; chmn. Europe com. Interdenominational Fgn. Missions Assn., Wheaton, 1988—. Office: Bible Christian Union Inc 2748 Hatfield Valley Rd Hatfield PA 19440

MURRAY, HUGH LEANDER, deacon; b. Galt, Ont., Can., Feb. 27, 1925; came to U.S., 1951; s. Douglas and Nora (Weiler) Murray. BA, Goddard Coll., 1970; MusB, St. Michael's Choir Sch., 1972; D Ministry, United Theol. Sem., 1990. Ordained deacon Roman Cath. Ch., 1980. Dir. music ministry, organist Rosary Cathedral, Toledo, Ohio, 1951—, cons. to restoration cathedral skinner pipe organ, 1991; part time staff Toledo Diocesan Ministry Program, 1981-88, mem. deacon coun. edn. com., 1991. Author: Deacon Ritual Handbook, 1989; also articles; editor, writer Toledo Diocese, 1983-88. Mem. Am. Guild Organists (choirmaster cert. 1956), Deanery Deacon Fraternity. Home: 4142 Harris St Toledo OH 43613

MURRAY, MONSIGNOR JAMES J., charitable organization administrator. Head Cath. Charities, N.Y.C. Office: Cath Charities 1011 1st Ave New York NY 10022*

MURRAY, SISTER JEAN CAROLYN, college president; b. Broadview, Ill., May 30, 1927. B.A., Rosary Coll., River Forest, Ill., 1949; Ph.D. in French Lang. and Lit., Fribourg, 1961. Instr. French Rosary Coll., 1961-66, asst. prof., 1966-68, assoc. prof., 1968—; pres. Rosary Coll., River Forest, Ill., 1981—; bd. dirs. Fenwick Prep. High Sch. Editor: La genese Dialogues des Carmelites, 1963; editor, translator: Correspondance, choisie et presentee, Vol. I, Combat pour la verite Vol. II, Comban pour la liberte, 1971. Mem. West Cook County Heart Assn., Leadership Greater Chgo. Assocs. Mem. MLA, Am. Assn. Tchrs. French, Ill. Fgn. Lang. Tchrs. Assn., Associated Colls. Ill., Univ. Club Chgo., Chgo. Network, Econ. Club, Fedn. Ind. Colls. and Univs. (vice chair). Home and Office: 7900 W Division River Forest IL 60305

MURRAY, LARRY JAMES, minister; b. Asheville, N.C., Dec. 31, 1945; s. James R. and Nell R. M.; m. Patricia Ann Burris, July 11, 1968; children: Cathy Elaine Murray Banty, Terri Diane. Diploma, Fruitland Bapt. Bible Inst., Hendersonville, N.C., 1977; B in Bible Theology, Internat. Bible Sem.,

1987. Ordained to ministry Bapt. Ch., 1978. Youth leader Bapt. Pole Creek Ch., Candler, N.C., 1974-75; with prison ministry Craggy Prison, Asheville, 1975-76; assoc. pastor, youth min. Hyland Heights Bapt., Lynchburg, Va., 1978-80, min., 1980-81; min. Antioch Bapt., Yale, Va., 1981—; evangelism com. Petersburg (Va.) Bapt. Assn., 1984—. Sgt. U.S. Army, 1965-67, Korea. Republican. Home: Rte 1 PO Box 1A Yale VA 23897 *The greatest challenge today is Christianity is for all who prefers Jesus as Lord is to let Him live through our lives each and every day as He wills.*

MURRAY, LEWELLYN ST. ELMO, minister; b. Colon, Panama, Mar. 25, 1926; came to U.S., 1957; s. Robert Murray and Ida (Samuels) Cunningham, m. Dorothy Adassa Hinds, Nov. 24, 1955; 1 child, Juan R. Murray. Student, Abel Bravo Coll., Colon, 1944-46; grad., George Mercer Sem., 1979. Ordained to ministry Episcopal Ch. as priest, 1981. Vicar St. Lydia's Episcopal Ch., Bklyn., 1981—, spiritual dir., 1992—; acct. Sumner Stores Corp., N.Y.C., 1961; mem. budget com. Episcopal Diocese of N.Y.; instr. lay readers course Diocese of L.I., Garden City, N.Y., 1982—; interim chaplain Bklyn. Psychiat. Ctr. Active east Bkyln. chs., 1982. Recipient Svc. award Chestnut and Crystal Sts. Block Assn., 1988. Office: St Lydia's Episcopal Ch 958 Glenmore Ave PO Box 214 Brooklyn NY 11208

MURRAY, MARTHA BOWMAN, missionary educator; b. Daretown, N.J., Mar. 22, 1951; d. William Redding and Carmela (Ricapito) Bowman; m. Stanley A. Murray, Aug. 4, 1973: children: Christopher Joseph K., Timothy David, Sarah Eileen, Katherine Elizabeth. Grad. Eastern Coll., St. Davids, Pa., 1973; MEd Pa. State U., 1975; MEd, Marywood Coll., 1977. Career missionary Am. Baptist Ch./U.S.A., Valley Forge, Pa., 1979—, currently in Okinawa, Japan. Contbr. articles to profl. jours. Bd. dirs. Okinawa Christian Sch., 1984—. Mem. Christian Women's Club. Home and Office: 1438-1 Uehara Maeda, Urasoe-shi, Okinawa 901 21, Japan

MURRAY, OBIE DALE, minister; b. Leesburg, Fla., Sept. 8, 1950; s. Calvin Obie and Doris Jean (Waddell) M.; m. Mary Donnette Horton, Dec. 21, 1969; children: Catina, Chad, Jeffrey. BS, Lee Coll., 1980. Ordained to ministry Ch. of God, 1986. Pastor Irondale (Ala.) Ch. of God, 1980-82; assoc. pastor Mt. Zion Ch. of God, Snead, Ala., 1982-84; pastor Bynum (Ala.) Ch. of God, 1984-86, Fellowship Ch. of God, Daphne, 1986-89, Winfield (Ala.) Ch. of God, 1989—; evangelism dir. Ch. of God Crossroads Dist., Bay Minette, Ala., 1986-89; dist. youth dir. Ch. of God Fayette (Ala.), 1990—. With U.S. Army, 1970-71. Mem. Winfield Ministerial Assn. (sec.-treas. 1990—), Pi Delta Omicron.

MURRAY, ROBERT EUGENE, religious organization executive; b. Aurora, Ill., July 28, 1926; s. Archie Alexander and Lucille Edith (Reising) M. BA, Loyola U., 1949; MA in Philosophy, West Baden (Ind.) Coll., 1951, MA in Theology, 1958; STD, Gregorian U., 1963. Tchr. St. Ignatius Coll. Preparatory, Chgo., 1951-54; prof. Christian ethics Jesuit Sch. Theology, Chgo., 1963-73, pres., 1965-73; exec. dir. Chgo. Bible Soc., Chgo., 1983—; dir. Chgo. Cluster Theol. Schs., 1966-73; pres., dir. Assn. Chgo. Theol. Schs., 1968-73. Editor, contbr, book revs. Rev. for Religious, 1963-66. Mem. Evang. Coun. for Fin. Accountability. Roman Catholic. Office: Chgo Bible Soc 104 S Michigan Ave Chicago IL 60603

MURRAY, VERNON GAY, minister; b. Keyser, W.Va., June 28, 1945; s. Paul Edward and Ethel Grace (Spessert) M.;m. Margaret Ann Scott, Aug. 14, 1971; children: Jessica Rennee, Rachel Lydia, Timothy Scott, Joel Russell. BA, W.Va. U., 1971; MDiv, Union Theol. Sem, 1988; postgrad., McCormick Theol. Sem., 1988—. Ordained to ministry Presbyn. Ch. (USA), 1988. Pastor Eagle Mills Assembly of God, Harmony, N.C., 1977-78, Washington (N.C.) Assembly of God, 1979-81, Jamesville (N.C.) Assembly of God, 1982-85, South Hill (Va.) Presbyn. Ch., 1988—; house parent Nat Greene Boys Home, Summersville, N.C., 1973-76; parole officer Div. Correction, Kingwood, W.Va., 1971-73; ; mem. Com. on Preparation for Ministry, 1989—. Contbr. articles to profl. jours. Chaplain Parkview Middle Sch. PTA, South Hill, Va., 1989—. Recipient prize 4th Ann. Harper/Collins Best Sermons Competition; Union theol. Sem. grantee, 1985-88; Presbytery of the Peaks, scholar, 1988—. Mem. Southside Clergy Assn. (pres. 1991—), Lions Club (chaplain 1988-91). Home: 808 Windham Ave South Hill VA 23970 Office: 914 N Mecklenburg Ave South Hill VA 23970 *In my life I have not experienced the extraordinary but quite often I have experienced the extra in the ordinary.*

MURRAY, WILLIAM JOSEPH, religious organization administrator; b. Mansfield, Ohio, May 25, 1946; s. William Joseph Murray and Madalyn (Mays) O'Hair; m. Susan Murray (div. 1966); 1 child, Robin; m. Valerie Murray (div.); 1 child, Jade Amber. DD, U.C.I. Bible Inst., 1981. Asst. to pres. WW Cribbing Co., San Francisco, 1965-67; airline agt. Am. Airlines, San Francisco, 1966; ops. agt. Quantas Airlines, Honolulu, 1967-68; ops. mgr. Braniff Airlines, Dallas, 1970-73; v.p. Am. Atheists, Austin, Tex., 1973-76; ops. mgr. Air Pacific, San Francisco, 1977-80; dir., evangelist Freedom's Friends, Dallas, 1981-89; gen. mgr. Dallas-Washington Travel Corp., Dallas, 1989—. Author: My Life Without God, 1982; editor: Bicentennial U.S. Constitutional Education, 1986, Nicaragua: Portrait of Tragedy, 1987, The Church is Not for Perfect People, 1988. Del. Rep. State Conv., Houston, 1988. With U.S. Army 1968-70. Republican. Baptist. Office: Freedom's Friends PO Box 319 Coppell TX 75019

MURREN, DOUGLAS EDWARD, pastor; b. Wenatchee, Wash., July 16, 1951; s. Virgil Edward and Gloria Mae (Humphres) M.; m. Debra Jean Landin, Mar. 27, 1971; children: Matthew Douglas, Raissa Anne. BA in Religion, Seattle Pacific U.; DD (hon.), Internat. Ch. of the Foursquare Gospel. Lic. pastor Internat. Ch. Foursquare Gospel. Asst. pastor Bethesda Christian Ctr., Wenatchee, 1974-79; founding pastor Eastside Christian Communion, Bellevue, Wash., 1979-80, Eastside Foursquare Ch., Kirkland, Wash., 1981—; conf. speaker, cons. various orgns., Poland, USSR, Norway, Fed. Republic Germany, Haiti, and U.S.; supt. div Foursquare Gospel Ch., N. King County, Wash., 1985—. Author: Iceman, 1986, Is It Real When It Doesn't Work?; editor Pastoral Resource, 1986—, Baby Boomerang, 1990, Is It Real When It Doesn't Work?, 1990; host (radio show) Growing Together; columnist Ministries Today; contbr. articles to profl. jours. Office: Eastside Foursquare Ch PO Box 536 Kirkland WA 98083-0536

MURTAUGH, JACK, ecumenical agency administrator. Exec. dir. Interfaith Conf. Greater Milw. Office: Interfaith Conf 1442 N Farwell Ave Ste 200 Milwaukee WI 53202*

MURTHA, JOHN FRANCIS, priest, academic administrator, history educator; b. Mt. Pleasant, Pa., May 28, 1930; s. Francis Regis and Margaret Ellen (Kearns) M. BA cum laude, St. Vincent Coll., 1953; MA, Columbia U., 1960; PhD, Cath. U. Am., 1964; M Div., St. Vincent Sem., 1985. Ordained priest Roman Cath. Ch., 1957. Assoc. prof. history St. Vincent Coll., Latrobe, Pa., 1977—, bd. dirs., 1977-82, 84—, pres., 1985—; prior St. Vincent Archabbey, Latrobe, 1980-85, mem. coun. srs., 1977-88. Editor: America 200, Essays in American History, 1976; contbr. articles to New Cath. Ency., 1963. Mem. Am. Benedictine Acad., Elks. Democrat. Office: St Vincent Coll Office of Pres Latrobe PA 15650-2690

MURYASZ, SISTER JACQUELINE MARIE, nun; b. Passaic, N.J., July 8, 1955; d. Stanley T. and Mary M. (Venit) M. BA in Elem. Edn., Felician Coll., 1984; MS, U. Notre Dame, 1988. Joined Felician Sisters. Tchr. Holy Cross Sch., Trenton, N.J., 1982-83; dir. admissions St. Mary's Hosp., Orange, N.J., 1983-84; tchr. Bishop Ahr High Sch., Edison, N.J., 1984-88; asst. dir. bus. Felician Coll., Lodi, N.J., 1988-89; prin. St. John Kanty, Clifton, N.J., 1989—; mem. salary com. Diocese of Paterson, Clifton, 1991-92; moderator Confraternity Christian Doctrine-Bishop Ahr High Sch., 1987-88, club moderator, 1984-88, edn. com., 1986-88. Vol. Straight and Narrow, Paterson, 1987—. Mem. ASCD, Nat. Cath. Edn. Assn., Spiritual Life Club (Lodi) (sec. 1987-89), Notre Dame Club North Jersey. Home: 61 Wesley St Clifton NJ 07013 Office: St John Kanty Sch 37 Speer Ave Clifton NJ 07013

MUSANTE, CATHERINE ANTOINETTE, nun; b. San Francisco, Mar. 24, 1911; d. Attilio Stephen and Antoinette Veronica (Draghicevich) M. BA, Stanford U., 1931, MA, 1932. Cert. tchr. Dir. novices Corpus Christi Monastery, Menlo Park, Calif., 1952-63, 82-85, procuratrix, 1963-65, subprioress, 1966-70, prioress, 1970-79, 82-91, subprioress, 1991—; del. Roman Commn., Rome, 1980, 82, Liturg. Commn., 1976. Translator various books. Mem. Conf. Nuns Order of Preachers of USA (sec. 1982). Home: 215 Oak Grove Ave Menlo Park CA 94025

MUSANTE, JACQUELINE MURIEL, religion educator, lay worker; b. N.Y.C., June 30, 1926; d. Frederick Arnold and Ellen Mary (Haggerty) Whitehead; m. Edward John Musante, June 5, 1948 (dec. Mar. 1986); children: Kathleen M. DeWalt, Susan E., Edward J. Jr., Andrea M. Parker, Ellen R. Musante-Saba, Michael J., Jacqueline M. Feldman. Cert. in Spiritual Direction. Dir. Chistian Formation Our Lady of Good Counsel Ch., Bridgeport, Conn., 1968-88; dir. youth svcs. Diocese Bridgeport, 1975-76; pastoral asst. Notre Dame Ch., Easton, Conn., 1988—; mem. faculty Catechist Certification Program, Diocese of Bridgeport, 1975—; co-chair Diocesan Ecumenical Interreligious, Diocese of Bridgeport, 1980—; speaker Nat. Evangelization Congress, Hartford, Conn., 1981; chairperson Anglican/Roman Cath. Dialogue, Diocese of Bridgeport, 1982-84, 90—. Contbr. articles to religious publs. Mem. Nat. Cath. Edn. Assn., Bridgeport Religious Edn. Dirs. Home: 95 Rock House Rd Easton CT 06612 Office: Notre Dame Ch of Easton 640 Morehouse Rd Easton CT 06612

MUSHEGAN-WATSON, JANET, pastor, personal growth specialist; b. Chattanooga, May 29, 1955; d. Harry Ararat and Myrtle O. (Paulk) M.; m. F. Daniell Watson Jr., July 26, 1977; children: Nathan, Noah. BA, Agnes Scott Coll., 1977; cert., Psychol. Studies Inst., 1986; MS, Ga. State U., 1986. Dir. family svcs. Gospel Harvester Ch., Marietta, Ga., 1983-85; asst. pastor Gospel Harvester Ch., Marietta, 1985—; personal growth specialist Gospel harvester Ch., Marietta, 1986—. Mem. Nat. Parents Resource Inst. for Drug Edn., Atlanta, 1989—. Recipient Good Citizenship award DAR, 1973. Mem. Am. Assn. for Counseling and Devel., Ga. Coun. on Child Abuse, Kappa Delta Pi. Republican. Avocations: singing, writing. Office: Gospel Harvester Ch 1521 Hurt Rd Marietta GA 30060

MUSIN, DONALD JELINE, minister; b. Tarentum, Pa., May 22, 1936; s. John Jeline and Helen Frances (Jeune) M.; m. Gloria Garman, Feb. 4. 1967; children: Michael Hanley, Tom Hanley, Jon, Christine Hanley Batten, Melissa Musin North. BA, Gannon U., 1964; STM, Freelandia Coll. Theol., Cassville, Mo., 1979, STD, 1983; PhD, Internat. Sem., Orlando, Fla., 1984; MRE, Whitefield Theol. Sem., Lakeland, Fla., 1985, M in Religion magna cum laude, 1986; postgrad., Whitfield Theol. Sem., 1991—. Lic. to ministry Presbyn. Ch. in Am., 1975; ordained Gospel Crusade, 1976, Ref. Presbyn. Ch. in U.S., 1986, Presbyn. Ch. in Am., 1989. Adminstr. New Life Ctr., De Kalb, Ill., 1977-78; pastor United Meth. chs., Clarksville, Ga., 1978-79; supply pastor Home Ch., Cape Coral, Fla., 1979-80; bibl. and counseling instr. Gospel Crusade, Inc., Bradenton, Fla., 1981-85, dir. ministries, dean schs., 1983-85; exec. dir., co-founder Dominion Sch. Edn., Lakeland, 1985-87; pastor The Rock Presbyn. Ch., Stockbridge, Ga., 1989—; co-founder, exec. v.p., acting pres. Atlanta Sch. Bibl. Studies, Decatur, Ga., 1989—; chmn. Christian edn. com. North Ga. Presbytery, Atlanta, 1989—. Author: Pastoral Internship/Counseling, 1984, Christian Ministry Development, 1988; contbr. articles to religious jours. Staff sgt. USAF, 1954-57. Mem. N.Am. Profs. Christian Edn., Nat. Christian Counselors Assn. (lic. pastoral counselor, cert. instr., examiner 1991—), Evang. Ch. Alliance, Acad. Parish Clergy, Henry County Vol. Chaplains Assn. (v.p. 1989-91), Am. Fedn. Christian Schs. and Colls. (bd. dirs., exec. v.p. Fla. chpt. 1991—), Ga. Fedn. Christian Colls. and Univs. (co-founder, pres. 1990—, lobbyist 1991). Home: 2420 Hwy 155 N McDonough GA 30253 Office: The Rock Presbyn Ch 33 White Dr Stockbridge GA 30281

MUSTAPHA, ALHAJI MOHAMED SANUSI, transportation executive; b. Freetown, Sierra Leone, June 1, 1903. Grad., Prince of Wales Sch., Freetown, 1925. With Sierra Leone Civil Service, 1926; joint sec. Foulah Town Mosque Com., 1933; founder Mustapha Bros., 1946; reader law Lincoln's Inn, London, 1947-50; minister Ministry of Works and Transport, 1953, Ministry of Natural Resources, 1957, Ministry of Fin., 1958-59; dep. prime minister Republic of Sierra Leone, 1959, mem. governing council, cen. com., 1978; minister Ministry of Trade and Industry, 1962, Ministry of Social Welfare, 1963-64; mem. Sierra Leone Parliament, 1969; acting 2d v.p. Sierra Leone Airlines, Freetown, 1979-80, chmn., 1982—; apptd. lic. buying agt. Sierra Leone Produce Mktg. Bd., 1950, pres. assn. lic. buying agts., 1967; del., advisor to Sierra Leone Constl. Conf., London, 1960. Asst. sec. Sierra Leone Muslim Congress, 1932, chmn. bd. govs. Secondary Sch., 1965-69, pres., 1974; hon. sec. East Ward Rate Payers Assn., 1935; nat. treas. sierra Leone Peoples' Party, mem. exec. com., 1950; mem. legis. council, exec. council Freetown East Electoral Dist., 1951; bd. govs. Ahmadiyya Secondary Sch., 1965-70; chmn. bd. govs. Prince of Wales Sch., 1967-70. Served as cpl. Sierra Leone Defence Corps, 1939-45. Decorated comdr. Brit. Empire, comdr. Order of Rokel; recipient Sierra Leone Independence medal, 1961. Mem. Old Prince Waleans Assn., Royal Commonwealth Soc. Office: Sierra Leone Airlines, 21/23 Siaka Stevens St, Freetown Sierra Leone also: PO Box 285, Freetown Sierra Leone

MUTO, SUSAN ANNETTE, religion educator, academic administrator; b. Pitts., Dec. 11, 1942; d. Frank and Helen (Scardamalia) M. BA in Journalism and English, Duquesne U., 1964; MA, U. Pitts., 1967, PhD in English Lit., 1970. Asst. dir. Inst. of Formative Spirituality, Duquesne U., Pitts., 1965-80, dir., 1980-88, faculty coordinator grad. programs in foundational formation, 1979-88, prof., 1981—; guest lectr. formative reading various colls. and community orgns., 1970—. Author: (with Adrian van Kaam) The Emergent Self, 1968, (with Adrian van Kaam) The Participant Self, 1969, Approaching the Sacred: An Introduction to Spiritual Reading, 1973, Steps Along the Way, 1975, A Practical Guide to Spiritual Reading, 1976, The Journey Homeward: On the Road of Spiritual Reading, 1977, Tell Me Who I Am, 1977, Celebrating the Single Life, 1982, Blessings That Make Us Be, 1982, Pathways of Spiritual Living, 1984, 89, Mediation in Motion, 1986, (with Adrian van Kaam and Richard Byrne) Songs for Every Season, 1989, (with van Kaam) Commitment: Key to Christian Maturity, 1989, Commitment: Key to Christian Maturity, A Workbook and Guide, 1990, John of the Cross for Today, 1990, Womanspirit, 1991; contbr. articles to religious and secular publs. Mem. Edith Stein Guild, Epiphany Assn. (exec. dir. 1988—), Phi Kappa Phi. Home: 2223 Wenzell Ave Pittsburgh PA 15216 Office: Epiphany Assn Pittsburgh PA 15206

MUTTI, ALBERT FREDERICK, minister; b. Hopkins, Mo., Feb. 13, 1938; s. Albert Frederick and Phyllis Margaret (Turner) M.; m. Etta Mae McClurg, June 7, 1959; children: Timothy Allen, John Frederick, Martin Kent. AB, Cen. Meth. Coll., 1960; MDiv., Garrett Theol. Sem., 1963; DMin., St. Paul Sch. Theology, 1975. Sr. pastor Union Star Charge, Mo., 1963-65, Crossroads Parish, Savannah, Mo., 1965-74; assoc. coun. dir. Mo. West Conf. UMC, Kansas City, 1974-80, coun. dir., 1980-82; sr. pastor First United Meth. Ch., Blue Springs, Mo., 1982-87; dist. supt. Cen. Dist. UMC, Mo., 1987-89; dist. supr. Kansas City N. Dist., 1989—. Chair. Savannah Community Betterment, 1971; bd. mem. St. Mary's Hosp. Blue Springs, 1986; dir. ARC, Savannah, 1968; dir. United Meth. Found., St. Louis, bd. Discipleship, Nashville, Tenn., bd. Global Ministries, N.Y.; pres. Mo. Coun. Chs., Jefferson City, Dean Mo. Area Ministers Sch., Fayette; curator Cen. Meth. Coll. Home: 607 Camelot Liberty MO 64068 Office: 1512 Van Brunt Blvd Kansas City MO 64127

MUYSKENS, JOHN DAVID, minister; b. Sheldon, Iowa, Apr. 19, 1934; s. George Bernard and Jannetta Eileen (Den Hartog) M.; m. Donna DeLaine Greenfield, Aug. 26, 1958; children: Mark Alan, Julia Muyskens Ostendorf, Deborah Muyskens DuMez. BA, Cen. Coll., Pella, Iowa, 1956; BD, Western Seminary, Holland, Mich., 1959; ThM, Princeton (N.J.) Seminary, 1962, D of Ministry, 1978. Pastor Pottersville (N.J.) Reformed Ch., 1959-67; pastor First Reformed Ch., Union City, N.J., 1967-75, New Brunswick, N.J., 1975—; pres. Synod of the Mid-Atlantics Reformed Ch. in Am., New Brunswick, 1981-82; trustee Northwestern Coll., Orange City, Iowa, 1980-88; mem. exec. com. Reformed Ch. in Am., N.Y.C., 1982-88; chmn. theol. students com. Classis of New Brunswick, N.J., 1988—. Author: Centennial History of the Church in Pottersville, 1965, Diary of Dina Van Bergh, 1991, Three Mile Run Church, 1991, History of First Reformed Church in New Brunswick, 1991. Vice-pres. Brunswick and Raritan Housing Corp., 1980—; trustee Housing Coalition of Middlesex County, New Brunswick, 1982—. Paul Harris Fellow, New Brunswick Rotary, 1989. Mem. Interfaith Leadership Assn. of Cen. N.J. (sec., treas. 1989—), Rotary (pres. elect 1991). Office: First Reformed Church 9 Bayard St New Brunswick NJ 08901

MYA HAN, ANDREW, archbishop. Archbishop of Myanmar, bishop of Yangon The Anglican Communion. Office: Bishopscourt, Dagon PO, 140 Pyidaungsu Yeiktha Rd, Yangon Myanmar*

MYERS, ALBERT EDWIN, clergyman, religious organization executive; b. Akron, Ohio, Sept. 18, 1931; s. Forrest D. and Marian H. (Conner) M.; m. Naomi Ann Paullin, Aug. 9, 1953; children: Paul T., Kathryn I., Deborah H., Forrest C. BA, Akron U., 1954; MDiv, Trinity Luth. Theol. Sem., 1955; STM, Oberlin Coll., 1959; D Ministry, Vanderbilt U., 1974. Ordained to ministry Evang. Luth. Ch. in Am., 1955. Pastor chs., Ohio, Wyo., Ont., Can., Pa., 1955-74; exec. dir. Pa. Coun. Chs., Harrisburg, 1974—; bd. mgrs. Pa. Bible Soc., 1979—; mem. Commn. on Religion in Appalachia, Knoxville, 1974—; mem. governing bd. Nat. Coun. Chs., 1976-81. Author: The Pastoral Epistles, 1970, A Family of the Bagaduce, 1976, Asa Williams and Direxa Dunn, 1976. Trustee Thiel Coll., Greenville, Pa., 1976-85, United Way Pa., 1974-76; mem. exec. com. planning div. Tri-County United Way, 1974-78; mem. dist. com. Keystone Area coun. Boy Scouts Am., 1974-78; moderator radio show Face the Issue, Harrisburg, 1974-82; bd. dirs. Pa. Citizens Svc. Project, 1988—, Pa. div. Am. Trauma Soc., 1985—, Harrisburg State Hosp., 1990—. Named hon. canon St. Stephen's Episcopal Cathedral, 1984; recipient leadership citation Pa. Senate, 1984. Mem. Nat. Assn. Ecumenical Staff, Soc. Descs. Colonial Clergy. Democrat. Home: 5341 Windsor Rd Harrisburg PA 17112 Office: Pa Coun Chs 900 S Arlington Ave Harrisburg PA 17109

MYERS, ALTON J., minister; b. Defiance, Ohio, Dec. 31, 1934; s. Herman A. and Stella Lucinda (Schubert) M. BS in Edn., Defiance Coll., 1959; MA, Bowling Green State U., 1970; MDiv, Dubuque Theol. Sem., 1975. Ordained to ministry Presbyn. Ch., 1977. Pastor Bloomingburg (Ohio) Presbyn. Ch., 1976-82, First Presbyn. Ch., Albion, Ind., 1982—. Author: (poem) A Winter Too Early, 1989. Active Friends Noble County Pub. Libr., Albion, 1988—. Mem. Albion Ministerial Assn. (pres. 1986—), Lions, Masons. Home: 208 W Highland Albion IN 46701 *I see life as a faith journey, in which to be active and optimistic about our gifts is to find that life as it is meant to be, glorifying God and serving others.*

MYERS, SISTER CORRINE, religious organization administrator; b. Latrobe, Pa., Dec. 1, 1936; d. James Hilary and Regina Alice (Quinn) M. BS in Edn., Carlow Coll., Pitts., 1963; cert. in spirituality religious studies, St. Louis U., 1976. Joined Sisters of Mercy, Roman Cath. Ch., 1960. Educator various Cath. schs., Pitts., 1957-75; dir. Sisters of Mercy Motherhouse, Pitts., 1976-80; min. religious edn. Glenmary Home Missioners Parishes, Va., 1980-85; dir. Nazareth House of Prayer, Gate City, Va., 1984—. Active Diocesan Tchrs. Orch., Pitts., 1964-67, Lee Theis Chorale, Pitts., 1967-75. Mem. Retreats Internat., Spiritual Dirs. Internat. Democrat. Home and Office: Rte 2 Box 277 Gate City VA 24251

MYERS, CRAIG ALAN, minister; b. Meyersdale, Pa., July 18, 1964; s. Fred William and L. Fern (Evans) M.; m. Laura Estelle Sanders, Dec. 29, 1990. BA, Pa. State U., 1985; MDiv, Ashland (Ohio) Theol. Seminary, 1990; Diploma, Evangel. Tchr. Tng. Assn., 1990. Ordained to ministry Ch. of the Brethren, 1991. Summer pastor Laughlin Ch. of the Brethren, Grantsville, Md., 1987-90, Dunnings Creek Ch. of the Brethren, New Paris, Pa., 1989; pastor Blue River Ch. of the Brethren, Columbia City, Ind., 1990—; dir. Brethren Revival Fellowship, York, Pa., 1989—; mem. Brethren Com. on Ministerial Leadership, Elgin, Ill., 1990—; tchr. Brethren Inst., Elizabethtown, Pa., 1990—. Contbr. poetry anthology, 1989. Mem. coord. Coll. Reps., University Park, Pa., 1984. Mem. No. Ind. Brethren Ministers Assn., Eta Beta Rho (pres. 1989-90). Home: 3070 East 700 North Columbia City IN 46725 Office: Blue River Ch of Brethren 3040 East 700 North Columbia City IN 46725

MYERS, ERIC LEE, minister; b. Washington, July 27, 1962; s. Russell and Virginia Lee (Jenkins) M.; m. Lisa Machel Sharp, July 20, 1985; 1 child, Brett Alan. Diploma, Word of Life Sch. Youth Ministries, 1982; BS, Liberty U., 1986; postgrad., Liberty Bapt. Theol. Sem., 1986-87, 91—, U. S.C., Spartanburg, 1989-90. Ordained to ministry Bapt. Ch., 1991. Intern Thomas Rd. Bapt. Ch., Lynchburg, Va., 1983; youth pastor Gospel Bapt. Ch., Salem, Va., 1985-86; minister of youth and edn. Met. Bapt. Ch., Greenville, S.C., 1987-90; asst. pastor Lighthouse Bapt. Ch., Quincy, Ill., 1990—; program dir. World of Life camps, summers 1981-83; club leader, mem. com. Young Life, Quincy, 1990—; assoc. area rep. Word of Life Clubs, Taylor, S.C., 1987-90; journey leader Holyland U.S.A., Bedford, Va., 1985-87; mem. Quincy Youth Net, 1991—. Mem. Nat. Christian Counselors Assn., Evang. Tchr. Tng. Assn., Nat. Network of Youth Ministries, Profl. Assn. Christian Educators. Republican. *But thanks be to God, who giveth us victory through our Lord Jesus Christ. Therefore my beloved brethren, be ye steadfast, immovable, always abounding in the work of the Lord, knowing that your labor is not in vain in the Lord. (I Corinthians 15:57,58).*

MYERS, GARY LYNN, clergyman; b. Lexington, N.C., Oct. 21, 1951; s. Malcolm Lewis and Edna Mae (Grubb) M.; m. Joyce Lorraine Everhart, Aug. 19, 1972; children: Misty Shannon, Joshua Daniel. Student, Davidson County Community Coll, 1970-71; Assoc. Div., Southeastern Theol. Sem., 1986. Ordained to ministry Bapt. Ch. Laity First Bapt. of Welcome (N.C.), 1970-81, Trinity Bapt. Ch., Arcadia, N.C., 1981-84; pastor Victory Bapt. Ch., Thomasville, N.C., 1984-89, Oak Hill Meml. Bapt. Ch., Thomasville, 1989—; del. to Nevis, West Indies for mission work Fgn. Mission Bd., summers 1987, 88. Mem. Midway (N.C.) Fire/Rescue, EMT, 1975-86, bd. dirs., 1983-85; coach basketball/baseball Little League, Midway Elem. Sch., 1985-91. Republican. Home: 400 Kennedy Rd Thomasville NC 27360 Office: Oak Hill Meml Bapt Ch 7 Raleigh Rd Thomasville NC 27360

MYERS, JOHN JOSEPH, bishop; b. Ottawa, Ill., July 26, 1941; s. M.W. and Margaret Louise (Donahue) M. BA maxima cum laude, Loras Coll., 1963; Licentiate in Sacred Theology, Gregorian U., Rome, 1967; Doctor of Canon Law, Cath. U. Am., 1977; DD (hon.), Apostolic See, Vatican City, 1987. Ordained priest Roman Cath. Ch., 1966, bishop, 1987. Asst. pastor Holy Family Parish, Peoria, Ill., 1967-70; asst. dept. internat. affairs U.S. Cath. Conf., Washington, 1970-71; asst. pastor St. Matthew Parish, Champaign, Ill., 1971-74; vice chancellor Cath. Diocese Peoria, 1977-78, vocation dir., 1977-87, chancellor, 1978-87, vicar gen., 1982-90, co-adjutor bishop, 1987-90; bishop of Peoria, 1990—; bd. govs. Canon Law Soc. Am., Washington, 1985-87; bd. dirs. Pope John XXIII Ctr. for Med.-Moral Rsch. and Edn., Boston; mem. sem. com. Mt. St. Mary's Sem., Md., 1989—. Author: (commentary) Book V of the Code of Canon Law, 1983; contbr. numerous articles to religious publs. Mem. Canon Law Soc. Am., Nat. Conf. Cath. Bishops. Roman Catholic. Office: Cath Diocese Peoria 607 NE Madison PO Box 1406 Peoria IL 61655

MYERS, KEVIN RICE, minister; b. Kokomo, Ind., June 5, 1956; s. Francis Asbury and Harriett B. (Clingenpeel) M.; m. Marjorie Rice, Sept. 19, 1981; 1 child, Christopher. BA in Polit. Sci., Ball State U., 1977; MDiv, Garrett-Evang. Theol. Sem., Evanston, Ill., 1981. Ordained to ministry United Meth. Ch. as deacon, 1978, as elder, 1982. Assoc. pastor 1st United Meth. Ch., Lowell, Ind., 1979-80; pastor Spring Prairie United Meth. Ch., Elkhorn, Wis., 1980-81; assoc. pastor Monroe (Wis.) United Meth. Ch., 1981-83; pastor chs. United Meth. Ch., Plover, Amherst and Buena Vista, Wis., 1983—; chairperson computer com. Wis. Conf. United Meth. Ch., Sun Prairie, 1987-91, mem. bd. ordained ministry, 1988, conf. sec., 1989—. Editor Wis. Conf. Yearbook and Jour., 1989-91. Office: Plover United Meth Ch 2104 Plover Springs Dr PO Box 35 Plover WI 54467

MYERS, LARRY WAYNE, religion educator; b. Cape Girardeau, Mo., Sept. 1, 1946; s. Willard Dickmann and Wilma Mabel (Biri) M.; 1 child, Christoph-Martin Mattias. MA in Religion, St. Louis U., 1973, PhD, 1990; MDiv, Concordia Sem., St. Louis, 1972; BA, Concordia Sr. Coll., Ft. Wayne, Ind., 1968. Ordained to ministry Luth. Ch.-Mo. Synod, 1972. Missionary Luth. Ch. in Korea, Seoul, 1972-77; asst. prof. Concordia Coll., St. Paul, 1977-80; pastor Trinity Luth. Ch., Frankfurt, Main, Fed. Republic Germany, 1980-86; asst. prof. Concordia Luth. Coll., Austin, Tex., 1986-88, Concordia Sem., St. Louis, 1988-90; interim staff Commn. on Theology and Ch. Rels., Luth. Ch.-Mo. Synod, St. Louis, 1990-91; instr. Milw. Luth. High Sch., 1991—; asst. scholarly rsch. subcom. Commn. on Church Lit., The Luth. Ch.-Mo. Synod, St. Louis, 1979-80, doctrinal reviewer, 1988—. Transl. monographs. Lt. col. USAFR, 1972—. Aid Assn. for Luths. grantee, St.

Louis, 1976-77, Am. Acad. in Rome, 1978; NEH fellow, 1988. Mem. Am. Acad. Religion, Soc. Bibl. Lit., Am. Philol. Assn., Am. Classical League, Vergil Soc., Res. Officers Assn. Republican. Office: Milw Luth High Sch 9700 W Grantosa Dr Milwaukee WI 53222

MYERS, RICHARD F., minister; b. Atlantic City, N.J., Nov. 15, 1944; s. Florian Elwood and Ruth (Mertz) M.; m. Helen Marie Mumford, Dec. 2, 1967; 1 child, Kristin Michelle. Student, Sacramento City, 1964-66, U. Md., Frankfurt, Fed. Republic Germany, 1966-67. Ordained to ministry Christian Ch., 1980. Adminstr. Merlin Carothers, Escondido, Calif., 1976-78; evangelist Christians United for Jesus, Escondido, 1978-86; pastor New Life Outreach, Millville, N.J., 1986—; pres. New Life World Outreach, 1985—, Christians United for Jesus, Calif., 1985—; bd. dirs., del. Christian Assembly Ministries, St. Martin, West Indies, 1983—. Author: Faith, Fear & Frustration, How Can I Believe?, Lifting Your Level of Faith; author (paper) The Answer. Mem. exec. bd. Greater Millville Celebration. With U.S. Army, 1963-66. Named as Outstanding Young Man, Rotary Internat., 1971. Mem. Charismatic Bible Ministries, Millville Ministerial Assn. Republican. Office: New Life World Outreach Ministries/Church Bluebird Ln Millville NJ 08332 *When living life in this world, one must constantly choose between things and people. Sometimes it seems people interrupt the things we feel we must get done. Let us always see "things" as intrusions into one's daily life...never the "people: who interrupt you.*

MYERS, THOMAS OSCAR, minister; b. Terre Haute, Ind., June 20, 1936; s. Oscar Lowell and Julia Sena (Hudson) M.; m. Ann Clayton Eddings, July 23, 1960 (div. Oct. 1982); children: Robyn Lynn Myers Hurley, Thomas O. II, Kerry Clayton; m. Sharon Sue Stewart, June 30, 1984. AB, Lincoln Christian Coll., 1959, Bethany Nazarene Coll., 1965; M Music Edn., U. Okla., 1971. Ordained to ministry Christian Ch., 1960. Youth min. First Ch. of Christ, Catlin, Ill., 1956-57; min. Success Christian Ch., Paris, Ill., 1957-61; prof. music Midwest Christian Coll., Oklahoma City, 1961-68; prof. of music Lincoln Christian Coll., Lincoln, Ill., 1968-84; min. of music Hillcrest Christian Coll., Granada Hills, Calif., 1984-86; min. First Christian Ch., Victorville, Calif., 1986—; pres. Assn. Christian Coll. Music Educators, 1980-81. Named Citizen of the Month Lincoln (Ill.) Courier, 1982. Mem. So. Calif. Mins. Assn. (pres. 1990-91), Kiwanis (pres. Lincoln club 1982). Home: 15225 Tuscola Rd Apple Valley CA 92307 Office: First Christian Ch 15548 6th St Victorville CA 92392 *Among all the positive influences in my life, none has been more profound than the example of Godly parents and their unshakeable faith in Christ and their undying commitment to the authority of scripture. I pray that I have done as much for my children.*

MYERS, WILLIAM CHARLES, youth minister; b. Honolulu, June 12, 1963; s. Jackie Charles Myers and Karen Kay (Pierceson) Collins; m. Margaret Elizabeth Kerr, May 25, 1985. Student, U. Iowa, 1981; BA, Monmouth Coll., 1985; MDiv, Princeton Theol. Sem., 1988. Student min. A Christian Ministry in the Nat. Parks, Grand Teton Nat. Park, summer 1985, 86; chaplain intern Presbyn. Home at 58th and Greenway, Phila., summer 1987, Presbyn. U. of Penn. Med. Ctr., Phila., 1988-89; youth min. Nassau Presbyn. Ch., Princeton, N.J., 1989—. Office: Nassau Presbyn Ch 61 Nassau St Princeton NJ 00542 *There is a place in our soul, the most deep and dark, which is forever wrought with the despair of our human condition. Here is kept the pain we feel when others near to us are suffering. Here is kept the guilt we feel when we uncontrollably strikeout and hurt those whom we love the most. Here is kept the fear when we look into the face of death and see ourselves. In this place, we are sickened and scared to death. In this place, we know we are naked. As we stand face to face with death, in this dark place of our soul, Christ is there. We are reminded, in his body fractured upon the cross and his blood shed upon the earth, death is not the final word.*

MYERS, WILLIAM GEORGE, minister; b. Faulkton, S.D., Aug. 29, 1938; s. William Edwin and Harriett Constance (Kuhl) M.; B.S. in Edn., No. State U., Aberdeen, S.D., 1956-60; M.Div. in Theology, Garrett-Evang. Theol. Sem., Evanston, Ill., 1965; M.A. in Liturgy, U. Notre Dame, 1984. Ordained elder United Methodist Ch., 1966. Asst. pastor Ingleside-Whitfield United Meth. Parish, Chgo., 1962-65; pastor-dir. Christ the Carpenter Parish and Christian Ctr., Rockford, Ill., 1965-76; chaplain, instr. St. Mary's Acad., Nauvoo, Ill., 1976-88; assoc. pastor Colusa/Dallas City/Nauvoo United Meth. Chs., Ill., 1976—; dir. Radio-TV Ministry, Rockford, 1967-71; sec. Midwest Religious Broadcasting Commn., 1967-71. Advisor southside youth council NAACP, 1962-64; bd. dirs. Central Day Care Ctr., Rockford, 1969-72, Protestant Welfare Services, Rockford, 1972-74; bd. dirs., pres. Family Consultation Services, Rockford, 1974-76; pres. Nauvoo Hist. Soc., 1979-84, dir. resource and research ctr., 1984—; treas. Hancock County Theatre for Performing Arts, Ill., 1979-84; mem. United Meth. Fellowship for Worship and Other Arts. Mem. Nat. Council Tchrs. English, Ill. Council Tchrs. English, Nat. Cath. Edn. Assn., Order of Saint Luke (formation officer), Nauvoo Ministerial Assn., Sigma Tau Delta. Democrat. Home: 290 N Page St Nauvoo IL 62354 Office: Saint Mary's Acad 105 N Necer Nauvoo IL 62354

MYHAND, DENNIS MONROE, minister; b. Monticello, Ark., June 10, 1957; s. Bert Zellner and Janet (Barry) M. BS in Psychology, U. Ark., 1986; MDiv, Presbyn. Theol. Sem., 1990. Ordained to ministry, Presbyn. Ch. (USA), 1990. Minister Dermott (Ark.) Presbyn. Ch., 1990—. With U.S. Army, 1974-77. Mem. Nat. Rifle Assn., Rotary. Republican. Home: 103 S School St Dermott AR 71638 Office: Dermott Presbyn Ch PO Box 188 Dermott AR 71638

MYRICK, STEVEN DALE, radio programming administrator; b. St. Louis, Aug. 29, 1956; s. John Dale and Louise Marie (Allman) M.; m. Virginia Theresa Berg, July 19, 1980; children: Justin, Allison. Grad., Broadcast Ctr., Clayton, Mo., 1982. Announcer Sta. KFVO, Clayton, Mo., 1987-89, asst. program dir., 1989—; mem. staff New Life Evangelistic Ctr., St. Louis, 1989—, KNLC-TV, St. Louis, 1990—. Home: 462 Pasadena Webster Groves MO 63119 Office: Sta KFVO-AM 85 Founders Ln Clayton MO 63105

NAAS, SISTER JOLINDA, school system administrator, nun; b. Haubstadt, Ind., May 14, 1937; d. Joseph Paul and Elizabeth Bertha (Brenner) N. BS, St. Benedict Coll., 1967; MA, Ball State U., 1976, cert. adminstrn. and supervision, 1982. Joined Sisters of St. Benedict, Roman Cath. Ch., 1953. Tchr. schs. Diocese Evansville, Ind., 1956-69, prin., 1972-90; tchr., prin. Archdiocese L.A., Huntington Beach, Calif., 1969-72, Diocese of Owensboro, St. Romuald Sch., Hardinsburg, Ky., 1990—. Mem. Sisters Senate, Evansville 1974-76. Nat. Assn. Elem. Sch. Prins. grantee, 1983. Mem. Nat. Cath. Ednl. Assn. Home and Office: St Romuald Convent N Main St Hardinsburg KY 40143

NABAKOWSKI, TIMOTHY JAY, minister; b. Amherst, Ohio, Jan. 12, 1947; s. James F. and F. Jane (Baird) N.; m. Anne Marie Racine, June 24, 1973; children: Naomi Joy, Blanca. BA, Wittenberg U., 1968. Ordained to ministry, 1975. Coord. Carlotta (Calif.) Mansion, Gospel Outreach; deacon Gospel Outreach Christian Ctr., Eureka, Calif., 1973-75; elder, house head Gospel Outreach Soc., Vancouver, Can., 1975-76; co-pastor Gospel Outreach Christian Fellowship, Seattle, 1986-89; assoc. pastor Gospel Outreach Christian Fellowship, 1989—; owner New Life Upholstery, Seattle, 1982—. Republican.

NABORS, CHARLOTTE DEVINNEY, minister; b. Charleston, W.Va., May 14, 1938; d. Dallas Harold and Bonita Baker (Blair) DeVinney; m. Oran Rogers Nabors, Dec. 20, 1959; children: Stacey Blair, Christopher Thomas, Charles Roger. BA, Furman U., 1960; M in Religious Edn., U. St. Thomas, 1980, Perkins Sch. Theology, Dallas, 1969-72, 88, 90; D in Ministry, Brite Div. Sch., Ft. Worth, 1991. Ordained to ministry Christian Ch., 1980. Ednl. asst. Northway Christian Ch., Dallas, 1964-72; prof. Thailand Theol. Sem., Chiang Mai, 1972-73, 76-78; dir. children's program Meml. Dr. Christian Ch., Houston, 1973-75; workshop leader various chs. and sems., Burma, Singapore, Thailand, 1976-78; founding pastor Lao Community of Christian Faith, Houston, 1980-82; assoc. min. Central Christian Ch., Dallas, 1983-91; co-pastor 1st Christian Ch., Denton, Tex., 1991—; mem. Greater Dallas Community of Chs. (bd. dirs. 1986-89, Faith and Life com. 1987—); parliamentarian North Tex. Area Christian Chs., Dallas, 1989-91; vice-moderator North Tex. Area Christian Chs., 1991-92; cons. Refugee Ministries. Contbr. articles to profl. jours., also sermons. Bd. mem. Houston Hunger Coalition, 1979-80, East Dallas Health Coalition, 1983—. Mem. Southwest Assn. Christian Ch. Educators (sec. 1990-91), Assn. Christian Church Educators (sec. 1991-92), Dallas Pastors' Assn. (pres. 1987-88), Theta Phi. Office: 1st Christian Ch 1203 N Fulton Denton TX 76201

NABORS, MICHAEL C. R., minister; b. Kalamazoo, Nov. 12, 1959; s. Clarence Lee and Kathleen (Whaling) N.; m. Needa Renetta Moore, July 6, 1980; children: Simone Charice, Lanez Dominic, Jarell Desmond. BS, Western Mich. U., 1982; MDiv, Princeton Theol. Sem., 1985, ThM, 1986. Ordained to ministry Bapt. Ch. Dean Christian edn. Progressive Nat. Bapt. Conv., Washington, 1987-89, dir. Christian edn., 1989-91, nat. tchr., 1990—; min. First Bapt. Ch., Princeton, N.J.; pres. Princeton Clergy Assn., 1989-90, v.p., 1988-89; mem., dir. edn. N.J. Progressive Nat. Bapt. Conv., Princeton, 1988—; dir. edn. Ea. Regional of Progressive Bapts., Washington, 1989-91; mem. Trenton Ecumenical Area Ministry, 1989. Pres., founder Concerned Black Parents and Citizens of Princeton, 1986; bd. dirs. Youth Employment Svcs., Princeton, 1989, Intergovtl. Drug Com., Princeton, 1989. Named one of Outstanding Young Men of Am., 1983, Outstanding Community Leader State of N.J. Dept. Human Svcs., Trenton, 1990, Youth of Yr. Optimists, Kalamazoo, 1977; United Theol. Sem. fellow, 1990. Mem. NAACP (pres. Cen. N.J. chpt. 1987), Coalition for Nuclear Disarmament. Democrat. Home: 28 Green St Princeton NJ 08540 Office: First Bapt Ch John St and Paul Robeson Pl Princeton NJ 08540

NADEAU, JAMES LEE, priest; b. Caribou, Maine, July 10, 1961; s. Reginald Joseph and Kathleen Marie (Roy) N. AB, Dartmouth Coll., 1983; STB, Gregorian Univ., Rome, 1986, STL, 1988. Ordained priest Roman Cath. Ch., 1988. Vicar St. Louis Parish, Fort Kent, Maine, 1988-89; coll. chaplain Univ. of Maine, Fort Kent, 1988-89; vicar St. Andre's Parish, Biddeford, Maine, 1989—; coll. chaplain Univ. of New England, Biddeford, 1989—; lectr. Univ. of New Engl., 1990—, St. Joseph's Coll., North Windham, Maine, 1988—. Chaplain KC, Fort Kent, 1988-89, York County Dist. Scouts, Maine, 1989—; bd. dirs. York County YMCA, Biddeford, 1990—; bd. dirs. Harbor Project, 1990-91. Recipient Outstanding Ednl. Achievement award as a Trio Student, New England Assn. Ednl. Opportunity Prog. Personnel, Mystic, Conn., 1991. Mem. Soc. Bibl. Lit., Cath. Bibl. Assn., Friends of the Vatican Libr. Democrat. Home: 73 Bacon St Biddeford ME 04005 Office: St Andres Parish 73 Bacon St Biddeford ME 04005

NADICH, JUDAH, rabbi; b. Balt., May 13, 1912; s. Isaac and Lena (Nathanson) N.; m. Martha Hadassah Ribalow, Jan. 26, 1947; children: Leah N. (Mrs. Aryeh Meir), Shira A. (Mrs. James L. Levin), Nahma M. Nadich (Mrs. David Belcourt). B.A., CCNY, 1932; M.A., Columbia U., 1936; rabbi, M.H.L., Jewish Theol. Sem. Am., 1936, D.H.L., 1953, D.D. (hon), 1966. Rabbi Temple Beth David, Buffalo, 1936-40; co-rabbi Anshe Emet Synagogue, Chgo., 1940-42; lecture tour U.S., South Africa and Rhodesia, 1946-47; rabbi Kehillath Israel Congregation, Brookline, Mass., 1947-57; rabbi Park Ave. Synagogue, N.Y.C., 1957-87, rabbi emeritus, 1987—; conducted first Bat Mitzvah in People's Republic of China, 1990. Author: Eisenhower and the Jews, 1953, Jewish Legends of the Second Commonwealth, 1983; Editor, translator: (Menachem Ribalow) The Flowering of Modern Hebrew Literature, 1959; editor: (Louis Ginzberg) Al Halakha v'Aggada, 1960. Pres. Rabbinical Assembly, 1972-74; pres. Jewish Book Council Am., 1968-72; bd. dirs., exec. com. Jewish Theol. Sem. Am.; formerly bd. dirs., mem. exec. com. Nat. Jewish Welfare Bd., Fedn. Jewish Philanthropies N.Y.; mem. hospice com. Beth Israel Med. Ctr.; mem. N.Y.C. Holocaust Meml. Com.; v.p. bd. dirs. Jewish Braille Inst.; past pres. Assn. Jewish Chaplains Armed Forces. Served to lt. col. as chaplain AUS, 1942-46, ETO. Decorated Order Brit. Empire; Croix de Guerre France; Ittur Lohamai Hamdinah Israel; fellow Herbert Lehman Inst. Talmudic Ethics, 1958. Mem. Mil. Chaplains Assn., Phi Beta Kappa. Lodge: Masons. Home: 1040 Park Ave New York NY 10028 Office: Park Ave Synagogue 50 E 87 St New York NY 10128

NADLER, ALLAN LAWRENCE, rabbi, educator; b. Montreal, Que., Can., May 8, 1954; came to U.S., 1976; s. Joseph Y. and Doris (Joselevsky) N. BA, McGill U., 1976; MA, Harvard U., 1982, PhD, 1988. Ordained rabbi, 1976. Rabbi Charles River Synagogue, Boston, 1980-84, Shaar Hashomayim, Montreal, 1984—; exec. dir Religious Zionists of Toronto, 1978-79; lectr. McGill U., Montreal, 1982-84, asst. prof., 1988—. Columnist Boston Jewish Times, 1984; contbr. articles to profl. jours. Govt. of Que. grad. fellow, 1976-78, Solomon fellow Harvard U., 1980. Mem. Rabbinical Coun. Am. Office: Shaar Hashomayim Congregation, 450 Kensington Ave, Westmount, PQ Canada H3Y 3A2

NAGEL, CHRIS B., JR., minister; b. Easton, Md., Oct. 14, 1952; s. Chris Brooks and Miriam (Todd) N.; m. Susan Myers, Dec. 29, 1973; children: Chris III, Amylin, Lauren. BBA, Western Ky. U., 1974; cert., Inst. Bibl. Studies, San Bernardino, Calif., 1977. Ordained minister, 1977. With Campus Crusade for Christ, Internat., 1974—; sr. staff high sch. ministry Campus Crusade for Christ, Internat., Washington, 1974-77; trainee Lay Tng. Ctr., Orlando, Fla., 1977-78; coord., dir. Singles Ministry, Washington, 1978-81; coord. Ch. Leadership Ministry, Washington, 1981-84; founder, exec. dir. Here's Life, Conn., Hartford, 1984—; Conn. state coord. Family Life Ministry, Boston, 1985-88, Nat. Day of Prayer Com., San Bernardino, 1985-88. Coach Little League Baseball, Arlington, Va., 1983, West Hartford, Conn., 1990; mem. adv. coun. on instrn. Tuckahoe Elem. Sch., Arlington, 1983-84; treas. PTA Norfeldt Sch., West Hartford, 1985-88. Named one of Oustanding Young Men in Am., Jaycees, 1981, 84. Republican. Avocations: tennis, golf. Home: 76 Hyde Rd West Hartford CT 06117 Office: Here's Life Conn 80 State House Sq #231456 Hartford CT 06123

NAGEL, DAVID CHARLES, monk, dietetic technician; b. Milw., Feb. 6, 1951; s. Harold Grover and Joyce Rita (Kaffka) N. AA, Cardinal Stritch Coll., Milw., 1974, BSBA, 1986; MST in Theol. Studies, Cath. Theol. U., 1989. Cert. dietary mgr., dietetic technician. Joined Bros. in Sacred Heart Fathers and Bros., Roman Catholic Ch., 1969. Asst. food service mgr. Sacred Heart Monastery, Milw., 1971-74; dir. food service St. Joseph's Indian Sch., Chamberlain, S.C., 1974-82, dir. ops., 1982—, dir. devel., 1990—; v.p. Dehon Industries, Chamberlain, 1982-85, Lakota Devel. Council, Chamberlain, 1982-85; dir. religious formation Sacred Heart Fathers and Bros., Chgo., 1986-90. State winner Nat. Chicken Council, 1979; winner recipe contest Food Mgmt. Mag., 1977. Mem. Am. Dietetic Assn., Am. Sch. Food Service Assn., Dietary Mgrs. Assn. (state pres. 1976, chpt. treas. 1984-85). Democrat. Avocations: computers; piano and organ. Home and Office: St Joseph's Indian Sch N Main St Chamberlain SD 57325

NAGELE, DANIEL ALAN, minister; b. Kingston, N.Y., Aug. 1, 1962; s. David Richard Sr. and Dorrene Carol (Askey) N.; m. Loretta Jean Marion, Oct. 17, 1987. Diploma in Bible, Counseling, Elim Bible Inst., Lima, N.Y., 1986, Teaching Cert., 1986. Pres. Genesis Outreach Ministries, Ridgway, Pa., 1985-87; youth pastor Utica Evangelistic Ctr., Sterling Heights, Mich., 1989—; advisor Students Taking Action Together in Christ, Sterling Heights. Home: 43720 Merrill Rd Sterling Heights MI 48314 Office: Utica Evangelistic Ctr 43700 Merrill Rd Sterling Heights MI 48314

NAGY, GYULA, bishop; b. Pelsőc, Gömör, Hungary, Sept. 22, 1918; s. Sandor Nagy and Vilma Benkő; m. Margit Schmidtbauer, Apr. 27, 1947; children: Gábor, Gyula, Éva Margit. Grad., Luth. Theol. Faculty, Hungary, 1940, U. Berlin, 1943; PhD, Artium Magister, Berlin, 1943; ThD, Hungary, 1946; ThD honoris causa, Debrecen, Hungary, 1988. Ordained to ministry Luth. Ch., 1940. Vicar Luth. Ch., Sopron, Győr, and Pécs, Hungary, 1944-50; dir. Diaconesses' Ctr. Luth. Ch., Győr, 1950; prof. systematic theology and philosophy Luth. Theol. Faculty, Budapest, Hungary, 1950-82; bishop No. Diocese, Evang. Luth. Ch. Hungary, Budapest, 1982-90, presiding bishop, 1987-90; bishop emeritus Evang. Luth. Ch. Hungary, 1990—; mem. ch. and soc. com. World Coun. Chs., 1968-75, mem. faith and order com., 1975-83, mem. cen. com., 1983—; sec. for higher theol. edn. Luth. World Fedn., Geneva, 1971-75; dir. theol. dept. Conf. European Chs., Geneva, 1975-80. Author: Theological Social Ethics, 1968, The Treasure of the Church, 1988; editor: Documentation Service of the Conference of European Churches, 1976-80. Mem. exec. com. UN Orgn. Hungary, Budapest, 1982—; mem. Hungarian Parliament, 1987-90, mem. fgn. affairs com., 1987-90, mem. constl. com., 1989-90. Decorated banner Order 1st Class of Hungary; recipient medal Evang. Luth. Ch. Hungary, 1983, medal Assn. UN Hungary, 1986. Home: Bakator u 10-12, H-1118 Budapest Hungary Office: Evang Luth Ch Hungary, Üllői ut 24, H-1085 Budapest Hungary Address: Evangelikus Egyhaz, Puskin u 12, 1088 Budapest Hungary

NAIRN, CHARLES EDWARD, pastor, religious educator; b. Columbus, Ohio, Aug. 26, 1926; s. William Elden and Hariette (Basbagill) N.; m. Margaret Lucille Prentiss, Aug. 2, 1952; children: Elizabeth, Barbara Kay, Stephen, Michael, Ronald. BA in Philosophy and Religion, Kent (Ohio) State U., 1950, MLS, 1951; BDiv in Philosophy and Religion, Oberlin (Ohio) Coll., 1958; MDiv in Philosophy and Religion, Vanderbilt U., 1972. With various chs., 1960-84; libr., tchr. philosophy and religion Lake Superior State U., 1968-88, ret., 1988. Leader Boy Scouts Am. With USN, 1944-46. Mem. Am. Acad. Religion, Am. Philosophy Assn., Soc. Bibl. Lit., Soc. Christian Philosophy, Metaphys. Soc. Am., Sault Ste. Marie Internat. Libr. Assn. (co-bd. dirs. 1968-88), Mich. Libr. Assn. (rep. Sault Ste. Marie and Lansing, Mich. chpt.). *Life is a gift from God. In life we discover and come to know that, as Jesus taught and lived, this Being in whom we live, and move and have our being is "Our Father." Thus we and all forms of life are one in the family of God.*

NAIRN, THOMAS ALLEN, priest; b. Cleve., Mar. 18, 1948; s. Francis Joseph and Patricia Alice (Jagelewski) N. BA, Quincy Coll., 1971; MDiv, Cath. Theol. Union, 1975, MA, 1976; PhD, U. Chgo., 1985. Ordained priest Roman Cath. Ch., 1975. Assoc. pastor St. Stanislaus Ch., Cleve., 1975; prof. Cath. Theol. Union, Chgo., 1980—; vis. lectr. Yarra Theol. Union, Melbourne, Australia, 1986; vis. scholar St. Edmund's Coll., Cambrige, Eng., 1989; med. ethics cons. Alexian Bros. Hosp., Elk Grove Village, Ill., 1985—; bd. dirs. Franciscan Herald Press, Chgo., 1987—. Contbr. articles to profl. jours. Chair Chgo. Area Faculty for Nuclear Issues Edn., 1984-88; vice-chair Chgo. Com. to Defend the Bill of Rights, 1981—. Mem. Soc. Christian Ethics, Cath. Theol. Soc. Am. Home: 5401 S Cornell Ave Chicago IL 60615 Office: Cath Theol Union 5401 S Cornell Chicago IL 60615

NAKASHIMADA, BONNIE CHARLENE, minister; b. Regina, Sask., Can., Aug. 12, 1960; came to U.S., 1982; d. Andrew Joseph and Audrey Mildred (Schmuland) Gouinchuck; m. David Nakashimada, Aug. 31, 1985. BRE, Can. Bible Coll., Regina, 1982. Lic. to ministry Christian Ch., 1982. Intern youth ministry Salem (Oreg.) Alliance Ch., 1982-83; youth minister Portland (Oreg.) Alliance Ch., 1983—; mem. Christian edn. dist. com. Christian and Missionay Alliance, Canby, Oreg., 1983—. Avocations: running, athletic teams. Office: Portland Alliance Ch 1832 NE 39th Ave Portland OR 97212

NAKAYAMA, FUJI, head of religious order. Head World Buddhist Fellowship, Tokyo. Office: Hozenji Buddhist Temple, 3-24-2 Akabane-dai, Kita-ku, Tokyo Japan*

NAKHJAVANI, ALI-YULLAH, church organization administrator; b. Haifa, Israel, Sept. 19, 1919; s. Ali-AKbar and Fatimah Nakhjavani; m. Violette Banani, Oct. 3, 1945; children: Bahiyyih, Mehran. BA, Am. U. Beirut, 1939. Mem. Nat. Assembly Bahá'is Iran, 1950-51, Nat. Assembly Bahá'is Cen. and East Africa, 1956-61; pres. Internat. Bahá'i Coun., 1961-63; mem. Universal House of Justice, Haifa.

NANCE, WILLIAM ROBERT (BILL NANCE), broadcast professional; b. Dayton, Ohio, May 21, 1950; s. William Robert Nance and Mary Lou (Gentry) Charles; m. Carol Anne Kaylow, Mar. 15, 1975; children: William Robert III, Jennifer Elaine. Grad. high sch., Dayton. Host Sta. WTJC-TV, Dayton, 1985-87; program dir. Sta. WFCJ-FM, Dayton, 1989—. Pres. Am. Cancer Soc., Montgomery County, Ohio, 1989—, trustee Ohio div., 1989—; bd. dirs. Jr. Achievement Dayton, 1987—. Recipient 2 awards Nat. Assn. Realtors, 11 awards Am. Cancer Soc., Paul S. Noblitt Sch. Bell award, Headliners award Atlantic City Press Club, 1979, others; named Dayton area Up and Comer, 1988. Mem. UPI (numerous awards), Nat. Acad. Family Physicians, Soc. Profl. Journalists (Queen City chpt.), Rotary (bd. dirs. Dayton club 1987—). Mem. Christian Chs. and Chs. of Christ. Office: Sta WFCJ-FM PO Box 93.7 Dayton OH 45449

NANNAN-PANDAY, R. M., head of religious order. Pres. Sanatan Dharm Hindu Faith, Paramaribo, Suriname. Office: Sanatan Dharm, New Delhi St 24, POB 1267, Paramaribo Suriname*

NAPIER, LONNIE L., religious organization publications administrator. Gen. sec. publs. Christian Meth. Episcopal ch., Memphis. Office: Christian Meth Episcopal Ch PO Box 2018 Memphis TN 38101*

NARAIN, SASE, religious center administrator. Pres. Hindu Religious Ctr., Georgetown, Guyana. Office: Hindu Religious Ctr, Maha, Sabha, 162 Lamaha St, Georgetown Guyana*

NARDI, THOMAS JAMES, psychologist; b. N.Y.C., Feb. 27, 1949. BA, Manhattan Coll., 1970; MS, St. John's U., 1972, PhD, 1977. Lic. psychologist, N.Y., N.J. Psychologist Bronx (N.Y.) Children's Psychiat. Ctr., 1973-80, Rockland County Bd. Coop. Edn. Svcs., N.Y.C., 1980-81, St. Dominic's Home, Blauvelt, N.Y., 1981-82; clin. dir. N.Y. Ctr. for Eclectic Psychotherapy, Nanuet, N.Y., 1982—; adj. prof. Pace U., Pleasantville, N.Y., 1979—, L.I. U. Mercy Coll., Dobbs Ferry, N.Y., 1978—. Co-author: (play) Somethings You Remember, 1986. Recipient Gran Croce al Merito del Lavoro Italian Acad. for Social and Econ. Improvement, 1985, George Stewart Meml. award for Literary Contbns. to Field of Hypnosis Assn. to Advance Ethic Hypnosis, 1982. Mem. Internat. Acad. Eclectic Psychotherapy, Am. Bd. Sexology, Am. Acad. Behavioral Medicine. *The questions are many but the answers are available to us. To find the solutions we must look within our souls. All answers, all change, all progress comes from within us. If there is to be peace it must be by one.*

NARROWE, MORTON HERMAN, rabbi; b. Phila., Mar. 15, 1932; arrived in Sweden, 1965; s. Morris and Sarah Ruth (Lisack) N.; m. Judith Luba Halpren, June 15, 1958; children: Joshua Avraham, Elizabeth Ann, David Isaac. BA, Yeshiva U., 1954; MA, Jewish Theol. Sem. Am., 1959, DD, 1984; DHL, 1990. Ordained rabbi, 1959. Rabbi Temple Beth Sholom, Satellite Beach, Fla., 1962-65; rabbi Jewish community Stockholm, 1965—; chief rabbi Jewish community, 1975—; v.p. World Council Synagogues, 1975—. Contbr. articles to theol. publs. Mem. Bible Commn. Sweden, bd. dirs., 1976—; v.p. Swedish br. Internat. Coun. Christians and Jews, 1980-88, pres., 1988-91; pres. Swedish Friends Red Star of David, 1983-87; bd. dirs. Zionist Fedn. Sweden, Jewish Community Ctr. Stockholm. Lt. USN, 1959-62. Lodge: B'nai Brith. Home: Torstenssonsgatan 4, S-11456 Stockholm Sweden Office: Judiska Forsamlingen Wahrendorffsgatan, 3 Box 7427, S-10391 Stockholm Sweden

NARUM, WILLIAM HOWARD KENNETH, philosophy and religion educator; b. Fargo, N.D., Aug. 22, 1921; s. William and Helen Clara (Fossum) N.; m. Jeanne Lois Kunau, Sept. 1, 1957; children: Paul, Peter, David. BA, St. Olaf Coll., 1943; BTh, Luther Theol. Sem., 1945; ThM, Princeton Theol. Sem., 1946, ThD, 1951. Instr. St. Olaf Coll., Northfield, Minn., 1947-49, asst. prof., 1949-53, assoc. prof., 1953-57, prof., 1957-91, prof. emeritus, 1991—; vis. prof. U. Iowa, 1957-58, U. Philippines, 1964-65. Co-editor, contbg. author: Quest for a Viable Saga, 1977; contbg. author: Christian Faith and the Liberal Arts, 1960; contbr. articles to profl. jours. Fulbright grantee, 1954-55, Rockefeller grantee, U. Philippines, 1964-65; fellow E.-W. Ctr., 1972, NEH, 1978-79; recipient Harbison award Danforth Found., 1963-64. Mem. Am. Acad. Religion, Am. Philos. Assn., Assn. for Asian Studies, Soc. Christian Philosophers, Metaphys. Soc. Am. Democrat. Home: 205 S Lincoln St Northfield MN 55057

NASH, NANCY TRICE, minister, director; b. San Francisco, Feb. 23, 1943; d. David Hale and Vera (Hume) Trice; m. Phillip Howard Nash, Dec. 29, 1962; children: Neil, Tiffany, Timothy. Student, Pepperdine U., 1961-63; BA, George Fox Coll., 1989. V.p. Dramatic Word, Salem, Oreg., 1976—; dir. women's ministries 1st Ch. of the Nazarene, Salem, 1984—. Author: newsletter Caring, 1984—. Bd. dirs. Victory House, Salem, 1985, N.W. Med. Teams, Salem, 1985-86. Recipient Outstanding Svc. award Sr. Svcs.

Assn., 1986. Republican. Avocations: hiking, friends, reading. Office: 1st Ch of the Nazarene 1550 Market St NE Salem OR 97303

NASH, RICHARD MARK, minister; b. Detroit, May 1, 1958; s. Richard Taylor and Joyce Elaine (Jansen) N.; m. Elizabeth Keller, June 21, 1980. BA in History cum laude, Harvard U., 1980; ThM, Dallas Theol. Seminary, 1985; postgrad., Trinity Evang. Divinity Sch., 1989—. Ordained minister Fellowship of Evang. Community Chs., 1985. Instr. in lay inst. Dallas Theol. Seminary, 1983; prof. Free Will Bapt. Bible Coll., 1985; minister of Christian edn. Cen. Free Will Bapt. Ch., Royal Oak, Mich., 1986-87; assoc. pastor for adult edn. Community Ch. of Greenwood, Ind., 1987—; curriculum writer Randall House, Nashville, 1985-86, cons., 1985; coord. Trinity Ins. Practical/Bibl. Studies, Indpls. Extension of Trinity Evang. Div. Sch.; adj. prof. Trinity Evang. Div. Sch., 1989—; cons. Scripture Press Publs., 1989—. Contbr. articles to profl. jours. and the Open Bible. Named One of Outstanding Young Men of Am., 1979, 80. Mem. Nat. Assn. Dirs. Christian Edn., Fellowship Evang. Community Chs. Avocations: shortwave radio, computers, internat. affairs, classical music, reading. Home: 1199 Pilgrim Rd Greenwood IN 46142 Office: Community Ch of Greenwood 1477 W Main St Greenwood IN 46142

NASH, RONALD HERMAN, philosophy educator; b. Cleve., May 27, 1936; s. Herman Nash and Viola McAlpin; m. Betty Jane Perry, June 8, 1957; children: Jeffrey A., Jennifer A. BA, Barrington (R.I.) Coll., 1958; MA, Brown U., 1960; PhD, Syracuse U., 1964. Instr. philosophy Barrington Coll., 1958-60, Houghton (N.Y.) Coll., 1960-62; prof. philosophy Western Ky. U., Bowling Green, 1964-91; prof. philosophy religion Ref. Theol. Sem., Orlando, Fla., 1991—; dept. head Western Ky. U., Bowling Green, 1964-84; mem. adv. bd. CEBA, Lynchburg, Va., 1989—. Author 23 book, including Poverty and Wealth, 1986, Faith and Reason, 1988, The Closing of the American Heart, 1990, The Gospel and the Greeks, 1991, Beyond Liberation Theology, 1992; mem. bd. editors Durell Jour. Money and Banking, 1988-91. Advisor U.S. Civil Rights Commn., Washington, 1988-91. Fellow NEH, 1969. Office: Ref Theol Sem PO Box 945120 Maitland FL 32794

NASH, STEVEN BOYD, minister; b. New Brunswick, N.J., Nov. 4, 1955; s. Boyd M. and Janice (Behun) N.; m. Mary Ann Kulakovich, Nov. 5, 1983; 1 child, Sarah. BA in Bibl. Lit., Northeastern Bible Coll., Essex Fells, N.J., 1984; MA in Religion, Westminster Theol. Sem., Phila., 1986, postgrad., 1986—. Ordained to ministry Conservative Bapt. Assn. Am., 1990. Interim preacher Jamesburg (N.J.) 1st Bapt. Ch., 1984-85; assoc. pastor Stelton Bapt. Ch., Edison, N.J., 1986; instr. in Bible Northeastern Bible Coll., Essex Fells, 1986-89; pastor Raritan Rd. Bapt. Ch., Cranford, N.J., 1988—; instr. in evangelism Sayre Woods Bapt. Ch., Old Bridge, N.J., 1986-87. Mem. Conservative Bapt. Assn. N.J. Republican. Home: 13 Harvard Rd Linden NJ 07036 Office: Raritan Rd Bapt Ch 611 Raritan Rd Cranford NJ 07016

NASH, SYLVIA DOTSETH, religious organization executive, consultant; b. Montevedio, Minn., Apr. 25, 1945; d. Owen Donald and Selma A. (Tollefson) Dotseth; divorced; 1 child, Elizabeth Louise; m. Thomas L. Nash, Dec. 20, 1986. Grad., Calif. Luth. Bible Sch., 1965. Office mgr. First Congl. Ch., Pasadena, Calif., 1968-75; adminstrv. asst. Pasadena Presbyn. Ch., 1975-78; dir. adminstrv. svcs. Fuller Theol. Sem., Pasadena, 1978-81; chief exec. officer Christian Mgmt. Assn., Diamond Bar, Calif., 1981—; bd. dirs. Gospel Lit. Internat., Rosemead, Calif.; mem. adv. com. Christian Mgmt. Rev., Chgo., 1986—; cons. various orgns., 1985—. Editor: The Clarion, 1975-78, The Christian Mgmt. Report, 1981-86; contbr. articles to profl. jours. Mem. Nat. Assn. Ch. Adminstrs. (sec. 1979-81), NAFE, Am. Soc. Assn. Execs. Office: Christian Mgmt Assn PO Box 4638 Diamond Bar CA 91765

NASSIF, BRADLEY LOUIS, research scholar; b. Cedar Rapids, Iowa, July 25, 1954; s. Louis Rustom and Lydia (Ferris) N.; m. Barbara Anne Strait, June 11, 1988. BA, Friends U., 1977; MA in New Testament, Denver Sem., 1981; MA in European Hist., Wichita State U., 1984; MDiv, St. Vladimir's Othodox Sem., Scarsdale, N.Y., 1985; PhD in Patristics and Ea. Christianity, Fordham U., 1991. Mentor SUNY, Nanuet, 1985; owner, operator Gt. Plains Smokemaster, Wichita, Kans., 1980—; adj. prof. Friends U., Wichita, Kans., 1986, St. Francis Coll., Bklyn., 1988; cons. editor Christianity Today mag., Carol Stream, Ill., 1981; guest preacher for joint ann. meeting Am. Missiology Soc., and Am. Assn. Mission Profs., 1989; speaker in field. Contbr. articles to religious mags. Paraprofl. Wichita Pub. Schs., 1982-84. Recipient Antiochian scholarship, Antiochian Orthodox Archdiocese N. Am., 1983-85, Presidential scholarship, Grad. Sch. Arts & Scis. Fordham U., 1987-88, Grad. Asst. Fellowship, Fordham U. Theology dept., 1987-88. Mem. Internat. Patristic Soc., N. Am. Patristic Soc., Orthodox Theol. Soc Am., Evang. Theol. Soc., Soc. Bibl. Lit., Am. Acad. Religion, Am. Soc. Ch. History, Soc. for Study Ea. Orthodoxy and Evangelicalism (founder, pres.). Republican. Home: 225 N Gow Wichita KS 67203 *The most valuable perspectives on the present are those which have carefully digested the past.*

NASSON, RONALD, religious organization administrator. Treas. Albanian Orthodox Archdiocese in Am., Jamaica Plain, Mass. Office: Albanian Orthodox Archdiocese Am 26 Enfield St Jamaica Plain MA 02130*

NATHAN, JOHNNIE ALMA, minister; b. Dayton, Ohio, Feb. 15, 1950; d. Conner and Mattie Lee (Clark) Brewer; m. Thomas Nathan (div. Apr. 1977); 1 child, Thomas James. Grad. high sch., Dayton. Ordained to ministry Pentecostal Ch. Min. St. Paul Ch., 1975-77, Mt. Olivet Ch., Dayton, 1990—. Home: 127 Crown Ave Dayton OH 45427

NATHANIEL, HIS GRACE BISHOP See POPP, NATHANIEL (WILLIAM GEORGE)

NATTIEL, CHRISTINE HENRY, minister; b. Orlando, Fla., Feb. 22, 1939; d. Frank and Willie (Lee) Henry; m. Willie Lee Nattiel; children: Gale Frances, Willie Jr., Frank Henry, Timothy David, Dorothy Jeanne, Elizabeth. Diploma, Mebane High Sch., Alachua, Fla., 1957. Ordained to ministry Baptist Ch., 1976. Minister Bapt. Ch., Gainesville, Fla., 1976—. Fundraiser, Citizens for Martin Luther King Day, Gainesville, 1986. Named Outstanding Fundraiser, Citizens for Martin Luther King, 1986. Republican. Avocations: helping elderly and children. Home: Rte 3 Box 170 Newberry FL 32669

NAU, ARLO, ecumenical agency administrator. Adminstr. Ariz. Ecumenical Coun., Phoenix. Office: Ariz Ecumenical Coun 4423 N 24th St Ste 750 Phoenix AZ 85016*

NAUSIN, FRANK GILBERT, minister; b. Albany, Calif., Mar. 13, 1948; s. Frank Jr. and Clara Lillian (Fadness) N.; m. Linda Irene Lewis, June 20, 1970; children: Timothy Frank, Jeremy Thomas. BA cum laude, Calif. Luth. U., 1970; MDiv, Pacific Luth. Sem., 1974. Ordained to ministry Luth. Ch., 1974. Asst. pastor Bethany Luth. Ch., Scottsdale, Ariz., 1974-75; pastor Mt. Cross Luth. Ch., Camarillo, Calif., 1975-82; sr. pastor Tanque Verde Luth. Ch., Tucson, 1982—; mem. profl. preparations com. Pacific S.W. Synod, Evang. Luth. Ch. Am., L.A., 1977-83, chmn. bd. outreach, 1983-88, mem. coun. bd. Grand Canyon Synod, Phoenix, 1988—. Bd. dirs. Camp Yoligawa, Yucapia, Calif., 1975-77; vol. YMCA, Tucson, 1989-90, Tanque Verde Little League, Tucson, 1987-90; chmn. Camarillo (Calif.) Ministerial Assn., 1977-79. Mem. Merilac Lodge (chmn. bd. dirs. 1989-90). Democrat. Office: Tanque Verde Luth Ch 8625 E Tanque Verde Rd Tucson AZ 85749

NAVARRO, CONRADO ENRIQUE, chaplain; b. Havana, Cuba, Oct. 25, 1954; s. Luis Lazaro and Gladys Alonso (Gamas) Belasquida; m. Nilda Lima, Dec. 28, 1974; children: Nelly, Elizabeth Ann, Conrado Enrique II. BA, U. S.C., 1978; MDiv, Southeastern Bapt. Theol., Seminary, Wake Forest, N.C., 1983. Lic./ordained to ministry So. Bapt. Conv., 1983. Commd. 2d lt. USAF, 1980, advanced through grades to capt., 1986; pastor Raleigh (N.C.) Spanish Mission, 1980-83; chaplain candidate USAF, 1980-83; pastor William Carey Bapt. Ch., Medford, N.Y., 1983-86; res. chaplain Dover (Del.) AFB, 1983-86; chaplain/capt. USAF, Patrick AFB, Fla., 1986-91, Upper Heyford, Eng., 1991—; 2d v.p. Bapt. Conv. of N.Y., Syracuse, 1984-86. Editor sports/entertainment: (newsletter) The Enquiry, 1982. Mem. Mil. Chaplains Assn. (treas. 1989-90), Air Force Assn. Republican. Home: 20 C SG/HC7 APO New York NY 09644 Office: USAF 20 CSG/HC APO New York NY 09644

NAYLOR, C. BRUCE, ecumenical agency administrator. Exec. dir. The Ch. Fedn. Greater Indpls. Inc. Office: Ch Fedn Greater Indianapolis 1100 W 42nd St Indianapolis IN 45208*

NAYLOR, JAMES LORA, JR., minister; b. Albany, Ga., July 24, 1927; s. James Lora Naylor Sr. and Mary Iona (Harrington) Halford; m. Mary Elizabeth Shirah, Apr. 6, 1947; children: Patricia Gayle, Deborah Joyce, Jackie Lou, James Lora III. BTh, MTh, Internat. Bible Sch. and Sem., 1980; ThD, Internat. Bible Sch. and Sem., Orlando, Fla., 1981. Ordained to ministry So. Bapt. Conv., 1980. Moderator Tucker Bapt. Assn., Camila, Ga., 1983-84; pres. Pastors' Fellowship, Fairburn Assn., Atlanta, 1987; pastor Mt. Pleasant Bapt. Ch., Vada, Ga., 1988—; moderator Bowen Bapt. Assn., Bainbridge, Ga., 1990-91; dir. Bowen Sr. Adults, Bainbridge, 1990-91; pres. Internat. Environ. Products, 1990—. Author: Twain Shall Be One Flesh, 1989; patentee in field. Chaplain Downtown Civic Club, Lakeland, Fla., 1950, Gideons Internat., Albany, Ga., 1959, Jr. C. of C., Albany, 1960; lay chaplain USS Tweedy, 1960. With USN, 1945-46, 50-51, 60-61. Home: Rte 2 Box 1057 Climax GA 31734 Office: Internat Environ Products 2610 Dawson Rd Albany GA 31707

NCAMISO NDLOVU, LOUIS, bishop. Bishop of Manzini Roman Cath. Ch., Swaziland. Office: Coun Swaziland Chs, POB 1095, Manzini Suriname*

NCOZANA, SILAS S., religious organization administrator. Gen. sec. Ch. of Cen. Africa (Presbyn.), Blantyre. Office: Ch Cen Africa, POB 413, Blantyre Malawi*

N'DAYEN, MONSIGNOR JOACHIM, archbishop. Archbishop of Bangui, pres. Bishop's Conf. Roman Cath. Ch., Cen. African Republic. Office: BP 798, Bangui Central African Republic*

NDINISA, JEREMIAH, clergy member, priest. Pres. United Christian Ch. of Africa, Mbabane, Swaziland. Office: United Christ Ch, POB 6, Mbabane Swaziland*

NEAL, ALBERT AIKEN, minister, educator; b. Camden, S.C., Aug. 4, 1945; s. James Peter DeVeaux Neal Sr. and Geneva E. (Outten) N.; m. Virgina Miller, Aug. 4, 1972; children: Erica Denise, ALeta LaValle. BS, Benedict Coll., 1966; BD, Fla. State Christian U., 1968; MEd, S.C. State Coll., 1968; PhD, Universal Life Ch., Modesto, Calif., 1981; cert. ednl. specialist, U. S.C., 1984; MDiv., Luth. Theol. Sem., 1988; EdD, U. S.C., 1988. Ordained minister, 1968. Tchr., counselor Fairfield High Sch., Winnsboro, S.C., 1966-70; instr. U. S.C., Columbia, S.C., 1970-88; asst. prof. U. S.C., Columbia, 1988—; interim pastor Macedonia Bapt. Ch., Ridgeway, S.C., 1969-70, St. Dorcas Bapt. Ch., North, S.C., 1970, 72, Zion Bapt. Ch., 1970-72; pastor Sutton Br. Bapt. Ch., Lugoff, S.C., 1970-87; sr. pastor Antioch Bapt. Ch. Koon Rd., Columbia, 1987—; assoc. dir. nat. youth sport program U. S.C., Columbia, 1986—; cons. U.S. Army Edn. Ctr, Ft. Jackson, S.C., 1969—, Dept. Edn., S.C., N.C., Fla., Va., Ky., 1970—, Stevens Co., Ga., 1975. Contbr. articles to profl. jours. Chaplain North Columbia Civic Club, Columbia, 1982—. Mem. Am. Pub. Health Assn., Am. Driver and Traffic Safety Educator Assn., Coll. and Univ. Safety Educator Assn., Nat. Safety Council, Bapt. Ednl. and Missionary Conv. S.C., Modern Music Master Soc., NAACP (life), Alpa Phi Omega, Omega Psi Phi. Avocations: electronic equipment, photography, woodworking. Home: 217 Cordova Dr Columbia SC 29203 Office: U SC 216-E Health Scis Columbia SC 29208

NEAL, ALBERT HARVEY, retired minister; b. Morganton, Ark., Apr. 4, 1925; s. Albert Wilburn ad Alma Fay (Bittle) N.; m. Barbara Jean Sly, Oct. 28, 1946 (div. Jan. 1984); children: Brenda L. Wood, Linda Caroll, Ronda Jean Easter; m. Betty Lu Dunn Beasley, Sept. 25, 1987. DD (hon.), Sch. Bible Theology, San Jacinto, Calif., 1989. Ordained to ministry Pentecostal Ch. of God, 1950. Pastor Yreka, Calif., Farmersville, Calif., 1949-55; dir. Indian missions, 1955-65; dist. supt. Pacific NW Dist., 1965-77; world missions field rep., 1977-79; pastor Longview, Wash., 1979-82, Grover City, Calif., Kelseyville, Calif., 1982-90; area sales dir. Bennie Harris Assocs., 1973-91; asst. gen. supt. Pentecostal Ch. of God, Joplin, Mo., 1973-77. With USN, 1942-46, PTO. Decorated Presdl. Unit Citation, Philippines Liberation with 2 stars, South Pacific ribbon with 9 stars. Republican. Home: PO Box 760 Ceres CA 95307

NEAL, BRUCE WALTER, minister; b. Belleville, Ont., Can., Jan. 27, 1931; s. Walter John and Harriet (Hammersley) N.; m. Barbara Lou Fennell, Aug. 29, 1953; children—Susan, Janice, Jeffrey, Sharon, Jennifer. B.A., McMaster U., Hamilton, Ont., 1951, B.D., 1954, D.D. (hon.), 1976; postgrad. U. Chgo., 1954-56; Th.M., Victoria U., 1978. Ordained to ministry Can. Bapt. Ch., 1954. Pastor, Queensway Bapt. Ch., Brantford, Ont., 1951-54; interim pastor Gurnee Community Ch., Ill., 1955-56; assoc. sec. Bd. Religious Edn., Bapt. Conv. of Ont. and Que., Toronto, Ont., 1956-61; assoc. minister Yorkminster Park Bapt. Ch., Toronto, 1961-65; pastor James St. Bapt. Ch., Hamilton, 1965-72; sr. pastor Walmer Rd. Bapt. Ch., Toronto, 1972-84, Lorne Park Bapt. Ch., Mississauga, Ont., 1984—; chmn. relief and devel. com. Can. Bapt. Fedn., Toronto, 1974-84, pres., 1982-85; chmn. bd. Can. Foodgrains Bank, Winnipeg, Man., Can., 1984-86; pres. Bapt. Mins. Credit Union, Ont., 1988—. Trustee McMaster Div. Coll., 1991—. Author: The Table is for Eating, 1966; Bite a Blue Apple, 1972, God's Ten Words For All of Us, 1987, Claim the Joy, 1989, What We Mean, 1991. Vice chmn. budget com. United Appeal, Hamilton, 1972. Avocations: model railroading; curling. Home: 1856 Truscott Dr, Mississauga, ON Canada L5J 2A2 Office: Lorne Park Bapt Ch, 1500 Indian Rd, Mississauga, ON Canada L5H 1S7

NEAL, MARJORIE ESTHER HERMAN, minister; b. Troy, N.Y., Aug. 9, 1935; d. George Albert and Elizabeth Alida (Dobert) Herman; m. Kenneth W. Neal, Sept. 18, 1962; children: Joan Elizabeth, Carol Marie, Linda Bennett, Jeffrey Kenneth. BS in Cultural Studies, SUNY, Buffalo, 1981; MDiv with distinction, Christ The King Sem., 1985, MA in Pastoral Ministry with distinction, 1987. Ordained to ministry United Ch. Christ and Christian Ch. (Disciples of Christ), 1985. Lay chaplain Williamsville (N.Y.) View Manor, 1979-80; supply pastor Christian Ch., United Ch. of Christ, Western Area Buffalo, 1981-85; interim pastor Pembroke Community Ch., Corfu, N.Y., 1985-86; pastor St. Paul's United Ch. of Christ, Alden, N.Y., 1986—; interim pastor Winger Ch. of Christ (Disciples), Wainfleet, Ont., Can., 1991—; adminstr. Christian women's fellowship N.E. region Christian Ch. (Disciples of christ), Buffalo, 1978-81, with dept. Ch. and Ministry, 1986—; moderator Western area United Ch. Christ, Christian Ch., Buffalo, 1989-90; cons. World Day of Prayer workshop, Wellsprings coord, forum coord., Ch. Women United, Buffalo, 1966—; with radio/TV dept. Buffalo Area Coun. Chs., 1985—. Host. local TV program Ch. Invitation, 1987—. Mem. planning bd. Maryvale Sch. System, Cheektowaga, N.Y., 1977-79. Mem. Internat. Assn. Women Mins. Home: 4778 Union Rd Cheektowaga NY 14225 *With God, all things are possible!.*

NEAL, MONTFORD LEE, minister; b. Clay City, Ky., Jan. 25, 1942; s. Howard Clay and Nannie (Drake) N.; m. Rita Denniston, Dec. 2, 1963; children: Robert, Randy, Melissa. BS in Elem. Edn., Ind. U., 1975; MA in Ednl. Psychology and Guidance, Tenn. Tech. U., 1978; MDiv, United Sem., Dayton, Ohio, 1982; D Ministry, Nazarene Theol. Sem., 1989. Ordained to ministry Ch. of God, 1966. Pastor 1st Chs. of God, Ohio, 1964-67, Ind., 1967-76, Tenn., 1976-85; prof. Mid-Am. Bible Coll., 1985-90; pastor Bristow (Okla.) 1st Ch. of God, 1989—; missionary S.Am., 1984-85; adj. prof. homiletics and communications Mid-Am. Bible Coll., 1990—; mem. Writers of Warner Press (Conf.), Anderson, Ind., 1983—; speaker S.W. and Mid-West confs; spiritual emphasis speaker Bay Ridge Christian Coll, Kenelleton, Tex., 1991; mem. Bd. Ch. Svc. Gen. Assembly, 1991—, Bd. Christian Edn. N.E. Dist. Ch. of God, 1991. Author: The Gospel of Mark, 1983, Inductive Studies to New Testament, 1988; contbr. articles to profl. jours. Mem. Okla. Ministerial Orgn. (1st v.p. 1990—), Bristow Ministerial Alliance (v.p. 1990-91, pres., 1991—), Okla. Assembly (v.p. 1990—), Program Com. of Okla. (chairperson 1990—, exec. bd. 2d v.p. 1990—). Avocations: fishing, golf, walking, history, travel. Home: 5 Sunset Ln Briston OK 74010

NEAL, PERRY DAVID, clergyman, evangelist; b. Montgomery, Ala., Jan. 15, 1941; s. Cameron M. and Alice (Perry) N.; m. Marcelene Spivey, June 18, 1961. BA, Stamford U., 1967; ThM, New Orleans Theol. Sem., 1970. Ordained to ministry 1960. Pastor Tunnell Chapel Bapt. Ch., 1960-64, Sister Springs Bapt. Ch., Selma, Ala., 1963-67; assoc. pastor, dir. evangelism First Bapt. Ch., Biloxi, Miss., 1968-70; pastor First Bapt. Ch., Bay St. Louis, Miss., 1970-73, Eastdale Bapt. Ch., Montgomery, 1973-75; evangelist, pres., chmn., bd. dirs. Perry Neal Evangel. Assn., Montgomery, 1975—. Mem. Ala. Conf. Full Time Evangelists, Conf. So. Bapt. Evangelists (parlimentarian, v.p.), So. Bapt. Conv., Ala. Bapt. Conv. Home: 4418 Wares Ferry Rd Montgomery AL 36109

NEAL, RANDALL STRANTON, minister; b. Kansas City, Kans., May 20, 1952; s. Howard Stranton and Bonnie Jean (Johnson) N.; m. Dee Anna Maynard, June 11, 1976; children: Bethany, Russell. AA, Broward Community Coll., Ft. Lauderdale, Fla., 1975; BA, Fla. Atlantic U., 1977; MDiv, S.W. Baptist Theol. Seminary, Ft. Worth, 1981, PhD, 1988. Pastor Atlantic Bapt. Ch., Margate, Fla., 1976; instr. Tarrant County Jr. Coll., Ft. Worth, 1983-84; teaching fellow S.W. Bapt. Theol. Seminary, Ft. Worth, 1982-84; pastor First Bapt. Ch., Alba, Tex., 1984-89, Dover Shores Bapt. Ch., Orlando, Fla., 1989—. Profl. coord. Am. Cancer Soc., Ft. Worth, 1981. Fellow Soc. Bibl. Religion, Am. Acad. Religion; mem. Greater Orlando Bapt. Assn. (dir. evangelism 1990—). Republican. Home: 1913 Excalibur Dr Orlando FL 32822 Office: Dover Shores Baptist Church 551 Gaston Foster Rd Orlando FL 32807

NEAL, TOM WRIGHT, JR., minister; b. Temple, Tex., Aug. 22, 1946; s. Tom Wright and Elsie Mae (Oates) N.; m. Linda Ann Jones, Apr. 9, 1965; children: Marshall David, Jeffrey Andrew. BA, Eureka Coll., 1971; MDiv, Brite Divinity Sch., Tex. Christian U., 1975, DMin, 1986. Ordained to ministry Christian Ch. (Disciples of Christ), 1975; cert. in active parenting, conflict mgmt. Yoke min. 1st Christian Chs., Seminole, Andrews, Tex., 1975-77; assoc. min. Woodlawn Christian Ch., San Antonio, 1977-78; min. Bethany Christian Ch., Jackson, Tenn., 1978-84, Sandy Ln. Christian Ch., Ft. Worth, 1984-87, 1st Christian Ch., Kingsville, Tex., 1987—; adj. prof. philosophy Park Coll., NAS, Kingsville, 1990—; pres. Regional Inter-Faith Assn., Jackson, 1980, 81; moderator Bluebonnet Area; rep. Regional Coun. Christian Chs. in Southwest. Author: The Prophets, 1983, Single Young Adult Ministry, 1986. Chaplain Tex. State Guard, Andrews, 1975-76; pres. Kingsville Coalition for Parent Edn., 1990-91; mem. long range planning com. Kingsville Adult Dependent Care, 1991. Recipient Conflict Mgmt. Rsch. award Christian Ch., San Francisco, 1991; Carter Ministerial Edn. Com. scholar Brite Div. Sch., 1972-74, Granville Walker Ministerial scholar, Brite Div. Sch., 1974-75. Office: 1st Christian Ch 1900 S Brahma Blvd Kingsville TX 78363

NEALL, RALPH EUGENE, religious educator; b. Hinsdale, Ill., Oct. 21, 1927; s. Virle R. and Nellie Marvelle (Eastman) N.; m. Beatrice Short, Aug. 11, 1949; children: Randolph E., Cheryl Neall Smith. BA, Atlantic Union Coll., South Lancaster, Mass., 1949; MDiv, Andrews U., Berrien Springs, Mich., 1971, PhD, 1982. Min. N.Y. Conf. Seventh Day Adventists, 1949-55, 56-57, Bermuda Mission Seventh Day Adventists, 1955-56, Cambodia Dist. Seventh Day Adventists, 1957-64; pres. Vietnam Mission Seventh Day Adventists, 1964-68; chair Bible dept. Southeast Union Coll., Singapore, 1971-74; prof. religion Union Coll., Lincoln, Nebr., 1977—. Author: How Long, O Lord, 1982; contbr. articles to profl. jours. Mem. Soc. Bibl. Lit., Andrews Soc. Religious Scholars. Republican. Home: 2001 Broadmoore Dr Lincoln NE 68506 Office: Union Coll 3800 S 48th St Lincoln NE 68506 *A Christian must make plans as though the Lord were not coming for a hundred years, and yet live faithfully as though He were coming tonight.*

NEATHERY, JAMES ARTHUR, religious organization administrator; b. Jamestown, N.Y., July 27, 1961; s. Thomas Howerton and Sally Jean (Saff) N.; m. Melissa Marie Barker, Aug. 25, 1990. BS, Cornell U., 1983; ThM, Dallas Theol. Sem. Summer missionary Navigators, Madiun, Indonesia, 1985; interim pastor Faith Community Ch., Dallas, 1987-88; founder, dir. Front Line Ministries, Dallas, 1988—; mem. staff Young Life Urban, Dallas, 1989—. Republican. Mem. Fellowship Bible Ch. Home: 6006 La Vista Dallas TX 75206

NEDDO, FRANCIS JACKSON, missionary; b. South Bend, Ind., Feb. 3, 1921; s. Gabriel Guy and Mamie Adeline (Annis) N.; m. Hazel Kline, Aug. 4, 1946; children: Mary, Michael, Jonathan, Joel, Faith, Flora, Carolee. BS, Bryan Coll., 1954. Pres. Christian Endeavor, St. Joseph County, Ind, 1940-43; asst. dir. New London (Conn.) Youth for Christ, 1945-46; exec. com. St. Joseph County Youth For Christ, South Bend, 1946-48; supt. Mishawaka (Ind.) Christian Youth Ctr., 1946-50; Bible Club dir. Rhea County Youth for Christ, Dayton, Tenn., 1952-55; community ministries dir. Cedine Bible Mission, Spring City, Tenn., 1955—; Bible club dir. Cedine Bible Mission, Spring City, 1955-88, Bible quiz dir., 1955-91; com. chmn. Child Evangelism, Chattanooga, 1961-81. With USN, 1944-46. Named Bible Quiz Dir. of Yr., Cedine Bible Quiz Coaches, Spring City, 1980-89. Mem. Christian Educators Assn. Internat., Wycliffe Assocs., Evang. Tchr. Tng. Assn., Assn. N.Am. Missions. Republican. Home: 15413 Dayton Pike Sale Creek TN 37373 Office: Cedine Bible Mission Rt 1 Box 2390 Spring City TN 37381

NEECE, EVELYN RUTH, church secretary, treasurer; b. Flat River, Mo., June 2, 1926; d. Albert Oscar and Mary Anna Johnson; m. Charlie Ott, Apr. 16, 1971 (dec. July 1975). Grad. high sch., Flat River. Youth dir. First Bapt. Ch., Desloge, Mo., 1953-71; sec.-treas. House of Hope, Tampa, Fla., 1985—, coord., 1985-90; bd. dirs. Faith-Pool Prayer Group Outreach, Inc., Tampa, 1988—. Author The Good Report bull., 1985-91. Office: House of Hope 4320 Bay to Bay Blvd Tampa FL 33629-6607 *Life is so precious when you realize the awesomeness of how God truly directs when we allow Him to. He places those individuals in our path whom He knows will influence us in the right direction always. Negatism is obsolete to a positive Christian.*

NEEL, PEGGY SUE, religious association executive, consultant; b. Kingston, Okla., Dec. 2, 1934; d. Grover Cleveland and Lorene (Findley) Lasiter; m. Johnny J. Easley, Jan. 4, 1954 (div. 1968); 1 child, Kathryn Sue. Student Murry Jr. Coll., 1953-54. Clk.-typist Tinker AFB, Oklahoma City, 1954-60, procurement clk., 1961-63, personnel clk., sec., 1964-69; exec. sec. Larry Jones Evangelical Assn., Oklahoma City, 1970-75; bookkeeper, sec., procurement clk. Ch. of New Life, Oklahoma City, 1976-78; bookkeeper, exec. sec. legal spl. asst. to pres. and adminstrv. v.p. for Larry Jones Internat. Ministeries, Oklahoma City, 1979—; v.p. counseling Women's Aglow, State of Okla., 1976-78, v.p. adminstrn., 1978-80. Author: How To Pray According to God's Will, 1982. Active Chickasaw Indian Tribe. Avocations: oil painting; studying history of American Indians. Home: 507 SW 55th St Oklahoma City OK 73109

NEELEY, MARK E., minister; b. Tyler, Tex., Sept. 7, 1952; s. Morris Earl and Margaret Ann (Maynor) N.; m. Peggy Jean Matthews, Dec. 7, 1979; children: Sarah Ann, Sally Elizabeth. BA, Baylor U., 1974; MDiv, Southwestern Bapt. Theol. Sem., 1977, D. Ministry, 1987. Ordained to ministry So. Bapt. Conv., 1977. Assoc. pastor 1st Bapt. Ch., Hitchcock, Tex., 1977-80, pastor, 1980-90; pastor 1st Bapt. Ch., Mineola, Tex., 1990—; mem. exec. bd. Bapt. Gen. Convention of Tex., Dallas, 1987-90.

NEFF, LESTER LEROY, administrator, minister; b. Medford, Oreg., Nov. 20, 1923; s. James Asher and Ruth (Turnbow) N.; m. Avon Maxine Bostwick, Aug. 15, 1942; children: Lawrence Dale, Carol Lee, Donald Leroy. BA, Ambassador Coll., 1959, MA in Theology, 1962. Inspector Retail Credit Co., Atlanta, 1946-55; dept. mgr. Worldwide Ch. of God, Pasadena, Calif., 1955-64, 1971-73; bus. mgr. Ambassador Coll., Big Sandy, Tex., 1964-71, 73-76; pastor Worldwide Ch. of God, Pasadena, Calif., 1976-79, ministerial adminstr., 1979-81; sec., treas. Ambassador Coll., Pasadena, Calif., 1981—. Sgt. USAAF, 1943-46. Office: Worldwide Ch of God 300 W Green St Pasadena CA 91105

NEFF, ROBERT WILBUR, church official; b. Lancaster, Pa., June 16, 1936; s. Wilbur Hildebr and Hazel Margaret (Martin) N.; m. Dorothy Rosewarne, Aug. 16, 1959; children: Charles Scott, Heather Lynn. B.S., Pa. State U., 1958; B.D., Yale Div. Sch., 1961, M.A., 1963, Ph.D., 1969; D.D., Juniata Coll., 1978, Manchester Coll., 1979; D.H.L., Bridgewater Coll., 1979. Asst. prof. Bridgewater Coll., 1964-65; mem. faculty dept. Bibl. studies Bethany Theol. Sem., 1965-77, prof., 1973-77; gen. sec. Ch. of the Brethren, Elgin, Ill., 1978-86; pres. Juniata Coll., 1986—; mem. faculty North Park Sem., No. Baptist Sem., Theol. Coll. No. Nigeria. Author works in field. Mem. governing bd. Nat. Council Chs. of Christ, 1976-86, mem. exec. com., 1979-86; mem. Mid-East panel, 1980, 2d v.p., 1985-86; cen. com. World Council of Chs., 1983—; rep. Assembly of World Council of Chs., 1983; exec. Com. on Interchurch Relations, 1980-84, mem. del. to China, 1981, chmn. presdl. panel, 1982-84; bd. dirs. Bethany Theol. Sem., 1978-86; bd. dirs. Mellon Bank (Cen.) Nat. Assn., 1987—, exec. com., 1989—; bd. dirs. Huntingdon County and IndustryInc., 1987—; campaign chmn. United Way, Huntingdon County, 1989. Danforth fellow, 1958-69. Mem. Soc. Bibl. Lit., Soc. Old Testament Study, Chgo. Soc. Bibl. Rsch., Soc. Values in Higher Edn., Coun. of Ind. Colls. (nat. bd. dirs. 1991), Pa. Coun. Ind. Colls. and Univs. (exec. com. 1988-90). Democrat. Home: RD 4 Box 37 Huntingdon PA 16652 Office: Juniata Coll 1700 Moore St Huntingdon PA 16652

NEGREPONTIS, MICHAEL (BISHOP TIMOTHY), bishop; b. Athens, Greece, June 7, 1928; s. Anastasios and Maria Negrepontis. Sacred Theology, U. Thessalonika, Greece; M.Div., Holy Cross Greek Orthodox Theol. Sch., Boston; B.A. with honors, Hellenic Coll. Ordained deacon Greek Orthodox Ch., 1950, ordained priest, 1952. Pastor St. Nicholas Ch., Bethlehem, Pa., 1955-61, Parish of Sts. Constantine and Helen, Middletown, Ohio, 1961-62; pastor Holy Trinity Ch., London, Ont., Can., 1962-67, Harrisburg, Pa.; pastor Dionysios Ch., Kansas City, Kans., St. Barbara; dean Holy Trinity Archdiocesan Cathedral, N.Y.C., until 1969; spl. asst. to chancellor and personnel dir. archdiocesan staff Archdiocesan Hdqrs., N.Y.C., from 1969; pastor St. Anargyroi Ch., Marlboro, Mass., until 1973, Ch. Holy Ascension, Fairview, N.J.; elevated to Titular Bishop of Pamphilos, 1973, consecrated bishop, 1974; bishop Greek Orthodox Diocese in S.Am., 1974-79; aux. bishop to the Archbishop 7th Archdiocesan Dist. Detroit, 1979; bishop Greek Orthodox Diocese of Detroit, 1979—; apptd. pastor Greek Orthodox Communities of Republic of Panama. Decorated Grand Master of Order of Vasco Nuñez de Balboa, Republic of Panama; Grand Taxiarch, Order Orthodox Crusaders of Holy Sepulcher. Address: 19405 Renfrew Rd Detroit MI 48221

NEGRÓN SANTANA, HERMIN, bishop; b. Naranjito, P.R., Nov. 10, 1937; s. Angel Negrón and Gracia Santana. B.A., Universidad Católica, Ponce, P.R., 1963; B.D., Regional Sem. St. Vincent de Paul, Boynton Beach, Fla., 1969. Ordained priest Roman Catholic Ch., 1969. Asst. pastor St. Mickael's Ch., Naranjito, 1969-70; asst. pastor St. Benito's Ch., Patillas, P.R., 1970-71; pastor Santo Cristo de la Salud Ch., Comerio, P.R., 1971-81; chancellor Diocese of Caguas, P.R., 1981; aux. bishop, vicar gen. Diocese of San Juan, P.R., 1981. Named adoptive son of Comerio, 1981. Home: Arzobispado de San Juan Apartado 1967 San Juan PR 00903

NEHER, JAMES EDWARD, minister; b. Huntington, N.Y., Mar. 5, 1953; s. Edward James and Elizabeth Jane (Garlough) N.; m. Judith Ann Vincent, May 12, 1980; children: Jeffrey, Benjamin, Daniel, Timothy. BA, SUNY, Stony Brook, 1975; MDiv, Biblical Theol. Sem., Hatfield, Pa., 1979. Ordained to ministry Bible Fellowship Ch., 1989. Archivist Biblical Theol. Sem., 1982-86; asst. pastor Graterford (Pa.) Bible Fellowship Ch., 1987-90; pastor Christian edn. Grace Bible Fellowship Ch., Reading, Pa., 1990—; lectr. in field. Author: A Christian's Guide to Today's Catholic Charismatic Movement, 1977. Mem. Evang. Theol. Soc., Interdisciplinary Biblical Rsch. Inst. (tape editor 1981-84). Avocations: arranging and performing sacred music. Office: Grace Bible Fellowship Ch 1128 Hampton Blvd Reading PA 19604 *God has not authorized preachers to devise brand-new thoughts, but to lovingly present the old ones.*

NEIDERHISER, FREDERICK GERALD, clergyman; b. Greensburg, Pa., Mar. 4, 1951; s. Charles Frederick and Lida Geraldine (Kabernick) N.; m. Debra Ann Jacobs, Aug. 18, 1973; children: Jonathan, Joel. BA in Psychology, Thiel Coll., 1973; MDiv, Luth. Theol. Sem., Gettysburg, Pa., 1977; D Ministry, Luth. Theol. Sem., Phila., 1990. Ordained to ministry Evang. Luth. Ch. in Am., 1977. Pastor Holy Trinity Luth. Ch., Pitts., 1977-81, St. James Evang. Luth. Ch., Pitts., 1977-81, 1st Evang. Luth. Ch., New Kensington, Pa., 1981-91, The Evang. Luth. Ch. of the Holy Trinity, Wildwood, N.J., 1991—; mem. Pitts. Area Mission Strategy Team, 1979-81; del. Luth. Ch. in Am. Conv., Toronto, Ont., Can., 1984; mem. com. on inclusiveness and diversity SW Pa. Synod. Designer, developer Lutheran Prayer Beads; composer several anthems. Bd. dirs. Beechview Meals on Wheels, Pitts., 1977-81, Arlington Meals on Wheels, Pitts., 1977-81. Mem. Greater New Kensington Clergy Assn., Luths. Concerned, Beechview C. of C. (charter, 1st pres. 1979-81). Office: The Evang Luth Ch of the Holy Trinity 2810 Atlantic Ave Wildwood NJ 08260

NEIDHARDT, WALTER JIM, religion editor, physics educator; b. Paterson, N.J., June 19, 1934; s. Walter Henry N.; m. Janet Williams; children: John, Jerome. ME, Stevens Inst. Tech., 1956, MS in Physics, 1958, PhD, 1962. Assoc. prof. physics N.J. Inst. Tech., Newark, 1968—. Author: (with others) The Christian Frame of Mind, 1989; contbr. articles to profl. jours. Fellow Am. Sci. Affiliation (cons. editor Perspectives on Sci. and Christian Faith 1968—, chairperson publs. com., 1982—, pres. met. sect. 1974-76, 80-82, 81-88); mem. Ctr. for Theology of Natural Sci., Inst. for Encounter with Sci. and Theology, Assn. Christians in the Math. Scis., Interdisciplinary Bibl. Rsch. Inst., Inst. for Religion in an Age of Sci., Michael Polanyi Soc. N. Am., Karl Barth Soc. N.Am. Mem. Presbyn., Free Meth. Ch. Home: 146 Park Ave Randolph NJ 07869 Office: NJ Inst for Tech Newark NJ 07102

NEIGHBOUR, RALPH WEBSTER, SR., minister, religious school executive; b. Salisbury, N.C., July 21, 1906; s. Robert Edward and Nellie Gertrude (Planck) N.; m. Ruth May Zimmerman, June 29, 1928; children: Ralph W., David Eugene, Carol Jane Neighbour Voss. BA, Wheaton Coll.; DD (hon.), Piedmont Bible Coll., 1968. Ordained to ministry Bapt. Ch., 1927. Min. First Bapt. Ch., Paw Paw, Mich., 1929-30, Northumberland, Pa., 1930-35, Elyria, Ohio, 1935-40; min. Ft. Wayne (Ind.) Gospel Temple, 1946-50, Ch. of the Open Door, Elyria, 1950-72; assoc. dir. Letourneau Evangelistic Ctr., N.Y.C., 1940-46; pres., broadcaster Ralph Neighbour Evangelistic Assn., Houston, 1949—; chaplain Northeastern Penitentiary, Lewisburg, Pa., 1930-35; radio evangelist, 1922—. Author books, novels, short stories; editor: Jour. Christian Conservative, Bapt. News. Mem. Nat. Religious Broadcasters (hon., exec. bd. dirs., Milestone award 1982), Internat. Religious Broadcasters (organizer). Republican. Home: 13851 Hollowgreen Dr Houston TX 77082 Office: Evangelistic Assn PO Box 19888 Houston TX 77224 *God is the source of all life; therefore, life is a gift from God. Be thankful regardless of the color, race or sex of your body. Which is only a temporary tabernacle. Life once begun never ends. Death is only a gateway into another creation and life continues forever. Life on Earth is only a school of preparation for another and better world.*

NEIHOF, JOHN ELDON, minister, association executive, educator; b. Melbourne, Ky., Oct. 5, 1934; s. Ernest Lewis and Blanche (Painter) N.; m. Agnes Pearl Creed, Aug. 30, 1958; children: John Eldon Jr., James Raymond, Marcia K. Neihof Warren, Mary Ann. AA, Ky. Mountain Bible Coll., 1956; BA, Asbury Coll., 1959. Minister U. Meth. Ch., Williamstown, Ky., 1957-58; tchr. math. Mt. Carmel High Sch., Vancleve, Ky., 1959-81; minister White Oak Ch., Vancleve, 1960-61, Mt. Carmel Ch., Vancleve, 1962-76; tchr. Ky. Mountain Bible Coll., Vancleve, 1976-90, pres., 1981-90; pres. Ky. Mountain Holiness Assn., 1981—, evangelist, 1981—. Named to Hon. Order of Ky. Cols., 1989. Home: PO Box 10 Vancleve KY 41385 Office: Sta WMTC 730 AM 400 Mt Carmel Rd Vancleve KY 41385 also: Ky Mountain Bible Coll Office of the Pres Box 10 Vancleve KY 41385

NELL, CRAIG ARTHUR, lay worker, social services administrator; b. Medina, Ohio, Mar. 22, 1952; s. Raymond Boyd Jr. and Alice Evelyn (Swales) N.; m. Pamela Erle Baldwin Boker, Mar. 23, 1978 (div. Sept. 1983); children: Tiana Faye, Jared Baldwin; m. Deborah Anne Sillas, Feb. 14, 1987. Student, U.S. Mil. Acad., 1970-72; BA in Ministry, Melodyland Sch. Theology, 1978; MS in Pastoral Counseling, Calif. Christian Inst., 1986, MA in Marriage, Family, Child Counseling, 1987. Christian psychotherapist Calif. Christian Inst. Counseling and Assessment Ctr., Orange, 1987-89; dir. Christian program Care Unit Hosp. Orange, Calif., 1989-90; dir. social svcs. Manor Care Nursing Ctr., Fountain Valley, Calif., 1990-91, Fullerton (Calif.) Residential Manor, 1991—, Fullerton Residential Manor, 1991—; singles' ministry leader Newport-Mesa Christian Ctr., Costa Mesa, Calif., 1980-84; counselor crisis intervention phone Hotline Help Ctr., Orange, 1986. Food distbr. Benevolence Ministry Vineyard Christian Fellowship of Anaheim, 1989-91; active Oper. Rescue, Garden Grove, Calif., 1989-91; block capt. Republican Party, Santa Ana, Calif., 1990-91. Home: 1300 N Clinton St Space 10 Santa Ana CA 92703 Office: Fullerton Residential Manor 2441 W Orangethorpe Ave Fullerton CA 92633

NELSEN, NEWELL STEWART, pastor; b. Mpls., Mar. 31, 1941; s. Ervin Newell and Margaret Elizabeth (Anderson) N.; m. Sandra Marilyn Svendsen, Dec. 28, 1963; children: Lisa Karyn, Scott Eric. BA, Gustavus Adolphus Coll., 1962; BD, Augustana Theol. Sem., 1966; MDiv, Luth. Sch. of Theology Chgo., 1971. Pastor East and West Union Luth. Parish, Carver, Minn., 1966-69, King of Glory Luth. Ch., Arvada, Colo., 1969-72, Luth. Ch. of the Resurrection, Lakewood, Colo., 1972-76; asst. to bishop Ind. Ky. Synod Luth. Ch. in Am., Indpls., 1976-78; pastor Grace Luth. Ch., Columbia City, Ind., 1978—; chaplain Arvada Colo. Police Dept., 1969-72, Lakewood Dept. Pub. Safety, 1972-76, Ind. State Police, Indpls., 1979—. Mem. Columbia City (Ind.) Pk. Bd., 1979-83; bd. dirs. Ind. Mental Health Assn., 1985—; various bd. and coms. Mem. Whitley County Art Guild, Whitley County Hist. Assn., Rotary. Home: 601 W Columbia Pkwy Columbia City IN 46725 Office: Grace Luth Ch 204 N Main St Columbia City IN 46725

NELSON, ALAN JAN, minister, evangelist; b. Los Angeles, Sept. 18, 1944; s. Arthur Leonard and Laura Nelson; A.A., Los Angeles Valley City Coll., 1965; B.S., San Franando Valley State Coll., 1967; M.S., Calif. State Coll., Los Angeles, 1969. Actor, 1962—, screen writer, 1978—, comic, 1965—, stuntman, 1975—, film producer, 1979—; asst. adminstr. Oak Hill Learning Services, Lakeview Terrace, Calif., 1970; dir. community services City of South El Monte (Calif.), 1971; v.p. Ev Gray Lighting Co., Van Nuys, Calif., 1972-75; hosp. adminstr. Los Angeles Met. Hosp., 1976; exec. dir. Search Consortium, West Los Angeles, 1977-79; pres. AGVA, N.Y.C., 1979-83; pres. L & N Prodns. Inc., Van Nuys, 1975—; pres. A.J.N. Hallelujah, Inc., 1981—; 4th v.p. Theatre Authority Inc., 1980-83; corp. cons. entertainment field, 1975-78; evangelist, 1975—. V.p. West Los Angeles Coordinating Coun., 1977; mem. El Monte Coordinating Coun., 1971. Recipient Mid-Wilshire Optimists Outstanding Service award, 1980, Outstanding Service plaque AGVA, 1981, citation for advancement of variety artist State of N.J., 1981, Golden Mask award Hollywood Appreciation Soc., 1982. Mem. Screen Actors Guild, Actors and Artists Am. Assoc. (5th v.p. 1980-83). Democrat. Club: Friars. Home: 6356 Ventura Canyon Van Nuys CA 91401 *I 've walked upon the mountain and lived in the desert of life. I found there is one path to truth, and there is a price you pay for standing in it. This great country will never have true peace until it has peace with God! Jesus is the truth.*

NELSON, BRENT ALAN, minister; b. Duluth, Minn., Sept. 16, 1962; s. Warren Leslie and Constance Emily (Peterson)N.; m. Kathryn Louise Hammerstrom, Sept. 21, 1985. BA, U. Minn., 1986; MDiv, Bethel Theol. Sem., 1990. Radio announcer Northwestern Coll. Radio Network, St. Paul, Minn., 1983-89; minister Bapt. Gen. Conf., Mpls., 1988—; leader worship team, Mpls., 1990—. Active Nat. Right to Life Com., Washington, 1989-90, Pro-Life Action Ministries, Mpls., 1989-90. Mem. Evang. Theol. Soc. Avocations: reading, writing, music, phys. exercise. Home: 2548 37th Ave S Minneapolis MN 55406 Office: Immanuel Bapt Ch 3620 E 26th St Minneapolis MN 55406

NELSON, BRYANT MCNEILL, Christian radio station manager; b. Tampa, Fla., Feb. 16, 1932; s. Laudies Ira and Nell (McNeill) N.; m. Grace Ann Moore, Aug. 30, 1958; children: Faith, Stephen, Mark, Hope, Peter. BA, Bob Jones U., 1960; postgrad., U. Del., 1961, Radford U., 1978. Pastor, founder Roseoak Bapt. Ch., Balt., 1960-68; missionary Costa Rica, 1970-72, P.R., 1972-73; pastor Cen. Bapt. Ch., Panama City, Fla., 1973-75, Ridgeview Bapt. Ch., Stuarts Draft, Va., 1975-79; coll. pres. Colonial Bapt. Coll., Chesapeake, Va., 1979-84; pastor Calvary Bapt. Ch., Tampa, Fla., 1984-89; sta. mgr. Bible Broadcasting Network, Chesapeake, 1989—. With USAF, 1949-52. Recipient Founders award Rosedale Bapt. Ch., Balt., 1989, Ridgeview Christian Sch., Stuarts Draft, 1976, Appreciation award Colonial Bapt. Coll., 1983. Mem. Fla. Christian Edn. Assn. (pres. 1984—). Republican. Office: Sta WYFL FM 120 E Belle St Henderson NC 27536

NELSON, DAVID C., minister; b. Chgo., Dec. 25, 1953; s. Jack Giamalva and Virginia Nelson. BA, U. Ill., Chgo., 1976; MDiv, Garrett Evangelical, Evanston, Ill., 1981, MST, 1983; postgrad., Luth. Sch. Theol., 1991—. Ordained to ministry Luth. Ch. in Am., 1983. Assoc. pastor Mt. Pleasant Luth. Ch., Racine, Wis., 1983-86; pastor Edgebrook Luth. Ch., Chgo., 1986—; v.p. Augustana Ctr. Bd. of Govs., Chgo., 1990—, speakers bur. Luth. Social Svcs. of Ill., 1990—. Author: (collection sermons) Ministers Annual 1987-89, Ministers Annual Manual, 1989-90; contbr. Faith and Ministry in Light of the Double Brain, 1991. Mem. Edgebrook-Sauganash Br. Am. Cancer Soc., Edgebrook-Sauganash Ministerial Assn. (treas. 1989). Home: 5835 Dakin St W Chicago IL 60634-2639 Office: Edgebrook Luth Ch 5252 W Devon Ave Chicago IL 60646-4145 *Even though I see myself as a preacher my goal is to help people realize that the faith is communicated to others not so much by what we say but by what we do. How we treat other people is the yardstick by which our faith can be measured.*

NELSON, DEANE FREDERICK, religion educator, minister; b. Missoula, Mont., Aug. 4, 1938; s. Joseph Richmond and Alice Ruth (Kipp) N.; m. Mildred Kay Scott, July 26, 1964; children: Teresa Rochelle, Gregory Scott. MA, Andrews U., Berrien Springs, Mich., 1962; MDiv, Andrews U., 1965; MPH, Loma Linda U., 1970; D Ministry, McCormick Theol. Sem., 1976. Ordained to ministry Seventh-day Adventist Ch., 1967. Dir. health programs Warburton (Victoria, Australia) Health Care Ctr., 1976-78; pastor So. Calif. Conf. Seventh-day Adventists, Glendale, 1978-81; asst. prof. ch. and ministry Sch. of Religion Loma Linda (Calif.) U., 1980-84; pastor Cen. Calif. Conf. Seventh-day Adventists, Clovis, 1984-90; assoc. prof. religious studies Can. Union Coll., College Heights, Alta., Can., 1990—; advisor, vis. prof. Bicol Christian Coll. Med., Legaspi City, Philippines, 1987-90. USPHS grantee, 1969-70; recipient Sylvia Besser award Kern County Dept. Mental Health, 1970. Mem. Am. Acad. Religion, Soc. Biblical Lit., Andrews Soc. Religious Studies. Office: Can Union Coll, Box 430, College Heights, AB Canada T0C 0Z0

NELSON, DIEDRIK ARLEN, minister; b. Sioux Falls, S.D., Jan. 14, 1934; s. Maurice Alvin and Gladys Ellen (Peterson) N.; m. Doris OnaLee Rollag, Dec. 23, 1956; children: Christopher, Jonathan, Stephanie. BA, Augustana, Sioux Falls, S.D., 1956; BD, Luther Theol. Sem., 1960; ThM, Union Sem. in Va., 1961, PhD, 1964. Ordained to ministry Luth. Ch., 1964. Teaching fellow Pitts. Theol. Sem., 1964; pastor Groton (S.D.) Luth. Parish, 1964-70; sr. pastor Luth. Meml. Ch., Pierre, S.D., 1970-78, Grace Luth. Ch., Watertown, S.D., 1978-88, Brandon (S.D.)-Split Rock Luth. Parish, 1988—; lectr. Luther Theol. Sem., 1967. Contbr. revs. to profl. jours. Mem. Soc. Bibl. Lit. Democrat. Home: 1116 Lark Dr Brandon SD 57005 Office: Brandon Luth Ch 600 E Holly Brandon SD 57005

NELSON, DOROTHY, religious organization administrator. Chairperson, judge Baha'i Faith, Wilmette, Ill. Office: Baha'i Faith 536 Sheridan Rd Wilmette IL 60091*

NELSON, DOROTHY WRIGHT (MRS. JAMES F. NELSON), federal judge; b. San Pedro, Calif., Sept. 30, 1928; d. Harry Earl and Lorna Amy Wright; m. James Frank Nelson, Dec. 27, 1950; children: Franklin Wright, Lorna Jean. B.A., UCLA, 1950, J.D., 1953; LL.M., U. So. Calif., 1956. Bar: Calif. 1954. Research assoc. fellow U. So. Calif., 1953-56; instr., 1957, asst. prof., 1958-61, assoc. prof., 1961-67, prof., 1967, assoc. dean., 1965-67, dean., 1967-80; judge U.S. Ct. Appeals for 9th Circuit, 1980—; cons. Project STAR, Law Enforcement Assistance Adminstrn.; mem. select com. on internal procedures of Calif. Supreme Ct., 1987—. Author: Judicial Administration and The Administration of Justice, 1973; Contbr. articles to profl. jours. Co-chmn. Confronting Myths in Edn. for Pres. Nixon's White House Conf. on Children, Pres. Carter's Commn. for Pension Policy, 1974-80; bd. visitors U.S. Air Force Acad., 1978; bd. dirs. Council on Legal Edn. for Profl. Responsibility, 1971-80, Constnl. Right Found., Am. Nat. Inst. for Social Advancement; adv. bd. Nat. Center for State Cts., 1971-73. Named Law Alumnus of Yr. UCLA, 1967; recipient Profl. Achievement award, 1969; named Times Woman of Yr., 1968; recipient U. Judaism Humanitarian award, 1973; AWARE Internat. award, 1970; Ernestine Stalhut Outstanding Woman Lawyer award, 1972; Coro award for edn., 1978. Fellow Am. Bar Found., Davenport Coll., Yale U.; mem. Bar Calif. (bd. dirs. continuing edn. bar commn. 1967-74), Am. Judicature Soc. (dir.), Assn. Am. Law Schs. (chmn. com. edn. in jud. adminstrn.), Am. Bar Assn. (sect. on jud. adminstrn., chmn. com. on edn. in jud. adminstrn. 1973—), Phi Beta Kappa, Order of Coif (nat. v.p. 1974-76), Jud. Conf. U.S. (com. to consider standards for admission to practice in fed. cts. 1976-79). Office: US Ct Appeals Cir PO Box 91510 Pasadena CA 91109

NELSON, DOTSON MCGINNIS, JR., clergyman; b. Clinton, Miss., Mar. 11, 1915; s. Dotson McGinnis and Mary (White) N.; m. Grace Elizabeth Philpot, Oct. 8, 1941; children—Carol Lois, Dotson McGinnis III, Mary Grace, William Philpot. B.A. summa cum laude, Miss. Coll., 1935; Th.M., So. Bapt. Theol. Sem., 1938, Ph.D., 1945; D.D., Furman U., 1958, Miss. Coll., 1973. Ordained to ministry Bapt. Ch., 1935; pastor Vinton Bapt. Ch., Roanoke, Va., 1941-42, Second Bapt. Ch., Richmond, 1942-44, Calvary Bapt. Ch., Kansas City, Mo., 1946-52, 1st Bapt. Ch., Greenville, S.C., 1952-61, Mountain Brook Bapt. Ch., Birmingham, Ala., 1961-81; now pastor emeritus. Mountain Brook Bapt. Ch.; Mem. fgn. mission bd. So. Bapt. Conv., 1942-43, 47-52, 54-60, 1st v.p., 1976-77; exec. com., 1977-88; chmn. exec. bd. Ala. Bapt. Conv., 1966-68, mem. exec. bd., 1966-72, 78—, pres. conv., 1973-74, 74-75, mem. ednl. adv. com., 1975-81, chmn. ednl. adv. com., 1975-79; chmn. (Edn. Commn.), 1979-81; mem. Commn. Religious Liberty and Human Rights, Bapt. World Alliance, 1970-75; Bus. activities dir. Home Savs. & Loan, Kansas City, Mo., 1949-52. Chmn. bd. dirs. Found. for Pastoral Counseling and Consultation; dir. Spastic Aid Ala., 1961; trustee So. Bapt. Theol. Sem., William Jewell Coll., 1948-52, Samford U., 1961-66; trustee Furman U., 1957-61, chmn. trustees, 1959-61; bd. visitors Mo. Bapt. Hosp., 1949-52; bd. dirs. YMCA, Birmingham, So. Bapt. Found., 1968-70, Bapt. Hosp. Found. Birmingham, So. Bapt. Hosps., 1968-70. Served to lt. Chaplains Corps USNR, World War II. Recipient Service to Humanity award Miss. Coll., 1976. Mem. So. Bapt. Sem. Alumni Assn. (pres. Ala. 1980-81), Greater Birmingham Ministers Assn. (pres. 1971). Lodge: Kiwanis. Home: 1202 Brookhill 2350 Montevallo Rd Birmingham AL 35223 Office: Mountain Brook Bapt Ch Montevallo Rd Birmingham AL 35213

NELSON, DUANE JUAN, minister; b. Urbana, Ill., Nov. 19, 1939; s. Elmer Andrew and Mabel Mae (Jones) N.; m. Marlys Mavis Klaustermeier, Aug. 30, 1974; children: Matthew, Joshua, Joel. BA, Wartburg Coll., Waverly, Iowa, 1961; MDiv, Wartburg Theol. Sem., Dubuque, 1965. Ordained to ministry Luth. Ch., 1966. Pastor St. Paul's Luth. Ch., Massillon, Ohio, 1966-67, Hope Luth. Ch., Indpls., 1967-69, Grace Luth. Ch., Westchester, Ill., 1977-78; sr. chaplain Minn. Rec./Diag. Ctr., Lino Lakes, 1970-75; criminal justice chaplain Luth. Social Svc., Washington, 1975-77; staff chaplain Unity Med. Ctr., Fridley, Minn., 1978-81; sr. chaplain Anoka (Minn.) Metro-Reg. Treatment Ctr., 1981—; sec. bd. Ch. in Soc., St. Paul Synod, 1986-90; mem. specialized pastoral com., bd. for ministry St. Paul Area Synod, 1991—; mem. chaplaincy adv. bd. HHS, 1990—; program chmn. Assn. of Mental health Chaplains, Midwest states, 1973-75. Writer, producer Multi-Media presentation, Celebrate Life, 1986, Your Part in God's World, 1988, others. Pres. Coalition for Criminal Justice Reform, Washington, 1976; co-founder Pastoral Care sect. Minn. Chem. Dependency Assn., St. Paul, 1983; lectr. health care workshops; v.p. Guardian Angel Corp., St. Paul; mem. State of Minn. AIDS Steering Com., 1985-86. Mem. Assn. for Clin. Pastoral Edn., Minn. State Chaplains Orgn. (chmn. 1990—), Anoka County Corrections Outpatient Treatment Program, Castle Singers (pres. 1960). Office: Anoka Metro-Reg Trtmt Ctr 3300 4th Ave N Anoka MN 55303

NELSON, EDWIN STERLING, biblical studies educator, administrator; b. Toledo, Ohio, Mar. 2, 1943; s. Edwin Henry and Grace Mildred (McCrory) N.; children from previous marriage: Ginger, Susan, Sarah, Edie; m. Marjorie Newman Burn, Dec. 25, 1986. BA, Platte Valley Bible Coll., 1964; MDiv, Lincoln Christian Sem., 1970; Th.M., Gordon-Conwell Theol. Sem., 1972; PhD, Boston U., 1982. Instr. Biblical studies Platte Valley Bible Coll., Scottsbluff, Nebr., 1966-69; lectr. Gordon-Conwell Theol. Sem., South Hamilton, Mass., 1974; dept. asst. Boston U., 1974; assoc. prof. Milligan Coll., Tenn., 1974-82, Pacific Christian Coll., Fullerton, Calif., 1982-85; faculty assoc. Ariz. State U., Tempe, 1983—; dir. extension program Pacific Christian Coll., 1982-85; minister Payson Christian Ch., 1985—; sec., bd. dirs. Rim Guidance Ctr., Payson, 1986—; chaplain Payson Police Force, 1985—; bd. dirs. Rim County Healthcare Found., 1985-86, mem. bicentennial commn., 1986-87. Named Danforth assoc. Danforth Found., 1981-87; Daad fellow Goethe Insts., 1979. Mem. Soc. Bibl. Lit., Cath. Bibl. Assn., Theta Phi, Alpha Chi. Republican. Home and Office: 645 W Orange Grove # 108 Tucson AZ 85704

NELSON, EULAH MAE, minister; b. Andrews, S.C., July 10, 1933; d. Ben and Alice (Wallace) Jackson; m. I.V. Nelson, Sept. 28, 1964; children: Joyce E. Nelson House, Carmalitta P., Wanda Michell Nelson-Robinson. Student, Mich. Bible and Arts Sem., Detroit, 1955-56, Moody Bible Inst., 1957-58, Aenon Bible Coll., 1982-83; ThB (hon.), Fla. Beacon Bible Coll., 1991. Ordained to ministry Pentacostal Ch., 1966. Evangelist S.C., 1946-51; with Gospel Singing Ministry, Detroit and Chgo., 1952-63; pastor, founder Bibleway Healing Temple, Inc., Rochester, N.Y., 1966—; mem. adv. bd. Rochester Sch. Dist., 1988—; vice chairperson N.Y. and Ont. dist. coun. Pentacostal Ch., 1986-88; internat. evangelist Living Witness and PAW, U.S. and abroad.; active Rochester Interfaith Jail Ministry. Auhto, pub. Deliverance of Flame mag., 1975-79. Bd. dirs. Aenon Bible Coll., Indpls., 1989—. Named Most Outstanding Woman Pastor Mayor of Rochester, 1975; recipient award Davenport Hatch Found., 1975, Meritorious Svc. award IMCWA/PAW, 1989. Mem. NAACP. Office: Bibleway Healing Temple Inc 660 W Main St Rochester NY 14603

NELSON, FRANS EDWARD, minister, theology and computer science educator; b. Herbert, Sask., Can., Jan. 29, 1933; s. Axel Bernhard and Anna Olive (Gulstein) N.; m. Joan Marie Hurley, Nov. 26, 1982. BA, St. Mary's U., San Antonio, 1960; MDiv, Concordia Theol. Sem., Ft. Wayne, Ind., 1964; STM, Luth. Theol. Sem., Gettysburg, Pa., 1975; PhD, NYU, 1980. Ordained to ministry Luth. Ch., 1965. Missionary Iglesia Cristo Rey-Spanish Luth. Mission, Orange, Calif., 1989—; instr. Christ Coll., Irvine, Calif., 1987, Rancho Santiago Coll., Santa Ana, Calif., 1990, Coastline Community Coll., Laguna Hills, Calif., 1991—. With USAF, 1955-59. Mem. Am. Acad. Religion, Assn. for Computing Machinery, Soc. Psychol. Study of Social Issues, UN Assn. (pres. Coastline chpt. 1989-92). Home: 980 El Camino Dr Ste 2 Costa Mesa CA 92626 Office: UN Assn Coastline Chpt 23521 Paseo de Valencia Ste 306-A Laguna Hills CA 92653 *Let us thank God for everything that he has given us. And we know that he has given us everything we have and that he would like to give us much more. Let us pray that he will show us how to share what he has given us. For we know that when we share what we have we make others happy and we make ourselves happy. May God make us into a people who love to give gifts! For we know that his Word says it is more joyous to give than receive gifts. We are never happier than when we are able to give gifts.*

NELSON, GAILON WALKER, minister; b. Andalusia, Ala., Jan. 20, 1931; s. James Monroe and Eunice (Walker) N.; m. Ruth Owens, Dec. 31, 1954; children: Ruth Maria Nelson Ulmer, Gailon Owens. Ordained to ministry So. Bapt. Conv., 1975. Enlisted U.S. Army, 1948; assigned to Fed. Republic Germany, Vietnam, Korea, Hawaii, ret.,, 1969; pastor New Chapel Bapt. Ch., 1974-81, Bethanyy So. Bapt. Ch., Kinston, Ala., 1981—. Mem. VFW, DAV (comdr. Andalusia), Am. Legion, Civitans. Democrat. Home and Office: Rte 3 Box 300 Andalusia AL 36420

NELSON, HUBERT JOHN ARTHUR, pastor; b. Rockford, Ill., Oct. 8, 1935; s. Ralph Arthur and Ruby Prunella (Johnson) N.; m. Joan Isabella Studlien, June 29, 1956; children: Laurie, Bruce, Denise, Mark, Joel. BA, Augsburg Coll., 1959; ThB, MDiv, Augsburg Theol. Sem., 1962; postgrad., Luther N.W. Theol. Sem. Pastor Bethany Luth. Ch., St. Paul, 1962-68; assoc. pastor Our Saviors Luth. Ch., Rockford, Ill., 1968-70, co-adminstrv. pastor, 1970-84; sr. pastor Bethlehem Luth. Ch., Mpls., 1984—; bd. dirs. Div. Social Ministry Orgn. E.L.C.A., Chgo.; bd. exec. com. Ebenezer Soc., Mpls. Luth. Bible Ministries, St. Paul. Contbg. author: Daily Readings From Spiritual Classics, 1990. Sec. Phalen Area Community Coun., St. Paul, 1964-68, Jail Reachout, Rockford, 1978-82; v.p. YMCA, St. Paul, 1965-68. Office: Bethlehem Luth Ch 4100 Lyndale Ave S Minneapolis MN 55409 *A* *congregation will forgive its pastor many sins and overlook many shortcomings if it has experieced that he or she loves them without reservation.*

NELSON, ISRAEL JAMES DOUGLAS, minister; b. Las Vegas, Aug. 16, 1944; s. Charles Erastus and Helen Virginia (Taub) Nelson Moore; m. Lynn Angus Unger, June 12, 1970; children: Heather Angus, Carmel Christiana. BA in Sociology, Stanford U., 1967; MDiv, San Francisco Theol. Seminary, 1971; D Ministry, Colgate Rochester Div. Sch., 1984. Credentialed alcoholism counselor, N.Y., nat. cert. counselor. Pastor First Presbyn. Ch., Orange Cove, Calif., 1971-74; asst. pastor First Presbyn. Ch., Akron, Ohio, 1974-75; pastor First Presbyn. Ch., Shortsville, N.Y., 1975-77; clergy cons. Alcohol Rehab. Program Clifton Springs (N.Y.) Hosp., 1976-78; alcoholism counselor Roanoke-Chowan Mental Health Ctr., Ahoskie, N.C., 1978-80, Park Ridge Chem. Dependency, Inc., Rochester, N.Y., 1980-83, Finger Lakes Alcoholism Counseling and Referral Agy., Newark, N.Y., 1983-85; rehab. supr. Daybreak Alcoholism Treatment Facility, Rochester, 1985-86; program dir. Mercy Hall Alcoholism Treatment Program, St. Jerome Hosp., Batavia, N.Y., 1988—; ptnr. Human Progress Enterprises, Geneva, N.Y., 1986-90; adminstrv. dir. Adult Child and Co-Dependency Ctr., Inc., Rochester, 1986-90; parish assoc. 1st Presbyn. Ch., LeRoy, N.Y., 1990—. Author: Awakening: Restoring Health Through the Spiritual Principles of Shalom, Jesus, and the Twelve Step Recovery Program, 1989. Mem. Presbytery of Genesee Valley. Democrat. Avocations: swimming, jogging, Scottish history, gardening. Home: 6 Pumpkin Hook West Henrietta NY 14586 Office: Mercy Hall Saint Jerome Hosp 16 Bank St Batavia NY 14020

NELSON, JAMES F., judge, religious organization administrator. BS, U. Calif., LLB, Loyola U., Los Angeles. Bar: Calif. 1954. Judge, Los Angeles Mcpl. Ct. Chmn. Baha'i Faith Nat. Spiritual Assembly Bahais of the U.S., Wilmette, Ill. Address: care Nat Spiritual Assembly Baha'i Faith 536 Sheridan Rd Wilmette IL 60091 Office: US Courthouse 110 N Grand Ave Los Angeles CA 90012

NELSON, JOHN DOUGLAS, elementary educator; b. Burbank, Calif., Aug. 9, 1951; s. Clarence Carl Henry and Shirley Isabel (Pierson) Nelson; m. Linda Ann Nelson, June 25, 1988; children: Kristen Marie, Jennifer Alicia, Michelle Elizabeth. BA, Occidental Coll., 1975; student, Fuller Theol. Sem., Pasadena, Calif. Cert. assoc. ch. musician, Presbyn. Assn. Musicians. Tchr. Hoover High Sch., Glendale, Calif.; asst. choral dir. Calif. Inst. Tech., Pasadena; tchr., music dept. chair Toll Jr. High Sch., Glendale; tchr. Calvary Christian Sch., Glendale; dir. Computer Ctr. Recipient Arion award in Choral Music. Mem. Choral Conductors' Guild, Am. Choral Dirs. Assn. Home: 1116 E Doran St Glendale CA 91206 *The greatest achievement we can hope to attain, although it is God who gives the ability, is to be like David, "a man after God's own heart."*

NELSON, JOHN ROBERT, theology educator, clergyman; b. Winona Lake, Ind., Aug. 21, 1920; s. William John and Agnes Dorothy (Soderborg) N.; m. Dorothy Patricia Mercer, Aug. 18, 1945; children: Eric Mercer, William John. A.B., DePauw U., 1941, L.H.D., 1960; B.D., Yale U., 1944; D. Theol., U. Zürich, Switzerland, 1951; LL.D., Wilberforce U., 1954; D.D., Ohio Wesleyan U., 1964; L.H.D., Loyola U., 1969; D.H., Hellenic Coll., 1985. Ordained to ministry Meth. Ch., 1944; dir. Wesley Found., Chapel Hill, N.C., 1946-48; assoc. dir. Wesley Found., Urbana, Ill., 1950-51; study sect. United Student Christian Council, N.Y.C., 1951-53; sec. commn. on faith and order World Council Chs., Geneva, Switzerland, 1953-57, chmn. working com., 1967-75; dean, prof. theology Vanderbilt Div. Sch., 1957-60; vis. prof. ecumenics Princeton Theol. Sem., 1960-61; vis. prof. United Theol. Coll., Bangalore, India, and Leonard Theol. Coll., Jabalpur, India, 1961-62; Fairchild prof. Christian theology Grad. Sch. Theology, Oberlin Coll., Ohio, 1962-65; prof. systematic theology Boston U. Sch. Theology, 1965-84, dean, 1972-74; Peyton lectr. So. Meth. U., 1961; Merrick lectr. Ohio Wesleyan U., 1964; Lowell lectr., 1966; Burke lectr. U. Calif.-San Diego, 1985; Willson lectr. Centenary Coll., 1985; vis. prof. Pontifical Gregorian U., Rome, 1968-69; Mendenhall lectr. DePauw, 1974; Russell lectr. Tufts U., 1976; cons. Pres.'s Commn. for Study Ethical Problems in Biomed. Research, 1980-82; dir. Inst. Religion, Tex. Med. Ctr., Houston, 1985—; adj. prof. medicine Baylor Coll. Medicine, 1985—, adj. prof. religious studies Rice U., 1987—; adj. prof. religion and health care U. Tex. Sch. Applied Health Scis., 1985—. Author: The Realm of Redemption, 1951, One Lord, One Church, 1958, Overcoming Christian Divisions, rev. edit, 1962, Criterion for the Church, 1963, Fifty Years of Faith and Order, (with J. Skoglund), 1963, Crisis in Unity and Witness, 1968, Church Union in Focus, 1968, Science and Our Troubled Conscience, 1980, Human Life: a Biblical Perspective for Bioethics, 1984; editor: The Christian Student and the World Struggle, 1952, Christian Unity in North America, 1958, No Man Is Alien, 1971; editor-at-large, The Christian Century; assoc. editor: Jour. Ecumenical Studies. Del. all 7 Assemblies World Council Chs., 4th World Conf. on Faith and Order, 1963, United Meth. Gen. Conf., 1968, 72; mem. commn. on faith and order Nat. Council Chs.; mem. U.S. Commn. for UNESCO, 1974-80; Bd. dirs. Value of Life com., Graymoor Ecumenical Inst. Fellow Kennedy Inst. Ethics Georgetown U. Fellow Am. Acad. Arts and Scis.; mem. Am. Theol. Soc. (past pres.), N.Am. Acad. Ecumenists (past pres.), Soc. Européenne de Culture (v.p.), AAUP, Phi Beta Kappa, Beta Theta Pi. Clubs: St. Botolph, Doctors, Country (Brookline, Mass.). Lodge: Rotary. Office: Inst of Religion Tex Med Ctr PO Box 20569 Houston TX 77225 *The sequence of my persuasions and commitments has been from Christian unity to human unity to basic concern for the value of human life itself; and these are cumulative convictions from which I cannot deviate.*

NELSON, KENNETH SIGURD, clergyman; b. Bklyn., Jan. 16, 1943; s. Arvid Bernard and Martha Sofia (Nilsson) N.; m. Judith Binner, June 15, 1975. BA with hons., Hartwick Coll., Oneonta, N.Y., 1965; MA, Colgate U., 1968; MDiv, Luth. Theol. Sem., 1974. Ordained to ministry, Luth. Ch. of Am., 1974. Dir. student activities Endicott Coll., Beverly, Mass., 1967-68; dean student affairs Davis & Elkins Coll., Elkins, W.Va., 1968-71; pastor Abiding Presence Luth. Ch., Trenton, N.J., 1974-76, Am. Luth. Ch. Brussels, 1976-80, United Christian Congregation of Stockholm, 1980-84; missionary in residence Southeastern Pa. Synod Luth. Ch. Am., Phila., 1984-85; sr. pastor Zion Luth. Ch., Spring City, Pa., 1985—. Contbr. articles to profl. jours. Mem. Sixteenth Century Soc., Rennaissance Soc., Acad. Preachers, Ea. Pa. Hist. Soc. Avocations: history, reading, hiking, travel. Office: Zion Luth Ch 39 Bonnie Brae Rd Spring City PA 19475-2401 *There is not greater demonstration of our need for a gracious God than the way humanity has acted towards itself in this century. There is no greater evidence of the graciousness of God than God's willingness to make connections with us in spite of ourselves.*

NELSON, MARJORIE ANN, lay minister; b. Benson, Minn., June 13, 1920; d. Hugh Joseph and Agnes Mary (Drinkwine) Doyle; m. Ralph Almer Nelson, Dec. 3, 1942; children: Dianne Wilmoth, Bruce, Dennis, Mary, Deborah Sheehan, Rebecca Simenson, Roberta Mattison. A in office mgmt., med. stenography, Mpls. Med. Bus. Coll., 1940. Tchr. religious edn. St. Mary's Cath. Ch., Willmar, Minn., 1970-84, eucharistic min., 1978—, usher, worship com. hostess, 1990—; mem. St. Mary's Ch. adv. com., 1964-67, bd. edn., 1964-69, bldg. com., 1976-79, parish coun., 1984-86, worship com., 1990—. Mem., officer VFW Aux., 1946— (25 Yr. award 1987), Minn. Hosp. and Home Assn. Aux. (mem. nom. com., 1991—); leader, counselor, dir. Girl Scouts Am., 1954— (Thanks badge 1984, religious awards dir.), Boy Scouts Am., 1954—; vol. Kandiyohi County March of Dimes, 1958-68; vol. Blood Mobile, 1971-76; chairperson Rice Meml. Hosp. Aux. 35th Anniversary, 1986; chairperson Rice Meml. Hosp. 50th Anniversary, 1987, bd. dirs., 1987—, pub. rels. coord., 1990—; Willmar Civ. Scholarship Com., 1991—; election judge City of Willmar, 1990—. Recipient cert. for faithful svc. Willmar Health Care Ctr., 1987, Diocesan Disting. Svc. medal, New Ulm Diocese, 1989. mem. Church Women United (bd. dirs. 1969—), Daughters of Isabella, 1942—, Coun. Cath. Women, St. Mary's Altar and Rosary Soc. (past pres., sec., treas., 1940—), Am. Field Svc., 1960-61, Kandiyoh County Hist. Soc., 1984—, Benevolent Patriotic Order Does, 1982—, Wilmar Area Retirees Chapt. AFL-CIO (sec., 1991-92), 1986—, Parents Call Parents U. Minn., U. Saint Cloud, Coll. Saint Benedict, 1962-87, Bus. and Profl. Women, 1941-45. Home: 720 Bonham Blvd Willmar MN 56201 *I believe children and young adults should have goals so they know where they are going in life. I think home, church, school and friends compliment the child's growing years. We make the effort to make the difference. I also believe never be satisfied and always try to improve.*

NELSON, MARY BERNICE, religious editor; b. Indpls., Oct. 24; d. Leonard Lester and Bernice Irene (Dalton) N. Student, Bapt. Bible Coll., Springfield, Mo., 1970; BA, Biola U., LaMirada, Calif., 1979. Sec. Indpls. Bapt. Temple, 1970-71; sec., adminstrv. asst. Inst. of Holy Land Studies, Jerusalem, 1971-72; personnel asst. Biola Coll., LaMirada, 1973; asst. to personnel dir. Biola Coll., 1977; editorial asst. Accent Pubs., Denver, 1983—; youth editor Accent Pubs., asst. to exec. editor curriculum, asst. to exec. editor books, exec. editor books, dir. media rels., all current. Author 2 books; co-author 2 books; ghostwriter; editor Christian Edn. Today; contbr. articles to profl. and consumer jours. Republican. Office: Accent Pubs 12100 W 6th Ave Denver CO 80215

NELSON, NORMAN AUGUSTINE, minister; b. Chgo., Feb. 11, 1926; s. Olof H. and Anna Victoria (Dahlquist) N.; m. Joan Lenore Thorp, June 18, 1955; children: Beth Lenore Nelson Smayda, Ruth Deborah, Karen Eileen Nelson Anderson, Donald Lars, Karl Erik. AB, Gustavus Adolphus Coll., 1949; MDiv, Luth. Sch. Theology, R.I., 1953; D Ministry, Luth. Sch. Theology, Chgo., 1977. Ordained to ministry Luth. Ch. in Am., 1953. Pastor Saron Luth. Ch., Chgo., 1953-61, Salem Luth. Ch., Chgo., 1961-70; sr. pastor Gloria Dei Luth. Ch., Downers Grove, Ill., 1970—; dean western Chgo. dist. Augustana Luth. Ch., 1960-61, mem. Ill. Synod. Luth. Ch. in Am., 1968-74, 83-87, cons., Phila., 1982—; with West Suburbs Counseling and Edn. Svc., 1978-90. Mem. com. on religious leaders Chgo. Urban League, 1962-68; bd. dirs. West Subruban Counseling and Ednl. Svcs., 1978—, Augustana Coll., Rock Island, Ill., 1980-83, ARC DuPage-Kane counties, Ill., 1983-85. Office: Gloria Dei Luth Ch 1005 Grant St Downers Grove IL 60515

NELSON, PAUL THOMAS, religion educator; b. Hinsdale, Ill., Nov. 29, 1952; s. Everett W. and Helen B. (Thomas) N.; m. Susan Jean Baker, May 15, 1977; children: Katherine, John. AB magna cum laude, Princeton U., 1974; MDiv, Yale U., 1977, MA, 1979, MPhil, 1981, PhD, 1984. Rsch. assoc. Luth. Ch. in Am., N.Y.C., 1982-84; vis. asst. prof. theology U. Notre Dame, South Bend, Ind., 1984-85; assoc. prof., chmn. dept. religion Wittenberg U., Springfield, Ohio, 1985—. Author: Narrative and Morality, 1987; contbr. articles to profl. jours. Mem. Am. Acad. Religion, Soc. Christian Ethics. Lutheran. Office: Wittenberg U PO Box 720 Springfield OH 45501

NELSON, PHILIP ADEL, retired lay worker; b. Elgin, Tex., May 13, 1903; m. Jno Nelson and Hilma Olson; m. Marion Hammer, Dec. 7, 1927; children: Philip Adel Jr., Bette (Mrs. Curtis Heinrich). Grad., Trinity Coll. (now Tex. Luth. Coll.). Pres. Luth. Bretherhood in Tex. Home: 2601 Jarratt Austin TX 78703-2434

NELSON, RICHARD EARL, minister; b. Marquette, Mich., May 10, 1926; s. Victor E. and Ethel Olive (McCullough) N.; m. Dorothy Louise Rawlings, Aug. 28, 1952; children: John Victor, Christine Louise. BA with honors, No. Mich. U., 1950; MDiv, McCormick Theol. Sem., 1953. Ordained to ministry Presbyn. Ch. (USA), 1953. Pastor Dafter, Donaldson, Neebish Island Presbyn. Chs., Mich., 1953-55; coll. pastor Presbyn. Student Ctr., Cedar Falls, Iowa, 1955-64; assoc. sec. Pakistan Student Christian Movement, Lahore, Pakistan, 1962-63; campus min. United Campus Ministry, Duluth, Minn., 1964-78, Superior, Wis., 1964-78; mem. staff Maj. Mission Fund United Presbyn. Ch. U.S.A., Fargo, N.D., 1978-79; mem. staff Maj. Mission Fund United Presbyn. Chs. U.S.A., Bloomington, Minn., 1979-80, Denver, 1981; interim pastor various Presbyn. chs., Wis., Minn., Ky., 1982-87; regional counselor Bicentennial Fund Presbyn. Ch. U.S.A., Duluth, Minn., 1988-91; stated clk. Duluth and No. Waters Presbyteries, Duluth, 1973-79; mem. Presbyn. Panel; commr. Gen. Assembly, 1963, 77; moderator Duluth Presbytery, 1971;.asst. clin. prof. U. Minn. Sch. Medicine, 1976-78. Contbr. to Papers of the Algonquian Confs. 1983, 84, 87, Homily Svc. The Liturgical Conf., 1986, 87; book reviewer Wis. Mag. History, 1983, 84. Mem. chorus Duluth-Superior Symphony Orch., 1977—. With USN, 1944-46. Mem. St. Louis County Hist. Soc. (bd. govs. 1989—), Native Am. Art Studies Assn., Marquette County Hist. Soc. Avocation: collecting old maps and prints of Great Lakes area, native Am. artifacts. Home: 2730 Branch St Duluth MN 55812

NELSON, ROBERT GEORGE, minister; b. Racine, Wis., Nov. 21, 1928; s. Harold George and Augusta Marie (Due) N.; m. Arlene Marie Sandberg, Dec. 30, 1951; children: Joel K., Karen L. Nelson Smith, Katherine L. Nelson Flahive, Roberta A. Nelson Bowie. BA, Cana Coll., 1952; BD, Trinity Theol. Sem., Blair, Nebr., 1955; MDiv, Wartburg Theol. Sem., 1977; D Ministry, San Francisco Theol. Sem., 1982. Ordained to ministry Evangelical Luth. Ch. Sr. pastor Our Savior's Luth. Ch., Lincoln, Nebr., 1961-66, Trinity Luth. Ch., Ft. Collins, Colo., 1966-77, Morningside Luth. Ch., Sioux City, Iowa, 1977-79, Peace Luth. Ch., Sterling, Colo., 1979-84, Our Savior's Luth. Ch., Colorado Springs, Colo., 1984—; mem. nat. stewardship com. Am. Luth. Ch., Mpls., 1962-74, mem. com. Internat. Yr. Disables, 1981—; mem. congl. life bd. Evangelical Luth. Ch. Am., Chgo. and Denver, 1988—. Bd. dirs. Eben-Eber Luth. Care Ctr., Brish, Colo., 1979-84. Capt. USAF, 1955-61. Mem. Mil. Chaplain Assn., Kiwanis. Home: 2537 N Bennett Colorado Springs CO 80909 Office: Our Savior's Luth Ch 1128 E Boulder Colorado Springs CO 80903

NELSON, ROBERTA JEAN, lay worker, animal health technician; b. Natrona Heights, Pa., Dec. 24, 1960; d. Robert James Jr. and Carolyn Dorothy (Henry) N. Student, Sch. of Computer Tech., 1983-84, Biscayne Paramed. Inst., 1978-79. Tchr. Sunday sch. 1st Evang. Luth. Ch., Apollo, Pa., 1980-84, 86-90, pres. Women of Evang. Luth. Ch. Am.,, 1988-89, bd. dirs., mem. bldg. and ground com., 1991—, instr. confirmation edn., 1982, 86-89, 91, mem. ch. choir, 1971—, mem. music and worship com., 1988—, chairperson Christian edn. com., 1989—, chairperson, fellowship com., 1990—, dir. youth, 1987—, sec., ch. coun., 1988—; animal health technician, office mgr. Keystone Vet. Svcs., Shelocta, Pa., 1990—. Democrat. Home: 415 N Fourth St Apollo PA 15613

NELSON, TERRELL MARK, minister; b. Atlanta, Aug. 25, 1960; s. Jim Minter and Anne (Foster) N.; m. Laurie Ellen Bray, May 21, 1983; 1 child, Meredith Grace. BA in Religion, Mercer U., 1982; MDiv, Southwestern Bapt. Theol. Sem., 1985. Ordained to ministry So. Bapt. Conv., 1985. Assoc. youth min. New hope Bapt. Ch., Fayetteville, Ga., 1980-82; youth min., assoc. pastor Preston Highlands Bapt., Dallas, 1982-87; min. to students First Bapt., Merrit Island, Fla., 1987-88, Calvery Bapt., Ga., 1987-88, First Bapt., Ft. Lauderdale, Fla., 1988-90; pastor Greentree Bapt. Ch., Tyrone, Ga., 1990—; home missionary Home Mission Bd. of So. Bapt. Conv., 1990—. Republican. Home: 402 Minton Way Peachtree City GA 30269 Office: PO Box 248 Tyrone GA 30290 *Perhaps the key word in life is "becoming". We ought always to be in the process of becoming the person God wants us to be, the citizen our country needs us to be, to churchman our congregations need us to be, and certainly not least of all, the loving leaders our families need us to be.*

NELSON, TERRY ELLAN ELISABETH, minister; b. Chgo., Nov. 17, 1954; d. Julius Paul Kastens and Janice Joy (Johnson) and Mary Ann (Reisner); m. Lee Alan Nelson, May 28, 1983. Student, Ea. Ill. U., 1976-78; BA, Valparaiso U., 1981; MDiv, Christ Sem., 1985. Ordained 1985. Clk., typist R. Cooper, Jr., Des Plaines, Ill., 1972-73; statis. typist A.B. Dick Co., Niles, Ill., 1973-76; nurse aide Hilltop Nursing Home, Charleston, Ill., 1977-78; crew trainer McDonald's Corp., Valparaiso, Ind., 1978-81; fieldwork pastor Luth. Ch. of the Living Christ, Florissant, Mo., 1981-83; intern pastor Wiley Luth. Ch., Ellisville, Ill., 1983-84; fieldwork pastor Immanuel Luth. Ch., Park Ridge, Ill., 1984-85; owner, operator Nelson Catering, St. Louis and Chgo., 1982-85; vacancy pastor Zion Luth. Ch., International Falls, Minn., 1985-86; exec. sec. Boise Cascade Corp., 1987; chaplain USN, Phila., 1987—. Contbr. articles to profl. jours. Mem. Canton (Ill.) Ministerial Assn., 1983-84, International Falls Ministerial Assn., 1985-86. Lt. USN, 1988. Mem. AAUW. Avocations: cooking, gardening, sewing, reading, music.

NELSON, WILLIAM HOYT, minister; b. Alexander City, Ala., Jan. 18, 1930; s. William Olin and Iula Vashti (Jones) N.; m. Gueldine Trussell, Jan. 21, 1951; children: Monya Deen Claborn, Kendall Hoyt. BA in Journalism, Psychology & History, Auburn U., 1951; postgrad., Ala. Christian Sch. Religion, 1951-53. Ordained to ministry Ch. of Christ, 1958. Min. Dadeville (Ala.) Ch. of Christ, 1958-68, College Ave. Ch. of Christ, Enterprise, Ala., 1968-73, Hartselle (Ala.) Ch. of Christ, 1973-75, Ozark (Ala.) Ch. of Christ, 1975-78, Moulton (Ala.) Ch. of Christ, 1978—; founder, bd. mem. Wiregrass Christian Youth Camp, Chancellor, Ala., 1968—; adv. bd. Leadership and Ch. Growth Internat., 1988. Chmn. Sharlene Jones Heart Transplant Dr., Moulton, 1987, Heart Assn. Fund Dr., Moulton, 1988-91, Carley Peters Liver Transplant Dr., Moulton, 1990. Named Local Citizen of Month, Moulton (Ala.) Advertiser, 1991. Mem. Civitan Internat. (bd. dirs. 1989—, Outstanding Ministry Svc. award 1991). Republican. Home: 13110 Court St Moulton AL 35650 Office: Moulton Church of Christ 597 Main St Moulton AL 35650 *Because of the brevity of life, we have but few opportunities to influence those with whom we live and serve. Therefore, we should grasp every such opportunity to share ourselves with all who are less fortunate than we.*

NELTING, GEORGE, religious and charitable organization executive. Territorial comdr., commr. cen. ter. The Salvation Army, Chgo. Office: Salvation Army 860 N Dearborn St Chicago IL 60610

NEMAPARE, ESAU THOMAS JAN, minister; b. Nemapare, Midlands, Zimbabwe, 1903; s. Jan and Mazvidza (Masiye) N.; m. Jane Vuyelwa Nkunzane, Feb. 3, 1931; children: Barbara, Elizabeth, Peter, Rose, Florence, Andrew; 1 adopted child, Prisca. Diploma in theology, Cliff Coll., Eng., 1965. Ordained to ministry African Meth. Ch. Zimbabwe, 1936; cert. tchr., Zimbabwe. Tchr. evangelist Waddilove Tng. Instn., nr. Marondera, Zimbabwe, 1923-28, Wesleyan Meth. Ch., from 1928. Address: African Meth Ch in Zimbabwe, Box 59, 635029 Shurugwi Zimbabwe

NESHEIM, OBED JOHN, minister; b. Vernon County, Wis., Mar. 5, 1929; s. Ole John and Vera Josepha (Snartemo) N.; m. Donna Lou Hanson, Aug. 22, 1959; children: Paul, Mark. BA, Luther Coll., 1950; cert. in theology, Luther Sem., St. Paul, 1954; postgrad., Calif. Grad. Sch. Theology, 1971-73. Ordained to ministry Am. Luth. Ch., 1954. Pastor local ch. Burr Oak, Iowa, 1954-57; instr. Luther Coll., Decorah, Iowa, 1957-61; sr. pastor Christ Luth. Ch., Preston, Minn., 1961-65, St. Mark's Luth. Ch., Hacienda Heights, Calif., 1965—; dean East San Gabriel conf. Am. Luth. Ch., 1971-74; founder, bd. dirs. Heights Luth. Schs., 1972-87, Luth. Credit Union, 1975—. Chmn. human resources San Gabriel Valley coun. Boy Scouts Am., 1973-76. Home: 2130 Las Lomitas Dr Hacienda Heights CA 91745 Office: St Mark's Luth Ch 2323 Las Lomitas Dr Hacienda Heights CA 91745

NESIUS, KAREN ELIZABETH, clergywoman; b. Chgo., July 21, 1961; d. Philip A. and Carol (Cummings) N. BA in Sociology, Ill. Wesleyan U., 1983; MDiv, Garrett Evang. Theol. Sem., 1988. Ordained to ministry Meth. Ch. Asst. pastor Williamston (Mich.) United Meth. Ch., 1986-87; pastor Edwardsburg (Mich.) United Meth. Ch., 1988—; co-dean West Mich. Conf. Camps Crystal Springs-Kalamazoo Dist., Davagiac, Mich., 1990, 91. Coauthor: (curriculum) Adventures of Paul, 1990. Sec. Cass County Coalition Against Domestic Violence, 1991; mem. Edwardsburg High Sch. Bldg. Improvement Commn., 1990-91. Mem. Gamma Upsilon. Home: 26841 Church St Edwardsburg MI 49112 Office: Edwardsburg United Meth Ch 26875 Church St Edwardsburg MI 49112

NESMITH, RICHARD DUEY, clergyman, theology educator; b. Belleville, Kans., Jan. 9, 1929; s. Eugene Gordon and Edith Mae (Duey) N.; m. Patricia N. Nichols, Aug. 24, 1985; children—Leslie Ann, Lisa Lorraine, Laurel Sue, Lana Louise. B.A., Nebr. Wesleyan U., 1950; M.Div., Garrett Evang. Sem., 1953; Ph.D., Boston U., 1957. Ordained to ministry United Methodist Ch., 1953; dean students MacMurray Coll., Jacksonville, Ill., 1957-61; prof. sociology of religion St. Paul's Sch. Theology, Kansas City, 1961-67; dir. planning Nat. div. Methodist Bd. of Global Ministries, N.Y.C., 1967-73; pastor Trinity Ch., Lincoln, Nebr., 1973-77; dean Sch. Theology Boston U., 1977-88, prof., 1988—; bd. dirs. State Line Farms, Inc.; pres. Nesmith Inc. Producer religious TV program, Perspectives. Office: Boston U Sch Theology 745 Commonwealth Ave Rm 438 Boston MA 02215

NESS, CHARLES ALLEN, minister; b. Hanover, Pa., Jan. 21, 1947; s. Reuben and Ruth Naomi (Kuhns) N.; m. Janet Louise Nauman, June 25, 1966; children: Andrew, Carlton, Charles Lamar, Arneda. Student, Rosedale Bible Inst., Irwin, Ohio, 1970-71, 78; N.E. Bible Inst., Green Lane, Pa., 1969, Ctr. Urban Theol. Studies, Phila., 1987, Westminister Sem., Phila., 1987. Lic. to ministry Mennonite Ch., 1969, ordained, 1971. Pastor Upper Skippack (Pa.) Mennonite Ch., 1969-89; itinerant evangelist, 1973—, prison min., 1976—; founding pastor (prison ministry) Liberty Ministries, Souderton, Pa., 1980—, ministries dir., 1985—; area supr. Choice Books, Souderton, 1978-85; pres. bd. dirs. Liberty Ministries, 1980-85; interim pastor Downing Hills Mennonite Ch., Downingtown, Pa., 1990, Perkiomenville (Pa.) Mennonite Ch., 1991. Editor: (newsletter) Liberty Letter, 1985—; producer-speaker (radio) Liberty Report, 1989—. Home: PO Box 228 Skippack PA 19474-0228 Office: Liberty Ministries P O Box 363 Souderton PA 18964 *I have found help in dealing with the complexities of life by remembering that many problems represent the conflict between the kingdoms of good and evil and that through faith I can know peace and share in the ultimate victory of God.*

NESSAN, CRAIG LEE, minister, university official; b. Lansing, Mich., June 9, 1952; s. Lee A. and Lucy E. (Welford) N.; m. Cathy Sue Gee, Dec. 16, 1972; children—Benjamin, Nathaniel, Sarah, Andrew, Jessica. B.A., Mich. State U., 1974; M.Div., Wartburg Theol. Sem., 1978, S.T.M., 1978. Ordained to ministry Am. Luth. Ch., 1978. Pastor Trinity Luth. Ch., Phila., 1978-82; pastor St. Mark Luth. Ch., Cape Girardeau, Mo., 1987—; univ. asst. U. Regensburg, Fed. Republic of Germany, 1982-86; instr. religion S.E. Mo. State U., Cape Girardeau, 1989—; assoc. chaplain Frankford-Torresdale Hosp., Phila., 1978-82, mem. desegregation team Phila Sch. System, 1979-82. Mem. Bread for the World, Washington. Mem. Fellowship of Reconciliation, Luth. Peace Fellowship. Phi Beta Kappa. Author: Orthopraxis or Heresy, 1989; contbr. articles to profl. jours. Office: 1900 Cape LaCroix Rd Cape Girardeau MO 63701

NESSEL, WILLIAM JOSEPH, priest; b. Phila., Feb. 2, 1929; s. William Joseph and Claire M. (Lynch) N. AB in Philosophy, Cath. U. Am., 1953, MA in Politics, 1958, JCD in Canon Law, 1961; MDiv, St. Charles Borromeo Seminary, 1988. Professed Oblate of St. Francis de Sales, 1947; Ordained priest Roman Cath. Ch., 1956. Tchr. various schs., Phila., 1949-51; dir. pers. Camp DeSales for Boys, Bklyn., Mich., 1960-65; dir. religion Marymount Coll., Va., 1963-69; dir. field edn. Ind. Theol. Schs., Washington, 1970-73; dir. deacon program DeSales Hall Sch. of Theology and Oblates, 1973-77; dir. pastoral ministry program Allentown Coll., 1977-81; hosp. chaplain Daytona Beach, Fla., 1981-82; pastor St. Francis de Sales Ch., Robesonia, Pa., 1982-87, Sacred Heart Ch., Lewisburg, Pa., 1988—; chaplain Wernersville State Hosp., 1984-87, Allentown Coll., 1978-79; dir. pers. Oblates of St. Francis de Sales, 1973-78, planning, 1973-76, continuing edn., 1972-74; founder, dir. pastoral ctr. for adult edn. Archdiocese of Washington, 1971-73, chmn. dept. canon law Washington Theol. Union, 1969-70, dir. pastoral field edn., 1969-70; faculty DeSales Sch. Theology, Washington, 1960-77. Author: First Amendment Freedoms, Papal Pronouncements and Concordat Practice, 1961, The Campus Parish, 1969, Catholic Origins in Buffalo Valley and Chillisquaque Township of Central Pennsylvania, 1990; contbr. articles to profl. jours. Edn. com. mem. INTER-MET Sem., Washington, 1972-73; canonical advisor Wilmington-Phila. Province O.S.F.S., 1973-85; bd. trustees Allentown Coll., 1983—, Salesianum Sch., Wilmington, 1977-78; bd. dirs. Nat. Assn. Cath. Pers. Adminstrs., 1975-78, Packwood Mus., Lewisburg. Mem. Canon Law Soc. Am., Lewisburg Ministerium (pres.). Home: 814 St Louis St Lewisburg PA 17837

NESSER, JOAN KAY, religious organization administrator; b. Litchfield, Minn., Jan. 11, 1938; d. Walter Clarence and Muriel Ilene (Paulson) Jacobson; m. Joseph Stevens Nesser, Mar. 6, 1962; children: Natalie C., Aaron D., Adrienne I., Stephen J. AA, North Hennepin Community Coll., Brooklyn Center, Minn., 1981; Cert., Shalem Inst. for Spiritual, Formation, Washington, 1984; MA in Pastoral Theology and Ministry, Luther Northwestern

Seminary, St. Paul, Minn., 1990. Vol. coord. North Heights Luth. Ch., Roseville, Minn., 1981-83; instr. Lay Ministry Tng. Ctr., Roseville, 1983-86; founder, dir. Praise of His Glory Prayer Ministries Inc. and Prayer Community, New Brighton, Minn., 1978—, Christos Prayer Center and Spiritual Meditation and Direction Program, Lino Lakes, Minn., 1978—; advisor Iona Ctr. for Spiritual Growth, Mpls., 1990—. Author: Prayer, Journey from Self to God, 1985, 4th edit. 1990, Deepening Prayer Through Meditation, 1987. Dist. chmn. local Rep. party, New Brighton, 1969. Mem. Circle Pines Clergy Assn., St. Paul Area Evangel. Luth. Ch. American Pastors and AIMS. Office: Christos Prayer Ctr 1212 Holly Dr Lino Lakes MN 55038

NESTOR, CHARLES BERNARD, clergyman; b. Washington, Aug. 6, 1947; s. Alfred Hanson and Dicie Thelma (Doyle) N.; m. Belinda Joyce Gibson, Aug. 6, 1966; children: Christine Lee, Charles Bernard II, Amy Catherine. BA, Southeastern Coll., Lakeland, Fla., 1972; MA, Wheaton (Ill.) Coll., 1981. Ordained to ministry Assemblies of God, 1975. Pastor First Assembly of God, Triangle, Va., 1972-73; assoc. pastor Arlington (Va.) Assembly of God, 1975-77; pastor First Assembly of God, Niagara Falls, N.Y., 1977-80; assoc. pastor Calvary Temple, Naperville, Ill., 1980-83; pastor Bethel Temple, Oak Park, Ill., 1985-88; sr. pastor Manassas (Va.) Assembly of God, 1988—; sec. Capital sect. Assemblies of God, Fairfax, Va., 1976; pres. Empire State Teen Challenge, Syracuse, N.Y., 1979-80; treas. Faith Walk, Buffalo, 1985-87. Producer, host: (TV program) New Life in Niagara Falls, 1978-80, (radio program) The Pastor's Study, 1980. Mem. Rotary Club, Delta Epsilon Chi. Home: 11902 Falling Creek Dr Manassas VA 22111 Office: Manassas Assembly of God 8515 Plantation Ln Manassas VA 22110

NESTOR, WAYNE ALLEN, missionary; b. Tacoma, Aug. 3, 1953; s. Ralph Albert and Ursula (Freund) N.; m. Diann Kay Snyder, Nov. 24, 1978; children: Beth, Sarah, Laura. BS in Pastoral Studies, North Cen. Bible Coll., 1984. Ch. planting missionary Fed. Republic of Germany; assoc. pastor Christian Life Assembly of God, Plymouth, Wis., 1984-85; founding pastor Liberty Assembly of God, Concord, N.H., 1985-89; sr. pastor Bayard (Nebr.) Assembly of God, 1989-91; missionary DFM-Assemblies of God, Springfield, Mo., 1991—; regional rep. Salvation Army, Bayard, 1990-91. Staff sgt. USAF, 1975-79, ETO. North Cen. Bible Coll. scholar, and others. Mem. Bayard Ministerial Alliance (sec., treas. 1990-91), S.E. N.H. Assemblies ofGod (sec., treas. Concord chpt. 1988-89). Republican. Office: NE Dist Coun Assemblies of God PO Box 1965 Grand Island NE 68802

NETTELHORST, ROBIN PAUL, lay worker; b. Lockbourne AFB, Ohio, Mar. 14, 1957; s. Paul Merrit and Naomi Jean (Saylor) N.; m. Ruth Williamson Nettelhorst, June 25, 1983. BA summa cum laude, L.A. Bapt. Coll., 1979; MA, UCLA, 1983. Ordained to ministry Bapt. Ch. as deacon, 1987. Lectr. Christian Heritage Coll., El Cajon, Calif., 1984; lectr. old testament and bibl. langs. L.A. Bapt. Coll., Newhall, Calif., 1984-87; novelist Palmdale, Calif., 1987—. Contbr. articles to profl. jours. Sunday sch. tchr. Placerita Bapt. Ch., Newhall, Calif., 1980-87, elder, treas., 1984-87; Bible and Hebrew tchr. Olivet Bapt. Ch., Lancaster, Calif., 1990. Mem. Soc. Bibl. Lit., Am. Acad. Religion, Am. Schs. Oriental Rsch., Small Press Writers and Artists Orgn. Home and Office: 38551 11th St E # 30 Palmdale CA 93550 *To hold the hand of God, to listen to his heart, to feel his pain, to taste his joys, to long for his happiness—that is to love God.*

NETTERVILLE, GEORGE BRONSON, minister; b. McComb, Miss., Dec. 31, 1929; s. George Irving and Eula Hazel (Bronson) N.; m. Mary Elbridge Bogie, Mar. 15, 1957. BA with honors, Southeastern La. U., 1951; BD, Lexington Theol. Sem., 1957, ThM, 1958; PhD, Sussex Coll. (Eng.), 1971. Ordained to ministry Christian Ch. (Disciples of Christ), 1952. Minister various chs. in Miss. and Ky., 1953-59; minister 1st Christian Ch., Clarksdale, Miss., 1959-64, Univ. Christian Ch., Starkville, Miss., 1964-68; assoc. regional minister Christian Ch. in Tenn., Nashville, 1968-80; regional minister, pres., 1980-90; ret.; bd. dirs. Christmount Christian Assembly, Black Mountain, N.C., 1975-90; mem. gen. bd. Christian Ch., Indpls., 1980-90; pres. Tenn. Assn. Chs., Nashville, 1982-84; bd. dirs. Ch. Fin. Council, Indpls., 1986-90; treas. So. Christian Services, Macon, Ga., 1986-88. Served as cpl. U.S. Army, 1951-53; Korea. Mem. Conf. Regional Ministers, Am. Acad. Religion, Soc. Bibl. Lit., Am. Schs. of Oriental Research, Council of Ministers of Christian Ch. Lodge: Masons.

NEUFELD, HERB, religious organization administrator. Moderator Can. Conf. Mennonite Brethren Chs., Abbotsford, B.C. Office: Mennonite Brethren Chs Can, 3-169 Riverton Ave, Winnipeg, MB Canada R2L 2E5*

NEUHAUS, RICHARD JOHN, priest, research institute president; b. Pembroke, Ont., Can., May 14, 1936; Came to U.S., 1950; s. Clemens Henry and Ella Carolina (Prange) N. M Div., Concordia Sem., 1960; DD (hon.), Benedictine Coll., 1985, Gonzaga U., 1985, Valparaiso U., 1986, Nichols Coll., 1986, Boston U., 1988. Ordained to ministry Luth. Ch., 1960; ordained priest Roman Cath. Ch., 1991. Pastor St. John The Evangelist, Bklyn., 1961-78; sr. editor Worldview Mag., N.Y.C., 1972-82; dir. Rockford Inst. Ctr. on Religion and Soc., N.Y.C., 1984-89, Inst. on Religion and Pub. Life, N.Y.C., 1989—. Author: Freedom for Ministry, 1979, The Naked Public Square, 1984, The Catholic Moment, 1987, America Against Itself, 1992. Office: Inst Religion & Pub Life 156 Fifth Ave Ste 400 New York NY 10010

NEUMAN, ISAAC, rabbi; b. Zd-Wola, Poland, Dec. 4, 1922; came to U.S., 1950; Diploma, Hebrew U. Jerusalem; B of Hebrew Letters, Hebrew Union Coll., 1958, MA in Hebrew Letters, 1969; BA, U. Cin., 1960; ordained rabbi, Hebrew Union Coll., DD (honoris causa), 1985. Ordained rabbi, 1960. Rabbi Kol Shearith Israel, Republic of Panama, 1957-59, Dothan, Ala., 1959-61, Temple Judah, Cedar Rapids, Iowa, 1961-74, Sinai Temple, Champaign, Ill., 1974-87; chief rabbi of Berlin and German Dem. Republic, 1987-88; vis. prof. Cornell Coll., Mt. Vernon, Iowa, 1963-68, Marymount Coll., Boca Raton, Fla., 1966-69; guest lectr. Sch. Religion, U. Iowa, Iowa City, 1964; with faculty dept. religious studies Coe Coll., 1969-72, Parkland Coll., Champaign, 1980-81, U. Ill., Urbana, 1982-83. Contbr. articles to Chgo. Tribune, L.A. Times, other newspapers and jours. aux. chaplain Chanute AFB, Rantoul, Ill., Ft. Rucker, Ala.; bd. dirs. Sch. Religion, U. Iowa; bd. dirs. Cedar Rapids-Marion Area Commn. on Human Rights; giver invocation U.S. Ho. of Reps., 1970, 83; mem. U.S. Holocaust Meml. Coun. Mem. Champaign-Urbana Ministerial Assn. (pres. 1977-79). Home: 2203 Clover Ln Champaign IL 61821 Office: 3104 W Windsor Rd Champaign IL 61821

NEUROTH, WILLIAM C., minister, ecumenical agency administrator. Exec. dir. N. Ky. Interfaith Commn. Inc., Covington. Office: No Ky Interfaith Commn Inc 501 Greenup St Covington KY 41011*

NEUSNER, JACOB, humanities and religious studies educator; b. Hartford, Conn., July 28, 1932; m. Suzanne Richter, Mar. 15, 1964; children: Samuel Aaron, Eli Ephraim, Noam Mordecai Menahem, Margalit Leah Berakhah. AB in History magna cum laude, Harvard U., 1953; postgrad. (Henry fellow), Lincoln Coll., Oxford, Eng., 1953-54; postgrad. (Fulbright scholar), Hebrew U., 1957-58; M.H.L., Jewish Theol. Sem. Am., 1960, DHL (hon.), 1987; Ph.D. in Religion (Univ. scholar), Columbia U., 1960; A.M. ad eudem, Brown U., 1969; L.H.D., U. Chgo., 1978; D.Phil. (hon.), U. Cologne, 1979. Instr. religion Columbia U., 1960-61; asst. prof. Hebrew U. Wis.-Milw., 1961-62; research asso. Brandeis U., 1962-64; asst. prof. religion Dartmouth Coll., 1964-66; assoc. prof. Dartmouth Coll., Providence, 1966-68; prof. religious studies Brown U., Providence, 1968-75, prof. religious studies, Ungerleider Disting. scholar Judaic studies, 1975-82, Univ. prof., Ungerleider Disting. scholar, 1982-90, Disting. Rsch. prof. religious studies, 1990—; vis. prof. Jewish Theol. Sem. Am., summer 1977, Iliff Sch. Theology, Denver, summer 1978; Hill vis. prof. U. Minn., 1978; pres. Max Richter Found., 1969—; mem. bd. advisors I. Edward Kiev Library Found., 1977—, Ancient Biblical Manuscript Center Library, Sch. Theology, Claremont, 1978—; mem. Nat. Council for the Humanities, governing bd. Nat. Endowment Humanities, 1978-84; lectr. various orgns. Author: A Life of Yohanan ben Zakkai, 1962 (Abraham Berliner prize in Jewish history), A History of the Jews in Babylonia, 1965-70, Development of a Legend: Studies on the Traditions Concerning Yohanan ben Zakkai, 1970, Aphrahat and Judaism: The Christian-Jewish Argument in Fourth Century Iran, 1971, The Rabbinic Traditions about the Pharisees before 70, 1971, Eliezer ben Hyrcanus: The Tradition and the Man, 1973, The Idean of Purity in Ancient Judaism, 1973, A History of the Mishnaic Law of Purities, 1974-80, Judaism: The Evidence of the Mishnah, 1981, others; author numerous textbooks including American Judaism, Adventure in Modernity, 1972, From Politics to Piety: The Emergence of Pharisaic Judaism, 1973, 78, Invitation to the Talmud: A Teaching Book, 1974, Between Time and Eternity: The Essentials of Judaism, 1976, Form-Analysis and Exegeis: A Fresh Approach to the Interpretation of Mishnah, 1980; editor numerous books including Studies in Judaism in Late Antiquity, 1973—, Studies in Judaism in Modern Times, 1975—, Library of Judaic Learning, 1975—, Brown Judaic Studies, 1976—, Chicago Studies in the History of Judaism, 1980—, Basic Jewish Ideas, 1981—; founder, editor-in-chief Brown Studies on Jews and their Societies, 1985—; mem. bd. cons.: Religious Traditions, 1977—; mem. editorial bd.: The Second Century, 1980—, Studies in Religion/Sciences Religieuses, 1981-83, Assn. for Jewish Studies Rev, 1981-83, Jour. Am. Acad. Religion, 1985—, Hebrew Ann. Rev., 1985—, Religious and Theol. Studies, 1985—; contbg. editor: Moment, 1977—, The Reconstructionist, 1983—. Kent fellow Nat. Council for Religion in Higher Edn., 1957-60; Lown fellow, 1962-64; Guggenheim Found. fellow, 1973-74, 79-80; Am. Council Learned Socs. fellow, 1966-67, 70-71; research grantee Am. Philos. Soc., 1965, 67; recipient Univ. Medal for Excellence Columbia U., 1974, Von Humboldt prize Von Humboldt Found., 1981, Disting. Humanitarian award Ohio State U., 1983. Fellow Royal Asiatic Soc., Am. Acad. Jewish Research (exec. com. 1976—); mem. Am. Acad. Religion (v.p., program chmn. 1967-68, pres. 1968-69, chmn. sect. on history of judaism 1979-81, dir. 1981—), Am. Oriental Soc., Assn. Jewish Studies, N.Am. Soc. Study of Religion (founding com. 1986—, exec. com.), Am. Hist. Assn., Soc. Bibl. Lit., Phi Beta Kappa. Home: 735 14th Ave NE Saint Petersburg FL 33701 Office: U South Fla Dept Religious Studies Tampa FL 33620 *What makes us different from animals is our mind, our capacity to reason, to ask why. That is how we are "like God" in the Biblical sense: knowing the difference between good and evil, but also between what is true and what is untrue. That is, further, how we know God. My life is spent in the places where people learn to use their minds as best they can, and I teach, as best I can, how my student can do so. What a privilege!.*

NEVINS, JOHN J., bishop; b. New Rochelle, N.Y., Jan. 19, 1932. Student, Iona Coll. (N.Y.), Cath. U. Washington. Ordained priest, Roman Catholic Ch., 1959. Ordained titular bishop of Rusticana and aux. bishop Diocese of Miami, Fla., 1979-84; first bishop Diocese of Venice, Fla., 1984—. Office: PO Box 2006 Venice FL 34284

NEWBERT, RUSSELL ANDERSON, minister; b. Gardiner, Maine, July 19, 1937; s. Russell Copeland and Gwen May (Anderson) N. BS, U. Maine, 1959; MDiv, Gen. Theol. Sem., N.Y.C., 1964; MA, U. Notre Dame, South Bend, Ind., 1989. Ordained to ministry, Episcopal Ch., 1964. Asst. minister St. Michael & All Angels Ch., Cin., 1964-72; rector Bel-Mar Episcopal Parish, Bellaire-Martins Ferry, Ohio, 1972-75, St. Simons Episcopal Ch., Buffalo, 1975—; chmn. Diocesan Commn. Ministry, Buffalo, 1986-90; mem. Diocesan Music Commn., Buffalo, 1987—, Diocesan Litury Commn., 1987—. Mem. S. Buffalo Ecumenical Assn., 1975—. Home: 202 Cazenovia St Buffalo NY 14210 Office: St Simons Episcopal Ch 200 Cazenovia St Buffalo NY 14210

NEWBORN, ERNEST, ecumenical agency administrator. Pres. Interreligious Found. for Community Orgn., N.Y.C. Office: Interreligious Found for Community Orgn 402 W 145th St New York NY 10031*

NEWBY, JAMES RICHARD, clergyman, educator; b. Mpls., July 8, 1949; s. Richard Prouty and Doris Irene (Prignitz) N.; m. Elizabeth Salinas, Dec. 21, 1969; 1 child, Alicia Marie. AB, Friends U., 1971; MDiv, Earlham Sch. Religion, 1977; DD (hon.), William Penn Coll., 1985; postgrad., Princeton Theol. Sem. Pastor Friends Ch., Central City, Nebr., 1971-73, Chester/New Burlington, Ohio, 1973-75, Cin., 1975-79; exec. dir. Yokefellow Acad. and Inst., Richmond, Ind., 1979-87, Trueblood Acad., Earlham Sch. Religion, Richmond, 1987—; pres. Trueblood Acad. Endowment, Richmond, 1985—; clk. First Friends Ch. Ministry and Oversight, Richmond, 1990—. Editor Quaker Life Mag., Friends United Meeting, 1990—; author: Religion-Between Peril and Promise, 1984, Religion-Reflections From the Light of Christ, 1980, Elton Trueblood: Believer/Teacher/Friend, 1990. Founding mem. Internat. Inst. for Christian Youth, Nat. Ctr. Juvenile Justice, Pitts., 1985—. Named Disting. Christian Scholar/Lectr., The Staley Found., 1983. Mem. Yokefellows Internat. (bd. dirs. 1979—). Avocations: golf, running. Home: 721 SW 18th St Richmond IN 47374 Office: Earlham Sch Religion 228 College Ave Richmond IN 47374

NEWBY, JOHN M., academic administrator. Pres. Cen. Wesleyan Coll., Central, S.C. Office: Cen Weslayan Coll 1 Weslayan Dr Central SC 19630-1020*

NEWBY, SARAH CLARK, lay church worker; b. Nicholasville, Ky., Sept. 8, 1936; d. Herbert Hoover and Nannie (Thompson) Clark; m. Louis A. Newby, Aug. 19, 1961; children: Sahara Alexine Newby Waiters, Teresa Anita. BA, U. Ky., 1958, MA, 1965; postgrad., Georgetown Coll., 1985. Choir mem., Sunday Sch. tchr., ch. clerk Macedonia Bapt. Ch., Keene, Ky., 1961-70; musician Davistown Bapt. Ch., Lancaster, Ky., 1970-75; ch. clerk First Corinthian Bapt. Ch., Frankfort, Ky., 1976—. Mem. NEA, Ky. Edn. Assn., Fayette County Edn. Assn. Democrat. Home: 372 Preakness Dr Lexington KY 40516 Office: First Corinthian Bapt Ch Second and Murray Sts Frankfort KY 40601 *The acquiring and practicing a firm belief and faith in the Almighty God will serve as bulwark against troubled times that one may encounter in his or her life.*

NEWCOMB, DOUGLAS DAVID, religious organization administrator; b. Tonawanda, N.Y., May 16, 1957; s. David Alfred and Lois Marie (Suchy) N.; m. Jan Dubois Shepherd, July 21, 1978; children: Laura, Stephen. BS in Fin., U. Colo., 1979; MBA with honors, Regis Coll., 1990. Bd. elders Faith Bible Chapel, Arvada, Colo., 1984—, adminstr., treas., 1988—. Mem. Bd. Elders Faith Bible Chapel, 1984—. Mem. Nat. Assn. Ch. Bus. Adminstrs. Republican. Office: Faith Bible Chapel 6210 Ward Rd Arvada CO 80004

NEWELL, ARLO FREDERIC, editor; b. Stafford, Kans., Feb. 22, 1926; m. Helen Louise Jones, Aug. 1, 1947; children: Rebecca S., Samme Le, Eric F. BA, Anderson U.; student, U. N.C., Duke U., Boston Coll.; MDiv, MRE, Eden Theol Sem.; DD (hon.), Mid-Am. Bible Coll. Ordained to ministry Ch. of God, 1950. Assoc. pastor Ch. of God, Akron, Ind.; pastor Ch. of God, High Point, N.C., 1951-60, St. Louis, 1960-72, Springfield, Ohio, 1972-77; editor in chief Warner Press, Inc., Anderson, Ind., 1977—; chmn. Gen. Assembly, Ch. of God, 1968-74, 76-77. Mem. Kiwanis. Home: 1927 Mark Ln Anderson IN 46012 Office: Warner Press Inc PO Box 2499 Anderson IN 46018

NEWELL, BYRON BRUCE, JR., clergyman, former naval officer; b. Long Beach, Calif., July 31, 1932; s. Byron Bruce and Eleanor Whitaker (Davis) N.; m. Ingrid Charlotte Asche, June 11, 1955 (dec. July 1989); children: Thomas, Susan, Robert, Michael; m. Theresa Ann Troncale, Sept. 1, 1990. Student, Wesleyan U., 1950-51; BS, U.S. Naval Acad., 1955; MSEE, U.S. Naval Postgrad. Sch. Monterey, 1962; postgrad. nuclear power tng., 1964-65; MDiv, Va. Theol. Sem., 1987. Ordained priest, Episcopal Ch., 1988. Commd. ensign U.S. Navy, 1955, advanced through grades to rear adm., 1980; weapons officer U.S.S. Lowry, Hull (destroyers), 1955-58; comdg. officer salvage ship, 1962-64, exec., comdg. officer nuclear cruisers, 1968-77, manpower/tng. surface ship personnel, 1977-79; with Nat. Mil. Command Center, Washington, 1979-80, chief navy info., 1980-82, chief navy legis. affairs, 1982-84; assoc. dean Trinity Episcopal Sch. for Ministry, Ambridge, Pa., 1990—. Decorated Legion of Merit, D.S.M. Mem. Naval Inst., Naval Hist. Soc., Met. Club. Home: 256 Thorn St Sewickley PA 15143

NEWLIN, JEFFREY JOHN, minister; b. Manitowoc, Wis., May 30, 1951; s. Roy Adolf and Jane (Specht) N.; m. Virginia Ann Tonnessen, June 18, 1977; children: James, Peter. BA, Northwestern U., 1973; MA with honors, U. Cambridge, Eng., 1975; MDiv, Yale U., 1977; DMin, McCormick Theol. Sem., 1987. Ordained to ministry Presbyn. Ch. (USA), 1977. Asst. pastor First Presbyn. Ch., River Forest, Ill., 1977-79; pastor Hagerstown (Md.) Presbyn. Ch., 1979-88, Riverside Presbyn. Ch., Jacksonville, Fla., 1988—. Mem. Rotary. Office: Riverside Presbyn Ch 849 Park St Jacksonville FL 32204

NEWMAN, GARY LEN, minister; b. Grand Saline, Tex., Aug. 12, 1947; s Leonard Bonn and Ruby Pearl (Joslin) N.; m. Janis Elain McClain, Jan. 28, 1966; children: Jerry Leonard, Kristi Paige, Kelli Jan, Kimberly Gail. BA, Criswell Coll., Dallas, 1979; postgrad., New Orleans Bapt. Theol. Sem., 1986, 87. Ordained to ministry, So. Bapt. Conv., 1972. Music and youth dir. Terrace Hills Bapt. Ch., Longview, Tex., 1974-76, Grace Temple Bapt. Ch., Terrell, Tex., 1976-79; pastor Minden (Tex.) Bapt. Ch., 1979-87; evangelist Dallas, 1987-88; pastor Tyland Bapt. Ch., Tyler, Tex., 1988—; dir. Sunday sch., Smith Bapt. Assn., Tyler, 1991—, evangelism dir., 1989-90; treas. Rusk/Panola Bapt. Assn., Henderson, 1987-88; chmn. mission builder, Tyler, 1986—; pres. Smith Bapt. Assn. Pastor's Conf., Tyler, 1991—. Republican. Home: 6202 Huntington Tyler TX 75703-4141 Office: Tyland Bapt Ch 2818 Silver Creek Tyler TX 75702

NEWMAN, HARRY ALEXANDER, church executive; b. Jacksonville, Fla., Sept. 3, 1928; s. Harry Alexander and Susie Mae (Aldrich) N.; m. Barbara Seiss Buck, June 10, 1950 (dec. 1985); children: Bruce, Beth, Scott, Tempe, Harry, Donald, Jane, Gary, Laura; m. Elizabeth Jane Tuttle, June 24, 1989. BSBA cum laude, U. Fla., 1954; BS in Health Scis., Duke U., 1973. Mgr. acctg. and cost div. Prudential Ins. Co. Am., Jacksonville, 1954-67; physician assoc. Piedmont Clinic, Lawndale, N.C., 1976-84; missionary United Meth. Ch., Bolivia, 1967-76; field rep. United Meth. Ch., Atlanta, 1984-89, Asheville, N.C., 1989—; chmn. med. work teams United Meth. Ch., Lawndale, 1980-84. Bd. dirs. Am. Cancer Soc., Jacksonville, 1963-66, Children's Home Soc., Jacksonville, 193-66; mem. Jacksonville Beach Dem. Com., 1960. With USN, 1946-48, 50-52. Mem. Beta Gamma Sigma. Avocations: golf, tennis, fishing, reading, painting. Home: 72 Crestwood Dr Asheville NC 28804 Office: United Meth Ch 1293 Hendersonville Rd 23 Asheville NC 28803

NEWMAN, ROBERT CHAPMAN, religion educator; b. Washington, Apr. 2, 1941; s. Allan L. C. and Lois May (Gardner) N. BS in Physics, Duke U., 1963; PhD in Astrophysics, Cornell U., 1967; MDiv, Faith Theol. Sem., 1970; MST in Old Testament, Bibl. Theol. Sem., 1975. Assoc. prof. math. and sci. Shelton Coll., Cape May, N.J., 1968-71; assoc. prof. N.T. Bibl. Theol. Sem., Hatfield, Pa., 1971-77, prof., 1977—; dir. Interdisciplinary Bibl. Rsch. Inst., Hatfield, 1981—; bd. dirs. Windward Ministries, Hatfield. Coauthor: Science Speaks, 3d edit., 1969, Genesis One and the Origin of the Earth, 1977; editor: Evidence of Prophecy, 1988; also articles. Bd. dirs. Pinebrook Jr. Coll., Coopersburg, Pa., 1984—. Woodrow Wilson hon. fellow, 1963-64, NSF fellow, 1963-67, A. D. White hon. fellow, 1963-64. Fellow Am. Sci. Affiliation; mem. Evang. Theol. Soc. Republican. Home: 115 S Main St Hatfield PA 19440 Office: Bibl Theol Sem 200 N Main St Hatfield PA 19440 *"When I consider your heavens, the work of your fingers, the moon and stars, which you have set in place, what is man that you are mindful of him, the son of man that you care for him?" (Psalms 8: 3-4).*

NEWMAN, SAMUEL TYLER, minister; b. Henderson, Ky., Sept. 24, 1964; s. Lee Tyler and Betty Jean (English) N.; m. Christina Diane Barron, Mar. 14, 1987; children: Emily Christine, Jonathan Tyler. MusB, Union Univ., 1986; M Christian Edn., So. Bapt. Theol. Seminary, Louisville, Ky., 1990. Minister of music and youth Beech Bluff (Tenn.) Bapt. Ch., 1983-85; minister of youth and recreation Highland Bapt. Ch., Pulaski, Ind., 1986-87; assoc. minister/edn., music and youth First Bapt. Ch., Morganfield, Ky., 1988—; dir. discipleship tng. Green Valley Bapt. Assn., Henderson, Ky., 1991-92. Named to Outstanding Young Men in Am., 1986. Mem. Phi Mu Alpha (chaplain 1985-86), Sigma Alpha Epsilon (emminent chronicler 1985-86). Home: Rte 5 Box 27N Morganfield KY 42437 Office: First Baptist Church 109 West McElroy Morganfield KY 42437

NEWMAN, SANDY KAY, minister; b. Salem, Ark., May 28, 1951; d. Richard and Geraldine Morney. AA, Cowley County Community Coll., 1976. Lic. to ministry Pentecostal Holiness Ch., 1991. Pres. Destiny Ministries, Arkansas City, Kans., 1984—. Home and Office: 126 Random Rd Arkansas City KS 67005

NEWMAN, THOMAS DANIEL, minister, school administrator; b. London, Eng., May 12, 1922; s. Frederick and Margaret (O'Leary) N.; m. Louise Johannah Albertano, Apr. 1, 1963; 1 dau., Susan (Mrs. Alan J. Rennie). Student, Glasgow Sch. Accounting, 1946, Unity Sch. Christianity, 1962-66, Harvard Div. Sch., 1967—; DSc, Alma Coll., 1975. Ordained to ministry Ch. of Christ, 1966. Mng. dir. Thomas Newman (Printers) Ltd., 1945-49; mng. dir. H. & M.J. Pubs. Ltd., 1947-49, Forget-Me-Not Greeting Cards Ltd., 1949-61, Diplomat Greetings Ltd., 1957-61, Nevill's Ltd., 1955-57; pastor Christ's Ch., Springfield, Mo., 1966-67, Longwood, Brookline, Mass., 1967—; adminstrv. dir. Am. Schs. Oriental Research, 1968, treas., 1970—, trustee, 1972—; founder Carthage Research Inst., Khereddine, Tunisia, 1975, Cyprus Archaeol. Research Inst., Nicosia, 1977; cons. Joint Archeol. Expdns. to, Ai, 1969-73, to; Tell-El-Hesi, 1970-73, to, Idalion, 1970-73; mem. Joint Archeol. Expdn. to, Caesarea Maritima, 1971, to; Carthage, 1975; dir. Logistics Survey Qu'Rayyah, Saudi Arabia, 1973; pub. cons. (Dead Sea Scrolls Com.), 1968-73; Trustee Allbright Inst. Archeol. Research, Jerusalem.; Am. Center Oriental Research, Amman, Jordan. Served with RAF, 1940-45. Mem. Archeol. Inst. Am., Soc. Bibl. Lit., Soc. O.T. Studies. Clubs: Mason, Harvard Faculty; University (Boston) (Sarasota). Home: 8 Club Acre Ln Bedford NH 03110 Office: Colchester and Chapel Sts Brookline MA 02146

NEWMAN, WILLIAM C., bishop; b. Balt., Aug. 16, 1928. Student, St. Mary Sem., Cath. U., Loyola Coll. Ordained priest Roman Cath. Ch., 1954. Aux. bishop Archdiocese of Balt., 1984—. Address: 5400 Roland Ave Baltimore MD 21210

NEWPORT, JOHN PAUL, educational administrator, philosophy of religion educator; b. Buffalo, Mo., June 16, 1917; s. Marvin Jackson and Mildred (Morrow) N.; m. Eddie Belle Leavell, Nov. 14, 1941; children: Martha Ellen Gay, Frank M., John P. Jr. BA, William Jewell Coll., Liberty, Mo., 1938; ThM, So. Bapt. Theol. Sem., Louisville, 1941, ThD, 1946; PhD, U. Edinburgh, Scotland, 1953; MA, Tex. Christian U., 1968; LittD, William Jewell Coll., 1967. Assoc. prof. Baylor U., 1949-51, New Orleans Bapt. Theol. Sem, 1951-52; prof. Southwestern Bapt. Theol. Sem, Ft. Worth, 1952-76, Rice U., 1976-79; vis. prof. Princeton Theol. Sem., 1982; v.p. acad. affairs, provost Southwestern Bapt. Theol. Sem., 1979-90, v.p. emeritus, spl. asst. to pres., 1990—, disting. prof. philosophy of religion, 1990—. Author: Theology and Contemporary Art Forms, 1971, Demons, Demons, Demons, 1972, Why Christians Fight over the Bible, 1974, Christ and the New Consciousness, 1978, Christianity and Contemporary Art Forms, 1979, Nineteenth Century Devotional Thought, 1981, Paul Tillich, 1984, What Is Christian Doctrine? 1984, The Lion and the Lamb, 1986, Life's Ultimate Questions, 1989; contbr. numerous articles to jours. and mags. Seatlantic fellowship Rockefeller Found., Harvard U., 1958-59. Mem. Am. Acad. Religion (pres. S.W. div. 1967-68), Soc. of Bibl. Lit. and Exegesis, Southwestern Philos. Assn., N.Am. Paul Tillich Soc. (dir. 1984-86), Southside C. of C. (Ft. Worth) (bd. dirs.), Downtown Rotary Club (Ft. Worth) (trustee), Ft. Worth Club. Democrat. Avocations: golf, swimming, tennis. Office: Southwestern Bapt Theol Sem PO Box 22000 Fort Worth TX 76122

NEWSON, DAVID HUGHES, minister; b. Edmonton, Alta., Can., Dec. 9, 1917; s. William Victor and Mamie Ethel (Hughes) N.; m. Margaret Louisa Daniels, May 28, 1950; children: Dale Elizabeth, Jill Rebecca, Graham Hughes, Owen John. BA, U. Alta., 1940, LLB, 1941; MDiv, Union Theol. Sem., N.Y.C., 1948. Ordained to ministry, Presbyn. Ch. USA 1949. Asst. minister Huguenot Meml. Ch., Pelham, N.Y., 1948-49; minister Watchung Presbyn. Ch., Bloomfield, N.J., 1950-89; ret.; moderator Newark Presbytery, 1961-62; pres Better Human Rels. Coun., Bloomfield, 1961-62; chaplain Bloomfield Coll., 1966-71; adj. prof. humanities, religion, philosophy of religion Fairleigh Dickinson U., 1972-84. With RCAF, 1942-45. Recipient Brotherhood award, B'nai B'rith, 1963, Mayor's award, 1969. Home: 81 Highland Dr Lancaster PA 17602 *Whether we like it or not, the idea of national sovereignty is becoming less feasible and the necessity for world community more apparent. I look forward to the time when world citizenship will provide the same duties, responsibilities and freedoms as are now present in the world's leading democracies.*

NEWSWANGER, CARL KEEPORT, minister; b. Bird-in-Hand, Pa., May 11, 1941; s. Willis Raymond and Alice Edna (Keeport) N.; m. K. Louise Myers, Aug. 19, 1967; children: Jon Christopher, Jill Allison. BA in History, Ea. Mennonite Coll., 1964; MDiv, Goshen Bibl. Seminary, Elkhart, Ind., 1969. Pastor Pueblo (Colo.) Mennonite Ch., 1969-72, Mennonite Ch., Normal, Ill., 1972-79, Orrville (Ohio) Mennonite Ch., 1979-85, Hartville (Ohio) Mennonite Ch., 1985—; exec. sec. Ohio Conf. of the Mennonite Ch., Kidron, 1983-85; pres. Ohio Inter-Mennonite Coun. on Aging, Kidron, 1984—. Editor Ill. Missionary Guide mag., 1975-79. Home: 1211 Glenview NE North Canton OH 44721 Office: Hartville Mennonite Church 1470 Smith Kramer Hartville OH 44632

NEWTON, BRADFORD CURTIS, minister; b. Arcadia, Calif., Dec. 4, 1957; s. Charles and Shirley Newton; m. Jennifer Lynette Christian, Aug. 123, 1981; children: Amanda, Tyler. BA, Andrews U., 1980, MDiv, 1983, postgrad., 1983—. Ordained to ministry Seventh-day Adventist Ch. , 1988. Pastor Ill. Conf. Seventh-day Adventists, Brookfield, 1983—, Monmouth (Ill.) Seventh-day Adventist Ch., 1983-87, Burr Ridge (Ill.) Seventh-day Adventist Ch., 1987-89, Bolingbrook (Ill.) Seventh-day Adventist Ch., 1989—; chmn. evangelism com. Ill. Conf. Seventh-day Adventists, Brookfield, 1991—. Mem. ethics com. Hinsdale (Ill.) Hosp., 1986—; chaplain Police Dept., Bolingbrook, 1990—. Mem. Bolingbrook Ministerial Orgn. Office: Seventh-day Adventist Ch 301 E Boughton Rd Bolingbrook IL 60440 *Contentment's flower germinates in the soil of commitment, blossoms with the dew of compassion, flourishes in the sunlight of service.*

NEWTON, HOWARD EDWIN, minister; b. Readsboro, Vt., Mar. 1, 1929; s. William Alfred and Florence Leslie (Walden) N.; m. Frances Margaret Perry, June 26, 1954; children: Bruce John, Wayne Stuart, Lisa Carol Newton Bagley. BA, Hope Coll., 1951; MDiv, New Brunswick Theol. Sem., 1954; STM magna cum laude, Union Theol. Sem., 1959, postgrad., 1957-59; postgrad., Columbia U., 1960-63. Ordained to ministry Ref. Ch. in Am., 1954; transferred to United Meth. Ch., 1971. Assoc. min. First Reformed Ch., Scotia, N.Y., 1954-57; min. First Reformed Ch., Long Island City, N.Y., 1960-64, Reformed Ch., Middletown, N.J., 1958-60, Christ Community Reformed Ch., Stony Brook, N.Y., 1964-71, Christ United Meth. Ch., Staten Island, N.Y., 1971-78, United Meth. Chs., Hobart and Township, N.Y., 1978-84, Mary Taylor Meml. United Meth. Ch., Milford, Conn., 1984—; sec. N.Y./Conn. Found. United Meth. Ch., White Plains, N.Y., 1988—; com. on min., supv. candidates for min. Conn. Cen. Dist. United Meth. Ch., Hamden, 1986—. Human resources devel. bd. dirs. City of Milford, Conn., 1990—; evaluation of agencies com. United Way, Milford, 1989—. Mem. Phi Alpha Theta. Home: 47 Commodore Pl Milford CT 06460 Office: Mary Taylor Meml Meth Ch 168-176 S Broad St Milford CT 06460

NEWTON, ROBERT D., JR., religion educator; b. Camden, Ark., Jan. 3, 1928; s. Robert D. and Ora Belle (Simmons) N.; m. Ann Kelly, Sept. 7, 1951; children: Beth Ann Newton Watson, Christopher David. BA, Yale U., 1950; MDiv, Union Theol. Sem., 1953; PhD, Columbia U./Union Theol. Sem., 1960. Ordained to ministry United Meth. Ch., 1961. Prof. religion DePauw U., Greencastle, Ind., 1956—, chair dept. philosophy and religion, 1977—, faculty devel. coord. for writing program, 1981—. With U.S. Army, 1946-48. Mem. AAUP, Am. Acad. Religion, Soc. Christian Ethics, Danforth Assoc. Office: DePauw U Asbury Hall Greencastle IN 46135

NEYHART, PHILLIP RAY, minister; b. Chgo., Apr. 29, 1956; s. O. Eugene and Muriel Jane (Reed) N.; m. Phyllis Jo Priddy, May 26, 1979; children: Jennifer Lynn, Brian Phillip. BA, Cin. Bible Coll., 1979; MA, Cin. Christian Sem., 1989. Ordained to ministry Christian Chs. and Chs. of Christ, 1978. Youth min. Greenfield (Ohio) Ch. of Christ, 1978-79; min. Jamestown (Ky.) Christian Ch., 1980-88; sr. min. Lyndon Christian Ch., Louisville, 1988—; chaplain Russell County Hosp. Chaplaincy, Russell Springs, Ky., 1983-88. Mem. local arrangement com. N.Am. Christian Conv., Louisville, 1989; dir., treas. White Mills (Ky.) Christian Camp, White Mills, 1982-86; mem. South Cen. Ky. Christian Mins. Assn., Columbia, 1980-88, pres., 1986-88; judge activity coord. Jamestown Independence Celebration, 1985-87; moderator quick recall Ky. Acad. Assn. Named Outstanding Young Men of Am. U.S. Jaycees, 1983. Mem. Greater Louisville Christian Mins. Assn., Evang. Tchr. Tng. Assn., Russell County Ministerial Assn. (sec.-treas., v.p., pres., cert. excellence 1988). Republican. Home: 8011 Osborne Dr Louisville KY 40222 Office: Lyndon Christian Ch 8125 LaGrange Rd Louisville KY 40222 *Life has more meaning when we are involved in caring for, and encouraging others. True contentment comes through faithfully serving others, to the honor and glory of Christ.*

NEYLON, MARTIN JOSEPH, bishop; b. Buffalo, Feb. 13, 1920; s. Martin Francis and Delia (Breen) N. PhL, Woodstock Coll., 1944, ThL, 1951; MA, Fordham U., 1948. Ordained priest Roman Cath. Ch., 1950. Bishop Roman Cath. Ch., 1970; mem. Soc. of Jesus; tchr. Regis High Sch., N.Y.C., 1952-54; master Jesuit novices Poughkeepsie, N.Y., 1955-67; chaplain Kwajalein Missile Range, Marshall Islands, 1967-68; superior Residence for Jesuit Students, Guam, 1968-70; coadjutor bishop Caroline and Marshall Islands, 1970-80; Vicar apostolic, 1971—; residential bishop New Diocese of Carolines-Marshalls, 1980—. Address: PO Box 250, Truk 96942, Federated States of Micronesia

NGHEAN, GREGORY YONG SOOL, religious organization administrator. Pres. Cath. Bishops' Conf. of Malaysia, Singapore and Brunei, Singapore. Office: Archbishop's House, 31 Victoria St, Singapore 0718, Singapore*

NGUELOUOLI, ABOUBAKAR, religious organization executive; b. Brazzaville, People's Republic of the Congo, Mar. 25, 1953; s. Yahaya and Amina; divorced, 1979; 1 child, Hafsah; m. Marié Nguelouoli, Oct. 6, 1991; 1 child, Salim. B.E.M.G., Brazzaville, 1972; diplome langue, U. Islamique, Saudi Arabia, 1978. Sec. gen. Jeunesse Musulnane, 1978-79; sec. gen. rels. exterieures Comité Islamique, 1979-88; pres. Comité Islamique du Congo, 1988—; fonctionnaire div. traduction interprètareat Ministere des Affairs Etraugèrs. Office: Conseil Islamique, Brazzaville BP55, People's Republic of the Congo

NIBBELINK, GARY WAYNE, minister; b. New Sharon, Iowa, July 3, 1944; s. Steven Evert and Gertrude Henriette (Vos) N.; m. JoAnne Ruth Vander Hart, Apr. 27, 1965; children: Steven, Susan, Darren, Allison. BA in Bible, Cen. Bible Coll., 1986; MA in Bible Lit., Assemblies of God Theol. Sem., 1988. Ordained to ministry Assemblies of God, 1990. Youth pastor Westport Assembly of God, Springfield, Mo., 1985-87; pastor 1st Assembly of God, Waterloo, Iowa, 1988—; dean acad. affairs, instr. Life Bible Inst., Waterloo, Iowa, 1991—; sect. III Sunday sch. rep. Iowa dist. Assemblies of God, Waterloo, 1990—. Staff sgt. Air NG, 1962-69. Mem. Black Hawk Assn. of Evangelicals (treas. 1990). Office: 1st Assembly of God 738 April St Waterloo IA 50702 *My greatest desire is to spend eternity with my children and grandchildren. If, during my ministry, I win hundreds to the Lord but lose one of them, I will feel I have failed.*

NICCUM, STEPHEN DUANE, minister; b. Muncie, Ind., Aug. 4, 1959; s. Donald Gordon Niccum and Margaret Ellen (Baker) Unger; m. Cheryl Diane Miller, Nov. 22, 1980; children: Benjamin Ryan, Stephanie Diane. BA, Anderson U., 1982; MDiv, Anderson Sch. Theology, 1988. Ordained to ministry Ch. of God, 1990. Assoc. pastor Shady Grove Ch. of God, Muncie, 1980-83, Eaton (Ind.) Ch. of God, 1983-86, First Ch. of God, East Wenatchee, Wash., 1989—. Office: 1st Ch of God 181 1st St SE East Wenatchee WA 98802 *It seems that so many exert such an awesome amount of energy trying to change the world. If we could focus that attention and energy on ourselves and our own families it would make for a better tomorrow for us and our families, and for all those whom we are so desperately seeking change.*

NICHOLAS, ARCHBISHOP, religious organization administrator. Adminstr. Russian Orth. Ch. Can., Edmonton, Alta. Office: Russian Orthodox Ch Can, 9566-101 Ave Ste 303, Edmonton, AB Canada T5H 0B4*

NICHOLAS, BISHOP (RICHARD G. SMISKO), bishop; b. Perth Amboy, N.J., Feb. 23, 1936; s. Andrew and Anna (Totin) S. Grad., Christ the Saviour Sem., Johnstown, Pa., 1959; student, Patriarchal Theol. Acad., Istanbul, Turkey; BA, U. Youngstown, 1961; BTh, U. Pitts. Ordained priest Am. Carpatho-Russian Orthodox Greek Cath. Diocese, 1959. Pastor Sts. Peter and Paul Ch., Windber, 1959-62; prefect of discipline, tchr. Christ the Saviour Sem., Johnstown, 1963-65; pastor Sts. Peter and Paul Ch., Homer City, 1965-71, St. Michael's Ch., Clymer, 1971-72, St. Nicholas Ch., N.Y.C., 1972-78; elevated to archimandrite Am. Carpatho-Russian Orthodox Greek Cath. Diocese, 1976; abbot Monastery of Annunciation, Tuxedo Park, N.Y., 1978-82; elected titular bishop of Amissos, aux. bishop Ukrainian Orthodox Diocese of Ecumenical Patriarchate, 1983; consecrated bishop Am. Carpatho-Russian Orthodox Greek Cath. Diocese, 1985, bishop, 1985—; asst. Christ the Saviour Cathedral, 1963-65; chmn. XIV Diocesan Coun., New Brunswick, N.J., 1985, XV Diocesan Coun., Pitts., 1991. Office: 312 Garfield St Johnstown PA 15906

NICHOLAS, DAVID ROBERT, minister, academic administrator; b. L.A., May 10, 1941; s. Robert Grant and Pearl Elizabeth (Pickard) N.; m. Donna Lynn Roberts, June 28, 1969; children: Joy Lynn, Faith Elizabeth. AB, Azusa Pacific U., 1963; MS, U. So. Calif., 1967; MDiv., L.A. Bapt. Theol. Sem., 1966; ThM, Talbot Theol. Sem., 1971; ThD, Grace Theol. Seminary, 1982. Ordained to ministry Gen. Assn. Regular Bapt. Chs., 1970. Dir. admissions, mem. faculty L.A. Bapt. Coll., Newhall, Calif., 1966-71; dean, pres. Van Nuys (Calif.) Christian Coll., 1972-76; pastor Tri-Lakes Bapt. Ch., Columbia City, Ind., 1977-78; acad. dean, assoc. prof. Southwestern Coll., Phoenix, 1978-80; sr. pastor, acad. supt. Grace Bapt. Ch., Yuba City, 1980-82; sr. pastor Placerita Bapt. Ch., Newhall, 1982-84; pres., prof. theology Shasta Bible Coll., Redding, Calif., 1985—; chmn. Greater Redding Area Christian Edn. Conv., 1988—; trustee Regular Bapt. Conf. So. Calif., 1983-85, pres. 1963-65; dir. Bapt. Youth Assn. So. Calif., 1969-71. Author: Foundations of Biblical Inerrancy, 1978, What's A Woman to Do...In The Church?, 1979, Church Discipline: Option or Obligation, 1991; contbr. articles to religious jours.; recordings include Trombone Testimonies, 1990; host broadcast program Truth for Today, 1988—, Bible Answer Man, 1978-80. Trustee Christian Heritage Coll., El Cajon, Calif., 1981-85; mem. steering com. Calif. Activists Network, Los Altos, Calif., 1991; del. Conf. on the Preservation of the Family, 1991; gov. Am. Coalition for Trad. Values, Washington, 1984; chaplain Los Angeles County Bd. Suprs., 1984. Recipient Svc. award Am. Legion, 1955. Mem. Evang. Theol. Soc., Creation Rsch. Soc., Kappa Tau Epsilon. Republican. Home: 8264 Taylor Ln Redding CA 96001 Office: Shasta Bible Coll 2980 Hartnell Ave Redding CA 96002

NICHOLS, ALBERT MYRON, minister; b. Creston, Iowa, Oct. 17, 1914; s. Albert Maurice and Lou (Myers) N.; m. Phyllis Cochran, June 28, 1939; children: Byron Albert, Phillip Garrett. AB, UCLA, 1936; BS, San Francisco Theol. Sem., 1940; DD, Occidental Coll., 1952. Ordained to ministry United Presbyn. Ch. in U.S.A., 1940. Pastor chs. North Hollywood, Calif., 1940-43; assoc. pastor Pasadena (Calif.) Presbyn. Ch., 1943-57; pastor 1st Presbyn. Ch., Pendleton, Oreg., 1957-82; ret. 1st Presbyn. Ch., Pendleton, 1982; chmn. gen. assembly com. on responsible marriage and parenthood United Presbyn. Ch. in U.S.A., 1959-62, mem. Bd. Christian Edn., 1969-72; mem. 1st coun. Synod of Pacific; moderator Oreg. Synod, 1968, 69; stated clk. Ea. Oreg. Presbytery, 1975—. Pres. Pasadena Child Guidance Clinic, 1955-57; trustee San Francisco Theol. Sem., 1963-84; life trustee Lewis and Clark Coll., Portland, Oreg.; mem. Pendleton City Recreation Commn., 1965—; founding bd. dirs. Presbyn. Intercommunity Hosp., Whittier, Calif.; mem. State of Oreg. Health Coun., 1985-88, State Trauma Adv. Bd., 1987—; chmn. City of Pendleton Capital Improvements Commn., 1983—. Named 1st Citizen of Pendleton, 1984. Home: 1013 NW 12th St Pendleton OR 97801

NICHOLS, BILLY NICK, minister; b. Monroe, La., Apr. 3, 1938; s. Wilburn F. and Carrie (Estes) N.; m. Jeanette Broussard, July 27, 1957; 1 child, Steven Felder. BA, Bapt. Christian Coll., 1975; MA, Faith Bapt. Coll., 1978; DD, Bapt. Christian U., 1981. Ordained to ministry Bapt. Ch., 1961. Pastor Trinity Bapt. Ch., Texas City, Tex., 1965-75, Victory Bapt. Ch., Texarkana, Tex., 1975-79, Hamill Rd. Bapt. Ch., Chattanooga, 1979—; pres. Family Conflict Seminar, Hixson, Tenn., 1980—, Tenn. Bapt. Coll., Hixson, 1989—, Hamill Rd. Christian Sch., Hixson, 1979—. Sgt. U.S. Army, 1957-60. Mem. Tenn. Assn. Christian Schs. (treas. Chattanooga chpt. 1986—), Nat. Assn. Marriage and Family Counselors, Ark. Travelers. Republican. Home: 1863 Thrasher Pike Hixson TN 37343 Office: Hamill Rd Bapt Ch 1928 Hamill Rd Hixson TN 37343 *When the sun forgets to shine for someone along the way, I want to be a bright light at the end of their day. My desire is to burn out being a light for those in darkness.*

NICHOLS, DANIEL JOSEPH, minister; b. Detroit, Nov. 10, 1948; s. Reeder Clayton and Estella (Griggs) N.; m. Johnnie Marie Lundy, Apr. 17, 1970; 1 child, Joanna Marie. AA in Bus., Internat., 1983, BRE, 1984, ThM, 1984, DD, 1984. Ordained to ministry, Bapt. Ch., 1978. Asst. pastor Midfield (Ala.) Bapt. Ch., 1977-78; pastor Pine Haven Bapt. Ch., Shannon, Ala., 1978-79, Belview Bapt. Ch., Mcalla, Ala., 1979-81, Open Acres Bapt. Ch., Montgomery, Ala., 1981-82, Mt. Calvary Bapt. Ch., Tarrant, Ala., 1982-90, Adamsville (Ala.) Bapt. Ch., 1990—; Mem. Cook Springs Camp, Birmingham, Ala., 1986—, Stoner Adult Community, 1988—. Mem. Lions. Home: 3328 Wentwood Circle Adamsville AL 35005 Office: Adamsville Bapt Ch PO Box 250 Adamsville AL 35005

NICHOLS, DAVID EUGENE, minister, parochial school educator; b. Charleston, W.Va., Sept. 9, 1953; s. Paul E. and Mary J. (Anderson) N.; m. Rhonda M. Nichols, Sept. 17, 1971; children: Jonathan D., Christina R., Jessica N., Christopher E. BTh, Internat. Sem., Orlando, Fla., 1984, DDiv, 1984. Ordained to ministry Ind. Full Gospel Ch., 1984. Acct. Kan County Bd. Edn., Charleston, W.Va., 1978-84; dir., founder Nichols Family Ministries, Elkview, W.Va., 1981—; adminstr. Victory Christian Acad., Clendenin, W.Va., 1986—; pastor Victory Chapel, Clendenin, 1987—; dir. Elk Valley Improvement Coun., Clendenin, 1990—. Mem. Clendenin Ministerial Assn. Avocation: musician, computer hobbyist. Home: 378 Frame Rd Elkview WV 25071 Office: Victory Chapel Elk River Rd S PO Box 1042 Clendenin WV 25045

NICHOLS, DAVID LAWRENCE, religion educator, religious institution executive; b. Elkhorn, Wis., Nov. 7, 1947; s. Lawrence W. and Athalie (Wedell) N.; m. Joyce I. Carr, Feb. 2, 1969 (div. Jan. 1984); children: Joshua D., Amanda J.; m. Linnea A. Berg, Jan. 2, 1988. BA cum laude, Harvard U., 1969; MDiv, No. Bapt. Sem., Lombard, Ill., 1977, postgrad., 1983—. Ordained to ministry Bapt. Ch., 1977. Bus. mgr. Good News Circle, Elgin, Ill., 1972-76; dir. recruitment/fin. aid No. Bapt. Sem., Lombard, 1978-80; pastor First Bapt. Ch., Westchester, Ill., 1980-84; asst. to pres. for devel. No. Bapt. Theol. Sem., Lombard, 1984-86, v.p. for bus. adminstrn., 1986—; treas. Soc. Profl. Ch. Leaders, Chgo., 1979-81. Treas. Cabrini Green Legal Aid Clinic, Chgo., 1988-91. Home: 2420 Mayfair Westchester IL 60154 Office: Northern Bapt Theol Sem 660 E Butterfield Lombard IL 60148 *Now is the time for vision and leadership: from the seminary for the church, from the church for the world.*

NICHOLS, DELTON, chaplain; b. Canton, Miss., Sept. 21, 1953; s. Walter Jr. and Jodie Irene (Barnes) N.; m. Laura Nadine McKoy, June 14, 1980; 1 child, Tiffany. BA, Morehouse Coll., 1975, MDiv, 1978; ThM, Princeton Theol. Seminary, 1988. Ordained to ministry Nat. Bapt. Conv., 1974. Commd. capt. U.S. Army, 1978, advanced through grades to maj., 1986; battalion chaplain U.S. Army, Fed. Republic Germany, 1978-86; brigade chaplain U.S. Army, Fort Jackson, 1986-87; instr. ethics U.S. Army Armor Sch., Fort Knox, Ky., 1988-91; brigade chaplaine 501st Mil Intelligence Brigade, Korea. Article editor: Turret, 1988-91; contbr. articles to jours. Mem. Assn. of U.S. Army. Office: US Army Armor School Command and Staff Dept Fort Knox KY 40121

NICHOLS, FRANCIS WILLIAM, religion educator; b. St. Paul, Aug. 3, 1930; s. Francis Wilber and Genevieve Cecile (Hoffmann) N.; m. Jane Therese Gillispie, June 19, 1969; children: Gregory, Matthew, Genevieve. BA, St. Mary's Coll., Winona, Minn., 1952, MA, 1955; MA, Loyola U., Chgo., 1959; LSR, Lateran U., Rome, 1964; D.esTh., Strasbourg (France) U., 1969. High sch. tchr. Roman Cath. schs., Chgo., Memphis, Glencoe, Mo., 1952-61; asst. prof. Christian Bros. Coll., Memphis, 1964-67; asst. prof. St. Louis U., 1969-75, assoc. prof., 1975—. Roman Catholic. Office: St Louis U 3634 Lindell Saint Louis MO 63108

NICHOLS, GEORGE LEON, JR., minister; b. Phila., Mar. 7, 1938; s. George Leon Sr. and Elva Grace (Berger) N.; m. K. Diane Hunt, Sept. 21, 1963; children: Katherine J., Stephen J. BS in Bible, Phila. Coll. Bible, 1961; postgrad., Reformed Episcopal Sem., Phila., 1961-63; DD, Fla. Bible Coll, Hollywood, 1976; D of Ministry, Luther Rice Sem., Jacksonville, Fla., 1979; MA, Liberty U., 1988. Ordained to ministry Bapt. Ch., 1961; cert. Christian counselor. Pastor Nicetown Bapt. Ch., Phila., 1961-64, 1st Bapt. Ch., Elmer, N.J., 1964-67; sr. pastor Pennsville Bapt. Ch., Mt. Pleasant, Pa., 1967-87, Faith Bapt. Ch., Wilmington, Del., 1987—; trustee Phila. Coll. Bible, Langhorne, Pa., 1987; trustee, v.p. Out-island Ministries, St. Petersburg, Fla., 1973; bd. dirs. Grace Ind. Bapt. Mission, Sellersville, Pa., 1987, Camp Haluwasa, Hammonton, N.J. Mem. AACD, United Assn. Christian Counselors (bd. dirs., pres. Harrisburg, Pa. chpt.), Bibl. Archeol. Soc., Evang. Theol. Soc. Home: 2707 Burnley Rd Wilmington DE 19808 Office: Faith Bapt Ch 4210 Limestone Rd Wilmington DE 19808 *To enjoy life we must have a theology that is practical and practiced.*

NICHOLS, HUEY PAUL, minister; b. Irwin County, Ga., Oct. 3, 1934; s. Grady Paul and Mary Mildred (Godwin) N.; m. Patricia Ann Starnes, Mar. 27, 1971; children: Keith Paul, Jeffery Scott, Karen Elaine, Tammy Leighann, Mark Stephen, Matthew Joel, Donna Jean. Student in acct., So. Bus. U., 1953; AA, Emmanuel Bapt. Coll., 1968, BA, 1969. Ordained to ministry So. Missionary Bapt. Ch., 1972. Pastor Irwinville (Ga.) Bapt. Ch., 1972-73, Bethlehem Bapt. Ch., Fitzgerald, Ga., 1974-75, 86-88, St. Illa Bapt. Ch., Douglas, Ga., 1976-83, 1st Freewill Bapt. Ch., Douglas, 1984, Pleasant Hill Bapt. Ch., Rebecca, Ga., 1989—; tchr. Bible class Atlanta City Stockade, 1965-68, Atlanta Fed. Prison, 1967-68; chmn. evangelism Smyrna Bapt. Assn., Douglas, 1980-81; missions vol. Ga. Bapt. Convention, India, Liberia, Africa, Panama, 1991. With U.S. Army, 1955-57. Recipient of Acommedation, So. Bapt. Convention, 1988—. Home: Rte 2 Box 2025 Fitzgerald GA 31750

NICHOLS, LARRY A., JR., minister, author; b. Providence, July 12, 1956; s. Larry A. and Joyce G. (Spendolini) N.; m. Zelia Marie Coelho, Mar. 27, 1976; children: Melissa Ann, Charissa Grace, Alicia Sadie. BA, Evangel Coll., Springfield, Mo., 1982; MDiv, Yale U., 1986; postgrad., Concordia Sem., Ft. Wayne, Ind., 1987. Vicar St. Peter's Luth. Ch., Norwalk, Conn., 1987-88; pastor Our Redeemer Luth. Ch., Greenville, R.I., 1988—; dir., chmn. Worship Commn. New England LCMS, 1990—.

NICHOLS, TERESA ANN, lay worker; b. Norfolk, Va., Oct. 8, 1956; d. Charles Edward and Mary Maxine (Blake) N. AS, Floyd Jr. Coll., 1987; BS in Recreation, W. Ga. Coll., 1991. Lic. therapeutic recreation specialist. Youth vol. Presbyn. Ch., Rome, Ga., 1984—, Sunday Sch. tchr., 1989-91; lay min. Cherokee Presbyn. Ch., Rome, Ga., 1990—; therapeutic recreation specialist Residential Treatment Unit, Drugs and Alcohol Rehab., Cedartown, Ga., 1991; intern Camp Catskills, Liberty, N.Y., summer 1991. Named. Vol. Yr., Muscular Dystrophy Assn., Birmingham, Ala., 1979, Children's Hosp., Birmingham, 1979, Cerebral Palsy, Anniston, Ala., 1980, Vol. of Month, Easter Seals, Birmingham, 1991. Fellow W. Ga. Pks. and Recreation Assn., W. Ga. Coll. Recreation Club, Presbyns. in Action. Home: 104 Forrest Ln Cedartown GA 30125 Office: Residential Treatment Unit US Hwy 27 N Cedartown GA 30125

NICHOLS, TIMOTHY ROBERT, minister; b. Barberton, Ohio, Oct. 19, 1956; s. Herbert Donald and Pearl Betty (Smith) N.; m. Libby Marie Sprout, Dec. 29, 1979; children: Ashley Marie, Robert Keith, Eric Timothy. BA, Harding U., 1981; MS, Frostburg State U., 1989. Minister Ch. of Christ, Barrackville, W.Va., 1981-83, Keyser, W.Va., 1983—; instr. Potomac State Coll. of W.Va. Univ., 1991—; supervised psychologist, pvt. practice of Stephen M. Townsend, Romney, W.Va., 1991—; bd. dirs. W.Va. Christian Youth Camp, Harrisville. Author: Affirmations that Cannot Stand, 1985; contbr. articles to profl. jours. Pres. Burlington, W.Va. Community PTA, 1990-91. With U.S. Army, 1975-78. Recipient Wilda Petenbrink Rsch. Assistantship, Frostburg State U., 1988-89, Scholastic All-Am. Nat. award in Psychology, U.S. Achievement Acad., 1988-89; named to Outstanding Young Men of Am., 1989. Mem. Am. Assn. Christian Counseling, Assn. for Rsch. in Values and Social Change, Am. Assn. for Counseling and Devel., Am. Mental Health Counselors Assn., Pres.'s Ambassador for Christian Edn. Republican. Home: Rte 1 Box 211 Burlington WV 26710 Office: Church of Christ PO Box 512 Keyser WV 26726 *Nothing in life is more important than the search for truth. Divine Truth is revealed in the Scriptures. This Truth is supported by all other "truths" and towers above them.*

NICHOLS, VANCE EVERETT, minister, principal; b. San Diego, Feb. 3, 1959; s. Kermit Don Nichols and Veora Rachel (Huffman) Nichols-Wilson; m. Janet Louise Perkins, June 9, 1984; children: Joel Vance, Joshua Paul. BS in Radio and TV, San Diego State U., 1986. Producer, creative cons. Horizon Gate Prodns., Spring Valley, Calif., 1985-86; prin. sch. ministries Calvary So. Bapt. Ch./Calvary Christian Schs., San Diego, 1986-89; elem. prin., dir. devel. Riverside (Calif.) Christian High Sch., 1989—; pastor Tamarind Ave. Bapt. Ch., Fontana, Calif., 1989-91; arbitrator Christian Conciliation Ct., San Diego, 1989; seminar leader Assn. Christian Schs. Internat., Anaheim, Calif., 1990—. Wrote, produced, and directed various motion pictures; author numerous short stories and poems. Active Nat. Right to Life, San Diego, Riverside, 1987—. Recipient numerous domestic, internat. film and scholastic journalism awards. Mem. Internat. Fellowship Christian Sch. Adminstrs., Calvary Arrowhead So. Bapt. Assn. (exec. bd. 1989-91). Republican. Home: 3635 Verde St Riverside CA 92504 Office: Riverside Christian High Sch 3532 Monroe St Riverside CA 92504 *If we as believers in the Lord Jesus Christ sincerely desire to make more and better disciples in the rising storm of these last days, we will only accomplish the mission if we have a faith that will walk on water.*

NICHOLS, WILLIAM HOWARD, JR., minister; b. Nashville, Sept. 6, 1942; s. William Howard Sr. and Helen Bernice (Jones) N.; m. Jacqueline Juanette Johnson, Feb. 3, 1968; children: Timothy Howard, Jerald Lorenzo (dec.), Erika Michelle, Eric David. BS, Ky. State U., 1965; MDiv, Memphis Theol. Sem., 1991. Ordained to ministry Presbyn. Ch., 1988. Host, producer Love Express Ministry Sta. WPTA-TV, Ft. Wayne, Ind., 1973-75; assoc. min. New Hope Bapt. Ch., Evansville, Ind., 1975-77; founder, pastor Love Chapel Ch. of God in Christ, Nashville, 1978-88; organizing pastor Whitehaven Second Cumberland Presbyn. Ch., Memphis, 1988—; co-chmn. bd. Christian edn. New Hopewell Presbytery, 1991—. With U.S. Army, 1965-67. Home: 3857 Apricot Cove Memphis TX 38115 Office: Whitehaven Second Cumberland Presbyn Ch 524 E Raines Rd Memphis TN 38109-8331 *There just may be a window in the next decade in which the nation can successfully address it's unresolved racial tensions. I am preparing to offer guidance for such an opportunity.*

NICHOLSON, BETTY, religious organization administrator. Sec. Fundamental Meth. Ch. Inc., Springfield, Mo. Office: Fundamental Meth Ch Inc Rte 2 Box 397 Ash Grove MO 65604*

NICHOLSON, JOHN WAYNE, JR., youth minister; b. Tuscaloosa, Ala., Feb. 1, 1967; s. John Wayne Nicholson, Sr. and Patricia Ann (Sherril) Parten; m. Vanessa Jean Junkin, Sept. 17, 1989; 1 child, Jeremy Wade. BA, Samford U., Birmingham, Ala., 1989. Interim min. of music Little Sandy Bapt. Ch., Tuscaloosa, Ala., 1985; interim min. of music and youth Eutaw (Ala.) Bapt. Ch., 1986-87; min. of youth Meadow Brook Bapt. Ch., Birmingham, Ala., 1987-89, First Bapt. Ch. of Pinson (Ala., 1989—; nat. conf. leader Ridgecrest Nat. Conf. Ctr., Nashville, 1989; conf. leader Ridgecrest Bapt. Ch., Birmingham, 1990. Chaplain Fellowship of Christian Athletes, Pinson, Ala., 1989—; vol. Chalkville Ala.) Youth Svcs. Sch., 1990—. Republican. Home: 4561 Bud Holmes Rd Pinson AL 35126 Office: First Baptist Ch of Pinson 4036 Spring St Pinson AL 35126 *I find that the essence of life is found in the simple gifts which God gives. Far too often we seek Him in the big and boisterous, yet I find Him consistently in the simple and quiet. It is unfortunate that we are all so busy doing things which have no eternal significance.*

NICHOLSON, ROY S., clergyman; b. Walhalla, S.C., July 12, 1903; s. Samuel Dendy and Beulah Young (Lindsay) N.; m. Ethel Macy, June 26, 1924 (dec. Dec. 1985); children: Roy S., Lee Huffman; m. Winifred Bisbing, Oct. 7, 1986. Student, Wesleyan Meth. Acad. and Coll., Central, S.C., 1918-24; D.D., Houghton Coll., 1944; Th.B., Central Sch. Religion, 1956; Litt.D., Central Wesleyan Coll., 1981; L.H.D., Bartlesville Wesleyan Coll., 1985. Ordained to ministry Wesleyan Meth. Ch., 1925; tchr. N.C., 1924; pastor East Radford, Va., 1925-26, Long Shoals, N.C., 1926-30, Kannapolis, N.C., 1930-35, Brooksville, Fla., 1969-74; supt. Wesleyan Youth Work, 1934-35, Sunday sch. sec. and editor, 1935-39, home missionary sec., 1939-43; mem. bd. adminstrn. Wesleyan Meth. Ch., 1935-59, 63-68, chmn., 1947-59; v.p. Wesleyan Meth. Ch. Am., 1939-47, pres., 1947-59, pres. emeritus, 1959-68; prof. Bible Central Wesleyan Coll., 1959-68, chmn. div. religion, 1959-68; Editor Wesleyan Meth., Wesleyan Youth, 1943-47; Am. counselor Immanuel Gen. Mission, Japan, 1964—; bd. dirs. Wesleyan Bible Conf. Assn., 1970—; gen. supt. emeritus Wesleyan Ch., 1972—, Wesleyan Bible Conf. Assn., 1981—. Author: Wesleyan Methodism in the South, 1933, History of the Wesleyan Methodist Church, 1951, Notes on True Holiness, 1952, Arminian Emphases, 1962, A Valid Theology for Our Day, 1963, Commentary on The Pastoral Epistles, 1965, Commentary on The First Epistle of Peter, 1969, Studies in Church Doctrine, True Holiness: The Wesleyan-Arminian Emphasis (revised edit.), 1985; also articles; contbr. to: Aldersgate Doctrinal Series, 1963; other publs. in field. Chmn. bd. trustees Houghton, Central, Miltonvale and Marion colls., 1947-59; adv. council Ky. Mountain Bible Inst., World Gospel Mission. Recipient Disting. Alumnus of Yr. award Central Wesleyan Coll. Alumni Assn., 1973. Mem. Nat. Holiness Assn. (bd. adminstrn. 1955-64, 70—, rec. sec. 1960-64). Home: 1905-K N Centennial St High Point NC 27262

NICHOLSON, SHIRLEY JEAN, editor; b. Little Rock, Jan. 8, 1925; d. Franc I. and Shirley (Parish) Mullen; m. William M. Nicholson, Feb. 17, 1957; children: Carol Ward, Patricia Nicholson-Hedberg. BA, UCLA, 1957; postgrad., Montclair (N.J.) State U., 1976. Cert. elem. tchr., N.J.; cert. tchr. spl. edn. Sr. editor Theosophical Publ. House, Wheaton, Ill., 1981—. Author: Ancient Wisdom—Modern Insight; compiler: Shamanism, The Goddess Reawakening, Karma: Rhythmic Return to Harmony. Vol. counselor Hospice of DuPage, Glen Ellyn, Ill., 1989—. Mem. Am. Acad. Religion, Noetic Inst., Assn. Transpersonal Psychology. Mem. Theosophical Soc. in Am. Office: Theosophical Publ House 306 W Geneva Rd Wheaton IL 60187

NICHTING, ANN LOUISE, religious education educator; b. Portsmouth, Ohio, Oct. 19, 1940; d. Bernard Anthony and Jane (McCormick) Glockner; m. Theodore William Nichting, July 19, 1969; children: Jennifer Ann, Stephen Christopher. BS in Elem. Edn., Ohio State U., 1967; MEd, Ohio U., 1989. Tchr. various Cath. schs., 1961-71; tchr. religious edn. various chs., 1968—; dir. religious edn. St. Bernadette Ch., Lancaster, Ohio, 1990—; mem. Diocese of Columbus Pastoral Plan, 1985-87. Author poetry. Bd. dirs. YMCA, Jackson, Ohio, 1975-85. Mem. Diocesan Assn. Religious Educators, Ohio Dir. Religious Educators Orgn., Jackson Women's League (pres. 1975-76). Home: 4 Pleasant View Jackson OH 45640 Office: St Bernadette Ch 1843 Wheeling Rd Lancaster OH 43130

NICKELSBURG, GEORGE WILLIAM ELMER, minister, religion educator; b. San Jose, Calif., Mar. 15, 1934; s. George William Elmer and Elsie Louise (Schwab) N.; m. Marilyn Luce Miertschin, Aug. 28, 1965; children: Jeanne Marie, Michael John. Student, Concordia Jr. Coll., Bronxville, N.Y., 1951-53; BA, Valparaiso U., 1955; postgrad., Washington U., St. Louis, 1956-57; BD, Concordia Sem., St. Louis, 1960; STM, Concordia Sem., 1962; postgrad., Am. Sch. Oriental Rsch., 1963-64; ThD, Harvard U., 1968. Ordained to ministry Luth. Ch., 1966. Pastor Good Shepherd Luth. Ch., Akron, Ohio, 1966-69; asst. prof. U. Iowa Sch. Religion, Iowa City, 1969, assoc. prof., 1972-77, prof., 1977—, dir. Sch. Religion, 1990—; vis. scholar Institum Judaicum Delitzschianum, Munster, Fed. Republic Germany, 1974. Author: Resurrection, Immortality and Eternal Life in Intertestamental Judaism, 1972, Jewish Literature between the Bible and the Mishnah, 1981; also articles. Guggenheim fellow, 1977-78, fellow NEH, 1984-85, Netherlands Inst. Advanced Study, 1980-81. Mem. Soc. Bibl. Lit. (chmn. pseudepigrapha group 1973-80), Soc. N.T. Studies, Cath. Bibl. Assn., Am. Acad. Religion. Home: 1713 E Court St Iowa City IA 52245 Office: U Iowa Dept Religion Iowa City IA 52242

NICKLE, DENNIS EDWIN, electronics engineer, church deacon; b. Sioux City, Iowa, Jan. 30, 1936; s. Harold Bateman and Helen Cecilia (Killackey) N. BS in Math., Fla. State U., 1961. Reliability mathematician Pratt & Whitney Aircraft Co., W. Palm Beach, Fla., 1961-63; br. supr. Melpar Inc., Falls Church, Va., 1963-66; prin. mem. tech. staff Xerox Data Systems, Rockville, Md., 1966-70; sr. tech. officer WHO, Washington, 1970-76; software quality assurance mgr. Melpar div. E-Systems, Inc., Falls Church, 1976—; ordained deacon Roman Catholic Ch., 1979. Chief judge for computers Fairfax County Regional Sci. Fair, 1964-88; mem. Am. Security Council; scoutmaster, commr. Boy Scouts Am., 1957—; youth custodian Fairfax County Juvenile Ct., 1973-87; chaplain No. Va. Regional Juvenile Detention Home, 1978-88; moderator Nocturnal Adoration Soc.; parochial St. Michael's Ch., Annandale, Va., 1979-89, Christ the Redeemer, Sterling, Va., 1990—. Served with U.S. Army, 1958-60. Recipient Eagle award, Silver award, Silver Beaver award, other awards Boy Scouts Am.; Ad Altare Dei, St. George Emblem, Diocese of Richmond. Mem. Assn. Computing Machinery, Computer Soc., Am. Soc. For Quality Control, CODSIA (mem. working group), ORLANDO II (Govt./industry working group), Old Crows Assn., Rolm Mil-Spec Computer Users Group (internat. pres.), Nat. Security Indsl. Assn. (convention com. 1985—, software quality assurance subcom., regional membership chmn. 1981-89, nat. exec. vice-chmn. 1989—), IEEE (sr., mem. standards working group in computers 1983—), Hewlett Packard Users Group, Smithsonian Assn., Internat. Platform Assn., NRA (endowment), Alpha Phi Omega (life), Sigma Phi Epsilon. Club: KC (4 deg.). Author: Stress in Adolescents, 1986; co-author: Handbook for Handling Non-Productive Stress in Adolescence, Standard For Software Life Cycle Processes, IMPEESA Junior Leader Training Guide. Office: 7700 Arlington Blvd Falls Church VA 22046

NICOLETTI, GEOFFREY LOUIS, educator; b. Phila., July 8, 1949; s. Louis Joseph and Rhoe Rosaria (Cirillo) N.; m. Marlene Evelyn Kurtz, Oct. 2, 1982; 1 child, Michael. BA in English, LaSalle Coll., 1975; MA in Theology, Villanova U., 1981. Educator Melrose Acad., Elkins Park, Pa., 1981-83, Our Lady Help of Christians, Abington, Pa., 1983-85, LaSalle Coll. High Sch., Wyndmoor, Pa., 1985—; lectr. Jung Inst., Kusnacht, Switzerland, 1984. Mem. com. Upper Moreland Sch. Bd., Montgomery County, Pa., 1990—; student Freedoms Found., Valley Forge, 1987-90; author Lancaster Mennonite Hist. Soc., 1987. Mem. Nat. Cath. Edn. Assn., Am. Acad. Religion, Montgomery County Community Coll. Writers Group. Office: LaSalle Coll High Sch 8605 Cheltenham Ave Wyndmoor PA 19118

NIDA, EUGENE ALBERT, minister, author; b. Oklahoma City, Nov. 11, 1914; s. Richard Eugene and Alma Ruth (McCullough) N.; m. Althea Lucille Sprague, June 19, 1943. AB, UCLA, 1936; MA, U. So. Calif., 1939; PhD, U. Mich., 1943; DD (hon.), Eastern Baptist Sem., Phila., 1956, So. Calif. Bapt. Sem., 1959; ThD, U. Muenster, Fed. Republic Germany, 1967; LittD (hon.), Heriot-Watt U., Scotland, 1974, Brigham Young U., 1979; PhilD (hon.), U. Chile, Santiago, 1980; LHD (hon.), La Salle U., Philippines, 1985; ThD (hon.), U. Iceland, 1986. Prof. linguistics Summer Inst. Linguistics U. Okla., 1937-53; ordained to ministry Bapt. Ch., 1943; exec. sec. translations Am. Bible Soc., 1943-80; coordinator research in translations United Bible Socs., 1970-80; cons. translations Am. Bible Soc. and; with United Bible Socs., since 1981. Author: Bible Translating, 1947, Morphology, 1949, Learning a Foreign Language, 1950, God's Word in Man's Language, 1952, Customs and Cultures, 1954, Message and Mission, 1960, Translator's Handbook of the Gospel of Mark, 1962, Toward a Science of Translating, 1964, Religion Across Cultures, 1968, Theory and Practice of Translation, 1969, Componential Analysis of Meaning, 1975, Exploring Semantic Structures, 1975, Language Structure and Translation, 1975, Good News for Everyone, 1977, Signs, Sense and Translation, 1982, Translating Meaning, 1983, Language, Culture, and Translating, 1991; co-author: Translator's Handbook of the Acts of the Apostles, 1972, Translator's Handbook on the Epistle to the Romans, 1973, Translator's Handbook on Ruth, 1973, Translator's Handbook on 1-2 Thessalonians, 1975, Translator's Handbook on Galatians, 1976, Translator's Handbook on Philippians, 1977, Translator's Handbook on Colossians and Philemon, 1977, Translator's Handbook on First Peter, 1979, Translator's Handbook on the Gospel of John, 1981, Meaning Across Cultures, 1981, Style and Discourse, 1983, On Translation, 1985, From One Language to Another, 1986, Lexical Semantics of the Greek New Testament, 1991; editor: Book of One Thousand Tongues, 1972; co-editor: Greek-English Lexicon of the New Testament: based on Semantic Domains. Recipient Diamond Jubilee award Inst. Linguistics, London, 1976; Alexander Gode medal Am. Translators Assn., 1977; named Fulbright Disting. Prof. Maurice Thorez Inst., Moscow, 1989. Mem. Am. Assn. Applied Linguistics, Linguistic Assn. Can. and U.S., Linguistic Soc. Am. (pres. 1968), Internat. Assn. Semiotic Studies, Am. Anthrop. Assn., Soc. for Textual Scholarship (pres. 1987-88), Soc. N.T. Studies, Soc. Bibl. Lit. and Exegesis, Phi Beta Kappa, Pi Gamma Mu. Home: 19 Ingleton Circle Kennett Square PA 19348 Office: 1865 Broadway New York NY 10023

NIEBUHR, RICHARD REINHOLD, theological educator; b. Chgo., Mar. 9, 1926; s. Helmut Richard and Florence Marie (Mittendorff) N.; m. Nancy Mullican, Oct. 14, 1950; children—Richard Gustav, Sarah Louise. A.B. magna cum laude, Harvard U., 1947; B.D. summa cum laude, Union Theol. Sem., N.Y.C., 1950; Ph.D., Yale U., 1955. Ordained to ministry United Ch. of Christ. Minister 1st Ch. of Chirst, Cornwall, Conn., 1950-52; lectr. religion Vassar Coll., Poughkeepsie, N.Y., 1954-56; asst. prof. Harvard Div. Sch., Cambridge, Mass., 1956-59; assoc. prof. Harvard Div. Sch., 1959-63, prof., 1963—, now Hollis prof. div., chmn. com. on study of religion, 1966-72, 73-78. Author: Resurrection and Historical Reason, 1957, Schleiermacher on Christ and Religion, 1964, Experiential Religion, 1972, Streams of Grace, 1983. Fulbright research scholar, Heidelberg, Fed. Republic Germany, 1958. Fellow Am. Acad. Arts and Scis.; mem. Am. Acad. Religion, Am. Theol. Soc., Phi Beta Kappa. Democrat. Avocation: photography. Office: Harvard U Div Sch 45 Francis Ave Cambridge MA 02138

NIEDERGESES, JAMES D., bishop; b. Lawrenceburg, Tenn., Feb. 2, 1917. Student, St. Bernard Coll., St. Ambrose Coll., Mt. St. Mary Sem. of West, Athenaeum of Ohio. Ordained priest Roman Cath. Ch., 1944. Pastor Our Lady of Perpetual Help, Chattanooga, 1962-73, Sts. Peter and Paul Parish, 1973-75; bishop of Nashville, 1975—; mem. personnel bd. Diocese of Nashville. Office: 2400 21st Ave S Nashville TN 37212

NIEDNER, FREDERICK ARTHUR, JR., theology educator; b. Lander, Wyo., May 5, 1945; s. Frederick Arthur and Esther Margaret (Harting) N.; m. Dawn Ellen Morgan May 13, 1972 (div. July 1983); m. Barbara Louise Crumpacker, July 26, 1986; children: Joshua Morgan, Rebekah Joy, Micah Frederick. BA, Concordia Coll., Ft. Wayne, Ind., 1967; MDiv, Concordia Sem., St. Louis, 1971, STM, 1973; DTh, Christ Sem., St. Louis, 1979. Assoc. prof. Valparaiso (Ind.) U., 1973—; bd. dirs. Internat. Walther League, Chgo., 1985-89, Wheat Ridge Found., Chgo., 1989—. Author: Keeping the Faith, 1980; contbr. articles to profl. jours. Recipient O.P. Kretzman award Wheat Ridge Found., Chicago, 1986. Mem. Soc. of Bibl. Lit., Chgo. Soc. Bibl. Rsch., Nat. Assn. Profs. of Hebrew, Lutheran Deaconess Assn. Democrat. Avocations: baseball and soccer coaching, gardening, cooking. Home: 1402 Cross Creek Rd Valparaiso IN 46383 Office: Valparaiso U Valparaiso IN 46383

NIELSEN, ALBERT KRAMER, clergyman; b. Muhlenburg Mission, Liberia, Nov. 5, 1920; s. Carl Henry and Dorothea Anna (Kramer) N.; m. Mabel Inez Ruffner, June 25, 1950; children: Karl, Dorothy, Hal. BS, Madison Coll., 1953; MA, George Peabody Coll. for Tchrs, 1955. Ordained to ministry Adventist Ch. as elder, 1956; lic. gen. radiotelephone FCC. Chaplain, religious educator, sec. governing bd. Rural Life Found., Inc., Savannah, Tenn., 1954—; chaplain Harbert Hills Nursing Home, Savannah, 1969—; sta. mgr. Sta. WDNX Ednl. Radio, Olive Hill, Tenn., 1973—. Explorer post advisor, com. mem. Boy Scouts Am., 1972—. With USAAF, World War II; pub. affairs officer Tenn. Def. Force, 1988—. Decorated Am. Theater ribbon, Victory medal. Mem. NSPE, Hardin Amateur Radio Emergency Svc. Office: Harbert Hills Acad Rte 2 Box 212 Savannah TN 38372 *We have not yet used all our strength until we allow God to help us. Don't bother to give God orders, just report for duty.*

NIELSEN, KIRSTEN, theology educator; b. Svendborg, Fyn, Denmark, Oct. 12, 1943; d. Verner Gustav Thorvald and Else Marie (Foss) Schroll; m. Leif Nielsen, July 29, 1967. MA in Religious Studies, French, Aarhus U., Denmark, 1970, PhD in Theology, 1976, ThD, 1985. Asst. prof. Inst. Religionsvidenskab, U. Aarhus, 1971-76; assoc. prof. Inst. Religionsstudier, U. Aarhus, 1976—; dean of faculty U. Aarhus, 1984-89; mem. Com. for Translating the Old Testament into Modern Danish, 1976-92. Mem. Dansk Teologisk Soc. (bd. dirs.), Religionsvidenskabeligt Tidsskrift (bd. dirs.). Lutheran. Avocations: literature, music. Home: Vågøgade 5, 8200 Aarhus Jutland, Denmark Office: Det Teologiske Fakultet, Nordre Ringgade, 8000 Aarhus Jutland, Denmark

NIELSEN, NIELS CHRISTIAN, JR., theology educator; b. Long Beach, Calif., June 2, 1921; s. Niels Hansen and Frances (Nofziger) N.; m. Erika Kreuth, May 10, 1958; children—Camilla Regina, Niels Albrecht. BA, George Pepperdine Coll., L.A., 1942; BD, Yale U., 1946, PhD, 1951. Ordained to ministry Meth. Ch., 1946. Pastor Woodbury (Conn.) Meth. Ch., 1944-46; instr. religion Yale U., New Haven, 1948-51; faculty Rice U., Houston, 1951—; now J. Newton Rayzor prof. religious studies. Rice U., 1982-83, prof. emeritus, 1991—; Amax presdl. prof. humanities Colo. Sch. Mines, Golden, 1982-83. Author: Philosophy and Religion in Contemporary Japan, 1957, Geistige Länderkunde USA, 1960, A Layman Looks at World Religions, 1962, God in Education, 1966, Solzhenitsyn's Religion (Nelson), 1975, The Religion of Jimmy Carter, 1977, The Crisis of Human Rights, 1978, Religions of the World, 1982, Revolution and Religious Roots in Eastern Europe, 1991; contbr. articles to profl. jours. Mem. Am. Acad. Religion, Am. Philos. Soc., Am. Soc. Study Religion (sec. 1977-89), Soc. for Values in Higher Edn. Democrat. Home: 2424 Swift St Houston TX 77030

NIELSON, JOHN WILLIAMS, minister; b. Shawnee Mission, Kans., Aug. 30, 1968; s. John M. and Janice (Williams) N.; m. Amy B. Krutenat, June 17, 1989. BA in Religion, Ea. Nazarene Coll., 1989; MDiv, Nazarene Theol. Sem., Kansas City, Mo. Lic. min. Ch. of the Nazarene, 1988. Min. music and drama St. Paul's Ch. of the Nazarene, Kansas City, 1989—. Mem. Phi Delta Lambda. Office: 8500 E 80th Terr Kansas City MO 64138

NIEMAN, FRANK BERNARD, dean; b. Cin., Oct. 16, 1932; s. Frank August and Marie Bernadine (Schoenfeld) N.; m. Mary Margaret Moore, Aug. 6, 1955; children: William, Francis, Ann, Matthew, Peter, Mary, John, Catherine. Lay evangelist Roman Cath. Ch., Fresno, Calif., 1962-66; acad. dean Sch. Applied Theology, Grad. Theol. Union, Berkeley, Calif., 1970-89, pres., dean, 1989—; dir. Inst. Lay Theology, San Francisco, 1972—; sec. Clergy Edn. Adv. Bd., Oakland, Calif, 1979-86; trainer Edn. for Ministry Program, Sewanee, Tenn., 1981-87; exec. dir. Formation for Christian Ministry, Berkeley, 1981-85. Author: (study books) Christian Awareness Program, 1980; contbr. articles to profl. publs. Mem. Soc. for Advancement of Continuing Edn. in Ministry, Nat. Orgn. Continuing Edn. of Roman Cath. Clergy. Home: 3022 Vessing Rd Pleasant Hill CA 94523 Office: Sch Applied Theology Grad Theol Union 5890 Birch Ct 5890 Birch Ct Oakland CA 94618-1626

NIEMINSKI, JOSEPH IGNATIUS, bishop; b. Hazleton, Pa., May 22, 1926; s. Ignatius and Mary (Pekala) N.; m. Marie Remian, Jan. 28, 1953; children: Robin, Renee Ann. Diploma in theology, Savonarola Theol. Sem., Scranton, Pa., 1946; BA, U. Toronto, Ont., Can., 1959; ThM, Christian Acad. Theology, Warsaw, Poland, 1977, DTh, 1981. Ordained priest Polish Nat. Cath. Ch., 1946. Asst. priest Holy Mother of Rosary Cathedral, Buffalo, 1946-47; rector St. Johns Parish, Toronto, 1947—; sec. Supreme Coun., Polish Nat. Cath. Ch., 1962-78, bishop Polish Nat. Cath. Ch. of Can., 1968—. Home: 296 Mill Rd # F-5, Etobicoke, ON Canada M9C 4X8 Office: 186 Cowan Ave, Toronto, ON Canada M6K 2N6

NIEPORTE, WILLIAM MICHAEL, minister; b. Middletown, Conn., Sept. 5, 1963; s. Dennis Lee and Julia (Bibisi) Kauffman; m. Billie Jeana Murray, Jan. 7, 1989; 1 child, Michelle Ann. BA, Stetson U., 1985; MDiv, So. Sem., Louisville, 1989. Ordained to ministry So. Bapt. Conv., 1987. Youth min. 1st Bapt. Ch., Palatka, Fla., 1985; pastor Salem United Ch. of Christ, New Middletown, Ind., 1986-89, Valley City (Ind.) Presbyn. Ch., 1987-89, Morattico Bapt. Ch., Kilmarnock, Va., 1989—; regional coord. Bapt. Peace Fellowship, Va., 1989—. Vol. Covenant Crafts, Louisville, 1986, Wayside Christian Mission, Louisville, 1987; intern Coun. on Peacemaking, Louisville, 1987. Recipient Abernathy Trust Fla.Bapt. Found., 1985, Order of Omega Stetson U., 1989; Patillo Found. grantee, 1988. Mem. Lancaster Ministerial Assn. (human rels. com. 1989—), Rappahanock Bapt. Assn. (dir. Sunday sch. div. 1989—), Seminarians Against Hunger (officer 1988). Democrat. Home and Office: Rte 1 Box 3401 Kilmarnock VA 22482 *If challenges such as poverty, hunger, war and the destruction of the environment are ever to be solved, then people of faith must first begin to see their involvement in such issues as being an act of worship and commitment to the ways of God.*

NIERMANN, THOMAS ARTHUR, minister; b. Alamosa, Colo., May 17, 1941; s. Henry William and Edna Ida (Krumm) N.; m. Helen Ruth Walker, Aug. 5, 1966; children: Andrew, Anne, Sally, Matthew, Adam, Luke, Noah. AA, St. John's Coll., Winfield, Kans., 1963; BA, Concordia Sr. Coll., Ft. Wayne, Ind., 1965; MDiv, Concordia Sem., St. Louis, 1969. Licensed Pastor, Mo. Pastor Platte Valley Luth. Ch., Saratoga, Wyo., 1969-76, Grace Luth. Ch., Hanna, Wyo., 1969-76, Calvary Luth. Ch., Wood Dale, Ill., 1976-87; sr. pastor St. John's Luth. Ch., Elgin, Ill., 1987—. Lutheran. Home: 715 Wright Ave Elgin IL 60120 Office: St John's Luth Ch 115 N Spring St Elgin IL 60120

NIGRO, ARMAND MICHAEL, priest, theology and philosophy educator; b. Spokane, Wash., Mar. 29, 1928; s. Frank Anthony and Margaret Mary (Vecchio) N. BA, Gonzaga U., 1950, MA, 1951; Licentiate in Theology, Alma Coll., 1957; PhD, Gregorian U., Rome, 1963. Joined S.J., Roman Cath. Ch., 1944, ordained priest, 1965. Prof. philosophy Seattle U., 1960-65, Gonzaga U., St. Michael's Inst., Spokane, 1965-75; prof. theology Gonzaga U., Spokane, 1975—, bd. dirs., 1982-86, trustee, 1983-86; founder Mater Dei Inst., Spokane, 1981, rector-pres., 1986-87; prof. philosophy Kachebere Maj. Sem., Mchinji, Malawi, 1991—; dir. religious retreats, spiritual dir., min. various Cath. parishes and instns. Columnist various Cath. newspapers; author 2 books; contbr. articles to religious jours. Co-founder Caritas, Seattle, 1963, Spokane chpt. Am. Indian Movement, 1966, Inst. Contemporary Spirituality, 1972—, New-Life, Villa Maria, 1977, N.W. Cath. Charismatic Bibl. Inst., 1981; pres. Spokane Human Rels. Coun., Frank and Rose Steele Charitable Trust, 1981; active Spokane Housing Coalition; trustee Gonzaga bd. dirs. House of the Lord Retreat Ctr., Tum Tum, Wash., 1983-88; asst. chaplain Fairchild AFB, 1980-88; founder, pres. Marriage Assocs. Toward Congenial Homes. Mem. NAACP. Home: N 1107 Astor St Spokane WA 99202 Office: Gonzaga U E 500 Boone Ave Spokane WA 99258

NIKKEL, RONALD WILBERT, social services administrator; b. Lethbridge, Alta., Can., June 8, 1946; came to U.S., 1978; s. Henry Peter and Katharine (Penner) N.; m. Celeste Carisa Friesen, June 11, 1970. BA, U. Winnipeg (Can.), 1970; MPS, Loyola U., Chgo., 1983. Nat. dir. YFC/Youth Guidance, Toronto, Ont., Can., 1973-78, Chgo., 1978-82; field dir. Prison Fellowship Internat., Washington, 1982-84, v.p., 1984-88, pres., 1988—. Editor: Guidelines for Volunteer Programs in Justice, 1988. Chmn. Non Govtl. Orgns. Alliance in Crime Prevention and Criminal Justice, N.Y.C., 1988—; bd. dirs. Love and Action, Annapolis, Md., 1989—. Episcopalian. Avocations: photography, hiking, gardening. Office: Prison Fellowship Internat PO Box 17434 Washington DC 20041

NILSEN, NELS WILLIAM, minister; b. Ridgewood, N.J., Oct. 8, 1954; s. Arthur and Elizabeth Betrice (Touw) N. BA in Bibl. Lit., Northeastern Bible Coll., Essex Fells, N.J., 1978, ThB, 1979; MDiv, Trinity Evang. Div. Sch., Deerfield, Ill., 1983; postgrad., William Paterson Coll., Wayne, N.J., 1986. Pastoral intern Calvary Evang. Free Ch., Essex Fells, 1978-79; ministry Yellowstone Nat. Park, 1982, Lake Mohave Nat. Recreation Area, 1982-83, Lincoln Boyhood Nat. Meml. Pk., 1983, 84, The Blue Ridge Pkwy. at Rock Knob, 1983; ministry staff Metro Youth for Christ, Wayne, N.J., 1987—; substitute tchr. Hawthorne (N.J.) High Sch., 1987—. With U.S. Army, 1974. Republican. Home: 265 Mahwah Rd Mahwah NJ 07430 Office: Metro Youth for Christ 62 Sandra Ln Wayne NJ 07474 *To lead is to serve. Kids need to lead. Kids need to serve its prayer and its action.*

NILSON, JON, theology educator; b. Chgo., Sept. 3, 1943; s. John Edward and Rosemary Therese (Murnighan) Nilson Daniels; m. Kathryn Mary Hogan, Aug. 24, 1968; children: Julie, Amy, Daniel. AB, St. Mary of Lake Sem., 1965, STB, 1967; MA, U. Notre Dame, 1968, PhD, 1975. Assoc. prof. theology Loyola U., Chgo., 1975—. Author: Hegel and Lonergan, 1979, From This Day Forward, 1983; also articles. Recipient Publ. Subvention award Lonergan Trust Fund, 1978; grantee Loyola-Mellon Fund, 1980; Inst. Advanced Study Religion fellow U. Chgo., 1983. Mem. Cath. Theol. Soc. Am. Roman Catholic. Home: 2312 W Estes Ave Chicago IL 60645 Office: Loyola U 6525 N Sheridan Rd Chicago IL 60626

NIMOCKS, MICHAEL FREDERICK, deacon; b. Columbus, Ohio, May 10, 1942; s. Harry Arthur and Mary Therese (Brenner) N. Student, Ohio State U., 1960-61. Ordained deacon Roman Cath. Ch., 1977. Deacon Our Lady of Mt. Carmel Parish, Buckeye Lake, Ohio, 1977—. Trustee Buckeye Lake Civic Assn., 1986-88; cen. com. Dems., Buckeye Lake, 1978-82; village coun. Buckeye Lake, 1981-85; dir. scouting Diocese of Columbus, 1983—; asst. state fire marshal State of Ohio, 1981—. Mem. Ohio Fire Chiefs Assn., Permanent Deacon Assn. Region 6 (trustee 1978-88), Lions (pres. 1975-76). Home: PO Box 964 Buckeye Lake OH 43008 Office: Our Lake of Mt Carmel PO Box 45 Buckeye Lake OH 43008

NIMS, GARY ALAN, minister; b. Clinton, Iowa, Feb. 5, 1952; s. Harold Stanley and Betty McFarland (Wakefield) N.; m. Rita Kay Albrecht, July 12, 1980; children: Elisabeth Anne, Nathaniel Wesley, Rebecca Kay. BA magna cum laude, Morningside Coll., Sioux City, Iowa, 1974; MDiv cum laude, Emory U., 1977. Ordained to ministry United Meth. Ch. as deacon, 1976, as elder, 1980. Pastor Linden United Meth. Ch., Waterloo, Iowa, 1978-83, Dunkerton (Iowa) United Meth. Ch., 1983-86; assoc. pastor 1st United Meth. Ch., Indianola, Iowa, 1986-90; min. outreach St. Paul's United Meth. Ch., Cedar Rapids, Iowa, 1990—; dist. chair evangelism United Meth. Ch., Cedar Rapids, 1990—, conf. bd. evangelism, Des Moines, 1990—. Contbr. articles to mags. Mem. Lions. Office: St Pauls United Meth Ch PO Box 2065 Cedar Rapids IA 52406

NINEHAM, DENNIS ERIC, retired theology educator; b. Southampton, Eng., Sept. 27, 1921; s. Stanley Martin and Bessie Edith (Gain) N.; m. Ruth Corfield Miller, Aug. 13, 1946; children: Elizabeth, Clare, Hugh, Christopher. BA, Oxford U., 1943, MA, 1947; BD, Cambridge U., 1964; DD (hon.), Yale U., BDS, 1965; DD (hon.), U. Birmingham, Eng., 1972; DD, Oxford U., 1978. Fellow, chaplain Queen's Coll., Oxford, Eng., 1946-54; prof. London U., 1954-64; regius prof. Cambridge U., 1964-69; fellow Emmanuel Coll., Cambridge, 1964-69; warden Keble Coll., Oxford, 1969-79; prof. Bristol U., Eng., 1980-86. Author: The Gospel of St. Mark, 1963, The Use and Abuse of the Bible, 1976, Explorations in Theology, 1977; editor: Studies in the Gospels, 1955, 2d. edit. 1957, The Church's Use of the Bible, 1963. Proctor Ch. of Eng. Assembly, 1955-70, Ch. of Eng. Gen. Synod, 1970-76. Fellow King's Coll. U. London, 19631, hon. fellow Keble Coll. Oxford U., 1980, fellow King Edward VI Sch. Southampton, 1986, hon. fellow Queen's Coll., Oxford, 1991. Home: 4 Wootten Dr, Iffley Turn, Oxford OX4 4DS, England

NIPKOW, KARL-ERNST HEINRICH, theologian; b. Bielefeld, Fed. Republic Germany, Dec. 19, 1928; s. Ernst and Margarete (Spiekerkötter) N.; m. Rosemarie Ingrid Kowalzyk, June 4, 1954; children: Renate Dorothea, Markus Friedemann. PhD, U. Marburg, Fed. Republic Germany, 1959; ThD (hon.), U. Helsinki, Finland, 1990. Cert. tchr. Tchr., secondary, grammar schs. Bielefeld, 1955-61; lectr. U. Marburg, 1961-65; prof. Tchr. Tng. Coll., Hannover, Fed. Republic Germany, 1965-68, U. Tübingen, Fed. Republic Germany, 1968—; commr. World Council Chs., Geneva, 1968-83; chmn. Comenius Inst., Muenster, Fed. Republic Germany, 1969—; commr. edn. Evang. Ch. Germany, Hannover, 1969—. Author: Schule und Religionsunterricht im Wandel, 1971, Grundfragen der Religionspaedagogik, 3 vols., 1975-82, Bildůng als Lebensbegleitüng ünd Erneüerüng,

1990; contbr. articles to profl. jours. Mem. Deutsche Gesellschaft fuer Erziehungswissenschaft, Gesellschaft fuer Wissenschaftliche Theologie, The Religious Edn. Assn., Internat. Sem. on Religious Edn. and Values. Lutheran. Home: 49 Weiherstrasse, 7400 Tübingen 9, Federal Republic of Germany Office: Evangelical Theol Faculty, Hoelderlinstrasse 16, 7400 Tübingen Federal Republic of Germany

NISARI, JOSEPH, priest, social worker; b. Lahore, Pakistan, Aug. 6, 1942; s. Barkat Joseph and Regina Mariam (Bulanda) N. MA, Christ the King Sem., 1968; postgrad., Universitas Urbaniana, 1983; MSW, Fordham U., 1989. Ordained priest, Roman Cath. Ch. Pastor/prof. Most Rev. Armando Trindade, Lahore, rector of cathedral; asst. pastor Roman Cath. Ch., Bklyn., priest. Mem. Nat. Assn. Social Workers. Home: 2805 Fort Hamilton Pkwy Brooklyn NY 11210

NISHI, SHUNJI FORREST, priest, theology educator emeritus; b. Chino, Calif., Feb. 20, 1917; s. Forest Jintaro and Yoshie (Ueda) Nishibayashi; m. Marian Asako Koyama, Mar. 5, 1944; children: Barbara, Eleanor, John. AB, UCLA, 1938; BD, Episc. Theol. Sch., Cambridge, Mass., 1943; PhD, Columbia U., 1950; DD (hon.), Ch. Divinity Sch., Berkeley, Calif., 1985. Ordained to ministry Episcopal Ch., 1944. Acting chaplain Columbia U., N.Y.C., 1947-48; fellow, tutor Gen. Theol. Sem., N.Y.C., 1947-50; dean, prof. Cen. Theol. Coll., Tokyo, 1950-56; chaplain Iolani Sch., Honolulu, 1956-59; Episc. chaplain U. Calif., Berkeley, 1959-68; lectr. theology Ch. Divinity Sch. of Pacific, Berkeley, 1959-68, prof., 1968-85, prof. emeritus, 1985—; vis. prof. Gen. Theol. Sem., N.Y.C., 1985, St. Michael's Sem., Seoul, Republic of Korea, 1986; trustee St. Margaret's House, Berkeley, 1962-68, Grace Cathedral, San Francisco, 1972-77; mem. Diocesan Coun., San Francisco, 1966-68; del. World Conf. on Faith and Order, Montreal, Can., 1963, Anglican Congress, Mpls., 1955. Contbr. articles and revs. to profl. jours. Mem. Pacific Coast Theol. Soc. (exec. sec. 1967-68), Am. Acad. Religion, Conf. of Anglican Theologians (convenor 1972). Democrat. Home: 76 Parnassus Rd Berkeley CA 94708 Office: Ch Div Sch Pacific 2451 Ridge Rd Berkeley CA 94709 *What a devastating fallacy it is to think that the life of faith and the life of learning are irreconcilably opposed to each other!!!.*

NISHIMURA, KEN, minister, philosophy educator; b. Tokyo, Aug. 27, 1934; s. Keiichi and Mitsuru (Uchimura) N.; m. Yuko Sekiya, Mar. 19, 1989; 1 child, Atsuko Hope. BA, Pasadena Coll., 1958; MDiv., Asbury Sem., 1961; PhD, Emory U., 1966. Ordained to ministry United Meth. Ch. as deacon, 1962, as elder, 1964. Min. Monrovia (Ga.) Community Ch., 1956-58; chaplain, prof. philosophy Oglethorpe U., Atlanta, 1964—; mem. faculty coun. U. Ctr. Ga., Ogelthorpe U., 1968—, chair 1970-71; vis. prof. Tokai U., Tokyo, 1980-81, Tokyo Union Theol. Sem., 1987-88; Tokunin prof. Seigakuin U., Tokyo, 1988—. Author: Theology of T. Kagawa, 1966. Mem. Am. Philos. Assn., Ga. Philos. Soc. (sec., treas. 1968-69), Kagawa Soc. Home: 3 Brookhaven Dr NE Atlanta GA 30319-3003

NISI, VITTORIA EUFEMIA, religion educator, nun; b. Taranto, Puglia, Italy, Aug. 7, 1943. BA, Villa Maria Coll., 1985. Joined Oblate Sisters of Sacred Heart of Jesus, 1961. Tchr. Oblate Sisters, Rome, 1965-71; adminstr., bookkeeper Oblate Sisters, Parete, Italy, 1972-74; kindergarten tchr. St. Frances Cabrini Sch., Conneaut, Ohio, 1984-86, 4th grade tchr., 1987-88; kindergarten tchr., prin., del., superior Villa Maria Teresa Presch. and Oblate Sisters, Hubbard, Ohio, 1988-91. Office: Oblate Sisters 50 Warner Rd Hubbard OH 44425

NISSEN, CARL ANDREW, JR., minister, retired procurement analyst; b. Manhattan, Kans., June 26, 1930; s. Carl Andrew and Bernice Lydia (Varney) N. Student, Denison U., 1948-49; BA, Ohio State U., 1960; postgrad., Grad. Sch. Theology, Oberlin, Ohio, 1959, Berkeley Bapt. Divinity Sch., 1960-61. Ordained to ministry Ohio Bapt. Conv. Supply pastor Ohio Bapt. Conv., various, 1958-61, 82-85; pastor Sinking Creek Bapt. Ch., Springfield, Ohio, 1985-90; chaplain gen. SAR, Louisville, 1989-90; ret., 1990; procurement analyst Def. Electronics Supply Ctr., Dayton, Ohio, 1963-90, ret., 1990. Sgt. U.S. Army, 1950-53, Korea; lt. col. Ohio Mil. Res., 1984-91. Recipient George Washington Honor medal Freedom's Found., 1972, Minute Man medal SAR, 1991. Home: 1001 Fordham Dr Sun City Center FL 33573-5236 *Faith in the presence of Almighty God in our lives makes the challenges we face opportunities for change.*

NISSLEY, M. JOHN, religious organization administrator; b. Morgantown, Pa., Mar. 30, 1949; s. Ira and Ruth S. (Stoltzfus) N.; m. Lois C. Musselman, Oct. 24, 1970; children: Monica Dawn, Lara Nicole. BS, Pa. State U., 1974; MRE, Grand Rapids Bapt. Sem., 1983. Ordained to ministry Mennonite Ch., 1986. House parent Clayton Coll. for Boys, Denver, 1968-70; youth counselor Millersville (Pa.) Youth Village, 1975; camp dir. Tel-Hai Camp, Honey Brook, Pa., 1975-81; pastor Masonville Mennonite Ch., Washington Boro, Pa., 1984-90; assoc. dir. for evangelism Ea. Mennonite Bd. Missions, Salaunga, Pa., 1989—; mem. long range planning com. Locust Grove Mennonite Sch., Smoketown, Pa., 1986-89; campus pastor Millersville Christian Fellowship, 1986-88. Mem. program com. Millersville Internat. House, 1987-90; bd. dirs. Millersville Youth Village, 1987—. Office: Ea Mennonite Bd Missions Oak Ln and Brandt Blvd Salunga PA 17538

NIUKULA, PAULA NAYALA, minister; b. Dobuilevu, Fiji, Apr. 8, 1937; d. Epeli Taninamakadri Niukula and Ulamila Ana Nadeve; m. Sainimere Nasau, Dec. 6, 1967; children: Emosi Mace, Karalaini Kaloni, Jone Brian. Licentiate in theology, Melbourne Coll. Divinity, Davuilevu, Fiji, 1961; grad., Leonard Theol. Coll., Jabalpur, India, 1966; BDiv, Serampore (India) Coll., 1966; MA, U. of South Pacific, Suva, Fiji, 1977. Ordained to ministry Meth. Ch., 1966. Asst. min., tchr. Bible Sch. and Theol. Coll., Davuilevu, 1961-63; conf. sec. Meth. Ch., Suva, 1969-70, gen. sec., 1979-83, pres. conf., 1984-86; cir. and div. supt. Meth. Ch., Viseisei, Fiji, 1988-90, writer Christian perspective on social issues, 1990—; dir. family life program Pacific Conf. Chs., Suva, 1976-78; conf. del. Meth. World Coun., Nairobi, Kenya, 1986; del. World Coun. Chs., Nairobi, 1975, First Pacific Ecumenical Forum, Suva, 1990, World Meth. Conf., Singapore, 1991. Retranslator Fijian New Testament, 1966-71. Invited mem. Fiji Gt. Coun. Chiefs, 1984, 85, Somosomo, 1986; univ. coun. U. of the South Pacific, 1985-87, 91—. Office: Meth Ch in Fiji, GPO 357, Suva Fiji

NIX, ROBERT LYNN, minister; b. Belleville, Ark., Nov. 24, 1940; s. Huey Watson and Edna Mae (Johnson) N.; m. Patricia Sue Palmer, Aug. 27, 1961; children: Kevin Lynn, Robert Keith, Jonathan Kyle, Kelly Eugene. Diploma, Jackson (Miss.) Coll. Ministries, 1965. Ordained to ministry United Pentecostal Ch. Internat., 1963. Prof. Pentecostal Bible Inst., Tupelo, Miss., 1965-66; missionary to Peru, United Pentecostal Ch. Internat., 1966-69; missionary supt. United Pentecostal Ch., Peru, 1966-85; pres. United Pentecostal Sem., Peru, 1969-85; missionary supt. United Pentecostal Ch., Costa Rica, Cen. Am.; pres. United Pentecostal Sem. United Pentecostal Ch., Cen. Am., 1983-85; pastor United Pentecostal Spanish Ch., Hilsboro, Oreg., 1985-86, Christian Apostolic Ch., San Antonio, 1987—. Home and Office: 806 W Elsmere Pl San Antonio TX 78212-2655 *The Apostle Paul said, "For me to live is Christ." (Phil. 1:21). In this age of hedonism and materialism many believe that life consists of worldly goods and human achievements. How mistaken they are! People never really live until they die to self and allow Jesus Christ to become the Supreme Lord of their lives.*

NIX, WILLIAM GAINES, minister; b. Northport, Ala., Mar. 7, 1926; s. Robert Gaines and Iva Louise (Gay) N.; m. Evelyn Margaret Jost, July 23, 1949; children: Beverly Denise Nix Allen, Cynthia Lea. BSEE, U. Colo., 1955; D Religion, Sch. Theology at Claremont, 1971. Ordained to ministry United Ch. of Christ, 1968. Elec. engr., tech. mktg. GE, 1955-65; pastor Etiwanda (Calif.) Congl. Ch., 1968-70; min. camping and program devel. Cen. Pacific conf. United Ch. of Christ, Portland, Oreg., 1971-75; assoc. conf. min. Fla. conf. United Ch. of Christ, 1975-79; sr. min. Ormond Beach (Fla.) Union Ch., 1979-84, Venice (Fla.) United Ch. of Christ, 1984—; disaster coord. Fla. conf. United Ch. of Christ, 1986—; disaster cons. Ch. World Svc., N.Y.C., 1986—; chmn. disaster com. Fla. Coun. Chs., 1990—. Mem. com. Sarasota County (Fla.) Emergeny Ops., 1990—; mem. exec. com. Fla. VOAD, Tampa, 1990—; trustee S.W. Fla. Ret. Ctr., Venice, 1988—. With USN, 1944-52, PTO, Korea. Mem. Am. Radio Relay League, Venice Area Ministerial Assn. (pres., dir., other offices 1984—), Old Timer's Club, Tamiami Radio Amateurs Club, Warm Mineral Springs Archeol. Soc. (charter). Home: 1349 Cambridge Dr Venice FL 34293 Office: Venice United Ch of Christ 620 Shamrock Blvd Venice FL 34293 *Life is a precious incomplete gift intrusted to incomplete beings who are given the opportunity and responsibility to creatively pursue the realization of individual potential in loving relationships with the Creator and one's neighbors.*

NIXON, BARBARA ELIZABETH, clergy person; b. Detroit, Aug. 3, 1954; d. Glenn Curry and Irma Mary (Nisbet) N. BA, Kirkland Coll., Clinton, N.Y., 1976; MA, Columbia U., 1981; Dip.C.S., Regent Coll., Vancouver, B.C., 1983; MDiv, Yale U., 1987. Minister, dir. edn. A Christian Ministry in the Nat. Pks., Kings Canyon Nat. Park, Calif., 1975; dance instr. Kirkland and Hamilton Colls., Clinton, N.Y., 1976-77; adminstrv. asst. Christian Counseling & Psychtherapy Ctr., N.Y.C., 1978-80; ednl. and cultural programmer Columbia U., N.Y.C., 1980-81; ministry intern Christ Episcopal Ch., Wesleyan U., Greenwich and Middletown, Conn., 1984-85; seminarian asst. The Episcopal Ch. at Yale, New Haven, 1986-87; asst. chaplain and tchr. St. Paul's Sch., Concord, N.H., 1987-88; residence dir. Gordon Coll., Wenham, Mass., 1989-90; asst. rector Calvary Episcopal Ch., Danvers, Mass., 1989, St. John's Episcopal Ch., Vernon, Conn., 1990—; cons. in field; dancer Boston Liturgical Dance Ensemble, 1988-90, Cambridge Ct. Dancers, Boston, 1988-90. Dancer, choreographer Boston U. Sch. Theology, Women and the Word Conf., 1989. Panel mem. bicentennial conf. Christians for Bibl. Equality, Mpls., 1989; mem. Conn. Diocesan Commn. on Higher Edn. Mem. Hamilton Coll. Alumni Assn., Yale U. Alumni Assn., Rockville Clergy Assn. Avocations: ballet, folk and modern dance, music, theatre, travel. Office: St Johns Episcopal Ch PO Box 2237 Vernon CT 06066-1637

NOAH, SHERI LYNN, minister; b. LaRochelle, France, Dec. 16, 1954; came to U.S., 1956; d. Grover Carter Noah and Pauline Esther (Takach) Westaby; m. David Hacker, May 25, 1991; stepchildren: Hilary, Corey. AA, Yakima Valley Community Coll., Wash., 1975; BA, Whitworth Coll., 1977; student, Latin Am. Bibl. Sem., San Jose, Costa Rica, 1983; MDiv, McCormick Theol. Seminary, Chgo., 1985. Ordained to ministry Presbyn. Ch. (U.S.A.), 1986. Subsistence worker United Presbyn. Ch. U.S.A./Fedn. of Protestant Chs., Uruguay, 1979-81; minister Trinity Presbyn. Ch., Stockton, Calif., 1986—; chmn. Stockton Interfaith Sponsoring Com. for Ch.-based Community Organizing, 1989—; mem. Metro Ministries (co-chair Unity in Community Com., 1990-91), Stockton, 1986—, Latin Am. Support Com., Stockton, 1986—; supr. tutoring prog., Trinity Ch., 1989—. Office: Trinity Presbyn Church PO Box 6285 Stockton CA 95206

NOAKES, GEORGE, archbishop; b. Wales, Sept. 13, 1924; David John and Elizabeth Mary Noakes; m. Jane Margaretta Davies, 1957. BA, University Coll. of Wales, Aberystwyth; postgrad., Wycliffe Hall, Oxford U., Eng.; DD (hon.), U. Wales, 1989. Curate Lampeter, 1950-56; vicar Eglwyswrw, 1956-59, Tregaron, 1959-67, Cardiff, 1967-76; rector Aberystwyth, 1976-79; canon St. David's Cathedral, 1977-79; archdeacon Cardigan, 1979-82; vicar Llanychaearn, 1980-82. Avocations: cricket, angling. Office: Lys Esgob, Abergwili, Dyfed SA31 2JG, England*

NOBLE, MITZI MCALEXANDER, travel company executive; b. Kingsport, Tenn., Feb. 6, 1941; d. Buren and Ruby Estelle (Hodges) McAlexander; m. Paul Benjamin Noble, June 29, 1957; children: Michael B., James B. Student, Nat. Bus. Coll., 1958-59, U. Mich., 1958, Ind. U., 1963-65; RBA, Shepherd Coll., 1985; postgrad. Wesley Theol. Sem. and Howard U. Sch. Div., 1985-88; MDiv, Gen. Theol. Sem., 1990. Co-owner, dir. personnel, soloist All-Student Band, Winchester, Va., 1965-69; co-owner, gen. mgr., chmn. bd. Ednl. Tour Consultants, Winchester, 1967—, Noble's Travel World, Winchester, 1975—; sales and mktg. rep. Air France, Washington, 1970-75; pastor St. Luke's and Holy Trinity churches, Montego Bay, Jamaica, 1986—; asst. to rector St. John's of Lattingtown Episcopal Ch., Locust Valley, N.Y., 1990—; lectr. Shenandoah Coll. and Conservatory of Mus., Winchester, 1982. Chmn. Downtown Devel. Bd., Winchester, 1977-83; mem. selection and budget com. United Fund, Winchester, 1984—; bd. dirs. Wayside Found. for the Arts, Middletown, Va., 1981-84. Mem. Actor's Equity Assn., Retail Mchts. Assn. (officer, dir. 1970-81), Winchester C. of C. (officer, dir. 1979-83), Sigma Alpha Iota, Tau Beta Sigma. Episcopalian. Club: Quota (exec. bd.) (Winchester). Avocations: music; cantor and soloist; music theatre; church leadership; world travel. Home: 331 Lattingtown Rd Locust Valley NY 11560 Office: Noble's Travel World 16 N Braddock St Winchester VA 22601 *First we must learn to receive then we can give. We receive the love of God and then we give love to others. In this same way, we listen; then we share. This is the way we learn to live with others. We all have much to receive and learn from each other, then we pass it on.*

NOE, VIRGILIO CARDINAL, cardinal; b. Zelata di Bereguardo, Italy, Mar. 30, 1922. With titular ch. St. John Bosco; vicar gen. Vatican City State; archpriest St. Peter Basilica; with titular Ch. Voncaria; elevated to Sacred Coll. Cardinals, 1991. Office: Vatican City State 00120, Europe*

NOEBEL, DAVID ARTHUR, minister, educator; b. Oshkosh, Wis., Aug. 27, 1936; s. Arthur William and Dorothy Helen (Schaeffer) N.; m. Alice Maren Koch, Aug. 24, 1957; children: Brent David, Joy. BA, Hope Coll., 1959; postgrad., U. Wis., 1959-63; MA, U. Tulsa, 1971; LLD (hon.), Am. Christian Coll., Tulsa, 1974. Ordained to ministry Christian Ch., 1963. Pastor Grace Bible Ch., Madison, Wis., 1959-63, Christian Crusade Ch., Tulsa, 1963-71; v.p. Am. Christian Coll., Tulsa, 1971-74, pres., 1974-78; pres. Summit Ministries, Manitou Springs, Colo., 1978—. Author: The Marxist Minstrels, 1974, The Homosexual Revolution, 1977, Understanding the Times, 1991. Rep. candidate for Congress, Madison, 1962. Mem. Am. Philos. Assn., Assn. Christian Philosphers, Coun. Nat. Policy. Home: 928 Osage Ave Manitou Springs CO 80829 Office: Summit Ministries PO Box 207 Manitou Springs CO 80829

NOEL, LAURENT, bishop, educator; b. St. Just de Bretenieres, Que., Can., Mar. 19, 1920; s. Remi and Albertine (Nadeau) N. B.A., Coll. de Levis, 1940; L.Th., Laval U., 1944, L.Ph., 1948; D.Th., Inst. Angelicum, Rome, 1951. Ordained priest Roman Catholic Ch., 1944; prof. theology Laval U., 1946-48, 52-63, prof. ethics Med. Sch., 1952-63; vice rector Grand Sem., Sch. Theology, 1961-63; aux. bishop Que., 1963-74; apostolic adminstr. Diocese of Hauterive, 1974-75; bishop Diocese of Trois-Rivieres, Que., 1975—; Provincial chaplain Assn. des Infirmieres Catholiques, 1958—; chaplain Syndicat Profl. des Infirmieres Catholiques, 1958-63. Author: Precis de morale medicale, 1962. Address: Bishop's House, CP 879, Trois Rivières, PQ Canada G9A 5J9

NOLAN, JOHN GAVIN, bishop; b. Mechanicsville, N.Y., Mar. 15, 1924; s. Michael Edward and Teresa (Gavin) N. STD, Cath. U. Am., MLS; MA in History, Fordham U.; LHD (hon.), St. John's U., St. Joseph's Coll., Windham, Maine. Ordained priest Roman Cath. Ch. Assoc. pastor Annunciation Ch., Ilion, N.Y., 1949-50; prof. Mater Christi Sem., Albany, N.Y., 1954-60; sec. gen. Cath. Near East Welfare Assn., N.Y.C., 1966-88; pres. Pontifical Mission for Palestine, N.Y.C., 1966-88; aux. bishop Archdiocese for Mil. Svcs. U.S.A., Bonn, Fed. Republic Germany, 1988—. Office: Archdiocese for Mil Svcs, Kaiserstrasse 141, 5300 Bonn Federal Republic of Germany

NOLAN, RICHARD THOMAS, minister, educator; b. Waltham, Mass., May 30, 1937; s. Thomas Michael and Elizabeth Louise (Leishman) N. BA, Trinity Coll., 1960; cert. in clin. pastoral edn., Conn. Valley Hosp., 1962; diploma, Berkeley Divinity Sch., 1962; MDiv., Hartford Sem. Found., 1963; postgrad., Union Theol. Sem., N.Y.C., 1963; MA in Religion, Yale U., 1967; PhD, NYU, 1973; post doctoral, Harvard U., 1991. Ordained deacon Episcopal Ch., 1963, priest, 1965. Instr. Latin and English Watkinson (Conn.) Sch., 1961-62; instr. math. Choir Sch. of Cathedral of St. John the Divine, N.Y.C., 1962-64; instr. math. and religion, assoc. chaplain Cheshire (Conn.) Acad., 1965-67; instr. Hartford (Conn.) Sem. Found., 1967-68, asst. acad. dean, lectr. philosophy and edn., 1968-70; instr. Mattatuck Community Coll., Waterbury, Conn., 1969-70; asst. prof. philosophy and history Mattatuck Community Coll., Waterbury, 1970-74, assoc. prof., 1974-78, prof. philosophy and social sci., 1978-92, prof. emeritus, 1992—; rsch. fellow in med. ethics Yale U., 1978, rsch. fellow in profl. and bus. ethics, 1987; vicar St. Paul's Parish, Bantam, Conn., 1974-88; pastor emeritus St. Paul's Parish, Bantam, 1988—; pres. Litchfield Inst., Inc., Conn. and Fla., 1984—; mem. ethics com. Waterbury Hosp. Health Ctr., 1984-88; vis. and adj. prof. philosophy, theology and religious studies Trinity Coll., Conn., L.I. U., U. Miami, St. Joseph Coll., Conn., Pace U., Teikyo Post U., U. Conn. Hartford Grad. Ctr., Cen. Conn. State U., Barry U., Fla., Broward Community Coll., Fla., 1964—; adj. assoc. in continuing edn. Berkeley Div. Sch. Yale U., 1987-89; Rabbi Harry Halpern Meml. lectr., Southbury, Conn., 1987; guest speaker various chs. and orgns. including Cathedral of St. John the Divine, N.Y. and Trinity Cathedral, Miami; mem. faculty of consulting examiners Charter Oak State Coll., Conn., 1990—; fellow Associated Fellows for Counseling and Psychotherapy, Inc., 1990—; assoc. for edn. Christ Ch. Cathedral, Hartford Conn., 1988—, hon. canon, 1991—; liaison diploma and cert. program in religious studies, U. Cambridge, Eng., 1991—; cons. Dept. Def. Activity Non-Traditional Ednl. Support, Ednl. Testing Svcs., Princeton, 1990. Author: (with H. Titus and M. Smith) Living Issues in Philosophy, 7th edit., 1979, 8th edit., 1986, 9th edit., 1993, (with F. Kirkpatrick) Living Issues in Ethics, 1982; editor, contbr. Diaconate Now, 1968; host Conversations With..., 1987-89. Mem. Am. Acad. Religion, Am. Philos. Assn., Authors Guild, Inst. Soc., Ethics and Life Scis., Boston Latin Sch. Alumni Assn., Tabor Acad. Alumni Assn., Phi Delta Kappa. Address: PO Box 483 Bristol CT 06011-0483 also: 2121 W Oakland Park Blvd # 333 Fort Lauderdale FL 33311-1507 *Who am I? By baptism I am a resurrected child of God born to love and be loved; my pilgrimage among others is lived within this baptismal identity, more enduring than any achievement.*

NOLAND, DOUGLAS EUGENE, minister, educator; b. Pensacola, Fla., Sept. 12, 1957; s. Robert Edgar and Lena Vermelle (Lide) N.; m. Penelope Louise Goettsch, Jan. 22, 1959. BS in Bus. Adminstrn., Mobile Coll., 1980; MA in Rel. Edn., Southwestern Bapt. Theol. Sem., Fort Worth, 1984. Sales rep. Russ Berrie & Co. South, Hialeah, Fla., 1980-81; minister of youth and edn. First Bapt. Ch., Titusville, Fla., 1985-89; First Bapt. Ch., Atmore, Ala., 1989—; mem. Sunday sch. assisteam Brevard Bapt. Assn., Rockledge, Fla., 1988-89, Escambia Bapt. Assn., Flomaton, Ala., 1989—. Worker and Sunday sch. campaign coordinator Fla. Bapt. Conv., 1988—; scouting coordinator Troop 352, Titusville, 1988—. Mem. So. Bapt. Rel. Edn. Assn. Baptist. Avocations: cycling, water skiing, swimming, sailing. Office: First Bapt Ch 310 S Main St Atmore AL 36502

NOLD, DANIEL RAY, minister, educator; b. Downey, Calif., Aug. 18, 1962; s. Rodney Ray and Cheryl Louise (Duncan) N.; m. Lynn Susan Jacobson, June 10, 1984; children: Sarah Danielle, Katelyn Louise. BA, Bethel Coll., 1984; MDiv, Bethel Sem., 1989. Carpet installer Metro Carpet, Bklyn., 1984-86; football coach Bethel Coll., St. Paul, 1986-89; sr. pastor First Bapt. Ch., Grove City, Minn., 1989—; instr. in Greek Bethel Sem., St. Paul, 1988-89; pres. West Cen. Ministerial, Willmar, Minn., 1990—. Editor: Religious Newspaper, 1989—. County del. Meeker Rep. Caucus, Litchfield, Minn., 1989; chmn. Grove City Precinct Caucus, 1989. Mem. Evang. Theol. Soc. Bonhoeffer Soc., Eta Beta Rho. Republican. Baptist. Avocations: reading, sports, hunting, woodworking. Home: 409 S 2d St Box 322 Grove City MN 56243 Office: 1st Bapt Ch 321 N 5th St Grove City MN 56243

NOLDE, NANCY, ecumenical agency administrator. Exec. dir. Del. Valley Media Ministry, Phila. Office: Del Valley Media Ministry 1501 Cherry St Philadelphia PA 19102*

NOLT, DOUGLAS EUGENE, campus pastor; b. Lancaster, Pa., Mar. 19, 1957; s. Donald Eugene and Lois Winona (Davis) N.; m. Judith Irene Adams, June 27, 1981; children: Daniel Eugene, Jacob Adam. BA in Religion, U. Findlay, 1979; M of Div., Winebrenner Theol. Sem., 1983. Ordained to ministry Ch. of God, 1983. Assoc. in ministry, campus pastor Ch. of God Gen. Conf. U. Findlay, 1983—; pastor E. Pa. Conf. Chs. of God Gen. Conf. Mem. Nat. Assn. Coll. and Univ. Chaplains, Hancock County Ministerial Assn., Winebrenner Sem. Alumni Assn. (sec. 1984-85). Republican. Avocations: electronics, researching religious cults. Home: 251 Prospect Ave Findlay OH 45840 Office: U Findlay 1000 N Main St Findlay OH 45840-3695

NOLTING, EARL, academic administrator; b. Columbus, Ind., July 24, 1937; s. Earl Seeger and Gladys Marie (Veale) N.; m. Judith Lynn Tegeler, June 18, 1961; children: Susan, Matthew, David. BSBA, Ind. U., 1959, MS in Edn., 1961; PhD in Psychology, U. Minn., 1967. Lic. psychologist, Wis.; lic. consulting psychologist, Minn. Counselor, asst. prof. U. Minn., Mpls., 1966-68; assoc. dir. U. Wis., Madison, 1968-72, assoc. dean, assoc. vice-chancellor, 1970-74; assoc. prof. edn. Kans. State U., Manhattan, 1974-86, dean of students, 1974-86; dir. dept. counseling, continuing edn., extension U. Minn., Mpls., 1986—; cons. psychologist Alberg and Assocs., Shoreview, Minn., 1989—. Contbr. articles to profl. publs. Exec. bd. Adult Learner Svcs. Network, St. Paul, 1989-90. 1st lt. U.S. Army, 1961-62. Mem. AACD, Am. Psychol. Assn., Am. Coll. Pers. Assn. (news editor 1977-82, sen. 1982-85, Presdl. award 1982). Avocations: sailing, gardening, reading. Home: 3336 Lake Johanna Blvd Saint Paul MN 55112 Office: Continuing Edn/Extension 315 Pillsbury Dr SE Minneapolis MN 55455

NOONAN, GUY FRANCIS, priest; b. N.Y.C., Dec. 25, 1949; s. Daniel Francis and Eileen (Flynn) N. BA, Cath. U. Am., 1972, MA, 1976, post grad., 1976; French Immersion, L'U. Laval, Quebec, 1978. Tchr. John Kennedy High Sch., Warren, Ohio, 1972, 76-79; assn. adminstr. San Pedro Ctr., Orlando, Fla., 1979-82; dir. San Pedro Ctr., Orlando, 1982-84, St. Bridget Ch., Mpls., 1987—; bd. dirs. RENEW, Orlando, 1980-82, Justice and Peace Ministry, Washington, Mpls., 1986—. Author: Teresa: Image for Our Times, 1986, Re-Entry into Comm., 1988, Shame, 1990. Community organizer Joint Ministry Project, Mpls., 1989—. Office: Saint Bridget Ch 3811 Emerson Ave N Minneapolis MN 55412

NORDLIE, ROBERT LELAND, minister; b. Detroit, June 21, 1949; s. Fred A. Jr. and Elizabeth J. (Luke) N.; m. Diana Marie Schukowsky, June 19, 1971; children: Rebekah, MaryBeth. AA, Concordia Coll., Ann Arbor, Mich., 1969; BA with distinction, Concordia Coll., Ft. Wayne, Ind., 1971; MDiv, Concordia Theol. Sem., Springfield, Ill., 1975; D Ministry, Trinity Evang. Div. Sch., Deerfield, Ill., 1987. Pastor Messiah Luth. Ch., Sterling, Ill., 1975-81; sr. pastor Immanuel Luth. Ch., Hillside, Ill., 1981—. Office: Immanuel Luth Ch 2317 S Wolf Rd Hillside IL 60162

NORDQUIST, SANDRALEE RAHN, lay worker; b. Chgo., Dec. 5, 1940; d. Herbert Henry and Elinor Gertrude (Duben) Rahn; m. George Leczewski, Oct. 13, 1962 (div. Dec. 1968); 1 child, Peter George (dec.); m. David Arthur Nordquist, July 19, 1969; children: Kerilinn D., Sharianne R. AA, Harper Coll., 1982; BS in English, Elmhurst (Ill.) Coll., 1985, BS in Theology, 1988. Cert. English and history tchr., Ill. Tchr. English Luther High Sch., Chgo., summer 1990; confirmation tchr. Evang. Luth. Ch. of the Holy Spirit, Elk Grove, Ill., 1990-91, leader adult Bible study, 1991—; guild pres., adv. preaching Evang. Luth. Ch. of the Holy Spirit, 1990-91; tchr. Foreman High Sch., Chgo., 1990—; feature writer Daily Herald, Paddock Publs., 1991—. Columnist (newspaper) Pulitzer Pubs. Notebook, 1986-90. Leader Girl Scouts U.S., Chgo. and Elk Grove, 1968-70, 77-81; v.p. Dist. 59 Orch. Assn., Elk Grove Village, Ill., 1985-87; pres. Sch. Dist. 59 Project 444, Elk Grove Village, 1981. Mem. Nat. Coun. Tchrs. of English, Ill. Assn. Tchrs. of English, Sigma Tau Delta. Home: 639 Sycamore Dr Elk Grove Village IL 60007 Office: Foreman High Sch 3235 N LeClaire Ave Chicago IL

NOREN, PAUL HAROLD ANDREAS, retired clergyman; b. St. Paul, July 10, 1910; s. Andreas and Amanda Amelia (Olson) Noren; m. Linnea Swanson, Oct. 7, 1936 (dec.); children: Andrea Marie, Karen, Mary-Ellen Beth; m. Janice Herrick, Feb. 14, 1979; children: Craig Llewellyn, Karen, Brian Llewellyn. AB, Gustavus Adolphus Coll., 1931; MDiv, Augustana Theol. Sem., Rock Island, Ill., 1934; DD (hon.), Bethany Coll., Lindsborg, Kans., 1958. Ordained to Luth. ministry, 1934. Pastor St. Paul, 1934-38, Duluth, Minn., 1938-44, Mpls., 1944-53; sr. pastor Augustana Luth. Ch., Denver, 1953-68, Mt. Olivet Luth. Ch., Mpls., 1968-74; preacher biennial conv. Luth. Ch. in Am., Dallas, 1972, White House, 1969; mem. Bd. Christian Svc., Luth. Minn. Conf., 1938-41, chmn. budget com., 1940-51; mem. com. on liturgical theory and practice Augustana Luth. Ch., 1944-60, v.p. cen. conf., 1956-62, sec. Bd. Christian Higher Edn., 1952-62, chmn. joint com. on Luth. unity, 1961-62, mem. exec. bd., 1962-68, mem. commn. on Luth. chaplaincy for Colo. instns., 1961-62, v.p. Bd. Coll. Edn. and Ch. vocations, 1962-64, pres., 1964-66; mem. Bd. World Missions, 1968-70; del. Nat. Council of Chs., 1966; pres. Denver Area Council Chs., 1962-64; pres. Religious Council Human Rels. Met. Denver, 1965; pres. Colo. Council

Chs., 1967; chaplain Colo. Senate, 1963-68, 81-82, Rep. Nat. Conv., 1964; chmn. Billy Graham Colo. Crusade, 1965, gen. chmn. Upper Midwest Crusade, 1973; exec. bd. Minn. Synod Luth. Ch. in Am., 1968-76; mem. exec. coun. Luth. Ch. Am., 1966-68; condr. preaching missions Oreg., Colo., Minn., Tex., 1980-91. Author Profiles of the Passion, 1961; contbr. articles to profl. jours.; radio broadcaster, 1963-68, devotional telecast, 1968-78; speaker and conductor of missions in chs. Chmn. Gov.'s Com. on Respect for Law, 1964-68, Pres.'s Colo. Commn. Law Enforcement and Adminstrn. of Justice, 1966-68, Gov.'s Com. on Minorities and the Disadvantaged, 1968, Mt. Olivet Luth. Ch. Council, Mt. Olivet Sr. Citizen's Home, Mt. Olivet Careview Home, Mt. Olivet Rolling Acres and Sch. for Mentally Retarded, Cathedral of the Pines Youth Camp, Santal Mission Bd., 1970-72; mem. Mayor's Com. on City-Citizen Rels., 1965-68; trustee Swedish Med. Ctr., Englewood, Colo., 1953-68, Greater Mpls. Council Chs., 1948-53, v.p. 1952-53, chmn. weekly edn. for released time instrn. 1951-53; bd. dirs. Midland Luth. Coll., Fremont, Nebr., 1966-68. Recipient Disting. Alumni Citation Gustavus Adolphus Coll., 1962, Torch of Liberty award Anti-Defamation League of B'nai Brith, 1964. Mem. Rotary, Kiwanis, Probus Club of Fullerton (Calif.), Sigma Tau. Home: 839 Glenwood Circle Fullerton CA 92632

NORHEIM, NEIL MARTIN, minister; b. Green Bay, Wis., May 27, 1943; s. Erling H. and Mercedes Lucille (Huebner) N.; m. Karen F. Larson, May 28, 1964; children: Jennifer L. Cox, Angela D. BA in Ministry, Lincoln Christian Coll., 1967, B of Sacred Music, 1967; MS, Pittsburg (Kans.) State U., 1985. Ordained to ministry Christian Chs. and Chs. of Christ, 1967. Sr. min. Ch. of Christ, Orrville, Ohio, 1968-73; sr. min. First Christian Ch., Champaign, Ill., 1973-76, Kewanee, Ill., 1976-82, Miami, Okla., 1982-88; speech prof. Ozark Christian Coll., Joplin, Mo., 1988-89; pulpit min. Chapel Rock Christian Ch., Indpls., 1989—; bd. dirs. Nat. Ch. Growth and Rsch. Ctr., Washington, N.Am. Christian Conv., Cin.; trustee Lincoln (Ill.) Christian Coll., 1990—; dir. Christian TV Mission, Springfield, Mo., 1981-89. Contbr. articles to profl. jours. Mem. Rotary (Miami, Okla. pres. 1987-88). *In all my adult ministry I've discovered that personal integrity and a transparent/consistent lifestyle is necessary for long range influence in the church. In a world it is: faithfulness.*

NORIEGA, NORMAN JOSEPH, minister; b. Wareham, Mass., Aug. 28, 1942; s. Anthony and Irene E. (Grace) N. Diploma, Salvation Army, 1961; diploma (hon.), Zion Bible Inst., Barrington, R.I., 1987. Ordained to ministry Christian Ch., 1977. Founder, pastor Interdenominational Pentecostal Fellowship and Ch., New Bedford, Mass., 1974—. Republican. Home: 112 Harwich St New Bedford MA 02745 *Biblical Christianity is Man's greatest source of abundant living, value, fulfillment and hope for the future.*

NORMAN, ANTONY DILWORTH, music minister; b. Charlotte, N.C., June 29, 1963; s. Austin Donald and Nancy Lee (Irvin) N.; m. Susan Diane Matherly, Dec. 17, 1988; 1 child, Anais Dorian. BS in Psychology, Liberty U., Lynchburg, Va., 1984, MA in Counseling, 1986; PhD in Ednl. Psychology, U. Va., 1990. Ordained to ministry, Bapt. Ch. Minister of music Calvary Bapt. Ch., Holland, Mich., 1990—, counselor, 1990—; supt. Calvary Bapt. Sch., Holland, Mich., 1990—. Mem. Phi Delta Kappa. Office: Calvary Bapt Ch 517 W 32nd St Holland MI 49423

NORMAN, D. F., minister, religious organization administrator; b. Henderson, Ky., Apr. 3, 1935; s. Homer T. and Cordie Lee (McCormick) N.; m. Joyce Parrent, Dec. 22, 1956; children: Rhonda Norman Taylor, Joy, Leslie. BA, Baylor U., 1956, postgrad.; BD, So. Bapt. Theol. Sem., Louisville, 1959; ThM, Southeastern Bapt. Theol. Sem., Wake Forest, N.C., 1960. Ordained to ministry So. Bapt. Conv., 1956. Pastor Johnson Bapt. Ch., Warsaw, N.C.; assoc. pastor Moreland Ave. Ch., Atlanta; pastor 1st Bapt. Ch., Trion, Ga., White Oak Hills Bapt. Ch., 1970-84; dir. pastoral ministry dept. Ga. Bapt. Conv., Atlanta, 1984—; bd. dirs. Home Mission Bd., So. Bapt. Ch., Atlanta, 1980-88, v.p., 1986-87. Trustee Tift Coll., Forsyth, Ga., 1980-84. Mem. So. Bapt. Mins. of Aging (v.p. 1989-91), So. Bapt. Ch. Adminstrs. (pres. Bapt. sch. bd. 1991), Religious Conf. Mgmt. Assn. Office: Ga Bapt Conv 2930 Flowers Rd S Atlanta GA 30341

NORMAN, HOMER HOWARD, minister; b. Clendenin, W.Va., July 2, 1933; s. Otmer Clay Norman and Dulcie Ellen (Parsons) Guthrie; m. Nancy Carol Taulbert, Nov. 21, 1954; children: Dina Carol Vornberger, William Joseph, Rachael Ann Arvin, Jennifer Ellen. AA, Tallahassee (Fla.) Jr. Coll., 1968; BS, Fla. State U., 1970; MDiv, Asbury Theol. Seminary, Wilmore, Ky., 1986. Pastor United Meth. Ch., Monticello, Fla., 1967-70, Irvine, Ky., 1970-76, Perryville, Ky., 1983-86, Olive Hill, Ky., 1986—; welder SouthEast Coal Co., Irvine, 1974-79, Horn's Equipment, Irvine, 1979-83. Instr. Cumberland Hoedowners, Irvine, 1971-84; food crisis bd. Carter County Food Crisis Ctr., Grayson, Ky., 1988—; adv. bd. Bethany House, Olive Hill, 1988—; pastoral care St. Claire Med. Ctr., Morehead, Ky., 1987—. Named Ky. Col. Gov. of Ky., 1983; named to Hall of Fame Renfro Valley (Ky.) Barn Dance, 1983; recipient Appreciation award Estill County Clogging Assn., Irvine, 1977. Mem. Olive Hill Ministeral Assn. (sec. 1986-87), Carter County Ministeral Assn. Democrat. Avocations: square dancing, fishing, woodworking. Home: PO Box 465 Olive Hill KY 41164

NORMAN, RONNIE LEE, minister; b. Columbia, Tenn., Oct. 28, 1957; s. Clarence and Virginia (Medkeff) N.; m. Martha Louise Goodall, Aug. 2, 1980; children: Mary Beth, Ryan. BA in Bible, Freed-Hardeman U., Henderson, Tenn., 1979. Minister Highlands Ch. of Christ, Lakeland, Fla., 1981-85, First Colony Ch. of Christ, Sugar Land, Tex., 1985—; traveling speaker chs. in 25 states, 1981—. Steering com. Houston Help the Homeless Campaign, Houston, 1989. Home: 3103 Poplar Pl Sugar Land TX 77479 Office: 1st Colony Ch of Christ 3119 Sweetwater Blvd Sugar Land TX 77479

NORMAN, TIMOTHY JOE, youth pastor; b. Clinton, Iowa, Apr. 17, 1962; s. Dale Rolland and Bessie Elizabeth (Pruett) N.; m. Flora Christine Norman, May 8, 1981; children: Theresa, Jessica, Timothy, Alicia, Malinda. Student, Berean Coll., 1981-87. Youth pastor Assembly of God, Willcox, Ariz., 1985-87; sr. pastor Assembly of God, Leon, Iowa, 1987-90; youth pastor Assembly of God, Oskaloosa, Iowa, 1991—; youth rep. Assemblies of God, Willcox, 1985-87. Author: Cross Warrior Manual, 1991. Mem. Kiwanis (Oskaloosa). Home: 502 A Ave E Oskaloosa IA 52577 Office: First Assembly of God Hwy 63 Oskaloosa IA 52577

NORRIS, ARLYN C., minister; b. Sibley, Iowa, Sept. 9, 1949; s. Clyde H. and Helen R. (Hamann) N.; m. Wanda L. Schoon, June 3, 1972; children: Seth A., Aaron J., Rachel S.B. BA, Augustana Coll., Sioux Falls, S.D., 1971; MDiv, Luther-Northwestern Sem., 1975. Ordained to ministry Luth. Ch. Am. Pastor Zion Luth. Ch., Rake, Iowa; sec. stewardship com. W. Iowa Synod Evang. Luth. Ch. Am., Storm Lake, 1987—. Bd. dirs. Rake Pub. Libr., 1986—, Rake Community Ctr. Com., 1983-89. Mem. Lions (sec. Kenmare, N.D. chpt. 1980-82). Home and Office: Zion Luth Ch 4th St Rake IA 50464

NORRIS, CYNTHIA CLARICE, religious organization administrator; b. Balt., Nov. 16, 1956; d. Robert J. Sr. and Clarice Xavier (Gee) N. BA, Coll. of Notre Dame, Balt., 1978; MA, St. Mary's Ecumenical Inst., 1986. Cons. Nat. Office for Black Catholics, Washington; dir. religious edn. St. Bernardine Ch., Balt.; religious edn. cons. Silver Burdett and Co., Morristown, N.J.; exec. dir. Black Catholic Ministries, Archdiocese of Chgo.; transfer ctr. dir. Montay Coll., Chgo., until 1991; adminstrv. unit mgr. placement svcs. Aunty Martha's Youth Svc., Chgo., 1991—. Mem. Nat. Assn. Black Catholic Adminstrs., Boys' Hope, League of Black Women. *At birth we're given names by family; at work we're given titles by employers; in life were given labels by society. Aren't you glad to know your blessings and talents are God-given!.*

NORRIS, EARL RAY, minister; b. St. Joseph, Mo., July 28, 1937; s. George Edward and Carol Geneve (Buetzer) N.; m. Sharon Leigh Sullivan, July 9, 1966; children: Wesley Charles, Camille Leigh. B of Music Edn., U. Kans., 1959; MRE, Southwestern Bapt. Theol. Sem., 1970. Cert. music tchr., Kans., Md.; ordained to ministry Bapt. Ch., 1975. Min. of music 1st Bapt. Ch., New Carrollton, Md., 1963-68, Stadium Dr. Bapt. Ch., Ft. Worth, 1968-69; min. of edn. and music Derita Bapt. Ch., Charlotte, N.C., 1970-75, Woodlawn Bapt. Ch., Decatur, Ga., 1975-85; assoc. pastor/edn. Cen. Park Bapt. Ch., Birmingham, Ala., 1985—; band dir. Stone Mountain (Ga.) Christian Sch., 1981-84. Saxophone soloist Official USN Band, Washington, 1960-63; band dir. pub. sch., Prince Georges County, Md., 1964-68; saxophonist Birmingham Community Concert Band, 1985—. Mem. Birmingham Bapt. Assn. (exec. bd.), Birmingham Community Concert Band Assn. (bd. dirs.). Office: Cen Park Bapt Ch 1900 43rd St West Birmingham AL 35208 *All that we are and all that we ever hope to be, fulfilled in Jesus Christ.*

NORRIS, FREDERICK WALTER, theology educator; b. Chillicothe, Ohio, Mar. 13, 1941; s. William O. and Julia H. (Dowdy) N.; m. Carol Jean Brooks, Aug. 30, 1963; children: Lisa Carol, Mark Frederick. BA, Milligan Coll., Johnson City, Tenn., 1963; ThM, BD, Phillips U., Enid, Okla., 1967; PhD, MPhil, Yale U., 1970. Adj. asst. prof. Emmanuel Sch. Religion, Johnson City, 1970-72; asst. prof. Milligan Coll., 1970-72; from assoc. dir. to dir. Inst. zur Erforschung des Urchristentums, Tuebingen, Fed. Republic Germany, 1972-77; from assoc. prof. to prof. Emmanuel Sch. Religion, 1977—; dir. European Evangelistic Soc., Atlanta, 1982-91; Tuohy disting. vis. prof. religious studies John Carroll U., Cleve., 1988. Author: Faith Gives Fullness to Reasoning, 1991; editor: Encyclopedia of Early Christianity, 1990, North American Patristic Society Monograph Series. Andrew W. Mellon fellow, 1981-82, 86, Dumbarton Oaks summer fellow, 1987. Mem. Am. Soc. Ch. History, Am. Acad. Religion, North Am. Patristic Soc. Democrat. Mem. Christian Ch. Office: Emmanuel Sch Religion 1 Walker Dr Johnson City TN 37601

NORRIS, JOHN, school system administrator. Supt. schs., dir. child-youth ministry Archdiocese of Milw. Office: Schs and Child Youth Ministry PO Box 2018 Milwaukee WI 53201*

NORRIS, JOY COLE, music minister; b. Atlanta, Oct. 22, 1958; d. Benjamin Steven and Rachel Maxine (Montgomery) Cole; m. Ronald Timothy Norris, May 21, 1983. Grad., Jackson Coll. Ministries, 1979; postgrad., NE La. U. Min. music 1st Penntecostal Ch., West Monroe, La., 1981-83, 87-88, Durham, N.C., 1986-87; dir. children's choir and splty. groups 1st Penntecostal Ch., Jackson, Miss., 1983-86; min. music Apostolic Tabernacle, Atlanta, 1979-80, 88—; dir. Metro Atlanta Youth Choir, 1979-80; lectr. music Jackson Coll. Ministries, 1983-86; music conf. clinician, performer Tex. Music Ministries Conf., 1990; instr., performer, recording artist, song writer, 1991; music conf. clinician Nat. Music Ministries Conf.; pvt. tchr. vocal and keyboard music; pub. speaker, vocal performer; lectr. choir and vocal clinic. Singer Wayne Goodine Trip, JCM Chorale, 1976-79; dir. numerous mus. prodns.; co-author 4 dramas, Kid's Klub, 1991. Home: PO Box 686 Jonesboro GA 30237 Office: 9769 Tara Blvd Jonesboro GA 30236

NORRIS, JUNE, minister; b. Trinidad, Colo., June 30, 1922; d. Ernest Ellsworth and Bessie Mildred (Dawson) Rudolph; m. Willard M. Norris, Feb. 12, 1938 (div. Sept. 1966); children: Gene Curtis, Paul Martin, Dixie June. Student, East L.A. Coll., 1968-74, Samaritan Bible Sch., L.A., 1972-74. Lic. Universal Fellowship Met. Community Chs., 1973, ordained 1974. Staff clergy Met. Community Ch., L.A., 1972-80; pastor Met. Community Ch., Fayetteville, N.C., 1980-81, St. John's Met. Community Ch., Raleigh, N.C., 1981-88, Ch. Holy Spirit of Met. Community Ch., Des Moines, 1989—; office mgr. W.M. Norris Constrn., Orlando, Fla., 1961-66; clk. outpatient div. Fla. Hosp., Orlando, 1966-67; supr. White Meml. Med. Ctr., L.A., 1968-76. Contbr. articles to Front Page jour. Mem. team to testify state legis. com. for gay/lesbian rights St. John's Met. Community Ch., 1985. Recipient Disting. Svc. award Universal Fellowship Met. Community Ch., 1991, appreciation White People Healing Racism, 1991. Mem. Hosp. Credit Mgrs. Assn. (pres. 1970-71). Avocations: bowling, scrabble, sports. Office: Ch Holy Spirit MCC 6001 SW 14th St Des Moines IA 50315

NORRIS, ROBERT MICHAEL, minister; b. Evvw Vale, Wales, Jan. 11, 1951; came to U.S., 1980; s. Thomas Neil and Margo (Morley) N.; m. Caren Elizabeth McDade, Sept. 28, 1985; children: Sarah, Adam, Aaron. ThM, St. Andrews, Scotland, 1973, PhD, 1976. Ordained to ministry Presbyn. Ch., 1976. Asst. min. City Temple Ch., London, 1976-80; exec. pastor 1st Presbyn. Ch., Hollywood, Calif., 1980-83; sr. pastor 4th Presbyn. Ch., Bethesda, Md., 1983—. Editor: (journal) Themelios, 1976. Mem. Cosmos Club. Home: 6913 Persimmon Tree Rd Bethesda MD 20817 Office: 4th Presbyn Ch 5500 River Rd Bethesda MD 20816

NORRIS, RUSSELL BRADNER, JR., minister, religious organization administrator, educator; b. Hackensack, N.J., Mar. 3, 1942; s. Russell Bradner Sr. and Ann Mae (Dubanowitz) N.; m. Dixie K. Battistella, June 1, 1974; 1 child, Claire Ann Chanenchuk. BSEE, MIT, 1964; postgrad., U. Ill., 1964-65; MDiv, Luth. Sch. of Theology at Chgo., 1969; ThD with honors, U. Strasbourg, France, 1972. Ordained to ministry Luth. Ch., 1972. Editorial asst. Inst. for Ecumenical Research, Strasbourg, 1970-72; pastor Mt. Union (Pa.) Luth. Parish, 1972-78; sr. pastor Zion Luth. Ch., Hollidaysburg, Pa., 1978-85; exec. minister S.C. Christian Action Council, Columbia, 1985-89; adj. faculty mem. St. Francis Coll., Loretto, Pa., 1982-83, Cen. Wesleyan Coll., Central, S.C., 1989-90; prof. Luth. Theol. So. Sem., Columbia, S.C., 1989—; gen. chmn. 11th Nat. Workshop on Christian-Jewish Rels., Charleston. Author: God, Marx and the Future, 1974, (with others) Many Faces of Marxism, 1984; contbr. articles to profl. jours. Fellow Rockefeller Found., Chgo., 1965-66, World Council of Chs., Strasbourg, 1969-70. Mem. Am. Acad. Religion, Soc. Christian Ethics, S.C. Acad. Religion, Assn. for Clin. Pastoral Edn., Nat. Assn. of Ecumenical Staff, Assn. for Theol. Field Edn., Rotary. Avocations: model railroading, camping, backpacking. Office: Luth Theol So Sem 4201 N Main St Columbia SC 29203

NORRIS, VICTOR SNYDER, minister; b. Huntingdon, Pa., Sept. 29, 1944; s. Herman L. and Wanda (Snyder) N.; m. Inez M. Ramsey, Aug. 28, 1965; children: Todd, Jo De, Toby. BS in Edn., Shippensburg (Pa.) U., 1966; MDiv, Ea. Mennonite Sem., Harrisburg, Va., 1985. Ordained to ministry Ch. of Brethren, 1974. Mem. bd. mid. Pa. dist. Ch. of Brethren, Huntingdon, 1972-75, Ch. of The Brethren, Harrisburg, Va., 1986-88; pastor Nokesville (Va.) Ch. of Brethren, 1989—; rep. Va. Coun. Chs. to Ch. of Brethren, Harrisburg, 1987-88; mem. leadership devel. conf. Mid-Atlantic dist. Ch. of Brethren, Washington, 1989—. Mem. parade com. for Nokesville Day, Raritans, 1990. Mem. Ruritans. Democrat. Home and Office: Nokesville Ch of Brethren PO Box 56 Nokesville VA 22123

NORTH, ROSS STAFFORD, minister, religion educator, academic administrator; b. Abilene, Tex., Mar. 2, 1930; s. Lucas E. and Lala (Coppers) N.; m. JoAnne Boswell, June 10, 1955; children: David, Julia, Linda, Susan. BA, Abilene Christian U., 1950; MA, La. State U., 1952; PhD, U. Fla., 1957. Min. Chs. of Christ, 1948—; instr. Cen. Christian Coll., Bartlesville, Okla., 1952-58; dean Okla. Christian U. Sci. and Arts (formerly Okla. Christian Coll.), Oklahoma City, 1958-71, exec. v.p., 1971—. Author: Preaching: Men and Method, 1985, Armageddon Again?, 1991, Handbook on Church Doctrines, 1991; mem. adv. coun. Christian Chronicle, 1981—; contbr. numerous articles to religious jours. Recipient Alumni citation Abilene Christian U., 1971. Home: 2201 Reveille Edmond OK 73013 Office: Okla Christian U Sci and Arts Box 11000 Oklahoma City OK 73136

NORTHFELT, MERLYN WINFIELD, minister; b. Mpls., Dec. 16, 1915; s. Frank Ivar and Esther Emily (Eckgren) N.; m. Dorothy May Underwood, Oct. 11, 1938; children: Marilyn Ann Coffey, Sandra Lou Landon. AB, Seattle-Pacific, 1942; MDiv, Garrett Theol. Sem., 1946; LHD (hon.), North Cen. Coll., 1975; DD (hon.), Garrett Theol. Sem., 1980, Morningside Coll., 1968, Seabury-Western Theol. Sem., 1979. Ordained to ministry United Meth. Ch., 1945. Pastor United Meth. Ch., Yorkville, Ill., 1943-51, Lake Bluff, Ill., 1951-61; dist. supt. No. Ill. Conf., Rockford, 1961-65; chief staff No. Ill. Conf., Chgo., 1965-70; pres. Garrett-Evangelical Theol. Sem., Evanston, Ill., 1970-80; retired, 1980; del. Gen. Conf. United Meth. Ch., 1964, 68, 72, 76, 80. Bd. dirs. global mission United Meth. Ch., N.Y., 1968-80; pres. Home Owners Assn., Sarasota, Fla., 1981; chmn. adv. bd. Meadows Community, Sarasota, Parent Child Ctr., 1987-91. Mem. No. Ill. Conf. United Meth. Ch., Meadows Golf Club. Democrat. Home: 4802 Green Croft Sarasota FL 33580

NORTON, DARYL EDWARD, military professional, minister; b. Jefferson, Tenn., Sept. 5, 1957; s. Edward Franklin and Geneva Hollis (Curnutt) N.; m. Beverly Louise Pinkston, Dec. 3, 1977; children: Joshua Thomas, Esther Susanna. BA, Carson-Newman Coll., 1979; MDiv, So. Bapt. Theol. Sem., Louisville, 1987; grad. with distinction, Mil. Sch., Ft. Sill, Okla., 1989. Ordained to ministry So. Bapt. Conv., 1988. Pastor Riverview Bapt. Ch., 1984-86, Rolling Fork Bapt. Ch., Boston, Ky., 1986-87; enlisted U.S. Army, 1988, advanced through ranks to sgt., 1991; fire direction specialist U.S. Army, Ft. Sill, 1988—; vol. chaplain Operation Desert Storm U.S. Army, Saudi Arabia, 1991; dir. stewardship com. East Tenn. Bapt. Assn., Newport, 1985-86. Mem. Phi Alpha Theta, Pi Tau Chi. Home: 5532 A Hammel Rd Fort Sill OK 73503 Office: HHS 6/27 FA Fort Sill OK 73503

NORVELL, THOMAS VERNON, minister; b. Lake Charles, La., Oct. 19, 1955; s. Thomas Vern and Barbara Joyce (Grant) N.; m. Alica Nell Reynolds, Sept. 9, 1978; children: Thomas Vernon, Carey Lane. BS in Psychology/Religion, Ea. N.Mex. U., 1978; MDiv, Golden Gate Bapt. Theol. Sem., 1981. Ordained to ministry So. Bapt. Conv., 1982. Min. edn. Capital City Bapt. Ch., Sacramento, 1981-89; assoc. pastor edn. and adminstrn. First Bapt. Ch., Fair Oaks, Calif., 1989—. Bd. dirs., treas. Support Abused Victims Early, Sacramento, 1986-90. Recipient Award of Excellence Cosumnes River Coll., 1989; cert. appreciation Superior Ct., Calif., 1988. Mem. Western Bapt. Religious Educators Assn. (chmn. program 1986-88). Office: First Bapt Ch 4401 San Juan Ave Fair Oaks CA 95628

NORWALK, THOMAS KENT, minister; b. Toledo, May 14, 1954; s. Clifton O. and Lucille A. (Wilkins) N.; m. Rebecca L. Fleck, May 28, 1976; children: Seth T., Karlin R. AB, Heidelberg Coll., 1976; MDiv, Eden Theol. Sem., 1979. Ordained to ministry United Ch. of Christ, 1979. Pastor Immanuel United Ch. of Christ, Kettlersville, Ohio, 1979-86, St. John's United Ch. of Christ, Crown Point, Ind., 1986—; del. Gen. Synod, United Ch. of Christ, 1983, 85, chmn. N.W. Ind. com. on ministry, 1987—, NW Ind. Assn. coun. Bd. dirs., Pres. Contact Cares NW Ind., Merrillville, 1989—. Mem. Kiwanis (chmn. spiritual aims Crown Point). Office: Saint John's United Ch of Christ 1288 S Indiana Ave Crown Point IN 40307

NORWOOD, MATTHEW A., bishop. Mem. bd. of apostles, bishop Ch. of Our Lord Jesus Christ of the Apostolic Faith Inc., N.Y.C. Office: Ch Our Lord Jesus Christ Apostolic Faith Inc 2081 Adam Clayton Powell Jr New York NY 10027*

NOSTBAKKEN, ROGER WESLEY, theological educator, administrator, clergyman; b. Aneroid, Sask., Can., Sept. 7, 1930; s. Ole and Lillie Matilda (Owenson) N.; m. E. Andrea, Oct. 6, 1956; children—Kirsten, Randi, Inger, Mikkel. B.A., U. Sask., 1955; B.D., Luth. Theol. Sem., 1956; Th.M., Princeton Theol. Sem., N.J., 1958, Th.D., 1962. Ordained to ministry Evangelical Lutheran Ch., 1956. Pastor, Armena Luth. Parish, Sask., 1956-57, Sucasunna Luth. Parish, N.J., 1957-60, Kindersly Luth. Parish, Sask., 1961-63, Mt. Zion Luth. Parish, Edmonton, Alta., Can., 1963-65; prof. Luth. Theol. Sem., Saskatoon, Sask., 1965—, pres.-elect, 1984-85; dir. religious studies U. Sask., Saskatoon, 1973-85; v.p. Evangel. Luth. Ch. of Can., 1970-84; pres. Luth. Council in Can., 1975-78, 83-85; mem. exec. com. Luth. World Fedn., Geneva, 1977-90; bd. dirs. Inst. for Ecumenical Research, Strasbourg, France, 1978-90; pres. Luth. Theol. Sem., Saskatoon, 1985—. Mem. Can. Soc. for Study of Religion, Can. Theol. Soc. Club: Rotary (Saskatoon). Home: 33-455 Pinehouse Dr, East Saskatoon, SK Canada STK 5X1 Office: Luth Theol Sem U Sask, 114 Seminary Crescent, Saskatoon, SK Canada S7N 0X3

NOTERMAN, SISTER M. PATRICE, academic administrator. Pres. Mallinkrodt Coll. of the North Shore, Wilmette, Ill. Office: Mallinkrodt Coll North Shore Wilmette IL 60091*

NOTTINGHAM, WILLIAM JESSE, church mission executive, minister; b. Sharon, Pa., Nov. 22, 1927; s. Jess William and Alice May (Green) N.; m. Patricia Clutts, Feb. 1, 1949; children: Theodore Jess, Deborah Joan, Nancy Alice, Gregory Philip. BA, Bethany Coll., W.Va., 1949, DD (hon.), 1987; BD, Union Theol. Sem., N.Y.C., 1953; PhD, Columbia U., 1962; DD (hon.), Christian Theol. Sem., Indpls., 1984. Ordained to ministry Christian Ch. (Disciples of Christ). Pastor Ch. of Christ, Canoe Camp and Covington, Pa., 1949-50; field worker Ch. of the Master, N.Y.C., 1950-53; assoc. min. Nat. City Christian Ch., Washington, 1954-58; fraternal worker Coun. on Christian Unity, France, 1958-65; with youth dept. World Coun. of Chs., Geneva, 1965-68; exec. sec. for Latin Am. and Caribbean Div. Overseas Ministries, Christian Ch. (Disciples of Christ), Indpls., 1968-76, exec. sec. East Asia and Pacific, 1976-83, pres., 1984—. Author: Christian Faith and Secular Action, 1968, The Preaching and Practice of Liberation, 1986; translator: God's Underground, 1970, Prayer at the Heart of Life, 1975, Materialist Approaches to the Bible, 1985, Madeleine Barot, 1991. Fulbright scholar, 1953-54. Mem. Assn. Disciples for Theol. Discussion, Nat. Coun. of Chs. of Christ in USA (gen. bd.). Democrat. Office: Christian Ch (Disciples of Christ) Div Overseas Ministries PO Box 1986 Indianapolis IN 46206

NOVAK, DAVID, Judaic studies educator, rabbi; b. Chgo., Aug. 19, 1941; s. Syd and Sylvia (Wien) N.; m. Melva Ziman, July 3, 1963; children: Marianne, Jacob George. AB in Classics and Ancient History, U. Chgo., 1961; M in Hebrew Lit., Jewish Theol. Sem. Am., 1964; PhD, Georgetown U., 1971. Ordained rabbi, 1966. Rabbi Shaare Tikvah Congregation, 1966-69; dir. Jewish chaplaincy St. Elizabeth's Hosp., 1966-69; rabbi Emanuel Synagogue, Oklahoma City, 1969-72, Beth Tfiloh Congregation, Balt., 1972-77, Congregation Beth El, Norfolk, Va., 1977-81, Congregation Darchay Noam, Far Rockaway, N.Y., 1981-89; Edgar M. Bronfman prof. modern Judaic studies U. Va., Charlottesville, 1989—; lectr. philosophy Oklahoma City U., 1969-72, New Sch. for Social Rsch., 1982-84; lectr. Jewish studies Balt. Hebrew Coll., 1972-77; adj. asst. prof. philosophy Old Dominion U., 1977-81; vis. assoc. prof. Talmud Jewish Theol. Sem. Am., 1986-88; adj. assoc. prof. Baruch Coll., CUNY, 1984-88, adj. prof., 1989; founder, v.p., coord. panel Halakhic inquiry Union Traditional Judaism/Inst. Traditional Judaism. Contbg. editor Sh'ma, First Things; mem. editorial bd. Brown U. Studies in Judaism, Historians Press, Echad jour. V.p. Inst. on Religion and Pub. Life. Essay winner Hyman G. Enelow prize Jewish Theol. Sem. Am., 1975; recipient Rabbi Jacob B. Augus award Jewish Theol. Sem. Am., 1984. Fellow Acad. for Jewish Philosophy (dir. publs.); mem. Am. Theol. Soc., Assn. for Jewish Studies, Am. Acad. Religion, Am. Philos. Assn., Jewish Law Assn., N.Y. Bd. Rabbis, Leo Baeck Inst., Assn. for Religion and Intellectual Life (adv. bd.). Home: 5311 Cutshaw Ave Richmond VA 23226 Office: U Va Dept Religious Studies Cocke Hall Charlottesville VA 22903

NOVÁK, JOSEPH, minister; b. Pecs, Hungary, June 9, 1959; came to U.S., 1982; s. Sebestyen and Ilona (Kova'cs) N.; m. Georgie Kövesdi, July 11, 1981; children: Esther, Benjamin. MDiv, Conservative Bapt. Sem., Portland, Oreg., 1989. Ordained to ministry Bapt. Ch., 1989; registered chem. engr., Hungary. Min. Am. Hungarian Bapt. Ch., Alhambra, Calif., 1989—. Editor Gospel Messenger periodical, 1990—. Home and Office: Am Hungarian Bapt Ch 2212 S Fremont Ave Alhambra CA 91803-4316

NOVAK, MICHAEL (JOHN), religion educator, author, editor; b. Johnstown, Pa., Sept. 9, 1933; s. Michael John and Irene (Sakmar) N.; m. Karen Ruth Laub, June 29, 1963; children: Richard, Tanya, Jana. A.B. summa cum laude, Stonehill Coll., North Easton, Mass., 1956; B.T. cum laude, Gregorian U., Rome, 1958; M.A., Harvard U., 1966; LL.D., Keuka (N.Y.) Coll., 1970, Stonehill Coll., Mass., 1977; L.H.D., Davis and Elkins (W.Va.) Coll., 1971, LeMoyne (N.Y.) Coll., 1976, Sacred Heart U., 1977, Muhlenberg Coll., 1979, D'Youville Coll., 1981, Boston U., 1981, New Eng. Coll., 1983, Rivier Coll., 1984, Marquette U., 1987. Teaching fellow Harvard U., 1961-63; asst. prof. Stanford U., 1965-68; assoc. prof. philosophy and religious studies State U. N.Y., Old Westbury, 1968-71; assoc. dir. humanities Rockefeller Found., N.Y.C., 1973-75; provost Disciplines Coll., SUNY, Old Westbury, 1969-71; vis. prof. Jan. session Carleton Coll., Northfield, Minn., 1970, Immaculate Heart Coll., Hollywood, Calif., 1971; vis. prof. U. Calif., Santa Barbara, 1972, Riverside, 1975; Ledden-Watson disting. prof. religion Syracuse U., 1977-79; journalist nat. elections Newsday, 1972; writer in residence The Washington Star, 1976, syndicated columnist, 1976-80, 84-89; columnist Forbes Mag., 1989—; resident scholar in religion and public policy Am. Enterprise Inst., Washington, 1978—,

George Frederick Jewett chair pub. policy research, 1983—, dir. social and polit. studies, 1987—; chmn. working seminar on family and Am. welfare policy Ind., 1986; faculty U. Notre Dame, Ind., 1986-87, vis. W. Harold and Martha Welch Prof. Am. Studies, 1987, 88; judge Nat. Book awards, 1971, DuPont Broadcast Journalism awards, 1971-80; speechwriter nat. polit. campaigns, 1970, 72; mem. Bd. Internat. Broadcasting, 1983—; mem. Presdl. Task Force Project Econ. Justice, 1985-87, Council Scholars Library of Congress, 1986—; mem. monitoring panel UNESCO, 1984; vice chmn. Lay Commn. Cath. Social Teaching and U.S. Economy, 1984-86; U.S. Ambassador to Experts Meeting on Human Contacts of the Conf. On Security and Cooperation in Europe, Bern, Switzerland, 1986; U.S. rep. to human rights commn. UN, 1981-83. Author: novel The Tiber was Silver, 1961, A New Generation, 1964, The Experience of Marriage, 1964, The Open Church, 1964, Belief and Unbelief, 1965, A Time to Build, 1967, A Theology for Radical Politics, 1969, American Philosophy and the Future, 1968, Story in Politics, 1970, (with Brown and Herschel) Vietnam: Crisis of Conscience, 1967; Politics: Realism & Imagination, 1971, Ascent of the Mountain, Flight of the Dove, 1971, A Book of Elements, 1972, All the Catholic People, 1971, Naked I Leave, 1970, The Experience of Nothingness, 1970, The Rise of the Unmeltable Ethnics, 1972, Choosing Our King, 1974, The Joy of Sports, 1976, The Guns of Lattimer, 1978, The American Vision, 1978, Rethinking Human Rights I and II, 1981, 82, The Spirit of Democratic Capitalism, 1982, Confession of a Catholic, 1983, Moral Clarity in the Nuclear Age, 1983, Freedom with Justice, 1984, Human Rights and the New Realism, 1986, Will It Liberate? Questions About Liberation Theology, 1986, Character and Crime, 1986, The New Consensus on Family and Welfare, 1987, Taking Glasnost Seriously: Toward an Open Soviet Union, 1988, Free Persons and the Common Good, 1989, This Hemisphere of Liberty, 1990; numerous other articles and books transl. into all maj. langs.; assoc. editor Commonweal mag., 1966-69; contbg. editor Christian Century, 1967-80, Christianity and Crisis, 1968-76, Jour. Ecumenical Studies, 1967—, This World, 1982-89, First Things, 1990—; religion editor Nat. Rev., 1979-86; founder, pub. Crisis, 1982—. Decorated K.M.G., Sovereign Mil. Order of Malta, 1987; Kent fellow, 1961—; fellow Hastings Inst., 1970-76; named Most Influential Prof. Sr. Class Stanford U., 1967, 68; Man of Yr. Johnstown, Pa., 1978; recipient Faith and Freedom award Religious Heritage Am., 1978, Medal of Freedom, 1981; named Friend of Freedom, 1981; Newman Alumni award CCNY, 1984; George Washington Honor medal, 1984; award of Excellence, Religion in Media, 8th annual Angel Awards, 1985, Ellis Island Medal Honor, 1986, diploma as vis. prof. U. Francisco Marroquin, 1985; named acad. corr. mem. from U.S., Argentina Nat. Acad. Scis., Morals & Politics, 1985, others. Mem. Soc. Religion in Higher Edn. (cen. com. 1970-73), Am. Acad. Religion (prog. dir. 1968-72), Coun. Fgn. Relations, Cath. Theol. Soc., Soc. Christian Ethics, Inst. Religion and Democracy (dir. 1981—), Nat. Ctr. Urban and Ethnic Affairs (dir. 1982—). Office: Am Enterprise Inst 1150 17th St Washington DC 20036 *Many persons have found a certain emptiness at the heart of human life —an experience of nothingness. Hidden in it, implicit in it, are prior commitments to honesty, courage, freedom, community. To increase the frequency of such acts in our lives is to grow, and to feel them diminish is to wither.*

NOVOA, LUIS ERNESTO, minister; b. Bklyn., Jan. 26, 1958; s. Ernesto and Ana Delia (Ramos) N.; m. Rose Moreno, June 4, 1977; children: Samuel, Jonathan, Daniel, Benjamin. BA in Doctrianl Studies, Internat. Bible Inst., 1987-89; BS in Human Svcs., Boricua Coll., 1988—. Ordained to ministry Pentecostal Ch., 1986. Evangelist Chs. of God Good Shepherd, Bklyn., 1979-84; intern Coun. Pentecostal Chs. of Jesus Christ, 1984; pastor Pentecostal Ch. One in Christ, 1985—; pres. Hispanic Ministry Assn. Bklyn., 1988—; gen. sec. Coun. Pentecostal Chs. Jesus Christ, 1988—; deacon Ch. of God Good Shepherd, Bklyn., 1979-83, youth pastor, 1976-80. Office: PO Box 147 Brooklyn NY 11232

NOWACK, VIRGINIA BERGLUND, minister; b. Orange, N.J., Mar. 4, 1944; d. Lawrence Nils and Estelle Antonette (Pospisil) Berglund; m. Dennis Charles Nowack, June 29, 1968; children: Scott Dennis, Andrew LAwrence. BA, Cedar Creat Coll., 1966; Mdiv, Princeton Theol. Sem., 1982; postgrad., McCormick Theol. Sem. Ordained to ministry Presbyn. Ch. (U.S.A.), 1982; cert. tchr., N.J., N.Y. Asst. pastor 1st Presby. Ch., Red Bank, N.J., 1982-84; assoc. pastor 1st Presby. Ch., 1984-85; co-pastor Onondaga Valley Presby. Ch., Syracuse, N.Y., 1985-86; pastor Onondaga Valley Presby. Ch., 1986—; chairperson Evangelism com., Presby. Cayuga, Syracuse, 1989—; chaplain, vol., Community Gen. Hosp., Syracuse, 1988-91; mentor, Synod Northeast Presby. Ch., Syracuse, 1991—; del., 1984. Author (with others): Our Story: The Presbyterian Church U.S.A., 1983. Recipient Thompson Scholar award, Columbia Theol. Sem., 1989. Office: Onondaga Valley Presbyn Ch 275 W Seneca Tnpk Syracuse NY 13207

NOYCE, GAYLORD BREWSTER, religion educator, minister; b. Burlington, Iowa, July 8, 1926; s. Ralph Brewster and Harriett (Norton) N.; m. Dorothy Caldwell, May 25, 1949; children: Elizabeth, Karen, Timothy. BA, Miami U., Oxford, Ohio, 1947; MDiv, Yale U., 1952. Ordained to ministry United Ch. of Christ, 1952. Asst. min. Hancock Congl. Ch., Lexington, Mass., 1952-54; min. United Ch., Raleigh, N.C., 1954-60; mem. faculty Yale U. Div. Sch., New Haven, 1960—, prof., 1980—; mem. steering com. Ch. Union Conversations, United Ch. of Christ and Christian Ch. Author: The Church Is Not Expendable, 1969, The Responsible Suburban Church, 1970, Survival and Mission for The City Church, 1975, The Art of Pastoral Conversation, 1981, New Perspectives on Parish Ministry, 1981, Pastoral Ethics, 1988, The Minister as Moral Counselor, 1989. Chmn. Conn. Commn. on Race and Religion, 1965-68. With USN, 1944-46. Mem. Assn. Theol. Field Edn. (sec.-treas. 1971-73), Assn. for Profl. Edn. in Ministry (steering com., pres. 1980-82), Assn. for Case Teaching (sec.-treas. 1984-86). Democrat. Office: Yale U Div Sch 409 Prospect St New Haven CT 06510

NOYD, R(OY) ALLEN, religious organization administrator; b. Jamestown, N.Y., July 4, 1941; s. Roy Alvin and Carolyn Jane (Van Benthuysen) N.; m. Patricia Ruth Berg, June 2, 1962; children: Scott A., Jeffrey D., Noelle K. Student, Jamestown Community Coll., 1960-62. Ordained to ministry, 1972; cert. behavioral analyst. Assoc. pastor Jamestown (N.Y.) Revival Ctr., 1972-78; pastor Faith Assembly, Jamestown, 1984-85; sr. pastor New Covenant Assembly, Jamestown, 1985-88; gen. sec., treas. Christian Ch. of N.Am., Transfer, Pa., 1988—; pres., Jamestown N.Y. Chpt. of Pentecostal Fellowship North Am., 1987-88, v.p., 1985-87. Mem. Nat. Assn. Evangs. (fin. commn.), Nat. Christian Counselors Assn. (regional rep.), Carlson Learning Co. (assoc.), Religious Conf. Mgmt. Assn. Republican. Home: 2449 Romar Dr Hermitage PA 16148 Office: Christian Ch of North Am Rd #1 Box 141-A Transfer PA 16154 *Both Moses and Paul experienced a time in the desert. My own desert experience brought me from a religious mindset into a spiritual relationship with Jesus Christ.*

NOYES, DOROTHY RAE, missionary, educator; b. San Francisco, Feb. 17, 1927; *; d. Raymond Edward and Marjorie E. (Smith) Stannard; m. Alfred Frederic Noyes, Aug. 23, 1952 (dec.); children: Russell Edward, Alfred Frederic Jr., Kathryn Louise, James Duncan. BA, U. Redlands, 1949; cert. in social work, U. Calif., Santa Cruz, 1968. Commd. to ministry Am. Bapt. Fgn. Missionary Soc., 1978. Dir. religious edn. First Bapt. Ch., Yakima, Wash., 1950-51; adminstrv. clk. Am. Bapt. Assembly, Green Lake, Wis., 1976-78; missionary, tchr. Am. Bapt. Fgn. Mission Soc., Yokohama, Japan, 1978—. Republican. Home: 77 Kuritaya Kanagawa-ku, 221 Yokohama Japan Office: Soshin Girls Sch, 8 Nakamaru Kanagawa-ku, 221 Yokohama Japan

NSENGIYUMVA, VINCENT, archbishop. Archbishop of Kigali Roman Cath.Ch., Rwanda. Office: Archeveche, BP 715, Kigali Rwanda*

NUGENT, MIRIAM, religion educator; b. Elmira, N.Y., Aug. 30, 1940; d. John T. and Helen (Fitzpatrick) N. BA in English, Nazareth Coll., Rochester, N.Y., 1972; MS in Edn., Elmira Coll., 1978. Cert. tchr., N.Y. Tchr. St. Mary's Sch., Bath, N.Y., 1962-64, St. Rita's Sch., Webster, N.Y., 1964-67; tchr., prin. St. Patrick's Sch., Oswego, N.Y., 1967-83; prin. St. Louis Sch., Pittsford, N.Y., 1983—. Mem. Sisters of Mercy Elem. Network (liaison). Home: 64 S Main St Pittsford NY 14534 Office: Saint Louis Sch 11 Rand Pl Pittsford NY 14534

NULL, PAUL BRYAN, minister; b. Oakland, Calif., May 7, 1944; s. Carleton Elliot and Dorothy Irene (Bryan) N.; m. Renee Yvonne Howell, Aug. 23, 1969; children: Bryan Joseph, Kara Renee. BS, Western Bapt. Coll., 1973; MDiv, Western Conservative Bapt. Sem., 1979. Ordained to ministry Bapt. Ch., 1982. Asst. pastor Bethel Bapt. Ch., Aumsville, Oreg., 1972-74, sr. pastor, 1974-87; sr. pastor The Calvary Congregation, Stockton, Calif., 1987—; trustee Conservative Bapt. Assn. of Oreg., 1982-85, mem. Ch. extension com., 1975-85. Radio show commentator Food for Thought, 1987. Panel mem. Presdl. Anti-Drug Campaign, 1984. Served with U.S. Army, 1965-67. Named Outstanding Young Man Am., 1979. Mem. Conservative Bapt. Assn. of Am., Kiwanis, Lions, Delta Epsilon Chi. Avocations: lap swimming, bicycling. Home: 1320 W Acacia St Stockton CA 95203 Office: The Calvary Congregation 703 E Swain Rd Stockton CA 95207

NULMAN, SEYMOUR SHLOMO, rabbi, educator, author; b. Newark, June 9, 1921; s. Samuel and Nellie (Feder) N.; m. Miriam Weinberg, May 24, 1942; children: Shifra Nulman Zwick, Basheva Nulman Schreiber; m. Hilda Chill Leiter, Mar. 10, 1983. A.A., Isaac Elchanon Theol. Sem., 1942; B.A., Yeshiva U., 1942; M.A., Columbia U., 1944, postgrad., 1945—. Ordained rabbi, 1943. Rabbi East Side Torah Ctr., N.Y.C., 1943—; dean Yeshiva Konvitz, N.Y.C., 1945—; chmn. bd. dirs. Shlom Bonayich Grad. Inst. Israel, 1985—; pres. Yeshiva Bais Yisroel, Jerusalem, 1987—; dean Talmud Torah Jacob David, N.Y.C., 1941—; chaplain Slutzker Landsmanshaft Orgn. Am., 1960—, N.Y. Infirmary-Beekman Downtown Hosp., N.Y.C., 1973—, Bellevue Hosp. Ctr., 1974—, Meltzer Sr. Citizens' Tower, N.Y.C. Housing Authority, 1974—; pres. Yehudah Wolf Inst., N.Y.C., 1939-45, Jacob David Assn., 1948—; founder, dir. East Side Jewish Adult Studies Program, 1950—, Rabbanit Miriam Nulman Free Adult Inst. Judaic Studies, 1955—, Mobilization for Youth, Lower East Side, N.Y., 1958—; chmn. Am. com. Yeshiva Torah Ore, Jerusalem; chmn. Jewish Community Council East Side, N.Y.C., 1950-54, Youth Commn. East Side C. of C., 1959-70, Nat. Day Sch. Tchrs. Licensing Commn., Nat. Assn. Hebrew Day Schs., 1964—, Religious Instn. Commn., N.Y.C., 1964-70, Essex Delancey Neighborhood Assn., 1970—, Lower East Side Neighborhoods Assn., 1972—, Multi-Service Ctr., N.Y.C., 1973—; dir. Rabbanit Miriam Nulman Free Adult Inst. of Jewish Studies, Yeshivas Torea Moshe, Jerusalem, 1955, Massaryk Towers, N.Y.C., N.Y.C. Com. on Inter-Racial Conflicts; v.p. United Jewish Council of Eastside N.Y.; judge Jewish Conciliation Bd. Am. Author: Syllabus and Techniques for Hebrew Day School, 1953, Holiday Customs and Ceremonies, 1959, Torah Journal, 1959, The Memorial Book, 1965, Handbook for Jewish Parents, 1965, The Year of Jewish Holidays, Festivals and Ceremonies, 1982, Concise Guide to the Traditional Jewish Wedding, 1989, Slutzk/East Side Torah Center--100 Years in America, 1989; editor monthly letter, 1958—; contbr. articles to profl. jours. Del. White House Conf. Children and Youth, 1970; state supt. ch.-related schs. com. HEW, 1960-64; mem. planning bd. Borough Manhattan, 1960—, New Gov. Hosp., N.Y.C., 1972-74; mem. Jewish com. Manhattan coun. Boy Scouts Am., 1955—; mem. adv. coun. Joint Legis. Commn. Pub. Health, Medicine, Medicaid and Compulsory Health and Hosp. Inst. State N.Y., 1968—; mem. Joint Human Rsch. Med. Rsch. Com.; mem. Met. Com. on Talmud Torah Edn., 1969—, Health Systems Agy., N.Y.; founders com., bd. dirs. Coordinating Coun. Bikuz Cholim Socs. of Visitors to Sick and Home Bound. Recipient numerous merit awards; other awards Svc. Internat. Torah Schs., 1966, Outstanding Educator award Parents Assn., 1968, Shofar award Boy Scouts Am., 1969, Community Fedn. Jewish Philanthropies, 1971, Torah Leadership P'eylim, 1972, Community L.E.N.A. Assns., 1973, Disting. Svc. Jewish Conciliation Bd. Am., 1974, Pastoral Care Chaplaincy Sch., N.Y. Bd. Rabbis, 1975, State of Israel Bonds, 1982, Negev State of Israel, 1983; Israel award Nat. Synagogue Israel Bonds, 1985, Scroll Honor award State Israel Bonds, 1986, State of Israel Bonds Citations, 1990, Israel award for Leadership, 1989; Bronze Tablet commemorating 50 yr. svc. as dean and rabbi., 1990. Mem. Religious Instn. Assn. (pres. 1958-70), Nat. Conf. Day Sch. Prins. and Deans (chmn.), Rabbinical Bd. East Side (founder, v.p.), Union Orthodox Rabbis U.S. and Can. (exec. mem. adminstrv. bd.), Assn. Torah Edn., Nat. Assn. Jewish Chaplains (founding), Rabbinical Alumni Yeshiva U., Orthodox Jewish Congregations Am., Nat. Assn. Orthodox Jewish Scientists (mem. planning bd.), Rabbinical Sem. Am. Alumni Assn. (sec.), Nat. English Prins. Assn. (sec. 1960-70), Nat. Assn. Hebrew Day Schs.-Yeshivas (chmn. bd. dirs. 1967-69), Nat. Yeshiva Sch. Prins. (v.p.), N.Y.C. C. of C. (bd. dirs.), NEA, Jewish Community Rels. Coun. N.Y., Human Rsch. Med. Rev. Com. Club: B'nai B'rith. Home: 268 E Broadway New York NY 10002 Office: East Side Torah Ctr 313 Henry St New York NY 10002 *All my life I have strived to serve "In the Vineyard of the Lord", dedicating my efforts and work in the service between Man and God and between Man and fellowman.*

NUNN, DAVID OLIVER, minister; b. Dallas, Dec. 11, 1921; s. Henry Nathan and Eva (Law) N.; m. Leona Clementine Hagood, May 16, 1947; children: Rebecca Ann, Naomi Ruth, David Paul, Tommy Lee. Ordained to ministry Assemblies of God, 1953. Founder Bible Revival Evangelistic Assn., Inc., Dallas, 1952—, pres., 1952-90, also bd. dirs., 1952—; dir. Voice of Healing, Inc., Dallas, 1956-61, nat. radio speaker, 1958-62; internat. radio speaker Bible Revival, Inc., Dallas, 1963-90; evangelist crusades worldwide; founder various Bible Colls. and orphanages in third world countries. Editor: (mag.) Healing Messenger, 1965-90; author 23 books, 1962-82. Sgt. USAAF, 1941-45, ETO. Home: PO Box 3990 Dallas TX 75208

NUNN, GEORGE HARRY, minister, college president; b. Noranda, Que., Can., Nov. 29, 1935; s. George Harry and Shiela (Darwin) N.; m. Ruth Naomi Bohrer, Nov. 24, 1954; children: Ruth Ann, Harry, Timothy, Stephen. DD (hon.), Christianview Bible Coll., 1977; DMin, Can. Christian Coll., 1979. Ordained to Ministry Pentecostal Holiness Ch. of Can., 1955. Pastor Bethel Assembly, Tacoma, Wash., 1962-69, Ch. By The Side of the Road, Seattle, 1969-71; gen. supt. Pentecostal Holiness Ch. of Can., Waterloo, Ont., Can., 1971—; pres. Christianview Bible Coll., Ailsa Craig, Ont., 1975-90. Office: Pentecostal Holiness Ch, PO Box 442, Waterloo, ON Canada N2J 4A9

NUNN, WALTER GORDON, pastor; b. Covington, Ga., July 4, 1928; s. Walter Roy and Vinnie Rose (Gordon) N.; m. Margaret Elizabeth Harbin, May 29, 1951; children: Betsy Nunn Parham, Jon David, Cheryl, Robert. AB, Mercer U., 1949; MDiv, So. Bapt. Theol. Sem., Louisville, 1952; DD (hon.), Samford U., 1972. Ordained to ministry So. Bapt. Conv., 1951. Pastor Hokes Bluff 1st Bapt. Ch., Gadsden, Ala., 1952-54; pastor 1st Bapt. Ch., Haleyville, Ala., 1954-61, Gardendale, Ala., 1961-70, Jasper, Ala., 1970-82; pastor Univ. Bapt. Ch., Huntsville, Ala., 1982—; pres. Ala. Bapt. Conv., 1971-73; vice chmn. exec. com. So. Bapt. Conv., 1971-80; moderator Walker Bapt. Assn., 1974-76, Madison Bapt. Assn., 1987-89; mem. Madison Bapt. Mins. Conf., 1982—. Contbr. sermons to books; book rev. editor Ala. Bapt., 1962—; newspaper columnist. Mem. Jasper Cemetery Bd., 1972-74, Huntsville Mayor's Adv. Group, 1988-89; pres. Walker County Assn. for Retarded Citizens, 1975-78, Citizens Action Program, Birmingham, Ala., 1977-79, NW Ala. Mental Health Bd., 1979-82. Named Ala. Outstanding Large Ch. Pastor of Yr., Samford U., 1990. Mem. Greater Huntsville Mins. Assn. (pres. 1989-90), Masons. Home: 1007 Speake Rd Huntsville AL 35816 Office: Univ Bapt Ch 809 Jordan Ln Huntsville AL 35816

NUTT, NAN, church administrator; b. Pasadena, Calif., Dec. 25, 1925; d. Paul Geltmacher and Estelle Boggs (Love) White; m. David Ballard Norris, Jan. 8, 1944 (div. 1966); children: Teresa, Anita, Carol, Steven; m. Evan Burchall Nutt, July 12, 1969. AA, Chaffee Jr. Coll., Calif., 1967; BA, Pomona Coll., 1969. Adminstrv. asst to dept. head sch. elec. engring. U. Tenn., Knoxville, 1952-53; adminstrv. asst. to minister of ch. edn. United Congl. Ch., Claremont, 1955-62; adminstrv. asst. to personnel dir. Pomona Coll., Claremont, 1962-63; bus. mgr. 1st Congl. Ch., Long Beach, Calif., 1982-86, ch. adminstr., 1986—. Chmn. Nat. Women's Polit. Caucus, Tucson, 1972, nat. rep. Ariz., 1973-79, chmn. greater Long Beach, 1981, vice chmn., Calif., 1986-88; pres. Coalition for ERA, Ariz., 1973-79; commr. Cultural Heritage Commn., Long Beach, 1985-87, chair, 1987—; mem. adv. bd. Plymouth West Older Adult Svc. and Info. System, 1989—. Democrat. Avocation: politics.

NUTTING, JOHN E., minister, ecumenical agency administrator. Exec. sec. Vt. Ecumenical Coun. and Bible Soc., Burlington. Office: Vt Ecumenical Coun Bible Soc 285 Maple St Burlington VT 05401*

NUVEEN, JOHN SEPTIMUS, cultural affairs organization executive; b. Evanston, Ill., Feb. 21, 1934; s. John and Grace Bennet N.; children: John, Octavius, Nuveen. Pastor Amagansett (N.Y.) Presbyn. Ch., 1962-63; mem. Iona Community, Ch. of Scotland, Glasgow, 1959-60; pres. Ctr. for Arts, Religion, Edn., Berkeley, Calif., 1988—; bd. dirs. Soc. for Arts, Religion and Contemporary Culture, N.Y.C.; vis. scholar Grad. Theol. Union, Berkeley, 1981-82. Author: Poems for Dreamers, 1986. Active Saco Valley Environ. Svc. Project. Mem. Am. Acad. Religion. Home and Office: 1563 Solano Ave # 133 Berkeley CA 94707 *Since "the longer you are the way you are, the more you are that way, " (Nuveen's Laws, #2, 1982), and since there is an inverse proportionality between destructive personal involvement in a position and security in that position, it is good to cultivate forgiveness and thankfulness, early, if Hugo was right, in one's grandmother.*

NYBERG, WALTER LAWRENCE, psychology and religion educator emeritus; b. Mpls., Nov. 20, 1922; s. Knute Harold and Helga (Bergman) N.; m. Ruth Brewster Whitney, Dec. 15, 1944; children: Jane, James, Peter, Paul. BA, Macalester Coll., St. Paul, 1946; STB, Boston U., 1949, STM, 1953; PhD, NYU, 1964. Ordained to ministry Meth. Ch., 1949. Pastor Meth. chs. in Mass., Oreg., Kans., 1949-59; assoc. min. Community Ch., Great Neck, N.Y., 1959-61; prof. religious studies U. of the Pacific, Stockton, Calif., 1962-90, ret., 1990; therapist Human Achievement Counseling Ctr., Stockton, 1969-86. Bd. dirs. Wesley Found., 1951-59. Democrat. Avocations: carpentry, music, travel, literature, computer. Home: 420 Bristol Stockton CA 95204 also: 655 Browns Valley Rd Watsonville CA 95076

NYCKLEMOE, GLENN WINSTON, bishop; b. Fergus Falls, Minn., Dec. 8, 1936; s. Melvin and Bertha (Sumstad) N.; m. Ann Elizabeth Olson, May 28, 1960; children: Peter Glenn, John Winston, Daniel Thomas. BA, St. Olaf Coll., 1958; MDiv, Luther Theol. Sem., St. Paul, 1962; D of Ministry, Luth. Sch. Theology, Chgo., 1977. Ordained to ministry Am. Luth. Ch., 1962. Assoc. pastor Our Savior's Luth. Ch., Valley City, N.D., 1962-64; assoc. pastor Our Savior's Luth. Ch., Milw., 1964-67, co-pastor, 1967-73; sr. pastor Our Savior's Luth. Ch., Beloit, Wis., 1973-82, St. Olaf Luth. Ch., Austin, Minn., 1982-88; bishop Southeastern Minn. Synod, Evang. Luth. Ch. in Am., Rochester, 1988—; bd. dirs. Luth. Social Svcs. of Minn., Mpls., Bd. of Social Ministries, St. Paul, Minn. Coun. Chs., Mpls. Mem. bd. regents St. Olaf Coll., Northfield, Minn., 1988—. Avocations: skiing, trap shooting, golf. Office: SE Minn Synod Evang Luth Ch Am Assisi Heights Box 4900 Rochester MN 55903

NYE, ERIC WILLIAM, educator; b. Omaha, July 31, 1952; s. William Frank and Mary Roberta (Lueder) N.; m. Carol Denison Frost, Dec. 21, 1980. AB, St. Olaf Coll., 1974; MA, U. Chgo., 1976, PhD, 1983; postgrad., Queens' Coll., Cambridge, England, 1979-82. Tutor in coll. writing com. U. Chgo., 1976-79, teaching intern, 1978; supr., tutor in Am. Lit. Cambridge U., England, 1979-82; asst. prof. English U. Wyo., Laramie, Wyo., 1982-89, assoc. prof. English, 1989—; honorary visiting fellow U. Edinburgh (Scotland) Inst. for Advanced Studies in the Humanities, 1987; guest lectr. NEH Summer Inst., Laramie, Wyo., 1985, Carlyle Soc. of Edinburgh, 1987, Wordsworth Summer Conference, Grasmere, England, 1988; cons. NEH. Contbr. articles and reviews to profl. jours. Mem. Am. Friends of Cambridge U. Named Nat. Merit Scholar St. Olaf Coll., 1970-74; recipient Grad. Fellowship, Rotary Found., 1979-80, grant U. Wyo., 1984-85, Am. Coun. of Learned Socs., 1988, Disting. Alumnus award, Lincoln (Neb.) E. High Sch., 1986. Mem. MLA (del. assembly, 1990—), Assn. for Documentary Editing, Bibliographical Soc. London, Assn. for Computers and the Humanities, Assn for Literary and Linguistic Computing, Coleridge Soc. (life), Friends of Dove Cottage (life), Charles Lamb Soc., Carlyle Soc., Rsch. Soc. for Victorian Periodicals, The Victorians Inst., The Tennyson Soc., Am. Acad. of Religion-Soc. of Biblical Lit., Penn Club (London), Queens' Coll. Club (Cambridge), Phi Beta Kappa (v.p., sec. Wyo. chpt. 1988—). Home: 1628 Kearney St Laramie WY 82070 Office: U Wyo Dept English Box 3353 University Sta Laramie WY 82071

NYESTE, ISTVAN, minister; b. Berveni, Romania, Mar. 3, 1955; came to U.S., 1985; s. Istvan and Magdolna (Kádár) N.; m. Judit Miko, Mar. 11, 1978; children: Eva Judit, Steven László. Diploma in engring., Electro Mech. Coll., Romania, 1980; MDiv, New Brunswick Theol. Sem., 1990; postgrad., Trinity Luth. Sem., Columbus, Ohio, 1991—. Ordained to ministry Hungarian Ref. Ch. (United Ch. of Christ), 1990. Student pastor New Brunswick, N.J., 1986-89; student pastor Hungarian Reformed Ch., Columbus, Ohio, 1989-90; min. Hungarian Reformed Ch., Columbus, 1990—. Recipient Rev. Edward Lodewick prize New Brunswick Theol. Sem., 1990. Office: Hungarian Reformed Ch 365 E Woodrow Ave Columbus OH 43207 *The greatest blessing of my life is that I do not have to strain my brain to try to figure out everything about God, I only have to praise Him because in His saving love He has figured out everything about me. And then He said: You are forgiven.*

NYGREN, E(LLIS) HERBERT, theology educator; b. Bklyn., June 27, 1928; s. Erik H. and Jenny (Walaas) N.; m. Louise Whitton, June 9, 1951; children: E. Herbert, Steven E. BA, Taylor U., 1951; STB, Biblical Sem., N.Y.C., 1954; MA, NYU, 1954, PhD, 1960. Ordained min. Meth. Ch., 1951. Min. United Meth. Ch., various locations, 1951-60; prof. Emory (Va.) and Henry Coll., 1960-69; prof. Taylor U., Upland, Ind., 1969-91, prof. emeritus, 1991—. Contbr. articles to profl. publs., chpt. to book. Mem. Evangelical Theol. Soc., Am. Soc. Ch. History. Republican.

NYGREN, MALCOLM ERNEST, minister; b. Portsmouth, Ohio, Sept. 12, 1925; s. Gustav Henning and Alma Marie (Viberg) N.; m. Betty Sue Perry, May 14, 1950; children: Melinda (Mrs. Robert Pierce), Nancy. AB, Hanover Coll., 1949; BD, McCormick Theol. Sem., 1952; STD, San Francisco Theol. Sem., 1980. Ordained to ministry Presbyn. Ch. (USA), 1952. Sr. pastor 1st Presbyn. Ch., Champaign, Ill., 1952-90. Author: Lord of the Four Seasons, 1986; columnist Champaign News Gazette, Mattoon Jour. Gazette; contbr. religious and humorous articles to periodicals. Bd. dirs. Kemmerer Village, Assumption, Ill., 1976-82; pres., fellow Charles W. Christie Found., Champaign, 1975-86; mem. instl. rev. bd. U. Ill., Urbana-Champaign, 1991—. With inf. U.S. Army, 1943-46, ETO. Mem. Soc. for Sci. Study of Religion, Rotary. Office: 1818 Woodfield #201C Savoy IL 61874 *We are all citizens of two worlds-and the world we can't see is more significant than the one we do.*

NYQUIST, JOHN PAUL, minister; b. Oakland, Nebr., Jan. 1, 1954; s. Carroll Gordon and Rose (LaVonne) N.; m. Cheryl Ann Hutchins, May 16, 1981; children: Natalie Marie, John Taylor, Carson Andrew, Sawyer Paul. BS in Archtl. Studies, U. Nebr., 1976; ThM, Dallas Theol. Sem., 1981, ThD, 1984. Ordained to ministry Fellowship Evang. Bible Ch., 1983. Min. youth and music Paul's Union Ch., LaMarque, Tex., 1979-80; sr. pastor Evang. Bible Ch., Omaha, 1983—; mem. adv. bd. Grace Coll. of the Bible, 1985-89; mem. exec. com. Fellowship Evang. Bible Chs., Omaha, 1987—, chmn. commn. on chs., 1990—. Mem. NAE (rep. churchman's com. 1990—), Tau Sigma Delta, Phi Eta Sigma. Republican. Home: 7906 Arlington Dr Omaha NE 68134 Office: Evang Bible Ch 7820 Fort St Omaha NE 68134

NYQUIST, JOHN W., Christian school association administrator; b. Two Harbors, Minn., Dec. 28, 1944; s. George Victor and Ruby N.; m. Karen Sue Warneking, 1978; children: Kareen, Robert, George, Benjamin. Student, Portland (Oreg.) State U., 1972; AA, City Coll. San Francisco, 1975; BA, San Francisco State U., 1982; postgrad., S.F. State Graduate Sch., 1982-84. Cert. tchr., Calif. Served with USAF, 1962-68. Republican. Mem. United Pentecostal Ch. Office: 1970 Ocean Ave San Francisco CA 94127

NZE ABUY, RAFAEL MARIA, archbishop. Archbishop of Malabo, Roman Cath. Ch., Equatorial Guinea; pres. Bishops' Conf. Office: Arzobispado, Apdo 106, Malabo Equatorial Guinea*

OAKLEY, CHERI LYNN, missionary, educator; b. Winslow, Ariz., Oct. 1, 1957; d. Vernon L. and Kathryn Ann (Baynes) O. BS in Christian Edn. and Missions, Johnson Bible Coll., Knoxville, Tenn., 1980. Cert. EMT. Sunday sch. tchr. Christian Ch., Heyworth, Ill., 1974-87, coord. music, treas. missionary com., 1983-88; missionary tchr. Portugal Christian Mission, Lisbon,

1981-83, 88—, music min., 1988—; tchr. Am. Christian Internat. Acad. Cascais, Portugal, 1990—; campus ministry rep. Ill. State U., Bloomington, 1985-88. Mem. Ch. of Christ. Home: Rua Por do Sol 29, 2775 Carcavelos Portugal Office: Portugal Christian Mission RR 2 Box 288 Bloomington IL 61704

OAKLEY, JAMES EDWIN, minister; b. Highland Park, Mich., Apr. 29, 1948; s. Edward Detriot and Lois Christine (Lane) O.; m. Sherry Ellen Roach, June 18, 1971; children: Dayrol Edward, Kristine Nicol. Student in Bus. Mgmt., G.R. Community Sch., Auburn, Wash., 1975-77; AA in Bibl. Study, Nazarene Bible Coll., 1989. Ordained to ministry Ch. of the Nazarene, 1991. Pastor Tampa (Fla.) Grace Ch. of the Nazarene, 1989-91, Geneva (Fla.) 1st Ch. of the Nazarene, 1991—. Mem. Zone Mins. Assn. (sec. 1991—), Tri-City Mins. Assn. (treas. 1991—). Home: 225 W Hwy 46 PO Box 410 Geneva FL 32732 Office: 1st Ch Nazarene 205 W Hwy 46 PO Box 410 Geneva FL 32732

OAKLEY, ROBERT BRUCE, pastor; b. Moorestown, N.J., Feb. 14, 1959; s. David Robert and Eleanor (Gayman) O.; m. Lori Ann Lewis, July 30, 1988. BA in Bible Studies, Bob Jones U., Greenville, S.C., 1983, MA in Pastoral Studies, 1985, MDiv, 1987. Sr. pastor Landmark Bapt. Ch., Browns Mill, N.J., 1988—. Office: Landmark Baptist Ch Ridge Rd 8 South Lakeshore Box 33 Browns Mills NJ 08015 Home: 3 Lakeview Blvd Browns Mills NJ 08015

OAKMAN, DOUGLAS EDWARD, religion educator; b. Des Moines, Feb. 11, 1953; s. Virgil Lee and Dorothy Jean (Rastovac) O.; m. Deborah Lynn Sattler, Sept. 11, 1976; children: Justin Michael, Jonathan Edward. BA with honors, U. Iowa, 1975; MDiv, Christ Sem.-Seminex, 1979; PhD, Grad. Theol. Union, 1986. Ordained to ministry Evang. Luth. Ch. in Am., 1982. Assoc. pastor Bethlehem Luth. Ch., Oakland, Calif., 1982-86; asst. prof. Pacific Luth. U., Tacoma, 1988—. Author: Jesus and the Economic Questions of His Day, 1986; contbr. articles to profl. jours. Mem. Soc. Bibl. Lit., Cath. Bibl. Assn., The Context Group (Project on Bible in Its Cultural Environment), Phi Beta Kappa. Democrat. Lutheran. Home: 870 120th St S Tacoma WA 98444 Office: Pacific Luth U Religion Dept Tacoma WA 98447

OAKS, M(ARGARET) MARLENE, minister; b. Grove City, Pa., Mar. 30, 1940; d. Allen Roy and Alberta Bell (Pinner) Eakin; m. Lowell B. Chaney, July 30, 1963 (dec. Jan. 1977); children: Christopher Allen, Linda Michelle; m. Harold G. Younger, Aug. 1978 (div. 1986); m. Gilbert E. Oaks, Aug. 3, 1987. BA, Calif. State U., L.A., 1972; religious sci. studies with several instrs. Ordained to ministry Ch. Religious Sci., 1986. Tchr. Whittier (Calif.) Sch. Dists., 1972-74, Garden Grove (Calif.) Sch. Dist., 1974-78; instr. Fullerton Coll., 1974-75; founding min. Community Ch. of the Islands (now Ch. of Religious Sci.), Honolulu, 1978-80; min. Ch. of Divine Sci., Pueblo, Colo., 1980-83; founding min. Ch. Religious Sci., Palo Alto, Calif., 1983-86; min. Ch. Religious Sci., Fullerton, Calif., 1986—; workshop leader Religious Sci. Dist. Conv., San Jose, Calif., 1985, Internat. New Thought Alliance Conf., Las Vegas, 1984, Calgary, Alta., Can., 1985, Washington, 1988, Golden Valley Unity Women's Advance, Mpls., 1986, 87, Qume Corp., San Jose, 1985; instr. Fullerton Coll., 1974-75. Author: The Christmas in You, 1983, Ki Aikido the Inner Martial Art, 1984, Old Time Religion is a Cult, 1985, Beyond Forgiveness, 1985, Service the Sure Path to Enlightenment, 1985, Stretch Marks on My Aura, 1987, Beyond Addiction, 1990; contbr. articles to profl. publs. Del. Soviet and Am. Citizens Summit Conf., 1988, 89; pres. Soviet-Am. New Thought Initiatives, 1991; founder Op. K.I.D.S.; founder, bd. dir. Awakening Oaks Found., 1990. Named Outstanding Businesswoman, Am. Businesswomen's Assn., 1989. Mem. Fullerton Inerfaith Ministerial Assn. (sec. treas. 1987-89, pres. 1991-92), United Clergy of Religious Sci. (treas. 1991-92), Internat. New Thought Alliance (O.C. chpt. pres. 1990), Soroptimists (chair com. internat. coop. and goodwill 1987-88), Kappa Delta Pi. Republican. Avocations: painting, sewing, writing, dancing. Office: 1st Ch Religious Sci 117 N Pomona Ave Fullerton CA 92632

OBANDO BRAVO, MIGUEL CARDINAL, archbishop of Managua; b. La Libertad, Nicaragua, Feb. 2, 1926. Ordained priest Roman Cath. Ch., 1958. Titular bishop of Puzia di Bizavena and aux. bishop of Matagalpa, 1968—, archbishop of Managua, 1970—, elevated to Sacred Coll. of Cardinals, 1985. Address: Arzobispado, Apto 3058, Managua Nicaragua

OBESO RIVERA, SERGIO, archbishop; b. Jalapa, Mexico, Oct. 31, 1931. Ordained priest Roman Cath. Ch., 1954; named bishop Papantla, 1971-74; named titular bishop of Uppenna with personal title of archbishop, 1974-79, archbishop of Jalapa, Mexico, 1979—. Office: Arzobispado Ave Revolucion 2, Apartado 359, Jalapa Mexico

O'BIER, DON MICHEAL, minister; b. Bossier City, La., May 29, 1946; s. Theron Julius and Ruth Amanda (Sanderson) O'B.; m. Glenda Joyce Sturges, Aug. 9, 1974; children: Rebecca, Rachel, Robin. BS, Northwestern State U. of La., 1968; M. Religious Edn., Southwestern Bapt. Theol. Sem., 1977. Ordained to ministry So. Bapt. Conv., 1977. Minister of edn., youth and music 1st Bapt. Ch. Lakeside, Ft. Worth, 1976-77; minister of edn. 1st Southern Bapt. Ch., El Monte, Calif., 1977-79; minister of edn. and outreach Bammel Bapt. Ch., Houston, 1979-82, 1st Bapt. Ch., Huntsville, Tex., 1982-84; minister edn. and sr. adult edn. Grace Temple Bapt. Ch., Dallas, 1984-91; asst. pastor in personal evangelism 1st Bapt. Ch., Dallas, 1991—; mem. exec. bd. Bapt. Benevolent Ministries of Oak Cliff, Dallas, 1986-88; cons. on adult ministry Assn. Sunday Sch. Improvement Support Team, Dallas, 1984—. Chmn. community advisor com. John Peeler Elem. Sch., Dallas, 1990, 91. Capt. U.S. Army, 1969-75, Vietnam. Decorated Bronze Star, 4 Air medals, Vietnam Cross of Gallantry with palm. Mem. Dallas Bapt. Assn. (exec. bd. 1984—), So. Bapt. Religious Edn. Assn. Republican. Home: 339 Brookwood Duncanville TX 75116 Office: 1st Bapt Ch Ervay and San Jacinto Sts Dallas TX 75201

O'BRIEN, BETTY ALICE, theological librarian, researcher; b. Kingsburg, Calif., June 12, 1932; d. Robert Herbert and Alice Dorothy (Larson) Peterson; m. Elmer John O'Brien, July 2, 1966. AA, North Pk. Coll., 1952; diploma, North Pk. Theol. Sem., 1954; BA, Northwestern U., 1956; MLS, U. Calif., Berkeley, 1957. Asst. libr. North Pk. Theol. Sem., Chgo., 1957-69; libr. St. Leonard Coll., Dayton, Ohio, 1971-84; researcher United Theol. Sem., Dayton, 1986—, reference supr., 1991—. Editor: Religion Index 2: Festschriften 1960-69, 1980. Mem. Am. Theol. Libr. Assn. (bd. dirs. 1981—, editor Summary Proc. 1982—), Ohio Theol. Libr. Assn. (sec. 1972-76, chairperson 1978-79), Meth. Librs. Fellowship (v.p., pres. 1991—). Mem. United Meth. Ch. Office: United Theol Sem 1810 Harvard Blvd Dayton OH 45406

O'BRIEN, ELMER JOHN, educator, librarian; b. Kemmerer, Wyo., Apr. 8, 1932; s. Ernest and Emily Catherine (Reinhart) O'B.; m. Betty Alice Peterson, July 2, 1966. A.B., Birmingham So. Coll., 1954; Th.M., Iliff Sch. Theology, 1957; M.A., U. Denver, 1961. Ordained to ministry Methodist Ch., 1957; pastor Meth. Ch., Pagosa Springs, Colo., 1957-60; circulation-reference librarian Boston U. Sch. Theology, Boston, 1961-65; asst. librarian Garrett-Evang. Theol. Sem., Evanston, Ill., 1965-69; librarian, prof. United Theol. Sem., Dayton, Ohio, 1969—; abstractor Am. Bibliog. Center, 1969-73; dir. Ctr. for Evang. United Brethren Heritage, 1979—; chmn. div. exec. com. Dayton-Miami Valley Libr. Consortium, 1983-84; rsch. assoc. Am. Antiquarian Soc., 1990. Author: Bibliography of Festschriften in Religion Published Since 1960, 1972, Religion Index Two: Festschriften, 1960-69; pub. Meth. Revs. Index, 1918-85, 1989-91. Recipient theol. and scholarship award Assn. Theol. Schs. in U.S. and Can., 1990-91; Assn. Theol. Schs. in U.S. and Can. library staff devel. grantee, 1976-77, United Meth. Ch. Bd. Higher Edn. and Ministry research grantee, 1984-85. Mem. ALA, Acad. Libr. Assn. Ohio, Am. Theol. Libr. Assn. (head bur. personnel and placement 1969-73, dir. 1973-76, v.p. 1977-78, pres. 1978-79), Am. Antiquarian Soc. (rsch. assoc. 1990), Delta Sigma Phi, Omicron Delta Kappa, Eta Sigma Phi, Kappa Phi Kappa. Club: Torch Internat. (v.p. Dayton club 1981-82, pres. 1982-83). Home: 7818 Lockport Blvd Centerville OH 45459

O'BRIEN, JAMES RANDALL, minister; b. McComb, Miss., Aug. 29, 1949; s. Donald Ray and Irene (Allred) O'B.; m. Patricia Kay Donahoe, Dec. 21, 1975; children: Alyson, Shannon, Christopher. BS, Miss. Coll., 1975; MDiv, ThD, New Orleans Bapt. Theol. Sem., 1977, 82; postdoctoral studies, Yale U., 1986, STM, 1987. Ordained to ministry So. Bapt. Conv., 1977. Assoc. missionary Home Mission Bd., New Orleans, 1976-78; pastor Red Bluff Bapt. Ch., Greensburg, La., 1978-80, DeGray Bapt. Ch., Arkadelphia, Ark., 1980-83; asst. prof. religion Ouachita Bapt. U., Arkadelphia, 1980-87; sr. pastor Calvary Bapt. Ch., Little Rock, 1987-91; assoc. prof. Baylor U., Waco, Tex., 1991—; nat. treas. New Orleans Bapt. Theol. Sem., 1990-91, bd. trustees, 1989-90. Author: The Mosaic Messiah, 1983; editor: Journey in Faith, 1985; contbr. articles to profl. jours. Sgt. U.S. Army, 1970-71, Vietnam. Named Outstanding Faculty Mem. Ouachita Bapt. U., 1982-82, 84-85, Staley Disting. Christian scholar Miss. Coll., 1991. Home: 8606 Green Branch Waco TX 76712 Office: Baylor U Dept Religion Waco TX 76798

O'BRIEN, JOSEPH LEWIS, priest; b. Toledo, Sept. 28, 1929; s. Joseph Lewis and Mary Elizabeth (Daley) O'B. BA, U. Western Ont., London, Can., 1951. Ordained priest Roman Cath. Ch., 1955. Assoc. pastor St. Joseph Ch., Maumee, Ohio, 1955-62, St. Francis de Sales Ch., Toledo, 1962-68; pastor St. Thomas More U. Parish, Bowling Green, Ohio, 1968-70, Our Lady Mt. Carmel parish, Bono, Ohio, 1970-72, Immaculate Conception Parish, Toledo, 1972-79, St. Charles Parish, Toledo, 1979-82, St. Patrick Parish, Grand Rapids, Ohio, 1982—; diocesan dir. Cursillos in Christianity, Toledo, 1964-69, Papal Vols., Toledo, 1964-72, Evangelization, Toledo, 1978-85; diocesan del. pub. policy com. Ohio Coun. Churches, Columbus, 1978-83. Dir. aging project VISTA, Toledo, 1975-79; dir. FACT Neighborhood Orgn., Toledo, 1975-79; mem. Human Rights Commn., Toledo, 1991—. Mem. Nat. Fedn. Priests' Couns. (bd. dirs., rep. Cin. province 1988-91), Toledo Priests' Coun. (chair social action com. 1982-86), KC. Democrat. Avocations: golf, fishing, stamp collecting. Office: Saint Patrick Ch 14010 US Rte 24 Grand Rapids OH 43522

O'BRIEN, JUSTIN, theologian, philosopher, consultant; b. Chgo.; s. George J. O'Brien and June Drake. BA, U. Notre Dame, 1956; PhB, St. Albert's Coll., 1962, MA, 1963; MA, Marquette U., 1970; Doctor's degree, Nijmegen U., 1972, PhD, 1981. Cons. lifestyle mgmt. Justin O'Brien Assocs., St. Paul, 1989—; adj. prof. Coll. St. Catherine, St. Paul, 1988—, St. Mary's Coll., Mpls., 1989—. Author: Theory of Religious Consciousness, 1981, Running and Breathing, 1984, Christianity and Yoga, 1990, The Wellness Tree, 1990; co-author: Mirrors for Men, 1991. Sierra Found. grad. grantee, 1964-65, Vam Doren Found. grad. grantee, 1970. Mem. Am. Acad. Religion, Amnesty Internat . U.S. Psychotronic Assn. Home and Office: PO Box 75032 Saint Paul MN 55175

O'BRIEN, KATHLEEN MARY, lay worker; b. Fond du Lac, Wis., Sept. 22, 1951; d. John Francis and Marian (Goebel) O'B. BA in English, Marian Coll., 1973; MA in Religious Edn., Notre Dame Inst., 1983. Tchr. St. Michael's Sch., Ripley, Ohio, 1976-80, St. Patrick's High Sch., Maysville, Ky., 1980-83; dir. religious edn. Holy Trinity Parish, West Union, Ohio, 1976-87; pastoral assoc. St. Catherine Parish, Atlanta, Tex., 1987—, St. Mary of the Cenacle Parish, New Boston, Tex., 1988—. Home and Office: 205 W Miller St Atlanta TX 75551 *In the service of others it is often the little things that mean the most. A birthday or anniversary remembered, a quick call to let someone know you missed them, a little act of kindness or service, all the little things draw us closer to one another and to the Lord.*

O'BRIEN, MARY-MARGARET, church official, commercial artist; b. Derby, Conn., Feb. 26, 1946; d. John and Mary Ann (Kalasinsky) Hlywa; m. Michael Fleming O'Brien, Apr. 20, 1968; children: Heather Beth, Mathew Brenden. Student comml. art, Paier Coll. Art, Hamden, Conn., 1967. Comml. artist Sears Roebuck & Co., Orange, Conn., 1967-68; graphic artist Mark I Printers, Hamden, 1968-69; display mgr. Montgomery Ward, Junction City, Kans., 1969-70; tchr. Cabbage Hill Day Sch., Woodbridge, Conn., 1974-78; co-owner, mgr., buyer Odzookens-Craft Concern, Ltd., Woodbridge, 1979-83; sales cons. Princess House, Inc., North Dighton, Mass., 1983-86; adminstrv. asst., editor newsletter Trinity Evang. Free Ch., Woodbridge, 1987—; designer, buyer Woodbridge Stitchery, 1984; sec., bookkeeper Mark Assocs. Realtors, New Haven, 1985-86. Contbr. articles to various publs. Treas. Free Ch. Women's Ministry, Woodbridge, 1988-89; sec. 1900 Free Ch. Conf. Com., Mpls., 1989—. Democrat. Evangelical. Avocations: creative needlework, walking, reading, acting. Home: 175 Bethmour Rd Bethany CT 06525

O'BRIEN, ROGER GERARD, priest; b. Seattle, Aug. 3, 1935; s. Francis Thomas and Susan Elizabeth (Jurich) O'B. BA, Sulpician Sem. of Northwest, 1957, MDiv, 1961; MLS, U. Wash., 1961; Lic. in Theology, St. Mary's Sem., 1964; ThD, Cath. U., Louvain, Belgium, 1969. Ordained priest Roman Cath. Ch., 1961. Prof. systematic theology St. Patrick's Sem., Menlo Park, Calif., 1968-69, St. Thomas Sem., Kenmore, Wash., 1969-76; ecumenical and interfaith officer Archdiocese of Seattle, 1976-80, dir. office of worship, 1977-82; pastor St. Luke Parish, Seattle, 1982—; bd. dirs. Ch. Coun. Greater Seattle, 1976-82, Wash. Assn. Chs., 1976-82. Contbr. articles to profl. jours. Mem. Jewish/Christian Dialogue, Seattle, 1976—; bd. dirs. Archdiocese of Seattle Faith and Community Devel. Dept., 1982-86; mem. Archdiocesan Liturgical Commn., 1990-91. Mem. Nat. Assn. Diocesan Ecumenical Officers (bd. dirs. 1980-82). Democrat. Home and Office: St Luke's Ch 322 N 175th St Seattle WA 98133

O'BRIEN, THOMAS JOSEPH, bishop; b. Indpls., Nov. 29, 1935. Grad., St. Meinrad Coll. Sem. Ordained priest Roman Catholic Ch., 1961. Bishop of Phoenix, 1982—. Office: 400 E Monroe Phoenix AZ 85004

O'BYRNE, PAUL J., bishop; b. Calgary, Alta., Can., Dec. 21, 1922. Ordained priest Roman Catholic Ch., 1948; bishop of Calgary, 1968—. Office: Cath Pastoral Care Ctr, 1916 2d Ave SW Room 205, Calgary, AB Canada T2S 1S3

O'CALLAGHAN, JOHN JOSEPH, priest; b. New Rochelle, N.Y., Oct. 20, 1931; s. Francis Eugene and Marion Helen (O'Reilly) O'C. AB, Loyola U., Chgo., 1954, MA in Classical Langs., 1960; ThD, Gregorian U., Rome, 1967. Joined S.J., Roman Cath. Ch., 1949, ordained priest, 1962. Prof., rector Jesuit Sch. Theology, Chgo., 1967-76; sec. pers. Jesuit Conf., Washington, 1976-80, pres., 1980-83; gen. asst. S.J., Rome, 1983—. Contbr. articles to profl. jours. Mem. Cath. Theol. Soc., Soc. Christian Ethics. Address: Curia Generalizia Compagnia, di Gesu/Borgo Santo Spirito 5, 00195 Rome Italy

O'CHESTER, HAROLD EUGENE, clergyman; b. Bklyn., Aug. 19, 1927; s. John and Catherine Miriam (Johnson) O'C.; m. Barbara Jean Hostetter, Aug. 9, 1957; children: Jennifer, Shannon, Kathleen. BA, Miss. Coll., Clinton, 1954; ThM, New Orleans Bapt. Seminary, 1958; DD (hon.), Calif. Grad of Theology, L.A., 1981. Ordained to ministry Bapt. Ch., 1952. Pastor Bapt. Ch., Miss., 1952-69, Great Hils Bapt. Ch., Austin, Tex., 1969—; co-dir. Great Hills Retreat Ministry, Austin, 1969—. Author: Why Me Lord, 1985; author booklet How To Give Master Charge, 1988. With USN, 1945-47, 50-52. Named Pastor Fastest Growing Ch. in Tex., Moody Monthly, 1976, 77, 78, 80. Mem. Lions, Jaycees (Outstanding Man of Yr. award 1962). Republican. Avocations: skiing, traveling, hunting, reading. Office: Great Hills Bapt Ch 10500 Jollyville Rd Austin TX 78759

OCHNER, RONALD WILLIAM, pastoral counselor; b. East Orange, N.J., Aug. 23, 1935; s. Louis Karl and Elizabeth (Chiego) O.; m. Mae Marie Sisti, June 15, 1957; children: Cheryl Lynn, Robert, Richard, Christopher. BA, Montclair State Coll., Upper Montclair, N.J., 1957; MDiv, Steon Hall U., 1986. Ordained deacon Roman Cath. Ch., 1974. Founder, exec. dir. The Servants of the Holy Cross, Pompton Plains, N.J., 1971—, The Bros. of Jesus, Pompton Plains, 1988—, Still Point Counseling Ctr., Pompton Plains, 1989—; dir. religious edn. St. Clements Parish, Rockaway, N.J., 1978-80; dir. adult edn. Our Lady of Good Counsel, Pompton Plains, 1980-82; prayer counselor Pastoral Sch. Prayer Counseling, Winter Park, Fla., 1986—; co-liaison for bishop Cath. charismatic renewal Dioces of Paterson, N.J., 1987—; mem. adv. coun. Nat. Svc. Com.-Charismatic, Washington, 1987—; pres. Senate Enterprises Inc., fin. planning, Pompton Plains, 1974—. Capt. USMC, 1957-59. Mem. Assn. Christian Therapists, Nat. Liaison Assn. Republican. Home: 30 Ramapo Rd Box 366 Pompton Plains NJ 07444 Office: Still Point Counseling Ctr 30 Washburn Rd Box 32 Pompton Plains NJ 07444

OCHOA, ARMANDO, bishop; b. Oxnard, Calif., Apr. 3, 1943. Grad., Ventura (Calif.) Coll., St. John's Coll., Camarillo, Calif. Ordained priest Roman Cath. Ch., 1970. Titular bishop of Sitifi Calif.; aux. bishop L.A., 1987. Office: Chancery Office 1531 W 9th St Los Angeles CA 90015

OCHS, PETER WARREN, religion educator; b. Boston, Jan. 26, 1950; s. Sidney and Ruth (Adelman) O.; m. Vanessa Lynn Yablin, June 16, 1974; children: Juliana, Elizabeth. BA summa cum laude, Yale U., 1971, PhD, 1979; MA, Jewish Theol. Sem., 1974. Dir. Jewish Theol. Sem. Pre-High Sch., N.Y.C., 1972-74; counselor to Jewish students Colgate U., Hamilton, N.Y., 1979-86, asst. prof. religion, 1979-86; advisor Colgate-Hamilton Jewish Community, Hamilton, N.Y., 1979—; Wallerstein vis. assoc. prof. Jewish studies Drew U., Madison, N.J., 1988-90, Wallerstein assoc. prof. Jewish studies, 1990—; Fulbright sr. lectr. in philosopy The Hebrew U. of Jerusalem, 1988; lectr. in field. Author: Knowledge Under the Mast, 1970, Talk of the Sea—Oral Navigational Lore on Puluwat, 1971, Learning Sea Lore on Puluwat Atoll, 1975, (with others) Understanding the Rabbinic Mind: Essays on the Hermeneutic of Max Kadushin, 1990; mem. editorial bd. Cross Currents—Religion and Intellectual Life; contbr. articles to profl. jours. Mem. Labor Zionist Alliance, Israel, 1981—, Nitivot Shalom, Jerusalem, 1981—, edn. com. Sch. Bd. of Hebrew Acad. Morris County (chairperson). NEH grantee, 1971, 73, 74, Smithsonian Instn. fellow, 1969, Kent fellow, 1974, Yale U. fellow, 1977, Colgate U. rsch. grantee, 1980, 81, 82. Mem. Soc. for Values in Higher Edn., Am. Acad. Religion, Am. Philos. Assn., Charles S. Peirce Soc., Assocs. for Religion in Intellectual Life, Assn. for Advancement of Am. Philosophy, Acad. for Jewish Philosophy, B'nai Brith. Office: Drew U Dept Religion Madison NJ 07940

O'CONNELL, SISTER COLMAN, nun, college administrator, consultant. BA in English, Speech, Coll. St. Benedict, St. Joseph, Minn., 1950; MFA in Theater, English, Cath. U., 1954; PhD in Higher Edn. Adminstrn., U. Mich., 1979; student, Northwestern U., Birmingham U., Stratford, Eng., Denver U., Stanford U., Sophia U., Tokyo. Entered Order of St. Benedict. Tchr. English Pierz (Minn.) Meml. High Sch., 1950-53, Cathedral High Sch., St. Cloud, Minn., 1950-53; chairperson theater and dance dept. then prof. theater Coll. of St. Benedict, St. Joseph, 1954-74, dir. alumnae, parent relations, ann. fund, 1974-77, dir. planning, 1979-84, exec. v.p., 1984-86, pres., 1986—; cons. Augsburg Coll., Mpls., 1983-85, Assn. Cath. Coll. and Univs., 1982, Minn. Pvt. Coll. Council, 1982, SW (Minn.) State U., Marshall, 1980-82, Wilmar (Minn.) Community Coll., 1980-82, Worthington (Minn.) Community Coll., 1980-82, U. Minn., Morris, 1980-82; bd. dirs. Security Fin., St. Cloud, Minn. Publ Radio. Chair bd. Minn. Pvt. Coll. Coun., 1991—; bd. dirs. St. Cloud Community Found., 1991—. Mem. St. Cloud Area C. of C. (bd. dirs. 1987-90). Office: Coll St Benedict 37 College Ave Saint Joseph MN 56374-2099

O'CONNELL, NEIL JAMES, priest, academic administrator; b. Buffalo, May 21, 1937; s. Cornelius James and Marie Katherine (Schneider) O'C. BA, St. Bonaventure U., 1960; STB, Cath. U., Washington, 1964; MA, Siena Coll., 1967; PhD, U. Ga., 1970. Ordained priest Roman Cath. Ch., 1964. Instr. history and sociology St. Francis Coll., Rye Beach, N.H., 1965-67; asst. prof. history Prairie View (Tex.) A&M Coll., 1970-71; asst. assoc. prof. history Fisk U., Nashville, 1971-80, chmn. history, 1975-80, dir. div. fine arts and humanities, 1976-79; acad. dean Erie Community Coll., City Campus, Buffalo, 1980-86; dean faculty and instrn. Elizabeth Seton Coll., Yonkers, N.Y., 1986-89; dean Elizabeth Seton Sch. Assoc. Degree Studies of Iona Coll., Yonkers, N.Y., 1989-90; pres. St. Bonaventure U., St. Bonaventure, N.Y., 1990—. Contbr. articles to jours. in field. Trustee Archbishop Walsh High Sch., Olean, N.Y., 1990—, Bishop Timon High Sch., Buffalo, Trocaire Coll., Buffalo; bd. dirs. Econ. Devel. Zone, Olean, YMCA, Olean, 1990—, Industry, Bus., Commerce, Edn. Coalition, Olean, 1990—, Coll. Consortium for Internat. Studies. Mem. Olean C. of C. (bd. dirs. 1990—), Rotary, Phi Beta Sigma. Democrat. Avocations: walking, theater, music. Home: St Bonaventure U Saint Bonaventure NY 14778 Office: St Bonaventure U Office of President Saint Bonaventure NY 14778

O'CONNELL, PATRICK FRANCIS, psychiatrist, deacon; b. Toledo, Ohio, June 17, 1926; s. Francis Edward and Ruth Magdalen (Hayward) O'C.;m. Rita Josephine Marcil, Oct. 21, 1950; children: Carol, Ruthann, Beverly, Frank, Stephen, Sheila. BA, St. Leo's Coll., Fla., 1981; MD, St. Louis U., 1950. Diplomate Am. Bd. Psychiatry and Neurology. Psychiatrist in pvt. practice Pensacola, Fla., 1983—; deacon St. Ann's Ch., Gulf Breeze, Fla., 1985—. Capt. M.C., USN, 1944-83. Decorated Navy Commendation medal with combat V. Fellow Am. Psychiat. Assn. (life); mem. AMA, K.C. Office: 5043 Bayou Blvd Pensacola FL 32503 *While retaining respect for elders and peers, question everything to see if things can be looked at from another point of view.*

O'CONNOR, SISTER ANN PATRICIA, school system administrator. Supt. schs. Diocese of Santa Rosa, Calif. Office: Office Schs Supt PO Box 6654 Santa Rosa CA 95406*

O'CONNOR, BILLY KEITH, minister; b. Pomona, Calif., Nov. 19, 1942; s. Claude Willis and Judith M. (Anthony) O'C.; m. Cherith Joy Schoming, Feb. 14, 1981; children: Kevin, Kira. BTh., L.I.F.E. Bible Coll., 1964; MA, Azusa Pacific U., 1974. Ordained to ministry Foursquare Gospel Ch., 1965. Pastor Foursquare Gospel Ch., Salmon, Idaho, 1964-66; pastor Foursquare Gospel Ch., Royal Oak, Mich., 1966-69; min. edn. Foursquare Gospel Ch., Pomona, Calif., 1969-71; min. edn., youth Valley Community Drive-In Ch., San Dimas, 1971-74, Ch. of the Nazarene, Monrovia, Calif., 1974-77; sr. pastor Ch. of the Nazarene, Newberg, Oreg., 1977—; area chmn. Newberg premiere of Billy Graham film Joni, 1979; gen. chmn. Two Kroeze Bros. Crusades, Newberg, 1978, 88. Contbr. youth, adult materials to religious pubs. Parade chmn. Newberg Old Fashion of Festival, 1981-90, gen. chmn., 1983-90; bd. dirs. Newberg Sch. Dist., 1990—; pres., co-founder Salmon Ministerial Assn., 1964-65. Named Citizen of Yr. Newberg C. of C., 1988. Mem. Newberg Ministerial Assn. (pres. 1979-81, 88-89), Toastmasters Internat. (Able Toastmaster). Republican. Office: Ch of the Nazarene 1549 E 1st St Newberg OR 97132 *There is no greater joy than in being God's person in God's place doing God's bidding for God's glory. In that place is found the greatest sense of personal identity and life's deepest satisfaction.*

O'CONNOR, CHARLES E., religious organization administrator. Pres. Grace Gospel Fellowship, Grand Rapids, Mich. Office: Grace Gospel Fellowship 1011 Aldon St SW Grand Rapids MI 49509*

O'CONNOR, DANIEL WILLIAM, retired religious studies and classical languages educator; b. Jersey City, Mar. 17, 1925; s. Daniel William and Emma Pauline (Ritz) O'C.; m. Carolyn Lockwood, June 26, 1954; children—Kathlyn Forssell Beal, Daniel William III. B.A., Dartmouth Coll., 1945; M.A., Columbia U., 1956, Ph.D., 1960; M.Div., Union Theol. Sem., 1950. Ordained to ministry United Ch. of Christ, 1950. Mem. exec. com., bd. home missions Congl. Chs., 1946-51; pastor Paramus Congl. Ch., N.J., 1950-55; assoc. sec. Student Christian Movement YMCA, N.Y., 1947-48; exec. sec. Earl Hall Columbia U., N.Y.C., 1948-50; tutor asst., dept. N.T. Union Theol. Sem., N.Y.C., 1958-59; successively asst. prof., assoc. prof., prof. religious studies St. Lawrence U., Canton, N.Y., 1959-67, dir. summer session, 1966, assoc. dean coll., 1967-68, Charles A. Dana prof. religious studies and classical langs., 1967-89, chmn. dept. religious studies and classical langs., 1974-89, Charles A. Dana emeritus prof., 1989—. Author: Peter in Rome, 1969; contbr. articles to Ency. Britannica and profl. jours., also revs. Trustee Silver Bay Assn. YMCA, N.Y., 1978-85, 86-92, Lit. Vols. Am., St. Lawrence County, N.Y., 1991—; bd. dirs. U.S. Power Squadron, St. Lawrence Squadron, N.Y., 1972-75. Served with USNR, 1943-45. Grantee Lilly Found., Columbia U., 1969-70, Mellon Found., Am. Schs. Oriental Research, Jerusalem, 1979. Mem. AARP, Am. Soc. Oriental Rsch., Am. Soc. Bibl. Lit., Am. Acad. Religion (pres. Eastern Internat. region 1985-86), Nat. Audobon Soc., AAUP, Adirondack Mountain Club, Rotary (pres. Canton Club 1972-73, Rotary Found. scholarship selection com. dist. 704, 1983-87, gov. dist. 704 1987-88, dist. 704 ext. com. 1988-89, youth exchange com. dist. 704 1990—, lit. com. 1991—). Home: 3 Hillside Circle Canton NY 13617

O'CONNOR, EDWARD DENNIS, theology educator; b. Denver, Oct. 28, 1922; s. Edward James and Mary Alethaire (Spalding) O'C. A.B., Notre Dame U., 1944; sem. student, Holy Cross Coll., 1944-48; S.T.L., Institut catholique de Paris, 1950; S.T.D., Angelicum, Rome, 1959. Ordained priest Roman Catholic Ch., 1948; faculty U. Notre Dame, 1952—, now assoc. prof. theology. Author: The Dogma of the Immaculate Conception, 1958, Faith in the Synoptic Gospels, 1961, The Pentecostal Movement in the Catholic Church, 1971, The Gifts of the Spirit, 1973, Perspectives on Charismatic Renewal, 1975, Pope Paul and the Spirit, 1978, others. Address: Corby Hall Notre Dame IN 46556

O'CONNOR, SISTER GEORGE AQUIN (MARGARET M. O'CONNOR), college president, sociology educator; b. Astoria, N.Y., Mar. 5, 1921; d. George M. and Joana T. (Loughlin) O'C. B.A., Hunter Coll., 1943; M.A., Catholic U. Am., 1947; Ph.D. (NIMH fellow), NYU, 1964; LL.D. Manhattan Coll., 1983. Mem. faculty St. Joseph's Coll., Bklyn., 1946—; prof. sociology and anthropology St. Joseph's Coll., 1966—, chmn. social sci. dept., 1966-69, pres., 1969—; Fellow African Studies Assn., Am. Anthrop. Assn.; Bklyn. C. of C. (dir. 1973—), Alpha Kappa Delta, Delta Epsilon Sigma. Author: The Status and Role of West African Women: A Study in Cultural Change, 1964. Fellow African Studies Assn., Am. Anthrop. Assn.; mem. Bklyn. C. of C. (dir. 1973—), Alpha Kappa Delta, Delta Epsilon Sigma. Office: St Joseph's Coll 245 Clinton Ave Brooklyn NY 11205

O'CONNOR, HUBERT PATRICK, bishop; b. Huntingdon, Que., Can., Feb. 17, 1928; s. Patrick Joseph and Mary Stella (Walsh) O'C. B.A., St. Patrick's Coll., Ottawa, 1952; L.S.T., Holy Rosary Scholasticate, Ottawa, 1956. Joined Congregation Missionary Oblates Mary Immaculate, 1948; ordained priest Roman Cath. Ch., 1955; mem. staff Holy Rosary Scholasticate, 1956-61; pastor St. John's Parish, Lillooet, B.C., 1967-68; prin. Cariboo Indian Residential Sch., Williams Lake, B.C., 1961-67; sec.-treas. Order Oblates Mary Immaculate in B.C., Vancouver, 1968-71; dir. St. Paul's Provincial House, 1968-71, Western region Oblate Fathers Indian-Eskimo Commn., 1968-71; bishop Diocese of Whitehouse, Y.T., Can., 1971-86, Diocese of Prince George, B.C., Can., 1986—; nat. dir. Cath. Women's League Can., 1973-78; chmn. Missions Commn., Can. Conf. Cath. Bishops, 1985-87. Club: K.C. (state chaplain B.C. and Yukon).

O'CONNOR, JOHN JOSEPH CARDINAL, archbishop, former naval officer; b. Phila., Jan. 15, 1920; s. Thomas Joseph and Dorothy Magdalene (Gomple) O'C. M.A., St. Charles Coll., 1949, Catholic U. Am., 1954; Ph.D., Georgetown U., 1970; D.R.E., Villanova (Pa.) U., 1976. Ordained priest Roman Cath. Ch., 1945, elevated to monsignor, 1966, consecrated bishop, 1979, created cardinal, 1985; served in Chaplain Corps U.S. Navy, 1952, advanced through grades to rear adm.; assigned to Atlantic and Pacific fleets U.S. Navy, Okinawa and Vietnam; sr. chaplain U.S. Naval Acad.; chief of chaplains U.S. Navy, Washington; aux. bishop, vicar gen. Mil. Vicariate, 1979-83; apptd. bishop of Scranton Pa., 1983-84; archbishop Archdiocese of N.Y., 1984—; Exec. bd. Nat. USO, Georgetown Center Strategic and Internat. Studies, Marine Corps Found. Author: Principles and Problems of Naval Leadership, 1958, A Chaplain Looks at Vietnam, 1969, In Defense of Life, 1981, (with Elie Wiesel) A Journey of Faith, 1990. Decorated DMS, Legion of Merit (3), Meritorious Service medal. Mem. Am. Polit. Sci. Assn. Office: Archdiocese NY 452 Madison Ave New York NY 10022

O'CONNOR, JUNE ELIZABETH, religious studies educator; b. Chgo., June 3, 1941; d. Philip Kevin and Eva Marie (Ennis) O'C.; m. Harry Hood, Aug. 11, 1973; 1 child, Meagan Hood. BA in English Lit., Mundelein Coll., 1964; MA, Marquette U., 1966, Temple U., 1972; PhD, Temple U., 1973. Instr. theology Mundelein Coll., Chgo., 1965-69, Temple U., Phila., 1970-73; asst. prof. religion U. Calif., Riverside, 1973-79, assoc. prof., 1979—, chmn. program in religious studies, 1985—. Author: The Quest for Political and Spiritual Liberation: A Study in the Thought of Sri Aurobindo Ghose, 1977, The Moral Vision of Dorothy Day: A Feminist Perspective, 1991; assoc. editor Jour. Religious Ethics, 1978-82, mem. editorial bd. 1982-85; mem. editorial bd. Religion, 1990—; contbr. articles to profl. jours. Grantee U. Calif., Riverside, 1975—. Mem. Am. Acad. Religion (pres. Western region 1984-85, v.p., program chmn. 1983-84, mem. nat. com. on edn. study of religion), Soc. Christian Ethics (bd. dirs. 1979-83, 90-94, chmn. Pacific sect. 1977-78, vice chmn., program chmn. 1976-77), Coll. Theology Soc., Danforth Found. (assoc.), Pacific Coast Theol. Soc., Soc. Values in Higher Edn. Office: U Calif Program Religious Studies Riverside CA 92521

O'CONNOR, MICHAEL PATRICK, religious writer, editor; b. Lackawanna, N.Y., Apr. 7, 1950; s. John David and Anna Mariah (Crosta) O'C. AB, U. Notre Dame, 1970; MA, U. British Columbia, 1972, U. Mich., 1974; PhD, U. Mich., 1978. Editor Ann Arbor, Mich., 1978—. Author: Hebrew Verse Structure, 1980, An Introduction to Biblical Hebrew Syntax, 1990; editor: The Word of the Lord Shall Go Forth: Essays in Honor of David Noel Freedman in Celebration of His Sixtieth Birthday, 1983, The Bible and Its Traditions, 1983, Backgrounds for the Bible, 1987, Agrammatic Aphasia: A Cross-Language Narrative Sourcebook, 1990; contbr. chpts. to books and articles to profl. jours. Mem. Am. Oriental Soc., Soc. Bibl. Lit., Cath. Bibl. Soc. Roman Catholic. Home: 1012 E University Ann Arbor MI 48104

ODDI, SILVIO CARDINAL, Italian ecclesiastic; b. Morfasso, Piacenza, Italy, Nov. 14, 1910; s. Agostino and Esther (Oddi) O.; Doctorate in Canon Law, Rome, 1936; Dr. honoris causa, U. Buenos Aires, 1944, St. John's U., N.Y.C., 1981, St. Charles Sem., Phila. Ordained priest Roman Cath. Ch., 1933; named archbishop titular of Mesembria, 1953, cardinal, 1969. Mem. Vatican Diplomatic Service, Iran, Lebanon, Syria, Palestine, Egypt, France, Yugoslavia, Belgium and Luxembourg, 1936-69; spl. missions to Central Africa, Latin Am., Philippines, Cuba and Dominican Rep., 1961-74; mem. Congregations for Causes of Saints, Bishops, Oriental Chs. of Pub. Affairs of the Ch., Supreme Tribunal of Apostolic Segnatura, Amministrazionedel Patrimonio della Sede Apostolica, Congregation per l'Evangelizzazione dei Popoli, Sanctuaries of Loreto and Pompei; pontifical legate to Basilica and Convent of St. Francis (Assisi). Home: 21 Via Pompeo Magno, 00192 Rome Italy

ODEN, WILLIAM BRYANT, bishop, educator; b. McAllen, Tex., Aug. 3, 1935; s. Charles Alva and Evea (Bryant) O.; m. Marilyn Brown, July 12, 1957; children: Danna Lee Oden Bowen, William Dirk, Valerie Lyn Oden McCray, Charles Bryant. BA, Okla. State U., 1958; MDiv, Harvard U., 1961, postgrad., 1974; ThD, Boston U., 1964; DD (hon.), Oklahoma City U., 1980; LHD (hon.), Centenary Coll., 1990. Ordained to ministry Meth. Ch., 1981. Pastor Aldersgate United Meth. Ch., Oklahoma City, 1963-69, St. Stephen's United Meth. Ch., Norman, Okla., 1969-76, Crown Heights United Meth. Ch., Oklahoma City, 1976-83; prof. Phillips Grad. Sem., Enid, 1976-88; pastor 1st United Meth. Ch., Enid, 1983-88; bishop United Meth. Ch., Baton Rouge, 1988—; assigned to La. area; pres. SCJ Coll. of Bishops, 1989-90; del. Gen. Conf., 1976, 80, 84, 88; chmn. Okla. Del. to Gen. and Jurisdictional Confs., 1984, 88; Jackson lectr. Perkins Sch. Theology, So. Meth. U., 1975, Wilson lectr. SCJ Bishop's Week, 1989. Author: Oklahoma Methodism in the Twentieth Century, 1968, Liturgy as Life Journey, 1976, Wordeed: Evangelism in Biblical and Wesleyan Perspective, 1978. Trustee Oklahoma City U., 1980-88, Southwestern U., Winfield, Kans., 1983-88, Centenary Coll., 1988—, Dillard U., 1988—. Mem. Am. Acad. Homiletics. Avocations: writing, reading biographies, mountain climbing, backpacking. Home: 7344 Woodstock Baton Rouge LA 70809 Office: La United Meth Hdqrs 527 North Blvd Baton Rouge LA 70802

ODOM, DAVID RUSSELL, pastor; b. Rutherfordton, N.C., May 16, 1950; s. William Chivous and Rosie Sue (Arrowood) O.; m. Linda Ann Ard, Oct. 7, 1972; children: Crystal Gaye, David Jonathan, Curtis Jeremy, Stephanie Le. Student, Liberty U. Svc. dir. Full Gospel Revival Ch., Rutherfordton, 1969-72; pastor in tng. Fellowship Assembly Ch., Florence, S.C., 1972-86; pastor Shiloh Assembly Ch., Florence, 1986—, pres. bd., 1986—; svc. technician Sears, Florence, 1972—. Office: Shiloh Assembly Ch 1410 S Floyd Circle Florence SC 29501

ODOM, GEORGE COSBY, JR., retired religion educator; b. Sebree, Ky., Aug. 30, 1922; s. George Cosby and Connie Bell (Walker) O.; m. Harriet Aileen Zimmer, Mar. 18, 1944; children: Melodie Joy, Denis Lee, Georgette June and Gloria Jane (twins.). BTh, No. Bapt. Theol. Sem., Chgo., 1951; MA, Baylor U., 1952; LHD (hon.), Sioux Empire Coll., Hawarden, Iowa, 1966. Ordained to ministry Conservative Bapt. Assn. Am., 1950; cert. fgn. missionary. Missionary, tchr. Conservative Bapt. Fgn. Missionary Soc., Wheaton, Ill., 1952-87; prof. Theol. Sem. Batista do Nordeste, Floriano, Piaui, Brazil, 1957-68; tchr., ch. planter State of Piaui, 1969-87; ret., 1987; Bible tchr. Sunset Villa Nursing Home, Roswell, N.Mex., 1987—; acting chaplain Sub-Ets World War II, Roswell, 1988—. With USNR, 1942-45, PTO. Recipient plaque Brazilian Bapt. Conv., 1987. Mem. VFW, Pecos Valley U.S. Submarine Vets. World War II (life). Republican. Home: 802 S Plains Park Dr Roswell NM 88201-3619 *The one thing that has given spiritual strength in my personal life is the reality of God's presence from day to day.*

ODOM-GROH, LARRY LEA, minister; b. Quincy, Ill., May 28, 1942; s. Richard Gabreil and Dorothy Ida (Waddell) G.; m. Melanie Morene Odom, Sept. 8, 1978; children: Mrs. Katherine Ann Groh Marple, Laura Lea. BA, Tex. Christian U., 1972; MDiv, Episcopal Theol. Sem., 1976; postgrad., Lexington Theol. Sem., 1991—. Pastor S. Austin (Tex.) Christian Ch., 1973-77, Arlington Christian Ch., Jacksonville, Fla., 1977-80; pastor, developer Raymore (Mo.) Christian Ch., 1980-87; evangelist 1st Christian Ch., Seattle, 1987-90; pres., cons. Evangel. Cons. Svc., Boone Grove, Ind.; adj. cons. Nat. Evangel. Assn., Lubbock, Tex., 1989; v.p. Congress Disciples Clergy, Indpls., 1985-89; 1st v.p. Christian Ch. Mid-Am., Jefferson City, Mo., 1986-87. Author: Your Master Plan, 1991; contbr. articles to jours. in field. Chaplain Raymore Police Dept., 1981-87, Cass County Fire dist., 1985-87, Belton (Mo.) Rsch. Hosp., 1985-87; dir. Raymore Emergency Mgmt. Agy., 1984-87. Named Speaker of Yr., Toastmasters Internat., 1980; Larry Odom-Groh Day named in his honor, City of Raymore, 1987. Mem. Alban Inst., Optimists (pres. 1985-87). Home: PO Box 57 Boone Grove IN 46302-0057 Office: Evangel Cons Svc 360 Groveland Boone Grove IN 46302

O'DONNELL, CLETUS FRANCIS, bishop; b. Waukun, Iowa, Aug. 22, 1917; s. Patrick E. and Isabelle A. (Duffy) O'D. M.A., St. Mary of Lake Sem., Ill., 1941; J.C.D., Cath. U. Am., 1945. Ordained priest Roman Catholic Ch., 1941; asst. pastor Our Lady of Lourdes Ch., Chgo., 1941-42; vice chancellor Archdiocese of Chgo., 1947-60, vicar, gen. counsel, 1961; apptd. titular bishop Abrittum, aux. bishop Chgo., 1960-67; consecrated bishop, 1960; pastor Holy Name Cathedral, Chgo., 1966; bishop Diocese of Madison, Wis., 1967—; chmn. Am. Bd. Cath. Missions, from 1966, Nat. Catholic Edn. Assn., from 1977. Recipient C. Albert Koob award Nat. Cath. Edn. Assn., 1978. Office: Holy Name Sem High Point Rd RR2 Madison WI 53719

O'DONNELL, EDWARD JOSEPH, bishop, former editor; b. St. Louis, July 4, 1931; s. Edward Joseph and Ruth Mary (Carr) O'D. Student, Cardinal Glennon Coll., 1949-53; postgrad., Kenrick Sem., 1953-57. Ordained priest Roman Cath. Ch., 1957, consecrated bishop, 1984; asso. pastor in 5 St. Louis parishes, 1957-77; pastor St. Peter's Ch., Kirkwood, Mo., 1977-81; assoc. dir. Archdiocesan Commn. on Human Rights, 1962-70; dir. Archdiocesan Radio-TV Office, 1966-68, Archdiocesan Vocation Council, 1965; editor St. Louis Rev., 1968-81; vicar-gen. Archdiocese of St. Louis, 1981—, aux. bishop, 1984—; bd. dirs. Nat. Cath. Conf. for Interracial Justice, 1980-85, NAACP, 1964-66, Urban League St. Louis, 1962-68; chmn. Interfaith Clergy Coun. Greater St. Louis, 1963-67. Named to Golden Dozen Internat. Soc. Weekly Newspaper Editors, 1970, 77. Mem. Cath. Press Assn., Nat. Assn. TV Arts and Scis. Home: 8900 Clayton Rd Saint Louis MO 63117 Office: 4445 Lindell Blvd Saint Louis MO 63108

O'DONNELL, ROBERT PATRICK, priest; b. Gary, Ind., June 11, 1919; s. Liquori Alphonsus and Carolyn Emily (Senn) O'D. BA, U. Chgo., 1943; MA, Cath. U., 1945; postgrad., Gregorian U., Rome, 1980-81. Ordained priest Roman Cath. Ch., 1949. Asst. Sacred Heart Ch., Russellville, Ky., 1950-52; adminstr. Our Lady of Lourdes Ch., Otway, Ohio, 1953-55; dir. pub. rels. Glenmary Home Missioners, Glendale, Ohio, 1956-60; chaplain Glenmary Sisters, Fayetteville, Ohio, 1960-66; pastor Holy Redeemer Ch., Vancebury, Ky., 1966-80, St. Francis De Sales Ch., Idabel, Okla., 1987—; editor, photographer Glen Mary's Challenge, Cin., 1952-80; designer/builder seven chs., Ky., 1952-64. Founder/designer: Appalachian Studios-resident artist, gen. mgr., 1966-80; composer music, producer: (musical) From Sheeba They Came, 1990; producer: (movie) Glenmary Story, 1958; other. Recipient Thomas Jefferson award, U.S. Office of Pres., 1979, Four Chaplains Nat. award Office of Four Chaplains Found., Phila., 1981. Mem. Rotary. (internat. exch. chmn. 1989-91). Home: 13 SE Jefferson Idabel OK 74745

O'DONNELL, THOMAS JOSEPH, priest; b. Balt., Mar. 8, 1918; s. Thomas Joseph and May (Brophy) O'D. BA, MA, Georgetown Univ.; BTh, Woodstock (Md.) Theol. Coll. Ordained priest Roman Cath. Ch., 1950. Tchr. med. moral theology Woodstock Seminary, 1962-65; regent, prof. med. ethics Sch. of Medicine Georgetown U., Washington, 1966-76; dean of men, prof. ethics St. Pius X Seminary, Erlanger, Ky., 1975-80; med. moral cons. Tulsa (Okla.) Diocese, 1980-85; rector Lincoln Diocesan Sem., Waverly, Nebr., 1985—; dir. Good Counsel Retreat, Waverly, 1985—. Author: Medicine and Christian Morality, 1975, 91, Morals in Medicine, 1956, enlarged edit. 1960, Home Study Course, 1990; guest editor: Medical-Moral Newsletter. Recipient Gerald Kelly award Nat. Fedn. Cath. Phys. Guilds, 1981. Mem. Nat. Soc. Med. Rsch. (past v.p.), Nat. Kidney Found. (past v.p.), Nat. Conf. Cath. Bishops (cons.), AMA (cons.), Fellowship of Cath. Scholars (cons.). Home: Rte 1 PO Box 110 Waverly NE 68462 Office: Lincoln Diocesan Seminary 7303 North 112th RR No 1 Waverly NE 68462

O'DONOVAN, LEO JEREMIAH, university president, theologian, priest; b. N.Y.C., Apr. 24, 1934; s. Leo J. Jr. O'D. AB, Georgetown U., 1956; Licentiate in Philosophy, Fordham U., 1961; STB, Woodstock Coll., 1966, Licentiate in Sacred Theology, 1967; ThD, U. Münster, Fed. Republic Germany, 1971. Joined S.J., 1966, ordained priest Roman Cath. Ch., 1966. Instr. philosophy Loyola Coll., Balt., 1961-63; asst. prof. Woodstock (Md.) Coll., 1971-74; assoc. prof. Weston Sch. Theology, Cambridge, Mass., 1974-81, prof., 1981-89; pres. Georgetown U., Washington, 1989—; provincial asst. formation Md. Province of S.J., Balt., 1985-88; cons. Nat. Conf. Cath. Bishops, Washington, 1986—; vis. fellow Woodstock Theol. Ctr.; bd. dirs. The Riggs Nat. Bank. Co-editor: The Society of Jesus and Higher Education in America, 1965, (author preface) Faithful Witness: Foundations of Theology for Todays Church, 1989; asoc. editor Jour. Am. Acad. Religion, 1985—; mem. adv. bd. America mag., 1985—; contbr. numerous articles to America, Washington Post, Communio, Cross Currents, Religion in Life, other jours. Bd. dirs. U. Detroit, 1986—. Fulbright scholar Fulbright Found., U. Lyon, France, 1956-57; Danforth fellow Danforth Found., 1956-71; Assn. Theol. Schs. grantee on teaching, 1978-79. Fellow Soc. for Values in Higher Edn.; mem. Boston Theol. Soc., University Club . Office: Georgetown U Office of President Washington DC 20057

ODUYOYE, MERCY AMBA, religion educator; b. Asamankese, Ghana, Oct. 21, 1934; d. Charles Kwaw and Mercy Dakwaa (Turkson) Yamoah; m. Adedoyin Modupe Oduyoye, Dec. 9, 1968. BA in Religionwith honors, U. Ghana, Legon-Accra, 1963; BA in Theology with honors, Cambridge (Eng.) U., 1965, MA in Theology with honors, 1969. Cert. tchr. Tchr. Ministry Edn., Ghana, 1955-59; youth edn. sec. World Council Chs., Geneva, 1967-70; youth sec. All Africa Conf. Chs., Ibadan, Nigeria, 1970-73; tchr. States Schs. Bd., Ibadan/Oyo State, 1973-74; lectr. U. Ibadan, Ibadan/Oyo State, 1974-80, sr. lectr., 1980-86; Ford scholar Women's Studies in Religion Harvard Divinity Sch., Cambridge, Mass., 1985-86; vis. prof. Union Theol. Sem., N.Y.C., 1986-87; vis. lectr. Harvard U., 1985-86; commr. Faith and Order Commns., World Council Chs., Geneva, 1976-87, dep. gen. sec., 1987—. Author: Youth Without Jobs, 1972, Flight From the Farms, 1973, Church Youth Work in Africa, 1973, Christian Youth Work, 1979, And Women, Where Do They Come In:, 1980, Hearing and Knowing: A Theological Reflection on Christianity in Africa; editor: The State of Christian Theology in Nigeria, Who Will Roll The Stone Away?: Ecumenical Decade of the Churches in Solidarity with Women, 1990. Mem. Nigerian Assn. for the Study of Religions, West Africa Assn. Theol. Insts., Ecumenical Assn. African Theologians (former v.p.), Ecumenical Assn. Third World Theologians, Oxford Inst. Meth. Theol. Studies (mem. steering com.), Internat. Assn. Mission Studies. Avocations: handicrafts, reading. Home: 2 Alayande St Bodija Estate, Ibadan 0Y0 State Nigeria Office: care World Council of Churches, 150 route de Ferney POB 66, 1211 Geneva 20, Switzerland

OFFNER, STACY KAREN, rabbi; b. N.Y.C., Nov. 24, 1955; d. Charles David and Marilyn Pearl (Sommer) O.; life ptnr. Nancy Steinberg Abramson, June 1, 1987; children: Jill, Charlie. AB, Kenyon Coll., Gambier, Ohio, 1977; MAHL, Hebrew Union Coll., N.Y.C., 1982. Ordained rabbi, 1984. Rabbinic intern Temple Bethel, Great Neck, N.Y., 1981-82; student rabbi Beth Shalom, Toms River, N.J., 1982-84; asst. rabbi Mt. Zion Temple, St. Paul, 1984-87, assoc. rabbi, 1987-88; rabbi Shir Tikvah Congregation, St. Paul, 1988—; bd. dirs. Rabbinic Pension Bd., N.Y.C., 1987—; cen. planning and budgeting United Jewish Fund & Coun., St. Paul, 1984-85; adj. prof. Hamline U., St. Paul, 1984—. Contbr. articles to profl. jours. Founding mem. Feminists in Faith, Mpls.-St. Paul, 1984-88; mem. task force on sexual exploitation Minn. Dept. Corrections, St. Paul, 1985-87; mem. disability svcs. panel United Way, St. Paul, 1985-86; religious affairs com. Planned Parenthood, St. Paul, 1985-89. Recipient Clergy Appreciation award, Civitan, 1990, Founding Feminist award, Women's Polit. Caucus, 1988, Sherrill Hooker Meml. award, Lesbian and Gay Community, 1989. Mem. Women's Rabbinic Network (exec. bd., regional rep.), Cen. Conf. Reform Rabbis, Mid-West Assn. Reform Rabbis, Coalition for Advancement Jewish Edn., Minn. Rabbinic Assn. Office: Shir Tikvah Congregation 1671 Summit Ave Saint Paul MN 55105

O'FLAHERTY, EDWARD MARTIN, academic administrator; b. Boston, Oct. 29, 1934; s. Edward M. and Rose R. (Hagelstein) O'F. AB, Boston Coll., Chestnut Hill, Mass., 1959; PhL, Facultes S.J. Albert, Louvain, Belgium, 1959; MA, U. Pa., Phila., 1964, PhD, 1979. Joined Soc. of Jesus, 1952. Lectr. Boston Coll., 1973-76; rector Jesuit Sch. Theology, Berkeley, Calif., 1976-79; provincial superior New Eng. Province, Soc. Jesus, 1979-85; pres. Weston Sch. Theology, Cambridge, Mass., 1985—. Author: Iglesia y Sociedad en Guatemala, 1984. Trustee Boston Coll., 1986—, St. Joseph's U., Phila., 1986—. Mem. Assn. Theol. Schs. Roman Catholic. Office: Weston Sch Theology 3 Phillips Pl Cambridge MA 02138

OGDEN, SCHUBERT MILES, theologian, educator; b. Cin., Mar. 2, 1928; s. Edgar Carson and Neva Louetta (Glancy) O.; m. Joyce Ellen Schwettman, Aug. 26, 1950; children: Alan Scott, Andrew Merrick. AB, Ohio Wesleyan U., 1950, LittD (hon.), 1965; DB, U. Chgo., 1954, PhD, 1958, DHL (hon.), 1983. Ordained to ministry United Methodist Ch., 1958; mem. faculty Perkins Sch. Theology, So. Meth. U., 1956-69, assoc. prof. theology, 1961-64, prof., 1964-69; univ. prof. theology Div. Sch., U. Chgo., 1969-72; prof. theology Perkins Sch. Theology, So. Meth. U., Dallas, 1972-83, Univ. Disting. prof. theology, 1983—, dir. grad. program in religious studies, 1974-90; Merrick lectr. Ohio Wesleyan U., 1965; vis. fellow Coun. of Humanities, Princeton U., 1977-78; Sarum lectr. U. Oxford, 1980-81, Ferguson lectr. U. Manchester, 1990; Fulbright rsch. prof., also Guggenheim fellow Marburg (Germany) U., 1962-63. Fellow Am. Coun. Learned Socs., Johns Hopkins U., 1950-51. Mem. Am. Acad. Religion (pres. 1976-77), Am. Acad. Arts and Scis., Soc. Values in Higher Edn., Am. Philos. Assn., Am. Theol. Soc., Phi Beta Kappa, Omicron Delta Kappa, Phi Mu Alpha. Author: Christ Without Myth, 1961, 2d edit., 1979, The Reality of God, 1966, 3d edit., 1991, Faith and Freedom, 1979, 2d edit., 1989, The Point of Christology, 1982, 2d edit., 1991, On Theology, 1986, 2d edit., 1991, Is There Only One True Religion or Are There Many?, 1991; editor, translator: Existence and Faith, Shorter Writings of Rudolf Bultmann, 1960, New Testament and Mythology and Other Basic Writings of Rudolf Bultmann, 1984; mem. editorial bd. Jour. Religion, 1972—, Modern Theology, 1984—, Jour. Am. Acad. Religion, 1985—. Office: So Meth U Perkins Sch Theology Dallas TX 75275 *Of greater help to me than anything else in keeping my work and career in proper perspective are these questions of the Apostle Paul: "What have you that you did not receive? If then you received it, why do you boast as if it were not a gift?" (1 Cor. 4:7).*

OGIDA, MIKIO, history of religion educator; b. Akita, Japan, Jan. 20, 1938; s. Shigeji and Kiyono (Sato) O.; m. Noriko Yamamoto, May 3, 1966; 1 child, Satoshi. BD, Doshisha U., Kyoto, Japan, 1961; S.T.M., Doshisha U., 1963; ThM, Harvard U., 1969. Assoc. minister Heian Ch., United Ch. of Christ in Japan, Kyoto, 1963-66; lectr. Kobe Jogakuin U., Nishinomiya, Hyogo, Japan, 1969-72; assoc. prof. Kobe Jogakuin U., 1972-81, prof., 1981—, dean students, 1989—. Author: Religions of the World, 1981. Mem. Japan Soc. Christian Studies, Soc. Hist. Studies Christianity Japan, Classical Soc. Japan. Avocation: igo, skiing. Home: 4 11 1 108 Makami cho, Takatuki shi Osaka, Japan Office: Kobe Jogakuin U, 4 1 Okadayama, Nishinomiya Hyogo, Japan

OGILVIE, LLOYD JOHN, clergyman; b. Kenosha, Wis., Sept. 2, 1930; s. Vard Spencer and Katherine (Jacobson) O.; m. Mary Jane Jenkins, Mar. 25, 1951. B.A., Lake Forest Coll., 1952, Garrett Theol. Sem., 1956; postgrad., New Coll., U. Edinburgh, Scotland, 1955-56; D.D., Whitworth Coll., 1973; L.H.D., U. Redlands, 1974; D.Humanities, Moravian Coll., 1975; LLD, Ea. U., 1988. Ordained to ministry Presbyn. Ch., 1956; student pastor Gurnee, Ill., 1952-56; first pastor Winnetka (Ill.) Presbyn. Ch., 1956-62; pastor 1st Presbyn. Ch., Bethlehem, Pa., 1962-72, 1st Presbyn. Ch., Hollywood, Calif., 1972—; preacher Chgo. Sunday Evening Club, 1962—, also frequent radio and TV personality weekly syndicated TV program Let God Love You. Author: A Life Full of Surprises, 1969, Let God Love You, 1974, If I Should Wake Before I Die, 1973, Lord of the Ups and Downs, 1974, You've Got Charisma, 1975, Cup of Wonder, 1976, Life Without Limits, 1976, Drumbeat of Love, 1977, When God First Thought of You, 1978, The Autobiography of God, 1979, The Bush Is Still Burning, 1980, The Radiance of the Inner Splendor, 1980, Congratulations, God Believes in You, 1981, Life as it Was Meant to Be, 1981, The Beauty of Love, The Beauty of Friendship, 1981, The Beauty of Caring, The Beauty of Sharing, 1981, God's Best for My Life, 1981, God's Will in Your Life, 1982, Ask Him Anything, 1982, Commentary on Book of Acts, 1983, Praying with Power, 1983, Falling into Greatness, 1983, Freedom in the Spirit, 1984, Making Stress Work For You, 1984, The Lord of the Impossible, 1984, Why Not Accept Christ's Healing and Wholeness, 1984, If God Cares, Why Do I Still Have Problems?, 1985, Understanding the Hard Sayings of Jesus, 1986, 12 Steps to Living Without Fear, 1987, A Future and a Hope, 1988, Enjoying God, 1990, Silent Strength, 1990, The Lord of the Loose Ends, 1991; gen. editor: Communicator's Commentary of the Bible, 1982; host: (TV and radio program) Let God Love You. Office: 1760 N Gower St Hollywood CA 90028

O'GRADY, JOHN FRANCIS, priest, theology educator. BA, Mary Immaculate Coll., 1962; MDiv, Mary Immaculate Sem., 1966; Licentiate in Sacred Theology, Coll. St. Anselm, Rome, 1967; STD, U. St. Thomas, Rome, 1969; Licentiate of Sacred Scripture, Gregorian U., Rome, 1975, D of Sacred Scripture, 1978. Ordained priest Roman Cath. Ch., 1966. Asst. prof. theology Our Lady of Angels Sem., Niagara U., Albany, N.Y., 1968-71; dir. office clergy edn. Diocese of Albany, 1971-73, 73-75, dir. liturgy office, 1971-73; assoc. prof. Bibl. studies St. Bernard's Sem., Rochester, N.Y., 1977-81, dean acad. affairs, 1978-81; vis. prof. Duquesne U., Pitts., 1981, prof. Bibl. theology, chair dept. theology, 1982-87; prof., chair dept. theology and philosophy Barry U., Miami Shores, Fla., 1987—, assoc. dean for grad. studies Sch. Arts and Scis., 1988—; vis. prof. SUNY, Albany, 1970, Providence Coll., 1970-74, Coll. St. Rose, Albany, 1971-73, St. Joseph's Sem., Yonkers, N.Y., 1971-73, U. St. Thomas, Rome, 1974, Siena Coll., Loudonville, N.Y., 1975-77, St. Michael's Coll., Winooski, Vt., 1979-80, U. Rochester, 1981, Fairfield (Conn.) U., 1981, U. Pitts., 1984, St. Vincent's Sem., Pitts., 1986, U. St. Mary-of-the-Lake, Mundelein, Ill., 1987; lectr. Providence Coll., 1970, Siena Coll., Loudonville, 1971, 82, U. Innsbruck, Austria, 1976, other univs. and orgns.; mem. Ecumenical Bd. for Clergy Edn., Albany. Author: The Doctrine of Nature and Grace in the Writings of George Tyrrell, 1969, Jesus Lord and Christ, 1973, Christian Anthropology, 1975, Individual and Community in John, 1978, Models of Jesus, 1981, Mark: The Sorrowful Gospel, 1981, The Gospel of John: Testimony of the Beloved Disciple, 1981, Das menschliche Antlitz Gottes, 1983, The Story of the Apple Tree: A First Communion Book, 1985, The Jesus Tradition and the Four Gospels, 1989, Pillars of Paul's Gospel: Galatins and Romans, 1990, Disciples and Leaders: The Origin of Christian Ministry in the New Testament, 1991; also articles; editor Bibl. Theology Bull., 1975-80, assoc. editor, 1981—; assoc. editor Chgo. Studies, 1987—. Founding mem. Christians United in Mission, Albany, bd. dirs. edn. com. 1972-73; bd. dirs. Rochester Ctr. for Theol. Edn., 1978-81, Holocaust Ctr., Miami, 1987—; active Miami chpt. Global Co-operation for a Better World, 1988—. Columbia U. fellow, 1976-81. Mem. Cath. Bibl. Assn., Cath. Theol. Soc. Am., Soc. Bibl. Lit., Am. Acad. Religion. Home: 1000 Quayside Terr #

2104 Miami FL 33138 Office: Barry U 11300 NE 2d Ave Miami Shores FL 33161

O'HARA, RICHARD EDWARD, clergyman; b. Balt., Oct. 6, 1947; s. Richard Edward and Naomi Caroline (Wantz) O'H.; m. Marilyn Elizabeth Widmer, May 10, 1975; children: Joshua Douglas, Jesse Daniel, Jonathan David. BA, Washington Bible Coll., 1970; M Religious Edn., Golden Conwell Theol. Sem., South Hamilton, Mass., 1975; D Ministry, Trinity Theol. Sem., Newburgh, Ind., 1987. Ordained to ministry Conservative Congl. Christian Conf., 1976. Assoc. pastor The Coll. Ch., Northampton, Mass., 1974-77; pastor Union Ch., Tyringham, Mass., 1978-83; prof. Berkshire Christian Coll., Lenox, Mass., 1977-83; adj. prof. Gordon-Conwell Theol. Sem., South Hamilton, Mass., 1985—; pastor First Ch. of Christ Congl., Lynn, Mass., 1983—; bd. dirs. New Eng. Assn. Christian Edn., Lexington, Mass., 1980-86, Evangelistic Assn. New Eng., Boston, 1984-88; chaplain Berkshire County House of Correction, Pittsfield, Mass., 1981-83, Lynn Fire Dept., 1984—, Atlanticare Med. Ctr., Union Hosp., 1990. Author: God's Prophetic Calendar, 1981. Del. White House Conf. on Family, Washington, 1980; mem., chmn. Sch. Com. Union 29, Tyringham, 1980-83; bd. mem. Christian Action Coun., Boston, 1985; leader Lynn Coun. on Aging, 1984-89. Byington fellow Gordon-Conwell Theol. Sch., South Hamilton, 1975; recipient Community Svc. award, Lynn, 1987, 88, 89. Mem. Nat. Assn. Profs. Christian Edn., The Alban Inst., Rotary Club of LYnn (sgt. at arms 1990). Republican. Home: 83 York Rd Lynn MA 01904 Office: First Ch of Christ Congl 678 Lynnfield St Lynn MA 01904

O'HEARN, DANIEL P., mission worker; b. Canandaigua, N.Y., Apr. 10, 1963; s. Perry Franklyn O'Hearn and Glendora (Pimm) Jackson; m. Ina M. Jenkins, May 2, 1987; children: Luke Isaiah, Mathew Jerimiah. BA in Occupational Edn., Wayland Bapt. U., 1991; BA in Elem. Edn., U. Alaska, 1991; AA in Fire Sci., Community Coll. of A.F., Eielson AFB, Alaska, 1991. Lic. mission worker. Christian edn. staff, bd. dirs. Pentecostal Ch. God, Fairbanks, Alaska, 1985-90; christian edn. staff, bd. dirs., sec., treas. Pentecostal Holiness Ch., Fairbanks, 1990—; commd. 2nd lt. USAF, 1981, advance through grades to capt., 1991; sec., treas. Trinity Chapel Pentecostal, Fairbanks, 1990—. Active Citizens for Quality Edn., Fairbanks, 1990—. Decorated Accomadation Medal with Valor. Mem. Christian Youth (mem. organizer 1985—). Home and Office: Trinity Chapel Pentecostal PO Box 75463 Fairbanks AK 99707

O'HIGGINS, JAMES, priest, history educator; b. Birstal, Yorkshire, U.K.; Aug. 21, 1915; s. Thomas and Ellen (Ryan) O'H. Lic. Phil., Heythrop Coll., U.K., 1939, S.T.L., 1949; M.A., Oxford U., 1942, Ph.D., 1966. Joined Soc. Jesus, Roman Cath. Ch. Sr. history master Corby Sch., Sunderland, U.K., 1942-45, St. Ignatius Coll., London, 1950-61; sr. history tutor Campion Hall, Oxford U., 1962—, tutor for grads., 1972—. Author: Anthony Collins - The Man and His Works, 1970; Determinism and Freewill, 1976; Yves De Vallone-The Making of an Esprit Fort, 1982. Fellow Royal Hist. Soc., English Hist. Assn., Am. Cath. Hist. Assn. Roman Catholic. Avocations: reading; walking; cricket; academic detection. Home: Campion Hall, Oxford 0XI 1QS, England Office: Oxford U, Oxford 0XI 1QS, England

OHLERKING, DAVID PAUL, religious organization administrator; b. Eagle Grove, Iowa, Feb. 14, 1940; s. Fred Wilhelm and Leona Fern (Mosher) O.; m. Naomi Jean Bougher, Feb. 14, 1959; children: David Paul II, Daniel P., Susan J., Joshua S. Grad. high sch., Eagle Grove. Ordained to ministry Assemblies of God, 1972, World Evangelism Fellowship, 1988. Missionary Assemblies of God, Springfield, Mo., 1969-88; treas. Internat. Corr. Inst., Brussels, 1975-80; dir. devel. Far East Advanced Sch. Theology, Manila, 1982-84, Jimmy Swaggart Ministries, Baton Rouge, 1988—; dir. Childcare Internat., worldwide, Baton Rouge, 1984—; vice chmn. bd. dirs. Faith Acad., Manila, 1972-76, 82-84; chmn. bd. dirs. Internat. Christian Acad., Brussels, 1977-80. Author: Wordspeaker's Plan, 1982; editor Compassionate Heart mag., 1984—; contbr. articles to religious publs. Named Dir. of Yr., Youth for Christ, Omaha, 1967. Republican. Home: 7948 Wimbledon Baton Rouge LA 70810 Office: Childcare Internat PO Box 2550 Baton Rouge LA 70821 *The God I once called a fiction had a fantastic plan for my life. Stepping out of atheism into that plan changed everything for me.*

OHLINGER, MARIE EDNA, lay worker; b. Kutztown, Pa., Nov. 21, 1941; d. Robert William and Edna Mae (Rhode) Gift; married, June 12, 1965. Cert., Alvernia Coll., Reading, Pa., 1984-85, 87; cert. in ch. music, Lebanon Valley Coll., Annville, Pa., 1991. Organist, choir dir. Maidencreek United Ch. of Christ, Blandon, Pa., 1970—, Maidencreek Luth. Ch., Blandon, 1987—; sec. Met. Edison Co., Reading, Pa., 1973—; pianist Blandon Lions Club, 1972—. Recipient 20 Yr. Svc. Honor award Maidencreek United Ch. of Christ, 1990. Mem. Am. Guild Organists (dir. Reading chpt.), Lioness Club (pianist 1972—). Home: RD 3 Bernville PA 19506

OHMAN, ROBERT BAIRD, university chaplain, minister; b. Marietta, Okla., Nov. 19, 1934; s. Raymond Norman and Marion Margaret (Baird) O.; m. Carol Anne Bartel, June 21, 1958; children: Julie Amelia, Christopher Baird, Jonathan Robert. BS in History, Wheaton Coll., 1957; ThM, Dallas Theological Sem., 1962; D in Ministry, Fuller Theological Sem., 1976. Ordained to ministry Presbyn. Ch., 1968. Asst. minister Calvary Ch., Pacific Palisades, Calif., 1962-64, Westminster Presbyn. Ch., San Jose, Calif., 1964-68; assoc. minister Trinity United Presbyn. Ch., Santa Ana, Calif., 1968-75; chaplain Westmont Coll., Santa Barbara, Calif., 1977—; min. at large Santa Barbara Presbytery, 1986—. Republican. Avocations: skiing, photography. Office: 3938 State St Santa Barbara CA 93105

OHMART, DALE LYNN, minister; b. Coffeyville, Kans., Oct. 8, 1959; s. Theodore Hobart and Anita Belle (Hayden) O.; m. Cynthia Jean Bower, Aug. 16, 1980; children: Nathan, Natalie, Natina, Natasha. B in Bible Lit., Ozark Christian Coll., 1982; postgrad., Gordon Conwell Theol. Sem., 1987, Johnson Bible Coll., 1990—. Ordained to ministry Christian Ch., 1981. Min. Leanna Christian Ch., Savonburg, Kans., 1978-81; assoc. min. Londonderry (N.H.) Christian Ch., 1882-86, min., 1986—; music chmn. Ea. Christian Conv., Hartford, Conn., 1984, v.p., Hershey, Pa., 1989, registration chmn., 1991. Mem. Londonderry Clergy Assn. (chmn. 1988—). Home: 5 Miltimore Rd Derry NH 03038 Office: Londonderry Christian Ch 372 Mammoth Rd Londonderry NH 03053 *In my opinion, no statement better captures both the purpose and challenge of life than the words of Jesus: "Let your light shine before men in such a way that they may see your good works, and glorify you Father who is in heaven." (Matthew 5:16).*

OHRSTEDT, ROBERT JAMES, minister; b. Columbus, Ohio, Nov. 9, 1953; s. Robert James and Carneal Elsie (Layne) O.; m. Brenda P. Tokeinna, Sept. 17, 1979. BA, Capital U., 1975; MDiv, Trinity Sem., 1980, postgrad., 1984—. Ordained to ministry Evang. Luth. Ch., 1980. Pastor Our Saviors Luth. Ch., Cathlamet, Wash., 1980-84; counselor Vols. of Am., Columbus, 1984-86, community dir., 1985-87; pastor Grace Luth. Ch., Bessemer, Ala., 1987-90, Grove Chapel, Harmony Grove Luth. chs., Indiana, Pa., 1990—; dean Lower Columbia Luth. Conf., Longview, Wash., 1983-84; pres. Wahkiakum Ministerium, Cathlamet, 1980-81. Mem. steering com. AIDS Task Force, Birmingham, Ala., 1988, Leadership Bessemer, 1988; organizer Wahkiakum Food Bank, Skamakowa, Wash., 1983. Home: PO Box 827 Indiana PA 15701 Office: RD 6 Box 320 Indiana PA 15701 *The greatest difficulty in our modern world is to see that technique is not wisdom. There is a great deal of talk about training people for work, but that is the easy part. Each of us must also grapple with the deeper truths of the spirit. To refuse this amounts to resigning our humanity.*

OHSIEK, FREDERICK CHARLES, minister; b. Savannah, Ga., Apr. 11, 1937; s. John Henry and Marion Elizabeth (Knight) O.; m. Margaret Ann Reinsch, Jan. 12, 1966; children: Carol, Frederick, Peter. AB, Newberry Coll., 1959; MDiv, Luth. Theol. So. Sem., Columbia, S.C., 1962; postgrad., U. Tenn., 1965-67. Ordained to ministry Luth. Ch., 1964. Pastor Miller-Zion Luth. Parish, Knoxville, Tenn., 1964-67, Ascension Luth. Ch., Jackson, Miss., 1968-75, St. John's Luth. Ch., Nashville, 1975-80, Christ Luth. Ch., Prattville, Ala., 1980—; dean Cen. Ala. Luth. Cluster, 1989-90; bd. dirs. Luth. Ministeries Tutoring Ctr., Prattville, 1990. Bd. dirs. Assn. for Retarded Citizens, Prattville, 1985, Community Concern, 1983-85; trustee Newberry (S.C.) Coll., 1969-75, 77-83. Capt. USAR, 1961-69. Mem. Prattville Ministerial Alliance (pres. 1985), Kiwanis (pres. Prattville club 1989). Office: Christ Luth Ch 2175 Cobbs Ford Rd Prattville AL 36067-9008

OISHI, JITSOISHI, religious organization administrator. Pres. Buddhist Chs. Can. Office: Buddhist Chs Can, 220 Jackson Ave, Vancouver, BC Canada V6A 3B3*

O'KEEFE, FREDRICK REA, bishop, consultant, educator; b. Washington, Mar. 26, 1944; s. Roy Fox and Kathryn Isabelle (Rea) O'Keefe. Student, Fordham U., 1970-72; STD (hon.), StarReach Inst., Putnam Valley, N.Y., 1973; student, St. Augustines Sch. Theology, Fla., 1984; HHD (hon.), Trinity Hall Coll. & Sem., Santa Monica, 1987. Div. mgr. Sears Roebuck, Peekskill, N.Y., 1970-76; pres. Dreadnought Corp., Peekskill, 1974-76; gen. mgr. R. Shaw Co., Laguna Beach, Calif., 1977, N.D. Burger Co., L.A., 1980-84; v.p. mktg. Grand Am. Computers, Irvine, Calif., 1984; tchr. Confraternity Christian Doctrine, Myrtle Beach, S.C., 1967-68; deacon to priest Old Cath. Ch. in N.Am., Peekskill, 1975-82; consecrated bishop Old Episcopal Ch., Scotland, 1982; vicar gen. Lomita, Calif., 1982-83; presiding bishop Redondo Beach, Calif., 1983—; archibishop-abbot Incarnation Abbey Order of St. Benedict, 1987—; dir. Conlegium Spiriti Refulgentis, Redondo Beach, 1975—, Am. Bd. Examiners in Pastoral Counseling, Washington, 1986—, sec., treas. 1982—; exec. dir. Am. Coun. on Schs. and Colls., Washington, 1982—; chmn. Grad. Coll. Theology, L.A., 1983-87; chaplain L.A. Sheriff's Dept., 1983-86; cons. CSR Cons., Clearwater, Fla., 1975—. Assoc. editor, journalist City News Svc., 1984—. With USAF, 1964-70. Recipient John Philip Sousa award, 1963. Mem. Am. Ministerial Assn. (sec. 1982—, bd. dirs. 1985—), Anglican Soc. N.Am., The Confraternity of the Blessed Sacrament, Silicon Valley Computer Soc., Pinellas IBM-PC Users Group, Inc., Internat. Order of St. Luke the Physician, Soc. of Christian Letters, Small Press, Writers and Artists Orgn., Planetary Group Writers Club, Order of the Holy Redeemer, Ecumenical Ch. Fedn., Anglican Inst. Ecumenical Coun. of Cath. and Orthodox Bishops, Tampa Bay Skeptics Soc., Patrons of Husbandry. Avocations: composing, carpentry, screen-writing, liturgics. Office: 20505 US 19 N 12-266 Clearwater FL 34624-6010

O'KEEFE, GERALD FRANCIS, bishop; b. St. Paul, Mar. 30, 1918; s. Francis Patrick and Lucille Mary (McDonald) O'K. Student, St. Paul Sem., 1938-44; B.A., Coll. St. Thomas, 1945; LLD (hon.), St. Ambrose Coll., 1967, Loras Coll., 1967; LHD, Marycrest Coll., 1967. Ordained priest Roman Cath. Ch., 1944. Asst. St. Paul Cathedral, 1944, rector, 1961-67; chancellor Archdiocese of St. Paul, 1945-61, aux. bishop, 1961-67, vicar gen., 1962-67; bishop Diocese of Davenport, Iowa, 1967—; instr. St. Thomas Acad., St. Paul, 1944-45. Home: 1430 Clay St Davenport IA 52804 Office: Diocese of Davenport 2706 Gaines Davenport IA 52804

O'KEEFE, J. REDMOND, ecumenical agency administrator. Head Indsl. Cape Breton Coun. Chs., Sydney, N.S., Can. Office: Indsl Cape Breton Coun Chs, 56 Rosewood Dr, Sydney, NS Canada B1P 1P4*

O'KEEFE, JOSEPH THOMAS, bishop; b. N.Y.C., Mar. 12, 1919. Ed. Cathedral Coll., N.Y.C., St. Joseph's Sem., Yonkers, N.Y., Cath. U., Washington. Ordained Roman Catholic priest, 1948; ordained titular bishop of Tre Taverse and aux. bishop of N.Y., 1982-87; apptd. and installed bishop of Syracuse, 1987. Office: 240 E Onondaga St PO Box 511 Syracuse NY 13201

O'KEEFE, LLOYD F., minister. Exec. sec. Akron (Ohio) Area Assn. Chs. Office: Akron Area Assoc Chs 750 Work Dr Akron OH 44320*

O'KEEFE, VINCENT THOMAS, clergyman, educational administrator; b. Jersey City, Jan. 10, 1920; s. James and Sarah (Allen) O'K. A.B., Georgetown U., 1943; M.A., Woodstock Coll., 1945, Ph.L., 1944; Th.L., St. Albert de Louvain, Belgium, 1951; student, Muenster (Germany) U., 1951-52; S.T.D., Gregorian U., Rome, 1954. Ordained priest Roman Cath. Ch., 1950. Instr. Latin and math. Regis High Sch., N.Y.C., 1944-47; assoc. prof. fundamental theology Woodstock Coll., 1954-60; acad. v.p. Fordham U., Bronx, N.Y., 1960-62; exec. v.p. Fordham U., 1962-63, pres., 1963-65, rector Jesuit community, 1984-88; gen. asst. to superior gen. Soc. of Jesus, Rome, 1965-83; v.p. spl. projects Jesuit Conf. Soc. of Jesus, 1988-90; superior, writer provincial residence Soc. of Jesus, Bronx, 1990—; Mem. regents exams. and scholarship center N.Y. State Dept. Edn.; pres., dir., mem. exec. com. Council Higher Ednl. Instns. of N.Y.C. Author: The History and Meaning of Ex Attrito Fit Contritus, 1957; Contbr. articles to religious publs., also book reviews. Dir. N.Y. World's Fair, 1964-65; Corp. Bd. mgrs. New York Bot. Garden; dir., mem. bd. Center Intercultural Formation, Cuernavaca, Mexico; trustee Fordham U. Fellow Royal Soc. Encouragement Arts Mfrs. and Commerce (London); mem. Council Higher Edn. City N.Y., Religion Council Cath. Secondary Schs. Archdiocese of N.Y., Cath. Bibl. Assn., Cath. Theol. Assn. Am., Religion Ednl. Assn., NEA, Jesuit Ednl. Assn., Nat. Cath. Edn. Assn., Internat. Assn. Univs., Soc. Cath. Coll. Tchrs. Sacred Doctrine, Phi Beta Kappa. Office: Office of Provincial 501 E Fordham Rd Bronx NY 10458

OKOGIE, ANTHONY OLUBUNMI, archbishop. Pres., archbishop Cath. Bishops'Conf. Nigeria, Lagos. Office: PO Box 8, Lagos Nigeria*

OKOTH, YONA, archbishop. Archbishop of Uganda, bishop of Kampala The Anglican Communion. Office: POB 14123, Kampala Uganda*

OLAH, JAMES SANDER, minister; b. Muskegon, Mich., Sept. 24, 1946; s. William Alexander and Jessica Wilson (Windsor) O.; m. Nancy Beth Alberts, June 29, 1968; children: Heather Lynn, Heidi Beth. Student, Grand Rapids Sch. Bible & Mus., 1968, William Tyndale Coll., 1979-81, St. Clair Community Coll., Port Huron, Mich., 1982-83. Ordained to ministry Bapt. Ch., 1969. Youth pastor Calvary Bible Ch., Lapeer, Mich., 1972-77; pastor Wadhams Bapt. Ch., Port Huron, 1977—; sec. and treas. Ind. Fundamental Chs. Am., Mich., 1983-85, regional program chmn., 1987-90; ops. bd. Blue Water Family Life Svcs., Port Huron, 1987—; TV host Eye Opener Program, Port Huron, 1986—. Sec. Kimball Twp. (Mich.) Housing Adv. bd., 1983-85, Kimball Twp. Zoning Bd. Appeals, 1986-89; bd. dirs. Community Fedn. for Decency, Port Huron, 1985-88. Mem. Evang. Ministerial Fellowship Pastors (Evangelism leader 1978, v.p. 1983-84, treas. 1987-88), Mich. Theol. Soc. (bd. dirs. 1987—). Home and Office: Wadhams Bapt Church 5461 Lapeer Rd Port Huron MI 48060

O'LAUGHLIN, SISTER JEANNE, university administrator; b. Detroit, May 4, 1929. Pres. Barry U., Miami. Office: Barry U 11300 NE 2nd Ave Miami FL 33161

OLBRICHT, THOMAS HENRY, college administrator, biblical theology educator; b. Thayer, Mo., Nov. 3, 1929; s. Benjamin Joseph and Agnes Martha (Taylor) O.; m. Dorothy Jetta Kiel, June 8, 1951; children: Suzanne M., Eloise J. Olbricht Brown, Joel C., Adele L. Olbricht Foster, Erica M. BS, No. Ill. U., 1951; MA, U. Iowa, 1953, PhD, 1959; STB, Harvard U., 1962. Asst. prof., dir. forensics Harding Coll., Searcy, Ark., 1954-55; asst. prof., chmn. dept. U. Dubuque, Iowa, 1955-59; from instr. to assoc. prof. Pa. State U., University Park, 1962-67; assoc. prof. Bibl. theology Abilene Christian U., Tex., 1967-69, prof., 1969-86, dean Coll. Liberal and Fine Arts, , 1981-85, chmn. grad. studies Coll. Bibl. Studies, 1985—; chair religious div. Pepperdine U., Malibu, Calif., 1986—. Author: Informative Speaking, 1968; Power To Be, 1979; He Loves Forever, 1980; The Message of Ephesians and Colossians, 1983. Pres. 2d Century Bd., 1981. Mem. Am. Acad. Religion (pres. SW chpt. 1976-77). SW Com. on Religious Studies (pres. 1978-79, sec.-treas. 1982-86). Mem. Ch. of Christ. Lodge: Kiwanis (pres. local club 1972-73, chmn. Tex.-Okla. conv. 1981). Office: Pepperdine U Religion Div Malibu CA 90263

OLCZAK, JOSEPH MARIAN, priest; b. Rudnik nr. Lublin, Poland, Mar. 19, 1940; came to U.S., 1970; naturalized, 1976; s. John and Maria (Kedra) O. Licentiate in Sacred Theology, Cath. U., Lublin, 1970. Ordained priest Roman Cath. Ch., 1965. Sub-prior Pauline Fathers, Doylestown, Pa., 1971-75, prior, 1984-90; pastor St. Lawrence Parish, Cadogan, Pa., 1975-84; assoc. prof. dogmatic theology Holy Apostles Coll. and Sem., Cromwell, Conn., 1985—. Mem. Assn. Polish Priests (pres. 1984), Mariological Soc. Am. Address: PO Box 2049 Doylestown PA 18901

OLD, HUGHES OLIPHANT, research theologian, clergyman; b. Redondo Beach, Calif., Apr. 13, 1933; s. Shadburne Edward and Emma Coulter (Oliphant) O.; m. Mary Chase McCaw, June 12, 1982; children: Hannah Chase, Isaac Houghton Chambers. BA, Centre Coll., 1955; BD, Princeton Theol. Sem., 1958; postgrad., U. Tubingen, 1964-66; ThD, U. Neuchatel, 1971. Ordained to ministry Presbyn. Ch., 1959. Minister Presbyn. Ch., Atglen, Pa., 1959-64, Faith Presbyn. Ch., West Lafayette, Ind., 1972-85; mem. Ctr. for Theol. Inquiry, Princeton, N.J., 1985—. Author: Patristic Roots of Reformed Worship, 1975, Worship, 1984, Reformed Baptismal Rite in the Sixteenth Century, 1989; contbr. numerous articles to scholarly jours. Fellow N.Am. Acad. Liturgy; mem. Union League Phila. Republican. Avocations: painting, music. Office: 50 Stockton St Princeton NJ 08540

OLDENBURG, DOUGLAS W., academic administrator. Pres. Columbia Theol. Sem., Decatur, Ga. Office: Columbia Theol Sem Office of the President 701 Columbia Dr BOX 520 Decatur GA 30031*

OLDFIELD, JOHN STEWART, pastor; b. Oak Park, Ill., July 7, 1940; s. Stewart Singer and Sylvia (Beckwall) O.; m. Dagmar Rettedal, June 18, 1966; children: Kristie, David, Peter, Ingrid. BA, Coll. Wooster, 1963; MDiv, Conservative Bapt. Theol. Sem., 1967. Ordained to ministry Evangelistic Missionary Fellowship, 1968. Pastor Levant (Kans.) Community Ch., 1967-74, Yorktowne Chapel, York, Pa., 1974—; radio speaker, producer Sta. WSBA, York, 1982—; mgr., promoter The Melting Pot/The Looking Glass, coffee house ministry to youth, York, 1976-88. Capt., co-founder York City Police Chaplains Corps, York, 1983—; chmn. CityLight, 1986-90. Recipient Jefferson award Sta. WGAL-TV, 1984, award for promoting human dignity and social justice York City Human Rels. Commn., 1984, Liberty Bell award York County Bar Assn., 1985. Mem. Evang. Missionary Fellowship (bd. dirs. 1978—, chmn. credentials com. 1981—), Nat. Assn. Evangs., Nat. Religious Broadcasters, Internat. Conf. of Police Chaplains. Republican. Home: 428 Allegheny Dr York PA 17402 Office: Yorktowne Chapel 43 E College Ave York PA 17403

OLDHAM, WILLIAM EDWARD, minister, accountant, educator; b. Delhi, La., Aug. 10, 1948; s. Edward Lincoln and Meriam Galdys (Boze) O.; m. Lucille Takkordai Telukdharrie, Aug. 25, 1971; children: Kenneth Ganash, Brian Rajpaul, Indra Anita. BA, Anderson U., 1973, postgrad., 1985-86; postgrad., Ind. Bus. Coll., 1975. Ordained to ministry Ch. of God (Anderson, Ind.), 1990; cert. tchr. Ind., Ala. Assoc. pastor East 10th St Ch of God, Indpls., 1985-86; missionary Mercy Corp./Ch. of God, Honduras, 1986; sr. pastor Sheridan (Ind.) Ch. of God, 1987-88; sr. pastor First Ch. of God, Mobile, Ala., 1988-89, Shreveport, La., 1989—; pres. Right Hand Ministries, Inc., Indpls., 1986—. Author: A Study in John's Gospel, 1991; developer bd. game Power, 1975. With USAF, 1969-70, Vietnam. Named Outstanding Coach Fall Creek Little League, Indpls., 1983, 84, 85, 86. Mem. Assn. Govt. Accts., Lions (pres. Fall Creek chpt. 1983-84, Pres.'s award 1984). Office: First Ch of God 6808 Jefferson-Paige Rd Shreveport LA 71119 *The source of life is found in God. The joy of life is found in God. The meaning of life is found in God. All things point to God. When we use our lives for any purpose other than worship of and service to God, all we have is emptiness, vanity and futility.*

OLDS, JAMES HOWARD, minister; b. Owen County, Ky., Sept. 4, 1945; s. James H. and Sadie Mae (Stewart) O.; m. Sandra Lewis, Sept. 19, 1964; children: Wesley Howard, Bradley Stewart. BA, Asbury Coll., 1966; MDiv, Asbury Theol. Sem., 1970; D in Ministry, Lexington Theol. Sem., 1977. Ordained to ministry Meth. Ch., 1970. Pastor Woodlawn-Beech Fork United Meth. Ch., Bardstown, Ky., 1966-70, Eminence (Ky.) United Meth. Ch., 1970-75, Crestwood (Ky.) United Meth. Ch., 1975-84, Trinity Hill United Meth. Ch., Lexington, Ky., 1984-91, St. Paul United Meth. Ch., Louisville, 1991—; vice chairperson Ky. Conf. Coun. on Ministries, Lexington, 1988—; chairpersonKy. Conf. Vision 2000, Lexington, 1990—; pres. Ky. Conf. Retirement Home, inc., Lexington, 1989—; mem. Ky. State Wesley Found., Frankfort, 1982—, Southeastern Jurisdiction Communications, Atlanta, 1991—. Pres. Community Kitchen Bd. Dirs., Lexington, 1988—; mem. Mayors Task Force on Homelessness, Lexington, 1989-90; chmn. Gov.'s Commn. on Prison Chaplains, Crestwood, Ky., 1979. Named to Honorable Order of Ky. Colonels; recipient Harry Denman Evangelism award Ky. Conf. of United Meth. Ch., 1983. Mem. Rotary, Lions. Democrat. Home: 1605 Dundee Rd Louisville KY 40205 Office: St Paul United Meth Ch 2000 Douglas Blvd Louisville KY 40205

O'LEARY, SISTER DENNIS, nun, religious education director; b. Wheeling, W.Va., Nov. 17, 1934; d. Dennis Edward and Eleanor Elizabeth (Mullen) O'L. B of Elem. Edn., Duquesne U., 1970; MA, U. Dayton, 1988. Joined Sisters of St. Joseph, Roman Cath. Ch., 1952. Tchr. St. Vincent Grade Sch., Wheeling, 1954-55, 57-58, 1969-81; tchr. Corpus Christi Grade Sch., Wheeling, 1955-56, 66-67, St. Joseph Grade Sch., Huntington, W.Va., 1958-65, St. Francis Xavier Grade Sch., Moundsville, W.Va., 1967-69; dir. religious edn. St. Margaret Mary Parish, Parkersburg, W.Va., 1981—; dir. Christ Renews His Parish Renewal Program, Wheeling, 1980-81, Parkersburg, 1982—, Confraternity of Christian Doctrine, Parkersburg, 1981—; dir. Christian edn. for elem., jr. high and high sch. students, 1981—. Participant Pro-Life, Charleston, W.Va., 1989. Home: 1205 25th St Parkersburg WV 26101 Office: St Margaret Mary Parish Religious Edn Bldg 2508 Dudley Ave Parkersburg WV 26101

O'LEARY, EDWARD CORNELIUS, bishop; b. Bangor, Maine, Aug. 21, 1920; s. Cornelius J. and Annabel (McManus) O'L. B.A., Holy Cross Coll., Worcester, Mass., 1942; S.T.L., St. Paul's U. Sem., Ottawa, Can., 1946. Ordained priest Roman Cath. Ch., 1946, named monsignor, 1954, consecrated bishop, 1971; vice-chancellor, then chancellor of Diocese of Portland, Maine; diocesan consultor, pro-synodal judge of diocese, pres. priests senate, mem. finance com. of diocese, also dir. Commodity Service Corp., 1969-75; titular bishop of Moglaena, aux. bishop Portland, 1971-74; bishop Roman Cath. Diocese Portland, 1974-89, bishop emeritus, 1989—; mem. Maine Office Religious Coop., from 1973. Mem. Nat. Conf. Cath. Bishops. Address: 307 Congress St Portland ME 04101

OLEK, JOHN J., parochial school and church administrator; b. Moorhead, Minn., Feb. 24, 1953; s. Oscar A. and Helen G. (Flynn) O.; m. Nancy Ann Rockstad, Apr. 7, 1973; children: John Jr., Lisa, Amanda, Nicholas. Degree in banking and fin., U. Minn., Crookston, 1982. Dir. fin. and devel. Cathedral Parish and Elem. Sch., Crookston, 1983—. Asst. youth activities Fisher (Minn.) Pub. Schs., 1985—. Mem. Nat. Assn. Ch. Bus. Adminstrs. Home: 503 5th St S Fisher MN 56723 Office: Cathedral Parish 702 Summit Ave Crookston MN 56716

OLENDER, DAVID PAUL, minister; b. Buffalo, Mar. 18, 1967; s. Richard Martin and Barbara Marie (Hale) O.; m. Dawn Raneé Howard, Oct. 22, 1988. BA, Cin. Bible Coll., 1989. Youth min. Brownsburg (Ind.) Christian Ch., 1988-89; assoc. min. 1st Christian Ch., Tarpon Springs, Fla., 1989—; Bible study leader Fellowship Christian Athletes, Tarpon Springs, 1989—; youth motivator, leader drop out program East Lake High Sch., Tarpon Springs, 1989—. Mem. chs. of Christ. Republican. Home: 5215 Spike Horn Dr New Port Richey FL 34653 Office: 1st Christian Ch 2795 Keystone Rd Tarpon Springs FL 34689

OLERT, FREDERICK HERMAN, retired minister; b. Holland, Mich., Dec. 12, 1904; s. Henry John and Jane (Brink) O.; m. Aug. 21, 1929; children: Mary, Grace, Sarah, Fred, Susan Jane. AB, Hope Coll., 1926; postgrad., U. Chgo., 1928, U. Edinburgh; ThM, Louisville Theol. Sem., 1930; DD (hon.), Hope Coll., 1940, U. Edinburgh; degree, Western Sem., 1929; DD (hon.), Alma Coll., Hope Coll., 1960; 0DD (hon.), Alma Coll., 1940. Ordained to ministry Presbyn. Ch. (U.S.A.), 1930. Min. various chs., Ky., Ohio; min. various chs., Detroit, Richmond, L.A.; radio and TV ministry, ch. organist.

OLFORD, STEPHEN FREDERICK, religious organization administrator, minister; b. Kalene Hill, Northern Rhodesia, Mar. 29, 1918; came to U.S., 1959; s. Frederick Ernest Samuel and Bessie Rhoden (Santmier) O.; m. B. Heather Brown, June 30, 1948; children: Jonathan MacGregor, David Lindsay. Student, Oxford U., Eng.; Diploma in Theology, St. Luke's Coll. Mildmay, London, 1937; postgrad., Missionary Tng. Colony Upper

Norwood, London, 1939; ThD, Luther Rice Sem., 1978; DD (hon.), Dallas Bapt. U., 1983, Wheaton (Ill.) Coll., 1966; LittD (hon.), Houghton Coll., 1966; HHD (hon.), Richmond Coll., Toronto, Ont., Can., 1975. Ordained to ministry Bapt. Ch., 1953. Army chaplain Newport, South Wales, 1939-45; sr. min. Duke St. Bapt. Ch., Richmond, Surrey, Eng., 1953-59, Calvary Bapt. Ch., N.Y.C., 1959-73; pres. Encounter Ministries, Inc., Memphis, 1973—; mem. coun. reference Evang. Bible Sem., Republic South Africa, 1986—, Helps Internat. Ministries, Harlem, Ga., 1988—, S.Am. Mission, Lake Worth, Fla., 1989—, Women Alive Ministries, Collingswood, N.J., 1982—, Italy for Christ, Atlanta, 1984—; mem. adv. bd. Internat. Bible Reading Assn., Murfreesboro, Tenn., 1989—. Author 19 books, 14 booklets; contbr. articles to religious periodicals. Recipient award for 15th yrs. on Sta. WPIX-TV, 1975, Faith and Freedom award Religious Heritage of Am., 1983; Disting. Svc. award Nat. Religious Broadcasters, 1987, honor award So. Cen. chpt., 1991. Fellow Royal Geographic Soc., Philos. Soc. Great Britain (life). Office: Encounter Ministries Inc PO Box 757800 Memphis TN 38175

OLIPHANT, BEN R., bishop. Mem. presidium World Meth. Coun. Office: World Meth Coun PO Box 518 Lake Junaluska NC 28745*

OLIPHINT, BENJAMIN RAY, bishop; b. Hemphill, Tex., May 28, 1924; s. John H. and Tressie (Post) O.; m. Nancy Brooke Kelley, June 7, 1952; children: Mary Brooke, Stuart Ray, John Clayton, Kelley MacLauren. BA, So. Meth. U., 1944; BD, Duke U., 1946; S.T.M., Union Theol. Sem., 1947; PhD, U. Edinburg, 1951. On trial, ordained deacon La. Conf., United Meth. Ch., 1946; full connection, elder, 1949. Minister St. Luke's Meth. Ch., New Orleans, 1947-49; assoc. minister 1st Meth. Ch., Alexandria, La., 1951-52; minister St. Paul's Meth. Ch., Monroe, La., 1952-65, 1st Meth. Ch., Alexandria, La., from 1965; now bishop Tex. Conf. United Meth. Ch., Houston. Del. Gen. Conf. United Meth. Ch., 1964; mem. Gen. Bd. Edn., 1964,. Office: 5215 S Main St Houston TX 77002

OLIPHINT, (KENNETH) SCOTT, minister; b. Amarillo, Tex., Sept. 30, 1955; s. Varner Hulen Jr. and Patricia Anne (Kelly) O.; m. Margaret Elizabeth Clark, Dec. 21, 1977; children: Jared, Joel, Bonnie. BS, West Tex. State U., 1978; MA in Religion, Westminster Theol. Sem., Phila., 1983, ThM, 1984. Ordained to ministry Orthodox Presbyn. Ch., 1985. Dir. Pursuit Ministries, Amarillo, 1984—; pastor Christ Covenant Ch., Amarillo, 1988—. Contbr. chpt. to book. Pres. Amarillo Crisis Pregancy Ctr., 1988-90, mem. adv. bd., 1990—. Office: Pursuit Ministries 714 S Tyler St Ste 301 Amarillo TX 79101

OLITZKY, KERRY MARC, rabbi; b. Pitts., Dec. 22, 1954; s. Abraham Nathan and Frances (Reznick) O.; m. Sheryl Mandy Rosenblatt, Aug. 28, 1977; children: Avi Samuel, Jesse Michael. BA, U. South Fla., 1974, MA, 1975; MA in Hebrew Lit., Hebrew Union Coll., 1980, D in Hebrew Letters, 1985. Ordained rabbi, 1981. Asst rabbi, dir. religious edn. Congregation Beth Israel, West Hartford, Conn., 1981-84; dir. sch. edn. Hebrew Union Coll., N.Y.C., 1984—. Author, editor: We Are Leaving Mother Russia, Glossary of Jewish Life, A Jewish Mourner's Handbook, The Safe Deposit and Other Stories about Old Lovers, Grandparents and Crazy Old Men. Mem. Religious Edn. Assn., Assn. Reform Zionists of Am., Nat. Assn. Temple Educators, Cen. Conf. Am. Rabbis, Coalition for the Advancement of Jewish Edn., Gerontology Soc. Am., Joint Commn. on Jewish Edn., Assn. for Supervision and Curriculum Devel., Nat. Interfaith Coalition on Aging. Democrat. Office: Hebrew Union Coll Jewish Inst Religion 1 W 4th St New York NY 10012

OLIVER, HALLEY BROOKS, minister, retired; b. Tipton, Mich., June 2, 1921; s. Samuel Noble and Edith (MacBain) O.; m. Nan Christine Johnson, Dec. 27, 1945; children: Mary Huber, John Brooks, Timothy Dwight, Andrew. AA, Muskegon (Mich.) Jr. Coll., 1941; AB, Oberlin Coll., 1943, BD, 1945; DD (hon.), Olivet Coll., 1980. Ordained min. United Ch. of Christ, 1946. Pastor 1st Congl. Ch., Belding, Mich., 1946-48, Hart, Mich., 1948-53; pastor 1st Congl. United Ch. of Christ, Owosso, Mich., 1954-87, pastor emeritus, 1987—; chmn. bd. trustees Mich. Conf. Congl. Ch., Lansing, Mich.; moderator Mich. Conf. United Ch. of Christ, Lansing. Mem. Shiawassee Mid County Planning Commn., Owosso, 1968; bd. mem. Owosso Hist. Commn., Shiawassee Hospice. Recipient Owosso City Proclamation for 30 Yrs. Svc. in a City Pastorate, 1984, Legis. Tribute Mich. House of Reps., 1987; named Citizen of Yr., Owosso County C. of C., 1986. Mem. Kiwanis, Wigton Lodge, Masons. Home: 1200 Ward St Owosso MI 48867 *I give thanks for a family who taught us to laugh with them. The sharing of joy and laughter does not isolate; it fills fuller lives which can be lonely and barren, even to the point of forgetting the purposes of God. The trust laughter requires is akin to the faith evoked by grace. I may laugh at you if I don't know you or care. I will laugh and cry with you when I can walk beside you.*

OLIVER, HAROLD HUNTER, theologian, educator; b. Mobile, Ala., Oct. 9, 1930; s. Alonzo E. and Amelee (Dunaway) O.; A.B., Samford U., 1951; B.D., So. Bapt. Theol. Sem., 1954; Th.M. Princeton Theol. Sem., 1955; Ph.D., Emory U., 1961; m. Martha Ann Maddox, Aug. 12, 1951, 1 dau., Daphne Ann. Instr., Southeastern Bapt. Theol. Sem., Wake Forest, N.C., 1957-61, asst. prof., 1961-62, assoc. prof., 1962-65; assoc. prof. Boston U., 1965-70, prof. of philos. theology, 1970—, acting assoc. dean, 1984, dir. advanced professional studies, 1985-90; vis. fellow Inst. Theoretical Astronomy, Cambridge U., 1971-72; Chavanne vis. prof. religious studies Rice U., Houston, 1980-81. Nat. panelist Nat. Endowment for Humanities. A.T.S. faculty fellow, 1963-64; Danforth postdoctoral fellow, 1971-72. Fellow Royal Astron. Soc. (London); mem. Am. Acad. Religion, Am. Theol. Soc., Am. Philos. Assn., Metaphys. Soc. Am., Internat. Soc. Metaphysics Soc. Values in Higher Edn. Author: A Relational Metaphysic, 1981; Relatedness: Essays in Metaphysics and Theology, 1984; mem. editorial adv. bd. ZYGON: Jour. of Religion and Sci.; bd. editorial cons. The Personalist Forum; contbr. articles to profl. jours. Home: 7 Marshall Rd Winchester MA 01890 Office: Boston U 745 Commonwealth Ave Boston MA 02215

OLIVER, JOHN WILLIAM POSEGATE, minister; b. Vincennes, Ind., Apr. 9, 1935; s. Dwight L. and Elizabeth (Posegate) O.; m. Cristina Shepard Hope, Oct. 19, 1968; children: John William Posegate Jr., Sloan Christian Shepard. BA, Wheaton Coll., 1956; BD, Fuller Theol. Sem., 1959; ThM, So. Bapt. Theol. Sem., 1963. Ordained to ministry Presbyn. Ch. in Am., 1962. Asst. pastor Covenant Presbyn. Ch., Hammond, Ind., 1964-66, Trinity Presbyn. Ch., Montgomery, Ala., 1966-69; pastor 1st Presbyn. Ch., Augusta, Ga., 1969—; moderator Cen. Ga. Presbytery, Presbyn. Ch. in Am., 1976. Trustee Westminster Schs., Augusta, 1972—; chmn. clergy Augusta United Way Campaign, 1974; mem. exec. bd. clergy staff Univ. Hosp., Augusta, 1975-76; mem. bd. commmrs. Augusta Housing Authority, vice-chmn., 1976—; trustee, chmn. bd. Columbia Bible Coll. and Sem., 1978—; mem. ministerial adv. bd. Reformed Theol. Sem., 1978-85, 89—; bd. dirs. Mission to the World, Presbyn. Ch. in Am., 1984-89. Mem. Evang. Theol. Soc., Nat. Assn. Evangelicals. Home: 3205 Huxley Dr Augusta GA 30909 Office: 642 Telfair St Augusta GA 30901

OLIVER, MARY ANNE MCPHERSON, religion educator; b. Montgomery, Ala., Nov. 21, 1935; d. James Curtis and Margaret Sinclair (Miller) McPherson; m. Raymond Davies Oliver, Aug. 28, 1959; children: Kathryn Sinclair, Nathan McPherson. BA, U. Ala., Tuscaloosa, 1956; certificat, Sorbonne, Paris, 1958; MA, U. Wis., 1959; PhD, Grad. Theol. Union, Berkeley, Calif., 1972. Vol. tchr., preacher, counselor, 1972—; instr. U. Calif., Berkeley, St. Mary's Coll., Moraga, Calif., 1973; adj. faculty San Francisco Theol. Sem., San Anselmo, 1977-81; lectr. San Jose (Calif.) State U., 1980-81, San Francisco State U., 1985-86; adj. prof. dept. liberal arts John F. Kennedy U., Orinda, Calif., 1987—. Author: History of Good Shepherd Episcopal Mission, 1978; contbr. articles to profl. jours. Rep. Ala. Coun. on Human Rels., Mobile, Ala., 1958; active deanery, conv. Good Shepherd Episc. Ch., Berkeley, Calif., 1970-75; rep. U. Calif. Fgn. Student Hospitality, Berkeley, 1965-70; vol. tchr. Berkeley pub. schs., 1965-73; bd. dirs. Canterbury Found., Berkeley, 1972-75; chmn. bd. dirs. West Berkeley Parish, Berkeley, 1976-78. Recipient award French Consulate, New Orleans, 1956; Fulbright grantee, 1956, grantee Mabelle McLeod Lewis Found., 1969. Mem. Am. Acad. Religion, Conf. on Christianity and Lit. Democrat. Home: 1632 Grant St Berkeley CA 94703 Office: John F Kennedy U 12 Altarinda Rd Orinda CA 94563 *Wherever two are gathered, there is the Holy One.*

OLLER, MARK LOUIS, lay worker, small business owner; b. Fresno, Calif., Jan. 19, 1964; s. John William Jr. Oller and Lois Elaine (Klotz) White. BA, Hardin-Simmons U., 1986. Mgr., owner Western Insulators, Inc., San Andreas, Calif., 1986—. Office: 746 Church Hill Rd PO Box 1448 San Andreas CA 95249

OLLEY, JOHN WILLIAM, minister, educator; b. Sydney, Australia, July 26, 1938; s. John Jeffrey George and Dorothy Elizabeth Ellen (Allison) O.; m. Elaine Waugh, Jan. 20, 1962; children: David John, Linda Christine, Catherine Louise. BSc with honors, U. Sydney, 1959, PhD, 1964; BD with honors, Bapt. Theol. Coll., Eastwood, Australia, 1965; M in Theology, Melbourne (Australia) Coll. Div., 1975. Ordained to ministry Bapt. Ch. Pastor Bapt. Chs., New South Wales, Australia, 1963-68; missionary Am. Bapt. Chs., Hong Kong, 1968-78; head O.T. Dept. Bapt. Theol. Coll. Western Australia, Bentley, 1978—, vice prin., 1984-91, prin., 1991—; lectr. Chinese U. Hong Kong, 1968-78, chmn. dept. religion, 1974-77; mem. council Evangelical Alliance Western Australia, Perth, 1979—; lectr. Curtin U., Bentley, part-time, 1981-88; pres. Bapt. Chs. Western Australia, 1982-83; alt. mem. Lausanne Com. for World Evangelization, Singapore, 1983-90. Author: Righteousness in Isaiah LXX, 1979, What on Earth?, 1982; contbr. articles to profl. jours. Mem. Soc. Bibl. Lit., Australia and New Zealand Soc. for Theol. studies (com. mem. Western Australia chpt. 1981—), Am. Schs. Oriental Research (profl.), Internat. Assn. Mission Studies, Australian Bapt. Missionary Soc. (chmn. bd. dirs. 1990—). Home and Office: Bapt Theol Coll Western Australia, Hayman Rd, Bentley Western Australia 6102, Australia

OLLO, MICHAEL ANTHONY, educational coordinator, educator; b. Newark, Mar. 14, 1959; s. Mary Constance (Rotunda-Ollo) Buono; m. Maura Lucy Fitzmorris, Mar. 17, 1991. AA in Communications, Community Coll. of Air Force, 1979; student, U. Miami, 1978, Sch. Internat. Tng., Global Edn., Brattleboro, Vt., 1986; BS in Social Studies and Edn., Caldwell (N.J.) Coll., 1990. Cert. tchr., N.J. Tchr. math. and sci. Project Link Edn. Ctr., Newark, 1984-88, dir. student svcs., 1987-88; tchr. math. and sci., outdoor edn. coord. DOME Project, Inc., N.Y.C., 1989—; program coord., ednl. cons. for fgn. born students Edn. Resources Plus, Rutherford, N.J., 1988—; asst. dir. New Day Vacation Community for Retarded People, South Orange, N.J., 1984—. Hospice vol. Hospice Inc. of Hudson County, Jersey City, 1982-84; dir. Dominican Basketball League of N.J., 1986-88; coord. relief camp Appalachian Relief Project, Huntington, W.Va., 1988-90; coord. youth group St. Joseph's parish, East Orange, N.J., 1984-88. Staff sgt. USAF, 1977-82. Mem. ASCD, Nat. Sci. Tchrs. Assn., Phi Alpha Theta Internat. Roman Catholic. Avocations: basketball, reading, camping, lecturing on ecological and social awareness and tours. Home: 636 10th St Lyndhurst NJ 07071 Office: DOME Project Inc 486 Amsterdam Ave New York NY 10024

OLMSTEAD, GERALD EUGENE, minister; b. Fairview, Pa., Feb. 27, 1954; s. Floyd Eugene and Alice Bertha (Illig) O.; m. Linda Kathleen Sippy, Aug. 2, 1975; children: Jessica Lynn, Dane Jerod. BS in Art Edn. cum laude, Edinboro (Pa.) State U., 1976; MDiv, Pitts. Theol. Sem., 1987. Ordained to ministry United Meth. Ch. as elder, 1989. Pastor Stanton Heights and Pacific Ave. United Meth. Chs., Pitts., 1983-87, Falls Creek (Pa.) United Meth. Ch., 1987-91, Little Cooley and New Richmond United Meth. Chs., Centerville, Pa., 1991—; mem. vital congregations and faithful disciples coms. Indiana (Pa.) dist. Western Pa. Conf., United Meth. Ch., 1989—. Contbr. articles to religious jours.; creator multi-media and graphic art works for various ch. events. Speaker for Support of Scotopic Sensitivity Detection and Treatment, Pa., 1989—. Home and Office: RD 2 Box 204 Centerville PA 16404

OLMSTEAD, WILLIAM CARL, principal; b. Rock Island, Ill., Apr. 26, 1946; s. Carl Milo and Mary Ruth (James) O.; divorced, 1983; children: Deborah, Daniel. BRE, Life Bible Coll., 1969; MS, Western Ill. U., 1974. Min. of youth Foursquare Ch., Kokomo, Ind., 1969-72; prin. Temple Christian Acad., Moline, Ill., 1977—. Mem. Internat. Ch. of Foursquare Gospel. Home: 1835 18th Ave A Moline IL 61265 Office: Temple Christian Acad 2305 7th Ave Moline IL 61265

OLSBY, GARY ALLEN, minister; b. Lynwood, Calif., Feb. 3, 1956; s. Donald Eugene and Lucille Margaret (Stockwell) O.; m. Tamala RaNae Mattox, Sept. 2, 1978; children: Heather, Ryan. BA, Pacific Christian Coll., 1978; MA, Biola U., 1990. Ordained to ministry Ind. Christian Ch., 1978. Min. Christian Edn. West Valley Christian Ch., Canoga Park, Calif., 1977-84, Knott Ave. Christian Ch., Anaheim, Calif., 1984—; tchr. Pacific Christian Coll., Fullerton, Calif., 1988. Author: Bible History Overview—Old Testament, 1990. Bd. dirs. Leadership Tng. Inst., Fullerton, 1985—. Office: Knott Ave Christian Ch 315 S Knott Ave Anaheim CA 92804 *I find that I have a constant burden to give people the "big picture" of the scriptures.*

OLSEN, HAROLD CHARLES, minister; b. Elkhart, Ind., June 13, 1931; s. George Alfred and Reathel Malinda (Kamp) O.; m. Sally Anne Beadle, Aug. 13, 1954; children: Daniel Joseph, Michael John. BS in Edn., Taylor U., 1953; MA in Religious Edn., Winona Lake Sch. of Theology, Ind., 1955; Diploma in Colonial Studies, Royal Belgian Colonial Sch., Brussels, 1957; MEd, Grand Valley State U., 1977. Ordained to ministry Calvary Undenominational Ch., 1962; cert. elem./secondary tchr., Mich. Missionary Africa Inland Mission Internat., Pearl River, N.Y., 1957-88; minister of missions Calvary Undenominational Ch., Grand Rapids, Mich., 1988—; area com. mem. Africa Inland Mission Internat., 1985—; prof. of missions Grand Rapids Sch. of Bible and Music, 1981-83. Author: Africa Heroes of the Congo Rebellion, 1969, It Happened in Africa, 1972, Africa Myths About Christianity, 1972, Adventures in Nairobi, 1974; contbr. articles to profl. jours. Mem. YMCA, Grand Rapids, 1991. Named Missions Instr. of Yr., Grand Rapids Sch. of Bible and Music, 1983. Republican. Home: 761 Bradford Place NE Grand Rapids MI 49546 Office: Calvary Undenominational Ch 777 E Beltline Ave NE Grand Rapids MI 49546 *The only thing in this life that really matters is one's relationship to our very giver and sustainer of life - The Lord Jesus Christ.*

OLSEN, LESTER PAUL (LES OLSEN), minister; b. Valentine, Nebr., Aug. 10, 1945; s. Lloyd Lester and Marie (Schulz) O.; m. Linda Marie Knuth, Aug. 24, 1965; children: Mark, Misty, Gwen, Lacey. BS, Sioux Falls Coll., 1968; MA, Augustana Coll., 1984; D of Ministry, Univ. of Bibl. Studies, Bethany, Okla., 1991. Ordained to ministry Bapt. Ch., 1989. Mem. adv. bd. Maranatha Bible Camp, North Platte, Nebr., 1978-91; pastor Kilgore (Nebr.) Bapt. Ch., 1985—; case worker Nebr. Dept. Social Svcs., Valentine, 1987—; del. Berean Fund Ch. Coun., North Platte, 1979-80. Author: Cybernetics Come of Age, 1991. Chaplain Sandhills Composite Squadron, CAP, 1988-91. Recipient Charles Yeager Aerospace Edn. achievement award CAP, 1991; NSF grantee, Washington, 1972. Mem. Aircraft Owners and Pilots Assn., Nat. Ministers Coun., Nebr. Ministers Coun, Niobrara Ham Club. Republican. Home: PO Box 455 Valentine NE 69201 Office: Kilgore Baptist Church Kilgore NE 69216

OLSEN, MILES JEFFREY, religious educator, minister; b. Sidney, Nebr., Sept. 30, 1952; s. Harold Daniel and Genevieve Marie (Schwartz) O.; m. Carol Lynne Genuchi,. BBE, Western Bible Coll., 1984; MA in Bib. Studies magna cum laude, Criswell Coll., 1989. Youth pastor intern Friendly Hills Bapt. Ch., Morrison, Colo., 1983-84; tchr. bible Derby Hill Bapt. Ch., Loveland, Colo., 1984-85; minister of youth and christian edn. First Bapt. Ch., North East, Pa., 1985-86; tchr. bible First Bapt. Ch., Dallas, 1986—; teaching fellow in pedagogy Western Bible Coll., 1983-84. With U.S. Army, 1973-76, ETO. Baptist. Avocations: tennis, hiking, drama, music.

OLSEN, WESLEY, academic administrator. Pres. Southwestern Coll., Phoenix. Office: Southwestern Coll 2625 E Cactus Rd Phoenix AZ 85032*

OLSHANSKY, NORMAN, social work adminstrator; b. N.Y.C., May 6, 1946; s. Charles and Belle (Rottblatt) O.; m. Anne Barbara Levin, June 27, 1982; children: Matthew, Lauren, Jana, Benjamin. Student, Coll. William and Mary, 1964-66; BS, Va. Commonwealth U., 1969; MSW, Wayne State U., 1971. Vista vol., program dir. United South End Settlements, Boston, 1966-68; dir.-adminstr. Common Ground Inc., Birmingham, Mich., 1970-73; asst. dir. Jewish Community Ctr., Memphis, 1973-78; regional dir. Anti-Defamation League, Richmond, Va., 1978-82; dir. pers. Circuit City Stores, Inc., Richmond, 1982-85; exec. dir. United Jewish Community of the Va. Peninsula, Newport News, Va., 1985-88, Sarasota-Manatee Jewish Fedn., Sarasota, Fla., 1988—; cons. Office of Drug Abuse and Alcoholism, State of Mich., 1972, Jewish Fedns. of Va. and N.C. Legis. Affairs, 1978-85. Mem. NASW (unit chmn.), Assn. Jewish Community Orgn. Profls., B'nai Brith. Jewish. Avocations: fishing, tennis. Office: Sarasota Manatee Jewish Fed Fedn 580 S McIntosh Rd Sarasota FL 34232

OLSON, CAROL ANN, librarian; b. Chgo., Dec. 16, 1945; d. Kenneth Carlyle and Marion Heath (Barkway) Nygaard; m. Ray Alan Olson, June 15, 1974; children: Eric Robert, Peter Alan. BA in History, Jamestown (N.D.) Coll., 1968; MALS, U. Minn., 1970. Acquisitions libr. Luther Northwestern Sem. Library, St. Paul, 1971—. Mem. Minn. Libr. Assn., Libr. Rsch. Roundtable Div. of Minn. Libr. Assn. Lutheran. Home: 2724 N Griggs St Saint Paul MN 55113 Office: Luther Northwestern Sem Libr 2375 Como Ave Saint Paul MN 55108

OLSON, DARRYL RAYNOLD, minister, painter; b. Milaca, Minn., Feb. 18, 1940; s. Andrew Reinhold and Edla Mary (Reed) O.; m. Kathleen Christine, Jun. 10, 1961; children: Melody Rae, Dares Del, Charmel Dae Sancho. Student, North Central Bible Coll., 1958-63. Evangelist Assemblies of God, Milaca, Minn., 1963-67; pastor Assemblies of God, Park Rapids, Minn., 1972-76, Cokato, Minn., 1976-80, various locations, 1980--; pastor Twin Falls Christian Center, St. Croix Falls, Wis. Conducted radio program Without a Song 1975, contr. articles to local newspaper. World Bible Way Fellowship. Office: Twin Falls Christian Center PO Box 294 Taylor Falls MN 55084 *St. John 10:10 quotes Jesus as saying, "I am come that they might have life and that more abundantly." My aim in life is to share the "abundant life" with others and to inspire them to share it with someone else. There is no greater life than sharing "The Life," Jesus.*

OLSON, DAVID WENDELL, bishop; b. St. Paul, Apr. 4, 1938; s. Wendell Edwin and Eva Victoria (Edstrom) O.; m. Nancy Grace Evans, May 7, 1961; children: Kathryn, Jonathan, Justin. BA, St. Olaf Coll., 1960; MDiv, Luther Sem., St. Paul, 1964. Ordained to ministry Am. Luth. Ch.,1964. Dir. North Mpls. Luth. Coalition, 1978-82; asst. prof. Luther N.W. Sem., St. Paul, 1982-84; asst. to bishop S.E. Minn. dist. Am. Luth. Ch., St. Paul, 1984-87; bishop Mpls. area synod Evang. Luth. Ch. in Am., Mpls., 1987—. Chair Robbinsdale (Minn.) Sch. Bd., 1976-82; trustee Fairview Hosp., Mpls. Bush Found. fellow, 1975. Office: Evang Luth Ch in Am 122 W Franklin Ave Rm 600 Minneapolis MN 55404

OLSON, DENNIS THORALD, religion educator; b. Luverne, Minn., Jan. 6, 1954; s. Toby and Esther (Heaak) O.; m. Carol Joyce Andersen, June 3, 1978; children: Eric Leif, Kristen Esther. BA, Augustana Coll., Sioux Falls, S.D., 1976; MDiv, Luther Theol. Sem., 1980; MA, Yale U., 1981, PhD, 1984. Teaching fellow Yale Div. Sch., New Haven, 1981-84; parish pastor United Luth. Ch., Frost, Minn., 1984-87; instr. Luther Northwestern Theol. Sem., St. Paul, 1985-87; asst. prof. of Old Testament Princeton (N.J.) Theol. Sem. Author: The Death of the Old and the Birth of the New: The Framework of the Book of Numbers and the Pentateuch, 1985, Saints and Sajourners: An Old Testament Journey, 1990; contbr. articles to profl. jours. N.Am. Ministerial fellowship Fund for Theol. Edn., 1976-80, Grad. Alumni fellowship Yale U., 1983-84; resident scholar Ctr. for Theol. Inquiry, Princeton, 1990—, Nat. Merit scholar, 1972-76. Mem. Soc. of Bibl. Lit. Office: Princeton Theol Sem CN821 Princeton NJ 08542 *There is no Paradise, no Garden of Eden, no ideal Promised Land in this life. But there are momentary glimpses of such places, glimpses which give hope and encouragement to carry on.*

OLSON, GEORGE LEROY, minister, missionary; b. Gary, Ind., July 12, 1924; s. George and Marian (Lundgren) O.; m. Miriam Louise Burton, June 15, 1949; children—Tami Ann Haas, Timothy John, Christina Louise Gano. B.A., Augustana Coll., 1945; M.Div., Luth. Sch. Theology, Chgo., 1949. Ordained to ministry Lutheran Church in America, 1949. Missionary Japan Evang. Luth. Ch., Hiroshima, Japan, 1951-65; dir. Luth. Office Communication, Tokyo, 1966—, Luth. Communications Asia, Tokyo, 1983—; cons. Japan Luth. Hour, Tokyo, 1979—. Editor Japan Christian Quar., 1982—. Contbr. articles to profl. jours. Founder Forum Children's TV, Tokyo, 1977—; Asia coordinator TV Awareness Tng., Tokyo, 1982—. Recipient Alumni Service award Augustana Coll. Alumni Assn. 1982. Mem. Internat. House Japan, Internat. Advt. Assn., Fgn. Corr. Club Japan (assoc.), Japan Soc. Studies Journalism and Mass Communication. Club: Ai Shin Kai. Home: 1-14-20 Higashi Cho,, Koganei Shi, Tokyo Japan Office: Luth Office Communicatio, 1-1 Ichigaya Sadohara, Cho, Shinjuku-Ku, Tokyo 162, Japan

OLSON, GORDON W., religion educator; b. Brantford, N.D., Sept. 18, 1936; s. Lloyd A. and Alice I. (Black) O.; m. Mary L. Swenson, June 6, 1959; children: Laurie B., Linda M., Diane R., Erik G. BA, Concordia Coll., Moorhead, Minn., 1958; MA, U. Minn., 1972. Dir. music Univ. Luth. Ch. of Hope, Mpls., 1968-72; editor of music Augsburg Pub. House, Mpls., 1972-77; dir. music Calvary Luth. Ch., Golden Valley, Minn., 1972-87; exec. dir. Nat. Luth. Choir, Mpls., 1987-89; prof. Augsburg Coll., Mpls., 1989—; music specialist S.E. synod Am. Luth. Ch., Mpls., 1980-87. Active adminstrn. com. Golden Valley Bicentennial Com., 1975-76; coord. Music Arts of Golden Valley, 1980-88; mem. devel. bd. Villa Maria Ctr., Frontenac, Minn., 1988—. Mem. Am. Choral Dirs. Assn. (religion coord. Minn. chpt. 1982-88), Am. Guild English Handbell Ringers, Luth. Musicians Assn. (charter mem.). Home: 2425 Winfield Golden Valley MN 55422 Office: Augsburg Coll 731 21st Ave S Minneapolis MN 55454

OLSON, GRACE CAMERON, minister; b. Phila., May 15, 1940; d. Thomas Cameron and Grace (Worthington) Dudley; m. Royal Lloyd Olson, July 14, 1962; children: Cindy Grace, Royal Lloyd Jr., Gary Donald, Eric Douglas. BA, Wagner Coll., 1980; MDiv, Union Theol. Sem., N.Y.C., 1984. Ordained minister in Luth. Ch.; RN. Pastor St. Philip's Luth. Ch., Bklyn., 1984-86; pastor, chaplain Goldwater Meml. Hosp., Roosevelt Island, N.Y., 1985-86; pastor St. Barnabas Luth. Ch., Howard Beach, N.Y., 1986-88; asst. to the bishop Met. N.Y. Synod, N.Y.C., 1988—. Office: Met NY Synod 390 Park Ave S New York NY 10016

OLSON, HOWARD STANLEY, biblical studies and missiology educator; b. St. Paul, Minn., July 18, 1922; s. Oscar Ludwig and Clara Josephine (Peterson) O.; m. Anna Louise Anderson, June 17, 1946; children: Howard J., Sharon L., Timothy E., Linda H. BA, Gustavus Adolphus Coll., 1943; MDiv, Augustana Sem., Rock Island, Ill., 1946; PhD, Hartford Sem. Found., 1965; LLD (hon.), Gustavus Adolphus Coll., 1970. Missionary, prof. Augustana Luth. Ch., Luth. Ch. in Am./Evang. Luth. Ch. in Am., Tanzania, East Africa, 1946-88; prof. theology Luth. Theol. Coll., Makumira, Tanzania, 1964-88, prof. emeritus, 1988; prof. bibl. studies and missiology Wartburg Theol. Sem., Dubuque, Iowa, 1988-91; dir. of Music rsch. Luth. Theol. Coll., Makimura, 1967-88; abstractor Religious and Theol. abstracts, Myerstown, Pa., 1990. Author: Phonology and Morphology of the Rimi Language, 1964, First Swahili text for teaching Greek, 1972, rev. edit., 1985; compiler African ethnic hymns in English, 1977, in Swahili, 1967, 73, 87; editor Africa Theol. Jour., 1982-88;. Named Outstanding Alumnus, Luth Sch. of Theol., Chgo., 1978, Hartford (Conn.) Sem. Found., 1990; recipient Festschrift Luth. Theol. Coll. Makumira, 1988. Mem. Hymn. Soc. Am., Soc. of Bibl. Lit., Tanzania Soc. (life mem.). *The astounding diversity of cultures in our global village need not divide us, but rather can enhance our mutual enrichment, for no culture is too poor but what it can give, and none is too rich but what it can receive.*

OLSON, JERRY DEAN, JR., minister; b. Feb. 18, 1958; s. Jerry Dean and Nellie Ruth (Grimaud) O. MusB, Samford U., 1981; M in Ch. Music, The So. Bapt. Theol. Sem., 1983. Vol. pianist Bellevue Bapt. Ch., Grovetown, Ga., 1971-77; youth asst. Pike Ave. Bapt., Birmingham, Ala., 1977-78; minister music Fultondale (Ala.) First Bapt., 1978-80; assoc. minister music Beechwood Bapt., Louisville, 1982-84; minister music First Bapt. Ch., Belmont, N.C., 1984—; dir. Gaston Bapt. Music Ministry, Gastonia, N.C., 1985-88, 90—; mem. N.C. Singing Churchmen/Women, Cary, N.C., 1984—. V.p., bd. dirs. Community Concert Assn., Gastonia, 1988-91. Mem. N.C. Music Conf., Fedn. Music Clubs (study chmn. 1991), Am. Choral Dirs. Assn., Choristers Guild, Hymn Soc. Am., Am. Guild Organists (exec. com.

1990—). Home: 411 Dogwood Ln Belmont NC 28012 Office: First Bapt Ch 23 N Central Ave Belmont NC 28012

OLSON, JOHN A., ecumenical agency administrator. Exec. dir. Spokane Christian Coalition, Wash. Office: Spokane Christian Coalition E 245-13th Ave Spokane WA 99202*

OLSON, MARK JACK, minister; b. Fargo, N.D., Apr. 11, 1963; s. Norman Clifford and Inga (Larson) O.; m. Teresa Michelle Mickelson, Feb. 16, 1985. BS in Pastoral Studies, North Cen. Bible Coll., 1985. Youth pastor First Assembly of God, Kenosha, Wis., 1985; assoc. youth pastor Eden Prairie (Minn.) Assembly of God, 1986-87; youth pastor Mt. Olivet Assembly of God, Apple Valley, Minn., 1988—; rep. west twin cities sect. Minn. dist. Assemblies of God, Mpls., 1989—; mem. adv. bd. The Difference Youth Ministries, Eden Prairie, 1986—. Home: 7431 142 St Ct W Apple Valley MN 55124 Office: Mt Olivet Assembly of God 14201 Cedar Ave S Apple Valley MN 55124

OLSON, MATTHEW WAYNE, minister; b. Royal Oak, Mich., Oct. 11, 1960; s. Wayne Harry and Elinore (Green) O.; m. Elizabeth Ann Rhodes, Dec. 14, 1985. BA in Psychology, Mich. State U., 1982; MA in Psychology, Trinity Evang. Div. Sch., Deerfield, Ill., 1987, MDiv, 1988. Ordained to ministry Congregationalist Ch., 1988. Youth worker Pilgrim Congregationalist Ch., Bloomfield, Mich., 1982; intern Cen. Congregationalist Ch., Galesburg, Ill., 1982-83; intern First Congregationalist Ch., St. Johns, Mich., 1988-89, interium, 1989; pastor First Congregationalist Ch., Saugatuck, Mich., 1990—; co-dir. Heritage of Pilgrim Endeavor, Congl. Christian Chs./Nat. Assn., Oak Creek, Wis., 1990—. Mem. Nat. Assn. Counseling & Devel. Home: 67 Union Douglas MI 49408 Office: 1st Conglist Ch Corner Hoffman & Griffith Saugatuck MI 49453

OLSON, PAUL LEONARD, chaplain; b. Milaca, Minn., Apr. 19, 1952; s. Roland E. and Esther R. Olson; m. Marcella Catherine Grandy, July 6, 1974; children: Thomas Paul, Daralee Ann, Melissa Sue, Joshua Adam. BA in Theology, Internat. Sem., 1986, postgrad. Ordained to ministry Ind. Assemblies of God, 1979. Pastor Assembly of God Ch., Lisbon, N.D., 1973-75; instr. Shiloh House Ministries Inc., Anoka, Minn., 1977-80; evangelist Olson Ministries, Ellendale, N.D., 1980-82, Milaca, Minn., 1982-88; chaplain CAP, Sierra Vista, Ariz., 1989—; trainer Cochise County Med. Assistance, Bisbee, Ariz., 1988—. Recipient Comdr.'s commendation Ariz. wing CAP, 1990. Mem. Evang. Tchrs.' Tng. Assn.; Air Force Assn. Home: 650 Busby Dr # 18 Sierra Vista AZ 85635 *I have found that no matter what obstacles this life may throw in your path, you can make it through providing you place your trust in God and always look for something positive each day. A relationship with God plus a positive attitude equals success!.*

OLSON, STEVEN DARREL, minister; b. Fargo, N.D., Sept. 30, 1953; s. Jocelyn Darrel and Arlene Mabel (Aune) O.; m. Stephanie Ann Melstad, June 26, 1976; children: Kathryn, Janet. BA in Psychology, Whitworth Coll., 1975; diploma in Youth Leadership, Minn. Sem. Consortium, 1982; MDiv, Luther Theol. Sem., 1984. Ordained to ministry Luth. Ch., 1984. Youth worker Calvary Luth. Ch., Grand Forks, N.D., 1976-78; area dir. Young Life, Grand Forks, 1978-80; youth asst. Luth. Ch. of the Good Shepherd, Mpls., 1980-82; min. First English Luth. Ch., Wausau, Wis., 1984—; chmn. Dist. Youth Orgn. northern Wis., 1985-87; cons. Synod Youth Orgn. East-Cen. Wis., 1987—; mem. Task Force on Ministry East-Cen. Wis., 1990—. Youth bd. mem. Woodson YMCA, Wausau, 1985-89. Office: First English Luth Ch 402 N 3rd Ave Wausau WI 54401

OLSON, STEVEN FLOYD, pastor; b. Billings, Mont., May 20, 1953; s. Floyd William and Irene Eleanor (Matson) O.; m. Jill Denise Gambill, Jan. 19, 1974; children: Sara Michelle, Ryan Michael. BA, Whitworth Coll., 1975; MDiv, Luther Northwestern Theol. Sem., St. Paul, 1988. Ordained to ministry Evang. Luth. Ch. in Am., 1988. Adminstr. Presbyn. Ministries, Inc., Seattle, 1975-79, St. John's Luth. Home, Billings, Mont., 1983-85; pastor Messiah Luth. Ch., Auburn, Wash., 1988—; chaplain Bethesda Luth. Med. Ctr., St. Paul, 1987-88; mem. bd. synod extended ministries com. Evang. Luth. Ch. in Am., Tacoma, 1990—, mem. focus on youth ministries region I, Seattle, 1990—, mem. synod outreach com. SW Wash., 1991—, mem. social orgn. coun. region I, 1991—. Composer church music, 1973—. Coach Auburn Little League, 1989—. Mem. Auburn Ministerial Orgn., Columbia Luth. Home Corp. Home: 3014 15th St SE Auburn WA 98002 Office: Messiah Luth Ch 805 4th St NE Auburn WA 98002

OLSTAD, BRENT RAYMOND, music minister; b. Tokyo, Feb. 26, 1960; s. Raymond Milton and Lois (King) O.; m. Rachel Iola Shinn, June 20, 1987; 1 child, Bryce Raymond. BS in Music, Biola U., 1984. Organist Calvary Bapt. Ch., Whittier, Calif., 1980-84; minister of music Faith Bible Ch., Reno, Nev., 1988—, elder, 1989—, supt. Sunday sch., 1991—. Composer, arranger music book: The Faithful Flutist, 1989. Home: 1425 Dogwood Dr Sparks NV 89431

OLTZ, RICHARD JOHN, publishing executive, minister; b. Duluth, Minn., Sept. 20, 1945; s. Donald F. and Helen J. (Richardson) O.; m. Mary Jane Willman, June 1969; children: Shawn Richard, Jennifer Marie. Student, Olivet Coll., 1963-64; pastorial ministries, Berean Coll., 1980-83, counseling, 1984. Sr. pastor First Missionary Ch., Bad Axe, Mich., 1985-87; exec. dir. Bethel Pub., Elkhart, Ind., 1987—; sr. pastor Grace Chapel, N. Liberty, Ind., 1990—. Mem. Christian Booksellers Assn., Anabaptist Pubs., Christian Mgmt. Assn., Fellowship of Cos. for Christ, Protestant Ch. Publs. Assn. (dir. 1989—). Office: Bethel Pub Co 1819 S Main St Elkhart IN 46516 *No matter how successful life may appear to be, no matter what you may have accomplished, God must get all the glory or you will have labored in vain.*

OLUFOSOYE, TIMOTHY OMOTAYO, archbishop; b. Ondo, Nigeria, Mar. 31, 1918; s. Chief Daniel and Felecia (Akinduro) O.; widowed, 1945; 4 children. Degree in Theology, St. Andrew's Coll., Oyo, Nigeria, 1958; DD (hon.), U. B.C., Can. Archbishop Ch. Nigeria, Ibadan, 1979—; justice of the peace. Decorated Order of the Officer (Nigeria). Office: Bodija Estate, POB 1666, 12 Awosika Ave, GPO, Ibadan Oyo State, Nigeria

O'MAHONY, AUDREY MADELINE, religious order administrator; b. Tipperary, Ireland, May 17, 1938; came to U.S., 1957; d. Michael and Mary O'Mahony. BA, Incarnate Word Coll., San Antonio, 1963; MA, Cath. U. Am., 1967; EdD, U. San Francisco, 1986. Cert. secondary tchr., Tex., La.; joined Sisters of Charity of Incarnate Word, Roman Cath. Ch., 1956. Tchr. English, Incarnate Word High Sch., San Antonio, 1963-71, chmn. dept., 1969-71; tchr. Archbishop Chapelle High Sch., New Orleans, 1971-72, asst. prin., 1972-74; asst. registrar Incarnate Word Coll., 1974-80, asst. acad. v.p., 1984-86, acad. v.p., 1986-87, dean grad. studies, 1987-90; gen. councilor Sisters of Charity of Incarnate Word, San Antonio, 1990—; mem. Coll. Planning Commn., Incarnate Word Coll., 1986-91. Trustee Incarnate Word High Sch., 1977-80, 87-89, Spohn-Kleberg Meml. Hosp., Kingsville, Tex., 1988—, Santa Rosa Health Care Corp., San Antonio, 1991—; mem. steering com. IWC Brainpower Connection, San Antonio, 1989—; mem. pub. policy com. Inter-Congl. Leadership Group, San Antonio, 1990—, Archdiocesan Pastoral Council, 1991—. Grantee Nat. Ctr. for Higher Edn. Mgmt. Systems, 1980, Nat. Cath. Edn. Assn./Assn. Cath. Colls. and Univs., 1985, Cen. Am. Study Tour, 1988. Mem. Smithsonian Assocs., San Antonio Mus. Assn., Leadership Conf. Women Religious, Nat. Assn. of Women in Edn. Avocations: walking, African violets, antique shows and shops, attending horse shows and thoroughbred racing. Office: Incarnate Word Generalate 4503 Broadway San Antonio TX 78209

O'MALLEY, SEAN, bishop; b. Lakewood, Ohio, June 29, 1944. Ed., St. Fidelis Sem., Herman, Pa., Capuchin Coll. and Cath. U., Washington. Ordained priest Roman Cath. Ch., 1970. Espiscopal vicar of priests serving Spanish speakin Washington archdiocese, 1978-84; exec. dir. Spanish Cath. Ctr., Washington, from 1973; bishop Roman Cath. Ch., St. Thomas, V.I., 1985—. Address: PO Box 1825 Saint Thomas VI 00801

OMAR, IRFAN, church lay worker; b. Delhi, India, Dec. 20, 1965; came to U.S., 1989; BA, St. Stephen's Coll., Delhi, 1986; MRE, Unification Theol. Sem., Barrytown, N.Y., 1991. Joint sec. Nat. Youth and Students Forum, Delhi, 1985-89; coord. Islamic Friendship Found. Internat., 1988-89; exec. mem. Islamic Friendship Found., 1989—; sales exec. Islamic Ctr. Publs., New Delhi, 1987-88; exec. sec. Bus. and Employment Bur., New Delhi, 1988. Office: Islamic Friendship Found, 525 Jigar Villa, Chandni Chowk, Delhi 110006, India *Life is an event of time and space caught between the two great tragedies—birth and death. Wisdom of life thus would be to lift oneself above the level of tragedy and attempt to reach a higher state of consciousness.*

O'MARA, JOHN ALOYSIUS, bishop; b. Buffalo, Nov. 17, 1924; s. John Aloysius and Anna Theresa (Schenck) O'M. Student, St. Augustine's Sem., Toronto, Ont., Can., 1944-51; J.C.L., St. Thomas U., Rome, 1953. Ordained priest Roman Catholic Ch., 1951; mem. chancery Archdiocese of Toronto, 1953-69; pres., rector St. Augustine's Sem., Toronto, 1969-75; pastor St. Lawrence Parish, Scorboro, Ont., 1975-76; bishop Diocese of Thunder Bay, Ont., 1976—; pres. Ont. Conf. Cath. Bishops, 1986—. Bd. dirs. Ont. Hosp. Assn., 1961-65; mem. Ont. Hosp. Services Commn., 1964-69. Named hon. prelate of Papal Household with title monsignor, 1954. Address: PO Box 756, Thunder Bay, ON Canada P7C 4W6

O'MEARA, EDWARD THOMAS, bishop; b. St. Louis, Aug. 3, 1921; s. John and Mary (Fogarty) O'M. Student, Kenrick Sem., 1943-46; STD, Angelicum U., Rome, 1953. Ordained priest Roman Cath. Ch., 1946. Monseignor, then ordained bishop Roman Catholic Ch., 1972; asst. pastor St. Louis Cathedral, 1952-55; asst. nat. dir. Soc. for Propagation of the Faith, St. Louis, 1956-60, dir., 1960-67; nat. dir. N.Y.C., 1967-79; archbishop of Indpls., 1980—; apptd. titular bishop of Thisiduo and aux. bishop of St. Louis, 1972-80. Editor: World Mission mag.

O'MEARA, MARCIAN THOMAS, priest; b. Denison, Iowa, Mar. 4, 1929; s. Clarence Joseph and Elizabeth Ruth (Hassett) O'M. BA, Conception Sem., 1954, MA, 1959. Ordained priest, Roman Cath. Ch., 1959; prior St. Pius X Priory, Pevely, Mo., 1969, abbot, 1972-77; chaplain dir. St. Anthony Hosp., Denver, 1977-83; dir. Permanent Diaconate, Archdiocese of Denver, 1981-86, dir. Formation for Seminarians, dir. vocations, 1983-85. Vicar for Religious 1985—, vicar for Permanent Deacons, 1986—; chmn. Archdiocesan AIDS Task Force; chaplain Denver Serra Club. Office: Archdiocese of Denver 200 Josephine St Denver CO 80206

O'MEARA, THOMAS FRANKLIN, priest; b. Des Moines, May 15, 1935; s. Joseph Matthew and Frances Claire (Rock) O'M. MA, Aquinas Inst, Dubuque, Iowa, 1963; PhD, U. Munich, Federal Republic of Germany, 1967. Ordained priest Roman Cath. Ch., 1962. Assoc. prof. Aquinas Inst. of Theology, Dubuque, Iowa, 1967-69; prof. U. Notre Dame, South Bend, Ind., 1981-84, William K. Warren prof. of theology, 1985—. Author 14 books, including: Romantic Idealism and Roman Catholicism, 1983, Theology of Ministry, 1985, Church and Culture, 1991. Mem. Catholic Theol. Soc. Am. (pres. 1980). Office: U Notre Dame Dept of Theology Notre Dame IN 46556

O'NEAL, ELLIS ELDRIDGE, JR., retired theological librarian, consultant; b. Norfolk, Va., Dec. 18, 1923; s. Ellis Eldridge and Lelia Alice (McDaniel) O'N.; m. Helen Elizabeth Spivey, Aug. 12, 1961. BA, U. Richmond, 1946; postgrad., So. Bapt. Theol. Sem., Louisville, 1946-47; MDiv, Andover Newton Theol. Sch., 1949; MS, Simmons Coll., 1962. Ordained to ministry So. Bapt. Conv., 1948, Am. Bapt. Chs. in the U.S.A, 1961. Pastor Hillsboro Bapt. Ch., Crozet, Va., 1949-56, Chamberlayne Bapt. Ch., Richmond, Va., 1956-60; libr., faculty Andover Newton Theol. Sch., Newton Centre, Mass., 1960-86, ret., 1986; libr. cons. Zion Rsch. Found., Boston, 1976, Am. Bapt. Hist. Soc., Rochester, N.Y., 1977, Fla. Meml. Coll., Miami, 1977, Theol. Coll., Samford U., Birmingham, Ala., 1988—. Indexer, mem. editorial com. Baptist Life and Thought, 1983; indexer Andover Newton Quar., 1966-80; contbr. articles to profl. jours. Active 1st Bapt. Ch., Newton Centre, 1960—. Mem. Am. Theol. Libr. Assn. (Lilly Endowment scholar 1961-62), Am. Bapt. Hist. Soc. (sec. 1989—, 20 yr. cert. of svc. 1981). Home: 616 Westover Ave Apt 1 Norfolk VA 23507

O'NEIL, ERVIN RAYMOND, pastor; b. Tucson, July 16, 1959; s. James Virgil and Lorraine Agnes (Deyette) O'N.; m. Pamela Jean Foster, Apr. 22, 1978; 1 child, Ashlee Nicole. BS, Ariz. State U., 1983; ThM, Internat. Bible Sem., 1984; MA in Edn., No. Ariz. U., 1986. Ordained to ministry Dove Valley Ch., 1985. Asst. pastor Faith Christian Fellowship, Santa Cruz, Calif., 1980-82; interim dir. counseling The Valley Cathedral, Phoenix, 1984; bus. mgr. Dove Valley Ch., Glendale, Ariz., 1985—; assoc. pastor Dove Valley Ch., Glendale, 1985—; disability claims specialist State of Ariz., Phoenix, 1986—. Author: Old Testament Theology, 1984. Fellow Internat Assn. Christian Clin. Counselors (ordination); mem. World Ministry Fellowship (ministry lic.). Home: 2834 W Morten Phoenix AZ 85051 Office: Dove Valley Ch 6610 N 47th Ave #9 Glendale AZ 85301

O'NEIL, LEO E., bishop; b. Holyoke, Mass., Jan. 31, 1928. Ed. Mary-knoll Sem., St. Anselm's Coll., Manchester, N.H., Grand Sem., Montreal, Que., Can. Ordained Roman Cath. priest, 1955; ordained titular bishop of Bencenna and aux. bishop of Springfield (Mass.), 1980-89, co-adjutor bishop Manchester, N.H., 1989-90, bishop, 1990—. Office: Diocese of Manchester St Joseph Cathedral 145 Lowell St Manchester NH 03101

O'NEILL, ARTHUR J., bishop; b. East Dubuque, Ill., Dec. 14, 1917. Student, Loras Coll., Dubuque, Iowa, St. Mary's Sem., Balt. Ordained priest Roman Catholic Ch., 1943; bishop of Rockford Ill., 1968—. Office: Diocesan Chancery 1243 N Court St Rockford IL 61103

O'NEILL, BEVERLY LEWIS, college president; b. Long Beach, Calif., Sept. 8, 1930; d. Clarence John and Flossie Rachel (Nicholson) Lewis; m. William F. O'Neill, Dec. 21, 1952. AA, Long Beach City Coll., 1950; BA, Calif. State U., Long Beach, 1952, MA, 1956; EdD, U. So. Calif., 1977. Elem. tchr. Long Beach Unified Sch. Dist., 1952-57; instr., counsellor Compton (Calif.) Coll., 1957-60; curriculum supr. Little Lake Sch. Dist., Santa Fe Springs, Calif., 1960-62; women's advisor, campus dean Long Beach City Coll., 1962-71, dir. Continuing Edn. Ctr. for Women, 1969-75, dean student affairs, 1971-77, v.p. student svcs., 1977-88, supt.-pres., 1988—, exec. dir. Found., 1983—. Advisor Jr. League, Long Beach, 1976—, Nat. Coun. on Alcoholism, Long Beach, 1979—, Assistance League, Long Beach, 1982—; bd. dirs. NCCJ, Long Beach, 1976—, Meml. Hosp. Found., Long Beach, 1984—, Met. YMCA, Long Beach, 1986—, United Way, Long Beach, 1986—. Named Woman of Yr., Long Beach Human Rels. Commn., 1976, Disting. Alumni of Yr.,Calif. State U., Long Beach, 1985, Long Beach Woman of Yr. Rick Rackers, 1987, Assistance League Aux., 1987; recipient Hannah Solomon award Nat. Coun. Jewish Women, 1984, Outstanding Colleague award Long Beach City Coll., 1985, NCCJ Humanitarian award, 1991. Mem. Assn. Calif. Community Coll. Adminstrs. (pres. 1988-90, Harry Buttimer award 1991), Calif. Community Colls. Chief Exec. Officers Assn., Rotary, Soroptimists (Women Helping Women award 1981, Hall of Fame award 1984). Democrat. Office: Long Beach Community Coll 4901 E Carson St Long Beach CA 90808

ONEMA, FAMA, bishop, minister; b. Othuhi, Kasai, Zaire, Jan. 23, 1936; s. Jean Fama and Cathérine Walu; m. Ekoko Onema, June 5, 1952; children: Paul Fama, Muyala, Pende, Tawa, Walu, Shaumba, Otshudi, Omba, Shako. Diploma in theology, Mulungwishi, Zaire, 1959; BA, Morningside Coll., 1965, D (hon.), 1990. Ordained to ministry United Meth. Ch. Sec., dir. pastor sch. Cen. Zaire Ann. Conf., Lodja, 1965-72; bishop cen. Zaire United Meth. Ch., 1972—; pres. bd. dirs. Union Sem., 1973—, also mem. faculty; moderator Nat. Coun. Chs., 1973-85; mem. gen. com. All Africa Conf. Ch., Nairobi, Kenya, 1981-87; del. gen. conf. United Meth. Ch., St. Louis, 1971, African Cen. Conf., Botswana, Zambia, Malawi, 1968-72; dir. Gen. Bd. Global Ministries, N.Y.C., 1988—. Decorated officier Nat. Léopard, comdr. (Zaire). Home and Office: United Meth Ch, BP 560, Kananga Zaire

ONEY, ALVIN JAMES, minister; b. Longview, Tex., May 1, 1943; s. Aubrey Miller and Phoebe Adean (Nowlin) O.; m. Patricia Ann Morton, July 14, 1964; children: Vicky Jane, Alvin James, Paul Mark. BA, E. Tex. State U., 1978. Ordained to ministry, So. Bapt. Conv. Pastor Cave Springs Bapt. Ch., Marshall, Tex., Lassater Bapt. Ch., Jefferson, Tex., Emmanuel Bapt. Ch., Mims, Tex., Center Grove Bapt. Ch., Linden, Tex., Linwood Bapt. Ch., Shreveport, La. Democrat. Office: Linwood Bapt Ch 1622 Midway Shreveport LA 71108

ONG, SUE, religious organization administrator. Head World Fedn. Buddhists, Korea Regional Ctr., Seoul. Office: World Fedn Buddhists, 15-4 Chung-Dong, Chung-Ku, Seoul 100, Republic of Korea*

ONGARO, MARIO PETER, priest; b. Verona, Italy, Apr. 7, 1926; came to U.S., 1947; s. Giuseppe and Giulia (Bonfante) O. BA, Athenaeum of Ohio, 1951; MA, Xavier U., 1961; MLS, U. Mich., 1964. Ordained priest Roman Cath. Ch., 1951; lic. psychologist, Ohio. Pastoral ministry Pala Indians, San Diego, 1956-58; instr. classics Sacred Heart Sem., Monroe, Mich., 1952-56, instr. philosophy classics, 1961-64; instr. classics Sacred Heart Sem., Cin., 1958-61, sch. counselor, 1964-68; adminstr. Comboni Mission Ctr., Cin., 1968-83; psychologist, educator Casa Comboni, Los Angeles, 1983-87; vice provincial superior Provincial Hdqrs., Cin., 1987—, dir. personnel, 1981—; mem. com. re-writing constitutions Comboni Missionaries, Rome, 1976-79, provincial counselor, 1979-84. Mem. Am. Psychol. Assn., Ohio Psychol. Assn., Am. Orthopsychiat. Assn., Soc. Personality Assessment. Home and Office: 8108 Beechmont Ave Cincinnati OH 45255

ONLEY, ERNEST EDWARD, JR., minister, religious organization administrator; b. Norfolk, Va., May 21, 1932; s. Ernest Edward Sr. and Hazel Bernice (White) O.; m. June Fay Baker (dec. July 1983); children: Ernest Edward III, Karen, Kenneth, Steven, Edith, Elaine; m. Elaine Jones Herrin, May 25, 1984; stepchildren: Timothy, Jeffrey, Jon Herrin. BA, William Carey Coll., 1967; MRE, New Orleans Bapt. Theol. Sem., 1969; CPE, Mandeville State Hosp., La., 1969. Cert. in stress mgmt., conflict mgmt., transitional church study, clin. therapist. Regional dir. Pilot Life Ins. Co., Norfolk, 1960-62; pastor Avery Bapt. Ch., Green County, Miss., 1963-64, Derby Bapt. Ch., Poplarville, Miss., 1964-66, Ridgecrest Bapt. Ch., Hattiesburg, Miss., 1966-67, Springfield Bapt. Ch., Morton, Miss., 1967-70; dir. mission ministries Second Baptist Ch., Little Rock, 1970-72; dir. community ministries Capital Bapt. Assn., Oklahoma City, 1973-83; dir. Christian Ministries dept. Ga. Bapt. Conv., Atlanta, 1984—; mem. Sr. Adult Task Force, Atlanta, 1987—, clin. therapist Penfield (Ga.) Christian Home, 1985—; chaplain supr. Univ. Okla., Oklahoma City, 1975-80; dir. Social WorkInterns, Okla. Bapt. Univ., Shawnee, 1975-81. Contbr. articles to Urban Hearbeat, 1981, Prayer Power, 1979, Invitation to Life, 1981, Missions USA, 1975-84. 2nd v.p. Norfolk Jr. C. of C., 1960, 1st. v.p., 1961. With USMC, 1951-53, Korea. Recipient Most Outstanding Ch. of Yr. award Miss. Bapt. Conv., 1969-70, Nat. PACT award Home Mission Bd., Southern Bapt. Conv. USA, 1988. Mem. Transactional Analysis Assn., Masons. Republican. Avocation: gardening. Office: Ga Bapt Conv 2930 Flowers Rd South Atlanta GA 30341

ONLEY, SISTER FRANCESCA, college president; b. Phila., Mar. 4, 1933; d. Edward Patrick and Marie (Rice) O. B.A., Holy Family Coll., 1959; M.S., Marywood Coll., 1966; Ph.D., So. Ill. U., 1986. Cert. secondary counselor, Penn. Tchr. Nazareth Acad. Grade Sch., Phila., 1952-64; tchr. Nazareth Acad., Phila., 1964-67, vice prin., counselor, 1967-72, prin., 1972-80; asst. to pres. Holy Family Coll., Phila., 1980-81, pres., 1981—; bd. dirs. Comcast, Phila., 1983—; bd. dirs. NGA, Inc., 1990—, chmn. fin. com., 1990. Bd. officer, sec. N.E. br. ARC, Phila., 1984—, bd. dirs., 1983—. Recipient Alumni award Holy Family Coll. Alumni 1982, Woman of Yr. award Soroptimist Internat. N.E. Phila., 1991. Mem. Mid. State Assn. Schs. and Colls., Assn. Governing Bds., Coun. Ind. Colls., N.E. C. of C. (bd. dirs. 1983—). Roman Catholic. Office: Holy Family Coll Grant & Frankford Aves Philadelphia PA 19114

OOSTERWAL, GOTTFRIED, religion educator; b. Rotterdam, The Netherlands, Feb. 8, 1930; came to U.S., 1968; s. Hillebrand and Margaretha (Obrikat) O.; m. Emilie Tilstra, Oct. 31, 1957; children: Waronne, Dantar, Erik. Student, John Calvin Coll., Rotterdam; PhD in Theology, Religious Sci., U. Utrecht (The Netherlands), D.Litt. in Anthropology. Instr. religion Netherlands Theol. Sem., Zeist, 1950-56; pastor, pioneer missionary Seventh-Day Adventist Ch., West New Guinea, 1956-63; prof. theology, missions Philippines, 1963-68; dir. Ctr. for Intercultural Rels., Berrien Springs, Mich., 1987—; dir. Inst. of World Mission, Berrien Springs, 1969—. Contbr. articles to profl. jours. Rsch. grantee ZWO, WOTROP, 1957-63. Fellow ASAO; mem. Am. Acad. Religion, ASM. Office: Inst of World Mission Berrien Springs MI 49104

OPALINSKI, FRED STANLEY, minister; b. North Charleroi, Pa., Aug. 16, 1948; s. Fred and Margaret (Mihovich) O.; m. Janet Ruth Kepple, Sept. 4, 1971; children: Megan Ruth, Kristen Lucille. BA, Thiel Coll., 1970; MDiv, Luth Sem., Gettysburg, Pa., 1974. Ordained to ministry Luth. Ch. Am., 1974. Pastor Williamson-Upton Luth. Parish, Mercersburg, Pa., 1971-80; assoc. pastor Trinity Luth. Ch., Latrobe, Pa., 1980-87, sr. pastor, 1987-90; v.p. Latrobe Ministerium, 1987-90. Author: (text and music) Children's Praise, 1991, (text) Praise God, 1991; editor, contbr.: Called and Gathered, 1978. Pres. chpt. Am. Field Svc., Mercersburg, 1978-80; bd. dirs. Luth. Social Svcs., York, Pa., 1975-80, Thiel Coll., Greenville, Pa., 1984—. Democrat. Avocations: music, travel, photography. Home: 805 Fairmont St Latrobe PA 15650 Office: Trinity Luth Ch 331 Weldon St Latrobe PA 15650

ORANGE, LARRY FRANKLIN, minister; b. Ky., Feb. 1, 1943; s. Frank and Nettie (Barshars) O.; m. Janet Lou Smith, June 15, 1963; children: Jerry Paul, Terry Mark, Anna M. Orange Sales. BS, Campbellsville Coll., 1969; MA, Ea. U., Richmond, Ky., 1977; MDiv, MRE, So. Bapt. Sem., Louisville, 1983, postgrad. Ordained to ministry So. Bapt. Conv. Pastor Action Mission, Campbellsville, Ky., 1966-69, Gravel Switch (Ky.) Bapt. Ch., 1969-70, Thompsonville Bapt. Ch., Springfield, Ky., 1970-74, Hustonville (Ky.) Bapt. Ch., 1974-80, New Hope Bapt. Ch., Springfield, 1980-84, West Broadway Bapt. Ch., Louisville, 1984—. Office: West Broadway Bapt Ch 8420 Six Mile Ln Louisville KY 40220

ORENDORFF, DAVID EDWARD, minister; b. Eureka, Kans., Nov. 23, 1948; s. SinClair and Mary Katherine (Hamilton) O.; m. Margaret Victoria Egeland, Aug. 14, 1971; children: Erika Kristen, Johanna Elisabeth. AS, Northwest Coll., Powell, Wyo., 1969; BA, Rocky Mountain Coll., 1971; MDiv, MA, Meth. Theol. Sch., 1975; postgrad., Claremont Grad. Sch., 1975-77. Ordained to ministry Meth. Ch., 1978. Youth pastor Claremont (Calif.) Presybn. Ch., 1975-77; pastor United Meth. Ch., Sunburst, Mont., Kevin, Mont., Sweetgrass, Mont., 1977-81, First United Meth. Ch., Polson, Mont., 1981-85, St. Paul's United Meth. Ch., Helena, Mont., 1985—; past pres. coun. on finance and adminstrn. Yellowstone Conf. United Meth. Ch., chair coun. on ministries. Author: (with others) Word and Witness, 1983. Chair The Friendship Ctr. (homeless and domestic violence shelter), Helena, 1992, Helena Human Rights Task Force, 1991. Mem. Soc. Bibl. Lit. Democrat. Home: 536 N Warren Helena MT 59601

ORFILA, ANSLEY ULM, minister; b. Lafayette, La., May 10, 1940; s. James Lawrence and Eula Kate (Ulm) O.; m. Virginia Rose Hippler, June 2, 1962; children: Mark, Rebecca, Rachel, Sarah. BA, La. Coll., 1961; BDiv, New Orleans Bapt. Theol. Sem., 1964, DMin, 1979. Ordained to ministry Assemblies of God, 1963. Pastor Bethlehem Bapt. Ch., Mangham, La., 1959-62, Victory Assembly of God, Alto, La., 1962-63; Pastor First Assembly of God, Pittsburg, Tex., 1964-68, Slidell, La., 1968—; dist. bd. dirs., presbyter La. Dist. Assemblies of God, Alexandria, 1985—, sectional sec.-treas., 1969-85. Contbr. numerous articles to profl. jours. Mem. Slidell Ministerial Alliance (pres. 1973-74, 83-84), La. Coll. Ministerial Alliance (pres. 1960-61), Alpha Chi (v.p. 1960-61). Home: 1550 Lakewood Dr Slidell LA 70458 Office: First Assembly of God 1460 W Lindberg Dr Slidell LA 70458

ORMAN, ALAN R., religious organization administrator. Pres. Jewish Community Coun., Windsor, Ont., Can. Office: Jewish Community Coun, 1641 Ouellete Ave, Windsor, ON Canada N8X 1R9*

ORMOND, JOHN KEVIN, minister; b. Bath, N.C., Nov. 3, 1965; s. William Henry and Mildred (Sawyer) O.; m. Becky Sue Pryor, Aug. 2, 1986; children: Ashley Rebekah, Kristin Elizabeth. BA magna cum laude, Roanoke Bible Coll., Elizabeth City, N.C., 1988. Ordained to ministry Christian Ch., 1987. Youth min. Mt. Olive Ch. of Christ, Belhaven, N.C., 1985-86,

Athens Chapel Ch. of Christ, Bath, 1986-88; min. Sanford (N.C.) Christian Ch., 1988-90, Vinton (Va.) Ch. of Christ, 1990—. Republican. Office: Vinton Ch of Christ 2107 Feather Rd Vinton VA 24179 *In the age we now live, there are many people crying out for help. As a Christian leader my greatest task is to teach these people to direct their cries to the One that can help.*

ORMOS, CLAUDE PATRICK, priest; b. Paris, Feb. 22, 1951; came to U.S., 1990; s. Paul Stephan and Jacqueline (Cernat) O.; m. Kristine Helen Graunke, Jan. 30, 1982; 1 child, Daniel John. BA, Ind. U., 1975; MA, Chgo. Theol. Sem., 1977; Diploma in Ministry, Montreal Diocese Theol. Sem., Quebec, Can., 1978; postgrad., McGill U., Montreal, 1988-90, M Sacred Theology, 1989. Ordained to ministry Anglican Ch. of Can., deacon, 1978, priest, 1979. Curate St. Philip's Ch., Montreal, 1978-80; priest, assoc. St. Barnabas Ch., Pierrefonds, Quebec, 1980-82; rector St. Martin's Ch., Otterburn Pk., Quebec, 1982-88; teaching assoc. Montreal Inst. for Min., 1985-90; warden of lay readers Diocese of Montreal, 1985-90; interim priest Grace Episc. Ch., Freeport, Ill., 1990-91. Contbr. articles on preaching and ethics to profl. jours. Mem. Can. Assoc. Pastoral Edn., Alban Inst. Episcopalian. Home: PO Box 128 Avoca WI 53506 *A life lived with passion and depth and great love is a life lived well.*

O'ROURKE, CARL EDWARD, priest; b. Detroit, Nov. 6, 1935; s. Patrick Joseph and Marion (McCarthy) O'R. BS, U. Detroit, 1958; MSW, U. Mich., 1969; MDiv, Catholic Theol. Union, 1983. Cert. social worker, Mich., marriage counselor, Mich.; ordained priest Roman Cath. Ch., 1988. With Roman Cath. Diocese, Joliet, Ill.; priest St. Petronille Ch., Glen Ellyn, Ill.; past psychiat. social worker Harper Hosp., Detroit, 1972-78. Home and Office: 420 Glenwood Glen Ellyn IL 60137

O'ROURKE, EDWARD WILLIAM, bishop; b. Downs, Ill., Oct. 31, 1917; s. Martin and Mary (Hickey) O'R. Student, St. Henry's Coll., Belleville, Ill., 1935-38; B.A., St. Mary of the Lake Sem., Mundelein, Ill., 1940, M.A., 1942, S.T.L., 1944; Licentiate of Philosophy, Aquinas Inst., River Forest, Ill., 1960. Ordained priest Roman Catholic Ch., 1944, bishop, 1971; asst. chaplain Newman Found., U. Ill., 1944-59; exec. dir. Nat. Cath. Rural Life Conf., Des Moines, 1960-71; bishop of Peoria, Ill., 1971—; Dir. refugee resettlement Diocese of Peoria, 1948-59; chmn. arbitration com. Nat. Conf. Cath. Bishops, 1973-76. Author: Marriage and Family Life, 1955, Fundamentals of Philosophy, 1956, Gift of Gifts, 1977, Self Help Works, 1978, Living Like a King, 1979, Roots of Human Rights, 1981; Editor: Catholic Rural Life Mag, 1960-71. Chmn. priorities com. Peoria United Fund, 1972-73; Bd. dirs. Internat. Vol. Services, 1960-71; trustee Cath. Relief Services, 1978-80; chmn. bd. Am. Coll. Louvain, 1977-80. Recipient John Henry Newman award, 1959, Nat. Cath. Rural Life Conf. Distinguished Service award, 1973. Club: K.C. (4 deg.). Office: Chancery Office 607 NE Madison Ave PO Box 1406 Peoria IL 61655 also: 600 NE Monroe Ave Peoria IL 61603

ORR, JEFFERY LEE, minister; b. Honolulu, Sept. 10, 1961; s. Donald Ray and Sonja Faye (Winters) O.; m. Linda Fay Owen, Mar. 10, 1989; children: Adam Ross. A in Bible, Bellview Preacher Tng. Sch., Pensacola, Fla., 1982; A Ministry, Ala. Christian Sch. Religion, Montgomery, 1984, BA, 1986. Minister Canoe (Ala.) Ch. of Christ, 1981-82, Lynn Haven (Fla.) Ch. of Christ, 1987-88, Saucier (Miss.) Ch. of Christ, 1988-89; instr. N.W. Fla. Sch. Bibl. Studies, Pensacola, 1987-90; minister Fitzgerald (Ga.) Ch. of Christ; substitute tchr. Ben Hill/Fitzgerald Schs., 1991—; youth activities dir. Bellview Ch. Christ, Pensacola, 1984-85. Home and Office: Fitzgerald Ch of Christ 215 S Merrimac Dr Fitzgerald GA 31750

ORR, JOHN BERK, minister, educator, university official; b. Long Beach, Calif., Apr. 1, 1933; s. Robert McLeese and Esther A. (Broekema) O.; m. Thelma Hodson, Aug. 27, 1961; children: Steven, John. B.A., U. N.Mex., 1955; B.D., San Francisco Theol. Sem., 1958; M.A., Yale U., 1963, Ph.D., 1965. Ordained to ministry United Presbyn. Ch. in U.S.A., 1958; dir. Sch. Religion, U. So. Calif., 1967-81, 91—, Tansey prof. Christian ethics, 1974—, dean Sch. Edn., 1981-89. Author: The Radical Suburb, 1971, Moral Choice, 1972. Mem. Am. Soc. Christian Ethics, Am. Acad. Religion, Soc. Sci. Study of Religion. Home: 3702 Fenley Dr Los Alamitos CA 90720 Office: U So Calif Sch Edn Los Angeles CA 90007

ORR, LARRY G., pastor; b. Flint, Mich., Apr. 6, 1948; s. George J. and Florabell (Staley) O.; m. Janice Elaine Harns, Aug. 15, 1970; children: Angela Marie, Chad Michael. BS, John Wesley Coll., 1973; MDiv, Nazarene Theol. Sem., Kansas City, Mo., 1978. Ordained to ministry Wesleyan Ch. Min. of music and youth Wesleyan Ch., Eaton Rapids, Mich., 1970-72; asst. pastor Emanuel Grace Wesleyan Ch., Lansing, Mich., 1973; sr. pastor Cen. Wesleyan Ch., Kansas City, 1974-80, Wesleyan Ch., St. Peters, Mo., 1980—; sec. of evangelist Tri-State Dist., Kansas City, 1978-80; chaplain O'Fallon (Mo.) Police Dept., 1982-83, St. Peters Police Dept., 1982-83; mem. Dist. Bd. Ministerial Standing, Bartlesville, Okla., 1982-88; mem. Dist. Bd. Adminstrn., Bartlesville, 1985-88. Pres. PTO, St. Peters, 1984. With U.S. Army, 1966-68, Vietnam. Decorated Bronze Star, Purple Heart and Air medal. Office: Wesleyan Ch 250 Salt Lick Rd Saint Peters MO 63376

ORR, PATRICIA PEPPER, minister; b. Rocky Mt., N.C., Feb. 4, 1954; d. Alvin Frank and Mildred Juanita (Pittman) Pepper; m. William Elford Orr, Sept. 3, 1988. BA, Mars Hill Coll., 1976; MDiv, Southeastern Sem., 1979; D. Ministry, Erskine Sem., 1990. Ordained to ministry So. Bapt. Conv., 1979. Chaplain N.C. Bapt. Hosp., Winston-Salem, 1978, S.C. Bapt. Hosp., Columbia, 1979-80; child care counselor Presbyn. Children's Home, Wytheville, Va., 1982-83; exec. dir. Transylvania Christian Ministry, Brevard, N.C., 1983-90; vol. clin. chaplain McCormick (S.C.) Correctional Inst., 1990—; dir. crisis unit Connie Maxwell Children's Home, Greenwood, S.C., 1991—; participant N.C. Poverty Project, 1988, Commn. on Religion in Appalachia, 1989, Nat. Poverty Workshop, 1990. Chair bd. dirs. SAFE, Brevard, 1985-88; mem. family selection bd. Habitat for Humanity, Brevard, 1985-88; bd. dirs. Hospice/Home Care, Brevard, 1984-89; del. Protestant Health and Welfare, New Orleans, 1986. Mem. Assn. Christian Counselors, N.C. Chaplains Assn., Alban Inst. Home: PO Box 805 Brevard NC 28712 Office: Connie Maxwell Children's Home PO Box 1178 Greenwood NC 29648 *Life is not a combination of "if only's" and "just wait until tomorrows". Instead, life is to be lived and celebrated right here and now. I find Jesus to be a man who knew how to live here and now. He taught us not to be anxious about tomorrow, but let tomorrow take care of itself. In actuality the only real place is HERE and the only real time is NOW. This is ultimately where we touch life and life touches us, where the authentic vitalities of existence are to be found. Wise is the person, young or old, who makes this secret their own.*

ORSY, LADISLAS, theologian, educator; b. Pusztaegres, Hungary, July 30, 1921; came to U.S., 1966, naturalized, 1972; s. Joseph and Maria (Bujka) O. Student, Pazmany U., Budapest, Hungary, 1940-43; L.Ph., Gregorian U., Rome, 1948, D.C.L., 1957; L.S.T., Jesuit Theol. Coll., Louvain, Belgium, 1952; M.A. in Law, Oxford U., 1960. Joined Soc. of Jesus, 1943, ordained priest Roman Cath. Ch., 1951. Prof. canon law Gregorian U., Rome, 1960-66, Cath. U. Am., 1966-67, 1974-91, prof. emeritus, 1991—; prof. theology and canon law Fordham U., 1967-74; vis. prof. Boston Coll., 1967; vis. scholar Grad. Theol. Union, Berkeley, Calif., 1971-72; vis. prof. Georgetown U. Law Sch., 1981-82, 91—, U. Fribourg, Switzerland, 1983. Author: Open to the Spirit, 1968, The Lord of Confusion, 1970, Probing the Spirit, 1976, Blessed Are Those Who Have Questions, 1976, The Evolving Church and the Sacrament of Penance, 1978, From Vision to Legislation, 1985, Marriage in Canon Law, 1986, The Church: Learning and Teaching, 1987, Profession of Faith, 1990, Theology and Canon Law, 1992; contbr. articles to legal and theol. jours. Bd. dirs. Georgetown U.; trustee Marquette U. Recipient award excellence Nat. Cath. Ednl. Assn., 1974. Mem. Canon Law Soc. Am. (bd. govs. 1969-71), Soc. Internationale de Droit Canonique et de Legislation Religieuse Comparees, Cath. Theol. Soc. Am., Canon Law Soc. Gt. Britain, Can. Canon Law Soc., Internat. Assn. Study Canon Law., Canon Law Soc. Australia and New Zealand, Eastern Canon Law Soc. Office: Cath U Am Dept Canon Law Washington DC 20064

ORTEGA, ENCARNACION MARIA, principal; b. Piernigas, Burgos, Spain, Feb. 2, 1938; came to U.S., 1961; d. Cipriano and Encarnacion (Alonso) O. BA, Immaculate Conception, Segovia, Spain, 1961, Fresno State Coll., 1972; MA summa cum laude, Fresno State U., 1975; MA, San Francisco U., 1983, M Catechist (hon.), 1983. Joined Sisters of Immaculate Conception, 1958. Local superior, prin. Sisters of Immaculate Conception, Firebaugh, Calif., 1969-72; delegate, prin. Our Lady of Perpetual Help, Clovis, Calif., 1972-78; local superior, prin. St. Joachim, Madera, Calif., 1984—. Mem. Nat. Cath. Ednl. Assn., Nat. Fedn. Religious Edn., Assn. for Supervision and Curriculum Devel., Com. Religious Devel. Edn. (prin. adv. com.), Internat. Reading Assn., Kappa Delta Pi. Home: 224 N J St Madera CA 93637 Office: St Joachim Sch 400 W 4th St Madera CA 93637

ORTEGA Y ALAMINO, JAIME LUCAS, archbishop. Archbishop of San Cristóbal de la Habana, Roman Cath. Ch., Cuba. Office: Calle Habana 152, Apdo 594, Havana Cuba*

ORTIZ, MICHAEL GUADALUPE, priest; b. Salina, Kans., Feb. 10, 1929; s. Miguel and Petra (Jaurez) O. MA, L.I. Univ., 1976. Ordained as priest Roman Cath. Ch., 1956. Commd. 1st lt. U.S. Army, 1966, advanced through grades to col., 1985; asst. Our Lady of Guadalupe, East Chicago, Ind., 1956-62; advanced through grades to col. Our Lady of Guadalupe, 1985; asst. St. Mary's, Holly Springs, Mich., 1962-66; chaplain/col. U.S. Army, 1966—. Decorated Legion of Merit, Bronze Star, Air medal. Mem. Rotary. Office: US Army Attn AFKB-CH Fort Sam Houston TX 78218

ORTWEIN, JOHN LAWRENCE, religious organization administrator; b. Harlowton, Mont., June 14, 1944; s. Orton Orvis and Lorree Mae (Story) O.; m. Catherine M. Bownes, Nov. 27, 1971; children: Shamus, Maria, Teresa. BA, Carroll Coll., Helena, Mont., 1966; MEd, U. Mont., 1972. Exec. dir. Mont. Cath. Conf., Helena, 1984—. Active Campaign for Human Devel., Helena, 1987—; bd. dirs. Mont. Human Svcs. Found., Helena, 1987—, Mont. Hunger Coalition, 1989—, Helena, 1989—, Mont. Homeless Coalition, Helena, 1991—. With U.S. Army, 1969-70. Mem. Nat. Assn. State Cath. Conf. Dirs. Home: 429 S California Helena MT 59601 Office: Mont Cath Conf 530 N Ewing Helena MT 59601

ORVICK, GEORGE MYRON, church denomination executive, minister; b. Hanlontown, Iowa, Jan. 9, 1929; s. George and Mabel Olina (Mandsager) O.; m. Ruth Elaine Hoel, Aug. 25, 1951; children: Daniel, Emily, Mark, Kirsten. AA, Bethany Luth. Coll., Mankato, Minn., 1948, candidate of theology, 1953; BA, Northwestern Coll., Watertown, Wis., 1950. Ordained to ministry Evang. Luth. Synod, 1953. Pastor Our Saviour Luth. Ch., Amherst Junction, Wis., 1953-54, Holy Cross Luth. Ch., Madison, Wis., 1954-86; cir. visitor Evang. Luth. Synod, Mankato, 1964-69, pres., 1970-76, 1980—. Author: Our Great Heritage; columnist The Luth. Sentinel, 1982—. Home: 1117 Lori Ln Mankato MN 56001 Office: Evang Luth Synod 447 N Division St Mankato MN 56001

ORY, SUSAN SUMMER, religious education director, church secretary; b. Atlanta, May 22, 1951; d. John Henry and Dorothy Anne (Armstrong) Summer; m. Bruce Quintin Bartley, Sept. 12, 1950 (div. Apr. 1979); m. James William Ory, Aug. 20, 1982; 1 child, Jonathan. Student, North Ga. Coll., 1969-72, U. Alaska, 1979-80. Dir. Christian edn. Old St. Andrew's Parish, Charleston, S.C., 1989—; sec. planned giving office Episcopal Diocese of S.C., Charleston, 1990—.

OSACKY, JOHN (BISHOP JOB OF HARTFORD), bishop. Bishop of Hartford The Orthodox Ch. in Am., Cumberland, R.I. Office: Orthodox Ch Am 6 Clark Rd Cumberland RI 02864*

OSBORN, CHRISTOPHER RAYMOLN, JR., minister; b. Memphis, Aug. 13, 1950; s. Christopher Raymoln and Elsie Mae (Hatcher) O.; m. Judy Marie Moore, Oct. 5, 1968; children: Steven Ray, Richard Wayne, Brittany Anne. Assoc. Div., Mid-Atlantic Bible Inst., 1985; BA, Mid-Atlantic Bible Coll., 1987; M. Ministry, Mid-Atlantic Sem., 1987; D. Ministry cum laude, Covington Theol. Sem., 1988. Ordained to ministry So. Bapt. Conv., 1981. Pastor Bethel Meml. Bapt. Ch., Gaffney, S.C., 1981-87, Silver Creek Bapt. Ch., Mill Spring, N.C., 1987—. Foster parent Cherokee County DSS, Gaffney, 1984-87, 91—, Polk County DSS, Tryon, N.C., 1988-89, mem. foster care rev. bd., 1989—; mem. adv. bd. Cherokee Children's Home, Gaffney, S.C., 1986-87. Mem. Am. Assn. Christian Counselors, Am. Assn. Family Counselors, Polk Bapt. Assn. (dir. ch. tng. 1987-90, dir. evangelism 1990—, v.p. pastors' conf. 1990-91, dir. vacation Bible sch. 1990). Office: Silver Creek Bapt Ch 292 Silver Creek Rd Mill Spring NC 28756 *In my life, I find purpose as I put God first, value people more than things, and strive to make the world a better place by helping others. True success is to hear Jesus say, "Well done."*

OSBORN, JAMES ANDREW, lay church worker; b. St. Louis, Mar. 10, 1963; s. Richard Wendall and Janet Sue (Lucas) O.; m. Sherri Luann Keys, June 29, 1984; children: James Lucas, Nicholas Andrew, Samuel David. BS in Music Edn., S.W. Mo. State U., 1984. Music counselor Southside Assy. of God, St. Louis, 1981; interim music dir. Butler Hill Bapt. Ch., St. Louis, 1982, Grace Meth. Ch., Springfield, Mo., 1984; interim music/youth minister First United Meth. Ch., Lebanon, Mo., 1986-87; music dir. Cloverdale Assembly of God Ch., Little Rock, 1987—; ensemble dir. Concord Bapt. Ch., St. Louis, 1980-81; children's choir coord. First Bapt. Ch. of Lebanon, 1985-87, handbell dir., 1986-87. Writer, perform song: The Best in Me, 1990. Asst. dir. U. Ark. Little Rock Community Band, 1990—. Named Tchr. of the Yr., Cloverdale Christian Acad., 1988-89. Mem. Mo. Music Educators (S. Cen. Dist. pres. elect 1986-87), Assn. of Christian Schs. Internat. (del. S. Cen. dist. 1988-90). Republican. Home: 6022 Hinkson Little Rock AR 72209-4706 Office: Cloverdale Christian Acad 6111 W 83rd St Little Rock AR 72209-4706

OSBORN, JAMES LOWELL, pastor; b. Battle Creek, Mich., June 9, 1931; s. Horace R. and Edna L. (Cain) O.; m. Janet Robinson, May 30, 1959; children: Joan R., James Lowell Jr., Jill L. BSEE, Marquette U., 1953; BD, Southwestern Bapt. Theol. Sem., Ft. Worth, 1963, MDiv, 1973. Ordained to ministry So. Bapt. Conv., 1962. Pastor Caney (Okla.) Bapt. Ch., 1962-65, Saters Bapt. Ch., Lutherville, Md.d, 1967-73; assoc. Bapt. Conv. Md. and Del., Lutherville, 1973-87; pastor Potomac Heights Bapt. Ch., Indian Head, Md., 1988—; trustee Bapt. Home Md., Balt., 1968-75; mem. various ch. coms. Contbr. articles to Discipleship Tng. mag. Lt. USNR, 1953-56. Republican. Office: Potomac Heights Bapt Ch 37 Glymont Rd Indian Head MD 20640 *One of the saddest commentaries on American life, it seems to me, is the casual and superficial manner in which we view the activity of worship. Worship is the most important activity we do, and most religionists opt out on any given day of worship, Saturday, Sunday, or any other.*

OSBORN, JOHN WILLIAM, minister; b. Hillsdale, Mich., Jan. 4, 1936; s. John Kenneth and Delight Elizabeth (Evans) O. BA, Alma Coll., 1958; BD, San Francisco Theol. Sem., 1962. Pastor 1st Presbyn. Ch., Ubly, Mich., 1962-67, Fraser Ch., Ubly, Mich., 1962-67, First Presbyn. Ch., Decatur, Mich., 1967-69, Fraser Ch., Deckerville, Mich., 1969-75, Presbyn. Ch. Ctr. Junction, Scotch Grove, Iowa, 1975-79, Union Presbyn. Ch., Walton, Ind., 1979-80, Tri-City Parish, various cities, N.D., 1981-85, 1st Presbyn. Ch., Reinbeck, Iowa, 1985—. Mem. Lions Club, Masons, Odd Fellows. Home: 604 Park Reinbeck IA 50669 Office: 1st Presbyn Ch 405 Broad Reinbeck IA 50669

OSBORN, LA DONNA CAROL, clergywoman; b. Tulsa, Mar. 13, 1947; d. T.L. and Daisy (Washburn) O.; m. Cory A. Nickerson, Dec. ll, l98l; children: Tommy O'Dell, LaVona Hardesty, Daneesa Dolan, Donald O'Dell. Student, Assemblies of God Coll., 1963. Fgn. mission corr., purchaser, personnel agt. Osborn Found., Tulsa, 1969-75, exec. asst., 1975-76, internat. gen. mgr., 1976-8l, internat. editor-in-chief, 198l-86, corp. pres., 1986—; assoc. pastor Internat. Gospel Ctr., Tulsa, 1986-89, pastor, 1989—; motivational speaker Christian Women's Fellowship Internat., Nigeria, 1977, Internat. Women's Conf., Tulsa, 1988-89, correctional instns., Okla., 1988-89, S.W. Women's Conf., Albuquerque, 1989, Pastors Tng. Sem., Papua New Guinea, 19899, Internat. Conf. Bibl. Equality, Tulsa, 1990, Faith Conf., Paris, 1991; founder Believers' Network Internat. Author, editor Bible tng. courses. Republican. Avocations: Jewish Biblical history, computer science, skiing, motorcycling, women's issues. Office: Internat Gospel Ctr Box 70036l Tulsa OK 74170

OSBORN, LLOYD WILLIAM, clergyman; b. nr. Fenton, Iowa, July 15, 1929; s. Roy and Mabel Isabel (Cooper) O.; m. Lila Jean Belle Lidke, Nov. 26, 1950; children: Lora Kay Osborn Taylor, Diane Eline Osborn Fortney, Janell Louise. Student, Santa Ana Coll., 1952-53; BA, Winona State Coll., 1957; MDiv, Garrett Grad. Sch. Theology, 1961; postgrad., St. Johns U., 1982-83. Ordained to ministry Meth. Ch., as deacon, 1959, as elder, 1962. Mgr., co-owner Osborn Farm, Fenton, Stewartville, Iowa, Minn., 1947-51; chaplain's asst. USMC, 1951-53; splties. rep. & trainer, Cutco Div. Wearever, Olean, N.Y., 1952-54; pastor, Minn. Conf. United Meth. Ch., Mpls., 1954-91; writer, broadcaster KMRS-Radio, Morris, Minn., 1968-73; supr. Care Co. I, Sauk Centre, Minn., 1983-84; sec. Minn. Conf. Com. Religion & Race, 1990-91; mem. Minn. Ann. Conf. United Meth. Ch., 1962—, Conf. Bd. of Edn., 1962-65, Minn. Coun. Chs., 1979, numerous Ecumenical Ministerial Assns. Pres. Young Reps. Club, Winona State U., 1956; councilman, st. & lights commr., Herman, Minn. 1967-69; dist. dir. Jr. High Youth, 1962-64. With USMC, 1951-53. Grantee Estarl award, Minn. Eastern Star, 1954-57. Mem. West Sub-Dist. Mins. Assn., Lions, Kiwanis (rep. for Citizens Vol. Coordinating Com.); chaplain, Am. Legion. Avocations: old cars, mil. rifles, photography. Home and Office: 11925 42d St NE Spicer MN 56288 Office: United Meth Ch 301 3d St Moose Lake MN 55767

OSBORN, RONALD EDWIN, minister, church history educator; b. Chgo., Sept. 5, 1917; s. George Edwin and Alma Edith (Lanterman) O.; m. Naomi Elizabeth Jackson, Sept. 10, 1940 (dec.); 1 dau., Virginia Elizabeth (dec.); m. Nola L. Neill, Aug. 29, 1986. Student, Lynchburg Coll., 1934-35, Union Theol. Sem. in Va., 1936; A.B., Philips U., 1938, M.A., 1939, B.D., 1942, Litt. D., 1969; postgrad., U. Okla., 1940-41; Ph.D., U. Oreg., 1955; D.D., Bethany Coll., 1989. Min. Christian Ch., Lahoma, Okla., 1936-38, 1st Christian Ch., Geary, Okla., 1938-42, First Christian Ch., Jonesboro, Ark., 1942-43; editor youth publs. Christian Bd. Publ., St. Louis, 1943-45; prof. ch. history Northwest Christian Coll., Eugene, Oreg., 1946-50; min . Ch. of Christ, Creswell, Oreg., 1946-50; assoc. prof. ch. history Christian Theol. Sem. (formerly Butler U. Sch. Religion), Indpls., 1950-53, prof., 1953-73, dean, 1959-70; dir. ecumenical study Council Christian Unity, Disciples Christ, Indpls., 1954-57; vis. prof. ch. history and ecumenics Union Theol. Sem., Manila, Philippines, 1965; vis. prof. ch. history Sch. Theology, Claremont, Calif., 1970-71; prof. Sch. Theology, 1973-82; lectr. Grad. Sch. Ecumenical Studies, Chateau de Bossey, Switzerland, 1954-55; Del. World Conf. on Faith and Order, 1952, 63, 4th Assembly World Council Chs., Sweden, 1968; pres. Internat. Conv. Christian Chs., 1967-68; 1st moderator Christian Ch. (Disciples of Christ), 1968; staff Assembly World Council Chs., Evanston, Ill., 1954. Author: Toward the Christian Church, 1964, A Church for These Times, 1965, In Christ's Place, 1967, Experiment in Liberty, 1978, The Faith We Affirm, 1979, The Education of Ministers for the Coming Age, 1987, Creative Disarray: Models of Ministry in a Changing America, 1991; editor: Seeking God's Peace in a Nuclear Age, 1985, symposium The Reformation of Tradition, 1963, Encounter (formerly Shane Quar.), 1952-63. Mem. Disciples of Christ Hist. Soc. (trustee emeritus, past pres.), Am. Hist. Assn., Am. Soc. Ch. History, ACLU, Phi Kappa Phi, Theta Phi. Home: 85647 Bradbury Ln Eugene OR 97405 *"A person who doesn't think is a slave; a person who won't imagine is a prisoner." (Daniel Dyer, "Imagine the world without imagination," Cleve. Plain Dealer, Jan. 3, 1986.*

OSBORNE, H. PAUL, priest; b. Garrison, Ky., Sept. 19, 1914; s. Lee and Virginia Elizabeth (Hickman) O.; married; children: Ann Harlan Mitchell Osborne, Thomas Lee, John Holland. AB cum laude, Ky. Wesleyan, 1938; MDiv, Lexington (Ky.) Theol. Sem., 1941; MA cum laude, Incarnate Word Coll., 1955. Ordained to ministry Episcopal Ch., 1945. Rector Epiphany Ch., Kingsville, Tex., 1945-48, St. Paul's Ch., San Antonio, 1948-55; v.p Well's Orgn., Chgo., 1955-58; regional mgr. Bond Div./U.S. Treasury, San Antonio, 1958-61; minister various churches, S.C., Kans., Mass., Ark., 1961-80; fund raising cons. Garrison, Ky., 1980—; pres. Minister's Assn., San Antonio, 1953-54, Coun. of Churches, Great Bend, Kans., 1975-76, Kans. Ecumenical Body, 1978-80. Mem. housing commn. San Antonio Authority, 1952-54, Consortium on Seminaries, Boston, 1968-69. Mason. Democrat. Home: PO Box 577 Garrison KY 44141-0577 *The function of the clergy is to clarify the faith he/she professes, and establish its relevancy to the times in which he/she lives.*

OSBORNE, JAMES ALFRED, religious organization administrator; b. Toledo, July 3, 1927; s. Alfred James and Gladys Irene (Gaugh) O.; m. Ruth Glenrose Campbell, Nov. 26, 1945; 1 child, Constance Jean (Mrs. Donald William Canning). Grad., Salvation Army Sch. for Officers Tng., 1947; student, U. Chattanooga, 1954-55. Corps officer Salvation Army, Magness, Nashville, 1947, Southside, Memphis, 1948, Owensboro, Ky., 1949-54; comdg. officer Salvation Army, Chattanooga, 1954-61; city comdr. Salvation Army, Miami, Fla., 1961-65; divisional sec. Ky.-Tenn. Div. Salvation Army, 1965-68, gen. sec. N.C. and S.C. Div., 1966-70, pub. rels. sec. 15 so. states, D.C. and Mex., 1970-71, divisional comdr. Md. and No. W.Va. Div., 1971-73; divisional comdr. Nat. Capital and Virginias Div. Salvation Army, Washington, 1973-78; divisional comdr. Fla. Div. Salvation Army, 1978-80, chief sec. Western Ter., 1980-84; nat. chief sec. Salvation Army, Verona, N.J., 1984-86; territorial comdr. so. states Salvation Army, Atlanta, 1986-89; nat. comdr. Salvation Army USA, so. states, P.R., Virgin Islands Salvation Army, 1989—; chmn. Salvation Army Nat. Planning and Devel. Commn., 1974-76, 84—. Sec. Tenn. Conf. on Social Welfare, 1959, v.p., 1960; pres. Fla. Conf. on Social Welfare, 1965; pres. Ky. Welfare Assn., 1970. Mem. Chattanooga Pastors Assn. (pres. 1958), Va. and W. Va. Welfare Confs., Rotary. Home: 8328 Ft Hunt Rd Alexandria VA 22348 Office: 615 Slaters Ln Box 269 Alexandria VA 22348

OSBORNE, KENAN BERNARD, academic administrator, theology educator; b. Santa Barbara, Calif., May 29, 1930; s. Fredric Earle and Ida Louise (Lerg) O. BA, San Luis Rey Coll., 1952; STB, Old Mission Theol. Sem., 1956; Licentiate in Sacred Theology, Cath. U. Am., 1965; ThD, Ludwig Maximilians U., Munich, Fed. Republic Germany. Ordained priest Roman Cath. Ch., 1955. Instr. Greek and history St. Anthony's Sem. High Sch., Santa Barbara, 1956-57; asst. dir. Franciscan Communication Ctr., L.A., 1957-58; dir. admissions, dir. missions Franciscan Province of St. Barbara, Oakland, Calif., 1958-64; prof., dean Franciscan Sch. Theology, Berkeley, Calif., 1968—, acting pres., 1969-71, pres., 1971-85; prof. systematic theology Grad. Theol. Union, Berkeley, 1968—; faculty St. Marys Coll., Moraga, Calif., 1971, 74, 77, U. San Francisco, 1972-91, U. Seattle, 1974. Author: New Being, 1969, Sacraments of Initiation, 1987, Sacramental Theology, 1988, Priesthood, 1989, Reconciliation and Justification, 1990; assoc. editor Jour. Ecumenical Studies, 1973—; contbr. articles to profl. jours. Mem. Am. Acad. Religion (exec. sec. western region, nat. bd. dirs.), Cath. Theol. Soc. Am. (nat. bd. dirs., past pres.), Pacific Coast Theol. Conf., Kreis der Freunden Paul Tillich E.V. Address: 1712 Euclid Ave Berkeley CA 94709

OSBORNE, OTIS O., minister; b. Matewan, W.Va., Jan. 28, 1939; s. Thomas R. and Carrie L. (Ward) O.; m. Brenda A. Platt, Feb. 29, 1964; 1 child, Stephen O. BTh, Internat. Sem., 1985. Min. Schoharie Valley Gospel Ch., Sloansville, N.Y. Mem. Nat. Christian Counselors Assn., United Assn. Christian Counselors. Home: Rte 20 Box 7 Sloansville NY 12160 Office: Schoharie Valley Gospel Ch Rte 20 Box 7 Sloansville NY 12160

OSBURN, CARROLL DUANE, religious educator; b. Arkansas City, Kans., Sept. 2, 1941; m. Linda Carol Moore, July 31, 1966; children: Heather Denise, Valerie Michelle. MTh, Harding Grad. Sch. Religion, Memphis, 1968, MA, 1969; DMin, Vanderbilt U., 1970; PhD, St. Andrews U., Scotland, 1974. Asst. prof. Greek Harding Grad. Sch. Religion, 1973-77, assoc. prof. Greek, 1977-81, prof. Greek and New Testament, 1981-83; prof. religion Pepperdine U., Mailbu, Calif., 1983-87; Walling disting. prof. New Testament Abilene (Tex.) Christian U., 1987—; bd. dirs. Restoration Quarterly, Abilene, Pioneer Bible Translators, Duncanville, Tex., 1981-87. Contbr. articles to profl. jours. Named Christian Educator of Yr. 20th Century Christian, 1983. Mem. Soc. Bibl. Lit. (chmn. New Testament textual criticism sect. 1983-90), Assn. Internat. d'Etudes Patristiques, Optimist Club. Mem. Christian Ch. Office: Abilene Christian U Sta A Box 8425 Abilene TX 79699

OSGOOD, THEODORE JESSE, minister; b. Florence, Kans., Mar. 6, 1940; s. Jesse William and Cleo Marie (Hankins) O.; m. Sandra Kay

Wilkinson, Sept. 10, 1966; children: Eric Samuel, Dana Elizabeth. BA, Southwestern Coll., Winfield, Kans., 1963; MDiv, Asbury Theol. Sem., Wilmore, Ky., 1967. Ordained to ministry United Meth. Ch., 1968. Pastor Hicks Chapel Meth. Ch., Dexter, Kans., 1961-63, Clymers (Ind.)-Camden Charge, 1966-68, Clymers-Webb Chapel Charge, 1968-70, Trinity United Meth. Ch., Frankfort, Ind., 1970-74, Matoaka (W.Va.) Charge, 1976-80, Summit Valley United Meth. Ch., Williamstown, W.Va., 1980-83; chaplain, sch. counselor Navajo Mission Sch., Farmington, N.Mex., 1974-76; pastor, parish coord. 1st United Meth. Ch., Welch, W.Va., 1983—; youth coord. Bluefield (W.Va.) Dist., 1976-80, Parkersburg (W.Va.) Dist., 1980-83; parish coord. Welch Coop. Parish, 1983—; mem. evangelism com. Bluefield Dist. Coun., 1983—. Contbr. poetry to various publs. Bd. dirs. Glenwood Park Retirement Home, Princeton, W.Va., 1984-89. Recipient Outstanding Pres. award Kiwanis Club, Matoaka, 1980, Pastor of Yr. award Bluefield Dist., 1978, 89. Mem. McDowell Ministerial Assn. (sec. 1983-85, pres. 1985-87, treas. 1987-89), Rotary (pres. Welch 1990—). Republican. Home: 107 Lake Dr Welch WV 24801 Office: 1st United Meth Ch PO Box 416 Welch WV 24801

O'SHEA, PATRICK JOHN, priest; b. N.Y.C., Dec. 12, 1932; s. Patrcik and Anne (McCarthy) O'S. BA, St. Patricks Coll., Calif., 1952, MDiv, 1958. Ordained priest Roman Cath. Ch., 1958, monsignor, 1972. Asst. pastor Mission Dolores, San Francisco, 1958-70; sect. to bishop Mission Dolores, Stockton, Calif., 1970-72; dir. Propagation of The Faith, San Francisco, 1972—; pastor Holy Name Parish, San Francisco, 1978-90, St. Cecilia Parish, San Francisco, 1990—. Mem. Knights Holy Sepulchre, Seirra Club, Variety Club. Home: 2555 27th Ave San Francisco CA 94116 Office: Propagation of The Faith 445 Church St San Francisco CA 94114

O'SHIELDS, DALE ALVIN, pastor; b. Greenville, S.C., Nov. 7, 1955; s. Alvin B. and Jo Ellen (Rouda) O'S.; m. Teresa Bowen, May 28, 1977; children: Christian Marie, Jessica Dawn. AA, Anderson Coll., 1976; BS, Erskine Coll., 1978; MA, Regent U., 1983. Assoc. pastor Christian Fellowship, Belton, S.C., 1978-82; counselor, asst. campus min. Regent U., Va. Beach, Va., 1983, dir. campus ministries, 1984-86; sr. pastor, founder Ch. of Redeemer, Gaithersburg, Md., 1986—. Office: Ch of Redeemer 610 E Diamond Ave Gaithersburg MD 20877

OSIEK, CAROLYN ANN, religious sister; b. St. Charles, Mo., June 11, 1940; d. Omar Henry and Helen Mary (Broeckelmann) O. BA, Fontbonne Coll., St. Louis, 1962; MA in Teaching, Manhattanville Coll., Purchase, N.Y., 1966; ThD, Harvard U., 1978. Rsch./resource assoc. in women's studies dept. New Testament Harvard Divinity Sch., Boston, 1976-77; prof. New Testament Cath. Theol. Union, Chgo., 1987—, asst. prof. New Testament, 1977-83, assoc. prof. New Testament, 1983-87. Assn. Theol. Schs. grantee, 1984-85, NEH Seminar grantee, 1991. Mem. Soc. Bibl. Lit., Cath. Bibl. Assn., Chgo. Soc. Bibl. Rsch., North Am. Patristics Soc., Societas Novi Testamenti Studiorum. Democrat. Office: Cath Theol Union 5401 S Cornell Ave Chicago IL 60615

OSMAN, HERBERT EUGENE, minister; b. Manchester, Ohio, Sept. 13, 1931; s. Estel Meredith and Sarah Elizabeth (Foster) O.; m. Rosamond Blockinger, June 23, 1957; children: Mary Osman Henderson, Mark Herbert, Michael Eugene. BS in Social Studies, Ea. Ill. U., 1957; BDiv in Pastoral Work, Christian Theol. Sem., 1961. Ordained to ministry Meth. Ch., 1957. Pastor Remington (Ind.) United Meth. Ch., Red Mountain United Meth. Ch., Mesa, Ariz.; mem. Ariz. Ecumenical Coun. Conf. Congl. Devel. Bd.; mem. Hospice Corp. bd. East Valley Hospice, Mesa, 1985—; pres. corp. bd. Family Emergency Svc. Ctr., Mesa, 1989—; mem. com. Homeless Trust Fund Oversight Com., State Ariz., 1991—. Cpl. U.S. Army, 1953-55. Office: Red Mountain United Meth Ch 2936 N Power Rd Mesa AZ 85205

OST, WARREN WILLIAM, minister; b. Mankato, Minn., June 24, 1926; s. William Frederick and Margaret Avery (Denison) O.; m. Nancy Nesbitt, May 15, 1954; 1 child, Laura Margaret. BA, U. Minn., 1948; MDiv, Princeton U., 1951; DD (hon.), Moravian Theol. Sem., Bethlehem, Pa., 1971. Ordained to ministry Presbyn. Ch. (U.S.A.), 1951. Min. parishes, Phila., Scranton, Pa., N.J., 1948-51; resident min. Yellowstone Nat. Park, Wyo., 1950-52; dir. A Christian Ministry in Nat. Parks, N.Y.C., 1951—; bd. dirs. Ring Lake Ranch, Dubois, Wyo., 1964—; charter mem. Tourisme-Oecumenique, Geneva, 1967—; cons. Pontifical Commn. on Migration and Tourism, The Vatican, Rome, 1967—. Editor: Gospel, Freedom and Leisure, 1965. Bd. dirs. Prescott Neighborhood House, N.Y.C., 1961—; pres. East 49th Street Assn., N.Y.C., 1961-62. Recipient Pub. Svc. award U.S. Dept. Interior, 1977; named hon. park ranger Nat. Park Svc., 1977. Mem. Assn. Theol. Field Educators, Nat. Park Svc. Employees and Alumni Assn. (life), Conf. Nat. Park Concessioners (life), Denison Soc., Amis du Chemin St. Jacques, Union League Club, Princeton Club, Phi Mu Alpha. Home: 224 E 49th St New York NY 10017 Office: A Christian Ministry in Nat Pks 222 1/2 E 49th St New York NY 10017

OSTASZEWSKI, ALYCE VITELLA, religion educator; b. Chgo., Apr. 24, 1936; d. Peter Anthony and Cleta Earline (Chastain) Indelli; m. Gerald Earl Nelson (div. 1967); children: Peter J., Mary A., William P., Paula A.; m. Stanley Joseph Ostaszewski; children: Vinson Shaw, Stacean V. Grad. high sch., Chgo., 1954. Tchr. religious edn. St. John the Evangelist Ch., Streamwood, Ill., 1967-68; tchr. religious edn., facilitator Rite of Christian Initiation of Adults, St. Thomas More Ch., Elgin, Ill., 1980-86; tchr. religious edn., young adult min. St. Julie Billiart Ch., Newbury Park, Calif., 1987-89, confirmation coord., 1990—; confirmation asst. coord. St. Paschal Baylon Ch., Thousand Oaks, Calif., 1991—; master chatechist, basic faith formation educator L.A. Diocese, Santa Barbara Region, 1990—; com. mem. Santa Barbara Regional Conf., 1988—. Sec. Village of Streamwood Homeowners Assn., 1957-58; bd. dirs. Oak Ridge Estates Homeowners Assn., Newbury Park, Calif., 1986-88.

OSTER, MERRILL JAMES, entrepreneur, publisher, author, lecturer; b. Cedar Falls, Iowa, May 30, 1940; s. Harland James and Pearl Rosetta (Smith) O.; m. Carol Jane Dempster, June 1, 1962; children: David, Leah Jane. BS, Iowa State U., 1961; MS, U. Wis., 1962. Asst. radio-TV farm dir. Sta. WKOW, Madison, Wis., 1961-62; asst. editor Crops and Soils mag., Madison, 1962, Ford Farming and Ford Almanac mags., 1964-67; editor Top Farmer Intelligence, Woodstock, Ill., 1967-69; pres. Communication Cons., Cedar Falls, 1969—, Oster Farms and Pork Pro, Inc., Cedar Falls, 1971—; founder, pres. Profl. Farmers of Am., Inc., 1973—; pub. Futures Mag., Inc., 1975—; pres. Hometowner, Inc., 1976-84, Cedar Terrace Developers, Inc., 1977—, Oster Communications, Inc., 1981—; chmn. Future Source Inc., Lombard, Ill., 1981—; bd. dirs. Danish Mut. Ins. Co., Western Home Inc.; instr. U. Wis. Grad. Sch. Banking, 1976-82, Land Buying Strategies Seminar, 1977-86; mem. Nat. Yr. of the Bible Com., 1983. Author: How Farmers Use Futures for Profit, 1978, Multiply Your Money Through Commodity Trading, 1979, Multiply Your Money Trading Soybeans, 1981, Farmland Buying Strategies, 1983, Becoming a Man of Honor, 1986, Becoming a Woman of Purpose, 1989, Vision-Driven Leadership, 1991; also booklets and articles on future of agr.; contbg. editor: AgriFinance, Banking mag., Successful Farming, Soybean Digest, 1969-75. Bd. dirs. Emmaus Bible Coll., Dubuque, Iowa, 1976-79, 82-88, treas., 1977-79, vice chmn., 1979, chmn. instl. planning com., 1982-84; pres. Christian Heritage Sch. Bd., 1977-79, 81—; chmn. bd. trustees Downing Ave. Gospel Chapel, 1978-79, 83-84; pres. Ireland Outreach Internat., 1981—; bd. reference Campus Crusade for Christ, 1981—; bd. dirs. Here's Life Pubs.; mem. internat. exec. com. Here's Life World; bd. dirs. Iowa State U. Alumni Achievement Fund., 1978-82, Nat. Bus. Consortium for Gifted and Talented, 1983, Hawkeye Inst. Tech. Found., 1982-84, Interest Ministries ; bd. govs. Iowa State U., 1991—, Main St. Devel. Corp., 1991—; hon. adv. bd. mem. Fellowship of Christian Farmers Internat., 1991—; chmn. bd. dirs., founding mem. Metro Unity Coalition; chmn. Cedar Falls Long Range Planning Com., 1989-91. Named Outstanding Young Iowa State U. Alumnus, 1975; named an Iowa Entrepreneur of Yr., Inc. mag., 1989, Econ. Devel. Personality of Yr., 1991. Mem. Am. Assn. Agrl. Editors, Nat. Assn. Agrl. Marketers Assn., Mag. Pubs. Assn., Chief Execs.' Orgn., World Bus. Coun., Cedar Falls C. of C. (dir. 1975-76, v.p. 1989, pres. 1990-91), Athletic Congress of U.S., Alpha Zeta, Sigma Delta Chi. Republican. Clubs: Cedar River Runners; Sunnyside Country (Waterloo, Iowa). Lodge: Rotary (Cedar Falls, Iowa). Home: Rte 4 Cedar Falls IA 50613 Office: 219 Parkade Cedar Falls IA 50613

OSTHUS, MARK ADRIAN, minister; b. Mpls., Feb. 9, 1945; s. Raymond Stanward and Dagny Lillian (Osthus) Twedt; m. Christine Ann Salmon, Dec. 21, 1968; children: Liv, Kristoffer, Timothy, Anders. BS, Augustana Coll., 1967; MDiv, Luther Northwestern Theol. Sem, 1981. Assoc. dir. of admissions Augustana Coll., Sioux Falls, S.D., 1968-77; assoc. pastor Bethany Luth. Ch., Rice Lake, Wis., 1981-83; asst. to pres. Luther Northwestern Theol. Sem., St. Paul, 1983-88; pastor Bethlehem/Trinity Luth. Chs., Grand Marais, Minn., 1988—; chmn. Cook County Ministerium, Grand Marais, 1990, Cook County Child Protection Team, Grand Marais, 1991, mem., 1989—; dean Lake Superior Conf., Evang. Luth. Ch. in Am., 1990, 91—. Member stratetic planning team Cook County Sch. Dist., 1990; conf. presl. Northern Wis. Dist. Am. Luth. Ch., Wausau, Wis., 1982-83; trustee Carthage Coll., Kenosha, Wis., 1982-83; bd. dirs. Roseville (Minn.) Youth Football Assn., 1985-88; chair bd. dirs. Outreach for Christ, Internat., Sioux Falls, 1975-77. Augustana Coll. fellow, 1986—. Mem. N.E. Minn. Synod Luth. Men in Mission Constituting Assembly (chmn. task force 1990). Home: PO Box 158 Grand Marais MN 55604 Office: Bethlehem Luth Ch PO Box 638 Grand Marais MN 55604

OSTLING, RICHARD NEIL, journalist, author, broadcaster; b. Endicott, N.Y., July 14, 1940; s. Acton Eric Sr. and Christine Cathryn (Cumins) O.; m. Joan Elaine Kerns, July 8, 1967; children: Margaret Anne, Elizabeth Anne. BA, U. Mich., 1962; MS in Journalism, Northwestern U., 1963; MA in Religion, George Washington U., 1970; LittD (hon.), Gordon (Mass.) Coll., 1989. Reporter, copyreader Morning News and Evening Jour., Wilmington, Del., 1963-64; asst. news editor Christianity Today mag., Washington, 1965-67, news editor, 1967-69; staff corr. Time mag., N.Y.C., 1969-74, religion editor, 1975—; broadcaster Report on Religion, CBS Radio Syndication, Washington, 1979—; reporter MacNeil/Lehrer Newshour, PBS, 1991—. Author: Secrecy in the Church, 1974; co-author: Aborting America, 1979. Served with USNG, 1964-70. McCormick Found. fellow, 1962-63. Mem. Religion Newswriters Assn. (pres. 1974-76), Phi Beta Kappa. Mem. Christian Reformed Ch. Home: 280 Hillcrest Rd Ridgewood NJ 07450 Office: care Time Magazine Time and Life Bldg Rockefeller Ctr New York NY 10020

OSVATH, LUDOVIC LAJOS, minister; b. Lupoaia, Romania, July 22, 1938; came to U.S., 1980; s. Lajos and Anna (Feher) O.; m. Jolan Pacso, May 4, 1963; 1 child, Judith. Grad., Inst. Tech., Romania, 1954, Inst. Bus., Romania, 1957, Ady Endre Coll., Romania, 1978; student, Heritage Bapt. Inst., Cleve., 1986. Ordained to ministry Bapt.Ch., 1955. Preacher Bapt. Ch., Romania, 1955—; mem. coms. Bapt. Ch., Egrespatak, Romania, 1955-65; treas., mem. com. Bapt. Ch., Zalau, Romania, 1965-73; pres. Hungarian Missionary Soc. Inc., Cleve., 1989—; del. Romanian Bapt. Congress, Bucharest, Hungary, 1978; maintenance exec. Sponge, Inc., Cleve., 1985—. Underground rep. Amnesty Internat., Romania, 1977-80. Mem. Christian Mgmt. Assn., Bocskai Cultural Soc. (sec. 1988—). Office: Hungarian Missionary Soc PO Box 6327 Cleveland OH 44101-1327

OSWALD, HAROLD NICHOLAS, JR., lay worker; b. Joliet, Ill., Nov. 29, 1961; s. Harold N. and Judith D. (Taylor) O. Diploma, Waldron (Mich.) Area Schs., 1980. Asst. song leader Prattville (Mich.) Community Ch., 1987-91; mem. Christian Family Centre, Adrian, Mich., 1991—. Author: TOP Devotional Guide, 1991. Mem. Sons Am. Legion (West Unity, Ohio). Republican. Office: Christian Family Ctr 1800 W US 223 Adrian MI 49221

OSWALT, JOHN NEWELL, theology educator, religious writer; b. Mansfield, Ohio, June 21, 1940; s. Glenn Starr and Mildred LaVergne (Wachs) O.; m. Karen Suzanne Kennedy, Aug. 11, 1962; children: Elizabeth Greer, Andrew Clark, Peter Newell. AB, Taylor U., 1957-61; BDiv, Asbury Theol. Sem., 1961-64, ThM, 1965; MA, Brandeis U., 1966, PhD, 1968. Ordained to ministry, United Meth. Ch., 1978. Asst. prof. Barrington (R.I.) Coll., 1968-70; assoc. prof. Asbury Theol. Sem., Wilmore, Ky., 1970-78, prof., 1978-82; pres. Asbury Coll., Wilmore, 1983-86; prof. Trinity Evang. Div. Sch., Deerfield, Ill., 1986-89, Asbury Theol. Sem., Wilmore, Ky., 1989—. Author: Where are You, God?, 1982, Isaiah, Chapters 1-39, 1986, The Leisure Crisis, 1987. Cubmaster Wilmore Troop Boy Scouts Am., 1980-83. Nat. Def. Fgn. Lang. fellow Brandeis U., 1967-68, Univ. fellow Brandeis U., 1965-67. Mem. Soc. Biblical Lit., Wesleyan Theol. Soc., Inst. Biblical Research. Republican. Avocations: reading, gardening, scale-model trains. Home: 135 Lowry Ln Wilmore KY 40390 Office: Asbury Theol Sem Lexington Ave Wilmore KY 40390 *There is no more important question than this: "What must I do to inherit eternal life?" We pass through time like an arrow. May that passsing be such as to strike an eternal target squarely.*

O'TOOLE, EUGENE JOSEPH, priest, social services administrator; b. South Amboy, N.J., 1952. BA, St. Mary Sem. & U., Balt., 1975, MDiv, 1979, D. Ministry, 1990. Ordained priest Roman Cath. Ch., 1979. Parochial vicar, pastor Cath. Diocese of Raleigh (N.C.), 1978-80; staff chaplain, dept. head Fed. Bur. Prisons, U.S. Dept. Justice, Memphis and Lexington, Ky., 1980-84; chaplain N.J. State Prison, Trenton, 1986-89; supr. chaplaincy svcs. Albert C. Wagner Youth Correctional Facility, Bordentown, N.J., 1989—; adj. faculty mem. in pastoral theology St. Charles Sem., Phila., Seton Hall U., Newark; weekend asst. St. Anthony Cath. Ch., Trenton, N.J., Our Lady of Sorrows Ch., Mercerville, N.J. Home: 507 Grand St Apt 2-E Trenton NJ 08611 Office: A C Wagner Youth Facility PO Box 500 Bordentown NJ 08505

O'TOOLE, ROBERT FRANCIS, biblical studies educator, Jesuit priest; b. St. Louis, June 20, 1936; s. William Francis and Anastasia (Earner) O'T. A.B., St. Louis U., 1960, M.A. and Ph.L., 1961, S.T.L., 1968; S.S.L., S.S.D., Pontifical Biblical Inst., 1970, 1975. Tchr., prefect of discipline St. John's Coll., Belize, Central Am., 1961-64; tchr. Regina Mundi, Rome, 1972-74; instr. to assoc. prof. St. Louis U., 1973-84, chairperson theol. studies, 1982-87, prof., 1984-91, Pontifical Bibl. Inst., 1991—; trustee Rockhurst Coll., Kansas City, Mo., 1983-87. Author: Acts 26: The Christological Climax of Paul's Defense, 1978; The Unity of Luke's Theology: An Analysis of Luke-Acts, 1984, Who Is A Christian? A Study in Pauline Ethics, 1990; also articles. Mem. Soc. Biblical Lit., Catholic Bibl. Assn., Inst. Theol. Encounter with Sci. and Tech., Am. Acad. Religion, Studiorum Novi Testamenti Societas. Avocations: hiking, swimming, gardening. Address: Pontifical Bibl Inst, Via della Pilotta 25, 00187 Rome Italy Office: St Louis U 3634 Lindell Blvd Saint Louis MO 63108 *It is mercy I desire and not sacrifice. (Matt 9:13; 12:7) We are useless servants. We have done no more than our duty. (Luke 17:10).*

OTT, STANLEY JOSEPH, bishop; b. Gretna, La., June 29, 1927; s. Manuel Peter and Lucille (Berthelot) O. S.T.D., Pontifical Gregorian U., Rome, 1954. Ordained priest Roman Catholic Ch. Bishop Roman Catholic Ch., 1951, aux. bishop, 1976; assoc. pastor St. Francis Cabrini Parish, New Orleans, 1954-57; chaplain La. State U., Baton Rouge, 1957-61; ofcl. Marriage Tribunal, Diocese of Baton Rouge, from 1961; chancellor rector St. Joseph Cathedral, Baton Rouge, 1968-76; aux. bishop of New Orleans, 1976-83, bishop of Baton Rouge (La.), 1983—; liaison bishop Nat. Coun. Cath. Women. Bd. dirs. ARC, Boy Scouts Am. Mem. Nat. Conf. Cath. Bishops, U.S. Cath. Conf. Democrat. Club: K.C. (state chaplain), Cath. Daughters Am. Home: 3330 Hundred Oaks Ave Baton Rouge LA 70808 Office: 1800 S Acadian Thruway PO Box 2028 Baton Rouge LA 70821

OTTAWAY, LOIS MARIE, religious organization administrator; b. Wichita, Kans., Oct. 9, 1931; d. Albert Horace and Clare Marie (Russell) O. BS, Kans. State U., 1953; MA, U. Iowa, 1962; postgrad., Wheaton (Ill.) Coll., 1962-69. Advisor student publs., mgr. news svc. Wheaton (Ill.) Coll., 1959-81; asst. dir. vol. representation Med. Assistance Programs Internat., Wheaton, 1983-84, asst. dir. ch. relations, 1984-87; dir. devel. Cabrini Green Legal Aid Clinic, Chgo., 1988—; mgr. media relations World Relief Corp., Wheaton, 1982-83; sec.-treas. West Suburban Evang. Fellowship, Wheaton, 1984-85, v.p., 1985-86; deacon LaSalle St. Ch., Chgo., 1973-77, vice moderator, 1981-87. Contbr. articles to profl. jours. Election judge DuPage County, Wheaton, 1978—. Recipient Vol. of Yr. award Programmed Activities for Correctional Edn., Chgo., 1972. Mem. Evangs. for Social Action (bd. dirs. 1979-80), Christian Community Devel. Assn. Democrat. Club: Suburban Press of Chgo. (rec. sec. 1977-82, bd. dirs. 1982-85). Avocations: vol. service, geneal. research, growing African violets. Home: 201 N President # 3A Wheaton IL 60187 Office: Cabrini Green Legal Aid Clinic care LaSalle Found 300 W Hill Chicago IL 60610

OTTENWELLER, ALBERT HENRY, bishop; b. Stanford, Mont., Apr. 5, 1916; s. Charles and Mary (Hake) O. S.T.L., Cath. U. Am., 1943. Ordained priest Roman Catholic Ch., 1943, consecrated aux. bishop of Toledo, 1974; asso. pastor St. John's Parish, Delphos, Ohio, 1943-59, St. Richard's Parish, Swanton, Ohio, 1959-61; pastor St. Joseph's Parish, Blakeslee, Ohio, also mission Sacred Heart, Montpelier, Ohio, 1961-62, Our Lady of Mt. Carmel Parish, Bono, Ohio, 1962-68, St. John's Parish, Delphos, Ohio, 1968-76, St. Michael's Parish, Findlay, Ohio, 1976-77; consecrated aux. bishop of Toledo, 1974, bishop of Steubenville, 1977—. Mem. Ohio Gov.'s Com. on Migrant Labor, 1955-75; mem. governing bd. Retreats Internat., 1975; chmn. laity com. Nat. Conf. Cath. Bishops, 1978. Office: Chancery Office 422 Washington St PO Box 969 Steubenville OH 43952

OTTERSEN, ROGER W., religious organization administrator. Gen. overseer Christian Cath. Ch., Zion, Ill. Office: Christian Cath Ch Dowie Memorial Dr Zion IL 60099*

OTTLEY, JAMES H., bishop. Bishop of Panama Episcopalian Ch. Office: Bishop of Panama, Box R, Balboa Republic of Panama*

OTTO, A. STUART, JR., theologian, author; b. Mt. Vernon, N.Y., Apr. 20, 1915; s. Albert Stuart and Verna (Wilkens) O.; m. Catherine Ruth Gale, Dec. 14, 1968. D.D., Trinity Sch. Theology, 1967. Gen. mgr. Otto Program Mgmt., Akron, Ohio and Pomona, Calif., 1950-58; div. mgr. Nat. Assemblies, North Hollywood, Calif., 1958-64; dir. The Invisible Ministry, San Marcos, Calif., 1964—; pres. San Marcos Ministerial Assn., 1973; chmn. Com. for an Extended Lifespan, San Marcos, 1978-82. Author: How to Conquer Physical Death, 1968; The Fifth Kingdom, 1970; Poems of Praise, 1982, How to Be Secure In An Explosive World, 1987. Contbr. articles to profl. jours. Pres. Santa Monica Bay Optimist Club, 1949; co-founder San Marcos Hist. Soc., 1967; chmn. San Marcos Ministerial Assn., 1973. Served to 2d lt. U.S. Army, 1943-46. Mem. Bacon Soc., San Marcos C. of C. Ch. of the Trinity, Rotary (pres. San Marcos club 1968-69). Office: The Invisible Ministry Box 4608 Salem OR 97302-8608 *"If a man keep my saying, he shall never see death." (John 8:51). I take this literally and believe we are not intended to die. "Whosoever liveth and believeth in me shall never die. Believest thou this?" (John 11:26). Yes, I believe it!.*

OTTO, EDGAR JOHN, minister; b. Guthrie, Okla., Oct. 7, 1926; s. Edgar and Anna Hattie (Wendel) O.; m. Rosemarie Naig, July 23, 1949; children: Vicki, Deborah, Bunnie, Ole. BA, Macalester Coll., 1947; BTh, Concordia Sem., Springfield, Ill., 1951, BD, 1969, MDiv, 1971; MA in Religion, Concordia Sem., St. Louis, 1973. Ordained to ministry Luth. Ch.-Mo. Synod, 1951. Pastor Grace/Christ Luth. Ch., Pequot Lakes, Minn., 1951-54, Ea. Heights Luth. Ch., St. Paul, 1954-66, Immanuel Luth. Ch., Springfield, 1966-75, St. John's Luth. Ch., East Moline, Ill., 1975-80; adminstrv. asst. mission dept. South Wis. dist. Luth. Ch.-Mo. Synod, Milw., 1980—. Recipient Servus Ecclesiae Christi Concordia Theol. Sem., 1978. Republican. Home: 2528 N 124th # 231 Wauwatosa WI 53226 Office: Luth Ch Mo Synod South Wis Dist 8100 W Capital Dr Milwaukee WI 53222

OTTO, VIVIAN WICKEY, diaconal minister; b. Fargo, N.D., Aug. 16, 1925; d. Norman Jay Gould and Ethel Ruth (Bashoar) W.; m. N. Eugene Otto, Jan. 2, 1949 (dec. May, 1979); children: Barbara Jean Otto Wege, Ruth Ann Otto Peters. BA, Gettysburg Coll., 1946; MRE, Union Theol. Sem., 1947. Cert. Christian edn., evangelism. Asst. regional sec. Nat. Luth. Student Svc., Phila., 1947-49; dir. Christian edn. Chevy Chase (Md.) Meth. Ch., 1963-81; program dir. Washington West Dist. United Meth. Ch., 1981-91; regional curriculum cons. Cokesbury United Meth. Pub. House, 1991—. Trustee Gettysburg Coll., 1986-89; pres. Gettysburg Coll. Woman's League (pres. 1986-89, Outstanding Alumni 1991); past pres. Chevy Chase Jr. Woman's Club. Mem. Christian Educators Fellowship. Home and Office: 4948 Sentinel Dr Bethesda MD 20816

OTTO, WILLIAM HARVEY, minister; b. Milw., Feb. 5, 1936; s. Harvey Ewald and Vera Alta (Mehne) O.; m. Paula Louise Bierwagen, June 14, 1959; children: Pamela Lynn, Scott William. AA, Concordia Coll., Milw., 1956; BA, Concorida Sem., St. Louis, 1958, MDiv, 1961; postgrad., Trinity Div., Deerfield, Ill., 1990. Missionary So. Dist. Luth. Ch. Mo. Synod, Gulfport, Miss., 1961-65; pastor Zion Luth. Ch., Milw., 1965-68, Beautiful Savior Luth. Ch., Mequon, Wis., 1968—; bd. dirs. So. Wis. Dist. Luth. Ch., Milw., chmn. stewardship, 1978—, area coord. $40 million fund dr., 1978-81. Coach Little League, Mequon, 1970-78; mem. Crisis Intervention Com., Mequon, 1984—, student adv. coun. Homestead High Sch., Mequon, 1985—; chmn. bd. dirs. Luth. Child and Family Svcs., Wauwatosa, Wis., 1972-82. Recipient Spiritual Advisor award Optimists, Mequon, 1982. Home: 2311 W Ranch Rd Mequon WI 53092

OTTOSON, JOSEPH WILLIAM, clergyman; b. Chgo., June 12, 1929; s. Joseph Swenson and Lillian (Bennett) Ottoson; m. Clarice I. Warme, May 26, 1956; children: David, Cynthia, Paul. BA, Northwestern U., 1952, MA, 1957, PhD, 1967; MDiv, Augustana Sem., 1956. Ordained to ministry Luth. Ch., 1958. Pastor Our Saviour's Luth. Ch., Soderville, Minn., 1958-61; campus pastor St. Cloud (Minn.) State U., 1961-83, assoc. prof., 1968-70; dir. Ministries Unltd., Brainerd, Minn., 1983—; dir. extended ministries Luth. Ch. of Cross, Nisswa, Minn., 1985-87; chaplain, psychologist No. Pines Mental Health Ctr., Brainerd, 1985—; chaplain Crow Wing County Jail, Brainerd, 1984-86, St. Joseph's Med. Ctr., Brainerd, 1984-89; clin. social worker, 1990—. Bd. dirs. Vol. in Probation, Brainerd, 1985-88, Port, Brainerd, 1985-88, C.A.R.E.; pres. Am. Cancer Soc., Brainerd, 1984-86. Home: 7594 Interlachen Rd Lake Shore MN 56401

OTTOSON, R. STANLEY, religious organization administrator. Chmn. bd. dirs. Internat. Bible Soc., Colorado Springs, Colo. Office: Internat Bible Soc 1320 Jet Stream Dr Colorado Springs CO 80921*

OTTS, JAMES MITCHELL, minister; b. Stutgartt, Fed. Republic Germany, May 24, 1968; s. James A. and Ruby Jean (Suddeth) O. Student, Campbell U., 1987-88. Youth minister Turner Meml. Bapt. Ch., Garner, N.C., 1988; pastoral assoc. Glacier Valley Bapt. Ch., Juneau, Alaska, 1990-91; music and youth min. Oak Grove Bapt. Ch., Jemison, Ala., 1991—; freight supr. Lamonts, Juneau, 1990—. outreach leader Campbell U. Bapt. Student Union, Buies Creek, N.C., 1988; mem. rd. crew Elishah Ministry, Erwin, N.C., 1988; disc jockey WCCE-FM sta. Campbell U., 1988. With USAR, 1985-90. Republican. Home and Office: Oak Grove Bapt Ch 14052 County Rd # 51 Jemison AL 35085 *My main goal in life is to know Jesus better. This the key to a joy filled life with understanding that true joy is being able to believe in the mountain top while we are yet in the Valley.*

OTUNGA, MAURICE CARDINAL, archbishop of Nairobi; b. Chebukwa, Kenya, Jan. 1923; son of tribal chief. Ordained priest Roman Catholic Ch., 1950; formerly tchr. Kisumu Maj. Sem.; attaché apostolic del. Mombasa, 1953-56; titular bishop of Tacape, also aux. Kisumu, 1957; bishop of Kisii, 1961; titular archbishop of Bomarzo, 1969, coadjutor of Nairobi, 1969-71; archbishop of Baitobi, Nairobi, 1971—; elevated to Sacred Coll. of Cardinals, 1973; titular ch. St. Gregory Barbarigo; mil. vicar of Kenya, 1981; primate of Kenya, 1983—; dir. Castrense for Kenya; mem. Congregation of Sacraments and Divine Worship, Congregation of Religious and Secular Insts., Commn. Revision Code of Canon Law. Address: Archbishop's House, PO Box 14231, Nairobi Kenya

OUELLET, GILLES, archbishop; b. Bromptonville, Que., Can., Aug. 14, 1922; s. Joseph Adelard and Armande (Biron) O. B.A., Sherbrooke Sem. Ordained priest Roman Cath. Ch., 1946. Bishop of Gaspe, 1968-73; archbishop of Rimouski Que., 1973—; pres. Can. Conf. Cath. Bishops, 1977-79. Address: PO Box 730, 34 Ouest Rue de L'Eveche, Rimouski, PQ Canada G5L 7C7

OUELLETTE, SISTER GLORIA MARIANNE, nun; b. Eagle Lake, Maine, Apr. 14, 1925; d. Henry M. and Phoebe (Gagnon) Q. BA, St. Joseph's Coll., North Windham, Maine, 1962; MA in Counseling, Psychology, Boston Coll. U., 1968. Joined Sisters of Little Franciscans of Mary, Roman Cath. Ch., 1944. Mem. formation-vocation team Little Franciscans of Mary, Worcester, Mass., 1964-69, provincial counselor, 1973-76; charter mem., officer Adv. Counsel of Women Religious, Portland,

Maine, 1966-71; dist. supr. Maine SAD #27, Fort Kent, Maine, 1966-71; prin. St. Mary's Cath. Sch., Hartsville, S.C., 1971-79; mem. pastoral team staff St. Michael Cath. Ch., Garden City, S.C., 1979-87; coord. religious edn. Immaculate Conception Cath. Ch., Calais, Maine, 1988-91. Received Appreciation of Ministry award St. Mary's Cath. Ch., Hartsville, 1973, Exceptional Ministry to Youth award Diocesan Youth Conv., Portland, Maine, 1991. Mem. Nat. Pastoral Musicians Orgn., Today's Liturgy, Musicians, Liturgists. Home: 12 E Main St Fort Kent ME 04743 Office: 17 Calais Ave Calais ME 04619 *One of the greatest needs of our times is the openness and availability of the adult world to our youth. Our young people need a sense of unconditional acceptance and gentle guidance from us at this critical time of their lives; our sincere love and trust can help make a difference for them.*

OUTKA, GENE HAROLD, philosophy and Christian ethics educator; b. Sioux Falls, S.D., Feb. 24, 1937; s. Harold Irvin O. and Gertrude Anne (Elliott) Finch Outka; m. Carole Lee DeVore, June 26, 1960, (div. 1982); children: Paul Harold, Elizabeth Noelle; m. Susan Jane Owen, Dec. 29, 1984; 1 child, Jacqueline Elliott. B.A., U. Redlands, 1959; B.D., Yale U., 1962, M.A., 1964, Ph.D., 1967; L.H.D., U. Redlands, 1978. Instr. Princeton U., N.J., 1965-66, lectr., 1966-67, asst. prof., 1967-73, assoc. prof., 1973-75; assoc. prof. Yale U., New Haven, 1975-81, Dwight prof. philosophy and Christian ethics, 1981—; dir. resdl. seminar for coll. tchrs. NEH, New Haven, 1977-78; Mary Farnum Brown lectr. Haverford Coll., Pa., 1977; mem. faculty workshop on teaching of ethics Hastings Inst. of Soc., Ethics and Life Scis., Princeton, N.J., 1979; Merrick lectr. Ohio Wesleyan U., Delaward, Ohio, 1983; Williamson Meml. lectr. Meth. Theol. Sch. in Ohio, 1986. Author: Agape: An Ethical Analysis, 1972; co-editor and contbr.: Norm and Context in Christian Ethics, 1968, Religion and Morality, 1973; mem. editorial bd. Jour. Religious Ethics. Service fellow office of spl. projects Health Services and Mental Health Adminstrn., HEW, Washington, 1972-73; mem. adv. com. social ethics Inst. Medicine Nat. Acad. Scis., 1975-77. Fellow Am. Council Learned Socs., 1968-69; fellow NEH, 1979-80, Woodrow Wilson Internat. Ctr. for Scholars, 1983; vis. scholar Kennedy Inst. of Ethics, Georgetown U., 1972-73. Mem. Soc. for Values in Higher Edn., Am. Acad. Religion, Soc. Christian Ethics (mem. editorial bd.), Am. Theol. Soc. Office: Yale U Dept Religious Studies 320 Temple St New Haven CT 06520

OVA, WAYNE KEITH, pastor, principal; b. Kansas City, Kans., Mar. 21, 1953; s. Dwyane Keith Ova and Donna Lou (Horning) Foulk; m. Debbie Susan Davolt, June 23, 1979; children: Eric Jason, Justin Wayne, Christopher Ryan. BA in Music, Bapt. Bible Coll., 1975; BTh., Faith Bible Bapt. Coll., 1985. Assoc. pastor Elm Grove Bapt. Ch., Bonner Springs, Kans., 1977-84; pastor Faith Bapt. Ch., Osawatomie, Kans., 1986—. Republican. Home: 515 Retan Osawatomie KS 66064 Office: Faith Bapt Ch Brown at Retan Osowatomie KS 66064

OVERBECK, JAMES A., educator; b. Eau Claire, Wis., Sept. 11, 1940; s. Arwin Kubel O.; m. Lois Ellen More, June 11, 1966; children: Kristen, Andrew, Jonatan. BA, CArthage Coll., 1963, MDiv, 1967, MLS, 1975; PhD, U. Chgo., 1975. Ordained elder Presbyn. Ch. 1983. Instr. Ch. hist. Luth. Sem., Phila., 1969-71; dir. libr. Sch. Theol., Claremont, Calif., 1975-80, Columbia Theol. Sem., Campbell Libr., Decatur, Ga., 1980—; bd. dirs. U. Ctr. Ga. Libr. Group, Atlanta, 1990-91. Mem. Am. Theol. Libr. Assn. (bd. dirs. 1983-86), Am Soc. Ch. Hist., Am. Acad. Religion. Office: Columbia Theol Sem 701 Columbia Dr PO Box 520 Decatur GA 30031

OVERGAARD, ROBERT MILTON, religious organization administrator; b. Ashby, Minn., Nov. 6, 1929; s. Gust and Ella (Johnson) O.; m. Sally Lee Stephenson, Dec. 29, 1949; children: Catherine Jean Overgaard Thuleen, Robert Milton, Elizabeth Dianne Overgaard Almendinger, Barbara, Craig, David (dec.), Lori Overgaard Noack. Cert., Luth. Brethren Sem., 1954; BS, Mayville (N.D.) State U., 1959; MS, U. Oreg., 1970. Ordained to ministry Ch. Luth. Brethren Am., 1954. Pastor Elim Luth. Ch., Frontier, Sask., Can., 1954-57, Ebenezer Luth. Ch., Mayville, 1957-60, Immanuel Luth. Ch., Eugene, Oreg., 1960-63, 59th Street Luth. Ch., Bklyn., 1963-68, Immanuel Luth. Ch., Pasadena, Calif., 1969-73; exec. dir. world missions Ch. Luth. Brethren Am., Fergus Falls, Minn., 1973-86, pres., 1986—; Editor Faith and Fellowship, 1967-75. Home: 806 W Channing Ave Fergus Falls MN 56537 Office: Ch Luth Brethren Am Box 655 Fergus Falls MN 56537

OVERHOLT, DARWIN D., clergyman, mission executive; b. Buffalo, Aug. 12, 1943; s. Darwin J. and Shirley A. (Engelhart) O.; m. Christine Ann Schultz; children: Keith, Karen, Kristopher, Kelly. BS in Religion, Houghton Coll., 1969; MDiv, Trinity Sem., Newburgh, Ind., 1982, DMin, 1985. Ordained to ministry Bapt. Ch. Pastor West Portland Bapt. Ch., Westfield, N.Y., 1966-69, Hunt (N.Y.) Bapt. Ch., 1970-75, Prospect Avenue Bapt. Ch., Buffalo, 1975-86; exec. dir. City Mission Soc., Inc., Buffalo, 1986—; chmn. Child Evangelism Fellowship, Buffalo, 1982-84. Author: Biblical Leadership Training, 1985. Mem. Tri-County Ministers (pres. 1972-74), Fundamental Ministers (pres. 1983-85), Kiwanis (com. chmn. Buffalo). Avocations: fishing, hunting, woodwork. Home: 19 Wainwright Ct Williamsville NY 14221 Office: City Mission Soc Inc 100 E Tupper St Buffalo NY 14205

OVERHOLT, EDWARD LYNN, minister; b. Middlesboro, Ky., June 30, 1956; s. Estle Kenneth and Lillian Loretta (Sandefur) O. AA, Carson-Newman Coll., 1986; BA, Clear Creek Bapt. Bible Coll., 1989. Ordained to ministry Bapt. Ch., 1977; cert. funeral dir., Tenn. Pastor Cedar Grove Bapt. Ch., Tazewell, Tenn., 1976-85, Tazewell Bapt. Ch., 1985—; dir. pub. rels./alumni Clear Creek Bapt. Bible Coll., Pineville, Ky., 1990—; pres. Cumberland Gap of Bapt. Youth Fellowship, 1976-77, chmn. evangelism com., 1978-79. Editor newsletter The Mountain Voice, 1990—. Mem. Bapt. Pub. Rels. Assn., Order of Demolay (chaplain 1975-79). Home: 232 Todd Circle Tazewell TN 37879 Office: Clear Creek Bapt Bible Coll 300 Clear Creek Rd Pineville KY 40977

OVERLUND, ERVIN KENNETH, clergyman; b. Silverton, Oreg., May 6, 1928; s. Oscar Reinhart and Emma Charlotte (Johnson) O.; m. Sylvia Adrene Moe, Nov. 25, 1954; children: Ruth, Mary, Timothy, Joel, Rachel. BA, Augsburg Coll., 1956; BD, Luth. Theol. Sem., St. Paul, 1961. Ordained to ministry Am. Luth. Ch., 1961, Evang. Luth. Ch. Am., 1988. Minister Coulee (N.D.)-Lostwood Luth. Parish, 1961-65, Benedict (N.D.)-Ruso Luth. Parish, 1965-68, Fordville (N.D.)-Lankin Luth. Parish, 1969-78; chaplain Lake Region Luth. Home, Devils Lake, N.D., 1978-91, Good Samaritan Ctr., Devils Lake, 1981—; dean Grafton Conf., Am. Luth. Ch., 1973, mem. Dist. Coun. Ea. N.D., Fargo, 1973, del. 7th gen. conv., Detroit, 1974. V.p. Devils Lake Mayor's Com. for Employment of Handicapped, 1990. Mem. Assn. for Clin. Pastoral Edn., Am. Soc. on Aging, N.D. Chaplains Assn. (charter, sec.-treas. 1978-79), North Dakota Peace Coalition, Rotary (sec. Devils Lake 1982-91, del. N.D. Gov. con. libr. and info. svcs. 1990). Democrat. Home: 1213 5th Ave N Devils Lake ND 58301 Office: Good Samaritan Ctr 302 7th Ave Devils Lake ND 58301

OVERMAN, RICHARD HINSON, religion educator, minister; b. L.A., Jan. 20, 1929; s. Wallace Leroy and Ruth (Hinson) O.; m. Phyllis Chamberlin, June 28, 1958; children: Robert, Leah. BS, Stanford U., 1950, MD, 1954; ThM, Sch. Theology, Claremont, Calif., 1961; PhD, Claremont Grad. Sch., 1966. Ordained to ministry United Meth. Ch. Asst. prof. religion U. Puget Sound, Tacoma, 1965-68, assoc. prof., 1968-75, prof., 1975—. Author: Evolution and the Christian Doctrine of Creation, 1967. Capt. M.C., USAF, 1955-57. Dempster fellow Meth. Bd. of Higher Edn. and Ministry, 1962-64, Rockefeller fellow, 1963-65. Home: 2336 Sunset Dr W Tacoma WA 98466 Office: U Puget Sound 1500 N Warner St Tacoma WA 98416

OVERMYER, KENNETH WAYNE, minister, business owner; b. Kewanna, Ind., Dec. 9, 1931; s. Lloyd William and Nora Jane (Woodcox) O.; m. Madonna Kathryn Wilson, Aug. 24, 1952; children: Deborah Overmyer Good, David Lloyd. BS in Psychology, Manchester Coll., 1954; BD, Evang. Sem., Naperville, Ill., 1958; BS in Elem. Edn., Grace Coll., 1972; MDiv, Garrett Evang. Sem., Evanston, Ill., 1972. Ordained to ministry Evang. United Brethren Ch., 1958. Pastor Berne (Ind.) Trinity United Meth. Ch., 1959-66, Walnut Creek United Meth. Ch., Warsaw, 1966-76, Shipshewana (Ind.) First United Meth. Ch., 1976-81, Bethal United Meth. Ch., Elkhart, Ind., 1981-86, River Park United Meth. Ch., South Bend, Ind., 1986-91, St. Andrew's United Meth. Ch., Syracuse, Ind., 1991—; co-owner Overmyer Enterprises, 1975—; dir. evangelism Ind. Conf. No. Evang. United Brethren Ch., 1959-66. Recipient Cert. of Appreciation Evang. United Brethren, 1976. Mem. Ministerial Assn., Lions, Kiwanas, Masons (chaplain 1982-88), Blue Lodge. Democrat. Home: 1308 N Lond Dr Syracuse IN 46567 Office: St Andrew's United Meth Ch 1413 N Long Dr Syracuse IN 46567

OVERSTREET, R(EGINALD) LARRY, minister; b. Owosso, Mich., Aug. 17, 1941; s. Reginald and Nancy Ruth (Clifton) O.; m. Linda Darlene Sunday, Aug. 17, 1962; children: Lori Lea, Lois Ann, Reginald Lloyd. BA, Bob Jones U., 1963; MDiv, San Francisco Bapt. Theol. Sem, 1968; MA, Wayne State U., 1974, PhD, 1979. Ordained to ministry Bapt. Ch., 1963. Pastor Beulah Bapt. Ch., Roseville, Mich., 1968-72, Springwells Ave. Bapt. Ch., Detroit, 1972-74; asst. prof. Midwestern Bapt. Coll., Pontiac, Mich., 1974-75, Detroit Bapt. Theol. Sem., Allen Park, Mich., 1975-79; prof. Grace Theol. Sem., Winona Lake, Ind., 1979-91; pastor 1st Bapt. Ch., Warsaw, Ind., 1980-91; prof. Clearwater (Fla.) Christian Coll., 1991—. Contbr. articles to religious publs. Mem. Speech Communication Assn., Religious Speech Communication Assn., Cen. States Speech Assn., Ind. Speech Assn., Evang. Theol. Soc., Optimist (chaplain 1983-84). Republican. Home: 2225 Nursery Rd Clearwater FL 34624 Office: Clearwater Christian Coll 3400 Gulf-to-Bay Blvd Clearwater FL 34624 *True success in ministry, and in life, is pleasing God by allowing Him to use us to fulfill His purpose in our lives.*

OVERTON, EDWIN DEAN, campus minister, educator; b. Beaver, Okla., Dec. 2, 1939; s. William Edward and Georgia Beryl (Fronk) O. B.Th., Midwest Christian Coll., 1963; M.A. in Religion, Eastern N.Mex. U., 1969, Ed.S., 1978; postgrad. Fuller Theol. Sem., 1980. Ordained to ministry Christian Ch., 1978. Minister, Christian Ch., Englewood, Kans., 1962-63; youth minister First Christian Ch., Beaver, Okla., 1963-67; campus minister Central Christian Ch., Portales, N.Mex., 1967-68, Christian Campus House, Portales, N.Mex., 1968-70; tchr. religion, philosophy, counseling Eastern N.Mex. Univ., Portales, 1970—, campus minister, Christian Campus House, 1968—, dir., 1980—; farm and ranch partner, Beaver, Okla., 1963—. State dir. Beaver Jr. C. of C., 1964-65; pres. Beaver High Sch. Alumni Assn., 1964-65; elder Cen. Christian Ch., Portales, 1985-88, 1990—; chmn. Beaver County March of Dimes, 1966; pres. Portales Tennis Assn., 1977-78. Mem. U.S. Tennis Assn. Republican. Club: Lions. Home: 1129 Libra St Portales NM 88130 Office: 223 S Ave K Portales NM 88130

OVERWAY, KURT RANDALL, minister; b. Holland, Mich., Nov. 3, 1959; s. August J. and Mary Ann (Van Dyke) O.; m. Judith Marie Spencer, July 11, 1981; 1 child, Katelyn Marie. AA, Concordia Coll., Ann Arbor, Mich., 1980, BA, 1982; MDiv, Concordia Sem., 1987. Min. Luth. Ch.; pres. Chaplain Corps. SGMA, Wymore, Nebr., 1988-90.

OWEN, CARLOS J., minister; b. Dixon, Ill., Dec. 23, 1939; s. James Loal and Bessie (King) O.; m. Barbara Marie Jaynes, Nov. 4, 1958; children: Carlos Jr., Cynthia, James, Kimberly. B of Theology, Internat. Sem., 1982, DD, 1984. Ordained to ministry, 1982. Pastor Faith Tebernacle, Boston, 1981-85; asst. pastor 1st Ch. of New Jersulam, Rockland, Mass., 1985-90; carpenter, foreman Modern Continental Constrn. Co., Cambridge, Mass., 1979—; trustee, Hyde Park Pentecoastal, 1965-80; youth min., deacon, asst. pastor, Boston Ch. Scoutmaster, tng. com., commr. staff Boy Scouts Am., Boston, 1971-84, Silver award, 1977, Designated Wood Badge award, 1975. Mem. Masons, Scottish Rite. Home: 9 Lawrence Rd Plymouth MA 02360

OWEN, GEORGE EARLE, clergyman, religion educator; b. Christiansburg, Va., Mar. 26, 1908; s. George Elvy and Ethel (Berry) O.; m. Margaret Frances Richards, May 23, 1936; children—Mary Devon (Mrs. Christopher G. Smith), Anne Franklin (Mrs. A.M. Fountain II), Margaret Earle (Mrs. Gerald Daniel Clark, Jr.), Deborah Elizabeth. B.A. cum laude, Bethany (W.Va.) Coll., 1931, D.D., 1961; M.A., U. Chgo., 1938; B.D., Union Theol. Sem., N.Y.C., 1940; Ed.D., Columbia, 1943; D.H.L., Tougaloo Coll., 1984. Ordained to ministry Christian Ch., 1928; pastor in Bolivar, Pa., 1928-31, Tazewell, Va., 1931-35, Winchester, Va., 1935-37, N.Y.C., 1937-40, Buenos Aires, Argentina, 1944-45; v.p., head ch. history dept. Union Theol. Sem., Buenos Aires, 1943-48; vis. prof. Cambridge (Eng.) U., 1948; head philosophy dept. Union Theol. Sem., Manila, Philippines, 1951-55; dean Coll. Missions, also exec. sec. missionary selection and tng.; United Christian Missionary Soc, Indpls., 1955-57; ambassador Fla. chain missions United Christian Missionary Soc. 1956, exec. chmn. div. gen. depts., 1957-68; chmn. commn. coop. polity and practice internat. Conv. Christian Chs., 1960-70, chmn. com. long range planning, 1970 and beyond, 1967-69; mem. yearbook publ. com. World Call, 1958-70; asst. to gen. minister, pres. Christian Ch., 1968-73; elder emeritus First Christian Ch., Melbourne, Fla., 1987—; mem. U.S. conf. World Council Chs., 1961-69, accredited visitor constituting assembly, Amsterdam, 1948; mem. Nat. Council Family Relations, U. Geneva, Switzerland, 1966, Commn. on Brotherhood Restructure, 1960-70. Author: (with others) Alpha Kappa Pi Pledge Manual, 1931, Faith and Freedom, 1953, Education for Mission and Change, 1969, A Century of Witness, 1975, The Nature of Prayer, 1977; (poetry) Reflections, 1990; also articles; editor: (with others) Riverplate Reflections, 1943-48, Yearbook and Directory of the Christian Church, 1970-73. Mem. Marion County Assn. Mental Health, Indpls. Council World Affairs, Ind. Council Family Relations.; Mem. bd. Religion in Am. Life, 1967-73, Irvington Historic Landmarks Found., 1970-72, 75-76; trustee Colegio Ward, Buenos Aires, 1943-48; trustee Toulagoo (Miss.) Coll., 1962—, mem. exec. com., 1967-84. emeritus, 1984—; ; mem. interim ministries 1st Christian Ch., Vero Beach, Dayton Beach and Miami, Titusville, Fla., elder emeritus, Melbourne, Fla., 1984—. Recipient Distinguished Service award Disciples of Christ Chs., Tagalog area Philippines, 1954. Mem. Indpls. Mus. Art, Internat. Platform Assn., Am. Bible Soc. (adv. council 1969-73), Ind. Hist. Soc., Irvington Hist. Soc. (life, pres.), Disciples of Christ Hist. Soc. (life), Benton House Assn. (pres. 1975-76), Nat. Fedn. State Poetry Socs., Indpls. Athletic Club, Contemporary Club, Indpls. Lit. Club, Space Coast Poetry Club, Fla. State Poets Assn., Nat. Fed. State Poetry Socs., Brevard Art Ctr. and Mus., Masons, Alpha Kappa Pi (nat. grand chaplain 1932-42), Kappa Delta Pi, Phi Delta Kappa, Tau Kappa Alpha. Home: 5075 S AIA Hwy Melbourne Beach FL 32951 *The nature of love is such that you may love unwisely but you can never love too much.*

OWEN, RAYMOND HAROLD, minister; b. Gleason, Tenn., Apr. 21, 1932; s. Charlie Emerson and Lula (Page) O.; m. Lavell Coburn, Oct. 4, 1952; children: Dana (dec.), Darryl R., Dyton L. BA in Religion, Oklahoma City U., 1964; ThM, So. Meth. U., 1967; MA in Evangelism, Scarritt Coll., Nashville, 1972; DD (hon.), Oklahoma City U., 1979. Ordained to ministry United Meth. Ch., 1967. Pastor 1st United Meth. Ch., Hugo, Okla.; dist. supt. Meth. Ch., Bartlesville Dist., Okla., 1977-82; sr. min. Epworth United Meth. Ch., Oklahoma City, 1971-73, New Haven United Meth. Ch., Tulsa, 1973-77, 1st United Meth. Ch., Bartlesville, Okla., 1982—; del. Jurisdictional Conf. S.W. United Meth. Ch., 1976, 80, 84, 88—, Gen. Conf., 1980, 84, 88, 90; mem. exec. com. World Meth. Coun. 1986—; bd. dirs. Green Co. Retirement Villa, Bartlesville. Author: Probingins in Prayer, 1975, Seedtime and Harvest, 1980, Questions That Shape Destiny, 1983, Listening To Life, 1987. 2d lt. U.S. Army, 1954-60. Mem. Rotary. Office: First United Meth Ch 500 S Johnstone Bartlesville OK 74005 *It is never very far from the mediocre to the exceptional; it is just more painful.*

OWENS, CHANDLER DAVID, bishop. Bishop Ch. of God in Christ, Newark. Office: Ch of God in Christ 14 Van Velsor Pl Newark NJ 07112*

OWENS, CHARLES FRANKLIN, JR., minister; b. Loxley, Ala., Apr. 29, 1956; s. Charles Franklin Sr. and Virginia Louise (Berga) O. BA in Econ., U. South Ala., 1977; MDiv, New Orleans Bapt., 1980. Ordained to ministry So. Bapt. Conv., 1980. Youth min. First Bapt. Ch., Independence, La., 1979-80; min. of youth, edn. Va. Hills Bapt. Ch., Alexandria, 1980-84, Thomas Meml. Bapt., Bennettsville, S.C., 1984—; editor S.C. Bapt. Youth Min. Assn., Columbia, 1987-88; adv. coun. Charleston So. U., S.C., 1991—. Adv. mem. Marlboro Alcohol & Drug Abuse Commn., Bennettsville, 1987. Named one of Outstanding Young Men of Am., 1985. Home: 221 Cypress Ln Bennettsville SC 29512 Office: Thomas Meml Bapt Church 308 W Main St Bennettsville SC 29512 *The greatest gift that I can give to the future is to invest my life in the youth of today.*

OWENS, DONALD PHIL, priest; b. Ft. Worth, Feb. 14, 1942; s. Donald Phil Sr. and Marguerite Ione (Deal) O.; m. Barbara John, Apr. 9, 1966; children: Kathryn Gwyn (dec.), Meredith Lyn, Cynthia Dawn. BA, Trinity U., San Antonio, 1966; MDiv, Pitts. Theol. Sem., 1969; PhD, U. Okla., 1986. Ordained to ministry Presbyn. Ch., 1969, as deacon and priest Episcopal Ch., 1975; lic. profl. counselor; lic. marriage and family therapist. Pastor 1st Presbyn. Ch., United Presbyn., Ingram, Tex., 1969-71, 1st Presbyn. Ch., Clinton, Okla., 1971-75; curate, chaplain St. John's Episc. Ch., Diocese of Okla., Norman, 1975-81; chaplain U. Okla. St. Anselm U. Ctr., Norman, 1975—; chmn. Episc. Province VII Ministry in Higher Edn., 1986—, Nat. Adv. Com. to the Presiding Bishop in Ministry in Higher Edn., 1989—; mem. clin. pastoral care bd. Presbyn. Hosp., Oklahoma City, 1991. Mem. Bethesda Alternatives, Norman, 1991-93. Mem. Episc. Soc. in Ministry in Higher Edn. Republican. Office: St Anselm of Canterbury 800 Elm Norman OK 73069

OWENS, GLEN EDWARD, minister; b. El Dorado, Ark., Feb. 4, 1947; s. Glen E. and Vanessa (Thompson) O.; m. Susan Ruth Oakley, May 31, 1969; children: Kent, Kathleen. BSBA, La. Tech. U., 1969; postgrad., Southwestern Bapt. Theol. Sem, 1980-82, New Orleans Bapt. Theol. Sem., 1985. Ordained to ministry Bapt. Ch. 1976, lic. Gospel ministry Bapt. Ch., 1980, ordained to Gospel ministry Bapt. Ch. 1980; cert. ch. bus. adminstr., tchr., Evang. trainer, tchr. Cost acct. Tex. Eastman Co., Longview, Tex., 1969-70, asst. to ins. tax acct., 1970-73, ins. tax acct., 1973-79; assoc. pastor, adminstr. Oakland Heights Bapt. Ch., Longview, Tex., 1979-84; interim pastor Ellerbe Rd. Bapt. Ch., 1986-87; adminstr. Broadmore Bapt. Ch., Shreveport, La., 1984-87; min. young adult edn., dir. ch. ops. Roswell St. Bapt. Ch., Marietta, Ga., 1987-89; asst. exec. dir. Fla. Bapt. Conv., Jacksonville, 1989—; bd. dirs. Radio Station WFTD.AM, Marietta; adv. bd. Office Equipment Ctr., Atlanta; pres. Ark-La-Tex Signal Users Group, Shreveport, La., 1987, 88-89. V.p., sec. CAUS Inc., Dallas, 1982, 87; chmn. Properties and Ins. Coms. Northwest La. Assn., 1985-86, Computer Study Com. Northwest La. Assn., 1985-86. Named Outstanding Young Men Am., 1979, Outstanding Bapt. Men Tex., 1983. Mem. Nat. Assn. Ch. Bus. Adminstrs.(fellow 1983), Southern Bapt. Ch. Adminstrs. Assn. Bapt. Religious Educators Assn., Christian Ministries Assn.

OWENS, HAROLD ESTON, minister; b. Sussex, N.J., Feb. 8, 1943; s. Eston Cleveland and Hazel Elizabeth (Milhoan) O.; m. Cherie Ann Baughman, Feb. 8, 1964; children: Paul Scott, Rachel Elisabeth, Luke Eston. BA cum laude, Alderson-Broaddus Coll., 1967; MDiv, Crozer Theol. Sem., 1970; ThM, Princeton Theol. Sem., 1971. Ordained to ministry United Meth. Ch., 1970. Assoc. pastor Richardson Pk. United Meth. Ch., Wilmington, Del., 1967-69; pastor West Cecil Parish, North East, Md., 1969-71; co-pastor Peninsula-McCabe United Meth. Ch., Wilmington, 1971-73; pastor Janes United Meth. Ch., Rising Sun, Md., 1973-84; founder, bd. dirs. Yokefellow Soc., Inc. of Md., Rising Sun, 1984—, pres., 1990—. Mem. Christian Socratic Soc. Home and Office: 36 N Queen St Rising Sun MD 21911

OWENS, JAMES ROBERT, communications educator; b. Grove City, Pa., Jan. 3, 1957; s. Thomas W. and Frances Maureen (Bender) O.; m. Lynette Comstock Hendry, July 6, 1985. BA, Asbury Coll., Wilmore, Ky., 1979; MS, Ind. U., 1980, Specialist in Edn. degree, 1981; PhD, Southeastern U., 1983. Assoc. instr. Ind. U., Bloomington, 1980-81; pres. Worldwide News Service, Lexington, Ky., 1980-86; prof. Asbury Coll., 1981—; cons. OMS Internat., Indpls., 1980-83, Evang. U. of Bolivia, South Am., 1990; cons., TV producer Missionary Ch., Ft. Wayne, Ind., 1984-89; olympics exec. dir. Worldwide News Svc., L.A., 1984; radio reporter, sportcaster Winter Olympics in Lake Placid, Allied Ind. Press Assn., 1980; freelance TV ABC Sports, N.Y.C., 1986—; TV producer for Overseas Coun., Greenwood, Ind., 1989-90, African Leadership, Inpls., 1990—; commentator control stage mgr. Goodwill Games and internat. broadcasts TBS Sports, Atlanta, 1990; freelance videographer SportsChannel Am./Creative Sports Mktg., Charlotte, N.C., 1990; producer Downtown Prodns., Lexington, 1990—; gen. mgr. TV32, Wilmore, Ky., 1987—, bd. dirs., 1990—. Author: Basic Photography, 1977, Snow Photography, 1980; contbr. articles to profl. jours.; editor Intercollegiate Religious Broadcasters Faculty Sourcebook, 1988; producer 2 pilot TV programs for KET/PBS affiliate, 1988-91, TV documentaries in Honduras, 1983, France, 1985, Dominican Republic, 1986, Haiti, 1986, Kenya, 1989, Bolivia, 1990, Zaire, 1991. Tchr. 4-H, Boy Scouts Am., N.Y., Pa., Ky., Ind., 1980-86. Recipient Lens Gallery award Lens Mag., 1981, Philo T. Farnsworth video award, 1989, finalist, 1990, 91; finalist Hometown Video Festival award, 1989; named to Hon. Order Ky. Cols., 1985, one of Outstanding Young Men of Am., 1985, 86. Mem. Intercollegiate Religious Broadcasters (nat. chmn. 1985-88), Nat. Acad. Cable Programming (judge ACE awards 1990), Ky. Assn. Communications and Tech. (bd. dirs. 1986-88), Ky. Intercollegiate State Legis. (faculty advisor 1981-86), Nat. Fedn. Local Cable Programmers, Ford Philpot Assn. (bd. dirs. 1989—), Asbury Broadcast Communications (faculty advisor 1982—). Republican. Avocations: media lapel pin collecting, photography. Home: 700 N Lexington Ave Wilmore KY 40390 Office: Asbury Coll 201 N Lexington Ave Wilmore KY 40390

OWENS, JOSEPH, clergyman; b. St. John, N.B., Can., Apr. 17, 1908; s. Louis Michael and Josephine (Quinn) O. Student, St. Mary's Coll., 1922-27, St. Anne's Coll., Montreal, Que. Can., 1928-30, St. Alphonsus Coll., Woodstock, Ont., Can., 1930-34; M.S.D., Pontifical Inst. Mediaeval Studies, Toronto, 1951. Ordained priest Roman Cath. Ch., 1933; parish asst. St. Joseph's Ch., Moose Jaw, Sask., Can., 1934-35, St. Patrick's Ch., Toronto, 1935-36, Maria-Hilf Ch., Tomslake, B.C., Can., 1940-44; instr. philosophy St. Alphonsus Sem., Woodstock, Ont., Can., 1936-40, 48-51, 53, Assumption U., Windsor, Ont., Can., 1954; with Pontifical Inst. of Mediaeval Studies, Toronto, 1954—; prof. Pontifical Inst. of Mediaeval Studies, 1960—; instr. mediaeval moral doctrine Accademia Alfonsiana, Rome, Italy, 1952-53; mem. faculty dept. philosophy Sch. Grad. Studies, U. Toronto. Mem. editorial bd.: The Monist, 1961—; Contbr. numerous articles to religious and profl. jours. Mem. Canadian Philos. Assn. (pres. 1981-82), Am. Catholic Philos. Assn. (pres. 1965-66), Metaphys. Soc. Am. (councillor 1965-67, pres. 1971-72), Soc. Ancient Greek Philosophy (pres. 1971-72), Catholic Commn. Intellectual and Cultural Affairs, Royal Soc. Can. Home: 141 McCaul St, Toronto, ON Canada M5T 1W3 Office: 59 Queen's Park Crescent, Toronto, ON Canada M5S 2C4

OWENS, MICHAEL TED, minister; b. Gastonia, N.C., Nov. 29, 1952; s. Charles Ted and Frances (Black) O.; m. Jimmie Luke, Aug. 3, 1974; children: Jessica Ruth, Jennifer Lee, Janah Elizabeth. Student, East Coast Bible Coll., 1989—. Ordained to ministry Ch. of God, 1984. Assoc., ministerial intern Ch. of God (Cleveland, Tenn.), Rocky Mount, N.C., 1979-80; pastor Ch. of God (Cleveland, Tenn.), Elizabeth City, N.C., 1980-83, Salisbury, N.C., 1983—. Mem. adv. bd. Maple Prison Unit, Camden, N.C., 1980-83. Recipient Cert. of Appreciation, Gov. Jim Hunt State of N.C., 1981. Mem. Acts II Ministerial Assn. (v.p. 1987-88, pres. 1989-90), Lions. Republican. Home: 108 S Oak St Granite Quarry NC 27802 Office: Morlan Park Ch of God 121 Carolina Blvd Salisbury NC 28146

OWENS, PAMELA JEAN, minister; b. Dallas, Sept. 21, 1948; d. Thomas H. Jr. and Neva Mae (Helton) Owens; m. Richard John Ream Jr., Apr. 14, 1974; children: Johanna Ruth, Daniel Joseph, Richard John. BA magna cum laude, Vanderbilt U., 1969; MDiv with honors, Austin Presbyn. Seminary, 1980; postgrad., U. Chgo., 1984—. Ordained, 1980. Assoc. chaplain Brown Schs. Tex., Austin, 1975-76; assoc. pastor Koenig Lane Christian Ch., Austin, 1978-79; pastor Woodgrove Brethren Christian Parish, Woodland, Mich., 1981-84, Irving Park Christian Ch., Chgo., 1985—; bd. dirs. Love, Inc., Hastings, Mich., 1983-84. Contbr. articles to profl. jours. Organizer N.C. Polit. Prisoners Com., Charlotte, 1972-74. Disciples House scholar U. Chgo., 1984—. Mem. Soc. Bibl. Lit., Phi Beta Kappa. Democrat.

OWENS, RICHARD WILSON, pastoral counselor; b. Tampa, Fla., Apr. 29, 1941; s. Walter and Alene (Brown) O.; m. Ella Mae Phelps, Dec. 20, 1980; children: Richard Jr., Sonjia, Chez, Ila-Donnasanova, Contrina, Lester. BS, Ga. State U., 1982, MS, 1989; MDiv, Emory U., 1985. Student pastor North Ga. Conf. United Meth. Ch., Atlanta, 1983-85, pastor, 1985-89, pastoral counselor, 1989—; dir. and founder Hue Christian Counseling Ctr., East Point, Ga. Mem. North Ga. United Meth. Fellowship, Atlanta, 1986—. With U.S. Army, 1962-69, Korea. Mem. Am. Assn. Counseling and Devel. Office: Hue Christian Counseling 2147 Dodson Dr East Point GA 30344

OWENS, ROBERT F., ecumenical agency administrator. Exec. dir. S.E. Associated Ministries, Louisville. Office: SE Associated Ministries 3728 Taylorsville Rd Louisville KY 40220*

OWENS, ROBERT JESSEN, JR., minister, religion educator; b. Springfield, Ill., Oct. 20, 1947; s. Robert Jessen and Betty June (Taylor) O.; m. Mary Ann Johnson, Aug. 23, 1969; children: Monica Michele, Taylor Robert. AB magna cum laude, U. Ill., 1969; MA, MDiv, Lincoln Christian Sem., 1973; PhD, Johns Hopkins U., 1982. Ordained to ministry Christian Chs., 1972. Asst. prof. Bible Manhattan (Kans.) Christian Coll., 1974-76; adj. faculty sacred scripture St. Mary's Sem., Balt., 1978-83; assoc. prof. Emmanuel Sch. Religion, Johnson City, Tenn., 1980-87, prof. Hebrew Bible/Old Testament, 1987—; vis. scholar Wolfson Coll., U. Oxford, Eng., 1987-88. Author: Genesis and Exodus Citations of Aphrahat the Persian Sage, 1983. Mem. Soc. Bibl. Lit., Cath. Bibl. Assn., Fellowship of St. Alban and St. Sergius,. Home: 1805 Colonial Ridge Dr Johnson City TN 37604 Office: Emmanuel Sch Religion 1 Walker Dr Johnson City TN 37601-9989

OWENS, ROBIN SHANE, clergyman; b. Clinton, S.C., May 1, 1954; s. David Herbert Sr. and Doris Mabel (Wofford) O.; m. Susan Ann Modlin, Aug. 23, 1980; children: Wesley, Amy, Andrew. BA, Presbyn. Coll., 1975; MDiv, Columbia Sem., 1980, postgrad., 1990—. Ordained to ministry Presbyn. Ch., 1980. Pastor Wildwood Presbyn. Ch., Morehead City, N.C., 1980-84, Bixby Presbyn. Ch., Advance, N.C., 1984-88, Olney Presbyn. Ch., Gastonia, N.C., 1989—; moderator, evangelism com. Presbytery of Western N.C., Morganton, N.C., 1990—; vice-moderator Evangelism Network, Synod of Mid-Atlantic, Richmond, 1990—. Home: 232 Olney Church Rd Gastonia NC 28056 Office: Olney Presbyn Ch 251 Olney Church Rd Gastonia NC 28056 *In response to the question of why I am a minister, the answer is simple. I seek to show love for God by serving people.*

OWENS, RONNIE DAVID, minister; b. Jamestown, Tenn., Nov. 24, 1945; s. Blaine Gladys Owens; m. Judith Carol Cooper, Dec. 22, 1968; children: Melissa Dawn, Jill Elaine. BS, Tenn. Tech. U., 1968; MDiv, So. Bapt. Theol. Sem., Louisville, 1975. Ordained to ministry Bapt. Ch., 1973. Pastor Fairmont Bapt. Ch., Louisville, 1972-75, New Salem Bapt. Ch., Limestone, Tenn., 1975-79, Oak Hill Bapt. Ch., Jonesborough, Tenn., 1979-81, Skyline Heights Bapt. Ch., Johnson City, Tenn., 1981-86, Grace Bapt. Ch., Elizabethton, Tenn., 1986—; chaplain Sycamore Shoals Hosp., Elizabethton, 1990—; Mem. exec. bd., Christian svcs. com. Tenn. Bapt. Conv., Brentwood, Tenn., 1988—. Mem. policy rev. com. Elizabethton Bd. Edn., 1990-91. Mem. Watauga Assn. of Bapts. (chmn. com. on coms. 1990—), Assn. for Clin. Pastoral Edn. Home: 604 Ontario Dr Elizabethton TN 37643 *In a world filled with brokenness pain and suffering, a word from God brings courage, hope, forgiveness and comfort. It is the task of God's servants in ministry to be vessels thru which God touches human life with a loving presence and brings reconciliation..*

OWENSBY, EMMETT C., minister; b. Jasper, Mo., Mar. 18, 1918; s. Arthur D. and Ressie (Taylor) O.; m. Mary Newell O., Jan. 17, 1943; children: Mary Ann, Carolyn K., Emma Sue. BEd, Evansville U., 1966; BTh, So. Bapt. Seminary, Louisville, 1948; Teaching Credentials, U. Southeastern Ky., 1949. Ordained to ministry Bapt. Ch., 1942. Min. First Bapt. Ch., Monroe City, Mo., 1948-54, Montgomery City, Mo., 1954-56; min. Forest Ave. Bapt. Ch., Kansas City, Mo., 1956-62, Cornerstone Bapt. Ch., Evansville, Ind., 1962—; cons. State Welfare Dept., Ind., 1964-89; Pres. Pastor's Conf., Evansville, 1963-65, treas. 1965-69. Bd. dirs. Hannibal (Mo.) LaGrange U., 1951-54; treas. Girl Scouts U.S., Monroe City, 1951-54; active Mayor's Human Rels. Com., Evansville, 1978-82, Civil Defence, State of Ind., 1965—. Mem. local C. of C., Masons. Home and Office: 1300 Sheffield Dr Evansville IN 47710

OWEN-TOWLE, CAROLYN SHEETS, clergywoman; b. Upland, Calif., July 27, 1935; d. Millard Owen and Mary (Baskerville) Sheets; m. Charles Russell Chapman, June 29, 1957 (div. 1973); children: Christopher Charles, Jennifer Anne, Russell Owen; m. Thomas Allan Owen-Towle, Nov. 16, 1973. BS in Art and Art History, Scripps Coll., 1957; postgrad. in religion, U. Iowa, 1977. Ordained to ministry Unitarian-Universalist Ch., 1978. Minister 1st Unitarian Ch., San Diego, 1978—; pres. Ministerial Sisterhood, Unitarian Universalist Ch., 1980-82; mem. Unitarian Universalist Svc. Com., 1979-85, pres., 1983-85. Bd. dirs. Planned Parenthood, San Diego, 1980-86; mem. clergy adv. com. to Hospice, San Diego, 1980-83; mem. U.S. Rep. Jim Bates Hunger Adv. Com., San Diego, 1983-87; chaplain Interfaith AIDS Task Force, San Diego, 1988—. Mem. Unitarian Universalist Ministers Assn. (exec. com. 1988, pres. 1989-91). Avocations: freedom of choice, reading, walking, designing environments. Office: 1st Unitarian Ch 4190 Front St San Diego CA 92103

OWINGS, TIMOTHY LAWRENCE, minister; b. Hialeah, Fla., May 19, 1953; s. Neal Carey and Eileen (Maguire) O.; m. Kathleen Lynn Pignato, July 12, 1975; children: Nathan Thomas, Justin Neal, Lindsey Elaine. BA, Palm Beach Atlantic Coll., 1975; MDiv, So. Bapt. Theol. Sem., 1978, PhD, 1983. Ordained to ministry So. Bapt. Conv., 1973. Pastor Hiseville (Ky.) Bapt. Ch., 1977-79, Hillcrest Bapt. Ch., Frankfort, Ky., 1980-83, 1st Bapt. Ch., Mooresville, N.C., 1983-86, Calvary Bapt. Ch., Tuscaloosa, Ala., 1986-90, 1st Bapt. Ch., Augusta, Ga., 1990—. Author: A Cumulative Index to New Testament Greek Grammars, 1983; contbr. articles to religious jours. Mem. pres.'s coun. Mercer U., Macon, Ga., 1990; bd. dirs. ARC, Augusta, 1991. Named an Outstanding Alumnus, Palm Beach Atlantic Coll., 1980. Mem. Rotary. Home: 3521 Stevens Way Augusta GA 30907-9564 Office: First Bapt Ch 3500 Walton Way Augusta GA 30909-1822

OXTOBY, WILLARD GURDON, clergyman; b. Kentfield, Calif., July 29, 1933; s. Gurdon Corning and Miriam Burrell (White) O.; m. Layla Jurji, Sept. 27, 1968 (dec. June 1980); children: David Merrill, Susan Elizabeth; m. Julia Ching, July 25, 1981. BA, Stanford U., 1955; MA, Princeton U., 1961, PhD, 1962. Lectr., asst. prof. faculty divinity McGill U., Montreal, Que., Can., 1960-64; assoc. prof. religious studies Yale U., New Haven, 1966-71; prof. religious studies Trinity Coll. U. Toronto, Ont., Can., 1971—, dir. Centre for Religious Studies, 1976-81; Co-pres. 33d Internat. Congress Asian and North African Studies, 1990. Author: Some Inscriptions of the Safaitic Bedwin, 1968, Ancient Iran and Zoronstrianism, 1973, The Meaning of Other Faiths, 1983; editor: Religious Diversity, 1976; contbr. articles to encys. and dictionaries. Danforth Found. grad. fellow, St. Louis, 1955-58, Am. Coun. Learned Socs. study fellow, N.Y.C., 1964-65, sr. fellow, 1975-76, Shastri Indo-Canadian Inst. sr. fellow, Montreal, 1975-76, Social Scis. and Humanities Rsch. Coun. Can. rsch. grantee, Ottawa, Ont., Can., 1984-86. Mem. Am. Soc. for Study of Religion (pres. 1990-93), Am. Acad. Religion (monograph editor 1968-70), Can. Soc. for Study Religion, N.Am. Assn. for Study Religion, Am. Oriental Soc., Can. Asian Studies Assn. Office: Trinity Coll, 6 Hoskin Ave, Toronto, ON Canada M5S 1H8

OZOLINS, KARLIS LOTARS, retired library director; b. Riga, Latvia, Mar. 11, 1923; came to U.S., 1943; s. Karl and Alma (Cukste) O.; m. Sulamit I. Ivask, Nov. 10, 1945; children: Dina Ruth, Andrew Lynn, Peter Charles. BA, Augsburg Coll., 1951; BTh, Augsburg Theol. Sem., 1952; MLS, U. Minn., 1961, MEd, 1966; MDiv, U. Luther Northwestern Sem., 1970; PhD, U. Mich., 1972. Pastor Luth Free Ch., Barronett, Wis., 1951-55; instr. Augsburg Coll., Mpls., 1955-59, libr., 1959-61; lectr. U. Minn., Mpls., 1961-69; Fulbright prof. Nat. Taiwan U., Taipei, 1963-64; lectr. U. Mich., Ann Arbor, 1966-67; dept. head libr. sci. Ill. State U., Normal, 1971-73; dir. libr. Gustavus Adolphus Coll., St. Peter, Minn., 1973-80; dir. libr. U. St. Thomas, St. Paul, 1980-90, ret., 1990—. Editorial advisor Jour. of Baltic Studies; book reviewer in field. Mem. ALA, Minn. Libr. Assn., Am. Latvian Assn., Hist. Luth Conf., Beta Phi Mu. Lutheran. Home: 1905 N Fairview Ave Saint Paul MN 55113

PACALA, LEON, association executive; b. Indpls., May 3, 1926; s. John and Anna (Ferician) P.; m. Janet Lefforge, Dec. 28, 1947 (dec. July 1987); children: Mark, Stephen, James; m. Virginia Strasenburgh, Mar. 10, 1990. AB, Franklin (Ind.) Coll., 1949; BD, Colgate Rochester Div. Sch., 1952; PhD, Yale U., 1960; LLD (hon.), Nazareth Coll., 1980; LHD (hon.), Franklin Coll., 1987. Ordained to ministry Baptist Ch., 1952. Asst. prof. philosophy and religion DePauw U., 1956-61; participant study religion undergrad. coll. Lilly Found., 1957-59; assoc. prof. religion Bucknell U., 1961-68, prof., 1968-73, chmn. dept., 1961-64, dean, 1962-73; pres. Colgate Rochester (N.Y.) Div. Sch.; also Bexley Hall, Crozer Theol. Sem., 1973-80; exec. dir. Assn. Theol. Schs. in U.S. and Can., 1980-91; cons. acad. adminstrn. Beirut Coll. Women, 1972. Contbr. articles to profl. jours. Exec. com. Christian Faith in Higher Edn. Projects, 1965-68; trustee Franklin Coll. With USAAF, 1944-45. Internat. Rotary scholar, Louvain U., Belgium, 1952-53. Mem. Am. Conf. Acad. Deans (exec. com., treas., chmn., presiding officer 1973-74), Am. Assn. Higher Edn., Assn. Am. Colls. (commn. religion higher edn.), Assn. Theol. Schs. (com. accreditation), Ea. Assn. Coll. Deans and Advisers Students. Home: 3515 Elmwood Ave Rochester NY 14610 Office: 10 Summit Dr Pittsburgh PA 15275

PACHENCE, RONALD ANTHONY, priest; b. Miami, Fla., May 25, 1945; s. Anthony Michael and Rose Marie (Triano) P. BA in Philosophy, Conception Sem., 1967; MA in Religious Edn., Cath. U., 1972, PhD in World Religions and Cath. Studies, 1978. Ordained priest Roman Cath. Ch., 1974. Instr. St. Mary's Coll. Sem., Balt., 1976-77; asst. prof. D'Youville Coll., Buffalo, 1977-81; assoc. prof. U. San Diego, 1981—; founding dir. Inst. for Christian Ministries, U. San Diego, 1985—. Author: Speaking of Sacraments, 1988, (audioprodn.) Church Sacraments; writer, producer Cath. TV Network series on Cath. Ch., Advent, Lent, Islam; editor, theol. cons. Benziger Pub. Co. Writer, reporter San Diego Ecumenical Conf. TV: Sunday Focus, 1986—; vol. United Way of San Diego, 1987-88. Mem. Coll. Theology Soc., Nat. Assn. TV Arts and Scis., AAUP. Office: U San Diego Alcala Park San Diego CA 92110 *For Paul, love is the greatest of the Christian virtues. I've often wondered why he didn't give this honor to hope. As I have known the three things that last, hope must be the mother of faith and love. Without her, faith seeks the comfort of certitudes, and love makes no sense at all.*

PACHOW, WANG, religion educator; b. Chungking, China, June 1, 1918; came to U.S., 1968; naturalized, 1975; s. Wang High-shan and Mashih; m. Mavis de Silva, June 2, 1956; 1 child, Hsuan. BA, Mengtsang Coll., Shanghai, China, 1936; MA, Visva-Bharati U., Santiniketan, India, 1941; PhD, U. Bombay, 1948. Prof. religion U. Iowa, Iowa City, 1975-88, prof. emeritus, 1988—. Author: A Comparative Study of the Pratimoksha, 1955, Chinese Buddhism: Aspects of Interaction and Reinterpretation, 1980; contbr. to Ency. Britannica, profl. jours. Mem. Am. Acad. Religion, Mahabodhi Soc., Am. Oriental Soc., Assn. Asian Studies, Soc. Study Chinese Religions, Visva-Bharati Soc. (India). Home: 821 Iowa Ave Iowa City IA 52240 Office: U Iowa Sch Religion Iowa City IA 52240 *When one faces problems which concern the day-to-day life, let conscience be the guide. If everyone were considerate and appreciative of fair play, then there would be peace within and harmony without.*

PACK, WALTER FRANK, minister, religion educator emeritus; b. Memphis, Mar. 27, 1916; s. Joseph Walter and Mary Elizabeth (Gibson) P.; m. Della Carlton, June 22, 1947. A.A., David Lipscomb Coll., Nashville, 1935; B.A., U. Chattanooga, 1937; M.A., Vanderbilt U., 1939; Ph.D., U. So. Calif., 1948. Ordained to ministry Ch. of Christ, 1932. Minister various Chs. of Christ, 1932—; instr. David Lipscomb Coll., 1940-44; prof. religion Pepperdine U., Los Angeles, 1947-49, prof., chmn. dept. religion, 1963-76, disting. prof., 1978-86, disting. prof. emeritus, 1986—, dean Grad. Sch., 1967-78; chmn. div. religion Seaver Coll., 1980-83; prof. bible Abilene (Tex.) Christian U., 1949-63; Frank and Della Pack disting. prof. New Testament studies Abilene U., 1986. Staff writer: 20th Century Christian, Restoration Quarterly; Author: Great Preachers of Today, 1963, (with Prentice Meador) Preaching to Modern Man, 1969, Tongues and the Holy Spirit, 1973, The Living Word Commentary: Gospel according to St. John, 1975, The Book of Revelation, 1983; Editor: Our Bible, 1951. Mem. Soc. Bibl. Lit., Phi Beta Kappa, Phi Kappa Phi, Pi Gamma Mu, Alpha Chi. Home: 10858 Wagner St Culver City CA 90230 Office: 24255 Pacific Coast Hwy Malibu CA 90265 *From my youth I have been committed to New Testament Christianity. This faith I have shared with others. By Christ's standards I have endeavored to live and to serve.*

PACKARD, RUSSELL CALVERT, deacon; b. Alhambra, Calif., Apr. 10, 1946; s. Homer W. and Ruth Ellen Packard; m. Beverly Albert, Dec. 26, 1966 (div. Dec. 1976); children: Tara, Todd, Brent; m. Gretchen Myers, Feb. 25, 1978; children: Christine, Jennifer. MD, U. Calif., Irvine, 1971; BS in Religious Studies summa cum laude, St. Leo Coll., 1981. Ordained deacon Roman Cah. Ch., 1981; diplomate Am. Bd. Psychiatry and Neurology. Instr. pastoral counseling Permanent Diaconate Program, 1981-88; pastoral assoc. St. Paul Cath. Ch., Pensacola, Fla., 1984—; psychiat. cons. Diocese of Pensacola-Tallahassee, 1981—; adj. prof. psychology-psychiatry U. West Fla., 1988—; dir. Headache Mgmt. and Neurology, Pensacola, 1981—; bishop's rep. bd. dirs. Community Health Ctr., 1982-85; mem. Permanent Diaconate Bd., Diocese Pensacola-Tallahassee, 1981-88; chairperson bioethics com. Sacred Heart Hosp., Pensacola, 1988—. Author: Come, Journey with Me, 1984, The Psychiatric Wards, 1984; editor: Psychiatric Aspects Headache, 1989. Comdr. USN, 1970-80. Fellow ACP, Am. Acad. Neurology; mem. Am. Psychiat. Assn., Am. Assn. Study Headache, Escambia County Med. Soc. Republican. Home: 2040 Utica Pl Pensacola FL 32503 Office: 5500 N Davis Hwy Pensacola FL 32503

PACKENHAM, DANIEL J., academic administrator. Pres. St. Francis Sem., Milw. Office: St Francis Sem 3257 S Lake Dr Milwaukee WI 53207*

PACKER, BARRY DEAL, minister; b. Dallas, Mar. 17, 1956; s. Howard Lynn and Barbara (Bell) P.; m. Diane Carol Stephens, June 3, 1978; children: Collin Bell, Clark Stephen. BA, Abilene Christian U., 1978; ThM, Harding U., Memphis, 1981; D Ministry, Fuller Theol. Sem., Pasadena, Calif., 1991. Ordained to ministry, Ch. of Christ. Minister of involvement So. Hills Ch. of Christ, Abilene, 1981-88; minister of the word LaMesa (Calif.) Ch. of Christ, 1988—; trustee Bell Trust, Dallas, 1990—; chmn. vis. com. for Coll. Bibl. Studies, Abilene Christian U., 1988-91. Mem. Pres.'s Coun., Pepperdine U., 1989—. Named Alumnus of the Yr., Dallas Christian Schs., 1984. Office: La Mesa Ch of Christ 5150 Jackson Dr La Mesa CA 91941

PACZESNY, SISTER EDMUNETTE, college president, nun; b. Milw., Oct. 13, 1933; d. Edmund Michael and Edna (Jankowski) P. BA, Marquette U., 1955; MS in Edn., Fordham U., 1958, PhD, 1962; LHD (hon.), Canisius Coll., 1984, Niagara U., 1989. Joined Franciscan Sisters of St. Joseph, Roman Cath. Ch. Instr. Hilbert Coll., Hamburg, N.Y., 1962-89, acad. dean, 1968-74, pres., 1974—. Trustee St. Joseph Hosp., Cheektowaga, N.Y., 1982—, St. Francis High Sch., Athol Springs, N.Y., 1990—. Mem. Am. Assn. Higher Edn., Western N.Y. Consortium Higher Edn (sec.-treas. 1982—), Rotary (officer Hamburg chpt. 1990—).

PADBERG, JOHN W., educational administrator, history educator, writer; b. St. Louis, May 22, 1926; s. John Francis and Emily C. (Albrecht) P. A.B., St. Louis U., 1959, Ph.L., 1951, M.A., 1954; S.T.L., St. Mary's Coll., 1959; Ph.D., Harvard U., 1965. Ordained priest Roman Catholic Ch., 1957. Prof. history St. Louis U., 1964-75, acad. v.p., 1969-73; research assoc. Jesuit Conf., Washington, 1973-75; pres., prof. history Weston Sch. Theology, Cambridge, Mass., 1975-85; dir. Inst. Jesuit Sources, St. Louis, 1986—; exec. com. Internat. Conf. Catholic Theol. Insts., 1978-84, pres., 1984-87. Author: Colleges in Controversy: The Jesuit Schools in France from Revival to Suppression, 1815-80, 1969; (monographs) The General Congregations of the Society of Jesus: A Brief Survey of Their History, 1974; Personal Experience and the Spiritual Exercises: The Example of St. Ignatius, 1978; The Society True to Itself: A Brief History of the 32nd General Congregation of the Society of Jesus, 1983. Editor, partial translator: Documents of the Thirty-First and Thirty-Second General Congregations of the Society of Jesus, 1977. Recipient E. Harris Harbison award for Disting. Teaching, Danforth Found., 1969. Mem. Cath. Theol. Soc. Am., Am. Hist. Assn., Am. Soc. Ch. History, Am. Catholic Hist. Assn., Soc. Franch Historical Studies, Am. Acad. Religion, Soc. for Values in Higher Edn. Home: Jesuit Hall 3601 Lindell Blvd Saint Louis MO 63108 Office: Inst Jesuit Sources 3700 W Pine Blvd Saint Louis MO 63108

PADILLA LOZANO, JOSE GUADALUPE, bishop; b. San Miguel el Alto, Mexico, Dec. 12, 1920. Ordained priest Roman Cath. Ch., 1946; bishop of Veracruz Mexico, 1963—. Office: Insurgentes Veracruzanos 470, Paseo del Malecon, Veracruz Mexico 91700

PADIYARA, ANTHONY CARDINAL, archbishop; b. Changanacherry, India, Feb. 11, 1921. Ordained priest Roman Cath. Ch., 1945. Consecrated bishop, 1955, prefect to Changanacherry dei Siro-Malabaresi,, 1970, transferred to Ernakulani,, 1985, created cardinal,, 1988. Office: PO Box 2580 Ernakulam, Cochin 682 031 Kerala, India

PADOVANO, ANTHONY THOMAS, theologian, educator; b. Harrison, N.J., Sept. 18, 1934; s. Thomas Henry and Mary Rose (Cierzo) P.; m. Theresa Lackamp, 1974; children—Mark, Andrew, Paul, Rosemarie. B.A. magna cum laude, Seton Hall U., 1956; S.T.B. magna cum laude, Pontifical Gregorian U., Rome, Italy, 1958, S.T.L. magna cum laude, 1960, S.T.D. magna cum laude, 1962; Ph.L. magna cum laude, St. Thomas Pontifical Internat. U., Rome, 1962; M.A., NYU, 1971; Ph.D., Fordham U., 1980. Ordained priest Roman Cath. Ch., 1959. Asst. chaplain Med. Center, Jersey City, 1960; asst. St. Paul of the Cross Ch., Jersey City, 1962, St. Catharine Ch., Glen Rock, N.J., 1963; prof. systematic theology Darlington Sem., Mahwah, N.J., 1962-74; prof. Am. lit. Ramapo Coll., N.J., 1971—; adj. prof. theology and religious studies Fordham U., 1973—; mem. Archdiocesan Commn. Ecumenical and Interreligious Affairs, 1965, Commn. Instrn. Clergy in Documents Vatican II, 1966; del. Dialogue Group Luth.-Roman Cath. Theol. Conversations, 1969; del. at large Senate of Priests, Archdiocese of Newark; Danforth assoc., 1975—; lectr. in field, also appeared radio and TV; parish minister St. Margaret of Scotland, Morristown, N.J. Author: The Cross of Christ, the Measure of the World, 1962, The Estranged God, 1966, Who is Christ, 1967, Belief in Human Life, 1969, American Culture and the Quest for Christ, 1970, Dawn Without Darkness, 1971, Free to be Faithful, 1972, Eden and Easter, 1974, A Case for Worship, 1975, America: Its People, Its Promise, 1975, Presence and Structure, 1975, The Human Journey, 1982, Trilogy, 1982, Contemplation and Compassion, 1984, Winter Rain: A Play, 1985, His Name is John: A Play, 1986, Christmas to Calvary, 1987, Love and Destiny, 1987, Summer Lightening: A Play, 1988, Conscience and Conflict, 1989, Reform and Renewal, 1990, A Celebration of Life, 1990, The Church Today: Belonging and Believing, 1990; editor: Centenary Issue Roman Echoes, 1959; mem. editorial bd. The Advocate, 1966-73; contbr. articles to mags. Active Diocese Paterson Ecumenical Commn.; founding pres. Justice and Peace Commn., Diocese of Paterson, active Resigned Priests Com. Mem. Cath. Theol. Soc. Am., Mariological Soc. Am., Nat. Fedn. Priests Councils (ofcl. rep. to Constl. Conv., Chgo. 1968), Corpus (pres.), Fedn. Christian Ministries, Internat. Fedn. of Married Cath. Priests (v.p. for N.Am.). Home: 9 Millstone Dr Morris Plains NJ 07950 Office: Ramapo Coll New Jersey Mahwah NJ 07430 *People rather than ideas have been most formative in my life. More accurately, people, as they embodied certain ideals have proved most decisive. There is nothing more persuasive than an idea which becomes so vital that it transforms the person who proclaims it.*

PADRICK, RICHARD KEITH, religious organization administrator; b. Indpls., Dec. 5, 1939; s. Millard Douglas and Mary (Keith) P.; m. LaVerne Dubois, June 10, 1961; children: Michael Douglas, Keith Andrew. BA, U. Indpls., 1962; MDiv, Christian Theol. Sem., Indpls., 1966. Pastor Tuxedo Park Bapt. Ch., Indpls., 1969-73, First Bapt. Ch. No. Hills, Deadwood, S.D., 1973-75; exec. dir. Edna Martin Christian Ctr., Indpls., 1976-89, Milw. Christian Ctr., 1989—; mem. Ind. Mins. Coun., Indpls., 1972-75; mem. Urban Strategies-Indpls., 1982-85; mem. Neighborhood Aciton Program Am. Bapt. Ch., U.S.A., Valley Forge, Pa., 1976. Mem. Inner City Youth Serving Agys., Nat. Soc. Fund Raising Excs., Kiwanis. Office: Milw Christian Ctr 2137 W Greenfield Ave Milwaukee WI 53204

PADRO, PETER LOUIS, JR., theologian, historian, consultant; b. Bronx, N.Y., Apr. 6, 1945; s. Peter and Florence P.; m. Ramona James, June 26, 1971; children: Peter Jason, Daniel Ross. Student St. Benedict's Sem., 1965-71; MDiv, Fuller Theol. Sem., 1984. Ordained to ministry Spanish Reform Ch., 1974. Pastor Calvary Chapel, Hawaiian Gardens, Calif., 1973, Grace Orthodox Presbyn. Ch., Carson, Calif., 1980-81, 1st Bapt. Ch. Carson, 1981-83, Inglewood (Calif.) Friends Ch., 1989—; dir. Libr. Padro y Navarro, Carson, 1986—; cons. Fedn. Anti-Communist Entities Latin Am., Buenos Aires, 1985—. Fellow Caribbean Hist. Assn. (sec. 1983—); mem. Nat. Assn. Profl. Journalists, Interam. Fedn. Journalists. Avocations: numismatics, harmonica playing. Home: 207 Orchid Ln Long Beach CA 90805-2319

PAGANO, ANNA LOUISE REYNOLDS, priest; b. Indpls., Feb. 19, 1933; d. Wellington Wormuth Reynolds and Janice (Lillycrop) Thomas; m. Joseph Stephen Pagano, June 8, 1957; children: Stephen Reynolds, Christopher Joseph. BA, Antioch Coll., Yellow Springs, Ohio, 1955; MDiv with honors, Duke Div. Sch., 1979, MTh, 1981; Anglican Studies Cert., Gen. Theol. Seminary, N.Y.C., 1982. Ordained to ministry Episcopal Ch. as deacon, 1983, as priest, 1984. Asst. rector Ch. of the Holy Family, Chapel Hill, N.C., 1983-84; asst. rector Chapel of the Cross, Chapel Hill, N.C., 1983-85, assoc. rector, 1985—; pres. N.C. Episcopal Clergy Assn., Chapel Hill, 1989-91; budget chmn. Diocesan Coun., Raleigh, N.C., 1988-91; chmn. Diocesan Deacons' Tng. Com., Raleigh, 1987-90, Diocesan Comm. on Aging, Raleigh, 1984-87. Author poetry, sermon tapes. Vice-pres. Interfaith Coun. for Social Svc., Chapel Hill, 1988; bd. dirs. Coaltion for Battered Women, Durham, N.C., 1983-86, Orange County Women's Ctr., Chapel Hill, 1983-85, Instnl. Rev. Bd., Med. Sch., Univ. N.C., 1988-90. Democrat. Home: 114 Laurel Hill Rd Chapel Hill NC 27514

PAGE, CURTIS MATTHEWSON, minister; b. Columbus, Ohio, Oct. 24, 1946; s. Charles N. and Alice Matthewson P.; m. Martha Poitevin, Feb. 12, 1977; children: Allison, Charles, Abigail. BS, Ariz. State U., 1968; MDiv, San Francisco Theol. Sem., 1971, D Ministry, 1985. Ordained to ministry Presbyn. Ch., 1971. Pastor Ketchum (Idaho) Presbyn. Ch., 1972-80, Kirk O'The Valley Presbyn. Ch., Reseda, Calif., 1980-90; campaign dir. Kids 1st Edn. Reform Partnership, L.A., 1990-91; sr. pastor Orangewood Presbyn. Ch., Phoenix, 1991—; bd. dirs. Express Pub., Ketchum. Bd. dirs. Mary Magdalene Home, Reseda; moderator Kendall Presbytery, 1978; chmn. com. on preparation for the ministry, San Fernando, Calif., 1988-90; chmn. Ketchum City Zoning Commn., 1979-80; mem. Ketchum Master Planning Commn., 1974, Mayor's Citizen's Adv. Task Force on Ethics, 1990; co-chmn. Voice Community Orgn. in San Fernando Valley, 1988-90. Avocations: amateur radio, tennis, snow skiing. Office: Orangewood Presbyn Ch 7321 N 10th St Phoenix AZ 85020

PAGE, JEAN-GUY, priest, educator; b. Montreal, Que., Can., Jan. 17, 1926; s. Almanzor and Alice (Gauvin) P. BA, Laval U., 1948, lic. in Theology, 1964; diploma in pastoral, Lumen Vitae, Belgium, 1965; PhD, Gregorianum, Rome, 1967. Ordained priest, 1952. Priest St. Anselm Parish, Que., Can., 1952-55, Our Lady Parish, Que., 1955-59; chaplain Young Christian Students, Que., 1959-63; prof. theology Laval U., Que., 1967—; dir. Major Sem., 1969-72; mem. Diocesan Pastoral Coun., Que., 1967-68, 73-74, diocesan priests coun., 1968-72. Author: Reflections Sur L'Eglise du Quebec, 1976, Foi ou Liberte?, 1977, Qui EstL'Eglise?, 1977-79 (3 vols.), Une Eglise sans Laics?, 1980, Le Nautonier de Dieu, 1984, La Source, 1985, Regarde et tends l'oreille, 1986, Prêtre, un métier sans avenir?, 1989, Le Christ, avenir du monde, 1990, L'Eglise à son printemps, 1990; contbr. articles to profl. jours. Mem. Can. Soc. Religious Studies, Societe Canadienne de Theologie. Office: F A Savard Bldg 736, Laval Univ Ste Foy, Quebec, PQ Canada G1K 7P4

PAGE, JOHN IRWIN, college president; b. Ft. Scott, Kans., Oct. 2, 1930; s. John Ellis and Ava Leona (Brown) P.; m. Virginia Maxine Witt, Aug. 1, 1951; children: Brenda, Carma, Courtney, Jonathan. BA, Kans. City Coll. and Bible Sch., 1952; MS, Pitts. State U., 1955, EdS, 1969; PhD Kans. State U., 1989. Pastor Ch. of God (Holiness), Stockton, Mo., 1952-58, Ft. Scott, Kans., 1959-80; prin. Ft. Scott Christian Heights Sch., 1954-80; mgr. Ironquill Estates, Ft. Scott, 1975-80; pres. Kansas City Coll. and Bible Sch., Overland Park, 1980—; v.p. Witt Engring., Inc., El Dorado Springs, Mo., 1968-80, Plainview Farms, Inc., Ft. Scott, 1974—; pres. Bourbon County Police Chaplaincy, Ft. Scott, 1965-80. Pres. Multi-County 4-C, Ft. Scott, 1970; bd. dirs. Human Relations Com., Ft. Scott, 1971; precinct worker Republican Party, Bourbon County, 1963. Named Outstanding Alumnus, Ft. Scott Community Coll., 1980, Hon. Police Col. Bourbon County Police Chaplaincy, 1965. Mem. Phi Delta Kappa (Continuous Service award 1985), Overland Park C. of C. Avocations: hunting, golf, sports. Home: 5301 W 83d St Prairie Village KS 66208 Office: Kansas City Coll and Bible Sch 7401 Metcalf St Overland Park KS 66204

PAGE, MARILYLE SWEET, priest, counselor; b. St. Louis, July 10, 1942; d. Martin Pierce and Vera Fern (Bigings) Sweet; m. Robert Jeffress Page, Dec. 28, 1974. BS in Home Econs., Ohio U., 1964; MDiv, Bexley Hall, 1975, D of Ministry, 1986. Ordained to ministry Episcopal Ch. as deacon, 1975, as priest, 1977. Buyer Lazarus Dept. Store, Columbus, Ohio, 1964-72; mgr. Edn. Resource Ctr. Bookstore Episcopal Diocese of Rochester, N.Y., 1975-84; clergy cons., trustee Huther-Doyle Meml. Inst., Rochester, 1986-89; rector Episcopal Ch. of the Atonement, Westfield, Mass., 1989—; assoc. rector St. Stephens Episcopal Ch., Rochester, 1977-79; rector St. Peter's Episcopal Ch., Henrietta, N.Y., 1979-89; counselor, therapist Chili (N.Y.) Counseling Ctr., 1983-89; trustee Episcopal Ch. Home, Rochester, 1981-87, pres., 1985-87; trustee Westfield Area Mental Health Clinic, 1991. Trustee Westfield Area Mental Health Clinic, 1991. Mem. Am. Assn. for Marriage and Family Therapy (clin.), Am. Assn. Pastoral Counselors (pastoral counselor-in-tng. 1987). Home: 60 Western Ave Westfield MA 01085-2615 Office: Episcopal Ch of Atonement 36 Court St Westfield MA 01085

PAGE, ROBERT JEFFRESS, theologian, educator; b. Oswego, N.Y., Nov. 18, 1922; s. Alanson S. and Virginia (Haskins) P.; m. Elizabeth Jean McKown, Nov. 21, 1947 (div. Mar. 1974); 3 children; m. Marilyle Elizabeth Sweet, Dec. 28, 1974. A.B., Hamilton Coll., 1944; S.T.B. cum laude, Episcopal Theol. Sch., 1947; Ph.D., Columbia, 1955. Ordained priest Episcopal Ch., 1948; curate Trinity Ch., Binghamton, N.Y., 1947-49; rector St. Paul's Ch., Aurora, N.Y.; also chaplain to Episcopal students Wells Coll., 1949-52; asst. chaplain Columbia U., 1953-55; mem. faculty Kenyon Coll., 1955-68, prof. theology, 1962-68; prof. theology Colgate Rochester/Bexley Hall/Crozer Div. Schs., 1968-88; acting dean Bexley Hall, 1989; priest-in-charge St. Andrews's Ch., Caledonia, N.Y., 1970-73, 85, 87, Ch. of Incarnation, Penfield, N.Y., 1973-74, Zion Ch., Palmyra, N.Y., 1975, Christ Ch., Rochester, 1976-77, Ch. of the Epiphany, Rochester, 1978, Grace Ch., Lyons, N.Y., 1980, St. Luke's Ch., Fairport, N.Y., 1981, Trinity Ch., Greece, N.Y., 1983, Zion Ch., Avon, N.Y., 1984, Grace Ch., Scotsville, N.Y., 1985, St. Luke's Ch., Brockport, N.Y., 1986, St. John's Ch., Honeoye Falls, 1987-88; bd. dirs. Rochester Center Theol. Studies, 1968-84; mem. standing com. Diocese of Rochester, 1978-82, pres., 1980-82; dep. Gen. Conv. of the Episcopal Ch., 1979, 82, mem. commn. on ministry, 1983-88, chmn., 1985-88; priest assoc. Ch. of Atonement, Westfield, Mass., 1990—; vis. fellow St. Augustine's Coll., Canterbury, Eng., 1962-63; vis. prof. Grad. Theol. Union, Berkeley, Cal., 1967, U. Rochester, 1970-72, 74; vis. scholar Episcopal Theol. Sch., Cambridge, Mass., 1972; Faculty fellow Assn. Theol. Schs., 1962-63, 79; mem. Ecumenical Com., Diocese of Western Mass., 1991—, Bd. Examining Chaplains, 1991—. Author: Charles Gore, Anglican Apologist, 1955, Liberal Catholicism, 1964, New Directions in Anglican Theology, 1965. Mem. Conf. Anglican Theologians, Delta Kappa Epsilon. Club: Genesee Valley. Home: 60 Western Ave Westfield MA 01085

PAGE, RODNEY I., ecumenical agency adminisrator, minister. Exec. dir. Ecumenical Ministries Oreg., Portland. Office: Oreg Ecumenical Ministries 0245 SW Bancroft St Ste B Portland OR 97201*

PAGELS, ELAINE HIESEY, historian of religion, educator; b. Palo Alto, Calif., Feb. 13, 1943; d. William McKinley and Louise Sophia (van Druten) Hiesey; B.A., Stanford, 1964, M.A., 1965; Ph.D., Harvard, 1970; m. Heinz R. Pagels, June 7, 1969, (dec. July 23, 1988); children: Sarah Marie, David van Druten. Asst. prof. history of religion Barnard Coll., Columbia, 1970-74, from asso. prof. to prof., chairperson dept. religion, 1974-82; Harrington Spear Paine prof. religion Princeton U., 1982—. Nat. Endowment Humanities grantee, 1973; Mellon fellow Aspen Inst. Humanistic Studies, 1974, Hazen fellow, 1975; Rockefeller fellow, 1978-79; Guggenheim fellow, 1979-80; MacArthur prize fellow, 1981-87. Mem. Soc. Bibl. Lit., Am. Acad. Religion. Episcopalian. Club: Bibl. Theologians. Author: The Johannine Gospel in Gnostic Exegesis, 1973, The Gnostic Paul, 1975, The Gnostic Gospels, 1979, Adam, Eve and The Serpent, 1988.

PAGETT, BETTY STRATHMAN, minister; b. Long Beach, Calif., Nov. 24, 1941; d. Earl R. and Miriam E. (Kline) Strathman; m. John Mason Pagett (div. 1984); 1 child, Wendy Elizabeth. BA, U. Pacific, 1963; MRE, Union Seminary, 1965, MDiv, 1975. Ordained minister United Meth. Ch. Minister Eglise Methodiste, Paris, 1965-66; university programs staff Bd. of Global Ministries, N.Y.C., 1966-69; mem. internat. devel. team CCUN, N.Y.C., 1969-70; Auburn fellow Union Seminary, N.Y.C., 1970-71; lectr., cons. N.Y.C., 1971-78; minister various Meth. Chs., Oakland, Concord and San Rafael, Calif., 1979—; adj. prof. Am. Bapt. Sem. West, Berkeley, Calif., 1978-86; pres. Marin Interfaith Co., Marin County, Calif., 1987-88; chair Jurisdictional Com. on Ministry, 1984-88; bd. dirs., faculty mem. Western Jurisdiction Licensing Sch., Claremont Sch. Theology; vice-chair, del., Gen. Conf. Delegation, No. Calif.-Nev. United Meth., 1984-88. Contbr. articles to profl. jours. Bd. dirs. Canal Ministry, San Rafael, Calif., 1988—, Continuing Edn. Sets, San Anselmom Calif., 1988—; faculty So. Marin Leadership Inst., Marin City, 1988—. Avocations: camping, hiking. Office: First United Meth Ch 9 Ross Valley Dr San Rafael CA 94901

PAGOSA, DOROTHY CATHERINE, religious organization administrator, nun; b. Cleve., June 29, 1954; d. Richard Walter and Ruth Laverne (Schueszler) P. BBA, Cleve. State U., 1975. Joined Sisters of St. Joseph-TOSF, Roman Cath. Ch. Pastoral min. St. Jude Parish, Warrensville Heights, Ohio, 1984-86; staff person 8th Day Ctr. for Justice, Chgo., 1986—; dir. social justice Sisters of St. Joseph, TOSF, Chgo., 1988—. Mem. Bread for World, 1987—, Peru Peace Network-U.S.A., 1991—, Chgo. Coalition for Homeless, 1991—; mem. subcom. on hunger City of Chgo., 1990—; active Pledge of Resistance, Chgo., 1989—; v.p. Pub. Welfare Coalition, 1987—; sec. Ill. Hunger Coalition, 1989-91; pres. bd. Food Justice Programs, 1988—; treas. Chgo. Inter-Agy. Food Network. Recipient recognition award Ill. Hunter Coalition, 1991. Office: 8th Day Ctr for Justice 1020 S Wabash Ave Ste 680 Chicago IL 60605

PAINTER, WILLIAM RALPH, academic administrator. Pres. Evang. Theol. Sem. Inc., Goldsboro, N.C. Office: Evang Theol Sem Inc 2302-2400 E Ash St Goldsboro NC 27530*

PAISANT, SISTER IMMACULATA, school system administrator. Supt. Cath. schs. Diocese of Houma-Thibodaux, La. Office: Office Supt Cath Schs PO Box 9077 Houma LA 70361*

PALACIOS, GLORIA P., religious organization executive; b. Zaragoza, Mexico, May 29, 1965; came to U.S., 1968; d. Maria Gloria (Martinez) Garcia; m. Ricardo Palacios, July 6, 1985; 1 child, Victoria Marie. AA, Robert Morris Coll., Chgo., 1984. Bookkeeper The Advt. Agy., Inc., Chgo., 1984; adminstrv. asst. Archdiocese of Chgo., 1985—. Catechist tchr., coord. St. Josaphat Ch., Chgo., 1984—, sec. parish pastoral coun., 1989, sports com., 1990, Hispanic com., 1984—; active C.M.F. aux. Bishop Placido Rodriguez, 1988. Mem. NAFE. Democrat. Avocations: reading, bicycling, volleyball, softball, volunteer work. Office: Archdiocese of Chgo 1048 N Campbell Ave Chicago IL 60622

PALAU, LUIS, religious organization administrator, evangelist; b. Buenos Aires, Argentina, Nov. 27, 1934; came to U.S., 1960; s. Luis Sr. and Matilde (Balfour) P.; m. Patricia Marilyn Scofield, Aug. 5, 1961; children; Kevin and Keith (twins), Andrew, Stephen. BA, St. Alban's Coll., Buenos Aires, 1954; grad. cert. in Bible, Multnomah Sch. of Bible, 1961; DD (hon.), Talbot Theol. Sem., 1977, Wheaton Coll., 1985. Missionary Overseas Crusades, Inc., Santa Clara, Calif., 1961-71, field dir. Latin Am. sect., 1967-71, pres., 1976-78; pres. Luis Palau Evangelistic Assn., Portland, Oreg., 1978—. Author: Walk on Water, Pete, 1974, Sex and Youth, 1974, Whom Shall I Marry, 1976, The Schemer and the Dreamer, 1976, The Moment to Shout, 1977, Heart After God, 1978, Our God Reigns, 1981, Tough Questions, 1984, Time to Stop Pretending, 1985, So You Want to Grow, 1986 Say Yes! How to Renew Your Spiritual Passion, 1991; co-author: Scottish Fires of Revival, 1980, Luis Palau: Calling the Nations to Christ, 1983; author/editor numerous tracts, articles and booklets on current socio-religious topics; host radio program Heartbeat with Luis Palau, 1991. Mem. Nat. Religious Broadcasters. Office: Luis Palau Evangelistic Assn 1100 NW Murray Rd Portland OR 97229

PALAZZINI, PIETRO CARDINAL, Italian ecclesiastic; b. Piobbico, Italy, May 19, 1912; s. Giovanni and Luigia (Conti) P.; grad. Seminario Regionale Marchigiano, 1932; Th.D., U. Lateranense, 1937, J.C.L., 1942. Ordained priest Roman Cath. Ch., 1934; asst. Major Roman Sem., 1942-45; vice rector Pontifical Roman Sem. Juridical Studies, 1945-49; undersec. Vatican Dicastery Religious, 1956-58; sec. Vatican Dicastery for Clergy, 1958-73; created archbishop, 1962, cardinal, 1973; prefect of Sacred Congregation for Causes of Saints, 1980; prof. moral theology and canon law Ponticial Lateran U., 1945-56. Recipient Gold medal Italian Ministry Pub. Edn. Mem. Theol. Roman Acad., Marian Internat. Acad., Acad. Internat. S. Tommaso, Raffaello Acad., Tiberina delle Scienze di Ferrara, Sistina, Card. Bessarione Acad. Author works on moral theology, canon law, articles. Address: 83 Proba, Petronia, Rome Italy

PALMAS, ANGELO, clergyman; b. Villanova Monteleone, Italy, Dec. 21, 1914. Student, Pontifical Sem., Cuglieri, Italy; Doctorate in Theology, Pontifical Sem., Cuglieri, 1939; License in Philosophy, Gregorian U., Rome, 1942; Doctorate in Civil and Canon Law, Latran Pontifical U., Rome, 1946. Ordained priest Roman Cath. Ch., 1938, archbishop, 1964. Sec. Apostolic Nunciature, Belgium, 1947-52; auditor Apostolic Nunciature, Switzerland, 1952-54; auditor, counsellor Apostolic Nunciature, Lebanon, 1954-60; mem. Secreatariat of State, Vatican, 1960-64; apostolic del. to Vietnam and Cambodia, 1964-69; apostolic Nuncio Colombia, 1969-75; apostolic Pro-Nuncio Ottawa, Can., 1975-90. Address: Via Accursio 8, 00165 Rome Italy

PALMER, DONALD CURTIS, interdenominational missionary society executive; b. Nelson, Minn., Oct. 8, 1934; s. Roy August Adn Cora (Bergner) P.; m. Dorothy Mae Nordquist, Mar. 16, 1962; children: Jean Marie, John Eric. Student, U. Minn., 1952-55; degree in Bible, Briercrest Bible Coll., Caronport, Can., 1958; MA in Missions, Trinity Divinity Sch., Deerfield, Ill., 1967; D in Ministry, Trinity Divinity Sch., 1989. Missionary Colombia GMU Internat., Kansas City, Mo., 1959-71; dir. evangelism GMU Internat., 1969-71, field sec. Latin Am., 1971-73, v.p. field ministries for Latin Am., 1973-85, v.p. research and strategy, 1985—; vis. prof. Grace Coll. of the Bible, Omaha, 1982—; mem. Frontier People's Com., 1985—, Evang. Missiological Soc., 1991—. Author: Explosion of People Evangelism, 1974; (with others) Dynamic Religious Movements, 1978, Managing Conflict Creatively, 1990. Republican. Baptist. Avocations: golf, tennis, hiking. Home: 2230 NE 73rd St Kansas City MO 64118 Office: GMU Internat 10000 N Oak Kansas City MO 64155 *The greatest inner quality that a person can possess is a thankful, grateful spirit.*

PALMER, ELLSWORTH LEVI, pastor; b. Portland, Oreg., Mar. 19, 1910; s. Levi Ellsworth and Lydia Clara (Shuinard) P.; m. Hilaria Ursula Castillo, Nov. 19, 1919; 1 child, Paul Henry. Student, Western Bapt. Theol. Sem., 1933-34; BA, Anderson Coll. & Theol., 1946; postgrad., U. Miami, 1968-72; DDiv., Nebr. Christian Coll., 1971. Ordained to ministry Ch. of God, Anderson, Ind., 1946. Asst. to pastor Belvedere Spanish Ch. of God., L.A., 1935-43; pastor Prospect Hill Spanish Ch. of God, San Antonio, 1946-50; missionary dir. Ch. of God, Cuba, 1950-60; pres., radio and tv commn. Inter-Am. Conf., Ch. of God, 1973-75; pres. Spanish Am. Concilio Ch. of God, 1972-73; founder Spanish Concilio in Fla., 1989—; vocat. tchr., coord. Dade County Pub. Schs., Miami, 1963-78; active Cuban Refugee work, Ch. of God, Miami, 1960-72; planned and built Spanish Ch. Bldgs., Miami, 1966-68; tech. radio broadcasting Spanish Ch. of God, Miami, 1977-81; organizer Spanish tours to Israel, other holy lands, 1975-88. Editor La Trompeta Spanish Lang. Ch. mag., 1946-50; contbr. vocat. edn. materials, photos and films, 1965-78. Mem. Presdl. Task Force, Rep. Party, Miami, 1990—. Recipient Disting. award letter Pres. Ronald Reagen, Washington, 1984, Disting. Svc. plaque Spanish Ch. of God, Miami, 1984, 50 Yrs. Svc. award in Spanish Countries, Ch. Extension, Anderson, 1985, 1986 Disting. Svc. award Warner So. Coll. Fla.; (with Hilaria) Disting Svc. award in Spanish Missions, Internat. Fla. Missions Conv., 1991; Disting. Svc. plague Spanish Am. Concilio USA, 1991. Mem. Spanish Assn. Mins. and Chs. Miami, Fla. Mins. and Chs. Ch. of God. Home: 4611 SW 4th ST Miami FL 33134 Office: Spanish Ch of God 4180 SW 5th Terr Miami FL 33134 *God created man to become involved with other people as well as himself. Reach out a hand of love to those who say life has been very difficult to them. Let's use our talents, knowledge and our assets to help them. We can be an instrument of God's love that will give them hope. This is the will of God.*

PALMER, GAY B., music school director, musician; b. Cordele, Ga., Oct. 11, 1962; d. Cecil Stanley and Virginia (Hall) Bowen; m. J. Scott Palmer. MusB, Samford U., 1985. Founder, dir. sch. music and orch. Lakeside Bapt. Ch., Birmingham, Ala., 1985—. Writer, arranger music compositions. Mem. Music Tchrs. Nat. Assn., Ala. Music Tchrs. Assn., Birmingham Music Tchrs. Assn., Nashville Songwriters Assn. Inc. Republican. Avocations: traveling, running, reading, writing. Office: Lakeside Bapt Ch 2865 Old Rocky Ridge Rd Birmingham AL 35243

PALMER, GRETCHEN EVERILDE, music minister; b. Mankato, Minn., Sept. 5, 1945; d. John Jacob and Everilde Mary (Schultz) Stroebel; m. Kenneth Charles Palmer, July 15, 1968; children: Monica, Michael. BS in Music Edn., Mankato State U. Adult choir dir. Thief River Falls (Minn.) Luth. Ch., 1968-69; music dir. Rockland Community Ch., Golden, 1970-82; dir. worship Mountain Christian Fellowship, Golden, 1983—; pvt. piano instr. Arvada, Colo., 1970—. Mem. Choristers Guild (contbr. articles to newsletter, festival com. 1988-91), Am. Guild Handbell Ringers, Piano Guild. Home: 11680 W 72d Pl Arvada CO 80005 Office: Mountain Christian Fellowship 166 S Lookout Mountain Rd Golden CO 80401

PALMER, HARRY WILLIAM, retired minister; b. Marathon, N.Y., Dec. 18, 1919; s. Fred David and Ruth Estella (Squires) P.; m. J. Pearl Burleigh, Sept. 2, 1942; children: Harry W. Jr., Mark Allan, Nancy Ellen. BA, Houghton Coll., 1941; MTh, So. Bapt. Theol. Sem., Louisville, 1945. Ordained to ministry Am. Bapt. Assn., 1947, Presbyn. Ch., 1976. Pastor East Waterboro (Maine) Bapt. Ch., 1946-51, Blaisdell Meml. Bapt. Ch., Waterboro, 1946-51, North Alfred (Maine) Bapt. Ch., 1946-51, Federated Ch. (Am. Bapt.-Presbyn.), Masonville, N.Y., 1951-76, Trout Creek (N.Y.) Bapt. Ch., 1959-66; chaplain Camp Brace Youth Opportunity Camp, Masonville, 1963-76; pastor W.Va. Mountain Project (Presbyn.), Brush Creek, 1976-85; bd. dirs. N.Y. State Bapt. Conv., Syracuse, N.Y.; bd. dirs., sec. Rural Ch. Inst., Ithaca, N.Y., 1952-58; moderator Presbytery of Parkersburg, W.Va., 1983. Mem., capt. Masonville Fire Dept. & Ambulance, Masonville, 1955-76; scouter Boy Scouts Am., Masonville, 1956-76; mem. com. on institutional ministry N.Y. State Coun. of Chs., Syracuse, 1965-68; chmn. Masonville br. ARC, 1957-66. Mem. Presbytery of Geneva (peacemaking com. 1986-92), Golden Agers Club (pres. 1987-90), Community Chest (pres. 1989-91). Home: 2660 E Naples St Wayland NY 14572-9701 *The ultimate folly of the human family may be that we choose war and destruction instead of peace and cooperation. There is enough for all if we curb our greed and share with each other.*

PALMER, HELEN VIRGINIA, religious organization administrator; b. Isanti County, Minn., Apr. 11, 1928; d. Wesley B. and Mary (Haumiller) Hiller; m. Maurice L. Palmer, Apr. 3, 1948; children: Maureen, Mark, Mischelle. Grad. high sch., St. Francis, Minn.; cert. in ch. bus. adminstr., U. St. Thomas, 1988. Parish adminstr. St. Margaret Mary Ch., Golden Valley, Minn., 1975-85; parish bus. adminstr. St. William's Ch., Fridley, Minn., 1986—. Recipient Good Neighbor award Sta. WCCO and Northland Ford Dealers, Mpls., 1981. Mem. Nat. Assn. Ch. Bus. Adminstrs. (sec. N. Cen. chpt. 1986-87), Assn. Parish Adminstrs. Office: St William's Ch 6120 Fifth St NE Fridley MN 55432 *Through the classes and seminars that I have taken every quarter of every year, I have learned one important thing, that education is a life-long learning process. It is not enough to have a good mind, you must use it well as God intended each of us to do.*

PALMER, KIM RICHARD, minister; b. L.A., Nov. 30, 1950; s. Eugene Earl and Lloyd Fern (Martin) P.; m. Beverly Lynn Decker, Aug. 19, 1978; children: Ryan Eugene, Mark Russell. BFA in Music, Earlham Coll., 1973; AS in Dairy Sci., Ohio State U., Wooster, 1978; MA in Biblical Studies, Ashland Sem., 1982; MusM, Azusa Pacific U., 1988. Ordained minister Evang. Free Ch. Am. Youth dir. Ch. of God, Wooster, 1978-80; pastor Goodyear Heights Ch. Nazarene, Akron, Ohio, 1981-82, East Whittier (Calif.) Friends Ch., 1982-88, Evang. Free Ch., Yorba Linda, Calif., 1988—; guest musician chs. in Midwest, East and Pacific regions, 1978—; guest conductor S.W. Yearly Meeting of Friends, Yorba Linda, 1984, 87; ejudicator Festival of Youth, Akron, 1981. Presser Music scholar Earlham Coll., 1972, Earlham preaching grantee, 1973, Whittier Musicians Club scholar, 1968. Mem. Yorba Linda/Placentia Pastors Assn. Republican. Avocations: model railroading, photography, reading, camping, auto repair. Office: Evang Free Ch 5320 Richfield Rd Yorba Linda CA 92686

PALMER, LESTER DAVIS, minister; b. Augusta, Ga., Oct. 6, 1929; s. Lawton Evans and Gwendolyn (Ramsbotham) P.; m. Janelle Griffin, May 6, 1951; children: Gwen Palmer Chandler, Kathy, Sandra Palmer Wood, Leslie. BA, Johnson Bible Coll., 1952; MDiv, Lexington Theol. Sem., 1958; postgrad., Boston U., 1961-63; DD, Bethany Coll., 1989. Ordained to ministry Christian Ch. (Disciples of Christ), 1951; CLU, 1981, ChFC, 1984. Assoc. gen. min. Christian Ch. Ky., Lexington, 1957-61; assoc. prof. ch. adminstrn. Lexington Theol. Sem., 1963-66; v.p. Pension Fund of Christian Ch., Indpls., 1966-83, pres., 1983—. Editor Promotional and Interpretive Bull., 1984—; contbr. articles to profl. jours. Home: 5953 Manning Rd Indianapolis IN 46208 Office: Pension Fund of Christian Ch 155 E Market St Indianapolis IN 46204

PALMER, MILEY EMBRY, minister; b. Ft. Worth, Mar. 20, 1937; s. Guy Embry and Miley Guion (Griswold) P.; m. Janet Elaine Kuhlmann, June 27, 1959; children: Elizabeth Anne, Mary Kathryn, Michael Sean, Patricia Lynne. BA, McKendree Coll., 1958; MDiv, Garrett Theol. Sem., 1962; DMin, Christian Theol. Sem., 1977. Ordained to ministry Meth. Ch., 1959. Pastor Calvary United Meth. Ch., Normal, Ill., 1963-69, Faith United Meth. Ch., Champaign, Ill., 1969-73; directing min. Wesley United Meth. Ch., Charleston, Ill., 1973-79; supt. Peoria (Ill.) Dist., 1979-85; dir., min. The Wesley Found. and Ch., Urbana, Ill., 1985—; trustee Meth. Med. Ctr., Peoria, 1967—; del. Gen.-Jurisdictional Confs., 1980, 84, 88; chairperson bd. discipleship Cen. Ill. Conf., 1989—. Mem. Rotary (Urbana). Office: The Wesley Found 1203 W Green St Urbana IL 61801

PALMER, STEPHEN EUGENE, clergyman; b. Independence, Iowa, Aug. 2, 1896; s. Alanson Llewelyn and Mary (Clark) P.; m. Katharine Hoelzel Greenslade, June 28, 1922 (dec. Feb. 1976); children: Stephen Eugene, Robert John, David Clark; m. Helen Donner Whiley, Apr. 16, 1977. A.B., Coll. of Wooster, 1917; student, U. Rennes, France, 1919; M.Div., B.D. with honors, McCormick Theol. Sem., 1922; D.D., Coll. of Wooster, 1942. Ordained to ministry Presbyn. Ch., 1922; pastor First Ch., Superior, Wis., 1922-26, Waukesha, Wis., 1926-30; pastor Westminster Ch., Youngstown, Ohio, 1930-36, First Ch., Lockport, N.Y., 1936-62; interim pastor Lafayette Ave. Presbyterian Ch., Buffalo, 1962-63; interim pastor 1st Presbyn. Ch., Akron, Ohio, 1964-65, Sheridan, Wyo., 1966-67, Casper, Wyo., 1968-69, Skaneateles, N.Y., 1970-71; interim pastor Fairmount Presbyn. Ch., Cleve., 1974-75; Study and travel, Egypt, Palestine, 1928, 1936; Pres. Ministers Assn. Youngstown and Lockport. Author: Quisling and Others, 1981. Leader in orgn. of Youngstown Citizens' Assn. for Good Govt., 1933; vice moderator Gen. Assembly Presbyn. Ch. U.S.A.; also moderator Presbytery Western N.Y., 1943-44, 61-62; chmn. fgn. missions Synod of N.Y., 1950-56; bd. Fgn. Missions of Presbyn. Ch., 1946-52. Served as 1st lt. inf. U.S. Army, World War I. Fellowship visitation to Hungarian Ref. Chs. Yugoslavia, 1958; churches of twelve African nations, 1965-66; churches of fourteen nations West Africa, 1967-68; mission stas. and chs. Amazon River, 1971-72; United Ch. S. India, 1973; United Ch. S. India Far East, 1976. Mem. McCormick Theol. Sem. Alumni Assn. (pres. 1942-43), Am. Legion, Vets. Fgn. Wars. Clubs: Masons (Buffalo), Rotary (Buffalo), Torch (Buffalo) (dir.). Home: 819 Lakeside Ct Lakeland FL 33801

PALMER, THOMAS MONROE, minister, treasurer, administrative assistant; b. Muskogee, Okla., Aug. 31, 1931; s. Alvie Wilder and Virginia Lucille (Burgess) P.; m. Juanita Myrle Crawford, Aug. 21, 1953; children: Kathy J. Palmer Davis, Anita G. Palmer Willock, Melanie D. Palmer Garrett. Student, Muskogee Jr. Coll., 1949-50; BA, Okla. Bapt. U., 1953; BD, Southwestern Bapt. Theol. Seminary, 1956; D in Ministry, Luther Price Sem., 1984. Ordained to ministry Bapt. Ch., 1952. Pastor 1st Bapt. Ch., Jasper, Ark., 1956-59, Cotter, Ark., 1959-60, Panama, Okla., 1960-63, Collinsville, Okla., 1965-80; pastor Trinity Bapt. Ch., Ardmore, Okla., 1963-65; dir. Owasso (Okla.) Bapt. Retirement Village, 1980-85; pastor Faith Bapt. Ch., Broken Arrow, Okla., 1985—; sec., treas., bd. dirs. Northeastern Health Care, Inc., Owasso, 1986—. Chaplain Okla. State Senate, Oklahoma City, 1979; bd. dirs. Owasso Sr. Ctr., 1982-85, Owasso C. of C., 1984-86; pres. bd. dirs. Collinsville Meml. Hosp., 1985—. Recipient Achievement award Okla. State Senate, 1979, Ambassador award Collinsville C. of C., 1984. Mem. So. Bapt. Ministry to Aging (v.p. long term care), Tulsa Bapt. Assn. (moderator 1978-79), Bapt. Gen. Conv. Okla. (v.p. 1979-80), Kiwanis (pres. Collinsville chpt. 1983-84). Democrat. Avocations: travel, golf, reading. Home: 1708 W Yuma Ct Broken Arrow OK 74011 Office: 2800 S First Pl Broken Arrow OK 74012

PALMER, WILLIAM ARTHUR, clergyman, editor; b. Bklyn., Oct. 19, 1946; s. William Arthur and Julia Emmaline (Sievers) P.; m. Rose Carolyn Warfield, June 8, 1968; children: Ruth Anita, Genevieve Elizabeth. BA, Lincoln Christian Coll., Ill., 1968; MA, Union Theol. Sem., N.Y.C., 1978. Ordained to ministry Christian Ch., 1968. Pastor Glen Cove (N.Y.) Christian Ch., 1969-78, First Christian Ch., Upper Marlboro, Md., 1978-81, Good Shepherd Christian Ch., Upper Marlboro, 1981—; sec. Ea. Christian Conv., Pitts., 1978-79, treas. Valley Forge, Pa., 1985-86, Md. area rep., Hershey, Pa., 1991; vice chmn. bd. Christian Prison Ministry Chaplancy Svcs., Frederick, Md., 1985-89, chmn. bd., 1989-90; treas. Capital Concern, Washington, 1987-90, bd. dirs. 1987—. Author: Shepherding, 1986; copy editor: Rules for Leadership, 1986, Technicians Today Mag., 1990—; contbr. articles to mags. Bd. dirs., trustee Glen Cove Hist. Soc., N.Y., 1973-78; sec. Pastoral Counseling Greater Marlboro, Upper Marlboro, 1986-90. Recipient Tng. award Eastern Star, Washington, 1977. Mem. Marlboro Clergy Assn. (pres. 1984). Avocations: archeology, reading and writing about history. Home and Office: 10500 Angora Dr Cheltenham MD 20623

PALMS, ROGER CURTIS, magazine editor, clergyman; b. Detroit, Sept. 13, 1936; s. Nelson Curtis and Winifred Jessie (Bennett) P.; m. Andrea Sisson, Aug. 22, 1959; children—Grant Curtis, Andrea Jane. B.A., Wayne State U., 1958; B.D., Eastern Baptist Sem., Phila, 1961, M.Div., 1971, D.D., 1977; M.A., Mich. State U., 1971. Ordained to ministry Am. Bapt. Chs., 1961. Pastor Ronceverte Bapt. Ch., W.Va., 1961-64; pastor 1st Bapt. Ch., Highland Park, N.J., 1964-67; chaplain Am. Bapt. Student Found., Mich. State U., East Lansing, 1967-73; assoc. editor Decision mag. Billy Graham Evang. Assn., Mpls., 1973-76, editor, 1976—; guest lectr. at schs of evangelism and writers' confs. Author 12 books including: Living on the Mountain, 1985, Enjoying the Closeness of God, 1989, Let God Help You Choose, 1989; speaker nationally syndicated radio program Something for You. Trustee No. Bapt. Theol. Sem., 1973—. Mem. Evang. Press Assn. (pres. 1991—). Office: Decision Mag Billy Graham Evang Assn 1300 Harmon Pl Minneapolis MN 55403 *Investing in people's spiritual lives, giving time and counsel, will bring multiplied results for generations. It is one of the most far-reaching ways I can put faith to work.*

PALS, DANIEL L., religion educator; b. South Holland, Ill., Oct. 28, 1946; s. Herbert H. and Margaret B. (Vanderaa) P.; m. Phyllis Ross Balzer, Aug. 11, 1973. AB, Calvin Coll., 1968; BD, Calvin Theol. Sem., 1971; MA, U. Chgo., 1973, PhD, 1975. Asst. prof. history Trinity Coll., Deerfield, Ill., 1976-77; asst. prof. religion and history Centre Coll., Danville, Ky., 1977-80; chmn. dept. religion U. Miami, Coral Gables, Fla., 1980—, Outstanding Honors prof., 1983. Author: The Victorian Lives of Jesus, 1982; editorial asst. Church History, 1973-76; contbr. articles to profl. jours. Recipient Max Orovitz award U. Miami, 1980, 84, 90, Freshman Teaching award, 1989. Mem. Am. Soc. Ch. History, Am. Acad. Religion. Mem. Presbyn. Ch. (U.S.A.). Home: 1239 Dickinson Dr Coral Gables FL 33124 Office: U Miami Dept Religion PO Box 248264 Coral Gables FL 33124

PANAGORE, PETER BALDWIN, minister; b. Marlborough, Mass., Feb. 2, 1959; s. Peter and Janet Marie (Baldwin) Panagore; m. Michelle Louise Miclettie, June 29, 1985; 1 child, Alexandra Amelia. BA, U. Mass., Amherst, 1982; MDiv, Yale U., 1986. Ordained to ministry United Ch. Christ, 1987. Assoc. pastor Orange (Conn.) Congl. Ch. United Ch. Christ, 1986-89; pastorSunset Congl. Ch. and 1st Congl. Ch. United Ch. Christ,

Deer Isle, Maine, 1989—. Contbr. poetry to Hobo Jungle, Glassblower. Office: 1st Congl Ch PO Box 292 Deer Isle ME 04627

PANG, WING NING, researcher; b. Hong Kong, Jan. 14, 1942; came to U.S., 1963; s. Hok Ko and Shun Chun (Fong) P.; m. Elaine Chi-Ling Chan, July 18, 1970; children: Hannah Hsin-Sung, Jonathan Duncan. BArch, U. Calif., Berkeley, 1967; MCPUD, Harvard U., 1971; PhD, UCLA, 1978. Staff Chinese World Mission Ctr., Pasadena, Calif., 1981-84, dir., 1984-86; assoc. prof. William Carey Internat. U., Pasadena, 1981-86; exec. com. N.Am. Congress of Chinese Evangs., Pasadena, 1983-87; dir. Chinese Coordination Ctr. of World Evangelism, Pasadena, 1987—, chmn. rsch. com., 1987—; ptnr. South Seas Investments, Santa Monica, 1978—; dir. Edn. Svc. Exchange with China, Alambra, Calif., 1981—; chmn. rsch. com. N.Am. Congress of Chinese Evang., Pasadena, 1978-87; adj. prof. Alliance Theol. Sem., Nyack, N.Y., 1989—. Author: Chinese Awareness Seminar Handbook, 1985. Office: CCCOWE PO Box 7338 Alhambra CA 91802-7338

PANGERL, SUSANN M., psychotherapist; b. St. Paul, Jan. 14, 1951; d. Russell Charles and Evelyn Dorothy (Buehring) P.; m. John A. Gallagher, Aug. 4, 1978; children: Liam, Siobhan. BA, Gustavus Adelphus Coll., St. Peter, Minn., 1973; cert. ministry, U. Chgo., 1978, MA, 1978. Chaplain Hospice of Southeastern Mich., Southfield, 1979-83; lectr. Mercy Coll. Detroit, 1978-83; adj. faculty Meadville/Lombard Sem., Chgo., 1988—; sr. clin. staff Ctr. for Religion and Psychotherapy, Chgo., 1983—. Computer vol. Walt Disney Magnet Sch., Chgo., 1988—. Fellow Am. Assn. Pastoral Counselors; mem. Unitarian Universalist Soc. (steering com. 1988-1990), Am. Assn. Religions Persin Culture and Religion, Pastoral Theology Soc. Unitarian Universalist. Home: 1720 W Granville Chicago IL 60660 Office: Ctr Religion-Psychotherapy 30 N Michigan Ste 1920 Chicago IL 60602

PANIKKAR, RAIMON, priest; b. Barcelona, Spain, Nov. 3, 1918; came to U.S., 1967; s. Rammuni and Carmen (Alemany) P. Philosophy Licenciate, U. Barcelona, 1941, Chem. Sci. Licenciate, 1942; PhD, U. Madrid, 1946, D Chem. Scis., 1958. Ordained priest Roman Cath. Ch., 1946. Chaplain U. Madrid, 1946-50, U. Salamanca (Spain), 1950-53, U. Rome, 1950-63, Diocese Varanasi (India), 1964—; prof. U. Calif., Santa Barbara, 1971-87, prof. emeritus, 1987—. Author: Intrareligious Dialogue, 1978, Vedic Experience, 1989, Blessed Simplicity, 1982, The Silence of God, 1989. Mem. Teilhard de Chardin Centre (v.p.), Am. Acad. Religion, Internat. Inst. Philosophy. Office: U Calif Santa Barbara CA 93106

PANKEY, RONALD ARTHUR, minister; b. Salinas, Calif., June 20, 1956; s. Charles Herbert Pankey and Winnie Ruth (Durham) Irvin; m. Kathrine Anne Kisseé, Aug. 6, 1977; children: Charles Jonathan, Sara Ruth. Student, Golden Oaks Bible Coll., Roseville, Calif., 1972-76, Mid-Am. Nazarene Coll., Olathe, Kans., 1979-81, Point Loma Nazarene Coll., San Diego, 1985-86. Ordained to ministry Ch. of the Nazarene, 1988. Assoc. pastor Ch. of the Nazarene, Carmichael, Calif., 1983-85; pastor Ch. of the Nazarene, Rogue River, Oreg., 1985-88, Chapel of the Cross, Anchorage, 1988-89, Ch. of the Nazarene, Webb City, Mo., 1989-91, Cen. Ch. of the Nazarene, Coffeyville, Kans., 1991—; v.p. Ministerial Alliance, Webb City, 1990-91. Mem. Sex Edn. Adv. Panel, Rogue River, 1986, Sch. Bd., 1987; crisis intervention counselor, Rogue River, 1986-88. Named Great Commn. Leader, Great Commission Fellow, Oreg. Pacific Dist. Ch. of the Nazarene, 1989. Mem. Christian Holiness Assn., Am. Family Assn., Serotoma (Colorado Springs), Lions. Republican. Office: Cen Ch of the Nazarene 1501 W 9th Coffeyville KS 67337 *It may be easy for me to converse with people. I may even have an excellent gospel proclamation and plan, but if I do not love them and accept them as they are, my evangelism has no integrity. People don't care how much I know until they know how much I care.*

PANNELL, RANDALL J., minister, educator; b. Dallas, Apr. 2, 1950; s. Dan M. and Betty J. (Cook) P.; m. Janet P. Davies, May 21, 1971 (div. Oct. 1983); children: Karen Marie, Nathan Andrew; m. Estella Lillian Kelley, Aug. 18, 1984. BA, Baylor U., 1972; MDiv, Southwestern Bapt. Theol. Sem., Ft. Worth, 1975; PhD, Southwestern Bapt. Theol. Sem., 1979; cert. in lang., Inst. de Lengua Espanol, San Jose, Costa Rica, 1980. Instr. Southwestern Bapt. Theol. Sem., Ft. Worth, 1976-79; asst. prof. Sem. Internat. Teol. Bapt., Buenos Aires, Argentina, 1980-83; acad. dean Am. Christian Coll., Houston, Tex., 1984-87; pastor Calvin Presbyn. Ch., Houston, 1987—; instr. Ammerman Enterprises, Stafford, Tex., 1986—. Author: (book) A Word from the Lord Just for You, 1987; book reviewer: Southwest Jour. Theology, 1977-79, Jour. Bibl. Lit. 1983-85; contbr. articles to profl. jours. Mem. Soc. Bibl. Lit., Cath. Bibl. Assn., Nat. Assn. Bapt. Profs. Religion. Home: 3916 Heathersage Ct Houston TX 77084 Office: Calvin Presbyn Ch 1782 W Sam Houston Pkwy N Houston TX 77043

PANNING, ARMIN, academic administrator. Pres. Wis. Luth. Sem., Mequon. Office: Wis Luth Sem 11831 N Seminary Dr 65W Mequon WI 53092*

PANOWICZ, SISTER MARY KAY, print shop executive, health care administrator; b. Grand Island, Nebr., Mar. 29, 1948; d. Albin Eugene and Barbara (Pysczynski) P. BA with honors, Mt. Marty Coll., 1971; Master of Selected Studies, U. S.D., 1979. Adminstrv. asst. Mt. Marty Coll., Yankton, S.D., 1971-74, asst. dir. pub. rels., 1974-81, instr. art. dept., 1980-85; mgr. print shop Sacred Heart Monastery, Yankton, 1981—; graphic art cons. Fedn. St. Gertrude, Crookston, Minn., 1979—. Two-person show of photographs, Mount Marty Coll., 1976, Bede Art Gallery, 1985. Trustee Sacred Heart Hosp., Yankton, 1982-89, chmn. bd. trustees, 1987-89; sec.-treas. bd. dirs. Benedictine Health System, Yankton, 1987—; sec. bd. dirs. Benedictine-Presentation Health Alliance, Yankton, 1987—; trustee Benedictine Health Ctrs., Canon City, Colo., 1990—. Democrat. Avocation: original fabric art work. Home: 1005 W 8th St Yankton SD 57078 Office: Convent Print Shop 1005 W 8th St Yankton SD 57078

PANTIN, GORDON ANTHONY, archbishop. Archbishop of Port of Spain Roman Cath. Ch., Trinidad and Tobago. Office: 27 Maraval Rd, Port of Spain Trinidad and Tobago*

PANUSKA, JOSEPH ALLAN, university president; b. Balt., July 3, 1927; s. Joseph William and Barbara Agnes (Preller) P. B.S., Loyola Coll., Balt., 1948; Ph.D., St. Louis U., 1958; S.T.L., Woodstock Coll., 1961; LL.D. (hon.), U. Scranton, 1974. Joined Society of Jesus, 1948; ordained priest Roman Catholic Ch., 1960; instr. dept. physiology Emory U. Sch. Medicine, 1962-63; asst. prof. biology Georgetown U., 1963-66, assoc. prof., 1966-72, prof., 1973; provincial, bd. dirs. Jesuit Conf. Md. Province (S.J.), 1973-79; acad. v.p., dean faculties, prof. biology Boston Coll., 1979-82; pres. U. Scranton, Pa., 1982—; mem. Pa. Commn. Ind. Colls. and Univs., 1982—, mem. exec. com., treas., 1987—, vice chmn., 1988-89, chair, 1990-91; mem. Pres.'s Commn., NCAA, 1989-90. Mem. editorial bd. Cryobiology, 1968-88, editor in chief, 1971-74; contbr. chpts. to books, articles to sci. research jours. Mem. corp. Am. Found. Biol. Rsch., 1967-85, pres. bd. dirs., 1974-79, v.p., 1979-83; trustee Loyola Coll., 1979-85, St. Joseph's U., 1979-84, U. Scranton, 1970-73, St. Peter's Coll., 1971-72, Woodstock Coll., 1973-76, Fordham U., 1982-88, Cambridge Ctr. for Social Studies, 1973-79 (pres. 1973-79), Corp. Roman Cath. Clergymen, 1973-79 (pres. 1973-79); bd. dirs., rector Jesuit Community at Georgetown U., 1970-73; bd. dirs. United Way Pa., 1985-87, Scranton Preparatory Sch., 1984-90; chmn. Pa. Commn. for Ind. Colls. and Univs., 1990-91. NIH postdoctoral trainee, 1962-63; Danforth Found. Harbison prize for disting. teaching, 1969; vis. fellow St. Edmunds Coll., Cambridge U., 1969. Mem. Am. Physiol. Soc., Soc. for Cryobiology, Soc. Exptl. Biology and Medicine, Assn. Jesuit Colls. and Univs. (bd. dirs. 1982—), Pa. Assn. Colls. and Univs. (exec. com., adv. com. to State Bd. Edn. 1990-91), Scranton C. of C. Office: U Scranton Office of Pres Scranton PA 18510 *In order to be happy in a leadership role and to succeed in it, I have to possess a sense of coherence with my life values. I also need to recognize that my own activity makes a real difference in the empowerment of others so that there is a multiplier effect which extends me beyond my own person and activity.*

PANZETTA, JOHN COSMO, clinical chaplain; b. Pulsano, Apulia, Italy, Feb. 22, 1941; came to U.S., 1970; s. Gaetano Cosimo and Maria Giuseppa (Barletta) P.; m. Joanne Panzetta, Mar. 14, 1970; children: Maria Grazia, John Cosmo Jr. BA in Bible, Cen. Bible Coll., Springfield, Mo., 1972; MA in Pastoral Studies, Fairfield (Conn.) U., 1977; MDiv, Yale U., 1979. Interpreter Lido Sylvana Camping, Pulsano, 1956-64, Recreation Motel, Pulsano, 1965-67; spl. interpreter Monopole De La Gare Hotel, Milano, Italy, 1968-69; quality control inspector Nat. Can., Danbury, Conn., 1972-79; sr. chaplain Sumter Correctional Inst., Bushnell, Fla., 1979—; adminstrv. chaplain Sumter Detention Ctr., Bushnell, 1987—; ministerial cons. Sumter Ministerial Assn., Bushnell, 1979—; cons. prison ministry Morris Cerullo World Evangelism, San Diego, 1990—; mem. commn. of chaplaincy Assemblies of God, Springfield, Mo., 1986-88. Vol. Fed. Correctional Inst., Danbury, 1972-79; mem. Sumter County Sheriff Dept., 1988—. Mem. Am. Chaplaincy Assn., Fla. Chaplaincy Assn., Fla. Coun. on Crime and Delinquency, Clin. Pastoral Edn. Assn. Republican. Avocations: bocci, golf, hiking, visiting historical places, museums. Home: Rte 1 Box B-3 Bushnell FL 33513-9744 Office: Sumter Correctional Inst PO Box 667 Hwy 476-B Bushness FL 33513-0667 *Right or wrong, apologize. If you are right, you gain a friend back. If you are wrong, you make peace with your friend. Either way you win.*

PAPADEMETRIOU, GEORGE CONSTANTINE, priest, director, educator; b. Thasos, Greece, Apr. 11, 1932; came to U.S., 1947; s. Constantine G. and Ourania C. (Katsifas) P.; m. Athanasia Antoniou, June 26, 1960; children: Dean, Jane, Tom. BTh, Holy Cross Orthodox Sem., 1959; MTh, Tex. Christian U., 1966; PhD, Temple U., 1977; MLS, Simmons Coll., 1983. Pastor Greek Orthodox Archdiocese, 1960—; libr. dir. Hellenic Coll., 1981—; assoc. prof. theology and philosophy Holy Cross Orthodox Sem., Brookline, Mass., 1978—. Mem. AHEPA, Mass. Commn. on Christian Unity, Orthodox Theol. Soc. Am., Am. Acad. Religion, Am. Theol. Libr. Assn. Office: Hellenic Coll 50 Goddard Ave Brookline MA 02146

PAPAFIL, THEODORE NICHOLAS, priest; b. Norfolk, Va., Jan. 16, 1958; s. Nicholas Theodore and Carolyn (Anthoulis) P.; m. Drucilla Arakas, Aug. 23, 1980; children: Kyriaki, Elizabeth, Nicholas. BA, Old Dominion U., 1979; MDiv, Holy Cross Seminary, Brookline, Mass., 1982. Ordained to ministry Greek Orthodox Ch. as deacon, 1981, as priest, 1982. Asst. priest Annunciation Cathedral, Atlanta, 1982-84; parish priest St. Paul, Savannah, Ga., 1984-86, Holy Trinity, Asheville, N.C., 1986-89; diocese youth dir. Diocese of Atlanta, 1989—; parish priest Holy Trnasfiguration, Marietta, Ga., 1989—. Home: 2376 Netherstone Dr Marietta GA 30066 Office: Holy Transfiguration PO Box 669834 Marietta GA 30066

PAPANDREA, FRANK DEMETRIO, minister, religion educator, college dean; b. Roselle, N.J., Feb. 25, 1947; s. Frank William and Alice (Dunham) P.; m. Georgette Balasic, July 18, 1970; children: Dawn, Franky. BA, Rutgers U., 1972; MDiv, Liberty Bapt. Theol. Sem., Lynchburg, Va., 1976; PhD, Calif. Grad. Sch. Theology, 1982. Ordained to ministry Ind. Bapt. Ch., 1976. Founder, pastor Union County Bapt. Ch., Clark, N.J., 1976—; prof., dean faculty Bible Coll. and Sem., India Theol. Sem., Clark, 1990—; dir. Priority One India, USA Missions, Clark, 1980—; speaker Sta. WAWZ Bapt. Beacon, Zarapheth, N.J., 1984—; TV ministry speaker Suburban Cable, East Orange, N.J., 1991—; dir. Christian Family Counseling Ctr., Clark, 1990—; gospel soloist Union County Bapt. Ch., N.J., 1976—; pres. N.J. Bapt. Bible Fellowship, 1988-89, sec., 1986-87. Author: Ecclesiology, 1986. With inf. U.S. Army, 1966-68, Vietnam. Classroom named in his honor India Theol. Sem., Bramavar, 1990. Republican. Office: Union County Bapt Ch 4 Valley Rd Clark NJ 07066

PAPE, ARNIS WESTON, minister; b. Portales, N.Mex., Dec. 24, 1950; s. Arnis Wilson and Lella Mae (Berry) P.; m. Lucena Ann Molzen, May 31, 1975; children: John Dayton, Jennifer Marie. BA in Psychology, U.N.Mex., 1974. Ordained to ministry Church of Christ, 1972. Assoc. minister Ch. of Christ, Plainview, Tex., 1974-76; pulpit minister Ch. of Christ, Artesia, N.Mex., 1976-85, Ft. Collins, Colo., 1985—; tchr. Pepperdine U., Malibu, 1991. Editor bull. Meadowlark Messenger, 1985—; contbr. articles to profl. jours.; author booklet: Happy Though Married, 1988. Co-founder Am. Children's Transplant Fund, Ft. Collins, 1987; mem. Parent Adv. Bd., Artesia, 1983-84; mem. pres.'s coun. Lubbock Christian U., 1985—. Recipient award for outstanding svc. Ch. of Christ, 1985. Avocations: photography, biking, camping, woodworking. Home: 2212 Shawnee Ct Fort Collins CO 80525 Office: Church of Christ 2810 Meadowlark Ave Fort Collins CO 80526 *A principle I have tried to hold to in my adult life is found in the old axiom, "Attitude is Everything". A positive mind brings a brighter idea, a more noble solution, and a happier day.*

PAPPALARDO, SALVATORE CARDINAL, archbishop of Palermo; b. Villafranca, Sicula, Sicily, Sept. 23, 1918. Ordained priest Roman Cath. Ch., 1941; entered diplomatic secretariat of state, 1947; titular archbishop of Miletus, 1966; pro-nuncio in Indonesia, 1966-69; pres. Pontifical Ecclesiastical Acad., 1969-70; archbishop of Palermo, 1970—; elevated to Sacred Coll. of Cardinals, 1973; titular ch. St. Mary Odigitria of the Sicilians; mem. Congregation of Oriental Chs., Congregation of Clergy. Address: Arcivescovado via Mateo, Bonello 2, 90134 Palermo Italy

PAPROCKI, THOMAS JOHN, priest, lawyer; b. Chgo., Aug. 5, 1952; s. John Henry and Veronica Mary (Bonat) P. BA, Loyola U., Chgo., 1974; student Spanish lang. study, Middlebury Coll., 1976, student Italian lang. study, 1987; M in Divinity, St. Mary of the Lake Sem., 1978; student Spanish lang. study, Instituto Cuannahuac, 1978; Licentiate in Sacred Theology, St. Mary of the Lake Sem., 1979; JD, DePaul U., 1981; JCD, Gregorian U., Rome, 1991. Bar: Ill. 1981, U.S. Dist. Ct. (no. dist.) Ill. 1981. Assoc. pastor St. Michael Ch., Chgo., 1978-83; pres. South Chgo. Legal Clinic, 1981-87, 91—, bd. dirs., 1987—, exec. dir., 1981-85; adminstr. St. Joseph Ch., Chgo., 1983-86; vice-chancellor Archdiocese of Chgo., 1985—; senator Presbyteral senate Archdiocese of Chgo., 1985-87; bd. dirs. Cath. Conf. Ill., 1985-87. Editorial Adv. Bd. Chicago Catholic Newspaper, 1984-85; contbr. articles to profl. jours. Bd. dirs. United Neighborhood Orgn., Chgo., 1982-85, S.E. Community Youth Svc. Bd., Chgo., 1985, Ctr. for Neighborhood Tech., Chgo., 1986-87. Fellow Leadership Greater Chgo.; mem. ABA, Ill. Bar Assn., Chgo. Bar Assn. (Maurice Weigle award 1985), Advs. Soc. Lawyers, Cath. Lawyers Guild, The Chgo. Jr. Assn. Commerce and Industry (Ten Outstanding Young Citizens award 1986), Pi Sigma Alpha, DePaul U. Alumni Assn. Avocations: hockey, running, reading. Home: 2315 W Augusta Blvd Chicago IL 60622 Office: Archdiocese of Chgo 155 E Superior PO Box 1979 Chicago IL 60690

PAQUETTE, MARIO, priest; b. Montreal, Que., Can., Apr. 9, 1938; s. Rynaldo and Antoinette (Venne) P. BA, U. Montreal, 1959, STL, 1963; JCD, Gregorian U., Rome, 1971. Ordained priest Roman Cath. Ch., 1963. Sec. to archbishop of Montreal, 1963-68; asst. Office for Ethnic Communities, Montreal, 1971-72; adv. Eccles. Regional Tribunal, Montreal, 1971-75, judge, 1975—; vice chancellor Archdiocese of Montreal, 1975-84, episcopal vicar and dir. Office for Ethnic Communities, 1984—; rep. Cath. bishops to Internat. Cath. Migration Commn., Geneva, 1977-80; pres. Standing Conf. Cath. Orgns. Concerned for Refugees, 1978-80, Cath. Immigration Svcs., Montreal, 1982-85, Can. Found. for Refugees, Ottawa, Ont., 1981-84; mem. consultative bd. Min. Immigration, Que., 1979-82; named prelate of honor Holy See, The Vatican, 1988. Author: Priests' Senates in Quebec (in French), 1973; contbr. articles to periodicals and newspapers. Mem. Can. Canon Law Soc. Home: 1071 rue Cathedrale, Montreal, PQ Canada H3B 2V4 Office: Roman Cath Archdiocese, 2000 Sherbrooke St W, Montreal, PQ Canada H3H 1G4

PARDEE, LENORA MAXINE, minister, director; b. Ravenswood, W.Va., July 1, 1937; d. Ross Erwin and Leora Inez (Brewer) Grimes; m. Pierre James Pardee, Sept. 4, 1957 (div. 1972); children: James, Martha Pardee Carlson, Robert. BS in Edn., Youngstown (Ohio) State U., 1967; MDiv, Pitts. Sem., 1986. Ordained to ministry Presbyn. Ch., 1986. With J.G. Pardee Co., Youngstown, 1967-72; tchr. East Liverpool (Ohio) City Sch., 1972-74; with computer dept. Hall China Co., East Liverpool, 1974-84; ministry, dir. Lake Erie Presbytery-Presbyn. Area Ministry, Sugargrove, Pa., 1985-87, Lehigh Presbytery-N.W. Ministry, Mahanoy City, Pa., 1987—; bd. dirs. ecumenical com. for continuing edn. MOravian Sem., Bethlehem, Pa., 1988—, Micah Project, Allentown, Pa. Commr. Boy Scouts Am., E. Liverpool, 1976-83. Mem. Mahanoy Area Administerial Assn. (pres. 1989—), AAUW. Democrat. Avocations: camping, painting. Home and Office: 38 W Mahanoy Ave Mahanoy City PA 17948

PARE, MARIUS, bishop; b. Montmagny, Que., Can., May 22, 1903; s. Joseph and Lucie (Boulet) P. BA, Laval U., 1927. Ordained priest Roman Cath. Ch., 1927. Tchr. dir. Coll. Sainte Anne de la Pocatiere, 1927-52, rector, 1952-56, aux. bishop, 1956, coadjutor bishop, 1960; bishop Chicoutimi, Que., 1961-79; ret., 1979; mem. commn. for clergy Can. Conf. Caths.; mem. commn. edn. 2d Vatican Coun.; mem., cons. Sacred Congregation Cath. Edn., Rome. Decorated knight grand cross Order Equestre du St. Sepulchre de Jerusalem. Mem. KC (4th degree). Home: 927 E Jacques-Cartier St, Chicoutimi, PQ Canada G7H 2A3

PARIS, PETER JUNIOR, religion educator, minister; b. New Glasgow, N.S., Can., May 30, 1933; s. Freeman Archibald and Violet Agatha (Jewell) P.; m. Shirley Ann McMillen, May 13, 1961; children: Valerie Lynn ToKunbo, Peter Brett. BA, Acadia U., Wolfville, N.S., 1956, BD, 1958; MA, U. Chgo., 1969, PhD, 1975; DD (hon.), McGill U., 1989, Acadia U., 1990. Ordained minister African United Bapt. Assn. N.S. Gen. sec. U. Alta. chpt. Student Christian Movement Can., Edmonton, 1958-61, spl. travelling sec., Toronto, 1964-65; nat. travelling sec. Student Christian Movement Nigeria, Ibadan, 1961-64; instr. urban studies Associated Coll. of Mid-West, Chgo., 1969-70; instr. ethics and soc. Howard U. Div. Sch., Washington, 1970-72; asst. prof. ethics and soc. Vanderbilt U. Div. Sch., Nashville, 1972-77, assoc. prof., 1977-83, prof., 1983-85; Elmer G. Homrighausen prof. Christian social ethics Princeton (N.J.) Theol. Seminary, 1985—; sr. fellow Mathey Coll., Princeton U., 1988—; cons. Assn. Theol. Schs., Indpls., 1986—, W.E.B. DuBois Inst., Harvard U., 1988—; lectr. U. S.Africa, Pretoria, Aug., 1988; fellow W.E.B. DuBois Inst., Harvard U., 1990. Author: Black Leaders in Conflict, 1978 (excerpts in Congrl. Record May, 1981), The Social Teaching of the Black Churches, 1985; co-editor: Justice and the Holy, 1989; mem. editorial bd. Soundings: An Interdisciplinary Jour., The Jour. Religion; author essays, chpts. in books. Ford Found. fellow Ctr. Urban Studies, U. Chgo., 1968-70, Woodrow Wilson fellow, 1990; rsch. grantee Lilly Endowment, Vanderbilt U., NRC, Princeton Theol. Seminary. Fellow Soc. for Values Higher Edn.; mem. Am. Acad. Religion (assoc. dir. 1983-85), Soc. Christian Ethics (bd. dirs. 1977-82, v.p. 1990, pres. 1991), Soc. Study of Black Religion (founding mem.). Democrat. Office: Princeton Theol Sem Dept of Theology CN 821 Princeton NJ 08542

PARIZO, KEVIN DOUGLAS, church organist, educator; b. Burlington, Vt., Dec. 28, 1952; s. Matthew Mayo and Elizabeth Ann Parizo; m. Garreth Ann Lundrigan, June 26, 1987; children: Coughlan, Tierney. BA, Johnson (Vt.) Coll., 1974; MusM, Montreal Conservatory Music, Que., Can., 1974; Mus M, U. Mass., 1975. Cert. tchr., Vt. Organist, dir. music Ch. of Assumption, Middlebury, 1975—; organist, accompanist chorale, adj. faculty St. Michael's Coll., Winooski, Vt., 1975—; pvt. tchr., Middlebury, 1975—; mem. Diocesan Luturgical Commn., Burlington, 1991—. Composer: Mass of Assumption, 1984, also numerous ch. choral and organ works, 1975—. Bd. dirs. French Cultural Commn. Vt., Montpelier, 1988—, Humane Soc. Addison County, Middlebury, 1989-91. Memm. Am. Guild Organists, Nat. Assn. Pastoral Musicians (dir. music ministries div.), Royal Can. Coll. Organists, KC. Roman Catholic. Home: 57 Seymour St Middlebury VT 05735 Office: Ch of Assumption 19 College St Middlebury VT 05753

PARK, ANDREW SUNG, religion educator; b. Woolsan, Korea, Dec. 29, 1951; s. Jae Ki and Chong Hui (Kim) P.; m. Sun Ok Myong, Apr. 29, 1985; children: Amos Daniel, Thomas Micah. BTh, Seoul Meth. Sem., 1973; MDiv, Iliff Sch. Theology, 1977; MA, Claremont Sch. Theology, 1980; PhD, Grad. Theol. Union, 1985. Minister Korean Christian Ch., Colorado Springs, Colo., 1973-77, Calvary Korean United Meth. Ch., San Francisco, 1985-87; asst. prof. Sch. Theology, Claremont, Calif., 1987—; trustee Clinebell Inst., 1987—. Contbr. articles to profl. jours. Mem. Am. Acad. Religion, Buddhist-Christian Studies, Korean Studies, The Korean Soc. for Religious Studies in N.Am. Democrat. Office: Sch Theology Claremont 1325 N College Ave Claremont CA 91711

PARK, DABNEY GLENN, JR., management consultant; b. Electra, Tex., Aug. 21, 1941; s. Dabney Glenn and Georgia J. (Johnson) P.; m. Betty Kirksey, Aug. 31, 1963; children: Morgan Elizabeth, Province Elizabeth. BA, U. Tex., 1963; MA, Tulane U., 1965, PhD, 1971. Asst. prof. history U. Cin., 1967-72; exec. asst. to pres. S.I. Community Coll., N.Y., 1972-73; exec. dir. external degree program Fla. Internat. U., Miami, 1973-77; exec. v.p. Higher Edn. Mgmt. Inst., Coconut Grove, Fla., 1977-83; v.p. Thoughtware, Inc., Coconut Grove, 1983-84; pres. Performance, Inc., Coral Gables, Fla., 1984—; cons. Nat. Episcopal Ch., various colls. and univs., businesses. Author: The Care of Learning: Stewardship of Resources for Theological Education in the Episcopal Church, 1990; co-author: Strategic Decision Making, 1988, Strategic Analysis, 1990; author pamphlets, articles, exec. tng. materials. Trustee, St. Stephen's Sch., Coconut Grove, 1978-82, Seabury-Western Theol. Sem., Evanston, Ill., 1983—; mem. standing com. Episcopal Diocese S.E. Fla., 1980-82, exec. officer, 1991—; founding chmn. Trinity Episcopal Sch., Miami, 1982-86. Fulbright fellow, Italy, 1966-67. Mem. Assn. Governing Bds., Assn. Higher Edn., Medieval Acad. Am., Dante Soc. Am., Am. Soc. Ch. History. Episcopalian. Avocations: tennis, racquetball. Home: 3920 Durango St Coral Gables FL 33134 Office: Performance Inc Ste 302 4649 Ponce de Leon Blvd Coral Gables FL 33146

PARK, EUNG-CHUN, religious educator; b. Seoul, July 21, 1958; came to U.S., 1984; s. Young-Hwan and Jung-Sun (Chung) P.; m. Young-Hee Kim, Sept. 25, 1982; children: Eui-Sun, Eun-Gyul. BA, Seoul Nat. U., 1981; MDiv, Presbyn. Theol. Seminary, Seoul, 1984; STM, Yale U., 1986; PhD, U. Chgo., 1991. Lectr. Presbyn. Theol. Coll., 1983-84; interim min. New Haven (Conn.) Presbyn. Ch., 1984-86; youth pastor Sae-Kwang Presbyn. Ch., Des Plaines, Ill., 1986—; libr. staff Yale Divinity Libr., New Haven, 1984-86; adj. prof. McCormick Theol. Seminary, Chgo., 1989—. Honorary pres. fellow Prebyn. Theol. Seminary, 1983, Two Bros. fellow Yale U., 1986; Century scholar U. Chgo., 1986. Mem. Soc. Bibl. Lit. Office: McCormick Theol Seminary 5555 S Woodlawn Ave Chicago IL 60637 *For those to whom life is a pilgrimage, every day is replete with newness because each day is part of the untrodden road that leads to what they are ultimately heading toward.*

PARK, FRANCIS WOOD, III, minister; b. Rochester, Pa., Aug. 15, 1932; s. Francis Wood and Regina Ruth (Rees) P.; m. Marie Suzane Jacobs, Aug. 29, 1953; children: Andrew Wood, Ann Margaret, Catherine Jane. BA, Coll. of Wooster, 1954; MDiv, Pitts. Theol. Sem., 1957. Ordained to ministry Presbyn. Ch., 1957. Pastor 1st Presbyn. Ch., Fredericktown, Ohio, 1957-60, Northminster Presbyn. Ch., North Canton, Ohio, 1960-65; pastor, head of staff 1st Presbyn. Ch., Elmira, N.Y., 1965-70, Covenant Presbyn. Ch., Columbus, Ohio, 1970-83; pastor Faith Presbyn. Ch., Sun City, Ariz., 1984—; bd. dirs. Pitts. Theol. Sem., 1989—, Austin Presbyn. Theol. Sem. Ctr. for Ministry with Older Adults, Sun City, 1989; mem. presbytery coun. Grand Canyon Presytery, Ariz., 1986—, chmn. planning, 1986—; mem. Gen. Assembly spl. com. on structure rev., 1991—. Author: Pray With Me, 1987. Chmn. adv. coun. for Urban Renewal, North Canton, 1964-65, dir. Young Citizens Found., 1964-65; chmn. County Coun. on the Aging, Elmira, 1967-70; dir. Newtown Towers, Elmira, 1969-70; mem. NW Mental Health Svcs. Bd., Columbus, 1975; v.p. Sun Cities Area Children's Found., Sun City, 1991—. Mem. Rotary (chmn. well-being com. Sun City-Lakeview club). Home: 10113 Pine Spring Dr Sun City AZ 85373 Office: Faith Presbyn Ch 16000 Del Webb Blvd Sun City AZ 85351 *Someday we may mature enough to acknowledge the true value of maturity. The most valued resource of our nation, next to the Library of Congress, is the wisdom, skill and experience of America's older adults...and it's to be found in every community. Anyone who tells an older adult he is over the hill and has nothing to contribute is committing homicide. Any older adult who says he is over the hill and has nothing to contribute is committing suicide.*

PARK, HOWARD MITCHELL, priest; b. International Falls, Minn., Jan. 27, 1922; s. Mike and Lydia (Pullianen) P.; m. Shirley Danielson, Sept., 1952; children: Sharman, Diedre, Karl, Erik, Kirsten; m. Dorothy Lew Wallace, July, 1983. Student, U. Alaska, 1950-52, U. B.C., 1952-56; BS, SUNY, Albany, 1974; diplomate in divinity, Ch. Divinity Sch. of the Pacific, 1981. Ordained priest Episcopal Ch., 1982. Engr. Dept. Aviation, Terr. of Alaska, 1951-53; project engr. Morrison-Knudsen Co., 1950-60; v.p., gen. mgr. Saunders, Inc., Anchorage, 1961-65, No. Ventures, Inc., Anchorage, 1961-65; mgr. heavy constrn. Braund, Inc., Anchorage, 1968-73; spl. asst. Occupational Safety and Health Adminstrn., State of Alaska, Anchorage, 1973-74, Dept. Health, State of Alaska, Anchorage, 1974-75; vicar St. Barnabas Mission Ch., Mt. Shasta, Calif., 1982—; chmn. Commn. on Stewardship, Episcopal Diocese No. Calif., 1983-85. Served to 1st lt. USAF, 1942-50, ETO. Decorated D.F.C., Purple Heart with cluster, Air medal with 18 clusters; recipient Presdl. citation with cluster, 1944-45. Mem. Order St. Luke (chaplain 1985-88). Democrat. Lodges: Shriners, Masons. Avocations: woodworking, shop, writing. Office: St Barnabas Episcopal Ch PO Box 1350 Mount Shasta CA 96067

PARK, JOHN FAIRCLOTH, cantor; b. Greenville, S.C., Apr. 15, 1930; s. John Andrew and M. Inez (Faircloth) P. Student, Furman U., 1947-50; BA, U. N.C., 1951, MA, 1954; student, Cin. Conservatory of Music, 1954-55; EdD, Columbia U., 1962. Cantor Temple Emanuel, Kingston, N.Y., 1967—; chmn. div. humanities and social scis. Ulster County Community Coll., Stone Ridge, N.Y., 1963-85. Composer various works for cantor and cantor and choir. Mem. Am. Conf. Cantors. Home: 69 Wilson Ave Kingston NY 12401-2111 Office: Temple Emanuel 243 Albany Ave Kingston NY 12401

PARK, TAYLOR RICHARD, clergyman; b. Quincy, Fla., Aug. 7, 1959; s. Edwin Taylor and Oneida (Shaw) P.; m. Deborah Marie Park, July 11, 1981; children: Joshua, Elizabeth, Caleb, Hannah. BS, Southeastern Bible Coll., 1983. Ordained to ministry, 1983. Youth pastor Grace Bible Ch., Birmingham, Ala., 1981-83; personnel dir. Inner City Impact, Chgo., 1983-86, ctr. dir., 1986-87; interim pastor Logan Square First Bapt. Ch., Chgo., 1987; assoc. pastor/youth Springville Rd. Community Ch., Birmingham, Ala., 1987—; area coord. Sonlife Ministries, Chgo., 1988—; chaplain Hewitt-Trussville High Sch. Football, Birmingham, Ala., 1988—.

PARKE, CLIFFORD THOMAS, minister; b. Kansas City, Mo., Jan. 24, 1936; s. Edgar Lloyd and Lula (Cox) P.; m. Alma Nell Logsdon, June 26, 1955; children: Susan N. Meyer, Janice L. Saleheshtehardi, Deborah Ruth, Sarah Kay. BA, Eureka (Ill.) Coll., 1958; MDiv, Christian Theol. Sem., Indpls., 1963; MA, St. Mary's U., 1986; postgrad., Drew U., 1990—. Ordained to ministry Christian Ch. (Disciples of Christ), 1963. Minister Bellflower (Ill.) Christian Ch., 1964-72, First Christian Ch., Knoxville, Ill., 1972-78; sr. minister First Christian Ch., Great Bend, Kans., 1978-81, Woodlawn Christian Ch., San Antonio, Tex., 1981-86; dir. devel. Helping Hands Lifeline Found., San Antonio, 1986-88; sr. minister First Christian Ch., Wilmington, Del., 1988—; cons. Inman Christian Ctr., San Antonio, 1986-88; v.p. N.E. Parish Coun., Wilmington, 1990-91, pres., 1991—; sec. Christian Coun. Del., Wilmington, 1990—; mem. outreach com. Christian Ch., Capital Area, Chevy Chase, Md., 1989—. Columnist: Knoxville (Ill.) Journ., 1973-78; writer: (advt. material) Bloomington (Ill.) Broadcasting (Pen and Mike award for Outstanding Radio Script 1971); contbr. articles to profl. jours. Cons. Message To The Media, Inc., Montchanin, Del., 1990-91. Recipient Canfield Meml. scholarship Christian Theol. Seminary, Indpls., 1962; named to Outstanding Young Men of Am., 1968. Mem. Capital Area Ministers Assn., Nat. Assn. Christian Counselors, Nat. Evangelism Assn. of Christian Ch. Republican. Home: 241 Plymouth Rd Fairfax Wilmington DE 19803 Office: First Christian Church 2848 Grubb Rd Wilmington DE 19703

PARKER, BARRY LYNN, minister; b. San Marcos, Tex., July 2, 1958; s. Leonard Keith and Yvonne (Dennis) Parker; m. Mary Ann McCarn, May 23, 1980; children: Timothy, Darwin. Cert. Religious Theology, Ala. Christian Sch. Religion, Montgomery, 1986. Minister Ch. of Christ, Baytown, Tex., 1985-86, Tishomingo, Okla., 1986-87, Tyler, Tex., 1987-88; minister/missionary Ch. of Christ, Roanoke, Va., 1988-91, Mathis, Tex., 1991—. Author: (tract) Divorce and Remarriage: Some Emotional Arguments Considered, 1986, 90; contbr. articles to profl. jours. Home: Rte 11 PO Box 194a Roanoke VA 24019-9803 Office: Church of Christ 407 E Rockport Mathis TX 78368

PARKER, CAROLINE JANE FAIRCHILD, church secretary; b. Moselle, Miss., Feb. 23, 1938; d. Eleven Everett and Marie Antionette (Sellers) Fairchild; m. James Gary Parker Sr., June 5, 1958; children: Dianna Lynn Parker Perez, James Gary Jr. Student, Jones Jr. Coll., Ellisville, Miss., 1955-57. Sec. West Ellisville Bapt. Ch., Ellisville, 1975—; pres. Jones County Bapt. Secs. Assn., Laurel, Miss., 1989-91. Mem. Miss. Bapt. Assn. Republican. Office: West Ellisville Bapt Ch 1108 B Ave Ellisville MS 39437-2014

PARKER, CHARLES ARTHUR, association executive; b. Mpls., July 2, 1961; s. John Elliot and Susan Harriet (Flemming) P.; m. Constance Angela Wilkinson, June 9, 1985. BA, George Washington U., 1983; MDiv., Wesley Theol. Sem., 1987. Assoc. pastor Cape St. Claire United Meth. Ch., Annapolis, Md., 1985-88; exec. dir. Bread for the City, Washington, 1988—. Mem. Mayor's Commn. on Food, Nutrition and Health, Washington, 1988—. Democrat. Office: Bread for the City 1305 14th St NW Washington DC 20005

PARKER, EVERETT CARLTON, clergyman; b. Chgo., Jan. 17, 1913; s. Harry Everett and Lillian (Stern) P.; m. Geneva M. Jones, May 5, 1939; children: Ruth A. (Mrs. Peter Weiss), Eunice L. (Mrs. George Kolczun, Jr.), Truman E. A.B., U. Chgo., 1935; B.D. magna cum laude, Chgo. Theol. Sem., 1943, Blatchford fellow, 1944-45, D.D., 1964; D.D., Catawba Coll., Salisbury, N.C., 1958; L.H.D., Fordham U., 1978, Tougaloo Coll., 1987. Pastor Waveland Ave. Congl. Christian Ch., 1943; asst. pub. service and war program mgr. NBC, 1943-45; founder-dir. Protestant Radio Commn., 1945-50; lectr. communication Yale Div. Sch., 1946-58, dir. communications research project, 1950-54; dir. Office Communication United Ch. Christ, 1954-83; N.Y. corr. Christian Century mag., 1956-63, editor-at-large, 1963-71; editor-at-large Channels of Communication Mag., 1983-84; sr. research assoc., adj. prof. Fordham U., 1983—; chmn. broadcasting and film commn. Nat. Coun. Chs., 1969-72, mem. gen. bd., 1966-72; chair Study Commn. on Theology, Edn. and Electronic Media, 1985-87; treas. Found. for Minority Interests in Media, 1985—, Hispanic Telecommunications Network, 1986—; mem. adv. com. on advanced TV svcs., Consumer Adv. Group FCC, 1988—. Producer-dir.: nat. TV programs including series Off to Adventure, 1956, Tangled World, 1965; producer: motion pictures Tomorrow?, 1962, The Procession, 1961, The Pumpkin Coach, 1960; originator: series Six American Families, PBS-TV, 1977; Author: Religious Radio, 1948, Film Use in the Church, 1953, The Television-Radio Audience and Religion, 1955, Religious Television, 1961, (with others) Television, Radio, Film for Churchmen, 1969, Fiber Optics to the Home: The Changing Future of Cable, TV and The Telephone, 1989. Recipient Human Relations award Am. Jewish Com., 1966, Faith and Freedom award Religious Heritage Found., 1966, 77, Alfred I. DuPont-Columbia U. award pub. service in broadcasting, 1969; Roman Cath. Broadcasters Gabriel award pub. service, 1970; Lincoln U. award significant contbn. human relations, 1971; Racial Justice award Com. for Racial Justice, United Ch. Christ, 1973; Ch. Leadership award Council for Christian Social Action, 1973; Public Service award Black Citizens for a Fair Media, 1979, Pioneer award World Assn. for Christian Communication, 1988. Club: Yale (N.Y.C.). Home: 11 Midland Ave White Plains NY 10606 Office: Fordham University Dept Communications Bronx NY 10458

PARKER, HAROLD W., minister; b. Ruffin, N.C., Oct. 28, 1924; s. James Burlie and Sallie Mae (Dove) P.; m. Blanche Allene, Mar. 7, 1931 (dec. 1983); children: Harold Lane, Karen, Trudy; m. Vivian King, Aug. 1, 1985. Student, Peidmont Bible Coll., Winston-Salem, Fruitland Bible Coll., Hendersonville, N.C.; DSL, Bethany Bible Coll., Dothan, Ala. Ordained to ministry, Bapt. Ch. Minister North Coolzemer (N.C.) Bapt. Ch., 1946-49, Antioch Bapt. Ch., Linoolton, N.C., 1949-50, Torentine Bapt. Ch., Mocksville, N.C., 1950-52, Calvary Bapt. Ch., Toccoa, 1952-55, Westside Bapt. Ch., Maiden, N.C., 1952-57, Landis (N.C.) Bapt. Ch., 1957-62, Grove St. Bapt. Ch., Danville, Va., 1962-67, Amity Hills Bapt. Ch., Asheboro, N.C., 1967-83, Unity Bapt. Ch., Kannapolis, N.C., 1984—. With USN, 1942-44. Home: 1721 Raleigh Rd Lexington NC 27292

PARKER, JAMES FLOYD, minister, pension fund executive; b. Ann Arbor, Mich., Nov. 2, 1946; s. Ivan William and Elnor (Coles) P.; m. Sharon Kay Metty, June 14, 1969; children: Ryan Christopher, Brent Eugene, Scott Coles. B in Bus. Adminstrn., U. Mich., 1968; MDiv, Garrett-Evang. Theol. Sem., Evanston, Ill., 1971; postgrad., U. Pa., 1981; DD (hon.), Adrian Coll., 1987. Campus minister, intern Northwestern U., Evanston, 1968-69, U. Ill. at Chgo., 1969-70; asst. minister Batavia (Ill.) United Meth. Ch., 1970-71; adminstrv. trainee United Meth. Ch. Gen. Bd. Pensions, Evanston, 1971-72, asst. gen. sec., 1972-75, asst. actuary, 1976-78, assoc. gen. sec., 1978-81, treas., 1982-86, gen. sec., 1987—. Sec. MABC Credit Union, Evanston, 1972-78; chair investment com. 1st United Meth. Ch., Arlington Heights, Ill., 1989—; mem. exec. com. Ch. Pensions Conf., 1987—; mem. steering com. Ch. Alliance, 1987—. Mem. U. Mich. Alumni Assn., Phi Kappa Phi, Beta Gamma Sigma. Avocations: church choir, volleyball, soccer coaching. Home: 2529 RFD Long Grove IL 60047 Office: Gen Bd of Pensions United Meth Ch 1200 Davis St Evanston IL 60201

PARKER, MATTHEW, organization administrator; b. Cin., Nov. 14, 1945; s. Matt and Ruth Parker; m. Karon Lanier, Aug. 8, 1981; children: Matthew Jr., Tiffany, Michael. Diploma in Gen. Gigle, Grand Rapids Sch. Bible-Music, 1969; BA in Sociology, Wheaton Coll., 1977; MA in Edn. Adminstrn., U. Detroit, 1987. Mem. staff Black campus ministry and athletes in action Campus Crusade for Christ, 1971-72; dir. summer program Detroit Afro Am. Mission, 1978-79; adminstr. J. Allen Caldwell Pvt. Schs., 1979-81; founder, dir. urban ministry program, instr. cross culture William Tyndale Coll., 1981-84, assoc. v.p. urban acad. affairs, asst. prof. urban affairs, 1985-88; pres. Inst. for Black Family Devel., Detroit, 1989—; founder, pastor Great Commission Community Ch. (name now Hamilton Missionary Bapt. Ch.), 1979-85; founder, dir. Nat. Summit on Black Ch. Devel., 1984, 86, 90; chmn. Congress on Evangelizing Black Am., Atlanta, 1985-88; Bible tchr. Southfield Bible Study; bd. dirs. Christian Rsch. and Devel., 1986-87; mem. devel. of ch. planning strategy Calvary Bapt. Ch. and Afro Am. Mission, 1979-85; devel. mgmt. and fin. systems Mendelhall Ministries, 1979-85; active Detroit Youth for Christ; conf. in field. Pub. book: Black Church Development, 1986; editor: The Black Family: Past, Present, Future, 1991. Trustee Bryan Coll.; mem. Religious Alliance Against Pornography. Mem. Nat. Religious Broadcasters. Home: 15151 Faust Detroit MI 48223 Office: Inst for Black Family Devel 16776 Southfield Rd Detroit MI 48235

PARKER, PIERSON, minister, religion educator; b. Shanghai, China, May 27, 1905; s. Alvin Pierson and Susie Estelle (Williams) P.; m. Mildred Ruth Sorg, June 12, 1933; 1 son, Peter Pierson. A.B., U. Calif., 1927; student, So. Meth. U., 1928-29; M.A., Pacific Sch. Religion, 1933, Th.D. magna cum laude, 1934; S.T.D., Ch. Div. Sch. of Pacific, 1964. Ordained to ministry Congregational Ch., 1936, Episcopal Ch., 1944; instr. Bibl. lang. and lit. Pacific Sch. Religion, 1934-36; pastor North Congl. Ch., Berkeley, Calif., 1936-44; St. Andrew's Episc. Ch., Oakland, Calif., 1944-47; pres. No. Calif. Congl. Conf., 1938-39; lectr. Bibl. lit. Ch. Div. Sch. Pacific, 1940-43, instr., 1943-44, asst. prof., 1944-47, assoc. prof., 1947-49; Glorvina Rossell Hoffman prof. N.T. lit. and interpretation Gen. Theol. Sem., N.Y.C., 1949-74; sub-dean Gen. Theol. Sem., 1972-74; chaplain to seminarians Diocese of Los Angeles, 1974-83; disting. prof.-in-residence Cathedral of St. John the Divine, N.Y.C., 1975; prof. N.T. Grad. Sch. Theology, U. of South, 1951-52, 54-55, 56-57, 58-60, 67-69, 71-74; priest-in-charge Trinity Cathedral, Newark, 1953-54; research scholar Oxford U., 1957; lectr. N.T., St. Augustine's Coll., Canterbury, Eng., 1955; seminar asso. Columbia U.; vis. prof. Pacific Sch. of Religion, Ch. Div. Sch. Pacific, 1965, 1966, Seminario del Caribe, 1970, U. of South, 1975, Bloy Episc. Sch. Theology, 1978-79; priest-in-charge Ch. of Holy Spirit, Nice, France, 1962, St. Helena's Ch., Istanbul, Turkey, 1969; canon Cathedral Ch. of St. Paul, Los Angeles, 1977-81, Diocese of Los Angeles, 1981—; assoc. rector St. Ambrose Ch., Claremont, Calif., 1990—. Author: Interpreters' Bible (vol. on Deuteronomy), 1951, (with H.H. Shires, G. E. Wright) The Gospel Before Mark, 1953, Inherit the Promise, 1957, Christ Our Hope, 1958, Meditations on the Life of Christ, 1959, Good News in Matthew, 1976; co-author: New Synoptic Studies, 1983; mem. editorial bd.: Anglican Theol. Rev., 1949, Jour. Bibl. Lit., 1960-74; contbr. religious publs., Ency. American. Mem. Studiorum Novi Testamenti Societas, Soc. Bibl. Lit. (pres. Pacific Coast sect. 1946-48, mem. council 1944, v.p. Middle Atlantic sect. 1959-60, pres. 1960-61, archivist 1976-83, nat. hon. pres. 1978), Pacific Theol. Group, Inst. Antiquity and Christianity, Pacific Sch. Religion Alumni Assn. (pres. 1943-46), Alpha Sigma Phi. Home: 650 W Harrison Ave Claremont CA 91711

PARKER, RICHARD GARLAND, minister; b. Decatur, Ala., Feb. 15, 1956; s. Charles Garland and Helen Ruth (Pruitt) P.; m. Celinda Kay Wilkerson, May 14, 1983; children: Andrew Joseph, Hannah Catherine. BA, Samford U., 1978; MA, Southwestern Bapt. Theol. Sem., 1983. Ordained to ministry Bapt. Ch., 1990. Min. youth activities 1st Bapt. Ch., Monroeville, Ala., 1978-80; min. youth 1st Bapt. Ch., Henrietta, Tex., 1981-83; min. to single adults Colonial Hts. Bapt. Ch., Jackson, Miss., 1983-91; min. to singles/internats. Olive Bapt. Ch., Pensacola, Fla., 1991—; recreation com. mem. Bapt. Assn., Jackson, 1987-88. Named Outstanding Young Man in Am., 1985. Mem. Miss. Bapt. Religious Edn. Assn. Republican. Home: 4111 Lyric Ln Pensacola FL 32514 Office: Olive Bapt Ch 1836 Olive Rd Pensacola FL 32514

PARKER, THOMAS C., minister; b. Endicott, N.Y., Apr. 27, 1959; s. Charles H. and Phylis T. (Trenberth) P.; m. Gayle Behan, Nov. 26, 1979; children: Luke, Benjamin, Zachary. BA, U. Ariz., 1981; MDiv, Princeton Theol. Sem., 1984; PhD, ABD, U. Sheffield, Eng. Assoc. pastor Scottsdale (Ariz.) Presbyn. Ch., 1984-87; area dir. Fuller Theol. Sem. Ariz. Extension, Phoenix, 1988—. Internat. Rotary scholar, 1987-88. Mem. Soc. Bibl. Lit., Nat. Assn. of Profs. of Hebrew. Office: Fuller Theol Semluary 3300 W Camelback Phoenix AZ 85017

PARKER, THOMAS DUNKLIN, religion educator; b. L.A., Dec. 22, 1931; s. Thomas Dunklin and Elizabeth (Jacobi) P.; m. Geraldine Jeffery, Aug. 1, 1952 (div. 1976); children: Katherine, David, Jeffery, John, Michael; m. Katherine Eudora Campbell, Sept. 16, 1978. BA, L.A. State Coll., 1954; BD, San Francisco Theol. Sem., 1957; PhD, Princeton Theol. Sem., 1965. Ordained to ministry Presbyn. Ch., 1957. Minister Orenco (Oreg.) Presbyn. Ch., 1957-60, United Presbyn. Ch. of Millstone, Perrineville, N.J., 1961-64; faculty McCormick Theol. Sem., Chgo., 1965—; mem. theology com. Caribbean and North Am. chpt. World Alliance Reformed Chs., 1970-90. Editor: Christian Theology: A Case-Method Approach, 1976, Peace, War, and God's Justice, 1989. Rockefeller Doctoral fellow, 1964, Faculty fellow Am. Assn. Theol. Schs., 1970. Mem. Am. Theol. Soc. (former pres.), Am. Acad. Religion. Office: McCormick Theol Sem 5555 S Woodlawn Chicago IL 60637

PARKS, DAVID SCOTT, clergyman; b. Hagerstown, Md., Jan. 1, 1963; s. William L. and Ann (Moon) P.; m. Tamela Geohagan, May 26, 1990. BA in Bus. Mgmt., N.C. State U., 1985, BA in Econs., 1985; MDiv with Christian Edn., Southeastern Bapt. Theol. Sem., 1989. Ordained to ministry Bapt. Ch., 1987. Summer missionary So. Bapt. Ch. Home Mission Bd., San Francisco, 1984; summer youth worker Arlington Bapt. Ch., Charlotte, N.C., 1987; assoc. pastor Flat Rock Bapt. Ch., Louisburg, N.C., 1987-89; assoc. minister The Hill Bapt. Ch., Augusta, Ga., 1989—; associational youth cons. Tar River Bapt. Assn., Louisburg, 1988-89; associational fin. com. Augusta (Ga.) Bapt. Assn., 1989—, chmn. campus ministry com., 1990—. Mem. So. Bapt. Religious Edn. Assn., Augusta Bapt. Religious Edn. Assn. Home: 305 Indian Trail Ct Augusta GA 30907 Office: The Hill Bapt Ch 2165 Kings Way Augusta GA 30904

PARKS, ELMER L., minister emeritus; b. New Brighton, Pa., Mar. 6, 1916; s. Elmer Lewis Parks and Helen (Roberts) Reich; m. Esther E. Parks, Nov. 25, 1944; children: Mary Kathleen Young, Eleanor Ann Chain, Richard Lewis. AB, Geneva Coll., 1937, DD (hon.), 1950; BD, Drew U., Madison, N.J., 1940, MA, 1945. Assoc. pastor Emory United Meth. Ch., Pitts., 1941-43; pastor Mars (Pa.) United Meth. Ch., 1943-49, Smithfield United Meth. Ch., Pitts., 1949-52, Ingomar United Meth. Ch., Pitts., 1952-82; pastor emeritus Ingomar United Meth. Ch.; patient rep. Passavant Hosp., Pitts., 1982—; mem. Bd. of Ordained Ministry, 1970-84; mem. United Meth. Found., Pitts., 1982—. Mem. Northland Libr. Bd., McCandless, Pa., 1986-89, YMCA Bd. Mgmt., McCandless, 1984—; mem. corp. bd. Passavant Hosp., McCandless, 1964—. Recipient Disting. Svc. award Geneva Coll., 1988. Mem. North Hill Ministerium. Home: 9621 Hilliard Rd Pittsburgh PA 15237 Office: Passavant Hosp 9100 Babcock Blvd Pittsburgh PA 15237

PARKS, JAMES WILLARD, minister; b. Canton, Ohio, May 25, 1927; s. Sherman and Anne Bell (Watkins) P.; m. Caselta J. Parks, June 1962 (dec. 1972); m. Jeanette C. Parks, Nov. 1974; children: Sheryl, Gordon, Jamye, Carl, Cynthia, Laren, Stacy and Tracy (twins), Dawn and Shawn (twins), James S., Anthony, Cynthia, Jeannette, Lavia, James W.; m. Phyllis Greene; 1 stepchild, Bryan Talwin. AS, Ind. Coll., Indpls., 1968; cert., U. Md., Wiesbaden Campus, Fed. Republic Germany, Brigham Young u., Multnomah Bible Coll., Portland, Oreg. Ordained to ministry Christian M.E.Ch., 1957. Commd. Christian M.E.Ch., Wiesbaden; pastor Flint Hill Christian M.E.Ch., Mineral Springs, Ariz., 1990—; tchr. Nashville High Sch., 1989—; chaplain CAP, Cambridge, Ohio, 1972-78; del. Gen. Conf. Christian M.E.Ch., Birmingham, Ala.; rep. Haiti Conf.; speaker Black C. of C., Texachana, Tex., 1984—, Easter Sunrise Svc., Nashville, 1991—. Author: Window Into Yesterday, 1979. Candidate Quarum Ct., Nashville, 1990. Sgt. USAF. Recipient clergy appreciation Civitan Club; named to Ky. Cols. Mem. NAACP, Nashville Mins. Fellowship (sec. 1989—). Democrat. Home: 518 W Hempstead Nashville AR 71852

PARKS, LARRY JOSEPH, minister; b. Jersey City, May 4, 1955; s. Joseph Wilson and Ann (Harmon) P.; m. Delories Andrea Baxter, June 8, 1983; 1 child, David. Student, Southeastern Coll., 1982084. Ordained to ministry Internat. Ch. of Foursquare Gospel. Music dir. Teen Challenge, Rehrersburg, Pa., 1978-81; assoc. pastor St. Peters F.B.H. Ch., Paterson, N.J., 1981-82, Freedom Assembly of God, Sanford, Fla., 1983-88; sr. pastor Sonlight Christian Ctr., Orlando, Fla., 1989—; dir. Straight St. Ministries, Orlando, 1991—. With U.S. Army, 1972-74. Mem. NAACP. Republican. Home: 215 Loch Low Dr Sanford FL 32773 Office: Sonlight Christian Ctr 126 N Hart Blvd Orlando FL 32811

PARKS, MICHAEL WILLIAM, minister; b. Cleve., Aug. 7, 1947; m. Glenda Sue Fink, Aug. 19, 1967; children: Aaron, Lisa. ThB, Mt. Vernon Bible Coll., 1969; postgrad., Gaston Coll., 1969. Ordained to ministry Foursquare Gospel Ch., 1976. Minister Foursquare Gospel Ch., S.E. Harrisburg, N.C., 1969-83; minister, outreach evangelism Holy Spirit Harvest Ch., Macon, Ga., 1984—; dir. outreach Holy Spirit Harvest Ch., Macon, 1984—; state bd. dirs. Ga. Literacy Coalition, Atlanta, 1991—. Author: (booklet) Ministering to the Poor, 1988, A Better World Begins With Me, 1988. Editor newsletter Southside Lions Club, Macon, 1981-84, bd. dirs., 1982-84. Recipient Grant to Fund Edn. in the Innter City Peyton Anderson, 1990, Grant to Fund Food and Feeding Program Bonner Found., 1990-91. Office: Holy Spirit Harvest Ch 2254 Rocky Creek Rd Macon GA 31206

PARKS, ORLANDO ALVIN, II, minister; b. Washington, Mar. 7, 1961; s. Orlando Allen and Minnie Marie (Cabell) P.; m. La Vonne Denyse Rawles, Mar. 25, 1989; 1 child; 6 foster children. Student, Prince George's Community Coll., Largo, Md., 1981-83, Bowie State U., 1985, Washington Bible Coll., Lanham, Md., 1985. Lic. to ministry Bapt. Ch., 1985. Min. youth Mt. Enon Bapt. Ch., Washington, 1987—; dir. United for Harvest Outreach Ministeries, Lanham, 1989—; counselor, asst. spl. edn. Richardson Elem. Sch., Washington; pres., dir. Prince George's Community Gospel Choir, Largo, 1981-88, advisor, 1988-90; mem. Bowie State Gospel Choir, 1985-87. Mem. PTA, Ft. Washington, 1989-91; counselor Prince George's County ARC, 1991—, Assn. for Retarded Citizens of Prince George's County, 1991—; dir. Richardson Elem. Gospel Choir, boys group leader Champs. Named to Outstanding Young Men of Am., 1989, 90, Counselor of the Yr., Sta. WYCB, Washington, 1987-88. Mem. Coun. of Exceptional Children, Toastmaster Internat., Phi Beta Sigma. Office: United for Harvest Outreach Ministries PO Box 1026 Lanham MD 20703 *As we endeavor to bring about change by God's word, we in our own life have to remember to keep the bread fresh.*

PARKS, R(OBERT) KEITH, missionary, religious organization administrator; b. Memphis, Tex., Oct. 23, 1927; s. Robert Crews and Allie Myrtle (Cowger) P.; m. Helen Jean Bond, May 24, 1952; children: Randall, Kent, Eloise, Stanley. BA, U. North Tex., 1948; BD, Southwestern Bapt. Theol. Sem., 1951, ThD, 1955; LittD (hon.), Hardin-Simmons U., 1976; D Missions (hon.), Calif. Bapt. Coll., 1980; STD (hon.), S.W. Bapt. Coll., Bolivar, Mo., 1981; DD (hon.), U. Richmond, 1987. Ordained to ministry So. Bapt. Conv., 1950. Pastor Red Springs (Tex.) Bapt. Ch., 1950-54; instr. Bible Hardin-Simmons U., Abilene, Tex., 1953-54; missionary Fgn. Mission Bd., So. Bapt. Conv., Indonesia, 1954-68; area dir. S.E. Asia Fgn. Mission Bd., So. Bapt. Conv., Richmond, Va., 1968-75, dir. div. mission support, 1975-79, pres., 1980—; mem., past chmn. Inter-Agy. Coun., So. Bapt. Conv., 1980—; trustee Bapt. Joint Com. on Pub. Affairs, Washington, 1980-91. Author: Crosscurrents, 1966, World in View, 1987; also numerous articles. Recipient Disting. Alumnus award Southwestern Bapt. Theol. Sem., 1980, U. North Tex., 1991, E.Y. Mullins Denominational Svc. award So. Bapt. Theol. Sem., 1989. Office: So Bapt Conv Fgn Mission Bd 3806 Monument Ave Richmond VA 23230

PARLETTE, THOMAS JOSEPH, minister; b. San Antonio, Nov. 1, 1963; s. Thomas Alfred and Barbara Jean (Grafton) P. BA, Eastern Ill. U., 1986; MDiv, Princeton Seminary, 1990. Ordained to ministry Presbyn. Ch., 1990. Asst. min. Atlantic Highlands (N.J.) Navesink United Meth. Chs., 1988-90; assoc. pastor for Christian edn. and youth Westmont Presbyn. Ch., Johnstown, Pa., 1990—; mem. communications com. Redstone Presbytery, Greensburg, Pa., 1990—. Actor Penn Wood Players, Johnstown, Pa., 1991. Office: Westmont Presbyn Ch 601 Luzerne St Johnstown PA 15905

PARNELL, WILLIAM MICHAEL, minister; b. Florence, S.C., June 27, 1956; s. William Preston and Sarah Vermelle (Pope) P.; m. Wanda Lynn Jones, Jan. 18, 1980; children: Michael Scott, Joshua Adam, Amber Lynn. Cert. O.T., Hartsville Community Coll., 1981. Lic. to ministry Pentecostal Holiness Ch., 1982. Pastor Piney Plains Ind. Free Will Bapt. Ch., Hartsville, S.C., 1979-80; evangelist S.C. Conf. Pentecostal Holiness Chs., Lake City, S.C., 1982—; agt. Capital Holding Co., Cheraw, S.C., 1984—. Author numerous Christian music compositions. Home: 204 Willow Ln Cheraw SC 29520

PARONT, GEORGE JOHN, priest; b. Flushing, N.Y., Feb. 28, 1953; s. George Henry and Harriet Ann (Warner) P. BA in Scholastic Philosophy, Sacred Theology, St. Mary's U., 1967, MA in Sacred Theology, 1968; postgrad., St. John's U., 1971; cert. human resources devel., Cornell U., 1985. Ordained priest Roman Cath. Ch., 1977, consecrated bishop, 1990; awarded canonical mission Archdioceses San Antonio, 1967. Chmn. dept. sci. Cath. Youth Orgn. Diocese Bklyn., Cresthaven, N.Y., 1959-71; instr. theology Incarnate Word Acad., San Antonio, 1967-68; tchr. Holy Cross High Sch., San Antonio, 1968-69; asst. pastor St. Gregory's Ch., Ronkonkoma, N.Y., 1977-78; pastor St. John the Evangelist Ch., Brookhaven, N.Y., 1978—; bd. dir. Inst. Roman Cath. Studies, Brookhaven, 1978—; mem. nat. adv. bd. Am. Christian Coll., Tulsa, 1973. Author: Experiments in Electricity, 1962, Experiments in Lights, 1962, The Invalidity of the ThucConsecrations, 1988; editor: The Armorer, 1972-74, The Guardsman, 1972-74; contbr. articles to profl. jours. Sustaining mem. Rep. Nat. Com., 1974—; treas. local 253 AFL-CIO AFSCME, 1971-75, pres. CSEA local 1000-253, 1980-89; mem. labor mgmt. coms. N.Y. State Gov.'s Office Employee Rels., 1987-88. With N.Y.N.G., 1971-83. Author: Experiments in Electricity, 1962, Experiments in Light, 1962, The Invalidity of the Thuc Consecrations, 1988; editor: The Armorer, 1972-74, The Guardsman, 1972-74; contbr. articles to profl. jours. Mem. Found. for Christian Theology, Queens Inst. Anthropology, Archaeol. Inst. Am., Am. Bible Soc., Epsilon Delta Chi, KC. Republican. Avocations: biblical archaeology, numismatics, public speaking.

PARR, DARRYL ALAN, minister; b. Bremerton, Wash., Nov. 19, 1960; s. Charles Sheldon and Clarice Opal (Mosbarger) P. BA, Seattle Pacific U., 1983; MDiv, Lexington (Ky.) Theol. Sem., 1986; postgrad., U. Geneva, Switzerland, 1986-87. Minister Smithfield (Ky.) Christian Ch., 1983-86, 1st Christian Ch., Bethany, Ill., 1987—; pres. Bethany Ministerial Alliance, 1988—. Community rep. In-Touch Drug Edn. Program, Bethany, Ill., 1987; v.p. Sheridan Neighborhood Planning Assn., Bremerton, 1982; bd. dirs. Coalition Against Domestic Violence, Charleston, Ill., 1988—; mem. adv. coun. Partnership Adult Literacy, 1989—. Beasley scholar Lexington Theol. Sem., 1983-86, Bossey scholar, 1986-87; recipient Christian Bd. of Publ. award, 1986, Montgomery award Lexington Theol. Sem., 1986, Pres.'s Citation, Seattle Pacific U., 1988. Mem. Coll. Profl. Christian Ministers, Disciples of Christ Hist. Soc., Coun. on Christian Unity, Nat. Wildlife Fedn. Democrat. Avocations: reading, guitar, travel. Home: 214 S St John PO Box 81 Bethany IL 61914-0081 Office: 1st Christian Ch 312 W South Water Bethany IL 61914-0289

PARR, THOMAS RANDALL, minister; b. San Antonio, Jan. 2, 1957; s. Tom Ray and Grace Elizabeth (Brashear) P.; m. Pamela Sue Parr, Jan. 4, 1986; children: Lauren Elise, Candace Elaine. MDiv, San Antonio Sem., 1985, D Ministry, 1987; ThD cum laude, Kingsway Theol. Sem., 1988. Ordained to ministry The N.T. Ch., 1983, Ch. on the Rock, 1990; lic. World Ministry Fellowship. Assoc. pastor The New Testament Ch., San Antonio, 1982-83; sr. pastor The Upper Room Ch., San Antonio, 1983-87; commd. lt. (j.g.) USN, 1988; chaplain USN, Washington, 1988—; advanced through grades to lt. USN, 1990; pres. Randall Parr Ministries, San Antonio, Dallas, 1982-88. Producer/dir. (film) Chaplains With The Fleet Marine Force, 1991, Integrated Combat Ministry, 1990, Women in the Navy Chaplain Corps, 1991; author: American Home Cell Groups, 1990; contbr. articles to profl. jours. Mem. Ch. Growth Internat. Republican. *Two simple words have revolutionized my life. They have brought the living God onto the scene and allowed me to watch Him make my life a continual pageant of triumph in Christ. They have caused me to be the above and not the beneath, the head and not the tail, and have turned confusion into confidence, impossibility into reality, religion into revelation, and law into life. Valued as pearls from Heaven, I have inscribed them upon my heart and would advise the same to anyone seeking to rise above mediocrity and make the most out of their brief visit to this earth. Handle them with loving care, rehearse them with diligence and do not restrain them with human intellect: PRAY and OBEY.*

PARRENT, ALLAN MITCHELL, dean, religion educator, academic administrator; b. Frankfort, Ky., Dec. 27, 1930; s. Overton Crockett and Lillian (Mitchell) P.; m. Carol Armistead, Sept. 21, 1957; children: Elizabeth Armistead, Ann Beauchamp, Katherine Crockett. BA, Georgetown (Ky.) Coll., 1952; MA, Vanderbilt U., 1955, MDiv, 1961; PhD, Duke U., 1969. Fgn. svc. officer U.S. Dept. of State, Washington, 1962-64; asst. dir. student affairs Duke U., Durham, N.C., 1964-67; dir. Washington program Nat. Coun. of Chs., Washington, 1967-72; prof. Christian ethics Episcopal Theol. Sem. in Va., Alexandria, 1972—, assoc. dean acad. affairs, v.p., 1983—; Clinton S. Quin prof. Episcopal Theol. Sem. in Va., 1984. Contbr. articles to profl. jours. Lt. USN, 1956-59. Danforth Found. fellow, 1952-62, Rockefeller Found. fellow, 1959-60; Fulbright scholar Durham (Eng.) U., 1952-53; named to hon. Order of Ky. Cols., 1963. Mem. Internat. Inst. of Strategic Studies, Coun. on Christian Approaches to Def. and Disarmament (co-chair 1971-89), Soc. Christian Ethics (bd. dirs. Episc. com. religion and freedom). Avocation: singing. Home: 3979 Seminary Rd Alexandria VA 22304 Office: Episc Theol Sem 3737 Seminary Rd Alexandria VA 22304

PARRIS, GREGORY LEROY, minister; b. Fernandina Beach, Fla., Nov. 1, 1953; s. Alvin and L. Edith (Simmons) P.; m. Myra Eugenia Plummer, May 23, 1987. Student, U. Md., 1971-74; diploma, Gen. Motors Dealer Devel. Acad, Detroit, 1986-87. Salesman Heinrich Chevrolet, Rochester, N.Y., 1974-76; salesman Dreschel Buick, Toyota, Isuzu, Rochester, 1976-80, bus. mgr., 1980-85; prin. Greg Parris, Inc., Covington, Tenn., 1987-88; pastor Ch. of Love, Rochester, N.Y., 1981-87, Bibleway Temple, Deerfield Beach, Fla., 1987—. Mem. Classified Civil Svc. Bd., City of Deerfield Beech, Fla., 1988, Preservation of Pub. Edn. Com. Recipient Cert. of Merit, Ch. of the Holy Trinity, Washington, 1973. Democrat. Avocation: music. Home and Office: Bibleway Temple, Inc. 877 SW 2nd Terr Deerfield Beach FL 33441

PARRISH, RON, minister; b. Big Spring, Tex., May 9, 1942; s. Earl and Edith (Higgs) P.; m. Jerrill Ann Stephenson, May 27, 1962; children: Beverlee Jo Parrish McClure, Josh Jonathan, Matthew Michael. Diploma in Bible, Tex. Bapt. Inst. and Sem., Henderson, 1977. Ordained to ministry Am. Bapt. Assn., 1974. Pastor Union Cross Bapt. Ch., Nacogdoches, Tex., 1973-75, 1st Bapt. Ch., Lone Star, Tex., 1975-79, Mt. Pleasant Bapt. Ch., Denison, Tex., 1979-86, 2d Bapt. Ch., Malvern, Ark., 1987—; advisor Am. Bapt. Assn. Nat. Women's Aux., 1981—; moderator Saline Dist. Men's Fellowship, 1990-91; asst. moderator Saline Miss. Bapt. Assn., Hot Spring, 1990—; min. of the day Ark. State Legislature, Little Rock, 1991. Contbr. numerous articles to profl. jour. Mem. Kiwanis (Kiwanian of Yr. award 1987). Office: 2d Bapt Ch 210 W Mill St Malvern AR 72104

PARRISH, SUSAN BURGESS, minister, educator; b. New Orleans, Dec. 10, 1958; d. Truman Floyd and Ruby Lee (Bell) Burgess; m. Rodney Gene Parrish, Apr. 11, 1981. BA, Samford U., 1981; MA in Christian Edn., So. Bapt. Theol. Sem., Louisville, 1984. Min. youth and activities Westmont Bapt. Ch., Birmingham, Ala., 1981-82, Rineyville (Ky.) Bapt. Ch., 1982-83; min. edn. and youth 1st Bapt. Ch., Huntingburg, Ind., 1983-84, Bapt. Temple, Reidsville, N.C., 1985-90; min. edn. Siloam Bapt. Ch., Marion, Ala., 1990—; dir. Christian ministries and counseling svcs. Judson Coll., Marion, 1990—; dir. Sunday sch. Cahaba Bapt. Assn., Marion, 1990—; dir. discipleship tng. Dan Valley Bapt. Assn., Reidsville, 1986-89, dir. youth ministry, 1985-88; clinician Sunday sch., sr. adult work and discipleship tng., 1985—. Mem. So. Bapt. Women in Ministry, So. Bapt. Religious Edn. Assn., So. Bapt. Assn. of Ministries to the Aging, So. Bapt. Alliance. Home: 703 Moore St Marion AL 36756 Office: Siloam Bapt Ch 505 Washington St Marion AL 36756 also: Judson Coll Bibb St Marion AL 36756 *I believe the most important thing in one's spiritual life is to think for one's self. We are influenced by our family and background, peers, society, education and relationships. It is very easy to let someone tell you what to believe and think and to let life make choices for us. This happens when we let things that influence us become the deciding factor in our decisions, especially in the matters of faith. Indoctrinated faith is not true faith for it does not give persons the strength of foundation to be able to withstand the difficult days of life. It only gives what someone else helds true, not what you have worked through for yourself. I believe our God gave us a brain to be used to its fullest capacity. We have much potential to fulfill. This will not be done when we rely on others to do the thinking and decision making for us.*

PARRISH-HARRA, CAROL WILLIAMS, minister, author, lecturer; b. Nettleton, Ark., Jan. 21, 1935; d. Claremce Elmer and Corinne (Parrott) Williams; m. Charles Clayton Harra, Dec. 2, 1975. Accounts control mgr. Caledesi Nat. Bank, Dunedin, Fla., 1963-66; analysis coordinator Capital Formation Counselor Co., Clearwater, Fla., 1966-71; ordained to ministry Spiritual Center St. Petersburg (Fla.), 1971; assoc. minister Temple of Living God, St. Petersburg, 1971-75; pres. Fla. Humanistic Inst., St. Petersburg, 1974-75; dir. Villa Serena Spiritual Community, Sarasota, 1976-81; pres. Light of Christ Community Ch., Tahlequah, Okla., 1981—; acad. dean. Sancta Sophia Sem., 1990—; mem. faculty Internat. Coll. Nat. Health Scis., 1977-82; moderator, speaker Sarasota chpt., NCCJ, 1979-81; workshop leader, lectr. retreats Spiritual Frontiers Fellowship; trustee Nat. Council Community Chs., 1980-84; trustee, Internat. Assn. Near Death Studies, regional trustee Internat. Council of Community Chs., 1983-86, 87-90. Author: New Age Handbook on Death and Dying, 1982, Messengers of Hope, 1983, The Aquarian Rosary, 1988, The Book of Rituals: Personal and Planetary Transformation, 1990, Tapping the Power of Ritual, 1990; contbr. articles to religious jours. Mem. NOw, Am. Bus. Women's Assn., Assn. for Past-Life Rsch. and Therapies. Democrat. Address: 101 Summit Ridge Dr Tahlequah OK 74464

PARROTT, DEAN ALLEN, minister; b. Cass City, Mich., Aug. 24, 1922; s. Earl Watts and Anna Lura (Smith) P.; m. Ione Elizabeth Kneeshaw, Apr. 18, 1942; children: Jean Parrott Dunsford, Keith, Dale. AB, Adrian (Mich.) Coll., 1953; ThB, Owosso Bible Coll., 1957; MA, Mich. State U., 1960; postgrad., Wayne State U., 1960-63, Western Mich. U., 1967-68; D Ministry, Calif. Grad. Sch. Theology, 1985. Ordained to ministry Free Meth. Ch., 1944; psychologist ltd. lic. Mich., marriage counselor, Mich. Pastor Free Meth. Ch., Rose City, Mich., 1944-45, Sandusky, Mich., 1946-50; sr. min. Free Meth. Ch., Adrian, Mich., 1950-53, Hillsdale, Mich., 1953-59, Lincoln Park, Mich., 1959-66, Kalamazoo, 1966-76; sr. pastor Free Meth. Ch., Westland, Mich., 1976-87, ret., 1987; min. counseling Cen. Wesleyan Ch., Holland, Mich., 1988—; del. Free Meth. Ch. N.Am. Gen. Conf., 1964, 74, 79, 85, Conf. Prophesy, Jerusalem, 1971; host daily radio Question Hour Sta. WKPR, Kalamazoo, 1966-72; counselor Christian Found. Emotional Health, Detroit, 1964-66. Contbr. articles profl. jours. Mem. Mental Health Council, Lincoln Park, 1960-66, Pastor's Adv. Bd. Planned Parenthood, Detroit, 1963-66, Kalamazoo Community Relations Bd., 1969-71, South Mich. Conf. Bd. Adminstrs. Mem. Am. Psychol. Assn., Kalamazoo Ministerial Assn. (pres. 1971-73), Wesleyan Theol. Soc., Nat. Council Family Relations, Acad. Religion and Mental Health, Am. Inst. Family Relations, Christian Assn. Psychol. Studies. Avocations: ham radio, antique radios restoration, photography, workshop, gardening. Home: 683 Hayes Holland MI 49424 Office: Cen Wesleyan Ch 446 W 40th St Holland MI 49423

PARROTT, DOUGLAS MORRIS, religion educator; b. Utica, N.Y., July 16, 1927; s. William Clinton and Helen Elizabeth (Morris) P.; m. Anne Ethel Elder, July 13, 1957 (div. 1983); children: Elizabeth, Kirk; m. Christine Elaine Petzar, July 30, 1988. BA, Hamilton Coll., 1949; MDiv, Union Theol. Sem., 1952, MST, 1965; PhD, Grad. Theol. Union, Berkeley, Calif., 1970. Ordained to ministry United Presbyn. Ch. (U.S.A.), 1953. Pastor various chs., N.Y., N.J., 1953-65; rsch. assoc., then rsch. fellow Inst. Antiquity and Christianity, Claremont, Calif., 1968-71; assist. prof. religious studies U. Calif., Riverside, 1971-77, assoc. prof., 1977-87, prof., 1987—, chmn. program religious studies, 1981-85. Editor: Nag Hammadi Codices V-VI, 1978, Nag Hammadi Codices III, 3-4, and V, 1 (Euguostos and the Sophia of Jesus Christ), 1991. Mem. Soc. Biblical Lit., Soc. for New Testament Studies, Cath. Biblical Assn. Home: 5253 Falkirk Ave Riverside CA 92506 Office: U Calif Program Religious Studies Riverside CA 92521

PARROTT, RICHARD LESLIE, minister; b. Kelso, Wash., Oct. 5, 1952; s. A. Leslie and Lora Lee (Montgomery) P.; m. Carol Rose Wells, June 3, 1974; children: Andrew Leslie, Justin Richard. BS in Psychology, Ea. Nazarene Coll., Wollaston, Mass., 1974; MA in Psychology, U. Mo., Kansas City, 1975; MDiv, Nazarene Theol. Sem., Kansas City, 1977; PhD in Edn., Oreg. State U., 1982. Ordained to ministry Ch. of the Nazarene, 1978. Pastor Ch. of the Nazarene, Corvallis, Oreg., 1977-83, Detroit Ch. of the Nazarene, 1983-88; sr. pastor Salem (Oreg.) Ch. of the Nazarene, 1988—; bd. regents N.W. Nazarene Coll., Nampa, Idaho, 1989—. Author: (mission book) Double Vision, 1985; (membership book) Welcome to the Church of the Nazarene, 1988. Office: 1st Ch of the Nazarene PO Box 7075 Salem OR 97303

PARROTT, RODNEY LEE, religious educator; b. Ontario, Oreg., Mar. 26, 1942; s. Floyd Irwin and Doris Sue (Blair) P.; m. Mary Anne Helseth, June 12, 1964; 1 child, Joshua Stephen. BTh, N.W. Christian, 1965; MDiv, Phillips U., 1969, ThM, 1970; PhD, Claremont Grad. Sch., 1980. Pastor First Christian Ch., Carmen, Okla., 1966-69; campus minister United Campus Ministry, Alva, Okla., 1970-73; minister of Christian nurture First Christian Ch., Pomona, Calif., 1974-76; asst. dean Disciples Sem. Found., Claremont, Calif., 1979-89, assoc. dean, 1989—; mem. Faith and Order Commn. South Calif. Ecumenical Coun., L.A., 1989—, Interfaith Coalition on Racism, Pomona, Calif., 1980-89. Co-author: The Ministry of Elders, 1990. Recipient Ecumenical Svc. award Pomona Valley Coun. Chs., 1983; scholarships/fellowships, 1961-79. Fellow Jesus Sem.; mem. Soc. Bibl. Lit., World Future Soc., Assn. Religious Futurists, Disciples of Christ Hist. Soc., Rotary, Theta Phi. Democrat. Office: Disciples Sem Found 1325 N College Ave Claremont CA 91711 *Although we are only here for a short while, each of us can do something to make human life in society better in the long term. That is servant leadership.*

PARRY, WALTER P., minister. Exec. dir. Fresno (Calif.) Met. Ministry. Office: Fresno Met Ministry 1055 N Van Ness Ste H Fresno CA 93728*

PARSLEY, ROBERT CHARLES, minister; b. Tulsa, Aug. 11, 1956; s. Victor Bernard and Margery Sue (Mathews) P.; m. Carole Ellen McKenzie, Oct. 2, 1982; children: Robert McKenzie, Timothy James, Kelly Mathews. BA in Religion with high honors, Ouachita Bapt. U., 1978; MDiv, So. Bapt. Theol. Sem., 1982; D Ministry, Southwestern Bapt. Theol. Sem., 1990. Ordained to ministry Bapt. Ch., 1978. Youth minister First Bapt. Ch., Leithfield, Ky., 1979-80; chaplain Bapt. Med. Ctr., Little Rock, 1980-81; pastor Lula (Miss.) Bapt. Ch., 1982-84; pastor First Bapt. Ch., Prescott, Ark., 1984-88, Dardanelle, Ark., 1988—; chmn. adv. bd. Bapt. Student Union, Ark. Tech. U., Russellville, 1988-90. County chmn. Ark. Sesquicentennial Commn., Prescott, 1986. Mem. Ark. Alumni So. Bapt. Theol. Sem. (pres. 1986), Dardanelle Ministerial Alliance (pres. 1989-90), Rotary. Home: Rt 3 Box 96 Dardanelle AR 72834 Office: First Bapt Ch PO Drawer S Dardanelle AR 72834 *I refuse to accept the idea that the church and Christianity are irrelevant in the modern world. I find my greatest satisfaction in assisting others in spiritual formation.*

PARSONS, DONALD D., bishop. Bishop of Alaska Evang. Luth. Ch. in Am., Anchorage. Office: Synod of Alaska 4201 Tudor Center Rd Ste 315 Anchorage AK 99516*

PARSONS, DONALD JAMES, retired bishop; b. Phila., Mar. 28, 1922; s. Earl and Helen (Drabble) P.; m. Mary Russell, Sept. 17, 1955; children—Mary, Rebecca, Bradford. B.A., Temple U., 1943; M.Div., Phila. Div. Sch., 1946, Th.D., 1951, D.D. (hon.), 1964; postgrad., U. Nottingham, Eng., 1968; D.C.L., Nashotah (Wis.) House, 1973. Ordained priest Episcopal Ch., 1946, consecrated bishop, 1973; curate Immanual Ch., Wilmington, Del., 1946-49; rector St. Peter's Ch., Smyrna, Del., 1949-50; prof. N.T., Nashotah House, 1950-73, pres., dean, 1963-73; bishop Diocese of Quincy, Ill., 1973-88. Author: A Life-time Road to God, 1966, In Time with Jesus, 1973, Holy Eucharist: Rite Two, 1976. Home: 308 W Edgevale Peoria IL 61604 Office: Diocese of Quincy 3601 N North St Peoria IL 61604

PARSONS, EDWIN SPENCER, clergyman, educator; b. Brockton, Mass., Feb. 16, 1919; s. Edwin Webber and Ethel Faunce (Marsh) P.; m. Eleanor Millard, Nov. 3, 1944; children: William Spencer, Ellen, James Millard, Bradford Delano. A.B., Denison U., 1941, D.D., 1967; B.D., Andover Newton Theol. Sch., 1945; D.D., Kalamazoo Coll., 1966; L.H.D., Chgo. Coll. Osteo. Medicine, 1978. Ordained to ministry Am. Baptist Ch., 1944; asst. minister First Bapt. Ch., Newton Centre, Mass., 1945-47; exec. dir. Bapt. Student Found., Inc., Cambridge, Mass., 1947-59; pastor Hyde Park Union Ch., Chgo., 1959-65; assoc. prof. ethics U. Chgo. Div. Sch., 1965-78, prof., 1978-81; dir. ministerial field edn., 1977-79, asst. to dean, 1981-88; dean Rockefeller Meml. Chapel, 1965-79; v.p., dir. New Eng. office Health Resources Ltd., Kansas City, Mo., 1979-89; cons. dept. ch. and soc. Am. Bapt. Chs. of Mass., 1979-86, also editor Mass. Bapt. News, 1983-85; chmn. strategy and action com., bd. dirs. Mass. Council Chs., 1983-85; adj. prof. Andover Newton Theol. Sch., 1981-85. Author: The Christian Yes or No, 1964; contbr.: Belief and Ethics, 1978. Pres. Council Hyde Park-Kenwood Chs. and Synagogues, 1963; chmn. Abortion Rights Assn. Ill., 1974-79; founder, chmn. Ill. Religious Coalition for Abortion Rights, 1975, Ill. Clergy Consultation Services on Problem Pregnancies, 1971-79; bd. dirs., chmn. clergy adv. com. Planned Parenthood Assn., Chgo., 1977-79; bd. dirs. Hyde Park YMCA, Facing History and Ourselves Nat. Found., 1983-87; bd. govs. Internat. House, Chgo., 1969-79; trustee Packard Manse (Mass.), Bapt. Theol. Union, 1960-70, 81—; pres., bd. mgrs. Ministers and Missionaries Benefit Bd., 1975-81; mem. policy council Religious Coalition for Abortion Rights of Mass., 1980-86; sec., treas. Bolton Inst. for Sustainable Future, 1983-87; mem. gen. bd., mem. exec. com., mem. commn. on Christian unity Am. Bapt. Chs., 1963-72, 74-81; bd. dirs. Planned Parenthood League of Mass., 1984—; interim assoc. dir. Mass Coun. Chs., 1988-89. Democrat. Home: 69 Fort Point Rd North Weymouth MA 02191

PARSONS, ELMER EARL, retired clergyman; b. Cloverland, Wash., Oct. 4, 1919; s. Claud Solomon and Bessie Lillian (Campbell) P.; m. Marjorie Emma Carlson, Aug. 29, 1942; children—Karl Elmer, James Myron, Helen Joy, Ann Elizabeth, Lois Marie, Louise Melba. B.A., Seattle Pacific U., 1942; S.T.B., N.Y. Theol. Sem., 1945; S.T.M., Asbury Theol. Sem., Wilmore, Ky., 1955; D.D. (hon.), Greenville (Ill.) Coll., 1958. Ordained to ministry Free Methodist Ch., 1944; acad. dean Wessington Springs (S.D.) Coll., 1945-47; missionary to China, 1947-49, missionary to Japan, 1949-54; supt. Japan Free Meth. Mission, 1950-54; pres. Central Coll., McPherson, Kans., 1955-64, Osaka (Japan) Christian Coll., 1964-74; Asia area sec., Free Meth. Ch., 1964-74; bishop Free Meth. Ch. N.Am., 1974-85. Author: Witness to the Resurrection, 1967. Named Alumnus of Year Seattle Pacific U., 1976. Mem. Wesleyan Theol. Soc.

PARSONS, RALPH L., II, deacon, small business owner; b. Columbus, Ohio, June 7, 1936; s. Ralph L. and Bessie C. (Writsel) P.; m. Mary Thompson, Oct. 11, 1953; 1 child, Ralph L. III. BBA, Otterbein Coll.; grad., Ohio State U.; postgrad., Pontifical Coll. Josephinum. Assoc. dir. rural life Diocese of Columbus, 1989—. Patentees in field. Home: Box 28 1795 Olmstead Rd West Jefferson OH 43162-0028

PARSONS, TIMOTHY JOHN, minister; b. Altoona, Pa., Dec. 12, 1962; s. George Emerson and Lenore Betty (Barley) P.; m. Susan Lois Fry, July 6, 1985. BS, Liberty U., 1985. Intern Thomas Rd. Bapt. Ch., Lynchburg, Va., 1983-85; youth pastor Bethel View Bapt. Ch., Bristol, Tenn., 1985-86, Bible Bapt. Ch., Paducan, Ky., 1986—; part-time min. Angel of Mercy, Paducan, 1988—; chaplain Angel of Mercy, Paducan, 1989—. Mem. Paducah Amateur Radio Assn., West Ky. EMT Assn. (chaplain 1990—), Network of Youth Mins. Office: Bible Bapt Youth 1915 N 10th St Paducah KY 42001

PARTHENIOS, patriarch, religious order leader; b. Port-Said, Egypt, Nov. 30, 1919; s. Minas Coinidis and Heleni Lahanas. Degree in theology, Theol. Sch. Halki Constantinople, Istanbul, 1939. Ordained to ministry Greek Orthodox Ch. as deacon, 1939, as priest, 1948. Chief sec., patriarchal vicar Greek Orthodox Ch., Alexandria, Egypt, 1954-58; bishop Met. of Carthage, Tripoli-Libya-Tunis and Casablanca, 1958-87; patriarch Greek Orthodox Patriarchate Alexandria, 1987—; rep. World Coun. Chs., main speaker for Orthodox Ch., Canberra, Australia, 1991; mem. for dialogues Roman Cath.-Mid. East Coun. Chs. Home: Rue El Attarine 104, PO Box 2006, Alexandria Arab Republic of Egypt

PARTIN, MILTON DOUGLAS, minister; b. North Richland Hills, Tex., Sept. 15, 1962; s. Melvin Edward Partin Jr. and Patrica (Hanna) Davis; m. Marci Brown, Oct. 5, 1985. BA, Dallas Christian Coll., 1985; MDiv, Emmanuel Sch. Religion, Johnson City, Tenn., 1988. Intern Northside Christian Ch., San Antonio, 1983, Los Alamos (N.Mex.) Christian Ch., 1984; youth dir. Munsey Meml. United Meth. Ch., Johnson City, Tenn., 1986-88; assoc. min. Raintree Christian Ch., Lubbock, Tex., 1988—; dir. West Tex. Teen Conv., Midland, 1988—; mem. curriculum com. Guadalupe Christian Camp, Queens, N.Mex., 1988—; regent Dallas Christian Coll., Dallas, 1988—. Contbr. articles to profl. publs. Named to Outstanding Young Men of Am., 1986. Mem. Delta Epsilon Chi. Home: 4601 40th St Lubbock TX 79414 Office: Raintree Christian Church 3601 82nd St Lubbock TX 79423

PARTIN, WINFRED, clergyman; b. Whitley County, Ky., Oct. 19, 1946; s. Orville and Mary (Partin) P.; student Am. Sch., Chgo., Buford Ellington Vocat. Sch., Morristown, Tenn.; m. Lucille Davis, Sept. 28, 1966; children: Patsy Gail, Pamela Kaye, Paul Timothy. Ordained to ministry So. Bapt. Ch., 1966; pastor chs. in S.E. Ky. and N.E. Tenn., 1966-77; pastor Anthras Bapt. Ch., Duff, Tenn., 1977-79, King's Settlement Bapt. Ch., Clairfield, Tenn., 1981—; coin collector, 1960—; owner Partin's Coins and Stamps, Morristown, 1970—. Mem. Campbell County Bapt. Assn. Democrat. Writer for various hobby publs.; contbr. publs. including Rural Kentuckian, Scott's Stamp Jour., Stamp World, Pulpit Helps, Farm Life News, Linn's Stamp News, Danville Times-Examiner (Ky.). author poetry, fiction and non-fiction. Address: 414 Oak St Morristown TN 37814

PASCHANG, JOHN LINUS, retired bishop; b. Hemingford, Nebr., Oct. 5, 1895; s. Casper Paschang and Gertrude Fischer. D of Canon Law, Cath. U. Am., Washington, 1925, MA, 1926, PhD, 1927; JD (hon.), Creighton U., 1960. Pastor St. Rose Ch., Hooper, Nebr., 1921-23, Holy Cross Ch., Omaha, 1927-51; bishop Grand Island, Nebr., 1951-72; ret., 1972. Author: The Sacramentals, 1925, The Popes and Revival of Learning, 1927. Mem. KC (state chaplain 1938-42). Republican. Roman Catholic. Avocation: missionary work. Home: 505 S Arthur St Grand Island NE 68802

PASCO, TITO E., bishop; b. Town Balasan, Iloilo, The Philippines, Jan. 4, 1930; s. Hermogenes and Bernardina (Esquillo) P.; married 1969; 1 child, Tito E. Jr. BTh, St. Andrew's Theol. Sem., Quezon City, The Philippines, 1957, MDiv, 1989. Ordained to ministry Philippine Ind. Ch. Missionary bishop Diocese of Antique and Palawan, Philippine Ind. Ch., 1964-66; bishop of Antique, Romblon and Or. Mindoro, 1966-75; nat. coord. Stewardship Program Philippine Ind. Ch., 1975-81, gen. sec., 1981-89, supreme bishop Obispo Maximo, 1989—; chmn. Paglingap Ministry, Met. Manila, 1981-86, vice chmn., 1989—; vice chmn. Nat. Coun. Chs., The Philippines, 1981-83, chmn., 1989-91; mem. cen. com. World Coun. Chs., 1991—. Spiritual adviser Circulo Balaseñes, Met. Manila, 1988—; trustee Trinity Coll., 1989—; mem. bd. advisors, vice chairperson St. Andrew's Sem., 1989—. Recipient cert. of appreciation Nat. Coun. Chs., 1981. Mem. Christian Lit. Soc., Kiwanis (cert. of merit Pasay City club 1988, spiritual adviser 1989—). Home: 21 Tramo St, Pasay City, Manila The Philippines

PASKAI, LASZLO CARDINAL, archbishop; b. Szeged, Hungary, May 8, 1927. Grad. high sch., Szeged. Joined Franciscan Order, Roman Cath. Ch., 1949, ordained priest, 1951. Episcopal liturgist Szeged, 1952-55; prof. philosophy Theol. Acad., Szeged, 1955-65; lectr., then prof. philosophy Theol. Acad., Budapest, Hungary, 1965-78; apptd. titular bishop of Bavagaliana, apostolic gov. of Veszprem, 1978; diocesan bishop of Veszprem, 1979, coadjutor with right succession to archbishop of Kalocsa,, 1982, archbishop of Esztergom and primate of Hungary, 1987—, created cardinal, 1988; mem. Hungarian Parliament; apostolic prefect Cen. Sem. Budapest, 1955-62, spiritual, 1962-65, spiritual prefect, 1965-69, rector, 1973-78; chmn. Hungarian Cath. Bench of Bishops, 1986—. Address: Vatican City Vatican City Also: Berenyi Zsigmond utca 2, 2500 Esztergom Hungary

PASKOW, SHIMON, rabbi; b. Newark, 1932; m. Carol Bauman; 1 child, Michele. BA, CUNY Bklyn. Coll.; MA, Hebrew Union Coll.-Jewish Inst. Religion, 1959, hon. doctorate; hon. doctorate, Jewish Theol. Sem. Am. Rabbi, 1959. Assoc. rabbi Valley Jewish Community Ctr./Temple Adat Ari El, 1965-69; rabbi, spiritual leader Temple Etz Chaim, Thousand Oaks, Calif., 1969—; lectr. in field. Contbr. numerous articles to profl. jours. and newspapers. Mem. community rels. com. San Fernando Valley (Calif.) Area Coun., community adv. com. of 12th dist. City of L.A.; hon. trustee So. Calif. Coun. for Soviet Jews; chmn. campaigns United Jewish Welfare Fund, State of Israel Bonds; past bd. dirs. Gregor Mendel Bot. Found., Inc., Greater Conejo Valley, Calif. Chaplain U.S. Army, 1960; col. USAR. Recipient Shalom award Govt. of Israel. Mem. Cen. Conf. Am. Rabbis, Rabbinical Assembly, Mil. Chaplains Assn., Assn. Jewish Chaplains, Soc. Bibl. Lit., Am. Jewish Hist. Soc. Home: 42 Verde Vista Dr Thousand Oaks CA 91360 Office: Temple Etz Chaim 1080 Janss Rd Thousand Oaks CA 91360

PASS, THOMAS EMERY, clergyman; b. Ft. Oglethorpe, Ga., Feb. 28, 1945; s. Albin G. and Harriet Kerth(Hanauer) P.; m. Suzanne Sandoz; children: Garrick Thomas, Christiane Kathleen. BA, La. State U., 1967; ThM, New Orleans Theol. Sem., 1970; postgrad., Austin Presbyn. Theol. Sem., 1970-71; DMin, McCormick Theol. Sem., Chgo., 1977. Ordained to ministry, Presbyn. Ch. Assoc. pastor Grace Presbyn. Ch., Houston, 1971-75; pastor First Presbyn. Ch., Post, Tex., 1975-88, Greenville, Tex., 1988—; mem. Marriage Svc. com., Office of Worship, Presbyn. Ch. USA, Louisville, 1984-86; moderator Palo Duro Union Presbytery, 1979-80, 80-81. Contbr. articles to profl. jours.; author prayers: Presbyterian Mission Yearbook, 1986. Home: Rte 6 Box 315 A6 Greenville TX 75401 Office: First Presbyn Ch 5905 Stonewall Greenville TX 75401

PASTILLE, CATHERINE L., youth minister; b. Providence, Apr. 15, 1958; d. Alfred G. and Louiise R. (Cimaglio) P. BS in Mgmt., R.I. Coll., 1986, postgrad. Life cert. coach Am. Coaches Effectiveness Program; cert. youth ministry Diocesan Youth Ministry Inst. Program coord. Providence County Regional Cath. Youth Orgn., Cranston, R.I., 1987-89; youth min., coord. religious edn. Our Lady of Grace Ch., Johnston, R.I., 1989—; coord. grades 7-10 religious edn. St. Michael's Ch., Smithfield, R.I., 1990—; exec. asst. Travelers Aid Soc. R.I., Providence, 1990—; mem. evangelization planning team Diocese of Providence, 1987-89; chmn. adult com. Young Life in R.I., 1987-89; bd. dirs. Providence County Regional Cath. Youth Orgn., 1989—. Named Volleyball Coach of Yr., Providence County Regional Cath. Youth Orgn., 1990. Mem. AACD, Am. Mental Health Counseling Assn., Assn. for Religion and Value Issues in Counseling. Democrat.

PASTUKHIV, SERHIJ KINDZERIAVYJ, clergyman, artist, musician; b. Ukraine, July 4, 1924; came to U.S., 1950, naturalized, 1960; s. Jacob and Kateryna (Buniak) P.; m. Julia Lytwynenko, Jan. 27, 1952; children: Olga, Irene, Larissa. Ed., U. Erlangen, Germany, 1949. Ordained to ministry Holy Ukranian Autocephalic Orthodox Ch. in Exile, 1965; rector Holy Trinity Cathedral, Bklyn., 1969—; adminstr. Holy Ukranian Autocephabic Orthodox Ch. in Exile, 1969—; archpriest-protopresbyter, 1976—; Mem.

Standing Conf. of Canonical Orthodox Bishops Am., 1969—; mem. eccles. endorsing agts. Armed Forces Chaplains Bd. Author numerous publs. on theology, philosophy, also translator biblical material into Ukrainian. Exhibited one-man shows, N.Y.C., Phila., Scranton, Washington, Chgo. Home: 103 Evergreen St W Babylon NY 11704

PATAKI, ANDREW, bishop; b. Palmerton, Pa., Aug. 30, 1927. Student, St. Vincent Coll., St. Procopious Coll., Lisle, Ill., Sts. Cyril and Methodius, Byzantine Cath. Sem., Grigorian U., Rome. Ordained priest Roman Cath. Ch., 1952. App. aux. bishop of Passaic, N.J. Byzantine Cath. diocese, 1983; bishop of Parma Ohio, 1984—. Home: 8924 Stover Ln Brecksville OH 44141 Office: 1900 Carlton Rd Parma OH 44134

PATE, GARY RAY, minister; b. Ottawa, Ill., May 26, 1957; s. William Ray and Glena Ray (Blanchard) P.; m. Linda Sue Lane, July 2, 1976; children: Tonika Rae, Jeffrey William. Student, Rend Lake Coll., 1975-77; Diploma in Christian Ministry, Boyce Bible Sch., 1988; BTh., Internat. Sem., 1991. Lic. to ministry Bapt. Ch., 1984, ordained, 1988. Sr. adult minister Clifton Bapt. Ch., Louisville, 1986-87; assoc. pastor Ridgeview Bapt. Mission, Taylorsville, Ky., 1987; pastor Ridgeview Bapt. Mission, Taylorsville, 1988-89, Hurricane Bapt. Ch., Cadiz, Ky., 1989—; camp pastor Land Between the Lakes Area Ministry, 1989—; dir. family ministries Little River Bapt. Assn., Cadiz, 1989—; evangelist Ky./Brazil Mission Link, Esperito Santos, Brazil, 1990. Mem. Trigg County Ministerial Alliance (pres. 1991—). Home: 4177 Hurricane Rd Cadiz KY 42211 Office: Hurricane Bapt Ch 4177 Hurricane Rd Cadiz KY 42211 *Two Thoughts: The Great Commission has never been cancelled, Cause needed change to be suggested.*

PATE, KENNETH RANDALL, minister; b. Wharton, Tex., May 24, 1968; s. Kenneth Rayburn and Sharon Kay (Allison) P.; m. Jena J. Ramsey, July 9, 1988. Student, Tex. Bible Coll., 1986-87. Ordained to ministry Pentecostal Ch. Evangelist United Pentecostal Ch., Charleston, Ill., 1987-88, youth pastor, 1988-89; pastor United Pentecostal Ch., Champaign, Ill., 1989-91; sectional youth leader, sect. 8 Ill. Dist. United Pentecostal Ch., 1989—. Home: 1006 Scottsdale Dr Champaign IL 61821 Office: United Pentecostal Ch 1511 N McKinley Champaign IL 61821

PATE, LARRY DALE, missionary leader; b. Oakland, Calif., Sept. 28, 1946; s. Alvin James and Maxine Evelyn (Ward) P.; m. Mary Ethel Reed, Aug. 26, 1967; children: Stephen Timothy, Shauna Danean. BS in Theology/Missiology, Bethany Coll., 1968; MA in Missiology, A/G Theol. Sem., 1979, Fuller Theol. Sem., 1988; D of Missiology, Fuller Theol. Sem., 1990. Pastor Tranquility (Calif.) Community Ch., 1971-74; missionary Div. of Fgn. Missions A/G, Bangladesh, Asia, 1974-80; missionary to Brazil Div. of Fgn. Missions A/G, Springfield, Mo., 1982-84; missions prof. So. Calif. Coll., Costa Mesa, 1980-82; dir. two-thirds world missions ministries OC Internat., Milpitas, Calif., 1984—, dir. internat. ministry team, 1991—; cons. World Evang. Fellowship Missions Commn., Singapore, 1986—, various orgns., Latin Am., Africa, Asia, 1985—; internat. dir. Two-Thirds World Missions Project-Lausanne Com. for World Evangelism, London, 1988—; del., speaker Lausanne II, Manila, 1989; cons. Confraternidad de Misiones de Latin Am., coord. com., 1984-87; cons., evaluation com. Asian Missions Congress, 1990. Author: (missiology textbook) Misionologia (in Portugese/Spanish), 1987, (handbook) From Every People, 1989 (named one of five best mission books, 1989); contbr. articles to profl. jours. Mem. Internat. Soc. Frontier Missions (leader task groups, 1989—).

PATE, RONALD EVERETT, minister; b. Pensacola, Fla., Dec. 21, 1952; s. Everett and Mary Jo (Anglin) Sunday; m. Patricia Ann Johnson, Aug. 4, 1973; childen: J. Christopher, Caitlin Rachel. BA in Religion, Samford U., Birmingham, Ala., 1976; MDiv, New Orleans Bapt. Theol. Sem., 1980, ThD, 1988. Ordained to ministry So. Bapt. Conv., 1977. Minister of evangelism and youth Second Bapt. Ch., Bessemer, Ala., 1973-74; assoc. pastor Phila. Bapt. Ch., Birmingham, 1974-77; assoc. pastor music and youth Ames Blvd. Bapt. Ch., Marrero, La., 1977-80, pastor, 1980-86; sr. pastor Hillcrest Bapt. Ch., Country Club Hills, Ill., 1986—; teaching fellow New Orleans Bapt. Theol. Sem., 1980-84; adminstrv., fin. com. Chgo. Met. Bapt. Assn., 1987-90, dir. evangelism, 1987—. Home: 19207 Center Ave Homewood IL 60430 Office: Hillcrest Bapt Ch 17300 Pulaski Rd Country Club Hills IL 60478

PATINO, ARTHUR, JR., deacon; b. San Antonio, Apr. 27, 1927; s. Arthur and Martha P.; m. Marie Patino, Aug. 26, 1951; children: Anthony, Roland, Diane. Deacon St. Leo's Ch., San Antonio, 1985—. With U.S. Army, 1945-46. Home: 502 W Malone San Antonio TX 78214

PATON, RUSSELL EMERSON, clergyman; b. Kansas City, Mo., June 13, 1960; s. Harold Russell Jones and Sharon Lea (Davis) Paton; m. Sarah Elizabeth, Feb. 20, 1989; 1 child, Joshua Ross. BS in Journalism, U. Mo., 1982; MDiv, St. Paul Sch. Theology, Kansas City, Mo., 1990. Ordained to ministry Meth. Ch. as deacon, 1990. Dir. youth ministry Leawood (Kans.) United Meth. Ch., 1987-88; pastor Southern Heights/Jarbalo United Meth. Ch., Leavenworth, Kans., 1988—; chmn. Communication Com./Kans. East, Topeka, 1990—; bd. dirs. United Meth. Reporter, Dallas, 1990—; deacon Kans. East Conf., 1990—. Contbg. author: Landmark Bible Commentary, 1991; editorialist Leavenworth Times, 1990. Publicity coord. Mike Hayden for Gov., Topeka, 1988; bd. mem. Child Abuse Prevention Team, Leavenworth, 1990. Recipient Leadership award Eastern Star Lansing, Kans., 1989. Mem. United Meth. Assn. Communicators, Video Producers/Mktg. Network, Leavenworth Clergy Assn., Lions. Republican. Home and Office: So Heights/Jarbalo Meth Ch 726 Muncie Rd Leavenworth KS 66048

PATRICK, ANNE ESTELLE, nun, theologian, religion educator; b. Washington, Apr. 5, 1941; d. William Davis and Estelle (Flynn) P. BA, Medaille Coll., 1969; MA, U. Md., 1972, U. Chgo., 1976; PhD, U. Chgo., 1982. Joined Sisters of the Holy Names, 1958. Prof. religion Carleton Coll., Northfield, Minn., 1980—. Editor Religious Book Club, 1989—; mem. editorial bd. Jour. Religious Ethics, 1989-91; contbr. articles to various publs. Assoc. Park Ridge Ctr. Mem. AAUP, Cath. Theol. Soc. Am. (pres. 1989-90, dir. 1985-91), Soc. Christian Ethics (dir. 1987-91), Am. Acad. Religion, Coll. Theology Soc., Nat. Assembly Religious Women (dir. 1972-75), D.C. Coun. Women Religious (founding pres. 1971-73). Office: Carleton Coll Northfield MN 55057

PATTEN, BEBE HARRISON, minister; b. Waverly, Tenn., Sept. 3, 1913; d. Newton Felix and Mattie Priscilla (Whitson) Harrison; m. Carl Thomas Patten, Oct. 23, 1935; children: Priscilla Carla and Bebe Rebecca (twins), Carl Thomas. D.D., McKinley-Roosevelt Coll., 1941; D.Litt., Temple Hall Coll. and Sem., 1943. Ordained to ministry Ministerial Assn. of Evangelism, 1935; evangelist in various cities of U.S., 1933-50; founder, pres. Christian Evang. Chs. Am., Inc., Oakland, Calif., 1944—, Patten Acad. Christian Edn., Oakland, 1944—, Patten Bible Coll., Oakland, 1945-83; chancellor Patten Coll., Oakland, 1983—; founder, pastor Christian Cathedral of Oakland, 1950—; held pvt. interviews with David Ben-Gurion, 1972, Menachim Begin, 1977, Yitzhak Shamir, 1991; condr. Sta. KUSW world-wide radio ministry, 70 countries around the world, 1989-90, Stas. WHRI and WWCR world coverage short wave, 1990—. Founder, condr.: radio program The Shepherd Hour, 1934—; daily TV, 1976—, nationwide telecast, 1979—; Author: Give Me Back My Soul, 1973; Editor: Trumpet Call, 1953—; composer 20 gospel and religious songs, 1945—. Mem. exec. bd. Bar-Ilan U. Assn., Israel, 1983, internat. bd. overseers, trustee Bar-Ilan U., 1991. Recipient numerous awards including medallion Ministry of Religious Affairs, Israel, 1969; medal Govt. Press Office, Jerusalem, 1971; Christian honoree of yr. Jewish Nat. Fund of No. Calif., 1975; Hidden Heroine award San Francisco Bay council Girl Scouts U.S.A., 1976, Golden State award Who's Who Hist. Soc., 1988; Ben-Gurion medallion Ben-Gurion Research Inst., 1977; Resolution of Commendation, Calif. Senate Rules Com., 1978; hon. fellow Bar-Ilan U., Israel, 1981; Dr. Bebe Patten Social Action chair established Bar-Ilan U. Mem. Am. Assn. for Higher Edn., Religious Edn. Assn., Am. Acad. Religion and Soc. Bibl. Lit., Zionist Orgn. Am., Am. Assn. Pres. of Ind. Colls. and Univs., Am. Jewish Hist. Soc., Am.-Isreal Pub. Affairs Com. Address: 2433 Coolidge Ave Oakland CA 94601 *He that labors in any great or laudable undertaking has his fatigues first supported by hope, and afterwards rewarded by joy. To strive with difficulties, and to conquer them, is the highest human felicity. I am not afraid of tomorrow for I have seen yesterday and I love today.*

PATTEN, BEBE REBECCA, college dean, clergywoman; b. Berkeley, Calif., Jan. 30, 1950; d. Carl Thomas and Bebe (Harrison) P. BS in Bible, Patten Coll., 1969; BA in Philosophy, Holy Names Coll., 1970; MA in Bibl. Studies New Testament, Wheaton Coll., 1972; PhD in Bibl. Studies New Testament, Drew U., 1976; MA in Philosophy, Dominican Sch. Philosophy & Theology, 1990. Ordained to ministry Christian Evang. Ch., 1963. Dean Patten Coll., Oakland, Calif., 1978—; presenter in field. Author: Before the Times, 1980, The World of the Early Church, 1990; contbg. author: Internat. Standard Bibl. Ency., rev. edit., 1983. Active Wheaton Coll. Symphony, 1971-72, Drew U. Ensemble, 1971-75, Young Artists Symphony, N.J., 1972-75, Somerset Hill Symphony, N.J., 1973-74, Peninsula Symphony, 1977, 80-81, Madison Chamber Trio, N.J., 1973-75. Named one of Outstanding Young Women of Am., 1976, 77, 80-81, 82; St. Olaf's Coll. fellow, 1990. Mem. AAUP, Am. Acad. Religion, Soc. Bibl. Lit., Internat. Biographical Assn., Christian Assn. for Student Affairs, Assn. for Christians in Student Devel., Inst. for Bibl. Rsch., Phi Delta Kappa.

PATTEN-BENHAM, PRISCILLA CARLA, religion educator, academic administrator; b. Berkeley, Calif., Jan. 30, 1950; d. Carl Thomas and Bebe (Harrison) Patten; m. Donald W. Benham, Mar. 30, 1986; 1 child, Charmaine P. Benham. BS, Patten Coll., 1969; BA in Psychology, Coll. Holy Names, 1971; MA in New Testament, Wheaton Coll., 1972; PhD in New Testament, Drew U., 1976. Prof. religion Patten Coll., Oakland, Calif., 1975—, pres., 1983—; v.p. Christian Evang. Chs. Am., Oakland; dir. Cathedral Chorale, Oakland, 1976—. Co-author: Before the Times, 1980, The World of the Early Church, 1991; also articles. Violinist Redwood Symphony. Mem. AAUP, Assn. Ind. Calif. Colls. and Univs., Soc. Bibl. Lit., Am. Acad. Religion, Bar-Ilan Assn. of the Greater Bay Area, Oakland C. of C. Office: Patten Coll 2433 Coolidge Ave Oakland CA 94601

PATTERSON, ANITA CAROL, religion educator; b. Henryetta, Okla., May 10, 1944; d. Seth Owen Christy and Helen Tessie (Davis) Best; m. William E. Patterson, Mar. 31, 1969. BA in Edn., Southwestern State U., 1967; MRE, Cen. Bapt. Theol. Sem., 1989. Coord. Christian edn. First Bapt. Ch., Paola, Kans., 1988-91; min. evangelism and ch. growth 1st Bapt. Ch., Coffeyville, Kans., 1991—. Mem. Coalition Against Substance Abuse, Order Eastern Star. Home: 2402 Pkwy Coffeyville KS 67337 *Jesus Christ has made and is still making a significant difference in my life, and my heart's desire is that I will live my life in such a way that I will lead others to know Him personally as Savior and Lord.*

PATTERSON, ARTHUR LAWRENCE, minister; b. Bradford, Pa., Mar. 9, 1934; s. Glenn M. and Alice Mae (Carl) P.; m. Jeanette Irene Benson, Nov. 14, 1954 (dec. Dec. 1978); children: Nancy, Alicia, Laurie. BA, Baylor U., 1957; BD, So. Bapt. Theol. Sem., 1961. Ordained to ministry Bapt. Ch., 1955. Pastor First Bapt. Ch., College Hill, Ohio, 1960-66, North Park Bapt. Ch., Pitts., 1966-68, First Mason (Ohio) Ch., 1968—; trustee Bapt. Sunday Sch. Bd., So. Bapt. Conv., 1969-78, So. Bapt. Home Mission Bd., 1982-90; moderator Cin. Bapt. Assn. 1976-78; bd. dirs. Ohio State Bapt. Conv., 1980—, mem. exec. com. 1980—, pres. 1982-84; mem. coms. So. Bapt. Conv., 1978. Contbr. articles to publs. Mem. Mason Sch. Bd., 1977-89, Warren County Youth Svcs. grant bd.; pres. Mary Haven Youth Ctr., Warren County, 1974-84, Lebanon Citzens Adv. Coun., 1974-84; bd. dirs. Countryside YMCA, Lebanon, Ohio, 1981—. Named Citizen of Yr., Mason, Ohio, 1982. Mem. Kiwanis (pres. 1977-78), Masons (32 degree), Shriners. Home: 735 Reading Rd Mason OH 45040 Office: First Bapt Ch 745 Reading Rd Mason OH 45040

PATTERSON, B. LEROY, clergyman; b. Lubbock, Tex., Jan. 28, 1935; s. B. W. and Jewel Elizabeth (Wilson) P.; m. Ada Pearl Reynolds (dec. 1981); children: Connie, Lenita; m. Martha Jean Seaton, 1984. BA, Hardin-Simmons U., Abilene, Tex., 1956; MDiv, S.W. Bapt. Theol. Sem., Ft. Worth, 1961; postgrad., Tex. A&M U., Bryan, 1973; DDiv, Houston Bapt. U., 1984. Pastor Graham St. Bapt. Ch., Abilene, 1955-56, Mustang Bapt. Ch., Denton, Tex., 1956-60, First Bapt. Ch., Van Vleck, Tex., 1961-62, Calvary Bapt. Ch., Rosenburg, Tex., 1963-65, First Bapt. Ch., Caldwell, Tex., 1965-74, Meml. Bapt. Ch., Houston, 1975—; mem. state exec. bd. Bapt. Gen. Conv. Tex., 1976-82, 84-90; moderator Union Bapt. Assn., Houston, 1985-87; bd. trustees, chmn. Highland Lakes Bapt. Encampment; vice-chmn. STate Exec. Bd., Bapt. Gen. Conv. Tex., 1988-89; preacher crusades in Japan, Australia, Hong Kong, Indonesia, Taiwan. Bd. dirs. Tex. Alcohol and Narcotic Edn., 1980-85; bd. trustees Houston Bapt. U., 1982-89, chmn. com. to elect trustees, 1985-86; chmn. Falls-Independent-Robertson-Milam Assns. Home: 254 Branding Iron Houston TX 77060 Office: Meml Bapt Ch 9101 Airline Dr Houston TX 77037

PATTERSON, DONIS DEAN, bishop; b. Holmesville, Ohio, Apr. 27, 1930; s. Raymond J. and Louella Faye (Glasgo) P.; m. JoAnne Nida, Dec. 22, 1951; children: Christoper Nida, Andrew Joseph. BS, Ohio State U., 1952; STB, Episcopal Theol. Sch., 1957; M Div, Episcopal Divinity Sch., 1972; DD (hon.), Nashotah House Sem., 1984, U. of South, 1986. Rector St. Andrews Ch., Washington Court House, Ohio, 1957-63, St. Marks Ch., Venice, Fla., 1963-70, All Sts. Ch., Winter Park, Fla., 1970-83; bishop Episcopal Diocese Dallas, 1983—; trustee Seabury Western Theol. Sem., Evanston, Ill., 1981-82, U. of South, 1983—, Episcopal Theol. Sem. S.W., 1983—. Chmn. Episcopal Ch. House of Bishops Armed Forces Com., 1989—. Officer U.S. Army, 1952-54, Korea; chaplain (col.) USAR, 1954-84. Office: Episcopal Diocese Dallas 1630 N Garrett St Dallas TX 75206

PATTERSON, EDWIN, minister; b. Andalusia, Ala., Sept. 6, 1921; s. Walter Levi and Kate Edline (Aughtman) P.; m. Margaret Alice Hall, May 14, 1966. Degree, Brennan Bus. Sch., 1940; postgrad., Samford U., 1950-57. Ordained to ministry So. Bapt. Conv., 1947. Pastor various chs. Ala., 1947—; including Hopwell, 1949-67, Harmony Bapt. Ch., Andalusia, 1967-80, Searight Bapt. Ch., Dozier, Ala., 1980—; acct. C.G. Tomberlin, M.D., Andalusia, 1985—. Home: 407 Lakeview Dr Andalusia AL 36420 Office: PO Box 486 Andalusia AL 36420 *In Him, we live and move and have our being. Therefore, my heart's desire is to honor Christ in all things, for He is the way, the truth, and the life.*

PATTERSON, J. O., bishop. Presiding bishop Ch. of God in Christ, Memphis. Address: Ch of God in Christ PO Box 320 Memphis TN 38101

PATTERSON, JIMMY DALE, minister; b. Brownwood, Tex., Oct. 2, 1958; s. Josie Mildred (Lee) P.; m. Amy Elizabeth Crutchfield. BA, Howard Payne U., 1982; MA in Religious Edn., Southwestern Sem., 1987. Ordained to ministry Bapt. Ch., 1981. With Coggin Ave. Bapt. Ch., Brownwood, 1979—; min. Downing Bapt. Ch., De Leon, Tex., 1981-87; min. students Parkwood Bapt. Ch., Jacksonville, Fla., 1987-90; pastor Ft. Caroline Bapt. Ch., Jacksonville, Fla., 1990—. Named one of Outstanding Young of Am., 1985. Mem. Williamson Bapt. Assn. (dir. of youth 1987—). Avocations: photography, oil painting, basketball. Home: 8335 Calento St Jacksonville FL 32211-6326 Office: Ft Caroline Bapt Ch 11428 McCormick Rd Jacksonville FL 32225 *I my life I have found that sparrows fly in flocks, but eagles fly alone. Although there is safety in numbers true courage is tested when alone.*

PATTERSON, LEIGHTON PAIGE, college president, minister; b. Ft. Worth, Oct. 19, 1942; m. Dorothy Jean Kelley, June 22, 1963; children: Armour Paige, Carmen Leigh. BA, Hardin-Simmons U., 1965; ThM, New Orleans Bapt Theol Sem, 1968, ThD, 1973. Ordained to ministry So. Bapt. Conv., 1959. Pastor Sardis Bapt. Ch., Rotan, Tex., 1962-63, 2d Bapt. Ch., Abilene, Tex., 1963-65, Bethany Bapt. Ch., New Orleans, 1966-70, 1st Bapt. Ch., Fayetteville, Ark., 1970-75; pres. The Criswell Coll., Dallas, 1975—; trustee Fgn. Mission Bd., So. Bapt. Conv.; mem. Bapt. World Alliance; panelist TV broadcast Am. Religious Town Hall. Author: A Pilgrim Priesthood-An Exposition of 1 Peter, 1982, The Troubled Triumphant Church-Exposition of 1 Corinthians, Everyman's Bible Commentary. 1983, Song of Solomon, Commentary on Revelation, 1986; cons. editor The New American Commentary. Mem. Coun. for Nat. Policy, Internat. Policy Forum. Mem. Evang. Theol. Soc., Nr. East Archaeol. Soc. Office: The Criswell Coll 4010 Gaston Ave Dallas TX 75246 *Man's adversities are God's universities.*

PATTERSON, RICKEY LEE, clergyman; b. Indpls., Sept. 24, 1952; s. William Irving and Wanda Lou (Calbert) P.; B.A., Ind. U., 1976; postgrad. U. Miami, 1976-80; M.Theology, Internat. Bible Inst. and Sem., 1983; m. Sharon Rose Leonard, May 4, 1974. Pres. Pat-Cat Enterprises, Inc., Miami, 1977—; pastor, 1972—; founder, pres. Jesus Students Fellowship, Inc., 1973—, pastor, 1979—, radio broadcast speaker, 1978—, dir. J.S.F. Cassette Ministries, 1978—; pres. Jesus Fellowship, Inc., 1981—; ordained to ministry Internat. Conv. Faith Chs. and Ministers, Inc., 1980; coll. unit dir. Northwestern Mut. Life Ins. Co., Milw., 1980-83; founder, supt. Jesus Fellowship Christian Sch., 1983—; pres. Dade County Pvt. Sch. Systems, Inc., 1983—; instr. Bible, Ind. U., 1973-76; instr. Bible, U. Miami, 1976—, also guest lectr. dept. religion; pres. Miami Bible Inst., 1984—; guest lectr. Miami North Community Correctional Center, Dade County Correctional Inst., Fed. Inst. Corrections; adv. Miami chpt. Women Aglow, 1980-82; campus minister Ind. U., U. Miami, Fla. Internat. U., Miami-Dade Community Coll., U. P.R.; exec. bd. mem. Internat. Congress of Local Chs., 1988—; dir. Christian Benefactor, 1990—. Charter mem. Rep. Presdl. Task Force; sustaining mem. Rep. Nat. Com.; bd. govs. Am. Coalition Traditional Values, 1984—; mem. exec. bd. Internat. Congress of Local Chs., 1988—. Mem. Bur. Bus. Practice, Nat. Audubon Soc., Am. Entrepreneurs Assn., Inst. Cert. Fin. Planners., Am. Security Council, U.S. Senatorial Club, Zool. Soc. Fla., Adult Congregate Living Facility (pres. Naples chpt. 1988—), Christian Booksellers Assn., Nat. Assn. Life Underwriters, Miami Assn. Life Underwriters, Am. Mktg. Assn., Full Gospel Businessmen's Fellowship Internat., Internat. Coalition of Local Chs. (mem. exec. bd. 1988—), Ind. U. Alumni Assn., Sigma Pi. Republican. Editor: Spirit of Life Mag., 1980-82; chief editor Miami Jour., 1984—, monthly newsletter The Christian Benefactor, 1990. Home and Office: 9775 SW 87th Ave Miami FL 33176

PATTERSON, RONALD PAUL, publishing company executive, editor, clergyman; b. Ashland, Ohio, Dec. 4, 1941; s. Donald Edward and Mildred (Niswender) P.; m. Marlene Pfahler, Sept. 1, 1962; children: Paul Edward, Mark Loren. BA, Malone Coll., 1963; MDiv, United Theol. Sem., Dayton, Ohio, 1967; MA, Syracuse U., 1970; DD, Cen. Meth. Coll., 1988. Ordained to ministry United Methodist Ch. Editor youth publs. Otterbein Press, Dayton, 1964-68; editor The Upper Room, Nashville, 1970-74, Word Books, Waco, Tex., 1974-77; book editor, editorial dir. Abingdon Press, Nashville, 1977-88; v.p. United Meth. Pub. House, 1984-88, sr. editor Ch. Resources, 1988—, dir. pub., 1985-86; v.p. Religious Pub. Rels. Coun. Nashville, 1970-74; jr. coll. instr. creative writing, Waco; leader writers' workshops. Author: (with others) The Kyle Rote Story, 1975; editor: Come On, Let's Pray, 1972; compiler: The Coming of Easter, 1973; founding editor Alive Now! devotional publ.; editorial dir. Quar. Rev., 1980-87; contbr. articles to mags. Tchr. Tenn. State Prison, Nashville, 1984-88; vice chmn. pastor-parish com., Hermitage, Tenn., 1984-86; v.p. YMCA, Dayton; bd. dirs. Combined Health Appeal, 1988; treas. United Way. Recipient George Washington Honor medal Nat. Freedom Found., Valley Forge, Pa., 1960, Paul M. Hinkhouse award Religious Pub. Relations Council, N.Y.C., 1973; named one of Outstanding Young Men Am., 1972. Mem. Am. Acad. Religion, Religion Pub. Group, Christian Publs. Assn., Southeastern Pubs. Assn. (exec. com. 1985-88), Pubs. Assn. of South (treas.), Robertson Assn., Evang. Christian Pubs. Assn. (bd. dirs. 1987-88), Nashville Soccer Assn. Democrat. United Methodist. Club: Capitol. Avocations: boating; refinishing furniture; golf; tennis; racquetball. Home: 4060 Port Cleburne Ln Hermitage TN 37076 Office: Abingdon Press Div of United Meth Pub House 201 8th Ave S Nashville TN 37202

PATTERSON, VIRGINIA CATHARINE, religious organization executive; b. N.Mex., Jan. 23, 1931; d. Edward Cecil and Edith Elizabeth (Roweton) P. B.A., U. Tulsa, 1953; M.A. Bible/Missions, Columbia Bible Coll. (S.C.), 1956; M.S. Elem. Ed., Okla. State U., 1963; Ed.D., No. Ill. U., DeKalb, 1978. Tchr., recreation dir. Girls Indsl. Sch., Columbia, S.C., 1954-57; tchr., prin., Kent Acad., Nigeria, 1958-68; publ. dir. Pioneer Girls, Inc., Wheaton, Ill., 1969-70; pres. Pioneer Clubs and Pioneer Ministries, Inc., Wheaton, Ill., 1970—; adj. prof. Wheaton Coll. Grad. Sch. (Ill.), 1979—. Author: A Touch of God, 1979. Presbyterian. Office: Pioneer Clubs 27W130 St Charles Rd Wheaton IL 60187

PATTERSON, WINDELL RAY, minister; b. Martinsville, Va., Feb. 1, 1930; s. John Pedigo and Erma Hope (Bennett) P.; m. Edith Turner, Sept. 22, 1950; 1 child, Stephen Wayne. AA, Bluefield Coll., 1955; BA, Concord Coll., 1959; MDiv, Southeastern Bapt. Theol. Sem., 1984. Ordained to ministry So. Bapt. Conv., 1951. Pastor Braimwell (W.Va.) Bapt. Ch., 1957-60, New Hope and Zoar Bapt. Chs., Orange County, Va., 1960-65, North Pamunkey Bapt. Ch., Lahore, Va., 1965-68, Tazewell Bapt. and Bundy's Chapel Bapt. chs., Tazewell, Va., 1968-79, Mayo Bapt. Ch., 1979-85, Roberts Chapel Bapt. Ch., Pendleton, N.C., 1985—; moderator East River Bapt. Assn., Dublin, Va., 1976-77; mem. joint adv. com. Highlands Bapt. Assn., 1973-79; mem. bds. and coms. Va. Bapt. Gen. Assn., Richmond, 1978-81; chmn. continuing theol. edn. com. Henry County Bapt. Assn., Martinsville, Va., 1983-84. Chaplain, 1st lt. Tazewell Rescue Squad, 1976-77; pres. Tazewell County Assn. for Retarded Citizens, 1974-76; chmn. Tazewell County Devel. Corp., 1972-73;. Recipient Cert. of Appreciation, East River Bapt. Assn., 1973-79. Fellow West Chowan Bapt. Assn. (bd. dirs. 1987-90, pres. 1988-90, chmn. continuing theol. edn. com. 1990—), Ruritan (pres. Severn/Pendleton chpt. 1989-90), Rotary (pres. Tazewell club 1989-90, Past Pres. award 1979). Democrat. Home: PO Box 128 Pendleton NC 27862

PATTESON, ROY KINNEER, JR., administrator, clergyman; b. Richmond, Va., Oct. 27, 1928; s. Roy Kinneer and Mary (Anderson) P.; m. Edna Pauline Cox, Apr. 15, 1950; children: Stephen, David. B.A., U. Richmond, 1957; B.D., Union Theol. Sem., 1961; Th.M., Duke U., 1964, Ph.D., 1967. Ordained to ministry Presbyterian Ch. in U.S.A., 1961. Fellow Duke U. Inst. Medieval and Renaissance Studies, 1968; pres. So. Sem. Jr. Coll., 1970-72; v.p. Mary Baldwin Coll., 1972-77; pres. King Coll., Bristol, Tenn., 1977-79; asst. to pres. Va. Wesleyan Coll., 1979-81, v.p., 1981-85; v.p. Westminster-Canterbury of Hampton Rds., Inc., Virginia Beach, Va., 1985-88; asst. sec. bd. trustees Westminster-Canterbury of Hampton Rds., Inc., 1986-88; dir. Norfolk (Va.) Sr. Ctr., 1987-88; cons. Marts & Lundy Inc., Rockbridge Baths, Va., 1988—; pastor Pittsboro and Mt. Vernon Springs Presbyn. chs., Pittsboro, N.C., 1962-65; mem. mission council and chmn. budget com. Shenandoah Presbytery, 1973-77; chmn. com. on higher edn. Norfolk Presbytery, 1980-82; mem. community adv. bd. Madison Coll., 1975-77; bd. dirs. Tenn. Ind. Coll. Fund; v.p. Mid-Appalachian Coll. Council, 1978-79. Vice pres. Rockbridge Hist. Soc., Lexington, Va., 1970-77; chmn. edn. com. Staunton-Augusta C. of C. Served with U.S. Army, 1948-49; with U.S. N.G., 1949-52. Recipient Grad. Scholar award Duke U., 1966. Office: Box 130 Rockbridge Baths VA 24473

PATTISON, FRED LEWIS, minister, academic administrator; b. N.Y.C., Sept. 14, 1932; s. George Wilson and Florence Augusta (Cross) P. Ordained to ministry, 1955. Pastor Bethel Bible Christian Ch., Garden City Park, N.Y., 1954-58, Faith Bapt. Ch., Tucson, Ariz., 1958-70, Casa De Cristo Evang. Ch., Phoenix, 1976—; pres. Phoenix Evang. Bible Inst., 1981—; exec. sec. The Evang. Network, Phoenix, 1988—; presiding overseer Conf. Evang. Christian Chs., Phoenix, 1991—; pres. Cristo AIDS, Phoenix, 1986—. Republican. Home: 1731 E Griswold Rd Phoenix AZ 85020 Office: Casa De Cristo Evang Ch 1029 E Turney Phoenix AZ 85014

PATTISON, GEORGE LINSLEY, minister; b. Cambridge, Eng., May 25, 1950; s. George William and Jean (Allan) P.; m. Hilary Christine Cochrane, Feb. 25, 1971; children—Charlotte Ann, Neil John Robert, Elisabeth Linsley. M.A., Edinburgh U., Scotland, 1972, B.D., 1977; Ph.D., Durham U., Eng., 1983. Ordained to ministry Ch. of Eng., 1977. Curate, Ch. of Eng., Newcastle-Upon-Tyne, 1977-80; parish priest Ch. of Eng., Suffolk, 1983-91, dean of chapel King's Coll., Cambridge, 1991—. Author: Art, Modernity and Faith, 1991, Kierkegaard: The Aesthetic and the Religious, 1991; contbr. articles to learned jours. Travelling scholar U. Edinburg, in Tubingen, Fed. Republic Germany, 1976, U. Durham, in Copenhagen, 1982. Avocations: yoga, music, running, reading, writing. Home: 15, Eltisley Ave, Cambridge CB3 9JG, England *Religion should not seek to absorb all other forms of life but instead must affirm with reverence and wonder the rich plurality of life in its human and non-human manifestations, abondoning forever the attempt to answer all questions.*

PATTON, GARY LLOYD, pastoral care administrator; b. Cin., July 23, 1954; s. Herman Lloyd and Nora Irene (Garrett) P.; m. Mabel Larraine McCowan, Aug. 16, 1974; children: Monica Larraine, Kyle Lloyd. BA,

Anderson U., 1976; MA, La. Tech. U., 1979; cert. in clin. pastoral edn., Med. Coll. Ohio, Toledo, Cabell Huntington (W.Va.) Hosp.; postgrad., Ohio U., 1990—. Tchr. Bethel Christian Sch., Ruston, La., 1976-77; pastor Ruston Ch. of God, 1976-80, 1st Ch. of God, Wauseon, Ohio, 1980-86, Trinity Ch. of God, Huntington, W.Va., 1986-90; dir. pastoral care St. Mary's Hosp., Huntington, 1990—; bd. mem. Hope Hill Children's Home, Hope, Ky., 1988—. Mem. Assn. of Clin. Pastoral Edn. (clin. mem.), Assn. of Mental Health Clergy. Mem. Ch. of God. Avocations: horses, guns, farming. Office: St Marys Hosp 2900 1st Ave Huntington WV 25701

PATTON, GEORGE MALLORY, medical technician, missionary; b. Camden, Ark., Apr. 20, 1930; s. Charles Holley and Mary Hanna (Moore) P.; m. Alice Belle Silmon, Sept. 26, 1959 (div. Aug. 1960); m. Martha Ann Messinger, Apr. 16, 1983. BS in Sci. Edn., N.E. La. U., 1955; postgrad., Presbyn. Sch. Christian Edn., Richmond, Va., 1968-9, 72-73. Missionary Presbyn. Ch. U.S., Chonju, Republic of Korea, 1964-78; lab. technician Morehouse Gen. Hosp., Bastrop, La., 1978—. Sgt. U.S. Army, 1948-52. Mem. Soc. Bibl. Lit. Democrat. Home: 2022 Gemini Dr Bastrop LA 71220

PATTON, KENNETH ROGER, minister; b. Frankfurt, Fed. Republic Germany, Oct. 16, 1957; (parents Am. citizens); s. Roger G. and Carol J. (Baker) P.; m. Isabel Aurelia Tortora, Nov. 26, 1982; children: Mary Elizabeth, William Kenneth. AS, Yuba Coll., Marysville, Calif., 1977; BA in Social Sci., Calif. State U., Sacramento, 1985. Ordained to ministry So. Bapt. Conv., 1985. Assoc. pastor Wheatland (Calif.) So. Bapt. Ch., 1983-85; sr. pastor Palermo (Calif.) Bapt. Ch., 1985—; vice chmn. adv. bd. Salvation Army, Oroville, Calif., 1991—. Mem. Kiwanis (sec. Oroville 1986—, Outstanding Sec. award Calif.-Nev.-Hawaii Dist. 1990). Republican. Home: 7796 Irwin Ave Palermo CA 95968

PATTON, ROBERT THOMAS, minister, finance and economics consultant; b. Toledo, Aug. 16, 1940; s. Thomas Laton and Doris Caroline (Tabbert) P.; m. Carol Anne Yount, June 9, 1962 (div. June 1970); 1 child, Elizabeth; m. Elizabeth Chamberlain, Feb. 8, 1975. BSME, U. Mich., 1962; MBA, U. Minn., 1966; PhD, U. Wash., 1969; D Ministry, Western Conservative Bapt. Sem., Portland, Oreg., 1985. Commd. to ministry Assemblies of God, 1979. Prof. fin. Western Wash. U. Coll. Bus. and Econs., 1970-79; assoc. pastor Hillcrest Chapel, Bellingham, Wash., 1979—, treas., bd. dirs., 1981—; treas., bd. dirs. Greater Bellingham Ministries, 1981—. Author: A Manual for Operating a Church Corporation in the State of Washington, 1984; contbr. articles to profl. jours. Treas. Bellingham area crusades, 1979, 81. Mem. Nat. Assn. Forensic Economists. Home: 1100 Chuckanut Crest Dr Bellingham WA 98226 Office: Hillcrest Chapel 1414 Larrabee Ave Bellingham WA 98225

PATTON, RONALD L., minister, communication educator; b. Covington, Ky., Dec. 10, 1941; s. Charles Milton and Florence A. (De Voss), P., m. Donna Jean Avery, July 18, 1964; children: Andrew Charles, Kirk Richard. AB in Early European History, U. Cin., 1964; Min Div., MA in Edn., McCormick Theol. Sem., Chgo., 1968; D of Ministry, San Francisco Theol. Sem., San Anselmo, Calif., 1985. Ordained to ministry Presbyn. Ch., 1968. Pastor Earl Park (Ind.) Presbyn. Ch., 1968-70; assoc. pastor 1st Presbyn. Ch., Grand Haven, Mich., 1970-73; pastor Westport Presbyn. Ch., Kansas City, Mo., 1973-86; dir. Kansas City progams, instr. mass communications Mo. Valley Coll., Kansas City and Marshall, Mo., 1986-87; dir. Midwest Presbyn. Media Services, Kansas City, 1987—; sales exec. Coldwell Banker Residential Real Estate Services, 1987-88; minister Christ Presbyn. Ch., Kansas City, 1987—; instr. pub. speaking Met. Community Colls., Kansas City, 1987—; mem. Heartland Presbytery, Kansas City, 1973—, budget com., 1981-86, racial ethnic com., 1987—. Author: Every Sunday at 11: The Disciplined Art of Preaching, 1991. chaplain Boy Scouts Am., Kansas City, 1973-86, scoutmaster, 1985-86, cubmaster, Westwood, Kans., 1977-78; residential chmn. Am. Cancer Soc., Johnson County, Kans., 1984-85. Avocations: tennis, swimming, skiing, private pilot.

PAUL, FELIX, bishop. Bishop of Port Victoria Roman Cath. Ch., Victoria, Seychelles. Office: Bishop's House, Olivier Maradan Rd, POB 43, Victoria Seychelles*

PAUL, GARRETT EDWARD, religion educator; b. Chicago Heights, Ill., Nov. 10, 1949; s. Gilbert Herbert and Eleanor Tribune (Jenne) P.; m. Martha Elizabeth Styers, Oct. 13, 1979; children: Christopher Leland, Jonathan Friedrich. AB, Wabash Coll., Crawfordsville, Ind., 1971; MA, U. Chgo., 1973, PhD, 1980. Assoc. prof., chair dept. religion Gustavus Adolphus Coll., St. Peter, Minn., 1983—; mem. ch. coun., pres. Living Word Luth. Ch., Laurinburg, N.C., 1977-83; mem. ch. coun. First Luth. Ch., St. Peter, 1990—. Translator: Jungel, Karl Barth, 1986, Troeltsch, The Christian Faith, 1991. Fulbright faculty devel. grantee, 1977. Mem. Am. Acad. Religion, Soc. Christian Ethics, Soc. Bus. Ethics, Ernst Troeltsch Gesellschaft, Phi Beta Kappa. Democrat. Office: Gustavus Adolphus Coll Saint Peter MN 56082 *Our headlong rush towards individualism now shows some signs of abating, but only after it has destroyed more communities-cultural and ecological-than we can ever imagine. Will we now learn again from our religious traditions that there is something greater than ourselves?.*

PAUL, JOEL H., religious organizations consultant and administrator; b. Brookline, Mass., Sept. 4, 1942; s. Samuel Murray and Doris (Mochine) P.; m. Lillian Amcis, Nov. 14, 1974; children: Nachman, Elie, Heshy, Shulamit. BS, Boston U., 1964; MS, Yeshiva U., 1967; postgrad., U. Pa., 1973-74. Founding dir. New Eng. Region, Nat. Conf. Synagogue Youth, 1952-64; dir. Youth Bur. Community Search Div., Yeshiva U., N.Y.C., 1966-71; dir. B'nai B'rith Hillel/Founds. of Greater Phila., 1971-73, exec. dir., 1973-85; pres. Joel H. Paul & Assocs., N.Y.C., 1985—; v.p. Religious Zionists; bd. govs. Union of Orthodox Jewish Congregations of Am., N.Y.C., 1989—. Recipient Service Award for Decade of Svcs. to Coll. Youth, Jewish Campus Activities Bd., 1981. Mem. Assn. Jewish Community Orgn. Profls., Nat. Soc. Fund Raising Execs. Office: Joel H Paul & Assocs 241 W 30th St New York NY 10001-2801

PAUL, JOHN JOSEPH, bishop; b. La Crosse, Wis., Aug. 17, 1918; s. Roland Philip and Louise (Gilles) P. B.A., Loras Coll., Dubuque, Iowa, 1939; S.T.B., St. Mary's Sem., Balt., 1943; M.Ed., Marquette U., 1956. Ordained priest Roman Catholic Ch., 1943; prin. Regis High Sch., Eau Claire, Wis., 1948-55; rector Holy Cross Sem., La Crosse, 1955-66, St. Joseph's Cathedral, La Crosse, 1966-77; aux. bishop Diocese of La Crosse, 1977-83, bishop, 1983—. Office: PO Box 4004 La Crosse WI 54602-4004

PAUL, ROBERT SCOTT, minister; b. Poplar Bluff, Mo., Mar. 24, 1958; s. Robert Leon and Lois Jean (Albright) P.; m. Jennifer Sue Jackson, Aug. 11, 1979; children: Rachel Elizabeth, Kristen Hope. BA, Johnson Bible Coll., Knoxville, 1980; MA, Cin. Christian Sem., 1991. Ordained to ministry, Ind. Christian Ch. Sr. minister Cen. Christian Ch., Richmond, Ind., 1980—; bd. dirs. Christian Counseling Svcs., Muncie, Ind., 1986—; ministerial advisor Christian Student Found., Ball State U., Munice, 1981—; coun. of seventy Johnson Bible Coll., Knoxville; founder E. Cen. Ind. Christian Youth Fellowship, Richmond, 1982-84. Bd. dirs. Citizens for Community Value of Hope County, 1987—; campaign com. Seal for Prosecutor, Richmond, 1990. Republican. Office: Cen Christian Ch 4511 National Rd W Richmond IN 47374

PAULIEN, JON, religion educator; b. N.Y.C., June 5, 1949; s. Kurt Emil and Gertrude (Ludwig) P.; m. Pamella Gulke, Dec. 23, 1973; children: Tammy Kaye, Joel Jonathan, Kimberly Kaye. BA, Atlantic Union Coll., South Lancaster, Mass., 1972; MDiv, Andrews U., Berrien Springs, Mich., 1976, PhD, 1987. Ordained to ministry Seventh-day Adventist Ch., 1978. Assoc. pastor German Brooklyn Seventh-day Adventist Ch., Ridgewood, N.Y., 1972-73, sr. pastor, 1978-81; pastor Port Jervis (N.Y.) Seventh-day Adventist Ch., 1976-78; asst. prof. theology Andrews U., 1984-85, asst. prof. N.T., 1985-88, assoc. prof. N.T., 1988—; Mem. Adventist approach to contemporary culture com. Seventh-day Adventist, Washington, 1985—, mem. ministerial tng. study com., Washington, 1989—. Author: Decoding Revelation's Trumpets, 1988; assoc. editor Andrews U. Sem. Studies, 1990—; contbr. articles to religious jours. Mem. Soc. Bibl. Lit., Chgo. Soc. Bibl. Rsch., Andrews Soc. Religious Study. Republican. Home: 8756-1 N Ridge Berrien Springs MI 49103 Office: Andrews U Theol Sem Berrien Springs MI 49104 *It isn't who you know or what you know, but who you are that really counts. Just as pitching is 90% of success in baseball, character is 90% of success in life.*

PAULK, EARL PEARLY, pastor; b. Appling County, Ga., May 30, 1927; s. Earl Pearly and Addie Mae (Tomberlin) P.; m. Norma Lucille Davis, July 5, 1946; children: Rebecca Mae, Susan Joy, Roma Beth. BA, Furman U., 1947; BDiv, Candler Sch. Theology, 1951; MDiv, Emory U., 1972; DD, New Covenant Internat. Bible Coll., New Zealand, 1990; DD (hon.), Oral Roberts U., Tulsa, 1987. Ordained to ministry Ch. of God. Tchr. Lee Coll., Cleveland, Tenn., 1947-48; pastor Moultrie (Ga.) Ch. of God, 1948-49, Buford (Ga.) Ch. of God, 1949-50; youth dir. Dorabille (Ga.) Ch. of God, 1950-51; pastor Hemphill Ave Ch. of God (now Mt. Paran Ch. of God), Atlanta, 1951-60; sr. pastor Chapel Hill Harvester Ch. (Cathedral of the Holy Spirit), Decatur, Ga., 1960—; presiding bishop Internat. Communion of Charismatic Chs., Atlanta, 1982—; trustee Charismatic Bible Ministries, Tulsa, 1985—; mem. steering com. Global Mission , L.A., 1989—; counselor, human svc. minister to chemically addicted, AIDS patients, single parents, sr. citizens. Author: Your Pentecostal Neighbor, Forward in Faith, The Divine Runner, Satan Unmasked, Subltle Doors to Satanism, The Wounded Body of Christ, Ultimate Kingdom, Sex Is God's Idea, Held in the Heavens Until, To Whom Is God Betrothed?, Thrust in the Sickle and Reap, That the World May Know, 101 Questions Your Pastor Hopes You Never Ask, The Church: Trampled or Triumphant?, The Local Church Says Hell No!. Trustee, regent Oral Rroberts U., Tulsa, 1986—; mem. steering com. Community APPEAL to the Homeless, Atlanta, 190—; mem. adv. bd. Bd. Edn.-Ben Jones, Atlanta, 1990. Recipient Disting. Svc. award Empire Real Estate Bd., 1989. Mem. Network of Christian Ministries (exec. Bd. 1980—), Tikkun Ministries of Refernce (bd. dirs.), Rambo-McQuire (Nashville, bd. dirs. 1988—), Found. for the Discovery Am. (Gaithersburg, Md., bd. dirs. 1990—), Lord's Day Alliance (Atlanta, bd. dirs. 1989—). Avocations: golf, tennis. Office: Chapel Hill Harvester Ch 4650 Flat Shoals Pkwy Decatur GA 30034

PAULSELL, WILLIAM OLIVER, seminary president, minister; b. Miami, Fla., Aug. 26, 1935; s. Oliver Otto and Dorothy Ann (Eason) P.; m. Sally Myers Atkins, Aug. 22, 1957; children: Stephanie Ann, Diane Carole. BA, Tex. Christian U., 1957; BD, Vanderbilt U., 1959, MA, 1961, PhD, 1965; DD (hon.), Bethany Coll., Bethany, W.Va., 1990. Ordained to ministry Christian Ch. (Disciples of Christ), 1959. Prof. religion Atlantic Christian Coll., Wilson, N.C., 1962-81; dean Lexington (Ky.) Theol. Sem., 1981-87, pres., 1987—. Author: Taste and See, 1976, Letters from a Hermit, 1978, Tough Minds, Tender Hearts, 1990; editor: Sermons in a Monastery, 1983. Mem. Am. Soc. Ch. History, Disciples of Christ Hist. Soc. Office: Lexington Theol Sem 631 S Limestone Lexington KY 40508

PAULSEN, JAN, clergyman, church administrator; b. Narvik, Norway, Jan. 5, 1935; came to Eng., 1968; s. Reidar A. and Alfhild K. (Kirstensen) P.; m. Kari Trykkerud, July 1, 1955; children—Laila, Jan-Rune, Rein Andre. B.A., Andrews U., Berrien Springs, Mich., 1957, M.A., 1958, M.Div., 1962; Dr.Theol. Tubingen U. (W.Ger.), 1972. Ordained to ministry Seventh-Day Adventist Ch., 1963. Minister, Seventh-Day Adventist Ch., Arendal and Haugesund, Norway, 1959-61; lectr. Bekwai Tchr. Tng. Coll. (Ghana), 1962-64; lectr., coll. pres. Adventist Coll. of West Africa, Ilishan, Nigeria, 1964-68; lectr. Newbold Coll., Bracknell, Eng., 1968-76, pres., 1976-80; gen. sec. Seventh-day Adventist Ch. Hdqrs. for No. Europe, St. Albans, Hertfordshire, Eng., 1980—, pres., 1983—. Author: When the Spirit Descends, 1977; contbr. articles to various jours. Mem. bd. Newbold Coll., Bracknell, 1976—. Mem. Internat. Assn. Mission Studies. Home: 43 Cunningham Hill Rd, Saint Albans Hertfordshire AL1 5BX, England Office: Seventh-day Adventist Church, Headquarters Northern Europe, 119 Saint Peters St, Saint Albans Hertfordshire AL1 3EY, England

PAULSEN, WAYNE MERRILL, minister; b. Carroll, Iowa, Feb. 18, 1941; s. Henry Arthur and Edna Lucille (Nelson) P.; m. Julia Ann Cormack, Aug. 15, 1965; children: Lisa Beth, Lori Ann. BS, N.W. Mo. State U., 1963; BD, Cen. Bapt. Theol. Sem., 1966, MDiv, 1972; D of Ministry, McCormick Theol. Sem., 1985. Ordained to ministry Am. Bapt. Ch., 1966. Assoc. minister 1st Bapt. Ch., Wichita, Kans., 1966-69; pastor 1st Bapt. Ch., Colby, Kans., 1969-77, Garden City, Kans., 1977-88; sr. pastor 1st Bapt. Ch., North Platte, Nebr., 1988—. Trustee Ottawa (Kans.) U., 1991—. Mem. Am. Bapt. Ministers Coun., Rotary (dist. gov. 1984-85). Office: 1st Bapt Ch 100 McDonald Rd North Platte NE 69101

PAULSON, HENDRIK PIETER, religious organization administrator; b. Dinteloord, North Brabant, The Netherlands, May 18, 1948; s. Pieter Simon Marius and Margaretha Antonia (Stoltink) P.; m. Mona Delene Messenger, Nov. 18, 1978; children: Larissa, Michael. Grad., Dutch Agr. Inst., Gorinchem, The Netherlands, 1966; cert., Capernwray Bible Sch., Carnforth, Eng., 1971. European dir. Open Doors, Ermelo, The Netherlands, 1975-78; founder, gen. dir. St. Antwoord, Roosendaal, The Netherlands, 1979-90; founder, gen. dir. Ea. European Bible Mission, Colorado Springs, Colo., 1971—, Delta, B.C., Can., 1972—; also chmn. bd. dirs. Ea. European Bible Mission; bd. dirs. Bibl. Edn. by Extension, Vienna and Dallas, 1985—, Nova Nadeja, Brno, Czechoslovakia, 1991—, Noua Sperante, Timisoara, Romania, 1991—, Ost Europaische Bibel Mission, Vienna, Austria, 1991—, St. Hoop voor Oost Europa, Roosendaal, The Netherlands, 1991—; mem. exec. com. Mission Forum, Vienna, 1984—.; Author: Beyond The Wall, 1982, Huil Niet Om de Winnaars, 1984, Tegen De Verdrukking In, 1987; author, editor Focus newsletter, 1979—; scriptwriter film More Than Meets the Eye, 1978. Home: Albrectsgasse 32A, A2500 Baden Austria Office: Ea European Bible Mission PO Box 110 Colorado Springs CO 80901-0110

PAULSON, SCOTT, minister; b. Topeka, Feb. 24, 1953; s. Stuart Glenn and Laura (Gage) P.; m. Patricia Zarullo, Nov. 15, 1980; children: Glenn, Joseph, Monica. BA in English, U. Iowa, 1975; BD, Evang. Theol. Sem., 1980, MDiv, 1982. Ordained to ministry Ch. of Christ, 1980. Asst. min. Ch. of Christ, Seattle, 1980-84; min. Ch. of Christ of Bellevue, Wash., 1984-89, Ridgewood Werik Ch., Albany, N.Y., 1990—. Democrat. Office: Ridgewood Werik Ch 21 N Gate Dr Albany NY 12203-5101

PAULSON, WARREN LEE, minister; b. Racine, Wis., Nov. 18, 1932; s. Harvey Leonard and Gertrude Cecilia (Anderson) P.; m. Ruth Esther Pedersen, Apr. 4, 1959; children: Joy Ruth, Katherine Esther, David Warren. AA, Concordia Jr. Coll., Ft. Wayne, Ind., 1954; MDiv, Concordia Theol. Sem., Ft. Wayne, 1988; BTh., Concordia Theol. Sem., Springfield, Ill., 1958; advanced cert. in clin. pastoral tng., Inst. Pastoral Care, 1966. Ordained to ministry Luth. Ch.—Mo. Synod, 1958. Pastor Trinity Luth. Ch., Newberry, Mich., Grace Luth. Ch., Germfask, Mich., 1958-63, Faith Luth. Ch., Germantown, Wis., 1963-65; with clin. tng. dept. prison, mental and univ. hosps., 1965-66; coordinating chaplain Mich. Corrections Camps, Grass Lake, 1966—; svc. to deaf Mich. Upper Peninsula, 1960-62; cir. counselor No. Wis. dist. Luth. Ch.—Mo. Synod, 1962-63; chaplains' rep. Chaplaincy Adv. Com., Mich. Dept. Corrections, 1976-79; com. mem. to various denom. convs.; chaplaincy cons. County Jail, Jackson, Mich., 1982-88. Mem. Am. Protestant Correctional Chaplains Assn. (regional v.p. 1981), Am. Correctional Chaplains Assn., Am. Correctional Assn., Mich. Statewide Chaplains Assn. (v.p. 1989-91, pres. 1991—). Home: 4839 Sequoia Jackson MI 49201 Office: Corrections Camps 6000 Maute Rd Grass Lake MI 49240 *The most important thing in serving people is to love them.*

PAULY, NANCY MARIE, pastoral associate; b. Bayville, N.Y., Nov. 2, 1936; d. Salvatore and Angelina (Turano) Meringolo; children: James, Matthew, Edward, Jennifer Cavendar, Gregory, Andrew. BA in Pastoral Ministry, Marylhurst (Oreg.) Coll., 1987; MA in Theology cum laude, Mount Angel Sem., St. Benedict, Oreg., 1990. Dir. religious edn. St. Francis Ch., Sherwood, Oreg., 1979-85; dir. faith formation St. Luke Ch., Woodburn, Oreg., 1989-91; pastoral assoc. St. Vincent de Paul Ch., Salem, Oreg., 1991—; prof. catechetics Mount Angel Sem., St. Benedict; religious edn. cons. Archdiocese of Portland, Oreg., 1985-88; adj. prof. Marylhurst Coll., 1990, mem. adv. bd., 1989-91; mem. adv. bd. Benedictine Sisters, Mt. Angel, 1988—; mem. Archdiocesan Evangelizatoin Com., Portland, Oreg. Friends of C.G. Jung, Portland; mem. Pastoral Assocs. of Oreg., Portland. Named AAUW Outstanding Woman, 1987; recipient Tng. award for religious leadership, Order Eastern Star, 1987. Democrat. Home: 780-D Lockhaven Dr NE Keizer OR 97303

PAUPINI, GIUSEPPE CARDINAL, former archbishop; b. Mondavio, Italy, Feb. 25, 1907. Ordained priest Roman Cath. Ch., 1930; titular archbishop of Sebastopolis in Abasgia, 1956; served in Vatican Diplomatic Corps, 1956-69; internuncio to Iran, 1956-57; nuncio to Guatemala and El Salvadtor, 1958-58, to Colombia, 1959-69; created cardinal, 1969; titular ch. All Saints Ch.; major penitentiary, 1973; mem. Congregation of Causes of Saints, Commn. State of Vatican City. Address: Via Rustirucci 13, Rome Italy

PAVAN, PIETRO CARDINAL, Italian ecclesiastic; b. Treviso, Italy, Aug. 30, 1903. ordained Roman Cath. Ch., 1928. Proclaimed cardinal, 1985; deacon San Francesco da Paola ai Monti. Address: Ponte Galeria, Via della Magliana 1240, 00050 Rome Italy

PAVEY, NORMAN CURTIS, minister; b. New Britain, Conn., Nov. 10, 1943; s. Fred and Ruth Elizabeth (Larson) P.; m. Sybil Joyce Brown, July 2, 1967; children: Sarah Elizabeth, Christopher James. BA, Cen. Conn. State U., 1965; MDiv, United Seminary, New Brighton, Minn., 1969; ThM, United Sem., New Brighton, Minn., 1974, D Ministry, 1984. Ordained to ministry United Ch. of Christ, 1969. Minister Minnewashta United Ch. of Christ, Excelsior, Minn., 1969-74, Granite Falls United Ch. of Christ and 1st Presbyn. Ch., Maynard, Minn., 1974-82; sr. minister First Congregational United Ch. of Christ, Fremont, Nebr., 1982—; chmn. Western Assn. Ch. and Ministry, Minn., 1980-82, Omaha Assn. Ch. and Ministry, 1986-90, Commn. on Ministry, Lincoln, Nebr., 1988—; del. Gen. Synod, United Ch. of Christ, 1986-89. Chmn. Granite Falls Health Care Com., 1974-82, Jail Study Com., Granite Falls, 1974-78,; bd. dirs. Meml. Hosp. of Dodge County Found., Fremont, 1987—. Named to Outstanding Young Men of Am., 1978. Mem. Alban Inst., Rotary (chaplain 1990-91). Office: First Congregational Ch UCC 1550 North Broad PO Box 910 Fremont NE 68025 *Only the Spirit of God can save us from our personal and social ills.*

PAWLIKOWSKI, JOHN THADDEUS, priest; b. Chgo., Nov. 2, 1940; s. Thaddeus John and Anna Mary (Mizera) P. AB, Loyola U., Chgo., 1963; PhD, U. Chgo., 1970. Ordained priest Roman Cath. Ch., 1967. Tchr., adminstr. Cath. Theol. Union, Chgo., 1968—, prof. social ethics; bd. dirs. Nat. Cath. Conf. Interracial Justice, Chgo., 1982-90; mem. Justice and Peace Commn., Eastern Province Svcs., Chgo., 1980-90. Author: Jesus and the Theology of Israel, 1989; editor: Economic Justice: CTO's Pastoral Commentary on the Bishops Pastoral Economics, 1988. Bd. dirs. Ill. Humanities Coun., Chgo., 1988-91, U.S. Holocaust Meml. Coun., Washington, 1980-91. Recipient Interfaith award Am. Jewish Com., Chgo., 1972, Wallenbourg award in religion Raoul Wallenbourg Com., Chgo., 1990. Mem. Am. Acad. Religion, Cath. Theol. Soc., Soc. Christian Ethics. Home: 1420 E 49th St Chicago IL 60615-2002 Office: Cath Theol Union 5401 S Cornell Ave Chicago IL 60615-5698

PAWLOWICZ, MICHAEL WILSON, gospel broadcaster, minister; b. Balt., Oct. 25, 1938; s. Sigmund S. and Mary Elizabeth (Esterline) P. BD, Ravenna Sch. Ministerial, 1968; DD (hon.), So. Calif. Grad. Sch. Theology, 1988. Ordained to ministry, 1960. Assoc. dir. Youth for Christ, Balt., 1959-61; dir. Youth for Christ, Morgantown, Pa., 1965-68; bd. dirs. Youth for Christ, Huntsville, Ala., 1971—; dir. youth Meml. Presbyn. Ch., Lancaster, Pa., 1966-68; news dir. Sta. WMHR, Christian radio, Syracuse, N.Y., 1969; mgr. gospel Sta. WGNR, Oneonta, N.Y., 1970; program mgr., news dir. Sta. WNDA, gospel radio, Huntsville, 1970—; student supr. Lancaster (Pa.) Bible Sch., 1964-66; bd. dirs. Madison County Child Evangelism Fellowship, 1971-76; elder Calvary Bible Ch., 1974—. Contbr. articles to various religious jours. Mem. Mayor of Ontonta's Adv. Com., 1970. Recipient Presdl. commendation, 1970, Lefty Gomez Sports award, 1976; named Huntsville Gospel Mus. Amb., 1976. Mem. Gospel Music Assn., Huntsville Ministerial Assn. (pres. 1990-91), Huntsville Press Club (pres. 1979-80). Home: 2819 Newby Rd Box 7 Huntsville AL 35805 Office: 2407 9th Ave Huntsville AL 35805

PAYNE, DAVID SETH, clergyman, accountant; b. Stowe Twp., Pa., Apr. 3, 1934; s. Seth Harry and Eva Retta (Over) P.; m. Nancy Judith Worsnop, July 18, 1959; children: David Seth II, Cynthia E. Payne Van Pelt, Donald J. Student Robert Morris Bus. Sch., 1954-56, 59-60; AA, Nazarene Bible Coll., 1973; BA, Mid-Am. Nazarene Coll., 1975; M.A.R., Asbury Theol. Sem., 1978; postgrad. Denver Sem., 1979—. CPA, Pa., Colo.; ordained to ministry Nazarene Ch., 1979. Staff acct. various pub. acctg. cos., Pitts. and Pensacola, Fla., 1961-66; mgr. budgets and measurements Escambia Chem. Corp., Pensacola, 1966-68, parent co. Ebasco Industries, N.Y.C., 1968-69; internal auditor Air Products & Chem. Corp., Allentown, Pa., 1969; pub. acct., Pensacola, 1969-70, Lexington, Ky., 1976-78; sr. acct. Nygren Sears and Co., CPAs, Colorado Springs, Colo., 1970-73, 80-82, Fred Marting, CPA, Colorado Springs, 1979; instr. acctg. Lexington Tech. Inst., 1974-75; bus. office mgr. Mid-Am. Nazarene Coll., Olathe, Kans., 1973-74; pastor First Ch. of Nazarene, Nicholasville, Ky., 1976-78, Black Forest Ch. of Nazarene, Colorado Springs, 1978-82, Forestdale Ch. of Nazarene, Birmingham, Ala., 1982—; acct. Nazarene Bible Coll., Colorado Springs, 1978-79, instr. Bible, fall 1979-80; aux. chaplain U. Ala. Hosps., Birmingham, 1982-83; sec. standing ways and means com. Ala. North dist. Ch. of Nazarene, 1982-83, chmn., 1983—, mem. Ala. North dist. bd. orders and relations, 1983-84, mem. Ala. North Dist. Bd. Ministerial Studies, 1983-84. Bd. dirs. Ala. Citizens Action Program, 1983—; mem. textbook com., Jefferson County, Ala., 1983. Served with USN, 1956-59. Mem. Am. Inst. C.P.A.s, Am. Sch. Oriental Research, Bibl. Archaeology Soc., Wesleyan Theol. Soc., Hon. Order Ky. Cols. Republican. Office: PO Box 236 Cottondale AL 35453

PAYNE, DONALD GLEN, clergyman; b. Pontotoc, Miss., Nov. 21, 1956; s. Marion Monroe and Inez (Mathis) P.; m. Charlotte Sue Rowan, Oct. 27, 1974; children: April Suzanne, Lauren Nicole. BS, Blue Mountain Coll., 1980; MDiv, New Orleans Bapt. Sem., 1984, D Ministry, 1989. Ordained to ministry So. Bapt. Conv., 1978. Interim pastor Ellistown Bapt. Ch., Blue Springs, Miss., 1978-79; pastor 1st Bapt. Ch. of Biggersville, Rienze, Miss., 1979-81; interim pastor Temple Bapt. Ch., Myrtle, Miss., 1982; pastor Sylvarena Bapt. Ch., Wesson, Miss., 1984-89, Forest Lake Bapt. Ch., Tuscaloosa, Ala., 1989—; cons. interfaith witness Home Mission Bd., Atlanta, 1985-91; pres. minister's conf. Copiah Bapt. Assn., Hazlehurst, Miss., 1987-89, dir. family ministry, 1985-89; dir. family ministry Tuscaloosa Bapt. Assn., Northport, Ala., 1990—, mem. exec. com., 1989—. Author: People Reaching People, 1988. Mem. adv. com. Single Parent Program - Co-Lin Coll., Wesson, Miss., 1986-89. Home: 3005 11th Ave E Tuscaloosa AL 35405 Office: Forest Lake Bapt Ch 107 18th St Tuscaloosa AL 35401

PAYNE, EDWARD CARLTON, minister; b. Hartford, Conn., Aug. 4, 1928; s. Robert Carlton and Margaret Ilon (Bodnar-Donovan) P. Lic.Th., Santa Maria del Gracia, 1947; Lic.Sac.Th., St. Francis Sem., 1966; B.S., Peoples U., 1973, M.Div., 1976, D.S.M., 1971, D.A.E.H., 1973; D.D., St. Ephrem's Inst., 1974. Ordained deacon, 1947, archdeacon, 1951, presbyter, 1953, priest, 1966, archpriest, 1967; rector's asst. Grace Episcopal Ch., Hartford, Conn., 1947-51; asst. chaplain St. Mary and All Saints Episcopal Ch., Higganum, Conn., 1947-50; chaplain's asst. St. Elizabeth's Episcopal Chapel, Hartford, Conn., 1947-55; dir., prior Order of the Cross, Hartford, Conn., 1951—; rector's asst. Ch. of the Good Shepherd, Hartford, 1951-55, St. James Episcopal Ch., Hartford, 1956-57; rector Holy Cross Old Roman Cath. Ch., Hartford, 1966—; canon Old Cath. Cathedral Ch. of Christ-on-the-Mount, Mariavite-Russian Orthodox Ch., Woodstock, N.Y., 1967-68; sr. pastor Old Roman Cath. Cathedral Ch. of the Holy Saviour, Niagra Falls, N.Y., 1971-81; dean of Conn.-R.I. Old Roman Cath. Ch., 1968-69, bishop of Conn.-R.I., 1969-72, archbishop of New Eng., 1972—, metropolitan, exarch of Ugro-Finnic Peoples,, 1975—; patriarch Old Roman Cath. Hungarian Orthodox Ch. Patriarchate of N. Am., 1975—; pastor West Community Ch., East Granby, Conn., 1976—; pres. Council of Bishops, Am. World Patriarchates of Byelorussian-Ukrainian Orthodox Cath. Ch., 1975-78; staff mem. Open Hearth Mission, Hartford, 1985-91; moderator United Cath. Conf., Boston, 1967-69; interim pastor Christ Cath. Ch. of the Transfiguration, Boston, 1970-72; instr. Independent Cath. Seminarium, 1970—; mem. Synod of No.Am. Old Roman Ch., 1966-85; mem. Commn. on Liturgy and Music, 1968-70; hon. chaplain N.S.K.K. Motorcycle Club, Hartford, Conn., 1974-75; interim organist Our Saviour's Polish Nat. Cath. Ch., Hartford, Conn., 1957, Warburton Community Congregational Ch. (United Ch. of Christ), Hartford, Conn., 1959-60, Hartford Elks Lodge, 1962-64, organist, 1964—; chaplain, organist, counselor Culbro Tobacco Co., Windsor and Simsbury,

Conn., 1967, 77-78. Editor: The Silver Cross, 1951—, The Independent Catholic, 1970—, The Associated Traditionalist, 1974-75; Asst. editor: The Augustinian, 1966-70. Chmn. Hartford Area Peter A. Reilly Def. Com., 1974-76; chmn. Bradley J. Ankuda Def. Com., 1977-78. Recipient God and Country award First Hartford Council Area, 1949; recipient cert. of appreciation Quirk Middle Sch., Hartford, Conn., 1978; prelate Order of St. Nicholas, Kent, Eng., 1971; nominee Cmdr. Orthodox Order of St. Gregory the Illuminator, Holy Russian Orthodox Ch. in Exile. Mem. Traditionalist Clergy Assn. (sec. 1974-75), Red Men Club, Elks. Republican. Performer, instr., composer, arranger tenor banjo, mandolin, bugle, piano, organ, and carillon. Office: PO Box 290261 Wethersfield CT 06129-0261 *Be "Furchtlos und Treu" ("Fearless and Faithful"). Never consider yourself to be a failure or you'll be one. Keep on keeping on, no matter what the odds. Go onward and upward, using all stumbling blocks as stepping stones, even though you have to burn bridges so that you don't retreat. And, above all, offer many prayers of thanks to God every day, for that's what the Eucharist means: THANKSGIVING.*

PAYNE, JEFFREY FORD, minister; b. Starkville, Miss., Feb. 24, 1958; s. Earnest Clifford and Emma Lou (Johnston) P.; m. Cynthia Lynn Allen, Aug. 25, 1979; children: Andrew Johnston, Taylor Allen. BA in Bible, Harding U., 1980; MA in Ministry, Okla. U. Arts and Scis., 1991. Ordained to ministry Ch. of Christ, 1980. Minister Magness (Ark.) Ch. of Christ, 1976-80, Ann Arbor (Mich.) Ch. of Christ, 1980-82, Northeast Ch. of Christ, Greenville, S.C., 1985-89, Del City (Okla.) Ch. of Christ, 1989—; campus minister Western Ky. U., Bowling Green, 1982-85; speaker TV and radio spots; host talk show Forum, Oklahoma City, 1990; mem. adv. bd. mag. The Christian Chronicle, 1989—; chaplain Okla. Senate and Ho. of Reps., 1991. Editor ch. bull. Sharing the Promise, 1988—; contbr. articles to mags.

PAYNE, KEVIN CLARK, minister; b. Humansville, Mo., Dec. 13, 1957; s. Theo Granville and Rachel Ann (Jackson) P.; m. Tamera Joyce Siegel, May 31, 1980; children: Heather Nicole, Holly Rachelle. BA in Religion, Psychology, S.W. Bapt. U., 1980; MDiv, Midwestern Bapt. Sem., Kansas City, Mo., 1985, postgrad., 1990—. Ordained to ministry So. Bapt. Conv., 1981. Pastor First Bapt. Ch., Kidder, Mo., 1981-84, Cowgill, Mo., 1984-86; Pastor Salem Ave. Bapt. Ch., Rolla, Mo., 1987—; moderator Phelps County Bapt. Assn., Rolla, Mo., 1990—; chmn. subcom. Mo. Bapt. Nominating Com., Jefferson City, 1989-90. Host Choose Life radio program, 1991—. Spurgeon fellow William Jewell Coll., 1991—. Home: 807 Wakefield Rolla MO 65401 *It is important that people be led to challenge traditional ways of thinking about our world. In a society that is inundated with rapid change and technological advances, creative and well thought-out approaches to moral and ethical issues and problems are a necessity in achieving credibility and effectiveness.*

PAYNE, MARGARET BERNETA, religious association executive, educator, consultant; b. Colville, Wash., Nov. 15, 1935; d. Daniel Grinim and Doris Evelyn (Thing) Knauss; m. Donald Lewis Payne, Oct. 30, 1959; children—Kathryn Doris, Diane Lynda. B.A. in Edn., Seattle Pacific U., 1957; postgrad. Eastern Wash. U., 1958-59, Seattle U., 1972-73, U. South Fla., 1965-66, Fla. State U., 1963-64. Tchr. elem. schs., Wash., 1957-60, Fla., 1962-70; tchr. Head Start of Stevens County, Chewelah, Wash., 1970-72, dir., 1972-74, dir. Home Start and Mobile Presch. Programs, 1973—; cons. Region X HEW, 1972-79; ednl. specialist Dist. 105 Yakima (Wash.) County, 1976-80; asst. dir. N.E. Wash. Rural Resource Devel. Assn., Colville, 1974-76; curriculum specialist, editor Free Methodist World Hdqrs., Winona Lake, Ind., 1980-81, dir. children's ministries, 1981—; part-time instr. Yakima (Wash.) Valley Coll., 1977-79; cons. in field. Mem. Wash. Futures, 1970-72; mem. Tri County State Planning Com., Wash. Dept. Social and Human Services, 1973-74; mem. Stevens County (Wash.) Planning Comm., 1974-76; mem. Stevens County Council for Children, 1974-76; bd. dirs. Neighborhood Forums, Stevens County, 1975-76; mem. Yakima Valley Coll. Services for Handicapped Com., 1978-79; dir. Christian edn. Yakima Free Meth. Ch. Mem. Exec. Women's Service Orgn., Lakeland Community Concert Assn. Republican. Author tng., instrnl. and curriculum guides for tchr. use. Office: Free Methodist World Hdqrs 901 College Ave Winona Lake IN 46590

PAYNE, PAULA MARIE, minister; b. Waukegan, Ill., Jan. 13, 1952; d. Percy Howard and Annie Maude (Cashing) P. BA, U. Ill., 1976; MA, U. San Francisco, 1986; MDiv, Wesley Theol. Sem., 1991. Ordained to ministry United Meth. Ch., 1990. Chaplain for minority affairs Am. U., Washington, 1988-89; chaplain, intern NIH, Bethesda, Md., 1989-90; pastor Asbury United Meth. Ch., Charles Town, W.Va., 1990—; supt. ch. sch. United Meth. Ch., Oxon Hill, Md., 1989-90; mem. AIDS task force Wesley Theol. Sem., Washington, 1988-89; mem. retreat. com. Balt. Conf., 1990—; chair scholarship com. Asbury United Meth. Ch., 1990—. Bd. dirs. AIDS Task Force Jefferson County, Charles Town, 1991—, Community Ministries, Charles Town, 1991—. Tech. sgt. USAF, 1984-88. Ethnic Minority scholar United Meth. Ch., 1988-89, Brandenburg scholar, 1988-89, Tadlock scholar, 1989-90, Calvary Fellows scholar Calvary United Meth. Ch., 1989-90; recipient Cert. of Recognition Ill. Ho. of Reps., 1988. Mem. U. Ill. Alumni Assn. (bd. dirs. 1987-88), Alpha Kappa Alpha (pres. local chpt. 1974-76, v.p. 1973). Democrat. Home: PO Box 816 Charles Town WV 25414 *What good is excellence in scholarship, if one cannot lead souls to Christ.*

PAYNE, PHILIP BARTON, religion educator; b. Rockville Centre, N.Y., July 2, 1948; s. John Barton and Dorothy Dean (Dosker) P.; m. Nancy Catherine Anderson, Sept. 5, 1976; children: David Barton, Kimiko Ruth, Brendan John. BS with high honors, Wheaton (Ill.) Coll., 1969; MA in New Testament summa cum laude, Trinity Evang. Divinity Sch., Deerfield, Ill., 1972, MDiv summa cum laude, 1973; PhD in New Testament, Cambridge U., 1976. Ordained, 1973. Missionary, dir. Kyoto Christian Studies Ctr. Evang. Free Ch. Japan Mission, 1976-84; vis. prof. New Testament Gordon Conwell Theol. Seminary, South Hamilton, Mass., 1985-87, Bethel Theol. Seminary, St. Paul, 1987; pres. Linguist's Software, Inc., Edmonds, Wash., 1988—; vis. prof. New Testament Trinity Evang. Divinity Sch., 1976; adj. prof. New Testament Fuller Theol. Seminary, Seattle, 1988-90; supr. New Testament studies Cambridge U., 1974-75. Author: (computer programs) Laser Greek, 1986, Laser Hebrew, 1986, MacGreek New Testament, 1986. Higgins scholar Nat. Coun. Chs., 1973. Fellow Tyndale Fellowship; mem. Soc. Bibl. Lit., Inst. for Bibl. Rsch., Evang. Theol. Soc., Japan Evang. Theol. Soc. (Regius com. 1979-83). Republican. Home: PO Box 580 Edmonds WA 98020 Office: Linguist's Software Inc PO Box 580 Edmonds WA 98020

PAYNE, RODERICK AUSTIN, minister; b. Ft. Worth, Tex., Feb. 3, 1955; s. Robert Austin and Jo Ann (McCord) P.; m. Vicky Jean Payne, Mar. 4, 1976; children: Brandon Austin, Sharon Jean. BA in Communications, E. Cen. U., Ada, Okla., 1979; MA, Southwestern Bapt. Theol. Sem., Ft. Worth, 1987. Ordained to ministry, So. Bapt. Conv., 1987. Minister of music and youth New Bethel Bapt. Ch., Ada, 1977-85; houseparent Buckner Bapt. Children's Home, Dallas, 1985-87; minister of media First Bapt. Ch., Wichita Falls, Tex., 1987—; mem. nat. coun. Am. Christian TV Systems, Ft. Worth, 1990—; faculty Nat Drama Festival, Nashville, 1990; program participant Nat. Religious Broadcasters Conv., Washington, 1991. Contbr. articles to profl. jours. Recipient Angel award for Excellence in Media, L.A., 1990. Mem. Nat. Religious Broadcasters. Home: 1649 Ardath Wichita Falls TX 76301 Office: First Bapt Ch 1200 9th St Wichita Falls TX 76301

PAYNE, SIDNEY STEWART, archbishop; b. Fogo, Nfld., Can., June 6, 1932; s. Albert and Hilda May (Oake) P.; m. Selma Carlson Penney, Oct. 11, 1962; children—Carla, Christopher, Robert, Angela. B.A., Meml. U. Nfld., 1958; L.Th., Queen's Coll., Nfld., 1958; B.D., Gen. Synod, 1966; D.D. (hon.), Univ. of King's Coll., Halifax, 1981. Ordained to ministry Anglican Ch., 1957; parish pastor Happy Valley Labrador, 1957-65, Bay Roberts, Nfld., 1965-70, St. Anthony, Nfld., 1970-78; bishop Anglican Diocese of Western Nfld., 1978-90; met. Ecclesiastical Province of Can., archbishop Western Nfld., 1990—. Home: 13 Cobb Ln, Corner Brook, NF Canada A2H 2V3 Office: Nfld Light and Power Bldg, 83 West St, Corner Brook, NF Canada A2H 2Y6

PAYNE, WILLIAM LAMAR, minister; b. Cartersville, Ga., Sept. 10, 1966; s. William Roy Jr. and Sara Jane (Gearhart) P.; m. Ashley Paige Brooks, May 26, 1990. MusB, Samford U., 1988. Music intern Roswell St. Bapt. Ch., Marietta, Ga., 1985; orchestra dir. West Rome (Ga.) Bapt. Ch., 1986-87; assoc. minister of music Calvary Bapt. Ch., Clearwater, Fla., 1988-89, Winston-Salem, N.C., 1989—. Arranger: (orchestral arrangements) Awesome God, 1989, Heaven Medley, 1989, I am a Promise, 1990, The Baptist Hymnal, 1991, Communion Hymns, 1991, Praise and Worship Collection, 1992. Mem. Metro Instrumental Dirs., Christian Instrumental Dirs. Assn., Phi Mu Alpha. Republican. Home: 801 Braehill Blvd Winston-Salem NC 27104 Office: Calvary Baptist Church 5000 Country Club Rd Winston-Salem NC 27104

PAZDAN, MARY MARGARET, sister, educator; b. Chgo., July 2, 1942; d. Edward Sylvester and Eugenia Josephine (Ziemba) P. BA, Rosary Coll., River Forest, Ill., 1967; MA, Providence (R.I.) Coll., 1972; PhD, St. Michael's Coll., Toronto, 1982. Asst. prof. religious studies Edgewood Coll., Madison, Wis., 1981-84; facilitator theol. reflection groups St. Louis U., 1986—; assoc. prof. Bible studies Aquinas Inst. Theology, St. Louis, 1987—; chairperson dept. religious studies Edgewood Coll., 1982-85; assoc. tour dir. U. Wis. Madison Bible Tour, 1983; dir. Sinsinawa (Wis.) Bibl. Inst., 1984-88; Midwest promoter of preaching Sinsinawa Dominicans, 1988—. Author: Collegeville Biblical Commentary, 1986, Jesus as Son of Man, 1990; contbr. articles and book revs. to profl. jours. Menorah Inst. in Jewish Studies scholar, 1970; Shalom Hartman Inst. fellow, 1987, Brandeis-Bardin Inst. fellow, 1988. Mem. Cath. Bibl. Assn., Soc. Bibl. Lit. (chair New Testament sect. cen. states region 1988-90), Seminary Jewish-Christian Dialogue. Office: Aquinas Inst Theology 3642 Lindell Blvd Saint Louis MO 63108

PEACHEY, KEITH ALBERT, minister; b. Lewistown, Pa., Aug. 6, 1956; s. Loren Jacob and Jean Darles (Knepp) P.; children: Jennifer Dawn, Joshua Ryan. BA in Bible/Psychology (cum laude), Asbury Coll., 1978; MDiv (cum laude), Oral Roberts U., 1986; DMin, United Theol. Sem., 1991. Lic. to ministry United Meth. Ch., 1982; ordained as deacon, 1984, elder, 1987. Assoc. minister First United Meth. Ch., Coffeyville, Kans., 1978-82; pastor Epworth United Meth. Ch., Chelsea, Okla., 1982-83; assoc. minister First United Meth. Ch., Claremore, Okla., 1983-86; pastor Cache (Okla.)/Indiahoma United Meth. Chs., 1986-87, First United Meth. Ch./New Creation Fellowship, Martins Ferry, Ohio, 1987—; chair Dist. Mission Strategy Com., St. Clairsville, Ohio, 1989-91; vice-chair, publicity chair Bethesda Learning Ctr., 1991; pres. Ministerial Assn., Martins Ferry, 1989-90. Developer (church growth program) New Congregation Within a Congregation, 1990. Bd. dirs. Camp Fire Girls, Coffeyville, 1979; mem. Community Corrections Bd., Coffeyville, 1980; co-dir. CROP Walk, Claremore, 1983; adv. bd. mem. Salvation Army, Martins Ferry, 1987-91; bd. dirs. Head Start, Martins Ferry, 1989-90. Named to Nat. Dean's List, 1981-84. Mem. St. Clairsville Dist. Parsonage Fellowship (pres. 1989-90), Lions (dir. 1979-80), Kiwanis (v.p. 1989-91). Republican. Home: 407 S Third St Martins Ferry OH 43935 Office: First United Meth Ch PO Box 585 Martins Ferry OH 43935

PEACOCK, JOSEPH N., minister. Exec. dir. Evansville Area (Ind.) Coun. Chs. Inc. Office: Evansville Area Coun Chs Inc 103 NW 10th St Evansville IN 47708*

PEAK, PAUL E., music minister, educator; b. Bluefield, W.Va., May 18, 1953; s. B. C. and Margaretta Rose (Murray) P.; m. Donna Lou Quintana, June 6, 1975; children: Benjamin, Jenness, Anthony. AS in Music, S.W. Va. Community Coll., 1973; B in Music Edn., MusB in Ch. Music, Shenandoah Conservatory Music, 1976; MusM, Cinn. Conservatory Music, 1983. Lic. to ministry Ch. of the Nazarene as deacon, 1991. Min. of music Trinity Ch. of the Nazarene, Louisville, 1985-88, 1st Ch. of the Nazarene, Lexington, Ky., 1988—; music prof. God's Bible Coll., Cinn., 1978-85, 89—; music dir. Nazarene dist. events, Ky., 1988—. Mem. Am. Choral Dirs. Assn. Home: 1617 Thirlstane Ct Lexington KY 40505

PEAKE, WILLIAM ALFRED, minister; b. Schenectady, Apr. 26, 1953; s. William Alfred and Louise Irene (Biasi) P.; m. Susan Ellen Wiggins, Aug. 17, 1974; children: Matthew William, Benjamin Brian, Jonathan Claire. BA, Cen. U. Iowa, 1975; MDiv, U. Dubuque, 1980. Ordained to ministry Ref. Ch. in Am., 1980; cert. in clin. pastoral edn. Supply pastor Coal Ridge Community Ch., Knoxville, Iowa, 1975-79; pastor Faith Community Ch., Eddyville, Iowa, 1980-82, 1st German Ref. Ch., Buffalo Center, Iowa, 1982—; chmn. Buffalo Ctr./Rake Ministerium, Buffalo Center, 1984-85; founder Good Grief Bereavement Svcs., Buffalo Center, 1986-89; chaplain, coord. bereavement Hospice North Iowa, Forest City, 1990; com. mem. Ecumenical Ministries Iowa, 1991—. Contbr. articles to Masonic publ. Speaker Iowa Meml. Day Activities, Rake, 1987, Am. Legion Aux., Rake, 1989, 91; guest chaplain Iowa Ho. of Reps., Des Moines, 1987; lectr., trainer Faribault County Hospice, Blue Earth, Minn., 1988, 90; bd. dirs. Centre Stage Players, 1987, Caring Hearts Hospice, Forest City, 1988-90; bd. dirs. Ecumenical Ministries of Iowa, 1991. Study grantee Ref. Ch. in Am., 1990. Mem. Am. Bible Soc. (vol. speaker, coord. scripture courtesy ctr.), N.Am. Short Wave Assn., Masons (sec. 1985-87), Lions.. Home: 402 2d St SW Buffalo Center IA 50424-0414 Office: 1st German Ref Ch 401 1st St SW Buffalo Center IA 50424 *Every human being encounters loss daily. While some losses have a minimal impact, many losses begin a grueling process which must be worked. One loss is particularly tragic—the loss of a sense of self. God alone grants our identity. God helps our rediscovery, daily.*

PEALE, NORMAN VINCENT, minister; b. Bowersville, Ohio, May 31, 1898; s. Charles Clifford and Anna (DeLaney) P.; m. Ruth Stafford, June 20, 1930; children: Margaret (Mrs. Paul F. Everett), John, Elizabeth (Mrs. John M. Allen). AB, Ohio Wesleyan U., 1920, DD, 1936; STB, Boston U., 1924, AM, 1924, DD (hon.), 1986; DD, Syracuse U., 1931, Duke U., 1938, Cen. Coll., 1964; LHD (hon.), Lafayette Coll., 1952, U. Cin., 1968, Wm. Jewell Coll., 1952; LLD (hon.), Hope Coll., 1962, Brigham Young U., 1967, Pepperdine U., 1979; STD, Millikin U., 1958; LittD, Iowa Wesleyan U., 1958, Ea. Ky. State Coll., 1964, Jefferson Med. Coll., 1955; LHD (hon.), Northwestern U., 1984, Pace U., 1984, Milw. Sch. Engring., 1985, St. John's U., 1985, Marymount Manhattan, 1985; DD (hon.), Boston U., 1986, Mt. Union Coll., 1988; LHD (hon.), Judson Coll., 1988. Ordained to ministry M.E. Ch., 1922; pastor Berkeley, R.I., 1922-24, Kings Hwy. Ch., Bklyn., 1924-27, Univ. Ch., Syracuse, N.Y., 1927-32, Marble Collegiate Ref. Ch., N.Y.C., 1932-84; founder, pub. (with Mrs. Peale) Guideposts mag. Author: A Guide to Confident Living, 1948, The Power of Positive Thinking, 1952, The Coming of the King, 1956, Stay Alive All Your Life, 1957, The Amazing Results of Positive Thinking, 1959, The Tough-Minded Optimist, 1962, Adventures in the Holy Land, 1963, Sin, Sex and Self-control, 1965, Jesus of Nazareth, 1966, The Healing of Sorrow, 1966, Enthusiasm Makes the Difference, 1967, Bible Stories, 1973, You Can If You Think You Can, 1974, The Positive Principle Today, 1976, The Positive Power of Jesus Christ, 1980, Treasury of Joy and Enthusiasm, 1981, Positive Imaging, 1981, The True Joy of Positive Living, 1984; Have a Great Day, 1985; Why Some Positive Thinkers Get Powerful Results, 1986; Power of the Plus Factor, 1987, The American Character, 1988; co-author: (with Ken Blanchard) The Power of Ethical Management, 1988, The Power of Positive Living, 1990, My Favorite Quotations, 1990, This Incredible Century, 1991, My Christmas Treasury, 1991; co-author: chpt. in Am's. 12 Master Salesmen; writer for various secular and religious periodicals; Tech. adviser representing Protestant Ch. in filming of motion picture: motion picture One Man's Way, based on biography, 1963; film What It Takes To Be A Real Salesman. Trustee Ohio Wesleyan U., Central Coll.; mem. exec. com. Presbyn. Ministers Fund for Life Ins.; mem. Mid-Century White House Conf. on Children and Youth, Pres.'s Commn. for Observance 25th Anniversary UN; pres. Protestant Council City N.Y., 1965-69, Ref. Church in Am., 1969-70; lectr. pub. affairs, personal effectiveness; chaplain Am. Legion, Kings County, N.Y., 1925-27. Recipient numerous awards including: Freedom Found. award, 1952, 55, 59, 73, 74; Horatio Alger award, 1952; Am. Edn. award, 1955; Gov. Service award for Ohio, 1955; Nat. Salvation Army award, 1956; Disting. Salesman's award N.Y. Sales Execs., 1957; Salvation Army award, 1957; Internat. Human Relations award Dale Carnegie Club Internat., 1958; Clergyman of Year award Religious Heritage Am., 1964; Paul Harris Fellow award Rotary Internat., 1972; Disting. Patriot award Sons of Revolution, N.Y. State, 1973; Order of Aaron and Hur Chaplains Corps U.S. Army, 1975; Christopher Columbus award, 1976; All-Time Gt. Ohioan award, 1976; Soc. for Family of Man award, 1981; Disting. Achievement award Ohio Wesleyan U., 1983; Religion in Media Gold Angel award, 1984; Presdl. Medal of Freedom, 1984; 2d Ann. Family Weekly Nat. Treasure award, 1984; Disting. Am. award Sales and Mktg. Execs. Internat., 1985; Theodore Roosevelt Disting. Service award, 1985; World Freedom award Shanghai Tiffin Club, 1985; Napolean Hill Fedn. Gold medal for Literary Achievement, 1985; St. George Assn. Golden Rule award, 1985, Old Hero award NFL, 1987, Adele Rogers St. John Round Table award, 1987, Communicator of the Yr. award Sales and Mktg. Exec. Internat., Little Rock, 1987, Disting. Achievement award Am. Aging, 1987, Grand Cross award Supreme Council, Mother Council of World of 33d and last degree Masons, 1987, Magellan award Circumnavigators Club, 1987, Van Rensselaer Gold medal Masonic Temple Cin., Silver Buffalo award Boy Scouts Am., 1988, Outstanding Alumnus award Ohio Found. of Ind. Coll., 1989, Merit award in Humanities N.Y. Acad. Dentistry, 1989, Pope John XIII award Viterbo Coll., 1989, George M. and Mary Jane Leader Healthcare award, 1989, John Y. Brown award, 1989, Humanitarian of Yr. award Women's Nat. Rep. Club, 1990, Hance award St. Barnabas Health System, 1990, The Samaritan Inst. award, 1990, Caring Inst. award, 1990, Eleanor Roosevelt Val-Kill medal, 1991, Soaring Eagle award Brethren Home Fedn., 1991. Mem. SAR, Blanton-Peale Inst. (founder), Ohio Soc. N.Y. (pres. 1952-55), Episcopal Actors Guild, Am. Authors Guild, Alpha Delta, Phi Gamma Delta. Republican. Clubs: Metropolitan, Union League, Lotos. Lodges: Rotary, Masons (past grand prelate), Shriners, K.T. Office: 1025 Fifth Ave New York NY 10028

PEALE, RUTH STAFFORD (MRS. NORMAN VINCENT PEALE), religious leader; b. Fonda, Iowa, Sept. 10, 1906; d. Frank Burton and Anna Loretta (Crosby) Stafford; m. Norman Vincent Peale, June 20, 1930; children: Margaret Ann (Mrs. Paul F. Everett), John Stafford, Elizabeth Ruth (Mrs. John M. Allen). AB, Syracuse U., 1928, LLD, 1953; LittD, Hope Coll., 1962; LHD (hon.), Judson Coll., 1988. Tchr. math. Cen. High Sch., Syracuse, N.Y., 1928-31; nat. pres. women's bd. domestic missions Ref. Ch. Am., 1936-46; sec. Protestant Film Commn., 1946-51; chmn. Am. Mother's Com., 1948-49; pres., editor-in-chief, gen. sec., chief exec. officer Found. for Christian Living, 1940—; nat. pres. bd. domestic missions Ref. Ch. in Am., 1955-56; mem. bd. N. Am. Missions, 1963-69, pres., 1967-69; mem. gen. program council Ref. Ch. in Am., 1968—; mem. com. of 24 for merger Ref. Ch. in Am. and Presbyn. Ch. U.S., 1966-69; v.p. Protestant Council N.Y.C., 1964-66; hon. chancellor Webber Coll., 1972—; co-editor, pub. Guideposts, N.Y.C., 1945—, pres., 1985—; pres. Fleming H. Revell, Old Tappan, N.J., 1985—. Appeared on: nat. TV program What's Your Trouble, 1952-68; Author: I Married a Minister, 1942, The Adventure of Being a Wife, 1971, Secrets of Staying in Love, 1984; founder, pub. (with Dr. Peale) Guidepost mag., 1957—; co-subject with husband: film One Man's Way, 1963. Trustee Hope Coll., Holland, Mich., Champlain Coll., Burlington, Vt., Stratford Coll., Danville, Va., Lenox Sch., N.Y.C., Interchurch Center Syracuse U., 1955-61; bd. dirs. Cook Christian Tng. Sch., Lord's Day Alliance U.S.; mem. bd. and exec. com. N.Y. Theol. Sem., N.Y.C.; sponsor Spafford Children's Convalescent Hosp., 1966—; bd. govs. Help Line Telephone Center, 1970—, Norman Vincent Peale Telephone Center, 1977; mem. nat. women's bd. Northwood Inst., 1981. Named New York State Mother of Yr., 1963, Disting. Woman of Yr. Nat. Art Assn., Religious Heritage Am. Ch. Woman of Yr., 1969; recipient Cum Laude award Syracuse U. Alumni Assn. N.Y., 1965, Honor Iowans' award Buena Vista Coll., 1966, Am. Mother's Com. award religion, 1970, Disting. Svc. award Coun. Chs., N.Y.C., 1973, Disting. Citizen award Champlain Coll., 1976, Disting. Svc. to Community and Nation award Gen. Fedn. Women's Clubs, 1977, Horatio Alger award, 1977, Religious Heritage award, 1979, joint medallion with husband Soc. for Family of Man, 1981, Soc. Family of Man award, 1981, Alderson-Broaddus award, 1982, Marriage Achievement award Bride's Mag., 1984, Gold Angel award Religion in Media, 1987, Adela Rogers St. John Roundtable award, 1987, Disting. Achievement award Am. Aging, 1987, Paul Harris award N.Y. Rotary, 1989. Mem. Insts. Religion and Health (bd. exec. com.), Am. Bible Soc. (dir., v.p.), United Bible Soc. (v.p.), The Interchurch Ctr. (bd. dirs. 1957—, chair 1982-90), Nat. Coun. Chs. (v.p. 1952-54, gen. bd.; treas. gen. dept. United Ch. Women, vice chmn. broadcasting and film commn. 1951-55, program chmn. gen. assembly 1966), N.Y. Fedn. Women's Clubs (chmn. religion 1951-53, 57-58), Home Missions Coun. N.A. (nat. pres. 1942-44, nat. chmn. migrant com. 1948-51), Nat. League Am. Pen Women (hon. life), PEO, Alpha Phi (Frances W. Willard award 1976). Clubs: Sorosis (N.Y.C.) (pres. 1953-56, hon. life pres. 1975—); Lotos; Women's Nat. Republican (N.Y.C.). Office: Peale Ctr Christian Living 66 E Main St Pawling NY 12564

PEARCE, GARY DOUGLAS, minister; b. Baton Rouge, Dec. 1, 1952; s. Ray Douglas Pearce and Marcile Dockery Worsham; m. Deborah Betts, Feb. 21, 1975 (div. Feb. 1991); children: Douglas Ray, Kelli Elizabeth; m. Catherine Ann Walton, Aug. 31, 1991; stepchildren: Matthew Walton, Wendi Walton. BA in Religion, Miss. Coll., 1974; MRE, Southwestern Bapt. Theol. Sem., 1976, MDiv., 1980. Ordained to ministry So. Bapt. Conv., 1974; cert. clin. chaplain, La. Pastor Shepherd's Way Bapt. Ch., Grand Island, Nebr., 1980-85, Southminster Chapel, Baton Rouge, 1985-86; chaplain La. Tng. Inst., Bridge City, La., 1986, 1990—; pastor Wardline Bapt. Ch., Hammond, La., 1986-90; sec. exec. com. Dept. Corrections Chaplains, Baton Rouge, 1991; vice chmn. bd. dirs. Platte Valley Youth for Christ, Grand Island, 1982-83; moderator Ea. Nebr. Bapt. Assn., Omaha, 1983. Pres. Wasmer Elem. Sch. PTA, Grand Island, 1983-84, Grand Island PTA, 1984-85; chaplain, firefighter Natalbany Vol. Fire Dept., 1987-89. Mem. Am. Corr. Chaplains Assn., Am. Protestant Chaplains Assn., La. Chaplains' Assn., Chappapeela Bapt. Assn. (chmn. missions com. 1987-90). Republican. Home: 724 Heavens Dr # 5 Mandeville LA 70448-6726 Office: La Tng Inst 3225 River Rd Bridge City LA 70094 *It is said that the true test of a person's character is not if he can be knocked down but what he does when he gets there. A person of vision and faith will climb back up by the grace of God.*

PEARCE, GEORGE HAMILTON, archbishop; b. Boston, Jan. 9, 1921; s. George Hamilton and Marie Louise (Duval) P. BA, Marist Coll. and Sem., Framingham, Mass., 1943. Tchr. Marist Coll. & Sem., Bedford, Mass., 1947-48, St. Mary's High Sch., Van Buren, Maine, 1948-49; missionary Roman Catholic Vicariate of Samoa, 1949-67, vicar apostolic of Samoa, 1956-66; bishop Diocese of Samoa, 1966-67; archbishop Archdiocese of Suva, Suva, Fiji, 1967-76; apostolic adminstr. Diocese of Agana, Guam, 1969; pres. Episcopal Conf. of the Pacific, 1969-71; staff mem. Bethany House of Intercession, Hastings-on-Hudson, N.Y., 1977-83; asst. to bishop Diocese of Providence, 1983—. Home: 30 Fenner St Providence RI 02903

PEARCE, TIMOTHY HAROLD, minister; b. Flora, Ill., Mar. 11, 1958; s. Harold William and Gladys Aliene (Davis) P.; m. Cheri Lynn Trostle, June 30, 1990. Student, Mc Kendree Coll., 1976-77; BA in Christian Edn. and Religion with honors, Greenville Coll., 1981; MDiv, Asbury Theol. Sem., Wilmore, Ky., 1985. Ordained to ministry United Meth. Ch. as elder, 1987. Pastor Dogwood and Prairie United Meth. Chs., Oblong, Ill., 1985-88, Trinity and Golden United Meth. Chs., Flora, Ill., 1988—, Xenia United Meth. Ch., 1991—; founder, bd. dirs. The Solid Rock—Family Ministry Ctr., Flora; bd. dirs. Southeastern Ill. Family Counseling Ctr., Olney, Ill. Fellow Clay County Ministerial Alliance (pres. 1990). Home: 427 W Third Flora IL 62839 Office: Trinity United Meth Ch 430 W Third Flora IL 62839

PEARL, CHAIM, rabbi, author; b. Liverpool, Lancashire, Eng., Nov. 25, 1919; came to U.S., 1964; s. Alexander and Rebecca (Epstein) P.; m. Anita Newman, Nov. 16, 1941; children: David, Jonathan, Simon, Judith. BA, U. London, 1947, PhD, 1956; MA, U. Birmingham, Eng., 1952; DD (hon.), Jewish Theol. Sem. Am., 1981. Ordained rabbi, 1964. Asst. min. Birmingham Hebrew Congregation, 1945-49, chief min., 1949-60; min. The New West End Synagogue, London, 1960-64; rabbi Conservative Synagogue Riverdale, N.Y.C., 1964-80, ret., 1980; lectr. Buber Inst., Hebrew U., Jerusalem, 1991, also various Jewish religious instns., Jerusalem. Author: The Guide to Jewish Knowledge, 1956, The Medieval Jewish Mind, 1974, Rashi, 1988, Sefer Ha-Aggadah, 1988, others; assoc. editor The Jewish Bible Quar. Home: 1, Mavo Harari, Jerusalem 97886, Israel

PEARLSON, JORDAN, rabbi; b. Somerville, Mass., Sept. 2, 1924; s. Jacob and Freda (Spivak) P.; m. Geraldine S. Goldstein, Jan. 19, 1958 (div. 1989); children: Joshua Seth, Nessa Yocheved, Abigail Sara. BA in Econs. with honors, Northeastern U., 1948, JD, 1950; B Hebrew Letters, Hebrew Union Coll., 1954, M Hebrew Letters, 1958; DD (hon.), Union Coll., 1981. Ordained rabbi, 1956. Mem. faculty grad. program for Jewish religious educators Hebrew Union Coll., Cin., 1955-56; chmn. nat. religious adv. com. CBC, 1974-75; nat. chmn. joint pub. rels. com. Can. Jewish Congress, 1974, mem. nat. exec. com., 1974—, mem. nat. bd. Can.-Israel com., 1974—; rabbi

Temple Sinai Congregation, Toronto, Ont., Can.; mem. exec. com. bd. govs. Hebrew Union Coll.; Can. sr. del. Internat. Commn. on Interreligious Consultation, Geneva, 1973, London, 1975; founding mem. Nat. Christian-Jewish Consultation of Can. Jewish Congress, Can. Coun. Chs., Can. Conf. Cath. Bishops, Toronto Top Level Clerical Interreligious Luncheon Group; mem. Can. Jewish Congress, Anglican Ch. Consultation; participant internat. exploratory meetings with evangs. and fundamentalists, L.A., Houston; participant World Co. Chs. Gen. Assembly; commentator CBC TV religious programs. Columnist editor Toronto Star; corr. editor Christian-Jewish Rels.; contbr. articles to various publs. Nat. pres., bd. govs. Friends Ben Gurion U., Can. Coun. Christians and Jews, Juvenile Diabetes Rsch. Found., Crusade against Leukemia, Dysautonomia Found. Can., Found. against Addictive Gambling; chaplain Variety Club, Toronto. Recipient Scroll of Honour Toronto, Nat. Humanitarian award Can. Coun. Christians and Jews, 1990; named hon. citizen Municipality of Met. Toronto; Samuel Abrams fellow Hebrew Union Coll., Cin., 1951; scholar-in-residence N.Y. Sch. of Hebrew Union Coll., Jewish Inst. Religion, 1981; Rabbi Jordan Pearlson outreach program named in his honor Ben Gurion U., Negev, Israel. Mem. Cen. Conf. Am. Rabbis (fin. sec. 1976-79), Toronto Bd. Rabbis (past pres.), Hebrew Union Coll. Rabbinic Alumni Assn. (pres. 1976-77). Home: 55 Ravenscroft Cir, Willowdale, ON Canada M2K 1X1 Office: Temple Sinai Congregation, 210 Wilson Ave, Toronto, ON Canada M5M 3B1

PEARS, EDWARD RICHARD, religious organization administrator; b. New Castle, Pa., Nov. 20, 1951; s. Harold William and Ruth (Owrey) P.; m. Eileen Jane Maloney, Aug. 9, 1975; children: Nathanial, Sarah, Jesse. BS, Indiana U. of Pa., 1978. Program dir. Corning (N.Y.) Community YMCA, 1979-80; dir. Camp Hayo-Went-Ha YMCA, Central Lake, Mich., 1980-82; assoc. dir. YMCA of the Ozarks, Potosi, Mo., 1982-86; exec. dir. YMCA Camp High Harbour, Atlanta, 1986—; whitewater river guide Laurel Highland River Tours, Ohiopyle, Pa., 1975-79; owner, mgr. Trek Outfitters, Inc., Indiana, Pa., 1977-79. Mem. Am. Camping Assn., Assn. Profl. Dirs., Rabun County C. of C. Democratic. Protestant. Lodge: Lions (Central Lake v.p. 1982). Avocations: whitewater kayaking, canoeing, rockclimbing, photography, woodworking. Office: YMCA Camp High Harbour Rt 2 Box 2134 Clayton GA 30525

PEARSON, ANTHONY ALAN, minister; b. Tucson, Feb. 21, 1954; s. Arthur and Evelyn Virginia (Horne) P.; m. Marsha Lee Emory, May 3, 1985; children from previous marriage: Jonathan A., David N., Timothy A., Mark A., Monty B. Grad., Bapt. Bible Coll., Springfield, Mo., 1975; ThM, Tabernacle Bible Inst., Dedham, Mass., 1978; BA, Houston Bapt. U., 1988; postgrad., Southwestern Bapt. Theol. Sem., 1991—; DD (hon.), Homestead Coll., 1979. Ordained to ministry Baptist Ch. Pastor, founder Calvary Met. Tabernacle, Norwood, Mass., 1976-79; prin. Calvary Bapt. Sch., Arcola, Tex., 1979-80; pastor Grace Bapt. Ch., Tri-Cities, Tex., 1981-82, Meadowbrook Bapt. Ch., Houston, 1983—; cons. Bapt. Outpost Missions, LaCieba, Honduras, 1984-88. Author: (booklets) Biblical Spotlight on Tongues Movement, 1975, Short History of Baptists in the North East, 1978, God's Love Letter: The Bible, 1979, The Unforgivable Sin. Life mem. Houston Livestock Show and Rodeo. 1st lt. Tex. SG, 1985-87. Presdl. scholar Southwestern Bapt. Theol. Sem., 1988, 90. Mem. Biblical Archeology Soc., Am. Assn. Christian Counselors, Am. Schs. of Oriental Research, Am. Hist. Soc., Archaeol. Inst. Am., Meadowbrook Civic Club, Meadowbrook Karate Club, Alpha Chi, Theta Alpha Kappa. Democrat. Avocations: horses, Karate, archaeology, hunting. Office: 8202 Howard Dr Houston TX 77017

PEARSON, BIRGER ALBERT, religion educator; b. Turlock, Calif., Sept. 17, 1934; s. Yngve A. and Mildred C. (Anderson) P.; m. Karen L. Heurlin, Sept. 9, 1956; children: Ingrid, David, Kristin, Daniel, Sven, Anders. BA, Upsala Coll., 1957; MA, U. Calif., Berkeley, 1959; MDiv, Pacific Luth. Theol. Sem., 1962; PhD, Harvard U., 1968. Asst. prof. Duke U., Durham, N.C., 1966-69; prof. U. Calif., Santa Barbara, 1969—; researcher Am. Philos. Soc., Vatican Libr., 1986, Am. Rsch. Ctr. in Egypt/Smithsonian Inst., Cairo, Arab Republic of Egypt, 1974, Am. Philos. Soc., Cairo, 1972. Author: Gnosticism, Judaism, and Egyptian Christianity, 1990; editor: The Roots of Egyptian Christianity, 1986; editor, translator: Nag Hammadi Codices IX and X, 1981; co-translator: The Nag Hammadi Library in English, 1977, 81, 88. Conf. organizer NEH, Claremont, Calif., 1983. Mem. Soc. Bibl. Lit., Am. Soc. for the Study of Religion (elected mem.), Cath. Bibl. Assn. (elected mem.), Studiorum Novi Testamenti Societas (elected mem.), Internat. Assn. for Coptic Studies (charter). Lutheran. Office: U Calif Dept Religious Studies Santa Barbara CA 93106

PEARSON, CHARLES WARREN, minister; b. Winston-Salem, N.C., June 5, 1952; s. Charles Warren Pearson and Florence W. (Mitchell) Fauck; m. Patricia Susan Ipock, July 26, 1975; children: Aaron Benjamin, Courtney Rhea. B Music Edn., Mars Hill (N.C.) Coll., 1974; MusM, Southwestern Bapt. Theol. Sem., Ft. Worth, 1977. Ordained to ministry So. Bapt. Conv., 1976. Min. music 1st Bapt. Ch., Saluda, N.C., 1972-74, Taylor MMeml. Bapt. Ch., Hobbs, N.Mex., 1977-86; min. music and edn. Highland Bapt. Ch., Denton, Tex., 1974-77; min. worship and music Southcliff Bapt. Ch., Ft. Worth, 1986—; dir. N.Mex. Singing Churchmen, 1985, 86; trustee Southeastern Bapt. Sem., Wake Forest, N.C., 1981-86. Bd. dirs. Community Concert Series, Hobbs, 1981. Mem. Am. Choral Dirs. Assn., Am. Guild English Handbell Ringers. Office: Southcliff Bapt Ch 4100 SW Loop 820 Fort Worth TX 76109

PEARSON, ELIZABETH MARIA, religious consultant; b. Wauchula, Fla., Apr. 22, 1953; d. Walter Morgan and Naomi (Marsh) P. BS, Carson-Newman Coll., 1975; M.Religious Edn., So. Bapt. Sem., 1979. Youth minister Stock Creek Baptist Ch., Knoxville, Tenn., 1975, First Bapt. Ch., Bartow, Fla., 1976; cons. Woman's Missionary Union, Ga. Bapt. Conv., Atlanta, 1979—; intern Bapt. Goodwill Ctr., Knoxville, 1972-73; conf. leader N.Y. Bapt. Conv., 1980, Ridgecrest Bapt. Ctr. (N.C.), 1983; dir. Camp Pinnacle, Clayton, Ga.; vol. Briarcliff Bapt. Ch., Atlanta; pianist chapel services Ga. Mental Health, Atlanta. Named Carson-Newman Coll. Miss Tenn. Jenkins, 1975; So. Bapt. Sem. Joyce scholar, 1978. Mem. Ky. Bapt. Religious Edn. Assn. Democrat. Office: Georgia Baptist Convention 2930 Flowers Rd S Atlanta GA 30341

PEARSON, ROY MESSER, JR., clergyman; b. Somerville, Mass., Mar. 10, 1914; s. Roy Messer and Bessie M. (Ricker) P.; m. Ruth Simmons, July 12, 1936; children: Beverly, Bradford; m. Barbara K. Cerello, Sept. 1, 1990. AB magna cum laude, Harvard U., 1935; BD cum laude, Andover Newton Theol. Sch., 1938; DD, Amherst Coll., 1957, Brown U., 1971; LLD, Emerson Coll., 1966, Colby Coll., 1967; LHD, Norwich U., 1968; DSO, Curry Coll., 1969. Minister Southville (Mass.) Federated Ch., 1936-38; ordained to ministry Congl. Ch., 1938; minister First Congl. Ch. Swanzey, N.H., 1938-40, Amherst, Mass., 1940-47; minister Hancock Congl. Ch., Lexington, Mass., 1947-54; lectr. Andover Newton Theol. Sch., 1951-54, dean, 1954-65, pres., 1965-79, also trustee; pres. Andover Theol. Sem., 1954-65, Bartlett prof. sacred rhetoric, 1954-79 ; preacher Nat. Council Chs. in Brit. Isles, 1951; regular radio preacher Mass. Council Chs., 1952-57; preacher Internat. Congl. Council Brit. Isles, 1957; interim minister, Peterborough, Newport, New London, Hanover, Hopkinton, and Warner, N.H., 1979-87. Author: Here's Faith for You, 1953, This Do-And Live, 1954, The Hard Commands of Jesus, 1957, Seeking and Finding God, 1958, The Ministry of Preaching, 1959; Contbg. Author: (ed. G. Paul Butler) Best Sermons of 1955, 1955, Hear Our Prayer, 1961, The Preacher: His Purpose and Practice, 1963, The Believer's Unbelief, 1963, Best Sermons of 1964, 1964, Best Sermons of 1968, 1968, Prayers for All Occasions, 1990; also articles religious periodicals. Served as 1st lt. Chaplains Corps AUS, 1944. Recipient Churchman award for best sermon of the year, 1948; Am. Assn. Theol. Schs. fellow, 1960. Mem. Phi Beta Kappa. Club: University (Boston). Home: 31 Stony Brook Rd PO Box 870 New London NH 03257 *With the advance of my age and the growth of my faith I find myself a Christian agnostic. It is not that I believe less. Rather, that I believe more. God is too great for me to comprehend his immensities.*

PEARSON, STEVEN EARL, religious broadcast executive; b. Council Grove, Kans., May 12, 1953; s. Melvin E. and Doris Jane (Hanson) P.; m. Eleanor M. Converse, May 24, 1975; children: Hilary Abigail, Nathanial Aaron, Kristian Adam. BS in Radio/TV, Kansas State U., 1975. Founder Christian Action Team, Inc., Emporia, Kans., 1986-87; gen. mgr. Sta. KNGM Radio, Emporia, 1987—; bd. dirs. Heritage Family Bookstore, Emporia.; tchr. Flint Hills Christian Ch., 1980—. Contbr. articles to local publs. Cpt. U.S. Army, 1975-80. Decorated Army Commendation medal U.S. Army, 1979, 80. Mem. Two Rivers Soccer Assn. Republican. Home: 910 Woodland Emporia KS 66801 Office: Christian Action Team Inc Sta KNGM 115 W 5th St Emporia KS 66801 *I have found that prayer and bold action both bring mighty forces to my aid.*

PEASE, EDWIN CHAPMAN, JR., minister; b. Phila., Aug. 18, 1938; s. Edwin Chapman and Rebecca Elizabeth (Reeves) P.; m. Linda Jane Clark, Oct. 6, 1984. BA, U. Man., Winnipeg, Can., 1963; MDiv, Episcopal Div. Sch., 1979. Ordained to ministry Episcopal Ch. as deacon, 1979, as priest, 1980. Curate St. Anne's Episcopal Ch., Lowell, Mass., 1979-81; rector Christ Episcopal Ch., Medway, Mass., 1981—; mem. congregation resources and devel. commn. Episcopal Diocese of Mass., Boston, 1991; adj. prof. homiletics Episcopal Div. Sch., 1991. Office: Christ Episcopal Ch 14 School St PO Box 156 Medway MA 02053

PEASE, SARA GOODING, lay worker; b. Berlin, N.H., Nov. 12, 1918; d. Willard Merrill and Dorothy Quincy (Gay) Gooding; m. Donald Frederick Pease; children: Nancy Gay (dec.), Janet Meserve Pease Moore, Marcia Merrill Pease Lebhar. B in Religious Communications, George Mason U., 1987. Pres. Ch. Women United Frederick (Md.) County, 1981-82; ctr. assoc. Lancaster (Pa.) Theol. Sem., 1985-91; mem. task force Frederick Sch. Religion, 1984-90; sec. fellowship of faiths Mt. Holyoke Coll., South Hadley, Mass., 1937-38; mem. ministerial com. Hospice of Frederick County, 1983-84. Contbg. author: Advent Devotionals, 1981; editor newsletter Covenant Call, 1975-77, Ch. Women United in Frederick County, 1982, Ch. Woman in Md., 1988-90; contbr. articles, litany in field. Sherman scholar Mt. Holyoke Coll., 1936-39, Charles Merrill Smith scholar Ill. Wesleyan U. Writer's Conf., 1986. Mem. Nat. Assn. Parliamentarians (profl. registered parliamentarian 1968-91), LWV (dir. Frederick County chpt. 1980-81). Presbyterian.

PEASLEY, LYLE JAMES, lay worker; b. Bloomington, Ill., Nov. 9, 1954; s. Clarence Edward and Ada Marie (Oesch) P.; m. Patricia Ann Jones, Aug. 5, 1974; children: Jincey, Gabriel, Nicholas, Damian, Jonathan. AA, Southwestern Community Coll., 1974. V.p., cashier First State Bank, Stuart, Iowa, 1979—; Sun. sch. supt. 1st Congl. Ch., Stuart, 1979—, adult choir dir., 1980—, vacation Bible sch. dir., 1980—; dir. annual musicals Area Chs., Stuart, 1983—. Treas. Stuart C. of C., 1979—; dir. GILEAD, Des Moines, 1984-86. Named to Jr. Colls. Tital Honor Soc., 1974. Republican. Home: 411 N Western Stuart IA 50250 Office: First State Bank 215 N Division Stuart IA 50250

PECK, ALFRED DENNIS, minister; b. Milw., Nov. 8, 1953; s. Donald Allen and Ann Mary (Scarvasci) P. BS, Fort Wayne Bible Coll., 1986. Ordained to ministry, 1987. Pastor Clarksville (Pa.) Missionary Ch., 1986—; instr. Bible Time Def. Program, Greene County, Pa., 1986-88; pres. Jefferson-Morgan Ministerium, Greene County, 1988-89. Home: PO Box 204 Clarksville PA 15322 Office: Clarksville Missionary Ch PO Box 204 Clarksville PA 15322

PECK, ELBERT EUGENE, religious editor; b. Salt Lake City, Feb. 20, 1954; s. Eugene Lincoln and Elda (Shafer) P. BA in Polit. Sci. and Philosophy, Brigham Young U., 1978, MPA, 1981. Editor Sunstone Mag., Salt Lake City, 1986—. Mem. Mormon History Assn., Assn. for Mormon Letters, Assn. Mormon Counselors and Psychotherapists, Soc. Bibl. Lit., Am. Acad. Religion. Democrat. Home: PO Box 11122 Salt Lake City UT 84147 Office: Sunstone Found 331 S Rio Grande St #30 Salt Lake City UT 84101

PECK, PAUL LACHLAN, minister; b. Glens Falls, N.Y., Sept. 11, 1928; s. Paul Lee and Caroline Jeannette (Stanton) P.; children: Paul Barrett, Kathryn Elizabeth Peck Kadick. BS, U. Conn., 1952; ThD, Bernadean U., 1976; MEd, Westfield State Coll., 1983. Ordained to ministry Truth Ctr., 1972. With Proctor and Gamble Co., Watertown, N.Y., 1956-60; dir. deferred giving programs Syracuse (N.Y.) U., 1960-68, v.p., 1968-70; v.p. Fairleigh-Dickinson U., N.J., 1970-71, Manhattan Coll., Bronx, N.Y., 1971-75; founder, pastor Arete' Truth Ctr., San Diego, 1975—. Author: Footsteps Along the Path, 1978, Inherit the Kingdom, 1978, Milestones of the Way, 1978, Freeway to Health, 1980, Freeway to Work and Wealth, 1981, Freeway to Human Love, 1982, Freeway to Personal Growth, 1982, Your Dreams Count, 1990, Heroic Love Poems, 1990. Bd. dirs. Girl Scouts U.S.A., Syracuse, 1967-70; trustee, bd. dirs. Erickson Ednl. Found., 1970-75; vol. chaplain Auburn (N.Y.) State Prison, 1967-68; mem. chaplains' coun. Syracuse U., 1960-70; co-founder suicide and drug abuse prevention program Syracuse U., 1968-71, Fairleigh-Dickinson U., 1970-71, Manhattan Coll., 1971-75. Staff sgt. USNG, 1947-50. Mem. Internat. New Thought Alliance, SAR, Rotary, Knights of Malta (svc. award 1973), Masons, Shriners, Spiritual Frontiers Fellowship. Avocations: golf, book collecting. Home and Office: 6996 Camino Revueltos San Diego CA 92111

PECTOL, RICHARD WILLIAM, JR., minister; b. Claremore, Okla., Nov. 6, 1931; s. Richard W. and Hazel (Cash) P.; m. Ruby Vedagay Havens, Sept. 12, 1953; children: Thomas William, Sylvia Lynn Pectol Jinkerson. BA, Abilene Christian U., 1964, MA, 1966. Ordained to ministry Ch. of Christ, 1951. Min. Ch. of Christ, Munday, Tex., 1963-67, 10th and Broad Ch. of Christ, Wichita Falls, Tex., 1967-73, South Fork Ch. of Christ, Winston-Salem, N.C., 1973-79, Downtown Ch. of Christ, Searcy, Ark., 1979-88, Cen. Ch. of Christ, Claremore, Okla., 1988—; bd. dirs. Western Christian Found., Wichita Falls, 1967-85; mem. lectureship com. Abilene (Tex.) Christian U., 1972, Harding U., Searcy, 1980-87. Author: Sermons for the Seventies, 1974. Bd. dirs. Wichita Coun. on Alcoholism, Wichita Falls, 1968-73. Mem. Lions (pres. Munday 1972-73, chmn. interclub visits Searcy 1984-85, lion tamer Claremont 1990-91). Home: 1315 N Choctaw Claremore OK 74017 Office: Cen Ch of Christ 319 E Blue Starr Dr Claremont OK 74017

PEDDER, GLENN CURTISS, clergyman, army officer; b. Los Angeles, Sept. 3, 1942; s. Glenn Gibson Pedder and Julia Ida (Curtiss) Pedder Kee; m. Cathie Rachel Golnick, Apr. 10, 1965; children—Bethany Ann, Donna Marie. B.A., Calif. Lutheran Coll., 1965; B.D., M.Div., Wartburg Theol. Sem., 1969; D.Min., Colgate-Rochester Div. Sch., 1981. Ordained to ministry Lutheran Ch., 1969. Cert. marriage and family therapist, N.C. Pastor Ascension Luth. Ch., Ogden, Utah, 1969-72; commd. 2d lt. U.S. Army, 1972, advanced through grades to lt. col.; hosp. chaplain Lyster Army Hosp., Fort Rucker, Ala., 1972-73; asst. div. chaplain 2d Inf. Div., Republic of Korea, 1973-74; bn. chaplain 307th Engr. Bn., 82d Airborne Div., Fort Bragg, N.C., 1974-78; family life chaplain Fort Knox, Ky., 1979-82, brigade chaplain 22d Signal Brigade, Hoechst, Fed. Republic Germany, 1982-85; pastoral coordinator Fort Polk, La., 1985—; pres. Greater Ogden Ministerial Assn., 1971-72. Bd. dirs. Head Start Program, Ogden, 1970-72, March of Dimes, Ogden, 1970-72; convocator Calif. Luth. Coll., Thousand Oaks, 1971-72. Mem. Am. Assn. Marriage and Family Therapy (clin. mem.; approved supr. 1983—, bd. dirs. Ky. div. 1980-82), Hon. Order of Ky. Colonels. Home: 72 Apple St De Ridder LA 70634 Office: Office of Installation Chaplain HQ USAG Fort Polk LA 71459

PEDERSEN, WALTER, minister; b. Bklyn., Apr. 7, 1924; s. Oswald and Inga (Olsen) P.; m. Solveig Dahl, Jan. 19, 1951; children: Russell, Dianne, Dean. Student, CCNY, 1948; BS in Theology, North Cen. Bible Coll., 1953. Ordained to ministry Fellowship of Christian Assemblies, 1953. Pastor Evang. chs. N.Y., N.J., 1953-58; pastor Calvary Gospel Assembly, Estherville, Iowa, 1958-64, Rock Ch., Rockford, Ill., 1964-69, Homewood Full Gospel Ch., Homewood, Ill., 1969—; pres., bd. dirs. Homewood Full Gospel, 1988—; supt., founder Homewood Christian Acad., 1975—, Homewood Bible Inst., 1986—; bd. dirs. Global PLAN, Inc., Homewood, 1987—; talk show host WYCA Radio, 1987-89; internat. lectr. in field; speaker in field. Contbr. articles to profl. jours. Bd. dirs. South Suburban Hosp., Hazelcrest, Ill., 1986—; com. mem. Mayor Richard Daley Com. for Gospelfest, Chgo., 1990—, Mayor Daley Com. for M.L. King Day, Chgo., 1990—; bd. dirs. GRS Systems Internat., Homewood, 1990—. With USCG, 1942-46. Named Israel Tourism Del., 1983, Fact Finding Mission Del. U.S. Dept. Agriculture, 1987. Mem. Fellowship Christian Assemblies. Home: 3704 Poplar Pl Flossmoor IL 60422 Office: Homewood Full Gospel Ch 18620 Kedzie Ave Homewood IL 60430 *Life is to short to waste valuable time on pettiness. If we channel our energies into truly important lasting efforts, and keep a positive and joyful attitude with Jesus being central in all of lifes circumstances, not only will we be enriched, but others will also benefit because of our influence on them.*

PEDERSON, CLIFTON, academic administrator. Pres. Luth. Bible Inst. in Calif., Anaheim. Office: Luth Bible Inst Calif 641 S Western Ave Anaheim CA 92804*

PEDERSON, WAYNE ALLEN, broadcasting executive; b. Crookston, Minn., June 10, 1947; s. Ellsworth Benser and Helen Elizabeth (Logosz) P.; m. Norma Jane Ness, Sept. 14, 1968; children: Christina, Michelle. BA, U. Minn., 1969; MTh, Free Luth. Sem., Mpls., 1972. Mgr. Sta. KTIS AM-FM, Mpls., 1980—; program dir. Sky Light Network, St. Paul, 1985-88; freelance writer, voice-over, producer St. Paul, 1975—; tchr. adult class Calvary Bapt. Ch., St. Paul, 1980—; bd. dir.s Mpls. Assn. of Evangs., 1990—. Contbr. articles to profl. jours. Mem. Christian Mgmt. Assn. (seminar speaker), Nat. Religious Broadcasters (pres. Midwest chpt. 1987-89, coord. workshops 1980—, Regional Chpt. of Yr. award 1989, bd. dirs.), Suburban Area C. of C. (bd. dirs.). Office: Sta KTIS AM-FM 3003 N Snelling Saint Paul MN 55113

PEDNEAULT, ROCH, bishop; b. Alma, Que., Can., Apr. 10, 1927; s. Leonard and Marie-Ange (Tapin) R. BA, Laval U., Que., 1949, BTh, 1953, L of Scis., 1959. Ordained priest Roman Cath. Ch., 1953. Prof. chemistry Coll. of Chicoutimi, Que., 1953-67, rector, 1967-74; aux. bishop Roman Cath. Diocese Chicoutimi, 1974—; mem. social communications commn. Can. Conf. Cath. Bishops, 1976—, also mem. liturgy commn. Address: 602 Racine Est, Chicoutimi, PQ Canada G7H 6J6

PEELE, LUTHER MARTIN, minister; b. Laurel Hill, N.C., Jan. 20, 1929; s. Luther Martin and Mary Susanna (Falls) P.; m. Emma Lee Hayes; children: Luther Martin, Raymond Hampton, Audrey Melinda. Student, N.C. State U., 1947-49; BA in Philosophy and Religion, U. N.C., Wilmington, 1974; MDiv, Duke U., 1979. Ordained to ministry Meth. Ch. Min. Wrightsboro Meth. Ch., Wilmington, N.C., 1972-81, Devon Park and Oleander Meth. Chs., Wilmington, N.C., 1981-85, Zion Meth. Ch., Leland, N.C., 1985—. Home: Rt 2 Box 436 Leland NC 28451

PEEREY, RICHARD LEE, minister; b. Martin, Tenn., Oct. 25, 1948; s. Clifford Lee and Dorothy Jean (Shelby) P.; m. Jill Amy Morse, Nov. 24, 1972; children: Joel Lee, Amy Noelle. BA, Mobile Coll., 1971; MDiv, New Orleans Bapt. Theol. Sem., 1976; D. Ministry, Southeastern Bapt. Theol. Sem., 1984. Ordained to ministry So. Bapt. Conv., 1969. Pastor Bonner Creek Bapt. Ch., Franklinton, La., 1973-76, Beaver Dam Bapt. Ch., Franklin, Va., 1981—80; assoc. pastor, minister of edn. 1st Bapt. Ch., Danville, Va., 1976-80. chmn. student ministry com. Va. Bapt. Gen. Bd., 1991, chmn. ministerial edn. com., 1990. Mem. Isle of Wight (Va.) County Sch. Bd., 1989; bd. dirs. Gov.'s Magnet Sch., Norfolk, Va., 1990. Lt., chaplain USNR, 1980-81. Mem. Blackwater Bapt. Assn. (vice moderator 1987-89, moderator 1989-90), Am. Assn. Pastoral Counselors. Home: 3575 Carrsville Hwy Franklin VA 23851 Office: Beaver Dam Bapt Ch 3593 Carrsville Hwy Franklin VA 23851

PEERS, MICHAEL GEOFFREY, archbishop; b. Vancouver, B.C., Can., July 31, 1934; s. Geoffrey Hugh and Dorothy Enid (Mantle) P.; m. Dorothy Elizabeth Bradley, June 29, 1963; children: Valerie Anne Leslie, Richard Christopher Andre, Geoffrey Stephen Arthur. Zert.dolm., U. Heidelberg, Fed. Republic Germany, 1955; BA, U. B.C., Vancouver, 1956; Licentiate in Theology, Trinity Coll., Toronto, Ont., 1959, DD (hon.), 1977; DD (hon.), St. John's Coll., Winnipeg, Man., 1981, Wycliffe Coll., Toronto, 1987, Kent U., Canterbury, Eng., 1988, Montreal Diocesan Coll., Que., Can., 1989, Coll. of Emmanual and St. Chad, Sask., Can., 1990, Vancouver Sch. Theology, 1991, Thorneloe U., 1991. Ordained to ministry Anglican Ch. as deacon, 1959, as priest, 1960, consecrated bishop, 1977. Asst. curate St. Thomas Ch., Ottawa, 1959-61; chaplain U. Ottawa, 1961-66; rector St. Bede's Ch., Winnipeg, 1966-72, St. Martin's Ch., Winnipeg, 1972-74; dean of Qu'Appelle, Regina, Sask., 1974-77; bishop Qu'Appelle, 1977-82, archbishop, 1982-86; primate The Anglican Ch. Can., 1986—; instr. Ottawa Tchrs. Coll., 1962-66, St. Paul's High Sch., Winnipeg, 1967-69. Office: Anglican Ch Can, Church House 600 Jarvis St, Toronto, ON Canada M4Y 2J6

PEGORSCH, DENNIS WILLIAM, minister; b. Shawano, Wis., Dec. 13, 1941; s. William and Myrtle (Haeuser) P.; m. Grace Marie Droegemueller, June 30, 1969; children: David, Christine, Kim, Jeffrey. Student, Concordia Coll., Milw., 1959-61; BA, Concordia Sr. Coll., Ft. Wayne, Ind., 1961-63; BTh, Concordia Sem., St. Louis, 1963, MDiv, 1967; M in Social Work, U. Wis., 1972. Ordained to ministry Luth. Ch.-Mo. Synod, 1967. Pastor St. Peter-Immanuel Luth. Ch., Milw., 1967-74; adminstrv. pastor St. John Luth. Ch., Plymouth, Wis., 1974—; cir. youth rep. South Wis. dist. Luth. Ch.-Mo. Synod, Milw., 1968-74, cir. edn. rep., Plymouth, 1974—, camping com. mem., 1986-87, mem. older adult com., 1991—. Adv. bd. Willowglen Acad., Plymouth, 1986—; bd. dirs. Campfire, Inc., Plymouth, 1986-89, Luth. Family and Counseling Svcs., Milw., 1988—; mem. Plymouth Hist. Soc., 1990—. Home: 216 Division St Plymouth WI 53073 Office: St John Evang Luth Ch 222 N Stafford St Plymouth WI 53073

PEGRAM, DENNIS JAMES, financial administrator; b. Des Moines, Nov. 12, 1954; s. Joseph Norman Pegram and Norma Jean (Hooper) Smith; m. Ina Kay Carson, June 5, 1976; children: Joanie Joy, Joshua Neal, Audrey Beth, Bryce Elliot, Alana Marie, Clark-Everett Carson. BS in Bus. Mgmt., Bob Jones U., 1977, MS in Edn. Adminstrn. and Supervision, 1980. Bus. mgr. Tabernacle Bapt. Ch. and Christian Sch., Virginia Beach, Va., 1977-79; fin. adminstr. Hampton Park Bapt. Ch. and Christian Sch., Greenville, S.C., 1980—; treas. Charleston Christian Relief Fund, Greenville, S.C, 1989. Mem. Coun. Govts. Ednl. Adv. Com., Greenville, 1988—; pres. Rep. precinct com. orgn., 1985-88; regular ch. soloist, Greenville. Home: 101 Thompson Rd Taylors SC 29687 Office: Hampton Park Bapt Ch 875 State Park Rd Greenville SC 29609

PEGUES, W. WESLEY (WES PEGUES), youth minister; b. Tupelo, Miss., Nov. 22, 1956; s. William Edward and Norma (Crockett) P.; m. Terri Ann Rigsbee, June 12, 1982; children: Ashley, Jonathan, Stuart. B.Recreation Leadership, U. Miss., 1980; MRE, Southwestern Bapt. Theol. Sem., Ft. Worth, 1983. Ordained to ministry So. Bapt. Conv., 1983. Minister youth edn. Second Bapt. Ch., Levelland, Tex., 1983-85; minister of youth/activities Audubon Pk. Bapt. Ch., Memphis, 1985—; chmn. Shelby County Bapt. Family Ministry Coun., 1988—; dir. youth Shelby County Discipleship Tng., 1990—. Mem. Shelby County Bapt. Assn. (mem. coun. 1988—), So. Bapt. Religious Educators Assn., Tenn. Bapt. Youth Ministers Assn. Home: 3750 Briar Rose Memphis TN 38111 Office: Audubon Pk Bapt Ch 4060 Park Ave Memphis TN 38111

PEIFER, JANET MARIE, minister; b. Manheim, Pa., Apr. 13, 1945; d. Paul Milton and Mabel Kathryn (Myers) Witmer; m. Elvin Herr Peifer, Sept. 4, 1965; children: Loreen Renea, Scott Douglas. BA in Religious/Bibl. Studies, Messiah Coll., 1988; MDiv, Ea. Bapt. Theol. Sem., Phila., 1988—. Lic. to ministry Brethren in Christ Ch., 1990. Interim asst. pastor Refton (Pa.) Brethren in Christ Ch., 1988, pastoral asst. for pastoral care and counseling, 1989—; dir. music Refton Brethren in Christ Ch., 1988-91, dir. prayer, missions and outreach, 1984-89. Contbr. articles to profl. jours. Mem. Brethren in Christ Hist. Soc., Christians for Bibl. Equality. Republican. Home: 134 Sprecher Rd Willow Street PA 17584

PEINE, OLLIE CAMPBELL, pastor; b. St. Louis, Dec. 2, 1945; s. Lawrence J. and Gladys (Jacobsen) P.; m. Joyce Lee Eadie, Oct. 23, 1970; children: Crystal Lanette, Joy Janette. BA, Charleston Southern U., 1986. Ordained to ministry So. Bap. Conv., 1986. Pastor Emmanuel Bapt. Ch., Holly Hill, S.C., 1984-85, Southside Bapt. Ch., Charleston, S.C., 1986—; asst. dir. maint. Charleston Southern U., 1990—. With USN, 1964-68. Mem. NACUBO, APPA, SCAPPA, S.C. Energy Mgrs., Charleston Bapt. Assn. (clk. 1990—). Home: 121 Poplar Circle Summerville SC 29483

PEJZA, JOHN PHILIP, priest, school principal; b. Neshkoro, Wis., Aug. 5, 1934; s. Philip Peter and Regina Rosalie (Dombrowski) P. BA, Villanova U., 1957, MA, 1961, MSSS, 1964; MA, U. San Francisco, 1981; postgrad., U. San Diego, 1982, EdD, 1987. Joined Order of St. Augustine, Roman

Cath. Ch., 1952; ordained priest, 1961; cert. tchr. and adminstr., Calif. Tchr. Malvern (Pa.) Prep Sch., 1961-63; tchr. St. Augustine High Sch., San Diego, 1963-64, 70-75, prin., 1983-88; tchr., asst. prin. Villanova Prep. Sch., Ojai, Calif., 1964-70, pres., 1988—; prin. Cen. Cath. High Sch., Modesto, Calif., 1975-80, Marian High Sch., San Diego, 1981-83; secondary cons. Diocese of Stockton, Calif., 1977-80; exec. sec. province planning commn. Province of St. Augustine, Los Angeles, 1974-75; counselor Province of St. Augustine, Order of St. Augustine, Los Angeles, 1975-79; mem. priests' senate Diocese of San Diego, 1983-85. Contbr. articles to profl. jours. Mem. Nat. Cath. Ednl. Assn. (regional assoc. secondary div. 1987—), Augustinian Secondary Edn. Assn. (exec. sec. 1989—), Assn. Calif. Sch. Adminstrs., Nat. Assn. Secondary Sch. Prins., Internat. Radio Club Am. (pres. 1977-79), Phi Delta Kappa. Avocations: backpacking, reading, photography, shortwave radio. Home: 185 St Thomas Dr Ojai CA 93023 Office: Villanova Prep Sch 12096 Ventura Ave Ojai CA 93023-3999

PEKARSKY, DANIEL, religious organization administrator. Pres. Jewish Fedn. of Greater Vancouver, B.C., Can. Office: Jewish Fedn, 950 W 41st St, Vancouver, AB Canada V5Z 2N7*

PELÁEZ, ARMANTINA R., religious educator; b. Havana, Cuba, Apr. 21, 1948; came to U.S., 1962; d. Armando and Argentina (Pérez) P. BA, Ladycliff Coll., Highland Falls, N.Y., 1973; MA in Religious Edn., Fordham U., 1977; Cert. Tng. in Psychoanalysis and Psychotherapy, Weschester Inst., 1987. Asst. child care worker St. Joseph's Home of Peekskill (N.Y.), 1968-70; assoc. dir. religious edn. St. Joseph's of Palisades Parish, Western N.Y. and N.J., 1973-75; sec. evangelization Diocese of Paterson (N.J.) Roman Cath. Ch., 1975-80; Hispanic Apostolate coordinator, asst. adminstr. to vicar of Hispanic ministries, 1980-84; coord. catechesis and religious edn. U.S. Dept. Edn., Washington, 1984-90; dir. tng. Poly. Inst. Fla., Miami, 1990—; vol. team mem. pastoral Hispanic youth ministry St. Augustine's Parish, Union City, N.J., 1979-84; cons. Latin Am. Program Wilson Ctr., Washington, 1982, Ctr. for Applied in Apostolate, 1981; authorized instr. parent and tchr. effectiveness tng., N.J.; psychotherapist Palisade Counseling Ctr., Rutherford, N.J., 1982-87, Lakeland Counseling Ctr., Dover, N.J., 1985-87; co-dir., psychotherapist Eirene Counseling Ctr., Union City, N.J., 1987-90. Contbr. numerous articles in English and Spanish. Chmn., nat. bd. dirs. Nat. Planning Council, 1974-75. Mem. Nat. Assn. for Women Religious, Found. of Thanatology (assoc.), Am. Soc. Psychical Research, Las Hermanas Nat. Orgn. (N.Y. coordinator 1970-72, N.Y. Upstate coordinator 1972-73, N.J. coordinator 1978-79), Nat. Assn. Advancement of Psychoanalysis and Am. Bds. for Accreditation and Certification Inc., Nat. Counseling and Devel. Assn. Clubs: N.Y. Road Runners, N.Y. Race Walking; N.J. Shore Athletic, N.J. Athletics Congress. Home: 7935 SW 8th St #68 Miami FL 33144 Office: Poly Inst Fla 11865 (H3) Coral Way Miami FL 33175

PELFREY, LLOYD MARVIN, college president; b. Hamilton, Ohio, June 13, 1931; s. Addie Herbert and Vina Marie (Miller) P.; m. Mary Irene Rohrer, Feb. 9, 1957; children: Rhonda, Theda, Brenda. BA, Cin. Bible Coll., 1953; MA, Cin. Christian Sem., 1955, BD, 1956. Ordained to ministry Ch. of Christ/Christian Chs., 1953. Min. Ch. of Christ, Eaton, Ohio, 1951-56; min. Christian Ch., Englewood, Tenn., 1957, Prairie Hill, Mo., 1958-62; acad. dean Cen. Christian Coll., Moberly, Mo., 1957-73, pres., 1973—; mem. N.Am. Christian Conv., 1971-73, 84-86; mem. adv. com. Chaplaincy Endorsement Commn., 1973—; chmn. Christian Educators Conf., 1973; mem. convening com. Open Forum, 1989—. Contbr. articles to religious jours. Chmn. Citizens' Involvement and Human Devel. Com., Moberly, 1974, 75. Mem. Evang. Theol. Soc., Presdl. Assn. Christian Colls. (pres. 1981-82, sec. 1984-85), Midwest Conf. Christian Colls. (sec. 1967-70, 72-73, pres. 1970-72), Kiwanis (pres. 1973-74). Home: 418 Woodland Ave Moberly MO 65270-2234 Office: Cen Christian Coll 911 Urbandale Dr E Moberly MO 65270-1997

PELIKAN, JAROSLAV JAN, history educator; b. Akron, Ohio, Dec. 17, 1923; s. Jaroslav Jan and Anna (Buzek) P.; m. Sylvia Burica, June 9, 1946; children: Martin, Michael, Miriam. Grad. summa cum laude, Concordia Jr. Coll., Ft. Wayne, Ind., 1942; BD, Concordia Theol. Sem., St. Louis, 1946; PhD, U. Chgo., 1946; MA (hon.), Yale U., 1961; DD (hon.), Concordia Coll., Moorehead, Minn., 1960, Concordia Sem., 1967, Trinity Coll., Hartford, Conn., 1987, St. Vladimir's Orthodox Theol. Sem., 1988, Victoria U., Toronto, 1989; LittD (hon.), Wittenberg U., 1960, Wheeling Coll., 1966, Gettysburg Coll., 1967, Pacific Luth. U., 1967, Wabash Coll., 1988, Jewish Theol. Sem., 1991; HHD (hon.), Providence Coll., 1966, Moravian Coll., 1986, Jewish Theol. Sem., 1991; LLD (hon.), Keuka Coll., 1967, U. Notre Dame, 1979; LHD (hon.), Valparaiso U., 1966, Rockhurst Coll., 1967, Albertus Magnus Coll., 1973, Coe Coll., 1976, Cath. U. Am., 1977, St. Mary's Coll., 1978, St. Anselm Coll., 1983, U. Nebr.-Omaha, 1984, Tulane U., 1986, Assumption Coll., 1986, LaSalle U., 1987, Carthage Coll., 1991, U. Chgo., 1991; ThD (hon.), U. Hamburg, 1971, St. Olaf Coll., 1972; STD, Dickinson Coll., 1986. Faculty Valparaiso (Ind.) U., 1946-49, Concordia Sem., St. Louis, 1949-53, U. Chgo., 1953-62; Titus Street prof. eccles. history Yale U., 1962-72, Sterling prof. history, 1972—, William Clyde DeVane lectr., 1984-86, dir. div. humanities, 1974-75, chmn. Medieval studies, 1974-75, 78-80, dean Grad. Sch., 1973-78; Gray lectr. Duke U., 1960, Ingersoll lectr. Harvard U., 1963, Gauss lectr. Princeton U., 1980, Jefferson lectr. NEH, 1983, Richard lectr. U. Va., 1984, Rauschenbusch lectre. Colgate-Rochester Divinity Sch., 1984, Gilson lectr. U. Toronto, 1985, Hale lectr. Seabury-Western Sem., 1986, Mead-Swing lectr. Oberlin Coll., 1986, Gross lectr. Rutgers U., 1989; bd. dirs. Nat. Humanities Ctr., 1984-90; adv. bd. Ctr. Theol. Inquiry, 1984-90; mem. coun. The Smithsonian Instn., 1984-90; U.S. chmn. U.S. Czechoslovak Commn. on Humanities and Social Scis., 1987—. Author: From Luther to Kierkegaard, 1950, Fools for Christ, 1955, The Riddle of Roman Catholicism, 1959 (Abingdon award 1959), Luther the Expositor, 1959, The Shape of Death, 1961, The Light of the World, 1962, Obedient Rebels, 1964, The Finality of Jesus Christ in an Age of Universal History, 1965, The Christian Intellectual, 1966, Spirit Versus Structure, 1968, Development of Doctrine, 1969, Historical Theology, 1971, The Christian Tradition, 5 vols., 1971-89, Scholarship and Its Survival, 1983, The Vindication of Tradition, 1984, Jesus through the Centuries, 1985, The Mystery of Continuity, 1986, Bach Among the Theologians, 1986, The Excellent Empire, 1987, The Melody of Theology, 1988, Confessor Between East and West, 1990, Imago Dei, 1990, Eternal Feminines, 1990, also introductions to works of others; editor, translator: Luther's Works, 22 vols., 1955-71, The Book of Concord, 1959; editor: Makers of Modern Theology, 5 vols., 1966-68, The Preaching of Chrysostom, 1967, Interpreters of Luther, 1968, Twentieth-Century Theology in the Making, 3 vols., 1969-70, The Preaching of Augustine, 1973, The World Treasury of Modern Religious Thought, 1991; mem. editorial bd. Collected Works of Erasmus, Classics of Western Spirituality, Evangelisches Kirchenlexikon, Emerson's Nature, 1986, The World Treasury of Modern Religious Thought, 1990; departmental editor Ency. Britannica, 1958-69; adminstrv. bd. Papers of Benjamin Franklin; chmn. publs. com. Yale Univ. Press, 1979-90, v.p. bd. govs., 1988—; contbr. to many symposia, jours., encys. Pres. 4th Internat. Congress for Luther Research, 1971, New Eng. Congress on Grad. Edn., 1976-77. Recipient Abingdon award, 1959, Pax Christi award St. John's U., Collegeville, Minn., 1966, John Gilmary Shea prize Am. Cath. Hist. Assn., 1971, Nat. award Slovak World Congress, 1973, Religious Book award Catholic Press Assn., 1974, Christian Unity award Atonement Friars, 1975, Bicentennial award Czechoslovak Soc. Artsd Scis., 1976, Wilbur Cross medal Yale Grad. Sch. Assn., 1979, Profl. Achievement award U. Chgo. Alumni Assn., 1980, Shaw medal Boston Coll., 1984, Comenius medallion Moravian Coll., 1986, Alumnus of Yr. award Div. Sch. U. Chgo., 1986, Bicentennial medal Georgetown U., 1989, award for excellence Am. Acad. Religion, 1989, Umanità award Newberry Libr., 1990; sr. fellow Carnegie Found. Advancement Teaching, 1982-83; recipient Festschrift: Schools of Thought in the Christian Tradition, 1984. Fellow Medieval Acad. Am. (Haskins medal 1985, councillor); mem. Am. Hist. Assn., Am. Soc. Ch. History (pres. 1965), Internat. Congress of Luther Research (pres. 1971), Am. Acad. Arts and Scis. (v.p. 1976—), Am. Philos. Soc. (councillor 1984-87), Council of Scholars of Library of Congress (founding chmn. 1980-83), Phi Beta Kappa (united chpts. senator 1985-90), Elizabethan Club, Mory's. Home: 156 Chestnut Ln Hamden CT 06518 Office: Yale U Dept History 1504A Yale Sta New Haven CT 06520-7425

PELKONEN, J(OHN) PETER, minister; b. Boston, May 28, 1937; s. Frank Alexander andEffie Lydia (Mattson) P.; m. Nancy Lee Sprinkle, June 28, 1964. BA, Wittenberg U., 1958; MDiv, Hamma Sch. Theology, 1961; PhD in Religion, Duke U., 1972. Ordained to ministry, Luth. Ch. Am., 1962. Pastor Holy Trinity Luch. Ch., Ft. Walton Beach, Fla., 1962-65; prof. ch. history Hamma Sch. Theology, Springfield, Ohio, 1968-70; pastor 1st Luth. Ch., Beach City, Ohio, 1970-74; sr. pastor Faith Luth. Ch., Akron, Ohio, 1974-81; pastor St. John's Luth. Ch., Dayton, Ohio, 1981—; dir. Trinity Luth. Sem.; chmn. Ohio Synod Profl. Leadership Com., 1974-78, sec., 1987—; pres. Luth. Coun. Greater Akron, 1976-78; mem. instl. rev. bd., Wright State U., 1988—. Contbr. sermons to Clergy Jour., 1979—, articles to profl. jours.; translator Practical Theology, 1962. Luth. World Fedn. Exch. scholar, Finland, 1961-62, Duke U., 1965-67; G.H. Kearns fellow, 1967. Home: 3207 Allendale Dr Dayton OH 45409 Office: St John's Luth Ch 141 S Ludlow St Dayton OH 45402

PELLETIER, FREDERICK H., deacon; b. Superior, Wis., Nov. 26, 1916; s. Albert J. and Marianne Louise (Hertlein) P.; m. Mary Jane Elkerton, Aug. 16, 1939; children: Frederick Paul, Franklyn David, Joseph George, Marilyn Ann Pelletier Robins, Carolyn Jane Pelletier Kerker. Student, Superior State Coll. Ordained deacon Roman Cath. Ch., 1985. Deacon Holy Family Ch., Glendale, Calif., 1985—; pres., chief exec. officer Columbian Retirement Home Inc., L.A., 1987—. Pres. Greater Glendale Coun. on Aging, 1986-89, gen chmn. sr. fair, 1989-91. Named Outstanding Col., County of L.A., 1987. Mem. Elks, Golden Age Club (bd. dirs. 1984-91). Republican. Home: 321 E Stocker St Glendale CA 91207

PELLICANE, MARY, nun; b. Bklyn., Jan. 11, 1922; d. Joseph and Catherine Cecilia (Cuccia) P. BA, CUNY, 1943; postgrad., Rome. Joined Congregation Our Lady of Retreat in Cenacle, Roman Cath. Ch., 1946. Spiritual dir. Cenacle Retreat House, Boston, N.Y.C., N.Z., L.I., N.Y., 1948-77; dir. Cenacle Retreat House, Rochester, N.Y., 1961-64, Pitts., 1967-77, Charleston, W.Va., 1977—. Contbr. articles to profl. jours. Home and Office: Cenacle Retreat House 1114 Virginia St Charleston WV 25301

PELOTTE, DONALD EDMOND, bishop; b. Waterville, Maine, Apr. 13, 1945; s. Norris Albert and Margaret Yvonne (LaBrie) P. AA, Eymard Sem. and Jr. Coll., Hyde Park, N.Y., 1965; BA, John Carroll U., 1969; MA, Fordham U., 1971, PhD, 1975. Ordained priest Roman Cath. Ch., 1972. Provincial superior Blessed Sacrament, Cleve., from 1978; ordained coadjutor bishop Diocese of Gallup, N.Mex., 1986-90, bishop, 1990—; nat. bd. dirs. Maj. Superiors of Men, Silver Spring, Md., 1981—, Tekakwitha Conf., Great Falls, Mont., 1981—. Author: John Courtney Murray: Theologian in Conflict, 1976. 1st native Am. bishop. Mem. Cath. Theol. Soc. Am., Am. Cath. Hist. Soc. Address: Bishop of Gallup PO Box 1317 Gallup NM 87305-1317

PELTIER, SISTER MARY ANNE, religion educator; b. New Orleans, Sept. 16, 1936; d. Hobson and Lucille (De Long) P. BA, Our Lady of Holy Cross, New Orleans, 1961; MEd, Our Lady of the Lake, San Antonio, 1974. Prin. St. Agnes Sch., New Orleans, 1972-77; tchr. Sts. Peter & Paul Sch., New Orleans, 1977-78, prin., 1978-79; prin. St. Alphonsus Sch., Ocean Springs, Miss., 1979-90; asst. supr. student tchrs. Our Lady of Holy Cross Coll., 1991—; eucharistic min. Dioceses New Orleans, Biloxi, Miss., 1972-80; leader Parish Renew Group, Ocean Springs, 1987; gen. chpt. del. Marianites of Holy Cross. Contbr. articles to profl. jours. Mediator Ocean Springs Mcpl. Sch. Dist., 1979-90; sch. mediator DAR, Biloxi, 1979-90. Recipient Nat. Disting. Prin. award U.S. Dept. Edn., 1987, Svc. award Biloxi Bishop's Diocesan, 1985. Mem. Fort Maurepas Miss. Reading Coun., Nat. Cath. Educators Assn. (Adminstr's Exch. grand prize 1989), Cath. Diocese Prins. Assn. (pres. 1980-82), Delta Kappa Gamma (Golden Apple award). Home: Our Lady of Fatima Convent 314 Jim Money Rd Biloxi MS 39531

PELUSA, JOAN-ELLEN MICHELLE, Christian radio director; b. Baldwin, N.Y., June 21, 1960; d. Dominick Frank and Laura Mildred (Interranté) P. Cert., Columbia Sch. Broadcasting, Hollywood, Calif., 1979. Lic. 3d class radio broadcasting FCC. Music dir. Sta. WLPJ FM, New Port Richey, Fla., 1985—. Vol. with physically-challenged children in classes Richey Fundamental Elem. Sch., New Port Richey, 1987—. Republican. Roman Catholic. Home: 8033 Laurel Vista Lane Port Richey FL 34668 Office: Sta WLPJ FM Radio 8410 US Hwy 19 Ste 107-A New Port Richey FL 34668

PEMBERTON, JOHN, III, religion educator; b. New Brunswick, N.J., Feb. 16, 1928; married; 1 child. A.B., Princeton U., 1948; B.D., Duke U., 1952; M.A. (hon.), Amherst Coll., 1967. Asst. prof. religion Randolph-Macon Woman's Coll., 1954-58; assoc. prof. religion Amherst (Mass.) Coll., 1958-64, prof. religion, 1964—, Crosby prof. religion, Andrew Mellon prof. humanities, 1983-86. Author: (with W. Fagg) Yoruba Sculpture of West Africa, 1982, (with N. Drewal and R. Abivdeen) Yozuba: Nine Centuries of African Art and Thought, 1989; contbr. numerous articles and monographs on Yoruba religion and art. Mem. AAUP, Am. Acad. Religion, African Studies Assn. Office: Amherst Coll Dept Religion Amherst MA 01002

PENA, RAYMUNDO JOSEPH, bishop; b. Corpus Christi, Feb. 19, 1934; s. Cosme A. and Elisa (Ramon) P. D.D., Assumption Sem., San Antonio, 1957. Ordained priest Roman Catholic Ch., 1957; asst. pastor St. Peter's Ch., Laredo, Tex., 1957-60, St. Joseph's-Our Lady of Fatima, Alamo, Tex., 1960-63, Sacred Heart, Mathis, Tex., 1963-67, Christ the King and Our Lady of Pillar Parishes, Corpus Christi, 1967-69; pastor Our Lady of Guadalupe Parish, Corpus Christi, 1969-76; v.p. Corpus Christi Diocesan Senate of Priests, 1970-76; aux. bishop of San Antonio, 1976-80; bishop of El Paso, 1980—. Mem. Nat. Conf. Cath. Bishops, U.S. Cath. Conf. Home: 481 St Matthews St El Paso TX 79907 Office: 499 St Matthews St El Paso TX 79907

PENCE, JERRY GLENN, denominational executive; b. Twin Falls, Idaho, June 22, 1953; s. Grover Glenn Wilson and Lela Christine (Norris) Sharp; m. Calene Rose Mueller, May 24, 1975; children: Kristin, Kory. BA in Religion, Bartlesville Wesleyan Coll., 1975; MDiv, Nazarene Theol. Seminary, Kansas City, Mo., 1986. Ordained to ministry Wesleyan Ch., 1977. Asst. pastor Mitchell (S.D.) Wesleyan Ch., 1975-78; pastor Junction City (Kans.) Wesleyan Ch., 1978-80; sr. pastor Immanuel Wesleyan Ch., Kansas City, Kans., 1980-84, Concordia (Kans.) Wesleyan Ch., 1985-90; dir. of ch. growth The Wesleyan Ch.-Internat. Ctr., Indpls., 1990—; dist. sec. evangelism Kans. Dist. of The Wesleyan Ch., Salina, 1988-90; bd. dirs. Kans. Dist. Bd. Adminstrn., 1989-90; ch. growth assoc. Inst. for Am. Ch. Growth, Monrovia, Calif., 1987—. Editor: (book) A Greater Work to Do, 1990, (mag.) Mandate, 1990—; contbr. articles to profl. jours. Trustee Frank Carlson Libr., Concordia, 1987-90; curriculum com. Unified Sch. Dist. 333, 1989, master planning com., 1989-90. Mem. North Am. Soc. for Ch. Growth, Concordia Ministerial Assn. (pres., treas. 1986-89). Republican. Office: Dept Evangelism/Ch Growth 6060 Castleway Dr W Indianapolis IN 46250-0434

PENCHANSKY, DAVID, educator; b. Bklyn., Dec. 3, 1951; s. Charles and Mimi (Black) P.; m. Joyce Eileen Grigsby, Feb. 29, 1980; children: Simon Graham, Maia Lucy. BA cum laude, Queens Coll., 1974; MA, Assemblies of God Grad. Sch., 1980; PhD, Vanderbilt U., 1988. Asst. prof. U. St. Thomas, St. Paul, 1989—. Author: The Betrayal of God, 1990; contbr. articles to profl. jours. Mem. Soc. Bibl. Lit., Cath. Bibl. Assn., Phi Beta Kappa, Phi Alpha Theta. Home: 1480 Blair Ave Saint Paul MN 55104 Office: U St Thomas 2115 Summit Saint Paul MN 55105

PENDER, WILLIAM CLARK, minister; b. Rock Hill, S.C., Dec. 23, 1955; s. Robert Gibbon and Nelle (Clark) P.; m. Sheri Armitage; children: Joshua, Amelia. BA, Dartmouth Coll., 1977; MDiv, Columbia Theol. Sem., 1980; PhD, Duke U., 1984. Ordained to ministry Presbyn. Ch. (U.S.A.), 1980. Parish assoc. 1st Presbyn. Ch., Durham, N.C., 1981-84; pastor 1st Presbyn. Ch., Live Oak, Fla., 1984-89, Oakland Ave. Presbyn. Ch., Rock Hill, S.C., 1989—. Contbr. articles to profl. jours. Bd. dirs. Assn. for Retarded Citizens, Live Oak, 1987-89. Gurney Harris Kearns fellow Duke U., 1980-83, Friends of Columbia fellow Columbia Theol. Sem., 1977-78, Alumni/ae fellow Columbia Theol. Sem., 1980. Mem. Rotary (bd. dirs. Live Oak chpt. 1988-89). Democrat. Office: Oakland Ave Presbyn Ch 421 Oakland Ave Rock Hill SC 29730 *Fanny Crosby said it with sentiment; Dietrich Bohoeffer said it with courage. I say it in shallow emulation and in prayer: "I am thine, O Lord."*

PENDLETON, GLORIA BELL, lay worker; b. Washington, Dec. 30, 1927; d. Alton and Helen P. (Williams) Bell; m. Calvin Pendleton, Dec. 7, 1950; 1 child, Mark Alton. B in Gen. Studies, George Washington U., 1977; MDiv., Howard U., 1991. Vol. positions including elder, supt. ch. sch., tchr., others. various Presbyn. chs.; Protestant chaplain intern Commn. of Mental Health, St. Elizabeth campus, Washington. Advocate fair housing Neighbors, Inc., Washington, 1965-69; mgr. fed. program Dept. Navy, Washington, 1983-87. Mem. AAAW, Federally Employed Women, Chevy Chase Bus. and Profl. Women. Democrat. Home: 7425 9th St NW Washington DC 20012 Office: Nat Capital Presbytery 4915 45th St NW Washington DC 20016

PENFIELD, JANET G. HARBISON, editor; b. East Orange, N.J., Apr. 19, 1916; d. Harold Richardson and Evangeline (Dalrymple) German. AB, Smith Coll., 1937; postgrad., Princeton Theol. Sem., 1958. Assoc. editor Presbyn. Life mag., Phila., 1959-72; mem. Com. on Statement of Faith, Phila., 1960-67, Com. on Human Sexualtiy, N.Y.C., 1968—; del. Presbyn. Ch. to Consultation on Ch. Union, 1962—. Contbr. articles to religious jours. Mem. Assoc. Ch. Press (life). Home: 3120 Monroe Village Jamesburg NJ 08831

PENN, C(ECIL) RAY, religion educator; b. Loda, Ill., Sept. 16, 1948; s. Elmo and Lavane Belmont (Phillips) P. BA cum laude, McKendree Coll., 1970; MDiv cum laude, Wesley Theol. Sem., 1973; MA, U. Ill., 1981; PhD in Rhetorical Theory, Northwestern U., 1987; STM cum laude, Christian Theol. Sem., 1989. Ordained to ministry Meth. Ch., 1974. Asst. minister 1st Christian Ch., Alexandria, Va., 1971-74, Springfield (Va.) United Meth., 1974-75; pastor Cen. Ill. Meth. Conf., 1975-81; asst. prof. Radford (Va.) U., 1986—. Contbr. article to publs. Mem. Religious Speech Communication Assn., Speech Communication Assn. Home: 666 Auburn Ave Apt 700-J Radford VA 24141 Office: Radford U Dept Communication Box 5784 Radford VA 24141 *Looking at religious language enables us to see the paradoxical power in reconciling metaphors as well as the boundaries and barriers other metaphors create between believers. God oozes around our great and fragile symbols.*

PENN, DAVID C(LYDE), sales professional, clergyman; b. Chgo., Jan. 23, 1953; s. Robert Worth and Edmonia Alice (Kennedy) P.; m. Brenda Joyce Martin, May 18, 1974; children—Dortricia Kenyatta, Danielle Edmonia. A.A., Mich. Christian Coll., 1972; B.S., Heed U., 1978; M.R.E., Internat. Sem., 1981. Ordained to ministry Ch. of Christ, 1978. Assoc. minister 79th St. Ch., Chgo., 1975-78, Sheldon Heights Ch., Chgo., 1978-81, 82—; resident minister Beecher St. Ch., Cin., 1981-82; salesperson Sheldon Heights/Jays Foods, Chgo., 1975—; counselor, Sheldon Heights Ch., 1978—; co-chairperson Tri-State Youth Conf., Ill., Ind., Wis., 1979-81. Recipient Police award Chgo. Patrolmen's Assn., 1974; Stewardship award Sheldon Heights Ch., 1981. Fellow Mich. Christian Alumni Assn. Democrat. Club: VIP (pres. 1970-71). Home: 432 W 102d St Chicago IL 60628 Office: 11325 S Halsted St Chicago IL 60628 also: 1540 W 44th St Chicago IL 60637

PENN, DAVID JOSEPH, pastor; b. Yuba City, Calif., June 14, 1944; s. Joseph Francis and Ellen Letta (Pittenger) P.; m. Ruth Elizabeth Hetrick, Dec. 27, 1968; children: Lisa, Cristy, David II. BA, Pasadena Coll./Point Loma Nazarene Coll., 1967; MDiv., Nazarene Theol. Sem., 1971. Ordained to ministry Ch. of Nazarene, 1974. Pastor Jacobe Chapel Presbyn. Ch., Warrensburg, Mo., 1969-71; assoc. pastor Victory Hills Ch. of Nazarene, Kansas City, Mo., 1971-73; pastor Jacksonville (Ill.) Ch. of Nazarene, 1973-76, Kingwood (W.Va.) Ch. of Nazarene, 1976-82, Community Ch. of Nazarene, Racine, Wis., 1982-89, Hesperia (Calif.) Ch. of Nazarene, 1989—; sec. Ill. dist. Nazarene Youth Internat., 1974-76; chmn. Christian Life and Sunday Sch., 1985-89; mem. Wis. dist. Ministerial Credentials, 1984-89, adv. council, 1986-89; mem. fin. com. Wis. Ch. of Nazarene, 1983-89. Trustee Mt. Vernon Nazarene Coll., 1981-82; exec. sec. Clyde Dupin Crusade, Kingwood, W.Va., 1979-82; chaplain Morgan County Jail, Jacksonville, 1974-76; mem. Jacksonville Welfare Bd., 1976, Jacksonville Red Cross, 1976; pres. Kingwood Ministerial Fellowship, 1980-82. Recipient Leaders Fellowship award. Mem. Racine Pastor's Fellowship (pres. 1987-89). Avocations: photography, fishing, people, cars. Office: Hesperia Ch of Nazarene 8518 Maple Ave Hesperia CA 92345

PENNELL, WILLIAM WAYNE, minister; b. Boone, N.C., Sept. 15, 1939; s. Thomas Milton and Luna Mabel (Payne) P.; m. Betty Jane Sullivan, Aug. 15, 1959; children: Beverly, Becky, Bethany, William Wayne Jr. Student, Mars Hill Jr. Coll., 1960; BA, East Tenn. State U., 1964; DD (hon.), Clarksville Sch. Theology, 1968, Hyles/Anderson U., 1976. Ordained to ministry Bapt. Ch. Pastor Clear Branch Bapt., Erwin, Tex., 1958-62, Temple Bapt. Ch., Kingsport, Tenn., 1962-74, Rochester Hills Bapt. Ch., 1974-77, Forrest Hills Bapt. Ch., Decatur, Ga., 1977—; moderator Southwide Bapt. Fellowship, 1979, vice moderator, 1989. Mem. Ga. Assn. Christian Schs. (del.). Home: 3872 Samaria Ct Tucker GA 30084 Office: Forrest Hills Bapt Ch 923 Valley Brook Rd Decatur GA 30033

PENNELLA, JOSEPH, minister; b. Avellino, Napoli, Italy, Mar. 19, 1947; came to U.S., 1969; s. Geraldo Pennella and Grazia Grippo; m. Tina Sica, July 27, 1969; children: Sara, Jonathan, Jerry, Melania. Student, Bereano, Rome, 1963, Liberty Home Bible Inst., 1990. Ordained to ministry Christian Ch. N.Am., 1980. Asst. pastor Italy, 1963-69; pastor Evang. Christian Ch., 1974—.

PENNER, ROBYN ROXANNE, minister, social worker; b. Virden, Man., Can., Feb. 9, 1968; d. Ron and Ruth (Sawatzky) P. BA in Social Work, Ea. Mennonite Coll., 1989. active various ch. vol. positions, 1988—. Min. youth Parkview Mennonite Ch., Harrisonburg, Va., 1988—; caseworker Big Bros./Big Sisters Am., Harrisonburg, 1989—. Home: 1241 A Lincolnshire Dr Harrisonburg VA 22801 Office: Parkview Mennonite Ch 1600 Park Rd Harrisonburg VA 22801

PENNEY, ALPHONSUS LIGUORI, archbishop; b. St. John's, Nfld., Can., Sept. 17, 1924; s. Alphonsus Liguori and Catherine (Mullaly) P. L.Ph., U. Ottawa, 1945, L.Th., 1949; LL.D., Meml. U. Nfld., 1980. Ordained priest Roman Cath. Ch., 1949. Named vicar forane Roman Cath. Ch., 1960, vicar gen., 1971, prelate of honour, 1971, asst. priest, then parish priest, 1949-72; bishop Roman Cath. Ch., Grand Falls, Nfld., 1973-79; archbishop Roman Cath. Ch., St. John's, Nfld., 1979-91, archbishop emeritus, 1991—; chmn. Cath. Edn. Com., 1979-91. Served with RCAF, 1952-57. Address: PO Box 145, Saint John's, NF Canada A1C 5H5

PENNINGTON, ANNA RUTH, minister; b. Newport News, Va., Apr. 6, 1948; d. Henry Clay and Martha Anna (Vittletoe) P. BA, Baylor U., 1969; M of Ch. Music, Southwestern Bapt. Theol. Sem., 1975, postgrad., 1990—. Ordained to ministry Bapt. Ch., 1987. Secondary tchr. San Antonio Ind. Sch. Dist., 1970-72; music missionary Fgn. Mission Bd. of So. Bapt. Conv., Sao Paulo, Brazil, 1976-80; organist, choirmaster St. Mary's Cath. Ch. of Assumption, Waco, Tex., 1981—; chmn. music St. Mary's Cath. Sch., Waco, 1982-89; protestant chaplain Regis/St. Elizabeth Ctrs., Waco, 1987—; chaplain intern Bapt. Meml. Hosp., San Antonio, 1991—; bd. dirs. Tex. Ch. Conf. of Blind, treas., 1986-88. Recipient 3rd Place Enid Markham Organ Competition, 1982. Mem. Southwestern Sem. Theol. Fellowship, Am. Guild Organists (Cen. Tex. chpt., sub-dean 1986-89). Democrat. Avocations: traveling, reading, singing, playing piano, spectator sports. Home: 2724 Columbus Ave Waco TX 76710

PENNINGTON, JOHN ELTON, minister; b. Abbott, Ark., Nov. 4, 1929; s. John Calton and Stella Lucille (Snider) P.; m. Retha Ellen Willians, Jan. 9, 1948; 1 child, Brenda Dian Pennington Carbonia. Student, Ouchita Bapt., 1957-58, West Arkansas Coll., Ft. Smith, Sch. Theol., New Orleans, 1959-63. Ordained to ministry So. Bapt. Ch. Pastor Winfield Bapt. Ch., Waldron, Ark., 1955-57, Dayton Bapt. Ch., Mansfield, Ark., 1957-61, Glendale Bapt. Ch., Booneville, Ark., 1961-67, Charleston (Ark.) North Side, 1967-72, Temple Bapt., Ft. Smith, 1972—; v.p. Ark. Bapt. State, Little Rock, 1975-76, Ark. Bapt. Pastor's Conf., Little Rock, 1978. Pres. Ministerial Alliance, Ft. Smith, 1983-85; chmn. pastoral care com. St. Edwards Hosp., 1976-83; disaster relief com. Sparks Hosp., 1975—. Mem. Concord Bapt. Assn. (moderator 1975-78, treas. 1980—). Office: Temple Bapt Church 5100 S 31st Fort Smith AR 72901

PENNINGTON, VICKI DAVIS, music director; b. Corsicana, Tex., Aug. 7, 1951; d. James Henry and Violet Mae (Carey) Davis; m. James Edward Pennington, July 23, 1985; 1 child, Andrew. BM in Edn., East Tex. State U., 1973; MM in Edn., Midwestern State U., 1979. Music dir. 1st United Meth. Ch., Vernon, Tex., 1983—; music instr. Vernon Regional Jr. Coll., 1981—. Mem. Jr. Svc. League, Vernon, 1987—; bd. dirs. Community Concert Assn., Vernon, 1991, Coun. of the Arts, Vernon, 1986—. Mem. Am. Choral Dirs. Assn., Am. Guild of English Handbell Ringers, Fellowship of United Meths. in Worship, Music, and Other Arts, Musicians Club of Vernon (pres. 1990-92). Home: 2020 Stephens Vernon TX 76384 Office: PO Box 1602 Vernon TX 76384

PEOPLES, DWAYNE ROBERT, pastor; b. Lawson, Mo., Feb. 6, 1962; m. Robert and Juanita (Oberkrom) P.; m. Susan Annette Atkins, July 28, 1984; 1 child, Danae Annette. BA, Mid Am. Nazarene Coll., 1984; MDiv, Nazarene Theol. Sem., 1988. Ordained elder Nazarene Ch., 1990. Sr. pastor 1st Ch. of the Nazarene, York, Nebr., 1988—. Mem. York Planning Com., 1991. Mem. York County Ministers Alliance. Home: 949 East 4th York NE 68467 Office: 1st Ch of the Nazarene 11th and Beaver York NE 68467

PEPPARD, PATRICK FRANCIS, priest, theology educator, drama director; b. Cleve., Feb. 14, 1942; s. Joseph Paul and Rosemary (Schepley) P. BA, Loyola U., Chgo., 1965, MA, 1970, MDiv, 1973. Cert. secondary sch. tchr., Mich. Dir. drama St. John's High Sch., Toledo, 1966-69, 73-79, St. Thomas High Sch., Chgo., 1972-73, Jesuit High Sch. U. Detroit, 1979—. The Peppard award for sr. making most outstanding contribution to Campion Hall Theater was named in his honor St. John's High Sch., 1985. Mem. S.J. (best one act play performance award 1985). Avocations: reading, hiking, cooking. Home: 8400 S Cambridge Detroit MI 48221 Office: U Detroit Jesuit High Sch 8400 S Cambridge Detroit MI 48221

PERCELL, EMERY A., minister; b. Bayfield, Colo., June 21, 1933; s. Dan I. and Laura O. (Knight) P.; m. Betty Ann Percell, Nov. 2, 1954; children: David, Deborah, Douglas, Diane. BA, Colo. Coll., 1956; MDiv, Iliff Sch. Theology, Denver, 1961; DMin, U. Chgo., 1980. Ordained to ministry United Meth. Ch. as elder, 1961. Pastor Harding/Serena Meth. Chs., Ill., 1961-67, St. Stephens Meth. Ch., Chgo., 1967-69, United Ch. Hyde Park, Chgo., 1969-79; sr. pastor Wesley United Meth. Ch., Aurora, 1979-88, 1st United Meth. Ch., Evanston, Ill., 1988—; chair coun. on fin. No. Ill. Conf., 1974-70, registrar bd. ordained ministry, 1982-88; bd. dirs. Meth. Mins. Pension Fund. mem. Soc. Bibl. Lit., Kiwanis (pres. Chgo. chpt. 1971-79), Rotary. Home: 310 Church Evanston IL 60201 Office: 1st United Meth Ch 1630 Hinman Evanston IL 60201 *Secular individualism dissolves the social fabric of political and moral life. At the same time, however, it opens a window of opportunity for the Gospel Story. My imagination leaps at the chance of a century for the Church.*

PERCESEPE, GARY JOHN, philosophy educator, religious lay worker; b. Yonkers, N.Y., Feb. 9, 1954; s. Arnold R. and Rosalia (DeFrancesco) P.; m. Suzanne Marie Hale, June 8, 1975; children: Jae Marie, Vincent. BA, Cedarville Coll., 1975; MA, Denver Sem., 1978, U. Denver, 1978; PhD, St. Louis U., 1986. Assoc. prof. philosophy, dir. honors program Cedarville (Ohio) Coll., 1983—; bd. dirs. Habitat for Humanity, Springfield, Ohio, 1989—; advisor Students for Social Justice, Cedarville, 1989—. Author: Future(s) of Philosophy, 1989, Philosophy: An Introduction to the Labor of Reason, 1990; gen. editor series in philosophy, 1988—; contbr. articles to profl. jours. Mem. MLA, Am. Philos. Assn., Am. Acad. Religion, Soc. Christian Philosophers, Am. Cath. Philos. Assn., Nat. Collegiate Honors Coun., Evangs. for Social Action. Democrat. Baptist. Home: 350 Moorefield Rd Springfield OH 45502 Office: Cedarville Coll Dept of Philosophy Box 601 Cedarville OH 45314 *The most serious tasks require the lightest touch.*

PERDUE, DANIEL STEPHEN, clergyman; b. Sharon, Pa., Apr. 30, 1952; s. James Harold and Ruth Elizabeth (Whitmire) P.; m. Tina Marie Roberts, June 15, 1973; children: Chad Stephen, Jennifer Lynn, Stephanie Marie. G-rad. music, Bapt. Bible Coll., 1973. Ordained to ministry Bapt. Ch. Minister music, asst. pastor Calvary Bapt. Ch. and Sch., Leesburg, Fla., 1973-75; minister music, minister youth Temple Bapt. Ch., Titusville, Fla., 1975-80; minister music, minister youth, asst. pastor Palm Springs Dr. Bapt. Ch., Altamonte Springs, Fla., 1981-85; youth dir., Bible tchr. Bethlehem Bapt. Ch. and Sch., Fairfax, Va., 1985-89; asst. pastor, minister music Bethel Bapt. Ch. and Sch., Cocoa, Fla., 1989—. Named Educator of Yr., Seminole County C. of C., 1982; recipient Football and Basketball Coach award Scholastic Coach mag., 1984-85. Home: 1950 Michigan Ave Cocoa FL 32922 Office: Bethel Bapt Ch and Ch Acad 1950 Michigan Ave Cocoa FL 32922

PERDUE, LEO G., academic administrator. Pres. Brite Div. Sch., Tex. Christian U., Ft. Worth. Office: Brite Div Sch Tex Christian U PO Box 32923 Fort Worth TX 76129*

PERDUE, RICHARD DALE, lay worker, accountant; b. Eugene, Oreg., Mar. 16, 1955; s. Robert J. and Naomi Mae (Duren) P.; m. Sherry Lynn (Halstead) P., June 19, 1976; children: Michelle Anne, Shannon Renee. BS, U. Oreg., 1978, N.W. Christian Coll., 1978; postgrad., Boise State U., 1979-81. CPA, Oreg. Youth pastor Junction City (Oreg.) First Christian Ch., 1976-78; mem. steering com. S.W. Christian Ch., Boise, Idaho, 1978-81; charter mem. Orchards Christian Ch., Lewiston, Idaho, 1982-84; treas., choir dir., Sunday sch. tchr. Eastside Christian Ch., Albany, Oreg., 1984—, also bd. dirs.; owner Richard D. Perdue, CPA, Albany, 1988—; mem. exec. bd., treas. Linn-Benton Celebration, Corvallis, Oreg., 1990—. Treas. Mighty Oaks Devel. Ctr., Albany, 1990—; parade chmn. Linn County Vet.'s Day Celebration, Albany, 1989, 90. Mem. ACPAs, Oreg. State Soc. CPAs, Benton-Linn Soc. CPAs, Albany C. of C. (treas. 1988—, Jr. First Citizen award 1990), Kiwanis (pres. Takena club 1990-91), Optimist (bd. dirs. Albany club 1990—), Springhill Golf Club, Albany Athletic Club. Home: 3503 Chicago St SE Albany OR 97321 Office: PO Box 785 Albany OR 97321

PEREIRA, A. NICOLAU GRACIAS, priest, educator; b. Majorda, India, Sept. 25, 1926; s. Rogaeiano Jose Gracias Pereira and Maria Josefina Rodrigues. BSc, St. Xavier's Coll., Bombay, 1955; PhD, St. Louis U., 1963. Ordained priest Roman Cath. Ch., 1950. Instr. Webster (Mo.) Coll., 1962; grad. asst. chemistry dept. St. Louis U., 1963; rsch. assoc., Inst. Molecular Physics U. Md., College Park, 1963-64; prin. St. Xavier's Coll., Mapusa, India, 1965—; postgrad. tchr. U. Bombay and Goa, 1967—; mem. Goa Edn. Coun., 1968-79, Goa Planning Commn., 1984—; chmn. ednl. subcom. of Goa Planning Commn., 1984—. Author: Water and Its Nature, 1972; contbr. articles to profl. jours.; editor: Renovacao, 1979-83. Recipient State award as Educationist, Goa Govt., 1986. Fellow Inst. Menezes Braganza (pres. 1975-80, editor jour. 1975-80); mem. Am. Chem. Soc., AAAS, Indian Sci. Congress, Sigma Xi. Roman Catholic. Home and Office: St Xaviers Coll, Xaviernagar, Mapusa 403 525, India

PEREIRA, PETER, minister; b. Hyderabad, India, Oct. 19, 1952; s. Raymond Anthony and Lily (Isaac) P.; m. Esther Geethanjali, Aug. 25, 1979; children: Rebekah Sujatha, Jonathan Raj, Philip Deepak. BSIE, Indsl. Engring. Coll., Chgo., 1978; MDiv, No. Bapt. Theol. Sem., Lombard, Ill., 1986, MA in Urban Studies, 1986. Ordained to ministry United Meth. Ch. as deacon, 1986, as elder, 1988. Pastor India Christian Fellowship Ch., Chgo., 1981—, Faith United Meth. Ch., Elmhurst, Ill., 1986-90, Alden (Ill.) United Meth. Ch., 1985-86; evangelist, 1991—; mem. Asian-Am. Pastoral Counseling Ctr., Chgo., 1984—, Billy Graham Ctr., Wheaton, Ill.; lectr. in field. Recipient Evangelism award, No. Bapt. Theol. Sem., 1986. Mem. Nat. Assn. United Meth. Evangelists, Fedn. of Indo-Am. Christians of Chgo., Soc. Internat. Ministries, Mission Soc. for United Meth. 1st Asian Indian apptd. as conf. approved evangelist in U.S.A. Home: 192 S Kenilworth Elmhurst IL 60126 Office: India Christian Fellowship 606 E Ashland Chicago IL 60611

PEREIRA, ROBERT WILLIAM, religious school administrator; b. N.Y.C., July 25, 1947; s. Manuel G. and Judy (Norat) P.; m. Kathy E. Falknor, June 29, 1974; children: Jay, Angela. BA in Elem. Edn., Cedarville Coll., 1969; MA in Sch. Adminstrn., Wright State U., 1972. Adminstr. Blackhawk Christian Sch., Ft. Wayne, Ind., 1975-78; prin. then asst. supr. Heritage Christian Schs., Milw., 1980—; served various chs. as deacon, asst. Sunday sch. supr., Sunday sch. tchr. Named Outstanding Educator of Yr. Beavercreek (Ohio) Jaycees, 1972. Mem. Assn. Christian Schs. Internat. (Wis. rep. 1989—).

PERELMUTER, HAYIM GOREN, rabbi, educator; b. Montreal, Que., Can., June 2, 1914; s. Benjamin and Tillie (Goren) P.; m. Nancy Goodman, July 20, 1940; children: Mayer, Michael. BA, McGill U., 1935; MHL, Jewish Inst. Religion, 1939; MA, Harvard U., 1940; DHL, Hebrew Union Coll., 1979. Rabbi Beth Israel, Waltham, Pa., 1939-41, Beth Zion Temple, Johnstown, Pa., 1941-57; rabbi KAM Isaiah Israel Congregation, Chgo., 1957-80, rabbi emeritus, 1980—; prof. of Jewish studies Cath. Theol. Union, Chgo., 1967—; vis. prof. Jewish studies Pacific Luth. Theol. Sem., Berkeley, Calif., 1980—. Author: David Darshan, 1984, Siblings, 1989, (with others) Women and Priesthood, 1974, This Immortal People, 1983, Worship and Prayer, 1988. Mem. Am. Jewish Hist. Soc. (acad. adv. coun. 1985—), Cen. Conf. of Am. Rabbis, Soc. Bibl. Lit., Am. Assn. of Religion, N.Am. Acad. of Liturgy, Standard Club. Home: 5000 S East End Ave Chicago IL 60615

PEREZ, JOSE MANUEL, minister; b. Pharr, Tex., July 11, 1954; s. Paula (Gonzalez) P.; m. Delilah L. Perez, Nov. 30, 1974; children: Jason Troy, Lesli Joy. Diploma, Bethel Bible Inst., 1983; BA, SAGC, 1990. Ordained to ministry Assemblies of God Ch., 1990. Assoc. pastor Templo Bethel, Pharr, 1980-83; pastor Bethel Assembly of God, Grand Rapids, Mich., 1984-88, Primera Asamblea de Dios, Corpus Christi, Tex., 1988—; youth dir. Midwest Latin dist., Grand Rapids, 1968-88; sec., treas. Corpus Christi sect. Assemblies of God, 1989—. Mem. Pres.'s Coun. on Aging, Holland, Mich., 1976-77; vice chmn. Holland Migrant Coun., 1977-78, chmn. 1978-79. Home: 6238 Beechwood Ave Corpus Christi TX 78412 Office: Primera Asamblea de Dios 402 Cheyenne St Corpus Christi TX 78405

PERKINS, ANTHONY LEE, minister, educator; b. Port Arthur, Tex., Oct. 18, 1942; s. Bertis Olin and Lola Lee (Elmore) P.; m. Elva Jean Perkins, July 22, 1959; children: Lana Darlene Perkins Monzingo, Anthony Lee Jr. BTh, Internat. Sem., 1980; BA, Metro State U., 1983; MS in Psychology, Emmanuel Bapt. U., 1991; PhD in Psychology, Caroline U. Theology, 1991. Ordained to ministry Pentecostal Ch., 1965. Pastor Word Aflame Ch., Corsicana, Tex., 1978-81, Weches United Pentecostal Ch., Crockett, Tex., 1962-63, Allentown United Pentecostal Ch., Lufkin, Tex., 1965-68, Westside United Pentecostal Ch., Ft. Worth, 1976-77, Echoes of Calvary Ch., St. Paul, Minn., 1981—; vol. chaplain Tex. Dept. of Corrections, Huntsville, 1977-79, Sheriffs Dept. Anoka County, 1991—; pres. Calvary Christian Inst., St. Paul, 1987—; tchr. pastoral counseling to Soviet mins., USSR, 1991. Mem. Nat. Christian Counselors Assn. (cert.). Home: 1017 127th Ln NE Blaine MN 55434 Office: Echoes of Calvary Ch PO Box 155 Circle Pines MN 55014 *It takes all of my inner strength plus all the good people I meet along the way to attain the goal in life that I feel I must.*

PERKINS, FLOYD JERRY, theology educator; b. Bertha, Minn., May 9, 1924; s. Ray Lester and Nancy Emily (Kelley) P.; m. Mary Elizabeth Owen, Sept. 21, 1947 (dec. June 1982); children: Douglas Jerry, David Floyd, Sheryl Pauline; m. Phyllis Genevra Hartley, July 14, 1984. AB, BTh, N.W. Nazarene Coll., 1949; MA, U. Mo., 1952; MDiv, Nazarene Theol. Sem., 1952; PhD, U. Witwatersrand, Johannesburg, South Africa, 1974. Ordained to Christian ministry, 1951. Pres. South African Nazarene Theol. Sem., Florida Transvaal, Africa, 1955-67; pres. Nazarene Bible Sem., Lourenzo Marques, Mozambique, 1967-73, Campinas, Brazil, 1974-76; prof. missions N.W. Nazarene Coll., Nampa, Idaho, 1976; prof. theology Nazarene Bible Coll., Colorado Springs, Colo., 1976—; chmn., founder com. higher theol. edn. Ch. of Nazarene in Africa, 1967-74; sec. All African Nazarene Mission Exec., 1967-74; ofcl. Christian Council Mozambique, 1952-74. Author: A History of the Christian Church in Swaziland, 1974. Served with USN, 1944-46. Mem. Soc. Christian Philosophers, Evang. Theol. Soc., Am. Schs. Orientan Rsch., Am. Soc. Missiology, Assn. Evang. Missions Profs. Republican. Avocation: golf. Office: Nazarene Bible Coll 1122 Chapman Dr Colorado Springs CO 80935 *Personal philosophy: Be cheerful, hopeful, courageous, honest, candid, faithful, committed, loyal, and the whole world will be yours!.*

PERKINS, LARRY HOWARD, minister; b. Mayfield, Ky., Dec. 11, 1955; s. Ervin Lawrence and Betty Jean (Wylie) P.; m. Eva M. Clark, Nov. 18, 1977; children: William Brian, Kristin Marie. Student, U. Ky., 1974-76. Ordained to ministry Ch. of Christ. Youth dir. 7th & College Ch. of Christ, Mayfield, 1977-79; minister Bardwell (Ky.) Ch. of Christ, 1979-83, Elkton Rd. Ch. of Christ, Greenville, Ky., 1985—; elder Elkton Rd. Ch. of Christ, Greenville, 1990—. Founder-pres. Muhlenberg County Children's Fund, Inc., Greenville, 1987—. Recipient Ky. Col. cert. Wallace Wilkinson, Gov. of Ky., 1989. Republican. Office: Elkton Rd Ch of Christ Hwy 181 S PO Box 619 Greenville KY 42345

PERKINS, OTTIS LAWRENCE, minister; b. Caledonia, Miss., Jan. 5, 1936; s. Ottis Posey and Birdie Ann (Adams) P.; m. Jessie Grace Pridmore, July 16, 1954; children: Dennis Lawrence, Larenda Kay, Karen Lane. Degree in Pub. Acctg., Miss. State U., 1957. Ordained to ministry Pentecostal Ch., 1966. Pastor Pentecostal Holiness Ch., San Benito, Tex., 1968-61; dist. Lifeliner dir., dir. ch. edn. Pentecostal Holiness Ch., San Benito, 1960-61; pastor Pentecostal Ch. God, Columbus, Miss., 1964-74, dist. youth dir., 1964-66, dist. supt., 1966-74; gen. sec., treas. Pentecostal Ch. God, Joplin, Mo., 1974-77; pastor Pentecostal Ch. God, Greenwood, Miss., 1977—, dist. supt., 1980—; Mem. Commn. on Chaplains Nat. Assn. Evangelicals, 1974-77; dir. Media Ministries, Pentecostal Ch. God, 1987-91, mem. gen. bd., 1966-77, 80—. Mem. bd. regents So. Bible Coll., 1964-77, pres. 1974-75, bd. dirs., 1974-77; chmn. Drug Abuse Action Com., C. of C., Columbus, 1971-73, chmn. youth activities, 1971-73; mem. drug abuse edn. seminar, U. Miami, 1972; chaplain CAP, Tombigbee Sq., Columbus AFB, 1972-74. Capt. USAF, 1958-63. Mem. Am. Assn. Retired Persons., Nat. Assn. Pvt. Enterprise. Home: Rte 1 Box 565 Greenwood MS 38930

PERKINS, ROBERT REX, minister; b. Shelbyville, Ind., Aug. 15, 1940; s. Hallie T. and Marjorie Frances (Muir) P.; m. Carolyn Sue Jones, Aug. 25, 1962 (div. Oct. 1968). BA, Olivet Nazarene U., 1962; MA, Butler U., 1968. Ordained to ministry Pentecostal Holiness Ch. Internat., 1990. Pres. Universal Printing & Pub. Co., Charleston, S.C., 1983-87; min. edn., counseling Life Christian Assembly Ch., Charleston, 1987—; founder, dir. Red Sea Ministries-Exodus Internat., Charleston, Preparing the Bride, Charleston, 1991—. Author: Steps for Preparing the Bride, 1991, (tapes and video) Steps for Preparing the Bride, 1991.

PERKINS, SHIRLEY M., lay worker; b. Orange, Calif., Feb. 6, 1926; d. Andrew George and Dorlena Mary (Koelling) Edwards; m. Robert L. Perkins, Nov. 23, 1944 (dec. Sept. 1980); children: Vicky, Katherine, Leonard, Rena Lea. Grad. high sch., Orange, 1943. Sec. Immanuel Luth. Ch., Orange, 1988—; sec. Ch. Planning Coun./Voters, Orange, 1989—. Office: Immanuel Luth Ch 802 E Chapman Ave Orange CA 92666

PERKINS, SISTER VICTORIA MARIE, school system administrator; b. Dodge City, Kans., June 27, 1942; d. Ward and Mamie (Lavery) P. BA, St. Mary Coll., Leavenworth, Kans.; MA, Ohio State U.; postgrad., U. Mo., Kansas City. Joined Sisters of Charity of Leavenworth, Roman Cath. Ch. Tchr. St. Daniel the Prophet Sch., Chgo., 1962-63; tchr. math Bishop Ward High Sch., Kansas City, Kans., 1965-76; tchr. Bishop Hogan High Sch., Kansas City, Mo., 1976-77, prin., 1977-87; assoc. supt. sch.s Diocese Kansas City-St. Joseph (Mo.), 1987-88, supt. schs., 1988—; del. Nat. Congress for Cath. Schs. for 21st Century, 1991. Named Career Woman of Yr. Career Club Kansas City and The Jones Store Co., 1985; recipient UMOJA award Black Cath. Caucus, 1987. Mem. Nat. Cath. Ednl. Assn., Nat. Coun. Tchrs. Math., Chief Adminstrs. Cath. Edn., Mo. Coun. Am. Pvt. Edn., Mo. Cath. Conf., Greater Kansas City Literacy Task Force, Harmony in a World of Difference. Democrat. Avocations: running, crocheting, needlepoint. Home: 520 Garfield Kansas City MO 64124-1514 Office: Schs Supt PO Box 419037 300 E 36th Kansas City MO 64141

PERKS, ROGER IAN, minister; b. Wellington, New Zealand, Dec. 26, 1921; came to U.S., 1974; s. Thomas Edgar and Gertrude Elsie (Trezise) P.; m. Patricia Helen Rickett, Feb. 26, 1945; children: Anne Francis Rickett, Jennifer Jane Kirk. MDiv, Ashland Coll., 1976. Ordained to ministry United Ch. of Christ, 1975. Pastor Eighth United Ch. of Christ, Cleve., 1974-77; interim pastor Bethany Presbyn. Ch., Cleve., 1977-78; pastor Immanuel Presbyn. Ch., Cleve., 1978-81; supply pastor various chs. in Cleve. area., 1982-84; pastor Trinity Presbyn. Ch., Cleve., 1985—. Wing comdr. RAF, 1940-46, 48-74. Fellow Acad. of Parish Clergy (adminstrv. v.p. 1981—); mem. Rotary (pres. Cleve. club 1981-82, sec. 1989-91). Office: Trinity Presbyn Ch 22111 Chagrin Blvd Cleveland OH 44122

PERLMAN, LAWRENCE, rabbi; b. Montreal, Aug. 23, 1952; s. Philip and Marilyn (Miller) P.; m. Sharyn Sue Steinberg, Sept. 10, 1978; children: Ariela, Hannah. BA, Middlebury (Vt.) Coll., 1974; PhD, Brandeis U., Waltham, Mass., 1987. Ordained rabbi 1982. Rabbi Shaare Zion Congregatoin, Montreal. Author: Abraham Heschel's Idea of Revelation, 1989. Wasserman fellow, Am. Jewish Hist. Soc., 1985. Mem. Assn. Jewish Studies, Rabbinical Assembly. Home: 39 Ellerdale Rd, Montreal, PQ Canada H3X 1T1 Office: Shaare Zion Cong, 5575 Cote St Luc Rd, Montreal, PQ Canada H3X 2C9

PERLMAN, SUSAN GAIL, organization executive; b. N.Y.C., Dec. 29, 1950; d. Philip and Pearl Perlman; ed. Hunter Coll., N.Y.C., 1967-71. Copywriter, Blaine Thompson Advt., N.Y.C., 1968-71; copywriter J.C. Penney Co., N.Y.C., 1971-72; assoc. exec. dir. Jews for Jesus, San Francisco, 1972—, bd. dirs., also editor Issues mag.; speaker, cons. in field; steering com. mem. Lausanne Consultation on Jewish Evangelism, Copenhagen, Denmark; del. Bapt. Gen. Conf.; mem. Lausanne Com. for World Evangelization, Oxford, Eng. Mem. Am. Jewish Congress. Democrat. Baptist. Office: 60 Haight St San Francisco CA 94102

PERMAR, RAYMOND THOMAS, minister; b. Balt., Sept. 13, 1933; s. Henry Jacob and Nora Elizabeth (Meekins) P.; m. Ida Sheila Davis, Sept. 3, 1955; children: Robert Thomas, Stephen William, John Temple. BA, Fla. State., 1972, ThM, 1974; D of Div., U. Bible Inst., 1975, PhD, 1976; DD (hon.), Christ Coll., 1990. Ordained to ministry Congregation of Christ Ch. Asst. pastor Antioc Full Gospel Ch., Sembach, Germany, 1967-68, Bapt. Ch., Wichita Falls, Tex., 1969-70; pastor Calvary Bapt. Ch., Frankfort, Ill., 1972; evangelist Permar Evangelistic Assn., Wichita Falls, 1972-77; pastor Christ Christ Assembly, Wichita Falls, 1977—; presiding bishop Congregation of Christ, Wichita Falls, 1990—; commd. 2nd lt. USAF, 1952, advance through grades to master sgt., 1972; field rep. and faculty mem. Christ Body Bible Sch., Texarkana, Tex., 1990—. Author: Husband Heal ur Home, 1973. V.P. Full Gospel Businessmen Inter, Wichita Falls, 1975, chaplain, 1983-88; chaplain Civil Air Patrol, Wichita Falls, 1974-76, Tex. State Guard, Wichita Falls, 1976; v.p. Jaycee, Omaha, 1962-63. Mem. VFW (chaplain 1989), United Assn. Christian Clin. Counselors (cert.), Assn. Christian Marriage Counselors, Inst. Motivational Living Cons., Charismatic Bible Ministries. Republican. Home: 3210 Euel St Wichita Falls TX 76305 Office: Congregation of Christ 3212 Euel St Wichita Falls TX 76305

PERRIN, JAC DEAN, JR., religious educator; b. Kankakee, Ill., Jan. 25, 1957; s. Jack Dean Perrin and Kathryn Gale (Woods) Ferguson; m. Bonnie Jean Kinney, Nov. 23, 1973; children: April Michelle, Aimee May. Lic. in cosmetology, Americana Acad., Des Moines, 1976; BA in Pastoral Studies magna cum laude, North Cen. Bible Coll., Mpls., 1986. Trainer evangelism dept. Summit Ave. Assembly of God, St. Paul, 1981-87, min. to youth, 1983-87; min. to collegians, min. of missions Calvary Temple, Naperville, Ill., 1987-89; youth specialist, faculty, dir. youth ministries North Cen. Bible Coll., 1990—. Mem. Soc. Bibl. Lit., Delta Epsilon Chi. Home: 830 Portland Ave Saint Paul MN 55105 Office: North Cen Bible Coll 910 Elliot Ave S Minneapolis MN 55404

PERRY, ALEXANDER, church treasurer, bookkeeper; b. Aiken, S.C., Oct. 31, 1939; s. Alexander Perry Sr. and Lenora (Gadsden) Tutt; m. Sarah Bell Waller, May 30, 1959; children: Pamela Elizabeth, Paula Marie, Bruce Calvin, Camisha Lynn. Ed. high sch., Greenwich, Conn., 1954-58. Asst. treas. Bethel Am. Ch., Greenwich, 1976-82, treas., bookkeeper, 1982—, trustee, 1976—. Mem. A.M.E. Ch. Home: 4 Kellee Circle Norwalk CT 06854 Office: Bethel Am Ch 42-44 Lake Ave Greenwich CT 06830

PERRY, CHARLES EDGAR, JR., pastor; b. Chillicothe, Ohio, July 10, 1942; s. Charles Edgar Sr. and Kathleen Louise (Vla) P.; m. Martha Louise Dennewitz, July 21, 1963; 1 child, Phillip Eugene. BA, Lexington Bapt. Coll., 1972; MDiv, Grace Theol. Sem., 1975; D of Ministry, Luther Rice Sem., 1991. Ordained to ministry Bapt. Ch., 1975. Youth pastor Tabernacle Bapt. Ch., Chillicothe, Ohio, 1968-69; assoc. pastor N. Middletown (Ky.) Bapt. Ch., 1970-72; sr. pastor Whitestown (Ind.) Bapt. Ch., 1975-81, Sierra Bapt. Ch., New Castle, Calif., 1981—. Author: Why Christians Burn-out, 1982. Mem. Sierra Writer's Club, Psi Beta Nat. Honor Soc. Republican. Home: 6134 Woodside Dr Rocklin CA 95677 Office: Sierra Bapt Ch 2215 Auburn Folsom Rd Newcastle CA 95658

PERRY, CHARLES WAYNE, minister; b. Montgomery, Ala., July 25, 1948; s. Collin Wade and Belle (Ray) P.; m. Joyce Marie Summers, Apr.. 12, 1968 (div. May 1981); m. Donna Jean Boyer, Nov. 22, 1987; Christopher Warren, Christiana Marie Boller, David Allen Boller. BA, Campbell U., 1970; MDiv, Wesley Theol. Sem., 1974; DMin, Emory U., 1980; cert. in family therapy, Valdosta State Coll., 1990. Pastor Morgan Circuit United Meth. Ch., Berkeley Springs, W.Va., 1971-74, Zion Circuit United Meth. Ch., Cumberland, Md., 1974-75, Pine Level Circuit United Meth. Ch., Prattville, Ala., 1975-77; chaplain Plattsburgh AFB, Plattsburgh, N.Y., 1977-80, Oasan Air Base, Republic of Korea, 1980-81, Bergstrom AFB, Austin, Tex., 1981-85; sr. Protestant chaplain Clark Air Base, Republic of the Philippines, 1985-87, Moody AFB, Valdosta, Ga., 1987-90; div. chief, lt. col. basic tng. Chaplain Svc., Lackland AFB, San Antonio, 1990—. Vol. Boy Scouts Am., 1980—. Mem. Am. Assn. Marriage and Family Therapy (clin. mem., supr.-in-tng.), Am. Assn. Christian Counselors, Hastings Inst., Natl. Eagle Scout Assn. Avocations: running, private pilot, camping, hiking. Office: Lackland AFB Chapel 3700 ABG/HCFC Lackland AFB TX 78236-5000

PERRY, DAVID, minister. Exec. dir. edn. for mission and ministry Episcopal Ch., N.Y.C. Office: Episcopal Ch Office Edn Mission and Ministry 815 2nd Ave New York NY 10017*

PERRY, DONALD CHARLES, minister, vocal music educator; b. Alexandria, Ind., Mar. 17, 1925; s. John Wesley and Bernice (Board) P.; m. Jean Soles, Aug. 30, 1946; children: Judith Ann, Janet, Joan. BM, Baylor U., 1949, MS, 1954; postgrad., Colo. Coll., 1953, E. Stroudsberg State U., 1977. Cert. tchr.; ordained to ministry Bapt. Ch., 1981. Tchr. choral music Colorado Springs (Colo.) High Sch., 1950-54; Bethany Bapt. Ch., Colorado Springs, 1950-54; minister music and edn. Trinity Bapt. Ch., Kerrville, Tex., 1954-56, Oak Forest Bapt. Ch., Houston, 1956-58, 1st Bapt. Ch., Weatherford, Tex., 1958-61, Walnut St. Bapt. Ch., Owensboro, Ky., 1961-63, Lockeland Bapt. Ch., Nashville, 1963-67, 1st Bapt. Ch., Erwin, Tenn., 1967—; v.p. Tenn. Bapt. Chorale, 1973, pres. 1976; pres. Unicoi County Ministerial Assn., Erwin, 1974, 89, Upper Ea. Tenn. Ch. Music Conf., 1982, 90-91; dir. Colo. Bapt. All-State Chorus, Colorado Springs, 1953, Kerrville (Tex.) Civic Chorale, 1954-56, Erwin Community Chorale, 1968-70, Erwin Youth Chorale, 1968-78. Minister of music Bethany Bapt. Ch., Colorado Springs, Colo., 1950-54; pres. Unicoi County Ministerial Assn., 1989. Served with USN, 1943-46. Mem. Am. Choral Dirs. Assn., Am. Guild English Handbell Ringers, Tenn. Bapt. Ch. Music Conf., Phi Mu Alpha (sinfonia). Democrat. Avocations: photography, record collecting, motorcycling, video. Home: 244 1st St Erwin TN 37650 Office: 1st Bapt Ch Main at Love Sts Erwin TN 37650 *The pursuit of excellence and consistant dedication to the proper tasks will keep life challenging and in focus.*

PERRY, DWIGHT ARNOLD, denominational missions executive; b. Chgo., Feb. 7, 1955; s. Edward and Bernice (Pulliam) P.; m. Cynthia Laverne Weems, May 25, 1979; children: Dwight Jr., David, Cynthia, Danyelle. BA in History Edn., U. Ill., 1977, MEd in Ednl. Psychology, 1978; D of Ministries, Covington Theol. Sem., 1984. Ordained pastor Temple Universal Orthodox Ch., 1980, Evangelical Ch. Alliance of Bradley, Ill., 1980. Student leader, discipleship trainee The Navigators, 1973-78; elders team, dir. home bible study ministry Grove Heights Bapt. Ch., Chgo., 1978-80; campus rep. Conservative Bapt. Home Mission Soc., 1979-80; exec. dir., founder Agape Gosepl Mission, Inc., Chgo., 1980-86; founder, pastor Chicagoland Bible Ch., Chgo., 1982-88; midwest regional coord., evening sch. Moody Bible Inst., Chgo., 1989; nat. coord. black ministries Bapt. Gen. Conf., 1989—. Home: 9523 S Parnell Ave Chicago IL 60628

PERRY, E. EUGENE, communications educator; b. Martins Ferry, Ohio, Dec. 25, 1957; s. Edwin Ray and Sally Lou (Youst) P. BS in Edn., Ohio U., 1979; MDiv, U. Dubuque, 1982. Asst. chaplain U. Dubuque, Iowa, 1981-82; instr. theater U. Dubuque, 1984; asst. sem. rels. Theol. Sem., 1982-83; deacon Westminster Presbyn. Ch., Dubuque, 1986-87; instr. communications N.E. Iowa Community Coll., Peosta, 1989—; youth adv. del. Gen. Assembly, United Presbyn. Ch. in U.S.A., 1977; substitute tchr. Dubuque Community Schs., 1982-85; advisor drama and speech dept. Western Dubuque Community Schs., Epworth, Iowa, 1989-91. Author: (plays) It Works for Everybody Else, 1984, Wanted: A Cook, 1990, Just a High School Play, 1991; contbr. articles to profl. jours. Chmn. play-selection com. Barn Community Theater, Dubuque, 1981-83; active Dubuque County Dem. Cen. Com., 1984-87, 89-91, office mgr. hdqrs., 1984; del County Dem. Conv., Dubuque, 1984, 86, 90; del., sec. 2d Dist. Dem. Conv., 1984, 86, 90; mem. 5 Flags City Civic Ctr. Commn., Dubuque, 1989—, chmn., 1991—; founding bd. dirs. Dubuque County Habitat for Humanity, 1991. Home: 473 1/2 Locust St Dubuque IA 52001

PERRY, EDWARD K., bishop. Bishop upstate N.Y. region Evang. Luth. Ch. in Am., Syracuse. Office: Evang Luth Ch in Am 3049 E Genessee St Syracuse NY 13224*

PERRY, EUGENE ADDISON, minister; b. Bartlesville, Okla., Dec. 6, 1940; s. Eugene Addison and Mary Elizabeth (Beddoe) P.; m. Raneal Ivey, May 17, 1964; children: Mark Edward, Suzanne Elizabeth, Rebecca Raneal. BA, Okla. Bapt. U., 1962; BD, Southwestern Bapt. Theol. Sem., 1966, MDiv, 1966, M in Religious Edn., 1968, MA, 1983; D of Ministry, Luther Rice Sem., 1978. Ordained to ministry, 1961. Pastor First Bapt. Ch., Ashland, Okla., 1960-61; office adminstr., staff evangelist Evangelistic Assn., Ft. Worth, 1963-67; pastor First Bapt. Ch., Konawa, Okla., 1969-72, Brookhaven Bapt. Ch., Norman, Okla., 1972-76; pastor First Bapt. Ch., Lone Grove, Okla., 1976-80, Tonkawa, Okla., 1980-88; pastor Westport Bapt. Ch., Cleve., 1988—; with speakers bur. Tex. Alcohol Narcotics Edn., Inc., Dallas, 1964-68; missionary speaker fgn. mission bd. So. Bapt. Conv., Mindanao, Philippines, 1981, Sabadell, Spain, 1983, Manresa, Valencia, Spain, 1985, Northeast Arctic, Alaska, 1976, Nigeria, W. Africa, 1991; missionary speaker Youth for Christ of Portugal, Lisbon, 1985; adj. faculty So. Bapt. Ctr. for Biblical Studies, Jacksonville, Fla., 1982-85, Okla. Bapt. U., Shawnee, 1984—. Author: Directives for Godly Living, 1978. Chaplain Okla. Ho. of Reps., Oklahoma City, 1986; governing bd. Blackwell (Okla.) Regional Hosp., 1986-88; bd. dirs. Tonkawa C. of C., 1984, Tonkawa United Way, 1981-88; bd. trustees Okla. Bapt. U., 1989—; bd. dirs. Sooner Alcohol Narcotics Edn., 1990—. Mem. Am. Assn. Christian Counselors, Bapt. Gen. Conv. of Okla. (bd. dirs. 1986-88), Okla. Bapt. Hist. Soc. Republican. Avocations: travel, golf, fishing, reading.

PERRY, FLOYDE E., bishop. Bishop of So. Ohio Ch. of God in Christ, Shaker Heights. Office: Ch of God in Christ 3716 Rolliston Rd Shaker Heights OH 44120*

PERRY, H. WILLIAM, minister; b. Live Oak, Fla., Feb. 7, 1941; s. Harvey W. and Kathryn (Milligan) P.; m. Margaret Huyck, June 26, 1964; children: Laura, Gayla. BA, Stetson, U., 1963; MTh., So. Bapt. Theol. Sem., 1967, DMin., 1976. Ordained to ministry in Bapt. Ch. Pastor English Bapt. Ch., Carrollton, Ky., 1965-67, Powell's Chapel Bapt. Ch., MUrfreesboro, Tenn., 1967-69; pastor 1st Bapt. Ch., Pelham, Ga., 1969-74, Hawkinsville, Ga., 1974-81, Statesboro, Ga., 1981—; pres. bd. dirs. Christian Index, Atlanta, 1981-83; pres. trustees Ga. Bapt. Children's Homes, Atlanta, 1988-90; mem. Ga. Bapt. Exec. Com., Atlanta, 1970-74, 77-81. Chmn. bd. dirs. Ogeechee Home Health Agy., Statesboro, 1986-88; bd. dirs. United Way of Bulloch County, Statesboro, 1982-84, Statesboro Regional Libr., 1990—; charter dir. Hawkinsville C. of C., 1976-77. Named Master of Ceremonies, Heart Fund Telethon, Statesboro, 1990, 91. Mem. Statesboro Ministerial Assn. (pres. 1987-89), Ogeechee River Bapt. Assn. (moderator 1987-89), Rotary. Home: 504 Park Ave Statesboro GA 30458 Office: 1st Bapt Ch 108 N Main Statesboro GA 30458

PERRY, JANE ELLEN, minister; b. Cozad, Nebr., Aug. 31, 1958; d. Allen Leroy and Mamie Bernice (Griffith) P. BA, Kearney State Coll., 1979. Ordained to ministry Ch. of God; cert. elem. tchr., Nebr. Minister of edn. First Ch. of God, Kearney, Nebr., 1980—; treas. Nebr. Christian Edn. Assn., Kearney, 1984—; state Christian edn. chmn. Nebr. Chs. of God, 1983-84; trustee First Ch. of God, Kearney. County del. Buffalo County Rep. Party, Nebr., 1980—. Office: First Ch of God Academy 4310 17th Ave Kearney NE 68847-8246

PERRY, NORMAN ROBERT, priest, magazine editor; b. Cin., Dec. 17, 1929; s. Joseph Sylvester and May Ann (Hafertepe) P. B.A. cum laude, Duns Scotus Coll., 1954. Joined Franciscan Order, Roman Cath. Ch., 1950, ordained priest, 1958. Assoc. pastor St. Clement Ch., St. Bernard, Ohio, 1959-61; assoc. pastor St. Therese Ch., Fort Wayne, Ind., 1961-62; tchr. Bishop Luers High Sch., Fort Wayne, 1961-62; preaching band Franciscan Friars, 1962-66; definitor St. John the Baptist Province, Cin., 1972-75; vicar provincial St. John the Baptist Province, 1975-81; editor St. Anthony Messenger, 1981—; visitator gen. Order of Friars Minor, Commissariat of the Holy Land, Washington, 1980, Acad. Am. Franciscan History, Washington, 1981; mem. office of due process Archdiocesan Adminstrv. Review Bd.; trustee Franciscan Terrace; pro-syndol judge Cin. Archdiocesan Tribunal. Author: Best of the Wiseman, 1981; assoc. editor St. Anthony Messenger, 1966-81. Recipient numerous awards for reporting, editorials, opinion and review writing. Home: St Francis Friary 1615 Vine St Cincinnati OH 45210 Office: St Anthony Messenger 1615 Republic St Cincinnati OH 45210

PERRY, PAUL F., minister; b. Bklyn., July 9, 1932; s. Foster Best and Rosalie Esther (Carlson) P.; children: Julia Kay, David Butler. Student, Trinity U., San Antonio, 1951-53; BBA, Southwestern U., Georgetown, Tex., 1954; MDiv, Garrett-Evang. Theol. Sem., 1958; MA, Northwestern U., 1958; D of Ministry, So. Meth. U., 1977. Ordained to ministry United Meth. Ch. Pastor 1st United Meth. Ch., Rocksprings, Tex., 1958-61, Hunt (Tex.) United Meth. Ch., 1961-64, 1st United Meth. Ch., Pearsall, Tex., 1964-69, Oak Pk. United Meth. Ch., Corpus Christi, Tex., 1969-72; sr. pastor Trinity United Meth. Ch., San Antonio, 1972-80; pastor 1st United Meth. Ch., Rockport, Tex., 1989—; chair commn. on Christian unity and interreligious concerns S.W. Tex. conf. United Meth. Ch., San Antonio, 1988—, del., sec. commn. on Christian unity and interfaith rels. Tex. conf., Austin, 1990—. Contbr. articles to religious jours. Coord. Hemisfair, Frio County C. of C., Pearsall, 1968; organizer events CROP, Tex., 1983—. With USAF, 1951-54. Named Man of Yr in community svc. Frio County C. of C., 1968. Mem. Acad. Homiletics, Am. Acad. Religion, Soc. Bibl. Lit., Soc. for Sociology of Religion, Lions. Home: 1414 Shadyside Dr Rockport TX 78382 Office: First United Meth Ch 801 Main St Rockport TX 78382

PERRY, RICKEY L., religious organization administrator; b. Cedar City, Utah, Jan. 31, 1949; s. Anthon and Anna Mae (Peterson) P.; m. Lori Sanders, Mar. 17, 1972; children: Rachel, Rebekah, Naomi, Daniel, Eve, Sarah. Student, Dixie Coll., 1967-68; BA, So. Utah State Coll., 1972; MSW, U. Utah, 1974. Lic. social worker, Ohio. Caseworker Latter-day Saints Social Svcs., Spokane, Wash., 1974-77; practitioner Latter-day Saints Social Svcs., Nashua, N.H., 1977-78; dir. N.Y. agy. Latter-day Saints Social Svcs., Fishkill, 1978-87; S.D. zone rehab. mgr. Latter-day Saints Social Svcs., Rapid City, 1987-89; dir. Ohio agy. Latter-day Saints Social Svcs., Columbus, 1989—; cons. Bldg. Families Through Adoption, S.D., 1987-89, Carlsen Learning Ctr., Columbus, 1989—. Mem. Dutchess County Rep. Com., Fishkill, 1975-77; soccer coach Pickerington (Ohio) Youth Athletic Assn. Mem. Nat. Assn. Social Workers, Acad. Cert. Social Workers. Home: 12095 Woodstock Ave Pickerington OH 43147 Office: LDS Social Svcs Box 367 Groveport OH 43125

PERRY, ROBERT HAYNES, minister; b. Hattiesburg, Miss., Jan. 1, 1933; s. Matthew Eudious and Edna Inez (Haynes) P.; m. Doris Helen Warnock, June 7, 1953; children: Robert Haynes, Peggy Ann, Mary Lynn, Marcia Kay. BA, Miss. Coll., 1955; ThM, Luther Rice Sem., 1968, ThD, 1971. Pastor Forkland Bapt. Ch., Winterville, Miss., 1951-56, Parkview Bapt. Ch., Leland, Miss., 1956-58, Emmanuel Bapt. Ch., Greenville, Miss., 1958-67, New Palestine Bapt. Ch., Picayune, Miss., 1967-69, Crestwood Bapt.Ch., Jackson, Miss., 1969-70, Hanging Moss Bapt. Ch., Jackson, 1970-75; pastor 1st Bapt. Ch., Raleigh, Miss., 1975-80, Waynesboro, Miss., 1980-88; pastor Macedonia Bapt. Ch., Brookhaven, Miss., 1988—; assn. moderator Washington County Bapt. Assn., Greenville, 1964, Pearl River County Bapt. Assn., Picayune, 1968, Smith County Bapt. Assn., Raleigh, 1975-76, Wayne County Bapt. Assn., Waynesboro, 1980-84. Author: Brief Studies in I and II Peter, 1969, Evangelism Manual, 1971, Brief Studies in Prophecy, 1974; editor: Smith County History, 1976. Pres. Raleigh High Sch. Band and Athletic Booster Club, 1976-77; bd. dirs. Christmas Parade City of Raleigh, 1977-78; bd. dirs. Smith County Hist. Soc., 1976-80. Recipient scholarship Rotary, 1958. Mem. Lions (pres. Waynesboro club 1986-87, 100% Pres. award Brookhaven Noonday chpt. 1988-89). Avocations: sports, running, writing, art. Office: Macedonia Bapt Ch Rte 3 Box 585 Brookhaven MS 39601

PERRY, SHARON LYNN, religious organization administrator, educator; b. Logan, W.Va., Aug. 14, 1952; d. Charles Everett and Annis Rae (Dyer) York; m. Bartholomew Perry, May 24, 1975. Student, Bible Inst., Parkersburg, W.Va., Elkins, W.Va., 1970-80; B. in Cosmetology, Mamie Scott, Parkersburg, 1974. State evangelist, soloist, pianist Ch. of God, Beckley, W.Va., 1976-78, 81-83; soloist, pianist Ch. of God, White Sulphur Springs, W.Va., 1988-90, dist. ladies ministries pres., 1988-90; state ladies ministries bd. mem. Ch. of God, Beckley, W.Va., 1990—; ch. music dir., ladies Bible tchr. Mallory (W.Va.) Ch. of God, 1990—, tchr. Sunday sch., 1991—; state seminar speaker Ch. of God, Huntington, W.Va., 1991, Parkersburg, 1991, Logan, W.Va., 1991, dir. music, Mallory, 1990—, ladies choir dir., Beckley, 1991. Contbg. author: Women of Devotion, 1991. Area fund collector Children's Cancer Soc., Beckley, 1990; dist. l.m. pres. Anti-Aboratonist Campaign, White Sulphur Springs, 1988-90, Fight Against Child and Adult Pornography, White Sulphur Springs, 1989. Office: Mallory Ch of God PO Box 63 Mallory WV 25634-0063 *In my life I have found that people are searching for genuineness in a world which seems full of pretense and imitation.*

PERRY, WILLIAM HAROLD, church elder; b. Phila., Aug. 23, 1952; s. Harold Frances and Joyce Truscott (Miller) P.; m. Jennifer Sue Greene, May 3, 1980; children: David, Brian, Rachel, Linda, Christine, Stephanie. BA, Fla. Bible Coll., 1976; BA in Edn., Fla. Atlantic U., 1982. Cert. secondary educator English, Fla. 010sr. elder Lauderdale Community Ch., Ft. Lauderdale, Fla., 1982—; internat. student worker Internat. Students Inc., Ft. Lauderdale, 1987—; bd. dirs. A Woman's Pregnancy Ctr., Ft. Lauderdale, 1985—. Author: The Storyteller's Bible Study, 1991. Republican. Home: 3130 SW 21 St Fort Lauderdale FL 33312-3736 Office: Internat Students Inc 3130 SW 21 St Fort Lauderdale FL 33312-3736 *Life can be meaningful and understood only when one is in proper relationship with the Creator through the Lord Jesus Christ, the One who bridged the gap between the eternal and finite.*

PERRY-DANIEL, ANNIE VEE, minister; b. Rocky Mount, N.C., May 26, 1940; d. Levi Parson and Annie Mary (Powell) Perry; m. Jan. 23, 1965 (div. 1985); children: Dana Charlette, Corlisa Eugene, Barbara Ann. BA in Sociology, Morgan State U., Balt., 1980; MDiv, Howard U., Washington, 1983. Ordained to ministry, United Meth. Ch., 1983. Rsch. asst. Balt. City Schs., 1972-75; youth ministries coord. Christ United Meth. Ch., Balt., 1978-80; pastor Boundary United Meth. Ch., Balt., 1980-81; intern Simpson-Hamline United Meth. Ch., Washington, 1981-82; pastor Lewin United Meth. Ch., Balt., 1982-85, John Wesley United Meth. Ch., Glen Burnie, Md., 1985—; chaplain's asst. Morgan Christian Ctr., Balt., 1978-80; broadcaster Sta. WANN, Annapolis, Md., 1988; cons. in field; mem. Dist. Bd. Ordained Ministries, 1985—, Interfaith Com. on Jewish Christian Rels., 1988—, Bd. Higher Edn. and Campus Ministry, 1989—; featured writer Jour. Religious Thought, 1989; religious affairs editor Balt. Times, 1989—. Editor Annapolis Anchor, 1986-88; contbg. editor, A Jour. for Ministers, Sermon Starters, 1988. Charter mem. Meth. United for Peace with Justice, Balt., 1987. Cornish scholar, 1980, meritorious scholar Howard U., 1981, 82, United Meth. Crusade scholar, 1981, 82; Howard Stone Anderson fellow, 1981, 82. Democrat. Methodist. Avocations: photography, nature walks, gourmet cooking. Office: John Wesley United Meth Ch 6922 Ritchie Hwy Glen Burnie MD 21061

PERSELL, DAVE MATTHEW, clergyman; b. Trenton, Mo., Jan. 5, 1954; s. Lloyd Arthur and Mable Marie (Sprague) P.; m. Deborah Jean Selfridge, Jun. 20, 1981; children: Micah Beth, Nathan Andrew. BA, Mid-America Nazarene Coll., 1976; MRE, Nazarene Theol. Sem., 1979. Ordained Ch. of Nazarene, 1987. Organist Church of the Nazarene, Trenton, Mo., 1968-72; singles min. dir./organist Church of the Nazarene, Olathe, Kans., 1981-82; assc. pastor Church of the Nazarene, Bel Air, Md., 1982—; dir. IMPACT(1985-90), youth camp(1983-86) Church of Nazarene, Bel Air, Md.; del. Nazarene Youth Intl., Indpls. 1990. Author: play Sound of the Shofar, 1989; artist various religious works. Recipient Distinguished Service award Ch. of Nazarene, 1986, Outstanding Young Men of Am., 1988. Mem. Dist. Coun. Nazarene Youth Intl., Nazarene Multiple Staff Assc. Church of the Nazarene. Home: 1608 Cass Dr Bel Air MD 21014

PERSELL, WILLIAM DAILEY, priest; b. Rochester, N.Y., May 6, 1943; s. Charles Bowen Jr. and Emily Elizabeth (Aldrich) P.; m. Nancy Ellen Pollard, May 5, 1973; children: Jeffrey, Mark, Karen Gazis, Kathleen, Lisa, Kristen Helsing. BA cum laude, Hobart Coll., Geneva, N.Y., 1965; MDiv cum laude, Episcopal Theol. Sch., Cambridge, Mass., 1969. Teaching fellow Internat. Coll., Beirut, Lebanon, 1967-68; asst., priest-in-charge, assoc. rector St. Paul's Ch., Tustin, Calif., 1969-72; assoc. rector St. John's Ch., L.A., 1972-73, rector, 1973-82; rector St. Ann and The Holy Trinity Ch., Bklyn., 1982-91; dean Trinity Cathedral, Cleve., 1991—; pres. St. Ann Ctr. for Restoration and the Arts, Inc., Bklyn., 1983-91; sec. bd. Pastoral and Ednl. Svcs., Inc., Bklyn., 1982-91. Mem. adv. bd. Downtown Drop-in Ctr. for Homeless, Bklyn., 1988-91; mem. Diocesan Commn. on Social Concerns and Peace, L.I., N.Y., 1983-91, Diocesan Racial Justice Commn., L.I., 1985-91, Bklyn. Ecumenical Coops., 1986-91; bd. govs. Bklyn. Heights Assn., 1990-91; mem. Episcopal Peace Fellowship, Ohio, 1991—; bd. dirs. Trinity Presch., 1991—, Music and Performing Arts at Trinity, 1991—. Proctor fellow The Episcopal Div. Sch., Cambridge, 1981. Mem. Episcopal Div. Sch. Alumni Assn. (co-pres. 1991), Rembrandt Club. Democrat. Avocations: travel, reading, arts. Office: Trinity Cathedral 2021 E 22d St Cleveland OH 44115 *The church must advocate for the voiceless, hear the cries of the poor and oppressed, and empower men and women for abundant life in Christ Jesus.*

PERSSON, PHYLLIS-ANN, religious organization administrator; b. Providence, R.I., Feb. 4, 1945; d. Domenic Thomas and Ida (Cherubino) DeNucci; m. Robert Carlton Persson, Sr.; children: Robert C. Jr., David A., Eric C., Krista M. BA, Annhurst Coll., 1966; MA, Providence Coll., 1985. Dir. religious edn. Med. technologist II R.I. Hosp., Providence, 1966-70, 72-74; coordinator religious edn. St. Ann's Church, Cranston, R.I., 1978-79; feature writer Italian Echo, Providence, 1978-80; dir. religious edn. St. Mary's Church, Cranston, 1979—; cons. Office of Religious Edn., Diocese of Providence, 1987-88; bd. dirs. R.I. Chpt. Com. for the Prevention of Child Abuse, Pawtucket, 1980—. Contbr. articles to religious publs. Co-chmn. Celebration of the Internat. Yr. of the Child, 1979. Mem. Profl. Religious Educators of Providence, (chmn. advocacy com. 1986-89), Nat. Catholic Edn. Assn., Assn. for Supervision and Curriculum Devel., Nat. Assn. Parish Coordinators/Dirs. of Religious Edn., GFWC R.I. State Fedn. Women's Clubs (pres.-elect 1988— and other offices), GFWC Cranston Jr. Women's Club (pres. 1977-78, v.p. 1976-77). Roman Catholic. Avocations: crafts, cake decorating, gardening. Office: St Marys Religious Edn 85 Chester Ave Cranston RI 02920

PERSSON, WALTER HELGE, church official; b. Göteborg, Sweden, May 8, 1928; s. Helge and Elisabeth Persson; m. Maj Gunnel; children: Anders, Pergunnar, Tomas, Jonas. MEd, Göteborg Folkskolesem, 1950; postgrad. in theology, Lidingö Sem., Sweden, 1953; diploma, Colonial Sch., Brussels, 1954; DD (hon.), North Park Sem. and Coll., 1984. Sch. insp. Swedish Missions, The Congo, 1955-58, high sch. dir., 1958-60; edn. sec. Mission Covenant Ch., Sweden, 1961-75, sec. world missions, 1976-83, pres., 1983—; bd. mgrs. World Council Christian Edn., 1967-72; mem. edn. unit World Council Chs., 1972-80; mem. area com. World Alliance Reformed Chs., 1987—; gen. sec. Internat. Fedn. Free Evang. Chs., 1971-86, pres., 1987—; v.p. Swedish Ecumenical Coun., 1984—; pres.Swedish Free Ch. Coun., 1990—. Office: Mission Covenant Ch4, Tegnérgatan 8, PO Box 6302, S-11381 Stockholm Sweden

PERVO, RICHARD IVAN, minister, religion educator; b. Lakewood, Ohio, May 11, 1942; s. Alexander Ivan and Elizabeth (Kline) P.; m. Karen E. Moreland, Apr. 2, 1967. BA, Concordia Coll., Fort Wayne, Ind., 1964; BD, Harvard U., 1971, ThD, 1979. Instr. Episcopal Theol. Sch., Harvard U., Cambridge, Mass., 1971-75; asst. prof. Seabury-Western Theol. Seminary, Evanston, Ill., 1975-79, assoc. prof., 1979-89, prof., 1989—; treas., bd. dirs. Anglican Theol. Rev., Evanston, 1984-89. Author: Profit With Delight, 1987, Luke's Story of Pl, 1990; contbr. numerous articles and revs. to profl. jours. Mem. Soc. Bibl. Lit., North Am. Patristics Soc., Studiorum Novi Testamenti Societas, Midwest Patristics Seminar, Chgo. Soc. Bibl. Rsch. Home: 638 Haven Evanston IL 60201 Office: Seabury Western Theol Sem 2122 Sheridan Evanston IL 60201

PESSAGNO, J. MERIC, Islamic theology educator; b. Balt., Apr. 7, 1933; s. Allan D. and Pola Irene (Pokszywka) P.; m. Betty Cacciapaglia, Nov. 21, 1971; children—Eric, Claudia. B.A., Cath. U. Am., 1957, M.A., 1964; Ph.D., Yale U., 1973. Prof. Xarerian Bros., N.Y.C., 1951-69, prof. Islamic theology NYU, N.Y.C., 1974-77; prof. Islamic studies Pace U., White Plains, N.Y., 1988—. Contbr. articles to profl. jours. NEH grantee, 1976, 79. Fellow Conn. Acad. Arts Scis.; mem. Am. Acad. Religions (chmn. Islamic studies group 1980-85), Am. Oriental Soc. (book rev. editor 1985-87), Internat. Soc. Neo-Platonism, Columbia U. Arabic Studies Group. Democrat. Club: New Haven Oriental (Conn.). Home: 9 Buena Vista Dr Westport CT 06880 Office: Pace U N Broadway White Plains NY 10601

PESSIA, WAYNE JOSEPH, minister; b. Bradford, Pa., July 30, 1963; s. Lawrence Ralph and June Elizabeth (Koehler) P.; m. Anne Marie Dexter, July 28, 1984; children: Katelyn May, Jacob Lawrence. BS, Valley Forge Christian Coll., 1987. Ordained to ministry Internat. Ch. of the Foursquare Gospel, 1991. Intern pastor Bradford (Pa.) Foursquare Ch., 1986; asst. pastor Easton (Mass.) Foursquare Ch., 1987-89; sr. pastor Charlestown (N.H.) Foursquare Ch., 1989—; pioneered and chartered 1st Foursquare Ch. in N.H.

PETER, ARCHBISHOP See L'HUILLIER, PETER

PETER, VAL JOSEPH, social service administrator, educator, priest; b. Omaha, Nov. 20, 1934. PhB, Lateran U., Rome, 1956; Licentiate in Sacred Theology, U. St. Thomas, Rome, 1960, STD, 1965; JCD, Lateran U., Rome, 1967. Ordained priest Roman Cath. Ch., 1960. Defender of bond Archdiocese of Omaha, 1966—; chmn. dept. theology Coll. of St. Mary, Omaha, 1966-70; prof. theology Creighton U., Omaha, 1970-84; exec. dir. Father Flanagan's Boys Home, Boys Town, Nebr., 1984—. Bd. dirs. League for Civil Rights. Recipient Disting. Faculty award Creighton U., 1983, Presdl. citation, 1984, Archbishop Gerald T. Bergan award, 1986, Svc. to Mankind award Sertoma Internat., 1987, Creighton Prep Alumnus of Yr. award, 1988, Person of Yr. award U. Notre Dame, 1991. Mem. Nat. Assn. Homes and Svcs. for Children (bd. dirs.), League Civil Rights (bd. dirs. 1986—), Our Sunday Visitor Inst. (bd. dirs. 1986—). Roman Catholic. Home and Office: Boys Town 14100 Crawford St Boys Town NE 68010

PETERLIN, MICHAEL LESLIE, minister; b. Calumet, Mich., Feb. 15, 1945; s. John Michael and Rhoda Eliza (Donald) P.; m. Anne Lucille Carlyon, July 18, 1970; children: Aaron, Zachariah. BA, Mich. Tech. U., 1969; MDiv, Meth. Theol. Sch., Delaware, Ohio, 1974; DMin, Meth. Theol. Sch., 1978. Ordained to ministry, Meth. Ch. Sales rep. Peterlin Bros., Inc., Calumet, 1956-65; minister Mich. Tech. U. and Republic Meth. ch., Houghton, 1967-70, Sharon United Meth. Ch., Manchester, Mich., 1970-76; minister 1st United Meth. Ch., Manistique, Mich., 1976-80, Escanaba, Mich., 1980—; pres. Peterlin Mgmt. Co., Escanaba, 1981—; minister Detroit Annual Conf. United Meth. Ch., 1967—; pres., chmn. bd. dirs. Covenant Creations, Inc., Escanaba, 1985—; v.p. bd. dirs. John Peterlin & Sons Corp., Calumet, 1984—. Chmn. retail com. Downtown Devel. Authority, Escanaba, 1988—; pres. adv. bd. St. Francis Hosp., Escanaba, 1989. Mem. Christian Booksellers Assn., Nat. Sch. Supply and Equipment Assn., Nat. Office Products Assn. Office: Peterlin Mgmt Co 1001 Ludington St Escanaba MI 49829

PETERS, A. G., bishop. Bishop N.S. Diocese, Anglican Ch. Can., Halifax. Office: Anglican Ch Can 5732 College St, Halifax, NS Canada B3H 1X3*

PETERS, CLAY ETHA, II, minister; b. Roanoke, Va., Apr. 27, 1962; s. Clay Etha and Audrey Lera (Quinn) P.; m. Catherine Ann Oliver, Aug. 13, 1988. Counseling cert., Cornerstone Christian Ministry, Hunstville, Ala., 1988; pastoral ministries diploma, Southwestern Bapt. Sem., 1989; BTh, Internat. Bible Inst. and Sem., 1989; student, Liberty H. Bible Inst., 1989—, Va. Inst. Pastoral Care, 1990—. Ordained to ministry So. Bapt. Conv., 1989; lic., 1990. Interim pastor Gravel Hill Bapt. Ch., Hardy, Va., 1989-90, bi-vocat. pastor, 1990, pastor, 1990—; co-youth coord. Thaxton (Va.) Bapt. Ch., 1981-82; counselor Clyde Dupin Crusade, Bedford, Va., 1983; co-chair music Youth Joy Explosion Crusade, Bedford, 1985; pastor Jr. High youth Cornerstone Ch., Roanoke, 1989. Recipient Safety award Vocat. Indsl. Clubs Am., 1979, Ops. Improvement award Appalachian Power Co., 1986. Republican. *It's been said, quite correctly, that there are two types of people in God's kingdom here on this earth: watchers and workers. I want to be known as one of the workers for the Lord Jesus Christ.*

PETERS, DAVID FARR, minister; b. Meriden, Conn., Aug. 18, 1958; s. David Farr and Barbara Louise (Goldstien) P.; m. Susan Zappulla, 1985; 1 child, Kyla Elizabeth. BS, Cen. Conn. State Coll., 1981; MDiv, Andover Newton Theol. Sch., 1984. Ordained to ministry United Ch. of Christ, 1985. Min. Christian edn. 1st Congl. Ch., Waltham, Mass., 1981-84; assoc. min. 1st Congl. Ch., Danbury, Conn., 1984-86; min. Roxbury (Conn.) Congl. Ch., 1986—; mem. staff Silver Lake Conf. Ctr., Sharon, Conn., 1975-82; del. gen. synod United Ch. of Christ, N.Y.C., 1979, 81, 85; bd. dirs. Bd. for World Ministries, 1979-86, Conn. Conf. United Ch. of Christ, 1988—. Editor: Teaching for You, 1980. Home: 28 Church St Roxbury CT 06783 Office: Roxbury Congl Ch 24 Church St Roxbury CT 06783

PETERS, DAVID WALTER, minister; b. Davenport, Iowa, May 15, 1935; s. Walter L. and Charlotte H. (Grimes) P.; m. Judith Belle Brokate, Jan. 19, 1964; children: Daniel W., Karen L. BA, Augustana Coll., 1958; MDiv., Chgo. Luth. Theol. Sem., 1962. Ordained to ministry United Luth. Ch. in Am., 1962. Pastor St. John Luth. Ch., El Paso, Tex., 1962-66, Trinity Luth. Ch., Canon City, Colo., 1969-72; asst. pastor Advent Luth. Ch., Westminister, Colo., 1966-69, Messiah Luth. Ch., Denver, 1972—; dir. Rainbow Trail Luth. Camp, Hillside, Colo., 1969-72, chair, 1974-80; chair Park Hill Clergy, Denver, 1988-89. Pres. Eben Ezer Luth. Found., Brush, Colo., 1986-89; pres. bd. dirs. Eben Ezer Luth. Care Ctr., Brush, 1989—. Recipient Faith in God award Westminster Jaycees, 1968. Republican. Home: 1300 Quince St Denver CO 80220 Office: Messiah Luth Ch 1750 Colorado Blvd Denver CO 80220

PETERS, EARL LOUIS, minister; b. Green Bay, Wis., Jan. 25, 1934; s. William Carl and Eliese Olga (Behneke) P.; m. Sharon Mae Behrens, July 25, 1959; children: William, Laura, Susan, Mary. BA, Wartburg Coll., Waverly, Iowa, 1956; BD, Wartburg Sem., Dubuque, Iowa, 1960, MDiv, 1977; D Ministry, Luth. Sch. Theology, Chgo., 1984. Ordained to ministry Luth. Ch., 1960. Pastor St. Paul Evang. Luth. Ch., Tampico, Ill., 1960-65, Shepherd of Hills Luth. Ch., Bridgeton, Mo., 1965-71; sr. pastor Our Savior's Luth. Ch., Burbank, Ill., 1971—. Chaplain Timber Trails coun. Boy Scouts Am., 1990; mem. So. Stickney Adv. Mental Health Bd., 1973—. Named Man of Yr., Lions, 1982. Mem. Burbank C. of C., Burbank Clergy Assn. (pres. 1979—). Home: 6510 W 83rd Rd Burbank IL 60459 Office: Our Savior's Luth Ch 8607 S Narragansett Burbank IL 60459

PETERS, JACK RICHARD, chaplain; b. Grandfield, Okla., Aug. 2, 1930; s. Andrew jackson and Lvis (Thomas) P.; m. Norma Regina Black, Dec. 21, 1954; children: Jacque Marie Peters Hogue, Janice Irene Peters Stout. BA, Okla. Bapt. U., 1958; BDiv, Golden Gate Bapt. Sem., 1962; M in Family and Child Counseling, Chapman Coll., 1975. Ordained to ministry So. Bapt. Conv., 1958; cert. abuse counselor. Min. 1st Bapt. Ch., Monitor, Wash., 1958-60, Oluster, Okla., 1962-65, Shattuck, Okla., 1965-66; commd. ensign USN, 1966, advanced through grades to capt., 1981; chaplain COMDESRON 7, San Diego, 1966-68; various assignments, 1968-76; assigned to USS Canopus, 1976-78, 2D MARDIV, Camp Pendleton, N.C., 1978-81, NAS Whidbey Island, Oak Harbor, Wash., 1981-84, 3D MARDIV, Okinawa, Japan, 1984-85, Balboa hosp., San Diego, 1985, Amphibious Base, Coronado, Calif., 1985-87, 3D MAW, MCAS, 1987—. With USN, 1950-54. Decorated Bronze Star, Silver Star, Nat. Def. Svc. Medal, Combat Action Ribbon. Mem. Masons. Home: 21282 Bishop Mission Viejo CA 92692 Office: Office of Wing Chaplain 3D MAW MCAS El Toto Santa Ana CA 92709

PETERS, KELLY BOYTE, clergywoman; b. Bartlesville, Okla., Oct. 12, 1958; d. Robert Howard and Barbara Ann (Stout) B.; m. David Alan Peters, June 18, 1983; children: Michael Eugene, Anne Elizabeth. BA, Kalamazoo Coll., 1980; MDiv, Vanderbilt U., 1983. Ordained minister Disciples of Christ Ch. Assoc. minister Cen. Christian Ch., Waco, Tex., 1983-85; edn. coord. Waco Rape Crisis Ctr., 1985-86; pastor First Christian Ch., Henry, Ill., 1986-88; assoc. minister Lakewood (Ohio) Congl. Ch., 1988—; freelance writer United Ch. News, Cleve., 1989—, Disciple mag., 1990—; com. mem. Continuing Edn. for Clergy, Cleve., 1988—. Co-author: Spiritual Growth, 1988; author: Holy Ground, 1990, Study Guide Ethics and Genetics, 1985. Pres. Inner City Ministry Bd. Dirs., Waco, 1986; sec. Bd. Dirs. Caritas of Waco, 1986. Democrat. Avocations: reading, writing, exercise. Office: Lakewood Congl Ch 1375 W Clifton Blvd Lakewood OH 44107

PETERS, LANNY LEE, minister; b. Lexington, N.C., Mar. 31, 1952; s. Marcus Eugene and Gladys Mills (Neighbors) P.; m. Karen Jean Bridgman, Aug. 30, 1956. BS in Edn. magna cum laude, Western Carolina U., 1956; MA in Edn., East Carolina U., 1976; postgrad., Pacific Sch. Religion, 1979-81; MDiv, Southeastern Bapt. Theol. Sem., 1982. Ordained to ministry Bapt. Ch., 1983. Campus min. Unitas, Berkeley, Calif., 1980-81, First Bapt. Ch., Washington, 1981-89; sr. pastor Oakhurst Bapt. Ch., Decatur, Ga., 1989—. Home: 331 Winnona Dr Decatur GA 30030 Office: Oakhurst Bapt Ch 222 E Lake Dr Decatur GA 30030

PETERS, LARRY ALBUR, pastor; b. Norfolk, Nebr., May 9, 1954; s. Albur George and Florence Mae (Monson) P.; m. Amy Christine Brune, May 20, 1978; children: Joseph Albur, Andrew Christian, Rachel Allyson. AA, St. John's Coll., Winfield, Kans., 1974; BA, Concordia Sr. Coll., Ft. Wayne, Ind., 1976; MDiv, Concordia Sem., Ft. Wayne, Ind., 1980. Pastor Resurrection Luth. Ch., Cairo, N.Y., 1980—; cir. counselor Atlantic dist. Luth. Ch.-Mo. Synod, Bronxville, N.Y., 1982-85, chmn. commn. on worship Atlantic dist., 1987—, mem. fin. bd. Atlantic dist., 1986—, editor worship notes newsletter Atlantic dist., 1988—; presenter conf. on worship and ch. growth Luth. Ch.-Mo. Synod, St. Louis, 1989. Contbr. articles to profl. jours.; editor (newsletter) Worship Notes. Mem. Am. Guild of Organists. Republican. Office: Resurrection Luth Ch Rte 23B PO Box 563 Cairo NY 12413-0563 *Luther said, "Something must be dared in the Name of Christ." However tragic our mistakes, the greater tragedy is not to try at all. There is no regret worse than failing to act or speak because you are afraid you will be found inadequate. God forgive me, but something must be dared in the Name of Christ.*

PETERS, MICHAEL WAYNE, minister; b. Grand Rapids, Mich., July 16, 1952; s. Eugene Thomas and Thedora (Sowers) P.; m. Patricia Lou Clements, Oct. 14, 1973; children: Aubrey Lee, Shawn Michael. AA, Ferris State Coll., 1973. Ordained to ministry Assemblies of God Ch., 1986. Dir. Christian Life Nazarene Ch., Grand Rapids, 1976-80; fellowship group leader 1st Assembly of God, Grand Rapids, 1984; sr. pastor Native Am. Assembly of God, Grand Rapids, 1987—; pre-teen camp dir. Mich. dist. Assemblies of God, 1990—, bd. dirs. Indian youth counsel, 1989—; speaker Convocation of Christian Indian Leadership, 1990, 91. Bd. dirs. Title V (Indian Edn.), Grand Rapids, 1991. Recipient Merit of Achievement award U.S. Dept. Agr., 1978-86, Disting. Svc. award U.S. Dept. Agr., 1986. Home: 730 St Clair NW Walker MI 49504 Office: Native Am Assemblies of God 17 S Division Grand Rapids MI 49503

PETERSEN, BETTY L., minister, retired personnel manager; b. Portsmouth, Ohio, Jan. 3, 1921; d. John B. and Nancy (Darragh) Frostick; divorced; 1 child, Marianne Kent. Cert., Faith Bible Inst., 1983; student, Ohio State U., Mt. Vernon Nazarene Coll. Minister, evangelist Christian Bapt. Conf., Portsmouth, 1951-86; pastor Christian Bapt. Conf., Briary, Ky., 1959-61; youth leader Christian Bapt. Conf., tri-state, 1959-61, 63-65; editor paper Christian Bapt. Conf., 1958-62; tchr., asst. tchr. New Boston (Ohio) Christian Bapt. Ch., 1983-86, pres., 1984-86; editor New Boston (Ohio) Christian Bapt. Ch., Portsmouth, 1984-86; treas. Wheelersburg (Ohio) Christian Bapt. Ch., 1984-86; freelance writer. Mem. aux. bd. Scioto Meml. Hosp., Portsmouth, 1987-88. Recipient Cert. Appreciation Scioto Joint Vocat. Sch., 1981, Shawnee State Coll., 1982. Mem. Bus. and Profl. Women's Club, Nazarene Ministerial Assn., U.S. Health Assn. (hospice vol. Portsmouth chpt. 1986—), Am. Assn. Ret. Persons (v.p., pres. 1983-86), Ch. Women United (pres. Scioto chpt. 1988—), Svc. Guild of U.S. Health (pres. Portsmouth chpt. 1986-87), Green Triangle Garden Club (sec. 1985—), Homemakers. Republican. Home: 2403 Grandview Ave Portsmouth OH 45662

PETERSEN, BRUCE LEE, minister; b. Brainerd, Minn., Nov. 18, 1942; s. Roy I. and Nora (Christianson) P.; m. Jacquelyn Rae Stone, Dec. 18, 1965; children: Heather Ann, Erik David. BA, Olivet Nazarene U., 1965; MDiv, Nazarene Theol. Sem., 1971; D Ministry, Trinity Evang. Div. Sch., 1982. Ordained to ministry Ch. of Nazarene, 1971. Assoc. pastor Coll. Ch. of the Nazarene, Olathe, Kans., 1967-71, Nampa, Idaho, 1987—; sr. pastor First Ch. of the Nazarene, Saginaw, Mich., 1971-79, Springfield, Ohio, 1979-87; min.-in-residence Nazarene Theol. Sem., 1985; trustee Olivet Nazarene Coll., Kankakee, Ill., 1978-84, Mt. Vernon (Ohio) Nazarene Coll., 1984-87, Nazarene Bible Coll., Colorado Springs, Colo., 1989—; mem. pastoral denomination com. Ch. of Nazarene, Kansas City, Mo., 1985-89; pres. Saginaw County Evang. Mins. Assn., Saginaw, 1975-78, Clark County Evang. Mins. Assn., Springfield, 1982-85, Clark County Prayer Breakfast, 1986-87; bd. dirs. Springfield (Idaho) Christian Schs., 1979-84. Author: (sermon series) Focus On Worship, 1985; contbg. author: A Pastor's Workshop Resource, 1987, Biblical Resources For Holiness Preaching, 1990. Pres. Clark County Evang. Mins. Assn., Springfield, Ohio, 1982-85, Clark County Prayer Breakfast, 1986-87, SaginawCounty Evang. Mins. Assn., 1975-78; bd. dirs. Springfield Christian Schs., Springfield, 1979-84. Mem. Nampa Ministerial Assn. Home: 1015 S Canyon Nampa ID 83686 Office: Coll Ch of the Nazarene 504 E Dewey Ave Nampa ID 83686 *I am constantly amazed that God would choose me for special service. Achievement in life is thus measured, not by the acclaim of others, but by what the One who has called me sees as significant.*

PETERSEN, DAVID LEE, religious studies educator; b. Elgin, Ill., Mar. 21, 1943; s. Kermit Wesley and Charlotte (McClelland) P.; m. Sara Joyce Myers, May 5, 1990; children: Naomi K., Joshua E. BA, Coll. Wooster (Ohio), 1965; BD, Yale U., 1968, MPhil, 1970, PhD, 1972. Prof. religious studies U. Ill., Urbana, 1972-83; prof. O.T. Iliff Sch. Theology, Denver, 1983—; Fulbright Commn. sr. lectr., Denmark, 1977-78. Author: Late Israelite Prophecy, 1977, The Roles of Israels Prophets, 1981, Prophecy in Israel, 1987, Haggai and Zechariah, 1984; editor: Harper's Bible Commentary, 1988, Canon, Theology and Old Testament Interpretation, 1988. NEH fellow, 1989-90. Mem. Soc. Bibl. Lit., Am. Schs. Oriental Rsch. Office: Iliff Sch Theology 2201 S University Blvd Denver CO 80210

PETERSEN, GERALD LEE, minister; b. Hustisford, Wis., Feb. 7, 1946; s. Byron H. and C. Lorraine (Wogsland) P.; m. Catherine Anne Yuscka, Aug. 17, 1968; children: Kimberly A., Matthew E., Nathan A. BA, Luther Coll., 1968; MDiv, Luther Theol. Sem., St. Paul, 1971. Ordained to ministry Am. Luth. Ch., 1972. Pastor Christ Luth. Ch., Spring Green, Wis., 1972-78, Sugar Creek Luth. Ch., Elkhorn, Wis., 1978—; bd. dirs. Isidore Interfaith Organizing, Milw., 1984-87, Ecumenical Ministry with Mature Adults, Elkhorn, 1979-83; chmn. Dodgeville Conf. Am. Luth. Ch., Spring Green, 1974-77. Bd. dirs., sec. Wis. Farmers Found., Inc., Milw., 1988-91. Mem. Alban Inst., Lakeland Med. Ctr. Chaplaincy (sec.-treas. 1986-87), Lions (bd. dirs. Spring Green chpt. 1974-77), Rotary (bd. dirs. Elkhorn chpt. 1982-85, 90—). Office: Sugar Creek Luth Ch Rte 2 Box 46 Elkhorn WI 53121

PETERSEN, NORMAN RICHARD, JR., religious studies educator; b. Chgo., Aug. 25, 1933; s. Norman Richard and Mildred May (Wilson) P.; m. Antoinette DeRosa, Jan. 28, 1956; children: Kristen, Mark, Joanna. B.F.A., Pratt Inst., 1957; S.T.B., Harvard U., 1961, Ph.D., 1967. Instr., asst. prof. Wellesley Coll., Mass., 1963-69; asst. prof., then assoc. prof. religion Williams Coll., Williamstown, Mass., 1969-77; prof. Williams Coll., 1978-79, Washington Gladden prof. religion, 1980—. Author: Literary Criticism for New Testament Critics, 1978, Rediscovering Paul. The Sociology of Paul's Narrative World, 1985 (Bibl. Archeology Soc. book award 1986, Am. Acad. Religion book award 1987); assoc. editor: Semeia, 1974-82. Mem. Mt. Greylock Regional High Sch. Com., Williamstown, 1980-85. Served with AUS, 1952-54. Mem. Soc. Bibl. Lit., Studiorim Novi Testamenti Societas. Office: Williams Coll Dept Religion Williamstown MA 01267

PETERSEN, W. W., academic administrator. Pres. Bethany Luth. Theol. Sem., Mankato, Minn. Office: Bethany Luth Theol Sem 447 N Division St Mankato MN 56001*

PETERSEN, WILLIAM JAMES, publishing executive; b. Chgo., Aug. 19, 1929; s. Elmer Niels and Edna Helen (McAlpine) P.; m. Ardythe I. Ekdahl, Dec. 20, 1952; children: Kenneth W., J. Randall, Kathryn A. BA, Wheaton Coll., 1950; LittD (hon.), Ea. Coll., St. David's, Pa., 1975. Editorial dir. Christian Life mag., Chgo., 1953-57; exec. editor Eternity mag., Phila., 1957-75; editor Eternity mag., 1975-86; v.p., editorial dir. Fleming H. Revell Co., Tarrytown, N.Y., 1986—. Author: Another Hand on Mine, 1966, Those Curious New Cults, 1972, The Discipling of Timothy, 1981, Husbands and Wives, 1990; exec. dir. The Bible Study Hour, Phila., 1975-86. Trustee Conservative Bapt. Theol. Sem., Denver, 1974-80. With U.S. Army, 1951-53. Mem. Evang. Press Assn. (v.p. 1976-78, pres. 1978-80). Office: Revell Pub 120 White Plains Rd Tarrytown NY 10591

PETERSEN, WILLIAM LAWRENCE, theology educator; b. Laredo, Tex., Jan. 19, 1950; s. Elizabeth M. Petersen. BA, U. Iowa, 1971; MDiv, Luth. Theol. Sem., Saskatoon, Can., 1975; postgrad., McGill U., 1975-77; D in Theology, Rijksuniversiteit te Utrecht, The Netherlands, 1984. Lectr. Meml. U., St. John's, Newfoundland, Can., 1977; vis. asst. prof. U. Notre Dame, Ind., 1985-86, asst. prof., 1986-90; asst. prof. Pa. State U., 1990—. Author: The Diatessaron and Ephrem Syrus As Sources of Romanos the Melodist, 1985; editor: Origin of Alexandria, His World and His Legacy, 1988, Gospel Traditions in the Second Century, Origins, Recensions, Text and Transmission, 1989; mem. editorial bd. Internat. Greek N.T.; contbr. articles to scholarly jours. Mem. Soc. of Biblical Lit. (mem. editorial bd. The N.T. in the Greek Fathers 1985—), Studiorum Novi Testamenti Soc. Club: Alpine Français (Chamonix sect.). Avocations: Alpine mountaineering, skiing, music, travel. Office: Pa State U Religious Studies Dept 215 Sparks Bldg University Park PA 16802

PETERSON, CARLOS RANDALL, minister; b. Erwin, Tenn., Apr. 7, 1947; s. Clyde Woodward and Virginia (Runion) P.; m. Julia Tugwell, Aug. 8, 1969; children: April Beth, Ginny Margret, Emily Rebekah. BA, Carson-Newman Coll., 1969; postgrad., Southeastern Bapt. Theol. Sem., Wake Forest, N.C., 1969-71; MRE, Luther Rice Sem., Jacksonville, Fla., 1987, D Ministry, 1990. Lic. to ministry So. Bapt. Conv., 1965; ordained, 1969. Pastor Greene Hills Bapt. Ch., Greeneville, Tenn., 1971-75, Bowersville (Ga.) Bapt. Ch., 1975-77; pastor 1st Bapt. Ch., Warrenville, S.C., 1977-80, Kingstree, S.C., 1980-85; assoc. pastor 1st Bapt. Ch., Tallahassee, 1985-89; pastor 1st Bapt. Ch., Athens, Tenn., 1989—; mem. gen. bd. S.C. Bapt. Conv., 1978-80, chmn. nominating com., 1982-84; pres. ACTS Bd., Tallahassee, 1988-89. Contbr. articles to profl. jours.; host (radio programs) New Light-New Hope, 1975-85, Good News, 1989—, (TV svc.) 1st Bapt. Ch./Worship, 1985-89. Chaplain Bowersville Citizen's Com., 1976-77; pres. Warrenville Community Christian Coun., 1978-80; mem. ch. initiative com. Carson-Newman Coll., Jefferson City, Tenn., adv. com. Cleveland State Community Coll., Cleveland, Tenn. Named Outstanding Young Man Jaycees Internat., 1979-81; Menninger Inst. fellow, 1985—. Mem. Internat. Platform Assn., Athens/McMinn Ministerial Assn. (pres. 1990—), Kiwanis. Home: 1505 Brentwood Dr Athens TN 37303 Office: 1st Bapt Ch 302 Washington Ave Athens TN 37303

PETERSON, ERNEST WESLEY, minister; b. Twin Falls, Idaho, Mar. 30, 1926; s. Ernest Ludwig and Esther Louise (Johnson) P.; m. Evelyn Christine Edie, Aug. 28, 1965; children: Ellen Louise, Amy Ruth. BS, Coll. of Idaho, 1961; MDiv, Pitts. Theol. Sem., 1965. Ordained to ministry Presbyn. Ch. (U.S.A.), 1965. Min. Burgess Presbyn. Ch., Aledo, Ill., 1965-70, Sunbeam United Presbyn. Ch., Aledo, 1965-75, Media (Ill.) United Presbyn. Community Ch., 1975-91, Stronghurst (Ill.) Presbyn. Ch., 1975-91; ret., 1991. Cpl. U.S. Army, 1953-55.

PETERSON, FREDRIC DAHLIN, lay worker, insurance administrator; b. Waterbury, Conn., Feb. 12, 1937; s. Philip Fredric and Frances (Dahlin) P.; m. Edith Arline Nilsen, Mar. 31, 1961; children: Philip, Lori. BA, Tufts U., 1958. Fin. sec. Wethersfield (Conn.) Evang. Free Ch., 1973-77, chmn. missions bd., 1978-82; sec. overseas missions bd. Evang. Free Ch. Am., Mpls., 1983-89, 91—, chmn. nat. conf. com., 1991; adminstr. Aetna Life Ins. Co., Hartford, Conn., 1958—; chmn. fin. com. Wethersfield Evang. Free Ch., 1989-91. Home: 51 Wildwood Rd Wethersfield CT 06109

PETERSON, GENE RICHARD, minister; b. Columbus, Ohio, Apr. 21, 1949; s. Lauritz Irving and Genevieve Roberta (Arnold) P.; m. Gail Lynette Simon, Nov. 26, 1990. BA, Capital U., 1971; MDiv, Trinity Sem., Columbus, Ohio, 1977. Ordained to ministry Luth. Ch., 1977. Pastor Peever (S.D.) Luth. Ch., 1977-82, Our Savior Luth. Ch., Highmore, S.D., 1982-86; sr. pastor Trinity Luth. Ch., Madison, S.D., 1986-90; synod interim specialist Evang. Luth. Ch. in Am. S.D. Synod, Sioux Falls, 1990—; chmn. bd. dirs. Lutherans Outdoors in S.D., Sioux Falls, 1983-86, Bethel Luth. Home, Madison, S.D., 1986-90; interim pastor Grace Luth. Ch., Sturgis, S.D., 1990-91. Co-author: (tng. manual) Evangelism Partners, 1984. Exec. dir. Trinity Organ Fund Dr., Madison, 1989-90. Mem. Assn. Luth. Interim Pastors (S.D. dir.), Interim Ministry Network (Ecumenical), Kiwanis Club (spiritual aims chmn.). Democrat. Office: ELCA SD Synod Augustana College Sioux Falls SD 57197

PETERSON, GILBERT A., college president; b. Newark, Apr. 30, 1935; s. Frederick Julius and Elsie Elizabeth (Anderson) P.; m. Dolores Allen; children: Craig Alan, Jeffrey Todd, Phillip Mark, Steven Paul. BA in Philosophy, Shelton Coll.; MA, NYU, EdD in Adminstr. and Higher Edn. Dir. Christian edn. Reformed Ch. Westwood (N.J.), 1956-60; chmn. Christian edn. Phla. Coll. Bible, 1960-69, acad. dean, 1969-74; dir. Christian edn. Trinity Evang. Divinity Sch., Deerfield, Ill., 1974-79; pres. Lancaster (Pa.) Bible Coll., 1979—; pres. Creative Leadership in Mgmt., Lancaster, 1977—; adj. mem. faculty Northeastern Bible Coll., Essex Fells, N.J., 1956-60. Author: Bible Study Skills, 1967, (with others) Churches in Crisis, 1981; editor, author: Christian Education of Adults, 1984; author, presenter (8 video tapes) Biblical Principles of Management, 1981. Bd. dirs. Lancaster Family YMCA, 1985-91. Recipient Founder's Day award NYU, 1971. Mem. Soc. Advancement Mgmt., Assn. Higher Edn., Nat. Assn. Profs. Christian Edn., Evang. Theol. Soc., Lancaster C. of C. (found. bd. dirs.), Rotary, Phi Delta Kappa, Kappa Delta Phi. Republican. Baptist. Avocations: photography, woodworking, swimming, gardening, golf. Home: 2104 Millstream Rd Lancaster PA 17602 Office: Lancaster Bible Coll 901 Eden Rd Lancaster PA 17601

PETERSON, JOHN EDWARD, minister; b. Seattle, Aug. 12, 1953; s. Wilbur Glen and Donna Jean (Nielsen) P.; m. Judith Arlene Coleman, Dec. 19, 1975; children: Bjorn Karl, Christine Anna, Joel Thomas. BA in Polit. Sci., Bethel Coll., 1976; MDiv. in Ch. History, Bethel Theol. Sem., 1980, postgrad., 1989—. Ordained min. Bapt. Ch., 1982. Pastor Bethel Bapt. Ch., Hartford, Conn., 1980-83, Ord, Nebr., 1983—; chmn. bd. trustees Great Plains Bapt. Conf., Omaha, 1990—; bd. regents Bethel Coll. and Sem., St. Paul, 1990—. Unit commr. Boy Scouts Am., Ord, 1988—. Mem. Am. Soc. Ch. History. Republican. Home: 1819 N Street Ord NE 68862 Office: Bethel Bapt Ch 212 N 21st St PO Box 144 Ord NE 68862 *My success is measured only by my devotion to God and obedience to His Word.*

PETERSON, JOHN EVERETT, missionary; b. Mankato, Minn., June 12, 1937; s. Elmer Harvey Peterson and Anna Johanna (Rasmussen) Stanley; m. Iva Jean Miles, Aug. 12, 1960; children: Sara Ann, James Harvey. BA, Pillsbury Bapt. Bible Coll., Owatonna, Minn., 1959; BD, Temple Bapt. Sem., Chattanooga, 1961; MA, Bob Jones U., 1962, PhD, 1964. Ordained to ministry Bapt. Ch., 1961. Missionary Assn. Bapts. for World Evangelism, Inc., Cherry Hill, N.J., 1964—; dir. deaf works Assn. Bapts. for World Evangelism, Inc., Sao Paulo, Brazil, 1979—. Editor, co-author: Communicating with Your Hands (in Portuguese), 1987. Republican. Home: Rua Barao de Jaguara 504, 13015 Campinas Brazil Office: Assn Bapts World Evangelism, Rua Alvares Machado 480, 13013 Campinas Brazil *Man's profoundest needs are spiritual. When these needs are fulfilled by Christ's redemptive plan, all other aspects of human existence are influenced.*

PETERSON, JOHN WILLARD, composer, music publisher; b. Lindsborg, Kans., Nov. 1, 1921; s. Peter Ephraim and Adlina Mary (Nelson) P.; m. Marie Alta Addis (Feb. 11, 1944); children: Sandra Lynn Peterson Catzere, Candace Kay Peterson Strader, Pamela Lee Peterson Cruse. Student, Moody Bible Inst., 1947-48; MusB, Am. Conservatory Music, 1952; MusD (hon.), John Brown U., 1967; DD (hon.), West Bapt. Sem., 1970; DFA (hon.), Grand Canyon U., 1979. Radio broadcaster Sta. WMBI, Chgo., 1950-55; editor in chief, pres. Singspiration, Inc., Grand Rapids, Mich., 1955-71; exec. composer Singspiration, Inc., Carefree, Ariz., 1977-83; pres. John W. Peterson Music Co., Scottsdale, Ariz., 1983—; pres. Good Life Prodns., Scottsdale, 1977-83; bd. dirs. Gospel Films, Inc., Muskegon, Mich., Family Life Radio. Co-author: (autobiography) The Miracle Goes On, 1976; composer works include numerous cantatas, musicals, gospel songs, hymns and anthems. 1st lt. USAAF 1942-45, CBI. Decorated Air medal; recipient Sacred Music award Nat. Evang. Film Found., 1966, Music Achievement award Christian Artists, 1985; Honor Cert. Freedoms Found., 1975; winner Internat. Gospel Composition of Yr., Soc. European Stage, Authors and Composers, 1986. Mem. ASCAP, Hump Pilots Assn. Inductee Gospel Music Hall of Fame, 1986. Home: 11668 N 80th Pl Scottsdale AZ 85260

PETERSON, KENNETH CURTIS, JR. (CASEY PETERSON), editor; b. St. Paul, May 20, 1941; s. Kenneth Curtis and Katherine M. (Moss) P.; m. Deborah Ann Swan, Apr. 8, 1961 (div. May 1988); children: Theresa Marie, Steven Kenneth, Thomas George; m. Eileen Marie Forrester, Sept. 30, 1989. BA, U. Minn., 1968. Editor Internat. Marriage Encounter, St. Paul, 1984—. Contbr. articles to Marriage Encounter, 1984—. Office: Marriage Encounter 955 Lake Dr Saint Paul MN 55120

PETERSON, KENNETH RICHARD, minister; b. Stambaugh, Mich., July 15, 1946; s. Bertal Richard and Eria Kay (Hendrickson) P.; m. Pamela Honan, May 31, 1970; children: Brian, Kristin. BA, Mich. State U., 1968; MDiv, Luth. Sch. Theology Chgo., 1973. Ordained to ministry Luth. Ch., 1972. Pastor St. John's Luth. Ch., North Liberty, Ind., 1972-82, Augustana Luth. Ch., Elkhart, Ind., 1982-90, Good Shepherd Luth. Ch., South Bend, Ind., 1990—. Office: Good Shepherd Luth Ch 1021 Manchester Dr South Bend IN 46615

PETERSON, LESLIE ERNEST, bishop; b. Noranda, Que., Can., Nov. 4, 1928; s. Ernest Victor and Blanch (Marsh) P.; m. Yvonne Hazel Lawton, July 16, 1953; children—Shauna Peterson Van Hoof, Tom, Jennifer Peterson Glage, Kathryn Peterson Scott, Jonathan. B.A., U. Western Ont., London, Ont., Can., 1952; L.T.H., Huron Coll., London, Ont., Can., 1954, D.D. (hon.), 1984; tchr.'s cert., North Bay Tchrs. Coll., Ont., 1970. Ordained to ministry Anglican Ch., 1954. Priest Diocese of Algoma, Coniston, Ont., 1954-58; priest Diocese of Algoma, Elliot Lake, Ont., 1959-63, rural dean, 1961-63; priest Diocese of Algoma, North Bay, 1963-78; priest Diocese of Algoma, Parry Sound, Ont., 1978-83, archdeacon, 1980-83; bishop Diocese of Algoma, Sault Ste. Marie, Ont., 1983—; tchr. North Bay Elem. Sch., 1970-78. Avocations: canoeing, cross country skiing, gardening. Home: 134 Simpson St, Sault Sainte Marie, ON Canada P6A 3V4 Office: Diocese of Algoma, PO Box 1168, Sault Sainte Marie, ON Canada P6A 5N7

PETERSON, MARIE KATHERINE, director of music ministries; b. Hartford, Wis., May 21, 1942; d. Nicholas Frank and Lucille Katherine (Schwartz) Schnitzler; m. George Allen Peterson, Apr. 24, 1965; children: Margie, Greg. B of Music Edn., U. Wis., Oshkosh, 1964. Dir. adult choir St. Anne's Cath. Ch., Escanaba, Mich., 1966-70, 71—, dir. youth choir, 1979-84, dir. jr. choir, 1984—, dir. music ministries, 1976—; screen printer Weisserts Screen Printing, Escanaba, 1987—; charter mem. Diocesan Liturgical Commn., Marquette, Mich., 1976-78; mem. Parish Liturgical Commn., Escanaba, 1971—. Composer various choral works, 1966—. Musical dir. Players De Noc, Inc., Escanaba, 1966—, Kiwanis Bicentennial Men's Chorus, Escanaba, 1975-77. Named to Outstanding Young Women of Am., 1967, Hon. Kiwanis Mem., Escanaba, 1977. Mem. Nat. Pastoral Musicians, Diocesan Music Assn., The BrightSpots, Lady Elks (Lady Elk of Yr. 1990, pres. 1979-80), Keyboard Guild Assn., Eagles Aux. Home: 217 South Lincoln Rd Escanaba MI 49829 Office: St Anne's Cath Ch 817 S Lincoln Rd Escanaba MI 49829-1137

PETERSON, RALPH EDWARD, clergyman; b. Duluth, Minn., Apr. 12, 1932; s. Harold Edward and Muriel (Miller) P.; m. Karen Birgitta Esselius, May 31, 1969; 1 son, Kristofer Amandus Esselius. B.A., U. Minn., 1954; M.A.T., Harvard U., 1955; grad., Advanced Mgmt. Program, 1977; student, Episcopal Theol. Sch., Cambridge, Mass., 1955-56; M.Div., Lutheran Sch. Theology, Rock Island, Ill., 1960; postgrad., Columbia U., 1962-63; D.D., Gettysburg Coll., 1971. Ordained to ministry Luth. Ch. in Am., 1960, Ch. of Sweden, 1983, Episcopal Diocese of N.Y., 1989. Pastor Christ Ch., Hammond, Ind., 1960-62; exec. dir. dept. ministry Nat. Coun. Chs. of Christ, 1962-64; exec. dir. dept. ministry, vocation and pastoral services Nat. Coun. Chs., 1965-66; pastor St. Peter's Ch., N.Y.C., 1966-80; dir. study on health and society Luth. Ch. in Am., 1981-82; assoc. dir. Dept. Health and Hosps., Archdiocese of N.Y., 1981-82; dir. Ctr. for Health Mission, New Haven, 1982-84; pres. Open Congregation, Inc., N.Y.C., 1984-89; head religion dept. and dir. pastoral counseling The Masters Sch., Dobbs Ferry, N.Y., 1989—, Henry Sloan Coffin chair bibl. studies, 1990—; lectr. N.Y. Theol. Sem., 1965-67; Mem. Citizens Com. N.Y.C.; Mem. bd. theol. edn. Luth. Ch. Am., 1967-72; adv. com. Christian ministries Episcopal Ch., 1965-68; exec. bd. Met. N.Y. Synod, Luth. Ch. Am., 1966-70; del. assembly World Council Ch., Uppsala, 1968, Appeal of Conscience, Romania, 1980; chmn. religion and vocation sect. Nat. Vocat. Guidance Assn., 1965; pres. The Common at the Intersection, 1977-79. Trustee, chmn. N.Y. Theol. Sem., 1966-78; trustee Inst. Advanced Pastoral Studies, Bloomfield Hills, Mich., 1967-71, Gettysburg Theol. Sem., 1968-74; mem. Am. com. for Mansfield Coll., Oxford (Eng.), U., 1965-74; bd. dirs. Religious Communities for the Arts, 1975-82; exec. bd. The Healing Community, 1978-84; bd. dirs., treas. African Soc. Equal Opportunities for the Handicapped, 1986-88; mem. organizing bd. Internat. Ctr. Study Social Rels., 1986-88, dir. Am. Summer Insts., Uppsala, Sweden, 1985—; mem. adv. bd. Inst. Theology, N.Y., 1988—. Fellow Soc. of Arts, Religion and Contemporary Arts; mem. Inst. Religion and Mental Health (profl. bd. 1964-76), Am. Scandinavian Found., Forum on Investment Responsibility, Societas Sanctae Birgittae, Acad. Parish Clergy (pres. 1967-71), Phi Delta Kappa. Clubs: Harvard (N.Y.C.), University (N.Y.C.). Office: The Masters School 49 Clinton Ave Dobbs Ferry NY 10522

PETERSON, ROBERT ANTHONY, JR., educational administrator; b. Hammonton, N.J., Apr. 12, 1956; s. Robert Anthony and Nancy B. (Henschel) P.; m. Susanna A. Allen, June 13, 1981; children: Rebecca, Robert Anthony III, Joseph, James. BA, Bryan Coll., Dayton, Tenn., 1978; MA, Grace Sem., Winona Lake, Ind., 1982. Cert. tchr., N.J. Tchr. Pilgrim Acad., Egg Harbor, N.J., 1978-81, headmaster, 1981—; tchr. Garden State Bible Sch., Pleasantville, N.J., 1979—; journalist Gannet News, Vineland, N.J., 1983-87. Author: A Goodly Heritage, 1991; columnist Our South Jersey Heritage, Egg Harbor News, 1982-87; contbr. articles to The Freeman, Nat. Rev., other publs. Lectr. to chs., local civic groups; deacon Emmanuel Congl. Ch., Egg Harbor, 1980—. Named oratorical contest coach of yr. Am. Legion, citizen of yr. Egg Harbor City Kiwanis Club, 1988. Mem. Atlantic County Hist. Soc., Presbyn. Hist. Soc. Avocations: writing, swimming, soccer, basketball, collecting South Jerseyana. Home: 413 White Horse Pike Egg Harbor City NJ 08215 Office: Pilgrim Acad Egg Harbor City NJ 08215

PETERSON, STEPHEN LEE, librarian, education administrator; b. Lindsborg, Kans., Jan. 31, 1940; s. Donald Gordon and Grace (Forsberg) P.; m. Mabel Jean Moen, Aug. 31, 1963; children: Anne Davina, Matthew Robert Moen. BA, Bethel Coll., 1962; BD, Colgate Rochester Div. Sch., St. Paul, 1965; AMLS, U. Mich., 1967, AM, 1968; PhD, Vanderbilt U., 1975. Asst. dir. for bibliog. svcs. Vanderbilt U., Nashville, 1971-72; head libr. Yale Div. Sch., New Haven, 1972—; libr. Beinecke Rare Book Libr. Yale U., 1978-80; asst. to dean Yale Div. Sch., New Haven, 1984-87, assoc. dean for adminstrn., 1987-89; mem. adv. com. Christianity in China Resources Project, 1982-84. Contbr. articles to profl. jours. Info. sci. fellow Xerox Corp., 1967-68, fellow Coun. on Libr. Resources, 1975-76. Mem. Am. Theol. Libr. Assn. (joint com. on libr. resources 1984-89, pres. 1986-87), Assn. Theol. Schs. (libr. staff devel. grantee 1975-76, commn. on accrediting 1982-84, task force on info. systems 1985-88). Home: 57 Northside Rd North Haven CT 06473 Office: Yale Div Sch 409 Prospect St New Haven CT 06511

PETERSON, THOMAS CHARLES, minister, pastoral counselor and therapist; b. San Francisco, Mar. 16, 1955; s. Roy Joseph and Grace Jeannette (Burns) P.; m. Melody Rose Clarkson, Aug. 17, 1985; 1 child, Shannon Nicole. BA, Living Word Sem., Maryland Heights, Mo., 1986; MS, Carolina Christian U., Linwood, N.C., 1990; postgrad., U. Bibl. Studies, Bethany, Okla., 1990, Carolina U. Theology, Charlotte, N.C., 1991—. Ordained to ministry Full Gospel Assemblies, 1984, Internat. Conf. Faith Ministries, 1986, Assn. Evang. Assemblies, 1989. Elder, tchr. Joy of Lord Fellowship, Buckley, Wash., 1980-81, By His Word Christian Ctr., Tacoma, 1982-88; assoc. pastor Valley Christian Ctr., Sumner, 1988-89; founder, pres. Joyful Life Ministries, Tacoma, 1985—; dir., therapist Christian Counseling and Family Outreach, Tacoma, 1990—; chaplain Tacoma Police Dept., 1988-90; dir. Inst. for Personal Devel., Tacoma, 1991. Sgt. USAF, 1973-77. Mem. Nat. Christian Counselors Assn. (profl. affiliate, lic. pastoral counselor and temperament therapist), United Assn. Christian Counselors, Internat. Assn. Christian Clin. Counselors, U.S. Chaplaincy Assn. Republican. Home: 5615 S Verde Tacoma WA 98409 Office: Joyful Life Ministries/ CCFO PO Box 98198 Tacoma WA 98498 *Life can sometimes throw us a curve ball. We may not always know the "why's" in life, but if we maintain faith in God, faith in ourselves and press ahead, something better usually lies right around the corner. The human potential is limited only by our ability to believe.*

PETERSON, WALTER FRITIOF, university official; b. Idaho Falls, Idaho, July 15, 1920; s. Walter Fritiof and Florence (Danielson) P.; m. Barbara Mae Kempe, Jan. 13, 1946; children: Walter Fritiof III, Daniel John. BA, State U. Iowa, 1942, MA, 1948, PhD, 1951; HHD (hon.), Loras Coll., 1983; LHD (hon.), Clarke Coll., 1991. Instr. State U. Iowa, 1949-51, Buena Vista Coll., 1951-52; asst. prof. history, chmn. dept. history Milw. Downer Coll., 1952-57, assoc. prof. history, chmn. social sci. div., 1957-64; assoc. prof. history Lawrence U., Appleton, Wis., 1964-67; prof. history, Alice G. Chapman libr. Lawrence U., 1967-70; pres. U. Dubuque, 1970-90, chancellor, 1990—; Vis. lectr. summers Ball State U., Muncie, Ind., 1954, 56, Drake U., Des Moines, 1962, U. Wis.-Milw., 1959, 61, 63, 64; regional tng. officer Peace Corps, 1965-68; dir. India project, 1965; cons. history Allis-Chalmers Mfg. Co., 1959—, Home Mut. Ins. Co., 1968—, Wm. C. Brown Pub. Co., 1981—, Secura Ins., Dubuque Packing Co. Editor: Transactions of Wis. Acad. Scis., Arts and Letters, 1965-72, The Allis-Chalmers Corporation: An Industrial History, 1977; Contbr. articles to profl. jours. Mem. exec. com. coun. theol., edn. com. Presbyn. Ch. U.S.A.; chmn. assoc. theol. faculties of Iowa, 1975-76; advisor Templeton Prize for Progress in Religion, 1986—; bd. dirs. Finley Hosp., pres., 1983-84; chmn. Finley Health Found., 1986—; bd. dirs. Dubuque Symphony Orch., Dubuque Art Assn., Jr. Achievement, Nat. Rivers Hall of Fame, 1984; chmn. Iowa Assn. Coll. and Univ. Pres.'s, 1975-76; chmn. Iowa Coll. Found., 1982-83. With USAAF, 1942-45, PTO. Recipient Dubuque Citizen award, 1990, Disting. Civic Svc. award, 1991; named to Dubuque Bus. Hall of Fame, 1990. Mem. Am. Hist. Assn., Orgn. Am. Historians, Iowa Assn. Ind. Colls. and Univs. (chmn. 1988-89), Dubuque County Hist. Soc. (bd. dirs.), Dubuque C. of C. (bd. dirs.), Phi Alpha Theta, Kappa Delta Pi, Phi Delta Kappa. Office: U Dubuque Office of Chancellor 2000 University Ave Dubuque IA 52001

PETIT, PATRICIA JEAN, religious ministry administrator; b. Pierre, S.D., Jan. 21, 1935; d. Benjamin Franklin and Betty Edna (Ward) Padilla; m. Irvin William Petit, Jr., June 4, 1955 (dec. June 1980); children—Theresa Marie (dec.), Michelle Jean Petit Porvasnik, Marcia Anne Petit Rank, Sharon Rose Petit Ames. Certificate, Nettleton Comml. Coll., Sioux Falls, S.D., 1955. Sec., Downtown Clinic, Pierre, S.D., 1953-54, John Morrell, Sioux Falls, 1954-55, Wilson Sch., Rapid City, S.D., 1966-68, S.D. Sch. Mines, Rapid City, 1968-73; sec., asst. editor West River Catholic paper, Rapid City, 1973-81; dir. Ministry to Separated, Divorced and Widowed Diocese of Rapid City, 1981-88; dir. pastoral lay ministries/spirituality, OLPH Cathedral, 1988—. Author newspaper column: Pat's Prayers for Peons, 1977-81. Democrat. Roman Catholic. Club: Catholic Daus. of the Am. (state and local officer 1958-78). Office: Our Lady of Perpetual Help Cathedral 520 Cathedral Dr Rapid City SD 57701

PETRILLO, DENNIS DALE, religious educator; b. Denver, Mar. 25, 1954; s. Jerry and Neva Ilene (Storm) P.; m. Kathy Diane Roberts, Jan. 14, 1978; children: Lance, Brett, Laura. AA, York Coll., Nebr., 1974; BA, Harding U., Searcy, Ark., 1977; MA, Harding Grad. Sch., Memphis, 1981; PhD, U. Nebr., 1989. Minister Como Ch. of Christ, Miss., 1976-81; prof. religion York (Nebr.) Coll., 1981-85, Bear Valley Sch. Bibl. Studies, Denver, 1985—; minister Parker Ch. of Christ, Parker, Colo., 1988—; Contbr. articles to profl. jours. Reg. dir. Cystic Fibrosis, Como, 1978; editor Christian Devel. Pub., Denver, 1989—. Named Tchr. of the Yr., York Coll. 1984. Mem. Soc. Bibl. Lit. Republican. Ch. of Christ. Avocations: weight lifting, racquetball, bowling, skiing, basketball. Office: Bear Valley Sch Bibl Study 2707 S Lamar Denver CO 80227

PETRO, THOMAS CARLTON, minister; b. Flint, Mich., Sept. 13, 1962; s. David James and Patricia Anne (McClain) P.; m. Brenda Joy Fincham, Aug. 10, 1985; children: Timothy David, Rachel Lee Anne. BA, Faith Bapt. Bible Coll., 1986; postgrad., Faith Bapt. Theol. Sem., 1986-87. Lic. to ministry Gen. Assn. Regular Bapt. Chs., 1988. Pastor Open Door Bapt. Ch., Prescott Valley, Ariz., 1987—; mem. coun. Ariz. Assn. Regular Bapt. Chs., Peoria, 1989—, treas., 1990—; asst. camp dir. Camp Tishomingo, Mesa, Ariz., 1988-91, treas., 1991—. Vol. Bible tchr. Las Fuentes Care Ctr., Prescott, Ariz., 1989—. Republican. Home: 8449 E Stevens Dr Prescott Valley AZ 86314

PETRUCELLI, FRANK, school system administrator. Supt. schs. Diocese of Paterson, Clifton, N.J. Office: Schs Div Supt 777 Valley Rd Clifton NJ 07013*

PETRY, RAY C., church history educator emeritus; b. Eaton, Ohio, July 2, 1903; s. Benjamin F. and Jennie (Kitterman) P.; m. Ruth Mertz, May 29, 1930 (dec. Feb. 1965). A.B., Manchester Coll., 1926, LL.D., 1948; A.M., U. Chgo., 1927, Ph.D. (fellow), 1932. Asst. prof. history McPherson (Kans.) Coll., 1929-30, prof. religion, 1933-37; faculty Manchester Coll., 1930-31; asst. prof. ch. history Duke Div. Sch., 1937-43, assoc. prof., 1943-45, prof., 1945-72, James B. Duke prof. ch. history, 1964-72, emeritus, 1972—; Sr. fellow Southeastern Inst. Medieval and Renaissance Studies, U. N.C., 1965; prof. ch. history summers Union Theol. Sem., also Columbia, 1947, 55, Iliff Sch. Theology, 1949, 75, So. Meth. U., 1953; found. lectr. Crozer Theol. Sem., 1948; Lilly Found. lectr. Goshen (Ind.) Coll., 1958; lectr. ch. history U. Oreg., West Coast colls., 1959; European editorial researcher Library Christian Classics, 1954; Gheens hist. lectr. So. Bapt. Theol. Sem., 1966; Centennial lectr. U. Chgo. Div. Sch., 1967; guest mem. Mansfield Coll., Oxford (Eng.) U., 1968; lectr. ch. history U. Edinburgh, Scotland, 1968; Carver-Barnes Meml. lectr. Southeastern Bapt. Theol. Sem., 1971; James A. Gray lectr. Duke, 1972; vis. prof. Pacific Luth. U., 1977-81; mem. Collegium, 1976—; Mem. council Duke, 1952-54, acad. council, 1963-65, Duke library council, 1957-60, exec. com., 1958-60; numerous other lectrs. and seminars; participant Roman Cath.-Protestant Colloquium, Harvard U., 1963. Author: Francis of Assisi, 1941, 2d edit., 1964, No Uncertain Sound, 1948, Preaching in the Great Tradition, 1950, Christian Eschatology and Social Thought, 1956, Late Medieval Mysticism, 1957, 80, History of Christianity, vol. I, 1962, 81, (with others) Medieval and Renaissance Studies, 1966, The Impact of the Church Upon Its Culture, 1968; Contbr. to: (with others) jours. Commissio Internationalis Bonaventuriana Centenary, Vol. II, 1973, Festschrift Duke University, 1974, Ency. Brit. Joint grantee Duke U. Research Council; Joint grantee Carnegie Found. for Advancement Teaching. Mem. Am. Soc. Ch. History (pres. 1951, hon. mem. council 1952—, editorial bd. 1947-74), Phi Beta Kappa. Home: 4879 Northgate Ct Dayton OH 45416

PETTIGREW, CAROLYN LANDERS, theological school official, minister; b. Columbus, Ohio, Sept. 30, 1945; d. Wayman and Mary Gerldine (Lambert) Landers; m. Grady L. Pettigrew, Jr., Jan. 27, 1968; children: Dawn Karima, Grady Landers. BSc in Edn., Ohio State U., 1967; MDiv, Meth. Theol. Sch., Delaware, Ohio, 1987; postgrad., Washington Theol. Union, 1991—. Ordained to ministry United Ch. of Christ, 1988; lic. speech and hearing therapist, Ohio. Youth min., dir. Christian edn. 1st Congl. Ch., Columbus, 1983-86; assoc. chaplain Grant Med. Ctr., Columbus, 1987-90; ednl. asst. to acad. dean for MA in alcohol and drug abuse ministry and continuing edn. Meth. Theol. Sch., 1990—; trustee United Ch. of Christ House, Chautauqua, N.Y., 1990—, Chautauqua Inst. Arts, 1990—; chmn. new clergy orientation Met. Area Ch. Bd., Columbus, 1990-91, co-convenor drug abuse task force. Compiler, author: African American Spirituality: A Bibliography, 1991. Mem. women's bd. Martin Luther King Ctr. for Performing Arts, Columbus, 1987—; mem. docent alumni group Columbus Mus. Arts; evaluator pub. reports AIDS Task Force, Columbus, 1990—; mem. women's agenda on human svcs. Ohio Gov.'s Task Force, Columbus, 1990—. Recipient 11 Kudos, Grant Med. Ctr., 1987-90, Humanitarian award Columbus chpt. Alpha Kappa Alpha, 1990. Mem. Women's Theol. Group, Cen. S.E. Assn. United Ch. of Christ (chair dept. Christian edn. 1985-90), Jr. League Columbus, Zora Lit. Club (founder, convenor), Ladies of Lambda. Home: 1780 Halleck Pl Columbus OH 43209 Office: Meth Theol Sch Delaware OH 43015-0931

PETTIT, DAVID STARLING, clergyman; b. Martins Ferry, Ohio, Aug. 26, 1942; s. Walter Henry and Elizabeth Louise (Carroll) P.; m. Charlotte Rosemary Vrotsos, Jan. 7, 1961; children: Mary, Vonda, Heather, Teresa, Rebecca. BA, Kentucky Christian, 1964, BTh, 1965; MEd, Central State U., Edmond, Okla., 1978. Ordained Christian Ch., 1964; lic. profl. counselor, Okla. Min. Medora (Ind.) Christian Ch., 1964-68, Farmdale Ch. Christ, Barboursville, W.Va., 1968-72; missionary, educator Coll. World Mission, San Juan, P.R., 1972-74; prof., dean Midwest Christian Coll., Okla. City, 1975-85; min. Forest Hill Christian Ch., Okla. City, 1985—; cons. Outreach Internat., Evansville, Ind., 1978-85. Editor: Somemore, 1984. Mem. Am. Assn. Counseling and Devel. Avocation: fishing. Home: 10900 N Florida Ave Oklahoma City OK 73120 Office: Forest Hill Christian Ch 2121 N MacArthur Blvd Oklahoma City OK 73127

PETTIT, PETER ACKER, minister; b. Bethlehem, Pa., Mar. 9, 1955; s. Alfred Wells and Betty Adelaide (Acker) P.; m. Lynn Freund, Aug. 8, 1976; children: Jennifer Leigh, Sarah Freund. AB with honors, Princeton U., 1975; MDiv, Luth. Theol. Sem., Phila., 1980; MA, Claremont Grad. Sch., 1990. Staff asst. Luth. Ch. in Am., N.Y.C., 1975-76; seminarian asst. New Hanover Luth. Ch., Gilbertsville, Pa., 1979-80; teaching fellow Luth. Theol. Sem., 1980-81; text analyst Inst. for Antiquity and Christianity, Claremont, Calif., 1982-83; cataloguer, interim dir. Ancient Bibl. Manuscript Ctr., Claremont, 1983-84, dir., 1985-89; pastor Hope Luth. Ch., Riverside, Calif., 1990—; theol. cons. NCCJ, Inc., N.Y.C. and L.A., 1984-86, mem. adj. staff Nat. Program Office, 1988-89; instr. Sch. Theology, Claremont, 1986—, U. Judaism, 1988—, UCLA, 1988-90, U. Calif., Riverside, 1991—; vis. prof. Hebrew Union Coll., 1989. Co-author: An Inventory of Race Relations: The Lutheran Church in America, 1976; editor: Christ Alone, The Hidden God, and Lutheran Exclusivism, 1991; translation editor: Am. Bible Soc., N.Y.C., 1983-84; editor The Folio, 1983-89. Named One of Outstanding Young Men of Am., U.S. Jaycees, 1979; Nat. Merit scholar, 1972-75; Timken-Sturgis fellow Claremont Grad. Sch., 1982-83, Finkelstein fellow U. Judaism, 1989-90. Fellow Weissberg Family Ctr. for Religious Pluralism, Shalom Hartman Inst.; mem. Soc. Bibl. Lit., Cath. Bibl. Assn., Am. Schs. Oriental Research, Sigma Xi (assoc.), Nat. Assn. Profs. of Hebrews, Assn. for Jewish Studies (So. Calif. regional steering com.), Rotary (Found. Grad. scholar 1984-85). Democrat. Avocation: golf. Office: Hope Luth Ch 2882 Arlington Ave Riverside CA 92506-4599

PETTIT, STEPHEN JOHN, minister; b. Carthage, Ill., Mar. 19, 1959; s. John Dennis and Sharon Su (Soland) P.; m. Julia Kaye Thompson, May 13, 1979. BS, St. Louis Christian Coll., 1984. Ordained to ministry Christian Ch., 1985. Min. Fouts Christian Ch., Centralia, Ill., 1978-84; sr. min. Southside Christian Ch., Bloomington, Ind., 1984—. Named one of Outstanding Young Mins., 1989.

PETTIT, VINCENT KING, bishop; b. New Brunswick, N.J., Aug. 31, 1924; s. John Mervin and Marion (King) P.; m. Virginia Sorensen, June 17, 1950; children—Joan Anders, Ann, Vincent, Jr. B.S., Rutgers U., 1950; M.Div., Phila. Div. Sch., 1958; M.S.T., Temple U., 1963, N.Y. Theol. Sch., 1981; D.D. (hon.) Gen. Sem., N.Y.C., 1984. Ordained bishop Episcopal Ch., 1984. Rector St. George's Ch., Pennsville, N.J., 1961-67, St. Mary's Ch., Keyport, N.J., 1967-72, Trinity Ch., Cranford, N.J., 1972-81, Christ Ch., Toms River, N.J., 1981-83; bishop Diocese of N.J., Trenton, 1983—; mem. exec. coun. Episcopal Ch., N.Y.C., 1983-88 ; chmn. standing liturgical com., 1983—. With U.S. Army, 1942-46. Home: 104 Pilger Ct Lakehurst NJ 08733 Office: Diocese of NJ 808 W State St Trenton NJ 08618

PETTY, DOUGLASS, minister; b. Aliceville, Ala., Mar. 29, 1953; s. Joseph and Willie (Hood) P.; m. Renay Saddie Durley, Oct. 31, 1980; 1 child, Riebeil. AS in Phys. Edn., Lawson Community Coll., 1977; BA in Psychology, Talladega (Ala.) Coll., 1979; MA in Psychology, Wash. U., Saint Louis, 1980; PhD in Christian Counseling, Christian Bible Coll., 1991. Lic. pastoral counselor; cert. pastoral counselor. Asst. to the pastor West Presbyn. Ch., St. Louis, 1985-87; dir. God's Word is for Today, St. Louis, 1982—; area rep. Nat. Christian Counselors Assn., Kittaning, Pa., 1989—; singles ministry advisor Mt. Zion Bapt. Ch., 1987—, assoc. dir. Christian edn., 1987—; counselor U. Mo., Saint Louis, 1991—; bd. pres. Greater Outreach Evangelistic Ctr., St. Louis, 1987-90; bd. v.p. Workshop Enterprises, St. Louis, 1986-90, Living Inc., St. Louis, 1988-90. Bd. dirs. St. Louis Jobs Corps Adv. Bd., 1988—, Forest Park Children's Ctr., St. Louis, 1988—, VAEL St. Louis Community Coll., 1987—, RSVP St. Louis Community Coll., 1984—. Mem. AACD, Nat. Christian Counselors Assn., Assn. of Multicultural Counseling and Devel. (bd. dirs. Mo. chpt. 1990-91, pres. elect 1991—). Home: 3123 Rauschenbach Saint Louis MO 63107 *When the "big picture" is clearly understood, it is quite apparent as to just how futile some inappropriate pursuits are.*

PETTY, H. MICHAEL, SR., minister; b. Tifton, Ga., Oct. 27, 1961; s. henry Lee Petty and Helen B. (Hall) Chafin; m. Sue Ellen McAllister, Mar. 20, 1982; children: Mallory Lee, Henry Michael Jr. AA, Brewton-Parker Coll., 1990, B of Ministry, 1991. Ordained to ministry So. Bapt. Conv., 1985. Pastor Mt. Olive Bapt. Ch., Fitzgerald, Ga., 1984-89, Rocky Creek Bapt. Ch., Lyons, Ga., 1989-91, Olivet Bapt. Ch., Dublin, Ga., 1991—. Recipient Starr Miller award Brewton-Parker Coll., 1991, Brewton-Parker Religious Leadership award, 1991. Mem. Brewton-Parker Ministerial Assn. (pres. 1990-91), Lyons Ministerial Assn. Republican. Home and Office: Rte 4 Box 55 Dublin GA 31021

PETTY, JOHN STUART, minister; b. Kansas City, Mo., Dec. 20, 1949; s. Harold Thomas and S. Marie (James) P.; m. Lynn Annette Nebergall, Feb. 27, 1971; 1 child, Erika Vanessa. MS, Ft. Hays State U., 1975; MDiv, Wartburg Sem., 1987. Ordained to ministry Evang. Luth. Ch. Am., 1987. Pastor Zion Luth. Ch., Montrose, Colo., 1987—; staff psychologist Dubuque (Iowa)-Jackson County Mental Health, 1984-87. Contbr. articles to profl. pubs. Commr. City of Hays (Kans.), 1977-83, mayor, 1981-82; mem. Kans. Crime Victims' Reparations Bd., Topeka, 1980-83; mem. state com. Kans. Dem. State Com., Topeka, 1977-83. With USNG, 1971-77. Mem. Am. Group Psychotherapy Assn., Western Kans. Psychol. Assn. (pres. 1980), Kans. Orgn. Profl. Psychologists (bd. dirs. 1981-82). Office: Zion Luth Ch 701 S Junction Montrose CO 81402

PETTY, THOMAS RAMSEY, minister; b. Evanston, Ill., June 13, 1949; s. Thomas Berry and Dorothy Mae (Miller) P.; m. Linda Suzanne Blosser, June 8, 1974; children: Carrie Augusta, John Thomas, William Berry. AB, Brown U., 1971; MDiv, Garrett-Evang. Theol. Sem., 1975; cert., Coll. Fin. Planning, Denver, 1990. Ordained to ministry United Meth. Ch. as elder, 1977. Assoc. pastor Roselle (Ill.) United Meth. Ch., 1974-81; pastor Yorkville and Millbrook (Ill.) United Meth. Chs., 1981-86, Wesley United Meth. Ch., Sterling, Ill., 1988—; chairperson No. Ill. Conf. Bd. Trustees, Chgo., 1988—, mem. adminstrn. com., 1988—, episcopal residence com., 1988—, configuration task force, 1989—. Adj. chaplain CGH Med. Ctr, Sterling, 1989—; chaplain Whiteside County Hospice Assn., Sterling, 1990—. Office: Wesley United Meth Ch 2200 16th Ave Sterling IL 61081

PETTY, WALLACE EUGENE, minister; b. Slater, Mo., June 22, 1935; s. James Wallace and Marybell (Anderson) P.; m. Evelyn Dolores Petty, Aug. 13, 1954; 1 child, Edwin Eugene. Student, Cen. Mo. State, 1967, Assemblies of God Grad. Sch., Springfield, Mo., 1978. Pastor Winona (Mo.) Assembly of God, 1969-75, First Assembly of God, East Prairie, Mo., 1975-77, Searsport (Maine) Free Gospel Ch., 1977-81; dep. sec., trainer No. New Engl. Dist. Assemblies of God, Portland, 1979—; dir. child min. No. New Engl. Dist. Assemblies of God, Portland, Maine, 1981-89; dir. child ministries No. New Engl. Dist. Assemblies of God, Portland, 1981-89, dist. presbyter, 1987—, dir., sec., 1989—; dist. presbyter So. Mo. Dist. Assemblies of God, Springfield, Mo., 1970-75. With U.S. Army, 1953-62. Office: No New Eng Dist PO Box 3775 501 River Rd Portland ME 04104

PETUSKEY, JOHN ALBERT, priest; b. Elizabeth, N.J., Dec. 9, 1938; s. John Albert Sr. and Helen Ursula (Grisckis) P. BA in Philosophy, St. Joseph Coll., Rensselaer, Ind., 1964; MA in Theology, U. Dayton, 1967; MA in Teaching, Oklahoma City U., 1972. Ordained priest Roman Cath. Ch., 1966. Dir. edn., supt. schs. Archdiocese Oklahoma City, 1975-81; acad. dean deacon program Archdiocese Oklahoma City and Diocese Tulsa, 1975-80; dir. ecumenical and interreligious affairs Archdiocese Oklahoma City, 1981; pastor St. Francis of Assisi, Oklahoma City, 1977-87, St. John the Bapt. Cath. Ch., Edmond, Okla., 1989—; dir., v.p. Okla. Conf. Chs., Oklahoma City, 1981—; chmn. Archdiocesan Coun. Priests, Oklahoma City, 1984-90; dir. Assoc. Cath. Charities, Oklahoma City, 1985—; mem. Natural Family Planning Bd., Archdiocese Oklahoma City, 1984-89; prs. Agy. Christian Coop. Ministries, Oklahoma City, 1984-88; mem., chair Faith and Order Commn., Okla. Conf. Ch., Oklahoma City, 1984—. Mem. bd., officer Mental Health Assn. Oklahoma County, Oklahoma City, 1984—. Mem. Nat. Cath. Edn. Assn., Mariological Soc. Am., Fellowship Cath. Scholars, Newman Soc. Am., Nat. Cath. Stewardship Assn., Nat. Assn. Dirs. Ecumenism, Edmond Ministerial Assn. (pres. 1989—). Republican. Home and Office: St John the Bapt Cath Ch 924 S Littler St Edmond OK 73034 *Generosity is the only response to a loving God. The marvel is that the Lord is never outdone in generosity.*

PEUGH, ROGER DENNIS, religion educator; b. Yakima, Wash., June 17, 1943; s. Harold F. and Laura L. (Lowe) P.; m. Nancy Sue Orndorf, June 5, 1965; children: Ryan, Philip, Lamar, Lynae. BA in History, Grace Coll., Winona Lake, Ind., 1965; MDiv, Grace Theol. Sem., Winona Lake, 1968; cert. German proficiency, Goethe Inst., Berlin, 1970. Ordained to ministry Fellowship Grace Brethren Chs., 1969. Assoc. pastor Grace Brethren Ch., Elkhart, Ind., 1965-68; missionary Grace Brethren Fgn. Missions, Stuttgart, Fed. Republic Germany, 1969-89, field supt., 1976-89, regional dir. Europe, 1986-90; prof. missions Grace Theol. Sem., Winona Lake, 1989—; moderator Fellowship Grace Brethren Chs., Winona Lake, 1989-90. Named Alumnus of Yr., Grace Coll., 1983. Mem. Evang. Missiological Soc., Evang. Theol. Soc. Office: Grace Theol Sem 200 Seminary Dr Winona Lake IN 46590

PEURIFOY, ROBERT CLAUDE, minister; b. Concord, N.C., May 6, 1951; s. Robert Eugene and Hazel Maziele (Staton) P.; m. Virginia Frances Byrd, Sept. 4, 1980; children: Rebekah Ann, Nathan Daniel. AS, Montreat-Anderson Coll., 1971; BA, Scarrit Coll., 1973; MDiv, Wesley Sem., Washington, 1978; D Ministry, Drew U., 1991. Ordained to ministry United Meth. Ch. as deacon, 1975, as elder, 1980. Min. Marriottsville Cir., Sykesville, Md., 1975-77, Shooting Creek Cir., Hayesville, N.C., 1977-81, Robbinsville (N.C.) United Meth. Ch., 1981-86, Bethlehem United Meth. Ch., Advance, N.C., 1986—; bd. dirs. Dist. Mission/Outreach, Lexington Dist., 1990—; del. 16th World Meth. Conf., Singapore, 1991. Mem. Robbinsville Fire Dept., 1981-86; chaplain Graham County Rescue Squad, Robbinsville, 1981-86; chaplain, fireman Smith Grove Fire Dept., Advance, 1986—. Mem. Cir. Rider Motorcycle Club Internat., Christian Motorcycle Assn. Home: Rte 1 Box 137 Redland Rd Advance NC 27006-9712 Office: Bethlehem United Meth Ch Redland Rd Advance NC 27006-9712

PEVEC, ANTHONY EDWARD, bishop; b. Cleve., Apr. 16, 1925; s. Anton and Frances (Darovec) P. MA, John Carroll U., Cleve., 1956; PhD, Western Res. U., Cleve., 1964. Ordained priest Roman Catholic Ch., 1950. Assoc. pastor St. Mary Church, Elyria, Ohio, 1950-52, St. Lawrence Ch., Cleve., 1952-53; rector-prin. Borromeo Sem. High Sch., Wickliffe, Ohio, 1953-75; adminstrv. bd. Nat. Cath. Edn. Assn., 1972-75; pastor St. Vitus Ch., Cleve., 1975-79; rector-pres. Borromeo Coll., Wickliffe, 1979-82; aux. bishop Diocese of Cleve., 1982—; cons. Nat Conf. Cath. Bishops Com. on Pro-Life Activities, 1990—; mem. U.S. Cath. Conf., 1982—, Ohio Cath. Conf., 1982—, Papal Visitation Team, 1982-87; mem. Bishops' Com. on Vocations, 1984-86. Mem. v.p. Slovenian-Am. Heritage Found., Cleve., 1975—. Honoree, Heritage Found., Cleve., 1982; named Man of Yr., Fedn. Slovenian Nat. Homes, Cleve., 1985; inducted into Hall of Fame, St. Vitus Alumni Assn., 1989. Democrat. Roman Catholic. Avocations: reading; music. Home and Office: Diocese of Cleve 28700 Euclid Ave Wickliffe OH 44092-2585 *Ultimately I must always remember that the Lord is totally in control of my life, no matter how complicated it may seem to be. I am here to do the Lord's will., and wherever I go I come to do His will.*

PEYTON, PATRICK, priest; b. Carracastle Village, County Mayo, Ireland, Jan. 9, 1909; s. John Peyton and Mary Gillard. Grad. from sem., U. Notre Dame, 1929, AB, 1937; postgrad., Bengalese Fgn. Missions Sem., Holy Cross Coll., Washington, 1937; LLD (hon.), Stonehill Coll., 1962. Joined Congregation of Holy Cross, Roman Cath. Ch., 1929, ordained priest, 1941. Founder Family Rosary Crusade, 1942, host radio program, 1945—; founder Family Theater, Inc., 1947, Diocesan Family Rosary Crusades, London, Ont., Can., 1948, Crusade for Family Prayer, Inc., 1954; participant nationwide celebration of Marian Year The Philippines, 1984; participant crusades worldwide, 1954—; participant Internat. Eucharistic Congress, Phila., 1976, Peru Eucharistic Congress, 1988. Producer (TV shows) The Triumphant Hour, 1950, The Joyful Hour, 1950, Hill Number One, 1951, That I May See, 1951, A Star Shall Rise, 1952, Visitation, 1981, The Annunciation, 1991, Rosary Around the World with Father Peyton, 1991; (radio programs) The Joyful Mysteries of the Rosary, 1947, The Glorious Mysteries of the Rosary, 1948 (films) Resurrection, 1981, Nativity, 1982, Seven Last Words, 1982, Ascension, 1985, Descent of the Holy Spirit, 1985, Presentation, 1985, Finding at the Temple, 1985, Annunciation, 1985; author: The Ear of God, 1951, Father Peyton's Rosary Prayer Book, 1954, All For Her, 1968, A Man of Faith, 1983; subject of TV documentary A Dedicated Man, 1990. Founder All For Her Fund, 1969, FRC Found., Manila, 1976. Recipient George Washington Honor medal Freedom Found., 1954, Nat. Mass Media award Thomas Alva Edison Found., 1955, hon. 4th degree KC, 1956, Pro Ecclesia et Pontifice award Pope John XXIII, 1959, Pro Piis Meritis cross Knights of Malta, 1979, Maximilian Kolbe award Roman Cath. Ch., 1989, papal letters of commendation from Pius Xii, John XXIII, Paul VI, John Paul II; named Mayo Man of Yr., Govt. of Ireland, 1988. Address: Family Theater Prodns 7201 Sunset Blvd Hollywood CA 90046 also: The Family Rosary Inc Executive Park Dr Albany NY 12203 also: Family Rosary Crusade, Unit 502 Midtown Executive Homes, United Nations Ave, Paco Manila 1007, The Philippines

PFAFF, NANCY WATSON, religious ministry professional, consultant; b. Reno, Nev., Nov. 15, 1942; d. Kenneth James and Dorothy Emma (Palmer) Watson; m. Donald Chesley Pfaff, July 4, 1964; children: Kristina, Nicholas. BS, U. Nev., 1964; postgrad., Fuller Theol. Sem., 1985-88, Internat. Sch. Theology, 1989-90. Adminstrv. asst. Four Square Ch. Sparks, Nev.,

1981-83; owner Lifestyle Mgmt., Reno, 1983-90; staff cons. Ch. Resource Ministries, Fullerton, Calif., 1990—; pres. Nev. Ch. Growth, Reno, 1985—; del. Lausanne II in Manila Prayer Team, 1989. Editor Nev. Ch. Growth Newsletter, 1985—. Developer support group for Christian leaders Leader's in Fellowship Together, 1990—; coord. voluntary action ctr. United Way No. Nev., Reno, 1986. Mem. N.Am. Soc. for Ch. Growth (cert. ch. growth cons.), Aglow Club (pres. 1975-77), Toastmasters (membership chair 1985-86). Democrat. Office: Ch Resource Ministries 271 E Imperial Hwy #621 Fullerton CA 92635-5189

PFATTEICHER, PHILIP HENRY, minister, English educator; b. Phila., Oct. 29, 1935; s. Ernst P. and Esther T. (Linaka) P.; m. Lois Sharpless, June 24, 1961; children: Carl, Carolyn, Sarah, Linda. BA, Amherst Coll., 1957; BD, Luth. Theol. Sem., Phila., 1960; MA, U. Pa., 1960, PhD, 1966; STM, Union Theol. Sem., 1968. Ordained to ministry Evang. Luth. Ch. in Am., 1960. Asst. pastor Trinity Ch., Phila., 1960-64; pastor Bethany Ch., Bronx, N.Y., 1964-68; campus pastor East Stroudsburg (Pa.) U., 1968—, prof. English, 1968—, chmn. dept., 1978-83; mem. Liturgical Text Com., 1968-78, Task Force on Occasional Svcs., 1978-82; interim pastor Faith Luth. Ch., Pitts., 1989-90; Mellon Found. vis. scholar NYU, N.Y.C., 1985; lectr. in Christian Instns., Union Theol. Sem., N.Y.C., 1991—; adj. prof. Luth. Theol. Sem., Phila., 1991-92. Author: Lesser Festivals, 1975, Festivals and Commemorations, 1980, Commentary on Occasional Services, 1983, Foretaste of the Feast To Come, 1987, Commentary on the Lutheran Book of Worship, 1990, Dictionary of Liturgical Terms, 1991. Mem. MLA, Am. Acad. Religion, Hymn Soc. Am., Am. Acad. Liturgy, Soc. Bibl. Lit., Liturgical Conf., Nat. Coun. Tchrs. English, Classical Club (Phila.). Democrat. Home: 127 Village Dr Stroudsburg PA 18360 Office: East Stroudsburg U East Stroudsburg PA 18301 *It is in maintaining faith with the past that we are best prepared to be open to the future.*

PFAU, JOANN GRACE, youth ministry coordinator; b. Longview, Wash., June 2, 1967; d. Dalton Charles and Paula Grace (Kalanick) P. BA in Religious Studies, St. Martins Coll., Lacey, Wash., 1989. Religious edn. asst. St. Mary's Ch., Kelso, Wash., 1986-88 summers; youth ministry coord. St. Cecilia's Ch., Bainbridge Island, Wash., 1989—; bd. dirs. CHANNEL Ministry Tng. Program, Seattle, 1990—. Recipient Eagle of the Cross award Archdiocese of Seattle, 1894. Mem. Archdiocesan Assn. of Youth Mins. (regional rep. 1989-91). Office: St Cecilias Ch 1310 Madison Ave N Bainbridge Island WA 98110

PFAUTCH, ROY, minister, public affairs consultant; b. St. Louis, June 24, 1936; s. Floyd and Bertha Edna (Berghoefer) P. AB, Washington U., St. Louis, 1957; BD, Princeton Theol. Sem., 1961. Ordained to ministry Presbyn. Ch., 1961. Asst. to pres. Princeton Theol. Sem., 1961-63; pres. Civic Service, Inc., St. Louis and Washington, 1963—; mem. adv. com. on voluntary fgn. aid, U.S. Dept. State, 1981-83, Nat. Service Council, 1982-83. Del. Rep. Nat. Conv., Dallas, 1984; co-chmn. Nat. Day Prayer, 1985, 89, hon. co-chmn. Presdl. Inaugural, Washington, 1985, 89; chmn. Salute to Pres. Dinner, Washington, 1986; bd. overseers Reagan scholars program Eureka (Ill.) Coll., 1982-89; mem. presbytery Elijah Prish Lovejoy, United Presbyn. Ch., 1961—; bd. dirs. St. Louis Pub. Library System, 1980-86; del. XXIV Olympics, Seol, 1988. Mem. Internat. Assn. Polit. Cons., Am. Assn. Polit. Cons. (v.p., sec., pres. 1980-84) Am. Assn. Pub. Opinion Research, Mktg. Research Assn., Council Pub. Polls. Clubs: St. Louis, Noonday, Racquet (St. Louis), University (Washington). Avocations: horse riding, gardening, reading. Home: 52 Portland Pl Saint Louis MO 63108 Office: Civic Service Inc 1 Mercantile Ctr Room 2612 Saint Louis MO 63101 also: Civic Service Inc 1050 Connecticut Ave NW Suite 870 Washington DC 20036

PFEIFER, MICHAEL DAVID, bishop; b. Alamo, Tex., May 18, 1937; s. Frank and Alice (Savage) P. Student, Oblate Sch. Theology. Ordained priest Roman Cath. Ch., 1964, bishop, 1985; mem. Missionary Oblates of Mary Immaculate. Priest Roman Cath. Ch., Mexico City, 1964-1981; provincial-superior of Oblate So. U.S. Province Roman Cath. Ch., San Antonio, 1981-85; bishop Roman Cath. Ch., San Angelo, Tex., 1985—. Address: PO Box 1829 San Angelo TX 76902

PFNÜR, VINZENZ, theology educator; b. Berchtesgaden, Bavaria, Germany, June 16, 1937; s. Vinzenz and Sophie (Brandner) P.; m. Brigitte Birkenstock, Feb. 25, 1969; children: Vinzenz, Martin, Johannes, Maria. Diploma in Theology, U. Bonn, Fed. Repubic of Germany, 1963; D in Theology, U. Münster, Fed. Repubic of Germany, 1970. From asst. to prof. in theology U. Münster, 1969—. Editor Theologische Revue, 1971—; contbr. articles on late-Medieval and Reformation history and on ecumenical theology (instification by faith). Mem. Joint Luth.-Roman Cath. Internat. Commn. Office: U Münster Cath Theol Sem, Johannisstr 8-10, D-4400 Münster Federal Republic of Germany

PHAN, PETER CHO, theology educator, reseacher; b. Nha Trang, Viet Nam, Jan. 5, 1943; came to U.S., 1975, naturalized, 1982; s. Hien Van Phan and So Thi Le. BA, U. London, 1968, PhD, 1986; BD, Salesian Pontifical U., Italy, 1971, S.T.L., 1972, S.T.D., 1978. Asst. prof. theology U. Dallas, Irving, 1975-80, assoc. prof., 1980-86, prof., 1986—, chmn. dept. theology, 1980—, dir. PhD program theology, 1980-85. Author: Social Thought, The Message of the Fathers of the Church, 1984, Culture and Eschatology, 1985, Grace and the Human Condition, 1988, Eternity in Time: A Study of Karl Rahner's Eschatology, 1988. Arthur Vining Davis faculty devel. grantee U. Dallas, 1979; NEH faculty devel. grantee, 1985, King fellow, 1987. Mem. Cath. Theol. Soc. Am., Coll. Theology Soc., Am. Acad. Religion, Council S.W. Theol. Schs. (v.p. 1984—), Sch. Theology Laity (bd. dirs. 1984—).

PHARIS, WILLIAM HENRY, III, pastor; b. Ft. Worth, Apr. 10, 1953; s. W.H. Jr. and Jeanne Anne (Marti) P.; m. Sherry McLune, Jan. 4, 1975; children: William Henry IV, Jonathan Edward. BA, TCU, 1974; ThM, Dallas Theol. Sem., 1980. Youth pastor St. Luke United Meth. Ch., Halton City, Tex., 1972-76; asst. pastor Indian Hills Community Ch., Lincoln, Nebr., 1984-88; sr. pastor Trinity Bible Ch., Aledo, Tex., 1988—. Mem. Evang. Theol. Soc., Conf. on Faith & History. Home: 103 Black Forest Weatherford TX 76086 Office: Trinity Bible Ch PO Box 213 Aledo TX 76008

PHELAN, CAROLE MARY ROSS, minister, writer; b. Sydney, New South Wales, Australia, Dec. 30, 1925; came to U.S., 1962; d. Henry James and Elizabeth Maud (Shaw) Stevens; m. Christopher Joseph Phelan, Dec. 23, 1953; 1 child, Colin Michael Ross. BBA, Clarks Coll., London, 1942; DD, Philpots Sem., London, 1956. Sec. to dir. Archers Film Prodns., London, 1943-45; editorial asst. Hutchinson & Co., London, 1945-50; sec. to gen. mgr. Kemsley Newspapers, London, 1951-53; tchr. Philpots Sem., 1956-62; dir. edn. Universal Mind Sci. Ch., Long Beach, Calif., 1971-72; adminstr. Mountain View, Calif., 1972-74; treas.-sec., minister, tchr. Aquarian Horizon Centre, Los Angeles, Cupertino and Santa Barbara, Calif., 1975-86; pres., sec., minister, tchr. Los Angeles, 1987—. Author: Why Meditation?, 1988; contbr. articles on self-devel. and metaphysics to profl. jours. Home and Office: Aquarian Horizon Ctr 10760 Rose Ave Ste 304 Los Angeles CA 90034

PHELAN, MARY BENEDICT, religious administrator, editor, researcher, consultant; b. Galesburg, Ill., Mar. 4, 1902; d. John Francis and Ellen Victorine (Malone) P. BA, Clarke Coll., 1924; MA, U. So. Calif., 1928; PhD, Cath. U. Am., 1941; LittD (hon.), Loras Coll., 1967; LLD (hon.), U. Dubuque, 1969, Clarke Coll., 1974. Joined Sisters of Charity, B.V.M., Roman Cath. Ch., 1931. Tchr., adminstr. Burbank (Calif.) Pub. Schs., 1925-31; prof., chmn. dept. psychology and edn. Mundelein Coll., Chgo., 1934-57; pres. Clarke Coll., Dubuque, Iowa, 1957-69; corp. rep. Sisters of Charity, B.V.M., Dubuque, Iowa, 1970-79; editor, researcher, cons. Sisters of Charity, B.V.M., 1970—; mem. Gov's. Commn. on Status of Women, Des Moines, 1964-68; cons. HEW div. Coll. Support, Washington, 1968, 69; various commns. Arts, religion. Author: Report of the President for Twelve Years, 1969 (Merit award 1969); contbr. articles to profl. jours. Vol. letter writter Amnesty Internat., Nederland, Colo., 1970—, tutor Lit. Vols. Chgo., 1975—. Recipient George Washington Honor medal Freedoms Found., 1965, Disting. Civil Service award Dubuque Area C. of C., 1967, 1970 Am. Alumni Achievement award in Edn. Cath. U. Am., 1970; Mary Benedict Hall named in her honor Clarke Coll., 1974. Mem. Am. Psychol. Assn. (emeritus mem.). Home and Office: 6364 N Sheridan Rd Chicago IL 60660

PHELAN, THOMAS, clergyman, educator; b. Albany, N.Y., Apr. 11, 1925; s. Thomas William and Helen (Rausch) P. A.B. (N.Y. State Regents scholar 1942, President's medal 1945), Coll. Holy Cross, Worcester, Mass., 1945; S.T.L., Catholic U. Am., 1951; postgrad., Oxford (Eng.) U., 1958-59, 69-70. Ordained priest Roman Cath. Ch., 1951; pastor, tchr., adminstr. Diocese of Albany, 1951-58; resident Cath. chaplain Rensselaer Poly. Inst., Troy, N.Y., 1959-72; prof. history, dean Sch. Humanities and Social Scis. Rensselaer Poly. Inst., 1972—; pastor Christ Sun of Justice Univ. Parish, Troy, 1971—; chmn. architecture and bldg. commn. Diocese Albany, 1968—; cons. in field. Author Hudson Mohawk Gateway, 1985; author monographs, articles, revs. in field. Pres. Hudson-Mohawk Indsl. Gateway, 1971-84, bd. dirs., exec. com., 1984—; mem. WMHT Ednl. Telecommunications, 1966-77, 84-90, chmn., 1973-77; chmn. Troy Hist. Dist. and Landmarks Rev. Commn., 1975-86, chmn. adv. com., 1987—; v.p. Preservation League N.Y. State, 1979-82, mem. trustees council, 1982-87; pres. Preservation League N.Y. State, 1987-89; sec. and bd. dirs. Partners for Sacred Places, 1989—; bd. dirs. Hall of History Found., 1983-87. Served with USN, 1943-46. Recipient Paul J. Hallinan award Nat. Newman Chaplains Assn., 1967; ann. award Albany Arts League, 1977; Disting. Community Service award Rensselaer Poly. Inst., 1979; Edward Fox Demers medal Alumni Assn. Rensselaer Poly. Inst., 1986; Disting. Service award Hudson-Mohawk Consortium of Colls. and Univs., 1988; named Citizen Laureate of the N.Y. State U. Found. at Albany, 1988; Danforth Found. fellow, 1969-70; grantee Homeland Found., 1958-59; grantee Dorothy Thomas Found., 1969-70. Fellow Soc. Arts, Religion and Contemporary Culture; mem. Ch. Soc. Coll. Work (dir., exec. com. 1970—), Am. Conf. Acad. Deans, Liturgical Conf., Soc. Indsl. Archaeology, Assn. Internat. pour l'Etudes des Religions Prehistoriques et Ethnologiques, Cath. Campus Ministry Assn., Cath. Art Assn., Assn. for Religion and the Intellectual Life (bd. dirs. 1987—). Clubs: Ft. Orange, Troy Country; Squadron A (N.Y.C.). Home: 5 Whitman Ct Troy NY 12180 Office: Rensselaer Poly Inst Troy NY 12180 *Service and community building have motivated most of my business and personal actions. I received these values from my parents and from the church. I work to make positive contributions towards a world in which there is more justice and consequent hope of peace.*

PHELPS, C. RONALD, chaplaincy training director; b. Flint, Mich., Mar. 31, 1930; s. Maurice Edwin and Iva Pauline (McCullough) P.; m. Audrey Eleanor Hormel, Apr. 22, 1955; children: Diane, Donna, Deborah. BA, Grand Canyon Coll., 1958; BD, Southwestern Bapt. Theol. Sem., Ft. Worth, 1961, MDiv, 1973. Ordained to ministry So. Bapt. Conv., 1959. Pastor 1st Bapt. Ch., Lingleville, Tex., 1959-61; assoc. pastor Cen. Bapt. Ch., Flint, Mich., 1961-63; chaplain trainee Fed. Bur. Prisons, El Reno, Okla., 1963-64; staff chaplain VA Med. Ctr., Allen Park, Mich., 1964-86; dir. chaplain tng. and devel. Dept. Vets. Affairs, Hampton, Va., 1986—; dept. chaplain Mich. dept. Am. Legion, Lansing, 1979-80. Staff sgt. USAF, 1948-52. Mem. Nat. VA Chaplains Assn., Mil. Chaplains Assn. U.S.A. (Disting. Svc. award 1991). Office: Nat VA Chaplain Tng Ctr VA Medical Ctr (004) Hampton VA 23667

PHELPS, DENNIS LANE, minister, educator; b. Monroe, La., July 23, 1955; s. Vaughn Lavelle and Vestal (Humphreys) P.; m. Robbin Jean Loewer, May 27, 1979; 1 child, Kristen Lane. BA, La. Coll., 1978; MDiv, New Orleans Bapt. Theol. Sem., 1981; PhD, Southwestern Bapt. Theol. Sem., 1990. Ordained to ministry Bapt. Ch., 1978. Coord. ch. ministries La. Moral and Civic Found., Baton Rouge, 1973-79; staff evangelist Dennis Phelps Evangelistic Ministries, 1979—; pastor Brownfields Bapt. Ch., Baton Rouge, 1981-82; grader/teaching fellow Southwestern Bapt. Theol. Sem., Ft. Worth, 1982-87; pastor St. Francis Village Protestant Fellowship, Crowley, Tex., 1986-88; asst. prof. of preaching Bethel Theol. Sem., St. Paul, 1988—; cert. instr. MasterLife Discipleship Tng. of So. Bapt. Conv., 1983. tchr. adult Sunday sch. U. Bapt. Ch., Ft. Worth, 1983-86. Named Outstanding Young Men of Am., U.S. Jaycees, 1983-85, 89. Mem. Inst. of Bibl. Rsch., Religious Speech Communications Assn., Acad. of Homiletics, Am. Assn. of Religion, Soc. Bibl. Lit., Assn. Practical Theology. Office: Bethel Theol Sem 3949 Bethel Dr Saint Paul MN 55112

PHELPS, DOUGLAS ALAN, music and worship minister; b. Kewanee, Ill., Jan. 2, 1951; s. Ray Edward and Donna Rachael (Williamson) P.; m. Marcia Sue Hall, May 20, 1972; children: Stephanie Sue, Christopher Alan, Rebecca Sue. Student, Ozark Christian Coll., Joplin, Mo., 1969-70; B of Music Edn., Nebr. U., 1973; MMus, Southwestern Bapt. Theol. Sem., Ft. Worth, 1978. Ordained to ministry Christian Ch., 1978. Prof. Dallas Christin Coll., 1975-81, Ozark Christian Coll., 1981-85; min. music and worship Gateway Christian Ch., Aurora, Colo., 1985—; com. mem. N.Am. Christian Conv., Cin., 1991-93; officer Assn. Christian Coll. Educators, Joplin, 1975-85. Co-author: Let's Make a Joyful Noise . . . Together, 1989; contbr. articles on music ministry to mags.; producer albums Revelation, 1978-80. Office: Gateway Christian Ch 14700 E Mississippi Ave Aurora CO 80012

PHELPS, JUSTIN ANDREW, deacon, retired surgeon; b. Bergenfield, N.J., May 7, 1925; s. Chester Arthur and Marie Annette (Mesereau) P.; m. Charlotte Rose Kistka, Feb. 27, 1954; children: Marie Anne, Barbara Jean, Angela Rose, Paul Andrew. BA, Canisius Coll., Buffalo, 1944; MD, U. Buffalo, 1947. Diplomate Am. Bd. Surgery. Deacon Cathedral of Our Lady of Lourdes, Diocese of Spokane (Wash.), 1980—. Capt. USAF, 1954-56. Fellow ACS. Home: N 14711 Gleneden Dr Spokane WA 99208 Office: Cathedral Our Lady Lourdes W 1115 Riverside Spokane WA 99201 *I never cease to recognize similarities and parallels between the good and bad in the practice of medicine and ministry in the church. I am convinced medical care and practice and humanity's spiritual and material lot would both be improved by increased humility, compassion and love of God and neighbor.*

PHERIGO, LINDSEY PRICE, religion educator; b. Miami, Fla., Dec. 29, 1920; s. Ezekiel Lindsey and Dorothy Price (Richardson) P.; m. Viola May Schmitt, Feb. 22, 1942; children: Linda Jane, Stephen Albert, Ruth Armet, Robert Price. BAE, U. Fla., 1942; STB, Boston U., 1945, PhD, 1951. Reader in Biblical history Wellesley (Mass.) Coll., 1947-49; instr. in religion Syracuse (N.Y.) U., 1949-51; asst. prof. religion Scarritt Coll., Nashville, 1951-53, prof. of Bible, 1953-56, Clara Perry prof. Christian life and thought, 1956-59, acad. dean, 1957-59; vis. instr. in New Testament Vanderbilt Divinity Sch., Nashville, 1954-59; prof. New Testament and early ch. history St. Paul Sch. Theology, Kansas City, Mo., 1959-86, prof. emeritus, 1986—; cons. in Bible and theology The Village Ch., Prairie Village, Kans., 1977-91. Author: The Great Physician, 1983, revised edit. 1991; contbr. articles to profl. publs. Edmund M. Beebe fellow, 1946, Ford Found. fellow, 1952; Lindsey P. Pherigo chair in New Testament named in his honor, 1986. Mem. Soc. Biblical Lit. Democrat. Methodist. Avocations: classical music, photography, stamps, coins, books. Home: 4960 Westwood Rd Kansas City MO 64112 Office: St Paul Sch Theology 5123 Truman Rd Kansas City MO 64127

PHIBBS, GARNETT ERSIEL, engineer, educator, minister, religious organization administrator; b. Clinchfield, Va., Oct. 12, 1922; s. Willie McDonald and Alma Irene (Horton) P.; m. Aug. 18, 1945 (div. 1972); children: Gerald Edwin, David Miller, Robert Lee. BA, Bridgewater (Va.) Coll., 1943; MRE, Bethany Theol. Sem., 1945; BDiv, Yale U., 1952, STM, 1954; postgrad., Boston U., Princeton U., St. Louis U. Cert. tchr., Calif. Pastor Ch. of the Brethren, Bassett, Va., 1945-50, Champaign, Ill., 1955-56, Wilmington, Del., 1956-57, Glendale, Calif., 1969-70; pastor Niantic (Conn.) Bapt. Ch., 1950-51, Congl. Ch., Killingworth, Conn., 1951-55; exec. dir. Coun. of Chs., Trenton, N.J., 1957-62, Toledo, 1962-69; exec. dir. Citizens Aiding Pub. Offenders, Toledo, 1974-76; engr. Beverly Hills (Calif.) Hotel, 1981-91; mem., cons., leader Parents Without Ptnrs., 1972-90, ; mem. Habitat for Humanity, 1989-91; cons. North Toledo Community Orgn., 1977; co-founder Rescue Crisis Svc.; founder Interfaith Housing Corp., Toledo. Author: Bethel Memory Makers, 1977; contbr. articles to profl. jours. Mem. Toledo Bd. of Community Rels., 1962-69, Ohio State Civil Rights Commn. of N.W. Ohio, Toledo, 1966-68, U.S. Civil Rights Commn., Toledo, 1965-69, Planned Parenthood Bd., Fraternal Com. Toledo, Spain; mem., past pres. Kiwanis Internat., 1945-69; founding bd. dirs. West Hollywood Homeless Orgn. Recipient Community Svc. award NAACP, 1960, So. Calif. Regional award Parents Without Parents, 1980; named Man of the Yr., ACLU, 1969. Mem. Internat. Union Oper. Engrs., Am. Correctional Assn., Am. Assn. for Pub. Adminstrs., Calif. Assn. Marriage and Family Counselors, Halfway House Assn, Parents and Friends of Gays and Lesbians. Democrat. Avocations: gardening, theater, camping. Home: 1136 N Larrabee # 304 West Hollywood CA 90069-2050 also: care The Mulls 2364 Robinwood St Toledo OH 43620

PHILBRICK, ANN MATHEWS, minister; b. Phila., May 22, 1956; d. John Alden III and Marion Francis (Broadbent) P. Student, Vassar Coll., 1974-76; BA in Geography, U. N.C., Chapel Hill, 1978; MDiv, Princeton Theol. Sem., 1982. Ordained to ministry Presbyn. Ch. Assoc. pastor Covenant Presbyn. Ch., Madison, Wis., 1982-90; pastor Christ United Presbyn. Ch., Carnegie, Pa., 1990—; chairperson United Christian Resource Ctr., Sun Prarie, Wis., 1987-90, bd. dirs. Mem. Great Lake Assn. of Ch. Educators (state rep. 1983-86, treas. 1986-89), Pi Beta Phi (chmn. alumni com. adv. club 1988-90). Office: Christ United Presbyn Ch 428 Washington Ave Carnegie PA 15106-2729

PHILIPP, THOMAS J., minister; b. Des Moines, Feb. 20, 1936; s. William Bernard and Martha Adele (Mack) P. BA, Macalester Coll., St. Paul, 1958; MDiv, Union Theol. Sem., N.Y.C., 1962; MA, SUNY, Albany, 1966. Ordained to ministry, Presbyn. Ch. USA. Asst. minister Jermain Meml. Presbyn. Ch., Albany, N.Y., 1962-65; campus minister Oswego (N.Y.) Protestant Campus Ministry, 1965-72; asst. prof. SUNY, Oswego, 1968-72; pastor Community Presbyn. Ch., Merrick, N.Y., 1982—; minister higher edn. L.I. United Campus Ministries, Merrick, N.Y., 1972—; v.p. Middle Earth Crisis Counseling, Bellmore, N.Y., 1982—; treas. Ctr. for Family Resources, Hempstead, N.Y., 1985—. Bd. dirs. Planned Parenthood of Nassau, Hempstead, 1985—, Fedn. Justice Agencies, Hempstead, 1982; bd. dirs., former pres. Nassau Citizens Budget Com., 1972—. Mem. Nat. Campus Ministers Assn. (sec. 1979-81), Presbyn. Ministers in Higher Edn. Democrat. Home: 34 Wynsum Ave Merrick NY 11566

PHILIPPE, SISTER PAULITA, nun; b. Livingston, Ill., May 12, 1937; d. Paul and Emma (Martinelli) P. BA, DePaul U., Chgo.; MA in Religious Edn., Aquinas Inst., Grand Rapids, Mich. Entered Dominican Sisters, Roman Cath. Ch. Tchr. various cath. schs., Springfield, Ill., 1959-78; dir. religious edn. various chs., 1978—, St. Thomas the Apostle Ch., Decatur, Ill. Mem. Ill. Parish Coord. & Dirs. Assn. Home: 4002 Lourdes Dr Decatur IL 62526 Office: St Thomas Apostle Ch 2160 N Edward St Decatur IL 62526

PHILIPS, JAMES DAVISON, minister; b. Peason, La., May 22, 1920; s. Volney Graham and Eleanor Margaret (Davison) P.; m. Katherine Wright; children: James Davison Jr., June Eleanor, Graham Gordon. BA, Hampden-Sydney Coll., 1940; BD, Columbia Theol. Seminary, 1943; PhD, U. Edinburgh, Scotland, 1955; (hon.) DD, Presbyn. Coll., Hampden-Sydney, 1962, 63. Ordained to ministry, Presbyn. Ch., 1943. Asst. pastor First Presbyn. Ch., Atlanta, 1947-50; pastor First Presbyterian Ch., Thomasville, Ga., 1950-54, Decatur (Ga.) Presbyn. Ch., 1954-75; pres. Columbia Theol. Seminary, Decatur, 1975-86; also, bd. dirs., Columbia Theol. Seminary; trustee, Presbyn. Coll., Agnes Scott Coll. Chmn. Mayor's Adv. Com., Decatur, 1962-70. Chaplain USNR, 1943-46. Named Mr. DeKalb, Am. Red Cross, Decatur, 1987, Sr. Citizen of the Yr., Lions Club, Decatur, 1987. Mem. Rotary, Druid Hills Golf Club. Avocations: golf, fishing, travel. Home: 133 Pinecrest Ave Decatur GA 30030

PHILLIP, MALCOLM IRVING, minister; b. Basseterre, St. Christopher and Nevis, Apr. 26, 1934; came to U.S., 1980; naturalized, 1988; s. Glennis Phillip and Maisie (Walters) P.; m. Chessie Perlina Constant, Aug. 28, 1958; children: Randoline, Randolph, Alden. Ministerial cert., Caribbean Wesleyan Coll., 1958; BTh, God's Bible Sch. Coll., 1978; ThM, Internat. Sem., 1983, ThD, 1984, DD (hon.), 1985. Ordained to ministry Ch. of God, 1965. Pastor Wesleyan Ch., St. Christopher and Nevis, 1958-63; pastor Ch. of God, St. Christopher and Nevis, 1963-72, Antigua, 1978-80, Cin., 1980-89; evangelist St. Christopher and Nevis, 1972-76. Author: Reflections of Excellent Spirits, 1983, Developing and Delivering a Sermon, 1983, Bible Theology Made Simple, 1983. Mem. North Avondale Neighborhood Assn., Cin., 1984. Mem. United Assn. Christian Counselors (cert.). Home: 759 Clinton Springs Ave Cincinnati OH 45229

PHILLIPS, ALAN LEROY, minister; b. Rome, N.Y., May 17, 1949; s. Francis Elliot and Allie Mae (Jones) P.; m. Sharon Leah Porter, Aug. 22, 1970; children: Rachel, Luke, Chelsea. BS, Abilene (Tex.) Christian U., 1971, MDiv, 1982, postgrad., 1990—. Ordained to ministry Ch. of Christ, 1973. Youth minister Ch. of Christ, Clyde, Tex., 1974-75; assoc. minister Ch. of Christ, Brownsville, Tex., 1975-76; dir. Internat. Mission, N.Y.C., 1978-89; minister Ch. of Christ, Temple Hills, Md., 1989—; affiliate UN, N.Y.C., 1978—; deacon Manhattan Ch. of Christ, N.Y.C., 1979-89. Co-author: Eyewitness News, 1980. Area coord. Rep. party, N.Y.C., 1980-89. With USN, 1971-73. Mem. Tchrs. English as Second Lang., N.Y. Road Runners. Home: 4005 Beachcraft Ct Temple Hills MD 20748 Office: Oxon Hill Ch of Christ 4201 Brinkley Rd Temple Hills MD 20748

PHILLIPS, ALFRED PATRICK, educator, priest; b. Mobile, Ala., Mar. 17, 1927; s. Alfred Yancey and Rosa Layet (Parker) P. BS, Spring Hill Coll., 1952; Licentiate in Philosophy, MA, St. Louis U., 1958, STL, 1963; ThM, St. Mary's U., 1969. Joined Soc. of Jesus, 1952; ordained priest Roman Cath. Ch., 1963. Prof. philosophy and theology Loyola U., New Orleans, 1963-76, dir. religious studies program, 1969, dean campus ministries, 1973-76; dir. Jesuit Spirituality Ctr., rector St. Charles Coll., Grand Coteau, La., 1976—; rector, sr. tchr. Jesuit Coll. Preparatory Sch., 1986—, trustee 1986—; lectr. theology and philosophy St. Patrick's Coll., Ottawa, Ont., Can., 1967-68, U. Ibero-Americana, Mexico City, Mexico, 1966; lectr. theology and spirituality local community; co-founder Christian Friends for Social Action in La., 1972. Mem. La. Coalition Campus Mins., Jesuit Campus Ministry Assn., Sigma Alpha Kappa. Office: St Charles Coll Grand Coteau LA 70541

PHILLIPS, ANNABELLE W., religion educator, elementary school principal; b. Charleston, W.Va., Feb. 13, 1926; d. Richard and Anna (Littleton) Ward; m. Edward Eugene Phillips, Jan. 7, 1949; c1 child, Twyla Phillips Johnson. BA, Trevecca Nazarene Coll., 1948; MA, U. So. Miss., 1968. Sun. sch. tchr. Ch. of the Nazarene, Ala., 1944-91, music minister, 1988-91, ch. organist, 1971-91; prin. Nazarene Elem. Sch., Ala., 1988—, ch. pianist, missionary pres., 1949-89; elem. sch. prin. Mobile (Ala.) County Pub. Schs., 1951-88; elem. sch. bd. dirs. First Ch. of the Nazarene, Mobile, 1988—, mem. official bd., 1978-90. Edn. rep. United Way, Mobile, 1968-88; vol. Am. Heart Assn., Mobile, 1986-88. Named Mother of the Yr. City of Mobile, 1971. Mem. NEA, Ala. Edn. Assn., Mobile County Edn. Assn., Nazarene Internat. Edn. Assn. Home: 709 Oak Field Dr PO Box 91447 Mobile AL 36691 Office: First Ch of the Nazarene 669 Azalea Rd Mobile AL 36609-1515

PHILLIPS, BEVERLY GAY, lay worker; b. Wilmington, N.C., July 31, 1954; d. Quince Joshua and Mary Ila (Butler) P.; m. David Thomas Phillips, Nov. 5, 1978; children: Beverly Lynn, Quincy Thomas, Nickolas Mark. BA in Physical Edn. and Recreation, U. N.C., Wilmington, 1975. Youth leader Dublin (N.C.) Pentecostal Free Will Bapt. Ch., 1970-75; tchr. Sunday sch. Delco (N.C.) Pentecostal Free Will Bapt. Ch., 1978—; choir leader Delco Pentecostal Free Will Bapt. Ch., 1980—, youth leader, 1981—. Home: Rte 1 Box 548 Delco NC 28436

PHILLIPS, CALVIN L., academic administrator. Pres. Emmanuel Sch. Religion, Johnson City, Tenn. Office: Emmanuel Sch Religion 1 Walker Dr Johnson City TN 37601*

PHILLIPS, CHRIS ALLEN, youth minister; b. Princeton, W.Va., Aug. 24, 1962; s. Harold and Betty Jane (Cooper) P.; m. Kari Yvonne Wade, May 24, 1986; 1 child, Aaron Todd. BA in Theology & Youth Ministry, Berkshire Christian Coll., 1985. Youth min. Advent Christian Ch., New Albany, Ind., 1986-91, Mechanicsville, Va., 1991—; nat. youth bd. chmn. Advent Christian Gen. Conf. Am., Charlotte, N.C., 1990—. Vol. football coach New Albany Youth Football League, 1986, 87. Mem. Nat. Network of Youth Mins. Home: 6317 Studley Rd Mechanicsville VA 23111

PHILLIPS, DOROTHY ALEASE, lay church worker, educator; b. Durham, N.C., May 11, 1924; d. Clarence Robert and Addie Lee (Outen) Hicks; m. Chester Raymond Phillips, Oct. 10, 1942; children: Cynthia Kaye, Dean Hayward, Kent Vincent. BS in Edn. and English, Bob Jones U., 1954; M in Edn., East Carolina U., 1970. Cert. secondary tchr., N.C. Former writer, illustrator Sunday sch. lit. Ayden (N.C.) Press.; former nat. youth chmn. women's aux. Free Will Bapts.; dir. pub. rels. and Christian edn. Heritage Bapt. Ch., Johnson City, Tenn., 1980-91; participant Blue Ridge Mountain Christian Writers Conf., Black Mountain, N.C.; former tchr. journalism Rose High Sch., Greenville, N.C.; mem. choirs, Sunday sch. tchr. various Bapt. chs. Home: 1601 Paty Dr Johnson City TN 37604 *My dual role, as a high school teacher and a minister's wife, has afforded me wonderful opportunities to know and love many people. I have found joy in serving others.*

PHILLIPS, HAROLD L., clergyman; b. Wichita Falls, Tex., May 4, 1955; s. Harry and Bea (Rountree) P.; m. Cindy Johnson, Aug. 13, 1977; children: Jeff, Cory, Mark. BA in Ministry, Dallas Christian Coll., 1977. Ordained to ministry. Minister First Christian Ch., Davis, Okla., 1977-78; youth minister Meml. Park Christian Ch., Tulsa, 1978-82; assoc. minister Draper Park Christian Ch., Oklahoma City, 1982-86, Littleton (Colo.) Christian Ch., 1986-91; minister Mt. Branson (Mo.) Christian Ch., 1991—; pres. Okla. Christian Youth Conv., 1986, Colo. Christian Youth Conv., 1990; trustee Colo. Christian Svc. Camp, 1989-91. Republican. Home and Office: Mt Branson Christian Ch PO Box 5052 Branson MO 65616

PHILLIPS, JAMES ALLEN, clergyman; b. Monahans, Tex., Aug. 21, 1952; s. James Allen and Margeret (Webb) P.; divorced; 1 child, Amber Mashea. Assoc. in Bibl. Studies, Nazarene Bible Coll., Colorado Springs, Colo., 1980; student U. Colo., 1981. Ordained to ministry Ind. Holiness Ch., 1985. Registered evangelist Ch. of Nazarene, Colorado Springs, 1979-81; assoc. pastor Trinity Ch. of Nazarene, Abilene, Tex., 1982-83, Moore Ch. of Nazarene, Okla., 1984; founder. dir. S.O.L.O. Sch. Ministry, Moore, 1985; founder, dir. Bet-Limud Biblical Inst., Moore, 1986—; dir. edn. Bet Ami, Oklahoma City, 1987—; ednl. dir. Congregation Bet Ami, 1987—. Mem. Simon Wiesenthal Ctr., Internat. Christian Embassy Jerusalem. Served with USN, 1971-77. Mem. Am. Assn. Counseling and Devel., Wesleyan Theol. Soc., Union of Councils for Soviet Jews, Simon Wiesenthal Ctr. Avocations: technical rock climbing; ice climbing; mountaineering. Office: 3629 NW 19th St Oklahoma City OK 73107

PHILLIPS, JAMES MCJUNKIN, mission organization administrator; b. Pitts., Mar. 21, 1929; s. Harry Pursell and Ruth (McJunkin) P.; m. Ruth Henning, June 29, 1957; children: Catherine Ann, Marjorie Ruth. AB, Princeton U., 1949, PhD, 1959; BDiv, Yale U., 1955. Missionary, instr. Presbyn. Mission, Korea, Seoul, 1949-52; missionary, prof. Presbyn. Ch. U.S.A. in Japan, Tokyo, 1959-75; vis. prof. San Francisco Theol. Sem., San Anselmo, Calif., 1975-82; assoc. dir. Overseas Ministries Study Ctr., New Haven and Ventnor, N.J., 1983—. Author: From the Rising of the Sun, 1981; assoc. editor Internat. Bull. Missionary Rsch., Ventor, New Haven, 1983—. Mem. organizing com. Coun. Asian Policies, Tokyo, 1970-72. Mem. Am. Soc. Ch. History, Am. Acad. Religion, Assn. Profs. of Mission (pres. 1986-87), Am. Soc. Missiology. Democrat. Presbyterian. Avocations: jogging, gardening, traveling. Home: 76 Jaenicke Ln Hamden CT 06517 Office: Overseas Ministries Study Ctr 490 Prospect St New Haven CT 06511-2196

PHILLIPS, JOHN ANDREW, minister; b. Wichita Falls, Tex., Dec. 3, 1951; s. Harry and Bea (Rountree) P.; m. Marie Aclin, Dec. 15, 1973; children: Joshua, David. B of Sacred Lit., Dallas Christian Coll., 1976. Ordained to ministry Christian Ch. (Disciples of Christ), 1979. Min. Antioch Christian Ch., Odessa, Tex., 1981-86; min. North Side Christian Ch., Oklahoma City, 1986—; pres. Odessa Ministerial Alliance, 1985-86. Named one of Outstanding Young Men in Am., 1983. Office: North Side Christian Ch 2526 NW 122d St Oklahoma City OK 73120-7004

PHILLIPS, KEITH WENDALL, minister; b. Portland, Oreg., Oct. 21, 1946; s. Frank Clark and Velma Georgina (Black) P.; m. Mary Katherine Garland, July 16, 1973; children: Joshua, Paul, David. BA, UCLA, 1968; MDiv, Fuller Theology Sem., 1971, D. of Ministries, 1972; LHD (hon.), John Brown U., 1990. Dir. Youth For Christ Clubs, L.A., 1965-71; pres. World Impact, L.A., 1971—; mem. urban ministries resources svcs. editorial adv. bd. Zondervan Pub. House; commencement speaker Tabor Coll., 1969, 91, John Brown U., 1990. Author: Everybody's Afraid in the Ghetto, 1973, They Dare to Love the Ghetto, 1975, The Making of a Disciple, 1981, No Quick Fix, 1985. Chmn. L.A. Mayor's Prayer Breakfast Com., 1985—. Named Disting. Staley lectr., 1969. Mem. Evangelistic Com. of Newark (pres. 1976—), World Impact of Can. (pres. 1978—), The Oaks (pres. 1985—), Faith Works (pres. 1987—). Baptist. Office: World Impact 2001 S Vermont Ave Los Angeles CA 90007 *Our knowledge of God's Word outruns our obedience. The challenge for Christians is to live what we know.*

PHILLIPS, LLOYD AUSTIN, minister; b. Utica, N.Y., Mar. 20, 1928; s. Harold H. and Margaret Patience (Jenkins) P.; m. Iva Jean Scott, June 19, 1948; children: John Lloyd, David Lane, Linda Marie Baker. BA, Houghton (N.Y.) Coll., 1951; BDiv, Calvin Sem., 1958, ThM, 1978. Ordained elder Meth. Ch. Pastor Oakdale Meth. Ch., Grand Rapids, Mich., 1953-61, Bronson (Mich.) First Meth. Ch., 1961-69, Stevensville (Mich.) United Meth. Ch., 1969-79, Mt. Hope United Meth. Ch., Lansing, Mich., 1979-84, Wesley United Meth. Ch., Niles, Mich., 1984—; pres. bd. dirs. Samaritan Counseling Ctr., Benton Harbor, Mich., 1977-79; co-dir. counseling svc. Programs for Prison Inmates, Lansing, Mich., 1982-84; dir. religious TV program Cornerstone, Lansing, 1980-83. Precinct chmn. Dem. Party, Stevensville, 1976; chmn. bd. Bronson (Mich.) Cemetary Assn., 1965-69. Ingham County Bd. of Suprs. grantee, 1984. Mem. Bibl. Archaeology Soc., Niles (Mich.) Area Ministerial Assn. (pres. ministers group 1990-91), Optimists (pres. elect Niles chpt. 1990-91, pres. 1991—), Rotary (song leader Bronson chpt. 1965-69). Home: 2486 US # 12 E Niles MI 49120 Office: Wesley United Meth Ch 302 Cedar Niles MI 49120-2612

PHILLIPS, MELVIN ROMINE, minister; b. Parkersburg, W.Va., July 10, 1921; s. Chester Corliss and Julia Augusta (Romine) P.; m. Carolyn Beckner, Aug. 12, 1944; children—Ann Elizabeth, Ruth Elaine, Ralph, Beth Carol. B.A., Alderson-Broaddus Coll., 1944; B.D., Colgate Rochester Div. Sch., 1946; postgrad. Marshall U., 1949-50. Ordained to ministry, Am. Bapt. Ch. U.S.A., 1946. Pastor, Mumford, N.Y., 1944-46, Kingwood-Masontown Bapt. Parish, W.Va., 1946-49; univ. pastor Marshall U., Huntington, W.Va., 1949-50; pastor First Bapt. Ch., Shelbyville, Ind., 1950-57; Anderson, Ind., 1957-67, Jamestown, N.Y., 1967-73; exec. minister Assoc. Chs. of Fort Wayne and Allen County, Ind., 1973-88; chaplain Towne House Retirement Ctr., 1989—; cons. Endowment Horizons, Inc. Bd. dirs. East Wayne St. Ctr., Ft. Wayne Rescue Mission, F.W. Com. of 24. Named Man of Yr., Jaycees, 1954; recipient Ecumenical citations in Anderson and Jamestown, Community Svc. award NAACP, 1966, A. Philip Randolph Humanitarian award, 1988. Mem. Ind. Council Chs. (bd. dirs., recipient Ecumenical citation 1964, pres. 1962-64), Am. Bapt. Hist. Soc., Clergy United for Action, N.Am. Acad. Ecumenists, Nat. Assn. Ecumenical Staff, Bibl. Archaeology Soc., Amnesty Internat. Club: Rotary. Home: 4616 Tacoma Ave Fort Wayne IN 46807 Office: Towne House Retirement Ctr 2209 St Joe Center Rd Fort Wayne IN 46825

PHILLIPS, NAT, JR., minister; b. Cleveland, Tenn., June 12, 1930; s. Nat Sr. and Grace (Quinn) P.; m. Dolores Cornett, Dec. 26, 1950; children: Stephen Quinn, Michelle Phillips Cole. BA, Carson-Newman Coll., 1950; MDiv, Southwestern Bapt. Theol. Sem., 1955; MA, Vanderbilt U., 1961; PhD, U. Tenn., 1967. Pastor Little Hope Bapt. Ch., Clarksville, Tenn., 1955-61; assoc. pastor First Bapt. Ch., Balboa, C.Z., 1961-63; pastor Fairview Bapt. Ch., Oak Ridge, Tenn., 1963-67, Evang. Bapt. Ch., Weirton, W.Va., 1967-68; assoc. prof. Tenn. Temple U., Chattanooga, 1968—; pastor South Dalton Bapt., Dalton, Ga., 1975-82; assoc. pastor Kingwood Bapt. Ch., Chattanooga, 1985—. Author: numerous corr. courses in pastoral studies, 1988-90; editor: The Evangelical, 1955-68, 1975-82. Avocations: woodwork, carpentry, hiking. Home: 3259 Ozark Circle Chattanooga TN 37415

PHILLIPS, RANDALL CLINGER, minister, university administrator; b. Santa Maria, Calif., Dec. 3, 1924; s. Glenn Randall and Ruth (Clinger) P.; children—Ruth Ann Phillips McKercher, Janet Lee Phillips Kessler, Melinda Lee. B.S. cum laude, U. So. Calif., 1946, M.Th., 1951, Th.D., 1966; D.Arts, Willamette U., 1963; D.D., Calif. Western U., 1964. Ordained to ministry Meth. Ch., 1947; minister Sherman Oaks, Calif., 1949-55, Burbank, Calif., 1955-59; minister Wilshire United Meth. Ch., 1959-78; sr. v.p. U.S. Internat. U., San Diego, 1978—; mem. exec. com. nat. bd. publs. United Meth. Ch.; pres. Inter-religious Council Los Angeles. Vice pres. bd. trustees Sch. Theology, Claremont, Calif.; bd. dirs., v.p. Portals House, Los Angeles; pres., chmn. bd. dirs. Midnight Mission Los Angeles, Wilshire YMCA; chmn. bd. Pacific Homes. Served to lt. (j.g.) USNR, 1943-47. Recipient Freedoms Found. award, 1967, 68. Mem. Los Angeles Council Chs. (pres. 1970-71), People to People Internat. (pres., trustee San Diego chpt.), Sertoma (chaplain, pres. Wilshire area club), Rotary, Masons (33 degree), Shriners, Kappa Alpha. Republican. Home: 10347 Caminito Goma San Diego CA 92131 Office: 10455 Pomerado Rd San Diego CA 92131

PHILLIPS, ROYCE WAYNE, pastor, educator; b. Abilene, Tex., June 26, 1953; s. Royce Lavalle and Velma Violet (Dixon) P.; m. Cindy Ruth Badman, June 13, 1977; children: Ruth Ann, Royce Alan, Alice Renee, David Wayne. ThG, Bapt. Bible Coll., 1975, BA, 1976; postgrad., U. Iowa, 1988-90; grad. of theology, Bapt. Bible Coll.; postgrad., Bapt. Christian U., Shreveport, Las., 1991—. Ordained to ministry Ind. Bapt. Ch., 1984. Asst. bus. dir. High St. Bapt. Ch., Springfield, Mo., 1975-76; asst. pastor Bapt. Tabernacle, Albany, N.Y., 1976-77, Bethel Bapt. Ch., Mt. Bethel, Pa., 1977-80; tchr., adminstr. Bethel Bapt. Ch., Santa Ana, Calif., 1980-83; pastor Tabernacle Bapt. Ch., Coralville, Iowa, 1983—; adminstr. Cornerstone Christian Sch., Coralville, 1986—; mem., del. Bapt. Bible Fellowship, Springfield, Mo., 1971—, Iowa Bapt. Bible Fellowship, Des Moines, 1983—. Twp. trustee County Govt., West Lucas Twp., Johnson County, 1988; mem. county cen. com. Rep. Orgn., Johnson County, 1984—. Republican. Home: 1413 Sycamore St Iowa City IA 52240 Office: Tabernacle Bapt Ch 1705 Second St Hwy 6 Coralville IA 52241 *So often the greatest attribute is endurance, the greatest characteristic perseverance. So often the problem is conquered simply by hammering at it until it crumbles.*

PHILLIPS, THOMAS KENT, minister; b. Corinth, Miss., Oct. 19, 1947; s. John Thomas and Dorothy Lorene (Conn) P.; m. Quida Jean Jobe, July 20, 1968; children: Cara Elizabeth, Molly Faith, Mathew Thomas. BA magna cum laude, U. Miss., 1970; MDiv, So. Bapt. Theol. Seminary, Louisville, Ky., 1974; DM, So. Bapt. Theol. Seminary, 1978. Ordained minister. Pastor Octuckalofa Bapt. Ch., Water Valley, Miss., 1969-70; street evangelist Walnut St. Bapt. Ch., Louisville, 1971; coordinator counseling and follow-up Billy Graham Evangelistic Assn., Mpls., 1975, asst. dir. counseling and follow-up, 1976-88, crusade dir., 1978-80, 81-86, sr. crusade dir., 1987—, program dir., 1987-89, dir. counseling and follow-up, 1989—; doctoral cand. supr. So. Bapt. Theol. Seminary, Louisville, 1982—; founder ARISE, Tacoma, Wash., 1988-89; lectr. spiritual awakening, 1985-89. Author: Prescription for a Slumbering Church, 1988; editor 30 Discipleship Exercises, 1981, Teen Scene, 1982, Roots, 1983; compiler: Jesus Loves Me, 1990. Bd. dirs. Greater Tacoma (Wash.) Christian Outreach Fellowship, 1984-89; v.p. Follow-Up Ministries, 1985—; bd. dirs. Creative Lifestyle Internat., 1988-89, Youth for Christ, 1989—. Mem. N. Am. Ch. Growth Soc., N.Am. Evangelists Network, Horizon Internat. Baptist. Avocations: speaking, jogging, assisting third world endavors, skiing, reading. Home: 5709 69th Ave Ct West Tacoma WA 98467 Office: Billy Graham Evangelistic 1300 Harmon Pl Minneapolis MN 55403 *All important values in life are built around relationships, one's relationship with God being the priority.*

PHILOTHEOS, bishop; b. Istanbul, Turkey, Sept. 1, 1924; came to U.S., 1960, naturalized, 1965; s. George and Lambrini Karamitsos. M.S.T., U. Athens, 1959; postgrad., Hunter Coll., N.Y.C., 1960-61, U. Scranton, 1962-64, Latin Am. Inst., N.Y.C., 1966-67. Ordained deacon Greek Orthodox Ch., 1950, priest, 1961; consecrated bishop, 1971; priest Annunciation Ch., Scranton, Pa., 1961-65, St. Eleftherios Ch., N.Y.C., 1965-71; aux. bishop to Archbishop Iakovos, N.Y.C., 1971—; dir. Eccles. Ct.; also bishop of Meloa; chief sec. Greek Orthodox Synod of Bishops in Ams.; former v.p. Greek Orthodox Clergy Fellowship Greater N.Y. Trustee, former gen. dir. St. Basil's Acad., Garrison, N.Y.; gen. dir. Archdiocese Registry and Philanthropies. elected to episcopate by Holy Synod of Ecumenical Patriarchate of Constantinople, 1971. Address: 8-10 E 79th St New York NY 10021

PHILPOT, FORD, minister, evangelist; b. Manchester, Ky., June 16, 1917; s. Granville and Wilamena (Reid) P.; m. Virginia, July 24, 1940; children: Timothy N., Daniel. Student, Asbury Coll., 1950, Asbury Sem., 1951; AB, BD, Emory U., 1952. Ordained to ministry Meth. Ch. Pres. Ford Philpot Evangelistic Assn., Lexington, Ky., 1954—, The Story Inc., Lexington, 1959-89. Author: Truth in the Morning, 1969, So You Want a MT?, 1964. 1st sgt. USMC, 1946. Republican. Home: 798 Cindy Blair Way Lexington KY 46503 Office: Ford Philpot Evangelistic Assn Inc Box 3000 Lexington KY

PHINNEY, FREDERICK WARREN, priest; b. Lawrence, Mass., May 15, 1922; s. Arthus Osgood and Lucile Snow (Flagg) P.; m. Eleanor Sanburn, May 31, 1947; children: Benjamin, Joanna, Frederick Jr., John, Martha, Harriet. AB, Harvard U., 1943; MDiv, Episc. Theol. Sch., Cambridge, Mass., 1948. Ordained priest Episcopal Ch., 1948. Rector Ch. of Our Saviour, Brookline, Mass., 1950-56, St. John's Ch., Beverly Farms, Mass., 1956-63, Ch. of the Holy Spirit, Lake Forest, Ill., 1963-81; warden St. Julian's Retreat & Tng. Ctr., Limuru, Kenya, 1981-83; asst. to bishop of Mass. Boston, 1984; priest in charge St. Paul's Within the Walls, Rome, 1985; interim priest Christ Ch., Cambridge, 1986-87, St. Andrew's, Wellesley, Mass., 1989-90; canon St. Luke's Cathedral, Butere, Kenya, 1987—; dean Waukegan deanery Diocese of Chgo., 1971-81; chmn. Iran Diocesan Assn./USA, 1973-78; mem. standing com. Diocese of Chgo., 1969-72, pres., 1970-72; pres. trustees Episcopal Chaplaincy Harvard/Radcliffe, 1988-90. Assoc. editor The Living Ch. mag., 1984—.

PHIPPS, LAWRENCE HENRY, minister; b. Knoxville, Tenn., June 28, 1954; s. Paul D and May Alice (Oestriech) P.; m. Karen Denise McMoy, Aug. 28, 1976; children: Heather Denise, Lauren Brooke. BA, Auburn U., 1976; M in Divinity, So. Bapt. Sem., Louisville, 1979, D in Ministry, 1983. Pastor Moreland (Ky.) 1st Bapt. Ch., 1977-80, Franklin Crossroads Bapt. Ch., Cecilia, Ky., 1980-84; pastor 1st Bapt. Ch., Oneonta, Ala., 1984-90, Enterprise, Ala., 1990—; field supr. So. Bapt. Sem., 1985—. Mem. com. on bds. Ala. Bapt. Conv., 1985-87; trustee Samford U., 1986—. Named one of Outstanding Young Men Am., 1985. Mem. Nat. Eagle Scout Assn., Friendship Bapt. Assn. (chmn. fin. com. 1984-88), Coffee Bapt. Assn. (chmn. pers. com. 1990—), Academic Boosters Club (Oneonta), Quaterback Club (Enterprise), Lions. Office: 1st Bapt Ch 302 N Main St Enterprise AL 36330

PHIPPS, WILLIAM EUGENE, religion and philosophy educator; Waynesboro, Va., Jan. 28, 1930; s. Charles Henry and Ruth LaVell (Patterson) P.; m. Martha Ann Swezey, Dec. 21, 1954; children: Charles, Anna, Ruth. BS, Davidson Coll., 1949; MDiv, Union Theol. Sem., 1952; MA, U. Hawaii, 1963; PhD, U. St. Andrews (Scotland), 1954; hon. M.H.L., Davis and Elkins Coll., 1972. Ordained to ministry Presbyterian Ch., 1952. Prof. Bible Peace Coll., Raleigh, N.C., 1954-56; prof. religion and philosophy Davis and Elkins Coll., Elkins, W.Va., 1956—, pres. faculty assn., 1973-75, 1986-87. Author: Paul Against Supernaturalism, 1986, Death: Confronting the Reality, 1987, Genesis and Gender, 1989, Cremation Concerns, 1989, The Sheppards and Lapsley, 1991. Recipient Scholarly and Creative Accomplishments award Davis and Elkins Coll., 1980. Mem. Am. Acad. Religion. Democrat. Home: Lincoln Ave Elkins WV 26241 Office: Davis and Elkins Coll Elkins WV 26241

PHREANER, DAVID GRAY, minister; b. Great Neck, N.Y., Nov. 12, 1946; s. C. Edgar and Hester (Gray) P.; m. Lisa Rothermich. AB, Amherst Coll., 1969; MA, U. Chgo., 1971; D Ministry, Meadville-Lombard Theol. Sch., 1973. Ordained to ministry Unitarian Universalist Assn., 1973. Asst. min. Unitarian Universalist Soc. Germantown, Phila., 1974-76; min. Unitarian Universalist Ch. Farmington, Mich., 1976-79; extension min. Prairie Star Dist., Mpls., 1979-84; interim min. chs. in Pa., Maine, N.Y., 1984-88; min. Unitarian Universalist Ch. Manchester, N.H., 1988—. Mem. Unitarian Universalist Mins. Assn. Office: Unitarian Universalist Ch Manchester 669 Union St Manchester NH 03104

PIATT, RICHARD C., II, missionary pastor, educator; b. Dayton, Ohio, Nov. 5, 1953; s. Richard C. and Mildred E. (Hahn) P.; m. Susan E. Kreitzer, July 17, 1976; children: Eileen, Emily, Rich. BS in Biology, Wright State U., Dayton, 1976; MDiv, Grace Theol. Sem., Winona Lake, Ind., 1979, ThM, 1981. Ordained to ministry Gen. Assn. Regular Bapts., 1982. Pastor Palestine (Ind.) Ch., Wildwood Chapel, Upper Sandusky, Ohio; pastor, missionary Amb. Bapt. Ch., Jacksonville, Fla., 1988—; tchr. Univ. Christian Sch., Jacksonville, 1988—; prof. Luther Rice Sem., Jacksonville, 1991—; interviewer Sta. WJFR, Jacksonville, 1990—. Home and Office: Amb Bapt Ch 13825 Windjammer Ln Jacksonville FL 32224

PICACHY, LAWRENCE TREVOR CARDINAL, archbishop of Calcutta; b. Darjeeling, India, Aug. 7, 1916; s. Edwin and May (McCue) P.; ed. St. Joseph's Coll. Ordained to ministry Roman Cath. Ch.; rector, headmaster St. Xavier's Coll., Calcutta, India, 1954-60; bishop of Jamshedpur, India, 1962-69; archbishop of Calcutta, India, 1969—; v.p. Cath. Bishop's Conf. of India, 1972-76, pres., 1976-81; cardinal Sacred Consistory of Pope Paul VI, 1976—. Club: Rotary. Address: Archbishops House, 32 Park St, Calcutta 700 016, India

PICIRILLI, ROBERT EUGENE, clergyman, college dean, writer; b. High Point, N.C., Oct. 6, 1932; s. Eugene and Lena (Harrell) P.; m. Clara Mae Lee, June 14, 1953; children: Annina Jean, Myra Jane, Mary June, Celina Joy, Roberta Jill. B.A., Free Will Bapt. Bible Coll., Nashville, 1953; M.A., Bob Jones U., 1955, Ph.D., 1963, D.D., 1967. Ordained to ministry Free Will Bapt. Ch., 1952; grad. asst. Bob Jones U., 1954-55; prof. N.T., Free Will Bapt. Bible Coll., 1955—, registrar, 1960-79, dean, 1979—, dean grad. sch., 1982-86; clk. Nat. Assn. Free Will Baptists, 1961-65, moderator, 1966-71, treas. hist. commn., 1974—, mem. bd. of retirement and ins., 1978-89, sec., 1979-89; mem. testing com. Am. Assn. Bible Colls., 1959-72, research commn., 1982—, chmn., 1989—; sec.-treas. So. region Evang. Theol. Soc., 1964-68, vice chmn., 1972-73, 84-85 chmn., 1973-74, 85-86. Author: Paul, the Apostle, 1986, 1,2 Corinthians, 1987. Ephesians and Philippians, 1988, 1, 2 Thessalonians, 1990. Pres. Ransom Elementary Sch. P.T.A., 1965-67. Fellow Inst. for Bibl. Research; mem. AAHE, Nashville Philatelic Soc. (treas. 1980-81, pres. 1981-82, 1st v.p. 1982-88), Delta Epsilon Chi. Home: 301 Greenway Ave Nashville TN 37205

PICKARD, WILLIAM MARSHALL, JR., minister; b. Jackson, Ala., Oct. 19, 1920; s. William Marshall Sr. and Lilla Vea (Avinger) Pickard; m. Mary Ann Martin, June 25, 1946; children: Mary Susan, Henry Martin, William Marshall III, Jamie Earl, Paul Wesley. AB, Randolph Macon Coll., 1942; B Divinity, Emory U., 1945, PhD, 1966; postgrad., Harvard U., 1971. Ordained to ministry United Meth. Ch. as elder, 1947. Pastor United Meth. Ch., Ala., 1945-54; missionary United Meth. Ch., Philippines, 1954-71; prof. Huntingdon Coll., Montgomery, Ala., 1971-86; gen. sec. United Christian Ashrams Internat., Montgomery, Ala., 1986—. Author: Rather Die Than Live-Jonah, 1974; contbr. articles to profl. jours. Mem. Am. Acad. Religion, Am. Soc. Missiology, Internat. Assn. Mission Studies, Ala. Phil. Soc., Masons. Avocations: photography, fishing. Home: 3037 Lansdowne Dr Montgomery AL 36111 Offfice: United Christian Ashrams 1500 E Fairview Ave Montgomery AL 36106

PICKEL, A. W., III, religious organization administrator; b. Flora, Ill., Nov. 11, 1955; s. A.W. Jr. and Rosalind B. (Cole) P.; m. Diane R. Poel, Aug. 15, 1981; children: Lara Michelle, Alissa Christine, Jessica Nicole, Rebecca Ashley. BS in Acctg., U. Ill., 1977; postgrad., Wheaton Coll., 1978, 79. Mem. staff The Navigators, Iowa State U., 1979-81, The Navigators, Kansas State U., 1981-87, The Navigators, Kansas City, 1987—.

PICKELL, CHARLES NORMAN, clergyman, educator; b. Haddonfield, N.J., Dec. 18, 1927; s. William Norman and Ada Marie (Kelley) P.; m. Sarah Mitchell Harlow, Nov. 20, 1982; children by previous marriage: Rachel Grace, Stuart Charles, Arthur John, Luke Andrew, Heather Lee; step-children: Ellen Landon Harlow, Ethan John Harlow. BA, Juniata Coll., 1949; MDiv, Pitts. Theol. Sem., 1952, ThM, 1957; DD, Sterling Coll., 1964; postgrad. Harvard U., 1959-60, Andover-Newton Theol. Sch., 1960-61, No. Va. Community Coll., 1973, George Mason U., 1982. Ordained to ministry Presbyterian Ch. U.S.A., 1952. Pastor Chelsea Presbyn. Ch., Atlantic City, 1952-55, 1st Presbyn. Ch., Monongaleha, Pa., 1955-57, United Presbyn. Ch., Newton, Mass., 1957-63, Wallace Meml. United Presbyn. Ch., Hyattsville, Md., 1963-70, Vienna Presbyn. Ch., Va., 1970-80, Ashburn Presbyn. Ch., Va., part-time 1980-85, full-time, 1985—; mem. adminstrv. faculty George Mason U., Fairfax, Va., 1980-83; mgr. adminstrv. and support svcs. Creative Mgmt. Systems, McLean, Va., 1983-84; adj. prof. Gordon Div. Sch., Wenham, Mass., 1958-63; moderator Presbytery Boston, United Presbyn. Ch. U.S.A., 1959, chmn. ministerial rels., 1961-63; moderator Synod New Eng., 1960; asst. stated clk. Presbytery Washington City, 1969; chmn. nominating com. Nat. Capital Union Presbytery of United Presbyn. Ch. U.S.A. and Presbyn. Ch. U.S., 1974-77, moderator, 1978; mem. council Synod of Vas., Presbyn. Ch. U.S., 1976-82, chmn. council, 1980-82; mem. adv. bd. Salvation Army, Fairfax, 1981-83; mem. governing bd. United Coll. Ministries in No. Va., 1982—, chmn. 1987—; mem. hunger com. Nat. Capital Presbytery, 1984-86; mem. New Ch. Devel. Com. Nat. Capital Presbytery, 1988, chair, 1989—; trustee Westminster Coll., New Wilmington, Pa., 1957-61, Gordon Div. Sch., Wenham, Mass., 1959-70; trustee Gordon Coll., Wenham, 1959-82, chmn. acad. affairs, 1965-82; mem. governing bd., incorporator Gordon-Conwell Theol. Sem., Hamilton, Mass., 1969-71. Author: Preaching to Meet Men's Needs, 1957, Colossians, A Study Manual, 1965, Works Count Too!, 1966, also ch. sch. curricula, poetry and numerous articles in religious periodicals; author, editor: Presbyterianism in New England, 1960. Mem. Vienna Vol. Fire Dept., 1973-83, pres., 1978-80; chief chaplain Fairfax County Fire and Rescue Dept., 1974-81; mem., chaplain Burke Vol. Fire Dept., Va., 1983-88; mem. Asburn (Va.) Vol. Fire Dept., 1988—, bd. dirs., sec., 1991—. Mem. Hymn Soc. Am., Presbyn. Hist. Soc., Alban Inst. Republican. Avocations: writing, history, hymnody, spectator sports, theatre. Home: 44173 Bristow Circle Ashburn VA 22011 Office: Ashburn Presbyn Ch PO Box 275 Ashburn VA 22011 *Amid the shifting sands of contemporary thought one does best to be rooted in the scriptures of the Judeo-Christian tradition and to focus on the person of Jesus Christ as the source for the formation of sound ethical systems and values.*

PICKELMANN, HENRY MICHAEL, minister; b. Frankenmuth, Mich., June 27, 1947; s. Edmund Ernest and Edna Katherine (Zimmerman) P.; m. Janet Marie Baacke, June 24, 1972; children: Jennifer, Jonathon. BA, Concordia Tchrs. Coll., River Forest, Ill., 1970; MA, Saginaw Valley State U., 1980. Commd. to ministry Luth. Ch., 1969. Minister of edn. Zion Luth. Ch., Summit, Ill., 1969-73, Trinity Luth. Ch., Bay City, Mich., 1973—; pres. bd. dirs. Valley Luth. High Sch., Saginaw, Mich.; sec. Bd. of Christian Care for Mich. Dist., Ann Arbor. Mem. Bay Community Found., Bay City, 1991—. Mem. Luth. Edn. Assn., ASCD. Office: Trinity Lutheran Sch 20 E Salzburg Rd Bay City MI 48706

PICKERING, GREGORY HALEY, minister; b. Orange, Tex., Jan. 12, 1960; s. Charles Walker Sr. and Ollie V. (Haley) P.; m. Kathy Sue Smith, May 28, 1983; children: Michael Hoffmann, Jeffrey Haley. BBA in Fin., Tex. A&M U., 1982; MRE in Youth, Southwestern Bapt. Theol. Sem., Ft. Worth, 1987. Lic. to ministry So. Bapt. Conv., 1985, ordained, 1990. Summer missionary Bapt. Student Union, Baytown, Tex., 1980; youth dir. 1st Bapt. Ch., College Station, Tex., 1980-82; min. youth and music 1st Bapt. Ch., Hemphill, Tex., 1982-85; min. youth and activities 1st Bapt. Ch., Orange, 1987—; conf. leader Glorieta Summer Youth Celebration, 1986, 87; asst. dean Super Summer Youth Evangelism Sch., Waco, Tex., 1989—; mem. student work com. Bapt. Student Union Lamar U., Beaumont, Tex., 1990—. Founder United Christian Svcs., Hemphill, 1984. Mem. Golden Triangle Assn. of Youth Mins. (fin. chair Hot Hearts conf. 1987—), Nat. Network Youth Mins., Lions. Office: 1st Bapt Ch 602 Green Ave Orange TX 77630

PICKERING, WILLIAM TODD, minister; b. Pitts., May 24, 1946; s. Thomas Edwin and Lucile Hutchinson (Todd) P.; m. Lee Ann Bunnell, Sept. 5, 1970; children: Matthew Todd, David Merrill, Amy Noreen. BA, Randolph/Macon Coll., 1968; MDiv, Gen. Theol. Sem., 1971. Ordained to ministry Episcopal Ch. as deacon, 1971, as priest 1971. Vicar St. Alban's Episcopal Ch., Murrysville, Pa., 1971-76; rector Christ Episcopal Ch., Greensburg, Pa., 1976-83, St. Paul's Episcopal Ch., Mt. Lebanon, Pa., 1983—; bd. dirs. Sheldon Calvary Camp, Conneaut, Ohio, 1985-91; chmn.

worship dept. Diocese of Pitts., 1988—; bd. dirs. Commn. on Ministry, Pitts., 1985—; bd. chmn. St. Paul's Episcopal Nursery Sch., Mt. Lebanon, 1986—. Pres. bd. dirs. Interfaith Re-employment Group, Pitts., 1990—; bd. dirs. Parent & Child Guidance Ctr., Pitts., 1987—, Outreach South Hills, Inc., Mt. Lebanon, 1986—. Mem. Pitts. Athletic Assn. Republican. Home: 126 Boxfield Rd Pittsburgh PA 15241 Office: St Pauls Episcopal Ch 1066 Washington Rd Pittsburgh PA 15228 *The rediscovery of being a community of God's people who are mutually responsible and interdependent is the greatest challenge to the Church and culture in the '90s.*

PICKERN, MALCOLM E., clergyman; b. Atmore, Ala., July 12, 1955; s. Horace Eugene and Agnes Pauline (McCall) P.; m. Julie Ann Hush, Aug. 12, 1977; children: Joshua Paul, Christie Ruth. BA in Religion, La. Coll., 1977; postgrad., Southwestern Bapt. Sem., 1981-82, New Orleans Bapt. Sem., 1985. Ordained to ministry Bapt. Ch. Minister to youth New Hope Bapt. Ch., Calcasieu, La., 1974-77; pastor Harmony Bapt. Ch., Glenmore, La., 1978-80, Murray St. Bapt. Ch., Lake Charles, La., 1980-83, Flactor Bapt. Ch., Hicks, La., 1983-85, Unity Bapt. Ch., Atmore, Ala., 1986—; evangelism dir. Escombia Bapt. Assn., Atmore, 1987—; chairperson South Ala. Jay Struck Crusade, Flomcton, Ala., 1989-90. Mem. Atmore Ministerial Assn. (pres. 1990-91). Home: Rt 4 Box 484F Atmore AL 36502

PICKETT, RAYMOND WALLACE, JR., pastor; b. Mansfield, Ohio, Apr. 8, 1955; s. Raymond W. and Phyllis (Ballenger) P.; m. Leah Baxter, Aug. 16, 1980; children: Benjamin, Sarah. BA, Oral Roberts U., 1978, MA, 1982; MDiv, Wartburg Seminary, Dubuque, Iowa, 1989; PhD, U. Sheffield, England, 1990. Adj. lectr. in New Testament St. John's Coll., Nottingham, England, 1984-86, Wartburg Seminary, 1987-88; assoc. pastor Bethany Luth. Ch., Tulsa, 1988—. Mem. Soc. Bibl. Lit. Office: Bethany Luth Ch 5324 E 46th St Tulsa OK 44135

PICKHOLZ, MORRIS, rabbi; b. Stryj, Poland, Dec. 1, 1919; came to U.S., 1924; s. Berisch and Golda Pickholz; m. Esther M. Tendler, Feb. 2, 1947; children: Rochelle Lynn, Cheryl Eileen, Gary Robert. BS, Columbia U., 1955; EdM, Temple U., 1965. Ordained rabbi, 1944. Pres. Bd. Rabbis Phila., 1960-62; bd. mem. Zionist Orgn. Phila., 1962-65; asst. prof. Bible LaSalle U., Phila., 1970-71; asst. prof. Talmud Herzeliah Coll., N.Y.C., 1975-77; instr. Yiddish Baruch Coll., N.Y.C., 1978-79; rabbi Temple Bnai Jacob, West Palm Beach, Fla., 1987—. Mem. Rabbinical Assembly. Home: 3040 Lillian Rd West Palm Beach FL 33406 Office: Temple Bnai Jacob 2177 S Congress Ave West Palm Beach FL 33406

PICKLE, JOSEPH WESLEY, JR., religion educator; b. Denver, Apr. 8, 1935; s. Joseph Wesley and Wilhelmina (Blacketor) P.; m. Judith Ann Siebert, June 28, 1958; children: David E., Kathryn E., Steven J. BA, Carleton Coll., 1957; B.D., Chgo. Theol. Sem., 1961; MA, U. Chgo., 1962, PhD, 1969. Ordained to ministry Am. Bapt. Conv., 1962. Asst. pastor Judson Meml. Ch., N.Y.C., 1959-60; acting dean summer session Colo. Coll., Colorado Springs, 1969-70, from asst. prof. to prof. religion, 1964—; vis. prof. theology Iliff Sch. Theology, Denver, 1984; vis. prof. religious studies U. Zimbabwe, Harare, 1989; cons. Colo. Humanities Program, Denver, 1975-89; coord. Sheffer Meml. Fund, Colo. Coll., Colorado Springs, 1983—. Co-editor Papers of the 19th Century Theology Group, 1978, 88. Pres. bd. dirs. Pikes Peak Mental Health Ctr., Colorado Springs, 1975, Colo. Health Facilities Rev. Coun., Denver, 1979-84; mem. Colo. Health Facilities Rev. Coun., Denver, 1976-84, Colo. Bd. Health, Denver, 1986-91. Am. Bapt. Conv. scholar, 1953-59; Fulbright Hays Grad. fellow Fulbright Commn., U. Tübingen, Fed. Republic Germany, 1963-64, Danforth fellow, 1957-63. Fellow Soc. for Values in Higher Edn.; mem. Am. Theol. Soc., Am. Acad. Religion (regional pres. 1983-84), Cath. Theol. Soc. Am. Democrat. Home: 20 W Caramillo Colorado Springs CO 80907 Office: Colo Coll 14 E Cache la Poudre Colorado Springs CO 80903

PIECHOCINSKI, THOMAS ANTHONY, priest; b. N.Y.C., Apr. 26, 1934; s. Anthony Joseph and Genevieve Bernice (Godlewski) P. BA in History, St. Francis Coll., Loretto, Pa., 1957; MA in Edn., Seton Hall U., 1961; EdD, Pacific States U., 1977. Ordained priest Roman Cath. Ch., 1961; lic. marriage counselor, N.J. Counselor Wildwood Cath. High Sch., North Wildwood, N.J., 1961-65, Camden Cath. High Sch., Cherry Hill, N.J., 1965-66; dir. student personnel svcs Holy Spirit High Sch., Absecon, N.J., 1966-75; counselor chaplain Cabrini Coll., Radnor, Pa., 1975-77; divorce therapist Diocese of Camden, Ventnor, N.J., 1983—; pastor St. Cecilia, Monmouth Junction, N.J.; adj. faculty Seton Hall U., South Orange, N.J., 1973-74. Recipient sports photojournalism award Look mag., 1954, commendation USAF Recruitment Svc., 1965, cert. N.J. Sch. Counselor's Assn., 1975; named Counselor of Yr., N.J. Assn. Coll. Admission Counselors, 1976. Fellow Am. Orthopsychiat. Assn.; mem. Am. Assn. Marriage and Family Therapy (clin.), N.J. Assn. Marriage and Family Therapy, Nat. Coun. Family Rels., ACCD (life), Nat. Vocat. Guidance Assn. (profl.), Assn. for Religious and Values Issues in Counseling (assoc.), Am. Coll. Personnel Assn. (assoc.), N.Y. Acad. Sci. Republican. Home: 46 Kingston Ln Monmouth Junction NJ 08852

PIEPER, THOMAS ALLEN, minister; b. Camp Lejeune, N.C., Mar. 23, 1956; s. Thomas Leroy and Mary Sue (Adams) P.; m. Martha Gail Surface, Aug. 6, 1983; children: Kristen, Katherine, Andrew. B in Music Edn., Okla. Bapt. U., 1979; MDiv, Southwestern Bapt. Theol. Sem., Ft. Worth, 1985. Ordained to ministry So. Bapt. Conv., 1989. Asst. pastor Lane Prairie Bapt. Ch., Cleburne, Tex., 1983-87; dir. outreach Birchman Bapt. Ch., Ft. Worth, 1987-89; pastor, tchr. 1st Bapt. Ch., Quemado, N.Mex., 1989—; moderator Mountain Assn. of N.Mex., Quemado, 1990—, youth cons., 1989—. Contbr. articles to mags. Mem. Internat. Trumpet Guild, Phi Mu Alpha Sinfonia. Home: PO Box 75 Quemado NM 87829 Office: 1st Bapt Ch PO Box 102 Quemado NM 87829

PIERARD, RICHARD VICTOR, history educator; b. Chgo., May 29, 1934; s. John Perkins and Diana Florence (Russell) P.; m. Charlene Burdett, June 15, 1957; children: David, Cynthia. BA, Calif. State U., L.A., 1958, MA, 1959; PhD, U. Iowa, 1964. Prof. history Ind. State U., Terre Haute, 1964—; vis. prof. Greenville (Ill.) Coll., 1972-73; Free Theol. Acad., Seeheim, Fed. Republic Germany, 1971, 78, Regent Coll., Vancouver, B.C., Can., 1975, Trinity Evang. Div. Sch., Deerfield, Ill., 1982, No. Bapt. Theol. Sem., Lombard, Ill., 1987, Fuller Theol. Sem., Pasadena, Calif., 1988, 91; Fulbright prof. U. Frankfurt, Fed. Republic Germany, 1984-85; Fulbright prof. U. Halle, German Dem. Republic, 1989-90; mem. nat. adv. coun. Ams. United for Separation of Ch. and State, 1985—; pres. Greater Terre Haute Ch. Fedn., 1987-88; del. Lausanne II Congress on World Evang., Manila, Philippines, 1989; mem. Bapt. Heritage Study Commn., Bapt. World Alliance, 1990—. Author: The Unequal Yoke: Evangelical Christianity and Political Conservatism, 1970, Bibliography on the Religious Right in America, 1986; co-author: Twilight of the Saints: Biblical Christianity and Civil Religion, 1978, Civil Religion and the Presidency, 1988; contbr. articles to religious publs. Del. White House Conf. on Librs., Washington, 1979, Ind. Dem. Party Convention, Indpls., 1980, 88; precinct committeeman Dem. Party, Terre Haute, 1978-80, 90—; mem. Ind. Gov.'s Adv. Com. on Librs., 1980-81. With U.S. Army, 1954-56. Recipient Terre award Bapt. World Alliance, 1991; Fulbright scholar U. Hamburg (Fed. Republic Germany), 1962-63; rsch. fellow U. Aberdeen (Scotland), 1978; Chavanne scholar Baylor U., 1988. Mem. Conf. on Faith and History (sec.-treas. 1967—), Evang. Theol. Soc. (pres. 1985), Am. Hist. Assn., Am. Soc. Ch. History, Ind. Assn. Historians, Am. Soc. Missiology, Internat. Assn. Mission Studies, Soc. for Encouragement and Preservation of Barbershop Quartet Singing in Am. Home: 550 Gardendale Rd Terre Haute IN 47803 Office: Ind State U Dept History Terre Haute IN 47809

PIERCE, DARYL EUGENE, radio station administrator; b. Youngstown, Ohio, Aug. 2, 1963; s. Donald Ward Pierce and Delores Jean (Bowers) Falasco; m. Julie Ann Duncan, Dec. 10, 1988. Student, Mt. Vernon Nazarene Coll., 1984-89. Sta. mgr. Mt. Vernon (Ohio) Nazarene Coll., 1989—; music dir. Sta. WNZR Radio, 1987. Mem. Ch. of the Nazarene. Home: 205 E Vine St Mount Vernon OH 43050 Office: 16279 Glen Rd Mount Vernon OH 43050

PIERCE, JAMES ERIC, minister; b. St. Louis, Feb. 23, 1940; s. Erie F. and Virginia (Fears) P.; m. Anita Moss, June 3, 1961 (div. 1974); children: Pamela Elizabeth, Heather Anita; m. Kimberly L. Townsend, Aug. 31,

1989. BA, Miss. State U., 1961; MDiv, Candler Sch. Theology, 1963; PhD, Emory U., 1977. Ordained to ministry United Meth. Ch. as deacon, 1962, as elder, 1964. Prof. Lambuth Coll., Jackson, Tenn., 1969-72; prof.; campus min. Pfeiffer Coll., Misenheimer, N.C., 1972-84; sr. chaplain, exec. dir. The Chapel of Four Chaplains, Valley Forge, Pa., 1984-90, assoc. chaplain, 1990—; pastor Bethel United Meth. Ch., East Coventry, Pa., 1990—. Chaplain Phila. VA Med. Ctr., 1986—. Col. USAR, 1957—, Vietnam vet. Decorated Bronze Star, Purple Heart, Meritorious Svc. medal; recipient Legion of Honor award Order of De Molay, 1990; named Man of Yr. Jewish War Vets. Am. Phila. Coun., 1988,. Mem. Vietnam Vets. Meml. Soc. (adv. bd. 1984-90), Greater Phila. Wallenberg Soc. (adv. bd. 1984-90), U.S. Army Chaplain Mus. Assn. (pres. bd. govs. 1989-91), Scottish-Am.Mil. Soc. (nat. chaplain 1987—), Internat. Order of Rainbow for Girls (chmn. bd. advisors Phila. assembly 1987-90, Grand Cross of Color award 1989). Home: 950 Bethel Church Rd Spring City PA 19475 Office: Bethel United Meth Ch 952 Bethel Church Rd Spring City PA 19475

PIERCE, NATHANIEL W., minister; b. Boston, Aug. 18, 1942; s. Alvah Nathaniel and Anne (Whicher) P.; m. Audrey Byam, Oct. 18, 1975; stepchildren: John J. Buchanan, Rebecca Ruth Hermanson, Alice Ann Ebbers. BS in Engring., Cornell U., 1966; MDiv, Ch. Div. Sch. of Pacific, Berkeley, Calif., 1972; MA in Theology, Grad. Theol. Union, Berkeley, Calif., 1972. Ordained deacon Episcopal Ch., 1972, priest, 1973. Rector Grace Episcopal Ch., Nampa, Idaho, 1975-84, All Saints Parish, Brookline, Mass., 1984-89; interim exec. dir. Interfaith AIDS Ministry, West Newton, Mass., 1990; interim chaplain Children's Hosp., Boston, 1990; rector Great Choptank Parish Christ Ch., Cambridge, Md., 1991—; trustee Ch. Div. Sch. of Pacific, Berkeley, 1971-72; dep. Gen. Conv., Episcopal Ch., 1979; chmn. Standing Commn. on Peace, Nat. Episcopal Ch., 1986-88. Author: The Voice of Conscience, 1989. Vice pres. Brookline Vis. Nurses Assn., 1988-90, Planned Parenthood of Idaho, Boise, 1983-84. Home: 107 High St Cambridge MD 21613 Office: Great Choptank Parish 601 Church St Box 456 Cambridge MD 21613 *If one assumes that one can make a difference, one will make a difference.*

PIERCE, PAUL LESLIE, missionary; b. Lowell, Mass., Nov. 26, 1944; s. Harold James and Edna Louise (Holden) P.; children: F. Benjamin, Christopher Jacob. AA, Mt. Wachusetts Community Coll., 1969; BTh, Internat. Bible Inst. & Sem., 1983, MTh, 1984. Pastor First Bapt. Ch., Watertown, Mass., 1984-88; dir. Gospel Outreach Ministries, Haiti, W.I., 1988—. Del. Nat. Rep. Conv., New Orleans, 1988, Mass. Rep. Conv., Boston, 1990; State coord. Pat Robinson for pres., Mass., 1988; sec. Watertown Rep. Town Com., 1989-90. Mem. Freedom Coun. (exec. bd. dirs. Virginia Beach, Va. chpt. 1984-86), Watertown Ministerial Assn. (pres. 1984-86), Bapt. Conv. of Mass., Internat. Ministries Assn. Office: Gospel Outreach Ministries PO Box 396 Boston MA 02272-0396

PIERCE, ROBERT L., church council director; b. Northeast, Pa.; s. Elton Leon and Ruth Henrietta (Goodrich) P.; m. Martha Carol Gardner, Dec. 1958; children: Nathan Robert, Daniel Allen. Student, Pa. State U., 1954-56; BA, Franklin (Ind.) Coll., 1958; M in Divinity, Andover Newton Theol. Sch., Newton Centre, Mass., 1962; postgrad., New Eng. Tng. Inst., Ashway, R.I., Univ. Assocs., San Anselund, Calif., Nat. Humanistic Edn. Ctr., Saratoga Springs, N.Y., Sch. Allied Health, SUNY, Stony Brook. Ordained Bapt. Ch., 1962. Youth dir. 1st Bapt. Ch., Anderson, Ind., 1958; asst. pastor 1st Bapt. Ch., Erie, Pa., 1959, Pilgrim Congl. Ch., Nashua, N.H., 1960-61; adminstrv. asst. Am. Bapt. Home Missions, N.Y.C., 1961-63; assoc. dir. youth dept. Nat. Council Chs., N.Y.C., 1963-69; dir. Schenectady (N.Y.) Inner City Ministry, 1969-85; exec. dir. L.I. Council Chs., Rockville Centre, N.Y., 1985—; U.S. del. East Asian Youth Assembly, 1964; dir. Youth Leadership Tng. Sem., Syracuse U., 1965; cons. FOCUS Chs., Albany, N.Y., Planned Parenthood, Schenectady, Inter-Met. Sem., Washington, Boys Club Am., Schenectady and N.Y.C., Y.W.C.A., Schenectady, Schenectady Police Dept., numerous local congregations Am. Bapt. Chs. U.S.A., Mass. Conf. United Ch. of Christ, Amnesty Internat., N.Y.C. Editor: Jour. of Assn. for Creative Change, 1983—, mem. editorial com. N.Y. Times, L.I. Edit. Founding dir. Schenectady Community Dispute Settlement Project, 1978; charter mem. Human Svc. Planning Coun., Schenectady, Eugene Dix Meml. Scholarship Fund, 1972, Schenectady County Youth Bur., 1973, Pres.'s Citizens' Task Force Against Child Abuse and Neglect, 1983-85; councilman Cobbleskill (N.Y.) Coll., 1984-85; mem. bd. dirs. and personnel com. Parish Resource Ctr.; mem. exec. com. Nassau County (N.Y.) Health and Welfare Coun.; chmn. Sr. Svc. Com., Suffolk Inter-Agy. Coord. Coun., Suffolk County Exec.'s HIV/AIDS Adv. Panel; mem. L.I. Regional HIV/AIDS Planning Coalition; commr. Nassaud County HIV/AIDS Commn.; founding mem. Suffolk and Nassau Habitat for Humanity; bd. dirs. Parish Resource Ctr., Rocky Point, L.I.; mem. long range planning com. East End Hope for Hospice; bd. dirs. Project REAL. Recipient Partnership in Ministry award Am. Bapt. Chs. Met. N.Y., 1990; named Patroon Schenectady City Coun., 1985. Mem. Schenectady Profl. Clergy Support Group (convenor), Interfaith Assn. Religious Leaders Nassau County (exec. com.), Suffolk Interfaith Clergy Coun. (past pres.). Avocations: hiking, sailing, gardening, music. Office: Long Island Coun Chs 249 Merrick Rd Box 105 Rockville Centre NY 11571

PIERCE, WILLIAM JOSEPH, minister; b. Mobile, Ala., Sept. 23, 1954; s. John Higdon and Zoie (Burnett) P.; m. Dawn Allene, Sept. 13, 1959; 1 child, John Joseph. AA, Brevard Community Coll., Cocoa, Fla., 1976; BA, U. Cen. Fla., 1985; postgrad., New Orleans Bapt. Theol. Sem., 1985-87, Southeastern Sem., Wake Forest, N.C., 1988—. Lic. to ministry Bapt. Ch. With security First Bapt. Ch., Orlando, Fla., 1982; lit. and Bible tchr. Eastland Christian Sch., Orlando, 1985; youth, singles minister Westview Bapt. Ch., Sanford, Fla., 1985-86; coll. campus dir. Bapt. Campus Ministries, Orlando, 1986—; Christian disciple Pierced Heart Ministries, Orlando, 1986—; youth minister New Life Fellowship, Orlando, 1987; sub. tchr. Orange County (Fla.) Sch. Bd., Orlando; crusade counselor Billy Graham Evangelical Assn., Mpls.; bd. dirs. Polk Correctional Inst. chapel Bd., Inc., Winter Haven, Fla. Named one of Outstanding Young Men of Am., 1984, 85, 86. Republican. Avocations: tennis, golf, surfing. Home and Office: 324 Railroad St Wake Forest NC 27587 Also: Southeastern Sem PO Box 3719 Wake Forest NC 27587

PIERRE, MARIE-JOSEPH, patristics educator; b. Argentan, Normandy, France, Nov. 12, 1945; arrived in Israel, 1977; s. Louis and Brigitte (Lepetit) P. Lic. philosophy, 1971; ThD, Cath. Inst., Paris, 1985; Dr. Sci. of Religions, Sorbonne U., Paris, 1985. Prof. patristics Ecole Biblique & Archeologique Francaise, Jerusalem, 1983-89; prof. Centre Etudes Juives Ratisbonne, Jerusalem, 1989-90, Syriac Inst. Catholique de Paris, 1990—. Author: (with J. Rousee) Catalogue de la bibliotheque de l'Ecole Biblique, 1983-89, Aphraate Le Sage Persan, Les Exposes Paris, 1988-89. Mem. Assn. pour l'Étude de la Litterature Apocryphe Chétienne. Address: Saint-Martin-Des-Champs, 61200 Argentan France

PIERSEE, CHARLES RALPH, religious organization executive; b. Denver, Aug. 8, 1931; s. Charles Ross and Bula Elizabeth (Turner) P.; m. Carolyn Ellen Moors, June 13, 1954; children: Kimberly A. Gardell, Rene Elaine (dec.), Shelly A. Schmidt, Dean A. BA, U. Wash., 1955. Commd. ensign USN, 1955, advanced through grades to capt.; asst. dir. logistics USN 7th Fleet, Yokosuka, Japan, 1965-68; comdg. officer USN Tng. Ctr., Wilkes Barre, Pa., 1968-70; dir. S.E. dir. U.S. Recruiting/Manpower, Charleston, S.C., 1970-73, Pers. Plans Div. Bur. Naval Pers., Washington, 1973-76, Mobilization Pland Directorate CNO Staff, Washington, 1978-80; dep. comdr. Naval Res. Readiness Command # 22, Seattle, 1980-83; comdr. Naval Res. Readiness Command # 7, Charleston, 1983-85; dir. Asia/Pacific area Assn. Chris. Confs. Teaching and Svc., Denver. Chairman task force Seattle C. of C., 1987-88. Decorated Legion of Merit. Mem. Naval Res. Assn. (exec. coun. 1989—), Navy Assn. U.S. Wash. Alumni Assn. Republican. Presbyterian. Home: 9314 21st Ave NW Seattle WA 98117-2707 Office: PO Box 27239 Denver CO 80227-0239

PIERTSE, HENDRIK JOHANNES CHRISTOFFEL, theologian, educator; b. Brits, Republic South Africa, June 11, 1936; s. Barend Jacobus and Magdalena (Van Greunen) P.; m. Louisa Maria DeBruyn, Apr. 8, 1961; children: Louise, Barend Jacobus; m. 2d, Johanna Bouwman, Sept. 5, 1990. BA, U. Pretoria, 1958, BDiv, 1961; Dth, U. Stellenbosch, 1978. Ordained to ministry, Dutch Reformed Ch., 1962. Pastor Dutch Reformed

Ch., Shabani, Zimbabwe, 1962-66, Pretoria, Republic South Africa, 1965-72, Johannesburg, Republic South Africa, 1973-75; lectr. U. Pretoria, 1976-79; prof. practical theology U. South Africa, Pretoria, 1980—; chmn. Marriage Council South Africa, 1968-73; sec. Nationwide Cong. on Ch. in the 80s in South Africa, 1982. Author: Huweliks Pastoraat, 1977, God's Word for Today, 1980, Communicative Preaching, 1987, A Primer in Practical Theology; contbr. articles to jours. Recipient Pro Arte medal, U. Pretoria, 1961. Mem. Inst. Contextual Theology, Co. Practical Theology (v.p. 1981—), Arbeitsgemeinshaft für Homiletick, Internat. Biog. Assn. Avocations: walking, poetry. Office: Practical Theology U, South Africa Muckleneukrand, Pretoria 0001, Republic of South Africa

PIETRZAK, DANIEL M., priest, academic administrator; b. Buffalo, Mar. 12, 1939; s. Thaddeus S. and Stella G. (Cybulski) P. BA, St. Hyacinth Coll., 1961; STL, Seraphicum, Rome, 1965; MS, South Conn. State U., 1968; PhD, Fordham U., 1981. Joined Order Friars Minor (Franciscans) Roman Cath. Ch., ordained priest, 1964. Tchr. Kolbe High Sch., Bridgeport, Conn., 1965-67; prof. philosophy and psychology St. Hyacinth Coll.-Sem., Granby, Mass., 1967-76, registrar, 1968-76, acad. dean, 1973-76, pres., 1991—; sem. rector Seraphicum, Rome, 1977-82; min. provincial Franciscan Order, St. Anthony Province, Balt., 1982-91; asst. gen. Order Friars Minor Conventual, Rome, 1976-82. Fordham U. fellow, 1969. Mem. APA, Nat. Cath. Edn. Assn., So. Sci. Study of Religion. Home and Office: 66 School St Granby MA 01033

PIGOTT, CHARLES SEDGIE, minister; b. Tylertown, Miss., Sept. 29, 1920; s. Charles Collier and Ollie (Yarborough) P.; m. Ruth Gertrude Graupner, June 2, 1945; children: Wayne, Candace, Timothy. BA, Miss. Coll., 1942; BD, Andover Newton, 1946; MST, Harvard U., 1952. Chaplain USN, 1942-62; pastor 1st Congl. Ch., Bristol, R.I., 1962-74, Ventnor Community Ch., N.J., 1974-80, 1st Congl. Ch., Thetford, Vt., 1980-82, Riverpoint Congl. Ch., West Warwick, R.I., 1982—. Commd. USN, 1942-62. Decorated Purple Heart. Home and Office: 73 Providence St West Warwick RI 02893

PIKE, GEORGE HAROLD, JR., religious organization executive, clergyman; b. Summit, N.J., Jan. 14, 1933; s. George Harold and Ann Aurelia (Brewer) P.; m. Pauline Elizabeth Blair, Aug. 27, 1955; children: Elizabeth, George 3d, James. BA, Trinity Coll., Hartford, Conn., 1954; MDiv, Dubuque (Iowa) Theolog. Sch., 1957. Ordained to ministry Presbyn. Ch. USA., 1957. Pastor 1st PResbyn. Ch., Kasson, Minn., 1956-59, 3d Presbyn. Ch., Dubuque, 1959-64; sr. pastor Presbyn. Ch., Bettendorf, Iowa, 1964-68; sr. pastor 1st Presbyn. Ch., Vancouver, Wash., 1968-78, Cranford, N.J., 1978-88; exec. chair Presbyn. Ch. USA, Louisville, 1988—; mem. exec. com. Consultation on Ch. Union, Princeton, 1980-89, pres., 1984-88. Dir. Bettendorf Bd. Edn., 1964-68, pres. 1967-68; bd. dirs. Southwest Wash. Hosps., Vancouver, 1969-78. Named Citizen of Yr., Jaycees, Bettendorf, 1967, Citizen of Yr., B'nai B'rith, Cranford, 1988; named to Honorable Order of Ky. Cols., 1989. Avocations: golf, photography. Home: 10086 Brookwood Cr Louisville KY 40223 Office: Presbyn Ch USA 100 Witherspoon St Louisville KY 40202

PIKELNY, DOV BURYL, rabbi, educator; b. Chgo., Apr. 16, 1933; s. Jacob and Adeline (Lerman) P.; m. Barbara Davida Bromberg, Oct. 15, 1977; children: Gary D. Pomerantz, Glen H. Pomerantz. BA, Yeshiva U., 1953; MA, Columbia U., 1955; rabbinate, Hebron Yeshiva, Jerusalem, Israel, 1955. Ordained rabbi, 1955. Educator Mesivta Tifereth Jerusalem, N.Y.C., 1953-55, Associated Talmud Torahs, Chgo., 1955-63; headmaster Beth El Acad., Akron, Ohio, 1963-68, Hillel Acad., Swampscott, Mass., 1968-74; rabbi-educator Temple Shalom, Salem, Mass., 1970-80, Beth El Congregation of Rogers Park, Marblehead, Mass., 1980—. Pres. North Shore Educators Assembly, Boston, 1975-77; bd. dirs. Jewish Fedn. of the North Shore, Jewish Family Svc. of the North Shore. Mem. New Eng. Rabbinical Assembly, Mass. Bd. Rabbis, New Eng. Jewish Educators Assmbly, Salem Clergy Assn. (pres. 1977-79), Peabody Clergy and Ministerial Assn. Freemasons (Mount Carmel Lodge, 32 degree, Aleppo Shrine). Democrat. Avocation: computers. Home and Office: 345 Atlantic Ave Marblehead MA 01945

PILARCZYK, DANIEL EDWARD, archbishop; b. Dayton, Ohio, Aug. 12, 1934; s. Daniel Joseph and Frieda S. (Hilgefort) P. Student, St. Gregory Sem., Cin., 1948-53; PhB, Pontifical Urban U., Rome, 1955, PhL, 1956, STB, 1958, STL, 1960, STD, 1961; MA, Xavier U., 1965; PhD, U. Cin., 1969; LLD (hon.), Xavier U., 1975, Calumet Coll., 1982, U. Dayton, 1990, Marquette U., 1990, Thomas Moore Coll., 1991. Ordained priest Roman Catholic Ch., 1959; asst. chancellor Archdiocese of Cin., 1961-63; synodal judge Archdiocesan Tribunal, 1971-82; mem. faculty Athenaeum of Ohio, St. Gregory Sem., 1963-74; v.p. Athenaeum of Ohio, 1968-74, trustee, 1974—; also rector St. Gregory Sem., 1968-74; archdiocesan dir. ednl. services, 1974-82, aux. bishop of Cin., 1974-82, vicar gen., 1974-82, archbishop of Cin., 1982—; bd. dirs. Pope John Ctr., 1978-85; trustee Cath. Health Assn., 1982-85, Cath. U. Am., 1983-91, Pontifical Coll. Josephinum, 1983-; v.p. Nat. Conf. Cath. Bishops, 1986-89, pres., 1989—; U.S. rep. Episc. Bd. Internat. Commn. on English in Liturgy 1987—; chmn., 1991—. Author: Praepositini Cancellarii de Sacramentis et de Novissimis, 1964-65, Twelve Tough Issues, 1988, We Believe, 1989, Living in the Lord, 1990, The Parish: Where God's People Live, 1991. Ohio Classical Conf. scholar to Athens, 1966. Mem. Am. Philol. Assn. Home and Office: 100 E 8th St Cincinnati OH 45202

PILCH, JOHN JOSEPH, biblical scholar, international speaker, author; b. Bklyn., Aug. 7, 1936; s. John Joseph Sr. and Anna Mary (Wypych) P.; m. Jean Peters. BA, St. Francis Coll., Burlington, Wis., 1959; MA, Marquette U., 1968, PhD, 1972. Chair and lectr. religion St. Francis Coll., Burlington, 1965-71; vis. lectr. U. St. Mary of the Lake, Mundelein, Ill., 1971-72; asst. prof. Hebrew Bible U. St. Mary of the Lake, 1972-74; lectr. social sci. Milw. Area Tech. Coll., 1974-76; program dir., sr. planner S.E. Wis. Health Systems Agy., Milw. 1974-77; asst. prof. preventive medicine Med. Coll. Wis., Milw., 1976-88; program coord. community health U. Wis. Extension, Milw., 1977-79; vis. prof. Bible Mercy Coll., Dallas, 1987; speaker and author, Biblical scholar Catonsville, Md., 1979—; Polish lang. abstractor New Testament Abstracts, Cambridge, Mass., 1963—; prof. adv. com. Interurban Health Careers, MPS, Milw., 1980-88. Author: Wellness: Invitation to Life, 1981, Galatians & Romans Commentary, 1983, Wellness Spirituality, 1985, Hear the Word!, vols. 1-2, 1991, Dictionary of New Testament Values, 1991; book rev. editor Bibl. Theology Bull., Jamaica, N.Y., 1979—; author: (cassette tapes) Aging in Grace and America, 1988. Bd. dirs. St. Mary's Nursing Home, Milw., 1980-86. Fellow Social Facets Seminar of Westar Inst. (charter); mem. Cath. Bibl. Assn. Am. (nominating com. 1982-86), Soc. Bibl. Lit., Soc. for Ancient Medicine and Pharmacy, The Context Group (press officer 1989—). Avocations: singing professionally in the opera, cooking, internat. travel. Home and Office: 1318 Black Friars Rd Catonsville MD 21228

PILCHIK, ELY EMANUEL, rabbi, writer; b. Russia, June 12, 1913; came to U.S., 1920, naturalized, 1920; s. Abraham and Rebecca (Lipovitch) P.; m. Ruth Schuchat, Nov. 20, 1941 (dec. 1977); children: Susan Pilchik Rosenbaum, Judith Pilchik Zucker; m. Harriet Krichman Perlmutter, June, 1981. A.B., U. Cin., 1935; M.Hebrew Lit., Hebrew Union Coll., 1936, D.D., 1964. Ordained rabbi, 1939; founder, dir. Hillel Found. at U. Md., 1939-40; asst. rabbi Har Sinai Temple, Balt., 1940-41; rabbi Temple Israel, Tulsa, 1942-47, Temple B'nai Jeshurun, Short Hills, N.J., 1947-81; prof. Jewish Thought Upsala Coll., 1969—; pres. Jewish Book Council Am., 1957-58. Author: books, including Hillel, 1951, From the Beginning, 1956, Judaism Outside the Holy Land, 1964, Jeshurun Essays, 1967, A Psalm of David, 1967, Talmud Thought, 1983, Midrash Memoir, 1984, Touches of Einstein, 1987, Luzzatto on Loving Kindness, 1987, Prayer in History, 1989; author: play Toby, 1968; lyricist 6 cantatas; contbr. articles to profl. and gen. jours. Bd. dirs. Newark Mus.; mem. ethics com. N.J. Bar Assn. Served as chaplain USNR, 1944-46. Mem. N.J. Bd. Rabbis (pres. 1955-57), Central Conf. Am. Rabbis (pres. 1977-79). Office: 1025 S Orange Ave Short Hills NJ 07078 *I have been influenced by the teaching of the 1st sage Hillel who said: "If I am not for myself, who will be for me? And if I am for myself only, what am I? And if not now, when?".*

PILGRIM, WALTER EDWARD, minister; b. St. Paul, Mar. 26, 1934; s. Walter John and Theresa Amelia (Bensamen) P.; m. Jeanette Marie

Schmierer, Aug. 11, 1957; children: Kathryn, Kristen, Karyn. BA, Wartburg Coll., Waverly, Iowa, 1956; BD, Wartburg Theol. Sem., Dubuque, Iowa, 1960; ThM, Princeton Theol. Sem., 1966, PhD, 1971. Ordained to ministry Evang. Luth. Ch., 1960. Minister Our Savior Luth., Edmonton, Alta., 1960-65; tchr. Pacific Luth. U., Tacoma, Wash., 1971—; dir. Luth. Inst. for Theol. Edn., Tacoma, 1973—. Author: Good News to the Poor, 1981. Luth. World Fedn. scholar, West Germany, 1978-79, Pacific Luth. U. regents scholr, 1986. Mem. Soc. Bibl. Lit., Soc. for Advancement Continuing Edn. for Ministry. Home: 2410 Western Rd Steilacoom WA 98388 Office: Luth Inst Theol Edn Pacific Luth U Tacoma WA 98447

PILKENTON, KENNETH L., real estate agent, minister; b. Tulsa, Aug. 23, 1943; m. Martha Lamb, Sept. 14, 1968. Student, Sam Houston State U., Huntsville, Tex., 1961-62, U. Houston, 1963, So. Bible Coll., Houston, 1967-68, Collin County Community Coll., 1986—. Ordained minister Full Gospel Fellowship of Chs., 1968; lic. real estate broker. Founder, pres., evangelist, tchr. Spiritual Life Ministries, Inc., McKinney, Tex., 1972—; rd. mgr. McDuff Bros. Ministry, Pasadena, Tex., 1968-72; assoc. min. Roger McDuff Evangelistic Assn., Inc., Pasadena, Tex., 1982-84; office mgr. Merritt-Ammons Real Estate, McKinney, 1985-87; owner, mgr. Pilkenton Real Estate & Property Mgmt., 1987-90; broker, mgr. Century 21, Field & Assocs., 1990—; co-founder, mgr. The Timesmen Gospel Singing Quartet, 1964-68. Recipient Cert. of Appreciation Rotary Club, 1976. Avocation: photography. Home: PO Box 141 McKinney TX 75069 *The most important decision a man could make is to learn the words and character of God and pattern his own life as God directs.*

PILLA, ANTHONY MICHAEL, bishop; b. Cleve., Nov. 12, 1932; s. George and Libera (Nista) P. Student, St. Gregory Coll. Sem., 1952-53, Borromeo Coll. Sem., 1955, St. Mary Sem., 1954, 56-59; B.A. in Philosophy, John Carroll U., Cleve., 1961, M.A. in History, 1967. Ordained priest Roman Cath. Ch., 1959. Assoc. St. Bartholomew Parish, Middleburg Hts., Ohio, 1959-60; prof. Borromeo Sem., Wickliffe, Ohio, 1960-72; rector-pres. Borromeo Sem., 1972-75; mem. Diocese Cleve. Liturgical Commn., 1964-69, asst. dir., 1969-72; sec. for services to clergy and religious personnel Diocese Cleve., 1975-79; titular bishop Scardona; and aux. bishop of Cleve. and vicar Eastern region Diocese of Cleve., 1979-80, apostolic adminstr., from 1980; bishop of Cleve., from 1981; trustee Borromeo Sem., 1975-79, Cath. U., 1981-84; trustee, mem. bd. overseers St. Mary Sem., 1975-79; mem. adv. bd. permanent diaconate program Diocese of Cleve., 1975-79, hospitalization and ins. bd., 1979; bd dirs. Cath. Communications Found., 1981—. Bd. dirs. NCCJ, 1986—. Mem. Nat. Cath. Edn. Assn. (dir. 1972-75), U.S. Cath. Conf., Nat. Conf. Cath. Bishops, Cath. Conf. Ohio., Greater Cleve. Roundtable (trustee from 1981). Home and Office: Chancery Office 350 Chancery Bldg 1027 Superior Ave Cleveland OH 44114

PILOT, DOUGLAS MONTGOMERY, pastor; b. North Wildwood, N.J., Sept. 25, 1945; s. Milton Pilot and Norma Mae (Bardo) Pilot Keller; m. M. Gail Loftin, Aug. 11, 1966; children: David Douglas, Andrea Michelle. BS in Secondary Edn., John Brown U., 1969; MDiv, Southwestern Bapt. Theol. Sem., 1976; D of Ministry, Luther Rice Theol. Sem., 1983. Pastor Barron (Okla.) Bapt. Ch., 1966-71, Greencastle (Pa.) Bapt. Ch., 1976-86, Wyoming Valley Bapt. Ch., Wilkes-Barre, Pa., 1986—; community rep. Greencastle-Antrim Sr. Ctr., 1976-86; evangelism dir. N.E. Pa. Bapt. Assn., Scranton, Pa.; assoc. youth camp dir. Keystone Bapt. Assn., Mechanicsburg, Pa., 1979-86, missions com. chmn., 1980-86. Chaplain Wilkes-Barre Gen. Hosp., 1987—; chaplain, fireman West Pittston (Pa.) Hose Co. #1, 1987—. Office: Wyoming Valley Bapt Ch 233 N River Rd Wilkes-Barre PA 18702-1829 *More than ever in this busy and hectic world in which we live, we need an anchor. For me that anchor is Jesus Christ. While everything around us changes, He is always the same: Dependable.*

PIMENTA, SIMON IGNATIUS CARDINAL, bishop; b. Bombay, Mar. 1, 1920. Ordained to priest Roman Cath. Ch., 1949. Elected to titular Ch. of Bocconia, 1971; consecrated bishop, 1971, coadjutor bishop,, 1977, bishop of diocese,, 1978, created cardinal,, 1988. Address: Archbishops House, 21 Nathalal Parekh Marg, Bombay 400039, India

PINA-CABRAL, DANIEL, bishop; b. Gaia, Portugal, Jan. 27, 1924; s. Joaquim and Maria Pina-Cabral; m. Ana Avelina Pina-Cabral, Aug. 6, 1951; children: João Paulo, Ana Isabel, Joana, Daniel José. Licenciature in Law, U. Lisbon, Portugal, 1947. Named canon of Gibraltar; archdeacon Lusitanian Ch., Portugal, 1965-67; asst. bishop of Lebombo Anglican Ch., Mozambique, 1967-68, bishop of Lebombo, 1968-76; archdeacon of Gibraltar Anglican Ch., Portugal and Spain, 1987—. Address: Ch Eng, Rua Fernao Lopes, Castanheda 51, 4100 Porto Portugal

PINK, MICHAEL QUENTIN, religion educator; b. Toronto, Ont., Can., Sept. 23, 1955; came to U.S., 1985; s. Peter and Edith Jean (Wilson) P.; m. Brenda Davis, Jan. 25, 1986. Grad., North Delta Sr. Secondary Sch., 1973. Elder, treas., tchr. Abundant Life Ch., Mt. Juliet, Ind., 1987—; pres. Hidden Manna Inc., Mt. Juliet, 1988—; speaker in field. Author: The Bible, Inc.-In Your Life, Job. and Business, 1988 (Best Seller award), The Lord's Prayer, 1989, The Words in Red, 1989, Psalm 91, 1990 (Best Seller award), (booklets) Love Lifters, 1989. Mem. Fellowship of Cos. for Christ (co-founder local chpt., bd. dirs. Tenn. region). Office: Hidden Manna Inc PO Box 807 Mount Juliet IN 37122

PINKERTON, EDITH CHARLENE, communications executive; b. Saltville, Va., July 15, 1953; d. Charles Edgar Hunt and Dorothy Grace (Whitehead) Vance; m. Jerry Wayne Pinkerton, June 19, 1971; children: April Michelle, Lydia Grace. Student, SVC Coll., 1986-87. Sales mgr. Sta. WGTH Radio, Richlands, Va., 1979—. Presbyterian. Office: Rt 3 Box 359 Cedar Bluff VA 24641

PINKSTON, ISABEL HAY, minister, religious organization administrator; b. Cambridge, Ohio, Oct. 30, 1922; d. Wilmer Martin and Mary Nola (Clark) Hay; m. Benedict George Dudley, Mar. 12, 1969 (dec. Feb. 1974); m. Robert Sherrill Pinkston, May 1, 1984. BA cum laude, Monmouth (Ill.) Coll., 1944; postgrad. in Christian edn., Wheaton (Ill.) Coll., 1948-49. Ordained to ministry Nat. Assn. Congl. Chs., 1985. Instrumental and vocal music tchr. United Presbyn. Mission Sch., Frenchburg, Ky., 1944-48; dir. Christian edn. United Presbyn. Ch., Zanesville, Ohio, 1949-51; Christian edn. dir. A.R. Presbyn. Ch., Augusta, Ga., 1952-55; mem. staff Koinonia Found., Pikesville, Md., 1956-66; min., pres. bd. dirs. Ch. Religious Rsch., Inc., Grand Island, Fla., 1988—; del., participant Internat. Conf. Paranormal Rsch., Ft. Collins, Colo., 1988-89; tchr. psychography course Sancta Sophia Sem., 1991. Author: (biography) Seed-Sower for God's Kingdom, 1987; co-editor: Psychography , 1990; editor (newsletter) Koinonia Epistle, 1957-66, Religious Rsch. Jour., 1988—, Religious Rsch. Press, 1988—. Mem. Internat. Coun. Community Chs. (del. 1988—), Assn. for Past-Life Rsch. and Therapy (workshop leader 1989), Internat. Forum on New Sci. Home: PO Box 208 Grand Island FL 32735 Office: Ch Religious Rsch Inc 11134 CR 44 Leesburg FL 34788

PINKSTON, MOSES SAMUEL, minister; b. Camden, N.J., Jan. 14, 1923; s. William Lincoln and Benena (McDonald) P.; m. Esther Miller, Nov. 18, 1951; children: Moses S. Jr., Steven Alan. BA, Gordon Coll., 1949; MDiv, Temple U., 1952; MSW, Rutgers U., 1968; PhD, Calif. Grad. Sch. Theology, 1977. Ordained to ministry Am. Bapt. Chs. in the U.S.A., 1949. Area min., dir. urban ministries Am. Bapt. Chs., West Oakland, Calif., 1970-74; pastor Antioch Bapt. Ch., San Jose, Calif., 1974—; ret., 1988. Author: Black Church Development, 1977. Commr. Human Rels. Commn., Santa Clara County, Calif., 1975-77; mem. Urban Task Force, San Jose, 1980-82, San Jose Minority Com., 1984—. Lt. U.S. Army, 1943-46, ETO. Recipient Disting. Citizen award San Jose City, 1981. Mem. NAACP, NASW, Ministerial Alliance Santa Clara (pres. 1981), Masons. Democrat. Home: 1120 Silver Breeze Ct Stockton CA 95210

PINKSTON, RICHARD L., JR., minister; b. Memphis, July 26, 1955; s. Richard L. and Jewel Lee (Wilson) P. BA, Lambuth Coll., Jackson, Tenn., 1977; MDiv, Memphis Theol. Sem., 1980. Ordained deacon United Meth. Ch., 1978, elder, 1981. Pastor chs., Gibson County, Tenn., 1978-80, Caroll County, Tenn., 1980-83, Haywood County, Tenn., 1983-86; 0assoc. pastor lst United Meth. Ch., Jackson, 1986-87; pastor Georgian Hills United Meth. Ch., Memphis, 1987—; bd. dirs. Memphis Conf. Found., 1987—; mem. com. on worship Memphis Conf., 1987—; mem. work area on worship Asbury Dist., 1987—, mem. com. on ordained ministry, 1987—. Recipient award United Meth. Ch. Bd. Discipleship, 1988-90. Mem. Frayser Ministerial Alliance. Home: 1726 Georgian Dr Memphis TN 38127-4313 Office: Georgian Hills United Meth Ch 3925 Overton Crossing Memphis TN 37127-4099

PINKWASSER, D., rabbi; s. Edward Irwin and Selma Judith (Frakt) P.; m. Ann Jacqueline Rosenzweig, Aug. 8, 1971; children: Joshua, Aaron. BA, Bklyn. Coll., 1970; MA, NYU, 1971; DD, Rabbinical Assembly Coll., 1973. Cert. tchr., Ariz. Tchr. N.Y.C. Pub. Schs., 1968-75, Scottsdale (Ariz.) Pub. Schs., 1975-84; rabbi Temple Emanuel, Tempe, Ariz., 1978—. V.p. Religious Adv. Com., Dept. Corrections, 1987-88 (prison chaplain 1985—); bd. dirs. Chem. People Task Force, 1986-87. Recipient placque Desert Cross Lutheran Ch., Tempe, 1988. Mem. Rabbis of Greater Phoenix (bd. dirs., pres. 1986—, sec. treas. 1984-86), Jewish Fedn. Phoenix (bd. dirs. 1986—), Bur. Jewish Edn. (bd. dirs. 1986—). Avocations: skiing, traveling, music, foreign languages. Office: Temple Emanuel 5801 S Rural Rd Tempe AZ 85283

PIN-MEI, IGNATIUS KUNG (GONG) CARDINAL See KUNG (GONG) PIN-MEI, IGNATIUS CARDINAL

PINSKY, STEPHEN HOWARD, rabbi; b. N.Y.C., May 11, 1944; s. Simon and Ruth Rita (Rosenberg) P.; m. Elisabeth Leone Eisen, June 16, 1968; children: Seth William, Kira Sharon. BA cum laude, Franklin & Marshall Coll., Lancaster, Pa., 1966; BHL, Hebrew Union Coll., N.Y.C., 1968; MHL, Jewish Inst. Religion, N.Y.C., 1971. Ordained rabbi, 1971. Asst. rabbi Temple Beth-El of Great Neck (N.Y.), 1971-74, assoc. rabbi, 1974-76; rabbi Temple Sinai of Bergen County, Tenafly, N.J., 1976-81; assoc. rabbi Temple Israel, Mpls., 1981-85, sr. rabbi, 1985—; vis. lectr. Augsburg Coll., Mpls., 1983—; mem. Joint Commn. on Rabbinic Placement, N.Y.C., 1987—, Task Force on Interfaith Activities, 1987—, Joint Task Force on Synagogue Music, N.Y.C., 1983-86. Vice chmn. Ctr. for Victims of Torture, Mpls., 1990—; bd. dirs. Planned Parenthood of Minn., Mpls., 1981-89, Children's Theatre Co., Mpls., 1987—, Alfred Adler Inst. Minn., Mpls., 1981-85. Mem. Cen. Conf. Am. Rabbis, Minn. Rabbinical Assn. (pres. 1985-86). Home: 4615 Gaywood Dr Minnetonka MN 55345 Office: Temple Israel 2324 Emerson Ave S Minneapolis MN 55405

PINSON, DAVID CRAIG, minister; b. Sidney, Ohio, Oct. 22, 1954; s. Frank and Betty Jean (Whitt) P.; m. Kathy Jean Higginbotham, May 28, 1977; children: Brian Christopher, Priscilla Danielle. BA, Mt. Vernon (Ohio) Nazarene Coll., 1979; MA, Ashland (Ohio) Theol. Sem., 1981; postgrad., Bethany Theol. Sem., Dothan, Ala. Ordained to ministry Ch. of the Nazarene, 1979. Min. Warsaw (Ohio) Ch. of the Nazarene, 1977-79, Bellevue (Ohio) Ch. of the Nazarene, 1979-82, Buffalo (W.Va.) Ch. of the Nazarene, 1982-84, Seth (W.Va.) Ch. of the Nazarene, 1986-87, Campbell's Creek Ch. of the Nazarene, Charleston, W.Va., 1987—; instr. Nazarene Bible Sch., South Charleston, W.Va., 1985—. Mem. Phi Delta Lambda. Office: Campbell's Creek Ch of the Nazarene 543 Campbell's Creek Dr Charleston WV 25306 *No one person's life is exempt from the struggle of obstacles. All too many face these obstacles angry and alone, failing to learn the valuable lessons that they provide. The chiefest of those lessons is that all obstacles are surmountable, once a person realizes that God is with him or her, and that He transforms obstacles into opportunities.*

PINSON, WILLIAM MEREDITH, pastor, writer; b. Ft. Worth, Aug. 3, 1934; s. William Meredith and Ila Lee (Jones) P.; m. Bobbie Ruth Judd, June 4, 1955; children: Meredith Pinson Creasey, Allison Pinson. BA, U. N. Tex., 1955; BD, Southwestern Bapt. Theol. Sem., Ft. Worth, 1959, ThD, 1963, MDiv, 1973; LittD (hon.), Calif. Bapt. Coll., Riverside, 1978; DD (hon.), U. Mary Hardin-Baylor, Belton, Tex., 1984; LHD, Howard Payne U., Brownwood, Tex., 1986; LittD (hon.), Dallas Bapt. U., 1990. Ordained to ministry Bapt. Ch., 1955. Assoc. sec. Christian Life Commn., Dallas, 1957-63; prof. Christian ethics Southwestern Bapt. Theol. Sem., Ft. Worth, 1963-75; pastor First Bapt. Ch., Wichita Falls, Tex., 1975-77; pres. Golden Gate Bapt. Theol. Sem., Mill Valley, Calif., 1977-82; chmn. program com. Christian Life Commn., Southern Bapt. Conv., spl. rsch. for home mission bd., mem. nat. task force planned growth in giving, 1984—, stewardship commn., 1986—, adj. prof. Southwestern Bapt. Theol. Sem., 1976-77; v.p. Bapt. Gen. Conv. Tex., 1972-73; mem. state missions commn., 1976-77, vice chmn. urban strategy com., chmn. order of bus. com., 1976, chmn. steering com. Good News Texas, 1976-77, chmn. resolutions com.; speaker in field. Contbr. articles to numerous theological publs. Named Lilly Found. scholar Southwestern Bapt. Theol. Sem., 1960-62; Recipient Mosaic Missions award Home Mission Bd., 1984. Avocations: travel, reading. Office: Bapt Gen Conv Tex 333 N Washington Dallas TX 75246

PINT, SISTER ROSE MARY, nun, religious order administrator, health care executive. BS in Nursing, Marillac Coll. Nursing, 1966; MA in Human Rels., St. Louis U., 1971, cert., 1977. Joined Franciscan Sisters, Daus. of Sacred Hearts of Jesus and Mary, Roman Cath. Ch., 1959. Staff nurse St. Anthony's Hosp., St. Louis, 1966-67, dir. staff devel., 1971-73; coord. alcohol outpatients dept. St. Michael Hosp., Milw., 1967-68, dir. outpatient clinic, 1968-69; with hosp. task force Franciscan Sisters, Wheaton, Ill., 1969-71; v.p. ops. St. Elizabeth Hosp., Appleton, Wis., 1973-76; v.p. clin. svcs. Marianjoy Rehab. Ctr., Wheaton, 1976-78; dir. Franciscan Sponsorship Commn., Wheaton, 1979-83; chairperson, chief exec. officer Wheaton Franciscan Svcs., Inc., 1983-86, chairperson bd., 1986—; provincial directress Franciscan Sisters, Daus. of Sacred Hearts of Jesus and Mary, Wheaton, 1988—; mem. Chgo. Archdiocesan Collaboration Task Force, Commn. on Cath. Health Care Ministry Network. Author: (with others) Catholic Health Care Systems: A Prescription for Success, 1988. Recipient Harold M. Coon, MD Award of Merit Wis. Hosp. Assn., 1975; named Outstanding Young Woman of Yr., Appleton (Wis.) Jaycees, 1975, Outstanding Bus. and Profl. Woman Leader of DuPage County, DuPage YWCA, 1990. Fellow Am. Coll. Hosp. Adminstrs.; mem. Am. Hosp. Assn., Ill. Hosp. Assn., Cath. Health Assn. U.S. (trustee), Cath. Health Assn. Wis., Ill. Cath. Conf. Hosps., Leadership Conf. Women Religious, Franciscan Fedn., Chgo. Cath. Health Care Alliance. Address: 26W171 Roosevelt Rd PO Box 667 Wheaton IL 60189-0667

PIOVANELLI, SILVANO CARDINAL, former archbishop of Florence; b. Feb. 21, 1924. ordained Roman Cath. Ch., 1947. Consecrated bishop Titular Ch. Tubune, Mauritania, 1982; archbishop Florence, Italy, 1983-87; proclaimed cardinal, 1985. Address: Arcivescovado, Piazza S Giovanni 3, 50129 Florence Italy

PIPE, MURRAY A., religious organization head. Pres. Fellowship Evang. Bapt. Chs. in Can., Guelph, Ont. Office: Evang Bapt Chs Can, 3034 Bayview Ave, Willowdale, ON Canada M2N 6J5*

PIPER, THOMAS SAMUEL, minister, consultant; b. Racine, Wis., Feb. 26, 1932; s. Wallace William and Margaret Alice (Lahr) P.; m. Mary Alice Smith, Mar. 12, 1955; children: Daniel Thomas, David Michael, Grace Susan Piper Gonzales. BS, Lawrence U., 1954; ThM, Dallas Theol. Sem., 1969. Ordained to ministry Christian Ch., 1982. Mng. editor Good News Broadcaster mag., Lincoln, Nebr., 1969-82; pastor adminstrn. Faith Bible Ch., Sterling, Va., 1982-86; pres., cons. Ministries in Sync, Sterling, 1986—; mem. writers conf. faculty Mt. Hermon (Calif.) Christian Conf., 1978-80, Christian Writers Inst., Wheaton, Ill., 1980; mem. pres.'s coun. Loudon County, Good News Jail and Prison Ministry, Arlington, Va., 1984-86; pres. Christian Ministries Mgmt. Assn., Washington, 1987, 88; mem. Christian Mgmt. Assn., 1989-90, Nat. Assn. Ch. Bus. Adminstrs., 1986-90. Contbr. numerous articles to profl. jours. With USN, 1956-58. Mem. Voice of Bibl. Reconciliation (bd. dirs. 1991—), Dallas Theol. Sem. Assn. (pres. local chpt. 1991—), Internat. Assn. Bus. Communicators (life, pres. 1977-79). Republican. Home and Office: Ministries in Sync 1307 E Holly Ave Sterling VA 22170 *The strategic result of our calling today is helping churches in a me-centered high-tech age to synchronize their ministries to produce a pleasing and efficacious impact before a watching world.*

PIPKIN, H. WAYNE, religion educator; b. Houston, Aug. 10, 1939; s. Henry W. and Lillie (Kuehn) P.; m. Arlene L. Schenk, June 12, 1965; children: Nancy Gail, Heather Michelle. BA, Baylor U., 1961; MA, U. Conn., 1963; PhD, Hartford Sem., 1968. Ordained to ministry Am. Bapt. Ch., 1990. Missionary Fgn. Mission Bd., So. Bapt. Conv., Richmond, Va., 1978-89; prof. Anabaptist and sixteenth century studies Associated Mennonite Bibl. Sem., Elkhart, Ind., 1989—; assoc. dir. Inst. Mennonite Studies, Elkhart, 1989—; advisor Mennonite Hist. Libr., 1990—. Author: A Zwingli Bibliography, 1972, Christian Meditation, 1976; translator, editor: Huldrych Zwingli, Writings, II, 1984, Balthasar Hubmaier, 1989; mem. editorial bd. Mennonite Quar. Rev., 1989—; contbr. articles to profl. publs. Del. State Dem. Party, Tex., 1972; coord. Bread for the World, Ohio, 1976-78; trustee Franklin County Hunger Task Force, Columbus, Ohio, 1975-78. Fulbright scholar, 1968-69. Mem. Am. Acad. Religion, Am. Soc. Ch. History, 16th Century Studies Conf., Ecclesiastical History Soc., Mennonite Hist. Soc., Zwingli Verein. Democrat. Office: Associated Mennonite Sems 3003 Benham Ave Elkhart IN 46517

PIRAINO, PAUL LYNN, minister; b. Mount Morris, N.Y., July 31, 1964; s. Peter and Phyllis Irene (Dodson) P.; m. Christine Balent, Sept. 27, 1986; children: Jessica Christine, Angela Marie, Lauren Nicole. B in Pastoral Ministry/Christian Edn., United Wesleyan Coll., 1986. Asst. pastor Bayview Wesleyan Ch., Traverse City, Mich., 1987-89, Victory Hwy. Wesleyan Ch., Painted Post, N.Y., 1989—; dist. exec. youth bd. Wesleyan Dist. Cen. N.Y., 1989—; youth network assoc. Traverse City, 1989—. Named Outstanding Young Men of Am., 1990. Republican. Home: 14 Charles St Corning NY 14830

PIRKLE, ESTUS WASHINGTON, minister; b. Vienna, Ga., Mar. 12, 1930; s. Grover Washington and Bessie Nora (Jones) P.; m. Annie Catherine Gregory, Aug. 18, 1955; children: Letha Dianne, Gregory Don. BA cum laude, Mercer U., 1951; BD, MRE, Southwestern Bapt. Sem., 1956, ThM, 1958; DD, Covington Theol. Sem., 1982. Ordained to ministry So. Bapt. Conv., 1949. Pastor Locust Grove Bapt. Ch., New Albany, Miss.; speaker Camp Zion, Myrtle, Miss. Author: Preachers in Space, I Believe God, Sermon Outlines Book, Who Will Build Your House?; producer religious films: If Footmen Tire You, What Will Horses Do?, 1973, The Burning Hell, 1975, Believer's Heaven, 1977. Home: PO Box 721 New Albany MS 38652 Office: PO Box 80 Myrtle MS 38650

PIROMGRAIPAKD, SOMCHAI, minister; b. Ubol, Thailand, Feb. 7, 1945; came to U.S., 1970; s. Prachak Thongin and Wandee (Sawangngarm) P.; m. Boonpin Choikiatkul, May 30, 1971; children: Bruce, Michael. AS, East L.A. Coll., 1977; BA, Loma Linda U., 1987. Ordained to ministry Seventh-day Adventist Ch., 1989; registered respiratory therapist, Calif. Assoc. chaplain Bangkok Adventist Hosp., 1965-67; assoc. pastor Bangkok Adventist Hosp. Ch., 1967-69; founder, pastor Thai Seventh-day Adventist Ch., Redlands, Calif., 1974—; mem. coordinating com. Asian South Pacific Ministry, Pacific Union Conf. Seventh-day Adventist, Westlake Village, Calif., 1989-91. Home: 4450 Belair Dr La Canada CA 91011 Office: Thai Seventh-day Adventist Ch 10855 New Jersey St Redlands CA 92373

PIRONIO, EDUARDO CARDINAL, Argentinian ecclesiastic; b. Buenos Aires, Argentina, Dec. 3, 1920; ed. Diocesan Sem. La Plata, Pontifical U. Angelicum, Rome. Ordained priest Roman Cath. Ch., 1943; prof. maj. Diocesan Sem. Mercedes; rector Sem. Metropolitano Buenos Aires Sem. Buenos Aires-Villa Devoto; vicar gen. of Mercedes; dean Faculty of Theology, Cath. U. Argentina; aux. bishop of La Plata, 1964; sec.-gen. CELAM, 1968-71, pres., 1971-75; bishop of Mar del Plata, 1975; pro-prefect Sacred Congregation for Religious and Secular Insts., 1975; cardinal prefect SCRIS, 1976-84, mem. Pontifical Council for Laity (pres. 1984—). Participant in synods of bishops, 1967, 69, 71, 74, 78, 80; dir. retreats for priests, men religious, women religious; dir. retreat for Pope Paul and Roman Curia, 1974. Office: Piazza del S Uffizzio 11, 00193 Rome Italy

PISCOPO, RICH, executive director; b. N.Y.C., Oct. 21, 1955; s. Joseph and Grace (Scauso) P.; m. Ruth Chei, Mar. 27, 1976. Cert. of bibl. studies, So. Bapt. Extension, 1975. Ordained to ministry So. Bapt. Ch., 1975. Youth pastor Grace Bapt. Ch., Lake Grove, N.Y., 1974-80; assoc. evangelist Billy Graham Assn., Holliston, Mass., 1981; crusade evangelist Evangelistic Team, Inc., N.Y.C., 1982-90; exec. dir. Scripture Gift Mission/USA, 1990—; chmn. Rich & Ruth Evangelistic Team, N.Y.C., 1982—; bd. dirs. Internat. Evangelism, N.Y.C. Author (tract) Am. Tract Soc., 1987; contbr. articles to religious mags. Speaker Outreach Say No to Drugs programs, 1981—. Mem. Conf. of So. Bapt. Evangelists (pres. N.Y. chpt. 1981—). Republican. Office: Scripture Gift Mission PO Box 250 Willow Street PA 17584 also: Scripture Gift Mission, 3 Eccleston St, London SW1W9LZ, England *I have travelled around the world to almost 40 countries. I have found people have the same heart need. Jesus Christ is the only one who can meet that heart need.*

PISHAW, KARL JOSEPH, pastor; b. Seattle, June 5, 1953; s. Joseph Junior and Shirley Lois (Johnson) P.; m. Jean Mae Buckley, May 26, 1984; 1 child, Abigail Lynn. Diploma Bibl. studies, Luth. Bible Inst., Seattle, 1973, BS, 1976; BA, U. Dubuque, 1980; MDiv, Wartburg Theol. Sem., Dubuque, 1984. Ordained to ministry Am. Luth. Ch., 1984. Youth dir. Renton (Wash.) Luth. Ch., 1974-76; guitarist RADIANCE music team Luth. Bible Inst., 1976; youth min. Bethlehem Luth. Ch., Sedro-Woolley, Wash., 1976-79; assoc. pastor Fron and Minnewaska Luth. Chs., Starbuck, Minn., 1984-90, Luth. Ch. of Master, Brooklyn Center, Minn., 1990—; clergy rep., mem. adv. bd. Early Childhood/Family Edn., Starbuck and Glenwood, Minn., 1985-90; conf. del. Augustana Coll. Assn., Sioux Falls, S.D., 1985-89; pastoral advisor Women's Aglow Fellowship, Morris, Minn., 1987-90; bd. advisors Luth. campus ministry U. Minn., Morris, 1988-90. Musician, singer, guitarist, songwriter (cassette tape) Songs of the New Covenant, 1976; guitarists record album RADIANCE, 1976. Mem. entertainment com. Starbuck Heritage Days, 1988. Mem. Brooklyn Center-Brooklyn Park Ministerial Assn., Gt. Comm. Network. Republican. Office: Luth Ch of Master 1200 69th Ave N Brooklyn Center MN 55430

PITRONE, MARGO RAE, minister; b. Toronto, Ont., Can., Nov. 22, 1960; came to U.S., 1965; d. Henry Floyd and Frieda Jo (Baethke) Mattson; m. Lawrence R. Pitrone, Apr. 25, 1984. BSW, Andrews U., 1983; MDiv, Princeton Theol. Sem., 1988. Assoc. pastor Tierrasanta Seventh-day Adventist Ch., San Diego, 1988-89; v.p. North Pk. Christian Svc. Agy., San Diego, 1989, pres., 1990; chair Ministerial Adv. Com., Riverside, 1990-91. Contbr. articles to profl. jours. Vol. chaplain Paradise Valley Hosp., San Diego, 1988—; pres. Women Mins. of Southeastern Conf. of Seventh-day Adventists, Riverside, 1989-90, mem. Justice Commn., 1991. Mem. Adventist Assn. of Women, Adventist Women's Inst., San Diego Seventh-day Adventist Ministerial Assn., Tierrasanta Ministerial Assn. Home: 532 Canyon Dr PO Box 941 Bonita CA 91908

PITTELKO, ROGER DEAN, clergyman; b. Elk Reno, Okla., Aug. 18, 1932; s. Elmer Henry and Lydia Caroline (Nieman) P.; A.A., Concordia Coll., 1952; B.A., Concordia Sem., St. Louis, 1954, M.Div., 1957, S.T.M., 1958; postgrad. Chgo. Luth. Theol. Sem., 1959-61; Th.D., Am. Div. Sch., Pineland, Fla., 1968; D.Min., Faith Evang. Luth. Sem., Tacoma, 1983; m. Beverly A. Moellendorf, July 6, 1957; children—Dean, Susan. Ordained to ministry, Lutheran Ch.-Mo. Synod, 1958; vicar St. John Luth. Ch., S.I., N.Y., 1955-56; asst. pastor St. John Luth. Ch., New Orleans, 1958-59; pastor Concordia Luth. Ch., Berwyn, Ill., 1959-63; pastor Luth. Ch. of the Holy Spirit, Elk Grove Village, Ill., 1963-87; chmn. Commn. on Worship, Luth. Ch.-Mo. Synod; asst. bishop Midwest region English dist., 1983; pres. and bishop English dist., 1987—. Mem. Luth. Acad. for Scholarship, Concordia Hist. Inst. Republican. Clubs: Maywood (Ill.) Sportsman; Itasca (Ill.) Country. Author: Guide to Introducing Lutheran Worship. Contbr. articles to jours. Home: 19405 Stamford Livonia MI 48152 Office: 23001 Grand River Ave Detroit MI 48219

PITTMAN, MATTHEW DALE, minister; b. Proctorville, Ohio, Oct. 3, 1969; s. Garland Jerry and Carolyn Delores (Saunders) P. AA, Ohio Valley Coll., 1990. Asst. minister Hurricane (W.Va.) Ch. of Christ, 1990—. Mem. Sigma Epsilon Chi. Republican. Home: 2904 1/2 Virginia Ave Hurricane WV 25526

PITTS, DANNY CARROL, minister; b. Soso, Miss., Aug. 21, 1950; s. Elvin Jonah and Betty Lou (Parker) P.; m. Helen Ruth Cole, Oct. 6, 1972; children: Lee Jefferson, Nancy Carol. BS, U. So. Miss., 1972; MDiv, Bapt. Missionary Assn. Theol. Sem., 1981. Ordained to ministry Bapt. Missionary Assn. Am., 1977. Pastor, ch. planting missionary Bapt. Missionary Assn. of Miss., Lakeland, Fla., 1981-84; pastor Bethel Bapt. Ch., Port Arthur, Tex., 1985—; trustee Tex. Bapt. Home for Children, Waxahachie, 1988—. Contbr. articles to profl. jours. Home: 6247 Garnet Ave Port Arthur TX 77640

PITTS, ROBERT DUANE, religion educator, minister; b. Rockford, Mich., Feb. 16, 1932; s. Ralph Hays and Mildred (Jewell) Pitts; m. Marsha E. Weir, Aug. 15, 1952; children—Debra, Gregory, Sheila. Student Moody Bible Inst., 1950-52; A.B., Greenville Coll., 1955; M. Div., No. Bapt. Theol. Sem., 1958; M.A., U. Mich., 1964; D. Ed., Ind. U., 1969. Ordained to ministry Baptist Ch., 1958. asst. pastor Temple Bapt. Ch., St. Paul, 1959-61; asst. supt. Lydia Children's Home, Chgo., 1961-62; tchr. English, Greenville High Sch., Mich., 1962-63; dir. pub. relations and devel. Oakland City Coll., Ind., 1964-67; asst. dean, assoc. prof. Geneva Coll., Beaver Falls, Pa., 1969-73; prof. religion Taylor U., Upland, Ind., 1973—, v.p. acad. affairs, 1973-82, assoc. dean div. of letters, 1990—; pastor Mt. Gilead Bapt. Ch., Hemlock, Ind., 1987—; trustee AuSable Trails Inst. of Environ. Studies, Mancelona, Mich., 1973-86; post-doctoral fellow Ecumenical Inst. for Theol. Research, Jerusalem, 1986-87. Contbr. articles to profl. jours. Mem. Evang. Mennonite Ch., Upland. Mem. Evang. Theol. Soc., Nat. Assn. Profs. Christian Edn., Bibl. Archaeology Soc. Republican. Baptist. Avocations: golf; hunting; photography. Home: 915 S Second St Upland IN 46989 Office: Taylor U Dept Bibl Studies Upland IN 46989

PITTS, WILLIAM LEE, JR., religion educator; b. Winfield, Kans., Dec. 27, 1937; s. William Lee and Berniece Irene (Beck) P.; m. Ruth Eleanor Landes, Sept. 15, 1961; children: William Robert, James Lee. BA, Baylor U., 1960; MDiv, Vanderbilt U., 1963, PhD, 1969. Instr. Mercer U., Macon, Ga., 1966-69; asst. prof. Houston Bapt. U., 1969-70, Dallas Bapt. U., 1970-75; prof. Baylor U., Waco, Tex., 1975—, dir. grad. studies in religion, 1988—. Editor Jour. Tex. Bapt. History, 1981—; book rev. editor Jour. of Ch. and State, 1983-85; contbr. articles, book revs. to profl. jours. Co-organizer Waco Soccer Assn., 1976. Mem. Am. Soc. Ch. History (host, program chmn. 1981), Am. Acad. Religion (chmn. regional sessions 1976, 90), Conf. on Faith and History, Popular Culture Assn., Nat. Assn. Bapt. Profs. of Religion (pres. S.W. div. 1986-87), Oral History Assn., Independence Bapt. Assn. (pres. 1984—, mem. selection com. Tex. Bapt. elder statesman). Home: 717 Ivyann Dr Waco TX 76712 Office: Baylor U Dept Religion Waco TX 76798

PIZZIMENTI, DAVID MICHAEL, minister; b. Chicago Heights, Ill., Mar. 9, 1954; s. Louis John and Carolyn Dean (Morgan) P.; m. Judy Ann Konkol, Apr. 1974 (div. 1980); children: Jessica Marie, Joshua Michael; m. Kelly Elise Burden, Oct. 24, 1981. AA, Enterprise (Ala.) Jr. Coll., 1985. Ordained to ministry, 1986. Founding pastor Glory to Him Fellowship, Inc., Ozark, Ala., 1987—; Ala. dist. dir. Rhema Ministerial Assn., Tulsa, 1989—. With U.S. Army, 1981-86. Office: Glory to Him Fellowship 3501 E Andrews Ave Ozark AL 36360

PLACHER, WILLIAM CARL, philosophy and religion educator; b. Peoria, Ill., Apr. 28, 1948; s. Carl Henry and Louise Ellen (Swanson) P. AB, Wabash Coll., 1970; M. Philosophy, Yale U., 1974, PhD, 1975. Prof. philosophy and religion Wabash Coll., Crawfordsville, Ind., 1974—; mem. Ctr. Theol. Inquiry, Princeton, 1987-88; vis. scholar dept. religious studies Stanford U., 1980-81. Author: A History of Christian Theology, 1983, Readings in the History of Christian Theology, 1988, Unapologetic Theology, 1989. Mem. com. to draft brief statement of faith Presbyn. Ch. USA, 1984—. Danforth fellow Danforth Found., 1970. Mem. Am. Acad. Religion (chair narrative group 1986-89). Home: 1107 S Grant Crawfordsville IN 47933 Office: Wabash Coll Dept Philosophy & Religion Crawfordsville IN 47933

PLAGENZ, GEORGE RICHARD, minister, journalist, columnist; b. Lakewood, Ohio, Dec. 11, 1923; s. George William and Edith Louise (Fenner) P.; m. Faith Hanna, Sept. 12, 1953 (div.); children—Joel, George William II, Nicole, Sarah. B.A. cum laude, Western Res. U., 1945; S.T.B., Harvard, 1949. Ordained to ministry Unitarian Ch., 1951. Sports writer Cleve. Press, 1943-46; asst. minister King's Chapel, Boston, 1951-54; news broadcaster Radio Sta. WEEI, Boston, 1955-63; writer Boston Sunday Advertiser, 1963-70; religion editor Cleve. Press, 1970-82; syndicated columnist Scripps-Howard Newspapers, 1974-80, Newspaper Enterprise Assn., 1980—. Mem. Beta Theta Pi. Club: Harvard (Boston). Home: 239-B East Beck St Columbus OH 43206

PLANK, FRANK BENJAMIN, III, minister; b. Phila., Dec. 16, 1942; s. Frank Benjamin Jr. and Jeanne (Wright) P.; m. Barbara Lynn Pearce, June 5, 1965; children: Kristen Lynn, Kelly Lynn, Kara Lynn. BA, Furman U., 1965; MDiv magna cum laude, New Brunswick Theol. Sem., 1981; D Ministry, Ashland Sem., 1990. Ordained to ministry Nat. Assn. of Congl. Christian Chs., 1981. Elder 1st Congl. Ch., Chester, N.J., 1978-81; sr. pastor Plain Congl. Ch., Bowling Green, Ohio, 1981-90, Community Ch., Plantation, Fla., 1990—. Chmn. Mazahoa Mission Adv. Bd., Bowling Green, 1987-90. bd. mem. at large, 1990—; bd. dirs., trustee God's Garden, Bowling Green, 1981—; co-dir. Tortola Work Camp Mission Outreach, Manchester, Conn., 1985—. Mem. Nat. Assn. Evangelicals, Ohio Assn. Congl. Christian Chs., Fla. Assn. Congl. Christian Chs. Home: 901 SW 68th Ave Plantation FL 33317 Office: Plantation Community Ch 6501 W Broward Blvd Plantation FL 33317

PLANK, KARL ANDREWS, theology educator; b. Raleigh, N.C., Nov. 18, 1951; s. Charles Andrews and Joyce Cecelia (Clayton) P.; m. Mary Elizabeth Jacobs, Aug. 3, 1974 (div. Oct. 1983); m. Kathleen Blackwell, Dec. 22, 1989. BA, Hanover Coll., 1974; Master Divinity, Vanderbilt U., 1977, MA, 1980, PhD, 1983. Instr. Davidson (N.C.) Coll., 1982-83, asst. prof. Theology, 1983-88, assoc. prof. Theology, 1988—. Author: Paul and the Irony of Affliction, 1987; contbr. articles to profl. jours. mem. Internatn. Thomas Merton Soc., Am. Acad. Religion, Soc. Bibl. Lit. Episcopalian. Avocations: Celtic and Early Am. folk music, baseball, photography. Home: P O Box 946 Davidson NC 28036 Office: Davidson Coll P O Box 1719 Davidson NC 28036

PLANTE, SISTER MARY MICHAELINDA, school system administrator; b. Providence, Dec. 13, 1934; d. Albert Adlaide Plante and Helen Maude (Willey) Caron. BS in Edn., Mercy Coll., 1957; MA in Edn., R.I. Coll., 1969; EdD, Boston Coll., 1991. Cert. family counselor Boston Family Inst. Tchr. Diocese Fall River, Mass., 1957-65, assoc. supt, 1985—; tchr. Diocese Providence, 1957-65; dir. Carter Day Nursery, Providence, 1968-73; asst. registrar Salve Regina Coll., Newport, R.I., 1973-74, exec. housekeeper, 1965-68; prin. St. Mary's Parish, Winchester, Mass., 1974-84; religious edn. coord. St. Bartholomew Parish, Providence, 1985—. V.p. Mercy Elem. Edn. Network, 1987-89, pres., 1989-92; mem. New Eng. Dept. Chief Administrs. Mem. Nat. Cath. Edn. Assn., N.E. Assn. Cath. Devel. Dirs. (exec. bd. dirs. 1988—), Fall River C. of C. (Pub. Safety award 1990), Delta Kappa Gamma, Phi Delta Kappa. Democrat. Avocations: reading, sewing, walking, listening classical music. Office: Diocese Fall River 423 Highland Ave Fall River MA 02720

PLANTINGA, ALVIN, philosophy educator, author; b. Ann Arbor, Mich., Nov. 15, 1932; s. Cornelius A. and Lettie Gertrude (Bossenbroek) P.; m. Kathleen Ann DeBoer, June 16, 1955; children: Carl, Jane, Harry, Ann. A.B., Calvin Coll., 1954; M.A., U. Mich., 1955; Ph.D., Yale U., 1958; D.D. hon., Glasgow U., Scotland, 1982. Instr. Yale U., New Haven, 1957-58; assoc. prof. Wayne State U., Detroit, 1958-63; prof. Calvin Coll., Grand Rapids, Mich., 1963-82; John A. O'Brien prof. philosophy U. Notre Dame, Ind., 1982—; dir. summer seminar Coun. Philosophic Studies, Grand Rapids, 1973; dir. summer seminars NEH, Grand Rapids, 1975, 76, 78, co-dir., 1986; dir. Notre Dame Ctr. Philosophy of Religion. Author: God and Other Minds, 1967, The Nature of Necessity, 1974, God, Freedom and Evil, 1974, Does God Have A Nature?, 1980. Fellow Ctr. Advanced Study in Behavioral Scis., 1968-69; Guggenheim fellow, 1971-72; fellow NEH, 1975-76, 87; vis. fellow Balliol Coll., Oxford, Eng., 1975-76, Gifford Lectr., 1987, Wilde lectr., 1988. Mem. Am. Philos. Assn. (pres. western div. 1982), Soc. Christian Philosophers (pres. 1983-86). Home: 50505 Hollyhock Rd South Bend IN 46637 Office: U Notre Dame Dept Philosophy Notre Dame IN 46556

PLASTERER, GEORGE MICHAEL, minister; b. Bemidji, Minn., Dec. 4, 1951; s. Albert Owen and Alwra (Knee) P.; m. Cheryl Ann Bellmere, June 6, 1978 (div. Sept. 1990); children: Michael, David. AA, Miltonvale (Kans.) Wesleyan Coll., 1972; BA, Ind. Wesleyan Coll., 1974; MDiv, Asbury Theol. Sem., 1979; D Ministry, McCormick Theol. Sem., Chgo., 1987. Ordained to ministry as deacon United Meth. Ch., 1983, as elder, 1985. Pastor Greenville (Ind.) Parish, 1979-82, Brownstown (Ind.) Parish, 1982-87; assoc. pastor Plainfield (Ind.) Parish, 1987—. Mem. Spiritual Formation Com., Bloomington, Ind., 1987; chairperson chaplaincy com. Hendricks Community Hosp., Danville, Ind., 1991. Home: 320 S Vine St Plainfield IN 46168 Office: Plainfield United Meth Ch 600 Simmons St Plainfield IN 46168

PLASTOW, JOHN ROBERT, religion writer, publisher, musician; b. Blue Island, Ill., June 22, 1958; s. Robert Lewis and Dorothea Isabel (Kidwell) P.; m. Karen Marie Andrews, June 23, 1979; children: John Robert II, Melody Elizabeth. BA in Music and Theatre, U. Redlands, 1979. Dir. theatre Crystal Cathedral Music Ministry, Garden Grove, Calif., 1979-82; dir. Family Arts Ctr. Grace United Meth. Ch., Long Beach, Calif., 1982-83; exec. dir. Plastow Ministries/Prodns., Orange City, Calif., 1985—, Plastow Publs., Orange, Calif., 1988—, The Drama Store, Orange, 1989—; cons. various chs. and pubs., 1980—, including Crystal Cathedral, Garden Grove, 1986-88, Alexandria House, Nashville, 1988-91, Sparrow, Nashville, 1990-91; speaker, clinician MusicCalif., Music Minn., Music Tex., Mus. Fla., other nat. confs. Author: Football, Pizza and Success!, 1987; script writer over 50 dramas, 1988-91, musicals Can't Say It Loud Enough, 1991, The Majesty and Glory of Christmas, 1991; contbr. articles to religious and musical publs. Republican. Mem. Evang. Free Ch. Am. Avocations: cooking, animals, baseball.

PLATT, ALBERT THOMAS, religious organization administrator, clergyman; b. Atlantic City, May 17, 1927; s. Raymond and Florence Mildred (Hitchner) P.; m. Gladys Ann Hage, June 17, 1948; children: Elizabeth Gayle Platt Sandoval, Roberta Ann Platt Friesen, Brenda Joann. BA, Wheaton Coll., 1947; ThM, Dallas Theol. Sem., 1951, ThD, 1962. Ordained to ministry Ind. Bapt. Ch., 1951. Adminstr. programming Sta. TGNA, Guatemala City, Guatemala, 1952-60; prof., adminstr. Cen. Am. Bible Inst., Guatemala City, 1960-67; founder, pres. Cen. Am. Theol. Sem., Guatemala City, 1967-73; pres. Cen. Am. Mission Internat., Dallas, 1974—. Office: Cen Am Mission Internat 8625 La Prada Dr Dallas TX 75228

PLATT, WINSTON ALAN, minister; b. Cuba, N.Y., Aug. 15, 1948; s. Alfred Carlton and Felice Freda (Schuyler) P.; m. Sandra Sue Davis, July 12, 1969; children: Sharon Dawn, John Daniel, Gloria Joy, Anna Faith. Diploma in pastoral tng., Moody Bible Inst., 1969; BA in Sociology, Trinity Coll., 1971. Ordained to ministry Bible Ch., 1974. Pastor Eagleville Bible Ch., Jefferson, Ohio, 1972-81, North Bingham (Pa.) Community Ch., 1981-82; interim pastor various chs., N.Y., 1982-85; pastor Oatka Bapt. Ch., Warsaw, N.Y., 1985-90, Birdsall Community Ch., Angelica, N.Y., 1990—; vol. chaplain Ashtabula (Ohio) Gen. Hosp., 1976-78, Ashtabula County Jail, 1977-80; mem. com. Inst. Basic Life Principles, Cleve., 1977-80; missionary-pastor Village Missions, 1990—. Vol. fireman Angelica Hose Co., 1982-85. Mem. Intercounty Bible Bapt. Fellowship (pres. 1987-88).

PLAUT, JONATHAN VICTOR, rabbi; b. Chgo., Oct. 7, 1942; s. W. Gunther and Elizabeth (Strauss) P.; m. Carol Ann Fainstein, July 5, 1965; children: Daniel Abraham, Deborah Maxine. BA, Macalester Coll., 1964; postgrad., Hebrew Union Coll., Jerusalem, 1967-68; BHL, Hebrew Union Coll., Cin., 1968, MA, 1970, DHL, 1977. Ordained rabbi, 1970. Rabbi Congregation Beth-El, Windsor, Ont., Can., 1970-84; sr. rabbi Temple Emanu-El, San Jose, Calif., 1985—; lectr. Assumption Coll. Sch., 1972-84, St. Clair Coll., 1982-84; adj. asst. prof. Santa Clara U., 1985—. Editor: Through the Sound of Many Voices, 1982; contbr. articles to profl. jours.; host weekly program Religious Scope Sta. CBET-TV, Religion in the News Sta. CKWW Radio, 1971-84. Chmn. bd. Jewish Nat. Fund Windsor, 1981-84; chmn. United Jewish Appeal Windsor, 1981-83, State of Israel Bonds, Windsor, 1980; nat. bd. dirs. Jewish Nat. Fund Can., 1972-84; pres. Reform Rabbis of Can., 1982-84; bd. dirs. Can. Jewish Congress, 1978-84, Jewish Family Svc. Santa Clara County, 1987-90, Jewish Fedn. Greater San Jose, 1986—; chaplain San Jose Fire Dept., 1987—; mem. exec. cabinet United Jewish Appeal, Windsor, 1971-84; mem. exec. com. Windsor Jewish Community Coun., 1970-84, chmn. 1975-84; mem. adv. coun. Riverview unit Windsor Hosp. Ctr., 1972-81; pres. Credit Counselling Svc. Met. Windsor, 1977-79. Mem. Can. Jewish Congress (nat. exec. bd. 1978-84), Can. Jewish Hist. Soc. (nat. v.p. 1974-84), Rabbinic Assn. Greater San Jose (chmn. 1986-87), Cen. Conf. Am. Rabbis, Nat. Assn. Temple Educators, Can. Assn. Temple Educators, Can. Coun. Christians and Jews (Windsor chpt.), Rotary. Office: 1010 University Ave San Jose CA 95126

PLAUT, WOFL GUNTHER, minister, author; b. Muenster, Germany, Nov. 1, 1912; emigrated to U.S., 1935, arrived in Canada, 1961; s. Jonas and Selma (Gumprich) P.; m. Elizabeth Strauss, Nov. 10, 1938; children: Jonathan, Judith. LLB, U. Berlin, 1933, JD, 1934; MHL, Hebrew Union Coll., Cin., 1939, DD, 1964; LLD, U. Toronto, 1978; DLitt, Cleve. Coll. Jewish Studies, 1979; LLD, York U., 1987. Ordained rabbi, 1939. Rabbi B'nai Abraham Zion, Chgo., 1939-48, Mt. Zion Temple, St. Paul, 1948-61; sr. rabbi Holy Blossom Temple, Toronto, Ont., Can., 1961-77; sr. scholar Holy Blossom Temple, 1978—; adj. prof. York U., 1979—. Author: Mount Zion, 1956, The Jews in Minnesota, 1959, The Book of Proverbs - A Commentary, 1961, Judaism and the Scientific Spirit, 1962, The Rise of Reform Judaism, 1963, The Growth of Reform Judaism, 1964, The Case for the Chosen People, 1965, Your Neighbour is a Jew, 1967, Page 2, 1971, Genesis, A Modern Commentary, 1974, Time to Think, 1977, Hanging Threads, 1978, U.S. title The Man in the Blue Vest, 1980, Numbers, A Modern Commentary, 1979; editor, chief author The Torah, A Modern Commentary, 1981, 7th edit., 1990, Unfinished Business; autobiography, 1981; Refugee Determination in Canada, 1985, The Letter, 1986, The Magen David: How The Six Pointed Star Became The Jewish Symbol, 1991, The Man Who Would Be Messiah, 1988, 2d edit., 1990; co-author: The Rabbi's Manual, 1988; editorial contbr. Toronto Globe and Mail, Can. Jewish News; editor: Affirmation, 1981-87; bibliography pub. in Through the Sound of Many Voices, 1982; contbr. to encys., anthologies, other books, articles to mags., newspapers. Chmn. Minn. Gov.'s Commn. on Ethics in Govt., 1958-61 ; pres. St. Paul Gallery and Sch. Art (name changed to Minn. Mus.), 1953-59, World Federalists Can., 1966-68; nat. pres. Can. Jewish Congress, 1977-80; vice chmn. Ont. Human Rights Commn., 1978-85; bd. govts. World Union for Progressive Judaism, 1970— pres. Central Conf. Am. Rabbis, 1983-85, bd. inquiry human rights cases, 1987—. Capt. AUS, 1943-46. Decorated Bronze Star; officer Order of Can.; Plaut Chair for Project Mgmt. established in his honor at Ben-Gurion U., Israel, 1991. Clubs: York Racquets, Oakdale Golf and Country. Office: 1950 Bathurst St, Toronto, ON Canada M5P 3K9

PLAVIN, RICHARD JEFFREY, rabbi; b. Perth Amboy, N.J., May 15, 1946; s. Herman and Ella (Blake) P.; m. Lisa Schnitzer, June 27, 1971; children: Aviva Rahel, Ariel Adina, Ilana Tamar. BS, Columbia U., 1968; M. Hebrew Letters, Jewish Theol. Sem., 1971; EdD, Tchrs. Coll., N.Y.C., 1975. Ordained rabbi, 1973. Rabbi Jewish Community Ctr. of Verona (N.J.), 1974-79, Temple Beth Sholom, Manchester, Conn., 1979—; bd. dirs. Solomon Schechter Day Sch., West Hartford, Conn., 1984-90, Greater Hartford Jewish Fedn., West Hartford, 1984—; mem. rabbinic cabinet United Jewish Appeal, 1990—; mem. rabbinic adv. bd. Jewish Nat. Fund, 1989—. Mem. mktg. bd. Marc, Inc., Manchester, 1990-91. Mem. Zionist Orgn. of Conservative Movement (bd. dirs. 1986—). Office: Temple Beth Sholom 400 E Middle Turnpike Manchester CT 06040

PLEMING-YOCUM, LAURA CHALKER, religion educator; b. Sheridan, Wyo., May 25, 1913; d. Sidney Thomas and Florence Theresa (Woodbury) Chalker; m. Edward Kibbler Pleming, Aug. 25, 1938 (dec. Nov. 1980); children: Edward Kibbler,lam Rowena Pleming Chamberlin, Sidney Thomas; m. William Lewis Yocum, Dec. 19, 1989. BA, Calif. State U., Long Beach, 1953, MA in Speech and Drama, 1954; postgrad., U. So. Calif., L.A., 1960-63; D Religion, Grad. Sch. Theology, Claremont, Calif., 1968. Internat. lectr. Bibl. studies, 1953—, adult seminar resource person, 1953—; Bibl. lectr. Principia Coll., Elsah, Ill., 1968-90; Bible scholar 1st Ch. of Christ, Scientist, Boston, 1970-75; tchr. adult edn. Principia Coll., summers, 1969-71; tour lectr. to Middle East, 1974—; mem. archaeol. team, Negev, Israel. Author: Triumph of Job, 1979; editor (newsletter) Bibleletter, 1968-84. Mem. AAUP, Am. Acad. Religion, Soc. Bibl. Lit. and Exegesis, Am. Schs. Oriental Rsch., Inst. Mediterranean Studies, Religious Edn. Assn., Internat. Platform Assn., Congress Septuagint and Cognate Studies, Religious Edn. Assn., Zeta Tau Alpha (alumni pres. Long Beach chpt. 1960), Gamma Theta Upsilon (prs. Long Beach chpt. 1952).

PLETT, HARVEY G., religion educator, minister; b. Winniped, Man., Can., Nov. 23, 1933; s. Isaac and Augusta Plett; m. Pearl Francis Dueck, Aug. 22, 1958; children: Michael, Kaylene, Emery, Timothy. BA, Goshen Coll., 1959; MA, U. Minn., 1963; MDiv, Goshen Coll. Bibl. Sem., 1970; PhD, U. Man., 1991. Cert. tchr., Can. Assoc. min. Evang. Mennonite Conf., Landmark, Man., 1958—; dean of students Steinbach (Man.) Bible Coll., 1962-67, 85—, pres., 1967-82, acad. dean, 1982-85; chmn. bd. missions Evang. Mennonite Conf., Can., 1983-89, moderator, 1989—. Home: Box 3271, Steinbach, MB Canada R0A 2A0

PLETT, LESLIE P., mission educator; b. Lorette, Man., Can., Dec. 14, 1943; came to U.S., 1986; s. Peter Koop and Elizabeth Plett; m. Sandra Bayne Nehrboss, May 19, 1967; children: Stacy Bayne, Suzanne Joy. BA in Bible/Missions, Fla. Bible Coll., 1986; MA in Adminstrv. Studies, Briercrest Grad. Sch., 1991. Ch. planter New Tribes Mission, Philippines, 1969-77, field dir., 1966-67; assoc. dir. Internat. Cross-Culture Inst., Kissimmee, Fla., 1986-89; missions program dir. Fla. Bible Coll., Kissimmee, 1989—. Author: (manual) Missionary Planning Program, 1982, Language and Culture Learning Guidelines, 1981, (handbook) Bible Doctrine, 1990. Home: 1701 Poinciana Blvd Kissimmee FL 34758 Office: Fla Bible Coll 1701 Poinciana Blvd Kissimmee FL 34758

PLOIESTEANUL, NIFON, religious organization administrator. Sec. Holy Synod Romanian Orthodox Ch., Bucharest. Office: Holy Synod, Str Antrim 29, 70666 Bucharest Romania*

PLOMP, TEUNIS (TONY PLOMP), minister; b. Rotterdam, The Netherlands, Jan. 28, 1938; arrived in Can., 1951; s. Teunis and Cornelia (Pietersma) P.; m. Margaret Louise Bone, July 21, 1962; children: Jennifer Anne, Deborah Adele. BA, U. B.C. (Can.), Vancouver, 1960; BD, Knox Coll., Toronto, Ont., Can., 1963, DD (hon.), 1988. Ordained to ministry Presbyn. Ch., 1963. Minister Goforth Meml. Presbyn. Ch., Saskatoon, Sask., Can., 1963-68, Richmond (B.C.) Presbyn. Ch., 1968—; clerk Presbytery of Westminster, Vancouver, 1969—; moderator 113th Gen. Assembly Presbyn. Ch. Can., 1987-88, dep. clk., 1987—; chaplain New Haven Correctional Centre, Burnaby, B.C. Contbr. mag. column You Were Asking, 1982-89. Avocations: record collecting, audiophile, biking, swimming. Office: Richmond Presbyn Ch, 7111 #2 Rd, Richmond, BC Canada V7C 3L7

PLOTKIN, ALBERT, rabbi; b. South Bend, Ind., Sept. 9, 1920; s. Samuel and Sophie (Novak) P.; m. Sylvia Pincus, Aug. 28, 1949; children: Janis, Debra Ruth. BA magna cum laude, U. Notre Dame, 1942; B in Hebrew Letters, Hebrew Union Coll., Cin., 1947, M in Hebrew Letters, 1948; D in Hebrew Letters, Hebrew Union Coll., L.A., 1967; LLD (hon.), Ariz. State U., 1989. Ordained rabbi, 1948. Asst. rabbi Temple DeHirsch, Seattle, 1948-49; rabbi Temple Emanuel, Spokane, Wash., 1949-55; sr. rabbi Temple Beth Israel, Phoenix, 1955—; instr. Ariz. State Univ., Phoenix, 1957—; pres. Pacific Assn. Reformed Rabbis, L.A., 1967-68; bd. mem. Hebrew Union Coll., Cin., 1968-70; sec. Cen. Conf. Am. Rabbis, N.Y.C., 1969-71; bd. mem. UJA of N.Y.C., 1974-77. Contbr. numerous articles to publs. Bd. mem. Ariz. Commn. on Humanities, Phoenix, 1974-77, Phoenix (Ariz.) Symphony, 1979-82, Ariz. Opera Co., Phoenix, 1986-88; chmn. Mayor's Com. for Homeless, Phoenix, 1988-91. Recipient Disting. Achievement award Ariz. State U., 1988; named Man of the Yr. Spokane (Wash.) Jr. C. of C., 1953, United Fund, Phoenix, 1961, City of Hope, Phoenix, 1963, Nat. Conf. on Christians and Jews, Phoenix, 1972, Red Cross, Phoenix, 1981, Cen. Corridor of Chs., Phoenix, 1982, Man of State, Wash., 1954, Jr. C. of C., Phoenix, 1966. Home: 930 W Catalina Dr Phoenix AZ 85013 Office: Temple Beth Israel 3310 N 10th Ave Phoenix AZ 85013

PLOTKIN, PAUL, rabbi; b. Toronto, Ont., Can., May 22, 1950; came to U.S., 1978; s. Issac and Goldie (Lefkowitz) P.; m. Lea Greenberg, Dec. 21, 1971; children: Tal, Tamar, Orit. BA, York U., Toronto, 1971; MA, Jewish Theol. Sem., 1974. Ordained rabbi, 1976. Rabbi Congregation Beth Israel, Vancouver, B.C., Can., 1976-78, Temple Beth Israel, Miramar, Fla., 1978-83, Temple Beth Am, Margate, Fla., 1983—. Bd. dirs. N.W. Regional Hosp., Margate, 1988—, Hospice, Inc., Ft. Lauderdale, Fla., 1983-85. Recipient Scroll of Honor, Israel Bonds, 1982. Mem. North Borward Bd. Rabbis (pres. 1987-88), Rabbinical Assembly (pres. S.E. region 1988-90, nat. trustee 1990—). Home: 7901 NW 20th St Margate FL 33063 Office: Temple Beth Am 7205 Royal Palm Blvd Margate FL 33063 *My greatest challenge as a rabbi is to instill into a congregation of secularists the feeling of being commanded. For out of that acknowledgement will flow the sense of holiness.*

PLOWMAN, EDWARD E(ARL), editor; b. Hanover, Pa., Sept. 27, 1931; s. Edward E. Sr. and Roberta G. (Geiman) P.; m. Rose M. Orazi; children: Gail E., Gary E., Beth Anne, J. Philip. Diploma, Phila. Coll. Bible, 1952; BA, Wheaton Coll., 1954; ThM, Dallas Theol. Sem., 1958. Ordained to ministry Am. Bapt. Ch., 1958. Pastor Park Presidio Bapt. ch., San Francisco, 1960-70; news editor, then sr. editor Christianity Today mag., Washington, 1970-80; dir. communications overseas ministries Billy Graham Evang. Assn., Mpls., 1980-87; editor Nat. and Internat. Religion Report, Springfield, Va., 1987—. Author: the Jesus Movement, 1971, Washington: Christians in the Corridors of Power, 1975; also book series and TV scripts on Billy Graham's ministry in Communist countries. Recipient Spl. award Religious Heritage Found. Am., 1983, numerous 1st pl. awards in journalism. Mem. Evang. Press Assn. (1st pl. awards). Office: Religion Report PO Box 5139 Springfield VA 22150

PLUIMER, ROBERT PETER, minister; b. Belle Fourche, S.D., Jan. 30, 1941; s. Fred Henry and Grace Edith (Atkins) P.; m. Rebecca Card, Dec. 17, 1966; children: Roman, Bridgette. BTh, Eugene (Oreg.) Bible Coll., 1963; ThD (hon.), Fla. Beacon Coll., Largo, 1984. Sr. pastor Colonial Bible Ch., Tustin, Calif., 1970—. Mem. Open Bible Standard Chs. Office: Colonial Bible Ch 14451 Franklin Ave Tustin CA 92680

PLUM, ANN THERESE, nun; b. Aachen, Ger., June 5, 1921; d. John and Mary Eva (Senden) P. BA, St. Francis Coll., Ft. Wayne, Ind., 1963; postgrad., Manhattanville of Sacred Heart, Purchase, N.Y., 1970, St. Louis U., 1980-81. Entered O.L.V. Missionary Sisters, Roman Cath. Ch. Diocesan supr. high sch. religion L.A., 1958-63; field cons. Diocesan Office Religion, Detroit, 1969-71; dir. religious edn. St. Therese Parish, Midvale, Utah, 1971-74; dir. religious edn. and pastoral ministry St. Pius X Parish, Moab, Utah, 1981-84; coord. religious edn. Our Lady Perpetual Help Parish, Glendale, Ariz., 1984—; dir. postulants O.L.V. Missionary Sisters, Huntington, Ind., 1963-69, councilor, area coord., 1973-74, v.p., area coord., Victory Noll, Huntington, 1974-80. Mem. Network, Washington. Mem. Coords. and Dirs. Religious Edn. Office: Religious Edn Office 7515 N 57th Ave Glendale AZ 85301

PLUMB, RALPH EDWARD, minister, religious organization executive; b. Waterbury, Conn., Apr. 7, 1953; s. Chauncey Raymond and Louise (Lord) P.; m. Ann Ainsworth, Jan. 25, 1976; children: Bristol Michelle (dec.), Chelsea Joy, Misty Nicole. Student, U. Bridgeport, 1971-73; BA, Oral Roberts U., 1975; MDiv, Fuller Theol. Sem., Pasadena, Calif., 1979; postgrad., Calif. State Poly. U., Pomona, 1980-81. Ordained to ministry Conservative Congl. Christian Conf., 1981. Dir. communications and mktg. World Vision, Monrovia, Calif., 1978-82; dir. internat. rels. World Vision Internat., Monrovia, 1982-86; dir. gifts in kind World Vision Relief and Devel., Monrovia, 1986-89; pres. Internat. Aid Inc., Spring Lake, Mich., 1990—; owner, pres. Commodity Resource Mgmt., Upland, Calif., 1986—. Bd. dirs. Christian Outreach Appeal, Long Beach, Calif., 1985—, Good News for India, San Dimas, Calif., 1987—. Lt., chaplain USNR, 1985-89. Mem. Christian Mgmt. Assn., Rotary. Office: Internat Aid Inc 17011 W Hickory Spring Lake MI 49456

PLUMMER, JOHN DENNIS, lay worker; b. Orange, Calif., June 11, 1943; s. Samuel Bernard and Barbara (Watson) P.; m. Linda Laurnell, Sept. 10, 1963 (div. Jan. 1972); 1 child, Barbara Diane; m. Katherine Brewer, Mar. 31, 1973; children: Scott Jackson, David Brewer. BA, Western State Coll., Gunnison, Colo., 1969. Elder Presbyn. Ch., Upland, Calif., 1985-88, trustee, 1987-88, youth leader, 1989—; sr. contracts adminstr. CEC Instruments, San Dimas, Calif., 1989—. Home: 12627 Verdugo Ave Chino CA 91710-3742

PLYMALE, STEVEN FREDERICK, religion educator, minister; b. Huntington, W.Va., Oct. 24, 1946; s. Robert Lee and Catherine (Turina) P.; m. Barbara Ann Rave, Mar. 19, 1966; children: Lisa Michelle Henjes, Emily Ellen. BA, Marshall U., 1969; MDiv, Garrett Evang. Theol. Sem., 1972; PhD, Northwestern U., 1986. Assoc. prof., campus minister Morningside Coll., Sioux City, 1981—; mem. clergy Cedar Grove United Meth. Ch., 1972-76, Lubeck United Meth. Ch., 1976-77; campus minister Morningside Coll., Sioux City, 1981—; mem. Spritual Formation Leadership Team-Iowa Ann. Conf., 1985-88. Author: The Prayer Texts of Luke-Acts. Fin. chair Coun. on Sexual Assault and Domestic Violence, Sioux City, 1986-89, mem. speakers bur., 1989—. Grantee Gen. United Meth. Ch., 1988. Mem. Soc. Bilb. Lit., Nat. Assn. Campus Ministers, Iowa Peace Inst. (speaker), Assn. for the Scientific Study of Religion. Home: 3322 Dodge Ave Sioux City IA 51106 Office: Morningside Coll 1501 Morningside Ave Sioux City IA 51106

PODHORETZ, NORMAN, magazine editor, writer; b. Bklyn., Jan. 16, 1930; s. Julius and Helen (Woliner) P.; m. Midge Rosenthal Decter, Oct. 21, 1956; children: Rachel, Naomi, Ruth, John. A.B., Columbia, 1950; B.H.L., Jewish Theol. Sem., 1950, LL.D. (hon.), 1980; B.A. (Kellett fellow), Cambridge (Eng.) U., 1952, M.A., 1957; LHD (hon.), Hamilton Coll., 1969, Yeshiva U., 1991. Assoc. editor Commentary, 1956-58, editor in chief, 1960—; editor in chief Looking Glass Library, 1959-60; Mem. U. Seminar Am. Civilization, Columbia, 1958. Author: Doings and Undoings, The Fifties and After in American Writing, 1964, Making It, 1968, Breaking Ranks, 1979, The Present Danger, 1980, Why We Were in Vietnam, 1982; The Bloody Crossroads, 1986; editor: The Commentary Reader, 1966. Chmn. new directions adv. com. USIA, 1981-87. Served with AUS, 1953-55. Fulbright fellow, 1950-51. Mem. Council on Fgn. Relations, Com. on the Present Danger., Com. for the Free World. Office: Commentary 165 E 56th St New York NY 10022

PODOLL, LYNN ALLAN, minister; b. Aberdeen, S.D., Aug. 18, 1941; s. Melvin Tobias and Maxine Eleanor P.; m. Karla Elizabeth Wegner, May 28, 1967;children: Nathan, Steven, Elizabeth, Anne. BA, Concordia Sr. Coll., Ft. Wayne, Ind, 1963; MDiv, Concordia Sem., St. Louis, 1967. Ordained to ministry Luth. Ch.-Mo. Synod, 1967. Pastor St. John's Luth. Ch., South Whitley, Ind., 1967-71, Shepherd of the Ridge Luth. Ch., North Ridgeville, Ohio, 1971-76; campus pastor Univ. Luth. Ch., West Lafayette, Ind., 1976-85; pastor Redeemer Luth. Ch., Newton, N.J., 1985—; mem. Luth. Campus Ministers Orgn., Ill., 1976-85. Contbr. articles and devotions to profl. jours. Bd. mem. Chancel Players, Lafayette, Ind., 1979-82, Opera de Lafayette, 1983-85. Home: 21 Elm St Newton NJ 07860 Office: Redeemer Luth Ch 37 Newton-Sparta Rd Newton NJ 07860 *If your god is not big enough to handle your problems or your anger, you'd better get a new god.*

POE, HARRY LEE, minister; b. Greenville, S.C., Nov. 16, 1950; s. William Nelson and Katherine Cureton (Little) P.; m. Mary Anne Whitten, July 11, 1981; children: Rebecca Whitten, Mary Ellen Whitten. Student, Georgetown U., 1970; BA, U. S.C., 1975; MDiv, So. Bapt. Theol. Seminary, 1978, PhD, 1982; postgrad., Oxford U., England, 1979. Ordained to ministry Bapt. Ch., 1982. Fin. dir. S.C. Rep. Party, Columbia, 1974; chaplain Ky. State Reformatory, LaGrange, 1978-82; pastor Simpsonville (Ky.) Bapt. Ch., 1982-86; assoc. dir. evangelism dept. Ky. Bapt. Conv., Middletown, 1986-88; asst. prof. So. Bapt. Theol. Sem., Louisville, 1988-91; assoc. prof. evangelism, assoc. dean for acad. affairs, dir. D Ministry Program Bethel Theol. Sem., St. Paul, 1991—; bd. dirs. Ky. Council of Jail and Prison Ministry, Louisville, 1986—. Author: The Fruit of Christ's Presence, 1990; contbg author: Handbook for Youth Evangelism, 1988, Evangelism in the Twenty-First Century, 1989, Baptist Theologians, 1990; contbg. editor The Southern Partisan; book reviewer Rev. and Expositor; contbr. articles and poems to popular and profl. jours. Mem. Whitney Young Job Corps Ctr. Community Relations Council, Simpsonville, 1982-86, treas., 1985; chmn. Neighborhood Watch, Simpsonville, 1983, St. Jude Children's Hosp. Bike-A-Thon, Simpsonville, 1984; adv. bd. The South Found.; dir. evangelism Shelby Bapt. Assn., 1984-86, Long Run Bapt. Assn., 1989—. Garret fellow, 1978-81; recipient Outstanding Service award Whitney Young Job Corps Ctr., 1985. Mem. St. Andrew's Soc. of Upper S.C. Acad. for Evangelism in Theol. Edn., Ky. Bapt. Hist. Soc. Avocations: violin, fiddle, woodworking, painting, farming. Office: Bethel Theol Sem 3949 Bethel Dr Saint Paul MN 55112

POE, JAMES L., minister; b. Ft. Lauderdale, Fla., Oct. 13, 1950; s. James T. and Elizabeth M. (Pearson) P.; m. Toby L. Bonar, Mar. 3, 1972; children: Mark C., Sara E., Daniel J. BA, Palm Beach Atlantic Coll., 1972. Min. music Wilton Manors Bapt. Ch., Ft. Lauderdale, 1967-72; instr. St. Francis Sch., Riviera Beach, Fla., 1972-78; min. music 1st Bapt. Ch., Boynton Beach, Fla., 1976—; dir. music Palm Lake Bapt. Assn., West Palm Beach, Fla., 1985-90. Composer, arranger numerous choral and orchestral works. Pianist Adult Spl. Edn., Palm Beach County, Fla., 1980—. Mem. So. Bapt. Music Conf., Fla. Bapt. Music Conf. Republican. Avocations: history, golf. Home: 130 SW 14th Ave Boynton Beach FL 33435 Office: 1st Bapt Ch 301 N Seacrest Blvd Boynton Beach FL 33435

POELLOT, LUTHER, minister; b. Palatine, Ill., Oct. 23, 1913; s. Sigfried Daniel and Lisette (Brueggemann) P.; m. Esther Maaser, May 23, 1942; children: Sharon Ruth, Carolyn May (Mrs. Ray Gluesenkamp), Marion Kay, Celia Louise (Mrs. Allen Thomas). Student, Concordia Coll., Milw., 1927-33, Concordia Sem., St. Louis, 1933-37. Ordained to ministry Luth. Ch.-Mo. Synod, 1942. Head clk. Concordia Sem. Libr., St. Louis, 1937-39; missionary Ft. Myers, Fla., 1940; pastor various chs. Dallas, 1940-50, Mercedes, Tex., 1950-52, Pitcairn, Pa., 1952-62, Waterloo, Ont., Can., 1962-64; indexer, editor Concordia Pub. House, St. Louis, 1964-78. Author: Revelation, 1972, 76, reprinted in Concordia Classic Commentary Series, 1987; translator: The Nature and Character of Theology, 1986, Ministry, Word, and Sacraments, 1981; contbr. articles to profl. jours.; composer poetry, hymns. Home: 753 Buckley Rd Saint Louis MO 63125 *Hope fills the heart and drives all fear away, of hell and of death that ends life's little day. Faith soars beyond the grave. We hasten home. Our Savior rose—we are not here to stay.*

POESNECKER, GERALD E., religious organization head. Dir. Ch. of Illumination, Quackertown, Pa. Office: Ch of Illumination PO Box 220 Quackertown PA 18951*

POETHIG, EUNICE BLANCHARD, clergywoman; b. Hempstead, N.Y., Jan. 16, 1930; d. Werner J. and Juliet (Stroh) Blanchard; m. Richard Paul Poethig, June 7, 1952; children—Richard Scott, Kathryn Aileen, Johanna Klare, Margaret Juliet, Erika Christy. B.A., De Pauw U., 1951; M.A., Union Theol. Seminary, 1952; M.Div., McCormick Theol. Sem., 1975, S.T.M., 1977; Ph.D., Union Theol. Seminary, 1985. Ordained to ministry Presbyterian Ch., 1979; missionary United Presbyn. Ch. USA to United Ch. of Christ in Philippines, 1956-72; mem. faculty Ellinwood Coll. Christian Edn., Manila, 1957-61; mem. faculty, campus ministry Philippine Women's U., Manila, 1962-68; bd. dirs. Jane Addams Conf., Journey's End Refugee Resettlement Agy., Coun. of Bishops and Execs. of Buffalo Area Met. Ministries; trustee Presbyn. Found., 1991—; editor New Day Pubs., Manila, 1969-72; curriculum editor Nat. Council Chs., Manila, 1962-72; assoc. exec. Presbytery Chgo., 1979-85; exec. Presbytery of Western N.Y., 1986—; speaker Presbyn. Women, 1973, 76, 79, 81, 85, 88; mem. Council Execs., Ill. Council Chs., 1980-85. Author: Bible Studies in Concern, Response, A.D., 1975, (book) Good News Women, 1987, Sing, Shout, and Clap for Joy: Psalms in Worship, 1989, Friendship Press Study on Philippines, 1989, Liturgy 9:1, 1990, Hunger Program Workbook, 1991; editor Hymn book-series: Everybody, I Love You, 1971-72, 150 Plus Tomorrow: Churches Plan for the Future, 1982, 85. Mem. organizing bd. Asian Center Theology and Strategy, Chgo., 1974; bd. dirs. Ch. Women United, Chgo., 1974-79; mem. Environ. Def. Fund, Women's Ordination Conf. Nat. Presbyn. Ch. Com., planning com. Celebrate Adult Curriculum, 1987—, Presbyn. Gen. Assembly Challenge to the Ch. Fund., 1989; trustee McCormick Theol. Sem., Chgo., 1974-75; mem. Erie County Environ. Mgmt. Coun., 1990—. Recipient Walker Cup, DePauw U., 1951. Nettie F. McCormick fellow in Old Testament Hebrew, McCormick Sem., Chgo., 1975. Mem. Soc. Bibl. Lit., Soc. Ethnomusicology, Assn. of Exec. Presbyters (bd. dirs., chairperson, 1991—), Am. Schs. Oriental Research, Witherspoon Soc., Nat. Assn. Religious Women, Internat. Assn. Women Mins., Nat. Assn. Presbyn. Clergywomen. Office: Presbytery of Western NY 2450 Main St Buffalo NY 14214 *I do not pray that people will come "back to church" but that the church will help us go forward to God.*

POETTCKER, HENRY, retired seminary president; b. Rudnerweide, Russia, Mar. 27, 1925; s. John and Margaretha (Voth) P.; m. Aganetha Baergen, July 4, 1946; children—Victoria (Mrs. D. Ross McIntosh), Ronald, Martin. A.B., Bethel Coll., North Newton, Kans., 1950; B.D., Mennonite Bibl. Sem., Chgo., 1953; Th.D., Princeton Theol. Sem., 1961, converted Ph.D., 1973. Ordained to ministry Mennonite Ch., 1948; instr. Can. Mennonite Bible Coll., Winnipeg, Man., 1954-59; pres. Can. Mennonite Bible Coll., 1959-78; pres. Mennonite Bibl. Sem., Elkhart, Ind., 1978-90, assoc. for devel., 1991—; interim dean Bluffton (Ohio) Coll., 1965-66; vis. lectr. Taiwan Theol. Coll. and Tainan Theol. Coll., Taiwan, 1973-74. Editor: (with Rudy A. Regehr) Call to Faithfulness, 1972, Alumni Bull. Can. Mennonite Bible Coll, 1960-73. Pres. Gen. Conf. Mennonite Ch., Newton, Kans., 1968-74. Mem. Soc. Bibl. Lit. and Exegesis, Can. Soc. Bibl. Studies. Home: 527 Borebank St, Winnipeg, MB Canada R3N 1E8 Office: Assoc Mennonite Bibl Sem 3003 Benham Ave Elkhart IN 46517 *The secret of happiness lies not in doing what one likes, but in liking what one does.*

POHL, GLYN WILLIAM, priest; b. Dubuque, Iowa, June 11, 1913; s. William and Myrtle Genevieve (Glynn) P.; m. Jessie Edith Manifold, July 8, 1939 (dec. May 1976); m. Charlean Moss Kengla, Mar. 5, 1977. BA, U. Iowa, 1938; grad., U.S. Army C. and G.S. Sch., Ft. Leavenworth, Kans., 1944; cert. in Efficiency, U.S. Army Arty. Sch., Ft. Sill, Okla., 1948. Ordained to ministry Episcopal Ch., 1968. Commd. 2d lt. U.S. Army, advanced through ranks to lt. col., ret.; deacon Ch. of the Nativity, San Rafael, Calif., 1963-68; priest Ch. of the Nativity, San Rafael, 1968-77, Ch. of the Redeemer, San Rafael, 1977-86, 90—, St. Aidan's Ch., Bolinas, Calif., 1986-90; cursillo spiritual dir., San Francisco, Marin County, 1969—. Republican.

POHL, LEIF ALAN, minister; b. Milw., Sept. 22, 1940; s. Neil Alan and Frieda (Radtke) P.; m. Janice Jean Forsyth, May 28, 1966; children: Eric, Jennifer, Andrew, Thomas. BA, U. Colo., 1962; MDiv, Luth. Sch. Theology Chgo., 1966. Ordained to ministry Luth. Ch. Am., 1966. Campus pastor Ball State U., Muncie, Ind., 1966-69; pastor Holy Trinity Luth. Ch., Muncie, 1966-69, Faith Luth. Ch., Owensboro, Ky., 1969-76, Our Saviour Luth. Ch., Valparaiso, Ind., 1976-85, Grace Luth. Ch., Muscatine, Iowa, 1985—; pres. Porter County Coun. Luth. Chs., Valparaiso, 1982-84; pastor, supr. Luth. Sch. Theology, Chgo., 1986—; bd. dirs. Porter County Luth. Relief Fund, Portage, Ind. Contbr. articles to ch. publs. Bd. dirs. Muscatine County Commn. on Aging, 1987—. Office: Grace Luth Ch 2107 Cedar St Muscatine IA 52761

POHLHAUS, GAILE MARGARET, religious studies educator; b. Jamaica, N.Y., Nov. 4, 1938; d. Melvin Bernard and Marjorie (McKeough) Benson; m. William Gerard Pohlhaus, Dec. 27, 1969; children—Gaile, William. B.A. in Math., Coll. of St. Elizabeth, 1961; M.A. in Math., Boston Coll., 1965; M.A. in Theology, Villanova U., 1978; postgrad., Temple U., 1979—. Tchr. St. Vincent Acad., Newark, 1961-63; tchr., dept. chmn. Bayley Ellard High Sch., Madison, N.J., 1963-69; asst. prof. practical theology Villanova U., 1987—; lectr. Speakers Bur., 1982—. Book reviewer: Jour. Ecumenical Studies, Horizons; author Manual for Small Group Pre-Marital Counselling, 1974-76. Mem. AAUP, Coll. Theology Soc., Cath. Theol. Soc. Am., Am. Acad. Religion. Roman Catholic. Avocations: reading; computers. Home: 341 S Devon Ave Wayne PA 19087 Office: Villanova U Dept Religious Studies Villanova PA 19085 *If education was more cooperative and less competitive, we might produce men and women capable of global peace.*

POINDEXTER, RICHARD GROVER, minister; b. Carthage, N.C., June 9, 1945; s. Romie Dallas and Mollie (Underwood) P.; m. Glenda Joyce Tudor, Feb. 23, 1968; children: Tonya Joyce, Amanda Caroline. BA in Sociology, N.C. State U., 1967; MDiv., New Orleans Bapt. Theol. Sem., 1973. Ordained to ministry So. Bapt. Conv., 1972. Assoc. pastor, youth dir. Amite Bapt. Ch., Denham Springs, La., 1971-72; Sunday sch. cons. Canal Blvd. Bapt. Ch., New Orleans, 1973; pastor First Bapt. Ch., LaGrange, N.C., 1973-77, Anderson Grove Bapt. Ch., Albemarle, N.C., 1977-86, Rankin Bapt. Ch., Greensboro, N.C., 1986—; cons. Challenge to Build, Bapt. State Conv. of N.C., Cary, 1977—; mem. Brazil Mission Trip, Piedmont Bapt. Assn., Greensboro, 1989. Chaplain N.C. Army Nat. Guard, Greensboro, 1976—; trustee Christian Action League of N.C., Raleigh, 1985—. Office: Rankin Bapt Ch 3317 Summit Ave Greensboro NC 27405

POLETTI, UGO CARDINAL, Italian ecclesiastic; b. Omegna, Italy, Apr. 19, 1914. Ordained priest Roman Catholic Ch., 1938. Served in various diocesan offices, Novara, Italy; consecrated titular bishop of Medeli and aux. of Novara, 1958; pres. Pontificial Mission Aid Soc. for Italy, 1964-67; archbishop of Spoleto, 1967-69; titular archbishop of Cittanova, from 1969; served as 2d vice-regent of Rome, 1969-72; pro-vicar gen. of Rome, 1972; elevated to cardinal, 1973; vicar gen. of Rome, 1973—; now pres. Bishops' Conf.; archpriest Patriarchal Lateran Archbasilica, from 1973; grand chancellor Lateran U. Mem. Congregations of Clergy, Sacraments and Divine Worship, Oriental Chs., Religious and Secular Insts., Council for Laity. Office: Vicariato di Roma, Piazza, San Giovanni, Laterano 6, 00184 Rome Italy

POLHILL, JOHN BOWEN, religion educator; b. Americus, Ga., Jan. 6, 1939; s. Lucius McLendon and Elizabeth Bowen Polhill; m. Nancy Louise Carmack, Dec. 23, 1966; children: Marian Elizabeth, John Bowen Jr. BA, U. Richmond, 1960; MDiv, So. Bapt. Theol. Sem., 1963, PhD, 1968. Ordained to ministry So. Bapt. Conv., 1963. Prof. N.T. So. Bapt. Theol. Sem., Louisville, 1968—, assoc. dean over PhD Program, 1991—. Mem. Soc. Bibl. Lit., Assn. Bapt. Profs. Religion. Office: So Bapt Theol Sem 2825 Lexington Rd Louisville KY 40280

POLIN, MILTON HAROLD, rabbi; b. Chgo., Oct. 7, 1930; s. Abraham Noah and Dorothy (Blacher) P.; m. Shainee Fagy Sachs, Aug. 15, 1954; children: Kenneth Saul, Dorothy Anne, Rena Beth, Gail Menucha, Nechama Bea. MA, U. Chgo., 1953; B. Hebrew Letters, Hebrew Theol. Coll., 1954. Ordained rabbi, 1954. Rabbi Mt. Sinai Congregation, Cheyenne, Wyo., 1954-56, Keneseth Israel Congregation, Louisville, 1956-66, Tpheris Israel Chevra Kadisha Congregation, St. Louis County, Mo., 1966-74, Kingsway Jewish Ctr., Bklyn., 1974—; bd. govs. Orthodox Union, N.Y.C., 1986—; pres. Greater N.Y. Coun., Rel Zionists Am., N.Y.C., 1988—. Contbr. articles to profl. publs. Mem. Rabbinical Coun. Am. (pres. 1986-88), Vaad Harabbanim of Flatbush (pres. 1979-81). Office: Kingsway Jewish Ctr 2810 Nostrand Ave Brooklyn NY 11229

POLING, KERMIT WILLIAM, minister; b. Elkins, W.Va., Oct. 1, 1941; s. Durward Willis and Della Mae (Boyles) P.; m. Patricia Ann Groves, June 12, 1965; children: David Edward Elson, Mikael Erik. Diploma in Bible, Am. Bible Sch., 1966; BRE, Am. Bible Coll., 1991; BA in Bible, Reed Coll. Religion, 1968; AA, W.Va. U., 1970; ThD, Zion Theol. Sem., 1971; postgrad., Wesley Theol. Sem., 1974; LLD, Geneva Theol. Coll., 1980; DSL (hon.), Berean Christian Coll., 1981; postgrad., Mansfield Coll., U. Oxford, Eng., 1986, 90, 91; D Ecumenical Rsch., St. Ephrem's Inst. for Oriental Studies, 1989. Ordained to ministry United Meth. Ch., 1967. Pastor Parkersburg-Crossroads (W.Va.) Cir., 1967-70; asst. sec. W.Va. Ann. Conf., 1967-69; pastor Hope-Halleck Morgantown Cir., 1970-76, Trinity-Warren Grafton (W.Va.) Charge, 1976-83, 1st Trinity Pennsboro (W.Va.) Charge, 1983—; editor local ch. news; instr. Bible, Bodkin Bible Inst., 1972-75; mem. staff Taylor County Coop. Parish, 1976-83; coord. Hughes River Coop. Parish, 1983—; mem. chaplains com. Grafton City Hosp., 1976-82; mem. coun. Centre d'Etudes et d'Action Oecumeniques, 1972-74. Author: A Crown of Thorns, 1963, A Silver Message, 1964, History of the Halleck Church, 1970, Eastern Rite Catholicism, 1971, From Brahmin to Bishop, 1976, Cult and Occult: Data and Doctrine, 1978; contbr. articles and poems to religious jours. Decorated Royal Afghanistan Order of Crown of Amanullah; Order of Polonia Restituta; Mystical Order of St. Peter; knight Grand Cross of the Order of St. Dennis of Zante, 1990; recipient Good Citizenship award Doddridge County, 1954, Silver medal Ordre Universel du Merit Humain, Geneva, 1973, Commendation for Outstanding Achievement in Ministry Ohio House Reps., 1988; named Chief of Dynastic House of Polanie-Patrikios, 1988. Mem. SAR, Internat. Platform Assn., Sovereign Order St. John Jerusalem, Ritchie County Ministerial Assn. (pres. 1984—), Order Sacred Cup, Knights of Malta. Home: 118 Ray Ave Pennsboro WV 26415 Office: 302 Lincoln St Grafton WV 26354

POLING, WAYNE ALLEN, minister; b. Amarillo, Tex., July 29, 1950; s. Clifford Harold and Ruby Lorena (McClellan) P. BA, Hardin Simmons U., 1972; MRE, S.W. Baptist Theol. Sem., 1976. Ordained to ministry So. Baptist Conv., 1982. Min. youth Colonial Bapt. Ch., Dallas, 1973-76; min. edn. Lamar Bapt. Ch., Wichita Falls, Tex., 1976-81; leader, tng. cons. Bapt. Sunday Sch. Bd., Nashville, 1981—. Mem. Am. Soc. Tng. and Devel., So. Baptist Religious Edn. Assn., S.W. Bapt. Religious Edn. Assn. Office: Baptist Sunday Sch Bd 127 9th Ave N Nashville TN 37234

POLISH, DANIEL FRIEDLAND, rabbi; b. Ithaca, N.Y., Mar. 25, 1942; s. David and Aviva (Friedland) P.; children: Jonathan, Ariel. BA, Northwestern U., 1964; B. Hebrew Letters, Hebrew Union Coll., 1966, MA Hebrew Letters, 1967; PhD, Harvard U., 1973. Ordained rabbi, 1968. Dir. edn. Interfaith Met. Theol. Edn., 1973-77; assoc. exec. dir. Synagogue Coun. Am., Washington, 1977-81; sr. rabbi Temple Israel, L.A., 1981-88, Temple Beth El, Birmingham, Mich., 1988—; mem. exec. bd. Cen. Conf. Am. Rabbis, 1973-75. Editor: Formations of Social Policy in the Catholic and Jewish Traditions, 1980, Liturgical Foundations of Social Policy in the Catholic and Jewish Traditions, 1983; contbr. articles and revs. to religious and gen. jours. and books. Chmn. Friedns of Labor Israel, Jerusalem, 1990—; mem. exec. bd. United Way, Detroit, 1989—, Interfaith Round Table of Greater Detroit, 1990—, New Detroit, 1990—. Mem. Union Am. Hebrew Congregations (chmn. leadership devel. 1983—). Office: Temple Beth El 7400 Telegraph Rd Birmingham MI 48010

POLK, DAVID PATRICK, editor; b. Oaktown, Ind., Mar. 8, 1940; s. Raymond and Oeta Alicia (Fleener) P.; m. Kitty Marie Southard, May 29, 1960. AB with honors, Ind. U., 1963; M.Th., Claremont Sch. Theology, 1966; PhD, Claremont Grad. Sch., 1983; postgrad., U. Munich, 1969. Ordained minister in Christian Ch., 1978. Asst. prof. religion Drury Coll., Springfield, Mo., 1969-70; asst. prof. history of theology Lexington (Ky.) Theol. Sem., 1970-74; sr. pastor First Christian Ch., Cedar Rapids, Iowa, 1975-83; Brown prof. pastoral ministry Brite Divinity Sch., Tex. Christian U., Ft. Worth, 1983-90; editor Chalice Press, St. Louis, 1990—; v.p. Christian Bd. Publ., St. Louis. Author: On the Way to God, 1989; editor: The Education of the Practical Theologian, 1989, What's A Christian to Do? 1991. Mem. Assn. Practical Theology (pres. 1987-90), Am. Acad. Religion, Ctr. for Process Studies. Democrat. Office: Christian Bd Publ PO Box 179 Saint Louis MO 63166 *We require a vision of the whole conjoined with the discernment of particularities close at hand. Practical theology is seeing through bifocals.*

POLLACK, STUART ALAN, rabbi; b. Syracuse, N.Y., Dec. 4, 1951; s. Alex and Rose P.; m. Robin, Nov. 17, 1974; 1 child, Max. BA in Psychology, Pa. State U., 1972; MA in Hebrew Laws, Hebrew Union Coll., 1975; MS in Edn., Johns Hopkins U., 1980. Ordained rabb. 1977.

POLLARD, ALTON BROOKS, III, religion educator, minister; b. St. Paul, May 5, 1956; s. Alton Brooks Jr. and Lena Laverne (Evans) P.; m. Jessica Juana Bryant, July 14, 1979; children: Alton Brooks IV, Asha Elise. BA, Fisk U., 1978; MDiv, Harvard U., 1981; PhD, Duke U., 1987. Ordained to ministry Am. Bapt. Conv., Progressive Bapt. Conv., 1979. Pastor John Street Bapt. Ch., Worcester, Mass., 1979-82, New Red Mountain Bapt. Ch., Rougemont, N.C., 1984-86; asst. prof. religion St. Olaf Coll., Northfield, Minn., 1987-88, Wake Forest U., Winston-Salem, N.C., 1988—; vis. asst. prof. U. N.C., Greensboro, 1991; assoc. min. Emmanuel Bapt. Ch., Winston-Salem, 1988; bd. dirs. Crisis Control Ministry, Winston-Salem; mem. South Africa Crisis Coordinating Com., Winston-Salem, 1989—. Assoc. editor Black Sacred Music, 1987—; contbr. articles to religious jours. Mem. adv. bd. Worcester County Sch. Bd., 1980-82; mem. Community AIDS Awareness Campaign, Winston-Salem, 1991; mem. community problem solving com. United Way, Winston Salem and Forsyth County, 1990—. Pew grantee Wake Forest U., 1990. Mem. Soc. for Study Black Religion, Religious Rsch. Assn., Am. Acad. Religion, Assn. for Sociology Religion, Soc. for Sci. Study Religion. Home: 2026 Storm Canyon Rd Winston-Salem NC 27106 Office: Wake Forest U PO Box 7212 Winston-Salem NC 27109

POLLARD, FRANKLIN DAWES, minister, seminary president; b. Olney, Tex., Feb. 25, 1934; s. Daniel Spurgeon and Ova Roena (Boone) P.; m. Jane Shepard, Sept. 1, 1955; children—Brent, Suzanne. BBA, Tex. A&M U., 1955; BD, Southwestern Bapt. Theol. Sem., Fort Worth, 1959; D.Min., New Orleans Bapt. Theol. Sem., 1983; D.D. (hon.), Miss. Coll., Clinton, 1977; L.H.D., Calif. Bapt. Coll., Riverside, 1983. Ordained to ministry So. Bapt. Conv., 1956. Pastor First Bapt. Ch., Seagraves, Tex., 1961-64; pastor First Bapt. Ch., Dimmitt, Tex., 1964-66, Tulia, Tex., 1966-70; pastor Shiloh Terr. Bapt. Ch., Dallas, 1970-74; pastor First Bapt. Ch., Jackson, Miss., 1974-80, San Antonio, 1980-83; pres. Golden Gate Bapt. Theol. Sem., Mill Valley, Calif., 1983-86; preacher The Bapt. Hour radio show, Fort Worth, 1976-86; pastor 1st Bapt. Ch., Jackson, Miss., 1986—; host, Bible tchr. At Home with the Bible, radio and TV show, 1978-83; nat. TV preacher nat. The Bapt. Hour, So. Bapt. Conv., 1990—; v.p., exec. bd. Bapt. Gen. Conv., Tex., 1973; exec. bd. Miss. Bapt. Conv., 1977-80. Author: How to Know When You're a Success, 1973; The Bible In Your Life, 1978; After You've Said I'm Sorry, 1982; Keeping Free, 1983. Recipient Disting. Service award Jaycees, 1966, Valley Forge Freedom Found. award, 1982; named one of Seven Outstanding Preachers, Time mag., 1979. Lodge: Rotary. Home: 2332 Southwood Rd Jackson MS 39211-6212

POLLARD, TERRY WAYNE, minister; b. Kansas City, Mo., Oct. 7, 1958; s. Raymond Eliot Pollard and Eva Lavonne (Triplett) Maddox; m. Patty Jo Weir, Mar. 22, 1980; children: Chadric, Lance, Leandra. BA in Religion, Kansas City Coll./Bible Sch., 1980; postgrad., Moody Bible Inst., Chgo., 1989—. Pastor/sch. adminstr. Ch. of God Holiness, Seattle, 1980-84, Hallsville, Mo., 1984-86; editor Herald and Banner Press, Overland Park, Kans., 1986-91; sr. pastor Lakewood Bible Fellowship, Lake Charles, La., 1991—; v.p. Gen. Youth Coun., Overland Park, 1985—, Pierce County Holiness Assn., Tacoma, Wash., 1981-84; bd. dirs. Amb. Found. Inst., Dayspring Ministries, 1991—, Oceanic Gospel Pub. Mission, 1991—. Editor-in-chief: (Sunday Sch. curriculum) Way, Truth and Life series, 1986—; contbr. articles to profl. jours. Vol. Peery for Rep., Overland Park, 1990; mem. Kansans for Life, 1988—, Comm. of 200/Interchurch Holiness Conv., 1988—. Named to Outstanding Young Men of Am., 1987; recipient Outstanding Ministry award Kansas City Coll. and Bible Sch., 1980. Mem. Alumni Assn. Kansas City Coll. and Bible Sch. (pres. 1986—). Republican. Home: 6031 W 76th St Prairie Village KS 66208 Office: 111 W LaGrange Lake Charles LA 70605

POLLEY, MAX EUGENE, clergyman, educator; b. South Bend, Ind., June 3, 1928; s. Maynard Ernest and Helen Bertha (Moore) P.; m. Jacquelyn Bertha Vander Ven, June 11, 1950; children: Vance Ernest, Lynn Anita. AB, Albion Coll., 1950; BD, Duke Div. Sch., 1953; PhD, Duke U., 1957. Ordained to ministry Presbyn. Ch., 1953. Prof. religion Davidson (N.C.) Coll., 1956—. Author: Amos and the Davidic Empire, 1989. Gurney Harris Kearns fellow, 1954-56; Southern fellow, 1959; Lilly postdoctoral fellow, 1964-65; NEH grantee, 1978. Mem. Soc. Bibl. Lit. Democrat. Presbyterian. Avocations: tennis, golf, trout fishing. Home: 243 Ney Circle Davidson NC 28036 Office: Davidson Coll Davidson NC 28036

POLOMÉ, EDGAR CHARLES, language educator; b. Brussels, Belgium, July 31, 1920; came to U.S., 1961, naturalized, 1966; s. Marcel Félicien and Berthe (Henry) P.; m. Julia Joséphine Schwindt, June 22, 1944 (dec. May 1975); children: Monique (Mrs. John Ellsworth), Laure, André Robert; m. Barbara Baker Harris, July 11, 1980 (div. Jan. 1991); m. Sharon Looper Rankin, Feb. 8, 1991. B.A., Université Libre de Bruxelles, 1941, Ph.D., 1949; M.A., Cath. U. Louvain, 1943. Prof. Germanic lang. Athénée Ville de Bruxelles, 1942-56; prof. Dutch Belgian Nat. Broadcasting Corp., Brussels, 1954-56; prof. linguistics U. Belgian Congo (now Zaire), 1956-61; prof.

Germanic, Oriental, African langs. and lits. U. Tex., Austin, 1961—, dir. Ctr. for Asian Studies, 1962-72, Christie and Stanley Adams Jr. Centennial prof. liberal arts, 1984—; chmn. dept. U. Tex., 1969-76. Author: Swahili Language Handbook, 1967, Language in Tanzania, 1980, Language, Society and Paleoculture: Essays, 1982, Essays on Germanic Religion, 1989; editor: Old Norse Literature and Mythology, 1969, The Indo-Europeans in the 4th and 3rd Millennia, 1982, Guide to Language Change, 1990; co-editor Jour. Indo-European Studies, 1973—, The Mankind Quar., 1980—; mng. editor Jour. Indo-European Studies, 1987—. Served with Belgian Aux. Aerodrome Police, 1945. Fulbright prof. U. Kiel, 1968; Ford Found. team dir. Tanzania survey, 1969-70. Mem. Linguistics Soc. Am., Am. Oriental Soc., MLA, African Studies Assn., Am. Anthrop. Assn., Indogermanische Gesellschaft, Societas Linguistica Europea, Société de Linguistique de Paris, Am. Inst. Indian Studies (chmn. lang. com. 1972-78). Home: 2701 Rock Terrace Dr Austin TX 78704-3843 Office: U Tex 2601 University Ave Austin TX 78712 *Having taught and done research on four continents—Europe, Africa, America and Asia—I feel gratitude that my experience has enabled me to discover the richness of man's intellectual and artistic heritage. It has especially allowed better appreciation of the perennial aesthetic, ethical and social values that make us all part of the great human brotherhood, whatever our language, creed or ethnic background.*

POLSON, SAMUEL LEWIS, pastor; b. New Castle, Ind., Feb. 19, 1956; s. Luther Clendon and Eunice Agee (Sidwell) P.; m. Susan Lynn Bittner, June 2, 1978; 1 child, Ruth Alice. BA in Theology, Bob Jones U., Greenville, S.C., 1978, MA in Theology, 1980. Min. of youth Calvary Bapt. Ch., Findlay, Ohio, 1980-86; sr. pastor West Park Bapt. Ch., Knoxville, Tenn., 1986—; founder, pres. East Tenn. Youth Outreach, Knoxville, 1987-88; co-founder, pres. Brazil Bible Mission, Knoxville, 1988—; exec. com. Internat. Conf. on World Evangelism, Fairfax, Va., 1991—. Republican. Office: West Park Bapt Ch 8833 Middlebrook Pike Knoxville TN 37923

POLSTER, STEPHEN JAMES, minister; b. Fish Creek, Wis., July 7, 1953; s. Martin Arno and Dorothy Ellen (Stephenson) P.; m. Caroline Grace Fenner, June 12, 1976; children: Sarah Elizabeth, Rachel Ann. BA, CArroll Coll., 1975; MDiv, U. Dubuque, 1978. Ordained to ministry United Meth. Ch. as deacon, 1976, as elder, 1979. Assoc. pastor New Hope Parish, Union Grove, Wis., 1978-80, parish dir., 1980-86; pastor Fennimore (Wis.) United Meth. Ch., 1986-90; sr. pastor Trinity Ch., Beaver Dam, Wis., 1990—; pres. Ministerial Assn., Fennimore, 1988-90; chairperson program and arrangements com. Wis. Conf. United Meth. Ch., 1990—. Mem. Sesquicentennial Com., Beaver Dam, 1990-91; pres. Kiwanis, Fennimore, 1989-90; bd. dirs. Fennimore Scholarship Found., Inc., 1987-90, Schmitt-Woodland Hills Retirement Ctr., Richland Ctr., Wis., 1989-90. Mem. United Meth. Found. (bd. dirs. 1988—). Office: Trinity Ch 308 Oneida St Beaver Dam WI 53916

POMA, EUGENIO, bishop; b. Ancoraimes, La Paz, Bolivia, Feb. 2, 1944; s. Pedro P. and Gregoria Anaguaya; m. Antonia Callisaya, Dec. 29, 1968; children: Gabriel, Marco, Alex. Grad., Normal S. Bolivar, La Paz, 1974; BA in Edn., Nat. Coll. Edn., 1977; MA, Govs. St. U., 1979. Pres. Youth League, Ancoraimes, 1968-70; La Paz Meth. Ch., La Paz, 1974-76; nat. sec. Meth. Ch., Bolivia, 1980-85, bishop, 1986-90; ednl. dir. Meth. and Ministry Edn., La Paz, 1990—; prin. Ministry of Edn. and Meth. Ancoraimes, 1968-70; tchr. Meth. Schs., La Paz, 1971-74, Ministry of Agr. and Edn., 1975-76; bilingual coord. Ill. Bilingual Edn., Chgo., 1975-77, bilingual tchr., Chicago Heights, 1977-79. Author: Aymara Spanish and English Dictionary, 1966, co-author: Aymara Learning, 1966.

POMPUSCH, SISTER ANITA, academic administrator. Head Coll. St. Catherine, St. Paul. Office: Coll St Catherine Saint Paul MN 55105*

PONDER, CATHERINE, clergywoman; b. Hartsville, S.C., Feb. 14, 1927; d. Roy Charles and Kathleen (Parrish) Cook; student U. N.C. Extension, 1946, Worth Bus. Coll., 1948; BS in Edn., Unity Ministerial Sch., 1956; 1 child, Richard. Ordained to ministry, Unity Sch. Christianity, 1958; minister Unity Ch., Birmingham, Ala., 1956-61; founder, minister Unity Ch., Austin, Tex., 1961-69, San Antonio, 1969-73, Palm Desert, Calif., 1973—. Mem. Assn. Unity Chs., Inc. (hon. DD 1976), Internat. New Thought Alliance, Internat. Platform Assn. Clubs: L.A., St. James (Hollywood, Calif.), Petroleum of L.A., Cardinal (Raleigh, N.C.). Author: The Dynamic Laws of Prosperity, 1962, The Prosperity Secret of the Ages, 1964, The Dynamic Laws of Healing, 1966, The Healing Secret of the Ages, 1967, Pray and Grow Rich, 1968, The Millionaires of Genesis, 1976, The Millionaire Moses, 1977, The Millionaire Joshua, 1978, The Millionaire from Nazareth, 1979, The Secret of Unlimited Prosperity, 1981, Open Your Mind to Receive, 1983, Dare to Prosper!, The Prospering Power of Prayer, 1983, The Prospering Power of Love, 1984, Open Your Mind to Prosperity, 1984, The Dynamic Laws of Prayer, 1987. Office: 73-669 Hwy 111 Palm Desert CA 92260

PONDER, JAMES ALTON, clergyman, evangelist; b. Ft. Worth, Jan. 20, 1933; s. Leo A. and Mae Adele (Blair) P.; BA, Baylor U., 1954; MEd, Southwestern Bapt. Theol. Sem., 1965; m. Joyce Marie Hutchison, Sept. 1, 1953; children: Keli, Ken. Ordained to ministry Baptist Ch., 1953; pastor Calvary Bapt. Ch., Corsicana, Tex., 1953-57, First Bapt. Ch., Highlands, Tex., 1957-62, Ridglea West Bapt. Ch., Ft. Worth, 1963-66, First Bapt. Ch., Carmi, Ill., 1966-67; dir. evangelism Ill. Bapt. State Conv., 1968-70, Fla. Bapt. Conv., 1970-81; pres. Jim Ponder Ministries, Inc., 1981—; dir. Inst. World Evangelism div. Jim Ponder Ministries; preacher Crossroads radio program; fgn. mission bd. evangelist in various countries of Asia, Central Am., Middle East, 1960—; project dir. Korea Major Cities Evangelization Project, 1978-80; evangelist ch. revivals, area crusades and evangelism confs., 1951—; mem. faculty Billy Graham Schs. Evangelism, 1970—; co-founder Ch. Growth Inst. Fla., 1976; co-dir. Ch. Growth Crusades, 1978-79; founder, dir. Inst. World Evangelism (I-Owe), 1987—; pres. Conf. Fla. Baptist Evangelists, 1986-87; sports announcer Sta. KIYS, Waco, Tex., 1950-54; speaker worldwide missionary radio broadcast Crossroads with Jim Ponder. Bd. dirs. N. Fla. chpt. Leukemia Soc. Am. Mem. Internat. Platform Assn., Fellowship Christian Athletes, Smithsonian Instn., N. Am. Soc. Church Growth, Acad. Evangelism in Edn., Acad. Evangelism Profs. Democrat. Club: Kiwanis. Author: The Devotional Life, 1970; Evangelism Men...Motivating Laymen to Witness, 1975; Evangelism Men...Proclaiming the Doctrines of Salvation, 1976; Evangelism Men...Preaching for Decision, 1979; author, video tchr. Becoming a Witness; contbr. articles to religious publs.; speaker in field. Home: 2000 Countryside Cir N Orlando FL 32804 Office: PO Box 547995 Orlando FL 32854

PONDER, REGINALD WALLACE, minister, church administrator; b. Nashville, June 30, 1937; s. Speers Gordon and Lucy E. (Davis) P.; m. Carrie Naomi Davis, July 20, 1958; children: Katherine Elisabeth, Reginald Wallace, Jr., Ruth Lynette. BS in Rural Sociology, N.C. State U., 1958; MDiv, Duke U., Durham, N.C., 1961; Doctor of Ministry, Emory U., Atlanta, 1977. Ordained to ministry Meth. Ch. as deacon, 1959, as elder, 1961. Min. various chs., N.C., 1958-78; dist. supt. New Bern Dist., N.C., 1978-80, Raleigh Dist., N.C., 1980-83; min. First United Meth. Ch., Rocky Mount, N.C., 1983-86; exec. sec. S.E. Jurisdictional Coun. on Ministries, Lake Junaluska, N.C., 1986-88; exec. dir. S.E. Jurisdictional Adminstrv. Coun., Lake Junaluska, N.C., 1988—; del. Gen. Conf. and S.E. Jurisdictional Conf., 1980, 1984, 1988. Bd. dir. Gen. Bd. of Global Ministries, 1983-88, N.C. Internat. Folk Festival, Waynesville, 1988—; founder and chmn. Lee Co. Coun. on Aging, N.C., 1972-74; chmn. Lee Co. Coun. on Alcoholism, 1974-76; active Hinton Rural Life Cen., 1970—. Recipient Sanford Jaycee Dist. Ser. award, 1972; named Rotarian of the Year, Sanford Rotary Club, 1978. Mem. Gen. Coun. on Ministries, Rotary Internat. Democrat. Avocations: golf, tennis, investing, travel. Home: 109 Glendale Dr Lake Junaluska NC 28745 Office: SEJ Administrative Council 1 N Lakeshore Dr PO Box 67 Lake Junaluska NC 28745

PONET, JAMES EDWARD, rabbi; b. Hartford, Conn., Oct. 29, 1946. BA, Yale U., 1968; MA, Hebrew Union Coll., Cin., 1973. Ordained rabbi, 1973. Fellow Shalom Hartman Inst., Jerusalem, 1974-81; Jewish chaplain Yale U., New Haven, 1987—; dir. Yale Hillel Found., New Haven, —; chmn. bd. Interns for Peace, N.Y.C., 1988—; pubr. Orim: A Jewish Jour. at Yale, 1986-88; tchr. Edgar M. Broneman Youth Fellowship in Israel, 1989—. Weekly columnist Nat. Jewish Post and Opinion, 1987—. Mem. steering com. Am. Israel Com.f or Israeli-Palestinian Peace, 1983—. With U.S. Army, 1979-87. Mem. Cen. Conf. Am. Rabbis. Home: 35 High St New Haven CT 06511 Office: 1904-A Yale Sta New Haven CT 06521

PONTOLILLO, BROTHER PETER A., school system administrator. Supt. schs. Archdiocese of San Antonio. Office: Archdiocesan Schs Office PO Box 28410 San Antonio TX 78228*

POOL, TERRY FRANKLIN, minister; b. San Diego, Nov. 25, 1953; s. Troy Felix and Lois Lucille (Townlin) P.; m. Joyce Wray Hodges, Nov. 24, 1973; John Franklin, Joshua Raymond. BA, Southeastern Bible Coll., Lakeland, Fla., 1977. Assoc. pastor Northside Assembly of God, Biloxi, Miss., 1981-82; pastor First Assembly of God, Monticello, Fla., 1982-85, Lighthouse Assembly of God, Eufaula, Ala., 1985-87, First Assembly of God, Brewton, Ala., 1987-89; assoc. pastor First Assembly of God, Valparaiso, Fla., 1989—; bd. dirs. Noah's Ark Daycare, Valparaiso, Fla., 1989—. Republican. Office: Valparaiso Assembly of God Hwy 190 PO Box 638 Valparaiso FL 32580

POOLE, BRENDA SHARON, secretary, bookkeeper; b. Mobile, Ala., Mar. 29, 1960; d. James Hayward Odom and Lois Eugenia (Allgood) Elms; m. Randy Earl Poole, Sept. 24, 1976; children: Melissa, Melody, Miranda. Student, Mobile Coll. Sec. First Assembly of God Ch., Saraland, Ala., 1980-84, ch. bookkeeper, 1984-90, pianist, 1986—, pastor's sec., 1990—; tchr. Sunday sch. dept., Saraland, 1989—. Mem. Women's Joy Fellowship (bd. dirs. Saraland chpt. 1991—). Office: First Assembly of God Ch Hwy # 43 PO Box 660 Saraland AL 36571

POOLE, EDWARD OTTO, minister; b. Phila., Feb. 17, 1931; s. Robert Jr. and Anna K. (Kolbe) P.; m. Marian Ruby Barr, Aug. 9, 1958; children: Ellen Poole Morgan, Alice Poole Temnick, Leah Poole Greenwood, Sara Barr Poole. AB, Wheaton (Ill.) Coll., 1953; MST, Temple U., 1956; ThM, Princeton (N.J.) Sem., 1959. Ordained to ministry Presbyn. Ch. (U.S.A.), 1956. Asst. pastor Glading Meml. Presbyn. Ch., Phila., 1956-59; pastor 1st Presbyn. Ch., Port Kennedy, Pa., 1959-64, Hillsborough Presbyn. Ch., Belle Mead, N.J., 1964-69, Sherwood Presbyn. Ch., Washington, 1970-76; area counselor Major Mission Fund, Presbyn. Ch. (U.S.A.), Butler, Pa., 1977-79; area min. Beaver-Butler Presbytery, Zelienople, Pa., 1980-89; interim pastor Livingston (N.J.) Presbyn. Ch., 1990-91; supply min. Newark and Phila. Presbyteries, 1991—. Mem. Presbytery of Newark. Home: 130 Davis Rd Doylestown PA 18901-3804 Office: Presbytery of Newark 9 S Munn Ave East Orange NJ 07018 *The things of this world carry a mixed blessing. Jesus was surely right when he said, "From everyone to whom much has been given, much will be required..." (Luke 12:48, NRSV).*

POOLE, THOMAS GEORGE, religion educator; b. Indiana, Pa., June 15, 1952; s. Russell Edward and Mildred Mae (Lipsie) P.; m. Anne Katherine Ard, June 14, 1986; 1 child, Katherine Lacy. BA, Roberts Wesleyan Coll., 1974; MDiv, Colgate Rochester Div. Sch., 1977; PhD, Pa. State U., 1984. Ordained to ministry United Ch. of Christ, 1983. Asst. prof. Pa. State U., University Park, 1986—, dir. religious affairs, 1986—; bd. dirs. United Ch. Christ, Pa. Cen. Conf., 1985-88; chmn. theol. commn., 1985-88, del. Gen. Synod, 1989-91; pres. No. Assn., United Ch. Christ, State College, Pa., 1989-91. Author: (with others) Black Families, 1990; contbrs. articles and revs. to relious publs. Sec. Forum on Black Affairs, State College, Pa., 1984—; cons. ethics com. Centre Community Hosp., State College, 1984—; bd. dirs. United Campus Ministry, State College, 1989—. Israel summer program student B'nai Brith Hillel Fedn., 1985; Crozer scholar Crozer Theol. Sem., Rochester, 1988, 91. Mem. Am. Acad. Religion, Soc. Christian Ethics, Assn. Coll. and Univ. Religious Affairs (exec. com. 1986—), Am. Coll. Pers. Assn. Democrat. Office: Pa State U 105 Eisenhower Chapel University Park PA 16802

POOVEY, WILLIAM ARTHUR, theology educator; b. Balt., Sept. 20, 1913; s. William Arthur and Opal (Holl) P.; m. Mary Virginia Smith, June 29, 1940. B.A., Capital U., Columbus, Ohio, 1934; certificate, Evang. Lutheran Sem., Columbus, 1939; M.A., Northwestern U., 1939; D.D., Wartburg Coll., Waverly, Iowa, 1972. Ordained to ministry Am. Luth. Ch., 1939; instr. speech Capital U., 1935-39; pastor in Monterey Park, Cal., 1939-45, San Antonio, 1945-53, Memphis, 1953-57; prof. homiletics Wartburg Theol. Sem., Dubuque, Iowa, 1957-76; acting pres. Wartburg Theol. Sem., 1970, 71; mem. commn. research and social action Am. Luth. Ch., 1960-72, chmn., 1963-72, mem. bd. pensions, 1972-83. Author: Hymn Dramatizations, 1942, Questions That Trouble Christians, 1946, Problems That Plague Saints, 1950, No Hands But Ours, 1954, Your Neighbor's Faith, 1961, And Pilate Asked, 1965, Cross Words, 1967, Lenten Chancel Dramas, 1967, What Did Jesus Do?, 1968, Chancel Dramas for Lent, 1968, The Christian in Society, 1969, Mustard Seeds and Wine Skins, 1972, Let Us Adore Him, 1972, Stand Still and Move Ahead, 1973, Signs of His Coming, 1973, Six Faces of Lent, 1974, Banquets and Beggars, 1974, the Power of the Kingdom, 1974, Celebrate with Drama, 1975, The Days Before Christmas, 1975, The Wonderful Word Shalom, 1975, The Days Before Easter, 1976, The Prayer He Taught, 1976, Letting the Word Become Alive, 1977, Six Prophets for Today, 1977, Planning a Christian Funeral, 1978, The Days of Pentecost, 1979, Faith is the Password, 1979, Prodigals and Publicans, 1980, We Sing Your Praise, O Lord, 1980, How to Talk to Christians about Money, 1982. Home: 10418 Applegate San Antonio TX 78230

POPE, MARVIN HOYLE, retired language educator; b. Durham, N.C., June 23, 1916; s. Charles Edgar and Bessie Cleveland Sorrell P.; m. Helen Thompson Bretana, Sept. 4, 1948 (dec. Feb. 5, 1979); m. Ingrid Brostrom Bloomquist, Mar. 9, 1985. AB, Duke U., 1938, AM, 1939; PhD, Yale U., 1949. Instr. dept. religion Duke U., Durham, 1947-49; asst. prof. Hebrew Yale U., New Haven, 1949-55, assoc. prof., 1955-64, prof. Semitic langs. and lit., 1964-86, prof. emeritus, sr. rsch. scholar, 1986—; Haskell lectr. Oberlin Coll., 1971, vis. lectr. Cath. U. Lublin, Poland, 1977, Fulbright lectr. U. Aleppo, Syria, 1980; Wickenden lectures Miami U., Oxford, Ohio, 1982; Fulbright Rsch. scholar Inst. Ugaritforschung U. Muenster, Fed. Republic Germany, 1986, 90; Hooker disting. vis. prof. McMaster U., Hamilton, Ont., Can., 1986; bd. dirs. Am. Sch. of Oriental Rsch., Jerusalem, Hebrew Union Coll. Bibl. and Archeol. Sch., Jerusalem; trustee Albright Inst. Archeol. Rsch., Jerusalem; fellow Pierson Coll. Yale U. Author: El in the Ugaritic Texts, 1955; The Book of Job, 1973, Song of Songs, 1977 (Nat. Religious Book award 1978), Syrien Die Mythologie der Ugariter und Phoenizier, 1962; contbr. articles to scholarly jours. and dictionaries. Mem. rev. standard version Bible com. Nat. Coun. of Chs., 1960—; mem. 1st Ch. Round Hill. With USAAF, 1941-45, PTO. Nat. Endowment for Humanities Rsch. grantee, 1980—. Mem. Am. Oriental Soc., Am. Schs. Oriental Rsch., Soc. Bibl. Lit., Am. Soc. Study Religions, Columbia U. Seminar for Study of Hebrew Bible, Yale Club, Oriental Club New Haven, Mory's Club, Stanwich Country Club, Phi Beta Kappa. Home: 538 Round Hill Rd Greenwich CT 06831

POPE, NATHAN REINHART, pastor; b. Marinette, Wis., Oct. 15, 1949; s. Reinhart John and Carol Jean (Negley) P.; m. Patrice Ann Felgenhauer, Aug. 15, 1976; children: Gregory, Melanie, Nicholas, Natalie. BA, Northwestern Coll., Watertown, Wis., 1972; MDiv, Wis. Luth. Sem., 1977; D Ministry, Luther Rice Sem., Jacksonville, Fla., 1990. Ordained to ministry Wis. Evang. Luth. Synod, 1977. Asst. pastor St. Mark's Luth. Ch., Citrus Heights, Calif., 1977-80; assoc. pastor 1st Luth. Ch., Racine, Wis., 1980-83, sr. pastor, 1983—; mem. dist. coun. Wis. Evang. Luth. Synod, dist. del., Milw., 1980—, synod del., New Ulm, Minn., 1991; registered agt. Wise Penny-Welstores Inc., Racine, 1983—; cir. pastor So. Pastoral Conf.; mem., sec. Shoreland Luth. High Sch. Found.; voting mem. Shoreland Luth. High Sch. Fedn. Contbg. author: Sermon Studies on the Gospels, 1990, Soli Deo Gloria, 1991. Republican. Home and Office: 735 Grand Ave Racine WI 53403

POPE, WILLIAM KENNETH, bishop; b. Hale, Mo., Nov. 21, 1901; s. William Mumford and Victoria (LaRue) P.; m. Kate Sayle, Mar. 16, 1930; children—Katherine Victoria, Kenneth Sayle. Student, Clarendon (Tex.) Coll., 1917-20; B.A., So. Methodist U., 1922, B.D., 1924, LL.D., 1964; student, Yale Grad. Sch., 1927-29; D.D. (hon.), Southwestern U., Georgetown, Tex., 1937, Hendrix Coll., 1961. Ordained to ministry Methodist Ch., 1925, consecrated bishop, 1960; pastor in Milford, Tex., 1924-26, Breckenridge, Tex., 1929-33, Georgetown, Tex., 1933-36, Springfield, Mo., 1936-40, Austin, Tex., 1940-49, Houston, 1949-60; bishop Ark. area Meth. Ch., 1960-64, Dallas-Ft. Worth area, 1964—; bishop-in-residence Perkins Sch. Theology, So. Meth. U., 1972-76; Mem. gen. bd. evangelism, bd. Christian social concerns Meth. Ch.; mem. program council United Meth. Ch.; chmn. bd. Western Meth. Assembly, Fayetteville, Ark., 1960-64; vis. lectr. Perkins Sch. Theology, So. Meth. U., 1949; del. World Conf. on Life and Work, Oxford, Eng., 1937, World Meth. Conf., Oxford, 1951; vis. preacher Gen. Conf. Meth. Ch. in, Mexico, 1946; rep. Meth. Ch. in U.S. to centennial celebration Methodism in, India, 1956. Author: A Pope at Roam, the Confessions of a Bishop, 1976; Contbr.: Prayer for Today. Pres. Tex. Council Chs., 1968; pres. Tex. Conf. Chs., 1969; Chmn. bd. trustees So. Meth. U., 1971-72. Mem. Lambda Chi Alpha, Theta Phi, Tau Kappa Alpha. Office: So Meth Univ Perkins Sch Theology Dallas TX 75205

POPKO, SISTER KATHLEEN MARIE, company executive; b. Holyoke, Mass., Oct. 28, 1943; d. Peter Anthony and Phyllis (Kisiel) P. BS in Nursing, Marillac Coll., 1968; Masters in Social Welfare, Brandels U., 1973, PhD, 1975. Research assoc. Levinson Policy Inst., Brandels U., Waltham, Mass., 1974-75; adj. asst. prof. Heller Sch., Brandels U., Waltham, 1975-79; v.p. planning Mercy Hosp., Springfield, Mass., 1975-81; v.p. Sisters Providence, Holyoke, Mass.; project dir. Devel. Sisters Providence Health System, Holyoke, 1980-84; pres. Sisters Providence, 1985—. Author: Regulatory Controls, 1976. Chmn. bd. dirs. Consolidated Cath. Health Care, Chgo., 1985-88; bd. dirs. Cath. Health Assn., 1985-88; exec. com. Leadership Conf. Women Religious, 1986—, pres. 1990—. Home: 53 Mill St Westfield MA 01085 Office: Sisters Providence Gamelin St Holyoke MA 01040

POPLACK, KENNETH DAVID, rabbi; b. Seattle, June 2, 1926; s. Abraham E. and Helen (Trakenisky) P.; m. Deborah Raab, June 27, 1950; children: Yosef, Naomi. BS, St. Joseph's U., 1963. Ordained rabbi, 1949. Rabbi Mesivta Rabbi Chaim, Berlin, 1949, Temple Israel, Lehighton, Pa., 1953-55, B'Nai Jacob Synagogue Ctr., Phoenixville, Pa., 1955-63, Bethpage (N.Y.) Jewish Community Ctr., 1963-78, Congregation Ahavas Israel, Passaic, N.J., 1978—; v.p. L.I. Bd. Rabbis, 1974-75. Mem. Passaic-Clifton Bd. Rabbis (chmn. 1990-91), N.Y. Bd. Rabbis, Rabbinical Assembly, B'nai Brith. Home: 40 Belmont Pl Passaic NJ 07055 Office: Congregation Ahavas Israel 181 Van Houten Ave Passaic NJ 07055

POPP, BERNARD F., bishop; b. Dec. 6, 1917. Ordained priest Roman Cath. Ch., 1943. Bishop San Antonio, 1983—. Address: PO Box 28410 San Antonio TX 78228

POPP, NATHANIEL (WILLIAM GEORGE) (HIS GRACE BISHOP NATHANIEL), bishop; b. Aurora, Ill., June 12, 1940; s. Joseph and Vera (Boytor) P. BA, Ill. Benedictine-St. Procopius Coll., 1962; MDiv, Pontifical Gregorian U., Vatican City, 1966. Ordained priest Romanian Greek Catholic Ch., 1966; consecrated bishop Romanian Orthodox Episcopate of Am., 1980. Asst. pastor St. Michael Byz Ch., Aurora, 1967; parish priest Holy Cross Romanian Orthodox Ch., Hermitage, Pa., 1975-80; aux. bishop Romanian Orthodox Episcopate of Am., Orthodox Ch. in Am., Jackson, Mich., 1980-84; ruling bishop Romanian Orthodox Episcopate of Am., Orthodox Ch. in Am., Detroit, 1984—; mem. Holy Synod Orthodox Ch. in Am., Syosset, N.Y., 1980—; mem. participant Monastic Consultation, Cairo, 1979, Seventh Assembly, Vancouver, Can., 1983. Author: Holy Icons, 1969; editor newspaper Solia. Chmn. Romanian-Am. Heritage Ctr., Grass Lake, Mich.; organizer, chmn. Help for Romania Nat. Relief Fund and Help the Children of Romainia Relief Fund. Republican. Home and Office: Romanian Orthodox Episcopate Am 2522 Grey Tower Rd Jackson MI 49201-9120

POPPE, LEONARD BRUCE, minister; b. Corpus Christi, Tex., Oct. 23, 1959; s. Clarence Henry and Lucile Lesterly (Bethke) P.; m. Karin Sue Hafermann, May 8, 1982; children: Jennifer Diane, Brian Daniel. BA in Religion, U. Fla., 1983; MDiv, Concordia Theol. Sem., 1987. Ordained to ministry Luth. Ch.-Mo. Synod, 1987. Min. Our Savior Luth. Ch., Columbus, Miss., 1987—. Vol. chaplain Golden Triangle Reg. Med. Ctr., Columbus, 1988—; pastoral counselor Recovery House, Columbus, 1989—. Mem. Cir. Pastors Conf. (sec. 1988-89, pres. 1989-90), Dist. Pastors Conf. (sec. 1989-91). Office: Our Savior Luth Ch 1211 18th Ave N Columbus MS 39701 *Many of the personal burdens people carry are the result of one's focussing too intently on their failures and weaknesses. While we must acknowledge our human weaknesses, we also have a Savior who died for those weaknesses and failures—and overcame them. Don't take yourself so seriously; take Christ seriously.*

PORATH, JEROME RICHARD, school system superintendent; b. Milw., July 31, 1946; m. Andrea J. Valentine; children: Judith Christine, James Christian, Jennifer Elizabeth, Joanna Helen, Julie Margaret. Student, Marquette U., 1963-67; BA in Philosophy, St. Louis U., 1969, MA in Philosophy, 1972, PhD in Edn., 1982. Tchr., adminstr. St. Francis Xavier Grade Sch., St. Louis, 1969-72; dir. govt. programs Archdiocese of St. Louis, 1972-76, asst. supt. of schs., 1976-78; exec. dir. Fairness in Edn., St. Louis, 1976; supt. of schs. Diocese of Albany, N.Y., 1978-85, Archdiocese of Washington, 1985-91, Archdiocese of L.A., 1991—; lectr. St. Louis U., 1974, 76, 78, Inst. for Cath. Edn., St. Louis, 1975, N.J. Summit on Cath. Sch. Edn., Convent Station, 1988, Cath. Edn. Inst., 1990; cons. planning Archdiocese of Mobile, Ala., 1990—; adj. lectr. Grad. Sch. Arts and Scis., Cath. U. Am., Washington, 1991; chair com. on profl. and fin. affairs Commn. on Elem. Schs., Mid. States Assn. colls. and Schs. Active Susbstance Abuse Coun., Prince George's County, Md., parish coun. St. Camillus Cath. Ch., Silver Spring, Md.; chmn. Cath. sch. sect. United Way Greater St. Louis, 1975-78; del. Conf. on Edn., Office of Gov. of Mo., 1976; mem. Adv. Coun. for Chpt. II of ECIA, Office of Gov. of N.Y., 1983-85; mem. adv. com. Office of Edn. Commr. of N.Y. State, 1983-85. Recipient Headstart Vol. award, 1976. Mem. Chief Adminstrs. Cath. Edn. of Nat. Cath. Ednl. Assn. (bd. dirs. rsch. ctr., exec. com., adv. com. schs. div. 1987-90), U.S. Cath. Conf. (com. on Cath. schs. and pub. policy), Md. Cath. Conf. (chair edn. dept.), Am. Assn. Sch. Adminstrs., Alpha Sigma Nu. Office: 1520 W 9th St Los Angeles CA 90015

PORATH, JONATHAN DAVID, college administrator, rabbi, educator; b. Atlantic City, N.J., Oct. 22, 1944; s. Tzvi Hyman and Esther (Levin) P.; m. Deena Geller, Mar. 18, 1975; children: Yehuda, Batsheva, Akiva, Yael, Shlomo Reuven. BA, Brandeis U., 1966; MA, Columbia U., 1969; M in Hebrew Lit., Jewish Theol. Sem., N.Y.C., 1970. Ordained rabbi, 1970. Dir. Hillel Found., U. Okla., Norman, 1970-72; assoc. dir. dept. edn. United Synagoga of Am., N.Y.C., 1972-75; rabbi Temple Beth Or, Clark, N.J., 1975-84; dir. Israel office Rockland Community Coll., Jerusalem, 1985—. Author: Jews of Russia, 1972. Founder, co-chmn. Soviet Jewry Resettlement Project, Jerusalem, 1990—. Mem. Rabbinical Assembly (exec. bd. 1972-75). Home: Nerot Shabbat, Jerusalem 623/10, Israel Office: Rockland Community Coll, 97 Yaffo #228, Jerusalem Israel

PORCELLO, JACK SAMUEL, minister; b. Rochester, N.Y., Sept. 10, 1960; s. Jack R. Porcello and Josephine M. (Gange) Haak; m. Susan Elaine Van Vessem, Aug. 16, 1986; children: Maureen S., Bethany E., Abigail J. Grad. high sch., Rochester. Ordained to ministry Dayspring Fellowship , 1989. Elder Dayspring Fellowship, Spencerport, N.Y., 1986—, asst. pastor, children's pastor, 1989-90; sr. pastor Calvary Chapel of Caledonia, N.Y., 1990—; trustee, children's activities dir. Dayspring Fellowship, 1986—. Pub. rels. dir. Youth Devel. Inc., Rochester, 1990. Mem. Loving Edn. at Home (chpt. leader 1990). Republican. Office: Calvary Chapel Caledonia 137 North St Caledonia NY 14423

PORT, ROBERT STANLEY, rabbi; b. N.Y.C., Jan. 19, 1927; s. Philip and Evelyn (Schulberg) P.; m. Deborah Fisch, June 23, 1953; children: Reva, Andrew, Joan, Lisa. Student, Yavne Hebrew Theol. Sem., 1950-53; BA, NYU, 1950, MA, 1952. Ordained rabbi, 1954. Rabbi Jeannette, Pa., 1953-56, Whitestone, N.Y., 1956-58; rabbi Farmingdale (N.Y.) Jewish Ctr., 1958-62, Beth Jacob Synagogue, Norwich, Conn., 1962-68, Temple Sinai, Middletown, N.Y., 1968-76, Temple Ohav Shalom, Sayreville, N.J., 1976—; chaplain N.Y. State Police, 1968—, Mid-Hudson Psychiat. Ctr., New Hampton, N.Y., 1972—. Bd. dirs. Jeannette (Pa.) Dist. Hosp., 1955-57, Norwich chpt. NAACP, 1963-68, Thames Valley Coun. for Community Action, Norwich, 1964-68, Thames Valley Mental Health Orgn., Norwich, 1965-68; active Marriage Encounter, Inc., 1973—. Mem. Interfaith Coun., Mensa, Rotary (bd. dirs. 1972—). Home: 29 Frederick Pl Parlin NJ 08859

PORTALES, ALFREDO, pastor; b. Allende, Coah., Mex., Apr. 10, 1946; came to U.S., 1971; s. Simon Jose and Maria Louisa (Martinez) P.; m. Mapy Isabel Gonzales, Dec.28,1968; children: Alfredo Jr., Nohemi, David, Sarita. AAS in Automated Systems, Tarrant County Jr. Coll., Ft. Worth, 1991. Ordained minister. Bible tchr. Bapt. Mex. Ch., Allende, Mex., 1962-67; tchr. deacon Mex. Bapt. Ch., Ft. Worth, 1971-77; tchr. deacon Interdenominational Ch., Ft. Worth, 1977-86, founder, pastor, 1986—; technician Bell Helicopter Textron, Ft. Worth, 1978—; trustee Confraternity of Full Gospel Chs., Dallas,Ft. Worth, 1988—. Republican. Home: 2316 Refugio Ave Fort Worth TX 76106

PORTER, ANDREW PEABODY, theology educator, physicist; b. Boston, Oct. 5, 1946; s. Phil and Joan (Peabody) P. AB, Harvard U., 1968; MS, U. Calif., Davis, 1968, PhD, 1976; MTS, Ch. Divinity Sch., 1980. Physicist Lawrence Livermore (Calif.) Nat. Labs., 1968—; instr. in theology Sch. for Deacons, Castro Valley, Calif., 1980-88. Mem. Cath. Theol. Soc. Am. Home: 774 Joyce St Livermore CA 94550

PORTER, EMERSON LEON, music minister, administrator; b. Snyder, Tex., Aug. 17, 1949; s. Leon and Jo Ann (Stevens) P.; m. Cynthia Beth Gann, June 10, 1972; children: Marcy, Holly. BS in Zoology, Tex. A&M U., 1971; M in Ch. Music, S.W. Bapt. Theol. Sem., 1974. Music dir. Samuel's Ave. Bapt. Ch., Ft. Worth, 1971-72; min. music, youth 1st Bapt. Ch., Justin, Tex., 1972-75; min. music, adminstrn. 1st Bapt. Ch., Allen, Tex., 1975—. Mem. community task force Allen (Tex.) Ind. Sch. Dist., 1990; coach Allen Sports Assn., 1990-91. Fellow Nat. Assn. Ch. Bus. Adminstrs., So. Bapt. Assn. Bus. Adminstrs.; mem. So. Bapt. Ch. Music Conf. (West rep. 1989-91), Singing Men of Tex. North Cen. (treas. 1988—), Allen Ministerial Alliance. Home: 906 Lake Highlands Allen TX 75002-2021 Office: 1st Bapt Ch PO Box 8 204 E Main Allen TX 75002-0008

PORTER, GARY STEPHAN, minister; b. Bangor, Maine, Nov. 23, 1952; s. Leo Gilman and Gloria May (Getchell) P.; m. Jo Ann Sturm, Sept. 7, 1974; children: Matthew, Lisa. B in Eng. Bible, Rockford (Ill.) Sch. Theology, 1977. Ordained to ministry Fellowship of Christian Assemblies, 1982. Min. Open Bible Ch., Palo, Ill., 1976-79; adminstr. Neues Leben Ill., Polo, 1979; min. Faith Ctr., Rockford, 1981-90; founding min. Vineyard Ministries, Roscoe, Ill., 1990—; bd. dirs. Mobile Love, Rockford, 1976-81; pres. Polo Ministerial Assn., 1977-78; No. Ill. area advisor Women Aglow Internat., 1988—; seminar lectr., 1990—; chaplain Rockford Police Dept., 1987-90. Author: The Dream Journal, 1990, Dreams: A Way God Speaks, 1991, The Biblical Dream Dictionary, 1991; contbr. articles to mags. Twp. coord. Rep. party primary election, 16th Congl. Dist., 1978; mem. precinct com. Rep. party, Rockford, 1982-86. Mem. Assn. Christian Therapists. Office: Vineyard Ministries 11364 2d St Roscoe IL 61073

PORTER, H(ARRY) BOONE, Episcopal priest; b. Louisville, Jan. 10, 1923; s. Harry Boone and Charlotte (Wiseman) P.; m. Violet Monser, June 28, 1947; children: Charlotte M., H. Boone III, Michael T., Gabrielle R., Clarissa, Nicholas T. BA, Yale U., 1947; STB, Berkeley Div. Sch., 1950; STM, Gen. Theol. Sem., N.Y.C., 1952; PhD, Oxford U., 1954. Ordained to ministry Episc. Ch., 1950. From asst. to assoc. prof. Nashotah (Wis.) House, 1954-60; prof. liturgics Gen. Theol. Sem., N.Y.C., 1960-70; exec. dir. Roanridge Found., Kansas City, 1970-77; editor The Living Church, Milw., 1977-90, sr. editor, 1990—; rector St. Peter's Ch., North Lake, Wis., 1980-90; pres. New Directions Ministries, Inc., N.Y., 1980-85. Author: Ordination Prayers, 1967, Keeping the Church Year, 1977, Jeremy Taylor: Liturgist, 1979, A Song of Creation, 1986, Day of Light, 1988. Active Porter Charitable Found., Inc. Tech. sgt. U.S. Army, 1943-45, PTO. Named McMath Lectr., Diocese of Mich., 1965, Sheridan Lectr., Nashotah House, 1986. Fellow North Am. Acad. Liturgy; mem. Associated Parishes, Inc. (council, pres. 1973-75). Clubs: Yale (N.Y.C.); Pendennis (Louisville); Pequot Yacht (Southport, Conn.). Avocations: gardening, sailing. Office: Living Ch 816 E Juneau Ave Milwaukee WI 53202

PORTER, LEE, religious organization administrator; b. Mexico, Mo., June 13, 1929; s. Chaston and Hazel (Martin) P.; m. Pat Long, May 12, 1956; children: Lee II, Lane. AA, Hannibal-LaGrange Coll., Hannibal, Mo., 1951; BA, William Jewell Coll., Liberty, Mo., 1953; BD, Southwestern Sem., Ft. Worth, Tex., 1956; ThD, Southwestern Sem., 1965; DD, William Jewell Coll., Liberty, Mo., 1970. Dir. recreation Glorieta Bapt. Assy., Glorieta, N.Mex., 1953-56; pastor First Bapt. Ch., Glen Rose, Tex., 1956-59, Calvary Bapt. Ch., Casa Granada, Ariz., 1959-60, Winbourne Ave. Bapt. Ch., Baton Rouge, 1960-64, First Bapt. Ch. Bellaire, Houston, 1964-72; dir. orgn. Christian Life Commn. So. Bapt. Conv., Nashville, 1972-75; sr. adult cons. Bapt. Sun. Sch. Bd., Nashville, 1976-79; design editor Bapt. Sun. Sch. Bd., 1979—; regis. sec. So. Bapt. Conv., 1977—, 1st v.p., 1969-70, 2d v.p., 1968-69, chmn. order of bus. com., 1971-72; lectr. in field. Author: Mission Vaction Bible School, 1970, Great Doctrines of The Bible, 1975; contbr. articles to profl. jours. Baptist. Avocations: sports. Home: 1201 Longstreet Cir Brentwood TN 37027 Office: Bapt Sunday Sch Bd 127 9th Ave N Nashville TN 37234

PORTER, MYRON JOSEPH, minister; b. Pampa, Tex., Nov. 1, 1948; s. Myron Joseph and Dorothy Viola (Stone) P.; m. Suzanne Thomas, Dec. 26, 1969; children: Jennifer Kathleen, Rebecca Lynne, Deborah Ann, Amanda Suzanne. BS in Physics, West Tex. State U., 1971; MDiv., Southwestern Bapt. Theol. Sem., 1974; D. Ministry, Golden Gate Bapt. Theol. Sem., 1981; Student, USAF Acad., 1967-68. Ordained to ministry Bapt. Ch., 1971. Dir. Bapt. student union Western Tex. Coll., Snyder, 1974-77, women's basketball coach, 1974-77, prof. Bible, 1974-77; dir. Bapt. student union U. Alberta, Edmonton, Can., 1977-82, U. Calgary (Can.), 1982-86, Del Mar Coll., Corpus Christi, Tex., 1986-89, Corpus Christi State U., 1986-89; prof. Bible Del Mar Coll., Corpus Christi, 1986-89; dir. Bapt. student union Southwest Tex. State U., San Marcos, 1989—; adj. prof. Bible, Houston Bapt. U., 1989—. Author: Developing a Ministry to the Temporary Summer Employees of Yellowstone Park, 1981. Moderator Midwest Bapt. Assn., Alberta, Can., 1983-85. With USAF, 1967-73. Mem. Assn. So. Bapt. Campus Ministers (nominating com.), Southwestern Bapt. Theol. Sem. Alumni (Can. pres. 1984-85), NRA, North Am. Hunting Club, North Am. Fishing Club. Avocations: hunting, fishing, golf, camping, bridge. Office: Bapt Student Union 518 W LBJ Dr San Marcos TX 78666

PORTER, NANCY JEAN, minister, religious organization administrator; b. Cleve., Mar. 10, 1930; d. Harold J. and Ruth (Marquardt) P. BA, U. Mich., 1952; MRE, N.Y. Theol. Sem. Ordained to ministry Ind. Assemblies of God, 1957. Missionary Global Frontiers, Global Missions, Atlanta, 1955-71; missionary, evangelist Mex., Nigeria, Ghana, Indonesia, The Philippines, 1973-81; prin. Bible Sch.-Christ Ascension Ch., Enugu, Nigeria, 1982-84; dir. African Heartbeat, Phoenix, 1985-91, Harvest Heartbeat, Phoenix, 1991—; tchr. seminars in Pakistan, India, Nigeria, Cameroon. Editor African Heartbeat newsletter, 1976-91, Harvest Heartbeat newsletter, 1991—. Mem. Assemblies of God Internat., Internat. Conv. of Faith Chs. and Mins., Charismatic Bible Mins., Sweetwater Ministries, End Time Handmaidens, Phi Beta Kappa. Home: 11811 N 19th Ave # 2 Phoenix AZ 85029 Office: Harvest Heartbeat Glendale AZ 85312-5745 *In my life I have tried to follow the Master wherever he guided me, despite inconveniences and difficulties. Nothing is worthwhile unless done for Him.*

PORTER, RALPH FRANKLYN, pastor; b. Long Beach, Calif., Sept. 28, 1942; s. Lowell Dean and Phyllis (Martin) P.; m. Helen Laura Young, Sept. 4, 1964; children: Deanna Marcy, Melinda Stimpson, R. Michael, Jonathan. BA, Biola U., 1964; postgrad., Talbot Theol. Sem., 1964-65; ThM, Dallas Theol. Sem., 1969, postgrad., 1978-83. Ordained to ministry Am. Bapt. Chs., 1964. Prof. Bible exposition Cen. Am. Theol. Sem., Guatemala, 1970-78, 83-88; pres. Guatemala Bible Inst., Chimaltenango, 1979-82; pastor Evang. Free Ch., Salt Lake City, 1989—; bd. dirs. Guatemala Bible Inst., 1975-82, Huehue Acad., Guatemala, 1980-87, Cen. Am. Theol. Sem., Guatemala, 1981; v.p. Intermountain West Region Evang. Free Ch., Salt Lake City, 1990—. Author, editor Ediciones Las Americas, Puebla, Mexico, 1978-91; editor series Estudios Biblicos ELA, 1985—; author Spanish booklets, commentaries. Mem. Evang. Free Ch. Ministerial Assn. Office: Evang Free Ch 6515 S Lion Ln Salt Lake City UT 84121

PORTER, SAMUEL RICHARD, minister; b. Gainesville, Tex., Mar. 17, 1952; s. Roy Wilson P. and Claudia Mae (Helton) Hamilton; m. Sheryl Denise Peters, June 22, 1974; children: Aaron Neal, Joshua Jared. BA in Religion, Baylor U., 1975; MDiv, Southwestern Bapt. Theol. Sem., 1977. Ordained to ministry So. Bapt. Conf., 1974. Assoc. pastor First Bapt. Ch., Marietta, Okla., 1975-77; pastor First Bapt. Ch., Eakly, Okla., 1977-84, Bartlesville (Okla.) So. Bapt. Ch., 1984—; bd. dirs. Okla. Bapt. Gen. Conv., 1989—, chmn. family care com., 1989—, mem. exec. com., 1990—; pres. Agrimission Fellowship, 1985-86. Pres. Okla. Tex. Longhorn Assn., 1989-90. Office: Bartlesville So Bapt Ch PO Box 3367 Bartlesville OK 74006

PORTER, STANLEY EARL, religion educator; b. Long Beach, Calif., Nov. 23, 1956; s. Stanley Earl and Lorraine (DeHaan) P. BA, Point Loma Coll., 1977; MA, Claremont (Calif.) Grad. Sch., 1980, Trinity Evang. Div. Sch., 1982; PhD, U. Sheffield, Eng., 1988. Assoc. prof. Greek Biola U., LaMirada, Calif., 1988—; cons. The Dictionary of Classical Hebrew, U. Sheffield, Eng., 1988—; coun. of theologians, Evang. Affirmations 89, Deerfield, Ill., 1989. Author: Verbal Aspect in the Greek of the New Testament, 1989, Katallassō in Ancient Greek Literature with Reference to the Pauline Writings, 1991; editor: The Bible in Three Dimensions, 1990, The Language of the New Testament, 1991; contbr. articles to profl. jours. Vis. scholar St. Johns Coll., 1989; faculty rsch. grant Biola U., 1989, 90; vis. rsch. fellow U. Sheffield, 1988; Tyndale fellowship, 1984-86. Fellow Inst. for Bibl. Rsch.; mem. MLA, Tyndale Fellowship for Bibl. and Theol. Rsch., Evang. Theol. Soc., Soc. of Bibl. Lit., Am. Acad. Religion, Inst. for Antiquity and Christianity, Am. Philological Assn., Am. Soc. Papyrologists, Assn. Internat. de Papyrologues. Republican. Office: Biola U 13800 Biola Ave La Mirada CA 90639

PORTER, SUSAN GIFT, evangelist, singer; b. Jackson, Mich., July 21, 1948; d. Aldon Kerrigan and Mildred Lois (Curren) Gift; m. Daniel Robert Porter, Mar. 26, 1977; 1 child, Jonathan. BA, Cedarville Coll., 1970. Ordained to ministry Masterpiece Gospel Ch. Corp., 1982. Missionary Bethel Bapt. Ch., 1974; v.p., corp. sec., Christian edn. cons. Masterpiece Gospel Inc., Oak Harbor, Wash., 1977—. Author: Puppets for Safe Kids, 1984; recording artist, singer. Mem. Nat. Assn. Evangs. Avocations: counted cross stitch, bowling, reading, bicycling. Office: Masterpiece Gospel Inc PO Box 100 Oak Harbor WA 98277-0100

PORTER, THOMAS J., music educator, religious organization director; b. Bismarck, N.D., Sept. 4, 1958; s. Kenneth C. and Patricia A. (Undem) P.; m. Jenifer M. Frank, May 2, 1987; children: Hannah Jocelyn, Joel Christian. BA in Music, U. of Mary, 1979; MA in Music, DePaul U., 1980; MA in Theology, U. Notre Dame, 1986. Ind. musician, 1980-90; dir. of worship Diocese of Bismarck, 1982—; instr. music U. Mary, Bismarck, 1987-91. Contbr. articles to profl. jours. Musician Bismarck-Mandan Symphony, 1977-89; vol. United Way, Bismarck, 1988-89, Young Life, 1980-84. Mem. Nat. Fedn. Musicians, Nat. Pastoral Musicians Assn., Am. Guild Organists, Fedn. of Diocesan Liturgical Com. (nat. bd. dirs. 1990-91). Roman Catholic. Avocations: gardening, cycling downhill and cross country skiing. Home: 302 6th Ave NW Mandan ND 58554 Office: Diocese of Bismarck 520 N Washington St Bismarck ND 58502

PORTER, W. L., bishop. Bishop of Cen. Tenn., Ch. of God in Christ, Memphis. Office: Ch of God in Christ 1235 East Pkwy S Memphis TN 38114*

PORTERA, ALAN AUGUST, religion educator; b. Buffalo, Jan. 29, 1951; s. Albert Andrew and Adele Beatrice (Pecorella) P.; m. Marcia Jean Urbaniak, May 16, 1975; 1 child, Alanna Jachelene. BS, State U. Coll. N.Y., Buffalo, 1974; MS in Edn., Niagara U., 1981; doctoral candidate, SUNY, Buffalo, 1984. Cert. nursery sch., kindergarten, grades 1-6, and art grades K-12, N.Y. Tchr. St. Gregory's, Williamsville, N.Y., 1974-75, St. Mark's, Buffalo, 1975-76, St. James, Depew, N.Y., 1977-79, St. Teresa's, Niagara Falls, N.Y., 1979-89; dir. religious edn. St. Joseph's, North Tonawanda, N.Y., 1978—, Niagara Falls, N.Y., 1990—; cons. edn. sales Knowledge Nest, Chgo., 1989-90; religious edn. moderator Region 26, 29, 30, Diocese of Buffalo, 1981-83. Author: Concern for Peace and Justice, 1981, Foundations for Faith Formation, 1989, Fundamental Building Blocks of Faith, 1991. Named Religious Educator of the Year Diocese of Buffalo, 1979. Mem. ASCD, Nat. Assn. for Core Curriculum, Western N.Y. Assn. Dirs. and Coords. of Religious Educators (v.p. 1985-87). Democrat. Roman Catholic. Home: 8420 Troy Ave Niagara Falls NY 14304 Office: St Joseph's Catechetical Ministries 1451 Payne Ave North Tonawanda NY 14120 also: 625 Tronolone Pl Niagara Falls NY 14301 *Learning is a womb to tomb experience. I believe it truly is a lifelong process of change that permits the learners to apply the knowledge that they have acquired to their own life experience.*

PORTLAND, PAUL JAMES, priest, religious order administrator; b. Hazleton, Pa., Nov. 14, 1946. BA in English and Philosophy summa cum laude, Mt. St. Paul Coll., 1969; MA in English Lit. and Lang., U. Wis., Milw., 1971, postgrad., 1971-73; postgrad., Washington Theol. Coalition, 1973-76. Joined Soc. Divine Order, Roman Cath. Ch., 1964, ordained priest, 1976. Rsch. asst. U. Wis., Milw., 1969-70, teaching asst., 1970-73; mem. internal ministry team Soc. Divine Savior, 1973-76, provincial sec., dir. communications, 1979-88, dir. renewal, 1979-85; pres. gen. chpt. Soc. Divine Savior, Steinfeld, Fed. Republic Germany, 1981; vicar provincial Soc. Divine Savior, 1982-88, dir. planning, 1985-88; 1st vice chair gen. chpt. Soc. Divine Savior, Steinfeld, 1987; provincial N.Am. province Soc. Divine Savior, 1988—; asst. prof. English, dir. campus ministry Brescia Coll., Owensboro, Ky., 1977-79; with Salvatorian Assocs., 1967-79; instr. confraternity of Christian doctrine St. Pius X Parish, Wauwatosa, Wis., 1969-70; with staff Wis. Sch. for Girls, Oregon, 1974; campus min. Robert Morris Coll., Point Pk. Coll., Pitts., 1976-77; pres. Synod N.Am. Province of Salvatorians, 1976-79; facilitator gen. chpt. Salvatorian Sisters, Rome, 1989. Edn. Professors' Devel. Act fellow, 1969-71. Mem. Phi Kappa Phi, Sigma Tau Delta, Alpha Mu Gamma. Home and Office: 1735 Hi-Mount Blvd Milwaukee WI 53208

PORTON, GARY G., history and religion educator. BA in History, UCLA, 1967; MA in Judaic Studies, Hebrew Union Coll., L.A., 1969; PhD in Religious Studies, Brown U., 1973. Asst. prof. U. Ill., Urbana, 1973-79, assoc. prof., 1979-84, prof. religion, 1984—, prof. comparative lit., 1987—, prof. history, 1991—; lectr. Ariz. State U., 1975, U. Ariz., 1975, U. Iowa, 1976, So. Ill. U., 1978, Danville Jewish Community Ctr., 1984, U. Fla., 1985, Sinai Temple, 1985, Temple Benei Abraham, 1986, 88, Temple Anshei Emet, 1988, Coll. William and Mary, 1988, Tulane U., 1989; Philip S. Bernstein lectr. U. Rochester, 1979, Solomon Goldman lectr. Spertus Coll. Judaica, Chgo., 1982; scholar-in-residence Congregation Ner Tamid, 1991. Author: The Traditions of Rabbi Ishmael, Part One: The Non-Exegetical Materials, 1976, The Traditions of Rabbi Ishmael, Part Three: Exegetical Materials in Tannaitic Collections, 1977, The Traditions of Rabbi Ishmael, Part Three: The Exegetical Materials in Amoraic Collections, 1979, The Traditions of Rabbi Ishmael, Part Four: The Materials as a Whole, 1982, Understanding Rabbinic Midrash: Texts and Commentary, 1985, Goyim: Gentiles and Israelites in Mishnah-Tosefta, 1988; also articles; (with others) The Formation of the Babylonian Talmud, 1970, The Modern Study of the Mishnah, 1973, Christianity, Judaism and Other Greco-Roman Cults: Studies for Morton Smith at Sixty, 1975, Approaches to Ancient Judaism: Theory and Practice, 1978, Aufstieg und Niedergang der römischen Welt, 1979, The Study of Ancient Judaism, 1981, To See Ourselves as Others See Us: Christians, Jews, "Others" in Late Antiquity, 1985, Early Judaism and Its Modern Interpreters, 1986, Midrash as Literature: The Primacy of Documentary Discourse, 1987, New Perspectives on Ancient Judaism Volume One: Religion, Literature, and Society in Ancient Israel Formative Christianity and Judaism, 1987, Sifra: An Analytical Translation, 1988; contbr. to: World Book Encyclopedia, 1988, The Encyclopedia of Religion, 1988; assoc. editor for Jewish history: Dictionary of Biblical Judaism; mem. editorial bd. Shofar. U. Ill. fellow, 1975, 78, NEH fellow, 1977, Ctr. for Advanced Study, U. Ill., 1982, Guggenheim fellow, 1982; grantee Max Richter Found., U. Ill., 1976, 77, 78, Am. Philos. Soc., 1977, Rsch. Bd., U. Ill., 1989. Home: 605 S Prospect Champaign IL 61820 Office: U Ill Program for Study Religion 3014 Fgn Langs Bldg 707 S Mathews Urbana IL 61801

POSADAS OCAMPO, JUAN JESUS CARDINAL, cardinal, archbishop; b. Salvatierra, Mexico, Nov. 10, 1926. Ordained priest Roman Cath. Ch., 1950. Named bishop of Tijuana Mexico, 1970-82, bishop of Cuernavaca, 1982-87, archbishop of Guadalajara, 1987—; named cardinal Roman Cath. Ch., 1991—. Office: Archdiocese Roman Cath Ch, Guadalajara Mexico

POSEY, MARK NICHOLS, minister; b. Feb. 2, 1965; s. Glenn Appleton and Iris Jean (Halcomb) P.; m. Pauli Jean Dixon, Aug. 15, 1987; 1 child, Kayla Ruth. BS in Bible, Freed-Hardeman U., Henderson, Tenn., 1988. Ordained to ministry, Ch. of Christ. Minister Lynn (Ala.) Ch. of Christ, Big Sandy (Tenn.) Ch. of Christ, 1987-88; assoc. minister, youth minister Arab (Ala.) Ch. of Christ, 1988—; dir., coord. Multi-County Youth Bible Bowl, Arab, 1988—. Contbr. religious articles to various religious pubs.; editor Sun. sch. matl./vacation Bible sch. matl. and curriculum. Home: 75 12th Ave NE Arab AL 35016 Office: Arab Ch of Christ PO Box 376 Arab AL 35016

POSEY, WILLIAM MARVIN, minister; b. San Antonio, May 22, 1954; s. Marvin Richard and Mary Louise (Wrba) P.; m. Krystin Lovella Van Riper, Jan. 14, 1978; 1 child, Nathan Glenn. B Gen. Studies, Wichita State U., 1986; MDiv, Asbury Theol. Sem., Wilmore, Ky., 1989. Ordained to ministry United Meth. Ch., 1989. V.p. Wichita (Kans.) Street Ministry, 1983-85; pastor Ebenezer-Hayes United Meth. Ch., Clay Center, Kans., 1989—; dir. Lighthouse for Christ, Clay Center, 1989—; mem. steering com. Festival of Sharing, Beloit, Kans., 1989—. With USN, 1973-74. Mem. Wesleyan Theol. Soc. Home and Office: 627 Prospect St Clay Center KS 67432

POSFAY, GEORGE, minister; b. Budapest, Hungary, June 18, 1921; s. Gyula and Hermine (Toth) P.; m. Emese E. Koppanyi, Apr. 19, 1959; children: Eva S., Clara M. Diploma, Elizabeth U., Hungary, 1943; postgrad. U. Uppsala and Lund, Sweden, 1947-49; MA, Western Res. U., 1959; Licentiale in Theology, Lund U., 1970; ThD, Evang. Luth. Sem., Budapest, 1991. Ordained to ministry Luth. Ch. of Hungary, 1943. Asst. pastor Evang. Ch., Szeged, 1943-44, Budapest, 1944-46, First Hungarian Luth. Ch., Cleve., 1950-52; pastor Resurrection Evang. Luth. Ch., Caracas, Venezula, 1952-71; exec. sec. Dept. Ch. Coop., Luth. World Fedn., Geneva, 1971-86. Editor: Hungarian Program, Trans World Radio, Monte Carlo, Monaco, 1986—; chaplain Scout Orgn., Caracas, 1952-71. Contbr. articles to profl. jours. Nathan Soderblom Found. Curatorium scholar Stockholm, 1964; Luth World Fedn. scholar 1964-65. Mem. Am. Soc. Missiology. Home and Office: 4 Chemin de la Bride, 1224 Chene-Bougeries, Geneva Switzerland

POSSEHL, CARL LOUIS, minister; b. Elkader, Iowa, Feb. 20, 1945; s. Ralph Carl Louis and Lenora Olivia (Olson) P.; m. Andrea Louise Hoover, June 2, 1967; children: Lois Lenora Possehl Keen, Leah Lenora Possehl Wyatt, Sara Sue Possehl Hanson, Jonathan David. BS, Upper Iowa U., 1968; postgrad., Asbury Theol. Sem., Wilmore, Ky., 1974-76; M in Ch. Mgmt., Olivett Nazarene U., Kankakee, Ill., 1991. Ordained to ministry Wesleyan Ch., 1971. Lay missionary Wesleyan World Missions Wesleyan Acad., Guynabo, P.R., 1968-70; pastor Lebanon (Ky.) Wesleyan Ch., 1974-79; asst. pastor Trinity Wesleyan Ch., Elizabethtown, Ky., 1979-81, pastor, 1981-85; sr. pastor Plantation Wesleyan Ch., Summerville, S.C., 1985—; sec. evangelism and ch. growth bd. S.C. dist. Wesleyan Ch., 1990-91. Chaplain Hardin Meml. Hosp., Elizabethtown, 1983-84, Trident Meml. Hosp., North Charleston, S.C., 1987-89. Mem. Wesleyan Theol. Soc. Home: 219 Kennington Dr Goose Creek SC 29445 Office: Plantation Wesleyan Ch 2301 N Main St Summerville SC 29483

POST, AVERY DENISON, church official; b. Norwich, Conn., July 29, 1924; s. John Palmer and Dorothy (Church) P.; m. Margaret Jane Rowland, June 8, 1946; children: Susan Macalister Post Ross, Jennifer Campbell, Elizabeth Post Elliott, Anne Denison Post Proudman. B.A., Ohio Wesleyan U., 1945; B.D., Yale U., 1949, S.T.M., 1952; L.H.D. (hon.), Lakeland Coll., Sheboygan, Wis., 1977; D.D. (hon.), Chgo. Theol. Sem., 1978, Middlebury Coll. (Vt.), 1978, Defiance Coll. (Ohio), 1979; LL.D. (hon.), Heidelberg Coll. (Ohio), 1982, Chapman Coll.; Litt.D. (hon.), Elmhurst Coll. Ordained to ministry, 1949; pastor chs. in Vt., Ohio, Conn. and N.Y., 1946-63; sr. minister Scarsdale (N.Y.) Congl. Ch., 1963-70; minister, pres. Mass. conf. United Ch. Christ, 1970-77; pres. United Ch. Christ, N.Y.C., 1977-89; mem. central com. World Council Chs., 1978—; exec. com., bd. govs. Nat. Council Chs., 1977-89; moderator, planning com. 7th Gen. Assembly World Coun. Chs.; lectr. Bible Adelphi Coll., Garden City, N.Y., 1958-59; Luccock lectr. Yale U. Div. Sch., 1961; lectr. homiletics Union Sem., N.Y.C., 1967-69, bd. dirs., 1967-77; trustee Andover Newton Theol. Sem., 1970-80; del. numerous internat. ch. meetings; sr. fellow Hartford Sem., 1989—. Bd. dirs. Bridges for Peace, 1990—, Bangor Theol. Sem., Hanover, N.H., 1991—; life mem. PTA, Norwich, N.Y. With USNR, 1943-45. Decorated Comdr.'s Cross (Federal Republic Germany), 1990; recipient 1st Ecumenical award Mass. Coun. Chs., 1976; Disting. Achievement award Ohio Wesleyan U., 1983. Fellow Soc. Arts, Religion and Contemporary Culture; mem. Boston Athenaeum, Randolph (N.H.) Mountain Club, Phi Beta Kappa, Omicron Delta Kappa. Democrat. Home: PO Box 344 Meadowbrook Rd Norwich VT 05055

POTARACKE, SISTER ROCHELLE MARY, nun, educator; b. La Crosse, Wis., Mar. 27, 1935; s. John and Theodora Sibylla (Kreibich) P. B.S., Viterbo Coll., 1964; M.A., Cath. U., 1969. Joined Franciscan Sisters of Perpetual Adoration, Roman Cath. Ch., 1952. Tchr. Sacred Heart Sch., Eau Claire, Wis., 1956-68; tchr. Our Lady Fatima, Spokane, Wash., 1958-60; tchr. Cathedral Sch., La Crosse, 1960-76; instr. Viterbo Coll., La Crosse, 1976-81, asst. prof., 1981—, Mem. Nat. Assn. Edn. Young Child, Great Rivers Assn. Edn. Young Child, Wis. Assn. Tchr. Edn., Am. Assn. Colls. for Tchr. Edn.

POTEAT, JAMES DONALD, diaconal minister; b. Spindale, N.C., Feb. 27, 1935; s. Albert Carl and Daliah Elizabeth (Freeman) P.; m. Clara Walker Yelton, Oct. 12, 1957; children: Deborah Poteat Emmons, Clara Poteat Frederick, James Donald Jr., Teresa Poteat Morris. BA, The Citadel, Charleston, S.C., 1957; MA, Kans. State U., 1973. Ordained to ministry United Meth. Ch. Commd. U.S. Army, 1957, advanced through grades to col., ret., 1983; chmn. parish rels. coun. U.S. Army Protestant Chapel, Okinawa, Japan, 1977-79, chmn. fin. com., 1977-79; chmn. parish rels. coun., chmn. fin. com. U.S. Army Protestant Chapel, Ft. McPherson, Ga., 1981-83; pastor's adminstrv. asst. Prospect United Meth. Ch., Covington, Ga., 1988—; youth dir. U.S. Army Protestant Chapel, various location, 1977-81, Sun. sch. supt., Ft. McPherson, 1981-83; Sun. sch. supt. Prospect United Meth. Ch., 1991—. Author: Long Range Planning, Prospect United Methodist Church, 1990, others. Mem. Ret. Officers Assn., Army Aviation Assn. Am., United Meth. Ch. Bus. Adminstrs. Assn. (cert.). Office: Prospect United Meth Ch 6752 Hwy 212 N Covington GA 30209

POTTER, A. WAYNE, worship and music minister; b. San Antonio, Dec. 9, 1953; s. Leslie Richard and Ruby Nell (Horn) P.; m. Cynthia Lynne Howe, Aug. 18, 1974; children: Ladonna, Larissa. B. Min., Luther Rice Bible Coll., 1981; M.M., No. Arizona U., 1983. Mus. dir. Eternity, Inc., Austin, Tex., 1973-79, Fla. Bible Ch., Hollywood, Fla., 1979-81; min. music First So. Baptist Ch., Scottsdale, Ariz., 1983-84; min. music/worship Jacksonville Chapel, Lincoln Park, N.J., 1984-87, First So. Baptist Church, Topeka, Kans., 1988–; sales rep. Century Cos. of America, Topeka, Kans., 1990–; exec. dir. Heartland Christian Artists Assc., Topeka, 1990--. Composer various songs. Mem. Kansans for Life, Topeka, 1989--. Mem. Kansas-Nebraska Singing Men, Life Underwriters Training Coun., Topeka Musicians Union, Intl. Assc. Jazz Educators. Republican. Southern Baptist. Home: 3300 SW 35th Terr Topeka KS 66614 Office: Century Companies of Am 1020 S Kansas Ave Ste 220 Topeka KS 66612

POTTER, JAMES ALBERT, minister; b. Hopkinton, Mass., Mar. 16, 1927; s. Francis Cyrus and Edith Louella (Kimball) P.; m. Joan Evelyn Miller, Aug. 6, 1949; children: Kenneth E., Marcia A., Marilyn J. Tufts Coll., 1945-49, Bangor Theol., 1951-54, Tufts U., 1954-55. Ordained minister United Ch. of Christ, 1963. Pastor Danville (Vt.) Congl. Ch., 1954-59; asst. pastor Community Congl. Ch., Villa Park, Ill., 1959-64; pastor First. Congl. Ch., Bunker Hill, Ill., 1964-67; sr. pastor United Ch. of Hardwick, Vt., 1967-82, Valley Community Ch., Feeding Hills, 1982-89; chaplain Heritage Hall Nursing Home, Agawam, Mass., 1988—; chaplain Noble Hosp., Westfield, Mass., 1991—. Contbg. author: Manual For Ministry, 1986. Founder, first pres. Sr. Citizen Ctr., Hardwick, 1970; pres. Orleans County Coun. Social Agencies, Newport, Vt., 1977-80, N.E. Transit Authority, Newport, 1977-78. Recipient Svc. award Vt. Samaritan, 1982. Mem. Kiwanis Club (pres. 1970-71). Home: 82 S Maple St #33 Westfield MA 01085

POTTER, JAMES VINCENT, educator; b. Walla Walla, Wash., July 17, 1936; s. James Floyd and Dorothy May (Turner) P.; m. Margaret Mae Fogerson, July 4, 1954 (div. Apr. 1970); children: Deborah Ann, David Allan, Rebecca Lynn, Mary Michelle, Jonathon James; m. Paula Maureen Brutsman, Feb. 28, 1986; stepchildren: Carolyn June, Catherine Doreen, Paul Clayton, Connie Lynn. BA in Bibl. Studies, Logos Bible Coll., 1989; MA in Theology, Logos Grad. Sch., 1989; PhD, Vision Christian U., 1990, postgrad., 1991. Lic. pastoral counselor; cert. temperament therapist; cert. substance abuse counselor and program adminstr., marriage and family therapist. Lectr., lit. evang. Seventh-day Adventist Ch., Idaho, 1956-60, Oreg., 1960-61; staff mem. U. of the Nations Family Ministries, Kailua-Kona, Hawaii, 1989; pastor Gospel of Salvation Ministries, 1989—; dean Coll. Christian Counseling, Vision Christian U., Hilo, Hawaii, 1990—; pres. Family Care Svcs. Internat., 1990—; v.p. Vision Christian U., Ramona, Calif., 1991—; adminstr., clinician Hawaii Family Care Ctrs., Hilo, 1989—; vice chmn. Teen Challery of Hawaii, 1991—, govtl. apptd. mem. Hawaii Area Svc. on Mental Health and Substance Abuse, 1991—; pres., Profl. Assn. Christian Therapists, 1989—, Internat. Christian Counselors Assn., 1988—; lectr. western states, 1989—. Author: Soul Care, 1989, Untwisting Twisted Temperaments, 1991; co-author: Family Care Center Manual, 1991, Christian Character Alinement, 1991; (newsletter) Gem-State Surveyor, 1976. Dem. nominee Idaho State Legis., House Rep., Boise, 1976, 78; vice chmn. Idaho Tech. Adv. Coun., Boise, 1976-83; pres. Idaho Assn. Land Surveyors, Boise, 1976-77; chmn. Western Fedn. Profl. Land Surveyors, 12 western states, 1979-80; nat. dir. Am. Congress Surveying Mapping, Washington, 1981-83; state del. Hawaii State Rep. Conv., Turtle Bay, 1988. With USN, 1953. Am. Congress Surveying Mapping fellow, Washington, 1980. Mem. Am. Bd. Christian Psychologists, Am. Assn. Family Counselors, Am. Assn. Christian Counselors, Nat. Christian Counselors Assn (bd. dirs. 1988—), Christian Assn. Psychol. Studies, Nat. Soc. Profl. Land Surveyors (gov.). Office: Vision Christian U PO Box 1690 Keaau HI 96749 *Sin, which separated man from God, is the "distortion" from all that which God intended man to be. Jesus Christ "became sin" (2 Corinthians 5:21), assuming in His flesh the distortion of humanity, that we might in Him have "the right to become children of God." (John 1:12). The Church is called to minister this healing to a sin sick world. (Isiah 61: 1,2).*

POTTER, KENNETH ROY, minister; b. Pittsfield, Mass., Dec. 29, 1919; s. Roy Wilder and Lillian Bertha (Clark) P.; m. Julia Helen Morris, June 12, 1943; children: Susan Elaine Potter Goslin, Terry LaVerne Potter Rowe, Ronald Duane. Student, Anderson (Ind.) U., 1946-48; BTh, Warner Pacific Coll., 1950. Ordained to ministry Ch. of God (Anderson, Ind.), 1956. Min. music Church of God, Couer d'Alene, Idaho, 1950-51; pastor various Chs. of God in Utah, Ill., Oreg., Mont. and Calif., 1951-70, Eastgate Ch. of God, Fresno, Calif., 1970-71, Southlake First Ch. of God, Merrillville, Ind., 1971-78, Ch. of God, Mt. Ayr, Ind., 1979-81, Oakview Community Ch. of God, Scio, Oreg., 1984-86, First Ch. of God, Coquille, Oreg., 1986—; pres. Laton (Calif.) Ministerial Assn., 1958-59; treas. Missoula (Mont.) Evang. Ministerial Alliance, 1961-62; counselor Gary Contact-Help, Gary-Merrillville, 1973-75; pres. Scio Ministerial Assn., 1985-86, Coquille Ministerial Assn., 1990—; former mem. Napa, Calif. Art Assn. Crafted model automobile, Fisher Body Craftsman's Guild competition (2nd prize state award, Va.), 1937. Staff sgt. USAF, 1941-45, PTO. Mem. Coquille Valley Art Assn. Home: 845 E 14th St Coquille OR 97423 Office: First Ch of God 696 N Collier St Coquille OR 97423 *Although I know that things will not always be so, yet I always hope for and expect the best. To seek God's kingdom and His righteousness first is my aim. I fully believe the Bible, and its instructions result overall in the best possible life.*

POTTER, RALPH BENAJAH, JR., theology and social ethics educator; b. Los Angeles, May 19, 1931; s. Ralph Benajah and Vivian Irene MacNabb (Borden) P.; m. Jean Ishbel MacCormick, Aug. 15, 1953; children: Anne Elizabeth, Ralph Andrew, James David, Margaret Jean; m. Christine Iva Mitchell, Aug. 25, 1985; children: Charles Benajah Mitchell Potter, Christopher Ralph Mitchell Potter. B.A., Occidental Coll., 1952; postgrad., Pacific Sch. Religion, 1952-53; B.D., McCormick Theol. Sem., 1955; Th.D. (Presbyn. Grad. fellow 1958-63, Rockefeller fellow 1961-62, Kent fellow 1963-64), Harvard, 1965. Ordained to ministry Presbyn. Ch., 1955; dir., pastor Clay County Presbyn. Larger Parish, Manchester, Ky., 1955-58; sec. social edn. Bd. Christian Edn., United Presbyn. Ch. in U.S.A., Phila., 1963-65; asst. prof. social ethics Harvard Div. Sch.; mem. Center for Population Studies, Harvard U, Cambridge, Mass., 1965-69; prof. social ethics Harvard Divinity Sch., 1969—; mem., prof., Ctr. for Population Studies, Harvard U., 1969-89; theologian-in-residence Am. Ch. in Paris, 1975; sr. rsch. scholar Kennedy Inst. for Bio-ethics Georgetown U., 1974; assoc. Lowell House, Harvard U.; founding fellow Hastings Ctr. Author: War and Moral Discourse, 1969; contbr. chpts. to The Religious Situation, 1968, 1968, Religion and the Public Order, 1968, Toward a Discipline of Social Ethics, 1972, The Population Crisis and Moral Responsibility, 1973, Community in America, 1988, also scholarly articles. Mem. Soc. Christian Ethics, Soc. for Values in Higher Edn., Société Européene de Culture, Am. Acad. Religion, Tocqueville Soc. Office: 45 Francis Ave Cambridge MA 02138

POTTMEYER, HERMANN JOSEF, theology educator; b. Bocholt, Germany, June 1, 1934; s. Ernst and Hermine (Veelken) P. Lic. in philosophy, U. Gregoriana, Rome, 1957, ThD, 1964; Habilitation, U. Münster, Fed. Republic Germany, 1974. Ordained priest Roman Cath. Ch., 1960. Vicar Diocese of Münster, 1964-67; sci. asst. U. Münster, 1967-72, scholar, 1972-74, univ. lectr., 1974; prof. theology U. Bochum, Fed. Republic Germany, 1974—; cons. Synod German Dioceses, 1971-75, German Bishops Conf., 1980—, Cen. Com. German Caths., 1987—; vis. prof. U. Gregoriana, Rome, 1989, U. Notre Dame, Ind., 1991. Author: Der Glaube von dem Anspruch der Wissenschaft, 1968, Unfehlbarkeit und Souveränität, 1975; editor: Kirche im Wandel, 1982, Handbuch der Fundamentaltheologie, 4 vols., 1985-88, Die Rezeption des 2 Vatikanischen Konzils, 1986, Die Bischofskonferenz, 1989, Kirche im Kontext der modernen Gesellschaft, 1989. Office: U Bochum, Universitätsstrasse 150, D-4630 Bochum Federal Republic of Germany

POTTORFF-ALBRECHT, PHYLLIS DEMETER, minister; b. Mullen, Nebr., Mar. 21, 1942; d. William Thomas and Winnie Lily (Cook) Pottorff; children: Charles William, David Andrew. Student, Cen. Bus. Coll., 1960, Nat. Guild Hypnotists, 1991, Real Estate Tng. Ctr., 1991, Am. Soc. Appraisers, 1991. Ordained to ministry Universalist Life-Unity Assn., 1960; cert. clin. hypnotherapist. Minister First Women's Ch. Colo., Broomfield, 1979—; resident mgr. Safehouse, Colo., 1990—. Chairperson Dem. party, 1979-82. Mem. Friends of Metaphysics (pres. 1985-91), Colo. Holistic Health Help for Helpers. Home and Office: Help for Helpers/The Farmer's Daughter-Wagon Wheel Realty 10623 Van Gordon Way # 73601 Broomfield CO 80021

POTTS, DONALD RALPH, religion educator, minister; b. St. Louis, June 10, 1930; s. Benjamin Sedwick and Ethel Dorothy (Dietz) P.; m. Jeanne Daugherty, June 10, 1951; children: Cynthia Diane Chamberlin, Donald Mark. AA, S.W. Bapt. Coll., 1950; BA in Psychology, Okla. Bapt. U., 1952; BD, Southwestern Bapt. Theol. Sem., 1955, ThD in Homiletics, 1959, M.Div., 1973. Instr. Southwestern Bapt. Theol. Sem., Fort Worth, 1959-60; pastor Cen. Bapt. Ch., Lawton, Okla., 1960-64; prof. religion Cameron Coll., Lawton, 1960-64; pastor First Bapt. Ch., Groves, Tex., 1964-76; prof., chmn. dept. religion East Tex. Bapt. U., Marshall, 1976—. Contbr. to Holman Bible Dictionary, 1991; contbr. articles to ch. publs. Pres. Lawton-Fort Sill Ministerial Alliance, 1963, Groves Ministerial Alliance, 1968. Oxford U. grantee, 1980. Mem. Am. Acad. Religion, Assn. Bapt. Tchrs. Religion, Bibl. Archeol. Soc., Nat. Geog. Soc., Smithsonian Inst. Lodge: Rotary (dir. 1984-85, pres. 1986-87, Paul Harris fellow 1987). Avocations: reading, travel, hunting, numismatics, fishing. Home: 702 Ambassador Marshall TX 75670 Office: East Tex Baptist U Dept Religion 1209 N Grove Marshall TX 75670

POUNDERS, GREGORY K., superintendent; b. Salina, Kans., Oct. 12, 1960; s. Jerry Dean and Valerie Darlene (Bonds) P.; m. Mary Katherine, June 20, 1981; children: Jonathan, Holly. ABS, Trinity Coll., 1984; BS, Commonwealth Bapt. Coll., 1986. Cert. in early childhood teaching strategies. Supt. Valley Christian Sch., Mission, Tex.; educator Gethsemane Bapt. Sch., Evansville, Ind. Contbr. articles to profl. jours. Mem. Internat. Fellowship Christian Sch. Adminstrs. (cert.), Am. Assn. Christian Sch. Adminstrs. (cert.).

POUNDS, ELTON WILLIAM, pastoral care administrator; b. Smith Ctr., Kans., June 27, 1935; s. Elton Lee and Thelma (Wookey) P.; children from previous marriages: Jan, Mark, Kimberly, Andrew, christopher, Kyra, Chandra. AB, Hastings Coll., 1957; MDiv, Seabury-Western Theol. Sem., 1960. Rector Grace Ch., Columbus, Nebr., 1965-69, Holy Trinity Parish, Gillette, Wyo., 1969-72; dir. Trinity Ranch Diocese of Colo., Wetmore, 1972-77; curate Grace Ch., Colorado Springs, Colo., 1977-85; dir. pastoral care AMI-St. Luke's Hosp., Denver, 1985—; dir. pastoral care and edn. P/SL Health Care System, Denver, 1985—; chmn. bd. examining Chaplains, Diocese of Colo., 1968—. Editor: Large Print Book of Common Prayer, 1982. Judge Campbell County, Wyo., 1970-72; pres. Chaplaincy Corps Colorado Springs Police Dept., 1980-81; mem. Civil Rights Commn., 1965-67; del. Gov.'s Conf. on Aging, Colo., 1980. Fellow Seabury, 1971, 78, Citizens' Goals, 1981. Mem. AAAS, Am. Assn. Clin. Pastoral Edn., Gerontol. Soc. Am., Western Gerontol. Soc. Am. (presenter model program on aging 1981), Amnesty Internat., Episcopal Soc. Ministry on Aging (bd. dirs. 1980-82), N.Y. Acad. Scis. Republican. Episcopalian. Avocations: tennis, skiing. Home: 2657 S University E Denver CO 80210 Office: St Lukes Hosp 601 E 19th Ave Denver CO 80203

POUPARD, PAUL CARDINAL, archbishop; b. Aug. 30, 1930. ordained Roman Cath. Ch., 1954. Titular bishop Usula, 1979, archbishop, 1980, proclaimed cardinal, 1985; deacon San Eugenio; pres. Pontifical Coun. for Dialogue with Non-Believers, 1985; pres. Pontifical Coun. for Culture, 1988. Address: Piazza San Calisto 16, 00153 Rome Italy

POVISH, KENNETH JOSEPH, bishop; b. Alpena, Mich., Apr. 19, 1924; s. Joseph Francis and Elizabeth (Jachcik) P. A.B., Sacred Heart Sem., Detroit, 1946; M.A., Cath. U. Am., 1950; postgrad., No. Mich. U., 1961, 63. Ordained priest Roman Catholic Ch., 1950; asst. pastorships, 1950-56; pastor in Port Sanilac Mich., 1956-57, Munger, Mich., 1957-60, Bay City, Mich., 1966-70; dean St. Paul Sem., Saginaw, Mich., 1960-66; vice rector St. Paul Sem., 1962-66; bishop of Crookston Minn., 1970-75; bishop of Lansing Mich., 1975—; bd. consulators Diocese of Saginaw, 1966-70; instr. Latin and U.S. history St. Paul Sem., 1960-66. Weekly columnist Saginaw and Lansing diocesan newspapers. Bd. dirs. Cath. Charities Diocese Saginaw, 1969-70. Mem. Mich., Bay County hist. socs. Lodges: Lions, KC (pres. Mich. Cath. Conf. 1985—). Office: Chancery Office 300 W Ottawa Lansing MI 48933

POWELL, CHARLES WILLIAM, minister; b. Gilman, Colo., May 9, 1937; s. Harold Hayes and Rosella Charlotte (Collins) B. BS Colo. State U., 1970; postgrad., Western Conservative Bapt. Sem., 1982. Ordained to ministry Evang. Ch. Alliance, 1976; cert. sec. tchr., Wash. Team leader The Navigators, Colorado Springs, 1966-72; sr. pastor Albion (Wash.) Community Ch., 1972-76; hon. v.p. Am. Missionary Fellowship Portland, Oreg., 1979-81; itinerant preacher Oreg., 1976—; field rep. Internat. Messengers, 1989-91. Contbr. articles to religious jours. Res. policeman Whitman County Sheriff's Office, Colfax, Wash., 1975-76. With USN, 1956-62. Mem. Am. Legion, U.S. Naval Inst., Mensa. Avocations: reading, computer science, amateur magic, square dancing. Home and Office: 2220 SE Taylor St Portland OR 97214 *Nothing is all of anything. We never have all the story, sometimes just enough to bother us, to tangle our mind and leave us chewing on it.*

POWELL, DAVID WAYNE, minister; b. Paducah, Ky., May 9, 1957; s. Joe Wayne and Delores (Wicker) P.; m. Cathy Ann Dublin, Aug. 18, 1979; 1 child, Katie Louise. BA, Freed-Hardeman U., 1981; ThM, Harding Grad. Sch. Religion, Memphis, 1986. Min. youth and assoc. Henderson (Tenn.) Ch. of Christ, 1981-86; pulpit min. Ramer (Tenn.) Ch. of Christ, 1986-88, 1988—; assoc. min. North Jackson Ch. of Christ, 1989—. Author: Gospel Advocate Mag., 1984, 87, Spiritual Sword Mag., 1985, Lectureship Book, 1985, 90; author, broadcaster Words from the Heart, 1986-88. Mem. Jackson Christian Sch. PTF (treas. 1989-90), Freed-Hardeman U. Alumni Assn. (pres. 1986-88), Alpha Psi Omega. Avocations: fishing, sports, reading, painting. Home: 36 Parchman Dr Jackson TN 38305 Office: Jackson Christian Sch 832 Country Club Ln Jackson TN 38305

POWELL, DENNIS DUANE, church planter; b. Evansville, Ind., Mar. 21, 1961; s. Gilbert and Anna Rose (Kirby) P.; m. Pamela Joyce Noel, May 10, 1986; children: Austin Duane, Amy Rose. BA, Oakland City Coll., 1983, MAR, 1985, MDiv, 1986. Ordained to ministry Gen. Bapt. Ch., 1980. Field coord. Youth Evangelism Svc., Bradenton, Fla., 1980-83; assoc. pastor Mt. Vernon (Ind.) Gen. Bapt. Ch., 1980-83; sr. pastor Sharon Gen. Bapt. Ch., Newburgh, Ind., 1983-86; ch. planter Cen. Southern Ill. Mission, O'Fallon, 1986—; adj. instr., Oakland City (Ind.) Coll., 1985-86; bd. dirs., Gen. Bapt. Home Missions, Poplar Bluff, Mo., 1984-86; asst. moderator, United Assn. Gen. Bapts., Boonville, Ind., 1985; mem. GROW team, Gen. Bapt. Evangelism Coun., Poplar Bluff, 1988-89; pres., Marion Meml. Hosp., Chaplains Corp., Ill., 1988-89. Chaperone Graduation Spree, Marion, 1988-89; mem. Nat. Right to Life. Mem. O'Fallon Clergy Coun., Bibl. Archaeology Soc. Home: 201 Ruth Dr O'Fallon IL 62269 Office: Cen Southern Ill Missions PO Box 448 O'Fallon IL 62269

POWELL, EARL DEAN, clergyman; b. San Antonio, Feb. 20, 1959; s. Charles Edward and Ellen Ethel (Stewart) P.; m. Denise Lee Edgar, July 25, 1981; children: Ryan Christopher, Reid Michael. BBA, Hardin-Simmons U., 1981; MDiv, Southwestern Bapt. Theol. Sem., 1988, postgrad., 1988—. CPA, Tex. Auditor Condley and Co., CPA's, Abilene, Tex., 1980-82; v.p. fin. B.S.J.V., Inc., Abilene, 1982-84; corp. acctg. mgr. Pengo Industries, Inc., Ft. Worth, 1984-86; div. controller Pengo Industries, Inc., Joshua, Tex., 1986-88; co-founder Megalomania Investment Group, Abilene, 1983-84; mem. Acctg. Issues Symposium, Abilene, 1981. Editor newsletter Singleminded, 1986-87. Vice-moderator Salt Fork Bapt. Assn., 1989-90; mem. exec. bd. Bi-Fork Bapt. Area, 1989—, Newcastle Ministerial Alliance, 1988—; area fund raiser chmn. St. Jude's Children's Hosp.; youth worker Hendrick Home for children, Abilene, 1983; incorporator Illusions and Reality Inc., Crowley, Tex., 1986; minister single adults 1st Bapt. Ch., Everman, Tex., 1986-88. Named one of Outstanding Youth Worker, Hendrick Home for Children, 1984, one of Outstanding Young Men Am., 1987. Mem. AICPA's, Tex. Soc. CPA's. Avocation: translating koine Greek New Testament. Office: First Baptist Church Box 100 Newcastle TX 76372

POWELL, FRED EARL, III, pastor; b. Newark, Apr. 30, 1930; s. Frederick Earl Jr. and Helen May (Willis) P.; m. Donna Joyce MacArthur, Dec. 10, 1949; children: David, Linda Battagler, Jeffrey, Judy Battagler, Daniel, Todd, Beth. BA, Faith Bapt. Coll., BTh, 1978, ThM, 1980, D of Ministry, 1982. Ordained to ministry So. Bapt. Conf., 1970. Pastor First Bapt. Ch., Camden, Mo., 1969-74, Pisgah Bapt. Ch., Excelsior Springs, Mo., 1974-84; sr. assoc. pastor First Bapt. Ch., Atlanta, 1984-90, Moore, Okla., 1990—. Author: Deacon - Baptist Tradition or Biblical Truth, 1991, Things You Didn't Learn in Seminary-But Wish You Had, 1990. Mem. So. Bapt. Conv. (editor-in-chief Communicator Mag., 1990—, pastor's conf. sec. treas. 1983-84, nominating com. del. 1983, calendar com. chmn. 1984-86), Communicator Ministries Inc. (pres. 1990—). Home: 21 SW 103 St Oklahoma City OK 73139 Office: First Bapt Ch 201 S Howard Ave Moore OK 73160

POWELL, H(AROLD) GRANT, minister, educator; b. Tampa, Fla., Sept. 18, 1957; s. Harold Grant and Joan Lamar (Lundgren) P.; m. Jennifer Suzanne Thomas, June 22, 1985; 1 child, Joshua Grant. B Christian Edn., Anderson (Ind.) U., 1980; MDiv, Anderson Sch. Theology, 1985. Ordained to ministry Ch. of God (Anderson, Ind.), 1986. Min. youth and Christian edn. Kokomo (Ind.) 1st Ch. of God, 1980-82; min. youth and music Palm Beach Gardens (Fla.) Ch. of God, 1983-84; min. Christian edn. Vero Beach (Fla.) 1st Ch. of God, 1985—; adj. prof. Warner-So. Coll., Lake Wales, Fla., 1990—; condr. Tchrs.-Are-Great workshops Nat. Bd. Christian Edn., Anderson, 1989—. Contbr. article to religious jour. Office: 1st Ch of God 1590 27th Ave Vero Beach FL 32960 *On his death bed, my father spoke the words by which I model my life: "Stay on your knees, be humble, be a man of love, and let God take care of His church."*

POWELL, JAMES DIXIE, minister; b. Moultrie, Ga., Nov. 14, 1938; s. Leslie W. Sr. and Nannie L. (Barker) P.; m. Mary Louise Hearn, Sept. 14, 1963; 1 child, Richard David. BA, U. South Fla., 1976; MBA, Fla. Inst. Tech., Melbourne, 1983; MDiv, New Orleans Bapt. Sem., 1985. Ordained to ministry Bapt. Ch., 1984. License examiner Fla. Highway Patrol, Orlando, 1961-64; fleet service rep. Fla. Power Corp., St. Petersburg, 1965-67, acct., 1967-79, systems analyst, 1979-83; dean edn. night div. Cameron Coll., New Orleans, 1985; min. edn. 1st Bapt. Ch., Bradenton, Fla., 1986-90, East Brent Bapt. Ch., Pensacola, Fla., 1990—; Stewardship chmn. Manatee chpt. So. Bapt. Assn., Bradenton, 1986-89. Chmn. St. Petersburg Citizens' Budget Rev. Com., 1977-80; bd. dirs. Selective Service St. Petersburg, 1982-83. Mem. U.S. Jaycees. Republican. Avocations: reading, swimming, gardening. Home: 8186 Squire Rd Pensacola FL 32514 Office: East Brent Bapt Ch 4801 N Davis Hwy Pensacola FL 32503

POWELL, JAMES RICHARD, religious organization administrator; b. Jacksonville, Fla., May 27, 1944; s. Ernest A. and Thelma B. (Carrico) P.; m. Peggy A. Baker, June 26, 1965; children: Pamela, Stephen, Nathan, Jennifer. Diploma in Christian Edn., Moody Bible Inst., Chgo., 1968; BA in Bus., Elmhurst Coll., 1969. Publishing exec. Youth For Christ USA, Wheaton, Ill., 1966-74; mktg. rep. Thomas Nelson Bible Pub., Nashville, 1974-78; pres. Christian Bible Soc., Nashville, 1978-82; v.p. Internat. Bible Soc., East Brunswick, N.J., 1982-83; pres. Internat. Bible Soc., Colorado Springs, 1983—. Mem. Christian Mgmt. Assn., Evangel. Christian Pubs. Assn., Internat. Conf. Evangel. Bible Socs. Office: Internat Bible Society 1820 Jet Stream Drive Colorado Springs CO 80921

POWELL, JOHN PAUL, minister; b. Eugene, Oreg., Feb. 9, 1950; s. Robert Vincent and Marilyn Powell Lorenz (Mowe) P.; m. Pamela Baker, Aug. 20, 1977; children: Stewart Baker Jefferson, Elliott Hamilton Jefferson, Jennifer Rebecca. BA, N.W. Christian Coll., 1972; MDiv, Fuller Theol. Sem., 1977, DMin, 1982. Ordained to ministry Presbyn. Ch. Youth minister Christian Ch., Dallas, Oreg., 1969-70; intern Peachtree Christian Ch., Atlanta, 1971; student pastor Christian Ch., Elkton, Oreg., 1971-72; asst. min. Park Ave. Christian Ch., Des Moines, 1972-74; assoc. minister South Pasadena (Calif.) Christian Ch., 1974-75, Glendale (Calif.) Presbyn. Ch., 1977-83; co-pastor First Presbyn. Ch., Sherman Oaks, Calif., 1983-88; sr. pastor Westminster Presbyn. Ch., Lubbock, Tex., 1988—; soloist/world tour Continental Singers, Thousand Oaks, Calif., 1970; soloist/waylighters Northwest Christian Coll., Eugene, Oreg., 1970-71; soloist/opera/recording Crystal Cathedral, Garden Grove, Calif., 1976-77; faculty Campell Hall Episcopal Sch., North Hollywood, 1985-88. Author: (journal) Leadership, 1990; lectr. Western Spirituality, 1982-88. Bd. dirs. Mo Ranch, Kerrville, Tex., 1990, Presbyn. Ctr. Doctor's Clinic, East Lubbock, 1990; exec. dir. PACE Presbyn. Across Calif. Event, San Diego, 1988; chair Bicentennial Fund Synod of the Sun, S.W. Tex., 1989. Named Outstanding Young Men of Am. Jaycees, 1972; Oreg. Scholar Pub. Secondary Edn., 1968. Mem. Presbyn. For Renewal (network moderator 1985-90), Nat. Covenant Group, Palo Duro Presbytery, Synod of the Sun (commr. 1989-90), Rotary. Presbyterian. Avocations: music/voice, guitar, violin, golf, watercolors. Home: 9317 Salisbury Ave Lubbock TX 79424 *The healing of persons begins with that touch of grace, when the Face of the Universe is known to be Love, the hands of spouse and friends to be Trust, and the Destiny of Nations tied to Blessed Hope.*

POWELL, PETER JOHN, priest, scholar; b. Bryn Mawr, Pa., July 2, 1928; s. William and Helena (Teague) P.; m. Virginia Lee Raisch, June 13, 1953; children: Katherine, Christine, John, Stephen. BA, Ripon Coll., 1950, LittD, 1982; MDiv, Nashotah House Sem., 1953, DD, 1971; LLD, Muskingum (Ohio) Coll., 1982; DD, Seabury-Western Theol. Sem., 1984. Ordained to ministry priest Episcopal Ch. as priest, 1953. Priest in charge Holy Cross-Immanuel Ch., Chgo., 1953-54, St. Timothy's Ch., Chgo., 1953-61; founder, dir. St. Augustine's Ctr. for Am. Indians, Chgo., 1962-71; scholar in residence Newberry Libr., Chgo., 1972—, rsch. assoc., 1975—; sr. postdoctoral fellow Smithsonian Instn., Washington, 1988-89; bd. dirs. D'Arcy McNickle Ctr. for History Am. Indian, Newberry Libr., Chgo., rsch. assoc.; pres. Found. Preservation Am. Indian Art and Culture, Chgo.; mem. adv. bd. Mitchell Indian Mus. Kendall Coll., Evanston, Ill. Author: Sweet Medicine: The Continuing Role of the Sacred Arrows, the Sun Dance and the Sacred Buffalo Hat in Northern Cheyenne History, 1969, People of the Sacred Mountain: A History of the Northern Cheyenne Chiefs and Warrior Societies, 1830-79: With an Epilogue 1969-74, 1981, The Cheyennes, Ma'heo'o's People: A Critical Bibliography, 1980; mem. editorial adv. bd. Am. Indian Art mag., Scottsdale, Ariz.; contbr. articles to profl. jours. Recipient Ann. award Chgo. Commn. Human Rels., 1961; knighted by King Peter of Yugoslavia, 1968; fellow Nat. Endowment for Humanities, John Simon Guggenheim Meml. Found., Bollingen Found. Mem. Phi Beta Kappa. Home: care St Augustine's Center 4512 N Sheridan Rd Chicago IL 60640 Office: Newberry Libr 60 W Walton St Chicago IL 60610

POWELL, SISTER RITA, nun, religious order superior; b. Phila., Nov. 30, 1922; d. Arthur C. and Mary C. (Sullivan) P. BA, Villanova U., 1951; MA, Cath. U. Am., 1954. Joined Sisters of Mercy, Roman Cath. Ch.; cert secondary sch. tchr., Pa. Tchr. various schs. Pa., 1943-48; tchr. Acad. Sisters of Mercy, Gwynedd Valley, Pa., 1948-49, 50-55, 56-70, Mater Misericordiae Acad., Merion, Pa., 1949-50, 55-59; tchr. Gwynedd-Mercy Coll., Gwynedd Valley, 1951-54, 56-62, also chmn. bd. dirs.; prin. Gwynedd-Mercy Acad., Gwynedd Valley, 1962-70; mem. gen. coun. Sisters of Mercy Coun., Merion, 1970-85, superior gen., 1985—; chmn. Mercy Health Corp., Bala Cynwyd, Pa., 1985; pres. Sisters of Mercy Corp., Merion, 1985. Chmn. bd. dirs. Walsingham Acad., Williamsburg, Va., 1985. Mem. Leadership Conf. Women Religious (region III).

POWELL, ROBERT EVERETT, minister; b. Montgomery, Ala., Feb. 6, 1934; s. Robert Powell and Gracie Lee (Auls) P.; m. Eugenia Sarah Powell, Sept. 23, 1967; children: Michael, David, Kevin. BS in Elem. Edn., Montgomery Coll., Ala., 1960; MA in Edn., William Paterson Coll., 1975; EdD, NYU, 1975-77; MDiv, New Brunswick (N.J.) Theol.Sem, 1981; doctorate adminstrn. and supervision, NYU. Ordained to ministry, Bapt. Ch., 1979, Presbyn. Ch., 1982. Tchr. Paterson (N.J.) Bd. Edn., 1967-79, vice prin., 1980-88; pastor Ascension Presbyn. Ch., 1980-83, St. Augustine Presbyn. Ch., Paterson, 1984—, Beth Salem Presbyn. Ch., Columbus, Ga., 1989—. Named Alpha Man of the Yr. for community svc., 1977. Mem. N.J. Adminstrs. Assn., N.J. Edn. Assn., Alpha Phi Alpha. LDemocrat. Presbyterian. Address: 3964 Scarlet Oak Ct Doraville GA 30340

POWELL, STEVEN LOYD, minister; b. Dixon, Ill., Feb. 27, 1954; s. Elmer Loyd and Eleanor Mae (Ritchey) P.; m. Kathryn Ann Benda, Nov. 25, 1975; children: Julie Ann, Phillip Loyd, Stephanie Michelle. Student, Cen. Bible Coll., 1972-75. Ordained to ministry Assemblies of God, 1980. Co-pastor Peace Chapel Assembly of God, Morris, Ill., 1975-77; pastor Mt. Vernon (Ill.) First Assembly of God, 1977-80; sr. pastor First Assembly of God, Hammond, Ind., 1980-89, Bethel Temple Assembly of God, Tampa, Fla., 1989—; youth rep. southeastern sect. Ill. Dist. Assemblies of God, Carlinville, Ill., 1978-80; adviser Joy Fellowship, Northwest Ind. Dist., 1980-82; presbyter Ind. dist. Assemblies of God, Indpls., 1982-89; founder, exec. producer, host "Come Alive" program First Assembly of God, Hammond, Ind., 1983-85. Local adviser Women's Aglow, Morris, Ill., 1975-77, Homewood, Ill., 1982-87; area bd. adviser Women's Aglow Chgo., 1988-89; area exec. chmn. World Wide Pictures, Mt. Vernon, Ill., 1978-79; bd. regents North Cen. Bible Coll., Mpls., 1986-89; nat. bd. govs. Am. Coalition for Traditional Values, 1984-88; bd. dirs. Lake County Econ. Opportunity Coun., Hammond, 1985-88, mayor's rep., 1988-89; founder, exec. dir. soup kitchen Caring Hands, Hammond, 1986-89; task force mem. Project Self-Sufficiency, Hammond, 1987-89; com. mem. Hammond Long-Range Planning Commn., Hammond, 1988-89. Named for Svc. with Distinction, Revivaltime Choir, 1972-74, one of Outstanding Young Men of Am., U.S. Jaycees, 1979; recipient Disting. Svc. Award Hammond Jaycees, 1988, Good Samaritan award 1st Assembly of God Caring Hands, 1989, Key to City of Hammond, Mayor of Hammond, 1989. Office: Bethel Temple Assembly of God 1510 W Hillsborough Ave Tampa FL 33603 *In the quest for God's excellency in our lives, we must be acutely aware of the necessity of our genuine willingness to give up what we are now in order to become all that God would desire.*

POWELL, WILLIAM ROGER, minister; b. Cambridge, Ohio, June 7, 1953; s. Marquis Clifford and Linnie Pearl (Smith) P.; m. Teresa Kay Hursey, June 7, 1975; children: Clinton Matthew, Magdalene Marie. BA (summa cum laude), Roberts Wesleyan Coll., 1983; MDiv, Asbury Theol. Sem., 1987. Ordained to ministry Free Meth. Ch. as deacon, 1986, as elder, 1988. Minister Kent (Ohio) Free Meth. Ch., 1987-90, First Free Meth. Ch., Gloversville, N.Y., 1990—; pres. Ministerial Assn. Roberts Wesleyan Coll.,

Rochester, 1982-83; sec. Kent Ministerial Assn., 1988-90. Chaplain Mountain Valley Hospice, 1991—. Mem. Fulton County Clergy Assn. (sec. 1991—), Kappa Alpha Chi. Home: 1200 County Hwy 122 Gloversville NY 12078 Office: 1st Free Meth Ch 205 Kingsboro Ave Gloversville NY 12078

POWER, CORNELIUS MICHAEL, archbishop; b. Seattle, Dec. 18, 1913; s. William and Kate (Dougherty) P. Student, St. Patrick Sem., 1933-35, St. Edward Sem., 1935-39; J.C.D., Cath. U. Am., 1943. Ordained priest Roman Catholic Ch., 1939; asst. pastor St. James Cathedral, Seattle, 1939-40; resident chaplain Holy Names Acad., Seattle, 1943-52; adminstr. Parish of Our Lady of Lake, Seattle, 1955-56; pastor Parish of Our Lady of Lake, 1956-69; vice chancellor Archdiocese of Seattle, 1943-51, chancellor, 1951-69; apptd. domestic prelate, 1963, 2d bishop of Yakima, 1969, bishop of Yakima, 1969-74; archbishop Portland, Oreg., 1974-86; ret., 1986. Address: Archdiocese of Portland 2838 E Burnside Portland OR 97214

POWER, JACK, JR., clergyman; b. Littlefield, Tex., Apr. 26, 1945; s. Larkin Jackson and Eva L. (Cole) P.; m. Jo Beth Pettus, Aug. 14, 1965; children: Jack, III, Jacquelyn. Student, Howard County Jr. Coll., 1963-64, Arlington Bapt. Coll. and Sem., 1965-66. Ordained to ministry Bapt. Ch., 1966; dept. mgr. J.C. Penney Co., Big Springs, Tex., 1961-64, Fort Worth, 1965-66; assoc. pastor Rolling Hills Bapt. Ch., Fort Worth, 1966-67, First Bapt. Ch., Englewood, Colo., 1967-69; pastor Houston Bapt. Temple, Houston, 1969—. Rotarian (sec.). Home: 2603 Wood River Dr Spring TX 77373 Office: 15620 Sellers Rd Houston TX 77060 also: PO Box 60967 Houston TX 77205

POWER, SISTER MARY CLAUDE, school system administrator. Supt. schs. Diocese of Santa Jose, Calif. Office: Edn Dept Diocese San Jose 841 Lenzen Ave San Jose CA 95126*

POWER, WILLIAM EDWARD, bishop; b. Montreal, Que., Can., Sept. 27, 1915; s. Nicholas Walter and Bridget Elizabeth (Callaghan) P. B.A., Montreal Coll., 1937; student, Grand Sem., Montreal.; LLD (hon.), St. Francis Xavier U., 1989. Ordained priest Roman Catholic Ch., 1941; parish asst. Montreal, 1941-47; vice-chancellor Diocese Montreal, 1947-50; diocesan chaplain Young Christian Workers and Christian Family Movement, 1950-53; nat. chaplain Young Christian Workers, 1953-59; chaplain, mgr. Cath. Men's Hostel, Montreal, 1957-59; pastor St. Barbara's Ch., Lasalle, Que., 1959-60; bishop of Antigonish N.S., 1960-87; bishop emeritus Diocese of Antigonish, N.S., 1987—; chancellor St. Francis Xavier U., 1960-87; pres. Can. Conf. Cath. Bishops, 1971-73. Address: St Francis Xavier, UPO 155, Box 1330, Antigonish, NS Canada B2G 1C0

POWER, WILLIAM LARKIN, religion educator; b. Biloxi, Miss., Aug. 2, 1934; s. Ellis Candler and Lauraine (Barbour) P.; m. Margaret Joan Holloway, Dec. 23, 1957 (dec. 1969); children: William Keith, Richard Kevin; m. Mildred Amburn Huskins, Dec. 30, 1970. BA, U. Miss., 1956; BD, Emory U., 1959, PhD, 1965. Ordained to ministry United Meth. Ch., 1959. Assoc. dir. United Christian Fellowship, Bowling Green, Ohio, 1959--62; asst. prof. philosophy Lambuth Coll., Jackson, Tenn., 1965-67; mem. faculty U. Ga., Athens, 1967—, assoc. prof., 1976—; lectr. numerous profl. groups; bd. dirs. Felton Williams Mission, Atlanta, 1968—. Bd. dirs. Friends of Ga. Mus. Art, 1980—, v.p., 1982-83, pres., 1983-84; bd. dirs. Hope Haven Sch., 1981—, sec., 1982-83; bd. dirs. United Fund Athens, 1974-80, Athens YMCA, 1974—; cons. Com. Humanities Ga., 1975—; mem. scholarship bd. Army ROTC, U. Ga., 1976—; trustee Athens Acad., 1982—. Named Outstanding Honors Prof., U. Ga., 1976, 83, 84. Mem. Am. Acad. Religion (editorial bd. 1980—), Soc. Philosophy of Religion (editorial bd. 1990), Athens Country Club. Democrat. Home: 525 W Cloverhurst Ave Athens GA 30606 Office: U Ga Dept Religion Athens GA 30602 *For those who desire to live, live well, and live better, there is still no substitute for knowledge and wisdom.*

POWERS, BRUCE POSTELL, educator, clergyman; b. Savannah, Ga., May 25, 1940; s. Bruce and Lila (Goynes) P.; m. Barbara Jean Clark, July 3, 1965; children: Bruce, Jason. AB, Mercer U., 1964; MRE, So. Bapt. Theol. Sem., 1967, EdD, 1971. Ordained to ministry So. Bapt. Conv., 1978. Staff minister Tattnall Sq. Bapt. Ch., Macon, Ga., 1959-65, Melbourne Heights Ch., Louisville, 1965-70; cons. Sunday Sch. Bd., Nashville, 1971-77; prof. Christian edn. Southeastern Bapt. Theol. Sem., Wake Forest, N.C., 1978—. Author: Christian Leadership, 1979, Growing Faith, 1982, How to Handle Conflict in the Church, 1991; editor: Christian Education Handbook, 1981, Adventures in Christian Service, 1983, Church Administration Handbook, 1985. Recipient Citation for Faculty Excellence, Southeastrn Bapt. Theol. Sem., 1989. Mem. World Future Soc., Ea. Bapt. Religious Edn. Assn., So. Bapt. Religious Edn. Assn. (pres. bd. dirs. 1984—), N.C. Religious Edn. Assn. (bd. dirs. 1982-85), Religious Edn. Assn. Office: Southeastern Sem Box 1889 Wake Forest NC 27588

POWERS, EDWARD ALTON, minister, educator; b. Jamestown, N.Y., Oct. 26, 1927; s. Leslie Edgar and Mabelle Florence (Alton) P.; children: Randall Edward, Christopher Alan, Ann Lynn. BA, Coll. of Wooster, 1948; MDiv, Yale U., 1952; EdD, Columbia U., 1973. Ordained to ministry Congregational Ch., 1951; pastor Hamden, Conn., 1949-53, Pleasant Hill, Ohio, 1953-56; sec. dept. youth work Congl. Christian Ch. Bd. Home Missions, 1956-60; gen. sec. div. Christian edn., bd. home missions Congl. and Christian Chs., 1960-61; div. Christian edn., bd. homeland ministries United Ch. of Christ, 1962-73; gen. sec., div. evangelism, edn., ch. extension United Ch. Bd. Homeland Ministries, 1973-79; mem. faculty Inst. Mgmt. Competency, Am. Mgmt. Assn., N.Y.C., 1980-87; sr. lectr. Grad. Sch. Mgmt. New Sch. for Social Research, 1981—; mem. program bd. div. edn. and ministry Nat. Council Chs., 1963-80; mem. edn. working group World Council Chs.; chmn. Peace Priority Team, United Ch. of Christ, 1970-75, adminstr., editor sexuality study, 1977; ptnr. Cane Powers Cons., and Powers, Wayno & Assocs. Author: Journey Into Faith, 1964, Signs of Shalom, 1973, (with Rey O'Day) Theatre of the Spirit, 1980, In Essentials Unity, 1982, Youth in the Global Village, 1982; also articles. Home: 215 E 24th St Apt 712 New York NY 10010 Office: Graybar Bldg 420 Lexington Ave Ste 300 New York NY 10170

POWERS, JAMES B., religious organization administrator. Pres. Am. Bapt. Assn., Greenwood, Miss. Office: The Am Bapt Assn 607 N Aubrey Cir Grenwood MS 38390*

POWERS, PATRICK J., ecumenical agency administrator. Exec. dir. Christian Svc. Ctr. for Cen. Fla., Inc., Orlando. Office: Christian Svc Ctr Cen Fla Inc 808 W Central Blvd Orlando FL 32805*

POWNALL, MELVIN JORDAN, evangelist; b. Coatesville, Pa., Jan. 6, 1923; s. Jacob Elsworth and Alta May (Jordan) P.; m. Emily Jane Rutledge, Aug. 7, 1946; children: William Timothy, Thomas Clayton (dec.), Gary Lee. BA, Pepperdine U., 1949, MA, 1959; MA, Fuller Theol. Sem., 1980. Missionary Chs. of Christ, Italy, 1950-55, 59-65, 73-78, 80-84; local evangelist Hollywood, Calif., 1957-59, Berkley, Calif., 1957-59, Santa Rosa, Calif., 1965-70, L.A., 1970-73; local evangelist Conejo Valley Ch. of Christ, Thousand Oaks, Calif., 1985—; owner, pres. Tele-jo Svcs., Newbury Park, Calif., 1990—. Author several tracts; contbr. articles to profl. jours. Active Friendly Visitor program Sr. Concerns, Inc., Thousand Oaks, 1990—. 1st lt. A.C., U.S. Army, 1944-46. Recipient (with wife) Disting. Christian Svc. award Pepperdine U., 1985. Mem. Am. Parkinson Disease Assn. Home: 540 Artisan Rd Newbury Park CA 91320 Office: Conejo Valley Ch of Christ 2525 E Hillcrest Dr Thousand Oaks CA 91362

POYDOCK, MARY EYMARD, nun, educational administrator, biologist, educator; b. Sykesville, Pa., Dec. 3, 1910; d. John Andrew and Anna Mary (Dryna) P. B.A. (NSF grantee), Mercyhurst Coll., 1943; M.A., U. Pitts., 1947; Ph.D. (Sperti fellow), St. Thomas Inst., 1965. Joined Sisters of Mercy, Roman Cath. Ch.; tchr. elementary sch. Erie Diocese, 1935-41; tchr. high sch. Pitts. Diocese, 1941-47; instr. biology, 1947-49, Mercyhurst Coll., Erie, Pa.; asst. prof. biology, assoc. prof. biology Mercyhurst Coll., 1949-55, prof., 1955-64, prof., chmn. dept. biology, 1964-70; dir. Mercyhurst Coll. (Undergrad. Research), 1960-65, Mercyhurst Coll. (Cancer Research), 1960—; also artist. Author: Outline of Histology, 1956, Guidelines for Biotechnique, 1970, Guidelines for Microbiology, 1971, and others.; Contbr. articles to profl. jours. Recipient disting. alumna award, 1985. Mem. AAAS, Pa. Acad. Sci., Am. Assn. Cancer Research, Am. Cancer Soc. (mem. exec. bd. Erie Unit 1966-75), Cancer Prevention Study (gen. chmn. Erie unit 1973-74), Zonta Club of Erie II, Sigma Xi, Beta Beta Beta. Home and Office: 501 E 38th St Erie PA 16546

POYTHRESS, VERN SHERIDAN, religion educator, minister; b. Madera, Calif., Mar. 29, 1946; s. Ransom Huron and Carola Eirene (Nasmyth) P.; m. Diane Marie Weisenborn, Aug. 6, 1983. BS, Calif. Inst. Tech., 1966; PhD, Harvard U., 1970; MDiv, ThM, Westminster Theol. Sem., 1974; MPhil, Cambridge (Eng.) U., 1977; ThD, U. Stellenbosch, Republic of South Africa, 1981. Ordained to ministry Presbyn. Ch. in Am., 1981. Asst. prof. N.T., Westminster Theol. Sem., Phila., 1976-81, assoc. prof., 1981-87, prof., 1987—. Author: Philosophy, Science and the Sovereignty of God, 1976, Understanding Dispensationalists, 1987, Symphonic Theology, 1987, Science and Hermeneutics, 1988, The Shadow of Christ in the Law of Moses, 1991; assoc. editor Westminster Theol. Jour., 1981—. Fellow NSF, 1966-70, Ned B. Stonehouse fellow, 1974. Mem. Linguistic Assn. Can. and U.S. Home: 510 Twickenham Rd Glenside PA 19038 Office: Westminster Theol Sem Chestnut Hill Philadelphia PA 19118

POZZA, LARRY ALLEN, minister; b. Akron, Ohio, June 21, 1957; s. Layton Wray and Charlotte Phillis (Robinson) P.; m. Estera Madjar, Mar. 12, 1983; 1 child, Kevin Layton. B, Malone Coll., 1981; M, Dallas Theol. Sem., 1987. Ordained to ministry Christian Ch., 1986. Dir. Christian edn. Redeemer Bapt. Ch., Cleve., 1981-83; pastor Erieside Ch. on the Blvd., Willowick, Ohio, 1988—; instr. Moody Bible Inst., Cleve., 1988—. Office: Erieside Ch on Blvd 221 E 320th St Willowick OH 44095

PRACHT, RONALD JOE, minister; b. Parsons, Kans., Aug. 28, 1951; s. Henry Ray and Dorothy (Koenig) P.; m. Cindy Louella Shaffer, Aug. 4, 1972; children: Rachel, Priscilla, Faith. BA, S.W. Bapt. U., Bolivar, Mo., 1974; postgrad., Southwestern Bapt. Theol. Sem., Ft. Worth, Tex. Ordained to ministry, So. Bapt. Ch. Youth pastor First So. Bapt. Ch., Independence, Kans., 1971; interim pastor Friendship Bapt. Ch., Parsons, Kans., 1972; music and youth pastor Golden Ave. Bapt. Ch., Springfield, Mo., 1972-73; assoc. pastor Olivet Bapt. Ch., Wichita, Kans., 1973-89, pastor, 1989—; chmn. Bapt. Student Union Com., Wichita, 1982—; mem. Youth Evangelism Team, Kans-Nebr. So. Bapt., 1976-82, mem. exec. bd., 1990—. Chaplain Wichita State U. Football Team, 1974-79, Wichita Police Dept., 1978—. Office: Olivet Bapt Ch 3440 W 13th St Wichita KS 67203

PRAMUK, MARY THERESA, youth minister; b. Lexington, Ky., Dec. 7, 1967; d. John Charles and Gladys Marion (Doherty) P. Student, Transylvania U., 1985-87; BA in English and Psychology, U. Ky., 1989. Youth minister Mary Queen of the Holy Rosary Ch., Lexington, 1990—. Mem. Phi Beta Kappa. Roman Catholic. Office: Mary Queen of Holy Rosary 601 Hill-N-Dale Dr Lexington KY 40503

PRATER, JOHN L., minister, educator; b. Granite City, Ill., Feb. 28, 1939; s. Roy J. and Doris Marie (Hensley) P.; m. Eloise Grace Crum, Apr. 6, 1963; children: Timothy Lee, James Robert. BA, Los Angeles Pacific, 1963; MDiv, Asbury Theol. Sem., 1967. Lic. psychologist counselor, Mo.; cert. addictions therapist. Educator Free Meth. Ch., Winona Lake, Ind., 1959-74; supr. adminstrn. Pacific Telephone and Telegraph, Los Angeles, 1963-64, Sorenson Engring., Yucaipa, Calif., 1974-75; minister Pentecostal Ch. of God, Joplin, Mo., 1976; educator, adminstr. Assemblies of God, Springfield, Mo., 1976-87; chaplain, counselor Prescott (Ariz.) VA Med. Ctr., 1987—; chaplain, cons. City of Duarte, Calif., 1967-69, City of Barstow, Calif., 1973-74; psychol. counselor San Bernadino County, Barstow, 1973-74; chaplain, counselor Sheriff's Dept., Mohave County, Ariz., 1981-85. V.p. Prescott chpt. ARC. Recipient cert. appreciation Duarte City Council, 1969, Barstow City Council, 1974,Asst. Sec. Def., Dept. of the Army (Res. Affairs). Mem. Assn. Christian Schs. Internat., Christian Camping Internat., Ch. Bus. Adminstrs., Nat. Assn. VA Chaplains, Mil. Chaplains Assn., Soc. Preservation and Encouragement of Barber Shop Quartet Singing in Am. Republican. Club: Bullhead City (treas. 1981-84) Lodge: Lions. Avocations: electronics, aviation. Home and Office: 1840 Iron Springs Rd A4J Prescott AZ 86301 Office: VA Med Ctr Chaplain Svc #125 Prescott AZ 86313

PRATER, LAWRENCE ARNOLD, evangelist; b. Evanston, Ill., Feb. 1, 1917; s. James Dotrie and Beulah (Arnold) P.; m. Martha Frances Crigler, May 22, 1941; children: Kenneth Lee, Judy Ann. BS in Edn., NE Mo. State U., 1940; DD (hon.), Asbury Theol. Sem., Wilmore, Ky., 1969. Ordained to ministry Meth. Ch. Pastor United Meth. Ch., Corder, Mo., 1955-57, Belton, Mo., 1957-59, Lebanon, Mo., 1959-65; dist. supt. United Meth. Ch., Joplin, MO., 1965-72; approved evangelist United Meth. Ch., Lantana, Fla., 1972—. Author: Learning to Pray, Prayer Partners. Mem. Nat. Assn. United Meth. Evangelists. Republican. Home: 6910 Kingston Dr Lantana FL 33462

PRATOR, LLOYD EUGENE, priest; b. Martinez, Calif., Nov. 11, 1944; s. James Olen and Hortense (Rives) P. BA, Stanford U., 1966; MDiv, Episcopal Theol. Sch., 1974. Ordained priest Episcopal Ch., 1974. Curate Transfiguration Parish, San Mateo, Calif., 1974-77; asst. to Bishop of Calif. Episcopal Ch., San Francisco, 1977-79; rector All St.'s Ch., San Francisco, 1979-88, St. John's Ch., N.Y.C., 1988—; mem. ministries commn. Diocese of Calif., San Francisco, 1980-88, mem. edn. dept., 1974-78; dean Lower Manhattan Clergy, N.Y.C., 1989—. Trustee Haight Ashbury Alcohol Treatment Svcs., San Francisco, 1984-88, Calif. Counseling Svcs., San Francisco, 1985-88; mem. inst. rev. bd. Columbia Presbyn. Hosp., N.Y.C., 1988—; bd. dirs. People With AIDS Coalition, N.Y.C., 1990—; mem. Concerned Reps. for Individual Rights. Capt. USAF, 1966-69. Mem. Associated Parishes, Assn. Anglican Musicians (planning com. 1989-91), The Club. Office: St John's Ch 224 Waverly Pl New York NY 10014-2405

PRATT, ANDREW LEROY, religion educator; b. Elmhurst, Ill., Jan. 22, 1959; s. LeRoy George and Vervia Stella (Probst) P.; m. Pamela Jean Knight, May 14, 1981; children: Lydia Grace, Abigail Christian. BA, William Jewell Coll., 1981; MDiv, So. Bapt. Theol. Sem., 1984, PhD, 1988; postgrad., U. Chgo., 1986. Ordained to ministry So. Bapt. Conv., 1981. Pastor Bear Creek Bapt. Ch., Westport, Ind., 1984-88; adj. instr. religion studies S.E. Mo. State U., Cape Girardeau, 1988—; Bible chair Bapt. Student Ctr., Cape Girardeau, 1988—; dir. Ctr. for Faith and Learning, Cape Girardeau, 1988—; pulpit supply, interim pastor S.E. Mo. region So. Bapt. Ch., 1988—. Contbr. articles, book revs. to profl. publs. Mem. Am. Soc. Ch. History, Am. Acad. Religion, So. Bapt. Hist. Soc., S.E. Mo. State Campus Ministers Fellowship. Office: Bapt Student Ctr 909 Normal Ave Cape Girardeau MO 63701

PRATT, HENRY BROOKS, minister; b. Colliers, W.Va., Apr. 6, 1933; s. William H. and Bertha May (Brooks) P.; m. Betty Lou Burget, June 9, 1957; children: Kelly Pratt Dinsmore, Barry. BA, Milligan Coll., 1955; BD, Christian Theol. Sem., 1959; MA, Butler U., 1959. Ordained to ministry Christian Ch., 1955. Min. Kempton (Ind.) Christian Ch., 1956-61, Boswell (Ind.) Christian Ch., 1961-66; sr. min. 1st Christian Ch., Rolla, Mo., 1966-77, Madison Park Christian Ch., Quincy, Ill., 1978-83; mem. N.Am. Christian Conf. Com., Cin., 1968-90; bd. dirs. Nat. Ch. Growth Rsch. Ctr., Washington, 1972—; mem. founders com. Emmanuel Sch. Religion, Johnson City, Tenn., 1975. Producer album of sacred music, 1978. Mem. Adams County Cancer Soc., Quincy, 1982-89, Great River Barbershop chorus, Quincy (pres. 1991). Office: Faith Christian Ch 4115 North 12th St Quincy IL 62301

PREBISH, CHARLES S., religion educator; b. Chgo., Oct. 11, 1944; s. Jacob L. and Sydelle (Grossman) P.; m. Susan Lee Kodicek, Aug. 31, 1968; children: Jared Berkeley, Robinson Ashley. BA, Western Res. U., 1966; MA, Case-Western Res. U., 1968; PhD, U. Wis., 1971. Assoc. prof. religious studies Pa. State Univ., University Park, 1971—. Author: Buddhist Monastic Discussion, 1975, Buddhism: A Modern Perspective, 1975, American Buddhism, 1979. Pa. State Univ. grantee, 1972-73, 77. Mem. Am. Oriental Soc., Assn. Asian Studies, Am. Acad. Religion (chmn. Buddhism group 1981-86), Internat. Assn. Buddhist Studies (assoc. sec. 1976-81, bd. dirs. 1981-90), Nittany Valley Track Club (University Park), Pa. State Wrestling Club, State Coll. Wrestling Club. Office: Religious Studies Program Pa State Univ University Park PA 16802

PREGNALL, WILLIAM STUART, priest; b. Charleston, S.C., Mar. 26, 1931; s. Alexander Howard and Marion Lockwood (Lewis) P.; m. Gabrielle Joye Uzzell, Dec. 20, 1952; children: William Stuart, A. Marshall, Garielle Joye Ford. BA, U. N.C., 1952; MDiv., Va. Theol. Sem., 1958, DD (hon.), 1987; DMin., U. of the South, 1975. Ordained priest Episcopal Ch., 1959. Vicar Holy Trinity Episcopal Ch., Grahamville, S.C., 1958-59; dir. christian edn. Diocese of S.C., Charleston, 1960; asst. rector St. John's Ch., Charleston, W.Va., 1961-62, rector, 1962-65; episcopal chaplain La. State U. St. Albans Chapel, Baton Rouge, 1965-70; rector St. Augustine's Ch., Washington, 1970-73; prof. field edn. Va. Theol. Sem., Alexandria, 1973-81; dean, pres. Ch. Div. Sch. of the Pacific, Berkeley, Calif., 1981-89; rector St. Mary's Parish, Washington, 1989—; vicar Ch. of the Cross, Bluffton, S.C., 1958-59, St. Luke's Ch., Hilton Head Island, S.C., 1958-59. Author (books) Laity and Liturgy, 1975, The Episcopal Seminary System During the Decline of the American Empire, 1988. Chair Citizens Com. Against Police Violence, Baton Rouge, 1972. Lt. USN, 1952-60. Named to Order of Holy Grail U. N.C.-Chapel Hill, 1951, Order of Golden Fleece, 1952. Mem. Associated Parishes Inc., Episcopal Peace Fellowship, Phi Eta Sigma, Phi Beta Kappa. Democrat. Avocation: fishing. Home: 1730 Arch St Berkeley CA 94709 Office: Ch Div Sch of the Pacific Office of the Pres 2451 Ridge Rd Berkeley CA 94709

PREHEIM, VERN QUINCY, religious organization administrator, minister; b. Hurley, S.D., June 27, 1935; s. Jacob Roy and Selma (Miller) P.; m. Marion Kathryn Keeney, Aug. 28, 1958; children: Jay, Janette, Beth, Brian, Lorie. AA, Freeman Jr. Coll., 1956; BA, Bethel Coll., 1957; BD, Mennonite Bibl. Sem., 1960. Algeria program dir. Mennonite Cen. Com. Mennonite Ch., Algiers, 1960-62; Peace sec. Gen. Conf. Mennonite Ch., Newton, Kans., 1962-65, gen. sec., 1980—, dir. Africa and Middle East, 1965-75, Asia dir., 1975-80; mission bd. sec. Gen. Conf. Mennonite Ch., 1968-72, chmn. gen. bd. dirs., 1974-80. Home: 1112 Lorna Ln Newton KS 67114 Office: Gen Conf Mennonite Ch 722 Main St Newton KS 67114 *To maintain a sense of direction with a vibrant hope in an uncertain world is imperative for the religious community. Our challenge is also to help others find direction and maintain hope.*

PREMASAGAR, P. VICTOR, religious organization administrator. Moderator Ch. of South India, Madras. Office: Ch of South India, Cathedral Rd, POB 4906, Madras 600 086, India*

PREMAWARDHANA, SHANTA DEVADASA ELLAWALA, minister; b. Colombo, Sri Lanka, June 3, 1952; came to U.S., 1981; s. Cyril Devadasa Ellawala and Mercy (Lekamge) P.; m. Dhilanthi Charmina Fernando, June 4, 1977; children: Charith, Devaka, Amali. BTh, Serampore Coll., West Bengal, India, 1977, BD, 1978; MA, Northwestern Univ., Evanston, Ill., 1985, postgrad. Ordained to ministry Bapt. Ch., 1984. Minister Chgo. Ashram of Jesus Christ, Skokie, Ill., 1983—, Cornell Bapt. Ch., Chgo., 1989—; resident chaplain Rush-Presbyn./St. Luke's Med. Ctr., Chgo., 1984-85; instr. world religions Southwest Bapt. Univ., Bolivar, Mo. (Chgo. campus), 1985—; moderator Chgo. Met. Bapt. Assn., Oak Park, Ill., 1990—; bd. dirs. Synapses, Inc., Chgo. Co-author: (seminar) Growing Up in America, 1987. Mem. Am. Acad. Religion. Baptist. Office: Cornell Bapt Church 5001 S Ellis Ave Chicago IL 60615

PREMNATH, DEVADASAN NITHYA, biblical literature educator; b. Chittoor, India, Oct. 21, 1950; s. Easter Rakshnya and Saraswathy Kamala (Samuel) Das; m. Roslyn Ann Karaban, May 15, 1982; children: Deepa Lynn, Micah Rayan. BA, Arts and Sci. Coll., Chittoor, 1970; MA, S.V. U. Coll., Tirupati, India, 1972; MDiv, United Theol. Coll., Bangalore, India, 1977; ThD, Grad. Theol. Union, Berkeley, Calif., 1984. Ordained to ministry Ch. South India, 1978. Asst. pastor St. James Ch., Madras, 1972-73; dir. youth work Diocese of Vellore, India, 1977-78; lectr. United Theol. coll., 1984-87; registrar, asst. prof. St. Bernard's Inst., Rochester, N.Y., 1988—; dir. clergy continuing edn. Diocese of Vellore, India, 1985-86; ecumenical minister in residence St. John's Ch., Berkeley, Calif., 1979-83; dir. clergy continuing edn. Diocese of Madras, 1986-87. Contbr. articles to profl. jours. Grantee World Coun. Chs., Geneva, 1979-82, British Sch. Archaeology Jerusalem, London, 1981. Mem. Soc. Bibl. Literature. Avocations: tennis, music. Office: St Bernard's Inst 1100 S Goodman St Rochester NY 14620

PRENTIS, JOHN BROOKE, III, theological seminary administrator; b. St. Louis, Feb. 12, 1937; s. John Brooke and Olivia Valeska (Mohrstadt) P.; m. Nancy Jane Bland, June 25, 1960; children: Mary B., John B., Samuel J.B., Nancy B. BA, Yale U., 1959. Asst. sec.-treas. Tower Grove Bank & Trust Co., St. Louis, 1963-67; pres. Arnold (Mo.) Savs. Bank, 1967-71; chmn. Bank of Ferguson (Mo.), 1971-75; exec. v.p. United Mo. Bancshares, Kansas City, Mo., 1971-75; pres. United Mo. Bank of St. Louis, 1973-75, Pranour Corp., St. Louis, 1976-82, Duraflex-Omega Corp., Whittier, Calif., 1978-81, Westminster Christian Acad., St. Louis, 1982-85; pubr. St. Louis Globe-Democrat, St. Louis, 1985-87; v.p. Covenant Theol. Sem., St. Louis, 1989—; dir. God's World Pubs., Asheville, N.C., Chs. Vitalized, Inc., St. Louis, Friendshp Villages, St. Louis. Contbr. editorials to newspapers. Com. mem. Rep. Party, St. Louis, 1960-68; mem. Mo. Edn. Commn., 1990—. With U.S. Army, 1961-66. Mem. Mo. Athletic Club, Univ. Club St. Louis. Presbyterian. Avocations: fishing, reading, speaking, travel. Home: 9054 Fair Oaks Crescent Saint Louis MO 63117

PRENZLOW, ELMER JOHN-CHARLES, JR., minister; b. Norfolk, Nebr., Apr. 4, 1929; s. Elmer Edward and Alvinia C. (Henning) P.; m. Karen McHarg DeMoss, July 4, 1980; 1 child, Elmer Carl III. BA, Northwestern Coll., Watertown, Wis., 1950; BD in Theology, WELS Luth. Sem., Mequon, Wis., 1953; MA in English and Philosophy, U. Minn., 1961; MS in Edn. Psychology, U. Wis., 1969; PhD in Psychology and Criminal Justice, Walden U., 1975. Pastor St Paul's Lutheran Ch., Bloomer, Wis., 1953-62; chaplain, instr. U. Wis., Milw., 1962-79; dir. devel. and pub. relations Luth. Ch.-Mo. Synod, Southern Wis. Dist., Milw., 1979-82; dir. devel. and fin. resources Adult Christian Edn. Found. Bethel Series, Madison, Wis., 1988-89; major gifts counselor Luth. Ch.-Mo. Synod Internat. Hdqrs., St. Louis, 1982-88, world relief devel. counselor, 1989—; vice chmn. Standing Com. Dept. Campus Ministry Luth. Coun. U.S.A., N.Y., 1964-83; chmn. Milw. Religious Counselors, 1965-72, dept. humanities Spencerian Bus. Coll., 1967-77; v.p. Patricia Stevens Career Coll.; speaker, lectr. in field. Contbr. articles to profl. jours. Mem. Wis. State Legis. Com for Kerner Report, Madison, 1968-69, Nat. Adv. Commn.U.S. Justice Dept. on Law Enforcement standards and goals, Washington, 1971-73, ad hoc com. for establishing U.S. Bur. Prisons Nat. Inst. for Corrections, Washington, 1973-75, 19th congr. dist. Wis. svc. acad. review bd., Milw., 1975-82. Named Outstanding Prof. Spencerian Bus. Coll., Milw., 1972. Mem. Assn. of Luth. Devel. Execs., Optimists, Wis. Club. Republican. Avocations: travel, music, auto racing, golf, fishing. Home: 715 Windy Ridge Dr Manchester MO 63021 Office: LCMS Internat Ctr 1333 S Kirkwood Rd Saint Louis MO 63122 *Nothing communicates to others what we believe more loudly and effectively than the measure of those principles they witness being personally carried out in our own lives!.*

PRESCOTT, ALLIE, ecumenical agency administrator. Exec. dir. Met. Inter Faith Assn., Memphis. Office: Met Inter Faith Assn PO Box 3130 Memphis TN 38173*

PRESCOTT, WILLIAM BRUCE, minister; b. Denver, Dec. 30, 1951; s. William Rex and Betena Naomi (Fletcher) P.; m. D. Kylene Winters, Nov. 24, 1973; children: William Doyle, Candice Joy. BS in Corrections, U. Albuquerque, 1973; MDiv, Southwestern Bapt. Sem., 1978, PhD, 1986. Ordained minister in Bapt. Ch., 1976. Youth minister Sandia Bapt. Ch., Albuquerque, 1974-75; pastor Clairette (Tex.) Bapt. Ch., 1976-79; instr. philosophy and religion Tarrant County Jr. Coll. NW Campus, Ft. Worth, 1984-86; pastor Easthaven Bapt. Ch., Houston, 1987—; adj. prof. Southwestern Bapt. Theol. Sem., HBU Extension, Houston, 1987—; police chaplain Houston Police Dept., 1987—; trustee Southeast Area Ministries, Houston, 1988—. Book reviewer to Southwestern Jour. Theology; contbr. articles to profl. jours. Named one of Outstanding Young Men of Am., Jaycees, 1984. Mem. Am. Acad. Religion, Nat. Assn. Bapt. Profs. of Religion, So. Bapt. Alliance, Baptists Committed. Democrat. Home: 2203 Bisontine Friendswood TX 77546 Office: Easthaven Bapt Ch 9321 Edgebrook Houston TX 77075

PRESS, SAMUEL BELOFF, rabbi; b. Middletown, Conn., June 6, 1936; s. Isador Morris and Pearl (Beloff) P.; m. Phyllis L. Ledewitz, Dec. 19, 1964; children: Daniel, Deborah, Adam. BA, Yeshiva Coll., 1957; M. Hebrew Letters, Yeshiva U., 1960. Ordained rabbi, 1960. Rabbi Agudat Achim, Hartford, Conn., 1962-64, Oyster Bay (N.Y.) Jewish Ctr., 1964-78; rabbi Beth Abraham Synagogue, Dayton, Ohio, 1978—, chmn., 1991; trustee Jewish Fedn., Dayton, 1978—; bd. dirs. Anti-Defamation League, Ohio and Mich., 1978—; pres. Synagogue Forum Dayton, 1989—. Contbr. articles, sermons to religious publs. Trustee Black White Racial Forum, Dayton, 1989—, Community Rels. Coun., Dayton, 1978—; mem. Black Jewish Forum, Dayton, 1989—; founding mem. Interfaith Forum, 1991. Chaplain USAF, 1960-62. Recipient tribute United Jewish Appeal. Mem. N.Y. Bd. Rabbis, Rabbinical Assembly, Chgo. Bd. Rabbis. Home: 3499 Gorman Ave Dayton OH 45415 Office: Beth Abraham Synagogue 1306 Salem Ave Dayton OH 45406 *We strive so earnestly to find the mystery and transcendent... And we need but look in the eye of a neighbor, a lover, a needful soul... We can never discover the Why, but we can choose the attitude for our response...*

PRESSLER, HERMAN PAUL, III, judge, lay church worker; b. Houston, June 4, 1930; s. Herman P. and Elsie (Townes) P.; m. Nancy Avery, Feb. 28, 1959; children: Jean Townes Pressler Visy, Anne Lyle Pressler Csorba, Herman Paul IV. AB, Princeton U., 1952; JD, U. Tex., 1957; LLD (hon.) Criswell Coll., 1988. Bar: Tex. 1957, U.S. dist. ct. (so. dist.) Tex. 1957. Assoc. Vinson & Elkins, Houston, 1958-70; judge 133d Dist. Ct., Houston, 1970-78; justice 14th Ct. Appeals, Houston, 1978—. Mem. Tex. Legislature, rep. Harris County, 1957-59; mem. Pres.'s Drug Adv. Coun.; exec. com. Coun. for Nat. Policy; chmn. bd. Sta. KHCB-FM, Evang. Christian Ednl. Found., Houston, 1966—; vice-chmn. trustee bd. exec. com. So. Bapt. Conv. Lt. (j.g.) USN, 1954-56. Named Outstanding Young Man of Houston, Jr. C. of C., 1957; recipient Faith in God award, 1976, medal of honor, DAR, 1976. Mem. various profl. assns. Republican. Baptist. Home: 282 Bryn Mawr Circle Houston TX 77024 Office: 14th Ct Appeals 1307 San Jacinto Houston TX 77002

PRESSLEY, TED KERMIT, minister; b. Gastonia, N.C., Dec. 20, 1938; s. Hazen K. and Grace Roberta Pressley; m. Jacqueline Jo Parks, Nov. 25, 1986; children: Russell, Angela, Richelle. Diploma, Southwestern Bapt. Sem., 1972. Ordained to ministry So. Bapt. Conv., 1968. Pastor Yucca Bapt. Ch., Ft. Worth, 1968-70, Jesus Temple, Ft. Worth, 1970-71; pres., founder Cowboys for Christ Internat., Ft. Worth, 1971—. Editor Christian Ranchman, 1972—; writer syndicatated newspaper column, 1984—. With USAF, 1956-60. Office: Cowboys for Christ PO Box 7557 Fort Worth TX 76111

PRESSMAN, JACOB, rabbi; b. Phila., Oct. 26, 1919; s. Solomon David and Dora (Levin) P.; m. Marjorie Steinberg, June 14, 1942; children: Daniel Joseph, Joel David, Judith Sharon. BA, U. Pa., 1940; MHL, Jewish Theol. Sem., 1944, Dr.Hebrew Letters, 1960, Dr. Humane Letters, 1979. Ordained rabbi, 1945. Rabbi Forest Hills Jewish Ctr., N.Y.C., 1944-46, Congregation Sinai, L.A., 1946-50, Temple Beth Am, L.A., 1950—; dir. Bonds of Israel, L.A., 1988-90, city chmn., 1990-91; vice chmn. bd. govs. L.A. Jewish Fedn. Coun., 1988—; founder U. Judaism, L.A. Hebrew High Sch., Herzl Sch., Camp Ramah at Ojai, Akiba Acad., Rabbi Jacob Pressman Acad. Mem. Rabbinical Assembly Western Region (pres. 1954-56), Bd. Rabbis So. Calif. (pres. 1958-61). Office: Temple Beth Am 1039 S La Cienga Blvd Los Angeles CA 90035 *God is. God is good. His creation is good, and so, mankind, being of His creation is good. As an act of grace, God gives man the power to choose between good and evil in his ways, and with even greater grace gives man the awareness that he has this choice. Man is perfectible. His perfect stage, the Messianic era, is coming; but it will always be coming, never at a moment in time to arrive, but always inviting us to progress to newer and higher goals personally and as a society, each new mountaintop of human progress toward that nobler future merely opens our eyes to visions of even greater and more God-like human life.*

PRESTON, ALDON EMORY, minister; b. Antioch, Calif., Mar. 17, 1960; s. Albert Emory and Mary Lucille (ISbell) P. BA, Oral Roberts U., 1983; ThM, Pacific Coast Bible Coll., 1990. Ordained to ministry Pentecostal Ch. Youth/music min. Garden Acres Community Ch., Stockton, 1983-85; founding pastor New Life Fellowship, Oakley, Calif., 1987—; min. Christian edn. Calif. Pentecostal Holiness Ch., Sacramento, 1984—; counselor, advisor Antioch chpt. Women's Aglow, Calif., 1991. Office: New Life Fellowship PO 1387 3641 E Main Oakley CA 94561 *One's primary purpose is to worship our Creator—everything else persued should help make that possible.*

PRESTON, JAMES HERMAN, clergyman; b. Bethany, Mo., Mar. 21, 1951; s. Wilbur A. and Mary (Bartlett) P.; m. Betty Jo A. Witman, Jan. 18, 1970; children: Melinda, Lori, Daniel, Rebekah, Jennifer. Grad. Theology, Bapt. Bible Coll., 1973; BS in Secondary Edn., Sauk Village Bapt. Bible Coll., 1980; MTh, Temple Bapt. Bible Sem., 1989, ThD, 1991. Ordained to ministry Bapt. Ch., 1973; cert. EMT. Youth dir. Alpha Bapt. Ch., Denver, 1973; pastor Greenland Bapt. Ch., Beecher City, Ill., 1973-74, Effingham (Ill.) Bapt. Temple, 1974-85, Lighthouse Bapt. Ch., Cortez, Colo., 1985—; Trustee Fellowship Bapt. Coll., East Peoria, Ill., 1978-82; v.p. Internat. Fellowship Bapts., East Peoria, 1982-90; pres. Ill. Fellowships Bapts., Effingham, Ill., 1978-82. Author: Giving Birth to New Churches, 1976, Church Staff Handbook, 1978, Pauline Epistles, 1979, Simple Lessons on the Tabernacle, 1980, Revelation commentary, 1981, Names and Titles of Christ for Every Day, 1981, Teaching Teachers, 1986, Dealing with Church Problems, 1988, Dealing with Stress in Our Churches, 1989, Iraq in Prophecy, 1991. Home and Office: Lighthouse Bapt Ch 11502 Hwy 145 Cortez CO 81321

PRETTI, BRADFORD JOSEPH, lay worker, insurance company executive; b. Glenwood Springs, Colo., Oct. 11, 1930; s. Joseph John and Ethel Elizabeth (Roe) P.; m. Nancy Ann Clayton, Mar. 30. 1951 (div. 1971); children: Kristi Pretti Micander, Terice Pretti Brownson, Bradford Joseph, Holli; m. Sarah Jane Rupp, Aug. 8, 1974. BA, U. Colo., 1952. Pres. Pub. Adv. Ins. Com., Chaves County, N.Mex., 1965-72; sr. warden St. Thomas á Beckett Ch., Roswell, N.Mex., 1978-79, St. Andrew's Ch., Roswell, N.Mex., 1991—; mem. Progam Coun. Diocese of Rio Grande, Albuquerque, 1981-84, mem. Venture in Mission Commn., 1980-84, pres. Standing Commn., 1981-85, chmn. Bishop Search Commn., 1987, dep. to Gen. Conv., 1985-88; ptnr. Cathedral chpt. Roswell, N.Mex., 1988-91; pres. Roswell Ins. & Surety Agy., RBS Ins., 1974—; sr. warden St. Andrews Ch., Roswell, 1991; instr. Ea. N.Mex. U., Roswell, 1970—. Contbr. articles to jours. in field. Pres. Assurance Home Found., Roswell, 1984—; campaign chmn. United Way of Chaves County, Roswell, 1982, v.p., 1984; bd. dirs. Roswell Hospice Inc., 1984; trustee Roswell Mus. and Art Ctr., 1985, pres. bd. trustees, 1990—. Mem. N.Mex. Ind. Ins. Agts. Assn. (Outstanding Svc. award 1964), Roswell C. of C. (treas. 1984, pres. elect 1985, pres. 1986, Pres.'s Club citation 1983), Mus. Trustees Assn., Am. Contract Bridge League (pres. #382 sect. 1965-68), C Club (Boulder, Colo.). Republican. Episcopalian. Avocation: duplicate bridge. Home: 317 Sherrill Ln #14 Roswell NM 88201 Office: RBS Ins 1510 W Second St Roswell NM 88201 *Without a deep, abiding faith our lives are essentially meaningless.*

PRETTO, FRANKLIN DAVID, priest; b. Colon, Panama, Jan. 27, 1946; came to U.S., 1966; s. David Elias Pretto and Hilda Louise (Ferro) De Pretto. BA, St. Thomas Theol., Denver, 1969; MDiv, St. Patrick Theol., Menlo Park, Calif., 1971. Ordained priest Roman Cath. Ch., 1972. Assoc. dir. Aquinas Newman Ctr., Albuquerque, 1970-75; dir. St. Paul Newman Ctr., Las Vegas, Nev., 1975-77; assoc. pastor Our Lady of Guadalupe Ch., Santa Fe, 1980-82; pastor San Isidro Ch., Santa Fe, 1982—. Entertainer various restaurants; record album Tamboritos Panamenos, 1981, Cosa Buena, 1988; appeared on the Cristina TV talk show, Miami, 1990, as Salsa Padre in Noticias y Mas Univision, Miami, 1991. Bd. mem. 375th Anniversary of Santa Fe, 1986; mem. Congressman Bill Richardson's Com. Hispanic Artists, Santa Fe, 1986. Named Young Citizen of Yr., Santa Fe C. of C., 1981; Frank Pretto Day proclaimed by City of Santa Fe, 1981. Avocations: swimming, acting, movie poster collecting, travel. Office: San Isidro Cath Ch Rt 6 Box 111 Santa Fe NM 87501

PREUETT, DANNY GENE, minister; b. Carson City, Nev., Oct. 14, 1959; s. Robert Austin and Oneta Marie (DeBusk) Mannon; m. Dawn Marie Richendollar, Dec. 8, 1978; 1 child, Tiffany Marie. Dir. youth mins. Collingdale (Pa.) Ch. of Nazarene, 1980-83; asst. pastor Colonial Ch. of Nazarene, Orlando, Fla., 1986-89, assoc. pastor, 1989-90; youth min. Bartow (Fla.) Ch. of Nazarene, 1990-91; pastor Tampa (Fla.) Grace Ch. of the Nazarene, 1991—; mem. prodn. control staff Gen. Engines, Co., Inc., Lake Wales, Fla., 1990-91. With USN, 1977-83. Home: 2711 W Wallace Ave Tampa FL 33611 Office: Grace Ch of the Nazarene 3706 Wyoming Ave Tampa FL 33611 *I believe that for any ministry to thrive, there must be outreach, incorporation, discipleship and leadership. Above all else, we must exhibit genuine love for others.*

PREUS, DAVID WALTER, bishop, minister; b. Madison, Wis., May 28, 1922; s. Ove Jacob Hjort and Magdalene (Forde) P.; m. Ann Madsen, June 26, 1951; children: Martha, David, Stephen, Louise, Laura. BA, Luther Coll., Decorah, Iowa, 1943, DD (hon.), 1969; postgrad., U. Minn., 1946-47; BTh, Luther Sem., St. Paul, 1950; postgrad., Union Sem., 1951, Edinburgh U., 1951-52; LLD (hon.), Wagner Coll., 1973, Gettysburg Coll., 1976; DD (hon.), Pacific Luth. Coll., 1974, St. Olaf Coll., 1974, Dana Coll., 1979; LHD (hon.), Macalester Coll., 1976. Ordained to ministry Luth. Ch., 1950; asst. pastor First Luth. Ch., Brookings, S.D., 1950-51; pastor Trinity Luth. Ch., Vermillion, S.D., 1952-57; campus pastor U. Minn., Mpls., 1957-58; pastor Univ. Luth. Ch. of Hope, Mpls., 1958-73; v.p. Am. Luth. Ch., 1968-73, pres., presiding bishop, 1973-87; exec. dir. Global Mission Inst. Luther Northwestern Theol. Sem., St. Paul; Disting. vis. prof. Luther-Northwestern Sem., St. Paul, 1988—; Luccock vis. pastor Yale Div. Sch., 1969; chmn. bd. youth activity Am. Luth. Ch., 1960-68; mem. exec. com. Luth. Council U.S.A.; v.p. Luth. World Fedn., 1977-90; mem. cen. com. World Council Chs., 1973-75, 80-90; Luth. del. White House Conf. on Equal Opportunity. Chmn. Greater Mpls. Fair Housing Com., Mpls. Council Chs., 1960-64; Mem. Mpls. Planning Commn., 1965-67; mem. Mpls. Sch. Bd., 1965-74, chmn., 1967-69; mem. Mpls. Bd. Estimate and Taxation, 1968-73, Mpls. Urban Coalition; sr. public adv. U.S. del. Madrid Conf. of Conf. on Security and Cooperation in Europe, 1980-81; bd. dirs. Mpls. Inst. Art, Walker Art Center, Hennepin County United Fund, Ams. for Childrens Relief, Luth. Student Found., Research Council of Gt. City Schs., Urban League, NAACP; bd. regents Augsburg Coll., Mpls. Served with Signal Corps AUS, 1943-46, PTO. Decorated comdr.'s cross Royal Norwegian Order St. Olav, Order of St. George 1st deg. Orthodox Ch. of Georgia (USSR), 1989; recipient Regents medal Augustana Coll., Sioux Falls, S.D., 1973, Torch of Liberty award Anti-Defamation League, 1973, St. Thomas Aquinas award St. Thomas U. Office: 2481 W Como Ave Saint Paul MN 55108

PREUS, JACOB AALL OTTESEN, former seminary president and church executive; b. St. Paul, Jan. 8, 1920; s. J. A. O. and Idella (Haugen) P.; m. Delpha Holleque, June 12, 1943; children: Patricia (Mrs. Gerhard Bode), Delpha (Mrs. George Harris), Carolin (Mrs. Jerold Misner), Sarah (Mrs. Dennis Schwab), Idella (Mrs. Mark Moberg), Mary (Mrs. William Churchill), Jacob, Margaret (Mrs. Steve Jones). B.A., Luther Coll., 1941; B.D., Luther Sem., 1945; M.A., U. Minn., 1946, Ph.D., 1951. Ordained to ministry Luth. Ch., 1945. Pastor South St. Paul, Minn., 1945-46; prof. Bethany Coll., Mankato, Minn., 1947-50, 56-58; pastor Luverne, Minn., 1950-56; prof. Concordia Theol. Sem., Springfield, Ill., 1958-69; pres. Concordia Theol. Sem., 1962-69, Luth. Ch. Mo. Synod, 1969-81; mem. constituting com. Luth. Coun. in U.S.A. Translator: Chemnitz: The Lord's Supper, The Two Natures of Christ, On Justification, Loci Theologici; contbr. chpt. to The Doctrine of God, 1962; articles to theol. jours. Home: 705 Laclede Station Rd Apt 369 Saint Louis MO 63119

PREUS, ROBERT DAVID, educational administrator, minister; b. St. Paul, Oct. 16, 1924; s. Jacob A.O. and Idella (Haugen) P.; m. Donna Mae Rockman, May 29, 1948; children—Daniel, Klemet, Katherine, Rolf, Peter, Solveig, Christian, Karen, Ruth, Erik. B.A., Luther Coll., Decorah, Iowa, 1944; B.D., Bethany Luth. Sem., Mankato, Minn., 1947; Ph.D., Edinburgh U. (Scotland), 1952; D.Theol., Strasbourg U. (France), 1969. Pastor, First Am. Luth. Ch., Mayville, N.D., Bygland Luth. Ch., Fisher, Minn., 1947-49, Harvard St. Luth. Ch., Cambridge, Mass., 1952-55, Mt. Olive Luth. Ch., Cross Lake Luth. Ch., Clearwater Luth. Ch., Trail, Minn., 1955-57; prof. systematic theology Concordia Sem., St. Louis, 1957-74; pres., prof. Concordia Theol. Sem., Springfield, Ill. and Ft. Wayne, Ind., 1974—. Author: The Inspiration of Scripture, 1955; The Theology of Post-Reformation Lutheranism, vol. 1, 1970, vol. 2, 1972; Getting Into the Theology of Concord, 1977. Republican. Avocation: Cross country skiing. Home: 2829 Fox Chase Run Fort Wayne IN 46825 Office: Concordia Theol Sem 6600 N Clinton St Fort Wayne IN 46825

PRICE, ALVIN HELM, minister, sociology and gerontology educator; b. Oakland, Miss., Apr. 11, 1941; s. Alvin T. and Christine (Helm) P.; m. Josephine Connell, June 14, 1963; children: Don Allen, Bethany Rose. AA, Freed-Hardeman Coll., 1962; BA, Abilene Christian U., 1963; MA, U. Tenn., 1974; cert. in gerontology, U. Ala., 1979, U. North Tex., 1983. Minister Liberty Ch. of Christ, Dennis, Miss., 1963-64, Capitol St. Ch. of Christ, Jackson, Miss., 1964-67, Ch. of Christ, Greenville, Miss., 1967-69, Broadway Ch. of Christ, Knoxville, Tenn., 1969-73, Ch. of Christ, Wildersville, Tenn., 1974—; assoc. prof. sociology and gerontology Freed-Hardeman U., Henderson, Tenn., 1974-87; presenter workshops, 1979—. Chmn. bd. Chester County Sr. Citizens, Henderson, 1985. Mem. So. Gerontol. Soc., Tenn. Assn. for Gerontology/Geriatric Edn. (pres. 1986, exec. com. 1987—), Christian Aging Network. Democrat. Home: 456 Galbraith Ave Henderson TN 38340 Office: Freed-Hardeman U 158 E Main Henderson TN 38340

PRICE, CECIL EDWARD, youth minister; b. Houston, Sept. 14, 1956; s. Frank Edward and Dorothy Louise (Russell) P.; m. Annick Elizabeth Metayer, Aug. 14, 1982; children: Frank, John-Michael, Elizabeth. BA, Harding U., 1978. Youth min. Sunset Ch. of Christ, Dallas, 1979-80, Cockrell Hill Ch. of Christ, Dallas, 1980-86, Webb Chapel Ch. of Christ, Dallas, 1986-88, 8th and Harrison Ch. of Christ, Harlingen, Tex., 1988—. Composer, writer various hymns and songs. Organizer Rio Grande Valley Summer Youth Series, Tex., 1989-90, South Tex. Christian Teen Night, 1989-90; trustee, tchr. Found. Sch. of Ch. Music, Austin, Tex., 1990; trustee Valley Christian Heritage Sch., Alamo, Tex., 1990. Mem. Chs. of Christ. Home: 725 E Carrol Harlingen TX 78550 Office: 8th and Harrison Ch of Christ 801 E Harrison Harlingen TX 78550 *In working with teens, I have found that they want to know how much I care before they care how much I know.*

PRICE, DENNIS JOE, minister; b. Rocky Mount, N.C., Apr. 24, 1955; s. Tom Lewy and Jane (Rhodes) P. AA, Louisburg (N.C.) Jr. Coll., 1976; BRE, Campbell U., 1978; student, Southeastern Bapt. Sem., Wake Forrest, N.C., 1979-83. Ordained to ministry So. Bapt. Conv., 1983. Youth min. Oakdale Bapt. Ch., Rocky Mount, 1975-80, Guess Rd. Bapt. Ch., Durham, N.C., 1980-82; assoc. pastor Guess Rd. Bapt. Ch., Durham, 1990—, Ebenezer Bapt. Ch., Durham, 1982-85; dir. Kids' Alive Ministries, Durham, 1985-90; dir. Kids' Kountry, Durham, 1985—. Author: Children's Sermon, 1988. N.C. State Rep. Del., 1974; active N.C. Right to Life, 1986—. Mem. Ruritans (pres. 1990). Home: 2207 Peppertree St Durham NC 27705 Office: Guess Rd Bapt Ch 3102 Guess Rd Durham NC 27705 *With little effort, we can have a big impact in the lives of others. Let God use you as a vessel of blessings to others.*

PRICE, EARNEST, JR., religious educator, minister; b. Ellisville, Miss., Mar. 6, 1919; s. Earnest and Vivian (Jordan) P.; m. Catherine Upchurch, May 9, 1941; 1 child, Catherine Elizabeth. BS, Miss. State U., 1940; MA, Columbia U., Union Theol. Sem., 1948; postgrad., Union Theol. Sem., 1945-51. Ordained to ministry, United Ch. of Christ. Assoc. exec. dir. YMCA, Miss. State U., 1940-42, exec. dir., 1943-47; exec. dir. YMCA, coord. religious activities La. State U., Baton Rouge, 1948-53; exec. dir. YMCA, dir. religious life Miss. State U., 1953-56; assoc. exec. dir. Cen. Atlantic Area Coun. YMCA, Newark, 1956-61; assoc. exec. dir. coll. and univ. div. Nat. Coun. YMCA's, N.Y.C., 1961-69, dir. manpower planning, 1969-73, dep. dir. nat. pers. svcs., 1973-77; Kearns prof., dir. human rels. studies High Point (N.C.) Coll., 1977-85; pastoral care pastor 1st United Meth. Ch., High Point, 1985—; cons. personell adminstrn. S.E. Region Coun. YMCAs, Atlanta, 1977-81, YMCA Greater N.Y., N.Y.C., 1977-78; trustee Am. Humanics, Inc., Kansas City, Mo., 1972—; pres. Nat. Assn. Coll. & Univ. YMCA Dirs., 1953-56. Contbr. articles to profl. jours. Pres. Community Chest, 1960, United Fund, 1961, both Glen Ridge, N.J.; bd. dirs. United Way Greater High Point, 1981-87, High Point Drug Action Coun., 1981-87, Vol. Action Ctr., High Point, 1988-90; bd. dirs., vice-chair Urban Ministry, High Point, 1989—, chair, 1990—; bd. dirs. Habitat for Humanity, High Point, 1990—, vice-chair, 1991—. With U.S. Army, 1942-43. Mem. Kiwanis (bd. dirs. Glen Ridge chpt. 1976-77), Rotary (bd. dirs. Starkville, Miss. chpt. 1955-56), ACLU, Common Cause, Amnesty Internat., People for Am. Way, Clergy and Laity Concerned, Ams. for Dem. Action, Omicron Delta Kappa, Alpha Phi Omega. Democrat. Avocations: golf, classical music, money markets, gardening, travel. Home: 4402 Oak Hollow Dr High Point NC 27265 Office: First United Meth Ch 512 N Main St High Point NC 27760

PRICE, FREDERICK KENNETH CERCIE, minister; b. Santa Monica, Calif., Jan. 3, 1932; s. Fred Cercie and Winifred Bernice (Ammons) P.; m. Betty Ruth Scott, Mar. 29, 1953; children: Angela Marie Price Evans, Cheryl Ann Price Crabbe, Stephanie Pauline Price Buchanan, Frederick Kenneth. Diploma (hon.), Rhema Bible Tng. Ctr., Tulsa, 1976; DD (hon.), Oral Roberts U., 1982; student (hon.), Pepperdine U., 1990. Ordained to ministry Bapt. Ch., 1955, African Meth. Episcopal Ch., 1957, Kenneth Hagin Ministries, 1975. Asst. pastor Mt. Sinai Bapt. Ch., Los Angeles, 1955-57; pastor African Meth. Episcopal Ch., Val Verde, Calif., 1957-59; pastor, Christian Missionary Alliance W. Washington Community Ch., Los Angeles, 1965-73; pastor Crenshaw Christian Ctr., Los Angeles, 1973—; founding mem. bd. trustees Internat. Conv. Faith Ministers, Inc., Tulsa, 1979—; chmn. bd., pres. Fellowship of Inner City Word of Faith Ministries. Author: How Faith Works, 1976, How to Obtain Strong Faith, 1977, Thank God for Everything, 1977, Ingredient, 1978, Faith: Foolishness or Presumption, 1979, Explanation to Receiving Your Healing by the Laying on of Hands, 1980, Now Faith Is, 1983, High Finance, God's Financial Plan, Tithes and Offerings, 1984, How to Believe God for a Mate, 1987, Marriage and the Family, Practical Insight for Family Living, 1988, The Origin of Satan, 1988, Living in the Realm of the Spirit, 1989, Concerning Them Which are Asleep, 1989, Homosexuality: State of Birth or State of Mind, 1989, Prosperity on God's Terms, 1990, Practical Suggestions for a Successful Ministry, 1991. Democrat. Avocation: scuba diving. Office: Crenshaw Christian Ctr Attention Angela Evans Mailing PO Box 90000 Los Angeles CA 90009

PRICE, J. P., minister; b. Houston, May 6, 1947; s. Dewey H. Price and Florence Helfrich Senulis; m. Hollie J. Brewer, June 25, 1966; children: Paula Jo, Joseph Paul. BA, Houston Bapt. U., 1978, MA, 1981; PhD, U. Houston, 1983. Ordained to ministry Christian Life Ministries, 1978. Youth pastor Freeway Forest Bapt. Ch., Houston, 1975-77, Victory Bapt. Ch., Houston, 1977-78; co-founder, prof. Gethsemane Internat. Bible Inst., Houston, 1989—; pastor First Ch. N.W., Houston, 1978—. Author: Inner Healing, 1988, Process of Salvation, 1990. Trustee Christian Life Ministries, Houston, 1978—, Gethsemane Inst. Bible Inst., Houston, 1989—, Plantation Estates Homeowners Assn., Porter, Tex., 1979—; del. Rep. Party, Montgomery, 1987. With USMC, 1964-68. Decorated Purple Heart. Recipient Pastor Achievement award, Union Bapt. Assn., 1983. Mem. Lone Star Bow Hunters, Nat. Assn. Counseling Psychologist, Houston Bapt. U. Alumni Assn. Home: 104 Plantation Ave Porter TX 77365 Office: First Church of NW 6730 W Tidwell Houston TX 77365 *The tragedy of human history is that man never seems to learn from his mistakes or the mistakes of those who have gone before him.*

PRICE, JOHN EDWARD, religion educator; b. Chgo., Mar. 7, 1942; s. Edward F. Price and Carolyn Maxine Polachek; children: Larissa Marie, James Thomas,s Elizabeth Suzanne. BA, Univ. of St. Mary of the Lake, 1964, STB, 1966, STL, 1968. Lic. dir. religious edn. Tchr. Mother of God Sch., Waukegan, Ill., 1968-69; tchr., chmn. religion dept. Holy Trinity High Sch., Chgo., 1969-70; coord. religious edn. Transfiguration Ch., Wauconda, Ill., 1970-75; dir. religious edn. St. Athanasius Ch., Evanston, Ill., 1975-91, Ch. of St. Mary, Lake Forest, Ill., 1991—; catechist resource person Archdiocesan Office of Religious Edn., Chgo., 1977-80; field supr. Mundelein Coll. and Inst. Pastoral Studies, Chgo., 1979-80, 84; team mem. North Cen. Evaluation, Chgo., 1984; presenter, lectr. Archdiocese of Chgo., 1979, 80, 84, 85. Author: (filmstrip) Learning Right and Wrong, 1978, (testing svc.) Religious Education Diagnostic Survey, 1983; contbr. articles to religious publs. Del. Ill. White House Conf. on Librs. and Info. Svcs., Springfield, 1978. Mem. Cath. Theol. Soc. Am., Religious Edn. Assn., Nat. Assn. Parish Coords. and Dirs., Ill. Assn. Parish Coords. and Dirs., Chgo. Assn. Religious Educators (treas. 1979-82, Care award 1983), Book Discussion Club. Avocations: photography, fishing, scuba diving, bicycling, poetry. Office: St Mary's Religious Edn Ctr 201 E Illinois Rd Lake Forest IL 60045

PRICE, JOHN WHEATLEY, religious organization head. Brit. chaplain Anglican Ch., Amsterdam, The Netherlands. Office: Christ Ch, Greonburgwal 42, 1011 HW Amsterdam The Netherlands*

PRICE, JOHN WILSON, priest; b. Corpus Christi, Tex., Nov. 24, 1938; s. W. Armstrong and Evelyn (Wilson) P.; m. Arlene Bruchmiller, June 25, 1966; children: Robert Lancaster, Frederick William, Helen Catherine. BA, U. Tex., 1961; MDiv, Va. Theol. Sem., 1964. Ordained priest Episcopal Ch., 1964. Curate Trinity Episcopal Ch., San Antonio, 1964-65; asst. rector St. Mark's Episcopal Ch., San Antonio, 1965-68; rector St. George's Episcopal Ch., Austin, Tex., 1968-88, Holy Comforter Ch., Spring, Tex., 1988—; exch. rector Hanwell Parish Ch., London, 1975-76; founder, pres. bd. St. George's Ct., Austin, 1980-88; mem. exec. bd. Episcopal Diocese of Tex., 1989—; state chaplain Tex. N.G., 1991—. Home: 19418 Craigchester Spring TX 77388 Office: Holy Comforter Ch 2322 Spring-Cypress Rd Spring TX 77388

PRICE, NELSON, interfaith cable company executive; b. Valley City, N.D., Oct. 4, 1928; s. Nelson Allen and Charlotte (King) P.; m. Ann Freeman, Mar. 27, 1954; children: Donna Lynn, David Brent, Debra Leah, Dara Gwen. BA, Morningside Coll., 1951, D Communications (hon.), 1988; postgrad., U. Chgo., 1957-58; MA, Goddard Coll., 1975. Dir. communication Ind. area The Meth. Ch., Indpls., 1952-57; dir. communication No. Ill. Conf., Chgo., 1957-59; dir. pub. rels. and field work TV, Radio and Film Commn., Nashville, 1959-61, dir. prodn., 1961-64, dir. programming, 1964-75; dir. pub. media div. United Meth. Communications, N.Y.C., 1975-90; pres. Media Action Rsch. Ctr., Inc., N.Y.C., 1975-90; sec.-treas. Nat. Interfaith Cable Coalition, Inc., N.Y.C., 1988-90, pres., chief exec. officer, 1990—; pres., chief exec. officer Vision Interfaith Satellite Network, N.Y.C., 1990—; treas., past. pres. Communication Commn., Nat. Coun. Chs., N.Y.C., 1961—; trainer TV Awareness Tng., N.Y.C., 1977—; pres. bd. dirs. Ecumedia News Svc., N.Y.C., 1985-88. Exec. producer Night Call, 1969 (Faith and Freedom award 1969), Begin with Goodbye, 1979 (Cine award 1979), A Fuzzy Tale, 1977 (Asifa-East award 1977), Children's Growing, 1980 (Am. Film Fest award 1980), TV series Catch the Spirit, 1985-90 (Angel awards, 1985-89, Cine award 1989); producer Breakthru, 1966 (Ohio State award 1966). Bd. dirs. Nat. Coalition Against TV Violence, 1980-90; mem. New City United Meth. Ch. Recipient Gabriel award Cath. Broadcasters Assn., 1969, 76-77, Brotherhood award NCCJ, 1969, Paul M. Hinkhouse award Religious Pub. Rels. Assn., 1973-74, 77, 79, 82, 84, 87. Mem. NATAS, Internat. Radio and TV Soc., Religious Pub. Rels. Coun. (past bd. dirs.), Internat. Transactional Analysis Assn., World Assn. Christian Communications. Democrat. Home: 120 N Broadway Nyack NY 10960 Office: VISN Cable TV Network 74 Trinity Pl Ste 915 New York NY 10006 *We have a choice—of affirming that which is healthy and holy and positive in each person—or affirming that which is destructive and violent. Violence begets violence, love begets love.*

PRICE, ROBERT LESLEY, minister; b. Paducah, Ky., Aug. 11, 1941; s. William Orman and Evelyn (Kersey) P.; m. Janett Ann Giles, Aug. 26, 1961; children: Jeffrey Marshall, Pamela Evelyn. BSME, U. Ky., 1964, MSME, 1965; MDiv, Southwestern Bapt. Theol. Sem., 1978, D Ministry, 1991. Ordained to ministry So. Bapt. Conv., 1976. Sr. engr. Pratt & Whitney Aircraft Co., West Palm Beach, FL, 1964-72; Mem. field staff Campus Crusade for Christ, West Palm Beach, Fla., 1972-75; pastor Chisholm (Tex.) Bapt. Ch., 1976-78, Emmanuel Bapt. Ch., Terrell, Tex., 1978-81, Cornerstone Bapt. Ch., Terrell, 1981—; chaplain Tri-City Hosp., Dallas, 1989—; prof. engrng. drafting Trinity Valley Community Coll., 1985—. Inventor integrated control for turbopropulsion system, 1974. Chmn. Terrell Say No to Drugs program, 1988. Home: 322 Rash Ln Terrell TX 75160 Office: Cornerstone Bapt Ch 113 Hwy 205 Terrell TX 75160 *I believe that the Christian life should be lived such that walking by faith is not an option but an absolute necessity.*

PRICE, ROSS EUGENE, minister; b. Culbertson, Mont., Apr. 15, 1907; s. Ernest Eugene and Lydia Ann (Cuff) P.; m. Irene Elizabeth Taylor, Aug. 4, 1933; children: Dorothy Lois, Patricia Louise, Michael Kennedy. AB, N.W. Nazarene Coll., 1932; MA, Pasadena Coll., 1944, BD, 1945, DD (hon.), 1949; ThM, McCormick Sem., 1950; PhD, U. So. Calif., 1966. Ordained to ministry Ch. of the Nazarene, 1933. Pastor various chs. Wyo., Mont. and Ill., 1932-48; prof. dean grad. studies Pasadena (Calif.) Coll., 1948-61, prof., 1961-69; prof. theology Olivet Nazarene Coll., Kankakee, Ill., 1969-75; prof. Bible and theology Nazarene Bible Coll., Colorado Springs, Colo., 1978-80; evangelist, 1980—; dist. supt. Rocky Mountain dist. Ch. of the Nazarene, Mont., Wyo., 1970-78; lectr. Nazarene Theol. Sem., Bethany Nazarene Coll., N.W. Nazarene Coll., Point Loma Nazarene Coll., Can. Nazarene Coll. and Nazarene Coll., 1962-85. Author: (with Olive M. Winchester) Crisis Experience in the Greek New Testament, 1953; Dynamic Evangels, 1966, Some Absolutes From Jesus, 1984, others; contbr. articles to encys. and dictionaries. Mem. Evang. Theol. Soc. (past pres. Pacific Coast sect.), Wesleyan Theol. Soc., Phi Delta Lambda, Pi Epsilon Theta. Republican. Home: 1540 Hiawatha Dr Colorado Springs CO 80915 *We should never be reluctant to invest a lifetime of preparation into one single hour of service.*

PRICE, ROY CANTRELL, minister; b. L.A., May 23, 1935; s. Walter and Wilma Harlan (Nance) P.; m. Sandra Lee Burns, Aug. 27, 1957; children: Steven R., Cynthia Price Long. BA, Westmont Coll., 1957; ThM, Luther Rice Sem., Jacksonville, Fla., 1977, D Ministry, 1978; DPhil, Oxford Grad. Sch., Dayton, Tenn., 1988. Ordained to ministry Christian and Missionary Alliance, 1962. Youth pastor Grace Ch., Santa Barbara, 1957-58; pastor Valley Neighborhood Ch., San Jose, 1958-60, Williams Community Ch., Williams, Oreg., 1960-63; assoc. pastor Portland Alliance Ch., 1963-64; pastor Arbor Hts. Alliance Ch., Seattle, 1964-68; asst. pastor Allegheny Ctr. Alliance Ch., Pitts., 1968-71; sr. pastor Christian and Missionary Alliance, Wadsworth, Ohio, 1971-75; pastor Internat. Protestant Ch., Saigon, Vietnam, 1975; sr. pastor First Alliance Ch., Louisville, 1975-81, Paradise (Calif.) Alliance Ch., 1981—; bd. mgrs. Christian and Missionary Alliance, Colorado Springs, 1985-91, mem. dist. exec. com., Oakland, Calif., 1982-86; guest lectr. Pippert Alliance Theol. Sem., 1984; adj. lectr. Pastoral Theology and Ch. Polity, 1988. Contbr. articles to profl. jours. Trustee Feather River Health Found., Paradise, 1986-91; mem. Community Drug Abuse Task Force, Paradise, 1987; bd. dirs., trombonist Paradise Symphony Orch. Mem. Nat. Assn. Evangelicals, Ministerial Assn. of Paradise (pres. 1987), Paradise C. of C., Lions (1st v.p. 1974-75), Rotary. Republican. Avocations: golf, tennis, singing. Home: 333 Circlewood Dr Paradise CA 95969 Office: Paradise Alliance Ch 6491 Clark Rd Paradise CA 95969 *The basic issue in religion is not moral code, ritual, symbolism, or history. It is truth. Jesus of Nazareth claimed to be truth and validated his claim when he rose from the dead. No one else in history has ever equaled that achievement.*

PRICE, SUE ELLEN, lay worker; b. Gordo, Ala., May 25, 1948; d. J.D. and Charline (Bryant) Yearby; m. Marvin Locke Price, Mar. 25, 1966; children: Rodney Clayton, Sidney Blaine. Dipl., Satsuma (Ala.) High Sch., 1966. Sun. sch. tchr. Saralnd (Ala.) Ch. of God, 1972-85, ch. sec., 1974-85; Sun. sch. tchr. Chickasaw Ch. of God, Mobile, Ala., 1986—, ch. sec., 1988—. Vice pres. Dixie Youth Baseball, Saraland, 1978-81, 83-87; treas. Satsuma Quarterback Club, 1986-87. Home: 1121 Alvarez Dr Saraland AL 36571 Office: Chickasaw Ch of God 455 Iroquois St Chickasaw AL 36611

PRICHARD, JOHN DAVID, minister; b. Burnwell, W.Va., July 19, 1948; s. Joseph and Agnes Arvada (Fisher) P.; m. Drema Kay Clark, Apr. 11, 1970; children: Angela Kay, John David II. AB, Nazarene Bible Coll., 1980; postgrad., U. Bibl. Studies, Bethany, Okla., 1989. Ordained minister Ch. of the Nazarene, 1981. Pastor, zone youth dir. Dille (W.Va.) Ch. of the Nazarene, 1975-77; pastor Craigsville (W.Va.) Ch. of the Nazarene, 1980-82, Walton (W.Va.) Ch. of the Nazarene, 1982-84, Marion (Va.) Ch. of the Nazarene, 1984-88, Beckley (W.Va.) First Ch. of the Nazarene, 1988—; ch. planter Va. Dist., Wytheville, 1985-86; area coord. Va. Nazarene Dist., Marion, 1987-88; dist. adult dir. W.Va. South Dist., Summersville, 1990—; cafeteria mgr. W.Va. Dist. Campgrounds, 1990—; dist. coll. recruiter Nazarene Bible Coll., Colorado Springs, Colo., 1990—. Chmn. Libr. Commn., Walton, W.Va., 1983-84; dir. Weekday Religious Edn. Program, Marion, 1985-86. With USN, 1966-70, Vietnam. Recipient Great Commn. Leadership award W.Va. South Dist., Charleston, 1990; named Alumnus of Yr., W.Va. South Dist., Nazarene Bible Coll., Colorado Springs, 1990. Mem. Beckley Ministerial Assn. Democrat. Home: 605 Johnstown Rd Beckley WV 25801 Office: First Ch of the Nazarene 607 Johnstown Rd Beckley WV 25801

PRICKETT, T. A., minister; b. Verbena, Ala., July 31, 1934; s. Elmer Marshall and Catherine (Strength) P.; m. Helen Marlene Holland, Dec. 1, 1957; 1 child, Panda Prickett Krouse. BA, Samford U., 1957; MDiv, So. Bapt. Sem., 1965, D. Ministry, 1980. Ordained to ministry So. Bapt. Ch., 1953. Pastor Haysop Bapt. Ch., Centreville, Ala., 1954-57, Mt. Carmel Bapt. Ch., West Blocton, Ala., 1957-58, Bethabara Bapt. Ch., Philpot, Ky., 1961-65, Seven Hills Bapt. Ch., Owensboro, Ky., 1965—; asst. pastor Forest Lake Bapt. Ch., Tuscaloosa, Ala., 1958-61; pres. Ky. Bapt. Pastors' Conf., 1973; 1st v.p. Ky. Bapt. Convention, 1974, chmn. bus./fin. com., 1984, 85; bd. dirs. Western Recorder, 1980-86, chmn., 1986. Contbr. articles to profl. publs. Pres. Civitan Club, Owensboro, 1971-72; mem. Audubon Area Community Svcs. RSVA Adv. Coun., 1987-89; bd. dirs. Widowed Persons Svc., 1984—; pres. Owensboro-Daviess County Com. on Aging, Inc., 1975-76, 89-91, v.p., 1988; vol. United Way, 1980; vice chmn. bd. dirs. Elizabeth Munday Sr. Ctr., 1982-89; mem. Chautauqua Community Ctr. Adv. Commn., 1990, 91; mem. Mayor's Citizens Adv. Com. on Cable TV, 1989-91. Named Ky. Col., Commonwealth of Ky., 1972. Mem. Daviess-McLean Bapt. Assn. (moderator 1970-71, chmn. trustees 1989, chmn. program com. 1990, chmn. spl. constn. com. 1987-89, Sunday sch. dir. 1970-75, 79-80, chmn. stewardship and budget com., chmn. nominating com.). Democrat. Home: 209 W Legion Blvd Owensboro KY 42301 Office: Seven Hills Bapt Ch 1709 Alexander Ave Po Box 2222 Owensboro KY 42302-2222 *Those who are frustrated with life usually have not given much to life. Success and happiness is in giving. This understanding of life may be hard and demanding, but it's rewards are satisfying and encouraging.*

PRIDE, DOUGLAS SPENCER, minister; b. Latrobe, Pa., Jan. 13, 1959; s. Spencer MacVeagh and Kathleen (Tidd) P.; m. Elizabeth Armstrong, June 5, 1982; children: Kathryn Elizabeth and Jennifer Suzanne (twins), Pamela Campbell. BA, Westminster Coll., 1980; MDiv, Pitts. Theol. Sem., 1983, postgrad., 1988—. Ordained to ministry Presbyn. Ch., 1983. Asst. pastor Shadyside Presbyn. Ch., Pitts., 1983-85, assoc. pastor, 1985-91; pastor Presbyn. Ch. of Clearfield, Clearfield, Pa., 1992—; chaplain palliative care program West Penn Hosp., 1983-86. Bd. dirs. Pitts. Theol. Sem., 1983-86; mem. alumni coun. Westminster Coll., New Wilmington, Pa., 1986—, pres., 1989-90; bd. dirs. Bethesda Ctr., Pitts.; lst v.p. Spina Bifida Assn., Pitts., 1987-89, pres., 1989—, bd. dirs. 1984, sec. bd., 1985-87. Mem. Pitts. Presbytery, Longue Vue Club, Jewish Community Ctr., Univ. Club. Republican. Avocations: tennis, racquetball, reading. Home: 2538 Meadow Rd Clearfield PA 16830

PRIES, KENNETH KARL, minister; b. Oakland, Calif., Mar. 19, 1946; s. Karl Henry and Gertrude (Salter) P. BS, Cin. Bible Coll., 1968; MDiv, Phillips U., 1976; postgrad., Cin. Christian Sem. Ordained to ministry United Ch. of Christ. Min. 1st Christian Ch., Stanberry, Mo., 1977-79; interim min. Mendon-Bosworth (Mo.) Christian Parish, 1979-80; min. 1st Christian Ch., Colusa, Calif., 1980-85; assoc. min. Eastside Ch. of Christ, Turlock, Calif., 1985-86; min. Union Congl. United Ch. of Christ, Gregory, S.D., 1989—; sec. Ministerial Alliance, Okla. and Calif., 1976-77, 81-85, pres., Stanberry, Mo., 1977-79; camp coord. Heavenly Hills Christian Camp, 1981-86; bd. dirs. Christian Ch. (Disciples of Christ) No. Calif.-Nev., 1983-86. V.p. Assn. for Retarded Citizens, Stanberry, Mo., 1978-79; mem. Friends of Libr., Colusa, Calif.; bd. dirs. ARC, Yuba City, Calif., 1981-85, Modesto, Calif., 1985-87. Broadhurst scholar, 1976. Mem. Profl. Assn. Clergy, Young Ams. for Freedom, Sertoma Club, Comml. Club, Kiwanis (pres. Modesto club 1985-87), Rotary (bd. dirs. Gregory club 1990—). Republican. Home: 209 E 6th St PO Box 206 Gregory SD 57533 Office: Union Congl United Ch of Christ 519 Rosebud Ave Gregory SD 57533

PRIESAND, SALLY JANE, rabbi; b. Cleve., June 27, 1946; d. Irving Theodore and Rosetta Elizabeth (Welch) P. B.A. in English, U. Cin., 1968; B.Hebrew Letters, Hebrew Union Coll.-Jewish Inst. Religion, 1971, M.A. in Hebrew Letters, 1972; D.H.L. (hon.), Fla. Internat. U., 1973. Ordained rabbi, 1972. Student rabbi Sinai Temple, Champaign, Ill., 1968, Congregation B'nai Israel, Hattiesburg, Miss., 1969-70, Congregation Shalom, Milw., 1970, Temple Beth Israel, Jackson, Mich., 1970-71; rabbinic intern Isaac M. Wise Temple, Cin., 1971-72; asst. rabbi Stephen Wise Free Synagogue, N.Y.C., 1972-77; assoc. rabbi Stephen Wise Free Synagogue, 1977-79; rabbi Temple Beth El, Elizabeth, N.J., 1979-81, Monmouth Reform Temple, Tinton Falls, N.J., 1981—; chaplain Lenox Hill Hosp., N.Y.C., 1979-81. Author: Judaism and the New Woman, 1975. Mem. commn. on synagogue relations Fedn. Jewish Philanthropies N.Y., 1972-79, mem. com. on aged commn. synagogue relations, 1972-75; mem. task force on equality of women in Judaism pub. affairs com. N.Y. Fedn. Reform Synagogues, 1972-75; mem. com. on resolutions Central Conf. Am. Rabbis, 1975-77, com. on cults, 1976-78, admissions com., 1983-89; chmn. Task Force on women in rabbinate, 1977-83, chmn. 1977-79, mem. exec. bd., 1977-79, com. on resolutions, 1989—; mem. joint commn. on Jewish edn. Central Conf. Am. Rabbis-Union Am. Hebrew Congregations, 1974-77; mem. task force on Jewish singles Commn. Synagogue Relations, 1975-77; mem. N.Y. Bd. Rabbis, 1975—, Shore Area Bd. Rabbis, 1981—; mem. interim steering com. Clergy and Laity Concerned, 1979-81; bd. dirs. NCCJ, N.Y.C., 1980-82, Jewish Fedn. Greater Monmouth County, trustee; trustee Planned Parenthood of Monmouth County, also chair religious affairs com., Brookdale Ctr. for Holocaust Studies, Monmouth Campaign for Nuclear Disarmament; v.p. Interfaith Neighbors, 1988—. Cited by B'nai Brith Women, 1971; named Woman of Yr. Temple Israel, Columbus, Ohio, 1972, Woman of Yr. Ladies Aux. N.Y. chpt. Jewish War Vets., 1973, Woman for All Seasons N. L.I. region Women's Am. ORT, 1973, Extraordinary Women of Achievement NCCJ, 1978, Woman of Achievement Monmouth County Adv. Commn. on Status Women, 1988; recipient Quality of Life award Dist. One chpt. B'nai B'rith Women, 1973, Medallion Judaic Heritage Soc., 1978, Eleanor Roosevelt Humanities award Women's div. State of Israel Bonds, 1980, Rabbinical award Coun. Jewish Fedn., 1988, Woman of Leadership award Monmouth Coun. Girl Scouts U.S., 1991. Mem. Hadassah (life), Central Conf. Am. Rabbis, NOW, Am. Jewish Congress, Am. Jewish Com., Assn. Reform Zionists Am., B'nai B'rith Women (life), Jewish Peace Fellowship, Women's Rabbinc Network. Home: 10 Wedgewood Circle Eatontown NJ 07724 Office: 332 Hance Ave Tinton Falls NJ 07724

PRIEST, RUTH EMILY, music minister, choir director, composer; b. Detroit, Nov. 7, 1933; d. William and Gertrude Hilda (Stockley) P. Student, Keyboard Studios, Detroit, 1949-52, Wayne State U., Detroit, 1953, 57, Ea. Pentecostal Bible Coll., Peterborough, Ont., 1954-55, Art Ctr. Music Sch., Detroit Inst. Mus. Arts, 1953-54. Organist, pianist, vocalist Berea Tabernacle, Detroit, 1943-61; organist Bethany Presbyn. Ch., Ft. Lauderdale, Fla., 1961-67, 69-72; choir dir., organist Bethany Drive-in Ch., Ft. Lauderdale, Fla.; organist First Bapt. Ch., Pompano Beach, Fla., 1967-68, St. Ambrose Episcopal Ch., Ft. Lauderdale, 1969-72; music dir., organist Grace Brethren Ch., Ft. Lauderdale, 1972-75; ch. organist, pianist Bibletown Ch., Boca Raton, Fla., 1975-85; min. music, organist Warrendale Community Ch., Dearborn, Mich., 1985—; ptnr. Miracle Music Entertainment; concert and ch. organist/pianist; organist numerous weddings, city-wide rallies of Detroit and Miami Youth for Christ, Christ for Labor and Mgmt., Holiness Youth Crusade, numerous other civic and religious events; pvt. tchr. piano, organ, music theory; featured weekly as piano soloist and accompanist on Crusade for Christ, Detroit, 1950-60, CBC-TV, Windsor, Ont., Can.; staff organist Enquire Hotel, Galt Ocean Mile, Ft. Lauderdale, Fla., 1962-67; mem. faculty div. fine arts Franklin Rd. Christian Sch., Southfield, Mich., 1991—; tchr. piano adult edn. evening sch. program Mich. Pub. Sch. System, 1991—. Recording artist: Ruth Priest at the Organ, Love Notes from the Heart, Christmas with Ruth. Mem. Am. Guild Organists (past mem. exec. bd. Detroit chpt.). Office: Miracle Music Ent PO Box 554 Southfield MI 48037-0554 *I agree with Martin Luther that music is one of God's greatest gifts to mankind. At a very early age my natural response to life was, and still is, an outflow of love to God through the musical gifts with which He has blessed me.*

PRIM, RICHARD DOUGLAS, pastor; b. Indpls., Feb. 14, 1954; s. Harold E. and Martha F. Prim; m. Eleanor B. Prim, Feb. 5, 1978; children: Joy, Richard II, Whitney. A, Bayridge Christian Coll., 1976; BS, Ind. Christian U., 1980; postgrad., Cen. Bapt. Coll., 1987-89, Nazarene Theol. Sem., 1988-90. Lic. counselor, Kans. Ast. treas. Nat. Inspirational Youth Conv. Ch. of God, 1986-89, treas., 1990—; 1st v.p. Interstate Assn., Topeka, 1987-89; state credential com. Kans. State Ch. of God, 1987—. Mem. Wheels for Freedom (bd. dirs.). Office: Freeman Ave Ch of God 1060 Freeman Ave Kansas City KS 66102

PRIMATESTA, RAUL FRANCISCO CARDINAL, archbishop of Córdoba (Argentina); b. Capilla del Señor, Argentina, Apr. 14, 1919. Ordained priest Roman Catholic Ch., 1942; formerly tchr. minor and maj. seminaries, La Plata; titular bishop of Tanais, also aux. of La Plata, 1957; bishop of San Rafael, 1961-65; archbishop of Córdoba, 1965—; elevated to Sacred Coll. Cardinals, 1973; titular ch., St. Mary of Sorrowful Virgin; mem. Congregation of Bishops, Congregation of Religious and Secular Insts., Congregation Sacraments and Divine Worship, Commn. Revision Code Canon Law. Address: Hipolito Yrigoyen 98, 500 Córdoba Argentina

PRIMO, QUINTIN EBENEZER, JR., bishop; b. Liberty County, Ga., July 1, 1913; s. Quintin Ebenezer and Alvira Wilhemenia (Wellington) P.; m. Winifred Priscilla Thompson, July 5, 1942; children: Cynthia Priscilla, Quintin Ebenezer, Susan Alvira. BA, Lincoln U., 1934, STB, 1937; MDiv, Va. Theol. Sem., 1941, DD (hon.), 1973; DD (hon.), Seabury-Western Sem., 1972; LHD (hon.), St. Augustine's Coll., 1972; STD (hon.), Gen. Theol. Sem., 1973. Curate St. Agnes' Ch., Miami, Fla., 1941-42; vicar St. Gabriel's Ch., Rutherfordton, N.C., 1942-44; priest-in-charge St. Stephen's Ch., Winston-Salem, N.C., 1944-45; vicar St. Timothy's Ch., Bklyn., 1945-47; vicar St. Simon's Ch., Rochester, N.Y., 1947-61, rector, 1961-63; priest-in-charge St. Matthew's Ch., Wilmington, Del., 1963-66, rector, 1966-69; rector Detroit, 1969-71, St. Matthew's and St. Joseph's Ch., Detroit, 1971-72; suffragan bishop Diocese of Chgo., 1972-84; interim bishop Del., 1985-86. Past bd. dirs. Bexley Hall Theol. Sem., Episc. Charities, Domestic and Fgn. Missionary Soc. of P.E. Ch.; chmn. Diocese of Chgo. Commn. on Met. Affairs; chmn. com. urban affairs Ho. of Bishops; chmn. Nat. Mission in Ch. Soc.; co-founder Union Black Episcopalians; life trustee Rush-Presbyn.-St. Luke's Med. Ctr., Chgo., St. Augustine's Coll., Raleigh, N.C.; mem. steering com. Episc. Urban Bishops; bd. dirs., past pres. Chgo. Conf. on Religion and Race; former bd. dirs. Nat. Safety Council; bd. dirs. Chgo. chpt. NCCJ, Peninsula United Meth. Country Home Inc., Kalmar Nyckel Found. Mem. Clergy Assn. of Diocese of Chgo. Home: 3322 Morningside Rd Wilmington DE 19810

PRINCE, ROBERT WILLIAM, III, minister; b. Covington, Ga., Feb. 7, 1955; s. Robert William Prince Jr. and Peggy Ann (Bates) Dunn; m. Patricia Lee Andrews, May 26, 1979; children: Preston Jay, Elizabeth Ann. BA, Baylor U., 1977; MDiv, Southwestern Bapt. Theol. Sem., Ft. Worth, 1981, PhD, 1985. Ordained to ministry So. Bapt. Conv., 1976. Pastor Cego (Tex.) Bapt. Ch., 1976-77; youth min. 1st Bapt. Ch., Marietta, Ga., 1978-79; pastor 1st Bapt. Ch., Bryson, Tex., 1980-85, Hot Wells Bapt. Ch., San Antonio, 1985-87, N.W. Hills Bapt. Ch., San Antonio, 1987—; cons. Christian edn. coordinating bd. Bapt. Gen. Conv. of Tex., 1990—. Contbr. articles to profl. jours. Com. mem. Bryson Sr. Citizens' Coun., 1980-85; mem. nominating com. Bapt. Meml. Hosp. System, San Antonio, 1989-90. Named one of Outstanding Young Men Am. U.S. Jaycees, 1983. Mem. San Antonio Bapt. Assn. (missions devel. coun. 1986—, vice moderator, 1989—), Lions (pres. Bryson club 1984-85). Home: 6133 Ridge Glade San Antonio TX 78250 Office: Northwest Hills Bapt Ch 6585 Heath Rd San Antonio TX 78250

PRINCIPE, WALTER HENRY, priest, theology educator; b. Rochester, N.Y., Oct. 15, 1922; s. Arthur S. and Louise (Masnaghetti) P. BA with honors, U. Toronto, Can., 1946; MA in Philosophy, U. Toronto, 1951; postgrad., St. Basil's Sem., Toronto, 1946-50; Mediaevorum Studiorum Licentiatus summa cum laude, Pontifical Inst. Mediaeval Studies, 1951, Mediaevorum Studiorum Doctoratus summa cum laude, 1963; Diplôme de l'École Pratique des Hautes Études, U. Sorbonne, Paris, 1954; DHL (honoris causa), St. John Fisher Coll., 1988. Joined Congregation St. Basil, Roman Cath. Ch., 1940, ordained priest, 1949. Lectr. U. St. Michael's Coll., Toronto, 1949-51, assoc. prof. faculty theology, 1953-64, prof., 1964-79, dean, 1955-65, adj. prof., 1980—; jr. fellow history of theology Pontifical Inst. Mediaeval Studies, Toronto, 1962-64, sr. fellow, 1964-88, Inst. prof., 1988—; assoc. prof. Sch. Grad. Studies, U. Toronto, 1963-64, prof., 1964—; lectr. Inst. for Rsch. on World Religions, Chinese Acad. Social Scis., Beijing, 1983; apptd. mem. Internat. Theol. Commn., Sacred Congregation for Doctrine of the Faith, Vatican City, 1980-85, U.S. Luth.—Roman Cath. Dialogue, Nat. Conf. Cath. Bishops U.S., 1988—; mem. Cath. Commn. on Intellectual and Cultural Affairs; bd. dirs. Humanities Rsch. Coun. Can., 1975-78, exec. bd., 1976-78, chair, 1976-77. Author: The Theology of the Hypostatic Union in the Early Thirteenth Century, Vol. 1, 1963, Vol. 2, 1967, Vol. 3, 1970, Vol. 4, 1975, Introduction to Patristic and Medieval Theology, 1980, 2d edit., 1982, Faith, History and Cultures: Stability and Change in Church Teachings, 1991; also articles. John B. Guggenheim fellow, 1967. Fellow Royal Soc. Can.; mem. Assn. Internat. d'Études Patristiques, Can. Patristics Soc., Can. Soc. for Study of Religion, Can. Theol. Soc. (v.p. 1969-70, pres. 1970-71, past pres. 1971-72, hon. mem. 1987), Cath. Theol. Soc. Am. (v.p. 1988-89, pres.-elect 1989-90, pres. 1990-91, past pres. 1991—, John Courtney Murray award 1987), N.Am. Patristic Soc., La Soc. Canadienne de Théologie, La Soc. Internat. pour l'Étude de la Philosophie Médiévale. Home and Office: 59 Queen's Park Cres, Toronto, ON Canada M5S 2C4

PRITCHETT, JOSEPH ALLEN, minister; b. Mountain View, Calif., Oct. 22, 1962; s. James Homer and Helen Rebecca (Kimble) P.; m. Robin Frances Hubert, May 26, 1984; children: Rebecca, Benjamin. Student, Concord Coll., 1981; BA in Theology, Berkshire Christian Coll., 1985. Ordained to ministry Advent Christian Gen. Conf., 1987. Interim pastor 1st and 2d Congl. Ch., Chester, Mass., 1984; pastoral intern Oak Hill Bible Ch., Oxford, Mass., 1984; interim pastor Corbin (Ky.) Advent Christian Ch., 1985-86; pastor 1st Advent Christian Ch., Barbourville, Ky., 1985-87; assoc. pastor United Advent Christian Ch., Wilmington, N.C., 1987—; so. regional rep. Nat. Youth Bd. Advent Christian Gen. Conf., 1989—; chmn. So. Advent Christian Youth Bd., 1989—. Contbr. articles to Christian youth jours. Mem. So. Advent Christian Assn. (bd. dirs. 1991—), Ea. N.C. Coastal Dist. Advent Christian Min.'s Fellowship (sec.-treas. 1989—), Berkshire Christian Coll. Alumni Assn. (v.p. 1991—), Operation Outreach. Republican. Office: United Advent Christian Ch 4912 S College Rd Wilmington NC 28412 *Knowing that the impossible may be overcome with God always gives me hope. I can face anything because my God can face anything.*

PRIVETTE, WILLIAM EDWARD, minister; b. Hartsville, S.C., June 29, 1949; s. Junius Gordon and Thelma Edward (Slade) P.; m. Eleanor Ruth Tyson, Aug. 29, 1968; children: Matthew Edward, William Mark, Amy Marie. AA, Louisburg Coll., 1969; BA, Atlantic Christian Coll., 1971; MDiv, Duke Div. Sch., 1975; postgrad., Asbury Theol. Sem. Min. Hebron United Meth. Ch., Mebane, N.C., 1971-75, Fairview United Meth. Ch., Altamahaw, N.C., 1975-78, Apex (N.C.) United Meth. Ch., 1978-81, So. Pines (N.C.) United Meth. Ch., 1981-87, Queen St. United Meth. Ch., Kinston, N.C., 1987—; chair Greenville (N.C.) Dist. Com. on Superintendency, 1990—. Office: Queen St United Meth Ch 500 N Queen St Kinston NC 28501

PRIVITERA, LINDA FISHER, priest; b. Pitts., Oct. 30, 1946; d. Cecil Blaine Fisher and Jean Elisabeth (Morton) Kasten; children: Eileen, Laura, Christine. BSN, Va. Commonwealth U., 1968; MDiv, Yale U., 1986. Ordained deacon Episcopal Ch., 1987; priest, 1988. Chaplain Masonic Home, Hosp., Wallingford, Conn., 1984-85; seminarian St. Marks Episc. Ch., New Britain, Conn., 1985-87; asst. rector All Saints Episc. Ch., Meriden, Conn., 1987-90; assoc. rector All Saints Episc. Ch., Worcester, Mass., 1990—; mem. Diocesan Task Force on Initiation, Conn. Liturgical Commn., 1988-90; chaplain Companions of the Cross, New Haven, 1988-90, Hospice Team, N.W. Conn.. Vis. Nurses Assn., 1989-90, Meriden Hospice Team, Wallingford Hosp., 1989-90; mem. Province I AIDS Task Force, Springfield, Mass., 1989—; dir. retreats Trinity Camp, Conf. Ctr., West Cornwall, Conn. 1990—, St. Luke's in the Fields, N.Y.C, 1990—. Bd. dirs. Religious Coalition for Abortion Rights, Hartford, Conn., 1989-90; mem. NOW, 1986—. Mem. Alban Inst., Cen. Worcester Clericus. Office: All Saints Episc Ch 10 Irving St Worcester MA 01609 *Most of my saints are women of color, those who keep on keepin' on, who refuse to give up, who know what it is to partner with God.*

PROBASCO, WILLIAM LEE, clergyman; b. Paducah, Tex., Sept. 23, 1937; s. Grover Cleveland and Victoria Louise (Jordan) P.; m. Janette Sue Jones, Aug. 8, 1957 (dec. Nov. 1990); children: Vicki, Chrisi, Rebecca, Timothy. BS, Dallas Bapt. Coll., 1957; postgrad., Dallas Theol. Sem., 1963-67; BTh, Luther Rice Sem., Jacksonville, 1964, MDiv, 1978, D Ministry, 1980. Ordained to ministry Baptist Ch. Pastor Rock Hill Bapt. Ch., Bowie, Tex., 1956-59; pastor First Bapt. Ch., Oden, Ark., 1959-63, Josephine, Tex., 1963-67, Stamps, Ark., 1967-69; pastor Meadows Bapt. Ch., Plano, Tex., 1969-72, First Bapt. Ch., Conway, Ark., 1972-83, Meadowbrook Bapt. Ch., Gadsden, Ala., 1985—; v.p. Ark. Bapt. State Conv., Little Rock, 1981, 82; trustee, exec. com. So. Bapt. Sunday Sch. Bd., 1991—. Author, contbr.: A Passion for Preaching, 1989. With U.S. Army, 1953-61. Fellow Victoria Soc. Gt. Britain; mem. Am. Assn. Family Counselors. Republican. Baptist. Avocations: amateur archaeology. Home: 219 6th St Rainbow City AL 35901 Office: Meadowbrook Bapt Ch 2525 Rainbow Dr Gadsden AL 35901

PROBST, JOHN ELWIN, chaplain, minister; b. Klamath Falls, Oreg., Apr. 3, 1940; s. John Albert and Jocelyn Marlia (Tunnell) P.; m. Patty P. Maness, Jan. 13, 1975; children: Marla, Joni, Jessica. BTh, Internat. Bible Sem., Orlando, Fla. Ordained to ministry So. Bapt. Conv., 1969. Pastor 1st Bapt. Ch., Dorris, Calif., 1968-72; evangelist, Tex., 1972-74; youth pastor Salem Bapt. Ch., Rocky, Okla., 1974-75; pastor Retrop Bapt. Ch., Carter, Okla., 1975-79; supply pastor 1st Bapt. Ch., Hobart, Okla., 1975-79; interim pastor Mountain Heights So. Bapt. Ch., Leadville, Colo., 1979; missionary-evangelist, interim pastor Skyway Bapt. Ch., Glendale, Ariz., 1979-82; pastor 1st So. Bapt. Ch., Monrovia, Calif., 1982-85; chaplain Media Focus, Duarte, Calif., 1982—; interim pastor United Community Ch., Glenday, Calif., 1988-90; revival leader; former mem. evangelism and search com. Estrella Assn., Ariz.; former br. mgr. Sherwin Williams Co.; writer, casting dir., producer Seven Star Prodn.; assoc. producer, writer, casting dir. Castel Prodns.; writer Esses Films; researcher, writer, asst. producer Nunn Prodns.; telemarketer White Horse Prodns; pres. L.A. So. Bapt. Pastors Conf., 1983; ch. planter Philippine Crusade, 1983, 85; numerous others. With USAF, 1959-64. Mem. So. Calif. Motion Picture Coun. (life, Golden Halo awards 1985). Office: PO Box 618 Duarte CA 91010 *If I am able through sensitivity in prayer and loving devotion, to stay each day in the center of God's Will for my life-then I will accomplish exactly and only what He plans for me to do.*

PROBST, WALTER CARL, JR., minister; b. Kerrville, Tex., Apr. 4, 1937; s. Walter Carl Sr. and Selma Adela (Pfluger) P.; m. Marilyn Faye Jorgensen, Dec. 7, 1963; children: Christie Ann, Michelle Renee. BS, Tex. Luth. Coll., 1960; BD, Wartburg Theol. Sem., 1963. Ordained to ministry Am. Luth. Ch., 1963. Pastor Salem Luth. Ch., Roscoe, Tex., 1964-67; pastor St. John Luth. Ch., Rutersville, Tex., 1967-75, Cat Spring, Tex., 1975-90; pastor Lake Livingston Luth. Ch., Onalaska, Tex., 1990—; bd. dirs. Luther League, Brenham Conf., 1972-75; chaplain Cat Spring Vol. Fire Dept., 1976—; dean Cat Spring Deanery, 1983—. Mem. Brenham Conf. Mission Soc. (sec. 1981—). Home and Office: Lake Livingston Luth Ch Box 1688 Onalaska TX 77360

PROCTER, JOHN ERNEST, former publishing company executive; b. Gainesboro, Tenn., July 23, 1918; s. Leon and Mary (Poteet) P.; m. Jane Sprott, May 23, 1941; children: Mary Carol, Valere Kay. Student, Vanderbilt U., 1940-41, U. Miami (also extension div.), 1943-44, U. Tenn., 1946-50; LL.D. (hon.), Ohio No. U., 1971; D.L. (hon.), Ky. Wesleyan Coll., 1981. With Methodist Pub. House, Nashville, 1945-83; v.p., pub. Methodist Pub. House, 1964-70, pres., pub., 1970-83; dir. 3d Nat. Bank, Nashville. Bd. dirs. Tenn Council on Econ. Edn. Served to capt. USAAF and USAF, 1944-45, 50-52. Decorated Certificate of Valor; Air medal with 7 oak leaf clusters;

D.F.C. Mem. Adminstrv. Mgmt. Soc. (past pres. Nashville, area. sec.-treas. 1967-68, Merit Key award 1961, Diamond Merit award 1967), Nashville C. of C. (past mem. bd. govs.), Assn. Am. Pubs. (past dir.). Clubs: Rotary, Belle Meade Golf & Country. Office: 201 8th Ave S Nashville TN 37203 *The modest success I have achieved is the result of an intense commitment to intellectual honesty, sensitivity to the needs of my associates, the setting of challenging and realistic goals, striving for efficiency by doing things right and being effective by doing the right things, always with faith in myself and my associates.*

PROCTOR, DENNIS VERNON, minister, consultant; b. Buffalo, N.Y., May 7, 1954; s. Emory Clement and Rose Thelma (Gray) P.; m. Deborah Diane Wilson, Oct. 6, 1979; children: Emory C. II, Dennis Vernon Jr. BA, Livingstone Coll., Salisbury, N.C., 1976; JD, Ohio State U., 1979; MA in Religion, Ashland (Ohio) Theol. Sem., 1984-86; postgrad., Western Res. Psychiat. Ctr., Northfield, Ohio, 1985-86. Sr. min., pastor St. James African Meth. Episcopal Zion Ch., Wilmington, N.C., 1979-86, St. Luke African Meth. Episcopal Zion Ch., Wilmington, 1986—; pres. Proctor, Clement & Co., Wilmington and Washington, 1986—; del. World Meth. Coun., Lake Junaleska, N.C., 1990-91, N.C. Coun. Chs., Raleigh, 1987—; appointee Employment Security Commn. Adv. Coun., Human Rels. Task Force, N.C., 1989. Fellow N.C. Inst. of Politics, 1989. Fellow Nat. Assn. Pastoral Counselors; mem. Masons, Phi Delta Phi. Home: 709 Church St Wilmington NC 28401

PROCTOR, SAMUEL DEWITT, clergyman; b. Norfolk, Va., July 13, 1921; s. Herbert Quincy and Gladys Velma (Hughes) P.; m. Bessie Louise Tate, Sept. 23, 1944; children—Herbert, Timothy, Samuel, Steven. A.B., Va. Union U., 1942; postgrad., U. Pa., 1944-45; B.D., Crozer Theol. Sem., 1945; student, Div. Sch., Yale U., 1945-46; Th.D., Alfred U., Beaver Coll., Boston U., 1950; hon. degree, Bucknell U., Davidson Coll., Ottawa U., Dillard U., Rider Coll., Stillman Coll., N.C. A&T State U., Fisk U., Howard U., U. R.I., Atlanta U., Wilberforce U., Va. Union U., St. Peters Coll., N.J., Coe Coll., Central Mich. U., U. Md., Bloomfield Coll., Bryant Coll., Morehouse Coll., N.C. State U., Southeastern Mass. U., Va. State U., Boston U., Bethune-Cookman Coll., Fairleigh Dickinson U., Colgate U., Columbia U., Mount Union Coll., Livingston Coll., Monmouth Coll., Jewish Theol. Sem., Johnson C. Smith U., Kean State Coll., U. D.C., Rutgers U., U. Louisville, Tuskegee U. Ordained to ministry Bapt. Ch., 1943; pastor Pond Street Ch., Providence, 1945-49; prof. religion and ethics Va. Union U., 1949-50; dean Sch. Religion, 1950-53, v.p., 1953-55, pres., 1955-60; pres. A&T State U. N.C., 1960-64; assoc. dir. Peace Corps, 1963-64; assoc. gen. sec. Nat. Council Chs., 1964-65; dir. N.E. region, later spl. asst. to nat. dir. OEO, 1965-66; pres. Inst. for Services to Edn., 1966-68; univ. dean spl. projects U. Wis., Madison, 1968-69; prof. edn. Grad. Sch. Edn., Rutgers U., New Brunswick, N.J., 1969-84; sr. minister Abyssinian Bapt. Ch., N.Y.C., 1972-89; vis. lectr. edn. Emory U., Atlanta, 1967-69; Anne Potter Wilson vis. prof. Vanderbilt U. Div. Sch., 1990-91; prof. United Theol. Sem., Dayton, Ohio, 1991—; Lyman Beecher lectr. Yale Div. Sch., 1990; mem. visitors com. Harvard Div. Sch., 1991—. Author: The Young Negro in America, 1960-1980, 1966, Sermons from the Black Pulpit, 1985, Preaching about Crises in the Community, 1988, My Moral Odyssey, 1989, How Shall they Hear?, 1992. Trustee United Negro Coll. Fund, Colgate Rochester/Crozer Theol. Sem., Middlebury Coll., Overseas Devel. Council, Vt. Christian Children's Fund. Recipient Outstanding Alumnus award Boston U., 1964; Distinguished Service award State U. N.Y. at, Plattsburgh, 1966. Mem. Kappa Alpha Psi, Sigma Pi Phi. Home: 63 MacAfee Road Somerset NJ 08873 *The good life is more than the abundance of things that we possess, or the applause that we may receive, pleasant and deserving as these may be. It is the satisfaction that one finds living in pursuit of and in obedience to the truth about God.*

PROFEIT-LEBLANC, LOUISE FRANCES, religious organization administrator; b. Whitehorse, Y.T., Can., Nov. 16, 1951; d. Richard Alfred and Dorothy Ellen (Profeit) Dickson; m. Robert Francis LeBlanc, Oct. 9, 1982; children: Ellenise, Krystal, Tanana. Nursing asst. diploma, Y.T.T.C., Can., 1971. Cert. nursing asst. Chmn. Nat. Spiritual Assembly of Bahá'ís of Can., Thornhill, Ont., Can., 1989—. Writer, co-producer videos. Bd. dirs. Friends of No. Storytelling Festival, 1988—. Short story named Best Short Story, CBC, 1986; video named Best Docu-Drama, Nat. Native Film Assn., 1989. Mem. Soc. Yukon Artists Native Ancestry (bd. dirs. 1989-91), Assn. Bahá'í Studies. Office: Can Bahá'í Community, 7200 Leslie St, Thornhill, ON Canada L3T 6L8

PROFFITT, THURBER DENNIS, III, minister, educator; b. Richmond Heights, Mo., Nov. 18, 1943; s. Thurber D. and Patricia Louise (Howard) P.; m. Janet Grace Ogburn, 1985. AA, Cerritos Coll., 1963; BA, Calif. State U., Fullerton, 1965, MA, 1972; postgrad., Inter-Mission Lang. Sch., Bolivia, 1969-70; MDiv, Fuller Theol. Sem., 1971; postgrad., Biola Coll., 1972; PhD, UCLA, 1988. Ordained to ministry Conservative Bapt. Assn., 1976. Missionary intern Andes Evang. Mission, Bolivia, 1969-70; youth pastor Latin Am. Meth. Ch., Pasadena, Calif., 1970-72; tchr. Inland Christian Sch., San Bernardino, Calif., 1972-73, Hazel Ave. Ch. Sch., 1973; with Missionary InterServe, India, 1976-77; tchr. Cherry Valley Brethren Sch., 1977-78, 1st Ch. of God Ch. Sch., 1978-79; instr. Ch. Heritage Coll., 1983-88, U. San Diego, 1988, San Diego Community Coll. Dist., 1989—, Point Loma Nazarene Coll., 1990—; instr. naval extension ctr. Chapman U., 1990—. Author: Tijuana, 1992. OAS fellow, 1984. Mem. Evang. Theol. Soc., Near East Archaeol. Soc., Assn. Borderlands Scholars, Pacific Coast Coun. on Latin Am. Studies (H.B. Herring award 1988). Home: 468 S Anza St El Cajon CA 92020

PROIETTI, GARY LEO, minister; b. Bklyn., Aug. 29, 1952; s. Elias Leo and Esther Rose (Bassetta) P.; m. Faith Ann Richardson, Nov. 30, 1974; children: Michael Ryan, Valerie Elise, Lauren Kay. BA, Northwest Coll., Kirkland, Wash., 1977; MDiv, Tex. Christian U., 1984; postgrad. studies, Boston U., 1985. Youth pastor Hempstead (N.Y.) Assmbly of God, 1973-74; minister of youth First Assembly of God, Elizabeth, N.J., 1974-76; assoc. minister First Christian Ch., Fort Worth, 1983-84; minister First Christian Ch., Lynn, Mass., 1984-87, Hiram (Ohio) Christian Ch., 1987—; carpenter various bldg. contractors, Ft. Worth; v.p. Lynn (Mass.) Coun. of Chs., 1985-87; pres. Greater Lynn Clergy Assn., 1986-87; trustee Ecumenical TV Channel, Canfield, Ohio, 1989—; sec./treas. District III Ministers' Fellowship, Akron, Ohio, 1990-91. Office: Hiram Christian Ch 6868 Wakefield Rd Hiram OH 44234

PROPES, MAJOR THOMAS, pastor; b. Nicholls, Ga., Oct. 1, 1957; s. Hoke Smith and Jewll (Davis) P.; m. Laquita Joy Perkins, July 10, 1976; children: Matthew Thomas, Summer Joy. BS, Lee Coll., 1980. Ordained to ministry, 1984. Evangelist Ch. of God, Tifton, Ga., 1980-84; dist. overseer Ch. of God, Hinesville, Ga., 1984—; chmn. state music bd. Ch. of God, 1984-87; pastor Live Oak Ch. of God, Hinesville, 1984—. Author: Healing for the Whole Man...Accomplished and Applied, 1983. Chaplain Liberty County Sheriff's Dept., Hinesville, 1984—; bd. dirs. Liberty County YMCA, 1989. Named one of Outstanding Young Men of Am., 1983-86. Mem. Liberty County Ministerial Assn. (treas. 1988), Ch. of God State Coun. Ga., Ch. of God Gen. Benevolence (bd. dirs. 1988). Republican. Avocations: dog training, racquetball, outdoor activities. Home: Rte 3 Box 95 Hinesville GA 31313 Office: Live Oak Ch of God Live Oak Ch of God Hinesville GA 31313

PROSSER, BRUCE REGINAL, JR. (BO PROSSER), minister; b. Milledgeville, Ga., Sept. 23, 1953; s. Bruce R. Prosser Sr. and Sarah (Dukes) Ellington; m. Gail Ford, June 26, 1976; children: Jamie Lynn, Katie Beth. BBA, Ga. Coll., 1975; MRE, So. Sem., 1979, MDiv, 1980; postgrad., U. Ga., 1988-89, N.C. State U., 1990. Ordained to ministry Hardwick Bapt. Ch., 1978. Assoc. pastor Shepherdville (Ky.) First Bapt. Ch., 1979-82, Cen. Bapt. Ch., Warner Robins, Ga., 1982-84; min. edn., adminstr. First Bapt. Ch., Roswell, Ga., 1984-89; assoc. pastor Forest Hills Bapt. Ch., Raleigh, N.C., 1989—; chaplain Phi Delta Theta Frat., Ga. Coll., 1974-75, North Roswell PTA, 1985-87; pres. Met. Religious Educators, Atlanta, 1987-88. Author: (with others) Single Adult Leadership, 1991; contbr. articles to profl. publs. Assoc. dir. Met. Enlargement Campaign, Atlanta, 1988-89; facilitator N.C. State Leadership Devel. in Creativity and Humor. Mem. So. Bapt. Religious Edn. Assn. Office: Forest Hills Bapt Ch 3110 Clark Ave Raleigh NC 27607 *We have been called by our Divine God to be vessels of his Love, Grace and Redemption. May your day be filled with rainbows and watermelons and blessed with His love and laughter.*

PROSSER, JOHN ROBERT, pastor; b. Kingston, N.Y., Sept. 23, 1959; s. Robert Vernon and Shirley Mae (Wiegert) P.; m. Ruth Ann Gingerich, Aug. 8, 1981. BS in Bible, Valley Forge Christian, 1984; MS in Counseling, Carolina Christian U., 1990; PhD in Counseling Psychology, Emmanuel Bapt. U., 1990. Ordained to ministry Evang. Ch. Alliance, 1985. Pastor Cyclone (Pa.) Community Ch., 1985-86; pre-sch. tchr., pastor Rochester (N.Y.) Christian Ch., 1986-88; supr. Open Door Mission, Rochester, 1988; asst. to pastor Assembly of God, East Aurora, N.Y., 1988-91; v.p. in charge of ministry Christian Fellowship, Inc., Kingston, 1978-80. Home: 1683 Two Rod Rd Marilla NY 14102

PROSSER, PETER EDWARD, priest, educator; b. Birminghan, Eng., Dec. 16, 1946; came to U.S., 1983; s. Norman Albert and Lily May (Taylor) P.; m. Elfriede Biermayer, May 2, 1970; children: Nathalie Lorraine, Andrea Gwynneth. Diploma in Theology, Ea. Coll., 1970; BA, Bethel Coll.; MDiv, U. Montreal, Que., Can., 1975, MA, 1978, PhD, 1989. Ordained to ministry Assemblies of God, 1973; ordained priest Anglican Ch., 1975. Pastor Assemblies of God, Montreal, 1970-75; asst. parish priest Anglican Ch., Montreal, 1975-77, parish priest, 1978-83; parish priest Episcopal Ch., Springfield, Mo., 1977-78; prof., extended univ. coord. Regent U. Grad. Sch., Virginia Beach, Va., 1983—; interim rector Episcopal Ch., Chesapeake, Va., 1984; asst. rector Galilee Ch., Virginia Beach, 1984—; organizing mem. Ministry to Prisons, Montreal, 1972. Co-author: Death and Dying, 1981; also articles. With RAF, 1962-67. U. Montreal fellow, 1980, 81. Mem. Soc. Pentecostal Studies, Am. Acad. Religion, Soc. Bibl. Lit., Ch. History Soc., Scandinavian Christian U., Rotary. Home: 3341 King Richard Ct Virginia Beach VA 23452 Office: Regent U Virginia Beach VA 23452

PROUDFOOT, WAYNE LEE, religion educator; b. Peterborough, N.H., Nov. 17, 1939; s. Raymond Stanley and Sarah Alice (King) P. BS, Yale U., 1961; BD, Harvard U., 1964, ThM, 1966, PhD, 1972. Asst. prof. philosophy of religion Andover-Newton Theol. Sch., 1969-70; asst. prof. religion Fordham U., N.Y.C., 1970-72; prof. Columbia U., N.Y.C., 1972—; bd. dirs. Fund for Theol. Edn. Kent fellow, 1965-68. Mem. Am. Acad. Religion, Soc. for Values in Higher Edn. Home: 315 W 106th St New York NY 10025 Office: Columbia U 506 Kent Hall New York NY 10028

PROULX, AMEDEE WILFRID, bishop; b. Sanford, Maine, Aug. 31, 1932. s. Francis Adelard and Rose Anna (Sevigny) Grad. B.A. St. Hyacinthe Sem., Quebec, S.T.L., St. Paul U. Sem., Ottawa, J.C.L., Cath. U., Washington. Ordained priest Roman Catholic Ch., 1958; ordained titular bishop of Clipia and aux. bishop of Portland, Maine, 1975—. Office: Diocese of Portland 510 Ocean Ave PO Box 6750 Portland ME 04101

PRUITT, JIMMY D., minister; b. Lubbock, Tex., Jan. 30, 1962; s. Jimmy D. P.; m. Cindy Hart, Oct. 2, 1981. BA, Howard Payne U., 1988; postgrad., Southwestern Bapt. Theol., Seminary, Ft. Worth, 1989—. Minister of youth First Bapt. Ch. Lake Brownwood (Tex.), 1987-89, East Side Bapt. Ch., Comanche, Tex., 1989—; assn. youth ministry coord. Comanche Bapt. Assn., 1989-91. Republican. Home: PO Box 1162 Blanket TX 76432 Office: East Side Baptist Church 207 FM 3381 Comanche TX 76442

PRUITT, TIMOTHY CAROL, minister; b. Beech Grove, Ind., June 12, 1956; s. Carol Merrill Roger and Martha Jean (French) P.; m. Rita Jo Helms, June 14, 1980. BS in Physics, Rose-Hulman Inst. Tech., 1978; Degree in Missions, Jackson Coll. Ministries, 1981; MBA, U. Indpls., 1990. Lic. to ministry United Pentecostal Ch., 1983. Assoc. missionary United Pentecostal Ch. Internat., Leeward Islands, 1982-83; tchr. coll. career Calvary Tabernacle, Indpls., 1983-85; electronics engr. Naval Avionics Ctr., Indpls., 1983—; mem. youth com. Calvary Tabernacle, Indpls., 1983-84, team min., 1984-85, chmn. home Bible study advt., 1984-85. Dir. Thanksgiving meal for needy, Calvary Tabernacle, Indpls., 1990—. Mem. Pi Mu Epsilon, Delta Mu Delta. Republican. Home: 8621 Greta Dr E Indianapolis IN 46239 Office: Naval Avionics Ctr B 463 6000 E 21st St Indianapolis IN 46219-2189

PRUITT, WILLIAM CHARLES, JR., minister, educator; b. Reed, Okla., May 31, 1926; s. William Charles and Helen Irene (Sanders) P.; m. Ellen Ruth Palmer, Aug. 25, 1953; children: Philip, Suzanne, John. BS, Stephen F. Austin State U., 1956, MEd, 1958; BD, MRE, Bapt. Missionary Assn. Theol. Sem., 1959, DRE, 1963; MLS, East Tex. State U., 1963. Ordained to ministry Bapt. Missionary Assn. Am., 1955. Pastor Mt. Pleasant Bapt. Ch., Bedias, Tex., 1955-60, Calvary Bapt. Ch., Commerce, Tex., 1960-63, Glenfawn Bapt. Ch., Laneville, Tex., 1963-66, New Hope Bapt. Ch., Winkler, Tex., 1966-70, Pleasant Ridge Bapt. Ch., Centerville, Tex., 1970-74, Redland Bapt. Ch., Centerville, 1970-79, Concord (Tex.) Bapt. Ch., 1983—; dir. libr. svc., instr. Bapt. Missionary Assn. Theol. Sem., 1958-67, prof. missions and religious edn., 1967-72; instr. psychology Jacksonville Coll., 1971-76; asst. dir. East Tex. Adult Edn. Coop., 1973—. Tex. wing chaplain CAP, 1971-77; exec. dir. Armed Forces Chaplaincy Com., Bapt. Missionary Assn. Am., Jacksonville, Tex., 1965—. Mem. Mil. Chaplains Assn. U.S., Tex. Assn. for Continuing Adult Edn., Lions. Home: Rte 8 Box 327 Jacksonville TX 75766 Office: PO Box 912 Jacksonville TX 75766

PRUITT, WILLIAM KEITH, minister; b. Colorado Springs, Colo., Apr. 18, 1964; s. William Joseph and Mary Agnes (Griffin) P.; m. Sonya Rachelle Adkison, Mar. 17, 1990. AA, Okaloosa-Walton Community Coll., 1985; BS in Mgmt., U. West Fla., 1987; MDiv, New Orleans Bapt. Theol. Sem., 1989. Lic. to ministry So. Bapt. Conv., 1987; ordained, 1990. Min. youth Shalimar (Fla.) Bapt. Ch., 1988; assoc. pastor youth Warrington Bapt. Ch., Pensacola, Fla., 1989—; mem. com. Bapt. Campus Ministry, Pensacola, 1991—. Home: 114 Country Rd Pensacola FL 32507 Office: Warrington Bapt Ch 103 W Winthrop Ave Pensacola FL 32507 *If we would be more concerned with our love for others than concerned with their violations of our love then we could be not who others want us to be, but rather who we are.*

PRUTER, KARL HUGO, bishop; b. Poughkeepsie, N.Y., July 3, 1920; s. William Karl and Katherine (Rehling) P.; m. Nancy Lee Taylor, 1943; children: Hugo Jr., Robert, Karl, Stephen, Maurice, Katherine, Nancy Goodman. B.A., Northeastern U., 1943; M.Div., Lutheran Theol. Sem., Phila., 1945; M.A. in Edn., Roosevelt U., 1963; M.A. in History, Boston U., 1968. Guest lectr. Landerziehungsheim, Stein, West Germany, 1964-65; ordained priest Christ Catholic Ch., 1965; pastor Ch. of the Transfiguration, Boston, 1965-70; suffragan bishop Christ Cath. Ch. Author: The Theology of Congregationalism, 1953, The Teachings of the Great Mystics, 1969, A History of the Old Catholic Church, 1973, The People of God, 1975, The Jewish Christians in the United States, 1985. Address: Cathedral Ch Prince of Peace Highlandville MO 65669

PRYFOGLE, MARION LEE, minister; b. South Gate, Calif., Oct. 4, 1944; s. William L. and Mary E. (Campbell) P.; m. Pamela Dee Parson, Dec. 28, 1963; children: Michael, Mark, Daniel, Andrew, Mary. BA, Calif. State U., Dominguez Hills, 1973; MDiv, Golden Gate Bapt. Sem., Mill Valley, Calif., 1979. Ordained to ministry So. Bapt. Conv., deacon, 1970, minister, 1977. Deacon, dir. edn. 1st Bapt. Ch., Signal Hill, Calif., 1970-75; min. edn. and youth 1st Bapt. Ch., Rodeo, Calif., 1975-76; pastor 1st Bapt. Ch., San Leandro, Calif., 1977—; sales rep. L.L. Sams & Sons, Waco, Tex., 1986—; instr. extension program Golden Gate Bapt. Sem., Oakland, Calif., 1983-90; moderator East Bay Bapt. Assn., Oakland, 1984-86. Bd. dirs. Washington Manor Homeowners, San Leandro, 1990—; candidate for San Leandro City Coun. and San Lorenzo Sch. Bd., 1990. With U.S. Army, 1963-66. Scholar Art Ctr. Sch., L.A., 1962, 3d Armored Div., 1966. Mem. Nat. Assn. Evangs. Republican. Home: 1286 Brown Ct San Leandro CA 94579 Office: 1st Bapt Ch 14797 Farnsworth St San Leandro CA 94579

PRYOR, FRED HOWARD, small business owner; b. Excelsior Springs, Mo., Feb. 22, 1934; s. Charlie Arthur and Mary Malissa (Tinkle) P.; m. Shirley Jean Pryor, Dec. 16, 1955; children: Sherilyn Jean Pryor Coulter, Rebecca Ann Pryor Phillips. BA, William Jewell Coll.; BTh, So. Bapt. Theol. Sem.; MA, U. Mo. Pastor So. Bapt. Conv., Kansas City, Mo., 1960-69; tchr. Dale Carnegie Courses, Kansas City, Mo., 1970—; pres. Fred Pryor & Assocs., Kansas City, Mo., 1970-75, Fred Pryor Seminars, Kansas City, Mo., 1975—. Bd. dirs. Baptist Health Systems, Kansas City, 1984—. Recipient Achievement award, William Jewell Coll., 1980. Mem. Nat. Speaker Assn. Office: 2000 Johnson Dr Shawnee Mission KS 66205

PRYSTOWSKY, SEYMOUR, rabbi; b. N.Y.C., July 10, 1936; s. David and Florence (Rebowsky) P.; children: Elan H., Donna L. BA, Hunter Coll., 1957; B in Hebrew Letters, MA, Hebrew Union Coll.-Jewish Inst. Religion, N.Y., 1961; DD (hon.), Hebrew Union Coll.-Jewish Inst. Religion, 1986; PhD, Dropsie Coll., 1973. Ordained rabbi, 1961; cert. family therapy. Chaplain U.S. Army, Ft. Lewis, Wash., 1961-63; rabbi Congregation Or Ami, Lafayette Hill, Pa., 1963—. Mem. Am. Family Therapy Assn., Cen. Conf. Am. Rabbi. Office: Congregation Or Ami 708 Ridge Pike Lafayette Hill PA 19444

PRZYBILLA, SISTER CARLA, religious organization administrator; b. Buckman, Minn., July 14, 1935; d. Charles and Teresa (Gangl) Przybilla. BA, Coll. St. Catherine, St. Paul, 1959; PhD, Cath. U. Am., 1984. Joined Franciscan Sisters, Roman Cath. Ch., 1953. Dir. novice and formation Franciscan Sisters, Little Falls, Minn., 1968-72, v.p., 1970-76, gen. superior, 1984-88; assoc. dir. New Life Ctr., The Plains, Va., 1989—; exec. dir Nat. Religious Formation Conf., 1976-80; prof. theology and ministry Cath. U. Am., Washington Theol. Union; mem. Union Internat. Superiors, Rome, 1984-88; chairperson bd. for hosps. and nursing homes Franciscan Sisters Health Care. Writer, editor newsletters Franciscan Sisters. Chairperson bd. Parents Without Ptnrs. and Day Activities for Mentally Handicapped, Morrison County, Minn., 1972-76; mem. numerous Franciscan bds. on mission. Mem. Cath. Theol. Soc. Am., Am. Dietetic Assn. (pres. Minn. chpt. 1963-64, Romuald award), Pi Gamma Mu. Home: 206 Maple St #2 PO Box 1876 Middleburg VA 22117 Office: New Life Ctr PO Box 467 The Plains VA 22171

PUCCETTI, PATRICIA IRENE, religious and cultural organization administrator; b. Torrance, Calif., Nov. 9, 1956; d. Victor Francis and Helen Grace (Wise) P. BA in Liberal Arts, Thomas Aquinas Coll., 1978; MA in Religious Edn., St. John's U., 1983. Editor, corp. sec. Caths. United for the Faith, New Rochelle, N.Y., 1982-90, bd. dirs.; adminstrv. coord. Homeland Found., N.Y.C., 1990—; tchr., cons. Narnia Clubs, Manhattan, N.Y., 1983—; tutor Newman Tutorial Program, So. Conn., 1985-86. Editor Faith and Life series, 24 vols., 1984-87, Lay witness, 1986-90; producer religious art calendar, 1987—. Mem. N.Y. Cath. Forum (founding bd. dirs. 1983—), Fellowship of Cath. Scholars. Avocations: calligraphy, clothing design, dance. Home: 74 Warren St New Rochelle NY 10801 Office: Homeland Found 230 Park Ave # 1528 New York NY 10169

PUCHY, JAMES JOHN, chaplain; b. Elizabeth, N.J., Nov. 25, 1956; s. Julius John and Gloria Annette (Lasky) P.; m. Rebecca Lynn Genshaw, May 24, 1980. BA in Econs./English, Rutgers Univ., 1978; MS in Systems Mgmt., Univ. So. Calif., 1981; MDiv in Theology, Alliance Theol. Seminary, N.Y.C., 1988; postgrad., U. So. Calif., 1991—. Ordained to ministry Christian and Missionary Alliance, 1988. Asst. pastor New City (N.Y.) Alliance Ch., 1986-88; commd. 2d lt. U.S. Army, 1978, advanced through grades to capt., 1982; ranger chaplain, 1st Batt. 75th Ranger Regiment U.S. Army, Hunter Army Air Field, Ga., 1988-91; dep. group chaplain, 45th Support Group U.S. Army, Schofield Barracks, Hawaii, 1991—; pastor Hunter Army Air Field Chapel, 1988-91; founding pastor Helemano Community Chapel, Helemano Mil. Reservation, Hawaii, 1991. Home: 12 A Circle Dr Wahiawa HI 96786 Office: HHC 45th Support Group Schofield Barracks HI 96857 *If you invest in people your return will be immeasurably great and will last for eternity.*

PUDAITE, ROCHUNGA, minister, publisher; b. Senvon, India, Dec. 4, 1928; s. Chawnga Pudaite; m. Lalrimawi Pakhuongte, Jan. 1, 1958; children: Paul, John, Mary. Student, St. Paul's Coll., 1949-52, Wheaton (Ill.) Coll., 1955-58; BA, Allahabad (India) U., 1954; MA, No. Ill. U., 1961; JD, Malone Coll., Canton, Ohio, 1977. Ordained to ministry Evangelical Free Ch., 1959. Exec. dir. Indo-Burma Pioneer Mission, 1958-67; pres. Partnership Mission Inc., Wheaton, 1968-72; moderator Evang. Free Ch. of India, 1972—; pres. Bibles for the World, Inc., Wheaton, 1973—; speaker in field. Author: Hmar-English Grammar, 1958, The Education of the Hmar People, 1961, My Billion Bible Dream, 1982, The Dime That Lasted Forever, 1985, The Book that Set My People Free, 1986, The Greatest Book Ever Written, 1989; editor: Kristien, 1957-63, Khawnvar, 1970-72, Bibles For The World News, 1973. Mem. Evang. Press Assn., Internat. Platform Assn. Lodge: Rotary. translated Bible into Hmar tribal language of India. Home: 1555 E Forest Ave Wheaton IL 60189-0805 Home: Box 805 Wheaton IL 60189

PUESAN KHOURY, CESAR A., minister, Spanish language coordinator, educator; b. Santo Domingo, Dominican Republic, June 3, 1938; s. César C. Puesán and Aurora Khoury; m. Nercy C. Frómeta, Oct. 15, 1958; children: César Jr., Nilda, Myrna A. AA in Bus., Colegio Las Antillas, Cuba, 1959; BBA, Antillian Coll., P.R., 1969; MBA, Inter-Am. U., P.R., 1975; MA in Edn., Loma Linda U., 1977, EdS, 1977, EdD, 1982. Pres. Dominican Coll., Santo Domingo, 1960-65; sec., treas. Dominican Conf., Dominican Republic, 1965-69; auditor Antillian Union, Puerto Rico, 1970-74; Spanish coordinator Wis. Conf. Seventh Day Adventist Ch., Milw., 1975—; also bd. dirs. Wis. Conf. Seventh Day Adventist Ch. Bd. dirs. Wis. Acad., Columbus, 1976—; bd. dirs. Spanish Seventh Day Adventist Ch., Milw., 1977—. Mem. Nat. Soc. Pub. Accts., Nat. Assn. Accts. Avocation: music. Home: 2301 W Vogel Ave Milwaukee WI 53221 Office: Wis Conf SDA 2324 S 24th St Milwaukee WI 53221

PUETT, TERRY LEE, pastor; b. Gary, Ind., Dec. 5, 1943; s. Ralph E. and Leone I. (Hatton) P.; m. Linda Lee Tuinstra, Feb. 6, 1965; children: Stephen, Matthew, Phillip, Andrew. Student, Grand Rapids Bible Coll., 1968; ThM, Internat. Bible Sem., Plymouth, Fla., 1981, ThD, 1987; DD (hon.), Bethany Bible Sem., Dothan, Ala., 1982. Ordained to ministry Ind. Fundamental Chs. Am., 1972. Pastor Allen (Mich.) Bapt. Ch., 1966-68; sr. pastor Goodells (Mich.) Bible Ch., 1968-72, Dreckerville (Mich.) Bible Ch., 1972-76, Lake Ctr. Bible Ch., Portage, Mich., 1976—. Author: So You've Become a Christian, 1973, Basic Bible Doctrine, 1976, Bible Study Manual, 1978, A Study of Deacons, 1980. Home: 225 Larkspur Portage MI 49002 Office: Lake Ctr Bible Ch 805 E Osterhout Portage MI 49002

PUFFE, PAUL, minister; b. Crookston, Minn., May 22, 1953; s. Esthel Royal and Elaine Amelia (Radi) P.; m. Eleanor Ann Billmeyer, Dec., 1974; children: P. Alexander, Daniel, Timothy. BS, MIT, 1975; MDiv, Concordia Seminary, St. Louis, 1979; MA, U. Mich., 1984. Ordained to ministry Luth. Ch.-Mo. Synod, 1979. Pastor St. Thomas Luth. Ch., Ann Arbor, Mich., 1979-84; asst. prof. Concordia Luth. Coll., Austin, Tex., 1984—, dir. preseminary program, 1985—, chmn. religion div., 1985-87. Mem. Soc. Bibl. Lit. Office: Concordia Luth Coll 3400 N I35 Austin TX 78705

PUGH, JESSIE TRUMAN, minister; b. Noble, La., Oct. 28, 1923; s. Jessie Trulonzer and Lucy (Sanderson) P.; m. Bessie Byrl Halbrooks, Aug. 10, 1944; children: James Terry, Datha Jo, Nathanael Brent. BTh, Tex. Bible Coll., 1971; DD, Berean Christian Coll., 1973; D Christian Lit., Christian Life Coll., 1985. Ordained to ministry United Pentecostal Ch. Internat. Youth sec. Tex. Dist., 1940, pres. youth camps, 1954; instr. Tex. Bible Coll., Houston, 1962-67; pastor various chs., 1944-67; gen. dir. home missions U.S. and Can., 1967-74; pastor 1st Pentecostal Ch., Odessa, Tex., 1974—; pres. Christian Life Coll., Stockton, Calif., 1980-82; dist. supt. Tex. dist. United Pentecostal Ch., 1983—; speaker camp meetings and convs.; overseas lectr. Contbr. articles to profl. jours. Home: 1500 Tangelwood St Odessa TX 79760 *I am increasingly impressed that the real issues of life are moral. All racial and physical maladies have roots in neglected moral and spiritual principles. Thus to uphold and propagate such is to have lived well.*

PUGH, JOHN E., clergyman; b. Norfolk, Va., Mar. 16, 1928; s. Charles Shafter Pugh and Mary (Musselman) Nelson; m. Jerre Sharp, July 31, 1976; children: John Mark, Lydia Elizabeth, Beth Marie Jacobson. BSBA, Am. U., 1984; MDiv, Union Theol. Sem., 1957. Ordained to ministry, Meth. ch. Pastor Meth. Ch., Libby, Mont., 1957-61; assoc. pastor 1st Meth. Ch., Great Falls, Mont., 1961-62; pastor Meth. Ch., Shelby, Mont., 1962-68; sr. pastor United Meth. Larger Parish, Butte, Mont., 1968-72; pastor United Meth. Ch., Havre, Mont., 1972-78, Worland, Wyo., 1978-=81; organizing pastor Hope United Meth. Ch., Billings, Mont., 1981-87; pastor United Meth. Ch., Laurel, Mont., 1987—; chmn. Conf. of Evangelism, Mont., 1954-56, Conf. Com. for Ch. Extension, Mont. and Wyo., 1985-87. Home: PO Box 481 Laurel MT 59044 Office: Laurel United Meth Ch 701 3d Ave Laurel MT 59044

PULICE, DEANO SALVATORE, minister; b. Uniontown, Pa., Feb. 11, 1957; s. Sam and Beatrice (Owen) P.; m. Darlene Ann Sampey, Aug. 15, 1981; children: Deanna, Christopher, Janelle. MusB, Roberts Wesleyan Coll., 1986. Ordained to ministry Free Meth. Ch. N.Am. as elder, 1991. Assoc. staff mem. Fay West Youth for Christ, Uniontown, Pa., 1978-79; asst. pastor Brockport (N.Y.) Free Meth. Ch., 1984-86; founding pastor Bridgeport (W.Va.) Free Meth. Ch., 1986-89; sr. pastor Monacrest Free Meth. Ch., Monaca, Pa., 1989—; sec., bd. adminstrn. W.Va. Conf., Morgantown, 1987-89; bd. dirs. evangelism Pitts. Conf., 1989—. Home: 1000 Elm St Monaca PA 15061 Office: Monacrest Free Meth Ch Elmire & Walnut St Monaca PA 15061

PULLEY, TRISH BASS, religion educator; b. Nashville, June 13, 1962; d. George Harold and Lorena Yates (Johnson) Bass; m. Daniel Russell Pulley III, Aug. 22, 1987. AS in Criminal Justice, BA in Sociology, Tenn. Tech. U., Cookeville, 1984; MA in Christian Edn., Scarritt Grad. Sch., Nashville, 1987. Min. youth Brentwood (Tenn.) United Meth. Ch., 1986-87; dir. day camp ministry Nat. Christian Mission Program, Tenn. Outreach Project, Inc., Nashville, 1987-88, assoc. dir. leadership and tng. devel., 1988-89, assoc. exec. dir. overall daily mgmt., also dir. svc. project, dir. day camp, 1989—; mem. staff parish com. bd. higher edn. and ministry Forest Hills United Meth. Ch., Brentwood, 1990—; leader seminars, youth retreats, 1989—. Tchr. adult Sunday sch. class The Seekers, Forest Hills United Meth. Ch., 1989—. Named Outstanding Young Religious Leader, Jaycess, 1985. Mem. Christian Camping Internat., Christian Educators Fellowship (pres. 1985-86), United Meth. Women, Zeta Tau Alpha. Home: 3037 High Rigger Dr Nashville TN 37217 Office: Mountain TOP Inc 2704 12th Ave S Nashville TN 37204

PULLIAM, MARTINA ANNE, minister; b. Santa Barbara, Calif., Nov. 7; d. Julio Jimenez Vasquez and Mildred (Wilson) Ford; m. Michael Cassiba, May 19, 1978 (div. Feb. 1982); m. Roy Vester Pulliam, Oct. 5, 1984. Student, Paris Jr. Coll., 1987-88. Asst. chaplain Choctaw County Jail, Hugo, Okla., 1991; disc jockey min. Keor Christian Radio, Atoka, Okla., 1991. Tutor Laubach Lit. Action, Hugo, 1990-91. Democrat. Home: 214 E Rosewood St Hugo OK 74743

PULLIAM, RUSSELL BLEECKER, columnist, editorial writer, elder; b. Indpls., Sept. 20, 1949; s. Eugene S. and Jane B. Pulliam; m. Ruth Eichling, Nov. 26, 1977; children: Christine, Daniel, John, Sarah, David. BA, Williams Coll., 1971. Reporter, editor AP, N.Y.C. and Albany, N.Y., 1971-76; editorial writer, columnist Indpls. News, 1978-; deacon Second Reformed Presbyn. Ch., Indpls., 1983-89, elder, 1989—. Contbr. articles to religious jours. Bd. dirs. Community Outreach Ctr., Noble Ctrs. Marion County Assn. for the Mentally Retarded, Indpls., 1984—; participant Stanley K. Lacey Leadership Series, 1980—; mem. adv. bd. Youth as Resources. Recipient Casper award Community Svc. Coun., 1980, 81, 82, 86; 1st place editorial writing Hoosier State Press Assn., 1979, 80, 3d place editorial writing UPI, 1983, 2d and 3d place, 1986; named Sagamore of the Wabash Gov. of Ind., 1980. Mem. Prison Fellowship, Ind. Assn. for Home Educators, Indpls. C. of C., Soc. Profl. Journalists (treas. Ind. chpt. 1982—, found. bd. 1991—, 2d place editorials and columns 1984, 85, hon. mention editorials 1988, 3d place columns 1989), Nat. Conf. Editorial Writers. Home: 1241 N New Jersey Ave Indianapolis IN 46202 Office: Indpls News 307 N Pennsylvania St Indianapolis IN 46204

PULLIAM, STANLEY RUSSELL, minister; b. Clovis, N.Mex., June 17, 1952; s. Howard Mervin and Avice Lovinia (Clayton) P.; m. JoAnn Gilbert, May 27, 1974; children: Gayla Joy, Christa Noel, Aaron Michael. BA, Ea. Nazarene Coll., 1975; MS, U. Ga., 1979, postgrad., 1979-84. Asst. pastor Wollaston Ch. of the Nazarene, Quincy, Mass., 1975-77; assoc. pastor Athens (Ga.) Ch. of the Nazarene, 1979-83; exec. dir., chmn. WORD Teaching and Outreach Ministries of Athens, 1983—; bd. dirs. Athens Chap. Full Gospel Bus. Men, 1985-89; sec. Wesleyan Holiness Charismatic Fellowship, 1983—. Pub., editor: (newsletter) Wesleyan Holiness Charismatic Fellowship, 1983—. Precinct chmn. Clarke County (Ga.) Rep. Orgn., 4th Ward, 1987-91, precinct rep. Dist. 5C, 1991—; area vice-chmn. Ga. 10th Congl.. Dist. Rep. Orgn., 1989-91; mem. State Rep. Com., 1991—. Mem. So. Soc. for Philosophy and Psychology, Phi Delta Lambda. Republican. Home: 348 Knottingham Dr Athens GA 30601 Office: WORD Teaching and Outreach Ministries PO Box 454 Athens GA 30601 *The ultimate essence of life is this: that I come to the place where I am clearly hearing what God is saying today, and then I yield myself completely to become fully obedient to it.*

PULSE, JEFFREY HOWARD, minister; b. Storm Lake, Iowa, Mar. 20, 1958; s. Howard Leslie and Joann Celeste (Schoening) P.; m. Sara Louise Bunz, Aug. 10, 1985; children: Nathaniel David, Jonathan Christian. BS in Elem. Edn., Concordia Coll., 1980; MDiv, Concordia Theol. Sem., 1984, STM, 1991. Minister St. John's Luth. Ch., Burt, Iowa, 1985—; spiritual advisor Kossuth Luths. for Life, Algona, Iowa, 1988—; bd. govs. Camp Okoboji, Milford, Iowa, 1987—. Author: (with others) Compendium of Hebrew Morphology, 1982. Chmn. Pub. Sch. Phase III Com., Burt, 1987—. Mem. Iowa Dist. Luth. Ch.-MS (chmn. youth bd., bd. dirs. Ft. Dodge, Iowa chpt. 1988—), Ducks Unltd. (com. Algona chpt. 1988—), Lions (pres. Burt chpt. 1990-91). Republican. Home: 502 Walnut Burt IA 50522 Office: St Johns Luth Ch 109 Maple Burt IA 50522

PUMP, PHILLIP MYRON, religion educator; b. Marion, Ohio, Mar. 14, 1947; s. Franklin Edward and Lily Arlene (Paddock) P.; m. Mercy Ann Brookshire, Dec. 12, 1969; 1 child, David Matthew. BA, Calif. State U., Northridge, 1971; MA, Calif. Grad. Sch. Theology, 1986. Tchr. Van Nuys (Calif.) Bapt. Day Sch., 1974-80, adminstr., 1980-88; Christian day sch. assn. dir. L.A. Bapt. City Mission Soc., Sepulueda, Calif., 1988-91; dir. Christian edn. The Ch. on the Way, Van Nuys, Calif., 1991—; bd. dirs. White Oak Counseling Ctr., Granada Hills, Calif., 1989—. Republican. Home: 22912 Banyan Pl # 194 Saugus CA 91350 Office: The Ch on the Way 14800 Sherman Way Van Nuys CA 91405

PUMPHREY, ROGER MACK, minister; b. Milw., Aug. 25, 1947; s. Andrew and Daisy (Smith) P.; m. Evelyn Greer, June 14, 1980; children: Khyana, Jamil. AA, BA, Concordia Coll., River Forest, Ill., 1972; MEd, Faith Bapt. Sem., 1977; D Ministry in Pastoral Counseling, Berean Sem., 1981; MA in Christian Counseling, Liberty U., 1991. Ordained to ministry Anglican Rite Synod, Holy Cath. Ch. in Ams. Asst. chaplain Milw. Luth. Hosp., 1974-75; pastor St. Martin's Chapel, Milw., 1975—; pres. St. Martin's Sem., Milw., 1975—; tchr. Milw. Pub. Schs., 1977—; chaplain Milw. Psychiat. Hosp., 1990—. Co-author: Manual for Ministry, 1986; contbr. Black Family mag., 1983, Community Jour., 1987. Mem. Gov.'s Task Force, 1984. With USAF, 1966. Office: St Martin's Sem 412 E Burligh St Milwaukee WI 53206

PUOPOLO, ROCCO NICHOLAS, priest; b. Norwood, Mass., Dec. 15, 1949; s. Rocco A. and Angelina C. (Marinelli) P. BA in Theology, St. Francis De Sales, 1972; MDiv, Cath. Theol. Union, 1977. Ordained priest Roman Cath. Ch., 1977. Tchr. Kolenten Secondary Sch., Sierra Leone, West Africa, 1973-74; assoc. pastor Kabala Cath. Mission, Makeni Diocese, Sierra Leone, West Africa, 1978-80; edn. sec. Diocese of Makeni, Freetown, Sierra Leone, West Africa, 1980-84; nat. chaplain Young Christian Students, Sierra Leone, West Africa, 1982-84; chaplain Fourah Bay Coll., Sierra Leone, West Africa, 1982-84; formation dir. Xaverian Missionaries, Franklin, Wis., 1985—; pres., bd. dirs. Fedn. of Returned Overseas Missionaries, Detroit, 1990-91; vice provincial Xaverian Missionary Fathers, Wayne, N.J., 1987—; mem. Midwest Mission Task Force, Milw., 1984—. Home and Office: 6838 S 51st St Franklin WI 53132

PURCELL, JOHN M., minister, teacher; b. New Orleans, Feb. 2, 1939; s. Malcolm Lee and Mary Inez (Ratchford) P.; m. Juanita Quinn, June 10, 1962; children: Paul M., Melanie C. BA, Austin Coll., 1961; MDiv, Austin Presbyn. Theol. Sem., 1965. Cert. secondary schs. tchr. Assoc. pastor First Presbyn. Ch., El Dorado, Ark., 1965-66; campus minister Lamar U., Beaumont, Tex., 1970-74; pastor Robbins Meml. Presbyn. Ch., Beaumont, 1966-74; pastor First Presbyn. Ch., Commerce, Tex., 1974-79, Denison, Tex., 1979-90; pastor Lakeview Presbyn. Ch., New Orleans, 1990—; mem. Permanent Judicial Com. Presbyn. Ch. (USA), Louisville, 1983-89. Bd. dirs. Vol. Action Ctr. Greenville, Tex., 1976-79, Home Hospice of Grayson County, Sherman, Tex., 1981-90, Denison (Tex.) Helping Hands, 1984-90. Recipient Appreciation award, Texoma Mental Health and Mental Retardation Bd., Denison, Tex., 1985, Home Hospice, Sherman, Tex., 1989. Mem. Rotary Club (bd. dirs. Denison, Tex. 1984-90). Avocations: apiarist, skiing. Home: 6312 Perlita New Orleans LA 70122 Office: Lakeview Presbyn Ch 5914 Canal Blvd New Orleans LA 70124

PURCHASE, THOMAS JOSEPH, minister; b. Rochester, N.Y., July 28, 1949; s. Frederick Joseph and Jean T. (Mahaney) P.; m. V. Julianne Misja, Nov. 6, 1976; children: Timothy, Shaun. BA, Siena Coll., Loudonville, N.Y., 1971; MS, Rochester Inst. Tech., 1976; M in Div., Nazarene Theol. Sem., 1982. Ordained to ministry Nazarene Ch., 1984. Audio-visual aide Hoover Dr. Jr. High Sch., Rochester, 1971-72; TV engrng. asst. Rochester Inst. Tech., 1972-73; salesman J.B. Hunter, Rochester, 1972-75; curriculum materials specialist Nat. Tech. Inst. for the Deaf, Rochester, 1975-79; pastor Ch. of the Nazarene, Waterville, Vt., 1982-91, Keene, N.H., 1991—. Bd. dirs. Draft Info. Ctr. Rochester Area, 1971-73; sec. Blemheim Neighborhood Assn., Kansas City, Mo., 1981-82; 2d v.p. Ithiel Falls camp meeting, Johnson, Vt., 1983-91; mem. adv. bd. Lamoille County Interagy. Network for Kids, 1988-91. Mem. Wesleyan Theol. Soc. Home: 57 Maple Keene NH 03431 Office: 55 Maple Keene NH 03431 *The most productive use of my time and energy is telling people about Jesus Christ and the radical change He performs in a life fully yielded to Him.*

PURDY, CHARLES MICHAEL, minister; b. Rome, Ga., May 23, 1951; s. Charles Edward and Oline Allie (McCord) P.; m. Deborah Anita Allgood, Oct. 8, 1952; children: Michael Shane, Isaac Benjamin, Stephen Jeremy. BA in Art Edn., Shorter Coll., 1974; BA in Bible Studies, Criswell Bible Coll., 1977; postgrad., New Orleans Bapt. Sem., 1983-86. Tchr. art Adairsville (Ga.) High Sch., 1974-75; comml. artist Wilson Engraving, Dallas, 1975-76; computer operator 1st Nat. Bank, Dallas, 1976; courier Thompson, Simmons, Knight & Bullion, Dallas, 1976-77; assoc. pastor youth Point View Bapt. Ch., Combine, Tex., 1976-77; assoc. pastor edn. First Bapt. Ch. Kennesaw, Ga., 1977-79; minister youth activities First Bapt. Ch. Center Point, Birmingham, Ala., 1979-80; pastor Calvary Bapt., Wilburton, Okla., 1980-83, Spring Pl. Bapt., Chatsworth, Ga., 1983-86; assoc. pastor youth Abilene Bapt. Ch., Augusta, Ga., 1986—; mission speaker Bapt., Haiti, 1978; camp tchr., counselor Kiamichi Bapt. Assembly, Okla., 1980-82; assoc. outreach leader San Bois Assn., Okla., 1981-82. Recipient Certification Evang. Dept. Home Mission Bd., 1984; named one of Outstanding Young Men in Am., 1985; listed in Official Register Outstanding Young Am. So. Bapt. Conv., 1986. Republican. Avocations: art, football, softball, basketball, tennis, golf. Home: 334 Forest Ct Martinez GA 30907 Office: Abilene Bapt Ch 3917 Washington Rd Martinez GA 30907

PURINTON, BARBARA DE BONCOEUR ALLEN, minister; b. Mineola, N.Y., July 12, 1949; d. Charles Maxwell and Barbara (Wiltbank) Allen; m. Charles Murray Purinton, Jr., July 29, 1978; children: Malcolm Forrest, Pamela Eleanor, Caitlin Allen. BA, Hamilton Coll., 1971; MDiv cum laude, Andover-Newton Theol. Sem., 1978; D Ministry, Ea. Bapt. Theol. Sem., Phila., 1991. Ordained to ministry United Ch. of Christ, 1978. Dir. religious edn. Newton Highlands (Mass.) United Ch. of Christ, 1976-78; co-pastor 2d Congl. Ch., Jeffersonville, Vt., 1978-83; assoc. pastor Danville (Vt.) Congl. Ch., North Danville Bapt. Ch., 1983-85; pastor chs., Danville, North Danville, 1986-89, Richmond (Vt.) Congl. United Ch. of Christ, 1989—. Vol. Richmond Rescue. Fellow Roothbert Fund Inc., 1974-78, 90; Teagle grantee Ea. Bapt. Sem., 1989-90. Home: PO Box 302 Richmond VT 05477 Office: Richmond Congl Ch of Christ Bridge St PO Box 302 Richmond VT 05477

PURKISER, WESTLAKE TAYLOR, emeritus theology educator, author, editor; b. Oakland, Calif., Apr. 28, 1910; s. Jacob W. and May F. (Naismith) P.; m. Arvilla M. Butler, July 24, 1930; children: Joyce Mae (dec.), Joanne Lois, Sharon Lee. A.B., Pasadena Coll., 1930; A.M., U. So. Calif., 1939, Ph.D., 1948. Ordained to ministry Ch. of the Nazarene, 1932; pastor Riverside, Calif., 1930-34, Bellflower, 1934-35, Corning, 1935-37; prof. philosophy Pasadena Coll., 1937-43, dean, 1943-45, v.p., 1945-49, pres., 1949-57; prof. English Bible Nazarene Theol. Sem., 1957-60; editor Herald of Holiness, 1960-75; prof. Bibl. theology Point Loma Nazarene Coll., San Diego, 1975-77; prof. emeritus Point Loma Coll., San Diego, 1977—. Author: Know Your Old Testament, 1947, Some Concepts of the Datum in American Realism (abstract), 1948, Conflicting Concepts of Holiness, 1953; Editor: Exploring the Old Testament, 1956, Security: The False and the True, 1956, Beliefs that Matter Most, 1959, Adventures in Truth, 1960, Exploring Our Christian Faith, 1960, Sanctification and Its Synonyms, 1961, The Message of Evangelism, 1963, Spiritual Gifts: The Charismatic Revival, 1964, Search the Scriptures: First and Second Samuel, 1965, Give Me an Answer, 1968, The New Testament Image of the Ministry, 1969, When You Get to the End of Yourself, 1970, Search the Scriptures: Genesis, 1970, Search the Scriptures: Psalms, 1970, Interpreting Christian Holiness, 1971, Adventures in Bible Doctrine, 1971, The Paradox of Prayer, 1974, Our Wonderful World, 1974, Beacon Bible Expositions: Hebrews, James and Peter, 1974, God's Spirit in Today's World, 1974, Gifts of the Spirit, 1975, God, Man, and Salvation, 1977, Exploring Christian Holiness, vol. 1: The Biblical Foundations, 1983, Called into Holiness: The Second Twenty-five Years, 1983, These Earthen Vessels, 1985, The Lordship of Jesus: A Study in Christian Discipleship, 1986, A Primer on Prayer, 1987. Mem. Phi Beta Kappa, Pi Epsilon Theta, Phi Delta Lambda, Kappa Phi Kappa. Address: 12839 Sutter Creek Volcano Rd PO Box 336 Sutter Creek CA 95685

PURSCH, SUSAN MARIE, religious organization administrator; b. Mpls., Jan. 8, 1948; d. Delroy Paridan and Janice Marie (Johnson) P.; m. Russell Motter Long, Apr. 25, 1981; stepchildren—Christopher, Jonathan. A.A., Waldorf Coll., 1968; B.A., Augsburg Coll., Mpls., 1970. Keypunch and computer operator Fairview Hosp., Mpls., 1968-70; youth and Christian edn. dir. 1st Lutheran Ch., Litchfield, Minn., 1970-73; dir. Christian edn. Gloria Dei Lutheran Ch., Huntingdon Valley, Pa., 1973-74; sec. for youth Global Hunger Concers, Div. for Parish Services Luth. Ch. in Am., Phila., 1974—. Mem. Nat. Assn. Female Execs. Democrat. Lutheran. Avocations: Downhill skiing; travel. Home: 387 E Gowen Ave Philadelphia PA 19119 Office: Div Parish Services 2900 Queen Ln Philadelphia PA 19129

PURSELL, CLEO WILBURN, church offical; b. Ft. Worth, Feb. 16, 1918; d. Charles P. and Eltrie Lee (Tice) Dalton; m. Paul Edgar Pursell, Feb. 16, 1939 (dec. 1973). Grad. high sch. Ordained to ministry Nat. Assn. Free Will Bapts., 1939. Asst. pastor various chs., Okla., 1939-57; pres. Okla. State Aux., First Okla. and First Mission Dists.; officer Calif. State Aux., 1960; 2nd v.p., youth chmn. Woman's Nat. Aux. Conv. 1946-48, 52-55, nat. study chmn., 1955-57, exec. sec.-treas., Nashville, 1963-85. Author: Missionary Education of Our Youth, 1955, Woman's Auxiliary Manual, 1965, Triumph Over Suffering, 1982, Death and Dying, 1982, Anne: You're Super, 1990; column Words for Women in Contact mag., 1966-70; editor: Co-Laborer, 1963-85; contbr. articles to profl. jours. Prominent in youth work, Okla., 1939-57; tchr. dist. and state Sunday Sch. workshops. Mem. Women's Fellowship Federated Women's Missionary Socs. (treas. Bristow, Okla., 1955). Home: 1148 Vultee Blvd Apt 12 Nashville TN 37217

PURSER, ROBERT DUANE, chaplain, naval officer; b. Oklahoma City, Feb. 9, 1957; s. Robert Earl and Lillian Irene (Shenuski) P.; m. Frances Wydnes Fisher, Sept. 3, 1983; children: Rebecca Christine, Andrew Thompson. BA, Taylor U., 1979; MDiv., Denver Theol. Sem., 1985. Ordained to chaplaincy Full Gospel Chs., 1985. Coll. intern pastor South Fellowship, Denver, 1984-85; commd. lt. USN, 1985; chaplain USN 2d Marine Div., Camp Lejenne, N.C., 1985-87, USN Naval Tng. Ctr., Orlando, Fla., 1987-89, USN USS Worden, Pearl Harbor, Hawaii, 1990—, Persian Gulf War, 1990-91. Editor: (ship mag.) Worden Jour., 1990—. Office: USS Worden CG-18 FPO AP HI 96683-1142

PURSLEY, GEORGE WILLIAM, religion educator; b. Parker City, Ind., Jan. 9, 1954; s. George Oscar and Billie Faye (Baker) P.; m. Rebecca Lynn Mathias, June 10, 1978; children: Ashley Danielle, Tristan Bonar. Student, U.S. Mil. Acad., 1972-73; AB, Asbury Coll., 1976; MDiv, Asbury Theol. Sch., 1979; postgrad., Ohio State U., 1982—; MSS, Ohio U., 1989. Ordained to ministry Chs. of Christ in Christian Union, 1983. Intern The Christ Hosp., Conn., 1977, United Meth. Chs., Ind., Ohio, Ky., 1974078; pastor Ch. of Christ in Christian Union, Richland Center, Wis., 1979-80; dir. fin. aid Circleville (Ohio) Bible Coll., 1980-85, asst. prof. history, 1981, assoc. prof. history, 1981—, interim libr., 1989-90; chaplain Ohio N.G., 1989—. Contbr. articles to profl. jours. Cub Scout leader, Boy Scouts Am., 1989—. Home: 538 Westview Dr Lancaster OH 43130 Office: Circleville Bible Coll 1476 Lancaster Pike Circleville OH 43113

PURVIS, CLINTON CLIFFORD, III, lay worker; b. Chataue Vienne, France, July 17, 1954; (parents Am. citizens); s. Clinton Clifford Jr. and Jenny M. P. BA in Bible, Miss. Coll., 1977; MRE, Southwestern Bapt. Theol. Sem., 1979; postgrad., Troy State U., 1984. Min. of youth First Bapt. Ch., Edwards, Miss., 1975-77; min. of youth Hillcrest Bapt. Ch., Columbus, Ga., 1978-79, Myrtle Grove Bapt. Ch., Pensacola, Fla., 1979-86; min. to students First Bapt. Ch., Tallahassee, Fla., 1986—; counsel Campus Ministry Assn., Tallahassee, 1987—; team chaplain Fla. State football and baseball, 1989—. Named Outstanding Young Man Am., Jaycees. Home: PO Box 905 Tallahassee FL 32302 Office: First Bapt Ch PO Box 710 Tallahassee FL 32302

PURVIS, WILLIAM JESSE JR., minister; b. Okinawa, Japan, May 16, 1956; came to U.S., May, 1957; s. William Jesse Sr. and Ethelda Kay (Kirkland) P.; m. Deborah Michelle Raybon, July 1, 1980; children: William Jesse III, Adam Brent, Caleb Blake. BTh, Clarksville Sch. Theology, 1980; postgrad., Luther Rice Sem., 1991. Ordained to ministry So. Bapt. Conv. Radio pastor Truth for Youth Ministries, Columbus, Ga., 1977-80; min. to youth Pinehurst Bapt. Ch., Columbus, 1980-82; pastor Cascade Hills Bapt. Ch., Columbus, 1983—; mem. credentials com. Ga. Bapt. Conv., Savannah, 1990—, adv. com. Watchman Fellowship, Columbus, 1990—. Office: Cascade Hills Bapt Ch 4510 Oates Ave Columbus GA 31904

PURYEAR, MARION BROOKS, minister; b. El Paso, Tex., June 3, 1951; s. Edward Wade Puryear and Lola Loree (Hemperley) Chailaire); m. Aleathea Voncille Raburn, Mar. 8, 1972; 1 child, Jeremy Brooks. AA, Clarke Coll., 1979; BA, Miss. Coll., 1981; MDiv, New Orleans Bapt. Theol. Sem., 1986, postgrad., 1990—. Ordained to ministry Bapt. Ch., 1977. Pastor Holmesville Bapt. Ch., McComb, Miss., 1985-86; pastor 1st Bapt. Ch., Walnut Grove, Miss., 1986-87, Blountsville, Ala., 1987-90, Cordova, Ala., 1990—; stewardship dir. Leake County Bapt. Assn., Carthage, Miss., 1986-87; mem. nominating com. Walker County Bapt. Assn., Jaspe, Ala., 1990—; evangelism dir. Friendship Bapt. Assn., Oneonta, Ala., 1987-89. Patient-care giver Hospice of Cullman County, Cullman, Ala., 1989; co-sponsor Food-Share Program of Ala., Blountsville, 1989; coach, bd. dirs. Blountsville Little League, 1988; dir. area Mental Health Ala. Fund, Blountsville, 1989; fellow mem. Jr. Coll. Adv. Com., Newton, Miss., 1977-78. With U.S. Army, 1969-71, Vietnam. Fellow Lions. Republican. Home: 110 Cliff St Cordova AL 35550 Office: 1st Bapt Ch PO Box 12 Cordova AL 35550 *Life is a constant process of decision-making between choices that are either good or bad, helpful or harmful, or beneficial or detrimental. Right choices should encourage while wrong choices should instruct.*

PUSATERI, JOSEPH MICHAEL, priest; b. Iowa City, Iowa, June 23, 1939; s. Gus A. and Anne Magdalene (Cira) P. BA, Cath. U., 1962, MS in Liberal Studies, 1967. Libr. Chanel High Sch., Bedford, Ohio, 1966-68; missionary Diocese Samoa and Tokelau, Apia, Western Samoa, 1968-86; libr. Pacific Regional Sem., Suva, Fiji, 1987-89, Holy Spirit Sem., Port Moresby, Papua, New Guinea, 1990—. Recipient Paul Harris fellow, 1986. Mem. Cath. Libr. Assn., Rotary Club (Pago Pago pres. 1973-74, Apia pres. 1979-80, Suva East dir. 1988-89). Home and Office: Holy Spirit Sem, PO Box 1717 Boroko, Bomana Papua New Guinea *What is more useless than a used match? If useless matches working together can form something beautiful, how much more can we?.*

PUSCAS, LOUIS, apostolic bishop; b. Sept. 3, 1915. Attended, Quigley Preparatory Sem., Chgo., Oradea-Mare, Roumania, Propaganda Fide Sem., Rome, Benedictine Coll., Lisle, Ill. Ordained priest Roman Cath. Ch., 1942. Titular bishop Leuce; apostolic exarchate, 1983, appointed firs eparch, 1987. Office: 1121 44th St NE Canton OH 44714

PUSKAS, CHARLES BARTO, JR., editor, religion educator; b. Youngstown, Ohio, Nov. 3, 1951; s. Charles Barto and Eve Laura (Minoff) P.; m. Susan Elaine Best, July 29, 1972; children: Rita Marie, Charles Barto III. Student, Youngstown State U., 1970-72; BA, Cen. Coll., Springfield, Mo., 1974; MA, Wheaton (Ill.) Coll., 1975; PhD, St. Louis U., 1980. Asst. prof. Bibl. studies Evang. Coll., Springfield, 1977-80; adj. prof. religious studies So. Mo. State U., Springfield, 1981-88; assoc. min. Schweitzer United Meth. Ch., Springfield, 1988-90; adj. prof. religious studies Drury Coll., Springfield, 1989-90; acad. editor Fortress Press, Mpls., 1990—. Author: Introduction to the New Testament, 1989, Essential Christianity, 1981, Campus Ambassador Magazine, 1980. Bd. dirs. Dem. Alliance, Springfield, 1987—; pres. South Golden Property Owners, Springfield, 1985-87. Recognized for religious leadership Order of Eastern Star, 1972-76. Mem. Soc. Bibl. Lit., Cath. Bibl. Assn. (assoc.), Am. Acad. Religion (convenor Hebrew Bible/New Testament Midwest regional 1984-87). Home: 6994 W Shadow Lake Dr Lino Lakes MN 55014

PUSLECKI, EDWARD, minister, academic administrator; b. Katowice, Poland, Jan. 28, 1951; s. Walenty and Czeslawa (Schmidt) P.; m. Boguslawa Barbara Mroczynska, Nov. 16, 1974; 1 child, Marcin. MTh, Christian Acad. Theology, Warsaw, Poland, 1978; postgrad., Ecumenical Inst. World Coun. Chs., Geneva, 1985-86, Haggai Inst., Somgare, 1991. Ordained to ministry Meth. Ch. Poland. Pastor Meth. congregations, Lukta, Slonecznik, Elblag, Poland, 1973-86; youth leader Meth. Ch. Poland, 1973-86; dist. supt. Meth. Ch. in Poland, 1986-89, gen. supt., 1989; pastor Meth. Congregation, Bydgoszcz, Poland, 1986-89; lect. Meth. Theol. Sem., Warsaw, 1986; dir. English Lang. Coll., Warsaw, 1990—; mem. Samaritan Found., Warsaw, 1990. Contbr. articles to jours. in field. Home: Mokotowska 12/9, 00-561 Warsaw Poland Office: United Meth Ch, Mokotowska 12, 00-561 Warsaw Poland

PUTNAM, FREDERICK WARREN, JR., bishop; b. Red Wing, Minn., June 17, 1917; s. Frederick W. and Margaret (Bunting) P.; m. Helen Kathryn Prouse, Sept. 24, 1942; children—James Douglas, John Frederick, Andrew Warren. B.A., U. Minn., 1939; M.Div., Seabury-Western Theol. Sem., 1942, D.D., 1963; postgrad., State U. Iowa, 1946-47. Ordained to ministry Episcopal Ch. as deacon, priest, 1942. Pastor in Windom and Worthington, Minn., 1942-43, Iowa City, 1943-47, Evanston, Ill., 1947-59, Wichita, Kans., 1960-63; Episcopalian chaplain State U. Iowa, 1943-47; suffragan bishop Episcopal Diocese, Okla., 1963-79; bishop Episc. Ch. in, Navajoland, 1979-83; assisting bishop Diocese of Minn., 1983-89; acting rector St. George's, Pearl Harbor, Hawaii, 1984-85, St. Clement's, Honolulu, 1986, St. John's, Kula, Maui, Hawaii, 1988, St. Elizabeth's, Honolulu, 1990; interim rector St. Stephen's Episcopal Ch., Edina, Minn., 1991—; bd. dirs. Kiyosoto Ednl. Experiment Program, 1954—, v.p., 1989—; cons. Oklahoma City Community Relation Commn., 1966-70; Pres. Okla. Conf. Religion and Race, 1963-67; v.p. Greater Oklahoma City Council Chs., 1966-67; nat. chaplain Brotherhood of St. Andrew, 1967-79, mem. brotherhood legion, 1972—; priest assoc. Order Holy Cross, 1942—; exec. com. Conf. Diocesan Execs., 1969-76, pres., 1972-74; mem. Okla. Commn. United Ministries in Higher Edn., 1970-79, pres., 1973-75; mem. nat. com. on Indian work Episc. Ch., 1977-80; chaplain Okla. Assn. Alcoholism and Alcohol Abuse, 1974-78; hon. life mem. Oklahoma City and County Criminal Justice Council, 1978—. Author articles.; editor, pub.: Shareres mag, 1957-63. Founder, pres. Oklahoma City Met. Alliance for Safer City, 1971-78; Trustee Seabury-Western Theol. Sem., 1959-65, Episcopal Theol. Sem. Southwest, 1966-69, St. Simeon's Episcopal Home, 1963-79, St. Crispins Episcopal Conf. Center, 1963-79, Casady Sch., 1963-79, Holland Hall Sch., 1963-79, Episcopal Soc. Cultural and Racial Unity, 1967-70; trustee Neighborhood Services Orgn., treas., 1969; founder, 1st pres. Friends of Wichita Pub. Library, 1962; bd. dirs. Minn. Photographic Exbn.; chmn. Mpls.-St. Paul Internat. Photographic Exhbn., 1987, 89; State Bd. Minn. Common Cause, 1989—. Recipient Disting. Service award Evanston Jr. C. of C., 1952; Merit award Photog. Soc. Am. Fellow Coll. Preachers; mem. ACLU, Assoc. Parishes (pres. 1960-64), Mpls. Soc. Fine Arts (mem. photo coun.), Photog. Soc. Am., Am. Com. for KEEP (v.p. 1961-70, 90), Walker Art Ctr., Sierra Club, Met. Sr. Fedn., Audubon Club, Am. Assn. Ret. Persons, Minn. Hort. Soc., Hist. Soc. Episcopal Ch., Archaeol. Conservancy, World Future Soc., Photographic Soc. Am. (assoc. 1989—), Twin Cities Assn. Camera Clubs (v.p. 1987), U. Minn. Alumni Assn., Minn. Hist. Soc., St. Paul Camera Club, N.Am. Rights Found., People for the Am. Way, Episcopal Peace Fellowship, Amnesty Internat., Greenpeace, Nat. Pks. and Conservation Assn., Friends Photography, Liturgical Conf., Living Ch. Found., Worldwatch Inst., Clan Douglas Soc., Phi Kappa Psi. Clubs: Normandale Tennis and Swim. Home: 5229 Meadow Ridge Minneapolis MN 55439

PUTNAM, J. WESLEY, evangelist; b. Dallas, Aug. 31, 1951; s. James William and Jewell (Perry) P.; m. Felicia Mangum, Jan. 21, 1972; children: James Wesley II, Philip Mangum, Timothy Luke. BMus, N.E. La. U., 1973; MDiv., Asbury Theol. Sem., 1978. Ordained to ministry United Meth. Ch., 1979. Pastor Grayson and Kelly (La.) United Meth. Ch., 1972-74, Jonesville (Ky.) and Mt. Pisgah United Meth. Ch., 1974-78, Lazbuddie (Tex.) United Meth. Ch., 1978-79, Hale Center (Tex.) United Meth. Ch., 1979-81; evangelist Wesley Putnam Ministries, Bedford, Tex., 1981—; affiliate mem., bd. discipleship United Meth. Ch., mem. coun. on evangelism. Contbr. articles to profl. jours. Mem. Nat. Assn. United Meth. Evangelists (pres. 1989-91, Philip award 1991). Republican. Office: Wesley Putnam Ministries 2107 B Greenbriar Dr Southlake TX 76092 *There is no one who has ever lived who knew God any better than you or I can know Him...We must simply pay the same price in building that relationship as they did.*

PUTNAM, LEON JOSEPH, philosophy and religion educator; b. Kalamazoo, Dec. 7, 1928; s. Forrest Elmer and Hazel Effie (Dresselhouse) P.; m. Phyllis Irene Millspaugh, May 17, 1955; children—Mark, Lee. A.A. (Tompkins scholar), 1948; A.B., U. Mich., 1950, A.M., 1951; B.D. (fellow), Colgate Rochester Div. Sch., 1955; Ph.D. (fellow), Harvard, 1962. Ordained to ministry Baptist Ch., 1955; asst. prof. Heidelberg Coll., Tiffin, Ohio, 1959-62, assoc. prof., 1962-66, prof. philosophy and religion, 1966—; instr. Winebrenner Theol. Sem., Findlay, Ohio, part time 1970-71. Author: The Future of Faith, 1967. Recipient Swedenborg Essay award, 1958. Mem. Am. Philos. Assn., Am. Acad. Religion, Soc. For Sci. Study Religion, AAUP. Home: 16 Park Pl Tiffin OH 44883

PUTT, B. KEITH, religion educator; b. Corinth, Miss., May 26, 1955; s. Billy C. and Era Mae (Spencer) P.; m. Sherry R. Burns, Aug. 3, 1974; children: Jonathan, Christopher. BA, Blue Mountain Coll., 1977; MDiv, Southwestern Sem., 1980, PhD, 1985; MA, Rice U., 1990. Doctoral adj. Southwestern Sem., Ft. Worth, 1981-83; asst. prof. religion Houston Bapt. U., 1984-90; asst. prof. philosophy of religion Southwestern Bapt. Theol. Sem., Ft. Worth, 1990—; interim pastor Lakeside Bapt. Ch., Houston, 1986-88, First Bapt. Ch. Alief, Houston, 1989-90. Mem. Am. Acad. Religion, N.Am. Paul Tillich Soc., Nat. Assn. Bapt. Profs. of Religion. Home: 5806 Melstone Dr Arlington TX 76016 Office: Southwestern Sem PO Box 22000 Fort Worth TX 76122-0176 *Is it not wonderful that in God's abundant grace he has decided not to give us all the answers? Sometimes redemption is in asking the questions.*

PUTT, ROBERT ALLEN, minister; b. Bedford, Va., Oct. 29, 1952; s. Melvin Allen and Zelda Mae (Johns) P.; m. Vicky Anne Humphreys, June 8, 1974; children: Ashley, Jami. AS, Bluefield (Va.) Coll., 1973; BS, Radford (Va.) U., 1975; MDiv, Southeastern Bapt. Sem., Wake Forest, N.C., 1980; D Ministry, Drew U., Madison, N.J., 1988. Ordained to ministry, So. Bapt. Conv., 1978. Youth minister Reedy Creek Bapt. Ch., Cary, N.C., 1977-79; assoc. pastor Salem Bapt. Ch., Apex, N.C., 1979-83; minister of edn. WEstover Bapt. Ch., Richmond, Va., 1984; assoc. pastor Grove Park Bapt. Ch., Burlington, N.C., 1984-89; pastor Pearisburg (Va.) Bapt. Ch., 1989—; field supr. Southeastern Bapt. Sem., Wake Forest, 1982-86; mem. curriculum bldg. team Bapt. Sun. Sch. Bd., 1985-86. Pres. Giles County Shelter, Inc., Pearisburg, 1990-91; founder Western Wake Crisis Ctr., Apex, 1983. Mem. Giles County Ministerial Assn. (pres. 1990-91), Highlands Ministerial Assn. (v.p. 1990-91), Giles County Chess Club (pres. 1990-91). Office: Pearisburg Bapt Ch 600 S Tazewell St Pearisburg VA 24134 *If one can see life as it can be, then work to move toward that goal, not with the goal as an end unto itself but as a means for shaping one's steps in that direction.*

PYATT, CLYDE DWIGHT, minister; b. Marion, N.C., Nov. 26, 1928; s. James Davis and Carrie Estella (Shaver) P.; m. Hilda Viola Arndt, Oct. 5, 1955; children: James Lattimore, Timothy Dwight, Andrew Clyde. AB, Duke U., 1949, MDiv, 1952. Ordained deacon and elder, United Meth. Ch. Pastor Pine Grove United Meth. Ch., Winston-Salem, N.C., 1973-78, Pleasant Garden (N.C.) United Meth. Ch., 1978-82, New Salem United Meth. Ch., Statesville, N.C., 1982-84, Cole Meml. United Meth. Ch., Charlotte, N.C., 1984-88, Wesley Heights-St. Timothy, Lexington, N.C., 1988-90; sr. pastor Midway United Meth. Ch., Lexington, 1990—; sec. com. on rules, Western N.C. Conf., 1960-68; mem. bd. mgrs. N.C. Pastor's Sch., Durham, 1978-82; disaster response coord., Western N.C. Annual Conf., 1976-84; exec. com. Bd. Global Ministries, WNC Annual Conf., 1980-84. Contbg. author publs. in field. Pres. various PTAs, Lake Junaluska and Winston-Salem, N.C., 1969-71, 74-78; chaplain South Fork Vol. Fire Dept., Winston-Salem, 1975-78; bd. dirs. WNCC Meth. Credit Union, 1970-90, pres. 1991—. Democrat. Office: Midway United Methodist Ch Rte 12 PO Box 2930 Lexington NC 27292

PYATT, WILLIAM GORRELL, minister; b. Noblesville, Ind., Sept. 15, 1953; s. Edward Monroe and Margaret S. (Shone) P.; m. Brenda Joyce Gorrell, July 19, 1980; children: Lauren Marie, Scott Monroe. BA, Monmouth Coll., 1975; MDiv, Methesco, Delaware, Ohio, 1981, MA in Christian Edn., 1981. Ordained to ministry United Meth. Ch., 1981. Youth minister St. John's United Meth., Edwardsville, Ill., 1978, Grace United Ch. of Christ, Lancaster, Ohio, 1978-79, North Broadway United Meth., Columbus, Ohio, 1980-81; assoc. pastor First United Meth., Carbondale, Ill., 1981-86, Union United Meth., Belleville, Ill., 1986-91, 1st United Meth. Ch., Carterville, Fla., 1991—; local coord. Youth Ministry TV Network, Belleville, 1988-90; conf. rep. UMC Forum, Nashville, Tenn., 1984, 86, 89; seminar leader Scarritt Grad. Sch., Nashville, 1987; small group leader Youth '88, Macomb, Ill., 1988. Chmn. St. Clair County Walk for CROP, Belleville, 1987-88; mem. Belleville Area Clergy Assn., 1986-90; pastoral care bd. Meml. Hosp. of Carbondale, Ill., 1982-86; sec. So. Ill. Bd. Diaconal Ministry, 1984-90. Mem. Christian Educators Fellowship, So. Ill. Coun. on Youth Ministries (dist. coord. 1982-85, 87-90), Rainbow Riders (dir. continuing edn. 1982-89). Office: 1st United Meth Ch 201 Main St Carterville IL 62918

PYLE, FLOYD HASKELL, minister; b. Bernie, Mo., Oct. 26, 1946; s. Charlie Everett and Gertie Mae (Stocks) P.; m. Sheila Lynne Alcorn, June 18, 1977; children: Erica Malyn, Charles Aaron. Student, Midwestern Bapt. Theol. Sem., 1986—. Ordained to ministry So. Bapt. Conv., 1981. Pastor Pascola (Mo.) Bapt. Ch., 1981-82, Catron (Mo.) Bapt. Ch., 1983-85, 1st Bapt. Ch., Edgar Springs, Mo., 1985—. Mem. Adult Abuse Bd. of Phelps County, Rolla, Mo., 1991. Home: PO Box 487 Edgar Springs MO 65462 Office: 1st Bapt Ch PO Box 487 Edgar Springs MO 65462-0487

PYLE, MARTIN WAYNE, minister; b. Manchester, Tenn., May 27, 1959; s. Billy Wayne and Carol Dean (Martin) P.; m. Rachel Johnson Murphree, June 6, 1980; children: Rebekah, John Paul, David. BA, David Lipscomb U., 1981; MA in Religion, Harding Grad. Sch., 1986. Ordained to ministry Ch. of Christ, 1981. Minister Como (Miss.) Ch. of Christ, 1981-83, Northside Ch. of Christ, Blytheville, Ark., 1986-90, Mandarin Ch. of Christ, Jacksonville, Fla., 1990—; youth minister Kaufman (Tex.) Ch. of Christ, 1983-86; advisor Sardis (Miss.) Lake Christian Camp, 1981-83; mem. steering com. Dallas Summer Youth Series, 1983-86. Author: (study guide) Book of Nehemiah, 1985, A Life That Shines, 1985. Sec. Como Vol. Fire Dept., 1982-83; co-founder Parent/Teen Drug Awareness Program, Kaufman, 1985-86; pres. Miss. County Community Coll. Booster Club, Blytheville, 1988-89. Mem. Mandarin Clergy Assn. Home: 5231 W Gathering Oaks Ct Jacksonville FL 32258 Office: Mandarin Ch of Christ 12791 Old St Augustine Jacksonville FL 32258 *Worldly accomplishment is a noble goal, but real success is found as we trust God to provide insight and direction in life. Following His path, there cannot be failure.*

PYNE, DONALD EUGENE, priest; b. San Francisco, Dec. 24, 1929; s. Thomas Francis and Marcia Aileen (Worth) P. BA, St. Patrick's Coll., 1952, MDiv, 1977; postgrad., San Francisco Theol. Sem., 1979, Calif. State U., Dominquez Hills, 1980. Ordained priest Roman Cath. Ch., 1956. Tchr. Marin Cath. High Sch., Kentfield, Calif., 1957-66; parish priest Archdiocese of San Francisco Bay Area, 1966—; pastor St. Charles Ch., San Carlos, Calif., 1982—; dean Deanery G, So. San Mateo County, 1983—; faculty Coll. Notre Dame, Belmont, Calif., 1981-83; cons. Archdiocese San Francisco, 1983—; vice chmn. San Francisco Coun. Priests, 1984-85; mem. Com. On-Going Edn. of Priests. Address: 880 Tamarack Ave San Carlos CA 94070 *Life is worth living. Live it according to the best we have.*

QABBANI, MUHAMMAD RASHID, religious leader. Grand mufti of Lebanon Sunni Muslims, Beirut; pres. Malagasy Luth. Ch., Antananarivo, Madagascar. Office: Sunni Muslims, Dar el-Fatwa, Ilewi Rushed St, Beirut Lebanon*

QUALLEY, RONALD GENE, minister; b. Warren, Minn., Feb. 1, 1946; s. John and Mildred (Nygren) Q.; m. Sandra Lee Treffy, Feb. 24, 1968; children: David Allen, Mark Stephen. BA in Chemistry and Math., Concordia Coll., Moorhead, Minn., 1968; MDiv, Evang. Luth. Theol. Sem., 1972. Ordained to ministry Luth. Ch., 1972. Intern pastor Grace Luth. Ch., Miami Springs, Fla., 1970, pastor, 1970-86; pastor Lord of Life Luth. Ch., Fairfax, Va., 1986—; spiritual dir. Nat. Cursillo Movement, 1984-86; mem. bd. Miami (Fla.) Coalition Religious Leaders, 1986-87; chmn. Luth. Coun. in the USA, 1984-86; cons. seminars Ch. Mgmt. for Parish Leadership, 1984—. Bd. mem. Upjohn Health Svcs., 1986—; mem. Task Force on Urban Devel. in North Va., 1988—, Nat. Hemophilia Soc., 1990; bd. regents Capt. U., Columbus, Ohio, 1981-83. Mem. Nat. Acad. Evangelists. Republican. Office: Lord of Life Luth Ch 5114 Twinbrook Rd Fairfax VA 22032

QUALLS, CHARLES LEE, minister; b. Roswell, Ga., Nov. 23, 1964; s. James Winston Sr. and Julie (Womack) Q. BS in Sociology, West Ga. Coll., 1987. Summer intern Roswell First Baptist Ch., 1984-85; instr. Centrifuge Youth Camps, Ridgecrest, N.C., 1986-87; admissions rep. West Ga. Coll., Carrollton, 1987; edn. intern Roswell First Baptist Ch., 1987-88; asst. dir. Centrifuge Youth Camps, Greenville, S.C., 1988-89; intern dept. family ministry Ky. Bapt. Conv., 1990—; retreat leader So. Baptist Churches, Ga., Ala., N.C., 1986-89; conf. leader, Ga. Baptist Conv., Atlanta, 1988—. Co-author: Sex Role Content in Music Videos (1985). Mem. Roswell 1st Baptist Ch., 1974—, Student League, West Ga. Coll., 1985-87; pres. Christian edn. coun. So. Bapt. Theol. Sem. Named to Oustanding Young Men of Am., 1988. Mem. Baptist Student Union (editor 1984-85), Alpha Beta Lambda, Omicron Delta Kappa, Pi Gamma Mu. Republican. Avocations: reading, photography, collectibles, sports. Home: SBTS Box 606 2825 Lexington Rd Louisville KY 40280

QUARRACINO, ANTONIO CARDINAL, cardinal; b. Pollica, Italy, Aug. 8, 1923. Ordained priest Roman Cath. Ch., 1945. Bishop of Nueve de Julio, 1962, bishop of Avellaneda, 1968-85, archbishop of La Plata, 1985-90, archbishop of Buenos Aires, 1990—, elevated to the Sacred Coll. of Cardinals, 1991, with titular ch. of St. Mary of Heath. Office: Archdiocese Roman Cath Ch, Rivadaria 415, 1002 Buenos Aires Argentina*

QUATTLEBUM, DONALD LEE, minister; b. Hayward, Calif., Sept. 19, 1957; s. Chester James and Bonnie (Powers) Q.; m. Deborah Jean Stillwaggon, June 3, 1978; children: Donald Lee II, David John. Diploma of ministry, Zion Bible Inst., Barrington, R.I., 1978; BA, Southeastern Coll., Lakeland, Fla., 1989; postgrad., Liberty U., Lynchburg, Va., 1989—. Ordained to ministry Bethel Temple, 1979; lic. to preach Assemblies of God, 1983, ordained to ministry, 1988. Asst. pastor Bethel Temple, Antioch, Calif., 1978-79; assoc. pastor Calvary Temple, Klamath Falls, Oreg., 1979-82, Brentwood (Calif.) Assembly of God, 1985-86; asst. pastor 1st Assembly of God, Antioch, 1982—; youth pastor Heirborn Youth Ministries, Antioch, 1989—. Mem. Nat. Network Youth Ministries, Rotary. Office: 1st Assembly of God PO Box 2117 Antioch CA 94531 *For our life to count or have meaning, it must be lived to the fullest. A full life is never spent alone, but shared with those who are loved, those found unloved, and even those who are unlovely.*

QUAY, PAUL MICHAEL, priest, theology and philosophy of science educator; b. Chgo., Aug. 24, 1924; s. Eugene and Effie (Alley) Q. A.B. in Classics, Loyola U., Chgo., 1950; Ph.L., West Baden Coll., Loyola U., Ind., 1952; B.S., MIT, 1955, Ph.D. in Physics, 1958; S.T.L., West Baden Coll., 1962. Joined Soc. of Jesus, 1946, ordained priest Roman Catholic Ch., 1961. Research assoc. physics Case Inst. Tech., Cleve., 1962-63; vis. prof. physics Loyola U., Chgo., 1965-67; asst. prof. physics St. Louis U., 1967-70, assoc. prof. physics-theology, 1970-83; research prof. philosophy Loyola U., Chgo., 1981—; external reader dept. physics Birla Inst. Tech., Mesra, Ranchi, India, 1971-81; cons. physics Nat. Bur. Standards, Boulder, Colo., summers 1966, 67. Mem. bd. advisors Am. Pro Life Assurance Soc., adv. bd. Citizens United Resisting Euthanasia. Author: The Christian Meaning of Human Sexuality; mem. editorial adv. bd. Linacre Quar.; contbr. articles to profl. jours. Served with Signal Corps, U.S. Army, 1942-46, PTO. NSF fellow, 1956-58. Mem. Am. Phys. Soc., Inst. for Theol. Encounter with Sci. and Tech., Philosophy of Sci. Assn., Fellowship of Cath. Scholars (bd. dirs. 1977-79), Soc. Christian Culture, Am. Cath. Philosophical Assn., Jesuit Philosophical Assn., Sigma Xi. Home: Jesuit Residence Loyola U 6525 N Sheridan Rd Chicago IL 60626 Office: Dept Philosophy Loyola U 6525 N Sheridan Rd Chicago IL 60626 *At the heart of the universe one finds the Heart of Christ.*

QUESENBERRY, ROBIN ELAINE, minister; b. Columbia, S.C., Oct. 18, 1957; d. Oden Robert and Wilma (McLeod) Q. BA in Religion, Carson Newman Coll., Jefferson City, Tenn., 1979; MRE, So. Bapt. Theol. Sem., Louisville, 1981. Lic. to ministry So. Bapt. Conv., 1981. Min. youth Ch. of the Bretheren, Dandridge, Tenn., 1977-79, Jefferson (S.C.) Bapt. Ch., summers 1978-79, Pleasant Grove United Meth. Ch., Sellersburg, Ind., 1979-81, Calvary Bapt. Ch., Fairfax, Va., summer 1980; min. youth and discipleship 1st Bapt. Ch., Dade City, Fla., 1981-91; min. youth and singles 1st Bapt. Ch., Moncks Corner, S.C., 1991—. Contbr. articles to mag. Office: 1st Bapt Ch Moncks Corner 112 E Main St Moncks Corner SC 29461 *I find Matthew 6:33 and Romans 12:1-2 to be the true secret to happiness. When we aren't conformed to the pattern of this world but we seek God's kingdom first, God will give us everything we need to be truly happy.*

QUICK, NORMAN, bishop. Bishop of R.I. Ch. of God in Christ, Bklyn. Office: Ch of God in Christ 1031 E 215th St Brooklyn NY 11221*

QUICK, WILLIAM KELLON, pastor; b. Marlborough County, S.C., May 20, 1933; s. Douglas and Virginia (Stubbs) Q.; m. Barbara Elizabeth Campbell, Jan. 15, 1955; children: Stephen Kellon, Kathryn Elizabeth, David Christopher, Paul Sanders. AA, Pfeiffer Coll., 1952; BA, Randolph Macon Coll., 1954; MDiv, Duke Div. Sch., 1958; DDiv (hon.), Pfeiffer Coll., 1972, Albion Coll. and Union Coll., 1984. Ordained to ministry as deacon United Meth. Ch., 1956, as elder, 1958. Assoc. pastor Broad St. Meth., Richmond, Va., 1953-54; pastor Camp Glenn Circuit, Morehead City, N.C., 1954-55, Bahama (N.C.) Circuit, 1955-59, First United Meth., Zebulon, N.C., 1959-63; sr. pastor St. James United Meth., Greenville, N.C., 1963-69, Trinity United Meth., Durham, N.C., 1969-74, Met. United Meth., Detroit, 1974—; bd. visitors Duke U. Div. Sch., Durham, 1982—; mem. adv. bd. United Theol. Sem., Dayton, 1989—; chmn. Evangelism Detroit Ann. Conf., 1987—; mem. Commn. on the Gen. Conf., Louisville, 1988—. Author: Signs of Our Times, 1989 (Silver Angel award 1990). Trustee Henry Ford Hosp., Detroit, 1988—; chmn. Detroiters Uniting, 1987-91; v.p. Christian Communications Coun., Detroit, 1988-92; bd. dirs. New Center Area Coun., Detroit, 1980—; mem. adv. bd. United Theol. Sem., Dayton, 1989—, trustee, 1991—; mem. Martin Luther King Birthday Commn., State of Mich. Recipient Religious Leader of Mich. award, 1982, William Booth award Salvation Army, 1986, Disting. Alumnus award Randolph-Macon Coll., 1987, Humanitarian award North Detroit U. Med. Ctr., 1988, Disting. Alumnus award Duke U. Div. Sch., 1990, Merit award Christian Communication Coun. Detroit, 1990, Disting. Alumni award Pfeiffer Coll., 1991; named Father of Yr. and Outstanding Leader YMCA, 1987. Mem. Wranglers, Rotary. Office: Met United Meth Ch 8000 Woodward Ave Detroit MI 48202 *Road signs exhort passers-by "Prepare to Meet God", meant obviously to remind us that life will one day end. We should begin now to live in such a way that we are prepared to meet God. I suggest that people are better counseled to prepare to meet God in the next person one meets or the next event in one's life instead of waiting for some final moment of death and judgment.*

QUIGLEY, THOMAS HARRY, JR., minister, religious organization administrator; b. Cin., Aug. 4, 1942; s. Thomas Harry and Ruth (Raleigh) Q.; m. Helen Jane Wertz, July 9, 1966; children: Christine Amy, Thomas Charles. BA, Ohio State U., 1964; BDiv, U. Chgo., 1967. Ordained to ministry Christian Ch. (Disciples of Christ), 1967. Assoc. min. 1st Christian Ch., Louisville, 1967-72; exec. dir. Louisville Area Interch. Orgn., 1972-78, Ind. Interreligious Commn. on Human Equality, Indpls., 1978-80, Greater Mpls. Coun. Chs., 1980-88, Greater Dallas Community Chs., 1988—. Mem. Nat. Assn. Ecumenical Staff, Beta Theta Pi. Democrat. Home: 9453 Meadowknoll Dr Dallas TX 75243 Office: Greater Dallas Community Chs 2800 Swiss Ave Dallas TX 75204

QUILL, JOHN DANIEL, religion educator; b. Chgo., Dec. 22, 1943; s. Cornelius John Quill and Virginia Hix Harry; m. Mary Gay Wallenborn, June 10, 1967; children: Anne-Marie Gonzalez, Mary Beth, Patrick M., Daniel J. BS in Edn., Loyola U., Chgo., 1968; MS in Edn., No. Ill. U., 1974. Tchr. St. Thomas of Villanova Sch., Palatine, Ill., 1964-72; prin. St. Therese Sch., Aurora, Ill., 1972-76, St. Nicholas Sch., Aurora, Ill., 1973-76; tchr. St. Joseph Acad., Brownsville, Tex., 1976-80; dir. religious edn. St. Mary's Ch., Brownsville, Tex., 1977-79; prin. St. Anthony Sch., Casper, Wyo., 1980-83, St. Mary's Sch., Brownsville, Tex., 1983—; religion cons. Silver Burdett & Ginn Pubs., Brownsville, 1988-91; del. Nat. Congress for Cath. Schs., Nat. Cath. Edn. Assn., 1991. Mem. ASCD, Nat. Cath. Edn. Assn. Home: 335 Honey dr Brownsville TX 78520 Office: St Marys Sch 1300 Los Ebanos Blvd Brownsville TX 78520 *A spiritual person is one who has achieved an awareness of him/herself and understands relationships. Be aware of your burdens, your trials and stresses, and then let them go. Be aware of them but don't identify with them. Your life cannot become your frustrations.*

QUINN, ALEXANDER JAMES, bishop; b. Cleve., Apr. 8, 1932. Attended, St. Charles Coll., Catonsville, Md., St. Mary Sem., Cleve., Lateran Sem., Rome, Cleve. State U. Ordained priest Roman Cath. Ch., 1958. Titular, bishop, aux. bishop Cleve. Diocese, 1983, vicar western region. Office: 2500 Elyria Ave Lorain OH 44055

QUINN, FRANCIS A., bishop; b. Los Angeles, Sept. 11, 1921. Ed., St. Joseph's Coll., Mountain View, Calif., St. Patrick's Sem., Menlo Park, Calif., Cath. U., Washington, U. Calif., Berkeley. Ordained priest Roman Cath. Ch., 1946; ordained titular bishop of Numana and aux. bishop of San Francisco, 1978, apptd. bishop of Sacramento, 1979. Office: 1119 K St PO Box 1706 Sacramento CA 95812-1706

QUINN, JAMES PETER, SR., deacon, newspaper manager; b. Waterbury, Conn., May 9, 1934; s. Henry Bernard and Minnie (Christopher) Q.; m. Ann Louise Urillo, Nov. 17, 1956; children: Louise, Margaret and James (twins), Mark and Matthew (twins). Grad. high sch., Waterbury, 1951. Lector Roman Cath. Ch., Southington, Conn., 1967-80, eucharistic min., 1980-83, deacon, 1983—; foreman newspaper composing rm. Middletown (Conn.) Press Pub. Co., 1962—. Republican. Home: 5 Lincoln Dr Southington CT 06489

QUINN, JOHN R., archbishop; b. Riverside, Calif., Mar. 28, 1929; s. Ralph J. and Elizabeth (Carroll) Q. Student, St. Francis Sem., Immaculate Heart Sem., San Diego, 1947-48; Ph.B., Gregorian U., Rome, 1950, Licentiate in Sacred Theology, 1954, S.T.L., 1954. Ordained priest Roman Cath. Ch., 1953, as bishop, 1967. Assoc. pastor St. George Ch., Ontario, Calif., 1954-55; prof. theology Immaculate Heart Sem., San Diego, 1955-62, vice rector, 1960-62; pres. St. Francis Coll. Sem., El Cajon, Calif., 1962-64; rector Immaculate Heart Sem., 1964-68; aux. bishop, vicar gen. San Diego, 1967-72; bishop Oklahoma City, 1972-73, archbishop, 1973-77; archbishop San Francisco, 1977—; provost U. San Diego, 1968-72; pastor St. Therese Parish, San Diego, 1969; apptd. consultor to Sacred Congregation for the Clergy in Rome, 1971; pres. Nat. Conf. Cath. Bishops, 1977-80, chmn. Com. of Liturgy; chmn. Ccom. on Family Life U.S. Cath. Conf.; chmn. Bishops' Com. on Pastoral Rsch. and Practices, Bishops' Com. on Doctrine; mem. Bishops' Com. on Sems., Pontifical Commn., Seattle, 1987-88, Bishops' Com. for Pro-Life Activies, 1989—; apptd. pontifical del. for religious in U.S., 1983; pres. Calif. Cath. Conf., 1985. Chmn. Com. of Liturgy of Nat. Conf. Cath. Bishops, Com. on Family Life of the U.S. Cath. Conf.; chmn. Bishops' Com. on Pastoral Rsch. and Practices, Bishops' Com. on Doctrine; mem. of Bishops' Com. on Sems., Pontifical Commn., Seattle, 1987-88; mem. Bishops' Com. for Pro-Life Activities, 1989—. Mem. Cath. Theol. Soc. Am., Canon Law Soc. Am., Am. Cath. Hist. Soc. Address: 445 Church St San Francisco CA 94114-1799

QUINN, RANDY L., pastor; b. North Kingston, R.I., Apr. 7, 1956; s. Kenneth J. and Carol J. (Miller) Q.; m. Ronda K. Watson, Feb. 14, 1986. BS in Bldg. Constrn., U. Wash., 1978; MDiv, Garrett-Evang. Theol. Sem., 1988. Assoc. pastor Sherman United Meth. Ch., Evanston, Ill., 1984-85; intern pastor Twin Valley Parish, Fredonia, Kans., 1985-87; pastor First United Meth. Ch., Saint John, Wash., 1988—; mem. conf. Town & Country Network, Seattle, 1989—, dist. coun. on ministries, 1988-90. Lic. foster home, Dept. Social and Health Svcs., Colfax, Wash., 1990—; mem. ad hoc com. for AIDS curriculum, St. John Sch. Dist., 1989, steering com. for sch. dist. self-study, 1990-91; mem. Saint John Vol. Fire Dept., 1988—; cubmaster Cub Scout Pack 3590, 1990—; commr. North Whidbey Water Dist., Oak Harbor, Wash., 1977-79. Lt. USN, 1978-83, Res. 1983—; vol. Big Bros., Seattle, 1977-79, Athens, Ga., 1979, Vallejo, Calif., 1981-83; bd. dirs. Big Bro./Big Sisters of Napa and Solano Counties, Calif., 1982-83. Mem. Bread for the World, Naval Res. Assn., Alban Inst., O'Hara Rural Ministry Inst., U. Wash. Alumni Assn., Community Club. Office: 1st United Meth Ch PO Box 236 Saint John WA 99171

QUINTERO ARCE, CARLOS, archbishop; b. Etzatlan, Jalisco, Mexico, Feb. 13, 1920; s. Silverio Quintero and Lucrecia Arcede Q. S.T.D., Gregorian U., Rome, Italy, 1946. Ordained priest Roman Cath. Ch., 1944; mem. faculty Guadalajara Sem., 1947-54, prefecto of studies, 1954-61; bishop of Ciudad Valles, 1961-66; titular archbishop Tysdro, Mexico, 1966-68; archbishop Hermosillo, Mexico, 1968—; mem. Conf. Latin Am. Bishops, Medellin, 1968, Puebla, 1979. Pres. Commn. on Edn. and Culture in Mexico, 1969-72; mem. Synod Rome; pres. Dept. Edn., Consejo Episcopal Latino Americano, 1976-78. Mem. Mexican Bishop's Conf. Office: 1 Apartado P, Hermosillo Sonora, Mexico *Mi ideal fué anunciar el Misterio de Jesús de Nazareth Hijo de Dios porque 'en sus palabras hay Vida eterna' (Jn, 61 6.68). Del conocimiento de Jesús nace el vigor de la Fe y la fuerte adhesión a la Iglesia y por consiguiente la presencia activa en la sociedad para formar una humanidad nueva. La Educación humaniza y personaliza al hombre, lo acerca a Cristo y lo integra al proceso social latino americano para lograr los cambios necesarios en America.*

RAAB, MENACHEM, rabbi, day school administrator; b. Phila., July 9, 1923; s. Sara Hammer, June 12, 1949; children: David, Moshe Shmuel, Tikva, Noam, Yaron. BA, Yeshiva U., 1944; MA, Columbia U., 1948; D., Yeshiva U., 1970. Ordained rabbi, 1947; cert. prin. Rabbi congregation Phila., 1951-55, Rochester, N.Y., 1955-63, N.J., 1965-73; dean Jerusalem Coll. of Tech., 1973-77; dir. day sch. dept. Cen. Agy. for Jewish Edn., Miami, Fla., 1978-88; dean Hillel Community Day Sch., North Miami Beach, Fla., 1988—. Author: Understanding the Siddur, 1980; contbr. articles to mags. and newspapers. Recipient Rabbi Herzog Gold medal Religious Zionists Am., 1964, Brotherhood award NCCJ, 1971, Bonds for Israel Jerusalem award, 1972, Yeshiva U. Alumni award, 1985. Mem. Rabbinical Coun. Am. (pres. Fla. region 1979-85), Educators Coun. Am., Nat. Coun. for Jewish Edn. Home: 1110 NE 170 St North Miami Beach FL 33162 Office: Hillel Community Day Sch 19000 NE 25 Ave North Miami Beach FL 33180

RAABE, PAUL RICHARD, educator; b. Fairview, Kans., Apr. 9, 1953; s. Bernard Otto and Evelyn Louise (Wessler) R. BS, Concordia, 1975; MDiv, Concordia Sem., 1979; MA, Wash. U., St. Louis, 1979; PhD, U. Mich., 1989. Ordained to ministry Luth. Ch., 1979. Instr. Concordia Coll., Ann Arbor, Mich., 1979-83; asst. prof. Concordia Sem., St. Louis, 1983-91, assoc. prof., 1991—. Author: Psalm Structures: A Study of Psalms with Refrains, 1990; contbr. articles to profl. jours. Walther fellowship Concordia Sem., 1983. Mem. Am. Schs. of Oriental Rsch., Bibl. Archaeology Soc., Soc. Bib. Lit.,

Cath. Bibl. Assn. Office: Concordia Sem 801 DeMun Ave Saint Louis MO 63105

RAAFLAUB, VERNON ARTHUR, religion educator; b. Magnetawan, Ont., Can., Apr. 30, 1938; s. Arthur Frederick and Olga Elizabeth (Hoerner) R. Diploma in electronics, Radio Electronics TV Schs., North Bay, Ont., 1959; diploma in theology, Concordia Theol. Sem., Springfield, Ill., 1965, BTh, 1972; MDiv, Concordia Theol. Sem., Ft. Wayne, Ind., 1987; postgrad., Wilfrid Laurier U., Waterloo, Ont., 1974-75; MA in Adminstrn., Briercrest Bible Coll., Caronport, Sask., 1985. Ordained to ministry Luth. Ch., 1965. Pastor Nipawin (Sask.) Choiceland Luth. Parish, 1965-76; instr. Can. Luth. Bible Inst., Camrose, Alta., 1976-77, acad. dean, instr., 1977-85, prof. Old Testament studies, acad. dean, 1985—; Counsellor Luth. Ch. Mo. Synod, Carrot River Cir., 1971-75. Co-editor: The Creation Alternative, 1970; contbr. numerous articles to profl. jours. Chmn. Easter Seal Campaign, Nipawin; mem. Can. council World Mission Prayer League, 1980-85; bd. dirs. Concordia Coll., Edmonton, Alta., 1975-78. Grantee Luth. Ch. Can., Zion Found., 1975. Mem. Nat. Assn. Profs. Hebrew, Am. Schs. Oriental Research, Near East Archeol. Soc., Am. Sci. Affiliation (assoc.), Creation Rsch. Soc. (assoc.), Assn. Psychol. Type, Histadruth Ivrith Am., Rotary (pres. Nipawin chpt. 1972-73, bd. dirs. 1968-71). Avocations: electronics, multitrack recording, music, waterskiing, swimming. Office: Can Luth Bible Inst, 4837 52A St, Camrose, AB Canada T4V 1W5 *A commitment to people in their hurts and needs, both spiritual and physical, to the defence and protection of the unborn, and to a "caretaker" responsibility to the natural environment is, in my understanding, a natural working out of Christian faith. It is God's world; we live under Him and for Him, in service to Jesus Christ.*

RAASCH, RANDOLPH HOWARD, minister; b. Milw., May 16, 1956; s. Howard William and Elizabeth Lucille (Templeton) R.; m. Diana Streit, Sept. 3, 1983; children: Elizabeth, Sarah. AA, Concordia Coll., Milw., 1976; BA, Concordia Coll., Ann Arbor, Mich., 1978; MDiv, Concordia Sem., St. Louis, 1982; postgrad., Concordia Theol. Sem., Fort Wayne, Ind., 1988—. Ordained to ministry Luth. Ch.-Mo. Synod, 1982. Assoc. pastor Pinnacle Luth. Ch., Rochester, N.Y., 1982-89, First Immanuel Luth. Ch., Cedarburg, Wis., 1989—; instr. Concordia U. Wis., Mequon, 1990—; pres. Rochester (N.Y.) Luth. Mission Soc., 1985-86, bd. dirs., 1983-85; chmn. Evangelism Com. of Luth. Ch.-Mo. Synod Ea. Dist., Buffalo, N.Y., 1986-89; bd. drs. Bd. for Parish Svcs., Luth. Ch.-Mo. Synod Ea. Dist., Buffalo, 1986-87, Bd. for Mission Svcs., Luth. Ch.-Mo. Synod Ea. Dist., Buffalo, 1987-89; com. mem. Evangelism Com. Luth. Ch.-Mo. Synod So. Wis. Dist., Milw., 1990—. Contbr. articles to profl. publs. Mem. Concordia U. Wis. Alumni Assn. (chmn. grand reunion 1990). Home: W67 N786 Evergreen Blvd Cedarburg WI 53012-1137 Office: First Immanuel Luth Ch W64 N640 St John Ave Cedarburg WI 53012

RABBANI, RÚHÍYYIH (MARY MAXWELL RABBANI), religious organization official, writer; b. N.Y.C., Aug. 8, 1910; d. William Sutherland and May Ellis (Bolles) M.; m. Shoghi Effendi Rabbani, Mar. 24, 1937. Student, McGill U., Can. Mem. staff Bahá'í Faith World Ctr., 1957-63; mem. Internat. Bahá'í Teaching Ctr.; named Hand of the Cause Bahá'í Faith; rep. Can. Bahá'í Conf. for Indians and Eskimos, 1986; Universal House of Justice del. to meeting of Internat. Soc. for Gen. Systems Rsch., Budapest, Hungary, 1987; guest speaker European Bahá'í Women's Conf., Madrid, 1990, Bahá'í Mediterranean Conf., Corsica, 1990; Universal House of Justice rep. to Nat. Spiritual Assembly of Bahá'ís of Romania, Bucharest, 1991. Author: Prescription for Living, 1950, The Priceless Pearl, 1969, Manual for Pioneers, 1974, The Desire of the World, 1982; producer (documentary films) The Green Light Expedition, 1976, The Pilgrimage, 1980; contbr. articles to religious jours. Hon. pres. Sacred Lit. Trust, Manchester, Eng., 1989—; hon. mem. internat. support com. Internat. Ctr. for Peace, Peace Mus., Verdun, France, 1991—. Office: Bahá'í World Ctr, PO Box 155, Haifa 31 001, Israel

RABE, VIRGIL WILLIAM, minister, religion educator; b. Monroe, Wis., Nov. 3, 1930; s. Albert and Beulah (Davidson) R.; m. Nancy Ann Fay, July 9, 1955; children: Jonathan Paul, Laurie Fay. BA, U. Wis., 1954; BS, McCormick Theol. Sem., 1957; ThD, Harvard U., 1963. Ordained to ministry United Presbyn. Ch. in USA, 1957. Pastor First Presbyn. Ch., Waltham, Mass., 1957-59; prof. religion and philosophy Mo. Valley Coll., Marshall, 1961—. Contbr. articles to profl. jours. Rockefeller doctoral fellow Harvard U., 1959-61. Mem. Soc. Bibl. Lit., Mo. Union Presbytery, Alpha Sigma Phi. Home: 316 E Black St Marshall MO 65340 Office: Mo Valley Coll Marshall MO 65340

RABENIRINA, REMI, bishop. Bishop of Antananarivo The Anglican Communion, Madagascar. Office: Eveche Anglican, Ambohimanoro, 101 Antananarivo Democratic Republic of Madagascar*

RABENSTEIN, MANFRED, rabbi; b. Tann, Hesse, Germany, July 13, 1911; came to U.S., 1938; s. Hugo and Lina (Fichtelberger) R.; m. Flora Plaut, Mar. 31, 1936; children: Aaron A., Bernard H., Naomi D. Rabenstein Miller, Jacob S. BEd, Jewish Cantorial & Tchrs. Sem., Cologne, Germany, 1932. Chaver, Rabbinical Coll. Kol Torah, Jerusalem, 1971. Pub. sch. and Hebrew tchr. Darmstadt, Germany, 1932-38; rabbi Congregation New Hope, Cin., 1939—. Mem. Orthodox Union N.Y.C. Home: 7866 Greenland Pl Cincinnati OH 45237

RABINOVITCH, CELIA MILDRED, art historian, religion writer; b. Morden, Man., Can., Aug. 26, 1954; d. Milton and Shaela (Cohen) R. BFA in Painting, U. Man., 1974, BA in History of Religions, 1975; MFA in Painting, U. Wis., 1980; PhD in History of Religions and Art History, McGill U., Montreal, 1984. Lectr. history of religions McGill U., Montreal, Que., Can., 1982; asst. prof. fine arts U. Colo., Denver, 1983-90; vis. prof. Dept. Religion U. Colo., Boulder, 1988; adj. prof. Grad. Sch. Architecture and Planning U. Colo., Denver, 1988-90; vis. artist and grad. faculty Syracuse U., 1989-90; instr. Emily Carr Coll. Art and Design, Vancouver, B.C., Can., 1990-91. One person shows include U. Wis., 1980, The Grotto Cycle, U.M.C. Fine Arts Ctr., U. Colo., Boulder, 1988, Regis Coll., Denver, 1989; exhibited in group shows at Springfield Art Assn. Gallery, Ill., 1979, U. Wis.-Madison Art Gallery, 1979, 80, McGill U., 1980, Winnipeg Art Gallery, 1981, U. So. Colo., Pueblo, 1985, U. Colo. Denver/Emanuel Gallery, 1983, 84, 85, 87, others; author: The Surreal and the Sacred: Archaic, Occult and Daemonic Elements in Modern Art, 1914-40, 1992; contbr. articles to profl. jours. Mem. coll. adv. com. Denver Art Mus., 1987-90. Recipient Peter L. Coultry Meml. Book prize, U. Man., 1973, Isbister award in fine arts, U. Man., 1973, Univ. Gold medal, 1974, U. Colo. Found. Faculty award, 1984, others; grantee, Man. Arts Coun., 1981, McGill Humanities Rsch. Coun., 1983, The Can. Coun. for the Arts, 1984, U. Colo. grantee, 1989. Mem. Coll. Art Assn. Am., Univ. Art Assn. Can., Internat. Assn. of Art Critics of Can., Am. Acad. Religion. Avocations: swimming, biking, making jewelry. Home: 150 Madrone Ave Larkspur CA 94939

RABINOWITZ, MAYER ELYA, religion educator, librarian; b. N.Y.C., Jan. 31, 1939; s. Simcha Rabinowitz and Dvorah (Resnikoff) Masovetsky; m. Renah Lee Levine, June 16, 1965; children: Oded Simcha, Dalya Adina, Ayelet Zviyah. BA, B in Hebrew Lit., Yeshiva U., 1960, MA, 1961; M Hebrew Lit., Jewish Theol. Sem., 1965, PhD, 1974. Ordained rabbi, 1967. Instr. Talmud Jewish Theol. Sem., N.Y.C., 1970-74, asst. prof., 1974-76, assoc. prof., 1976—, dean students Sem. Coll., 1974-76, assoc. dean Grad. Sch., 1976-79, dean Grad. Sch., 1979-87, libr., 1987—, chmn. Joint Ben Din of Conservative Movement, 1989—; mem. com. on Jewish law and standards Rabbinical Assembly, N.Y.C., 1978—. Author: Sefer Hamordekhai-Tractate Gittin, 1990; also articles. Grantee U.S. Govt., 1960-61, Meml. Found. for Jewish Culture, 1977-78; Herbert Lehman fellow Jewish Theol. Sem., 1963-70. Mem. Assn. Jewish Studies, Assn. Jewish Librs., Judaica Conservancy Found. Office: Jewish Theol Sem 3080 Broadway New York NY 10027

RABINOWITZ, STANLEY SAMUEL, rabbi; b. Duluth, Minn., June 8, 1917; S. Jacob Mier and Rose (Zeichik) R.; m. Anita Bryna Lifson, June 24, 1945; children: Nathaniel Herz, Sharon Deborah, Judith Leah. B.A., State U. Iowa, 1939; M.A., Yale U., 1950; M. Hebrew Lit., Jewish Theol. Sem., 1944, Doctor Hebrew Lit., 1971. Ordained rabbi, 1943; dir. United Synagogue, N.Y.C., 1943-46; rabbi B'nai Jacob Synagogue, New Haven, Conn., 1946-53, Adath Jeshurun Synagogue, Mpls., 1953-60; rabbi Adas Israel Synagogue, Washington, 1960-86, rabbi emeritus, 1986—; v.p. Rabbinical Assembly, N.Y.C., 1974-76, pres., 1976-78; vice chmn. B'nai B'rith Youth Commn., 1965-76; pres. Mercaz, 1977-83. Club: Cosmos (Washington). Home: 3115 Normanstone Terr NW Washington DC 20008 Office: Adas Israel Synagogue 2850 Quebec St NW Washington DC 20008

RABY, TEDDY LEE, clergyman; b. Kingston, Tenn., May 26, 1928; s. Sanie David and Jessie (Gordon) R.; m. Mable Zora Nelson, Feb. 4, 1947; children: Betty Jean, Evelyn L. (dec.), Edward, Samuel, Denise, Robin, Teddy Lee II, Lisa, Donna. Grad. Theology, Pioneer Theol. Sem., 1952, DTh, 1958; MTh, Colonial Acad., 1954, D Bible Philosophy, 1960; DD (hon.), Bapt. Christian Coll., Shreveport, La., 1988; D Ministry (hon.), Theol. Sem. Bowling Green, Ky., 1989, ThD (hon.), 1991. Ordained to ministry Bapt. Ch., 1951. Pastor Swan Pond Bapt. Ch., Kingston, Tenn., 1951-52, Little Valley Bapt. Ch., Blaine, Tenn., 1952-53, Union Valley Bapt. Ch., Oliver Springs, Tenn., 1953-55, Victory Bapt. Ch., Maryville, Tenn., 1959-79, New Fairview Bapt. Ch., Oliver Springs, 1955-79, 83—; chair bd. Bapt. Internat. Bible Inst., Harriman, Tenn., 1983—; trustee World Bapt. Coll., Ft. Worth, 1950-52, Colonial Theol. Sem., Rockford, Ill., 1950-54. Author: Christ is Conqueror, 1958, He is Coming Again, 1959; author sermon: Jerusalem, A Burdensome Stone, 1991—. Sgt. U.S. Army, 1946-49. Home: RR 2 Box 144A Oliver Springs TN 37840 Office: New Fairview Bapt Ch RR 2 Oliver Springs TN 37840 *If we are to be a blessing to mankind now, present, we must embrace a firm hope in the future. By our devotion to Christ we can have both.*

RACHLIS, ARNOLD ISRAEL, rabbi, religion educator; b. Phila., Apr. 25, 1949; s. Burech and Pauline (Glanzberg) R.; m. Robin Claire Goldberg, July 4, 1974; children: Adam, Michael. B.A., U. Pa.; 1970; M.A., Temple U., 1972; Ordination, Reconstructionist Rabbinical Coll., 1975; B.A. (hon.) Central High Sch., Phila., 1966. Ordained rabbi, 1975. Asst. dir. Hillel Found., Temple U., Phila., 1972-74; lectr. with Temple U., 1974-76; mem. faculty Spertus Coll., Chgo., 1976-85; rabbi Jewish Reconstructionist Cong., Evanston, Ill., 1976—; host Hayom (Today) Syndicated Cable TV Show Sta. WJUF-TV, Chgo., 1982—; host Of Cabbages and Kings Program ABC-TV, Chgo., 1982—; sr. fgn. affairs advisor Dept. State, Washington, 1985-86; internat. bd. dirs. New Israel Fund; bd. dirs. U. Ill. Fund for Gerontology Rsch.; mem. adv. bd. China Judaic Studies Assn., Nanjing U., People's Republic of China. Contbr. articles to profl. jours.; regular columnist Chgo. Jewish Sentinel; columnist Phila. Jewish Exponent, 1974-76.; cons. for Jucaica section Compton's Ency. Recipient Leadership Citation Jewish Reconstructionist Found., 1980; White House fellow, 1985-86, Leadership Greater Chgo. fellow, 1988-89; subject of award winning documentary film, The Legacy. Mem. Reconstructionist Rabbinical Assn. (pres. 1977-79); Chgo. Bd. Rabbis (pres. 1990-91), Chgo. Action for Soviet Jewry (adv. council), Chevra. Avocations: theater, writing, hiking, foreign travel. Home: 708 Judson Evanston IL 60202 Office: Jewish Reconstructionist Congregation 303 Dodge St Evanston IL 60202

RACKMAN, JOSEPH ROBERT, lawyer; b. N.Y.C., Mar. 29, 1948; s. Emanuel and Ruth Sylvia (Fischman) R.; m. Eliane Norris, June 28, 1972; children: Sophia, Anya, David, Alexander. BA summa cum laude, Yeshiva U., 1969; JD, Harvard U., 1972; LLM in Taxation, NYU, 1978. Bar: N.Y. 1973, U.S. Tax Ct. 1975, Fla. 1980, U.S. Ct. Appeals (5th and 11th cirs.) 1982, U.S. Supreme Ct. 1982. Assoc. Graubard Moskovitz et al, N.Y.C., 1974-76, Weil Gotshal & Manges, N.Y.C., 1976-80; ptnr. Tew, Critchlow et al, Miami, Fla., 1980-82, Finley Kumble et al, Miami, 1983-87, Tew, Jorden & Schulte, Miami, 1988-89, Squadron, Ellenoff, Plesent & Lehrer, N.Y., 1989—. Contbr. articles to profl. and religious jours. Vice pres. Cen. Agy. for Jewish Edn., Miami, 1986-88, Hebrew Acad., Miami, 1985-88; bd. dirs. Am. Jewish Com., Miami, 1985-88, bd. dirs. N.Y. chpt., 1990—, mem. Jewish communal affairs commn., 1990—; mem. bd. Westchester Day Sch., 1990—. Office: 551 Fifth Ave New York NY 10176

RADA, HEATH KENNETH, school president; b. Richmond, Va.; s. Joseph C. and Grace (Miller) R.; m. Peggy Joyce Fish; children: Margaret Grace, Mary Talmage. Student, St. Andrews Presbyn. Coll., 1962-64; BS, Va. Commonwealth U., 1967; MA, Presbyn. Sch. Christian Edn., 1970; EdD, N.C. State U., 1976. Cert. Christian educator, N.C., Va. Tchr. 5th grade Henrico County, Va. Pub. Schs., Richmond, 1969-70; instr. sociology, chmn. social sci. dept., acting dean students, dir. Spl. Svcs. Upward Bound fed. programs Southeastern Community Coll., Whiteville, N.C., 1970-74; assoc. prof., founding dir. Ctr. for Community Edn. Appalachian State U., Boone, N.C., 1975-80; pres. Presbyn. Sch. Christian Edn., Richmond, 1980—; dir. recreational and cultural program for sr. citizens Sr. Ctr., William Byrd Community Ctr., Richmond, Adult Edn. Bd. Va. Commonwealth U., Consumer Credit Counseling Svc. Richmond; part-time dir. Christian edn. First Presbyn. Ch., Whiteville, 1970-74, rep. to assemblies, South Africa, Kenya, Zaire, Geneva; mem. Richmond City Schs. Supt. Search Com.; tchr. adult edn. Tri-Nat. Inst., Chorley, Eng., 1978; del. First Internat. Community Ednl. Workshop, La Paz, Bolivia, 1976; bd. dirs., mem. exec. com. Collegiate Schs.; bd. dirs., v.p. Sheltering Arms Rehab. Hosp. Author: Blessed are the Debonair: The Wit and Wisdom of Charles E. S. Kraemer, 1990. Mem. Lakeside Presbyn. Ch., Richmond, com. theol. edn. Presbyn. Ch. U.S.A., worship ministry unit and theology, spl. com. theol. instns., Budget Work Group, Hanover Presbytery Task Force Higher Edn., planning com. Montreat Christian Edn. Conf., 1991, adv. bd. N.C. Govs. Office Citizens Affairs, adv. bd. N.C. Govs. Interagy.; bd. dirs. Richmond AIDS Info. Network; guidance worker emotionally disturbed children Meml. Found., Richmond. Recipient Margaret Bowen award St. Andrews Presbyn. Coll., 1983; named Community Educator of Yr., State of N.C., 1979. Mem. Nat. Conf. Christians and Jews (bd. dirs., chmn. ann. Richmond interfaith breakfast), Rotary (bd. dirs. Richmond chpt.). Democrat. Avocations: music, skiing, swimming, traveling, drama. Office: Presbyn Sch Christian Edn 1205 Palmyra Ave Richmond VA 23227

RADCLIFFE, ROBERT JAMES, minister, educator; b. Joliet, Ill., Oct. 8, 1940; s. George L. and Vera L. (Linscott) R.; m. Stephanie Anne Schoenhals, July 10, 1990; children: Richard James, Robyn Suzanne. BA, Wheaton (Ill.) Coll., 1962, MA, 1964; PhD, Claremont (Calif.) Grad. Sch., 1982. Ordained to ministry Bapt. Ch., 1969. Dir. Christian edn. Temple Bapt. Ch., Lodi, Calif., 1964-69; assoc. pastor Grosse Pointe Bapt. Ch., Grosse Pointe Woods, Mich., 1969-71, Sunkist Bapt. Ch., Anaheim, Calif., 1971-76; assoc. prof. Biola U., La Mirada, Calif., 1976-89; prof. ednl. ministry Western Conservative Bapt. Sem., Portland, Oreg., 1989—; cons. David C. Cook Pub. Co., Elgin, Ill., 1981—. Contbr. articles to profl. jours. Mem. N.Am. Profs. Christian Edn., Religious Edn. Assn. Office: Western Conservative Bapt Sem 5511 SE Hawthorne Blvd Portland OR 97215

RADDE, LEONARD CARL, minister; b. Big Spring, Tex., Sept. 27, 1935; s. Samuel Carl and Rebecca Doris (Dickerson) R.; m. Elizabeth Ann Poteet Oglesby, May 31, 1969; children: Timothy Lynn, James Allen. AS, Tarleton State U., 1955; BS, Tex. Wesleyan Coll., Ft. Worth, 1958; M in Theol., So. Meth. U., 1964; D of Ministry, Drew U., 1987. Ordained to ministry Meth. Ch. Pastor Springtown (Tex.) Meth. Ch., 1964-66; placement supr. Tex. Employment Commn., Waco, 1966-70; pastor Itasca (Tex.) United Meth. Ch., 1970-74; pastor 1st United Meth. Ch., Coleman, Tex., 1974-78, Ennis, Tex., 1978-83; sr. minister 1st United Meth. Ch., Killeen, Tex., 1983-89; sr. pastor 1st United Meth. Ch., Burleson, Tex., 1989—; chmn. bd. Wesley Voice Ministries Internat., Floyd Knobs, Ind., 1984-88, stat. sec. Cen. Tex. Conf. of Meth. Ch., 1982—; chmn. Com. Edn. and the Advance, United Meth. Ch., 1984-88. Author: Loving: A Bible Study in Moral Decision, 1977. Chmn. Ennis Airport Zoning Bd., 1981-82. Recepient Am. Farmer Degree award, Future Farmers of Am., 1953; named one of Outstanding Young Men of Am., 1970. Mem. Ennis C. of C. (bd. dirs. 1979-81). Lodges: Lions (pres. Meridian, Tex., bd. dirs. Itasca, Coleman, Ennis, Killeen). Avocations: Western and landscape painting, flying. Office: 1st United Meth Ch Box 399 Burleson TX 76028

RADECKI, DANE JOSEPH, principal; b. Green Bay, Wis., Nov. 17, 1950; s. Richard John and Theresa Ann (Villeneuve) R. BA, St. Norbert Coll., DePere, Wis., 1973; MDiv, Cath. Theol. Union, 1977; MSA, U. Notre Dame, 1981; EdD, U. San Francisco, 1987. Joined Canons Regular of Premontre, Roman Cath. Ch., 1968; ordained priest, 1977; cert. sch. adminstr., Wis. Tchr. math. Premontre High Sch., Green Bay, 1972-73, tchr. math. and religion, 1977-79, dir. devel., 1979-81, campus min., 1981-82; prin. Premontre/Notre Dame Acad., Green Bay, 1987—. Mem. Nat. Cath. Edn. Assn., Wis. Assn. Prins. Cath. Secondary Schs. (treas. 1991—), Phi Delta Kappa. Office: Notre Dame de la Baie Acad 610 Maryhill Dr Green Bay WI 54303-2092

RADEMACHER, ROBERT PAUL, minister; b. Omaha, Sept. 21, 1942; s. Heye J. and Johanna (Stoehr) R.; m. Darlene Edna Haecker, June 9, 1968; children: Jonathan, Jeffrey, Jeremy, Jennifer. BA, Dana Coll., 1964; MDiv, Wartburg Sem., 1968; D Ministry, McCormick Sem., Chgo., 1985. Ordained to ministry Evang. Luth. Ch. in Can., 1968. Pastor Kyle Luth. Parish, Sask., Can., 1968-70, Midale (Sask.) Luth. Parish, 1970-81, Christ Luth. Ch., Neudorf, Sask., 1981—; mgr., treas. Luth. Bible Camp, Midale, 1970-81; mem., sec., chmn. St. Paul Luth. Home Bd., Melville, Sask., 1981-90. Editor Sask. Synod News, 1991—. Sec. supervisory com. Midale Credit Union. Home and Office: Christ Luth Ch, Box 10, Neudorf, SK Canada S0A 2T0

RADER, DICK ALLEN, religion educator, university dean; b. Oklahoma City, Nov. 30, 1940; s. Nash Moore and Inez Cecil (Skaggs) R.; m. Norma Sue Harris, June 11, 1961; children: Michael, Darrel, Steven, Gregory, Jeffrey. BA, Okla. Bapt. U., 1963; BD, MDiv, Southwestern Bapt. Theol. Sem., Ft. Worth, 1966, PhD, 1980. Ordained to ministry So. Bapt. Conv., 1963. Youth min. 1st Bapt. Ch., Midwest City, Okla., 1961-63; pastor 1st Bapt. Ch., Mill Creek, Okla., 1963-64, Little City Bapt. Ch., Madill, Okla., 1964-67; missionary Fgn. Mission Bd., So. Bapt. Conv., Zambia, Republic of South Africa, 1967-80; prof., dean Okla. Bapt. U., Shawnee, 1980—. Author: Responding to God's Call, 1985, Travelin' in Style, 1991, Christian Ethics in an African Context, 1991. Pres. local chpt. PTA, Shawnee, 1981-82; deacon 1st Bapt. Ch., Shawnee, 1983. Mem. Nat. Assn. Bapt. Profs. of Religion, Am. Soc. Missiology, Assn. Evang. Profs. of Missions. Democrat. Home: 701 W 39th Shawnee OK 74801 Office: Okla Bapt U 500 W University Shawnee OK 74801

RADER, PAUL ALEXANDER, minister, administrator; b. N.Y.C., Mar. 4, 1934; s. Lyell M. and Gladys Mina (Damon) R.; m. Kay Fuller, May 29, 1956; children: Edith Jeanne, James Paul, Jennifer Kay. BA, Asbury Coll., Wilmore, Ky., 1956; BD, Asbury Theol. Sem., 1959; LLD (hon.), Asbury Coll., Wilmore, Ky., 1984; ThM, So. Bapt. Theol. Sem., Louisville, 1961; D Missiology, Fuller Theol. Sem., 1973. Ordained to ministry Salvation Army, 1961. Tng. prin. The Salvation Army, Seoul, 1973-74, edn. sec., 1974-77, chief sec., 1979-83; tng. prin. The Salvation Army, Suffern, N.Y., 1983-86; divisional comdr. for Ea. Pa. and Del. The Salvation Army, Phila., 1986-88; chief sec. ea. ter. The Salvation Army, N.Y.C., 1988; territorial comdr. U.S.A. western ter. The Salvation Army, Rancho Palos Verdes, Calif., 1989—; adj. prof. Seoul Theol. Sem., 1980-82; trustee Asian Ctr. for Theol. Studies and Mission, 1980-83, Asbury Coll., 1988—; pres. The Salvation Army Calif. Corp., Rancho Palos Verdes, 1989—. Recipient Alumnus A award Asbury Coll., 1982, Disting. Alumni award Asbury Theol. Sem., 1989; Paul Harris fellow Rotary Internat., 1989. Mem. Am. Soc. Missiology, Internat. Assn. Mission Studies. Office: The Salvation Army 30840 Hawthorne Blvd Rancho Palos Verdes CA 90274

RADER, SHARON ZIMMERMAN, minister; b. Battle Creek, Mich., Oct. 7, 1939; d. Elmer John and Lucille Ivalene (Koteskey) Zimmerman; m. Blaine B. Rader, June 30, 1962; children: Matthew Scott, Mary Ruth. BA, North Cen. Coll., 1961; MDiv, Garrett Evang. Theol. Sem., 1976; DD (hon.), Adrian Coll., 1989. Ordained to ministry United Meth. Ch. Pastor Mayfair United Meth. Ch., Chgo., 1976-78, Baseline United Meth. Ch., Battle Creek, 1978-81, Univ. United Meth. Ch., East Lansing, Mich., 1986-89; program coord. West Mich. Conf. United Meth. Ch., Grand Rapids, Mich., 1981-86, dist. supt., 1989—; trustee Albion (Mich.) Coll., 1985-88; del. gen. confs. United Meth. Ch., 1984, 88, researcher gen. commn. status and role of women, Evanston, 1974-76, chair rsch., planning and futuring, Gen. Coun. on Ministries, Dayton, Ohio, 1984—. Editor jour. Wellsprings, 1990; contbr. articles to mags. and newspapers, introduction to book. Pres. Sch. Coun., Chgo., 1977-78; bd. dirs. Habitat for Humanity, Grand Rapids, Mich., 1986-88; pres. NOW, Battle Creek, 1980-81. Mem. World Futures Soc. Office: Grand Rapids Dist United Meth Ch PO 6247 Grand Rapids MI 49516

RADHA, SIVANANDA (URSULA SYLVIA HELLMAN), spiritual teacher; b. Berlin, Mar. 20, 1911; came to Can., 1952. Photography diploma Berlin Sch. Photography, 1942; grad. Berlin Sch. Advt., 1940. Initiated into Sanyas, Saraswati Order of Sanyas, 1956. Dir. Divine Life Soc., Burnaby, B.C., Can., 1957-63; dir. Yasodhara Ashram Soc., Kootenay Bay, B.C., 1963—; adj. faculty Antioch Coll., Seattle, Los Angeles, 1979-80, 82-84; mem. faculty C.I.T.P., Menlo Park, Calif., 1975-82; founder Assn. for Devel. Human Potential, Idaho, 1970—; founder 7 Radha Houses, 1982—. Author: Kundalini Yoga for the West, 1978; Mantras Words of Power, 1980, Seeds of Light, 1980, Radha: Diary of a Woman's Search, 1981, Hatha Yoga: The Hidden Language, 1987, Divine Light Invocation, 1990, In the Company of the Wise, 1991. Mem. Assn. for Humanistic Psychology, Assn. for Transpersonal Psychology, Divine Life Soc., Internat. Transpersonal Assn., Am. Soc. for Psychical Research. Address: PO Box 9, Kootenay Bay, BC Canada V0B 1X0

RADINSKY, JOSEPH RUBEN, rabbi; b. Seattle, Oct. 9, 1936; s. Jack and Lillian (Silver) R.; m. Juliette Mizrahi, Mar. 23, 1958; children: Devorah Radinsky Urkowitz, Eliezer, Dena Radinsky Lipsky. Student, Yeshiva U., 1954-56; BA in English, U. Wash., 1958; MA in Comparative Lit., Harvard U., 1959; Rabbinic degree, Hebrew Theol. Coll., 1969. Ordained rabbi. Tchr. Seattle Hebrew Acad., 1959-61; rabbi Congregation Sons of Abraham, Lafayette, Ind., 1963-76, United Orthodox Synagogues, Houston, 1976—; Pres. Tex. Kallah of Rabbis, Houston, 1981-82, Houston Rabbinic Assn., 1979-81. Author: Torah Concepts: The Source of Jewish Values, 1982, Book II, 1985, Book III, 1988, Book IV, 1991. Chmn. Mayor's Commn. on Human Rels., Lafayette, 1968-72. Recipient Heritage award Israel Bonds, Builders aware AMIT Women, Man of Yr. award Jewish Herald Voice, Scholarship Grantor award Zionist Orgn. Am. Mem. Rabbinical Coun. Am. (exec. com. 1972—), Nat. Rabbinic Cabinet of Israel Bonds, Chgo. Rabbinical Coun., Houston Kashruth Assn. (Rabbinic chmn. 1976—), B'nai Brith (v.p., sec. 1965-75). Home: 9311 Greenwillow Houston TX 77096 Office: United Orthodox Synagogues 9001 Greenwillow Houston TX 77096

RADKE, DALE LEE, religious organization administrator, deacon, editor; b. Sheboygan, Wis., July 9, 1933; s. Alfred and Viola (Aschenbach) R.; m. Diane Jean Simon, Aug. 16, 1958; children: Laura Lee, Jay Ryan. AA, Concordia Wis., 1954. Store mgr. Badger Paint Stores, Milw., 1958-65; with sales dept. Hilton Co., Butler, 1965-67; with sales and customer service depts. Century Hardware, Milw., 1967-72; exec. dir. Greater Milw. Fedn. Luth. Chs., Mo. Synod., Milw., 1973-87, 90—, Luth. of Wis., Milw., 1982-89; Wis. affiliate Am. Heart Assn., Milw., 1989; editor Badger Luth. newspaper, Milw., 1990—; voice of God-Love Prayer Telephone, 1973—. Editor The Milw. Luth., 1982-89; contbr. articles to clown mags. Mem. Milw. Citizenship Commn., 1960-63; mem. religious leaders div. Nat. Safety Coun., Chgo., 1980-91, bd. dirs., 1987-89; mem. Milw. Safety Commn., 1970—, chmn., 1983-89; mem. community svc. dir. Nat. Safety Coun., 1990—. Mem. Milw. Advt. Club, Milw. Press Club, Milw. Jaycees (Outstanding Young Man of Yr. 1962), Variety Club, Nat. Speakers Assn., Wis. Profl. Speakers Assn., Kiwanis, various clown orgns. Lutheran. Home: 6410 W Melvina St Milwaukee WI 53216 Office: PO Box 18024 Milwaukee WI 53218-9998

RADUA, MAIKALI, priest. Head Anglican Ch., Apia, Western Samoa. Office: Anglican Ch, POB 16, Apia Western Samoa*

RAFFEL, CHARLES MICHAEL, educator; b. Boston, Aug. 28, 1950; s. Milton Henry and Mildred (Parad) R.; m. Rivka Z. Gruber, Jan. 1, 1978; children: Aliza, Joshua. BA, Wesleyan U., 1972; MA, Brandeis U., 1977, PhD, 1983. Asst. prof. Yeshiva U., N.Y.C., 1981—; Erna S. Michael chair in Jewish studies Yeshiva U., 1983—. Contbr. articles to religion and ethics publs. Mellon Found. grantee. Mem. Assn. Jewish Studies, Found. for Jewish Culture, Meml. Found. Jewish Culture. Avocations: running, tennis. Home: 190 Norman Rd New Rochelle NY 10804

RAFTERY, WILLIAM JOHN, priest; b. Somerville, Mass., July 16, 1916; s. William Francis and Beatrice Mary (Cody) R. BA, Cath. U., 1945; MA, Villanova U., 1953. Ordained priest Roman Cath. Ch., 1945. Tchr. St. Mary's Prep. Sch., Penndel, Pa., 1945-58; rector, prin. Immaculate Sem., Lafayette, La., 1958-64; rector, pres. Grad. Sch. Notre Dame Sem. Coll., New Orleans, 1964-67; parish priest Diocese Worcester, Mass., 1968—; chaplain Lafayette Serra Club. Mem. Sch. Prins. Assn., Coll. Pres's. Assn. Home and Office: Box 307 Manomet MA 02345

RAGAN, JOHN CHARLES, minister; b. Blair, Nebr., Feb. 15, 1960; s. Gilbert Charles and Joyce Marie (Neilson) R.; m. Tamra Lynn Hohwieler, June 14, 1986; 1 child, Philip. BA, Dana Coll., 1982; MDiv, Wartburg Sem., 1986. Ordained to ministry Luth. Ch., 1986. Pastor 1st Luth. Ch., Lake Andes, S.D., 1986-90, East Lake Andes Luth. Ch., Lake Andes, 1986-90, Wilmot (S.D.) Luth. Ch., 1990—; vol. Springfield (S.D) Correction Facility, 1986-89; co-chair Charles Mix County Interagy., Lake Andes, 1986-87; pres. Lake Andes Area Kinship Bd., 1987-89; treas. S.D. Kinship Coun., Mitchell, S.D., 1988-89. Lectr. Keystone Outreach Ctr., Watertown, S.D., 1990-91; firefighter Wilmot Fire Dept., 1990—; emergency medicine technician Lake Andes Ambulance Assn., 1987-90; foster parent Dept. Social Svcs., Pierre, S.D., 1988—; asst. state dir. Mil. Affiliate Radio Svc., Wilmot, 1990. Recipient Community Svc. award VFW Aux., 1988, The Shepherd Staff award S.D. Synod Devel. Office, 1988. Mem. Alban Inst., Assn. Clin. Pastoral Edn., Coll. Chaplains (affiliate), Jaycees (sec., treas. 1990-91, pres. 1991—). Republican. Home: Box 130 Wilmot SD 57279-0130 Office: Wilmot Luth Ch Ordway and 5th Ave Box 130 Wilmot SD 57279-0130 *The complexities of life along with our advances in technology can overwhelm us and draw our attention away from God. By living life one day at a time and becoming morally responsible for our individual and societal actions, we can concentrate on God's will for our lives and strive to be the best that we can possibly be.*

RAGLAND, WYLHEME HAROLD, minister, health facility administrator; b. Anniston, Ala., Dec. 19, 1946; s. Howard and Viola (Pearson) R.; children from previous marriage: Frederick, Seth. BA, Jacksonville State U., 1973; MDiv., Emory U., 1975; D in Ministry, Vanderbilt U., 1978. Ordained to ministry United Meth. Ch. Pastor Center Grove United Meth. Ch., Huntsville, Ala., 1975-77, King's Meml. United Meth. Ch., Decatur, Ala., 1977—; dir. pastoral svcs. North Ala. Regional Hosp., Decatur, 1984—, also employee assistance ofcl.; bd. dirs. Bd. of the Ordained Ministry, Birmingham, Ala., Ethnic Minority Ministries, Commn. on Ch. and Safety, Birmingham; del. North Ala. Ann. Conf., Birmingham, 1991. Contbr. articles to various publs. Mem. adv. bd. The Albany Clinic, Decatur, 1989—; mem. N.W. Counseling Ctr., Decatur, 1990—, Community Unity of Decatur, 1989—, Morgan County Hist. Commn., Decatur, 1988—. Protestant fellow Rockefeller Found., 1973-75. Mem. Decatur Dist. Mins. Assn., Employee Assistance Soc., Sigma Tau Delta, Pi Gamma Mu, Phi Alpha Theta. Home: 511 Walnut St NE Decatur AL 35601 Office: North Ala Regional Hosp Hwy 31 S Decatur AL 35601

RAHAMAN, HAJI ABDOOL, religious organization administrator; b. Georgetown, Guyana, Apr. 2, 1931; s. Abdool Wahab and Noorjehan Khan; m. Kadija Ali, Sept. 12, 1951; children: Raheema, Ryhanna, Zulaika, Hafiz, Shashudeen, Khadija, Rafina. Owner, operator K. Rahaman & Sons Gen. Stores; pres. Guyana United Sad'r Islamic Anjuman, Georgetown, 1982—. former chmn. People's Dem. Movement, Guyana. Home: 51, Russel & Evans Sts, Charlestown, Georgetown 4, Guyana Office: 157 Alexander St, Kitty, PO Box 10715, Georgetown 4, Guyana

RAHER, RICHARD RAY, minister; b. Denver, May 29, 1949; s. Ralph Gerald and Teresina M. (Jaramillo) R.; m. Robbi Louise Seagle-Simpson, Dec. 16, 1977; children: Aaron, Nathan. AS in Elec. Tech., San Diego Mesa Coll., 1977, AA in Mid. Mgmt., 1980. Elder Calvary Chapel, San Diego, Calif., 1976-80; asst. pastor Calvary Chapel, Poway, Calif., 1980-84; founder, sr. pastor Calvary Chapel, Ramona, Calif., 1984—; co-founder, asst. pastor Calvary Chapel, Julian, Calif., 1988-90; pres. Ramona Ministerial Assn., 1988-89. Author: (booklet) Love in Action, 1989. Mem. Ramona Substance Abuse Com., 1988—; co-founder, chmn. Ramona Crisis Pregnancy Ctr., 1989-90. with USN, 1969-72, Vietnam. Grantee ADAPT Found., 1990. Mem. Calvary Chapel Outreach Fellowship. Office: Calvary Chapel 709 D St Ste 202 Ramona CA 92065 *The legacy I hope to leave in this life: if any mark can be made upon the culture where I dwell it is the undeniable fact of my love for Jesus Christ. The marvelous privilege it has been to serve Him as a "fisher of men."*

RAHFELDT, DARYL GENE, minister; b. Ames, Iowa, Feb. 16, 1947; s. Edward DeLos and Anna Henrietta (Borchert) R.; m. Marjorie Kay Johnson, Mar. 18, 1973; children: Emily Kathryn, Gretchen Amanda. BS in Forestry, Iowa State U., 1969; MA in New Testament, Wheaton (Ill.) Coll., 1975; PhD in Bibl. Theology, Marquette U., 1987. Ordained to ministry Community Ch., 1988. Lay leader, tchr. Christian and Missionary Alliance, Wheaton, Ill., 1973-75; asst. pastor, youth pastor Christian and Missionary Alliance, Fremont, Nebr., 1975-78; ch. planter, founding pastor Christian and Missionary Alliance, Pullman, Wash., 1978-80; lay leader, tchr. Bapt. Gen. Conf., Brown Deer, Wis., 1981-88; sr. minister Community Ch., Rolling Meadows, Ill., 1988—; seminar leader religion Marquette Continuing Edn. Program, Milw., 1983; instr. N.T. Carroll Coll., Waukesha, Wis., 1983; tchr. adult bible class Capitol Dr. Luth. Ch., Milw., 1986-87. With U.S. Army 1969-72. Fellowship Arthur J. Schmitt Found., 1983-84. Mem. Rolling Meadows Ministerial Assn., Xi Sigma Pi. Home: 2508 W Fremont St Rolling Meadows IL 60008 Office: Community Ch 2720 Kirchoff Rd Rolling Meadows IL 60008 *What we must believe if we are to have any hope for this life or the next is that God exists, and that he is in the business of turning evil into good.*

RAHTJEN, BRUCE DONALD, minister; b. Rochester, N.Y., May 14, 1933; s. Donald Fellows and Anne Elizabeth (Miller) R.; m. Jeanne Marie Hamilton, June 5, 1954 (div. 1972); children: Donald Bruce, Nancy Jeanne, James Robert; m. Irma L. McCormac, July 21, 1973. BA cum laude, U. Rochester, 1955; BD, Colgate Rochester Div. Sch., 1958; PhD, Drew U., 1964. Ordained to ministry Meth. Ch., 1958, priest Episcopal Ch., 1979. Pastor Meth. Ch. of Holley, N.Y., 1955-58, Brown Meml. Meth. Ch., Jersey City, 1958-60; instr. Colgate Rochester Div. Sch., 1960-62; prof. St. Paul Sch. Theology, Kansas City, Mo., 1962-81; coll. chaplain Episcopal Diocese W. Mo., Kansas City, 1981-83; rector Trinity Episcopal Ch., Independence, Mo., 1983-89; dean sch. ministerial tng. Episcopal Diocese of West Mo., 1990—; vicar St. Mary's Episcopal Ch., Kansas City, Mo., 1990—; del. Gen. Conv. of the Episc. Ch., 1985, 88; adj. prof. Park Coll. Grad. Sch. of Religion, Independence, Mo. Author: Scripture and Social Action, 1966, Biblical Truth and Modern Man, 1968, Workbook in Experiential Theology, 1973; contbr. articles to profl. jours. Mem. Human Rels. Commn., Independence, 1983-87; bd. dirs. Hospice Care Mid-Am., Kansas City, 1978-90. Mem. Assn. for Creative Change (pres. 1978), Phi Beta Kappa. Democrat. Episcopalian. Avocations: gardening, fishing, cooking. Home: 3412 W Coleman Rd Kansas City MO 64111 Office: St Mary's Ch Box 156748 Kansas City MO 64106

RAIBLE, PETER SPILMAN, minister; b. Peterborough, N.H., Nov. 22, 1929; s. Robert Jules and Mildred (Galt) R.; m. Dee Dee Rainbow, June 18, 1950 (div. 1968); children: Stephen M., Robin S., Robert R., Deborah R.; m. Marcia McClellan Barton, June 5, 1987. PhB, U. Chgo., 1949; BA, U. Calif., Berkeley, 1952; MDiv, Starr King Sch. Ministry, 1953, D in Sacred Theology (hon.), 1974. Ordained to ministry Unitarian Ch. Asst. minister First Unitarian Ch., Providence, 1953-55; minister Unitarian Ch., Lincoln, Nebr., 1955-61, Univ. Unitarian Ch., Seattle, 1961—; bd. pres. Starr King Sch., Berkeley, 1967-68; mem. exec. com. Council Chs., Seattle, 1982-88; adj. prof. Meadville Lombard, 1987-88, Northwest Theol. Union, 1989. Author: How to Case a Church, 1982; book editor Jour. Liberal Ministry, 1965-71. Bd. dirs. Council Planning Affiliates, Seattle, 1969-73, Wash. State chpt. ACLU, Seattle, 1963-67; chmn. ministerial adv. com. Planned Parenthood Ctr., Seattle, 1963-68; pres. United Nations Assn., Lincoln, 1959-61. Served as cpl. USAF, 1948-49. Merrill fellow Harvard U., Cambridge, Mass., 1972. Mem. Unitarian Universalist Ministers Assn. (pres. 1973-75, Pacific N.W. dist. exec. 1962-64, pres. 1985-87, mem. commn. on appraisal 1977-81). Office: U Unitarian Ch 6556 35th Ave NE Seattle WA 98115

RAINBOW, PAUL ANDREW, educator; b. Mpls., July 19, 1955; s. James Robert and Miriam Bonnie (Herbold) R.; m. Alison Jane Muff, June 25, 1988; 1 child, Daniel John. BA, U. Minn., 1977; MDiv, Trinity Evang. Div. Sch., 1980; ThM, Harvard Div. Sch., 1983; DPhil, U. Oxford, Oxon, U.K., 1988. Asst. prof. N.T. N.Am. Bapt. Sem., Sioux Falls, S.D., 1988—. Rsch. grantee Tyndale House, 1984-86. Mem. Soc. Bibl. Lit., Inst. for Bibl. Rsch. Office: NAm Bapt Sem 1321 W 22nd St Sioux Falls SD 57105

RAINER, THOMAS SPRATLING, pastor; b. Union Springs, Ala., July 16, 1955; s. Samuel Solomon Sr. and Amelia Nan (Keller) R.; m. Nellie Jo King, Dec. 17, 1977; children: Samuel III, Arthur, Jess. BS summa cum laude, U. Ala., Tuscaloosa, 1977; MDiv, So. Bapt. Theol. Sem., 1985, PhD, 1988. Ordained to ministry So. Bapt. Conv., 1984. Pastor Hopewell Bapt. Ch., Madison, Ind., 1984-86, Louisville, 1986-88; sr. pastor Azalea Bapt. Ch., St. Petersburg, Fla., 1988-90; pastor Green Valley Bapt. Ch., Birmingham, Ala., 1990—; trustee Bay Area Pregnancy Ctr., Clearwater, Fla., 1988-90; mem. bd. overseers Criswell Coll., Dallas, 1991—; adj. prof. Beeson Div. Sch. Samford U., Birmingham, 1991—. Author/editor: Evangelism in the 21st Century, 1989; contbr. revs. and articles to profl. jours. Garrett fellow So. Bapt. Theol. Sem., 1986-88. Mem. Acad. for Evangelism in Theol. Edn., Beta Gamma Sigma, Omicron Delta Epsilon. Home: 3595 Burntleaf Ln Birmingham AL 35226 Office: Green Valley Bapt Ch 1815 Patton Chapel Rd Birmingham AL 35226 *Life is a series of never-ending choices which compete for our limited resource of time. I have found that my life takes on its fullest meaning when my priorities for time are my God, my family, and my church.*

RAINES, JAMES RAY, academic administrator, minister; b. DeWitt, Ark., Sept. 21, 1937; s. Tony Madison and Hazel (York) R.; m. Ann M. Oldnar, June 2, 1957; children: James T., Michael R., Kimberly Ann. BA, Cen. Bapt. Coll., Conway, Ark., 1960. Ordained to ministry Bapt. Ch. Pastor Zion Bapt. Ch., Fordyce, Ark., 1954-63, First Bapt. Ch., Gurdon, Ark., 1963-73, Immanuel Bapt. Ch., Camden, Ark., 1973-84; pres. Cen. Bapt. Coll., Conway, Ark., 1984—. Mem. Kiwanis (spiritual leader 1990), Masons (chaplain 1982). Baptist. Avocations: golf, fishing, hunting, travelling. Office: Cen Bapt Coll 1501 Coll Ave Conway AR 72032

RAINES, JERRY RICHARD, minister; b. Lamesa, Tex., Sept. 29, 1946; s. Hershel Edwin and Dorothy Louise (Painter) R.; m. Sue Ann Davis, Aug. 17, 1968; children: Jay Richard, Rebecca SuAnn, Hannah Maryelle. BA, Howard Payne Coll., 1969; MDiv, Southwestern Bapt. Theol. Sem., 1972, D Ministry, 1987. Ordained to ministry So. Bapt. Conv., 1968. Pastor Ireland Bapt. Ch., Gatesville, Tex., 1968-69; youth min. Calvary Bapt. Ch., Harlingen, Tex., 1969-70; pastor 1st Bapt. Ch., Lometa, Tenn., 1971-73, Live Oak Bapt. Ch., Gatesville, 1973-78, Canyon Creek Bapt. Ch., Temple, Tex., 1978—. Mem. Bell Bapt. Assn. Office: Canyon Creek Bapt Ch 4306 S 31st St Temple TX 76502

RAINIERO, JOSEPH W., clergyman; b. Port Chester, N.Y., May 24, 1939; s. William Joseph and Margaret (Defiance) R.; m. Dorothy A. Rende, Sept. 14, 1958; 1 child, Debra A. Rainiero Pinto. Student, Fairfied Bible Sch., 1976, Breane Coll. of Bible, 1982. Ordained to ministry Assemblies of God Ch. Asst. pastor Trinity Ind. Assemblies of God Ch., Harrison, N.Y., 1982—; traffic mgr. Texaco Inc. Hdqrs., White Plains, N.Y., 1981—. With USAF, 1957-61. Home: Trinity Ind Assemblies of God Ch 11 Purdy St Harrison NY 10528-3705

RAINS, DARREL, minister; b. Okemah, Okla., Aug. 10, 1945; s. Lee Ray and Mary Ellen (Douglass) R.; m. Suzanne Hunter, Nov. 9, 1968; children: Nathan, Amy. Student, U. Okla., 1963-65; BA, Okla. Bapt. U., 1968; MDiv, Southwestern Bapt. U., Ft. Worth, Tex., 1971, D Ministry, 1978. Ordained to ministry, So. Bapt. Conv., 1967. Pastor 1st Bapt. Ch., Moyers, Okla., 1967-68, Midway Bapt. Ch., Pernell, Okla., 1968-71, Agnew Ave. Bapt. Ch., Oklahoma City, 1971-77, Sandia Bapt. Ch., Albuquerque, 1977-85, 1st Bapt. Ch., Pampa, Tex., 1985—; trustee McCarley Found., Pampa, 1985-91; nominating com. Bapt. Gen. Conv. Tex., 1991. Bd. dirs. United Way, Pampa, 1986-90. Republican. Home: 1220 Christine Pampa TX 79065 Office: First Bapt Ch 203 N West St Pampa TX 79066 *In a day of rapidly depleting natural resources, we need to remember that the human soul and spirit are the only renewable resources known to man. The world needs the presence of the Greatest Man—Jesus—again in human hearts.*

RAINS, HENRY THOMAS, minister; b. St. Louis, Aug. 2, 1955; s. Allie Thomas and Donna Louise (Baugh) R.; m. Catherine Elizabeth Fitzsimmons, Apr. 7, 1979; children: Amanda Marie, Elizabeth Lynn, Andrew Travis. AA, So. Bapt. Coll., 1975; BA, S.W. Bapt. Coll., 1977; MDiv, Midwestern Bapt. Theol. Sem., 1991. Ordained to ministry So. Bapt. Conv., 1977. Pastor Creve Coeur (Ill.) So. Bapt. Ch., 1979-81, Broadway Bapt. Ch., St. Louis, 1981-85, Witt's Chapel Bapt. Ch., Maynard, Ark., 1985-86, Allen Pk. Bapt. Ch., Galesburg, Ill., 1986-91, Hoosier Prarie Bapt. Ch., Louisville, Ill., 1991—. Chmn. adv. bd. The Salvation Army, Galesburg, 1989-90, vice chmn. 1990-91; trustee Ill. Bapt. Coll., Galesburg, 1989-90. Named to C.H. Spurgeon Soc. William Jewell Coll., 1984. Mem. Metro-Peoria Bapt. Assn. (assoc. evangelism dir. 1987-91). Home: RR 2 Box 308 Clay City IL 62824 Office: Hoosier Prarie Bapt Ch RR 2 Louisville IL 62858

RAINS, VANCE CLIFTON, church director; b. Orlando, Fla., July 12, 1967; s. Clark Clifton and Linda Mary (Haman) R.; m. Kelly McFarlane, Aug. 18, 1990. BA, U. Cen. Fla., 1989. Dir. youth ministry 1st United Meth. Ch. Orlando, 1990—. Home: 1700 Gurtler Ct # 2 Orlando FL 32804 Office: 1st United Meth Ch 142 E Jackson Orlando FL 32801

RAINWATER, JOHN VICTOR, JR., minister; b. Ft. Worth, Dec. 15, 1942; s. John Victor and Wilda Jean (Griffith) R.; m. Miriam Elizabeth Williams, Dec. 23, 1965; children John V. III, Joseph Allen. MusB, Hardin-Simmons U., 1966; M in Ch. Music, Southwestern Bapt. Theol. Sem., Ft. Worth, 1970. Min. music and youth Hillcrest Pk. Bapt. Ch., Arlington, Tex., 1966-68, 1st Bapt. Ch., Gilmer, Tex., 1968-72, Winbourne Ave. Bapt. Ch., Baton Rouge, 1973-76, 1st Bapt. Ch., Marshall, Tex., 1976-80; min. music and adminstrn., founding charter member Celebration Bapt. Ch., Tallahassee, Fla., 1980-90; sec. Fla. Bapt. Assn. Ministry Music, Tallahasse, 1990—. Fellow Nat. Assn. Ch. Bus. Adminstrs., So. Bapt. Ch. Bus. Adminstrn. Assn.; mem. So. Bapt. Ch. Music Conf. Republican. Home: 4007 Kilmartin Dr Tallahassee FL 32308 Office: Celebration Bapt Ch 3737 Shamrock E Tallahassee FL 32308 *One of the most meaningful statements for me was from Fred Smith at a lecture series when I was in college at Hardin Simmons University. "How can you find God's will? Answer your mail!". Many times we worry and say "Oh what would God have me to do?". When we need to get busy with the things that God has put on our desk! To find God's will Answer your Mail!.*

RAINWATER, NATHAN RANDY, minister; b. Maryville, Tenn., Nov. 15, 1955; s. Halloce Palmer and Etta Louise (Myers) R.; m. Priscilla Christine Myers, Oct. 11, 1980; children: Sarah Nicole, Nathan Philip, Joel Scott. BS, U. Tenn., 1979; MDiv, New Orleans Bapt. Theol. Sem., 1985. Ordained to ministry Bapt. Ch., 1985. Assoc. pastor Cen. Bapt. Ch., New Orleans, 1985-86; ch. planter apprentice Home Mission Bd., Taos, Mo., 1986-88; mission pastor Liberty Road Bapt. Chapel, Taos, Mo., 1988—; moderator Dixon Bapt. Assn., Bland, Mo., 1989-91, youth camp dir., 1990, 91. Citizens adv. input group Blair Oaks Sch. Dist., Wardsville, Mo., 1990. Mem. New Orleans Bapt. Theol. Sem. Alumni Assn. (sec. Mo. chpt. 1986-87). Home: 7115 Redbird Rd Jefferson City MO 65101 *The day to day trials of life will bring a clearer vision of the hope of the Glory of God or they will bring the clouds of discouragement and defeat. The choice is ours.*

RÄISÄNEN, HEIKKI MARTTI, theology educator; b. Helsinki, Dec. 10, 1941; s. Martti Olavi and Saara Ilona (Itkonen) R.; m. Leena Marjatta Wright, Oct. 19, 1974; children: Ilkka, Markku, Päivi, Tuomo. ThM, U. Helsinki, 1965, MA, 1968, ThD, 1969; DD (hon.), U. Edinburgh, Scotland, 1990. Ordained to ministry Luth. Ch., 1965. Minister Luth. Ch., Espoo, Finland, 1965-66; asst. prof. N.T. studies U. Helsinki, 1968-70, lectr., 1969-74, acting assoc. prof., 1972-74, prof., 1975—; rsch. fellow Finnish Acad., Helsinki, 1971-72, rsch. prof., 1984—. Author: Die Mutter Jesu im Neuen Testament, 1969, Paul and the Law, 1983, The Torah and Christ, 1986, The Messianic Secret in Mark's Gospel, 1990, Beyond New Testament Theology, 1990, others; chief editor Vartija, 1989—; contbr. numerous articles to profl. jours. Mem. Finnish Acad. Scis., Soc. N.T. Studies, Finnish Exegetical Soc. (chmn. 1980-85). Home: Vantaanjänne 1 B 11, SF-01730 Vantaa 73, Finland Office: U Helsinki Theol Faculty, Neitsytpolku 1 B, SF-00140 Helsinki Finland

RAITT, JILL, educator; b. Los Angeles, May 1, 1931; d. Arthur Taylor and Lorna Genevieve (Atherton) R.; B.A., in Philosophy, San Francisco Coll. Women, 1953, M.A. in English, 1964; M.A. in Theology, Marquette U., 1967; M.A., U. Chgo, 1967, Ph.D., 1970. Instr., then asst. prof. theology San Francisco Coll. Women, 1963-64, Immaculate Heart Coll., Hollywood, Calif., 1967-68, St. Xavier Coll., Chgo., 1966-68; asst. prof. program religious studies U. Calif.-Riverside, 1969-73; assoc. prof. history theology Duke Div. Sch., 1973-81; prof., chmn. dept. religious studies U. Mo., Columbia, 1981-87, 90—, Middlebush prof. humanities, 1990—; Alexander Robertson lectr. U. Glasgow, Scotland, 1985. Contbr. articles and revs. to profl. religious jours. U. Chgo. fellow, 1968-69, Faculty fellow U. Calif., Riverside, 1970, NEH fellow, 1975-76, Radcliffe Inst. fellow, 1975-76, Duke Research Coun. fellow, 1975, Nat. Humanities Ctr. fellow, 1987-88; Humanities Inst. grantee, 1972-73. Mem. Am. Acad. Religion (sec. Western region, 1972-73, nat. sec., 1972-75, nat. pres. 1980-81, assoc. dir. 1981-83), Calvin Studies Soc. (v.p. 1985-87, pres. 1987-89). Roman Catholic. Office: U Mo Dept Religious Studies 405 GCB Columbia MO 65211

RAKESTRAW, ROBERT VINCENT, theology educator; b. Phila., Nov. 16, 1943; s. Arthur Jesse and Mary Anne (Stenella) R.; m. Judy Kay Engevik, July 22, 1967; children: Joan Marie, Laureen Dawn. Student, St. Joseph's Coll., Phila., 1961-63; diploma, Prairie Bible Coll., 1967; BS, MA, Calvary Bible Coll., Kansas City, Mo., 1970; M.Phil., PhD, Drew U., 1985. Ordained minister in Bapt. Ch., 1967. Pastor Harmony Bapt. Ch., Kansas City, Mo., 1968-69; instr. Prairie Bible Coll., Three Hills, Alberta, Can., 1970-75; sr. pastor Calvary Bapt. Ch., Flemington, N.J., 1976-80; prof. theology The Criswell Coll., Dallas, 1985-88; assoc. prof. theology Bethel Theol. Sem., St. Paul, 1988—. Author: (with others) Baptist Theologians, 1990, Nelson's Illustrated Bible Dictionary, 1986; newspaper columnist Red Deer Advocate, Red Deer, Alberta, 1973-75; contbr. articles to profl. jours. Scholar St. Joseph's Coll., Phila., 1961-63; teaching fellow in ethics Drew U., 1983. Mem. Am. Acad. Religion, Am. Theol. Soc., Soc. Christian Ethics, Wesleyan Theol. Soc., Evang. Theol. Soc. (sec.-treas. eastern region 1978-80), Rotary. Home: 1281 80th Ave NE Spring Lake Park MN 55432 Office: Bethel Theol Sem 3949 Bethel Dr Saint Paul MN 55112

RAKOW, THOMAS CHARLES, minister; b. Richland Center, Wis., Nov. 27, 1956; s. Robert David and C. Marie (Flamme) R.; m. Elizabeth Susan Wahlbeck, Nov. 26, 1988; 1 child, Abigail. AA, U. Wis., Richland Center, 1980; BA, Moody Bible Inst., Chgo., 1984; MA in Religion, Asbury Theol. Sem., 1987. Pastor Beulah Wesleyan Ch., Gillingham, Wis., 1987-89, Silver Lake (Minn.) Congl. Ch., 1989—. Contbr. articles to profl. jours. Home: 217 Queen Ave NW Silver Lake MN 55381 *Christ deserves our complete service—even if those we are ministering to do not.*

RALPH, MARGARET NUTTING, religious education educator; b. Lincoln, Nebr., Mar. 23, 1941; d. Charles Bernard and Mary Agnes (Flannagan) Nutting; m. Donald Edward Ralph, July 20, 1963; children: Daniel, John, Anthony, Kathleen. BA, St. Mary's of Notre Dame, 1963; MA, U. Mass., 1970; PhD, U. Ky., 1980. Tchr. religion faculty Lexington (Ky.) Cath. High Sch., 1974-83; instr. dept. English, religious studies program U. Ky., Lexington, 1980-88; sec. of ednl. ministries Cath. Diocese of Lexington, 1988—; dir. MA in Religious Edn. for Roman Catholics program Lexington Theol. Sem., 1988—; cons. adult faith devel. Diocese of Covington, Ky., 1982-88; bd. dirs. Ky. Coun. Churches, Lexington, 1989—. Author: And God Said What?, 1986, Willie of Church Street, 1989, Plain Words About Biblical Images: Growing in Our Faith Through Scripture, 1989, Discovering the Gospels: Four Accounts of Good News, 1990, Discovering the First Century Church: The Acts of the Apostles, Letters of Paul and the Book of Revelation, 1991. Discovered The First Century Ch., 1991. Office: Cath Diocese of Lexington 1310 Leestown Rd Lexington KY 40508

RALSTON, TIMOTHY JOHN, religion educator; b. Toronto, Ont., Can., Apr. 2, 1956; came to U.S., 1988; s. Henry William and Iva Eileen (Riddolls) R.; m. Carol Anne Bigelow, May 5, 1979; 1 child, Briana Leigh. BS, U. Waterloo, Ontario, Canada, 1978; ThM, Dallas Theol. Seminary, 1983, postgrad., 1988—; postgrad., U. Toronto, 1985-86. Ordained to ministry Fellowship of Evang. Bapt. Chs., 1985. Pastor Hockley Valley Bible Chapel, Orangeville, Ont., 1983-85; assoc. pastor Chartwell Bapt. Ch., Oakville, Ont., 1985-87; instr. Cen. Bapt. Seminary, Toronto, 1987, Dallas Theol. Seminary, 1988—; corp. mem. Inter-Varsity Christian Fellowship, 1987—. Mem. Evang. Theol. Soc., Soc. Bibl. Lit. Office: Dallas Theol Seminary 3909 Swiss Ave Dallas TX 75204 *Life is best savored in the company of friends who know the dangers, see the opportunities, share the risks and enjoy the victory together.*

RAMAGE, DAVID, JR., academic administrator. Pres. McCormick Theol. Sem., Chgo. Office: McCormick Theol Sem Office of Pres 5555 S Woodlawn Ave Chicago IL 60637*

RAMBO, LEWIS RAY, psychology and religion educator; b. Stephenville, Tex., Dec. 29, 1943; s. Harold Jack and Dorothy Gwendolyn (Gibson) R.; m. Pamela Moser, Aug. 30, 1967 (div. Feb. 1981); m. Hsifei Helen Chen, Sept. 30, 1988 (div. Aug. 1991); 1 child, Anna Catherine. BA, Abilene Christian U., 1967; MDiv, Yale U., 1971; MA, U. Chgo., 1973, PhD, 1975; postgrad., Grad. Theol. Union, Berkeley, Calif., 1978—. Prof. Trinity Coll., Deerfield, Ill., 1975-78, San Francisco Theol. Sem., San Anselmo, Calif., 1978—; mem. faculty Grad. Theol. Union, Berkeley, Calif., 1978—. Author: The Divorcing Christian, 1983, Conversion, 1991; co-author: (bibliography) Psychology of Religion, 1976; editor Pastoral Psychology, 1984—; bd. dirs. Internat. Jour. of the Psychology of Religion, 1990—. Lady Davis fellow Hebrew U. of Jerusalem, 1985; rsch. grantee Lilly Endowment and Christian Theol. Sem., Indpls., 1989, interdisciplinary seminar grantee Lilly Endowment, Grad. Theol. Union, 1989-90. Mem. Am. Acad. Religion, Am. Psychol. Assn., Soc. for the Sci. Study of Religion, Am. Soc. Missiology. Mem. Chs. of Christ. Office: San Francisco Theol Sem 2 Kensington Rd San Anselmo CA 94960-2905

RAMEY, GEORGE GROVER, theology educator, university administrator; b. Dixon, Mo., Aug. 17, 1938; s. Donald Edward and J. Ruth (Crum) R.; m. Patricia Ann Perkins, June 7, 1959; children: Jonathan Edward, Steven Wesley. AA, S.W. Baptist Coll., 1958; BA, William Jewell Coll., 1960; BDiv, Midwestern Baptist Sem., 1963; M. Theology, So. Bapt. Sem., 1965, PhD, 1968. Pastor Hopewell Bapt. Ch., Barnett, Mo., 1958, New Hope Bapt. Ch., Bethany, Mo., 1961-63; asst. prof. Cumberland Coll., Williamsburg, Ky., 1968-72, assoc. prof., 1972-82, prof. religion, 1982—, dir. bus. affairs, treas., 1976-88, v.p. for bus. affairs, treas., 1988—; field supr. Joint Archaeol. Expdn. to Ai, Jordon, 1966, lab. technician, 1971. Cubmaster Williamsburg Pack 15, Boy Scouts Am., 1973-80. Mem. Soc. Bibl. Lit., Am. Sch. Oriental Rsch., Nat. Assn. Profs. Hebrew (mem. nat. exec. com. 1974—), Coun. Ind. Ky. Coll. and Univ. Bus. Officers, Nat. Assn. Coll. and Univ. Bus. Officers. Home: 75 Hemlock St Williamsburg KY 40769-1793 Office: Cumberland Coll Bus Office Williamsburg KY 40769-1372

RAMEY, JOHN MICHAEL, clergyman; b. Beaumont, Tex., Feb. 11, 1958; s. John Wilburn and Mary Jo (Blair) R.; m. Laura Lee Heerten, Aug. 24, 1980; children: Laura Elizabeth, Ana Lea, Sara Justina, Josiah John. A in Religion, Concordia Luth. Coll., 1978; B in Ch. History, Concordia Coll., 1980, MDiv, 1984; ThD, Trinity Theol. Sem., 1988. Ordained to ministry Luth. Ch. Vicar Shepher of the Lake Luth. Ch., Garrison, Minn., 1982-83; pastor Zion/Trinity Luth. Chs., Upland/Campbell, Nebr., 1984-87; pastor, missionary Highlands Luth. Ch., Lincoln, Nebr., 1987-91; mission developer Family of Faith-Copperfield, Houston, 1991—; chaplain Tex. Army Nat. Guard, Houston, 1991—; cir. edn. dir. Hastings Circuit (Nebr.) Luth. Ch.-Mo. Synod, 1984-87; counselor Hastings Zone LWML, 1984-87; cir. sec. Lincoln Cir. Luth. Ch.-Mo. Synod, 1988-89. Author: Doctrine of the Church According to St. John, 1988. Mem. Campbell (Nebr.) Jaycees, 1988. Recipient Individual Achievement award Nebr. Army Nat. Guard, 1990, Army Commendation, 1991, Nat. Def. Svc. medal, 1991. Republican. Office: Copperfield Mission LCMS 16313 Wellers Way Houston TX 77095 *The* *call of Christ is to make disciples, not members: that requires the commitment of love and time and effort. It brings the reward of knowing you have fulfilled Christ's commission as one of His own.*

RAMIREZ, RICARDO, bishop; b. Bay City, Tex., Sept. 12, 1936; s. Natividad and Maria (Espinosa) R. B.A., U. St. Thomas, Houston, 1959; M.A., U. Detroit, 1968; Diploma in Pastoral Studies, East Asian Pastoral Inst., Manila, 1973-74. Ordained priest Roman Catholic Ch., 1966; missionary Basilian Fathers, Mex., 1968-76; exec. v.p. Mexican Am. Cultural Ctr., San Antonio, 1976-81; aux. bishop Archdiocese of San Antonio, 1981-82; bishop Diocese of Las Cruces, N.M., 1982—; cons. U.S. Bishop's Com. on Liturgy, from 1981; advisor U.S. Bishop's Com. on Hispanic Affairs, from 1981. Author: Fiesta, Worship and Family, 1981. Mem. N.Am. Acad. on Liturgy, Hispanic Liturgical Inst., Padres Asociada Derechos Religiosos Educativos y Sociales. Lodges: K.C; Holy Order Knights of Holy Sepulcher. Office: Diocese of Las Cruces 1280 Med Park Las Cruces NM 88004

RAMSAY, DEVERE MAXWELL, religious educator; b. Tuscaloosa, Ala., Sept. 2, 1925; d. J. Alston and Lucille (DeVere) Maxwell; m. William M. Ramsay, Apr. 27, 1954; children: William M. Jr., John A. BA, U. Ala, 1946; MA, Presbyn. Sch. Christian Edn., 1948; postgrad., Tchrs. Coll., N.Y.C., 1966-67. Cert. dir. Christian Edn. Presbyn. Ch. Dir. Christian Edn. 1st Presbyn. Ch., Anderson, S.C., 1948-51; assoc. regional dir. Christian Edn. Synod of Ala., Birmingham, 1951-54; instr. Christian Edn. Bethel Coll., McKenzie, Tenn., 1980—; cons. in Christian Edn. Cumberland Presbyn. Ch., Memphis, 1981—, Presbyn. Ch. (US), 1981—. Author: God's Promises, 1964, God's Son, 1965, God's People, Our Story, 1984, God's People, Our Story, Old Testament, 1985, Glimpses of the Gospel Through Art, 1990. Mem. exec. com. Carroll County Dem. Orgn., McKenzie, Tenn., 1984. Avocations: grandmothering. Home: Rt 2 Box 235 McKenzie TN 38201 Office: Bethel Coll McKenzie TN 38201

RAMSAY, KARIN KINSEY, lay worker; b. Brownwood, Tex., Aug. 10, 1930; d. Kirby Luther and Ina Rebecca (Wood) Kinsey; m. Jack Cummins Ramsay Jr., Aug. 31, 1951; children: Annetta Jean, Robin Andrew. BA, Trinity U., 1951. Cert. assoc. ch. edn., 1980. Youth coord. Covenant Presbyn. Ch., Carrollton, Tex., 1961-76; dir. ch. edn. Northminster Presbyn. Ch., Dallas, 1976-80, Univ. Presbyn. Ch., Chapel Hill, N.C., 1987-90, Oak Grove Presbyn. Ch., Bloomington, Minn., 1990—; mem. Presbytery Candidates Com., Dallas, 1977-82, Presbytery Exams. Com., Dallas, 1979-81; clk. coun. New Hope Presbytery, Rocky Mount, N.C., 1989-90. Author: Ramsay's Resources, 1983-91; contbr. articles to jours. in field. Design cons. Brookhaven Hosp. Chapel, Dallas, 1977-78; elder Presbyn. Ch., Carrollton, 1982—; coord. Lifeline Emergency Response, Dallas, 1982-84. Mem. Assn. Presbyn. Ch. Educators. Home: 9725 Pleasant Ave S 3-B Bloomington MN 55420 Office: Oak Grove Presbyn Ch 2200 W Old Shakopee Rd Bloomington MN 55431 *Yesterday taught me the lessons which made today possible. Today is the challenging link between yesterday and tomorrow. Tomorrow is an opportunity built on the foundation of today. Today is special.*

RAMSAY, FATHER KENNETH A., pastor; b. Jamaica, W.I.; s. Stephen and Rhoda (Bedward) R. BA in Philosophy, St. John's Sem., 1959, MD, 1985; CAGS, St. Joseph Coll., 1987; postgrad., The Grad. Theol. Found. Pastor Roman Cath. Archdiocese of Jamaica, Kingston. Mem. AACD, Am. Mental Health Counseling Assn. Home: Saint Bonaventure 114058 170th St Jamaica NY 11434

RAMSAY, NANCY JEAN, theology educator; b. Salisbury, Md., June 22, 1949; d. Thelbert H. and Marilyn Jean (Douglas) R. BA, U. N.C., Greensboro, 1971; D Ministry, Union Theol. Sem. Va., 1975; PhD, Vanderbilt U., 1987. Ordained to ministry Presbyn. Ch. (U.S.A.), 1975. Assoc. pastor 1st Presbyn. CCh., Rocky Mount, N.C., 1975-79; asst. prof. pastoral theology Louisville Presbyn. Theol. Sem., 1983-87, assoc. prof., 1988—, dir. field edn., 1983-87; chair com. on women's concerns Presbyn. Ch. (U.S.A.), 1976-78, chair div. corp. and social mission, 1978-79, mem. gen. assembly coun., 1983-85, mem. com. to write brief statement ref. faith, 1984-91; speaker denominationally-sponsored meetings and workshops; mem. Mid. Tenn. Presbytery. Contbr. articles to religious jours., chpts. to books. Salem Ch. fellow Union Theol. Sem. Va., 1975, George Mayhew fellow Vanderbilt U., 1981-82. Mem. Soc. for Pastoral Theology, Am. Acad. Religion, Am. Assn. Pastoral Counselors, NOW, Phi Beta Kappa. Democrat. Office: Louisville Presbyn Theol Sem 1044 Alta Vista Rd Louisville KY 40205-1798

RAMSEY, CHARLIE BANKS, JR., minister; b. Harrisonburg, Va., Nov. 9, 1965; s. Charlie Banks Sr. and Rita Sue (McCraw) R. BS in Bibl. Edn., Lee Coll., 1989. Youth minister Roswell (Ga.) Ch. of God, 1989—; spiritual dir. Tres Dias, Atlanta, 1990—. Vice pres. Upsilon Xi Men's Christian Fraternity, Lee Coll., 1987, pres. student body, 1986-87. Named to Outstanding Young Men of Am., 1987. Mem. Nat. Youth Leaders Assn. Home: 723 Jett Woodstock GA 30188 Office: Roswell Church of God 410 Rucker Rd Alpharetta GA 30201

RAMSON, RONALD W., academic administrator. Pres. Kenrick-Glennon Sem., St. Louis. Office: Kenrick-Glennon Sem Office of Pres 5200 Glennon Dr Saint Louis MO 63119*

RAMUNDO, THOMAS JOSEPH, JR., minister; b. Chgo., Sept. 7, 1948; s. Thomas Joseph Sr. and Mary Rachel (Casurella) R.; m. Noni Audrey Graz, Aug. 23, 1969; children: Theresa Marie, Samuel Mark (dec.), Christy May. BA, Spring Arbor Coll., 1970; postgrad., Trinity Div. Sch., 1971-73, Garrett Sem., 1980-81; MA, Bethel Coll., 1984. Ordained to ministry Free Meth. Ch. as elder, 1974. Pastor Irving Park Free Meth. Ch., Chgo., 1970-73, Rapid City (S.D.) Free Meth. Ch., 1973-78, Woodstock (Ill.) Free Meth. Ch., 1978-81, 1st Free Meth. Ch. Warsaw, Ind., 1981-87; sr. pastor Jackson (Mich.) Free Meth. Ch., 1987—; mem. bd. adminstrn., So. Mich. Conf., Free Meth. Ch., 1989—, chmn. bd. Christian edn., 1989—; bd. dirs. Light and Life, Indpls., 1990—; campus and conf. speaker in field.; preaching prof. in field. Author: Stewardship Preaching Resources, 1982; contbr. articles to profl. jours. Bd. dirs. Jackson County Citizens for Life, 1988—. Office: Jackson Free Meth Ch 2829 Park Dr Jackson MI 49203 *Claiming Christ as my Risen Savior and crowning Christ as my Reigning Sovereign, I purpose to live exalting His Kingship and Extending His Kingdom.*

RAND, HOWARD BENJAMIN, religious organization administrator, educator, editor, lawyer; b. Haverhill, Mass., June 13, 1889; s. Frank Nathenial and Letty May (Lepper) R.; m. Hazel Gertrude Smith, July 23, 1913 (dec. 1982). LLB, U. Maine, 1912. Instr., lectr. on Bibl. truths Anglo Saxon Fedn. Am., Haverhill, 1928-46, nat. commr., 1946—; treas., editor Destiny Pubs., Haverhill and Merrimac, Mass., 1928—. Author: The Story the Bible Tells, 1953, Study in Revelation, 1951, Digest of the Divine Law, 1943, Study in Hosea, 1955, The Challenge of the Great Pyramid, 1943, others; also editor. With Mass. Army N.G., 1909-1912. Mem. Phi Alpha Delta. Home and Office: 43 Grove St Merrimac MA 01860 *My thoughts are that I should live righteously in accord with what God requires of a man who so elects to live.*

RANDALL, BENJAMIN F., religious organization administrator; b. Albert Lea, Minn., June 7, 1946; s. Benjamin F. and Rose Elein (Chilson) R.; m. Linda Ferry, July 12, 1969 (div. Sept. 1976); m. Roberta Hensley, July 5, 1980; children: Jason, Sean, Christopher. AA, Solano Community Coll., 1972; BA, U. San Francisco, 1976, MA, 1978. Bus. adminstr. Vaca Valley Christian Life Ctr., Vacaville, Calif., 1984—; single ministry dir. Christian Life Ctr., Vacaville, 1988—. Contbr. articles to profl. jours. Asst. recorder Solano County, Fairfield, Calif., 1982. With U.S. Army, 1966-68, Vietnam. Mem. Nat. Assn. Ch. Bus. Adminstrs., Nat. Assn. Single Leadership, Single Adult Ministries Assn.(No. Calif. and Nev. dists.). Mem. Assemblies of God. Office: Vaca Valley Christian Life Ctr 6391 Leisure Town Rd Vacaville CA 95687

RANDALL, CHANDLER CORYDON, church rector; b. Ann Arbor, Mich., Jan. 22, 1935; s. Frederick Stewart and Madeline Leta (Snow) R.; m. Marian Archias Montgomery, July 2, 1960; children: Sarah Archais, Elizabeth Leggett, Rebekah Stewart. AB in History, U. Mich., 1957; S.T.B. in Theology, Yale U., 1960; PhD in Hebraic Studies, Hebrew Union Coll., 1969; D.D. (honoris causa), Yale U., 1985. Rector St. Paul's Episcopal Ch., Richmond, Ind., 1967-71; rector Trinity Episcopal Ch., Ft. Wayne, Ind., 1971-88, St. Peter's Episcopal Ch., Del Mar, Calif., 1988—; bd. dirs. Living Ch. Found., Milw.; bibl. theologian Episcopal Ch. Stewardship, N.Y.C., 1985; alumni coun. Berkeley Divinity at Yale, New Haven, Conn., 1981-87; bishop's cabinet Diocese of No. Ind., South Bend, 1983-87. Author: Satire in the Bible, 1969, An Approach to Biblical Satire, 1990; contbr. articles to profl. jours. Founder Canterbury Sch., Ft. Wayne, 1977; commr. Ind. Jud. Qualifications Commn., Indpls., 1981-87; pres. Ft. Wayne Plan Commn., 1977; bd. dirs. Ft. Wayne Park Found., 1983-88; platform com. Ind. Republican Party, Indpls., 1974. Recipient Disting. Svc. medal U. Mich., 1981, Scheuer scholar Hebrew Union Coll., 1963-66, Liberty Bell award Ft. Wayne Bar Assn., 1988; named Sagamore of the Wabash, Gov. Ind., 1987. Mem. Am. Schs. Oriental Research, Yale U. Alumni Club (pres. 1982-88), Quest Club (pres.), Chi Psi (nat. chaplain 1982). Republican. Avocations: college recruiting, genealogy. Office: St Peters Episcopal Church PO Box 336 Del Mar CA 92014

RANDALL, CLAIRE, church executive; b. Dallas, Oct. 15, 1919; d. Arthur Godfrey and Annie Laura (Fulton) R. A.A., Schreiner Coll., 1948; BA, Scarritt Coll., 1950; DD (hon.), Berkeley Sem., Yale U., 1974; LHD (hon.), Austin Coll., 1982; LLD, Notre Dame U., 1984. Assoc. missionary edn. Bd. World Missions Presbyterian Ch., U.S., Nashville, 1949-57; dir. art Gen. Council Presbyterian Ch., U.S., Atlanta, 1957-61; dir. Christian World Mission, program dir., assoc. dir. Ch. Women United, N.Y.C., 1962-73; gen. sec. Nat. Council Ch. of Christ in U.S.A., N.Y.C., 1974-84; nat. pres. Ch. Women United, N.Y.C., 1988—. Mem. Nat. Commn. on Internat. Women's Yr., 1975-77, Martin Luther King Jr. Fed. Holiday Commn., 1985. Recipient Woman of Yr. in Religion award Heritage Soc., 1977; Empire State Woman of Yr. in Religion award State of N.Y., 1984; medal Order of St. Vladimir, Russian Orthodox Ch., 1984. Democrat. Presbyterian. Avocations: golf, swimming; painting; reading; music. Home: 155 W 68th St New York NY 10023

RANDALL, LAURA HELEN, librarian; b. Atlanta, May 29, 1950; d. Luther Hill and Louella Whorley (Higgins) R. BA cum laude, Vanderbilt U., 1972; MDiv, Va. Theol. Sem., 1976; MLS, Emory U., 1981. Catalog libr. Bridwell Libr. So. Meth. U., Dallas, 1981-88, sr. reference libr. Bridwell Libr., 1988—. Mem. Am. Theol. Libr. Assn., Jr. League of Dallas, Beta Phi Mu. Episcopalian. Office: So Meth U Bridwell Libr Dallas TX 75275

RANKIN, GARY LABAN, minister; b. Charlotte, N.C., Feb. 18, 1948; s. Julius Lucius and Lillie Belle (Graves) R.; m. Selina Joy Brendle, Oct. 10, 1971; children: Cliff, Trent. AA, Gaston Coll., Dallas, N.C., 1968; AB, Belmont (N.C.) Abbey Coll., 1970; clin. pastoral diploma, Gaston Meml. Hosp., Gastonia, N.C., 1980. Ordained to ministry So. Bapt. Conv., 1979. Assoc. pastor Sunset Forest Bapt. Ch., Gastonia, 1975-78, Ridge Bapt. Ch., Gastonia, 1978-79; pastor Craig Meml. Bapt. Ch., Stanley, N.C., 1979—; sec.-treas. Pastor's Conv., 1980; mem. ordination com. South Fork Bapt. Assn., 1981-83, mem. fin. com., 1985-87, mem. exec. com., 1987-89, mem. program com., 1989-91. Pres. Springfield Sch. PTO, Stanley, 1980-82, East Gaston Band Booster Club, Mt. Holly, N.C., 1988—; chmn. adv. bd. Springfield Sch., 1981; mem. adv. bd. East Gaston High Sch., 1989—. Republican. Home and Office: Craig Meml Bapt Ch 1246 Mariposa Rd Stanley NC 28164

RANNABARGAR, MARVIN RAY, minister; b. Kansas City, Mo., Jan. 6, 1939; s. Arthur McDonald and Grace B. (Clements) R.; m. Lola I. Bailey, Aug. 10, 1960 (div. Oct. 1980); children: Paul, Ruth; m. Mary Ruth Yulich, 1984. BA, Culver-Stockton Coll., 1961; MDiv, Drake U., 1964. Ordained minister Christian Ch., 1964. Assoc. pastor 1st Christian Ch., Hannibal, Mo., 1966-68; sr. pastor 1st Christian Ch., DuQuoin, Ill., 1969-71, Brookfield, Wis., 1971-75; sr. pastor Univ. Christian Ch., Normal, Ill., 1975-80, Emerson Park Christian Ch., Kansas City, Kans., 1980-87, Ridgewiew Christian Ch., Kansas City, 1987—; chmn. bd. UMHE, U. Wis., Milw., 1974-75; chmn. Hosp. Chaplaincy, Bloomington-Normal, 1977. Contbr. articles to Disciple mag., 1970—. Chmn., mem. Human Relations Commn., Kansas City, 1984-87; mem. adv. bd. Public Utilities Bd., Kansas City, 1985-87; mem. bd. Planned Parenthood, Bloomington, 1978, Crosslines, Kansas City, 1987—. Psyche M. Gooden scholar, 1962-63. Mem. Tau Kappa Epsilon. Democrat. Home: 8643 E 50 St Kansas City MO 64129 Office: Ridgeview Christian Ch 8640 Sin-A-Bar Rd Kansas City MO 64129 *Life is too short to be trivialized. I celebrate each movement and give thanks for each remembrance.*

RANSOM, DAVID P., minister; b. New Haven, Conn., Nov. 22, 1932; s. Howard Stephen Ransom and Mabel Lorraine (Soden) Ransom-Foley; m. Louise Freeman Swett, June 16, 1956; children: Stephen Barre, Sarah Elisabeth, Geoffrey Jon, Peter William. BA, Dartmouth Coll., 1954; BD, Andover Theol. Seminary, Newtown Centre, Mass., 1960, D of Ministry, 1973. Chaplain's asst. Base Chapel/U.S. Army, Camp Rilmer, N.J., 1955-56; interim pastor East Barre (Vt.) Congregational Ch., summer 1957; student asst. Second Congregational Ch., Medfield, Mass., 1957-58; pastor Shrewsbury Community Ch., Cuttingsville, Vt., 1958-60, Federated Ch., Avon, Ill., 1961-63; dir. and minister of Christian edn. First Congregational Ch., Willimantic, Conn., 1964-67; assoc. pastor, minister of Christian edn. First Congregational Ch., Stoneham, Mass., 1968-73; various others to pastor Pilgrim United Ch. of Christ, New Bedford, Mass., 1973-83, The Second Congregational United Ch. of Christ, Jeffersonville, Vt., 1988—. Mem. Assn. for Clin. Pastoral Edn., Am. Assn. Pastoral Counselors. Republican. Home and Office: PO Box 40 Main St Jeffersonville VT 05464-0040

RANSOM, ROBERT LOUIS, minister; b. Jeffersonville, Ind., June 22, 1950; s. William Roberty Ransom and Ruthanna (Moore) Ransom Dodd; m. Donna Evelyn Pottschmidt, Aug. 12, 1972; children: Matthew Robert, Sarah Elizabeth. BA, Ft. Wayne Bible Coll., 1972; MDiv, Asbury Theol. Sem., 1975. Ordained to ministry, Missionary Ch., 1977. Pastor 1st Missionary Ch., Bluffton, Ohio, 1975-79, Newson Missionary Ch., Saint Paris, Ohio, 1979-84; dir. Christian Edn. ministries Mich. Dist. Missionary Ch., Burton and Flint, Mich., 1984-89, mem. children's, youth and Christian Edn. bds., bd. dirs.; asst. to pres. Missionary Ch., Ft. Wayne, Ind., 1989—. Contbr. articles to profl. jours..; rep. constl. commn. Missionary Ch., Ft. Wayne, Ind., 1981—, dist. rep. ednl. ministries com., 1978—; dist. youth dir. East Cen. dist. Missionary Ch., Troy, Ohio, 1978-84; pres. Lima chpt. Nat. Assn. Evangs., Ohio, 1978-79; chmn., fundraiser Christian Rural Overseas Program, 1977. Bd. dirs. Cystic-Fibrosis, Northwest Clark County, Ohio, 1981. Scholar State of Ind., 1968; grantee Fort Wayne Bible Coll. Women's Aux., 1971. Mem. Kappa Kappa Kappa. Republican. Home and Office: 3822 Live Oak Blvd Fort Wayne IN 46804

RANSON, GUY HARVEY, clergyman, religion educator; b. Godley, Tex., Nov. 26, 1916; s. Jake Mincer and Willie Ann (Hardesty) R.; m. Rose Ellen Clark, May 24, 1949; children: Kenneth Clark, Kelly Maurice, Diana Louise. BA, Hardin-Simmons U., 1939; MA, U. Ky., 1944; postgrad., U. Cambridge, Eng., 1947-48; PhD, Yale U., 1956. Ordained to ministry Presbyn. Ch., 1961. Asst. prof. philosophy William Jewell Coll., Liberty, Mo., 1948-49, prof., chmn. dept. philosophy, 1949-52; asst. prof. ethics So. Bapt. Theol. Sem., Louisville, 1952-53, assoc. prof., 1953-58; assoc. prof. Div. Sch., Duke U., Durham, N.C., 1959-60, Princeton (N.J.) Theol. Sem., 1960-61; prof. religion Trinity U., San Antonio, 1961-82, prof. emeritus, 1982—, chmn. dept. religion, 1961-77, mem. curriculum council, 1961-77, chmn. curriculum council, 1967-68, mem. faculty senate, 1964-69, chmn. faculty senate, 1968-69; mem. com. ecumenical rels. Alamo Presbytery and Synod of Tex., 1967-70; mem. gen. coun. Alamo Presbytery, 1967-73, vice moderator, chmn. ministerial com., 1973. Author: F.D. Maurice's Theology of Society, 1956; mng. editor: Rev. and Expositer, 1957, 58; contbr. articles to profl. jours. Chmn. social action com. San Antonio Council Chs., 1968-70; mem. cen. priorities com. Community Welfare Council, San Antonio, 1968-69, Com. to Study San Antonio Sch. Dist., 1966-67; bd. dirs. Inman Christian Ctr., 1964-70, chmn. bd., 1969-70. Recipient research grant Trinity U. for archeol. excavation Hebron, Jordan, summer 1966. Mem. AAUP (chpt. pres. 1962-63), Am. Soc. Ch. History, Am. Philos. Assn., Am. Soc. Christian Ethics, Am. Acad. Religion, Am. Inst. Archaeology, Southwestern Philos. Soc. Club: South Tex. Yale U. (pres. 1977). Home: 115 Irvington Dr San Antonio TX 78209

RANUM, PAUL ARTHUR, minister, religious organization executive; b. Starbuck, Minn., Feb. 22, 1929; s. Arthur R. and Agnes C. (Kirkwold) R.; m. Sylvia H. Almlie, Sept. 7, 1956; children: Eric, Heidi, Gretchen, Ingrid. BA, Luther Coll., 1952; BTh, Luther Theol. Sem., 1956. Ordained to ministry, Am. Luth. Ch., 1956. Pastor Am. Luth. Ch., Newport, Wash., 1956-62, Our Saviour's Luth. Ch., Spirit Lake, Idaho, 1956-62, Our Savior Luth. Ch., Laurel, Mont., 1962-69, Bethesda-Our Savior's Parish, Alexandria and Nelson, Minn., 1969-79; dist. min., asst. to bishop S. W. Minn. Dist. Am. Luth. Ch., Willmar, Minn., 1979-87; synod min. Southwestern Minn. Synod, Evang. Luth. Ch. in Am., Redwood Falls, Minn., 1988—. Home: 2800 N W 12th Ave Willmar MN 56201 Office: Southwestern Minn Synod Evang Luth Ch Am Box 277 Redwood Falls MN 56283

RANZAHUER, GUILLERMO GONZALEZ, bishop; b. Huatusco, Veracruz, Mex., Mar. 12, 1928; s. Edmundo Rauzahuer Cércamo and Lucia (Gonzélez) Lecuona. Ordained priest Roman Catholic Ch.; consecrated bishop of Diocese of San Andres Tuxtla; pres. Comision Episcopal de Ministerios laicalos y diaconado permanente. Office: Constitucion Y Morelos, San Andres Tuxtla, Veracruz CP, Mexico 95700

RAPHAEL, MARK ROSS, rabbi; b. N.Y.C., Oct. 25, 1952; s. Paul and Norma (Silverman) R.; m. Diane E. Spitz, Oct. 28, 1984; 1 child, Tali Elitov. BA, Clark U., 1974; MA in Jewish Edn., Jewish Theol. Sem., 1980, MA in Jewish Studies, 1981. Ordained rabbi, 1981. Rabbi, prin. Congregation Beth Ahm, Windsor, Conn., 1981-87; rabbi Temple Israel, Vestal, N.Y., 1987—; pres. Conn. Valley Rabbinical Assembly, Hartford, 1985-87, Conn. Valley Educators Assembly, Hartford, 1986-87. Mem. Rabbinical Assembly, Broome County Bd. Rabbis (pres. 1989-90). Office: Temple Israel 4737 Deerfield Pl Vestal NY 13850

RAPPAPORT, ROY ABRAHAM, anthropologist, educator; b. N.Y.C., Mar. 25, 1926; s. Murray and Judith (Israelson) R.; m. Ann Allison Hart, Aug. 15, 1959; children: Amelia, Georgiana. B.S., Cornell U., 1949; Ph.D. (Burgess hon. fellow), Columbia U., 1966. Owner, operator Avaloch Inn, Lenox, Mass., 1951-59; mem. faculty, dept. anthropology U. Mich., Ann Arbor, 1965—; chmn. U. Mich., 1974-80, dir. program on studies in religion, 1991—; participant archaeol. fieldwork Society Islands, 1960, ethnol. fieldwork, New Guinea, 1962-64, 81-82; sr. scholar East-West Center, 1968-69; cons. ERDA, 1976, Dept. Energy, 1977-80, State of Nev., 1986—, Nat. Acad. Scis., 1988—. Author: (with others) Archaeology on Moorea, French Polynesia, 1967, Pigs for the Ancestors, 1968, The Sacred in Human Evolution, 1971, The Flow of Energy in an Agricultural Society, 1971, Liturgies and Lies, 1976, Ecology, Meaning and Religion, 1979; contbr. articles to anthrop. jours. Guggenheim fellow, 1969; Am. Council Learned Socs. fellow, 1972-73. Fellow AAAS; mem. Am. Acad. Arts and Scis., Am. Anthrop. Assn. (pres.-elect 1985-87, pres. 1987-89). Jewish. Home: 2360 E Delhi Rd Ann Arbor MI 48103

RAPPORT, JOE ROOKS, rabbi; b. Columbus, Ohio, May 26, 1957; s. James Louis and Karlyn Ann (Israelson) R.; m. Gaylia R. Rooks, Oct. 8, 1980; children: Yael, Lev. BA, Coll. of Wooster, 1979; MA in Hebrew Lit., Hebrew Union Coll., 1982; AM/PhD, Washington U., St. Louis, 1988. Ordained rabbi, 1984; cert. secondary sch. tchr. Interim rabbi B'nai El, St. Louis, 1984-85; assoc. rabbi The Temple, Louisville, 1988—; lectr. in Judaic thought U. Louisville/Bellarmine Coll., 1988—; bd. dirs. Jewish Community Ctr., Louisville, 1988-91; del. Nat. Assn. Jewish Community Rels. Couns., Miami, Fla., 1991; mem. inter-agy. com. on Soviet resettlement Jewish Family and Vocat. Svcs., Louisville, 1990—; ptnr. MAZON: A Jewish Response to Hunger, 1988—. Contbr. articles to profl. pubs. Co-chair Louisville Coalition for homeless, 1990—, Many People-One Community (Mayor's Commn. on Prejudice), Louisville, 1990—; chair social action Community Rels. Coun., Louisville, 1991—. Rsch. fellow Washington, 1987; recipient Julie Linker Young Leadership award Jewish Community Fedn., 1990. Mem. Cen. Conf. Am. Rabbis (mem. task force on cults 1984—), Louisville Bd. Rabbis, Religious Action Ctr. of Reform Judaism, NCCJ (chair edn. com. 1990-91), Phi Beta Kappa. Office: The Temple 5101 Brownsboro Rd Louisville KY 40241

RASCHKE, CARL ALLAN, humanities educator, college program director, author, educator; b. N.Y.C., Sept. 11, 1944; s. Charles Frederick and Grace Evelyn (Van Nostrand) R.; m. Lorita Elaine Lagiglia, Mar. 2, 1968 (div.); 1 child, Erik; m. Susan Kay Doughty, Sept. 9, 1981. BA, Pomona Coll., 1966; MA, Grad. Theol. Union, 1969; PhD, Harvard U., 1973. Staff reporter Livermore (Calif.) Herald and News, 1967-68; teaching asst. U. Mass., Boston, 1970-71; asst. prof. religious studies U. Denver, 1972-77, prof. religious studies, 1984—, dir. Inst. for the Humanities, 1987—; mem. adv. group on pub. humanities Nat. Endowment for the Humanities, Washington, 1988. Author: Interruption of Eternity, 1980, Theological Thinking, 1988, Painted Black, 1990; editor: Lacan and Theological Discourse, 1989. Sr. fellow Independence Inst., Golden, Colo., 1986—; columnist Colorado Springs Gazette Telegraph, 1987-90; pres. Omega Found., 1981-84. Fellow German Acad. Exch. Svc., 1974-75, Nat. Endowment for the Humanities, 1978-79. Mem. Am. Acad. Religion (pres. Denver chpt. 1977-78, editor 1982—), Am. Philos. Assn., Am. Assn. for Advancement Core Curriculum (pres.), Inst. for Advanced Philos. Rsch. (advisor), Colo. Innovation Soc. Avocations: music, tennis, travel, computers. Office: U Denver Dept Religious Studies Denver CO 80208

RASER, HAROLD EUGENE, religion educator; b. Altadena, Calif., Mar. 9, 1947; s. John and Bernice Irene (Deemy) R.; m. Joy Eloise Atteberry, Mar. 14, 1968; children: Erika Dawn, Derren John. BA, Pasadena Coll., 1968, MA, 1970; MDiv, Nazarene Theol. Sem., 1974; PhD, Pa. State U., 1986. Ordained to ministry Ch. of the Nazarene, 1979. Assoc. pastor, min. of youth 1st Ch. of the Nazarene, San Jose, Calif., 1970-72; instr. humanities Pa. State U., University Park, Pa., 1976-77; instr. religion Asbury Coll., Wilmore, Ky; prof. history of Christianity Nazarene Theol. Sem., Kansas City, Mo., 1980—; adj. lectr. in ch. history St. Paul Sch. Theology (Meth.), Kansas City, 1984-87; adj. prof. ch. history Fuller Theol. Sem., Pasadena, 1988-89; vis. prof. European Nazarene Bible Coll., Büsingen, Fed. Republic Germany, 1986-87. Author: Phoebe Palmer, Her Life and Thought, 1987; editor The Tower, 1989—; contbr. articles to profl. jours. Mem. Am. Acad. Religion, Am. Soc. Ch. History, Wesleyan Theol. Soc. Office: Nazarene Theol Sem 1700 E Meyer Blvd Kansas City MO 64131

RASMUSSEN, MARVA JEAN, music educator; b. Kansas City, Mo., Nov. 21, 1957; d. Leon and Mildred Lenore (Partner) Nungester; m. Gary Dean Rasmussen, June 20, 1981; children: Lauren Danae, James Garrison. B Music Edn., U. Mo., Kansas City, 1980, M Music Edn., 1984. Cert. tchr., Kans. Elem. tchr. strings Kansas City (Kans.) Pub. Schs., 1980-81; elem. and secondary tchr. strings Olathe (Kans.) Pub. Schs., 1981-85; pvt. violin and viola tchr. Prairie Village and Olathe, Kans., 1981-87; instrumental music dir. 1st Christian Assembly of God, Cin., 1988—; dir. Jr. High Pops Orch., Olathe, 1983-85, All-City Elem. Orch., Olathe, 1984-85. Dir. bell choir Evangel Temple, Kansas City, Mo., 1978-85, asst. dir. sanctuary choir, 1978-87; dir. Alpha Ringers, 1st Christian Assembly of God, 1989—, dir. adult vocal ensemble and orch.; mem. Kansas City (Mo.) Civic Orch., 1986-87, Hamilton-Fairfield Symphony Orch.; dir. Chamber Orch. at Ursuline Acad., Cin., 1991—. Mem. Mortar Bd., Mu Phi Epsilon (pres. 1978-79, historian 1979-80, rec. sec. 1991—, Outstanding Sr. 1980), Pi Kappa Lambda. Republican. Mem. Assemblies of God Ch. Home: 732 Windfield Dr Loveland OH 45140

RASOLONDRAIBE, PÉRI, theology educator; b. Ambovombe, Androy, Dem. Republic of Madagascar, June 29, 1947; s. Jean Hary Rasolondrainy and Berthe Barclay Rahagoharivelo; m. Ernestine Razanaivo, Aug. 27, 1965; children: Lalahery, Maminiaina, Norohirina, Andrimpifaliana. Diploma in Theology, Luth. Sem., Fianarantsoa, Dem. Republic Madagascar, 1969; ThM, Luther Sem., 1973; PhD, Princeton U., 1984. Ordained to ministry, Luth. Ch., 1969. Tchr. elem. sch. Malagasy Luth. Ch., Fort-Dauphin, Madagascar, 1964-65, youth pastor, 1969-71; tchr. secondary pvt. sch., coll. Fianarantsoa, Madagascar, 1966-69; instr. theology Luth. Sem., Fianarantsoa, 1973-75, prof. theology, 1983-87, sem. pres., 1984-87; cons. urban mission Luth. World Fedn., Geneva, 1975-78; interim parish pastor Am. Luth. Ch., Jersey City, 1979-81; prof. theology Luther Northwestern Theol. Sem., St. Paul, 1987—, dir. cross-cultural studies, 1990—; Contbr. articles to profl. jours. Chmn. Blood Donors Assn., Fianarantsoa, 1985-87.

Scholar Am. Luth. Ch., St. Paul, 1971-73, Princeton, N.J., 1978-83; grantee Luth. World Fedn., Africa, 1975. Mem. Soc. Sci. Study of Religion, Am. Acad. Religion, Consortium Theol. Schs., Ptnrs. of Conscience. Avocations: photography, computer graphics, gardening, conversation. Office: Luther Northwestern Theol Sem 2481 Como Ave Saint Paul MN 55108

RAST, WALTER EMIL, archaeology educator; b. San Antonio, July 3, 1930; s. Alfred Otto and Edith Gertrude (Jordan) R.; m. Susanna Marie Droege, June 5, 1955; children: Joel, Timothy, Rebekah, Peter. AA, St. John's Coll., Winfield, Kans., 1950; BA, Concordia Sem., St. Louis, 1952, MDiv, 1955, MS in Theology, 1956. Hebrew instr. Concordia Sem., St. Louis, 1956-57; min. Luth Ch. of The Savior, Bedford, Mass., 1957-61; asst. prof. Valparaiso U., Valparaiso, Ind., 1961-67; assoc. prof. Valparaiso U., Valparaiso, 1967-72, prof., 1972—; staff excavator Tell Ta'annek, Jordan, 1963-68, Tell er-Rumeith, 1967; dir. archaeology expdn. to Dead Sea Plain, Jordan, 1975—. Author: Tradition History and the Old Testament, 1972, Taanach: Iron Age Pottery, 1978; co-author: Bab edh-Dhra: Excavations in the Cemetery, 1989; editor Bull. Am. Schs. Oriental Rsch., 1984-90. Pres. Valparaiso Builders Assn., 1976-80. Grantee NEH, Nat. Geog. Soc.; fellow Rockefeller Found., N.Y., 1963-65, Am. Coun. Learned Societies, N.Y., 1971-72, NEH, Washington, 1983, Gertrude Henkel Stiftung Düsseldorf U. Tübingen, Fed. Republic Germany, 1989-90. Mem. Am. Schs. Oriental Rsch. (2d v.p. 1988—), Soc. Bibl. Lit., Chgo. Soc. Bibl. Rsch., Israel Exploration Soc., Brit. Sch. Archaeology in Jerusalem, Archeol. Inst. Am. Democrat. Lutheran. Avocations: gardening, woodwork, hiking, bicycling. Office: Valparaiso U Dept Theology Valparaiso IN 46383

RATCLIFF, DONALD EARL, minister, educator; b. Pomeroy, Ohio, Apr. 6, 1951; s. Clarence Earl and Lois Anna (Harris) R.; m. Brenda Sue Campbell, Dec. 16, 1978; children: John Wesley, Stephen Earl, Emma Beth. BA, Spring Arbor Coll., 1973; MA, Mich. State U., 1975; EdS, U. Ga., 1986. Ordained to ministry Christian Nation Ch., 1978. Asst. prof. dept. chair Circleville Bible Coll., 1975-78; tchr., adminstr., dean of men Christian Union Bible Sch., Roseau, Dominica, W.I., 1978-79; dir. Christian edn. Vinton Bapt. Ch., Ohio, 1981-82; interim pastor Mt. Pleasant Bapt. Ch., Toccoa, Ga., 1983-84; asst. prof. Toccoa Falls (Ga.) Coll., 1982—. Author: Using Psychology in the Church, 1984, Handbook of Preschool Religious Education, 1988, Handbook of Youth Ministry, 1991, Introduction to Psychology and Counseling, 1991; contbr. articles to profl. jours. Mem. Soc. for the Sci. Study of Religion, Assn. Profs. and Rschrs. in Religious Edn., Christian Assn. Psychol. Studies. Office: Toccoa Falls Coll PO Box 800840 Toccoa Falls GA 30598 *Children are perhaps the most undervalued treasure of the church. They are the key to both short-term and long-term growth of the church; the are the church of the future.*

RATCLIFF, HOWARD DUANE, minister; b. Coffeyville, Kans., Aug. 10, 1950; s. Howard Franklin and Fern Marie (Shamblin) R.; m. Myrtle Nadine McCormac, Aug. 7, 1969; children: Natalie, Derek, Eric. Student, Hutchison (Kans.) Jr. Coll., 1971, Southwestern Coll., Oklahoma City, 1974; B.Bile Theology, Internat. Bible Inst., Orlando, 1985, M.Bible Theology, 1985. Ordained to ministry Assembly of God Ch., 1975. Sr. pastor Assembly of God Ch., Iola, Kans., 1978, Baytown, Tex., 1979-86, Indianola, Iowa, 1986-88, Tulsa, 1988—; chmn., pres. Eastland Assembly of God, Tulsa, 1988—, First Assembly of God, Indianola, 1986-88; del., teller com. Gen. Coun. of Assemblies of God, Indpls., 1989. Coach, mem. YMCA, Baytown, 1983-85. With U.S. Army, 1967-70. Named Trophy Coach of Yr., YMCA, 1984. Me. Light for the Lost (Gold Pen 1989, 90), Tulsa Area Ministerial Alliance, Concerned Women of Am. Office: Eastland Assembly of God Ch 12310 E 21st St Tulsa OK 74129

RATH, GEORGE EDWARD, bishop; b. Buffalo, Mar. 29, 1913; s. Edward F. and Eudora Pearl (Chadderdon) R.; m. Margaret Webber, Apr. 7, 1934; children: Peter F. (dec.), Gail (Mrs. Richard M. Sherk). A.B., Harvard U., 1933; B.D., Union Theol. Sem., 1936; S.T.D., Gen. Theol. Sem., 1964. Ordained deacon Episcopal Ch., 1938, priest, 1939; asst. to chaplain Columbia, 1936-39; asst. chaplain, 1939-41; vicar All Saints' Ch., Millington, N.J., 1941-49; rector All Saints' Ch., 1949-64; suffragan bishop Episcopal Diocese Newark, 1964-70; bishop coadjutor, 1970-73, bishop, 1974-78, ret., 1978; archdeacon Morris County, 1959-64; assisting bishop Episcopal Diocese of Mass., 1982-89. Chmn. bd. trustees Christ Hosp. Jersey City, 1966-79; trustee Cape Cod Mus. Natural History, 1980-85; bd. dirs. Nauset Workshop, 1981-86, 88—. Mem. Cape Cod (Mass.) Bird Club, Harvard Club of Cape Cod, Montclair (N.J.) Bird Club. Home: 2 Cedar Land Rd PO Box 996 East Orleans MA 02643

RATKIN, ANNETTE LEVY, library director; b. Louisville, July 8, 1927; d. David and Leah (Fishgall) Rose; m. Ralph Z. Levy, Sept. 14, 1949 (dec. Nov. 1976); children: Ralph Z. Jr., David William, Gail Levy Seibold; m. Rubin S. Ratkin, Dec. 14, 1986. BA, Vanderbilt U., 1948, MLS, 1975. Dir. librs., archives Jewish Fedn. of Nashville and Mid. Tenn., 1978—. Editor booklet: A Guide for Teaching the History of the Jews of Nashville, Tennessee, 1985; editor slide, cassette program: The History of the Jewish Community of Nashville, Tennessee, 1983. Mem. ALA, Assn. Jewish Librs. (rec. sec. 1988), Tenn. Archivists, Soc. Am. Archivists. Office: Jewish Fedn Nashville 801 Percy Warner Blvd Nashville TN 37205

RATLIFF, RONALD D., minister; b. Bethany, Mo., Mar. 29, 1950; s. Darrell D. and Delores Jean (Marshal) R.; m. Iva Gail Bascom, July 2, 1967; children: Stacey Lane, Shannon Wayne. A in Divinity, Mid-Western Theol. Sem., Kansas City, Mo., 1991. Ordained to ministry So. Bapt. Conv. Min. Ridgeway (Mo.) Bapt. Ch., 1983-86, Pilot Grove 1st Bapt. Ch., Gilman City, Mo., 1986—; mem. Mid-west Missions, Kansas City, 1991; rancher, welder, Gilman City. Vol. fireman, chief City of Gilman City, 1979—, mem. city coun., 1987—, mem. community betterment bd., 1990—. Home: Box 91 Gilman City MO 64642

RATLIFF, RONALD EUGENE, minister; b. Piqua, Ohio, Dec. 13, 1947; s. Vernon Knox and Joanne Constance (Covault) R.; m. Sherri Lynn Ross, Apr. 2, 1977; children: Ronald Jr., Michelle Renee, Roderick Preston, Meredith Simone, Geoffrey Kristian. Diploma, Pacific Bible Coll., 1975; AB, Calif. State U., 1982; MDiv, Princeton Theol. Sem., 1986; EdD, Fla. Internat. U., 1991. Ordained to ministry Am. Bapt. Ch., 1986. Asst. prin. Calvary Christian Sch., Yorba Linda, Calif., 1974-79; founding pastor New Covenant Community Ch., Anaheim Hills, Calif., 1979-83; student chaplain Princeton Med. Ctr., Princeton, N.J., 1983-86; spl. mission pastor Am. Bapt. Chs. U.S.A., Valley Forge, Pa., 1986-89; founding pastor Old Cutler Community Ch., Miami, Fla., 1989—; mem. rsch. faculty Fla. Internat. U., 1991—. Editor: Theological Journal, 1988. Recipient scholarship Princeton Sem., 1983-86, scholarship, fellowship Fla. Internat. U., 1987-91. Mem. ASCD, Am. Acad. Religion, Soc. Bibl. Lit., The Alban Inst., Assn. for Religious and Value Issues in Counseling, Mins. Counsel Am. Bapt. Ch. U.S.A., Phi Kappa Phi. Home: 19555 SW 87th Pl Miami FL 33157 *I am learning that both dereliction and mastery present the believer with times of intoxication out of which she or he must find space for soberness, because time-space is multidimensional and the senses, assisted by deity, may guide one through the narrow course.*

RATZINGER, JOSEPH ALOIS CARDINAL, prefect, former archbishop; b. Marktl, Germany, Mar. 16, 1927; s. Joseph and Maria (Peintner) R. Ed., U. Munich. Prof. theology U. Freising, 1951, U. Bonn, 1958, U. Munster, 1963, U. Tubingen, 1966, U. Regensburg, 1969; Ordained priest Roman Cath. Ch.; chaplain, 1951; archbishop, 1977; cardinal, 1977 former archbishop of Munich-Freising, chmn. Bavarian Bishops Conf., 1977-82; now Prefect Sacred Congregation for the Doctrine of Faith. Author books and articles. Office: Piazza del St Uffizio 11, I-00120 Vatican City Vatican City

RATZLAFF, DAVID EDWARD, minister; b. Kansas City, Mo., Mar. 12, 1938; s. John Henry and Amy May (Cathcart) R.; m. Shiela Paige Hickerson, June 9, 1958; children: Perry Dean, Kevin Lee, Kalista Kay. BA in Ministry, Nebr. Christian Coll., 1961; MDiv, Memphis Theol. Sem., 1991. Ordained to ministry Christian Ch., 1962. Minister Christian Ch., Neligh, Nebr., 1959-67; owner, mgr. Kordsman Evangelistic Assn., Hiawatha, Kans., 1967-75; sr. minister Christian Ctr., Hiawatha, Kans., 1970-72; salesman Saladmaster Co., Springfield, Mo., 1975-76; ops. coordinator Blackwood Bros. Quartet, Memphis, 1976-79, 85; mgr. sales and service Elliot Impression Products, Memphis, 1980-85; minister Bethany Christian Ch., Eads, Tenn., 1986—; program chmn. exec. com. Western Area Christian Chs.; mem. commn. on ministry com. for Christian Chs. (Disciples of Christ), Tenn., 1988—; western area moderator, mem. gen. and exec. bds. Region of Christian Ch. of Tenn., 1991—. Co-author: (songbook) Kordsman Presents, 1966; recorded and produced 6 long play albums, 1966-74. Bd. dirs. Memphis Family Link, 1985-86; mem. United Cerebral Palsy, 1983-86; asst. police chief City of Neligh, 1962-67, coordinator, 1965-67. Mem. Nat. Arts and Recording Artists, Collierville Ministerial Assn., Christian Ch. Ministers Memphis. Republican. Mem. Disciples Christ. Avocations: fishing, weight lifting, basketball, coaching baseball and softball. Home: 441 Bethany Rd Eads TN 38028 Office: Bethany Christian Ch 421 Bethany Rd Eads TN 38028

RATZLAFF, RUBEN MENNO, religion educator, minister; b. Burrton, Kans., Jan. 8, 1917; s. Henry and Julia (Foth) R.; m. Frances Irene King, Sept. 7, 1941; children: Keith Lowell, Paul Dennis, Mark Henry, Loren Lee. BA, Johnson Bible Coll., 1940; BD, Butler U., 1955, MA, 1959. Ordained to ministry Chs. of Christ, 1938. Min. Pleasant Hill Christian Ch., Hall, Ind., 1948-50; min. Christian Ch., Clermont, Ind., 1950-55, Kennard, Ind., 1955-59; prof. San Jose (Calif.) Christian Coll., 1959—; ann. vis. lectr. Springdale Coll., Birmingham, Eng., 1985—. Author: Ezra Nehemiah, 1982; contbr. articles to profl. jours. Recipient Hebrew award Hebrew Synagogue, 1950. Mem. Theta Phi. Home: 1567 Willowdale Dr San Jose CA 95118 also: 72 Wellman Croft, Selly Oak, Birmingham B29 6NS, England Office: San Jose Christian Coll 790 S 12th St San Jose CA 95112 *What amazes me most is that God the Almighty sends His Son to knock at our door, and wait with His hat in His hand while we decide whether to follow Him.*

RAUCH, CARL THOMAS, III, minister; b. Cadillac, Mich., Apr. 11, 1942; s. carl Thomas Jr. and Kathryn (Anderson) R. AAS in Bldg. Constrn. Tech., Ferris State Coll., 1975, BS in Bus. Mgmt., 1977; Mdiv, Ch. God Sch. Theology, 1984; postgrad., Ga. State U., 1985-89. Min. outreach elderly Mission Ch. of God, Atlanta, 1984-87; min. outreach orphanage Tijuana Christian Orphanage, San Ysidro, Calif., 1991—. Mem. Ga. State U. Gerontology Club. Home and Office: Tijuana Christian Orphanage PO Box 435247 San Ysidro CA 22700

RAUCH, W(ILLIAM) ERIC, pastor; b. Columbus, Ohio, June 10, 1935; s. William and Rozsika (Tumbaz) R.; m. Ruth Elaine Benson, June 28, 1958; children: Holly Pike, Adam. BA, Capital U., 1957; BD, Evang. Luth. Theol. Sem., 1961; MST, Union Theol. Sem., 1962; D Ministry, Trinity Luth. Sem., 1982. Ordained to ministry Evang. Luth. Ch., 1962. Founding pastor Christ the King Luth. Ch., Youngstown, Ohio, 1962-65, Huntington, W.Va., 1965-70; dir., tv, radio, films Am. Luth. Ch., St. Paul, 1970-74; co-pastor First Luth. Ch., Manatowoc, Wis., 1974-77; sr. pastor St. Paul Luth. Ch., Berea, Ohio, 1977—; chmn. Luth. Communications Ministry Northeastern Ohio, Cleve., 1988—. Host, producer: (weekly radio program) Silhouette, 1970 (Gabriel award 1974). Recipient Cert. of Indebtedness, The Am. Luth. Ch., 1974. Mem. Assn. for Psychol. Type. Office: St Paul Luth Ch 276 E Bagley Rd Berea OH 44017

RAUDSEPP, KARL, bishop; b. Puurmanni, Estonia, Mar. 26, 1980; came to Can., 1948; naturalized, 1950; s. Jaan and Liisa (Gruner) R. m. Ellen Feldmann, July 20, 1935; 4 children. Cand. theol. U. Tartu, Estonia, 1933. Ordained to ministry Estonian Evang. Luth. Church, 1933, dean, 1958, bishop, 1976. Pastor St. Michael Ch., Vandra, Estonia, refugee camps, Fed. Republic Germany; pastor Luth. World Fedn. Svc. to Refugees, St. John's Estonian Ch., Montreal, Que., Can. Author: Marked by Cross, 1982; monographies R.G. Kallas, Arthur Võõbus; author 3 edits. of sermons in Estonian.

RAUFF, EDWARD ALLEN, clergyman; b. N.Y.C., July 19, 1929; s. Edward and Olga (Keene) R.; m. Elaine Carol Schacht, June 16, 1956 (div. Sept. 1982); children: Pauline, David, Dawn, Kathryn, Mark, Caitlin; m. Naomi Kathryn Gutheil, Apr. 9, 1983. BA, MDiv, Concordia Sem., St. Louis, 1956; MA, Columbia U., 1958. Ordained to ministry Luth. Ch.-Mo. Synod, 1956. Pastor Gethsemane Luth. Ch., Columbus, Ohio, 1956-62, St. John Luth. Ch., Detroit, 1962-67, Emanuel Luth. Ch., Patchogue, N.Y., 1967-70, Christ Luth. Ch., Burbank, Calif., 1984-86; adminstr. Luth. Coun. U.S.A., N.Y.C., 1970-80; exec. dir. SE Luth. High Sch., L.A., 1981-84; pastor Mt. Olive Luth Ch., Pasadena, Calif., 1986—; pres. Census Access for Planning in the Ch., 1975-77. Co-author: Lutheran Church Statistics, 1975; author: Why People Join the Church, 1979. Mem. Religious Rsch. Assn. (treas. 1977-79). Home: 1805 Harding Ave Altadena CA 91001 Office: Mt Olive Luth Ch 1118 N Allen Ave Pasadena CA 91104

RAUSCH, GERTRUDE MARIE (POLLY RAUSCH), religious educator; b. Harvard, Nebr., Nov. 23, 1940; d. Richard Frederick and Christina Louise (Haller) Miller; m. David John Rausch, Aug. 11, 1962; children: Catherine, David, John, Lorraine, Cheryl, Theresa. BA, Ill. Benedictine Coll., 1977; MA in Religious Studies, Mundelein Coll., 1990. Youth minister St. Margaret Mary Parish, Naperville, Ill., 1983-85; religious edn. coord. St. Joseph Parish, Downers Grove, Ill., 1985-87, Our Lady of Mt. Carmel Parish, Darien, Ill., 1987—. Election judge DuPage County Election Commn., Naperville, 1972-86; mem. Naperville Art League, 1970-71; organizer Girl Scouts U.S., Naperville, 1971-76. Mem. Nat. Cath. Edn. Assn., Ill. Parish Coords. and Dirs. (diocesan rep. 1987-89, sec. 1989—), N.E. DuPage Religious Edn. Cluster. Democrat. Home: 101 Devon Ln Naperville IL 60540 Office: Our Lady Mt Carmel Parish 8404 Cass Ave Darien IL 60559

RAUSCH, THOMAS PETER, priest, theologian, educator; b. Chgo., Feb. 12, 1941; s. Charles J. and Imelda C. (Claffy) R. BA, Gonzaga U., 1966, MA, 1967; STM, Jesuit Sch. Theology, 1972; PhD, Duke U., 1976. Joined S.J., Roman Cath. Ch., 1960. Instr. philosophy Loyola U., L.A., 1967-69; prof. theology Loyola Marymount U., L.A., 1976—, dir. campus ministry, 1981-85, rector Jesuit Community, 1988—; Cath. tutor to Ecumenical Inst., Bossey, Switzerland, 1983-84. Author: The Roots of Catholic Tradition, 1986, Authority and Leadership in the Church, 1989, Radical Christian Communities, 1990. Mem. theol., ecumenical commns. Archdiocese L.A.; mem. L.A. Cath.-Evang. Dialogue. Kearns fellow Duke U., 1973-75. Mem. Cath. Theol. Soc. Am., N.Am. Acad. Ecumenists, L.A. Luth.-Cath. Com. Office: Loyola Marymount U Jesuit Community Los Angeles CA 90045

RAVE, JAMES A., bishop. Bishop of Northwestern Ohio, Evang. Luth. Ch. in Am., Toledo. Office: Evang Luth Ch Am 241 Stanford Pkwy Ste A Toledo OH 45840*

RAVINDRA, RAVI, religion educator; b. Patiala, Punjab, India, Jan. 14, 1939; came to Can., 1961; s. Dalip Chand and Purna Devi (Aggrawal) Gupta; m. Sally Lee Bambridge, Aug. 30, 1965; children: Munju Monique, Kabir Paul. BSc, M Tech., Indian Inst. Tech., Kharagpur, 1959, 61; MSc., U. Toronto (Ont., Can.), 1962, PhD, 1965; MA, Dalhousie U., Halifax, N.S., Can., 1968. Prof. religion Dalhousie U., Halifax, 1966—; sr. rsch. fellow Killam Found. Inst. Advanced Study, Princeton, 1977, Shastri Indo-Can. Inst., Indian Inst. Advanced Study, 1977-78. Author: Theory of Seismic Head Waves, 1971, Whispers From the Other Shore, 1984, The Yoga of the Christ, 1990, Science and Spirit, 1991; contbr. articles to profl. jours. Can. Coun. fellw, Princeton, 1968-69, Soc. for Values in Edn. postdoctoral fellow, 1973-74. Mem. Am. Soc. for Study of Religion, Am. Acad. Religion, Can. Soc. Study Religion. Hindu. Home: 12 Pottery Ln, Halifax, NS Canada B3P 2P5 Office: Dalhousie U, 6209 University Ave, Halifax, NS Canada B3H 3J5 *In the midst of the vastness, charged with life, beauty and energy, most of us spend our time imagining the world to be a big bazaar and making our little bargains. Thus we remain on the surface of the cosmos and of ourselves. Real life is possible only when we abandon the mystery—within and without.*

RAWLINGS, JOHN A., minister; b. Randolph County, Ind., June 19, 1925; s. Earl and Lina Alma (Johnson) R.; m. Barbara Joyce Wilcox, Aug. 2, 1968; children: Jonna Kay Rawlings MacRae, Michael, Stuart, Dru Rawlings Kraft, Barbara Rawlings Baker. BA, Ind. Cen. Coll., 1950; MST, Garrett Theol. Sem., Evanston, Ill., 1955; D Ministry, Butler U., 1972. Ordained to ministry United Ch. of Christ. Min. Phila.-Ingalls Meth. Ch., Greenfield, Ind., 1948-50, Ambridge Meth. Ch., Gary, Ind., 1950-57, Danville (Ind.) 1st Meth. Ch., 1958-59, Montrose Meth. Ch., Terre Haute, Ind., 1959-63, Grace Meth. Ch., South Bend, Ind., 1963-68, St. Paul United Ch. Christ, Indpls., 1969-75, Pioneer United Ch. Christ, San Diego, 1976—; del. jurisdictions No. Cen. Jurisdiction Meth. Ch., 1964, synod United Ch. Christ, Ames, Iowa, 1985; moderator San Diego Assn. United Ch. Christ, 1984. Bd. dirs. Meth. Hosp., Gary, 1955-63; mem. Citizens Coun. San Diego Community Coll. Dist. Sgt. maj. U.S. Army, 1944-46. Mem. So. Calif. Conf. United Ch. Christ. Home: 1355 Inspiration Dr PO Box 1985 La Jolla CA 92037 Office: Pioneer United Ch Christ 2550 Fairfield St San Diego CA 92110

RAWLS, FRANK MACKLIN, lawyer; b. Suffolk, Va., Aug. 24, 1952; s. John Lewis and Mary Helen (Macklin) R.; m. Sally Hallum Blanchard, June 26, 1976; children: Matthew Christopher, John Stephen, Michael Andrew. B.A. cum laude in History, Hampden Sydney Coll., 1974; J.D., U. Va., 1977. Bar: Va. 1977, U.S. Dist. Ct. (ea. dist.) Va. 1977, U.S. Ct. Appeals (4th cir.) 1977. Assoc. Rawls, Habel & Rawls, Suffolk, 1977-78, ptnr., 1978-91; ptnr. Ferguson & Rawls, 1991—; bd. dirs. Suffolk Title Ltd., 1986—. Deacon Westminster Reformed Presbyn. Ch., Suffolk, 1979-83, elder, clk. of session, 1984—; chmn. bd. dirs. Suffolk Crime Line, 1982-90, Suffolk Cheer Fund, 1982—, Covenant Christian Schs., Suffolk, 1982-84; bd. dirs. Norfolk Christian Schs., 1990—; mem. adv. bd. dirs. Salvation Army, Suffolk, 1977—, chmn., 1989—; chmn. Suffolk Com. on Affordable Housing, 1989-90; bd. dirs. Suffolk YMCA, 1988-90. Mem. ABA, Suffolk Bar Assn., Va. State Bar, Va. Bar Assn., Christian Legal Soc., Va. Trial Lawyers Assn., Assn. Trial Lawyers Am., Suffolk Bar Assn., Rotary. Home: PO Box 1458 Suffolk VA 23434

RAY, DAN ALAN, minister; b. Sumner County, Tenn., Oct. 14, 1933; s. James Bernice and Arizona (Brown) R.; m. Martha Bomar, July 26, 1936; children: Dan A. Jr., Barry Dean, David Andrew, Robin Ann. BA, Furman U., 1955; MA, Calif. Grad. Sch. Theology, 1971. Pastor Sylvia Circle Bapt. Ch., Rock Hill, S.C., 1954-59, Coll. Park Bapt. Ch., Phoenix, 1959-61, Palo Verde Bapt. Ch., Phoenix, 1961-66, First So. Bapt. Ch., Orange, Calif., 1966-71, Bethel Bapt. Ch., Greenville, S.C., 1974-77; dir. assn. missions Beaverdam Assn., Seneca, S.C., 1974-77; dir. evangelism and stewardship Penn.-South Jersey Conv., Harrisburg, 1977-80; dir. stewardship S.C. Bapt. Conv., 1980—. Del. Rep. Nat. Conv., Kansas City, 1976. Avocation: gardening. Home: 125 Killian Rd Columbia SC 29203 Office: SC Bapt Conv 907 Richland St Columbia SC 29201

RAY, H. RICHARD, JR. (RICK RAY), minister; b. Greenboro, N.C., Nov. 5, 1953; s. Herman Richard and Cynthia Rachael (Cox) R.; m. Rosa Lea Pine, July 20, 1974; Courtney Miran, Adam Richard. BRE, Piemont Bible Coll., 1980; M in Ministry, Trinity Theological Seminary, 1990. Assoc. pastor Centerview Bapt. Ch., Kannapolis, N.C., 1977-79; min., music and edn. Hunter Hills Bapt. Ch., Greensboro, N.C., 1979-83; min. edn. Allandale Bapt. Ch., Austin, Tex., 1983-88; min. edn. and ch. growth Grove Ave. Bapt. Ch., Richmond, Va., 1988-89. Contbr. articles to profl. jours. Mem. Greenboro Hist. Preservation Soc., Greensboro, N.C., 1972-73. Mem. Min. Edn. Growth Assn. Baptist. Office: First Bapt Ch 201 S Howard St Moore OK 73160

RAY, JONATHAN DAVID, minister; b. Madisonville, Ky., Dec. 25, 1963; s. Erwin Douglas and Ora Jean (Miller) R. MusB, Johnson Bible Coll., 1986. Ordained to ministry Ind. Christian Ch. Keyboardist Christ in Youth, Joplin, Mo., 1983-85; assoc. mus. min. Eastside Christian Ch., Fullerton, Calif., 1985; min. youth and music Bowling Green (Ky.) Christian Ch., 1987—. Named Outstanding Young Min., N.Am. Christian Conv., Cin., 1989. Republican. Home: 1569 Virginia Ave Bowling Green KY 42101 Office: Bowling Green Christian Ch 1912 Smallhouse Rd Bowling Green KY 42104

RAY, MICHAEL LYNN, minister; b. Hopkinsville, Ky., Apr. 12, 1965; s. Jerry Max and Nancy Carolyn (Wilkerson) R.; m. Susan Lee Burgess, Aug. 20, 1988. BA, David Lipscomb U., 1988. Ordained to ministry Ch. of Christ, 1988. Min. Ch. of Christ, Portsmouth, Ohio, 1988—. Republican. Home: 2140 Grandview Portsmouth OH 45662 Office: Ch of Christ 1423 Summit St Portsmouth OH 45662

RAY, RICHARD ARCHIBALD, clergyman, editor; b. New Orlean, Jan. 22, 1936; s. Archibald Cole and Eliza Owen (Britt) R.; m. Lila Frances McGeachy, Aug. 26, 1959; children: Lila English, Roderick Archibald, Alison Britt. A.B., Dartmouth Coll., 1958; postgrad., Princeton Theol. Sem., 1958-59; B.D., Union Theol. Sem. in Va., 1961; Ph.D., U. St. Andrews, Scotland, 1964. Ordained to ministry Presbyn. Ch.; minister Presbyn. Ch., Crossett, Ark., 1963-66, Tyler Meml. Presbyn. Ch., Radford, Va., 1966-68; prof. Stephens Coll., Columbia, Mo., 1968-71; editor, mng. dir. John Knox Press, Atlanta, 1971—; sr. pastor First Presbyn. Ch., Bristol, Tenn., 1981—. Co-pub., editor: Jour. of Social Philosophy, 1971-81. Pres. bd. dirs. Grandfather Home for Children, 1987-90; v.p. Missionary Emergency Fund, bd. dirs.; trustee King Coll.; bd. dirs. Calvin Studies Soc. Rockefeller Bros. fellow. Mem. Am. Acad. Religion, Am. Philos. Assn. Home: 105 Oak Forrest Dr Bristol TN 37620 Office: 701 Florida Ave Box 762 Bristol TN 37620

RAYBURN, CAROLE ANN, psychologist, researcher, writer; b. Washington, Feb. 14, 1938; d. Carl Frederick and Mary Helen (Milkie) Miller; m. Ronald Allen Rayburn (dec. Apr. 1970). BA in Psychology, Am. U., 1961; MA in Clin. Psychology, George Washington U., 1965; PhD in Ednl. Psychology, Cath. U. Am., 1969; MDiv in Ministry, Andrews U., 1980. Lic. psychologist, D.C., Md., Mich. Psychometrician Columbian Prep. Sch., Washington, 1963; clin. psychologist Spring Grove State Hosp., Catonsville, Md., 1966-68; pvt. practice, 1968, 71—; staff clin. psychologist Instl. Care Svcs. Div. D.C. Children's Ctr., Laurel, Md., 1970-78; psychologist Md. Dept. Vocat. Rehab., 1973-74; psychometrician Montgomery County Pub. Schs., 1981-85; lectr. Strayer Coll., Washington, 1969-70; forensic psychology expert witness, 1973—; guest lectr. Andrews U., Berrien Springs, Mich., 1979, Hood Coll., Frederick, Md., 1986-88; instr. Johns Hopkins U., 1986, 88-89; adj. faculty Profl. Sch. Psychol. Studies, San Diego, 1987; adj. asst. prof. Loyola Coll., 1987; cons. Julia Brown Montessori Schs., 1972-78, 82—, VA Ctr., 1978, 91—. Editor: (with M. J. Meadow) A Time to Weep and a Time to Sing, 1985; contbg. author: Montessori: Her Method and the Movement (What You Need to Know), 1973, Drugs, Alcohol, and Women: A National Forum Source Book, 1975, The Other Side of the Couch: Faith of the Psychotherapist, 1981, Clinical Handbook of Pastoral Counseling, 1985, An Encyclopedic Dictionary of Pastoral Care and Counseling, 1990, Religion, Personality, and Mental Health, 1991; author copyrighted inventories Religious Occupations and Stress Questionnaire, 1986, Religion and Stress Questionnaire, 1986, Organizational Relationships Survey, 1987, Attitudes Toward Children Inventory, 1987, Child Care Workers Inventory, 1987, State-Trait Morality Inventory, 1987; cons. editor Profl. Psychology, 1980-83; assoc. editor Jour. Pastoral Counseling, 1985-90, guest editor, 1988; contbr. numerous articles to profl. jours. Recipient Svc. award Coun. for Advancement Psychol. Professions and Scis., 1975, cert. D.C. Dept. Human Resources, 1975, 76, cert. recognition D.C. Psychol. Assn., 1976, 1985; AAUW rsch. grantee, 1983. Fellow Am. Orthopsychiat. Assn., Md. Psychol. Assn. (editor newsletter 1975-76, cert. recognition 1978, chair ins. com. 1981-83, pres. 1984-85, exec. adv. com. 1985—), APA (chair equal opportunity affirmative action div. clin. psychology 1980-82, mem. editorial. bd. Jour. Child Clin. Psychol., 1978-82, pres. clin. psychol. women sect., 1984-86, program chair, 1991, div. psychol. women chair task force on women and religion, 1980-81, div. psychol. interested in religion issues chair, reg. affairs com., 1989-91, liaison APA com. on women in psychology 1978-80, mem. task force on religious issues in grad. end. and clin. tng. 1988—, mem.-at-large 1990—); mem. Assn. Practical Psychologists Montgomery-Prince George's Counties (pres. 1986-88, editor newsletter 1990—), Balt. Assn. Cons. Psychologists (pres. 1976-78), Internat. Torch (pres. 1991—), Psi Chi. Research on stress in religious profls., women and stress, women and religion, pastoral counseling, psychotherapy, children. Address: 1200 Morningside Dr Silver Spring MD 20904

RAYFIELD, GARY GENE, minister; b. Shelby, N.C., May 22, 1947; s. Otto Floyd and Maggie Levada (Black) R.; m. Judy LaVerne Roper, Apr. 17, 1967; children: Christopher, Carrie, Kimberly, Sara. BA in Religion, Gardner-Webb Coll., Boiling Springs, N.C., 1982; MDiv, Southeastern Bapt. Theol. Sem., Wake Forest, N.C., 1987. Lic. to ministry So. Bapt. Conv., 1978, ordained, 1986. Bus min. Sierra Bapt. Ch., Alamagordo, N.Mex.,

1972-73, 1st So. Bapt. Ch., Peoria, Ariz., 1973-74; pastor children's ch. Anthony Grove Bapt. Ch., Crouse, N.C., 1978-80; dir. Sunday sch., youth min. 2d Bapt. Ch., Cherryville, N.C., 1980-83; pastor South Creek Missionary Bapt. Ch., Aurora, N.C., 1986-87, Harvey Bapt. Ch., Marquette, Mich., 1989—; security officer Glaxo Pharms., 1987; truck driver various cos., 1988-89; dir. Bible teaching Upper Peninsula Assn., Mich. So. Bapts., Gladstone, 1989—, mem. nominating com., 1989-91. Staff sgt. USAF, 1965-74. Decorated Air medal with eight oak leaf clusters, DFC with four oak leaf clusters. Mem. Kiwanis (pub. rels. com. Marquette 1989). Home and Office: Harvey Bapt Ch 224 Silver Creek Rd Marquette MI 49855

RAYL, GRANVILLE MONROE, religious association executive, founder; b. Sedalia, Mo., Aug. 21, 1917; s. Burley and Cordelia (Swope) R.; m. Hazel Arlene Gruver, June 8, 1952; children: Janet Arlene, Granville Alan. BTh, Faith Bible Coll. and Theol. Sem., 1964; DD, The Evang. Evangelism Crusades, 1962; ThD, Faith Bible Coll. and Theol. Sem., 1965. Ordained to ministry Fundamental Ministers and Chs., 1957. Regional dir. Fundamental Ministers & Chs., Inc., Kansas City, 1957-62; pres. Internat. Bible Coll. & Sem., DeSoto, Mo., 1963—, Assn. Internat. Gospel Assemblies, Inc., DeSoto, 1962—. Republican. Avocation: gardening. Office: Assn Internat Gospel Assemblies Inc 411 S Third St DeSoto MO 63020

RAYMOND, ROBERT EARL, minister, consultant; b. Denver, Mar. 12, 1926; s. Elbert Harold and Mary Josephine (Hassan) R.; m. Carol Hathaway, June 9, 1947; children: Michael Leslie, Barbara Lee. BA, U. Denver, 1950; Diplomate in Divinity, McCormick Theol. Seminary, Chgo., 1954; DD, Carroll Coll., 1971. Ordained to ministry Presbyn. Ch., 1954. Minister of edn. First Presbyn. Ch., Kirkwood, Mo., 1954-58, Oklahoma City, Okla., 1958-61; field dir. of ch. edn. Synod of Wis., Waukesha, 1961-70; dir. ecumenical devel. St. Benedict Ctr., Madison, Wis., 1970-73; assoc. synod exec. Synod of Lakes and Prairies, Bloomington, Minn., 1973-91; ret., 1991; pvt. cons. Preferred Futures Now, Edina, Minn., 1991—; bd. dirs. North Cen. Career Devel. Ctr., New Brighton, Minn., Ctr. and Network for Ch. Edn., Mpls.; adv. commn. on profl. devel. Presbyn. Ch., Louisville, Ky., 1965—. Contbr. articles to profl. jours. Bd. dirs. Oklahoma City Community Coun., 1959-60, Okla. Planned Parenthood, 1959-60, various YMCAs, Denver, Oklahoma City, Kirkwood, 1950-61; chief Protestant advisor Boy Scouts of Am., St. Louis, 1954-58. With USN, 1943-46, ETO, ATO. Recipient First prize in Rabbinical Lit., U. Denver, 1950, Farwell Preaching prize McCormick Theol. Seminary, 1954. Mem. Acad. of Parish Clergy, World Future Soc., Global Futures Network, Minn. Futurists, Planetary Soc, Space Studies Inst., St. Andrews Soc., Twin Cities Scottish Club, Phi Beta Kappa, Kappa Delta Pi. Home: 4819 Maple Rd Edina MN 55424

RAYNOR, ROBERT LAYTON, minister; b. Shelby, N.C., Apr. 4, 1954; s. Bruce Layton and Coleen Virginia (Dorsey) R.; m. JoAnn Farris, Aug. 25, 1975; children: Kelly, Paige, Lindsay. BS, Atlanta Christian Coll., 1979. Ordained to ministry Ind. Christian Ch., 1979. Youth minister Bethel Christian Ch., Conyers, Ga., 1975-79, Northside Ch. of Christ, Newport News, Va., 1979-82, First Christian Ch., Cumming, Ga., 1982-86; sr. minister Covington (Ga.) Christian Ch., 1986-89; founding minister Grace Fellowship Ch., Covington, 1989—; bd. dirs. So. Christian Youth Conv., Gateway Acad., Covington; radio disc jockey Sta. WWEV, Cumming, Ga., 1985-86. Contbr. articles to local newspaper; contbr. TV program channel 8/ABC, 1982. Active Food Outreach, Covington, 1986—. Named to Outstanding Young Men of Am., 1984. Mem. Masons. Republican. Mem. Christian Ch. Avocations: hunting, fishing, softball, music, tennis. Home: 166 Deep Step Rd Covington GA 30209 Office: Grace Fellowship PO Box 2502 Covington GA 30209

RAZAFIMAHATRATRA, VICTOR CARDINAL, archbishop of Tananarive; b. Ambanitsilena-Ranomansina, Madagascar, Sept. 8, 1921; Joined S.J., 1945, ordained priest Roman Cath. Ch., 1956; rector of Fianarantsoa Minor Sem., 1960-63; superior Jesuit residence at Ambositra, 1963-69; rector of Tananarive Maj. Sem., 1969-71; bishop of Farafangana, 1971; archbishop of Tananarive, 1976—; elevated to Sacred Coll. Cardinals, 1976; titular ch. Holy Cross in Jerudalem; pres. Madagascar Episcopal Conf.; mem. Congregation Evangelization of Peoples, Commn. Revision Code Canon Law. Address: Archeveche Andohalo, Tananarive Democratic Republic of Madagascar

READ, ALLAN ALEXANDER, minister; b. Toronto, Ont., Can., Sept. 19, 1923; s. Alec P. and Lillice (Matthews) R.; m. Mary Beverly Roberts, Sept. 28, 1949; children—John Allan, Elizabeth Anne, Peter Michael, Martha Ruth. B.A., U. Toronto, Can., 1946; Licentiate in Theology, Trinity Coll., Toronto, 1948, D.D., 1972; D.D., Wycliffe Coll., Toronto, 1972; D.S.T. (hon.), Thornloe Coll., Sudbury, Ont., 1982. Ordained diaconate, 1948, priest, 1949, Anglican Ch. of Canada. Rector Diocese of Toronto-Anglican Ch., Parish of East and West Mono, Ont., Can., 1947-54, Diocese of Toronto-Trinity Anglican Ch., Barrie, Ont., Can., 1954-72; Suffragan bishop Diocese of Toronto-Anglican Ch., Toronto, Ont., Can., 1972-81; bishop Diocese of Ont., Kingston, Ont., Can., 1981—; canon St. James Cathedral, Toronto, 1957-61; archdeacon of Simcoe, Diocese of Toronto, 1961-72, Can. churchman bd. trustees; dir. Anglican Found., Toronto. Author: Unto The Hills, 1951; Shepherds in Green Pastures, 1953. Hon. Reeve, Black Creek Pioneer Village, 1981-82. Recipient Rural Workers Fellowship award Episcopalian Ch. of U.S., 1952; named Citizen of Yr., City of Barrie, 1967. Office: Diocesan Centre, 90 Johnson St, Kingston, ON Canada K7L 1X7

READ, DAVID HAXTON CARSWELL, clergyman; b. Cupar, Fife, Scotland, Jan. 2, 1910; came to U.S., 1956; s. John Alexander and Catherine Haxton (Carswell) R.; m. Dorothy Florence Patricia Gilbert, 1936; 1 son, Rory David Gilbert. Student, Daniel Stewart's Coll., Edinburgh, 1927; M.A. summa cum laude, U. Edinburgh, 1932, D.D., 1957; student, Montpelier, Strasbourg, Paris, 1932-33, Marburg, 1934; B.D., New Coll., Edinburgh, Scotland, 1936; D.D., Yale U., 1959, Lafayette Coll., 1965, Hope Coll., 1969; Litt.D., Coll. Wooster, 1966; L.H.D., Trinity U., 1972, Hobart Coll., 1972, Knox Coll., 1979; D.H.L., Japan Internat. Christian U., 1979, Rockford Coll., 1982. Ordained to ministry Ch. Scotland, 1936; minister Greenbank Ch., Edinburgh, 1939-49; chaplain to U. Edinburgh, 1949-55; chaplain to Her Majesty the Queen, Scotland, 1952-56; minister Madison Ave. Presbyn. Ch., 1956-89, minister emeritus, 1989—. Author: The Spirit of Life, 1939, Prisoners' Quest, 1944, The Communication of the Gospel, 1952, The Christian Faith, 1956, I Am Persuaded, 1962, Sons of Anak, 1964, God's Mobile Family, 1966, Whose God is Dead?, 1966, The Pattern of Christ, 1967, Holy Common Sense, 1966, The Presence of Christ, 1968, Christian Ethics, 1968, Virgina Woolf Meets Charlie Brown, 1968, Religion without Wrappings, 1970, Overheard, 1971, Curious Christians, 1972, An Expanding Faith, 1973, Sent from God, 1974, Good News in the Letters of Paul, 1976, Go . . . And Make Disciples, 1978, Unfinished Easter, 1978, The Faith is Still There, 1980, This Grace Given, 1984, Grace Thus Far, 1986, Preaching About the Needs of Real People, 1988, Christmas Tales for All Ages, 1989; translator (from German): The Church to Come, 1939; Contbr. articles religious jours., periodicals, U.S. and Eng. With Coldstream Guards, 1936-39; chaplain Brit. Army, 1939-45. Clubs: Century Assn. (N.Y.C.); Pilgrims. Prisoner of war, 1940-45. Home: 750 Columbus Ave #2H New York NY 10025

READ, HARRISON ANDREW, religious organization administrator; b. Phila., Sept. 27, 1950; s. Harrison Wilfred and Margaret (Bolf) R.; m. Brenda Joyce Hamrick, Jan. 26, 1974; children: Bryan Andrew, Joseph Benjamin. AS in Tech., Temple U., 1971; BS, Pepperdine U., 1979, MBA, 1981. Various positions Campus Crusade for Christ, San Bernardino, Calif., 1972-84; dir. of devel. Devel. Assn. for Christian Instns., Dallas, 1984-86, U.S. nat. dir., 1986-88; dir. Evang. Devel. Ministry, Inc., Dallas, 1987—; pres., chief exec. officer Devel. Assn. for Christian Instns., Dallas, 1988—; mem. adv. bd. Scripture Film Internat., Lubbock, Tex., 1989—; chmn. bd. Keystone Acad., Plano, Tex., 1989—; mem. adv. bd. Global Missions Fellowship, Dallas, 1990—, The Little Ch., Laguna Beach, Calif., 1990—. Author: (with others) Money for Ministries. Mem. Christian Mgmt. Assn. Office: Evang Devel Ministry Inc 3870 Antigua Dr Dallas TX 75244

READ, SISTER JOEL, college president. BS in Edn., Alverno Coll., 1948; MA in History, Fordham U., 1951; hon. degrees, Lakeland Coll., 1972, Wittenburg U., 1976, Marymount Coll., 1978, DePaul U., 1985, Northland Coll., 1986, SUNY, 1986. Former prof., dept. chmn. history dept. Alverno Coll., Milwaukee, Wis.; pres. Alverno Coll., 1968—; pres. Am. Assn. for Higher Edn., 1976-77; mem. coun. NEH, 1977-83; bd. mem., Edn. Testing Service, Neylan Commn.; past pres., Wis. Assn. Ind. Colls. and Univs.; chmn., Commn. on the Status of Edn. for Women, Am. Assn. Colls., 1971-77; mem. exec. com. Greater Milw. Com., GMC Edn. Trust; bd. dirs. F and M Bank. Exec. bd. Milw. YMCA. Recipient Anne Row award Harvard U. Grad Sch. Edn., 1980. Mem. Rotary. Office: Alverno Coll 3401 S 39th St Milwaukee WI 53215-4020

READ, MARVIN, JR., pastor; b. Ripley, Tenn., July 27, 1936; s. Marvin Read Sr. and Gertie B. Reeves; m. Margaret A. Jointer, Oct. 13, 1979; children: Doris B., Joyce A., Kathy D., Marvin III. A in Gen. Studies, Ind. U. N.W., 1989. Ordained to ministry Bapt. Ch., 1985. Pastor Providence Bapt. Ch., Gary, Ind., 1986—; turn foreman Inland Steel Co., East Chicago, Ind.; trustee 1st Bapt. Ch., East Chicago, 1963-77, tchr. Sunday sch., 1978-79; tchr. Sunday sch. 1st Bapt. Ch., Gary, 1980-81. Pres. 1300 Wallace St. Block Club, Gary, 1990. Home: 1360 Wallace St Gary IN 46404 Office: New Providence Bapt Ch 640 E 45th Ave Gary IN 46409

READ, MELINDA RUTH BOUCHER, broadcasting executive; b. Lynnwood, Wash., July 18, 1957; d. George Wade and Ruthlea (Eberhart) B.; m. Thomas Wilmot Read. AAS, Fashion Inst. Tech., N.Y.C., 1978; BA, Seattle Pacific U., 1979. V.p. Read Broadcasting, Spokane, 1980—. Republican. Office: Read Broadcasting Box 683 Spokane WA 99210

READY, JACK WESLEY, religious educator, administrator; b. Dothan, Ala., Nov. 22, 1943; s. J.B. and Irene Cornelia (Kirkland) R.; m. Judy Gayle Branton, Nov. 25, 1964; children: Marty, Chris, Keli. Diploma in choral coordination, Fla. Bapt. Coll., 1973; BA, Mobile Coll., 1977; MRE, New Orleans Bapt. Theol. Sem., 1979. Cert. ch. bus. adminstr. Min. music and youth Grandview Bapt. Ch., Dothan, 1972-75, 1st Bapt. Ch., Fairhope, Ala., 1975-82; assoc. pastor, adminstr. 1st Bapt. Ch., Dothan, 1982—. Mem. adv. coun. Ala. Inst. for Deaf and Blind, Dothan, 1986—, Wiregrass Rehab. Ctr., 1989—; pres. Northview Band Boosters, Dothan, 1988-89; bd. dirs. Northview Quarterback Club, 1987-88. Sgt. Ala. Army N.G., 1960-66. Mem. Nat. Assn. Ch. Bus. Adminstrs., So. Bapt. Religious Educators, Ala. Edn. and Music Assn., C. of C., Kiwanis. Office: 1st Bapt Ch PO Box 2025 Dothan AL 36302

REAL, SISTER CATHLEEN CLARE, college president; b. Kewanee, Ill., June 1, 1934; d. John Thomas and Catherine Cecelia (Breen) R. BA in Math. and Chemistry, Marycrest Coll., Davenport, Iowa, 1957, LHD (hon.), 1985; MA in Math., St. Louis U., 1959; PhD in Math., U. Iowa, 1968. From instr. to asst. v.p. for acad. affairs to pres. Marycrest Coll., 1958-75; chair dept. math. Schenectady (N.Y.) County Community Coll., 1975-77; asst. acad. dean Barat Coll., Lake Forest, Ill., 1977-79; v.p. for acads. Coll. of St. Mary, Omaha, 1979-84, acting pres., 1983-84; pres. Siena Heights Coll., Adrian, Mich., 1984—; bd. dirs. Adrian State Bank. Bd. dirs. United Way, Adrian, 1985-, Goodwill-LARC, Adrian, 1986-, legatus Mich. chpt., 1988-, Citizens Gas, Adrian, 1990—. Recipient Anti-Defamation award Omaha Anti-Defamation League, 1983. Mem. Am. Assn. Higher Edn. Democrat. Roman Catholic. Lodge: Zonta. Office: Siena Heights Coll 1247 E Siena Heights Dr Adrian MI 49221-1796

REAMER, SHIRLEY JEAN, minister; b. South Bend, Ind., Aug. 15, 1935; d. John Lewis and Vivian Leora (Hammer) Helvey; m. Thomas Charles Reamer, June 22, 1956; children: Thomas Darwin, Trent Alan, Terry Michael, Traci Sue, Tricia Ann. Grad. high sch., South Bend, 1953. Ordained to ministry Full Gospel Fellowship, 1974. Dir. children's ministry Calvary Temple, South Bend, 1972-73; evangelist Full Gospel Fellowship, 1976—; founder, pastor Maranatha Temple, South Bend, 1981—; founder, pres. Women's Aglow Fellowship, Michiana, Ind., 1976-79; founder, dir. Prison Ministry-Aglow, Westville, Ind., 1976-77; founder, dir. Soup Kitchen/Care Ctr., Maranatha Temple, 1982—, Supplied Facilities for Ctr. for Homeless, 1984-87, dir. City March, 1989; mem. United Religious Community Task Force, South Bend, 1985. Author: Ministerial Ethics, 1984, Teaching Syllabus, 1985, Recruits for Christ, 1987. Recipient Spirit of Am. Women award J.C. Penneys, South Bend, 1988; named one of 16 Best Pastors, Charisma Mag., 1988. *Life, when valued like our most treasured possessions, will be held as sacred and will always be found on a lighted path to direct the way of another.*

REAMES, CHERYL WALLACE, religion educator, writer; b. Houston, Dec. 23, 1945; d. Dickson Elliott Wallace and Frances Pauline (Dold) Breaux; m. Waverly Grant Reames, June 3, 1967; children: Matthew David, Andrew Christopher. BA in Behavioral Sci., Scarritt Coll., 1969; MRE, Wesley Theol. Sem., Washington, 1975; BS in Elem. Edn., Shenandoah Coll. & Conservatory, 1990. Cert. elem. tchr., Va. Asst. in dean's office Meth. Theol. Sch., Delaware, Ohio, 1967-68; caseworker Delaware County Welfare Dept., 1968-71; instr. creative dramatics Arlington (Va.) Recreation Dept., 1972; writer curriculum and articles United Meth. Pub. House, Nashville, 1976—; instr. Lord Fairfax Community Coll., Middletown, Va., 1979-80; tchr. Powhatan Sch., Boyce, Va., 1986-88; educator early childhood sect. Northwestern Regional Ednl. Programs, Winchester, Va., 1990—; cons. in religious edn., 1975—; cons. reading, 1989—; tchr. reading Winchester City Schs., 1990. Contbr. numerous articles to religious edn. publs. Active local chpt. Boy Scouts Am., Lynchburg, Va., 1982-83, den leader local chpt., Stephens City, Va., 1990—. Mem. ASCD, Christian Educators Fellowship, Va. Christian Educators Fellowship, Religious Edn. Assn. U.S. and Can., Internat. Reading Assn., Va. State Reading Assn., Wesley Sem. Grads. Assn. (pres. 1980-82), Apple Valley Reading Coun., Phi Theta Kappa. Mem. United Meth. Ch. Office: PO Box 428 Stephens City VA 22655

REAP, SISTER MARY MARGARET, college president; b. Carbondale, Pa., Sept. 8, 1941; d. Charles Vincent and Anna Rose (Ahern) R. BA, Marywood Coll., Scranton, Pa., 1965; MA, Assumption Coll., Worcester, Mass., 1972; PhD, Pa. State U., 1979. Elem. tchr. St. Ephrem's, Bklyn., 1966-67; secondary tchr. South Catholic High, Scranton, Pa., 1967-69, Maria Regina High Sch., Uniondale, N.Y., 1969-72; mem. faculty Marywood Coll., Scranton, Pa., 1972-86, dean, 1986-88, pres., 1988—; vis. tchr. Mainland China, Wuhan, 1982, Marygrove Coll., Detroit, 1979; bd. dirs. Moses Taylor Hosp.; bd. dirs., exec. com. Lourdesmont Sch. Contbr. articles to profl. jours. Recipient bilingual fellowship Pa. State U., 1976-79, Local Chpt. Svc. award UN, 1984; named Northeast Woman, Scranton Times, 1986, Outstanding Alumna, Pa. State Coll. Edn., 1989. Mem. Coun. Ind. Colls., Am. Assn. Cath. Colls., C. of C. (bd. dirs.), Phi Delta Kappa (Educator of Yr. award 1990). Office: Marywood Coll Office of Pres Scranton PA 18509-1598

REAPSOME, JAMES WILLIS, editor; b. Mt. Joy, Pa., Oct. 16, 1928; s. Willis James Reapsome and Mary Esther (Brechbill) Glasford; m. Evelyn Duffy, Mar. 17, 1953 (dec. Oct. 1960); children: Sara, John; m. Martha Viola Gray, Feb. 3, 1962. AB, Franklin and Marshall Coll., 1950; ThM, Dallas Theol. Sem., 1957. Ordained to ministry, 1957. Mem. campus staff Inter-Varsity Christian Fellowship, 1950-51; dir. pub. rels. Inter-Varsity Christian Fellowship, Chgo., 1957-61; editor-in-chief Sunday Sch. Times, Phila., 1961-67; chaplain, asst. prof. of religion Malone Coll., Canton, Ohio, 1967-69; pastor Congl. Bible Ch., Marietta, Pa., 1973-79; mng. editor Christianity Today, Inc., Wheaton, Ill., 1979-82; exec. dir. Evang. Missions Info. Svcs., Wheaton, Ill., 1982—; editor Evang. Missions Quarterly, Wheaton, 1964—, World Pulse newsletter, Wheaton, 1982—; tchr. journalism Phila. Coll. of Bible, 1961-67; tchr. journalism, Old Testament and New Testament survey Malone Coll., 1967-69; tchr. Christian writing Trinity Evang. Div. Sch., 1981—; tchr. communications theory Bethany Coll. of Missions, 1990, 91; speaker in field; trustee Greater Europe Mission Bd., Manarah Bookshop Ministries, Amman, Jordan. Founding editor, writer, Youthletter, 1969-86, Discern the Times, 1970-73; author weekly newspaper column The Lamplighter; editor: This Day, The Untapped Generation, Saturation Evangelism, Indonesia Revival, the Church the Body of Christ; contbr.: The Great Commission Handbook, 1988; contbr. articles to profl. pubs; co-author: Discipleship: The Growing Christian's Lifestyle, Mariage: God's Design for Intimacy. Office: PO Box 794 Wheaton IL 60189

REARDON, DANIEL FRANCIS, priest; b. Chgo., Jan. 24, 1932; s. James Joseph and Ann Valeria Reardon. BS, Loyola U., Chgo., 1954; MS, Marquette U., 1961; MST, Jesuit Sch., Berkeley, Calif., 1981. Cert. secondary sch. tchr., Ill. Instr. Viatorian Schs. Cathedral High Sch., Spalding Inst., St. Viator, Springfield, Peoria, Arlington Heights, Ill., 1954-73; pastor Holy Cross Ch., Morgan city, La., 1974-79; assoc. pastor Maternity B, Bourbonnais, Ill., 1981-83; pastor St. Mary, St. Martin, St. John, Iroquois County, Ill., 1983-89; assoc. pastor St. Viator Ch., Chgo., 1989—. Democrat. Address: 4770 W Addison St Chicago IL 60641

REAUGH, JACK LOGAN, JR., minister; b. Greenville, Pa., Apr. 20, 1944; s. Jack Logan and Dorothy Ellen (Williams) R.; m. Carol Jean Morgan, Aug. 3, 1966; children: John Allen, Mary Ellen, James Michael. BS in Edn., Edinboro (Pa.) U., 1972; MDiv, Meth. Theol. Sch. in Ohio, Delaware, 1976. Ordained to ministry United Meth. Ch. Pastor Phillipsville-Lowville (Pa.) United Meth. Ch., 1968-69, Bethel-White Oak United Meth. Ch., Titusville, 1969-73, Hickernell-Norrisville United Meth. Ch., Springboro, 1973-77, South Fork (Pa.) 1st United Meth. Ch., 1977-86, Evang. United Meth. Ch., Corry, Pa., 1986—; sec. com. on ordained ministry Erie Meadville dist. Western Pa. Conf., United Meth. Ch., 1987—; pres. Wesley Woods United Meth. Camp, Grand Valley, Pa., 1990—, Corry Area Ministerium, 1990-91. Mem. Corry Area Juvenile Diversion Com., 1988—. Recipient cert. of appreciation Johnstown (Pa.) dist. United Meth. Ch., 1986, Foxview (Pa.) Manor, Inc., 1988. Office: Evang United Meth Ch 911-921 N Center St Corry PA 16407

REAVES, KENNETH MARTIN, minister; b. Nashville, Nov. 9, 1954; s. Johnnie Taylor and Viola Cathrine (Arnold) R.; m. Diane Young, Aug. 20, 1977; children: Travis Michael, Katrina Dawn. BS, Miami Christian Coll., 1978; MDiv., Southwestern Theol. Sem., 1980, D in Ministry, 1987. Ordained min. So. Bapt. Ch. Assoc. min. youth First Bapt. Ch., Perrine, Fla., 1975-77; sr. pastor Southside Bapt. Ch., Ft. Pierce, Fla., 1981-86, Immanuel Bapt. Ch., Ft. Lauderdale, Fla., 1986-88, First Bapt. Ch., Clewiston, Fla., 1988—; moderator Indian River Bapt. Assn., Ft. Pierce, 1982-84, Big Lake Bapt. Assn., Clewiston, 1990-91; mem. Credentials Com. Fla. Bapt. Conv., 1989-91, com. on nominations So. Bapt. Conv., 1990-91. Office: First Bapt Ch 102 E Ventura Clewiston FL 33440

REAVIS, HERBERT M., JR., clergyman, evangelist; b. Wellington, Tex., June 8, 1956; s. Herbert M. Reavis and Effie (Spear) Smith; m. Lisa M. Buck, Dec. 17, 1977; children: Joshua, Jonathan, Joseph. Diploma in evangelism, Moody Bible Inst., Chgo., 1977; BA, Milligan (Tenn.) Coll., 1979; MA, So. Bapt. Ctr. Bibl. Studies, Jacksonville, Fla., 1982, D Ministry, 1989. Ordained to ministry Bapt. Ch., 1978. Assoc. evangelist evangelistic team, 1974-76; pastor Newark Bapt. Ch., Thomasville, Ga., 1979-81, Calvary Bapt. Ch., Moultrie, Ga., 1981-83, Westwood Bapt. Ch., Live Oak, Fla., 1983-88, 1st Bapt. Ch., Ormond Beach, Fla., 1988-89, Springhill Bapt. Ch., Fernandina Beach, Fla., 1989—; speaker ann. meetings numerous ch. assns., Fla. and Ga., 1976—. Named Urban Minister of Yr., Suwannee Bapt. Assn., 1985; recipient award for outstanding accomplishments and excellence in pastoral leadership So. Bapt. Ctr. for Bibl. Studies, 1990. Mem. Fla. Bapt. Assn. (mem., chmn. coms. 1988-89). Republican. Home: RR 1 Box 116A Fernandina Beach FL 32034 Office: Springhill Bapt Ch RR 1 Box 116 Fernandina Beach FL 32034

REBECK, DAVID PAUL, minister; b. Cleve., Mar. 6, 1950; s. Paul C. and Ruth E. (Berger) R.; m. Jeanette Elaine Barber, May 26, 1973; children: John D., Ann E. AA, Concordia Jr. Coll., Ann Arbor, Mich., 1970; BA, Concordia Sr. Coll., Ft. Wayne, Ind., 1972; MDiv, Christ Sem.-Seminex, St. Louis, 1976. Ordained to ministry Evang. Luth. Ch. Am., 1977. Asst. pastor Pilgrim Luth. Ch., St. Paul, 1977-81; pastor Peace Luth. Ch., Cedar Rapids, Iowa, 1981—; bd. dirs. Iowa Inter Ch. Forum, Des Moines, 1984-87; deam Iowa conf. English Synod, A.E.L.C., Cedar Rapids, 1985-88; rep. S.E. Iowa transition team Evang. Luth. Ch. Am., 1986-87, chair congl. life program bd., Iowa City, 1988—. Co-author: Scriptural and Topical Indices to LBW, 1985. Chaplain Cedar Rapids Police Dept., 1985—. Democrat.

REBELL, WALTER, theologian, educator; b. Herten, Fed. Republic Germany, Apr. 26, 1951. Diploma in Pedagogy, Pädagogische Hochschule Dortmund, 1976; Diploma in Psychology, U. Bochum, 1979, ThD, 1982. Prof. theology U. Siegen, Fed. Republic Germany, 1986—. Author: Gehorsam und Unabhängigkeit, 1986, Gemeinde als Gegenwelt, 1987, Psychologisches Grundwissen für Theologen, 1988, Alles ist möglich dem, der glaubt, 1989, Zum neuen Leben berufen, 1990, Erfüllung und Erwartung, 1991. Avocation: sports. Home: 59 Forellstrasse, D-4350 Recklinghausen Federal Republic of Germany Office: Univ Siegen FB1, PF 10 1240, 59 Siegen Federal Republic of Germany *The exegesis of the New Testament must point out, that a fascinating life of freedom is possible—possible for those, who accept Jesus Christ as the middle of the symbolic universe (or semantic universe) in which people live.*

REBER, SIDNEY CRAFT, JR., religious organization executive; b. Jackson, Miss., June 12, 1918; s. Sidney Craft and Robbie Edna (Merrill) R.; m. Alwilda Montgomery, Dec. 4, 1943; children: Rebecca Alwilda Reber Washington. BS, Trinity U., San Antonio, 1950; postgrad. Trinity U., 1950-52, Miss. Coll., Clinton, 1952-53, Southwestern Bapt. Theol. Sem., 1967-68. With War Dept., Washington and Atlanta, 1940-43; classification analyst U.S. Civil Svc. Commn., Dallas, 1945-46; personnel officer VA, Dallas, San Antonio, Jackson, Miss., 1946-53; regional tng. officer, taxpayer assistance officer IRS, Dallas, 1953-63; bus. mgr., treas. Malaysia-Singapore Bapt. Mission, So. Bapt. Conv., Fgn. Mission Bd., Singapore, 1963-69; dir. mgmt. svcs. div. So. Bapt. Fgn. Mission Bd., Richmond, Va., 1969-80, v.p. mgmt. svcs., 1980—. Served to 2d lt. USAAF, 1943-45. Mem. Am. Mgmt. Assn., Soc. Advancement Mgmt. Baptist. Lodge: Rotary. Home: 23 James Close Woodlands, Golders, London England Office: Fgn Mission Bd So Bapt Conv 3806 Monument Ave Richmond VA 23230

RECHENBERG, BASIL WILLIAM, priest, psychologist, educator; b. Memphis, June 27, 1928; s. Harry William and Clothilde Louise (Meacham) R.; B.A., So. Meth. U., 1948; L.Th., Seabury-Western Theol. Sem., 1952, B.D., 1953; M.A., Immaculate Conception Sem., 1967; postgrad. U. Chgo., 1948-49, 57-60. Joined Order St. Benedict; ordained priest Roman Cath. Ch., 1968; lic. psychologist, Mo. Psychologist Iowa State Penitentiary, Ft. Madison, 1953-57, psychologist Des Moines Child Guidance Ctr., 1960-63, Conception Sem. Coll., Mo., 1965—, dir. psychol. services, 1972—; prof. psychology and Latin, 1970-81, prof. Latin, 1970—; cons. Benedictine Counseling and Cons. Inst., Maryville, Mo., 1979-86. Contbr. articles to profl. jours. Vicar Abbot-Pres., Swiss-Am. Benedictine Congregation, Ditll River, Mass., 1986—. Fellow Am. Orthopsychiat. Assn.; mem. Am. Classical League, Am. Psychol. Assn. (assoc.), Classical Assn. Middle West and South, Soc. Personality Assessment (assoc.), Mo. Classics Assn. Republican. Home: Conception Abbey Conception MO 64433 Office: Conception Sem Coll Conception MO 64433 Office: PO Box 67 Still River MA 01467

RECHTMAN, CYNTHIA, minister; b. N.Y., Nov. 28, 1946; d. Albert and Sophie (Rifkes) Spanner; m. Marvin Michael, Aug. 22, 1964; 1 child, Lisa Beth. Student, Bradley Coll., 1964, Aldelphi U., 1982. Sec. Old Westbury (N.Y.) Hebrew Congl., 1983-85; v.p. Old Westbury Hebrew Congl., 1985-87, pres., 1987—. Bd. trustees, exec. com. Old Westbury Hebrew Congl., N.Y., 1983—. Home: 86 Oakdale Ln East Hills NY 11577

RECK, SISTER CARLEEN, school system administrator. Supt. schs. Diocese of Jefferson City, Mo. Office: Office Sch Supt PO Box 417 Jefferson City MO 65102*

RECKARD, EDGAR CARPENTER, JR., retired minister, educator, college official; b. Huntington, W.Va., Dec. 20, 1919; s. Edgar Carpenter and Nanny Lois (Musselwhite) R.; m. Susanna Laing McWhorter, June 26, 1948; children—Edgar Scott, Francis Laing, Matthew Kinsley, Charles William, Mark Alan. B.A., Yale, 1942, M.Div., 1948; M.A. (ad eundem), Brown U., 1958; D.H.L., Westminster Coll., Mo., 1978; postgrad., U. Cambridge, Eng., U. Edinburgh, Scotland, 1948-50. Ordained to ministry Presbyn. Ch., 1948; chaplain, adviser to overseas students U. Edinburgh, 1948-50; chaplain, prof. Westminster Coll., Mo., 1950-52, Brown U., 1952-58; chaplain, prof.-at-large, gen. sec., dir. Ctr. Ednl. Opportunity Claremont Coll., Calif., 1958-72; v.p., dean of coll., prof. Centre Coll. of Ky., Danville, 1972-85; prof. emeritus Centre Coll. of Ky., 1985—, provost, 1976-83, pres. pro tem, 1981-82; sr. cons. Council on Founds., 1983-84, Assn. Am. Colls., 1983-84; vis. mem. Sr. Common Room, Mansfield Coll., Oxford, 1964-65; Underwood fellow, 1971-

72, ednl. cons., India, 1971-72. Named Claremont, Calif. Citizen of Yr., 1967; recipient Human Rights award Pomona Valley UN Assn., 1968, Golden Goblet award for svcs. to youth Los Angeles County, 1969, Gov.'s citation for outstanding svc. to Ky. Gov.'s scholar program, 1986. Mem. AAUP, Am. Acad. Religion, Am. Inst. Archaeology, Elizabethan Club Yale U., Yale Club of N.Y.C., Faculty House of Claremont U. Ctr., Phi Beta Kappa, Omicron Delta Kappa. Home: 560 W 8th St Claremont CA 91711-4222

REDAL, RUEBEN H., religious organization administrator. Pres. World Confessional Luth. Assn., Tacoma, Wash. Office: World Confessional Luth Assn 409 N Tacoma Ave Tacoma WA 98403*

REDD, AARON HERSHALL, pastor; b. Wilcoe, W.Va., Apr. 24, 1928; s. Walter Harrison and Viola Shelton (Malone) R.; m. Shelby Frances Williams, May 31, 1953; children: Aaron Jr., James Michael, Karl F. Errol W., Terry D., Mark A. BRE, Aenon Bible Coll., 1956. Ordained to ministry Pentecostal Ch., 1966. Various positions Grace Temple Ch., Johnson City, Tenn., 1948-66, pastor, 1972—, elevated to dist. elder, 1978; 1st vice chmn. W.Va. and East Tenn., Coun., Keystone, W.Va., sec. exec. bd., trustee, dist. elder bishop's cabinet. Mem. Mayor's com. to integrate Johnson City, 1958-62; mem. Juvenile Home Bd. Johnson City Commn., 1970-74; mem. City Mgr.'s Yr. of Constn., 1986. Helped build four churches, 1944, 65, 80, 86. Home: 303 Jackson Ave Johnson City TN 37604 Office: Grace Temple Ch Eternal Life Ctr 208 Garden Dr PO Box 1463 Johnson City TN 37605

REDDICK, JOHNNIE ERVIN, religious order administrator, bishop; b. Kinston, N.C., Apr. 21, 1935; s. James Lister and Junnie (Parker) R. Student, Arts and Tech. State U., Greensboro, N.C., 1955-60, Hampton Inst., 1955-60; DD (hon.), Shaw U., 1987; LHD (hon.), United Christian Sem., Goldsboro, N.C., 1988. Ordained to ministry United Am. Free Will Bapt. Denomination, Inc., 1953. Pastr. Free Will Bapt. Denomination, Kinston, 1953—, dist. elder, 1962-65, ann. bishop, 1965—, gen. bishop, 1984—; nat. pres. Free Will Bapt., USA, Kinston, 1984—; social worker Lenoir County Schs., Kinston, 1966—; founder, builder Mt. Calvary Free Will Bapt. Ch., LaGrange, N.C., 1959——; founder, dir. Free Will Bapt. Bible Corr. Class, Kinston, 1967-87. Trustee Shaw U. Div. Sch., Raleigh, N.C., 1984—; bd. dirs. Shelter for Homeless, Kinston, 1991—, Assn. for Retarded Citizens, Kinston, 1996—. Recipient Legion of Hoonor, Nat. Chaplains Assn., 1976, Key of City, City of Newark, 1985; col. gov.'s staff State of La., 1985. Mem. NAE, NAACP, Alpha Psi Omega. Democrat. Home: 705 Cameron Dr Kinston NC 28501 Office: Free Will Bapt Hdqrs 1011 University St Kinston NC 28501

REDDING, MARY LOU, religious press organization head. Pres., mng. editor Associated Ch. Press, Nashville. Office: Assoc Ch Press The Upper Rm 1908 Grand Ave Nashville TN 37202*

REDDISH, MITCHELL GLENN, religion educator; b. Jesup, Ga., Aug. 13, 1953; s. Warren Glenn and Coy Juanita (Griffis) R.; m. Barbara Susan Waters, July 6, 1975; children: Timothy Glenn, Elizabeth Ann, Michael Jerrell. BA in English, U. Ga., 1975; MDiv, So. Bapt. Theol. Sem., Louisville, 1978, PhD in New Testament Studies, 1982. Ordained to ministry So. Bapt. Conv., 1978. Pastor Mt. Hermon Bapt. Ch., Bedford, Ky., 1978-83; instr. So. Bapt. Theol. Sem., 1980-82; asst. prof. religion Stetson U., DeLand, Fla., 1983-89, assoc. prof. religion, 1989—; adj. prof. N.T., So. Bapt. Theol. Sem., 1982-83; faculty advisor Stetson Habitat for Humanity, DeLand, 1989-91. Book rev. editor: Pulpit Digest, 1986-90; editor: Apocalyptic Literature: A Reader, 1990; co-author: An Introduction to the Bible, 1991; contbr. articles to profl. jours. Bd. dirs. West Volusia Habitat for Humanity, DeLand, 1989—; active People Helping People, DeLand, 1983—, pres. 1990—. Mem. Am. Acad. Religion, Soc. Bibl. Lit., Nat. Assn. Bapt. Profs. of Religion, Phi Beta Kappa, Phi Kappa Phi, Phi Eta Sigma, Omicron Delta Kappa. Democrat. Home: 537 E Compton Ct De Land FL 32724 Office: Stetson Univ Campus Box 8354 DeLand FL 32720

REDINGTON, JAMES DUGGAN, priest, theology educator; b. Scranton, Pa., Jan. 12, 1945; s. Joseph Girard and Ann Mary (Dempsey) R. BA in Philosophy, Boston Coll., 1968; MA in Indian Studies, U. Wis., 1970, PhD in South Asian Langs. and Lit., 1975. Joined S.J., Roman Cath. Ch., 1962, ordained priest, 1978. Assoc. prof. dept. theology Georgetown U., Washington, 1978—. Author: Vallabhacarya on the Love Games of Krsna, 1983. Fulbright fellow, 1973-74, Am. Inst. Indian Studies, 1986-87. Mem. Am. Acad. Religion, Coll. Theology Soc. Democrat. Office: Georgetown U Dept Theology Washington DC 20057

REDINGTON, PATRICK EDWARD, religion educator; b. Galesburg, Ill., Sept. 30, 1946; s. Edward Patrick and Aileen (Lee) R.; m. Deirdre Eileen Aukward, Aug. 19, 1972; children: Maura Eileen, Edward Patrick. BA in History cum laude, Loras Coll., 1969; MA in Religious Edn., Cath. U. Am., 1972. Grad. teaching asst. Cath. U. Am., Washington, 1971; dir. religious edn. St. Clement Parish, Balt., 1972-74; tchr. Good Counsel High Sch., Wheaton, Md., 1974-81; dir. religious edn. St. Malachy Parish, Geneseo, Ill., 1981-88; dir. Ctr. on Work and Christian Life, Geneseo, Ill., 1986-90; assoc. dir. religious edn. Office of Cath. Edn., Diocese of Peoria, Ill., 1990-91; dir. evangelization Cath. Diocese of Peoria, Ill., 1990-91; dir. religious edn. St. Mary Parish, Evanston, Ill., 1991—; mem. religion curriculum com. Peoria Diocese, 1982-83; coord. Geneseo Christian Rural Overseas Program. Author: Catholics in America, 1979, Our Church History, 1980; also articles. Mem. congl. intern selection com. Md. 8th Congl. Dist., 1978. Mem. Nat. Cath. Edn., Religious Edn. Assn., Ill. Parish Coords. and Dirs. Religious Edn., Christian Assn. Peace Fellowship. Democrat. Office: 1421 Oak Ave Evanston IL 60201-4296

REDMON, WILLIAM E., minister, religious organization administrator; b. Atlanta, Mar. 18, 1940; s. James Cyrus and Irma Belle (Brown) R.; m. Margaret E. Dance, June 30, 1961; children: William Scott, Rex Edward. BA, Atlanta Christian Coll., 1962, BTh, 1963. Min. youth 1st Christian Ch., Carrollton, Ga., 1962-63; min. North DeKalb Christian Ch., Doraville, Ga., 1963-67, Palma Ceia Christian Ch., Tampa, Fla., 1967-72; dir. Lake Aurora Christian Assembly, Lake Wales, Fla., 1972—; treas. Fla. Christian Conv., 1970. Editor Christian Progress, 1972-73. Mem. Nat. Christian Camp Leaders Conf. (nat. pres. 1978), Am. Camping Assn., Christian Camping Internat. (cons. S.E. region 1980-86, pres. Fla. sect. 1987-89, pres. elect, 1991—). Home: 922 Strathmore Pl Lake Wales FL 33853 Office: Lake Wales Christian Assembly 237 Golden Bough Rd Lake Wales FL 33853

REDMOND, THOMAS PAUL, minister; b. Pitts., Dec. 11, 1954; s. John Harris and Rose (Polansky) R.; m. Deborah Jeanne Hoekstra, Aug. 13, 1977; 1 child, Phoebe Rose. BA in English, Bard Coll., 1977; MDiv, Western Sem., Portland, Oreg., 1982, MA in Pastoral Counseling, 1987, diploma in teaching, 1987. Ordained to ministry Conservative Bapt. Ch., 1984; cert. emergency med. tech., 1989, trauma life support, Wyo., 1990. Acting pastor Vly chapel, Stone Ridge, N.Y., 1977; pastor Cowlitz Way Bapt. Ch., Kelso, Wash., 1982-83; assoc. pastor Calvary Bapt. Ch., Longview, Wash., 1983-84; pastor 1st Bapt. Ch., Chugwater, Wyo., 1988-91; vol. chaplain Wovlitz County Sheriff's Chaplaincy, Kelso, 1983-88; chaplain Platte County Meml. Hosp., Wheatland, Wyo., 1988-91. Columnist Chugwater Prairie Press, 1989-91, Platte County Record-Times, 1991; contbr. articles to mags. Emergency med. tech. Chugwater Ambulance Svc., 1989-91; instr. ARC, Cheyenne, Wyo., 1990-91; sec. Chugwater Econ. Devel., 1991-91. Mem. N.Am. Assn. Ventriloquists, Fellowship Christian Magicians, Wyo. Ambulance and Emergency Med. Svc. Assn., Wyo. Associated State Incident Stress Team (peer debriefer, chaplain 1990-91). Republican. Home: 4 Pin Oak Dr Lawrenceville NJ 08648 *God is still most important, even though our lives are busy.*

REDMOND, VIRGIL BLAIR, minister; b. Curtisville, Ark., Sept. 22, 1928; s. Alvin Orrie and Lorraine (Barnes) R.; m. Nyladine Jeanette Deyarmond, Apr. 14, 1951; children: Thomas, Richard, Mary. Student, Grand Rapids Bible Inst., Mich., 1952-58. Ordained to ministry, Bapt. Ch. Gen. Sun. sch. supt. N. Park Bapt. Ch., Grand Rapids, 1957-59; missionary pastor Bapt. Mid-Missions, Cleve., 1959—; missionary pastor Bapt. Mid-Missions, State of Alaska, 1960—. Chmn. Econ. Devel. Com., Port Nikiski, Alaska, 1970; mem. com. White House Conf. on Families, Fairbanks, 1980. Office: Calvary Bapt Ch Box 1329 Kenai AK 99611-1329

REDMONT, JANE CAROL, religious writer, pastoral minister; b. Neuilly sur Seine, France, May 7, 1952; d. Bernard Sidney and Joan (Rothenberg) R. BA, Oberlin (Ohio) Coll., 1972; MDiv., Harvard U., 1976. Cert. Theological Field Edn. Supr. Instr. English as a Second Lang. Lanser Language Services, Paris, 1972-73; teaching asst. Harvard U., Cambridge, Mass., 1974-75, editor, devel. assoc. Harvard Divinity Bulletin, 1980-83; media coordinator Women's Theol. Coalition Boston Theol. Insti., Newton Ctr., Mass., 1975-76; asst. Cath. chaplain SUNY, Stony Brook, 1976-77; chaplain St. Paul's U. Cath Ctr., Madison, Wis., 1977-80; religion writer The Capital Times, Madison, Wis., 1980; social justice minister Paulist Ctr. Community, Boston, 1983-86; freelance writer, devel. cons., Cambridge, 1986—; capital campaign dir., program developer Hospice West Inc., Waltham, Mass., 1988-89; dir. devel. The Family Ctr., Inc., Somerville, Mass., 1990-91; regional dir. NCCJ, Boston, 1991—; co-host Paulist Ctr., Authors Forum, Boston, 1988—; mem. adv. bd. James E. Annand Ctr. for Spiritual Growth, Berkeley Div. Sch., Yale U. Contbr. articles to profl. jours., mags., newspapers. Bd. dirs. Am. Com. Human Rights, Social Action Ministries Greater Boston, Fellowship in Israel for Arab-Jewish Youth; justice of peace, Mass.; mem. Cath.-Jewish Com. Archdiocese of Boston, 1983-86, 91—; mem. Harvard Div. Sch. Alumni Assn. and Coun., 1988—, v.p. 1989-91, bd. dirs. 1991—. Mem. Women in Communications, Nat. Writers' Union, Am. Acad. Religion, Soc. Bibl. Lit., Nat. Soc. Fund-Raising Execs., Harvard Div. Sch. Alumni Assn. (v.p. 1989-90, rep. 1991—, bd. dirs. 1991—). Democrat. Roman Catholic. Avocation: music. Home: 2130 Massachusetts Ave Cambridge MA 02140 Office: NCCJ 15 Broad St Ste 505 Boston MA 02109

REECE, DONALD J., bishop. Bishop of St. John's-Basseterre, Roman Cath. Ch., Antigua and Barbuda. Office: Office of Bishop, of St John's-Basseterre, Saint John Antigua and Barbuda*

REECE, MAX G., minister; b. Boonville, N.C., Mar. 12, 1931; s. Joe and Deette (Johnson) R.; m. Virginia Weaver, July 1, 1950; children: Max G., Frederick Joel, Deborah Lynn. Student, Piedmont Coll., 1952-56; AA, Wingate (N.C.) Coll., 1961; student, Crisswell Coll., Dallas. Ordained to ministry So. Bapt. Conv., 1961. Pastor Allen Jay Bapt. Ch., High Point, N.C., 1981—; missionary, active revival crusades, 1969—; faculty So. Bapt. Sem. Extension Prog., 1983—. Home: 145 Old Mill Rd High Point NC 27265-1221

REECE, RICHARD TERRANCE, religious organization administrator; b. Phila., Sept. 5, 1935; s. George and Jennie (Devlin) R. BS in Chemistry, Niagara U., 1961; MS in Chemistry, Cath. U., 1965; MA in Theology, DeSales Sch., 1965. Tchr. chemistry Salesianum High Sch., Wilmington, 1956-58; camp medic Camp DeSales, Bklyn., 1958-61; tchr. chemistry N.E. Cath. High Sch., Phila., 1965-66, vice prin., 1966-77; vice prin. Bishop Ireton, Alexandria, Va., 1977-83; chair Oblates of St. Francis DeSales Inc., Wilmington, Del., 1983—. Chair Data Processing Com., Phila., 1966-77; bd. dirs. Allentown Coll., Center Valley, Pa., 1983—; chmn. bd. DeSales Sch. of Theology, Washington, 1983—, Salesianum High Sch., Wilmington, 1983—. Mem. Assn. Supervison and Curriculum Devel., Coun. Maj. Supt. of Men (bd. dirs.). Roman Catholic. Home: 2200 Kentnene Pkwy Wilmington DE 19806 Office: Oblates St Francis De Sales PO Box 1452 Wilmington DE 19899

REECE, ROBERT DENTON, educator; b. Bonham, Tex., Oct. 25, 1939; s. Clovis D. and Bonnie (Hyatt) R.; m. Donna Reece, June 5, 1965; children: Gwendolyn, Gregory, David, Emily. BA, Baylor U., 1961; BD, So. Bapt. Theol. Sem., 1964; MA, Yale U., 1966, MPhil, 1968, PhD, 1969. Asst. prof. Wright State U., Dayton, Ohio, 1969-75, assoc. prof., 1975-87, prof., 1987—. Author: Studying People: A Primer in the Ethics of Social Research, 1986; contbr. articles to profl. jours. Elder Westminster Presbyn. Ch., Dayton, 1986—. Danforth found. fellow, 1961-68. Mem. Am. Acad. Religion, Med. Ethics Consultation (chmn. 1983-85), Soc. for Health and Human Values (chmn. program dirs. group 1982-84), Soc. of Christian Ethics. Avocation: tennis. Home: 333 Volusia Ave Dayton OH 45409 Office: Wright State U Dept Community Health PO Box 927 Dayton OH 45401 *Gratitude may be the most basic of the virtues. Most of us are the recipients of important gifts which we cannot claim as our just desert—gifts which are ours by virtue of the accident of our birth into our particular historical time and social place. Who we are and what we accomplish depends in no small measure on our biological, social and intellectual heredity. Gratitude for our heritage does not mean the denigration of our own achievements as we build on those gifts. But it may make us more compassionate and more tolerant and it may help keep our pride in check.*

REECK, DARRELL, religious ethics educator; b. Tacoma, Jan. 25, 1939; s. Clarence and Orleen Lois (Colburn) R.; m. Lucille Ruth Wonderly, June 23, 1963; children—David Laurens Augustine, Christina Lucille. B.A., Seattle Pacific U., 1960; B.D., Garrett Evang. Theol. Sem., 1965; Ph.D., Boston U., 1970. Ordained elder United Methodist Ch., 1965; chartered fin. analyst, 186; asst. prof. religion U. Puget Sound, Tacoma, 1969-74, asst. acad. dean, 1974-76, assoc. prof., 1974-81, chmn. dept. religion, 1976-84, prof., 1981-91; portfolio mgr. Progressive Securities, Portland, oreg., 1989—; cons. Franklin Research and Devel. Corp., Boston, 1983-88, dir., 1984-88; dir. Franklin Insights, Boston. Author: Ethics for the Professions, 1982; Deep Mende, 1976. Contbr. articles and revs. to profl. jours. Bd. dirs., pres. Tacoma Community House, 1974-75, co-chmn. diamond jubilee com., 1983-84; mem. Gen. Commn. on Archives and History, United Meth. Ch., Madison, N.J., 1980-88; chmn. fin. com., 1984-88. Fellow Soc. for Values in Higher Edn.; mem. Soc. Christian Ethics, Am. Acad. Religion, Fin. Analysts Assn., Phi Kappa Phi. Democrat. Office: Progressive Securities 2435 SW Fifth Ave Portland OR 97201

REED, CYNTHIA KAY, minister; b. Amarillo, Tex., July 10, 1952; d. Carlos Eugene and Marjorie Marie (Daughetee) R. B of Music Edn., McMurry Coll., Abilene, Tex., 1976; MDiv, Perkins Sch. Theol., Dallas, 1991. Ordained to ministry Meth. Ch., 1989; cert. dir. music. Dir. music and Christian edn. Oakwood United Meth. Ch., Lubbock, Tex., 1978-84; dir. music and Christian edn. 1st United Meth. Ch., Childress, Tex., 1976-78, Littlefield, Tex., 1984-86; intern min. 1st United Meth. Ch., Lubbock, 1989-90, assoc. min., 1990—; extern chaplain Meth. Hosp., Lubbock, 1989—, Walk to Emmaus Renewal Movement, Lubbock, 1990—. Com. mem. Life Gift-Organ Donation, Lubbock, 1991; mem. Arthritis Found., Lubbock, 1991. Georgia Harkness scholar Div. Ordained Ministry, 1989. Mem. Christian Educators & Musicians Fellowship, Am. Guild Organists.

REED, DAVID BENSON, bishop; b. Tulsa, Feb. 16, 1927; s. Paul Spencer and Bonnie Frances (Taylor) R.; m. Susan Henry Riggs, Oct. 30, 1954 (div.); children: Mary, Jennifer, David, Sarah, Catherine; m. Catherine Camp Luckett, Apr. 15, 1984. A.B., Harvard U., 1948; M.Div., Va. Theol. Sem., 1951, D.D., 1964; D.D., U. of South, 1972, Episc. Theol. Sem., Ky., 1985. Ordained priest Episcopal Ch., 1952; missionary priest in Panama and Colombia, 1951-58; with Nat. Ch. Exec. Office, 1958-61; mission priest S.D., 1961-63; bishop of Colombia, 1964-72, Ecuador, 1964-70; bishop coadjutor Diocese of Ky., Louisville, 1972-74; bishop of Ky. Diocese of Ky., 1974—; 1st pres. Anglican Council Latin Am., 1969-72; chmn. standing commn. on ecumenical relations Episcopal Ch., 1979-82; pres. Ky. Coun. Chs., 1988-91; mem. governing bd. Nat. Coun. of Chs. of Christ in U.S.A., 1982—, mem. exec. com., 1985—, sec., 1988-91; Anglican co-chmn. Anglican Orthodox Theol. Cons., 1984—. Bd. dirs. Alliant Health Systems (formerly Norton Kosair Children's Hosp.), Louisville; trustee U. of South, 1972—, regent, 1979-82; chmn. Louisville United Against Hunger, 1980-84, 1986-87. Democrat. Home: 5226 Moccasin Trail Louisville KY 40207 Office: Episcopal Diocese of Ky 600 E Main St Louisville KY 40202

REED, DAVID LARUE, minister; b. Muncy, Pa., Feb. 1, 1949; s. Samuel Perry and Doris May (Foust) R.; m. Diane Marie Hinson, Jan. 24, 1971; children: Heather Marie, Philip Andrew. BA, Lycoming Coll., 1971; MDiv, United Theol. Sem., 1974; EdD, Pa. State U., 1982. Ordained to ministry United Meth. Ch. as deacon, 1972, as elder, 1976; cert. elem. tchr., Pa. Pastor Fairview United Meth. Ch., Montoursville, Pa., 1975-82, Otterbein United Meth. Ch., Boiling Springs, Pa., 1982—; chaplain to Meth. students Lycoming Coll., Williamsport, Pa., 1978-81; trustee Wesley Found., State College, Pa., 1978—; chmn. Task Force on United Meth. Higher Edn. in Pa., 1987—; mem. Pa. Commn. for United Ministries in Higher Edn., 1980—, chmn., 1988-90. Mem. Key Communicators, Boiling Springs, 1989—, South Middleton Area Resource Team, Boiling Springs, 1988—, Boiling Springs Sesquicentennial Com., 1991. Mem. Carlisle Flying Club (v.p. 1990—), Lions (pres. Boiling Springs 1988-89), Phi Kappa Phi. Democrat. Home: 839 Lindsey Rd Carlisle PA 17013 *Most of us would be better off if we spent less time worrying about what others think of us and more time doing what we know is the right thing to do.*

REED, DON WAYNE, mission organization administrator; b. Post, Tex., June 15, 1940; s. Roy W. and Eureka (Gollehon) R.; m. Wanda J. Reed, June 3, 1960; children: Stephen, Luanda, Lana. BA, Ouachita Bapt. U., 1962; BD in Lang., Southwestern Sem., 1967; DMin, Golden Gate Bapt. Sem., 1986. Ordained to Ministry So. Bapt. Conv., 1959. Pastor, missionary Ark., Tex., Okla., Peru, 1963-79; dir. missions Union Bapt. Assn., Norman, Okla., 1979-86; assoc. dir. vols. in missions dept. Fgn. Missions Bd., So. Bapt. Conv., Richmond, Va., 1986-88; dir. missions Kans. City Kans. Bapt. Assn., Overland Park, 1988—. Mem. Kiwanis. Office: Kans City Kans Bapt Assn 8745 Ballentine Ste A Overland Park KS 66214 *The cooperation of God's people leverages dramatically what can be accomplished in His Kingdom. I have dedicated my life to the enhancement of that cooperation.*

REED, DONALD LEWIS, minister; b. Fillmore, N.Y., Oct. 24, 1940; s. Lewis Merritt and Martha Mary (Shumaker) R.; m. Rachel Miriam Paulson, May 17, 1964; children: Rodney, Michelle. BA, Bryan Coll., Dayton, Tenn., 1963; ThM, Dallas Theol. Sem., 1967; MA, No. Am. Bapt. Sem., Sioux Falls, S.D., 1976; DMin, Bethel Sem., St. Paul, 1991. Ordained to ministry Bapt. Gen. Conf., 1970. Assoc. pastor Cen. Bapt. Ch., Sioux Falls, 1968-75; exec. minister Dakota Bapt. Conf., Sioux Falls, 1975-79; sr. pastor Faith Bapt. Fellowship, Sioux Falls, 1979-89; pastor Bethel Bapt. Ch., Santa Rosa, Calif., 1989—. Mem. Nat. Assn. Dirs. of Christian Edn. (pres. 1973-75). Home and Office: Bethel Ch 1577 Guerneville Rd Santa Rosa CA 95403-4108

REED, GERARD ALEXANDER, theology educator, history educator; b. Colorado Springs, Colo., Jan. 19, 1941; s. Paul Alexander and Lula (Taylor) R.; m. Roberta Kay Steininger, May 26, 1963. BA, So. Nazarene U., 1963; MA, Okla. U., 1964, PhD, 1967. Ordained to ministry Nazarene Ch., 1977. Asst. prof. So. Nazarene U., Bethany, Okla., 1966-68; prof. MidAm. Nazarene Coll., Olathe, Kans., 1968-82; prof., chaplain Point Loma Nazarene Coll., San Diego, 1982—. Contbr. articles to prof. publs. Parriott Found. fellow, 1964; summer seminar grantee NIH, 1979. Mem. Am. Maritain Assn., Am. Soc. Environ. History, Conf. of Faith and History, Wesleyan Theol. Soc., Western History Assn. Avocations: skiing, backpacking. Office: Point Loma Nazarene Coll 3900 Lomaland San Diego CA 92106

REED, JAMES EVERETTE, church administrator, former Christian education educator; b. Mathiston, Miss., July 3, 1944; s. Joseph Everette and Mary Ann (Johnson) R.; m. Jane Pickens, Nov. 29, 1948; children: David, Amanda. AA, Clarke Coll., Newton, Miss., 1967; BS, Samford U., Birmingham, Ala., 1972; MDiv, New Orleans Bapt. Theol. Sem., 1976, EdD, 1980. Mgr. New Orleans Bapt. Theol. Sem. Student Store, 1975-80; assoc. dir. Sem. Extension, Nashville, 1979-81; prof. Miss. Coll., Clinton, 1981-84; prof. Christian edn. New Orleans Bapt. Theol. Sem., 1984-90; ch. adminstr. 1st Bapt. Ch., Dothan, Ala., 1990—. Author: Church Administration, Search; co-author: A History of Christian Education. Bd. dirs. YMCA, Clinton, Miss., 1982-84, Joe Brown Recreational Pk., New Orleans, 1985-89. Named Tchr. of the Yr., Civitans, 1983-84. Mem. Nat. Assn. Prof. Christian Edn., Nat. Assn. Dirs. Christian Edn., So. Bapt. Religious Edn. Assn., Religious Edn. Assn., Assn. for Philosophy of Edn. Democrat. Baptist. Avocations: baseball coaching, reading. Office: 1st Bapt Ch 300 W Main St Dothan AL 36301

REED, MELVIN, lay worker; b. Atlanta, May 15, 1933; s. Wallace and Emma G. Reed; m. Vera L. Reed, Aug. 6, 1958; children: Pat Marian, Kelvin, Wallace, Alan, Trina. Hon. degree, Rose Crois U., San Jose, Calif., 1975. Assembly worker GM, Atlanta, 1965—. Lay worker Bread of World Covenant Chs., Washington, 1982, Presbyn. Ch.; mem. Rep. Presdl. Task Force. Sgt. U.S. Army, 1951-54. Mem. Soc. Bibl. Archaeology, Am. Arab Com., Coun. Notaries, Masons. Home: 1899 Goddard St SE Atlanta GA 30315

REED, MICHAEL KAMIN, minister; b. Lakeland, Fla., Apr. 1, 1962; s. Raymond and Elizabeth (Harvey) R.; m. Rhonda Estelle Croder, Dec. 15, 1984; children: Daniel Kamin, Stephen Michael. BA, Bapt. Coll. Charleston (S.C.), 1984; M.Ch. Music, So. Bapt. Theol. Sem., 1987. Ordained to ministry, So. Bapt. Conv., 1985. Minister of music Folly Beach (S.C.) Bapt. Ch., 1983-84; minister youth Warsaw (Ky.) Bapt. Ch., 1984-85; minister music and edn. Summerville Bapt. Ch., Phenix City, Ala., 1987-89; minister music and youth Berea Bapt. Ch., Lake City, Fla., 1989—; evangelism dir. Russell Bapt. Assn., Phenix City, 1988—; youth activities dir. Beulah Bapt. Assn., 1990—. Home: Rte 13 Box 838A Lake City FL 32055 Office: Berea Bapt Ch Hwy 47 S PO Box 1694 Lake City FL 32056

REED, RONALD DAVID, clergyman; b. Ashland, Ohio, Jan. 22, 1945; s. David Martin and Mary Katherine (Scott) R.; m. Deanna Ruth Pullins, Mar. 19, 1966; children: Jeffrey, Alicia. BSc in Agrl. Econs., Ohio State U., 1967; BSc in English Bible, Cin. Bible Coll., 1976; M Religious Edn., Cin. Christian Sem., 1978; MBA, U. Indpls., 1986. Ordained deacon Ch. of Christ, 1974, elder, 1978. Minister West Side Ch. of Christ, Lebanon, Ohio, 1975-78, Southport Heights Christian Ch., Indpls., 1978—; dir. Alexander Christian Found., Indpls., 1980—, Fellowship Christian Ministers, Indpls., 1980—; trustee Cin. Bible Coll. and Sem., 1989—; mem. N.Am. Christian Conv., Cin., 1988-90. Capt. U.S. Army, 1967-69, Vietnam. Named Salesman of Yr., Sales and Mktg. Execs., Milw., 1971. Mem. Am. Legion. Home: 3347 Gravelie Dr Indianapolis IN 46227 Office: Southport Heights Christian 7154 McFarland Rd Indianapolis IN 46227

REED, WILLIAM LAFOREST, religion educator emeritus; b. Defiance, Ohio, Jan. 9, 1912; s. Harold E. and Margaret (Schlotter) R.; m. Annetta Doria Pendergast, Dec. 31, 1935; 1 son, Russell Maurice. B.A., Hiram Coll., Hiram, Ohio, 1934; B.D., Yale, 1937, Ph.D., 1942; fellow, Am. Sch. Oriental Research, Jerusalem, 1937-38. Mem. faculty Tex. Christian U., 1946-56, 68-80, prof. religion, chmn. dept., 1968-75, Weatherly prof. religion, 1974-80, emeritus prof. religion, 1980—; prof. O.T., Lexington Theol. Sem., 1956-68; dir. Am. Sch. Oriental Research, 1951-52; sr. archaeologist AID, Amman, Jordan, 1964; archaeologist and/or dir. excavations in Jordan, Jericho, 1952, Dibon, 1952, Qumran Caves, 1952, Gibeon, 1959, 62, Elealeh, 1962, Saudi Arabia, 1962, 67, Yemen, 1972; Ordained to ministry Christian Ch., 1939. Author: The Old Testament Asherah, 1949, The Excavations at Dibon in Moab, 1964; co-author: Ancient Records from North Arabia, 1970; Co-editor: Translating and Understanding the Old Testament; Contbr. editor jours. in field. Trustee Am. Sch. Oriental Research, 1953-56, 63-69, exec. asst. to pres., 1956-66, treas., 1966-68; mem. council Soc. Bibl. Lit., 1963-69. Served to maj. Chaplains Corps AUS, 1942-46. Decorated Bronze Star.; Distinguished prof. Tex. Christian U., 1953-56; faculty grantee Am. Assn. Theol. Schs., 1961-62; research grantee Am. Philos. Soc., 1962, 67, 72; Garfield fellow Hiram Coll., 1973. Mem. Am. Acad. Religion, Am. Oriental Soc., Soc. Bibl. Lit., Theta Phi. Home: 6212 Whitman Ave Fort Worth TX 76133

REEDER, DAVID FRANKLIN, clergyman, broadcasting company executive; b. Aurora, Mo., Sept. 27, 1951; s. John Franklin and Laura Frances (Campbell) R.; m. Maureen K. Reeder, May 7, 1988; 1 child, MacKenzie Marie. BS, Mo. So. State Coll., Joplin, Mo., 1973; AA, Radio Engring. Inst., Kansas City, Mo., 1974, So. Bible Coll., Houston, 1976. Cert. broadcast engr.; ordained to ministry Pentecostal Ch. God, 1976. Pastor Pentecostal Ch. of God, Joplin, 1976-81; assoc. pastor Christ Ch., Washington, 1981-85; gen. mgr. WDCT, KYCR Marsh Broadcasting Co., Washington, Mpls., 1987—; lay leader Eternal Hope Luth. Ch., Brooklyn Park, Minn., 1990—. Fellow Soc. Broadcast Engrs., Aircraft Owners and Pilots Assn., Am. Radio Relay League, Minn. Broadcasters Assn., Washington Area Broadcasters; mem. Lions Club (pres. 1985-86, Lion of Yr. 1979). Office: Marsh Broadcasting KYCR 5730 Duluth St Minneapolis MN 55422

REEDER, JOHN P., JR., religious studies educator; b. Charlotte, N.C., July 11, 1937; s. John Pickens and Vestal (Hawkins) R.; m. Jane Clark, June 26, 1965; children—Nicholas Clark, Katherine Whitworth. B.A., Yale U., New Haven, 1960, B.D., 1964, Ph.D., 1968. Instr. dept. religion Princeton U., N.J., 1967-68, asst. prof. dept. religion, 1968-71; asst. prof. dept. religious studies Brown U., Providence, 1971-72, assoc. prof. dept. religious studies, 1973-79, prof. dept. religious studies, 1979—, chmn. dept. religious studies, 82-84, 85—. Author: Source Sanction and Salvation; co-editor (with Gene Outka) Religion and Morality; contbr. articles to profl. jours. Home: 51 Barnes St Providence RI 02906 Office: Brown U Dept Religious Studies Providence RI 02912

REEHER, JAMES IRWIN, minister; b. Sharon, Pa., Dec. 6, 1948; s. James William and Lillian (Irwin) R.; m. Marian Powell, Oct. 25, 1969; children: Elizabeth Margret, James Michael. BA, U. Tampa, 1975; MDiv, Emory U., 1978; DD, Boston U., 1989. Ordained to ministry United Ch. Ch. Min. Christ United Meth. Ch., Tampa, Fla., 1972-75, Lamar United Meth. Ch., Barnesville, Ga., 1975-78, 1st United Meth. Ch., Seffner, Fla., 1986-90; asst. min. Grace United Meth. Ch., Venice, Fla., 1978-79; founding min. 1st United Meth. Ch., Sarasota, Fla., 1980-86; min. Forest Hills United Meth. Ch., Tampa, 1990—; del. bd. ordained ministry Tampa Dist., 1987—; del. stewardship com. Fla. United Meth. Ch., Tampa, 1988—; bd. dirs. Jim Russo Prison Ministries, Bradenton, Fla., 1990—; chmn. anti-gambling campaign Fla. United Meth. Conf., 1986. Founding chmn. East Hillsborough Orgn., Seffner, 1988; bd. dirs. Life Enrichment Sr. Ctr., Tampa, 1990—. Recipient Outstanding Religious Leader award Sarasota Jaycees, 1985. Mem. Assn. for Clin. Pastoral Edn., Alban Inst., North Tampa Ministerial Assn. Democrat. Home: 3020 St Charles Dr Tampa FL 33618 Office: Forest Hills United Meth Ch 904 W Linebaugh Ave Tampa FL 33612

REES, ALFRED WILLIAM, minister, religious organization administrator; b. Toronto, Ont., Can., Dec. 29, 1925; s. William and Elizabeth Ann (Gates) R.; m. Lela Lucille Prosser, July 19, 1947; children: Lynda, Dianne, Mark, Marlene, Judi. Diploma in theology, Emmanuel Bible Coll., Kitchener, Ont., 1949; DD (hon.), Emmanuel Coll., Kitchener, Ont., 1987. Ordained to ministry Missionary Ch. Can., 1952. Pastor Missionary Ch. Can., Port Elgin, Ont., 1949-54; missionary World Ptnrs., Ft. Wayne, Ind., Calcutta, India, 1954-66; sr. pastor Banfield Meml. Ch., Toronto, 1967-91; nat. evangelist, pres. Missionary Ch. Can., North York City, Ont., 1982—; evangelist Crusade Evangelism Internat., London, Ont., 1971-81; pres. Gospel Lit. in Nat. Tongues, North York City, 1970—. Flight sgt. RCAF, 1943-46, CBI. Mem. Pi Alpha Mu. Home: 11 Ruddington Dr Apt 1427, Willowdale, ON Canada M2K 2J6 Office: Missionary Ch Can, 89 Centre Ave, Willowdale, ON Canada M2M 2L7

REES, PAUL STROMBERG, clergyman; b. Providence, Sept. 4, 1900; s. Seth Cook and Frida Marie (Stromberg) R.; m. Edith Alice Brown, June 3, 1926; children: Evelyn Joy Rees Moore (dec.), Daniel Seth, Julianna Rees Robertson. A.B., U. So. Calif., 1923, D.D. (hon.), 1944; D.D. (hon.), Asbury Coll., 1939, North Park Coll., Chgo., 1965, Warner Pacific Coll., 1982; Litt.D., Houghton Coll., 1953; L.H.D., Seattle Pacific U., 1959. Ordained to ministry Wesleyan Ch., 1921, Evangel. Covenant Ch., 1940. Assoc. pastor Pilgrim Tabernacle, Pasadena, Calif., 1920-23; ministerial supt. Detroit Holiness Tabernacle, 1928-32; pastor 1st Covenant Ch., Mpls., 1938-58; v.p. at large World Vision Internat., Monrovia, Calif., 1958-75; bd. dirs. World Vision Internat., 1960-85, now hon. life mem.; dir. Pastors' Conf. Ministry, 1964-75; editor World Vision Mag., 1964-72, contbg. editor, 1972-74, editor at large, 1974-87; internat. lectr. and preacher; moderator Evang. Covenant Ch. Am., 1948, v.p., 1950-55; v.p. World Evang. Fellowship; minister to ministers Billy Graham Crusades, London, 1954, Glasgow, 1955, N.Y.C., 1957, Sydney, Australia, 1959; columnist Covenant Companion, 1959-72; adviser World Council of Chs. Assembly, New Delhi, India, 1961, Uppsala, Sweden, 1968; speaker World Congress on Evangelism, Berlin, 1966, Nat. Congress on Evangelism, Mpls., 1969; lectr. Staley Disting. Scholar Found.; guest tchr. Congress on Japanese Evangelism, 1985. Author: Seth Cook Rees: The Warrior Saint, 1934, If God Be For Us, 1940, Things Unshakable, 1947, The Radiant Cross, 1949, The Face of Our Lord, 1951, Stir Up the Gift, 1952, Prayer and Life's Highest, 1956, Christian: Commit Yourself, 1957, The Adequate Man, 1958, Stand Up in Praise to God, 1960, Triumphant in Trouble, 1962, Proclaiming the New Testament—Philippians, Colossians, Philemon, 1964, Men of Action in the Book of Acts, 1966, Don't Sleep Through the Revolution, 1969; editor: Nairobi to Berkeley, 1967; assoc. editor: The Herald, 1955-75; contbg. editor, 1975-81, Christianity Today, 1958-75; cons. editor: Eternity mag, 1960-77; speaker Staley Lectr. Series George Fox Coll., 1972, Olivet Nazarene U., 1973, Houghton Coll., 1976, Mt. Vernon Nazarene Coll., 1977, Warner Pacific Coll., 1977, Asbury Coll., 1977, Cen. Wesleyan Coll., 1984. Trustee Asbury Coll., 1935-65; trustee Asbury Theol. Sem., 1967-80, now hon. life mem.; bd. dirs. William Penn Coll., 1950-58; bd. dirs. Christianity Today, 1958-81, now hon. life mem.; bd. dirs. Paul Carlson Found., 1965-72, Bread for the World, 1974-81, World Vision Inc., 1959-85, now hon. life mem. Recipient Freedoms Found. award, 1951. Mem. Nat. Assn. Evangs. (bd. adminstrn. 1942—, pres 1952-54, now emeritus mem.), Phi Beta Kappa. Home: 2121 N Ocean Blvd Boca Raton FL 33431 *I am convinced that the Christian world-view answers more questions, resolves more doubts, subdues more fears, meets more needs, humbles more pride, preserves more dignity, holds more hope than any other.*

REESE, BOYD TURNER, JR., librarian; b. Augusta, Ga., Jan. 14, 1945; s. Boyd T. Sr. and Anna Mary (Payne) R.; m. Hedy Lynette Eisenbraun, June 28, 1975; children: Emily Marie, Jessica Anne. BS in Indsl. Mgmt., Ga. Inst. Tech., 1967; MA in Theol. Studies, McCormick Sem., 1976; MS in Info. Studies, Drexel U., 1987; PhD, Temple U., 1990. Assoc. editor Sojourners mag., Chgo., 1971-74; asst. prof., dir. Phila. campus Messiah Coll., 1976-80; assoc. libr. history dept. Presbyn. Ch. U.S.A, Phila., 1988—. Temple U. fellow, 1980-82, 84. Mem. Am. Theol. Libr. Assn. (archivist 1989—), Am. Soc. for Ch. History, Conf. on Faith and History, Beta Phi Mu. Mem. Mennonite Ch. Office: Presbyn Ch USA Dept History 425 Logan St Philadelphia PA 19147

REESE, KERRY DAVID, minister; b. Kennewick, Wash., Dec. 17, 1953; s. Walter Theodore and Arline Winifred (Botz) R.; m. Robin Marie Harm, Aug. 18, 1978; children: Michelle, Benjamin, Emily. AA, Concordia Coll., 1974; BA, Concordia Sr. Coll., 1976; MDiv, Concordia Sem., 1980, STM, 1987. Asst. pastor St. Peter-Immanuel Luth. Ch., Milw., 1982-83; pastor Messiah Luth. Ch., Highland, Calif., 1983-90, Shepherd of the Hills Luth. Ch., Snohomish, Washington, 1990—. Mem. Luth. Ch.-Mo. Synod (del. Wichita, Kans. chpt. 1989). Office: Shepherd of the Hills Luth Ch 9225 212th St SE Snohomish WA 98290 *A single life span on earth seems hardly time enough to embrace the enormous spectrum of pleasures and intellectual pursuits that our Creator must certainly have wished for us to enjoy. It is the greatest consolation that by the grace of God through Jesus Christ, we shall be permitted continued growth in wisdom and character for all eternity.*

REESE, MARTHA GRACE, minister, lawyer; b. Newark, Ohio, Feb. 27, 1953; d. John Gilbert and Louella Catherine (Hodges) R.; 1 child, Elizabeth Lang Harman. BA with high distinction, DePauw U., 1975; JD magna cum laude, Ind. U., 1980; MDiv magna cum laude, Christian Theol. Sem., 1989. Bar: Ind. 1980, U.S. Dist. Ct. (so. dist.) Ind. 1980, U.S. Ct. Appeals (7th cir.) 1981. Law clk. U.S. Dist. Ct. (so. dist.) Ind., 1980-82; ordained to ministry Christian Ch. (Disciples of Christ), 1989; assoc. Baker & Daniels, Indpls., 1982-83; ptnr. Wilson, Hutchens & Reese, Greencastle, Ind., 1984-86; interim assoc., regional minister , The Christian Ch. in Ind. (Disciples of Christ), 1988-89; sr. pastor Carmel (Ind.) Christian Ch. (Disciples of Christ), 1989—; cons. Lilly Endowment, Inc., 1989, 90. Steering com. Ind. Leadership Celebration, 1983—. Mem. Carmel Ministerial Assn., Phi Beta Kappa, Theta Phi. Home: 3942 N Delaware St Indianapolis IN 46205

REESE, MICHAEL PAUL, minister; b. Parkersburg, W.Va., Oct. 11, 1959; s. Paul Francis and Nita Ruth (Freed) R.; m. Linda Darlene McCullough, May 17, 1980; children: Sarah Elizabeth, Benjamin Michael. BS in Bible, Freed-Hardeman U., 1981; BS in Biology, Fairmont State Coll., 1983; MA in Religion (magna cum laude), Ala. Christian Sch. Religion, 1989; postgrad., Cin. Bible Sem., 1989—. Ordained to ministry Ch. of Christ, 1979. Minister Topsy (Tenn.) Ch. of Christ, 1979-81, Oakwood Rd. Ch. of Christ, Fairmont, W.Va., 1981-89, Mannington (W.Va.) Ch. of Christ, 1989—; staff, tchr. Barbour County Youth Camp, Philippi, W.Va., 1984-90; tchr. Stark County Youth Rally, Canton, Ohio, 1985—. Vol. tchr. Marion County Sr. Citizens Ctr., Fairmont, 1984-89, Fairmont Arbors Retirement Home, 1984—, Mannington Sr. Citizens Ctr., 1989—. Recipient Study Grant Nat. Audubon Soc., 1977. Mem. Pres.'s Ambassadors Christian Edn. Home: Rte 2 Box 231 B Fairmont WV 26554 Office: Ch of Christ 706 E Main St Mannington WV 26582

REESE, ROY CHARLES, missionary; b. Cin., Sept. 29, 1949; s. Robert LeRoy and Mary Louise (Pragar) R.; m. Pauline Virginia Kerr, June 23, 1975; children: Amy Pauline, Daniel Roy, Samuel Joseph. B.A. in Math., U. Sask., Regina, Can., 1971, M.A. in Math., 1974; M.Div., Can. Theol. Sem., 1974. Ordained to ministry Christian and Missionary Alliance Ch., 1976. Lectr. math. U. Saskatchewan, 1971-74; asst. pastor Glen Oaks Alliance Ch., Troy, Mich., 1974-76; pastor Mt. Clemens Alliance Ch., Mich., 1976-78; tchr. Swanton Christian Sch., Ohio, 1978-79; missionary Christian and Missionary Alliance, Argenteuil, Pau, Martigues, France, 1979—; mem. Christian Edn. com. West Central Dist. Christian and Missionary Alliance, Mt. Clemens, 1976-78; mem. translations com. Christian and Missionary alliance, Martigues, 1985—. Mem. Alliance Evangelique Francaise, Math. Assn. Am. Avocations: math. research, computer sci., reading in history and philosophy. Home and Office: La Pastorale-Bat G, Rue Robert Desnos, 13500 Martigues France

REESER, DONALD M., pastor; b. Orangeville, Ill., Mar. 30, 1931; s. Martin Van Buren and Gladys L. (Schulz) R.; m. Joan Ellen Kurtz, Aug. 27, 1991; stepchildren: Mari Ellen, Renate Anne, Donald Martin. Diploma, Moody Bible Inst., 1954; AB in Psychology and Religion, Greenville (Ill.) Coll., 1956; MRE, No. Bapt. Theol. Sem., 1958; MA in German, So. Ill. U., 1975. Missionary tchr. Greater Europe Mission, Wheaton, Ill., 1960-69; asst. prof. Greenville Coll., 1969-79; pastor Bethany Bapt. Ch., Highland, Ill., 1983—; vice moderator area V Gt. Rivers region Am. Bapt. Chs., 1991—. Mem. Area V Am. Bapt. Chs. of the Great Rivers Region (vice moderator 1991—). Republican. Home: 704 N Locust Greenville IL 62246-1233 Office: Bethany Bapt Ch RR 3 Highland IL 62249

REESER, JAN E., magazine editor; b. Coatesville, Pa., Jan. 2, 1948. Student, Phila. Coll. Bible, 1965-69, U. Nebr., 1973-76, U. Bibl. Studies. Proofreader Grand Island Daily Ind., 1969-72; editorial asst., sec. Good News Broadcaster, Back to the Bible, 1972-79; graphics/editorial asst. Good News Broadcaster, 1979-81, asst. editor, 1981-83; copywriter Back to the Bible, 1983-84, supr. copy and lit. editing, 1984-88, mng. editor Confident Living mag., 1988—. V.p. Raptor Recovery Ctr., Lincoln, Nebr.; publicity chair Lincoln Community Concerts Assn. Mem. Evang. Press Assn. Office: Box 82808 Lincoln NE 68501

REEVES, DONALD BUSTER, minister; b. Seymour, Tex., Sept. 30, 1945; s. Donald Buster and Lillian Lauraine (Hughes) R.; m. June Marie Weaver, Aug. 4, 1967 (dec. 1973); 1 child, Carece Marie; m. Sandra Fay Teague, Nov. 10, 1973; children: Charity Christine, Joshua Kevin. BA, Hardin-Simmons U., Abilene, Tex., 1968; postgrad., Southwestern Sem., Ft. Worth, Tex., 1969. Ordained to ministry So. Bapt. Conv., 1967. Youth pastor Belmont Bapt. Ch., Abilene, Tex., 1965-67; youth evangelist, spreader, 1965-68; pastor various chs. various locations, 1969-73; evangelist and conf. speaker, 1970-90; pastor Temple Bapt Ch., Redlands, Calif., 1979-86, Mt. Franklin Bapt. Ch., El Paso, Tex., 1986—; bd. dirs. Sta. KSCE-TV Christian TV, El Paso, 1990—; pres. Calif. State Ministers Conf., Fresno, 1985; exec. bd. Calif. So. Bapt. Con., Fresno, 1982-86; evangelism chmn. El Paso Bapt. Assn., 1989-91; chmn. Here's Hope City-Wide Crusade, El Paso, 1990; sec.-treas. Pastors Conf., Bapt. Gen. Conv. Tex., 1991-92. Mem. Com. to Re-elect Judge Jose Troche, El Paso, 1990; founding mem. Helping Other People Eat (HOPE), Redlands, 1984-86; bd. dirs. Westside YMCA, 1989-91. Mem. Rotary. Republican. Home: 848 Brisa Del Mar Dr El Paso TX 79912

REEVES, GEORGE PAUL, bishop; b. Roanoke, Va., Oct. 14, 1918; s. George Floyd and Harriett Faye (Foster) R.; m. Adele Beer, Dec. 18, 1943; children—Cynthia Reeves Pond, George Floyd II. B.A., Randolph-Macon Coll., 1940; B.D., Yale U., 1943; D.D., U. of South, 1970, Nashotah House, 1970. Ordained priest Episcopal Ch., 1948, consecrated bishop, 1969; chaplain U.S. Naval Res., 1943-47, Fla. State U., 1947-50; rector All Saints Ch., Winter Park, Fla., 1950-59, Ch. of Redeemer, Sarasota, Fla., 1959-65, St. Stephens Ch., Miami, Fla., 1965-69; bishop of Ga., Savannah, 1969-85; ret., 1985. Mem. Phi Beta Kappa.

REEVES, LARRY ALAN, minister; b. Waynesville, N.C., Aug. 11, 1952; s. Ted Liner and Pansy (Bryson) R.; m. Shirley June Humphrey, May 26, 1974; children: Rebecca Joye, Sara Grace. BA, Berea Coll., 1974; MA in Religious Edn., So. Bapt. Sem., 1976, M of Divinity, 1977. Ordained to ministry Bapt. Ch., 1974. Pastor Gilead Bapt. Ch., Cottonsburg, Ky., 1974-75; intern campus ministry U. Louisville Bapt. Student Union, 1975-77; Bapt. campus minister U. Tenn., Knoxville, 1979-81; pastor Little Flat Creek Bapt. Ch., Corryton, Tenn., 1977-79, First Bapt. Ch., Jackboro, Tenn., 1981—; mem. exec. bd. and com. Tenn. Bapt. Conv., 1984—. Contbr. articles to profl. jours. State pres. Bapt. Student Union of Ky., Middletown, 1973-74; mem. senate joint Resolution No. 176 State of Tenn., Nashville, 1984, student summer mission fgn. mission bd. So. Bapt. Conv., Malaysia/Singapore, 1972. Mem. Campbell County Ministerial Assn. Democrat. Avocations: collecting folk stories, writing, fishing, golf. Home: PO Box 166 Jacksboro TN 37757 Office: First Bapt Ch PO Box 220 Jacksboro TN 37757

REGAN, DENNIS MARTIN, priest, former seminary president; b. Rockville Centre, N.Y., July 11, 1937; s. W. Kenneth and Isabella (Martin) R. BA, St. Bernard Sem., Rochester, N.Y., 1964; S.T.L., Pontifical Lateran U., Rome, Italy, 1968, S.T.D., 1970. Ordained priest Roman Catholic Ch., 1964; assoc. pastor Sacred Heart Ch., North Merrick, N.Y., 1964-67; professorial asst. N. Am. Coll., Rome, Italy, 1968-70; academic dean Seminary of Immaculate Conception, Huntington, N.Y., 1971-78, rector, pres., 1979-85, prof. moral theology, 1970—; pastor Infant Jesus Ch., Port Jefferson, N.Y., 1989—; adj. prof. moral theology, Fordham U., 1986-90. Author: Violent Revolution, 1970; contbr. articles and papers. Mem. com. for revision of Standards Assn. Theol. Schs., 1982-85; mem. Commn. on Justice and Peace, Diocese of Rockville Ctr., 1982—, chmn. Diocesan Commn. on Med. Ethics; trustee Cathedral Coll., Douglaston, N.Y., 1979-85, St. John Seminary, Boston, 1982-88. Named Prelate of Honor by Pope John Paul II, 1980. Mem. Cath. Theol. Soc. Am., Am. Acad. Religion, Am. Soc. Christian Ethics. Home and Office: Infant Jesus Ch Port Jefferson NY 11777

REGAN, FRANCISCO ANTONIO, priest; b. N.Y.C., Apr. 22, 1941; s. Frank Joseph and Katherine Theresa (Ward) R. BA in Philosophy, St. Columban's Major Sem., Boston, 1963. Ordained priest Roman Cath. Ch., 1966. Chaplain Young Christian Workers Movement, Lima, Peru, 1968-89, nat. chaplain, 1982-89; editor Religious Life Bull., Conf. Religious Life Peru, Lima, 1972-76; pastoral cons. Missionary Soc. St. Columban, Lima, 1975-89; gen. councillor Missionary Soc. St. Columban, Dublin, Ireland, 1989—. Contbr. numerous articles on religion, sociology, politics, and econs. to profl. jours. Cons. Trade Union Domestic Workers, Lima, 1975-78.

REGAN, MICHAEL GIBSON, organist, choir director, musician; b. Richmond, Va., Nov. 1, 1956; s. William Whitfield and Peggy Elizabeth (Gibson) R.; m. Meggi James (div. Dec. 27 1989); m. Martha Carol Gillette, Jan. 25, 1991. MusB, MusM, East Carolina U., 1981; postgrad., Eastman Sch. Music. Dir. bands Pender County Schs., Burgan, N.C., 1981-83; organist, choir dir. 1st Christian Ch., Wilmington, N.C., 1983-84, Queen St. Meth. Ch., Kinston, N.C., 1984-86; organist 1st Presbyn. Ch., Pittsford, N.Y., 1986-87; organist, choir dir. Larchmont Meth. Ch., Norfolk, Va., 1987—. Winner Young Artists Competition East Carolina U., 1981, Music Tchrs. Nat. Assn., 1977, 81. Mem. Am. Guild Organists (sub dean 1985-86, winner young artists competition 1987), Am. Guild English Handbell Ringers, Lions. Office: Larchmont Meth Ch 1106 Larchmont Crescent Norfolk VA 23508

REGAN, PATRICK JOHN, abbot; b. New Orleans, Jan. 18, 1938; s. John Edward and Helen Anna (Barnes) R. MA, St. John's U., Collegeville, Minn., 1966; STD, Inst. Catholique, Paris, 1971. Joined Benedictine Monks, Roman Cath. Ch., 1959, ordained priest, Roman Cath. Ch., 1965. Instr. St. Joseph Sem. Coll., St. Benedict, La., 1971—; abbot St. Joseph Abbey, St. Benedict, 1984—; pres. Swiss-Am. Benedictine Congregation, 1987—. Assoc. editor Worship, 1973-77. Mem. N.Am. Acad. Liturgy, Alliance for Internat. Monasticism (chmn. bd. 1987—). Office: St Joseph Abbey Saint Benedict LA 70457

REGAN, TOM, ecumenical agency administrator. Pres. Cornwallis Dist. Inter-Ch. Coun., Kings County, N.S., Can. Office: Cornwallis Dist Inter-Ch Coun, Centreville RR 2, Kings County, NS Canada N0T 1J0*

REGELE, MICHAEL BRUCE, minister, information and strategic planning services professional; b. Corvallis, Oreg., Mar. 30, 1952; s. William and Geneva (Chapman) R.; m. Debra S. Brog, June 26,1976; children: Jonathan, Justin, Jordan, Kiersten, Elissa. BA, Seattle Pacific U., 1975; MDiv, Fuller Theol. Sem., 1986. Ordained to ministry Presbyn. Ch. U.S.A., 1987; cert. tchr., Wash. Child care worker Griffin Home for Boys, Renton, Wash., 1973-74; tchr. Grace Acad., Kent, Wash., 1975-76, Columbia Sch., Seattle, 1976-78; assoc. pastor Mariners Ch., Newport Beach, Calif., 1980-84; exec. dir. Congress on Bibl. Exposition, Irvine, Calif., 1984-86; cons. Ministry Consulting, Irvine, 1986-87; pres. Ch. Info. and Devel. Svcs., Costa Mesa, Calif., 1987—; adj. faculty So. Calif. Coll., Costa Mesa; bd. dirs. Com. on Bibl. Exposition, Wheaton, Ill., 1983-88; mem. Com. on Preparation for Ministry, Anaheim, Calif., 1989—. Author: Your Church and Its Mission, 1988; co-author study guides. Bd. dirs. Irvine Unified Sch. Dist., 1990—. Mem. N.Am. Soc. Ch. Growth. Republican. Office: Ch Info and Devel Svcs 151 Kalmus Ste A-104 Costa Mesa CA 92626

REGES, MARIE STEPHEN, religion educator; b. Washington, Mar. 27, 1915; d. George Henry and Mary (Gately) R. BA, Trinity Coll., 1937, Catholic U. Am., 1938, Providence Coll., 1952; MA, U. Wis., 1970; LHD (hon.), Rosary Coll., 1984, Edgewood Coll., 1990. Prof. religious studies and math. River Forest, Ill., 1940-47, Edgewood Coll. Libr., Madison, Wis., 1959-62; prof. religious studies and Hebrew scriptures Edgewood Coll. Libr., Madison, 1970—; bd. jewish social svcs. Madison, Wis., 1990—; lectr. Outreach Programs, Madison, 1959—. Author: The New Catholic Encyclopedia, 1975, Womens Encyclopedia, 1991. Coord. Jewish-Christian Dialogue, Madison, 1987—; dir. Edn. for Parish Svc., Madison, 1981—; coord., lectr. Continuing Edn. of Edgewood, Madison, 1965—. Recipient City of Jerusalem Peace award Madison Jewish Coun., 1975, Swarsensky Svc. award Rotary, Madison, 1990. Mem. Cath. Bibl. Soc., Assn. Hebrew Lang. Prof., Wis. Acad. Arts and Sci., Hadassah Sinsinawa Dominicans. Office: Edgewood Coll Library 855 Woodrow Madison WI 53711

REGIER, JON LOUIS, clergyman; b. Dinuba, Calif., May 24, 1922; s. John and Adeline (Roth) R.; m. Joyce Palmer, June 12, 1948; children—Jon Denniston, Marjorie Grace, Susan Marie, Luke Roth. A.B., Huntington (Ind.) Coll., 1944; B.D., McCormick Theol. Sem., 1947; student, U. Mich. Sch. Social Work; D.D., Payne Theol. Sem., Wilberforce, Ohio, 1959. Ordained to ministry Presbyn. Ch., 1947; asso. dir. Dodge Christian Community House, Detroit House, Detroit, 1947-49; head resident Howell Neighborhood House; pastor Howell Meml. Ch., Chgo., 1949-58; lectr. social group work McCormick Theol. Sem., Chgo., 1952-58; exec. sec. div. home missions Nat. Council Chs., 1958-64; asso. gen. sec., chief exec. officer div. of Christian life and mission, 1965-73; exec. dir. N.Y. State Council Chs., Syracuse, 1973-87; pvt. profl. cons. non-profit orgns.; del. to Assembly of Div. World Mission and Evangelism, World Council Chs.; mem. exec. com. world mission and evangelism, del. World Conf. Ch. and Soc., Geneva, 1966; founding mem. IDOC, Internat., Rome, pres., 1972; founding mem. IDOC/N. Am., 1967; exec. council div. edn. and recreation Welfare Coun. Met. Chgo., 1953; mem. hard-to-reach youth rsch. com., 1953-58; mem. Chgo. Youth Commn., 1954-58; chmn. spl. study on delinquency, 1956-58; exec. com. Citizens' Crusade Against Poverty, 1964—, Citizens Adv. Ctr., 1967—; adv. mem. div. criminal justice State N.Y., 1977; mem. adv. coun. minimum wage standards for agriculture workers, adv. coun. minimum wages State Dept. Labor, 1978—, task force on child and family abuse N.Y., 1980—; mem. inter religious govtl. relations com., 1973—; mem. Religious Adv. Coun. Commn., N.Y. State, 1973; founding chmn. Religious Coalition for Abortion Rights, N.Y. State, 1974. Trustee Turtle Island Trust, 1978—, North Conway Inst.; bd. dirs. Literacy Vols. Greater Syracuse, 1976, Urban League Onondaga County, 1976; mem. Human Rights Commn. Syracuse and Onondaga County, N.Y., N.Y. State Human Rights Com., 1978—; N.Y. State Commr. Edn. Interfaith Adv. Council, 1973-88; founding bd. mem. Westminster Village (retirement village), 1984, Canterberry House (skilled nursing facility, 1986. Recipient Religious Freedom award, 1980. Mem. Nat. Fedn. of Settlements and Neighborhood Centers (dir. 1954-58), Nat. Assn. Social Workers (exec. council Chgo. chpt. 1955-58), Soc. Propagation of Gospel Among Indians and Others of N.Am., Nat. Assembly for Social Policy and Devel. (founding mem.). Home: 5251 Wethersfield Rd Jamesville NY 13078 Office: NY State Council Chs 3049 E Genesee St Syracuse NY 13224

REGISTER, CHARLES LEON, SR., clergyman; b. Starke, Fla., Dec. 29, 1959; s. Lennard Bernard and Ernestine (Young) R.; m. Charlene Beam, June 26, 1982; children: Charles Leon Jr., Christina Marie. BA, U. Fla., 1982; MDiv, New Orleans Bapt. Theol. Sem., 1984, ThD, 1991. Ordained to ministry Bapt. Ch., 1984. Youth min. First Bapt. Ch., Starke, 1981-82; ch. planter Home Mission Bd., So. Bapt. Conv., Atlanta, 1983; evangelism fellow New Orleans Bapt. Theol. Sem., 1986-89; pastor Riverview Bapt. Ch., Buras, La., 1984-89, First Bapt. Ch., Cantonment, Fla., 1989—; chaplain, lt. USNR, 1987—; asst. to dir. New Orleans Fedn. Chs., La. World's Fair Ministries, 1984; chmn. evangelism com. Plaquemines Bapt. Assn., Buras, La., 1985-86, vice-moderator, 1986-87, moderator, 1987-88; sec. missions com. Pensacola Bay Bapt. Assn., 1990—. Host daily radio ministry, Moments of Encouragement, 1990-91; preacher weekly TV ministry Moments of Encouragement, 1990—. Chaplain Cantonment Vol. Fire Dept., 1990-91. Mem. Kappa Alpha (undergrad. chmn. Fla. 1979-80). Republican. Home: 620 Cooley Rd Cantonment FL 32533 Office: First Bapt Ch 118 Morris Ave Cantonment FL 32533

REGISTER, MILTON DEAN, minister; b. Madison, Fla., Aug. 2, 1951; s. Carlton E. and Margaret E. Register; m. Sharon Giddens, Mar. 18, 1972; children: Heather, Wes. BA, Valdosta State Coll., 1973; MDiv, New Orleans Bapt. Theol. Sem., 1976, ThD, 1984. Ordained to ministry Bapt. Ch., 1972. Assoc. pastor First Bapt. Ch., Brunswick, Ga., 1976-79; pastor Enon Bapt. Ch., Franklinton, La., 1979-82; pastor First Bapt. Ch., Franklin, N.C., 1982-85, Gulfport, Miss., 1985—; edn. commn. Miss. Bapt. Conv. Bd., Jackson, 1989-91; ethics commn. Bapt. World Alliance, Washington, 1990—; nominating com. So. Bapt. Conv., Nashville, 1989. Author: Advanced Bible Study: Paul, 1988, Holman's Bible Dictionary, 1990; contbr. articles to profl. jours. Coach Dixie Youth League Baseball, Gulfport, Miss., 1988, 90; chaplain Gulfport High Sch. Football Team, 1990; bd. dirs. Unicare Home Health, Gulfport, 1990-91. Named Outstanding Religious Leader of Greater Gulfport, Gulfport Jaycees, 1988; recipient Best Pub. Speaker award Miss. Coast Mag., Gulfport, 1990-91. Office: First Bapt Ch 2120 14th St Gulfport MS 39501

REGNER, SIDNEY LAWRENCE, rabbi; b. N.Y.C., Sept. 25, 1903; s. Martin and Kate (Lichtman) R.; children: Norman (dec.), Babette Regner Melmed, James. BA, U. Cin., 1924; DD, Hebrew Union Coll., Cin., 1954. Ordained rabbi, 1927. Rabbi Reform Congregation Oheb Sholom, Reading, Pa., 1927-54; exec. v.p. Cen. Conf. Am. Rabbis, 1954-71, exec. v.p. emeritus, 1971—. Contbr. articles to profl. jours. Mem. Cen. Conf. Am. Rabbis. Home: 205 West End Ave New York NY 10023

REHBEIN, EDWARD ANDREW, minister, geologist, consultant; b. Portland, Oreg., Aug. 13, 1947; s. Edward Louis and Marjorie Ann (Simshaw) R; m. Phyllis Jean Boyer, June 23, 1973; children: Matthew Louis, Angela Mae. BS in Geology, Calif. Inst. Tech., 1969. Geologist U.S. Forest Svc., Elkins, W.Va., 1972-74, U.S. Geol. Survey, Billings, Mont., 1974-76; coal geologist W.Va. Geologic Survey, Morgantown, 1977; cons. Morgantown, 1978; geologist Allied Corp., Beckley, W.Va., 1979; sr. exploration geologist Kerr-McGee Corp., Beckley, 1980-82, regional mgr. exploration, Reno, Nev., 1983-85; exploration geologist, Oklahoma City, 1985-88; assoc. min. Ch. of Christ, Beckley, W.Va., 1989-90, min., 1990—; pres. M&R Computer Sales and Svc., Inc., Beckley, W.Va., 1989-90. Author: Remembering God's Word, 1991; contbr. articles to profl. jours. and mags. Mem. Am. Assn. Petroleum Geologists. Club: Shotokan Karate Am. Office: N Beckley Ch of Christ PO Box 951 Beckley WV 25801 *So God created man in his own image. (Genesis 1:27). Search the Scriptures, find the full meaning of this, and your life will never be the same.*

REHKOPF, CHARLES FREDERICK, church executive; b. Topeka, Dec. 24, 1908; s. Frederick A. and Mary G. (Jennings) R.; m. Dorothy A. Getchell, July 30, 1936; children: Frederick, Jeanne, Susan. B.S., Washburn Coll., 1932; cert. Episcopal Theol. Sch., 1935. Civil engr. Kans. Engring. Co., Topeka, 1927-30; rector Trinity Episc. Ch., El Dorado, Kans., 1935-44, St. John's Episc. Ch., St. Louis, 1944-52; archdeacon and exec. sec. Diocese Mo., Protestant Episc. Ch., St. Louis, 1953-76; chmn. dept. rsch.and planning Met. Ch. Fedn. Greater St. Louis, 1954-64; chmn. div. adminstrn. Mo. Coun. Chs., 1965-68, chmn. div. communications, 1970-72, chmn. div. Christian unity, 1972-73; registrar Diocese of Mo., 1949—; staff Episc. Ch., Webster Groves, Mo., 1976—. Editor The Historiographer's News Letter. Author articles pub. profl. jours. Trustee Episcopal Presbyn. Found. for Aging, Inc., mem. Religious Pub. Rels. Coun. Mem. Soc. Am. Archivists, Hist. Soc. Protestant Episc. Ch. (dir. 1973-89). Home: 642 Clark Ave Webster Groves MO 63119 Office: 1210 Locust St Saint Louis MO 63103

REHWALDT, TIMOTHY JON, minister; b. Hampton, Iowa, Aug. 25, 1958; s. Harold Oscar and Mary Ellen (Trahms) R.; m. Judith Elaine Sunness, June 20, 1981; children: Jon Steven, Thom Anthony, Audrey Christine. BA, Concordia Coll., 1980; MDiv., Concordia Sem., 1984. Ordained min. Luth. Ch.-Mo. Synod, 1984. Min. Grace Luth., Iola, Kans., 1984-87, Trinity Luth., Hampton, Iowa, 1987—. Office: Trinity Ev Luth Ch 16 12th Ave NE Hampton IA 50441

REICH, MARK CARLTON, minister; b. Burlington, N.C., Mar. 4, 1964; s. Gaither Britton and Elizabeth Mason (Burger) R.; m. Deborah Lynn Klein, July 19, 1986; 1 child, Emily Nicole. BA, Malone Coll., 1987. Lic. to ministry Evang. Friends Ch., 1990. Coord. youth Ypsilanti (Mich.) Evang. Friends Ch., 1987-89; asst. pastor, youth pastor Hanover Evang. Friends Ch., Mechanicsville, Va., 1990—; Va. area youth rep. Evang. Friends Ch. Eastern Region, Mechanicsville, 1990—. Robbins (N.C.) Area Civic Orgn. scholar, 1982. Home: 8180 Walnut Grove Rd Mechanicsville VA 23111 *Joy in life comes from a selfless unconditional love for Christ first, others second, and ourselves last.*

REICH, SEYMOUR DAVID, lawyer, fraternal organization executive; b. Bklyn., Apr. 23, 1933; s. James and Esther (Reich) R.; m. Helyn Brenner; children: Keith E., Leslie B., Jaime Reich Amiram. BA, U. Pa., 1954; LLB, Harvard U., 1957. Sr. ptnr. Dreyer and Traub, N.Y.C. Pres. B'nai Brith Internat., 1986-90; chmn. Conf. of Pres.'s Major Am. Jewish Orgn., 1989-90. Mem. Phi Beta Kappa. Office: Dreyer and Traub 101 Park Ave New York NY 10178

REICHL, SISTER MARY THOMAS, nun, health center chaplain; b. Marathon County, Wis., Nov. 29, 1928; d. George Joseph and Susan (Rauen) R. BA, Cardinal Stritch Coll., Milw., 1960; MA, Marquette U., 1964. Joined Order of Holy Cross Sisters, 1946. Tchr. Holy Cross High Sch., Merrill, Wis., 1955-64; tchr., asst. prin., guidance counselor Mater Dei High Sch., Breese, Ill., 1964-72; provincial superior Holy Cross Sisters, Merrill, 1972-78; chaplain Good Samaritan Health Ctr., Merrill, 1978—; bd. dirs. North Cen. Community Action Program, Merrill, 1974-84. Vol., Wausau (Wis.) Pregnancy Hotline, 1974-86. Mem. Am. Pers. and Guidance Assn., Wis. Assn. Cath. Chaplains, Nat. Assn. Cath. Chaplains. Roman Catholic. Avocations: listening to music, cross-country skiing, reading. Home: 601 W 10th St Merrill WI 54452 Office: Good Samaritan Health Ctr 601 Center Ave S Merrill WI 54452

REICHTER, ARLO RAY, minister; b. Eagle Grove, Iowa, May 22, 1947; s. Verven Leonard and Marvyl Nellie (Harvey) R.; m. Dianne Kristine Stueland, June 22, 1968; children: Kristi, Kari. BA, Sioux Falls Coll., 1969; MDiv, Am. Bapt. Sem., 1971; M of Liberal Arts, U. So. Calif., 1976; D Ministry, Jesuit Sch. Theology, 1980. Ordained to ministry Am. Bapt. Chs. in U.S.A., 1971. Co-pastor 1st Bapt. Ch. L.A., 1971-83; v.p. program Am. Bapt. Assembly, Green Lake, Wis., 1983—; mem. cen. sectional Christian edn. team Am. Bapt. Chs. in U.S.A., 1983—, chmn. exec. com. nat. continuing edn. team; bd. dirs. Am. Bapt. Chs. Wis., 1988-90, also moderator Christian Edn. Commn., 1988-90; mem. Am. Bapt. Camp and Conf. Team, 1983—; leader all major Am. Bapt. Nat. Youth Gatherings, 1972—; frequent conf. speaker and workshop leader on youth ministry, Christian edn. and spirituality. Author: The Group Retreat Book, 1983, also devotionals; contbr. articles to profl. jours. Vice chmn. study com. L.A. Unified Sch. Dist., 1981-83; chmn. Com. on Protestant Scouting, L.A., 1981-83; mem. Fond du Lac County 4-H Exec. Bd., 1987—. Mem. Ripon Area Clergy Assn. Home: Nordane Ave Ripon WI 54971 *Life is a great gift from a great God which can be vastly enriched through continual learning about ourselves, widening circles of relationships with other persons and deepening spiritual encounters with the living God.*

REID, BARBARA ELLEN, religion educator; b. Detroit, May 26, 1953; d. Charles Ralph and Christine Frances (O'Brien) R. BA, Aquinas Coll., 1975, MA, 1981; PhD, Cath. U. Am., 1988. Cert. secondary edn., Mich.; joined Dominican Sisters, Roman Cath. Ch., 1974. Tchr. St. Mary Cathedral High Sch., Saginaw, Mich., 1976-82; asst. prof. New Testament Cath. Theol. Union, Chgo., 1988—; mem. Pax Christi USA, Erie, Pa., 1989-90. Editor: Pastoral Dictionary of Biblical Theology; contbr. articles to religious jours. Mem. Amnesty Internat., N.Y.C., 1986-90. Mem. Cath. Bibl. Assn. Am., Soc. Bibl. Lit., Chgo. Soc. Bibl. Rsch. Office: Cath Theol Union 5401 S Cornell Chicago IL 60615

REID, BENJAMIN FRANKLIN, bishop; b. Bklyn., Oct. 5, 1937; s. Noah W. Sr. and Viola Reid; m. Anna Pearl Batie, June 28, 1958; children: Benjamin Jr., Sylvia, Angela, Natalie. Student, U. Pitts., 1955-56, No. Bapt. Theol. Sem., 1956-58; DD, Am. Bible Inst., Kansas City, Mo., 1971; PhD, Calif. Western U., 1975; LittD (hon.), Calif. Grad. Sch. Theology, Glendale, 1981; DD (hon.), Anderson U., 1982. Ordained to ministry Ch. of God (Anderson, Ind.), 1960; consecrated bishop, 1987. Pastor Adams St. Ch. of God, Springfield, Ill., 1958-59, 1st Ch. of God, Junction City, Kans., 1959-63; sr. pastor Southwestern Ch. of God, Detroit, 1963-71, 1st Ch. of God, L.A., 1971—; presiding bishop 1st Ch. of God, Nigeria, 1981—, Interstate Assoc. Ch. of God, Alaska, Ariz., Calif., Oreg., Wash., Nev., 1987—; pres. So. Calif. Sch. Ministry, L.A., 1985—; chmn. So. Calif. Mins.' Network, Inglewood, 1990. Author: Confessions of a Happy Preacher, 1971, Another Look at Other Tongues, 1974, rev. edit., 1981, Glory to the Spirit, 1990; contbg. editor Vital Christianity Mins. mag. Bd. dirs. L.A. Coun. Chs., 1974—, Inner City Found.-Excellence in Edn., L.A., 1987—, Urban League, L.A., SCLC, L.A., Ecumenical Ctr.-Black Ch. Studies, L.A.; chaplain Inglewood (Calif.) Police Dept. Recipient Mayor's award City of L.A., 1981, 86, Community Svc. award U. So. Calif., 1982, Supr.'s Com. award County of L.A., 1986, Mayor's award City of Compton, Calif., 1987. Mem. NAACP (life mem. South Bay br.), Inter-Denominational Mins. Alliance (pres. 1974-76, Svc. award 1976), Concerned Clergy of L.A., Shepherd's Prayer Gathering, Fellowship Ind. Chs. (founder, pres. 1989—). Democrat. Office: First Ch of God 9550 Crenshaw Blvd Inglewood CA 90305 *The greatest experience in life is to be committed to a cause greater than yourself and to have a challenge so great that only God can accomplish it.*

REID, DONALD MICHELE, minister; b. Macon, Ga., Aug. 20, 1958; s. John William Reid and Christine Quick Harper. BS, Ga. Coll., 1982; ThM, Dallas Theol. Sem., 1987. Ordained to ministry So. Bapt. Conv., 1987. Asst. pastor Fellowship Bible Bapt. Ch., Warner Robins, Ga., 1987-88; home missionary Home Mission Bd., Atlanta, 1988-90; pastor, ch. planter Aletheia Bapt. Ch., Macon, Ga., 1988—. Home: 3314 Mercer University Dr Macon GA 31204 Office: Aletheia Bapt Ch 1711 Oglesby Pl Macon GA 31204

REID, JAMES M., minister; b. Detroit, Aug. 25, 1953; s. James W. and Gladys (Eboff) R.; m. Bridget A. Reid, Apr. 7, 1977; children: Rachel, Nicole. Student, Mott Community Coll., Flint, Mich., 1990. Ordained to ministry Bapt. Ch. Youth minister Calvary Bapt. Ch., Flint, 1988—; ch. tng. tchr., Sunday sch. tchr. Calvary Bapt. Ch., Flint. Bd. dirs. Westside Teen Ctr. Office: Calvary Bapt Ch 1213 W 2d St Flint MI 48503

REID, RICHARD, academic administrator. Pres. Protestant Episcopal Theol. Sem. in Va., Alexandria. Office: Protestant Episcopal Theol Sem Office of Pres Alexandria VA 22304*

REID, THOMAS FENTON, minister; b. Buffalo, Sept. 9, 1932; s. Albert E. and Helen Gertrude (Rice) R.; m. Wanda Darlene Bousum, July 7, 1968; 1 child, Aimee Linette. Diploma, Cen. Bible Coll., Springfield, Mo., 1953; DD (hon.), Calif. Grad. Sch. Theology, 1981; LHD (hon.), Oral Roberts U., 1987. Ordained to ministry Assemblies of God, 1956. Missionary, evangelist Assemblies of God, Springfield, 1953-63; pastor Bethel Temple, Manila, 1959-60; st. pastor Full Gospel Tabernacle, Orchard Park, N.Y., 1963—; pres. Buffalo Sch. Bible, 1976—; pres. Nat. Ch. Growth Conf., Washington, 1984; sec., bd. dirs. Ch. Growth Inc., Seoul, Republic of Korea, 1979—. Author: The Exploding Church, 1979, Kingdom Now But Not Yet, 1988, Ethics, Excellence and Economics, 1989. Mem. Nat. Assn. Evangelicals (bd. dirs. 1979—), Nat. Religious Broadcasters, Friends of Anwar Sadat, Christians for Friends in Middle East. Republican. Home: 701 Willardshire Orchard Park NY 14127 Office: Full Gospel Tabernacle 3210 Southwestern Blvd Orchard Park NY 14127 *The very center of my belief system is that God made man in His own image. Man has great value, dignity and purpose. It is my responsibility to lead men to God, and help them find their true purpose and potential through Jesus Christ.*

REID, WILLIAM ALEXANDER, minister; b. Balt., July 19, 1943; s. Woodrow Wilson and Ruby Addie (Smith) R.; m. Andrea Claudette Rowan, Apr. 2, 1966; children: William Alexander II, Warren Anthony. AA, Lee Coll., Cleveland, Tenn., 1963; BA, U. Md., 1966; MS, Loyola Coll., Balt., 1987. Ordained to ministry Ch. of God, 1974. Pastor Damascus (Md.) Ch. of God, 1967-70, Bridgevile (Del.) Ch. of God, 1970-72; state youth and Christian edn. dir. Ch. of God, Columbia, Md., 1972-76, Ch. of God, Ind. br., Greenwood, 1976-80; pastor Essex Ch. of God, Balt., 1980-87; state youth and Christian edn. dir. Ch. of God, Columbia, 1987—; mem. state coun. Ch. of God, Delmarva (D.C.) div., 1980-84, 86-87, chmn. edn. bd., 1982-87, dir. youth and Christian edn., 1987—. Contbr. articles to profl. jours. Office: Ch of God State Office PO Box 98 Simpsonville MD 21150

REID-KING, RICHARD DOUGLASS, minister; b. Dayton, Ohio, Jan. 23, 1962; s. Christopher Middleton and Marilyn Sue (Jackson) King; m. Mary Courtney Reid, Aug. 26, 1989. BA, Mount Union Coll., Alliance, Ohio, 1984; MDiv, Yale Div. Sch., New Haven, 1989. Ordained to ministry United Ch. of Christ., 1990. Assoc. pastor St. Paul United Ch. of Christ, Palatine, Ill., 1989-91; interim pastor Bethel United Ch. of Christ, Elmhurst, Ill., 1991—; adj. instr. Old Testament, Coll. St. Francis, Joliet, Ill., 1991; convener Religious Assn. of Palatine, Ill., 1991; bass Community Renewal Chorus, Chgo., 1990-92. Democrat.

REIERSON, GARY BRUCE, religious organization administrator, minister; b. Mpls., Nov. 4, 1948; s. Clarence Newton and Hope Elizabeth (Nichols) R.; m. Pamela Jane Matson, July 10, 1970; children: Katharine Kim Matson, Elizabeth Lee Matson. BA magna cum laude, U. Minn., 1977; MDiv (with honors), United Theol. Sem. of the Twin Cities, 1978, D of Ministry (with distinction), 1986. Ordained to ministry United Ch. of Christ, 1978. Assoc. min. United Ch. of Christ, New Brighton, Minn., 1975-77, Plymouth Congl. Ch., Mpls., 1977-87; v.p. for devel. Greater Mpls. Girl Scout Coun., 1987-89; exec. dir. Greater Mpls. Coun. of Chs., 1989—, also bd. dirs.; founder, sec., bd. dirs. Ctr. and Network for Ch. Educators, 1977-81; bd. dirs. Minn. Coun. Chs., St. Paul Area Coun. Chs.; chairperson ministry of outreach Minn. conf. United Ch. of Christ, 1986-89, former bd. dirs. conf. Author: The Art in Preaching, 1988; co-author: The Plymouth Heritage, 1979, The Gift of Administration, 1981 (named one of Top Ten Books of 1981, Acad. Parish Clergy); also articles. Bd. dirs., chairperson ednl. ministries coun. Twin Cities Met. Ch. Commn., 1982-84; active religious affairs com. Planned Parenthood, 1985-87, Mayor's Task Force on Teen Pregnancy, City of Mpls., 1987-88, Met. Collaborative on Teen-Aged Pregnancy Prevention, 1987-89; mem. adv. bd. dirs. Abbott-Northwestern Ctr. for Pastoral Counselling, Mpls., 1988-91; bd. dirs. Hennepin County Bd., Fed. Emergency Mgmt. Agy., 1989—, Met. Interfaith Coun. on Affordable Housing, 1991—; mem. Coun. Agy. Execs., United Way Mpls. Area, 1989—. Recipient Joseph Jones Russell Sermon award Nat. Assn. Congl. Chs., 1986. Mem. Nat. Soc. Fund Raising Execs., Nat. Assn. Ecumenical Staff, Mpls. Ministerial Assn., Mpls. Club, Calhoun Beach Club. Mem. Democratic Farm Labor Party. Avocations: trains, travel, the arts, music, walking. Home: 2725 Toledo Ave S Saint Louis Park MN 55416 Office: Greater Mpls Coun Chs 122 W Franklin Ave Ste 218 Minneapolis MN 55416

REIFF, LEE HERBERT, religion educator; b. Newton, Kans., July 6, 1929; s. Tillman Erb and Ione Vera (Austin) R.; m. Geraldine Long, Aug. 22, 1950; children: Joseph Tillman, James Nathan. BA, So. Meth. U., 1951, BD, 1954; MA, Yale U., 1956, PhD, 1963; postgrad., Miss. Coll. Sch. Law, 1990—. Ordained elder United Meth. Ch., 1956. Min. Bakerville Meth. Ch., New Hartford, Conn., 1954-57; asst. prof. Millsaps Coll., Jackson, Miss., 1960-64, assoc. prof., 1965-69, prof. religion, 1969—; asst. prof. McMurry Coll., Abilene, Tex., 1964-65. Del. Dem. Nat. Conv., Chgo., 1968; trustee Communications Improvement Trust, Jackson, Miss., 1969—; mem. Instl. Rev. Bd., U. Miss. Med. Ctr., 1981-88. John M. Moore grad. fellow So. Meth. U., 1954, Dempster grad. fellow Meth. Bd. Edn., Nashville, 1957-58, Danforth Found. assoc., 1966-86. Mem. AAUP, ACLU, Christian Legal Soc., Am. Acad. Religion, Soc. Bibl. Lit., Phi Beta Kappa. Home: 810 Fairview Jackson MS 39202-1626 Office: Millsaps Coll Box 150383 Millsaps Jackson MS 39210

REIGSTAD, RUTH ELAINE, lay worker, retired physical therapy consultant; b. Mpls., Apr. 26, 1923; d. Olin Spencer and Amanda Sophia (Fjelstad) R. BA, St. Olaf Coll., Northfield, Minn., 1945; cert., U. Minn., 1947. Lic. phys. therapist, Wash. Phys. therapist Crippled Children's Sch., Jamestown, N.D., 1948-52; phys. therapist, clin. instr. Shriners Hosp., U. Minn., Mpls., 1955-58; phys. therapist Rehab. Center, Albuquerque, N.M., 1958-60, Brit. Nat. Health Svc., London; phys. therapy cons. Wash. State Health Dept., Olympia, 1961-73, cons., 1961-74; lay worker Good Shepherd Luth. Ch., Olympia, 1972-75; mem. various coms. Christ Luth. Ch., Tacoma, 1980—; Vol. Children Health Svcs. and Pub. Health of Wash. 1974—; bd. dirs. Morningside Rehab. Orgn., Olympia, Wash., PAVE rehab. orgn. Bd. dirs. Wash. State Phys. Therapy Assn., 1965-68. With USCG, 1943-45. Recipient Fellowship award Nat. Easter Seal Soc. Chgo. 1949; Scholarship award US Pub. Health Service Wash. 1962-64. Mem. Am. Phys. Therapy Assn. (life), Am. Pub. Health Assn., Am. Acad. Religion, Luth. Brotherhood Fraternity and Benevolent Orgn. (bd. dirs. Pierce County), Air Force Assn. (exec. coun. Pierce County, 1985—). Mem. Evang. Luth. Ch. Am. Avocations: volunteer work, travel, gardening, public speaking, creative writing. Home: 8808 1/2 Frances Folsom SW Tacoma WA 98498

REILING, CECILIA POWERS, hospital chaplain; b. Boston, Mar. 23, 1926; d. Edward Thomas and Delia (Hehir) Powers; m. Thomas Leonard Reiling, Nov. 11, 1960; stepchildren—Elizabeth, Kathleen, Mary, Eileen. B.A., Northeastern U., 1964, M.A., 1973; M.Ed., Boston U., 1979. Instr., advisor Chamberlayne Jr. Coll., Boston, 1964-73; instr. Bryant Coll., North Smithfield, R.I., 1973-79; chaplaincy vol. Sherrill House, Boston, 1972-79, researcher, 1977-79; program dir., v.p. College Club, Boston, 1970-72; chaplaincy vol. Martin Meml. Hosp., Stuart, Fla., 1980—. Mem. Am. Sociol. Assn., Mass. Sociol. Soc., Christian Sociol. Soc., Assn. for Clin. Pastoral Edn. Republican. Roman Catholic. Clubs: Stuart Yacht and Country (Fla.); Kittansett (Marion, Mass.). Avocations: golf, music. Home: 4264 SE Fairway E Stuart FL 34997

REILLY, DANIEL PATRICK, bishop; b. Providence, May 12, 1928; s. Francis E. and Mary (Burns) R. Student, Our Lady of Providence Sem., 1943-48, Grand Seminaire, St. Brieuc, France, 1948-53, Harvard U., 1954-55, Boston Coll., 1955-56; D. (hon.), Providence Coll., St. Michael'sColl., Holy Apostles Coll. and Sem., Salve Regina Coll., Our Lady of Providence Coll., Sacred Heart U. Ordained priest Roman Catholic Ch., 1953; asst. pastor Cathedral Saints Peter and Paul, Providence, 1953-54; asst. chancellor Diocese of Providence, 1954-56, sec. to bishop, 1956-64, chancellor, 1964-72, adminstr., 1971-72, vicar gen., 1972-75; became monsignor, 1965, consecrated bishop, 1975; bishop of Norwich, Conn., 1975—; Conn. state chaplain K.C., 1976—; Episcopal moderator Nat. Cath. Cemetery Corp., 1977-87; mem. ad hoc com. to aid ch. in Ea. Europe NCCB/U.S. Cath. Conf., also mem. adminstrv. com.; mem. pro-life com. NCCB, 1989—; past pres. New Eng. Consultation Ch. Leaders; mem. drafting com. U.S. Cath. Conf. Pastoral Letter, mem. com. on communications; mem. Holy See Pontifical Coun.-Cor Unum, 1984-1989. Trustee Cath. Mut. Relief Soc. Omaha, 1979—, St. John's Sem., Brighton, Mass., 1987—; bd. dirs. United Way Southeastern Conn., 1976—, Conn. Drug and Adv. Coun., 1978-80; chmn. bd. Cath. Relief Svcs., 1978-86; mem. fin. and budget com. U.S. Cath. Conf., 1985-87; chancellor Holy Apostles Coll. and Sem., Cromwell, Conn., 1985; mem. Conn. Cath. Conf., Christian Conf. Conn.; pres. Conn. Interfaith Housing. Lodge: Rotary. Home: 274 Broadway Norwich CT 06360 Office: 201 Broadway Box 587 Norwich CT 06360 *If you would make a true success of your life for time and for eternity, never forget that it will be achieved by your willingness to make countless efforts that will be known only to God.*

REILLY, THOMAS AUGUSTINE, priest, religious order superior; b. Springfield, Mass., Nov. 4, 1943; s. William Patrick and Mildred Catherine (Dudley) R. BA, Gregorian U., Rome, 1966, Licentiate in Philosophy, 1967. Joined Missionaries of LaSalette, Roman Cath. Ch., 1964, ordained priest, 1972. Dir. formation Missionaries of LaSalette, Ipswich, Mass., 1972-76; assoc. pastor Missionaries of LaSalette, Fitchburg, Mass., 1976-79; pastor Missionaries of LaSalette, Fairburn, Ga., 1979-81; superior Missionaries of LaSalette, Ipswich, 1981-85; provincial superior Missionaries of LaSalette, Hartford, Conn., 1985—. Home and Office: 85 New Park Ave Hartford CT 06106 Mailing Address: PO Box 260127 Hartford CT 06126-0127

REIMER, ELMER ISAAC, minister, educator; b. Drake, Sask., Can., May 18, 1922; came to U.S., 1947; s. Frank Ensz and Gertrude (Boese) R.; m. Catharina Peters, Sept. 26, 1943; 1 child, David Elmer. Student, Grace Coll. of Bible, 1947-48, 54-57. Ordained to ministry Evang. Mennonite Brethren Ch., 1949. Pastor Jansen (Nebr.) Evang. Mennonite Brethren Ch., 1948-53; pulpit supplier, 1954-57; pastor Kingsburg Ch., Springfield, S.D., 1957-62, Carter (S.D.) Gospel Fellowship, 1963-91; pres. Associated Gospel Ministries, Winner, S.D., 1973—; freelance piano tuner, Carter, 1958—. Address: Associated Gospel Ministries 924 Spruce St Newton KS 67114

REIMNITZ, ELROI, minister; b. Porto Alegre, Brazil, June 20, 1948; s. Elmer and Kordula Luise (Schelp) R; Ruth Weimer, June 1973; children: Patrick, Kristeen, Nicholas. Diploma, Seminario Concordia, Porto Alegre, 1966; postgrad., Faculdade Porto-Alegrense E.C.L., 1968; MDiv, Concordia Sem., St. Louis, 1971, ThD, 1975; postdoctoral studies, Faculdade de Direito I.R.R., Canoas, Brazil, 1976-77, Faith Luth. Sem., Tacoma, 1990—. Ordained to ministry Luth. Ch.-Mo. Synod, 1975. Vicar Immanuel Luth. Ch., Bristol, Conn., 1969-70; asst. to pastor Our Savior's 1st Luth. Ch., Granada Hills, Calif., 1974-75; pastor Zion Luth. Ch., Alamo, Tex., 1975, St. John's Luth. Ch., Canoas, 1976-78; pastor, dir. ministries Trinity Luth. Ch., Grand Island, Nebr., 1978-86; pastor Redeemer Luth. Ch., Thousand Oaks, Calif., 1986—; instr. U. Luterana do Brasil, Canoas, 1976-78; adminstrv. dir. Cultural Lang. Inst., Canoas, 1976-78; supt. Trinity Luth. Sch., Grand Island, 1978-86; treas. Grand Island cir. Nebr. dist. Luth. Ch.-Mo. Synod, 1984-86; chaplain police, sheriff and fire depts. City of Grand Island, 1985-86; counselor campus ministry Calif. Luth. U., Thousand Oaks, Calif., 1986—. Contbr. articles to religious jours. Adv. mem. Grand Island Luth. Family and Social Svcs., 1985-86; mem. programs com. Cen. Platte Natural Resources Dist., 1985-86; mem. site coun. Cypress Elem. Sch., Newbury Park, Calif., 1987-88; bd. dirs. Casas De La Senda Homeowners Assn., Newbury Park, 1986—; alt. mem. ad hoc com. Newbury Park Libr., 1987-90; active Community Devel. Allocation Com., Thousand Oaks, 1991—. Mem. Am. Assn. Christian Counselors, United Assn. Christian Counselors Internat. Home: 3883 San Marcos Ct Newbury Park CA 91320 Office: Redeemer Luth Ch 667 Camino Dos Rios Thousand Oaks CA 91360-2399

REINEKE, MARTHA JANE, religion and women's studies educator; b. Kalamazoo, Mich., May 25, 1954; d. Lester Morrison and Mary Elizabeth (Kugler) R.; m. William Cozart, May 19, 1979; 1 child, Elizabeth Jane. BA, Earlham Coll., 1976; MA, Vanderbilt U., 1980, PhD, 1983. Asst. prof. religion, dir. women's studies U. No. Iowa, Cedar Falls, 1984—. Contbr. articles to profl. publs. Mem. Am. Acad. Religion, Am. Philos. Assn., Am. Theol. Soc., Soc. Phenomenology and Existential Philosophy, Nat. Women's Studies Assn., Friends Soc. Higher Edn. Mem. Religious Soc. Friends. Office: U No Iowa Dept Philosophy & Religion Cedar Falls IA 50614-0501 *A gender-sensitive perspective is essential in a university. The success of women's quest for equality is based on noticing diversity among us. Women's studies provides all disciplines with the tools required to recognize diversity.*

REINES, ALVIN JAY, rabbi, religion educator; b. Paterson, N.Y., Sept. 12, 1926; s. Louis E. and Cecelia G. (Ruben) R.; m. Hera Carol Ginzberg, June 17, 1962; children: Jennifer, Kip, Adam. Grad., Hebrew Union Coll.-Jewish Inst. Religion, Cin., 1952; PhD, Harvard U., 1958. Ordained rabbi, 1952. From instr. to prof. Hebrew Union Coll.-Jewish Inst. Religion, Cin., 1959—; chmn. bd. trustees Inst. Creative Judaism, Cin. Author: Maimonides and Abrabanel on Prophecy, 1970, Polydoxy: Explorations in a Philosophy of Liberal Religion, 1988. Office: Hebrew Union Coll Jewish Inst Religion 3101 Clifton Ave Cincinnati OH 45220-2488

REISCHMAN, CHARLES J., religious organization administrator, minister; b. Westlake, Ohio, Mar. 22, 1955; s. Paul L. and Jean (Gabor) R.; m. Gina B. Reischman, Aug. 9, 1989. BA in Edn., U. Akron, 1980; MDiv, Episcopal Theol. Sem. S.W., 1990. Cert. secondary tchr., Ohio, Pa. Min. youth Episcopal Ch.; mem. staff Episcopal Renewal Ministries, Evergreen, Colo.; dir. Order of St. Philip the Evangelist, Evergreen. Home: 4380 Independence Trail Evergreen CO 80439 Office: Order of St Philip the Evangelist 2942 State Hwy 74 Ste 205 Evergreen CO 80439

REISEN, MILTON R., bishop. Bishop of S.E. Mich., Evang. Luth. Ch. in Am., Detroit. Office: Evang Luth Ch Am 19711 Greenfield Rd Detroit MI 48236*

REISMAN, BERNARD, theology educator; b. N.Y.C., July 15, 1926; s. Herman and Esther Sarah (Kavesh) R.; m. Elaine Betty Sokol, Aug. 26, 1951; children: Joel Ira, Sharon Fay, Eric K., Robin Sue. B in Social Sci, CCNY, 1949; M in Social Sci. and Adminstrn., Western Res. U., 1951; PhD, Brandeis U., 1970. Agy. dir. Jewish Community Ctr., Chgo., 1951-67; prof. Brandeis U., Waltham, Mass., 1969—, dir. Hornstein program in Jewish communal svc., 1971—; lectr. in field; vis. prof. Baerwald Sch. Social Work, Hebrew U., Jerusalem, 1978, Ctr. Jewish Edn. in Diaspora, 1978; sr. cons. Josephtal Found., Jerusalem, 1978; cons. European coun. Am. Joint Distbn. Com., 1978, Inst. for Jewish Life, N.Y.C., 1972-76; cons. on orgnl. theory Boston U. Med. Sch., 1969-70; rsch. assoc. on future of religion Nat. Coun. Chs., 1972-73; Arnulf Pins meml. lectr. Hebrew U., Jerusalem, 1983, 84. Author: Reform Is a Verb, 1972, The Jewish Experiential Book: Quest for Jewish Identity, 1978, The Chavurah: A Contemporary Jewish Experience, 1977; contbr. articles to profl. jours. With AUS, 1944-46, ETO. Recipient Farfel Jewish Family Svc. award, 1984; Whiting Found. grantee, 1977. Mem. Conf. Jewish Communal Svc. (chmn. publs. com. 1980—), Nat. Jewish Family Ctr., Am. Jewish Com. (1st chmmn. acad. adv. com. 1979-82, 75th Anniversary award 1981), Am. Jewish Hist. Soc. (acad. coun. 1979—), Radius Inst. (bd. dirs. 1980—), Assn. for Jewish Studies. Home: 28 Fairway Dr West Newton MA 02165 Office: Brandeis Univ Hornstein Prog in Jewish Communal Svc Waltham MA 02254

REISS, JOHN C., bishop; b. Red Bank, N.J., May 13, 1922; s. Alfred and Sophia (Telljohan) R. Student, Immaculate Conception Sem., 1941-46; B.A., Seton Hall U., 1947; S.T.L., Catholic U., 1947, J.C.D., 1953. Ordained Priest Roman Catholic Ch., 1947. Asst. chancellor Diocese of Trenton, 1954, sec., master ceremonies, 1953-62, vice chancellor, 1956-62, officialis, 1962-80, aux. bishop, 1967-80, bishop, 1982—. Mem. Trenton Mayor's Adv. Commn. on Civil Rights, 1962-68. Office: 701 Lawrenceville Rd Trenton NJ 08648 also: PO Box 5309 Trenton NJ 08638

REIST, WILLIAM HENRY, religious organization administrator; b. Lancaster, Pa., Dec. 24, 1951; s. Henry E. and Hazel (Nolt) R.; m. Judy M.

Markle, May 19, 1978; children: Jonathan M., Benjamin W. BA, Findlay Coll., 1973; MDiv, Winebrenner Theol. Sem., 1976. Ordained to ministry Chs. of God, Gen. Conf., 1976. Pastor Marysville (Pa.) Ch. of God, 1976-81, Elizabethtown (Pa.) Ch. of God, 1981-87; adminstr. Chs. of God, Gen. Conf., Findlay, Ohio, 1987—. Contbr. articles to Ch. Adv. mag. Trustee Bd. Pensions, Findlay, 1983—, U. Findlay, 1985—; trustee, sec. bd. Winebrenner Theol. Sem., Findlay, 1987—.

REISZ, H(OWARD) FREDERICK, JR., minister; b. Balt., May 13, 1939; s. Howard Frederick and Kathryn (Gwynn) R.; m. May Martin, June 6, 1965; children: Lisa Katherine, Heather Lynn. AB, Gettysburg (Pa.) Coll., 1961; BD, Luth. Sem., Gettysburg, 1965; AM, U. Chgo., 1967, PhD, 1977. Ordained to ministry Evang. Luth. Ch. Am., 1969. Assoc. campus minister Pa. State U., 1969-72; pastor Wittenberg Univ., Springfield, Ohio, 1973-78; sr. pastor Univ. Luth. Ch., Cambridge, Mass., 1978—; chmn. Luth. Coll. Chaplains, 1974-76; ecumenical officer New Eng. Synod Luth. Ch., 1988—, del. conv., 1986, 89; chmn. bd. ministry Harvard U., 1989-91. Contbr. articles to profl. jours.; author booklet for college. Chmn. Harvard Sq. Chs. Meal Program, Cambridge, 1986-91; mem. bd. dirs. Mass. Coun. Chs., 1985—; mem. Mayor's Adv. Com. on Homelessness, Cambridge, 1987-89; performer Hsp. Charity Magic Shows, Boston, 1985—. U. Chgo. fellow, 1968-69, Underwood fellow, Danforth Found., 1972-73; recipient Disting. Svc. award, Nat. Luth. Campus Ministry, 1990. Mem. N. Am. Paul Tillich Soc. (pres. 1990-91), Am. Acad. Religion, Boston Ministers Club, Harvard Sq. Clergy Assn. (sec. 1988-91), Soc. Am. Magicians (charity chmn. 1987-91), Phi beta Kappa. Democrat. Home: 48 Davis Ave Arlington MA 02174 Office: Univ Luth Ch 66 Winthrop St Cambridge MA 02138

REITH, LOUIS JOHN, church musician, librarian; b. Deloit, Iowa, Sept. 11, 1939; s. Ferdinand Henry John and Elsie Ida (Roschke) R. BA, Concordia Sr. Coll., Ft. Wayne, Ind., 1961; MDiv, Concordia Sem., St. Louis, 1966; MA, Washington U., St. Louis, 1967; MSLS, U. Ill., 1976; PhD, Stanford U., 1976. Organist, lay preacher St. John's Luth. Ch., Allegany, N.Y., 1979-85; asst. organist Pilgrim Luth. Ch., Bethesda, Md., 1985—; rare book cataloger Georgetown U. Libr., Washington, 1985—; substitute ch. organist various congregations, Washington, 1985—; speaker on East German chs., Washington, 1985—. Editor, translator German-pub. works on Martin Luther; contbr. book revs. and articles to profl. jours. Kent fellow Danforth Found., St. Louis, 1969; DAAD fellow Coun. for Internat. Edn., N.Y.C., 1969-71. Fellow Soc. Values in Higher Edn.; mem. ALA, Assn. Coll. and Rsch. Librs., Am. Guild Organists, Am. Hist. Assn., Soc. Reformation Rsch., Am. Theol. Libr. Assn. Home: 3201 Wisconsin Ave NW # 505 Washington DC 20016 Office: Georgetown U Libr PO Box 37445 Washington DC 20013-7445

REITZELL, HANS ULRICH, priest. Pastor Evang. Ch., Casablanca, Morocco. Office: Evang Ch, 22 rue d'Azilal, Casablanca Morocco*

REKLAU, TECLA SUND, ecumenical agency administrator. Exec. dir. Evanston (Ill.) Ecumenical Action Coun. Office: Evanston Ecumenical Action Coun PO Box 1414 Evanston IL 60204*

REMBERT, SANCO K., bishop. V.p., bishop Ref. Episcopal Ch., Charleston, S.C. Office: Ref Episcopal Ch PO Box 2079 Charleston SC 29403*

REMICK, OSCAR EUGENE, college president; b. Ellsworth, Maine, Aug. 24, 1932; s. Horace and Blanche (Rich) R.; m. Emma L. Lorance, Dec. 18, 1959; children: Mark Stephen, John Andrew, Paul Thomas. A.B., Ea. Coll., 1954; B.D. magna cum laude, Ea. Bapt. Theol. Sem., 1957; M.A., U.Pa., 1957; Ph.D., Boston U., 1966; student, Columbia U., 1959-61, Andover Newton Theol. Sem., 1957-58, Heidelberg (Germany) U., 1958-59; postdoctoral study, India, 1967; D.D., Assumption Coll., 1971, Allegheny Coll., 1974; LL.D. (hon.), Alma Coll., 1987, Davis and Elkins Coll., 1991; HHD (hon.), Carroll Coll., 1991. Ordained to ministry Presbyn. Ch. (U.S.A.), 1957. Ordained minister United Presbyn. Ch. U.S.A.; minister United Baptist Ch., Topsham, Maine, 1961-63; part-time instr. philosophy Bates Coll., 1962-63; minister First Congregational Ch., Paxton, Mass., 1963-66; asst. prof. philosophy and theology Assumption Coll., 1966-67, assoc. prof., 1967-71, prof. religious studies, 1969-71, v.p., acad. dean, coordinator acad. affairs, 1968-71; co-dir. ecumenical Inst. Religious Studies, 1967-71; Minister theol. studies First Baptist Ch., Worcester, Mass., 1966-71; pres. Chautauqua (N.Y.) Instn., 1971-77; lectr. State U. N.Y., 1972-77, prof. philosophy, dean for arts and humanities, dir. internat. edn., 1977-80; theologian-in-residence First Presbyn. Ch., Jamestown, N.Y., 1974-80; pres. Alma (Mich.) Coll., 1980-87, prof. philosophy and religion, 1980-87; pres., prof. philosophy Westminster Coll., New Wilmington, Pa., 1987—; mem. Com. on Higher Edn., Presbyn. Ch. (USA); bd. dirs. Integra North Bank, Titusville, Pa. Author: Value in the Thought of Paul Tillich; Christianity and Other Major Religions, 1968, India and Hinduism, 1968, Responding to God's Call, 1970, The Hidden Crisis in Education, 1971. Pres. Worcester Area Council Chs., 1970-71; mem. N.Y. State Council on Arts, 1974-80; chmn. Mich. Coun. for Arts, 1983-87; mem. Pa. Coun. on Arts, 1990—; trustee Mich. Colls. Found.; bd. dirs. No. Chautauqua County YMCA, CAPS, Concerned Citizens for Arts in Mich., Found. for Arts in Mich.; mem. Hoyt Inst. for Arts; mem. Lawrence County Econ. Devel. Corp.; mem. Com. on Higher Edn. of the Presbyn. Ch., U.S.A. Mem. Am. Philos. Assn., Soc. Advancement Continuing Edn. for Ministry, Am. Assn. for Advancement of Humanities, Mich. Intercoll. Athletic Assn., Assn. Ind. Colls. and Univs. Mich., Am. Friends of Jerusalem Soc. World Fellowship (pres.), Paul Tillich Soc. N. Am., Deutsche Paul-Tillich-Gesellschaft, Am. Assn. Higher Edn., Soc. Sci. Study Religion, Am. Acad. Religion, N.Am. Acad. Ecumenists, Soc. for Arts, Religion and Contemporary Culture, Nat. Assn. Ind. Colls. and Univs. (chair commn. on state rels.), Greater New Castle C. of C. (1st v.p.). Home: 521 New Castle St New Wilmington PA 16142 Office: Westminster Coll South Market St New Wilmington PA 16172-0001 *The striving for excellence cannot be limited to a single discipline, task, or job. It involves a commitment of such intensity that the quest for excellence must be regarded as a way of life. I have taken a great deal of inspiration from both great artists and athletes whose achievements tell us that even if excellence cannot be readily defined, there is no way it can be approximated or achieved without self-discipline, dedication and commitment.*

REMICK, ROBERT HAROLD, minister; b. Boston, Feb. 11, 1947; s. Frank E. and Irene B. (Doucette) R.; m. Brenda M. Dobson, Oct. 7, 1967; children: Kellie, Christopher, Kimberly. Ordained to ministry Bapt. Ch., 1983. Ch. planter/pastor Fellowship Bapt., Hanover, Mass., 1983-87; pastor Victory Bapt. Ch., Brant Rock, Mass., 1987—; ins. salesman, ind. agt., Duxbury, Mass., 1976—; bd. dirs. Bapt. Conv. New Eng., Northboro, Mass., 1986-89; pres. Marshfield (Mass.) Clergy Assn., 1989-90. Pres. Duxbury Music Promoters, 1990-91, v.p., 1988-90; mem. Republican Presdl. Task Force, 1985—. Mem. Nat. Assn. Life Underwriters. Home: 994 Franklin St Duxbury MA 02332

REMMERS, MARVIN HENRY, minister; b. Adams, Nebr., June 15, 1935; s. John Benjamin and Grace (Busboom) R.; m. Geraldine Ann Bauer, June 22, 1958; children: John, Julia, Joel. BA, Wartburg Coll., 1957, B of Divinity, 1961, MDiv, 1977. Pastor St. Paul's Evangel. Luth. Ch., Cole Camp, Mo., 1961-65, Evangel. Luth. Ch. of the Cross, Chgo., 1965-71; sr. pastor Am. Luth. Ch., Rantoul, Ill., 1971—; vice-pres. Ill. Dist. Am. Luth. Ch., Chgo., 1977-81; bd. dirs. Oaks (Okla.)-Cherokee Oaks Indian Mission, 1962-65, nat. stewardship com. Am. Luth. Ch., 1970-71, congregational life com./Evangel. Luth. Ch., 1989—, hospice com. Venany Hosp., Urbana, Ill., 1989—; chaplain Ill. State Senate, 1968; others. Chmn. Human Rels. Com., Rantoul, Ill., 1973-76; bd. dirs. Champaign County Community Svcs., Rantoul, 1973-77; pres. Rantoul Ministerial Assn., 1976, 81. Mem. Exch. Club. Republican. Home: 504 Church Drive Rantoul IL 61866 Office: American Lutheran Church 500 Church Drive Rantoul IL 61866

REMONT, ROY, minister; b. Cut Off, La., Oct. 3, 1929; m. Bettye Williams; children: Rebecca, Deborah, Martha. BA, Northwestern State U., 1950; MDiv, New Orleans Bapt. Theol. Sem., 1955; postgrad., Centary Coll., 1977, U. Ark., Little Rock, 1983. Ordained to ministry Bapt. Ch., 1948. Student pastor Union Bapt. Ch., Pleasant Hill, La., 1947-49; pub. sch. tchr. Natchitoches Parish (La.), 1949-51; pastor Pine Ridge Bapt. Ch., Goldonna, La., 1949-51; student pastor Gallman (Miss.) Bapt. Ch., 1951-55; missionary pastor Moreauville, La., 1955-63; pastor Westside Bapt. Ch., Alexandria, La., 1963-79; chaplain Hot Springs (Ark.) Rehab. Ctr., 1978—. Author: Saints and Sinners, T.A Is for You, I Was in Prison; contbr. articles to denominational publs. Major, squadron comdr. Civil Air Patrol; bd. dirs. Cenla Community Action Com., La., chmn. Parish Prison Rehab. Com., Alexandria. Named Optimist of Yr. Optimist Club, Alexandria; recipient Outstanding Community Svc. award Cenla Community Action Com. Mem. La. Bapt. Conv. (exec. bd.). Office: PO Box 1358 Hot Springs AR 71901

RENDALL, TED SEATOR, clergyman; b. Edinburgh, Scotland, Aug. 18, 1933; came to Can., 1953; s. James and Jane (Rendall) R.; m. Norline Hope, June 14, 1958; children—Stephen James, David Paul. Diploma Prairie Bible Inst., 1956; D.Div. (hon.), Winnipeg Theol. Sem., Man., Can., 1984. Ordained to ministry Associated Gospel Chs., 1963. Pastor Bethel Fellowship Ch., Three Hills, Alta., Can., 1955-75; pastor of preaching Prairie Tabernacle Congregtion, Three Hills, 1975—; vice prin. Prairie Bible Inst., Three Hills, 1960-66, prin., 1967-80, v.p. Biblical ministries, 1980—. Author books, including: Elisha: Prophet of the Abundant Life, 1969; In God's School, 1971; Discipleship in Depth, 1981; Fire in the Church, 1982. Give Me That Book!, 1982. Editor The Prairie Overcomer, 1972—, Young Pilot, 1960—. Home: 230 5th Ave N, Three Hills, AB Canada T0M 2A0 Office: Prairie Bible Inst, Three Hills, AB Canada T0M 2A0

RENEGAR, GEORGE ELMO, minister; b. Surry County, N.C., May 29, 1921; s. Charles Lee and Lela Levoria (Hardy) R. BA, Guilford Coll., Greensboro, N.C., 1951; ThB, Piedmont Bible Coll., Winston-Salem, 1955; MTh, Berean Sch. Theology, Linter, Ind., 1957, ThD, 1960. Ordained to ministry Bapt. Ch., 1940. Pastor Beaver (W.Va.) Bapt. Ch., 1972—; trustee Bob Jones U., Greenville, S.C., 1965-72, Piedmont Bible Coll., 1965-75, Va. Bible Coll., Norfolk, 1963-75, Berean Sem., Linton, Ind., 1961-76; pres. Va. Bible Coll., 1965-70; asst. home dir. Bapt. Mid-Missions, Cleve., 1961-65; dir. Evangelism Missions, Chattanooga, 1989—. Author: 10 Reasons, Family Alter, 1970, Man As He Is, 1979, Baptism Bible Way, 1980, Stop, Look, Listen, 1982. Bapt. Bible Fellowship, Evangelism Fellowship (dir.). Home: 300 Airport Rd #200 Beaver WV 25813

RENNEBOHM, J. FRED, religious organization administrator; b. 1927; married. With Robert W. Baird Co., until 1953, Allis-Chalmers Corp., 1953-70; sec. Heritage Wis. Corp., Milw., 1970-85, v.p., until 1985; exec. sec. Nat. Assn. Congl. Christian Chs., Oak Creek, Wis., 1985—. Office: 8473 S Howell Ave PO Box 1620 Oak Creek WI 53154

RENO, STEPHEN JEROME, provost, academic dean; b. Oxnard, Calif., Feb. 27, 1944; s. Warren Jerome and Marie Louise (Fischer) R.; m. Catherine Royce Motley, Sept.7, 1974; children: Matthew Stephen, Catherine Hamlen. AB, St. John's Coll., Camarillo, Calif., 1965; MA, U. Calif., Santa Barbara, 1968, PhD, 1975. Provost and dean of faculty So. Oreg. State Coll., Ashland, 1989—; bd. mem. SALT Ctr. for Field Studies. Author: The Sacred Tree, 1975; author, contbr.: Penguin Dictionary of Religion, 1981; jour. editor Gen. Theol. Ctr. Maine, 1988-89; contbr. articles to religious jours. Mem. CSC, Portland, Maine, 1985-88. Recipient Rsch. awards The British Acad., London, 1976-77, 78-79. Mem. British Assn. for History of Religion, Am. Acad. Religion. Roman Catholic. Home: 600 Neil Creek Rd Ashland OR 97520 Office: So Oreg State Coll 1250 Siskiyou Blvd Ashland OR 97520

RENQUIST, THOMAS ARN, minister; b. Ft. Dodge, Iowa, Mar. 3, 1947; s. Harris Clemens and Gretchen Margaret (Bertram) R.; m. Kathleen E. Schmidt, Sept. 29, 1968 (div. Mar. 1980); children: Seth Aaron, Raili Kirsten; m. Christine Larson, June 21, 1980; children: Jacob Vinod, Peter Daniel. BA, U. Iowa, 1969; MDiv, Yale U., 1972. Ordained to ministry Evang. Luth. Ch. Am., 1973. Pastor St. Paul Luth. Ch., Remsen, Iowa, 1973-76, Grace Luth. Ch., Davenport, Iowa, 1976-79, Good Shepherd Luth. Ch., Rochester, Minn., 1980—; mem. Southeastern Minn. Synod Coun., Rochester, 1987—; del. constituting conv. Evang. Luth. Ch. Am., Columbus, Ohio, 1987; mem. coun. Commn. on Ministry in N.Am., Mpls., 1981-87; chair Profl. Leadership Coun., Des Moines, 1977-79. Chair United Way of Olmsted County, Rochester, 1985—, Channel One, Inc., Rochester, 1981-90, Iowa East Cen. T.R.A.I.N., Davenport, 1976-79; bd. dirs. Mid-Sioux Opportunity, Inc., Remsen, 1975-76. Mem. Phi Beta Kappa. Home: 2824 Pinewood Rd SE Rochester MN 55904 Office: Good Shepherd Ch 559 20th St SW Rochester MN 55902

RENSHAW, GEORGIE GORDON, minister; b. Chickasha, Okla., Apr. 22, 1927; s. James Otis and Bessie Telah (Moody) R.; m. LaJuana Jo Dean, Aug. 18, 1950; children: Richard Curtis, Rhonda Gail Renshaw Irvin, Regina Sue Renshaw Hodnett. AA, Jacksonville Bapt. Coll., 1953, BA, 1954; BTh, Bapt. Missionary Assn. Theol. Sem., 1955, BD, 1958, ThM, 1965. Ordained to ministry Bapt. Missionary Assn. Am., 1950. Pastor various chs., Tex., 1950-60, Unity Bapt. Ch., Hope, Ark., 1960-80, Farmington Bapt. Ch., Corinth, Miss., 1980-82, College Avenue Bapt. Ch., Levelland, Tex., 1982—; writer adult dept. Golden Words Publs., 1966; pers. committeman Bapt. Missionary Assn. Am., 1976-78, pres., 1981-82. Trustee Cen. Bapt. Coll., Conway, Ark., 1961-63, Bapt. Missionary Assn. Theol. Sem., Jacksonville, Tex., 1962-64, Ark. Children's Home, Magnolia, 1978-80; pres. Hope Concerned Citizens, 1968; chmn. S.W. Ark. Devel. Coun., Hope, 1974-75, Hempstead County chpt. Ark. Regional Blood Svcs., 1977-80. With USN, 1948-49. Mem. Kiwanis (pres. 1970-71). Republican. Office: College Avenue Bapt Ch 213 N College Ave PO Box 1244 Levelland TX 79336 *I promise to do all within my power to let God be in control of my life. That He will be the Lord and Master of my life.*

RENTZ, WILLIE DERRELL, minister; b. Jacksonville, Fla., July 5, 1942; s. Willie George Rentz and Mattie May Louise (Cannady) Felberg; m. Virginia Inez Baxley, Dec. 7, 1963; children: Sheryl Lynn, Kelley Michelle, Karen Renee, Julie Ann. BA in Bibl. Studies, Luther Rice Sem., 1971, STM, 1974, EdD in Religion, 1977, MA in Counseling, 1986; grad. in Theology, Bapt. Bible Coll. Ordained to ministry So. Bapt. Conv., 1967. Pastor Beaumont, Pa., 1967-68, Faith Bapt. Ch., Boston, Ga., 1968-69, Fellowship Bapt. Ch., Jacksonville, 1970-77, Hickox Bapt. Ch., Nahunta, Ga., 1977—; sec. Fla. Regional of Ind. Fundamental Chs. Am., 1972-74. Pres. PTA, Nahunta, 1981-82; chaplain Soil Conservation for Brantley County, Ga., 1988—; mem. adv. com. Charter-By-The-Sea, St. Simons Island, Ga., 1988—. Recipient Pastoral Leadership award So. Bapt. Ctr. for Bibl. Studies, 1990. Mem. Piedmont-Okefenokee Bapt. Assn. (chmn. exec. com. 1978-81, chmn. missions com. 1978—, vice moderator 1983-85, moderator 1985-87, mem. budget com., 1989, clk. 1990), United Assn. Christian Counselors (cert.). Democrat. Avocations: tennis, reading. Home: Rte 1 Box 84A Nahunta GA 31553 Office: Hickox Bapt Ch PO Box 656 Nahunta GA 31553 *The agony of mankind is located in a nature depraved; the joy of mankind is found in a nature renewed, hence the necessity of recreation or being born-again through faith in Jesus Christ the Lord.*

REPKA, JOAN ANN, director; b. Jersey City, Jan. 1, 1948; d. Joseph and Agnes (Hanê) R. BA in History, Coll. of St. Elizabeth, 1971; MA in Social Sci., Montclair (N.J.) State Coll., 1977. Tchr. Acad. of St. Aloysius, Jersey City, 1971-79, asst. prin., 1980-85, prin., 1985-91, exec. dir., 1991—; pres. No. Province Assembly-Sisters of Charity, Jersey City, 1974-76, del. 1985, 88, 91, Archdiocesan Prin.'s Coun., Newark Archdiocese of N.J., 1991—. President North Jersey Cath. Baseball League, 1977-85; dir. North Jersey Cath. Softball League, 1981-85. Named Coach of the Yr., Hudson (N.J.) Dispatch Newspaper, 1980; recipient Woman's Network Commendation, Senator Bill Bradley, 1990. Mem. Nat. Cath. Ednl. Assn., Nat. Coun. for Social Studies, Nat. Assn. Secondary Sch. Prins., N.J. Prin.'s and Supr.'s Assn. Office: Acad of St Aloysius 2495 Kennedy Blvd Jersey City NJ 07304

RESH, JAMES, missionary; s. Wesley and Frances Resh; m. Ellen Welty; children: Sharon, Dorcas, Laurel, Becky, James Martin Jr. Founder Four States Christian Missions, Inc., Hagerstown, Md., 1955—. Address: Four States Christian Missions Inc 125 N Prospect St PO Box 685 Hagerstown MD 21741-0685 also: 72 N Main St Chambersburg PA 17201 *Trust in the Lord with all thine heart and lean not unto thine own understanding; in all thy ways acknowledge Him and He shall direct thy paths. (Proverbs 3:5,6).*

RESLER, ROGER A., lay worker, radio station manager; b. Wheatridge, Colo., Jan. 13, 1964; s. Wendell Lee and Dee Ann (Dickey) R.; m. Marcia Hernández, June 24, 1988. BS, John Brown U., 1988. Prodn. dir. Campus Radio Sta. KLRC, John Brown U., Siloam Springs, Ark., 1987-88; sta. mgr. Sta. KGCR-FM, Goodland, Kans., 1988—. Republican. Mem. Assemblies of God. Office: Sta KGCR FM Box 948 Goodland KS 67735

RESSEGUIE, JAMES LYNN, religion educator; b. Buffalo, Jan. 1, 1945; s. Leon Arthur and Mabel (Vary) R.; m. Dianne Laverne Paulson, Oct. 24, 1970; children: Timothy, Carin, Jay. AB, U. Calif., Berkeley, 1967; MDiv, Princeton Theol. Sem., 1972; PhD, Fuller Theol. Sem., Pasadena, Calif., 1978. Asst. prof. N.T. Winebrenner Sem., Findlay, Ohio, 1976-78, assoc. prof. N.T., 1979-83, J. Russell Bucher prof. N.T., 1984—; registrar, dean acad. and student affairs Winebrenner Sem., 1990—; tchr. Peace Corps Vol., Cameroon, 1967-69. Contbr. to theol. publs. USIA Fulbright grantee, U. Iceland, 1990. Mem. Am. Acad. Religion, Soc. Bibl. Lit., Inst. Bibl. Rsch. Presbyterian. Office: Winebrenner Theol Sem 701 E Melrose Ave Findlay OH 45840

REST, FRIEDRICH OTTO, minister; b. Marshalltown, Iowa, Aug. 28, 1913; s. Karl and Bertha (Leisy) R.; m. Dorothy Evelyn Schummacher, Aug. 20, 1940; children: Paul Frederick, Elizabeth Rest Bean, John Marvin. AB, Elmhurst Coll., 1935; BD, Eden Theol. Sem., 1937; DD (hon.), Mission House Theol. Sem., 1962. Ordained to ministry United Ch. of Christ, 1937. Pastor St. Paul United Ch. of Christ, Hermann, Mo., 1948-55; sr. pastor St. Paul United Ch. of Christ, Evansville, Ind., 1955-64, Salem United Ch. of Christ, Rochester, N.Y., 1964-70; pastor St. Peter United Ch. of Christ, Houston, 1970-75; assoc. pastor 1st Protestant Ch., New Braunfels, Tex., 1975-85; interim pastor San Antonio, Hawaii, 1985—; part-time chaplain Chandler Meml. Home, San Antonio; minister of visitation, First Protestant Ch., N. Braunfels, 1991—. Author: Our Christian Symbols, 1954 (11 printings), The Cross in Hymns, 1961, Funeral Handbook, 3rd printing, 1982, Fourteen Messages of Hope: Thoughts for Funerals and Other Occasions, 1985, A Month of Family Prayers, 1989, Prayers for Families of Today, 1989, Our Christian Worship, 3rd printing, others; contbr. articles to religious jours.; former host TV program Pastor's Study. Home: 827 W Merriweather St New Braunfels TX 78130 *Something I didn't put in any of my books, but equally reflecting my views: "Fear less, hope more; hate less, love more; talk less, say more; worry less, trust more." (modified from an ancient Scottish proverb.).*

RETZER, SISTER JEANINE, religious order administrator; b. Milw., Jan. 27, 1938; d. Alvin Martin and Sophie Rose (Becker) R. BA, Mt. Mary Coll., 1968; MA, St. John's U., Cleve., 1974. Tchr. Cath. Sch. Systems, Wis., Iowa and Pa., 1957-73, prin., 1966-71; dir. religious edn. St. Olaf's Parish and St. Mary's Parish, Wis., 1973-77; mem. pastoral team St. Mary's Parish, Menomonee, Wis., 1977-82; adminstr. motherhouse Mother of Sorrows Convent, Milw., 1981-82; provincial Sisters of the Sorrowful Mother, Milw., 1982—; adminstr. Gen. Lay Ministry Program, Menomonee Falls, Wis., 1980-82; mem. planning com. Gathering, Chgo., 1980; mem. Major Superior, Leadership Conf. of WOmen Religious. Mem. Cath. Health Assn., Nat. Cath. Edn. Assn., Religious Edn. Assn., Cath. Health Assn. Wis. Address: Sisters of Sorrowful Mother 6618 N Teutonia Ave Milwaukee WI 53209

RETZER, SISTER MARY JANE, librarian; b. Milw., Mar. 4, 1931; d. Alvin M. and Sophie (Becker) R. BS in Edn., Mt. Mary Coll., Milw., 1960; cert. in religious edn., Marquette U., 1961, MA in Edn., 1967. Joined Sisters of the Sorrowful Mother, Roman Cath. Ch., 1945. Primary tchr. St. Louis Sch., Wichita, Kans., 1950-52, St. Francis Borgia Sch., Cedarburg, Wis., 1952-54, Our Lady of Guadalupe Sch., Wichita, 1954-60; prin. St. Anthony's Pewaukee, 1960-66, St. Patrick's Sch., Estherville, Iowa, 1966-70; primary tchr. Mother of Perpetual Help Sch., Milw., 1970-90, libr., 1990—. Named Tchr. of Yr., Diocese of Milw., 1977. Mem. ALA, Nat. Cath. Educators Assn., Am. Math. Assn. Avocations: gardening, visiting sick and elderly, caring for elderly. Home: 444 W Bradley Milwaukee WI 53217

REUSCH, DONALD CARL, minister; b. Savanna, Ill., Nov. 12, 1956; s. Harlan Eugene and Rowline Marie (Perry) R. AS, Highland Community Coll., Freeport, Ill., 1976; BA, So. Ill. U., 1978; cert., Urban Ministry Program, Chgo., 1980; MDiv, Wartburg Theol. Sem., 1982. Ordained to ministry Evang. Luth. Ch. Am., 1983. Pastor Lily Butler (S.D.) Luth. Parish, 1983-87, Messiah Luth. Ch., Sioux Falls, S.D., 1987-90, St. Francis and St. Clare Met. Community Ch., Sioux Falls, 1990—; chairperson S.D. Synod Worship Com., Sioux Falls, 1987-90; mem. East Side Ministerial Assn., Sioux Falls, 1988-90; mem., del. Elca Regional Worship Leaders, 1989—. Mem. Butler Centennial Com., 1985; v.p. Sioux Empire Gay/Lesbian Coalition, Sioux Falls, 1989, pres. 1990; mem. Ea. Dakota AIDS Network, 1990—. Mem. Liturgical Conf. Democrat. Home: 704 E 20th St Sioux Falls SD 57105-0923 Office: St Francis & St Clare MCC 9th St and Cliff Ave Sioux Falls SD 57104 *If AIDS is God's judgement upon any particular segment of society, I find it amazing that the wrath of God can be thwarted by a thin layer of latex!.*

REUSS, CARL FREDERICK, sociologist; b. Phila., June 7, 1915; s. Charles Frederick and Marie Anna (Kick) R.; m. Thelma Steinmann, June 24, 1938; children: Paula Schanz, Ellen Jeppesen, Betty Shovelin. BS, U. Va., 1934, MS, 1935, PhD, 1937. Asst. rural sociologist Wash. State Coll., Pullman, 1937-44; prof. sociology Capital U., Columbus, Ohio, 1944-48; dean faculty Wartburg Coll., Waverly, Iowa, 1948-51; exec. sec. Bd. Christian Social Action, Am. Luth. Ch., Columbus, 1951-60; dir. Commn. on Rsch. & Social Action, Am. Luth. Ch., Mpls., 1961-80; asst. for rsch. coordination Office of Presiding Bishop, Am. Luth. Ch., Mpls., 1981-87; ret.; sec. Commn. on Inner Missions, Luth. World Fedn., Geneva, 1955-63; v.p. religious leaders Nat. Safety Coun., Chgo., 1973-78; rsch. adviser Commn. New Luth. Ch., Mpls., 1984-87; rsch., planning and evaluation standing com. Evang. Luth. Ch. in Am., Chgo., 1987-89; exec. dir. Luths. for Religious and Polit. Freedom, 1988—. Author: Profiles of Lutherans in the U.S.A., 1982; editor: Conscience and Action, 1971, Luth. Commentator, 1989—; contbr. articles to profl. jours. Active Citizens League, Mpls., 1961—. Recipient Citation as "pioneer mem.", 50th Ann. Mtg. Nat. Council on Family Relations, 1988. Mem. Nat. Coun. Family Rels., Soc. Sci. Study of Religion, Religious Rsch. Assn., Am. Sociol. Assn. (emeritus), Rural Sociol. Soc. Lutheran. Avocations: reading, travel. Home: 4425 Dunberry Ln Edina MN 55435 *Our freedom to make informed, responsible choices along the pathways of life, in accountability to God rather than to the pressures of peers or of special interests, is a major religious value crucial also to the quality of American public life.*

REUSS VON PLAUEN, ARCHBISHOP HEINRICH XXVI, metropolitan; b. Greiz, Plauen, Germany, Feb. 3, 1942; s. Prince Heinrich XXV and Princess Maria (Obrenovic-Brankovic) Reuss von Plauen. BSN, U. der Heiligen Dreifaltigkeit, Fed. Republic Germany, 1968, S.T.L., 1972; PhD, STD (hon.), U. Heil. Drei., Fed. Republic Germany, 1974, JD, 1984; AB, San Francisco State U., 1970, MS, 1980; LLD (hon.), South East U., Hong Kong, 1973; MS in Nursing, San Jose (Calif.) State U., 1989. Ordained priest Ea. Cath. Archdiocese (Chaldean-Syrian), 1968. Priest, missionary, RN Ea. Cath. Archdiocese, 1968-74, archimandrite, 1974, co-adjutor archbishop, 1974-76, met., primate of Ams., 1976—. Author: The History of the Eastern Catholic Liturgy, 1979. Rector Holy Trinity U., Phoenix, 1978—. Decorated prince-grand master Order St. Thomas the Apostle, Ea. Cath. Order of the Holy Sepulchre; knight grand cross Order Royal Crown Balearica, Order St. Agatha (Spain); knight grand cross Order of Black Eagle, bailiff grand cross Knights of the Holy Sepulchre (Fed. Republic Germany); knight grand cross Order St. Constantine (Greece); knight grand cross of justice Order St. George (Eng.); named Knight Grand Cross of Justice, Order St. John of Knights of Malta, 1963; named grand prelate Sovereign Hospitaller Order St. John of Knights of Malta, 1979. Address: Eastern Cath Archdiocese (Chaldean-Syrian) PO Box 3337 Daly City CA 94015 *The purpose of the Church is to serve and to love Christ's flock, especially the poor, needy, sick and the dying, in accordance with the Holy Scriptures. The Church must maintain the Apostolic Traditions and Canons of the Historic Church, in order to bring mankind up to God's level, not bring God down to mankind's level.*

REVELY, WILLIAM, minister; b. Charlottesville, Va., Jan. 20, 1941; s. William E. and Reaver (Carter) R.; m. Eleanora B. Fisher, 1991 (div. 1976); 1 child, Christana Re. BA in Sociology/History, Howard U., 1962, MDiv, 1967, MA in Social Work, 1971, DMin., 1982. Ordained to ministry Bapt. Ch., 1962. Pastor Union Bapt. Ch., Easton, Md., 1965-78, Mt. Gilead Bapt. Ch., Washington, 1979-89, Messiah Bapt. Ch., Detroit, 1989—; chmn. bd. dirs. Greater Opportunities Industrialization Ctr. Met. Detroit, Detroit, 1990—. Bd. dirs. Bagley Community Coun., Detroit; trustee Shaw U., Washington. Mem. SCLC, Bapt. Conv. USA Inc., Nat. Prog. Bapt. Conv., Am. Bapt. Ch. of the South, Lott Carey Fgn. Missions Conv., Nat. Citizens Band Assn., Mich. Dist. Assn., B.M. & E. State Conv., Wolverine State Conv., Coun. GBpt. Pastors of Detroit and Vicinity, Prince Hall Social Lodge. Office: Messiah Bapt Ch 8100 W Seven Mile Rd Detroit MI 48221

REVESZ, MARIE B., religion educator; b. Scranton, Pa., Feb. 1, 1952; d. William Stephen and Edna I. (Grella) Kluchinskas; m. Raymond P. Revesz, Oct. 27, 1973; children: Eric, Stephen, Karen. BA in Religious Studies, Marywood Coll., 1988, MS in Religious Edn., 1990. Theology educator Bishop Hoban High Sch., Wilkes Barre, Pa., 1988—; catechist, pro-life chmn., retreat dir., Sts. Peter and Paul Ch., Avoca; instr. religious edn. Inst. Diocese of Scranton; speaker at various parishes and workshops; moderator Christian Life Community, Wilkes Barre, 1990-91, Clown Ministry, Wilkes Barre, 1988-91; mem. Fellowship of Reconciliation, Scranton. Mem. Theta Alpha Kappa, Kappa Gamma Pi. Roman Catholic. Home: Box 600 Avoca PA 18641 Office: Bishop Hoban High Sch 159 S Penn Blvd Wilkes-Barre PA 18702

REVOLLO BRAVO, MARIO CARDINAL, bishop; b. Genoa, Italy, June 15, 1919. Ordained priest Roman Cath. Ch., 1943. Elected to titular Ch. of Tinisa di Numidia,, 1973; consecrated bishop, 1973; prefect, Nueva Pamplona, 1978; transferred to Bogota, Colombia, 1984—; created cardinal, 1988. Address: Carrera 7A No 10-20, Bogota Colombia

REX, LONNIE ROYCE, religious organization administrator; b. Caddo, Okla., May 11, 1928; s. Robert Lavern and Lennie Cordy (Gilcrease) R.; m. Betty Louise Sorrells, Apr. 8, 1949; children: Royce DeWayne, Patricia Louise, Debra Kaye. MusB, Oklahoma City U., 1950; DD (hon.), Am. Bible Inst., 1970. Advt. mgr. Oral Roberts Evang. Assn., Tulsa, 1955-57; bus. mgr. T.L. Osborn Found., Tulsa, 1957-69; gen. mgr. Christian Crusade, Tulsa, 1969-80; sec.-treas. David Livingstone Missionary Found., Tulsa, 1970-80, pres., 1980—; dep. dir. gen. Internat. Biog. Assn.; bd. dirs. Intra-Ch. Pension Fund, Bethany, Okla.; speaker internat. confs. Eng., Hungary, Korea, Singapore, Spain, N.Y.C. Author: Never a Child, 1989. Recipient Merit award Korea, 1975, Moran medal Republic of Korea, Humanitarian award Senator Hugh Scott, 1983, Svc. to Mankind award Internat. Biog. Congress, Spain, 1987, Internat. Lions Club award; named Outstanding Humanitarian of Yr., Am. Biog. Inst., 1987, Man of Yr., 1990. Mem. Phi Beta Kappa. Home: 6919 S Columbia Tulsa OK 74136 Office: David Livingstone Missionary Found 6555 S Lewis Tulsa OK 74136 *In my work among the starving in Ethiopia, I walked into a tent of over 100 mothers, lying on mats, who had given birth during the last three days. It was silent! Morbid silence! That haunting silence lives with me since that moment. I asked why? I was informed the babies did not have the strength to cry. I'm thankful my children could cry.*

REYES, ADRIEL, theology educator, tax consultant; b. Bronx, N.Y., Aug. 20, 1970; s. Ernesto and Teresa (Velez) R. BS in Theology, Liberty U., 1990. Registered tax cons. Chief dir. Youth Alive Ministries, Bklyn., 1987—; chancellor, prof. theology Youth Alive Bible Inst., Bklyn., 1991—; pres. Reyes Revelation, Inc., 1991—; counselor Office of State Senator Chris Mega, 1990; tax cons. Parkview Terr. Real Estate, Bklyn., 1991—. Sec. Ebenezer Ch. Coun., Bklyn., 1988-89; trustee Believers in Action, Bklyn., 1990—; counselor Office of Congressman Solartz, 1990. Mem. Am. Mgmt. Assn., TRW Credentials. Republican. Home: 5301 6th Ave Brooklyn NY 11220 *It's time for the Church to go through another reformation. One that would return it to the power and glory it had before the rise of the Roman Church.*

REYES, ANDRES JESUS, priest, family therapist; b. Santiago, Cuba, May 20, 1943; s. Andres and Ernestina (Aguiar) R.; 1 adopted child. Postgrad., Havana U., 1962, Roman Cath. Sem., Tegucigalpa, Honduras, 1966, U. Javeriana, Bogota, Colombia, 1970; MSW, Yeshiva U., N.Y.C., 1988. Ordained priest Roman Cath. Ch., 1970. Counselor Union Exiled Cubans, Union City, N.J., 1963-64; tchr. religious edn. dept. Instituto Tecnico Cen. High Sch., Bogota, Colombia, 1968-69; counselor Latin Am. Pastoral Team, Bogota, 1967-70; tchr. social sci. electronic engring. dept. Universidad Javeriana, Bogota, 1970; counselor Roman Cath. Archdiocese Newark, 1975; nat. dir. family life for Honduras Bishops' Nat. Conf., 1977-78; convener, chmn. Cuban prisoner refugee program Roman Cath. Archdiocese Newark, 1978-79; therapist psychiat. dept. Elizabeth (N.J.) Gen. Med. Ctr., 1986-88; pvt. practice individual and family therapy Bergenfield, N.J., 1988—; parish priest Roman Cath. Archdiocese Newark, 1971—; mem. bd. Welfare Dept., Borough of Bergenfield, 1987-90. Roman Catholic. Office: 560 A Main St Hackensack NJ 07601

REYES, JOSE ANTONIO, minister; b. Canovanas, P.R., May 24, 1940; s. Dionisio Reyes and Antonia (Rodriguez) R.; m. Olfa R. Martinez, May 30, 1964; 1 child, Jose A. BA in Edn., U. P.R., 1962; MA, Sch. Theology, Cleveland, Tenn., 1984; D Ministry, Logos Sch., 1985. Ordained to ministry Ch. of God of Prophecy, 1969. Youth dir. Ch. of God of Prophecy, Rio Piedras, P.R., 1956-58, pastor, 1963-68; mission rep. for Latin Am. Ch. of God of Prophecy, Cleveland, Tenn., 1969-75, internat. radio speaker, 1969—, internat. asst. gen. overseer, 1981—; pres. Hispanic Nat. Religious Broadcasting, Parsippany, 1985-88; v.p. Nat. Orgn. Advancement of Hispanic, 1983-86; com. mem. Hispanic Task Force of Am. Bible Soc., 1985-87; mem. Hispanic Commn., Nat. Assn. Evangelicals, Carol Stream, Ill., 1988—; exec. com. Nat. Religious Broadcasters, 1990—. Author: The Hispanics in USA - A Challenge, An Opportunity for the Church, 1984; author 10 Bible Study Guides on books of the Bible, 1985-90. Recipient Excellence in Hispanic Program Producer award Nat. Religious Broadcasters, 1988, Excellence in Ministry award Internat. Ministry Com., 1990. Mem. Spanish Voice of Salvation Sponsorship Club (pres.). Republican. Home: 3816 Northwood Cleveland TN 37311 *Equalling our Lord is an impossible task, but imitating Him is our supreme duty.*

REYES, LONNIE C., priest; b. Lockhart, Tex., June 1, 1942; s. Jose M. and Angela (Contreras) R. ThM, U. St. Thomas, 1969. Ordained priest Roman Cath. Ch., 1969. Parachial vicar St. Louis Ch., Waco, Tex., 1969-70; exec. sec. Hispanic Ministry Diocese of Austin, Tex., 1970-73; chancellor Diocese of Austin, 1975-86; pastor St. Julia Cath. Ch., Austin, 1986—; pastor Cristo Rey Parish, Austin, 1978-82. Trustee Laguna Gloria Art Mus., Austin, 1984-87; mem. integrity task force Travis County Dem. Party, 1984-85; chmn. Austin Police and Fire Commn., 1976-89; chmn. Father Joe Znotas Community Scholarship, Austin, 1984—; mem. blue ribbon ethics rev. com. City of Austin, 1985; mem. ad hoc com. on fgn. nats. Austin Police Dept. Apptd. monsignor by Pope Paul VI, 1976. Mem. Nat. Assn. Ch. Pers. Adminstrs., Diocesan Fiscal Mgmt. Conf., Canon Law Soc. Am., Austin Charro Assn.. Home: 900 Tillery Austin TX 78702 Office: St Julia Cath Ch 3010 Lyons Rd Austin TX 78702

REYNOLDS, FRANK EVERETT, religious studies educator; b. Hartford, Conn., Nov. 13, 1930; s. Howard Wesley and Caroline Mills Roys R.; m. Mani Bloch, Mar. 28, 1959; children—Roy Howard, Andrew Everett, Roger Frank. Student, Princeton U., 1948-51; B.A., Oberlin U., 1952; B.D., Yale Div. Sch., 1955; M.A., U. Chgo., 1963, Ph.D., 1971. Ordained to ministry Am. Baptist Ch., 1955. Program dir. Student Christian Ctr., Bangkok, Thailand, 1956-59; minister to fgn. students U. Chgo. Ecumenical Ministries, 1961-64; instr. U. Chgo., 1967-69, asst. prof. then assoc. prof., 1969-79, prof. history of religions and Buddhist studies, 1979—; co-dir. Liberal Arts and Study of Religions Project, NEH, Berkeley, Calif., 1985-90, NEH Sangitivavamsa Transl. Project, 1990—. Author: Guide to Buddhist Religion, 1981; (with others) Religions of the World, 1983; editor, co-translator: 3 Worlds According to King Ruang, 1981; co-editor: Anthropology and the Study of Religion, 1984, Cosmology and Ethical Order, 1985, Myth and Philosophy, 1990, Beyond the Classics: Religious Studies and Liberal Education, 1990; co-editor History of Religion Jour., 1977—; assoc. editor Jour. Religion, 1976—, Jour. Religious Ethics, 1981—. Jacob Fox Found. fellow, 1952, Danforth Found. fellow, 1960, 64; sr. rsch. grantee Fulbright Commn., 1973-74, NEH, 1978-79, 91—. Mem. Am. Soc. Study Religion, Am. Acad. Religion, Assn. Asian Studies (co-editor monograph series 1978-86), Internat. Congress History of Religions, Internat. Assn. Buddhist Studies. Home: 5433 S Blackstone Ave Chicago IL 60615 Office: U Chgo Swift Hall 1025 E 58th St Chicago IL 60637

REYNOLDS, FRANK MILLER, minister; b. Trumansburg, N.Y., Sept. 11, 1921; s. George Andrew and Beth (Miller) R.; m. Gladys May Richards, June 15, 1946; children: Daniel, Stephen, Timothy, Mark, THomas. BS in Agriculture, Cornell U., 1944. Ordained to ministry, 1949. Pastor Assembly of God Ch., Canandaiga, N.Y., 1947-52, Medford, N.J., 1952-58; pastor El Bethel, Staten Island, N.Y., 1958-62; founder, dir. Teen Challenge Tng., Rehrersburg, Pa., 1962-73, 87-88; nat. rep. Teen Challenge USA, Springfield, Mo., 1973-87; ret., 1988; sect. sec. Assemblies of God Cen. N.Y., 1948-52; dist. home missionary Assemblies of God N.J., 1953-59; sec. Teen Challenge, Bklyn., 1959-68. Co-author: Drug Bug, 1970, Somebody Help Me, 1970; contbr. articles to profl. jours. Republican. Avocation: gardening. Home: 4626 S Crescent Ave Springfield MO 65804 Office: Teen Challenge 1525 Campbell Ave Springfield MO 65803

REYNOLDS, GARY W., radio station manager; b. Semour, Mo., Aug. 18, 1948; s. Richard James and Rachael E. (Cornelious) R.; married; children: Tracy Lee, Richard James. Student, U. So. La., 1970-73. Sta. mgr. Sta. KSJY Radio, Lafayette, La., 1987—; cons. Exec. Consultants, Lafayette, 1988—; v.p. La. Christian Broadcasting Assn., Baton Rouge, 1990; sec.-treas. Lafayette Ednl. Broadcasting Found., 1987-90. Mem. La. Family Lobby, Lafayette, 1990. Staff sgt. U.S. Army, 1965-69. Named Officer of the Yr., 100 Club, Lafayette, 1985. Home: PO Box 31086 Lafayette LA 70593

REYNOLDS, GEORGE LAZENBY, JR., bishop; b. Opelika, Ala., Aug. 18, 1927; s. George Lazenby and Marion Banks (Barnett) R.; m. Barbara Clark, June 9, 1962; children: George III, Katherine. BA, U. South, 1950, DD (hon.), 1985; MDiv, Va. Theol. Sem., 1954, DD (hon.), 1984; PhD, NYU, 1973. Chaplain Sewanee (Tenn.) Mil. Acad., 1954-55; asst. to rector St. Paul's Episcopal Ch., Mt. Lebanon, Pa., 1955-56; priest-in-charge St. Christophers Episcopal Ch., Warrendale, Pa., 1956-62; assoc. sec. leadership tng. div. dept. Christian edn. Exec. Coun. of Episcopal Ch., N.Y.C., 1962-66, adminstr. tng. svcs., 1966-68; rector Christ Episcopal Ch., Glendale, Ohio, 1968-76, St. Stephens Episcopal Ch., Edina, Minn., 1976-85; bishop Episcopal Diocese Tenn., Nashville, 1985—. Chmn. adv. bd. Faith Orgn. in Covenant for Understanding and Svc., Nashville, 1988, 89; mem. Leadership Nashville, 1986—; bd. dirs. St. Andrew's (Tenn.) Sewanee Sch., 1985—; trustee U. South, 1985—. With USN, 1945-46. Mem. Assn. for Creative Change (pres. 1970-72). Home: 4115 Legend Hall Nashville TN 37215 Office: Episcopal Diocese Tenn 42 Rutledge Hill Nashville TN 37210

REYNOLDS, LEWIS DAYTON, religious organization administrator; b. Charleston, W.Va., July 26, 1937; s. James Shelby and Sybil Catherine (Lanham) R.; m. Ann Kathryn Reynolds, Aug. 25, 1962; children: John, Daniel. BBA, Marshall U., 1959; BTh., Aurora U., 1961; MDiv, Evang. Theol. Sem., Naperville, Ill., 1962. Ordained to ministry Advent Christian Ch., 1962. Pastor Advent Christian Ch., Mendota, Ill., 1961-64, Clendenin, W.Va., 1964-72; pastor New Covenant Fellowship, Penfield, N.Y., 1972-89; gen. overseer, elder Elim Fellowship, Lima, N.Y., 1989—; advisor Am. Bible Soc.; bd. dirs. Elim-Can., Paris, Ont. Bd. dirs. Elim Bible Inst., Lima. Mem. Pentecostal Fellowship N.Am. (bd. dirs.), Nat. Assn. Evangs. (bd. dirs.). Office: Elim Fellowship Inc 7245 College St Lima NY 14485

REYNOLDS, PATRICIA ANN, church official; b. Ft. Worth, Sept. 8, 1946; d. Thomas Joseph and Celestia Ella (Stogner) Free; m. Charles Evan Reynolds, July 2, 1966; children: Daman Scott, Thomas Howard. Student, Howard Payne Coll., 1967-68. Sec. to assoc. pastor, min. youth Highland Bapt. Ch., Dallas, 1974-76; adminstrv. asst., tchr. Bible, 1st United Meth. Ch., Snyder, Tex., 1985—. Speaker, singer civic clubs. and chs. Home: 3107 Ave T Snyder TX 79549 Office: 1st United Meth Ch 2700 College Ave Snyder TX 79549

REYNOLDS, PAUL V., religious organization administrator. Dist. supt. United Pentecostal Ch. in Can., Surrey, B.C. Office: United Pentecostal Ch Can, 1344-112th Ave, Surrey, BC Canada V3R 2E7*

REYNOLDS, ROBERT LESTER, church official; b. Webster, Mass., Nov. 27, 1917; s. Joseph and Lillian Mabel (Brown) R.; m. Beatrice Nelson, Aug. 17, 1941; children—Carole (Mrs. Richard Clark), Robert Craig. B.A., Atlantic Union Coll., 1941; M.A., Boston U., 1949, Ph.D., 1970. Dean of boys Shenandoah Valley Acad., New Market, Va., 1941-43; dean men Atlantic Union Coll., 1943-46; dean men, asst. bus. mgr., dir. devel. and pub. relations, dean students Pacific Union Coll., Angwin, Calif., 1946-59; pres. Atlantic Union Coll., 1960-68, Walla Walla Coll., College Place, Wash., 1968-76; gen. field sec. Gen. Conf. Seventh-day Adventists, Washington, 1976-80; exec. sec. Bd. Higher Edn. Gen. Conf. Seventh-day Adventists, 1980-88; mem. Gen. Conf. com. Seventh-day Adventists; also mem. bd. higher edn. and bd. regents Seventh-day Adventists (Gen. Conf.). Mem. Am. Hist. Assn., Phi Alpha Theta, Phi Delta Kappa. Club: Rotarian.

REYNOLDS, W. RONNIE, pastor, consultant; b. Huntington, W.Va., Sept. 23, 1939; s. Woodrow C. and Lucille (Nicely) R.; m. Glenda C. Arton, July 10, 1961; children: Ronnie Jr., Nona, Lollis, Rebecca. BBA, Marshall U., 1972; MDiv, Southeastern Bapt. Theol. Sem., 1975. Ordination to Gospel Ministry. Pastor Palestine Bapt. Ch., Ashton, W.Va., 1969-71, Mt. Union Bapt. Ch., Lesage, W.Va., 1971-72, Lea Bethel Bapt. Ch., Prospect Hill, N.C., 1972-75; career missionary Fgn. Mission Bd., So. Bapt. Conv., Argentina, South Am., 1975-86; pastor South Fork Bapt. Ch., Winston-Salem, N.C., 1986-88, Friends Bapt. Ch., Clemmons, N.C., 1988—; missionary Home Mission Bd., So. Bapt. Conv., Atlanta, 1989—; ch. growth cons. Bapt. State Conv. of N.C., Cary, 1988— (ch. planter of yr. 1989). Author: Home Cell Group Ministry, 1989, Spiritual Gifts Discovery, 1990. Chaplain Civitan Club, Winston-Salem, 1989-90. Sgt. U.S. Army, 1961-63. Mem. Ch. Growth Am. Democrat. Avocations: gardening, writing, reading. Home: 605 Greenvine Circle Winston-Salem NC 27103 Office: Friends Bapt Church 605 Greenvine Circle Winston-Salem NC 27103

REYNOLDS, WILLIAM JENSEN, church musician, hymnologist, composer; b. Atlantic, Iowa, Apr. 2, 1920; s. George Washington and Ethel (Horn) R.; student Okla. Baptist U., 1937-39; AB, Southwest Mo. State Coll., 1942; MSM, Southwestern Bapt. Theol. Sem., 1945; M.M., N. Tex. State U., 1946; EdD, George Peabody Coll. Tchrs. 1961; m. Mary Lou Robertson, July 6, 1947; children: Timothy Jensen, Kirk Mallory. Min. music 1st Bapt. Ch., Ardmore, Okla., 1946-47, 1st Bapt. Ch., Oklahoma City, 1947-55; music editor ch. music dept. Bapt. Sunday Sch. Bd., Nashville, 1955-80; guest prof. Southwestern Bapt. Theol. Sem., Ft. Worth, 1980—, prof. ch. music Sch. Ch. Music, 1981—; music dir. So. Bapt. Conv., Houston, 1958, Phila., 1972, Portland, Oreg., 1973, Dallas, 1974, Miami Beach, 1975, Norfolk, 1976, Kansas City, 1977, 83, 84, Atlanta, 1978, 86, Houston, 1979, St. Louis, 1980, Los Angeles, 1981, New Orleans, 1982, Pitts., 1983, Dallas, 1985, Atlanta, 1986; music dir. Bapt. World Alliance, Rio de Janeiro, 1960, Stockholm, 1975, Toronto, 1980, Los Angeles, 1985; music dir. Bapt. World Youth Conf., Toronto, 1958, Beirut, 1963, Berne, 1968; nat. cons. Ctr. for Study of So. Culture, U. Miss.; cons. rev. The Sacred Harp, 1991; mem. hymnal com. Baptist Hymnal, 1956; chmn. hymnal com., gen. editor Baptist Hymnal, 1975; gen. editor New Broadman Hymnal, 1977; composer: Ichthus, 1971; Reaching People, 1973; Share His Word, 1973; Bold Mission, 1977; more than 700 choral anthems, hymn tunes, songs, etc.; dir. Sacred Harp Pub. Co.; lectr., clinician, condr. seminars and workshops in ch. music; adjudicator music festivals. Author: A Survey of Christian Hymnody, 1963, 3d edit., 1987; Hymns of our Faith, 1964; Christ and the Carols, 1967; Congregational Singing, 1975; Companion to the Baptist Hymnal, 1976; Songs of Glory, 1990; co-author: A Joyful Song: Christian Hymnody, 1977, A Survey of Christian Hymnody, 1987; compiler: Building an Effective Music Ministry, 1980; contbr. to Hymns of the United Methodist Hymnal, 1989; weekly newspaper columnist History of Hymns. Recipient B.B. McKinney Found. award, 1960. Mem. Hymn Soc. Am. (pres. 1978-80), Ch. Music Pubs. Assn. (v.p. 1973-75), ASCAP, Nat. Acad. Rec. Arts and Scis., Gospel Music Assn., So. Bapt. Ch. Music Conf., Harpeth Valley Sacred Harp Singing Assn. (pres. 1966-80). Home: 6750 Cartagena Ct Fort Worth TX 76133-5449

RHOADES, KATHRYN ANN, youth minister; b. Huntington, N.Y., May 1, 1960; d. Arthur Karl August and Hildegarde Beulah (Kauz) Leseberg; m. Thomas David Rhodes, Jan. 7, 1989; children: Stephanie, Danielle. AA, Ventura (Calif.) Jr. Coll., 1982; BA with honors, Calif. State U., Northridge, 1984. Ordained to ministry Evang. Luth. Ch. Am. Dir. child/youth ministries Trinity Luth. Ch., Hemet, Calif., 1990—, assoc. in ministry, 1990—. Office: Trinity Luth Ch 25825 Columbia St Hemet CA 92344

RHODE, PAUL GERALD, minister; b. Boulder, Colo., Dec. 17, 1953; s. Ronald Henry and Delores Leona (Heermann) R.; m. Jayne Lynn Nuss, Aug. 8, 1975; children: Jeremy, Anna, Karl, Chloe. BS, Concordia Coll., Seward, Nebr., 1977; MDiv, Concordia Theol. Sem., 1981. Vicar Zion Luth. Ch., Brainerd, Minn., 1979-80; pastor St. Paul's Luth. Ch., Jerome, Idaho, 1981-89; sr. pastor Zion Evang. Luth. Ch., Tacoma, 1989—; chmn. Idaho Conf. Youth Bd., Jerome, 1982-88, Cir. Pastor's Conf., Jerome, 1988-89, sec. 1982-85. Organizer Peer Helper's Program, Jerome High Sch., 1986. Recipient Luth. Brotherhood scholarships. Office: Zion Luth Ch 3410 6th Ave Tacoma WA 98406

RHODES, ALAN CHARLES, minister; b. Plattsburgh, N.Y., July 25, 1951; s. Charles Oliver and Lillian Mary (Cromie) R.; m. Holly C. Craver, June 14, 1975 (div. July 1987); m. Nancy Lichtenhan, June 18, 1988. BA, Lycoming Coll., Williamsport, Pa., 1973; MDiv, Boston U., 1976. Ordained to ministry United Meth. Ch. as deacon, 1974, as elder, 1977. Assoc. pastor Shenendehowa United Meth. Ch., Clifton Park, N.Y., 1976-79; pastor Ft. Plain (N.Y.) and Freysbush United Meth. Chs., 1979-83, St. Paul's United Meth. Ch., Castleton-on-Hudson, N.Y., 1983-87, Grace United Meth. Ch., Ravena, N.Y., 1987—; chair fin. com., bd. mem., exec. com. Albany (N.Y.) United Meth. Soc., 1991-92; mem. fin. and nomination coms. Capital Area Coun. Chs., Albany, 1991-92; program chmn. Troy Ann. Conf. Sessions, Poultney, Vt., 1990-92. Bd. mem. Sr. Projects of Ravena, 1990-91; mem. Ravena-Coeymans-Selkirk Community Svcs. Comm., Ravena, 1990-91, R.C.S. Sch. Dist. Drug and Alcohol Adv. Com., Ravena, 1990-91; chairperson Albany Med. Ctr. Community Religious Com.; mem. Regional Clin. Pastoral Edn. Planning Task Force. Mem. Lions. Republican. Home: 20 Hillcrest Dr Ravena NY 12143 Office: Grace United Meth Ch 16 Hillcrest Dr Ravena NY 12143

RHOE, KENNETH ROLAND, minister; b. Annandale, Minn., Sept. 20, 1926; s. George Everett and Ruth Valentine (Johnson) R.; m. Elsie Mae Walberg, Apr. 26, 1947 (div. 1979); children: Llewellyn, Larry, Mark, Nancy, Carl, Holly; m. Barbara Ann Watkins, Nov. 16, 1979. Student, Angsburg Coll., 1956-57, cert. of theology, 1960. Ordained to ministry. Minister Barronette (Wis.) Luth. Parish, 1960-62, Cen. Luth. Ch., Salem, Oreg., 1962-72, Silverdale (Wash.) Luth. Ch., 1972-78, First United Ch. of Christ, Tacoma, 1986—, Plymouth Congl. Ch., Tacoma, 1988—; salesperson Spot Realty, Silverdale, 1988—. With seabees USN, 1943-46, PTO. Democrat. Home and Office: 17197 Clear Creek Rd NW Poulsbo WA 98370

RHYMES, BEVERLY GUYTON, religious organization official; b. Shawnee, Okla., May 2, 1931; d. Albert J. and Birma (Pool) Guyton; m. James Robinson (dec. Jul. 1962); m. Pete Rhymes, Nov. 12, 1964; children: Judy, Jill, Pete II, Libby, Kathy, Jim, Ray. BA, Blue Mountain Coll., 1951; MA, Loyola U., Balt., 1984. Chair retreats Episcopal Diocese of La., 1989—. Bd. dirs. MacDonell's Children's Home, Houma, La., 1984-90; nat. pres. Nat. Assn. Jr. Auxs., 1961; pres. Big Spring (Tex.) State Mental Hosp. Aux., 1970, Friends of the Libr., 1987; chair County Reps., Winston County, Miss., 1963. Recipient La Grande Dame award local hosp. and parish, 1987, Vol. Activist award Tri Parish Area, 1989. Mem. Episcopal Women of Vision (presenter 1990—). Home: 503 Central Ave Houma LA 70364

RIAN, EDWIN HAROLD, retired minister, religion educator; b. Mpls., Apr. 27, 1900; s. John Peter and Gunda (Songli) R.; children: Roanne, Abigail, Marian, Edwin Harold, Marian Schall. AB, U. Minn., 1924; ThB, Princeton Theol. Sem., 1927; AM, Princeton U., 1927; LLD (hon.), Bob Jones U., 1948; STD (hon.), Huron (S.D.) Coll., 1955; DD (hon.), Jamestown (N.D.) Coll., 1960; LHD (hon.), Moravian Coll., 1961. Ordained to ministry Presbyn Ch. (U.S.A.), 1927. Asst. min. Presbyn. Ch., Westfield, N.J., 1928-30; field sec. Westminster Theol. Sem., Phila., 1932-36, chmn. bd. trustees, 1937-47; mem. faculty Inst. Theology, Princeton Theol. Sem., 1948; asst. to pres. Princeton Theol. Sem., 1967-80; v.p. Trinity U., San Antonio, 1948-50, Beaver Coll., Jenkintown, Pa., 1950-54; pres. Jamestown Coll., 1954-60, Bibl. Sem., N.Y.C., 1960-63, Inst. for Ednl. Planning, N.Y.C., 1964-67; cons. Nat. Capital Union Presbytery Presbyn. Ch. U.S.A., Washington, 1980-81; mem. Presbytery San Diego. Author: A Free World, 1947, The Presbyterian Conflict, 1940, Christianity and American Education, 1949; co-editor, contbr.: A Christian Philosophy of Higher Education, 1957; contbr. articles to religious publs. Princeton fellow U. Berlin, Marburg U., Germany, 1927-78; career (books, articles, interviews, activities, pictures, etc.) selected by Princeton Theol. Sem. to be placed in permanent Archives of the Sem., 1991. Mem. Nassau Club (Princeton), Princeton Club of San Diego. Republican. Home: 5171 Manhasset Dr San Diego CA 92115 *In my retirement since 1982, I have tried my best to help individuals, especially young people, find their niche in life and to act as consultant for educational organizations to enlarge their usefulness.*

RIBBLE, DALE RAYMOND, minister; b. Neenah, Wis., Feb. 21, 1952; s. Ralph Raymond and Ruth Lorraine (Kling) R.; m. Caroline Ann Foat, May 26, 1973; children: Jonathan D., Daniel J., Joshua A., Raychel-Ann R., Elisabethann M. Diploma in pastoral studies, Briercrest Bible Inst., 1973, diploma in Evangelical Tch. Tng., 1973; diploma in Theology, Grace Theol. Sem., Winona Lake, Ind., 1977. Ordained to ministry Ind. Fundamental Chs. Am., 1978. Pastor North Dupo Bible Ch., Dupo, Ill., 1978-87; tchr. Brookes Bible Inst., St. Louis, 1985-87; sr. pastor Newton (Kans.) Bible Ch., 1988—; sec.-treas. Greater St. Louis Regional Ind. Fundamental Chs. Am., 1982-85; sec. Kans. Ch. Extension, Sedgwick, Kans.,a 1990—. Mem. adv. bd. Calvary Bible Coll., Kansas City, Mo., 1989—. Mem. Ind. Fundamental Chs. Am., Brookes Bible Inst. Soc. Home: 109 SE 9th Newton KS 67114-4321 Office: Newton Bible Ch 900 Old Main Newton KS 67114 *Life has a way of placing many obstacles before us and throwing many curves along the way. It is a constant comfort to know that the Lord Jesus Christ goes with us on the path, never changing. He is the sure foundation upon which I am building my life!.*

RIBBLE, TERRY LEE, minister; b. Neenah, Wis., Jan. 8, 1950; s. Ralph Raymond and Ruth Loraine (Kling) R.; m. Madeline Carol Forrer, Sept. 13, 1970; children: Tanya Charline, Shawn Nathan, Lisa Chantal. BTh, Inst. Biblique Bapt. Toulouse, Toulouse, France, 1972; MA in Bibl. Counseling, Grace Grad. Sch., Long Beach, Calif., 1983. Ordained minister Bapt. Ch., 1974. Minister Bethel Bapt. Ch., Topeka, 1972-75, Eglise Bapt. Evangelique, Shawinigan-Sud, Que., Can., 1975-84, Union Bapt. Ch., St. Johnsbury, Vt., 1984—; bd. dirs., prof. Ecole Théologique Bapt. de Québec, 1979—; prof. Séminaire Bapt. de Québec, Montreal, 1976—. Author: La Vie Nouvelle, 1977. Home: RFD 3 Box 272AA Saint Johnsbury VT 05819 Office: Union Bapt Ch 130 Railroad St Saint Johnsbury VT 05819

RIBEIRO, ANTONIO CARDINAL, patriarch of Lisbon (Portugal); b. Gandarela, Basto, Archdiocese of Braga, May 21, 1928; s. Jose and Ana (Goncalves) R. Student Sem. of Braga and Pontifical Univ., Rome. Ordained priest Roman Cath. Ch., 1953, appointed Patriarch of Lisbon, 1971, proclaimed cardinal, 1973; aux. bishop of Braga, 1967, Lisbon, 1969; prof. U. of Lisbon, 1965-67. Author: The Aevum According to Thomas Aquinas, 1958, The Socialization, 1964. Address: Campo de Santana 45, 1198 Lisbon Portugal

RICARD, JOHN H., bishop, educator; b. Baton Rouge, Feb. 29, 1940; s. Maceo and Albanie (St. Amant) R. BA, St. Joseph Sem., 1962, MA, 1968; MS, Tulane U., 1970. Ordained priest Roman Cath. Ch., 1968. Pastor Holy Redeemer Ch., Washington, 1972-75, Holy Comforter Ch., Washington, 1975-84; ordained titular bishop of Rucuma, 1984; aux. bishop Balt., 1984;

assoc. prof. Cath. U. Am., Washington, 1973—; mem. priest's senate Archdiocese of Washington, 1974—, mem. shc. bd., 1976—. Mem. Secretariat of Black Caths. Office: St Francis Xavier Rectory 1501 E Oliver St Baltimore MD 21213

RICARDS, PHILIP CLAYTON, philosophy educator; b. Pasadena, Calif., Oct. 13, 1944; s. John Day and Dorothy (du Fief) R.; m. Marlys Annette Miller, June 23, 1966 (div. Oct. 1980); 1 child, Luke Philip; m. Susan Celeste DeLand, Dec. 2, 1989. BA in Anthropology, U. Calif., Santa Barbara, 1969; MA in Religious Studies, Claremont Grad. Sch., 1980, PhD in Philosophy of Religion, 1987. Cert. community coll. lifetime teaching credential, Calif. Asst. prof. philosophy Pasadena (Calif.) City Coll., 1986—; dir. libr. Ctr. for Process Studies, Claremont, 1979-84. Contbr. articles to profl. jours. Claremont Univ. fellow Claremont Grad. Sch., 1978-79. Mem. Am. Acad. Religion, Am. Philos. Assn., Ctr. for Process Studies. Episcopalian. Office: Pasadena City Coll 1570 E Colorado Blvd Pasadena CA 91106

RICE, H. CRAIG, evangelist; b. Hallettsville, Tex., Nov. 21, 1945; s. H. M. and Emily Ann (Schmidt) R.; m. Bonnie L. Babcock, Mar. 15, 1980; children: Brent, Kristen, Scott. AA, Santa Rosa (Calif.) Jr. Coll., 1965; BS, Bethany Bible Coll., 1972. Pres. Current Evangelism Ministries, Cloverdale, Calif., 1967—; treas. Current Charities, Lodi, Calif., 1989—. Author: The Gospel Afloat, 1990. With USN, 1965-67. Mem. Sons of the Rep. of Tex., First Families of Ohio. Avocations: genealogy, stamp collector. Office: Current Evangelism Ministry 91 Church Ln Cloverdale CA 95425

RICE, JAMES LEONARD, minister; b. Decatur, Ill., Dec. 2, 1944; s. Leonard Baker and Zada Iris (Agers) R.; m. Carol Sue Hall, Sept. 22, 1963; children: Atina Sue Rice Snyder, Trent James, Todd Eric. AA, Hannibal-LaGrange Coll., 1973; BA, Mo. Bapt. Coll., St. Louis, 1977; MDiv, Mid-Am. Bapt. Sem., Memphis, 1983; DMin, Luther Rice Sem., Jacksonville, Fla., 1992. Ordained to ministry So. Bapt. Conv., 1971. Pastor Boody (Ill.) Bapt. Ch., 1971, First Bapt. Ch., Perry, Mo., 1972-73, Pleasant Grove Bapt. Ch., Gorin, Mo., 1973-75, First Bapt. Ch., Pleasant Hill, Ill., 1975-78, Yellow Leaf Bapt. Ch., Oxford, Miss., 1978-83, First Bapt. Ch., Memphis, Mo., 1983-85; pastor North Alton (Ill.) So. Bapt. Ch., 1985—; stewardship, evangelism dir. Pleasant Grove Assn., Memphis, 1984-85; vice moderator Alton-Indsl. Bapt. Assn., 1985-87, moderator, 1987-89, missions com. chmn., 1990—. Fellow Alumni Assn. of Mo. Bapt. Coll., Alumni Assn. Mid-Am. Sem. (state pres. 1989-90), Charles Hadden Spurgeon Soc. of William Jewell Coll. Republican. Home: 2251 State St Alton IL 62002 Office: N Alton So Bapt Ch 2245 State St Alton IL 62002

RICE, JERRY L., lay worker; b. Coeur d'Alene, Idaho, Apr. 12, 1954; s. Ray Francis and Helen Jean (Swink) R.; m. Jill Hardman, July 10, 1976 (div. 1979); 1 children: Jeanna Marie. Student, Bartlesville Wesleyan Coll., Okla., 1986-88. Mem. choir, ch. bd. Clarkston (Wash.) Wesleyan Ch., 1984-86; chaplain adult singles ministry, singles again 1st Wesleyan Ch., Bartlesville, 1989-90; security officer IPC Internat., Bartlesville, Okla., 1990; with Christian Missions to the Communist World, 1991—; active in evangelism, jail, hosp. and visitation ministries. Home: Christians Missions to the Communist World PO Box 443 Bartlesville OK 74003 Office: IPC Internat Inc Washington Park Mall Bartlesville OK 74003 *The two greatest challenges to humanity today are to return to the Godly moral and ethical standards established by our Creator in the beginning and to show genuine love to our fellow man. A commandment from our Creator direct to us.*

RICE, MAX MCGEE, business executive, lay religious administrator; b. Belton, S.C., Aug. 19, 1928; s. Max and Janie (Grier) R.; m. Vivian Barker Rice, Feb. 18, 1956; children: Vivian Ann, Carolyn, Eunice. BA, Furman U., 1949. V.p. Rice Mills., Belton, S.C., 1953-61; pres. Rice Corp., Travelers Rest, S.C., 1961—; pres. Christian Camping Internat., U.S.A. Div., 1990-91; exec. dir. Lay Christian Assocs.; founder, exec. dir. Look-Up Lodge, Christian Retreat Ctr. Author: Commonsense Christianity, 1974, When Can I Say "I Love You?," 1977, Your Rewards in Heaven, 1981, First String, 1987. Served with USAF, 1950-53. Baptist. Home: Look-Up Lodge 100 Old Hwy 11 Travelers Rest SC 29690-9146

RICE, RUBY LEE, lay worker; b. Balt., July 8, 1929; d. Benjamin Oscar and Hallie (Merks) Johnson; m. James Edward Blue, Apr. 18, 1948 (wid. Nov. 1962); children: Saundra, Anthony, Ruby, Diane; m. Herbert Archer Rice, Jan. 28, 1978. Diploma, Balt. Sch. of the Bible, 1968; AA in Law Enforcement, Community Coll. of Balt., 1972; BA in Sociology, Morgan State U., 1976, MS in Edn., 1977. Cert. tchr. social studies, personnel. Tchr. New Unity Bapt. Ch., Balt., supt., 1983-90, coord., 1990—; dir. United Christian Ashram, PennYam, N.Y., 1990—; tchr. Dept. Edn., Balt., 1974—; coord. Ch. Food Bank Distbn., Balt., 1979; dir. children's ministry Keuka (N.Y.) Christian Ashram, 1980-90; coord. church-wide missions prog., New Unity Bapt. Ch., 1990—; mem. Balt. Sch. of the Bible, 1968, sec. 1970-72; mem. Balt. Tchrs. Union, 1975. Charter mem. Threshold Halfway House for Ex-Offenders, Balt., 1966; bd. dirs., pres. Project P.L.A.S.E., Balt., 1975-85. Recipient Svc. award Vol. Action Ctr., Balt., 1975, Balt.'s Best award Mayor and City Coun., Balt., 1978, Meritous Svc. award Project P.L.A.S.E., Balt., 1985, Unsung Heroine award Mayor and Women's Commn., Balt., 1991. Home: PO Box 31646 Baltimore MD 21207 Office: New Unity Baptist Church 2654 Polk St Baltimore MD 21218

RICH, ELAINE SOMMERS, writer; b. Plevna, Ind., Feb. 8, 1926; d. Monroe and Effie (Horner) Sommers; m. Ronald L. Rich, June 14, 1953; children; Jonathan, Andrew, Miriam, Mark. BA, Goshen Coll., 1947; MA, Mich. State U., 1950. Asst. prof. Goshen (Ind.) Coll., 1947-49, 1950-5; instr. Bethel Coll., Newton, Kans., 1953-66; lectr. Internat. Christian U., Tokyo, 1971-78; instr. English U. Findlay, 1986-90; free-lance writer; adviser to internat. students Bluffton Coll., 1979-89; mem. Commn. on Edn. Gen. Conf. Mennonite Ch., 1980—. Author: Breaking Bread Together, 1958, Hannah Elizabeth, 1964, Tomorrow Tomorrow Tomorrow, 1966, Am I This Countryside?, 1981, Mennonite Women: A Story of God's Faithfulness, 1983, Spiritual Elegance: A Biography of Pauline Krehbiel Raid, 1987, Prayers for Everyday, 1990; religion columnist Mennonite Weekly Rev., 1973—; contbr. articles to jours. Democrat. Home: 112 S Spring St Bluffton OH 45817

RICH, JERRY LYNN, minister; b. Robinson, Ill., Dec. 12, 1951; s. George Jr. and Marjorie Ellen (Morehead) R.; m. Linda Jean Kratzer, June 4, 1977; children: Jeremiah, Charis. BA, Greenville Coll., 1974; MDiv, Asbury Theol. Sem., 1977; BS, Okla. Bapt. U., 1981; MBA, Cen. State U., Edmond, Okla., 1985. Ordained to ministry Free Meth. Ch. Pastor Bradbury Free Meth. Ch., Toledo, Ill., 1973-74; writer, researcher dept. info. and stewardship Free Meth. Hdqrs., Winona Lake, Ind., 1974-75; admissions counselor Greenville (Ill.) Coll., 1975-76; pastor Mooresville (Ind.) Free Meth. Ch., 1977-79; communications coordinator Deaconess Hosp., Oklahoma City, 1979-82, dir. materials mgmt., 1983-89; assoc. pastor in adminstrn. First Evangelical Free Ch., Manchester, Mo., 1990—. Author Stewardship series booklets, 4 vols., 1976; editor young teen publs. Light and Life Press, Winona Lake, 1977. Bd. mgrs. YMCA Oklahoma City, 1986-89; sec. Okla. Ann. Conf. Free Meth. Ch., Oklahoma City 1985-90, chmn. bd. adminstrn., 1986-89; trustee Cen. Coll., McPherson, Kans., 1987-90. Purchasing scholarship Nat. Assn. Purchasing Mgmt., 1983. Mem. Kiwanis (pres. Bethany, Okla. chpt. 1987-88). Republican. Lodge: Kiwanis (pres. Bethany, Okla. chpt. 1987-88). Home: 1501 Ploma Dr Manchester MO 63021 Office: First Evang Free Ch 1375 Carman Rd Manchester MO 63021

RICH, THERESE ANN, religious education director; b. Conneaut, Ohio, June 26, 1948; d. Jay R. and Catherine M. (White) R. BS in Edn., Youngstown State U., 1973; MA in Religious Studies, John Carroll U., 1985. Cert. pastoral studies, family ministry, art grades 7-12. Tchr. Diocese of Youngstown, Ohio, 1966-80; religion edn. tchr. Ursuline High Sch., Youngstown, 1980-85; dir. religious edn. St. Charles Borromeo, Youngstown, 1985-91, Our Lady of Perpetual Help, Aurora, Ohio, 1991—; chair prayer and worship com. Ursuline Srs., Youngstown, 1980-90, renovation team Ursuline Sisters, Youngstown, 1985-89; facilitator Loyola Univ., New Orleans, 1985—. Mem. Nat. Assn. Separated and Divorced, Nat. Assn. Ch. Mins., Family Coalition. Roman Catholic. Office: St Charles Religious Edn 7345 Westview Dr Youngstown OH 44512

RICH, THOMAS BLAISE, health facility administrator, deacon; b. Queens, N.Y., Nov. 25, 1951; s. Thomas M. and Louise (Nunziata) R.; m. Anne Rich, Nov. 24, 1977; children: Thomas F., Robert. AS in Nursing, SUNY, Albany, 1975; BS in Nursing, SUNY, 1982; MA in Health Edn., Adelphi U., 1985; MS in Nursing, Herbert H. Lehman Coll., 1987. Critical care supr. Winthrop-U. Hosp., Mineola, N.Y.; dir. nursing Bayview Nursing Home, Island Park, N.Y.; asst. dir. nursing Mercy Hosp., Rockville Centre, N.Y.; assoc. dir. nursing Parkway Hosp., Forest Hills, N.Y. Tchr. religious edn. Corpus Christi Roman Cath. Ch., Mineola, 1977—, organist, choir dir., 1977-88, deacon, 1988—, moderator, 1989-90, chmn. liturgy com., 1990—; canonical counselor tribunal Diocese of Rockville Ctr., 1990—. Mem. N.Y. State Recovery Room Nurse Assn., Am. Heart Assn., Sigma Theta Tau. Home: 394 Bauer Pl Mineola NY 11501 Office: Corpus Christi Roman Cath Ch 155 Garfield Ave Mineola NY 11501

RICHARD, EARL JOSEPH, educator; b. Arnaudville, La., Dec. 19, 1940; s. Lawrence and Wilma (Miller) R.; m. Mary Ann Richter, Dec. 20, 1985; children: Elizabeth, Marie-Anne, Joseph. BA in Philosophy/Lang., Cath. U. Am., 1963; MTh, MA in French Lit., U. Ottawa, Ont., Can., 1967; MA in Ancient Nr. Eastern Lang., Johns Hopkins U., Balt., 1972; PhD in N.T. Studies, Cath. U. Am., 1976. Asst. prof. Marycrest Coll., Davenport, Iowa, 1967-70; assoc. prof. Berea (Ky.) Coll., 1974-79; vis. prof. Boston U., 1979-81; from assoc. prof. to prof. Loyola U., New Orleans, 1981—. Author: Acts 6:1-8:4, 1978, Jesus One and Many, 1988, New Views on Luke and Acts, 1990; contbr. articles to profl. jours. Mem. Cath. Bibl. Assn., Soc. Bibl. Lit. (pres., pres. S.E. region 1990-91), Coll. Theology Soc. Home: 508 Walnut St New Orleans LA 70118 Office: Loyola U 6363 St Charles St New Orleans LA 70118

RICHARDS, BETH ANN, religious association executive; b. Weatherford, Tex., Oct. 18, 1951; d. Ted Taylor and Edna Mildred (Cox) R.; m. Kurt F. Schatz, July 28, 1973 (div. 1983); children: Christian Taylor, Richard Benjamin. Student, Weatherford Coll., 1970-73, Cen. Tex. Coll., 1979-82. Stenographer Parker County Probation Office, Weatherford, 1969-70; stenographer U.S. civil Service, Ft. Wolters, Tex., 1970-73, Illeshiem, Fed. Republic of Germany, 1976-79; stenographer Kelly Services, Tacoma, Washington, 1973-75; clk. sec. Centel of Tex., Killeen, 1979-80, adminstrv. supr., 1980-86; asst. dir. Annuity Bd., then purchasing agt. Support Services Dept. So. Baptist Conv., Dallas, 1986—. Mem. Nat. Assn. Female Execs., In-Plant Printing Mgmt. Assn., Nat. Assn. Printers and Lithographers, Am. Bus. Woman's Assn., Parents Without Ptnrs. 9dir. 1985-86). Baptist. Avocations: music. Home: 1676 Choteau Circle Grapevine TX 76051 Office: So Bapt Conv Annuity Bd 511 N Akard Dallas TX 75201

RICHARDS, CHARLES JACK, minister; b. Mason, Mich., Feb. 13, 1937; s. William Ferguson and Helen Eileen (Palmer) R.; m. Phyllis Ruth Veltman, June 12, 1960; children: Paul, Philip, Carrie Jo. BS, Western Mich. U., 1962; BD, Colgate Rochester Div. Sch., 1966; D of Ministry, Drew Theol. Sch., 1984. Ordained to ministry United Ch. of Christ, 1966. Pastor Reed Corners Federated Ch., Canandaigua, N.Y., 1962-66; pastor First Congl. United Ch. of Christ, Coloma, Mich., 1966-70, Ada, Mich., 1970-85; assoc. conf. min. Mich. Conf. United Ch. of Christ, East Lansing, Mich., 1985—. Chmn. Kent County Community Action Project, Lowell, Mich., 1976-80. Sgt. USMC, 1955-58. Mem. Toastmaster Internat. (cert.), Jaycees (v.p. 1969). Office: United Church of Christ E Area Office 15325 Gratiot Ave Detroit MI 48205

RICHARDS, HERBERT EAST, minister emeritus, commentator; b. Hazleton, Pa., Dec. 30, 1919; s. Herbert E. and Mabel (Vannaucker) R.; m. Lois Marcey, Jan. 1, 1942; children: Herbert Charles, Marcey Lynn, Robyn Lois, Fredrick East, Mark Allen. AB, Dickinson Coll., 1941; BD, Drew U., 1944; MA, Columbia, 1944; DD, Coll. of Ida., 1953; postgrad., Union Theol. Sem., 1941-48, Bucknell U., 1943-44. Accredited news reporter Nat. Assn. Broadcasters. Ordained to ministry Methodist Ch., 1944; pastor in Boiling Springs, Pa., 1937-40, Westchester, Pa., 1940-41, Basking Ridge, N.J., 1941-47; mem. faculty Drew U. and Theol. Sem., 1944-51, asso. prof. homiletics and Christian criticism, chmn. dept., asst. dean, 1947-51; spl. lectr. religion Howard U., 1947; minister 1st Meth. Cathedral, Boise, Idaho, 1951-69, 1st United Meth. Ch., Eugene, Oreg., 1969-78, Tabor Heights United Meth. Ch., Portland, Oreg., 1978-86; minister emeritus Tabor Heights United Meth. Ch., 1986—; weekly radio broadcaster Sta. KBOI, Sta. KIDO, 1941—; weekly TV broadcaster CBS, 1945—, ABC, 1969—, NBC, 1973; pres. Inspiration, Inc., TV Found., 1965—, TV Ecology, 1973; producer Life TV series ABC, 1974-75; also BBC, Eng., Suise Romande, Geneva, Switzerland; Chmn. Idaho bd. ministerial tng. Meth. Conf., 1954-60; chmn. TV, Radio and Film Commn., 1954-62, Oreg. Council Public Broadcasting, 1973; del. Idaho Conf. Meth. Gen. Conf., 1956, Jurisdictional Conf., 1956, World Meth. Council, 1957, 81, World Meth. Conf., 1981; mem. Gen. Conf., 1956-60, Jurisdictional Conf., 1956, 60; meml. chaplain Idaho Supreme Ct., 1960; chaplain Idaho Senate, 1960-68; mem. Task Force on TV and Ch., 1983. Author: In Time of Need, 1986; contbr. articles to religious publs.; composer: oratorios Prophet Unwilling, 1966, Meet Martin Luther, 1968, Dear Jesus Boy, 1973. Mem. Commn. on Centennial Celebration for Idaho, 1962-63; committeeman Boy Scouts Am. Bd.; dirs. Eugene chpt. ARC, 1954-73; trustee Willamette U., Cascade Manor Homes; adv. bd. Medic-Alert Found. Recipient Alumni citation in religious edn. Dickinson Coll., 1948, Golden Plate award Am. Acad. Achievement, Jason Lee Mass Media TV award, 1983; named Clergyman of Year Religious Heritage Am., 1965. Mem. Am. Acad. Achievement (bd. govs. 1967—), Am. Found. Religion and Psychiatry (charter gov.), Greater Boise Ministerial Assn. (pres.), Eugene Ministerial Assn. (pres. 1978), AAUP, Civil Air Patrol (chaplain Idaho wing, lt. col.), Eugene Country Club (Oreg.), Masons (editor Pike's Peak Albert That Is), Shriners, Elks, Rotary (editor Key and Cog, pres. dist. 510 Pioneer club). Home: 10172 SE 99th Dr Portland OR 97266 Office: Tabor Heights United Meth Ch 6161 SE Stark St Portland OR 97215 *When a person presses his face against the window pane of life, he becomes as a child waiting for his father's return; simple, trusting and infinitely wiser. In our present time of growth/conflict, such a face-pressing is essential to get us safely from where we are to where we ought to be.*

RICHARDS, JERRY LEE, religion educator, university administrator; b. Lawrenceville, Ill., Nov. 4, 1939; s. Russell O. and Elvessa A. (Goodman) R.; m. Susan Richards, Apr. 25, 1986; children: Mark, Renee, Teresa, Angela. B.A., Lycoming Coll., 1965; B.D., Evang. Congregational Sch. Theology, 1967; M.Div., Garrett Theol. Sem., 1968; D.Ministry, St. Paul Sch. Theology, 1975. Ordained to ministry Methodist Ch., 1968; pastor chs. Pa., 1960-65, Williamsport, Iowa, 1965-70; mem. faculty Iowa Wesleyan U., Mt Pleasant, 1970-85; prof. religion, dir. responsible social involvement Iowa Wesleyan U., Mt. Pleasant, 1975-85, v.p. for acad. affairs, 1975-82, pres., 1982-85. Pres. Mental Health Inst. Aux., Mt. Pleasant, 1976; dir. spl. gifts U. Wis.-Eau Claire, 1985—. Mem. Phi Alpha Theta. Office: U Wis Office of Devel 213 Schofield Hall Eau Claire WI 54701

RICHARDS, KENT HAROLD, religion educator; b. Midland, Tex., July 6, 1939; s. Eva E. Richards; m. Kristen A. Becker, Dec. 30, 1960; children: Lisken Lynn, Lisanne Elizabeth. BA, Calif. State U., 1961; MTh., Claremont Sch. Theology, 1964; PhD, Claremont Grad. Sch., 1969. Rsch. assoc. Inst. for Antiquities & Christianity, Claremont, Calif., 1967-68; asst. prof. Old Testament U. Dayton (Ohio), 1968-72; prof. Old Testament Iliff Sch. Theology, Denver, 1972—; vis. prof. Sch. of Theology/Grad. Sch., Claremont, 1969; mem. bd. of ordained ministry UMC, Rocky Mt. Conf., Denver, 1976-82, bd. of diaconal ministry, 1976-78. Editor: Biblical Scholarship in North America (annual publ.), 16 vols., 1981—, , Writings in the Ancient World. Chmn. Colo. Gov.'s award in Edn. Com., Denver, 1989-91. Rsch. grantee NEH, 1985-91, Lilly Found., 1985-86. Mem. Internat. Meeting Program (chair 1973—), Cath. Bibl. Assn. (program com. 1976-80), Soc. Bibl. Lit. (exec. sec. 1981-87), Am. Coun. Learned Socs. (coun. sec. 1981-87). Office: Iliff Sch of Theology 2201 S University Blvd Denver CO 80210

RICHARDS, PERRY SAMUEL, minister; b. Columbus, Ohio, May 20, 1953; s. Samuel Gelfer and Katheryn Jane (Brandon) R.; m. Lacinda Ann Whipple, Nov. 10, 1984. BA in History, Otterbeing Coll., Westerville, Ohio, 1976; MDiv, Christian Theol. Sem., Indpls., 1982, postgrad., 1989—. Ordained to ministry Christian Ch. (Disciples of Christ) as elder, 1983; ordained to ministry United Meth. Ch. as deacon, 1989, as elder, 1991. Pastor Orange (Ind.) Christian Ch., 1982-86, Columbia & Orange United Meth. Chs., Connersville, 1986-88, Laurel and Metamora United Meth. Chs., Laurel, Ind., 1988-90, Moores Hill & Mt. Sinai United Meth. Chs., Ind., 1990—; pres. Religion Coun., Otterbein Coll., Westerville, Ohio, 1975-76; vice moderator Area 10, Disciples of Christ, Fayette and Rush counties, Ind., 1987; mem. Helping Hands, Moores Hill, Ind., 1990—, pres., 1991. Pres. Ret. Sr. Citizens Vol. Program, Fayette County, 1987; bd. dirs. Town Bd. of Laurel, Ind., 1989-90, John Conner Players, Connersville, Ind., 1987. Luth. scholar grante, 1973, 74, 75. Home and Office: PO Box 337 Moores Hill IN 47032 *I believe in the tradition of John Wesley, that the world is our parish. God has given humanity the tool of education to minister to the world. The proper use of it ensures a dignified life style lived and the road to God through the redemption of the cross.*

RICHARDS, STEPHENS, cantor; b. N.Y.C., May 9, 1935; s. Sidney Solomon and Edna (Jacobs) R.; m. Barbara Winter, Jan. 15, 1965 (div. Jan. 1985); children: Paul Sidney, Jay Philip, William Michael; m. Marjorie Diane Morse, June 9, 1985. BA in Music, NYU, 1957; MA in Music Composition, Columbia U., 1960; B. Sacred Music, Hebrew Union Coll., 1969. Cantor Temple B'rith Kodesh, Rochester, N.Y., 1969-71, Indpls. Hebrew Congregation, 1971-77; editor Transcontinental Music of Union Am. Hebrew Congregations, N.Y.C., 1977-80; faculty Hebrew Union Coll., N.Y.C., 1977-80; cantor Temple Beth Israel, Phoenix, 1980-91, Temple Kol Ami, Phoenix, 1991—; mem. Joint Commn. on Synagogue Music, 1986—; chmn. Guild of Temple Musicians, 1971-73, 77-78; prin. Reform Temple, Suffern, N.Y., 1979-80. Composer (opera) Ballad of Ruth, 1959. Bd. dirs. ACLU, Phoenix, 1990—. Mem. ASCAP, Am. Conf. Cantors (v.p. 1976-80, exec. bd. 1971-74, 76-80, 91—). Home: 4602 N Arcadia Dr Phoenix AZ 85018 Office: Temple Kol Ami 10210 N 32d St Phoenix AZ 85028

RICHARDS, STEVEN PAUL, clergyman; b. Seattle, May 17, 1947; s. Donald Safar Richards and Elsa (Hageman) Pelly; m. Carolyn Sue Hibbard, Feb. 17, 1973; children: Sarah, Jeffrey, Daniel. Bible diploma, Spokane (Wash.) Bible Coll., 1976; BA, Whitworth Coll., 1982. Ordained to ministry Free Meth. Ch., 1982. Assoc. pastor 1st Evang. Free Ch., Spokane, 1974-78; sr. pastor Queen Ave. Free Meth. Ch., Spokane, 1979-84; program dir. World Relief, Seattle, 1984-85; missions pastor Overlake Christian Ch., Kirkland, Wash., 1985—; del. Lausanne II, Manila, 1989. Home: 14815 113 Ave NE Kirkland WA 98034 Office: Overlake Christian Ch 9051 132 Ave NE Kirkland WA 98033

RICHARDSON, AVIS JUNE, minister; b. Burlington, Colo., June 20, 1931; d. Elvis Guy Foley and Sarah Margaret (Yale) Smith; m. David W. Richardson, May 19, 1949; children: Angelia J. Richardson Pfeifer, John W., Alisa J. Richardson Hoffman. AA, McKendree Coll. Ordained deacon United Meth. Ch., 1971. Minister United Meth. Ch., Beckemeyer, Ill., 1968-71, Hamburg, Ill., 1971-73, Saint Jacob, Ill., 1973-77, Waltonville, Ill., 1977-78, Patoka, Ill., 1978-85, 1985-86, Staunton, 1985-87. Home: 513 W Main Staunton IL 62088

RICHARDSON, CHARLES RAYMOND, pastor; b. Pittsburg, Tex., Sept. 12, 1934; s. Earl Roscoe and Dora Mae (Keeling) R.; m. Betty Ruth Birdsong, Aug. 14, 1959; children: Christi, David, Mark. BA, Baylor U., 1957; BD, Southwestern Bapt. Theol. Sem., 1961. Ordained to ministry So. Bapt. Conv. Ch., 1954. Pastor 1st Bapt. Ch., Canton, Tex., 1966—; moderator Van Zandt Bapt. Assn., Van Zandt County, Tex., 1978-80; mem. exec. bd. Bapt. Gen. Conv. Tex., Dallas, 1968-77. Mem. Salvaion Army Svc. Unit, Pittsburg, 1960-65, Canton, 1966-70. Mem. Lions. Office: 1st Bapt Ch 303 S Athens St Canton TX 75103

RICHARDSON, C(LYTA) FAITH, church association executive; b. Tacoma, Dec. 10, 1915; d. James Moore and Allie Blanche (Marshall) Simpson; m. Henry Neil Richardson, Apr. 9, 1939 (dec. Dec. 1988); children: Joan Christine Richardson Wrenn, Marsha Ruth, Marla Faith. Student, U. Puget Sound, Tacoma, 1935-39, Syracuse U., 1948-52; LHD (hon.), Columbia Coll., S.C., 1985. Sec. to Bishop James K. Mathews, United Meth. Ch., Boston and Washington, 1967-80, Albany, 1990-92, sec. northeastern jurisdictional commn. archives and history, 1972-76, adminstrv. asst. Coun. of Bishops, 1980-84, mem. gen. com of archives and history, Madison, N.J., 1984-88, sec. Gen. Conf., United Meth. Ch., 1984-88; adminstr. Commn. on Pan-Meth. Coop., 1978-91; sec. adv. bd. Anna Howard Shaw Ctr., 1986—, mem. Women's Oral History Project, 1986—; treas. Hist. Soc. United Meth. Ch., 1989—. Editor: From Ivied Walls, 1989; translator: Pettinato's Ebla: A New Look at History, 1991; chair editorial com. The Book of Discipline, United Meth. Ch., 1980, 84; contbr. articles to profl. jours. Chmn. Commn. on Archives and History, So. New Eng. Conf., 1988—, sec. Coun. on Ministries, 1989—. Recipient Bean Pot award Boston U. Sch. Theology, Anna Howard Shaw Disting. Woman award, 1990. Mem. World Meth. Coun. (exec. com. 1986-91), World Meth. Hist. Soc. (editor Hist. Bull. 1991—), New Eng. Meth. Hist. Soc. (pres. 1988-90). Avocations: translating, research. Home: 168 Mt Vernon St Newtonville MA 02160

RICHARDSON, DOROTHY HOOD, minister; b. Clayton, N.C., Aug. 2, 1943; d. Gillis Jr. and Malissie (Sanders) Hood; m. James Richardson, Aug. 19, 1961; children: Linda Faye, Beverly Ann, Geraldine, Debra. BTh, United Christian Coll., 1983. Ordained to ministry African Meth. Episcopal Ch. as elder, 1983. Pastor St. Peter African Meth. Episcopal Ch., Warsaw, N.C., 1984-86, St. Paul African Meth. Episcopal Ch., Kenly, N.C., 1986—, Lee's Chapel African Meth. Episcopal Ch., Selma, N.C., 1986—. Recipient plaque Natvar, Inc., Clayton, 1982, pin Natvar, Inc., 1987, cert. recognition Missionary Soc., Smithfield, N.C., 1988. Mem. Clayton Ministerial Alliance (v.p. 1989—), Kenly Area Minister (exec. bd. 1987—), Johnston County Ministerial Alliance, Order Ea. Star (chaplain 1984—). Democrat. Build Fellowship Hall at St. Paul Ch., Kenly, N.C., 1991. Home: 2221 Peele Rd Clayton NC 27520

RICHARDSON, EDWARD ALLEN, minister; b. Woodlawn, Va., June 9, 1936; s. Claude Marvin and Mary Alice (Alderman) R.; m. Lillian Antionette Fogus, Oct. 15, 1957; children: Stanley (dec.), Rachel, Karen. BS, Holmes Coll. of the Bible, Greenville, S.C., 1956. Ordained to ministry Pentecostal Holiness Ch., 1957. Circuit pastor Greenbrier County, White Sulpher Springs, W.Va., 1956-61; pastor Bluefield (W.Va.) Pentecostal Holiness Ch., 1961-1967, Flomaton (Ala.) Pentecostal Holiness Ch., 1967-70, Lincoln Ave. Pentecostal Holiness Ch., Staunton, Va., 1982-90, Wytheville (Va.) Pentecostal Holiness Ch., 1970-82, 90—; dist. coord. Va. Conf. Pentecostal Holiness Ch, Dublin, 1972-90; officer Wythe County Ministerial Assn., Wytheville, 1974-82; chaplain Wythe County Community Hosp., Wytheville, 1974-82; radio speaker, Pentecost Today, 1974-82; treas., pres. Shenandoah Valley Pentecostal Fellowship, Staunton, 1982-90; bd. dirs. Staunton Ministerial Assn., 1986-90, Valley Mission, Staunton, 1990; writer newspaper column Pastor's Paragraph, 1990. Vol. Flomaton Fire Dept., 1967-70. Recipient Outstanding Svc. award, Wythe County Ministerial Assn., 1982, Shenandoah Valley Pentecostal Fellowship, Staunton, 1990. Office: Pentecostal Holiness Ch W Ridge Rd PO Box 527 Wytheville VA 24382 *What we do for ourselves is soon forgotten. What we do for others is remembered for a lifetime. What we do for God is remembered forever.*

RICHARDSON, GARY JOE, minister; b. Joplin, Mo., Oct. 14, 1945; s. Jimmy Joe and Norma Jean (Smith) R.; m. Ruthie Cheryl Hillhouse, Jan. 29, 1966; children: Melinda Snelson, Michael Richardson, Marci, Mark. BGen. Studies, Mo. So. State Coll., 1975; MMin, Bethany Theol. Sem., Dothan, Ala., 1984, DMin, 1985. Ordained to ministry So. Bapt. Conv., 1967. Pastor Northside Bapt. Ch., DeQuency, La., 1978-82; pastor First Bapt. Ch., Newkirk, Okla., 1982-85, Chelsea, Okla., 1985-89; pastor Va. Ave. Bapt. Ch., Bartlesville, Okla., 1989—; preacher Spanish Evang. Crusade, 1983. With USAF, 1965-68. Office: Va Ave Bapt Ch 132 S Virginia Ave Bartlesville OK 74003 *In this up and down, around and around world, I am thankful I serve the God who is always the same. Only He can give life stability.*

RICHARDSON, G(EORGE) PETER, religion educator; b. Toronto, Ont., Can., Jan. 6, 1935; s. George Grainger and Margaret Louise (Everett) R.; m. Nancy Jean Cameron, Dec. 22, 1959; children—Mary Rebekah, Susan Elizabeth, Jonathan Peter, Ruth Anne. B.Arch., U. Toronto, 1957; B.Div., Knox Coll., 1962; Ph.D., Cambridge U., 1965. Design architect John B. Parkin & Assocs., Don Mills, Ont., Can., 1957-59; campus minister Knox Ch., Toronto, 1965-69; asst. prof., assoc. prof., asst. to academic v.p. Loyola

Coll., Montreal, Que., 1969-74; assoc. prof., chmn. humanities dept. Scarborough Coll., U. Toronto, 1974-77, prof. religion, 1977—, prin. Univ. Coll., 1977-89; v.p. Can. Corp. for Studies in Religion. Author: Israel in the Apostolic Church, 1969, Paul's Ethic of Freedom, 1979; co-author: Law in Religious Communities in the Roman Period, 1991; editor: From Jesus to Paul, 1984, Anti-Judaism in Early Christianity, 1986; mng. editor Studies in Religion/Sciences Religieuses; assoc. editor Wilfrid Laurier U. Press. Chmn. Joint Practice Bd. Architects and Engrs., 1984—. Mem. Can. Soc. Bibl. Studies (pres. 1984-85), Inst. Bibl. Research, Soc. Bibl. Lit., Studiorum Novi Testamenti Societas. Avocations: antiques; carpentry; photography. Home: 42 St Andrews Gardens, Toronto, ON Canada M4W 2E1 Office: U Toronto, 15 Kings College Cir, Toronto, ON Canada M5S 1A1

RICHARDSON, JAMES CLAUDE, minister; b. Stuart, Va., Jan. 20, 1946; s. Robert Lee and Carolyn Annie (Haynes) R.; m. Carol Anne Quattlebaum, Aug. 1, 1970; children: Marcus David, Emily Haynes. B.M., Mars Hill Coll., 1968; M.C.M., So. Bapt. Theol. Sem., Louisville, 1971. Ordained to ministry Bapt. Ch., 1978. Assoc. minister, organist, choirmaster First Bapt. Ch., Savannah, Ga., 1971—; organist for various local, state and nat. meetings So. Bapt. Conv. Contbr. articles and book rev. in ch. music publs. Mem. Am. Guild Organists, Choristers' Guild, Am. Choral Dir.'s Assn., So. Bapt. Ch. Music Conf., Hymn Soc. North Am. Office: First Bapt Ch 223 Bull St Savannah GA 31412-9551

RICHARDSON, JAMES TROY, sociology educator, consultant; b. Charleston, S.C., Aug. 25, 1941; s. Lylse Vega and Vera Veda (King) R.; m. Sept. 2, 1966; 1 child, Tamatha Lea. BA in Sociology, Tex. Tech U., 1964, MA in Sociology, 1965; PhD in Sociology, Wash. State U., Pullman, 1968; JD, Old Coll. Law Sch., 1986. Bar: Nev. 1986. Instr. Tex. Tech U., Lubbock, 1965-66; NIMH fellow Wash. State U., 1966-68; asst. prof. sociology U. Nev., Reno, 1968-71, assoc. prof. sociology, 1971-76, prof. sociology, 1976-88, prof. sociology and jud. studies, 1988—, dir. Master of Jud. Studies Degree Program; v.p. Market Systems Rsch., Reno, 1981—; pres. Litigation Techs., Reno, 1986—; prof. U. Nev.-Reno Found., 1989; visitor London Sch. Econs., 1974-75. Author: Conversions Careers, Organized Miracles, The Brainwashing/Deprogramming Controversy, Money and Power in the New Religions, The Satanism Scare; contbr. numerous articles to profl. jours. Chair Washoe County Dems., 1976-78, State Group Ins. Com., Nev., 1984-90. Fulbright fellow The Netherlands, 1981. Mem. ABA, Nev. Bar Assn., Assn. for Sociology of Religion (pres. 1985-86), Am. Sociol. Assn., Soc. for Sci. Study of Religion, Internat. Soc. for Sociology of Religion (coun. mem. 1989—). Avocations: travel, fishing. Home: 2075 Marlette Ave Reno NV 89503 Office: U Nev Dept of Sociology Reno NV 89557

RICHARDSON, JENNIFER ROBERTS, religious administrator; b. Florence, Ala., Dec. 5, 1960; d. Clyde Harrison and Martha Penney (Long) Roberts; m. John Dowland Richardson, May 12, 1984. BS in Bus., U. Ala., 1983. Lic. securities dealer Nat. Assn. Securities Dealers. Mktg. rep. Cen. Bank of the South, Birmingham, Ala., 1983-85, jr. analyst, 1985-86, asset/liability officer, 1986-88, liability trader, 1988; lay missionary Amistad, Cochabamba, Bolivia, 1988-89; exec. dir. St. Mary's Episcopal Ctr., Inc., Sewanee, Tenn., 1990—. Vol. Cathedral of the Advent, Birmingham, 1983-88. Mem. Cochabamba Women's Club (sec. 1988-89). Republican. Episcopalian. Avocations: catering, reading, boating, entertaining.

RICHARDSON, JOHN JACOB, minister; b. Poteau, Okla., Feb. 24, 1940; s. John Spurgeon and Della Black R.; m. L. Jane White, Aug. 10, 1963; children: Julie Beth, John Clinton. MusB, Okla. Bapt. U., 1963; B in Ch. Music, Southwestern Bapt. Theol. Sem., Ft. Worth, 1968. Lic. to ministry Bapt. Ch., 1958. Minister of music First Bapt. Ch., Pauls Valley, Okla., 1966-68, West Memphis, Ark., 1968-74; minister of music East Hill Bapt. Ch., Tallahassee, 1974—; dist. dir. Ark. Bapt. Conv., West Memphis, 1968-74; instr. adult leaders Ch. Music Conf., Ridgecrest, N.C., 1984; regional dir. Fla. Bapt. Singing Men, 1985—; dir. master ringers handbell choir Fla. Music and Ministry Clinic, ch. music dept. Fla. Bapt. State Conv., 1985-86; instr. Young Musicians Music Conf., Shocco Springs, Ala., 1989; choral adjudicator and clinician state sponsored choral festivals, Ark., Fla., Ga.; dir. East Hill Bells; handbell clinician Fla. Handbell Festival. Mem. Fla. Bapt. Ch. Music Conf. (pres. 1986-87), So. Bapt. Ch. Music Conf. Democrat. Avocations: woodworking, photography. Home: 1523 Coombs Dr Tallahassee FL 32308 Office: East Hill Bapt Ch 912 Miccosukee Rd Tallahassee FL 32308-6499

RICHARDSON, JOHN MACLAREN, JR., Christian school administrator; b. Plainfield, N.J., Nov. 6, 1942; s. John MacLaren and Lucy Lenox (Baker) R.; m. Sharon Rae Kellogg, June 20, 1964; children: Elizabeth R. Updike, John M. III, James Kellogg. AA, George Washington U., 1965, BA, 1969; postgrad., Grace Theol. Sem., 1990—. Bus. mgr. ComMission, Inc., Harrisonburg, Va., 1983-84; prin. The Norman A. Whitesel Christian Sch., Mt. Crawford, Va., 1988-90; prin., founding mem. Blue Ridge Christian Sch., Bridgewater, Va., 1990—; bd. dirs. Trinity Christian Sch., Mt. Crawford, Va., 1985-88. Elder Grace Covenant Ch., Harrisonburg, 1988—. Lt. comdr. USNR, 1962-83. Decorated Nat. Def. medal, USN, 1964, Navy Good Conduct medal, USN, 1966, Armed Forces Reserve medal, USN, 1976. Mem. Internat. Fellowship Christian Sch. Adminstrs., Christian Mgmt. Assn., Naval Reserve Assn., Reserve Officers Assn., Am. Legion. Republican. Home: 551 Presidential Cir Penn Laird VA 22846 Office: Blue Ridge Christian Sch 100 Dinkel Ave PO Box 207 Bridgewater VA 22812 *I am convinced that an education which is not based upon the unchanging truth of the Holy Bible is, at best, irrelevant and, at worst, entirely misleading and without legitimate foundation.*

RICHARDSON, JOSEPH JOHN, SR., minister, realtor; b. La Grange, Ill., Feb. 6, 1930; s. Ansel and Pauline (Silvan) R.; m. Rita L. Sharp, Mar. 14, 1953; children: Cheryl Lynn, Joseph John Jr., Denise Michelle, Leonard Michael, Anthony Lawrence, Kenneth Scott. BA, Elmhurst Coll., 1989; MDiv, No. Bapt. Theo. Sem., Lombard, Ill., 1989; cert. graduation, Moody Bible Inst., 1979. Licensed realtor, Ill. Supr. Commonwealth Edison, Maywood, Ill., 1953-85; realtor Donora Realty Co., Maywood, 1965—; pastor St. James Community Bapt. Ch., Broadview, Ill., 1960—; advisor Black Student Union, Elmhurst Coll., Ill., 1988—, mem. Campus Ministry, 1989—, asst. chaplain, 1989—, mem. chaplain adv. com., 1989—. Mem. E.W. Corridor Assn., Downers Grove, Ill., 1990, Ill. Com. on Black Concerns in Higher Edn., U. Chgo., 1990; mem. West Suburban Consortium of Multi-cultural Coll. Adminstrs., 1990, spl. advisor to minority students, 1991; deacon African Meth. Episcopal Ch., 1965, elder, 1967; spl. adviser to minority student Elm Hurst Coll. With U.S. Army, 1948-52, Korea. Mem. Nat. Assn. Realtors, Ill. Assn. Realtors, W. Suburban Bd. Realtors, VFW (life mem.), Am. Legion (life), Alpha Phi Alpha (life, parliamentarian, chpt. advisor, recipient profl. achievement award 1990), Masons. Avocations: preaching, reading, football team chaplain Elmhurst Coll. Office: St James Community Bapt Ch PO Box 6607 Broadview IL 60153

RICHARDSON, MARIANNE BRIGGS, religious organization administrator; b. Wilkes-Barre, Pa., Sept. 14, 1942; d. Sterling Kenneth and Mildred (Helfrich) Briggs; m. James Albert Richardson, Dec. 28, 1963; children: Christine, Paula, Kenneth, Kate, Scott. BS in English and history, Fla. State U., 1963. Vol. in various parishes, 1963-82; tchr. English Pensacola (Fla.) Cath. High Sch., 1963-66; columnist So. Cross newspaper, 1970-72; dir. religious edn. Holy Spirit Cath. Ch., Tuscaloosa, Ala., 1982-84; youth min. St. Bede's Cath. Ch., Montgomery, Ala., 1984-86; dir. office of youth ministry Diocese of Birmingham, Ala., 1987—. Co-author: Competency-Based Standards for the Youth Ministry Coordinator, 1990. Mem. NCCJ (adv. bd. Birmingham chpt. 1988—), Nat. Fedn. Cath. Youth Ministry (com. 1988—). Office: Diocese of Birmingham 8131 4th Ave S Birmingham AL 35206 *In a world where personal, professional and diplomatic relationships fail on a daily basis, each of us must use all our energies to create a climate of open communication and genuine caring in all of our environs; we truly must be a beacon, the light of the world, a God-bearer to all whom we meet.*

RICHARDSON, RUSSELL MCCLELLAN, minister; b. Nashville, Aug. 22, 1952; s. Haskell D. and Dorothy Ava (Shipman) R.; m. Gayle Ann Richardson, May 11, 1973; children: Keith McClellan, Nathan Sean, Kevin Aaron Haskell. BA, Belmont Coll., 1974; MDiv, So. Bapt. Theol. Sem., 1977. Ordained to ministry So. Bapt. Convention Ch. Minister of music Brookside Bapt. Ch., Nashville, 1973-74; minister of music and youth Pleasant Ridge Bapt. Ch., Charlestown, Ind., 1975-79, Calvary Bapt. Ch., Clinton, Iowa, 1980-84; pastor Grace Bapt. Ch., Murfreesboro, Tenn., 1985—. Contbr. poetry to Tenn.-Ky. Soc. of Poets Anthology, 1977. Mem. Concord Bapt. Assn. (dir. sem. extension program 1987—), Phi Mu Alpha Synfonia. Office: Grace Bapt Ch 610 Dill Ln Murfreesboro TN 37130

RICHE, BEAU AARON, lay worker, office manager; b. Harlan, Iowa, Feb. 18, 1967; s. Bret Riley and Pamela Sue (Andersen) R. Youth worker Concord (Calif.) Valley Christian Ch., 1986-89; counselor South Valley Christian Ch., San Jose, Calif., 1989—, dir. jr. high activity, 1990—; office mgr. Aptronix, Inc., Santa Clara, Calif., 1990—. Home: 200 Hollis Ave #31 Campbell CA 95008

RICHERSON, JOHN HENRY, deacon, music minister; b. Hornsby, Tenn., Oct. 19, 1926; s. Alexander A. and Lillie Pearl (Burnett) R.; m. Martha Lorene Robley, Oct. 19, 1947; children: Thomas Anthony, Paul Randell, James Robley. Student music, various schs., Tenn., 1940-70. Ordained deacon So. Bapt. Ch., 1962. Tng. union dir. 1st Bapt. Ch., Rutherford, Tenn., 1958-62, 63-73, Sunday sch. supt., 1962-63; deacon 1st Bapt. ch., Rutherford, Tenn., 1962—, min. of music, 1966—; maintenance mgr. Five-M Apparel Mfg. Inc., Trenton, Tenn., 1986—. Composer gospel songs He Is My Savior, 1984, I'll Sing in Gloryland, 1985, I Found Jesus, 1985. Pres. PTA, Rutherford, 1960-63; mem. bd. Edn., Rutherford, 1968-69, chmn., 1969-72. Mem. Tenn. Credit Union League (chpt. pres. 1984-91, vice chmn., bd. dirs. 1985-91, Svc. award 1991). Home: PO Box 33 531 W Knox St Rutherford TN 38369-0033

RICHERSON, STEPHEN WAYNE, minister; b. Jackson, Tenn., Sept. 15, 1951; s. Claude Burnette and Mary Cathryn (Greathouse) R.; m. Rebecca Sue Darnell, Sept. 19, 1970; children: Mary Rebecca, Susan Virginia, James Stephen. BSBA, U. Richmond, 1973; MDiv, Southeastern Bapt. Theol. Sem., Wake Forest, N.C., 1979, DMin, 1984. Ordained to ministry Bapt. Ch., 1978. Minister music Hampton (Va.) Roads Bapt. Ch., 1974-76; assoc. minister music and youth Rolesville (N.C.) Bapt. Ch., 1976-78; minister Lea Bethel Bapt. Ch., Prospect Hill, N.C., 1978-80, Menchville Bapt. Ch., Newport News, Va., 1980-87, Westover Bapt. Ch., Richmond, Va., 1987—; br. mgr. Old Point Nat. Bank, Hampton, Va., 1973-76; trustee Va. Bapt. Children's Home, Salem, 1984-85, 87—, v.p., 1990-91, pres. 1991—; bd. dirs. Va. Bapt. Gen. Bd., Richmond, 1986-87; faculty Boyce Bible Sch. So. Bapt. Sem., Louisville, 1984-89. Author: Developing a Ministry Dream, 1984. Bd. dirs., swim and dive dir. Shenandoah Community Assn., Richmond, 1990—; soccer coach Reams Rd. Athletic Assn., Richmond, 1988-89; mem. PTA Providence Mid. Sch., Richmond, 1989—, PTA Reams Rd. Elem. Sch., Richmond, 1987—. Mem. Richmond Bapt. Ministers Conf., Peninsula Bapt. Ministers Conf. (v.p. 1980-87, moderator 1985-86, Pastor of Yr. 1986), Ministerial Support Group Richmond, Chaplain Assn. Chippenham Med. Ctr. Richmond. Office: Westover Bapt Ch PO Box 13048 Richmond VA 23225 *Of all the opportunities and experiences of life that demand our attention and involvement, I have discovered that time spent for oneself and one's family is the best investment I can make towards a fulfilling life in the ministry.*

RICHES, LEONARD W., bishop. Bishop Ref. Episcopal Ch., Pipersville, Pa. Office: Ref Episcopal Ch Smithown Rd RD 1 Box 501 Pipersville PA 18947*

RICHES, PIERRE PIETRO, priest, educator; b. Alexandria, Egypt, Nov. 30, 1927. Student, Victoria Coll., Alexandria, 1946; MA, Cambridge (Eng.) U., 1949; STD, Lateran U., Rome, 1959. Ordained priest Roman Cath. Ch., 1959. Pastor Diocese of Porto-S. Rufina, Rome, 1959-64, 78-84, canon, 1960—; theologian 2d Vatican Coun., Rome, 1963-65; conclavist papal election, Rome, 1963; vis. prof. Loyola U. Rome Campus, 1960-78, U. Santa Clara (Calif.), 1964-65, Coll. of Holy Cross, Worcester, Mass., 1968, Pastoral Inst. East Africa, Kampala, Uganda, 1970-71, Major Sem., Karachi, Pakistan, 1975, U. Calif., San Diego, 1987, 90; del. Afro-Europe Meeting on Culture, Brazzaville, Congo, 1972, Perspectives of Culture, Coun. of Europe, France, 1973; Fulbright vis. scholar, Chgo., 1964. Author: Note di Catechismo per ignoranti colti, 1982 (transl. into English as Back to Basics 1984), La leggerezza della Croce, 1991. Home: Il Brolo, Gargnano, 25084 Brescia Italy Office: Corso Vittorio Emanuele 282, 00186 Rome Italy

RICHEY, EVERETT ELDON, religion educator; b. Claremont, Ill., Nov. 1, 1923; s. Hugh Arthur and Elosia Emma (Longnecker) R.; m. Mary Elizabeth Reynolds, Apr. 9, 1944; children: Eldon Arthur, Clive Everett, Loretta Arlene Fincher, Charles Estel. ThB, Anderson U., 1946; MDiv, Sch. Theology, Anderson, Ind., 1956; ThD, Iliff Sch. of Theology, Denver, 1960. Pastor Ch. of God, Bremen, Ind., 1946-47, Laurel, Miss., 1947-48; pastor First Ch. of God, Fordyce, Ark., 1948-52; prof. Arlington Coll., Long Beach, Calif., 1961-68; pastor Cherry Ave. Ch. of God, Long Beach, 1964-68; prof. Azusa Pacific U., Azusa, Calif., 1968—; mem. Greater L.A. Sunday Sch. Assn., 1968—; mem., chmn. Commn. on Christian Higher Edn./Ch. of God, 1982—; pres. Ch. Growth Investors, Inc., 1981—. Author: ednl. manual Church Periodical--Curriculum, 1971-83. Mem. Nat. Assn. Profs. Christian Edn., Assn. Professor and Researchers of Religious Edn., Gen. Assembly (mins. of the Ch. of God). Republican. Avocation: gardening. Home: 413 N Valencia Glendora CA 91740 Office: Grad Sch of Theology Azusa Pacific U 901 E Alosta Azusa CA 91702

RICHMOND, JOANNE SUE, minister; b. Rockford, Ill., Sept. 1, 1958; d. Wendell Earl and Jean Fola (Meyer) R. BA, CArthage Coll., 1980; MDiv with honors, Pacific Luth. Theol. Sem., 1985. Ordained to ministry Evang. Luth. Ch. Am., 1986. Teaching asst. in religion Carthage Coll., Kenosha, Wis., 1978-80; intern pastor Calif. Luth. U., Thousand Oaks, Calif., 1983-84; assoc. pastor Westby (Wis.)-Coon Prairie and Vang Chs., 1986—; mem. camp staff Bethel Horizons, Dodgeville, Wis., 1978-86; dean South Cluster, LaCrosse Area Synod Evang. Luth. Ch. Am., Westby, 1990—, del. nat. assembly, 1991, mem. profl. candidacy com., LaCrosse, Wis., 1987—. Author ednl. curriculum materials; contbr. essays to Handbook of American Women's History, 1990. Mem. adv. coun. Norseland Nursing Home, Westby, 1987—; facilitator grief group Vernon Meml. Hospice, Viroqua, Wis., 1988—. Mem. Am. Camping Assn., World Wildlife Fund.

RICHTER, JAMES EDWARD, clergyman; b. Cullman, Ala., Oct. 27, 1949; s. Franklin Kiem and Jane Marcelle (South) R.; m. Linda Louise Leary, Dec. 15, 1973; children: David James, Karen Ruth. Student, George C. Wallace Jr. Coll., 1968-69; BCE, Auburn U., 1972, MS, 1974; MDiv, Reformed Theol. Sem., 1982. Ordained to ministry Presbyn. Ch. in Am., 1982. Pastor Meadow Creek Presbyn. Ch., Greeneville, Tenn., 1982-89; sr. pastor First Presbyn. Ch., Biloxi, Miss., 1989—. Dir. Abortion Alternative Christian Svcs., Johnson City, Tenn., 1987-89. Mem. Rotary (bd. dirs. Biloxi 1991). Home: 1337 Father Ryan Ave Biloxi MS 39530 Office: First Presbyn Ch 1340 Beach Blvd Biloxi MS 39530

RICHTER, ROBERT LAWRENCE, minister; b. Memphis, Oct. 20, 1934; s. Edwin Michael and Hettie Elizabeth (Meek) R.; m. Suzanne Doretha Landry, Aug. 14, 1960; children: Rachael, Christian, Ingrid. BA, Concordia Seminary, 1957; MDiv, Concordia Sem., 1972; D of Ministry, Wartburg Sem., 1981. Ordained to ministry Luth. Ch., 1960. Asst. pastor Gethsemane Luth. Ch., St. Paul, 1960-62; pastor Holy Cross Luth. Ch., Tuscaloosa, Ala., 1962-64, Grace Luth. Ch., Pensacola, Fla., 1967-75; chief, chaplain service VA Hosp., Madison, Wis., 1975—. Author: The Last Enemy, 1983, also articles. Served with USN, 1964-67, to lt. comdr. Res. Recipient St. Martin of Tours Medal Mo. Synod Luth. Ch. Am., 1983. Republican. Lutheran. Avocations: skiing, biking. Home: 5866 Roanoke Dr Madison WI 53719 Office: VA Hosp 2500 Overlook Terr Madison WI 53705

RICKETT, GENE, author, lay worker; b. Tinsley, Ky., Dec. 6, 1931; s. Elmer Oscar and Mary Ellen (Slusher) R.; m. Virginia May Johnson, Jan. 27, 1971. Student pub. schs., Washington. Pres. Poets for Christ, Seymour, Ind., 1965—. Author: Poems of Inspiration, 1964, Poetic Post Cards, 1972. With USAF, 1950-70. Mem. Masons. Address: 224 Tennessee Circle Seymour TN 37865

RICKETTS, MAC LINSCOTT, religion educator; b. St. Petersburg, Fla., Dec. 25, 1930; s. Ray Bashford and Fauna Lucille (Linscott) R.; m. Janis L. Harrington, Feb. 10, 1952; children: Scott, Martin, Ruth Lynn. AA, St. Petersburg Coll., 1950; AB, U. Fla., 1952; MDiv, Emory U., 1954; MA, PhD, U. Chgo., 1964. Pastor Meth. Ch., Ft. Lauderdale, Fla., 1954-57, Gulfport, Fla., 1957-59, Lovington, Ill., 1959-64; vis. instr. Millikin U., Decatur, Ill., 1964-65; asst. prof. religion Duke U., Durham, N.C., 1965-71; prof. religion Louisburg (N.C.) Coll., 1971—. Author: Mircea Eliade: The Romanian Roots, 1988; translator, editor: Autobiography 1 & 2 of Mircea Eliade, 1981, 89, Journal 1 and 4 of Mircea Eliade, 1989, 90; translator: The Forbidden Forest (by Eliade), 1978. Pres. Louisburg Civitan Club, 1975. Recipient Fulbright Hayes rsch. award for study in Romania, 1981; grantee NEH, 1984-85. Mem. Am. Acad. Religion, Am.-Romanian Acad. Arts and Scis. Democrat. Methodist. Avocations: gardening, music. Office: Louisburg Coll 501 N Main St Louisburg NC 27549

RICKMAN, CLAUDE ROGER, retired college official, clergyman; b. Brevard, N.C., Nov. 10, 1917; s. Andrew Cornelius and Flora Pearl (Powell) R.; m. Evelyn Thornton Tucker, Jan. 1, 1942; children: Claude Merideth, Sharon Carol Rickman Wallace, Bryan Cary. AB, BS, Marion Coll., 1941; MA, U. N.C., 1952, PhD, 1956; LLD (hon.), Central (S.C.) Wesleyan Coll., 1982. Ordained elder Wesleyan Meth. Ch., 1947. Pastor Ragan Wesleyan Ch., Gastonia, N.C., 1946, 48-50; dean Cen. Wesleyan Coll., 1946-68, pres., 1968-79, asst. to pres., 1980-89, dir. Alumni Assn., 1980-88; ret., 1989; pres. ministerial standing, N.C. dist. Wesleyan Ch., 1946-87, N.C. dist. Wesleyan Youth, Colfax, 1951-56; del. Gen. Conf. Wesleyan Ch., 1956-80, 88; mem. Wesleyan Coun. Edn., 1968-79. Mem. Pickens County (S.C.) Sch. Bd., 1983—; trustee Hephizibah Children's Home, Macon, Ga., 1989—; bd. dirs. Pickens, Oconee, Anderson Mental Health, 1986—. With USNR, 1942-45, lt. comdr. Res. ret. Mem. Lions. Republican. Home: Central Wesleyan Coll Box 458 Central SC 29630 *The advanced degrees and experience cause me to realize I have a vast field to learn in and serve in for the country, church, colleges and Christ. I agree with Peter Marshall that "the meaning of life is not in duration but donation."*

RIDDLE, EARL WALDO, retired church official, small business owner; b. St. Joseph, Mo., Jan. 29, 1920; s. Roderick Edwin and Nannie Myrtle (Albertson) R.; m. Etta Kathryn McGauhey, Aug. 23, 1942; children: Martha Anne Riddle Moretty, Mary Janet Riddle Switzer, David Earl. AS, Mo. Western Coll., 1940; AB, U. Kans., 1942; MDiv, Boston U., 1945, postgrad., 1946-50; D Ministry, San Francisco Theol. Sem., 1976. Ordained to ministry United Meth. Ch. as elder, 1945; cert. leader in sex edn. for youth. Assoc. pastor College Ave. Meth. Ch., West Somerville, Mass., 1946-50; dir. Wesley Found. Oreg. State U., Corvallis, 1950-54; pastor Forest Grove (Oreg.) Meth. Ch., 1954-60; sr. pastor 1st Meth. Ch., Twin Falls, Idaho, 1960-65, Caldwell, Idaho, 1965-68; coun. dir. Oreg.-Idaho Conf., United Meth. Ch., Portland, Oreg., 1968-85; owner, operator Riddle Enterprises, Portland, 1968—; dir. youth work Morgan Meml. Ch. All Nations, Boston, 1942-45; cons. on fin. and ministerial tax; ptnr. Riddle Engring. Co.; dir. Stewardship Enterprises; exec. dir. local com. Gen. Conf., United Meth. Ch., Portland, 1976, mem. Gen. Conf., 1964, 66, 68, 70, Western Jurisdictional Conf., 1964, 68, Gen. Bd. Edn., 1966-72; mem. Interbd. Com. on Missionary Edn., 1968-72; mem. exec. com. Conf. Program Dirs. Assn., 1968-72, Conf. Officers Assn., 1973-76; pres. Nat. Assn. Conf. Coun. Dirs., 1982-84, Nat. Assn. Stewardship Leaders, 1983-84; conf. sec. Oreg.-Idaho Ann. Conf., 1985-88; chmn. com. on correlation and edit. revision The Gen. Conf. of United Meth. Ch., 1988—. Editor: History of National Association of Conference Council Directors, 1974, Oreg.-Idaho Conf. jour., 1985-88, Tax Talk for Ministers, 1976-90; chmn. com. on correlation and editorial revision The Discipline, 1988; contbr. numerous articles to profl. jours. Coun. officer, scoutmaster Boy Scouts Am., 1942-45, 60-65, 68-76; exec. sec. Oreg.-Idaho United Meth. Found., 1970-85; bd. dirs., chmn. Forest Grove Union High Sch., 1955-60; mem. Oreg. Gov.'s Com. on Sexual Preference, 1976-78; mem. human rsch. com. Oreg. Health Scis. U., 1975—; bd. dirs. Planned Parenthood Assn., 1984-89, Samaritan Counseling Ctr., 1985-88; mem. fin. devel. com. Ecumenical Ministries Oreg., 1970-86, mem. Edn. Commn., 1970-85; mem. clergy com. on Oreg. Health Decisions, 1983-85; mem. health edn. curriculum development com. Oreg. Dept. Edn., 1985-88. Chaplain USNR, 1945-46. Recipient plaques and awards Boy Scouts Am., Exceptional Svc. Jason Lee award for excellence in communications, 1977, Exceptional Svc. award Parents and Friends of Lesbians and Gays, 1986, civil liberties award ACLU, 1989, spl. svc. award for Russian refugee work, 1990. Mem. Nat. United Meth. Assn. Communicators. Home: 465 NW 95th St Portland OR 97229-6309 *It is my hope that the world would be a better place because I traveled here.*

RIDDLE, STURGIS LEE, minister; b. Stephenville, Tex., May 26, 1909; s. Lee and Linda (McKinney) R.; m. Elisabeth Pope Sloan, Oct. 14, 1939. B.A. magna cum laude, Stanford U., 1931; student, Gen. Theol. Sem., N.Y.C., 1931-32; B.D. cum laude, Episcopal Theol. Sch., Cambridge, Mass., 1934; D.D., Seabury Western Theol. Sem., Evanston, Ill., 1957. Ordained deacon P.E. Ch., 1934, priest, 1935; Episcopal chaplain U. Calif., 1934-37; instr. church Div. Sch. of Pacific, 1934-37; rector Caroline Ch., Setauket, L.I., 1937-40; asst. minister St. Thomas Ch., N.Y.C., 1940-46; rector St. James Ch., Florence, Italy, 1947-49; dean Am. Cathedral of Holy Trinity, Paris, France, 1949-74; dean emeritus Am. Cathedral of Holy Trinity, 1974—; exchange preacher Trinity Ch., N.Y.C., 1956-57, 62, St. Bartholomew's Ch., N.Y.C., 1958, 63, 73, St. John's Cathedral, Denver, 1959, Grace Cathedral, San Francisco, 1960, Nat. Cathedral, Washington, 1961, Trinity Ch. Boston, 1964, St. Andrew's Cathedral, Honolulu, 1965, St. John's Ch., Washington, 1966, 67, 68, 70, 73, St. Thomas' Ch., N.Y., 1968, 73, St. Paul's Cathedral, Boston, 1969; clerical dep. Europe to Gen. Conv. P.E. Ch., 1949-60, 64, 70. Author: One Hundred Years, 1950; contbg. Author: We Believe in Prayer, 1958, That Day with God, 1965. Hon. gov. Am. Hosp. in Paris; fellow Morgan Library, N.Y.C., trustee bd. fgn. parishes; chmn. Friends of the Am. Cathedral in Paris. Decorated Legion of Honor France; grand cross and grand prelate Sovereign Order St. John of Jerusalem Knights of Malta; grand cross Ordre du Milice de Jesus Christ; Patriarchal Order Mt. Athos. Mem. Nat. Inst. Social Sci., Am. Soc. French Legion of Honor, Phi Beta Kappa. Clubs: Union, University, Pilgrims. Home: 870 Fifth Ave New York NY 10021

RIDENOUR, ALLEN CLYDE, minister; b. Fellowsville, W.Va., May 21, 1947; s. Clyde William and Helena Katherine (Matlick) R.; m. Rita Rae Cox, May 13, 1967; children: Misti Leann, Brian Allen, Jason Andrew. BA, W.Va. U., 1970; MDiv, Duke U. Div. Sch., 1974; D of Ministry, Trinity Theol. Sem., 1987. Ordained to ministry United Meth. Ch., 1971. Pastor Burlington (N.C.) United Meth. Ch., 1970-74, Crumper (W.Va.)-McDowell United Meth. Ch., 1974-77, Carr Meml. United Meth. Ch., Princeton, W.Va., 1977-81, St. Paul's United Meth. Ch., Oakland, Md., 1981-89; sr. pastor First United Meth. Ch., South Charleston, W.Va., 1989—; coord. New Life Missions/Key Events, Charleston, W.Va., 1988—. Author: The Personal Computer: An Aid in Pastoral Ministry, 1987. Named Pastor of Yr. Romney (W.Va.) Dist. United Meth. Ch., 1985. Home: 907 Glendale Ave South Charleston WV 25303 Office: First United Meth Ch 905 Glendale Ave South Charleston WV 25303

RIDER, DEBRA ALICE, minister; b. Oklahoma City, Apr. 5, 1965; d. John C. and Mary H. (Matthews) R. BME cum laude, Cen. State U., 1988; MDiv summa cum laude, Midwestern Bapt. Theol. Sem., 1991. Summer missionary Bapt. Student Union, Okla., 1987, Home Mission Bd., Okla., 1988; evangelism praxis Home Mission Bd., Kansas City, Mo., summer 1989, multi housing intern, 1989-90; minister to single adults Tiffany Springs Bapt. Ch., Kansas City, 1988—; with Tompkins Ins. Agy., 1991—. Dr. George W. Shirley Meml. scholar Midwestern Sem., Kansas City, 1988-89, Mr. & Mrs. L.F. Richardson Ministerial scholar, 1989-90, Dunwoody Bapt. Ch. Found. scholar, 1990-91. Office: 6504-A NW Prairie View Rd Kansas City MO 64151

RIDGEWAY, PATRICIA FLYNN, religion educator; b. Rochester, N.Y., Jan. 29, 1952; d. John Michael and Dorothy Cathryn (Lavell) Flynn; m. Robert Stephen Ridgway, May 2, 1987. BS, SUNY, Brockport, 1974; MPA, Golden Gate U., 1983. Tchr. 7th and 8th grades St. Andrews Sch., Rochester, N.Y., 1974-80; CCD/LEM tchr. Nellis AFB, Las Vegas, Nev., 1980-84; LEM tchr. Kunsan AB, Kunsan City, Korea, 1984-85; CCD/LEM tchr. RAF Lakenheath, U.K., 1985-88; CCD tchr. Hill AFB, Ogden, Utah,

1988—. Capt. USAF, 1988—. Democrat. Home: 6310 S 1575 E Ogden UT 84405-5201

RIDGWAY, CHARLES B., clergyman; b. Star City, Ark., Aug. 28, 1930; s. Walter R. and Essie (McNeal) R.; m. Dorothy Mae Jett, Jan. 26, 1951; children: Charla Karen, Angela Joy, Cecilia Lilleen, Priscilla Alice. BA, Anderson U., 1956, MDiv, 1964. Ordained to ministry, Ch. of God, 1958. Pastor Stringtown Ch. of God, Covington, Ind., 1957-59; pastor First Ch. of God, Paragold, Ark., 1959-61, LaGrange, Ga., 1961-67, Madisonville, Ky., 1967-79; pastor Oaklawn First Ch. of God, Hot Springs, Ark., 1979—; chmn. Hopkins County Ministerial Alliance, Madisonville, 1977, Hot Springs Ministerial Alliance, 1988-89; state chmn., Ch. of God in Ark., 1987-89. Organizer, bd. dirs. Hopkins County Sr. Citizens Ctr., Madisonville, 1973-79. Named Ky. Col., 1977. Mem. Gen. Assembly Ch. of God. Home: Rte 2 Box 578 Hot Springs AR 71901 Office: Oaklawn First Ch of God 2110 7th St Hot Springs AR 71913

RIDLEN, JUDITH ELAINE, minister; b. Champaign, Ill., Nov. 10, 1948; d. Samuel Franklin and Helen Louise (Camp) R. BS in Home Econs., Ill. State U., 1970; M. Religious Edn., Lexington Theol. Sem., 1974; D. Ministry, McCormick Theol. Sem., 1984. Ordained to ministry Christian Ch. (Disciples of Christ). Assoc. regional minister Christian Ch. in Ill.-Wis., Bloomington, Ill., 1974-84; sr. minister Northside Christian Ch., Knoxville, Tenn., 1984—; 1st vice-moderator Christian Ch. in Tenn., Nashville, 1988—; bd. dirs. Christmount Christian Assembly, Black Mountain, N.C., 1986—, Div. Homeland Ministries, Indpls., 1975-81; sec. Assn. Christian Ch. Educators, Indpls., 1983-84. Mem. Ch. Women United (officer Knox County unit 1986—). Office: Northside Christian Ch 4008 Tazewell Pike Knoxville TN 37918

RIDLEY, BETTY ANN, educator, church worker; b. St. Louis, Oct. 19, 1926; d. Rupert Alexis and Virginia Regina (Weikel) Steber; m. Fred A. Ridley, Jr., Sept. 8, 1948; children: Linda Drue Ridley Archer, Clay Kent. BA, Scripps Coll., Claremont, Calif., 1948. Christian sci. practitioner, Oklahoma City, 1973—; tchr. Christian sci., 1983—; mem. Christian Sci. Bd. Lectureship, 1980-85. Trustee Daystar Found. Mem. Jr. League Am. Home: 7908 Lakehurst Dr Oklahoma City OK 73120 Office: 3000 United Founders Blvd Suite 100-G Oklahoma City OK 73112 *What makes life a continuing joy and free of all fear is to know that God who is the only Creator is infinitely good. He is our Father and our Mother, our Judge and our best friend. He is our great Physician, caring for us tenderly and uninterruptedly. We have but to know this and live according to His law in order to enjoy His blessings.*

RIDLEY, DANIEL CARLYLE, music minister; b. Flint, Mich., May 16, 1953; s. Robert K. and Lois (Mamie) R.; m. Angelia Broom, Oct. 23, 1983. MusB, SW Bapt. Coll., 1975; M Ch. Music, So. Bapt. Theol. Sem., 1978. Minister of music 18th St. Bapt. Ch., Louisville, 1976-79, Swope Park Bapt. Ch., Kansas City, Mo., 1983—; minister of music and youth Matthews (N.C.) Bapt. Ch., 1979-83; dir. Messiah Community Chorus, Matthews, 1979-82, Mo. Bapt. Brass, 1983—; pres. Choristers Ghild, Charlotte, N.C., 1983, Mo. Music Men, 1991; state approved worker-instrumental music Mo. Bapt. Convention, 1985—. Contbr. articles to profl. publs. Mem. So. Bapt. Ch. Music Conf. Republican. Home: 8705 Stark Ave Raytown MO 64138 Office: Swope Park Bapt Ch 10415 Chestnut Dr Kansas City MO 64137

RIDLEY, GARY JOHN, college president; b. Worcester, Mass., Nov. 1, 1951; s. Wayne Douglas and Helen (Case) R.; m. Carol Corinne Gagnon, Mar. 17, 1973; children: Corinne Joy, Gary John Jr., Kevin Douglas. AB, Gordon Coll., 1973; MDiv, Trinity Evang. Div. Sch., Deerfield, Ill., 1977, D of Missions, 1990. Ordained to ministry Bible Ch., 1978. Instr. Alaska Bible Coll., Glennallen, 1978-87, pres., 1987—; bd. dirs. SENO Internat. Alaska, Glennallen. Vol. EMT, ambulance driver Copper River Emergency med. Svcs., Glennallen, 1984-88; bd. dirs. Cross Rd. Med. Ctr., Glennallen, 1990—. Office: Alaska Bible Coll Office of President Box 289 Glennallen AK 99588

RIDLEY, HUBERT DALE, minister; b. Dumas, Tex., Oct. 3, 1966; s. Hubert Hale and Mary June (Lackey) R. BBA in Fin., Tex. Tech. U., 1989. Youth intern Trinity Ch., Lubbock, Tex., 1989-91; youth minister St. Luke United Meth. Ch., Lubbock, 1991—. Republican. Home: 3708 44th Lubbock TX 79413 Office: St Lukes United Methodist 3717 44th St Lubbock TX 79413

RIDLEY, ROBERT HENDERSON, minister; b. Campbell, Tex., Jan. 27, 1911; s. Fred Reginald and Chloe Wan (Henderson) R.; m. Margaret Elizabeth Low, June 9, 1939; 1 child, Robert Low. Student, Wesley Coll., 1930, Dallas Theol. Sem., 1930-33; BA, East Tex. State U., 1935. Ordained to ministry United Meth. Ch., 1938. Pastor South Wilcox Ch., McKinney, Tex., 1940-44, 1st Meth. Ch., Carrollton, Tex., 1944-50, Trinity Ch., Dallas, 1950-74; interim pastor Brashear Charge, Hopkins County, Tex., 1975-91; Mem. reference com. Am. Bd. Missions to the Jews, Dallas, 1970-74; trustee North Tex. Conf. United Meth. Ch., 1959-70, chmn. bd., 1962-63; speaker Colonial Lodge Retirement Inn, Greenville, Tex., 1991—. Author: (with Margaret Low Ridley) Candles at Dusk, 1954, (with Margaret Low Ridley) Another Dawn, 1967,. Recipient Cert. Achievement East Tex. State U. Alumni Assn., 1974. Home: Box 118 Campbell TX 75422 *Allowed of God to be entrusted with the Gospel. Immortal tidings in mortal hands.*

RIECHERS, DONALD FRANK, minister, retired military officer; b. Platteville, Wis., Aug. 5, 1925; s. Emil Johann Dietrich and Ada Amanda Marie (Wise) R.; m. Wanda Ruth Frevert, May 21, 1955; children: Carl, Sarah, Ann. BA, Carthage Coll., 1951; BD, MDiv, N.W. Luth. Sem., St. Paul, 1955; postgrad., U. Ohio, 1953-54, Luth. Theol. S. Sem., Columbia, S.C., 1968-73. Ordained to ministry Luth. Ch., 1955. Intern, student pastor Nat. Luth. Coun., Ohio U., Athens, 1953-54; commd. 1st lt. USAF, 1955, advanced through grades to lt. col., 1973, chaplain, 1955-75, retired, 1975; pastor St. Paul's Luth. Ch., Mass City, Mich., 1975-84, Lord of the Lake Luth. Ch., Diamond City, Ark., 1984—; chair edn. com. Ark./Okla. Synod, Evang. Luth. Ch. Am.; del. Luth. Ch. in Am. to Luth. Coun. USA, 1984-87, chairperson div. for svc. to mil. pers., 1984-87. Treas. Sugarloaf Ind. Devel. Corp., North Boone County, Ark., 1988—; chaplain Long Lake Camp, Boy Scouts Am., Merrifield, Minn., summer 1953; ambulance driver Diamond City/Lead Hill Rescue Squad, 1988—. Recipient Community Svc. award Diamond City C. of C., 1989. Mem. Am. Legion (chaplain Diamond City post 1984—). Democrat.

RIECK, CAROLE ANN, librarian; b. Windsor Heights, W.VA., Jan. 27, 1937; d. Frank Wilhelm Rieck and Elsie Louise (Guegold) Stomps. BA, Kent State U., 1962; MLS, Case Western Res. U., 1964. Cert. edнl. media specialist, Ohio. Head libr. St. Augustine Acad. Libr., Lakewood, Ohio, 1980—; vol. St. Luke Ch. Libr., Lakewood, 1988-91. Author: (poems) American Poetry Anthology, 1984 (Golden Poet award 1985), Our World's Most Beloved Poems, 1984 (Silver Poet award 1986, 90), Hearts on Fire, vol. II, 1985. Ward leader Cuyahoga County Rep. Orgn., Cleve., 1983-89, mem. cen. com., 1981-89, precinct committeeperson, 1974-82. Mem. Cath. Libr. Assn. (bd. dirs. no. Ohio chpt. 1980—, recognition high sch. sect. treas. 1991—), Ohio Ednl. Libr. Media Assn., West Shore Librs., Lakewood Rep. Club (membership com., v.p. newsletter), Zeta Tau Alpha (alumnae chpt.). Home: 12520 Edgewater Dr #1207 Lakewood OH 44107 Office: St Augustine Acad 14808 Lake Ave Lakewood OH 44107 *Write down short and long term goals for your life, a plan for reaching each goal, and then do it. Your energy will be focused on meaningful activities and you will be pleased at how much more you are able to accomplish.*

RIEDEL, WALTER ROBERT, minister; b. Bklyn., Oct. 6, 1945; s. Robert Joel Martin and Dorothy Adele (Jacobsen) R.; m. Ruth Martha Pullmann, June 22, 1976; children: David Robert, Christopher Daniel, Jonathan Paul. BA, Yale U., 1969, MDiv, 1971; STM, Concordia, St. Louis, 1973. Ordained minister in Luth. Ch., 1975. Dir. youth ministry Ascension Luth. Ch., East Lansing, Mich., 1974-75; pastor Peace Luth. Ch., Taft, Calif., 1975-78; circuit missionary Am. Luth. Ch./Evang. Luth. Ch., Papua, New Guinea, 1978-82; prof., acad. dean Sr. Flierl Luth. Sem., Finschhafen, Papua, New Guinea, 1983-86; pastor Nativity Luth. Ch., Palm Beach Gardens, Fla., 1986—; sec. Tradewinds Conf., Fla. Synod, Evang. Luth. Ch. Am., 1988—, mem. global missions task force, Fla. Synod, 1988—, commn. on ecumenical rels., Fla. Synod, 1988—. Contbr. articles to profl. jours. Mem. Ministerial Assn. Northern Palm Beaches (pres. 1989-90). Office: Nativity Luth Church 4075 Holly Dr Palm Beach Gardens FL 33410

RIEDL, ROSE MARIE, religious education director; b. Chgo., Jan. 18, 1940; d. Michael and Alexandria (Babel) Welzien; widowed; children: Cate, Cindi, Robert. BS, George Williams Coll., 1973; MA, Mundelein Coll., 1981. Coord. religious edn. St. Mary Ch., Downers Grove, Ill., 1981-83; dir. religious edn. St. Peter Ch., East Troy, Wis., 1986-88, St. Gilbert Ch., Grayslake, Ill., 1988—; dir. religious edn. Archdiocese of Chgo. Contbr. articles to religious jours. Home: 1168 Lake Geneva Blvd Lake Geneva WI 53147

RIEGEL, ROBERT H., charitable organization administrator. Exec. dir., sec. Cath. Charities, Indpls. Office: Cath Charities 1400 N Meridian St PO Box 1410 Indianapolis IN 46206*

RIEGNER, GERHART MORITZ, religious organization executive; b. Berlin, Sept. 12, 1911; arrived in Switzerland, 1934; s. Heinrich and Agnes (Arnheim) R. Law degrees, Germany and France, 1932-34; LHD (hon.), Jewish Theol. Sem. of Am., 1982; ThD (hon.), Humboldt U., Berlin, 1988; D of Sacred Letters (hon.), U. St. Michael's Coll., Toronto, Can., 1990. With World Jewish Congress, Geneva, 1936—, sec. gen., 1965-83, co-chmn. governing bd, 1983-91, hon. v.p., 1991—; chmn. Internat. Jewish Com. on interreligious consultations, 1982-84. Contbr. articles to profl. jours. Chmn. Conf. on Non-Govtl. Orgns. in consultative status with UN, 1953-55, in consultative status with UNESCO, 1956-58, World Univ. Svc., Geneva, 1949-55. Recipient Nahum Goldmann medal, World Jewish Congress, 1981, Roger Joseph prize Hebrew Union Coll., 1984, Patriarch Abraham award, Brazilian Bishops Conf., 1989. Mem. Internat. Coun. Christians and Jews (hon. v.p. 1988—, humanitarian award 1981), Internat. Coun. Yad Vashem (Jerusalem), Meml. Found. for Jewish Culture (bd. dirs.), Beth Hatefutsdth-Mus. of the Jewish Diaspora (Tel Aviv). Office: World Jewish Congress, 1 Rue Varembe, Geneva 1211, Switzerland

RIEL, RUTH ELLEN, youth director; b. Dover, Ohio, July 19, 1957; d. Robert Elwood and Eleanor Alice (Stanley) R. BS in Edn., Asbury Coll., 1979; MS in Adminstrn. and Supr., Nova U., 1986. Cert. tchr. Fla. Tchr., drop-out prevention specialist Pinellas County Sch. Bd., Clearwater, Fla., 1984—; youth dir. 1st United Meth. Ch., Pinellas Park, Fla., 1985—; FCA sponsor Desoto High Sch., Arcadia, Fla., 1981-84; mem. PRAISE singing group, United Meth. Ch., St. PEtersburg, Fla., 1984-85; sr. high Sunday sch. tchr., United MEth. Ch., Brandenton, Pinellas Park, St. Petersburg, 1979-90. Mem. Nat. Coun. Tchrs. Math., Alternative Educators Assn., Christian Educators Fellowship. Office: 1st United Meth Ch 9025 49th St N Pinellas Park FL 34666

RIEMENSCHNEIDER, DAN LAVERNE, religious organization administrator; b. Pontiac, Mich., July 21, 1952; s. Henry LaVerne and Sarah Lou R.; m. Rebecca Joy Fruth, June 26, 1976; 1 child, Derek Henri. BA in Social Work, Mich. State U., 1974, PhD in Family Ecology, 1985; MA in Religion Edn., Asbury Seminary, Wilmore, Ky., 1976. Min. of Edn. Spring Arbor (Mich.) Free Meth. Ch., 1977-85; asst. prof. social work and family sci. Spring Arbor Coll., 1985-87; exec. dir. dept. edn. Free Meth. Ch. of North Am., Indpls., 1987—; chmn. Samaritan Counseling Ctr., Jackson, Mich., 1985-87. Bd. dirs. Mich. Council on Family Relations, Lansing, Mich., 1985-87. Mem. Nat. Council Family Relations, Nat. Assn. Evangelicals, Nat. Christian Edn. Assn. (bd. dirs.), Nat. Task Force on Family (bd. dirs.). Office: Free Meth World Hdqrs PO Box 535002 770 N High School Rd Indianapolis IN 46253-5002

RIESER, MICHAEL LEE, lay minister; b. Columbus, July 25, 1954; s. Theodore Carl and Marjorie Alice (Stockslager) R.; m. Cheryl Ann Mimm, June 26, 1976; children: John-Mark, Esther. AA, Christ for The Nations Inst., 1975; BS, S.W. Assembly of God Coll., 1983; postgrad., Assembly of God Theol. Sem., 1984, United Theol. Sem., 1990—. Pastor Living Water Assembly of God, Cadiz, Ohio, 1983-84; asst. adminstr. New Beginnings Sch., Columbus, 1985; asst. min. Ch. of Living Word, Columbus, 1987-90; pastor Appleton-Bennington United Meth. Ch., 1991—; chaplain Carriage Inn Nursing Home, Columbus, 1987-91; quality technician Crane Plastics, Columbus, 1985—. Mem. Nat. Assn. Evangelicals, Soc. for Pentecostal Studies. Republican. Home: 2743 Thorndale Columbus OH 43207 *Jesus Christ is the foundation of my life. When everything else crumbles away, I know the foundation is still there.*

RIGDON, V. BRUCE, minister; b. Phila., Feb. 23, 1936; s. Vernon L. and Mabel G. (Ailes) R.; m. Mary Elizabeth Shaw, June 20, 1959; children: Sarah, Mark, Gregory. BA, Coll. of Wooster, 1958; BD, Yale U., 1962, MA, 1963, PhD, 1968. Ordained to ministry Presbyn. Ch. (U.S.A.). From instr. to prof. in ch. history McCormick Theol. Sem., Chgo., 1965-88; sr. pastor Grosse Pointe (Mich.) Meml. Ch., 1988—. Office: Grosse Pointe Meml Ch 16 Lakeshore Dr Grosse Pointe Farms MI 48236

RIGEL, WILLIAM MALCOLM, minister; b. Athens, Ala., Oct. 6, 1926; s. Samuel Edward and Daisy Ezma (Rhinehart) R.; m. Martha Louise Haynes, June 9, 1946; children: William Jr., James, Paul, Robin, Angela. BA, Anderson U., 1967; MA, U. So. Fla., 1972; MST, U. Dubuque, 1974; STD, Emory U., 1981. Ordained to ministry Ch. of God (Anderson, Ind.), 1949; cert. rehab. counselor. Pastor South Lake Wales Ch. of God, Lake Wales, Fla., 1968-75; pastor, state min. Ga. Chs. of God., Marietta, 1986—; pastor Town Ctr. Community Ch. of God, Marietta, 1988—; prof. Warner So. Coll., Lake Wales, 1968-87; v.p. Mid-Am. Bible Coll., Oklahoma City, 1990-91. Home: 4041 May Breeze Rd NE Marietta GA 30066

RIGGS, JOHN T., II, minister; b. Oklahoma City, Aug. 24, 1947; s. John T. Riggs Sr. and Evelyn L. (Jones) Price; m. Linda Collins, Feb. 9, 1968 (div. 1980); children: John III, Regina, Donnell, Shardan, Julius, Treasure Tenisha, Carlors; m. Stacy Jones, Mar. 29, 1991. AA, Midwest Christian Coll., 1985; BS, Mid Am. Bible Coll., 1988; postgrad., Phillis Grad. Sem., Tulsa, 1989-91. Ordained to ministry. Assoc. pastor Pleasant Ridge Bapt. Ch., Oklahoma City, 1980-89; student asst. Apostolic Ch. Jesus Christ, Oklahoma City, 1983; student pastor Osage Ave. Christian Ch., Oklahoma City, 1989—; substitute tchr. Tulsa high schs., 1990—. Vol. chaplain Children's Meml. Hosp., Oklahoma City, 1984-88, Glenpool Police Dept., 1991. Phillis Grad. Sem. grantee, 1989-91, 1st Christian Ch., Tulsa grantee, 1989-91, 1st Christian Ch., Coffeeville, Kans. grantee, 1989-91. With U.S. Army, 1966-68, Vietnam. Mem. Full Gospel Bus. Men, Internat. Chaplains Assn. Home: 1152 E 137 Pl Glenpool OK 74033 Office: Osage Ave Christian Ch 1101 E Smith Okmulgee OK 74447

RIGHETTI, ROBERT SILVIO, editor, engineer; b. Upland, Calif., Aug. 24, 1949; s. Joseph Tony and Alice Pauline (Hiner) R.; m. Susan Beverly Broersma, July 2, 1972; children: Erin Nicol, Ryan Jared, Robert Joseph. Student, Mt. San Jacinto Coll., 1976-82, Calif. State U., Long Beach, 1982, Coll. of the Desert, 1979-82, U. Calif., Riverside, 1990—. Minister Jehovah's Witnesses Ch., So. Calif., 1967-88; editor, pub. Christian Quest, Idyllwild, Calif., 1988—; sr. project mgr. Willdan Assocs., Anaheim, Calif., 1987—. Editor Danney Ball Prodns.; artist, illustrator for books, newspapers. Mem. Soc. Biblical Lit., Cartoonist/Animators Profl. Soc. Republican. Home and Office: PO Box 1431 Idyllwild CA 92349

RIGHI-LAMBERTINI, EGANO CARDINAL, deacon; b. Cassalecchio di Reno, Bologna, Italy, Feb. 22, 1906. Ordained priest Roman Cath. Ch., 1929. Titular archibishop of Docles, 1960-79; elevated to Sacred Coll. of Cardinals, 1979; mem. Council for Pub. Affairs of the Church, Sacred Congregation for the Bishops, Secretariat for Non-Christians; hon. pres. Commn. for Sacred Art in Italy; deacon of S. Giovanni Bosco in Via Tuscolana. Address: Piazza della Citta, Leonina 9, 00193 Rome Italy

RIGHTER, WALTER CAMERON, bishop; b. Phila., Oct. 23, 1923; s. Richard and Dorothy Mae (Bottomley) R.; m. Marguerite Jeanne Burroughs, Jan. 26, 1946 (div.); children: Richard, Rebecca; m. Jane Elizabeth Meyer, Feb. 13, 1988. BA, U. Pitts., 1948; MDiv, Berkeley Div. Sch., New Haven, 1951, DD, 1972; DCL, Iowa Wesleyan U., 1982; DD, Seabury Western Sem., 1984. Ordained priest Episcopal Ch., 1951, consecrated bishop, 1972; lay missioner St. Michael's Ch., Rector, Pa., 1947-48; priest-in-charge All Saints Ch., Aliquippa, Pa., 1951-54, St. Luke's, Georgetown, Pa., 1952-54; rector Ch. of Good Shepherd, Nashua, N.H., 1954-71; bishop Diocese of Iowa, Des Moines, 1972-89; asst. bishop Dio. of Newark, 1989-91; exec. council Protestant Episcopal Ch. U.S.A., 1979-85; asst. bishop Newark, 1989, ret., 1989. Mem. N.H. com. White House Conf. on Youth, 1962, Regional Crime Commn., Hillsboro County, N.H., 1969-71; trustee Nashua Library, 1968-71, Seabury Western Sem., 1986-89; founding trustee The Morris Fund, Des Moines. Fellow Coll. Preachers, Washington Cathedral.

RIGHTS, GRAHAM HENRY, minister; b. Winston-Salem, N.C., Jan. 14, 1935; s. Douglas LeTell and Cecil Leona (Burton) R.; m. Sybil Critz Strupe, Sept. 7, 1963; children: Susan Elizabeth, John Graham. BA, U. N.C., 1956; BD, Yale U., 1959; postgrad., Moravian Theol. Sem., 1959-60, U. Edinburgh, Scotland, 1965-66; DD (hon.), Wofford Coll., 1989. Ordained to ministry Moravian Ch., 1960. Pastor Union Ch., Managua, Nicaragua, 1960-63, Managua Moravian Ch., 1960-65, Mayodan (N.C.) Moravian Ch., 1966-72, Messiah Moravian Ch., Winston-Salem, 1972-81; exec. dir. Bd. World Mission Moravian Ch., Bethlehem, Pa., 1981-83; pres. exec. bd. provincial elders' Moravian Ch., Winston-Salem, 1983—; pres. exec. bd. world-wide Moravian Chs., 1991—. Author: On the Roof of the World, 1961. Trustee Moravian Coll., Bethlehem, 1983—, Moravian Theol. Sem., Bethlehem, 1983—; bd. dirs. Crisis Control Ministry, Winston-Salem, 1976—. Home: 120 Cascade Ave Winston-Salem NC 27127 Office: Moravian Ch in Am Drawer O 459 S Chruch St Winston-Salem NC 27108

RIKER, DONALD ALLEN, health care facility administrator; b. Glen Ridge, N.J., Nov. 8, 1958; s. Kenneth Allen and Margaret (Corbyon) R.; m. Cynthia Joy Geiger, Aug. 21, 1982; children: Bethany, Sean. BA, Kean Coll., 1983. Cert. elem. tchr., N.J. Dir. Friendship Pregnancy Ctr., Morristown, N.J., 1985-88; coord. crisis pregnancy tng. Christian Action Coun., Falls Church, Va., 1988-90; exec. coun. Greater St. Louis Crisis Pregnancy Ctrs., 1990—; assoc. field staff Christian Action Coun., Falls Church, 1986-88. Baptist. Office: Greater St Louis Pregnancy Ctr 13010 C Manchester Rd Saint Louis MO 63131

RILEY, CAROLE A., religious institute director, music educator; b. Pitts.; d. Francis King and Gertrude (Daube) R. Student, Carlow Coll., 1959-61, Royal Conservatory, Montreal, Ont., Can., 1966-67; BS in Music Edn., Duquesne U., 1968, MusM, 1972, MA in Formative Leadership, 1978, PhD in Formative Spirituality, 1983; cert. in pastoral counseling, Pitts. Pastoral Inst., 1972-74; studies with Gregory Sebok, Adirondack Inst., 1972; postgrad., U. Pitts., 1978, Slippery Rock U., 1984. Joined Congregation Divine Providence, Roman Cath. Ch., 1959; cert. tchr., Pa. Mem. staff, spiritual dir. Cenacle Retreat House, Pitts. and Charleston (W.Va.), 1972—; adj. prof. Duquesne U., Pitts., 1980—, prof. piano, 1982—, asst. dean Sch. Music, 1982-85, exec. dir. Inst. Formative Spirituality; adj. prof. U. Charleston, Parkersburg, W.Va., 1983-88, St. Mary Coll., Moraga, Calif., 1983, U. San Diego, 1984, 86. Mem. Coll. Theology Soc., Coll. Music Soc., Music Tchrs. Nat. Assn., Pa. Music Tchrs. Assn., Pitts. Piano Tchrs., Soc. for Sci. Study of Religion, Religious Rsch. Assn. Avocations: sewing, walking, cooking. Home: 700 Forbes Ave Pittsburgh PA 15219 Office: Duquesne U 600 Forbes Ave Pittsburgh PA 15282

RILEY, CHARLES HOMER (SABBA MARC CHARLES RILEY), clergyman; b. Phila., Jan. 25, 1932; s. James Henry and Mary Idell (Bullock) R.; m. Doris Mae Bracey, 1955 (div. 1955); children—Charles, Jr., Leslie, William, Patience; m. Maedell Jacqueline Vera Luke Miller, 1966; children—Calvin, Ritajo, Jonathan, Adrienne, Naatasha, Immanne, L'Latanyya, Ariuss, Lé aquar. A.A., Vallejo Jr. Coll., Calif., 1963; A.B., Community Coll. Phila., 1976; B.A., U. Pa., 1977; B.A., Thomas Edison Coll., Princeton, N.J., 1976. Ordained priest, Eastern Orthodox Ch. Co-pastor Mt. Calvary Missionary Baptist Ch., Suisun/Fairfield, Calif., 1962-64; inspirator The Ch. of the New Life, Phila., 1966-80; primate and apostolic adminstr. African-Am. Orthodox Apostolate, Phila., 1980-82; patriarchal vicar Greek Orthodox Patriarchate of Alexandria and All Africa, Egypt, 1983—, pres., dean St. Simon's Holy Eastern Orthodox Sem., Phila., 1980—; apostolic dir. African-Am. Holy Eastern Orthodox Apostolic, 1983; pastor and overseer African Am. Holy Eastern Orthodox Chs. of the New Life, 1983. Contbr. articles to newspapers. First black Am. to be Eastern Orthodox priest. Dir. New Life and New Horizins Inc., Phila., 1969—. Served as staff sgt. USAF, 1951-64, PTO, ETO. Recipient award as Gang Prevention Leader Crisis Invention Network, Phila. 1966-71. Mem. Nat. Black M.B.A. Soc., U. Pa. Black Alumni Soc. Office: African-Am Holy Eastern Orthodox Apostolate 631 N 37th St Philadelphia PA 19104

RILEY, JOHN DAVID, engineer; b. Oakdale, Ky., May 24, 1933; s. John Martin and Edna Leora (Butler) R.; m. Annie Louise Robinson, June 25, 1954; children: Judyth Anne, Teresa Jeanne, Susan Eileen, Eric David. AB, Greenville Coll., 1956. Lic. radiotelephone operator, Tex. Prin. tchr. tng. Kans. Yearly Meeting of Friends, Kibimba, Burundi, 1959-61; ch. planting worker Kans. Yearly Meeting of Friends, Kwisumo, Burundi, 1961-63; engr., transl., tech. educator Sta. Radio Cordac, Bujumbura, Burundi, 1963-74; operator World Gospel Mission, Marion, Ind., 1980—; engr., tech. educator Sta. Radio Lumiere, La Jeune, Haiti, 1982-86; engr., chief operator Sta. KVMV-FM, McAllen, Tex., 1988-91; missionary Friends Africa Gospel Mission, Burundi, 1958-74, Wichita, Kans., 1957-75. Contbr. articles to orgn. jours. Mem. Evang. Friends Alliance. Home and Office: World Gospel Mission 2108 W Jackson Ave Mc Allen TX 78501 *Under the "grafted in" relationship through Jesus Christ I see no reason why an Arab Gentile could not claim God's endorsement to his being deemed a citizen of the Holy Land. In Jesus, he would no longer be a mortal threat to the Jew who is there.*

RILEY, JOHN ROBERT, minister; b. Flushing, N.Y., Apr. 6, 1954; s. Robert Harold Riley and Mary Cone Williams; m. Dana Powell Charles, Mar. 18, 1978; children: Abraham Robert, Thomas Jackson, Mary Christina. BS in Psychology, Ga. State U., 1978; MDiv, So. Sem., Louisville, 1982. Ordained to ministry So. Bapt. Conv., 1982. Interim assoc. pastor Lyndon Bapt. Ch., Louisville, 1982-83; assoc. pastor Severn (Md.) Bapt. Ch., 1983-87; minister of edn. and youth First Bapt. Ch., Carrollton, Ga., 1987—; assoc. Interfaith Witness Dept., Home Mission Bd., Atlanta, 1990—; dir. Carrollton Bapt. Assn. Youth Program, 1989—. Pres. Friends of the Libr., Carrollton, 1990—. Home: 120 N Fairlawn Dr Carrollton GA 30117 Office: First Bapt Ch 102 Dixie St Carrollton GA 30117 *I believe that the most neglected commandment in the late 20th century church is the foundational Love one another." Now, more than ever, there is a desperate need to heed this command.*

RILEY, KENNETH GENE, minister, camp director; b. LaGrande, Oreg., Mar. 26, 1959; s. John Newton and Janet Marie (Pederson) R.; m. Margaret Ann Smith, Sept. 5, 1981; children: Cherise Joy, Candace Sue, Christine June. BA, Faith Bapt. Bible Coll., 1981. Ordained to ministry Bapt. Ch., 1982. Asst. pastor Fundamental Bible Chapel, Pilot Mound, Iowa, 1979-81; assoc. pastor Silverdale (Wash.) Bapt. Ch., 1981-86; camp dir. Lake Ann (Mich.) Bapt. Camp, 1986—. Recipient Agriculture Accomplishment award DeKalb Agrl. Rsch. Inc., 1977, Tchrs. Cert. Evang. Tchr. Tng. Assn., 1981. Mem. Christian Camping Internat. Home: PO Box 109 Barber Rd Lake Ann MI 49650 Office: Lake Ann Bapt Camp Barber Rd Lake Ann MI 49650

RILEY, KENNETH LOYD, JR., lay worker; b. McGregor, Tex., July 2, 1957; s. Kenneth Loyd Sr. and Tince (Robinson) R.; m. Theresa LaVerne Colwell, Aug. 29, 1080; children: Averie, Arielle. Grad. high sch., Hewitt, Tex., 1975. Svcs. technician Southwestern Bell Telephone Co., Waco, Tex., 1975—; praise and worship leader Assembly of God Ch., McGregor, Tex., 1982-85; youth pastor Bethel Assembly of God Ch., Temple, Tex., 1987—. Home: 4314 Oak Bluff Cir Temple TX 76502

RILEY, LAWRENCE JOSEPH, bishop; b. Boston, Sept. 6, 1914; s. James and Ellen (Ryan) R. A.B., Boston Coll., 1936, LL.D., 1965; S.T.B., Gregorian U., 1939; S.T.D., Catholic U. Am., 1948; LL.D., Stonehill Coll., 1957. Ordained Priest Roman Cath. Ch., 1940; prof., rector St. John's Sem., Boston, 1941-66; prof. Emmanuel Coll., 1965-66; chaplain Harvard Cath. Club, 1950-54; vice officialis Met. Tribunal, Archdiocese of Boston, 1950-76;

sec. Archbishop of Boston, 1951-58; aux. bishop emeritus of Boston; asst. at Pontifical Throne, 1986—; vicar. gen. Archdiocese of Boston; pastor emeritus Most Precious Blood Parish, Hyde Park, Mass. Decorated Knight Comdr. with star Holy Sepulchre of Jerusalem; decorated Knight Order of Star of Italian Solidarity. Mem. Cath. Theol. Soc. Am. (past pres.), Mariological Soc. Am., Canon Law Soc. Am., Dante Alighieri Soc. Mass. (past v.p.), Nat. Cath. Edn Assn. Address: 43 Maple St Hyde Park MA 02136

RILEY, LINDA MARIE, religious organization administrator; b. Redwood City, Calif., May 1, 1953; d. Charles Robert and Ruth Louise (Toothman) Dalton; m. James William Riley, Aug. 12, 1973; children: Autumn, Amanda, Alexandra, Stephen. AA, El Camino Coll., 1977. Regional dir., bd. dirs. Open Arms, Federal Way, Wash., 1985-87; dir. Called Together Ministries, Torrance, Calif., 1987—. Author: One at a Time, 1986, Guide to Clergy Support Services, 1990; contbr. articles to profl. jours. Republican. Home and Office: Called Together Ministries 20820 Avis Ave Torrance CA 90503

RILEY, MEG AMELIA, religion educator; b. Houston, Nov. 20, 1955; d. Charles Woodson and Martha (Moore) Wilson; m. Kendrick Wronski, Sept. 7, 1991. BA, Reed Coll., Portland, Oreg., 1977; MA, United Theol. Sem., New Brighton, Minn., 1987. Cons. religious edn. 1st Unitarian Soc., Mpls., 1983-85; dir. religious edn. 1st Universalist Ch., Mpls., 1985-89; youth program dir. Unitarian Universalist Assn., Boston, 1989—. Editor: How to be a Con Artist, Conference Planning Handbook, 1991; creator, editor, team mgr. curriculum for adults: Ministry with Youth, 1991. Mem. Women Against Violence Against Women, Mpls., 1979-83; mem. Empowerment Group, Women Against Mil. Madness, Mpls., 1984-89; mem. Lesbian Feminist Organizing Com., Mpls., 1979-82. Recipient Ellie Morton award, Prairie Star Dist. Unitarian Universalist Assn., 1989. Mem. Soc. Larger Ministry, Unitarian Universalist Ministers Assn., Liberal Religious Educators Assn. Democrat. Office: Unitarian Universalist Assn 25 Beacon St Boston MA 02108 *I believe that our theology is much more grounded in our actions than our thoughts. I pay a great deal more attention to people's actions than words—how do they spend their money? time? life energy? This is faith.*

RILEY, PERRY EUGENE, minister; b. Houston, Oct. 14, 1950; s. Perry Eugene and Betty Eloise (Barlow) R.; m. Carolyn Joyce Womack, Aug. 15, 1969; children: Nathan Donnell, Angela Joyce. Houston Bapt. U., 1969-73; ThM, Southwestern Sem., 1982. Pastor Townley Pl. Bapt. Ch., Houston, 1970-73; evangelist Perry Riley Evanglistic Assn., Houston, 1973-78; pastor Elliott Bapt. Ch., Hearne, Tex., 1978-81, First Bapt. Ch., Rosebud, Tex., 1981-87, Eastside Bapt. Ch., Marianna, Fla., 1987—; dir. Latham Springs Bapt. Encampment, West, Tex., 1979-87; dir. evangelism Robertson Assn., 1979-81, moderator, 1980-81. Pres. Fla. Right to Life, Marianna, Fla., 1989—, state del., 1990-91; dir. Marianna Lions Club, 1988-89, v.p., 1990-91. Named Vol. of the Yr. Fla. Dept. Corrections, 1989, Outstanding Seminar Leader Prison Fellowship Ministries, 1990. Mem. Chapels for Prisons (pres. 1989—), Prison Fellowship Ministries, Chipola Ministerial Assn., Marianna Ministerial Assn. Republican. Home: 5053 Hwy 90E Marianna FL 32446 Office: Eastside Bapt Ch 4878 Hwy 90 E Marianna FL 32446

RILEY, RANDALL ALAN, minister; b. Warren, Ohio, June 21, 1949; s. Martin Earl and Ruth Marie (Baber) R.; m. Donna Marie Lynn, July 18, 1987; children: Jeremy, Stefanie, Joshua. BA in Psychology, Asbury Coll., Wilmore, Ky., 1971; BA in Bible, Lancaster Bible Coll., 1972; MA in Clin. Psychology, Akron U., 1975. Ordained to ministry, Christian Ch. 1973. Pastor Brady Lake Chapel, Kent, Ohio, 1972-75, Southington (Ohio) Christian Ch., 1975—. Author ency. Audience Hypnosis, 1977; author book: Miracles, 1990; contbr. articles to profl. jours. Trustee YMCA-Trumbull, Warren, 1986-88; pres. New Life Maternity Home, Warren, 1991—; coach Girls Softball, Southington, 1985-91. Recipient Gold award, N. Am. Assn. Ventriloquists, 1974, 75. Mem. Evang. Ministerial Fellowship (pres.), Ohio Mental Health Counselors Assn., Ohio Assn. Evangelicals. Home: 3290 Barclay Messerly Suthington OH 44470 Office: SCC PO Box 70 Southington OH 44470

RINAS, ERNIE EMIL, minister; b. Waverly, N.Y., Sept. 18, 1955; s. Adolph Julius and Lydia Tina (Dalke) R.; m. Rita June Terry, July 3, 1983; 1 child, Melody Marie. BA, Mobile (Ala.) Coll., 1981; MDiv in Pastoral Ministries, New Orleans Bapt. Theol. Sem., 1984. Ordained to ministry So. Bapt. Conv., 1977. Pastor Cedar City Bapt. Ch., Jefferson City, Mo., 1984-89, New Hope Bapt. Ch., Fulton, Mo., 1989—; messenger So. Bapt. Conv., 1977—; chmn. Callaway Assn., Fulton, 1985—, chmn. annuity and stewardship, 1985—; ex-officio mem. com. New Hope Bapt. Ch., 1989—. Home and Office: 907 Southwest Blvd Jefferson City MO 65109

RINCU, ION, religious organization administrator. Gen. sec. Bapt. Ch. (Union) Romania, Bucharest. Office: Bapt Ch, Bd N Titulescu 56/1, 78152 Bucharest Romania*

RINDEN, DAVID LEE, editor; b. Lake Mills, Iowa, Aug. 1, 1941; s. Oscar Henry and Iva (Stensrud) R.; m. Gracia Elizabeth Carlson, Sept. 11, 1966; children: Jonathan, Elizabeth, Amy. BA, Moorhead State U., 1964; diploma, Luth. Brethren Sem., 1966; postgrad., Seattle Pacific U., 1973. Ordained to ministry Luth. Ch., 1967. Pastor Bethesda Luth. Ch., Eau Claire, Wis., 1968-72, Maple Pk. Luth. Ch., Lynnwood, Wash., 1972-79; v.p. Ch. of the Luth. Brethren, Fergus Falls, Minn., 1991—; editor Faith & Fellowship, Fergus Falls, Minn., 1979—; exec. dir. ch. svcs. Ch. of the Luth. Brethren, Fergus Falls, 1979—; chmn. com. on commitment Ch. of Luth. Brethren, Fergus Falls, 1981-82, com. on role of women in ch., 1984-86, chmn. com. on 90th anniversary, 1989—, chmn. bd. publs., 1968-78. Editor: Explanation of Luther's Small Catechism, 1988; author: Biblical Foundations, 1981. Founding com. JAIL, Inc., Fergus Falls, 1991; pres. bd. dirs. Fergus Falls Fed. Community Credit Union, 1987—. Mem. Fergus Falls Ministerial Assn (sec. 1989-90, v.p. 1991—), Kiwanis. Home: 701 W Channing Fergus Falls MN 56537 Office: Ch of the Luth Brethren 704 W Vernon Fergus Falls MN 56537

RINEHART, DENNIS OLIVER, minister; b. Mansfield, Ohio, Apr. 27, 1946; s. Irvin Oliver and Eleanor Gladys (Gages) R.; m. Deborah Kay Lay, May 20, 1972; children: Benjamin Todd, Jennifer Eileen. BA, Spring Arbor (Mich.) Coll., 1968; MDiv, Asbury Theol. Sem., Wilmore, Ky., 1971. Ordained to ministry United Meth. Ch., 1971. Min. youth and edn. Dueber United Meth. Ch., Canton, Ohio, 1971-74; min. Rural Chapel United Meth. Ch., Galena, Ohio, 1974-79, Coshocton (Ohio) Park United Meth. Ch., 1979-88, Otterbein United Meth. Ch., Warren, Ohio, 1988—; dean Jr. High Sch. Christian Youth Festival Camp, Perrysville, Ohio, 1971-75, 5th-6th Grade Bible Bowl Camp, Painesville, Ohio, 1988-90. Resource leader grief recovery program Hospice, Warren, 1988—, Recovery from Loss, Warren, 1988—. Mem. Fellowship Merry Christians (min. of humor), Rotary (coord. meml. parade Champion Twp., Warren 1988—, Fellowship Champion 1990). Office: Otterbein United Meth Ch 1128 State Rd W Warren OH 44481

RINEHART, JOETTA FEEZOR, church denominational administrator; b. Denton, N.C., Feb. 24, 1933; d. Ernest Ray and Mary (Martin) Doby; m. Paul M. Feezor, Oct. 6, 1951 (dec. Aug. 1970); m. Bill L. Rinehart, June 15, 1975. Grad., Ashmore Bus Coll., 1953; student, U. N.C., Charlotte, 1971-72. Pres. United Meth. Women Western N.C. Conf., 1975-80; dir. Bd. Global Ministries, 1977-84; v.p. Southeastern Jursidiction United Meth. Women, 1980-84; fin. chmn. Gen. Commn. Status and Role Women, 1984-88, v.p., 1989-90, pres., 1990—; dir. pub. rels., mktg. and devel. Southeastern Jurisdiction Adminstrv. Coun., Lake Junaluska, N.C., 1986-90; trustee Pfeiffer Coll., Misenheimer, N.C., 1975-92, Givens Estates, Asheville, N.C., 1990—. Pres. N.C. Bus. and Profl. Womens Clubs Inc., Raleigh, N.C., 1975-76 (Women of Yr. 1975). Named Outstanding Woman N.C., 1985. Mem. Gen. Coun. Ministries, World Meth. Coun. Democrat.

RING, RODNEY EVERETT, religion educator; b. Sioux City, Iowa, May 13, 1927; s. Everett Irwin and Pearl Olive (Rubeck) R.; m. Naomi Ruth Korn, Sept. 11, 1949; children: Alexander Everett, Angela Catherine. MA, U. Chgo., 1950, PhD, 1954. Prof. Muhlenberg Coll., Allentown, Pa., 1950-51, 55-90, Thiel Coll., Greenville, Pa., 1954-55. Author: Solving Biblical Problems, 1988; editor ELNA bull., 1970-72; contbr. articles to religious jours. Sgt. U.S. Army, 1946-48. Grantee Muhlenberg Coll., 1964, Mack Trucks Inc., 1967. Mem. Soc. Bibl. Lit., Am. Acad. Religion. Home: 250 Deer Run Rd Kutztown PA 19530

RINGENBERG, WILLIAM CAREY, historian, minister; b. Ft. Wayne, Ind., Aug. 18, 1939; s. Loyal Robert and Rhoda (Roth) R.; m. Rebecca Helen Lehman, Aug. 18, 1962; children: Matthew, Mark, Peter, Melodie. BS, Taylor U., 1961; MA, Ind. U., 1964; PhD, Mich. State U., 1970. Ordained to ministry Evang. Mennonite Ch., 1979. From asst. prof. to prof. history Taylor U., Upland, Ind., 1968—, assoc. dean acad. affairs, 1974-79, chmn. dept. history, 1982—, dir. honors program, 1983—; min. Bailey Chapel United Meth. Ch., Anderson, Ind., 1979-80, Mt. Carmel United Meth. Ch., Hartford City, Ind., 1980-85, Cammack United Meth. Ch., Hartford City, Ind., 1985-89; v.p. Conf. on Faith and History, 1987-88, pres., 1989-90. Author: Taylor University: The First 125 Years, 1973, The Christian College: A History of Protestant Higher Education in America, 1984; mem. editorial bd. Christian Scholar's Rev., 1970-74; contbr. articles and revs. to religious publs. Lilly fellow Ind. U., 1962-63; scholar Inst. for Advanced Christian Studies, 1981, others. Mem. Am. Hist. Assn., Am. Soc. Ch. History, Orgn. Am. Historians, Chi Alpha Omega. Mennonite/Methodist. Office: Taylor U Dept History Reade Ctr Upland IN 46989 *What you are is more important than what you do. Wisdom is of greater value than knowledge, character than craft, love and kindness than manipulation.*

RINGER, EUGENE, pastor; b. Carrolltown, Ga., Jan. 22, 1937; s. Floyd and Ollie (Veal) R.; m. Bronis Lee Clark, June 13, 1954 (dec. May 1980); children: Alfred, Belvis, Laketha, Karen, Pamela, Kevin; m. Darlene Barrow, June 19, 1982; children: Janelle, Javon. Grad., Miracle Valley Bible Coll., 1967; DD, U. Bible Coll., 1978. Presiding jr. Bishop, nat. supt. Sharon Pentecostal Ch. God, Cleve., 1966-76; jr. Bishop Pentecostal True Holiness Ch. God, Birmingham, Ala., 1977-80; dist. Bishop Greater Emmanuel Apostolic Faith, Columbus, Ohio, 1980-87; pastor Faith Temple Pentecostal Ch. God, Dayton, Ohio, 1965-90; trustee Faith Temple Pentecostal Ch. God, Dayton, 1970-90. Home: 31 Knollview Pl Dayton OH 45405 *"For what is a man profited, if he shall gain the whole world, and lose his own, or what shall a man give in exchange for his soul?." St. Matthew 16:26.*

RINGLEBEN, JOACHIM, theologian; b. Flensburg, Fed. Republic Germany, July 7, 1945; s. Herbert and Lotte (Schweizer) R.; m. Heidrun Koch, 1970; children: Anselm, Almut. ThD, U. Kiel, Fed. Republic Germany, 1977, Habilitation, 1981. Asst. Theol. Faculty, Kiel, Fed. Republic Germany, 1973-83; prof. systematic theology U. Göttingen, Fed. Republic Germany, 1984—. Author: Hegel's Theory of Sin, 1977, Appropriation Kierkegaards Speculative Theology, 1983, The Nearness of God by Augustin, 1988. Mem. Sci. Soc. Theology, Internat. Hegel Soc., Kierkegaard Acad. Kopenhagen. Lutheran. Home: Dahlmannstrasse 24, 3400 Göttingen Federal Republic of Germany Office: Vereinigte Theologische, Seminare Platz der, Seminar Platz Göttinger, Sieben 2, 3400 Göttingen Federal Republic of Germany

RINGLER, STANLEY ARTHUR, rabbi; b. N.Y.C., Nov. 8, 1941; s. Jacob E. and Joan K. Ringler; m. Marlene F. Smith, June 18, 1967; children—Yaakov, Ami, Elana. B.A., U. Cin., 1965; B.H.L., Hebrew Union Coll., Cin., 1966, M.A.H.L., 1969. Ordained rabbi, 1969. Dir. U. Miami B'nai B'rith Hillel Found., Coral Gables, 1970-73; area dir. B'nai B'rith Hillel Founds. Greater Miami, 1973-79; Fla. area dir. B'nai B'rith Hillel Founds. of Fla., 1975-79; nat. dir. dept. community affairs B'nai B'rith Hillel Founds., Washington, 1979—; bd. dirs. Am. Jewish Congress, Council South Fla., 1975-77, Am. Jewish Com. Fla., 1978-79; mem. Nat. Rabbinic Cabinet, United Jewish Appeal, 1980—; mem. profl. com. on campus service Council of Jewish Fedns., 1981—; mem. campus adv. com. Nat. Jewish Communal Relations Adv. Com., Israel Task Force, 1982—; nat. dir. B'nai B'rith Hillel Acad. Assocs., Washington, 1984—; bd. dirs. Am. Friends of Beit Lohamei Hagetaot, Israel, 1984—, Givat Haviva Ednl. Found.; mem. U.S. adv. com. Shilo Adv. Service in Israel, 1983—. Contbr. articles to profl. jours. Mem. Central Conf. Am. Rabbis (nat. bd. dirs. 1977-79), Labor Zionist Alliance, Americans for Progressive Israel, Assn. Reform Zionists. Democrat. Jewish. Lodge: B'nai B'rith. Avocations: reading; writing. Office: B'nai Brith Hillel Founds 1640 Rhode Island Ave NW Washington DC 20036

RINKER, CRAIG WAYNE, pastor; b. Phila., Aug. 9, 1945; s. Berl Leroy and Maxene Betsy (Abshier) R.; m. Kathlyn Louise Waugh, Dec. 19, 1970 (div.); children: Sheri Lou, Amy Kathlyn, Craig Wayne II; m. Bonita Lee Dupre, Feb. 16, 1991. AA, St. Johns Coll., Winfield, Kans., 1965; BA in Philosophy, Concordia Sr. Coll., 1967; M of Divinity, Concordia Sem., 1971; MST, Luth. Sch. of Theology, 1975; PhD, U. Okla., Norman, 1979. Ordained pastor Luth. Ch., 1972. Vicar Messiah Luth. Ch., Oklahoma City, 1969-70; pastoral asst. Luth. Ch. of Our Savior, Bethany, 1972-75; assoc. pastor Good Shepherd Luth. Ch., Hayward, Calif., 1975-78; pastor Grace Luth. Ch., Houma, La., 1978—; cir. counselor Greater New Orleans #2-LCMS, 1979-88; vicar supr. Concordia Sem., Ft. Wayne, Ind., 1981-82; adj. asst. prof. U. Southwestern La., Lafayette, 1984-86; chmn. sect. So. Speech Communication Conv., Baton Rouge, 1984, Birmingham, 1990. Contbr. articles to profl. jours. Mem. bd. commrs. Terrebonne Gen. Hosp., Houma, La., 1987—, chmn. credentials com.; v.p. Bayouland YMCA, 1986-90; treas. Dulac Community Ctr., 1988-90; mem. Rep. Nat. Com. Mem. So. States Speech Communication Assn. (sect. chmn. conv. Baton Rouge, 1984, Birmingham 1990, panelist New Orleans 1988), Speech Communication Assn., Terrebonne Assn. Mins. (officer 1978—), Rotary (bd. dirs. 1980—), Krewe of Christopher. Republican. Lutheran. Avocations: bowling, reading. Home: 106 Mobile Estates Dr Gray LA 70359 Office: Grace Luth Ch PO Box 1246lvd Houma LA 70360

RIOS, DEBORAH CHARMAYNE, principal; b. Waco, Tex., Sept. 18, 1954; d. Arthur William and Johnnie Lucille (Collins) Hoff; m. Rudolph Guadalupe Rios Jr., July 12, 1975; children: Jason Rudolph, David Arthur. BS, Incarnate Word Coll., San Antonio, 1977; postgrad., Calif. State U., Fullerton, 1979, Luther Rice Seminary, Jacksonville, Fla. Dir. children's worship Village Parkway Bapt. Ch., San Antonio, 1985-88; kindergarten tchr. Village Parkway Christian Sch., San Antonio, 1987-89, dir., 1989-90, prin., 1990—; vacation Bible sch. tchr. Shearer Hills Bapt., San Antonio, 1976, Village Parkway Bapt., 1985-89, Sunday sch. tchr., 1983-85; presch. tchr. 1st Bapt., Orange, Calif., 1979-81. Coord. pack 127 Boy Scouts Am., 1989—; chmn. community action San Antonio Dog Tng. Club, 1987-88, trophy chmn., 1987-88. Mem. Internat. Fellowship Christian Sch. Adminstrs., Am. Home Econs. Assn., Tex. Assn. Bapt. Schs. (mem. at large), Bexar County Kennel Club, Golden Retriever Club Am., Field Spaniel Soc. Am. (chmn. nominating com. 1990). Office: Village Parkway Christian 3002 Village Pkwy San Antonio TX 78251 *During times when I have felt like giving up, I remember 1 Timothy 1:12, "I thank Christ Jesus our Lord, who has strengthened me, because He considered me faithful, putting me into service."*

RIPPIN, ANDREW LAWRENCE, religious studies educator; b. London, May 16, 1950. B.A., U. Toronto, Can., 1974; M.A., McGill U., Can., 1977, Ph.D., 1981. Lectr. Mich. State U., East Lansing, 1979-80; asst. prof. U. Calgary, Can., 1980-84, assoc. prof. religious studies, 1984-91, prof., 1991—; vis. prof. Inst. Islamic Studies, McGill U., 1991—. Author: (with J. Knappert) Textual Sources for the Study of Islam, 1986; editor: Approaches to the History of the Interpretation of the Qur'ān, 1988, Muslims: Their Religious Beliefs and Practices, Vol. I, The Formative Period, 1990; contbr. articles to profl. jours. Mem. Am. Oriental Soc., Am. Acad. Religion, British Soc. Middle Eastern Studies, Can. Soc. Study Religion. Office: U Calgary Dept Religious Studies, Calgary, AB Canada T2N 1N4 *To be, in the twentieth century, a popular novelist of the seventeenth seemed to him a diminution. To be, in some way, Cervantes and reach the Quixote seemed less arduous to him—and, consequently less interesting—than to go on being Pierre Menard and reach the Quixote through the experiences of Pierre Menard.*

RISCHAR, SISTER ANNE MARY, manager, retirement residence; b. Quincy, Ill., Aug. 21, 1937; d. George Maxmillan and Mildred (Cramsey) R. BA in English, Cardinal Stritch Coll., 1967; MEd, U. Wis., Milw., 1971; MBA, U. Notre Dame, 1985. Tchr. Archdiocese of Milw., 1957-58, 60-67, prin., 1967-75; tchr. Archdiocese of Chgo., 1958-60; consol. sch. adminstr. Diocese of Peoria, Ill., 1976-83; adminstr. St. Francis Convent, Milw., 1985-91; project mgr., mgr. sr. housing Canticle Ct., Inc., Milw., 1991—; facilitator for mgmt. Sisters of Divine Savior, Milw., 1990; facilitator for decision making Cursillo Leadership, Archdiocese of Milw., 1987, spiritual advisor, 1985—; bd. dirs. Project Equality, 1987—, pres., 1990. Roman Catholic. Avocations: cooking, baking, walking, reading. Home: 2339-A E Malvern Pl Milwaukee WI 53207 Office: Canticle Ct Inc 3201 S Lake Dr Saint Francis WI 53207

RISING, RICHARD LINN, retired priest; b. Columbus, Ohio, May 7, 1920; s. Francis Russell and Cicely Fay (Rodgers) R.; m. Charlotte Elizabeth Drea, Sept. 20, 1969; children: John Reed, Cynthia Anne, Caroline Fay, Stephen Reed, Catherine Reed, William Reed. BA, Williams Coll., 1942; MA, Harvard U., 1949; MDiv, Episc. Theol. Sch., Cambridge, Mass., 1952. Ordained priest Episcopal Ch., 1952. Seminary dean in P.R.; pastor various chs. in The Philippines; pastor chs. in Mass., the Caribbean, 1952-68; staff assoc. Am. Assn. Theol. Schs., Dayton, Ohio, 1968-70; assoc. dir. Episc. Bd. Theol. Edn., 1070-76; coord., editor Episc. Study Com. Preparation Ordained Ministry, 1974-76; rector St. Barnabas Parish, Cortez, Colo., 1976-80; ret., 1980; mem. adv. bd. St. Andrew's Theol. Sem., Manila, 1959-60; mem. Episc. Joint Commn. on Edn. for Holy Orders, 1965-68. Mem. editorial bd. Overseas Mission Rev., 1956-68; contbr. articles to religious jours. Mem. Phi Beta Kappa. Home: 560 Weller Ln Ashland OR 97520

RISTUCCIA, MATTHEW PAUL, minister; b. Newton, Mass., Nov. 2, 1952; s. Bernard J. and Elinor M. (Koonz) R.; m. Karen J. Holditch, June 18, 1977; children: Joel Stephen, Nathan John. BA in English Lit. cum laude, Princeton U., 1975; MDiv summa cum laude, Grace Sem., 1978; D Ministry, Dallas Sem., 1991. Ordained to ministry, 1979. Campus min. Princeton (N.J.) Evang. Fellowship, 1978-85; sr. pastor Westerly Road Ch., Princeton, 1985—; dir. Princeton Evang. Fellowship, 1986—; mem. U.S. coun. Arab World Ministries, Upper Darby, Pa., 1990—. Office: Westerly Rd Ch 25 Westerly Rd Princeton NJ 08540

RITCHIE, WYMAN, minister; b. Middle Granville, N.Y., July 8, 1929; s. John Arthur and Florence Eva (Farrar) R.; m. Mona Lou Klinger, June 21, 1949; children: Mona Lou, Nancy Arlene, Patricia Marie, Timothy David. BA in Bible, Cedarville Coll., 1971; ThM in Theology, Dallas Theol. Sem., 1971. Ordained to ministry Bapt. Ch., 1951. Pastor Lakeville Bapt. Ch., Cossayuna, N.Y., 1951-53, Grapeville Bapt. Ch., Climax, N.Y., 1953-57, East Lindley Bapt. Ch., Corning, N.Y., 1957-61, Marsh Corner Community Ch., Methuen, Mass., 1961-63, Calvary Bapt. Ch., Wellsville, N.Y., 1963-65; ch. planter, pastor Grace Bapt. Fellowship, Barre, Vt., 1973-90; carpenter, Barre, Vt., 1973-91. Republican. Home and Office: Grace Bapt Fellowship 8 Balsam Dr RR 4 Barre VT 05641

RITTENHOUSE, WILLIAM HENRY, minister; b. Macon, Ga., Apr. 6, 1922; s. William Henry and Forence (Perry) R.; m. Nell Crider, Dec. 20, 1944; children: Sherie, JoAnn, Nancy. BS, Stetson U., 1942; MA, U. N.C., 1947, PhD, 1949; postgrad., Duke U., 1949; PhD in Div., William Jewel Coll., 1949; LLD, U. Kuwait, 1974. Pastor Southside Bapt. Ch., Miami, Fla., 1949-55, Sylvan Hills Bapt. Ch., Atlanta, 1955-62, Roswell St. Bapt. Ch., Marietta, Ga., 1962-64; pres. High Flight Found., Colorado Springs, Colo., 1972-77; pastor First Bapt. Ch., Tupelo, Miss., 1977-82, Nassau Bay Bapt. Ch., Houston, 1965-72, 83—. Author: Barbed Wire Preacher, 1955. Served to lt. col. USAF, 1942-46, ETO, with res. to 1955. Decorated D.F.C., Legion of Merit, Air medal with oak leaf cluster, Bronze Star, Purple Heart, Presdl. Citation, USAF, 1942-45. Baptist. Lodge: Rotary. Office: Nassau Bay Bapt Ch 18131 Nassau Bay Dr Houston TX 77058

RITTER, BRUCE, priest, former administrator; b. Trenton, N.J., Feb. 25, 1927; s. Louis Charles and Julia Agnes (Morrissey) R. S.T.D., Seraphicum Pontifical U. of St. Bonaventure, Rome, 1958; L.H.D. (hon.), Niagara U., 1979, Lemoyne Coll., 1980, Fairfield U., 1981, Iona Coll., Amherst Coll., St. Francis Coll., 1982, Fordham U., 1983, Bellarmine Coll., 1984, Drew U., St. Peter's Coll., Pace U., U. Medicine and Dentistry, N.J., 1985; H.H.D. (hon.), Stonehill Coll., St. Francis Coll., Loretto, Pa., 1981, Franciscan Community; D.Ministry honoris causa, Immaculate Conception Sem., 1981; D.Pub. Service (hon.), Villanova U., 1981; LL.D., Chestnut Hill Coll., 1981; D.Humanitarian Services (hon.), Duquesne U., Providence Coll., 1982; D.Sc. (hon.), Boston Coll., 1983, Quincy Coll., 1985. Joined Order Minor Conventuals (Franciscan); ordained priest Roman Catholic Ch., 1956. Prof. theology Manhattan Coll., N.Y.C., 1963-68; founder, pres. Covenant House, N.Y.C., 1972-90. Commr. Atty. Gen.'s Commn. on Pornography, Dept. Justice, 1985; mem. adv. com. N.Y. State Clergy; bd. dirs. Americares Found., New Canaan, Conn. Served with USN, 1945-46. Recipient numerous awards including Elizabeth Ann Seton medal Coll. Mt. St. Vincent, 1978, Elliot Black award Am. Ethical Union of Boston, 1978, Golden Doughnut award Salvation Army, 1979, Franciscan Internat. award, 1979, Robert E. Gallagher award Cath. Charities Family and Children's Services, 1980, Kewetanda award Camp Fire Council Greater N.Y., 1981, Msgr. Lester Quinn Community and Humanity award, 1981, youth activity award N.J. State council K.C., 1982, Dr. Luke Mulligan Met. award Carmelite Scholarship Dinner, 1982, Pub. Service medal N.Y. State Bar Assn., 1982, St. Francis award St. Francis Boys' Homes, Inc., 1984, Jefferson Cup Exec. Forum, 1984, Cardinal Gibbons award Cath. U. Am., 1984. Life mem. Nat. Chaplain's Assn. (Legion of Honor award 1980). Office: care Covenant House 460 W 41st St New York NY 10036

RITTER, WALTER ADOLF, minister, educator; b. Edmonton, Alta., Can., June 24, 1932; s. Carl and Natalie (Gliege) R.: m. Doris Pauline Elizabeth Andres, June 11, 1957; 1 child, Libby (dec. Nov. 1984). BA, Concordia Sem., 1954, BD, 1957; STM, Luth. Theol. Sem., 1985. Ordained to ministry Luth. Ch., 1957. Pastor Christ Luth. Ch., MacNutt, Sask., Can., 1957-60, Faith Luth. Ch., Winnipeg, Man., Can., 1960-67, Bethel Luth Ch., Edmonton, 1967-76; instr. Augustana Univ. Coll., Camrose, Alta., 1976—, coord. Coll. Theology and The Arts, 1988—, coord. for theol. lecture series, 1990—; nat. coord. coll. and univ. work for Luth. Ch. Can., 1966-70; mem. joint commn. Inter-Luth. Rels., 1961-67; chmn. Edmonton bd. control, Concordia Coll. 1973-75, chmn. master plan com., 1975-76; participant 1st Nat. Luth.-Roman Cath. ch. dialogue, 1969. Contbr. articles to religious jours. Home: 6109 Marler Dr, Camrose, AB Canada T4V 2R3 Office: Augustana Univ Coll, 4901 46th Ave, Camrose, AB Canada T4V 2R3 *I have found that the call for open-mindedness often comes from those who wish nothing more than affirmation of their own biases, and their own firm convictions often deny the same right to those who disagree.*

RIVAS, ROBERT, bishop. Bishop of Kingstown Roman Cath. Ch., St. Vincent and the Grenadines. Office: Bishop's House, POB 860, Kingstown Saint Vincent and the Grenadines*

RIVERA, VICTOR MANUEL, retired bishop; b. Penuelas, P.R., Oct. 30, 1916; s. Victor and Filomena (Toro) R.; m. Barbara Ross Starbuck, Dec. 1944; 3 children. Student, Modern Bus. Coll. P.R., 1937, DuBose Meml. Ch. Tng. Sch., 1938; B.D., Ch. Div. Sch. Pacific, 1944, D.D., 1965; postgrad., St. Augustine Coll., Eng., 1957. Ordained deacon Episcopal Ch., 1943, priest, 1944; curate St. John's Cathedral, Santurce, P.R., 1944; rector St. Paul's Ch., Visalia, Calif., 1945-68; bishop San Joaquin, Fresno, Calif., 1968-88.

RIVERA Y DAMAS, ARTURO, archbishop. Archbishop of San Salvador, Roman Cath. Ch., El Salvador. Office: Seminario San Jose Montana, la Calle Poniente 3412, San Salvador El Salvador*

RIVERO, FATHER JULIO B., music educator; b. N.Y.C., Dec. 24, 1929; s. Rogelio and Carmen (Blanco) R. BS, Columbia U., 1952; MA, NYU, 1960, NYU, 1980. Asst. pastor St. Mary's Ch., St. Petersburg, Fla.; choir dir. St. Patrick Ch., Tampa, Fla.; dir. ESL, asst. headmaster St. Francis Prep., Spring Grove, Pa.; music dir. St. Patrick Ch. and Sch., Tampa, Fla.; spiritual dir. Our Lady of Divine Providence, Clearwater, Fla., 1991—. Mem. ASCD, Lang. Tchrs. Assn., Spanish Am. Ctr. (bd. dirs.). Home and Office: Our Lady of Divine Providence 702 Bayview Ave Clearwater FL 34619

RIVERS, DAVID BUCHANAN, priest; b. New Haven, May 22, 1937; s. Burke and Phyllis (McCausland) R.; m. Elizabeth Lee Zeller, Aug. 5, 1961; children: Christina, Julia, Diana, John. AB, Haverford Coll., 1959; STB, Episcopal Theol. Sch., 1964. Ordained to ministry Episopal Ch. as deacon, 1964, as priest 1965. Vicar St. Elizabeth's Episcopal Ch., Allentown, Pa., 1964-68; priest in charge St. Stephen's Ch., San Pedro de Macorís, Dominican Republic, 1968-71; rector Gloria Dei Ch., Phila., 1972—. Contbr. articles to profl. jours. Mem. Old Phila. Congregations (pres. 1990—). Democrat. Home: 916 S Swanson St Philadelphia PA 19147 Office: Gloria Dei Church Delaware Ave and Christian Philadelphia PA 19147

RIVERS, HORACE WILLIAM, minister; b. Chesterfield, S.C., Sept. 4, 1941; s. Horace Legett and Tessie Isabell (Burr) R.; m. Betty Faye Raffaldt, May 30, 1964; children: William Anthony, Horace Kevin, Jan Annette. AA, North Greenville Coll., 1975; BA, Lander Coll., 1976; M in Bibl. Studies, Friendship Coll., 1984, ThD, 1985. Ordained to ministry So. Bapt. Conv., 1968. Pastor Friendship Bapt. Ch., Honea Path, S.C., 1975-78, Calvary Bapt. Ch., Anderson, S.C., 1978-80, Philippi Bapt. Ch., Union, S.C., 1980-82, Arrowwood Bapt. Ch., Chesnee, S.C., 1982-88; pastor, pres. Bel Forest Bapt. Ch. and Christian Acad., Bel Air, Md., 1988—. Active Nat. Write Your Congressman, 1990. With USN, 1960-64. Mem. S.E. Accrediting Assn., Susquehanna Bapt. Assn. (vice moderator 1990-91, moderator 1991—), Am. Legion. Home and Office: Bel Forest Bapt Ch and Christian Acad 603 Vale Rd Bel Air MD 21014 *I can never get over the fact that God loved me so much that he sent His only Son to die for me. His love is transforming. The world needs to hear this news. I am committed to telling it in my little corner.*

RIVERS, SHANE, publisher, writer; b. Savannah, Ga., Nov. 6, 1941; m. Marissa Cagney (dec. Mar. 1983); m. Mary Antkowiak, 1989. BA, Ohio State U., 1963; MA, Toledo U., 1970. Reporter The Press Newspapers, Millbury, Ohio, 1963-65; corr. Cleve. Citizen, Columbus, Ohio, 1965-68; asst. editor Cleve. Citizen, 1977-82; corr. Toledo Blade, 1968-77; pub. Werik Christian News, Cleve., 1983—. Contbr. articles to religious jours. With U.S. Army, 1963-65. Office: Werik Christian News 3424 Helen Rd Cleveland OH 44122-3871

RIVES, THOMAS NELSON, minister; b. Memphis, May 18, 1946; s. Malcomb Eldridge and Dorothy Bell (Nelson) R.; m. Dianne Saleeby, Dec. 17, 1967; children: Thomas N. Jr., Ashley Dianne. BS in Edn., Memphis State U., 1971; postgrad., Southwestern Sem., 1977-79. Ordained to ministry Bapt. Ch., 1975. Min. youth Whitehaven Bapt. Ch., Memphis, 1970-74, 1st Bapt. Ch., Cleve., 1974-77; assoc. pastor 1st Bapt. Ch., Hurst, Tex., 1977-79; min. recreation Red Bank Bapt. Ch., Chattanooga, Tenn., 1979-83; assoc. pastor 1st Bapt. Ch., Tampa, Fla., 1983-86, Bay Area Bapt. Ch., Tampa, 1986—. Author: (pamphlet) Bring on the Clowns, 1990; contbr. articles to profl. jours. Sgt. U.S. Army, 1967-70. Recipient Army Commendation medal U.S. Army, 1969, Gov.'s Religious Commnedation, 1982. Mem. Recreation Assn. Fla. Bapt. (pres. 1986-89), Fellowship Christian Magicians, Clowns of Am., World Clown Assn. Home: 2306 Lila Ln Tampa FL 33629 Office: Bay Area Bapt Ch 9218 N 26th St Tampa FL 33612 *I believe when Jesus said, "I've come that you might have abundant life" He wanted us to enjoy the Christian life and not just endure it.*

RIZOR, AMELIA MARGARET, lay worker; b. Hopkinsville, Ky., July 14, 1963; d. Webb Claude and Margaret (Hadley) Rizor. BA, Belhaven Coll., 1986. Youth dir. jr. and sr. high sch. Faith Presbyn. Ch., Goodlettsville, Tenn., 1986—; stock specialist Castner Knott Inc., Goodlettsville, 1988—; coord. LUG Group Jackson (Miss.) Youth for Christ, 1984, 86, skit supr., 1984-86, Bahamas del., 1990; chmn. Outreach, Faith Presbyn. Ch., 1988-89, Vacation Bible Sch. dir, 1988-89; dir. Mex. mission trip World Servants, Reynosa, 1991. Author: Devotionals for Every Occasion, 1986. Chairperson 69th St. Adopt A Hwy. team, Goodlettsville, 1990. Named Miss Island in the Son, Sonshine Club, 1990, Stock Person of Yr., Castner Knott Inc., 1990. Home: 612 Dorothy Dr Goodlettsville TN 37072 Office: Faith Presbyn Ch 372 Caldwell Dr Goodlettsville TN 37072

ROA, DORIE CORRECES, church organist, nurse; b. Iligan City, Mindanao, The Philippines, Aug. 12, 1952; came to U.S., 1980; d. Guillermo Ramirez and Ambrosia Dalisay (Loyola) Correces; m. Antonio Baril Roa, Nov. 17, 1975; children: Ginnie Ann, Edsel. BS in Nursing, Mountain View Coll., Malaybalay, The Philippines, 1975; M in Nursing, U. The Philippines, Manila, 1979. Pianist So. Mindanao Acad., Davao, 1965-69; ch. pianist Seventh-day Adventist Ch., Davao City, The Philippines, 1966-75; pianist Mountain View Coll., 1969-73, MVC Coll. Nursing, Iligan City, 1973-75; pianist, organist Pasay City Seventh-day Adventist Ch., Manila, 1975-79; pianist Glendora (Calif.) Seventh-day Adventist Ch., 1980-82; pianist, organist Loma Linda (Calif.) Filipino Seventh-day Adventist Ch., 1982-83; pianist, organist Walker Meml. Seventh-day Adventist Ch., Avon Park, Fla., 1984—, mem. music com., 1988—, ch. organist coord., 1991; cardiac rehab. nurse Lake Placid (Fla.) Family Care Ctr., 1990—; organist, choir accompanist 1st United Meml. Meth. Ch., Lake Placid, 1985-87. Mem. Assn. Seventh-day Adventist Nurses, Am. Guild Organists, Asian Am. Assn., Lake Placid C. of C., Newstart Club, Rotary. Home: 2222 N Oleander Dr Avon Park FL 33825 Office: Lake Placid Family Care Ctr 201 US Hwy 27 S Lake Placid FL 33852

ROACH, SISTER ANN DOMINIC, school system administrator. Supt. schs. Archdiocese of Boston. Office: Office Schs Supt 468 Beacon St Boston MA 02115*

ROACH, JOHN ROBERT, archbishop; b. Prior Lake, Minn., July 31, 1921; s. Simon J. and Mary (Regan) R. B.A., St. Paul Sem., 1946; M.A., U. Minn., 1957; L.H.D. (hon.), Gustavus Adolphus Coll., St. Mary's Coll., St. Xavier U., Villanova U. Ordained priest Roman Catholic Ch., 1946; instr. St. Thomas Acad., 1946-50, headmaster, 1951-68; named domestic prelate, 1966; rector St. John Vianney Sem., 1968-71; aux. bishop St. Paul and Mpls., 1971; consecrated bishop, 1971; pastor St. Charles Borromeo Ch., Mpls., 1971-73, St. Cecilia Ch., St. Paul, 1973-75; archbishop of St. Paul, 1975—; appointed vicar for parishes, 1971, vicar for clergy, 1972—; Episc. moderator Nat. Apostolate for Mentally Retarded, 1974; Mem. Priests Senate, 1968-72; pres. Priests Senate and Presbytery, 1970; chmn. Com. on Accreditation Pvt. Schs. in Minn., 1952-57; mem. adv. com. Coll. Entrance Exam. Bd., 1964; Episc. mem. Bishops and Pres.'s Com.; chmn. Bishops Com. to Oversee Implementation of the Call to Action Program, 1979-80; chmn. priestly formation com.; mem. Cath. Charity Bd. Trustee St. Paul Sem. Sch. Div., 1971—, now chmn.; trustee Cath. U. Am., 1978-81, Coll. St. Catherine; chmn. bd. trustees St. Thomas Acad., U. St. Thomas, St. John Vianney Sem.; v.p. Nat. Conf. Cath. Bishops, 1977-80; pres., 1980-83, chmn. ad hoc com. on call to action, 1977. Mem. Am. Coun. Edn. (del. 1963-65), Minn. Cath. Edn. Assn. (past pres.), Assn. Mil. Colls. and Schs. U.S. (past pres.), North Cen. Assn. Colls. and Secondary Schs., Nat. Conf. Cath. Bishops (adminstrv. com., priestly formation com., chmn. vocations com., priorities and plans com.), U.S. Cath. Conf. (com. on social devel. and world peace, priorities and plans com., chmn. internat. policy com. 1991), Nat. Cath. Edn. Assn. (chmn. bd. dirs.), Nat. Cath. Rural Life Conf. (past chmn. task force on food and agr. 1987-89). Address: Chancery Office 226 Summit Ave Saint Paul MN 55102

ROACH, RICHARD RUSSEL, priest; b. Seattle, Oct. 12, 1934; s. Russel A. and Ruth (Hall) R. BA in Drama, U. Wash., 1955; MA in Philosophy, Gonzaga U., 1964; MDiv, Regis Coll., Toronto, Ont., 1969; M of Philosophy, PhD, Yale U., 1971, 75. Joined S.J., Roman Cath. Ch., 1958, ordained priest, 1969. Tchr. Jesuit High Sch., Portland, Oreg., 1964-66; asst. prof. Regis Coll./Toronto Sch. Theology, 1971-76; asst. to assoc. prof. moral theology Marquette U., Milw., 1976—; speaker TV, radio, various pub. forums. Bd. dirs. Christendom Coll., 1986-89. 1st lt. U.S. Army, 1958; capt. res., 1958-75. Mem. Soc. Christian Ethics of the U.S. and Can., Am. Acad. of Religion, Cath. Theol. Soc. Am., Fellowship of Cath. Scholars (bd. dirs. 1978-89), Inst. Theol. Encounters of Sci. and Tech., Cath. Theol. Alliance. Home and Office: Marquette U Jesuit Residence 1404 W Wisconsin Ave Milwaukee WI 53233

ROBB, JOHN WESLEY, religion educator; b. Los Angeles, Dec. 1, 1919; s. Edgar Milton and Alta (Boger) R.; m. Ethel Edna Tosh, June 13, 1942; children: Lydia Joan Robb Durbin, Judith Nadine. A.B., Greenville Coll., 1941; Th.M., U. So. Calif., 1945, Ph.D., 1952; L.H.D., Hebrew Union Coll.-Jewish Inst. Religion, 1977. Asst. prof. philosophy and religion Dickinson Coll., Pa., 1948-51; fellow Fund for Advancement Edn., 1951-52; asso. prof. U. So. Calif., Los Angeles, 1954-62; chmn. dept. religion U. So. Calif., 1954-67, prof., 1962-87, prof. bioethics Sch. Medicine, 1981-87, prof. emeritus, adj. prof. bioethics Sch. Medicine, 1988-91, prof. emeritus, 1991—, assoc. dean humanities Coll. Letters, Arts and Scis., 1963-68, Leonard K. Firestone prof., 1974, 75; vis. Disting. prof. USAF Med. Ctr., Wilford Hall, Tex., 1985. Author: Inquiry Into Faith, 1960; co-editor: Readings in Religious Philosophy; The Reverent Skeptic, 1979. Served as lt. (j.g.) USNR, 1945-47; to lt. 1952-54. Recipient award for excellence in teaching U. So. Calif., 1960, 74, Dart award for acad. innovation, 1970, Raubenheimer Disting. Faculty award, div. humanities, 1980, Outstanding Faculty award Student Senate, 1981; Robert Fenton Craig award Blue Key, 1980. Fellow Soc. for Values in Higher Edn.; mem. Am. Acad. Religion (v.p. 1966, pres. 1967), Am. Philos. Assn., AAUP (v.p. Calif. Conf. 1977, pres. 1978-79), Phi Beta Kappa (hon.), Phi Kappa Phi, Phi Chi Phi. Methodist. Home: 8001 Sand Point Way NE # C-35 Seattle WA 98115

ROBB, THOMAS BRADLEY, minister; b. Chgo., May 5, 1932; m. Shirley Mae Kolouch, Aug. 21, 1953 (div. June 1982); children: Marcia R. Bergen, J. Scott, Judith R. Walton, James D., Rebecca R. Hastings.; m. Elizabeth Lee Wilbanks, Nov. 2, 1982. BA, Ariz. State U., 1953; BD, San Francisco Theol. Sem., 1957, ThM summa cum laude, 1965, ThD, 1970. Ordained to ministry, Presbyn. Ch., 1957. Pastor First Presbyn. Ch., Madison, Kans., 1957-59, Fredonia, Kans., 1959-64; dir. adv. pastoral studies San Francisco Theol. Sem., San Anselmo, Calif., 1969-70; asst. prof. Iliff Sch. Theology, Denver, 1970-74; adminstr. Westminster-Canterbury House, Richmond, Va., 1974-76; program dir. Nat. Coun. on Aging, Washington, 1976-80; dir. Presbyn. Office on Aging, Atlanta, 1981-89; exec. dir. Nat. Interfaith Coalition on Aging, Athens, Ga., 1988—; trustee Nat. Ch. Residences, Columbus, Ohio, 1988—; adv. bd. Living-at-Home Program, N.Y.C., 1985-89; exec. com. Nat. Voluntary Orgns. for Ind. Living for the Aging, Washington, 1983-87. Author: The Bonus Years, 1968; co-author, editor: Older Adult Ministry, 1987; co-author: Senior Center Operation, 1978, Senior Center Administration, 1978. Mem. Nat. Coun. on Aging, Am. Soc. on Aging, Gerontol. Soc. Democrat. Presbyterian. Home: 624 Avery St Decatur GA 30030 Office: Nat Interfaith Coalition 298 S Hull St PO Box 1924 Athens GA 30603

ROBBINS, ANDREW JOSEPH, minister; b. Morgantown, W.Va., Nov. 19, 1910; s. Strawn Murphy and Oakie Urbana (Christner) R.; m. Ollie Mae Robertson, July 28, 1931; children: David Bruce, Linda Jean. BTh, Columbia Union Coll., 1931; MA, U. Chgo., 1942. Ordained to ministry Seventh-day Adventist Ch., 1935. Pastor Seventh-day Adventist Ch., Johnstown, Pa., 1931-35; overseas missionary Seventh-day Adventist Ch., China, 1935-41; tchr. Columbia Union Coll., 1942-50; pres. W. Pa. Conf. Seventh-day Adventis, 1950-58, pres. N. Philippine Union Mission, 1958-63, pres. Hong Kong-Macao Mission, 1964-69; dept. sec. Ariz. Conf. Seventh-day Adventists, 1969-71; chaplain Tempe (Ariz.) Community Hosp., 1971-77; vol. Tsuen Wan Adventist Hosp., Hong Kong. Pres. Tempe Ministerial Assn., 1975-76, Ariz. Assn. Hosp. Chaplains, 1976-77; sec.-treas. Tri-City Evangelicals, 1975-76. Address: 22724 De Soto St Grand Terrace CA 92324

ROBBINS, BRYAN THOMAS, JR., minister; b. Laurel, Miss., Apr. 30, 1957; s. Bryan Thomas and Nan Elizabeth (Warren) R.; m. Donna Sue Maze, May 24, 1980; children: Bryan T. III, Bethany H. MusB, Miss. Coll., 1979, MusM, 1984. Ordained to ministry, 1983. Min. music Whitesand Baptist Ch., Prentiss, Miss., 1978-80, Lake Forest Baptist Ch., New Orleans, La., 1980-81, FBC-Terry, Terry, Miss., 1982-83; min. music-asst. pastor Monticello Baptist Ch., Monticello, Miss., 1983--. Composer various church music; regional finalist Natl. Assc. Tchr. Singing, 1977-79. Presser scholar, 1978; recipient Disting. Svc. award Who's Who Miss., 1990. Mem. Phi Mu Allpha Sinfonia, Omicron Delta Kappa, Mortar Board, Miss. Singing Churchmen, One Voice Ensemble, Lawrence Cty. Ministers Conf. Southern Baptist. Office: Monticello Baptist Church Broad at Caswell Monticello MS 39654

ROBBINS, DALE ALAN, minister; b. Noblesville, Ind., Jan. 6, 1953; s. Myron Foulk and Cora Irene (Brown) R.; m. Jerri Judith Keller, Dec. 6, 1974; 1 child, Angela. Student, Ind. Christian U., 1973; BA in Bible, Spring Valley Bible Coll., 1983; MDiv, Golden State Sch. Theology, 1985; postgrad., Laney Coll., 1986; DHL (hon.), Golden State Sch. Theology, 1985. Ordained to ministry Assemblies of God Ch., 1978. Nat. evangelist Assemblies of God, Sheridan, Ind., 1973-81; sr. pastor Porter Assembly of God, Porter, Ind., 1981-82, Calvary Christian Ctr., Alameda, Calif., 1982-90, Christian Life Ctr., Grass Valley, Calif., 1990—; bd. dirs. Golden State Sch. of Theology, Oakland, Calif., 1984-86; co-chmn. Bay Area Christian TV Coalition, Alameda, Calif. 1987-88; tv personality Family Christian Broadcasting , Concord, Calif., 1985-90. Author: Ways Toward a More Effective Prayer Life, 1985; tv host Pathway to Calvary, 1984-90, producer, 1984-90; tv producer Dynamic Living, 1990. Contact pastor U.S. Naval Air Sta., Alameda, 1983-90. Republican. Office: Christian Life Ctr 13010 Hwy 49 Grass Valley CA 95949 *Through the years I've come to realize that no one is perfect, but I've also discovered that imperfect lives can be dramatically changed and improved by the simple virtues of love and encouragement.*

ROBBINS, DEBORAH RUTH, communications director; b. Shreveport, La., May 21, 1960; d. Luther Marvin and Barbara Anne (Cudd) R. BS, Wayland Bapt. U., 1982; postgrad., Auburn U., 1982-84. Worship sec. Bethany Bible Ch., Phoenix, 1985-87, dir. communications, 1987—; adj. prof. Southwestern Bible Coll., Phoenix, 1990—; owner Home Team Cards, Phoenix, 1989—; bd. dirs. Christian Vision Sound Systems, Phoenix, 1989—; social dir. New Life Singles, Phoenix, 1987-89, coun. mem., 1987-89. Editor: (newsletter) Window on Bethany, 1987 (Outstanding Newsletter award 1990). Official Valley Christian Officials Assn., Phoenix, 1988-90; fund raiser North Pop Warner Assn., Phoenix, 1987. Named Outstanding Historian Wayland Bapt. U., 1982. Mem. Ariz. Christian Writers Assn., Theta Alpha Psi, Phi Alpha Theta. Home: 7226 N 21st Ave Phoenix AZ 85021 Office: Bethany Bible Ch 6060 N 7th Ave Phoenix AZ 85013 *Understanding who I am is significant. Being willing to submit who I am to others—in love, kindness and compassion—is understanding who I am in God.*

ROBBINS, GREGORY ALAN, pastor; b. Santa Ana, Calif., Oct. 9, 1965; s. Vern Theodore and Marilyn May (Nienaber) R.; m. Christina Ann Kelly, May 18, 1985; children: Alyssa Nicole, Kyle Philip. BA summa cum laude, Pacific Christian Coll., 1988. Children's and youth min. First Christian Ch. of Westminster, Calif., 1988-91; pastor First Christian Ch. of Westminster, 1991—; key contact person Orange County Concerts of Prayer, Westminster, 1991—. Recipient honors scholarship Pacific Christian Coll., Fullerton, 1983. Mem. So. Calif. Ministerial Assn., Westminster Coun. of Mins. Republican. Office: First Christian Ch 13421 Edwards Westminster CA 92683 *Life is the vehicle to serve our life-giving Lord and Savior, Jesus Christ!.*

ROBBINS, GREGORY ALLEN, religion educator; b. Bloomington, Ind., July 7, 1952; s. William Kenneth and Delores Evelyn (Hesler) R. AB, Ind. U., Bloomington, 1974; MDiv, Yale U., 1977; PhD, Duke U., 1986. Asst. prof. dept. religious studies U. Denver, 1988-91, assoc. prof., chair dept., 1991—; lay campus chaplain Episcopal Ch. at Wichita (Kans.) State U., 1985-87; mem. commn. on ministry Episcopal Diocese Kans., Topeka, 1982-88. Co-author: Exploring the New Testament, 1986; editor, co-author: Intrigue in the Garden, 1988. Bd. mem. Colo. Endowment for Humanities, 1989—. NEH grantee, 1982, 86, Am. Coun. Learned Socs. travel grantee, 1987. Mem. Soc. for Values in Higher Edn., Soc. Bibl. Lit. (program chair 1982—, regional v.p. 1990-91, regional pres. 1991—), N.Am. Patristics Soc. Democrat. Episcopalian. Office: U Denver Dept Religion 2150 S Race Denver CO 80208

ROBBINS, JO ANN, minister; b. Ft. Dodge, Iowa, Apr. 27, 1932; d. Leland Arthur and Doris Ruby (Green) Whitted; m. Clifford Whitaker, Nov. 17, 1948 (div. Aug. 1964); m. William Vernon Robbins, Oct. 25, 1964; stepchildren: Billie Laverne Meeks, Donald Wayne Robbins, Lauri Ann Marshall. Diploma in Ministerial Studies, Berean Bible Sch., Springfield, Ill., 1983, Evangel. Ch. Alliance, Bradley, Ill., 1984. Bible study coord., counselor Aglow, Inc., Placerville, Calif., 1979; v.p. Women's Aglow, Inc., Placerville, 1979-80; pres. Calif. Gold Area, Women's Aglow, Inc., 1982-84; coord. Women's Ministries, Placerville, 1982-84; pastor, founder Feed My Sheep Ministries, Placerville, 1985—; owner JoAnn's Fashion Apparel, Placerville, 1990-91; mem. Foothill Ministerial Assn., El Dorado County, Calif., 1985-91; dir. 1st Assembly tape ministry, Placerville, 1981-83; tour host to Israel, Agape Love Tours, Placerville, 1988-89. Author: (short stories) Spiritual Warfare, 1990, Occult, 1970, (booklet) That I Might Know Him, 1981. Poll judge El Dorado Election Bd., 1988-91. Recipient Vol. Appreciation award El Dorado Convalescent Hosp., 1984-85. Mem. Evangel. Ch. Alliance, Women's Aglow. Republican. Office: Feed My Sheep Church 341 Placerville Dr Placerville CA 95667 *The best thing in my life is the peace and forgiveness that I have through Christ my Lord. He's my best friend, my brother, redeemer and Lord. I'm so grateful.*

ROBBINS, THOMAS LANDAU, humanities researcher; b. N.Y.C., Oct. 13, 1943; s. Manuel Lee and Elly (Landau) R. AB, Harvard U., 1965; MA, U. N.C., 1968, PhD in Sociology, 1973. Instr. Queens Coll., 1971-78, Cen. Mich. U., 1982-83; NIMH postdoctoral trainee in sociology Yale U., New Haven, 1979-81; sr. rsch. assoc. Santa Barbara (Calif.) Ctr. for Humanistic Studies, 1990—. Author: Cults, Converts and Charisma, 1988; co-editor: In Gods We Trust, 1981, 2d edit., 1990, Cults, Culture and the Law, 1985, Church-State Relations, 1987; assoc. editor Sociol. Analysis, 1984-90; contbr. articles to various publs. Mem. Soc. for the Sci. Study of Religion (exec. coun. 1988-91), Assn. for the Sociology Religion, (exec. coun. 1985-87), Am. Sociol. Assn., Soc. for the Study of Social Problems, Internat. Havana Brown Club, Havana Preservation Club. Meher Baba. Home and Office: 427 SW 4th St Apt A-8 Rochester MN 55902 *I am becoming concerned these days about threats to freedom of religion in the United States.*

ROBBINS, VERNON KAY, religion educator; b. Wahoo, Nebr., Mar. 13, 1939; s. Earl Willard and Mildred Irene (Hanson) R.; m. Deanna Shirley Moritz, Aug. 6, 1960; children: Rick Anthony, Chimene Alise. BA, Westmar Coll., 1960; BD, United Theol. Sem., Dayton, Ohio, 1963; MA, U. Chgo., 1966, PhD, 1969. Asst. prof. religion and classics U. Ill., Urbana, 1968-75, assoc. prof. religion and classics, 1975-84; prof. religion Emory U., Atlanta, 1984—; dir. religious studies U. Ill., Urbana, 1978-81; dir. pronouncement stories work group Soc. Bibl. Lit., 1981-87; chair dept. classics Emory U., Atlanta, 1985-86, chair dept. religion, 1988-89, chair dept. near eastern, Judaic langs. and lit., 1991-92. Author: Jesus the Teacher, 1984, Patterns of Persuasion, 1989, Ancient Quotes and Anecdotes, 1989; gen. editor Emory Studies in Early Cchristianity, 1991—; contbr. articles to profl. jours. Rsch. fellow Inst. for Ecumenical and Cultural Rsch., Collegeville, Minn., 1975, Soc. Bibl. Lit.-Claremont Fellowship, 1981, Fulbright Rsch. fellow U. Trondheim (Norway), 1983-84. Mem. Studiorum Novi Testament Societas (editorial bd. 1990—), Soc. Bibl. Lit. (editorial bd.), Cath. Bibl. Assn., Chgo. Soc. for Bibl. Rsch., Internat. Soc. for the History of Rhetoric, Emory Studies in Early Christianity (gen. editor 1991—), Fulbright Alumni Assn. Home: 1634 Stonecliff Dr Decatur GA 30033 Office: Emory U 312 Physics Bldg Atlanta GA 30322

ROBBINS, WILLIAM RANDOLPH, minister; b. West Hartford, Conn., May 22, 1912; s. Harry E. and Matilda Sydney (Franklin) R.; m. Sarah Craig Wright, June 6, 1942 (dec. Dec. 25, 1986); children: Henry Craig, Sarah Franklin Robbins Jenks, Thomas Nelson. BA, Princeton U., 1934; MDiv, Yale U., 1941, STD (hon.), 1984; postgrad., Oxford U., Eng., 1946-47, 82. Ordained priest Episcopal Ch., 1942. Asst. min. St. George's Ch., N.Y.C., 1941-43; rector St. Peter's Ch., Cazenovia, N.Y., 1943-49, St. Thomas's Ch., New Haven, 1949-84; founder St. Thomas's Day Sch., 1956, pres. sch. corp., 1956-84, headmaster emeritus, 1984—; chaplain Mil. Order Fgn. Wars U.S., past chaplain gen.; chaplain in chief Mil. Order Loyal Legion U.S.; chaplain le comite francais de Souvenir de laFayette, Civil Def. New Haven area, Old Guard City of N.Y., 2d co. Gov.'s Foot Guard, Conn., New Haven County Sheriff's Assn. Founder Christian Community Action, New Haven; sec. New Haven Archdeaconry; mem. Berkeley Divinity Sch. coun., Yale U.; bd. dirs. Lord's Day Alliance, New Haven Vis. Nurse Assn. 1st lt. U.S. Army, to lt. col. N.Y. N.G., to capt. USCG Aux. Recipient Alumni Disting. Ministry award Berkeley Div. Sch., Disting. Mil. Svc. award N.Y. State Guard, Outstanding Achievement award Princeton U. Class of 1934; assoc. fellow Trumbull Coll., Yale U. Mem. Soc. Descendants Colonial Govs. (chaplain gen.), Soc. Descendents Colonial Clergy (past chaplain gen.), The Soc. the Cin. (chaplain), Soc. Colonial Wars (chaplain), Soc. Descendents Knights of Garter, The Pilgrims, Dartmouth House English-Speaking Union, Most Venerable Order St. John's Hosp. Jerusalem, Berkeley Divinity Sch. Alumni (past pres.), Order of Knighthood, St. John of Jersulaem (sub-chaplain), Order of Hist. Mil. Commands (chaplain), Union Club of N.Y., Royal Tennis Court (Hampton Court Palace, Eng.), Oxford U. Club (life), Royal Tennis Ct. Club, Hampton Ct. Palace Club, Princeton Club, Union Club (N.Y.C.), Elizabethan of Yale Club, Royal Bermuda Yacht Club, Grad. Club (New Haven). Home: 24 Battis Rd Hamden CT 06514

ROBELOT, MILTON PAUL, deacon, architect; b. New Orleans, Oct. 31, 1909; s. Amedeé William and Eva (Trepagnier) R.; m. Mary Lucille Bright, July 20, 1938; 1 child, Katherine Marie Robelot Floyd. BArch, Tulane U., 1932; postgrad., Tex. A&M U., 1939; MS, Miss. State U., 1943. Registered architect, Tenn., Va., Mo.; ordained to ministry Roman Catholic Ch. as deacon, 1974. Deacon St. Dominic Ch., Kingsport, Tenn., 1974—; architect Mark Freeman & Assocs., Kingsport, Tenn.; chaplain Civitan, Kingsport, 1991—. Mem. AIA (emeritus), Tenn. Soc. Architects (emeritus), Moose, Elks. Home: 98 Crown Colony Kingsport TN 37660 *We cannot expect our future generations to have a sense of morality when they see immorality and crime depicted on TV and in our movies as a way of life. "It can't be wrong, everybody does it." No! Not everybody-I have been married 54 years to the same lady and we have many friends who also have a sense of responsiblity, integrity, duty, faithfulness and seriously adhere to the commandment; "Thou shall not commit adultry". Unless these despicable stories glorifying crime, rape, incest, immorality, etc., are removed altogether and replaced with wholesome stories depicting good morals and degrading crime, rape, and immorality as despicable, we cannot expect our future generations to have a sense of duty, integrity, responsibility and morality. We need God back in education and family life.*

ROBERTS, ARTHUR OWEN, religion and philosophy educator, clergyman; b. Caldwell, Idaho, Jan. 7, 1923; s. Owen Lawrence and Bertha (Jansonius) R.; m. Fern Lucile Nixon, Nov. 7, 1943; children: Lloyd Owen, Patricia Mae Nielsen, Teresa Mae Rogers. BA, George Fox Coll., 1944; BD, Nazarene Theol. Sem., 1951; PhD, Boston U., 1954. Ordained to ministry Soc. of Friends, 1945. Minister Everett (Wash.) Friends Ch., 1944-48, Kansas City (Mo.) Friends Ch., 1948-51, Meth. Ch., Grasmere, N.H., Goffstown, N.H., 1951-53; prof. philosophy and religion George Fox Coll., Newberg, Oreg., 1953-87, prof. at large, 1987—; dean of faculty George Fox Coll., Newberg, 1968-762; elder NW Yearly Meeting of Friends Ch., Newberg, 1986—; ethics commn. Christian Coll. Consortium, 1984-87; guest instr. Earlham Sch. Religion, 1960, 68, 72, Malone Coll., 1960; founding pastor Tigard Friends Ch., 1956-58; pastoral resource person Reedwood Friends Ch., Portland, Oreg., 1983-89; lectr. at various orgns. Author: Through Flaming Sword, 1959, Move Over, Elijah, 1967, Listen to the Lord, 1974, History of the Association of Evangelical Friends, 1975, Tomorrow is Growing Old: Stories of Quakers in Alaska, 1978, Sunrise and Shadow, 1984, Back to Square One: Handling Losses, 1990; co-author: (with Hugh Barbour) Early Quaker Writings, 1973; (with others) On the Edge of a Truth, 1980, Beacon Dictionary of Theology, 1983, Evangelical Dictionary of Theology, 1984, Great Christian Leaders, 1987; editor: Handbook of Church History, 1977, 2d edit., 1990, also several other books; editor Quaker Religious Thought, 1990—; contbr. articles to profl. jours. Mem. planning commn. City of Newberg, 1982-86; councilor City of Yachats, Oreg., 1988—. NEH rsch. grantee, Alaska, 1975. Mem. Am. Acad. Religion, Friends Hist. Soc. (editorial com.), Am. Soc. Ch. History, Soc. Christian Philosophers, Friends Assn. Higher Edn. Democrat. Home: Box 215 Yachats OR 97498

ROBERTS, AUGUSTINE (BRUCE), abbot; b. Nanking, Kiangsu, China, Oct. 23, 1932; (parents Am. citizens); s. William Payne and Dorothy (Mills) R. Licentiate in Theology, Angelicum U., Rome, 1961; LLD (hon.), Coll. of Our Lady of Elms, 1984. Joined Cistercian Order of the Strict Observance (Trappists), Roman Cath. Ch., 1953, ordained priest Roman Cath. Ch., 1959. Novice master Monasterio Trapense, Azul, Argentina, 1962-67, titular superior, 1968-83; abbot St. Joseph's Abbey, Spencer, Mass., 1984—; mem. Cistercian Publs. Corp., Kalamazoo, 1984—; vice-moderator Cistercian Gen. Chpt., Rome, 1984—. Author: Centered on Christ, 1977; also articles. Home: St Joseph's Abbey Spencer MA 01562

ROBERTS, DANNY KENT, minister; b. Bellair, Ill., Nov. 24, 1952; s. Harley Glen and Bertha Fae (Collins) R.; m. Ceselie Marie Northen, June 22, 1973; children: Daron Kent, Nathan John, Micah Timothy. BA, Johnson Bible Coll., Knoxville, Tenn., 1979; MA, Sangamon State U., Springfield, Ill., 1986. Ordained to ministry Christian Ch.-Ill., 1980. Min. Allerton (Ill.) Ch. of Christ, 1981-84, Mt. Auburn (Ill.) Ch. of Christ, 1984-87; sr. min. South Shores Christian Ch., Decatur, Ill., 1987—; chmn. God's Shelter of Love, Inc., Decatur, 1990—. Author: Evangelism Training, 1988, God's Word in Your Life, 1988, The Life of Christ, 1989, Leadership Training, 1990. With USAF, 1971-75. Mem. Chi Sigma Iota. Home: 136 Bristol Dr Decatur IL 62521 Office: South Shores Christian Ch 230 Bristol Dr Decatur IL 62521

ROBERTS, DAVID STONE, bishop; b. New Haven, Mar. 20, 1943; s. Harold Lucullus and Marie Ellen (Carlson) R. BA in French, Barrington (R.I.) Coll., 1966. Ordained bishop Faith Family Fellowship, 1976, Worldwide Gospel Ch., 1986. Dir. Intermountain Christian Ministries, Salt Lake City, 1984—; advisor Am./Soviet Christian Alliance, Salt Lake City, 1990—; founder S. Salt Lake Valley Pastors Prayer Group, Sandy, Utah, 1986—; chaplain Holy Trinity Mission, Sandy, 1990—; founder Ch. of the Risen Christ, 1991. Editor Intermountain Christian Ministry mo. newsletter, 1978—, Russian Lang. newsletter, 1991—. Vol. Utah State Penitentiary, Draper, 1987-90. Office: Holy Trinity Mission PO Box 21322 Salt Lake City UT 84121-0322

ROBERTS, DELBERT E., JR., minister; b. Spokane, Wash., Sept. 3, 1947; s. Delbert Earl and Florence Marie (Schmautz) R.; m. Linda Marie Wayman, Sept. 19, 1970; children: James Earl, Jonathan Del. BSEE, Wash. State U., 1969. Ordained to ministry Assemblies of God, 1974. Asst. pastor Arlington (Wash.) Assemblies of God, 1972-75; youth pastor Peoples Ch., Salem, Oreg., 1975-78; founding pastor Grace Community Ch., Greenwood Village, Colo., 1982—; founder Jesus N.W., Salem, 1977-78; pres., founder World Life Outreach, Denver, 1978—; presbyter Assemblies of God, Denver, 1986-91. Bd. dirs. Christmas For Needy Children, Greenwood Village, 1987-88. Mem. Kiwanis (v.p. 1987, bd. dirs. 1989-90). Office: Grace Community Ch 5455 S Valentia Way Greenwood Village CO 80111

ROBERTS, DONALD EUGENE, minister; b. Marion, Ind., Mar. 28, 1942; s. Frank M. and Nellie Margaret (Hegwood) R.; m. Linda Lou Fultz, Apr. 10, 1965; children: Jacquelyn Ann, Jeffrey Kyle. BS in Edn., Ball State U., 1965, MA in Edn., 1969; MDiv, Bethany Theol. Sem., 1977. Ordained to ministry Ch. of the Brethren, 1977. Elem. sch. tchr. Marion (Ind.) Community Schs., 1965-74; pastor Ch. of the Brethren, Portland, Ind., 1973-74; family life prog. dir. Bethany Union Ch., Chgo., 1974-76; pastor Nettle Creek Ch. of the Brethren, Hagerstown, Ind., 1977-79; pastor Ch. of the Brethren, Lanark, Ill., 1979-84, Topeka, 1984—; co-founder, bd. dirs. Topeka Peace Resource Ctr., 1985—; co-founder Topeka Religious Leaders Against the Death Penalty, 1987. Co-author: The Death Penalty/Statement of the Ch. of the Brethern, 1987. Democrat. Home: 3205 NW Rochester Rd Topeka KS 66617 Office: Ch of the Brethren 3201 NW Rochester Rd Topeka KS 66617 *We are living in a day when it is becoming increasingly clear that what we do individually not only has an impact on the rest of humanity but also on the rest of God's creatures and the whole of God's creation as well. Our survival will depend upon our willingness to base our decisions and our actions on this fact.*

ROBERTS, EUGENE EDWARD, minister; b. Catskill, N.Y., Apr. 7, 1945; s. Edward E. and Emma Louise (Guilzon) R.; m. Carol Sue Rajsky, Oct. 21, 1967; 1 child, Steven Christopher. BA in History, Hope Coll., 1967; MDiv, New Brunswick (N.J.) Theo. Sem, 1981. Ordained to ministry Reformed Ch. in Am., 1981. Pastor Franklin Reformed Ch., Nutley, N.J., 1981-89, Harlingen Reformed Ch., Belle Mead, N.J., 1989—; pres. Nutley Clergy Fellowship, 1982-84. Contbr. articles to profl. jours. Vice pres. Community Coun., Nutley, 1986-87; bd. dirs. Nutley Family Svc. Bur., 1983-86. Capt. USAF, 1967-72, Vietnam. Mem. Bread for the World, Nat. IMPACT (bd. dirs. Trenton, N.J. chpt. 1982-86), Rotary (v.p. Nutley chpt. 1987-88). Democrat. Home and Office: 34 Dutchtown Rd Belle Mead NJ 08502

ROBERTS, GRANVILLE ORAL (ORAL ROBERTS), clergyman; b. nr. Ada, Okla., Jan. 24, 1918; s. Ellis Melvin and Claudius Priscilla (Irwin) R.; m. Evelyn Lutman, Dec. 25, 1938; children: Rebecca Ann (dec.), Ronald David (dec.), Richard Lee, Roberta Jean. Student, Okla. Bapt. U., 1942-44, Phillips U., 1947; LLD (hon.), Centenary Coll., 1975. Ordained to ministry Pentecostal Holiness Ch., 1936, United Meth. Ch., 1968. Evangelist, 1936-41; pastor Fuquay Springs, N.C., 1941, Shawnee, Okla., 1942-45, Toccoa, Ga., 1946, Enid, Okla., 1947; began worldwide evangelistic ministry thru crusades, radio, TV, printed page, 1947; founder Oral Roberts Evangelistic Assn., Inc., Tulsa, 1948, Univ. Village Retirement Center, 1970, City of Faith Med./Research Ctr., 1981, Healing Outreach Ctr., 1986; founder, pub. Abundant Life mag., Daily Blessing (quar. mag.); founder pres. Oral Roberts U., Tulsa, 1963—; founding chmn. Charismatic Bible Ministries. Author: over 50 books including: If You Need Healing, Do These Things, 1947, God is a Good God, 1960, If I Were You, 1967, Miracle of Seed-Faith, 1970, autobiography The Call, 1971, The Miracle Book, 1972, A Daily Guide to Miracles, 1975, Better Health and Miracle Living, 1976, How to Get Through Your Struggles, 1977, Receiving Your Miracle, 1978, Don't Give Up, 1980, Your Road to Recovery, 1986, Attack Your Lack, 1986, How I Learned Jesus Was Not Poor, 1989, How to Resist the Devil, 1989, Fear Not!, 1989, A Prayer Cover Over Your Life, 1990; also numerous tracts and brochures, Bible commentaries. Recipient Indian of Yr. award Am. Broadcasters Assn., 1963; Okla. Hall of Fame, 1973; Oklahoman of Yr., 1974. Club: Rotary. Office: Oral Roberts U 7777 S Lewis Ave Tulsa OK 74171

ROBERTS, LINDA A., minister; b. Bryn Mawr, Pa., Dec. 1, 1959; d. John B. and Joan Isabel (Turner) R. BA in Journalism/Religion, Trinity U., 1981; MDiv., Princeton Theol. Sem., 1984. Ordained min. Presbyn. Ch., 1986. Asst. min. Second Presbyn. Ch., Albuquerque, 1984-87; religious studies instr. Menaul Sch., Albuquerque, 1985-87; interim chaplain Princeton (N.J.) Univ., Wesley-Westminster Found., 1987-88; univ. chaplain Vanderbilt Univ., Nashville, Tenn., 1989—; hunger action enabler Presbytery of Santa Fe, Albuquerque, 1985-87, budget com. 1986-87, group leader women's assn. 1986-87; chair, family selection com. Habitat for Humanity, Nashville, 1990—. Editor, pub.: (literary arts mag.) The Trinity Review, 1979-81, (newletters) The Mustard Seed, 1987-88, Into the World, 1989—. Vol. Jimmy Carter Work Project, Tijuana, Mexico, 1990; group leader Habitat for Humanity, Loahomma, Miss., 1990. Recipient Poetry award Exec. Com. of the Assn. Writing Program, San Antonio, 1981. Mem. Presbytery of Middle Tenn. (Congl. Life com. 1990—). Office: Vanderbilt Univ Presbyn Campus Ministry Box 6311 Sta B Nashville TN 37235

ROBERTS, ORAL See ROBERTS, GRANVILLE ORAL

ROBERTS, PHILIP LEE, communications executive; b. Jasper, Ala., Apr. 25, 1953; s. C. Herman and Theela Laura (Nunnelly) R.; m. Beverly Mae Chatfield, July 19, 1985; 1 child, Clark Alan. AAS, DeVry Inst. Tech., Atlanta, 1973; postgrad., Triton Coll., 1990—. Technician GTE Automatic Electric, Northlake, Ill., 1974-75; mem. tech. staff GTE Communication Systems, Northlake, 1975-86; v.p. engring. Com Systems Corp., Palatine, Ill., 1986-87; sr. staff engr. AG Communication Systems, Northlake, 1987—. Composer handbell music. Choir dir. 1st Bapt. Ch., Maywood, Ill., 1984—; musical dir. West Suburban Ringers, 1989—; chmn. bd. trustees Bapt. Inst. Ch. Arts, Oak Park, Ill., 1988-90. Recipient Good Citizenship award Walker County Bd. Edn., Jasper, Ala., 1970. Mem. Fellowship Am. Bapt. Musicians, Broadview Tennis Club (v.p. 1985-86). Democrat. Office: AG Comunication Systems 400 N Wolf Rd Northlake IL 60164

ROBERTS, R. PHILIP, religion educator, dean; b. Danville, Ky., Aug. 22, 1950; s. Ray Everett and Margaret L. (Mooneyham) R.; m. Anna Fierenczuk, June 29, 1980; children: Naomi Ann, Mark Everett. BA cum laude, Georgetown (Ky.) Coll., 1972; MDiv, So. Bapt. Theol. Sem., 1976; ThD, Free U. Amsterdam, The Netherlands, 1989. Pastor Immanuel Bapt. Ch., Wiesbaden, Fed. Republic Germany, 1975-78; asst. prof. evangelism So. Bapt. Sem., Louisville, 1982-85; pastor Internat. Bapt., Brussels, 1985-89; assoc. prof. evangelism Southeastern Sem., Wake Forest, N.C., 1989-91; acad. dean Bapt. Inst. Bibl. Studies, Orodea, Romania, 1991—; lectr. Evang. Theol. Faculty, Leuven, Belgium; trustee Inst. Bibl. Studies, Warsaw, Poland, 1990—. Author: Continuity and Change, 1989. Mem. Acad. Evangelism in Theol. Edn., Evang. Theol. Soc. Office: Southeastern Bapt Theol Sem South Wingate Wake Forest NC 27587-1889

ROBERTS, RAYMOND ROHRER, minister; b. St. Louis, Aug. 2, 1958; s. Raymond R. and Ruth Amanda (McHaney) R.; m. Sallie Ashlin Rowe, Jan. 14, 1984; children: Harrison McHaney, Katherine MacDonald. BA, Westminster Coll., 1980; MDiv, Columbia Theol. Sem., 1984. Ordained to ministry Presbyn. Ch. (U.S.A.), 1984. Pastor Amherst (Va.) Presbyn. Ch., 1984—; del. Synod of Mid-Atlantic, Presbyn. Ch. (U.S.A.), 1985; chair Youth Work unit Blue Ridge Presbytery, 1988-89. Chair Citizen's Involvement Team, Amherst, 1986—, Strategic Town Evaluation Planning Com., Amherst, 1989. Recipient McDearmon Community Svc. award Amherst-Nelson Pub. Co., 1989. Mem. Rotary. Democrat. Home: 223 Garland Ave Amherst VA 24521 Office: Amherst Presbyn Ch 2d St Amherst VA 24521 *Do everything that you do in the name of our Lord and Savior Jesus Christ.*

ROBERTS, RICHARD OWEN, clergyman, theological publisher, library consultant; b. Schenectady, N.Y., Sept. 9, 1931; s. John Earl and Mildred Hazel (Barden) R.; m. Margaret Ann Jameson, Sept. 8, 1962; children—Robert Owen, Gwynne Margaret. Student Gordon Coll., 1949-50; B.A., Whitworth Coll., 1955; postgrad. Fuller Theol. Sem., 1955-57. Ordained to ministry Congregational Ch. Pastor, evangelist University Park Congl. Ch., Portland, Oreg., 1957-61; minister-at-large Conservative Congl. Conf., Scotia, N.Y., 1961-65; pastor Evang. Community Ch., Fresno, Calif., 1965-75; dir. library Billy Graham Ctr., Wheaton, Ill., 1975-80; internat. evangelist, 1980—; owner Richard Owen Roberts, Pubs., Booksellers, 1961—; pres. bd. dirs. Internat. Awakening Ministries, Inc.; bd. dirs. Oxford Assn. for Research in Revival, Concerts of Prayer Internat. Author: Revival, 1982; Revival Literature, 1985; Whitefield in Print: A Preliminary Bibliography, 1985; The Solemn Assembly, 1989; Backsliding, 1990; Lord I Agree, 1990; Sanctify the Congregation, 1991. Home: 5 N 740 Dunham Rd Wayne IL 60184 Office: 391 Wegner Dr Box 786 West Chicago IL 60186 *A person who entertains a low view of God will suffer from an inordinately high view of himself, a mistaken view of sin and an absurd view of salvation.*

ROBERTS, RONALD ELDRIDGE, minister, educator; b. Mt. Holly, N.J., Jan. 30, 1942; s. Benjamin Charles and Juanita Odessa (Jacobs) R.; m. Gertrude Inez Timpson Carney, Jan. 30, 1965; children: Ronald E. Jr., Reginald E. BS, Phila. Coll. Bible, 1970; ThM, Dallas Theol. Sem., 1975, D.Min., 1985. Ordained to ministry Bethany Bap. Assn. Assoc. minister Mt. Calvary Bapt. Ch., Camden, N.J., 1965-70, 75-77, Golden Gate Bapt. Ch., Dallas, 1970-71; minister Christian edn. St. John Bapt. Ch., Dallas, 1972-75; dean students, faculty Manna Bible Inst., Phila., 1975-77; sr. pastor Baldwin Hills Bapt. Ch., L.A., 1977—; mem. adj. faculty Talbot Sch. Theology of Biola U., La Mirada, Calif., 1982-86, 87—, full faculty, 1986; bd. dirs., co-founder Black Evangelistic Enterprise, Dallas, 1972—. Contbr. articles to profl. jours. With USAF, 1960-64. Mem. S.W. Bapt. Conf. Missions (bd. dirs. 1980-82, 84-87), Evang. Tchrs. Tng. Assn., Nat. Black Evang. Assn. (past dir. Christian edn. dept. 1975-77), S.W. Bapt. Conf. Trustees (bd. dirs. 1991—), Camera Club. Democrat. Office: Baldwin Hills Bapt Ch 4700 W King Blvd Los Angeles CA 90016 *In our generation of often heated debates in ethical, philosophical, theological and other areas, it is a sobering thought to know that God by His Son, Jesus Christ, will carefully evaluate our motives and actions and recompense us for the deeds done in the body whether good or bad. Therefore, it matters what we believe, why we believe and how we behave.*

ROBERTS, ROY RONALD, minister; b. L.A., Apr. 2, 1945; s. Roy Roudney and Thelma E. (Tippie) R.; m. Patricia Ann Hendricks, June 16, 1974; 1 child, Dawn Marie. BA, Biola U., 1968; BD, Talbot Grad. Sch., Biola U., 1971, MRE, 1972; PhD, Calif. Grad. Sch., 1973; DRE, Grace Coll. Grad. Sch., 1976. Ordained to ministry Nat. Fellowship Grace Brethren Chs. Youth pastor Grace Brethren Ch., Long Beach, Calif., 1965-71; sr. pastor Grace Brethren Ch., Seal Beach, Calif., 1971-79; prof., chaplain Grace Coll. and Theol. Sem., Winona Lake, Ind., 1987-90; sr. pastor Grace Brethren Ch., New Holland, Pa., 1990—; officer, cons. Prison Fellowship Ministries, Washington, 1977—, trainer, 1990—; chaplain at large NFL, 1976—; chaplain Major League Baseball, 1975—; prof. Lancaster (Pa.) Bible Coll., 1990—; speaker in field. Author: God Has A Better Idea-The Home, 1975, The Game of Life: The Epistle of James, 1975, The Passionate Heart: The Epistle of II Timothy, 1992. Home: 215 Cindalyn Dr New Holland PA 17557 Office: Grace Brethren Ch 415 S Kinzer Ave New Holland PA 17557 *There are only two things in this world that will last forever: God's Word and people. He values His Word above His Name and more precious to the Lord Jesus than the universe are those He purchased with His own blood. We who serve Him must share the same passion.*

ROBERTS, STANLEY LEROY, minister, academic administrator, musician; b. Tifton, Ga., Jan. 4, 1962; s. Willie L. and Clarice (Carter) R.; m. Marie Jarriel, May 5, 1984. BA, Mercer U., 1984; M in Christian Ministry, So. Bapt. Theol. Sem., 1989, postgrad, 1989—. Min. music and youth Midway Bapt. Ch., Macon, Ga., 1982-85; min. music Evergreen Bapt. Ch., Frankfort, Ky., 1986—; assoc. dir. admissions So. Bapt. Theol. Sem., Louisville, 1986—; asst. dir. admissions Mercer U., Macon, 1984-86. Mem. Am. Choral Dirs. Assn. (v.p. 1988-89). Home: 2007 Grasmere Dr Louisville KY 40205

ROBERTS, THOMAS KEITH, minister; b. Meridian, Miss., Nov. 30, 1947; s. Jordan Luke and Myrtle Lucille (Long) R.; m. Judy Marie Andrews, Mar. 20, 1971; children: Angela Joy, Kevin Andrew. AA in Data Processing, Meridian Jr. Coll., 1967; A of Sacred Lit., Whites Ferry Rd Sch Bibl Study, 1975; BA, Faulkner U., 1976; MA, Am. Christian Coll., 1988. Ordained to ministry Ch. of Christ, 1975. Min. Ch. of Christ, Mansfield, La., 1975-77, Earle, Ark., 1977-80; min. Bawcomville Ch. Christ, West Monroe, La., 1980-81, Ch. of Christ, Calhoun, La., 1981—; pres. alumni assn. White;s Ferry Rd. Sch. Bibl. Studies, West Monroe, 1982-83, mem. faculty, 1985—, staff writer Sch. Bibl. Studies Report. Contbr. articles to profl. jours. Mem. Calhoun Civic Club (pres. 1985, v.p. 1991—), Mensa. Office: Ch of Christ 1288 Hwy 151 N, PO Box 159 Calhoun LA 71225 *This next century will challenge us to advance spiritually, as the last one challenged us technologically. "Man does not live by bread alone."*

ROBERTS, WESLEY A., minister; b. Tweedside, Jamaica, Jan. 3, 1938; came to U.S., 1972; s. Ignatius and Rayness (Wong) R.; m. Sylvia Y. Forbes, Sept. 1, 1962; children: Paul, Carolyn, Suzanne, Michael. BA, Wilfrid Laurier U., Ont., Can., 1965; MDiv, Toronto Bapt. Sem., Can., 1965; ThM, Westminster Theol. Sem., 1967; MA, PhD, U. Guelph, Ont., Can., 1968,72. Ordained to ministry Bapt. Conv. of Ont. and Que., 1967. Asst. prof. Christian Thought Gordon-Conwell Theol. Sem., South Hamilton, Mass., 1972-77, assoc. prof. ch. history, 1977-84, prof. ch. history, 1984-85; sr. pastor Peoples Bapt. Ch. Boston, Mass., 1982—; trustee Stony Brook (N.Y.) Sch., 1988—, Black Ecumenical Commn., Boston, 1983-86; mem. exec. com. Assn. Theol. Schs., Vandalia, Ohio, 1980-84. Author: book chpt. Reformed Theology in America, 1985; contbr. articles in profl. jours. Grad. fellowship Govt. Ontario, 1968-70; doctoral fellowship Govt. Can., 1970-72. Mem. Conf. Faith and History, Am. Soc. Ch. History, Soc. for Study of Black Religion. Democrat. Home: 1 Enon Rd Wenham MA 01984 Office: Peoples Bapt Ch Boston 134 Camden St Boston MA 02118

ROBERTS, WILLIAM THOMAS, minister; b. Wilkes-Barre, Pa., Jan. 21, 1944; s. William and Helen Agnes (Thomalonis) R.; m. Lynna James, Jan. 31, 1962; children: William T. Jr., Kelly Jane, Cary Chris. BA in Psych., Marian Coll., 1973; MPA, U. Mo., 1980; diploma, U.S. Army Command Coll. and Staff, 1980, Berean Coll. the Assembly God, 1987. Ordained to ministry Assembly of God., 1988; lic. adminstrn. Bus. adminstr., assoc. pastor First Assembly of God, Puyallup, Wash., 1983-88; sr. pastor, bd. elders Christ Chapel, Woodbridge, Va., 1988—. Contbr. articles on ch. mgmt. to profl. jours. Combined Fed. Campaign dir. U.S. Army, Alaska and Europe, 1969-83, dir. youth sports program, Redstone Arsenal, Ala., 1973. Maj. U.S. Army, 1983. Decorated Bronze Star, Air medal. Mem. Gen. Coun. of the Assembly God, Nat. Assn. Ch. Bus. Adminstrn. (regional v.p. 1986-88), Rotary. Republican. Office: Christ Chapel 13909 Smoketown Rd Woodbridge VA 22192

ROBERTSON, CHARLES ALFRED STUART, minister; b. Lockport, N.Y., Jan. 10, 1933; s. Montraville Charles and Dorothy Elizabeth (Nicholls) Stuart; m. Leah Ann Kronmann, June 9, 1979; children: Miriam, Edward, Charles, Philip, Stephen, Anna. Private pilot's license, Hyde Flight Sch., Md., 1953; BA, George Washington U., 1957; MDiv, Phila. Luth. Theol. Sem., 1960; MA, George Washington U., 1965. Ordained in United Luteran Ch. in Am., 1960. Pastor St. Matthew Luth. Ch., Richmond, Va., 1960-64, Nativity Luth. Ch., Alexandria, Va., 1965-68; missionary Luth. Ch., Lima, Peru, 1969-74; pastor Spanish Ministry, Washington, D.C., 1975-76; sr. pastor St. Peters Luth. Ch., Miami, Fla., 1977-90; pastor St. Marks Luth. Ch., Coral Gables, Fla., 1990—; bd. dirs. Andean Devel. Inst., 1970-73, Christian Community Svc. Agy., Miami, 1980—, Fla. Coun. of Chs., Orlando, 1983-85, Luth. Ministry of Fla., Tampa, 1987—; bd. chmn. Campus Ministry U. Miami, Fla., 1982-83; bd. pres. Luth. Coalition of Dade County, 1982-83; cons. N.Y. Theol. Sem., 1985-86. Author: (book) South American Mission History, 1973; contbr. articles to profl. jours. Bd. dirs. Gum Springs Community, Richmond, Va., 1960, Regional Planning Alexandria, Va., 1964, Hyde Park Community Orgn., Chgo., 1968; mediator Dade County Cts. 1989—; reg. dir. Boy Scouts Am., 1971-73. With U.S. Navy, 1950-54,. Decorated with Medal of Honor, Peruvian Nat. Govt., Lima, 1972; recipient Miami King's Day award Little Havana Community, Miami, 1982, cert. of appreciation City of Coral Gables, 1990. Mem. Airplane Owners and Pilots Assn., Kiwanis. Democrat. Home: 1417 Tunis St Coral Gables FL 33134 Office: St Marks Luth Ch 3930 Lejeune Rd Coral Gables FL 33134

ROBERTSON, DALE WAYNE, minister; b. Anderson, S.C., Apr. 6, 1954; s. William Eural and Avis Louise (O'Barr) R.; m. Beth Brown, Nov. 21, 1978; children: Miranda Renee, Christi Alisha. BTh, Brainerd Theol. Seminary, Spartanburg, S.C., 1985; MTh, Immanuel Bapt. Theol. Seminary, Peachtree City, Ga., 1988, MDiv, 1989, DD, 1990. Lic. and ordained to ministry So. Bapt. Conv., 1981. Assoc. evangelist Greater Life Evangelism Assn., Owasso, Okla., 1978-81; minister First Bapt. Ch., Colcord, Okla., 1981-83, Bowman (Ga.) Bapt. Ch., 1983-85, Morningside Bapt. Ch., Valdosta, Ga., 1985—; chmn. evangelism com. Hebron Assn., Elberton, Ga., 1984, Valdosta (Ga.) Assn., 1989; mem. com. or order of bus. Ga. Bapt. Conv., Atlanta, 1989, v.p. 1990, moderator, 1990, vice-moderator, 1991, mem. pers. com., 1991, various other offices; mem. com. on coms. So. Bapt. Conv., 1991; mem. resolutions com. Ga. Bapt. Conv., 1991. Home: 938 Madison Ave Valdosta GA 31602-2011 Office: Morningside Baptist Church PO Box 2445 Valdosta GA 31604 *In a day of questioned morality and extreme permissiveness, the greatest challenge we face is to remain faithful in sharing the never-changing truths of Scripture to an ever changing world.*

ROBERTSON, DONALD ERIC, minister; b. North Sydney, N.S., Can., Sept. 30, 1934; s. Alvin Gordon and Marjorie Helen (Mason) R.; m. Cairine Anne Fraser, Aug. 15, 1964; children: Iain, Leslie. BA, Acadia U., Wolfville, N.S., 1955, MDiv, 1957. Ordained to ministry Atlantic United Bapt. Conv., 1956. Pastor Margaree (N.S.) Bapt. Ch., 1956-57, Caledonia (N.S.) Bapt. Ch., 1957-62, Barss Corner (N.S.) Bapt. Ch., 1962-68, Digby (N.S.) Bapt. Ch., 1968-74, Grace Meml. Bapt. Ch., Fredericton, N.B., Can., 1974-80, 88—, Middleton (N.S.) Bapt. Ch., 1980-88; served Bd. Home Missions, Bd. Ministerial Standards. Trustee Acadia Div. Coll. Home: 120 Connaught St, Fredericton, NB Canada E3B 2A9

ROBERTSON, DOUGLAS JAMES, religious organization administrator; b. Amityville, N.Y., Oct. 6, 1955; s. Harry Leonard and Ida Agnes (Rooseland) R.; m. Patricia Louise Buechner, Mar. 27, 1976; children: Douglas James II, Joseph William, Christine Elaine. AA in Broadcasting, Columbia Sch. Broadcasting, 1974. Youth pastor Park Ave. Ch. of God, Portland, Maine, 1986-89; program dir. Sta. WLOB, Portland, Maine, 1982-84, Sta. WDCI, Portland, Maine, 1981-82; news dir. Sta. WLIX, L.I., N.Y., 1979-81; gen. mgr. Alien Christian Ministries, Windham, Maine, 1989—; telephone technician Nynex Meridian Systems, Portland, Maine, 1984—; drummer Alien Christian Band, Portland, 1989--. Songwriting lyricist. Republican. Home and Office: Alien Christian Ministries 412 Pope Rd Windham ME 04062 *No greater decision will anyone have in life than where they will spend eternity.*

ROBERTSON, ERNEST GARLAND, pastor; b. Richmond, Va., Nov. 26, 1931; s. William Thomas and Ruth Elanor (Reiben) R.; m. Patsy Ruth Day; children: Sharon, Gwen, Garland. BA, Bob Jones U., 1954; DST (hon.), Bapt. Christian Coll., Shreveport, La., 1975. Pastor Calvary Bapt. Ch., Landrum, S.C., 1954-57, Grace Bapt. Ch., Kinston, N.C., 1957-63, Faith Bapt. Ch., Easley, S.C., 1963-73, Connersville (Ind.) Bapt. Temple, 1973-77, New Testament Bapt. Ch., Hialeah, Fla., 1977—. Recipient Key to Miami, Mayor of Hialeah, 1986. Republican. Office: New Testament Bapt Ch 6601 NW 167th St Hialeah FL 33015

ROBERTSON, MARTIN WESLEY, JR., minister; b. Hawesville, Ky., July 13, 1962; s. Martin Wesley and Thelma Lee (Bruner) R.; m. Stephanie Wayne Touchton, Aug. 10, 1985. BA, Campbellsville Coll., 1985; postgrad. Luther Rice Sem. Lic. So. Bapt. Conv., 1980; Ordained to ministry So. Bapt. Conv., 1983. Assoc. pastor, minister youth Cloverport Bapt. Ch., Ky., 1982; pastor Tell St. Bapt. Ch., Tell City, Ind., 1983-85, Flint Missionary Bapt. Ch., Murray, Ky., 1985-86, Strongsville (Ohio) Bapt. Ch., 1986—. Page, Ky. State Senate; Ky. col. Fellow Blood River Bapt. Assn., Am. Psychol. Assn., Am. Assn. Counseling and Devel., Assn. Religious Values in Counseling, Greater Cleve. Bapt. Assn.; mem. So. Bapt. Conv. Republican. Avocations: fishing, golf, literature, physical fitness.

ROBERTSON, PAT (MARION GORDON ROBERTSON), evangelist, religious broadcasting executive; b. Lexington, Va., Mar. 22, 1930; s. A. Willis and Gladys (Churchill) R.; m. Adelia Elmer; children: Timothy, Elizabeth, Gordon, Ann. BA, Washington and Lee U., 1950; JD, Yale U., 1955; MDiv, N.Y. Theol. Sem., 1959; ThD (hon.), Oral Roberts U., 1983. Ordained minister So. Bapt. Conv., 1961. Founder, pres. Christian Broadcast Network, Virginia Beach, Va., 1960—; host 700 Club, 1968—; founder, pres. CBN Univ., 1977—, Continental Broadcasting Network, 1978—; bd. dirs. United Va. Bank, Norfolk; mem. Pres. Task Force on Victims of Crime, Washington, 1982. Author: (with Jamie Buckingham) Shout It From the Housetops: The Story of the Founder of the Christian Broadcasting Network, 1972, My Prayer for You, 1977, The Secret Kingdom, 1982, Answers to 200 of Life's Most Probing Questions, 1984, Beyond Reason, 1984, America's Date with Destiny, 1986, Beyond Reason: How Miracles Can Change Your Life, 1986, The Plan, 1989. Candidate for Rep. nomination for Pres. U.S., 1988. Recipient Disting. Merit citation NCCJ, Knesset medallion Israel Pilgrimage Com., Faith and Freedom award Religious Heritage Am., Bronze Halo award So. Calif. Motion Picture Council, Humanitarian award Food for the Hungry, 1982, George Washington Honor medal Freedoms Found. at Valley Forge, 1983; named Internat. Clergyman of Yr. Religion in Media, 1981, Man of Yr. Internat. Com. for Goodwill, 1981. Mem. Nat. Broadcasters (bd. dirs. 1973—). Office: The Christian Broadcasting Network CBN Ctr Virginia Beach VA 23463

ROBERTSON, PAUL, social agency administrator; b. N.Y.C.; s. Charles Robertson. Student, Howard U., 1961-63, Tex. So. U., 1966-67. Supr. maintenance G-D Maintenance Svc., Houston, 1973-76; mem. outreach staff Walnut Bapt. Ch., Jackson, Miss., 1976-78; with maintenance dept. City of Jackson, 1978-79; supr. Hannah & Stone Repair Co., Louisville, 1979-83; vol. worker Habitat for Humanity, N.Y.C., 1983-84; coord. Werik Shelter, Buffalo, 1985—. Mem. ch. choir local Bapt. ch., Louisville, 1981-82; vol. Afric Theatre Co., N.Y.C., 1984, Community Playhouse, Buffalo, 1986-87. Office: Werik Shelter 2289 Delaware Ave Buffalo NY 14216-2632

ROBERTSON, WILLIAM HUGH, JR. (BILL ROBERTSON), minister; b. Oak Grove, La., Nov. 13, 1952; s. William Hugh and Violet Marie (Womack) R.; m. Linda Gail Ezell, May 25, 1972; children: William Hugh III, Jennifer Morgan. BA, La. Coll., 1980; postgrad., Bapt. Christian U., 1991, Luther Rice Sem, 1991—. Ordained to ministry So. Bapt. Conv., 1971. Pastor Lismore Bapt. Ch., Jonesville, La., 1973-76, Bistineau Bapt.

Ch., Heflin, La., 1976-78, Trinity Bapt. Ch., Oak Grove, 1978-82, Fellowship Bapt. Ch., Jena, La., 1982—; chaplain Home Mission Bd., La. State Police, 1984—; mem. com. on coms. La. Bapt. Conv., Alexandria, La., 1991. Republican. Home: PO Box 1736 Jena LA 71342 Office: Fellowship Bapt Ch Rte 1 Box 311 Trout LA 71371

ROBIE, JOAN HAKE, religion writer, publishing company executive; b. Columbia, Pa.; d. Carl William and J. Helen (Raver) Hake; m. Charles William Robie, Oct. 9, 1954; children: David A., Daniel Keith. BS in Bible, Valley Forge Christian Coll., Phoenixville, Pa., 1976; cert. graphoanalyst, Sch. Graphoanalysis, Chgo., 1969. Pastoral asst., music dir. Littlestown, Pa., 1954-56; ch. pianist, organist on east coast, 1957-82; lectr., teacher Joan Robie Ministries, Lancaster, Pa., 1990—; pres., editor-in-chief Starburst, Inc., Lancaster, 1982—; TV host, N.Y.C., 1970-71; radio and TV personality, N.Y.C., Balt., Phila., Boston, also others, 1985—. Republican.

ROBILLARD, EDMOND, priest; b. St.-Paul-l'Ermite, Que., Can., Dec. 20, 1917; s. William and Marie (Lachapelle) R. B Arts and Scis., Coll. de l'Assomption, 1936; postgrad., Couvent Dominicain d'Ottawa, 1938-41; Licentiate in Theology, Cath. U. Am., 1943; ThD, U. Montreal, Can., 1944-45. Joined Dominican Order, Roman Cath. Ch., ordained priest, 1941. Prof. theology Coll. Dominicain, Ottawa, Ont., Can., 1943-50; prof. U. Montreal, 1955-83, prof. titulaire, 1970—; pres. Soc. des Ecrivains canadiens, 1973-77; sec. de l'Acad. candienne francaise, 1977-83. Author: De l'analogie et du concept d'etre, 1963, John Henry Newman: L'idee d'universite, 1968, John Henry Newman: Conferences sur la Doctrine de la justification, 1980, Reincarnation: Illusion or Reality, 1982, Quebec Blues, 1983, Nos Racines chrétiennes, 1985, La messe catholique de tous les dimanches de l'année sur des chorals de J. S. Bach, 1986, Tout ce qu'il vous dira, Faites-le, 1987, S. Justin: Itinéraire philosophique, 1989, Qui aime connaît Dieu, 1989, Le Discours poétique, 1991, La sagesse et les 1050 sentences du mime syrien Publilius Lochius, 1991; mem. editorial bd. jour. Carrefour Chretien, 1984—; contbr. articles to profl. jours. Mem. Soc. canadienne de theologie, Assn. canadienne francaise pour l'avancement des scis. Address: Les Péres Dominicains, 2715 Côte Sainte-Catherine, Montreal, PQ Canada H3T 1B6

ROBINS, LARRY WAYNE, music minister; b. Norman, Okla., Sept. 10, 1959; s. Rual Wayne and Billie Louise (Bagwell) Robins; m. Janell Marie Richey, Sept. 25, 1981. Grad. high sch., Oklahoma City, 1977. Asst. mgr. Postal Fin. Corp., Moore, Okla., 1980-81; ins. agt. Richey Ins. Agy., Oklahoma City, 1981-84; v.p. Gen. Builders Supply Inc., Oklahoma City, 1984-86; min. of music Broadway Assembly, Lorain, Ohio, 1986-89, Norman (Okla.) Tabernacle, 1989—; founder, dir. Norman Community Mass Choir, 1991—. Author, dir.: (stage prodn.) It Is Finished, 1984, Beyond Calvary's Shadow, 1989. Republican. Mem. Pentecostal Assemblies of God Ch. Avocations: calligraphy, racquetball, tennis, water and snow skiing, swimming. Home: 2209 SW 61st Terr Oklahoma City OK 73159-1813 Office: Norman Tabernacle 3650 E Robinson St Norman OK 73071

ROBINS, MILTON FRANKLIN, minister; b. Mount Ida, Ark., Aug. 5, 1922; s. Claud and Cora Bethel (Ragan) R.; m. Betty Lee Ayres, Mar. 11, 1950; children: Norbert, Lynda, Jamie, Eugene, Betty, Philip, Marilyn, Roger. Student, pub. schs., Tex. Ordained to ministry, 1953. Founder, pastor Pentecostal Ch. God, Jacksonville, Tex., 1953-55; pastor First Pentecostal Ch. God, Irving, Tex., 1955—; evangelist Irving, 1955—; organizer, bd. dirs. So. Bible Coll., Houston, 1957-90; sect. presbyter Dallas, Pentecostal Ch. God of Am., 1955-67, 74—, mem. gen. bd., 1967-73, chmn. resolutions com., 1957—, Dist. sec.-treas., 1985—, chmn. fin. com., 1985—. Contbr. articles to newspapers and religious jours. Home: 2209 W 11th StSt Irving TX 75060 Office: First Pentecostal Ch of God 1201 Maryland Irving TX 75060 *Life is a gift bestowed upon us by the Creator. What life becomes depends on the choices we make, the value we put upon ourselves, the convictions which steer us towar our goals and the priorities we put in place.*

ROBINSON, BARBARA AITKEN, lay church worker; b. Melrose, Mass., Dec. 8, 1928; d. Robert Hall and Laura Castle (Aitken) B.; m. Ross Utley Robinson, Oct. 3, 1953; children: Brian H., Emily C., Judith A., Ross Stuart, Rachel A., John W. BS, Simmons Coll., 1950. Elder Presbyn. Ch. (U.S.A.), Libertyville, Ill., 1972-74; deacon Presbyn. Ch. (U.S.A.), Pasadena, Calif., 1980-82; elder Presbyn. Ch. (U.S.A.), Santa Fe, 1986-88; pres. United Presbyn. Women, Pasadena, 1976-78; pres. Inter-Faith Coun. Santa Fe, 1988-90, exec. sec., 1990—. Active Commn. on Status of Women, Pasadena, 1982-85. Named Churchperson of Yr., Ecumenical Coun., 1980. Mem. Ch. Women United (pres. Pasadena unit 1977-79, Santa Fe unit 1987-89, N.Mex. region 1989—), LWV (pres. Santa Fe chpt. 1988-90, bd. dirs. 1991—). Home: 2393 Botulph Rd Santa Fe NM 87505 Office: Inter-Faith Coun 818 Camino Sierra Vista Santa Fe NM 87501

ROBINSON, BRYANT, SR., bishop. Bishop Ch. of God in Christ, Springfield, Mass. Office: Ch of God in Christ 1424 Plumtree Rd Springfield MA 01119*

ROBINSON, CLAYTON DAVID, minister, educator; b. Pasadena, Calif., Oct. 30, 1955; s. Gary Garth and Gay Elizabeth Clara (Guilmette) R.; m. Kimberly Ann Cole, June 18, 1977; children: Christina Mary, Kathleen Joy, Jonathan David. BA, So. Calif. Coll., 1975; MA, Azusa (Calif.) Pacific U., 1976; MDiv, Fuller Theol. Sem., 1978, D in Ministry, 1986. Co-pastor Foursquare Gospel Ch., Huntington Beach, Calif., 1975-82; pastor, founder Foursquare Gospel Ch., Mission Viejo, Calif., 1982-88; pastor Foursquare Gospel Ch., Arcadia, Calif., 1988-91; pastor, founder Foursquare Gospel Ch., Laguna Niguel, Calif., 1991—; mem. faculty Life Bible Coll., L.A., 1985—; mem. adj. faculty So. Calif. Coll., Costa Mesa, 1985; dir. Pacific Pines Camp, summer 1977-82; youth dir. Orange County (Calif.) Foursquare Chs., 1974-86; founder, dir. The Net Coffee House, Huntington Beach, 1981-82. Author: The Revelation, 1976, 2d edit. 1991, The Antichrist, 1980, A Strategy for Church Growth and Renewal, 1986; editor, author: Church Planting, 1991; contbr. numerous articles to profl. jours.

ROBINSON, DONALD FAY, minister emeritus; b. Boston, Feb. 6, 1905; s. Thomas Pendleton and Ethel Lincoln (Fay) R.; m. Carol Howard, May 9, 1942; children: Mary Howard Robinson Rizzotto, Thomas Howard. AB, Harvard U., 1926; postgrad., Crozer Theol. Sem., 1937-38. Ordained to ministry Unitarian Universalist Assn., 1957. Min. Second Parish, Hingham, Mass., 1957-77; emeritus, 1977—; dir. Unitarian Universalist Christian Fellowship, Boston, 1970-71, v.p. 1971-73, pres. 1973-75. Author: Out of the East (poems), 1927, Harvard Dramatic Club Miracle Plays, 1928, In Search of a Religion, 1938, Jesus Son of Joseph, 1964, Two Hundred Years in South Hingham, 1746-1946, 1980, Poems for People, 1982; contbr. articles to religious jours. Pres. Hingham Hist. Soc., 1960-63; trustee Wilder Charitable and Ednl. fund, Hingham, 1966—. Recipient Christian Rsch. Found. award, 1961. Mem. Internat. Platform Assn., Soc. Bibl. Lit., Unitarian Universalist Mins. Assn. Home: 114 East St Hingham MA 02043 Office: 685 Main St Hingham MA 02043 *The function of religion is to explain the experiences of life; and the role of the minister is to help the individual to understand and adjust to that explanation.*

ROBINSON, DONALD LEE, clergyman, educator; b. Pleasant Hill, Ohio, Nov. 29, 1929; s. John Amos and Nora Edna (Minnich) R.; m. Eleanor Jane Judy, June 7, 1952; children: John Raymond, Jane Diane, James Edward. BA, Juniata Coll., 1951; MDiv, Bethany Theol. Sem., 1954; DMinistry, Lancaster Theol. Sem., 1986. Ordained to ministry, Ch. of Brethren, 1951. Pastor Wilmington (Del.) Ch. of Brethren, 1954-57; dir. fin. Ch. Fedn. Greater Dayton, Ohio, 1957-61; pastor First Ch. of Brethren, Reading, Pa., 1961—; cons., Carr & Assocs., North Manchester, Ind., 1956-59, Ch. of Brethren, Elgin, Ill., 1965—; mem. faculty, Reading Area Community Coll., 1974—, Pace Inst., Reading, 1972—; pres. Family Guidance Ctr., Reading, 1978-86. Pres. HELP crisis intervention ctr., Reading, 1972-80; mem. White House Conf. on Problems of Youth in Am., 1974; cons. various sch. dists., Phila., Washington and Reading, 1978—, Reading Domestic Rels. Ct., 1982—. Mem. Rotary. Republican. Home: 1803 Salem Dr Reading PA 19610 Office: First Ch Brethren 2200 Bern Rd Reading PA 19610

ROBINSON, FISHER JOSEPH, priest; b. Abbeville, La., Aug. 12, 1929; s. Fisher Joseph and Winnie (Smith) R. BA, Divine Word Coll., Epworth, Iowa, 1952; MA, Cath. U. Am., 1959. Joined Soc. of Divine Word, Roman Cath. Ch., 1950, ordained priest, 1958. Dir. formation St. Augustine Sem., Bay St. Louis, Miss., 1959-61; assoc. pastor Notre Dame Cath. Ch., St. Martinville, La., 1961-63; dir. formation Divine Word Sem., Riverside, Calif., 1963-66, instr., 1963-67; prin. Verbum Dei High Sch., L.A., 1967-80; pastor St. Malachy's Ch., L.A., 1980-89; vicar Black Caths., African-Am. Vicariate, L.A., 1986—; mem. Archdiocesan Coun. Priests, L.A., 1976-80; cons. Archdiocesan Bd. Consultors, L.A., 1979; bd. dirs. Ecumenical Ctr. Black Ch. Studies, L.A., 1980; chair L.A. Archdiocesan Team of Nat. Black Cath. Pastoral Plan on Evangelization L.A., 1987. Co-author: Pastoral of African-American Catholics in the Archdiocese of Los Angeles, 1987. Commr. L.A. County Probation Com., 1976; trustee St. Anne's Maternity Home, L.A., 1978; bd. dirs. Community Care and Devel., L.A., 1983; mem. task force Respect for Life, L.A. Archdiocese, 1987; sec., bd. dirs. St. John's Major Sem., L.A., 1988. Mem. Nat. Bd. Black Cath. Adminstrs. (bd. dirs., rep. western regional div. 1988). Home: 6028 Victoria Ave Los Angeles CA 90043 Office: African-Am Vicariate 1530 W 9th St Los Angeles CA 90015 *Life is a great gift from God and we reflect His image in our likeness of Him. He graces us with the strength to grow in His image daily and share our gifts with all of our sisters and brothers whom He also created in His likeness.*

ROBINSON, FRANK WILLIAM, minister; b. Phila., July 9, 1937; s. Frank Ellis and Helen Ellen (Miller) R.; m. Barbara Jean Stevenson, Aug. 18, 1962; children: Steven, David, Kimberly, Deborah, Sheri. BA, Gordon Coll., 1965; MDiv, Reformed Episcopal Sem., Phila., 1967. Ordained to ministry Ind. Fundamental Chs. Am., 1968. Youth dir. J.R. Miller Presbyn. Ch., Upper Darby, Pa., 1960-63, 1st Bapt. Ch., Lowell, Mass., 1963-65; dir. Youth for Christ Lakeside Youth, Bucks County, Pa., 1965-68; sr. pastor Folcroft (Pa.) Union Ch., 1969-73, Bethlehem Ch., Randolph, N.J., 1973—; bd. dirs. Bible Basics Internat., Northeastern Bible Coll. (v.p. 1979—). Mem. Juvenile Conf. Com., Randolph, N.J., 1986-91. Mem. Morris County Evang. Ministerium (pres. 1979-80). Republican. Home: 23 Gilmar Rd Randolph NJ 07869 Office: Bethlehem Ch 758 Rte 10 Randolph NJ 07869

ROBINSON, GAY ELIZABETH CLARA, clergywoman; b. Stamford, Conn., Aug. 13, 1933; d. Theodore Alfred, Sr. and Elizabeth (Majher) Guilmette; student L.I.F.E. Coll., 1951-52; A.A., Orange Coast Coll., 1966; B.A., Calif. State U., 1968, M.A., 1970; postgrad., Golden State U., 1980—; m. Gary Garth Robinson, Feb. 3, 1952; children—Joy Leah Robinson, Clayton David. Asst. credit mgr. Phelps-Terkel, 1951-52; exec. adminstrv. asst. Pozzo Constrn. Co., 1952-53; ordained to ministry Internat. Ch. Foursquare Gospel, 1962; assoc. pastor Perris, Calif., 1955-58, SW Dist., 1958-60, Worldwide Mission rep. 70 countries, 1965—; pastoral staff Ch. by the Sea, Huntington Beach, Calif., 1960-84; founder Breath of Life, 1975; instr. Dynamic Life Seminars; instr. Irvine Coll., 1976-78; SW dist. sec., 1960-78; broadcaster sta. KYMS, 1979-84; tour dir., 1977—; participant exec. mgmt. seminars, 1976-78. Mem. Republican Women's Nat. Com. Scholarship Chapman Floating Coll. of the Seas, 1966; Pepperdine U. scholar, 1951. Mem. Nat. Assn. Evangelicals, Western Psychol. Assn., United Foursquare Women (past program chmn., publicity chmn.), L.I.F.E. Alumni Assn. (past alumni sec.). Club: Temple City Jr. Women's (devotion leader, sec., 1957-60). Contbr. book revs., articles to publs. in field.

ROBINSON, GEORGE MCKINSEY, minister; b. Chgo., Mar. 20, 1947; s. George Clark and Majel Jane (McKinsey) R.; m. Betty Jean Stenerson, Sept. 4, 1972; children: Gretchen Marie, Charles Clark, Michael McKinsey. BA, Harding U.; MPA, U. N.D. Min. Bismarck (N.D.) Ch. of Christ, 1978-80, Torrance (Calif.) Ch. of Christ, 1981—; bd. dirs. World Bible Sch. Inc., Austin; pres. Calif. Christian Children's Svcs., Santa Fe Springs, 1980-88, West Coast Christian Publ. Inc., Palos Verdes Estates, Calif., 1991—; missionary trip to The Philippines, 1986-88, Am. Samoa, 1989, Caribbean, 1989-91, Ghana, 1991. Author: Of Family, Farm & Friends, 1983. Mem. adv. bd. N.W. div. ARC, Mpls., 1979-80. Mem. Assn. for Regulatory Adminstrn. (life, founder). Office: Ch of Christ 3525 Maricopa St Torrance CA 90503 *If silence is golden, then laughter is priceless.*

ROBINSON, HADDON WILLIAM, education educator; b. N.Y.C., Mar. 21, 1931; s. William Andrew and Anna (Clements) R.; m. Bonita Vick, Aug. 11, 1951; children—Vicki Robinson Hitzges, Torrey William. B.A., Bob Jones U., 1951; Th.M., Dallas Theol. Sem., 1955; M.A., So. Meth. U., 1960; Ph.D., U. Ill., 1964. Prof. homiletics Dallas Sem., 1958-79; chmn. pastoral ministries dept., 1972-79; gen. dir. Christian Med. Soc., Dallas, 1970-79; assoc. pastor First Bapt. Ch., Medford, Oreg., 1956-58; pres. Denver Conservative Bapt. Sem., 1979-91; disting. prof. preachers Gordon-Conwell Theol. Sem., 1991—; Harold John Ockenga Distin. prof. preaching Gordon-Conwell Theol. Sem., South Hamilton, Mass., 1991—. Author: Psalm 23; Grief, 1976; Biblical Preaching, 1980; co-editor: Recent Homiletical Thought, 1983, The Christian Salt and Light Company, 1989, The Solid Rock Construction Company, 1989, Mastering Contemporary Preaching, 1989, Biblical Sermons, 1990, Decision-Making By the Book, 1991, What Jesus Said About Successful Living, 1991. Mem. Evang. Theol. Soc. (v.p. 1982-83, pres. 1983-84), Christian Med. Soc. (hon.). Office: Gordon-Conwell Theol Sem 130 S Essex St South Hamilton MA 01982

ROBINSON, HAROLD BARRETT, bishop; b. Nelson, Eng., June 14, 1922; came to U.S., 1922, naturalized, 1945; s. Harold and Mary (Barrett) R.; m. Marie A. Little, May 17, 1952; children—Mary Elizabeth, Martha Marie Anne Victoria, Jane Barrett. B.A., U. Calif. at Los Angeles, 1943; S.T.B., Gen. Theol. Sem., 1946, S.T.D., 1967, L.H.D. (hon.), 1979. Ordained priest Episcopal Ch., 1946. Curate, rector in San Diego, 1946-62; dean St. Paul's Cathedral, Buffalo, 1962-68; bishop coadjutor Diocese Western N.Y., Buffalo, 1968-70, bishop, 1970-87, ret., 1987; chaplain QE2, 1988, 89, asst. bishop N.Y., 1989—; chmn. bd. Epis. Radio/TV Found.; chaplain Buffalo Fire Dept. Mem. Mayor Buffalo Adv. Com.; Chmn. Bd. De Veaux Sch., Ch. Home, Ch. Mission of Help. Club: Saturn (Buffalo). Home: 9731 Knoll Rd Eden NY 14057

ROBINSON, HAROLD LEONARD, rabbi; b. Boston, Jan. 29, 1947; s. Milton and Evelyn (Wunsch) R.; m. Miriam Gariani, Dec. 28, 1970; children: Yair Dan, Dori Avigyle. BA in Polit. Sci., Coe Coll., 1968; BHL, Hebrew Union Coll., 1972, MA, 1974. Ordained rabbi, 1974. Rabbi Temple Israel, Gary, Ind., 1974-77, The Cape Cod Synagogue, Hyannis, Mass., 1977—; mem. Nat. Rabbinic Cabinet, 1986—, UAHC Resolutions Com., 1983—, Joint Social Action Commn. of Reform Judaism, 1980—; mem. Cen. Conf. Am. Rabbis, Mass. Bd. Rabbis. Chmn. Mass. Commn. Against Discrimination/Southeast Mass. Adv. Coun., 1991. Comdr. USNR, 1987—. Mem. Barnstable Clergy Assn. (past pres.), Rotary, Hyannis Yacht Club. Home: 226 Gleneagle Dr Centerville MA 02632 Office: The Cape Cod Synagogue 145 Winter St Hyannis MA 02601

ROBINSON, IDA LAFOSSE, minister, broadcaster; b. Phila., July 27, 1934; d. Charles and Alma Elizabeth (Johnson) B.; m. Benjamin H. LaFosse; children: Andre, Marcel, Benita, Tania. DD, Trinity Hall Coll. & Sem., Denver, 1985. Ordained to ministry Pentacostal Ch., 1963. Min. Ch. of God in Christ, Phila., 1959-63; evangelist Ch. of the Open Door, Phila., 1963-66; pastor Miracle Tabernacle, Camden, N.J., 1966-67, Salvation Tabernacle, Phila., 1967—; broadcaster Move of God Inc., Phila., 1967-73, overseer, 1985—; pastor Move of God Cathedral, N.Y.C., 1968—, broadcaster, 1985—. Editor Amb. mag., 1973. Avocation: youth counselor. Office: Move of God Cathedral 501-503 W 152 St New York NY 10031

ROBINSON, J. KENNETH, religious organization administrator, minister; b. Ft. Smith, Ark., Sept. 27, 1932; s. John B. and Jessie Mary (Ledbetter) R.; m. Addie Muriel Thompson, Nov. 22, 1956; children: J. Mark, Elizabeth Robinson Clifton, Robin Robinson Newman, Price. AA, Westark Coll., 1951; BS, Okla. Bapt. U., 1954; MRE, Southwestern Bapt. Theol. Sem., 1956. Ordained to ministry So. Bapt. Conv., 1975. Min. music/edn. San Jacinto Bapt. Ch., Amarillo, Tex., 1964-67, First Bapt. Ch., Carlsbad, N.Mex., 1967-71, Meadows Bapt. Ch., Plano, Tex., 1971-81, First Bapt. Ch., Carlsbad, N.Mex., 1981-86; dir. missions Pecos Valley Bapt. Assn., Artesia, N.Mex., 1987—; mem. com. on coms. So. Bapt. Conv., Nashville, 1971; v.p. Bapt. Conv. N.Mex., Albuquerque, 1970-71, bd. dirs., 1984-85; dir. Sunday sch. Pecos Valley Bapt. Assn., 1983-87; adj. prof. Sch. Ch. Music, Southwestern Bapt. Theol. Sem., Ft. Worth, 1979-80. Co-author: Music Making with Younger Children, 1971, Ministry of Religious Edn., 1978; contbr. articles to various jours. V.p. Plano Assn. for Retarded Citizens, 1979-81; bd. dirs. Community Concert Assn., Carlsbad, Artesia Community Concert Assn. Democrat. Home: 1470 W Cannon Artesia NM 88210 Office: Pecos Valley Bapt Assn 304 N 7th Artesia NM 88210 *There is no greater joy in life than the joy of seeing men and women come into a right relationship with their Lord; there is no greater satisfaction than to see them mature in that relationship. For whatever days God gives me, I am committed to these all important ministries.*

ROBINSON, JACK F(AY), clergyman; b. Wilmington, Mass., Mar. 7, 1914; s. Thomas P. and Ethel Lincoln (Fay) R.; A.B., Mont. State U., 1936; D.B., Crozer Theol. Sem., 1939; A.M., U. Chgo., 1949, postgrad., 1950-52; m. Eleanor Jean Smith, Sept. 1, 1937 (dec. 1966); 1 dau., Alice Virginia Dungey; m. Lois Henze, July 16, 1968. Ordained to ministry Bapt. Ch., 1939; minister Bethany Ch., American Falls, Idaho, 1939-41, 1st Ch., Coun. Grove, Kans., 1944-49; ordained (transfer) to ministry Congregational Ch., 1945; minister United Ch., Chebanse, Ill., 1949-52, 1st Ch., Argo, Ill., 1954-58, Congl. Ch., St. Charles, Ill., 1958-64; assoc. minister Plymouth Congregational Ch., Lansing, Mich., 1964-66; tchr. Chgo. Pub. Schs., 1966-68; minister Waveland Ave. Congl. Ch., Chgo., 1967-79, interim pastor Chgo. Met. Assn., 1979—, First Congl. Ch., Des Plaines, Ill., 1979, Bethany Congl. Ch., Chgo., 1980, Eden United Ch. of Christ, Chgo., 1983-84, St. Nicolai Ch., Chgo., 1984, Grace United Ch. of Christ, Chgo., 1985-86, Christ Ch. of Chgo., 1987-87, First Congl., Evanston, Ill., 1987-88, First Congl. Ch., Brookfield, Ill., 1988-89, 1st Congl. Ch., Steger, Il., 1990—; assoc. pastor, calling, People's Ch., Chgo., 1990—; hist. cons. Bell & Howell Co., Chgo., 1981-82. Assoc. Hyde Park dept. Chgo. YMCA, 1942-44. U. Chgo. Libr. 1952-54; chmn. com. evangelism Kans. Congl. Christian Conf., 1947-48; city chmn. Layman's Missionary Movement, 1946-51; trustee Congl. and Christian Conf. Ill., v.p., 1963-64; mem. exec. coun. Chgo. Met. Assn. United Ch. of Christ, 1968-70, sec. ch. and ministry com., 1982-88 ; mem. gen. bd. Ch. Fedn. Greater Chgo., 1969-71; mem. Libr. Bd. Coun. Grove, 1945-49; city chmn. NCCJ, 1945-49; dean Northside Mission Coun. United Ch. of Christ, 1975-77, sec. personnel com. Ill. Conf. United Ch. of Christ, 1986-88. Recipient Pres'. award Congl. Christian Hist. Soc. Mem. Am. Soc. Ch. History, Am. Acad. Polit. Sci., Am. Hist. Assn., C. of C. (past dir.), Internat. Platform Assn. Author: The Growth of the Bible, 1969; From A Mission to a Church, 1976; Bell & Howell Company: A 75 Year History, 1982, (co-author) Harza: 65 Years, 1986, History of the Illinois Conference, United Church of Christ, 1990. Home: 2614 Lincolnwood Dr Evanston IL 60201 Office: PO Box 4578 Chicago IL 60680

ROBINSON, JAMES BURNELL, religious educator; b. Indpls., Sept. 7, 1944; s. James Paul and Mary Jane (Groff) R.; m. Carol Ann Turner, Aug. 27, 1969 (div. May 1975); m. Linda Ann Turner, Dec. 4, 1978; 1 child, Darius Paul Rama. BA, Wabash Coll., 1966; MA, U. Wis., 1969, PhD, 1975. Prof. religion U. No. Iowa, Cedar Falls, 1971—; bd. dirs. Hermetic Acad. Author: Buddha's Lions. Sr. warden vestry St. Luke's Episcopal Ch., Cedar Falls, 1990. NEH scholar, 1987. Mem. Am. Acad. Religion, Internat. Assn. Buddhist Studies, Tibet Soc., Constantian Soc., Sarmatian Soc. Home: 1204 Clay St Cedar Falls IA 50613 Office: U No Iowa Dept Philosophy & Religion Cedar Falls IA 50614-0501 *Events have causes; the more we understand them, the greater our ability to sympathize. Actions have consequences; small kindnesses make for a better world.*

ROBINSON, JAMES EDWARD, minister; b. Lancaster, Pa., Oct. 7, 1954; s. James Edward and Thelma Lee (Weathers) R.; m. Ellen Louis Williams, Sept. 5, 1981; children: Brendan, Alexandra, Sarah. BA, Pa. State U., State College, 1976; MDiv, Colgate Rochester Div. Sch.-Bexley Hall-Crozer Theol. Sem., 1981; postgrad., Drew U., 1986—. Ordained to ministry Am. Bapt. Chs. in U.S.A., 1982. Pastor Bottskill Bapt Ch., Greenwich, N.Y., 1981-87, 1st Bapt. Ch., Troy, N.Y., 1987—. Mem. Mins. Coun., Downtown Clergy Assn. (convener 1987—), Troy Area United Ministries (v.p. 1989—), Rotary (pres. Troy club 1991—). Democrat. Office: 1st Bapt Ch 82 3d St Troy NY 12180 *It has been said that we are more receivers than we are achievers in this world. It has certainly been true in my life as I have encouraged and sustained by many people and in many ways. How we understand such blessings makes a difference- whether we see them as gifts of God, or somehow as our due because they are the work of our hands. I see them as gifts and my response is to return thanks.*

ROBINSON, JANICE MARIE, priest, former health association executive; b. Phila., June 6, 1943; d. Calvin C. and Leola O. (Edwards) R. BS in Nusing, U. Bridgeport, 1965; MA in Nursing, NYU, 1970; MDiv, Yale U., 1988. Ordained priest Episcopal Ch., 1988. Dir. nursing and outreach program Mid-Westside Neighborhood Health Services St. Luke's Hosp., N.Y.C., 1970-72; exec. dir. William F. Ryan Community Health Center, N.Y.C., 1972-79, Nat. Assn. Community Health Centers, Washington, 1979-85; asst. rector St. John's Episc. Ch., Norwood Parish, Chevy Chase, Md., 1988—; mem. study panel Inst. Medicine, Nat. Acad. Scis.; mem. ambulatory care standards Task Force Congressional Black Caucus Health Brain Trust; mem. nominating com. for Diocesan Bishop, 1989-90, Diocesan Fin. Com., 1990-91, chmn. 1992. Contbr. articles to profl. jours. Mem. Nat. Health Council, Am. Public Health Assn., Nat. Assn. Health Services Execs., Nat. Assn. Community Health Centers (pres. 1976-77), Washington Clergy Assn. (chmn. program com. 1990-92, bd. dirs. 1990-92), Sigma Theta Tau. Office: St Johns Episc Ch 6701 Wisconsin Ave NW Chevy Chase MD 20815 *Each person has a talent, and that talent must be exploited and shared. The more it is shared, the greater the depth is uncovered, always providing more to be shared.*

ROBINSON, JEROME STANCIL, minister; b. Birmingham, Ala., Nov. 22, 1924; s. Charlsie Chisenhall Robinson; children: Jerome, James. BS, U. Ala., 1961, MA, 1963, MS, 1965; DM, Luther Rice Sem., Jacksonville, Fla., 1984. Ordained to ministry So. Bapt. Conv., 1953. Pastor Mt. Olive Bapt. Ch., Tuscaloosa, Ala., 1953-61, Liberty Hill Bapt. Ch., Clanton, Ala., 1961-63, Skyland Bapt. Ch., Tuscaloosa, 1963-88, Hargrove Rd. Bapt. Ch., Tuscaloosa, 1990—; substitute tchr. Tuscaloosa City Schs., 1989-90; pastor emeritus Skyland Bapt. Ch., Tuscaloosa, 1988, moderator, 1961-62; tchr. Samford U. Ext., Tuscaloosa, 1991. Author: My Seven FAvorite Sugar Sticks, 1984, Church and State, 1984, History of Mt. Olive, 1959. Advt. chmn. Anti-Alcoholic Orgn., Tuscaloosa, 1968-69. With U.S. Army, World War II, ETO. Decorated Purple Heart, Bronze Star, World War II victory medals. Mem. Tuscaloosa Bapt. Pastors Conf., Springhill Lake Club. Home: 4330 Bass Dr Springhill Lk Tuscaloosa AL 35405

ROBINSON, JOHN H., minister; b. Oklahoma City, May 14, 1934; s. James Robinson; m. Mayotis Washington, Aug. 28, 1969; children: Donna, Angela, Toni, Adriann. BA, Lane Coll., 1964; BD, I.T.C., 1967, MDiv, 1971; DD (hon.), Miles Coll., 1985. Master counselor Rehab. Svcs., Little Rock, 1969-73; city adminstr. City of North Little Rock, Ark., 1973-75, E.O. adminstr., 1976-77; recruiter Urban League, Little Rock, 1975-76; adminstrv. asst. Shorter Coll., North Little Rock, 1977-81; minister Christian M.E.Ch., Oklahoma City, 1982—. Bd. dirs. HOPE, Inc., North Little Rock, 1971-75. With U.S. Army, 1955-56. Democrat. Avocation: horticulture. Home: 1609 NE 48th Oklahoma City OK 73111

ROBINSON, KERRY BRENT, pastor; b. Greenfield, Ind., Feb. 25, 1958; s. Forrest Robert and Peggy JoAnn (Toney) R.; m. Rebecca Ann Meyer, July 12, 1980; children: Kyle Brent, Kameron Blake. BA, Anderson U., 1980, MDiv, 1983; postgrad., Emory U., 1991—. Ordained to ministry Ch. of God, 1982. Min. of youth Meridian St. Ch. of God, Indpls., 1979-80, North Anderson (Ind.) Ch. of God, 1980-83; sr. pastor Scott Meml. Ch. of God, Chattanooga, 1983—; mem. Anderson U. Alumni Coun., 1987—; chmn. Tenn. State Assembly of Ch. of God, Anderson, 1990-91; conf. leader Internat. Youth Conv. of Ch. of God, Anderson, 1990; sec. So. Conf. of Ch. of God, Anderson, 1986-88. Contbr. articles to profl. jours. Mem. Chattanooga Assn. of Pastoral Care, Tri-State Evangelistic Assn. (steering com. 1990), East Ridge Mins. Assn. (chmn. 1990), Alpha Chi. Office: Scott Meml Ch 1620 Waterhouse Ave Chattanooga TN 37412 *The demand upon humanity in any age is for consistency and integrity within the realms of behaviour and personality. Answering this demand is the consuming goal of my life.*

ROBINSON, MARK BRYAN, minister; b. Yuba City, Calif., Feb. 29, 1960; s. Pike Calton Robinson; m. Juanita Rose Houtman, Sept. 12, 1981; children:

Rochelle, Briana, Kristen. BA in Bibl. Lit., NW Coll., Kirkland, Wash., 1982. Ordained to ministry Assemblies of God. Assoc. pastor Cen. Valley Ch., Halsey, Oreg., 1981-82; youth pastor Assembly of God, Midland, Mich, 1982-85, Evergreen Christian Ctr., Olympia, Wash., 1985-89; sr. assoc. pastor Calvary Temple, Bellingham, Wash., 1989—; founder, pres. For Parents Only Ministries, Bellingham, 1986—. Republican. Home: 2101 C St Bellingham WA 98225 Office: Calvary Temple 2014 C St Bellingham WA 98225

ROBINSON, MARS RAY, minister; b. Martin, Ky., Aug. 30, 1956; s. Mars and Thelma Grace (Hughes) R.; m. Karen Marie Beer, Jan. 1, 1977; children: Mars Stephen, Sarah Marie, Shawn Micheal, John Scott, Jessica Stacey. BA in Christian Ministry/Counseling, Ky. Christian Coll., 1979. Sr. minister Slate Valley Christian Ch., Owingsville, Ky., 1978-81; youth pastor Mt. Pleasant Christian Ch., Greenville, N.C., 1981-83; child care worker Christian Children's Home of Ohio, Wooster, 1983-85; youth pastor Greenwood Christian Ch., Canton, Ohio, 1985—. Scoutmaster Boy Scouts Am., 1978-81. With USN, 1975. Home: 4521 Frazer Ave NW Canton OH 44704 Office: Greenwood Christian Church 4425 Frazer Ave WW Canton OH 44709

ROBINSON, MILTON BERNIDINE, clergyman, editor; b. Forest City, N.C., June 29, 1913; s. Plato and Connie (McEntire) R.; m. Lois Mosley, Oct. 18, 1933; children: Evelyn Robinson Mercer, Essie Robinson McDaniel, Connie Robinson Foust (dec. Dec. 1983), Milton Bernidine, Arthur, Charles, Annie Robinson Evans, Bettie Robinson McKesson, Priscilla Robinson McKinney, Phylias, Kenneth. AB, Johnson C. Coll., 1963; MS, A&T State U., 1967; DD (hon.), Livingstone Coll., 1973. Ordained to ministry African Meth. Episcopal Zion Ch., 1949. Former farmer, sch. bus driver, Pullman porter, editor, brick mason, builder.; pastor St. John A.M.E. Zion Ch., Rutherford, N.C., 1965-76; tchr. Carver High Sch., Rutherford County, 1965-69; del. gen. conf. African Meth. Episcopal Zion Ch., 1960, 64, 68, 72, 76-80; del. World Meth Conf., 1971; connectional mem. bd. dirs. home-ch. div. Christian Edn., 1968-72; mem. governing bd. nat. Coun. Chs. Christ in U.S.A., 1972—. Editor Star of Zion, 1969-80. Chmn. Rutherford County Human Rels. Coun., 1968-69; 2d vice chmn. Rutherford County Dem. Exec. Com., 1970-74, 81—; chmn. trustees Doggett Grove African Meth. Episcopal Zion Ch., Forest City, N.C.; trustee Isothermal Community Coll., Spindale, N.C., 1983—. Mem. NAACP, Mason. Home: Rte 6 Box 600 Forest City NC 28043

ROBINSON, NANCY ANNE, religious school administrator; b. MIddletown, N.Y., Jan. 2, 1940; d. Derk and Dorothy Maretta (Adams) Zwart; m. William D. Robinson Jr., June 30, 1962 (div. June 1982); children: Sheryl, Jodi, William Douglas III. BA, The King's Coll., 1961. Cert. Assn. Christian Schs. Internat., 7-12 social studies tchr., Mass. Tchr. Atlantic Christian Sch., Ocean City, N.J., 1978-89; prin. Atlantic Christian Sch., Ocean City, 1989—. Home: 1453 Old Stagecoach Rd Ocean View NJ 08230 Office: Atlantic Christian Sch Box 271 10th & Wesley Ocean City NJ 08226

ROBINSON, NANCY DRUE, lay church worker, librarian; b. Auburntown, Tenn., Aug. 9, 1930; d. William M. and Mary G. (Higgins) R. BA, Carson-Newman Coll., 1953; MLS, Vanderbilt U., 1954. Catalog libr. So. Bapt. Theol. Sem., Louisville, 1954—. Mem. Am. Theol. Libr. Assn. Home and Office: 2825 Lexington Rd Box 294 Louisville KY 40280

ROBINSON, OTIS BERNARD, minister; b. Bennettsville, S.C., July 15, 1961; s. Otis Chester and Virginia Lee (Monroe) R.; m. Pamela Laveece Best, July 20, 1985; 1 child, Dana Reneé. BA, E. Carolina U., 1983; student, Hood Theol. Sem. Lic. FCC announcer. Assoc. minister Mt. Zion Christian Ch., Durham, N.C., 1983-85; assoc. minister, elder New Covenant Ch., Winston-Salem, N.C., 1985-89; sr. pastor Cedar Grove African Meth. Episcopal Zion Ch., New London, N.C., 1989—; counselor Telamon Corp., Raleigh, 1983-84, Joint Orange-Chatham Community Action, Pittsboro, N.C., 1985; chmn. bible tchr. Fountain of Life Christian Fellowship, Greenville, N.C., 1981-82; mem. W. Central N.C. Conf. of AME Zion Ch. Campaign worker Ams. for Robertson, Charlotte, N.C., 1987; mem. adv. bd. Community Christian Ch., Inc., Greenville. Mem. Nat. Christian Counselors Assn. (profl. assoc.), E. Carolina U. Alumni Assn. Republican. Avocations: traveling, sports, reading, meeting people. Office: Camp Barnhardt Rd Route 2 Hwy 740 New London NC 28127

ROBINSON, RONALD GUILFRED, minister; b. St. Louis, Nov. 9, 1955; s. Jack G. and Leoma Jean (Nelson) R.; m. Terri Jean O'Bryan, July 22, 1978; children: Joshua G., Tabitha Jean. BA, Ouachita Bapt. U., 1978; student, Midwestern Bapt. Sem., 1982-86. Ordained to ministry Bapt. Ch., 1976. Pastor Walnut St. Bapt. Ch., Arkadelphia, Ark., 1976-78; assoc. pastor Rock Hill Bapt. Ch., St. Louis, 1978-80; pastor 1st Bapt. Ch. of Cobden, Ill., 1980-82; assoc. pastor Tower Grove Bapt. Ch., St. Louis, 1982-86; pastor Bayless Bapt. Ch., St. Louis, 1986—; pastor, leader Continuous Witness Tng., St. Louis, 1982—; trainer Prayer for Spiritual Awakening, 1983—. Author: T.N.T., 1984, Show Me I'll Believe, 1984. 2d in state in baptisms Ill. Bapt. Conv., Cobden, 1981; recipient Sunday sch. growth awards Ill. State Bapt. Conv., 1981; led state in baptisms, Mo. Bapt. Conv., 1983, 84. Mem. Clear Creek Bapt. Assn. (Sunday sch. growth award, 1981), Fellowship Christian Magicians. Avocations: fishing, hunting, basketball, golf, writing. Office: Bayless Bapt Ch 8512 Morganford Saint Louis MO 63123

ROBINSON, TONI-ANN, religious writer; b. Stockton, Calif., May 19, 1944; d. Oliver Ulmont and Lucretia Minerva (Flentge) R. BA in Journalism, Calif. State U., L.A., 1975; MA in Religion, Claremont (Calif.) Coll., 1981. Freelance writer. Roman Catholic. Home and Office: 647 Colby Cir #A Claremont CA 91711

ROBINSON, VIVIAN U., religious organization administrator. Pres. Consultation on Ch. Union, Augusta, Ga. Office: 1256 Hernlen St Augusta GA 30901 also: care Sixth Episcopal Dist 2780 Collier Dr NW Atlanta GA 30318*

ROBINSON, WILLIAM JAMES, SR., lay worker; b. Erie, Pa., Aug. 17, 1896; s. William James and Margaret Fraser (Sweatman) R.; children: Nancy Robinson Weaver, William J. BA, Yale U., 1918; JD, Harvard U., 1923. Ordained elder Presbyn. Ch., 1946. Elder Presbyn. Ch., Lake Erie, Pa., 1946—. 1st lt. U.S. Army, 1917-19. Mem. Hemlock Nat. (life), Rotary (life), Masons (life). Home: 960 E Foothills Dr Tucson AZ 85718 *Love is the dominant force, so it will ultimately prevail over evil.*

ROBITSCHER, JAN BONDI, liturgical consultant; b. Washington, Jan. 16, 1954; d. Jonas Bondi Robitscher and Jean (Begeman) Robitscher-Bergmark. MusB, DePauw U., 1976; MA in Liturgy, MDiv, Nashotah House, 1983. Liturgical cons. Cathedral of St. James, South Bend, Ind., 1976-78, St. Patrick's Episc. Ch., Atlanta, 1978-80; liturgist, musician Cath. Ctr. Emory U., Atlanta, 1983-87; music asst. Ch. Divinity Sch. of the Pacific, Berkeley, Calif., 1988—; liturgical cons. Sch. for Deacons Diocese of Calif., 1990—; oblate Order of Holy Cross, 1990; retreat leader, spiritual dir., instr. liturgy, ch. music, Sch. for Deacons, 1991—. Mem. St. Mark's Episc. Ch., P.E.O. Sisterhood; vol. hospice chaplain. Recipient Visually Handicapped Student of Yr. award, 1972. Democrat. Avocations: photography, collecting religious art. Office: CDSP 2450 Le Conte Ave Berkeley CA 94709

ROBLES JIMENEZ, JOSE ESAUL, bishop; b. Jalpa, Zacatecas, Mexico, June 4, 1925. Ordained priest Roman Cath. Ch., 1949; bishop of Tulancingo, 1962-74, Zamora, Mexico, 1974—. Office: Obispado Apartado Postal 18, Zamora Michoacan, Mexico

ROBLYER, KATHLEEN ANNE CASEY, minister, nurse; b. Los Angeles, May 11, 1955; d. Donald F. and Marie A. (Round) Casey; m. Dwight A. Roblyer, Nov. 29, 1985. AA in Nursing, De Anza Coll., Cupertino, Calif., 1976; BS in Nursing, SUNY, Albany, 1981; MDiv, Golden Gate Bapt. Theol. Sem., Mill Valley, Calif., 1985, D Ministry, 1990; MS, U. Calif., San Francisco, 1987. RN; lic. to ministry Bapt. Ch., 1983. Nurse clin. cancer research ctr. M.D. Anderson Hosp. and Tumor Inst., Houston, 1977-79; nurse emergency dept. Kaiser-Permanente Hosp., Santa Clara, Calif., 1979-81; emergency specialist Emergency Specialists Corp., San Jose, Calif., 1981-83; coordinator Cambodian ministries 19th Ave. Bapt. Ch., San Francisco, 1982-84, asst. pastor, 1984-85; nurse emergency dept. and ICU St. Mary's Hosp., San Francisco, 1983-85; nurse emergency dept. Community Hosp. Los Gatos (Calif.)-Saratoga, 1985-87, Penrose Hosp., Colorado Springs, 1987-88; ethnic missions cons. Pikes Peak Park Bapt. Ch., Colorado Springs, Colo., 1987-90; cons. for outreach and leadership devel. programs, First Bapt. Ch., Cupertino, 1985-87; mem. metro evangelism adv. council Home Mission Bd. So. Bapt. Conv., Atlanta, 1985-87. Editor: In God's Image, 1983-84. Bd. dirs. S.E. Asian Sch. Theology, Mill Valley, 1984-87; mem. urban tng. coop. steering com So. Bapt. Conv. Home Mission Bd., 1988-90. Named Outstanding Young Woman of Am., 1982-84. Mem. So. Bapt. Women in Ministry, Council on Nursing and Anthropology, Bread for the World, Christians for Bibl. Equality, Mothers and Others for a Livable Planet. Democrat.

ROBU, IOAN, archbishop. Archbishop of Bucharest Roman Cath. Ch., Romania. Office: Archdiocese Bucharest, Str Nuferilor 19, 70749 Bucharest Romania*

ROBY, JASPER, bishop. Sr. bishop, exec. head Apostolic Overcoming Holy Ch. of God, Inc., Birmingham, Ala. Office: Apostolic Overcoming Holy Ch of God Inc 1120 N 24th St Birmingham AL 35234*

ROCHE, SISTER DENISE ANN, college president; b. Buffalo, Sept. 17, 1942; d. Vincent Joseph and Mary Elizabeth (Crehan) R. BA, D'Youville Coll., 1967; MA, Boston U., 1968; PhD, U. Mass., 1977; LHD (hon.), Niagara U., 1986. Tchr., Our Lady of Fatima Grade Sch., L.I., N.Y., 1964-66; instr. D'Youville Coll., Buffalo, 1968-71, asst. prof., 1975-78, assoc. dean for continuing studies, 1978-79, pres., 1979—; teaching assoc. U. Mass.-Boston, 1972-75; mem. adv. bd. Business First, Buffalo, 1985—; bd. dirs. Key Bank Western N.Y. Trustee Marygrove Coll., Detroit, 1981-87; bd. dirs. Child and Family Svcs., 1985—, City of Buffalo Bd. of Ethics, 1989; chmn. coll. and univ. div. United Way Appeal, Buffalo, 1983—; chairperson Buffalo chpt. ARC, Erie County Sheriff's Found. Com. Named Citizen of Yr. N.Y. Soc. Profl. Engrs., 1984, Woman of Yr. Girl Scouts U.S., 1987; recipient Pub. Service award SUNY-Buffalo Alumni Assn., 1985, Brotherhood award in religion NCCJ, 1986, Recognition award SUNY, 1986, Chancellor Charles P. Norton award , 1988, Edn. award So. Christian Leadership Conf., 1989, Equity award Western N.Y. Coun. for Edn. and Employment Equity, 1989, Susan B. Anthony award Interclub Coun. Western N.Y., 1989. Mem. Ind. Coll. Fund N.Y., Western N.Y. Consortium Higher Edn. (v.p.), Western N.Y. Regional Edn. Ctr. for Econ. Devel., Greater Buffalo Area C. of C. (bd. dirs.), Zonta. Roman Catholic. Home: 320 Porter Ave Buffalo NY 14201

ROCHE, JAMES JOSEPH, minister, columnist; b. Ludlow, Mass., May 17, 1953; s. William Burke and Lorraine (Parent) R.; children: Richrd, Alexandra, Bjorn; m. D. Grubb, 1989. BA with honors, Clark U., 1976; MA, Vt. Coll., 1983; MDiv, Union Theol. Sem., 1987; postgrad., Columbia U.; PhD, Union Inst., 1991. Lic. marriage and family therapist, clin. mental health counselor, profl. counselor; cert. counselor. Program dir. Mountainview Family Svcs., Nev., 1978-84; pastoral life liaison The Riverside Ch., N.Y.C., 1984-86; asst. min. Mid. Collegiate Ch. of N.Y., N.Y.C., 1986-88; min. Unitarian Ch. of Norfolk, Va., 1988-89; nat. syndicated columnist human sexuality, 1988-89. Mem. adv. bd. United AIDS Relief Effort, N.Y.C., 1987-89, Youth Out and United, Norfolk, 1988-89. Mem. Am. Assn. Sex Edn., Counselors and Therapists, Am. Assn. for Counseling and Devel., AAAS, Nat. Writers Union, Nat. Press Photographers Assn., Nat. Bd. Cert. Counselors, Am. Assn. for Adult Continuing Edn. Democrat. Home and Office: 747 Union St Brooklyn NY 11215

ROCHELLE, JAY COOPER, minister, theology educator; b. Southampton, Pa., Dec. 28, 1938; s. Norman Harold and Marion Emma (Sommer) R.; m. Cynthia Ann Hull, June 16, 1962 (div. 1981); m. Susan Etta Steinhaus, Nov. 26, 1983; children: Leah, Peter, Glynis, Micah, Caleb. AA, St. John's Coll., Winfield, Kans., 1959; BA, Concordia Sr. Coll., Ft. Wayne, 1961; postgrad., Luth. Sch. Theol., 1961-63; MDiv, Concordia Sem., St. Louis, 1965; ThM, Pitts. Theol. Sem., 1968; postgrad., Yale U., Valparaiso U., Claremont U. Ordained to ministry Luth. Ch., 1965. Pastor Ascension Luth. Ch., Pitts., 1965-68, St. John's Ch., Allentown, Pa., 1968-70; campus pastor Bloomsburg U., Pa., 1970-77, Yale U., New Haven, 1977-81; prof. Luth. Sch. Theology, Chgo., 1982—. Author: Create and Celebrate, 1971, The Revolutionary Year, 1973, I'm Not the Same Person I Was Yesterday, 1974, Spiritual Care, 1985, Attender at the Altar, 1988, Yielding to Community, 1991; contbr. articles to profl. jours. Adv. bd. New Haven Ctr. for Peace, Edn. and Action, 1978-81; pres. New Haven Calligraphers' Guild, 1978-81, Chgo. Calligraphy Collective, 1987-88; bd. dirs. Soc. of Scribes, N.Y.C., 1981. First vis. faculty Gruenewald Guild, Ctr. for Art and Rels., Leavenworth, Wash., 1982; invited mem. 1st conf. on Thomas Merton, 1975. Mem. Internat. Dietrich Bonhoeffer Soc. (mem. transl. team), Am. Acad. Religion, N.Am. Acad. Liturgy, Soc. Buddhist-Christian Studies. Home: 527 E 112th St Chicago IL 60628 Office: Luth Sch Theology 1100 E 55th St Chicago IL 60615

ROCK, CLINTON ANDREW, JR., pastor; b. Guthrie, Okla., July 25, 1915; s. Clinton Andrew and Effie May (Brown) R.; m. Golda Marie Krey, May 23, 1937; children: Mildred Mae Rock Paris, Gayla Ferne Rock Meroniuk, Clinton Andrew III. 2-yr. cert., Bresee Jr. Coll., Hutchinson, Kans., 1935-36; BTh, Bethany (Okla.) Nazarene Coll., 1946; MA in Teaching, Cen. State U., Edmond, Okla., 1962. Ordained to ministry Ch. of Nazarene, 1946; ordained elder Ch. of God (Anderson, Ind.), 1975. 1st pastor May Avenue Ch. of Nazarene, Oklahoma City, 1943-49; pastor Ch. of Nazarene, Tonkawa, Okla., 1949-50, Guthrie, 1950-52, Watonga, Okla., 1952-54; 1st pastor Grace Ch. of Nazarene, Cheyenne, Wyo., 1954-57; tchr. pub. schs., 1957-88; pastor 1st Ch. of God, Herington, Kans., 1988—; zone chmn. Ch. of Nazarene, Watonga, 1952-54, dir. youth camp Rocky Mountain dist., Big Timber, Mont., 1955, travelling evangelist, Basin, Wyo., 1957-58. Contbr. poetry to various publs. Recipient Useful Citizen award Am. Vets., Rawlins, Wyo., 1967. Mem. World of Poetry Assn.. Republican. Home: 1021 W Walut St Herington KS 67449 Office: 1st Ch of God 10th and W Walnut Sts Herington KS 67449

ROCKLAGE, SISTER MARY ROCH, health system executive; b. St. Louis, Mar. 5, 1935; d. Henry B. and Catherine (Lohman) R. RN, St. John's Sch. Nursing, St. Louis, 1959; BS in Nursing, St. Xavier Coll., Chgo., 1961; MHA, St. Louis U., 1963; LLD (hon.), Maryville Coll., 1983. Supr. Mercy Villa, Springfield, Mo.; tng. coord. St. John's Hosp., St. Louis; dir. cen. dispatch St. John's Mercy Hosp., St. Louis, 1962-65, supr. intensive care unit, 1965-67; dir. nursing svc. St. John's Mercy Hosp., 1967-69; adminstr., pres. ST. John's Mercy Med. Ctr., St. Louis, 1969-79; provincial adminstr. Sisters of Mercy, St. Louis, 1979-85; chief exec. officer Sisters of Mercy Health System, St. Louis, 1985—; vice chairperson bd. dirs. Holy Cross Health System, South Bend, Ind.; asst. prof. health care adminstn. Washington U., St. Louis, 1970-79; preceptor Washington U., St. Louis, 1970-79, St. Louis U., 1970-79, U. Mo., Columbia, 1976-79; bd. dirs. Health Care for the Homeless, St. Louis, 1984—; mem. health commn., govt. comm. Sisters of Mercy, Province St. Louis, local coord. St. Joseph's Convent of Mercy, St. Louis, 1969-76, 77-79, province personnel bd. 1973-75, health adv. bd., 1973—. Bd. trustees Maryville Coll, St. Louis, 1972-75, Mercy Hosp., Mercy Hosp., New Orleans, 1974-75; governing bd. St. John's Med. Ctr., Joplin, Mo., 1973-77, Mo. Hosp. Assn., Jefferson City, 1974-78, St. Edward Mercy Med. Ctr., Ft. Smith, Ark., 1975-80, Mercy Health Ctr., Oklahoma City, 1975-80, McAuley Hall, St. Louis, 1977-83, Mercy Hosp., Laredo, Tex., 1978-80, St. Anthony's Hosp., Alton, Ill., 1985—; pres. Greater St. Louis Health System Agy., 1976-77, bd. dirs. 1978-79. Named Woman of Achievement, St. Louis Globe-Democrat, 1974, to Nat. Register Prominent Citizens, 1975; recipient A.C.H.E. Kenrick award. Mem. Am. Nurses' Assn., Am. Coll. Hosp. Adminstrs., Catholic Health Assn. (bd. trustees 1980—, chairperson 1984-85, sec. 1981-84, bylaws, fin. and mission svcs. coms.), Catholic Hosp. Assn. (coun. on hosp. orgn. and adminstrn.),. Home: Sisters of Mercy 2039 N Geyer Rd Saint Louis MO 63131

ROCKLAGE, NORMA, SR., college administrator; b. St. Louis, July 18, 1933; d. Herry Bernard and Catherine (Lohmann) R. BA, Marian Coll., 1962, ArtsD (hon.), 1988; MA, St. Louis U., 1963, PhD, 1965. Assoc. prof. of classical langs. Marian Coll., 1965-70, acad. dean, 1970-74, v.p. for mission effectiveness, 1989—; exec. councilor Srs. of St. Francis, Oldenburg, Ind., 1974-82; noviee dir. Srs. of St. Francis, Oldenburg, 1987-89; mem. formation team Fraciscan Friars, Cin., 1983-87; trustee Marian Coll., 1974-82; adv. bd. Brebeuf Prep Sch., Indpls., 1990—. Active Sanctuary, Cin., 1983-89; dep. registrar Coalition of Women Voters, Cin., 1983-89. 3 Grants Lilly Endowment, 1989-90. Mem. Am. Assn. Higher Edn., Am. Coun. on Edn., Nat. Cath. Edn. Conf., Amnesty Rex Christi, Ind. Religious Hist., Indpls. Women Club. Home: 3200 Cold Spring Rd Indianapolis IN 46222 Office: Marian Coll 3200 Cold Spring Rd Indianapolis IN 46222

ROCKWELL, BRUCE ALLEN, religious association administrator; b. Syracuse, N.Y., May 31, 1943; s. James A. and Elizabeth (Peddie) R.; m. Cristine Vankirk Grey, June 1, 1976; 1 child, Jennifer. AB, Hamilton Coll., 1965; Savs. Banking degree, Brown U., 1976. Sr. profl. in human resources. Various positions Monroe Savs. Banks, Rochester, N.Y., 1965-78, v.p., mgr. human resources, 1978-86; Bishop's asst. Episcopal Diocese of Rochester, 1986—; stewardship area rep. Exec. Council of Episcopal Ch., N.Y.C., 1984—. Author newspaper column, 1987-89. With USNR, 1965-67. Democrat. Office: Episcopal Diocese Rochester 935 East Ave Rochester NY 14607

ROCKWELL, HAYS HAMILTON, bishop; b. Detroit, Aug. 17, 1936; s. Walter Francis and Kathryn (McElroy) R.; m. Linda Hullinger, Sept. 7, 1957; children: Keith, Stephen, Sarah, Martha. AB, Brown U., 1958; BD, Episcopal Theol. Seminary, Cambridge, Mass., 1961; DD (hon.), Episcopal Theol. Seminary SW, Austin, Tex., 1984, Kenyon Coll., 1965. Ordained to ministry Episcopal Ch. as deacon, 1961, as priest, 1962; ordained bishop, 1991. Chaplain St. Geroge's Sch., Newport, R.I., 1961-69, Univ. of Rochester, N.Y., 1969-71; dean Bexley Hall, Rochester, 1971-76; rector St. James' Ch., N.Y.C., 1976-91; bishop coadjutor Diocese of Mo., St. Louis, 1991—; dir. Union Theol. Seminary, N.Y.C., 1976, 87, 91. Author: Steal Away, Steal Away Home, 1985. Mem. Coun. on Fgn. Rels., N.Y.C., 1988; trustee U. Rochester, N.Y.C. Mem. Century Assn. (N.Y.C.). Office: Diocese of Missouri 1210 Locust St Saint Louis MO 63103

ROD, JANICE MARIE, librarian, pastor; b. Mason City, Iowa, Aug. 13, 1955; d. Herbert L. and C. Norene (Kaasa) R. BA, Luther Coll., 1977; MDiv, Luther Sem., 1981; MTh, Luther Northwestern Sem., 1983; MLS, U. Iowa, 1989. Ordained to ministry Am. Luth. Ch., 1985. Intern pastor Gloria Dei Luth. Ch., Tomah, Wis., 1979-80; pastor East Clermont Luth. Ch., Clermont, Iowa, 1985-86; libr. theology catalog St. John's U., Collegeville, Minn., 1989-91, head cataloger, libr. theology catalog, 1991—. Mem. Am. Theol. Libr. Assn., Minn. Theol. Libr. Assn., Beta Phi Mu. Office: St Johns U Alcuin Libr Collegeville MN 56321

RODDA, JAMES ERWIN, minister; b. St. Paul, Sept. 25, 1934; s. Gustave Earl and Elfrieda Anna Claussen; m. Joyse Marlene Hess, Sept. 21, 1958; children: Eric, Elliott, Gustave. AB, Park Coll., Parkville, Mo., 1956; postgrad., U. Chgo., 1956-59; BD, McCormick Theol. Sem., Chgo., 1963; postgrad., The Menninger Found., 1965-67. Ordained to ministry United Presbyn. Chs. (U.S.A.), 1962. Pastor 1st Presbyn. Ch., Dimondale, Mich., 1962-65; asst. pastor 1st Presbyn. Ch., Topeka, 1967-68; pastor 1st Presbyn. Ch., Wellington, Kans., 1981—; interim assoc. pastor Westminster Presbyn. Ch., Topeka, 1965-66; interim pastor Oakland Presbyn. Ch., Topeka, 1966-67; dir. emergency svc., chaplain Genesee County Community Mental Health Svcs., Flint, Mich., 1969-75; pastor Faith United Presbyn. Parish, Grandin, N.D., 1975-81; cons. Pub. Health Dept., Flint, 1970-75, Probate Ct., Flint, 1972-75, Youth Assistance Program, Flint, 1973-75; lectr. Flint Substance Abuse Tng. Program, 1973-75; lectr. chaplaincy dept. St. Luke Hosps., Fargo, N.D., 1977-81. Contbr. articles to profl. jours. Bd. dirs. Methodone Treatment Ctr., Flint, 1972-75, Fedn. of the Blind, Flint, 1972-74, Mental Health Adv. Bd., 1978-79, Presbyn. Manor, Arkansas City, Kans., 1986-87, 90-91; chmn. bd. Sumner County Hospice, Wellington, Kans., 1986-91. Home: 1101 N Park St Wellington KS 67152

RODGERS, DAVID MARLIE, principal; b. Johnstown, Pa., Sept. 6, 1945; s. Marlie Martin and Beatrice A. (Simmons) R.; m. Mary-Elizabeth Schnieders, Dec. 27, 1975; 1 child, Jonathon David. BA in Speech Edn., Grace Coll., 1976; cert. EMT, Indian River Community Coll., 1977; MA in Christian Sch. Adminstrn., Grace Sem., 1982. V.p., tchr. Grace Christian Schs., Okeechobee, Fla., 1977-78, prin., 1978-79; tchr. Evang. Christian Sch., Ft. Myers, Fla., 1979-84; prin. Grace Brethren Christian Sch., Ft. Lauderdale, Fla., 1990—; mem. com. South Fla. dist. Grace Brethren Ch., Okeechobee, 1990—. Republican. Home: 1442 Avon Ln # 13 North Lauderdale FL 33068 Office: Grace Brethren Christian Sch 1800 NW 9th Ave Fort Lauderdale FL 33311 *Paul the Apostle said, "For me to live is Christ, to die is gain." I feel that the most important thing for me to do is live like Christ and and to share my faith in Christ at all cost. The world is dying around us and we as Christians are doing nothing about it. The world needs to accept Christ as Savior before there is no more time to do so.*

RODGERS, KYLE L., youth minister; b. San Antonio, Oct. 1, 1958; s. Bernie E. and Janet (Dowell) R.; m. Pamela Mae Baker, June 16, 1979; 1 child, Andrew Kyle. BA, Bapt. Bible Coll., 1983. Youth pastor Park Hill Bapt. Ch., Pueblo, Colo., 1983-85, Temple Bapt. Ch., Odessa, Tex., 1985—. Republican. Home: 2737 Perryville Dr Odessa TX 79701

RODIMER, FRANK JOSEPH, bishop; b. Rockaway, N.J., Oct. 25, 1927; s. Frank Grant and Susan Elizabeth (Hiler) R. Student, St. Charles Coll., Catonsville, Md., 1944-45; B.A., St. Mary's Coll.-Sem., Balt., 1947; postgrad., Immaculate Conception Sem., Darlington, N.J., 1947-50; S.T.L., Cath. U. Am., 1951, J.C.D., 1954. Ordained priest Roman Catholic Ch., 1951; asst. chancellor, 1954-64, chancellor, 1964-77, apptd. papal chaplain, 1963; apptd. 6th Bishop of Paterson, N.J., 1977; consecrated 6th Bishop of Paterson, 1978, ordained, 1978—. Office: 777 Valley Rd Clifton NJ 07013

RODISCH, ROBERT JOSEPH, minister; b. Phila., Sept. 22, 1919; s. Edward and Isabelle (Dugan) R.; m. Ruth M. Weisner, Aug. 14, 1943; children: Ruth E. Rodisch Knudson, Lynda J. A.B., Grove City Coll., 1941, L.H.D. (hon.), 1980; B.Th., Princeton Theol. Sem., 1943; postgrad., Union Sem., 1944, Temple U., 1946-48; D.D., Tarkio Coll., 1962. Ordained to ministry Presbyn. Ch., 1943; pastor First Ch., Galeton, Pa., 1943-45, Langhorne, Pa., 1945-51; dir. S.E. Okla. Larger Parish, 1951-53; pastor Second Ch., Tulsa, 1953-62; moderator Muskogee Presbytery, 1952-53, Tulsa Presbytery, 1957-58; chmn. nat. missions com. Okla. Synod; synod exec. Mo. Synod, United Presbyn. Ch. U.S.A., 1962-69, Synods Mo. of United Presbyn. Ch. U.S.A. and Presbyn. Ch. in U.S., 1969-72; exec. Synods of Mid-Am., 1972-78; gen. dir. Support Agy. United Presbyn. Ch. U.S.A., N.Y.C., 1978-87, ret.; mem. gen. assembly mission council United Presbyn. Ch. U.S.A.; pres. Mo. Council of Chs., 1971-72. Sec. bd. trustees Interchurch Center, N.Y.C. Mem. Pi Gamma Mu. Clubs: Rotary, Masons. Home: PO Box 625 Duarte CA 91010

RODRIGUEZ, GLORIA G., educational foundation administrator; b. San Antonio, July 9, 1948; d. Julian Garza and Lucy (Villegas) Salazar; m. Salvador C. Rodriguez, June 17, 1972; children: Salvador Julian, Steven Rene, Gloria Vanessa. BA, Our Lady of the Lake U., 1973, MEd, 1973; MEd, U. Tex., San Antonio, 1979, postgrad. Cert. in bilingual edn. Bilingual tchr. Northside Ind. Sch. Dist., San Antonio, 1970-73; child devel. educator AVANCE, San Antonio, 1973-79, prin. investigator Project C.A.N. Child Abuse and Neglect, 1979-83, exec. dir. Project for Parent and Child, 1973—, project dir. Research and Evaluation Project, 1987—. Author: Parents Guide to Selection of Child Care, 1978; mem. editorial bd. (film strip series) El Mañana es Hoy, 1977; contbr. articles to profl. jours. Del. White House Conf. on Families, Los Angeles, 1980; mem. San Antonio Leadership, 1980-81, Wingspread II Conf., Racine, Wis., 1981, U.S./United Kingdom Literacy Bd., Family Resource Coalition Exec. Bd., Las. Familias, Leadership Tex., Harvard Family Research Project; vice-chmn., bd. dirs. San Antonio Devel. Agy., 1982-85; bd. dirs. San Antonio Local Devel. Co., 1982-84; chmn. Family Task Force Target 90, 1983-85; speaker U.S. Ho. Reps. com. Children, Youth and Family, Dallas, 1984, Presdl. com. on Child Safety, Austin, Tex., 1986. Named Woman of Yr., San Antonio Light Newspaper, 1980; named to Edgewood Hal of Fame Ind. Sch. Dist., 1983, San Antonio Hall of Fame, Women in Tex. Today, 1984; recipient Ednl. Achievement award Women in Communications, 1987. Mem. Hispanas Unidas. Democrat. Roman Catholic. Home: 203 E Quill San Antonio TX

78228 Office: AVANCE Ednl Programs for Parents & Children 301 S Frio Ste 378 San Antonio TX 78207 also: Diocese Corpus Christi 1119 W Santa Gertrudis Kingsville TX 78363

RODRIGUEZ, MIGUEL, bishop; b. Mayaguez, P.R., Apr. 18, 1931. Student, St. Mary's Minor Sem., Pa. Ordained priest Roman Cath. Ch., 1958. Bishop Arecibo, P.R., 1974-90; resident St. Charles of Borromeo Parish, Aguadilla, P.R., 1990—. Address: St Charles of Borromeo Parish PO Box 238 Aguadilla PR 00605

RODRIGUEZ, MOISÉS, minister; b. Carrizo Springs, Tex., June 1, 1958; s. Nicolas and Felicitas (Contreras) R.; m. Abigail Dominguez, Dec. 15, 1984; 1 child, Josué Moisé. BS, Howard Payne U., 1981; MDiv, S.W. Bapt. Theol. Sem., 1986; postgrad., Baylor U. Ordained to ministry So. Bapt. Conv., 1983. Pastor Mission Bautista Hispana, Dublin, Tex., 1981-85; assoc. pastor First Mex. Bapt. Ch., Ft. Worth, 1985-87; pastor Templo Bautista del Salvador, Waco, Tex., 1988-90; asst. dir.-lang. ch. extension Home Mission Bd. So. Bapt. Conv., Decatur, Ga., 1990—; v.p. La Hora Bautista, Brownwood, Tex., 1980-81, Hispanic Orgn. of Theol. Sem., Ft. Worth, 1984-85, pres., 1985-86. Active Waco Habitat for Humanity. Latin Am. Bapt. Scholar Bapt. Gen. Conv. Tex., 1977. Mem. Am. Acad. Religion, Soc. Bibl. Lit. Democrat. Home: 2503 Lawrenceville Hwy #4 Decatur GA 30033 Office: So Bapt Conv Home Mission Bd 862 Columbia Dr Decatur GA 30030

RODRIGUEZ, PLACIDO, bishop; b. Celaya, Mex., Oct. 11, 1940; came to U.S., 1953; s. Eutimio and Maria Concepcion (Rosiles) R. STB, STL, Cath. U., Washington, 1968; MA, Loyola U., 1971. Ordained priest Roman Cath. Ch., 1968, ordained to bishop, 1983. Pastor Our Lady Guadalupe Ch., Chgo., 1972-75, Our Lady of Fatima Ch., Perth Amboy, N.J., 1981-83; vocat. dir. Claretians, Chgo., 1975-81; bishop aux. Archdiocese of Chgo., 1983—. Office: 1048 N Campbell Chicago IL 60622

RODRIGUEZ, REYNALDO, JR., chaplain; b. Refugio, Tex., Mar. 5, 1944; s. Reynaldo Galindo and Fransica (Hernandez) R.; m. Maria Nynfa Hernandez, June 2, 1963; children: Eliza, Christina, Daniel Ray. Grad. high sch., Woodsboro, Tex. Ordained deacon Roman Cath. Ch., 1983. Pastoral min. St. Therese Parish, Woodsboro, 1983—; diocesan chaplain Cath. scouting Diocese of Corpus Christi (Tex.), 1985—; grocery clk. H-E-B Foods, Refugio, 1977—. Pres. Woodsboro PTA, 1968-72; scoutmaster Boy Scouts Am., Woodsboro, 1967-83; tchr. CCD St. Therese Parish, Woodsboro, 1967-90. Named Outstanding Young Man in Am. Jr. C. of C., Regugio, 1971. Home: PO Box 249 Woodsboro TX 78393 Office: Cath Com on Scouting 517 Pugh St Woodsboro TX 78393

ROE, EARL DEFOREST, religious organization administrator, minister; b. Endicott, N.Y., Sept. 12, 1918; s. Henry Thurston and Marian Lura (West) R.; m. Eunice Alline Harris, June 2, 1943 (div. 1950); 1 child, Joyce Alline Fishel; m. Thelma Rose Kiser, Sept. 1, 1951. Grad., Missionary Tng. Inst., Nyack, N.Y., 1940. Ordained to ministry Christian and Missionary Alliance, 1943. Asst. pastor Gospel Tabernacle, High Point, N.C., 1940-41; pastor Christian and Missionary Alliance Ch., Lexington, N.C., 1941-42, Madera, Pa., 1942-44, Peckville, Pa., 1944-47, Secretary, Md., 1947-48; bus. mgr. Northport Bapt. Ch., East Northport, N.Y., 1981—. Republican. Office: Northport Bapt Ch Elwood and Clay Pitts Rds East Northport NY 11731 *It has been very interesting to see events working toward the things which God prophesied in the Bible, including the reestablishment of Israel as a nation. Even the pollution of the environment is forecast of the judgments which the book of Revelation tells us will take place during the Great Tribulation.*

ROELS, EDWIN DALE, college president, clergyman; b. Zeeland, Mich., Feb. 2, 1934; s. John P. and Bertha (Kloosterman) R.; m. Bertie L. Klamer, Dec. 16, 1955; children: Dawn, Dick, Karen, Dale, Cheryl. AB, Calvin Coll., Grand Rapids, Mich., 1955; BD, Calvin Sem., Grand Rapids, 1958; ThD, Free U. Amsterdam, The Netherlands, 1962. Ordained to ministry Christian Reformed Ch., 1972. Instr. Calvin Coll., 1960-62; prof. Trinity Christian Coll., Palos Heights, Ill., 1962-67, dean students, 1970-72; dir. Servicemen's Home, Seoul, 1967-70; pastor Cottage Grove Christian Ref. Ch., South Holland, Ill., 1972-78, Unity Christian Ref. Ch., Prinsburg, Minn., 1984-87; Africa coord. World Home Bible League, South Holland, 1978-84; pres. Ref. Bible Coll., Grand Rapids, Mich., 1987—. Author: God's Mission, 1962, Someone Cares, 1970, God Understands, 1981, Answers To Live By, 1983. Fulbright scholar, 1958, Centennial Missions scholar Christian Ref. Ch., 1959, scholar Grand Rapids Found., 1962. Office: Ref Bible Coll 3333 E Beltline NE Grand Rapids MI 49505

ROELTGEN, KENNETH W., academic administrator. Head Mt. St. Mary's Sem., Emmitsburg, Md. Office: Mt St Mary's Sem Emmitsburg MD 21727*

ROG, FRANCIS S., priest; b. Chgo., Jan. 12, 1930; s. Frank and Stella (Madej) R. BS in Commerce, St. Louis U., 1951, MS in Commerce, 1953; PhD, Northwestern U., 1973. Ordained priest Roman Cath. Ch., 1955. Tchr. Gordon Tech. Sch., 1955-58, dir. vocations, 1955-61; tchr. Weber High Sch., Chgo., 1961-63, prin., 1990; assoc. pastor Our Lady of Loretto, St. Louis, 1963-65; dir. retreats Gordon Tech. High Sch., Chgo., 1967-73, asst. prin., 1973-74; pastor St. Stanislaus Kostka, Chgo., 1974-75; provincial superior Congregation of Resurrection U.S.A., Chgo., 1976-85; pastor St. Hyacinth, Chgo., 1985-90; prin. Weber High Sch., Chgo., 1990—; archdiocesan consultor Chgo., 1984, senator, 1965-87; chmn. senate, 1985-87; exec. mem. for religious ministry, 1983, ecclesiastical advocate and notary, 1979, dean, 1987-91. Home and Office: 2250 N Latrobe Ave Chicago IL 60639

ROGEBERG, THOMAS EDWARD, religious broadcasting company executive; b. Madison, Wis., June 25, 1943; s. Thorolf Edward and Alice (Dousman) R.; m. Karen Linda Ostenson; children: Timothy, John David. BA, U. Wis., 1965, MA, 1967. From film dir. to program supr. Sta. WHA-TV, Madison, 1964-68; dir. ops. Pub. TV Library, Bloomington, Ind., 1968-72; program mgr. Cen. Ednl. Network, Chgo., 1972-78; mgr. program scheduling Christian Broadcasting Network, Virginia Beach, Va., 1978-81; dir. Christian Broadcasting Satellite Network, Virginia Beach, 1981-82; v.p. ops. Christian Broadcasting Cable Network, Virginia Beach, 1982-84, sr. v.p. adminstrn. and ops., 1984-87, sr. v.p., gen. mgr., 1987-88; pres. Thorson & Co., Virginia Beach, 1988-89; exec. v.p. In Touch Ministries, Atlanta, 1990—. Elder Kempsville Presbyn. Ch., Virginia Beach, 1984-87. Research grantee Nat. Assn. Broadcasters, 1967; named one of 25 Who Count in the TV Industry, View mag., 1984. Mem. Nat. Religious Broadcasters (bd. dirs. 1991—). Avocations: videography and photography, family activities, church activities. Home: 4219 Allenhurst Dr Norcross GA 30092 Office: 3836 DeKalb Tech Pkwy Atlanta GA 30340

ROGERS, ADRIAN PIERCE, minister; b. West Palm Beach, Fla., Sept. 12, 1931; s. Arden and Rose (Purcell) R.; m. Joyce Gentry, Sept. 2, 1951; children: Steve, Janice, David, Gayle. BA, Stetson U., 1954; ThM, New Orleans Bapt. Theol. Sem., 1958; DD (hon.), Trinity Coll., Clearwater, Fla.; LittD (hon.), Calif. Grad. Sch. Theology, Glendale. Ordained to ministry Bapt. Ch., 1951. Pastor First Bapt. Ch., Fellsmere, Fla., 1951-54, Waveland (Miss.) Bapt. Chapel, 1955-58, Parkview Bapt. Ch., Ft. Pierce, Fla., 1958-64, First Bapt. Ch., Merritt Island, Fla., 1964-72, Bellevue Bapt. Ch., Memphis, 1972—; pres. So. Bapt. Conv., 1980, 87, 88, So. Bapt. Pastors' Conf., 1976. Author: The Secret of Supernatural Living, God's Way to Health, Wealth and Happiness, Mastering Your Emotions. Office: Bellevue Bapt Ch 2000 Appling Rd Cordova TN 38018

ROGERS, CARL ERNEST, religion educator; b. San Diego, Feb. 20, 1938; s. Carl Blair and Thelma Laraine (Peters) R.; m. Beverly Kay, June 20, 1965; children: Jacqueline Renee, Nathan Whitfield. BA, Oakland City Coll., 1970; MRE, So. Theol. Sem., Louisville, 1972. Cert. couples' communication/marriage enrichment. Minister Christian edn. Flint (Mich.) First Bapt. Ch., 1965-68, First Bapt. Ch., Oakland City, Ind., 1968-72; dir. Christian edn. Gen. Bapt. Hdqrs., Poplar Bluff, Mo., 1972-90, dir. ch. ministries, 1990—; assoc. in couples' communication Gen. Bapt. Hdqrs., Poplar Bluff, 1975—. Author: Sparks of Inspiration in Youth Ministry, 1975; contbr. articles to religious publs. Pres. Poplar Bluff Mcpl. Airport Bd., 1989-90; chairperson Poplar Bluff Area Pilots Assn., 1988-91. With USAF, 1956-60. Mem. Denomination Exec. in Christian Edn. (v.p. 1989-90), Masons. Home: 1502 Skyview Way Poplar Bluff MO 63901 Office: Gen Bapt Hdqrs 100 Stinson Dr Poplar Bluff MO 63901

ROGERS, CHRISTINE MARIE, minister; b. Forsyth, Ga., May 20, 1958; d. Oscar Franklin and Carol Elizabeth (Spear) R. BA in Music, Emory U., 1979, BA in Psychology, 1979; M of Church Music, Northwestern U., Evanston, Ill., 1980; MDiv, Garrett Evangel. Theol., Seminary, Evanston, 1983. Ordained to ministry United Meth. Ch. as deacon, 1982, as elder, 1985. Organist, dir. of music Lithania (Ga.) United Meth. Ch., 1974-78; organist, dir. of music/asst. pastor Edison Park United Meth. Ch., Chgo., 1979-82; asst. pastor Ch. of the Incarnation, Arlington Heights, Ill., 1982-83; pastor Earlville (Ill.) United Meth. Ch., 1983-87, Sharon United Meth. Ch., Plainfield, Ill., 1987—; coord. pastor care and bereavement, home health and hospice Ill. Masonic Hosp., 1991—; mem. Aurora (Ill.) Dist. Commn. on Ordained Ministry, 1987—, Dekalb (Ill.) Dist. Comm. on Ordained Ministry, 1984-87, No. Ill. Conf. Worship Com., 1984-87, Nor. Ill. Conf. Mission Com., 1984-87. Mem. Ill. Valley Youth Svc. Bd., Ottawa, 1984-87, Earlville Cert. Cities Prog.: Mktg., 1984-87, Mayor's Tornado Relief Com., Plainfield, Ill., 1990; coord./dir. Plainfield Tornado Relief: Foord/Meal Distbn., 1990. Named to Outstanding Young Women of Am., 1984; recipient Spiritual Leadership award Jr. Women's Club, Earlville, 1986. Mem. Plainfield Ministerial Assn. (pres. 1991). Democrat. Office: Sharon United Meth Church 216 W Lockport St Plainfield IL 60544

ROGERS, GARRY LEE, minister, medical technician; b. Asheville, N.C., May 29, 1950; s. Kenneth Ledbetter and Annie Faye (Freeman) R.; m. Judy Gaynelle Plemmons, Octo. 6, 1973; children: Angela Dawn, Andrea Gaynelle, Steffan Garry, Shaana Lynette. EMT-IV Tech., Asheville Buncombe Tech. Coll., 1984; B of Ministry, Internat. Bible Sem., Plymouth, Fla., 1985; student N.T. Study Series, Moody Bible Inst., 1985; M in Bible Theology, Internat. Bible Sem., Plymouth, Fla., 1986, DD (hon.), 1986. Lic. to ministry So. Bapt. Conv., 1969, ordained, 1973. Music dir. New Liberty Bapt. Ch., Asheville, 1967-73, assoc. pastor, 1975-76; pastor Mt. Pleasant Bapt. Ch., Hot Springs, N.C., 1973-74, Jones Valley Bapt. Ch., Leicester, N.C., 1976-90, Emmanuel Bapt. Ch., Clyde, N.C., 1990—; med. technician Tempoe Inc., Asheville, 1983—; sec. New Found Bapt. Sunday Sch. Conv., Asheville, 1983-85, moderator 1984-90; mem. gen. bd. Bapt. State Conv., Cary, N.C., 1984-87; trustee Christian Action League, Raleigh, N.C., 1987—; chaplain West Buncombe Fire Dept., 1985—, Erwin High Sch. Bus Drivers Assn., 1986. Author: Prayer and Praying, 1986. Vol. fireman and EMT West Buncombe Fire Dept., Asheville, 1983—; pres. Community Watch, Asheville, 1990—. Recipient Bold Mission 100% Increase in Giving award, Bold Mission 100% Increase in Baptisms award N.C. Bapt. Conv., 1977-82, 5 Yr. award West Buncombe Fire Dept., 1991. Mem. N.C. Firemans Assn., Buncombe County Sch. Bus Drivers Assn., N.C. Athletic Officials Assn. Democrat. Home: 520 Olivette Rd Asheville NC 28804 Office: Emmanuel Bapt Ch 26 Weaver Dr Clyde NC 28721 *One of the greatest joys a person can experience in this life is the receiving of others and the giving of oneself. Everyone should experience this joy in life.*

ROGERS, ISABEL WOOD, religious studies educator; b. Tallahassee, Aug. 26, 1924; d. William Hudson and Mary Thornton (Wood) R. BA, Fla. State U., 1945; MA, U. Va., 1947; MRE, Presbyn. Sch. Christian Edn., 1949; PhD, Duke U., 1961; DD (hon.), Austin Coll., 1986; LLD (hon.), Westminster Coll., 1988; LHD, Centre Coll., 1989. Campus min. 1st Presbyn. Ch., Milledgeville, Ga., 1949-52; campus chaplain Ga. Coll., Milledgville, 1952-61; prof. of applied Christianity Presbyn. Sch. Christian Edn., Richmond, Va., 1961—; elder Ginter Pk. Presbyn. Ch., Richmond, 1976-79, 89—; moderator of Gen. Assembly, Presbyn. Ch. U.S.A., 1987-88; lectr. Presbyn. chs. Author: The Christian and World Affairs, 1965, In Response to God, 1969, Our Shared Earth, 1980, Sing A New Song, 1981. Vol. Richmond Community Action Program, 1968-75, YWCA, Women's Advocacy Program, 1982—; bd. dirs. Presbyn. Outlook Found., Richmond, 1987—. Du Pont fellow U. Va., 1946. 47, Kearns fellow Duke U. Mem. Soc. Christian Ethics, Phi Kappa Phi, Phi Beta Kappa. Democrat. Avocations: hiking, jogging, tennis, gardening, stamp collecting. Home and Office: Presbyn Sch Christian Edn 1205 Palmyra Ave Richmond VA 23227

ROGERS, JAMES H., archbishop. Ordinary N.Am. Old Roman Cath. Ch., St. Albans, N.Y. Office: NAm Old Roman Cath Ch 118-09 Farmers Blvd Saint Albans NY 11412*

ROGERS, JERRY JAMES, minister; b. Lindsey, Okla., Nov. 1, 1943; s. Frank John and Sylvia Dell (Shelton) R.; m. Gloria Jean Moss, Nov. 21, 1964; children: Kent, Kevin, Korry. Grad. high sch., Oceanside, Calif. Ordained to ministry Ch. of Christ, 1965. Min. Eastside Ch. of Christ, Weatherford, Tex., 1966-67, Lynwood (Calif.) Ch. of Christ, 1968-69, Riverview Ch. of Christ, Bakersfield, Calif., 1970-77, Ashlan Ave. Ch. of Christ, Fresno, Calif., 1977-80, Elk Ave. Ch. of Christ, Duncan, Okla., 1980—; sec. Ministerial Alliance, Duncan, 1988-89; instr. Fresno (Calif.) Bible Prep., 1977-80. Author: (monthly mag.) Gospel Tidings, 1990; asst. editor (monthly youth mag.) Truth for Youth, 1967-72. Democrat. Office: Elk Ave Ch of Christ 2113 Elk Ave Duncan OK 73533

ROGERS, JIMMY DERYL, minister; b. Jan. 25, 1951; m. Diana Mullen; children: Angela Michelle, Jeremy Deryl. Student, East Tex. Bapt. Coll., 1971-72; Diploma, Luther Rice Seminary, Jacksonville, Fla., 1977. Ordained to ministry Bapt. Ch., 1968. Interim pastor First Bapt. Ch. of Lawson, Mesquite, Tex., 1981; minister Martin Springs Bapt. Ch., Sulphur Springs, Tex., 1985—; various demoninational activities including chmn. mission com. Cen.-West Tex. Assn. Bapt. Missionary Assn., 1979-80, mission com. Rehoboth Assn., So. Bapt. Conv., 1985-86, chmn. nominating com., 1985-87, moderator, 1987-89, Sunday Sch. Assist Team Dir., 1989-91; exec. com. BSU, 1987—. Pres. Ministerial Alliance, Sulphur Springs, 1990, Hopkins County Child Welfare Bd., 1988—, Hopkins County Foster Parent Assn., 1988-90; foster parent, 1983—; chmn. Region VII Child Welfare Adv. Bd., 1988-90; v.p. Sulphur Springs Soccer Assn., 1987-88; active Hopkins County Ministerial Alliance, 1985—; sec.-treas. DeSoto Area Minister's Assn., 1980; others. Nominated Rural Pastor of Yr., Tex. A&M U., Town and Country Ch. Conf./Progressive Farmer mag., 1978. Office: Martin Springs Bapt Church Rte 2 Box 259 Sulphur Springs TX 75482 *To walk with God - what a challenge! To walk in the footsteps of Christ - what a goal! To be limited by being human, yet freed by being in Christ - what grace and mercy!.*

ROGERS, JIMMY ROGER, minister; b. Grafton, W.Va., Sept. 22, 1938; s. Charles Donavan and Eleanora Pauline (Barcus) R.; m. Martha Sue Flannery, Mar. 1, 1958; children: Jimmy Lee, Cynthia Ann, William Allen, Darla Sue. AA, Spring Arbor (Mich.) Coll., 1962; student, Malone Coll., Canton, Ohio, 1962-66; B Bible, Universal Bible Inst., Kansas City, Mo., 1978; MDiv, Trinity Theol. Sem., Newburgh, Ind., 1988. Ordained elder Free Meth. Ch. N.Am., 1967. Pastor Mayfield Heights (Ohio) Free Meth. Ch., 1963-64, Alliance (Ohio) Free Meth. Ch., 1964-69, Center Free Meth. Ch., Sarahsville, Ohio, 1969-88, Living Water Free Meth. Ch., Dalton, Ohio, 1988-89, Urbana (Ohio) Free Meth. Ch., 1989—; mem. bd. evangelism Ohio Conf. Free Meth. Chs., Mansfield, 1971-75, young teen dir., 1974, trustee, 1986—; trustee Oakdale Christian High Sch., Jackson, Ky., 1973-78; chaplain Mary Rutan Hosp., 1990—, Mercy Meml. Hosp., 1990—. Bd. dirs. Guernsey, Monroe, Noble Tri-County Bd. Health, Caldwell, Ohio, 1979, Am. Cancer Soc., Urbana, 1991—. Recipient cert. of achievement Muskingum Joint County Bd. Mental Health, Mental Retardation and Drug Abuse, 1980. Memm. Champaign County Ministerial Assn., Light and Life Men. Home and Office: Urbana Free Meth Ch 630 E Ward St Urbana OH 43078

ROGERS, JOHN CHRISTOPHER, editor; b. Washington, June 24, 1962; s. Edwin Anthony Rogers and Carole Anne (Johnson) Dawson. BA in Psychology and English, U. Mass., 1986. Editor The Forerunner, Gainesville, Fla., 1989—. Author, assoc. editor: Holiness Herald, 1987. Home: PO Box 4103 Gainesville FL 32613 Office: The Forerunner PO Box 4103 Gainesville FL 32613

ROGERS, JOHN KEVIN, priest; b. San Francisco, Aug. 26, 1949; s. Donn E. and Marie T. (Scholtz) R. AB, Humboldt State Coll., 1971; MDiv, Pontifical Coll. Josephinum, 1976; D.Min., Grad. Theol. Found., Notre Dame, Ind., 1988. Ordained priest in Roman Cath. Ch. Assoc. pastor St. Bernard's Ch., Eureka, Calif., 1976-77, St. Joseph's Ch., Crescent City, Calif., 1977-78, St. James Ch., Petaluma, Calif., 1978-79; adminstr. St. Mary's Ch., Arcata, Calif., 1983-84; chaplain, lectr. religious studies Humboldt State U., Arcata, 1979—. Bd. trustees Dharma Realm Buddhist U., Talmage, Calif., 1989—; bd. dir.s Cath. Charities-Humboldt, Del Norte, Eureka, Calif., 1989—, Rhododendron Retreat Ctr., Rio Dell, Calif., 1987—. Fellow Grad. Theol. Found., Royal Asiatic Soc. of Gt. Britain and Ireland; mem. Am. Acad. Religion. Democrat. Decorated knight of the Equestrian Order of the Holy Sepulchre of Jerusalem. Home and Office: 700 Union St Arcata CA 95521

ROGERS, JOHN SAMUEL, pastor; b. Raleigh, N.C., Dec. 13, 1944; s. Ralph Wiley Sr. and Grace Butler (Harris) R.; m. Joyce Marie Thomas, Aug. 19, 1967; children: Brian John, Rebecca Louise. BA, Campbell U., Buies Creek, N.C., 1970; MDiv, Southeastern Bapt. Theol. Seminary, Wake Forest, N.C., 1973; postgrad., Drew U., Madison, N.J., 1985—. Cert. marriage enrichment leader. Chaplain Harnett Youth Ctr., Lillington, N.C., 1969-73; minister edn. 1st Bapt. Ch., Gaithersburg, Md., 1973-76; sr. pastor Buies Creek (N.C.) 1st Bapt. Ch., 1976—; gen. bd. mem. N.C. Bapt. Conv., Raleigh, 1978-79, place and preacher com. mem., 1983. Mem. Life and Family Resource Ctr., Buies Creek, 1979—, Harnett County (N.C.) Assn. Retarded Citizens, 1982—; pres. New Hope Group Home Bd., Angier, N.C., 1984-86. Served to sgt. U.S. Army, 1964-67, Vietnam. Decorated Air medal; recipient Service award Harnett chpt. ARC, 1982; named Pastor of Yr., Little River Woman's Missionary Union, 1982, 87. Mem. Little River Bapt. Assn. (pastor conf. pres. 1980, stewardship dir. 1986—). Democrat. Baptist. Avocations: golf, fishing.

ROGERS, LARRY, clergyman; b. Ft. Walton Beach, Fla., Feb. 23, 1961; s. Glen Allen and Dorothy Elizabeth (Rowell) R.; m. Tracey Lynn Guy, Aug. 14, 1982. BS, U So. Miss., Hattiesburg, 1985; MRE, New Orleans Bapt. Theol. Sem., 1989. Ordained to ministry So. Bapt. Conv. Minister music and youth Liberty (Miss.) Bapt. Ch., 1987-89; assoc. pastor edn. and youth Sherwood Bapt. Ch., Huntsville, Ala., 1989—; student coord. Madison Bapt. Assn. Assist Team, Huntsville, 1990—; mem. Disciple Youth Network, Nashville, 1988—. Vol. Salvation Army, Huntsville, 1989—. Mem. Fellowship Ala. Youth Ministers, Huntsville Student Ministers Fellowship. Home: 408 Arthur St NW Huntsville AL 35805 Office: Sherwood Bapt Ch 6600 Madison Pike NW Huntsville AL 35806

ROGERS, NELSON BURTON, religious organization executive; b. Bradford, Pa., Jan. 4, 1927; s. Burt H. and Florence G. (Theal) R.; m. Geraldine A. Merlau, Sept. 15, 1948; children: Bonnie, Brenda, Pamela. Student, Bryant and Stratton Bus. Inst., Buffalo, 1948. Traffic mgr. Mchts. Regrigerating Co., Buffalo, 1948-58; treas. Graoc Dairy Co., East Aurora, N.Y., 1958-60; asst. gen. mgr. Bapt. Life Assn., Buffalo, 1960-68, asst. treas., 1968-73, v.p., sec., 1973-79, pres., 1979-91, chief exec. officer, 1991—; pres. Am. Bapt. Chs. Niagara Frontier, 1974-76, Am. Bapt. Chs. N.Y. State, 1977-78; mem. gen. bd. Am. Bapt. Chs. U.S.A., Valley Forge, Pa., 1979-86. Mem. Rep. ins. adv. com. N.Y. State Assembly, 1986. Served with inf. U.S. Army, 1945-47. Named Man of Yr., Am. Bapt. Men. N.Y., 1981. Mem. Am. Soc. CLU's. Lodge: Masons. Home: 1558 Emery Rd East Aurora NY 14052 Office: Bapt Life Assn 8555 Main St Buffalo NY 14221

ROGERS, REX MARTIN, college official; b. Pasadena, Tex., Oct. 25, 1952; s. Ernest Bartholow and Yvonne Lee (Davis) R.; m. Sarah Lee Stone, Aug. 10, 1974; children: Elizabeth, Eric, Andrew, Adam. BA, Cedarville (Ohio) Coll., 1974; MA, U. Akron, Ohio, 1978; PhD, U. Cin., 1982. Vice prin., tchr. social studies Heritage Christian Schs., Cleve., 1974-77; tchr. social studies Cross Lanes Christian Schs., Charleston, W.Va., 1977-79; teaching asst. U. Cin., 1979-82; rsch. asst. Behavioral Sci. Lab., Cin., 1980-82; from asst. prof. to assoc. prof. polit. sci. Cedarville Coll., 1982-88, dir. planning, 1985-88; v.p. acad. affairs The King's Coll., Briarcliff Manor, N.Y., 1988-91; pres. Grand Rapids (Mich.) Bapt. Coll. and Sem., 1991—; trustee Christian Scholars Rev., 1989-91. Contbr. numerous articles to profl. jours. Grantee Wilder Found., 1981, 82, Cedarville Coll., 1988, The King's Coll., 1991. Mem. Am. Assn. for Higher Edn., Christian Mgmt. Assn. (pres. Dayton, Ohio chpt. 1988). Baptist. Avocations: reading, tennis. Home: 8960 Vincent Ave SE Alto MI 49302 Office: Grand Rapids Bapt Coll and Sem 1001 E Beltline NE Grand Rapids MI 49505

ROGERS, ROBERT GRANT, college dean; b. Columbus, Ohio, Apr. 13, 1938; s. Wilbur Grant and Ruby Nell (Huffman) R.; m. Gretchen L. Lalendorf, Aug. 28, 1960; children: Jennifer H. Rogers Hoheisel, Margot M. Rogers. BS, Ohio State U., 1960; S.T.B., Boston U., 1963, PhD, 1969. Instr. Bible and religion Wellesley (Mass.) Coll., 1967-68; lectr. Bible and religion lay Pastor's Sch., Boston U., 1970-73; asst. prof. religion Newton (Mass.) Coll., 1969-72, assoc. prof. religion, 1972-75; assoc. prof. religion Hampden-Sydney (Va.) Coll., 1975-81, prof. religion, 1981—, dean of freshmen, 1987—; vis. prof. religion Pine Manor Jr. Coll., Brookline, Mass., 1974-75; cons. several acad. colls.' honors programs. Author: (bibl. commentaries) The Gospel of John, 1975, The Exodus to the Monarchy, 1973, Behold Your King!, 1977; contbr. articles to profl. jours.; reviewer numerous books African Book Pub. Record, 1982—. Chair Piedmont Humanities Coun., Farmville, Va., 1988—, Va. Found. for the Humanities and Pub. Policy, Charlottesville, 1987-89, Va. Collegiate Honors Coun., Hampden-Sydney, 1986; mem. Prince Edward County Dem. Com., Farmville, 1985. Named Danforth Assoc., 1978-85; Lilly fellow in humanities Duke U., 1976-77. Mem. Theolog Group, Am. Acad. Religion, Nat. Acad. Advising Assn., Soc. Bibl. Lit., Sr. Citizens of Prince Edward (bd. dirs. 1991—), Rotary Internat. Avocations: gardening, ornithology. Office: Hampden Sydney Coll PO Box 685 Hampden-Sydney VA 23943

ROGERS, SCOTT BAILEY, minister; b. Jacksonville, Ill., July 16, 1955; s. Turner Alfred and Audrey (Bailey) R.; m. Shirley Moody, Dec. 20, 1975; children: Audrey, Adam, Nathan. BA, Lincoln Christian Coll., 1977; MA, Sangamon State U., 1980. Cert. Marital and Family Therapist, N.C.; ordained to ministry Christian Ch., 1976. Assoc. pastor Deland (Ill.) Christian Ch., 1974-77; min. Cornland (Ill.) Christian Ch., 1978-81; exec. dir. Asheville (N.C.) Buncombe Community Christian Ministry, 1981—. Participant Leadership Asheville; bd. dirs. Vis. Health Profls., Ashville, 1983-84; bd. dirs. Mental Health Assn. Buncombe County, 1983-87, pres. bd. dirs., 1986; bd. dirs. Home Health Care Adv. Bd.-Buncombe County Health Dept., 1984-86, Consumer Credit Counseling Svc., Asheville, 1984-86, Buncombe County Health Dept., 1984-86; bd. dirs. local chpt. United Way, 1988—; founding pres. Mountain Area Needs Alliance Food Bank, 1982-83, treas., 1990; adv. bd. Med. Pers. Pool, 1988-90; founding pres. Buncombe Emergency Assistance Coordinating Network, 1987, v.p., 1988—, treas., 1990; mem. cost and ethics com. Meml. Mission Hosp.; founding pres. Recycling Unltd., 1990—; founder, treas. So. Appalachian Mainstream Inc.; trustee Human Svc. Coun. 1990-91; mem. Community Problem-Solving Com. on Indigent Health Care, Asheville, 1989-91. Recipient Leadership award City of Lincoln, Ill., 1977, Gov.'s Vol. award Gov. N.C., 1982, 88, Coun. on Aging Leadership award, 1988. Mem. Am. Assn. for Marriage and Family Therapy, Fellowship Christian Athletes (bd. dirs. 1988-89), Interfaith Mins.' Fellowship of Asheville and Buncombe County, Ministerial Alliance, West Asheville Mins./Staff Assn., South Buncombe Mins. Assn., Leadership Asheville Alumni Assn., Kiwanis. Republican. Office: Asheville Buncombe Community Christian Ministry 24 Cumberland Ave Asheville NC 28801

ROGERS, TERRELL RANDOLPH, clergyman; b. Seminole, Okla., May 28, 1952; s. Terrell Chester and Joyce Welcome (Cheatwood) R.; m. Ida Marie Ables, June 3, 1978; children: Jeremy, Shekinah. BA, Baylor U., 1976; M.R.E., Southwestern Bapt. Theol. Sem., 1981. Ordained to ministry So. Baptist Ch., 1977. Youth minister Harris Creek Ch., Waco, Tex., 1976, Whispering Pines Ch., Conroe, Tex., 1977-78, Henderson Hills Ch., Edmond, Okla., 1978-80, Killarney Bapt. Ch., Winter Park, Fla., 1981-82, Calvary Bapt. Ch., Tulsa, 1983-85, First Bapt. Ch., Enid, Okla., 1985; pastor First Bapt. Ch., Porter, Okla., 1986—; founder, pres. Powerlife Ministries, 1981-85. Home: 4008 S Date Broken Arrow OK 74011 Office: PO Box 210 Porter OK 74454

ROGERS, THOMAS BRENT, minister; b. Richmond, Ky., May 6, 1962; s. Frank E. and Alberta (Whitaker) R.; m. Susan Lynne Van Dyke, Aug. 13, 1983; 1 child, Mary Beth. BBA with distinction, Ea. Ky. U., Richmond, 1984. Lic. to ministry United Meth. Ch., 1990. Pastor New Jasper United Meth. Ch., Xenia, Ohio, 1990—; internat. negotiator USAF, Wright Patterson AFB, Ohio, 1988—. Capt. U.S. Army, 1984-88, USAR, 1988—. Decorated Army Commendation medal. Home: 3060 Jasper Rd Xenia OH 45385 *The greatest challenge, especially for main line denominations, for the church today is keeping the Scriptures as the ultimate authority for the church and our faith. We must remember that we are called to transform society—not to be transformed by society. Without the authority of Scripture, we have no faith.*

ROGERS, WILLIAM DALE, minister; b. Alma, Ga., Oct. 29, 1945; s. Charles Edward and Rose A. (Burnam) R.; m. Launi Kay Manley, Dec. 2, 1979; children: Sarah Jayne and Hannah Lynn. BA, Azusa Pacific U., 1975, MA in Student Devel., 1977; MA in Counseling, Western Evang. Sem., 1983, MDiv, 1984. Ordained to ministry Soc. of Friends, 1989. Home: Rte 6 Box 115-C Astoria OR 97103 Office: Svensen Friends Ch Rte 6 Box 1016-A Astoria OR 97103

ROGERS-MARTIN, TIMOTHY LAWRENCE, clergyman; b. Russelville, Ky., Nov. 27, 1958; s. Henry Lawrence and Carolyn (Taylor) Martin; m. Julie Kaye Rogers, Sept. 1, 1985; children: Jared, Jacob. BA, U. Richmond, 1981; MDiv, Princeton Theol. Sem., 1985, MEd, 1988. Cert. Christian educator, Presbyn. Ch. (U.S.A.); ordained min. Presbyn. Ch. (U.S.A.). Dir. Christian edn. 1st Presbyn. Ch., Mendham, N.J., 1985-88; assoc. pastor Presbyn. Ch. of Liberty Corner, N.J., 1988—. Contbr. articles to profl. jours. Curriculum adv. Synod of N.E., Presbyn. Ch. (U.S.A.), 1986—; com. mem. Young Life, Basking Ridge, N.J., 1990—. Mem. Assn. Profl. Christian Educators, Christian Edn. Assocs. N.J., Ch. Edn. Cluster N.J. (steering com.), Phi Beta Kappa. Home and Office: Presbyn Ch ofLiberty Corner 45 Church St Liberty Corner NJ 07938 *Christian life is striving to do God's will, yet stumbling in sin, but never falling from God's grace.*

ROGGE, JOEL JAY, minister, lawyer, psychologist; b. N.Y.C., Dec. 15, 1934; s. Leo and Mollie Harrison; m. Virginia Alice Wilson, Dec. 27, 1959; children—Rebekah Leah, Michael Gabriel, Stephen Job; m. Cathy Louise Clark, Feb. 22, 1975; 1 child, Mary Elizabeth; m. Maryellen Gongas, Sept. 10, 1983; children: Sarah Alexandra, Hadrian Solomon. BS NYU, 1955; JD Columbia U., 1958; postgrad. Nashotah House, 1965-67; MDiv Episc. Theol. Sch., 1968; STM Andover Newton Theol. Sch., 1969, DMin, 1975; EdD Harvard U., 1976. Bar: N.Y. 1959, D.C. 1960, Wis. 1967, Mass. 1968, N.H. 1971; lic. psychologist, Mass. Atty. Office Gen. Counsel, HEW, 1959-60; individual practice law, Washington, 1960-61; assoc. firm Dickstein & Shapiro, Washington, 1961-62; atty. U.S. Commn. on Civil Rights, 1962-65; ordained to ministry Episcopal Ch. as deacon, 1968, as priest, 1969; pastor North St. Union Congl. Ch., Medford, Mass., 1968-70; vicar St. Martin's Chapel, Fairlee, Vt., 1971; counselor alcoholism clinic Contra Costa County Health Dept., Martinez, Calif., 1972-73; clin. dir. outpatient service North Shore Council on Alcoholism, Danvers, 1974-78; practice pastoral psychotherapy, 1977—; dir. Danvers Pastoral Counseling Center, 1977-82; clin. dir. Parish Pastoral Counseling Centers, Danvers, 1981-82; assoc. rector Calvary Episcopal Ch., Danvers, 1979-83; assoc. Andover Newton Theol. Sch., Newton Centre, Mass., 1980-82; sole practice law, Mass., 1984—. Episcopal Ch. Found. fellow, 1968-71. Mem. N.H. Bar Assn., Am. Assn. Pastoral Counselors (diplomate, gov., nat. legis. chmn., 1981-84, sec. N.E. region 1980-84),n., Mass. Psychol. Assn., Masons. Address: 74 County Rd Ipswich MA 01938

ROGNESS, PETER, bishop. Bishop of Greater Milw. Evang. Luth. Ch. in Am. Office: Evang Luth Ch Am 1212 S Layton Blvd Milwaukee WI 53215*

ROH, RAYMOND VINCENT, priest; b. Abie, Nebr., Oct. 9, 1932; s. Joseph F. and Mary A. (Shimerka) R. PhB, Little Rock Coll., 1955; MEd, Cath. U. Am., 1963; MRE, Creighton U., 1972. Ordained to ministry Roman Cath. Ch., 1959. Diocesan priest, pastor, sch. adminstr. Diocese of Lincoln, Nebr., 1959-76; evangelist, tchr, adminstr. Benedictine Abbey, Pecos, N.Mex., 1976-87; founder Monastery of the Risen Christ, San Luis Obispo, Calif., 1987—. Home: 1378 16th St Los Osos CA 93402 Office: Monastery of Risen Christ PO Box 3931 San Luis Obispo CA 93403 *I have found the greatest peace in my life in trying to live out a promise made to Jesus Christ, "I will do anything, go anywhere and suffer anything for you."*

ROHEN, SISTER JANE FRANCES, nun; b. Toledo, Ohio, Aug. 6, 1928; d. Edward I. and Grace Ann (Keil) R. Student, Toledo U., 1946-48. Joined Sisters of the Visitation, Roman Cath. Ch., 1954. Superioress Sisters of the Visitation, Toledo, 1972-78, 81-87, 1990—. Home and Office: 1745 Parkside Blvd Toledo OH 43607

ROHLFING, MARTIN HENRY, clergyman; b. Detroit, Sept. 4, 1932; s. Martin Henry and Gertrude (Schroeder) R.; m. Margaretha T. Angell, Dec. 27, 1960; children: Dorothy E. Kurtzweil, Mark Charles. STM, Concordia Sem., 1958; MEd, Washington U., 1959. Ordained to ministry Luth. Ch. Pastor St. John Luth. Ch., St. James, Mo., 1958-62, Luth. Ch. Resurrection, Portland, Oreg., 1962-74; internat. dir. Adult Christian Edn. Found., Madison, Wis., 1974-88; sr. pastor St. Stephen's Luth. Ch., Monona, Wis., 1988—; bd. dirs. Adult Christian Edn. Found., Madison, 1968-74, 88—. Named Hon. Citizen, Seoul, Korea, 1988.

ROHLFING, TIMOTHY B., minister, religious education administrator; b. Huntington, N.Y., Oct. 15, 1959; s. Richard E. and Gloria E. (Prince) R.; m. Gail E. Meyer, June 18, 1983: 1 child, Anna Nicole. BS in Edn., Concordia Tchrs. Coll., 1982. Lic. min. Luth. Ch.—Mo. Synod, 1982. Dir. youth and edn. mins. Beautiful Savior Luth. Ch., New Hope, Minn., 1982-89; youth min. Trinity Luth. Ch., Peoria, Ill., 1989—; pres. Minn.-South Dir. Christian Edn. Conf., 1986-87; chmn. 1990 Minn. South Dist. Youth Gatherings, Mpls., 1989-90. Contbr. articles to profl. jours. Mem. Theol. Educators and Associated Mins., Luth. Edn. Assn. Office: Trinity Luth Ch 135 NE Randolph Peoria IL 61606

ROHLFS, CARL W., pastor, educator; b. McKinney, Tex., May 2, 1951; s. Claus H. and Doris Myrle (Zirkel) R.; m. Barbara Jean Nelson, May 20, 1977; children: Randolph Nelson, Robert Sidney. BS, So. Meth. U., 1972, ThM, 1976. Ordained to ministry United Meth. Ch. Pastor youth Plymouth Park United Meth. Ch., Irving, Tex., 1975-77; pastor evangelism and adult edn. 1st United Meth. Ch., Victoria, Tex., 1977-78; founding pastor Asbury United Meth. Ch., Corpus Christi, Tex., 1978-84; sr. pastor 1st United Meth. Ch., Del Rio, Tex., 1984-88, San Angelo, Tex., 1988—; instr. Perkins Sch. Theology, So. Meth. U., Dallas, 1983—; del. World Meth. Conf., Nairobi, Kenya, 1986; chmn. dist. com. on ordained mins., United Meth. Ch., San Angelo, 1988—, mem. futures com. SW Tex. Conf., San Antonio, 1989—. Contbr. article and editorials to religious publs. Bd. dirs. Ct. Apptd. Spl. Advs., San Angelo, 1989—; fund raiser United Way, San Angelo, 1990—. Recipient Outstanding Pastor award Tex. United Meth. Colls. Assn., 1987, 89. Mem. San Angelo Ministerial Assn., Rotary. Home: 2711 Live Oak San Angelo TX 76901 Office: 1st United Meth Ch 37 E Beauregard San Angelo TX 76903

ROHM, ROBERT ALLAN, minister; b. Birmingham, Ala., Apr. 22, 1949; s. Mary Katherine (Barrett) R.; m. Donna Rea Lopez, July 26, 1970; children: Rachael, Esther, Elizabeth, Susanna. AA, Gordon Mil. Coll., Barnsville, Ga., 1969; BA, Fla. Bible Coll., 1971; MS, Pensacola (Fla.) Christian Coll., 1979; ThM, Dallas Theol. Seminary, 1985; PhD, North Tex. State U., 1988. Ordained to ministry Bapt. Ch., 1971. Youth dir. Hillside Bapt. Ch., Atlanta, 1971-72; tchr. Headland High Sch., East Point, Ga., 1972-73; prin. Clayton Christian Sch., Morrow, Ga., 1973-81; tchr., supr. curriculum First Bapt. Acad., Dallas, 1981-84; auditorium class pastor First Bapt. Ch., Dallas, 1984-86, minister to young married adults, 1986—. Author: Soul Winning Faith, 1972; contbr. articles to newspapers. Mem. Rep. Presdl. Task Force, Washington, 1981—. Recipient Disting. Service award Ga. Jaycees, 1976, Community Service award Sta. WSB, Atlanta, 1980; Hurley Found. grantee, 1982-85. Mem. Assn. Christian Schs. Internat. (cons. 1981-87). Avocations: jogging, tennis, softball. Office: First Bapt Ch 1707 San Jacinto Dallas TX 75201

ROHN, GORDON FREDERICK, religious organization administrator, minister; b. Fond du Lac, Wis., Feb. 4, 1939; s. Gordon F. and Janet (Reed) R.; m. Judith Amber Ciscel, June 11, 1960; children: Brian, Kevin, Grady, Nathan. MA in Mgmt., Webster Coll., 1981; BS in Polit. Sci., U. Wis., 1962, JD, 1965; MDiv, Trinity Evangel. Div. Sch., 1984. Bar: Wis., 1965. Commd. 2d lt. U.S. Army, 1962, advanced through grades to lt. col., ret., 1982; minister adminstrn. Fair Oaks Bapt. Ch., Concord, Calif., 1985-87; dir. internat. bur. Frontiers, Pasadena, Calif., 1988-90, dir. ch. rels., 1990—; pub. speaker in field; mgmt. cons. in field; founding bd. dirs. Tyndale Theol. Sem., Amsterdam, The Netherlands, 1983-85. Contbr. articles to profl. jours. Mem. Wis. Bar Assn., Officers Christian Fellowship (area coord. 1981-82), Christian Ministry Mgmt. Assn., Wycliffe Assocs. Republican. Baptist. Avocations: reading, computers, hiking, music, sports. Office: Frontiers PO Box 40159 Pasadena CA 91114

ROHRBACHER, PAUL DAVID, minister; b. Lancaster, Ohio, Aug. 9, 1950; s. Philip Arthur and Marjorie Sophia (Henkel) R.; m. Darhon Elaine Rees, June 14, 1974. BA, Capital U., 1973; MDiv, Evang. Luth. Theol. Sem., 1976. Ordained to ministry Am. Luth. Ch., 1978. Pastor St. Paul Evang. Luth. Ch., North Tonawanda, N.Y., 1978—; rep. coun. Upstate N.Y. Synod, Evang. Luth. Ch. in Am., Syracuse, 1987—, mem. exec. com., 1989—, pres. western N.Y. conf., 1984-87; del. gen. conv., San Diego, 1982. Contbr. articles to various jours. Master gardener Cornell Coop. Extension, Niagara County, N.Y., 1990—; active Camerata Singers Western N.Y., Buffalo, Crohn's and Colitis Found. Am., 1986—; bd. dirs. Hart Interfaith, Lewiston, N.Y., 1983-88. Samuel Trexler fellow Upstate N.Y. Synod, 1989. Mem. Twin Cities Ministerial Assn. (pres. 1982-84, v.p. 1987-90), Bread for the World. Home: 66 E Felton St North Tonawanda NY 14120 Office: St Paul Evang Luth Ch 64 E Felton St North Tonawanda NY 14120 *As I have grown I have found delight in letting the Holy Spirit take the lead. When I push one way, not the best, the Spirit prods the better direction. It is freeing to be prepared to go with the Spirit's flow.*

ROHRBAUGH, RICHARD LEANDER, minister, educator; b. Addis Ababa, Ethiopia, Dec. 12, 1936; (parents Am. citizens); s. James Leander and Marion (Walker) R.; m. Miriam Ruth Gathman, Apr. 11, 1960; children: Douglas Brian, Janet Marie. BA in Chemistry, Sterling Coll., 1958; MDiv, Pitts. Theol. Sem., 1961; STD, San Francisco Theol. Sem., 1977. Ordained to ministry Presbyn. Ch., 1961. Pastor Tri-City Presbyn. Ch., Myrtle Creek, Oreg., 1961-68, St. Mark Presbyn. Ch., Portland, Oreg., 1968-77; prof. religious studies Lewis and Clark Coll., Portland, Oreg., 1977—. Author: Into All the World, 1976, 80, The Biblical Interpreter, 1978, Une Bible Agraire Pour un Monde Industriel, 1981, Interpretation, 1985; contbr. articles to religious jours. Bd. dirs. Oreg. Mountain Rescue, Portland, 1980—; chmn. Mazama Climbing Program, 1982—; coun. mem. Friends of Seasonal Svc. Workers, Portland, 1983—. James Purdy scholar Pitts. Theol. Sem., 1971; fellow Fund for Theol. Edn., 1972. Mem. Am. Acad. Religion, Am. Schs. Oriental Rsch., Soc. Bibl. Lit. (pres. regional sect. 1990), The Context Group. Democrat. Home: 7010 SW 4th St Portland OR 97219 Office: Lewis & Clark Coll 0615 SW Palatine Hill Rd Portland OR 97219 *It is not so much what we know as what we care about that really matters. Caring about someone or something other than oneself changes everything in life and makes it worthwhile.*

ROHRS, BARBARA MASON, lay worker; b. Ypsilanti, Mich., Dec. 1, 1946; d. Wendell Dwight and Jane (Shutt) M.; m. Jonathan Edward Rohrs, Aug. 9, 1969; children: Stephanie, Christine, John, Rob. BS in Edn., Greenville (Ill.) Coll., 1969. Music dir. Holland (Ohio) Free Meth. Ch., 1974-87, dir. VBS, 1976, 77, dir. Christian edn., 1985-86, newsletter editor, mem. ofcl. bd., steward, mem. social action, music coms., devotional leader, sponsor; mem. Anthony Wayne Bd. Edn., Whitehouse, Ohio, 1984—. V.p., publicity dir. Anthony Wayne High Sch. Choir Boosters; mem. parent groups, mem. athletic coun. Anthony Wayne High Sch.; mem. bd. curriculum com. Anthony Wayne Bd. Edn. Republican. Home: 6637 S Mill Ridge Rd Maumee OH 43537-9659

ROJAS MENA, LUIS, bishop; b. Jalpa de Canovas Guanajuato, Mex., June 21, 1917; s. Francisco Rojas Soto and Severiana Mena Rivas. Student in, Mex., 1933; Licenciate Rome, 1938, Th.B., 1945. Ordained priest Roman Catholic Ch.; now bishop of Culiacan Diocese, Mex.; Mem. Episcopal Commn. of Dioceses; mem. Episc. Commn. of Canonization Causes. Office: Apartado Postal N 666, Culiacan Mexico 8000

ROLAND, CLARENCE HERREL, minister; b. Cedartown, Ga., May 7, 1933; s. Homer W. and Maude (Palmer) R.; m. Emily Lou Dyer, Apr. 23, 1955 (dec. Feb. 1990); 1 child, Mark Anthony. AB, Shorter Coll., 1959; MDiv, Southeastern Bapt. Sem., 1962; MEd, Ga. So. Coll., 1974; MA, L.I. U., 1975; MEd, Ga. State U., 1979. Dean of students Shorter Coll., Rome, Ga., 1963-66; commd. lt. U.S. Army, 1966, advanced through grades to lt. col., 1978, chaplain, 1966-89, ret., 1989; pastor Orchard Knob Bapt. Ch., Atlanta, 1990—; adj. instr. Ga. Mil. Coll., St. Leo Coll., 1988—; bd. dirs. Internat. Airport Chaplaincy, Atlanta, 1990—. Decorated Bronze Star, Legion of Merit; recipient Humanitarian Svc. award Chapel of Four Chaplains. Mem. Mil. Chaplaincy (life), Mil. Chaplains Assn. (life), Atlanta Bapt. Assn. (exec. com. 1990—), Ret. Officers Assn. (life). Home: 3330 Jonesboro Rd Fairburn GA 30213

ROLAND, EMMERETT WILBUR, minister; b. Red Bird, Okla., Oct. 24, 1931; s. Melvin Fred and Maggie Elizabeth (Wright) R.; m. Virginia Mae Bishop, Aug. 5, 1965. BD, St. Matthew U., 1956; DD, Mt. Sinai Theol. Sem., 1970. Ordained to ministry Am. Bapt. Conv., 1956. Pastor First St. Paul Bapt. Ch., North Oakland, Calif., 1961-66, St. Mary's Bapt. Ch., East Oakland, Calif., 1966-68; organizer and pastor Cornerstone Bapt. Ch., East Oakland, 1968-69; pastor 2d Bapt. Ch., Merced, Calif., 1969—. Editor Intermediate Quar., 1967-75; editorial staff writer Nat. Bapt. Publ. Bd., 1965-75. Mem. adv. bd. exec. opportunities program Merced Coll., 1972-74; mem. Koininia Scholarship Found., Oakland, 1964—. Mem. Shiloh Dist. Bapt. Assn. (moderator 1973), Gamma Chi Epsilon. Home: 396 E Brookdale Dr Merced CA 95340 Office: 2d Bapt Ch 501-515 Q St T Merced CA 95340

ROLLAND, DALE EVERETT, pastor; b. Sand Springs, Okla., Apr. 10, 1955; s. Bernice (Hines) Lewis; m. Robin Denise Scott, Aug. 9, 1975 (div. Sept. 1980); 1 child, Davina Lanise; m. Rubie Ann Wright, Aug. 6, 1988; children: Gene Williams, Donald Ray Williams. BA in Religion, Bishop Coll., Dallas, 1987; MRE, Phillips Sem., Enid, Okla., 1990. Ordained to ministry Bapt. Ch., 1986. Asst. pastor Midway Bapt. Ch., Dallas, 1985-87; youth pastor Antioch Bapt. Ch., Tulsa, 1988—; instr. Creek Dist. Assn./ Congress of Okla., 1989—, T. Oscar Chappelle Sch. of Religion, Tulsa, 1991—. Author: Journey of Life Thus Far, 1991; contbr. articles to publs. With U.S. Navy, 1973-74. Mem. North Tulsa Mins. Alliance. Democrat. Home: 828 S Wheeling # 203 Tulsa OK 74104-3627 *Many a person has decided to dance with the world and enjoy its pleasures and missed God's best plan for their lives. I have discovered that God's second best is wonderful and joyous still.*

ROLLER, DOUGLAS CHARLES, youth pastor; b. St. Louis, Oct. 27, 1961; s. Robert Charles and Ylene Harriet (Bridges) R.; m. Shelley Lynn Shores, Jan. 7, 1989. BA in Edn., Azusa Pacific U., 1984; MDiv., Fuller Sem., 1989. Youth pastor 1st Bapt. Ch., Downey, Calif., 1986—. Republican.

ROLLER, JOHN HERSCHEL, pastor; b. Orange, N.J., Nov. 7, 1949; s. Murray Ralph and Lorraine Winifred (Grosjean) R.; m. Mary Ellen Hegg, Aug. 25, 1973; children: Emily Jean, Sarah Elizabeth, Brian David. BA, Gordon Coll., 1976; ThM, Bethany Theol. Sem., Dothan, Ala., 1985, PhD, 1990. Ordained to ministry Advent Christian Ch., 1979. Pastor The Village Ch., Carpentersville, Ill., 1978-84, Advent Christian Ch. of Tallahassee, Fla., 1984-87, 1st Advent Christian Ch., Charleston, W.Va., 1987—; founder, dir. Internat. Christian Pen Pal Club, Charleston, 1975—; sec., treas. Mountaineers for Jesus, Charleston, 1989—. With U.S. Army, 1971-73. Democrat. Home: 617 Randolph St Charleston WV 25302-2020 Office: 1st Advent Christian Ch 615 Randolph St Charleston WV 25302-2020 *Four activities are indispensable to a Christian who wants to "grow up" spiritually: personal Bible study, personal prayer, person-to-person fellowship with other Christians, and person-to-person witnessing to non-Christian friends.*

ROLSTON, HOLMES, III, theologian, educator, philosopher; b. Staunton, Va., Nov. 19, 1932; s. Holmes and Mary Winifred (Long) R.; m. Jane Irving Wilson, June 1, 1956; children: Shonny Hunter, Giles Campbell. BS, Davidson Coll., 1953; BD, Union Theol. Sem., Richmond, Va., 1956; MA in Philosophy of Sci., U. Pitts., 1968; PhD in Theology, U. Edinburgh, Scotland, 1958. Ordained to ministry Presbyn. Ch. (USA), 1956. Pastor Walnut Grove Presbyn. Ch., Bristol, Va., 1959-67; asst. prof. philosophy Colo. State U., Ft. Collins, 1968-71, assoc. prof., 1971-76, prof., 1976—; vis. scholar Ctr. Study of World Religions, Harvard U., 1974-75; lectr. Yale U., Vanderbilt U., others. Author: The Cosmic Christ, 1966, John Calvin versus the Westminster Confession, 1972, Religious Inquiry: Participation and Detachment, 1985, Philosophy Gone Wild, 1986, Science and Religion: A Critical Survey, 1987, Environmental Ethics, 1988; assoc. editor Environ. Ethics, 1979—; mem. editorial bd. Oxford Series in Environ. Philosophy and Pub. Policy, Zygon: Jour. of Religion and Sci.; contbr. chpts. to books, articles to profl. jours. Recipient Oliver P. Penock Disting. Svc. award Colo. State U., 1983; Disting. Russell fellow Grad. Theol. Union, 1991. Mem. AAAS, Am. Acad. Religion, Soc. Bibl. Lit. (pres. Rocky Mountain-Gt. Plains region), Am. Philos. Assn., Internat. Soc. for Environ. Ethics (pres. 1989—), Phi Beta Kappa. Avocation: bryology. Home: 1712 Concord Dr Fort Collins CO 80526 Office: Colo State U Dept Philosophy Fort Collins CO 80523

ROLSTON, STEPHEN GARRY, radio station executive; b. Paraparaumu, Wellington, New Zealand, June 25, 1962; m. Kenneth Claude and Eva Elizabeth Maude (Edgecombe) R.; m. Michelle Lea Armitage, Sept. 27, 1986. Producer Radio Rhema, Christchurch, New Zealand, 1985-91, asst. sta. mgr., 1988-91, dominion councillor, 1988—; sta. mgr. Radio Rhema, Auckland, New Zealand, 1991—. Mem. Open Brethren Ch. Office: Radio Rhema Inc, 53 Upper Queen St, Auckland New Zealand

ROMAGOSA, ELMO LAWRENCE, clergyman, retired editor; b. Thibodaux, La., Jan. 11, 1924; s. Lawrence Gabriel and Lydie (Achee) R. Ed., St. Joseph Sem., Notre Dame Sem., New Orleans, 1947. Ordained priest Roman Cath. Ch., 1947. Asst. pastor Cut Off, La., 1947-50, New Orleans, 1950-58; chaplain Ursuline Convent and Nat. Shrine Our Lady of Prompt Succor, 1958-63; pastor St. John's Ch., New Orleans, 1963-70; asst. dir. Soc. for Propagation of Faith, 1950-60, dir., 1962; communications dir. Archdiocese New Orleans, 1962; founding editor Clarion Herald newspaper, 1963-74; priest in residence Sts. Peter and Paul Ch., New Orleans, 1970-72; pastor Holy Trinity Ch., New Orleans, 1972-74, St. Rose of Lima Ch., New Orleans, 1974-76, St. Clement of Rome Ch., Metairie, La., 1976-84; chaplain Port of New Orleans, 1984-88; pastor Ch. of Infant Jesus, Harvey, La., 1988—; nat. sec. Cath. Broadcasters Assn., 1963-65; mem. U.S. Cath. bishops subcoms. on Cath.-Jewish relations, 1965; named prelate of honor, 1980. Editor Airtime, 1963-64. Dir. Stella Maris Maritime Ctr., 1984-88; chaplain Harbor Police, Port of New Orleans, 1984-88, Propeller Club of U.S., Port of New Orleans, Council of Am. Master Mariners, Port of New Orleans, Greater New Orleans Council, Navy League of New Orleans, Maritime Council of Greater New Orleans, Maritime Trades dept. AFL-CIO; mem. Nat. Conf. Seafarers, 1984, pres., 1986—, mem. legal adv. com. Ctr. for Seafarers Rights, 1986; mem. Nat. Cath. Conf. for Seafarers, 1984, pres., 1986-88. Recipient First Place award for best editorial and best feature photo Press Club New Orleans, 1965, First Place award for best column Press Club New Orleans, 1972; named Prelate of Honor, Pope John II, 1980. Mem. Cath. Press Assn. (1st Place awards for gen. excellence 1963-65), Sociedad Espanola New Orleans (founding sec.-treas.). Republican. Lodge: Equestrian Order of Holy Sepulchre of Jerusalem (knight 1978, knight comdr. 1983, master of ceremonies 1986). Home and Office: Ch of the Infant Jesus 700 Maple Ave Harvey LA 70058

ROMAN, AGUSTIN A., clergyman; b. San Antonio de los Banos, Cuba, May 5, 1928; came to U.S., 1966; s. Rosendo and Juana (Rodriguez) R. BA, Sem. for Fgn. Missions, Montreal; M in Divinity, St. Vincent de Paul Regional Sem., Boynton Beach, Fla.; MA in Religious Studies, Barry U., Miami; MA in Human Resources, Biscayne Coll., Opa Locka, Fla. Ordained priest Roman Catholic Ch., 1959; pastor parishes Diocese of Matanzas, Cuba, 1959-61; spiritual dir. youth Diocese of Matanzas; expelled by Cuban Govt., 1961; pastor Holy Spirit Parish, Temuco, Chile, 1962-66; spiritual dir., prof. Inst. Humanities, 1962-66; spiritual dir. Cursillo Movement Diocese of Temuco, 1962-66; asst. pastor St. Mary's Cathedral, Miami, 1966-67, St. Kieran's Parish, Miami, 1967-68; chaplain Mercy Hosp., Miami, 1967-73, Shrine of Our Lady of Charity, Miami, 1967; named monsignor Archdiocese of Miami, 1974, named vicar for Hispanics, 1976, elected aux. bishop, 1979—; Episcopal ordination, 1979. Mem. Nat. Conf. Catholic Bishops (mem. ad hoc com. on migration and tourism 1980—, mem. ad hoc com. for hispanic affairs 1980—). Office: Archdiocese of Miami 9401 Biscayne Blvd Miami Shores FL 33138

ROMAN, CHESTER JOHN, deacon; b. New Britain, Conn., Aug. 18, 1924; s. Felix and Jozefa (Kolsut) R.; m. Frances Catherine Roligno, Oct. 14, 1950; children: Frances C., Josephine V., Angela M. Student, St. Thomas Sem., Bloomfield, Conn., 1981. Ordained deacon Roman Cath. Ch., 1981. Legionary Legion of Mary, New Britain, 1962-69, leader jrs., 1970-74; jr. curia leader Legion of Mary, Hartford, Conn., 1975-76; deacon St. Mary Ch., New Britain, 1981—. With USNR, 1943-46. Democrat. Home: 221 Willow St New Britain CT 06051-1359 Office: St Mary Ch 455 Main St New Britain CT 06051

ROMAN, SISTER GLORIA BELLE, nun, educator, educational administrator; b. Jackson, Mich., Dec. 19, 1941; d. Harry and Dorothy (Kracko) R. BA, Nazareth, 1967; MA, Notre Dame U., 1975, Boston Coll., 1988. Joined Sisters of St. Joseph of Nazareth, Roman Cath. Ch., 1960; cert. elem. educator, Mich.; cert. religious educator Diocese of Marquette, Mich. Mid. sch. tchr. St. Rita's Sch., Detroit, 1965; elem. tchr. St. Joseph Sch., Lake Orion, Mich., 1965-67, Our Lady of Fatima Sch., Michigan Center, Mich., 1967-69, St. Joseph Sch., Battle Creek, 1969-72, St. Mary Sch., Williamston, 1972-79, St. Therese Sch, Lansing, Mich, 1979-82; prin. Holy Angels Sch., Sturgis, Mich., 1982-83, St. Joseph the Worker Sch., Beal City, Mich., 1983-87; religious edn. coord., parish adminstr. Holy Name of Mary, Sault St. Marie, Mich., 1988—; com. mem. Pathways to the Chs., Sault Ste. Marie, 1989—. Vol. Kalamazoo (Mich.) COunty Jail, 1987-88. Recipient Grant Cen. Mich. U., 1980. Mem. Holy Name of Mary Parish Coun., Youth Group, Altar Soc. Home: Fontbonne Manor Nazareth MI 49074 Office: Holy Name of Mary 377 Maple Sault Sainte Marie MI 49783

ROME, CAROL ANN, religion educator; b. Romeville, La., Oct. 5, 1945; d. Audry Joseph and Frances Marie (Levet) R. BA, Nicholls State U., Thibodaux, La., 1967. Tchr. 1st grade St. James Parish Sch. Bd., Convent, La., 1967—; religious edn. coord. St. Michael, Convent, La., 1982—; sec. Cath. Daus. at St. Michael, 1973-75, 1st vice regent, 1975-79, regent, 1987-91, CCD tchr., 1967—. Named Tchr. of the Yr., St. James Parish Sch. Bd., 1987-88. Mem. NEA, St. James Assn. Edn., La. Edn. Assn., Nicholls Reading Coun., La. Coun. Tchrs. Math. Democrat. Home: 8196 LA 44 Convent LA 70723-2620

ROMER, CARL WILLIAM, clergyman, dairy goat breeder; b. nr. Bushong, Kans., July 28, 1904; s. C.H. William and Mary M. (Yount) R.; m. Violet Daisie Maxwell, June 1, 1930; children: Carl Louis, Francis William. Student Kans. State Coll., 1922-25; BS, State U. Iowa, 1928; LLB, Am. Extension U., 1929. Ordained to minisry Grace Christian Assemblies Ch., 1931. Instr. corr. study dept. math. Kans. State Coll., 1923-25; adminstr. pub. schs., Kans., 1925-27; head dept. engring. Rochester Jr. Coll., Minn., 1927-29; acting head dept. engring. Baker U., Baldwin, Kans., 1929-30, Ripon Coll., Wis., 1930-31; acct., adminstr. U.S. Post Office, Admire, Kans., 1935—; pastor Gospel Story Hour radio ministry Sta. KTSW-AM, Emporia, Kans., 1944—; justice of peace, Admire, 1951—; founder, tchr., evangelist Grace Bible Research Ctr., Kansas City, Kans., 1978—. Editor, pub.: Dairy Goat Year Book, 1942-68, Bible Expository volumes.Mem. Nat. Soc. Live Stock Record Assns. (hon.), Kans. Dairy Goat Soc. (co-organizer, pres.), Am. Goat Soc. (pres., bd. dirs.), French Alpine Breeders Assn. Am. (bd. dirs.), Nat. Alpine Breed Promotion Club (co-organizer, pres., nat. bd. dirs.). Home: Ivy Twp Admire KS 66830 Office: 7900 E 66th St Kansas City MO 64133

ROMERO, CLAUDE GILBERT, priest; b. Dixon, N.Mex., Feb. 15, 1936. BA, St. John's Coll., Camarillo, Calif., 1957; PhD, Princeton Theol. Seminary, 1982; postgrad., Harvard U., 1968-69. Ordained priest Roman Cath. Ch., 1961. Assoc. pastor Roman Cath. Diocese L.A., 1961-68, 86-90; from assoc. pastor to pastor Roman Cath. Diocese of El Paso, 1978-86; assoc. pastor Holy Spirit Cath. Ch., L.A., 1985—; adj. prof. U. Tex. El Paso, 1978-86, chaplain, 1978-86; adj. prof. Mt. St. Mary's Coll., L.A., 1987-88; vis. prof. Seminario Mayor San Carlos, Trujillo, Peru, 1985—. Author: Faith Beyond Boundaries; contbr. articles to profl. jours. Mem. Am. Acad. Religion, Soc. Bibl. Lit., Cath. Bibl. Assn., Am. Schs. Oriental Rsch., Acad. Cath. Hispanic Theologians U.S. (bd. dirs. 1988—). Home and Office: Holy Spirit Cath Ch 1421 S Dunsmuir Ave Los Angeles CA 90019

ROMERO, ENRIQUE A., diaconal music minister; b. Havana, Cuba, July 16, 1947; came to U.S., 1962; s. Alberto Rene and Ramona Maria (Leon) R.; m. Raquel Romero Hussey, Dec. 18, 1971 (div.); m. Amy S. Unger, Dec. 26, 1984; children: Angela Dawn Henderson, Gabriel Rene Romero. BA, Fla. Atlantic U., 1971; MA in Religion, Ashbury Theol. Sem., 1974. Music dir. Grace United Meth. Ch., Miami, Fla., 1965-70, First United Meth. Ch., West Palm Beach, Fla., 1970-71, Trinity Bapt. Ch., Lexington, Ky, 1971-76, First United Meth. ch., Warner Robbins, Ga., 1976-81, San Springs United Meth. Ch., Atlanta, 1981-84, St. Matthew United Meth. Ch., Belleville, Ill., 1984—; exec. dir. Sandy Springs UMC Performing Arts Ctr., Atlanta, 1982-84. Contbr. articles to profl. jours. Mem. Fellowship of United Meth. Musicians, Am. Guild of English Handbell Ringers. Avocation: racquetball. Home: 22 South 95th St Belleville IL 62223 Office: St Matthew United Meth Ch 1200 Moreland Dr Belleville IL 62223

ROMIG, EDGAR DUTCHER, clergyman; b. N.Y.C., July 6, 1921; s. Edgar Franklin and Ella Woodruff (Dutcher) R. BA, Princeton U., 1942; MDiv, Episcopal Theol. Sch., Mass., 1951; DD (hon.), Va. Theol. Sem., 1969. Ordained deacon Episcopal Ch., 1951, priest, 1952. Asst. minister Trinity Ch., Boston, 1951-53; rector Grace Ch., North Attleboro, Mass., 1953-58, St. Stephen's Ch., Lynn, Mass., 1958-64, Ch. of Epiphany, Washington, 1964—; dep. Episcopal Gen. Conv., 1973, 76, 79, 82, 85, 88, 91. Author: Trinity Church in the City of Boston, 1953; contbr. articles to various jours. Ambulance driver Am. Field Svc., 1942-43, NATOUSA; with AUS, 1943-45, ETO. Decorated Bronze Star, Purple Heart. Mem. Century Club (N.Y.C.), Princeton Club (N.Y.C.), Met. Club. Democrat. Home: 3006 32d St NW Washington DC 20008 Office: Ch of Epiphany 1317 G St NW Washington DC 20005

ROMM, J(UDAH) LEONARD, rabbi; b. Phila., May 27, 1946; s. Albert Benjamin and Laura Sarah (Lipsius) R.; m. Diane Linda Woodrow, Dec. 18, 1971; children: Zvi David, Gideon Zev. BA, Temple U., 1967; M.H.L., Jewish Theol. Sem., 1971. Ordained rabbi, 1972. Rabbi Temple Emanuel at Parkchester, Bronx, N.Y., 1972-76, Baldwin (N.Y.) Jewish Ctr., 1976-82, Temple Israel of Great Neck (N.Y.), 1982-87, Bellmore (N.Y.) Jewish Ctr., 1987—; chaplain Holly Patterson Home, Uniondale, N.Y., 1976-82. Author: (novel) The Swastika on the Synagogue Door, 1984; editor: (book of essays) Halakhah and the Modern Jew, 1989; contbr. articles, short stories, book revs. to profl. jours.; newsletter editor Union for Traditional Judaism, Mt. Vernon, N.Y., 1989—. Active AIDS curriculum Merrick-Bellmore (N.Y.) Sch. Dist., 1989; mem. L.I. Com. for Soviet Jewry, Carle Place, N.Y., 1976—. Mem. Rabbinical Assembly Nassau-Suffolk (pres. 1982-83), Union for Traditional Judaism (exec. bd.), The Rabbinical Assembly, N.Y. Bd. Rabbis (TV and radio commn.), L.I. Bd. Rabbis (sec. 1987-88). Democrat. Avocation: tropical fish. Home: 2517 Walters Ct Bellmore NY 11710 Office: Bellmore Jewish Ctr 2550 S Centre Ave Bellmore NY 11710 *Try to be a person.*

ROMNEY, JOSEPH BARNARD, educator, administrator; b. Salt Lake City, July 20, 1935; s. Junius Stowell and Ruth (Stewart) R.; m. Florence Black, May 1, 1959; children: Matthew Joseph, Suzanne, Aaron Stewart. BS, U. Utah, 1960, MA, 1967, JD, 1963, PhD, 1969. Commd. 2d lt. U.S. Army, 1960, advanced through grades to capt., ret., 1968; assoc. Romney and Boyer, Salt Lake City, 1963-68; asst. atty. gen. State of Utah, Salt Lake City, 1964-65; prof. history, assoc. dean Calif. Polytech. State U., San Luis Obispo, 1969-80; prof., assoc. dir. honors program, cello instr. Ricks Coll., Rexburg, Idaho, 1980—; cellist Utah Symphony Orch., Salt Lake City, 1954-56, 59-60, 66-68; pres. Millhollow Frozen Yogurt, Inc., Rexburg, 1982—. Author: A Research Guide to the History of San Luis Obispo County, California, 1983. Scoutmaster, dist. chmn. Boy Scouts Am., Utah, Calif. and Idaho, 1955-91. Recipient Dist. Merit award Boy Scouts Am., 1978. Mem. Utah State Bar Assn., Idaho Hist. Soc. (bd. editors 1988—), Mormon History Assn. (bd. editors 1979-81). Republican. LDS. Home: 53 S Millhollow Dr Rexburg ID 83440 Office: Ricks Coll Dept of Religion Rexburg ID 83460

ROMO, JOSE LEÓN, educator, library director; b. Roswell, N.Mex., July 16, 1930; s. Jose L. and Barbara (Romero) R. BA in Theology and Spanish, Coll. of Santa Fe, 1974; postgrad., Colegio Sant' Anselmo, Rome, 1975-76; MA in LS, U. Denver, 1980. Monk Order of St. Benedict, Pecos, N.Mex., 1970-75, 76-78, Rome, 1975-76; libr. dir. St. Vincent de Paul Sem., Boynton Beach, Fla., 1988—. Latin Am. Affairs scholar, U. N.Mex., 1948-50; U. Denver. Libr. Sci. fellow, 1979-80. Mem. ALA, Am. Coll. and Rsch. Librarians, Am. Theol. Libr. Assn. Office: St Vincent de Paul Sem Libr 10701 S Military Trail Boynton Beach FL 33436

ROMO GUTIERREZ, FERNANDO, bishop; b. Guadalajara, Mexico, June 18, 1915. Ordained priest Roman Cath. Ch., 1940; named bishop of Torreon Mexico, 1958—. Office: Apartado 430, Torreon, CP 27000 Coahuila Mexico

ROMOSER, BRUCE ALLEN, minister; b. San Francisco, Mar. 28, 1936; s. Albert Kolling and Thelma (King) R.; m. Auburn Lee Spencer, Sept. 3, 1959; children: Mark, David, Joy, Arthur, Matthew. BA, U. Md., 1962; MDiv, Southwestern Bapt. Theol., Seminary, Ft. Worth, 1973; DD, Am. Divinity Sch., Chgo., 1968. Ordained to ministry So. Bapt. Conv., 1962. Asst. to pastor Hillandale Bapt. Ch., Adelphi, Md., 1960-62; pastor Megargel (Tex.) Bapt. Ch., 1962-65; assoc. pastor Temple Bapt. Ch., Balt., 1965-68; missionary Fgn. Mission Bd., So. Bapt. Conf., Neuquen, Argentina, 1969-83; pastor Berwyn Bapt. Ch., College Park, Md., 1983-90, Bethel Bapt. Ch., Ellicott City, Md., 1990—; trustee Fgn. Mission Bd., So. Bapt. Conv., Richmond, Va., 1987—. Contbr. articles to profl. jour. Republican. Home: 3103 Ellicott Rd Beltsville MD 20705 Office: Bethel Bapt Ch 4261 Montgomery Rd Ellicott City MD 21043

RONESS, RONALD RALPH, rabbi; b. Montreal, Que., Can., Apr. 26, 1943; came to U.S., 1966; s. Abraham and Gertrude (Sommer) R.; m. Dina Farkas, Jan. 10, 1970; children: Raphael, David Jonah, Alexander Zev, Avi, Shoshana. BA, B in Commerce, Sir George Williams U., Montreal, 1964; MA, Yeshiva U., N.Y.C., 1969, MSW, 1978. Ordained rabbi, 1970; cert. pastoral counselor. Asst. rabbi Congregation Ohab Zedek, N.Y.C., 1969-70; rabbi Castle Hill Jewish Chapel, N.Y.C., 1970-83; rabbi of absorption ctrs. Jewish Agy., Jerusalem, 1983—; Hillel dir. Hofstra U., L.I., N.Y., 1970-78, CCNY, 1978-83; dir. community rels. Yeshiva U., N.Y.C., 1980-83; bd. dirs. Ethiopian Jewish Yeshiva, Jerusalem, 1989-91. Chmn. Har Nof Town Coun., Jerusalem, 1988-90, bd. dirs., 1990—. Mem. Rabbinical Coun. Am. (funeral standards com. N.Y.C. chpt. 1980-83, bd. dirs. Israel region 1983—). Home: 10 Barnet, Jerusalem Israel

RONIS, DERI JOY, religious studies educator; b. Bklyn., Mar. 31, 1951; d. Irving Theodore and Elsie (Lachow) R. BS, SUNY, N.Y.C., 1983; diploma in advanced studies, Unity Sch. for Religious Studies, 1984; PhD in Internat. Studies, Union Grad. Sch., 1987. Lic. tchr. unity. Mgr. spl. projects Advt. Community Times, Phila., 1978-79; coordinator fgn. lang. Bahamas Hotel Tng. Coll., Nassau, 1980-84; dir. pub. relations Mayflower Mgmt. Inst., Nassau, 1984; assoc. minister Unity Palm Beaches, West Palm Beach, Fla., 1984-86; coordinator youth edn. Jewish Community Ctr., West Palm Beach, 1986-87; adj. prof. Palm Beach Jr. Coll., Lake Worth, Fla., 1986—; cons. Palm Beach Bd. Edn., 1987—; counselor Unity Del Ray Beach, 1986—; coordinator Palm Beach County Beyond War, Palo Alto, Calif., 1985—. Vol. coordinator Tim Wirth campaign U.S. Senate, Boulder, Colo., 1986; campaigner Peace Edn. Week Fla. Mem. Nat. Assn. Female Execs., Ams. Dem. Action, Educators Social Responsibility, Consortium Peace, Research, Edn., Devel., Unity Bahamas (pres. bd. dirs. 1981-84). Democrat. Avocations: cycling, swimming, tennis, modern dance, travel. Office: Jewish Community Ctr 700 Spencer Dr West Palm Beach FL 33409

RONNOW, HELGE, minister. Pastor Moravian Brethren Ch., Christiansfeld, Denmark. Office: Moravian Brethren Ch, Brethren Community, 6070 Christiansfeld Denmark*

RONSISVALLE, DANIEL, minister; b. Washington, May 3, 1936; s. Benito Sebastian and Josefina (Castro) R.; m. Violet Fern Tidwell, June 8, 1956; children: Sheree Fern Ronsisvalle Johnson, Kenneth Daniel. BS, Southwestern Assemblies of God Bible Coll., Waxahachie, Tex., 1959. Ordained to ministry Assemblies of God, 1959. Dir. edn. Oak Cliff Assembly of God, Dallas, 1958-59; evangelist Assemblies of God, Dallas, 1959-61; pastor Lakeview Assembly of God, New Orleans, 1961-70, Cathedral of the Cross (formerly Huffman Assembly of God), Birmingham, Ala., 1970—; pres. 20th Century Guideline Christian TV Prodns., 1980—. Recipient Brother Bryan Humanitarian award City of Birmingham, 1976. Mem. Am. Assn. Bible Colls., Delta Epsilon Chi (hon.). Office: Cathedral of the Cross 1480 Center Point Pkwy Birmingham AL 35215 *The main objective in life should be to do what is right not necessarily what is good—for sometimes what is good may not be what is right. However, right is always right and in time will ultimately produce what is good.*

ROOKS, CHARLES SHELBY, minister; b. Beaufort, N.C., Oct. 19, 1924; s. Shelby A. and Maggie (Hawkins) R.; m. Adrienne Martinez, Aug. 7, 1946; children: Laurence Gaylord, Carol Ann. AB, Va. State U., 1949; MDiv, Union Theol. Sem., 1953; LHD (hon.), Howard U., 1981, Va. State U., 1984, Talladega Coll., 1989; DD (hon.), Coll. Wooster, 1968, Interdenominational Theol. Ctr., 1979, Va. Union U., 1980; LLD (hon.), Dillard U., 1986, Heidelberg Coll., 1990; LittD (hon.), Huston-Tillotson Coll., 1989. Ordained to ministry United Ch. of Christ, 1953. Pastor Shanks Village Ch., Orangeburg, N.Y., 1951-53; pastor Lincoln Meml. Congl. Temple, Washington, 1953-60; assoc. dir. Fund for Theol. Edn., Princeton, N.J., 1960-67, exec. dir., 1967-74; pres. Chgo. Theol. Sem., 1974-84; exec. v.p. United Ch. Bd. for Homeland Ministries, N.Y.C., 1984—; mem. exec. bd. dept. ministry Nat. Council Chs., 1962-70; chmn. bd. United Ch. of Christ Office of Communications, 1964-81, chmn. com. structure Central Atlantic Conf., 1970-72; mem. Union Theol. Sem. Alumni Council, 1968-70, Theol. Perspectives Commn. on Nat. Com. Black Churchmen, 1968-74; vis. fellow Episc. Theol. Sem. S.W., Austin, Tex., 1966; lectr. in field, 1960-74. Author: Rainbows and Reality, 1984, The Hopeful Spirit, 1987, Revolution in Zion, 1990; editor: Toward a Better Ministry, 1965; mem. editorial bd. Theology Today, 1966, New Conversations, 1977; contbr. articles to religious jours. Chmn. planning com. Nat. Consultation Negro in Christian Ministry, 1965; trustee Bexley Hall Theol. Sem., Colgate-Rochester Div. Sch., 1968-73, Lancaster Theol. Sem., Pa., 1969-74, Eastern Career Testing Ctr., Lancaster, 1969-74; mem. Princeton Regional Sch. Bd., 1969-70, exec. bd. Nat. Com. Religion and Labor, 1987-91; bd. dirs. The Africa Fund, 1987-91, Wash. Urban League, 1955-60, chmn. housing com., 1956-60; chmn. ednl. adv. com. Chgo. Urban League, 1978-84; pres. Communications Improvement, 1971-81; vice chair Nat. Com. for Full Employment, 1987-91. Served with AUS, 1943-46, PTO. Recipient Elizabeth Taylor Byrd Fund Outstanding Community Service award, 1969. Mem. Va. State U. Nat. Alumni Assn. (pres. 1966-67), Soc. for Study Black Religion (pres. 1970-74, 80-84), Assn. Theol. Schs. (cons. Black ch. studies 1970-71, mem. commn. on accrediting, 1976-82, chmn. 1980-82, exec. com. 1982-84). Office: United Church Bd Homeland Ministries 700 Prospect Ave Cleveland OH 44115-1100

ROONEY, E. ASHLEY, youth minister; b. Greenwich, Conn.; d. Stanley Carter and Elizabeth (Meriwether) Schuler; m. Thomas P. Rooney, Feb. 27, 1965; children: Siobhan, Stephen. BS, Columbia U., 1964; MA, Lesley Coll., 1988; diploma, McLean Hosp., 1989. Youth dir. Ch. of Our Redeemer, Lexington, Mass., 1980-89; youth min. 1st Congl. Ch., Winchester, Mass., 1986—; mem. Winchester Interfaith, 1986—, sec., 1989—. Producer, writer documentary God Won't Mind: The Making of A Rock Benefit, 1988; producer, writer, group facilitator, editor video series Telling It Like It Is, 1985-86; contbr. articles to Boston Globe, Redbook, others. Bd. dirs. Parent to Parent, Winchester, 1990—. Grantee Ch. Home Soc., 1983, 86, Polaroid Corp., 1984, Jenks Outreach, 1987-90, ENKA, 1989-90. Office: 1st Congl Ch 21 Church St Winchester MA 01890

ROOP, EUGENE FREDERIC, religion educator; b. South Bend, Ind., May 11, 1942; s. G. Frederic and Lois Elizabeth (Berkebile) R.; m. Delora Ann Mishler, Aug. 24, 1963; children: Tanya Marie, Frederic John. BS, Manchester (Ind.) Coll., 1964; MDiv, Bethany Theol. Seminary, Oakbrook, Ill., 1967; PhD, Claremont (Calif.) Grad. Sch., 1972. Asst. prof. Earlham Sch. Religion, Richmond, Ind., 1970-74, assoc. prof., 1975-77; assoc. prof. Bethany Theol. Seminary, 1977-78, prof. Bibl. studies, 1978-86, Wieand prof. Bibl. studies, 1987—; dir. Ch. of Brethren Outdoor Ministries Assn., Elgin, Ill., 1982-88; bd. dirs. Ecumenical Ctr. for Stewardship Studies, N.Y.C., 1979—. Author: Coming Kingdom Teacher's Guide, 1982, Living the Biblical Story, 1979, Commentary on Genesis, 1987, Heard in our Hand, 1990, Let the Rivers Run, 1991. Active sch. bd. adv. com., Villa Park, Ill., 1981-85. So. Ohio Seminary Consortium summer fellow, 1975, Assn. Theol. Schs. summer fellow, 1974, Sea-Atlantic Fund rsch. fellow, 1978-79. Mem. Soc. Bibl. Lit., Chgo. Soc. Bibl. Rsch., Assn. Case Tchrs. Avocations: photography, travel, tennis. Office: Bethany Theol Seminary Meyers and Butterfield Rds Oak Brook IL 60521

ROORDA, ERVIN GLEN, minister; b. near Pella, Iowa, Sept. 21, 1938; s. Henry C. and Tena Henrietta (Van Roekel) R.; m. Andrea Marie Boat, June 8, 1960; children: Anne Marie, Mary Elizabeth, Lisa Jane, Jonathan Ervin. BA, Cen. Coll., 1960; BD, Western Theol. Sem., 1963; ThM, Princeton Theol. Sem., 1967; postgrad., San Francisco Theol. Sem. Pastor Cen. Ref. Ch., Muskegon, Mich., 1963-69; assoc. pastor Fremont Presbyn. Ch., Sacramento, 1969-76; sr. pastor Manito Presbyn. Ch., Spokane, Wash., 1976—; commr. to gen. assembly Presbyn. Ch., 1974,86; moderator Presbytery of the Inland Empire, 1985-87. Mem. Nat. Campaign Com. for Maj. Mission Fund. Democratic. Avocations: tennis, cross-country skiing, walking, bicycling, canoeing. Home: 134 W 12th St Holland MI 49423-3215 Office: Manito Presbyn Ch 402-29th Ave E Spokane WA 99203

ROOT, JOHN DAVID, history educator; b. Michigan City, Ind., Dec. 20, 1940; s. Joseph McKelvey and Margaret Rose (Biever) R. BA, U. Notre Dame, 1962; MA, Ind. U., 1964, PhD, 1974. Prof. history Ill. Inst. Tech., Chgo., 1969—. Contbr. articles to profl. jours. Capt. U.S. Army, 1966-68, Vietnam. NEH fellow, 1981; grantee Am. Philos. Soc., 1976-79. Mem. Am. Acad. Religion, Am. Soc. for Ch. History, Am. Cath. Hist. Soc. (exec. coun. 1985-87), Am. Hist. Assn. Office: Ill Inst Tech Dept of Humanities Chicago IL 60616

ROOT, MICHAEL JOHN, theologian, educator; b. Norfolk, VA, U.S.A., Apr. 27, 1951; arrived in France, 1988; s. Joseph Ernest and Inez Mildred (McGuire) R.; m. Sarah Elizabeth Duncan. BA, Dartmouth Coll., 1973; MA, Yale U., 1975, PhD, 1979. Instr. in religion Davidson (N.C.) Coll., 1978-80; assoc. prof. theology Luth. Theol. So. Sem., Columbia, S.C., 1980-88; prof. Inst. Ecumenical Rsch., Strasbourg, France, 1988—, dir., 1991—; mem. exec. coun. Luth. Ch. Am., 1984-87; cons. Anglican-Luth. Internat. Continuation com., 1988—. Contbr. articles to profl. jours. Mem. North Am. Acad. Ecumenists, Am. Acad. Religion. Office: Inst Ecumenical Rsch, 8 rue Klotz, 67000 Strasbourg France

ROOTE, TOM STAFFORD, JR., church organization executive; b. Covington, Tenn., Dec. 18, 1934; s. Tom Stafford Sr. and Mary Olga (Price) R.; m. Martha Lorraine Stoudenmier, Aug. 27, 1960; children: James Thomas, Patricia Denise Roote Lowe. BA, Mercer U., 1957; MRE, New Orleans Bapt. Sem., 1959, EdD, 1967. Dir. edn. New Orleans Bapt. Assn., 1960-63; prof. Bapt. Bible Inst., Graceville, Fla., 1963-69; dir. assn. mission Columbus (Ga.) Bapt. Assn., 1969-70; exec. dir. Jacksonvillve (Fla.) Bapt. Assn., 1970-74, Birmingham (Ala.) Bapt. Assn., 1974-84, Suncoast Bapt. Assn., Clearwater, Fla., 1984-87, Greater New Orleans Fedn. of Chs., 1987—; prof. ch. adminstrn. New Orleans Bapt. Theol. Sem., 1991—; mem. urban tng. coop. So. Bapt. Conv., 1975-80; pres. Nat. Conf. Dirs. of Mission, 1978. Contbr. articles to profl. jours. Active Mayor's Task Force Against Drugs, New Orleans, 1989; vol. United Way, New Orleans, 1988-89. Mem. Rotary. Republican. Avocations: golf, carpentry, stained glass. Home: 4209 Seminary Pl New Orleans LA 70126 Office: New Orleans Bapt Theol Sem 3939 Gentilly Blvd Box 280 New Orleans LA 70126

ROOZEN, PETER KIP, minister; b. Yankton, SD, Oct. 31, 1958; s. Merance William and Carol Sue (South) R.; m. Tammie Lynn Tripp, Dec. 27, 1980; children: Christopher William, Kerrie Lynn. Student, U. S.D., 1976-78; BA, Dakota Wesleyan U., 1980; MDiv, Iliff Sch. Theology, 1985. Ordained to ministry United Meth. Ch. as deacon, 1983, as elder, 1987. Min. United Meth. Ch., Doland and Frankfort, S.D., 1985-90, Gary and Clear Lake, S.D., 1990—; sec. north dist. Global Ministries/Conf. Bd. Global Ministries, S.D., 1987—. Mem. Clear Lake Ministerial Assn., Amnesty Internat., S.D. Peace and Justice Ctr., Dakota Wesleyan U. Alumni Assn. (bd. dirs. 1987—). Home: 711 5th Ave S Clear Lake SD 57226 Office: United Meth Ch 407 5th Ave S Clear Lake SD 57226

ROPER, BILL LEE, music minister; b. Christian County, Ky., Apr. 16, 1937; s. Willie Marian and Katherine (Fleming) R.; m. Patricia Ann Phillips, Aug. 25, 1961; children: Elizabeth Ann, Katherine Ann. BS, Austin Peay State U., 1959; M Ch. Music, So. Sem., Louisville, 1966. Min. music Guthrie (Ky.) Bapt. Ch., 1957-59, 1st Bapt. Ch., Hopkinsville, Ky., 1959-61, Lyndon Bapt. Ch., Louisville, 1963-72, 1st Bapt. Ch., Montgomery, Ala., 1972—; music fieldwork adviser So. Sem., Louisville, 1968-72, guest lectr., 1967, 68, 69, 76. mem. exec. coun. So. Bapt. Ch. Music, 1989-91; vis. prof. So. Bapt. Theol. Sem., summer 1990. Author, composer for Broadman Press, 1973—. Pres. Bapt. Student Union, Austin Peay State U., Clarksville, Tenn., 1958-59; mem. exec. com. Tenn. State Bapt. Student Union, 1958-59; mem. faculty Ridgecrest Bapt. Assembly, 1968, Glorieta Bapt. Assembly, 1974. Mem. Am. Guild Organists, Choristers Guild (pres. 1974-75), So. Bapt. Ch. Music Conf. Home: 2444 Winchester Rd Montgomery AL 36106 Office: 1st Bapt Ch 305 S Perry St Montgomery AL 36106

ROPER, JOHN DEE, minister, lawyer; b. Oklahoma City, Feb. 15, 1935; s. Clay M. and Hester Ann (Campbell) R.; m. Suzy Baldwin, Mar. 16, 1957; children: Jeffrey Howard, Peggy Lynn Roper Cook, Sally Jo Roper Morris. BBA, U. Okla., 1956, LLB, 1958; STM, So. Meth. U., 1990. Bar: Okla., 1958, Kans. 1970; ordained to ministry Episcopal Ch. as deacon, 1981. Deacon St. James Episcopal Ch., Dallas, 1989-90, St. John's Episcopal Ch., Wichita, Kans., 1983-88, 90—; pvt. practice, Wichita, 1990—; chmn. refugee com. Episcopal Ch., Kans., 1982-87. Author: Pathways to Leadership, 1991. Home and Office: 14802 Willowbend Circle Wichita KS 67230

ROPER, LARRY LESTER, pastor, school administrator; b. England, Ark., June 10, 1948; s. Lloyd Lester and Ruth Ella (White) R.; m. Linda Lou Hornbarger, May 15, 1971; children: Larry Lester Jr., Angelica Marie. BS, So. Bible Coll., Houston, 1973. Ordained to ministry Pentecostal Ch. of God., 1974. Pastor Pentecostal Ch. of God, Clio, Mich., 1974-77; state youth dir. Pentecostal Ch. of God, St. Johns, Mich., 1977-79; pastor Pentecostal Ch. of God, Clio, 1979-80; pastor, adminstr. Pentecostal Ch. of God, Antioch, Calif., 1980-86, 91—; sec.-treas. State Yuth Pentecostal Ch. of God, Camden, Mich., 1976-77; presbyter Pentecostal Ch. of God, Citrus Heights, Calif., 1986—; advisor Women's Aglow, Antioch, 1987—. Republican. Home: 415 W 6th St Antioch CA 94509 Office: Living Word Pentecostal Ch 415 W 6th St Antioch CA 94509 *Life never seems to go as planned. The one constant in this world is that nothing seems to remain the same. How important, in an everchanging world, to find the Creator of life, of whom He declares in His Word "never changes."*

ROPER, PAUL DUANE, minister; b. Glenwood, Colo., June 18, 1951; s. Roy Edwin and Georgia Dean (Strobbe) R.; m. Linda June Napier, Aug. 12, 1972; children: Jody, Sarah, John. BTh, Tenn. Temple U., 1973, BB, 1974; postgrad., Denver Sem., 1987. Ordained to ministry Ind. Bapt. Ch., 1974. Pastor Bay St. Bapt. Ch., Pine Bluff, Ark., 1974-78, Greenland Bapt. Ch., Beecher City, Ill., 1978-83; asst. pastor Calvary Bapt. Ch., Flora, Ill., 1983-84; pastor Elmwood Bapt. Ch., Brighton, Colo., 1984—; pres. Gospel Lit. Mission to India, 1988—; adminstr. Elmwood Bapt. Sch., 1984—. Author: From the Wells of Salvation, 1978, Principles of Hermenutics, 1982, Symphony of Psalms, 1985, A Divine Photo Album, 1988. Chaplain Jefferson County Sheriff's Dept., Pine Bluff, 1977. Mem. Am. Assn. Christian Schs., Southwide Bapt. Fellowship, Tenn. Temple Reg. Alumni Assn. (pres. 1988—). Home: 13100 E 144th Ave Brighton CO 80601 Office: Elmwood Bapt Ch 13100 E 144th Ave Brighton CO 80601

ROPER, STEPHEN ROBERT, minister; b. Franklin, N.C., Oct. 5, 1962; s. Terrel Robert and Mary Louise (Long) R.; m. Rhonda Jo Von Cannon. BS, Appalachian State U., 1983; postgrad., So. Baptist Theol. Sem. Cert. social worker; ordained to ministry Bapt. Ch., 1985. Minister youth Cross Meml. Bapt. Ch., Marion, N.C., 1980; dir. recreation N.C. Bapt. Childrens Homes, Thomasville, 1981; social worker Watauga County Dept. Social Services, Boone, N.C., 1983-84; minister youth First Bapt. Ch., Franklin, N.C., 1984-85; assoc. campus ministries Carson-Newman Coll., Jefferson City, Tenn., 1985-86; dir. youth ministries Christ Ch. United Meth., Louisville, 1986—; leader seminar Fgn. Missions Study, 1980-83, div. youth and campus ministries Bapt. State Conv., 1981-83, student work dept. Tenn. Bapt. Conv., 1986. Named one of Outstanding Young Men Am, U.S. Jaycees, 1984. Mem. Assn. So. Bapt. Campus Ministers, Bapt. Student Unions N.C. (state pres.). Democrat. Avocations: reading, fishing, hunting, tennis, softball. Office: Christ Ch United Meth 4614 Brownsboro Rd Louisville KY 40207

ROQUE, FRANCIS XAVIER, auxiliary bishop; b. Providence, Oct. 9, 1928; s. Warren Edward Roque and Mary Loretta Gallagher. B.A., Saint John's Sem., 1950. ordained priest Roman Catholic, 1953. Parish priest Diocese of Providence, 1953-61; army chaplain U.S. Army, 1961-83; bishop Mil. Vicariate, N.Y.C., 1983—. Served to col. U.S. Army, 1961-83, Vietnam. Decorated Bronze Star. Office: Archdiocese for the Mil Services USA 962 Wayne Ave Silver Spring MD 20910

ROSAZZA, PETER ANTHONY, bishop; b. New Haven, Feb. 13, 1935; s. Aldo Massimiliano and Agatha Dolores (Dinneen) R. Student, Dartmouth Coll.; A.A., St. Thomas Sem., Bloomfield, Conn., 1955; B.A., St. Bernard Sem., Rochester, N.Y., 1957; postgrad., Seminaire Saint Sulpice, Paris; M.A., Middlebury Coll., 1967. Ordained priest Roman Catholic Ch., 1961; consecrated bishop, 1978; asst. pastor St. Timothy Ch., West Hartford, Conn., 1961-63; instr. modern langs. St. Thomas Sem., 1963-72; co-pastor Sacred Heart Ch., Hartford, Conn., from 1972; dir. Apostolate to Hispanics for Archdiocese of Hartford, 1972-78; aux. bishop Archdiocese of Hartford and titular bishop of Oppido Nuovo, 1978—; bd. dirs. Archdiocesan Office Urban Affairs. Mem. Nat. Conf. Cath. Bishops, U.S. Cath. Conf. Office: Chancery Office 134 Farmington Ave Hartford CT 06105

ROSE, AUBERT VERNER, JR., minister; b. Cleve., Apr. 5, 1926; s. Aubert V. Sr. and Sophia D. (Meyer) R.; m. Katheren M. Rudd, Dec. 24, 1946; children: Ann, Esther, Sarah. B in Bible Studies, Mid-Continent Coll., 1953; BS, Bethel Coll., 1954; DRE, So. Bapt. Ctr., 1987. Ordained to ministry So. Bapt. Conv., 1951. Pastor Bapt. Chs., Ky., Tenn., 1950-77; evangelist, pres. Ch. Renewal Crusades, Inc., various locations, 1977—. Author: How to Double Your Church, 1987. Republican. Home: 110 Morningside Dr Benton KY 42025 Office: Ch Renewal Crusades 110 Morningside Dr Benton KY 42025

ROSE, BENJAMIN LACY, minister; b. Fayetteville, N.C., Dec. 12, 1914; s. Charles Grandison and Irene (Lacy) R.; m. Anne Claiborne Thompson, June 23, 1938; children: Anne C., Margaret R., Lucy A., Ben L. Jr. AB, Davidson Coll., 1935; BD, Union Theol. Sem., 1938, ThM, ThD, 1950, 55; DD, King Coll., 1952, Davidson Coll., 1974. Ordained to ministry Presbyn. Ch., 1938. Pastor Chinquapin (N.C.) Ch., 1938-41, Cen. Ch., Bristol, Va., 1946-55, First Ch., Wilmington, N.C., 1956-57; prof. Union Theol. Sem., Richmond, Va., 1957-73; pastor Chapel on Boardwalk, Wrightsville Beach, N.C., 1973-78; minister Hebron Presbyn. Ch., Manakin Sabot, Va., 1982—; pastor to pastors Wilmington Presbytery, 1973-78; trustee Peace Coll., Raleigh, 1957-63, St. Andrews Presbyn. Coll., Laurinburg, N.C., 1957-60, Union Theol. Sem., Richmond, 1952-55; moderator Gen. Assembly Presbyn. Ch., Massenetta Springs, Va., 1971. Author: Confirming Your Call, 1967, The Ten Commandments in Modern Life, 1985, On Your Way Rejoicing, 1991; editor Questions & Answers in Presbyterian Survey, 1959-89. Col.

U.S. Army, 1941-46. Recipient Lifetime Citizenship award, 1955, Disting. Alumnus award Davidson Coll., 1985, Bronze Star medal U.S. Army, 1944, Legion of Merit medal, 1946, Oak Leaf Cluster to Legion of Merit medal U.S. Army, 1984. Mem. Assn. Sem. Profs. in Practical Fields (sec., treas. 1960-64), Kappa Sigma Frat. Home and Office: 1221 Rennie Ave Richmond VA 23227

ROSE, DOUGLAS RAYMOND, minister; b. San Antonio, Sept. 26, 1942; s. Raymond Alvin and Paula (Schober) R.; m. Esther Copeland, May 14, 1966; children: Richard Douglas, Aimée Raeanne. AA, Southwestern Jr. Coll., 1963; student, Cen. Bible Coll. Sem., 1963-64; BS, Southwestern Assembly God Coll, 1965; postgrad., U. Iowa, 1982. Ordained to ministry Assemblies of God, 1967. Sr. pastor Bethel Assembly of God, DeKalb, Ill., 1967-69; sr. pastor 1st Assembly of God, Kankakee, Ill., 1969-76, Bettendorf, Iowa, 1976-83; sr. pastor Bethel Life Ctr., Wichita, Kans., 1983-85, 1st Assembly of God, Belleville, Ill., 1985—; sec. Ill. state missions com. Assemblies of God, 1987—, state music dir., Chgo., 1971-76; bd. dirs. Christian Youth Ctr., Berkley, W.Va., 1966-67; bd. dirs., pres. Bethel Life Sch., Wichita, 1983-85; leader Holy Land Tour, Israel and Rome, 1972; pres. Ministerial Assn., Kankakee, 1972-75; presbyter section VII, Assemblies of God, Davenport, Iowa, 1980-83; bd. dirs. Sedgewick County Prison Ministries, Wichita, 1983-85. Contbr. articles to religious publs. Mem. Ill. Task Force, 1989—. Named Journalist of Yr., Ford Motor Co., 1961, City's Favorite Pastor, Belleville Jour.-News, 1990, Pastor of the Week, KSIV Radio, 1991. Mem. Nat. Assn. Christian Counselors, Belleville Clergy Assn., Assemblies of God Christian Edn. Assn., Metro-East Clergy Assn. (asst. presbyter 1988—). Office: 1st Assembly of God 900 Fair Oaks Ave Belleville IL 62221 *The family is God's masterpiece. Family trees are likely to produce inferior fruit unless they are watchfully pruned of spurious growth and sprayed with the essence of the 10 Commandments. Home is the seminary of all other institutions.*

ROSE, GARY MICHAEL, minister; b. Galion, Ohio, July 9, 1957; s. Wilbur Ruskin Rose and Gwendoline Mary (Burton) Thompson; m. Ruth Elaine Varner, Aug. 30, 1986. Student, Ohio Inst. Tech., 1975, Hartnell Coll., 1978; BA, Ft. Steilacoom Coll., 1981, Pacific Luth. U., 1982. Corp. asst. mgr. Care Pharmacies, Salinas, Calif., 1976-81; packer, loader Kaiser Refractories, Moss Landing, Calif., 1981; counselor, program dir. Mt. Cross Bible Camp, Felton, Calif., 1982-84; vicar Bethlehem Luth. Ch., Chesterton, Ind., 1984-85; parish pastor Evang. Luth. Ch., Mankato, Kansas, 1986—. Chmn. Jewell County (Kans.) Drug and Alcohol Bd., 1987—; v.p., bd. dir. Mankato Library, 1987—, mem. book com., 1986—; asst. scoutmaster Mankato Troop 36 Boy Scouts Am., 1986—. Mem. United Luth. Ministries (pub. rels. 1987). Democrat. Avocations: chess, aikido, reading, fishing, golf. Home: 202 South Ctr Mankato KS 66956 Office: Evang Luth Ch 119 E South St Mankato KS 66956

ROSE, HERBERT HERMAN, rabbi; b. N.Y.C., Nov. 13, 1929; s. Morris M. and Etta (Millens) R.; m. Esther Burgin, June 5, 1955; children: Judah, Ben Zion, Eve, Regina. BA, U. Cin., 1950; BHL, Hebrew Union Coll., Cin., 1952, MHL, 1955, DHL, 1962. Ordained rabbi, 1955. Rabbi Temple Emanuel, Livingston, N.J., 1957-62, Temple Ohr Elohim, L.I., 1962-65, Beth Ohr, Bklyn., 1978-82, Congregation Har HaShem, Boulder, Colo., 1982—; pres. N.Y. Assn. Reform Rabbis, 1969-70. Author: Life and Thoughts of A.D. Gordon, 1964; contbr. articles to religious jours. Exec. bd. Interfaith Coun. of Boulder, 1989—; bd. dirs. Anti-Defamation League of Denver, 1985-91; chmn. L.I. Com. for Soviet Jewry, 1964; bd. dirs. Menorah - Adult Jewish Edn., Boulder, 1988—. Recipient State of Israel Bond award, 1967. Mem. Rocky Mt. Rabbinical Coun. (pres. 1987-88), L.I. Assn. Reform Rabbis, Rocky Mt. Am.-Israel Friendship League (bd. dirs. 1989-91), Rocky Mt. Rabbinical Coun. (bd. dirs. 1982-91). Home: 523 Aztec Boulder CO 80303 Office: Congregation Har HaShem 3950 Baseline Rd Boulder CO 80303

ROSE, JOSEPH HUGH, clergyman; b. Jewett, Ohio, Nov. 21, 1934; s. Joseph Harper and Lottie Louella (VanAllen) R.; m. Nila Jayne Habig, Feb. 14, 1958; children: J. Hugh II, Stephanie Jayne, David William, Dawnella Jayne. ThB, Apostolic Bible Inst., St. Paul, 1955, DD, 1990. Ordained United Pentecostal Ch. Assoc. min. Calvary Tabernacle, Indpls., 1956-73; Ind. youth sec. United Pentecostal Ch., 1958-60, Ind. youth pres., 1960-72; bd. edn. United Pentecostal Ch., Hazelwood, Mo., 1974—; presbyter Ohio dist. United Pentecostal Ch., 1975—; pastor Harrison Hills Ch., Jewett, Ohio, 1973—. Editor, Ind. Dist. News, 1959-70; narrator radio svc. Harvestime, 1961—. Republican. Avocations: travel, classical music. Office: United Pentecostal Ch 8855 Dunn Rd Hazelwood MO 63042

ROSE, MARTIN ENGELBERT, theology educator; b. Wuppertal, Fed. Republic Germany, Sept. 30, 1947; arrived in Switzerland, 1976; s. Eugen and Martha (Trube) R.; m. Friedgard Stursberg, Dec. 7, 1972; children: Eva-Maria, Sonja, Christian. Cert. theology, U. Muenster, Fed. Republic Germany, 1971, ThD, 1974; ThD, U. Zurich, 1979. Sci. collaborator Patristic Commn. of Acad. Sci., Muenster, 1971-73; asst. Kirchliche Hochschule Bethel, Bielefeld, Fed. Republic Germany, 1974-76; asst. U. Zurich, 1976-80, asst. prof., 1980-84; reverend Reformed Ch. Zurich, Dinhard, Switzerland, 1980-84; prof. U. Neuchâtel, Switzerland, 1984—; vis. prof. Kirchliche Hochschule Berlin, Fed. Republic Germany, 1983. Author: The Exclusivity of Yahveh, 1975, Yahveh: The quarrels about the name of God, 1978, Deuteronomist and Yahvist, 1981. Mem. Soc. Rsch. of Old Orient. Home: Plan de la Croix 38, CH-2123 Saint-Sulpice Switzerland Office: U Neuchâtel, Faubourg de l'Hôpital 41, CH-2000 Neuchâtel Switzerland

ROSE, MICHAEL ALLEN, minister; b. Evansville, Ind., Mar. 13, 1956; s. Harold Lee and M. Jean (Barnfield) R.; m. S. Dawn Clapp, June 23, 1990. Student, Austin Peay State U., 1974-78; MusB, Ky. Wesleyan Coll., 1979; M Ch. Music, So. Bapt. Theol. Sem. Ordained to ministry So. Bapt. Conv., 1980. Min. music Whitesville (Ky.) Bapt. Ch., 1978-81, Henderson Meml. Bapt. Ch., Hopkinsville, Ky., 1981-86; assoc. min. music Cadiz (Ky.) Bapt. Ch., 1986—. Contbr. articles to jours. in field. Chmn. Champions Against Drugs, Trigg County, Ky., 1988-90; treas., Pennyroyal Region, 1990-91. Mem. Ky. Bapt. Music Assn. Home: 38 Bay Colony St PO Box 1178 Cadiz KY 42211 Office: Cadiz Bapt Ch 82 Main St PO Box 606 Cadiz KY 42211

ROSE, NATHAN HOWARD, principal; b. Jersey City, Oct. 3, 1952; s. Albert and Dorothy (Levin) R.; m. Beverly Kahan, Dec. 28, 1975; children: Lauren, Steven, Jonathan. BA, Rutgers U., 1974; MS, Yeshiva U., 1980. Cert. tchr. Dir. edn. Huntington (N.Y.) Jewish Ctr., 1977-80; dir. edn., asst. rabbi Temple Beth Sholom, Haddon Heights, N.J., 1980-82; dir. edn. Temple Beth El, Rochester, N.Y., 1982—; prin. Midrasha Community Hebrew High Sch., Rochester, 1982—. Author: Response, 1988, Noah's Ark, 1989. Mem. N.Y. Bd. Rabbis, Rochester Bd. Rabbis, Jewish Educators Assembly, Coun. for Jewish Educators. Office: Temple Beth El 139 S Winton Rd Rochester NY 14610

ROSE, ROBERT JOHN, bishop; b. Grand Rapids, Mich., Feb. 28, 1930; s. Urban H. and Maida A. (Glerum) R. Student, St. Joseph Sem., 1944-50; B.A., Seminaire de Philosophie, Montreal, Que., Can., 1952; S.T.L., Pontifical Urban U., Rome, 1956; M.A., U. Mich., 1962. Ordained priest Roman Catholic Ch., 1955; dean St. Joseph Sem., Grand Rapids, 1966-69; dir. Christopher House, Grand Rapids, 1969-71; rector St. John's Sem., Plymouth, Mich., 1971-77; pastor Sacred Heart Parish, Muskegon Heights, Mich., 1977-81; bishop Diocese of Gaylord, Mich., 1981-89, Diocese of Grand Rapids, Mich., 1989—; sec.-treas. Mich. Cath. Conf., Lansing, 1983. Mem. Nat. Conf. Cath. Bishops.

ROSE, SUSAN A. SCHULTZ, retired theological librarian; b. Mountain Lake, Minn., Dec. 22, 1911; d. David. D. and Anna (Eitzen) Schultz; m. Delbert R. Rose, Dec. 27, 1986. BA, John Fletcher Coll., 1940; BSLS, U. Ill., 1946, MLS, 1949; LittD (hon.), Houghton Coll., 1974. Dean women John Fletcher-Kletzing Coll., University Park, Iowa, 1940-45; asst. libr. Bethany (Okla.) Coll., 1946-47; dir. libr. svcs. Asbury Theol. Sem., Wilmore, Ky., 1949-78, ret., 1978; cons. grad. schs. theology librs. The Philippines, 1978-80, Nairobi, Kenya, 1983-84, Zagreb, Yugoslavia, 1984, Taiwan, Korea, Japan, 1987, Allahabad, India, 1989, Kericho, Kenya, 1989, Manila, 1990; cons. grad. schs. theology librs. Wesley Bibl. Sem., Jackson, Miss., 1987—; mem. exec. com. 1st Alliance Ch., Lexington, Ky., 1958-61, 66-73; del. to nat. coun. Christian and Missionary Alliance, Columbus, Ohio, 1964, to Nat. Congress on Edn., St. Paul, 1970. Contbr. articles to profl. jours. Sunday sch. tchr. 1st Alliance Ch., Lexington, 1951-70; mem. libr. bd. Withers-Jessamine County Libr., Nicholasville, Ky., 1966-77. Recipient Outstanding Spl. Libr. of Yr. award Ky. Trustees Assn., 1967, Disting. Svc. award Asbury Theol. Sem., 1974, Emily Russell award Assn. Christian Librs. , 1974, Disting. Alumnus award Vennard Coll. (successor to John Fletcher-Kletzing Coll.), 1982. Mem. Am. Theol. Libr. Assn. (ret., exec. sec. 1967-71, dir. 1974-77), Wesley Theol. Soc. (ret.), Christian Holiness Assn., Ky. Libr. Assn. (bd. dirs. 1960—, sect. chair 1966-67). Mem. Christian and Missionary Alliance. Home: 6228 Tanglewood Dr Jackson MS 39213 *To me life is two-dimensional. Total commitment to God is basic, then, neither knowingly exploit another nor permit another to exploit me. By helping others set worthy goals and achieve them I have found fulfillment. What a joy, years later to hear: "You changed my life course for the better. Thank You!".*

ROSE, T. T., bishop. Bishop of Cen. Ill., Ch. of God in Christ, Springfield. Office: Ch of God in Crist 1000 Dr Taylor Rose Sq Springfield IL 62703*

ROSE-HEIM, WILLIAM BENTLEY, minister, mediator, mental health therapist; b. Syracuse, N.Y., Aug. 29, 1955; s. William Bentley and Marilynn Ann Rose; m. Irma Diana Ruiz, Jan. 4, 1975 (div. Oct. 1985); children: Daniel Joseph, Christina Marie, Elizabeth Ann; m. Donna Rae Heim, May 16, 1986; 1 child, Zachariah Shalom. AA, Riverside (Calif.) City Coll., 1979; BA, Rockhurst Coll., 1980; MDiv, St. Paul Sch. Theology, Kansas City, Mo., 1986. Ordained to ministry Christian Ch., 1987. Pastoral assoc. Curé of Ars Cath. Ch., Leawood, 1979-83, St. Francis Xavier Cath. Ch., Kansas City, 1983-85; pastoral asst. St. Luke Presbyn. Ch., Kansas City, 1985-87; co-pastor 1st Christian Ch., Odessa, Mo., 1987—; mental health therapist West Cen. Mo. Mental Health Ctr., Warrensburg, 1990—; instr. in theology Rockhurst High Sch., Kansas City, 1980-84; vol. chaplain intern VA Med. Ctr., 1986-89, asst. chief chaplain, 1988; chairperson dept. ch. and soc. Christian Ch. of Mid.-Am., Jefferson City, Mo., 1989—; founder, mediator Helping Hand Dispute Resolution Svcs., 1991—. Co-founder Odessa Alanon Family Group, 1987-90, Odessa R/7 Friends for Youth, 1987—; sec. bd. dirs. Odessa Habitat for Humanity, 1989-90; co-founder Odessa Outreach-West Cen. Mo. Mental Health Ctr., 1990; co-founder, acting exec. dir. Odessa Community Svc. Ctr., 1991—. Mem. AACD, Am. Mental Health Counselors Assn., Assn. Disciple Musicians, Acad. Family Mediators, Hymn Soc. Am. Avocations: rock-climbing, music composition, writing, woodcraft, guitarist. Home: 600 S 5th St Odessa MO 64076 Office: 1st Christian Ch 224 W Dryden Odessa MO 64076 *Travelers tread lightly, your soles unshod. All ground is holy and barefoot God.*

ROSEKOPF, THOMAS ARTHUR, minister; b. Grand Rapids, Mich., May 13, 1958; s. Arthur William and Ruth Ann (Hazewinkel) R.; m. Dana Denise Lineberry, May 26, 1979; children: Reuben, Jacob, Luke. BS, Faith Bapt. Bible Coll., 1981. Cert. lic. gospel ministry Bapt. Ch., 1981. Assoc. pastor Burton Ave. Bapt. Ch., Waterloo, Iowa, 1981-84; dir. telemktg. Regular Bapt. Ch., Schaumburg, Ill., 1984-86; assoc. pastor 1st Bapt. Ch., Pana, Ill., 1986—; mem. com. Ill., Mo. State Youth Com., 1989—; chmn. Cen. Ill. Regional Bapt. Youth, 1990-91. Office: 1st Bapt Ch 114 S Maple St Pana IL 62557

ROSEN, AVRAM ABBOT, lawyer, consultant, organization executive; b. N.Y.C., June 7, 1915; s. Bernard Jules and Augusta (Carton) R.; m. Charlotte Zion, Sept. 27, 1949; children: Bernard Joshua, Julie Beth. B.A., Yale Coll., 1934; LL.B., Columbia U., 1937. Bar: N.Y. 1937. Gen. practice law N.Y.C., 1937-42; atty. U.S. Dept. Justice, Washington, 1942-43; spl. asst. to atty. gen. Tom Clark N.Y., N.J. and Pa., 1946-47; chief civil rights sect. Dept. Justice, Washington, mem. U.S. del. to UN, 1947-48; Midwest dir. Anti-Defamation League of B'nai B'rith, Chgo., 1948-85. Served with AUS, 1943-46, ETO. Recipient Chgo. Commn. on Human Relations Thomas H. Wright award, 1958; recipient Founders' Day award Loyola U., 1965. Jewish.

ROSEN, DAVID MOSES, rabbi, religious community leader; b. Moinesti, Romania, July 23, 1912; s. Abraham Leib and Taube Rosen; m. Amalia Ruckenstein, June 14, 1949. Rabbinical studies, U. Bucharest, Romania; PhD (honoris causa), Yeshiva U. Ordained rabbi. Rabbi Falticeni, Romania, 1938-40, Suceava, Romania, 1940; rabbi Reschit-Daat and Beit Eil synagogues, 1940-45, Grand Synagogue, Bucharest; chief rabbi of Romania; pres. Fedn. Jewish Communities. Author: And the bush Was Not Burned, 1978, Dangers, Tests, Miracles, 1990. Recipient Shazar award; David Moses Rosen chair established in his honor, Bar Ilan U. Mem. Conf. European Rabbis (standing com.), World Jewish Congress (governing bd.). Home: St Maria Rosetti 12, Bucharest Romania Office: Fedn Jewish Communities, Sfinta Vineri, Bucharest Romania

ROSEN, MOISHE, religious organization administrator; b. Kansas City, Mo., Apr. 12, 1932; s. Ben and Rose (Baker) R.; m. Ceil Starr, Aug. 18, 1950; children: Lyn Rosen Bond, Ruth. Diploma, Northeastern Bible Coll., 1957; DD, Western Conservative Bapt. Sem., 1986. Ordained to ministry Bapt. Ch., 1957. Missionary Am. Bd. Missions to the Jews, N.Y.C., 1956; minister in charge Beth Sar Shalom Am. Bd. Missions to the Jews, Los Angeles, 1957-67; dir. recruiting and tng. Am. Bd. Missions to the Jews, N.Y.C., 1967-70; leader Jews for Jesus Movement, San Francisco, 1970-73, exec. dir., 1973—, founder, chmn., 1973—; speaker in field. Author: Saying of Chairman Moishe, 1972, Jews for Jesus, 1974, Share the New Life with a Jew, 1976, Christ in the Passover, 1977, Y'shua, The Jewish Way to Say Jesus, 1982, Overture to Armageddon, 1991. Trustee Western Conservative Bapt. Sem., Portland, Oreg., 1979-85, 86—, Bibl. Internat. Coun. on Bibl. Inerrancy, Oakland, Calif., 1979-89; bd. dirs. Christian Advs. Serving Evangelism. Office: Jews for Jesus 60 Haight St San Francisco CA 94102

ROSEN, SANFORD EDWARD, rabbi; b. Cleve., May 13, 1920; s. Sanford Edward and Helen Myrtle (Frank) R.; m. Melba Mary Mells, Mar. 19, 1944; children: Ronald Milton, Louise Judith Rosen-Garcia. BA, Western Res. U., 1941; B of Hebrew Letters, Hebrew Union Coll., Cin., 1943, M of Hebrew Letters, 1947, D of Hebrew Letters, 1975; DD (hon.), Hebrew Union Coll., L.A., 1972. Ordained rabbi, 1947. Founding rabbi Temple Beth El, Bakersfield, Calif., 1947-51; founding rabbi Peninsula Temple Beth El, San Mateo, Calif., 1951-82, rabbi emeritus, 1982—. Bd. govs. Jewish Inst. Religion, Hebrew Union Coll., Cin., 1962-66; mem. gov.'s adv. com. on children and youth, Sacramento, Calif., 1958-62; co-founder Conf. on Religion, Race and Social Concern, San Mateo County, 1963. Recipient Human Family award Conf. on Religion, Race and Social Concern, 1981. Mem. Cen. Conf. Am. Rabbis (exec. bd. 1968-70), Bd. Rabbis No. Calif. (pres. 1963-65), Pacific Assn. Reform Rabbis (several offices 1952-56). Office: Peninsula Temple Beth El 1700 Alameda de las Pulgas San Mateo CA 94403

ROSENBAUM, IRVING JOSEPH, rabbi, educational administrator; b. Omaha, Dec. 20, 1921; s. David and Rose (Lederman) R.; m. Ruth Groner, Feb. 27, 1944; children: Roy, Don, Susan, Alan. B.A., U. Chgo., 1943; B.H.L., Rabbi, Hebrew Theol. Coll., 1945, D.H.L., 1977. Rabbi, 1945; nat. dir. religious dept. Anti-Defamation League of B'nai B'rith, 1944-55; curator Lasker Fellowship Program in Civil Liberties and Civil Rights Brandeis U., 1959-60; exec. v.p. Chgo. Bd. Rabbis, 1960-63; also bd. dirs.; rabbi Chgo. Loop Synagogue, 1963-77; pres. Jewish U. Am., Skokie, Ill., 1977-80, Hebrew Theol. Coll., Skokie, 1977-80; exec. v.p. Inst. for Computers in Jewish Life, 1980—. Author: weekly column Rabbi at Random in Chgo; Sentinel and other Anglo-Jewish newspapers, 1963—; producer, dir.: motion picture Your Neighbor Celebrates, 1949; Author (with O. Tarcov) Your Neighbor Celebrates, 1955, The Holocaust and Halakha, 1974; Contbr. articles to profl. publs. Mem. Religious Edn. Assn. (dir.), Rabbinical Council Am., Chgo. Rabbinical Council. Home: 6725 N Mozart St Chicago IL 60645 Office: 845 N Michigan Ave Suite 843 Chicago IL 60611

ROSENBAUM, STANLEY NED, theology educator; b. Dec. 8, 1939; s. Stanley Menz and Wilma (Nussbaum) R.; m. Mary Helene Pottker, Sept. 2, 1963; children: Sarah Catherine, William David, Ephraim Samuel. BA, Tulane U., 1961; postgrad., U. Chgo., 1961-64; MA, Brandeis U., 1967, PhD, 1974. Assoc. prof. Dickinson Coll., Carlisle, Pa., 1970-90; counselor Dickinson Coll., Hillel, 1971—; prof. Dickinson Coll., Carlisle, 1990—. Author: Amos of Israel: A New Interpretation, 1990, Celebrating Our Differences: Living Two Faiths in One Marriage, 1991; contbr. articles to religious publs. Woodrow Wilson fellow, 1961. Mem. AAUP, Assn. Jewish Studies, Nat. Assn. Profs. Hebrew, Am. Acad. Religion. Home: 431 S College St Carlisle PA 17013 Office: Dickinson Coll Box 162 Carlisle PA 17013 *Biblical scholarship is a form of worship undertaken by those who cannot sing.*

ROSENBERG, HENRI, advocate, rabbinic barrister; b. Antwerp, Belgium, May 1, 1950; s. Salomon and Gerda (Tobias) R.; m. Anita Kaszirer, May 23, 1974; children: Natasha Bella, Amanda Ethel, David, Salomon, Gershon, Dimitri. Licenciate in polit. and social scis., Cath. U., Louvain, 1974; grad. Jewish legal studies, Cen. Talmudic Acad., Jerusalem and Boston, 1977; LLD, U. Antwerp, 1985; M of Rabbinic Law, United Israel Insts., Jerusalem, 1985; postgrad. in Am. law, Columbia U., 1986, Leyden U., 1986; postgrad. in port and maritime law, U. Ghent, 1986; grad. parapsychology, Acad. Paranormal Scis., 1986; postgrad. internat. banking and fin., City U., London, 1987, U. Ghent, 1987—; LLD, U. Somerset, 1989; JD, Columbia Pacific Univ., 1989; Dr., Kensington U., Glendale, Calif., 1989; PhD, Somerset (England) U., 1990. Ordained rabbi, 1974. Asst. mgr. Scientific Translation Internat., Jerusalem, 1974-76; mgr. chem. dept. McGison PVBA, Antwerp, 1976-78; mng. dir. Intra Diamond Co. NV, Antwerp, 1978-85; advocate, Rabbinic barrister, researcher Inter-Univ. Ctr. for State Law, Brussels, 1987—. Author: Israel and the USSR: 20 Years of Diplomatic Negotiations, 1947-67, 1974, Aspects of Jewish Law: A Compilation, 1984, Lex Regni lex Est, 1988, Chaim Lerosh, 1988, Chaim Beyad, 1990. Founder, adminstrv. pres. Belgian Jewish Students' Front, 1970; co-founder, mem. com., spokesman coordinating com. Belgian Jewish Youth Orgns., 1971; mem. Israelite Community of Antwerp; pres. Keren Tobias Found.; chmn. Jewish Consumer's Def. Assn., v.z.w. Goedkosjer-non profit assn., 1989—. Home: Belgielei 195, 2018 Antwerp Belgium Office: Belgielei 195B, 2018 Antwerp Belgium

ROSENBERG, ROY A., rabbi; b. Balt., Dec. 22, 1930; s. H. Harry and Sylvia (Caplan) R.; m. Ruth Herzberger, Aug. 26, 1956; children: Raoul, Risa, Rani, Rianne, Remi. BA, U. Pa., 1951; MA, Hebrew Union Coll., 1955, DHL, 1964, DD (hon.), 1980. Ordained rabbi, 1955. Rabbi Temple Emanu-El, Rochester, N.Y., 1953-56; chaplain U.S. Army, 1956-58; rabbi Temple Emanu-El, Honolulu, 1958-66, Temple Sinai, New Orleans, 1966-70; Beth Shalom Peoples Temple, Bklyn., 1972-75; rabbi Temple Universal Judaism, N.Y.C., 1970—, 1975—. Author, translator: The Anatomy of God, 1973; author: Who Was Jesus?, 1986, Happily Intermarried, 1988, The Concise Guide to Judaism: History, Practice, Faith, 1990. 1st lt. U.S. Army, 1956-58. Mem. Soc. Bibl. Lit., Cen. Conf. Am. Rabbis, B'nai B'rith Lodge (pres. 1964-66). Democrat. Office: Temple Universal Judaism 1010 Park Ave New York NY 10028 *Biblical faith is rooted in the sense of covenant that links nations to God. Because the Jewish people over its history has plumbed the depths of despair and survived, Jewish faith must teach its followers to choose life for the entire human family. Because the Jewish people seeks to know God, it must seek to make His moral law the possession of all people, for all have a share in God.*

ROSENBERGER, BERYL GUY, pastor; b. Scotland County, Md., Jan. 4, 1935; s. Guy and Elva (Stott) R.; m. Mary Emma Adams, Sept. 8, 1958; children: John, Richard, Peter, James, Thomas, Mary Elizabeth. Student, Occidental Coll., 1953-55, U. Md., 1956-57; BA, Ga. State U., 1960-61; BD, MDiv, Columbia Theol. Sem., 1962; postgrad., Fuller Theol. Sem., 1990—. Pastor Roberts/Linley Presbyn. Chs., Anderson, S.C., 1961-66, Ga. Ave. Presbyn. Ch., Atlanta, 1966-74, Midway Presbyn. Ch., Anderson, 1974-89; dir. Healing Ministries for Ch., Anderson, 1990—; commr. Gen. Assembly Presbyn. Ch. Am., Montreat, N.C., 1965, Ft. Worth, 1973. With U.S. Army, 1955-58, capt. USNR, ret. Home: 2207 Boulevard Heights Anderson SC 29621

ROSENBERGER, DALE BRIAN, minister; b. Detroit, Mar. 13, 1954; s. Burton Wayne and Margaret Dolores (Cottrell) R.; m. Patricia Hirt, Aug. 20, 1977; children: Greta, Lise. PhB, Thomas Jefferson Coll., 1974; MDiv, Yale U. Divinity Sch., 1979. Ordained to ministry, 1979. Interim minister St. Peter's United Ch. of Christ, Champaign, Ill., 1979-80; minister Trinity United Ch. of Christ, Westville, Ill., 1980-85; sr. minister First Congl. United Ch. of Christ, Columbus, Ohio, 1985—. Author (sermon): Christian Ministry, 1990, Pulpit Digest, 1991, Best Sermons III, 1990. Office: First Congl Ch 444 E Broad St Columbus OH 43215

ROSENBERGER, GLEN MOYER, religion counselor; b. Sellersville, Pa., Nov. 8, 1941; s. Leroy and Dorothy (Moyer) R.; M. Ruth Marie Ritterbusch, Aug. 4, 1965; children: Dawn Marie, Lisa Grace, Cara Renee. BA in Bible, Bob Jones U., 1964; MA, Columbia Pacific U., 2989, postgrad., 1989—. Dir. John 5:24 Gospel Rescue Mission, Phila., 1964—; founder, dir. Temple Student Life Ctr., Phila., 1975—; bd. dirs. Livingstone Meml. Mission, Quakertown, Pa. Mem. Pennridge Community Action Team, Sellersville, 1988—. Office: Student Life Ctr 507 Rte 113 Sellersville PA 18960

ROSENBLOOM, AVIVA KLIGFELD, cantor; b. N.Y.C., Dec. 19, 1947; d. Samuel and Channah (Amsterdam) Kligfeld; m. Ben Rosenbloom, Nov. 26, 1970; 1 child: Etan Amitai. BS cum laude, Brandeis U., 1968; cert. music edn., Boston U., 1972; MusM, Calif. State U., 1980. Cantor Temple Israel of Hollywood, L.A., 1975—; cantor Shechina Conf. on Jewish Women's Spirituality, L.A., 1984, Timbrels of Miriam, L.A., 1991. Composer religious songs including Therefore Choose Life, 1985. Recipient Silverman prize in cantorial studies Hebrew Union Coll., L.A., 1979. Mem. Am. Conf. Cantors. Office: Temple Israel of Hollywood 7300 Hollywood Ave Los Angeles CA 90046

ROSENBLOOM, NOAH HAYYIM, rabbi, educator; b. Sept. 29, 1915; s. Michael and Sarah Leah (Weingelb) R.; m. Pearl Cohen; children: Leah Marion Rosenbloom Kalish, Michele Nathanyah Rosenberg. B. Religious Edn., Yeshiva U., 1942, DHL, 1948; MA, Columbia U., 1945; PhD, NYU, 1958. Ordained rabbi, 1942. Rabbi B'nai Israel, Steubenville, Ohio, 1942, Montefiore Hebrew Congregation, N.Y.C., 1943-45, Tikvas Israel, Phila., 1945-48, B'nai Israel Jewish Ctr., Bklyn., 1949—. Author: Luzzatto's Ethico-Psychological Interpretation of Judaism, 1965, Tradition in an Age of Reform, 1976, The Threnody and the Threnodist of the Holocaust, 1980, The Exodus Epic of the Enlightenment and Exegesis, 1983, Malbim: Exegesis Philosophy Science and Mysticism in His Writings, 1988, Studies in Literature and Thought, 1989, others; translator: Luzzatto's Foundations of the Torah, The Song of the Murdered Jewish People, 1980. Recipient Friedman award Histadruth Ivrith of Am., 1983; Horeb award Yeshiva U. Alumni Assn., 1965. Fellow Am. Acad. Jewish Rsch.; mem. Rabbinical Coun. Am. (editorial bd. Tradition). Home: 1066 E 85th St Brooklyn NY 11236

ROSENFELD, HARRY LEONARD, rabbi; b. Cleve., June 25, 1955; s. Nathan and Frances (Skrall) R.; m. Michele Lynn Hope, May 29, 1988. BS in Psychology, John Carroll U., 1976; MA in Hebrew Letters, Hebrew Union Coll., 1980. Ordained rabbi, 1981. Asst. rabbi Temple Israel, Memphis, 1981-84; rabbi Congregation Beth Sholom, Anchorage, 1984—; adj. prof. Alaska Pacific U., Anchorage, 1987—; exec. com. Alaska, Am. Israel Polit. Affairs Com., Anchorage, 1986—. Bd. dirs. Cath. Social Svcs., Anchorage, 1991—; pres. United Way Anchorage, 1985-90; mem. Mcpl. Health & Human Svcs. Commn., Anchorage, 1986-88, Anchorage Mcpl. Equal Rights Commn., 1986. Mem. Cen. Conf. Am. Rabbis (ch. state com. 1985-86), United Jewish Appeal Rabbinic Cabinet, Assn. Reform Zionists. Office: Congregation Beth Sholom 7525 E Northern Lights Blvd Anchorage AK 99504

ROSENFIELD, SHARON MANETTE DONER, communal social worker; b. Graham, Tex., Aug. 8, 1950; d. Abraham Joshua and Cyril (Rothkop) Doner. BSW, Ariz. State U., 1981; MSW, U. Md., Balt., 1988; MA in Jewish History, Balt. Hebrew U., 1989. Dir. Jewish Info. and Referral Svc. United Jewish Appeal Fedn. Greater Washington, Rockville, Md., 1988—; v.p. youth Tifereth Israel Congregation, Washington, 1987-89, bd. dirs., 1989-90. Co-editor: North American Network of Jewish Information Services Manual, 1989, editor newsletter, 1989-90, vice chmn. N.Am. Network of Jewish Info. Svcs., 1991—; author: (manuals) Forsake Us Not in Our Old Age, 1988, To Care for Him Who Shall Have Borne the Battle, 1988. Dem. campaign worker Cohen for Md. Ho. of Dels., 1990. Mem. Assn. Jewish Communal Workers. Office: Jewish Info and Referral Svc 6101 Montrose Rd Rockville MD 20852

ROSENSTOCK, ELLIOT DAVID, retired rabbi, educator; b. Kansas City, Mo., Dec. 18, 1932; s. Gustav and Edna Viola (Straus) R.; m. Nancy Scharff, July 10, 1958; children: Emily, David Gustav. BA, Cornell U., 1953; BHL, Hebrew Union Coll., 1958, MAHL, 1961, DHL, 1976, DD (hon.), 1986. Ordained rabbi, 1961. Asst. rabbi Collinwood Ave. Temple, Toledo, Ohio, 1961-63, assoc. rabbi, 1963-67; rabbi Temple Beth-El, South Bend, Ind., 1967-87; ret.; mem. ethics com. Holy Cross Care Svc., South Bend, 1989—; vis. asst. prof. U. Notre Dame, 1967-76; com. mem. Centennary Statement, Cen. Conf. of Am. Rabbis, 1976. Pres., chmn. bd. REAL Services, South Bend, 1984-85. 1st lt. USAF, 1954-56. Recipient Harold Hodgin award, S. Bend Assn. Life Underwriters, 1990. Mem. Cen. Conf. Am. Rabbis (exec. com. 1980-82), Am. Soc. CLUs and Chartered Fin. Cons. Home: 5914 S Gotham Dr South Bend IN 46614 Office: Northwestern Mut Life 120 W LaSalle St Box 209 South Bend IN 46624

ROSENTHAL, MORTON M(ANUEU), rabbi, religious organization administrator; b. Cleve., Apr. 16, 1931; s. Samuel M. and Anna (Gordon) R.; m. Lila Belt, June 28, 1959; children: Sandra L., David S. BS, Ohio State U., 1953; B. Hebrew Lit., Hebrew Union Coll., 1958, MA, 1960, DD (hon.), 1985. Ordained rabbi, 1960. Rabbi Har Sinai Temple, Trenton, N.J., 1960-65; dir. Latin Am. affairs dept. Anti-Defamation League, N.Y.C., 1960—; mng. dir. Inst. Jewish Affairs, London, 1989-91. Editor Latin Am. Report newsletter; contbr. numerous articles to profl. and Jewish publs. worldwide. Lt. USAF, 1953-55. Mem. Americas Soc., Fgn. Policy Assn., World Union for Progressive Judaism (bd. dirs. 1986—). Office: Anti-Defamation League 823 UN Plaza New York NY 10017

ROSETT, ANN DOYLE, librarian, church lay worker; b. Valdosta, Ga., Jan. 9, 1955; d. David Spencer Doyle and Lois Annette Gray; m. Robert Allen Richardson, Aug. 1, 1976 (div. June 1981); children: Caitlin Ann, Brendan Wesley; m. John David Rosett, Aug. 6, 1983. Student, Kenyon Coll., 1972-75, U. Dayton, 1974, U. Ala., Birmingham, 1978; BA, Shepherd Coll., 1982; MLS, U. Wash., 1988. Cert. profl. libr., Wash. Head libr. D.V. Hurst Libr., N.W. Coll. of the Assemblies of God, Kirkland, Wash., 1988—. Mem. ALA, Assn. Christian Librs., Assn. Coll. and Rsch. Librs., N.W. Assn. Christian Librs. (treas. 1989-91, pres. 1991—). Democrat. Mem. Assemblies of God Ch. Office: NW Coll Assemblies of God DV Hurst Libr/PO Box 579 5520 108th Ave NE Kirkland WA 98083-0579

ROSIN, WALTER L., religious organization administrator. Sec. Luth. Ch.-Mo. Synod, St. Louis. Office: The Luth Ch-Mo Synod 1333 S Kirkwood Rd Saint Louis MO 63122*

ROSMAN, STEVEN MICHAEL, rabbi; b. Bronx, N.Y., May 7, 1956; s. Ronald and Elaine (Solomon) R.; m. Bari A. Ziegel, Sept. 8, 1984; 1 child, Michal Sima Ziegel. BA in History summa cum laude, Hofstra U., 1978; MA in Hebrew Lit., Hebrew Union Coll., 1981; MA in Edn., NYU, 1983. Ordained rabbi, 1983. Asst. rabbi Temple Sinai, Stamford, Conn., 1979-82; rabbi Jewish Family Congregation, South Salem, N.Y., 1982—; assoc. Jewish chaplain Vassar Coll., Poughkeepsie, N.Y., 1987-88; bd. dirs. Maimonides Acad. Western Conn., Danbury, 1982—, Jewish Fedn. Greater Danbury, 1982—; mem. N.Am. Bd. World Union for Progressive Judaism, 1988—; lectr. Bedford Hills (N.Y.) Correctional Facility, 1989. Mem. adv. com. on AIDS edn. Katonah-(Lewisboro (N.Y.) Sch. Dist., 1989, mem. adv. com. on substance abuse, 1990. Teaching fellow NYU, 1985-86. Mem. Coalition for Alternatives in Jewish Edn., Cen. Conf. Am. Rabbis (mem. joint commn. on Jewish edn. 1985—), Nat. Assn. Temple Educators, Nat. Assn. for Preservation and Perpetuation of Storytelling, Jewish Storytelling Ctr., Rabbinic Student Assn. (v.p. 1981-82), Religions Edn. Fellowship (v.p. 1981-82). Home: 11 Lawson Ln Ridgefield CT 06877 Office: Jewish Family Congregation PO Box 249 South Salem NY 10590

ROSS, BARRY A., pastor; b. Woodbury, N.J., May 31, 1954; s. Harris Browning and Rosemarie (Kelly) R.; m. Michelle Marie Maroney, Feb. 21, 1982. BA, Stockton State Coll., 1976; diploma, Rhema Bible Tng. Ctr., Broken Arrow, Okla., 1981. Ordained to ministry Ind. Charismatic Ch. Various positions Osborn Found., Tulsa, 1980-82; youth min. Praise Tabernacle, Pleasantville, N.J., 1982; childrens min. Abundant Life Faith Ctr., West Goshen, Pa., 1983; pastor, chmn. bd. dirs., chief exec. officer, founder Word of Life Christian Fellowship, Absecon Highlands, N.J., 1983—. Contbr. articles to newspaper. Mem. Absecon-Galloway Mins. Fellowship, Rhema Ministerial Assn. Republican. Home: 379 E Upland Ave Absecon NJ 08201

ROSS, BARRY LOWELL, religion educator; b. Horicon, N.Y., Oct. 25, 1938; s. Kenneth Harvey and Mayfred Doris (McClure) R.; m. Margaret Hazel Tysinger, Aug. 8, 1959; children: Barri Lynne, John Naoki, Elizabeth Patton. BS, Houghton Coll., 1961; BD, Asbury Theol. Sem., 1964, ThM, 1965; MA, U. Mich., 1967; PhD, Drew U., 1979. Missionary, tchr. Wesleyan World Missions, Japan, India, 1967-72, 83—; tchr. United Wesleyan Coll., Allentown, Pa., 1972-79, Azusa (Calif.) PAcific U., 1979-83; pastor Lebanon (Pa.) Wesleyan Ch., 1973-74; chmn. edn. coun. Azusa Pacific U., 1980-83; dir. Wesleyan Mission, Japan, 1985—. Co-author: Wesley Study Bible, 1990; editor Wesley BookClub, Japan, 1985—; cont br. articles to profl. jours. Drew U. fellow, 1975. Mem. Wesleyan Theol. Soc., Soc. Bibl. Lit., Bibl. Archeol. Soc., Theta Phi. Republican. Home and Office: 2135-1 Kita Hassaku Cho, Midori-ku 226, Japan *I began early in life to learn that the urging of the Psalmist to "trust in the Lord and do good," to "delight yourself in the Lord," to "commit your way to the Lord," and to "be still before the Lord and wait patiently for him" (Ps. 37, NIV), indeed are not merely the admonitions of a theorist. In all reality, to live thus gives a framework around which all other facets of life are brought into manageable perspective.*

ROSS, BYRON WARREN, minister; b. L.A., Apr. 22, 1920; s. Byron George and Ruth Nancy (Olson) R.; m. Letha Alice Ausherman, Apr. 13, 1941; children: Byron Leland, Myron Eldon, Nancy Lee Anne, Bryant Alan. AB, Master's Coll., 1943; postgrad., Nyack Missionary Coll., 1943-44; BD, L.A. Bapt. Theol. Sem., 1944; PhD, Temple Hall Coll., 1947. Ordained to ministry Christian and Missionary Alliance. Pastor Christian and Missionary Alliance Ch., Manhattan Beach, Calif., 1942-43, Faith Bible Ch., Ridgecrest, Calif., 1988—; missionary Christian and Missionary Alliance, 1948-63; pastor, prin. Christian Heritage Schs., various cities, Calif., 1966-76; prin. Valley Christian Sch., Ridgecrest, 1986-88, Immanuel Christian Sch., Ridgecrest, 1980-81; dir. overseas lay-worker tng. Christian and Missionary Alliance, Lancaster, Calif., 1961-63; supr. King's Valley Christian Sch., Concord, Calif., 1976-79. Author: Expository Preaching, 1954, Sarangani Lay-Worker's Inst., 1958; pastnett Tape-Mate, 1963, Art-A-Graph, 1976. Republican. Home: PO Box 576 Inyokern CA 93527 Office: Faith Bible Ch 305 C Panamint St Ridgecrest CA 93555

ROSS, CHESTER WHEELER, retired clergyman; b. Evansville, Ind., Nov. 3, 1922; s. Mylo Wheeler and Irma (Berning) R.; A.B. cum laude, Kans. Wesleyan U., 1952; M.Div., Garrett Theol. Sem., 1954; D. Ministry, St. Paul Sch. Theology, 1979; m. Ruth Eulaine Briney, Aug. 30, 1949; children—James W., Deborah R., Judith R., Martha S., John W. Ordained to ministry United Meth. Ch., 1953; enlisted pvt. USAAF, 1942, advanced through grades to lt. col., 1968; chaplain, Africa, Europe, Alaska, Greenland, Taiwan; installation chaplain, Columbus AFB, Miss., 1972-75; ret., 1975; pastor Unity Parish, Iuka, Kans., 1975-80, Ness City (Kans.) United Meth. Ch., 1980-88. Instr. Parent Effectiveness Tng., 1st aid ARC; cubmaster, scoutmaster, dist. chmn. Boy Scouts Am., recipient Silver Beaver award, 1975; vol. parolee counselor; mem. USD 303 Sch. Bd. Paul Harris fellow Rotary Internat.; Decorated Air medal (2), Meritorious Service medal (2). Mem. Ness City Ministers Assn., Conf. Council on Fin. and Adminstrn., Mil. Chaplains Assn., Acad. Parish Clergy, Ret. Officers Assn., Res. Officers Assn., Air Force Aid, Air Force Assn., Nat. Hist. Soc., Am. Assn. Christian Counselors, Appalachian Trail Conf., Menninger Found., Kans. Sheriffs Assn. Assn. Ret. Persons, Order Ky. Col., Am. Legion, VFW, Rotary. Address: 1102 Arcade Goodland KS 67735

ROSS, DOUGLAS H., religious organization executive. PhD, U. Ottawa, Ont., Can.; DD, Queens U. Conf. exec. sec. United Ch. of Can., London, Ont., moderator, 1990. Office: The United Ch of Can, 359 Windermere Rd, London, ON Canada N6G 2K3

ROSS, GEORGE E., clergyman; b. Kansas City, Mo., Nov. 20, 1933; s. Walter W. and Eugenia C. (Moeckel) R.; m. Joan M. Ruda, June 4, 1960 (div. 1981); children: Mary E., Joan M. BA, Ohio Wesleyan, 1955; M Div, Episcopal Theol. Sch., 1958. Ordained to priest Episcopal Ch., 1958. Asst. rector St. Stephen's Ch., Cals, Ohio, 1958-60; rector St. Peter's Ch., Delaware, Ohio, 1960-63; archdeacon Diocese of Idaho, Boise, 1963-65; dean St. Michael's Cathedral, Boise, 1965-72; rector St. Paul's Ch., Akron, Ohio, 1972—; trustee Wesleyan U., Delaware, Ohio, Trinity Sem., Ambridge, Pa. Chaplain Akron Bluecoats, 1973—; trustee Habitat for Humanity, 1986—; pres. Akron Assn. Chs., Akron Intrfaith Council. Mem. Akron City, Rotary. Episcopalian. Office: St Paul s Episcopal Ch 1361 W market St Akron OH 44313

ROSS, GERMAN REED, clergyman; b. Mart, Tex.; s. Ira and Mary (Lewis) R.; children: Merria A., Winston Reed, Ira Gerald. BBA, Golden Gate U., 1948; BDiv., Pacific Luth. Theol. Sem., 1966, MDiv, 1967. Fiscal accounts officer OPA, VA, San Francisco, 1946-48; inventory clk. O. Caspersons & Sons, San Francisco, 1947-49; internal revenue agt. Richmond, Calif., 1949-58; ordained to ministry Chs. of God in Christ, 1953; pastor Mt. Sinai, 1955-80, Good Samaritan Cathedral Ch. of God in Christ, Oakland, Calif., 1979—; gen. sec. Chs. of God in Christ, 1976—; bishop N. Central Calif., 1973—; sec. United Nat. Auxiliaries Conv., 1976—; mem. Congress Nat. Black Chs., 1979—. Author: Here Am I, History and Formative Years of Church of God in Christ. Co-chair, Nat. Assault On Illiteracy Program. Served with USN, 1942-45. Recipient Disting. Service award Religious Workers Guild, 1977; also numerous awards and citations from civic and religious groups. Address: PO Box 10013 Oakland CA 94610 also: PO Box 10013 Oakland CA 94610 *The guiding principles that have contributed to my success are a strong religious conviction, unalterable faith in God and an indefatigable dedication to duty. It is my belief that I can do all things through Christ who strengthens me. A deep love for humanity has been nourished in my heart. It has been a joy to expend time and effort to achieve goals that are challenging but redound to the benefit of mankind.*

ROSS, HENRY A., bishop. Bishop Ch. of Our Lord Jesus Christ of the Apostolic Faith, Inc., N.Y.C. Office: Ch Our Lord Jesus Christ Apostolic Faith Inc 2081 Adam Clayton Powell Jr New York NY 10027*

ROSS, HUGH NORMAN, minister; b. Westmount, Can., July 24, 1945; came to U.S., 1973; s. James Stewart Alexander and Dorothy Isabel (Murray) R.; m. Kathleen Ann Drake, July 30, 1977; children: Joel Stephen, David Michael. BS, U. B.C., Vancouver, Can., 1967; MS, U. Toronto, Ont., Can., 1968, PhD, 1973. Min. evangelism Sierra Madre (Calif.) Congl. Ch., 1975-86, min. apologetics, 1986—; pres. Reasons To Believe, Pasadena, Calif., 1986—. Author: The Fingerprint of God, 1989, 2d edit., 1991; also articles, videos, audiotapes and tape albums. Grantee Murdock Charitable Trust, 1990. Mem. Christian Edn. Assn., Am. Sci. Affiliation (cons. commn. for integrity in sci. edn. 1986—). Office: Reasons To Believe 154 W Sierra Madre Blvd Sierra Madre CA 91024 *What is needed in life is a healthy skepticism, the kind that is promoted in the Bible: "Test everything." In other words, belief is to be based on established facts.*

ROSS, JAMES ROBERT, minister; b. Clarksville, Tenn., Aug. 11, 1934; s. Clyde D. and Claudine Evelyn (Singleton) R.; m. Doris Naugle, Sept. 3, 1950; children: Joy, Thomas, Lisa. BS, Southeastern La. U., 1962; BD, Columbia Theol. Sem., 1962; PhD, Emory U., 1969. Ordained to ministry Christian Chs., 1962. Prof. Bible Southeastern Christian Coll., Winchester, Ky., 1960-64; prof. philosophy Ala. A&M U., Huntsville, 1968-70; campus min. Christian Campus House, Charleston, Ill., 1970-80, Purdue Christian Campus House, West Lafayette, Ind., 1984—; dir. Christian Counseling Svc., Mount Vernon, Ill., 1980-84. Author: The War Within, 1970; contbr. articles to scholarly jours. Dist. coord. Bread for the World, Washington, 1976-79. Mem. Am. Assn. Pastoral Counselors, Am. Assn. Marriage and Family Therapy, Rotary. Home: 602 Dodge St West Lafayette IN 47906 Office: Spearsville Ch of Christ Rte 4 Box 233 Morgantown IN 46160

ROSS, JOANN, ecumenical agency administrator. Dir. Paducah (Ky.) Coop. Ministry. Office: Paducah Coop Ministry 1359 S 6th St Paducah KY 42001*

ROSS, JOHN MACDONALD, theological researcher; b. Bothwell, Lanarkshire, Scotland, Mar. 31, 1908; s. Sir James Stirling and Christina MacDonald (Ross) R.; m. Helen Margaret Wallace, Oct. 8, 1932; children: Christina, Helen, Gavin, George, Catherine. Student Highgate Sch., 1917-26; BA, Wadham Coll., Oxford U., 1930, MA, 1938. Asst. prin. Home Office, London, 1930-37, prin., 1937-46, asst. sec., 1951-68; asst. sec. Gen. Register Office, London, 1946-51. Author: Four Centuries of Scottish Worship, 1972; Introduction to Cicero on the Nature of the Gods, 1972. Contbr. articles to profl. jours. Mem. Brit. Council of Chs., London, 1952-64, Faith and Order Commn. of World Council of Chs., Geneva, 1964-76. Decorated comdr. Order Brit. Empire, 1967. Mem. Studiorum Novi Testamenti Soc. Mem. United Reformed Ch. Club: Athenaeum (chmn. library com. 1981-85) (London). Avocations: music, drawing, painting, book repairing. Home: 64 Wildwood Rd, London NW11 6UU, England *The Trinity satisfies all our needs, because the one God is our judge, redeemer, and inspirer.*

ROSS, JOSEPH LANNY, minister; b. Phila., July 3, 1940; s. Jonathan David and Annie (Urquhart) R.; m. Anne Elizabeth Taylor, Sept. 1, 1963; children: Joseph, Darrin, Monnae. B of Prof. Studies, Elizabethtown Coll., 1975; ThM, Internat. Sem., 1986, ThD, 1989, PhD, 1990. Ch. coord. Deliverance Evangelistic Ch., Phila., 1975-84, assoc. min., 1975—, dean of bible inst., min. of Christian edn., 1977-84, bibl. counselor, 1978—, min. of adminstrn., 1984-90, min. of pub. rels., 1990—; bd. mem. Phila. Sunday Sch. Assn., 1985-89; clergyman Phila. Police Commn. Rels., 1987—. Exec. mgr. (quarterly publ.) Evangel Mag. and Newsletter, 1975. Recipient Legion of Honor award The Chapel of Four Chaplains, Phila., 1975, Christian Counselor's award 700 Club of CBN, Phila., 1983, Human Svcs. award City of Phila. Human Svc. Dept., 1987, Speaker's award MTI Bus. Schs. Grad., Phila., 1987. Mem. Nat. Christian Counselors Assn., Pa. Assn. Notaries (notary pub. 1987—), Evang. Tng. Assn. (bible tchr. cert. 1976—), Hope Plaza, Inc. (v.p. 1982-85). Democrat. Home: 6306 Ogontz Ave Philadelphia PA 19141

ROSS, MARK STEPHEN, pastor; b. Springfield, Mo., Jan. 15, 1957; s. Robert Norman and Norma Jean (Hembree) R.; m. Cynthia Elizabeth Private, Apr. 7, 1977; children: Travis Stephen, Dallas Justin, Tara Elizabeth. AS, Walker Jr. Coll., 1982; BA, Samford U., 1984; MDiv, So. Sem., Louisville, Ky., 1987; postgrad., So. Sem., 1988. Ordained to ministry Bapt. Ch., 1982. Pastor Calvary Bapt. Ch., Dora, Ala., 1982-84, Chaplin (Ky.) Fork Bapt. Ch., 1985-87, Pleasant Grove Bapt. Ch., Shepherdsville, Ky., 1987—; mem. Ky. Bapt. Exec. Com., Middletown, 1991—. Mem. Nelson Bapt. Assn. (dir. evangelism 1989—, chmn. here hope steering com. 1990). Office: Pleasant Grove Bapt Ch 5285 Hwy 44E Shepherdsville KY 40165

ROSS, PAMELA JEAN, church official; b. Santa Ana, Calif., Jan. 27, 1944; d. Alonzo Eugene Burnett and Eunice Irene (Jackson) Ballard; m. Phillip Wayne Ross, Apr. 3, 1961; children: Daniel Wayne, Debra Lynne Ross Cherry, Dianna Marie Ross Chamberlain, Donya Annette. Grad. high sch., Carthage, Mo. Ch. sec. 1st Bapt. Ch., Carthage, 1987—; v.p. Ross & Assocs., real estate, Carthage, 1978—. Office: 1st Bapt Ch 631 S Garrison Ave Carthage MO 64836

ROSS, ROBERT LEON, minister; b. Ponca City, Okla., June 20, 1936; s. Frank B. and Alta N. (Eaton) R.; m. Maurine Mae Snow, June 1, 1958; children: Michael F., Roger B., Robert L. Jr. BA, Okla. Bapt. U., 1959; BD, Southwestern Bapt. Theol. Sem., 1963, MDiv, 1968. Ordained to ministry So. Bapt. Conv., 1956. Pastor Greenwood Bapt. Ch., Weatherford, Tex., 1960-64, Calvary Bapt. Ch., San Antonio, 1964-67, First Bapt. Ch., Drumright, Okla., 1967-70, Knob Hill Bapt. Ch., Oklahoma City, 1970-77; v.p. The Bapt. Found. Okla., Oklahoma City, 1977-85, pres., 1986—; bd. dirs. So. Bapt. Conv. Found., Nashville, Bapt. Health Care Corp, Oklahoma City, Bapt. Gen. Conv. Okla., Oklahoma City, 1968-70; commr. So. Bapt. Conv. Stewardship Commn., Nashville, 1989—. Author: The Steps of a Good Man: A Biography of C. Fred Williams, 1985. Chaplain Oklahoma State Legis. House of Reps., 1969, Oklahoma State Senate, Oklahoma City, 1988. Recipient Joe L. Ingram Sch. of Christian Svc. award Oklahoma Bapt. U., Shawnee, 1989, Profile in Excellence award, 1986. Republican. Home: 11917 Autumn Leaves Oklahoma City OK 73170 Office: Baptist Found Okla 3800 N May Ave Oklahoma City OK 73112

ROSS, SCOTT, religious organization administrator. Pastor, chmn. Ch. of God Gen. Conf., Oregon, Ill. Office: Ch of God Gen Conf 7606 Jaynes St Omaha NE 68134*

ROSS, STEVEN WILLIAM, church representative, insurance company official; b. N.Y.C., Oct. 12, 1946; s. Eugene Alton and Vilma Marie (Skoog) R. BA, Rutgers U., 1968, EdM, 1972. Cert. tchr., N.J.; CLU; CPCU. Mgr. community initiatives The Prudential, Newark, 1974—; rep. World Ministries Friends United Meeting Soc. of Friends, Richmond, Ind., 1987-90; clk. Shrewsbury (N.J.) Monthly Meeting Soc. of Friends, 1985-87, rec. clk., rep. at large N.Y. Yearly Meeting, 1985, 87-89, asst. clk. N.Y. Yearly Meeting, 1991—, clk., ministry and counsel Shrewsbury and Plainfield (N.J.) Half Yearly Meeting, 1989—; rep. Friends World Conf. Soc. of Friends, Elspeet, The Netherlands, 1991; advisor, cons. Newark Collaboration Group, 1984—; instr. Hispanic Leadership Opportunity Project, Newark, 1988—; adj. prof. Ctr. for Pub. Svc., Seton Hall U., South Orange, N.J., 1990. Contbr. articles to religious jours. Bd. dirs. Bd. Mem. Inst. N.J., 1985—, pres., 1989-90; bd. dirs. Youth Svc. Opportunities Project, 1989—, Ctr. for Corp. Community Rels., Boston Coll., 1990—. Sgt. U.S. Army, 1969-70, Korea. Recipient Svc. award Vol. Ctr. Essex County, 1990. Mem. Jaycees (internat. senator 1982). Home: 400 Sairs Ave Long Branch NJ 07740

ROSS, MRS. VICTOR, ecumenical agency administrator. Head 1st Miramichi Inter-Ch. Coun., Boiestown, N.B., Can. Office: 1st Miramichi Inter-Faith, Coun, Boiestown, NB Canada E0H 1A0*

ROSS-BRYANT, LYNN, religious studies educator; b. Reno, Nev., Feb. 23, 1944; d. Kenneth Woodrow and Francis Carol (Bidleman) Ross; m. Elliott Ross-Bryant, Aug. 21, 1976; 1 child, Mark. BA, Occidental Coll., 1966; MA, U. Chgo., 1969, PhD, 1973. Assoc. prof. religious studies U. Colo., Boulder, 1987—. Author: Theodore Roethke: Poet of the Earth, Poet of the Spirit, 1981, Imagination & the Life of the Spirit, 1981; contbr. numerous articles to profl. jours. Mem. Am. Acad. Religion (pres. Western region 1980-81). Democrat. Office: U Colo Dept Religious Studies CB 292 Boulder CO 80309-0292

ROSSENBACH, MARC MERLIN, minister; b. Phoenix, Nov. 20, 1957; s. Charles Harold and Margie Louise (Thompson) R.; m. Teresa Clark, Nov. 29, 1980; children: Briana Noel, Joshua Marc. BA in Preaching, Pacific Christian Coll., 1980; postgrad., Fuller Theol. Sem., 1988—. Ordained to ministry Christian Ch. (Disciples of Christ, 1980. Youth min. Lakewood (Calif.) 1st Christian Ch., 1978, North Orange (Calif.) Christian Ch., 1978-81; assoc. pastor Glendale (Ariz.) Christian Ch., 1981—; pres. Ariz. Christian Youth Conv., Phoenix, 1990-91; chaplain Thunderbird Samaritan Hosp., Glendale, 1986. Republican. Office: Glendale Christian Ch 9661 N 59th Ave Glendale AZ 85302

ROSSI, AGNELO CARDINAL, former archbishop of Sao Paulo; b. Joaquim Egidio, Brazil, May 4, 1913. Ordained priest Roman Cath. Ch., 1937; bishop of Barra do Pirai, 1956; archbishop of Riberoa Preto, 1962-64, of Sao Paulo, 1964-70; cardinal, 1965; titular ch. Mother of God; prefect Congregation for Evangelism of Peoples 1970-84; bishop Subrubicarian Title of Sabina and Poggio Mirteto, 1984; pres. Adminstrn. Patrimony of Holy See, 1984; grand chancellor Pontifical Urban U.; mem. Council Public Affairs of Ch., Congregation of Clergy, Congregation Doctrine of Faith, Congregation of Bishops, Congregation Oriental Chs., Congregation Causes of Saints, Congregation Religious and Secular Insts., Congregation Cath. Edn., Commn. Revision Oriental Code Canon Law, Commn. Works Religion. Address: 00121 Vatican City Vatican City

ROSSI, OPILIO CARDINAL, archbishop; b. N.Y.C., May 14, 1910; Italian citizen. Ordained priest Roman Cath. Ch., 1933; served in nunciatures in Belgium, Netherlands and Fed. Republic Germany, 1938-53; titular archbishop of Ancyra, 1953; nuncio in Ecuador, 1953-59, in Chile, 1959-61, in Austria, 1961-76; cardinal, 1976; cardinal presbyter S. Lorenzo, Lucina, 1987; pres. Cardinalatial Com. Sanctuaries of Pompei and Loretto. Address: Via della Scrofa 70, 00186 Rome Italy

ROSSI, PHILIP JOSEPH, priest, theology educator; b. Mt. Vernon, N.Y., Apr. 30, 1943; s. PHilip J. and Mary (Scola) R. AB, Fordham U., 1967; BD, Woodstock Coll., 1971; PhD, U. Tex., 1975. Joined Soc. of Jesus, Roman Cath. Ch., 1962, ordained priest Roman Cath. Ch., 1971. Assoc. prof. Marquette U., Milw., 1982—, chairperson theology dept., 1985-91. Author: Together Toward Hope, 1983; contbr. philosophy and theology articles to profl. jours. Bd. dirs. Creighton U., Omaha, 1985—. Mem. Coll. Theology Soc. (bd. dirs. 1987-90), Soc. Christian Ethics, North Am. Kant Soc., Cath. Theol. Soc. Am., Am. Acad. Religion. Office: Marquette U Theology Dept Milwaukee WI 53233

ROSSI, ROBERT JOSEPH, priest, provincial; b. Braddock, Pa., May 17, 1942; s. Domenick and Theresa (Fiumara) R. BA in Philosophy, St. Francis Coll., Fort Wayne, Ind., 1978; STB, Cath. U. Am.; MA in Religious Studies, St. Louis U. Joined Crosier Fathers and Bros., Roman Cath. Ch., ordained priest, 1970. Prior, pres. Wawasee Prep. Sch., Syracuse, Ind., 1973-75; mem. U.S. Provincial Bd., 1977-82; gen. councillor Crosier Fathers and Bros., Rome, 1982-83; prior, chancellor Crosier Sem., Onamia, Minn., 1984-86; provincial Crosier Fathers and Bros., Mpls., 1986—; mem. Crosier Order Gen. Bd., Rome, 1986—; spiritual dir. Crosier Sem., Onamia, Minn., 1970-73; spiritual dir. Firmin Desloge Hosp., St. Louis, 1971-74, 75; dir. Crosier Renewal Ctr., Hastings, Nebr., 1976-78, Crosier Ministry Ctr., Fort Wayne, Ind., 1978-80; adminstr. St. Ann's, Doniphan, Nebr., 1976; assoc. pastor St. Joseph Ch., Phoenix, 1980-81; part-time assoc. St. Stephen Byzantine Rite Parish, Phoenix, 1980-81, St. John the Bapt. Byzantine Cath. Parish, Mpls., 1983—; part-time St. Matthew Parish, West St. Paul, 1983, Nativity Parish, St. Paul, 1984; chmn. Diocesan Task Force for Lay Ministries, Phoenix, 1980; coord. for Lay Ministries, Diocese of Phoenix, 1981-82. Contbr. articles to religious jours. Mem. Conf. Major Superiors of Men (bd. dirs., chmn. Region V 1991—), Nat. Assn. Ch. Pers. Adminstrs. Home: 711 Lincoln Ave Saint Paul MN 55105 Office: Crosier Province Offices 3204 E 43d St Minneapolis MN 55406

ROSSMANN, MICHAEL LOUIS, minister; b. Chgo., Sept. 7, 1954; s. Kenneth Wayne and Marie Rose (Maiello) R.; m. Kathy Ellen Olson, Feb. 18, 1978; children: Ashley Marie, Bethany Anne, Crystal Joy. BS in Polit. Sci., Ariz. State U., 1976; MDiv with honors, Denver Sem., 1983. Ordained to ministry Conservative Bapts., 1985, Evang. Free Ch. Am., 1989. Campus evangelist, v.p. Young Lions of Judah, Tempe, Ariz., 1974-78; campus dir. Am. Bd. Missions and the Jews, Tempe, 1978-80; minister young marrieds Mudson Meml. Bapt. Ch., Denver, 1982-84, assoc. pastor, 1984-88; pastor Cen. Orchard Mesa Community Ch., Palisade, Colo., 1988—. Mem. Pi Sigma Alpha. Republican. Home: 298 34th Rd Palisade CO 81526-9569 Office: Cen Orchard Mesa Comm Ch 298 34th Rd Palisade CO 81526-9569

ROSS TALBOT, SYLVIA, religious organization administrator; m. Frederick Hilborn Talbot. Student, Inter-Am. U., P.R., Yale U. Former Minister of Health, Guyana; pres. Ch. Women United in U.S.A., 1987—. Office: Ch Women United in the USA 475 Riverside Dr Room 812 New York NY 10115

ROTENBERG, RENA E(LSA), school system administrator; b. Suffern, N.Y., July 14, 1935; d. Herman Solomon and Mollie Rebecca (Schatzow) Rosenbaum; m. Wolfgang Rotenberg, July 3, 1960; children: Saul, Seth, Naomi (dec.), Ruth. BA, Bklyn., 1957; postgrad., Hunter Coll., 1958-59; MA, Balt. Hebrew Coll., 1977. Cert. early childhood tchr., N.Y., Md. Tchr. Bklyn. Jewish Ctr. Hebrew Sch., 1954-60; tchr. presch. dept. East Midwood Day Sch., Bklyn., 1958-60; tchr. Jewish Community Ctr. Nursery Sch., Balt., 1960-61; dir. Beth Israel Nursery Sch., Randallstown, Md., 1969-73; dir. early childhood edn. Bd. Jewish Edn. of Balt., Inc., 1973—; resource cons. Gan Yeladin Child Care Ctr., Balt., 1983—, Am. Jewish Com., Balt.,

1986—; mem. women's svc. adv. coun. Sinai Hosp., Balt., 1987—. Author: Shabbat and Holiday Curriculum Guides, 1986, 87; co-author: Torah Talk, 1989; contbr. articles to profl. publs. Recipient Harry Greenstein award Associated Jewish Community Fedn. Balt., 1989. Mem. Nat. Assn. for Edn. of Young Children, Nat. Jewish Early Childhood Network (v.p. 1982-84), Nat. Assn. Jewish Early Childhood Specialists (founding mem.), Md. Com. for Children. Office: Bd Jewish Edn 5800 Park Heights Ave Baltimore MD 21215

ROTH, DOYLE JACK KEY, minister; b. Eustis, Fla., Apr. 9, 1958; s. James Robert and Lena May (Wilson) R.; m. Anita Jean Bergman, July 28, 1979; children: Joseph Doyle, Joy Elizabeth. BS in Ch. Music, St. Louis Christian Coll., Florissant, Mo., 1980, BA in Ministry/Bible, 1981; MA in Ch. Growth, Cin. Bible Seminary, 1989. Ordained to ministry Christian Ch., 1982. Min. youth Parkwood Christian Ch., Maryland Heights, Mo., 1978-80, Willow St. Ch. of Christ, Effingham, Ill., 1980-82; assoc. min. 1st Christian Ch., Union, Mo., 1982-88, Harvester Christian Ch., St. Charles, Mo., 1988—; pastoral care min. Chem. Dependency Unit, Edgewood, Washington, Mo., 1988—; pres. High Hill (Mo.) Christian Svc. Camp, 1988—; mem. Nat. Planning Coun./Christ in Youth Conf., Joplin, Mo., 1988-91; coord. children's session Mo. Christian Conv., Osage Beach, Mo., 1988-90. Office: Harvester Christian Church 2950 Kings Crossing Saint Charles MO 63303

ROTH, DUANE ALVIN (DEWEY ROTH), minister; b. Bluffton, Ind., Aug. 2, 1957; s. Clarence E. and Georgina Della (Smith) R.; m. Debbie Ann Brewer, June 9, 1979; children: Angel Brooke, Shonda Diane, Curtis Emanuel, Kelly Jo. BS in English Bible, Cin. Bible Coll., 1984. Minister of youth/edn. Cedar Creek Ch. of Christ, Leo, Ind., 1984-90; youth minister Brownstown (Ind.) Christian Ch., 1990—; prog. com. Ind. Christian Youth Conv., Indpls., 1991—, Ind. Jr. High Christian Conv., 1989—. Recipient Golden Poet award World of Poetry, 1987, 90; named to Outstanding Young Men of Am., 1987, 89. Home: 715 West Spring St Brownstown IN 47220 Office: Brownstown Christian Church 702 West Spring St Brownstown IN 47220 *It's been said that all of life is merely prelude—an overture to "real" life in heaven. I agree, but, hey folks, if you don't enjoy the overture, what makes you think you'll love the play?.*

ROTH, ELISABETH DIETLIND WILMA, minister; b. Steinheim, Germany, July 12, 1947; d. Friedrich Mühlenberend and Erika Koetter; m. Wolfgang Roth, May 5, 1976; children: Deborah, Johanna, Alexander, Maria. PhD in Theology, Heidelberg, 1978. Vicar and PhD Heidelberg, 1975; clin. pastorate Mainz, 1976; spl. ministry for teaching religion Gymnasium Staatl. Mainz-Gonsenheim, 1976-91; tchr. paedagogic of religion Studienseminar, Mainz, 1991—. Author: Politische Pilgerfahrt nach Chatyn, 1989, Das Drama des Gottesdienstes—vor und hinter der Kirchentur, 1991; contbr. numerous articles to profl. jours. Mem. Evangelische Kirche in Hessen und Nassau. Home: Hildastr 12, Wiesbaden Federal Republic of Germany 6200

ROTH, RISÉ BETH, religious organization administrator; b. Bklyn., May 28, 1960; d. Frederick Monroe and Irene (Kline) Molod; m. Robert Alan Roth, Sept. 22, 1985. Student, Jewish Theol. Sem., 1975-78, Haifa U., Israel, 1980-81; BA in Polit. Sci., William Smith Coll., 1982. Dir. women's div. Jewish Fedn. of Greater Hartford, Conn. Mem. Friends of the Hartford Ballet, 1991—. Mem. Nat. Coun. Jewish Women, Assn. Jewish Community Orgns. Pers. Office: Greater Hartford Jewish Fedn 333 Bloomfield Ave West Hartford CT 06117

ROTH, ROBERT PAUL, seminary educator, writer; b. Milw., Dec. 8, 1919; s. Paul Wagner and Rose Marie (Schulzke) R.; m. Margaret Agnes Beckstrand, June 17, 1943; children—Erik, Maren, Maarja, John, Sonja. B.A., Carthage Coll., 1941; M.A., U. Ill., 1942; M.Div., Northwestern Lutheran Sem., 1945; Ph.D., U. Chgo., 1947; D.D. (hon.), Roanoke Coll., 1958. Ordained to ministry Luth. Ch. in Am. Prof. Luthergiri Sem., Rajahmundry, India, 1946-48; pastor St. Paul Ch., Red Wing, Minn., 1949-53; prof. Luth. So. Sem., Columbia, S.C., 1953-61; dean Northwestern Luth. Sem., Mpls., 1968-76; dir. grad. studies Luther Northwestern Sem., St. Paul, 1976-83, prof., 1983-90; pres. Minn. Consortium Sems. Minn., 1976-78; chmn. com. on worship Luth. Ch. Am., 1970-78, mem. Bd. Publ., Phila., 1978—. Author: Meaning and Practice of the Lord's Supper, 1961; Story and Reality, 1973; The Theater of God, 1985; editor: New International Bible, 1978; editor in chief Areopagus mag., 1990—. Research fellow: Am. Assn. Theol. Schs., 1966, Aid Assn. for Lutherans, 1976, 78, Luth. Brotherhood, 1983, Luth. Ch. Am. Div. for Profl. Leadership, 1983, Div. for Global Missions, 1983. Mem. Am. Acad. Religion. Avocations: Painting watercolors; poetry; sailing. Home: 4194 Hillcrest Ln Wayzata MN 55391

ROTH, RONALD STEWART, rabbi; b. N.Y.C., Oct. 12, 1948; s. Morton and Adelaide (Drobbin) R.; m. Rhonda Cass, Aug. 28, 1971; children: Gabriel, Deena. BA, Cornell U., 1970; MA, Jewish Theol. Sem. Am., 1977. Ordained rabbi, 1978. Rabbi Beth-El Synagogue, East Windsor, N.J., 1978-85, West End Synagogue, Nashville, 1985—; bd. dirs. Mercaz, 1987—, Jewish Fedn. Nashville, 1987-88, 90—, FOCUS, Nashville, 1987—. Mem. Rabbinical Assembly (v.p. nothern coun. of southeast region 1990), Nashville Assn. Rabbis, Priests and Ministers (pres. 1987). Office: West End Synagogue 3814 West End Ave Nashville TN 37205

ROTH, SOL, rabbi; b. Rzeszow, Poland, Mar. 8, 1927; came to U.S., 1934, naturalized, 1939; s. Joseph and Miriam (Lamm) R.; m. Debra H. Stitskin, Nov. 26, 1957; children: Steven, Michael, Sharon. B.A., Yeshiva U., 1948, D.D. (hon.), 1977; M.A., Columbia U., 1953, Ph.D., 1966; Rabbi, Yeshiva U. Theol. Sem., 1950. Ordained rabbi Orthodox Jewish Congregations, 1950; pres. Rabbinical Council Am., 1980-82, N.Y. Bd. Rabbis, 1976-79; chmn. Israel Commn. Rabbinical Council Am., 1976-78; dean Chaplaincy Sch., N.Y. Bd. Rabbis, 1976-79; Samson R. Hirsch prof. dept. philosophy Yeshiva U., N.Y.C.; rabbi Jewish Center Atlantic Beach, N.Y., 1956-86, Fifth Ave. Synagogue, 1986—. Author: Science and Religion, 1967, The Jewish Idea of Community, 1977, Halakhah and Politics: The Jewish Idea of a State, 1988 (Samuel Belkin Meml. Lit. award 1989); editor: Morasha. Recipient award Synagogue Adv. Council United Jewish Appeal, 1975. Mem. Am. Philos. Assn. The Rabbi Dr. Sol Roth Chair in Talmud and Contemporary Halakha established at Yeshiva U., 1989. Home: 30 E 62d St New York NY 10021 Office: Yeshiva U Dept Philosophy 500 W 185th St New York NY 10033

ROTHBERGER, JOSEPH MEYER, rabbi, educator; b. N.Y.C., Feb. 9, 1937; s. Kaufman and Lillian (Diller) R.; m. Deborah Grosberg; children: Elie Saul, Richard Evan, Gabriella Lily. BA, Yeshiva U., 1958; MHL, 1961; rabbinical ord., Yeshiva U., 1961, MS in Edn., 1967. Ord. rabbi, N.Y. Rabbi, prin. Congregation, Pawtucket, R.I., 1963-65, 1965-68; tchr. Hillel Sch., N.Y., 1967-76; day camp dir. Yeshiva, Forest Hills, N.Y., 1974-76; prin. Yeshiva Acad. of Harrisburg (Pa.), 1976-78; tchr. Ramaz Sch., N.Y.C., 1978-80, North, Great Neck, N.Y., 1980-85; prin. Yeshiva, Bklyn., 1985—. Active Young Israel of Hillcrest, Flushing, N.Y., 1982-86. Capt. USAR, 1961-63. Mem. Rabbinical Coun. Am., Educators Coun. Am., Nat. Conf. Yeshiva Prins. Home: 65-15 171st St Flushing NY 11365

ROTHBLATT, DANIEL MORRIS, fundraiser and community organizer; b. Racine, Wis., Dec. 31, 1958; s. Isaiah and Agnes Rothblatt. BA in Design and Industry, San Francisco State U., 1983; MSW, U. So. Calif., Los Angeles, 1986; M in Jewish Communal Service, Hewbrew Union Coll., 1986. Asst. dir. Shenson's Delicatessen, San Francisco, 1979-83; campaign assoc. San Francisco Jewish Community Fedn., 1983-84; asst. dir. San Fernando Valley Region Jewish Fedn. Council, Los Angeles, 1986—. Mem. Nat. Assn. Social Workers, Second Generation, Assn. Jewish Community Orgn. Personnel, So. Calif. Conf. Jewish Communal Service. Office: Jewish Fedn Council 22634 Vanowen St Canoga Park CA 91307

ROTHE-BARNESON, JUNE EMMA, lay worker; b. Chico, Calif., Feb. 27, 1931; d. William Edgar and Jean Blanch (Howe) Rothe; m. John L. Barneson Jr., Apr. 26, 1953 (div. 1986); children: John L. III, Jean LaVere Barneson Ponciano. BA in Elem. Edn., Calif. State U., Chico, 1952. Cert. elem. sch. tchr. Mem. United Meth. Gen. Bd. Global Ministries, N.Y.C., 1972-80, United Meth. Gen. Commn. on Communication, Nashville, 1981-87; del. United Meth. Gen. Conf., Indpls., 1980; newsletter editor United Meth., 1960-80; trustee Glide Found., San Francisco, 1977-85, Butte County Task Force on AIDS; trustee Chico Area Coun. Chs., 1990—, v.p., 1990-91, pres., 1991—; co-owner Perchè No! (coffee house-ice cream shop), Chico, 1986—. Author: Cabin On Quesnel, 1969, Airspeed & Godspeed, 1976, Dogs On the Roof, 1983; contbr. articles to United Meth. mags. "Most World Minded Citizen" Douglas McArthur Scholarship Found., Chico, 1977. Democrat. Home and Office: 738 Downing Ave Chico CA 95926

ROTHENBERGER, JACK RENNINGER, clergyman; b. Boyertown, Pa., Oct. 4, 1930; s. Stuart Henry and Beulah (Renninger) R.; m. Jean Delores Schultz, Sept. 8, 1951; children: Susan Marie, Bruce Wayne. BS, Juniata Coll., 1952; MDiv, Hartford Theol. Sem., 1955; STM, Temple U., 1962; D Ministry, Lancaster Theol. Sem., 1977. Ordained to ministry Schwenkfelder Ch., 1955. Pastor Palm and Lansdale (Pa.) Schwenkfelder Ch., 1955-63, 65-66; stated supply, interim pastor Pa. United Ch. of Christ, 1963-69; chaplain, tchr., coord., dir. admissions Perkiomen Sch., Pennsburg, Pa., 1955-56, 62-67, asst. headmaster, headmaster, coach football backfield, basketball, 1967-69; min. Christian edn. Cen. Schwenkfelder Ch., Worcester, Pa., 1969-74, sr. min., 1974—; pres. Internat. Christian Endeavor, Columbus, Ohio, 1983-87; v.p. World Christian Endeavor, 1990—; mem. cabinet and bd. Pa. Coun. Chs., 1957—; mem. Pa. Conf. Interch. Cooperation; mem. Schwenkfeld Mission Bd., 1957, Schwenkfelder Bd. Pubs., 1957—, Schwenkfelder Libr. Bd., 1957—, Schwenkfeldian in Exile Soc., 1955—, also others. Author: Casper Schwenkfeld and the Ecumenical Ideal, 1962; editor The Schwenkfeldion mag., 1964-87; contbr. articles to profl. jours. First v.p. Schwenckfeld Manor, Lansdale, 1973—; v.p. Meadowood Total Care Retirement Community, Worcester, Pa., 1983—. Mem. No. Pa. Assn. United Ch. of Christ Ministerium, No. Pa. Ministerium, Methacton Area Ministerium, United Schwenkfelder Youth Fellowship, Montgomery County Sunday Sch. Assn., also others. Republican. Home: 3914 Gate House Ln Skippack PA 19474 Office: Cen Schwenkfelder Ch Valley Forge Rd Worcester PA 19490 *I extend the hand of fellowship to all believers in the Living Christ regardless of their specific expression of that faith. In a world of constant rapid change we can find direction through faith in the Living God revealed by Jesus.*

ROTHENBERGER, VICTOR CONRAD IMMANUEL, minister; b. Rhein, Sask., Can., Feb. 14, 1923; s. Conrad and Amalia (Propp) R.; m. Martha Ida Redlich, July 9, 1947; children: Sharon Rothenberger Thomson, Wayne, Deborah Rothenberger Mick, Richard. AA, Luther Coll., 1942; BA, U. Sask., 1947; ministerial diploma, Capitol U. and Sem., Columbus, Ohio, 1947; BD, Knox Coll., Toronto, Ont., Can., 1965; MA, MEd, Wright State U., 1975. Ordained to ministry Evang. Luth. Ch. in Can., 1947. Pastor various chs. in Sask., B.C. and Alta., Can., 1947-56, Sharon Luth. Ch., Pasadena, Tex., 1956-59; pastor Peace Luth. ch., Linton, N.D., 1959-62, Pickering, Ont., Can., 1962-65; pastor Christ Luth. Ch., Dayton, Ohio, 1965-74; pastor Martin Luther Ch., Vancouver, B.C., 1974-88, ret., 1988; chmn. B.C. conf. Am. Luth. Ch., Vancouver, 1952-53, mem. stewardship com. Can. dist., 1951-53; mem. campus ministry bd. Evang. Luth. Ch. in Can., Vancouver, 1981-84. Bd. dirs. Luth. Bible Sch. of B.C., 1981—. With Can. Armed Forces, 1940-43. Mem. Phi Alpha Theta. Home: 535 E 46th Ave, Vancouver, BC Canada V5W 2A2

ROTHERMEL, FRED ALLEN, military officer, minister; b. Ft. Worth, Dec. 8, 1940; s. Arno Fred and Annie Lucille (King) R.; m. Dana Sue Powell, Aug. 31, 1962; children: Cindy L. Rothermel Brown, Alisa S., Julie A., Kevin A. BA, Okla. Bapt. U., 1963; MDiv, Southwestern Bapt. Theol. Sem., 1967. Ordained to ministry So. Bapt. Conv., 1962. Pastor First Bapt. Ch., Paoli, Okla., 1962-65, Irving Bapt. Ch., Ryan, Okla., 1965-67; commd. lt. (j.g.) USN, 1967, advanced through grades to capt., 1987; exch. chaplain Royal Navy-USN Pers. Exchange program USN, London, 1976-78; asst. div. chaplain 3d Marine div. USN, Okinawa, Japan, 1982-83; dir. chaplains sch. advanced course USN, Newport, R.I., 1983-87; dir. profl. devel. and religious programs div. chaplain corps USN, Washington, 1987-91; fleet chaplain U.S. Atlantice Fleet USN, Norfolk, Va., 1991—; trustee Westwood Bapt. Ch., Springfield, Va., 1989—. Contbr. articles, papers to navy jours.; pub. jour. The Navy Chaplain, 1987-91. Basketball coach Southwestern Youth Assn., Burke, Va., 1987-91; coach Fairfax County Little League, 1988; den leader local pack Cub Scouts Boy Scouts Am., 1988, counselor eagle scout program, Springfield, Va., 1989; rep. chief of chaplains nat. hdqrs. YMCA, 1989. Decorated Legion of Merit, Meritorious Svc. medal with star, Navy Commendation medal. Republican. Office: Fleet Chaplain US Atlantic Fleet Hdqrs Comdr in Chief Norfolk VA 23511-6001 *There is an automatic linkage of the ethics, reputation and destiny of each person, community and nation. In choosing a discipline to live by one chooses his or her destiny.*

ROTHFUSS, FRANKLIN EDWARD, JR., minister; b. Pigeon, Mich., Nov. 6, 1946; s. Franklin Edward and Maxine Naomi (Dodds) R.; m. Sandra Lynn Ohlrich, June 21, 1969; children: Erin Morrae, Jessica Lynn, Tisha Coreen. AA, Concordia Jr. Coll., 1966; BA, Concordia Sr. Coll., 1968; MDiv, Concordia Sem., St. Louis, 1972. Ordained to ministry Luth. Ch.-Mo. Synod, 1972; joined Luth. Ch. in Am., 1981, Evang. Luth. Ch. in Am., 1988. Pastor 1st Luth., 1st St.John's Chs., Phillipsburg, Kensington, Kans., 1972-78, All Saints Luth. Ch., Dallas, 1978-80, Bethany Luth. Ch., Dallas, 1980-81, Fridhem Luth. Ch., Funk, Nebr., 1981-88, Redeemer Luth. Ch., Wayne, Nebr., 1988—; trustee Midland Luth. Coll., Fremont, Nebr., 1987—; chmn. N.E. Conf., Nebr. Synod, Evang. Luth. Ch. Am., 1989—; sec. Agys. and Instns. Com., Omaha, 1988—; pres. Wayne Ministerial Assn., 1989—. Author: Journey to Jerusalem, 1981; contbr. articles to profl. jours. Mem. Bread for the World, 1984—, Common Cause, Washington, 1985—. Home: 315 W Fifth St Wayne NE 68787 Office: Redeemer Luth Ch 502 Lincoln Wayne NE 68787

ROTHMAN, ROBERT AARON, rabbi, educator, psychotherapist; b. N.Y.C., Mar. 31, 1931; s. Hyman and Eva (Esrig) R.; m. Sherran Blair (div.); children: Dee Kates, Kay; m. Miriam Buch, Mar. 17, 1977; 1 child, Jessica Nicole. BA, Yeshiva U., 1953; BHL, MA, Hebrew Union Coll., 1957, DHL, 1966, DDiv, 1982; STM, N.Y. Theol., 1972; MSW, Wurzweiler Sch., 1988. Rabbi Community Synagogue, Rye, N.Y., 1966—; therapist Cath. Charities, Yonkers, N.Y., 1987-89; prof. Manhattanville Coll., Purchase, N.Y., 1990—. Pres. N.Y. Assn. Reform Rabbis, N.Y. met. area, 1984-86, Westchester Bd. of Rabbis, Westchester County, N.Y., 1986-89; bd. dirs. Wainwright House, Rye, 1987-89, Rye YMCA, 1987-89, Samaritan Counseling Ctr., 1990—. Recipient George Washington medal Freedoms Found. at Valley Forge, 1967, Recognition award United Jewish Appeal, 1972, Fed. of Jewish Philanthropies award, 1974, B'nai Brith award, 1983, Boy Scouts Shofar award, 1991. Mem. AAUP, N.Y. State Jewish War Vets. (chaplain), Cen. Conf. of Am. Rabbis (pst chmn. com.), Westchester Jewish War Vets. (chaplain), Rye (chaplain). Avocations: stamps, coins, reading. Office: Community Synagogue 200 Forest Ave Rye NY 10580

ROTMAN, ARTHUR, social welfare administrator; b. Montreal, Que., Can., Nov. 29, 1926; came to U.S., 1968; s. Myer Rotman and Mollie Schachtman; m. Anita Schecter, Sept. 4, 1947; children: Stephen, Laurie, Carol. B.A., George Williams Coll., Montreal, 1947; M.S., Case Western Res. U., 1949. Various positions YM-YWHA, Montreal, 1949-66, assoc. exec. dir., 1966-68; exec. dir. Jewish Community Ctr., Pitts., 1968-76; exec. v.p. Jewish Community Ctrs. Assn. N.Am., N.Y.C., 1976—; lectr. Sch. Social Work, McGill U., Montreal, 1958-68. Contbr. chpts. to books, articles to profl. jours. Mem. Assn. Jewish Ctr. Workers (past v.p.), World Conf. Jewish Communal Service (pres., past treas.). Democrat. Jewish. Office: Jewish Community Ctrs Assn NA 15 E 26th St Ste 1404 New York NY 10010

ROTTER, HANS, theology educator; b. Hemhof, Germany, Oct. 6, 1932; s. Georg and Zäzilia (Daxenberger) R. Student, Philos. Coll. Munich, 1956-59, U. Innsbruck, Austria, 1961-65; ThD, U. Innsbruck, 1967, D Moral Theology, 1969. Lectr. moral theology U. Innsbruck, 1969-70, prof., head dept. moral theology, 1970, dean Faculty of Theology, 1974-75; rector Internat. Theol. Sem., Innsbruck, 1979-86. Author books; contbr. over 140 articles to religious jours.; co-editor: Innsbrucker Theologische Studien. Home: Sillgasse 6 Jesuitenkolleg, A 6020 Innsbruck Austria Office: Inst Moraltheologie, Karl Rahner Platz 1, A 6020 Innsbruck Austria

ROTTSCHAEFER, WILLIAM ANDREW, philosophy educator; b. Tulsa, June 20, 1933; s. Dirk and Clara (Linsmeyer) R.; m. Marie Therese Schickel. BA, St. Louis U., 1956, MA, 1957, Licentiate in Sacred Theol., 1966; MS, U. Ill., 1969; PhD, Boston U., 1973. Asst. prof. philosophy SUNY, Oswego, 1972-73, Plattsburgh, 1973-75; asst. prof. philosophy Lewis & Clark Coll., Portland, Oreg., 1975-79, assoc. prof. philosophy, 1979-85, prof. philosophy, 1985—. Contbr. articles and revs. to profl. jours.; referee for several scholarly periodicals. Mem. Philosophy of Sci. Assn., Am. Philos. Assn., Inst. for Religion in an Age of Sci., Ctr. for Theology and the Natural Scis. (assoc.), Am. Acad. Religion, Metaphys. Soc. Am. Office: Lewis and Clark Coll Dept Philosophy Portland OR 97219

ROUBEY, LESTER WALTER, rabbi, retired educator; b. Balt., Feb. 11, 1915; s. Abraham and Sara (Cordish) R.; A.M., Johns Hopkins, 1936, Ph.D., 1938; M.H.L. and Rabbi, Hebrew Union Coll., 1947, D.D. (hon.), 1972; m. Charlotte Helen Stern, June 1, 1947; 1 son, Robert Arthur. Rabbi, 1947; rabbi, Lancaster, Pa., 1947-53, Reading, Pa., 1954-64, East Orange, N.J., 1964-66, Baton Rouge, 1966-80, rabbi emeritus, 1980—; adj. prof. religion Franklin and Marshall Coll., Lancaster, 1951-53; asso. prof. Romance langs. Kutztown (Pa.) State Coll., 1961-64; lectr. Romance langs. La. State U., Baton Rouge, 1966-70, assoc. prof., 1970-82, assoc. prof. religious studies and bibl. Hebrew, 1982-85. Mem. civic com., Lancaster, 1950-53; mem. adv. bd. Baton Rouge Gen. Hosp., 1967—, trustee, 1972—; mem. religious com. Reading round table NCCJ; chmn. Reading com. Am. Jewish Tercentenary, 1954-55; bd. dirs. ARC, 1968-71, Mental Health Assn. Baton Rouge, 1980-83. Mem. Central Conf. Am. Rabbis, Hebrew Union Coll.-Jewish Inst. Religion Alumni Assn. (trustee 1953-56), Am. Assn. Tchrs. French, Am. Assn. Tchrs. Italian, AAUP, MLA, South Central Modern Lang. Assn. (chmn. Italian sect. 1969), Phi Sigma Iota. Mason (32 deg., Shriner), Rotarian. Club: Baton Rouge Country. Producer, conductor series of TV worship programs, Lancaster, 1951-53.

ROUGHTON, PHILIP HUGH, minister; b. Ft. Pierce, Fla., Mar. 24, 1949; s. William Wesley and Lounette (McCullough) R.; m. Mica Keller, Aug. 28, 1970; children: Keller Andrew, Collin Marshall. BA, Asbury Coll., 1971; MDiv, Asbury Theol. Seminary, 1974, MA in Religion, 1975. Ordained to ministry Meth. Ch., 1971; elder, 1977. Assoc. minister Trinity United Meth. Ch., Tallahassee, 1975-80; minister Boca Grande (Fla.) United Meth. Ch., 1980-83; sr. minister First United Meth. Ch., Largo, Fla., 1983-88, Ormond Beach, Fla., 1988—; supervising pastor United Meth. Ch., Fla., 1980—, bd. of ordained ministry, 1985—, elder. Named one of Outstanding Young Men of Am., 1976. Mem. Largo Ministerial Assn. (pres. 1985). Democrat. Avocations: woodworking, water skiing. Office: First United Meth Ch 336 S Halifax Dr Ormond Beach FL 32074

ROULSTON, JOHN FRANK CLEMENT, church official; b. Brisbane, Queensland, Australia, Aug. 12, 1941; s. Leon Clement and Nancy Isabelle (Short) R.; m. Lynette Catherine Burgess, Jan. 4, 1964; children: Catherine Anne, Nigel John. BEd, U. Queensland, 1967; LittB, U. New Eng., NSW, Australia, 1972; M in Edn. Adminstrn., U. New Eng., 1974; MLitt, U. New Eng., NSW, Australia, 1988; PhD, U. Idaho, Moscow, 1976. Tchr. Dept. Edn., Queensland, 1961-67, English subject master, 1968-69, dep. prin., 1969-71, prin., 1972-73; prin. Cromwell Coll., U. Queensland, 1973-75; sr. lectr. ednl. adminstrn. Brisbane Coll. Advanced Edn., Queensland, 1977-84; dir. edn. and communication Uniting Ch. Australia, Brisbane, Queensland, 1984—, moderator Queensland Synod, 1990—; mem. reference group Ctr. Ednl. Leadership, Brisbane Coll. Advanced Edn., Queensland, 1989—. Editor Ministry mag., 1989; contbr. articles to profl. jours. Elder St. Andrews-Ann St. Uniting Ch., Brisbane, 1977—; lay preacher Uniting Ch. Australia, 1959—. Nat. travel scholar Autralian Coun. Ednl. Adminstrn., 1988. Fellow Queensland Inst. Ednl. Adminstrn. (pres. 1980-86), Austrlaian Coun. Endl. Adminstrn., Australian Inst. Mgmt.; mem. Commonwealth Coun. Ednl. Adminstrn., Australian Coll. Edn. (exec. mem.), Phi Delta Kappa. Avocations: public speaking, writing, acupuncture, massage therapy. Home: 44 Bulcock Ave, Mount Nebo Queensland 4520, Australia Office: Uniting Ch Australia, 60 Bayliss St, Queensland, Auchenflower 4066, Australia *Leaders must have a clear vision, be able to articulate that vision clearly and precisely to others, and live that vision day by day. We need this sort of leader in the church as well as in society generally.*

ROUSSEAU, RICHARD WILFRED, priest, theology educator, publishing executive; b. South Dartmouth, Mass., Sept. 26, 1924; s. Wilfred Joseph and Margaret Isabella (Donaghy) R. AB, Boston Coll., 1947, MA in Philosophy, 1948, MA in English, 1950; Licentiate in Sacred Theology, St. Albert Coll., Louvain, Belgium, 1957; PhD, Ottawa (Ont., Can.) U., 1969; STD, St. Paul's U., Ottawa, 1974. Joined S.J., 1943; ordained priest Roman Cath. Ch., 1954. Asst. prof., chair Boston Coll., Chestnut Hill, Mass., 1956-60; assoc. prof. Fairfield (Conn.) U., 1960-68; assoc. dir. faith and order commn. Nat. Coun. Chs. U.S.A., 1969-72; dean Weston Sch. Theology, Cambridge, Mass., 1972-77; prof., chair dept. theology/religious studies U. Scranton, Pa., 1979—; dir. U. Scranton Press. Editor: (book series) Bruce Contemporary Theology Series, 1963-73. Founder, bd. dirs. Nat. Workshop on Christian Unity, 1963-70. Fulbright scholar, 1963. Mem. Am. Acad. Religion, Coll. Theology Soc. (bd. dirs. 1965-67), Cath. Bibl. Assn. Home and Office: U Scranton Linden and Monroe Scranton PA 18510

ROUSSOS, STEPHEN BERNARD, minister; b. Ft. Wayne, Ind., June 18, 1960; s. James Theodore and Louise Marie (Diller) R.; m. Tina Marie Priest, July 31, 1982; children: Stephanie Marie, Nathaniel David. BA, Summit Christian Coll. (formerly Ft. Wayne Bible Coll.), 1982, Diploma in Christian Edn., 1982. Lic. min. Missionary Ch., 1982, ordained to ministry, 1985. Assoc., youth pastor Community Bible Ch., Lomita, Calif., 1982-85, sr. pastor, 1985-91; sr. pastor Freeman (S.D.) Missionary Ch., 1991—; mem. pastoral com. Luis Palau Crusade, Redondo Beach, Calif., 1990-91. Mem. Lomita/Harbor City Ministerial Assn. (treas. 1988-89, pres. 1989-91). Republican. Office: Freeman Missionary Ch PO Box 460 Freeman SD 54029

ROWAN, ALBERT THEODORE, minister; b. Kansas City, Mo., May 15, 1927; s. Albert Thomas and Florence Marion (Diggs) R.; married Carrie Mae McBride, Feb. 15, 1948; children: Richard, Brenda, Stephen, Allana, Allan. B of Religious Edn., BTh, Western Bapt. Bible Coll., 1955, 56; MDiv, Ashland Theol. Sem., 1976; D of Ministry, Trinity Theol. Sem., 1987; DD (hon.), Va. Theol. Sem., 1975. Ordained to ministry Bapt. Ch., 1952. Min. 2d Bapt. Ch., Marceline, Mo., 1955-56; min. 1st Bapt. Ch., Brusnwick, Mo., 1956, Quincy, Ill., 1956-60; min. Zion Bapt. Ch., Springfield & Salem Bapt. Ch., Champaign, Ill., 1960-64, Bethany Bapt. Ch., Cleve., 1964—; 1st v.p., Bapt. Ministrial Conf., Cleve., 1972—; adj. prof. Trinity Theol. Sem., Newburgh, Ind., 1990—. Chmn. City Planning Commn., Cleve., 1976—; exec. dir. Ministrial Head Start Assn., Cleve., 1987—. Named Pastor of Yr., Bapt. Ministerial Conf. Cleve., 1983, Alumnus of Yr., Western Bapt. Bible Coll., 1984. Mem. Northern Ohio Dist. Assn. (2d vice moderator 1989—), Cleve. Bapt. Assn. (bd. dirs. 1988—). Home: 3716 Langston Rd Cleveland Heights OH 44121 Office: Bethany Bapt Ch 1211 E 105th St Cleveland OH 44108

ROWDEN, A(LPHRO) JOHN, minister; b. Brinktown, Mo., Mar. 15, 1906; s. Robert Hosea and Clara Opal (Williams) R.; m. Margaret Louise Henderson, Jan. 18, 1936 (dec. July 1982); 1 child, Roberta Louise Rowden Crane; m. Sandra Kay McFadden, Jan. 7, 1985. Student, U. Mo., 1927-28; grad., Evang. United Bretheren Corr. Sch., Kansas City, Mo., 1946. Lic. to ministry Evang. United Bretheren Ch. as itinerant elder, 1942, ordained, 1947; cert. tchr., Mo. Pastor Evang. United Bretheren Ch., Adrian, Mo., 1941-46, Jennings, La., 1947-48; founder, pastor Revival Ch., Houston, 1949-50; pastor Evangelistic Ctr. Ch., Nevada, Mo., 1950-53; founder, sr. pastor, pres. bd. The Evangelistic Ctr. Ch., Kansas City, 1954—; daily radio min. The Gospel, 1951-85; founder, trustee Evangelistic Ctr. Ch., Nevada, Mo., 1951—, Evangelistic Ctr. Ch./Living Waters Wroship Ctr., Amarillo, Tex., 1965—; founder, pres. bd. dirs. Pan Am. Missions, Portland, Oreg., 1959—; charismatic ch. rep. Ministries of New Life, Prairie Village, Kans., 1986—; chaplain City Coun. Kansas City, 1987-90; organized chs. in several states and Sidney, Australia; guest speaker in various charismatic chs. and confs. throughout the U.S., Can., Jamaica, Colombia, Mex., 1954—. Author: (booklets) The Ministry of the Holy Spirit in the Life of Rev. and Mrs. A.J. Rowden, 1966, God's Master Plan, 1970, Kingdom Blessings Now, 1978, Heart of God, 1985, and others. Co-founder, dir. programs using 3d step of Alcoholics Anonymous to minister in 6 secular substance abuse treatment ctrs. throughout the Greater Kansas City Area, 1986-90; vol. Salvation Army, Kansas City, Kans., 1988-90. Home: 6506 Barton Circle # 101 Shawnee KS 66203 Office: Evangelistic Ctr Ch 1024 E Truman Rd Kansas City MO 64106 *You need to know that you know that you know that He (Christ) lives in your heart and that He (Christ) is able to do exceedingly and abundantly above all that you ask according to the resurrection power that mightily worketh in you who believe.*

ROWDEN, MARK ALLEN, minister; b. St. Louis, Apr. 15, 1957; s. Paul Eugene and Edith Eloise (Allen) R.; m. Janet Virginia Geisz, Dec. 28, 1985; children: Jane Ellen, Peter Douglas. BA in Psychology, Covenant Coll., 1983; MDiv, Covenant Seminary, St. Louis, 1987. Ordained teaching elder Presbyn. Ch., 1988. Church planting intern Mo. Presbytery, St. Louis, 1987-88; asst. pastor for evangelism and discipleship McIlwain Meml. Presbyn. Ch., Pensacola, Fla., 1988—. Office: McIlwain Meml Presbyn Ch 1220 E Blount St Pensacola FL 32503

ROWE, STEPHEN CHRISTIAN, minister, educator. BA in Philosophy with honors, Colgate U., 1967; ThM, U. Chgo., 1969, MA, 1970, PhD, 1974. Asst. prof. William James Coll. and Grand Valley State Coll., Allendale, Mich., 1972-73, coordinator, 1973-74, faculty, 1974-83; minister Fountain St. Ch., Grand Rapids, Mich., 1976-77; prof. philosophy Grand Valley State Coll., Allendale, 1983—, also chmn. dept. liberal studies; lectr. Urban Tng. Ctr., Chgo.; cons. Chgo. Theol. Inst.; part-time faculty YMCA Community Coll., Chgo. Editor: Living Beyond Crisis, 1980. Contbr. articles to profl. jours. U. Chgo. fellow, 1971-72; Danforth Found. grantee, 1977-84. Mem. Am. Acad. Religion, Am. Philos. Assn., Am. Soc. Christian Ethics, Assn. Integrative Studies, Assn. Gen. and Liberal Studies, Ctr. Process Studies, Chgo. Social Ethics, Soc. for Values in Higher Edn., U. Chgo. Com. Religion and Am. Pub. Life, Mich. Assn. Governing Bds., Phi Kappa Phi. Home: 1625 Seminole SE Grand Rapids MI 49506 Office: Grand Valley State Coll Allendale MI 49401

ROWE, WILLIAM LEONARD, philosophy educator; b. Detroit, July 26, 1931; s. William Edlin and Olive (Julian) R.; m. Margaret Ann Moan. BA with distinction, Wayne State U., 1954; BD summa cum laude, Chgo. Theol. Sem., 1957; MA, U. Mich., 1958, PhD, 1962. Instr. U. Ill., Urbana, 1960-62; asst. prof. Purdue U., West Lafayette, Ind., 1962-65, assoc. prof., 1965-69, prof., 1969—, head dept. philosophy, 1981-91; dir. summer session for coll. tchrs. NEH, 1982. Author: Religious Symbols and God, 1968, The Cosmological Argument, 1975, Philosophy of Religion, 1978, Thomas Reid on Freedom and Morality, 1991. Guggenheim fellow, 1984-85; Nat. Humanities Ctr. fellow, 1984-85. Mem. Am. Philos. Assn. Cen. Div. (pres. 1986-87), AAUP, Soc. Philosophy of Religion. Avocations: jogging, canoeing. Office: Purdue U Dept of Philosophy West Lafayette IN 47907

ROWELL, ELDRIGE BATES (REGGIE ROWELL), minister; b. Augusta, Ga., Mar. 8, 1952; s. Marshall Eldrige and Lucylle (Mizzell) R.; m. Carolyn Marie Rudy, Sept. 2, 1984; children: Justin McCorcle, Rachel Rowell. BA, Wofford Coll., 1974; MDiv, Yale U., 1977, STM, 1980. Ordained to ministry United Meth. Ch. as deacon, 1975, as elder, 1979. Assoc. pastor Cen. United Meth. Ch., Spartanburg, S.C., 1977-78, Fairfield (Conn.) - Grace United Meth. Ch., 1979-81; pastor Jefferson (S.C.) United Meth. Ch., 1981-82, Christ United Meth. Ch., Bennettsville, S.C., 1982-84, St. Andrew United Meth. Ch., Easley, S.C., 1987—; mem. Dist. Com. on Continuing Edn., 1985-87, Dist. Coun. on Ministries, 1988—, Conf. Bd. of Ch. and Soc., 1988—. Pres. Pickens County Mental Health Assn., 1988-91; exec. com. Mental Health Assn. in S.C., 1991-93; vol. chaplain Bept. Med. Ctr., Easley and Greeville Hosp. System. Mem. Easley Ministerial Assn. Home: 435 Pelzer Hwy Easley SC 29642 Office: Saint Andrew United Meth Ch 309 Pelzer Hwy PO Box 27 Easley SC 29641

ROWINSKI, FRANCIS C., bishop. Bishop of Buffalo-Pitts. Diocese, Polish Nat. Cath. Ch. Am., Buffalo. Office: Polish Nat Cath Ch of Am 182 Sobieski St Buffalo NY 14212*

ROWLAND, FRANK R., lay worker; b. Yakima, Wash., May 15, 1964; s. Frank H. and Sandra (K.) R. BA in Mktg., Wash. State U., 1986; post-grad., Fuller Theol. Seminary. Head youth leader Young Life, Selah, Wash., 1987—; advisor Ross Point (Idaho) Camp/Youth, 1991—. Republican. Home: 111 Selah-Naches Rd Selah WA 98942 Office: First Baptist Church 515 E Yakima Ave Yakima WA 98901

ROWLAND, HARRY MANNING, JR., clergyman; b. Nashville, Nov. 12, 1957; s. Harry Manning and Margaret Jane (Blackwelder) R.; m. Lana Jeanne Johnson, Aug. 22, 1981; children: Melissa Jeanne, Harry Manning III. BA in Bus., Baylor U., 1980; MDiv, Southwestern Sem., 1983; D Ministry, New Orleans Sem., 1990. Ordained to ministry So. Bapt. Conv., 1983. Summer missionary So. Bapt. Mission Bd., Dominican Republic, 1979; youth min. Columbus Avenue Bapt. Ch., Waco, Tex., 1982-85; minister coll. Woodmont Bapt. Ch., Nashville, 1985-88, assoc. pastor, singles minister, 1988—; com. chmn. Waco Bapt. Assn., 1983-85; com. mem. Nashville Bapt. Assn., 1985-88; leader religious conf., Kazakhstan, USSR, 1991. Mem. Nat. Assn. Single Adult Leaders, Ministers with Single Adults. Home: 2008 Boxwood Dr Franklin TN 37064 Office: Woodmont Bapt Ch 2100 Woodmont Blvd Nashville TN 37215 *I have found that good people find that life is good, kind people beget kindness and loving people never lack for love. The simple truths are often the most relevant, but also the most neglected. One truly reaps what one sows.*

ROWLAND, JOHN ANDREW, music and youth minister; b. Jacksonville, Fla., Feb. 2, 1959; s. Cecil Horace and Mary Jean (Byrom) R.; m. Jennifer Paulette Midkiff, June 15, 1985; 1 child, Mills-Anne Rebekah, Ethan Andrew. BA, Samford U., 1982; M of Ch. Music, So. Bapt. Theol. Sem., 1986. Minister music/youth Livermore (Ky.) Missionary Bapt. Ch., 1983-86, First Bapt. Ch., Palm Coast, Fla., 1986—. Home: 159 Bridgehaven Dr Palm Coast FL 32137 Office: First Bapt Ch 301 Palm Coast Pkwy Palm Coast FL 32137

ROWLAND, WILLIAM FREDRICK RICK, religion and communication educator; b. Erick, Okla., Mar. 20, 1934; s. Roger Sherman and Elizabeth Ann (Houston) R.; m. Lildra Queen, June 8, 1956; children: Roxanne, William Rick, Randi Irene Nichols, Rodney Glen. BS in Speech Edn., Okla. U., 1957; MS in Speech Edn., Pepperdine U., 1960; MA in Religion, Calif. Grad. Sch. Theology, 1988, DMN in Religion, 1990. Cert. tchr., Calif. Youth minister Northside Ch. of Christ, Santa Ana, Calif., 1962-65; youth minister Cen. Ch. of Christ, Santa Barbara, Calif., 1965-66, campus minister, 1966-72; campus minister, chmn. com. Malibu (Calif.) Ch. of Christ, 1975—; assoc. prof. religion/communications Pepperdine U., Malibu, Calif., 1975—; elder Cen. Ch. of Christ, Santa Barbara, 1972-75, Malibu Ch. of Christ, 1976-91; preaching min. Hollywood Ch. of Christ, 1991—; bd. dirs. Campus Jour. Mag., Arlington, Tex. Author: Campus Ministries: A Historical Study of Churches of Christ Campus Ministries and Selected College Ministries, from 1706 to 1990, 1991; editor Western Campus News, 1984—; contbr. articles to profl. jours., book chpts. Rep. Calif. Rep. Assembly State Conv., San Diego, 1964; legis. com. mem., Orange County, Calif., 1963-65. Recipient Svc. award Nat. Chs. of Christ Campus Ministry, 1988; U. Calif. Santa Barbara Campus Advance for Christ, 1977; named Outstanding Young Men of Am. Nat. Jr. C. of C., 1969; The Rick Rowland Campus Ministry Endowment Fund named in his honor U. Calif., Santa Barbara Campus Advance for Christ, 1991. Mem. Religious Speech Communication Assn. (interpersonal commuunication com.), Am. Acad. Religion, Speech Communication Assn., Nat. Campus Ministries Assn. Office: Pepperdine U Malibu CA 90263

ROWLANDS, ALEXANDER ERIC, minister; b. Kingwilliamstown, Cape Province, Republic of South Africa, Aug. 19, 1948; came to U.S., 1966; s. Eric Lievesly and Johanna (De Witt) R.; m. Rita Rae Coleman, June 14, 1969; children: Vanessa, Kathryn. BA, Wittenberg U., 1970; MA, Miami U., Oxford, Ohio, 1975, Fuller Acad., Pasadena, Calif. Ordained to ministry Assemblies of God, 1980. Assoc. pastor Grand Ave Ch. of God, Springfield, Ohio, 1968-69; youth pastor St. Clair Ave Bapt. Ch., Hamilton, Ohio, 1969-72; v.p. Youth Devel. Inc., San Diego, 1972-75; assoc. pastor 1st Assembly of God, San Diego, 1975-80; sr. pastor 1st Assembly of God, Cedar Rapids, Calif., 1981-88, Westgate Chapel, Edmonds, Wash., 1988—; presbyter Iowa dist. coun. Assembly of God, Des Moines, 1986-88. Home: 20216 12th Ave NW Seattle WA 98177 Office: Westgate Chapel 22901 Edmonds Way Edmonds WA 98020

ROWLEY, ROBERT DEANE, JR., bishop; b. Cumberland, Md., July 6, 1941; s. Robert Deane Sr. and Alice Marquerite (Wilson) W.; m. Nancy Ann Roland, June 27, 1964; children: Karen Gordon Rowley Butler, Robert Deane III. BA, U. Pitts., 1962, LLB, 1965; LLM, George Washington U., 1970; MDiv, Episcopal Sem. of S.W., 1977, DD (hon.), 1989. Ordained deacon Episcopal Ch., 1977; priest, 1978; bishop, 1989. Bar: Pa. 1965, U.S. Supreme Ct. 1970. Dean of students St. Andrew's Priory Sch., Honolulu, 1977-80; canon St. Andrew's Cathedral, Honolulu, 1979-81; rector St. Timothy's Episcopal Ch., Aiea, Hawaii, 1981-83; canon to bishop Diocese of Bethlehem (Pa.), 1983-89; bishop Diocese of Northwestern Pa., Erie, 1989—. Capt. USN, 1966—. Mem. Erie County Bar Assn., Erie Club, Lake Shore Country Club. Home: 810 Huntington Dr Erie PA 16505 Office: Diocese of Northwestern Pa 145 W 6th St Erie PA 16501

ROY, CHARLES EDWARD, religion educator; b. Birmingham, Ala., July 15, 1917; s. Moses Eugene and Bessie (Bennett) R.; m. Brona Nifong, Dec. 20, 1947; children: Rebecca Roy Benfield, AA, Young Harris Coll., 1938; AB cum laude, Piedmont Coll., 1940; MDiv, Candler Sch. Theology, 1944; MA, George Peabody Coll., 1949; DD (hon.), Greensboro Coll., 1980. Ordained elder United Methodist Ch. Chaplain, prof. religion, chmn. div. humanities Brevard Coll., N.C., 1944-84, emeritus, 1984—, acting pres., 1968-69. Pres. Transylvania County Youth Assn., 1965-68; bd. dirs. Transylvania-Henderson Counties Justice Alternatives, 1981—; bd. mem. Community Relations Council, Schenck Job Corps, Brevard, 1980—; chmn. Transylvania County Human Rels. Coun., Brevard, 1965-85; chmn. Transylvania County United Way, Brevard, 1971-72; mem. steering com. Transylvania Hospice Care, past. pres, bd. dirs. Recipient Gov.'s Vol. Service award, 1984, Outstanding Sr. Citizen's award Brevard Jaycees, 1985, Pres.'s Outstanding Citizen's award Brevard C. of C., 1987. Mem. Soc. Bibl. Lit., Am. Schs. Oriental Rsch., Transylvania County Ministerial Assn. Democrat. Lodge: Lions (pres. Brevard 1973-74). Avocations: travel, archeology, gardening, woodworking.

ROY, KEVIN BRIAN, minister; b. Shreveport, La., Oct. 28, 1959; s. Robert Edwin and Patsy Ruth (Willis) R.; m. Tana Lynn Nunnally, May 19, 1984; 1 child, Brittany Lynn. BA, East Tex. Bapt. Coll., 1981. Lic. to ministry Bapt. Ch., 1979, ordained 1982. Minister of youth Ingleside Bapt. Ch., Shreveport, La., 1981-86, Denman Ave. Bapt. Ch., Lufkin, Tex., 1986—; trustee Pineywoods Bapt. Encampment, Woodlake, Tex., 1990—. Mem. Nat. Network Youth Ministers. Home: 907 Old Orchard Lufkin TX 75901 Office: PO Box 1351 Lufkin TX 75901

ROY, RALPH LORD, minister; b. St. Albans, Vt., Sept. 30, 1928; s. Howard Allen and Olive Lydia (Corliss) R.; m. Margaret Ellen Finlay, Feb. 12, 1960; 1 child, Joyce Victoria. BA, Swarthmore Coll., 1950; MA, Columbia U. and Union, Theol. Seminary, 1952. Ordained to ministry United Meth. Ch. as deacon, 1952, as elder, 1961. Asst. minister Met. Community United. Meth. Ch., N.Y.C., 1957-60; minister Grace United Meth. Ch., N.Y.C., 1960-63, Green Ave./Knickerbocker United Meth. Ch., Bklyn., 1964-68, Cuyler Warren St. Community Ch., Bklyn., 1968-70, United Meth. Ch., Clinton, Conn., 1970-74, Mary Taylor United Meth. Ch., Milford, Conn., 1974-79, First United Meth. Ch., Meriden, Conn., 1979—. Author: Apostles of Discord, 1953, Communism and the Churches, 1960; contbr. articles to profl. jours. Chaplain Meriden (Conn.) Police Dept., 1981—. Home: 185 David Dr Meriden CT 06450 Office: First United Methodist Ch 15 Pleasant St Meriden CT 06450 *When I consider the magnificence and vastness of the universe, I can be overwhelmed by childlike marvel. That's one key aspect of God's creation. Another is the almost infinite variety, complexity, and beauty of life on our planet, all of it interdependent, making it urgent that we dwell together in harmony, mutual respect and peace.*

ROY, RAYMOND, bishop; b. Man., Can., May 3, 1919; s. Charles-Borromé e and Zephirina (Milette) R. B.A. in Philosophy and Theology, U. Man., 1942; student, Philos. Sem., Montreal, 1942-43, Major Sem., Montreal, 1943-46, Major Sem. St. Boniface, 1946-47. Ordained priest Roman Catholic Ch. 1947. Asst. pastor, then pastor chs. in Man., 1947-50, 53-66; chaplain St. Boniface (Man.) Hosp., 1950-53; superior Minor Sem., St. Boniface, 1966-69; pastor Cathedral Parish, St. Boniface, 1969-72; ordained bishop, 1972; bishop of St. Paul, Alta., Can., 1972—. Club: K.C. Address: 4410 51st Ave, Box 339, Saint Paul, AB Canada T0A 3A0

ROY, THOMAS CLAYTON, III, religious organization executive; b. Sheyboygan, Wis., Nov. 21, 1949; s. Thomas Clayton Jr. and Lorraine (Dahmer) R.; m. Caroline Lindsay Brown, Aug. 29, 1970; children: Amy Lorraine, Lindsay Alice. BS, Grace Coll., 1974; postgrad., St. Francis Coll., 1976; DTh. (hon.), Bapt. U., 1989. Assoc. dir. admissions Huntington (Ind.) Coll., 1979-83, Grace Coll., Winona Lake, Ind., 1983-86; exec. dir. Unlimited Potential, Inc., Warsaw, Ind., 1980—. Named Outstanding Young Men. of Am., 1980; recipient Disting. Alumni of the Yr. award, Grace Coll., 1987. Mem. U.S. Baseball Fedn., Pro-Bd. Nat. Sports Coalition. Office: Unlimited Potential Inc 600 E Winona PO Box 1355 Warsaw IN 46581

ROYALL, BOB LEE, minister; b. Abilene, Dec. 2, 1956; s. Walter B. Royall and Melva J. (Rock) Henson; m. Deborah Moore Terhune, Dec. 30, 1978; children: Elizabeth, Stephanie, David. BA in History, U. Tex., Arlington, 1981; MDiv, Golden Gate Sem., 1985. Lic. to ministry Baptist, 1981, ordained, 1988. Campus min. Bapt. Student Union, Ogden, Utah, 1981-82; admissions counselor Golden Gate Sem., Mill Valley, Calif., 1985-87; campus min. Bapt. Student Ministries U. Idaho, Moscow, 1987—. Home: 412 S Cleveland St Moscow ID 83843 Office: Bapt Student Ministries 822 Elm St Moscow ID 83843

ROYCE, JAMES EMMET, clergyman, educator, counselor; b. Spokane, Oct. 20, 1914; s. James Emmet and Lucie F. (Reilly) R. BA, Gonzaga U., 1939, MA, 1940; PhD, Loyola U., Chgo., 1945; STL, Alma Coll. of Santa Clara U., 1948. Lic. psychologist, Wash. Ordained to priesthood, 1947. Instr. Gonzaga U., Spokane, 1940-41; teaching fellow Loyola U., Chgo., 1941-44; asst. prof. to prof. dept. psychology Seattle U., 1948-80, chmn. dept. psychology, 1950-65, prof. emeritus, 1980—; pres., dean Notre Dame Coll., Nelson, B.C., Can., 1954-55; vis. prof. U. Pacific, 1954, Loyola U. of L.A., 1957, State U. N.H., 1966, U. Alaska, 1977, Kodiak Community Coll., 1977. Author: Personality and Mental Health, 1955, 2d edit., 1964, Man and His Nature: A Philosophical Psychology, 1961, Man and Meaning, 1969, Alcohol Problems and Alcoholism: A Comprehensive Survey, 1981, rev. edit., 1989; co-author: Ethics for Addiction Professionals, 1987; contbr. articles to profl. jours. Bd. dirs. Nat. Coun. on Alcoholism, 1976—; trustee Seattle U., 1974-78; mem. Gov.'s Adv. Bd. on Alcoholism, 1958-71, chmn. edn. com. Fellow APA (pres. div. 24, 1964-65), Am. Assn. State Psychology Bds. (pres. 1970-71); mem. Acad. Religion and Mental Health. Roman Catholic. Avocations: hiking, music. Home: Seattle U Seattle WA 98122

ROYSTER, ROBERT (BISHOP DMITRI OF DALLAS), bishop. Bishop of Dallas The Orthodox Ch. in Am. Office: Orthodox Ch in Am 4112 Throckmorton Dallas TX 75219*

ROYSTON, JAMES HOWARD, minister; b. Johnson City, Tenn., Mar. 1, 1948; s. Howard H. and Ethel F. (Carder) R.; m. Wanda Jeannie Hoilman, July 1, 1966; children: Jeffrey, Jennifer. BA, Carson-Newman Coll., 1975; MDiv, Southeastern Bapt. Theol. Sem., Wake Forest, N.C., 1980, D Ministry, 1988. Ordained to ministry So. Bapt. Conv., 1971. Pastor Piedmont Bapt. Ch., Dandridge, Tenn., 1974-76, Green Level Bapt. Ch., Apex, N.C., 1976-78, Carolina Pines Bapt. Ch., Raleigh, N.C., 1978-81; dir. missions Mecklenburg Bapt. Assn., Charlotte, N.C., 1981-86; pastor 1st Bapt. Ch., Huntersville, N.C., 1986—; moderator Mecklenburg Bapt. Assn., 1989-91, pres. Pastors Conf., 1989-90; bd. dirs. Bapt. State Conv., 1991—; v.p. Master Design Assocs., Columbia, S.C., 1991. Contbr. articles to religious publs. Bd. dirs. Crisis Assistance, Charlotte, 1981-86, Emergency Housing, Charlotte, 1983-86, Huntersville Crisis, 1988-91, Am. Cancer Soc., Charlotte, 1989-91. Named Cons. of Yr., Home Mission Bd., 1986. Mem. Lions. Office: 1st Bapt Ch PO Box 331 Huntersville NC 28078

ROZZELL, BOBBY LEON, evangelist; b. Oklahoma City, July 13, 1956; s. Ronald Raniel and Helen Faye (Thurmond) R.; m. Linda Denise Merrell, Aug. 15, 1975; children: Ronald Dale, Holly Denise, Timothy David. BS, Okla. Christian Coll., 1979; postgrad., Harding Grad. Sch. Religion, Memphis, 1979-81. Ordained to ministry Ch. of Christ, 1981. Assoc. minister Cherokee Hills Ch. of Christ, Oklahoma City, 1981-83, Westside Ch. of Christ, Norman, Okla., 1983-89; evangelist Elpyco Ch. of Christ, Wichita, Kans., 1989—. Office: Elpyco Ch of Christ 1739 Elpyco Wichita KS 67218-4307 *I want all my relationships with my fellow human beings to be such that I never have to dodge them or cross the street to keep from meeting them.*

RUBENSTEIN, JACOB SAMUEL, rabbi; b. Rosenheim, Germany, July 17, 1949; came to U.S., 1951; s. David and Eva (Bergman) R.; m. Deborah Powell, Sept. 1, 1969; children: Shira, Daniel, Jonathan, Yoheved. BA, Hebrew U., Jerusalem, 1972; MA, Harvard U., 1976. Ordained rabbi, 1972. Chief justices Ashkenazic and Sephardic Rabbinic Cts., Jerusalem, 1972; rabbi Congregation Beth Sholom, Milford, Mass., 1975-77, Providence, 1977-84; rabbi Young Israel of Scarsdale, N.Y., 1984—; trustee Westchester Jewish Conf., White Plains, 1986—; vice chmn. rabbinic adv. bd. N.Y. Fedn., exec. officer Westchester Rabbinical Coun., 1986—; vice chmn. Nat. Rabbinic Cabinet of Jewish Am. Fedn., N.Y.C., 1990—; pres. Westchester (N.Y.) Bd. Rabbis, 1990—. Contbr. to: Rabbinical Council of America Sermon Manual, 1982, 6th edit., 1991, Torah for Today, 1990; mem. Congl. Acad. Rev. Bd., 1986-89. Mem. Blue Ribbon Panel on Anti-Bias Crime, Westchester County-White Plains, N.Y., 1988; mem. adv. bd. Washington Inst. for Jewish Leadership and Values, 1988—. Recipient City of Peace award Israel Bonds, 1978, Dr. and Mrs. Abraham Stern Svc. award Yeshiva U., 1983, Rabbinical Leadership award Ohr Hameir Theol. Sem., 1985, Rabbinic Svc. award United Jewish Appeal, 1987. Mem. Rabbinical Coun. Am. (exec. bd., chmn. legis. and pub. affairs coms. 1985—), Religious Zionists Am., Inst. for Pub. Affairs (chmn. rabbinical adv. com. 1990—). Office: Young Israel of Scarsdale 1313 Weaver St PO Box 103H Scarsdale NY 10583 *Physical and social forces govern my life. But in the area of moral freedom, no matter how strong and overwhelming the limitations and mysteries, I can be sovereign, and under the burden of conditioning and conflict motivate my life.*

RUBENSTEIN, RICHARD LOWELL, theologian, educator; b. N.Y.C., Jan. 8, 1924; s. Jesse George and Sara (Fine) R.; m. Betty Rogers Alschuler, Aug. 21, 1966; children by previous marriage: Aaron, Nathaniel (dec.), Hannah Rachel, Jeremy. Student, Hebrew Union Coll., Cin., 1942-45; AB, U. Cin., 1946; MHL rabbi, Jewish Theol. Sem., N.Y.C., 1952; DHL (honoris causa), Jewish Theol. Sem., 1987; STM, Harvard U., 1955, PhD, 1960. Rabbi in Brockton, Mass., 1952-54, Natick, Mass., 1954-56; chaplain to Jewish students Harvard U., 1956-68; univ. chaplain to Jewish students U. Pitts. and Carnegie Inst. Tech., 1958-70; adj. prof. humanities U. Pitts., 1969-70; prof. religion Fla. State U., Tallahassee, 1970-77; Disting. prof. religion Fla. State U., 1977-81, Robert O. Lawton Disting. prof. religion, 1981—; dir. So. Center for Study of Religion and Culture, 1973-82; co-dir. Inst. for Humanities, 1980—; pres. Washington Inst. for Values in Pub. Policy, 1982-91; Disting. vis. prof. Calif. State U., Chico, 1979; Edgar M. Bronfman vis. prof. U. Va., 1985; mem. presiding coun. Internat. Religious Fedn. for World Peace, 1991—, mem. editorial bd. Internat. Jour. of World Peace, 1983; mem. adv. bd. Washington Times, 1982-91, chmn. editorial adv. bd., 1991—; mem. exec. adv. bd. The World and I mag., 1986—; mem. exec. com. Internat. Jour. of The Unity of Sciences, 1987—; mem. adv. bd. Inst. for Study of Am. Wars, 1989—. Author: After Auschwitz: Radical Theology and Contemporary Judaism, 1966, The Religious Imagination, 1968 (Portico d'Ottavia lit. prize for Italian transl. 1977), Morality and Eros, 1970, My Brother Paul, 1972, Power Struggle: An Autobiographical Confession, 1974, The Cunning of History, 1975, The Age of Triage, 1983, (with John K. Roth) Approaches to Auschwitz, 1986; editor: Modernization: The Humanist Response to Its Promise and Problems, 1982, Spirit Matters: The Worlwide Impact of Religion on Contemporary Politics, 1987, The Dissolving Alliance: The United States and the Future of the NATO Alliance, 1987; regular columnist Sekai Nippo, Tokyo, 1987—; mem. adv. bd. Paragon House Pubs. Recipient Portico d' Ottavia lit. prize Rome, 1977; John Phillips fellow Phillips Exeter Acad., 1970; postdoctoral fellow Soc. Religion in Higher Edn.; Nat. Humanities Inst. fellow Yale U., 1976-77; Rockefeller Found. fellow Aspen Inst. for Humanistic Studies, 1979. Mem. Rabbinical Assembly Am., Am. Acad. Religion, Soc. Sci. Study Religion, Profs. World Peace Acad. (exec. com. 1980—, pres. 1981-82), Soc. for Bibl. Lit., Internat. Psychohist. Assn., Western Assn. for German Studies, Inst. for Study of Am. Wars (adv. bd. 1990—), Internat. House of Japan, Nat. Press Club (Harvard chpt.), Cosmos Club. Home: 751 Lake Shore Dr Tallahassee FL 32312 also: 8 Clam Shell Ave East Hampton NY 11937 Office: Fla State U Tallahassee FL 32306

RUBIN, BARRY ALAN, rabbi, consultant; b. N.Y.C., July 29, 1945; s. Sidney and Helen Rubin; m. Steffi Karen Geiser, July 4, 1975; children: Rebecca, Shira. Student, Trinity Evang. Div. Sch., 1976-77, Talbot Sem., 1979, Balt. Hebrew U., 1988; BA, Ohio U., 1967, MA, 1968. Ordained rabbi, 1983; CPA, Md. Instr. Howard U., Washington, 1968-71; acct., 1972-74; min. Hineni Ministries, San Francisco, 1974-80; exec. dir. Messianic Ministry to Israel, Chattanooga, 1980-82; rabbi Emmanuel Messianic Congregation, Balt., 1981—; nat. dir. ch. ministries Chosen People Ministries, Charlotte, N.C., 1982-87; pres. Rubin Assocs., Washington, 1987—; mgmt communications cons. for ministries, chief exec officer Jewish N.T. Publs., Inc., Clarksville, Md., 1988—; exec. dir. Lederer Messianic Ministries, Balt. Author: You Bring the Bagels, I'll Bring the Gospel: Sharing Messiah with Your Jewish Neighbor; contbr. articles to religious publs.; producer music recs. With USCG, 1969-75. Mem. Union of Messianic Jewish Congregations, Messianic Jewish Alliance Am., Fellowship Messianic Congregations. Avocations: crossword puzzles, golf. *The great failure of modern man is his avoidance of the truths of both the older and newer scriptures.*

RUBIN, S. SMELKA, rabbi; b. Reghin, Mures, Romania, Mar. 17, 1925; came to U.S., 1949; s. Jacob Israel and Malka (Dachner) R.; m. Sofia Rosenbaum, Dec. 4, 1949; 6 children. Grad., Rabbinical Coll., Timisuora, Romania, 1948. Ordained rabbi, 1948. Rabbi Congregation Shar Hashomaim, Bronx, N.Y., 1949-51; grand rabbi Congregation Kehilas Jakob, West Lawrence, N.Y., 1951—; dean Bnos Israel Sch., West Lawrence, 1958-78. Author: Minhagim, 1971, Tifereth Avos, 1986. Named Grand Rabbi, Jerusalem, 1962. Mem. Histadruth Admorim Am. (v.p. 1972-89). Office: Congregation Kehilas Jakob 612 Beach 9th St West Lawrence NY 11691-5297

RUBINSTEIN, KAREN, religious organization executive. Exec. dir. Am. Zionist Fedn., N.Y.C. Office: Am Zionist Fedn 515 Park Ave New York NY 10022*

RUBIN-TILLES, MAX ABRAHAM, cantor, educator; b. Colon, Germany, Dec. 7, 1922; s. Isidore David and Chaja Miriam (Beiderman) Rubin; m. Ann Leibowicz, Jan. 31, 1950; children: Larry, Sheldon, Carolyn Miriam. Degree., Conservatory of Music, Krakow, Poland, Yeshiva Keter Torah, Krakow. Cantor tchr. Beth Emeth Congregation, Phila., 1953-56, Beth Joseph Ctr., Rochester, N.Y., 1956-62, Fair Lawn (N.J.) Jewish Ctr., 1962—. Composer cantata based on book The Language of Judaism (by Simon Glustrom). Hon. fellow Jewish Theol. Sem., 1978. Mem. Cantors Assembly of N.J. (chmn. 1977-79), Cantors Assembly, Jewish Minister-Cantors Assn., Masons. Home: 13-15 Ellis Ave Fair Lawn NJ 07410

RUBLE, ANN, minister; b. Seattle, Oct. 26, 1953; d. Monte Rahe and Stella (Terefinko) R.; m. Francis Michael Trotter, Aug. 29, 1984. Cert. sec., Met. Bus. Coll., Seattle, 1972. Ordained to ministry Ch. of Scientology, 1980. Minister Ch. of Scientology, Seattle, 1980—, dir. pub. affairs, 1983; pres. Ch. of Scientology of Wash. State, Seattle, 1984-88, dir., 1989—. Bur. chief Jour. Freedom News, 1984-88. Mem. Citizen's Commn. Human Rights, Seattle, 1984—, Com. on Religious Liberties, Seattle, 1985—, Wash. Environ. Coun., 1989—. Office: Ch of Scientology of Washington State 2603 Third Ave Seattle WA 98121 *My deep concern is that our basic human rights are being constantly eroded. This includes our right to freedom of religious expression, freedom of speech and other rights agreed to and espoused by those signers of our country's Bill of Rights long ago and passed down to us. A quote from L. Ron Hubbard sums up my philosophy in protecting human* *rights: "Price of freedom: constant alertness, constant willingness to fight back. There is no other price."*

RUBLE, RANDALL TUCKER, theologian, educator, academic administrator; b. Greenville, Va., Apr. 15, 1932; s. William Cecil and Carrie Mae (Connor) R.; m. Martha L. Grant, Sept. 6, 1958; children: John, Jeffrey, Ellen. A.B., Erskine Coll., 1958, B.D., 1961; Th.M., Princeton Theol. Sem., 1962, Ph.D., U. Edinburgh, 1964. Prof. Hebrew and Old Testament Erskine Sem., Due West, S.C., 1965—, v.p., dean, 1976—; supply pastor Abbeville (S.C.) Assoc. Ref. Presbyn. Ch., 1967—; chmn. N.Am. and Carribean area World Alliance of Reformed Chs., 1979-80. Author: The Ten Commandents For Our Day, 1971; contbr. articles to jours., mags. Mem. Town Council, Due West, 1972-75; chmn. Christian Prison Ministries, 1987—. Served with USAF, 1951-55. Mem. Soc. Bibl. Lit., Brit. Old Testament Soc., Nat. Assn. Profs. of Hebrew, S.C. Acad. Religion, Atlanta Theol. Assn. (pres. 1990—). Presbyterian. Home: PO Box 172 Due West SC 29639 Office: PO Box 171 Due West SC 29639

RUDD, LEO SLATON, psychology educator, minister; b. Hereford, Tex., Feb. 20, 1924; s. Charles Ival and Susan Leola (Horton) R.; m. Virginia Mae Daniel, Nov. 17, 1943; children: Virginia Kaye, Leo Jr., Bobbie Ann. BA, William Jewell Coll., Liberty, Mo., 1947; MRE, Cen. Bapt. Sem., Kansas City, Kans., 1948; MS, E. Tex. State U., Commerce, 1957; PhD, N. Tex. State U., Denton, 1959. Ordained to ministry, Southern Bapt. Conv. Bapt. student dir./instr. Smith County Bapt., Tyler, Tex.; psychology instr. Tyler (Tex.) Jr. Coll.; dir. missions, Linn County, Mo. Author: Syllabus for New Testament Studies, Syllabus for Old Testament Studies. With U.S. Army, 1942-43. Named Tchr. of the Yr., Tyler Jr. Coll., 1987, 1986 Best Tchr. Alumni award. Mem. Tex. Jr. Coll. Tchrs. Assn., Southwestern Bible Tchrs. Assn., E. Tex. Counselors Assn., DAV. Home: 1913 E 5th St Tyler TX 75701 *The slight of our yesterdays are so soon forgotten in the tomorrow of God's grace and love. Nothing can out do or surpass His goodness to us.*

RUDEN, VIOLET HOWARD (MRS. CHARLES VAN KIRK RUDEN), religious educator, practitioner; b. Dallas; d. Millard Fillmore and Henrietta Frederika (Kurth) Howard; B.J., U. Tex., 1931; C.S.B., Mass. Metaphys. Coll., 1946; m. Charles Van Kirk Ruden, Nov. 24, 1932. Radio continuity writer Home Mgmt. Club broadcast Sta. WHO, Des Moines, 1934; joined First Ch. of Christ Scientist, Boston, 1929; C.S. practitioner, Des Moines, 1934—; C.S. minister WAC, Ft. Des Moines, 1942-45; 1st reader 2d Ch. of Christ Scientist, Des Moines, 1952, Sunday sch. tchr., 1934—; instr. primary class in Christian Sci., 1947—. Trustee Asher Student Found. Drake U., Des Moines, 1973. Mem. Women in Communications, Mortar Bd., Orchesis, Cap and Gown, Theta Sigma Phi (pres. 1931). Republican. Club: Des Moines Women's. Home: 5808 Walnut Hill Dr Des Moines IA 50312

RUDIN, ANDREW C., energy consultant; b. New Haven, Sept. 21, 1943; s. Harry Rudolph and Anna Louise (Falk) R.; m. Joyce Chin, Mar. 19, 1983; children: Heather, Erik, Katy. BA, Clark U., Worcester, Mass., 1965; MAT, U. Vt., 1971. Project coord. Interfaith Coalition on Energy, Phila., 1982—; editorial adv. bd. Your Ch. Mag., Carol Stream, Ill., 1990—. Property com. mem. Abington (Pa.) YMCA, 1983—. Mem. ASHRAE. Home and Office: 30D Lakeside Apts Melrose Park PA 19126

RUDIN, ARNOLD JAMES, rabbi; b. Pitts., Oct. 7, 1934; s. Philip Gordon and Beatrice (Rosenbloom) R.; m. Marcia Ruth Kapan, July 27, 1969; children: Eve Sandra, Jennifer Anne. BA, George Washington U., 1955; MA, Hebrew Union Coll., 1960, DD, 1985. Ordained rabbi, 1960. Mil. chaplain USAF, Japan, Korea, 1960-62; asst. rabbi Congregation B'nai Jehudah, Kansas City, Mo., 1962-64; rabbi Sinai Temple, Champaign, Ill., 1964-68; rabbi Am. Jewish Com., N.Y.C., 1968—, dir. interreligious affairs, 1983—; lectr. in field; guest speaker numerous TV/radio progs. nationwide; organizer confs. in field. Author: Israel for Christians: Understanding Modern Israel, 1983; co-author: (with Marcia Rudin) Prison Or Paradise? The New Religious Cults, 1980, Why Me? Why Anyone?, 1986; author, editor numerous books; contbr. articles to profl. jours. Nat. coord. Am. Jewish Emergency Relief Effort, Biafran Relief, 1968, 69; founder Nat. Interreligious Task Force on Black-Jewish Rels.; mem. Martin Luther King, Jr. Fed. Holiday Commn.; co-chmn. First Nat. Black-Jewish Seminarians Conf., Atlanta, 1986; mem. exec. coun. Am. Jewish Hist. Soc.; others. Recipient Joshua Evans award George Washington U., Nelson and Helen Glueck prizes. Avocations: photography, collecting baseball memorabilia, crosswords. Home: 129 East 82nd St New York NY 10028 Office: American Jewish Committee 165 East 56th St New York NY 10022

RUDOLPH, MARK EDWARD, minister; b. Herrin, Ill., July 31, 1921; s. James and Emma Flora (Black) R.; m. Geneva June Purvis, July 3, 1942; children: Marquita Lee Rudolph Sparks, Emma Jean Rudolph Zabel. Grad. high sch., Kokomo, Ind., 1937. Ordained to ministry United Pentecostal Ch. Internat., 1949; cert. ultrasonic insp. Pastor Pentecostal Assembly, Granite City, Ill., 1950-51; pastor 1st United Pentecostal Ch., Peru, Ind., 1958-90, sect. presbyter Ind. dist., 1985-90. With U.S. Army, 1942-45. ETO. Mem. 25 Yr. Club (chaplain 1985-90). Home: 360 N Fremont Peru IN 46970

RUEF, JOHN SAMUEL, educator; b. Chgo., Jan. 24, 1927; s. John E. and Leota A. (Rice) R.; m. Jane Margraves Holt, Oct. 11, 1951; children: Marcus, Adam, Seth, Sarah. BD, Seabury-Western, 1950, STM, 1955, DD, 1975; ThD, Harvard U., 1960. Faculty mem. Berkeley Div. Sch., New Haven, 1960-71; pres. Nashotah (Wis.) House, 1974-85; chaplain Chatham (Va.) Hall, 1985—. Author: Understanding the Gospels, 1967, The Gospels and Teachings of Jesus, 1967, The First Letter of Paul to Corinth, 1971. Bd. dirs. Pittsylvania County Community Action, Chatham, 1990. Home: PO Box 1143 Chatham VA 24531 Office: Chatham Hall Pruden Ave Chatham VA 24531

RUEGG, WALTER JOSEPH, deacon, retired personnel administrator; b. St. Louis, Aug. 1, 1920; s. Walter Ernst and Alvina (Salat) R.; m. Marie Agnes Waldbuser, Oct. 4, 1941; children: Walter F., Donald C., James R., Joan M., Michael J. Student, Colo. Coll., Air U., Paul VI Inst., St. Louis, 1982-88. Ordained deacon Roman Cath. Ch., 1986. Permanent deacon St. Aloysius Parish, St. Louis, 1986—; mem. coun. deacons Archdiocese of St. Louis, 1989—; pers. asst., pers. officer, program officer Dept. Def. and VA, St. Louis and Colorado Springs, 1947-76. Chaplain St. Louis Airport, Boy Scouts Am., St. Louis. With U.S. Army, 1944-45; PTO. Decorated Bronze Star, Purple Heart.

RUEGSEGGER, HARVEY ALCID, minister; b. Kalispell, Mont., Mar. 26, 1935; s. John Grover and Iola Madaline (Winn) R.; m. Bonnie Lou Van Doren, June 10, 1956; children: Debra Lynn, David John, Daniel Paul. BTh, N.W. Christian Coll., 1958; MDiv, Drake U., 1967. Ordained to ministry Christian Ch. (Disciples of Christ), 1958. Pastor The Christian Ch., Palouse, Wash., 1958-63, Clearfield, Iowa, 1963-67; pastor Woodmont Christian Ch., Kent, Wash., 1967-74; assoc. min. First Christian Ch., Loveland, Colo., 1974—; chmn. bd. dirs. Big Thompson Inter-Faith Flood Disaster Recovery Task Force, Loveland, 1976-78; moderator Christian Ch. Cen. Rocky Mountain Region, Colo. and Wyo., 1990—. Chmn. bd. dirs. Cert. Bd. for Treatment Providers of the Eighth Jud. Dist., Larimer County, 1988-90; comdr. Loveland Police Chaplains (Chaplain of Yr. 1983), 1984, 88. Mem. No. Dist. Mins. of Christian Ch. (pres. 1984-85), Loveland Ministerial Assn. (pres. 1982-83), Loveland Lions (pres. 1985-86). Home: 2457 Nyssa Dr Loveland CO 80538 Office: First Christian Ch 2000 N Lincoln Loveland CO 80538 *Remember yesterday, dream about tomorrow, but live today. (Original source unknown).*

RUETHER, ROSEMARY RADFORD, theologian; b. St. Paul, Nov. 2, 1936; d. Robert Amstrong and Rebecca Cresap (Ord) Radford; m. Herman J. Ruether, Aug. 31, 1957; children: Rebecca, David, Mimi. A.B., Scripps Coll., 1958; M.A., Claremont Grad. Sch., 1960, Ph.D., 1965. Assoc. prof. Howard U., Washington, 1966-76; Georgia Harkness prof. Garrett Sem., Evanston, Ill., 1976—; lectr. Princeton Theol. Sem., 1971, 73; prof. Roman Cath. studies Harvard U., Cambridge, Mass., 1972-73; lectr. Yale Div. Sch., 1973-74. Author: The Church Against Itself, 1967, Communion is Life Together, 1968, Gregory Nazianzus, Rhetor and Philosopher, 1969, The Radical Kingdom, 1970, Liberation Theology, 1972, Religion and Sexism: Images of Women in the Judeo-Christian Tradition, 1974, Faith and Fratricide, 1974, New Woman/New Earth, 1975, Mary, The Feminine Face of the Church, 1977, The Liberating Bond, 1978, Women of Spirit, 1979, (with Rosemary Keller) Women and Religion in America, 1981, To Change the World: Christology and Cultural Criticism, 1981, Disputed Questions: On Being a Christian, 1982, Sexism and God-talk, 1983, Women and Religion in America: The Colonial Period, 1983, Womanguides: Texts for Feminist Theology, 1985, Women and Religion in America, 1900-1968, 1986, Women-Church: Theology and Practice of Feminist Liturgical Communities, 1986, Contemporary Catholicism, 1987, The Wrath of Jonah: The Crisis of Religious Nationalism in the Israel-Palestinian Conflict, 1989, Beyond Occupation: American Jewish, Christian and Palestinian Voices for Peace, 1990, Gaia and God: An Ecofeminist Theology of Earth-healing, 1992; contbg. editor: Christianity and Crisis; contbr. articles to profl. jours. Kent fellow, 1962-65; Danforth fellow, 1960-61. Mem. Soc. Religion in Higher Edn., Am. Theol. Assn., Soc. Arts, Religion and Culture. Home: 1426 Hinman Ave Evanston IL 60201

RUFFCORN, KEVIN EDWARD, minister; b. Minneapolis, Minn., Aug. 19, 1951; s. William Edward and Evelyn (Baldwin) R.; m. Faye Ann Iverson, Sep. 24,; c. BA in Speech/History, Concordia Coll., 1973; MDiv, Luther/Northwestern Sem., 1979. Min. Peace Luth. Ch., Dunseith, N.D., 1979-82; pastor/developer Grace Luth. Ch., East Dubuque, Ill., 1982-86; min. Grace Luth. Ch., Oconto Falls, Wis., 1986--; Synod editor The Lutheran, Chicago, Ill., 1989--. Author various religious books and articles. Bd. mem. County Health Bd., Oconto, Wis. Mem. Acad. Evangelists (bd. mem. 1988-90), fellow Acad. Parish Clergy (bd. mem. 1990--). Evangelical Lutheran Church. Office: Grace Lutheran Ch PO Box 144 Oconto Falls WI 54154-0144

RUGAMBWA, LAUREAN CARDINAL, archbishop of Dar es Salaam; b. Bukongo, Tanzania; July 12, 1912; s. Domitian Rushubirwa and Asteria Mukaboshezi; student Rutabo, Rubya Sem., 1926-33, Katigondo Sem., 1933-43; D.Canon Law, U. Propaganda, Rome, 1951; LL.D. (hon.), Notre Dame U., 1961, Georgetown U., 1961, Rosary Coll., Buffalo, 1965; LH.D. (hon.) Coll. of New Rochelle, 1961, also others. Ordained priest Roman Cath. Ch., 1943; bishop of Rutabo, 1952-60; elevated to Sacred Coll. Cardinals and bishop of Bukoba, 1960; archbishop of Dar es Salaam, 1969—; mem. congregation of Causes of Saints. Mem. Knights of St. Peter Claver, KC. Office: Archbishop's House, POB 167, Dar es Salaam Tanzania

RUHE, DAVID SIEGER, religious organization administrator, medical educator; b. Allentown, Pa., Jan. 3, 1914; arrived in Israel, 1968; s. Percy Bot and Amy Catherine (Sieger) R.; m. Margaret Rosa Kunz, Sept. 7, 1940; children: Christopher Kunz, Douglas Frederic. BS, Mich. State Coll., 1936, MS, 1937; MD, Temple U., 1941, ScD (hon.), 1956. Commd. intern USPHS, 1941, advanced through grades to sr. surgeon, 1954; audiovisual assoc. Assn. Am. Med. Colls., 1949-53; prof. med. communication, assoc. prof. preventive medicine U. Kans. Coll. Medicine, 1954-63; sec. Nat. Spiritual Assembly Baha'is of USA, Wilmette, Ill., 1963-68; mem. Universal House of Justice Baha'i Internat. Community, Haifa, Israel, 1968—; past med. acad. appointments Emory U. Coll. Medicine, N.Y. Coll. Medicine, U. Ill. Coll. Medicine; cons. in field. Author: Door of Hope, 1983; (with others) Films in Psychiatry and Mental Health, 1953, Films in the Cardiovascular Diseases, 1953; writer, dir. and producer 29 films in medicine and health (Golden Reel award 1956, Gold medal Venice Film Festival 1956, TV Raster award 1967). Mem. Com. Am. VA's, 1946-48; mem. Human Rights Council Wilmette, 1964-68. Fellow Am. Pub. Health Assn.; mem. United World Federalists, AMA, Phi Kappa Phi, Alpha Omicron Alpha. Avocations: artist, naturalist, sportsman. Office: Baha'i World Ctr, PO Box 155, Haifa Israel

RUINI, CAMILLO CARDINAL, cardinal; b. Sassuolo, Italy, Feb. 19, 1931. With titular Ch. of St. Agnes; vicar gen. of Rome, titular bishop of Nepte, archbishop, 1991—, elevated to Sacred Coll. Cardinals, 1991. Office: Diocese Roman Cath Ch, Office of Vicar Gen, 00120 Vatican City State Europe*

RUIZ, JOSE, minister; b. Havana, Cuba, May 22, 1925; came to U.S., 1958; s. Jose Ruiz and Conception Reluzco; m. America Alfonso, Dec. 25, 1947; children: Conception, Elda, Teresa. AA, Dade Coll.; BA, Fla. Internat. U.; MEd, U. Miami, New Orleans Bapt., Theol. Seminary; EdD, Calif. Coast U. Ordained to ministry Bapt. Ch., 1960; cert. tchr., Fla. Tchr. Miami (Fla.) High Adult Edn. Ctr., 1974—; pastor Buenas Nuevas Bapt. Ch., 1979—; prof. New Orleans Bapt. Theol. Seminary, 1980-90. Author: Jesus, The Exorcist, 1974. Republican. Home: 281 NW 59th Ct Miami FL 33126

RULAND, VERNON JOSEPH, priest, theology educator; b. Erie, Pa., Oct. 28, 1931; s. Vernon Joseph and Nell Marie (Driscoll) R. MA in English, Licentiate in Philosophy, Loyola U., Chgo., 1957, Licentiate in Theology, 1964; PhD in Theology and Lit., U. Chgo., 1967; MA in Counseling, U. Detroit, 1972. Joined S.J., Roman Cath. Ch., 1950, ordained priest, 1963; lic. marriage-family-child counselor, Calif. Tchr. English St. Xavier High Sch., Cin., 1958-60; prof. fundamental theology Jesuit Sch. Theology, Chgo., 1967-69; prof. theology U. Detroit, 1969-74; prof. theology, pastoral min. U. San Francisco, 1974—; vis. prof. U. Chgo., 1975-76. Author: Horizons of Criticism, 1975 (Book of Yr. award Conf. on Christianity and Lit. 1976), Eight Sacred Horizons, 1985; editor: Prose and Poetry of America, 1965. Home and Office: U San Francisco Jesuit Community San Francisco CA 94117

RUMPH, ARNOLD, minister; b. DeWyk, Drente, The Netherlands, Aug. 6, 1929; s. Albert and Lutina (Kwant) R.; m. Ann Marie Van Helden, Sept. 3, 1954; children: Albert Gerald, Ann Marie, Robert Luis, Edward Philip, Lucinda Grace, Christina Elizabeth. BA, Calvin Coll., 1954; BD, Calvin Theol. Sem., 1957; ThM, Princeton Theol. Sem., 1964. Ordained to ministry Christian Ref. Ch., 1957. Pastor Cobourg (Ont., Can.) Christian Ref. Ch., 1957-60, Fruitland (Ont.) Christian Ref. Ch., 1960-63, Mt. Hamilton (Ont.) Christian Reformed Ch., 1964-66; founder, mgr. La Peña Evangelistic Bookstore, La Plata, Argentina, 1967-73; missionary Christian Ref. World Missions, 1967-86; founder, rector, prof. theology Ref. Evang. Sem., Rio Piedras, Puerto Rico, 1973-78; dean, prof. theology and Christian ethics Sch. Theology, Mariano Galvez Univ., Guatemala City, 1978-81; dir. grad. studies, prof. theology Juan Calvino Sem., Mexico City, 1982-84; acad. dean, prof. theology and Christian ethics Internat. Theol. Sem., Pasadena, Calif., 1984-86; prof. theology and Christian ethics Internat. Theol. Sem., Pasadena, 1986-88; pastor Trinity Christian Reformed Ch., Chula Vista, Calif., 1988—; spiritual counselor Christian Trade Union Can., 1964-66; elder, moderator-elect Evang. Union Ch., Guatemala City, 1978-81. Co-editor Base Firme, denomination mag., 1970-73; contbr. articles to mags. Mem. Soc. for the Promotion Internat. Reformed Evangelism (founder, pres. 1991—). Home: 1040 Maple Dr No 31 Chula Vista CA 91911

RUMSCHEIDT, HANS-MARTIN, educator, minister; b. Leuna, Germany, July 24, 1935; arrived in Can., 1952, naturalized, 1957; s. Carl Friedrich and Edith Marie (Oeckinghaus) R.; m. Barbara Lawrence Guild, Dec. 28, 1962; children: Peter, Robert, Heidi. BA, McGill U., 1958, BD, 1961, STM, 1963, PhD, 1967. Ordained to ministry United Ch. Can., 1961. Min. chs., Montreal, Que, Can., 1962-65, United Ch. Can., Enterprise, Ont., Can., 1965-67; asst. min. Deer Park United Ch., Toronto, Ont., 1967-70; prof. hist. theology U. Windsor, Ont., 1970-75; prof. systematic theology Atlantic Sch. Theology, Halifax, N.S., Can., 1975—; sec. Can. Theol. Soc., 1968-70, pres., 1972-73. Author: Revelation and Theology-An Analysis of the Barth Harnack Correspondence of 1923, 1972, Adolf von Harnack—Liberal Theology at Its Height. 1989; editor: Fragments Grave and Gay (Karl Barth), 1971; Footnotes to a Theology—The Karl Barth Colloquium of 1972, 1974, Karl Barth in Re-View: Posthumous Works Reviewed and Assessed, 1981, The Way of Theology in Karl Barth—Essays and Comments, 1985; translator: The Theology of Dietrich Bonhoeffer, 1985. Mem. Am. Acad. Religion, Can. Soc. for Study Religion (sec. 1988-90, pres. 1990—), Karl Barth Soc. N.Am. Home: 5342 Kaye St, Halifax, NS Canada B3K 1Y3

RUNCIE, ROBERT ALEXANDER KENNEDY, retired archbishop of Canterbury; b. England, Oct. 2, 1921; s. Robert Dalziel and Anne R.; m. Angela Rosalind Turner, 1957; children: James, Rebecca. MA 1st class honors Litterae Humaniores, Brasenose Coll., Oxford (Eng.) U.; MA in Theology with distinction, Westcott House, Cambridge (Eng.) U., 1948, DD (hon.), 1980; DD (hon.), Oxford U., 1980, Cambridge U., 1981, U. South Sewanee, 1981, New Raday Coll., Budapest, 1987, U. S.C., 1987, St. Andrew's U., 1989; DLitt (hon.), U. Keele, 1981; LittD (hon.), Liverpool U., 1983, Rikkyo U., Tokio, 1987; DCL (hon.), U. Kent, 1982, U. West Indies, 1984; DD (hon.), Yale U., 1989. Ordained priest, Ch. of England, 1949. Curate All Saints Ch., Gosforth, 1950-52; chaplain, vice prin. Westcott House, 1953-56, vice prin., 1954-56; fellow, dean, asst. tutor Trinity Hall, Cambridge U., 1956-60, hon. fellow, 1975—; prin. Cuddesdon Coll., also vicar of Cuddesdon, 1960-69, bishop of St. Albans, 1970-80, archbishop of Canterbury, 1980-91, ret., 1991; Teape lectr. U. Delhi, 1962, William Nobel lectr. Harvard U., 1987. Editor: Cathedral and City--St. Albans Ancient and Modern, 1978, Seasons of the Spirit, 1983, Windows onto God, 1983, One Light for One World, 1988, Theology, University & the Modern World, 1988, Authority in Crisis? An Anglican Response, 1988, The Unity We Seek, 1989; created Baron Runcie of Cuddesdon, 1991. Served with Brit. Army, 1939-45. Decorated Mil. Cross; Order St. Vladimir class II, Russian Orthodox Ch., 1975; Cross of the Order of Holy Sepulchre, Patriarch Diodoros of Jerusalem, 1986; recipient Patron of Christian Unity award coun. on Christian Unity's Yale U., 1986; Squire Minor scholar; hon. fellow Brasenose Coll., Oxford U., 1979, Merton Coll. Oxford, 1991; holder Royal Victorian Chain, 1991, High Steward of Cambridge U., 1991. Mem. Athenaeum Club (London), Cavalry and Guards Club, Marylebone Cricket Club. Address: 26a Jennings Rd, Saint Albans, Hertfordshire AL1 4PD, England

RUNIA, KLAAS, theology educator; b. Oudeschoot, Netherlands, May 7, 1926; s. Douwe and Boukje (Koopmans) R.; m. Hendrika Jacoba Feenstra, Feb. 27, 1951; children: David T., D. John, Nynke D., Calvin N., Anthony P. BD, Free U. Amsterdam, 1948, ThM, 1949, ThD, 1955. Ordained to ministry, Reformed Ch. Netherlands, 1949. Minister of religion Reformed Ch. in Netherlands, 1949-56; prof. theology Reformed Theol. Coll., Geelong, Australia, 1956-71; prof. practical theology Theol. U., Kamper, The Netherlands, 1971—, rector of univ., 1975-79, 86-90. Author: The Theologische Tijd in de Theologie van Karl Barth, 1955, Het Christelijk Recht van de Friese Beweging, 1956, Reformed Dogmatics: Its Essence and Method, 1957, Karl Barth's Doctrine of Holy Scripture, 1962, I Believe in God, 1963, The Importance of the Reformation for the Discussion Between the Churches, 1964, The Interpretation of the Old Testament by the New, 1965, Calvijns betekenis in onze tijd, 1970 Prediking en Historisch-Kritisch Onderzoek, 1972 Nairobi in perspectief, 1976, Vragen van onze tijd, 1976, De Wereldraad in Discussie, 1978, Eigentijdse vragen, 1978, Theologiseren in Kampen, 1980, Heeft preken nog zin, 1981, The Sermon under Attack, 1983, Evangelisch, Reformatorisch, Gereformeerd, 1984, The Present-day Chridtological Debate, 1984, Het hoge woord in de lage landen, 1985, Waar blijft de kerk?, 1988, Het evangelie en de vele religies, 1991; editor, contbr. Das Himmelreich hat schon begonnen, 1977; mng. editor Centraal Weekblad, 1972—; chmn. editorial bd. Christian daily newspaper Fries Dagblad, 1978—. Mem. Fellowship European Evang. Theologians (chmn.), Ref. Ecumenical Coun. (v.p. 1988—). Avocations: reading, sailing. Home: Ysselkade 35, 8162 AC Kampen The Netherlands Office: Theol Univ, Koornmarkt 1, 8260 GA Kampen The Netherlands

RUNNER, GEORGE CYRIL, JR., minister, educational administrator; b. Scotia, N.Y., Mar. 25, 1952; s. George Cyril and Kay Carol (Cooper) R.; m. Sharon Yvonne Oden, Jan. 13, 1973; children: Micah Stephen, Rebekah Kay. Student, Antelope Valley Coll., Lancaster, Calif., 1970-88; grad. mgmt. cert., Azusa Pacific U., 1988; student, U. Redlands. Lic. to ministry Am. Bapt. Chs. in USA, 1977. Exec. pastor 1st Bapt. Ch. Lancaster, 1973—; founder, exec. dir. Desert Christian Schs., Lancaster, 1977—; founder, internat. dir. Supporting Ptnrs. in Christian Edn., Lancaster, Guatemala City, Guatemala, 1989—; seminar leader Internat. Ctr. for Learning, Ventura, Calif., 1972-82; curriculum cons. Gospel Light Publs., Glendale, Calif., 1974-80; bd. dirs. Greater L.A. Sunday Sch. Assn., 1978-79. Bd. dirs. Lancaster Econ. Devel. Corp.; mem. Salvation Army, Lancaster. Mem. Internat. Fellowship Ch. Sch. Adminstrs., Assn. Christian Schs. Internat., Christian Mgmt. Assn., Lancaster Ministerial Assn. Republican. Office: Desert Christian Schs 1st Bapt Ch 44648 15th St W Lancaster CA 93534

RUNNING, LEONA GLIDDEN, religion educator; b. Mt. Morris, Mich., Aug. 24, 1916; d. Charles Comstock and Leona Bertha (Boat) Glidden; m. Leif H. Running, May 17, 1942 (dec. 1946). BA, Emmanuel Missionary Coll., Berrien Springs, Mich., 1937; MA, Seventh-day Adventist Theol. Sem., Takoma Park, Md., 1955; PhD, Johns Hopkins U., 1964. Tchr. French and German Laurelwood Acad., Gaston, Oreg., 1937-41; sec. Pacific Union Conf. Seventh-day Adventists, Glendale, Calif., 1942-44; lang. sec. Voice of Prophecy Radio, Glendale, 1944-48; sec. to pres. Carolina Conf. Seventh-day Adventists, Charlotte, 1949-50; copy editor Ministry Mag., Takoma Park, 1950-54; prof. Bibl. langs. Seventh-day Adventist Theol. Sem., from 1955, now prof. emerita. Author: 36 Days and a Dream, 1953, From Thames to Tigris, 1958 (with David Noel Freedman) W.F. Albright, a 20th Century Genius, 1975, 2d edit., 1991; contbr. articles to profl. jours. Named Alumnus of Distinction Andrews U. Alumni Assn., 1977, Alumna of Yr. Adelphian Acad., 1978. Mem. Soc. Bibl. Lit., Chgo. Soc. Bibl. Rsch. Home: 9126 4th St Berrien Springs MI 49103 Office: Andrews U Seminary Berrien Springs MI 49104

RUNNION-BAREFORD, DAVID GEORGE, minister; b. Englewood, N.J., Nov. 11, 1947; s. George William and Grace Barbara (Keefer) Runnion; m. Lauren Elizabeth Kulp, Dec. 23, 1977; children: Benjamin, Park, Chad, Joseph, Piper, Jesse. BA in English, Wheaton (Ill.) Coll., 1969; MDiv, Gordon Conwell Theol. Seminary, South Hamilton, Mass., 1972, postgrad. Ordained to ministry Congl. Ch., 1973. Pastor Union Congregational Ch., Magnolia, Mass., 1971-75; coord. Project Image, Gloucester, Mass., 1975-77; pastor Gilead Congregational Ch., Hebron, Conn., 1977-82, Candia (N.H.) Congregational Ch., 1982—; vice pres. Bibl. Witness Fellowship, Knoxville, Tenn., 1990—, bd. dirs.; regional adv. Evangel. Assn. of N.E., Burlington, Mass., 1990—; co-organizer Bibl. Witness Fellowship-Missions Renewal, Hatfield, Pa., 1988—. Home: 169 High St PO Box 62 Candia NH 03034 Office: Candia Congregational Ch 1 South Rd PO Box 62 Candia NH 03034

RUNYAN, CYNTHIA MILDRED, religious organization administrator; b. Riverside, Calif., Dec. 18, 1951; d. Merrill Martin and Virginia Lucille (Killian) Meyer; m. Harold G. Phillips, Aug. 21, 1971 (div. 1981); children: Martin Wayne, Timothy Patrick, Steven Harold, Richard Charles. BS magna cum laude, Calif. Bapt. Coll., 1986. Supr. order entry dept. Here's Life Pub., San Bernardino, Calif., 1981-83; office mgr. Mgmt. Devel. Assocs., Orange, Calif., 1984; office adminstr. Newcastel Co., Orange, Calif., 1985-87; owner CMP Cons., Riverside, Calif., 1987-90; dir. devel. svcs. Fred Jordan Missions, Covina, Calif., 1990—; dir. mgmt. systems Ministry Stewardship, Inc., Moreno Valley, Calif., 1987-90; cons. in field. Dir. pub. rels. Victoria Ave Christian Ch., Riverside, 1989. Mem. NAFE, Perfect Heart Ladies Ensamble, Calif. Bapt. Coll. Alumni (citizen com.). Republican. Avocations: group singing, travel. Office: Fed Jordan Missions 915 Grand Covina CA 91711

RUNYON, THEODORE HUBERT, JR., religion educator, minister; b. Tomahawk, Wis., Mar. 20, 1930; s. Theodore H. Sr. and Carol Louise (Jett) R.; m. Cynthia Margaret Guild, June 25, 1955; children: Margaret, David, Stephen. BA, Lawrence U., 1952; BD, Drew U., 1955; ThD, U. Goettingen, Fed. Republic Germany, 1958. Ordained to ministry United Meth. Ch. as deacon, 1953, as elder, 1955. Min. to youth Hanson Pl. Cen. United Meth. Ch., Bklyn., 1952-54; pastor Christ United Meth. Ch., Phila., 1954-55; prof. systematic theology Candler Sch. Theology Emory U., Atlanta, 1958—; co-chmn. Oxford (Eng.) Inst. of Meth. Theol. Studies, 1976-80; mem. exec. com. World Meth. Coun., 1976-81; pres. Emory U. Senate, 1983-84; mem. gen. conf. commn. on Our Theol. Task, 1984-88. Editor: Hope for the Church, 1979, Sanctification and Liberation, 1981, Wesleyan Theology Today, 1985, Theology, Politics and Peace, 1989. Trustee CRISIS INC., Atlanta, 1968-72, Atlanta Assn. for Internat. Edn., 1979-82; mem. exec. com. Japanese Students Assn., Atlanta, 1986—. Recipient Disting. Alumnus award Lawrence U., 1986; named One of Outstanding Educators Am., 1975; Danforth Found. grantee, 1971-72, Assn. Theol. Schs. grantee, 1987-88; Fulbright fellow, Fed. Republic Germany, 1955-57. Mem. AAUP, Am. Acad. Religion, Bonhoeffer Soc., Soc. for Values in Higher Edn., Fla. Conf. United Meth. Ch. (ministerial mem.). Democrat. Home: 780 Houston Mill

Rd Atlanta GA 30329 Office: Emory U Candler Sch Theology Atlanta GA 30322

RUNZO, JOSEPH JOHN, religion educator; b. Flagstaff, Ariz., Nov. 11, 1948; s. Joseph V. and Ruth O. (Boehm) R.; m. Jean Goodban, Sept. 8, 1968. BA in Philosophy, U. Calif., Irvine, 1970; MA in Philosophy, U. Mich., 1973, PhD in Philosophy, 1974; MTS in Theology, Harvard U., 1976. Prof. religion and philosophy Chapman U., Orange, Calif., 1978—; vis. prof. religion Claremont Grad. Sch., 1989; vis. scholar St. Edmund's Coll., Cambridge U., Eng., 1990; vis. asst. prof. philosophy U. Mich., Ann Arbor, 1978. Author: Reason, Relativism and God, 1986; co-editor: Religious Experience and Religious Belief, 1986; editor: Ethics, Religion and the Good Society: New Directions in a Pluralistic World, 1992, Is God Real, 1992; contbr. articles to profl. jours. NEH grantee, 1979, 87, fellow, 1981, 90. Mem. Am. Acad. Religion, Am. Philos. Assn. (program com. 1990—), Soc. Christian Philosophy (editorial bd. 1988—), Soc. for Philosophy Religion, Philosophy of Religion Soc. (pres. 1983—). Office: Chapman U Depts Religion and Philosophy Orange CA 92666

RUOF, RICHARD ALAN, clergyman; b. Lancaster, Pa., Oct. 11, 1932; s. Robert Jacob and Geneva May (Devers) R.; A.B., Franklin and Marshall Coll., 1954; M.Div., Lancaster Theol. Sem. and Union Theol. Sem. Va., 1960; STM Luth. Theol. Sem., Gettysburg, Pa., 1974; D.Min., McCormick Theol. Sem., 1981; m. Anne Margaret Demos; children: Mark Alan Demos Ruof, Anne Tracy Demos Ruof, Richard James Demos Ruof. Ordained to ministry United Ch. Christ, 1960; pastor Harrisville (Va.) Charge of United Ch. Christ, 1959-62, Thurmont (Md.) Charge, 1962-67, First Congl. Ch., Cortland, N.Y., 1967-77, St. Paul's United Ch. Christ of Hamlin, Fredericksburg, Pa., 1977-81, St. John's United Ch. of Christ, Egg Harbor City, N.J., 1982-87, St. John's United Ch. of Christ, Friedensburg, Pa., 1987—. Registrar-treas. Susquehanna Assn., N.Y. Conf., United Ch. Christ, 1968-74; mem. Egg Harbor City Bd. Edn., 1984. Served with USNR, 1954-56. Home: 1215 Geronimo Dr Lake Wynonah RR #1 Auburn PA 17922

RUPEL, LAWRENCE MICHAEL, priest, psychotherapist; b. South Bend, Ind., Sept. 5, 1948; s. Maurice Eugene and Mary Elizabeth (Tamplen) R.; B.A., U. Tex., Austin, 1971; M.Div., Josephinum Sch. Theology, 1975. Ordained priest Roman Catholic Ch., 1975; mem. staff Marriage Tribunal Diocese Corpus Christi, 1975—; chaplain Incarnate Word Sisters, 1975-76; asso. pastor Our Lady of Guadalupe Ch., Corpus Christi, 1976-77; asso. pastor St. Paul Cath. Ch., Corpus Christi, 1977-79; asso. pastor St. Elizabeth Cath. Ch., Alice, Tex., 1979—; chmn. dept. measurement and evaluation Office Cath. Schs., 1976-78; alcoholism and drug abuse counseling, 1979; cons., primary therapist Coastal Bend Rehab. for Alcoholics; cons. Coastal Bend Council Alcoholism. Lic. profl. counselor. Mem. Am. Personnel and Guidance Assn., Canon Law Soc. Am., Nat. Cath. Guidance Assn., Am. Measurement and Evaluation in Guidance, Tex. Psychotherapy Assn. Democrat. Office: 3350 S Alameda Corpus Christi TX 78411

RUPERT, DAVID ANDREW, religious organization superintendent, minister; b. Oil City, Pa., Aug. 16, 1940; s. John Reuben and Wealtha Audrey (Smoyer) R.; m. Lois Martha Annable, June 30, 1962; children: Glenn David, Martha Jean. BA, Roberts Wesleyan Coll., 1962; BD, Western Evang. Sem., 1967, MDiv, 1972; D Ministry, Fuller Theol. Sem., 1980. Asst. pastor Free Meth. Ch., Herkimer, N.Y., 1962-63, Portland, Oreg., 1963-64, Salem, Oreg., 1964-67; pastor Free Meth. Ch., Redmond, Oreg., 1967-71; sr. pastor Willow Vale Community Ch.-Free Meth., San Jose, Calif., 1971-79; sr. pastor Free Meth. Ch., Sacramento, 1979-84, conf. supt., 1984—; Lifo cons., trainer Stuart Atkins, Inc., Beverly Hills, Calif., 1981; del., mem. Gen. Conf. Free Meth. Ch., Winona Lake, Ind. and Seattle, 1985, 89, mem., sec. youth conf., Winona Lake, 1969, Gen. Bd. Adminstrn./Adminstrn. Com., Indpls., 1989—; trustee Seattle Pacific U., 1987—; trustee Western Evang. Sem., Portland, 1985—. Editor: Celebrating one Hundred Years, 1983. Member adminstrv. and exec. coms. Greater Sacramento Billy Graham Crusade, co-chair fin. com., 1983; pres. Redmond Ministerial, 1968-69, Greater Sacramento Assn. of Evangs., 1981-83; founder, pres. Greater San Jose Assn. of Evangs., 1974-78; bd. dirs. Redmond United Way Fund, 1969-71. Mem. Calif. Coun. on Alcohol Problems, Northern Calif. Assn. Evangs. (v.p. 1986-88, pres. 1988-91), Rotary (editor bull. Redmond chpt. 1969-71, 2d Pres.' award 1971). Republican. Avocations: travel, photography, swimming, sports. Home: 9241 Linda Rio Dr Sacramento CA 95826-2209 Office: Calif Conf Free Meth Ch 9750 Business Park Dr # 212 Sacramento CA 95827-1716

RUPERT, (LYNN) HOOVER, minister; b. Madison, N.J., Nov. 3, 1917; s. Lynn Hoover and Hazel L. (Linabary) R.; m. Hazel Pearl Senti, June 22, 1941; children—Susan (Mrs. Max Unland), Elizabeth (Mrs. Warren W. Wright). A.B., Baker U., 1938; A.M., Boston U., 1940, M.Div. cum laude, 1941; student (summers), Garrett Bibl. Inst. and Northwestern U., 1942, Union Theol. Sem., 1943; D.D., Adrian Coll., 1952, Baker U., 1966; L.H.D., Milliken U., 1974. Ordained to ministry Methodist Ch., 1940; asst. pastor First Meth. Ch., Baldwin, Kans., 1936-38, St. Mark's Meth. Ch., Brookline, Mass., 1938-41; pastor Thayer-St. Paul, Kans., 1941-43, First Ch., Olathe, Kans., 1943-45; dir. youth dept. Gen. Bd. Edn. Meth. Ch., Nashville, 1945-50; pastor 1st Meth. Ch., Jackson, Mich., 1950-59; pastor 1st United Meth. Ch., Ann Arbor, Mich., 1959-72, Kalamazoo, 1972-83; faculty dept. religion Fla. So. Coll., Lakeland, 1983-89; adj. faculty Wesley Theol. Sem., Washington, 1989—; dean Mich. Meth. Pastors Sch., 1959-65; mem. Jud. Council United Meth. Ch., 1968-88 , sec., 1976-88, sec. emeritus, 1988. Author: Prayer Poems on the Prayer Perfect, 1943, Christ Above All (editor), 1948, Youth and Evangelism, 1948, Youth and Stewardship, rev, 1960, Your Life Counts (editor), 1950, What Methodists Believe, rev, 1959, John Wesley and People Called Methodists, 1953, I Belong, 1954, And Jesus Said, 1960, Enjoy Your Teen-Ager, 1962, A Sense of What is Vital, 1964, The Church in Renewal, 1965, My People are Your People, 1968, Where is thy Sting?, Christian Perspectives On Death, 1969, What's Good about God?, 1970, Woodstock, Main Street and the Garden of Eden, 1971, Some Idiot Raised the Ante, 1975, God Will See You Through, 1976, An Instrument of thy Peace, 1982, The High Cost of Being Human, 1986, Anthology of Pulpit Humor, 1990; writer: syndicated weekly mag. column Accent on Living; newspaper series Prayer for Today; newspaper feature Talking to Teens; contbr. to: newspaper feature Prayer for Today; other 1 publs., periodicals and newspapers. Testament of Faith, 1942. Trustee Bronson Hosp., 1972-83, Adrian Coll.; pres. bd. dirs. Youth For Understanding, 1970-83, Ann Arbor United Fund, YMCA-YWCA. Recipient Distinguished Alumnus award Boston U., 1969; Lucinda Bidwell Beebe fellow Boston U., 1941. Mem. World Meth. Council, Nat. Council Chs., Mark Twain Soc., Nat. Forensic League, Pi Kappa Delta, Alpha Psi Omega. Lodges: Mason, Rotary (Paul Harris fellow 1983). Home: 403 Russell Ave Gaithersburg MD 20877

RUPERT, TIMOTHY NEWTON, lay worker; b. Bethlehem, Pa., Nov. 20, 1966; s. Thomas N. and Faith (Eshbach) R. BA in Econs., Westminster Coll., 1989. Counselor Summers Best Two Weeks, Boswell, Pa., 1987-90; campus ministry vol. Coalition for Christian Outreach, Kent, Ohio, 1989-90; dir. youth ministries Bower Hill Ch., Pitts., 1990—. Home: 262 Mabrick Ave Pittsburgh PA 15228 Office: Bower Hill Community Church 70 Moffett St Pittsburgh PA 15243

RUPP, DAVID CARROLL, priest, systems analyst; b. Phila., Aug. 2, 1935; s. Jacob Carroll and Rebecca Elizabeth (Wescott) B.; m. Jacqueline Lois Waldon, May 14, 1959; children: Sarah Evangeline Rupp Kahl, Jacob-Aaron B., Adam-Michael A. BS in Edn., Ind. U., 1959, MS in Edn., 1967; cert., Salvation Army Sch. Officers, Chgo., 1966. Ordained priest Anglican Cath. Ch., 1975. Asst. field dir. Nat. ARC, Ft. Knox, Ky., 1960-61; officer Salvation Army, Kans., Wis, 1964-69; mgmt. intern GSA, Chgo., 1969-70; asst. tng. officer GSA, 1970-72; program mgr. GSA, Washington, 1972-86; parish rector Anglican Cath. Ch., Washington, Centreville, Va., 1976—; sr. systems analyst L.D. Research, Falls Church, Va., 1986—; mng. dir. Patch O'Green Resources, Inc., Nokesville, Va., 1987—; standing com. Anglican Cath. Ch. Diocese Mid Atlantic States, 1979-82, chmn. youth commn., 1982-86, diocesian ct., 1986—. Author proposed mil. tng. programs, fault insertion programs, manpower and hardware integration; editor numerous publs.; contbr. articles to profl. publs. With U.S. Army, 1954-57. Decorated Commendation medal, Meritorious Svc. medal; Fee Remission fellow, 1959. Mem. Res. Officers Assn., Vint Hill Officers, Bester G. Brown #433, Valley Of Alexandria Lodge. Republican. Home: PO Box 418 11118 Lonesome Rd Nokesville VA 22123-0418

RUPP, GEORGE ERIK, university president; b. Summit, N.J., Sept. 22, 1942; s. Gustav Wilhelm and Erika (Braunoehler) R.; m. Nancy Katherine Farrar, Aug. 22, 1964; children: Katherine Heather, Stephanie Karin. Student, Ludwig Maximilians U., Munich, Germany, 1962-63; A.B., Princeton U., 1964; B.D., Yale U., 1967; postgrad., U. Sri Lanka, Peradeniya, 1969-70; Ph.D., Harvard U., 1972. Ordained to ministry Presbyn. Ch. U.S.A., 1971; faculty fellow in religion, vice chancellor Johnston Coll., U. Redlands, Calif., 1971-74; asst. prof. Harvard Div. Sch., Harvard U., Cambridge, Mass., 1974-76, asso. prof., 1976-77, prof., dean, 1979-85; prof., dean acad. affairs U. Wis., Green Bay, 1977-79; prof., pres. Rice U., Houston, 1985—; bd. dirs. Tex. Commerce Bank, Houston, Panhandle Ea. Corp. Author: Christologies and Cultures: Toward a Typology of Religious Worldviews, 1974, Culture Protestantism: German Liberal Theology at the Turn of the Twentieth Century, 1977, Beyond Existentialism and Zen: Religion in a Pluralistic World, 1979, Commitment and Community, 1989; contbr. articles to profl. jours. Bd. dirs. Amigos de las Americas, Consortium on Financing Higher Edn., Inst. Internat. Edn., Meth. Hosp., St. John's Sch., Houston Symphony Orch., Houston Partnership. Danforth Grad. fellow, 1964-71. Mem. AAAS, Soc. for Values in Higher Edn., Am. Acad. Religion, Tex. Philos. Soc., Forum Club Houston (bd. dirs.). Office: Rice U PO Box 1892 Houston TX 77251

RUPWATE, D. D., minister, religious organization administrator. Gen. supt. Brit. Meth. Episcopal Ch. Can., Toronto, Ont. Office: Brit Meth Episcopal Ch Can, 460 Shaw St, Toronto, ON Canada M6G 3L3*

RUSACK, ROBERT CLAFLIN, bishop; b. Worcester, Mass., June 16, 1926; s. Roy Leonard and Dorothy (Claflin) R.; m. Janice Morrison Overfield, June 26, 1951; children—Rebecca Morrison, Geoffrey Claflin. B.A., Hobart Coll., 1946, D.D., 1970; priest-scholar, St. Augustine's Coll., Canterbury, Eng., 1957-58; S.T.D., Gen. Theol. Sem., 1965. Ordained deacon, priest Episcopal Ch., 1951; vicar in Deer Lodge and Philipsburg, Mont., 1951-57; rector in Santa Monica, Calif., 1958-64; suffragan bishop Los Angeles P.E. Ch., 1964-72; bishop coadjutor of P.E. Ch., Los Angeles, 1973-74, bishop of, 1974—. Pres. Los Angeles City Mission Soc., 1964—; Bd. dirs. Episcopal Home for Aged, Alhambra, Calif., 1964, Los Angeles World Affairs Council, 1974—, Neighborhood Youth Assn., 1965—, Seaman's Ch. Inst., San Pedro, Calif., 1964—; bd. dirs., pres. ex officio Gooden Home for Alcoholics; chmn. bd. trustees Bloy Episcopal Sch. Theology, Claremont, Calif.; hon. chmn. bd. Hosp. Good Samaritan, Los Angeles; chmn., trustee Harvard Sch., North Hollywood, Calif.; trustee Gen. Theol. Sem., Occidental Coll., Los Angeles; chmn. St. Paul's Cathedral Corp., 1962—. Clubs: Los Angeles Country, California. Home: 13828 Susnset Blvd Pacific Palisades CA 90272 Office: PO Box 2164 Los Angeles CA 90051 also: 1220 W 4th St Los Angeles CA 90051

RUSCH, FREDERICK ALBERT, religion educator; b. Ft. Wayne, Ind., Nov. 16, 1938; s. Wilbert H. Sr. and Margaret (Kogge) R.; m. Suzanne H. Lahrman, June 25,1 961; children: Elisabeth J., David E., Deborah A., Rachael J. BA, Concordia Sr. Coll., Ft. Wayne, 1959; MDiv, Concordia Sem., St. Louis, 1962; MA, Northwestern U., 1964, PhD, 1968. Ordained to ministry Luth Ch., 1965. Asst. prof. Concordia Coll., Ft. Wayne, 1965-71, assoc. prof., 1971-76; assoc. prof. Augustana Coll., Sioux Falls, S.D., 1976-88, prof., 1988—; pastor Trinity Luth. Ch., Hartford, S.D., 1978-83; mem., chair Shalom Bd. Dirs., Sioux Falls, 1985-90; chair dept. religion, philosophy and classics Augustana Coll., Sioux Falls, 1983-91. Contbr. articles to profl. jours. Mem. Soc. for Bibl. Lit., Am. Philol. Assn., Am. Inst. Archaeology, Assn. Luth. Coll. Faculties (pres. 1988-89), Classical Assn. Midwest and South. Democrat. Office: Augustana Coll Humanities Ctr Sioux Falls SD 57197 *I find life to be lived on the edge between community nurture and responsibility and the questing of the individual for excellence and identity. Each gives the other definition and importance.*

RUSCH, WILLIAM GRAHAM, religious organization administrator; b. Buffalo, Dec. 23, 1937; s. William Godfrey and Hope (French) R.; m. Thora Joan Ellefsen, Sept. 2, 1967. BA, SUNY, Buffalo, 1959, MA in Classical Langs., 1960; MDiv, Luth. Theol. Sem., Phila., 1963; PhD, U. Oxford, 1965. Ordained to ministry Evang. Luth. Ch., 1966. Assoc. pastor Evang. Luth. Ch. of the Holy Trinity, N.Y.C., 1966-68; asst. prof., chmn. dept. classical langs. Augsburg Coll., Mpls., 1968-71; assoc. exec. dir. div. Theol. Studies Luth. Coun. in the USA, 1971-78; adj. prof. The Gen. Theol. Sem., N.Y.C., 1978-82; exec. dir., asst. to Bishop Evang. Luth. Ch. in Am., Chgo., 1987—; vis. lectr. Waterloo Luth. Theol. Sem., 1969; adj. prof. Theology Fordham U., N.Y.C., 1984-86; mem. cen. com. World Coun. Chs., 1991—. Author: The Trinitarian Controversy, Ecumenism: A Movement Toward Church Unity; contbr. articles to profl. jours. Samuel Trexler fellow of N.Y. Synod Luth. Ch. in Am., 1964, 65. Mem. Am. Acad. Religion, Am. Soc. Christian Ethics, Am. Soc. Ch. History, Internat. Assn. Coptic Studies, Gen. Bd. Nat. Coun. Chs. Avocations: book collecting, chess, tennis. Office: Evang Luth Ch in Am 8765 W Higgins Rd Chicago IL 60631

RUSCHE, BRIAN, ecumenical agency administrator. Exec. dir. Joint Religious Legis. Coalition, Mpls. Office: Joint Religious Legis Coalition 122 W Franklin Ave Minneapolis MN 55404*

RUSH, BOB ROY, minister; b. Thomasville, Ala., May 7, 1942; s. Leroy and Bertha (Huggins) R.; m. Margaret Baugh, June 11, 1966; children: Samantha Anne, Paula Denise, Matthew Cory. BA, Mobile Coll., 1973; MDiv, New Orleans Bapt. Theol. Sem., 1977. Ordained to ministry So. Bapt. Conv., 1967. Pastor 2d Bapt. Ch., Uniontown, Ala., 1967-70, Beatrice (Ala.) Bapt. Ch., 1971-73, New Zion Bapt. Ch., Covington, La., 1974-77, Winbourne Ave. Bapt. Ch., Baton Rouge, 1978-82, Spring Bank Bapt. Ch., Silas, Ala., 1983-86, Lancaster (Ky.) Bapt. Ch., 1986—. Mem. Ky. Bapt. State Exec. Bd. Home: 115 Maplewood Dr Lancaster KY 40444 Office: Lancaster Bapt Ch 201 Richmond St Lancaster KY 40444

RUSH, KIP JOHN, minister; b. Austin, Tex., Aug. 31, 1964; s. Johnny Fred and Cheryl Darlene (Wiley) R.; m. Jodi Lyn Hearn, June 15, 1985. BA, Bethel Coll., McKenzie, Tenn., 1986; MDiv cum laude, Memphis Theol. Sem., 1990. Ordained to ministry Presbyn. Ch., 1990. Staff New Salem Cumberland Presbyn. Ch., Sharon, Tenn., 1984-86; youth dir. Colonial Cumberland Presbyn. Ch., Memphis, 1987-90; min. edn. Elmira Chapel Cumberland Presbyn. Ch., Longview, Tex., 1990—; asst. advisor young adults S. Tex. Presbyn. Youth, Austin, 1982-84; mem. youth planning coun. W. Tenn. Presbyn. Youth, Memphis, 1988-90, Bd. Christian Edn. Trinity Presbytery, Longview, 1990—, pastoral advisor Trinity Presbyterial Youth, Longview, 1990—. Vol. YWCA Wife Abuse Ctr. (Vol. Yr. award 1989), Memphis. Home: 3505 Elmira Dr Longview TX 75605 Office: Elmira Chapel Cumberland Presby Ch 3501 Elmira Dr Longview TX 75605

RUSH, WILLIAM EDWARD, minister; b. Cullman, Ala., Dec. 31, 1942; s. Curtis Edward and Edith Winnell (Buckalew) R.; m. Bobbie Louise Goodwin; children: Sherri Louise, Steven Edward. MusB in Ch. Music, Samford U., 1966; MusM in Ch. Music, Southern Sem., 1973. Minister of music Grove Hill (Ala.) Bapt. Ch., 1966-71, Lakeview Bapt. Ch., Auburn, Ala., 1974-76; minister music and youth Southside Bapt. Ch., Montgomery, Ala., 1976—; conductor Ala. Singing Men Brass Ensemble, Montgomery, 1976—, Montgomery Singing Ministers, 1977-83, 86—; composer, arranger Bapt. Sunday Sch. Bd., Nashville, Lorenz Pub. Co. Composer: In the Stillness, 1978, A Little Child, 1981, To Be a Blessing, 1983; arranger of instrumental Angels We Have Heard, 1985. Trombonist Montgomery Pageant Orch., 1982-83, Community Theatre Orch., 1985. Mem. Ala. Singing Men (area dir. 1978-87), Am. Soc. Composers, Authors and Pubs. Avocations: fishing, golf.

RUSHDIE, SALMAN, author; b. Bombay, June 19, 1947; s. Anis Ahmed and Negin Rushdie; m. Clarissa Luard, 1976 (div. 1987); m. Marianne Wiggins, 1988; 1 child, Zafar. Ed., Cathedral Sch., Bombay; MA in History with honors, King's Coll., Cambridge U., Eng., 1968. Author: Grimus, 1975; Midnight's Children (Booker McConnell prize for fiction, James Tait Black Meml. Book prize, E.SU Lit. award), 1981; Shame, 1983, The Jaguar Smile: A Nicaraguan Journey, 1987, The Satanic Verses, 1989 (Whitbread award 1988); Haroun and the Sea of Stories, 1991; contbr. to Firebird 1: Writing Today, 1982, London Rev. of Books, Anthology One, 1982, Shakespeare Stories, 1982, Authors Take Sides on the Falklands, 1982. Fellow Royal Soc. Lit.; mem. Internat. PEN, Soc. Authors, Nat. Book League (exec. com.). Office: care Deborah Rogers Ltd, 49 Blenheim Crescent, London W11, England

RUSHING, RAYBURN LEWIS, evangelist; b. Leonard, Tex., Sept. 18, 1922; s. John Sidney and Ollie May (Hunt) R.; m. Wilene Mozelle Dawson, Sept. 15, 1947; children: Gail Rushing Brigham, Gene, Tim, Joe. Student, East Tex. Bapt. Coll., 1947-49, Ouachita Bapt. Coll., 1950-52; DD, Defender's Theol. Sem., 1972. Ordained to ministry So. Bapt. Conv., 1947. Pastor So. Bapt. Ch., Tex., Ark., 1947-54; evangelist Youth for Christ Internat., Chgo., 1952-53; dir. Dallas Youth for Christ, 1954-56, United Temperance League, Mitchell, S.D., 1956-60; evangelist Ray Rushing Evangelistic Assn., Dallas, 1963-88. Editor, pub. The Nat. Voice, 1965-78; broadcaster: (radio and TV) Temperance Time, 1960-78. Chaplain Civil Air Patrol, Dallas, 1954; lobbyist United Temperance League, Pierre, S.D., 1958, Temperance Time, Washington, 1961, The Nat. Voice, Austin, Tex., 1965. With U.S. Army, 1941-45, ETO. Named to Honorable Order of Ky. Colonels, Honorary Dep. Sheriff Dallas County, 1976. Republican.

RUSNAK, MICHAEL, bishop; b. Beaverdale, Pa., Aug. 21, 1921; arrived in Can., 1951; s. Andrew and Maria (Sotak) R. Student, Slovak U. Bratislava, Oberište. Ordained priest Slovak Cath. Byzantine Rite Ch., 1949, joined Redemptorist Fathers, 1949. Founder Maria publ., 1953; dean Slovak parishes Byzantine Rite, Ukrainian Eparchy Toronto, Can., 1957; apptd. titular bishop Diocese of Cernik, 1964; apptd. apostolic visitator for Slovak Caths. of Byzantine Rite in Can., 1964, consecrated bishop, 1965; named eparch Diocese of Sts. Cyril and Methodius, Slovak Byzantine Cath. Eparchy in N.Am., Can., 1980. Address: Slovak Cath Ch in Can, 223 Carlton Rd, Unionville, ON Canada L3R 2L8

RUSSELL, CHARLES ALLYN, retired religion educator, clergyman; b. Bovina Center, N.Y., Sept. 3, 1920; s. Charles James and Hildreth (Tuttle) R.; m. Elizabeth Jane Vigh, June 9, 1947. AB, Houghton Coll., 1942; BD, Ea. Bapt. Theol. Sem., Phila., 1944, ThM, 1946; MA, U. Buffalo, 1955; PhD, Boston U., 1959. Ordained to ministry Bapt. Ch., 1945. Clergyman Osbornville (N.J.) Bapt. Ch., 1943-45, 1st Bapt. Ch., Northampton, Mass., 1946-50, Fredonia (N.Y.) Bapt. Ch., 1950-56, 1st Bapt. Ch., Pawtucket, R.I., 1959-60; asst. prof. ch. history So. Bapt. Theol. Sem., 1959; instr. then asst. prof. religion Boston U., 1959-67, assoc. prof., 1967-73, prof., 1973-88, prof. emeritus, 1988—. Author: A History of the Fredonia Baptist Church, 1808-1955, 1955, Voices of American Fundamentalism: Seven Biographical Studies, 1976. Recipient Solon J. Buck award Minn. History, 1972, Metcalf cup and prize Boston U., 1982, Humanitarian award New Eng. Inst., 1983. Mem. AAUP, Am. Acad. Religion, Am. Soc. Ch. History, Lincoln Group Boston, Boston Philatelic Group. Avocations: tennis, philately, deltiology, professional sports, baseball. Home: PO Box 39 Concord MA 01742-0039

RUSSELL, CHARLES WAYMAN, minister; b. Paducah, Ky., Apr. 15, 1938; s. Charles Thomas and Mildred Idelria (Jenkins) R.; m. Mary Ellis Jones, Sept. 4, 1956; children: Diana Darlene, Lovell Eugene. BA in Bible, N.W. Bible Coll., 1986. Assoc. minister Minot (N.D.) AFB Chapel, 1981-86; dir. Christian edn., asst. pastor Harrison St. Missionary Bapt. Ch., Paducah, 1988—; exec. dir. Project Best, Paducah, 1988—; dean Christian edn. 1st Dist. Assn. Sunday Sch. and Bapt. Tng. Union Congress of Christian Edn., 1990—. Mem. Adjustment Bd. Zoning Ordinance, Paducah, 1990, Census adv. com., Paducah, 1990. Named Duke of Paducah City of Paducah, 1989. Mem. NAACP (2d v.p. 1990). Democrat. Office: Harrison St Bapt Ch 1126 Harrison St PO Box 2523 Paducah KY 42002

RUSSELL, DONALD LEE, minister; b. Franklin, Pa., May 28, 1946; s. Arthur and Viola (Hepler) R.; m. Patricia Pruitt, Aug. 24, 1969; 1 child, Carrie Rebecca. Student, Frostburg (Mo. U., 1973, United Theol. Sem., Dayton, Ohio, 1976. Ordained to ministry United Meth. Ch., 1977. Min. United Meth. Ch., Princess Anne, Md., 1968-70, Eckhart Mines, Md., 1970-73; min. youth United Meth. Ch., Arcanum, Ohio, 1973-74; min. United Meth. Ch., Pa., 1974-79; dir. ch. devel. 4 Corners Native Am. Ministry, Shiprock, N.Mex., 1991—; assoc. admissions officer United Theol. Sem., Dayton, 1976—. Maj. USAF, 1979-90. Recipient Air Force Commendation award, Meritorious Svc. award. Home: PO Box 747 Kirtland NM 87417 Office: Four Corners Native Am Min PO Box 400 Shiprock NM 87420 *It is important to share the love of Christ totally—mind, body, and spirit—to all that we meet.*

RUSSELL, GARY E., minister; b. Detroit, Feb. 10, 1950; s. Billy Eugene Russell and Betty Mae (Harden) Berzley; m. Diane L. Rendel, Aug. 9, 1970; children: Chad M., Kurt L., Tara N., Bret M. BA in Theology, Andrews U., 1972, MDiv, 1974; MPH, Loma Linda U., 1981; postgrad., Andrews U., 1990. Ordained to ministry Seventh-day Adventist Ch., 1979. Assoc. min. Fla. Conf. of Seventh Day Adventists, Winter Park, 1975-77; min. Fla. Conf. of Seventh Day Adventists, Okeechobee, 1977-79, Vero Beach, 1977-81; min. Mich. Conf. of Seventh Day Adventists, Boyne City, 1981-85, Traverse City, 1985-88, Dowagiac, 1988 ; chaplain Cass County (Mich.) Sheriff's Dept., 1990—, Dowagiac Police Dept., 1990—, Wayne Twp. Vol. Fire Dept., 1991—. Asst. editor (newsletter) Adventist Baby Bommer Awareness, 1991; contbr. articles to profl. jours. Active Cass County Coalition Against Domestic Violence, 1989 ; edn. dir. World Vision/Crop Walk for Hunger, Dowagiac, 1989. Named Man Who Affirms Women, Assn. of Adventist Women, Berrien Springs, 1990; recipient Recognition of Honor, Cass County Civitans, 1990. Mem. Internat. Conf. Police Chaplains, Mich. Police Chaplains Assn., Dowagiac Ministerial Assn. (vice chair 1989-90, chmn. 1990—), Theta Alpha Kappa (v.p. 1991—). Avocations: reading, computers, sports, photography, writing. Home: 208 Cross St Dowagiac MI 49047 *Within the past few years I have begun to realize that I will probably not make a major impact on the world. I cannot feed all the hungry, clothe all the naked, free all the imprisoned. But I can do something for those within the sphere of my life. If I do this, and others do as well, together we will make a major impact on our world.*

RUSSELL, GEORGE AUSTIN, JR., minister; b. Birmingham, Ala., Jan. 22, 1948; s. George Austin Sr. and Betty Lorene (Forrester) R.; m. Judy Lynn Bruton, Mar. 28, 1970; children: Joshua, Kristina, Shannon, Ashley. BA, N.Mex. Highlands U., 1973. Asst. pastor 1st Bapt. of Ctr. Point, Birmingham, Ala., 1969, Lakeside Bapt. Ch., Birmingham, Ala., 1970-71; pastor Emmanuel Bapt. Ch., Las Vegas, N.M., 1971-73; missionary Liberty Ch., Mex., 1973-81; pastor Liberty Ch., Meridian, Miss., 1982-85, Chapel of Valley, Farmington, N.M., 1985-90, Jesus Chapel, El Paso, Tex., 1990—; v.p. Ministerial Assn., Meridian, 1983-85; adv. Shalom Ministries, Santa Fe, 1986—. Columnist Noticias newspaper, 1978-80; daily radio host El Camino de Amor, Mex. to Panama. Vice chmn. Juvenile Reintegration Ctr., N.Mex. Corrections Dept., 1987; Rep. city coun. candidate, Meridian, 1985, state Senate candidate, Farmington, 1988; Rep. organizational chmn., San Juan County, N.Mex., 1988. Home: 3961 Breckenridge El Paso TX 79936

RUSSELL, JOHN JOSEPH, JR., lay worker; b. Wilmington, Del., Mar. 27, 1957; s. John Joseph and Mary Jane (Schofield) R. Student, Liberty U. Assoc. mem. staff Inter-Varsity Christian Fellowship, 1987—; supr. State of Del. Home: 930 Kiamensi Rd Apt 2 Wilmington DE 19804 *I want my life to have an eternal focus. This life is short. The only two things that will last in the end, will be God's Word and people. What better way to have and keep this focus than to invest my life in both?.*

RUSSELL, KEITH A., academic administrator. Pres. N.Y. Theol. Sem., N.Y.C. Office: NY Theol Sem 5 W 29th St New York NY 10001*

RUSSELL, NORMAN, clergyman; b. Belfast, No. Ireland, Sept. 5, 1945; s. George and Elizabeth (Moraitis) R. B.A. with honours in English, London U., 1968, diploma in pastoral theology, 1976; B.A. with honours in Theology, Oxford U., 1970, M.A., 1973. Joined Oratory of St. Philip Neri, Roman Catholic Ch., 1972, ordained priest, 1976. Deacon, Ch. of England, London, 1971; deacon Roman Cath. Ch., London, 1975; chaplain London Oratory Sch., 1976-82, vice-provost, 1984-85. Co-editor Sobornost

Incorporating Eastern Churches Rev., 1979—; translator: Lives of the Desert Fathers, 1980; Climacus, Spiritual Ladder, 1983; Nellas, The Vocation of the Human Person, 1986; Philokalia, 1979—; contbr. articles to publs. in field. Home: The Oratory, London SW7 2RP, England

RUSSELL, PATRICK JAMES, priest; b. Boise, Idaho, May 10, 1959; s. Glenn Edward and Doralea (Trumble) R. BA, Boise U., 1982; MDiv, St. Patrick's Sem., 1986. Ordained priest Roman Catholic Ch., 1986. Assoc. pastor St. Marks Cath. Ch., Boise, 1986-91. Named Outstanding Young Man of Am. 1983, 84, 86, 87, Outstanding Youth in Achievement, Cambridge, U.K. Mem. Am. Film Inst., Amnestry Internat., Internat. Biog. Ctr., Right to Life/Spl. Olympics, Sigma Phi Epsilon. Democrat. Avocations: writing, painting, music, public speaking, acting. Office: St Marks Cath Ch 7503 Northview St Boise ID 83704

RUSSELL, ROBERT JOHN, religion educator; b. L.A., Aug. 23, 1946; s. John K. and Arden (Swanson) R.; m. Charlotte Ann Stott, Dec. 20, 1969; children: Christina Marie, Elizabeth Arden. BS in Physics, Stanford U., 1968; MS in Physics, UCLA, 1970; MDiv and MA in Theology, Pacific Sch. Religion, 1972; PhD in Physics, U. Santa Cruz, 1978. Ordained to ministry United Ch. Christ, 1978. Asst. prof. physics Carleton Coll., Northfield, Minn., 1978-81; founder, dir. Ctr. Theology and Natural Scis., Berkeley, Calif., 1981—, asst. prof. theology and sci. in residence, 1981-85, assoc. prof. theol. union, 1986—; ministerial standing United Ch. Christ No. Calif. Confs., 1981—. Co-editor: Physics, Philosophy and Theology, 1988, John Paul II on Science and Religion, 1990. Mem. AAAS, Am. Acad. Religion, Am. Phys. Soc. Office: Ctr for Theology and Natural Scis 2400 Ridge Rd Berkeley CA 94709

RUSSELL, ROBERT M., clergyman; b. Indpls., Oct. 13, 1943; s. Robert M. Russell Sr. and Deloris J. (Rice) Kennedy; m. Linda M. Russell, Nov. 3, 1961; children: Katherine, Larry, Karen, Penny. Student, Intermountain Bible Coll., 1978-81. Ordained to ministry Ch. of Christ. Minister Christian Ch., Parachute, Colo., 1979-81, Holly, Calif., 1981-84; minister Ch. of Christ, Pueblo, Colo., 1984—; trustee Platte Valley Bible Coll., Scottsbluff, Nebr., 1989—. With USN, 1961-64. Home: 1514 Horseshoe St Pueblo CO 81001 Office: Ch of Christ 2901 High St Pueblo CO 81008

RUSSELL, WILLIAM FOLSOM (JIM RUSSELL), minister; b. Tyler, Tex., Sept. 20, 1963; s. Wallace Delroy and Mildred Louise (Folsom) R.; m. Leah Lennon, July 2, 1982; children: Derek, Krista, Courtney. SBS, Harding Sch. Bibl. Studies, 1986; BS, Harding U., 1989; postgrad., Harding Grad. Sch. Religion, 1990-91. Ordained to ministry Ch. of Christ, 1986. Preacher Ch. of Christ, Des Arc, Ark., 1986-89, Atkins, Ark., 1989—. Author: His Majesty, Meditations, 1988. Mem. Lions. Home: 305 Ne 2d Atkins AR 72823 Office: Ch of Christ 105 N Ch Atkins AR 72823

RUSSER, MAXIMILIAN F., lay worker; b. Rochester, N.Y., Oct. 5, 1939; s. Max Oren and Marion Helen (Hampel) R.; m. Dolores H. Sharrock, Nov. 23, 1967 (div. Sept. 1974) 1 child, Sabrina; m. Edna Rita Vesjunas, May 22, 1976. AA, St. Michael's Coll., 1960; postgrad., St. Mary's Sem., 1960-61, Genesee Abbey, 1961-63; BA in Sacramental Theology, St. Bernard's Sem., 1967. Registered investment adviser, health underwriter. Trappist monk Genesee Abbey, Piffard, N.Y., 1961-63; asst. dir. St. Martin De Porres Ctr., Rochester, N.Y., 1965-67; cantor Assumption Ch., Jacksonville, Fla., 1977-85; tchr., bibl. theology Assumption Ch., 1977-89; writer, lectr., author freelance, Jacksonville, 1989—; seminarian, St. Joseph's Sem., Bordentown, N.J., 1955-56, St. Michael's Ch., Conesus, N.Y., 1956-58, St. Michael's Coll., 1958-60. Author: Authority In the Roman Catholic Church: The Corporate Rejection of Jesus, 1991. Named to Million Dollar Round Table, 1978. Mem. Nat. Assn. Life Underwriters (bd. dirs. 1986, Nat. Sales Achievement 1977-90), Nat. Assn. Securities Dealers, Nat. Small Bus. Assn., Jacksonville Life Underwriters Assn. (chmn. 1987), Life Underwriters Tng. Coun., Chmn.'s Coun. (leader 1985-91), Jacksonville C. of C., Toastmasters (bd. dirs. Rochester chpt. 1968-70). Republican. Home and Office: 745 Old Hickory Rd Jacksonville FL 32207 *It is not the expression of critisim and diversity that turns people away from religion, but rather the supression of criticism, the stifling of fresh data, and the distain for diversity, as well as the failure of religious people to practice what they preach.*

RUSSO, DIANE LUCILLE, evangelist; b. Springville, N.Y., Jan. 9, 1961; d. Bernard Lawrence and Pamela Lucille (Peacock) R.; 1 child, Rachael Susan Lminggio. Cert. in Basic Scis., Houghton Coll., 1985. Choir singer, altar worker women's dept. Bethesda Full Gospel Ch., Buffalo, 1981-85; min. youth and prison, sec. Urban Christian Ministries, Buffalo, 1981-86; street min. New Life Assembly of God, Buffalo, 1984; mem. worship team, child care helper New Creation Fellowship, Buffalo, 1988-89; tchr. Sunday sch. Restoration Deliverance Tabernacle, Buffalo, 1990-91. Home: 453 Perry St Apt 4 Buffalo NY 14204 *It is a joy serving Jesus. He's the author and finisher of my faith. Although I am not perfect the perfect one abides in me. He is a treasure worth living for.*

RUSSO, JOYCE CHASSE, parish librarian; b. Augusta, Maine, Nov. 4, 1938; d. Albert Joseph and Helen Marie (Raymond) Chasse; m. David Mark Russo, Nov. 25, 1960; children: Margaret, T. Mark, Miriam, Mary Beth. BA in English, St. Joseph's Coll., 1960. Parish libr. St. James Resource Ctr., Arlington Heights, Ill., 1979—. Mem. Cath. Libr. Assn. (no. Ill. chpt.), Ch. and Synagogue Libr. Assn. (v.p. N.E. Ill. chpt. 1987-88, pres. 1988-89, treas. 1991—). Roman Catholic. Office: St James Resource Ctr 820 N Arlington Heights Rd Arlington Heights IL 60004

RUSSO, ROBERT JOSEPH, minister; b. Bainbridge, Md., Sept. 4, 1955; s. Anthony Henry and Frances (Haithcock) R.; m. Lesa Lynn Starkes, Nov. 21, 1980. BA, Bapt. Bible Coll., Springfield, Mass., 1978. Ordained to ministry Bapt. Ch., 1978. Interim pastor Brean Bapt. Ch., Augustine, Fla., 1978; assoc. pastor St. Augustine Ch., 1979-80, Bethel Bapt. Ch., Melbourne, Fla., 1980; min. edn. Jupiter Rd. Bapt. Ch., Garland, Tex., 1981-84, assoc. pastor, 1984-91, pastor, 1991—. Editor yr. book Sojourner, 1978. Apptd. Garland Performing Arts Com.; dir. Youth Camp, Lone Star, Tex., 1984; vol. numerous activities. Journalism scholar Bapt. Bible Coll., 1978. Avocations: reading, music, racquet sports, golf, photography. Home: 4548 Chaha Rd #102 Garland TX 75043 Office: Jupiter Rd Bapt Ch 2422 N Jupiter Rd Garland TX 75042 *The most important thing in life is relationships, and not to build relationships to me seems to be a violation of one's existence.*

RUST, JAMES H., minister; b. Huntingdon, Tenn., Nov. 10, 1940; s. James Randolph and Bernice Marie (Lane) R.; m. Telitha Sue Russell, Dec. 23, 1961; stepchildren: Farrell, Walter, Brent, Janet; 1 child, James A.; 1 adopted child, Paul. Grad., Fruitland Bapt. Bible Inst., Hendersonville, N.C., 1977. Ordained to ministry So. Bapt. Conv., 1977. Pastor 1st Bapt. Ch., South Coffeyville, Okla., 1977-83, Harmony Bapt. Ch., Hallsville, Tex., 1983—. With U.S. Army, 1957-60. Recipient leadership awards Bapt. Gen. Conv. Tex. Home and Office: Harmony Bapt Ch PO Box 491 Hallsville TX 75650

RUST, LARRY DUWAYNE, minister; b. Kansas City, Mo., Mar. 27, 1947; s. Dewey Lee and Leora (Shaw) R.; m. Hilda Marie Clanton, June 11, 1970; children: Eric Duwayne, Adam Ryan. BS in Pastoral Theology, Bethany Coll., Santa Cruz, Calif., 1978. Ordained to ministry Assemblies of God, 1978. Pastor Assembly of God, Pinole and Hercules, Calif., 1982-85, Susanville, Calif., 1985—; mem. exec. bd. New Era Ministries, Red Bluff, Calif., 1980—, Lassen Camp, Mineral, Calif., 1988—. Bd. dirs. family life com. local high sch., Susanville, 1987—; chaplain Hercules/Pinole Police Dept., 1981-84. With U.S. Army, 1967-69, Vietnam. Mem. Evang. Ministerial Fellowship (pres. 1990—), Lassen Ministerial Fellowship (pres. 1987-89). Republican. Office: Susanville Assembly of God 473-465 Richmond Rd N Susanville CA 96130

RUST, STEPHEN CARL, minister; b. Bryan, Ohio, July 25, 1952; s. Harold Carl and Anna Marie (Heller) R.; m. Joy M. Harrison, June 21, 1975; children: Jennifer Ann, John Carl, Joel William. BA, Capital U., 1974; MDiv, Trinity Luth. Sem., Columbus, Ohio, 1978. Ordained to ministry Luth. Ch. Chaplain Fairfield Sch. for Boys, Lancaster, Ohio, 1974-75, Grant Hosp., Columbus, Ohio, 1975; vicar Holy Cross Luth. Ch., Sarasota, Fla., 1976-77; pastor Nativity Luth. Ch., Palm Beach Gardens, Fla., 1978-86, Redeemer Luth. Ch., Woodstock, Ill., 1986—; nat. del. Evang. Luth. Ch. Am., Chgo., 1989, mem. mission fund No. Ill. Synod, Rockford, 1988-89; nat. del. Am. Luth. Ch., Mpls., 1984; pastoral youth advisor Fla.-Bahamas Conf., Palm Beach Gardens, 1979-83. Bd. dirs. Am. Cancer Soc., Woodstock, 1989—. Mem. Woodstock Ministerial Assn. Republican. Home: 255 Ridgewood Dr Woodstock IL 60098 *I like virtually everything about my life. I am comfortable doing just about anything and I waste no time in complaining or wishing that things were otherwise. I celebrate and am enthusiastic about life and I want all that I can get out of it in order to give back to others.*

RUST, THOMAS JOSEPH, religious organization administrator; b. Lima, Ohio, Aug. 17, 1948; s. Millard Devon and Mildred Floretta (Tucker) R.; m. Fran Rust, Aug. 15, 1970. BS in Christian Edn., Ft. Wayne Bible Coll., 1972. Dir. youth guidance Youth for Christ, Lansing, Mich., 1972-76, ministry dir., 1976-79; founder Youth for Christ, Cin., 1979-82, Columbus, Ind., 1982—; broadcaster various local radio and TV stas., Columbus, 1982—. Founder, sponsor Fellowship Christian Athletes Mich. State U., 1972-79, football program chaplain, 1977-79; asst. coach Forest Park High Sch., Cin., 1979-82. Republican. Lutheran. Avocations: softball, golf, running, reading, travel. Home: 1772 Prairie Dr Columbus IN 47203 Office: Youth for Christ 442 1/2 5th St Columbus IN 47201

RUSTERHOLZ, HEINRICH RAINER, minister, religious association executive; b. Zürich, Switzerland, Oct. 10, 1934; s. Heinrich and Elisabeth (Fischer) R.; m. Ursula Schaub, Mar. 25, 1961; children: Andreas, Johannes, Barbara, Thomas. ThM, U. Zürich, 1963. Ordained to ministry. Parish pastor, 1964-65; missionary Basel Mission, Sabah, East Malaysia, 1966-69; ecumenical officer Ch. of Zürich, 1970-86; pres. Fedn. Swiss Protestant Chs., Berne, 1987—. Office: Fedn Swiss Protestant Chs, Sulgenauweg 26, PO Box 36, 3000 Berne 23, Switzerland

RUTBERG, ARTHUR SIDNEY, rabbi; b. N.Y.C., Dec. 21, 1956; s. Albert and Helen (Dubester) R.; m. Sara Eugenia Diaz, May 6, 1984; children: Pamela Eve, Raquel Katherine. BA, NYU, 1978; MA in Hebrew Lit., Jewish Inst. Religion, N.Y.C., 1981. Ordained rabbi, 1983. Religious sch. tchr. Stephen Wise Synagogue, N.Y.C., 1979-81; rabbi Temple Beth El, Augusta, Maine, 1981-82, Temple Sinai, Saratoga Springs, N.Y., 1982-83, Temple Beth Israel, Steubenville, Ohio, 1983-85, Temple Beth El, Brownsville, Tex., 1985-91; chaplain U.S. Army, Ft. Benning, Ga., 1991—. Del. Tex. Dem. Conv., 1990; chmn. Palmer Drug Abuse Prog., Brownsville, 1990, The Shepherd's Ctr. for Sr. Citizens, Brownsville, 1988-89. Mem. Cen. Conf. Am. Rabbis, S.W. Assn. Reform Rabbis, Kallah of Tex. Rabbis (pres. 1990-91), Brownsville Ministerial Assn. (pres. 1986-88), Rotary (program dir. 1986). Home: 2922 Mary Ann Dr Columbus GA 31906 Office: US Army Ind Tng Ctr PO Box 2232 Fort Benning GA 31905-0832

RUTHERFORD, EDWARD ARNOLD, clergyman; b. Fresno, Calif., Feb. 20, 1945; s. Edgar Lee and Lena (Dabbs) R.; m. Mary Helen Blackburn, July 22, 1967; children: Roben Renee, Michele Lenise. BS in Acctg., Calif. State U., Bakersfield, 1973, MS in Bus., 1976; postgrad. in religion, Berean Coll., Springfield, Mo., 1977; DD (hon.), So. Calif. Theol. Sem., 1985. Ordained to ministry Assemblies of God Ch., 1980. Various mgmt. positions Pacific Telephone Co., Bakersfield, 1966-77; sr. pastor Wofford Heights (Calif.) Assembly, 1977-81, Cerritos (Calif.) Assembly, 1982-87; pastor Calvary Christian Ch., Buena Park, Calif., 1987-88, Harbor Calvary Ch., San Pedro, Calif., 1989—; bd. dirs. World Wide Missions, Bellflower, Calif., 1985-86; ministerial rep. Forest Lawn, Long Beach, Calif., 1987-88; sec., bd. dirs. Tri Care Plus, Bell Gardens, Calif., 1987—; sec.-treas., bd. dirs. Missions Internat., Sacramento, 1988—; adj. prof. So. Calif. Coll., Costa Mesa, 1980-85, So. Calif. Theol. Sem., Stanton, 1985-87. Author: Church Business Administration, 1983; contbr. articles to religious mags. and newspaper. Mem. Bell Gardens Homeless Coalition, 1988; bd. dirs. Tri Care Ctrs., Bell Gardens, 1988. With USN, 1962-66. Fellow Nat. Assn. Ch. Bus. Adminstrs.; mem. Performex (assoc.). Democrat. Avocations: computers, photography. Office: Harbor Calvary Ch 867 W 10th St San Pedro CA 90731

RUTHERFORD, JOEL STEVEN, minister; b. Wichita, Kans., Dec. 18, 1959; s. James King R. and Norma Jean (Burden) Mendoza; m. Kelly Annette deSousa, July 31, 1982; children: Megan, Lindsey, James, Emily. Diploma, Rhema Bible Tng. Ctr., Broken Arrow, Okla., 1982. Ordained to ministry Christian Ch., 1982. Pastor Adair (Okla.) Christian Ch., 1981-84; pastor First Christian Ch., Charlestown, Ind., 1984—. Mem. North Clark County Ministerial Assn. (pres. 1989-91). Office: First Christian Ch 999 Water Charlestown IN 47111-1430 *There is no doubt in my mind that the summation of life's purpose is "to know God". Apart from Jesus Christ, there can be no hope for solving the world's problems. Only "born again" individuals can bring about a reborn nation and earth.*

RUTLEDGE, BETTY LOUISE, school administrator; b. Sparta, Ill., Sept. 24, 1937; d. Raymond Edgar and Hazel Aileen (Harriman) Thompson; m. Norman Rutledge Jr., Jan. 11, 1957; children: Janice Breazeale, Sharla Rawson, Lori Ladd. AA, Meridian (Miss.) Jr. Coll., 1972; BS in Elem. Edn. with highest honors, Miss. State U., 1976, MEd with distinction, 1983, cert. elem. adminstrn., 1986. 1st grade tchr. Calvary Christian Sch., Meridian, 1976-86, asst. prin., 1984-87, 8th grade tchr., 1986-87, prin., 1987—. Treas. Long Creek Bapt. Ch., Meridian, 1967—, pianist, 1975—. Office: Calvary Christian Sch 3917 7th St PO Box 4238 Meridian MS 39304

RUTT, HARRY WEAVER, minister; b. Ephrata, Pa., June 24, 1948; s. Harry N. and Anna May (Weaver) R.; m. Julia Ann Zimmerman, Jan. 6, 1968; children: Michelle, Keith, Christine, Stacy, Anthony. MA in Ch. Ministries, Ea. Mennonite Sem., Harrisonburg, Va., 1991. Ordained to ministry Lancaster Conf. Mennonite Ch., 1982. Pres., dir. New Life Tape Ministry, Stevens, Pa., 1972-82; ch. planter, pastor Christian Community Fellowship, Manchester, Pa., 1982-89; program coord. Ctr. for Evangelism and Ch. Planting, Ea. Mennonite Sem., 1990-91; bd. dirs. Jesus Ministries, Shirleysburg, Pa., 1975-81, Mennonite Renewal Svcs., Goshen, Ind., 1975-90; chmn. New Life for Girls, Dover, Pa., 1982-86. Home: 859 College Ave Harrisonburg VA 22801

RUX, BRUCE MACKENZIE, minister, chaplain; b. Stamford, Conn., Dec. 12, 1946; s. Frederic MacKenzie and Doris Loise (DeForest) R.; m. Carol Anne Osborne, May 14, 1977; children: Stephanie Lynne, Joshua MacKenzie. BS, Quinnipiac Coll., 1969; MDiv, Pittsburgh Sem., 1974. Ordained to ministry Presbyn. Ch. (U.S.A.), 1975. Pastor Margaret Park United Presbyn. Ch., Akron, Ohio, 1974-79; chaplain U.S. Army, Dallas, 1989—; pastor Hooks (Tex.)/Atlanta 1st Presbyn. Ch., 1989-91. Maj. U.S. Army, 1979—. Mem. Ministerial Alliance, Jacksboro, Tex., Amateur Radio Club New Boston. Republican. Home: 706 N Fifth St Jacksboro TX 76458 Office: The Parish of Jacksboro PO Box 716 Jacksboro TX 76458

RYAN, DANIEL LEO, bishop; b. Mankato, Minn., Sept. 28, 1930; s. Leonard Bennett and Irene Ruth (Larson) R. BA, Ill. Benedictine Coll., 1952; JCL, Pontificia Università Lateranense, Rome, 1960. Ordained priest Roman Cath. Ch., 1956, consecrated bishop, 1981. Parish priest Roman Cath. Diocese, Joliet, Ill, 1956-82, chancellor, 1965-78, vicar gen., 1977-79, aux. bishop, 1981-84; bishop Roman Cath. Diocese, Springfield, Ill., 1984—. Trustee Kendrick-Glennon Sem., St. Louis, 1988—. Office: Diocese of Springfield PO Box 3187 Springfield IL 62708-3187

RYAN, HERBERT JOSEPH, theology educator, priest; b. Scarsdale, N.Y., Feb. 19, 1931; s. Herbert J. and Elizabeth Angela (Gallagher) R. AB in Classical Langs., Loyola U., Chgo., 1954, PhL, 1955, MA in History, 1960; STL, Woodstock Coll., 1963; STD, Gregorian U., Rome, 1967; STD (hon.), Gen. Theol. Sem., N.Y.C., 1973. Joined S.J., 1949, professed, 1966; ordained priest Roman Cath. Ch., 1962. Assoc. prof. theology Woodstock Coll. and Union Theol. Sem., N.Y.C., 1967-74; prof. hist. theology Loyola Marymount U., L.A., 1974—; cons. on ecumenical and interreligious affairs to Vatican and Nat. Conf. Cath. Bishops, 1966-88; mem. Anglical Roman Cath. Consultation U.S.A., N.Y.C., Washington, 1969-84, Anglican Roman Cath. Internat. Commn., London, Vatican City, 1969-83, N.Y. Archdiocesan Ecumenical Commn., 1969-74, L.A. Archdiocesan Ecumenical Commn., 1974-86; DeBose lectr. U. of South, Sewanee, Tenn., 1974. Author: De Praedestinatione of J.S. Eriugena, 1967, Anglicans and Roman Catholics, 1973; editor series Documents on Anglical-Roman Catholic Relations, 1970-84; mem. editorial bd. Thought, 1982—; contbr. articles on ecumenism to profl. jours. Recipient Christian Unity award Graymoor Ecumenical Inst., London, 1973, medal of St. Augustine, Archbishop of Canterbury, London, 1981. Mem. Cath. Hist. Soc., Ch. Hist. Soc., Cath. Theol. Soc. Am., Am. Acad. Religion, N.Am. Acad. Ecumenists, Coun. on Study Religion (charter), Mediaeval Acad. Am., Fellowship Cath. Scholars, Mariological Soc. Home: 7101 W 80th St Los Angeles CA 90045 Office: Loyola Marymount U Xavier Hall Los Angeles CA 90045

RYAN, JAMES SMITH, minister; b. Green Bay, Wis., July 8, 1931; s. Harry Ivan and Helen Leota (Stewart) R.; m. Ila C. Attrill, May 30, 1953; children: Rick J., Ranae J., Rachelle J. Diploma, Cen. Bible Coll., 1953; BA in Bible Studies, North Cen. Bible Coll., 1967; MRE, Cen. Sem., 1970. Ordained to ministry Assemblies of God, 1956. Resident dean, men North Cen. Bible Coll., Mpls., 1966-67; mem. faculty Eugene (Oreg) Bible Coll., 1970-72; pastor, evangelist various chs. Assemblies of God, 1950-84; pastor Praise Fellowship Ch., Phoenix, 1984—; credit mgr. Sparrow Records, Canoga Park, Calif., 1981-84; mem. youth and Christian edn. coms. Assemblies of God. Author Open Bible Nat. Mag., 1971-72. Bd. dirs. Townhouse Assn. Am., Scottsdale, Ariz., 1990-91. Mem. Pentecostal Studies Assn. N.Am. Republican.

RYAN, SISTER JANICE E., college adminstrator. BA in English, Trinity Coll., 1965; MEd in Spl. Edn., Boston U., 1967; postgrad., U. Minn., 1968, U. Lund, Sweden, 1971, Harvard U., 1974-76, 80. Joined Sisters of Mercy, Roman Cath. Ch., 1954. Dir. pub. relations Trinity Coll., Burlington, Vt., 1967-71, asst. prof. spl. edn., 1967-74; lobbyist Vt. Legis., 1974-79; chair spl. edn. div., pres. Trinity Coll., Burlington, Vt., 1979—; mem. Am. Council on Edn.'s Govtl. Relations Commn. on Nat. Challenges in Higher Edn.; corporator, dir. Bank of Vt., trustee Vt. Law Sch.; task force on econ. devel. infrastructure, edn. and tng. NE-Midwest Leadership Council. Exec. com. Campus Compact, chair fed. initiatives task force; active Vt. Higher Edn. Coun.; lobbyist Vt. Legislature (chmn. spl. edn. div.), 1974-79. Mem. NACU (bd. dirs. 1990), Am. Assn. Higher Edn. (participant Spring Hill Conf. 1987). Office: Trinity Coll 208 Colchester Ave Burlington VT 05401

RYAN, JOHN BARRY, religion educator, writer; b. Bronx, N.Y., Apr. 7, 1933; s. John Michael and Winefred Mary (Barry) R.; m. Jeanette Calvo, June 12, 1976; 1 child, John Barry Jr. BA in English Lit., Cath. U., 1955; MA in English Lit., Manhattan Coll., 1961; BTh., U. Strasbourg, France, 1966; Licencié Theology, Strasbourg, France, 1969; STD, Inst. Catholique, Paris, 1973. Cert. peritus in liturgy. Tchr. elem. sch. Christian Bros. Schs., N.Y.C., 1955-58; tchr. secondary sch. Christian Bros. Schs., Syracuse, N.Y. and Detroit, 1958-65; tchr. Manhattan Coll., Bronx, 1972, asst. prof., 1973-81, assoc. prof., 1981-89, prof., 1989—, chmn. dept. religious studies, 1986-90; assoc. dir. Murphy Ctr. for Liturgical Rsch., U. Notre Dame, Ind., 1976-78. Author: The Eucharistic Prayer, 1974; co-author: Commentaries on the Rites, 1982; co-editor: Symbol: The Language of Liturgy, 1982; assoc. editor Worship, 1978-82; contbr. articles to profl. jours. Active schs. and neighborhood orgns., N.Y.C., 1983—; fund raiser local parish campaign. NEH grantee, 1981. Mem. AAUP, N.Am. Acad. Liturgy (founding mem., sec.-treas. 1975-83, pres. 1986), Societas Liturgica, Cath. Theol. Soc. Am., Alcuin Club, Phi Beta Kappa. Roman Catholic. Avocation: travel. Home: 235 E 234th St Bronx NY 10470 Office: Manhattan Coll Bronx NY 10471

RYAN, JOSEPH THOMAS, archbishop; b. Albany, N.Y., Nov. 1, 1913; s. Patrick J. and Agnes (Patterson) R. B.A., Manhattan Coll., 1935, LL.D., 1966; student, St. Joseph's Sem., Yonkers, N.Y., 1939; D.H.L., Siena Coll., 1964. Ordained priest Roman Cath. Ch. 1939; consecrated bishop. Diocesan dir. radio/TV, also diocesan dir. vocations Albany, 1954-57; chancellor Mil. Ordinariate, 1957-58; nat. sec. Cath. Near East Welfare Assn., 1960-65; also pres. Pontifical Mission for Palestine, 1960-66; archbishop of Anchorage, 1966-75; titular bishop of Gabi, coadjutor archbishop mil. vicar U.S. Armed Forces, 1975-85; mil. vicar U.S. Mil. Vicariate, 1985—. Served as chaplain USMCR, 1943-46. Named Papal Chamberlain, 1957; knight comdr. Equestrian Order Holy Sepulchre, 1958; comdr. with star, 1960; grand cross, 1966; grand ofcl. Order Independence Jordan, 1964. Home: 832 Varnum St NE Washington DC 20017 Office: Archdiocese for MilSvcs 962 Wayne Ave Silver Spring MD 20910

RYAN, KATHLEEN MARIE, religious education director; b. Covington, Ky., Dec. 12, 1937; d. Patrick Henry and Margaret Elizabeth (Fleissner) R. BA, Villa Madonna Thos More Coll., 1967; MEd, Xavier U., 1972, MA, 1985. Cert. tchr., life, Ky. Tchr. Diocesan Schs., Covington, Ky., 1958-90; dir. religion edn. St. Barbara, Erlanger, Ky., 1973-75, St. Paul, Florence, Ky., 1977-84, St. Timothy Parishes, Union, Ky., 1990—. Ministry dir. St. Walburg Monastery, Villa Hills, Ky., 1986—. Named Catechist of Yr. Diocese of Covington, 1984. Mem. Benedictine Fedn. (del. to Fedn. of St. Scholastica gen. chpt.). Democrat. Home: 2500 Amsterdam Rd Villa Hills KY 41017 Office: Saint Timothy Parish PO Box 120 Union KY 41091 *Because what I do as a DRE seems "so ordinary", I am both honored and humbled to even be considered for Who's Who. "We only pass this way once" so I hope that whatever I do will help make the world a better place for my having been here.*

RYAN, SISTER PATRICIA ANN, nun; b. Oakland, Calif., June 25, 1931; d. John Francis and Kathleen Cecilia (Gill) R. BA, San Francisco Coll. for Women, 1953; MS, Seattle U., 1967; Sec. Life Credential, U. San Francisco, 1969. Joined Sisters of Mercy, Roman Cath. Ch., 1955. Tchr. Mercy High Sch., Burlingame, Calif., 1956-58, 68-77, San Francisco, 1958-61, 67-68; tchr. Marian High Sch., Imperial Beach, Calif., 1961-67; asst. superior gen. Sisters of Mercy, Burlingame, 1977-81; pastoral assoc. St. Bruno's Parish, San Bruno, Calif., 1982-89; pres. Sisters of Mercy, Burlingame, 1989—; mem. San Francisco Archdiocesan Justice Commn., 1985-89. Trustee Mercy High Sch., San Francisco, 1978-80, Burlingame, 1978-80, St. Mary's Hosp., San Francisco, 1979-80, Mercy Hosp., San Diego, 1980-81, St. John's Hosp., Oxnard, Calif., 1981-83; treas. San Mateo County Organizing Project., 1984-86. Shell Merit fellow Stanford U., 1964. Mem. Leadership Conf. of Women Religious (global concerns com.), Cath. Healthcare West Corp. Mems. (chairperson 1990—). Address: 2300 Adeline Dr Burlingame CA 94010

RYAN, PATRICK DANIEL, clergyman, educator; b. St. Louis, June 5, 1944; s. Harold D. and Laverne M. (Boultes) R. BA, Cardinal Glennon Coll., 1966; MA, St. Louis U., 1970; MDiv, Kenrick Sem., 1973; CAES, Boston Coll., 1986. Ordained priest Roman Cath. Ch., 1970. Assoc. pastor St. Justin Parish, St. Louis, 1970-75; field edn. supr. Kenrick Sem., St. Louis, 1970-75; assoc. pastor St. Monica Parish, Creve Coeur, Mo., 1975-77; chair dept. religion St. Dominic's High Sch., O'Fallon, Mo., 1977-84; dir. adult edn. programs Archdiocese of St. Louis, 1986—; chair St. Louis Consortium Theol. Schs. Field Edn., 1973-75; presenter DeSales Nat. Workshop Team, Portland, Oreg., 1988—; exec. bd. Ecumenical Commn., 1988—, Office of Lay Formation, 1990. Author: Catechist Certification and Adaptation of De Sales Program, 1990. Mem. Religious Edn. Assn., Nat. Cath. Edn. Assn., Nat. Conf. Diocesan Dirs. Home: 3635 Union Rd Saint Louis MO 63125 Office: Cath Edn Office 4140 Lindell Blvd Saint Louis MO 63123

RYAN, THOMAS A., school system administrator. Supt. schs. Diocese of Grand Island, Nebr. Office: Office Schs Supt 311 W 17th PO Box 996 Grand Island NE 68802*

RYAN, THOMAS PATRICK, priest, ecumenical institute director; b. Mpls., Aug. 9, 1946; s. Francis William and Genevieve (Schmelz) R. BA in Philosophy and English Lit. magna cum laude, Don Bosco Coll., 1970; MA in Theology summa cum laude, Washington Theol. Union, 1974; cert., Canterbury Ecumenical Summer Sch., 1980, Grad. Sch., Ecumenical Inst. of World Coun. Chs., Switzerland, 1981, Henry Martyn Inst. for Islamic Studies, 1991. Joined Paulist Fathers, 1971; ordained priest Roman Cath. Ch., 1975 . Tchr. St. John Bosco High Sch., Bellflower, Calif., 1970-71, Stone Ridge Country Day Sch., Bethesda, Md., 1972-74; chaplain Ohio State U., Columbus, 1974-77; dir. Newman Ctr. McGill U., Montreal, Que., Can., 1977-80, guest prof., 1985; assoc. dir. Can. Ctr. for Ecumenism, 1980-84, dir., 1984—; co-sec. Nat. United Ch. of Can.—Roman Cath. Dialogue, 1982-87; del. 6th gen. assembly World Coun. Chs., Vancouver, Can., 1983, 7th gen. assembly, Canberra, Australia, 1991; ecumenical officer Archdiocese of Montreal, mem. priests' senate exec., 1985-89; apptd. Roman Cath. rep. communications team staff World Anglican Lambeth Conf., Canterbury, Eng., 1988. Author: Fasting Rediscovered: A Guide to Health and Wholeness for Your Body-Spirit, 1981, Tales of Christian Unity, 1983, Sur les Chemins de l'Unité, 1985, Wellness, Spirituality, and Sports, 1986, A Survival Guide for Ecumenically-Minded Christians, 1989; also articles; editor Ecumenism quar., 1984—; columnist for various newspapers, Can. Home: 3484 Peel St, Montreal, PQ Canada H3A 1W8 Office: 2065 Sherbrooke St W, Montreal, PQ Canada H3H 1G6

RYAN, WILLIAM FRANCIS, priest; b. Renfrew, Ont., Can., Apr. 4, 1925; s. William Patrick Ryan and Helen Mary Doneg. BA, Montreal U., 1951; MA in Labor Rels., St. Louis U., 1953; postgrad., Heythrop Coll., Oxon, Eng.; STL, St. Albert Coll., 1958; PhD in Econs., Harvard U., 1964. Ordained priest Roman Catholic Ch., 1957. Asst. prof. econs. Loyola Coll., Montreal, Que., Can., 1963-65; nat. dir. Social Justice Office Can. Conf. Cath. Bishops, Ottawa, Ont., 1964-70, gen. sec., 1984-90; founding dir. Ctr. of Concern, Washington, 1970-78; nat. supr. Jesuit Order, Toronto, Ont., Can., 1978-84; chancellor Sch. Theology Regis Coll., 1978-84; vis. sr. rsch. fellow Can. Inst. for Internat. Peace and Security, Ottawa, 1990-91; chair on Cath. social thought St. Paul U., Ottawa, 1991—; exec. sec. Inter-religious Peace Colloquim, Washington, 1975-78; bd. dirs. Roncalli Internat. Found., Montreal, 1979-83, North/South Inst., Ottawa, 1979-91; lectr. in field. Author: The Clergy and Economic Growth in Quebec, 1966; co-author: Religious as Contemplatives in the 80's, 1984; translator: The Primacy of Charity in Moral Theology, 1961; contbr. articles to profl. jours. Mem. Am. Econs. Assn., Club of Rome (U.S. assoc.). Avocations: hiking; skiing. Office: 169 Sunnyside Ave, Ottawa, ON Canada K1S 0R2

RYANT, BRADLEY ERVEN, retired clergyman, publishing company executive; b. Lowell, Mass., July 5, 1935; s. Charles Ervin and Jessie Maud (Gillman) R.; m. Anna Mae Fellows, June 13, 1959; children: Kenneth Nolan, Timothy Alan. MDiv, Bangor Theol. Sem., 1970; BA, Fla. Atlantic U., 1973. Ordained minister Unitarian Universalist Ch., 1973. Musician Oneida, N.Y., 1955-65; pastor Universalist Ch., Central Square, N.Y., 1974-76, Cortland, N.Y., 1976-84; street minister Syracuse, N.Y., 1984-87; owner, mgr. Snowbound Press, West Monroe, N.Y., 1988—. Author: (poetry under the name J.J. Snow) Strange Whispers in the Night, 1988, The Moving Darkness, 1989, the Night the Flowers Died, 1990, A Curious Mixture of Hope and Dispair, 1991; editor Poetry Peddler, 1988—; bi-monthly poetry columnist, 1988—; contbr. articles to various publs. Mem. Poets in Residence Writers Group (founding), Comstock Writers Group (hon., honored poet). Republican. Avocation: camping.

RYBOLT, JOHN E., academic administrator. Head St. Thomas Theol. Sem., Denver. Office: St Thomas Theol Sem Office of Pres 1300 S Steele St Denver CO 80210*

RYDEN, ERNEST EDWIN, JR., minister; b. St. Paul, Mar. 9, 1931; s. Ernest Edwin and Agnes Elizabeth (Johnson) R.; B.A., Augustana Coll., 1953; grad. Communications Sch., U.S. Navy, 1954; M.Div., Augustana Sem., 1959; postgrad. R.I. Coll., 1972; m. Lois Elizabeth Beck, Aug. 19, 1956; children—Paul Howard, Janice Beth, David Beck. Blood plasma researcher Moline (Ill.) Luth. Hosp., 1955-59; ordained to ministry Lutheran Ch. Am., 1959; pastor Bethany Luth. Ch., Orange, Mass., 1959-66, St. James Luth. Ch., Barrington, R.I., 1966—; dir. communications, editor Council Highlights, R.I. State Council Chs., 1971-82; producer, host The Week Starts Here, on NBC TV affiliate, Providence, 1971—, weekly cable TV ministry, 1982—; mem. governing bd., exec. bd. R.I. State Council Chs., 1971—; dean R.I. Dist., Luth. Ch. Am., mem. com. on Am. missions and communications com. New Eng. Synod; mem. bd. global missions New Eng. Synod, Evang. Luth. Ch. in Am., 1988—. Coord. establishment of inner-city health care center, Providence, 1968. Served with USN, 1953-55. Recipient Community Achievement award R.I. Dept. Community Affairs, 1982. Mem. R.I. Bible Soc. (pres. 1982-88), Aircraft Owners and Pilots Assn., Overseas Yacht Club, various clergy assns. Producer numerous TV programs, religious TV spots and filmstrips, and films, including: The Holocaust (Gabriel award for best locally produced religious TV program in U.S. 1977); Love Serving All (1st prize R.I. Film Commn. 1983); participant archaeological excavation Lachish, 1985, Caesarea, 1987. Home: 3 Blount Circle Barrington RI 02806 *After years of seeking positions which seemed to offer roads to achievement, I realized that not other place offered the scope of opportunities as did the place where I already was.*

RYER, MICHAEL EDWARD, minister; b. Dallas, Apr. 26, 1959; s. Edward Henry and Betty ann (Singleton) R.; m. Dana Lynn Butman; 1 child, Ashlie Michelle. B in Gen. Studies, U. Tex., Tyler, 1989; postgrad., Southwestern Bapt. Theol. Sem., 1989—. Min. music and youth Boyd Bapt. Ch., Bonham, Tex., 1979-81, Owentown Bapt. Ch., Tyler, 1981-83; min. music 1st Bapt. Chandler, Tyler, 1987-89; min. music and edn. Baylor Bapt. Ch., Ennis, Tex., 1990—; gen. mgr. Tex. Aluminum Industries, Longview, 1982-86. Mem. Nat. Assn. Remodeling Industry (pres. Tex. chpt. 1987—). Avocations: golf, racquetball. Office: Baylor Bapt Ch 210 N Preston Ennis TX 75119

RYLE, EDWARD JOSEPH, priest, religious organization administrator; b. Chgo., Dec. 23, 1930; s. John J. and Irene (Evans) R. MSW, Cath. U. Am., 1963, MA, 1974; MDiv, Pontifical Coll. Josephinum, Columbus, Ohio, 1973. Ordained priest Roman Cath. Ch., 1956. Asst. pastor St. Thomas the Apostle Ch. Roman Cath. Ch., Phoenix, 1956-61; asst. dir., dir. Cath. Charities Ariz., Tucson, 1963-71; dean grad. sch. social work Marywood Coll., Scranton, Pa., 1977-84; exec. dir. Ariz. Cath. Conf., Phoenix, 1984—; mem. social policy com., Cath. Charities USA, Alexandria, Va., 1975—. Author: (with others) Justice and Health Care, 1985; contbr. articles to jours. in field. Bd. dirs. Phoenix Urban League, 1985-89, Community Coun., Phoenix, 1988—; mem. Gov.'s Coun. on Children, Phoenix, 1986-87; chmn. Indsl. Commn. Ariz., Phoenix,1990—. Recipient Outstanding Achievement in Social Work award Cath. U. Am. Alumni Assn., 1984, Disting. Citizen citation, Phoenix Union High Sch. Dist., 1991. Mem. Cath. Theol. Soc. Am., Am. Pub. Welfare Assn. Office: Ariz Cath Conf 400 E Monroe St Phoenix AZ 85004

RYNEARSON, EARL, minister; b. South Bend, Ind., Feb. 19, 1938; s. Earl Herbert and (Mahler) R.; m. Kathryn Jane Mahler, Apr. 28, 1956; children: Pamela Sue, Debra Ann, Jeffrey A. Grad. high sch., South Bend, Ind. Pastor Abundant Life Fellowship, South Bend, Ind., 1984—; mgr. Fairview Cemetery, Mishwaka, Ind., 1978-90. Home: 51936 Portage Rd South Bend IN 46628 Office: Abundant Life Fellowship 51980 Portage Rd South Bend IN 46628

RYNEARSON, RODNEY RICHARD, church consultant, clergyman; b. Omaha, June 1, 1935; s. Wesley Welling and Helen Dorothy (Brock) R.; m. Rhoda Jean Ryan, June 22, 1958; children: Timothy John, Stephen Paul, Peter Mark. BA, Concordia Coll., St. Louis, 1956; MDiv, Concordia Sem., St. Louis, 1959; EdM, U. Rochester, 1972; EdD, Wayne State U., 1985. Ordained to ministry Luth. Ch.-Mo. Synod, 1959. Missionary to deaf Luth. Ch.-Mo. Synod, Spokane, Wash., 1959-67; pastor Alpha Luth. Ch. (for deaf), Rochester, N.Y., 1967-74; dir. Luth. Sch. for Deaf, Detroit, 1974-87; cons. blind and deaf ministry Luth. Ch.-Mo. Synod, St. Louis, 1987—; interim dir. No. Am. Mission; chaplain, mem. faculty Nat. Tech. Inst., Rochester Inst. Tech., 1968-74; mem. faculty Concordia Coll., Ann Arbor, Mich., 1980-87, Concordia Theol. Sem., Ft. Wayne, Ind., 1981-82; transcriber Luth. Libr. for Blind; pres. Ephphatha Conf., Luth. Ch., St. Louis, 1965-73; cons. on spl. edn. and rehab., Ghana, 1989. Editor: Deaf Child's Adv., 1974-85, The Adv., 1985-87, Eyes that Hear, 1987—. Recipient Christus Primus award Concordia Coll., Ann Arbor, 1988. Mem. Internat. Luth. Deaf Assn. (pastoral advisor St. Louis 1966-74, 87—, counselor, Svc. plaque 1974), Nat. Assn. for Blind, Coun. Luth. Ministries (pres. 1984-86), Calif. Educators and Transcriberts Assn., Kiwanis (life, pres. Detroit 1983, lt. gov. Mich. dist. 1985-86, Disting. Lt. Gov. award 1986). Avocations: camping, reading, golf. Office: Luth Ch-Mo Synod 1333 S Kirkwood Rd Saint Louis MO 63129

RYSZ, ANTHONY M., bishop. Bishop of Cen. Diocese, Polish Nat. Cath. Ch. Am., Scranton, Pa. Office: Polish Nat Cath Ch Am 529 E Locust St Scranton PA 18505*

SABATELLI, JOHN RAYMOND, minister; b. Bklyn., Mar. 26, 1946; s. Leonard Richard S. and Lucille Helena (Fischer) Bjanes; m. Jane Lenore Glassey, June 24, 1972; children: Elissa MArie, Andrew Christian. BA, Queens Coll., 1967; MDiv, Luth. Theol. Sem., 1971. Assoc. pastor Christ Luth. Ch., Wantagh, N.Y., 1971-75; pastor Christ Luth. Ch., Islip Terrace, N.Y., 1975-83, Balt., 1983—; chmn. bd. Deaton Hosp. and Med., Ctr., Balt., 1983—, Christ Ch. Harbor Apts., Balt., 1983—. Bd. dirs. Harbor Hosp. Ctr., Balt., 1989—, chmn. bd. Charles Light PArking Inc., Balt., 1983—; mem. Community Mobilization, Balt., 1989—. Mem. Phi Beta Kappa. Democrat. Office: Christ Luth Ch 701 S Charles St Baltimore MD 21230

SABATINI, LAWRENCE, bishop; b. Chgo., May 15, 1930; s. Dominic and Ada (Piloi) S. Ph.L., Gregorian U., Rome, 1953, S.T.L., 1957, J.C.D., 1960; M.S. in Edn., Iona Coll., 1968. Ordained priest, Roman Catholic Ch., 1957, bishop, 1978. Prof. canon law St. Charles Sem., S.I., N.Y., 1960-71; pastor St. Stephen's Parish, North Vancouver, B.C., Canada, 1970-78; provincial superior Missionaries of St. Charles, Oak Park, Ill., 1978; aux. bishop Archdiocese Vancouver, B.C., Can., 1978-82; bishop Diocese Kamloops, B.C., Can., 1982—; procurator, adviser Matrimonial Tribunal, N.Y.C., 1964-71; founder, dir. RAP Youth Counseling Service, S.I., N.Y., 1969-71; vice ofcl. Regional Matrimonial tribunal of Diocese Kamloops, 1978-82; chmn. Kamloops Cath. Pub. Schs., 1982—. Named Man of Yr. Confratellanza Italo-Canadese, 1979. Mem. Can. Canon Law Soc., Canon Law Soc. Am., Can. Conf. Cath. Bishops. Office: Diocese of Kamloops, 635A Tranquille Rd, Kamloops, BC Canada V2B 3H5

SABATTANI, AURELIO CARDINAL, church administrator; b. Casal Fiumanese, Italy, Oct. 18, 1912. Ordained priest Roman Catholic Ch., 1935. Various assignments, Imola, Italy; judge ofcl. ecclesiastical tribunal, Bologna, Italy; prelate auditor Roman Rota, 1955; ordained titular archbishop of Justinian Prima, 1965; prelate of Loreto, 1965-71; sec. Supreme Tribunal of Apostolic Signatura, 1971, pro-prefect, 1982-83, prefect, 1983; consultor Secretariat of State, 1971; elevated to Sacred Coll. of Cardinals, 1983; archpriest St. Peter's Basilica, Vatican, 1983; deacon St. Apollinaris. Mem. Council for Pub. Affairs of Ch., Congregation Bishops. Address: Piazza S Marta, 00120 Vatican City Vatican City

SABBAH, MICHAEL, religious leader. Patriarch of Jerusalem; pres. Bishop's Conf. Latin Rite, Roman Cath. Ch., Jerusalem. Office: Patriarch of Jerusalem, POB 14152, Jerusalem Israel*

SACHS, WILLIAM LEWIS, minister; b. Richmond, Va., Aug. 22, 1947; s. Lewis S. and Dorothy M. (Creasy) S.; m. Elizabeth Austin Tucker, May 17, 1986. BA, Baylor U., 1969; MDiv, Vanderbilt U., 1972; STM, Yale U., 1973; PhD, U. Chgo., 1981. Ordained to ministry Episcopal Ch., 1973; curate Emmanuel Episc. Ch., Richmond, 1973-75; asst. rector St. Chrysostom's Ch., Chgo., 1975-80, St. Stephen's Ch., Richmond, 1980—; mem. bd. Richmond Clericus, 1981; exam. chaplain Diocese of Va., 1981—; dir. Episc. Book Store, Richmond, In-Home Health Care, Inc.; program chmn. Richmond Episc. Clergy; chaplain Boston State Hosp., 1972; vis. lectr. Rikkyo U., Tokyo, 1985, 88, Duke U., 1991; adj. faculty U. Richmond; vis. prof. Union Theol. Sem. Bd. dirs. Va. Planned Parenthood, 1981-84. Stevenson fellow, 1971-72; Episc. Ch. Found. fellow, 1976-80. Mem. Arts Club Chgo., Vanderbilt Club Chgo. (pres. 1978-80). Author: One Body, 1986, The Transformation of Anglicanism, 1992; contbr. articles to theol. jours.; researcher Huntington Library; producer cable TV documentaries. Home: 718 St Christophers Rd Richmond VA 23226 Office: 6004 Three Chopt Rd Richmond VA 23226

SACK, DANIEL EDWARD, college chaplain; b. Dayton, Ohio, Feb. 27, 1962; s. Robert Jeremy and Ann (Chamberlain) S. BA in History, Northwestern U., 1984; MDiv, McCormick Theol. Sem., 1989; postgrad., Princeton U., 1991—. Ordained to ministry United Ch. of Christ, 1989. Intern Faith United Ch. of Christ, State College, Pa., 1987-88; asst. chaplain Austin Coll., Sherman, Tex., 1989-91; bd. dirs. United Ministry, Pa. State Coll., State College, 1987-88, United Campus Christian Ministry, Chgo., 1988-89. Trustee McCormick Theol. Sem., Chgo., 1986-87. Fellow Soc. for Values in Higher Edn.; mem. Am. Acad. Religion, United Ch. of Christ Ministers in Higher Edn. Address: Princeton U Dept Religion 3414 New Graduate Coll Princeton NJ 08544

SACKETT, GLENN CHARLES, minister; b. Caldwell, Idaho, Sept. 11, 1951; s. Glenn Clarence and Iva Blanche (Bonde) S.; m. Gail Lynn Peery, May 4, 1950; children: Michelle Lynn, Amy Lee, Jill Marie. BA, Boise Bible Coll., 1972; MDiv, Lincoln Christian Seminary, Ill., 1982; D of Ministry, Trinity Evangel. Divinity Sch., Deerfield, Ill., 1989. Ordained to ministry Christian Chs. and Chs. of Christ, 1972. Minister Garibaldi (Oreg.) Ch. of Christ, 1973-77, Pontoon Beach Ch. of Christ, Granite City, Ill., 1977-83; prof. Lincoln Christian Coll., 1983—; part-time prof. St. Louis Christian Coll., Florissant, Mo., 1982-83; trustee Boise Bible Coll., 1974-77; bd. dirs. Bond Christian Svc. Camp, Mulberry Grove, Ill., 1978-82; cons. Team Expansion, Cin., 1986-89. Contbg. author: My Favorite Missionary Sermon, 1981. Pres. Lady Railer Booster Club, Lincoln Community High Sch., 1990-91. Recipient Disting. Svc. award Boise Bible Coll., 1987. Mem. Acad. Homiletics, Nat. Assn. Evangelicals, Evang. Missiological Soc., Miss. Valley Evangelizing Assn. (bd. dirs. St. Louis 1979-82). Office: Lincoln Christian Coll 100 Campus View Dr Lincoln IL 62656

SACKMANN, ROBERT CARL, religious organization executive; b. Newark, Jan. 27, 1932; s. Charles Henry and Mildred Edith (Williams) S.; m. Helene Shirra Ewing, Sept. 19, 1953; children: Paul Frederick, Robert Bruce, Mark William, Kimberly Ann. BS in Biology, Rutgers U., New Brunswick, 1953; MDiv, Princeton Sem., 1956; DMin, McCormick Sem., Chgo., 1978. Pastor Lakeview Presbyn. Ch., Paterson, N.J., 1956-62; organizing pastor Christ United Presbyn. Ch., Marlton, N.J., 1962-68; ednl. cons. Synod of Tex., Denton, 1968-73; exec. presbyter Presbytery of Ohio Valley, Bloomington, Ind., 1973—; adj. prof. Louisville Presbyn. Theol. Sem., 1982—; bd. dirs. ENglishton Park, Lexington, Ind., 1973—; conflict mgmt. cons., Bloomington, 1978—; ch. orgn. devel. specialist, Bloomington, 1975—; workshop tchr., leader, 1973—. Author: Manual for Pastor Nomination, 1981, A Sensitive Presence, 1981, Moving Through the Maze, 1985, For the Sake of Conscience, 1986, A Gathering of Presbyters, 1987. Mem. Exec. Collegium (convenor 1983-84). Presbyterian. Home: 4401 Cambridge Ct Bloomington IN 47401 Office: Presbytery of Ohio Valley 1514 E 3rd St Bloomington IN 47401

SACON, KIYOSHI KINOSHITA, biblical studies educator; b. Yokohama, Japan, Jan. 2, 1931; s. Shigeru and Iku (Yoshida) K.; m. Kazuko Sacon; children: Joshua, Tom, Elijah, Rebekah. BA, Tokyo Union Theol. Sem., 1952, MDiv, 1955; ThD, Union Theol. Sem., N.Y.C., 1963. Ordained minister. Instr. Tokyo Union Theol. Sem., 1963-66, asst. prof., 1966-71, prof., 1971—, pres., 1987—; vice chmn. CoC Related Schs.' Coun., Tokyo, 1987-89; moderator Coun. Cooperative Mission, Tokyo, 1989—; chairperson CoC Related Schs.' Coun., Tokyo, 1989—; pres. Japan Assn. Theol. Edn., Tokyo, 1989—. Editor, translator common Bible project Japan Bible Soc., Tokyo, 1970-87; editor: Shinkyoōdoōyaku Seisho, 1987; reviewer Book List, London, 1974—. Fulbright grantee Fulbright Com., Japan, U.S., 1958, 60-63. Mem. Soc. for Old Testament Studies Japan (pres. 1981-85, bd. dirs. 1968—), Soc. for Old Testament Studies in Gt. Britain (assoc.), Soc. for Christian Studies in Japan, Japan Bibl. Inst. Mem. United Ch. of Christ. Home: 1 9 12 Gakuenmachi, Higashikurume-shi, Tokyo 203, Japan Office: Tokyo Union Theol Sem, 3 10 30 Osawa, Mitaka 181 Tokyo, Japan

SADECK, LORRAINE JEANNE, religion educator; b. New Bedford, Mass., Mar. 25, 1949; d. Wilfrid Joseph and Juliette Jeanne (Lemire) Pothier; m. Paul George Sadeck, June 14, 1969; children: Amy Jeanne, Julie Anne. BA in Math., Southeastern Mass. U., 1971; postgrad., U. Mass., Dartmouth Coll. Cert. secondary math. tchr., Mass. Catechist, coord. grade 2 St. John Neumann Ch., East Freetown, Mass., 1983-85, coord. 1-8 religion edn., 1985-89, dir. religious edn., 1989—, ex-officio mem. pastoral coun., 1991—. Author religious materials. Home: 90 Doctor Braley Rd East Freetown MA 02717 Office: St John Neumann Ch 157 Middleboro Rd East Freetown MA 02717 *I have come to realize that trust in God is utmost for those of us who labor in His vineyard. God has consistently provided the time, energies, insights, and people—oftentimes unexpected and most needed gifts—in my ministry to spread the Gospel.*

SADLER, IVAN, principal; b. New London, Conn., Feb. 19, 1950; s. Sol H. and Lillian (Lubchansky) S.; m. Andrea Sadler, Dec. 28, 1975; children: Brady Joshua, Hannah. BA, Hartwick Coll., Oneonta, N.Y., 1972; MS, So. Conn. State U., 1974, postgrad., 1981; postgrad., U. Ibero-Americana, Mexico City. Tchr. State of Conn. Adult Edn., New London, New London Bd. Edn.; asst. prin. Ledyard (Conn.) Bd. Edn.; prin. Chariho Reg. Sch. Dist., Hope Valley, R.I. Mem. R.I. Assn. Sch. Prins., Nat. Assn. Elem. and Middle Sch. Prins., R.I. Reading Coun., ASCD, Phi Alpha Theta. Office: Hope Valley Sch Main St Hope Valley RI 02832

SAEBOE, MAGNE, theology educator; b. Fjelberg, Norway, Jan. 23, 1929; s. Samson and Malla (Oelfaernes) S.; m. Mona Uni Bjoernstad, June 27, 1953; children: Snorre, Lars Arnljot, Jan Eystein. Cand. theol., Free Faculty of Theology, Oslo, 1956; D. Theol., U. Oslo, 1969. Tchr. Hebrew U. Oslo, 1961-70; lectr. O.T. Free Faculty of Theology, Oslo, 1969-70, prof. O.T., 1970—, dean, 1975-77, 1988-90. Author: Sacharja 9-14. Untersuchungen von Text und Form, 1969, Gjennom alle tider, 1978, Ordene og Ordet. Studies, 1979, Kommentar til Ordsprakene, Forkynneren, Hoysangen, Klagesangene, 1986; contbr. articles to profl. jours. Chmn. Lut. European Consultation on the Ch. and Jewish People, Hannover, Fed. Republic Germany, 1979-82. Mem. Wiss. Gesellschaft fur Theologie, The Royal Norwegian Soc. of Scis. and Letters, Norwegian Acad. Scis. and Letters, Nathan Soderblom-Sallskapet, Norwegian Bible Soc. (chmn. Old Testament translation com. 1968-78). Home: Lars Muhles vei 34, N-1300 Sandvika Norway Office: The Free Faculty of Theology, Gydas vei 4, Oslo 3, Norway *The religious and moral values of the Jewish-Christian heritage are more needed in the community of today than ever before.*

SAFSEL, JOSEPH SOLOMON, rabbi; b. N.Y.C., Mar. 8, 1932; s. Jacob and Norma (Garfinkel) S. MA, Fordham U., 1971. Ordained rabbi, 1956. Rabbi Young Israel, Cin., 1956-57, Congregation Anshe Sholom, New Rochelle, N.Y., 1958-60, Shomre Habrith, Reading, Pa., 1960-65, Congregation Anshe Amas, Bronx, N.Y., 1965-79; chaplain Albert Einstein Hosp., Bronx, 1965—; adminstr. rabbinic ct. Beth Din of Am., affiliated with Rabbinical Coun. Am., N.Y.C., 1979—. Home: 72-30 137th St Flushing NY 11367

SAGARIN, JAMES LEON, rabbi, author, editor; b. Oceanside, N.Y., Dec. 31, 1951; s. Lawrence and Ethel (Wallace) S.; m. Lori Beth Baumblatt, Aug. 31, 1986. BA, SUNY, Albany, 1974; MA in Hebrew Letters, Hebrew U. Coll. Jewish Inst. Religion, 1978. Ordained rabbi, 1979. Hillel dir., congl. rabbi So. Ill. U., Carbondale, 1979-80; dir. Young Judaea Jewish Community Ctrs. Assn., St. Louis, 1980-82; sr. adult coord., chaplain, dir. contg. edn. Cen. Agy. for Jewish Edn., St. Louis, 1982-88; prof. Hebrew langs. and lit. Washington U., St. Louis, 1985-88; assoc. rabbi Temple Beth-El, Chgo., 1988-91; rabbi Temple Menorah, Chgo., 1991—. Author: Hebrew Noun Patterns, 1987, Chicago Jewish Star, 1991; co-author: Oseh Shalom, 1990; youth editor Sagarin Rev., 1991. Mem. Cen. Conf. of Am. Rabbis, Nat. Assn. Professors of Hebrew. Lodge: B'nai Brith. Avocations: running, weight-lifting, writing. Home: 6434 Kimball Lincolnwood IL 60645 Office: Temple Menorah 2800 W Sherwin Ave Chicago IL 60645 *Happiness begins in the center and emanates outward. If a person can begin to see the fulfillment of his dreams both personally and professionally, it makes living ever the more so enjoyable and worthwhile.*

SAGER, ALLAN HENRY, minister, educator; b. Boerne, Tex., Aug. 29, 1934; s. Gustav W. and Estella I. (Szillat) S.; m. Erline S. Hohmann, Aug. 9, 1959; children: Denise, Monica. BA, Tex. Luth. Coll., 1955; BD, MDiv, Wartburg Theol. Sem., 1959; MA, Northwestern U., 1960, PhD, 1963. Ordained to ministry Evang. Luth. Ch. Am., 1963. Assoc. pastor Trinity Luth. Ch., Ft. Worth, 1963-65, sr. pastor, 1965-72; prof. for contextual edn. Luth. Theol. Sem., Columbus, Ohio, 1972-78, Trinity Luth. Sem., Columbus, 1978—; bd. regents Tex. Luth. Coll., Seguin, 1970—; spiritual dir. Nat. Luth. Secretariat, St. Paul, 1991. Author: Gospel-Centered Spirituality, 1990; contbr. to book: Daily Readings from Spiritual Classics, 1990. Named Disting. Alumnus, Tex. Luth. Coll., 1984. Mem. Assn. Theol. Field Educators, Luth. Contextual Edn. Dirs., Speech Assn. Am. Home: 117 S Roosevelt Ave Columbus OH 43209 Office: Trinity Luth Sem 2199 E Main St Columbus OH 43209

SAGER, ALVIN DOUGLAS, minister; b. Bessemer, Ala., Sept. 8, 1939; s. Clyde Sager; m. Elizabeth Faye Thompson, Dec. 18, 1959; children: Traci Sager Robinson, Tim, Cathy. AB, Samford U., 1961; ThM, New Orleans Bapt. Sem., 1965; D Ministry, Luther Rice Sem., Fla., 1975. Ordained to ministry So. Bapt. Conv., 1959. Pastor 28th Street West Bapt. Ch., Birmingham, Ala., 1955-57, Wilkes Bapt. Ch., Midfield, Ala., 1957-58, Trinity Bapt. Ch., Birminghamm, 1959-64; Gray's Creek Bapt. Ch., Denham Springs, Ala., 1964-66, North Pompano Beach (Fla.) Bapt. Ch., 1966-71, 1st Bapt. Ch., Alcoa, Tenn., 1971-84, Roebuck Park Bapt. Ch., Birmingham, 1984—; mem. adv. bd. Pastors for Life, Birmingham; trustee Bapt. Sunday Sch. Bd.; co-founder Ala. Bapts. for Life; pres. Inner-Change Ministries, Nashville; 1st v.p. Ala. Bapt. Pastor's Conf., 1988, pres., 1989; mem. search com. for dean Beeson Div. Sch.; mem. strategic planning com. Ala. Bapt. Conv.; pastor advisor Conf. Ala. Bapt. Evangelists, 1986-89; chmn. Christian life com. Birmingham Bapt. Assn. Author: A Scriptural Guide to Spiritual Gifts, 1988. Trustee Samford U., Birmingham; bd. dirs. Ala. Citizens Action Program, Birmingham. Office: Roebuck Park Bapt Ch 216 Roebuck Dr Birmingham AL 35215

SAGER, CRAIG A., SR., evangelist; b. Buffalo, Feb. 25, 1944; s. George Albert and Zeta Theresa (Schramn) S.; m. Linda Rose Simmons, Jan. 29, 1963 (div. June 1965); children: Frederick, Shiela, Melisa, Arnold; m. Donna Jean Mapes, Oct. 28, 1970 (dec. Sept. 1989); children: Edward, Theresa, Donna, Craig Jr., Zeta, Matthew, Sarah, Michael. Student in bus., Medina Cen. Coll., 1955-61, Genesee Community Coll., 1966-69. Ordained to ministry Israelite Worldwode Ch. of God. Pastor Open Bible Evangelistical Ch., Batavia, N.Y., 1976-85; evangelist Israelite Full Bible Congregation, Lockport, N.Y., 1985—; owner, operator Donna's Home Showcase, Lockport, 1989—, Donna's Cabinets and Custom Woodwork, Lockport, 1989—. State bd. dirs. Christians Organized for Decent Econ., Lockport, 1974—; asst. state dir. Citizens to Eliminate Poverty, Lockport, 1973—. Home: PO Box 158 Lockport NY 14095

SAGO, PAUL EDWARD, college administrator; b. Mo., July 5, 1931; s. John and Mabel S.; m. Donna; children: Bruce, Brad. Student, Mineral Area Coll., 1949-51; BS, Findlay Coll., 1953; postgrad., Winebrenner Theol. Sem., 1953-55; MS, St. Francis Coll., 1964; PhD, Walden U., 1976. Dir. devel. Findlay (Ohio) Coll., 1964-67, Hiram (Ohio) Coll., 1967-68; v.p. fin. affairs, treas. Anderson (Ind.) Coll., 1968-76; pres. Azusa Pacific U., Azusa, Calif., 1976-90, Woodbury U., Burbank, Calif., 1990—; participant seminars and insts. Trustee Findlay Coll., 1958-64; mem. Ind. adv. council SBA, 1972-76. Mem. Assn. Governing Bds. (pres.'s coun.), Internat. Platform Assn., Coun. for Advancement and Support Edn., Nat. Assn. Ind. Colls. and Univs., Assn. Ind. Calif. Colls. and Univs., Rotary. Office: Woodbury U 7500 Glenoaks Blvd Burbank CA 91510-7846

SAHAGUN DE LA PARRA, JOSE DE JESUS, bishop; b. Cotija, Mexico, Jan. 1, 1922. Ordained priest Roman Cath. Ch., 1946; named bishop of Tula Hidalgo, Mexico, 1961—. Office: Diocese of Tula, 5 de Mayo 5, Apartado Postal N 31, CP 42800 Tula Hidalgo, Mexico

SAHAS, DANIEL JOHN, religion educator; b. Athens, Greece, Apr. 18, 1940; moved to Can., 1969; s. John and Ioanna (Livadas) S.; m. Myrta Evelina, June 8, 1968; children—Ioanna-Maria, John Daniel. Ptychion, U. Athens, Greece, 1963; S.T.M., Ch. Theol. Sem., Indpls., 1966; Ph.D., Harford Sem. Found., Conn., 1969. Asst. prof. U. Waterloo, Ont., Can., 1969-75, assoc. prof., 1975-91, prof., 1991—; vis. prof. Vancouver Sch. Theology, B.C., 1983, Wilfrid Laurier U., Waterloo, 1984; dir. Middle E. Studies, U. Waterloo. Author: John of Damascus on Islam, 1972; Icon and Logos, 1986, 2d edit., 1988; also articles. Pres., Greek Orthodox Community, Kitchener-Waterloo, 1973-74, 85-86; gen. bd. Can. Council Chs., 1982-87; trustee Hellenic Coll., Holy Cross S., Brookline, Mass., 1980-82. Hon. fellow St. Paul's Coll., 1978-81. Greek Orthodox. Home: 136 Briarcliffe Cres, Waterloo, ON Canada N2L 5T8 Office: U Waterloo, Waterloo, ON Canada N2L 3G1

SAILORS, JAN DEE, minister; b. Palisade, Nebr., July 6, 1949; s. Lloyd and Georgia Tomina (McPherson) S.; m. Teresa Gail Ramsey, Aug. 14, 1970; children: Charles Lloyd, Benjamin Russell. Student, So. Nazarene U., 1967-70; AB in Religion, MidAm. Nazarene Coll., 1973; MDiv, Nazarene Theol. Sem., 1977. Ordained to ministry Ch. of the Nazarene, 1979. Min. of children First Ch. of the Nazarene, Salina, Kans., 1977-78; pastor Ch. of the Nazarene, Redford, Mo., 1978-80; ch. planter Ch. of the Nazarene, Bowling Green, Mo., 1980-82; pastor First Ch. of the Nazarene, Forrest City, Ark., 1983-85, Jonesboro, Ark., 1985-89; pastor Trinity Ch. of the Nazarene, Corpus Christi, Tex., 1989—; dist. NYI pres., South Ark. Dist. Ch. of the Nazarene, 1982-85, North Ark. Dist. Ch. of the Nazarene, 1987-89; treas. South Cen. Region NYI, 1983—; teen Bible quiz dir., South Cen. Region NYI, 1989—. Author: Luke Study Questions, 1992. Home: 5926 Del Starr Corpus Christi TX 78413 Office: Trinity Ch of the Nazarene 6225 Weber Rd Corpus Christi TX 78413 *The fellowship of kindred minds has been the most pleasant surprise of the Christian journey. I thank God for every benefit in Christ and the great resource of His Word, but finding joy in my traveling companions and Christian family is a greater boon than ever could be imagined.*

SAINT, JAMES GILES, JR., retired minister; b. Pitts., Oct. 26, 1913; s. James Giles and Amelia Mary (Staver) S.; m. Marie Elizabeth Carlson, June 29, 1937; children: Jean Marie, Dorothea Louise, Mary Anna, Ellen Amelia, Hazel Mathilda, Kathleen Victoria, James Giles IV. BA, Maryville (Tenn.) Coll., 1936; MDiv, Louisville Presbyn. Sem., 1939; postgrad., U. Chgo., 1939-42; D Ministry, McCormick Sem., 1980. Ordained to ministry, Presbyn. Ch. Pastor First Presbyn. Ch., Onarga, Ill., 1941-46, Gilman, Ill., 1943-46, Sheboygan, Wis., 1946-57, Elwood, Ind., 1964-69; pastor Second Presbyn. Ch., Oak Park, Ill., 1969-76; assoc. pastor, minister Christian edn. Calvin West Presbyn. Ch., Detroit, 1957-64; stated supply pastor First Presbyn. Ch., Willow Springs, Ill., 1976-79; temporary supply pastor 1st Presbyn. Ch., Brookfield, Ill., 1989-91; pres. ednl. insts., Wis. and Mich., 1948-64; youth adviser, Synod of Wis., Presbyn. Ch. U.S.A., 1950-55; strategy com., Presbytery of Chgo., 1979-89. Author booklets on Christianity; contbr. articles, photographs to numerous publs. Mem. Mayor's Com. on Kohler Strike, pres., Sheboygan. Mem. Wis. Ministerial Assn., Mich. Ministerial Assn. (Detroit chpt.), Ind. Ministerial Assn. (Elwood chpt.), Kiwanis, Pi Kappa Delta, Order of the Arrow. Avocations: photography, gardening, video production, carpentry, genealogy. Home: 845 Thomas Ave Forest Park IL 60130

ST. ANDREWS, BARBARA (FITTERER TROMBLEY), minister. A.B. in English, magna cum laude, U. Rochester, 1966, M.A. in English Lit., 1967; M.Div. magna cum laude, Wesley Theol. Sem., 1979; postgrad. Princeton Theol. Sem., 1983-84, Grad. Theol. Union, Berkeley, 1989. Ordained to ministry Episcopal Ch. as deacon, 1979, as priest, 1979. Tchr. English, Pittsford High Sch., N.Y., 1967-68; instr. English, U. Rochester, N.Y., 1967-68; editor, nat. cons. Houghton Mifflin Pub. Co., 1968-75, mgr. Washington office, 1976-79; Presidential fellow President's Exec. Exch. Program, Washington, 1975-76; assigned U.S. Travel Svc. Dept of Commerce; curate Parish of St. John the Evangelist, Hingham, Mass., 1979-80; with Bishop's staff Episcopal Diocese Calif., 1980-83; assoc. rector St. Stephen's Episcopal Ch., Belvedere, Calif., 1983-84, St. John's Episcopal Ch., Ross, Calif., 1984-86; host Mosaic program Sta. KPIX-CBS/TV, San Francisco, 1989; dir. medicine and philosophy Calif. Pacific Med. Ctr., San Francisco, 1990—; bd. dirs. ecumenical ministry First Bapt. Ch. Washington, 1976-78; liturgist U.S. Naval Chapel, Washington, 1977-79; clin. pastoral Sibley Hosp., Washington, 1978; offered opening prayers U.S. Ho. of Reps. and U.S. Senate, 1982-83, 85, 87-91 (first ordained woman to do so). Mem. coun. U. Rochester, 1975-85; mem. standing com. Diocese of Calif., 1983-84. With Chaplain's Res. Corps, USN, 1978-80. Named to Outstanding Young Women Am.; Reading fellow Coll. Preachers, Washington, 1983. Mem. Am. Bus. Women's Assn. (hon.), Rockefeller Found. (Bellagio 1987). Office: Pacific Presbyn Med Ctr 2485 Clay St San Francisco CA 94115

SAINT-ANTOINE, JUDE, bishop; b. Montreal, Que., Can., Oct. 29, 1930; s. Avila Saint-Antoine and Eva Vermette. B.A., U. Montreal, 1954, Licence Theologie, 1956, Licence sci. edn., 1965; D.Theology, U. Gregorienne, Rome, 1963. Ordained priest Roman Cath. Ch., 1956. Prof. religion Coll. St. Paul, Montreal, 1957-61, 63-67, Coll. Bois-de-Boulogne, Montreal, 1968-75; curé Diocese of Montreal, 1975-79, Episcopal vicar, 1979—, aux. bishop, 1981—. Author: Paul Ragueneau et ses lettres spirituelles, 1975. Recipient Silver medal for doctoral thesis U. Gregorienne, Rome, 1963. Mem. Conf. Cath. Bishops of Can., Assembly of Bishops of Quebec. Office: Diocese de Montreal, 2000 W Sherbrooke, Montreal, PQ Canada H3H 1G4

ST. CLAIR, HOWARD BARRY, religious organization administrator; b. Washington, Mar. 10, 1945; s. Elias Howard and Virginia Catherine (Scott) St. C.; m. Virginia Carol Price, June 14, 1970; children: Wesley Scott, Katherine Sterling, Jonathan Barry, Virgina Beurette. BA, Davidson (N.C.) Coll., 1967; MDiv, So. Sem., 1971; D in Ministry, Southwestern Sem., 1980. Mem. staff Campus Crusade for Christ (AIA), San Bernardino, Calif., 1967-68, Bethlehem Bapt. Ch., Louisville, 1969-71; dir., youth evangelist So. Bapt. Home Mission Bd., Atlanta, 1971-77; dir. Reach Out Ministries, Atlanta, 1978—; pastor Christ Community Ch., Atlanta, 1981-88. Author: Moving Toward Maturity Series, 1985, Buidling Leaders, 1987, Love, Sex & Dating, 1989. Mem. Nat. Network Youth Mins. (chmn. bd. San Diego chpt. 1979-91). Office: Reach Out Ministries 3961 Holland Br Rd Norcross GA 30092

ST. JOHN, SEYMOUR, priest; b. New Haven, Feb. 29, 1912; s. George Clare and Clara Hitchcock (Seymour) St. J.; m. Margaret Gordon Spencer, June 20, 1936 (dec. Oct. 1986); children: Gordon Webb, Margaret Seymour; m. Marie Annette Landry, June 24, 1989; children: Frederick Race, Laura Hasty, Margaret Rogers, Marie Kafus. BA, Yale U., 1935; MA, Columbia U., 1945; postgrad., Va. Theol. Sem., 1940-42; LHD (hon.), Tufts U., 1952; DD (hon.), Va. Theol. Sem., 1967. Ordained priest Episcopal Ch., 1942. Headmaster Choate Sch., Wallingford, Conn., 1947-73; assoc. min. Christ Meml. Chapel, Hobe Sound, Fla., 1975—. Contbr. articles to religious jours. Trustee, headmaster emeritus Choate Rosemary Hall, Wallingford, 1973—. Mem. Jupiter Island Club, Hobe Sound Yacht Club (commodore 1988-90). Home: 469 S Beach Rd Hobe Sound FL 33455 Office: Christ Chapel Box 582 Hobe Sound FL 33475

SAKAYIMBO, CIBULENU ROBERT, church denomination executive, minister; b. Kambalwanzo, Kahemba, Zaire, Oct. 7, 1946; s. Mwamunika Paul Kambalwanzo and Yamuno (Mwatonde) Pauline; m. Kazangne Nasola Constantine, Aug. 13, 1966; children: Kuwaha, Yamuno, Upale, Matondo, Tshikema, Mahango, Keji, Tshilengwa, Francis. Grad., Kinshasa (Zaire) Theol. Sch., 1970. Ordained to ministry Mennonite Ch. Zaire. Prof. theology Kamayala, Zaire, 1970-86; evangéliste communautive Zaire, 1984-87; pres. representant légal Mennonite Ch. Zaire, Tshikapa, 1987—. Home: B.P. 4557, 2 Kinshasa Zaire Office: B.P. 18, Tshikaya Zaire

SAKRISSON, RICHARD E., religious organization administrator. Pres. Apostolic Luth. Ch. Am., Vancouver, Wash. Office: Apostolic Luth Ch Am 7606 NE Vancouver Mall Dr Ste 14 Vancouver WA 98662*

SALA, HAROLD JAMES, minister; b. Denver, July 15, 1937; s. Delmar Harold and Ruby Edith (Irby) S.; m. Darlene Starr Duffield, Dec. 23, 1959; children: Bonnie, Steven, Nancy. BA magna cum laude, Bob Jones U., 1958, MA, 1959, PhD, 1963. Ordained to ministry, 1958. Assoc. pastor Calvary Temple, Denver, 1960-63; grad. asst. Bob Jones U., Greenville, S.C., 1963-66; pastor So. Bay Bible Ch., Redondo Beach, Calif., 1966-74; founder, pres. Guidelines, Inc., Laguna Niguel, Calif., 1963—; bd. dirs. Orinoco River Mission, L.A., 1972-74, Revival Prayer Fellowship, Laguna Niguel, 1984—, G.L.A.S.S., L.A., 1970-74, Hosp. Chaplain Ministries Am., L.A., 1970-74; adv. bd. Harvesting in Spanish, Denver, 1982—. Author: Guidelines for Living, 1967, Guidelines for Successful Living, 1972, A Love to Live By, 1973, They Shall be One Flesh, 1978, Train Up a Child, 1978, Science and God in the 80's, 1980, The Power of Positive Parenting, 1982, You Can Live Successfully, 1982, Something More Than Love, 1983, How to Enjoy Raising Your Children, 1984, Today Can Be Different, 1988, Coffee Cup Counseling, 1989, Your Family and the Ten Commandments, 1989; columnist Sidestreets, 1976—; contbr. articles to profl. jours. Columnist, Sidestreets, 1976—. Recipient Civic award L.A. County, 1973; named Outstanding Citizen, City of Redondo Beach, 1974. Mem. Nat. Religious Broadcasters, Western Religious Broadcasters. Republican. Office: Guidelines Inc 26076 Getty Dr Laguna Niguel CA 92677

SALAH AN SHIWEI, IMAM AL-HADJI, religious organization administrator. Chmn. Beijing Islamic Assn. Office: Beijing Islamic Assn, Dongsi Mosque, Beijing People's Republic of China*

SALAS, SISTER MARY CARMEN, chaplain; b. Laredo, Tex., Feb. 7, 1937; d. Hipolito L. and Encarnación (Sánchez) S. MA in Communication, U. Andres Bello, Caracas, Venezuela, 1971; BS, Loyola Coll., Balt., 1974; MA in Spanish, Boston Coll., 1990. Joined Mission Helpers of Sacred Heart, Roman. Cath. Ch., 1961. Dir. Dept. of Catechesis SPEV Permanent Secretariat, Caracas; Hispanic Affairs specialist Archdiocese of Detroit; chaplain Good Samaritan Hosp., Balt.; chaplain, campus min. Palo Alto Coll., Archdiocese of San Antonio. Author: Teaching Manuals for Catechist (K-8 grades). Recipient New Detroit, Boston Coll., Mexican Am. Cultural Ctr. scholarships. Mem. Cath. Campus Ministry Assn., Tex. Cath. Campus Ministry Assn. (chair), Conf. Religious for Hispanic Ministry. Home: 1707 Centennial San Antonio TX 78211

SALAS, RAUL RAMIRO, priest; b. Brownsville, Tex., Sept. 9, 1953; s. Raul and Juana (Treviño) S. BA, U. Dallas, Irvine, Tex., 1975; MDiv, Oblate Sch. Theology, San Antonio, 1979. Ordained priest Roman Cath. Ch., 1980. Tchr., coach, dean, retreat master St. Anthony High Sch. Sem., San Antonio, 1980-88; parochial vicar Our Lady of Gulf Ch., Port Lavaca, Tex., 1988—; dir. Rite of Christian Initiation of Adults, Port Lavaca, 1989—; sec. Edna (Tex.) Deanery, Diocese of Victoria, 1990—. Bd. dirs. United Way, Port Lavaca, 1990—; mem. Concerned Citizens for Youth, Port Lavaca, 1990—. Office: Our Lady of Gulf Ch 415 W Austin PO Box 87 Port Lavaca TX 77979

SALATKA, CHARLES ALEXANDER, archbishop; b. Grand Rapids, Mich., Feb. 26, 1918; s. Charles and Mary (Balun) S. Student, St. Joseph's Sem., Grand Rapids, 1932-38; M.A., Cath. U. Am., 1941; J.C.L., Inst. Civil and Canon Law, Rome, 1948. Instr. St. Joseph's Sem., Grand Rapids, Mich., 1945; ordained priest Roman Catholic Ch., 1945; assigned chancery office Diocese of Grand Rapids, 1948-54, vice chancellor, 1954-61; aux. bishop, 1961, vicar gen., 1961, consecrated bishop, 1962; pastor St. James Parish, Grand Rapids, 1962-68; titular bishop of Cariana and aux. bishop of Grand Rapids, 1962-68; bishop of Marquette, 1968-77; archbishop of Oklahoma City, 1977—. Mem. Canon Law Soc. Am. Office: PO Box 32180 7501 Northwest Expwy Oklahoma City OK 73123

SALAZAR, ALDEMAR MARTINEZ, mission director; b. Bogota, Colombia; s. Horacio Martinez Marucanda and Virgelina S. De Martinez; m. Elizabeth Gomez Lindo, June 23, 1990; children: Samuel Martinez Gomez. Bachillerato, Coll. Venecia, Colombia; grad., Colegio S. de Telecommunicación, Colombia; direccion de medios, Nat. U., Colombia; diploma in systematic theology, Inst. Biblico Mizpa, Colombia. Leader, pres. youth sect. Iglesia Cuadrangular, Bogota; dir. radio and TV Govt. of Colombia; fundador, dir. corp., missionary dir. Buenas Noticias, Colombia; mgr. Radio Nacional, Colombia. Mem. Cristiana Evangelica Ch. Office: Buenos Noticias, A.A. 3115, Bogota Colombia

SALAZAR, ARTURO, deacon; b. L.A., May 2, 1958; s. Antonio Alvarado and Victoria (Obregon) S.; m. Margaret Lujan, Sept. 6, 1980; 1 child, Michael Anthony. BSCE, U. So. Calif., 1980. Deacon 1st Fundamental Bible Ch., Monterey Park, Calif., 1982-85, 87—; exec. bd. First Fundamental Bible Ch., Monterey Park, 1983-85, sec., 1990, chmn., deacon, 1987-89, treas., 1985, 89, 91. Alt. 60th Assembly Dist. Rep. Com., El Monte, Calif., 1989-90; mem. Caltrans Hispanic Adv. Com., L.A., 1990—. Recipient Sustained Superior Accomplishment award, Caltrans, 1988, Cert. of Excellence, 1991. Republican. Home: 14045 Brookport St Baldwin Park CA 91706 *Give everything your best effort, irregardless of the return of your efforts. When you least expect it, your work will be rewarded.*

SALAZAR LOPEZ, JOSE CARDINAL, former archbishop; b. Ameca, Mex., Jan. 12, 1910. Ordained priest Roman Cath. Ch., 1934; named titular bishop of Prusiade, 1961, named bishop of Zamora, 1967-70, named archbishop of Guadalajara, 1970-88, created cardinal, 1973. Address: Arzobispado Apartado, Postal 1-331, Guadalajara Jalisco 44100, Mexico

SALDARINI, GIOVANNI CARDINAL, cardinal; b. Cantu, Italy, Dec. 11, 1924. Ordained priest Roman Cath. Ch., 1947. Titular bishop of Gaudiaba, aux. bishop of Milan, 1984, archbishop of Turin, 1989, elevated to the Sacred Coll. of Cardinals, 1991, with titular ch. of the Sacred Heart. Office: Archdiocese Roman Cath Ch, Via Arcivescovado 12, 10121 Turino Italy*

SALES, EUGENIO DE ARAUJO CARDINAL, archbishop of Rio de Janeiro; b. Acari, Brazil, Nov. 8, 1920; d. Celso Dantas and Josefa de A.S.; student Seminary Fortaleza City. Ordained priest Roman Catholic Ch., 1943, consecrated bishop, 1954, elevated to cardinal, 1969; Sede Plena apostolic adminstr., Natal, 1962, Salvador, 1964; archbishop, Salvador, 1968-71, Rio de Janeiro, 1971—; mem. Coun. Pub. Affairs, Sacred Congregations, Bishops, for Divine Cult, clergy, Evangelization, Oriental Chs., Cath. Edn., Couns. for Social Communication and Culture, Cardinal Coun. Organic and Econ. Problems. Editor: The Pastors Voice. Address: Gloria 446, 20241 Rio de Janeiro Brazil

SALIBA, JOHN ALBERT, educator, priest; b. Valletta, Malta, Apr. 16, 1937; came to U.S. 1966; s. Michael A. and Maria (Pace) S. L Phil, Heythrop Coll., Eng., 1960, S T L, 1966; diploma in Anthropology, Oxford (Eng.) U., 1962; PhD, Cath. U. Am., 1971. Joined S.J., 1954, ordained priest Roman Cath. Ch. 1965. Instr. religious studies U. Detroit Mercy, 1970, asst. prof. religion, 1971-87, prof., 1987—. Author (bibliography) Psychiatry and the Cults: An Annotated Bibliography, 1987, Social Science and the Cults: An Annotated Bibliography, 1990. Rsch. fellow Santa Barbara Ctr. Humanistic Studies, 1990-91. Mem. Am. Acad. Religion, Assn. Sociol. Religion, Soc. Sci. Study Religion, Coll. Theology Soc., Internat. Conf. Sociology Religion. Office: U Detroit Mercy 4001 W McNichols Rd Detroit MI 48221

SALIBA, PHILIP E., archbishop; b. Abou-Mizan, Lebanon, 1931; came to U.S., 1956, naturalized, 1961; s. Elias Abdallah and Salema (Saliba) S. B.A., Wayne State U., 1959; M.Div., D.D., St. Vladimir's Sem., N.Y., 1964; DHL, Wayne State U., 1986. Became sub-deacon Antiochian Orthodox Christian Ch. N.Am., 1945-49, ordained deacon, 1949-59, priest, 1959-66, consecrated archbishop, 1966, now primate; chmn. Standing Conf. Am.-Middle Eastern Christian and Moslem Leaders; chmn. Orthodox Christian Edn. Commn.; vice chmn. Standing Conf. Canonical Orthodox Bishops in Ams. Vice-chmn. St. Vladimir's Orthodox Theol. Sem. Address: 358 Mountain Rd Englewood NJ 07631

SALNAVE, GEORGE MICHAEL, minister; b. Flint, Mich., Sept. 3, 1949; s. George A. and Madaline Y. (Luhrs) S.; married, 1972; 1 child, Kyla Jane. Student, Flint Community Jr. Coll., 1967-69; AB in Sociology, U. Mich., Flint, 1972; MDiv, Fuller Theol. Sem., Pasadena, Calif., 1975, D of Ministry, 1987. Assoc. youth dir. 1st Presbyn. Ch., Flint, 1969-72; intern min. to young adults Immanuel Presbyn. Ch., L.A., 1972-73; intern 1st Presbyn. Ch., Hollywood, Calif., 1973-75; assoc. pastor 1st Presbyn. Ch., Santa Rosa, Calif., 1975-86; pastor 1st Presbyn. Ch., Montezuma, Iowa, 1986—. Mem. Kiwanis, Lions.

SALONEK, EUGENE WILLIAM, JR., lay worker, electrical engineer; b. Orange, Tex., June 11, 1957; s. Eugene William and Melba Opal (Brown) S.; m. Carol Ann Smith, Aug. 1, 1981; 1 child, Morgan Stafford. Registered profl. engr., Tex. Sr. engr. E.I. Du Pont, Victoria, Tex., 1979—; class pres. adult class United Meth. Ch., Victoria, Tex., 1991, class tchr., 1991; pres. United Meth. Men, 1st United Meth. Ch., 1986-87, Victoria dist., 1987. Asst. scoutmaster Boy Scouts Am., Victoria, 1979-84; dir., chmn. Jr. Achievement, Victoria, 1983-86. Mem. ASME, Victoria Amateur Club (treas. 1988), Radio Club. Home: 365 A Carefree Victoria TX 77901 Office: El DuPont PO Box 2626 Victoria TX 77902

SALSMAN, BERNEY, III, minister; b. Fayettville, N.C., Aug. 27, 1958; s. Berney Jr. and Jessie Marie (Underwood) S.; m. Rebecca Irene Salsman, Oct. 2, 1961; children: Erica Lenn, Lindsey Beth. BA in Bible, Cen. Bible Coll., Springfield, Mo., 1981. Ordained to ministry Assemblies of God. Pastor youth Calvary Temple Assembly of God Ch., Flossmoor, Ill., 1981-82; pastor youth 1st Assembly of God Ch., Bessemer, Ala., 1982-83, Griffin, Ga., 1983—; chaplain football team Griffin High Sch., 1984-89. Dir. religious activities Griffin Sesquicentennial Celebration, 1990. Mem. Griffin Ministerial Assn. (sec., v.p., pres. 1981-89), Kiwanis (chmn. Key Club Griffin 1989—). Home: 1912 Bonnieridge Griffin GA 30223 Office: 1st Assembly of God Ch 2000 W McIntosh Rd Griffin GA 30223

SALT, ALFRED LEWIS, priest; b. Hackensack, N.J., Apr. 30, 1927; s. Alfred John and Lily (Tittle) S.; m. Elizabeth May Loveland, June 18, 1949; children: Richard John, Michael Rob, Christopher William, Katharine Anne. BA with honors, Bishop's U., Lennoxville, Can., 1949, MA in History, 1951, BD, 1960; grad. advanced mgmt. program, Harvard U., 1970; D Ministry, Grad. Theol. Found., 1988. Ordained to ministry Episcopal Ch. as deacon, 1951, as priest, 1952. Incumbent St. Philip's, Sawyerville, Que., Can., 1951-52, St. John the Evangelist, Portneuf, Que., 1952-54; rector Christ Ch., Stanstead, Que., 1954-62, St. Michael's Ch., Sillery, Que., 1962-72, All Sts.' Ch., Millington, N.J., 1972—; bishop's chaplain Diocese of Que., 1962, hon. canon, 1970; pres. Morris Convocation, Morris County, N.J., 1974-78; retreat condr., 1979—; with Victorious Ministry Through Christ, Orlando, Fla., 1981—, dir., 1986—, v.p., 1989—, internat. coord.-elect, 1990—. Contbr. articles to religious jour. Mem. Superior Coun. Edn., Que., 1964-70; commr. Que. Protestant Sch. Bd., 1970-72; trustee Heath Village, Hackettstown, N.J., 1974-76; mem. Passaic Twp. Welfare Bd., Millington, 1977-78, 82. With USN, 1945-46. Mem. Somerset Hills Ministerial Assn., Order St. Luke (chaplain 1980—). Home: 15 Cross Hill Rd Millington NJ 07946 *The more I come to know Jesus, the more I come to know myself. The more I submit myself to Him, the less I depend upon myself.*

SALTARELLI, MICHAEL A., priest; b. Jersey City, N.J., Jan. 17, 1933; s. Angelo Michael and Caroline (Marzitello) S. BA, Seton Hall U., 1956; MA, Manhattan Coll., 1975. Ordained to ministry Roman Cath. Ch., 1960. Assoc. pastor Holy Family Ch., Nutley, N.J., 1960-77; pastor Our Lady of Assumption, Bayonne, N.J., 1977-82; exec. dir. Archdiocesan Pastoral Svcs., Newark, N.J., 1982-85; pastor St. Catherine Of Siena Ch., Cedar Grove, N.J., 1985-90; aux. bishop Archdiocese of Newark, 1990—; vicar for priests, Archdiocese of Newark, 1987—. Home and Office: 89 Ridge St Newark NJ 07104

SAMANIEGO BARRIGA, MANUEL, bishop; b. Angamacatiro, Mexico, Oct. 10, 1930. Ordained priest Roman Cath. Ch., 1953; named titular bishop of Passo Corese, 1969, named bishop of Ciudad Altamirano, 1971-79; named bishop of Cuautitlan Mexico, 1979—. also: Apartado Postal 14, CP 54800, Cuautitlan de Romero Rubio, Mexico City Mexico

SAMET, SEYMOUR, community relations consultant; b. Newark, N.J., Dec. 3, 1919; s. Isadore and Sylvia (Birn) S.; m. Elaine Rosenberg, Oct. 3, 1943; children: Anita Samet Rechler, Roberta. BA, Montclair State Coll., 1941; MEd, U. Miami, Coral Galbles, Fla., 1954. Asst. dir. Jewish Community Rels. Coun., Essex County, N.J., 1948-52; dir. Southeast Area Am. Jewish Com., 1952-64; chief intergroup rels. officer Community Rels. Svc., U.S. Dept. Justice, 1964-68; nat. dir. domestic affairs Am. Jewish Com., N.Y.C., 68-84; exec. dir. Dade County Community Rels. Bd., Fla., 1963-64; pres. H.R. Factor Assocs., Ft. Lee, N.J., 1984—. Trustee United Jewish Community, Bergen County, N.J., 1988—, dir. Jewish community rels. com., 1989-90; active Conf. Jewish Communal Svc. Staff sgt. signal corps U.S. Army, 1942-46, PTO. Mem. Soc. for Psychol. Study of Social Issues (chair N.Y.úN.J. chpt. rsch. project 1987—). Seymour Samet Human Rels. Libr. Collection estab. in honor Dade County (Fla.) Sch. System, 1964. Home and Office: 5 Horizon Rd Fort Lee NJ 07024

SAMLAN, ARNOLD D., rabbi, educator; b. Chgo., June 13, 1955; s. Raymond and Gertrude (Kooperman) S.; m. Deborah Lynn Schottland, July 1, 1979; children: Yoni, Hillel. BS, Loyola U., Chgo., 1977; B. Hebrew Lit., Hebrew Theol. Coll., 1979; MSW, U. Ill., Chgo., 1979; postgrad. in edn., St. Louis U., 1987—. Ordained rabbi, 1980. Youth dir. Lincolnwood (Ill.) Jewish Congregation, 1977-79; rabbi Congregation B'nai Shalom, Buffalo Grove, Ill., 1977-79; asst. rabbi, dir. edn. and youth Congregation Shearith Israel, Atlanta, 1979-86; dir. dept. secondary and community edn. Cen. Agy. for Jewish Edn., St. Louis, 1986-91; exec. dir. Bur. Jewish Edn. R.I., Providence, 1991—; chair Atlanta Jewish Youth Workers' Coun., 1984-85, Atlanta Jewish Edn. Dirs.' Coun., 1985-86. Contbr. articles to religious publs. Mem. Coun. for Jewish Edn. (nat. bd. dirs. 1990—), Coalition for Advancement of Jewish Edn. (nat. bd. dirs. 1983-85, 90—), Religious Edn. Assn., ASCD, Nat. Havurah Com. Home: 114 Lauriston St Providence RI 02906 Office: Bur Jewish Edn RI 130 Sessions St Providence RI 02906

SAMMONS, DAVID G., minister; b. Chgo., Feb. 11, 1938; s. Joseph Albert and Helen Louise (Leonard) S.; m. Rosemary Louise Sturtz, Aug. 30, 1959 (div. 1973); children: Donna, David, Michal Ann, Benjamin; m. Janis Miller, Jan. 24, 1974; 1 child, Matthew. AB, Dartmouth Coll., 1960; postgrad., Meadville/Lombard Coll., 1961-62; MDiv, Starr King Sch. Ministry, 1965; D in Min., Pacific Sch. Religion, 1978. Ordained to ministry, Unitarian Universalist Ch., 1965. Assoc. min. First Unitarian Ch., Rochester, N.Y., 1965-67; min. St. John's Unitarian Ch., Cin., 1967-78; sr. min. Unitarian Ch. of Evanston, Ill., 1978-84, Mt. Diablo Unitarian Universalist Ch., Walnut Creek, Calif., 1984—; bd. dirs. Beacon Press, Boston, 1969-75, Urban Ch. Coalition, N.Y.C., 1983, Unitarian Universalist Svc. Com., Boston, 1983, Starr King Sch. for the Ministry, 1984-89, v.p. 1988-89; pres. Pacific Cen. Dist. Unitarian Universalist Mins. Assn., 1985-86; mem. Unitarian Universalist Commn. on Appraisal, 1985-91, chair 1987-90. Author: The Marriage Option, 1977; contbr. articles to profl. jours. Pres. Cin. Action for Peace, 1968, Lake Geneva Summer Assembly, 1971, No. Shore Peace Initiative, Evanston, Ill., 1981-83; coord. Clergy Cons. Svc., Cin., 1969-71; convenor Clifton Clergy Group, Cin., 1974-76; scribe Downtown Clergy Assn., Evanston, 1980-82; chmn. Ill. Nuclear Freeze Adv. Com., Chgo., 1983; bd. dirs. Mt. Diablo Peace Ctr., 1984—, East Bay AIDS Interfaith Network, 1985-87, Shasta/Diablo Planned Parenthood, 1986-90; chmn. Walnut Creek Clery Assn., 1990—; various other orgns. Recipient Award of Honor, North Shore Peace Initiative, 1983, Mt. Diable Peace Ctr., 1989. Mem. Unitarian Universalist Mins. Assn. (25 Yr. Honor Speaker award), Phi Beta Kappa. Democrat. Home: 829 Hutchinson Walnut Creek CA 94598 Office: Mt Diablo Unitarian Univ Ch 55 Eckley Ln Walnut Creek CA 94596 *People of faith must always resist the temptation to privatize religion. The only faith worth having is the one that compels us into action.*

SAMMONS, WILLIAM HENLEY, pastor; b. Panola County, Tex., July 17, 1929; s. George Henley and Betty Elizabeth (Johnson) S.; m. Betty L. Ratley, Apr. 5, 1953; children: David Henley, Donna Elizabeth, Luther Daniel, Deborah Lyn. Student, East Tex. Bible Coll., 1956-57, various colls., Tex., La., 1949-69. Ordained to ministry So. Bapt. Conv., 1964. Pastor Christal Bapt. Ch., Tatum, Tex., 1964-66, Cedar Springs Bapt. Ch., Ore City, Tex., 1966-70, Bushnell Bapt. Ch., Galera, Okla., 1971-72; nursing home min. Terrace Hills Bapt. Ch., Longview, Tex., 1976-80; pastor Gladeview Bapt. Ch., Gladewater, Tex., 1974-76, 81—; estimator Brown & Root, U.S.A., Inc., Longview, 1985—. With U.S. Army, 1952-53, Korea. Decorated Bronze Star. Home: PO Box 14 Judson TX 75660 Office: Gladeview Bapt Ch 901 Culver St Gladewater TX 75647

SAMPIER, JACK MARTEL, minister; b. Aromas, Calif., Sept. 23, 1939; s. Leonard C. and Frances M. (Alexander) S.; m. Dixie Kay Bonds, Aug. 16, 1963; children: Karen Kay, Jack Jr. BA in Religion, So. Calif. Coll., 1971. Ordained to ministry Assemblies of God, 1989. Asst. pastor Glad Tidings Assembly of God, Newport Beach, Calif., 1965-70; chaplain decedent affairs Santa Anna (Calif.) Community Hosp., 1970-72; tchr. Berwick (La.) Assembly of God, 1976-82, Faith Chapel, LaMesa, Calif., 1983-86; pastor The Lighthouse Christian Ctr., El Cajon, Calif., 1987—; chmn. bd. dirs. Valley Hosp. Chaplains, El Cajon, 1990—. chmn. adv. bd. for disabled students St. Mary Parish (La.) Sch. Bd., 1974-80. Mem. Lions (pres. 1979-80). Republican. Home: PO Box 146 El Cajon CA 92022-0146 Office: Light House Christian Ctr 205 Lento Ln El Cajon CA 92021

SAMPLASKI, TERRY LEE, clergyman; b. Milw., Aug. 1, 1958; s. Robert Edward and Rachel (Rincon) S.; m. Sharon Lynn Mills, Dec. 17, 1983; children: Jeremy Randall, Jeffrey Ryan, Jamie Renee. Student, U. Tex., 1976-78; MusB, Hardin-Simmons U., 1981; postgrad., Southwestern Theol. Sem., 1983-85. Ordained to ministry So. Bapt. Conv., 1985. Mem. Eternity contemporary music group, 1981-83; assoc. minister music First Bapt. Ch., Euless, Tex., 1983-85; minister music Congress Ave Bapt. Ch., Austin, Tex., 1985-88; assoc. pastor/music College Hills Bapt. Ch., San Angelo, Tex., 1988-91; min. of music Bapt. Temple, McAllen, Tex., 1991—. Bd. dirs. pub. rels. Concho Valley Assn. for Blind, San Angelo, Tex., 1989—. Republican. Home: 6104 N 31st St McAllen TX 78504 Office: Bapt Temple 2001 Trenton McAllen TX 78504

SAMPSON, FRANKLIN DELANO, minister; b. Houston, Jan. 31, 1947; s. Harry Burney and Annie Belle (Lenzia) S.; m. Fannie Marie Iles, Mar. 12, 1972; children: De Anza Michelle, Franklin Delano, Jr., Frederick Dwayne. BA, U. Houston, 1970; D of Ministries (hon.), Mt. Hope Bible Coll., 1978. Ordained to ministry So. Bapt. Conv., 1969. Pastor Friendship Missionary Bapt. Ch., Houston, 1972—; moderator Unity Missionary Bapt. Gen. Assn., Houston, 1985—; chmn. Minister's Conf. of Missionary Bapt. Gen. Conv., Dallas, 1987—, Commn. on Orthodoxy of Nat. Bapt. Conv. of Am., Inc., Shreveport, La., 1987—; chief exec. officer Visions of Faith Ministries, Inc., Houston, 1985—. Mem. Bapt. Mins. Assn. of Houston and Vicinity (v.p. 1990—), Masons. Democrat. Home: 12947 Wincrest Ct Cypress TX 77429 Office: Friendship Missionary Bapt Ch 4812 Bennington Houston TX 77016

SAMRA, NICHOLAS JAMES, bishop; b. Paterson, N.J., Aug. 15, 1944; s. George H. and Elizabeth L. (Balady) S. BA, St. Anselm Coll., 1966; BD, St. John Sem., Brighton, Mass., 1970. Ordained priest Melkite-Greek Cath. Ch., 1970, bishop, 1989. Assoc. pastor St. Anne Ch., North Hollywood, Calif., 1970-78; pastor Holy Cross Ch., Anaheim, Calif., 1973-78, St. John The Bapt. Ch., Northlake, Ill., 1978-81, St. Michael Ch., Hammond, Ind., 1978-81, St. Anne Ch., West Paterson, N.J., 1981-89; aux. bishop Diocese of Newton, Mass., 1989—; chaplain Police Athletic League Supporters, North Hollywood, 1970's; vicar gen., corp. v.p., and regional bishop of Midwest region, Diocese of Newton; translator articles on Melkite subjects; mem. Ecumenical Commn., L.A., 1974-78. Mem. Cath. Archives Assn. Home and Office: 8525 Cole Warren MI 48093-5239

SAMS, DAVID MARCELLE, minister; b. Bedford, Ind., Feb. 2, 1968; s. Ronald Wayne and Dee Ann (Burkholder) S.; m. Melinda Elaine Wingfield, Oct. 13, 1990. BS in Bible, Johnson Bible Coll., Knoxville, Tenn., 1990. Ordained to ministry Christian Ch., 1990. Min. youth Centerville (Ind.) Christian Ch., 1990—. Home: 109 E Plum St Centerville IN 47330 Office: Centerville Christian Ch 111 N Morton Ave Centerville IN 47330

SAMS, JOHN ROLAND, retired mission executive, missionary; b. Whatcheer, Iowa, Nov. 1, 1922; s. Bert Willian and and Vesta Leora (Wilkins) S.; m. Frances Elizabeth McCluney, July 3, 1924; children: Phyllis Jean, Georgia Ann, Bert Franklin. BS, Iowa State U., 1949; MA, Drake U., 1952; student, Hartford Sem., 1952-54; MA, Chapman Coll., 1972; HHD (hon.), Philippine Christian U., Manila. Tchr. Paullina (Iowa) Pub. Schs., 1949-51; missionary Christian Ch. (Disciples of Christ), Thailand, 1954-67, Philippines, 1968-71; v.p. Am. Leprosy Missions, N.Y.C., 1972-76; exec. v.p. Am. Leprosy Missions, Bloomfield, N.J., 1976-84; pres. Am. Leprosy Missions, Elmwood Park, N.J., 1984-89. Served with USAAF, 1942-46. Mem. United Ch. of Christ. Avocations: travel, reading.

SAMUEL, ATHANASIUS YESHUE, archbishop; b. Hilwah, Syria, Dec. 25, 1907; s. Sowmey Malkey and Khatoun Malkey (Hido) S. Student, St. Mark's Sem., Jerusalem, 1923-27, 29-31, Cairo Theol. Coll., 1927-29; DD (hon.), Gen. Theol. Sem., N.Y.C., 1989. Ordained priest Syrian Orthodox Ch. of Antioch, 1932; sec. to Syrian orthodox patriarch of Antioch, 1931-32; father superior St. Mark's Monastery, Jerusalem, 1933-43; patriarchal vicar of Jerusalem, 1943-46; archbishop, 1946-52; patriarchal del. to U.S.A. and Can., 1949-57; archbishop to U.S.A. and Can., 1957—. Author: Treasure of Qumran, 1966, Liturgy of St. James, 1967, Rites of Baptism, Holy Matrimony and Burial, 1974, Book of Church Festivals, 1984. Decorated by Emperor Haile Selassie I gold cross and papal medallion Pope Paul VI, cross Knights of St. John of Jerusalem., Grand Cross of St. Ignatius Theophoros; proclaimed Dean of Bishops of the Holy See of Antioch, 1989. Mem. World Council Chs., Nat. Council Chs. of Christ in U.S.A. Home and Office: 49 Kipp Ave Lodi NJ 07644

SAMUEL, JAMES RAY, minister, dean; b. Florence, S.C., Apr. 2, 1952; s. Joseph and Jannie (Allen) S.; m. Dellyne Cypress, Aug. 17, 1974; 1 child, Brian James. BA in English, Livingstone Coll., 1975; MDiv, Duke U., 1982; Clin. Pastoral Edn., N.C. Sch. Pastoral Care, 1982; D Ministry, Drew U., 1990. Ordained to ministry A.M.E. Zion Ch., 1979. Sr. pastor Third Creek A.M.E. Zion Ch., Cleveland, N.C., 1980-82, Marable Meml. A.M.E. Zion Ch., Kannapolis, N.C., 1982-84, Soldiers Meml. A.M.E. Zion Ch., Salisbury, N.C., 1984-89, Little Rock A.M.E. Zion Ch., Charlotte, N.C., 1989—; dean Hood Theol. Sem., Salisbury, 1990—; trustee A.M.E. Zion Camp Dorothy Walls, Blue Mountain, N.C., 1982-91; del. 42d Gen. Conf. A.M.E. Zion Ch., St. Louis, 1984, 43d Gen. Conf. A.M.E. Zion Ch., Charlotte, 1988, World Meth. Conf., Singapore, 1991; mem. connectional budget bd. A.M.E. Zion Ch., 1988—. mem. Charlotte Community Rels. Coun., 1989—, Charlotte Minority Affairs Commn., 1989—, Charlotte Area Clergy Assn., 1989—. Recipient Keeper of Dream award Charlotte Community Rels. Coun., 1991. Mem. Assn. Theol. Schs., Assn. Theol. Deans, Masons. Home: 4811 Easthaven Dr Charlotte NC 28212 Office: AME Zion Ch 401 N McDowell St Charlotte NC 28212 *When faith emerges out of one's struggle for justice, it takes on an eschatological dimension. This eschatological faith allows the believer to experience a higher reality which operates above the historical reality of injustice and oppresion, bringing about the assurance of liberation and freedom.*

SAMUEL, KENNETH LANDON, minister; b. Jeffersonville, Ind., Dec. 26, 1961; s. Kenneth Elmer and Carolyn Dean (Triplett) S.; m. Sherry Ann Hart, June 17, 1982; children: Jessica Elaine, Ashley Mignon, Landon Alexander. BA in Bible, Freed-Hardeman Coll., Henderson, Tenn., 1983; MDiv, Lexington Theol. Sem., 1991. Minister Paris (Ky.) Ch. of Christ, 1983—; chaplain U. Ky. Med. Ctr., Lexington, 1989-90; guest lectr. Korea Bible Corres. Ctr. Winter Bible Sch., Seoul, 1985. Adv. bd. God's Pantry Crisis Food Ctr., Lexington, 1986; vol. Hospice for the Bluegrass, Bourbon County, Ky., 1988—; adv. com. Paris City Sch., 1989; Friend of Children, Childplace, Jeffersonville, Ind., 1983—; mem. clin. pastoral edn. profl. consultation com. U. Ky. Med. Ctr., 1991—. Office: Paris Ch of Christ 1923 S Main St Paris KY 40361 *It seems to me that the kindest people I have ever met are those to whom I have been kindest.*

SAMUEL, SUBRAMANIAN JOHNSON, religion educator; b. Nallamangalam, Tamil Nadu, India, Apr. 3, 1958; came to U.S., 1989; s. Kandaswami Subramanian and Mary Kamalammal. B of Commerce, Madurai Kamarajar U., 1978; BD, Serampore (India) U., 1981, MTh, 1985; M of Commerce, Sri Venkateswara U., Tirupati, India, 1984; MDiv summa cum laude, So. Meth. U., 1990—; cert. ind. theol. studies, Episcopal Theol. Sem., 1990. Ordained priest Meth. Ch. Lectr. Hindustan Bible Coll., Madras, India, 1981-83, Leonard Theol. Coll., Jabalpur, India, 1985-86, Bishop's Theol. Coll., Calcutta, India, 1986-88, Trulock Theol. Sem., Imphal, India, 1988-89; minister Diocese of Durgapur, CNI, Bankura, India, 1986-88. Contbr. articles to profl. publs. Home: Ch St Pottal Patty Post, Via Muhavur 626 111, Tamil Nadu 626 111, India Office: Episcopal Theol Sem PO Box 2247 Austin TX 78768 *In my life I have discovered that when we come to realize that we are identical with one another in essence as the Ultimate Reality, we transcend all our external marks and ideologies, and become one human community in which freedom, love and happiness are actualized.*

SAMUELS, JOE A., religious organization administrator. Pres. Seventh-day Bapt. Gen. Conf. U.S.A. and Can., Plainfield, N.J. Office: Seventh-day Bapt Gen Conf USA and Can 511 Central Ave Plainfield NJ 07060*

SAMUELS, THOMAS WILLIAM, minister; b. Miami, Fla., Feb. 27, 1934; s. Henry Cornelius and Cora Anna (Waters) S.; m. Juanita Iona Gibson, Oct. 8, 1954; children: Gennita Renae, Synovia Louise, Henry Jethro, Thomas William II. BS, Bethune Cookman Coll., Daytona Beach, Fla., 1955. Ordained to ministry Primitive Bapt. Ch., 1957. Pastor St. John Primitive Bapt. Ch., Mt. Dora, Fla., 1957-59, Mt. Zion Primitive Bapt. Ch., Eustis, Fla., 1957-73, Zion Hill Primitive Bapt. Ch., Lakeland, Fla., 1959-73, Mt. Moriah Primitive Bapt. Ch., Charlotte, N.C., 1973—; sec. Nat. Primitive Bapt. Conv., 1971-89, pres., 1989—; pres. N.C.-Va. Primitive Bapt. State Conv., E. Spencer, N.C., 1977—, S.W. Dist. Sunday Sch. Conv., Charlotte, 1977—; chmn. bd. dirs. Nat. Primitive Bapt. Conv., 1989—; instr. Christian Doctrin, Nat. Primitive Bapt. Sun. Sch. Congress, 1972—; mem. Echoes curriculum adv. bd. David C. Cook Pub. Co., 1988-91. Contbg. editor: The Story of Civil Rights, 1972. Chmn. ch. com. United Negro Coll. Fund of Johnson C. Smith U., 1984, 85, 87; bd. dirs. Charlotte Area Fund and Uptown Day Shelter, 1989-91. Mem. NAACP , Bapt. Ministers Conf. of Charlotte, Christian Ministers Fellowship. Democrat. Office: Mt Moriah Primitive Bapt Ch 747 W Trade St Charlotte NC 28202

SAMUELSON, NORBERT M., rabbi, religion educator; b. Chgo., Feb. 15, 1936; s. Albert and Mary (Okil) S.; m. Eileen Serelle Levinson, Aug. 18, 1957; children: Jeffrey David, Miriam Rachel. BA, Northwestern U., 1957; M. Hebrew Letters., Hebrew Union Coll., 1962; PhD, Ind. U., 1970. Ordained rabbi, 1970. Dir. Hillel Found. Ind. U., Bloomington, 1962-67, Princeton (N.J.) U., 1968-73; asst. prof. U. Va., Charlottesville, 1973-75; prof. of religion Temple U., Phila., 1975—; vis. fellow Oxford (Eng.) Ctr. for Postgrad. Hebrew Studies, 1987. Author: Gersonides on God's Knowledge, 1977, The Exalted Faith of Abraham Ibn Daud, 1986, An Introduction to Modern Jewish Philosophy; editor: Creation and the End of Days, 1986, Studies in Jewish Philosophy, 1987. Fulbright-Hayes rsch. fellow NEA, 1967-68. Fellow Acad. for Jewish Theol. Soc. (chair 1979-88, sec. 1989—); mem. Am. Theol. Soc., Am. Acad. Religion, Assn. for Jewish Studies. Democrat. Home: 7304 N 12th St Melrose Park PA 19126 Office: Temple U Dept Religion Philadelphia PA 19126

SAMUELU, TEL II, religious organziation administrator. Pres. Ch. of Tuvalu, Funafuti. Office: Ch Tuvalu, POB 2, Funafuti Tuvalu*

SANBORN, HUGH WIEDMAN, religion educator, administrator, pastoral therapist; b. Albany, N.Y., Nov. 29, 1939; s. Hugh Wallace and Elizabeth (Wiedman) S.; m. Barbara Ann Mortensen, June 16, 1962; children: Elisabeth, Daniel. BA in Psychology, Muhlenberg Coll., 1962; BD, Andover Newton Theol. Sch., 1966, MST, 1967; PhD in Religion and Personality, U. Iowa, 1975. Ordained to ministry United Ch. of Christ, 1965; lic. profl. counselor, Tex. Chaplain Iowa Security Med. Facility, Coralville, 1969-71; pastoral therapist St. Peter United Ch., Houston, 1978—; dir. campus ministries Houston United Campus Christian Life Com., 1980—; adj. asst. prof. Rice U., Houston, 1973—, dir., v.p., then pres. Meeting House West Counseling Ctr., 1980-85; vis. lectr. San Francisco Theol. Sem., 1982; Houston liaison World Coun. Chs., 1982-83; sec. ch. and ministry com. Houston Assn. United Ch. of Christ, 1983-85, 87-89; pastoral relator to clergy So. Cen. Conf., Austin, Tex., 1984-88; mem. Spl. Commn. Ministry in Higher Edn., Tex. Conf. of Chs., Austin, 1984-86. Author: Mental-Spiritual Health Models, 1979. Trustee Houston Rape Crisis Coalition, 1977-80; mem. Interfaith Peaceforce Houston, 1981-88; Houston coord. Union Concerned Scientists Peace Conv., 1981; organizer Peace Studies Ctr., U. Houston, 1982—; convener Intefaith Forum on Global Issues, 1989. Page fellow Andover Newton Theol. Sch., 1966-67. Mem. Assn. Clin. Pastoral Edn. (clin. mem.), Am. Acad. of Religion. Democrat. Home: 3711 Glen Haven Houston TX 77025 Office: U Houston United Campus Christian Life Com 208 A D Bruce Religion Ctr Houston TX 77204-3621 *The world longs for the integrity and transforming power of mature faith. When faith matures, the earth is seen as garden, the world's population as community, and the care and enhancement of both as the natural consequence of enacted love, peace and justice.*

SANCHEZ, JOSE T. CARDINAL, cardinal; b. Pandan, The Philippines, Mar. 17, 1920. Ordained priest Roman Cath. Ch., 1946. Prefect Congregation for Clergy; titular bishop of Lesvi, coadjutor bishop of Lucena, 1968, bishop of Lucena, 1976-82, archbishop of Nueva Segoria, 1982, resigned, 1986; sec. Congregation for Evangelization of Peoples, 1985-91; elevated to the Sacred Coll. of Cardinals, 1991, with titular ch. of St. Pius V. Office: Congregation for the Clergy, Office of Prefect, 00120 Vatican City Vatican City*

SANCHEZ, JUAN RAMON, JR., music and youth minister; b. Rio Piedras, Puerto Rico, July 29, 1965; came to U.S., 1973; s. Juan Ramon and Laura Rosa (De Jesus) S.; m. Jeanine Marie Dell, June 29, 1990; 1 child, Alexandra Dell. Student, U. Fla., 1990—. Ordained to ministry Bapt. Ch., 1991. Youth, music min. Orange Heights Bapt. Ch., Hawthorne, Fla., 1985-86; religious programs specialist USN, 1986-87; youth, music min. First Bapt. Ch., Baldwin, Fla., 1988-89, Newberry, Fla., 1989—; founder, dir. Family Life Ministries, Gainesville, Fla., 1990—; water safety instr. ARC, Jacksonville, Fla., 1988—; co-founder, trombonist Tropical Brass Quintet, Gainesville, 1988—; guest faculty Fla. Bapt. Conv., Jacksonville, 1982—, Bapt. Sunday Sch. Bd., Nashville, 1988—; dir. evangelism Bapt. Campus Ministries, Gainesville, 1986. Author: American Red Cross Communications, 1987, Burials at Sea, 1987. With USN, 1983-87. Nominated to U.S. Naval Acad., Congressman Tom Lewis, Avon Park, Fla., 1984; recipient Letter of Commendation, USS Detroit, Norfolk, Va., 1986; Friends of Music scholar, U. Fla., 1988-89. Mem. Phi Mu Alpha (pres. 1988-89). Office: First Bapt Ch 512 W Central Ave PO Box 309 Newberry FL 32669 *If there is one thing that is certain in this life we live, it is the incredible passage of time. It is our responsibility during our short time here to understand the two most important things: The love for God and the love for other human beings.*

SANCHEZ, PAUL, minister; b. Whittier, Calif., Oct. 21, 1964; s. Eloy Sanchez and Esther Rebecca (Randall) Brusuelas; m. Robyn Otelia (Nelson), Jan. 30, 1988; 1 child, Joshua Christopher. Student, Rio Hondo Coll., Whittier, 1982-84; AA, Word of Faith Bible Inst., Dallas, 1986. Ordained to ministry Assembly of God Ch. Youth worker First Family Assembly of God Ch., Whittier, 1983-86; asst. pastor Derby Acres (Calif.) Community Tabernacle, 1986-87; youth pastor Vaca Valley Christian Life Ctr., Vacaville, Calif., 1989—. Home: 902 Southdown Ct Winters CA 95694 Office: Vaca Valley Christian Life Ctr 6391 Leisure Town Rd Vacaville CA 95687-9405

SANCHEZ, ROBERT FORTUNE, archbishop; b. Socorro, N.Mex., Mar. 20, 1934; s. Julius C. and Priscilla (Fortune) S. Student, Immaculate Heart Sem., Santa Fe, 1954, N.Am. Coll., Gregorian U., Rome, 1960. Ordained priest Roman Cath. Ch., 1959; prof. St. Piux X High Sch., Albuquerque, 1960-68; dir. extension lay vols. Archdiocese Santa Fe, 1965-68, chmn. priest personnel bd., 1968-72, vicar gen., 1974, archbishop, 1974—; rep. instl. ministry pastoral care N.Mex. Council Chs., 1968; pres. Archdiocesan Priests Senate, 1973-74; rep. region X Nat. Fedn. Priests Councils, 1972-73; bd. dirs. Mexican Am. Cultural Center; mem. regional com. Nat. Conf. Catholic Bishops, N.Am. Coll., Rome; pres. N.Mex. Conf. Chs. Mem. U.S. Cath. Conf. (chmn. ad hoc com. Spanish speaking). Office: The Cath Ctr Archdiocese of Santa Fe St Joseph's Pl NW Albuquerque NM 87120

SANCHEZ, RUBEN DARIO, minister, parochial school educator, writer; b. Buenos Aires, Feb. 13, 1943; s. Ramon Jose and Maria Concepcion (Pardino) S.; m. Lina Alcira Tabuenca, Feb. 7, 1966; children: Adrian Nelson, Vivian Ethel. BA, River Plate Coll., Puiggari, Argentina, 1969; postgrad., Andrews U., 1971-72, MA, 1975; PhD, Calif. Sch. Theology, 1979. Ordained to ministry Seventh-day Adventist Ch., 1976. Pastor, tchr. River Plate Coll., Puiggari, 1969; min. lit. So. Calif. Conf., Glendale, 1970-71, Ill. Conf., Brookfield, 1972-77, Oreg. Conf., Portland, 1977-80; dir. Bible sch., assoc. speaker Voice of Prophecy, Thousand Oaks, Calif., 1980-84; dir. devel. Written Telecast, 1985—; founder Pacific N.W. Christian Sch., Woodburn, Oreg., 1979; founder, dir. Instituto Biblico Christiano, 1979-80; dir. Escuela Radiopostal (Corr. Bible Sch.), 1980-84; mem. Religious Broadcasters. Editor: Antologia Poetica, 1976; author: (textbook) Apasionante Exploration de la Biblia, 1977, Introduction to the Old Testament, 1979; (doctrinal devotional) Hungary Heart, 1984; contbr. articles to publs. Recipient Outstanding Service to Spanish Community in Oreg. award Sta. KROW, 1980; Andrews U. scholar, 1972. Mem. Assn. Christian Counselors, Christian Mgmt. Assn. Home: 2983 Elinor Ct Newbury Park CA 91320 Office: Adventist Media Ctr 1100 Rancho Conejo Blvd Newbury Park CA 91320

SANDBERG, GARY ALLEN, minister; b. Toledo, June 26, 1962; s. Arthur Ronald and Geraldine Ann (Pachalski) S.; m. Karen Lynn Westphal, Aug. 9, 1986. BA, Capital U., 1984; MDiv, Trinity Luth. Sem., Columbus, Ohio, 1988. Ordained to ministry Evang. Luth. Ch. Am., 1988. Assoc. pastor Trinity Luth. Ch., Monticello, Minn., 1988—; adult advisor Mpls. area synod Luth. Youth Orgn., Mpls., 1990—; chaplain Monticello Fire Dept., 1990—. Active Youth Task Force, Monticello, 1989, Early Childhood Family Edn, Monticello, 1990-91. Democrat. Home: Rte 3 Box 116 A Monticello MN 55362 Office: Trinity Luth Ch 449 W Broadway Box 776 Monticello MN 55362 *If every adult would accept the challenge to be a long-term positive influence to just one youth outside of their own family the benefits they receive would only be surpassed by the benefits our youth would receive.*

SANDEFER, IRA LEE, pastor; b. Royce City, Tex., Apr. 8, 1944; s. Ira Eugene and Irella Trella Martina (Smith) S.; m. Mary Paulette Hoover, Aug. 13, 1965; 1 child, Tommy Lee. AA, Claremore (Okla.) Jr. Coll., 1976; BA, Northeastern Okla. State U., 1979. Ordained to ministry Ch. of God, 1974. Evangelist Ch. of God, Tex., 1966-67, pastor, 1967-73; pastor Ch. of God, Okla., 1974-82; state youth and Christian edn. dir. Ariz., 1982-86; pastor Ch. of God, Ohio, 1986-87, Tex., 1987-88, Okla., 1988—; various offices in ministerial assns., 1968—; adv. bd. West Coast Christian Coll., 1982-84. Contbr. articles to profl. publs. Sgt. USNG, 1964-69. Home and Office: 622 N Townsend Ada OK 74820

SANDEFUR, ROBERT DAVID, youth pastor; b. Shawnee, Okla., Feb. 18, 1959; s. Tommy Robert and Mary Leigh (Garis) S.; m. Rebekah Sue McCrary, Apr. 2, 1983; 1 child, Ryan Christopher Mark. Student, Grace Bible Inst., 1979. Youth pastor Cornerstone Ch., Ft. Worth, 1985-87, Arlington (Tex.) Christian Ctr., 1987—; leader Bible study Sam Houston High Sch., Arlington, 1987—, Mansfield (Tex.) High Sch., 1989-91, Gunn Jr. High, Arlington, 1990-91. Coach ACC Acad., Arlington, 1988. Republican. Office: Arlington Christian Ch 801 Bardin Rd Arlington TX 76017

SANDERS, ANDREW WILLIAM, JR., music minister; b. Monticello, Fla., Jan. 19, 1948; m. Wandra Lorraine Merritt, Nov. 6, 1982; children: Fionn, André, Adrian. AA, Santa Fe Community Coll., Gainesville, Fla., 1972; BA, U. Fla., 1976; ThM, Internat. Sem., Plymouth, Fla., 1987, DD (hon.), 1988. Cert. tchr., Fla. Tchr. Alachua County Sch. System, Gainesville, 1976-77, Marion County Sch. System, Ocala, Fla., 1977-78; agt., supr. Trailways, Inc., Jacksonville, Fla., 1978-79; sales rep. Delta Airlines, Inc., Jacksonville, 1979—; minister music, tchr. Bible, Ch. of Christ Riverside Park, Jacksonville, 1979-89; minister music Dean Rd Ch. of Christ, Jacksonville, 1989—; dir. Music Ministry Workshops, Jacksonville, 1990—. Mem. Jacksonville Urban League, 1986—. Recipient cert. of appreciation Fla. Health and Rehabilitative Svcs., 1977, Jacksonville Urban League, 1987, Riverside Park Ch. of Christ, 1989. Mem. Fellowship Christian Airline Pers., United Assn. Christian Counselors Internat. (assoc.), U. Fla. Nat. Alumni Assn., Am. Legion, NAACP, Phi Beta Lambda. Democrat. Avocations: reading, gardening, travel, body building, singing. Office: Music Ministry Workshops PO Box 2061 Jacksonville FL 32203-2061

SANDERS, BRICE SIDNEY, bishop; b. Nashville, Oct. 15, 1930; s. Walter Richard and Agnes Mortimer (Jones) S.; m. Nancy Elizabeth Robinson, Aug. 22, 1953; children—Richard Evan, Robert Wesley, Lynne Elizabeth. B.A., Vanderbilt U., 1952; M.S.T., Episcopal Div. Sch., Cambridge, Mass., 1955; D.D. (hon.), Va. Theol. Sem., 1980, U. South, Sewanee, Tenn., 1984. Ordained to ministry. Rector St. James Ch., Union City, Tenn., 1955-58, Good Shepherd Ch., Knoxville, 1958-61, Eastern Shore Chapel, Virginia Beach, Va., 1961-70; assoc. dean Va. Theol. Sem., Alexandria, 1970-75; dean St. Andrews Cathedral, Jackson, Miss., 1975-79; bishop Diocese of East Carolina, Kingston, N.C., 1979—. Home: 2112 Sparre Dr Kinston NC 28501 Office: Diocese of E Carolina PO Box 1336 Kinston NC 28501 also: PO Box 3807 Knoxville TN 37917

SANDERS, CARL JULIAN, minister; b. Star, N.C., May 18, 1912; s. Hugh T. and Annie Margaret (Crowell) S.; m. Eleanor Louise Lupo, Sept. 28, 1935; children: Lundi (Mrs. John R. Martin), Eleanor (Mrs. Paul E. Kasler). B.A., Wofford Coll., 1933, D.D. (hon.), 1973; B.D., Candler Sch. Theology, 1936; D.D. (hon.), Randolph Macon Coll., 1953, Athens (Ala.) Coll., 1972, Huntingdon Coll., 1975; L.H.D. (hon.), Birmingham-So. Coll., 1977. Ordained to ministry Methodist Ch., 1934; pastor Cheriton, Va., 1936-40, Chase City, Va., 1940-44, Roanoke, Va., 1944-48, Richmond, Va., 1948-55; supt. Petersburg (Va.) Dist., 1955-56, Richmond Dist., 1956-61, Norfolk (Va.) Dist., 1965-71; pastor Richmond, 1961-65, Arlington, Va., 1971-72; bishop Birmingham (Ala.) Area, 1972-80; exec. dir. Ala.-West Fla. United Meth. Found., 1980-85, Found. for Bibl. Studies, 1980—; pres. com. relief United Meth. Ch., 1972-76, v.p. bd. global ministries, 1972-76; mem. World Meth. Council, 1971-80. Trustee Emory U., 1973—, Carraway Med. Center, Birmingham, 1972-80, Athens Coll., 1972-80, Huntington Coll., Montgomery, Ala., 1972-80, Va. Wesleyan Coll., Norfolk, 1960-72. Mem. Masons (grand chaplain supreme coun. So. Jurisdiction U.S.A.), Omicron Delta Kappa. Home: 2235 Monument Ave # 2 Richmond VA 23220

SANDERS, CECIL MALLON, JR., minister; b. Birmingham, Ala., Jan. 29, 1961; s. Cecil Mallon and Doris (McKibben) S.; m. Lynn Michelle Forsythe, June 15, 1985. BA, Wheaton Coll., 1983. Coll. minister McKinney Meml. Bible Ch., Ft. Worth, Tx., 1985—. Home: 5820 Highland Pk Dr #2103 Fort Worth TX 76132 Office: McKinney Bible Ch 3901 S Hulen Fort Worth TX 76109

SANDERS, ERNEST LEVONDE, minister; b. Montgomery, Ala., Mar. 22, 1955; s. Eddie L. and Annie Lue (Waits) S.; m. Barbara, May 20, 1983; children: Na'im, Ernest. BS, Troy State, 1980, MS, 1982; JD, Miles Sch. Law, 1987. Ordained to ministry Episcopal Ch., 1978. Pastor AME Zion Ch., Montgomery, Ala., 1982-87, Episcopal Ch. of Jesus, Talladega, Ala., 1987—. Author: Your Pastor and You, 1987, Showing God Approval, 1989. With U.S. Army, 1974-76. Mem. Capital City Bar, Nat. Bar Assn., Birmingham Ministrial Alliance, Talladega Assn. Ministers. Office: Episcopal Ch 307 Bradford Ave Talladega AL 35160

SANDERS, GERALD MARTIN, minister; b. Chattannoga, Mar. 3, 1947; s. Wyatt Ewing and Ruth LaNeil (Martin) S.; m. Jana Kaye Hawkins, Oct. 30, 1967; children: Gerald William, James Martin. BA, East Tenn. State U., 1970, MA in Philosophy, 1975; postgrad., Duke U., 1972-73, Luth. Theol. Sem., 1981-83. Ordained to ministry United Ch. of Christ, 1975. Pastor Lakeview United Ch. of Christ, Burlington, N.C., 1970-75, Shallow Well United Ch. of Christ, Sanford, N.C., 1975-77, Ch. of the Master United Ch. of Christ, Hickory, N.C., 1977-84; exec. dir. Bibl. Witness Fellowship, United Ch. of Christ, Knoxville, Tenn., 1984-91; mem. Nat. Conf. of Renewal Execs., 1985-91; gen. synod del. United Ch. of Christ, Cleve., 1979-81; ministerial mem. Ala.-Tenn. Assn., S.E. Conf., United Ch. of Christ. Editor: (with others) Issue in Sexual Ethics, 1978; contbr. articles to profl. publs. Participant White Ho. Conf. on Human Rights, Washington, 1983. Republican. Office: Bibl Witness Fellowship PO Box 50384 Knoxville TN 37950-0384

SANDERS, GILBERT LEE, clergyman; b. Clifton Hill, Mo., Sept. 27, 1946; s. Edward N. and Muriel E. (Purdue) S.; m. Susan Coiner, June 29, 1968; children: Dale L., Muriel S. BA, William Jewell Coll., Liberty, Mo., 1968; MDiv, So. Bapt. Theol. Sem., Louisville, 1971, ThM, 1972, PhD, 1979. Ordained to ministry So. Bapt. Conv., 1964. Pastor Chariton Ridge Bapt. Ch., Atlanta, 1964-68; adminstrv. staff So. Bapt. Theol. Sem., Louisville, 1974-82; pastor Bethany Bapt. Ch., Godfrey, Ill., 1982-89, Livonia (Mich.) Bapt. Ch., 1989—. Contbr.: Good News Daily Devotion Guide, 1985. Mem. Soc. Bibl. Lit. Office: Livonia Bapt Ch 32940 Schoolcraft Rd Livonia MI 48150

SANDERS, HAROLD ARTHUR, clergyman, educator; b. Iowa Falls, Iowa, June 8, 1919; s. Jacob Glenn and Myrtle Lucille (Tarpenning) S.; m. Hazel Luverne Anderson, Apr. 5, 1941; children—Mavis Rae, Harold Arthur, Paul Sidney, David Joshua, John Glenn, James Franklin, Mark

Wallace, Alice Lucille, Thomas Ashley. Cert. and Grad. of Theology, Northwestern Schs., Mpls., 1940; B.R.E., Northwestern Theol. Sem., 1941. Ordained to Gospel Ministry, 1941. Pastor, Temple Bapt. Ch., Omaha, 1942-45, First Bapt. Ch., Loup City, Nebr., 1945-49, Rowan & Galt Congl. Ch., Rowan, Iowa, 1949-56, Baileyville Bapt. Ch., Ill., 1956-59, Tabernacle Bapt. Ch., Chgo., 1959-65, First Bapt. Ch., Stillwater, Minn., 1965-74, Grace Bapt. Ch., Des Moines, 1974-79; dean of men, pastoral ministries instr. Grace Coll. of the Bible, Omaha, 1979—; bd. dirs. Conservative Bapt. Fgn. Mission Soc., Wheaton, Ill., 1968-74; pres., bd. dirs. Sunday Sch. Assn., Des Moines, 1975-79; chmn. pastors fellowship Conservative Bapt. Assn. Iowa, 1970-72. Juvenile ct. chaplain Washington County Ct. Systems, Minn., 1967-72; chaplain Ho. of Reps., State of Minn., St. Paul, 1972. Recipient Seal of State of Minn. for dedication and service to Stillwater community and state, 1973. Republican. Avocations; fishing; reading. Home: 1517 S 8th St Omaha NE 68108 Office: Grace Coll of the Bible 1515 S 10th St Omaha NE 68108

SANDERS, JACK THOMAS, religious studies educator; b. Grand Prairie, Tex., Feb. 28, 1935; s. Eula Thomas and Mildred Madge (Parish) S.; m. M. Patricia Chism, Aug. 9, 1959 (dec. Oct. 1973); 1 son, Collin Thomas; m. Susan Elizabeth Plass, Mar. 3, 1979. B.A., Tex. Wesleyan Coll., 1956; M.Div., Emory U., 1960; Ph.D., Claremont Grad. Sch., 1963; postgrad., Eberhard-Karls U., Tuebingen, Germany, 1963-64. Asst. prof. Emory U., Atlanta, 1964-67, Garrett Theol Sem., Evanston, Ill., 1967-68, McCormick Theol. Sem., Chgo., 1968-69; assoc. prof. U. Oreg., Eugene, 1969-75, prof., 1975—, head dept. religious studies, 1973-80, 85-90. Author: The New Testament Christological Hymns, 1971, Ethics in the New Testament, 1975, 2d edit., 1986, Ben Sira and Demotic Wisdom, 1983, The Jews in Luke-Acts, 1987; editor: Gospel Origins and Christian Beginnings, 1990, Gnosticism and the Early Christian World, 1990; mem. editorial bd.: Jour. Bibl. Lit., 1977-83. Mem. policy bd. Dept. Higher Edn. Nat. Council Chs., N.Y.C., 1971-73. NDEA grad. study fellow, 1960-63; Fulbright Commn. fellow, 1963-64; Am. Council Learned Socs. travel grantee, 1981; NEH fellow, 1983-84. Mem. Studiorum Novi Testamenti Soc., World Union Jewish Studies, Religion and Ethics Inst., Soc. Bibl. Lit. (regional sec. 1969-76, sabbatical research award 1976-77), AAUP (chpt. pres. 1981-82), Archeol. Inst. Am. (chpt. pres. 1988-89), Soc. for Sci. Study of Religion, Assn. for Sociology Religion. Democrat. Home: 390 E 50th Ave Eugene OR 97405 Office: Dept Religious Studies U Oreg Eugene OR 97403

SANDERS, JAMES ALVIN, minister, biblical studies educator; b. Memphis, Nov. 28, 1927; s. Robert E. and Sue (Black) S.; m. Dora Cargille, June 30, 1951; 1 son, Robin David. BA magna cum laude, Vanderbilt U., 1948, BD with honors, 1951; student, U. Paris, 1950-51; PhD, Hebrew Union Coll., 1955; DLitt, Acadia U., 1973; STD, U. Glasgow, 1975; DHL, Coe Coll., 1988, Hebrew Union Coll., 1988. Ordained teacher Presbyn. Ch., 1955; instr. French Vanderbilt U., 1948-49; faculty Colgate Rochester Div. Sch., 1954-65, assoc. prof., 1957-60, Joseph B. Hoyt prof. O.T. interpretation, 1960-65; prof. O.T. Union Theol. Sem., N.Y.C., 1965-70, Auburn prof. Bibl. studies, 1970-77; adj. prof. Columbia, N.Y.C., 1966-77; prof. Bibl. studies Sch. Theology and Grad. Sch., Claremont, Calif., 1977—; ann. prof. Jerusalem Sch. of Am. Schs. Oriental Research, 1961-62; fellow Ecumenical Inst., Jerusalem, 1972-73, 85; Ayer lectr., 1971, 79, Shaffer lectr., 1972, Fondren lectr., 1975, Currie lectr., 1976, McFadin lectr., 1979, Colwell lectr., 1979; guest lectr. U. Fribourg, Switzerland, 1981, 90, Hebrew Union Coll., 1982, Oral Roberts U., 1982, Tulsa U., 1982, Ind. U., 1982, Coe Coll., 1983, Garrett Sem., 1984, Pepperdine U., 1985, Western Sem., 1985, Bethany Sem., 1986; lectr. Union Sem. Sesquicentennial, 1987, U. Wis., 1987, U. Chgo., 1987; Gray lectr. Duke U., 1988; guest lectr. Notre Dame U., Georgetown U., Tex. Christian U., 1989, Alexander Robertson lectr. U. Glasgow, 1990-91; assocs. program lectr. Smithsonian, 1990; mem. internat. O.T. text critical com. United Bible Socs., 1969—; exec. officer Ancient Bibl. Manuscript Ctr. for Preservation and Research, 1977-80, pres., 1980—; Gustafson lectr. United Theol. Sem., 1991. Author: Suffering as Divine Discipline in the Old Testament and Post-Biblical Judaism, 1955, The Old Testament in the Cross, 1961, The Psalms Scroll of Qumran Cave 11, 1965, The Dead Sea Psalms Scroll, 1967, Near Eastern Archaeology in the Twentieth Century, 1970, Torah and Canon, 1972, 74, Identité de la Bible, 1975, God Has a Story Too, 1979, Canon and Community, 1984, From Sacred Story to Sacred Text, 1987; also numerous articles; mem. editorial bd. Jour. Bibl. Lit., 1970-76, Jour. for Study Judaism, Bibl. Theology Bull., Interpretation, 1973-78, Rev. Standard Version Bible Com. Trustee Am. Schs. Oriental Research. Fulbright grantee, 1950-51, Lilly Endowment grantee, 1981, NEH grantee, 1980, 91-92; Lefkowitz and Rabinowitz interfaith fellow, 1951-53, Rockefeller fellow, 1953-54, 85, Guggenheim fellow, 1961-62, 72-73, Human Scis. Rsch. fellow, 1989. Mem. Soc. Bibl. Lit. and Exegesis (pres. 1977-78), Phi Beta Kappa, Phi Sigma Iota, Theta Chi Beta. Home: PO Box 593 Claremont CA 91711 Office: Ancient Bibl Manuscript Ctr PO Box 670 Claremont CA 91711

SANDERS, JOHN CLARKE, priest; m. Frances Jameson, 1955; children: Clarke, Scott, David. BBA in Pers. Mgmt., U. Tex., 1955; BD, Sem. of SW, Austin, Tex., 1955; STM cum laude, Va. Theol. Sem., 1969. Ordained priest Episcopal Ch., 1958. Victor Holy Trinity Ch., Port Neches, Tex., 1958-61, rector, 1961-63; rector St. James Ch., Houston, 1963-70, Christ Episcopal Ch., Shaker Heights, Ohio, 1975-86; dean St. John Cathedral, Wilmington, Del., 1970-75, St. Philip's Cathedral, Atlanta, 1986—; dean SE Conv., Diocese of Tex., 1963, mem. exec. bd., 1965-67, chmn. dept. society rels., 1965; chmn. Episcopal Loyalty Fund, East Harris County, Tex.; alumni trustee Sem. of SW, 1967-68; chmn. Episcopal Soc. Cultural and Racial Unity, 1964-65; chmn. area clergy Resources for Leadership in '70s Diocesan Fund Campaign; mem. exec. bd. Diocese of Del., 1970-75, co-chmn. dept. ministries, 1970, chmn. clergy support div., 1971-75; protestant chmn. clergy dialog group NCCJ, Wilmington;. Vice chmn. Mid County chpt. Am. Cancer Soc., 1960-63, Houston Housing Corp.; mem. governing bd. Negro Child Ctr., Houston, 1964-68; mem. steering com. Wilmington Housing Alliance; bd. dirs. Early Childhood Enrichment Ctr., Ohio, Shaker Heights (Ohio) Youth Ctr. Recipient Disting. Congregation award Living Chs., 1965; Rossiter scholar Bexley Hall, 1982. Mem. Cleve. Alathean Soc. (chmn.). Home: 2799 Andrews Dr NW Atlanta GA 30305 Office: St Philip's Cathedral 2744 Peachtree Rd NW Atlanta GA 30363

SANDERS, MARVIN CECIL, theologian; b. New Edinburg, Ark., Apr. 26, 1934; s. Walter Earnest and Ruby Lee (Chambers) S.; m. Geraldine McClellan, Dec. 20, 1952; children: Randy, Ray. BA, Free Will Bapt. Bible Coll., Nashville, 1959, Ark. Tech. U., 1964; ThD, Trinity Theol. Seminary, Newburgh, Ind., 1981. Ordained to ministry Bapt. Ch., 1953. Tchr. Warren (Ark.) High Sch., 1965-81, Hillsdale Free Will Bapt. Coll., Moore, Okla., 1981—; min. Free Will Bapt. Chs., 1952—. Author: The Future: An Amillennial Perspective, 1990, (with others) Basic Training, 1989. Democrat. Avocations: fishing, horseback riding, farming, deer hunting. Home: 1500 SE 8th Moore OK 73160 Office: Hillsdale Free Will Bapt Coll 3701 S I 35 Moore OK 73153

SANDERS, MAVIS, religious press association administrator. Pres. Evang. Press Assn., Wheaton, Ill. Office: Evang Press Assn Scripture Press 1825 College Ave Wheaton IL 60187*

SANDERS, SHERRY CHRISTINE, lay worker; b. Wolcott, Ind., Dec. 25, 1950; d. Beverly Jean S. Cert., New Tribes Bible Inst., Waukesha, Wis., 1971, New Tribes Bible Inst., Fredonia, Wis., 1972, New Tribes Lang. Inst., Camdenton, Mo., 1973. Fin. office clk. New Tribes Bible Inst., Waukesha, 1975, book store clk., 1975-85, rec. sec., 1975, dean of women, 1976-79; women's counselor Pacific Garden Mission, Chgo., 1979; Dom tribe-bush missionary Simbu Province, Papua New Guinea, 1982-84; youth sponsor, girl's and ladies' Bible Study tchr. 1st Christian Ch., Brook, Ind., 1987—. Home: PO Box 325 Brook IN 47922 Office: 1st Christian Ch PO Box 446 105 W Broadway Brook IN 47922

SANDERS, TERRELL C., JR., academic administrator. Pres. Nazarene Theol. Sem., Kansas City, Mo. Office: Nazarene Theol Sem 1700 E Meyer Blvd Kansas City MO 64131*

SANDERS, WILLIAM EVAN, bishop; b. Natchez, Miss., Dec. 25, 1919; s. Walter Richard and Agnes Mortimer (Jones) S.; B.A., Vanderbilt U., 1942; B.D., U. of South, 1945, D.D., 1959; S.T.M., Union Theol. Sem., 1946; m. Kathryn Cowan Schaffer, June 25, 1951; 4 children. Curate St. Paul's Episcopal Ch., Chattanooga, 1945-46; asst. St. Mary's Cathedral, Memphis, 1946-48, dean, 1948-62; bishop coadjutor Tenn., Knoxville, after 1962, now bishop Eastern Tenn., 1985— Address: PO Box 3807 Knoxville TN 37917

SANDERSON, BRIAN KEITH, minister; b. Henderson, Ky., Dec. 17, 1960; s. J.W. and Linda Sue (Futtrell) S.; m. Laurie Lynn Clayton, June 26, 1986; children: Clayton Alan, Kendra Joy. B of Church Music, Union U., Jackson, Tenn., 1982; M of Church Music, So. Bapt. Theol. Sem., Louisville, 1985. Ordained to ministry Bapt. Ch., 1985. Min. music Salem Bapt. Ch., Henning, Tenn., 1980-81; min. music and youth Mercer (Tenn.) Bapt. Ch., 1981-82, Robards (Ky.) Bapt. Ch., 1982-85, So. Heights Bapt. Ch., Lexington, Ky., 1985-88, Audubon Bapt. Ch., Henderson, 1988—; mem. Common Call, Henderson, 1989—. Mem. Lions (greeter 1989-91), Lambda Chi Alpha, Phi Mu Alpha. Republican. Home: 101 N Bob-o-Link Henderson KY 42420 Office: Audubon Bapt Ch 3440 Zion Rd Henderson KY 42420

SANDERSON, RON EUGENE, minister; b. Marion, Ohio, Sept. 15, 1939; s. James Calvin and Olive Mae (Upton) S.; m. Linda Lou Clark, May 4, 1958; children: Terry L., Randy E., Timothy A., Tracey Renee Sanderson Ball. B in Ministry, Internat. Bible Inst., Orlando, Fla., 1984; postgrad., Moody Bible Inst., Chgo., 1988. Ordained to ministry Gen. Assn. of Regular Bapt. Chs. Sr. pastor 1st Bapt. Ch., Spencerville, Ohio, 1980-87, Kings Creek Bapt. Ch., Urbana, Ohio, 1987-88, Struthers (Ohio) Bapt. Tabernacle, 1988—. Recipient Town and Country award Ohio Bapt. Conv., 1986. Republican. Home: 299 Elm St Struthers OH 44471

SANDERSON, STANLEY RAY, minister; b. Yuba City, Calif., Dec. 16, 1950; s. Walter Columbus and Faithe Elaine (Edwards) S.; m. Kathleen L. Looney, Mar. 11, 1973; children: Aaron, Sarah, Seth. BA, Harding Coll., Searcy, Ark., 1974; MS, Abilene Christian U., 1982. Ordained to ministry Ch. of Christ, 1975. Youth minister Ch. of Christ, Eugene, Oreg., 1975-77; pulpit minister Ch. of Christ, Keizer, Oreg., 1977-81; minister of evangelism Ch. of Christ, Texas City, Tex., 1981-84; pulpit minister Ch. of Christ, Springfield, Oreg., 1984—. Bd. dirs. Montessori Learning Ctr., Texas City, 1981-84, Camp Dorena, Eugene, 1987-88; chaplain Boy Scouts Am., Springfield, 1988—, com. chmn., 1991—. Office: N Springfield Ch of Christ 1305 N 5th St Springfield OR 97477

SANDFORD, JOHN LOREN, minister; b. Joplin, Mo., July 23, 1929; s. George Oliver and Zelma Edith (Potter) S.; Paula Ann Bowman, Jan. 12, 1951; children: Loren, Amilee, Mark, John, Timothy, Andrea. BA, Drury Coll., 1951; MDiv, Chgo. Theol. Sem., 1958. Ordained to ministry United Ch. of Christ, 1958. Pastor First Congl. United Ch. of Christ, Streator, Ill., 1956-61, Council Grove, Kans., 1961-65, Wallace, Idaho, 1965-73; writer, tchr., counselor Elijah House, Inc., Coeur D'Alene, Idaho, 1973—; tchr. Sch. of Pastoral Care, Whitinsville, Mass., 1961-70, Camps Farthest Out, 1961—. Author: (with Paula Sandford) The Elijah Task, 1977, Restoring the Christian Family, 1979, The Transformation of the Inner Man, 1983, Healing the Wounded Spirit, 1985, Why Some Christians Commit Adultery, 1989, The Renewal of the Mind, 1991. Home: E 2906 Cambridge Dr Hayden Lake ID 83835 Office: Elijah House Inc S 1000 Richards Rd Post Falls ID 83854

SANDIFER, JAMES STEPHEN, minister; b. Shreveport, La., June 13, 1948; s. James Wyatt Jr. and Virginia Rose (Seaton) S.; m. Jo Elaine Butler, May 12, 1970; children: Kenneth, Cody. BA, Abilene Christian U., 1970, MA, 1972. Ordained to ministry Ch. of Christ, 1970. Minister Ch. of Christ, Skelmersdale, England, 1972-77, S.W. Cen. Ch. of Christ, Houston, 1977—; producer audio-visual materials Photomedia, Houston, 1977—; mem. ministry coun. Sta. KSBJ Community Christian Radio, Houston, 1980—. Author: Deacons: Male & Female?, 1989; contbr. articles to profl. jours. Chmn. Houston unit clergy com. Am. Cancer Soc., 1984—, chmn. div. scholarship com. for clergy, Austin, Tex., 1990—; cabinet mem. Houston Campaign for the Homeless, United Way, 1988—; dir. Human Resources Devel. Found., Houston, 1989—. Recipient Ministry Recognition, African Christian Hosp. Found., 1982, Outstanding Contbn. award Assn. Multi-Image, Internat., 1986. Mem. S.W. Ministerial Assn., Canon Profl. Svcs. Republican. Office: SW Cen Ch of Christ 4011 W Bellfort Houston TX 77025 *The challenge is greater than ever for Christians to live the radical life of Jesus in the hostile pagan world we call America. Rather than conforming doctrine to the American dream, the minister must allow God to use him as prophet and priest in the sanctified community regardless of the risks.*

SANDIFER, MARK M., minister; b. Jackson, Miss., Oct. 17, 1956; s. C.A. and Dorthy Ann (Magee) S.; m. Deborah J. Lyons, June 4, 1988. BS, Miss. Coll., 1986; MRE, New Orleans Bapt. Theol. Sem., 1988. Sun. sch. dir. Harrisville (Miss.) Bapt. Ch., 1978-81; min. of activities Calvary Bapt. Ch., Jackson, 1982-84; min. of youth Parkway Bapt. Ch., Metainie, La., 1986-87; min. of edn. Pearson Bapt. Ch., Pearl, Miss., 1988—; youth dir. Rankin Assn., Pearl, 1990—, records chmn. 1989-90. Mem. L.C.H.C. (pres. 1985-89). Office: Pearson Bapt Ch 151 S Pearson Rd Pearl MS 39208

SANDLER, JOSEPH BERNARD, book service executive; b. Bklyn, Mar. 18, 1937; s. Nathan and Pauline (Sklar) S.; m. Paula Rimler, Jan. 8, 1976; 1 child Elisa. B.A., Bklyn. Coll., 1959; A. Applied Sci. Voorhees Tech. Inst., 1964. Prodn. Supr. Union of Am. Hebrew Congregations, N.Y.C., 1964-69; prod. mgr. Grosset & Dunlap, N.Y.C., 1969-82; dir. book service United Synagogue of Am., N.Y.C., 1982—. Vice pres. Congregation chevra Torah, Bklyn., 1983—. Democrat. Jewish. Office: United Synagogue Am 155 Fifth Ave New York NY 10010

SANDLIN, S. Z., minister; b. Lubbock, Tex., Aug. 10, 1949; s. Horace E. and Helen B. (Zeh) S.; m. Cheryl Anne Colclazer, July 17, 1971; childrenn, Summer, Suzanna. BBA, Tex. Tech. U., 1971; MDiv, Southwestern Bapt. Theol. Sem., Ft. Worth, 1975, D Ministry, 1980. Ordained to ministry So. Bapt. Conv., 1975. Dir. Bapt. Student Union Kilgore (Tex.) Coll., Panola (Tex.) Coll., 1974-76; pastor Midway Bapt. Ch., Big Spring, Tex., 1976-78, South Plains Bapt. Ch., Levelland, Tex., 1978-80, Faith Bapt. Ch., Wichita Falls, Tex., 1980-90, 1st Bapt. Ch., Beaumont, Tex., 1990—; mem. nominating com. Bapt. Gen. Conv. Tex., 1988-90. Bd. dirs. Wichita Falls YMCA, 1982-84; mem. So. Bapt. Conv., Wichita-Archer-Clay Bapt. Assn. (chmn. student work com., 1980-82, pers. com. 1983—). Recipient Order of Arrow Boy Scouts Am., 1967. Home: 1155 Brandywine Beaumont TX 77706 Office: 1st Bapt Ch Box 1352 Beaumont TX 77704

SANDOVAL, MOISES, magazine editor, writer; b. Sapello, N.Mex., Mar. 29, 1930; s. Jose Eusebio and Amada (Perea) S.; m. Penelope Ann Gartman, Nov. 5, 1955; children—Margaret Ann, Michael Joseph, Rose Patricia, James Christopher, Mary Ruth. B.S. in Journalism, Marquette U., 1955; Cert. in Internat. Reporting, Columbia U., 1964. Asst. editor Peshtigo (Wis.) Times, 1957-58; state editor Dubuque (Iowa) Telegraph Herald, 1958-59; investigative reporter Albuquerque Tribune, 1960-63; sr. editor Pflaum Pubs., Dayton, Ohio, 1964-70; mng. editor Maryknoll Mag., NY, 1970-79, editor, 1979-91. Author: (with others) Puebla and Beyond, 1979; editor: Fronteras: History of U.S. Hispanic Church, 1983, Revista Maryknoll, 1980—; contbr. articles to profl. jours. U.S. coordinator Commn. of Hist. Studies of Ch. in Ams., Mexico City, 1982—. Served to 1st lt. U.S. Army, 1955-57. Ford Found. fellow, 1963-64; Alicia Patterson fellow, 1977-78. Mem. Cath. Press Assn. U.S. and Can. (bd. dirs. 1977-86), Assn. for Rights for Caths. Avocations: tennis; wood-working. Office: Maryknoll Mag Maryknoll NY 10545

SANDQUIST, THEODORE RICHARD, minister; b. Beloit, Wis., Aug. 8, 1947; s. Richard Olaf and Isabell Elanore (Carlson) S.; m. Dawn Kristin Geckler, July 17, 1971; children: Jason Samuel, Jon-Mark Philip, Jordan Scott, Jena Dawn. BA in Anthropology, Wheaton Coll., 1969. Ordained minister. Dir., v.p. Jesus People, Inc., New Song Records and Pub., Freeville, N.Y., 1972-79; minister of the gospel Covenant Love Community Ch., Freeville, 1972—; pres., pub. Psalm of Life Ministries, Freeville, 1984—; owner, operator Lion of Judah Music, Freeville, Nashville, 1980—. Republican. Avocations: mountain climbing, tennis, racquetball, squash, golf. Office: Covenant Love Community 1768 Dryden Rd Freeville NY 13068

SANDS, CHARLES DOUGLAS, evangelism coordinator; b. Wilmington, Del., Aug. 30, 1964; s. Charles Douglas Sands and Barbara (Fogg) Sands Reynolds. Student in Theology, Grace Bible Sch., 1988. Ministerial aide Evang. Spiritfilled Ch. Am., Phila., 1985-88, coord. Evangelism, 1989—. Author: The Lord's Song, 1985. Republican. Avocations: fishing, reading, skiing. Office: Evang Spiritfilled Ch Am 4205 Spruce St Philadelphia PA 19104

SANDS, RANDALL LEE, minister; b. Centralia, Ill., Feb. 9, 1962; s. Jimmie Dean and Helen Joyce (Clopton) S.; m. Barbara Lynn Phillips, Oct. 2, 1981; children: Matthew Ryan, Mack Randall. BA, Greenville (Ill.) Coll., 1990. Ordained to ministry Free Meth. Ch., 1990. Assoc. pastor Free Meth. Ch., Salem, Ill., 1985-87; pastor Free Meth. Ch., Hillsboro, Ill., 1987—; co-coord. Hillsboro Share, 1989—. Home: 202 Walnut St Hillsboro IL 62049 Office: Free Meth Ch 202 Walnut St Hillsboro IL 62049-1119

SANDSTROM, MARK RAND, minister; b. Glendale, Calif., Dec. 31, 1954; s. Morris Rand and Margaret Genevive (Hogendyk) S.; m. Pamela Jean MacArthur, Sept. 4, 1976. BS with honors, Northwest Christian Coll., 1980; MDiv, Sch. Theology, Claremont, Calif., 1985. Ordained to ministry Christian Ch. (Disciples of Christ), 1985. Pastor Franklin (Oreg.) Christian Ch., 1978-80; assoc. pastor Mt. Hollywood (Calif.) Congl. Ch., 1980-82; campus min. Pasadena (Calif.) City Coll., 1982-84; youth pastor 1st Christian Ch. (Disciples), Pasadena, 1982-85; assoc. min. 1st Christian Ch. (Disciples), Torrance, Calif., 1985-88; sr. min. Covina (Calif.) Christian Ch. (Disciples), 1988—; v.p. Hollywood Mins.' Assn., 1980-82; pres. South Bay Ecumenical Cluster, Torrance, 1986-87; bd. dirs. So. Calif. Ecumenical Coun., 1986-89. Bd. dirs. Hollywood-Wilshire Fair Housing , 1980-82; Calif. Parks Ministry, 1987—, Assn. for Retarded Citizens of San Gabriel Valle, El Monte, Calif., 1989—. Mem. Order of DeMolay (master councilor 1972), Masons. Home: 239 E Juanita Ave Glendora CA 91740 Office: Covina Christian Ch 240 S Grand Ave Covina CA 91724

SANDY, D. BRENT, minister, religion educator; b. Lebanon, Pa., Mar. 19, 1947; s. A. Rollin and Omega V. (Hartman) S.; m. Cheryl J. Ackerly, June 26, 1971; children: Jason Brent, Jaron Chad. BA, Grace Coll., 1969; postgrad., SUNY, Binghamton, 1969-70; MDiv with honors, Grace Sem., 1970-73; PhD, Duke U., 1977. Ordained to ministry Fellowship of Grace Brethren Chs., 1988. Min. music Calvary Bapt. Tabernacle, Vestal, N.Y., 1969-70, Edgemont Bapt. Ch., Durham, N.C., 1973-77, Ghent Brethren Ch., Roanoke, Va., 1988—; asst. prof. Grace Coll. and Sem., Winona Lake, Ind., 1977-82, assoc. prof., 1982-86, prof., 1986-88; prof. N.T. Liberty U., Lynchburg, Va., 1988—; vis. scholar U. Mich., Ann Arbor, 1984; participant Conf. on Teaching in Ancient World NEH, Nashville, 1982, Judaism and Early Christianity Seminar, NEH Duke U., 1982. Author: The Production and Use of Vegetable Oils in Ptolemaic Egypt, 1989; contbr. articles to profl. jours., chpts. in books. Grad. fellow Duke U., 1977. Mem. Soc. Bibl. Lit., Evang. Theol. Soc., Am. Philos. Assn., Am. Soc. Papyrology, Am. Classical League, Assn. Ancient Historians, Assn. Internat. de Papyrologues. Republican. Home: 103 Sparrow Dr Lynchburg VA 24502 Office: Liberty U PO 20000 Lynchburg VA 24506

SANG, BARRY RAY, religion educator; b. Chgo., Dec. 4, 1951; s. Charles Ray and Elizabeth Grace (Stone) S.; m. Kathy Elizabeth Hanna, Aug. 16, 1980. BA, Carroll Coll., Waukesha, 1974; MDiv, Colgate Rochester Theol. Sem., 1977; M.Phil., Drew U., Madison, N.J., 1981; PhD, Drew U., 1983. Ordained to ministry, Am. Bapt. Chs., USA, 1977. Asst. minister Mt. Lebanon Bapt. Ch., Pitts., 1977-79; lectr. Drew U. Coll. of L.A., Madison, N.J., 1981, 83; instr. Drew Theol. Sem., Madison, 1982; landscape crew Woodfield Gardens Apts., Rolling Meadows, Ill., 1984-85; asst. prof. religion Catawba Coll., Salisbury, N.C., 1985—. Tchr., mem. Milford Hills Bapt. Ch., Salisbury, N.C., 1986—; mem. Salisbury Concert Choir. Drew U. teaching fellow, 1981. Mem. Soc. Bibl. Lit., Nat. Archery Assn. Democrat. Baptist. Avocations: archery, swimming, French horn, choral ensembles, gardening. Home: 117 Larch Rd Salisbury NC 28144 Office: Catawba Coll 2300 W Innes St Salisbury NC 28144

SANGARE, AUGUST, archbishop. Archbishop of Bamako Roman Cath. Ch., Mali. Office: Archeveche, BP 298, Bamako Mali*

SANGSTER, VERLEY GENE, youth ministry executive; b. South Bend, Ind., Nov. 20, 1933; m. Pearlean Barton; children: Michael, Anthony, Scott, Dimitri, Vanessa, Vera, Vermella, Darryl. Student, Holy Cross Jr. Coll., South Bend, Ivy Tech, South Bend, Gabriel Richard Inst., Cen. Theol. Sem. Ordained Evang. Ch. Alliance, 1976, Austin Bapt. Ch., 1979. Cons. City Planning Assocs., Inc., Mishawaha, Ind., 1972-73; area dir. Young Life Chgo. (Ill.) Cen., 1973-79; nat. urban dir. Young Life, Chgo., Denver, 1979-89; v.p. U.S. field ministries Young Life, Denver, 1989—; chmn. World Vision Nat. Urban and Rural Ministry Project Adv. Coun., Monrovia, Calif., 1989—; bd. dirs. The Navigators, Colorado Springs, 1991—. Chmn. bd. dirs., Denver (Colo.) Broncos Youth Fedn., 1987—. Recipient Cert. of Gratitude and Achievement, City of South Bend, Ind., 1972; recognized for outstanding svc. to black youth in Am., African Meth. Episcopal Ch., Christian Edn. Dept., 1989. Office: Young Life 2801 E Colfax Ave GL6 Denver CO 80206

SANJARE, AUGUST, archbishop. Ordained priest Roman Cath. Ch. Archbishop of Bamako (Mali) Roman Cath. Ch. *

SANKS, CHARLES RANDOLPH, JR., psychotherapist, clergyman; b. Yonkers, N.Y., Feb. 14, 1928; s. Charles Randolph and Myrtle Elizabeth (Bunn) S.; m. Jacquelyn Gibson, Nov. 11, 1949; children—Charlene Cynthia Saunders, Valeri Ann. B.A. cum laude, Stetson U., 1956; B.Div., Southeastern Sem., 1960; M.Th., Union Sem., 1961; postgrad., U. Salamanca, Spain, 1975; D.Ministry, Wesley Theol. Sem., 1977. Ordained to ministry Baptist Ch., 1957. Minister Judson Meml. Bapt. Ch., Fayetteville, N.C., 1957-60; interim minister First Bapt. Ch. of South Miami, Fla., 1961-62, Sunset Heights Bapt. Ch., Hialeah, Fla., 1962; sr. minister Starling Ave. Bapt. Ch., Martinsville, Va., 1963-69; assoc. pastor 1st Bapt. Ch., Washington, 1969-82, minister to Pres. U.S., 1976-80; developer ministry to community foster-care patients, 1975; dir. Pastoral Counseling Ctr. Greater Marlboro, Md., 1982-87 ; sr. counselor Washington Pastoral Counseling Service, 1982—; dir. clin. mgmt. Washington Pastoral Counseling Service, 1988—; ptnr. Pastoral Psychotherapy Assocs., Washington, 1984—; fellow Am. Assn. Pastoral Counselors, 1984—; trainer Journeyman Program, Fgn. Mission Bd., So. Bapt. Convention, 1968; mem. exec. com. D.C. Bapt. Conv., 1971-77; leader, speaker in liturgics and worship N.C. Bapt. Conv. Conf., 1972, 75; cons. Pastoral Psychotherapy Assocs., Washington, 1981-84; lectr. on worship and liturgics So. Bapt. Theol. Sem., Louisville, 1978; lectr. Stetson U., Deland, Fla., 1978, So. Ecumenical Conf., Atlanta, 1978. Bd. dirs. Uplift House, Washington, 1970-73, Day Care Ctr., Martinsville, Va., 1963-69, Big Brother Orgn. and Sheltered Workshop, Martinsville, Va., 1963-69. Served to cpl. USMC, 1946-49. Fellow Interpreters' House, Lake Junaluska, N.C., 1968-79; guest Oxford U., Eng., 1981. Mem. Am. Digestive Disease Soc. (bd. dirs. 1979-87). Democrat. Baptist. Avocations; travel; horseback riding; music; art. Home: 1090 Larkspur Terr Rockville MD 20850

SANNEH, LAMIN, religion educator; married; 2 children. MA in Arabic and Islamic Studies, U. Birmingham, Eng., 1968; postgrad., Near East Sch. Theology, Beirut, 1968-69; PhD in African Islamic History, U. London, 1974. Resident tutor Ctr. for Study of Islam and Christianity, Ibadan, Nigeria, 1969-71; vis. scholar U. Sierra Leone, Freetown, 1974-75; lectr. U. Ghana, Legon, 1975-78, U. Aberdeen, Scotland, 1978-81; asst. prof., then assoc. prof. history of religion Harvard U., Cambridge, Mass., 1981-89; prof., chmn. Coun. on African Studies Yale U., New Haven, 1989—; cons. World Coun. Chs., 1974-79, The Africans TV series, PBS, 1986, Program on Christian-Muslim Rels. in Africa, 1988—, Prof. Lamin Sanneh Found., Banjul, The Gambia; instr. San Francisco Theol. Sem., San Anselmo, Calif., 1987, Iliff Sch. Theology, Denver, 1988; Disting. Staley Christian lectr. Mennonite Brethren Bible Coll., Winnipeg, Can., 1988; lectr. Princeton (N.J.) Theol. Sem., 1988; guest lectr. Haverford (Pa.) Coll., 1988; Mars lectr. Northwestern U., 1988; Spriggs lectr. Protestant Episcopal Theol. Sem., Alexandria, Va., 1990; Cullum lectr. Augusta Coll., U. Ga., 1990; participant various acad. confs. Author: West African Christianity: The Religious Impact, 1983, Translating the Message: The Missionary Impact on Culture, 1989, The Jakhanke Muslim Clerics: A Religious & Historical Study of Islam in

Senegambia (c. 1250-1905), 1990; also articles; co-editor Jour. Religion in Africa, 1979-84; mem. adv. bd. Studies in Interreligious Dialogue; editor-at-large The Christian Century; contbg. editor Internat. Bull. Missionary Rsch. Recipient award Theol. Edn. Fund, 1971-74, award U. London, 1972, Carnegie Truste of Univs. of Scotland, 1980. Mem. Internat. Acad. Union (consultative mem. Africa com.), Ecumenical Assn. African Theologians (exec. com.), Royal African Soc. Home: 47 Morris St Hamden CT 06517 Office: Yale U Div Sch 409 Prospect Sch New Haven CT 06510

SANO, ROY I., bishop. Ordained to ministry United Meth. Ch., later consecrated bishop; appointed Bishop Rocky Mountain Conf., United Meth. Ch., Denver. Office: Rocky Mt Conf United Meth Ch 2200 S University Blvd Denver CO 80210

SAN PEDRO, ENRIQUE, bishop; b. Havana, Cuba, Mar. 9, 1926; s. Enrique and Maria Antonia (Fornaguera) San Pedro. MA in Classical Lit., Coll. St. Estanislao, Spain, 1947; Licentiate philosophy, Univ. Pontificia de Comillas, Santander, Spain, 1950; Licentiate theology, Leopold-Franzens Univ., Innsbruck, Austria, 1958, STD, 1965; postgrad., Franz -Joseph Univ., Vienna, Austria, 1958-59, 60-64, Pontificio Instituto Biblico, Rome, 1963. Ordained priest Roman Cath. Ch., 1957. Lectr. Hebrew Sch. Theology, Colegio de St. Francisco de Borja, Barcelona, Spain, 1963-64; prof. Old Testament St. Pius X Pontifical Coll., Dalat, Vietnam, 1965-75, asst. dean studies, sec. to faculty theology, 1967-72, editor theology digest, 1968-72; prof. Holy Scripture Pacific Regional Sem., Suva, Fiji, 1978-80, head libr., 1979; prof. Holy Scripture and Homiletics St. Vincent de Paul Sem., Boynton Beach, Fla., 1981-85; aux. bishop Diocese of Galveston-Houston, 1986—; titular bishop Siccesi, 1986—; bd. dirs. bishop's com. priestly formation, Nat. Cath. Conf. of Bishops-U.S. Cath. Conf., also liaison for Vietnamese migration and refugee svcs., chmn. Hispanic Affairs Com.; cons. Bishop's com. on liturgy, sub-com. Hispanic liturgy; mem. exec. bd. Nat. Cath. Conf. Interracial Justice, Nat. Adv. Coun.; lectr. Loyola U., Chgo., one semester, 1963-64, St. Thomas Univ., Houston, 1986-87; vis. prof. Sem. de Santo Tomás, Santo Domingo, Dominican Republic, 1976-77, 80-81; instr. permanent deacons program Archdiocese Miami, Fla., 1981-85; guest lectr. Pacific Theol. Coll., Suva, 1978-80; tchr. seminars and courses, Fiji, French Polynesia, Am. Samoa, Miami, Fla., 1978-85; participant Premier Cong. Cath. Internat. des Etudes Biblique, Louvain, Belgium, Congs. Internat. Soc. Study Old Testament, Oxford, Eng., Bonn, Fed. Republic Germany, Uppsala, Sweden. Author: Introducción a la Literatura Profética, 1982, Diez Años Dialogando, 1989, also articles in profl. publs., book revs. Mem. Mayor's AIDS Alliance Adv. Bd., Houston/Harris County; mem. Hispanic AIDS Coalition, Houston Area HIV Health Svcs. Planning Coun., crackdown edn. com. Houston Ind. Sch. Dist., Greater Houston Coalition for Ednl. Excellence, U. Houston Pres.'s Adv. Coun.; trustee Inst. of Religion, Tex. Med. Ctr., Inst. Hispanic Culture Bd. Voc. Guidance Svcs.; bd. dirs. CASA-Child Advocates, Inc. Mem. Hispanic Inst., Asia Soc., Nat. Trust for Historic Preservation, Vatican Libr. First Hispanic bishop appointed to Diocese of Galveston-Houston. Home: 1111 Pierce Ave Houston TX 77002 Office: 1700 San Jacinto St PO Box 907 Houston TX 77001

SANSOUCIE, LARRY ALLEN, pastor, theology educator; b. DeSoto, Mo., Dec. 23, 1951; s. John Joseph and Eileen Mae (Smith) S.; m. Cheryl Annette Burton, July 21, 1979. BS in Physics, U. Mo., Rolla, 1973; MDiv, Chgo. Theol. Sem., 1978; DMin, Christian Theol. Sem., 1983. Ordained minister United Ch. of Christ, 1979. Asst. pastor Living Peace Bapt. Ch., Chgo., 1974-77; supply preacher United Ch. Christ churches, Ill. and Mich., 1977-78; pastor Waterford United Ch. Christ, Goshen, 1978-79, Plymouth United Ch. Christ, Dunkirk, Ind., 1979-83, Pleasant Valley United Ch. Christ, Osceola, Ind., 1983-87, Nashville United Ch. of Christ, West Milton, Ohio, 1987—; bd. dirs. Ind.-Ken. Conf. United Ch. of Christ, 1978-79. Author: The Ecumenical Lectionary: Theological Foundations, Liturgical Use, Congregational Usefulness, 1985, Dandelions in the Castle: An Essay on Subjectivity in Science and Technology, 1988; contbr. articles to profl. jours. Vol. various hosps., Chgo., Ind., nursing homes, Ind. 1979—; coordinator Plymouth Community Concerns Fund, Dunkirk, Ind., 1980-83; mem. religious arts steering com. United Religious Community St. Joseph County, Ind., 1983-86; active Ind.-Ky. Conf. United Ch. of Christ, 1978-87, mem. Ch. in Soc. commn., 1979-83, peace and justice task force, 1981-83, exec. com. Ea. Assn., 1982-83; active Ohio Conf. United Ch. of Christ, 1987—, at-large mem. Christian Nurture Commn., 1988—. Mem. Jay County Chaplains, Dunkirk Ministerial Assn. (pres. 1979-83), Osceola Ministerial Assn., Phi Theta Kappa, Kappa Mu Epsilon, Sigma Pi Sigma. Avocations: geneology, aerobics, travel, writing, walking. Home and Office: 4665 West State Rd 571 West Milton OH 45383

SANTUYO, RICARDO TAYTAY, business educator, deacon; b. Lauigan, Iloilo, The Philippines, Aug. 19, 1931; came to U.S., 1955; s. Cipriano Serilla and Crisanta Dangan (Taytay) S.; m. Rufina Padua Cruz, Jan. 14, 1962; 1 child, Raymond. BS in Commerce, U. San Agustin, Iloilo City, The Philippines, 1954; postgrad., U. East, Manila, The Philippines, 1971; MSA, U. Guam, 1973; EdD, Western Mich. U., 1979. Ordained Deacon Diocese of Guam, 1974. Acctg. clerk to acct. Masdelco Inc., Agana, Guam, 1955-60, analyst, transportation specialist, 1960-68; auditor, acct., supr. Government of Guam, Agana, 1968-71, 73-78; acct., office mgr. Trans-Asia Inc., Tamuning, 1972-73; auditor U.S. Naval Air Station, Fallon, Nev., 1980-81; instr. Western Mich. U., Kalamazoo, 1978-79, Long Beach (Calif.) Coll. Bus., 1981—, Long Beach City Coll., 1982—; instr. U. Guam, Mangilao, 1973-75, El Camino Coll., Torrance, Calif., 1982—, Golden State U., L.A., 1985-88. With Cursillos in Christianity, Agana, 1970-77, asst. spiritual dir., 1974-75, lay dir., 1976-77; v.p. Legion of Mary, Agana, 1975-77; deacon various dioceses Roman Cath. Ch., L.A., 1982-88, San Bernardino, Calif., 1989—, Agana, Guam, 1974-77, Kalamazoo, 1978-79. Mem. NEA, Calif. Tchrs. Assn. Republican. Roman Catholic. Avocations: hiking, cooking, reading. Home: 22914 Dracaea Ave Moreno Valley CA 92553 Office: Long Beach City Coll Dept Bus Adminstrn 455 E Artesia Blvd Long Beach CA 90805

SAPERSTEIN, HAROLD IRVING, retired rabbi; b. Troy, N.Y., Dec. 9, 1910; s. David and Rose (Lasker) S.; m. Marcia B. Rosenblum, Dec. 22, 1940; children: Marc Eli, David N. BA, Cornell U., 1931; M. Hebrew Letters, Jewish Inst. Religion, 1935; DHL (hon.), Hebrew Union Coll., 1960; D. Humane Letters (hon.), St. Francis Coll., 1972. Ordained rabbi, 1935. Rabbi Temple Emanuel, Lynbrook, N.Y., 1933-80; vis. rabbi West London Synagogue, 1980-81, 82-83; interim sr. rabbi Cen. Synagogue, N.Y.C., 1986-87, Congregation Rodeph Sholom, N.Y.C., 1989-90; rabbi emeritus Temple Emanuel, Lynbrook, 1980—; lectr. St. Francis Coll., Bklyn., 1977; pres. N.Y. Bd. Rabbis, N.Y.C., 1969-71, Assn. Reform Rabbis, N.Y.C., 1961-63; chmn. bd. dirs. Internat. Synagogue, Kennedy Airport, N.Y.C., 1975-85; bd. govs. Hebrew Union Coll.-Jewish Inst. Religion, 1954-58; del. World Zionist Congress, Geneva, 1939; chmn. N.Am. bd. World Union for Progressive Judaism, 1959-61. Contbr. articles to profl. publs. Trustee Franklin Hosp. Med. Ctr., Valley Stream, N.Y., 1978—; mem. legal grievance com. 10th Jud. Dist., State of N.Y., 1980-88. Maj. U.S. Army, 1943-46, ETO. Named Lynbrookman of Yr., 1977; street named in his honor Village of Lynbrook, 1980. Mem. Phi Beta Kappa. Home: 170 Hempstead Ave Malverne NY 11565

SAPERSTEIN, MARC ELI, religious history educator, rabbi; b. N.Y.C., Sept. 5, 1944; s. Harold Irving and Marcia Belle (Rosenblum) S.; m. Roberta Shapiro, June 17, 1970; children: Sara Michal, Adina Ruth. AB, Harvard U., 1966, PhD, 1977; student, Pembroke Coll., U. Cambridge, Eng., 1966-67; MA, Hebrew U., Jerusalem, 1971, Hebrew Union Coll., N.Y.C., 1972. Ordained rabbi, 1972. Lectr. in Hebrew lit. Harvard U., Cambridge, Mass., 1977-79; lectr. in Jewish studies Harvard U. Divinity Sch., 1979-81, asst. prof. Jewish studies, 1981-83, assoc. prof., 1983-86; Gloria M. Goldstein prof. Jewish history and thought Washington U., St. Louis, 1986—; rabbi Temple Beth David, Canton, Mass., 1973-86; mem. exec. bd. Cen. Conf. Am. Rabbis, 1985-87. Author: Decoding the Rabbis, 1980, Jewish Preaching, 1200-1800, 1989, Moments of Crisis in Jewish-Christian Relations, 1989, also articles. Fellow Charles & Julia Henry Fund, 1966-67, Am. Coun. Learned Socs., 1983-84, Inst. Advanced Studies Hebrew U., Jerusalem, 1989; Danforth Found. Kent fellow, 1973-77. Mem. Assn. Jewish Studies (bd. dirs. 1983—), Phi Beta Kappa. Home: 7445 Oxford Dr Saint Louis MO 63105 Office: Washington U Dept History Saint Louis MO 63130

SAPINSLEY, ELBERT LEE, rabbi; b. N.Y.C., Nov. 17, 1927; s. Robert Browning and Jesamine (Moayon) S.; m. Dorothy Kaufman, June 15, 1952 (div. July 1973); children: Jesamine Leah Sapinsley Schiltz, David Jay; m. Susan Melton Fowler, June 12, 1978; children: Mark Daniel Fowler, Dianna Fowler-Shupe. BS, U. Louisville, 1949; B of Hebrew Letters, Hebrew Union Coll., 1952, M of Hebrew Letters with honors in History, 1954, DD, 1979. Ordained rabbi, 1954. Rabbi Temple Hesed Abraham, Jamestown, N.Y., 1956-58, Temple Beth Sholom, Topeka, Kans., 1958-68; Hillel counselor Kans. State U., Manhattan, 1968-70; counselor No. Ill. U., DeKalb, Ill., 1970-73; rabbi Congregation Ahavath Sholom, Bluefield, W.Va., 1975—; chaplain VA Hosp., Topeka, 1958-70, Menninger Psychiat. Hosp., Topeka, 1964-66; vis. asst. prof. Kans. Univ. Sch. of Religion, Lawrence, 1960-65; instr. Hebrew, No. Ill. U., DeKalb, 1970-73; pres. Mid-Atlantic Region/Cen. Conf. of Am. Rabbis, 1986-88, sec., 2d v.p, 1982-86; mem. internat. exec. bd. Cen. Conf. Am. Rabbis, 1986-88. Contbg. author: Rabbis in Uniform, 1962; contbr. articles to profl. jours. Founder, chmn. Topeka Interfaith Coun. for Racial Justice, 1961; bd. dirs. Kans. Vocat. Rehab. Policy Planning Bd., 1966-68; founding mem., area chmn. Assn. of Reform Zionists of Am., 1978; bd. dirs. Greater Bluefield United Way, 1985. 1st lt. U.S. Army, 1954-56. Merrill grantee (twice), 1969. Mem. Bluefield Ministerial Assn. (pres. 1984-85), Greater Carolinas Assn. of Rabbis (sec. 1985-86), Rotary (bd. dirs. 1983-85), B'nai Brith, Phi Alpha Theta. Home and Office: PO Box 1240 Bluefield WV 24701

SAPP, CARL ROBERT, church consultant; b. McLeansboro, Ill., June 27, 1914; s. John Edla and Carrie Ethel (Marshall) S.; m. Dorothy Pearl Angle, Dec. 22, 1937; children: David Gordon, Jean Carolyn Sapp Ingram. AB, George Washington U., 1941; MA, Am. U., 1962; postgrad., So. Bapt. Theol. Sem., 1971. Min. edn. Providence Bapt. Ch., Vienna, Va., 1971-75; dir. dept. Christian edn. D.C. Bapt. Conv., Washington, 1977-83; ch. cons. Arlington, Va., 1966-71, 76-77, from 1983; chmn. edn. com. Va. Bapt. Gen. Bd., Richmond, 1967-68; 2d v.p. Bapt. Gen. Assn. Va., Richmond, 1967-68; trustee So. Bapt. Sunday Sch. Bd., 1970-78. Recipient Sec.'s Superior Svc. award USDA, 1968. Fellow Soc. Religious Orgn. Mgmt. (bd. dirs. 1984); mem. Pi Sigma Alpha. Home: 5534 N 18th Rd Arlington VA 22205 Office: Westover Bapt Ch 1125 N Patrick Henry Dr Arlington VA 22205

SAPP, DONALD GENE, minister; b. Phoenix, Feb. 27, 1927; s. Guerry Byron and Lydia Elmeda (Snyder) S.; m. Anna Maydean Nevitt, July 10, 1952 (dec.); m. Joann Herrin Mountz, May 1, 1976; children: Gregory, Paula, Jeffrey, Mark, Melody, Cristine. AB in Edn., Ariz. State U., 1949; MDiv, Boston U., 1952, MST, 1960; D Ministry, Calif. Grad. Sch. Theology, 1975. Ordained to ministry Meth. Ch., 1950. Dir. youth activities Hyde Park (Mass.) Meth. Ch., 1950-52; minister 1st Meth. Ch., Peabody, Mass., 1952-54, Balboa Island (Calif.) Community Meth. Ch., 1954-57, Ch. of the Foothills Meth., Duarte, Calif., 1957-63; sr. minister Aldersgate United Meth. Ch., Tustin, Calif., 1963-70, Paradise Valley (Ariz.) United Meth. Ch., 1970-83; dist. supt. Cen. West Dist. of Desert S.W. Conf. United Meth. Ctr., Phoenix, 1983-89. Editor Wide Horizons, 1983-89; contbr. articles to profl. jours. Chaplain City of Hope Med. Ctr., Duarte, 1957-63; trustee Plaza Community Ctr., L.A., 1967-70; corp. mem. Sch. Theology at Claremont, Calif., 1972-80; pres. Met. Phoenix Commn., 1983-85; del. Western Jurisdictional Conf. United Meth. Ch., 1984, 88; bd. dirs. Coun. Chs., L.A., 1963-67, Orange County (Calif.) Human Rels. Coun., 1967-70, Interfaith Counseling Svc. Found., 1982-89, Gen. Conf., United Meth. Ch., 1988, Wesley Community Ctr., Phoenix, 1983-89. With USN, 1945-46. Mem. Ariz. Ecumenical Coun., Bishops and Exec. Roundtable, Rotary (pres.), Kappa Delta Pi, Tau Kappa Epsilon. Democrat. Avocation: overseas travel. Home: 5225 E Road Runner Rd Paradise Valley AZ 85253

SAPSOWITZ, MARNA HELENE, rabbi; b. N.Y., Mar. 1, 1959; d. Melvin and Barbara (Rubin) S. BA cum laude, Brandeis U., 1980; MEd, Seattle U., 1988; MA in Hebrew Letters, Reconstructionist Rabbinical Coll., Wyncote, Pa., 1989. Ordained rabbi, 1989. Rabbi Temple Shalom, Yakima, Wash., 1989-90; rabbi, dir. edn. Temple Beth Hatfiloh, Olympia, Wash., 1989—. Mem. Reconstructionist Rabbinical Assn., Coalition for Advancement Jewish Edn., Religious Coalition for Abortion Rights. Office: Temple Beth Hatfiloh PO Box 2442 Olympia WA 98507

SARAF, YOUSUF IBRAHIM, bishop. Bishop of Cairo, Roman Cath. Ch. Office: Sanctuaire Notre Dame Fatima, 141 Charia Nouzha, Heliopolis, Cairo Arab Republic of Egypt*

SARAH, ROBERT, archbishop. Pres. Bishops' Conf., Roman Cath. Ch., Conakry, Guinea. Office: Archeveche, BP 1006 bis, Conakry Guinea*

SARANDAN, LYDIA MARY, minister; b. Detroit, Aug. 19, 1938; d. Florence (Pascut) S. AA, Highland Park (Mich.) Jr. Coll., 1959; BS in Edn., Wayne State U., 1962; MDiv, Princeton Theol. Sem., 1970. Ordained to ministry Presbyn. Ch. (U.S.A.), 1970. Assoc. min. Covenant Presbyn. Ch., West Lafayette, Ind., 1970-81, St. Andrew's Presbyn. Ch., Newport Beach, Calif., 1981—. Trustee Princeton Theol. Sem., 1977-80; bd. dirs. Adult Christian Edn. Found., Madison, Wis., 1977-78, YWCA, Santa Ana, Calif., 1985-87. Recipient Outstanding award in religion Orange Country, 1985. Home: 425 Gloucester Pl Costa Mesa CA 92627 Office: St Andrew's Presbyn Ch 600 St Andrews Rd Newport Beach CA 92663-5325

SARASON, RICHARD SAMUEL, religious studies educator; b. Detroit, Feb. 12, 1948; s. C. Kenneth and Cornelia B. (Stein) S.; m. Anne Arenstein, Feb. 12, 1983; children: Jonathan Philip, Michael Solomon. AB, Brandeis U., 1969; postgrad., Hebrew U., Jerusalem, 1970-72; M of Hebrew Lit., Hebrew Union Coll., 1974; PhD, Brown U., 1977. Instr. Brown U., Providence, 1976-77, asst. prof. religious studies, 1977-79; asst. prof. Hebrew Union Coll., Cin., 1979-81, assoc. prof., 1981-90, prof. rabbinic lit. and thought, 1990—. Author: A History of the Mishnaic Law of Agriculture: A Study of Tractate Demai, 1979; contbr. articles on rabbinic lit. to profl. jours. Pres. Jewish Fedn. Leadership Council, Cin., 1984-85; mem. chorus Cin. May Festival. Recipient Kate S. Mack award Jewish Fedn., 1983; grantee NEH, 1978; fellow Brown U., 1974. Fellow Soc. for Values in Higher Edn.; mem. Am. Acad. of Religion, Soc. of Bibl. Lit., Assn. for Jewish Studies, Am. Schs. for Oriental Research, Cen. Conf. Am. Rabbis, Phi Beta Kappa. Avocations: music, theater, cinema. Home: 7405 Laurel Oak Ln Cincinnati OH 45237 Office: Hebrew Union Coll 3101 Clifton Ave Cincinnati OH 45220

SARAUSKAS, R. GEORGE, priest, program director; b. Bavaria, Germany, Apr. 2, 1945; came to U.S., 1949; s. Stanley and Mary (Lucinskaite) S. MPA, Ill. Inst. Tech., 1970; MDiv, U. St. Mary of the Lake, Mundelein, Ill., 1971, Licentiate of Sacred Theology, 1976; PhD, Northwestern U., 1979. Ordained priest Roman Cath. Ch. Adminstr. St. Anthony Ch., Chgo., 1983-90; exec. dir. aid to ea. Europe Nat. Conf. Cath. Bishops, Washington, 1990—; dir. rsch. and planning Archdiocese of Chgo., 1983-90; dir. Lithuanian apostolate, 1986-90; mem. fin. com. Archdiocese Chgo., 1988-90. Commr. CSC, City of Evanston, Ill., 1974-79. Named a Papal Knight, Equestrian Order of Knights of Holy Sepulchre of Jerusalem, 1990; White House fellow Pres. of U.S., 1979. Fellow White House Fellows Assn. Office: Nat Conf Cath Bishops 3211 4th St NE Washington DC 20017-1194

SARCHET-WALLER, PAUL ROBERT, missionary, minister; b. Barnsley, Yorkshire, Eng., Jan. 13, 1947; arrived in Hong Kong, 1974; s. Henry and Brenda (Luty) Waller; m. Diane Winifred Sarchet, Dec. 19, 1970; children: Dodie Victoria, Rachel Emma, Nathan Paul. D.Ph.Ed., Welsh Nat. Coll., Cardiff, Wales, 1969; Chinese diploma, Hong Kong Chinese U., 1980; BTh, Shiloh Bible Coll., Oakland, Calif., 1980; DD (hon.), So. Calif. Theol. Sem., 1991. Mem. team Welsh Nat. Colls. Swimming Team, 1967-68, capt., 1968-69; Tchr. Barnsley Edn. Authority, Eng., 1969-72; tchr. Munro Coll., Jamaica, 1972-74; tchr., missionary Diocesan Boys Sch., Hong Kong, 1974-78; founder, sr. pastor Elim Full Gospel Ch., Hong Kong, 1982—; founder, chmn. Elim Full Gospel Publs., Hong Kong, 1985—; founder, prin. Elim Discipleship Tng. Sch., Hong Kong, 1985—; founder Elim Asia Missions, 1987—; founder discipleship tng. schs. in SE Asia, Malaysia, Philippines and India; conf. speaker in New Zealand, Eng., U.S.A., Malaysia, Philippines, Egypt. Author: Foundation Doctrine, 1987, The Holy Spirit, 1985, Principles of Ministry, 1985, Praise and Worship, 1988, Principles of Discipleship, 1987, Principles of Missions, 1988, Lay Ministry, 1990, Life-Style Evangelism, 1990, Equipped to Serve, 1991; contbr. articles to profl. jours.; vocalist (album) In Praise of Jesus, 1981. Office: Elim Full Gospel Church, PO Box 68, Shatin NT, Hong Kong

SARDOU, JOSEPH-MARIE, archbishop. Archbishop of Monaco The Roman Cath. Ch., Monte Carlo. Office: Archeveche, 6 rue des Fours, BP 517, Monte Carlo 98015, Monaco*

SARFF, DONOHUE RAY, clergyman; b. Palisade, Minn., Apr. 27, 1928; s. Pierre and Betsey (Tyren) S.; m. Marilyn Wanda Wisian, June 11, 1954; children: Paul, Daniel, John, Philip, Ruth. BA, Augsburg Coll., Mpls., 1956; MDiv., Luther Theol. Sem., St. Paul, 1960. Ordained to ministry Evang. Luth. Ch., 1960. Pastor Vienna(S.D.)-Pleasant Luth. Parish, 1960-65, Morningside Luth. Ch., Sioux City, Iowa, 1965-69, Nazarene Luth. Ch., Armstrong, Iowa, 1969—; bd. mem. Learning Ministry Team, Western Iowa Synod, 1989—, chaplain Lakes Area Conf., 1989—. Author: Up From Captivity, 1982; contbr. articles to parish edn. jours. Cubmaster, scoutmaster Boy Scouts Am., Sioux City, Armstrong, Iowa, 1966-75; EMT Armstrong Med. Svc., 1983—; treas. Armstrong Heritage Mus., 1989—; bd. regents Waldorf Coll., Forest City, Iowa, 1985—. Mem. Kiwanis (pres. 1975-76). Republican. Home: 307 5th St Armstrong IA 50514-0024

SARGENT, CHARLES JACKSON, minister; b. Hampton, Va., Oct. 23, 1929; m. Evaleen Litman Talton. BA in History, Va. Union U., 1949; MDiv, Drew Theol. Sem., 1952; ThD, Trinity Theol. Sem., 1985. Ordained to ministry Bapt. Ch., 1952. Pastor First Bapt. Ch., Madison, N.J., 1952-55, Ebenezer Bapt. Ch., Poughkeepsie, N.Y., 1955-59, Union Bapt. Ch., Stamford, Conn., 1959-68; spl. field reps. Mins. and Missionaries Benefit Bd., Am. Bapt. Chs., 1968-71, asst. to exec. bd., 1971-74; dir. devel. Interdenominational Theol. Ctr., Atlanta, 1974-76, v.p. for devel., 1976-77, asst. to pres., 1977-79, v.p. adminstrv. svcs., 1979-82; min. Friendship Bapt. Ch., College Park, Ga., 1977—; faculty mem. Bapt. Ednl. Ctr. N.Y., 1960-74, Interdenominational Theol. Ctr., Atlanta, 1981, 84—. Contbr. articles to profl. jours. Active ARC, Family Svc. Assn. of Am., Urban League, Bd. Edn., Poughkeepsie, N.J., Corp. Info. Ctr., N.Y.C., City Housing Authority, College Park, Clayton Jr. Coll. Minority Recruitment/Retention Adv. Com.; bd. dirs. Stamford (Conn.) Hosp., Historically Black Coll. Campus Mag., Met. Atlanta Transit Authority; moderator Atlanta Bapt. Assn., pres. New Era State Bapt. Conv. of Ga.; treas. Coll. Park Pastors Fellowship; bd. pub. safety, Stamford, Conn. Mem. So. Christian Leadership Conf., NAACP, Rotary, Knights of Pythias, Omega Phi Phi. Office: 1971 W Harvard Ave College Park GA 30337*

SARGON, SIMON A., composer, music director; b. Bombay, Apr. 6, 1938; m. Bonnie Glasgow, Nov. 17, 1961. BA, Brandeis U., 1959; MS, Juilliard Sch. Music, 1962. Staff N.Y.C. Opera, 1960; assoc. condr. Concert Opera, N.Y.C., 1962-68; concert pianist J. Tourel, N.Y.C., 1963-71; faculty Juilliard Sch. Music, N.Y.C., 1967-69; chmn. dept. voice Rubin Acad., Jerusalem, 1971-74; faculty Hebrew U., Jerusalem, 1973-74; dir. music Temple Emanu-El, Jerusalem, 1974—; assoc. prof. Southwestern U., Dallas, 1983—. Composer: Patterns in Blue, 1976, Elul: Midnight, 1980, Praise Ye the Lord, 1980, Sing His Praise, 1981, The Queen's Consort, 1982, Lord Make Me To Know My End, 1985, Jump Back, 1990, Before the Ark, 1990; rec. artist (album) Music for French Horn and Piano; contbr. Dallas Opera mag., 1980-84. Recipient Gretchaninoff award, 1962; grantee Am.-Israel Cultural Found., 1970-74, Meadows Found., 1987. Mem. Phi Beta Kappa.

SARMAZIAN, YESSAYI, minister. Min. Armenian Evang. Ch., Toronto, Ont., Can. Office: Armenian Evang Ch, 42 Glenforest Rd, Toronto, ON Canada M4N 1Z8*

SARNA, NAHUM MATTATHIAS, educator emeritus; b. London, Eng., Mar. 27, 1923; came to U.S., 1951, naturalized, 1959; s. Jacob and Milly (Horonzick) S.; m. Helen Horowitz, Mar. 23, 1947; children: David E. Y., Jonathan D. BA, U. London, 1944, MA, 1946; minister's diploma, Jews Coll., London, 1947; PhD, Dropsie Coll., Phila., 1955; D Hebrew Letters (hon.), Gratz Coll., Phila., 1984; LHD (hon.), Hebrew Union Coll.-Jewish Inst. Religion, 1987; D Hebrew Lit., Hebrew Coll., Boston, 1991. Asst. lectr. Hebrew, Univ. Coll., London, 1946-49; lectr. Gratz Coll., Phila., 1951-57; librarian Jewish Theol. Sem.; also asst. prof. Bible Tchrs. Inst., 1957-63, assoc. prof. of Bible, 1963-65; asso. prof. Bibl. studies Brandeis U., Waltham, Mass., 1965-67; Dora Golding prof. Bibl. studies Brandeis U., 1967-85, prof. emeritus, 1985—, chmn. dept. Near Eastern and Judaic studies, 1969-75, chmn. humanities council, 1980-81; vis. prof. Bible Dropsie Coll., 1967-68; vis. prof. religion Columbia U., 1964-65. Author: Understanding Genesis, 1966, Exploring Exodus, 1986, Commentary to Genesis, 1989, Commentary to Exodus, 1991; co-author: A New Translation of the Book of Psalms, 1973, The Book of Job, A New Translation with Introductions, 1980; editor, translator: Jewish Publ. Soc. Bible, 1966-85; editorial bd. Jour. Bibl. Lit, 1973-75, Soc. Bibl. Lit. Monograph Series, 1975—; deptl. editor Ency. Judaica; gen. editor Jewish Publ. Soc. Bible Commentary series, 1974—; editor Proceedings of the American Academy for Jewish Research; mem. editorial adv. bd. Biblical Archaeology Rev., Moment Mag.; contbr. to Ency. Brit., 1974, also articles to scholarly jours. Assoc. trustee Am. Sch. Oriental Research; trustee, mem. exec. com. Boston Hebrew Coll.; acad. adv. coun. Nat. Found. Jewish Culture; trustee Annenberg Rsch. Inst., 1990—. Recipient Jewish Book Ann. award, 1967; Am. Council Learned Socs. fellow, 1971-72; Inst. Advanced Studies fellow Hebrew U., 1982-83. Fellow Royal Asiatic Soc., Am. Acad. Jewish Research; mem. Soc. Bibl. Lit. and Exegesis, Am. Oriental Soc., Israel Exploration Soc., Archons of Colophon, Palestine Exploration Soc. Bibl. Colloquium, Assn. for Jewish Studies (hon. sec.-treas. 1972-79, pres. 1983-85). Home: 39 Green Park Newton MA 02158

SARPONG, PETER KWASI, bishop; b. Maase-Offinso, Ashanti, Ghana, Feb. 26, 1933; s. Peter Donkor and Anna Yaa Nkansah. Student, St. Theresa's Maj. Sem., 1954-56, St. Peter's Maj. Sem., Cape Coast, Ghana, 1957-59; Licentiate in Sacred Theology, U. St. Thomas Aquinas, Rome, 1962, STD, 1963; Diploma in Anthropology, M of Letters in Social Anthropology, U. Oxford, Eng., 1965; DSc (hon.), U. Sci. and Tech., Kumasi, Ghana, 1979. Ordained priest Roman Cath. Ch., 1959. Chancellor Cath. Diocese of Kumasi, 1960-61; chaplain Okomfo Anokye Hosp., Kumasi; rector St. Peter's Maj. Sem., 1967-70; bishop of Kumasi, 1970—; chancellor Cath. Inst. West Africa, Port Harcourt, Nigeria, 1985—; Ghana rep. Synod of Bishops, Rome, 1971; rep. Bishops for Promotion of Christian Unity, Rome, 1972; consultor Papal Commn. for Justice and Peace, Rome, 1972-76, also West African regional corr.; West African regional liaison Secretariat for Christian Unity, Rome, Secretariat for Non-Believers; mem. com. for African internal affairs Pan African Bishop's Conf.; v.p. Cath. Bishops' Conf. of Ghana, 1982-88, pres., 1988—. Author: The Sacred Stools of the Akan, 1971, Ecumenical Relations in Ghana, 1973, Some Christian Reflections on Poverty, Ghana in Retrospect, 1974, The One Honest Man, Ashanti Girl's Nubility Rites, 1977, Culture and the Kingdom, Guidelines on Priestly Life and Ministry, 1981, Essays on the University Student and Other Topics, 1982, The African Experience, 1987, African Theology: A Simple Description, Justice and Development in Africa: The Challenge of the 1990s, 1988, The Ceremonial Horns of the Ashanti; translator ch. texts from English and Latin into Asante lang.; contbr. numerous articles to profl. jours. and mags. Chmn. coun. U. Sci. and Tech., Kumasi, 1972-77; chmn. Com. Planning for Pre-Univ. Edn., 1974-77, Authorship Devel. Fund, 1974-77; chmn. bd. govs. Nat. Cultural Centre, Kumasi, 1974-77; mem. Ghana Red Cross; mem. Coun. of State, 1980-81. Decorated by Govt. of Dahomey (now People's Republic of Benin), 1972; recipient Freedom award City of Tuskegee, Ala., 1973, prize for Disting. Writers, Ghana Book Devel. Coun., Asantoman award Asantehene, 1991. Avocations: chess, draught, football, writing, dancing. Address: Office of Bishop, PO Box 99, Kumasi Ghana

SASSER, THOMAS LYNN, minister; b. Beaumont, Tex., Feb. 23, 1946; s. T.J. and Edna Sasser; m. Sandra Sue Talley, Feb. 24, 1968; children: Tammi, Timothy, Tina. BA in History, La. Coll., 1968; MA in Religious Edn., Southwestern Bapt. Theol. Sem., 1971. Ordained to ministry So. Bapt. Conv., 1969. Assoc. pastor Richey St. Bapt. Ch., Pasadena, Tex., 1971-73; min. to youth 1st Bapt. Ch., Texarkana, Tex., 1973-76; missionary Fgn. Mission Bd., Richmond, Va., 1976-77; min. to students 1st Bapt. Ch., West Monroe, La., 1977-83; assoc. pastor Cen. Bapt. Ch., Livingston, Tex., 1983-91; pastor Bapt. Ch., Hitchcock, Tex., 1991—; super summer dir. Bapt. Gen. Conv. Tex., Dallas, 1979—. Founder Lake Livingston Right-to-Life Assn., 1984. Named Disting. Am. Recruiter, La. Coll., 1981. Republican. Home:

5842 Terrebone Hitchcock TX 77563 Office: 1st Bapt Ch 6601 FM 2004 Hitchcock TX 77563 *Today there is a vacuum of learning. Very few people are asking questions. The people who learn ask questions. I serve a God who is not afraid of any questions and enjoys answering them.*

SASSO, SANDY, rabbi; b. Phila., Jan. 29, 1947; d. Israel and Freda (Plotrick) Eisenberg; m. Dennis Sasso, June 25, 1970; children: David Aryeh, Debora Shoshana. BA magna cum laude, Temple U., 1969, MA in Religion, 1972. Ordained rabbi, 1974. Rsch. assoc. Jewish Reconstructionist Found., N.Y.C., 1974-76; rabbi Congregation Beth-El Zedeck, Indpls., 1977—; lectr. Jewish Welfare Bd. Lecture Bur., 1972-77. Bd. dirs. Julian Mission, 1978-79; mem. adm. coun. Women's Health Resource Ctr., 1983—. Recipient Woman of Yr. award Brith Sholom Women, 1975. Mem. Reconstructionist Rabbinical Assn. (pres. Wyncote, Pa. chpt.), Nat. Coun. Jewish Women (edn. and pub. affairs coms.), N.Y. Bd. Rabbis, Coalition for Alternatives in Jewish Edn., NCCJ (exec. bd. 1978-79). Office: Reconstructionist Rabbinical Assn Church Rd & Greenwood Ave Wyncote PA 19095*

SATOWAKI, JOSEPH ASAJIRO CARDINAL, archbishop; b. Shittsu, Japan, Feb. 1, 1904. Ordained priest Roman Cath. Ch., 1932; served in various pastoral capacities in Nagasaki (Japan) archdiocese after ordination; apostolic adminstr. Taiwan (Japanese possession), 1941-45; dir. Nagasaki temporary major sem., 1945-57; vicar gen. of Nagasaki, 1945; ordained 1st bishop of Kagoshima, Japan, 1955; archbishop of Nagasaki, 1968—; pres. Japanese Episcopal Conf., 1979—; elevated to cardinal, 1979; titular ch. St. Mary of Peace; mem. commn. Revision of Code of Canon Law. Mem. Congregation: Evangelization of Peoples; secretariat: Non-Christians. Office: Catholic Ctr, 10-14 Venomachi, Nagasaki-shi Japan

SATTERTHWAITE, JOHN RICHARD, bishop; b. Whicham, Cumberland, Eng., Nov. 17, 1925; s. William and Clare Elisabeth (Beck) S. BA, Leeds U., 1945. Ordained deacon Anglican Ch., 1950, priest, 1951. Curate, parish priest Carlisle, Eng., 1950-54; asst., then gen. sec. Coun. Fgn. Rels. Lambeth Palace, 1955-70; bishop Diocese Gibraltar in Europe, London, 1970—. Author: (with others) Year Book, Ency. Britannica, 1980—, Chamber Ency., 1970. Awarded CMG, 1991; recipient 18 awards from fgn. chs. Mem. Athenaeum Club (London, gen. coun. 1960-70). Home: 19 Brunswick Gardens, London W8 4AS, England Office: 5A Gregory Pl, Kensington W8 4NG, England

SATTERWHITE, DONALD THOMAS, minister; b. Tallahassee, Fla., Dec. 4, 1953; s. Norman Clifton and Erma Dean (Funderburk) S.; m. Marie Giliberti, Dec. 19, 1972; children: Paul Daniel, Jessica Lynn, Rachel Ann. BA in Bibl. Edn., Fla. Bible Coll., Kissimmee, 1975; MDiv, New Orleans Bapt. Theol. Sem., 1989. Ordained to ministry Bapt. Ch., 1975. Dir. Pembroke Pines (Fla.) Jr. High Youth Ranch, 1973-75; founder, dir. Tri-State Youth Ranch, Dothan, Ala., 1975-80; exec. dir. Tri-State Teens for Christ, Port Jervis, N.Y., 1980-83; pastor Maye River Bapt. Ch., Bluffton, S.C., 1983-86, Faith Bapt. Ch., Westminster, S.C., 1986-88, Lebanon Bapt. Ch., Anderson, S.C., 1988-90, Sardis Bapt. Ch., Swansea, S.C., 1991—; moderator Savannah River Bapt. Assn., Ridgeland, S.C., 1986; dir. Brotherhood-Savannah River Assn., Ridgeland, 1984-86; vice-chmn. Christian Life Com. of the Beaver Dam Bapt. Assn., Seneca, S.C., 1987-88; camp pastor McCall Royal Amb. Camp, Pickens, S.C., 1985, 87. Pres. Nat. Fedn. for Decency, Hilton Head, S.C., 1985. Timothy Student scholar Fla. Bible Coll., 1975. Mem. Grace Evang. Soc. Republican. Home and Office: 1144 St Matthews Rd Swansea SC 29160 *God often uses some of our most difficult times on earth to draw us into a closer relationship with Him. Keeping our eyes focused on Him, will always lift us up.*

SAUCEDO, JOSE GUADALUPE, bishop. Bishop Southeastern Mex. Episcopal Ch., Xalapoa. Office: Episcopal Ch, Avda de las Americas 73, Col Aguacatal, 91130 Xalapoa Mexico*

SAUCEMAN, TEDDY CARROLL, minister; b. Greenville, Tenn., Dec. 11, 1940; s. James Carl and Mary Lou (Smith) S.; m. Billie Diane Lewis, Dec. 6, 1962; children: William Carl, Shannon Margaret, Tiffany Lynn. Ordained to ministry World Evangelism Fellowship Ch. Sr. pastor Word of Life Ch., Donaldsonville, La., 1975-78; gen. mgr. Sonlife Radio Group, Baton Rouge, 1978-80; v.p. World Missions for Jesus, Baton Rouge, 1982; assoc. pastor Faith Tabernacle Ch., Gonzales, La., 1982-84; gen. mgr. WLUX radio sta., Baton Rouge, 1984—; sec. Baton Rouge sect. La. Assemblies of God, 1987-88; sec. credentials com. World Evang. Fellowship, Baton Rouge, 1988-89. Pres. Parent Tchr. Fellowship, Family Christian Acad., Baton Rouge, 1988-89. Cpl. U.S. Army, 1966-69. Mem. La. Christian Broadcasters Assn. (pres. 1989—). Republican. Home: 39297 Hwy 74 Gonzales LA 70737 Office: WLUX 1550 AM 8919 World Ministry Ave PO Box 2550 Baton Rouge LA 70821

SAUCIER, EDWARD ALVIN, pastor; b. Ft. Riley, Kans., May 12, 1956; s. Reginald Joseph and Joy Evelyn (Smithson) S.; m. Shara Monise Bettis, June 1, 1974; 1 child, Jennifer Diane. BA, Okla. Bapt. U., 1977; MA, Internat. Sem., 1981, D in Ministry, 1983. Pastor Sharon Bapt. Ch., Tecumseh, Okla., 1976-79, Immanuel Bapt. Ch., Poteau, Okla., 1979-84, Highland Park Bapt. Ch., Bartlesville, Okla., 1984-88, First Bapt. Ch., Elk City, Okla., 1988—; moderator Beckham-Mills Assn., Sayre, Okla., 1990; trustee Okla. Bapt. U., Shawnee, 1988—. Mem. Okla. Bapt. Pastor's Conf. (v.p. 1990—), Ministerial Alliance (pres. Elk City chpt. 1990—). Home: 1302 Dalton Elk City OK 73644 Office: First Bapt Ch 1600 W Country Club Elk City OK 73644

SAUER, ROBERT C., religious organization administrator. 3d v.p. Luth. Ch.-Mo. Synod, St. Louis. Office: 2716 Norwich Saint Charles MO 63301*

SAUL, ROGER STEPHEN, missionary, author, real estate consultant; b. N.Y.C., Oct. 23, 1948; s. Warren Elmer and Jean Francis (Chamberlain) S.; m. Alma Salazar Aliviado; 1 child, Bonnie. BS, SUNY, 1970. Pres. Saul Enterprises, Cortland, 1972-74, Saul Investment Realty, Albuquerque, 1974-76; founder, missionary Worldwide Interfaith Peace Mission, Albuquerque, 1988—. Author: Moneymaker, 1974, Fast Fielding of Tenant's Questions, 1974, International Happy Christian Bachelor Book, 1991; producer videos Peace Think, Father Figure; contbr. articles to mags. Fellow U.S. Drug Free Powerlifting Assn. Avocations: sports, reading, travel. Home: 1429 Columbia NE Albuquerque NM 87106

SAULS, DON, minister; b. Eureka, N.C.; m. Marie Brown; children: Donna, Dale. MSL, Holmes Sch. of the Bible, Greenville, S.C., 1967; MEd, N.C. State U., 1984; postgrad., N.C. Wesleyan Coll. Ordained to ministry Pentecostal Free Will Bapt. Ch., 1966. Pastor Pentecostal Free Will Bapt. Ch., Benson, N.C., 1967-74, gen. dir. Christian Edn. dept., 1971-84, gen. supt., 1984—; tchr. Heritage Bible Coll., Dunn, N.C., 1971—, also trustee; chmn. bd. dirs. , sec., mem. exec. bd. Pentecostal Fellowship N.Am., 1988-91; lectr. U.S. and abroad. Columnist Messenger, 1984—; contbr. articles to jours. in field. Mem. Kiwanis (former pres. Dunn club, bd. dirs.). Office: Pentecostal Free Will Bapt Ch PO Box 1568 Dunn NC 28334

SAUNDERS, ANGELA GILL, church musician; b. Newton Abbot, Devon, Eng., July 10, 1951; d. Arthur John and Patricia Kathleen (Mortlock) Gill; m. Mark Howard Saunders, May 21, 1983; children: Kristen Marie, Kerri Lynn. BA in Biology and Music, Macalester Coll., 1973; MusM in Organ Performance, U. Colo., 1979, DMA Organ Performance, 1983. Organist/choirmaster Chapel of the Intercession, Denver, 1977-78; dir. music Highlands United Meth. Ch., Denver, 1978-80, Christ Ch. United Meth. Ch., Denver, 1980-83, Larchmont United Meth. Ch., Norfolk, Va., 1983-87; parish musician St. Uriel the Archangel Episc. Ch., Sea Girt, N.J., 1989—; pvt. instr., recitalist, 1973—; founding pres. Choristers Guild Tidewater Chpt., Norfolk, Va., 1984-87. Mem. All Officers' Wives USN, NAEC, Lakehurst, 1987—; newsletter person PTA, Lakehurst, 1990—. Grantee U. Colo. Grad. Sch., 1982; Lienke scholar Macalester Coll., 1969-73, Raudenbusch scholar Macalester Coll., 1969-73, Wesley Meml. scholar Macalester Coll., 1969-73. Mem. Fellowship of United Meth Musicians, Presbyn. Assn. Musicians, Am. Guild English Handbell Ringers, Am. Guild Organists (winner S.W. Jersey competition), Pi Kappa Lambda. Home: Quarters E NAEC Lakehurst NJ 08733 Office: St Uriel the Archangel Episc Ch 3d Ave at Philadelphia Sea Girt NJ 08750

SAUNDERS, HERBERT EUGENE, minister; b. Nortonville, Kans., May 31, 1940; s. Francis Davis and Lila Margaret (Stephan) S.; m. Barbara Louise Crandall, June 24, 1962; children: Brian Eugene, Peggy Susan, Michael David. BA, Salem Coll., 1962, DD, 1988; MDiv, Colgate Rochester Div. Sch., 1966. Ordained to ministry Seventh Day Baptist Gen. Conf., 1966. Pastor Seventh Day Bapt. Ch., Little Genessee, N.Y., 1962-67, Hebron, Pa., 1964-67, Plainfield, N.J., 1967-75; dean Seventh Day Ctr. on Ministry, Plainfield, 1975-82; pastor Seventh Day Bapt. Ch., Milton, Wis., 1982-90, Congl. Ch., Milton, Wis., 1990—; chmn. Seventh Day Bapt. Com. on faith and order, Janesville, Wis., 1983-88. Author: Sabbath: Symbol of Creation and Re-Creation, 1971; editor: (ch. sch. helps) The Helping Hand, 1984. Home: 409 Rogers St Milton WI 53563

SAUNDERS, JAMES DALE, chaplain; b. Milw., Aug. 21, 1950; s. Jack L. and Betty J. (Werner) S.; m. Barbara Jean Gariepy, July 13, 1974; children: Daniel P.L., Timothy M.J. BA, Carthage Coll., 1973; MDiv, Concordia Sem., Ft. Wayne, 1977. Ordained to ministry Luth. Ch. Mo. Synod, 1977. Pastor Trinity Luth. Ch., Casey, Ill., 1977-79; commd. 2d lt. USAF, 1979, advanced through grades to lt. col., 1987; installation staff chaplain USAF, Gila Bend AFAF, Ariz., 1985-87; sr. Protestant chaplain OSAN AB, Republic of Korea, 1988-90, Tyndall AFB, Fla., 1990—. Mem. Air Force Assn., Am. Legion. Home: 6112 Stephanie Dr Callaway FL 32404 Office: USAF 325 FW/HC Tyndall AFB FL 32403

SAUNDERS, LESLIE DEWITT, minister; b. Seattle, Jan. 21, 1930; s. Leslie Eugene and Elizabeth Mae (Carson) S.; m. Natalie Claire Hooke, May 29, 1960; children: Scott Andrew, Angela Claire. BS, Portland State U., 1971; MA, Inst. Transpersonal Psychology, 1991. Ordained to ministry Unity Ch. Minister Unity Ch. of Valley, Yakima, Wash., 1961-65; sr. minister Unity Ch., Portland, Oreg., 1965-75, First Unity Ch., St. Petersburg, Fla., 1975—. Contbr. articles to profl. jours. Mem. Assn. Unity Chs. (co-chmn. licensing and ordination com. 1971-75, bd. dirs. 1975-78), Assn. Transpersonal Psychology, Assn. for Applied Psychophysiology and Biofeedback, Spiritual Emergence Network, Assn. Humanistic Psychology, Rotary, Masons. Avocations: fishing, sailing, bicycling. Home: 5400 Park St N 609 Saint Petersburg FL 33709 Office: First Unity Ch 469 45th Ave N Saint Petersburg FL 33703

SAUNDERS, MONROE RANDOLPH, JR., minister; b. Balt., July 20, 1948; s. Monroe Randolph and Alberta (Brockington) S.; m. Winsome Delores Ricketts, Aug. 28, 1971; children: Darwin, Duane. AB, Morgan State U., 1971; MA in Religion, Howard U., 1975. Ordained to ministry United Ch. Jesus Christ (Apostolic), 1975, consecrated bishop, 1989. Pastor Capitol Hill United Ch. Jesus Christ, Washington, 1983, 1st United Ch. Jesus Christ, Detroit, 1980; exec. pastor 1st United Ch. Jesus Christ, Balt., 1980—, gen. sec. bd. bishops, 1989—, v.p., 1991—; diocesan bishop State Fla. 1st United Ch. Jesus Christ, 1990—; v.p. Ctr. for More Abundant Life, Balt., 1986—, Abundant Life Towers II, 1987—. Bd. dirs. Monroe Saunders Sch./Ctr. for Creative Learning, Balt., 1979, Mayfield Ave Community Assn., Howard County, Md., 1986, Urban Cardiology Rsch. Ctr., Balt., 1989; commr. Howard County Housing Commn., 1990. Office: 1st United Ch Jesus Christ 5150 Baltimore National Pike Baltimore MD 21229

SAUNDERS, WILLIAM CLINTON, minister; b. Morristown, N.J., Mar. 18, 1945; s. Byron Winthrop and Miriam (Wise) S.; m. Susan Elizabeth Thrasher, Jan. 12, 1976; children: Peter Wheaton, Brynn Ellis. AB, Oberlin Coll., 1967; BD, Union Theol. Sem., 1970; PhD, Columbia U., 1979. Ordained to ministry Unitarian Universalist Ch., 1972. Min. Unitarian Universalist Ch., Brunswick, Maine, 1976-85; min. Unitarian Universalist Ch., Urbana, Ill., 1985—; trustee Unitarian Universalist Assn., Boston, 1983-85, chair Young Adult Ministry, 1989-90; v.p. bd. dirs. Cen. Midwest Dist. Unitarian Universalist Assn., Chgo., 1987-89; Good Offices person Cen. Midwest Dist. Minister's Assn., 1989—. Chair Maine Humanities Coun., 1981-82; bd. dirs. Maine Audubon Soc., 1982-85. Mem. Unitarian Universalist Minister's Assn., Unitarian Universalist Hist. Soc. Home: 415 W Indiana Ave Urbana IL 61801 Office: Unitarian Universalist Ch 309 W Green St Urbana IL 61801

SAVAGE, FRANK X., education administrator. Exec. dir. edn. Archdiocese of Indpls. Office: Edn Office Cath Ctr PO Box 1410 1400 N Meridian St Indianapolis IN 46206*

SAVAGE, RUSSELL WAYNE, minister; b. Birmingham, Ala., Apr. 8, 1963; s. Hubbard Raymond and Sara Louise (Hurd) S.; m. Stephanie Lorraine Olinger, July 23, 1982; children: Scarlett Louise, Russell Wayne Jr., Jessica Yvonne, Joshua Hubbard. BA, U. South Fla., 1985; MDiv with honors, Midwestern Bapt. Theol. Sem., 1991. Ordained to ministry Bapt. Ch., 1985. Assoc. pastor Reynolds Rd. Bapt. Ch., Lakeland, Fla., 1986-88; pastor Short Creek Bapt. Ch., Rushville, Mo., 1989—; v.p., trustee Ind. Life Teaching Facility, Rushville, 1990-91. Republican. Home: Rt 1 Box 93 Rushville MO 64484 Office: Short Creek Bapt Ch Rt 1 Box 93 Rushville MO 64484

SAVAGE, WILLIAM EARL, religion educator, seminary administrator, banker; b. Wilmore, Ky., Feb. 5, 1918; s. Earl Wilson and Mary Nell (Jones) S.; m. Dorothy Jane Dorrycott, Dec. 28, 1939; children: Sue Ann, William Earl II, Carolyn. AB, Asbury Coll., Wilmore, Ky., 1939. V.p. Pineland Coll., Deland, Fla., 1939-42; bus. mgr. Ky.-Wesleyan Coll., Owensboro, 1942-44; v.p. bus. adminstrn. Asbury Theol. Sem., 1946-76; pres. First Fed. Savs. and Loan, Lexington, Ky., 1982-85, vice chmn. bd. dirs., 1982—; mem. United Meth. Bd. Global Ministries, 1960-72; mem. adminstrv. bd. Park United Meth. Ch., Lexington, 1960—; mem. World Meth. Coun., 1961—, exec. com., 1975—; bd. dirs. Asbury Theol. Sem., Wilmore, 1945—; lay leader Ky. Conf. United Meth. Ch., 1964-68; treas. bd. dirs. Ky. Meth. Found., 1982—. Trustee Cardinal Hill Children's Hosp., Lexington, 1954-60, Good Samaritan Hosp., Lexington, 1964—; bd. dirs. Lexington Coun. Arts, 1980-86. Mem. Ky. Savs. Loan League, Nat. Assn. Cert. Revenue Appraisers, U.S. Savs. League, Ky. Crippled Children's Soc. Democrat. Home: 4111 Harrodsburg Rd Lexington KY 40513 Office: First Fed Savs and Loan 110 W Vine St Lexington KY 40507

SAVARIMUTHU, JOHN GURUBATHAM, bishop; b. Kulasekharapatnam, India, Nov. 29, 1925; s. John and Koilpillai Gurubatham; m. Catherine Puan Sri (dec. Jan. 1989); children: Mary Thangam Savarimuthu Das, Johnny Yesadian, Nathanael Gurubatham. Student, Madras U., 1943-47; BD, Tamilnad Theol. Coll., India, 1952; Diploma in Theology with distinction, St. Augustine's Coll., Canterbury, Eng., 1963. Ordained priest Anglican Ch., 1952. Asst. curate St. Mark's Ch., Seremban, 1952-55, vicar of Negri Sembilan, 1956-62; curate St. Mary's Ch., Portsmouth, Eng., 1963, St. George's Cathedral, Kingston, Ont., Can., 1963; vicar of South Johor St. Christopher's Ch., Johor Bahru, 1964-70; archdeacon of So. archdeaconry Diocese of West Malaysia, 1970; vicar St. James' Ch., Kuala Lumpur, 1971; archdeacon So. and Cen. Archdeaconries, 1971; archdeacon Diocese of West Malaysia, 1972, vicar gen., 1972; consecrated bishop of West Malaysia Anglican Ch., Kuala Lumpur, 1973—; examining chaplain to bishop of Singapore and Malaya, 1964-70; vis. lectr. St. Peter's Hall, Trinity Coll., Singapore; nat. sec. Ch. Union Negotiating Com. Malaysia and Singapore, 1970-73; nat. v.p. Coun. Chs. Malaysia and Singapore, 1973-75; nat. pres. Coun. Chs. Malaysia, 1979-83; provincial sec. Coun. Ch. East Asia, 1979-83, chmn. theol. commn., 1979-87, chmn., 1987—; mem. Anglican-Luth. Internat. Commn., 1986—; participant numerous Anglican and ecumenical confs. V.p. Assunta Hosp. Found. Bd., 1978—; mem. Nat. Unity Bd., Office of Prime Min., Govt. of Malaysia, 1980—; active Anglican Internat. Network on Refugee and Migrant Ministry, 1988—. Decorated tan sri Pangalima Setia Mahota (Malaysia). Home: Rumah Bishop, 14 Pesiaran Stonor, 50450 Kuala Lumpur Malaysia

SAVELLE, JERRY JUNIOR, minister; b. Vicksburg, Miss., Dec. 24, 1946; s. Jerry Wallace and Attie T. (Snow) S.; m. Carolyn Ann Creech, July 15, 1966; children: Jerriann Savelle Carlin, Terri Lynn. Student, La. Technol. U., 1964-65, Northwestern State U., Natchitoches, La., 1965-66, Bapt. Bible Coll., Shreveport, La., 1966-68; DD (hon.), Bethel Christian Coll., Riverside, Calif., 1983, Oral Roberts U., 1985. Ordained to ministry Faith Christian Fellowship, 1982. Assoc. min. Kenneth Copeland Ministries, Ft. Worth, 1970-73, bd. dirs., 1982—; pres. Jerry Savelle Ministries, Crowley, Tex., 1974—; pastor Overcoming Faith Ctr. Ch., Ft. Worth, 1976-81; founder Overcoming Faith Christian Sch., Crowley, 1977-82, Overcoming Faith Ctr. Chs. Kenya, 1979—; pres. Overcoming Faith Bible Tng. Ctr., Ft. Worth, 1979-82; v.p. Internat. Conv. Faith Ministries, Inc., 1979—; trustee Charismatic Bible Ministries, 1986—; mem. Network Christian Ministries, 1987—; bd. regents Oral Roberts U., Tulsa, 1982-88. Author: The Established Heart, The Fruits of Righteousness, Living To Give, Godly Wisdom for Prosperity, Right Mental Attitude, Giving Birth to a Miracle, Sowing in Famine, Living in Divine Prosperity, Giving...The Essence of Living, The Spirit of Might, Sharing Jesus Effectively, Is Satan Can't Steal Your Joy, He Can't Steal Your Goods, Man's Crown of Glory, The Nature of Faith, Energizing Your Faith, Force of Joy, Drawn by His Love; also numerous cassette teaching tapes and videos. Mem. Rep. Congl. Leadership Coun., Washington, 1982—. With U.S. Army, 1967-71. Office: PO Box 748 10255 W Cleburne Rd Crowley TX 76036

SAVIANO, BERNADETTE, clergywoman, graphic arts specialist; b. Fall River, Mass., May 10, 1948; d. Jesse Medeiros and Rosaline (Aguiar) Tavares. BA in Theology, Philosophy, Greensboro (N.C.) Coll., 1988. Lic. minister, 1984. Account exec. Co-Art Ad Agy., Providence, 1973-75; account exec., ptnr. Argentieri Assocs. Advt. Providence, 1975-77; mktg. cons. Christian's, Providence, 1977-78; mgr. graphics dept. Purvis Systems (Computer Systems Engring. Co.), Middletown, R.I., 1978-86; minister adult edn., outreach and evangelism Lawndale Bapt. Ch., Greensboro, N.C., 1986; jr. chaplain Greensboro Coll., 1986—. Author: (poems) Desert Songs, 1982; exhibited photographs Newport Art Mus., 1983. Woodruff fellow Emory U., 1988-89, N.Am. Ministerial fellow, 1988-89; recipient Young Am. Poets award, 1975. Mem. Nat. Contract Mgmt. Assn., Nat. Assn. Female Execs. Home: 1901G Ashwood Ct Suite 116 Greensboro NC 27408

SAVILLE, JOHN FLEMING, minister; b. Grinnell, Iowa, Oct. 22, 1939; s. Donavon H. and Kathleen N. (Fleming) S.; m. Penelope Louise Fitzsimmons, Sept. 1958; children: John F. II, Stephen Brett. BA, North Cen. Bible Sch., Minn., 1973; MDiv, United Theol. Seminary of the, Twin Cities, 1976. Pastor Koronis Parish, Belgrade, Minn., 1974-77, 1st Presbyn. Ch., Schaller, Iowa, 1977-83, Westminster Presbyn. Ch., Lawton, Okla., 1983—; stewardship com. Presbytery and Synod levels, 1974-89; del. Synod of the Sun, 1986-88; pastor mentor Presbytery of Indian Nations, 1986—; mem. Indian Nations Com. on Ministry, 1991—. Pres. Ministerial Alliance, Schaller, 1979-80, Lawton, 1989-90; clergy rep. Mayor's Task Force/Substance Abuse, Lawton, 1989-90. Sgt. USAF, 1958-70, Vietnam. Mem. Lions (pres. 1981-82). Republican. Home: 418 Woodland Dr Lawton OK 73505 Office: Westminster Presbyn Church 7110 West Gore Blvd Lawton OK 73505

SAVOY, DOUGLAS EUGENE, bishop, religion educator, explorer, writer; b. Bellingham, Wash., May 11, 1927; s. Lewis Dell and Maymie (Janett) S.; m. Elvira Clarke, Dec. 5, 1957 (div.); 1 son, Jamil Sean (dec.); m. Sylvia Ontaneda, July 7, 1971; children: Douglas Eugene, Christopher Sean, Sylvia Jamila. Student, U. Portland, 1947-8; DST, D Canon and Sacred Law, Jamilian U. of the Ordained, 1980; PhD in Theology, DD (hon.), Tech. Inst. Bibl. Studies, Nev., 1990. Ordained to ministry Internat. Community of Christ Ch., 1962, bishop, 1971. Cardinal head bishop Internat. Community of Christ Ch., 1971—; lectr. in ministerial tng. studies, 1972—; pastor Univ. Chapel, Reno, 1979—; founder Jamilian Parochial Sch., 1976; chancellor, founder Sacred Coll. of Jamilian Theology; pres., founder Jamilian U. of the Ordained, 1980; pres. Advs. for Religious Rights and Freedoms; chmn. World Coun. for Human Spiritual Rights, 1984—; head Jamilian Orders of Patriarchs, 1990—; engaged in newspaper pub. West Coast, 1949-56; began explorations in jungles east of Andes in Peru to prove his theory that high civilizations of Peru may have had their origin in jungles, 1967; pres., founder Andean Explorers Club, Found., Reno; pres., Advocates for Religious Rights and Freedoms; chmn., World Coun. for Human Spiritual Rights. Author: Antisuyo, The Search for Lost Cities of the High Amazon, 1970, Vilcabamba, Last City of the Incas, 1970, The Cosolargy Papers, vol. 1, 1970, vol. 2-3, 1972, The Child Christ, 1973, Arabic edit., 1976, Japanese edit., 1981, The Decoded New Testament, 1974, Arabic edit., 1981, The Millenium Edition of the Decoded New Testament, 1983, On The Trail of The Feathered Serpent, 1974, Code Book and Community Manual for Overseers, 1975, Prophecies of Jamil, First Prophecy to the Americas, Vol. 1, 1976, Second Prophecy to the Americas, 1976, The Secret Sayings of Jamil, The Image and the Word, Vol. 1, 1976, Vol. 2, 1977, Project X—The Search For the Secrets of Immortality, 1977, Prophecy to the Races of Man, Vol. 2, 1977, Solar Cultures of The Americas, 1977, Dream Analysis, 1977, Vision Analysis, 1977, Christoanalysis, 1978, The Essaei Document: Secrets of an Eternal Race, 1978, Millennium edit., 1983, The Lost Gospel of Jesus: Hidden Teachings of Christ, 1978, Millennium edit., 1983, Secret Sayings of Jamil, Vol. 3. 1978, Vol. 4, 1979, Prophecy to The Christian Churches, 1978, The Sayings, vol. 4, 1979, Solar Cultures of Oceania, 1979, Prophecy of The End Times, Vol. 4, 1980, The Holy Kabbalah and Secret Symbolism, Vols. 1 and 2, 1980, Solar Cultures of China, 1980, Christotherapy, 1980, Christophysics, 1980, Christodynamics, 1980, Code Book of Prophecy, 1980, The Sayings, vol. 5, 1980, vol. 6, 1981, Solar Cultures of India, 1981, Prophecy on the Golden Age of Light and the Nation of Nations, Vol. 5, 1981, Solar Cultures of Israel, vol. 3, 1981, The Counsels, 1982, Prophecy of the Universal Theocracy, vol. 6, 1982, Prophecy of the New Covenant, vol. 7, 1982, The Book of God's Revelation, 1983, Miracle of the Second Advent, 1984; over 300 audio tape rec. lectures, 1974—, numerous others.; documentary film on Gran Vilaya, 1989; contbr. articles on Peruvian cultures to mags., also articles on philosophy and religion; discoverer lost city of Incas at Vilcabamba Cuzco, numerous ancient cities in Amazonia including Gran Pajaten, Gran Vilaya, Monte Peruvia, Twelve Cities of the Condor. Trustee in Trust Episcopal Head Bishop Internat. Community of the Grand Christ. Served with AS USNR, 1944-46. Decorated officer Order of the Grand Cross (Republic of Peru), 1989; recipient numerous exploring awards including over 40 Flag awards Andean Explorers Club, 1958-85 and Explorer of the Century trophy Andean Explorers Found., 1988, Silver Hummingbird award Ministry Industry and Tourism of Peru, 1987, medal of Merit Andres Reyes, 1989. Mem. Geog. Soc. Lima, Andean Explorers Found, Ocean Sailing Club, World Coun. for Human Spiritual Rights, Advs. for Religious Rights and Freedoms,hors Guild. Clubs: Explorers (N.Y.C.); Andean Explorers Found. and Ocean Sailing. Home: 2025 La Fond Reno NV 89509 Office: 643 Ralston St Reno NV 89503 *One who makes dreams come true is that person who gets an idea, figures out how to make it work and then throws all of his energy into the project, stopping at nothing.*

SAWATZKY, LEONARD, minister. Moderator Evang. Mennonite Mission Conf., Steinbach, Man., Can. Office: Evang Mennonite Mission Conf, Box 2126, Steinbach, MB Canada R0A 2A0*

SAWICKI, MARIANNE, religion educator; b. Balt., Jan. 21, 1950; d. William and Helen Amanda (Nelson) S.; m. Robert Joseph Miller, June 11, 1983. BA in Philosophy, Loyola Coll., Balt., 1971; MA in Communications, U. Pa., 1974; MA in Religious Studies, Cath. U. Am., 1978, PhD in Religious Studies, 1984. Vis. asst. prof. Loyola Marymount U., L.A., 1981-84; assoc. prof. Lexington (Ky.) Theol. Sem., 1985-89; guest prof. Princeton (N.J.) Theol. Sem., 1989-90; teaching asst. dept. philosophy U. Ky., Lexington, 1990—. Author: The Gospel in History, 1988, Faith and Sexism, 1979; co-editor: Catechesis: Realities and Visions, 1977; editor Liturgy, 1978-80; news editor Balt. Jewish Times, 1971-72; copy editor Balt. Sun , 1972-73, Miami Herald, 1974-75. Mem. Cath. Theol. Soc. Am., North Am. Acad. Liturgy, Am. Acad. Religion. Home: 100 Chelan Ct Lexington KY 40503 Office: U Ky Dept of Philosophy Lexington KY 40508

SAWTELLE, ROGER ALLAN, minister, religious organization administrator; b. Cin., July 18, 1940; s. Allan Wiant and Bobbie Clara (Irion) S. BA, Ind. U., 1963; MDiv, Harvard Div. Sch., 1967. Ordained to ministry A.M.E. Ch. as deacon, 1980, as elder, 1982. Pastor N. Kingstown United Meth. Ch., 1967, Wareham-Marion (Mass.) United Meth. Parish, 1967-68, Brayton-Quarry United Meth. Parish, Fall River, Mass., 1968-70, Bethel AME Ch., Lowell, Mass., 1981-87; ch. sch. supt. New Eng. Conf., AME Ch., Lowell, Mass., 1987—; supr. Fitchburg (Mass.) Welfare Office, 1971-91. Pres. Fall River Brotherhood Ctr., 1970-74; foundr Citizens for Universal Peace, Fall River, 1968-70. Mem. NAACP (pres. 1983-84). Office: New England Conf 5 Kinsman St Lowell MA 01852 *"Keep your eyes on the Prize. Hold on." Either God is real or He isn't. If we believe that He is real, then His will and love must be the driving force of our lives.*

SAWYER, JEFFREY WAYNE, minister; b. Joplin, Mo., May 23, 1968; s. Kenneth Wayne and Carol Sue (Hoofnagle) S.; m. Gretchen Louise Peiffer, July 28, 1990. Student, Cen. Christian Coll., Moberly, Mo., 1988—. Assoc. min. Crossroads Christian Ch., Macon, Mo., 1988—; v.p. Campus Christian Fellowship, Kirksville, Mo., 1986-88.

SAWYER, LUCIEN AVILA, religious organization administrator; b. Lowell, Mass., July 7, 1924; s. Lionel A. and Irene R. (Houde) S. BA, Oblate Coll., 1945, MA in Theology, 1949; MA in English, Cath. U. Am., 1952. Chaplain St. Joseph Hosp., Bangor, Maine, 1971-76, Conn. Valley Hosp., Middletown, 1976-83, St. Joseph Hosp., Lowell, 1983-87; dir. Health Care Ministry Archdiocese of Boston, 1987—; chmn. Com. on Hosp. Chaplains, Norwich, Conn., 1979-83; cons. Diocesan Tribunal, Norwich, 1979-83; quality assurance coord. State Chaplains, Conn., 1982-83; mem. adv. com. Mass. Gen. Hosp., Boston, 1989—. Contbr. articles to profl. jours. Mem. Oblates of Mary Immaculate. Mem. Assn. Mental Health Clergy (nat. sec. 1984-86, pres. 1986-88), Mass. Chaplains Assn., Oblates of Mary Immaclate. Avocations: travel, hiking, computers, theatre. Home: 62 Kirkwood Rd Brighton MA 02135 Office: Health Care Ministry 736 Cambridge St Boston MA 02135 *Religion provides strength for the individual person's struggle towards a loving community under God, while enabling the community to struggle towards the individual person's God-given rights. Neither is fully attainable but both are indispensable.*

SAWYER, RAYMOND ETON, bishop; b. Woonsocket, R.I., Nov. 7, 1946; s. Edgar Bertrand Decelles and Juliette Laurence (Breault) Robbins. BA, St. Thomas Aquinas U., Houston, 1976; STL, Faculte Libre Theology, Paris, 1978; STM, STD, Sorbonne, 1980. Ordained priest Old Cath. Ch. (Utrecht) and Brazilian Cath. Apostolic Succession, 1974. V.p. Sawyersmith Wholesale Import Co., 1980-85; dir. psychology McLane Am., 1987-88; priest Old Cath. Ch. (Utrecht) and Brazilian Cath. Apostolic Succession, Fla., N.Y. and Tex., 1974-88; bishop Old Cath. Ch. (Utrecht) and Brazilian Cath. Apostolic Succession, Salt Lake City, 1988—; mem. Nat. U.S. Synod of Bishops, Highlandville, Mo., 1988—; instr. French lit. Salt Lake Community Coll., 1990. Decorated Chevaliers Hospitalier de Pomerol, France, 1982. Mem. Phi Alpha Theta. Avocations: reading, hiking, cross-country skiing. Home: St Stephen's Mission Rectory 1924 East 3900 S Salt Lake City UT 84124 Office: St Lukes Old Cath Cathedral 1910 East 3900 S Salt Lake City UT 84124

SAWYER, TIMOTHY RAY, minister; b. Texas City, Tex., Nov. 6, 1962; s. Evan Jones and Eula Van (Melton) S.; m. Seana Gale McKeg, Dec. 21, 1985. MusB, East Tex. Bapt. U., 1985. Ordained to ministry So. Bapt. Conv., 1986. Interim min. music Mulberry Springs Bapt. Ch., Hallsville, Tex., 1983-84; dir. music West End Bapt. Ch., Galveston, Tex., 1985; min. music and youth Friendship Bapt. Ch., Marshall, Tex., 1985-89, Hillcrest Bapt. Ch., Nederland, Tex., 1989—. Mem. Nat. Network Youth Mins., Soda Lake Bapt. Assn. (dir. music 1987-89). Office: Hillcrest Bapt Ch 3324 Park Dr Nederland TX 77627

SAXON, RANDALL LEE, pastor, author; b. Waverly, N.Y., Oct. 28, 1947; s. Sherman Kenyon and Velma Marie (Dunning) S.; m. Diane Louise Kennedy, June 23, 1973 (div. Feb. 1985); children: Heather Marie, David Arthur; m. Anna Louise Clock, Mar. 15, 1986; children: Jennifer Elizabeth, Austin Todd. BA, Mansfield U., 1969; MDiv, Princeton Sem., 1973; D of Ministry, Drew U., 1992. Ordained to ministry Presbyn. Ch. U.S.A., 1973. Asst. pastor United Meth. Ch., Flemington, N.J., 1970-71; intern pastor Wattsburg (Pa.) Presbyn. Ch., 1971-72, East Greene Presbyn. Ch., Erie, Pa., 1971-72; asst. pastor Fewsmith Presbyn. Ch., Bellville, N.J., 1972-73; assoc. pastor Presbyn. Ch., Gettysburg, Pa., 1973-78; sr. pastor 1st Presbyn. Ch., Southampton, N.Y., 1978-86, Presbyn. Ch. of the Covenant, Port Arthur, Tex., 1986-91, 1st Presbyn. Ch., Wilmette, Ill., 1991—; nat. chaplain Sigma Theta Epsilon, Mansfield, Pa., 1968-72; permanent clk. Presbytery of Carlisle, Camp Hill, Pa., 1975-77, Synod of the Trinity, Camp Hill, 1977-78; jour. clk. Presbytery of L.I., Commack, N.Y., 1980-84; mem. Presbytery of Chgo. Author: Voices in the Wilderness, 1985, Parables for People of God, 1992; also articles, poetry. Program dir. Camp Brule, Boy Scouts Am., Forksville, Pa., 1972; dir. Youth in Govt. Seminar, Harrisburg, Pa., 1977; v.p. Internat. Seamen's Ctr., Houston, 1987—; chairperson City Task Force on Edn. Summit, Port Arthur, 1990-91; active Presbyn. Hist. Soc. Recipient cert. Shinnecock Indian Tribe, 1981; named an Outstanding Young Man of Am., Jaycees, 1971; Susquehanna Collegiate Inst. grantee, 1972. Mem. Acad. Parish Clergy, Am. Soc. Ch. History, Presbyn. Writers Guild, Scottish Soc. S.E. Tex. (pres. 1991-92), Rotary (pres. 1977-78). Democrat. Avocations: numismatics, canoeing, white-water rafting, travel, gardening. Home: 816 Greenleaf Ave Wilmette IL 60091 Office: First Presbyn Ch 600 9th St Wilmette IL 60091

SAYLES, GUY GAINES, minister; b. Huntington, W.Va., Mar. 16, 1957; s. Guy Gaines Sr. and Nancy Carol (Linkfield) S.; m. Marilyln Anita Plunkett, July 8, 1978; children: Amanda, Eliot. BA, Ga. So. Coll., 1978; MDiv, So. Sem, 1981; DMin, Emory U., 1989. Ordained to ministry So. Bapt. Conv., 1977. Pastor First Bapt. Ch., Locust Grove, Ga., 1983-85, Montezuma, Ga., 1985-87; assoc. pastor First Bapt. Ch., Griffin, Ga., 1987-89; pastor Whitehall Bapt. Ch., Accokeek, Md., 1989—; chmn. Prince George's Pastoral Counseling, Lanham, Md., 1990—; stewardship cons. Md.-Del. Bapt. Conv., Columbia, Md., 1990—; mem. advanced studies com. Candler Sch., Emory U., Atlanta, 1987-89. Contbr. articles to profl. jours. Chmn. Greater Griffin Habitat for Humanity, 1988-89; mem. Task Force on Religion and Peace, so. Ind., 1980-82, Ga. Commn. on U.S. Constn. Celebration, Macon County, Ga., 1987; bd. dirs. Am. Cancer Soc., Macon County, 1985-87. Mem. Phi Kappa Phi. Office: Whitehall Bapt Ch 1205 Farmington Rd E Accokeek MD 20607 *Though we are born and die individually, alone, it is life's highest achievement to discern our essential connections to others, to Creation and to God.*

SAYLOR, DENNIS ELWOOD, hospital chaplain; b. St. Louis, Sept. 22, 1933; s. Clarence Claude and Maggie Dena (Beard) S.; m. Helen Lucile Howe, Aug. 9, 1953; children: Dennis Alan, Douglas Brian. ThB, Calvary Bible Coll., 1954; BA, Taylor U., 1956; MA, Ball State U., 1957; PhD, Clayton U., 1978. Asst. prof. Calvary Bible Coll., St. Louis, 1958-60; pastor 1st Presbyn. Ch., Tilden, Ill., 1960-68; asst. prof. Ill. Coll., Jacksonville, 1966-71; chaplain Passavant Hosp., Jacksonville, 1971-74; dir. chaplaincy Presbyn. Hosp., Albuquerque, 1974-88; dir. pastoral care San Diego Hosp. Assn., 1988—; with adv. coun. Bethel Sem., San Diego, 1989—. Author: And You Visited Me, 1979, Songs in the Night, 1980, A Guide to Hospital Calling, 1983; contbr. 30 articles to jours. Bd. dirs. Consumer Credit Counseling Svc., Albuquerque, 1978-88; mem. profl. edn. com. Am. Cancer Soc., San Diego, 1988—. Recipient Teagle Found. grant, 1985. Fellow Coll. Chaplains Am. Protestant Hosp. Assn. (state rep. 1984-88); mem. Assn. for Clin. Pastoral Edn., Pastoral Care Inst. (exec. dir. 1983-88). Presbyterian. Office: Sharp HealthCare 7901 Frost St San Diego CA 92123

SAYNE, V. LYNN, minister; b. Knoxville, Jan. 3, 1955; s. Virgil and Sarah Agnes (Connatser) S.; m. Sheila Kaye McClain, Feb. 15, 1985; children: Jeremy Lynn, Daniel Paul, Jessica Lynsey. BS, Arlington (Tex.) Bapt. U., 1977; MTh, Calvary Bapt. Sem., Waycross, Ga., 1982; ThD, Heritage Bapt. Sem., Akron, 1983. Youth dir. Meyers Rd. Bapt. Ch., Grand Prairie, Tex., 1974-75; asst. pastor Northside Bapt. Ch., Carrollton, Tex., 1975-77; youth dir., bus. dir., music and asst. pastor Drew Pk. Bapt. Ch., Tampa, Fla., 1977-79; pastor Calvary Bapt. Ch., Vidalia, Ga., 1979-84, Fla. Ave. Bapt. Ch., Tampa, 1988—; bd. dirs. Back on the Farm Bible Conf., Elk Park, N.C., 1977-84, Clowns for Christ, Cleburne, Tex., 1984—; pres. Heritage Bapt. Coll., Vidalia, 1974-84; chaplain Vidalia Police Dept., 1979-84. Author: Church History, 1982, Bible Doctrine, 1981, How to Build a Bus Ministry, 1979, Petra, Rose Red City, 1977. Chaplain Meadows Meml. Hosp., Vidalia, 197984, Vidalia City Coun., 1979-84; res. officer Grand Prairie Police Dept., 1976-78, chaplian,, Vidalia Police Dept., 1979-84. Named Office of the Yr. Vidalia Police Dept., 1984. Mem. Internat. Soc. Magicians, Internat. Brotherhood Magicians, Soc. Am. Magicians, Fellowship of Christian Magicians (pres. 1991). Republican. Home: 4805 E Regnas Ave Tampa FL 33617 Office: Fla Ave Bapt Ch 4208 N Florida Ave Tampa FL 33603

SAYRE, FRANCIS BOWES, JR., clergyman; b. Washington, Jan. 17, 1915; s. Francis Bowes and Jessie Woodrow (Wilson) S.; m. Harriet Taft Hart, June 8, 1946; children: Jessie Wilson, Thomas Hart, Harriet Brownson, Francis Nevin. A.B. cum laude, Williams Coll., 1937, D.D. (hon.), 1963; M.Div., Episcopal Theol. Sch., Cambridge, Mass., 1940; L.H.D. (hon.), Wooster Coll., 1956; D.D. (hon.), Va. Theol. Sch., 1957, Wesleyan U., Conn., 1958, Hobart Coll., 1966; S.T.D. (hon.), Queen's U., Belfast, 1966; Litt.D. (hon.), Lehigh U., Ursinus Coll., 1973. Ordained to ministry Episcopal Ch., 1940; asst. minister Christ Ch., Cambridge, 1940-42; indsl. chaplain Diocese of Ohio, Cleve., 1946-51; rector St. Paul's Ch., East Cleveland, Ohio, 1947-51; dean Washington Cathedral, 1951-78; asso. dir. Woodrow Wilson Internat. Center for Scholars, Washington, 1978-79; Chmn. bd. Detroit Indsl. Mission, 1956-68; chmn. U.S. Com. for Refugees, 1958-61; mem. Pres.'s Com. on Equal Employment Opportunity, 1961-65; chmn. Woodrow Wilson Meml. Commn., 1962-68; mem. adv. com. Bishop of Armed Forces, 1972-78. Bd. govs. Nat. Space Inst.; bd. dirs. Presbyn. Ministers Fund; pres. Martha's Vineyard Hosp., 1981-83. Served as chaplain USNR, 1942-46. Recipient Clergyman of Yr. award Religious Heritage Am., 1976; Disting. Pub. Service medal NASA, 1977. Mem. Sigma Phi.

SCAGLIONE, EDWARD JERRY, minister, educator; b. L.A., June 21, 1944; s. Samuel G. and Lillian (Battaglia) S.; m. Constance Ruth Minardo, Dec. 20, 1968; 1 child, Edward Anthony. AA, Inst. of Christ, Greenville, S.C., 1971; grad., Bob Jones U., Greenville, S.C., 1979. Ordained to ministry Gospel Fellowship Assn., 1976. Youth dir. Fellowship Bapt. Ch., Anderson, S.C., 1969-71; teaching elder Ind. Bible Fellowship, Greenville, S.C., 1975-79; pastor tchr. Dover (Ohio) Bible Ch., 1979—; sec. Ohio Bible Fellowship, Columbus, 1985-88; pres., v.p. chaplins com. Union Hosp., Dover, Ohio, 1990-91; bd. of visitors Found. Bible Coll., Dunn, N.C., 1980— . Pres. V.P. Civitan, Greenville, S.C., 1972-79, Kidney Found. Bd. of Dir., Greenville, 1972-79; pres. elect Kidney Found. of S.C., 1976-79. Recipient Outstanding Svc. Kidney Foundation, 1972 (outstanding vol. 1976-77, 77-78.). Republican. Home: 509 E Third St Dover OH 44622 Office: Dover Bible Church Rt 1 Box 193A Dover OH 44622

SCAGLIONE, PAUL ANTHONY, priest; b. Raritan, N.J., Feb. 3, 1947; s. Carmen P. and Grace M. (Corradino) S. BA in Polit. Sci., Brescia Coll., 1968; MDiv, St. Meinrad Sch. Theology, 1973; cert. in spiritual direction, Inst. Spiritual Leadership, 1982. Ordained priest Roman Cath. Ch., 1973. Assoc. pastor St. Joachim Ch., Trenton, N.J., 1973-75; spiritual dir. St. Meinrad (Ind.) Sch. Theology, 1975-85; assoc. pastor St. Benedict Ch., Holmdel, N.J., 1985-89; pastor St. Thomas More Ch., Manalapan, N.J., 1989—; mem. Clergy Continuing Com., Trenton, 1985-87. Trustee Samaritan Ctr., Englishtown, N.J., 1989—; chairperson pastoral care clergy com. Bayshore Community Hosp., Holmdel, 1985-89. Mem. Nat. Assn. Spiritual Dirs. Democrat. Home and Office: St Thomas More Ch 186 Gordons Corner Rd Manalapan NJ 07726

SCAMEHORN, JOHN ROBERT, JR., minister; b. Niles, Mich., Jan. 3, 1932; s. John Robert and Lois Irene (Lamberton) S.; m. Irma June Hassinger, Aug. 29, 1953; children: Sheryl Anne, Lynn Martine, John Robert III, Abby Kay. BA in Journalism, Mich. State U., 1954; MDiv, Wesley Theol. Sem., 1981. Ordained elder United Meth. Ch., 1982. Pastor Centenary and Zion United Meth. Chs., Cumberland, Md., 1977-83, Mt. Savage (Md.) United Meth. Ch., 1983-87, Bedington United Meth. Ch., Martinsburg, W.Va., 1987—. 1st lt. U.S. Army, 1954-56. Republican. Office: Bedington United Meth Ch 535 Scrabble Rd Martinsburg WV 25401

SCANLAN, MICHAEL, priest, academic administrator; b. Far Rockaway, N.Y., Dec. 1, 1931; s. Vincent Michael and Marjorie (O'Keefe) S. BA, Williams Coll., 1953; JD, Harvard U., 1956; MDiv, St. Francis Sem., Loretto, Pa., 1975; LittD (hon.), Coll. Stuebenville, 1972; LLD, Williams Coll., Williamstown, Mass., 1978; PdD, St. Francis Coll., Loretto, Pa., 1987. Ordained priest Roman Catholic Ch., 1964. Acting dean Coll. Steubenville, Ohio, 1964-66, dean, 1966-69; rector pres. St. Francis Major Sem., Loretto, Pa., 1969-74; pres. Franciscan U. Steubenville, 1974—; pres. FIRE Catholic Alliance for Faith, Intercession, Repentence and Evangelism, 1984—. Author: The Power in Penance, 1972, Inner Healing, 1974, A Portion of My Spirit, 1979, The San Damiano Cross, 1983, Turn to the Lord-A Call to Repentance, 1984, Titles of Jesus, 1985, Let the Fire Fall, 1986, Healing Principles, 1987, Appointment with God, 1987, Repentance, 1989, The Truth About Trouble, 1989; chmn. editorial bd. New Covenant mag. Mem. Diocese of Steubenville Ecumenical Commn., 1964-69; bd. dirs. Rumor Control Ctr., Steubenville, 1968-69, C. of C., Steubenville, 1976-79; trustee United Way, Steubenville, 1975-80. Staff judge adv. USAF, 1956-57. Mem. Assn. Ind. Colls. and Univs. Ohio (sec. 1980-82), Fellowship of Catholic Scholars, Legatus. Roman Catholic. Avocations: tennis, golf. Office: Franciscan U Franciscan Way Steubenville OH 43952 *If you are going to change something, you've got to live on vision, before you live on reality. You have to be so inspired by the vision, that you keep telling everybody until it gets in them, and they start living it with you.*

SCANLAN, THOMAS JOSEPH, college president, educator; b. N.Y.C., Mar. 5, 1945; s. Thomas Joseph and Anna Marie (Schmitt) S. BA in Physics, Cath. U. Am., 1967; MA in Math., NYU, 1972; PhD in Bus. Adminstrn., Columbia U., 1978. Prin. Queen of Peace High Sch., North Arlington, N.J., 1972-75; dir. fin., edn. N.Y. Province, Bros. of Christian Schs., Lincroft, N.J., 1978-81; vice chancellor Bethlehem (Israel) U., 1981-87; pres. Manhattan Coll., Bronx, N.Y., 1987—. Trustee Lewis U., Romeoville, Ill., 1987—. Recipient Pro Ecclesia et Pontifice medal, Pope John Paul II, Vatican City, 1986. Mem. Bros. of Christian Schs., Am. Council Edn., Assn. Cath. Colls. & Univs., Assn. Am. Colls., Nat. Cath. Edn. Assn., Nat. Assn. Ind. Colls. & Univs., Phi Beta Kappa, Beta Gamma Sigma. Avocations: tennis, reading, movies. Office: Manhattan Coll Manhattan Coll Pkwy New York NY 10471

SCANLAND, DENNIS LAWRENCE, religious organization administrator; b. Detroit, Oct. 28, 1947; s. Harry B. and Georgette B. (Bastien) S.; m. Jo Ann Mary Cortese, Oct. 21, 1972; children: Jennifer, Jerard, Jeanna. Sacred Heart Seminary, Detroit. Dir. refugee resettlement Archdiocese of Detroit. Deacon Our Lady of the Woods, Woodhaven, Mich. Staff sgt. USAF, 1966-70. Democrat. Roman Catholic. Home: 22115 Derby Rd Woodhaven MI 48183 Office: 305 Michigan Ave Detroit MI 48226

SCANLON, MICHAEL JOSEPH, theology educator, priest; b. N.Y.C., Aug. 1, 1937; s. Michael Joseph and Christine (Costello) S. BA, Villanova U., 1960; STL, Cath. U. Am., 1964, STD, 1969. Joined Augustinian Order, Roman Cath. Ch., ordained priest. Prof. theology Washington Theol. Union, 1968—; prior Augustinian Order, Washington, 1977-90. Contbr. articles to religious publs. Trustee Villanova (Pa.) U., 1988—, Merrimack Coll., North Andover, Mass., 1988—. Recipient Alumni medal Villanova U., 1986. Mem. Am. Acad. Religion, Cath. Theol. Soc. Am. (treas. 1976-82, pres. 1988). Democrat.

SCANNELL, ELNORA MARY, lay worker; b. Lanark, Ill., Jan. 7, 1908; d. Timothy F. and Ellen Margaret S. BA, U. Wis., 1930. vol. Centro Guadalupano, Gallup, N.Mex., 1986—, Casa San Martin, Gallup, 1973-86, St. Martin House, Madison, Wis., 1933-73.

SCARBROUGH, WILLIAM FRANKLIN, minister; b. Atlanta, Oct. 20, 1940; s. James Marion and Eunice Olean (Adams) S.; m. Suzanne Letson, Oct. 29, 1972; children: Susan Jennifer, James William, Samuel Franklin. BA, Mercer U., 1962; MDiv, So. Bapt. Theol. Sem., Louisville, 1965, D Ministry, 1980; MEd, U. Ga., 1971. Ordained to ministry So. Bapt. Ch., 1965. Min. music Flat Rock Bapt. Ch., College Park, Ga., 1960-62, Thixton Lane Bapt. Ch., Louisville, 1962-64; assoc. min. 1st Bapt. Ch., Abbeville, S.C., 1965-68, Jefferson, Ga., 1968-71; pastor National Heights Bapt. Ch., Fayetteville, Ga., 1971—; music dir. Ga. Bapt. Pastor's Conf., Atlanta, 1984; state coord. Bapts. Committed, Atlanta, 1987-91. Contbr. devotionals to Christian Index, Suburban Post. Music dir. Abbeville Community Theater, 1967; bd. dirs. Abbeville Christian Youth Ctr., 1966-68; chmn. Jackson County Beautification Program, Jefferson, 1970-71; mem. adv. bd. United Way Fayette County, Fayetteville, 1988-91, Stoneworth Annuity, Atlanta, 1990, Atlanta Task Force for Homeless, 1990-91. Mem. Fayette County Mins. Assn. (pres. 1987-88). Home: 4830 Stonewall-Tell Rd College Park GA 30349 Office: National Heights Bapt Ch 103 Old Norton Rd Fayetteville GA 30214

SCARLOTT, SHERREE DONEICE, religious organization administrator; b. Augusta, Ga., July 23, 1957; d. Raymond A. Jr. and Betty J. (Ingle) Gibson; m. Michael G. Collins, Mar. 18, 1978 (div. Feb. 1988); children: Courtney Rhea, Whitney Jayne; m. Stephen Paul Scarlott, Apr. 15, 1989; 1 stepson, Jeffery. BBA, Midwestern State U., Wichita Falls, Tex., 1989. Bus. adminstr. First United Meh. Ch., Wichita Falls, 1984—. Treas. Church World Svc. Crop Walk, Wichita Falls, 1988-90. Fellow Nat. Assn. Ch. Bus. Adminstrn. (v.p. Texoma chpt. 1990—). Office: First United Methodist Ch PO Box 2125 Wichita Falls TX 76307-2125

SCARVIE, WALTER BERNARD, clergyman; b. Story City, Iowa, July 23, 1934; s. Walter Bernard and Florence Emily (Thompson) S.; m. Korinne Mary Thompson, June 1, 1975; 1 child, Krista Ruth. BA, Luther Coll., Decorah, Iowa, 1956; BD, Luther Theol Sem., St. Paul, 1963; MA, Cath. U. Am., Washington, 1973, postgrad., 1973-79. Ordained to ministry Am. Luth. Ch., 1964. Pastor St. Peter Luth. Ch., St. Clair, Mich., 1964-67; campus pastor Luth. Campus Ministry of Washington, 1967-78; Protestant chaplain Georgetown U. Law and Med. Schs., Washington, 1978-81; pastor Community of Christ, Washington, 1984—; rsch. cons. The Alban Inst., Washington, 1978-79; leader various liturgical and theol. seminars, Washington, 1970—. Editor Jour. Religious Concern, 1976; contbr. articles to religious jours. Mem. St. Clair (Mich.) Housing Commn., 1965-67; mem. Choral Arts Soc. Washington, 1968—, Friends of the Kennedy Ctr. for Performing Arts, Washington, 1971—. With U.S. Army, 1957-58. Osterman fellow ea. dist. Am. Luth. Ch., 1975. Mem. D.C. Conf. Clergy, Nat. Acad. Recording Arts and Scis. Office: Community of Christ 3166 Mt Pleasant St NW Washington DC 20010

SCHAAF, JAMES LEWIS, church history educator, registrar; b. Sharon, Pa., July 28, 1932; s. Lewis Christian and Helen Louise (Weimer) Schaaf; m. Phyllis Ann Reeck, Sept. 13, 1959; children: Karen Elizabeth, Susan Ann. BA, Capital U., 1954, BD, 1958; ThD, Universität Heidelberg, Germany, 1961. Instr. Trinity Luth. Sem., Columbus, Ohio, 1961-62; prof. ch. history Trinity Luth. Sem., Columbus, 1965—; pastor St. John Luth. Ch., Ottawa, Ontario, Can., 1962-65; registrar Trinity Luth. Sem., Columbus, 1988—. Mem. Am. Soc. Ch. Hist., Am. Assn. Collegiate Registrars and Admissions Officers, Am. Translators Assn., Luth. Hist. Conf. (treas. 1972-78, newsletter editor 1978—, membership sec. 1982—, v.p. 1990—). Republican. Lutheran. Home: 713 Strawberry Hill Rd W Columbus OH 43213-3445 Office: Trinity Luth Sem 2199 E Main St Columbus OH 43209-2334

SCHAALMAN, HERMAN EZRA, rabbi; b. Munich, Apr. 28, 1916; came to U.S., 1935; s. Adolf and Regina Schaalman; m. Lotte Schaalman, May 25, 1941; children: Susan Youdovin, Michael. MA, U. Cin., 1938; BHL, Hebrew Union Coll., 1939, MHL, 1941, DD, 1966. Rabbi Temple Judah, Cedar Rapids, Iowa, 1941-49; regional dir. Union Am. Hebrew Congregations, Chgo., 1949-55; rabbi Emanuel Congregation, Chgo., 1955-86, rabbi emeritus, 1986—; adj. prof. Garrett Evang. Seminary, Evanston, Ill., 1957—, Chgo. Theol. Seminary, 1986—. Contbr. numerous articles to profl. jours. Mem. Jewish Fedn. Met. Chgo. (bd. dirs. 1987—), Cen. Cong. Am. Rabbis (chmn. ethics com., bd. dirs. 1983—), Am. Jewish Com. (bd. dirs. 1984—, v.p.), Assn. Reform Zionists Am. (bd. dirs. 1988—, v.p.), Jewish Coun. Urban Affairs (bd. dirs. 1989—, v.p.), Coun. Rel. Leaders Met. Chgo. (pres. 1988—). Office: Emanuel Congregation 5959 Sheridan Rd Chicago IL 60660

SCHACKMANN, RANDY B., minister; b. Portland, Oreg., Sept. 26, 1953; s. Malden Phillip and Edwina (Watt) S.; m. Anita Kay English, Mar. 13, 1976; children: Emily Faye, Bryon Phillip, Brent Alexander. BA, Columbia Christian Coll., Portland, 1975; MA, Pepperdine Univ. Missionary Ch. of Christ, Taipei, Taiwan, 1968-69; youth minister Sandy (Oreg.) Ch. of Christ, 1972-74; family life minister Glendale (Calif.) Ch. of Christ, 1977-90, sr. minister, 1990—; chaplain Pilgrim Sch., L.A., 1989-90; dir. West Coast Bible Encampment/Teen Group, L.A./Ventura County, Calif., 1980-90; mem./co-dir. L.A. County Teen Summer J.A.M. Coun., L.A., 1979-90; mem. chancellor's adv. coun./Pepperdine U., Malibu, Calif., 1981-83. Author: A Light for the Verdugos: History of Churches of Christ, 1987; contbr. articles to profl. jours. Project dir. Walk for World Hunger, Manna Internat. World Relief, San Fernando Valley, North L.A., 1988. Recipient Grad. Presdl. scholarship Pepperdine U., 1985-88. Mem. Christian Edn. Assn. Republican. Office: Glendale Ch of Christ 2021 W Glenoaks Blvd Glendale CA 91201

SCHACTER, JACOB JOSEPH, rabbi; b. N.Y.C., Dec. 11, 1950; s. Herschel and Pnina (Gewirtz) S.; m. Yocheved Weisbord, Sept. 4, 1972; children: Leah Tehilla, Sarah Ahuva. AB, Bklyn. Coll., 1973; MA, Harvard U., 1978, PhD, 1988. Ordained rabbi, 1973. Rabbi Young Israel of Sharon, Mass., 1977-81, The Jewish Ctr., N.Y.C., 1981—; instr. Stern Coll., N.Y.C., 1983-84; chmn. Midtown Bd. Kashruth, N.Y.C., 1983—. Editor The Torah u-Madda jour., 1989—; contbr. articles to profl. jours. Recipient Goodhartz award of excellence, Judaic Studies, Bklyn. Coll., 1973; Meml. Found. Jewish Culture grantee, 1973-75; Harvard U. grad. fellow, 1973-75. Mem. Jewish Nat. Fund (dir.), Union Orthodox Jewish Congregations of Am. (bd. govs.), N.Y. Bd. Rabbis (bd. govs. 1983—), Commn. on Synagogue Relations (exec. coun.), Phi Beta Kappa. Office: Jewish Ctr 131 W 86th St New York NY 10024

SCHAD, JAMES L., bishop; b. Phila., July 20, 1917. Grad. St. Mary's Sem., Balt. Ordained priest Roman Catholic Ch., 1943; ordained titular bishop of Panatoria and aux. bishop of Camden, Avalon, N.J., 1966—. Office: Diocese of Camden Cathedral Immaculate Conception 642 Market St Camden NJ 08102

SCHAEFER, MICHAEL ANTHONY, minister; b. Lawerance, Kans., Oct. 22, 1949; s. Paul Schaefer and Cella Blanch (Williams) Milavec; m. Sheriglen Johnson, May 20, 1972; children: Sarah Glen, Shaun Joseph. Student, Rhema Bible Tng. Ctr., Broken Arrow, Okla., 1982-84. Ordained to ministry Believers Ctr. of Albuquerque, 1986, Bible Ch., 1987. Layman, bd. dirs., Sunday-sch.-teen leader Calvary Assembly of God, Albuquerque, 1972-82; asst. minister Believers Ctr. of Albuquerque, 1985—. Mem. Rhema Ministerial Assn. Internat. Home: 10016 Academy Knolls NE Albuquerque NM 87111 Office: Beleivers Ctr Albuquerque 5000 Marble NE Ste 320 Albuquerque NM 87110

SCHAEFER, RICHARD GARY, minister; b. Mobile, Ala., May 11, 1952; s. Richard Temple and Irma (Bryars) S.; m. Paula Cherry, July 24, 1982. BA with distinction, Mobile Coll., 1974; M in Ch. Music, Southwestern Bapt. Theol. Seminary, 1977. Minister of music and activities First Baptist Ch., Halls, Tenn., 1977-80; minister of music and youth Presley St. Bapt. Ch., Atmore, Ala., 1980-82, Crosscreek Bapt. Ch., Pelham, Ala., 1982-86; minister of music First Baptist Ch., Boaz, Ala., 1986—. Organizer blood drives ARC, 1983, 84. Mem. Tenn. Bapt. Chorale, Ala. Singing Men, Edn. Music Assn., Mobile Coll. Alumni Singers. Avocations: sports, reading. Office: First Bapt Ch 225 S Main St Boaz AL 35957

SCHAEFFER, RICHARD CHARLES, priest; b. Grayling, Mich., Feb. 20, 1952; s. Richard Cradick and Donna Marie (Scott) S. AA, Kirtland Community Coll., 1972; BA, Oakland U., 1974; MDiv, St. John's Provincial Sem., 1983. Ordained priest Roman Cath. Ch., 1983. Assoc. pastor St. Peter's Cathedral, Marquette, Mich., 1983-84, St. Mary Queen of Peace, Kingsford, Mich., 1984-85; pastor St. Stanislaus Kostka, Goetzville, Mich., 1985—, Our Lady of the Snows, Hessel, Mich., 1985—, Sacred Heart, De Tour, Mich., 1985—, St. Florence, Drummond Island, Mich., 1985—; parochial adminstr. St. Mary's Parish, Big Bay, Mich., 1990—; charter mem. project Rachel Diocese of Marquette, 1985—, assoc. dir. vocations, 1987-88, dir. vocations, 1988—; trustee Sacred Heart Maj. Sem., Detroit, 1990—. Named Outstanding Alumnus of Yr. Kirtland Community Coll., 1990. Mem. Am. Friends of Vatican Library (charter), Oakland U. Alumni Assn. Lodge: KC. Avocations: study of patristics, foreign languages, travelling, jogging, swimming. Home: 416 Fisher # 2 Marquette MI 49855 Office: 347 Rock St Marquette MI 49855

SCHAFER, LEE GLENN, broadcasting executive; b. Bemidji, Minn., Apr. 4, 1946; s. Glenn W. and Ada (Fischer) S.; m. Beth Anne Coursey, Nov. 26, 1970; children: Leigh Ann, David. BA, NW Nazarene Coll., 1968. Gen. mgr. Sta. KSPD-KBXL Radio, Boise, Idaho, 1983—. Choir singer Coll. Ch.

of Nazarene, Nampa. Office: Sta KSPD-KBXL Radio 5201 Overland Rd Boise ID 83705

SCHÄFER, PETER, Judaic studies educator; b. Hückeswagen, Fed. Republic Germany, June 29, 1943; s. Josef and Agnes (Fischer) S.; m. Barbara Siems; children: Ruth, Eva, Simon Peter. PhD, U. Freiburg, Fed. Republic Germany, 1968; Habilitation, U. Frankfurt, Fed. Republic Germany, 1973. Asst. U. Tübingen, Fed. Republic Germany, 1969-74; asst. U. Cologne, Fed. Republic Germany, 1974, prof., 1974-82, prof. Judaic Studies, 1982-83; prof. Judaic Studies U. Berlin, Fed. Republic Germany, 1983—. Author: Die Vorstellung vom Heiligen Geist in der Rabbinischen Literatur, 1972, Rivalität zwischen Engeln und Menschen, 1975, Studien zur Geschichte und Theologie des Rabbinischen Judentums, 1978, (with J. Maier) Kleines Lexikon des Judentums, 1981, Italian transl., 1985, Der Bar Kokhba-Aufstand, 1981, Synopse zur Hekhalot-Literatur, 1981, Geschichte der Juden in der Antike, 1983 (French: Histoire des Juifs, 1989), Geniza-Fragmente zur Hekhalot-Literatur, 1984, Konkordanz zur Hekhalot-Literatur, vol. 1, 1986, vol. 2, 1988, vol. 4, 1991, Ubersetzung der Hekhalot-Literatur, vol. 2, 1987, vol. 3, 1989, vol. 4, 1991, Hekhalot-Studien, 1988, (with A. Carmel and Y. Ben Artzi) Jewish Settlement in Palestine (634-1881), 1990, Der verborgene und offenbare Gott, 1991, Synopse zum Talmud Yerushalma, vol. 1, 1991. Fellow Oxford Ctr. Postgrad. Hebrew Studies (sr. assoc.), Brit. Acad. (corr.). Office: Freie U Berlin Inst Judaistik, Schwendenerstrasse 27, 1000 Berlin 33, Federal Republic of Germany

SCHAFER, THOMAS ANTON, religion educator; b. East Liverpool, Ohio, July 22, 1918; s. Anton Edward and Ellen (Sleven) S.; m. Eudora Jones, Aug. 18, 1944; children: Michal Ann, Polly Ruth, David Anton, Daniel Evan. AB, Maryville Coll., 1940; BD, Louisville Presbyn. Sem., 1943; PhD, Duke U., 1951. Ordained to ministry Presbyn. Ch., 1943. Instr. Bible Duke U., Durham, N.C., 1946, asst. prof. hist. theol., 1950-57, assoc. prof., 1957-58; asst. prof. Bible Rhodes Coll., Memphis, 1946-50; assoc. prof. ch. history McCormick Theol. Sem., Chgo., 1958-62, prof., 1962-86, prof. emeritus, 1986—; mem. Presbytery of Chgo., 1958—. Contbr. articles to publs. Guggenheim fellow, 1956-57. Fellow Phi Beta Kappa; mem. Am. Soc. Ch. History, Am. Hist. Assn., Presbyn. Hist. Soc. (bd. dirs. 1961-70). Democrat. Home: 4826 N Winchester Ave Chicago IL 60640

SCHAFFER, HARWOOD DAVID, minister; b. Dayton, Ohio, Oct. 15, 1944; s. Phillip David and H. Ruth (Scheid) S.; BS in Math., Ohio State U., 1965; MDiv, Hartford Sem. Found., 1969; m. Polly Anna Francis, May 6, 1983; children: Rosita, Virginia, Chandra, Karen, Amy, Laura. Ordained to ministry United Ch. of Christ, 1969; chaplain, tchr. Austin Sch., Hartford, Conn., 1967-71; asst. pastor S. Congl. Ch., Middletown, Conn., 1967-71; pastor Trinity United Ch. of Christ, Hudson, Kans., 1971-79, Emma Lowery United Ch. of Christ, Luzerne, Mich., 1979-82, First Congl. United Ch. of Christ and Scambler Union United Ch. of Christ, Pelican Rapids, Minn., 1982-86, United Ch. of Mapleton, Minn., 1986-88, First Congl. United Ch. of Christ, Sherburn and St. John's United Ch. of Christ, Ceylon, Minn., 1988—; area counselor 17/76 Achievement Fund of United Ch. of Christ, 1974-75; co-owner, Polly's Printery, 1984—;co-pub. West Martin Weekly News, 1990—, United Ch. Christ Rural Jour., 1989—; mem. Western Assn. council Kans.-Okla. Conf., United Ch. of Christ, 1, 1971-74, 76-79, sec.-treas., 1971-74, chmn. ch. and ministry com., 1976-79; mem. various bds. Mich. Conf., United Ch. of Christ, 1979-82; mem. ch. devel. com. Minn. Conf. United Ch. of Christ, 1984-89; conf. and assn. ch. and minister coms, 1989—. Am. camp mgr. Joint Archaeol. Expdn. to Tel Aphek/Antipatris, Israel, 1978, 80. Bd. govs. Austin Sch., Hartford, 1970-71; mem. Stafford County Democratic Central Com., 1976-79, Dem. Farm Labor precinct chairperson House dist. 10B, 1984-86; Oscoda County Dem. Com., 1980-82; mem. Stafford Council Overall Econ. Devel. Planning Com., 1976-79, chmn., 1977-79; mem. Oscoda County Housing Commn., 1979-82, Pelican Rapids Library Com., 1986. Home: 19 E Second St Sherburn MN 56171 Office: 10 N Main St Box 395 Sherburn MN 56171 *I have a strong commitment to serving the rural church and community. Pastors in rural areas are more than religious leaders—they are community leaders.*

SCHAFFER, THEODORE RICHARD, clergyman; b. Phila., Apr. 30, 1932; s. Warren Holcomb and Anna Elizabeth (Hess) S.; m. Marian Suzanne Shaffer, Dec. 17, 1955; children—James Warren, Marian Elizabeth, Heather Ruth. B.A., Gettysburg Coll., 1958; B.Div., Luth. Sch. Theology, Gettysburg, 1961. Ordained to ministry Lutheran Ch., 1961. Pastor Calvary Luth. Parish, Hempstead, Md., 1961-64, St. Matthew Luth. Ch., Kitchener, Ont., Can., 1964-73, Emanuel Luth. Ch., Bradford, Pa., 1973-84; pastor, dir. pub. relations and devel. Shepherd of the Valley Luth. Home and Retirement Ctr., Niles, Ohio, 1984—; mem. faculty Waterloo Luth. Sem., Ont., part-time, 1968-72; pres. Kitchener-Waterloo Council Chs., 1967-71; campus pastor U. Pitts.-Bradford, 1973-83; sec.-treas. Coalition of Ohio Luth. Agys., 1984—; cons. for pub. relations and fund devel. Scoutmaster Boy Scouts Am., East Lansdowne, Pa., 1951-54; sec. Jr. C. of C., Hempstead, 1962-64; mem. Bradford Area Sch. Bd., 1978-82, Niles Recovery Coalition for Tornado Relief. Mem. Assn. Luth. Devel. Execs. Republican. Avocations: gardening; model trains; home handyman. Home: 1181 Churchill Hubbard Rd Youngstown OH 44595-1342 Office: Shepherd of the Valley Lutheran Home and Retirement Center 1462 Hillcrest Dr Apt 4 Niles OH 44446

SCHAGRIN, ELIHU, rabbi; b. Wilmington, Del., June 20, 1918; s. Charles Wolf and Frances (Schwartz) S.; m. Dorothy Wallach, June 17, 1945; children: Gail S. Isaacs, Charles Wolf, Judith Michal. BA, U. Pa., 1940; M. Hebrew Lit., Jewish Inst. Religion, 1946; DD (hon.), Hebrew Union Coll.-Jewish Inst. Religion, 1971. Ordained rabbi, 1946. Rabbi Beth Israel Congregation, Coatesville, Pa., 1945-53; rabbi Temple Concord, Binghamton, N.Y., 1953-85, rabbi-emeritus, 1985—; rabbi Norwich (N.Y.) Jewish Ctr., 1986—, Leo Baeck Centre, Melbourne, Australia, 1989-90; chaplain U.S. Vets. Hosp., Coatesville, 1945-53. Pres. Coatesville Interracial Com., 1949-53; pres. Metro-Interfaith Housing, Inc., Binghamton, 1976-78, 86-89, Family and Children's Svc. Soc., Binghamton, 1961-63; sec. United Way of Broome County, Binghamton, 1976-77. Recipient Broome County Med. Soc., 1967, Man of Yr. award Beth David Orthodox Congregation, 1981, Founder's award Hillel Day Sch., 1987. Mem. Cen. Conf. Am. Rabbis (mem. exec. bd. 1968-70, 80-82, mem. placement commn. 1978-84), Hebrew Union Coll.-Jewish Inst. Religion Alumni Assn. (exec. bd. 1965-68), Rotary (pres. local chpt. 1967-68). Democrat. Home: 5 Chapin St Binghamton NY 13905 *We are all young once—indeed many times in our lifespan. We are young at our birth, when we enter the teens. We are young again upon our entrance into adulthood and into our life' s work. Thus we are truly young at every stage of our lifetime. When we look, then, upon all new stages with the eyes of youth, we can enjoy them all.*

SCHAIVE, JAMES MOREKO, JR., lay worker; b. Springfield, Ill., Jan. 18, 1933; s. James M. Sr. and Francis I. (Gates) S.; m. Barbara S. Anderson, Aug. 18, 1956 (div. 1975); children: Karen Lynn, Chris; m. Joyce M. Danner, Oct. 9, 1976. BS in Edn., Western Ill. U., 1956, MS in Edn., 1961. Cert. ednl. adminstrn. Educator State of Ill., Sheridan, 1978—; chmn., staff parish, Ottawa Evang. United Meth. Ch., Ill., 1985—, lay leader, 1985—; lay speaker, United Meth. Ch., Ottawa, 1981—. Chmn. Prairie State Games Track & Field, Ill., 1987-88. Mem. Correctional Edn. Assn. (v.p. 1991—), Lions (past dist. gov.), Elks. Republican. Home: 1213 State St Ottawa IL 61350 Office: Sheridan Correctional Ctr PO Box 38 RR #1 Sheridan IL 60551

SCHARBERT, JOSEF, retired theology educator; b. Grosse, Moravia, Czechoslovakia, June 16, 1919; arrived in Germany, 1946; s. Oskar and Maria (Kammer) S. D Theology, U. Bonn, Fed. Republic Germany, 1953; lic. in Bible, Pontifical Bible Inst., Rome, 1954. Ordained priest Roman Cath. Ch., 1948. Extraordinary prof. Phil. Theol. Sem., Freising, Fed. Republic Germany, 1958-64, prof., 1964-67, rector magn, 1967-68; prof. theology U. Munich, 1968-84, prof. emeritus, 1984. Author: Die Propheten Israels, 2 vols., 1965, 67, Genesis-Kommentar, 1983, 86, Exodus-Kommentar, 1989, also numerous others. Named Pontif. Hon. Prelate, 1979. Mem. Sudetendeutsche Akademie d. Wissensch. u. Künste. Home: Pählstrasse 7, D-8000 Munich 70, Federal Republic of Germany

SCHARF, GREG ROARK, clergyman; b. Brazil, Ind., May 12, 1948; s. Carl Wayne and Stella Mae (Roark) S.; m. Ruth Mary Adlam, Apr. 3, 1976; children: Graham, Roger Gordon. AB, Rice U., 1970; MDiv, Trinity Evang. Div. Sch., 1973, D Ministry, 1991. Ordained to ministry Evang. Free Ch., 1974. Chaplain to students All Souls, Langham Pl., London, 1973-77; pastor to students Knox Presbyn. Ch., Toronto, Ont., Can., 1977-80; sr. pastor Salem Evang. Free Ch., Fargo, N.D., 1980—; sec. alumni bd. Trinity Evang. Div. Sch., Deerfield, Ill., 1984-88; chair Com. for Safeguarding Spiritual Heritage, Evang. Free Ch. Co-author: Food for Life, 1977; editor: A Living Legacy, 1990. Fellow Hanszen Coll., Rice U., 1965-66. Home: 1028 N University Dr Fargo ND 58102

SCHARFENBERG, JOACHIM, theology and psychoanalysis educator; b. Erfurt, Germany, May 10, 1927. Grad. in theology, U. Jena, 1951; grad. in psychology, U. Kiel, 1953, ThD, 1953; grad., Psychoanalytical Inst., Berlin, 1961. Pastor Berlin, 1954-58, counsellor, psychotherapist, 1958-68; lectr. U. Tübingen (Fed. Republic Germany), 1968-71; prof. practical theology and psychoanalysis U. Kiel (Fed. Republic Germany), 1971—. Author several books. Home: Hofteich 2,, New Königsförde, D-2371 Bredenbek Federal Republic of Germany

SCHARLEMANN, HERBERT KARL, minister; b. Lake City, Minn., Aug. 5, 1927; s. Ernst Karl and Johanna (Harre) S.; m. Elizabeth Mae Fahrmann, July 1, 1956; children: Lizbeth, Timothy, Nancy, Daniel, James, Mary, Benjamin. BA, Northwestern Coll., 1949; BD, Evang. Luth. Theol. Sem., 1953; CRM, Concordia Sem., 1954, D Ministry, 1978. Ordained to ministry Luth. Ch.-Mo. Synod, 1956. Pastor Grace Luth. Ch., Dodge Ctr., Minn., 1956-58, Trinity Luth. Ch., Hoffman, Ill., 1958—; staff mem. Kaskaskia Coll., Centralia, Ill., 1965—; chmn. South Ill. Dist. Worship Com., 1965-85; pres. Centralia Area Ministerial Alliance, 1962-64; chaplain Kaskaskia Coll., 1965-85. Contbr. articles to religious jours. Precinctman Dem. Party. Mem. Luth. Acad. for Scholarship (award 1963), Luth. Edn. Assn., Soc. Bibl. Lit., Luth. Soc. for Worship and Arts, Luth. Human Rels. Soc., Century Club. Home: 8700 Huey Rd Box 20 Hoffman IL 62250 Office: Trinity Ch Hoffman IL 62250

SCHARLEMANN, ROBERT PAUL, religious studies educator, clergyman; b. Lake City, Minn., Apr. 4, 1929; s. Ernst Karl and Johanna Meta (Harre) S. Student, Northwestern Coll., Watertown, Wis., 1946-49; B.A., Concordia Coll. and Sem., St. Louis, 1952; B.D., Concordia Coll. and Sem., 1955; Dr. theol., U. Heidelberg (Germany), 1957. Ordained to ministry, Lutheran Ch., 1960. Instr. philosophy Valparaiso U., 1957-59; postdoctoral fellow Yale U., 1959-60; pastor Bethlehem Luth. Ch., Carlyle, Ill., 1960-62, Grace Luth. Ch., Durham, N.C., 1962-63; asst. prof. religion U. So. Calif., 1963-64, assoc. prof., 1964-66; assoc. prof. religion U. Iowa, Iowa City, 1966-68, prof., 1968-81; Commonwealth prof. religious studies U. Va., Charlottesville, 1981—; Fulbright-Hayes prof. U. Heidelberg, 1975-76. Author: Thomas Aquinas and John Gerhard, 1964, Reflection and Doubt in the Thought of Paul Tillich, 1969, The Being of God, 1981, Inscriptions and Reflections, 1989, The Reason of Following, 1991; editor Jour. of Am. Acad. Religion, 1980-85; contbr. articles to profl. jours. Mem. Am. Acad. Religion, Am. Theol. Soc., Société Européenne de Culture, Soc. for Philosophy of Religion. Office: Dept Religious Studies U Va Charlottesville VA 22903

SCHARPER, STEPHEN BEDE, editor, writer; b. Port Chester, N.Y., Sept. 5, 1960; s. Philip Jenkins and Sarah Jane Scharper; m. Mary Hilary Cunningham, Aug. 25, 1984. BA in English, U. Toronto, Ont., Can., 1982; MA in Theology, St. Michael's Coll., 1988. Asst. editor Cath. New Times, Toronto, 1982-84; editor Orbis Books, Maryknoll, N.Y., 1984-86; acquisitions editor Twenty-Third Publs., Mystic, Conn., 1986—. Editor: (with others) Insight Guide, 1991; contbr. articles to profl. jours. Mem. Dem. Nat. Com., Hartford, Conn., 1988-91. Mem. Am. Acad. Religion, Religious Edn. Assn. of U.S. and Can. (nominating com. 1991—), Coll. Theology Soc., Am. Teilhard Assn., Religious Pubs. Group., Soc. Bibl. Lit. Office: Twenty-Third Pubs 185 Willow St Mystic CT 06355 *In the current swirl of declining cultural and economic life, religious ideas offer perhaps the greatest hope for social and spiritual transformation, combining as they do faith, vision and a belief in our collective future.*

SCHARTNER, ALBERT LYMAN, organization administrator; b. Wakefield, R.I., July 18, 1931; s. Albert Carl and Ella Mae (Cook) S.; m. Kathleen Doris McBride; children: Dale Edward, Carl William, Beth Anne. BA, Westminster Coll., 1953; M in Div., Pitts. Theol. Sem., 1956, M in Theology, 1962; MA, North Tex. U., 1979. Min. Bethel United Presbyn., Irwin, Pa., 1957-64; asst. adminstr. Presbyn. Homes Cen. Pa., Dillsburg, 1964-69; pres., chief exec. officer Presbyn. Homes, Inc., Camp Hill, Pa., 1969—. Mem. editorial bd. Planning and Financing Facilities for Elderly handbook, 1978, Empirical Fin. and Legal Analysis research Book, 1984. Pres No. York County Sch. Bd., Dillsburg, 1980-84; trustee bd. pensions Presbyn. Ch., 1978-89; bd. dirs. affordable housing coun. Third Dist. Fed. Home Loan Bank, 1990—. Fellow Am. Coll. Nursing Home Adminstrs.; mem. Am. Assn. Homes Aging (del., bd. dirs. 1973-79), Pa. Assn. Non-Profit Homes for Aging (past pres., disting. service award 1985), Am. Pub. Health Assn., Gerontol. Soc., Am. Coll. Healthcare Execs., Phi Kappa Tau. Democrat. Lodge: Rotary (pres. 1970). Avocations: hiking, sailing, music. Home: 304 N Baltimore St Dillsburg PA 17019 Office: Presbyn Homes Inc 1217 Slate Hill Rd Camp Hill PA 17011

SCHATTSCHNEIDER, DAVID ALLEN, religion educator; b. Phila., Mar. 30, 1939; s. Allen Wilbur and Naomi (Wartman) S.; m. Doris Jean Wood, June 2, 1962; children: Laura, Ellen. BA, Moravian Coll., Bethlehem, Pa., 1960; MDiv, Yale U., 1964; MA, U. Chgo. Div. Sch., 1966, PhD, 1975. Instr. in hist. theology Moravian Theol. Sem., Bethlehem, 1968-71, asst. prof., 1971-78, assoc. prof., 1978-86, S. Morgan Smith and Emma Fahs Smith prof., 1986—, dean, v.p., 1988—; mem. investment policy com. Moravian Ch. in Am., Bethlehem, 1981—; cons. Gateway Films, 1982, 87. Author: (with others) Penn's Example to the Nations: 300 Years of the Holy Experiment, 1987; also articles; mem. editorial bd. James Burnside Bull., 1989—. Chmn. bd. Pinebrook Svcs. for Children/Youth, Whitehall, Pa., 1989—. Assn. Theol. Schs. grantee, 1981-82. Mem. Am. Hist. Assn., Am. Soc. Ch. History, Am. Soc. Missiology, Moravian Hist. Soc. (bd. mgrs. 1980—). Home: 2038 Sycamore St Bethlehem PA 18017

SCHATZ, DALE ERROL, minister; b. Berlin Heights, Ohio, Sept. 27, 1936; s. Lawrence John and Elsie Ann (Knittle) S.; m. Gwendolyn Faye Bruce, Aug. 25, 1956; children: Twila Dawn, Kenneth Scott, Craig Allen, Dayle Joy Schatz Shewmaker. Student, Cedarville (Ohio) Coll., 1954-56; diploma, Grand Rapids Bapt. Coll.-Sem., 1961; postgrad., Liberty U., Lynchburg, Va., 1988-90. Ordained to ministry Gen. Assn. Regular Bapt. Chs., 1961. Missionary pastor Fellowship Bapts. for Home Missions, New Hartford, N.Y., 1961-63, Dallas, 1963-78; missionary pastor Heritage Bapt. Ch., Enid, Okla., 1978-90, Heritage Bapt. Mission, Bella Vista, Ark., 1991—; supr. Advance Meat Co., Enid, 1980-90; del. Nat. Conf. Gen. Assn. Regular Bapt. Chs., speaker youth camps, N.Y., Okla., 1961-80, counselor youth camps, Ohio, N.Y., Tex., 1961-80, dir. camp sports, Dallas, 1978; supr. practical ministry Dallas Theol. Sem., 1968-77. Author, editor tape ministry Growing in Grace, 1988—, radio broadcast Growing in Grace, 1988-91. Mem. textbook rev. com. Dallas Ind. Schs. City PTA, 1975-76, chmn. affirmative action com., 1976. Recipient 15-yr. Svc. award Fellowships for Home Missions, 1978, 25-yr. award Heritage Bapt. Ch., Enid, 1987. Mem. Mid-Continent Pastors Fellowship (missionary 1987—), Pastors and Wives Fellowship (clk. Tex. 1969). Republican. Home: 6 Kirkconnel Ln Bella Vista AR 72739 Office: Heritage Bapt Mission PO Box 5362 Bella Vista AR 72714

SCHATZMANN, SIEGFRIED SAMUEL, minister, religion educator; b. Uster, Zurich, Switzerland, Aug. 8, 1941; came to U.S., 1972; s. Karl Johann and Ida Maria (Gatzi) S.; m. Madi Hirzel, Apr. 21, 1962; children: Myriam, David Alan, Marcel Mark. BS, Bethany Bible Coll., 1974; MDiv, S.W. Bapt. theol. Sem., 1976, PhD, 1981. Ordained to ministry Swiss Pentecostal Mission, 1965, So. Bapt. Conv., 1984. Min. Swiss Pentecostal Mission, Glarus, Switzerland, 1963-66; missionary Lesotho, 1966-72; assoc. min. Rockwood Park Assembly of God, Ft. Worth, 1978-81; prof. N.T. Oral Roberts U., Tulsa, 1981-91; dir. studies Elim Bible Coll., Nantwich, Eng., 1991—. Recipient Systems Approach to Instructional Devel. award Oral Roberts U., 1983, Faculty of Yr. award, 1986, Scholar of Yr. award, 1990. Mem. Soc. Bibl. Lit. , Inst. Bibl. Rsch. Home: 20 Charcote Crescent, Wistaston Crewe, Cheshire CW2 6UH, England Office: Elim Bible Coll, London Rd, Nantwich CW5 6LW, England

SCHAUB, MARILYN MCNAMARA, religion educator; b. Chgo., Mar. 24, 1928; d. Bernard Francis and Helen Katherine (Skehan) McNamara; m. R. Thomas Schaub, Oct. 25, 1969; 1 dau., Helen Ann. B.A., Rosary Coll., 1953; Ph.D., U. Fribourg, Switzerland, 1957; diploma, Ecole Biblique, Jerusalem, 1967. Asst. prof. classics and Bibl. studies Rosary Coll., River Forest, Ill., 1957-69; prof. Bibl. studies Duquesne U., Pitts., 1969-70, 73—; participant 8 archeol. excavations, Middle East.; adminstrv dir. expedition to the Southeast Dead Sea Plains, Jordan, 1989—; hon. assoc. Am. Schs. Oriental Rsch., 1966-67, trustee, 1986—; Danforth assoc., 1972-80. Author: Friends and Friendship for St. Augustine, 1964; translator: (with H. Richter) Agape in the New Testament, 3 vols, 1963-65. Mem. Soc. Bibl. Lit., Catholic Bibl. Assn., Am. Acad. Religion. Democrat. Home: 25 McKelvey Ave Pittsburgh PA 15218 Office: Duquesne U Theology Dept Pittsburgh PA 15282

SCHAUB, RAYMOND THOMAS, religion educator; b. South Bend, Ind., Mar. 26, 1933; s. Raymond August and Catherine (Guthrie) S.; m. Marilyn McNamara, Oct. 25, 1969; 1 child, Helen. MA in Philosophy, Aquinas Inst., Dubuque, Iowa, 1958, MA in Theology, 1961; Licentiate in Sacred Scripture, Pontifical Bibl. Commn., Rome, 1967; PhD, U. Pitts., 1973. Prof. Indiana U. Pa., 1969—. Author: Bab Edh-Dhra, 1989; editor: Southeastern Dead Sea Plain Expedition, 1981; contbr. articles to profl. jours. NEH grantee, 1975, 77, 79, 81, 90; NEH fellow, 1982-83, Fulbright fellow, 1989—. Mem. Am. Schs. Oriental Rsch. (trustee 1990—), Am. Ctr. Oriental Rsch. (trustee 1986-89), Cath. Bibl. Assn., Soc. Bibl. Lit., Am. Inst. Archeology. Office: Indiana U of Pa 442 Sutson Hall Indiana PA 15705

SCHEB, NANCY MARIE, lay church worker; b. Scranton, Pa., Apr. 4, 1947; d. Robert B. and Dorothy M. (Wenzel) Skelton; m. Dale E. Scheb, July 22, 1972; children: Mende M., Stephanie L. Mem. adult choir Hollisterville United Meth. Ch., Moscow, Pa., 1986—, asst. dir. children's choir, 1987—, sec.-treas. United Meth. Women, 1988—, lay speaker, 1989—. Home: RD 5 Box 5589 Moscow PA 18444

SCHEBERA, RICHARD LOUIS, priest, educator; b. N.Y.C., Aug. 6, 1937; s. Richard John and Mary Ann (Boylan) S. BD, Montfort Theol. Sem., 1964; STL, Institut Catholique, Paris, 1967; PhD, Fordham U., 1974. Ordained priest, 1964. Dir. edn. Montfort Sem., St. Louis, 1967-70; asst. prof. St. Louis U., 1974-77, assoc. prof. religion, 1978—; assoc. prof. MaryKnoll Theolgate, N.Y., 1977-78; adj. prof. Paul VI Inst., St. Louis, 1978-84. Fordham U. scholar, 1970-72; Am.-Israel Cultural Found. grantee, 1970. Mem. Coll. Theology Soc. (nat. sec. 1975-77). Home: 10316 Conway Rd Saint Louis MO 63131 Office: St Louis U Dept Theol Studi 3634 Lindell Blvd Saint Louis MO 63108

SCHECK, DENNIS RANDALL, religion educator; b. Chgo., Apr. 30, 1951; s. Wilbur B. and Lucille H. (Weber) S.; m. Margaret M. Zoebl, Nov. 18, 1972; children: Jennifer, Timothy, Aleisha. BA in Edn., Concordia Coll., River Forest, Ill., 1972; MRE, Loyola U., Chgo., 1975; EdD, Calif. Coast U., 1991; cert. in vol. mgmt., U. Colo., 1986. Cert. tchr., Ill. Dir. Christian edn. various Luth. churches, Chgo., 1972-75, U.S. Army, Ft. Carson, Colo., 1975—; mem. U.S. Army Religious Edn. Planning and Strategy Group, Washington, 1980—; mem. Coop. Curriculum Selection group, Washington, 1989-91. Co-author handbook on vol. mgmt., 1983; producer local weekly radio program, 1984-85; contbr. articles to various publs. Mem. Assn. Vol. Adminstrn., Luth. Edn. Assn. Avocations: reading, gardening. Office: Office of Staff Chaplain US Army Fort Carson CO 80913-5006

SCHEDLER, GILBERT WALTER, religion educator; b. Vancouver, B.C., Can., Mar. 11, 1935; s. Oscar August and Margaret (Barth) S.; m. Nancy Dunkak, July 20, 1975 (div. 1981); children: Christopher, Rachel, Sara. BA, Concordia Coll., St. Louis, 1957; BD, Concordia Sem., St. Louis, 1960; MA, Washington U., St. Louis, 1963; PhD, U. Chgo., 1970. Prof. U. Pacific, Stockton, Calif., 1967—. Author: (poetry) Waking Before Dawn, 1978, Making Plans, 1980, That Invisible Wall, 1985. NDEA fellow, 1960-64; NEH grantee, 1987. Taoist. Home: 1781 Oxford Way Stockton CA 95204 Office: U Pacific Religious Studies Dept Stockton CA 95211

SCHEDLER, NORBERT OSCAR, educator; b. Milw., Mar. 30, 1933; s. Oscar A.A. and Margaret (Barth) S.; m. Carol E. Skeels, June 27, 1958; children: Karen, Ruthanne, David. BA, Concordia Coll., 1955; STM, Concordia Sem., 1958; MA, Wash. U., 1959; PhD, Princeton U., 1962. Pastor Pilgrim Luth. Ch., Elkins Park, Pa., 1962-63; assoc. prof. Concordia Sr. Coll., Ft. Wayne, Ind., 1963-67; vis. assoc. prof. Purdue U., Lafayette, Ind., 1967-68; chmn. dept. philosophy Concordia Sr. Coll., Ft. Wayne, Ind., 1968-69, Purdue U., Lafayette, Ind., 1969-76; rsch. assoc. U. Calif., Berkeley, 1975-76; chmn. dept. philosophy U. Cen. Ark., Conway, 1976-85, dir. hons. coll., 1982—; expert witness U.S. Senate, Washington, 1985. Author: Philosophy of Religion, 1974; contbr. articles to profl. jours. Fellow Danforth Found., 1979-85. Mem. Am. Acad. Religion, Am. Philos. Assn., Ark. Philos. Soc. (program chmn.), Ctr. for Process Studies, Soc. for Religion and Ecology, Environ. Ethics, Nat. Collegiate Hons. Coun., Ark. Hons. Assn. (founder 1983). Office: U Cen Ark Box 5024 Conway AR 72032

SCHEER, SCOTT A., minister; b. Grand Haven, Mich., May 22, 1950; s. William R. and Lois Rose (Recknagel) S.; m. Cheryl Lynn Cavanaugh; children: Rochelle, Kimberly, James. BS in Christian Edn., Concordia Coll., St. Paul, 1972. Pastor 1st Assembly of God, Baraboo, Wis., 1975-76; evangelist World Vision, Grand Haven, 1976-79; pastor Gaylord (Mich.) Community Ch., 1979-83, Our Fathers House, Holland, Mich., 1983-87; sr. pastor Ch. of The Living Waters, Stuart, Fla., 1987—. Mem. Ind. Full Gospel Ch. Address: Ch of The Living Waters 6540 SE Federal Hwy Stuart FL 33494

SCHEETS, LAWRENCE JOSEPH, 3D, clergyman; b. Centralia, Ill., May 10, 1954; s. Lawrence Joseph Jr. and Ruth Morgan (Baldwin) S.; m. Cynthia Anne Payne, July 19, 1980; 1 child, L.J. Scheets 4th. BA, Asbury Coll., 1976; MDiv, Emory U., 1980. Cert. nat. lab leader jr. high sch. Assoc. pastor 1st United Meth. Ch., Vandalia, Ill., 1980-84; pastor Christopher (Ill.) and Greenwood United Meth. Chs., 1984-86; pastor 1st United Meth. Ch., Chester, Ill., 1986-91, Wood River, Ill., 1991—. Bd. dirs. United Meth. Children's Home, Mt. Vernon, Ill., 1988, bd. pensions, 1989; bd. dirs. Wesley Found. So. Ill. U., Carbondale and Edwardsville, Ill., 1987, Voight Lecture Series, 1985; chmn. So. Ill. Conf. Div. Local Ch. Edn., 1989. Mem. Christian Educators Fellowship, Fellowship of Merry Christians, Nat. Youth Ministry Orgn. (steering com. 1987-89, 91—), Internat. Trumpet Guild, Vandalia Ministerial Alliance (pres. 1982-84), Rotary (chmn. internat. svc. Vandalia club 1983-84), Lions, Masons (chaplain 1989—). Republican. Avocations: photography, running, bicycling. Home: 526 E Lorena Wood River IL 62095 Office: 1st United Meth Ch 6th and Lorena Sts Wood River IL 62095

SCHEETZ, SISTER JOELLEN, academic administrator. Head St. Francis Coll., Ft. Wayne, Ind. Office: St Francis Coll Fort Wayne IN 46808*

SCHEFFLER, LEWIS FRANCIS, educator, pastor; b. Springfield, Ohio, Oct. 13, 1928; s. Lewis Francis and Emily Louise (Kloker) S.; m. Willa Pauline Cole, Aug. 9, 1949 (div. 1978); children: Lewis Francis III, Richard Thomas, Gary Arlen, Tonni Kay; m. Mary Lee Smith, Apr. 18, 1978. BA in Liberal Arts, Cin. Bible Seminary, 1950; AA in Bus., Jefferson Coll., 1989; MAT, Webster U., 1989. Quality assurance Tectum Corp., Newark, 1954-57; research group leader Owens-Corning Fiberglas, Granville, Ohio, 1957-64; research administr. Modiglas Fibers Corp., Bremen, Ohio, 1965-68; dir. R & D Flex-O-Lite Corp., St. Louis; pastor Christian Ch., St. Louis, 1971-75; police commns. Brentwood (Mo.) Police Dept., 1975-87; pastor Christian Ch., Potosi, Mo., 1988-89, Slater (Mo.) Christian Ch., 1989—; prof. English lang. and lit. Missouri Valley Coll., Marshall, 1989—; mem. exec. bd. Northwest Area Christian Ch. (Disciples of Christ); mem. Coun. of Areas of Mid-Am. Region Christian Ch. (Disciples of Christ); cons. in field. Contbr. articles to profl. jours. Patentee in field. Money raiser United Appeal Lancaster, Ohio 1969, chaplaincy Blessing Hosp. Quincy, Ill., 1974, vol. Ill. Div. Children & Family Svc., 1972-75; exec. com. NW Area Christian Ch. (Disciples of Christ), Coun. of Areas Mid.-Am. Region, Christian Ch. (Disciples of Christ). Avocations: philosophy and pomology. Home: 729 Elm St Slater MO 65349 *Now and then, God has so touched people in such a way that,* *recognizing it, we think "So that's what God must be like!" and our ethical and moral sensitivities are heightened.*

SCHEIBE, JEFFREY RICHARD, lay worker; b. Brookfield, Wis., Apr. 10, 1957; s. Fredrick Richard and Ruth Ellen (Gruenwald) S.; m. Susan Marie Ketelhohn, June 2, 1990. BBA, U. Wis., Milw., 1979. Sec. Wis. Evang.-Luth. Synod Southeastern Dist. Youth Ministry, Milw., 1988—; topic leader religion EXEC-PC Bull. Bd. System, Elm Grove, Wis., 1990—. Home: 3302 N 86th St Milwaukee WI 53222

SCHELL, JOSEPH OTIS, clergyman, philosophy educator; b. Port Huron, Mich., May 30, 1914; s. Otis D. and Marie (Trese) S. A.B., Loyola U., Chgo., 1936, A.M., 1941; Ph.L., W. Baden (Ind.) Coll., 1938, S.T.L., 1945; student, U. Toronto, 1938-39. Joined Soc. of Jesus, 1931; ordained priest Roman Catholic Ch., 1944; instr. philosophy John Carroll U., Cleve., 1946-50; asst. prof. John Carroll U., 1950-53, chmn. dept. philosophy, 1950-64, assoc. prof., 1953-59, headmaster residence halls, 1959-64, prof. philosophy, 1959-83, dean Coll. Arts and Scis., 1964-67, univ. pres., 1967-70, coordinator religious affairs, 1971-80, campus minister, 1980—, hon. trustee, 1974—. Mem. Cleve. Commn. Heigher Edn.; Vice chmn. univ. and colls. div. United Appeal Greater Cleve., 1968-70; mem. Greater Cleve. Growth Assn., Urban Coalition of Cleve.; mem. adv. bd. Greater Cleve. Safety Council.; Trustee U. Detroit, Lake Erie Opera Theatre, Cleve. Internat. Program for Youth Leaders; regional office NCCJ, Cleve.; mem. adv. bd. Martha Holden Jennings Found. Mem. Am. Cath., Jesuit philos. assns., Jesuit, Nat. Cath. ednl. assns., Assn. Higher Edn., Ohio Coll. Assn. (exec. com. 1970—), Cath., Jesuit campus ministry assns., Nat. Assn. Coll. and Univ. Chaplains. Address: John Carroll U Cleveland OH 44118

SCHELLBERG, MARTA GLEE, clergywoman; b. Bellingham, Wash., Nov. 16, 1948; d. Martin Gleason and Betty Jean (Newell) Addicott; m. William Robert Rupp, Apr. 26, 1969 (div. Jan. 1988); children: Jennifer Karissa, Mark William; m. Kenneth Herman Schellberg, June 22, 1989. AA in Music Edn., Saddleback Jr. Coll., 1978; BA in Counseling Adminstrn., Thomas Edison State U., 1991. Cert. singles leadership. Tchr., music dir. Shepherd of the Hills/Presch., Mission Viejo, Calif., 1980-83; tchr., chancel choir dir. Old Stone United Meth. Ch., Key West, Fla., 1983-84; religion educator Grace Luth. Ch., Key West, 1981-84; children's choir dir. Shepherd of the Hills United Meth. Ch., Mission Viejo, 1985-87; ednl. program dir. singles ministry Garden St. United Meth. Ch., Bellingham, Wash., 1987—; mem. Bellingham Christian Educators, 1987—, Program Facilitators Fellowship, Seattle, 1988—, Wash. State Chs. Assn. for AIDS Tng., Bellingham, 1990—; dir. Sapphire Joy Singers, Bellingham, 1987—. Co-author curriculum: Intergenerational Activities, 1991. Mem. Nat. Singles Leadership (speaker), Am. Orff-Schulwerk Assn., Christians Alone Reaching Out (pres. 1990—), Wash. State Choristers Guild (pres. 1991-92). Home: 3005 Daniels Ct Bellingham WA 98226 Office: Garden St United Meth Ch 1326 N Garden St Bellingham WA 98225 *In my life I have found that to look at my "cup" as hay full rather than hay empty makes all the difference in how my day unravels. This is a conscious choice I chose to make.*

SCHELLING, TIM A., minister; b. Lancaster, Pa., Sept. 23, 1950; s. Gerald Parke and Patsy Ruth (Gehman) S.; m. Vicki Lynn Latimer, Aug. 15, 1975; children: Andy, Kelly, Jessica. ThG, Tenn. Temple U., Chattanooga, 1973; BA, Trinity Theol. Sem., Newburgh, Ind., 1988. Pastor Second Bapt. Ch., Chatsworth, Ga., 1969-77, Southside Bapt. Ch., Goodview, Va., 1977-80; pastor founder No. Ky. Bapt. Ch., Lakeside Park, Ky., 1980-91; sec. Ky. Bapt. Bible Fellowship, Flo, Ky., 1988. Home and Office: No Ky Baptist Ch 2681 Turkeyfoot Rd Lakeside Park KY 41017

SCHELLMAN, JAMES, religious organization administrator. Pres. Liturgical Conf., Washington. Office: The Liturgical Conf 1017 12th St NW Washington DC 20005*

SCHENCK, PAUL HAIM, minister; b. Bellville, N.J., Oct. 1, 1958; s. Henry Paul and Marjorie (Apgar) S.; m. Rebecca Susan Wald, Mar. 27, 1977; children: Leah Naomi, Ariel David, Abraham Josef, Alizah Jordan, Miriam Michal and Marta Ruth (twins). BA, Luther Rice Coll., 1984; postgrad., Internat. Seminary, Plymouth, Fla., 1990; M of Philosophy, Southwestern U., Salt Lake City, 1985. Ordained to ministry Assemblies of God, 1982. Dir. Upstate N.Y. Teen Challenge, Buffalo, 1979-80; curriculum devel. dir. Buffalo Sch. of Bible, 1980-83; sr. pastor New Covenant Tabernacle, Town of Tonawanda, N.Y., 1980—; headmaster Covenant Acad., Town of Tonawanda, 1987—; prof. Elim Bible Inst., Lima, N.Y., 1990—; chmn. P&R Schenck Assocs., Buffalo, 1986—; mem. Nat. Jewish Com., Gen. Coun. Assemblies of God, Springfield, Mo., 1985—; pres. Nat. Clergy Coun., Atlanta, 1988—. Author: (book, tape series) The Condom Conspiracy, 1986. Hon. chaplain, U.S. Ho. Reps., 1979, 80, vis. chaplain Erie County Holding Ctr., Buffalo, 1980; chmn. bd. Charles Grandison Finney High Sch., 1990—. Republican. Office: New Covenant Tabernacle 345 McConkey Dr Buffalo NY 14223

SCHENCK, ROBERT LEONARD, minister; b. Montclair, N.J., Oct. 1, 1958; s. Henry Paul and Marjorie Mary (Apgar) S.; m. Cheryl Elizabeth Smith, Apr. 9, 1977; children: Anna Lynn, Matthew Jason. Ministerial diploma, Berean Coll., 1980; cert. bible and theology, Buffalo Sch. the Bible, 1982. Ordained to ministry Assemblies of God Ch., 1982. Exec. dir. Empire State Teen Challenge, Rochester, N.Y., 1976-80; assoc. min. Webster (N.Y.) Assembly of God., 1980-81; min. Evangelism Community Gospel Ch., Long Island City, N.Y., 1981-82; pres. P&R Schenck Assocs. in Evangelism, Buffalo, 1982—; adj. prof. Buffalo Sch. the Bible, 1980, 82-83; dir. Western N.Y. Leadership Found., Buffalo, 1983-84; chmn. Rochester Area Youth Impact, Rochester, 1980-81, World Outreach Conf., Buffalo, 1985; founder Operation Serve Med. Dental Mission, Mexico City, 1983, Hearts for the Homeless, Buffalo, 1990. Editor: Legal Structures of American Denominations, 1983, Covenant Mag., 1983-86; author: When God Speaks, 1985. Lead walker 2000 Mile Charity Faithwalk, Buffalo, 1988; coord. Justice For All Rally, Buffalo, 1990. Recipient Presdl. Commendation letter Pres. George Bush, Washington, 1989, Mayoral Commendation award Mayor James Griffin, Buffalo, 1988, Mayoral Proclamation award Mayor Sidwey Bartholomew, New Orleans, 1988, Legis. Commendation award Legis. Charles Swanick, Buffalo, 1988. Mem. Nat. Assn. Evangelicals, Christian Coalition N.Y., Nat. Clergy Coun., Assn. Internat. Mission Svc., Asesoria Profl. de Mexico. Home: 24 Leawood Dr Tonawanda NY 14150 Office: P&R Schenck Assoc 345 McConkey Dr Buffalo NY 14223 *In my life I have found that faith is not the denial of reality, but rather the interpretation of reality.*

SCHENEMAN, MARK ALLAN, minister; b. Washington, Oct. 13, 1948; s. William Allyn and Jeanne K. (Lorah) Scheneman; m. Dorothy Mary Hosauer, Aug. 15, 1970; children: Katherine E., Elisabeth C., Peter A. BA, Moravian Coll., 1970; MDiv, Gen. Theol. Sem., 1973; MA in Religion, Temple U., 1976; D Ministry in Pastoral Ministry, Eastern Bapt. Theol. Sem., 1983. Ordained to ministry Episcopal Ch. Asst. St. Mary's Episcopal Ch., Ardmore, Pa., 1973-75, St. Anne's Episcopal Ch., Abington, Pa., 1975-77; rector St. Peter's Episcopal Ch., Broomall, Pa., 1977-86, St. John's Episcopal Ch., Carlisle, Pa., 1986—; chair budget com. local diocese, Phila., 1984-83, mem. planning com., Harrisburg, 1986-88, mem. commn. on ministry, Harrisburg, 1990—; adj. faculty mem. Eastern Bapt. Theol. Sem., Phila., 1985; mem. adv. bd. Internat. Cult Edn. Program; dir. Jubilee Ministry Ctr., St. John's Ch. Editor liturgy booklet: Stations of the Cross, 1982. Bd. dirs. Delaware County chpt. ARC, Media, Pa., 1984-85. Mem. Cult Awareness Network, Rotary. Office: St John's Episcopal Ch Box 612 Carlisle PA 17013

SCHENK, RICHARD CHARLES, priest, editor; b. Glendale, Calif., June 27, 1951; s. Robert C. and Betty K. (Groschong) S. BA, St. Albert's Coll., 1974; MA, Dominican Sch. Philosophy and Theology, 1977; ThD, U. Munich, 1986. Ordained Dominican priest Roman Cath. Ch., 1978. Sci. asst. U. Munich, 1982-85; editor medieval texts Bavarian Acad. Scis., Munich, 1986-91; prof. Dominican Sch. Philosophy and Theology, Grad. Theol. Union, Berkeley, Calif., 1991—; dir. Forschungsinstitut für Philosophie Hannover, Fed. Republic Germany, 1991—; vis. prof. U. Fribourg (Switzerland), 1989-91. Author: Die Gnade vollendeter Endlichkeit, 1989; contbr. articles to profl. jours. Home: Postfach 1313, 3006 Burgwedel, 3006 Burgwedel Federal Republic of Germany Office: Forschungsinstitut für, Philosophie Hannover, Lange Laube 14, 3000 Hannover Federal Republic of Germany *"Be ready to answer anyone asking what reasons you have for the hope which is in you." (1 Peter 3, 15).*

SCHENKEL, BARBARA ANN, minister, social worker; b. Albuquerque, Mar. 17, 1951; d. Richard Henry and Mildred (Voth) S. BSN, U. N.Mex., 1972; MDiv, Iliff Sch. Theology, 1978; MSW, Ariz. State U., 1988. RN, N.Mex.; ordained to ministry Meth. Ch., 1979. Minister intern Christ Ch. U. Meth. Ch., Denver, 1975-77; parish minister Herman (Nebr.) Federated and Riverside Bapt. Ch., 1978-82, Cambridge (Nebr.) Bartley U. Meth. Ch., 1982-85; family minister Red Mountain U.M.C., Mesa, Ariz., 1987; Christ Ch. Caring Community Coordinator, Denver, 1975-77; advisor alcohol treatment program Immanuel Hosp., Washington County, Nebr., 1980-82; mem. task group to study Ministry Effectiveness in Nebr., 1981; vis. del. to World Meth. Conf., Honolulu, 1981; registrar for candidacy Bd. or Ordained Ministry, 1980-84, strategy com., 1984-85; drug and alcohol cons. Salvation Army Adult Rehab. Ctr., Phoenix, 1987-88, Adult Protective Svcs., 1988—. Chaplain Jackson-Peck Am. Legion Post, Herman, 1980-82. Served to 1st lt. USAF Nurse Corps, 1973-75. Mem. Nebr. Ann. Conf. United Meth. Chs., Cambridge Ministerial Assn. (pres. 1984), Tekamah-Herman Ministerial Assn. (pres. 1981), S.W. Dist. Coun. Ministries (past com. memberships), Sierra, Amnesty Internat., Nat. Assn. Social Workers, Phi Kappa Phi. Avocations: horseback riding, bowling, crochet, needlepoint, crewel. Office: Adult Protective Svcs 1122 N 7th St Ste 205 Phoenix AZ 85006

SCHEPERS, DONALD HERBERT, religious organization administrator; b. St. Louis, May 14, 1951; s. Herbert Joseph and Amelia Marie (Pohlmann) S. BA, St. Mary's U., San Antonio, 1974; MDiv, St. Michael's Faculty Theology, Toronto, Ontario, Can., 1981. Math and sci. instr. Vianney High Sch., St. Louis, 1974-78; campus minister sch. medicine St. Louis U., 1981-82; chaplain Marianist Retreat and Conf. Ctr., Eureka, Mo., 1982-84, pres., chief exec. officer, 1984—; trainer Office of Ministry, St. Louis, 1986—; exec. com. Archdiocesan Coun. of Priests, St. Louis, 1988-90. Editor for Marianist Resources Commn., Dayton, Ohio, 1984-88; author: (with others) Ministry Discernment, 1988. Active Regional Commerce and Growth Assn., St. Louis, 1988. Mem. Retreats Internat. (bd. trustees, coun. area reps.), Met. Assn. of Retreat and Conf. Ctrs. Democrat. Roman Catholic. Avocations: backpacking, biking, guitar, fishing, running. Home: 4528 Maryland Ave Saint Louis MO 63108 Office: Marianist Retreat and Conf Ctr 1280 Hwy 109 PO Box 718 Eureka MO 63025

SCHERBARTH, RAY EDWIN, minister; b. Stratford, Ont., Can., May 1, 1941; came to U.S., 1967; s. Edwin J. and Olive A. (Fischer) S.; m. Carol M. VanderLuitgaren, June 24, 1967; children: Crista D., Craig H. Diploma in lay ministry, Concordia Coll., Milw., 1967; student, San Francisco State U., 1976-80; MDiv, Concordia Theol. Sem., Ft. Wayne, Ind., 1984. Ordained to ministry Luth. Ch.-Mo. Synod. Minister of youth West Portal Luth. Ch., San Francisco, 1967-70, asst. to pastor, 1970-80; asst. pastor Our Shepherd Luth. Ch., Birmingham, Mich., 1984-87, adminstrv. pastor, 1988—; bd. dirs. Luth. Care for Aging, San Francisco, 1978-80, Psychol. Studies, Farmington, Mich., 1989—; chmn. nominations Mich. dist. Luth. Ch.-Mo. Synod, Ann Arbor, 1988-91. Office: Our Shepherd Luth Ch 2225 E 14 Mile Rd Birmingham MI 48009

SCHERCH, RICHARD OTTO, minister; b. Balt., Nov. 21, 1926; s. Richard Leopold and Anna Elizabeth (Finger) S.; m. Janice Marie Halbgewachs, June 24, 1951; children: Richard Paul, Leslie Carol, Lisa Beth, Jeremy Thomas. BA, Gettysburg Coll., 1948; BD, Luth. Sch. Theology, Phila., 1951; PhD, Johns Hopkins U., 1959; D Ministry, Lancaster Theol. Sem., 1975. Ordained to ministry Luth. Ch., 1951. Mission developer Wichita, Kans., 1951-53; pastor Trinity Luth. Ch., Manhattan beach, Calif., 1953-57; asst. pastor 1st Luth. Ch., Balt., 1957-59; pastor St. Mark's Luth. Ch., Birdsboro, Pa., 1961-65, Zion Luth. Ch., Lebanon, Pa., 1965-71, Shiloh Luth. Ch., York, Pa., 1972-75, Christ Luth. Ch., Paramus, N.J., 1976-81; sr. pastor Emmanuel Luth. Ch., Venice, Fla., 1981—; mission developer Kansas City, Mo., 1959-61; lectr. Chautauqua (N.Y.) Inst., 1963, 64, 65; instr. Johns Hopkins U., Balt., 1957-58, U. Balt., 1958-59; dir. Consult, Inc., Lebanon, Pa.; adj. faculty mem. Luther Coll., Teaneck, N.J., 1977-78, Bergen Community Coll., Paramus, 1979; chmn. profl. support com. Fla. Synod Luth. Ch. Am., Tampa, Fla., 1987—, ptnr. in evangelism, Chgo., 1985—. Comdr. USNR, 1956-77. Mem. Internat. Transactional Analysis Assn., Venice C. of C., Rotary. Republican. Office: Emmanuel Luth Ch 800 S Tamiami Trail Venice FL 34285

SCHERER, ALFREDO VICENTE CARDINAL, former archbishop of Porto Alegre, Brazil; b. Bom Principio, Rio Grande do Sul, Brazil, Feb. 5, 1903; s. Pedro and Ana Oppermann Scherer; student Seminario Central de Sao Leopoldo and Pontifical Gregorian U., Rome. Ordained priest Roman Catholic Ch., Rome, 1926; pvt. sec. to archbishop of Porto Alegre, Brazil, 1927-33; organizer of Parishes of Tapes and Barra do Ribeiro, 1933-35; parish priest Sao Geraldo, Porto Alegre, 1935-46; aux. bishop of Porto Alegre, 1946; archbishop, 1946-81; elevated to Sacred Coll. of Cardinals, 1969. Address: Residencia Arquiepiscopal, Rua Espirito Santo 95, Porto Alegre RS, Brazil

SCHERMAN, PAUL H., ecumenical agency administrator. Head Summerside (P.E.I.) Christian Coun. Office: Summerside Christian Coun, 181 Green st, Summerside, PE Canada C1N 1Y8*

SCHERTZ, MARY HELEN, religion educator; b. Washington, Ill., Apr. 27, 1949; d. Elson Arthur and Eileen Elizabeth (Bachman) S. BA in English, Goshen Coll., 1971; MDiv, Assoc. Mennonite Biblical Sems, 1983; postgrad. in religion, Vanderbilt U. Asst. prof. religion Goshen (Ind.) Coll., 1983-84; New Testament bibliographer, rsch. asst. Vanderbilt U., Nashville, 1984-87, teaching asst., 1985-87; asst. prof. New Testament Assoc. Mennonite Biblical Sem., Elkhart, Ind., 1987—. Contbr. articles to profl. publs. Chair elders Assembly Mennonite Ch., Goshen, 1989—. Home: 328 W Wolf Elkhart IN 46516 Office: Assoc Mennonite Bibl Sems 3003 Benham Ave Elkhart IN 46517

SCHEUER-SUEVEL, MARKAY LYNN, minister; b. Chgo., Dec. 16, 1959; d. Garry Albert and Carolyn Jo (Lukens) Scheuer; m. Eric Bernhardt Suevel, July 27, 1985; children: Korissa Lynn, Joshua Bernhardt. BA, Elmhurst Coll., 1983; MDiv, Chgo. Theol. Sem., 1986. Pastor St. John United Ch. of Christ, Arlington Heights, Ill.; sec. mission coun. Ill. Conf. United Ch. of Christ, 1990—. Office: St John United Ch of Christ 308 N Evergreen AVe Arlington Heights IL 60004

SCHIEDER, JOSEPH EUGENE, clergyman; b. Buffalo, Sept. 23, 1908; s. Robert and Mary Loretta (Quinn) S. B.A., Niagara U., 1931; M.A., St. Bonaventure U., 1935; Ph.D., U. Ottawa, Ont., Can., 1943; LL.D., St. Vincent's Coll., 1951; Litt.D. (hon.), Seaton Hall U., 1954; L.H.D. (hon.), LaSalle Coll., 1956, Canisius Coll., 1986; D. in Pedagogy, Niagara U., 1987. Ordained priest Roman Catholic Ch., 1935; dir. Youth Retreats Diocese of Buffalo, 1939-48; diocesan dir. Confraternity of Christian Doctrine, Buffalo, 1941-48; dir. youth bur. Buffalo Police Dept., 1942-48; nat. dir. Cath. Youth Am., Washington, 1948-61; also dir. youth dept. Nat. Cath. Welfare Conf., Washington; apptd. Papal Chamberlain, 1950, Domestic Prelate, 1953, Prothonatary Apostolic, 1968; pastor St. Andrew's Ch., Buffalo, 1963-76; founder, 1st dir. St. Andrew's Montessori Sch., 1973; mem. Mental Health Bd., 1968—; dean theology Marymount Coll., Arlington, Va., 1961-63; diocesan consultor, 1969—; regional coordinator Diocese of Buffalo, procurator diocesan properties, 1977—; founder Nat. Cath. Youth Week; chmn. Permanent Com. Pub. Decency, Buffalo, 1941-48; diocesan dir. financial drive Diocese of Buffalo, 1971; mem. White House Conf. Children and Youth, 1950; adviser on Youth Spl. Mission to Germany USAF, 1952; Spl. Mission to Tokyo, Japan for UNESCO, 1953; adviser on youth U.S. Sec. Labor, 1951-60; adviser on fitness of youth to Pres. Eisenhower, 1955-60; chmn. task force founding Stella Niagara Ednl. Parks, Niagara Falls, N.Y.; mem. exec. bd. Cantalician Center, Buffalo; mem. adv. bd. ARC, Kenmore Mercy Hosp. Author: Talks to Parents, 1954, Spiritual Lifts for Youth, 1956; Editor of: Youth mag, 1949-61. Mem. ho. of dels. United Way, 1973—, vice chmn., 1975; bd. dirs. Oral Sch., Ft. Lauderdale, Fla., 1977; vice chmn. Bicentennial Celebration; bd. trustees Erie County Library Assn., 1979—; bd. fin. Diocese of Buffalo, 1979—; chmn. Buffalo div. Christian Bros. Tricentennial World Anniversary, 1981; Founder, past bd. dirs. various Cath. youth assns.; bd. founders St. Andrew's Country Day Sch.; chmn. Drug Abuse Program, Ft. Lauderdale, Fla., 1981—; mem. adv. bd. Project Korle Bu Accra Ghana, West Africa, 1983. Served as adviser to Cath. chief chaplain USAF, 1953; chief chaplain AUS, 1954. Recipient award Christian Bros., 1947, award Mayor of Rome, Italy, 1950, Archdiocese award Hartford, Conn., 1954, De la Salle medal Manhattan Coll., 1958, Padre Youth award for U.S., 1961, Star Solidarity from Pres. Italy, 1969, Bishop McNulty Meml. award, 1973, Pres.'s medal St. John's Coll., Washington, 1973; also awards dioceses Charleston, S.C.; also awards dioceses Wichita, Kans.; Man of Yr. award Town of Tonawanda, 1977; award for prestigious service Buffalo Fire Dept., 1980; 1st recipient Outstanding Alumni award St. Joseph's Collegiate Inst., 1984; Spl. Gift award for outstanding service to Diocese of Buffalo, 1986; Outstanding Service to Diocese of Buffalo citation Office Bishop of Buffalo, Oustanding Assistance and Help citation United Cerebral Palsy Assn., 1987; named Man of Yr., Marian Guild St. Andrew's Ch., Kenmore, N.Y. Clubs: University (Washington); Niagara Falls Country; Park Country (Buffalo), Saturn (Buffalo); Amherst (N.Y.) Country; Tower (Ft. Lauderdale, Fla.). Lodge: K.C. (4th deg.). Address: 72 Somersby Ct Buffalo NY 14221 *Zeal for my position and my vocation, accompanied by hard labor, has contributed much to whatever success I have attained. Love of people and sincerity and the spirit of sacrifice where others are concerned has added to my happiness in life. My faith in God has made difficult undertakings much easier.*

SCHIERSE, PAUL J., priest, canon lawyer; b. Phila., June 28, 1928; s. Paul Joseph and Sophia Margaret (Boltersdorf) S. BA in Philosophy, St. Charles Sem., Phila., 1951; JCB in Canon Law, Cath. U. Am., 1960, JCL, 1961, JCD, 1963. Ordained priest Roman Cath. Ch. Assoc. pastor Cath. Diocese of Wilmington, Del., 1955-59; asst. chancellor Diocese of Wilmington, 1962-69, chancellor, 1969-74, vicar for adminstrn., 1974-77; pastor St. Joseph's/Brandywine, Greenville, Del., 1977—; tribunal Cath. Diocese of Wilmington, 1958—. Mem. Canon Law Soc. Am. Home and Office: St Joseph's/Brandywine 10 Old Church Rd Greenville DE 19807

SCHIESLER, ROBERT ALAN, pastor; b. Lancaster, Pa., Sept. 3, 1949; s. Robert Joseph and Rita Marie (Gross) S.; m. M. Antoinette Rodez, Oct. 20, 1973. BA, St. Mary's Coll., Bapt., 1971; MA, St. Mary's Sem., Bapt., 1973; MDiv, Inter/Met., Washington, 1977; D Ministry, Inst. Grad. Studies, Detroit, 1985. Ordained to ministry Episcopal Ch., 1978. Rector St. Paul's Episcopal Ch., Albany, N.Y., 1978-80, Trinity Episcopal Ch., Belleville, Mich., 1980-85, St. Stephen's Episcopal Ch., Phila., 1985-88, St. Andrew's Episcopal Ch., Wilmington, Del., 1988—; tchr., dept. chmn. Carroll High Sch., Washington, 1972-75; chmn. Pa. Clergy Assn., Phila., 1986-88; mem. pers. com. Episcopal Diocese of Del., 1989—, vice chmn. standing com., 1990—. Bd. dirs. United Way, Wilmington, 1988—, Limen House, Wilmington, 1990, Del. Food Bank, Newark, 1989; vice chmn. Sojourners Place, Wilmington, 1989—. Mem. Del. Clergy Assn. (exec. com. 1989). Office: St Andrew's Episcopal Ch 8th and Shipley Sts Wilmington DE 19801

SCHIESS, BETTY BONE, priest; b. Cin., Apr. 2, 1923; d. Evan Paul and Leah (Mitchell) Bone; m. William A. Schiess, Aug. 28, 1947; children: William A. (dec.), Richard Corwine, Sarah. B.A., U. Cin., 1945; M.A., Syracuse U., 1947; M.Div., Rochester Ctr. for Theol. Studies, 1972. Ordained priest Episcopal Ch., 1974; priest assoc. Grace Episc. Ch., Syracuse, N.Y., 1975; mem. Gov.'s Task Force on Life and Law, 1985—; chaplain Syracuse U., 1976-78, Cornell U., Ithaca, N.Y., 1978-79; rector Grace Episc. Ch., Mexico, N.Y., 1984—; instnl. rev. bds. Crouse-Irving Hosp. and Upstate Med. Ctr., Syracuse, 1986-90; cons. Women's Issues Network Episc. Ch. in U.S., 1987—; writer, lectr., cons. religion and feminism, 1979—. Author: Take Back the Church, Indeed The Witness, 1982, Creativity and Procreativity: Some Thoughts on Eve and the Opposition and How Episcopalians Make Ethical Decisions, Plumline, 1988. Bd. dirs. People for Pub. TV in N.Y., 1978, Religious Coalition for Abortion Rights; mem. infant care rev. com. Crouse-Meml. Hosp.; trustee Elizabeth Cady Stanton Found., 1979; mem. policy com. Coun. Adolescent Pregnancy. Recipient Gov.'s award Women of Merit in Religion, 1984, Ralph E. Kharas award ACLU Cen. N.Y., 1986 Goodall disting. alumna award & Hills Sch., 1988, Human Rightes award Human Rights Commn. of Syracuse and Orange County, N.Y., 1989; hon. life membership Na'amat U.S., 1987. Mem. NOW (Syracuse), Internat. Assn. Women Ministers (dir. 1978, pres. 1984-87), Assn. for Vol. Surg. Contraception (exec. com.), Am. Soc. Law and Medicine, Clergy Assn. Diocese of Cen. N.Y. (v.p. 1985—), Mortar Bd., Theta Chi Beta. Democrat. Home and Office: 107 Bradford Ln Syracuse NY 13224 Office: Grace Episcopal Ch Main St Mexico NY 13114

SCHIESSL, DANIEL MARK, elementary educator; b. LaCrosse, Wis., Feb. 24, 1959; s. David Robert and Ileen Violet (Gehrke) S. BS, Dr. Martin Luther Coll., New Ulm, Minn., 1982; MEd, Mich. State U., 1990. Tchr. St. James' Luth. Sch., Milw., 1982-83, Garden Homes Luth. Sch., Milw., 1982-83, St. Paul's Luth. Sch., Stevensville, Mich., 1983—; sec. Southwest Mich. Tchrs. Conf., Benton Harbor, 1985-87, arts chmn., 1989—. Active YMCA, St. Joseph, Mich., 1990—. Mem. ASCD, Mich. High Sch. Sports Assn. Republican. Lutheran. Avocations: volleyball officiating, singing, yard work, travel. Home: 2450 Marquette Woods Rd Stevensville MI 49127 Office: St Pauls Luth Sch 2673 W John Beers Rd Stevensville MI 49127

SCHIFF, GARY STUART, academic administrator, educator; b. Bklyn., Mar. 27, 1947; s. Jacob and Lillian (Grumet) S.; divorced; children: Jeremy Jay, Rina Joy. BA, Bin Hebrew Lit., Yeshiva U., 1968; MA, Columbia U., 1970, Cert. in Middle East Studies, 1973, PhD, 1973. Asst. prof. Jewish studies and polit. sci. CUNY, 1973-76; dir. Mid. East affairs Nat. Jewish Community Rels. Coun., N.Y.C., 1976-78; exec. asst. to pres. Acad. for Ednl. Devel., N.Y.C., 1978-83; pres. Gratz Coll., Melrose Park, Pa., 1983—. Author: Tradition and Politics: The Religious Parties of Israel, 1977, The Energy Education Catalog, 1981; contbr. articles to profl. jours. Grantee NEH, Ford Found., Danforth Found., Woodrow Wilson Found., William Penn Found., Pew Charitable Trusts. Mem. Assn. for Israel Studies (v.p.), Coun. for Jewish Edn. (bd. dirs.), Assn. for Jewish Studies, World Jewish Congress (gov. bd.), Am. Jewish Com. (N.Y. chpt. bd. dirs., Phila. chpt. communal affairs commn.). Avocations: liturgical music, boating, cats. Home: 130 Spruce St Philadelphia PA 19106 Office: Gratz Coll Old York Rd & Melrose Ave Melrose Park PA 19126

SCHIFFER, IRA JEFFREY, rabbi; b. Bklyn., July 21, 1951; s. Morton and Naomi (Marlowe) S.; m. Linda Shrier, Nov. 1, 1981; children: Rachel, Benjamin. BA in Philosophy cum laude, Temple U., 1973; MA in History of Religion, Brown U., 1975. Ordained rabbi, 1981. Rabbi Temple Beth El, Newark, Del., 1977-87, Beth Am Synagogue, Balt., 1987—; pres. Del. Bd. Rabbis, 1984-86. Mem. pastoral adv. bd. Planned Parenthood of Del., Wilmington, 1984-87; bd. dirs. Jewish Family Svc. of Del., Wilmington, 1984-87. Mem. Reconstructionist Rabbinical Assn. (treas. 1983-85, pres. 1985-87), NCCJ (bd. dirs. 1987—), Balt. Jewish Coun. (bd. dirs. 1990—), Balt. Bd. Rabbis (pres. 1991—). Democrat. Office: Beth Am Synagogue 2501 Eutaw Pl Baltimore MD 21217

SCHILIT, DIANE LIPSON, religious organization administrator, educator; b. Vineland, N.J., Oct. 13, 1956; d. Sol and Suzanne (Rosenstein) Lipson; m. Howard Mark Schilit, Jan. 1, 1981; children: Jonathan, Suzanne, Amy. Student, Hebrew U., 1976-77; BA in Edn., U. Fla., 1978; MS in Personnel Adminstrn., American U., 1983. Spl. educator Prince George's Pub. Schs., Adelphi, Md., 1978-79; dir. program and youth B'nai Israel Congregation, Rockville, Md., 1979—; bd. dirs. Spl. Edn. Dept. Bd. Jewish Edn., 1987—. Active Task Force on Drinking and Driving, Montgomery County, 1981-82, task force Jewish Found. for Group Homes, Greater Washington, 1982-83; seaboard region liaison Youth Commn. United Synagogue, Rockville, 1979—. Mem. Jewish Youth Dirs. Assn. (chair membership 1981-82), Coalition on Advancements in Jewish Edn. Office: B'nai Israel Congregation 6301 Montrose Rd Rockville MD 20852-4195

SCHILLER, JOHANNES AUGUST, clergyman, educator; b. Gaylord, Kans., June 17, 1923; s. Johann Carl and Adele Dorothea (Kirchoff) S.; m. Aleen B. Linhardt, Aug. 26, 1946; children: Paul Omar, Samuel Robert. BA, Capital U., 1945; cand. theology, Evangel. Luth. Theol. Sem., 1947; MA, U. Mo., 1959; PhD in Sociology, U. Wash., 1967. Ordained to ministry Am. Luth. Ch., 1947. Pastor Peace Luth. Ch., Sterling, Colo., 1947-49, Trinity-St. Paul Parish, Malcolm, Iowa, 1949-51, Emmanuel Luth. Ch., Beatrice, Nebr., 1951-56, Salem Luth. Ch., Lenexa, Kans., 1956-58; asst.

prof., assoc. prof., now prof. sociology Pacific Luth. U., Tacoma, Wash., 1958-91; prof. emeritus Pacific Luth. U., Tacoma, 1991—; regency prof. Pacific Luth. U., Tacoma, Wash., 1976—, chair dept. sociology, 1956-71, 86-88, dean div. social scis., 1969-76, 88-91, dir. grad. programs div. social scis., 1977-82, dir. Ctr. Social Rsch. and Pub. Policy, 1987-90; chaplain Beatrice State Home, 1953-56; adj. prof. San Francisco Theol. Sem., San Anselmo, Calif., 1978-89. Editor: The American Poor, 1982; contbr. articles to profl. publs. Mem. Am. Sociology Assn., Pacific Sociology Assn., Nat. Coun. Family Rels., Wash. State Sociol. Assn. Home: 1217 Wheeler St S Tacoma WA 98444 Office: Pacific Luth Univ Tacoma WA 98447

SCHILLING, FRIEDRICH, JR., minister; b. Lynchburg, Va., Aug. 2, 1934; s. Friedrich and Lillian (Siler) S.; m. Barbara Huey, Feb. 17, 1962; children: Thomas F., Kathryn M., Anne E., Jonathan S. BS, U. of South, 1956; M in Forestry, Yale U., 1957, MST, 1968; BDiv, Union Theol. Sem., 1967, DMin, 1976. Ordained to ministry Presbyn. Ch. (USA). Svc. forester Va. Div. Forestry, Farmville, 1957-58; extension forester Va. Tech. U., Blackstone, 1961-64; min. Providence Presbyn. Ch., Matthews, N.C., 1968-74; sr. min. Beckley (W.Va.) Presbyn. Ch., 1974-85; min. Westminster Presbyn Ch., Knoxville, Tenn., 1985—; dir. Camp Merriewodd Harrison, Richmond, Va., 1965, 67; chair Inter-church Action Bd., Charlotte, N.C., 1970-74; chair specialized ministries com. Presbytery of Charlotte, 1971-74, mem. coordinating coun., 1978-81; chair long range planning Massonetta Bd., Harrisonburg, Va., 1983-84. Chair organizing group Teen Age Parents Svc., Charlotte, N.C., 1970-73; bd. dirs. Davis-Stuart Home, Lewisburg, W.Va., 1979-83; mem. exec. com. Union Theol. Sem. in Va., 1979-83; human rels. coun. City of Beckley, 1979-82; organizer, bd. dirs. Women's Resource Ctr., Battered Women's Shelter, Beckley, 1979; organizer, cons. Shepherd's Ctr. for Older Adults, Beckley, 1979-84; organizer, mem. adv. bd. Teen Ctr., Beckley, 1980-84; community planning coord. Symposium to Plan Youth Mus., Beckley, 1983-84. Capt. USAF, 1958-61. Recipient Min. of Yr. award Raleigh County Soil Conservation Svc., 1981. Mem. Kiwanis (pres. Beckley club 1983-84). Democrat. Home: 309 Forest Oak Dr Knoxville TN 37919 Office: Westminister Presbyn Ch 6580 Northshore Dr Knoxville TN 37919

SCHILLING, HERBERT GLEN, minister, religious organization administrator; b. McComb, Miss., Nov. 21, 1929; s. Herbert Luther and Mamie Elizabeth (Potts) S.; m. Juanita Bond, Nov. 23, 1949; children: Connie Lynn Schilling Taylor, Bonnie Sue Schilling Jackson. BS, Miss. Coll., 1962. Ordained to ministry So. Baptist Conv., 1957. Pastor Oak Grove (Miss.) Bapt. Ch., 1958-62; pastor Cen. Bapt. Ch., Yazoo County, Miss., 1962-65, Brookhaven, Miss., 1975-78; pastor Shady Grove (Miss.) Bapt. Ch., 1965-72, Friendship Bapt. Ch., Pike County, Miss., 1972-75; dir. missions Simpson Assn., Mendenhall, Miss., 1978—; chaplain Miss. N.G., Hazlehurst, 1967-72, hosps. in McComb, Brookhaven, Mendenhall, Magee, 1978—, Mendenhall Police Dept., 1990—. Mem. Lions Club, Bentonia, Miss., 1962-65; chaplain Exchange Club, Brookhaven, 1975-78. Home and Office: Rte 4 Box 389 Mendenhall MS 39111

SCHILLING, LINDA KAYE, writer, office manager; b. Portsmouth, Ohio, Oct. 22, 1948; d. Lennis Raymond and Doris Elizabeth (Herrmann) Adkins; m. Kenneth L. Bagby, Dec. 21, 1968 (div. Mar. 1984); children: Arthur P., Paul M.; m. Nicholas R. Schilling, Dec. 22, 1984. Student, Ohio U., 1966-67, Wright State U., 1977-83; diploma, Miami Valley Hosp. Sch. Nursing, Dayton, Ohio, 1970; BA in Human Devel., Antioch U., 1988; postgrad., United Theol. Sem., 1988—. RN, Ohio. Office mgr. Schilling Cabinet Co., Kettering, Ohio, 1984—; student assoc. pastor Christ United Meth. Ch., Kettering, 1990-91. Student trustee United Theol. Sem., Dayton, 1990-91; trustee Alpha Sch., Dayton, 1986-88. Mem. Dayton Bach Soc. (pres. 1990—). Home: 4173 White Oak Dr Dayton OH 45432 *Individual human lives and collective human existence mark time along their respective journeys by the milestones of life events. Decisions made and choices enacted contribute to the unique character of each person and each era of history. It is the process of journeying that makes all the difference.*

SCHILLING, SYLVESTER PAUL, pastor, religion educator; b. Cumberland, Md., Feb. 7, 1904; s. Sylvester and Ida Christina (Weber) S.; m. Mary Elizabeth Albright, 1930; children: Robert Albright, Paula Carol Schilling Foreman. BS, St. John's Coll., 1923; AM, Boston U., 1927, STB, 1929, PhD, 1934. Ordained to ministry Meth. Ch., 1928. Pastor Meth. Ch., Vienna, Va., 1932-33; asst. pastor Mt. Vernon Pl. Meth. Ch., Balt., 1933-36; pastor Meth. Ch., Prince Frederick, Md., 1936-40, Brookland Meth. Ch., Washington, 1940-45; prof. systematic theology and philosophy of religion Westminster (Md.) Theol. Sem., 1945-53; prof. systematic theology Boston U., 1953-69, chmn., div. theol. studies, 1954-69, prof. emeritus, 1969—; chmn. bd. world peace com. Balt. Conf. Meth. Chs., Md., D.C., W.Va., 1939-47, pres., bd. of edn., 1948-53; vis. prof. theology Union Theol. Sem., Manila, 1969-70, Wesley Theol. Sem., Washington, 1970-73, Garrett-Evang. Theol. Sem., Naperville, Ill., 1974, Andover Newton (Mass.) Theol. Sch., 1978-81; chmn. world peace com. Washington Fedn. of Chs., 1942-45. Author: Isaiah Speaks, 1958, Methodism and Society in Theological Perspective, 1960, Contemporary Continental Theologians, 1966, God in an Age of Atheism, 1969, God Incognito, 1974, God and Human Anguish, 1977, The Faith We Sing, 1983, (with others) The Church and Social Responsibility, 1953, We Believe, 1962, Christian Mission in Theological Perspective, 1967, The Boston Personalist Tradition, 1986; contbr. articles to profl. jours. Mem. NAACP (exec. bd. Cape Cod, Mass. chpt. 1978-88, Cert. of Merit 1985), Am. Theol. Soc. (pres. 1968-69), Am. Philos. Assn. Home: 403 Russell Ave # 613 Gaithersburg MD 20877 *As I grow older, I am increasingly convinced that a major factor in the maintenance of health and vigor in later life is the motivation provided by continued involvement in tasks that express one's deepest interests and abilities, especially those that contribute to the needs and well-being of other people.*

SCHIMPF, HELEN K., music minister; b. Englewood, N.J., Mar. 17, 1930; d. Karl William and Bertha (Reinold) Schumacher; m. Sidney J. Schimpf, Jul. 28, 1951; children: William Sidney, John Ernest, Karl Max, Peter Wallace. BS, SUNY, 1985. Organist St. Paul's Meth. Ch., Nyack, N.Y., 1969-71, Germonds Presbyn. Ch., Germonds, N.Y., 1971-74, Warwick Dutch Reformed Ch., Warwick, N.Y., 1974-77; music dir./organist Drew United Meth. Ch., Port Jervis, N.Y., 1977-80, St. Paul's United Meth. Ch., Middletown, N.Y., 1980--; Organist Holy Name Roman Cath. Ch., Otisville, N.Y.; founder/accompanist Miessia Chorale, Port Jervis, N.Y. 1978-81; organist Mercy Community Hosp. Author: The History of Methodist Music in American from 1637-1960. United Methodist. Office: St Paul's United Meth Ch 60 W Main St Middletown NY 10940-5732 *Everyone has some talent.*

SCHINDEL, ROGER H., clergyman; b. Mayville, Wis., Sept. 4, 1942; s. Herman and Dorothy Mae (Walters) S.; m. Kathryn Jean Rasmussen, Nov. 25, 1967; children: Jon Roger, Anne Kathryn. BA, Carthage Coll., Kenosha, Wis., 1965; MDiv, Luther Northwestern Sem., St. Paul, 1969. Ordained to ministry Evang. Luth. Ch. Am., 1969. Minister Hope Luthern Ch., St. Charles, Mo., 1969-75, Christus Victor Luth. Ch., Elk Grove Village, Ill., 1975—; mem. evangelism com. Met. Chgo. Synod, Evang. Luth. Ch. Am., 1988—, mem. constitution com., 1988—. Bd. dirs. Elk Grove Village Community Svcs., 1977-87; pres. bd. Serve our Srs. Program, Arlington Heights, Ill., 1988-90; bd. dirs. Kenneth W. Young Ctrs., Elk Grove Village, 1987—, chairperson resource devel. com., 1987—. Named Vol. of Yr., Elk Grove Village, 1988, Greater Woodfield Man of Yr., Woodfield Conv. Bur., Schaumburg, 1990. Mem. Elk Grove Clergy Coun. (chairperson 1988—). Office: Christus Victor Luth Ch 1045 S Arlington Heights Rd Elk Grove Village IL 60007

SCHINDLER, ALEXANDER MOSHE, clergyman, organization executive; b. Munich, Germany, Oct. 4, 1925; s. Eliezer and Sali (Hoyda) S.; m. Rhea Rosenblum, Sept. 29, 1956; children—Elisa Ruth, Debra Lee, Joshua Michael, Judith Rachel, Jonathan David. B in Social Sci., CCNY, 1950; B in Hebrew Letters, Hebrew Union Coll., 1951, M in Hebrew Letters, 1953, DD (hon.), 1977; DHL (hon.), U. S.C., 1987, Lafayette U., 1988; DD (hon.), Hamilton Coll., 1990. Ordained rabbi, 1953. Asst. rabbi Temple Emanuel, Worcester, Mass., 1953-56; assoc., rabbi Temple Emanuel, 1956-59; dir. New Eng. council Union Am. Hebrew Congregations, 1959-63, nat. dir. edn., 1963-67, v.p., 1967-72; pres.-elect, 1972, pres., 1973—; Mem. exec. bd. Conf. Presidents of Maj. Am. Jewish Orgns., 1967—, chmn., 1976-78; exec. bd. Hebrew Union Coll./Jewish Inst. Religion, 1967—; v.p. Meml. Found. for Jewish Culture, 1967—; v.p. World Jewish Congress; mem. exec. com. World Zionist Orgn., 1973—, mem. exec. com., joint distbn. com., 1987—, sec., 1991—; bd. govs. Hebrew Union Coll., 1973—; v.p. World Union for Progressive Judaism. Author: From Discrimination to Extermination, 1950; lit. editor: CCAR Jour., 1959-63; founding editor: Dimensions, Reform Judaism's quar. religious thought, 1966—; editor: Reform Judaism's graded text book series, 1963-67. Served with AUS, 1943-46. Decorated Bronze Star, Purple Heart; recipient Solomon Bublick prize Hebrew U. Jerusalem, 1978; Townsend Harris medal CCNY, 1979. Mem. Am. Assn. Jewish Edn. (exec. bd. 1963-67), Central Conf. Am. Rabbis (exec. bd. 1967—). Home: 6 River Ln Westport CT 06880 Office: Union Am Hebrew Congregations 838 Fifth Ave New York NY 10021 *To live life fully, clinging to its many gifts with all my might—and then, paradoxically, to let go when life compels us to surrender what it gave.*

SCHINDLER, PESACH, rabbi, educator, author; b. Munich, Germany, Apr. 11, 1931; came to U.S., 1940; s. Alexander Moshe and Esther (Zwickler) S.; m. Shulamith Feldman, June 30, 1954; children: Chaya, Gita, Meyer, Nechama, Avi. BA, CCNY Bklyn. Coll., 1953; MS, Yeshiva U., 1964; PhD, NYU, 1972; D Pedagogy (hon.), Jewish Theol. Sem., N.Y.C., 1987. Ordained rabbi, 1956. Dir. edn. Congregation Adath Israel, Toronto, Ont., Can., 1959-65; asst. dir. edn. United Synagogue of Am., N.Y.C., 1965-72; dir. Ctr. for Conservative Judaism United Synagogue of Am., Jerusalem, 1972—; asst. prof. Hebrew U., Jerusalem, 1975—; faculty U. Toronto Sch. Theology Jewish Studies Program in Jerusalem, 1986—, Sem. Jewish Studies, Jerusalem, 1988—; mem. internat. bd. Yad Vashem, Jerusalem, 1980—. Author: Hasidic Responses to the Holocaust in the Light of Hasidic Thought, 1990; contbr. numerous articles to profl. jours. Founding mem. Hebrew U. Orch., Jerusalem, 1988. Mem. Rabbinical Assembly (rabbinic ct. on conversion 1988—, com. on Jewish law 1990—), Educators Assembly, Jerusalem Long Distance Running Club (chmn. 1984-87). Office: United Synagogue Am, PO Box 7456, Jerusalem 94205, Israel *Faith is confrontation with the incredulous and with doubt. The struggle for redemption is confrontation with the non-redemptive. Both represent a form of creation ex-nihilo—a marvelous gift from the Almighty to even the humblest human being, His partner in the constant drama in the response to life.*

SCHINSTINE, KENNETH BRUCE, church administrator; b. Easton, Pa., June 4, 1933; s. William Joseph and Ruth Elizabeth (Hahn) S.; m. Rachael Ann Harper, June 1957 (dec.); children: William Thomas, Karen Elaine Burgess; m. Margaret JoAnn Stearns, Nov. 25. 1961. Student, West Chester State U., 1951-54, U. Colo., Denver, 1955-56, U. So. Colo., 1957-58. Ch. adminstr. First United Meth. Ch., Colorado Springs, Colo., 1977-83; ch. adminstr. First Presbyn. Ch., Orlando, Fla., 1983-86, Colorado Springs, 1986—; pres. Colo. Chpt. Nat. Assn. Ch. Bus. Adminstrs., Colorado Springs, 1982-84, Fla. Chpt. Nat. Assn. Ch. Bus. Adminstrs., Orlando, 1984-85; bd. dirs. Nat. Assn. Ch. Bus. Adminstrs., Ft. Worth, 1984-88 (fellow 1982). Author profl. workbooks. With U.S. Air Force, 1954-76. Ch. Bus. Adminstrs. fellow. Mem. Rotary Club (dir. 1991—). Republican. Home: 3006 Chelton Dr Colorado Springs CO 80909 Office: First Presbyn Ch 219 E Bijou St Colorado Springs CO 80903

SCHLAEGEL, PHILLIP H., academic administrator. Head Great Lakes Bible Coll., Lansing, Mich. Office: Great Lakes Bible Coll PO Box 40060 Lansing MI 48901-7260*

SCHLARMAN, STANLEY GERARD, bishop; b. Belleville, Ill., July 27, 1933. Student, St. Henry Prep. Sem., Belleville, Gregorian U., Rome, St. Louis U. Ordained priest Roman Catholic Ch., 1958, consecrated bishop, 1979. Titular bishop of Capri and aux. bishop of Belleville, 1979-83; bishop of Dodge City Kans., 1983—. Office: Diocese of Dodge City 1608 Ave C Dodge City KS 67801 also: PO Box 849 910 Central Ave Dodge City KS 67801

SCHLEGEL, RONALD JOHN, communications executive, minister; b. Beloit, Kans., Nov. 16, 1933; s. Albert P. and Luella A. (Sigg) S.; m. Edith Esterly, Nov. 27, 1956; children: Joy, Faith, John, Paul. AA, Concordia Jr. Coll., Fort Wayne, Ind., 1953; BA, Concordia Sem., 1955, MDiv, 1971. Ordained to ministry Luth. Ch.-Mo. Synod, 1959. Pastor St. Philip's Luth. Ch., St. Louis, 1959-67, Berea Luth. Ch., Balt., 1967-69; free-lance writer, producer St. Louis, 1969-78; mgr. pub. relations Internat. Luth. Laymen's League, St. Louis, 1978-90, dir. communication, 1990—. Editor MEDI-AKIT, 1987-89, Concordia Hist. Quar., 1971-73; contbr. articles to periodicals. Mem. Religious Pub. Rels. Coun. (chpt. pres. 1987-88, program chmn. 1986-87, sec. 1988-89, Award of Merit 1987). Avocations: swimming, racquetball, traveling, bridge, gardening. Home: 7155 Princeton Ave University City MO 63130 Office: Internat Luth Laymen's League 2185 Hampton Ave Saint Louis MO 63139 *There is no life apart from Jesus Christ. This not just a theological truism. It is a reality, day by day. It is His love and He Himself that we are called on to share with others.*

SCHLIESSWOHL, SCOTT J., ecumenical agency administrator. Exec. dir. Ind. Coun. Chs., Indpls. Office: Ind Coun Chs 1100 W 42nd St Rm 225 Indianapolis IN 46208*

SCHLOSSBERG, HERBERT, writer; b. Bklyn., Apr. 8, 1935; s. Jack and Mildred Schlossberg; m. Terry Ann Benz, June 16, 1962; children: Stephen, Laurie, Thomas. BA, Bethel Coll., 1959; MA, U. Mo., Columbia, 1961; PhD, U. Minn., 1965; MPA, Am. U., 1970. Elder Presbyn. Ch., Mpls., 1983-86; project dir. Fieldstead Inst., Irvine, Calif., 1986—. Author: Idols for Destruction, 1983, Called to Suffer, 1990, A Fragrance of Oppression, 1991; co-author: Turning Point, 1987, Freedom, Justice and Hope, 1988. Sgt. U.S. Army, 1954-56. Alliance Française fellow, 1963-64, U. Minn. Grad. Sch. fellow, 1963-64. Mem. Am. Legion. Home and Office: 5916 Oakland Ave Minneapolis MN 55417

SCHLOSSER, SISTER BLANCHE MARIE, religious educator; b. Arkansaw, Wis., Feb. 13, 1919; d. William George Schlosser and Ella Catherine Denning. Grad., Viterbo Coll., 1950, BS, 1955; MEd, De Paul U., 1964. Cert. tchr., Wis.; joined Franciscan Sisters of Perpetual Adoration, Roman Cath. Ch., 1937. Tchr., cathechist elem. schs. Wis., Iowa, 1939-52, adminstr. elem. schs., 1953-70; music tchr., religious coordinator St. Mary's Assumption Parish and Sch., Durand, Wis., 1978-87, coord. Confraternity Christian Doctrine programs, 1978-85; dir. St. Mary's Assumption Parish and Sch., Durand, 1978-90, dir. parish choirs, parish grade and high sch. religious edn. programs, 1990—. Parish del. Deanery Pastoral Council, Durand, 1973-82; deanery del. Diocesan Pastoral Council, La Crosse, Wis., 1976-82; active Parish Council, Durand, 1973-85. Recipient Martha Peck award Music Assn., Durand, 1984. Mem. Music Tchrs. Nat. Assn., Inc., Wis. Music Tchrs. Assn., Nat. Cath. Edn. Assn. (tchr. assoc.). Avocations: fishing, art, music, travel. Home and Office: St Marys Assumption Parish and Sch 901 W Prospect St Durand WI 54736

SCHLUB, TERESA RAE, minister; b. Oak Park, Ill., July 11, 1946; d. Robert Carl and Shirley Rae (Listhartke) Grupe; m. George Jonas Schlub, Aug. 29, 1981; stepchildren: Kathy Bruns, Gary, Greg, Dean. BA, Westmar Teikyo U., 1971; MDiv, Garrett Evangel. Seminary, Evanston, Ill., 1974. Ordained deacon United Meth. Ch., 1973, elder, 1978. Asst. minister First United Meth. Ch., Morris, Ill., 1974-76; minister Leaf River (Ill.) German Valley United Meth. Ch., 1976-82, East Jordan United Meth. Ch., Sterling, Ill., 1982-86, Paw Paw (Ill.) United Meth. Ch., 1986-89, Community United Meth. Ch., LaMoille, Ill., 1989—; mem. alumni coun., sec. Garrett Evangel. Theol. Seminary, Evanston, 1974-76; mem. Conf. Bd. of Evangelism, 1974-76. Bd. dirs. Green Hills Coun. of Girl Scouts, Freeport, Ill., 1986-88, Lee County Red Cross, Dixon, Ill., 1986-89; mem. Ill. Home Extension Assn., Grundy, Ogle, Whiteside, Lee County, 1974-89. Home: 71 Main PO Box 270 La Moille IL 61330 Office: Community United Meth Ch 73 Main La Moille IL 61330 *Life becomes meaningful when one is able to become vulnerable and be willing to take risks. This becomes possible when one has faith in God and confidence in the self. It also helps to know and experience the love of others.*

SCHMALENBERGER, JERRY LEW, pastor, seminary administrator; b. Greenville, Ohio, Jan. 23, 1934; s. Harry Henry and Lima Marie (Hormel) S.; m. Carol Ann Walthall, June 8, 1956; children: Stephen, Bethany Allison, Sarah Layton. BA, Wittenberg U., 1956, DDiv (hon.), 1984; MDiv, Hamma Sch. Theology, Springfield, Ohio, 1959, D of Ministry, 1976. Ordained to ministry Luth. Ch., 1959. Dir. Camp Mowana, Mansfield, Ohio, 1958-59; pastor 3d Luth. Ch., Springfield, 1959-61, 1st Luth. Ch., Bellefontaine, Ohio, 1961-66; sr. pastor 1st Luth. Ch., Tiffin, Ohio, 1966-70, Mansfield, 1970-79; sr. pastor St. John's Luth. Ch., Des Moines, 1979-88; pres., prof. parish ministry Pacific Luth. Theol. Sem., Berkeley, Calif., 1988—; co-dir. Iowa Luth. Hosp. Minister of Health Program, Des Moines, 1986-88; Roland Payne lectr. Gbarnga (Liberia) Sch. Theology, 1987. Author: Lutheran Christians' Beliefs Book One, 1984, Book Two, 1987, Iowa Parables and Iowa Psalms, 1984, Saints Who Shaped The Church, 1986, Stewards of Creation, 1987, Nights Worth Remembering, 1989; columnist "Rite Ideas", 1987-88. Bd. dirs. Grand View Coll., Des Moines, 1980—, Wittenberg U., Springfield, Ohio, 1974-87, Luth. Social Services of Iowa, 1980-87, chmn. pre fund drive, 1988; bd. dirs. Planned Parenthood of Mid-Iowa, Des Moines, 1987-88; dir. Evang. Outreach/Luth. Ch. Am., 1983-85; mem. Iowa Luth. Hosp. Charitable Trust, 1986-88; chair Com. for Homeless Fund, Des Moines, 1986. Named Outstanding Alumni Wittenberg U., 1965, Young Man of Yr. Tiffin Jaycees, 1965, Man of Yr. Bellefontaine Jaycees, Disting. Alumni award Trinty Sem., Columbus, 1989. Mem. NAACP, Acad. Preachers, Acad. Evangelists (organizer 1986—), Kiwanis, Rotary. Avocations: historical research and writing, travel, boating. Home & Office: 2770 Marin Ave Berkeley CA 94708 *Personal philosophy: Not perfect, but forgiven, we find real life in living ours for others.*

SCHMEELCKE, ROBERT CARL, minister; b. Jersey City, Oct. 26, 1942; s. Carl and Edith (Melzer) S.; m. Grace Flanders, Aug. 28, 1965; children: Kristen Elizabeth, Robert Flanders. AB, Upsala U., 1965; MDiv, Luth. Sch. Theology Chgo., 1969; MST, N.Y. Theol. Sem., 1973. Ordained to ministry Luth. Ch. in Am., 1969. Pastor Trinity Luth. Ch., Dover, N.J., 1969-76, St. John's Luth., Westville, N.J., 1976-78; sr. pastor St. Stephen's Luth. Ch., Wilmington, Del., 1978-90, Grace Luth. Ch., Miami Springs, Fla., 1990—; dean Del. dist. Evang. Luth. Ch. Am., 1989, del. assembly, 1989; treas. Delmarva Ecumenical Agy., 1986-90. Treas. Del. Coalition for Homeless, Wilmington, 1988-90. Office: Grace Luth Ch 254 Curtiss Pkwy Miami Springs FL 33166

SCHMELZENBACH, TERRY LEE, minister; b. Marietta, Ohio, Mar. 8, 1954; s. William Harold S. and Dorthy (Carpenter) Moore; m. Susan Darlene Keyser, Dec. 29, 1972; children: Mandy M. and Jamie N. Assoc. Bible Studies, Nazarene Bible Coll., Colorado Springs, Colo., 1984. Mechanic R.C. Calls, Marietta, Ohio, 1972-74, Caldwell Motors Ford, Caldwell, Ohio, 1975-77; heavy equipment operator Sidwell Mining, Zanesville, Ohio, 1977-81; mechanic J C Penney's, Colorado Springs, Colo., 1981-84; pastor Winston Salem (N.C.) Nazarene Ch., 1984-86, Tallmadge (Ohio) Nazarene Ch., 1986—; camp bd. trustee, mem. fin. com. Akron Dist. Ch. of the Nazarene, Louisville, 1986; treas. Akron Zone Ch. of the Nazarene, 1987-89. Pres. Nazarene Soft League, 1986-89; rep. Akron zone Nazarene Bible Coll., 1986—; vol. Summit County Home, Munroe Falls, Ohio, 1987—, Sumner Home, Akron, 1989—, Akron Youth for Christ, 1988—. Named one of Outstanding Young Men of Am., 1987; recipient gold standard award N.C. Nazarene Dist., 1985, Akron Dist., 1987; alumnus of the year Nazarene Bible Coll., 1985. Avocations: archery, photography. Office: Tallmadge Ch Nazarene 191 S Munroe Tallmadge OH 44278

SCHMID, HANS HEINRICH, theology educator; b. Zurich, Switzerland, Oct. 22, 1937; s. Gotthard and Erika (Hug) S.; m. Christa Nievergelt, Jan. 6, 1962; children—Anna Regula, Konrad Heinrich, Ulrich Martin, Verena Elisabeth. Dr. Theol., U. Zurich, 1965; Dr. Theol. honoris causa, U. Leipzig, 1991. Asst. prof. U. Zurich, 1967-69, prof. Old Testament studies, 1976-88, rector, 1988—; prof. Kirchliche Hochschule Bethel, Bielefeld, Fed. Republic Germany, 1969-76. Author books, including: Wesen und Geschichte der Weisheit, 1966; Gerechtgkeit als Weltordnung, 1968; Alttorientalische Welt in der alttestamentlichen Theologie, 1974; Der Sogenannte Jahwist, 1976. Mem. Wissenschaftliche Gesellschaft fur Theologie (pres. 1984-90), Schweizerische Gesellschaft fur Orientalische Altertums wissenschaft (bd. dirs. 1976-89), Gelehrte Gesellschaft, others. Mem. Freisinnig-demokratische Partei. Presbyterian. Home: In der Halden 11, CH 8603 Schwerzenbach Switzerland Office: U Zurich, Raemistr 71, CH 8006 Zurich Switzerland

SCHMIDT, DARYL DEAN, religious educator; b. Sioux Falls, S.D., Aug. 12, 1944; s. Arnold A. and Jennie Frances (Glanzer) S. BA, Bethel Coll., North Newton, Kans., 1966; MDiv, Assoc. Mennonite Seminaries, Elkhart, Ind., 1970; PhD, Grad. Theol. Union, Berkeley, Calif., 1979. Assoc. prof. Tex. Christian U., Ft. Worth, 1979—; vis. prof. Pacific Sch. Religion, Berkeley, Calif. Author: Hellenistic Greek Grammar and Noam Chomsky, 1981, The Gospel of Mark: Scholars Bible 1 with Introduction Notes and Original Text, 1991; contbr. articles and revs. to profl. jours. Recipient Jr. Scholar Rsch. award Southwest Commn. on Religious Studies, 1986. Mem. Soc. Bibl. Lit., Studiorum Novi Testamenti Societas. Democrat. Episcopalian. Office: Pacific Sch Religion 1798 Scenic Ave Berkeley CA 94709

SCHMIDT, DOUGLAS JOHN, minister; b. Westbrook, Minn., Oct. 8, 1952; s. John Arthur and Verna LaVera (Reemstma) S.; m. Carolyn Norma Erb, June 22, 1974; children: Andrew, Christina, Teresa. BA, Maranatha Coll., 1970; MRE, Temple Bapt. Theol. Sem., 1976, DRE, 1980. Ordained to ministry Bapt. Ch., 1976. Dean students London (Ont.) Bapt. Bible Coll., 1979-86; sr. pastor Ross Bible Ch., Port Huron, Mich., 1986-91, Troy (Bapt.) Ch., 1991—. Contbr. articles to religious publs. Chmn. ad hoc com. Project 2000, St. Clair County, Mich., 1989-91. Mem. Evang. Ministerial Assn. (pres. St. Clair County chpt. 1988-91). Office: Troy Bapt Ch 3193 Rochester Rd Troy MI 48043

SCHMIDT, EUGENE EDWARD, minister; b. Freeland, Mich., July 19, 1929; s. Otto M. and Alma C. (Kloha) S.; m. Janice Alene Bockelman, (div. 1977); m. Carol Elaine Stutz, Dec. 12, 1980; children: Stephen, Sheryl, Suzanne. AA, Concordia Coll., Ft. Wayne, Ind., 1950; BA, Concordia Sem., St. Louis, 1955, MDiv, 1955; DLL (hon.), Concordia Coll., Seward, Nebr., 1986. Ordained to ministry Luth. Ch.-Mo. Synod. Tchr. Zion Luth. Sch., Granton, Wis., 1950-51; pastor St. Paul's Luth. Ch., Durango, Colo., 1955-60, Grace Luth. Ch., Kansas City, Kans., 1960-80; dir. missions Kans. dist. Luth. Ch.-Mo. Synod, Topeka, 1980-85, pres., 1985—; chmn. Greater Kansas City (Mo.) Pastoral Conf., 1970-72; bd. dirs. Luth. Social Svc., Wichita, 1985—. Contbr. articles to religious jours. V.p. Durango (Colo.) Jaycess, 1956; pres. Lyons Club, Kansas City, Kans., 1974; bd. dirs. Wyandotte County Mental Health Ctr., 1970-71. Home: 3617 SW Kings Forest Rd Topeka KS 66614

SCHMIDT, HERB FREDERICK, clergyman; b. Jefferson City, Mo., Aug. 7, 1930; s. Henry Tom and Bertha (Kousmeyer) S.; m. Grace Kitzman, July 1, 1956; children: Conrad, David, Richard, Raymond. BA, Concordia Coll., St. Louis, 1952; MST, Concordia Sem., St. Louis, 1955; postgrad., San Francisco Theol. Sem., 1970-72. Ordained to ministry Evang. Luth. Ch. in Am., 1955. Asst. to dean of students Calif. Concordia Coll., Oakland, 1955-60; pastor Messiah Luth. Ch., Santa Cruz, Calif., 1960-68; campus pastor U. Calif., Santa Cruz, 1968-78, U. Ariz., Tucson, 1978-86, Stanford U., Palo Alto, 1986—; regional campus coord. TRI-Luth. Calif. Agy., 1974-78; chair Stanford Associated Ministry, 1987—. Contbr. articles to profl. jours. Pres. Bicentennial Polit. Alliance, Santa Cruz, 1974-77; chair Tucson Legal Assts. Program, 1982-84, South Bay Sanctuary Organists, Palo Alto, 1986-89. Danforth fellow, 1973-74; hon. fellow U. Calif., Santa Cruz, 1969—. Mem. Luth. Campus Ministry Assn. (exec. com., editor newsletter), Witness for Mid. East (exec. bd., treas. 1989—). Democrat. Home: 675 Monte Rosa Dr #814 Menlo Park CA 94025 Office: University Luth Ch 1611 Stanford Ave Palo Alto CA 94306 *The mystery and miracle of human existence is to find life by loosing it in service for others and working for peace and justice in God's world.*

SCHMIDT, JOHN LOUIS, minister; b. Pitts., May 30, 1933; s. Ralph Pittock and Julia Elizabeth (Kroll) S.; m. Alice Stewart Wagner, June 16, 1956; children: Bradford Jon, Alison Kay, Peter Geoffrey. AB, Westminster Coll., New Wilmington, Pa., 1955; DD (hon.), Westminster Coll., 1991; BD, Pitts. Theol. Sem., 1958, ThM, 1959; ThD, San Francisco Theol. Sem., 1976. Ordained to ministry Presbyn. Ch., 1959. Assoc. minister 2d Presbyn. Ch., Balt., 1959-63; chaplain Johns Hopkins U., Balt., 1959-63; sr. minister 1st

Presbyn. Ch., Jamestown, N.Y., 1963-82; chaplain RAF, 1965; exch. minister Presbyn. Ch. of Norwich (Eng.), 1965; sr. minister Presbyn. Ch. of Barrington Hills (Ill.), 1982—; pres., bd. trustees Presbyn. Homes of Western N.Y.; founder, chmn. bd. dirs. Presyterian Home of Jamestown; mem. pres.'s roundtable Pitts. Theol. Sem. Mem. Bd. Edn., Jamestown; legislator Chautauqua County, N.Y.; pres. planning coun. United Fund of Chautauqua County. World Coun. fellow World Coun. Chs.-U. Basel (Switzerland), 1979, Harvard fellow Harvard U.,1 981. Mem. North Am. Paul Tillich Soc., Am. Acad. Religion, Barrington Hills Country Club. Home: 883 Georgetowne Ln Barrington IL 60010 Office: Presbyn Ch 6 Brinker Rd Barrington IL 60010 *We are all the children of God. To live with one another in the grace of God makes possible a life filled with the joy of love and faith, work and play. No matter what life holds for us we are sustained by God's presence through it all.*

SCHMIDT, JOHN LYNN, minister; b. Alliance, Nebr., Jan. 4, 1947; s. Dorrance Henry and LaVaughn (Williams) S.; m. Deanna M. Kuhlmann, Aug. 24, 1968; children: Steve, Dave, Carrie. BS in BA, U. Nebr., 1970; MDiv, Concordia Theol. Sem., Ft. Wayne, Ind., 1977. Ordained to ministry, Luth. Ch.-Mo. Synod, 1977. Assoc. minister St. Mark Luth. Ch., Omaha, 1977-79; minister Trinity Luth. Ch., Norman, Okla., 1979-88; sr. minister First Luth. Ch., Chattanooga, 1988—; supt. The Luth. Sch., Chattanooga, 1988—; mem. dist. youth bd. Okla. Dist., Luth. Ch.-Mo. Synod, Oklahoma City, 1981-86, dist. mission bd. Mid.-South Dist., 1991—. Office: First Luth Ch 2800 McCallie Ave Chattanooga TN 37404

SCHMIDT, JUNE LAUREL, minister; b. Benton Harbor, Mich., June 5, 1941; d. Laurie Hudspeth-Minton and Julia Montgomery (Rowland) Minton; m. Ronald Edward Rogers, May 28, 1967 (dec.); children: Ronald Edward, Rhonda June; m. Donald Fredrick Schmidt, Dec. 18, 1980; stepchildren: Donald, Karen, Darryl, Lori, Mark. Diplomas in ministry, Gospel Crusade Inst. Ministry, Brandenton, Fla., 1980, 81. Ordained to ministry, Gospel Crusade Ministerial Fellowship, Bradenton, Fla., 1980. Assoc. pastorial trainee Soul's Harbour Ch., Tulsa, Okla., 1980; internat. dir. City of Light Sch. of Mininstry, Houston, 1980-82; dir. missions World Bible Way Fellowship, Dallas, 1983-85; pres., chief exec. officer His Word to the Nations, Inc., Dallas, Perry (Kans.), Sacramento, and Orlando, Fla., 1983—; regional dir., Caribbean region and Venezuela Gospel Crusade Ministerial Fellowship, Brandenton, Fla., 1986—; bd. mem. Gospel Crusade Ministerial Fellowship, Brandenton, 1986—, His Word to the Nations, Inc., Dallas, Perry, Sacramento and Orlando, 1983—, The Encouragers, Nashville, 1988—; cons. various internat. ministries, 1980—. Editor: The Gospel Crusader; contbr. numerous articles to religious publs. Capt., counselor Little League Baseball, Mililani Town, Hawaii, 1970; mem. Internat. Women in Leadership; bd. dirs. various internat. ministries. Mem. Charismatic Bible Ministries, Network Christian Ministries, Gospel Crusade Ministerial Fellowship, World Bible Way Fellowship. Republican. Non-denominational Pentecostal. Avocations: biking, creative gardening, writing, interior decorating, travel. Home and Office: 10794 Spring Brook Ln Orlando FL 32825 Office: Rte 2 Box 279 Bradenton FL 34202 *Life without knowing Jesus Christ as Lord and Savior is not life. It is meaningless existance. There is abundant life available to all mankind. "I (Jesus) am come that you might have life, and that you might have it more abundantly (JN10:10)." I challenge you: choose the abundant life found only in Christ Jesus!.*

SCHMIDT, SISTER MARY SYLVIA (PATRICIA ELLA NORA SCHMIDT), nun; b. Devine, Tex., Feb. 8, 1937; d. George Martin and Ella Mary (Brieden) S. BS in Edn., Our Lady of the Lake Coll., 1956; postgrad., St. Mary's U., San Antonio, summers 1962-63, 83-86. Joined Sisters of Div. Providence, Roman Cath. Ch., 1950, Sisters for Christian Community, 1972. Tchr. St. Joseph's Elem. Sch., Shreveport, La., 1956-61, Bishop Forest High Sch., Schulenburg, Tex., 1961-62, St. Mary's High Sch., Fredericksburg, Tex., 1962-66, St. Louis High Sch., Castroville, Tex., 1966-67; tchr., head dept. religion Bishop Kelly High Sch., Tulsa, 1967-70; coord. youth worker program Tulsa, 1970-72; resource worker office of edn. Diocese of Tulsa, 1971-73; pastoral asst. St. Thomas More Cath. Ch., Tulsa, 1973-82; assoc. dir. Tulsa Met. Ministry, 1982-88, exec. dir., 1988—; exec. sec. pastoral coun. Diocese of Tulsa, 1981—. Chair Tulsa Fire and Police Chaplaincy Bd., 1983-85, Tulsa Human Rights Commn., 1984-91; bd. dirs. Family and Children Svcs., Tulsa, 1986-90. Recipient Pinnacle award Tulsa Commn. on Status of Women, 1989, City of Faith award Cascia Hall High Sch., 1990. Mem. Nat. Assn. Ecumenical Staff (chair 1989-90), LWV (bd. dirs. local chpt.). Democrat. Office: Tulsa Met Ministry 221 S Nogales Tulsa OK 74127

SCHMIDT, ROBERTA JEANNE, nun; b. Kansas City, Mo., May 9, 1928; d. Ernest Louis and Florence Marie (Noonan) S. BA, Avila Coll., 1949; MA, St. Louis U., 1958, PhD, 1964; LLD, Lindenwood Coll., 1968. Joined Sisters of St. Joseph of Carondelet, Roman Cath. Ch., 1950. Tchr. Archdiocese of St. Louis, 1952-61; mem. faculty Fontbonne Coll., St. Louis, 1961-66, pres., 1966-72; consortium dir. United Colls. San Antonio, 1973-75; v.p. acad. affairs So. Benedictine Coll., Cullman, Ala., 1975-79; supt. schs. Archdiocese of Atlanta, 1980-82, sec. for edn., supt., 1982-89, sec. for edn., 1989—. Democrat. Office: Dept Cath Edn 680 W Peachtree St NW Atlanta GA 30308-1984

SCHMIDT, STEVEN JAMES, minister; b. Grand Rapids, Mich., June 6, 1947; s. Clayton Joseph and Ruth Gladuce (Schlief) S.; m. Mary Jule Veldman, Dec. 11, 1970; children: Matthew, Nicholas, Kathleen, Laura. Student, No. Mich. U., 1965-67, Grand Rapids Jr. Coll., 1967-68, So. Theol. Sem., 1980-82, U. Bibl. Studies, 1980, Inst. for Motivational Living, 1988-89. Ordained to ministry Am. Bapt. Assn., 1982; cert. behavioral analyst, Ohio. Assoc. min., min. evangelism North Parkersburg (W.Va.) Bapt. Ch., 1980-82; sr. min. Porterfield Bapt. Ch., Little Hocking, Ohio, 1983-90, Tabernacle Bapt. Ch., Chillicothe, Ohio, 1990—; chaplain Camden-Clark Hosp., Parkersburg, 1981-90; pres. Mins. Fellowship, Parkersburg Assn., 1982-85; mem. mins. adv. coun. Alderson-Broaddus Coll., Philippi, 1984-87; trustee Ohio Bapt. Conv., 1985—, exec. com., 1988-90; pres. Ohio Bapt. Mins. Coun., 1989; nat. senator Am. Bapt. Assn. Mins. Coun., 1989—; mem. Bd. Regional Ministries, 1991—; founder, pres. cons. firm Solutions. Author: (tape and manual) Heart to Heart Evangelism, 1981, (study guide) The Enquirers, 1982; contbr. articles to various jours. 1st lt. U.S. Army, 1968-71, Vietnam. Decorated DFC (3), Silver Star, Bronze Star (5), Purple Heart, Air medal (45), Vietnamese Cross of Gallantry. Mem. Belpre Ministerial Alliance, Ohio Bapt. Conv., Parkersburg Ministerial Alliance (assoc.). Republican. Home: 98 Limestone Blvd Chillicothe OH 45601 Office: Tabernacle Bapt Ch 221 E Main St Chillicothe OH 45601 *Some speak to the issues, but I speak to the heart, because out of the heart come the issues of life.*

SCHMIDT, W. CARLEEN, music director; b. Belle Rive, Ill., Sept. 21, 1938; s. Carl C. and Wilma R. (Jenkins) Johnson; m. Dale G. Schmidt, July 18, 1959; children: Linda Robbins, Diane E. Schmidt, Karen Breitbarth, Anita Schmidt. BA in History, U. Chgo., 1975; MA in Sci. Teaching, Govs. State U., University Park, Ill., 1976, MA in Ednl. Adminstrn., 1990. Organist Peotone (Ill.) United Meth. Ch., 1953—, jr. choir dir., 1970-75, 90—, sr. choir dir., 1970—, handbell choir dir., 1978—, adminstrv. bd., Sunday sch. tchr., 1978—; tchr. Peotone Elem. Sch., 1976—; organizer Greater Peotone Sacred Choir Festival, 1978-89; dir. Community Sacred Choir, Peotone, 1979-88; sec., founder Peotone Coun. local #604 IFT/AFT, Peotone, 1978-84. Pres. Peotone Tchrs. Assn., 1986-89; dir. Peotone Bicentennial Chorus, 1976-78; mem. Peotone Hist. Soc. Mem. Am. Soc. for Curriculum Devel., Nat. Coun. for the Social Studies, Nat. Coun. Tchrs. of English, Ill. Assn. of Tchrs. of English, Am. Fedn. Tchrs., Ill. Fedn. Tchrs., Peotone Women's Softball League, DAR (Cahokia Mound chpt. 1980—). Republican. Office: Peotone Elem Sch Conrad & Mill St Peotone IL 60468

SCHMIDT, W. ROBERT, school system administrator. Supt. schs. Diocese of Davenport, Iowa. Office: St Vincent Ctr 2706 Gaines St Davenport IA 52804*

SCHMIDT, WALTER ALLAN, minister, educator; b. Romeo, Mich., Mar. 10, 1948; s. Walter Edward Schmidt and Laura (Erdman) Hillman; m. Carolyn R. Engelbrecht, Sept. 7, 1968; children: Walter N., Timothy A. BA, Mich. State U., 1970; MDiv, Trinity Luth. Sem., Columbus, Ohio, 1974; D Ministry, Drew U., 1982. Ordained to ministry Luth. Ch., 1974. Pastor Nyssa (Oreg.)-Vale Luth. Parish, 1974-77; co-pastor Zion Luth. Ch., Ann Arbor, Mich., 1977-80; sr. pastor Good Shepherd Luth. Ch., Royal Oak, Mich., 1980-89, First English Luth. Ch., Grosse Pointe Woods, Mich., 1989—; adj. prof. Oakland Community Coll., Bloomfield Hills, Mich., 1986—. Author: Recruiting Evangelism, 1984, Lay Evangelism Calling, 1986, Why God Why?, 1990. Mem. Acad. for Evangelists (bd. dirs.), Soc. Bibl. Lit. Office: 1st English Luth Ch 800 Vernier Grosse Pointe Woods MI 48236 *Our major goal in life is to worship and serve God; when God is properly served, we express love and care to one another.*

SCHMIDT, WAYNE ELMER, theology educator; b. Fond du Lac, Wis., Apr. 10, 1927; s. Elmer A. and Edna L. (Guerke) S.; m. Bonnie Louise Roeming, July 25, 1970; children: Jonathan Wayne, Tara Ann. Diploma in teaching, Martin Luther Coll., New Ulm, Minn., 1948; BA, Northwestern Coll., Watertown, Wis., 1952; diploma in theology, Wis. Luth. Sem., Mequon, 1955; MS, U. Wis., 1960, PhD, 1968, MusM, 1973. Ordained to ministry Luth. Ch.-Mo. Synod, 1955. Pastor Our Savior Luth. Ch., Lena, Wis., 1955-57, St. Paul Luth. Ch., Oconto Falls, Wis., 1955-57; prin. Luther High Sch., Onalaska, Wis., 1957-71; pastor Wis. Luth. Chapel, Madison, 1971-75; prof. Concordia Sem., St. Louis, 1975—; pulpit asst. 1st Luth. Ch., LaCrosse, Wis., 1963-71; campus pastor U. Wis., LaCrosse, 1966-69; organist, pulpit asst. Concordia Luth. Ch., Maplewood, 1979—. Home: 11 Seminary Terr Saint Louis MO 63105 Office: Concordia Sem 801 DeMun Ave Saint Louis MO 63105

SCHMIDT, WILLIAM CHARLES, JR., minister; b. Balt., June 9, 1939; s. William Charles Sr. and Mary A. (Gloss) S.; m. Eunice Ruth Zimmerman, June 8, 1963; children: Steven William, Susan Gayle. BA, The King's Coll., 1961; ThM, Dallas Theol. Sem., 1965; D Ministry, Westminster Theol. Sem., Phila., 1989. Ordained to ministry, 1965. Asst. pastor Calvary Ind. Ch., Lancaster, Pa., 1965-70; sr. pastor Evang. Bapt. Ch., Springfield, N.J., 1970-78, Calvary Bapt. Ch., Bristol, Pa., 1978—; mem. U.S. coun. Andes Evang. Mission, Plainfield, N.J., 1970-77, pres., 1975-77. Mem. Interdenominational Fgn. Mission Assn. (bd. dirs. Wheaton, Ill. 1978-82, 90—), SIM Internat. (mem. USA coun. 1973-91, internat. bd. govs. 1983—), UFM Internat. (bd. dirs. 1980—), Rotary (exec. com. 1987—, scholarship com. 1986—, pres. 1989-90). Office: Calvary Bapt Ch 250 Green Ln PO Box 704 Bristol PA 19007

SCHMIECHEN, PETER M., academic administrator. Head Lancaster (Pa.) Theol. Sem. of the United Ch. of Christ. Office: Lancaster Theol Sem 555 W James St Lancaster PA 17603*

SCHMIEL, DAVID GERHARD, clergyman, religious education administrator; b. Cedarburg, Wis., Dec. 10, 1931; s. Gerhard August and Frieda Helena (Labrenz) S.; m. Shirley Ann Friede, July 6, 1957; children: Mark, Peter, Steven, Daniel, Julia. BA, Northwestern Coll., 1953; ThD, Concordia Sem., 1967. Pastor St. Paul's Luth. Ch., Gresham, Nebr., 1958-60, Onalaska, Wis., 1960-62; prof. St. Paul's Coll., Concordia, Mo., 1962-70; prof., dean Concordia Coll., St. Paul, 1970-81; pres. Concordia Coll., Ann Arbor, Mich., 1983-91; acad. dean Concordia Sem., St. Louis, 1981-82; dir. theol. edn. svc. Luth. Ch.-Mo. Synod, St. Louis, 1991—. Author: Via Propria and Via Mystica...Gerson, 1969. Found. for Reformation Rsch. Jr. fellow, Southeastern Inst. for Medieval and Renaissance Studies, Jr. fellow, 1965, 66, 68. Office: Luth Ch Mo Synod 1333 Kirkwood Rd Saint Louis MO 63122

SCHMITT, FRANK JOSEPH, III, religion educator, minister; b. Montgomery, Ala., June 19, 1939; s. Frank J. Jr. and Louise A. (McGehee) S.; m. Barbara N. O'Daniel, Aug. 12, 1958; children: Michael J., Todd L., Christie A. BA, Samford U., 1961; MRE, New Orleans Bapt. Theol. Sem., 1964, EdD, 1970; MBA, Lynchburg Coll., 1984. Ordained to ministry So. Bapt. Conv., 1961. Pastor 1st Bapt. Ch., Baldwin, La., 1965-67; min. edn. Cen. Bapt. Ch., Port Arthur, Tex., 1967-69, Eisenhauer Road Bapt. Ch., San Antonio, 1969-72; assoc. pastor River Oaks Bapt. Ch., Houston, 1972-73; prof. ch. ministries Liberty Bapt. Theol. Sem., Lynchburg, Va., 1973—; pastor Staunton Bapt. Ch., Huddleston, Va., 1986—; adult coord. Thomas Road Bapt. Ch., Lynchburg, 1973-74, asst. min. children's div., 1974-79, coord. jr. Sunday sch., 1980-83; min. edn. Old Forest Road Bapt. Ch., part-time, Lynchburg, 1983-85. Author Sunday sch. curriculum materials fundamentalist ch. publs.; contbr. articles to religious jours. and mag. Mem. Profs. Christian Edn., Nat. Assn. Ch. Bus. Adminstrs., Va. Bapt. Religious Edn. Assn. Home: 407 Keywood Dr Lynchburg VA 24501 Office: Liberty Bapt Theol Sem Box 20000 Lynchburg VA 24506 *One can attempt to do the work of ten men, or devote himself to equipping ten men to work. I have chosen to devote my life to equipping others to serve God through local churches.*

SCHMITT, HOWARD STANLEY, minister; b. Waterloo, Ont., Can., Oct. 19, 1933; came to U.S., 1971; s. Delton Howard and Beulah (Weber) S.; m. Dorothy Jean West, May 20, 1960; children: Valerie Jean Schmitt Jones, Jeffrey Howard. B Theology, Toronto Bible Coll., Ont., Can., 1963. Ordained to ministry Mennonite Ch., 1963. Pastor Wanner Mennonite Ch., Cambridge, Ont., 1960-71, Calvary Mennonite Ch., Ayr, Ont., 1964-69, S. Union Mennonite Ch., West Liberty, Ohio, 1971-83; hosp. chaplain Mary Rutan Hosp., Bellefontaine, Ohio, 1983-85; dir. devel. Adriel Sch., West Liberty, Ohio, 1985-86; pastor Bay Shore Mennonite Ch., Sarasota, Fla., 1986-91; sec. Mennonite Conf. Ont., Cambridge, 1970-71; overseer Ohio Con. Mennonites, West Liberty, 1972-78, 84-86; moderator Southest Mennonite Conf., Sarasota, 1989-91; mem. Mennonite Ch. Gen. Bd., 1991. Vice chair Mary Rutan Hosp. Bd., 1978-83. Recipient 13 Yrs. Svc. award Vol. Chaplains Group, Mary Rutan Hosp., 1985. Mem. Sarasota Mennonite Mins. Fellowship (past, sec., chmn.).

SCHMITT, JOHN JACOB, religious educator; b. Milw., May 6, 1938; s. Silvester Joseph and Frances Josephine (Knar) S.; m. Roberta Ann O'Hara, July 8, 1967; children: Maria-Kristina, Tara Elizabeth. BA, Marquette U., 1966; AM, U. Chgo., 1970; PhD, 1977. Asst. prof. St. Bonaventure (N.Y.) U., 1972-80; asst. prof. Marquette U., Milw., 1980-87, assoc. prof., 1987—; vis. prof. U. Sheffield, Eng., 1991. Author: Isaiah and His Interpreters, 1986; contbr. articles to religious jours. Recipient NEH award, 1978, NCCJ award, Jerusalem, 1986; Fulbright fellow, 1968-69. Mem. Cath. Bibl. Assn., Soc. Bibl. Lit., Nat. Assn. Profs. Hebrew, Am. Acad. Religion. Home: 1843 N 84th St Wauwatosa WI 53226 Office: Marquette U Theology Dept Milwaukee WI 53233

SCHMITT, MARK F., bishop; b. Algoma, Wis., Feb. 14, 1923. Ed., Salvatorian Sem., St. Nazianz, Wis., St. John's Sem., Collegeville, Minn. Ordained priest Roman Cath. Ch., 1948; titular bishop of Ceanannus Mor and aux. bishop of Green Bay, 1970-78, bishop of Marquette (Mich.), 1978—. Office: Chancery Office 444 S 4th St PO Box 550 Marquette MI 49855

SCHMITT, THOMAS RICHARD, minister; b. Chgo., May 17, 1964; s. Thomas Richard and Christine Marie (Clarke) Menges; m. Sheila Ann Miller, Mar. 23, 1985; 1 child, Ridgeway James. Student, No. Ill. U., 1981-83; B.Th., Oreg. (Ill.) Bible Coll., 1986. Ordained to ministry Ch. of God, 1987. Youth minister East Oregon Chapel, Oregon, Ill., 1985-86, Valley View Bible Ch., Paradise Valley, Ariz., 1986-87; minister Ch. of the Open Bible, Bedford, Ohio, 1989—; bd. dirs. SystemServe Missions, Bedford, 1984—. Contbr. articles to mags. Mem. Ch. of God Pastors' Assn., Nat. Honor Soc. Democrat. Office: Ch of the Open Bible 689 Adams St Bedford OH 44146 *Life as a person of faith is lived in hope of God's bright future with a challenge to share that brightness with others today.*

SCHMITZ, CHARLES EDISON, evangelist; b. Mendota, Ill., July 18, 1919; s. Charles Francis Schmitz and Lucetta Margaret (Foulk) Schmitz Kaufmann; m. Eunice Magdalene Ewy, June 1, 1942; children: Charles Elwood, Jon Lee. Student, Wheaton Coll., 1936-37, 38, 39; BA, Wartburg Coll., Waverly, Iowa, 1940; BD, Wartburg Theol. Sem., Dubuque, Iowa, 1942, MDiv, 1977. Ordained to ministry Luth. Ch., 1942. Founding pastor Ascension Luth. Ch., L.A., 1942-48, Am. Evang. Luth. Ch., Phoenix, 1948-65; dir. intermountain missions, founding pastor 12 Evang. Luth. parishes, southwestern states, Ariz., N.Mex., Fla., 1948-65; staff evangelist Am. Luth. Ch., Mpls., 1965-73; sr. pastor Peace Luth. Ch., Palm Bay, Fla., 1973-89; pastor-at-large Am. Evang. Luth. Ch., Phoenix, 1989—; charter mem. Navqjo Luth. Mission, Rock Point, Ariz., 1960—; pastoral advisor Ariz. Luth. Outdoor Ministry Assn., Prescott, 1958-65, 89—; retreat master, chaplain Kogudus, Fla., 1972, U.S. and Marbach and Berlin, 1990; mem. transition team Fla. Synod, Egang. Luth. Ch. Am., 1985-89; founder, chmn. Ariz. Ch. Conf. Adult and Youth Problems, 1956-65; chmn. Space Coast Luth. Retirement Ctr., Palm Bay, 1985-89; nat. chaplain German-Am. Nat. Congress, 1991; chpt. chaplain Luth. Brotherood, 1991—. Author: Evangelism for the Seventies, 1970; co-author: ABC's of Life, 1968; assoc. editor Good News mag., 1965-71. Chaplain Greater South Brevard Area C. of C., Melbourne, Fla., 1984-89. Named Citizen of Yr., Palm Bay C. of C., 1979. Mem. Nat. Assn. Evangelicals, Lions (officer Phoenix and Palm Bay clubs 1952—), Kiwanis (bd. dirs. L.A. chpt. 1942-48). Republican. Home: 12444 Toreador Dr Sun City West AZ 85375-1926 *The truly modern person today who, like the scribes of old, would aspire to fulfillment in leadership would do well to remember Jesus' words: "Therefore every scribe who has been trained for the Kingdom of Heaven is like the master of a household who brings out of his treasure what is new and what is old." (Matt. 13:52).*

SCHMUNK, PHILIP PAUL, minister; b. Ann Arbor, Mich., Nov. 27, 1954; s. Robert Frank Schmunk and Elizabeth Ruth (Southern) Winters; m. Donna Lynn, Aug. 23, 1975; children: Philip Andrew, Daniel Aaron, Jennie Elizabeth. BA in Bible Lit., Taylor U., 1976; MA in Systematic Theology, Denver Seminary, 1980. Ordained to ministry Bapt. Ch., 1980. Intern Southwest Bapt. Ch., Denver, 1977-79; asst. pastor First Bapt. Ch., Mpls., 1979-85; campus minister Inter-Varsity Christian Fellowship/U. Minn., Mpls., 1985-87; assoc. pastor Longview (Wash.) Community Ch., 1988—; pastoral advisor Child Evangelism Fellowship, Longview, 1990—; treas. Ministerial Assn., Longview, 1990—. Mem. PACE, Toastmasters (sgt.-at-arms). Republican. Office: Longview Community Church 2323 Washington Way Longview WA 98632

SCHNATTERLY, MICHAEL DEAN, priest; b. Hays, Kans., Oct. 9, 1955; s. Harry Lee Schnatterly and Toya Ann Van Raden; m. Clare Lorelle Inman, July 21, 1984; 1 child, Ansel Jack. BA in Theatre, Furman U., 1979; MDiv, Seabury-Western Theol. Sem., 1989. Ordained to ministry Episcopal Ch. as deacon, 1989, as priest 1989. Curate Christ Ch., St. Michaels, Md., 1989—; examining chaplain, commn. on ministry Diocese of Easton, Md., 1990—, chmn. youth com., 1991—; del. Nat. Episcopal Youth Event, Missoula, Mont., 1990; del. Province III youth network Episcopal Ch., 1989—. Mem. Bay 100 Youth Task Force, St. Michaels, 1989—, Talbot County AIDS Task Force, Easton, 1990—; organizer St. Michaels Forum on Drugs in the Community, 1990; active Nat. Episcopal AIDS Coalition. Recipient Cotton Meml. award Seabury-Western Theol Sem., 1989; Muriel Mount Joy Miller-Hart Trust grantee, 1986. Mem. Mensa, Order St. Helena (assoc.), Liturgical Conf., Rotary (v.p. St. Michaels Club 1990-91, pres. elect 1991—). Home: 8974 Treesdale Dr Easton MD 21601 Office: Christ Ch PO Box S 103 Willow St Saint Michaels MD 21663 *Religious folk are often viewed as hypocrites who point accusing fingers at others, saying, "Thou shall not..." Jesus Christ challenges us to a new ethical life which calls others to His positive and forgiving model with the words, "Blessed are those who..."*

SCHNEEMELCHER, WILHELM, theologian, educator; b. Berlin, Fed. Republic of Germany, Aug. 21, 1914; s. Wilhelm and Paula (Sachse) S.; m. Eva Ackermann, May 31, 1940; children: Wilhelm Peter, Christiane, Thomas, Stefan. Degree in Theology, U. Berlin, 1938; habilitation, U. Göttingen, Fed. Republic of Germany, 1949, D of Theology, 1954; Doctorate (hon.), U. Strassburg, France, 1966. Pastor Sülbeck, 1947-49; lectr. Göttingen, 1946-49; prof. U. Göttingen, 1953; prof. U. Bonn, 1954, dean theology faculty, 1958-59, 63-64, rector, 1967-68; mem. faculty Rhein-Westfalisches Rsch. Acad., Düsseldorf, 1973, pres., 1982-85, prof. emeritus, 1979—. Author: Early Christianity, 1981; co-editor Evangelical City Lexicon, 2 vols., 1987; editor New Testament Apocrypha, 2 vols., 1987-89, Reden und Anpatre, 1991. Mem. Rotary. Home: Böckingstrasse 1, 5340 Bad Honnef Federal Republic of Germany

SCHNEIDER, DELWIN BYRON, minister, educator; b. Oshkosh, Wis., May 14, 1926; m. Katherine Louise Gesch; children: Kathi Del, Mark, Michael, Lisa. BA, Concordia Coll., 1948; BS, Concordia Sem., 1951; MA, Pepperdine U., 1950; postgrad., U. Chgo., 1954-56, Japanese Lang. Ctr., Tokyo, 1956-58; PhD, Rikkyo U., Tokyo, 1961; postgrad., Harvard U., 1961-62. Ordained to ministry Luth. Ch., 1951. Pastor St. Paul Luth. Ch., Oak Lawn, Ill., 1951-56; dir. Japan Luth. Hour, Tokyo, 1956-61; chaplain, lectr. Boston U., 1962-65; assoc. prof. Gustavus Adolphus Coll., St. Peter, Minn., 1965-70; asst. dean acad. affairs, coordinator internat. programs Gustavus Adolphus Coll., St. Peter, 1968-70; edn. TV lectr. World Religions KTCA-TV, St. Paul, 1967; dir. The Inst. of E. Asian Studies, 1967-70; prof. U. Minn., Mpls., 1968-69; coordinator U. San Diego Ecumenical Ctr. World Religions, 1972—; lectr. Ctr. Theol. Study, Pacific Luth. Theol. Sem., Berkeley, Calif., 1983. Author: Konkokyo: A Japanese Religion, 1962, Historical Perspectives in Christianity's Relation to Other Religions, 1983, No God But God; contbr. chpts. to books. Mem. Assn. Asian Studies, Am. Acad. Religion. Clubs: Harvard (San Diego), San Diego Yacht. Office: U San Diego Dept Religious Studies San Diego CA 92110

SCHNEIDER, DENNIS RAY, lay minister; b. Shattuck, Okla., Jan. 3, 1940; s. Raymond Jacob and Lucille Wilma (Cully) S.; m. Eva Gladys Burton, Aug. 25, 1963; children: Clay Brian, Zane Craig (dec. May 1988). B.M.E. in Edn., Panhandle State U., 1963; MA in Music Edn., Ea. N.Mex. U., 1967. Lay min. Ch. of Christ, Cimarron, N.Mex., 1963-65, 1971-91, Shiprock, N.Mex., 1967-69, Chama, N.Mex., 1970—; bus driver Swope Farm & Livestock, 1963-90; band dir. Cimarron Pub. Schs., 1971-91; farmer, Arnett, Okla., 1985-91. EMT Cimarron Ambulance Svc., 1978-91. Mem. NRA (life, Inst. for Legal Action), Santa Fe Trail Assn. (charter), N.Mex. Farm Bur., Masons (sec. local lodge 1986-91, master). Republican. Home: Rte 1 Box 8 Cimarron NM 87714 *Mankind was created for two principal reasons: to fulfill the purpose for which they were created, thus using their gifts and talents to the very best of their ability; and to prepare themselves for eternity with God while so doing.*

SCHNEIDER, LOUIS KING, minister; b. Phila., Mar. 26, 1934; s. Louis Ferdinand and Thelma Elizabeth (Street) S.; m. Margaret Jane Kennedy, Aug. 2, 1958; children: David, Ann, Kathryn, Stephen. BS, Pa. State U., 1956; postgrad., Dallas Theol. Sem., 1962, Fuller Theol. Sem. Ordained to ministry 1962. Youth dir. Bothany Bible Ch., Phoenix, 1962-66; sr. pastor N.W. Bible Ch., Dallas, 1966-75; exec. dir. Pagosa Family Life, Pagosa Springs, Colo., 1976-83; sr. pastor N.W. Hills. Bapt. Ch., Corvallis, Oreg., 1983-87, Crosso (Tex.) Bible Ch., 1987—; bd. dirs. Crosto Butto (Colo.) Family Life; exec. dir. Bus. Community for Christ, Dallas, 1967-78. Contbr. articles to mags. Chaplain Dallas Cowboys, 1970-74, So. Meth. U. Football Team, Dallas, 1972-75; bd. dirs. YMCA, Dallas, 1958-62. Lt. j.g. USN, 1956-58. Recipient Leadership medal U.S. Olympic Com., 1979. Fellow Kerr Found.; mem. Covenant Christian Schs. (advisor), Rotary (chaplain 1970-75). Republican. Home: 104 Braxton Bragg Conroe TX 77302 Office: Conroe Bible Ch 1202 Callahan Conroe TX 77301

SCHNEIDER, MICHAEL ALLEN, clergyman; b. Laredo, Tex., Sept. 4, 1966; s. Donald Arthur and Janice Marlene (Greving) S.; m. Kimberly Marie Adams, July 23, 1988. BA, Wheaton Coll., 1988; postgrad., Duke Div. Sch., 1990—. Counselor United Meth. Camps, Germantown, Ohio, 1985, resource person, 1986; youth pastor Aley United Meth. Ch., Beavercreek, Ohio, 1988-90. Home: 2132 Bedford St #9 Durham NC 27707

SCHNEIDER, STANLEY DALE, retired minister; b. Massillon, Ohio, Oct. 15, 1921; s. Orlando Eli and Odessa McMillan (Doughty) S.; m. Marcella Caroline Degen, Aug. 24, 1945; children: Philip James, Carolyn Jean. AB, Capital U., 1943, DD (hon.), 1964; BD, Luth. Theol. Sem., 1945; postgrad., U. St. Andrews, Scotland, 1954-55, Ecumenical Inst., Geneva, 1958. Ordained to ministry Luth. Evang. Ch. in Am., 1945. Pastor Christ Luth. Ch., Regina, Sask., Can., 1945-47; asst. pastor St. Paul's Luth. Ch., Toledo, 1947-49, sr. pastor, 1975-87, pastor emeritus, 1987—; pastor St. Paul Luth. Ch., Michigan City, Ind., 1949-54; prof. homiletics, liturgics Luth. Theol. Sem., Columbus, Ohio, 1954-75; chair commn. on evangelism Am. Luth Ch., Mpls., 1960-62, chair bd. for theol. edn. and ministry, 1976-87; sec. Com. on Lectionary and Calendar Reform, 1976-80. Author: As One Who Speaks for God, 1965; co-editor: Interpreting Luther's Legacy, 1969. Pub. mem. Toledo

Labor/Mgmt./Citizen's Com., 1980—; bd. dirs. St. Luke's Hosp., Maumee, Ohio, 1979-91; mem. adult svcs. com. Lucas County Health Bd., Toledo, 1989—. Recipient Disting. Alumnus award Trinity Luth. Sem., 1988. Mem. Kit Kat Club (pres. Columbus chpt. 1974-75), Rotary. Home: 4464 Indian Rd Toledo OH 43615 Office: St Paul's Luth Ch 428 N Erie St Toledo OH 43624

SCHNEIDER, THEODORE FRANK, minister; b. Portsmouth, Va., Oct. 16, 1934; s. Theodore and Grace Louise (Tatem) S.; m. Doris Lee Smith, Elisa Anne, Timothy Allen. B.A., Roanoke Coll., Va., 1956; B.D., Luth. Theol. Sem., Pa., 1959, postgrad., 1961-63; postgrad. Franklin and Marshall Coll., 1984; D.D., Susquehanna U., 1985. Ordained to ministry Lutheran Ch. Am., 1959. Pastor, St. John Luth. Ch., Millheim, Pa., 1959-65, Advent Luth. Ch., Lancaster, Pa., 1965-71; dir. Camp Juniata, Milroy, Pa., 1961-62, Mt. Luther Camp, Mifflinburg, Pa., 1963; dean Lancaster dist., Cen. Pa. Synod, Luth. Ch. Am., 1965-70, 81-82; sr. pastor Luth. Ch. of the Good Shepherd, Lancaster, 1971-86, 91—. St. Luke Lutheran Ch., Silver Spring, Md., 1986—; chmn. candidacy com. , Div.for Ministry of Met. Washington Synod Evang. Luth. Ch. Am., 1988-89, mem. Synod Coun. Met. Washington Synod, 1988—; mem. exec. com. of Synod Coun., Met. Washington Synod, 1991—; chmn. exec. bd. Central Pa. synod Luth. Ch. Am., 1977-86, mem. commn. mission and strategy, 1975-76, mem. Lancaster dist. cabinet, 1965-86, chmn. com. parish life, 1973-75, chmn. com. worship, 1973; del.-at-large Biennial Conv., Luth. Ch. Am., 1968, 70, 72, 76, 80, 82, 84. Mem. exec. com., trustee Tressler Luth. Children's Home, 1959-68; mem. student rev. bd. Conestoga Valley Sch. Dist., 1975-86; pres. United Cerebral Palsy Lancaster County, 1966-75, regional dir., 1974-76; bd. dirs. Lancaster Boys' Club, 1975-76), tng. staff CONTACT/Lancaster, 1976-79, The Gate House, Lititz, Pa., 1978; chaplain Lancaster chpt. Am. Guild Organists, 1967—; mem. Silver Spring chpt. Am. Guild of Organists, 1991—. Recipient Humanitarian Service award United Cerebral Palsy Pa., 1975. Mem. Am. Guild Organists (chaplain 1965-86). Republican. Lodge: Kiwanis (dir. Silver Spring chpt. 1970-78, pres. 1976, mem. Natl. Legion of Honor 1989—) (Silver Spring). Author: Until the King Comes, 1991. Home: 919 Highland Dr Silver Spring MD 20910 Office: 9100 Colesville Rd Silver Spring MD 20910

SCHNEIDER, THOMAS R(ICHARD), physicist; b. Newark, N.J., Nov. 14, 1945; s. Valentine William and Mary Bernadette (Scanlon) S.; m. Paula Doris Tulecko, June 8, 1968 (div. June 1984); 1 child, Laurie Ann. BS with high honors, Stevens Inst. Tech., Hoboken, N.J., 1967; PhD, U. Pa., 1971. Postdoctoral fellow U. Pa. Nat. Ctr. for Engergy Mgmt. and Power, Phila., 1971-72; prin. rsch. physicist Pub. Svc. Electric & Gas Co., Newark, 1972-77; various positions, dir. dept., exec. scientist Electric Power Rsch. Inst., Palo Alto, Calif., 1977—; pres. bd. dirs. Lighting Rsch. Inst., N.Y.C., 1990—; bd. dirs., chmn. energy task force Coun. on Superconductivity for Am. Competiveness, Washington, 1991—; coord. for Ad hoc Working Group Report on Power Applications of Superconductivity for Dept. Commerce, 1990-91. Mem. IEEE, Am. Phys. Soc., Illuminating Engrng. Soc., Am. Soc. Assn. Execs. Achievements include advanced research in energy storage, energy applications of superconductivity. Home: 40 Saddleback Portola Valley CA 94028 Office: Electric Power Rsch Inst 3412 Hillview Ave PO Box 10412 Palo Alto CA 94303

SCHNEIDERS, SANDRA MARIE, religion educator; b. Chgo., Nov. 12, 1936; d. Alexander Aloysius and Glen Elizabeth (Ogle) S. BA, Marygrove Coll., 1960; MA, U. Detroit, 1967; S.T.L., Inst. Catholique, Paris, 1971; S.T.D., Pontifical Gregorian U., Rome, 1975. Joined Sisters, Servants of Immaculate Heart of Mary, Roman Cath. Ch., 1955. Tchr. various grade schs., 1958, 60-62; tchr. Immaculate Heart of Mary High Sch., Westchester, Ill., 1962-65; asst. prof. Marygrove Coll., Detroit, 1965-67; tchr. St. Mary High Sch., Akron, Ohio, 1967-68; asst. prof. Marygrove Coll., Detroit, 1971-72; prof. Jesuit Sch. of Theology, Berkeley, Calif., 1976—; Madeleva lectr. St. Mary's Coll., Notre Dame, Ind., 1986; disting. faculty lectr. Grad. Theol. Union, Berkeley, 1988. Author: New Wineskins, 1986, Women and the Word, 1986, Beyond Patching, 1991, The Revelatory Text, 1991; contbr. articles to profl. jours. Rsch. grantee Assn. Theol. Schs., 1979. Mem. Cath. Theol. Soc. Am., Cath. Bibl. Assn. Am., Soc. Bibl. Lit. (pres. western region 1988), Am. Acad. Religion, Pacific Coast Theol. Soc., Soc. for New Testament Studies. Democrat. Roman Catholic. Avocations: reading, running, swimming. Office: Jesuit Sch of Theology 1735 LeRoy Ave Berkeley CA 94709 *Life is too short to allow fear, inertia, or lack of imagination to prevent us from speaking the truth we know and doing the good we can in this world.*

SCHNEIER, ARTHUR, rabbi; b. Vienna, Austria, Mar. 20, 1930; m. Elisabeth Nordmann; children: Marc, Karen Schneier Dresbach. BA, Yeshiva U., 1951; MA in Psychology and Edn., NYU, 1953; DHL (hon.), Fordham U., 1981, L.I. U., 1981; PhD (hon.), U. Budapest, 1984; DD (hon.), Yeshiva U., 1986; ThD (hon.), Reformed Ch. Theol. Sem., 1988; LLD (hon.), Susquehanna U., 1988. Ordained rabbi, 1955. Rabbi Park East Synagogue, N.Y.C., 1962—; founder Park East Day Sch., Sam and Esther Minskoff Cultural Ctr., N.Y.C.; founder, pres. Appeal of Conscience Found., N.Y., 1965; chmn. Am. sect. World Jewish Congress, 1979-84, hon. chmn., 1984—; alt. rep. of U.S. to Gen. Assembly of UN, 1988; mem. Coun. of Fgn. Rels.; mem. U.S. Presdl. Delegation for Return of Crown of St. Stephen to Hungary, 1978; chmn. bd. dirs. Am.-romanian Flood and Earthquake Relief, 1970-74; leader Armenian Earthquake Relief, 1988; founding trustee U.S.-Japan Found; apptd. chmn. U.S. Commn. for Preservation Am.'s Heritage Abroad. Bd. dirs. UN Devel. Corp., N.Y., 1973-80; mem. exec. com., bd. dirs. Am. Joint Distbn. Com.; bd. dirs. Hebrew Immigration Aid Soc.; vice chmn. Am. Gathering of Honocaust Survivors; hon. vice chmn. Jewish Nat. Fund. Leader 1st Jewish prayer svc. in Kremlin, 1990; only Jewish leader to address Millenium of Russian Orthodox Ch., Moscow, 1988; recipient Clergyman of Yr. award Protestant Coun. Chs., 1983, Religious Liberty award, 1989, Torch of Freedom award Internat. League for Repatriation of Russian Jews, 1989, Ellis Island medal of Honor, 1990, Defender of Jerusalem award Jabotinsky Found., 1990. Mem. Rabbinical Coun. Am., N.Y. Bd. Rabbis (bd. govs. 1966—), Union Orthodox Jewish Congregations (bd. dirs.), World Fedn. Hungarian Jews (spiritual leader). Home: 251 E 71st St New York NY 10021 Office: 163 E 67th St New York NY 10021

SCHNEK, M. GEORGES, religious organization administrator. Chmn. Cen. Coun. Jewish Communities of Belgium, Brussels. Office: Cen Coun Jewish Communities, 2 rue Joseph Dupont, Brussels Belgium*

SCHNELLE, RICHARD MAX, pastor; b. Norwood, Ohio, Aug. 5, 1937; s. Henry Daniel Geroge and Pearl Mae (Jones) S.; m. Rose Anne Murphy, Feb. 5, 1966 (div. Oct. 1973). BA, Elmhurst Coll., 1961; BD, Eden Sem., 1965, MDiv, 1970. Assoc. pastor Zion United Ch. Christ, Louisville, 1965-71; wxec. dir. Covington Protestant Childrens Home, Ky., 1971-79; pastor Trinity United Ch. Christ, Louisville, 1979—; chaplain Brooklawn Treatment Ctr., Louisville, 1982—. Home: 205 Flanders Ct Apt 1 Louisville KY 40218 Office: Trinity United Ch Christ 3309 E Indian Trail Louisville KY 40213

SCHNER, JOSEPH GEORGE, priest, college president, psychologist; b. Winnipeg, Man., Can., Jan. 1, 1942; s. Joseph George and Josephine (Poplick) S. AB, Fordham U., 1967; MA, U. Windsor, Ont., Can., 1970; MDiv, St. Mary's U., Halifax, N.S., Can., 1974; PhD, U. Toronto, Ont., 1978. Joined SJ., 1961; ordained priest Roman Cath. Ch., 1974; registered psychologist, Ont., Sask. (Can.). Superior Bellarmine Residence, Toronto, 1975-81; dir. studies upper Can. province S.J., 1979-84; superior Jesuit Fathers Sask., Regina, 1984—; pres. Campion Coll. of U. Regina, 1986—. Contbr. articles to profl. jours. Bd. govs. Regis Coll., Toronto, 1984-91, St. Paul's Coll., Winnipeg, 1986-89, 91—. Mem. Can. Register Health Svc. Providers in Psychology, Can. Psychol. Assn., Sask. Psychol. Assn. (treas. 1984-87), Assn. for Psychol. Type. Office: Campion Coll, U Regina, Regina, SK Canada S4S 0A2

SCHNITZER, JESHAIA, rabbi, marriage and family therapist; b. Phila., Jan. 25, 1918; s. Philip and Jennie (Galler) S.; m. Hilde Maier, Mar. 9, 1947; children: Jonathan Aaron, Lisa Judith. BA, U. Del., 1940; rabbi, Jewish Inst. Religion Hebrew Union Coll., 1944; MA in Social Work, Columbia U., 1949; EdD, Tchrs. Coll., Columbia U., 1954; M.H.L. (hon.), Hebrew Union Coll., 1969; D.Div. (hon.), Jewish Theol. Sem., 1975. Diplomate Am. Bd. Sexology. Rabbi B'nai Abraham, Hagerstown, Md., 1943-44; chaplain U.S. Army Chaplain Corps., Korea, 1944-47; rabbi Free Synagogue, N.Y.C., 1947-49, 92d St. YMHA, N.Y.C., 1949-51, Congregation Shomrei Emunah, Montclair, N.J., 1951-79; rabbi emeritus Congregation Shomrei Emunah, Montclair, 1979—; adj. prof. Seton Hall U., South Orange, N.J., 1978-88; chaplain Montclair State Coll. Author: New Horizons for the Synagogue-A Counseling Program for the Rabbi and the Synagogue, 1956; contbg. author: Marriage Counseling, 1967. Mem. Montclair Civil Rights Commn., 1960-68; bd. dirs. ARC, Montclair chpt., 1953-55, 80-85; mem. Mayor's Montclair Youth Com., 1953-56; pres. Essex County Bd. Rabbis, 1959-61; bd. dirs. Council Social Agys., Montclair, 1960-63; bd. dirs. Child Guidance Clinic, Montclair, 1955-60, N.J. chpt. UN Assn., Montclair, 1955-65, Council Social Agys., Montclair, 1957-60, Jewish Community Council Essex County, 1953-56, Sex Info. and Edn. Council U.S., N.Y.C., 1968-72, Urban Coalition Montclair and Vicinity, 1969-74; exec. bd. mem. Tri-State Family Relations Council, 1955-60; co-chmn. Joint Chaplaincy Com. Metrowest, 1959—; v.p. Coordinating Coun. Compassionate Care of the Sick, 1991—. Recipient award for meritorious svc. B'nai B'rith, 1955, Disting. Svc. award Nat. Jewish Welfare Bd., 1948, Samuel W. and Rose Horowitz award Fedn. Jewish Philanthropies N.Y.C., 1977, Saul Schwarz Disting. Svc. award N.J. chpt. Conf. Jewish Communal Svc., 1990. Fellow Am. Assn. Marriage and Family Therapy (approved supr.); mem. Am. Assn. Sex Educators, Counselors and Therapists, Nat. Assn. Social Workers, Rabbinical Assembly Am. (pres. No. N.J. chpt. 1962-64), N.J. Assn. Marriage and Family Counselors (pres. 1960-63, 80-83), Jewish War Vets, Jewish Chaplains Assn., Ministerial Assn. Montclair and Vicinity (pres. 1971-72), Am. Bd. Sexology (clin. supr.), Internat. Acad. of Profl. Counseling and Psychotherapy Inc. (diplomate in profl. psychotherapy). Avocations: covered bridges, model trains, classical music. Home and Office: 144 Midland Ave Montclair NJ 07042

SCHNOEBELEN, WILLIAM JAMES, evangelist; b. Cedar Rapids, Iowa, Aug. 24, 1949; s. Cletus Joseph and Helen Mae (Jayne) S.; m. Sharon Lee Dura, May 31, 1974. BA in Music, Lora Coll., 1971; M Theol. Studies, St. Francis Sem., 1980; MA, Liberty U., 1990. Ordained to ministry Mormons for Jesus Evangelistic Assn., 1987. Exec. Sts. Alive in Jesus, Issaquah, Wash., 1987—. Author: Wicca: Satan's Little White Lie, 1990, Whited Sepulchers, 1990, Masonry: Beyond the Light, 1991; co-author: Mormonism's Temple of Doom, 1987. *In my ministry I have noted that most problems in people's lives begin and develop through attitudes of prayerlessness and carelessness with the Bible as the inerrant Word of God. Prayer must be what empowers us for service. The Bible tells us whom and how we should serve.*

SCHNUCKER, ROBERT VICTOR, history and religion educator; b. Waterloo, Iowa, Sept. 30, 1932; s. Felix Victor and Josephine (Maasdam) S.; m. Anna Mae Englekes, Sept. 18, 1955; children: Sarai Ann, Sar Victor, Christjahn Dietrich. AB, NE Mo. State U., 1953; BD, U. Dubuque, 1956; MA, U. Iowa, 1960, PhD, 1969. Ordained to ministry Presbyn. Ch., 1956/. Pastor United Presbyn. Ch. USA, Springville, Iowa, 1956-63; asst. prof. NE Mo. State U., Kirksville, 1963-65, assoc. prof., 1963-65, prof., 1969—; dir. Thomas Jefferson U. Press; supr. Bible exam. Presbyn. Ch. USA, Louisville, 1977-89; bd. dirs. Ctr. for Reformation Rsch., St. Louis, 1984—. Author: Helping Humanities Journal Survive, 1985; editor: Calviniana, 1989; contbr. articles to profl. jours.; author (tests) History Assessment Test, 1990; editor Editing History, Conf. for Hist. Jours., 1985—, Historians of Early Modern Europe, 1980—; book rev. editor, mng. editor Sixteenth Century Jour., 1973—; pub. Sixteenth Century Essays and Studies, 1980—. Fellow Soc. Sci. Study of Religion, 1988; NEH grantee for jour. pubs., 1980. Mem. 16th Century Studies Conf. (exec. sec. 1972—), Am. History Assn. (chair Robinson prize com. 1987), Am. Soc. Ch. History, Soc. History Edn., AAUP, Am. Acad. Religion, Soc. Bibl. Lit., Conf. Faith & History, Soc. for Reformation Rsch., Ren. Soc. Am., Soc. SCholarly Pubs., Soc. for Values in Higher Edn., Conf. for Hist. Jours. Office: NE Mo State U LB 115 Kirksville MO 63501

SCHOCH, DAVID EDMUND, minister; b. Pasadena, Calif., Apr. 24, 1920; s. Chester Albert Schoch and Rose (Aurelia) Biedebach; m. Evelyn Audene Ward; children: Rose Ann McKee, Steven Earl. BA in Theology, Living Waters Bible Coll., 1980; DD, Word of Faith Sch. of Theology, 1988. Ordained to ministry Christian Ch., 1953. Assoc. pastor Immanuel Gospel Temple, L.A., 1950-52, evangelist, 1952-53; pastor Bethany Chapel, Long Beach, 1953-86; sr. pastor Bethany Missionary Assn., Long Beach, 1953-86; convs. min., counsellor, 1986—; chmn. Revival Fellowship, Pasadena, 1960-85; mem. Network of Christian Ministries Word of Faith, New Orleans, 1985-90. Author: The Precious Blood, 1964, Sarah, 1952, The Prophetic Ministry, 1978; compiler of scriptures set to music, 1966. Tech. sgt. U.S. Army, 1941-46. Republican. Office: Bethany Missionary Assn 2214 E 6th St Long Beach CA 90814

SCHOEFFLER, BRYAN, religious organization executive; b. Dec. 17, 1957. Grad., Christ Unltd. Bible Inst., Kansas City, Mo., 1978. Ordained to ministry, 1978. Youth worker Family Life Ministries, Bath, N.Y., 1978-88; founder, dir. Christian Camping Svcs., Bath, 1988—; youth speaker. Mem. Christian Camping Internat., Finger Lakes Trail Conf., Internat. Assn. Approved Basketball Ofcls. Home and Office: 5698A Nipher Rd Bath NY 14810 *My goal in life is to help the local churches and camps of America to have more effective outreaches to youth, as I seek to most effectively serve God with my life.*

SCHOENBORN, ROGER LEE, minister; b. Oregon City, Oreg., June 10, 1948; s. Arthur Frank and Doris Naomi (Brown) S.; m. Ili Bieler, Aug. 16, 1980; children: Helena Christine, Priscila Belle, David Lee. BS, Oreg. STate U., 1970; MDiv., Western Evang. Sem., 1982. Ordained to ministry Evang. Ch., 1982. Missionary tchr. OMS Internat., Londrina, Paraná, Brazil, 1973-77, missionary camp developer, 1978-82; sr. pastor Yakima (Wash.) Evang. Ch., 1982—; mem. com. missions and ch. extension Pacific Conf. Evang. Ch., Milwaukie, Oreg., 1982-86, com. on stewardship, 1988-90, com. on ways and means, 1991, dir. missions, 1991. Chmn. Yakima Christian Sch., 1982-86; mem. com. ministerial rels. Pacific Conf. Evang. Ch., 1986-88, ways and means, 1985-86, trustee, 1985—. Named one of Outstanding Young Men of Am., 1981, 82. Mem. Yakima Assn. Evangelicals (sec. 1987-90). Republican. Clubs: Associação Recreativa Esportiva Londrinese (Londrina Parana, Brazil); San Marino (Guaratuba, Paraná, Brazil). Avocations: stamp collecting, reading, gardening, travelling. Office: Yakima Evang Ch 301 S 7th Ave Yakima WA 98902

SCHOENECKER, WARREN KROY, minister; b. Fargo, N.D., Mar. 15, 1930; s. Andrew E. and Evelyn T. (Jahr) S.; m. Elizabeth Pratt, Mar. 22, 1952; children: Stephen, Kathleen. BA, Luther Coll., 1956; MA, Ball State U., 1980. Ordained to ministry Meth. Ch., 1989; cert. profl. contracts mgr. Commd. 2d lt.cer USAF, 1952, advanced through grades to lt. col., 1975; security officer USAF, various locations, 1952-56; adminstrv. officer USAF, Vietnam, 1966-67; missile contr. USAF, Great Falls, Mont., 1967-71; procurement officer USAF, various locations, 1971-78; chief contracting USAF, Spain, 1978-79; mgr. contracts USAF, Germany, 1979-81; ret. USAF, 1981; ops. mgr. GE, 1956-60; engring. analyst Martin Marietta Corp., 1960-66; min. 1st United Meth. Ch., Hamlin, Tex., 1989—. Counselor Mental Health Assn., Abilene, Tex., 1981, SCORE, Abilene, 1982. Decorated Bronze Star. Mem. APGA, Rotary. Avocations: hunting, fishing, travel, woodworking. Home: 1044 NW 4th St Hamlin TX 79520 Office: 1st United Meth Ch 48 SW Ave A Hamlin TX 79520

SCHOENHERR, WALTER JOSEPH, bishop; b. Detroit, Feb. 28, 1920; s. Alex M. and Ida (Schmitz) S. Student, Sacred Heart Sem., Detroit, 1935-42, Mt. St. Mary's Sem., Norwood, Ohio, 1942-44, S.S. Cyril and Methodius Sem., Orchard Lake, Mich., 1944-45. Ordained priest Roman Catholic Ch., 1945; asst. pastor Detroit Parishes of St. Davids, St. Leos, St. Roses, Presentation and St. Bedes, Southfield, Mich., 1959-61; pastor St. Aloysius Parish, Detroit, 1961-65, Blessed Sacrament Cathedral, 1965-68; aux. bishop of Detroit, 1968—; appointed to serve South region Archdiocese of Detroit, 1977—; mem. Permanent Diaconate and Pastoral Ministry to Correctional Instns., Archidocesan Liturgical Commn.; founding chaplain De LaSalle council K.C. Served with Mich. N.G., 1952-67. Home: 11350 Reeck Rd Southgate MI 48195 Office: 1234 Washington Blvd Detroit MI 48226

SCHOEPP, MARK LEONARD, religious organization administrator; b. Ponoka, Alta., Can., July 20, 1954; came to U.S., 1978; s. Walter Frank and Emerald Jacueline (Woodruff) S.; m. Rebecca Elizabeth Betke, Jan. 27, 1980; children: Jenica Jun, Isaac John, Samuel Reuben, Gideon Michael. BA, U. Alta., Edmonton, 1975; Dir. Christian Edn. cert., Concordia Coll., Seward, Nebr., 1979, M in Parish Edn., 1989. Dir. Christian edn. Hope Luth. Ch of the Deaf, Portland, Oreg., 1979-84, Messiah Luth. Ch., Seattle, 1985-87, St. John Luth. Ch., Seward, Nebr., 1987—; bd. dirs., bd. for youth svcs. Luth. Ch.-Mo. Synod, St. Louis, 1975-79, mem. planning team for Nat. Youth Gatherings, 1980, 86, 92; chmn., bd. dirs. Walther League Bd. Govs., Chgo., 1981-89; mem. com. Dist. Task Force on Ministry with Handicapped, Portland, 1981-85. Contbr. articles to religious jour. Mem. Luth. Edn. Assn. (mem. theol. educators and associated mins. 1985—). Office: St John Luth Ch 919 N Columbia Seward NE 68434 *What a precious gift God gave in giving families. A place to learn about love, commitment and service to others—all things that God showed us in the life, death and resurrection of Jesus Christ.*

SCHOFIELD, CALVIN ONDERDONK, JR., bishop; b. Delhi, N.Y., Jan. 6, 1933; s. Calvin O. and Mabel (Lenton) S.; m. Elaine Marie Fullerton, Aug. 3, 1963; children: Susan Elaine, Robert Lenton. B.A., Hobart Coll., 1959, S.T.D. (Hon.), 1980; M.Div., Berkeley Div. Sch., 1959, D.D. (hon.), 1979; D.D. (hon.), U. of the South, 1981. Ordained priest Episcopal Ch., 1962; curate St. Peter's Episcopal Ch., St. Petersburg, Fla., 1962-64; vicar St. Andrew's Episcopal Ch., Miami, Fla., 1964-70; rector St. Andrew's Episcopal Ch., 1970-78; bishop coadjutor Diocese S.E. Fla., Miami, 1978-79, bishop, 1980—; exec. bd. Presiding Bishops Fund for World Relief; exec. coun. Episcopal Ch., 1991—. Regent U. of the South, Sewanee, Tenn., 1988—. Capt. chaplain corps USNR, 1960-85; ret., 1985. Mem. Naval Res. Assn., Naval Inst. Republican. Office: 525 NE 15th St Miami FL 33132

SCHOFIELD, JOHN-DAVID MERCER, bishop; b. Somerville, Mass., Oct. 6, 1938; s. William David and Edith Putnam (Stockman) S. BA, Dartmouth Coll., 1960; MDiv, Gen. Theol. Sem., N.Y.C., 1963, DD (hon.), 1989. Joined Monks of Mt. Tabor, Byzantine Cath. Ch., 1978; ordained priest Episcopal Ch. Asst. priest Ch. of St. Mary the Virgin, San Francisco, 1963-65, Our Most Holy Redeemer Ch., London, 1965-69; rector, retreat master St. Columba's Ch. and Retreat House, Inverness, Calif., 1969-88; bishop Episcopal Diocese of San Joaquin, Fresno, Calif., 1988—; aggregate Holy Transfiguration Monastery, 1984—; bishop protector Order Agape and Reconciliation, Chemainus, B.C., Can., 1990—. Episcopal visitor to Community of Christian Family Ministry, Vista, Calif., 1991—; trustee Nashotah House Sem., Wis., 1991—. Mem. Episcopal Synod of Am. (founder 1989), Episcopalians United (bd. dirs. 1987—). Republican. Office: Diocese of San Joaquim 4159 E Dakota Ave Fresno CA 93726

SCHOLER, DAVID MILTON, religion educator; b. Rochester, Minn., July 24, 1938; s. Milton Norris and Bernice Gladys (Anderson) S.; m. Jeannette Faith Mudgett, Aug. 16, 1960; children: Emily Hancock, Abigail Anne. BA, Wheaton Coll., 1960, MA, 1964; BD, Gordon Div. Sch., 1964; ThD, Harvard U., 1980. Ordained to ministry Am. Bapt. Chs. U.S.A., 1966. Asst. prof., then assoc. prof. N.T. Gordon-Conwell Theol. Sem., South Hamilton, Mass., 1969-81; dean of sem., Julius R. Mantey prof. N.T. No. Bapt. Theol. Sem., Lombard, Ill., 1981-88; Disting. prof. N.T. and early ch. history North Park Coll. and Theol. Sem., Chgo., 1988—; mem. gen. bd. Am. Bapt. Chs. U.S.A., Valley Forge, Pa., 1989—; mem. Bapt. World Alliance-Mennonite World Conf. Dialogue, McLean, Va., 1989—; vis. scholar, theologian Am. Bapt. Chs. U.S.A., 1985-86. Author: Nag Hammadi Bibliography 1948-69, 1971, A Basic Bibliographic Guide for New Testament Exegesis, 1973, The Caring God, 1989; assoc. editor N.T. book revs. Jour. Bibl. Lit., 1991—; contbr. articles, book revs. to profl. publs. Mem. Assn. Theol. Schs. (chair com. on standards 1988-90), Nat. Assn. Bapt. Profs. of Religion (pres. 1986-87), Am. Acad. Religion, Chgo. Soc. Bibl. Rsch. (pres. 1991—), Inst. for Bibl. Rsch., N.Am. Patristic Soc., Soc. Biblical Lit., Studiorum Novi Testamentum Soc. Home: 266 S Myrtle Ave Villa Park IL 60181 Office: N Park Coll & Theol Sem 3225 W Foster Ave Chicago IL 60625

SCHOLL, FENTON THOMAS, JR., minister; b. Louisville, June 25, 1950; s. Fenton Thomas and Grace (Adair) S.; m. Darba Sue Bowers, Apr. 14, 1979. AAS, Lexington Tech. Inst., 1972; BA, Georgetown Coll., 1975; MDiv, Princeton Theol. Sem., 1978; postgrad., So. Bapt. Theol. Sem., 1979. Ordained to ministry So. Bapt. Conv., 1975, Am. Bapt. Chs. U.S.A., 1980. Min. Calvary Bapt. Ch., Dayton, Ohio, 1980-82, Madison Ave. Bapt. Ch., Albany, N.Y., 1982-90; assoc. for devel. and programming N.Y. State Coun. Chs., Albany, 1990-91; exec. dir. Ga. Christian Coun., Macon, 1991—; del. observer 5th assembly World Coun. Chs., So. Bapt. Conv., Nairobi, Kenya, 1975; scholar-in-residence Andover-Newton Theol. Sem., 1982; bd. dirs. Christians United in Mission, Albany, 1988-90, Capital Area Coun. Chs., Albany, 1982-89. Vol. chaplain Miami Valley Hosp., Dayton, 1980-82; founder, bd. dirs. Ethiopian Refugee Relief Program, Albany, 1983-90, East African Relief Fund of Albany, 1985-86; bd. dirs. Du Lac Community Devel. Corp., Albany, 1990-91. Office: Ga Christian Coun PO Box 7193 Macon GA 31209 *I become excited by the sight of churches cooperating with each other, for it is in ecumenism where one begins to see the framework for God's kingdom on Earth.*

SCHOLSKY, MARTIN JOSEPH, priest; b. Stafford Spring, Conn., Jan. 16, 1930; s. Sigmund Felix and Mary Magdalen (Wysocki) S. BA, St. John's Sem., 1952, MA in History, 1956; MA in Classical Greek, Cath. U. of Am., 1966. Ordained priest Roman Cath. Ch., 1956. Asst. pastor St. Peter's Ch., Hartford, Conn., 1956-61; prin. St. Peter's Sch., Hartford, 1956-58; instr. St. Thomas Sem., Bloomfield, Conn., 1961-67; admissions dir. St. Thomas Sem., Bloomfield, 1965-67; vocations dir. Archdiocese of Hartford, 1967-78; chaplain Newington (Conn.) Children's Hosp., 1961-78; weekend asst. St. Mary's Ch., Newington, 1961-78; pastor St. Bartholomew Ch., Manchester, Conn., 1978-90; dean Manchester Deanery, 1989-91; spiritual dir. St. Thomas Aquinas High Sch., New Britain, Conn., 1991—; weekend asst. St. Francis of Assisi Ch., South Windsor, Conn., 1991—; instr. Holy Apostle's Sem. & Coll., Cromwell, Conn., 1988—. Contbr. articles to profl. jours. Home: 36 Griswold St Manchester CT 06040 Office: St Francis of Assisi Ch South Windsor CT 06074 *Conscience is not our own personal feelings about things; rather, it is our innate awareness of the rightness and wrongness of our deeds as God sees them, an awareness, often denied, that still remains the measure by which God will ultimately judge us all.*

SCHOLTES, ELIZABETH FRANCES, religion educator; b. Durham, N.C., Apr. 24, 1962; d. William Edgar and Betty Frances (Miller) S. BA, U. N.C., 1984; MRE, Gordon-Conwell Theol. Sem., 1989. Intern Christian edn. Forest Presbyn. Ch., Charlotte, N.C., summer 1987; dir. children's ministries New Meadows Bapt. Ch., Topsfield, Mass., 1988-89; dir. Christian edn., youth 1st Presbyn. Ch., Orangeburg, S.C., 1989—. Home: 1142 Evergreen NE Orangeburg SC 29115 Office: 1st Presbyn Ch PO Box 582 Orangeburg SC 29116

SCHOMER, HOWARD, social policy consultant, clergyman; b. Chgo., June 9, 1915; s. Frank Michael and Daisy (Aline) S.; m. Elsie Pauline Swenson, Mar. 23, 1942; children: Karine, Mark, Paul, Ellen. B.S. summa cum laude, Harvard U., 1937, postgrad., 1939-40; student, Chgo. Theol. Sem., 1938-39, 40-41, D.D., 1954; LL.D., Olivet Coll., 1966. Ordained to ministry United Ch. Christ, 1941. Student pastor Fitzwilliam, N.H., Oak Park, Ill.; asst. dean U. Chgo. Chapel., 1940-41; counsellor Am. history Harvard U., 1939-40; civilian pub. service Am. Friends Service Com., 1941-45; Am. Bd. Mission fellow to chs. of Europe Chambon-sur-Lignon, France, 1946-55; history tchr., work camp dir. Coll. Cevenol; founder internat. conf. center Accueil Fraternel, Permanent Conf. Protestant Chs. in Latin Countries of Europe; asst. to rapporteur UN Commn. on Human Rights, UN Econ. and Social Council, 1947-48; inter-church aid sec. for Europe World Council Chs., Geneva, 1955-58; pres., prof. ch. history Chgo. Theol. Sem., 1959-66; exec. dir. dept. specialized ministries Div. Overseas Ministries, Nat. Council Chs., N.Y.C., 1967-70; participant integration demonstrations in Ala., Ga., Washington, Chgo., SCLC, 1960-66; world issues sec. United Ch. Bd. World Ministries, 1971-80; Indochina liaison officer World Council of Chs., 1970-71; United Ch. of Christ officer for social responsibility in investments, 1972-81; founder, dir. Corp. Adv. Services, 1980-90; founder, mem. United Ch. Christ Working Group with United Ch. in German Democratic Rep. and Fed. Rep. of Germany, 1977-86; vis. prof. religion and society Andover Newton Theol. Sch., 1981; vis. lectr. Manchester Coll., St. John's U.; Woodrow Wilson vis. fellow Drew U., 1981; pres. Internat. Fellowship of Reconciliation, 1959-63, v.p., 1963-65; participant 1st-3d assemblies World Council Chs., Amsterdam, 1948, Evanston, 1954, New Delhi, 1961; rep. UN non-govt. orgn. UNIAPAC, 1979-85; pastoral assoc. First Congl. Ch. (United Ch. Christ), Montclair, N.J., 1983-89; delegated observer Vatican Council II, 1963; v.p. Am. Friends Coll. Cevenol., 1981-89; bd. dirs. Interfaith Center for Corp. Responsibility, 1973-81; chmn. exec. com. Freedom of Faith - A Christian Com. for Religious Rights, 1978-81; mem. nat. adv. bd. N.Y. State Martin Luther King Jr. Inst. for Nonviolence, 1989—. Translator: The Prayer of the Church Universal (Marc Boegner), 1954; editor: The Oppression of Protestants in Spain, 1955, The Role of Transnational Business in Mass Economic Development, 1975; editor-at-large Christian Century, 1959-70; contbr.: Business, Religion and Ethics-Inquiry and Encounter, 1982; articles to religious and interdisciplinary publs.; corr. in U.S. for Évangile et Liberté, 1988—. Past co-chmn. Chgo. Com. for Sane Nuclear Policy; bd. dirs. World Conf. on Religion and Peace, 1974-84, sec. for Kampuchea issues, 1979-81; former trustee Am. Waldensian Aid Soc.; mem. internat. council Internat. Ctr. Integrative Studies, 1984-91, bd. dirs., 1987—; trustee Internat. Inst. for Effective Communication, 1987—. Mem. ACLU, Wider Quaker Fellowship, Fellowship Reconciliation, Ctr. for Theology and the Natural Scis., Outlook Club (Berkeley), Harvard Club San Francisco, Phi Beta Kappa. *The human capacity to hope and the power of hope to achieve either good or evil are astonishing. Reasonable hope for the better calls simply for dedicated effort. Mystical hope for the perfect demands consecrated surrender.*

SCHOMMER, TRUDY MARIE, pastoral minister, religion education; b. Wayzata, Minn., May 18, 1937; d. Edward and Gertrude (Mergen) S. BA, Coll. St. Catherine, St. Paul, 1966; MA, Manhattanville Coll., 1971. Joined Order of Franciscan Sisters of Little Falls, Minn., 1955. Dir. religious edn. St. Pius X, White Bear Lake, Minn., 1971-77; campus min., theology tchr. St. Cloud (Minn.) State Univ., 1977-81; pastoral min. St. Galls, St. Elizabeth, Milw., 1981-85; dir. religious edn. St. Alexander's, Morrisonville, N.Y., 1985-90; pastoral min. of religious edn. St. Mary's, Bryantown, Md., 1990-91; diocesan dir. religious edn. Diocese of New Ulm, Minn., 1991—; exec. bd. mem. Nat. Assembly Religious Women, Chgo., 1974-78. Book reviewer Sister's Today, 1988-91. Mem. Network, Washington, 1978—. Mem. Nat. Cath. Edn. Assn., Nat. Parish Coords. and Dirs., Community Catechetical Leaders of Washington. Democrat. Roman Catholic. Home: 116 8th Ave SE Little Falls MN 56345 Office: St Marys Parish Rt 232 Bryantown MD 20617 *Life is an adventure: a time each of us is given to explore and discover the many ways Christ's life and love permeates the whole world. Life is a challenge: together as Christians we face the many challenges and difficulties of life.*

SCHONFELD, FABIAN, rabbi; b. Poland, Dec. 14, 1923; came to U.S., 1950; naturalized, 1955; s. Samuel and Manja (Oskenhendler) S.; m. Charlotte Jakobovits, 1944 (dec. Aug. 1959); m. Ruth Liefer, Nov. 7, 1961. BA, U. London, 1945; grad., Yeshiva U., 1952. Ordained rabbi, 1952. Rabbi Young Israel of Kew Gardens Hills, Flushing, N.Y., 1951—; lectr. Judaic studies Yeshiva U., 1970—; mem. bds. edn. Jewish day schs. Contbr. articles to profl. jours. Recipient awards United Jewish Appeal, 1958, Fedn. Jewish Philanthropy, 1969. Mem. Rabbinical Coun. Am. (past pres.), Rabbinic Alumni Yeshiva U., Coun. Young Israel Rabbis, Queens Rabbinical Assn., Synagogue Coun. Am. (co-chmn. inter-religious affairs com.), Poale Agudath Israel (pres.), World Jewish Cong. (sec. Am. sect.). Home: 70-41 153d St Flushing NY 11367 Office: Young Israel Kew Gardens Hills 150-05 70th Rd Flushing NY 11367

SCHONHOFF, ROBERT LEE, marketing and advertising executive; b. Detroit, May 24, 1919; s. John Clement and Olympia Regina (Diebold) S.; m. Kathleen O'Hara, Dec. 24, 1971; children: Rita, Elise, Robert. Student, Wayne State U., 1940-41. Artist, J.L. Hudson, 1939-42; v.p. advt. and mktg. Dillard Dept. Stores, Little Rock and San Antonio, 1963-77; owner R.L. Schonhoff Advt. and Mktg., San Antonio, 1977-83; owner Ad Graphics, AMC Printers Inc.; co-owner New Orleans Saints football team; mem. faculty Bus. Sch., St. Mary's U., 1975-81; bd. dirs. Groos Bank, San Antonio. Permanent deacon Roman Catholic Ch., San Antonio Diocese. Served to 1st lt. USAF, 1942-46. Mem. Am. Mktg. Assn. (founding dir. San Antonio chpt.). Clubs: Tapatio Springs Country; Josef (San Antonio). Home: 501 Hillside Dr San Antonio TX 78212 Office: 1528 Contour St Ste 101 San Antonio TX 78212

SCHOOLEY, JENNIFER LYNN, broadcasting executive; b. Oakdale, Calif., Sept. 22, 1957; d. Irwin Ross and Elvira Janet (Brown) Hickman; m. William C. Lyons, June 21, 1981 (div. Oct. 1988); m. Bruce O. Schooley, Apr. 21, 1991. BS in Communications, Pacific Union Coll., 1981. On-air commentator Sta. KCDS, Angwin, Calif., 1983—, talk show host, 1986-88, script writer for Step Aside (formerly Mellow Majesty), 1988—, host Step Aside, 1989—. Seventh-day Adventist. Home: PO Box 324 Angwin CA 94508 Office: Sta KCDS Broadcast Ctr Angwin CA 94508

SCHOOLEY, WARREN CALVIN, evangelist; b. Foster, Mo., Aug. 24, 1923; s. William Ruben and Bessie Mae (Yeokum) S.; m. Ruth Elaine Creel, May 22, 1950; children: Rodney, Rebecca, Charlotte, Milton. Student, York (Nebr.) Coll., 1963-64, Abilene Christian U., 1966-68, Ala. Christian U., 1988-89, Dept. Christian Ministries, 1990-91. Evangelist Ch. of Christ, Seward, Nebr., 1964-66, Hot Springs, S.D., 1966-78, various cities, 1981-86, various cities, Ala., 1986—. With U.S. Army, 1942-45. Home: 2289 Morris Major Rd Morris AL 35116

SCHOON, NELSON ROY, lay church worker, financial company executive; b. Gary, Ind., July 21, 1954; s. Warren Lambert and Lillian (Teninga) S.; m. Sandra Kay Saggau, Mar. 10, 1979; children: Kelly Louise, Megan Lillian, Tricia Kay, Rebecca Rose. BA, Wabash Coll., 1976. Youth leader Range Line Presbyn. Ch., Hebron, Ind., 1972-76, Sunday sch. tchr., 1991—; various fin. positions Campus Crusade for Christ, San Bernardino, Calif., 1976-80; ruling elder Presbyn. Ch. in Am., Grand Terrace and, San Bernardino, Calif., 1979-89; ministry coord. Good Shepherd Presbyn. Ch., Valparaiso, Ind., 1990-91, inactive ruling elder, tchr. Sunday sch., 1990-91; v.p. trusts Delco Fin. Svcs., Lowell, Ind., 1991—. V.p. bd. dirs. Lake County Assn. for the Retarded, Gary, Ind., 1991-92. Republican. *What the church needs more than ever is risk-takers. People willing to take on responsibilities they may not be comfortable with, but do so for the benefit of the church.*

SCHOONE, RAYMOND LAWRENCE, priest; b. Harrison, Wis., Nov. 10, 1931; s. Lawrence and Cecelia Marie (Zuiker) S. BA, St. Francis Sem., Milw., 1954; JCL, Cath. U. Am., 1962. Ordained priest Roman Cath. Ch., 1958. Asst. pastor Cathedral of Christ the King, Superior, Wis., 1958-60; pastor St. Adalbert Ch., 1975-81, St. Louis Ch., 1982, St. Anthony Ch., Superior, 1976—; vice chancellor, sec. to bishop Diocese of Superior, 1962-66, chancellor, 1966-81, vicar for religious affairs, 1972—, vicar for canonical affairs, 1981—; presiding judge Matrimonial Tribunal, Superior, 1962—. Mem. Canon Law Soc. Am., Cath. Charities Bur. (membership bd. 1980). Home: 4315 E 3d St Superior WI 54880

SCHOONOVER, MELVIN EUGENE, seminary administrator; b. Francesville, Ind., Aug. 22, 1926; s. Charles and Alma Louise (Garrigues) S.; m. Diana Russell Sturgis, May 24, 1957; 1 child, Diana Russell. AB, Wabash Coll., 1951; MDiv, Union Theol. Sem., 1956, STM, 1969; D. Ministry, N.Y. Theol. Sem., 1971; LHD (hon.), Wabash Coll., 1972; DDiv. (hon.), N.Y. Theol. Sem., 1978. Ordained to ministry Am. Bapt. Ch. U.S.A., 1956. Pastor Chambers Meml. Bapt. Ch., N.Y.C., 1958-68, Cen. Bapt. Ch., Wayne, Pa., 1978-83; dean degree programs N.Y. Theol. Sem., N.Y.C., 1969-78, dir. Fla. extention, 1983-85; pres. S. Fla. Ctr. for Theol. Studies, Miami, 1985—; trustee N.Y. Theol. Sem., 1978-83. Author: Making All Things Human, 1969, Letters to Polly, 1971, What If We Did Follow Jesus, 1978. Office: So Fla Ctr for Theol Study 609 Brickell Ave Miami FL 33131

SCHORSCH, ISMAR, clergyman, Jewish history educator; b. Hannover, Germany, Nov. 3, 1935; m. Sally Korn; children—Jonathan, Rebecca, Naomi. BA, Ursinus Coll., 1957; MA, Columbia U., 1961, PhD, 1969; MHL, Jewish Theol. Sem. Am., 1962; LittD (hon.), Wittenberg U., 1989, Ursinus Coll., 1990. Ordained rabbi, 1962. Instr. Jewish history Jewish Theol. Sem. Am., N.Y.C., 1964-68, asst. prof., 1970-72, assoc. prof., 1972-76, prof., 1976—, dean Grad. Sch., 1975-79, provost, 1980-84; asst. prof. Jewish history Columbia U., N.Y.C., 1968-70; bd. dirs. Leo Baeck Inst., 1976, mem. exec. com., 1980, pres., 1985-86, 90—, mem. editorial bd. of yearbook, 1987. Contbr. articles to Judaism, also other profl. publs. Chancellor Jewish Theol. Sem., 1986—. Served as chaplain U.S. Army, 1962-64. Recipient Clark F. Ansley award Columbia U. Press, 1969; NEH fellow, 1979-80. Fellow Am. Acad. for Jewish Research. Office: Jewish Theol Sem 3080 Broadway New York NY 10027

SCHOTTER, RICHARD DANIEL, choir director, retired industrial engineer; b. Amsterdam, N.Y., Sept. 12, 1917; s. Alfred F. and Linna (Kilsch) S.; m. Ruth Elsie Schmidt, Oct. 14, 1940; children: Carl B., Richard D. Jr. BA in Indsl. Design, Stuttgart, Germany, 1935; BSME, MSME, Technishe Hochschule, Cologne, Germany, 1934-34; postgrad., U. Wis., 1975. Cert. mfg. engr., mfg. systems mgr. Bandmaster The Salvation Army, Newark, 1940-48; choir dir. The Salvation Army, Pitts., 1948-59; min. music Riverdale (N.D.) Bible Ch., 1960-87; choir dir. Free Meth. Ch, Canajoharie, N.Y., 1991—. Patentee in field. Mem. Rep. Presdl. Task Force, Washington, Canajoharie, 1980-91. Mem. Soc. Mfg. Engrs., Inst. Radio Engrs., Acad. Scis. Home and Office: 243 Moyer St Canajoharie NY 13317

SCHOWENGERDT, LOUIS W., bishop. Ordained to ministry United Meth. Ch., later consecrated bishop. Bishop N. Mex. Conf., United Meth. Ch., Albuquerque, also N.W. Tex. Conf., Lubbock. Office: United Meth Ch 8100 Mountain Rd NE # 114 Albuquerque NM 87110 also: 1415 Ave M Lubbock TX 79401

SCHRADER, DAVID ALAN, minister; b. South Bend, Ind., Dec. 14, 1954; s. Raymond Harvey and Arlene Elizabeth (Griminus) S.; m. Pamela Kay Knox, July 23, 1977; children: John David, Jacqueline Renee. AB, Ind. U., South Bend, 1976; M in Div., Garrett-Evang. Theol. Sem. at Northwestern U., 1982. Ordained to ministry United Meth. Ch. as deacon, 1980, as minister, 1984. Assoc. pastor Norwood Park United Meth. Ch., Chgo., 1980-82; pastor Door Village United Meth. Ch., LaPorte, Ind., 1982-86; assoc. pastor, Coll. Ave. United Meth. Ch. at Ball State U., Muncie, Ind., 1986-88; sr. pastor Lakeville (Ind.) United Meth. Ch., 1988-91, 1st United Meth. Ch., Elkhart, Ind., 1991—; rep. to No. Ind. Conf. of Bd. Global Ministries United Meth. Ch., Marion, Ind., 1983-86; cons. pastoral care program LaPorte Hosp., 1984-86, Muncie Substance Abuse Task Force, 1987—; chmn. Div. Stewardship, United Meth. Ch. of N. Ind. Author: A Problem Called Heaven, 1989. Mem. Rotary Club (Elkhart). Avocations: angler, naturalist, classical music, history, literature. Office: 1st United Meth Ch 400 W Mishawaka Rd Elkhart IN 46517

SCHRAG, CALVIN ORVILLE, philosophy educator; b. Marion, S.D., May 4, 1950; s. John J.A. and Katie (Miller) S.; m. Virginia Marie Fields, Aug. 9, 1964; 1 child, Heather. BA, Bethel Coll., North Newton, Kans., 1950; BD, Yale U., 1953; postgrad., Heidelberg U., Fed. Republic Germany, 1954-55, Oxford U., England, 1955; PhD, Harvard U., 1957. Teaching asst. Harvard U., Cambridge, Mass., 1956-57; asst. prof. philosophy Purdue U., West Lafayette, Ind., 1957-60, assoc. prof., 1961-63, prof., 1964—, George Ade disting. prof., 1982—; vis. lectr. U. Ill., Champaign, 1960-61; vis. assoc. prof. Northwestern U., Evanston, Ill., 1963-64; vis. prof. Ind. U., Bloomington, spring 1968; mem. editorial bd. Northwestern U. Press, 1970—, Ind. U. Press, 1979; mem. adv. bd. Franklin J. Matchette Found., San Antonio, 1969—. Author: Existence and Freedom, 1961, Experience and Being, 1969, Radical Reflection, 1980, Communicative Praxis, 1986; co-editor Man and World: Internat. Philos. Rev., 1968—. Recipient teaching award Standard Oil Found., 1969; Fulbright fellow, 1954-55, Guggenheim fellow, Freiburg, Fed. Republic Germany, 1955-56; grantee NEH, 1979, 90, 86. Mem. Am. Philos. Soc. (exec. com. 1984-87), Metaphys. Soc. Am. (chmn. nominating com. 1977-78), Soc. for Phenomenology and Existential Philosophy (exec. dir. 1977-80), Ind. Philos. Assn. (pres. 1967-68). Home: 1315 N Grant St West Lafayette IN 47906 Office: Purdue U Dept Philosophy West Lafayette IN 47907

SCHRAG, DELBERT J., minister; b. Parker, S.D., Oct. 13, 1921; s. John J. and Kathryn (Miller) S.; m. Stella Verline Waltner, Aug. 11, 1946; children: Kathryn, Janet, Margaret, Barbara, John. AA, Freeman (S.D.) Jr. Coll., 1941; BA, Bethel Coll., 1948; BD, Bethany Sem., 1952; MA, U. Chgo., 1952. Ordained to ministry United Ch. of Christ, 1952. Pastor Ivanhoe Congregational Ch., Mundelein, Ill., 1949-71; area conf. min. Ill. Conf. United Ch. of Christ, Chgo., 1971-89; min. Trinity Community Ch., Berwyn, Ill., 1990—. Home: 1842 Cherry St Wheaton IL 60187

SCHRECK, ALAN EDWARD, theology educator; b. Rochester, N.Y., Dec. 7, 1951; s. Karl Joseph and Irene Marguerite (Varga) S.; m. Nancy Elizabeth Pflug, May 15, 1982; children: Paul Alan, Jeanne Elizabeth, Mark Joseph, Margaret Mary. BA in English and Theology, U. Notre Dame, 1973; MA in Theology, U. St. Michael's Coll., 1975, PhD in Theology, 1979. Asst. prof. theology Franciscan U. Steubenville, Ohio, 1978-82, assoc. prof., 1982-88, prof., 1988—. Author: Catholic and Christian: An Explanation of Commonly Misunderstood Catholic Beliefs, 1984, The Compact History of the Catholic Church, 1987, Basics of the Faith: A Catholic Catechism, 1987, The Catholic Challenge: A Fresh Look at the Message of Vatican II, 1991; (with Wendy Leifeld) Your Catholic Faith, 1989. Office: Franciscan U Steubenville Franciscan Way Steubenville OH 43952

SCHREIBER, JOHANNES, theology educator; b. Gahlen, Rheinland, Fed. Republic Germany, Dec. 11, 1927; s. Johannes Georg Robert and Martha Johanna (Genaehr) S.; m. Jutta Elisabeth Schultheiss, Aug. 30, 1962; 1 child, Dagmar Margret. Student, U. Tuebingen, Fed. Republic Germany, 1953; Studienrat, Akademie Tutzing, Munich, 1958; ThD, U. Bonn, Bonn, Fed. Republic Germany, 1960; Pfarrer (hon.), Landeskirchenrat Bayern, Munich, 1959. Cert. theologian. Kandidat Bethel Konvikt, Düsseldorf, Fed. Republic Germany, 1953; stipendiate World Coun. Chs., Uppsala, Sweden, 1954; sci. asst. Theologisches Woerterbuch, Erlangen, Fed. Republic Germany, 1955; tchr. Evangelische Akademie Tutzing, Tutzing, Fed. Republic Germany, 1956-57, Gymnasium Christian-Ernestinum, Bayreuth, Fed. Republic Germany, 1957-63; sci. asst. U. Mainz, Mainz, Fed. Republic Germany, 1963-66; univ. prof. U. Bochum, Bochum, Fed. Republic Germany, 1966—; bd. dirs. Evangelisch-Theologisches Seminar, Bochum. Author: Unterrichtlicher Vollzug, 1966, Theologie des Vertrauens, 1967, Markuspassion, 1969, Kreuzigungsbericht, 1986. Mem. Synode of Lutheran Ch. Westphalia, Fed. Republic Germany, 1966-84. With German Army, 1943-45. Home: Hahnenfussweg 40, 4630 Bochum Federal Republic of Germany Office: Ruhruniversitaet Bochum, GA 7 159, 4630 Bochum Federal Republic of Germany

SCHREITER, ROBERT JOHN, priest, theology educator; b. Nebraska City, Nebr., Dec. 14, 1947; s. Robert Frank and Mildred Mary (Kreifels) S. BA, St. Joseph's Coll., 1968, 69; ThD, U. Nijmegen, The Netherlands, 1974. Ordained priest Roman Cath. Ch., 1975. Prof. theology Cath. Theol. Union, Chgo., 1974—, dean, 1977-86. Author: Constructing Local Theologies, 1985, In Water and in Blood, 1988; editor: The Schillebeeck Reader, 1984; editor jour. New Theology Rev., 1988. Trustee Maryknoll (N.Y.) Sch. Theology, 1986—, St. Francis Sem., Milw., 1988—. Mem. Am. Soc. Missiology (pres. 1990—), Assn. Profs. of Mission (pres. 1980-81), Am. Acad. Religion, Cath. Theol. Soc. Am. Office: Cath Theol Union 5401 S Cornell Chicago IL 60615

SCHRIEBER, PAUL LOUIS, theology educator; b. Red Bud, Ill., Apr. 29, 1949; s. Oliver Lee and Florence Anne (Mueller) S.; m. Betty Jean Koehler, Nov. 21, 1973; children: Katherine, Jonathan, Sarah, Deborah, Rachel, Rebekah, Matthew, Mark. AA, St. Paul's Coll., Concordia, Mo., 1969; BA, Concordia Sr. Coll., Ft. Wayne, 1971; MDiv, Concordia Theol. Sem., Springfield, Ill., 1975; ThD, Concordia Sem., St. Louis, 1983. Pastoral asst. Epiphany Luth. Ch., St. Louis, 1975-76; vis. instr. Concordia Sem., St. Louis, 1976, asst. prof., 1981-88, assoc. prof. exegetical theology, 1988—; instr., asst. prof. Concordia Coll., River Forest, Ill., 1976-81; mem. standing com. broadcast Sta. KFUO. Mem. Soc. Bibl. Lit., Am. Sch. Oriental Rsch., Evang. Theol. Soc. Office: Concordia Sem 801 DeMun Clayton MO 63105

SCHROCK, PAUL MELVIN, editor; b. Tangent, Oreg., Aug. 4, 1935; s. Melvin and Anna Magdalena (Roth) S.; m. June Darlene Bontrager, Sept. 7, 1957; children: Carmen Joy Schrock-Hurst, Brent Lamar, Andrea Denise Schrock Wenger. BA, Ea. Mennonite Coll., 1958; MA in Journalism, Syracuse U., 1963. With Mennonite Pub. House, Scottdale, Pa., 1959—, asst. editor Gospel Herald, 1959-61, asst. to Herald Press book editor, 1959-61; editor Words of Cheer, Scottdale, Pa., 1961-70; editor Herald Graded Sunday Sch. series Mennonite Pub. House, Scottdale, 1967-68; founding editor Purpose mag. Mennonite Pub. House, Scottdale, Pa., 1968-71, editor The Way, 1970-75, book editor Herald Press, 1972-88, dir., 1988—; instr. linguistics and rhetoric, creative writing and photojournalism Ea. Mennonite Coll., 1970-72; with Mennonite Bd. of Missions Media Ministries, Harrisonburg, Va., 1970-72, producer Mennonite Hour and Way to Life programs, 1971-72; editor Alive Mag., 1970-75; free-lance photographer. Home: 14 Park Ave Scottdale PA 15683 Office: Mennonite Pub House 616 Walnut Ave Scottdale PA 15683

SCHRODER, NATHANIEL LEE, minister; b. Austin, Minn., Oct. 23, 1956; s. John Lyle and Patricia Rose (Skogerbo) S.; m. Gail Ruth Livdahl, Dec. 18, 1976; children: Jessie Lee, Levi Travis, Amanda Marie, Jordan Thomas. AAS, U. Minn., Crookston, 1978; BS, Multnomah Sch. of the Bible, 1985. Ordained to ministry Conservative Bapt. Assn., 1987. Youth worker Calvary Bapt. Ch., Crookston, 1977-81; youth pastor Burlingame Bapt. Ch., Portland, Oreg., 1982-85; min. youth and Christian edn. Calvary Bapt. Ch., Muscatine, Iowa, 1985—; del. Nat. Task Force on Youth Ministry, Chgo., 1988-89; pres. youth ministry Conservative Bapt. Assn. Iowa, Des Moines, 1988—; asst. athletic trainer. Muscatine High Sch., 1987-90. religious rep. Drug Free Sch. and Community Com., Muscatine, 1987, Substance Abuse Task Force, Muscatine, 1989-91. Mem. Youth Evang. Assn. (pres. Muscatine chpt. 1989—). Home: 811 Woodlawn Muscatine IA 52761 Office: Calvary Bapt Ch 2900 Mulberry Ave Muscatine IA 52761

SCHRODT, PAUL RAYMOND, religion educator, librarian; b. Des Moines, Jan. 7, 1938; s. Raymond Carl and Irene (Graham) S.; 1 child from previous marriage, Liesel. PhD, U. Munich, 1975; MLS, Syracuse U., 1988; postgrad., Columbia U., 1988-91. Dir. grad. religious studies Spalding Coll., Louisville, 1971-73; asst. prof. hist. theology St. Thomas Sem., Denver, 1973-78; ref. info. staff libr. Syracuse (N.Y.) U., 1987-88; cataloger rare books Colgate Rochester Divinity Sch., 1988-89; asst. libr., assoc. prof. United Theol Sem., Dayton, Ohio, 1989—. Author: The Problem of Dogma in Recent Theology, 1978; contbr. articles to religious publs. NEH fellow U. Colo., 1978, rsch. fellow U. Colo., U. Ariz., 1982, grad. studies fellow Gaylord Bros. Syracuse U., 1987; travel to collections grantee NEH, 1989. Mem. ALA, Am. Theol. Libr. Assn. (chairperson publs. com. Chgo. chpt. 1990—), N.Am. Patristics Soc., Ohio Theol. Librarians Assn. Roman Catholic. Office: United Theol Sem 1810 Harvard Blvd Dayton OH 45406

SCHROEDER, CLINTON PAUL, religious organization executive; b. Altamount, Ill., Feb. 5, 1929; s. Ernst William and Alma Juliann (Schwardtfeger) S.; m. Joan Eileen Groves, Aug. 14, 1954; children: John, Kurt, Kirsten, Kris. Student, U. Md., London and Heidelberg (Germany), U. Ill. Ednl. coord. USAF, 1950-54; adminstrv. asst. Overseas program U. Md., London and Heidelberg, 1954-57; pub. The Altamont News, 1958-61, The Cassville (Wis.) Am., 1961-64; fundraising counselor Luth. Laity Movement, 1965-67, 76-82; v.p. devel. Grand View Coll., Des Moines, 1967-76; adminstr. Shepherd of the Valley Luth. Ch., Phoenix, 1982-84; from mem. exec. staff to exec. dir. Luth. Laity Movement for Stewardship, N.Y.C., Chgo., 1984-90, Evang. Luth. Ch. in Am., Chgo., 1990—. Office: Luth Laity Movement 8765 W Higgins Rd Chicago IL 60631-4181

SCHROEDER, PHILIP, minister; b. Lansing, Mich., Jan. 24, 1937; s. Philip and Esther Anna (Ude) S.; m. Sharon Ruth Scherer, June 11, 1960; children: Sarah J., Rachel E., Maria J. BD, MDiv, Concordia Sem., 1960; STM, Union Theol. Sem., 1965. Ordained to ministry Luth. Ch., 1961. Campus pastor Ohio State U., Columbus, 1965-74; asst. to exec. dir. Luth. Council in USA, Chgo., 1978-83; dir. Ctr. for Study of Campus Ministry, Valparaiso, Ind., 1974-83; campus pastor Augustana Coll., Rock Island, Ill., 1983-88; pastor Trinity Luth. Ch., Mt. Morris, Ill., 1988—; pres. Columbus Luth. Pastors Conf., 1972-73. Author: Ministry With The Community College: A Lutheran Perspective, 1982; editor CSCM Yearbooks, 1975-80. Mem. Luth. Campus Ministry Assn., Luth. Acad. Scholarship (v.p. 1977-83). Avocation: tennis. Home: 401 E Lincoln Mount Morris IL 61054 Office: Trinity Luth Ch 308 E Brayton Rd Mount Morris IL 61054 *Life is a gift to be cherished, not a problem to be solved.*

SCHROEDER, ROY PHILIP, minister; b. Caro, Mich., Sept. 8, 1929; s. Philip and Esther (Ude) S.; m. Phyllis Joy Helge, June 4, 1955; children: Paul, Stephanie, Deborah, Suzanne, John. BA, Concordia Sem., St. Louis, 1950, BDiv, 1954, M Sacred Theology, 1955, ThD, 1968. Ordained to ministry, Luth. Ch., 1955. Vicar Japan Luth. Ch., Sapporo, Hokkaido, 1951-53; pastor St. Peter's Luth. Ch., Vincennes, Ind., 1955-57, St. John Luth. Ch., Monroeville, Ind., 1957-59, Peace Luth. Ch., Sparta, Mich., 1959-71, Ascension Luth. Ch., East Lansing, Mich., 1971—; chmn. Grand Rapids Area Pastors' Conf., 1969-72, West Mich. Pastors' Conf., 1971-73. Contbr. articles to profl. publs. Bd. mgrs. YMCA, East Lansing, 1979-87; mem. Ann Arbor (Mich.) Dist. Bd. Dirs., 1970-74. Avocations: photography, travel. Home: 5190 Park Lake Rd East Lansing MI 48823 Office: Ascension Luth Ch 2780 Haslett Rd East Lansing MI 48823

SCHROEDER, W(ILLIAM) WIDICK, educator; b. Newton, Kans., Nov. 12, 1928; s. William Fredric and Irene (Widick) S.; m. Gayle Eadie, Sept. 1, 1956; children: Scott David, Carla Gayle. BA, Bethel Coll., 1949; MA, Mich. State U., East Lansing, 1952; BDiv, Chgo. Theol. Sem., 1955; PhD, U. Chgo., 1960. Ordained to ministry United Ch. of Christ, 1955. Instr. Mich. State U., East Lansing, 1953-54, U. Chgo., 1958-60; from asst. prof. to prof. Chgo. Theol. Sem., 1960—. Author: (with Victor Obenhaus) Religion in American Culture: Unity and Diversity in a Midwestern County, 1964; Cognitive Structures and Religious Research, 1970; (with Victor Obenhaus, Larry A. Jones and Thomas P. Sweetser), Suburban Religion: Churches and Synagogues in the American Experience, 1974; (with Keith A. Davis) Where Do I Stand? Living Theological Options for Contemporary Christians, 1973, rev. edit. 1975, 3d edit., 1978; Flawed Process and Sectarian Substance: Analytic and Critical Perspectives on the United Church of Christ General Synod Pronouncement, Christian Faith: Economic Life and Justice, 1990; co-edited: (with Philip Hefner) Belonging and Alienation: Religious Foundations for the Human Future , 1976; (with Gibson Winter) Belief and Ethics: Essays in Ethics, the Human Sciences and Ministry in Honor of W. Alvin Pitcher, 1978; (with John B. Cobb, Jr.) Process Philosphy and Social Thought, 1981; (with Perry LeFevre) Spiritual Nurture, Congregational Development, 1984, Pastoral Care and Liberation Praxis: Essays in Personal and Social Transformation, 1986, Creative Ministries in Contemporary Christianity, 1991; (with Franklin I. Gamwell) Economic Life: Process Interpretations and Critical Responses, 1988. Mem. Am. Acad. Religion, Am. Sociol. Assn., Soc. for the Sci. Study of Religion, Inst. for the Religion in an Age of Sci., Religious Research Assn., Ctr. for Process Studies, Soc. Christian Ethics. Home: 2738 Virginia Pl Homewood IL 60430 Office: Chgo Theol Sem 5757 University Chicago IL 60637 *The aims of existence are aesthetic satisfaction and intensity of feeling. In facilitating these aims, the Divine Reality is the locus of potentiality, the mediator of experience, the evoker of feeling and the ultimate recipient of all that has become.*

SCHROEPPEL, JOHN EARL, minister; b. New Ulm, Minn., Apr. 17, 1938; s. John Earl and Alice Emilia (Swenson) S.; m. Anne Elizabeth Jackson, Sept. 7, 1980; children: Stephen Casper, John Paul, Peter Karl, Sarah Elizabeth. BA in Zoology, U. Minn., 1960; BS in Edn., Mankato State U., 1963; grad. in theology, Luther Northwestern Sem., St. Paul, 1968; MDiv, Luther Northwestern Sem., 1976, D Ministry, 1986; grad., Theol. Found. Ordained to ministry Luth. Ch., 1968. Pastor Bethany and Grace Luth. Chs., Inglis and Russell, Man., Can., 1968-74, St. Mark Luth. Ch., Cape Girardeau, Mo., 1977-78, Zion and Bethesda Luth. Chs., Kinistino and Beatty, Sask., Can., 1979-83, Faith Luth. Ch., Griswold, Iowa, 1983-88, Bethlehem Luth. Ch., Manly, Iowa, 1988—. Home: 406 W North St Rte 1 Box 196 Manly IA 50456 Office: Bethlehem Luth Ch 428 W Walnut Box M Manly IA 50456 *What a different world this would be if people would take the teachings of Jesus seriously.*

SCHROLUCKE, MARVIN ELMER, minister; b. New Knoxville, Ohio, Dec. 16, 1930; s. Elmer George and Louisa Clara (Maneke) S.; m. Joanne Smilek, Mar. 13, 1982; children: Mark S., Matthew S., Martin P. BS in

Commerce, Internat. Bus. Coll., Ind., 1949; BA, Lakeland Coll., 1954; BD, United Theol. Sem. of Twin Cities, 1957, MDiv, 1971. Ordained minister United Ch. of Christ. Pastor St. Paul United Ch. of Christ, Oskaloosa, Iowa, 1957-63, First Congl. Ch., Eddyville, Iowa, 1958-62, Faith United Ch. of Christ, Iowa City, Iowa, 1963-66; assoc. pastor St. Paul United Ch. of Christ, Elgin, Ill., 1966-72; pastor Friedens United Ch. of Christ, Farina, Ill., 1972-78, St. Paul United Ch. of Christ, Bible Grove, Ill., 1972-78, Trinity United Ch. of Christ, Canal Fulton, Ohio, 1978-89, Salem United Ch. of Christ, Wanatah, Ind., 1989—.

SCHUCK, MICHAEL JOSEPH, religion educator; b. Fargo, N.D., Dec. 28, 1953; s. Peter Joseph and Bertha Alice (Bjugson) S.; m. Aloyzija Stanislava Babič, July 18, 1981; children: Mateja, Aloysius. AB, St. Louis U., 1975; AM, U. Chgo., 1978, M in Religious Studies, 1980, PhD with distinction, 1988. Asst. prof. Loyola U., Chgo., 1986—. Author: That They Be One, 1990. Mellon grantee Loyola U., 1987. Mem. Am. Acad. Religion, Assn. for Religion & Intellectual Life, Cath. Theol. Soc. Am., Coll. Theol. Soc., Soc. Christian Ethics. Roman Catholic. Home: 3423 S Hermitage Chicago IL 60608 Office: Loyola U 820 N Michigan Ave Chicago IL 60611

SCHUELLER, ANTHONY L., priest, editor; b. Belgium, Wis., Jan. 31, 1950; s. John Anton and Mary Behildis (Heilmann) S. BA in Religious Studies, John Carroll U., 1973; MDiv, Loyola U., Chgo., 1977. Ordained priest Roman Cath. Ch., 1977. Assoc. pastor St. Charles Borromeo Ch., Albuquerque, 1977-79; vocation dir. Congregation of the Blessed Sacrament, Cleve., 1979-85, cons., 1990—; dir. St. Paul's Cath. Ctr., Salt Lake City, 1985-91; editor Emmanuel Mag., Cleve., 1991—; senator Diocesan Presbyteral Senate, Salt Lake City, 1987-91; dir. Diocesan Eucharistic Yr., Salt Lake City, 1988-89. Mem. clergy bd. Ulster Project Utah, Salt Lake City, 1989-91. Mem. Cath. Press Assn. Home: 5384 Wilson Mills Rd Cleveland OH 44143 Office: Emmanuel Mag 5384 Wilson Mills Rd Cleveland OH 44143

SCHUESSLER FIORENZA, ELISABETH, theology educator; b. Tschanad, Romania, Apr. 17, 1938; came to U.S., 1970; d. Peter and Magdalena Schuessler; m. Francis Fiorenza, Dec. 17, 1967; 1 child, Christina. MDiv., U. Wuerzburg, Federal Republic of Germany, 1962; ThD, U. Muenster, Federal Republic of Germany, 1970; Lic.Theol, U. Wuerzburg, 1963. Asst. prof. theology U. Notre Dame, South Bend, Ind., 1970-75, assoc. prof., 1975-80, prof., 1980-84; instr. U. Muenster, 1966-67; Talbot prof. New Testament Episcopal Div. Sch., Cambridge, Mass., 1984-88; Krister Stendahl prof. div. in New Testament studies Harvard U., Cambridge, Mass., 1988—; Harry Emerson Fosdick vis. prof. Union Theol. Sem., N.Y.C., 1974-75; guest prof. U. Tuebingen, Federal Republic of Germany, 1987. Author: Der Vergessene Partner, 1964, Priester für Gott, 1972, The Apocalypse, 1976, Invitation to the Book of Revelation, 1981, In Memory of Her, 1983, Bread not Stone, 1984, Judgement of Justice, 1985, Revelation: Visions of a Just World, 1991; founding editor Jour. Feminist Studies in Religion; also editor other works. Mem. Am. Acad. Religion, Soc. Bibl. Lit. (past pres.). Office: Harvard Div Sch 45 Francis St Cambridge MA 02138

SCHULER, RICHARD JOSEPH, priest; b. Mpls., Dec. 30, 1920; s. Otto Henry and Wilhelmine Mary (Hauk) S. BA, Coll. St. Thomas, 1942; MA, U. Rochester, 1950; PhD, U. Minn., 1963. Ordained priest Roman Cath. Ch., 1945. Prof. music Nazareth Hall Seminary, St. Paul, 1945-54; assoc. prof. music Univ. St. Thomas, St. Paul, 1955-69; pastor Ch. St. Agnes, St. Paul, 1969—. Editor: Fourteen Liturgical Works of Giovanni Maria Nanino, 1969, Sacred Music, 1975—. Founder, condr. Twin Cities Cath. Chorale, 1955—. Named Hon. Papal Prelate (monsignor), 1970; recipient Gold Lassus medal Caecilia Soc., Fed. Republic Germany, 1973; Fulbright scholar, 1954-55. Mem. Ch. Music Assn. Am. (gen. sec. 1972-76, pres. 1976—), Consociatio Internat. Musicae Sacrae (v.p. 1967-77). Home and Office: 548 Lafond Ave Saint Paul MN 55103

SCHULLER, ROBERT ANTHONY, minister; b. Blue Island, Ill., Oct. 7, 1954; s. Robert Harold and Arvella (DeHaan) S.; m. Linda Jo Pursley, May 31, 1974 (div. Feb. 1983); children: Angie Rae, Robert Vern; m. Donna Michelle, Nov. 10, 1984; children: Christina Michelle, Anthony John. BA, Hope Coll., 1976; MDiv, Fuller Theol. Sem., Pasadena, Calif., 1980. Ordained to ministry Reformed Ch. in Am., 1980. Min. evening worship Crystal Cathedral, Garden Grove, Calif., 1976-80, min. evangelism, 1980-81; pastor Rancho Capistrano Community Ch, San Juan Capo, Calif., 1981—; bd. dirs., lectr. Hour of Power, Garden Grove, 1976—; pres. Crystal Cathedral Ministries, San Juan Capo, 1984—, Rancho Capistrano Renewal Ctr. Author: Getting Through the Going-Through Stage, 1986, Power to Grow beyond Yourself, 1987, The World's Greatest Comebacks, 1988, Strength for the Fragile Spirit, 1989, Just Become You're on a Roll...Doesn't Mean You're Going Downhill, 1990; editor: Robert H. Schuller's Life Changes, 1981, Be an Extraordinary Person in an Ordinary World, 1984. Bd. dirs. South County Community Clinic, San Juan Capo, 1985—. Republican. Office: Rancho Capistrano 29251 Camino Capistrano San Juan Capistrano CA 92675

SCHULLER, ROBERT HAROLD, clergyman, author; b. Alton, Iowa, Sept. 16, 1926; s. Anthony and Jennie (Beltman) S.; m. Arvella DeHaan, June 15, 1950; children: Sheila, Robert, Jeanne, Carol, Gretchen. B.A., Hope Coll., 1947, D.D., 1973; B.D., Western Theol. Sem., 1950; LL.D., Azusa Pacific Coll., 1970, Pepperdine U., 1976; Litt.D., Barrington Coll., 1977. Ordained to ministry Reformed Ch. in Am., 1950; pastor Ivanhoe Ref. Ch., Chgo., 1950-55; founder, sr. pastor Garden Grove (Calif.) Community Ch., 1955—; founder, pres. Hour of Power TV Ministry, Garden Grove, 1970—; founder, dir. Robert H. Schuller Inst. for Successful Ch. Leadership, Garden Grove, 1970—; chmn. nat. religious sponsor program Religion in Am. Life, N.Y.C., 1975—; bd. dirs. Freedom Found. Author: God's Way to the Good Life, 1963, Your Future Is Your Friend, 1964, Move Ahead with Possibility Thinking, 1967, Self Love, the Dynamic Force of Success, 1969, Power Ideas for a Happy Family, 1972, The Greatest Possibility Thinker That Ever Lived, 1973, Turn Your Scars into Stars, 1973, You Can Become the Person You Want To Be, 1973, Your Church Has Real Possibilities, 1974, Love or Loneliness— You Decide, 1974, Positive Prayers for Power-Filled Living, 1976, Keep on Believing, 1976, Reach Out for New Life, 1977, Peace of Mind Through Possibility Thinking, 1977, Turning Your Stress Into Strength, 1978, Daily Power Thoughts, 1978, The Peak to Peek Principle, 1981, Living Positively One Day at a Time, 1981, Self Esteem: The New Reformation, 1982, Tough Times Never Last, But, Tough People Do!, 1983, Tough Minded Faith for Tender hearted People, 1984, The Be-Happy Attitudes, 1985, Be Happy You Are Loved, 1986, Success is Never Ending, Failure is Never Final, 1988, Believe in the God Who Believes in You, 1989; co-author: The Courage of Carol, 1978. Bd. dirs. Religion in Am. Life; pres. bd. dirs. Christian Counseling Service; founder Robert H. Schuller Corr. Center for Possibility Thinkers, 1976. Recipient Disting. Alumnus award Hope Coll., 1970, Prin. award Freedoms Found., 1974; named Headliner of Year in Religion, Orange County, 1977, Clergyman of Year, Religious Heritage Am., 1977. Mem. Religious Guild Architects (hon.), AIA (bd. dirs. 1986—). Club: Rotary. Office: Religion in Am Life 12141 Lewis St Garden Grove CA 92640

SCHULTE, FRANCIS B., bishop; b. Phila., Dec. 23, 1926. Grad., St. Charles Borromeo Sem. Ordained priest Roman Catholic Ch., 1952. Apptd. titular bishop of Afufenia and aux. bishop of Phila., 1981-85; bishop Wheeling-Charleston, W.Va., 1985-89; archbishop New Orleans, 1989—. Office: 7887 Walmsley Ave New Orleans LA 70125

SCHULTENOVER, DAVID GEORGE, theology educator; b. Sauk Rapids, Minn., Aug. 19, 1938; s. Isadore Joseph and Frances Ludwina (Ohmann) S. BS in Chemistry, Spring Hill Coll., 1963; MS in Organic Chemistry, Loyola U., Chgo., 1966; PhD in Hist. Theology, St. Louis U., 1975. Joined Soc. of Jesus, Roman Cath. Ch., 1956. Mng. editor Theology Digest, St. Louis U., 1968-70; asst. prof. theology Marquette U., Milw., 1974-78; asst. dir. novices Jesuit Coll., St. Paul, 1978-83; assoc. prof. theology Creighton U., Omaha, 1985—; adj. asst. prof. theology Creighton U., Omaha, 1979-84. Author: George Tyrrell: In Search of Catholicism, 1981 (Alpha Sigma Nu Book award 1981); contbr. articles to profl. jours. Deutscher Akademischer Austauschdienst fellow DAAD-Fulbright, Tübingen, Fed. Republic Germany, 1973-74, NEH fellow, Rome, other western European locations, 1984-85. Mem. Am. Acad. Religion, Am. Soc. Ch. History, Cath. Theol. Soc. Am., Alpha Sigma Nu. Office: Creighton U Theology Dept Omaha NE 68178-0522

SCHULTHEIS, MICHAEL JAMES, priest, consultant, economist; b. Colton, Wash., May 9, 1932; s. Andrew Michael Schultheis and Winifred E. Moser. MA in Philosophy, Gonzaga U., 1959, MA in Econs., 1963; MA in Theology, Regis Coll., Toronto, 1966; PhD, Cornell U., 1976. Joined S.J., 1952, ordained priest Roman Catholic Ch., 1965. Rsch. assoc. Inst. Social Rsch. Makerere U., Kampala, Uganda, 1970-73; staff assoc. interreligious task force on U.S. Food and Fgn. Assistance Program, Washington, 1975-76; assoc. rsch. prof. U. Dar Es Salaam, Tanzania, 1976-81; staff assoc. Ctr. of Concern, Washington, 1980-84; assoc. dir. Jesuit Refugee Svc., Rome, 1984-88; dir. Jesuit Refugee Svc./Africa, Nairobi, Kenya, 1988—. Author: Catholic Social Theology, 1984, rev. edit., 1987, 88, 90; editor: Papers on African Political Economy, 1979; contbr. articles to profl. jours. Mem. Am. Econ. Assn., African Studies Assn., Assn. Concerned African Scholars (bd. dirs. 1984-86), U.S. Cath. Mission Assn. (bd. dirs. 1984-85). Democrat. Avocations: bird watching, kite flying, gardening. Home and Office: Jesuit Refugee Svc, PO Box 14877, Nairobi Kenya

SCHULTZ, ARTHUR LELAND, minister, author; b. Deep River, Iowa, Oct. 9, 1921; s. Arthur Henry and Frances Pauline (Kitzmann) S.; m. Norma Arlene Neunaber, June 4, 1946; children: Alan, Nathan, Deborah, Daniel, Paul. BTh, Concordia Sem., Springfield, Ill., 1946. Ordained to ministry, Luth. Ch.—Mo. Synod, 1946. Pastor various chs. Austin and Dunnell, Minn., 1946-53; pastor St. Matthew Ch., San Antonio, 1953-57; pastor various chs. Burt and Red Oak, Iowa, 1957-68; pastor Holy Ghost Ch., Monroe, Mich., 1968-75, Trinity Ch., Hinton, Iowa, 1975-80; chaplain various health care instns. Des Moines, 1980-86; dir. adult edn. Iowa Dist. West, Luth. Ch.—Mo. Synod, 1959-67, cir. counselor, 1976-85; past bd. dirs. Mich. Luth. Homes, Monroe, Cen. Iowa Luth. Homes, Des Moines. Author: A Life Full, 1990. Mem. com. Gov.'s Task Force on Aging, Des Moines, 1985. Recipient Servus Ecclesiae Christi award Concordia Sem., 1987. Home: 12 Eaton Circle Bella Vista AR 72714

SCHULTZ, ARTHUR LEROY, clergyman, educator; b. Johnstown, Pa., June 14, 1928; s. Elmer Albert Robert and Alice Lizetta (Flegal) S.; m. Mildred Louise Stouffer, Nov. 29, 1948; children: Thomas Arthur, Rebecca Louise. BA, Otterbein Coll., 1949; MDiv, United Theol. Sem., 1952; MEd, U. Pitts., 1955, PhD, 1963. Sr. min. Albright United Meth. Ch., Pitts., 1952-56; dir. pub. rels. Otterbein Coll., Westerville, Ohio, 1956-65, adj. prof. religion and philosophy, 1990—; pres. Albright Coll., Reading, Pa., 1965-77, Ashland (Ohio) Coll., 1977-80; exec. dir. Cen. Ohio Radio Reading Svc., Columbus, Ohio, 1980-84; parish min. Ch. Master United Meth., Westerville, 1984-89; pres. Pa. Assn. Colls. & Univs., Harrisburg, 1974-75. Trustee Reading Hosp., 1967-77; trustee Wyo. Sem., Kingston, Pa., 1971-80; v.p. Found. for Ind. Colls. Pa., Harrisburg, 1972-73; pres. Pa. Coun. on Alcohol Problems, Harrisburg, 1968-76; pres. Westerville (Ohio) Hist. Soc., 1986-89, Westerville Area Ministerial Assn., 1991—. Named Outstanding Young Man of the Year Jr. C. of C., Westerville, Ohio, 1960. Mem. Rotary (charter pres. 1959, dist. 669 gov. 1965-66, dist. 669 sec.-treas. 1982--), Masons, Shriners, Torch Club. Republican. Methodist. Avocations: collecting post cards, golf, tennis, travel. Home: 6464 Middleshire Columbus OH 43229

SCHULTZ, CARL, religion educator, clergyman; b. New Castle, Pa., Sept. 15, 1930; s. Carl and Elizabeth (McChesney) S.; m. Annalee Price, July 19, 1955; children: Barbara Ann, Esther Marie, Carl Daniel. BRE, Malone, 1952; BA, Houghton, 1953; MA, Wheaton (Ill.) Coll., 1955; PhD, Brandeis U., 1973. Ordained to ministry Wesleyan Ch., 1956. Pastor Cleveland Dr. Wesleyan Ch., Cheektowaga, N.Y., 1954-58, 1st Wesleyan Ch., Bradford, Pa., 1958-65; prof. Houghton (N.Y.) Coll., 1965-67; pastor Community Ch., Medway, Mass., 1967-71; prof., chair div. religion and philosophy Houghton Coll., 1971—; pastor Hinsdale/Ischua United Meth. Ch., Hinsdale, N.Y., 1971—; Author: Commentary Job/Ecclesiastes The Evangelical Commentary, Job/Ecclesiates The Asbury Bible Commentary, Psalms 73-150 Wesley Study Bible; author: (with others) Old Testament Theological Handbook, 1978, Scripture in Context, 1980, An Exegetical Study of Scripture Passages That Relate to Marriage, 1984. Pres. Ministerial Assn., Bradford, Pa., 1963; chmn. Dept. Religious Edn. of Coun. of Chs., Bradford, 1962. NEH grantee Yale U., 1978, 81. Mem. Soc. Bibl. Lit., Am. Acad. Religion, Nat. Assn. Profs. Hebrew, Rotary (pres. Fillmore, N.Y. 1981-82). Home: 17 Park Dr Houghton NY 14744 Office: Houghton Coll Div Religion & Philosophy Houghton NY 14744

SCHULTZ, ERICH RICHARD WILLIAM, minister, librarian, archivist; b. Rankin, Ont., Can., June 1, 1930; s. William Henry and Martha Frieda (Geelhaar) S. BA, U. Western Ont., 1951; BD, Waterloo Luth Sem., 1954; M.Th., U. Toronto, 1958, B.L.S., 1959. Ordained to ministry Evang. Luth. Ch. in Can., 1956. Pastor St. Paul's Luth. Ch., Ellice Twp., Ont., 1954-56; libr. Waterloo (Ont.) Luth. Sem., 1959-60, lectr., 1959-70; libr., archivist Waterloo Luth. U. (named changed to Wilfrid Laurier U. 1973), 1960-90; archivist Ea. Synod, Evang. Luth. Ch. in Can., 1961-90; ret., 1991. Editor, bibliographer: Ambulatio Fidei: Essays in Honor of Otto W. Heick, 1965, Vita Laudanda: Essays in Memory of Ulrich S. Leupold, 1975; translator: Getting Along with Difficult People (Friederich Schmitt, author), 1970. Bd. dirs. Kitchener-Waterloo Community Concert Assn., pres. 1988-90. Mem. Can. Library Assn. (convenor outstanding svc. award com. 1978-80), Assn. Can. Archivists, Can. Luth. Hist. Assn., Luth. Hist. Conf., Ont. Assn. Archivists, Waterloo Hist. Soc. (v.p. 1980-82, pres. 1982-84), Ont. Library Assn. (v.p. 1967-68, pres. 1968-69), Inst. Profl. Librarians Ont. (v.p., pres. 1969-70), Am. Theol. Library Assn. (v.p., pres. 1975-77, chmn. program com. 1982-85), Waterloo Regional Heritage Found. (bd. dirs. 1990—). Home: 235 Erb St E, Waterloo, ON Canada N2J 1M9 Office: 75 University Ave, Waterloo, ON Canada N2L 3C5

SCHULTZ, GUSTAV HOBART, religious organization administrator; b. Foley, Ala., Sept. 23, 1935; s. Gustav H. and Anna H. (Coaker) Schultz; m. Flora Redd, June 16, 1958; children: Gustav Hobart III, Timothy Martin, Locke Elizabeth, Bettina Pauley. BD, Concordia Sem., 1961; MST, Luth. Sch. Theology, 1977. Pastor Holy Trinity Luth. Ch., Rome, Ga., 1961-65; asst. pastor Ascension Luth. Ch., Riverside, Ill., 1965-69; pastor U. Luth. Chapel, Berkeley, Calif., 1969—; dean of chapel Pacific Luth. Sem., Berkeley, 1977-78; aux. bishop Southwest Province Assn. Evang. Luth. Chs., 1979-87; chmn. Nat. Sanctuary Def. Fund, San Francisco, 1985—, Salvadoran Humanitarian Aid, Rsch. and Edn. Found., Washington, 1984—. Mem. Berkeley City Planning Commn., 1981-83; bd. dirs. Berkeley Emergency Food Project, 1983—, No. Calif. Ecumenical Coun., San Francisco, 1984-87; founding mem. Internat. Com. for Peace and Reunification of Korea, 1989—. Recipient Annual Berkeley Peace Prize, Warwick and Assocs. and Mayor of Berkeley, 1985. Office: U Luth Chapel 2425 College Ave Berkeley CA 94704

SCHULTZ, JOSEPH PENN, rabbi; b. Chgo,, Dec. 2, 1928; s. Mordecai Abraham and Charlotte Deborah (Paradise) S.; m. Bella Esther Intrater, Aug. 2, 1955; children: Charlotte Deborah, Reena, Eric. BA, Yeshiva U., N.Y.C., 1951; M in Hebrew Lit., Jewish Theol. Seminary, N.Y.C., 1955; PhD, Brandeis U., 1962. Ordainer, 1955. Asst. rabbi Congregation Kehillath Israel, Brookline, Mass., 1955-57; rabbi Beth Jacob Synagogue, Norwich, Conn., 1957-60, Temple Beth Shalom, Cambridge, Mass., 1960-73; asst. prof. religion Boston U., 1963-73; assoc. prof. history and Judaic studies U. Mo., Kans. City, 1973-78, Oppenstein Bros. disting. prof. Judaic studies, 1978—. Author: Judaism and the Gentile Faiths, 1981; editor: Mid-America's Promise, 1982, From Destruction to Rebirth, 1978, Ze'enah O'Re-Enah Book of Genesis, 1985. Mem. Soc. Bibl. Lit., Am. Acad. Religion. Home: 1104 W 100th St Kansas City MO 64114 Office: U Mo Kans City 5100 Rockhill Rd Kansas City MO 64110

SCHULTZ, LORENZ MYRON, JR., pastor; b. Denver, Sept. 17, 1937; s. Lorenz M. Schultz Sr. BA in History, U. Colo., 1959; MDiv, Union Theol. Sem., N.Y.C., 1963. Ordained to ministry United Meth. Ch. as elder, 1964. Pastor Errol Heights United Meth. Ch., Portland, Oreg., 1963-64, Hughes Meml. United Meth. Ch., Portland, 1964-68; campus pastor United Christian Campus Ministry, Chico (Calif.) State U., 1968-69, United Christian Campus Ministry, San Francisco State U., 1969-78; pastor Davis (Calif.) United Meth. Ch., 1978-86, Sierra Vista United Meth. Ch., Fresno, Calif., 1986-88, Newman United Meth. Ch., Grants Pass, Oreg., 1988—; dir. worship Oreg.-Idaho Annual Conf. United Meth. Ch., Portland, 1988—; chair episcopacy com. Calif.-Nev. Annual Conf. United Meth. Ch., San Francisco, 1984-88. Profl. chorister San Francisco Opera, 1972-78; soloist Rogue Opera, Ashland, Oreg., 1990—, Fresno (Calif.) Lyric Opera, 1987; chorister So. Oreg. Rep Singers, 1988—; mem. Grants Pass Performing Arts Com., 1990—, Josephine County Mental Health Adv., Grants Pass, 1989—; bd. dirs. So. Oreg. Rep Singers, Ashland, 1989—; mem. adv. com. Grants Pass Teen Theatre, 1991—. Ford fellow Urban Tng. Ctr., Chgo., 1967. Mem. Alban Inst., United Meths. in Worship, Music and Arts, Am. Guild Musical Artists, Yolo Hospice Davis (founder), ACLU, Sierra Club, Phi Beta Kappa, Phi Alpha Theta. Democrat. Home: 920 NE Wesley Ln Grants Pass OR 97526 Office: Newman United Meth Ch 132 NE B St Grants Pass OR 97526

SCHULTZ, MARIE EVELYN, religious organization administrator; b. Lambert, Mont., Aug. 14, 1929; d. Albert H. and Adina (Boese) S. Student, Bethel Coll. Asst. to pres. Bapt. Gen. Conf., Arlington Heights, Ill., 1970-86; dir. ch. relations Bethel Coll. & Sem., St. Paul, 1986—. Mem. Religious Conv. Mgrs. Assn., Bapt. Gen. Conf. (moderator 1988—). Avocations: snow skiing, out-of-doors activities. Home: 4524 Bridge Ct Shoreview MN 55126 Office: 3900 Bethel Dr Saint Paul MN 55112

SCHULTZ, ROBERT JOHN, religious institution administrator, pastor; b. Harvey, Ill., Feb. 6, 1945; s. John Schultz and Cora (Lotz) S.; m. Joyce Ann Mahler, June 3, 1967; children: Jeffrey, Michael, Kristin, Rebekah. AA, Concordia Jr. Coll., Milw., 1965; BA, Concordia Sr. Coll., Ft. Wayne, Ind., 1967; MDiv, Concordia Sem., 1971; MS in Urban Edn., U. Nebr., 1978. Assoc. pastor St. Paulus Luth. Ch., San Francisco, 1971-74; pastor Mt. Calvary Luth. Ch., Omaha, 1974-79; assoc. pastor St. Peter Luth. Ch., Hemlock, Mich., 1979-80; pastor St. Mark Luth. Ch., Saginaw, Mich., 1980—; dir. Mich. Luth. Ministries Inst., Saginaw, 1989—; mem. adv. Bd. Mission Devel., Ann Arbor, Mich., 1984—, Bd. Evangelism and Ch. Growth, Ann Arbor, 1989—; panelist Ask the Pastor-Channel WAQP, Saginaw, 1990—. Speaker Meml. Day activities, Hemlock, 1990. 1st lt. U.S. Army, 1969-75. Home: 14880 Bosswell Dr Hemlock MI 48626 Office: St Mark Luth Ch 2565 N Miller Rd Saginaw MI 48603

SCHULTZ, ROBERT KENNETH, minister; b. Mpls., July 29, 1947; s. Kenneth Theodore and Lillian G. (Wohlfeil) S.; m. Pamela Jean Schmiesing, Nov. 11, 1966; children: Cindi Lee, Abi Elisabeth, Caleb Robert. Student, U. Minn., 1965-67; grad. with honors, Bear Valley Sch. Biblical Studies, 1976; student, Clemson U., 1976-77, U. Alaska, Soldotna, 1979-80. Minister Ch. of Christ, Clemson, S.C., 1976-77, Soldotna, 1977-80; minister and elder Ch. of Christ, Bismarck, N.D., 1982—; dir. Dakota Christian Camp, Bismarck, 1984—; lectr. in field. Active Y's Men Internat., Bismarck, 1984-87. Recipient Vol. Leader award YMCA, 1984. Mem. Western Christian Found., Bismarck/Mandan symphony Orch. Assn. (bd. dirs. 1986-88), Bismarck Chem. Health Found. (bd. dirs. 1986-88), Sons of Norway, 3 Crowns, Swedish/Am. Soc., Kiwanis (com. chmn. Bismarck chpt. 1985, bd. dirs. 1987-88). Republican. Avocations: golf, walking, cycling, volleyball, cross-country skiing. Office: Ch of Christ 1914 Assumption Dr Bismarck ND 58501

SCHULTZ, SAMUEL JACOB, clergyman, educator; b. Mountain Lake, Minn., June 9, 1914; s. David D. and Anna (Eitzen) S.; m. Eyla June Tolliver, June 17, 1943; children: Linda Sue, David Carl. AA, Bethel Coll., 1938; BA, John Fletcher Coll., 1940; BD, Faith Theol. Sem., 1944; MST, Harvard U., 1945, ThD, 1949. Ordained to ministry Christian and Missionary Alliance Ch., 1944; pastor First Meth. Ch., Pine River, Minn., 1940-41, Waldo Congl. Ch., Brockton, Mass., 1944-45, Evang. Bapt. Ch., Belmont, Mass., 1945-47; prof. Gordon Coll., Boston, 1946-47, Bethel Coll. and Sem., St. Paul, 1947-49, St. Paul Bible Inst., 1948-49; prof. Wheaton (Ill.) Coll., 1949-80, prof. emeritus, 1980—, Samuel Robinson prof. Bible and theology, 1955-80, chmn. Bible and philosophy dept., 1957-63, chmn. div. Bibl. edn. and philosophy, 1963-67, chmn. div. Bibl. studies, 1972-79; prof. Old Testament and Bible Exposition Trinity Coll. Grad. Sch. (name now Tampa Bay Theol. Sem.), Dunedin (now Holiday), Fla., 1987—; interim supply pastor Bible Ch. Winnetka, Ill., 1951, 60; resident supply pastor South Shore Bapt. Ch., Hingham, Mass., 1958-59. Author: The Old Testament Speaks, 1960, 3d edit., 1980, 4th edit., 1990, Law and History, 1964, The Prophets Speak, 1968, Deuteronomy-Gospel of Love, 1971, The Gospel of Moses, 1974, 79, Interpreting the Word of God, 1976, Leviticus-God Dwelling among his People, 1983, The Message of the Old Testament, 1986. Mem. bd. edn. Bethel Coll. and Sem., 1960-65; historian Conservative Congregation Christian Conf., 1980-86; bd. dirs. Inst. in Basic Youth Conflicts, 1965-80, Congl. Christian Hist. Soc., 1984—; trustee Gordon-Conwell Sem., South Hamilton, Mass., 1980—; trustee Lexington (Mass.) Christian Acad., 1987—. NYU study grantee Israel, 1966, Wheaton Coll. Alumni research grantee, 1958. Mem. Soc. Bibl. Lit., Evang. Theol. Soc. (editor Jour. 1962-75), Near East Archaeol. Soc. (sec., bd. dir.), Wheaton Coll. Scholastic Honors Soc., Phi Sigma Tau. Book the Living and Active Word of God dedicated in his honor, 1983. Home: 9 Forbes Pl #802 Dunedin Beach FL 34698 Home (summer): 143 East St Lexington MA 02173 *Love the Lord your God with all your heart and with all your soul and with all your strength and your neighbor as yourself.*

SCHULWEIS, HAROLD MAURICE, rabbi; b. N.Y.C., Apr. 14, 1925; s. Maurice and Helen (Rezak) S.; m. Malkah Muriel Savod, June 22, 1947; children: Seth, Ethan, Alissa. BA, Yeshiva Coll., 1945; MA, NYU, 1948; MHL, Jewish Theol. Sem., 1950, DD (hon.), 1975; ThD, Pacific Sch. Religion, 1970; HHD (hon.), Hebrew Union Coll., 1983. Rabbi Conservative Jewish Congregation, 1945, Temple Emanuel, Parkchester, N.Y., 1950-52, Temple Beth Abraham, Oakland, Calif., 1952-70, Valley Beth Shalom, Encino, Calif., 1970—; instr. philosophy CCNY, 1948-51; adj. prof. contemporary civilization U. Judaism, L.A., 1970—; lectr. Jewish theology Hebrew Union Coll., L.A., 1971—; guest of Govt. of Fed. Republic Germany to observe rehab. of German ednl. instns., 1966; mem. nat. rabbinical cabinet Rabbinical Assembly, 1968, sec. assembly, 1978; mem. faculty B'nai B'rith Adult Edn. Commn. Author: Evil and the Morality of God, 1983; also articles; co-author: Approaches to the Philosophy of Religion, 1952; mem. editorial bd. The Reconstructionist, 1970—, Moment, 1974—, Davka, 1974—, Sh'ma, 1974—. Founder Inst. for the Righteous Arts, Judah Magnes Mus., Berkeley, Calif., 1961; founder, chmn. Inst. for Righteous Acts—Documentation and Study Ctr. on Rescuers of Jews in the Nazi Era. Recipient Social Actions award United Synagogue Am., 1969, medal Prime Min. of Israel, 1975. Office: 15739 Ventura Blvd Encino CA 91316

SCHULZ, WILLIAM FREDERICK, religious association executive; b. Pitts., Nov. 14, 1949; s. William F. and Jean Smith; m. Linda Lu Cotney, Nov. 17, 1978; stepchildren: Jeneanne Pina, Jason Pina. AB, Oberlin Coll., 1971; MA, Meadville/Lombard Theol. Sch., 1973, DMin, 1975, DDiv, 1987; MA, U. Chgo., 1974. Minister First Parish Unitarian Universalist, Bedford, Mass., 1975-78; dir. social responsibility Unitarian Universalist Assn., Boston, 1978-79, exec. v.p., 1979-85, pres., 1985—. Editor, contbr. Transforming Words: Six Essays on Preaching, 1984. Bd. dirs. Ams. United for Separation of Ch. and State, Ams. for Religious Liberty, People for the Am. Way, Planned Parenthood Fedn. Am. Recipient Albert Francis Christie prize, 1973, 75, Albert Schweitzer medal First Unitarian Ch. of Berkeley, Calif., 1983. Mem. ACLU, Unitarian Universalist Ministers Assn., Unitarian Universalist Hist. Soc., Internat. Assn. Religious Freedom, Fortnightly Club (Newburyport, Mass.). Democrat. Home: 9 Louisburg Sq Boston MA 02108 Office: Unitarian Universalist Assn 25 Beacon St Boston MA 02108

SCHUMACHER, FREDERICK JOHN, minister; b. Bklyn., Mar. 8, 1939; s. Friedrich and Elizabeth Marie (Perley) S.; m. Joyce Elaine Morris, June 9, 1961; children: Frederick Eugene, John Frederick, Joy Elaine. BS, U. Okla., 1961; BD, Cen. Luth. Theol. Sem., 1964; MDiv, Luth. Sch. Theology, 1972; STM, N.Y. Theol. Sem., 1972; D Ministry, Princeton Theol. Sem., 1978. Ordained to ministry, Luth. Ch., 1964. Asst. pastor, dir. religious edn. and evangelism St. Matthew's Luth. Ch., White Plains, N.Y., 1964-66, pastor, 1966—; vice-chmn. cons. com. on aging Luth. Ch. Am., 1974-78; mem. exec. bd. Met. N.Y. Synod, 1974-77; trustee St. Agnes Hosp., White Plains, 1983-86; dean TAppan Zee dist. Luth. Ch. Am., 1983-88; chaplain White Plains Police and Fire Depts., 1986—; Protestant chaplain White Plains Extended Care and Nursing Facility, Inc., 1972—; bd. dirs. Am. Luth. Pub. Bur., 1989—. Contbr. articles to religious jours. Bd. dirs. White Plains YMCA,

1972-74. Recipient Pioneer Friendship award Unitd Cerebral Palsy of Westchester, 1970; parish minister's fellow Fund for Theol. Edn., Inc., 1971, Samuel Trexler scholar, 1973. Home: 79 Greenridge Ave White Plains NY 10605 Office: 3 Carhart Ave White Plains NY 10605

SCHUMAN, MARY ANNE, nun; b. Milw., Mar. 10, 1922; d. Raymond Alexander and Anita Sophia Matilda (Efflandt) S. BA, St. Mary of Woods Coll., 1943. Joined Discalced Carmelite Nuns, Roman Cath. Ch., 1943. Dir., comoposer liturgical music Discalced Carmelites, Eldridge, Iowa, 1950—, prioress, 1980—, also novice mistress formation dir., editor newsletter, archivist. Editor: Songs from Carmel, 1970; contbr. book revs. to religious publs. Mem. Assn. Contemplative Sisters, Carmelite Communities Associated. Home and Office: Carmelite Monastery 17937 250th St Eldridge IA 52748 *There is an amazing interest in deep, contemplative prayer. Carmelites have an obligation to assist in a better understanding of wholistic spirituality which includes reaching out to God in mystery and love.*

SCHUPP, RONALD IRVING, clergyman, missionary; b. Syracuse, N.Y., Dec. 10, 1951; s. George August and Shirley Louise (Mitchell) S. Ordained ministry, Old Country Church, 1972; ordained Baptist ministry, 1976; cert., Moody Bible Inst., 1986. Missionary, asst. pastor The Old Country Ch. Inc., Chgo., 1972-76; missionary Solid Rock Bapt. Ch., Chgo., 1976-89, Marble Rock Missionary Bapt. Ch., Chgo., 1990—; asst. dir. Uptown Community Orgn., Chgo., 1974-76; dir. Chgo. Action Ctr., 1978-80; mem. bd. dirs. West Englewood United Orgn./Clara's House Shelter, 1991—, assoc. chaplain, 1991—. Mem. Nat. Coalition for the Homeless; mem. Chgo. Coalition for the Homeless, 1988—, vol. organizer, 1988—, mem. empowerment adv. com., 1991—; mem. Homeless on the Move for Equality, 1990—, bd. dirs., 1991—; mem. Chgo. Peace Coun., 1984-87; rep. Chgo. Welfare Rights Orgn., 1986-88; activist Chgo. Clergy and Laity Concerned, 1981-87. Recipient letter of commendation Chgo. Fire Dept., 1983. Mem. Operation Push, Inc., 1985—, (citation 1990), NAACP, 1991—, ACLU, 1991—, Chgo. Free South Africa (steering com. 1984—), Transafrica, 1991—. Democrat. Avocations: bicycle riding, poetry. Home: 6412 N Hoyne Ave Apt 3A Chicago IL 60645 *Look inward and see your soul, look outward and serve humanity.*

SCHURTER, DENNIS DEAN, chaplain; b. Great Falls, Mont., Sept. 19, 1942; s. Orie Olin and Martha Mary (Priboth) S.; m. Sandra Carol Boehme, Aug. 21, 1965; children: Stephanie Ann, Kyle Christopher. BA, Concordia Sr. Coll., Ft. Wayne, Ind., 1964; MDiv, Concordia Seminary, St. Louis, 1968; D Ministry, Tex. Christian U., Ft. Worth, 1987. Pastor Christ the King Lutheran Ch., Waxahachie, Tex., 1968-72, Redeemer Lutheran Ch., Greenville, Tex., 1972-74; chaplain Denton (Tex.) STate Sch., Denton, Tex., 1975-88; dir. chaplaincy svcs. Denton (Tex.) State Sch., 1988—; past pres., treas. Denton Hosp. Chaplaincy Bd., 1980-89, chmn., 1989—. Contbr. to profl. jours. Asst. scoutmaster Denton area Boy Scouts Am., 1982-90; bd. dirs., treas. Assn. for Retarded Citizens, Denton County, 1988—. Capt. USAFR, 1966-75. Fellow Coll. Chaplains Am., Inc. (cert.); mem. Am. Assn. on Mental Retardation (religion div. sec. 1976-78), Tex. Mental Health-Mental Retardation Chaplains Assn. (sec. 1987-88, pres. 1988-89). Office: Denton State Sch PO Box 368 Denton TX 76202

SCHUTZ, JOHN HOWARD, religious studies educator; b. Orange, N.J., Mar. 11, 1933; s. John Paul and Virginia (Wolfe) S.; m. Barbara Jane Foster, June 20, 1953; children: Martha Anne, Amy Thorndike. B.S., Northwestern U., 1954; B.Div., Yale U., 1958, M.A., 1959, Ph.D., 1964. Acting instr. dept. religious studies Yale U., New Haven, 1961-64, instr., 1964-65, asst. prof., 1965-68; assoc. prof., chmn. dept. religion U. N.C., Chapel Hill, 1968-72, prof., 1972—, Bowman and Gordon Gray prof. religious studies, 1983—; dir. Program in Religious Studies for Journalists, 1981—; vis. prof. Duke U., Durham, N.C., 1977. Author: Paul and the Anatomy of Apostolic Authority, 1975; editor, transl.: The Social Setting of Pauline Christianity (Gerd Theissen), 1982; editor Bull. Council on Study of Religion, 1970-72. Fulbright scholar, 1958-59; Cross-Disciplinary fellow Soc. Religion in Higher Edn., 1972-73; recipient Tanner award U. N.C., 1981. Mem. Studiorum Novi Testamenti Soc., Soc. Bibl. Lit. Home: 300 Glandon Dr Chapel Hill NC 27514 Office: U NC Chapel Hill NC 27514

SCHWAMBACH, STEPHEN R., minister; b. Evansville, Ind., Sept. 13, 1948; s. Richard Robert and Geneva Irene (Hornbeck) S.; m. Judith Gayle Buchanan, June 9, 1968; children: Peter, Tabitha, Abigail, Rebekah, Abraham. BA Religion, Evang. Bible Coll., Chgo., 1972; MA in Theology, Evang. Sem., Denver, 1975; PhD in Psychology, Pacific Western U., Clayton, Mo., 1978. Ordained to ministry, Am. Evang. Christian Chs., 1970. Pastor Bethel Temple, Evansville, Ind., 1981—; chmn. Evansville Christian Sch., 1975—, Marriage Internat., Evansville, 1988—. Author: Harvest House, 1989—, Tough Talk to a Stubborn Spouse, 1990, For Lovers Only, 1991. Office: Bethel Temple 4400 Lincoln Ave Evansville IN 47714

SCHWANZ, KEITH DUANE, minister; b. Grand Island, Nebr., Jan. 21, 1954; s. LeRoy C. and Myrtle G. (Vannaman) S.; m. Judith Ann Munson, June 28, 1975; children: Karla, Jason. Student, Northwestern U., 1972-74; BA, North Pk. Coll., 1977; MA in Ch. Music, Western Sem., Portland, Oreg., 1985; PhD in Ch. Music, The Union Inst., Cin., 1991. Ordained to ministry Ch. of the Nazarene, 1986. Assoc. pastor Moreland Ch. of the Nazarene, Portland, 1977-79, 1st Ch. of the Nazarene, Olympia, Wash., 1979-82, Rose City Ch. of the Nazarene, Portland, 1982-88, Ch. of the Nazarene, Oregon City, Oreg., 1988—; adj. prof. Western Evang. Sem., Portland, 1988—; speaker, worship leader retreats, confs., 1977—; mem. hymnal com. Ch. of the Nazarene, Kansas City, Mo., 1989—. Contbr. articles to profl. jours.; composer, arranger ch. music. Home: 7700 SE Strawberry Ln Milwaukie OR 97267

SCHWARCZ, ROY NICHOLAS, minister; b. N.Y.C., Oct. 9, 1947; s. Richard Samuel and Ruth S. (Klienfeld) S.; m. JoAnne Margaret Tillman, July 8, 1972; children: Susannah, Aliza, Rachel, Jacqueline. Diploma in Jewish studies, Moody Bible Inst., 1980. Ordained to ministry Fellowship Messianic Congregations Ch., 1979. Founding pastor Olive Tree Congregation, Chgo., 1978-80; co-founder, sr. pastor Olive Tree Congregation, Toronto, Can., 1984-86; co-founder Fellowship Messianic Congregations, L.A., 1985; founding pastor Vineyard Congregation, Long Grove, Ill., 1982-88; regional dir. Chosen People Ministries, Chgo., 1985-91, Christian Jew Found., Buffalo Grove, Ill., 1991—; v.p. Fellowship Messianic Congregations, L.A., 1988—. Co-founder congl. planting program Chosen People Ministries, 1978. Mem. Lausanne Consultation for Jewish Evangelism. Office: Christian Jew Found PO Box 7122 Buffalo Grove IL 60089

SCHWARTZ, ALLEN EDWARD, religious organization administrator; b. Staunton, Ill., Jan. 1, 1959; s. Melvin Erwin William and Dorothy (Marcus) S. BA, Macalester Coll., St. Paul, 1981; MSW, Washington U., St. Louis, 1988; MA in Jewish Communal Svc., Hebrew Union Coll., L.A., 1988. Field rep. Hebrew Immigrant Aid Soc., N.Y.C., 1988-90; dir. REfugee Resettlement Program Jewish Family Svc. of Greater Miami, Fla., 1990—; bd. dirs. N.Am. Conf. on Ethiopian Jewry, N.Y.C., 1988—. Home: 2105 Brickell Ave Miami FL 33139 Office: Jewish Family Svc 420 Lincoln Rd Miami Beach FL 33139

SCHWARTZ, BARRY DOV, rabbi; b. Boston, July 22, 1940; s. Melvin and Frances (Polonsky) S.; m. Sonia Katz, July 6, 1970; children: Avi Dan, Jonathan Shalom, Tamar Chana. B Jewish Edn., Hebrew Tchrs. Coll., 1958; AB, Boston U., 1961; M. Hebrew Letters, Jewish Theol. Sem., 1963, PhD, 1980, DDiv (hon), 1991. Ordained rabbi, 1965. Rabbi Temple Beth Mordecai, Perth Amboy, N.J., 1967-73, Temple B'nai Sholom, Rockville Centre, N.Y., 1973—; mem. coun. United Jewish Appeal, Israel Bonds. Contbr. articles, book revs. to profl. publs., introduction to The Sunflower. Mem. Ethics Commn., Rockville Centre; mem. Ednl. Found. of Rockville Centre; mem. Human Rights Commn.; bd. dirs. Mercy Hosp. Capt. USAF, 1965-67, chaplain, lt. col. USAFR. Named Outstanding Citizen, Human Rights Commn., 1990. Mem. Rabbinical Assembly (past pres.), N.Y. Bd. Rabbis (exec.), L.I. Bd. Rabbis (exec.), Synagogue Coun. Am. (exec.). Home: 1 Irving Pl Rockville Centre NY 11570 Office: Temple B'nai Sholom 100 Hempstead Ave Rockville Centre NY 11570

SCHWARTZ, LAURE ANN, youth director; b. Marengo, Iowa, July 10, 1961; d. Jerry and Bess (Collins) Timm; m. Shawn Schwartz, May 31, 1987. MusB in Edn., N.E. Mo. State U., 1986. Youth staffer Luth. Ch.-Mo. Synod., Cleve., 1982-83; music min. Celebrate Singers, Seward, Nebr., 1983-84; youth staffer, choir dir. Faith Luth. Ch., Kirksville, Mo., 1984-86; dir. youth ministry Christ the King Luth. Ch., Bloomington, Minn., 1988—. Composer: (Christian music) Celebrate the Lord, 1985, Graceful Praise, 1990. Office: Christ the King Luth Ch 1317 W 86th St Bloomington MN 55420

SCHWARTZ, SIMON, social worker; b. Montreal, Que., Can., Dec. 29, 1947; came to U.S., 1980; s. Harry and Doris (Tucker) S.; m. Candy Brown, June 22, 1969. BA, McGill U., Montreal, 1968; MS in Social Work, U. Wis., Madison, 1971. Lic. social worker, Mass.; P.S.W., Que. Social worker Jewish Family Svcs., Montreal, 1971-80. Avocations: music, world travel, linguistics, movie critiquing, record collecting. Home: 9 Park Vale Ave # 7 Boston MA 02134

SCHWARTZ, SUSAN CHRISTINE, minister; b. Columbus, Ohio, Dec. 4, 1949; d. Francis Edward and Sara Alice (Montgomery) S. BA, Capital U., 1975; MDiv, Trinity Luth. Sem., Columbus, 1980. Ordained to ministry Am. Luth. Ch., 1980. Asst. pastor Our Savior's Luth. Ch., Burbank, Ill., 1980-90; pastor New Life Luth. Ch., Hoffman Estates, Ill., 1990—; mem. exec. bd. South Chgo. Conf. Am. Luth. Ch., 1982-85, mem. dist. faculty Ill. SEARCH Bible Studies, 1983-85; dist. bd. Ill. div. World Mission and Interchurch Cooperation, 1982-85; dean S.W. Conf., Metro Chgo. Synod, 1987-90, Synod Coun. 1989—; Call Study Task Force, 1988-91. V.p. Burbank (Ill.) Police and Fire Chaplains, 1981-83. Home: 505 Crossing Ct Rolling Meadows IL 60008 Office: New Life Luth Ch 1500 Algonquin Hoffman Estates IL 60195

SCHWARTZMAN, SYLVAN DAVID, rabbi; b. Balt., Dec. 8, 1913; s. Jacob and Rose Padve) S.; m. Sylvia Cohen, Sept. 22, 1940; children: Judith I. Palay, Joel R. BA, U. Cin., 1936; MHL, Hebrew Union Coll., Cin., 1941; PhD, Vanderbilt U., 1952; MBA, U. Cin., 1970; D.D. (Hon.), Hebrew Union Coll.-Jewish Inst. Religion, 1981. Ordained rabbi, 1941. Dir. religious edn. Temple Israel, Boston, 1939-40; rabbi Congregation Children of Israel, Augusta, Ga., 1941-47; dir. field activities Union of Am. Hebrew Congregations, N.Y.C., 1947-48; rabbi Vine St. Temple, Nashville, 1948-50; prof. Jewish religious edn. Hebrew Union Coll., Cin., 1950-81; rabbi Congregation Aaron, Trinidad, Colo., 1975—; adj. prof. Chapman U., Albuquerque, 1987—; trustee Alfred Freudenthal Found., Trinidad, 1983—; chmn. com. on contracts, salaries, and fin. Cen. Conf. Am. Rabbis, N.Y.C., 1989—. Author: Rocket to Mars, 1968, Into the Underground Kingdom, 1975, Reform Judaism, Then and Now, 1971; co-author Elements of Financial Analysis, 1984, The Living Bible, 1962, others. Mem. Cen. Conf. Am. Rabbis (B'Yad Chazaka award 1989, hon. mem. 1991), Nat. Assn. Temple Educators (Emanuel Gamoran award 1972), Nat. Assn. Ret. Reform Rabbis (pres 1990-92). Home: 5409 Rawlings Rd NE Albuquerque NM 87111 *I am ever impressed by the insights of the past. So the Book of Proverbs has left us with an observation that speaks to the America of our time. "For lack of vision," the writer declares, "a people lose restraint" (Proverbs 29:18). Indeed, a society that lacks restraint already indicates a loss of that vision which once contributed to the nation's greatness.*

SCHWARZ, HANS, theology educator; b. Schwabach, Germany, Jan. 5, 1939; came to U.S., 1967; s. Johann and Babette (Götz) S.; m. Hildegard Höfling; children: Claudia, Hans, Krista. Th.D., Erlangen U., 1963. Ordained to ministry Luth. Ch. Bavaria, 1966. Asst. pastor St. Peter's Ch., Erlangen-Bruck, 1965-66; instr. to Edward C. Fendt, Trinity Luth. Sem., Columbus, Ohio, 1967-81; prof. Protestant theology Regensburg U., Bavaria, Fed. Republic Germany, 1981—; adj. prof. systematic theology Luth. Theol. So. Sem., Columbia, S.C., 1985—; ecumenical rels. officer Griechisch-deutsche Initiative, Wurzburg, 1981—; pres. Redeemer Luth. Ch., Columbus, 1980-81. Author 20 theol. books in English and German. Contbr. articles to profl. jours. Recipient Frederik A. Schiotz award, Am. Luth. Ch., 1974. Mem. Am. Acad. Religion, Wissenschaftliche Gesellschaft für Theologie, Deutsche Skandinavische Gesellschaft für Religionsphilosophie, Karl Heim Gesellschaft (v.p. 1982—). Office: Universitat Regensburg, 8400 Regensburg Federal Republic of Germany

SCHWARZ, KAREN ANNE, psychotherapist; b. San Francisco, Mar. 15, 1957; d. George Joseph and Bernice Annette (Matulich) S. BA in Psychology, BA in Religious Studies magna cum laude, Mt. St. Mary's Coll., Los Angeles, 1980; MA in Counseling Psychology, U. Notre Dame, Ind., 1981; postgrad., Calif. Sch. Profl. Psychology, Berkeley, 1986—. Cert. psychol. asst., Calif. Clin. intern Cath. Social Services, Van Nuys, Calif., 1978-79; campus minister El Camino Coll., Los Angeles, 1979-80; clin. intern Family Counseling Services, Elkhart, Ind., 1980-81; clin. intern Tom Smith Substance Abuse Treatment Ctr. San Francisco Gen. Hosp., 1987-88; staff psychotherapist Ctr. for the Whole Person, San Carlos, Calif., 1981-88; psychotherapist Robert Kaye, MD Med. Corp., San Mateo, Calif., 1988-91, Foster City (Calif.) Counseling Svcs., 1991—; psychology intern Garfield Geropsychiatric Hosp., Oakland, Calif., 1989-90, Acute Adolescent Svcs., Don Lowe Pavillion, Valley Med. Ctr., Santa Clara, Calif., 1990-91. Mem. Nat. Assembly Religious Women, Women's Ordination Conf. Mem. Nat. Assembly Religious Women, Women's Ordination Conf. (adv. coun. 1991—), Mercy Justice Coalition (women's issues com.), Nat. Coalition Am. Nuns, Cath. for A Free Choice, NOW (profl.), Am. Psychol. Assn. (divs. of psychology of women, religious issues, counseling psychology, psychoanalytic psychology, psychotherapy), AACD, Am. Mental Health Counselors Assn., Assn. for Religious Issues and Values in Counseling, Assn. For Women in Psychology. Democrat. Roman Catholic. Avocations: feminist psychoanalytic theory, feminist theology and spirituality, reform of Cath. Ch. Office: Foster City Counseling Svcs 1289 E Hillsdale Blvd Foster City CA 94404

SCHWARZ, SIDNEY HOWARD, rabbi; b. N.Y.C., Oct. 8, 1953; s. Allan and Judy (Brand) S.; m. Sandra Perlstein, July 3, 1983; children: David, Joel, Jennifer. BA in Polit. Sci. summa cum laude, U. Md., 1974; MA in Modern Jewish and Am. History, Temple U., 1977, PhD in History, 1982. Ordained rabbi, 1980. Rabbi Congregatin Beth Israel, Media, Pa., 1976-83; mem. faculty Akiba Hebrew Acad., Merion, Pa., 1981-83, Gratz Coll., Wilmington and Phila., Pa., 1981-83, Reconstructionist Rabinnical Coll., Wyncote, Pa., 1982-84; exec. dir. Jewish Community Coun. of Greater Washington, 1984-87; founding rabbi Adat Shalom Reconstructionist Congregation, Bethesda, Md., 1988—; founder, pres. Washington Inst. for Jewish Leadership and Values, 1988—; adj. prof. of Jewish history U. Md., 1986-87; bd. dirs. Jewish Reconstructionist Found., Nat. INst. on Holocaust, Interfaith Conf. Met. Washington; mem. editorial bd. Reconstructionist mag.; mem. Washington Area Community Investment Fund; bd. govs. Reconstructionist Rabbinical Coll.; mem. steering com. Nat. Rabbinic Chevrah. Host. TV talk show Jewish Community Hour. Mem. Reconstructionist Rabbinical Assn. (founding editor jour. Raayonot, mem. nat. commn. on intermarriage, mem. long range planning com.). Home: 11707 Farmland Dr Rockville MD 20852 Office: Wash Inst Jewish Leadership 6101 Montrose Rd Ste 208 Rockville MD 20852

SCHWARZENTRAUB, ELIZABETH KEITH (BETSY SCHWARZENTRAUB), church consultant; b. San Francisco, Nov. 11, 1949; d. John Alden and Marjery (Sperry) Keith; m. Kenneth Keith Schwarzentraub, Feb. 13, 1983; children: Jana Brooks, Eric, Matt. BS magna cum laude, U. Redlands, Calif., 1971; MDiv, Pacific Sch. of Religion, 1976; D in Ministry, San Francisco Theol. Sem., 1988. Ordained deacon, 1975, elder, 1978. Pastor First United Meth. Ch., Richmond, Calif., 1975-77, Lakewood United Meth. Ch., Sunnyvale, Calif., 1977-80, Holy Cross United Meth. Ch., Stockton, Calif., 1980-85, Isleton (Calif.) Community United Meth. Ch., 1985-88; sr. pastor Marysville 1st United Meth. Ch., 1988-91; prin. Schwarzentraub & Assoc. ch. cons., Davis, Calif., 1991—; mem. Stewardship Assocs., United Meth. Ch., 1980-85, 88—; chairperson Conf. Div. of Stewardship, Calif. and Nev., 1974-80; counterpart, researcher stewardship devel. New Life Chs., 1986-90; chairperson Shasta Dist. Com. on Ordained Ministry, 1989-91. Contbr. articles to profl. jours. Founder Stockton United Meth. Ministries, 1983, Christian Interfaith Aid, Isleton and Rio Vista, Calif., 1986; pres. Ministerial Assn., Yuba and Sutter Counties, 1990-91. Mem. AAUW, Christian Writers Fellowship Internat., Suburban Writers Club,Calif.-Nev. Conf. Stewardship Fellowship. Home: 1402 Nutmeg Ln Davis CA 95616

SCHWEIKER, WILLIAM, theologian, ethicist; b. Des Moines, Dec. 29, 1953; s. William A. and C. Novello (Welsh) S.; m. E. Mary Ingberg, Aug. 25, 1979; 1 child, Paul Welsh. BA, Simpson Coll., Indianola, Iowa, 1976; MDiv, Duke U., 1980; PhD, U. Chgo., 1985. Ordained to ministry United Meth. Ch. Student minister Wesley's Chapel, London, 1978-79; asst. prof. theology and ethics U. Chgo., 1989—. Author: Mimetic Reflections, 1990; author, editor: World Views and Warrants, 1987; co-editor: Cities of Gods, 1986, Meanings in Texts and Actions, 1992; contbr. articles to profl. jours. Dempster fellow United Meth. Ch., 1982, 83, Newcombe fellow Newcombe/Wilson Found., 1984-85, Assn. Theol. Schs. rsch. grantee, 1990. Fellow Soc. for Values in Higher Edn.; mem. Am. Acad. Religion, Soc. Christian Ethics. Democrat. Methodist. Office: U Chgo Div Sch 1025 E 58th St Chicago IL 60637 *Perhaps the most pressing problem of our time is how to bring goodness from the distortions of our world and thus to insure a future for finite existence. The question for me is how the resources of the religious traditions might help us think and act in this situation.*

SCHWENZER, GERHARD, bishop. Bishop of Helsinki Roman Cath. Ch., Norway. Office: Katolske Bispedomme, Akersvn, 5, POB 8270, Hammersborg, 0177 Oslo 1, Norway*

SCHWERDTFEGER, CINDY KAY, religious education director; b. Davenport, Iowa, Oct. 8, 1963; d. Stephen Brownlie and Janet Kay (Utech) West; m. David Allan Schwerdtfeger, Aug. 16, 1986; children: Rachel Kay, Kyle August. BA in Sociology, Iowa State U., Ames, 1986; MA in Christian Edn., N.Am. Bapt. Sem., 1988. Cert. Evang. tchr., U.S. Dir. children and youth ministries Second Reformed Ch., Lennox, S.D., 1987-88; coll. career dir. Trinity Bapt. Ch., Sioux Falls, S.D., 1989; dir. christian edn. Redeemer Bapt. Ch., St. Paul, 1989—; tchr. Westminister Presbyn., Cedar Rapids, Iowa, 1979-84; youth leader Campus Life/Youth for Christ, Cedar Rapids, 1980-82; youth sponsor First Evang. Free, Ames, 1984-85; counselor Cen. Bapt. Camp, Lansing, Iowa, summers 1984-85; Bible study leader Inter Varsity Christian Fellowship, Ames, 1983-85. Recipient scholastic recognition award Nat. Assn. Profs. Christian Edn., 1988. Mem. Fellowship Christian Educators. Republican. Home: 1816 Birch St # 3 White Bear Lake MN 55110 Office: Redeemer Bapt Ch 2479 Geneva Ave N Saint Paul MN 55128

SCHWERIN, DANIEL WILLIAM, minister; b. Waukesha, Wis., Aug. 23, 1963; s. William Andrew Schwerin and Mary Grace (Werning) Schmidt; m. Deborah Kaye Harris, Dec. 20, 1986; children: Rachel, Lee Ann. BA, Carroll Coll., 1985; MDiv, So. Meth. U., 1989. Ordained to ministry Meth. Ch., 1991. Pastor Stephens United Meth. Ch., Duncan, Okla., 1985-90, Parfreyville United Meth. Ch., Waupaca, Wis., 1990—; dist. youth coord. Lawton Dist. United Meth. Ch., Duncan, 1989-90; mem. Ministerial Alliance, Waupaca, 1990. Office: Parfreville United Meth Ch N1983 Hwy K Waupaca WI 54981 *1. Live and learn. Learn and live. 2. Grace happens.*

SCHWERY, HENRI CARDINAL, cardinal; b. St. Leonard, Switzerland, June 14, 1932. Ordained priest Roman Cath. Ch., 1957; ordained bishop, 1977. With titular Ch. of the Holy Protamartyrs; rector Coll. Sion, 1977—; elevated to Sacred Coll. Cardinals, 1991. Office: Diocese of Roman Cath Ch, C P 2068 rue de la Tour 12, CH-1950 Sion, Nord 2, Switzerland*

SCHWICHTENBERG, WILLIS ROBERT, minister; b. Morristown, Minn., Nov. 21, 1946; s. Harold A. and Mabel (Fratzke) S.; m. Alice Marie Fischer, Sept. 2, 1967; children: Jonathan, Jennifer, Jason, Jodee. BS, Mankato (Minn.) State U., 1968; BDiv, Concordia Theol. Sem., 1972, MDiv, 1973; D in Ministry, Covington Theol. Sem., 1990. Ordained to ministry Luth. Ch., 1972. Pastor Trinity/Zion Luth. Chs., Sheldon and Gilman, Wis., 1972-76, Our Savior Luth. Ch., Milford, Ill., 1977-82, Immanuel Luth. Ch., Freeport, Ill., 1982—; speaker Introspect Radio Ministry, 1983—. Author: Life and Ministry of Elijah, 1988, What Are You Doing, Lord? 1990, The Degrees of Memory Work, 1991. Office: Immanuel Luth Ch 615 S Chicago Ave Freeport IL 61032

SCHWOCHOW, ALAN ARTHUR, minister; b. Castalia, Ohio, June 7, 1953; s. Eric Ernest and Lucille Mae (Norman) S.; m. Elizabeth Ann Tonn, Feb. 15, 1981; 1 child, Miriam Elyse. BA, Capital U., 1975; MDiv, Trinity Luth. Sem., Columbus, Ohio, 1979. Ordained to ministry Am. Luth. Ch., 1979. Pastor Martin Luther Luth. Ch., Bucyrus, Ohio, 1979-85, Atonement Luth. Ch., Cin., 1985-87, Groveport (Ohio) Zion Luth. Ch., 1990—; v.p. North Cen. Conf. Ohio Dist. Am. Luth. Ch., 1983-85; interim pastor for So. Ohio Synod, Evang. Luth. Ch. in Am., 1988-90. Chairperson Bucyrus Area CROP Walk for Hunger, Ohio, 1982, 83. Mem. Bucyrus Area Ministerial Assn. (sec. 1980-81, pres. 1981-83), Groveport Ministerial Assn., Liturgical Conf. Office: Groveport Zion Luth Ch 6014 Groveport Rd Box 305 Groveport OH 43125

SCIMONE, DIANA ELIZABETH, religious writer; b. White Plains, N.Y., Nov. 5, 1950; d. Thomas and Regina (Raneri) S. Student, U. Dayton, Ohio, 1970, U. Paris, 1974; BA, Cath. U. Am., 1972. Writer, editor Charles Simpson Ministries, Mobile, Ala., 1984-87; editor Integrity Music, Inc., Mobile, 1988-89; freelance writer Maitland, Fla., 1989—; pres. Mobile Coun. for Internat. Friendship, 1986-89. Editor (newsletters) HM Notes, Family Times; contbr. numerous articles to profl. jours. Mem. Am. Women in Radio and TV, 1972-74, Washington Ind. Writers, 1979-84, Press Club of Mobile, 1984-89, Pub. Rels. Coun. of Ala., 1988-89; pres. Mobile Coun. for Internat. Friendship, 1986-89. Recipient Allied Orgn. award, 1981, Nat. Communications award, 1982, Outstanding Journalistic Achievement award Press Club of Mobile, 1986, Pub. Rels. Coun. Ala., Medallion Excellence award, 1987, 88. Mem. AFS, Gospel Music Assn., Christian Advt., Mktg. and Media Assn. (chmn., pub. rels. com. 1989-91).

SCOATES, HARRY WILLIAM, JR., minister, consultant; b. Palatka, Fla., Sept. 13, 1920; s. Harry William and Orlene (Buffkin) S.; m. Grace Mary Patten, Nov. 8, 1942; children: Luellen, Gaylon, Dana Sue. BA, Emory U., 1949, ThM, 1952; student, Valdosta State U., 1971-72. Pastor First United Meth. Ch., Jeffersonville, Ga., 1950-55, Cross Keys United Meth. Ch., Macon, Ga., 1955-60, First United Meth. Ch., Vidalia, Ga., 1960-65, Trinity United Meth. Ch., Savannah, Ga., 1965-70; dist. supt. United Meth. Ch., Cordele, Ga., 1970-72; council dir. United Meth. Ch., St. Simons Island, Ga., 1972-76; dir. Bd. of Global Ministers, Fin. and Field Service, N.Y.C., 1976-80; cons. United Meth. Communications, Nashville, 1980-82; cons. fin. United Meth. Ch., Atlanta, 1982—; cons. Hinton Rural Life Ctr., Havesville, N.C. Author: Riding the Wire, 1964; producer of many TV films, 1955—. Chmn. ARC, Vidalia, Savannah, 1960-70, Nat. March of Dimes, Jeffersonville, Macon, 1950-65; mem. Boy Scouts Am. Vidalia, Savannah, Cordele councils, 1950-72. Served with USN, 1942-47, PTO. Recipient Rural Minister of the Yr. award Progressive Farm & Emory U., 1955; named to Eagle Scouts Boy Scouts Am. Mem. World Meth. Council. Methodist. Home and Office: Rt 1 Box 149 Bethlehem GA 30620

SCOBEY, JAMES RALPH, retired minister; b. Newbern, Tenn., Apr. 1, 1922; s. William L. and Minnie (Cook) S.; m. Darlis Rebecca Edwards, Sept. 4, 1949; children: Laurinda Kay, Patricia Ann. BA, Bethel Coll., McKenzie, Tenn., 1948; MDiv, Memphis Theol. Sem., 1951. Ordained to ministry Presbyn. Ch., 1948. Min. 1st Cumberland Presbyn. Ch., Lexington, Tenn., 1947-50, Morning Sun Cumberland Presbyterian Ch., Cordova, Tenn., 1951-70; chaplain USAF, 1951-70; pastoral lcounselor Farmington (Mo.) State Hosp., 1973-87; mem. Presbyn. Coun. for Chaplains and Mil. Pers., Washington, 1973-77. Pres. Mineral Area Hospice Inc., Farmington, 1989—. Lt. col. USAF, 1959-70. Mem. Mil. Chaplain's Assn., Kiwanis, Masons. Home: 105 Oak Hill Downs Farmington MO 63640

SCOFIELD, ROBERT VINCENT, II, minister; b. Hudson, N.Y., Nov. 27, 1954; s. Robert Vincent and Lillian (Navarra) S.; m. Barbara Anne Wild; 1 child, Lynn Elizabeth. BA, SUNY, Albany, 1976; MRE, Tex. Christian U., 1981; postrgrad., Austin (Tex.) Presbyn. Theol. Sem., 1987—. Assoc. minister Pleasant Grove Christian Ch., Dallas, 1981-82; sr. minister First Christian Ch., Lamesa, Tex., 1982-84, Lexington, Tex., 1985—; counselor, advisor Crossroads Samaritan Counseling Satellite Ctr., Lamesa, 1984.

Mem. S.E. Dallas Ministerial Alliance (Outstanding Service award 1981), Lamesa Ministerial Alliance (pres. 1983-84, Appreciation and Honor award 1985), Lexington Ministerial Alliance (officer 1986). Mem. Disciples of Christ Ch. Avocations: softball, golf, reading. Home and Office: 145 W 5th St Bonita Spring FL 33923

SCOGGIN, BLAINARD ELMO, religious educator; b. Harris, N.C., Oct. 17, 1915; ls. Johnnie E. and Julia Pearl (McEntyre) S.; m. Hannah Belle Pearlman, Jan. 30, 1941; 1 child, Scarlett. BA, Furman U., Greenville, S.C., 1942; ThM, So. Bapt. Sem., Louisville, 1945, ThD, 1954. Minister Bapt. Ch., Owensboro, Ky., 1943-48, Canal Point, Fla., 1948-49; Bapt. rep. Jerusalem Bapt. Community, Israel, 1949-54; prof. Hebrew and O.T. Southeastern Bapt. Theol. Sem., Wake Forest, N.C., 1955—. Contbr. articles to profl. jours. Chmn. Friends of Raleigh Wake, 1974, N.C. Coun. on Holocaust, 1980-90; trustee Am. Schs. Oriental Rsch., Phila., 1979. Named Disting. Alumnus, Gardner Webb Coll., 1964, Outstanding Alumnus award 1978. Mem. Rotary (pres. 1971). Avocations: flying, fishing, gardening, golf. Home: 2230 Lash Ave Raleigh NC 27607 Office: SE Bapt Theol Sem Dept Hebrew & OT Wake Forest NC 27587

SCOGGINS, RICHARD TODD, evangelist, missionary; b. Riverdale, Md., Aug. 11, 1949; s. Charles Robert Scoggins and Persis Christopher (Hicks) Mitchell; m. Catherine Jane Sherman, July 5, 1975; children: Nathan Richard, Joanna Catherine. BA in Chemistry, Wesleyan U., Middletown, Conn., 1971; postgrad. in chemistry, Brown U., 1971-73; teaching cert., Assumption Coll., Worchester, Mass., 1975; postgrad. in theology, Gordon Conwell Sem., Hamilton, Mass., 1979; postgrad. in Theology, Columbia (S.C.) Grad. Sch. Bible and Missions, 1982. Cert. secondary tchr., R.I.; ordained to ministry, 1980. Football coach Brown U., Providence, 1973-75; tchr. Cranston (R.I.) Schs., 1975-81; campus minister Cranston Christian Fellowship, 1975-82; pastor, ch. planter Warwick (R.I.) Christian Fellowship, 1981-85; ch. planter Fellowship of Ch. Planters, Cumberland (R.I.) Fellowship, 1985-87, Chepachet (R.I.) Christian House Church, 1987, East Providence (R.I.) Christian Fellowship, 1988; dir., founder Inst. Bibl. Ministries, Cranston, 1985-89; freelance writer Warwick, R.I., 1989—; cons. Frontiers Mission to Muslims, Pasadena, Calif., 1985, Harvest Ministries to Italy, Messina, Italy, 1985-88. Author: Phillippians Devotional Guide, 1977, Obedient Disciple, 1988, Covenanting Together, 1989; contbr. articles to jours. in field. Mem. Nat. Assn. Neuthetic Counselors, Fellowship Ch. Planters, Lincoln Fellowship (founder). Republican. Avocations: golf, flying (pvt. license), camping, hiking. Home and Office: 75 Capron Farm Dr Warwick RI 02886

SCOGGINS, ROBERT CONROY, deacon, employee benefits administrator; b. Houston, Apr. 29, 1935; s. Robert Conroy and Gertrude Adelle (Crenshaw) S.; m. Trula Delle Harrison, July 25, 1959; children: Robert C. III, Lynn Ann, Katherine Camille. BS, U. Houston, 1957; postgrad., U. Dallas, 1971-74. Permanent deacon St. Mark Roman Cath. Ch., Plano, Tex., 1974—; mgr. employee benefits Ben E. Keith Co., Dallas, 1977—; lector, reader St. Francis de Sales Ch., Houston, 1962-67; acolyte St. Mark Roman Cath. Ch., Plano, 1966-67. With USAF, 1958-64. Fellow Inst. Life Ins. Coun.; mem. Am. Coll. Life Underwriters (cert. 1971), K.C. (grand knight 1966-67). Republican. Home: 401 Valley Cove Richardson TX 75080-1844 Office: Ben E Keith Co 1805 Record Crossing Dallas TX 75235

SCOLLARD, ROBERT JOSEPH, priest, retired librarian, archivist; b. Toronto, Ont., Can., Aug. 15, 1908; s. Robert and Lillian (McFadden) S. BA, U. Toronto, 1928, BLS, 1939; AMLS, U. Mich., 1942; D in Sacred Lit. (hon.), U. St. Michael's Coll., Toronto, 1983; tchr.'s cert., Ontario Coll. Edn., 1930, St. Basil's Sem., Toronto, 1933. Joined Basilian Fathers, Roman Cath. Ch., 1928, ordained priest, 1932. Asst. libr. Pontifical Inst. Mediaeval Studies, 1931-32, libr., 1932-51; libr. St. Basil's Sem., 1951-59, 68-69; periodicals libr. U. St. Michael's Coll., 1969-75, archivist, 1975-86, archivist emeritus, 1986—; Sec. gen. Congregation of St. Basil, Toronto, 1954-68. Author: Dictionary of Basilian Biography, 1969; editor, founder The Basilian Annals, 1944-68, The Basilian Newsletter, 1961-68; editor The Basilian Hist. Bull., 1970-77. Recipient Crux Pro Ecclesia et Pontifice medal Pope John Paul II, 1987. Mem. Ont. Libr. Assn., Am. Theol. Libr. Assn., Ex Libris Libr. Assn., U. Toronto Sr. Alumni Assn. (alumni talent unltd. com. 1986, U. Toronto Arbor award 1989), Can. Cath. Hist. Assn. (sec. 1970-73, George Edward Clark medal 1975). Home: 81 Saint Mary St, Toronto, ON Canada M5S 1J4 *When the late Cardinal George Bernard Flahiff chose his episcopal motto from the Roman Catholic Liturgy for the Mass, Per Ipsum et cum Ipso et in Ipso, from the final doxology of the First Canon, I have reflected more frequently on the Blessed Trinity. "Through Him, with Him, in Him, in the unity of the Holy Spirit, all glory and honour is yours, almighty Father, forever and ever. Amen."*

SCONIERS, M. L., bishop. Bishop of Western Fla., Ch. of God in Christ, Orlando. Office: Ch of God in Christ PO Box 5472 Orlando FL 32805*

SCORZA, SYLVIO JOSEPH, religion educator; b. Zürich, Switzerland, Mar. 21, 1923; came to U.S., 1929; s. Joseph Peter and Helena Christina (Kopp) S.; m. Phyllis Joan VanSetters, June 6, 1952; children: Christine Marie, Philip Joseph, John Forrest. AA, Woodrow Wilson Jr. Coll., 1942; AB, Hope Coll., 1945; BD, Western Theol. Sem., Holland, Mich., 1953; ThD, Princeton Theol. Sem., 1956; PhD, U. Ill., 1972. Ordained to ministry Ref. Ch. in Am., 1955. Stated supply pastor Hickory Bottom Charge, Loysburg, Pa., 1957-58; prof. religion Northwestern Coll., Orange City, Iowa, 1959-90, prof. emeritus, 1990—; vis. prof. Lancaster (Pa.) Theol. Sem., 1956-57, Western Theol. Sem., Holland, Mich., 1958-59; v.p. Ref. Ch. in Am., N.Y.C., 1988-89, pres., 1989-90, moderator, exec. com., 1990-91. Co-editor: Concordance to the Greek and Hebrew Text of Ruth, The Computer Bible, Septuagint series, Vols. XXX, XXX-B, 1988-89; contbr. articles to profl. jours. County del. Iowa Dems., Ft. Dodge, 1984. Recipient Disting. Alumnus award Hope Coll., 1989, Homecoming Honors award Northwestern Coll. N Club, 1990, Handicapped Person of Siouxland award Siouxland Com. for the Handicapped, 1990, Gov.'s award Iowa Commn. of Persons with Disabilities, 1990. Mem. Internat. Orgn. for Septuagint and Cognate Studies, Smithsonian Instsn., Nat. Geog. Soc., Iowa State Chess Assn. (v.p. 1984-85, dir. postal tournament 1987). Avocations: chess, bridge. Home: 520 2d St SW Orange City IA 51041 Office: Northwestern Coll Orange City IA 51041

SCOTT, ALAN RAY, youth minister, evangelist; b. Gallup, N. Mex., May 2, 1960; s. Donald Boyd Scott and Mary Francis (Hartsock) Linville; m. Sherry Sue McCracken, May 9, 1987. Student, E. Ky. U., 1978-79; FCC 3rd class lic., Internat. Broadcasting Sch., Dayton, Ohio, 1980; BS in English Bible, Cin. Bible Coll., 1987. Youth min. Ferry Ch. of Christ, Wanesville, Ohio, 1985-88; evangelist Operation Evangelize, Chesapeake, Ohio, 1988—; youth min.. Plainville, Loogootee and Antioch Youth Ministry, Washington, Ind., 1988—. Author: Live It or Forget It, 1988; creator: PLA Youth Ministry, 1988. Home: 804 W Walnut Washington IN 47501 Office: PLA Youth Ministry 2008 Memorial Ave Washington IN 47501 *In ministering to youth, it seems futile to compete with the world and merely entertain a teenager. Youth ministry that challenges youth in worship, Bible study and service will develop kids with depth. Fun and games have their place in youth ministry, but they should only be the icing on the cake, not the whole cake.*

SCOTT, ALFRED JAMES, bishop; b. Gordon, Ala., Oct. 30, 1913; s. Benjamin Sidney and Mozell (Collins) S.; m. May Etta Hallaway, July 20, 1935 (dec. Nov. 1973); children: Rubbeanuion and Scylance Bruin (twins); m. Ruby Hill, Oct. 24, 1977. Cert., Theol. Ctr., Atlanta, 1970; student, Savannah State Coll., 1984-86. Ordained to ministry Christian Ch., 1941. Minister Triumph The Ch. and Kingdom of God in Christ, Atlanta, also U.S. and Africa, 1941—, dist. bishop, S.C., N.C. and Va., 1963—, presiding bishop, 17th and 3d Episc. dists., Savannah, and chief apostle, 1987—; pres. Evangel. Ministerial Alliance, Savannah, 1962-63, Interdenom. Ministerial Alliance, Savannah, 1972-73; founder Trikogic Inc., 1969; chief apostle Triumph the Ch. and King of God in Christ, 1987—, founder Sch. of Prophets, 1990. Author: Triumph As I Know It, 1989; starred in: (BBC series America) Firebell in the Night. Sec. Savannah Transi Authority, 1974-87; mem. Dem. Exec. Com., Savannah, 1974-87. Avocations: reading, current events and news. Home and Office: Triumph Ch Kingdom of God in Christ 1323 N 36th St Savannah GA 31404 *We teach life to come to the point where we may be transcended as Enoch and Elijah were. We also know (Cor. 15:51) that we shall not all sleep but we shall be changed.*

SCOTT, BERNARD BRANDON, religion educator; b. Louisville, Sept. 9, 1941; s. Bernard and Jennie Carol (Mitchell) S.; m. Marilyn Kay Henlein, Dec. 27, 1966; children: Mariah Jon, Jonathan Brandon. BA in Classics, St. Meinrad Sem., 1963; MA in Helllenistic Religion, Miami U., Oxford, Ohio, 1968; PhD in New Testament, Vanderbilt U., 1970. Prof. St. Meinrad (Ind.) Sem., 1971-88, Phillips Grad. Sem., Tulsa, 1988—; vis. prof. Yale Div. Sch., New Haven, 1986; mem. commn. on Hispanic edn. Assn. Theol. Schs., 1976-78. Author: Jesus Symbol-Maker for the Kingdom, 1981, The Word of God in Words, 1985, Hear Then the Parables, 1989; editor: The Gospel and the Church, 1981; editor SBL Sources for the Study of the Bible, 1986-90. Kendrich Gobel fellow, 1968-70, Woodrow Wilson fellow, 1970-71. Mem. Cath. Bibl. Soc. (assoc. editor 1989—), Soc. Bibl. Lit. (assoc. editor 1990—), Nat. Seminar on Sayings of Jesus, Soc. Novi Testamenti Studiorum. Home: 6306 E 78th St Tulsa OK 74136 Office: Phillips Grad Sem 600 S College Tulsa OK 74104

SCOTT, BLAKELY NELSON, clergyman; b. Columbia, S.C., Feb. 11, 1948; s. Blakely, Jr. and Lillie Mae (Neal) S.; m. Mary Cornell Brooks, Aug. 31, 1969. Student S.C. State Coll., 1965-68; A. in Acctg., Palmer Coll., 1974; BA, U. S.C., 1975; B.D., Morris Coll., 1980; M.Div. Lutheran Theol. Sem., 1987. Teller, So. Bell Co., Columbia, 1976-78; pastor Mill Creek Bapt. Ch., Columbia, 1977-79, Mt. Moriah Bapt. Ch., Hopkins, S.C., 1978—, 1st Nazareth Bapt. Ch., Columbia, 1979—; asst. dir. of aux. services Benedict Coll., Columbia, 1978—; moderator Wateree Bapt. Assn.-U.D., Columbia, 1982—, dean Young People's Christian Assembly, Benedict Coll., 1985—. Mem. Hospice Bd. Bapt. Med. Ctr., Columbia, 1983, Interdenominational Concert Choir Bd.; bd. dirs. Connie Maxwell Children's Home. Served with USAF, 1969-73. Recipient Living the Legacy award Nat. Council of Negro Women, 1982. Mem. Chamber of Bapt. Ministers, S.C. Bapt. Edn. and Missionary Conv., Nat. Bapt. Conv. of Am., Gethsemene Bapt. Assn. (exec. com. mem. 1983—, asst. sec.), Omega Psi Phi (chaplain 1983-84), Alpha Phi Omega (adv. 1981—). Lodge: Masons. Avocations: reading, fishing, carpentry. Home: 408 Portchester Dr Columbia SC 29203 Office: Benedict Coll Harden and Blanding Sts Columbia SC 29204

SCOTT, C. DOUGLAS, minister; b. Ft. Smith, Ark., Apr. 4, 1952; s. Clyde Daniel and Henretta (Stovall) S.; m. Deborah Diane Pearce, Feb. 15, 1975; children: Joseph D., Jared M. Student, Westark Jr. Coll. Minister United Pentecostal Ch., Coffeyville, Kans. Republican. Avocations: reading, hunting, fishing. Home: 3611 W 4th Coffeyville KS 67337 Office: 1st United Pentecostal Ch 3408 W 8th PO Box 248 Coffeyville KS 67337

SCOTT, DALE MONROE, minister; b. Childress, Tex., July 19, 1925; s. Ray William and Eula Lee (Hobbs) S.; m. Betty Lou, Aug. 10, 1951; children: Bonita Fae, Kenneth Dale, Ronald Keith. BA, Calif. Bapt. Coll., 1953; M of Religious Edn., Calif. Bapt. Theol. Seminary, Covina, 1955; PhD, Calif. Grad. Sch., Glendale, 1972. Tchr. Calif. State U., La Puente, 1955-56, Bapt. Day Sch., Van Nuys, Calif., 1956-64; pastor/counselor/youth dir. First Bapt. Ch., Van Nuys, 1964-78; prin. Bapt. Day Sch., Reseda, Calif., 1978-80; pastoral care minister Ch. at Rocky Peak, Chatsworth, Calif., 1980—; pres. Bapt. Day Sch. Orgn., So. Calif., 1958-64. With USN, 1944-46. Recipient Geri award L.A. County Coun., 1971, Tchr. of the Yr. award L.A. City Schs., 1979, Dionysion Class award Van Nuys High Sch. Class, 1972, Kiwanian of Yr. award., Van Nuys, 1974-75. Republican. Office: Church at Rocky Peak 22601 Santa Susana Pass Rd Chatsworth CA 91311

SCOTT, DALE PHILLIP, minister; b. Fresno, Calif., Dec. 25, 1955; s. Kenneth Milton and Zoe Zane (Schmuke) S.; m. Kimberly Joyce Bohigian, Nov. 18, 1978; children: Taylor Zane, Rachel Leigh. BA in Religion, Calif. State U., Fresno, 1978; MDiv, Princeton Theol. Sem., 1982. Ordained to ministry Presbyn. Ch., 1982. Program coord. Calvin Crest Conf., Oakhurst, Calif., 1978-80; intern Boonton (N.J.) Presbyn. Ch., 1980-81; chaplain Princeton (N.J.) Nursing Home, 1981-82; assoc. minister edn. Webster Groves Presbyn. Ch., Webster Grove, Mo., 1982-90; assoc. minister evangelism Second Presbyn. Ch., Bloomington, Ill., 1990—; del. Nat. Youth Workers Conf., 1982, 84, 87. Named Theologian of the Yr., Huguenot Soc., 1981. Republican. Office: Second Presbyn Ch 313 N East St Bloomington IL 61701

SCOTT, DOUGLAS GORDON, priest; b. Phila., Jan. 14, 1949; s. Robert Allen and Jean Hamilton (Torrey) S.; m. Jane Elizabeth Kirkby, Aug. 13, 1977; children: Claire Aileen, Mhari Gordon, Joy Francis. BA, Muskingum Coll., 1970; MDiv, Phila. Div. Sch., 1974; MST, Gen. Theol. Sem., 1979. Ordained priest Episcopal Ch., 1974. Asst. St. Mary's Ch., Wayne, Pa., 1974-75; staff assoc. Diocese of Pa., Phila., 1974-75; curate Ch. of Atonement, Tenafly, N.J., 1975-77; rector St. John the Divine, Hasbrouck Heights, N.J., 1977-80, Ch. St. Thomas of Canterbury, Smithtown, N.Y., 1980-84, St. Martin's Ch., Radnor, Pa., 1985—. Author: The Piobaireachd Index, 1978, Sharing the Faith, 1985, Managing Transitions, 1991; co-author: The Fast I Choose, 1976; contbr. articles to profl. jours. Chmn. Com. on Nutritional Alternatives, Phila., 1975; lectr. Alfred Noyes Med. Conf., Norristown, Pa., 1975; bd. dirs. R.E.A.C.H., Hasbrouck Heights, 1979, H.E.A.L., Smithtown, 1983-84; mem. community bd. St. John's Hosp., 1980-81, supr. Lay Chaplains Program, 1982-84; Episcopal chaplain St. Johnland Nursing Home, Kings Park, N.Y., 1980-84. Mem. Mensa, Intertel. Home: 400 King of Prussia Rd Radnor PA 19087 Office: St Martins Ch Radnor PA 19087

SCOTT, GAREY BAXTER, minister; b. Tucumcari, N.Mex., Jan. 13, 1942; s. William Henry and Hazel Lily (Young) S.; m. Paulette Greer, July 21, 1962; children: Cynthia Lynn, Garey Baxter Jr., Tammy Marie Scott Clausen. BS in Bus., Wayland Bapt. U., 1982; student, Southwestern Bapt. Theol. Sem., 1976-78. Assoc. pastor Travis Ave. Bapt. Ch., Ft. Worth, Tex., 1976-78; minister of edn., adminstrn. First Baptist Ch., Tulia, Tex., 1978-82, Forrest City, Ark., 1982-85; minister of edn., adminstrn. Immanuel Bapt. Ch., Pine Bluff, Ark., 1985—; asst. dir. Harmony Bapt. Assn., Pine Bluff, Ark., 1985—; cons. Ark. Bapt. State Conv., Little Rock, 1983—. Author: (booklet) New employee manual, 1975; editor Adminstrn. Jour., 1983—. Mem. Southern Bapt. Religious Educators, Nat. Assn. of Ch. Bus. Adminstn., Ark. Religious Educators (v.p., pres. 1985-86), Toastmasters Internat. Democrat. Avocations: hunting, fishing, backpacking, woodworking, computers. Home: 3616 Worth St #423-A Dallas TX 75246 Office: Immanuel Bapt Ch 1801 W 17th St Pine Bluff AR 71603

SCOTT, JAMES JULIUS, religion educator, clergyman; b. Decatur, Ga., Feb. 2, 1934; s. J. Julius and Tena Laverne (Schonert) S.; m. Florence Richardson, Sept. 2, 1958; children: Mary Eleanor, Julia Wymond, James Julius. BA, Wheaton (Ill.) Coll., 1956; BD, Columbia Theol. Sem., 1959; PhD, U. Manchester, Eng., 1969. Ordained to ministry Presbyn. Ch. in U.S.A., 1959. Asst. to pastor Westminster Presbyn. Ch., Atlanta, 1955-58; pastor Brandon (Miss.) Presbyn. Ch., 1959-61; prof., dept. chmn. Belhaven Coll., Jackson, Miss., 1963-70; prof. Western Ky. U., Bowling Green, 1970-77; prof. religion, chmn. dept. Wheaton Coll., 1977—. Contbr. articles to profl. jours. Named Tchr. of Yr., Belhaven Coll., 1969, Distinctive Tchr., Western Ky. U., 1976. Fellow Inst. Bibl. Rsch.; mem. Chgo. Soc. Bibl. Rsch., Evang. Theol. Soc., Soc. Bibl. Lit. Home: 924 Eddy Ct Wheaton IL 60187 Office: Wheaton Coll Grad Sch Dept Theol Studies Wheaton IL 60187

SCOTT, JEFFERY WARREN, minister; b. Akron, Ohio, Jan. 26, 1959; s. Homer and Edna Mae (Blanar) S.; m. Debbie Ann Barnwell, Nov. 1, 1980; children: Amy Beth, Brennan Marshall. BSBA, Georgetown U., 1980; MDiv, New Orleans Bapt. Theol. Sem., 1983, MRE, 1984; PhD in Religion, Baylor U., 1991. Ordained to ministry Am. Bapt. Chs., 1981. Assoc. pastor Wisconsin Ave. Bapt. Ch., Washington, 1980-81, pastor, 1988-90; asst. pastor Grace Temple Bapt. Ch., Waco, Tex., 1984-86; pastor First Bapt. Ch., Eddy, Tex., 1986-87, Broadman Bapt. Ch., Cuyahoga Falls, Ohio, 1990—; mem. nat. adv. coun. Americans United for Separation Ch. and State, Silver Spring, Md., 1989—. Contbr. articles and book revs. to profl. jours. Univ. scholar Baylor U., Waco, 1985-88. Mem. So. Bapt. Hist. Soc., Cuyahoga Falls Ministerial Assn. Home: 188 Sand Run Rd Akron OH 44313 Office: Broadman Bapt Ch 350 E Bath Rd Cuyahoga Falls OH 44223

SCOTT, LORINDA KAY, lay worker; b. Van Wert, Ohio, Mar. 17, 1964; d. James Dewey and Betty (Bell) McDowell; m. Arlen Jerome Scott, Oct. 4, 1980; 1 child, Arlen Jerome II. Caseworker/office mgr. Salvation Army, Marion, Ind., 1989—; coms. sec. Calvary Social Brethren Sun. Sch., Marion, 1989-90, jr. youth leader, 1990-91, piano player jr. ch., 1990-91, dir. vacation Bible sch., 1991. Office: The Salvation Army 2001 S Gallatin St Marion IN 46953

SCOTT, MARK ANDREW, clergyman; b. Kingsport, Tenn., Nov. 2, 1949; s. Herbert Andrew and Oneida (Covington) S.; m. Karen Greene, Aug. 24, 1974; children: Elise, Anna, Monica. BA, U. Va., 1971; MDiv, Luther Theol. Sem., Columbia, S.C., 1976. Ordained to ministry Evang. Luth. Ch., 1976. Pastor Gloria Dei Luth. Ch., Knoxville, Tenn., 1976-80, St. John's Luth. Ch., Atlanta, 1980—; chair North Ga. Conf., S.E. Synod Evang. Luth. Ch. Am., Atlanta, 1989—, Atlanta U. Luth. Campus Ministry, 1982-90; mem. program com. Luth. Theol. Ctr., Atlanta, 1988—; coord. for continuing edn. in region 9 Evang. Luth. Ch. Am., Atlanta, 1990—. Mem. Gwinnett Toastmasters (pres. 1985). Office: St Johns Luth Ch 1410 Ponce de Leon Ave Atlanta GA 30083

SCOTT, MICHAEL DEAN (MICK SCOTT), clergyman; b. Mpls., Mar. 2, 1957; s. Raymond W. and JoAnn E. (Rye) Scott; m. Kristin K. Johnson, June 6, 1981; children: Michael Jr., Angela, Rebecca, Jacob. AA, Normandale Coll., 1977; BS in Religious Edn., BA in Bible Theology, St. Paul Bible Coll., 1987; postgrad., Bethel Sem., St. Paul, 1987—, North Park Sem., Chgo., 1988—. Lic. to ministry Evang. Covenant Ch., 1986. Chaplain Peterson Funeral Homes, Buffalo, Minn., 1985-87, Retirement Ctr. Wright County, Buffalo, 1986—; pastor evangelism Buffalo Covenant Ch., 1987-90; mission pastor Monticello (Minn.) Covenant Ch., 1990—; Chem. dependency worker Buffalo Hosp., 1990—; grief issues speaker St. Paul Bible Coll., St. Cloud State U., Wright County Social Svcs.; conclave instr. N.W. Conf., Covenant Ch., Mpls., 1989, 91, small group cons., 1991. Author: Small Group Leaders, 1989. Bd. mem. State Mental Health Assn., Mpls., 1984-87; bd. chmn. Commn. on Adult Edn., Mpls., 1988-89; bd. mem. Monticello ECFE, 1990—, Buffalo Soccer Assn., 1987—. Pell grantee State of Minn., 1987; recipient Linnae Friberg scholarship Buffalo Covenant Ch., 1990, 91. Mem. Covenant Ministerial. Home: Rt 3 Box 100B Monticello MN 55362 Office: Monticello Covenant Ch PO Box 1405 Monticello MN 55362

SCOTT, MICHELE CATHERINE, minister; b. Cedar Rapids, Iowa, Nov. 7, 1954; d. Claude Joseph Jr. and Eileen Catherine (Fieth) Dellevar; m. John Taggert Scott, Sept. 11, 1953 (div. 1986). BA cum laude, Coe Coll., 1976; MA in Hebrew and Semitic Studies, U. Wis., 1979; MDiv, Andover Newton Theol., 1982. Ordained to ministry United Ch. Christ, 1984. Asst. minister First Congl. United Ch. Christ, Cedar Rapids, Iowa, 1983-84; minister Hope Congl. United Ch. Christ, Granville, N.D., 1984-87; campus minister Minot (N.D.) State U., 1984-87; minister Peace, United Ch. Christ, Walnut, Iowa, 1987—; lectr. Minot State U., 1985-86. chair youth and young adult com. Iowa United Ch. Christ, 1989—. Religious rels. com. Mid-Am. Coun. Boy Scouts, Omaha, 1990; dist. com. Wacampsa Dist. Mid-Am. Coun., Omaha, 1989; bd. trustees Peace Haven Retirement Home, Walnut, Iowa, 1987—; mem. Walnut Community Club, 1987—. Mem. Soc. for Bibl. Lit., Nat. United Ch. Christ Assn. of Scouters, Federated Garden Club. Office: Peace United Ch Christ 108 N Street Walnut IA 51577

SCOTT, NATHAN ALEXANDER, JR., minister, literary critic, religion educator; b. Cleve., Apr. 24, 1925; s. Nathan Alexander and Maggie (Martin) S.; m. Charlotte Hanley, Dec. 21, 1946; children: Nathan Alexander III, Leslie K. AB, U. Mich., 1944; BD, Union Theol. Sem., 1946; PhD, Columbia U., 1949; LittD, Ripon Coll., 1965, St. Mary's Coll., Notre Dame, Ind., 1969, Denison U., 1976, Brown U., 1981, Northwestern U., 1982, Elizabethtown Coll., 1989; LHD, Wittenberg U., 1965; DD, Phila. Div. Sch., 1967; STD, Gen. Theol. Sem., 1968; LHD, U. D.C., 1976; DD, The Protestant Episcopal Theological Seminary in Va., 1985; HumD, U. Mich., 1988; LHD, Wesleyan U., 1989, Bates Coll., 1990. Ordained priest Episcopal Ch., 1960; canon theologian Cathedral St. James, Chgo., 1967-76. dean of chapel, Va. Union U., 1946-47; instr. humanities, Howard U., 1948-51, asst. prof., 1951-53, assoc. prof., 1953-55; asst. prof. theology and literature, U. Chgo., 1955-58, assoc. prof., 1958-64, prof., 1964-72, Shailer Mathews prof. of theology and lit., 1972-76, prof. English, 1967-76; Commonwealth prof. religious studies, U. Va., 1976-81, William R. Kenan prof. religious studies, 1981—, prof. English, 1976—. Author: Rehearsals of Discomposure: Alienation and Reconciliation in Modern Literature, 1952, The Tragic Vision and the Christian Faith, 1957, Modern Literature and the Religious Frontier, 1958, Albert Camus, 1962, Reinhold Niebuhr, 1963, The New Orpheus: Essays toward a Christian Poetic, 1964, The Climate of Faith in Modern Literature, 1965, The Broken Center: Studies in the Theological Horizon of Modern Literature, 1966, Ernest Hemingway, 1966, The Modern Vision of Death, 1967, Adversity and Grace: Studies in Recent American Literature, 1968, Negative Capability: Studies in the New Literature and the Religious Situation, 1969, The Unquiet Vision: Mirrors of Man in Existentialism, 1969, The Wild Prayer of Longing: Poetry and the Sacred, 1971, Nathanael West, 1971, Three American Moralists: Mailer, Bellow, Trilling, 1973, The Poetry of Civic Virtue: Eliot, Malraux, Auden, 1976, Mirrors of Man in Existentialism, 1978, The Poetics of Belief: Studies in Coleridge, Arnold, Pater, Santayana, Stevens and Heidegger, 1985; co-editor Jour. Religion, 1963-77; adv. editor Religion and Lit., Literature and Theology, Callaloo, Modernist Studies: Literature and Culture; poetry editor First Things. Fellow Am. Acad. of Arts and Scis.; mem. Soc. Arts, Religion and Contemporary Culture, Soc. for Values in Higher Edn. (Kent fellow), MLA., Am. Acad. Religion (pres. 1986); mem. bd. govs. Horace H. Rackham Sch. Grad. Studies U. Mich., Century Assn. (N.Y.C.), Quadrangle Club, Arts Club (Chgo.), Greencroft Club (Charlottesville, Va.). Office: U Va Dept Religious Studies Charlottesville VA 22903

SCOTT, NATHAN TYLER, minister; b. Kansas City, Mo., Mar. 16, 1957; s. Harold Eldred and Alvina (Brink) S.; m. Sharon Elaine Osborn, Oct. 24, 1981; children: Noah Tyler, Jonathan Tyler, Zachary Tyler. BS in Pastoral Studies, North Cen. Bible Coll., Mpls., 1985. Pastor Elsberry (Mo.) Assembly of God, 1985-88; children's min. Northland Cathedral, Kansas City, Mo., 1987-89, youth min., 1989—; dist. alumni rep. North Cen. Bible Coll. Alumni Assn., 1987—; asst. dist. youth dir., No. Mo. Dist. Assemblies of God, Excelsior Springs, 1986—. Editor: (newspaper) YouthNews, 1989—. Instr. Red Cross, Kansas City, 1990. Office: Northland Cathedral 600 NE 46th St Kansas City MO 64116 *Zestful living comes from trusting God with our life, our happiness. Life can only be fully enjoyed by recognizing God does all things right.*

SCOTT, OLOF HENDERSON, JR., priest; b. Phila., May 13, 1942; s. Olof Henderson and Julia Irene (Rutroff) S.; m. Eva Jakowenko, Sept. 13, 1969; children: Lisa Ann, Christopher Olof, Timothy Nicholas. BA in Physics, Franklin and Marshall Coll., 1964; MS in Nuclear Engring., Pa. State U., 1966; postgrad., St. Vladimir's Orthodox Theol. Sem., 1975-76. Ordained deacon Antiochian Orthodox Christian Ch., 1975, priest, 1976, archpriest, 1988. Pastor St. George Orthodox Ch., Charleston, W.Va., 1976—; dean of clergy Appalachian-Ohio Valley Deanery, 1976—; spiritual advisor NAC-SOYO of Archdiocese, 1977-82; mem. exec. bd. W.Va. Coun. Chs., 1977—; bd. govs. Nat. Coun. Chs., 1977—, mem. nominating com., 1979-81, exec. com., 1985—, membership com., 1988—. Contbr. articles to profl. jours. Mem. long-range planning com. W.Va. State Rep. Exec. Com., 1985-87. Mem. Acad. Parish Clergy (pres. W.Va. chpt. 1983-85), Am. Nuclear Soc., St. Vladimir's Theol. Found., Charleston Ministerial Assn., Order of St. John of Jerusalem-Knights Hospitellers (chaplain 1985—), Soc. for Preservation and Encouragement Barbershop Quartet Singing in Am., Inc. (v.p. 1984-85), Pa. State Club W.Va. (pres. 1984-88), Sigma Pi Sigma. Avocations: camping, barbershop quartet, motorcycling. Home: 4409 Staunton Ave SE Charleston WV 25304 Office: St George Orthodox Ch Po Box 2044 Charleston WV 25327 *My thoughts on life are but mere recitations of the Holy Scripture and my feeble attempts at making Those words and Thoughts my own.*

SCOTT, PAUL, religious organization administrator. Pres. Internat. Coun. of Community Chs., Homewood, Ill. Office: Community Chs Internat Coun 900 Ridge Rd LL1 Homewood IL 60430*

SCOTT, RICHARD BAKER, minister; b. Scotts Bluff, Nebr., Nov. 10, 1928; s. John David and Ethel May (Baker) S.; m. Dorothy Mae Meline, Dec. 14, 1947; children: Rhonda Rae, Radene Fae, ReVona Marie, Ricarda Jolene. BSL, Boise Bible Coll., 1954; EMT, Trease Valley Community Coll., Ontario, Oreg., 1972. Ordained to ministry, Christian Ch./Ch. of Christ, 1954. Asst. minister Cen. Christian Ch., Colorado Springs, Colo., 1954-56; minister Ch. of Christ, Sturgis, S.D., 1956-63, Kingsford, Mich., 1963-65, Glendive, Mont., 1965-66, Vale, Oreg., 1966-76, Enterprise, Oreg., 1976-78, Garibaldi, Oreg., 1978-83, Pendleton, Oreg., 1983-88, Weiser, Idaho, 1988—; trustee Boise Bible Coll., 1978-90; bd. dirs., treas. N.W. Christian Camp, Boise; bd. dirs. Dakota Evangelism Assn., Sturgis, 1957-63; chaplain Ft. Mead VA Hosp., Sturgis, 1960-63, Civil Air Patrol, Ontario, 1970-76, others in past. Pres. Washington County Sr. Citizens, Weiser, 1991—; chaplain Oreg. N.G. Res., 1985—. Home: 1295 E 2nd St Weiser ID 83672 Office: Christian Ch 1299 E 2nd St Weiser ID 83672

SCOTT, RICKY LYNN, minister; b. McMinnville, Tenn., Nov. 5, 1958; d. Nealy Milburn and Charlene (Bain) S.; m. Teresa Kay Goodwin, Nov. 5, 1983; 1 child: Haleigh Alexandra. Student, Auburn (Tenn.) Bible Inst., 1981-82, Clear Creek Bapt. Bible Coll., 1986-87. Ordained to ministry So. Bapt. Conv., 1983. Pastor Welchland Bapt. Ch., Spencer, Tenn., 1982-84, Pleasant View Bapt. Ch., Woodbury, Tenn., 1985-86, New Hope Bapt. Ch., Alexandria, Tenn., 1986—; evangelism chmn. Cen. Bapt. Assn., McMinnville, 1983-84. Sec. Alexandria Neighborhood Watch, 1990—. Mem. Salem Bapt. Assn. (missions com. chmn. 1986-89, asst. clk. 1990-91). Home: 204 E Main St Alexandria TN 37012 Office: New Hope Bapt Ch Rte 1 Alexandria TN 37012 *I want to be faithful as a pastor, preacher, parent and person and one day hear those words from the lips of our Lord, "Well done, thou good and faithful servant."*

SCOTT, ROBERT HAL, minister; b. Floydada, Tex., Apr. 2, 1930; s. Samuel Price and Fannie (Miller) S.; m. Carolyn Weaver, July 31, 1950; children: Vicki Lynette Reese, Steven Robert Scott. BA, Pasadena Coll., 1950; DD, Point Loma Coll., 1983. Ordained to ministry Ch. of the Nazarene, 1953. Pastor various Chs. of the Nazarene, Calif., 1950-75; dist. supt. Ch. of the Nazarene/So. Calif. Dist., Orange, Calif., 1975-86; dir. world mission Ch. of the Nazarene, Kansas City, Mo., 1986—; trustee Pasadena (Calif.) Coll., 1964-75, Point Loma Coll., San Diego, Calif., 1975-86, Nazarene Bible Coll., Colorado Springs, 1976-80. Contbr. articles to World Mission mag., 1986-91. Office: Internatl Hdqtrs Ch of the Nazarene 6401 The Paseo Kansas City MO 64131

SCOTT, T. T., bishop. Bishop of No. Miss., Ch. of God in Christ, Clarksdale. Office: Ch of God in Christ 1066 Barnes Ave Clarksdale MS 38614*

SCOTT, TIMOTHY DEAN, minister; b. Council Bluffs, Iowa, Apr. 12, 1964; s. Robert A. and Cecil M. (Grice) S.; m. Julie Ann McClarnon, Aug. 21, 1987. 1990-91; BTh., Ozark Christian Coll., Joplin, Mo., 1987; postgrad., N.E. Mo. State U., 1990-91. Ordained to ministry Christian Ch., 1989. Sr. minister Countryside Christian Ch., West Plains, Mo., 1985-86; dir. Joplin Family Y, 1986-87; sr. minister Hornet Christian Ch., Joplin, Mo., 1987—; campus min. Campus Christian Fellowship, Kirksville, Mo., 1989-91; min. to football team Ind. U. Campus Christian Ministry, Bloomington, Ind., 1991—; min. Ind. U. Football Team, 1991—; traveling evangelist, musician. Composer Christian songs. Vol. Joplin United Way, 1986-87; leader S.W. 4H Club, 1988—; vol. in corrections State of Mo., 1989—; vol. hosp. chaplain Kirksville Hosps., 1990—. Republican. Home: 906 N Blair Ave Bloomington IN 47404 Office: Ind U Christian Campus Min 707 E 8th St Bloomington IN 47408

SCOTT, WALDRON, mission executive; b. Kansas City, Kans., July 14, 1929; s. Waldron and Audrean (Spurgeon) S.; m. Georgia Dyke; children by previous marriage—Melody, Cheryl, Gregory, Douglas, Linda. B.A., Am. U., Beirut, 1953. Dir. The Navigators, Washington, 1954-59, Middle East and Africa, 1960-66, Asia/Australia, 1967-72; internat. field dir. The Navigators, Colorado Springs, Colo., 1973-74; gen. sec. World Evang. Fellowship, Colorado Springs, 1975-80; pres. Am. Leprosy Missions, Elmwood Park, N.J., 1981-84, Holistic Ministries Internat., Paterson, N.J., 1985—; bd. dirs. Passaic County Cultural and Heritage Coun., Christian Leadership in Higher Edn., adv. coun. Passaic County Human Svcs., Paterson YMCA, Scheffelin Rsch. and Tng. Ctr., Ch. World Svc., Div. Overseas Ministries' Nat. Coun. Chs., Vellore Christian Med. Coll., Paterson Community Health Ctr. Author: Bring Forth Justice; Karl Barth's Theology of Mission; editor: Serving our Generation. Chmn. Paterson Council Social Services, Citizens Alliance for a Drug Free Paterson. Mem. Leadership Paterson Alumni Assn., Am. Soc. Missiology, Nat. Assn. Evangelicals, Evangelicals for Social Action. Mem. Christian Reformed Ch. Office: Holistic Ministries Internat PO Box 2288 Paterson NJ 07509

SCOVIL, LARRY EMERY, minister; b. Conneaut, Ohio, Dec. 1, 1950; s. Lynn Edgar and Shirley Jean (Cook) S.; m. Kristine Adell Schulz, Dec. 19, 1970; children: Jennifer, Jarin, Lindsay. B. Music Edn., U. Wis., Oshkosh, 1972; MDiv, Bethel Theol. Sem., 1987. Ordained to ministry Conservative Congl. Christian Conv., 1976. Pastor Zoar Congl. Ch., Mott, N.D., 1975-81, Calvary Evang. Congl. Ch., St. Paul, 1981-86, Emmanuel Congl. Ch., Scottsbluff, Nebr., 1986—; bd. dirs. Conservative Congl. Christian Conf., St. Paul, 1988-91, rec. sec., 1991—, Rocky Mountain area rep., 1989—. Writer, arranger musical: Joy To The World, 1990. Mem. Panhandle Evang. Ministerial Assn. (pres. 1990—). Republican. Office: Emmanuel Congl Ch 301 W 40th St Scottsbluff NE 69361

SCUDDER, ROBERT, minister, youth home administrator; b. Monroe, LA., May 1, 1926; s. Lee and Aldyth (Flenniken) S.; m. Mary Nichols, Oct. 28, 1967; children: Lee, Doug, Vicki, Dana. BA in Human Behavior, Newport U., Newport Beach, Calif., 1983. Ordained to ministry So. Bapt. Conv., 1979. Min., tchr. Books 'n Tapes, Shreveport, La., 1974—; counselor Shreveport Counsel Ctr., 1975-80; asst. pastor Woodlawn Bapt. Ch., Shreveport, 1976; exec. dir., adminstr. Joy Home for Boys, Greenwood, La., 1979—; bd. dirs. Johnny Robinson Youth Shelter, Monroe, 1980—; mem. licensing bd. Dept. Health and Hosps. for Group Homes and Adoptions, State of La., 1986-88, 89—. Author: Genesis, 1976, Cults Exposed, 1981, Customs and Prayer, 1983; also child care pamphlet. Served with USN, 1941-43, PTO. Mem. Am. Assn. on Mental Deficiency (religious v.p. 1984-86, Kiwanis (pres. 1971-72, Child Care award 1984). Home: Box 550 Greenwood LA 71033 Office: Joy Home for Boys Box 550 Greenwood LA 71033

SCULLY, TIMOTHY RICHARD, priest, political science educator; b. Evanston, Ill., Jan. 18, 1954; s. Thomas Francis and Elizabeth Ann (Joyce) S. BA in Econ., U. Notre Dame, 1976, MDiv in Theology, 1979; MA in Polit. Sci., U. Calif., Berkeley, 1985, PhD in Polit. Sci., 1989. Ordained priest Roman Cath. Ch., 1981. Treas. Holy Cross Fathers, Santiago, Chile, 1980-83; asst. rector St. George's Coll., Santiago, 1980-83; asst. pastor Christ Our Redeemor Parish, Santiago, 1980-83; asst. prof. dept. govt. U. Notre Dame, 1989; sr. fellow Kellogg Inst. for Internat. Studies, Notre Dame, 1989—. Author: Rethinking the Center, 1991; co-author: Building Democratic Institutions, 1992. Recipient award Social Sci. Rsch. Coun., N.Y., 1989; Fulbright fellow Dept. Edn., 1988; FMRD Found. grantee, 1990. Mem. Phi Beta Kappa. Office: Kellogg Inst Notre Dame IN 46556

SEABLOM, SARA IRENE (SIS), minister; b. Grand Rapids, Mich., June 16, 1947; d. Max Leland Eckert and Jean Evelyn Campbell; adopted d. Ralph Lamar Fitts and Catherine Stella Thomson; m. Larry Arnold Hill, June 16, 1967 (div. Feb. 1971); 1 child, Cindy Lynn; m. Gordon Thomas Seablom, Nov. 28, 1976; children: Samson Sabbath, John Lamar, Edward Thomas, David Gordon; 1 stepchild, Jennifer Lynn. Student, No. Mich. U., 1966, 76, Andrews U., 1979-82. Ordained to ministry, 1991. Founder, pres., pastor Sonshine Ministries, San Marcos, Tex., 1983—; assoc. chaplain Chapel at the Summit, Canyon Lake, Tex., 1989-90; head capt. Andrews, mem. counseling hotline Andrews U., Berrien Spring, Mich., 1980-81; owner Sonshine Answering Svc.; sec. Sonshine Plumbing; prin., tchr., libr. Sonshine Sch. Author: True Stories-My Life, Total Living With Christ, Sonshine Songbook, Sonshine Counseling Manual, Daily Double Sevens, 1991. Assoc. mem. Helpline 512-353 HELP, Ch. Mobile Ministries; active various community orgns. Mem. San Marcos Ministerial Assn. Home and Office: 702-A Harmons Way San Marcos TX 78666 *In total living with Christ, the King, we are princes and princesses in His healthy kingdom emotionally, mentally, and physically. His daily double 7's and Luke 9:23 are the way—live, share.*

SEABORN, JOSEPH WILLIAM, JR., religion educator; b. Pickens, S.C., Mar. 23, 1954; s. Joseph and Betty Seaborn; m. Mary Margaret Seaborn, June 6, 1975; children: Mary Joy, Joseph. BA, Cen. Wesleyan U., Central, S.C., 1976; MDiv, Asbury Theol. Sem., Wilmore, Ky., 1979; ThM, Harvard U., 1982; ThD, Boston U., 1984. Teaching asst. Asbury Theol. Sem., Wilmore, 1979; assoc. prof. Ea. Nazarene Coll., Quincy, Mass., 1980-84; prof., chair div. religion Ind. Wesleyan U., Marion, 1984—. Author: God Does Word Processing, 1989, Celebration of Ministry, 1991. Bd. dirs. Lifetouch Ministries, Marion, 1984-87, Lifetime Ministries, Marion, 1987—. Recipient Sears Teaching award Sears Roebuck Inc., 1990. Mem. Soc. Bibl. Lit., Wesleyan Theol. Soc. Wesleyan. Home: 6960 S Maple Dr Marion IN 46953 Office: Ind Wesleyan U 4201 S Washington Marion IN 46953

SEABRIGHT, RUSSELL FREDERICK, religion educator; b. Wheeling, W.Va., June 22, 1934; s. Russell Frederick and Helen Anna (Custer) S.; m. Bonnie Jean Holman, Apr. 24, 1965; children: Leanne Marie, Duane Holman, Dwight William. BA, Gettysburg Coll., 1956; MDiv, Luth. Theol. Sem., 1959; D Ministry, United Theol. Sem., 1984. Ordained to ministry Evang. Luth. Ch. Am., 1959. Pastor Resurrection Luth. Ch., Hilliard, Ohio, 1967-72; chaplain Luth. Social Svcs., Columbus, Ohio, 1972-75, Good Shepherd Home, Ashland, Ohio, 1975-78; assoc. prof. in contextual edn. Luth. Sem., Columbus, 1978-89; assoc. prof. in ministry and field edn. Union Theol. Sem., N.Y.C., 1989—. Contbr. articles, sermons to profl. publs. Mem. Assn. Practical Theology, Assn. for Theol. Field Edn. (vice chair 1987-89, chair, 1989-91). Democrat. Office: Union Theol Sem 3041 Broadway New York NY 10027

SEABROOK, BRADLEY M., deacon; b. Savannah, Ga., Mar. 12, 1928; s. Bradley and Katie Lou (Carpenter) S.; m. Minnie Lucile Long, May 14, 1951; children: Criss, Lilla, Tina, Lisa. B Tech. in Indsl. Tech., Fla. Internat. U., 1979. Ordained deacon Roman Cath. Ch., 1980; lic. mechanic-airframe power plant. Mem. Diocesan Stewardship Commn Diocese Pensacola-Tallahassee (Fla.), 1976-79, dir. Office Black Cath. Ministry, 1986—; pastoral minister St. Anthony of Padua Parish, Pensacola, Fla., 1980—. With USN, 1946-48, USAF, 1951-55. Mem. KC (grand knight 1975-76). Democrat. Home: PO Box 702 Cantonment FL 32533 Office: Diocese of Pensacola Tallahassee PO Drawer 17329 Pensacola FL 32522

SEABROOK, JOHN GUILDS, JR., minister; b. Charleston, S.C., June 12, 1946; s. John Guilds and Frances (Guilds) S.; m. Anne Donaldson, Aug. 30, 1969; children: Sean Donaldson, April Carson. AB in English, Wofford Coll., 1968; MDiv, Princeton Seminary, 1971; ThM, Columbia Seminary, Decatur, Ga., 1991. Assoc. pastor First Presbyn. Ch., Gainesville, Fla., 1971-75; pastor Allendale (S.C.) Presbyn. Ch., 1975-78, Northminster Presbyn. Ch., Huntsville, Ala., 1978—; moderator North Ala. Presbytery, 1991. Pres. Ala. Friends of Adoption, Huntsville, 1984, Meadow Hills Initiative Neighborhood Assn., Huntsville, 1987—; bd. dirs., v.p. The Key, Huntsville, 1986-87. Recipient Fulbright scholarship Univ. Edinburgh, 1968-69, Community Svc. award Community Action Agy., Huntsville, 1990, Martin Luther King, Jr. Unity award Alpha Phi Alpha, Huntsville, 1991. Home: 2425 Gaboury Lane NE Huntsville AL 35811 Office: Northminster Presbyn Ch 4901 Meml Pkwy NW Huntsville AL 35810

SEABURG, CURTIS IRVING, II, minister; b. Albany, N.Y., Oct. 10, 1965; s. Curtis Irving Sr. and Donna Lee (Froehlich) S.; m. Pamela Jean Wilson, Aug. 16, 1987; children: Elissa Jean, Kiersten Ashley. Diploma in Bible, Zion Bible Inst., Barrington, R.I., 1987; BS, Valley Forge Christian Coll., 1989. Minister of youth Evangel Assembly of God, Ephrata, Pa., 1987-90, Calvary Assembly of God, Dover, Del., 1990—; pastor Solid Rock Youth Ministry, Dover, 1990—; dir. Cornerstone Worship Band, Dover, 1990—. Author: (manuals) Reconstruction, Youth Alive: Where to Start. Bd. dirs. Nursing Home Ministry, Ephrata, 1988-90. Mem. Zion Alumni Assn., Valley Forge Alumni. Home: 848 Woodcrest Dr Apt B-3 Dover DE 19901 Office: Calvary Assembly of God 1141 E Lebanon Rd Dover DE 19901 *One of the greatest lessons a youth leader can learn is that youths do not want some to be like them, they want someone they can be like.*

SEALY, VERNOL ST. CLAIR, scientist; came to U.S., 1962; m. Josephine Doreen Nanton, May 8, 1965; children: Vernetta, Vernol Jr. Gen. cert. edn., U. London, 1962; LLB, La Salle Ext. U., Chgo., 1967; BS in Zoology, Howard U., 1968, Med. Tech. cert., 1969, MS in Microbiology, 1971; MPH, U. Mich., 1974; PhD in Religion summa cum laude, Trinity Theol. Sem., Newburgh, Ind., 1988; Cultural Doctorate in Sacred Philosophy, World U., Tucson, 1984. Ordained to ministry Seventh-day Adventist Ch. as elder, 1978; registered microbiologist. Elder Seventh-day Adventist Ch.; mem. adminstrv. bd. Seventh-day Adventist Ch., Ann Arbor, Mich., 1975-81, Ypsilanti, Mich., 1981-84; dir. personal ministries Seventh-day Adventist Ch., Ypsilanti, 1981-82; mem. adminstrv. bd. Oakwood Seven-day Adventist Ch., Melvindale, Mich., 1986—; med. technologist D.C. Gen. Hosp., 1970-73; clin. lab. hematologist St. Joseph Mercy Hosp., 1973—; with nursing, neuro-psychiatry unit Freedmen's Hosp., Howard U., Washington; conducted M.S. rsch. NIH, 1970-71. Past mem. Boy's Scout Assn.; commandant Brit. Red Cross Soc. Fellow Royal Soc. Health; mem. Adventist Theol. Soc., Am. Soc. Clin. Pathologists (cert. med. technologist, hematologist), N.Y. Acad. Scis., Internat. Biog. Assn. (life patron), Am. Biog. Inst. and Rsch. Assn. (rsch. bd. advisors, dep. gov. 1988—). Home: 3667 Helen Ave Ypsilanti MI 48197 *To know the Creator-Redeemer God and to be like Him, is man's highest destiny. To reveal His presence through a constant exhibition of His love, is to know Him, and to be like Him: For God is Love.*

SEAMAN, WILLIAM A., minister. Exec. dir. Lehigh County Conf. Chs., Allentown, Pa. Office: Lehigh County Conf Chs 36 S 6th St Allentown PA 18101*

SEARLE, HELEN WOODWARD, lay worker; b. Reno, Nev., Sept. 28, 1946; d. Orator Frank and Dorothy Ann (Reid) Woodward; m. James Albert Searle, Jan. 17, 1970 (div. May 1986); children: James Albert III, Jane Alexandra, Julie Ann. Student, U. of Geneva, Switzerland, 1964-66, Lancaster Community Coll., 1984, Greenbrier Community Coll., 1986, 88. Sunday sch. tchr. Emmanuel Ch., Geneva, Switzerland, 1965-66, Bethesda-By-The-Sea, Palm Beach, Fla., 1966-69; CCD tchr. St. Catherine's, Ronceverte, W.Va., 1972-74, St. Charles Borromeo Ch., 1983—; sales clk., ad rep. La Pasha, Palm Beach, Fla., 1967; asst. mgr. Gucci, Inc. of Palm Beach, 1967-69; pers. bus. Creations of Sorts, White Sulphur Springs, W.Va., 1990—; creative instr. Mountain Laurel Garden Club, Greenbrier East High Sch., 1986-90; contbg. writer, mktg. dir. Down Home Publs., 1991—. Columnist Weekly Saint Column, Herb columns The Mountain Messenger, Lewisburg, W.Va., 1985-91. Therapy asst. Crippled Children's Ctr., Palm Beach, 1967; den leader White Sulphur Springs (W.Va.) Cub Scouts, 1978-81; field day chmn. Area V Black Diamond Girl Scout Coun., 1984; SME chmn. White Sulphur Springs (W.Va.) Area Black Diamond Girl Scout Coun., 1984-86; bd. dirs. Black Diamond Girl Scout Coun., 1984-88, nominating com. 1986-90; pres. Old White Garden Club, White Sulphur Springs, 1974-76, 84-85, city coun. rep. 1988—; bd. sec. Greenbrier Valley Econ. Devel. Corp., 1989-90; chmn. ann. Show-Me-Hike Spring Wildflower Tour, 1983—; others. Mem. White Sulphur Springs (W.Va.) C. of C. (sec., corr. sec. 1984-89, corr. sec. 1990—). Roman Catholic. Home: Box 94 Big Draft Rd White Sulphur Spring WV 24986 *My thoughts on life—be true to yourself, be strong and your strength will carry you through.*

SEARS, WILLIAM BERNARD, religious organization leader; b. Duluth, Minn., Mar. 28, 1911; s. Frank Cyril and Ethel M. (Wagner) S.; m. Kathleen Fox (dec. 1938); m. Marguerite Reimer, Sept. 29, 1939; children: William, Michael. Student, U. Wis. Broadcaster Sta. WCAU; with local spiritual assemblies N.Y.C. and Johannesburg (Republic of South Africa), 1956-58; chmn. Nat. Spiritual Assembly, south and west Africa; hand of the cause, chief stewart Baha'i Faith. Author, producer internat. quiz BBC; author 10 books. Address: Nat Spiritual Assembly of Bahais of the US Bahai National Ctr Wilmette IL 60091

SEAY, FREDERICK NEWSOME, minister; b. Pascagoula, Miss., May 5, 1963; s. Houston Kendrick and Glenmary (Newsome) S.; m. Ruth Arriaga, Dec. 30, 1989. BA, U. So. Miss., 1985; postgrad., Reformed Sem., Jackson, Miss., 1985-87; MDiv, Austin Presbyn. Theol. Sem., 1989. Ordained to ministry Presbyn. Ch., 1991. Pastor Shepherd of the Hills Presbyn. (USA)-Am. Bapt. Ch., Morenci, Ariz., 1990—; vol. in mission Puentes de Cristo, McAllen, Tex., 1987-89. Home: 106 Turner Ave Clifton AZ 85533 Office: Shepherd of the Hills Ch PO Box 1212 Burro Alley Morenci AZ 85540

SEAY, JOSEPH CARLTON, III, minister, postal service worker; b. Moultrie, Ga., Apr. 12, 1949; s. Joseph Carlton Jr. and Ruthie Lee (Carswell) S.; m. Jacqueline Ardrey Gooden, Aug. 29, 1987; children; Kush, Ronald. BA, Richmond (Va.) Sem., 1982, MDiv, 1984, DD (hon.), 1988. Lic. to ministry Missionary Bapt. Chs., 1974, ordained, 1980. Spl. Delivery carrier U.S. P.O., Richmond, 1973—; pastor Mount Pleasant Bapt. Ch., Providence Forge, Va., 1983-87, Oak Hill Bapt. Ch., Buckingham, Va., 1985—; moderator North River Bapt. Assn., Buckingham, 1986—; pastor Slate River Bapt. Ch., Buckingham, 1987—, Chief Cornerstone Bapt. Ch., Dillwyn, Va., 1989—; mem. Bapt. Gen. Conv. Va., 1986—. Contbg. author: A Proverb a Day, 1984; contbr. articles to jours. in field. Bd. dirs. U.S. Army Chaplain Fund, Karlsrue, Fed. Republic Germany, 1971-73; chapel supr. USAR, Richmond, 1977-84; evang. chmn. Gospel Music Workshop, Richmond, 1979-83; trustee Richmond, Va. Sem., 1982—; mem. Historic Buckingham Inc., 1988; bd. dirs. Providence Court Townhouse Assn., Chesterfield, Va., 1988; pres. Buckingham Land Orgn., 1991. Sgt. U.S. Army, 1967-73; staff sgt. USAR/Va. N.G., 1977-84. Mem. DAV, Am. Postal Workers Union, Am. Legion, Odd Fellows (sec. 1973—). Home: 8170 Clovertree Ct Richmond VA 23235-5366 Office: North River Bapt Assn Box 547 Dillwyn VA 23936 *Communication is the key to understanding. Surely, if we would communicate with God and understand, our problems with mankind will be defeated.*

SEBESAN, DENNIS JOHN, minister; b. Wilmington, Del., Feb. 18, 1947; s. Ivan John and Mary Constance (Garchinsky) S.; m. Ann McKnight Breeze, June 12, 1970; children: Ashley Paige, Heather Carol. AA, Goldey Beacom Coll., Wilmington, 1966; BS, E. Carolina U., 1969; MS, U. Ark., 1973; D in Ministry, Union Theol. Sem., Richmond, Va., 1981. Ordained to ministry Presbyn. Ch., 1981. Acct. U.S. Gen. Acctg. Office, Norfolk, Va., 1969, Peat Marwick Mitchell & Co., Raleigh, N.C., 1973-75, State of N.C. Dept. Social Services, Raleigh, 1975-77; pastor 1st Presbyn. Ch., Andalusia, Ala., 1981-86; pastor, head of staff 1st Presbyn. Ch., Bluefield, W.Va., 1986—. Mem. Gov.' Council on Child Abuse, Montgomery, Ala., 1983-86; bd. dirs., sponsor Covington County Parents Anonymous, Andalusia, 1983-86. Served with USN, 1969-73. Mem. Greater Bluefield Ministerial Assn. (sec. 1987-88), Beta Gamma Sigma. Home: 1324 Whitethorn St Bluefield WV 24701 Office: 1st Presbyn Ch 208 Tazwell St Bluefield WV 24701

SECKEL, CAROL ANN, conference superintendent; b. Bklyn., Oct. 28, 1949; d. Leonard Immanuel and Anna Beth (Eggleston) Klotz; m. Richard Kevin Seckel, June 27, 1970; children: Joshua Allen, Jason Andrew, Jeremy Jacob. B in Edn., U. Toledo, 1971; MDiv, MA in Christian Edn, Meth. Theol. Sch. Ohio, 1978. With Stouffer's Restaurant, Toledo, 1971-72; pre-sch. tchr. Liberty Community Ctr., Delaware, Ohio, 1972-73; co-dir. work study program Early Childhood Ctr., Methesco, Delaware, 1977-78; co-pastor numerous chs., Middleburg, Ohio, 1975-78, Chiloquin, Oreg., 1978-82; pastor Sitka (Alaska) United Meth. Ch., 1982-86; dist. supt. Oreg. Idaho Conf. United Meth. Ch., Salem, Oreg., 1986-88; conf. supt. Alaska Missionary Conf. United Meth. ch., Anchorage, 1988—; co-presenter United Meth. Bishops Com. on Faithful Disciples-Vital Congregation, Nashville, 1987. Mem., pres. bd. dirs. Klamath County Women's Crisis Ctr., Klamath Falls, Oreg., 1979-82, Sitkans Against Family Violence, Sitka, 1983-86; trustee Willamette U., Salem, 1986-88, Alaska Pacific U., Anchorage, 1988—; mem. Community Choir, Sitka, 1983-85; v.p. Tongass coun. Girl Scouts U.S., 1984-86. Fellowship United Meths. in Worship, Music and Other Arts. Democrat. Avocations: hiking, music, cross-country skiing, cross-stitching. Office: 3402 Wesleyan Dr Anchorage AK 99508 *Too many times we have chosen to be satisfied with the way things are. Those who work for peace and justice must stay alert. By the grace of God I pray we will never lose our vision of hope.*

SEDGWICK, HAROLD BEND, minister; b. St. Paul, Feb. 13, 1908; s. Theodore and Mary Aspinwall (Bend) S. BA, Harvard U., 1930; BD, Episc. Theol. Sch., 1935. Ordained to ministry Episcopal Ch., 1935. Asst. Christ Ch., Cambridge, Mass., 1935-38; rector All Saints' Ch., Brookline, Mass., 1938-48, St. Thomas Ch., Washington, 1948-57, Emmanuel Ch., Boston, 1957-62; canon St. Paul's Cathedral, Boston, 1962-75, lectr., preacher, 1975—, trustee, pres., 1976—. Contbr. articles to religious jours. Mem. Soc. of Men for Ministry, Bostonian Soc., Friends of Boston Common, Soc. Colonial Wars, Order of Founders and Patriots Am., Descendants of Signers of Declaration of Independence (nat. chaplain gen. 1973—), New Eng. Hist. Geneal. Soc. Home: Brookhaven at Lexington 1010 Waltham St F 24 Lexington MA 02173

SEDGWICK, TIMOTHY FOSTER, religion educator; b. Melrose Park, Ill., Dec. 6, 1946; s. Roger Stanley and Virginia May (Karau) S.; m. Martha Wallace Wilkinson, Aug. 24, 1968; children: Sarah Wallace, Ellen Foster. AB, Albion Coll., 1969; PhD, Vanderbilt U., 1975. Asst. prof. Denison U., Granville, Ohio, 1975-76, Marshall U., Huntington, W.Va., 1976-77, Blackburn Coll., Carlinville, Ill., 1977-78; prof. Christian ethics and moral theology Seabury-Western Theol. Sem., Evanston, Ill., 1978—; mem. adv. bd. Westminster Libr. Theol. Ethics; mem. nat. couns. and coms. Episcopal Ch. Author: Sacramental Ethics, 1987; mem. editorial bd. Anglican Theol. Rev.; also articles. Mem. Soc. Christian Ethics, Conf. Anglican Theologians. Home: 2135 Orrington Evanston IL 60201 Office: Seabury-Western Theol Sem 2122 Sheridan Rd Evanston IL 60201

SEDINGER, KATHY JO, church lay worker; b. McKeesport, Pa., June 25, 1953; d. Alvin John Jr. and Pauline Katherine (Szubra) S. BS, Rio Grande (Ohio) U., 1975; postgrad., Liberty Home Bible Inst., Lynchburg, Va., 1989-90. Lic. lay reader Episcopal Diocese Pitts., 1989; cert. tchr., Ohio. Tchr. vacation Bible sch. Olivet Presbyn. Ch., West Elizabeth, Pa., 1970-73, St. Mary's Episcopal Ch., Charleroi, Pa., 1989-90; intermediate Sunday sch. tchr., editor monthly paper St. Mary's Episcopal Ch., Charleroi, 1986—; tertiary 3d order Soc. of Ft. Francis, San Francisco, 1987-90, assoc., 1990—; mem. Christian Edn. Commn., Cherleroi, 1991—; dir. vacation Bible Sch. Combined Chs. Charleroi, 1991—; 1st v.p. St. Mary's Episcopal Ch. Women's Group, 1990-91, pres., 1991—; vol. Christian Life Missions, 1990—; welder equipment maintenance repair journeyman Buick Oldsmobile Cadillac group GM, Pitts., 1983—. Rep. United Way, Pitts., 1984—. Contbr. article to Franciscan Times. Mem. UAW, Alpha Mu Beta (sec. 1974—). Democrat. Home: 231 Collins Ave Floreffe PA 15025 Office: St Mary's Episcopal Ch 509 6th St Charleroi PA 15022 *It is my prayer for all people that we may be witnesses of faith instead of doubt; that we as Christians may be the source of hope and not despair; that we may lead others onto the light and not bring about the aloneness and desperation of darkness; that from the depths of sadness and tribulation we may raise ourselves and others to the heights of joy in which no human tongue can speak or mind comprehend through the unconditional love of our Lord and Savior Jesus Christ. Then may we begin to reach out to one another in the true spirit of unity and brotherhood.*

SEEDORF, DONNA LYNN, minister; b. Monterey, Calif., Apr. 24, 1953; d. Robert H. and Edith (Mills) Anders; m. Kevin Tommy Seedorf, Jan. 7, 1989. B of Music Edn., U. Montevallo, 1975; M in Christian Music, Golden Gate Theol. Sem., Mill Valley, Calif., 1978. Music assoc. Petaluma (Calif.) Valley Bapt., 1978-82; minister of music First Bapt. Ch., Boulder City, Nev., 1982-83; music assoc. St. Andrew Bapt. Ch., Panama City, Fla., 1984-86; minister of music Woodlawn United Meth. Ch., Panama City, 1987-89, 1st Bapt. Ch., Cottondale, Fla., 1989—; pvt. music tchr.

SEEGAR, KENNETH MICHAEL, priest; b. Wilkes-Barre, Pa., Mar. 10, 1961; s. Kenneth Earl and Irene Frances (Ostrowski) S. BS in Sociology, U. Scranton, 1983; MDiv, Mary Immaculate Sem., 1986. Ordained priest Roman Cath. Ch., 1987. Parochian vicar, parish youth coord. St. Aloysius Parish, Wilkes-Barre, 1987—, also parish dir. rite Christian initiation of adults, 1988—; regional vocation dir. Diocese of Scranton, Pa., 1988—, asst. master ceremonies to bishop, 1989—. Democrat. Home and Office: St Aloysius Rectory 143 Division St Wilkes-Barre PA 18702

SEEGER, EDWARD BETHEL, religious organization director, minister; b. Mar. 26, 1945; s. Edward Bethel and Barbara (Buehler) S.; m. Deborah Ann Lackey, Sept. 5, 1987; children: Edward Bethel III, Catherine Atlee. BA, Cornell U., 1967; MDiv, Princeton Theol. Sem., 1971; postgrad., Bd. Interdenominational Tng., 1972-74, Inst. Religion, Tex. Med. Ctr., Houston, 1975-77. Ordained to ministry United Presbyn. Ch. (USA), 1971. Youth min. Brick Presbyn. Ch., Rochester, N.Y., 1969-70; pastor Presbyn. chs., Beverly and Watertown, Ohio, 1971-75; staff chaplain Harris County Hosp. Dist., Houston, 1975-77; dir. prisoner svcs. Houston Met. Ministries, 1978-81, assoc. fund raising counsel, 1983, dir. congl. and interfaith rels., 1982-89; creative writer Palantir, Inc., Houston, 1981-82; exec. dir. Corpus Christi (Tex.) Metro Ministries, 1989—; stated supply min. Good Shepherd Presbyn. Ch., Houston, 1976-78; clin. instr. Harris County Hosp. Dist., Houston, 1977-78; adj. lectr. U. St. Thomas/St. Mary's Sem., 1977-78, Gulf Coast Bible Coll., Houston, 1977-78; vis. lectr. Cath. Archdiocese Mex., Mexico City, 1977; interim supply min. San Pablo Presbyn. Ch., Houston, 1978-81; apptd. to Ecumenism and Interfaith Commn., Cath. Diocese Galveston-Houston; community organizer, cons. Braes Interfaith Ministries, Houston; cons. Mental Health Assn. Houston and Harris County; chair svc. com. Presbytery of New Covenant; mem. statewide planning group World Conf. on Mission and Evangelism, World Coun. Chs., San Antonio; mem. planning com. Faith and Order Conf., Tex. Conf. Chs. Vol. CARE, Honduras, 1965; active AIDS Interfaith Coun., Houston, 1985—; apptd. to Ch. Rels. Adv. Group, Tex. Dept. Human Svcs.; apptd. to Task Force on Illiteracy, Task Force on Healthcare for Homeless, City/County Task Force on the Homeless, Mayor of Houston; tchr. ch. sch., preacher St. Philip Presbyn. Ch., Houston, 1975—. Mem. Nat. Assn. Ecumenical Staff of Nat. Coun. Chs. (commn. on regional and local ecumenism), Alban Inst. Home: 14918 Tesoro North Padre Island Corpus Christi TX 78418 Office: Corpus Christi Metro Ministries 1919 Leopard St Corpus Christi TX 78408

SEEGER, EMILY ANN, religion educator; b. Portland, Oreg., June 7, 1947; d. William Clay and Emilena (Honegger) Hurn; m. Donald Allan Seeger, Aug. 8, 1971; children: Elizabeth Ann, Mary Katharine. BA, Whitworth Coll., 1969; MRE, Pitts. Theol. Sem., 1972. Ordained to ministry Presbyn. Ch. as elder. Dir. Christian Edn. Aspinwall (Pa.) Presbyn. Ch., 1971-72, Delmont (Pa.) Presbyn. Ch., 1973-74; dir. Christian Edn. 1st Presbyn. Ch., Huron, S.D., 1987-91, Algona, Iowa, 1991—. Mem. sch. bd. Wolsey (S.D.) Sch. dist., 1988-91. Mem. Assn. Christian Ch. S.D. (exec. bd.). Home: 117 N Ackley Algona IA 50511 Office: 1st Presbyn Ch 101 N Main St Algona IA 50511

SEEL, ROBERT EDWARD, minister; b. Santiago, Chile, Jan. 3, 1924; s. Edward George and Miriam Ann (Rood) S.; m. Jean Esther Almy, May 19, 1948 (dec. 1962); children: Barbara Jean, Robert James; m. Elizabeth May Heath, Aug. 2, 1963; children: Edward W., Laura R. BA, Maryville (Tenn.) Coll., 1945; MA, NYU, 1952; MDiv, Princeton Theol. Sem., 1948; Licenciado, Cen. U., Caracas, Venezuela, 1962. Ordained to ministry, Presbyn. Ch. Pastor First Presbyn. Ch., Whitestone, N.Y., 1948-52; missionary Bd. Fgn. Missions, Caracas, 1952-78; assoc. dir. communication Synod of Lakes & Prairies, Bloomington, Minn., 1979-81; exec. presbyter Presbytery de Cristo, Tucson, 1981—; interim dir. Spanish Lang. Sch., San Jose, Costa Rica, 1964; sci. tchr. Colegio Americano, Caracas, 1965-66; treas. L.A. Commn. for Christian Edn., Lima, 1964-78. Author: 'Breve Historia Prsbnos, 1972. Mem. Assn. Exec. Presbyters (steering com. 1989-91), Assn. Presbyn. Christian Educators. Democrat. Office: Presbytery de Cristo 3809 E Third St Tucson AZ 85716

SEELEY, DAVID WILLIAM, minister; b. Des Moines, May 21, 1944; s. William Amos S. and Margaret Rose (Owens) Young; m. Janet Kay Hill, Mar. 14, 1964; children: John David, Karen Anne. BA cum laude, Lincoln Christian Coll., 1972; MA, Lincoln Christian Seminary, 1973; postgrad., U. South Fla., 1973-74, Fla. Atlanta U., 1975. Ordained 1976; cert. pastorial counseling, Liberty Baptist Coll., Lynchberg, Va. Asst. mgr. Regal Svc. Station, San Jose, Calif., 1965-66; dep. sheriff Santa Clara County Sheriff's Dept., San Jose, 1966-69; minister Allerton (Ill.) Christian Ch., 1969-70, Arm Prairie (Ill.) Christian Ch., 1970-72, Edgewood (Ill.) Christian Ch., 1972-73; guidance counselor Alva (Fla.) Middle Sch., 1973-76; pres. Good News of Christ, Inc., Englewood, Fla., 1978—; minister Northside Christian Ch. of Christ, Englewood, 1976—. Contbr. articles to religious publs.; author/pub. newsletters. Mem. Englewood Boosters Club, 1985—. Mem. Englewood Ministerial Assn. (sec. 1978-80), Suncoast Christian Ministers Assn. (pres. 1977-79), Lincoln Christian Coll. Alumni Assn., Southwest Fla. Christian Men's Fellowship, Club Nautico. Republican. Avocations: golf, swimming, fishing, boating. Office: Northside Christian Ch of Christ 685 N Indiana Ave Englewood FL 34223

SEEMUTH, DAVID PAUL, minister, educator; b. Milw., Mar. 2, 1956; m. Karen Rowold; children: Daniel, Kristin. BS, U. Wis., Milw., 1978; MDiv, Columbia Biblical Sem., 1982; PhD, Marquette U., 1989. Assoc. pastor Elmbrook Ch., Waukesha, Wis., 1982—; lectr. Marquette U., Milw., 1989—. Mem. Soc. Biblical Lit., Evang. Theol. Soc. Office: Elmbrook Ch 777 S Barker Rd Waukesha WI 53186

SEERVELD, CALVIN GEORGE, aesthetics educator; b. Bayshore, N.Y., Aug. 18, 1930; s. Lester Benjamin and Letitia (Van Tielen) S.; m. Ines Cecile Naudin ten Cate, Sept. 8, 1956; children: Anya, Gioia, Lucas. BA, Calvin Coll., 1952; MA, U. Mich., 1953; PhD, Free U. Amsterdam, The Netherlands, 1958. Mem. faculty, prof. aesthetics Inst. for Christian Studies, Toronto, Ont., Can., 1972—. Author: Rainbows for the Fallen World, 1980, On Being Human, 1988; translator from Hebrew, author oratorio version: Song of Songs, 1967, rev. edit., 1988; editor: Opuscula Aesthetica Nostra, 1984. Mem. Soc. Canadienne d'Esthetique (co-pres.). Mem. Christian Ref. Ch. N.Am. Address: Inst Christian Studies, 229 College St W, Toronto, ON Canada M5T 1R4 *Psalm 115 says that humans become like the gods they worship. If the meek shall indeed inherit the earth, does being listed in "Who's Who" constitute a prayer to be disinherited?.*

SEEVERS, BRADLEY JAY, youth minister; b. Athens, Ohio, Aug. 13, 1964; s. Donald Franklin and Ruth Helen (Brafford) S.; m. Kimberly Kae Stepp, Aug. 16, 1986; 1 child, Jessica Leigh. BS, Cin. Bible Coll., 1987. Ordained to ministry Ch. of Christ, 1990. Min. youth Grape Grove Ch. of Christ, Jamestown, Ohio, 1982-83, Walnut St. Ch. of Christ, Belpre, Ohio, 1986-88; dir. pub. rels. Cin. Bible Coll., 1983-84; min. Rutland (Ohio) Ch. of Christ, 1985-86; min. youth 5th Avenue Ch. of Christ, Lancaster, Ohio, 1988—; rep. Ohio Teens for Christ, Columbus, 1991. Republican. Office: 5th Avenue Ch of Christ Corner 5th and Broad St Box 457 Lancaster OH 43130 *My contribution to the future will be to change the minds of our youth. If we redirect the moral fabric of young people to make good choices, then and only then, will we change the future of our world for the good!.*

SEFCIK, JOHN KAROL, minister; b. Johnstown, N.Y., Mar. 21, 1922; s. Karol and Johanna (Vach) S.; m. Delphine Marie Covington, July 7, 1954; children: Karolton, John D., Nathan. BA, Park Coll., 1950; BD, Princeton (N.J.) Theol. Sem., 1953, ThM, 1968. Pastor First Presbyn., Mays Landing, Tuckahoe, N.J., 1953-55, Christ Presbyn., Catskill, N.Y., 1955-58, John Hus Presbyn., Binghamton, N.Y., 1959-71; chaplain Broome County Jail, Binghamton, 1960-70; pastor S.W. United Presbyn., Detroit, 1971-87; parish assoc. First Presbyn., Dearborn, Mich., 1987-90; ret. First Presbyn., Dearborn; moderator Susquehanna Valley Presbytery, South Tier, N.Y., 1968; mem. task force on youth Binghamton, 1965, Triple Cities Urban Mission, Binghamton, 1966. Dir. Ecumenical Project SAVE, Detroit, 1978-84; mem. S.W. Detroit Mental Health Com., Detroit, 1973; developer S.W. Detroit Aging Coalition, 1984; dir. S.E. Mich. Food Coalition, 1985. Sgt. U.S. Army, 1942-45. Recipient Svc. to Community award Hubbard Richard Community Coun., 1984, Svc. to Frail Elderly Ecumenical Project SAVE, 1979-85. Mem. Presbytery of Detroit. Home and Office: 11306 Brady Ave Redford MI 48239-2059

SEGAL, ALAN FRANKLIN, religion educator; b. Worcester, Mass., Aug. 2, 1945; s. Bennett Perry and Rose (Sadowsky) S.; m. Meryl Denise Goldey, Nov. 7, 1970; children: Ethan Lewis, Jordan Benjamin Gabriel. AB, Amherst Coll., 1967; MA, Brandeis U., 1968; BHL, Hebrew Union Coll., 1970; MA, M.Phil., PhD, Yale U., 1975. From lectr. to asst. prof. Princeton (N.J.) U., 1974-78; assoc. prof. U. Toronto (Ont., Can.), 1978-80; assoc. prof. Barnard Coll., Columbia U., N.Y.C., 1980-83, prof., 1983—. Author: Two Powers in Heaven, 1975, Rebecca's Children, 1986, Paul the Convert, 1990, The Other Judaisms, 1988; co-author: Deus Ex Machina, 1986; contbr. articles to profl. jours. Guggenheim fellow J.S. Guggenheim Found., 1977-78, Wilson fellow Woodrow Wilson Found., 1967-68, Mellon fellow to Aspen Inst., Mellon Found., NEH fellow, 1985-86, Annenberg fellow, 1991-92. Mem. Soc. Bibl. Lit., Am. Acad. Religion, Am. Soc. Study of Religion, Assn. Jewish Studies, Studiorum Novum Testamentum Societas, Can. Soc. for Study of Religion, Can. Soc. for Bibl. Studies (pres. 1990-91), Soc. for Sci. Study of Religion. Home: 5 Beechwood Rd Ho-Ho-Kus NJ 07423-1606 Office: Barnard Coll 219c Milbank Hall 3009 Broadway New York NY 10027-6598

SEGARS, JOHN KELVIN, minister; b. Carnesville, Ga., Aug. 20, 1935; s. Erastus Earl and Octie Irene (Payne) S.; m. Reba Nell Williamson, Nov. 6, 1954; children: Karen Failyer, Jackie Wheat. BTh, Internat. Sem., 1984, ThM, 1984, ThD, 1988, DD, 1985. Ordained to ministry So. Bapt. Conv., 1967. Pastor East Side Bapt. Ch., Winder, Ga., 1967-71, Beacon Height Bapt. Ch., Madison, Ga., 1971-79, Bethlehem (Ga.) First Bapt., 1980-85, Edwards Chapel Bapt., Athens, Ga., 1985—; team leader mission trip to Indian reservation, Fla., 1984, Liberia, 1988, Republic of Panama, 1991; mem. exec. com. Ga. Bapt. Conv., 1972-77, tchr. edn. extension class, 1991-92; with tour of Israel, other countries, 1974; pres. Mins.' Conf., 1988; elected preacher various ann. associational meetings. Author: Pneumatologh, 1989. Chaplain Barrow County Jail, 1968-71; bd. dirs. Assn. Youth Camp, 1972-75; chmn. Area Aging Program, Athens, 1983-84, Sr. Citizen Adv. Com., Madison, 1975-78, Winder, 1983. Named Citizen of Month Hi-Y Club, Morgan County, 1979. Mem. Morgan County Bapt. Assn. (moderator 1974-76), Applachee Bapt. Assn. (fin. com. chmn. 1984-85, moderator 1983-85), Sarepta Bapt. Assn. (moderator 1989, personnel com. chmn. 1991), Masons (chaplain 1976-79). Office: Edwards Chapel Bapt Ch 105 Timothy Pl Athens GA 30606

SEGEL, KENNETH IAN, rabbi; b. Buffalo, Mar. 16, 1942; s. David and Ethel (Wernick) S.; m. Sandra Goodman, Aug. 10, 1969; 1 child, Bree Arlyn. BA, SUNY, Buffalo, 1963; MA in Hebrew Lit., Hebrew Union Coll., 1970. Ordained rabbi, 1970. Assoc. rabbi Rodet Shalom Temple, Pitts., 1970-75; rabbi Gates of Prayer Congregation, New Orleans, 1975-84, Temple Emanuel, Montreal, Que., Can., 1984-87, Temple Beth Israel, Fresno, Calif., 1987—; lectr. in philosophy Fresno (Calif.) State U., 1988—; co-chmn. Fresno Jewish Community Rels. Com., 1988—; mem. exec. com. Fresno Jewish Fedn., 1988—; bd. dirs. Nat. Rabbinic Cabinet, UJA, N.Y.C., 1989—. Author: A Personal Word, 1990; contbr. articles to profl. pubs. Mem. ethics com. St. Agnes Hosp. Valley Children's House, Fresno, 1990—; bd. dirs. Fresno Human Rels. Com., 1990—; co-chmn. Dr. Mlking Com., Fresno, 1988-90; mem. Gov.'s Com. on Aging, Sacramento, 1988-90. Recipient Righteous Man award Detroit Armenian Community, 1990, Man of Yr. award Fresno Armenian Community, 1990. Mem. Fresno Ministerial Assn. (pres. 1990—), Cen. Ctr. Am. Rabbis, Pacific Assn. Reform Rabbis, Am. Jewish Hist. Soc., Am. Reform Zionist Assn. (exec. coun. 1980—), Am. Jewish Com. (exec. coun. 1988—). Office: Temple Beth Israel 2336 Calaveras St Fresno CA 93721

SEGELBAUM, CHARLES JACOB, cantor, music director; b. London, Mar. 12, 1939; s. Ludwig and Regina (Tarnowski) S.; m. Vivienne S. Goldstein, Dec. 22, 1969 (div. 1987); children: Elliott, Rochelle, Erik. Cantorial Dipl., Yeshiva U., N.Y.C., 1961. Cantor, music dir. Congregation Ner Tamid of South Bay, Rancho Palos Verdes, Calif., 1971-76, Congregation Beth Sholom, Northbrook, Ill., 1976-82, Congregation Ahavath Sholom, Ft. Worth, Tex., 1982-85, Temple Beth Emet, Anaheim, Calif., 1985-88, Temple Adath Israel, Merion, Pa., 1988—. The Cantors Assy.(sec. 1974-75, 1990—). Home: 6100 City Ave # 814 Philadelphia PA 19131 Office: Temple Adath Israel Old Lancaster at Highland Merion PA 19066

SEGER, WARREN RICHARD, religious organization administrator; b. O'Neill, Neb., Mar. 31, 1936; s. Darwin Eugene and Pearl Evalyn (Burge) S.; m. Esther Elaine Kaiser, June 2, 1957; children: Mark Steven, Annette Kristine Seger Hagaman, Daniel James. BS, U. Neb., 1960. Chmn. fin. Meth. Ch., Gordon, Neb., 1976-78; chmn. fin. Meth. Ch., O'Neill, 1985-88, chmn. adminstrv. coun., 1988—; pres. Seger Oil Co., O'Neill, 1978—. Mem. Sheridan County Planning Commn., Gordon, 1977; pres. Gordon High Sch. Bd., 1976; precinct chmn. Republican Party, O'Neill, 1980-90. With U.S. Army, 1955-57, Korea. Mem. Masons. Home: 728 N 6th O'Neill NE 68763

SEGRAVES, DANIEL LEE, clergyman; b. St. Louis, Oct. 29, 1946; s. Glen and Agnes (Hodges) S.; m. Judy Kay Miller, June 14, 1964; children: Sharon Kay, Mark Alan. BA in Theol. Studies, Gateway Coll. Evangelism, 1981; B. Christian Edn., Freedom U., 1980, M. Christian Edn., 1981, D. Ministry, 1982; EdD, Calif. Coast U., 1991. Ordained to ministry United Pentecostal Ch. Internat., 1968,. Dir. promotions and publs. gen. Sunday sch. dept. U.P.C.I., St. Louis, 1968-70; minister Christian edn. 1st Pentecostal Ch., St. Louis, 1971-74; pastor 1st Pentecostal Ch., Dupo, Ill., 1975-82; exec. v.p. Christian Life Coll., Stockton, Calif., 1982—; chmn., bd. dirs. Sta. KCJH radio, Stockton, 1989—. Author: The Search for the Word of God, 1984, Insights for Christian Living, 1988, Hair Length in the Bible, 1989, Ancient Wisdom for Today's World, 1990. Office: Christian Life Coll 9023 West Lane Stockton CA 95210

SEIBERT, MARY ANGELICE, nun; b. Louisville, Jan. 16, 1922; d. William Karl and Catherine A. (Schmidt) S. BS in Chemistry, Ursuline Coll., 1947; MS in Biochemistry, Institutum Vivi Thomas, Cin., 1950; PhD in Biochemistry and Philosophy, Institutum Vivi Thomas, 1952. Joined Ursuline Sisters, Roman Cath. Ch., 1940. Pres. Ursuline Coll., Louisville, 1963-68; pres. Ursuline Sisters, Louisville, 1980-88, assoc. dir. Office of Advancement, 1989—; dir. Monseignor Pitt Learning Ctr., Louisville, 1974; trustee St. Mary Coll, Ky., 1975-77, Bellarmine Coll., Louisville, 1982-88, Coll. New Rochelle, N.Y., 1983-89; vis. scholar Pope John Medical-Moral Rsch. Ctr., Dedham, Mass., 1988-89; Fulbright-Hays lectr. Univ. Coll. Galway, Ireland, 1968-69; pres. Ursuline Congregation, Louisville, 1980-88. Damon Runyon fellow St. Louis U. Med. Sch., 1953-54; recipient Woman of Yr. in Edn. award, YWCA, Louisville, 1976, cert. Outstanding Svc. to Higher Edn., Louisville Phi Delta Kappa, 1977, cert. Meritorious Svc. Jefferson Community Coll., 1978; HEW fellow, N.Y., 1979-80; named Bellarmine Coll. Alumna of Yr., 1980. Mem. AAAS, Inst. Theol. Encounter with Sci. and Tech., World Future Soc., Brookline Commn. Study Women Religious and the Intellectual Life, Brookland Commn. Washington, Hastings Ctr. Democrat. Home and Office: Ursuline Campus 3105 Lexington Rd Louisville KY 40206 *Our world needs teachers with vision to assume roles of moral leadership in a milieu which is so desperately confused by changing values and disappearing goals.*

SEICOL, SAMUEL ROBERT, rabbi; b. N.Y.C., Feb. 23, 1951; s. Noel Herbert and Betty Jean S.; m. Jennifer Jane Lewis, Aug. 18, 1974; children: Abigail Dara, Rebecca Sara, Benjamin Joseph. BA, Harvard U., 1973; MAHL, Hebrew Union Coll., N.Y.C., 1978. Ordained rabbi, 1978. Ednl. dir. Woodlands Community Temple, White Plains, N.Y., 1976-78; asst. rabbi Temple Emanuel, Pitts., 1978-80; rabbi Temple Chai, Phoenix, 1980-82; chaplain Kivel Geriatric Ctr., Phoenix, 1982—; membership chmn. Forum for Religion and Aging, San Francisco, 1986—; membership steering com. of bd. dirs. Am. Soc. Aging, San Francisco, 1989—. Lectr. casette tape, Story Telling: An Aging Art, 1990, The Memory Lives On, 1989. Adv. coun. Grief Network Coun., Phoenix, 1987—. Mem. Nat. Assn. Jewish Chaplains (treas. 1989—), Cen. Conf. Am. Rabbis, Assn. Clin. Pastoral Edn., Harvard Club of Phoenix (treas. 1990—, bd. dirs. 1985-90). Democrat. Office: Kivel Geriatric Ctr 3020 N 36th St Phoenix AZ 85018 *Success may be measured in several ways. For me true success comes from the quality of relationship developed between oneself and one's world. Teaching and learning, sharing and caring, giving and receiving: these lead to success.*

SEIFERT, WILLIAM NORMAN, religion educator; b. Phila., Dec. 29, 1952; s. Walter R. and Lucy (Sandrock) S. BA in Philosophy and Theology, U. Scranton, 1977; MDiv, Mary Immaculate Sem., 1980; postgrad., Pontifical Inst., Washington, 1991—. Prof. theology Allentown (Pa.) Cen. Cath. High Sch., 1981-87, chairperson, theology, 1983-87, dir. youth ministry, 1986-91; cons. Dept. Youth Ministry Adv. Bd., Orwigsburg, Pa., 1986-91; prof. theology Bethlehem (Pa.) Cath. High Sch., 1987-91; regional dir Apostolate for the Deaf, Allentown, 1981-91; cons. Diocesan Bd. Edn., Allentown, 1985-91, Youth Leadership Inst., Diocese of Allentown, 1985-91; mem. Youth Ministry Retreat Bd., Diocese of Allentown, 1985-90. Mem. Internat. Cath. Deaf Assn., Nat. Cath. Edn. Assn. Home: 730 W Broad St Bethlehem PA 18018 Office: Bethlehem Cath High Sch Dewberry and Madison Aves Bethlehem PA 18017-4699 *The pursuit of excellence must include far more than any mere material sense, for we are far more than mere flesh. There is that spiritual reality, equally us and enfleshed as our unique self, which we must account for. Excellence is a quality of the whole person.*

SEIGEL, ROBERT ALAN, rabbi; b. Charleston, S.C., July 19, 1938; s. Frank and Ann (Lipman) S.; m. Faye Polis, July 15, 1943; children: Tamar, J. Daniel. Student, Coll. of Charleston, 1956-57; BA, U. Cin., 1961; BHL, Hebrew Union Coll. Jewish Inst, Cin., 1964; MAHL, Hebrew Union Coll. Jewish Inst, 1965; DD, Hebrew Union Coll., 1990. Ordained rabbi, 1965. Rabbi Temple Sinai, Rochester, N.Y., 1965-68; asst. dir. Jewish Coun. Urban Affairs, Chgo., 1968-70; dir. B'nai B'rith Hillel Found., Evanston, Ill., 1970-71, Chapel Hill, N.C., 1971-77, Miami, Fla., 1977-78; exec. dir. Carolina Agy. for Jewish Edn., Charlotte, N.C., 1983-86; sr. rabbi Temple Beth El V'Shalom, Charlotte, 1980—; v.p. Mecklenburg Ministries, Charlotte Coun. Chs. and Synagogues, 1987-88. Author: Intermarriage-Guide for Jewish Parents, 1978; artist-designer art cards, 1985. mem. Civic Index, Charlotte, 1988—; mem. steering com. Catholic-Jewish Dialogue, Charlotte, 1984—, Interfaith Inst., Charlotte, 1985—; mem. com. Program for Affordable Health Care for Elderly, Charlotte, 1986-88. Mem. Central Conf. of Am. Rabbis (regional bd. 1988—), Rochester Bd. Rabbis (pres. 1968), Greater Carolinas Assn. Rabbis, Charlotte Area Clergy Assn. (pres. 1986-87). Avocations: computers in education, art. Home: 8814 Rittenhouse Cir Charlotte NC 28270 Office: Temple Beth El V'Shalom PO Box 13400 Charlotte NC 28270

SEILHAMER, RAY A., academic administrator. Head Evang. Sch. Theology, Myerstown, Pa. Office: Evang Sch Theol 121 S College St Myerstown PA 17067*

SEILHEIMER, DAVID A., treasurer; b. Hamilton, Tex., Feb. 15, 1949; s. Edwin John and Tommie J. (Allison) S. BA, Tex. Wesleyan U., 1971; ThM, So. Meth. U., 1974; MBA, Baylor U., 1985. Assoc. pastor Arlington Heights United Meth. Ch., Ft. Worth, 1974-78; pastor Florence-Jarrell (Tex.) United Meth. Ch., 1978-79; assoc. pastor Overton Park United Meth. Ch., Ft. Worth, 1979-82; pastor First United Meth. Ch., Hewitt, Tex., 1982-84; treas., sec., statistician S.W. Tex. Conf. United Meth. Chs., San Antonio, 1984—. Mem. Nat. Assn. Corp. Cash Mgmt., United Meth. Assn. Ch. Bus. Adminstrs., Gen. Bd. Pensions United Meth. Ch. (benefit adv. com.), San Antonio Cash Mgmt. Assn. Office: SW Tex Conf United Meth Ch 535 Bandera Rd San Antonio TX 78228

SEITH, THOMAS KARL, deacon, small business professional; b. Yonkers, N.Y., Aug. 10, 1927; s. Ludwig Karl and Alice (Wood) S.; m. Virginia Seith, Sept. 7, 1961 (dec. July 1963); children: Courtney Karl, Kenneth David; m. Monique M. Seith, Sept. 7, 1964; 1 child, Anne Collette. Student, U. Pa., 1946. Mgr. IBM, White Plains, N.Y., 1955-89; deacon Our Lady of Fatima Roman Cath. Ch., Wilton, Conn., 1981—; lector Our Lady of Fatima Roman Cath. Ch., 1978-80. With USN, 1945-46. Home: 91 Longmeadow Rd Wilton CT 06897

SEITZ, LANE RICHARD, minister; b. Painesville, Ohio, Dec. 6, 1946; s. Tony Frank and Ruth Marie (Schaefer) S.; m. Donna Kae Lehrbass, Dec. 21, 1968; children: Jodi Lynn, Timothy John. AA, Concordia Coll., 1966; BA, Concordia Tchrs. Coll., 1970; MDiv, Concordia Sem., 1974; D of Ministry, Fuller Theol. Sem., 1991. Ordained to ministry Luth. Ch., 1974. Min. St. Timothy Luth. Ch., Bedford, Iowa, 1974-76, Faith Luth. Ch., Spooner, Wis., 1976-80, 80-85, Christ Luth. Ch., Lampson, Wis., 1976-80; asst. to the pres. Minn. South Dist. Luth Ch.-Mo. Synod, Burnsville, 1985-91, pres. Minn. South Dist., 1991—; dir. subdist. Forward in Remembrance Luth. Ch.-Mo. Synod, St. Louis, 1980-82; chmn. No. Wis. Dist. Bd. of Evangelism, Wausau, 1982-85; mem. Dist. Planning Coun., 1982-85; chmn. 1985 Great Commn. Convocation, 1984-85; mem. dist. bd. dirs. Spooner (Wis.) Ambulance Svc., 1980-85; chaplain Dist. 8, Wis. State Patrol, 1983-85 (Disting. Svc. award 1985). Mem. Spooner Vol. Fire Dept., 1980-82. Recipient EMT of Yr. award Spooner Ambulance Svc., 1983, Svc. Ecclesia Christi award Concordia Theol. Sem., Ft. Wayne, Ind., 1985. Mem. Nat. Assn. Emergency Med. Technicians (instr., coord.), Wis. Emergency Med. Technician Assn. Republican. Home: 14198 Ash Cir NE Prior Lake MN 55372 Office: 14301 Grand Ave So Burnsville MN 55337

SEITZ, SHAWN ELIOT, lay worker; b. Wyandotte, Mich., Mar. 2, 1955; s. Fredrick Charles and CArolyn Emily (Eliot) S.; m. Rosalind Jane Cacciola, June 10, 1989. BS, Mich. State U., 1982, DVM, 1984. Accredited veterinarian. Student Gordon-Conwell Theol. Sem., South Hamilton, Mass., 1989—; pres. Alpha Tech Pet, Inc., Lexington, Mass., 1989—. With Naval Air, 1973-75, Hawaii. Named to Nat. Dean's List Edn. Communications, Inc., 1989-90. Mem. Mich. Veterinary Med. Assn., Am. Boarding Kennel Assn. Home: 33 Taft Ave Lexington MA 02173 Office: Alpha Tech Pet Inc PO Box 1257 East Arlington MA 02174

SEITZ, STEPHEN RICHARD, minister; b. Evansville, Ind., May 24, 1944; s. Charles Lewis II Seitz and Helen Margaret (Hancock) Williams; m. Barbara Diane Byers, June 30, 1968; 1 child, Carrie Ann. BA, Oakland City (Ind.) Coll., 1981; MDiv, United Theol. Sem., Dayton, Ohio, 1984. Ordained to ministry United Meth. Ch. Pastor Petersburg (Ind.) Cir.: United Meth. Ch., 1978-81, Tanner Valley United Meth. Ch., 1981-88, Shiloh United Meth. Ch., Jasper, Ind., 1988—. With USN, 1962-66. Mem. Kiwanis (pres. 1968-77), Masons (worshipful master 1973), Shriners. Home: 1350 4th St Jasper IN 47546 Office: United Meth Ch 1971 West State Rd 56 Jasper IN 47546

SELBY WRIGHT, RONALD, chaplain, minister; b. Scotland, June 12, 1908. Student, Melville Coll. and Edinburgh Acad., Edinburgh, Scotland, New Coll., Edinburgh; MA, Edinburgh U., 1933, DD (hon.), 1956. Minister of the canongate Edinburgh, 1936-77; moderator Ch. of Scotland, 1972-73; chaplain HM Forces, 1936-45, sr. chaplain, 1945—; sr. chaplain 52nd Lowland Div., 10th Indian Div., HM Forces, 1961—. Author: Asking Them Questions, Take up God's Armour, Another Home. Chaplain to H.M. the Queen, Comdr. the Royal Victorian Order of St. John. Decorated Comdr. Royal Victorian Order, Territorial Decoration Endinburgh Acad. (hon. dir.). Fellow Royal Soc. of Edinburgh; Hon. Old Lorettonian, Fettsian; mem. New Club (Edinburgh) and Atheneum Club (London). Home and Office: The Queen's House, Moray Place, Edinburgh Scotland

SELF, JON ADRIAN, minister; b. Little Rock, Oct. 6, 1967; s. James Adrian and Elaine May (Grose) S.; m. Frances Lorene Barnett, Dec. 23, 1989. BA in Christian Ministries, Williams Bapt. Coll., Walnut Ridge, Ark., 1989; postgrad., Midwestern Bapt. Theol. Sem., Kansas City, Mo., 1989—. Ordained to ministry So. Bapt. Conv. , 1985. Missionary Fgn. Mission Bd. So. Bapt. Conv., Kuala Lumpur, Malaysia, 1987, So. Bapt. Sunday Sch. Bd., Cuiabá, Brazil, 1987; resort min. Ptnrs. Inc., Virginia Beach, Va., 1988; pastor New Bethel Bapt. Ch., Pocahontas, Ark., 1988-89; youth min. Calvary Bapt. Ch., North Little Rock, Ark., 1989—.

SELF, L. DOUGLAS, pastor, editor; b. Clovis, N.Mex., June 6, 1945; s. A.R. and Oleta (Bilberry) S.; m. Rebecca Ann Cheatheam, June 12, 1966; children: Daniel, Bethany, David. BD, Wayland U., 1967; DivM, Southwestern Sem., Ft. Worth, Tex., 1972; D in Ministry, Denver Sem., 1986. Pastor Ch. Redstone, Colo., 1977—; pres. Pastoral Ministry Resources, Carbondale, Colo., 1985—. Author: Consumer's Guide to Religious Beliefs, 1985; editor Pastoral Ministry Newsletter, 1985—. V.p. Redstone Community Assn., 1984, pres. 1985. Republican. Avocations: hiking, skiing. Home: 22995 Hwy 133 Redstone CO 81623 Office: Pastoral Ministry Resources Carbondale CO 81623

SELF, NANCY GRISSOM, minister, religious organization administrator; b. Akron, Ohio, May 18, 1929; d. Thomas Albert and Mary Kathryn (Patterson) G.; m. Norman Douglas Self, June 2, 1957 (div. July 1985). BSHEc, Ohio U., 1951; postgrad., Garrett Theol., 1953, Vanderbilt Div. Sch., 1955-

57; ThM, Sch. Theol., 1966. Ordained to ministry United Meth. Ch. as deacon, 1961, as elder 1989. Missionary Meth. Ch., Hollywood, Calif., 1951-53; assoc. dir. teenage program YWCA, Akron, 1953-54; field sec. Bd. Missions Meth. Ch., N.Y.C., 1954-55; campus min. Calif. State U., Long Beach, 1960-73; gen. sec. Gen. Commn. on Status and Role of Women in United Meth. Ch., Evanston, Ill., 1973-91; min. Univ. United Meth. Ch., Redlands, Calif., 1991—; summer dir. Wesley Found. Ohio U., Athens, 1950; jurisdictional del. Western Jurisdiction, Seattle, 1972; bd. dirs. univ. Christian movement Northwestern U., Evanston; com. of 24 Women's Div. Global Ministries, N.Y.C., 1972; mem. U.S. Com. World Coun. Chs. Ecumenical Decade for Women, 1988—; cons. Images Women in Transition, 1976. Recipient Kilgore award, 1983. Democrat. Home: 1579 Finch Ave Redlands CA 92374 Office: Univ United Meth Ch 940 E Colton Ave Redlands CA 92374

SELF, WILLIAM LEE, clergyman, financial planner; b. Winston-Salem, N.C., Jan. 10, 1932; s. Edgar G. Self and Della (Curry) Taylor; m. Carolyn Shealy, Aug. 2, 1953; children: W. Lee, Bryan E. BA, Stetson U., 1954, DDiv (hon.), 1969; BD, Southeastern Bapt. Theol. Sem., 1957; STD, Emory U., 1971; DDiv (hon.), Mercer U., 1970; LLD (hon.), Han Yang U., Seoul, Korea, 1975. Ordained to ministry Bapt. Ch., 1957. Pastor Edgemont Bapt. Ch., Rocky Mount, N.C., 1957-60, West Bradenton Bapt. Ch., Bradenton, Fla., 1960-64, Wieuca Rd. Bapt. Ch., Atlanta, 1964-90, John's Creek Bapt. Ch., Atlanta, 1991—; pres. Stoneworth Fin. Svcs., Atlanta, 1991—; chmn. Ga. Bapt. Exec. Com., 1975; pres. Ga. Bapt. Conv., 1976; pres. fgn. mission bd. So. Bapt. Conv., 1977, 2d v.p., 1978. Co-author: Survival Kit for Stranded, 1975, Learning to Pray, 1978, Survival Kit for Marriage, 1981, Confessions of a Nomad, 1983, Before I Thee Wed, 1989. Pres. Buckhead Bus. Assn., Atlanta, 1990. Named Author of Yr., Dixie Coun. Authors and Journalists, 1984, one of Ten Most Outstanding Bus. Men. in Buckhead, 1988; represented Pres. Gerald Ford at Inauguration of Pres. of Liberia, 1976.

SELIG, ALAN DEE, minister; b. Wichita, Kans., Mar. 23, 1952; s. Leonard W. and Frances M. (Shirley) S.; m. Karen Ann Kruskop, May 18, 1974; children: Jennette, Caroline. B in Gen. Studies, Kans. U., 1974; MDiv, Cen. Bapt. Theol. Sem., 1978. Ordained to ministry Am. Bapt. Chs. in U.S.A., 1978. Pastor 1st Bapt. Ch., Larned, Kans., 1978-82, Dubuque, Iowa, 1982—; adj. prof. Bapt. history and polity Theol. Sem., U. Dubuque, 1987—; mem. Hunger Task Force, Am. Bapt. Chs. Cen. Region, Kans., 1980-81; mem. gen. bd. Am. Bapt. Chs. in U.S.A., 1988-91, nominating and reference coms., 1990-91, bd. internat. ministries, 1988-91, chair budget com., 1990; mem. Mid-Am. Bapt. Chs. Social Concerns Com., 1983-88, chair, 1987-88; co-dir. Bapt. Friendship Tour to USSR, 1987. Walk coord. CROP-Ch. World Svc., Larned, 1979-81; mem. Dubuque Regional AIDS Coalition, 1988—, chair direct svcs. com., 1989—. Named Alumnus of Yr., Cen. Bapt. Theol. Sem., 1991. Mem. NAACP (chair religion affairs com. Dubuque chpt. 1989—), Am. Bapt. Chs. Mins. Coun., Bapt. Peace Fellowship N.Am., Mid-Am. Bapt. Peace Fellowship (pres. 1982-86), Dubuque Area Christians United (bd. dirs. 1983-88). Office: 1st Bapt Ch 2143 Judson Dr Dubuque IA 52001

SELL, ALAN PHILIP FREDERICK, theologian; b. Farncombe, Eng., Nov. 15, 1935; s. Arthur Philip and Freda Marion (Bushen) S.; m. Karen Elisabeth Lloyd, Aug. 1, 1959; children: Bridget Rebecca Karen, Judith Bronwen Amanda, Jonathan Patrick Alan. BA, U. Manchester, Eng., 1957, BD, 1959, MA, 1961; PhD, U. Nottingham, Eng., 1967; DD, Ursinus Coll., 1988. Ordained United Reformed Ch., 1959. Minister various Congl. Chs., Eng., 1959-68; lectr. West Midlands Coll. of Higher Edn., Eng., 1968-83; theological sec. World Alliance of Reformed Chs., Geneva, 1983-87; prof., chair Christian Thought U. Calgary, Alta., Can., 1988—; sec. youth and edn. Worcestershire Congl. Chs., 1966-68; pres. Worcester and Dist. Free Ch. Fed. Council, 1966-67; chmn. West Midlands Provincial Dept. World Ch. and Mission, 1977-83; mem. Doctrine and Worship Com., United Reformed Ch., 1979-83; dir. tng. auxiliary ministry, 1980-83. Author: Alfred Dye, Minister of the Gospel, 1974, Robert Mackintosh: Theologian of Integrity, 1977, God Our Father, 1980, The Great Debate: Calvinism, Arminianism and Salvation, 1982, Korean edn., 1989, Church Planting: A Study of Westmorland Nonconformity, 1986, Theology in Turmoil: The Roots, Course and Significance of the Conservative-Liberal Debate in Modern Theology, 1986, Saints: Visible, Orderly and Catholic. The Congregational Idea of the Church, 1986, Defending and Declaring the Faith: Some Scottish Examples 1860-1920, 1987, The Philosophy of Religion 1875-1980, 1988, Aspects of Christian Integrity, 1990, Dissenting Thought and the Life of the Churches. Studies in an English Tradition, 1990, A Reformed, Evangelical, Catholic Theology, 1991; editor: (with Ross T. Bender), Baptism, Peace and the State in the Reformed adn Mennonite Traditions, 1991; Rhetoric and Reality. Theological Reflections upon Congregationalism and Its Heirs, 1991; contbr. articles to profl. jours. Councillor Sedbergh Rural Dist. Council, Yorkshire, Eng., 1962-64. Recipient Gunning prize Victoria Inst., 1981. Fellow Royal Hist. Soc., Soc. Antiquaries of London; mem. Soc. for the Study of Theology (mem. com. 1984-87), Am. Theol. Soc., Soc. Tchrs. Speech and Drama, Brit. Fedn. Music Festivals (adjuicator). Avocations: speech, drama, music, walking, croquet. Office: U Calgary, Dept Religious Studies, 2500 University Dr NW, Calgary, AB Canada T2N 1N4 *In a threatened and divided world the churches must, together, discern the mind of Christ so that, overcoming sectarianism, they may witness effectively to the unity God has given them and wills for all.*

SELLARDS, LYLE DURKIN, minister; b. Centralia, Wash., Feb. 17, 1929; s. John Harrison and Lura Elizabeth (Cox) S.; m. Geraldine Virginia Updike, July 14, 1951 (div. Dec. 1968); m. Joyce Williams, Oct. 11, 1975; children: Sandra Lynn Riley, Carol Ann Walker, Catherine Marie, Janet Leade, Pamela Lehde, Gretchen Lucas. AA, Centralia Community Coll., 1949; BTh, N.W. Christian Coll., 1951; MDiv, Lexington (Ky.) Theol. Sem., 1955; MTh, Vancouver (B.C., Can.) Sch. Theology, 1981; M in Counseling, Idaho State U., 1981. Ordained to ministry, 1951. Youth pastor Univ. Christian Ch., Seattle, 1951-52; pastor to coll. youth Cen. Christian Ch., Lexington, 1952-55; assoc. pastor Univ. Pl. Ch., Champaign-Urbana, Ill., 1955-59; with United Campus Christian Found., Bellingham, Wash., 1959-68, Idaho State U. Ecumenical Ministry, Inc., Pocatello, 1975-85; pastor Little White Ch. Congl. United Ch. of Christ, Malta, Mont., 1988-90, Orem (Utah) Community Ch., 1990—; interim pastor First Congl. Ch., Colville, Wash., 1985-86, St. John United Ch. of Christ, Hebron, N.D., 1987-88; clergy Utah Christian Ch. (Disciples of Christ), 1951—. Mem. Am. Assn. Pastoral Counselors, Am. Assn. Marriage and Family Mediators, Interim Ministry, Phillips County Ministerial Assn. (pres. Malta chpt. 1989-90), United Ch. of Christ, Rocky Mountain Conf. United Ch. of Christ, Utah. Home: 140 N 400 East Orem UT 84057 Office: Orem Community Ch 130 N 400 East Orem UT 84057 *Be open to life and the direction of God's Spirit. Live life, insofar as possible, according to Matthew 25, and be God's Peace.*

SELLECK, DAVID JESSE, pastor; b. Towanda, Pa., Mar. 3, 1927; s. Jesse L. and Gertrude A. (Bierfreund) S.; m. Dorothy J. Mitchell, July 4, 1950; children: Deborah, David A., Stephen P., Melody J., Mark N. Student, Elim Bible Inst., 1943-44; diploma, Zion Bible Inst., 1950. Lic. to ministry Assemblies of God, 1951, ordained 1955. Interim pastor Independent, at Christ Mission, Saugus, Calif., 1950; pastor Community Ch., Forbes Road, Pa., 1951, Greensburg, Pa., 1951, Uniontown, Pa., 1952-60, Milesburg, Pa., 1960-64, Clarion, Pa., 1964—; sectional sec. N.C. sect. Assemblies of God, 1960-64, sectional treas. NCW sect., 1965-69, dist. presbyter Pa.-Del. dist., 1970-91. Pres. Clarion chpt. ARC, 1970-81. With U.S. Army, 1945-47. Republican. Home: RD 1 Box 369 Clarion PA 16214 Office: POB 228 Clarion PA 16214 *We've only one life, and it soon will be past; so let's render to Christ a service that will last!.*

SELLERS, BARRY CURTIS, clergyman; b. Atlanta, Sept. 21, 1952; s. Herman Eli and Vernell Gelene (Collins) S.; m. Barbra Ann Pennington, Apr. 18, 1975; children: Michelle Ann, Michael Brandon, Ivan Barak. BS, Trevecca Nazarene Coll., 1974; MDiv, Nazarene Theol. Sem., 1980; D Ministry, Drew U., 1988. Ordained to ministry Ch. of the Nazarene, 1981. Min. youth and music First Ch. of Nazarene, Orlando, Fla., 1974-75; assoc. min. Cen. Ch. of Nazarene, Miami, Fla., 1975-77; min. youth and music Highland Crest Nazarene Ch., Kansas City, Kans., 1977-80; sr. pastor Cen. Ch. of Nazarene, Newark, Ohio, 1980-82; sr. pastor First Ch. of Nazarene, Thomasville, Ga., 1982-88, Sumter, S.C., 1988—; sec. Ga. dist. Nazarene Youth Internat., Thomasville, 1982-86; advisor Bd. Ministerial Studies, Atlanta, 1983-88, chmn., Columbia, S.C., 1988—; bd. mem. Dist. Fin. Com., Columbia, 1988—; ministerial rep. At Risk Com., 1990—. Recipient Pres. award Ga. Dist. Ch. of Nazarene, Atlanta, 1987, Key to City of Albertville, Ala., 1974. Mem. Sumter County Ministerial Assn. (sec. 1989-90). Home: 966 Shadow Trail Sumter SC 29150 Office: First Ch of Nazarene 1010 N Guignard Dr Sumter SC 29150 *The only difference between men and boys is not found in the price of their toys. The difference is in the names of their heroes. As we grow older our heroes change but we shouldn't stop having them.*

SELLERS, FRANKLIN H., bishop. Pres., presiding bishop Ref. Episcopal Ch., Chgo. Office: Ref Episcopal Ch 1629 W 99th St Chicago IL 60643*

SELLERS, JESSE W., minister; b. Tampa, Fla., Mar. 15, 1961; s. Jesse W. Sellers and Inez (Carter) Grubbs; m. Nancy Hope Kee, Feb. 26, 1983; 1 child, Rachel Elizabeth. BA, So. Bapt. Ctr. for Bibl. Studies, 1988, M in Ministry, 1990, postgrad., 1990—; postgrad., Moody Bible Inst., Toccoa (Ga.) Falls Coll., Liberty U. Ordained to ministry So. Bapt. Conv.; cert. in Christian counseling. Evangelist City View 1st Bapt. Ch., Greenville, S.C., 1985-87; assoc.min. Oak Crest Bapt. Ch., Greenville, 1987-89; pastor Mountain Grove Bapt. Ch., Pickens, S.C., 1989—; cert. master life leader Sunday Sch. Bd. of So. Bapt. Conv., Nashville, Home Mission Bd., Atlanta. Composer religious songs including Make a Joyful Noise, He's My Jesus, The Man, the Magic of This Moment. Mem. Assn. Christian Counselors, Pickens-Twelve Mile Bapt. Assn. (dir. assn. youth discipleship 1989—, pres. 1990, time, place and preacher com. 1990—), Pickens Ministerial Coun. (v.p. 1990—). Republican. Home: 775 Meece Mill Rd Pickens SC 29671 Office: Mountain Grove Bapt Ch 644 E Preston McDaniel Rd Pickens SC 29671

SELLEW, PHILIP HARL, minister, religious educator; b. Milw., Aug. 16, 1953; s. Donald Edgar and Elgine Joyce (Harl) S.; m. Kathleen Susan Troxell, May 17, 1975; 1 child, Charles Samuel. BA summa cum laude, Macalester Coll., St. Paul, 1975; MDiv cum laude, Harvard U., 1978, ThD, 1986. Ordained, 1981. Asst. prof. U. Minn., Mpls., 1984-90, assoc. prof., 1990—; lectr. Harvard Div. Sch., 1981-84; chmn. com. on outreach Boston Presbytery, 1981-84; state rep. United Ministries Bds., Mass., 1983-84; bd. dirs. United Ministries in Higher Edn., 1985-88. Author: Dominical Discourses, 1991; editor: Gospel Traditions, 1991; contbr. articles to profl. jours. Fellow Soc. for Promotion Roman Studies; mem. Soc. Bibl. Lit., Cath. Bibl. Assn., Am. Philological Assn., Phi Beta Kappa. Democrat. Office: U Minn Dept Classics 9 Pleasant St SE Minneapolis MN 55105

SELLS, LUTHER RAY, minister, consultant; b. Detroit, Sept. 20, 1936; s. Luther O. and Delpha I. (Zachary) S.; m. Phyllis E. Rauth, Feb. 19, 1966; children: Yvonne L. Sells Tharp, Thomas Ray. BS, Ball State U., 1960; MDiv, Meth. Theol. Sem., 1963; D of Ministry, McCormick Sem., 1975. Assoc. pastor 1st United Meth. Ch., Warsaw, Ind., 1963-65; exec. dir. Fletcher Pl. Ch. and Ctr., Indpls., 1965-71; urban ministry dir. Calumet Region United Meth. Ch., Hammond, Ind., 1971-78; exec. sec. Gen. Bd. Discipleship, Nashville, 1978-88; ch. cons. Nashville, 1988—. Mem. Meth. Theol. Alumni Assn. (pres. 1973-74). Democrat. Avocations: hiking, running. Home: 836 Kendall Dr Nashville TN 37209

SELNICK, THOMAS CONRAD, priest; b. Bay Village, Ohio, Sept. 7, 1957; s. William Blake and Barbara Jane (Brennan) S.; m. Elizabeth Amy Eaton, June 16, 1984; children: Rebeckah Eaton, Susannah Katherine. BA, Johns Hopkins U., 1979; MDiv, Episc. Divinity Sch., Cambridge, Mass., 1983; cert., Harvard U., 1987. Ordained to ministry, Episcopal Ch., 1983; cert. chem. dependency counselor. Asst. rector St. Albans Ch., Bexley, Ohio, 1983-86; vicar St. Andrew's Ch., Pickerington, Ohio, 1985-90; substance abuse counselor Columbus, Ohio, 1984-90, Ashtabula, Ohio, 1990—; rector St. Peter's Ch., Ashtabula, 1990—; spirituality advisor Maryhaven Rehab. Ctr., Columbus, 1983-90; svc. provider Ohio Biodyne, 1990—; ecumenical officer Episc. Diocese of So. Ohio, 1989-90; field edn. supr. Pontifical Coll. Josephinum, Worthington, Ohio, 1986-90. Treas. Joshua House, Columbus, 1988; orginator Poverty/Plenty Art Show, Columbus, 1987; pres. bd. dirs. Cen. Buying Ctr., Columbus, 1983-90. Home: 1538 Cherry Ln Ashtabula OH 44004 Office: St Peters Ch 4901 Main Ave PO Box 357 Ashtabula OH 44004

SELVADURAI, P., religious organization administrator. Chmn. Hindu Adv. Bd., Singapore. Office: Ministry Community Devel, Pearl's Hill Terrace, Singapore 0316, Singapore*

SELZER, DAVID OWEN, minister; b. Portsmouth, Va., Sept. 13, 1951; s. Christian William Jr. and Betty Jean (Lochner) S.; m. Ann Eleanor Miller, Nov. 24, 1985. BA, U. Ky., 1972; MDiv cum laude, Nashotah House Theol. Sem., 1976. Ordained priest Episcopal Ch., 1977. Assoc. rector St. Matthew's Episc. Ch., Louisville, 1976-84; chaplain Univ. Episc. Ctr., U. Minn., Mpls., 1984—; active single adult ministry Episc. Ch., 1984—, young adult ministry, 1977-88; mem. Commn. on Ministry, Diocese of Minn., 1985—; dep. Gen. Conv., Episc. Ch., 1988, 91. Editor: Being Single, 1988; newsletter editor, 1979-82. Bd. dirs., chair religious affairs Planned Parenthood Minn., St. Paul, 1986—; chair North Suburban Youth Clinic, Robbinsdale, Minn., 1989-90; bd. dirs. Religious Coun. for Abortion Rights, Minn., 1989—. Avocations: swimming, fine arts. Office: U Episc Ctr 317 17th Ave SE Minneapolis MN 55414 *The Incarnation gives us as Christians the gift of seeing humanity and the world not as fallen but as saved and good. Our challenge is to see the presence of God in all of life and to honor this.*

SEMANCIK, JOSEPH FRANCIS, priest, social services administrator; b. Whiting, Ind., Mar. 3, 1929; s. Frank J. and Lillian (Duray) S. AB, St. Meinrad (Ind.) Coll., 1953; MSW, Loyola U., Chgo., 1960; PhD, U. Chgo., 1977. Ordained priest Roman Cath. Ch., 1953. Asst. dir. Cath. Charities, Gary, Ind., 1960-62, Diocesan dir., 1962—; pastor Sacred Heart Ch., East Chicago, Ind., 1960—. Author: The Diocesan Director of Catholic Charities, 1978; mem. editorial bd. Social Thought, 1978—; contbr. articles to profl. jours. Bd. dirs. Lake County Community Devel. Com., Hospice of Calumet Area, Munster, Ind., 1979—. Named Prelate of Honor, Pope John Paul II, 1984. Mem. Am. Acad. Cert. Social Workers (diplomate). Avocations: golf, skiing, piano. Home: 4423 Olcott Ave East Chicago IN 46312 Office: Catholic Charities 973 W 6th Ave Gary IN 46402

SEMONES, G. DAVID, clergyman; b. Selma, Ala., Sept. 20, 1961; s. Gary Ira and Levina Gail (Ward) S. BA, Chapman Coll., Orange, Calif., 1983; MDiv, Lexington (Ky.) Theol. Sem., 1987. Ordained to ministry Christian Ch. Assoc. min. 1st Christian Ch. Atlanta, Tucker, Ga., 1987-90; assoc. regional min. Christian Ch. in N.C., Wilson, 1990—; advisor youth activities commn. Christian Ch. in Ga., Macon, 1988—, gen. youth coun. Christian Ch. in U.S.A. and Can., Indpls., 1990—. Active AIDS Task Force, Wilson, 1990—. Mem. Assn. Christian Ch. Educators. Democrat. Office: Christian Ch in North Carolina Box 1568 Wilson NC 27894

SEMPLE, IAN CHALMERS, religious organization official; b. New Barnet, Hertfordshire, Eng., Dec. 2, 1928; s. Robert and Harriet (Henderson) S.; m. Louise Gloor, July 13, 1963; children: Michael Robert, Nicholas Jürg, Jennifer Isabel. BA, Oxford (Eng.) U., 1952, MA, 1955. Mem. Nat. Spiritual Assembly of Bahá'is of Brit. Isles, 1956-61, Internat. Bahá'í Coun., Haifa, Israel, 1961-63, Universal House of Justice, Haifa, 1963; mem. aux bd. for propagation of Bahá'í faith in Europe, 1957-61. 2d lt. Brit. Army., 1947-49. Fellow Inst. Chartered Accts. in Eng. and Wales. Office: Bahá'í World Ctr, 16 Golomb St, 33 382 Haifa Israel

SENGELAUB, MARY MAURITA, nun, educator; b. Reed City, Mich., June 28, 1918; d. Henry Robert and Cecilia Barbara (Kailing) S. RN diploma, Grand Rapids, Mich., 1940; B of Nursing Edn., Mercy Coll., 1949; MHA, St. Louis U., 1954; HHD (hon.), St. Michael's Coll., Winsooski, Vt., 1979; LHD (hon.), Coll. Misericordia, Dallas, Pa., 1984. Joined Sisters of Mercy, Roman Cath. Ch., 1945. Asst. head nurse St. Mary's Hosp., Grand Rapids, 1940-41, supr. orthopaedic fl., 1948, adminstr., 1957-61; gen. staff nurse Reed City Community Hosp., 1941-42; clin. instr. Mercy Hosp., Bay City, Mich., 1942-44, asst. dir. nursing svc., clin. instr., 1944-45; dir. dept. nursing arts, instr. Mercy Coll. Detroit, Bay City, Mich., 1948-51, supr. med. svc., 1953-54, adminstr., 1954-57; asst. mother provincial, coord. hosps. Mich., 1961-65; asst. to dir. dept. health affairs U.S. Cath. Conf., 1965-71; pres. Cath. Hosp. Assn., 1970-77, chairperson, 1977-83; asst. to pres. Sisters of Mercy Health Corp., 1983-84, sr. adviser to pres., 1984-88; pres. Mercy Collaborative, 1984-88; project dir. creation of health system for Sisters of St. John of God, 1988-90; interim exec. dir. St. John of Good Health System Mercy Internat. Health Svcs., Farmington Hills, Mich., 1990; spl. cons. Mercy Health Found., 1990—; Organizing mem. Saginaw (Mich.) Diocesan Coun. Cath. Nurses, 1942-43; adv. bd. Nat. Assn. Cath. Chaplains; cons. to St. Anne's Hosp., Mercy Internat. Health Svcs., 1988-89; coord. social responsibility concerns Sisters of Mercy Regional Community Detroit. Contbr. articles to various publs. Chmn. bd. Pope John XXI-XXII Ctr. for Med. Moral Rsch. & Edn. Recipient Newcomer award as med. adminstr. of yr. Am. Acad. Med. Adminstrs., Alumni Merit award St. Louis U., 1990. Fellow ACHA; mem. Cath. Health Assn., Nat. Migrant Worker Coun. (Founders award 1990), St. Louis U. Alumni Assn. (award 1990), Am. Coll. Health Care Execs., Mich. Hosp. Assn., Am. Hosp. Assn. (citation 1975), Nat. League for Nursing. Avocations: reading, cooking, playing cards, crossword puzzles. Home: House of Hesed 29000 Eleven Mile Rd Farmington Hills MI 48336 Office: Mercy Health Svcs 34605 Twelve Mile Rd Farmington Hills MI 48331-3221

SENIEUR, JUDE RICHARD, priest, teacher; b. Cin., Dec. 29, 1918; s. Charles Edward and Mildred Prudence (Hayden) S. Student, St. Fidelis Coll., 1937-41, Capuchin Coll., 1942-46, Cath. U., 1946, George Washington U., 1971-72. Dir. vocations Capuchin Franciscans, Pitts., 1946-51; prof., prefect St. Fidelis Coll., Herman, Pa., 1951-52; superior Sts. Peter and Paul Monastery, Cumberland, Md., 1952-55; pastor San Conrado, San Juan, P.R., 1956-58; rectro Seminario Capuchino, Trujillo Alto, P.R., 1959-63; commd. ensign USN, 1957—; chaplain USN, Reserve, 1957-63; tchr., cons. USN, San Diego, 1982—. Author: Vocational Replies, 1951, Pequena Guia, 1958, Finding My Catholic Faith, 1986; editor: mag. VIDA, 1958-63; contbr. articles to profl. jours. Democrat. Avocations: painting, carpentry. Home: 4972 Providence Rd San Diego CA 92117

SENIOR, DONALD PAUL, religious organization administrator; b. Phila., Jan. 1, 1940; s. Vincent Edward and Margaret (Tiernan) S. BA in Philosophy, Passionist Sem. Coll., Chgo., 1963; Licentiate in Sacred Theology, U. Louvain, Belgium, 1970, STD, 1972. Prof. New Testament Cath. Theol. Union, Chgo., 1972—, dir. Israel program, 1980-88, acting dean, 1986-87, acting pres., 1988, pres., 1988—. Author books and articles on New Testament; assoc. editor The Bible Today, New Theology Rev., New Testament Message (22 vols.); gen. editor The Cath. Study Bible; writer, commentator, host radio and TV programs, Chgo. Mem. Cath. Bibl. Soc. Am., Soc. Bibl. Lit., Soc. for New Testament Studies, Cath. Theol. Soc. Am., Chgo. Soc. Bibl. Rsch. Democrat. Home and Office: 5401 S Cornell Ave Chicago IL 60615-5698

SENKBEIL, HAROLD LEIGH, clergyman; b. Ortonville, Minn., Mar. 6, 1945; s. Harold Edward and Enid Mary (Wadleigh) S.; m. Jane Frances Nesset, Sept. 5, 1971; children: Michael Leigh, Katherine Jane, Timothy Nesset. BA, Concordia Sr. Coll., 1967; BDiv, Concordia Theol. Sem., Springfield, Ill., 1971; MDiv, Concordia Theol. Sem., Ft. Wayne, Ind., 1978, MST, 1986. Ordained to ministry Luth. Ch., 1971. Pastor Bethlehem Luth. Ch., Mahnomen, Minn., 1971-75, Zion Luth. Ch., Morris, Minn., 1975-80; missionary South Wis. dist. Luth. Ch.-Mo. Synod, Madison, 1980; pastor Luth. Ch. of the Living Christ, Madison, 1980-87; assoc. pastor Elm Grove (Wis.) Luth. Ch., 1987—; bd. dirs. South Wis. Dist. Luth. Ch.-Mo. Synod, 1989—, catechism task force, St. Louis, 1984-89. Author: Sanctification: Christ in Action, 1989. Mem. Rsch. Animal Ethics Adv. Bd., U. Wis., Madison, 1985. Recipient Servus Ecclessiae Christi Concordia Theol. Sem., Ft. Wayne, 1988. Office: Elm Grove Luth Ch 945 N Terrace Dr Elm Grove WI 53122

SENN, FRANK COLVIN, minister; b. Buffalo, Apr. 22, 1943; s. Max Frank and Katherine Ellen (Lichtenberger) S.; m. Mary Elizabeth Langford, May 15, 1976; children: Andrew, Nicholas, Emily. BA, Hartwick Coll., 1965; MDiv, Luth. Sch. Theology, 1969; PhD, U. Notre Dame, 1979. Ordained to ministry Luth. Ch., 1969. Asst. pastor Gloria Dei Luth. Ch., South Bend, Ind., 1969-75; pastor Fenner Meml. Luth. Ch., Louisville, 1975-77, Christ the Mediator Luth. Ch., Chgo., 1978-81, Holy Spirit Luth. Ch., Lincolnshire, Ill., 1986-90, Immanuel Luth. Ch., Evanston, Ill., 1990—; asst. prof. liturgics Luth. Sch. Theology Chgo., 1978-81; dir. Liturgy Conf., Washington, 1987—; bd. dirs. Dialog, St. Paul, 1975—; chair edn. com. Metro Chgo. Synod Evang. Luth. Ch. Am., Chgo., 1989—; mem. Luth.-Episcopal Dialogue in U.S.A., 1977-81. Author: The Pastor As Worship Leader, 1977, Christian Worship and its Cultural Setting, 1983; editor: Protestant Spiritual Traditions, 1986, New Eucharistic Prayers, 1987. Mem. N.Am. Acad. Liturgy, Soc. Liturgica, S.E. Lake County Clergy Assn. (pres. 1988-89). Office: Immanuel Luth Ch 616 Lake St Evanston IL 60201

SENSEL, CHARLES WERNER, minister; b. Newport, Ky., Aug. 27, 1932; s. Elmer Frererick and Evelyn (Roettger) S.; m. Sheila Gail Borell, Aug. 23, 1958; children: Sheryl, Lisa, Christopher. AB, Ky. Wesleyan, 1958; BD, Garrett Theol. Sem., 1961. Ordained to ministry Meth. Ch., 1962. Second prior Religious House, Chgo., Kansas City, 1970-72; pastor Cen. Ill. Conf., United Meth. Ch., Bloomington, Ill., 1961—; chairperson conf. nominees Cen. Ill. Conf., United Meth. Ch., 1980-84, Bloomington, 1980-84, conf. trustee, 1984, chairperson, 1991. Author: Black History as Christian Education, 1966, Who is Dietrich Bonhoeffer and John Wesley, 1990, A Periscope for Bonhoeffer's Theology, 1985. Mem. Community Ctr., Chillicothe, 1988. Mem. Internat. Bonhoeffer Soc., Chillicothe C. of C., Rotary, Kiwanis. Home: 1606 Summit Dr Pekin IL 61554 Office: Grace United Meth Ch 501 N 4th Pekin IL 61554

SENSI, GUISEPPE MARIA CARDINAL, Italian ecclesiastic; b. Cosenza, Italy, May 27, 1907; s. Francesco and Melania (Andreotti Loria) S. Ed. Lateran U., Rome. Ordained priest Roman Cath. Ch., 1929; elevated to Sacred Coll. Cardinals, 1976. Diplomatic service for the Holy See, 1934-76; ordained titular archbishop of Sardes, 1955; apostolic nuncio to Costa Rica, 1955; apostolic. del. to Jerusalem, 1956-62; nuncio to Ireland, 1962-67, Portugal, 1967-76; Hon. mem. Acad. Consentina. Address: 16 Piazza S Calisto, 00153 Rome Italy

SENTER, WILLIAM ROBERT, III, minister, counselor, community leader; b. Chattanooga, Sept. 18, 1935; s. William R. and Virginia (Mack) S.; m. Linda Anne Howard, Feb. 9, 1963; children—Lydia Elizabeth, Matthew Mack. B.S., U. South, 1957; postgrad. U. Chattanooga, 1955, U. Tenn., 1958; B.D., Bexley Hall Div. Sch. Kenyon coll., 1961; M.Div., Bexley Hall/Colgate Rochester/Crozer Theol. Sem., 1973; postgrad. Vanderbilt Div. Sch., 1969-71, Southeastern Sch. Alcohol and Drug Studies, Athens, Ga., 1976. Ordained to ministry Episcopal Ch. as deacon, 1961, as priest, 1962; cert. substance abuse counselor, Tenn. Asst. St. James Ch., Knoxville, Tenn., 1961-63; priest-in-charge St. Columba's Ch., Bristol, Tenn., 1963-68, Epiphany Episc. Ch., Lebanon, Tenn., 1968-84; rector Grace Episc. Ch., Canton, Miss., 1984—; chaplain Camp Allegheny for Girls, Lewisburg, W.Va., 1976; hon. chaplain for a day U.S. Senate, 1976; pres., treas. Senter Sch., Chatanooga, 1973-78. Founder "Hangout", Lebanon, 1968-71; originator, first chmn. Project Help (free clothing distbn. project), Lebanon, 1970-73; originator, mem. Lebanon-Wilson County Drug Abuse Commn., 1969-71, chmn., 1974-84; incorporater Lebanon-Wilson County Mental Health Ctr., 1972; mem. Wilson County Welfare adv. bd., 1974-84; chmn. Horizons com., mem. exec. com. Wilson County Bicentennial Commn., 1974-76; personnel and mgmt. tng. cons. Cracker Barrel Old Country Stores, Lebanon, 1974-76; mem. Gov.'s Commn. on Alcohol and Drug Abuse, 1972-77, vice chmn. 1975-77; bd. dirs. Lebanon YMCA, 1973-78. Mem. Tenn. Ornithol. Soc. (v.p. 1973-75), Alumni Council U. South, SAR, Nat. Model R.R. Assn., Am. Assn. Arts and Scis., Profl. Alcohol and Drug Counselors Tenn., Am. Iris Soc., Sound and Light Lebanon, Canton Community Players, Delta Tau Delta. Address: Grace Episcopol Church PO Box 252 Canton MS 39046-0252

SEPTAR, YACUB MEHMET, religious leader. Grand mufti Islam Faith, Constanta, Romania. Office: Bd Tomis 41, 8700 Constanta Romania*

SEPULVEDA RUIZ-VELASCO, JOSE TRINIDAD, bishop; b. Atotonilco El Alto, Mexico, Mar. 30, 1921. Ordained priest Roman Cath. Ch., 1948; named bishop of Tuxtla Gutierrez Chiapas, Mexico, 1965—. Office: Anexo Catedral de San Marcos, CP 29000 Chiapas Mexico

SEQUEIRA, JOHN EDWARD, deacon; b. San Francisco, Feb. 13, 1940; s. Edward Charles and Mary Josephine (McCarty) S.; m. Barbara Carol Coughlan, Aug. 22, 1964; children: Margaret Mary, Carol Louise. BA, U. San Francisco, 1964. Ordained deacon Roman Cath. Ch., 1990. Pastoral min. Roman Cath. Ch., 1964-90; risk mgr. Fritz Cos., San Francisco, 1988—; permanent deacon Archdiocese San Francisco, 1990—. Mem. Serra Club San Francisco (pres. 1987-88). Home: 2602 Monte Cresta Dr Belmont CA 94002 *I have always found that we find our greatest strengths at the time when we seem to be at our weakest. It is from our brokenness that we are strong. The greatest example of this is Jesus in the Garden of Gethsamane.*

SERELS, M. MITCHELL, rabbi; b. N.Y.C., Jan. 12, 1948; s. Abraham and Dorothy (Schiller) S.; m. Ruth H. Bendayan, June 24, 1979; children: Alain, Steven, Diana. BA, Yeshiva U., 1967, MS, 1970; MA, Hunter Coll., 1970; PhD, NYU, 1990. Ordained rabbi, 1970. Rabbi Beth El, Myrtle Beach, S.C., 1970-71, Petah Tikva, Toronto, Can., 1971-73; dir. Sephardic Community Program, N.Y.C., 1973—; rabbi Magen David Sephardic, Scarsdale, N.Y., 1983—. Author: Sephardim & Holocaust, 1985, Jews of Tangier, 1991. Mem. Am. Soc. Sephardic Studies (exec. sec. 1980—), Can. Sephardic Fedn. (founder), Am. Assn. of Sephardic (exec. sec. 1984—), Orgn. Sephardic Rabbinate (exec. sec. 1985—), Club Can. (faculty advisor), Sephardic Club (faculty advisor), Psi Chi, Pi Gamma Mu. Office: Yeshiva U 500 W 185 St New York NY 10033

SERGEANT, HILDEGARDE, minister; b. N.Y.C., Jan. 17, 1941; d. Otto Ernest and Gertrude (Schurmann) Lehmann; m. Bruce Herbert Sergeant, Dec. 21, 1984; 1 child, William Scott Tonsfeldt. Diploma, Rhema Bible Tng. Ctr., Broken Arrow, Okla., 1982-84, Sch. of the Psalmist, Ft. Worth, 1986; cert., Christian Family Inst., Tulsa, 1987. Ordained to ministry, 1988. Evangelist/psalmist Love of God Ministries, Broken Arrow, U.S., Jamaica, 1984—; marriage counselor Victory Christian Ctr., Tulsa, 1985—, tchr., 1987—; dir., founder Women Alive in Christ Internat., Broken Arrow, 1986—. Author: The Listening Heart, 1960. Tchr. Sunday Sch., marriage class, Victory Christian Ctr., communication skills workshop, Broken Arrow, 1988; dir. Cherub Choir, 1978-79. Republican. Avocations: music, ballet, racquetball, reading. Home and Office: Love of God Ministries 1604 W Knoxville Broken Arrow OK 74012

SEROTTA, GERALD, rabbi; b. Miami, Fla., July 6, 1946; s. Maurice and Dorothy Ann (Levin) S.; m. Cynthia J. Arnson, Aug. 4, 1985; 1 child, Zachary Jonah. BA, Harvard U., 1968; MA, Hebrew Union Coll., 1974; STM, N.Y. Theol. Sem., 1977. Ordained rabbi, 1974; cert. pastoral counselor. Hillel dir. City Coll., N.Y.C., 1974-76, Adelphi Coll., Garden City, L.I., N.Y., 1976-77, Rutgers U., New Brunswick, N.J., 1977-82, B'nai B'rith George Washington U., Washington, 1982—; founding co-chair New Jewish Agenda, N.Y.C., 1979-82. Editor Jewish Student Press Svc., Jerusalem, 1971-72, N.Y.C., 1972-73; mem. editorial bd. New Menorah, 1982—, Tikkun, 1985—; contbr. articles to mags. Adv. bd. Shalon Ctr., Phila., 1982—, Jewish Fund for Justice, N.Y.C., 1984; bd. dirs. Hesed Ctr., Cambridge, Mass., 1989—. Mem. Assn. Hillel Dirs. (pres. 1982-84, exec. bd. 1979-86), Cen. Conf. Am. Rabbis. Democrat. Office: B'nai Brith Hillel 2300 H St NW Washington DC 20037

SESSIONS, JAMES SCOTT, religious organization administrator; b. Ballinger, Tex., Jan. 30, 1936; m. Frances Lee Ansley; children: Elisha, Lee. BA, So. Meth. U., 1958; postgrad., Perkins Sch. Theology, 1958-59; BD, Drew Sch. Theology, 1962; MST, Union Sem., N.Y.C., 1968. Ordained to ministry as elder United Meth. Ch., 1962. Asst. chaplain Brown U., 1960-61; Meth. chaplain Princeton (N.J.) U., 1962-63; chaplain Drew U., 1963-66; Meth. chaplain Harvard U., MIT, Cambridge, Mass., 1967-69, dir. United Ministries in Higher Edn. program, 1969-72; dir. So. Appalachian Ministry in Higher Edn., 1972-78; exec. dir. Southerners for Econ. Justice, 1978-81, Commn. on Religion in Appalachia, 1981—; assoc. pastor Harvard-Epworth Ch., 1967-69; cons. Bd. Global Ministries, United Meth. Ch., 1987-88. Editor: Appalachian Issues and Resources, Land Development Rag, Atlas of the Church in Appalachia; contbr. articles to religious jours. Bd. dirs. N.J. Meth. Student Movement, 1962-68; dir. literacy project, Jamaica, 1966; active Chs.' Com. on Voter Registration; organizer Hollow Community Orgn., Morristown, N.J., Newark Tutorial Project, East Boston Youth Project, Somerville Youth Project, Cambridge Ministry in Higher Edn.; former bd. dirs. numerous civic groups. Address: PO Box 10867 Knoxville TN 37939-0867

SESSIONS, WILLIAM LAD, philosophy educator; b. Somerville, N.J., Dec. 3, 1943; s. William George and Alice Edna (Billhardt) S.; m. Vicki Darlene Thompson, Aug. 28, 1965; children: Allistair Lee, Laura Anne. BA magna cum laude, U. Colo., 1965; MA in Comparative Study of Religion, Union Theol. Sem., N.Y.C., 1967; postgrad., Oxford (Eng.) U., 1967-68; PhD, Yale U., 1971; postdoctoral studies, Stanford U., 1976, Harvard U., 1977-78. Teaching fellow Yale U., 1969; instr. U. Conn., Waterbury, 1970-71; asst. prof. philosophy Washington and Lee U., 1971-77, assoc. prof., 1977-83, prof., 1983—; instr. So. Sem., 1972; vis. prof. St. Olaf Coll., 1985-86. Contbr. articles to religious and philos. jours. Ruling elder Lexington (Va.) Presbyn. Ch., 1983-89, tchr. Sunday sch., 1984—. Glenn grantee Washington and Lee U., 1975—, Babcock Found. grantee, 1976, NEH grantee, 1977, 83, 86, Mellon Found. grantee, 1978-79, Mellon East Asian Studies grantee, 1990. Mem. Am. Philos. Assn., Va. Philos. Assn., Soc. for Philosophy of Religion (exec. coun. 1988-91, v.p. 1991-92), Soc. Christian Philosophers (steering com. ea. region 1986-90, exec. com. 1987-90), Phi Beta Kappa (exec. com. Va. chpt. 1986—, v.p. 1989-91, pres. 1991—). Office: Washington & Lee U Newcomb Hall Lexington VA 24450

SESSUM, ROBERT LEE, minister; b. Memphis, Feb. 17, 1943; s. William Calvin and Elaine Melba (Holt) S.; m. Donna Ann Snyder, July 8, 1967; 1 child, William Paul. BA, Rhodes Coll., 1965; MDiv, Va. Theol. Sem., 1970. Ordained to ministry Episcopal Ch. as priest, 1971. Asst. to rector St. Paul's Ch., Chattanooga, 1970-72; vicar Ch. of the Nativity, Ft. Oglethorpe, Ga., 1972-74; assoc. rector Christ Ch., Raleigh, 1974-79; rector All Saints' Parish, Concord, N.C., 1979—; mem. standing com. Diocese of N.C., Raleigh, 1984-87, 90—, del. to gen. conv., 1985, 88, 91, bd. dirs. Conf. Ctr., 1982-85, chmn. Communication Commn., 1983-88; mem. Cursillo Secretariat for Diocese of N.C., 1985-88. Founding pres. Hosp. Pastoral Care, Inc., Concord, N.C., 1979; chmn. bd. Piedmont Area Mental Health Authority, 1982-89; bd. dirs. Cabarrus Coop. Ministries, 1984—, Penick Home, 1984-92; founding father Cabarrus County Winter Night Shelter, 1984; chmn. profl. sect. United Way Campaign, 1990, 91; mem. task force, steering com. Greater Charlotte Regional HIV Consortium. Recipient Community Vol. Svc. award Cabarrus County United Way, 1984, Outstanding Vol. Svc. award Gov. N.C., 1988; named Sr. Man of the Yr., Concord Jaycees, 1984, Outstanding Young Man of Yr., Ft. Oglethorpe C. of C., 1974. Mem. Concord Ministerial Assn., Kannapolis Ministerial Assn. , N.C. Clergy Assn. Democrat. Home: 271 Palaside Dr NE Concord NC 28025 Office: All Saints Episcopal Ch 525 Lake Concord Rd NE Concord NC 28025

SETCHKO, EDWARD STEPHEN, minister, theology educator; b. Yonkers, N.Y., Apr. 27, 1926; s. Stephen John and Mary Elizabeth (Dulak) S.; m. Penelope Sayre, Nov. 18, 1950; children—Marc Edward, Kip Sherman, Robin Elizabeth, Jan Sayre, Dirk Stephen. B.S., Union Coll., 1948; M.Div. cum laude, Andover Newton Theol. Sch., 1953, S.T.M., 1954; Th.D., Pacific Sch. Religion, 1962. Ordained to ministry United Ch. of Christ, 1954; cert. profl. hosp. chaplain. Psychometrician, Union Coll. Character Research Project, Schenectady, N.Y., 1947-50; asst. pastor Eliot Ch., Newton, Mass., 1950-54; clin. tng. supr. Boston City Hosp., 1951-54; intern, chaplain Boston State Mental Hosp., 1953-54; univ. campus minister U. Wash., Seattle, 1954-58; Danforth grantee, 1958-59; grad. fellow in psychotherapy Pacific Sch. Religion, Berkeley, Calif., 1959-60, instr. dept. pastoral psychology, 1960-61, grad. fellow, lectr. theology and psychology, 1961-62, asst. prof. psychology and counseling, 1962-63, dir. continuing theol. edn., 1962-63; field research sec. laity div. United Ch. Christ, Berkeley, Calif. and N.Y.C., 1963-68; vis. prof. psychology Starr King Ctr. for Religious Leadership, Berkeley, 1967-69; assoc. prof. religion and soc. Starr King Ctr., Grad. Theol. Union, Berkeley, Calif., 1969-71, prof., 1971-83; career counselor The Ctr. for Ministry, Oakland, Calif., 1986-89; mem. faculty, chmn. curriculum and faculty com. Layman's Sch. Religion, Berkeley, 1960-67; cons. and lectr. in field. Mem. Peace Del., Mid-East, 1983; lectr. Internat. Conf. on the Holocaust and Genocide, Tel Aviv, 1982, Nuclear Disarmament Conf., W.Ger., 1980, 81, 82, Internat. Ctr. for Peace in the Middle East, Resource Ctr. for Non-Violence, Clergy & Laity Concerned, Ecumenical Peace Inst., Internat. Peace Acad.; World Policy Inst., Inst. Peace and World Order, Am. Friends Service Com. (bd. dirs.), Ristad Found., Am. Friends Golan Heights, Elmwood Coll. Criminal Justice; dir. The Project for Peace and Reconciliation in the Middle East (non-profit Calif. Found. 1983-89); vol. South Berkeley hunger project Alta Bates Hospice. Lt. (j.g.) USNR, 1944-46, WW II. Mem. Am. Psychol. Assn. (cert.), Calif. State Psychol. Assn., Assn. Clin. Pastoral Edn., World Future Soc., Soc. Sci. Study of Religion, Inst. Noetic Scis., Com. for Protection Human Subjects (U. Calif.-Berkeley). Democrat. Contbr. articles to profl. jours.; condr. seminars: Futurology; Intricacies of Being Human, Images of Women and Men; Changing Values in Roles Between the Sexes in a Technological Society, Cybernetics and Humanization of Man; developer curriculum: Peace and Conflict Studies (U. Calif., Berkeley).

SETELIK, JAMES JOSEPH, JR., priest; b. Balt., Oct. 16, 1952; s. James Joseph and Jacqueline (Reisinger) S. BA in Criminology, Fla. State U., 1974; M. Div., Cath. Theol. Union, Chgo., 1981. Ordained priest Roman Cath. Ch., 1984. Pastor Diocese Reno and Las Vegas, Nev. Co-author: (booklet/workbook) Before...The Death Experience, 1988. So. Research and Scholarship Found. scholar, 1973-74. Mem. K.C. Democrat. Avocations: hiking, wines, music. Address: St Joseph Cath Ch 1035 C St Elko NV 89801 *When all vanities have faded and paled, we will be judged only on whether we have lived life to its fullest by loving one another and seeking a close relationship with God.*

SETIAN, NERSES MIKAIL, bishop, apostolic exarchate; b. Zara, Turkey, Oct. 18, 1918; s. Nishan and Bayzar (Deveciyan) S. B. in Philosophy, U. Gregoriana, Rome, 1937, L.Theology, 1942, J.C.D., 1945. Ordained priest Armenian Catholic Ch., 1941. Ordained titular bishop of Ancira at the Armenians and 1st exarch of the apostolic exarchate for Armenian-Rite Catholics in Can. and U.S.A. Armenian Catholic Ch., N.Y.C., 1981—. Home and Office: St Ann's Armenian Cath Cathedral 110 E 12th St New York NY 10003

SETLALEKGOSI, BONIFACE TSHOSA, bishop. Bishop of Gaborone, Roman Cath. ch., Botswana. Office: Bishop's House, PO Box 218, Gaborone Botswana*

SETLIFFE, ANDREW BENTON, JR., education minister; b. Reidsville, N.C., June 24, 1922; s. Andrew Benton and Nannie (Dockery) S.; m. Dorothy Cardwell, Mar. 2, 1946; children: Dorothy Jean, Marianne, Andrea Leigh. BA, Baylor U., 1950; MRE, Southwestern Bapt. Theol. Sem., 1952, DRE, 1959. Ordained to ministry, 1956. Min. edn. and administrn. Parkside Bapt. Ch., Denison, Tex., 1952-55; min. edn. First Bapt. Ch., Cleburne, Tex., 1955-58; min. edn. and administrn. Cen. Bapt. Ch., Wycross, Ga., 1958-60, Grand Ave. Bapt. Ch., Ft. Smith, Ark., 1960-70; min. edn. Pulaski Heights Bapt. Ch., Little Rock, 1970-76; retired, 1976; mem. Ridgecrest faculty So. Bapt. Youth Week, 1964, Tng. Union Week, 1966, 67; chmn. nominationg com. Ark. Bapt. State Conv., 1973, pres. exec. bd., 1976-77; adult conf. leader Ark. Bapt. Sunday Sch. Conv.; pres. Ark. Bapt. Religious Edn. Assn., 1974. Contbr. articles to religious publs. With U.S. Army. Decorated Bronze Star; Recipient Distinguished Svc. award Sch. Religious Edn., Southwestern Bapt. Theol. Sem., 1989. Mem. Southwestern Bapt. Religious Edn. Assns. 1st non-pastor to serve as pres. exec. bd. Ark. Bapt. Conv. Home: 6700 Granada Dr Little Rock AR 72205 Office: 2200 Kavanaugh Blvd Little Rock AR 72205

SETTGAST, LELAND G., religion educator, minister; b. Columbus, Nebr., June 6, 1939; s. George E. and Dena (Henke) S.; m. Eunice Wurdeman, Apr. 29, 1964; children: Bradford Lee, Christine Renee. Student, U. Nebr., 1956-57, St. Paul's Coll., 1958-59; BTh, Concordia Sem., Ft. Wayne, Ind., 1964; MA in Psychology, Calif. Coast U., 1977; DD, So. Calif. Theol. Sem., 1990. Ordained to ministry Luth. Ch.-Mo. Synod, 1964. Pastor Immanuel Luth. Ch., Osceola, Iowa, 1964-66, Highland Park Luth. Ch., L.A., 1966-68; sr. pastor Christ Luth. Ch., Norfolk, Nebr., 1968-73; exec. dir. Luth. Bible Translators, Orange, Calif., 1974-75; dir. chaplains Christian Jail Workers, Inc., L.A., 1976—, Los Angeles County Sheriff and Probation Depts., L.A., 1976—; dir. pub. rels. English dist. Luth. Ch.-Mo.Synod, Detroit, 1978—; chaplain Calif. Instn. for Women, 1988-89; prof. So. Calif. Theol. Sem., 1990—; dir. vol. edn., Gleaners, Inc., 1991—; panelist radio talk show Religion on the Line, L.A., 1983—; participant TV talk shows, L.A., 1980—; official chaplain Al-impics Internat., Castaic, Calif., 1987-89; participant Nat. Prayer Breakfast, Washington, 1988, Nat. Leadership Conf., Washington, 1988; U.S. dir. Philippine Prison Ministry, Bohol, The Philippines, 1988—. Producer, dir. filmstrip Victory Is Sobriety, 1983 (award of merit 1984), radio broadcast Beyond Prison Walls, 1977-79; editor Broken Shackles newspaper, 1976-83; actor TV and motion pictures, 1989—. Bd. dirs. Highland Park Symphony, L.A., 1967-68, Big Bros. Am., Norfolk, 1972-73; v.p., sec. Nat. Found. for Rehab., San Clemente, Calif., 1987—; bd. dirs. Friends Christ Coll., Irvine, Calif., 1980-81. Mem. Am. Protestant Correctional Assn., Am. Film Inst., Religion in Media, So. Calif. Broadcasters Assn., Kiwanis. Republican. Home: 2875 E Virginia Ave Anaheim CA 92806 *Life on earth is a short walk when compared to eternity. It can seem like an eternal walk, however, unless it is walked hand-in-hand with the Master.*

SETTLAGE, ARTHUR CRAIG, minister; b. Ft. Worth, July 1, 1942; s. Arthur Charles and Audrey Thelma (Jennings) S.; m. Rachel Helena Naumann, July 24, 1965. BA, Valparaiso U., 1964; MDiv, Concordia Sem., 1968; M Sacred Theology, Yale U., 1969. Ordained to ministry Evang. Luth. Ch. in Am., 1969. Parish pastor Savior Divine Luth. Ch., Palos Hills, Ill., 1969-87; dir. candidacy Evang. Luth. Ch. Am., Chgo., 1988—; sec. English Synod Luth. Ch., 1976-87, Met. Chgo. Synod, 1987-90. Contbr. articles to profl. pubs. Pres. S.W. Cook County Family and Mental Health Svcs., 1988-89. Avocations: travel, cooking. Office: Evangelical Luth Ch Am 8765 W Higgins Rd Chicago IL 60631-4195

SETTLE, EDWIN THEODORE, religion educator; b. Covington, Ky., Sept. 27, 1901; s. Edwin Theodore and Mary Ella (McGill) S.; m. Mary Louise Stacy, Aug. 15, 1931; 1 child, Louise Carroll. BA, U. Cin., 1923; ThM, So. Bapt. Theol. Sem., 1926; PhD, Yale U., 1931; postgrad., Oxford (Eng.) U., 1966. Minister First Bapt. Ch., West Haven, Conn., 1931-43; prof. religion and philosophy Doane Coll., Crete, Nebr., 1946-48, Coe Coll., Cedar Rapids, Iowa, 1948-69. Author: Why Doesn't God Do Something?, 1988; contbr. articles to profl. jours. Pres. Civic Forum, West Haven, Conn., 1941, Coun. on World Questions, Cedar Rapids, 1948. Major, chaplain, U.S. Army, 1943-46, ETO, PTO. Fellow NYU, 1959, Danforth Found., 1962. Mem. Am. Acad. Religion (pres. midwest sect. 1964), Am. Philos. Assn. (sec. Iowa sect. 1962-64), Soc. for Sci. Study Religion), UNA (congl. liaison 1986), Rotary (chmn. internat. svc. projects India-Thailand-Japan, North Stockton Calif. chpt. 1975-77). Home: 1319 N Madison Stockton CA 95202 *As a Christian minister and professor of religion and philosophy I see God as the Spirit of Truth, Justice and Love. In every area of life the quest for truth, the support of justice, and love of others (concern for their welfare) constitutes the true worship of God and is the basis for peace and happiness.*

SETTLE, MARVIN B., JR., religious organization administrator; b. Washington, May 19, 1948; s. Marvin B. and Paulinge E. (Robey) S.; m. Betty S. Maggard, June 22, 1968; children: Ryan R., Kevin C., Jeffrey C. AA, Bluefield Coll., 1968; BA, U. Richmond, 1970; MRE, So. Sem., 1972. Assoc. pastor Immanuel Bapt. Ch., Colonial Hts., Va., 1973-75, First Bapt. Ch., Bluefield, W.Va., 1975-78; dir. Christian Social Ministries, Richmond, Va., 1978-84; dir. missions Yates Bapt. Assn., Durham, N.C., 1984-88; exec. dir. Norfolk (Va.) Bapt. Assn., 1988—; Trustee Va. Bapt. Children's Home, Salem, Va., 1984, U. Richmond, 1988—. Home: 1088 Elloree Ct Virginia Beach VA 23464 Office: Norfolk Bapt Assn 513 N Lynnhave Rd Virginia Beach VA 23452

SETZER, JOSEPH, minister, church consultant; b. New Brunswick, N.J., Sept. 28, 1950; s. George David and Jean Ann (O'Brien) S.; m. Deborah Lynn Livingston, June 24, 1972; children: Kim, Kelly. BA, Northeastern Bible Coll., Essex Fells, N.J., 1974; ThM, Bethany Sem., Dothan, Ala., 1991; postgrad., Regent U., Virginia Beach, Va., 1991—. Ordained to ministry Conservative Bapt. Assn. Am., 1976. Youth evangelist, cons. Y.F.C.I., Wheaton, Ill., 1973-80; mem. R & D staff ea. region, dir. campus life div., dir. tng. club personel Young for Christ Internat., Totowa, N.J., 1973-77; asst. pastor Pennsville Bapt. Ch., Scottdale, Pa., 1981-83; pastor Saltsburg (Pa.) Bapt. Ch., 1983-88; pastor 1st Bapt. Ch., Meredith, N.H., 1988—, cons., 1991—; v.p. Conservative Bapt. Assn. Pa., Enola, 1982-87; state dir. Conservative Bapt. Assn. N.H. and Vt., Meredith, 1990—. Fireman, chaplain Saltsburg Fire Dist., 1984-88; mem. curriculum com. Saltsburg Sch. Dist., 1985-87; com. mem. N.H. Gov.'s Commn., 1990—. Mem. Christian Mgmt. Assn. (regional bd. dirs.), Meredith C. of C. Republican. Home: PO Box 1462 Meredith NH 03253 Office: 1st Bapt Ch PO Box 55 Meredith NH 03253 *There are many things that give the appearance of satisfaction but fall far short. By knowing Jesus Christ, I have found more satisfaction but also, purpose, meaning, and direction as Matthew 16: 24-28 and Acts 17:27-28 reveals.*

SETZER, KIRK, religious leader. Pres. Amana (Iowa) Ch. Soc. Office: Amana Ch Soc Amana IA 52203

SEUNG, ALBERT SI-NGAI, minister; b. Hong Kong, Dec. 1, 1951; came to U.S., 1982; s. You-Shek and Hang Hon (Lau) Sheng; m. Hsing Yian Ching, Aug. 15, 1987; 1 child, Zephaniah. BS, U. Houston, 1983; MABS, D.T.S., 1986. Ordained to ministry, 1985. Pastor Arlington (Tex.) Chinese Ch., 1985—; bd. dirs., Christian Com. Inc., Houston, 1990—. Com. mem. Arlington Substance Abuse Project Report, 1990; trustee United Way, Tarrant, Tex., 1991; advisor Arlington Police Dept., Tarrant. Mem. Citizen Police Acad. Home: 1519 Coll # 204 Arlington TX 76010 Office: Arlington Chinese Ch 805 Oakwood Ln Arlington TX 76012

SEWELL, JAMES THOMAS, minister, educator; b. Lubbock, Tex., Jan. 8, 1942; s. O.D. and Mary Jane (McMahon) S.; m. Linda Kay Morgan, June 8, 1963; children: Kathryn, Mark, Sharon. Grad. theology, Bapt. Bible Coll., Springfield, Mo., 1963; BA, Garland (Tex.) Bible Coll., 1965; MRE, MDiv, Temple Bapt. Theol. Sem., Chattanooga, 1968; PhD, Bob Jones U., Greenville, S.C., 1972. Prof. Bapt. Bible Coll., 1972—, chmn. edn. dept., 1975-79, dir. div. bibl. studies, 1979—; minister edn. Park Crest Bapt. Ch., Springfield, 1973—; pastor Bethel Bapt. Ch., Arlington, Tex., 1991—. Author: The Lesser Lights, 1977, Degrees For The Christian Ministry, 1980. Recipient Alumnus of Yr. award Bapt. Bible Coll. Alumni Assn., 1991. Avocations: computers, fishing, camping. Home: 317 Lemon Dr Arlington TX 76018 Office: Bethel Bapt Ch 506 E Randal Mill Rd Arlington TX 76011

SEXSON, LYNDA, religion educator; b. Vancouver, Wash., Sept. 25, 1942; m. Michael Sexson, Feb. 2, 1964; children: Devin, Vanessa. PhD, Syracuse (N.Y.) U., 1982. Assoc. prof. Mont. State U., Bozeman, 1976—; artist-in-residence Djerassi Found., Calif., 1983-84. Author: Margaret of the Imperfections, 1988 (Pacific N.W. Booksellers award 1989), Ordinarily Sacred, 1982; co-editor Corona Jour.; contbr. numerous articles to profl. jours. Mont. Art Coun. fellow, 1989; recipient Mont. award Mont. Com. for Humanities, 1984, Betty Coffey award Mont. State U., 1988. Mem. Am. Acad. of Religion, Soc. for Values in Higher Edn., Nat. Fedn. State Humanities Coun. (Helen C. Martin Schwartz prize 1984). Home: 515 S 7th Bozeman MT 59715 Office: Mont State U Dept History & Philosophy Bozeman MT 59717

SEXTON, RICHARD, school system administrator. Supt. schs. Diocese of Fresno, Calif. Office: Office Supt Schs 1510 N Fresno St Fresno CA 93703*

SEYMOUR, DAVID MAURICE, minister; b. Valparaiso, Fla., Oct. 24, 1952; s. Collie and Cary Christine (Watson) S.; m. Marilyn Rose Dallman, June 1, 1975. BA, U. N.C., Charlotte, 1976; MDiv, Duke U., 1980; postgrad., Luth. Theol. So. Sem., Columbia, S.C., 1990—. Ordained to ministry United Ch. of Christ, 1980. Pastor Belews Creek (N.C.)-Salem Chapel, 1980-84, Holland United Ch. of Christ, Suffolk, Va., 1984—; commr. Commn. for Racial Justice, United Ch. of Christ, Clevel., 1985—; del. Gen. Synod, Ames, Iowa, 1985; bd. dirs. So. Conf., Graham, N.C., 1989—. Contbr. to Christian jours. Congl. dist. organizer United Ch. of Christ Office for Ch. in Society, Suffolk, Va., 1985-90; mem. religion and socialism commn. Dem. Socialists Am. Mem. Mercersburg Soc., Nature Conservancy, Ruritan Club (chaplain 1985-87, chmn. pub. svc. com.). Office: Holland United Ch of Christ 6733 S Quay Rd PO Box 7097 Suffolk VA 23437

SEYMOUR, PHILIP MERRITT, pastor; b. Detroit, June 4, 1945; s. Everett Kyes and Doris Eleanor (Merritt) S.; m. Rachel Virginia Townsend, July 15, 1967 (div. Mar. 1989); m. Julie Look MacLachlan, Nov. 11, 1989. Student, Albion (Mich.) Coll., 1963-66; BA, Wayne State U., 1967; MDiv cum laude, Wesley Theol. Sem., 1970; postgrad., Ecumenical Theol. Ctr., 1983—. With Ford Motor Co., Dearborn, Mich., 1963-67; pastor Novi (Mich.) United Meth. Ch., 1970-75; assoc. pastor 1st United Meth. Ch., Ypsilanti, Mich., 1975-77; pastor Warren Ave. and Sheridan Ave. United Meth. Ch., Saginaw, Mich., 1977-80, Good Shepherd United Meth. Ch., Dearborn, 1980-88, Embury United Meth. Ch., Birmingham, Mich., 1988—; counselor in field. Founder Sr. and Youth Employment Svc., S.W. Oakland County, 1979-75; pres. New Life Com. on Retardation, Detroit, 1981-82. Mem. Assn. Psychol. Type, Sierra. Democrat. Avocations: pack packer, miniature furniture. Home: 1720 Bradford Birmingham MI 48009 Office: Embury United Meth Ch 1803 E 14th Mile Rd Birmingham MI 48009

SHACKLEFORD, WILLIAM ALTON, SR., minister; b. Red Springs, N.C., Aug. 5, 1947; s. Purcell and Pearl (Walton) S.; m. Rebecca Belsches, Dec. 2, 1972; children: Kristal Lynn, William Alton Jr. Student, Hampton U., 1965-67, U. Richmond, 1969, 70; DD (hon.), Va. Sem. and Coll., 1990. Ordained to ministry Unity Bapt. Mins.' Conf., 1977. Pastor Cedar Grove Bapt. Ch., Charles City, Va., 1979-82, St. Paul High Street Bapt. Ch., Martinsville, Va., 1986—; past pres. Bapt. Sunday sch. and Bapt. Tng. Union Congress of Va., Sunday sch. Union of Hampton and Adjoining Cities, Unity Bapt. Mins.' Conf., Newport News, Va.; corr. sec., mem. Christian edn. aux. Va. Bapt. State Conv.; sr. technician tech. svc. Badishe Corp., Williamsburg, Va., 1967-81, asst. supr. corp. office svcs., 1981-86; vol. chaplain, chaplain hospice program Martinsville and Henry County Meml. Hosp. Contbr. articles to Martinsville Bull. Apptd. supt. Schs. Adv. Coun.; mem. Child Abuse and Neglect Multidiscipline Team; bd. dirs. Martinsville and Henry County Habitat for Humanity; mem. exec. bd. Martinsville Voter's League, 1987—; apptd. adminstrv. bd., overall econ. devel. com., ad hoc drug and alcohol abuse com. Martinsville Dept. Social Svcs.; mem. adv. coun. Good News Jail and Prison Ministries; chmn. bd. dirs., mem.. adv. com., mem. editorial bd. Patrick Henry Drug and Alcohol Coun. Named Outstanding Min. Nat. Hairston Clan, 1988; recipient Dedicated Svc. award Va.'s One Ch. One Child Program, 1989, numerous others. Mem. NAACP, Martinsville and Henry County Ministerial Alliance (various positions). Home: 405 3d St Martinsville VA 24112 Office: St Paul High Street Bapt Ch PO Box 1003 401 Fayette St Martinsville VA 24114 *I live with the assurance that the invisible hand of God works to bless and exalt those who commit the totality of their existence to serve God and benefit humanity.*

SHAEFFER, DAVID LEON, lay worker; b. Dayton, Ohio, Sept. 20, 1959; s. Leon E. and Kathryn Elaine (Young) S.; m. Deborah Darlene Clibbon, Aug. 27, 1984; children: Mikaela Joy, Jonathan David, Christian Bryant. BA, Southwestern Coll., Phoenix, 1986, BS, 1986. Min. edn. Paradise Valley Evang. Free Ch., Phoenix, 1988-89; tchr. Paradise Valley Unified Sch. Dist., Phoenix, 1988—; mem. worship com. Paradise Valley Evang. Free Ch., 1988-89, elder, 1988-89, mem. missions com., 1991—. Republican. Office: Paradise Valley Evang Free Ch 3344 E Hearn Rd Phoenix AZ 85032-5363 *In the rush and tumult of living in today's society one thing remains clear. In the final analysis, faith, family and mankind provide the only lasting and eternal benefit.*

SHAEFFER, LAURIE, ecumenical agency administrator. Coun. adminstr. Greater Flint (Mich.) Coun. Chs. Office: Greater Flint Coun Chs 927 Church St Flint MI 48502*

SHAFER, ERIC CHRISTOPHER, minister; b. Hanover, Pa., Apr. 10, 1950; s. B. Henry and Doris M. (Von Bergen) S.; m. Kristi L. Owens, Nov. 24, 1973. BA, Muhlenberg Coll., 1972; MDiv, Hamma Sch. Theology, 1976. Ordained to ministry Luth. Ch. Am., 1976. Pastor Holy Trinity Meml. Luth. Ch., Catasauqua, Pa., 1976-83; asst. to Bishop Northeastern Pa. Synod, Wescosville, $, 1983—; staff ELCA Commn. for Fin. Support, 1988—; del. 5th Assembly Luth. World Fedn., Evian, France, 1970, Luth. Ch. Am. Convs., 1972, 74, 84; trustee Muhlenberg Coll., Allentown, Pa., 1972-83; participant in Global Consultation, Larnaca, Cyprus, 1987. Editor: The Northeaster newsletter, 1984-87, Luth. Ch. Am. Conv. Summary, 1986, Evang. Luth. Ch. Am. Conv. Summary, 1987, Partners in The Spirit newspaper, 1988—, The Spirit of the Northeastern Pennsylvania Synod newsletter, 1989—, Synod Lutheran mag. insert, 1988—; contbr. to an interdenominational sermon series; contbg. editor The Lutheran mag., 1989—; exec. producer: (TV series) One in Spirit, 1990-91. Bd. dirs. Planned Parenthood of Lehigh Valley, Allentown, 1982-83. Mem. Smoke Free Valley, Muhlenberg Coll. Alumni Assn. Democrat. Avocations: running, computers, photography, travel. Home: 62 Wall St Bethlehem PA 18018-6014 Office: Northeastern Pennsylvania Synod 4865 Hamilton Blvd Wescosville PA 18106-9705

SHAFER, WAYNE L., minister; b. Charleston, W.Va., Aug. 7, 1950; s. Charles Everett and Charlotte (Robison) S.; 1 child, Austin Matthew. BS, Marshall U., 1972; M Ministry, Anderson Sch. Theology, 1976, MDiv, 1977. Ordained to ministry Ch. of God, 1977. Sales rep. Fidelity Union Life Ins., Huntington, W.Va., 1972-73; clin. chemist Cabell-Huntington Hosp., 1973-74; pastor, chaplain Shiloh Friends Ch., Elwood, Ind. and Camp Little Turtle, Pleasant Lake, Ind., 1974-77; pastor Bennington (Vt.) Ch. of God, 1979-84; dir. pastoral care Putnam Meml. Health Corp., Bennington, 1983-88; dir. Ctr. for Pastoral Care, Shaftsbury, Vt., 1986-88; sales rep. Prudential Fin. Svcs., Shaftsbury, 1988-; pastoral counselor Shalom Counseling Ctr. 1st Congl. Ch., West Springfield, Mass., 1982, Neruol. Cons. PC, Bennington, 1985-88; chaplain Meml. Hosp., Worcester, Mass., 1982, Vol. Fire Dept., Bennington, 1986-88; sec. Minister's Coun. N.E. area Ch. of God, 1981-82, 87-88, sec. camp bd., 1987-88; mem. Tri-State Evang. Minister's Fellowship; facilitator establishing pastoral care as allowable Medicaid cost, Vt., 1987; coord. various symposiums. Editor (newsletter) Pilgrimage, 1981. Unit vol. Northern New Eng. div. Salvation Army, 1987-88; chairperson steering com. Regional Planning Adv. Coun., Bennington County, Vt., 1987; bd. dirs. Project Ind., Bennington, 1985-88; mem. Bennington Adult Resource Team, Adolescent Childwatch Com., Bennington Elderly Action Com. Mem. Coll. Chaplains, Assn. for Clin. Pastoral Edn. (clin.), Greater Bennington Ecumenical Clergy Assn. Avocations: hunting, fishing, sports. Home: 27 Wilder St White River Junction VT 05001

SHAFER, WILLIAM LEWIS, JR., minister; b. Rock Tavern, N.Y., Feb. 10, 1933; s. William Lewis Sr. and Dorothea Alice S.; m. Katherine Juanita Smith, Jan. 31, 1952; 1 child, William Lewis II. Ordained deacon Meth. Ch., 1958, ordained elder, 1960. Parish minister The Meth. Ch./United Meth. Ch., Center Ossipee, N.H., 1952—; minister The United Meth. Chs., Moultonville and, South Tamworth, N.H., 1988—; disaster coord. N.H. United Meth. Conf., 1985—; chaplain N.H. Gen. Ct., Concord, 1963, 69, 71, Civil Air Patrol. Bd. dirs., chmn. REACT Internat., Inc., Northbrook, Ill., 1983-85; pres. The Windrifter Resort Assn., Wolfeboro, N.H., 1980—.

SHAFFER, DAVID ALAN, minister; b. Wellington, Kans., May 8, 1954; s. Elvis Henry and Mary Ellen (Neal) S.; m. Vickie W. Brock, Aug. 9, 1975; children: Stephanie, Teresa. GTh, Bapt. Bible Coll., Springfield, Mo., 1982. Ordained to ministry Bapt. Bible Fellowship, 1985. Assoc. pastor Glenville Bible Bapt. Ch., Wichita, Kans., 1982-85; pastor Fundamental Bapt. Ch., Glenrock, Wyo., 1985-87, First Bible Bapt. Ch., Oklahoma City, 1987—; chmn. Okla. Bapt. Bible Fellowship, 1989—, Wyo. Bapt. Bible Fellowship, 1986-87. Contbr. articles to profl. jours. Republican. Home: 2105 SW 71st St Oklahoma City OK 73159 Office: First Bible Bapt Ch 1140 SW 29th St Oklahoma City OK 73109

SHAFFER, DEWEY LEE, minister; b. Balt., June 19, 1952; s. Alvey B. Sr. and Aurel Louise (Chenoweth) S.; m. Norene Louise Miller, Sept. 30, 1972; children: Annette, Adam, Amy. Student, North Cen. Tech. Coll., Mansfield, Ohio, 1971-72; BA in Religion, Mt. Vernon Nazarene Coll., 1987; MDiv in Bibl. Studies, Ashland (Ohio) Theol. Sem., 1990. Ordained to ministry Bapt. Ch., 1991. Pastor Bryn Zion Bapt. Ch., Mt. Gilead, Ohio, 1984-91, Grand Prairie Bapt. Ch., Marion, Ohio, 1991—; substitute tchr. Mt. Gilead Exempted Schs., 1987—, asst. band dir., 1990-91; moderator Marion Bapt. Assn., Ohio, 1988-90, exec. trustee social concerns-outreach, 1986-88; del. Am. Bapt. Ohio, 1988-90; asst. prof. Greek Ashland Theol. Sem., 1989-90. Bd. dirs. ARC, Mt. Gilead, 1988-91; com. mem. Mt. Gilead High Sch. Levy, 1991-92; counselor Mil. Support Group, Mt. Gilead, 1991-92. Recipient Harry Manning award Am. Bapt. Chs. Ohio, 1990; Jetter grantee Mt. Vernon Nazarene Coll., 1987. Mem. Morrow County Ministerial Assn., Inter-Ch. Coun. Mt. Gilead Com., Masons (32d degree). Republican. Home: 5243 Wyandot Rd Nevada OH 44849 Office: Grand Prairie Bapt Ch 4893 Upper Rd Marion OH 43302

SHAFFER, DOUGLAS L., minister. Exec. dir. Reading (Pa.) Urban Ministry. Office: Reading Urban Ministry 230 N Fifth St Rm 300 Reading PA 19601*

SHAFFER, FRANCES ANNETTE, minister; b. Mauk, Ga., Sept. 22, 1946; d. Sam and Myrtice (McCrary) Jenkins; m. Thomas Shaffer, Apr. 26, 1976. Lic. practical nurse, Columbus (Ga.) Vocat. Tech., 1971; certificate, Wash. Bible Coll., Lanham, Md., 1975, Patricia Stevens Coll., Washington, 1976; BA in Rehab. Counseling, Faith Coll., 1978. Ordained to ministry A.M.E. Ch. as elder, 1977. Resource specialist Taylor County Bd. of Edn., Butler, Ga., 1969-73; family svc. counselor Atlanta Housing Authority, 1973-75; records supr. Assn. of Am. Med. Colls., Washington, 1975; dir. Middle Flint Coun. on Aging, Albany, Ga., 1977-78, Eviron. Protection Program, Albany, 1978-83; pastor A.M.E. Ch., Atlanta, 1986-90, Mt. Carmel A.M.E. Ch., Atlanta, 1991—; coord. first Internat. Women in Ministry Seminar of A.M.E. Ch., Turner Theol. Sem., Atlanta, 1983; first female to deliver annual sermon in the Atlanta N. Georgia Annual Conf. of A.M.E. Ch. Leader Nat. Girl Scouts of U.S., Macon, Ga., 1964-66; bd. dirs. Sr. Citizen Bd., Butler, Ga., 1977—; mem. adv. coun. Atlanta Recreation Assn., 1989—. Mem. NAFE, NAACP, African Meth. Episcopal Ministers Alliance, Smithsonian Inst., Les Jeun Bon Temps (pres. Atlanta 1979-84), Order of Eastern Star. Republican. Avocations: reading, jogging, teen rap sessions, hiking, creative dancing. Home: 2723 Penwood Pl Lithonia GA 30058 Office: Mt Calvary Ch 1473 Wellswood Dr SE Atlanta GA 30315

SHAFFER, JOHN JAY, clergyman; b. Ludlow, Ill., Nov. 23, 1937; s. George H and Bernice H. (Radley) S.; m. Barbara Marian Dadd, June 16, 1962. B.A. in Philosophy, Ill. Wesleyan U., 1959; M.Div., Garrett-Evang. Theol. Sch., 1962. Ordained elder United Meth. Ch., 1962. Pastor chs., Wapella, St. James and Danville, Ill., 1957-62; pastor Alaska Missionary Conf., Kenai, Chugiak, Juneau-Douglas, Nome, East Anchorage, Sitka, Alaska, 1962—, Nome Presbyn. Ch., 1975-81, United Meth. Ch. of Sitka, 1988—; sec. Alaska Missionary, 1985—; chmn. Hope Retreat Ctr. Com., Alaska, 1983-88; del. Gen. conf. United Meth. Ch., 1980, Western Jurisdictional Confs., United Meth. Ch., 1968, 80. Bd. dirs. Rural Alaska Community Action Agy., 1975-79; candidate for Alaska Ho. of Reps., 1968. Merrill fellow Harvard U., 1989. Mem. Rotary, Phi Kappa Phi. *The claims and counterclaims of nations and religions often lead to serious conflict. I keep reminding myself that final judgment of all ideas and beliefs is not in my hands. It is in God's hands. We need to let God be God!.*

SHAFFER, PAUL M., lay worker; b. Harmony Grove, Pa., Sept. 15, 1942; s. Glenn M. and Ruth Louise (Boyer) S.; m. Mary Louise Sechrist, Sept. 15, 1968; 1 child, Paula Marie. Grad. high sch., Dillsburg, Pa., 1961. Royal ambassador dir. Little Bethel Bapt. Assn., Madisonville, Ky., 1980-83, brotherhood dir., 1983—; maintenance profl. Penney Park Apts., Madisonville, 1991—; trustee Hanson (Ky.) Bapt. Ch., 1985—, treas., 1989—. Big brother Big Bros./Big Sisters, Madisonville, 1989—; commr. City of Hanson City Coun., 1982-83. Democrat. Home: 135 W Railroad Hanson KY 42413

SHAFFER, RICHARD JERRY, JR., minister; b. Des Moines, May 5, 1959; s. Richard Jerry and Karen Lee (Beattie) S.; m. Jaimie Jene Beers,Apr. 7, 1984; 1 child, Tyler. BA, Drake U., 1981; MDiv, U. Dubuque, 1988. Ordained to ministry Presbyn. Ch., 1988. With air talent/prodn. dept. Sta. KRNT-KRNQ div. Stauffer Communications, Des Moines, 1979-82; copywriter, account exec. Mills Fin. Mktg. and Advt., Storm Lake, Iowa, 1982-85; theology rsch. asst. U. Dubuque Theol. Sem., 1986-87, teaching asst. Hebrew Studies, 1986-88; pastor United Presbyn. Ch., Vail, Iowa, 1988—; student pastor Cleghorn (Iowa) Presbyn. Ch., summers 1986-87, Mt. Pleasant Presbyn. Ch., Marcus, Iowa, summers 1986-87; mem. com. on ministry Prospect Hill Presbytery, 1989—, mission interpretation com., 1988-89. Editor presbytery newsletter The Prospector, 1990—. Mem. adv. com. Ar-We-Va Community Sch. Dist., Westside, Iowa, 1989—, human growth and devel. com., 1989—. Mem. Sigma Alpha Epsilon. Democrat. Avocations: photography, hiking. Office: United Presbyn Ch Box 98 Vail IA 51465

SHAHINIAN, DEAN VAHAN, foundation administrator, lawyer; b. Washington, Jan. 30, 1953; s. Paul and Grace (Jelalian) S. BS, Yale U., 1974; JD, U. Va., 1977; MS, MIT, 1979. Bar: Va., U.S. Supreme Ct. Exec. dir. The Ararat Found., Mt. Vernon, 1985—; asst. chief counsel Office of Thrift Supervision, Washington, 1986—; chmn. Armenian Life Cultural Lectrs., Washington, 1988—; mem. recruitment adv. com. St. Nersess Sem., New Rochelle, N.Y., 1986-88; bd. dirs. Christian Conciliation Svc. Met. Washington, 1980-82; mem. Diocese Coun. Armenian Ch. Am. Del. Diocese of Armenian Ch. Assembly, N.Y.C., 1989—; trustee Mamigonian Found., Rockville, Md., 1982-84; mem. Alexandria (Va.)-Leninakan Sister City Com., 1989-91. Mem. Va. State Bar, Christian Legal Soc., Nat. Press Club, Yale Club Washington, Harvard Club Washington, MIT Club Washington. Armenian Orthodox. Home: 8909 Captains Row Alexandria VA 22308 *"For yours, God, is the kingdom and the power and the glory, forever. Amen."*

SHAKARIAN, STEPHEN DEMOS, association executive; b. Downey, Calif., July 12, 1947; s. Demos Dee and Rose S.; m. Debra G. Shakarian, Mar. 14, 1975; children—Stephanie Lynn, Stephen Demos. BSM, Pepperdine U., 1983; MBA, UCLA, 1985. Vice pres., Omega Advt., Los Angeles, 1973-74, exec. v.p., mgr., 1974-75, pres., 1975-82; dir. ministries Full Gospel Bus. Men's Fellowship Internat., Irvine, Calif., 1978-80, dir. ministries and ops., 1980, chief operating officer, Costa Mesa, Calif., 1980—, also dir. Mem. Nat. Religious Broadcasters. Republican. Office: Full Gospel Bus Mens Fellowship 3150 Bear St Costa Mesa CA 92626

SHAMAH, MOSHE S., principal, rabbi; b. Bklyn., Jan. 24, 1937; s. Solomon and Alice (Sutton) S.; m. Miriam Srour, Dec. 9, 1962; children: Alisa, Rochelle, Leah, Solomon. Student, Bklyn. Coll., 1954-56; MEd, Loyola U., Balt., 1961; student, Ner Israel Rabbinical Coll., Balt., 1960-61; postgrad., Beth Medrash Govoha, Lakewood, N.J., 1961-66. Ordained rabbi, 1969. Prin. Sephardic High Sch., Bklyn., 1973—; Talmud instr. Mirrer Yeshiva, Bklyn., 1966-68; dir., head rabbi Sephardic Inst., Bklyn., 1968—; cons. Sephardic Edn. Ctr., L.A., 1978—; guest lectr. Shehebar Study Ctr., Jerusalem, summers 1980—. Mem. prins. coun. Bd. Jewish Edn., N.Y. Mem. Nat. Conf. Yeshiva Prins. Office: Sephardic High Sch 511 Ave R Brooklyn NY 11223 *The inspiration derived from the pathos, patience and long-range vision of the prophets of Scripture, joined with human conscience, comprises our chief hope for world peace, brotherhood and social justice.*

SHAMAPANI, ENOCK, bishop; b. Kalomo, Zambia, 1952; s. Maambo Meleki Shamapani and Mariah Zandala Mubulu; m. Lastinah Namoomba, Nov. 14, 1877; children: Sharon, Eric, Susan, Gladys. Cert. Upper Primary Edn., David Livingstone Tchrs.' Tng. Coll., Livingstone, Zambia, 1975; ThD, Scott Theol. Coll., Machako, Kenya, 1983. Ordained to ministry Brethren in Christ Ch., 1986. Pastor Brethren in Christ Ch., Choma, Zambia, 1983-87; prin. Bikalongo Bible Inst., Choma, 1987, bishop, 1988—; trustee Evang. Fellowship Zambia, Lusaka, 1990—, vice chmn., 1990—; chmn. Internat. Brethren in Christ Fellowshp, 1990—, sec., treas., 1990—; co. mem. Nairobi Evan. Grad. Sch. Theology, 1991—. Home and Office: Brethren Christ Ch, POB 630115, Choma Zambia

SHAMBLIN, BROADDUS WADE, clergyman; b. Sidney, Ohio, July 6, 1964; s. Marlin Lee Sr. and Brenda Lou (Kiser) S.; m. Kimberly Sue Eshleman, Jan. 2, 1988; 1 child, Leah Michele. AAS in Criminal Justice, Edison State Community Coll., 1984; BA in Criminology, Ohio State U., 1986; student, United Theol. Sem., 1986-87, 90-91; MA in Counseling, Marshall U., 1989. Counselor Unied Meth. Camps, Bellefontaine, Ohio, 1984, 86, Easter Seal Soc., Bellefontaine, Ohio, 1985; asst. chaplain Childrens Med. Ctr., Dayton, Ohio, 1986-87; computer operator Price Bros. Co., Dayton, Ohio, 1987; studetn assoc. ministry Community United Meth. Ch., Brookville, Ohio, 1990—. Recipient Mikellar Found. award, 1982. Mem. AACD, Am. Coll. Pers. Assn., Assn. Religous Values in Counseling, Royal Order Our Days (counselor 1970—), Hombres de La Mancha (charter, founder, pres. 1989—), Ohio State U. Alumni Assn. (life), Marshall U. Alumni Assn. Republican. Avocations: Spanish, Mexican travel, geneaological research, Appalachian studies. Home: 5501-9 Autumn Wood Dr Trotwood OH 45426 Office: Community Unied Meth PO Box 172 Brookville OH 45309-0172

SHAMBLIN, DARRELL RAY, lay worker; b. Elkhurst, W.Va., Dec. 3, 1927; s. Holly Orville and Claris Marie (Gray) S.; m. Suzanne Jane Perkins May 17, 1958 (dec. Oct. 1990); children: Bryan Drake, Kevin Gray, Holly Anne. Student, W.Va. Wesleyan Coll., 1946-48; BA in Journalism, Marshall U., 1950; M Letters, U. Pitts., 1957; postgrad., Northwestern U., 1958-62, United Theol. Sem., 1974. Dir. Meth. info. Meth. Ch., Pitts., 1953-55; dir. Meth. Info. and Pub. Rels. Meth. Ch., Chgo., 1955-57; mng. editor The Meth. Story, Chgo., 1957-64, editor, 1967-68; editor The Interpreter, Dayton, Nashville, 1969-87; dir. publs., assoc. pub. United Meth. Communications, Nashville, 1988—; lay mem. No. Ill. Ann. Conf., United Meth. Ch., 1960-68, W. Ohio Ann. Conf., United Meth. Ch., 1969-86; mem. communications com. Calvary United Meth. Ch., Nashville, 1990—. Contbr. articles to religious jours. With U.S. Army, 1950-52. Mem. Associated Ch. Press (bd. dirs., treas. 1986-89), Religious Pub. Rels. Coun., United Meth. Assn. Communicators. Home: 1224 Charlton Dr Antioch TN 37013 Office: United Meth Communications 810 Twelfth Ave S Nashville TN 37203-4744

SHANER, DAVID WAYNE, minister; b. Portsmouth, Va., Apr. 11, 1953; s. David Fay and Claudie Elenor (Hines) S.; m. Katherine Cheryl Brown, Oct. 21, 1978; children: Zachary, Kurtis, Austin. BS in Bible, Harding U., Searcy, Ark., 1976. Ordained to ministry, Ch. of Christ. Minsiter Ch. of Christ, Mundelein, Ill., 1976-78, Pullman, Wash., 1978-79, Coeur d'Alene, Idaho, 1979—; bd. dirs. Northeastern Wash. Christian Camps, Spokane, 1986—; consortium mem. Columbia Christian Coll., Portland, Oreg., 1987—. Author: One on One Evangelism, 1985. Recipient Leadership award, Spl. Olympics, 1986, Appreciation award, Soc. of Disting. High Sch. Students, 1984, 87, Svc. award, Mental Health Assn. Ida., 1989. Mem. Toastmasters (pres. 1984-89). Home: 4404 Spiers Ave Coeur d'Alene ID 83814 Office: Dalton Gardons Ch of Christ 6439 N 4th St Coeur d'Alene ID 83814

SHANK, HAROLD, minister; b. Indiana, Pa., Sept. 5, 1950; s. Leroy and Emma Florence (Hall) S.; m. Sally Jane Tague, May 17, 1974; children: Daniel Burton, Nathan Alexander. BA, Okla. Christian Coll., 1972; MA, Harding Grad. Sch. Religion, 1976, MA in Religion, 1977; PhD, Marquette U., 1988. Ordained to ministry Chs. Christ, 1976. Youth min. Coll. Ch. of Christ, Oklahoma City, 1972-74; ednl. min. Highland St. Ch. of Christ, Memphis, 1974-76, min., 1986—; min. Northtown Ch., Milw., 1976-86; adj. prof. Harding Grad. Sch. Religion, Memphis, 1988—, mem. dean's coun., 1990-91; script writer Herald of Truth Television, Abilene, Tex., 1977-90; pres., bd. dirs. Milw. Bibl. Archaeology Soc., 1982-86. Contbg. editor UpReach mag., 1990; contbr. articles to profl. jours. Mem. Dist. 8 Adv. Coun. Tenn. Dept. Social Svc., 1991—. Mem. Soc. Bibl. Lit., Am. Schs. Oriental Rsch. Office: Highland St Ch of Christ 443 S Highland St Memphis TN 38111

SHANKEL, JACK EUGENE, minister; b. Mayport, Pa., Aug. 20, 1932; s. Fred Cameron and Chloie Irene (Huffman) S.; m. Joyce Joan Bish, June 15, 1957; 1 child, Christi-Le Shankel Tribby. AB in Religion, Ea. Nazarene Coll., 1961, ThB, 1963, DD (hon.), 1980; postgrad., Andover-Newton Theol. Sem., 1964-66. Ordained to ministry Ch. of the Nazarene, 1964. Enlisted USN, 1952, advanced through grades to petty officer, 1956; with USNR, 1956-72; pastor St. Paul's Ch. of the Nazarene, Duxbury, Mass., 1962-65, First Ch. of the Nazarene, Augusta, Maine, 1965-71; supt. Maine dist. Ch. of the Nazarene, Augusta, 1971-88; supt. Northwestern Ohio dist. Ch. of the Nazarene, St. Marys, 1988—. Contbr. articles to civic and religious publs. Trustee Ea. Nazarene Coll., Wollaston, Mass., 1969-88, Mt. Vernon (Ohio) Nazarene Coll., 1988—, Nazarene Bible Coll., Colorado Springs, Colo., 1980—; dir. Bible Soc. Maine, Portland, 1974-82; v.p. Christian Civic League Maine, Augusta, 1975-80. Recipient resolution Maine Senate and Ho. of Reps., 1988. Mem. Nat. Assn. Evangelicals (dir. 1990—). Democrat. Office: Ch of the Nazarene Northwestern Dist 272 Jack Oak Point Rd Saint Marys OH 45885

SHANKS, HERSHEL, lawyer, publisher, editor; b. Sharon, Pa., Mar. 8, 1930; s. Martin and Mildred (Freedman) S.; m. Judith Alexander Weil, Feb. 20, 1966; children: Elizabeth Jean, Julia Emily. B.A., Haverford (Pa.) Coll., 1952; M.A., Columbia, 1953; LL.B., Harvard, 1956. Bar: D.C. 1956. Trial atty. Dept. Justice, 1956-59; pvt. practice Washington, 1959-88; partner firm Glassie Pewett, Beebe & Shanks, 1964-88; editor Bibl. Archaeology Rev., Washington, 1975—; pres. Bibl. Archaeology Soc., 1974—, Jewish Ednl. Ventures Inc., 1987—. Author: The Art and Craft of Judging, 1968, The City of David, 1973, Judaism in Stone, 1979; also articles; co-editor: Recent Archaeology in the Land of Israel, 1984; editor Ancient Israel, A Short History, 1988, Bible Rev., 1985—; editor Moment mag., 1987—. Mem. Am., Fed., D.C. bar assns., Am. Schs. Oriental Research, Phi Beta Kappa. Clubs: Nat. Lawyers (Washington); Nat. Press. Home: 5208 38th St NW Washington DC 20015 Office: Bible Review 3000 Connecticut Ave NW Ste 300 Washington DC 20008 *I try to take time to identify what is important in my life, to focus on that and ignore the rest when it conflicts. It takes conscious effort not to dissipate energy on activities and attitudes that don't matter in the big picture of my priorities. Free to concentrate on what I value most, I try to accomplish something each day in a regular, habitual way.*

SHANKWEILER, CARL DAVID, minister; b. Butler Twp., Pa., Nov. 23, 1946; s. Carl Benfield and Grace Amanda (Starr) S.; m. Cynthia L.R. Herb, June 23, 1973. BA, Pa. State U., 1967, MA, 1971; MDiv, Luth. Theol. Sem., Phila., 1972; ThM, Princeton Theol. Sem., 1973. Ordained to ministry Luth. Ch. in Am., 1973. Assisting pastor St. Mark Luth. Ch., Birdsboro, Pa., 1973-78; pastor St. James Luth. Ch., Geigertown, Pa., 1973-78, Trinity Luth. Ch., Wernersville, Pa., 1978-83; editor div. for parish svcs. Luth. Ch. in Am., Phila., 1983-87; dir. Genesis ednl. program Luth. Welfare Svc., Hazleton, Pa., 1988—, dir. communications, 1990; pastor Trinity Luth Ch., Valley View, Pa., 1990—; del. to nat. conv. Luth. Ch. in Am., N.Y.C., 1970, 80; mem. various coms. Northeastern Pa. Synod, Luth Ch. in Am. and Evang. Luth. Ch. in Am., Wescosville, 1976—, dean West Berks dist., 1981-83; accredited visitor World Coun. Chs. Assembly, Vancouver, B.C., Can., 1983; del. to nat. assembly Evang. Luth. Ch. in Am., Chgo., 1989, 91. Author: My Work as a Christian, 1977, Spirit Together, 1980, Seasons of the Son, 1982, The Bible: A User's Manual, 1985, A Resource for Leaders in Evangelism Ministry, 1990. Mem. v.p. Daniel Boone Sch. Bd., Birdsboro, 1975-78; mem., treas. Am. Bd. for Syrian Orphanage at Jerusalem, Inc., 1980—; bd. dirs. Eckley (Pa.) Miners' Village Assocs., 1990-91. Scholar Luth. Brotherhood, 1972. Mem. Mid. East Inst., Religious Edn. Assn., Berks County Hist. Soc., Schuylkill County Hist. Soc., Am. Philatelic Soc. Democrat. Home and Office: 1444 W Maple St Valley View PA 17983 Office: Trinity Ch PO Box 153 Gap and W Maple Sts Valley View PA 17983 also: Genesis PO Box 310 910 Stacie Dr Hazleton PA 18201 *If you want to tell if a person is a success, do not consider his/her great deeds; look to the small. Do not notice how she/he treats superiors, but inferiors. For success, ultimately, is judged by God's standards, not ours; and God's standards turn our thinking upside down.*

SHANOR, CLARENCE RICHARD, clergyman; b. Butler, Pa., Dec. 26, 1924; s. Paul L. and Marion (McCandless) S.; B.A., Allegheny Coll., 1948; S.T.B., Boston U., 1951, Ph.D., 1958; m. Anna Lou Watts, June 23, 1948; 1 son, Richard Watts. Ordained to ministry Methodist Ch., 1950; pastor Meth. Ch., South Hamilton, Mass., 1951-54; research asso. Union Coll., Schenectady, 1954-55; prof. Christian edn. Nat. Coll., Kansas City, Mo., 1956-58; asso. minister First United Meth. Ch., St. Petersburg, Fla., 1958-61, First United Meth. Ch., Fullerton, Calif., 1961-66; coord. Metro dept. San Diego dist. United Meth. Union, San Diego, 1966-87, ret., 1987; pres. Human Svcs. Corp., 1972-77. Treas. San Diego County Ecumenical Conf., 1970-71, pres., 1975-77; chmn. Coalition Urban Ministries, 1970-71, Cultural and Religious Task Force Rancho San Diego, 1970-74; chmn. western jurisdiction Urban Network United Meth. Ch., 1978. Chmn. San Diego Citizens Com. Against Hunger, 1969-72; bd. dirs. Interfaith Housing Found., chmn., 1979, pres. 1988—; v.p. North County Interfaith Coun., 1987—; mem. Gaslamp Quarter Project Area Com., San Diego, 1978, mem. coun., 1980-84; chmn. bd. Horton House Corp., 1978; mem. Mayor's Task Force on the Homeless, 1983-84; chmn. Downtown Coordinating Coun., 1983-84; mem. regional Task Force on Homeless, 1986-87; vice-chmn. Community Congress, 1987. Recipient San Diego Inst. for Creativity award, 1969, Boss of Yr. award Am. Bus. Women's Assn., 1972, Christian Unity award Diocesan Ecumenical Commn., 1984, Congl. Disting. Svc. award, 1984, Helen Beardsley Human Rights award, 1986, Mayor O'Connor's Seahorse award 1989. Mem. Lions. Author: (with Anna Lou Shanor) Kindergartner Meet Your World, 1966. Home: 1636 Desert Glen Escondido CA 92026-1849

SHAPIRO, AVRAHAM, rabbi; b. Jerusalem, 1918. Faculty Merkaz Harav Yeshiva, Israel, for 30 years, dir., 1981—; chief rabbi Ashkenazic Community of Israel, 1983—. Office: Ashkenazi Community, Office of Chief Rabbinate, Jerusalem Israel

SHAPIRO, CHAIM, rabbi; b. New Haven, Nov. 29, 1931; s. Samuel Aaron and Miriam Rebecca (Einbinder) S.; m. Sheila Esther Rabinowitz, Mar. 15, 1955; children: Elliott, Alan, Neil, Jonathan. BA, Yeshive Coll., 1953; MEd, U. Pitts., 1958; D. Ministry, Boston U., 1990. Ordained rabbi, 1956. Rabbi Congregation Rodeph Shalom Homestead, Pitts., 1956-58, Briarwood Jewish Ctr., Queens, N.Y., 1958-60, Touro Synagogue-Congregation Jeshuat Israel, Newport, R.I., 1987—; rabbi, exec. dir. Temple Israel, Long Beach, N.Y., 1984-87; prin. Young Israel-Wavecrest & Bayswater Sch., Far Rockaway, N.Y., 1964-69, Atlantic Beach (N.Y.) Jewish Ctr., 1960-78; youth dir. Young Israel of Long Beach (N.Y.), 1962-66. Author: A Proposed Guide for Orthodox Jewish Conversion, 1990, (booklet) A Guide to Judaism for Chaplains, 1988, (article series) The Kaddish Question, 1961. Spiritual guide Newport County Hospice and Vis. Nurses Assn., 1979—; bd. dirs. Hedward King Sr. Citizens Ctr., Newport, 1988—. Mem. Yeshiva U. Rabbinical Alumni Assn., Rabbinical Coun. Asm., Aquidneck Clergy Assn., R.I. Bd. Rabbis. Office: Touro Synagogue 85 Touro St Newport RI 02840

SHAPIRO, MAX ANDREW, rabbi; b. Worcester, Mass., Jan. 31, 1917; s. Samuel and Clara (Wolfgang) S.; m. Bernice Clein, Dec. 31, 1944 (dec. Mar. 1984); children: Susan, Steven; m. Abby Lou Evans, Dec. 1989. AB, Clark U., 1939; MEd, Boston Tchrs. Coll., 1940; BHL, Hebrew Union Coll., 1953, MHL, 1955, DD (hon.), 1980; DEd, U. Cin., 1960; LHD (hon.), U. St. Thomas, 1990. Ordained rabbi, 1955. Sr. rabbi Temple Israel, Mpls., 1963-85, rabbi emeritus, 1985—; lectr. dept. religion and philosophy Hamline U., 1958—; adj. prof. United Theol. Sem., 1975—; bd. govs. Hebrew Union Coll., Jewish Inst. Religion; co-chmn. task force on reform outreach Union Am. Hebrew Congregations, Cen. Conf. Am. Rabbis, 1979-83; dir. Ctr. for Christian-Jewish Learning, U. St. Thomas, St. Paul, 1985—. State commr. against discrimination, 1961-65; bd. dirs. Mt. Sinai Hosp., Mpls., Mpls. United Way, Minn. Coun. on Religion and Race. Rabbi Max A. Shapiro Forest in Israel established in his honor Jewish Nat. Fund., 1976; recipient Humanitarian award Nat. Jewish Hosp., Denver, State of Israel Bonds award, 1972, Internat. Franciscan award, 1989; named Outstanding Citizen, United Way, 1970, City of Mpls., 1966. Mem. Midwest Assn. Reform Rabbis (pres. 1970-71), Rabbinic Alumni Assn. (pres. 1973-74), Cen. Conf. Am. Rabbis (sec.), Minn. Rabbinical Assn. (pres. 1962-64). Office: Temple Israel 2324 Emerson Ave S Minneapolis MN 55405

SHAPIRO, MORRIS, rabbi, psychology educator; b. Goraj, Poland, Mar. 20, 1920; came to U.S., 1948; s. Mendel and Hinda (Harmon) S.; m. Lydia Spiegelman; children: Meyer, Mendel, Hinda; m. Rochelle Ada Berliner, June 23, 1963; children: Jerome, Simcha. BS, U. N.D., 1960, MA, 1959; DD (hon.), Jewish Theol. Sem., 1975. Ordained rabbi, 1939. Rabbi Synagogue, Berlin, N.H., 1952-56, Greenport, N.Y., 1956-57, Grand Forks, N.D., 1957-

61; rabbi Agudath Jacob Synagogue, Waco, Tex., 1961-64, B'nai Israel Synagogue, Tome River, N.J., 1964-66, South Huntington Jewish Ctr., Melville, N.Y., 1966-88; prof. of psychology SUNY, Farmingdale, 1974—; pres. Suffolk Bd. Rabbis, Melville, N.Y., 1977-79, mem. Nat. Beth Din, 1988—. Recipient New Life award Israel Bond, 1983, Max Arzt Rabbinical Svc. award, 1990. Mem. Rabbinical Assembly (pres. Nassau-Suffolk chpt. 1975-77, mem. law com. 1983—). Home: 103 Clay Pitts Rd Greenlawn NY 11740

SHAPIRO, RAMI M., rabbi, consultant; b. Springfield, Mass., Apr. 26, 1951; s. Archie Jack and Shirley (Cohen) S.; m. Deborah J. Flanigan, Feb. 17, 1951; 1 child, Aaron Herschel. BA in Philosophy, U. Mass., 1973; MA in Jewish Studies, McMaster U., 1974; M in Hebrew Letters, Hebrew Union Coll., 1983; PhD in Jewish Studies, Union Grad. Sch., 1985. Ordained rabbi, 1981. Rabbi Wright-Patterson AFB, Dayton, Ohio, 1979-81, Temple Beth Or, Miami, Fla., 1981—; bd. dirs. EnR Wordsmiths, Miami; sr. cons. Deming Method Cons. Group, Miami, 1986—. Author: Alef-Bet, 1983, Messiah-Man, 1984, One Minuite Mentsch, 1985, Open Hands, 1987. Co-facilitator Snowmass (Colo.) Group for Inter-faith Dialogue, 1985; speaker Green Earth Peace Campaign, Miami, 1985, Peace Coalition, Miami, 1985-86, South Fla. Hist. Soc., Miami, 1987—; bd. dirs. Earthwise, Miami, 1982-84. Mem. Cen. Conf. Amercias Rassis, Reconstructionist Rassinical Assn., Nat. Assn. for Preservation of Storytelling. Avocations: storytelling, writing, performing guitar music, reading. Office: Temple Bet Or PO Box 160081 Miami FL 33116

SHARKEY, PAUL WILLIAM, philosopher, religious educator; b. Oakland, Calif., Mar. 22, 1945; s. Paul Raymond and Alama Shirley (Bach) S.; 1 child, Erin Kathleen. AA, Pasadena City Coll., 1963; BA with high honors, Calif. State U., L.A., 1969; PhD, U. Notre Dame, 1973. Assoc. prof. philosophy and religion U. So. Miss., Hattiesburg, 1975—; clin. asst. prof. psychiatry U. Miss. Sch. Medicine, Jackson, 1983—. Editor: Philosophy, Religion and Psychotherapy, 1982; contbr. articles to profl. jours. Served with USN, 1964-69. Mem. Inst. for Advanced Philosophic Rsch. (sr. adviser 1980—), Am. Philosophical Assn., Am. Soc. for Philosophy, Counseling and Psychotherapy (founding), Metaphysical Soc. Miss., Philos. Assn. (pres. 1980-81), Sigma Xi. Home: 128 E Lakeside Dr Hattiesburg MS 39401 Office: U So Miss Dept Philosophy/Religion Box 5015 Hattiesburg MS 39406

SHARMA, ANTHONY FRANCIS, priest, religious order superior; b. Tindharia, West Bengal, India, Dec. 12, 1937; arrived in Nepal, 1984; s. Tarunraj and Hima Angelica (Kumari) S. PhB, De Nobili Coll., Pune, Maharastra, India, 1962; MS in Psychology and Counseling, De La Salle U., Manila, 1973. Joined S.J., Roman Cath. Ch., ordained priest; cert. counselor. Headmaster St. Robert's Boys' High Sch., Darjeeling, 1976-80; prin., rector St. Joseph's Coll., North Point, Darjeeling, 1980-84; ecclesiastical superior Cath. Ch. of Nepal, Kathmandu, 1980—. Author: Vineyard "Jiwan Khaet", 1970. Home: St Xavier's Sch, GPO Box 50, Kathmandu Nepal

SHARP, ALLAN RHINEHART, minister, retired religion educator; b. Covington, Ky., Mar. 23, 1925; s. Rhine Hart and Sue Marie (Yelton) S.; m. Ava Glyn High, Aug. 20, 1949; children: Cindy, Rhine, Tim. AB, Transylvania U., 1949; BD, Lexington (Ky.) Theol. Sem., 1952; EdD, Duke U., 1963; LittD (hon.), William Woods Coll., 1978. Ordained to ministry Christian Ch. (Disciples of Christ), 1949. Min. Wendell (N.C.) Christian Ch., 1952-53; prof. Atlantic Christian Coll. (name now Barton Coll.), Wilson, N.C., 1953-91, chair dept. religion and philosophy, 1981-91; min. Dudley (N.C.) Christian Ch., 1954—; pres. Christian Chs. in N.C., 1963. Contbr. articles to religious jours. Founder Wilson Crisis Ctr., 1971. mem. Wilson County Ministerial Assn. (pres. 1985), Alpha Theta Zi, Kappa Delta Pi, Theta Alpha Kappa. Home: 1604 Grove St Wilson NC 27893

SHARP, DOUGLAS RICE, theology educator; b. Monte Vista, Colo., Mar. 1, 1949; s. W. Edward and Pauline M. (Settle) S.; m. Linda K. Wolfe, July 30, 1983; children: Michelle Lynn, Jason Douglas. BA, William Jewell Coll., Liberty, Mo., 1971; MDiv, Am. Bapt. Sem. of the West, Berkeley, Calif., 1975; PhD, Grad. Theol. Union, Berkeley, Calif., 1988. Ordained to ministry Bapt. Ch., 1975. Instr. Am. Bapt. Sem. of the West, Berkeley, 1975-84; assoc. prof. No. Bapt. Theol. Sem., Lombard, Ill., 1985—. Author: The Hermeneutics of Election, 1990. Mem. Am. Acad. Religion, Soc. Bibl. Lit., Am. Soc. Ch. History, Am. Theol. Soc. Home: 1105 Jane Ave Naperville IL 60540 Office: No Bapt Theol Sem 660 E Butterfield Rd Lombard IL 60148

SHARP, MICHAEL DALE, clergyman; b. Huntsville, Ala., Sept. 11, 1952; s. Elzer Jackson and Illa Jeanette (Buffaloe) S.; m. Debra Carroll Sims, Nov. 23, 1972; children: Jonathan, Shaylon. BS, U. Ala., 1975; MDiv, Assemblies of God Theol. Sem., Springfield, Mo., 1985. Ordained to ministry Assemblies of God Ch., 1986. Pastor Faith Assembly of God, Springfield, 1984-85, First Assembly of God, Bessemer, Ala., 1986—; sec.-treas. Birmingham sect. Assemblies of God, 1989—; sec. Ala. Dist. Decade of Harvest Task Force, Montgomery, 1989—; mem. Ala. Dist. Chi Alpha Com., Montgomery, 1990—. Mem. Soc. Pentecostal Studies. Office: First Assembly of God 830 Briarwood Dr Bessemer AL 35023

SHARPE, ROBERT JOHN, minister, consultant; b. Detroit, Aug. 18, 1948; s. Russell Ahrens and Mary Jean (Kinsvater) S.; m. Nancy Norton, Aug. 23, 1969; children: John, Kathleen, Karen. Student, Moody Bible Inst., 1966-67, Detroit Bible Coll., 1967-69, St. Paul Bible Coll., 1969-70. Ordained to ministry Bapt. Ch., 1972. Pastor Grace Bapt. Ch., River Rouge, Mich., 1976-77; founding pastor Victory Heights Bapt. Ch., London, Ont., Can., 1978-80; instr. Bapt. Bible Coll. Can., Simcoe, Ont., 1979; pastor Valley Bapt. Ch., Rowland Heights, Calif., 1983-88; cons. Diamond Bar, Calif., 1985—; music leader 1st Bapt. Ch., Bassett, Calif., 1990—; religious talk show host Radio Sta. WMUZ, Detroit, 1967-68; announcer, musician, Bible tchr. Radio Sta. KICY, Nome, Alaska, 1967. Author: New Life Kit, 1979, Basic Bible Doctrine, 1978, 79. Moderator State Senate Candidates' Forum, Walnut, Calif., 1990. Mem. Walnut Valley C. of C. (v.p. 1989-90, program chmn. 1989-91). Office: 23441 Golden Springs Dr Ste 334 Diamond Bar CA 91765

SHATKUS, LEONARD JOSEPH, JR., minister; b. Scranton, Pa., Jan. 10, 1955; s. Leonard Joseph Sr. and Gertrude Theresa (Wynne) S. BA in Philosophy, Wilkes U., 1976; MDiv, Toronto Sch. Theology, Can., 1981; STM, Regis Theol. Coll., Toronto, 1982. Ordained to ministry Roman Cath. Ch., 1982; lic. to ministry Evang. Luth. Ch. Am., 1989. Instr., coach Bishop Egan High Sch., Fairless Hills, Pa., 1979-80; chaplain Palmetto Gen. Hosp., Hialeah, Fla., 1983; missionary Prelacy of Borba, Amazon, Brazil, 1983-84; vicar superior St. Francis Sem., Toronto, 1984; instr., coach, pres. faculty senate St. Thomas Aquinas High Sch., Ft. Lauderdale, Fla., 1985-87; instr., coach St. Francis Prep. Sch., Spring Grove, Pa., 1987-88; pastor Sunrise Luth. Ch., Port St. John, Fla., 1989—; counselor Prepare/Enrich Inc., 1991—; ecumenical rep. Space Coast Conf., Fla. Synod, Evangel. Luth. Ch. Am. leader Webelos Boy Scouts Am., Deerfield Beach, Fla., 1986-87; v.p. community devel. Port St. John Jaycees, 1990-91; moderator Port St. John Polit. Forum, 1990, Modified Sch. Calendar, Port St. John, 1991. Recipient M.D. Brandwene award Wilkes U., Wilkes Barre, Pa., 1976. Democrat. Home: 6071 Waterloo Ave Cocoa FL 32927 Office: Sunrise Lutheran Church 4775-4 Fay Blvd Cocoa FL 32927

SHAULL, RICHARD, theologian, educator; b. Felton, Pa., Nov. 24, 1919; s. Millard and Anna (Brenneman) S.; m. Mildred Miller, May 17, 1941; children—Madelyn, Wendy. B.A., Elizabethtown Coll., 1938, D.D., 1958; B.Th., Princeton Theol. Sem., 1941, Th.M., 1946, Th.D., 1959. Ordained to ministry Presbyn. Ch., 1941; pastor in Wink, Tex., 1941-42; missionary in Colombia, 1942-50, U. Brazil, 1952-62; prof. ch. history Campinas (Brazil) Presbyn. Sem., 1952-60; v.p. Mackenzie Inst., São Paulo, Brazil, 1960-62; prof. ecumenics Princeton Theol. Sem., 1962-80, prof. emeritus, 1980—; cons. internat. programs, 1960—; chmn. N.Am. Congress Latin Am., 1966-89, World Student Christian Fedn., 1968-73; acad. dir. Instituto Pastoral Hispano, N.Y.C., 1983-89. Author: Encounter with Revolution, 1955, (with Carl Oglesby) Containment and Change, 1967, (with Gustavo Gutierrez) Liberation and Change, 1977, Heralds of a New Reformation, 1984, Naming the Idols, 1988, The Reformation and Liberation Theology, 1991, also 3 books in Portuguese. Home: 46 Morgan Circle Swarthmore PA 19081

SHAW, ANGUS ROBERTSON, III, minister; b. Charlotte, N.C., Oct. 7, 1932; s. Angus Robertson Jr. and Claudia (Morrison) S.; m. Carolyn Farmer, Aug. 14, 1965; children: Karen, Rob. BA, Bob Jones U., 1955; MDiv, Columbia Theol. Sem., 1958, DMin, 1989; DD (hon.), King Coll., 1965. Asst. pastor 1st Presbyn. Ch., Pulaski, Va., 1956-62; pastor Seagle Meml. Ch., Pulaski, 1956-62, Royal Oak Ch., Marion, Va., 1962-69; sr. pastor 1st Presbyn. Ch., Dothan, Ala., 1969-78, Johnson City, Tenn., 1978—; chmn. bd. Salvation Army, Johnson City, Tenn., 1986, Contact Teleministries, Johnson City, 1987-88. Trustee Lees-McRae Coll., Banner Elk, N.C., 1979-84; chmn. ch., coll. coun. Montreat (N.C.)-Anderson Coll., 1980; chmn. ann. fund King Coll., Briston, Tenn., 1985-86; mem. bd. United Way, 1991—. Mem. Watauga Mental Health Assn. (bd. dirs. 1990—), Kiwanis Club (pres. 1990-91), Soc. Theta Pi. Home: 1013 Somerset Dr Johnson City TN 37604 Office: 1st Presbyn Ch 105 S Boone St Johnson City TN 37604

SHAW, CLIFFORD DEAN, minister; b. Fairfield, Nebr., Feb. 17, 1943; s. Wesley and Velma (Hoyt) S.; m. Judith L. Losh, May 30, 1964; children: David, Suzanne, Pricilla, Lydia, Jonathan. BSL, Midwestern Sch. Evngelism, Ottumwa, Iowa, 1964; MA, Calif. Grad. Sch. Theology, Glendale, 1986. Ordained to ministry Christian Ch.. 1966. Minister Mid-County Christian Ch., Port Neches, Tex., 1965-67; assoc. minister First Ch. Christ, Lake Charles, La., 1967-70; minister Christ Ch., Lake Charles, La., 1970-83; student recruiter Platte Valley Bible Coll., Scottsbluff, Nebr., 1983-90; minister Christian Ch. at Chatfield, Littleton, Colo., 1990—; com. mem. N.Am. Christian Conv., Cin., 1983-86; vice chmn. Nebr. Christian Conv., Kearney, 1991. Pres. bd. Ward 1 Fire Dist., Lake Charles, 1980-83, Community Christian Sch., Scottsbluff, 1988-90, Moss Bluff Christian Acad., Lake Charles, 1977-82. Office: Christian Ch at Chatfield 8375 S Wadsworth Blvd Littleton CO 80123

SHAW, DANIEL GERALD, religion educator; b. Fond du Lac, Wis., June 1, 1957; s. James Edward Shaw and Judith (Ziegler) Peschke. BA, U. Wis., Eau Claire, 1979; MA, Northwestern U., 1981, PhD, 1987. Asst. prof. Lawrence U., Appleton, Wis., 1989—. Mem. Am. Acad. Religion, Middle East Studies Assn. Office: Lawrence U Appleton WI 54912

SHAW, EDWIN LAWRENCE, religious leader, educator; b. Emmett, Idaho, Nov. 17, 1938; s. Harold Wetherby Shaw and Genevieve T. (Knight) Shaffer; m. Marcella Mae Beecher, June 11, 1960; children: Rebecca, Pamela, Dawn. BA, Bob Jones U., 1961; MA, Mich. State U., 1964. Ordained to ministry Bapt. Ch.; cert. tchr., adminstr. Supt. Nampa (Idaho) Christian Schs., 1963-70; headmaster King's Schs., Seattle, 1970-74; asst. pastor Esperance Bapt. Ch., Edmonds, Wash., 1974-77; sr. pastor Grace Conservative Bapt. Ch., Seattle, 1977-89; gen. dir. S.W. Conservative Bapt. Assn., Phoenix, 1989—; co-owner Stas. KBGN/KBXL Radio, Boise, Idaho, 1976-90; speaker various confs., workshops, retreats, radio programs, 1963—. Bd. dirs. Southwestern Coll., Phoenix, 1989—; trustee Western Sem., Portland, Oreg., 1979-85. Avocations: travel, running, landscaping garden. Home: 19013 N 90th Way Scottsdale AZ 85255 Office: SWCBA 2535 E Cactus Phoenix AZ 85036

SHAW, EUNICE ELIZABETH, lay worker; b. Tuscaloosa, Ala., July 11, 1934; d. James Walter and Eunice Martell (Hooper) Darnell; m. Howard Vernon Shaw, Apr. 26, 1953 (dec. Nov. 1976); children; Donna Gail Shaw Entrekin, Kenneth Alan. Student, Birmingham Bus. Coll., 1953. Sec.-treas. Wesley Chapel United Meth. Ch., Sylacauga, Ala., 1976—, Sylacauga Dist. United Meth. Ch., 1984-87. Named Woman of Yr. United Meth. Women, 1971. Home: 228 S Davis Ave Sylacauga AL 35150 Office: Wesley Chapel Meth Ch PO Box 1333 Sylacauga AL 35150-1333

SHAW, JAMES WILLIAM, minister; b. Chgo., June 18, 1940; s. Walter Leroy S. and Antoinette Marie (Reingruber) Krajacki; m. Shirley Fay LeCureux, Dec. 8, 1962; children: Cynthia, James III, Susan, Sandra, John, Joel. BA, Pillsbury Bible Coll., 1962; PhD, Calif. Grad. Sch. Theol., 1991. Pastor, youth Ashburn Bapt. Ch., Chgo., 1962-75; pastor Emmanuel Ch., Bellevue, 1975—; pres. Emmanuel Sch. of the Bible, Bellevue, 1975—; prof. Cascade Bible Coll., Bellevue, 1976—, prof., coord. Seattle Extention-Calif. Grad. Sch. Theol., Bellevue, 1987—. Author: What's With This Kid?, 1970, Ending the Travelague Syndrome: A Balaneed Strategem of Bible Study Methods, 1991. Coord. ski swap, Newport PTSA, Bellevue, 1982-90. Mem. Bellevue Ski Club (pres. 1979—). Avocations: skiing, cycling, camping, boating. Office: Emmanuel Ch Box 3341 Bellevue WA 98009

SHAW, JOSEPH MINARD, retired religion educator; b. Estherville, Iowa, Apr. 21, 1925; s. Carl E. and Martha Elizabeth (Sunde) S.; Mary Virginia St. John, June 8, 1955; children: Nancy Joy, Elizabeth Ann, Margaret Jean, Mary Martha. BA cum laude, St. Olaf Coll., 1949; BTh., Luther Northwestern Theol. Sem., St. Paul, 1953; PhD, Princeton Theol. Sem., 1958. Instr. religion St. Olaf Coll., Northfield, Minn., 1957-59, asst. prof., 1959-62, assoc. prof., 1962-68, prof., 1968-91, prof. emeritus, 1991—, chmn. dept. religion, 1985-88. Author: Pulpit Under the Sky, 1955, If God Be For Us, 1966, Our New Testament Heritage, Vol. I, 1968, Vol. II, 1969, History of St. Olaf College, 1974 (Col. Koch award 1975), The Pilgrim People of God, 1990; co-author: (with R. William Franklin) The Case for Christian Humanism, 1991. Bd. dirs. Northfield Hist. Soc., 1986-89. Ensign USNR, 1944-46, PTO. Fulbright fellow, 1951, Blandin faculty fellow Minn. Pvt. Coll. Rsch. Found., 1989-90; NEH grantee, 1978. Mem. Norwegian-Am. Hist. Assn., Phi Beta Kappa (award Delta of Minn. chpt. 1984). Democrat. Lutheran.

SHAW, LEONARD RAY, minister; b. Dallas, Dec. 28, 1957; s. Lois Rollin and Sandra Ann (Searcy) S.; m. Janet Rebecca Lyle, Aug. 22, 1979; children: Lucas, Rebecca, Landon, Cory Anna. BS in Religion, Miss. Coll., 1981; MEd, Southwestern Bapt. Seminary, Ft. Worth, 1984. Lic. to ministry Bapt. Ch., 1978. Intern First Bapt. Ch., Ridgeland, Miss., 1978-80; minister of youth Briarwood Drive Bapt. Ch., Jackson, Miss., 1980-81; pres. Common Ground Ministries, Ft. Worth, 1982—; pastor Common Ground Ch./So. Bapt. Conv., Ft. Worth, 1984—; dir. Common Ground Div. Dave Roever Evangel. Assn., Ft. Worth, 1988—; pres. Metro Clean, Ft. Worth, 1984—; campus dir. Jackson Youth for Christ, 1978; adminstrv. staff Emmans Road Ministry Sch., Euless, Tex., 1988—; producer radio prog. KPBC, Irving, Tex., 1988-89, radio host, 1988-89; evangelist Inner Life Ministries, Internat., Richardson, Tex., 1981; speaker various confs., others. Recipient Zwilling scholarship Miss. Coll., Clinton, 1977-81, Gilbert scholarship, 1977-81, Manning scholarship, 1977-81, 1981 Presdl. award scholarship Southwestern Bapt. Theol. Seminary, 1981, others. Office: Common Ground Church SBC PO Box 331-222 Fort Worth TX 76163

SHAW, MARK HOWARD, lawyer, business owner, entrepreneur; b. Albuquerque, Aug. 26, 1944; s. Brad Oliver and Barbara Rae (Mencke) S.; m. Ann Marie Brookreson, June 29, 1968 (div. 1976); adopted children: Daniel Paul, Kathleen Ann, Brian Andrew; m. Roslyn Jane Ashton, Oct. 9, 1976; children: Rebecca Rae, Amanda Leith. BA, U. N.Mex., 1967, JD, 1969. Law clk. to presiding justice N.Mex. Supreme Ct., Santa Fe, 1969-70; ptnr. Gallagher & Ruud, Albuquerque, 1970-74, Schmidt & Shaw, Albuquerque, 1974-75; sr. mem. Shaw, Thompson & Sullivan P.A., Albuquerque, 1975-82; chief exec. officer United Ch. Religious Sci. and Sci. Mind Publs., L.A., 1982-91; atty., bus. owner, entrepreneur Santa Fe, N.Mex., 1991—. Trustee 1st Ch. Religious Sci., Albuquerque, 1974-77, pres. 1977; trustee Sandia Ch. Religious Sci., Albuquerque, 1980-82, pres. 1981-82; trustee United Ch. Religious Sci., Los Angeles, 1981-82, chmn. 1982; trustee Long Beach (Calif.) Ch. Religious Sci., 1983-86, chmn. 1983-86; chmn. Bernalillo County Bd. Ethics, Albuquerque, 1979-82. Served as sgt. USMCR, 1961-69. Mem. N.Mex. Bar Assn., Pres.'s Assn., Am. Mgmt. Assn. Avocation: sailing. Home and Office: 2724 Puerto Bonito Santa Fe NM 87505

SHAW, PEGGY NAHAS, clergywoman; b. Merced, Calif., Feb. 3, 1958; d. Edward Nahas and Edith Candler (Stebbins) Paxman; m. Albert A. Polhamas, Sept. 18, 1977 (div. 1979); m. Michael Steven Shaw, May 25, 1980; children: Danica, Brandy Rae, Adria. Grad. high sch., Davis, Calif. Dianetics counselor Ch. Scientology Mission of Davis (Calif.), 1975-76, dir. processing, 1976-77, registrar, 1977-78, dissemination dir., 1978-82; dir. pub. svcs. Ch. Scientology Mission of Sacramento Valley, Davis, 1982-83, orgnl. exec., 1983-84, HCO exec., 1984-85; exec. dir. Ch. Scientology Missions Sacramento Valley-River Park-Chico, Vacaville, Calif., 1985—; also pres. bd. dirs. Ch. Scientology Missions Sacramento Valley-River Park-Chico, Vacaville, 1985—. Mem. Internat. Assn. Scientology (honor roll 1987). Avocation: horseback riding. Home: 4343 Kenneth Blvd Fair Oaks CA 95628 Office: Ch of Scientology 1485 River Park Dr Sacramento CA 95815

SHAW, ROBERT EUGENE, minister, administrator; b. Havre, Mt., Apr. 8, 1933; s. Harold Alvin and Lillian Martha (Kruse) S.; m. Marilyn Grace Smit, June 14, 1957; children—Rebecca Jean, Ann Elizabeth, Mark David, Peter Robert. B.A., Sioux Falls Coll., 1955; M.Div., Am. Baptist. Sem. of West, 1958; D.D. (hon.), Ottawa U., 1976, Judson Coll., 1984. Ordained to ministry Am. Bapt. Chs. U.S.A., 1958; pastor First Bapt. Ch., Webster City, Ia., 1958-63, Community Bapt. Ch., Topeka, Kans., 1963-68; sr. pastor Prairie Bapt. Ch., Prairie Village, Kans., 1968-78; pres. Ottawa U, Kans., 1978-83; exec. minister Am. Bapt. Chs. Mich., East Lansing, 1983—; mem. gen. bd. Am. Bapt. Chs. U.S.A., Valley Forge, Pa., 1972-80, nat. v.p., 1978-80; nat. v.p. Am. Bapt. Minister Council, Valley Forge, 1969-72, nat. pres., 1972-75; nat. chair Am. Bapt. Evang. Team, 1988—; mem. Internat. Commn. on Edn. and Evangelism, Bapt. World Alliance, 1990—; mem. nat. exec. com. Am. Bapt. Adminstrs. Colls. and Univs., 1980-82; bd. dirs. Kans. Ind. Colls. Assn., 1980-82. Trustee No. Bapt. Theol. Sem., Lombard, Ill., 1983—, Kalamazoo Coll., Mich., 1983—, Judson Coll, Elgin, Ill., 1983—; dir. Webster City C. of C., 1961-62, Ottawa C. of C., 1980-82. Office: Am Baptist Chs of Mich 4578 S Hagadorn Rd East Lansing MI 48823

SHAW, SUSAN MAXINE, religion educator; b. Rome, Ga., Dec. 19, 1960; d. Max Donald and JoAnn (Johnson) S. BA, Berry Coll., 1981; MA, So. Bapt. Theol. Sem., 1983, EdD, 1987. Staff writer Western Recorder, Middletown, Ky., 1982-83; Garrett teaching fellow, news dir. So. Bapt. Theol. Sem., Louisville, 1984-87; asst. prof. religion, chair religious studies dept. Calif. Bapt. Coll., Riverside, 1987-91; asst. prof. Christian ministries George Fax Coll., Newberg, Oreg., 1991—. Contbr. articles to profl. jours. Vol. Shelter House, Louisville, 1987. Named one of Outstanding Young Women of Am., 1983, 85. Mem. Western Bapt. Religious Edn. Assn. (v.p. 1988-89, pres. elect 1989-90), So. Bapt. Religious Edn. Assn., Bapt. Pub. Rels. Assn., Religious Edn. Assn. Democrat. Avocations: reading, literature, photography, basketball, writing. Office: George Fox Coll Newberg OR 97132

SHAW-GIBSON, EUNICE MORRELL, minister, educator, counselor; b. Kansas City, Kans., Nov. 22, 1948; d. Howard Downton Jr. and Marguerite Justine (Herron) Easley; m. Stephen Ellis Shaw, Dec. 23, 1966 (div. 1972); children: Kimberle McGruder, Stephen Shaw, E. Christopher Shaw; m. Jerome Charles Gibson, Nov. 28, 1989. BBA, U. St. Thomas, 1985; MA in Christian Edn., Golden Gate Theol. Sem., 1990. Counselor Boys Clubs of Kansas City, 1977-79; sales rep. So. Bell Telephone Co., Houston, 1979-83; account exec. AT&T Communications, Houston, 1983-87; sr. svcs. cons. Beth Eden Housing, Oakland, Calif., 1990—; sr. svcs. cons. Allen Temple Arms, Oakland, Calif., 1988—; minister in tng. Allen Temple Bapt. Ch., Oakland, 1988—; instr. So. Marin Bible Inst., Marin City, Calif., 1990—. Vol. Dem. Party, Houston, 1984, Fort Bend City, Tex., 1984-86, Rainbow Coalition, Marin County, Calif., 1988-90. Mem. Nat. Coun. Negro Women. Avocations: reading, music, travel.

SHEA, FRANCIS RAYMOND, clergyman; b. Knoxville, Tenn., Dec. 4, 1913; s. John Fenton and Harriet (Holford) S. A.B., St. Mary's Sem., Balt., 1935; B.S.T., N.Am. Coll.- Gregorian U., Rome, 1939; M.A., Peabody Coll., Nashville, 1942; D.D., 1969. Ordained priest Roman Cath. Ch., 1939; tchr. Christian Bros. Coll. and Siena Coll., Memphis, 1940-45; prin. Father Ryan High Sch., Nashville, 1945-46; pastor Immaculate Conception Ch., Knoxville, 1956-69; named bishop Evansville, Ind., 1969; consecrated, 1970. Mem. planning bd. United Fund Agys., Knoxville, 1968-69; bd. dirs. Buffalo Trace council Boy Scouts Am., Evansville, Child and Family Services, Knoxville. Office: Cath Ctr 4200 N Kentucky Ave PO Box 4169 Evansville IN 47724 also: 3115 Bayard Park Dr Evansville IN 47714

SHEA, RICHARD DAVID, church administrator, former air force officer; b. Mason City, Nebr., Sept. 6, 1919; s. David Cornelius and Mabel Gladys (Armagost) S.; m. Nondus Budge, Feb. 14, 1942; children—Patricia Lynne, Richard David, Michael Budge. Student U. Utah, 1937, 38, 51, 52; grad. Air War Coll., 1968. Commd. pvt. U.S. Army Air Force, 1942, advanced through grades to lt. col. Air N.G. and U.S. Air Force, 1978; dir. material Utah Air N.G., State Staff, 1971-76, Comdr. 151st Supply Squadron, 1976-78; ret., 1978; emergency response officer Ch. of Jesus Christ of Latter-Day Saints, Salt Lake City, 1980—. Pres. Utah Air N.G. Welfare Assn., Salt Lake City, 1960-70; chmn. utilities adv. com. ARC, Salt Lake City, 1982—; com. mem. Utah Gov.'s Flood Task Force, Salt Lake City, 1983. Home: 185 NW Temple Apt 304 Salt Lake City UT 84103 Office: Ch of Jesus Christ of Latter-Day Saints Emergency Response/Welfare Svcs 50 E North Temple Salt Lake City UT 84150

SHEALY, WILLIAM ROSS, religion educator; b. Chgo., May 28, 1925; s. William Ross and Arabell (Booknight) S. PhB, U. Chgo., 1951; BD, Garrett Sem., Evanston, Ill., 1953; STM, Union Theol. Sem., N.Y.C., 1958; PhD, Drew U., 1966. Ordained to ministry United Meth. Ch., 1954. Pastor Meth. Ch. West Pullman, Chgo., 1954-60; grad. asst. Drew U., Madison, N.J., 1961-63, instr., 1965; asst. prof. Tufts U., Medford, Mass., 1966-68; prof. Va. Wesleyan Coll., Norfolk, 1968—; vis. scholar Nat. Mus. Am. Art, Washington, 1985; mem. judges panel Va. region Optimist Internat., 1991. Mem. pks. task force City of Virginia Beach, Va., 1989—. Recipient Samuel N. Gray Teaching award Va. Wesleyan Coll., 1980; Smithsonian Instn. fellow, 1983, Mednick fellow Va. Found. for Ind. Colls., 1985. Mem. AAUP, Am. Acad. Religion, Soc. Sci. Study of Religion, Assn. for Religion and Intellectual Life, Sumi-e Soc. Home: 3624 Royal Palm Arch Virginia Beach VA 23452 Office: Va Wesleyan Coll Wesleyan Dr Norfolk VA 23502

SHEAN, JEANNETTE MARY, school principal; b. Chgo., Dec. 13, 1923; d. John Sylvester and Mary Cecilia (White) S. BA, DePaul U., 1953, MA, 1958; EdD, Northern Ariz. U., 1977. Instr. English Procopius Coll. Loretto Ext., Wheaton, Ill.; prin. St. Mark Sch., Phoenix, St. Gregory Sch., Phoenix; asst. prof. Seattle U. Author poetry; contbr. articles to profl. jours. Cert. sch. adminstr., Ariz. Recipient Clover Internat. Poetry award, Disting. Prin. award Nat. Cath. Edn. Assn., 1989; St. Xavier scholar, 1941-44, No. Ariz. grad. asst., 1975-77. Mem. ASCD, Ariz. Adminstrs. Assn., Phi Delta Kappa.

SHEARER, D(EAN) H(OWARD), minister; b. Renton, Wash., Jan. 24, 1956; s. Charles F. and Janice Kathleen (Hitchcock) S.; m. Linda Kay Rader, Dec. 17, 1977; children: Peter, Laurie. BS, N.W. Christian Coll., Eugene, Oreg., 1978; MA, Pacific Christian Coll., Fullerton, Calif., 1983; D of Min., Calif. Grad. Sch. of Theology, Glendale, 1986. Ordained to ministry Christian Ch., 1978. Min. to youth Sweet Home (Oreg.) Ch. of Christ, 1976-78; assoc. min. First Christian Ch., El Cajon, Calif., 1978-81; min. First Christian Ch., Vista, Calif., 1981-87; sr. min. First Christian Ch., Tillamook, Oreg., 1987—; chaplain El Cajon Valley Hosp., 1978-81, Tillamook County Gen. Hosp., 1987—; bd. dirs. YMCA, Vista, 1984-87, Oreg. Christian Evangelistic Fellowship, Clackamas, 1987—, Wi-Ne-Ma Christian Camp, Cloverdale, Oreg., 1988—; pres. Tillamook County Ministerial Assn., 1989. Radio host Religion in the News, 1988—. Named Am's. Outstanding Young Min. North Am. Christian Conv., 1989. Mem. Kiwanis (bd. dirs. 1989—). Republican. Home: 8075 Long Prairie Rd Tillamook OR 97141 Office: First Christian Ch 2203 Fourth St Tillamook OR 97141

SHEARER, MARIAN PECK, clergywoman; b. Derby, Conn., Sept. 22, 1949; d. Laurence Elbert Jr. and Marjorie (Griffiths) Peck; m. James C. Shearer, Sept. 26, 1971; 1 child, Katherine. BS, Syracuse U., 1971; MDiv, Colgate Rochester Div. Sch.-Bexley Hall-Crozer Theol. Sem., 1977. Ordained to ministry United Ch. of Christ, 1977. Asst. to pastor Salem United Ch. of Christ, Rochester, N.Y., 1977; min. Parma Greece United Ch. of Christ, Hilton, N.Y., 1977-88, 1st Congl. United Ch. of Christ, Albany, N.Y., 1988—; moderator N.Y. Conf. United Ch. of Christ, 1984-85; del. United Ch. of Christ Gen. Synod, Pittsburgh, Rochester, 1981-83, N.Y. State Coun. Chs., 1989—; chaplain SUNY, Brockport, 1985-88; bd. dirs. (pres.) Genesee Area Campus Ministries, 1975-86. Contbg. author: Eco-Justice Lifestyle Assessment, 1976; mem. editorial bd. The Egg jour., 1990—. Mem. coordinating com. Eco-Justice Task Force and Network, Ithaca, N.Y., 1975-88; founder, pres. Tabitha, Inc., Women Mins., Rochester, 1977-88; coord. Crop Walks for Hilton Community Coun., 1981-88; mem. Support Ministries for Persons with AIDS, Inc., Albany, 1989—. Mem. Internat. Assn. Women Mins., Hudson Mohawk Assn. United Ch. of Christ (ch. and ministry com. 1989—), Capital Area Coun. Chs. (co-chair women in ministry network 1988—). Office: First Congl Ch 405 Quail St Albany NY 12208

SHEARIN, MORRIS LEE, minister; b. Garysburg, N.C., Dec. 11, 1940; s. Simon and Bernice (Porch) S.; m. Bertha Cotton, Mar. 29, 1964; children: Felicia S., Morris Lee Jr. BA, Shaw U., 1976, MDiv, 1976; DMin, Howard U., 1981. Ordained to ministry Bapt. Ch., 1971. Pastor Cedar Grove Bapt. Ch., Lawrenceville, Va., 1970-74, Pleasant Grove Bapt. Ch., Adams Grove, Va., 1972-74, Mt. Olive Bapt. Ch., Lewiston, N.C., 1974-88, Israel Bapt. Ch., Washington, 1988—. Commr. Northampton County, Jackson, N.C., 1982-86; organizer Nation Share Cropper Assn., Wadesboro, N.C., 1982-83; bd. dirs. Montana Terrace Boys/Girls Club, 1990—, Stoddard Bapt. Home, 1990—. Mem. NAACP (chaplain D.C. br., pres. Seaboard, N.C. chpt. 1980-88, 2d v.p. Charlotte, N.C. chpt. 1984-88, 1st v.p. 1986-88, Outstanding Performance award 1987), Shaw Theol. Alumni Assn. (cert. of approval 1977), Howard U. Theol. Alumni Assn. (pres. 1990—), Omega Psi Phi (scroll of honor 1979), Century Club. Democrat. Office: Israel Bapt Ch 1251 Saratoga Ave NE Washington DC 20018

SHEDD, A. GLENROY, minister; b. Lebanon, N.H., Jan. 10, 1939; s. Marshall Proctor and Alice Margaret (Taylor) S.; m. Shirley Ann Hanson, July 27, 1963; children: Bradley Dean, Timothy Allen, Christy Lynn. BA in English Edn., Evangel Coll., 1962; MA in Christian Edn., Assemblies of God Theol. Sem., 1983. Lic. to ministry Assemblies of God, 1983. Asst. pub. relationist Assemblies of God, Springfield, Mo., 1960-64, editor CA Herald, 1965-66, Sunday sch. promotion coord., 1967-73, editor SS Action, 1974-76; minister of edn. Cen. Assembly of God, Springfield, 1976—; chmn. adv. bd. Joyland Learning Ctr., Springfield, 1976—; chmn. bd. dirs. Univ. Christian Fellowship, Springfield, 1981-85, 88—. Contbr. articles to profl. publs. With USAR, 1962-68. Mem. Profl. Assn. Christian Educators, Univ. Club (1st v.p. Springfield 1984, pres. 1985). Home: 2540 W Swan Springfield MO 65807-4039 Office: Cen Assembly of God 1301 Boonville Ave Springfield MO 65802-1897

SHEDD, HUDSON PAUL, missions director; b. San Pedro, Potosi, Bolivia, Jan. 15, 1926; came to U.S., 1938; s. Leslie Martin and Della Wilson (Johnston) S.; m. Myra May James, Sept. 10, 1949; children: James, Paul, David, Daniel. BA, Wheaton (Ill.) Coll., 1947; MDiv, Faith Theol. Sem., 1950; DD (hon.), Fla. Bible Coll., 1981. Field dir. Gospel Mission of S.Am., Uruguay, 1973-79; gen. dir. Gospel Mission of S.Am., Ft. Lauderdale, 1979—. Republican. Home: 1730 SW 22d Ave Fort Lauderdale FL 33312

SHEEHAN, DANIEL EUGENE, bishop; b. Emerson, Nebr., May 14, 1917; s. Daniel F. and Mary Helen (Crahan) S. Student, Creighton U., 1934-36, LL.D. (hon.), 1964; student, Kenrick Sem., St. Louis, 1936-42; J.C.D., Cath. U. Am., 1949. Ordained priest Roman Cath. Ch., 1942; asst. pastor Omaha, 1942-46; chancellor Archdiocese Omaha, 1949-69; aux. bishop Archdiocese Omaha, Omaha, 1964-69; archbishop of Omaha, 1969—; Pres. Canon Law Soc. Am., 1953; chaplain Omaha club Serra Internat., 1950-64. Chmn. bd. Father Flanagan's Boys' Home, Boys Town, Nebr.; chmn. Cath. Mut. Relief Soc., Omaha. Office: Chancery Office 100 N 62nd St Omaha NE 68132

SHEEHAN, MICHAEL JARBOE, bishop; b. Wichita, Kans., July 9, 1939; s. John Edward and Mildred (Jarboe) S. S.T.L., Gregorian U., Rome, 1965; J.C.D., Lateran U., Rome, 1971. Ordained priest Roman Catholic Ch. 1964. Asst. gen. sec. Nat. Council Catholic Bishops, Washington, 1971-76; rector Holy Trinity Sem., Dallas, 1976-82; pastor Immaculate Conception Ch., Grand Prairie, Tex., 1982-83; bishop Diocese of Lubbock, Tex., 1983—; chmn. Am. bd. Cath. Missions, 1989—; Tex. state chaplain KC. Contbr. articles to New Cath. Ency. Trustee St. Mary Hosp., Lubbock, 1983—. Mem. Nat. Conf. Cath. Bishops (mem. adminstv. com.). Club: Serra (chaplain 1983—) (Lubbock). Avocations: snow skiing, racquetball. Home: 4301 52d St Lubbock TX 79499 Office: Diocese of Lubbock PO Box 98700 Lubbock TX 79499

SHEEHY, HOWARD SHERMAN, JR., minister; b. Denver, Mar. 19, 1934; s. Howard Sherman and Mildred Louise (Fishburn) S.; m. Thelma Florine Cline, Sept. 4, 1954; children: John Robert, Lisa Florine, Michael Howard. A.A., Graceland Coll., 1953; B.S., Central Mo. State Coll., 1955; M.S., U. Kans., 1960, postgrad. Youth dir. Reorganized Ch. Jesus Christ Latter-day Saints, Independence, Mo., 1960-64; pastor Des Moines, 1964-68; church supr. Haiti, 1968-70, Canada, 1970-74, Australia, 1970-75, N.Z., 1970-75, India, 1970-78, Japan, Korea, Republic of China, Philippines, 1976-78; mem. Council of Twelve Apostles, 1968-78, mem. 1st presidency, 1978—; mem. corp. body Outreach Internat. Health Care Systems Inc., Restoration Trail Found., Independence Regional Health Ctr. Editor-in-chief: Saints Herald. Mem. nat. Protestant com. on scouting Boy Scouts Am., 1964-66; trustee Independence Regional Health Ctr., 1979-88, 90—; dir. Health Care Systems, Inc., 1990—. Lt. USNR, 1955-59. Mem. Pi Omega Pi, Phi Delta Kappa, Phi Kappa Phi. Republican. Home: 3403 S Crane St Independence MO 64055 Office: The Auditorium PO Box 1059 Independence MO 64051

SHEERAN, MICHAEL JOHN LEO, priest, educational administrator; b. N.Y.C., Jan. 24, 1940; s. Leo John and Glenna Marie (Wright) S. A.B., St. Louis U., 1963, Ph.L., 1964, A.M. in Polit. Sci., 1967, A.M. in Theology, 1971, S.T.L., 1971; Ph.D., Princeton U., 1977. Joined Soc. Jesus, 1957; ordained priest Roman Catholic Ch., 1970; exec. editor Catholic Mind, N.Y.C., 1971-72; assoc. editor Am. mag., N.Y.C., 1971-72; assoc. chaplain Aquinas Inst., Princeton, N.J., 1972-75; asst. dean Regis Coll., Denver, 1975-77, dean of Coll., 1977-82, v.p. acad. affairs, 1982—, acting pres., 1987—; retreat dir., cons. on governance for religious communities, 1970—. Author: Beyond Majority Rule, 1984. Contbr. articles and editorials to publs. Trustee Rockhurst Coll., Kansas City, Mo., 1982-91, Creighton U., Omaha, 1985—, U. San Francisco, 1985—. Ford Found. scholar, 1963. Democrat. Home: 3333 Regis Blvd Denver CO 80221 Office: Regis U 3333 Regis Blvd Denver CO 80221

SHEETS, DOLORES SANTOS, minister; b. N.Y.C., Feb. 4, 1937; d. August A. and Carmella (Roland) Santos; m. William Ralph Massey, May 30, 1957 (dec. 1968); children: Ronald Wynn, Russell Warren, Randall Walter; m. Elton Craig Sheets, Mar. 6, 1974. BS, Iowa State U., 1982; MDiv, Meth. Theol. Sch., 1986. Ordained to ministry, United Meth. Ch., 1988. Interim pastor Quad-City Hispanic Ministry, Rock Island, Ill., 1986; pastor Clarence (Iowa) United Meth. Ch., 1986-88, Hansell (Iowa)-West Fork United Meth. Ch., 1988-90, St. Mark's United Meth. Ch., Camanche, Iowa, 1990—; mem. bd. of ordained ministry United Meth. Ch., 1988—; del. World Meth. Conf., Singapore, 1991. Mem. Kiwanis. Home: 1306 Hiawatha Ln Camanche IA 52730 Office: St Mark's United Meth Ch 808 3d St Camanche IA 52730

SHELBY, WILLIAM ALAN, clergyman; b. Kansas City, Mo., Dec. 7, 1958; s. Millard C. and Edna Jean (Keith) S.; m. Dalona Luann Litle, July 20, 1985; children: Alison, Jessica. BA, Calvary Bible Coll., 1983; MA, Luther Rice Sem., 1991. Ordained to ministry Bapt. Ch., 1981. Coll. pastor Blue Ridge Bapt. Temple, Kansas City, Mo., 1981-82, chaplain, 1983-84; coll. pastor Kansas City Bapt. Temple, 1985—; dir. Cultural Discovery Group, Kansas City, 1987—. Office: Kansas City Bapt Temple 5460 Blue Ridge Cutoff Kansas City MO 64133

SHELDON, ELI HOWARD, minister; b. Monroe, Mich., May 25, 1937; s. Clarence O. and Orean Lavon (Longdon) S.; m. Freida Orene Townsend, Feb. 17, 1962; children: Stefanie Ann, Todd Howard. BA, Dallas Bapt. U., 1970; MDiv, Southwestern Bapt. Theol. Sem., 1973, D. Ministry, 1976. Ordained to ministry So. Bapt. Conv., 1971. Minister Plain View Bapt. Ch., Chalk Mountain, Tex., 1969-70, Eastside Bapt. Ch., Marietta, Okla., 1970-73, 1st Bapt. Ch., Roosevelt, Okla., 1974-77, Crown Heights Bapt. Ch., Oklahoma City, 1978—; bd. dirs. Bapt. Gen. Convention Okla., Oklahoma City, 1989—; adj. prof. Okla. Bapt. U., Shawnee, 1986—. Editor, writer, artist Crown Heights Comics; contbr. articles to newspapers and mags. Chaplain Lions Club, Roosevelt, 1974-77; chmn. Bi-Centennial Com., Roosevelt, 1975-76. Mem. Capital Bapt. Assn. (chmn. continuing edn. com. 1982—, mem. exec. bd. 1978—), Cowboy Hall of Fame (life). Home: 5732 NW 46th Oklahoma City OK 73122 Office: Crown Heights Bapt Ch 4802 N Western Oklahoma City OK 73118 *Every ministry can be improved if we use three phrases with genuine sincerity and concern. We love you, you're my friend, and we care about you.*

SHELDON, GILBERT IGNATIUS, clergyman; b. Cleve., Sept. 20, 1926; s. Ignatius Peter and Stephanie Josephine (Olszewski) S. Student, John Carroll U.; M.Div., St. Theol. Sem., 1970; D.Min., St. Mary Sem. and Ohio Consortium of Sems., 1974. Ordained priest Roman Catholic Ch., 1953; assoc. pastor Cleve. Diocese, 1953-64, diocesan dir. propagation of faith, 1964-74; pastor, Episcopal vicar Lorain County, Ohio, 1974-76; aux. bishop Cleve., 1976—; vicar for Summit County, 1979-80, So. Region, 1980—; bd. dirs. Soc. Propagation of Faith, 1968-74; instr. theology St. John Coll.; clergy adv. bd. econ. edn. Akron U.; mem. Bishop's Com. Latin Am. Served with USAAF, 1944-45. Mem. Nat. Conf. Cath. Bishops (adminstrv. bd. 1985—), Am. Legion, Cath. War Vets. Club: K.C. Lodge: Rotary (Akron). Office: 40 University Ave Akron OH 44308

SHELDON, L. PHILIP, JR., marketing executive, foundation administrator; m. Kathleen M. Green; children: Philip William, Joshua Daniel. BA in Polit. Sci., Johns Hopkins U., 1983. Pres. Trinity Communicators, Anaheim, Calif., 1983-84; gen. mgr. Heritage Telemarketing, North Little Rock, Ark., 1984-88; pres. Diener Cons., Inc., Anaheim, 1988-90, Child Protection Program Found., Inc., Dallas, 1990—. Home: 6203 High Brush Cir Dallas TX 75249 Office: Child Protection Program Found 7441 Marvin D Love Fwy 200 Dallas TX 75237

SHELDON, TERRY LYNN, minister, small business owner; b. Hudson, N.Y., June 25, 1937; s. Gerald W. and Mildred R. Sheldon; m. Mary Anne Seeger, Sept. 5, 1959; children: Mary Lynn, Kathleen, Stephen. BS, Utica (N.Y.) Coll., 1959; diploma in theology, U. of the South, 1984. Draftsman Consol. Sheet Metal, Utica, 1956-64, estimator, 1964-89, gen. mgr., 1972-89, v.p., 1985-89; co-owner Sheldon Sheet Metal, Utica, 1989—; co-chair Diocesan Commn. on Aging, Syracuse, N.Y., 1986—; ESMA designee Diocese of Cen. N.Y., Syracuse, 1988—; bd. dirs. Coun. of Chs., Utica, Your Neighbors, Inc., Utica. Author: (handbook) Beginners Guide to Nursing Home Visiting, 1986. Chaplain Masonic Home, Utica, 1986, St. Joseph's Nursing Home, Utica, 1987, CAP, Utica and Rome, N.Y., 1989. Mem. Internat. Order of St. Luke the Physician (assoc.), Mil. Chaplains Assn., Associated Order or Holy Cross. Episcopalian. Avocations: mountian climbing, reading, walking. Office: All Saints Ch 40 Faxton St Utica NY 13501

SHELDON, WILLIAM A., religious organization administrator. Sec., coun. of apostles Ch. of Christ, Independence, Mo. Office: Ch of Christ PO Box 482 Independence MO 65071*

SHELEY, DALE, minister; b. Richmond, Calif., Apr. 2, 1953; s. Robert Hamilton and Charlcie Elverta (Witt) S.; m. Elizabeth Carol Brooding, May 16, 1981; children: Rebekah Ann, Stepen Robert. BA, UCLA, 1975; postgrad., Simpson Coll., 1977; lic., Berean Coll., 1980. Ordained to ministry Assemblies of God, 1980. Youth pastor Cen. Assembly, ElSobrante, Calif., 1979-83, Bethel Ch., Grass Valley, Calif., 1984-86; sr. pastor Pinole (Calif.) Valley Assembly, 1986—; tchr. Richmond Unified Sch. Dist., 1989—; sectional youth rep. Assemblies of God, East Bay, Calif., 1983, recreation/evangelism rep., No. Calif. and Nev., 1989—; guest speaker 1st Youth Workers Conv., Argentina, 1985; dir. N.W. County Share Project, Pinole, Calif., 1989-90. Named Most Valuable Player of Tournament, Calvary Temple/Yuba City Governing Bd., 1983; Calif. Scholastic scholar State of Calif., 1971, football scholar UCLA, 1971-75. Republican. Home: 1598 Marlesta Rd Pinole CA 94564 Office: Pinole Valley Assembly 2850 Estates Ave Pinole CA 94564

SHELLEY, MARSHALL BRUCE, editor; b. Pasadena, Calif., Oct. 16, 1953; s. Bruce Leon and Mary Elizabeth (Harrington) S.; m. Susan Janzen Shelley, May 28, 1983; children: Stacey, Kelsey, Mandy. BA in Journalism, Bethel Coll., 1975; MDiv, Denver Sem., 1982. Ordained to ministry Bapt. Ch., 1982. Assoc. editor David C. Cook Pub. Co., Elgin, Ill., 1975-79; editor Leadership Jour., Wheaton, Ill., 1982—; exec. editor Christian History Mag., Wheaton, 1990—; v.p. Christianity Today Inc., Wheaton, 1990—. Author: Well-Intentioned Dragons, 1985, The Health Hectic Home, 1988, Keeping your Kids Christian, 1990. Mem. Am. Tract Soc. (bd. dirs. 1990—). Office: Christianity Today Inc 465 Gunderson Dr Carol Stream IL 60188

SHELNUTT, DUMAS BROUGHTON, minister; b. Atlanta, Apr. 26, 1955; s. Dumas Broughton Sr. and Georgia Texana (Ruff) S.; m. Kandy Jackson, Sept. 6, 1980; children: Meredith Dawn, Emory, Wesley Jackson. BA, La Grange Coll., 1975; MDiv, Emory U., 1978. Ordained to ministry Meth. Ch. Assoc. pastor 1st United Meth. Ch., Fayetteville, Ga., 1977-80; pastor Rock Springs/McKendree, Lawrenceville, Ga., 1980-83, North Fayette United Meth. Ch., Lawrenceville, 1983—; mem. bd. global ministries North Ga. Conf. United Meth. Ch., Atlanta, 1988—. Bd. dirs. Early Years Sch., Fayetteville, 1989—, Child-Abuse Coun., Fayetteville, 1986—, Cancer Soc., Fayetteville, 1983—. Mem. Rotary. Democrat. Home: 135 Creekwood Ct Fayetteville GA 30214

SHELP, EARL EDWARD, religion educator; b. Louisville, Oct. 28, 1947; s. Gordon Earl and Dora (Smith) S. B.S.C., U. Louisville, 1969; MDiv, So. Bapt. Theol. Sem., 1972, PhD, 1976. Ordained to ministry Bapt. Ch., 1971. Fellow Inst. of Religion, Houston, 1976-88; prof. Baylor Coll. of Medicine, Houston, 1978-88; exec. dir., sr. fellow Found. for Interfaith Rsch. and Ministry, Houston, 1988—. Author: Born to Die?, 1986, AIDS and the Church, 1987, AIDS: A Manual for Pastoral Care, 1987; editor: Pastoral Ministry Series, 1985-91. Mem. Soc. Christian Ethics, Am. Acad. Religion, Internat. AIDS Soc. Office: Found for Interfaith Rsch and Ministry 701 N Post Oak Rd Ste 330 Houston TX 77024

SHELTON, L(OUIS) AUSTIN, clergyman, psychologist; b. Shreveport, La., July 28, 1927; s. Benjamin Lee and Hazel Mae (Russell) S.; m. Bonnie May Curry, July 25, 1952; children: Janice Lynn, Kristel Joy, Marc Austin Lee, Camille Caye. BS in Edn., U. S.D., 1962, MA, 1963, EdD, 1968. Pastor Assembly of God Ch., Vernonia, Oreg., 1954-58, Vermillion, S.D., 1959—; psychologist Area Edn. Agy., Sioux City, Iowa, 1965—. Author: An Analysis of C.H. Spurgeon's Lectures on the Art of Preaching, 1962, A Comparative Study of Educational Achievement in One-Parent and Two-Parent Families, 1968. Bd. dirs. Vermillion Ind. Sch. Dist., 1971-76; pres. PTA, 1971. Served with USNR. Mem. Am. Psychol. Assn., Iowa Psychol. Assn., Phi Delta Kappa. Republican. Avocations: hunting, tennis, racquetball. Home: 1218 Valley View Dr Vermillion SD 57069

SHELTON, MALCOLM WENDELL, biblical studies educator; b. Eckmansville, Ohio, Aug. 26, 1919; s. Charles Edward and Mary Ina (Suffron) S.; m. Muriel Payne Moore, Aug. 9, 1987. BS in Edn., Olivet Nazarene Coll., 1951, BTh, 1952; M in Religion, Pasadena Nazarene Coll., 1952; BD, Nazarene Theol. Sem., Kansas City, 1954, MDiv, 1972; MS in Edn., Cen. Mo. State U., 1965; D in Ministry, Philips U. Grad. Sem., 1977; postgrad., U. Kans., 1966-67, Hebrew U., Jerusalem, 1979, 81, Wheaton Grad. Sch., 1982. Prof. old testament So. Nazarene U., Bethany, Okla., 1967-85, Mid-Am. Bible Coll., Oklahoma City, 1985—; tchr. various pub. schs., Kansas City, Mo., 1954-65. Staff sgt. U.S. Army, 1941-45. Mem. Soc. Bibl. Lit., Am. Sch. Oriental Rsch., Brit. Sch. Archaeology, Wesleyan Theol. Soc., Evang. Theol. Soc., Am. Rsch. Ctr. in Egypt. Republican. Home: 6404 NW 35th Bethany OK 73008 Office: Mid-Am Bible Coll 3500 SW 119th St Oklahoma City OK 73170

SHELTON, MICHAEL PATRICK, minister; b. Indpls., Aug. 12, 1953; s. Robert S. and Mary Lou (Singpiel) S.; m. Linda Jane Yardumian, Dec. 27, 1980. BA in Religion, Olivet Nazarene U., Bourbonnais, Ill., 1984; MDiv, Nazarene Theol. Sem., Kansas City, Mo., 1988. Trace support agt. Emery Worldwide, Kansas City, Mo., 1984-88; pastor Stony Point Nazarene Ch., Kansas City, Kans., 1988—; counselor Kans. Alcohol and Drug Rehab., Kansas City, Kans., 1988—; adj. prof. Nazarene Bible Coll., Kansas City. Chaplain Kansas City police dept. Mem. Western Wyandotte Ministers Assn. Republican. Home: 800 N 78th St Kansas City KS 66112 Office: Stony Point Nazarene Ch 800 N 78th St Kansas City KS 66112

SHELTON, MURIEL MOORE, religious education administrator; b. Freeport, N.Y., May 29, 1921; d. Samuel Talbott and Agnes Jerolean (Trigg) Payne; m. Ernest William Moore, May 29, 1944 (dec. Apr. 2, 1978); children: Diana Moore Williams, David E. Moore, Cathi Moore Mount, Douglas L. Moore; m. Malcolm Wendell Shelton, Aug. 9, 1987. AB, Eastern Nazarene Coll., 1942; MusM, U. Tex., 1966. Cert. educator gen. and choral music, English, Tex., Tenn., Ark., Kans. Music dir. Coll. Ave. United Meth. Ch., Manhattan, Kans., 1969-71, Cen. United Meth. Ch., Lawrence, Kans., 1971-75, First United Meth. Ch., Horton, Kans., 1975-78; dir. Christian edn. St. Mark's United Meth. Ch., Bethany, Okla., 1980—; chmn. bd. dirs. Northwest Food Pantry, Oklahoma City, 1987-88; rep. St. mark's United Meth. Ch. Labor Link Ctr., 1989—; lectr. in field. Contbr. articles to quarterly mags.; author: Song of Joy, 1985, Promises of Good, 1989. Mem. Christian Educators' Fellowship. Home: 6404 NW 35th Bethany OK 73008 Office: St Mark's United Meth Ch 8140 NW 36th Bethany OK 73008 *A life for God is eternally significant.*

SHELTON, ROBERT LOREN, religious studies educator, minister; b. Minneola, Kans., July 6, 1934; s. Sidney Clarence and Mary Catherine (Tucker) S.; m. Elinor Suzanne Ebright, Aug. 5, 1955 (div. 1972); children: Heidi Marie, Wendi Noelle; m. Mary Carolyn Voss, June 29, 1974; children: Michael Jeffrey, David Andrew. BA, Baker U., 1956; MDiv, Boston U., 1959, PhD, 1970. Ordained to ministry Meth. Ch., 1960. Campus minister Wesley Found., Kans. State U., Manhattan, 1960-63, Wesley Found., Washburn U., Topeka, 1963-65; state dir. Meth. Student Movement of Kans., Topeka, 1962-65; staff New Eng. Student Christian Movement, Cambridge, Mass., 1965-67; prof. dept. religious studies U. Kans., Lawrence, 1967—, chmn. dept., 1978-88, univ. ombudsman, 1985—; bd. dirs. Found. for Community Pastoral Edn., Kansas City, Mo., 1980—, pres. bd. dirs., 1984—; chmn. div. campus ministry Kans. Coun. of Chs., Topeka, 1964-65; mem. Commn. on Standards for Wesley Founds., Nashville, nat., 1964-68; United Meth. team mem. Roman Cath.-United Meth. Dialogue (Nat.) on Ethical Issues in Care of Sick and Dying, 1986-89. Author: Loving Relationships, 1987; co-author: Handbook of Verbal Group Exercises, 1974, Holy Living—Holy Dying, 1989; contbg. author Theological Yearbook, 1991; contbr. articles to profl. jours. State bd. dirs. Kans. Adv. Coun. on Civil Rights, Topeka, 1963-65. Recipient James C. Baker Grad. award United Meth. Ch., 1965-66; fellow Boston U. Human Rels. Ctr., 1965-67; named Danforth Assoc., Danforth Found., 1971—, one of Outstanding Educators in Am., 1971. Mem. Soc. Christian Ethics, Univ. and Coll. Ombudsman Assocs., Am. Acad. Religion, AAUP. Democrat. Office: U Kans Dept Religious Studies Lawrence KS 66045-2164 *What others may say or do, I cannot control. My humanity requires, however, that I control how I choose to interpret what they say and do, and how I respond within my own life. Often that is a great influence over others.*

SHELTON, ROBERT RYAN, minister; b. Paris, Ark., July 22, 1952; s. Jack S. and Velta M. (Adams) S.; m. Janice E. Hatcher, Sept. 3, 1971; children: Robert Shawn, Tracy, Nicole. BA, Citadel Coll., Ozark, Ark., 1976; postgrad., Immanuel Theol. Sem., Peachtree, Ga., 1989—. Ordained to ministry So. Bapt. Conv., 1976. Founder, adminstr. Christian schs., Ft. Smith, Ark., 1978-80; co-pastor 1st Bapt. Ch., Stilwell, Okla., 1980-85; evangelist, crusade dir., 1986-88; pastor 1st Bapt. Ch., Branch, Ark., 1989-91, Alma, Ark., 1991—; mission dir. Guatemala Bapt. Conv., 1989—; bd. dirs. Guatemala/Ark. Project, Little Rock, 1989—; mem. exec. bd. Concord Bapt. Assn., Ft. Smith, 1988—. Co-author: Trailblazer of Truth, 1990; producer, recorder 9 gospel music albums, 1986-91. Bd. dirs. Pregnancy Crisis Ctr., Ft. Smith, 1989—. Mem. Nat. Order Eagle Scouts. Republican. Home: PO Box 1040 Rte 2 Alma AR 72921 Office: 1st Bapt Ch Hwy 64 E Mountain Grove Rd Alma AR 72921 *Bad things often happen to good people, it is best that we remember, "it's not what happens, but what we make of what happens that can make the difference in our lives."*

SHELTON, SARAH JACKSON, clergyperson; b. Birmingham, Ala., Aug. 2, 1956; d. James Lamar and Hermione (Dannelly) Jackson; d. Lloyd Carson Shelton, Jan. 17, 1987; 1 child, David Lloyd. BS magna cum laude, U. Ala., 1977; MRE, So. Bapt. Theol. Sem., 1979, MDiv, 1981. Ordained to ministry Bapt. Ch., 1982. Minister Brookwood Bapt. Ch., Birmingham, Ala., 1981—; workshop leader Golden Gate Bapt. Theol. Sem. Women in Ministry Week, 1988. Author Day of Prayer Program, Bapt. Young Women, 1985. Vol. reader WBHM Radio, Birmingham, 1985-86; vol. Planned Parenthood, Birmingham, 1982-83. Office: Brookwood Bapt Ch 3449 Overton Rd Birmingham AL 35223

SHELTON, THOMAS ALFRED, Christian education director; b. Kansas City, Mo., Dec. 6, 1951; s. Thomas and Savanna S.; m. Phyllis Annette White, Aug. 18, 1979; children: Thomas, Reginald, Veronica. AA, Penn Valley Community, 1975; BA, U. Mo. Kansas City, 1983; MDiv, Cen. Bapt. Theol. Seminary, 1988. Cert. secondary tchr., social scis., Mo. Dean MidWest Dist. Congress, Kansas City, Mo., 1984—; pres. Black Student Fellowship, Kansas City, 1985-87; regional v.p. Nat. Conf. Black Seminarians, N.Y.C., 1986-88; asst. pastor Kansas City, 1985—; resource tchr. Kansas City Sch. Dist., 1988—; pres. Mt. Sinai Day Care Bd., Kansas City, 1989—; tchr. Five State Laymens Meeting, St. Louis, 1989. Bd. dirs. Kansas City Youth Ct., 1989—. Master sgt. USAF Res., 1979—. Mem. Tchrs. Union, ASCD. Home: 1706 E 60th St Kansas City MO 64110 Office: Mount Sinai Bapt Ch 3700 Brooklyn Kansas City MO 64127

SHELTON, WILLIAM C., religious organization administrator, consultant; b. Washington, Pa., Apr. 25, 1942; s. Joseph M. and Edith C. (Cort) S.; m. Thalia Berry Shelton, Dec. 1, 1962; children: Kimberly Ann Pacilla, William Douglas. BA, Waynesburg (Pa.) Coll., 1964; MSW, U. Pitts., 1969. Lic. social worker, Pa. Caseworker, supr. Pa. Dept. Pub. Welfare, Washington, 1964-69; dir. tenant svcs., supr. Washington County Housing Authority/Bd. of Assistance, 1969-79; dir. tenant svcs. Washington County Housing Authority, 1980-81; adminstr. Thomas Campbell Christian Ctr., Washington, 1981—; med. social worker Vis. Nurse Assn., Washington, 1966—, Kade Nursing Home, Washington, 1973—, Physicians Home Care, Washington, 1987—. Pres. Family Svc. of Washington, 1985, 87. Presbyterian. Avocations: sailing, golf, travel. Home: 72 Hilltop Acres Rd Washington PA 15301 Office: Thomas Campbell Christian Ctr 850 Beach St Washington PA 15301

SHENOUDA, ANBA, III, Egyptian ecclesiastic; b. Cairo, Aug. 3, 1923; B.A., Cairo U.; B.D., Coptic Orthodox Theol. Coll. Theol. tchr. and writer; former Bishop and prof. theology Orthodox Clerical Coll., Cairo; 1st chmn. Assn. of Theol. Colls. in the Near East; 117th Pope of Alexandria and Patriarch of the See of St. Mark of Egypt, the Near East and All Africa (Coptic Orthodox Church), 1971-81, 85—; removed from post by Pres. Sadat and banished to desert monastery Wadi Natroun, Sept. 1981, released Jan. 1985. Office: Coptic Orthodox Patriarchate, Anba Ruess Bldg Ramstet St, Abbasiya Cairo Arab Republic of Egypt

SHEPHERD, GENE R., academic administrator. Head Dallas Christian Coll. Office: Dallas Christian Coll Office of the President 2700 Christian Pkwy Dallas TX 75234*

SHEPHERD, HARVEY LAWRENCE, religion reporter; b. St. Catharines, Ont., Can., Sept. 7, 1939; s. Herbert Lawrence and Elinor Elizabeth (Burrows) S.; m. Jean Anderson; children: Andrea Jane, Hugh Lawrence. BA, U. Toronto, Ont., Can., 1961, postgrad., 1964-66. Reporter The Globe and Mail, Toronto, Ont., Can., 1961-64, 67-79, The Gazette, Montreal, Que., Can., 1979—. Mem. Can. Assn. Journalists, Association Professionale des Journalistes du Quebec, C.J. Jung Soc. Montreal (planning com. 1986—). Home: 4361 Wilson Ave, Montreal, PQ Canada H4A 2V3 Office: The Gazette, 250 Rue St Antoine W, Montreal, PQ Canada H2Y 3R7

SHEPHERD, JAY CEE, clergyman; b. Dallas, Sept. 14, 1953; s. Benjamin Franklin and Marjorie (Allen) S.; m. Vivian Ann Wood, Sept. 22, 1979; children: Jamin Charles, Sarah Lindsay. AS, Kilgore Jr. Coll., 1973; BBA, Tex. Tech. U., 1975; MA, Southwestern Bapt. Theol. Sem., 1983. Ordained to ministry Bapt. Ch., 1984. Minister music and youth First Bapt. Ch., Blue Ridge, Tex., 1981-83; minister coll. students and single adults First Bapt. Ch., West Monroe, La., 1983-86; minister to single adults Village Bapt. Ch., Oklahoma City, 1986—; com. mem. Nat. Con. Single Adults, 1991; conf. leader So. bapt. Conv., 1985—. Active Am. Cancer Soc., Longview, Tex.,

1978, YMCA, Longview, 1977-79. Recipient Pres. award Young Reps., Kilgore, 1973. Mem. Nat. Assn. Single Adult Leaders, So. Bapt. Assn. Single Adult Ministers, Capitol Bapt. Assn. Assist Team. Home: 6900 Talbot Canyon Rd Oklahoma City OK 73162 Office: Village Bapt Ch 10600 N May Ave Oklahoma City OK 73120-2604 *The essence of life revolves around our relationship with Jesus. In living life however, we have choices, and "...the peace of Christ which passes all understanding..." (Philippians 4:7) is a choice that we must make as life deals us many sorrows and disappointments.*

SHEPHERD, JOHN BARRIE, minister; b. Halifax, Yorkshire, Eng., Feb. 25, 1935; came to U.S., 1960; s. John Jenkinson and Florence (Woodhead) S.;m. Mhairi Catherine MacFarlane Primrose, May 16, 1938; children: Alison Catherine, Kirstin Fiona, Nicola Mairi, Ailsa Catriona. MA, U. Edinburgh, Scotland, 1960; MDiv cum laude, Yale U., 1964, MA in O.T., 1965; MA in Bibl. Studies, Hartford Theol. Sem., 1972; DLitt, Muskingum Coll., 1986. Ordained to ministry Presbyn. Ch., 1965. Dir. Campus Christian Found., U. Conn., Storrs, 1965-67; chaplain, asst. prof. religion Conn. Coll., New London, 1967-72; chaplain, sr. minister Coll. Wooster (Ohio), Westminster Presbyn. Ch., 1972-76; sr. minister Swarthmore (Pa.) Presbyn. Ch., 1976—; vice moderator Synod of New Eng., 1969-70; moderator Presbytery of Muskingum Valley, Ohio, 1976; mem. com. on worship United Presbyn. Ch., 1980-85, chmn., 1985-87; exec. bd., faculty Acad. Preachers, Phila., 1980—; adj. faculty Luth. Sem. Phila., 1991—; guest preacher Harvard U., Yale U., Duke U., Cornell U., Dartmouth Coll., Mt. Holyoke Coll., Agnes Scott Coll., USCG Acad., Kenyon Coll., Dickinson Coll., St. Giles Cathedral, Edinburgh, Scotland, and other univs. and sems. Author: Diary of Daily Prayer, 1975, A Diary of Prayer, 1981, Ecounters, 1983, Prayers from the Mount, 1986, Praying the Psalms, 1987, A Child Is Born, 1988, A Pilgrim's Way, 1989, A Moveable Feast, 1990, Seeing with the Soul, 1991; contbr. poems and articles to profl. jours. With RAF, 1953-55. Named Newlands orator Bathgate, Scotland, 1980, Somerville lectr. Luth. Sem. Phila., 1991; Aurelia Hoover grad. fellow Yale U., 1964, Am. Assn. Theol. Schs. fellow Yale U., 1962. Mem. Presbytery Phila., Fellowship Reconciliation, Presbyn. Writers Guild, St. Andrew's Soc. Phila. (chaplain). Avocations: swimming, fishing, sailing, music. Home: 107 Yale Ave Swarthmore PA 19081 Office: Swarthmore Presbyn Ch 727 Harvard Ave Swarthmore PA 19081

SHEPHERD, R. F., bishop; b. July 15, 1926; s. Herbert George and Muriel (Grant) S.; m. Ann Alayne Dundas, 1952; 6 children. BA with honors, U. B.C., 1948; postgrad., King's Coll., London; DD (hon.), St. John's Coll., Winnipeg, 1988. Curate St. Stephen's, London, 1952-57; rector St. Paul's, Glanford, Ont., 1957-59, All Sts., Winnipeg, 1959-65; dean, rector All Sts. Cathedral, Edmonton, Alta., 1965-69, Christ Ch. Cathedral, Montreal, 1970-83; rector St. Matthias, Victoria, B.C., 1983-84; Anglican Bishop of B.C., 1985—. Fellow Coll. of Preachers. Home: 1256 Beach Dr, Victoria, BC Canada V8S 2N3 Office: Diocese of B C, 912 Vancouver St, Victoria, BC Canada V8V 3V7

SHEPHERD, VICTORIA ELIZABETH, religion educator; b. Des Moines, Nov. 13, 1954; d. Arthur Ernest and Mary Joan (Taylor) Cutler; m. James Kent Shepherd, Nov. 26, 1975; children: Jennifer Anne, Jessica Joy, Virginia Joan. Grad. high sch., Des Moines. Cert. catecist Roman Cath. Ch., 1988. Rite of Christian Initiation of Adults team mem. Holy Family Ch., Council Bluffs, Iowa, 1984-90, tutor, 1985—, tchr. Vacation Bible Sch., 1985—, religion educator, 1985—. Home and Office: 4036 Rawlins Dr Council Bluffs IA 51501 *When our children look into the future, have we left them anything to see?.*

SHEPHERD, WILLIAM HENRY, JR., religion educator; b. Indpls., Sept. 20, 1957; s. William H. and Joycelyn (DeVaney) S. MusB, U. Ga., 1979; MDiv, Yale U., 1982. Ordained to ministry Episcopal Ch.as priest, 1983. Asst. rector St. Christopher's Episcopal Ch., Carmel, Ind., 1982-83; assoc. rector St. Paul's Episcopal Ch., Indpls., 1984-86; asst. rector St. Catherine's Episcopal Ch., Marietta, Ga., 1989-90; asst. prof. homiletics Va. Theol. Sem., Alexandria, 1991—. Contbr. articles to profl. jours. Mem. Soc. for Bibl. Lit., Acad. Homiletics. Office: Va Theol Sem Alexandria VA 22304

SHEPPARD, DARRELL KEITH, minister; b. Houston, June 18, 1965; s. Earl John and Nora Eunice (Watson) S.; m. Tami Sue Hopkins, Aug. 9, 1986. BS in Behavioral Sci., Mid-Am. Bible Coll., Oklahoma City, 1988. Ordained to ministry Ch. of God (Anderson, Ind.). Assoc. pastor Tanner St. Ch. of God, Sikeston, Mo., 1988—; state youth advisor Mo. Ministries Ch. of God, 1988—, mem. state bd. Christian edn., 1988—; exec. coun. S.E. dist. Ch. of God, 1991. Bd. dirs. Sikeston (Mo.) Little League Basketball, 1988—; mem. drug edn. com., athletic com. Sikeston Pub. Schs., 1990—. Recipient Sikeston Bell Vol. award Southwestern Bell and United Way, 1990-91, Outstanding Accomplishment to Fund Raising award Mid-Am. Bible Coll., 1991. Mem. Sikeston Area Ministerial Alliance, Sikeston Christian Businessmen's Fellowship. Office: Tanner St Ch of God 619 Tanner St Sikeston MO 63801

SHERIDAN, DANIEL PATRICK, religion educator; b. Bklyn., Mar. 9, 1946; s. William Aloysius and Loretta (Kenmelly) S.; m. Mary Ann E. Kaminski, Mar. 15, 1975; children: Daniel C., Timothy A. MA, St. Johns U., 1971; PhD, Fordham U., 1976. Asst. prof. Duquesne U., Pitts., 1978-82; assoc. prof. Loyola U., New Orleans, 1982—. Author: Advaitic Theism, 1986. Mem. S.W. Conf. of Assn. for Asian Studies (pres. 1990), Coll. Theology Soc., Am. Acad. Religion, Assn. for Asian Studies. Office: Loyola U 6363 St Charles Ave New Orleans LA 70118 *Twixt the saddle and the ground mercy sought and mercy found.*

SHERIDAN, WILLIAM COCKBURN RUSSELL, bishop; b. N.Y.C., Mar. 25, 1917; s. John Russell Fortescue and Gertrude (Magdalene) Hurley) S.; m. Rudith Treder, Nov. 13, 1943; children—Elizabeth Sheridan Noak, Margaret Sheridan Wilson, Mary Sheridan Janda, Peter, Stephen. Student, U. Va.; B.A., Carroll Coll., 1939; S.T.M., Nashotah House Sem., 1968, D.D., 1966, D.C.L., 1984. Ordained priest Episcopal Ch., 1943, consecrated bishop, 1972; asst. priest St. Pauls Ch., Chgo., 1943-44; rector Gethsemane Ch., Marion, Ind., 1944-47, St. Thomas Ch., Plymouth, Ind., 1947-72; Anglican chaplain Culver Mil. Acad., Ind., 1953-58, 70-72; bishop Diocese of No. Ind., South Bend, 1972-87, ret., 1987; clerical dep. to Gen. Conv., Nat. Synod, 1952-70. Author: Journey to Priesthood, 1950, For High School Boys Only, 1955, Between Catholics, 1968. Pres. bd. trustees Howe Mil. Sch., Ind., 1972-86, Nashotah House Sem., 1972-87. Mem. Alumni Assn. Nashotah House Sem. (pres. 1953-55, pres. bd. trustees 1985-87).

SHERLIN, CLAY HARVEY, minister; b. Knoxville, Tenn., Aug. 8, 1947; s. William Harvey and Mabel Dean (Jones) S.; m. Brenda Sue McCormack, Jan. 31, 1969; children: Leslie Harvey, Jennifer Brooke. AS in Mgmt., Draughon's Jr. Coll., Knoxville, 1978; BS in Acctg., Tenn. Wesleyan Coll., 1985. Ordained to ministry So. Bapt. Conv., 1973. Evangelist, Powell, Tenn., 1973-85; pastor Pleasant Hill Bapt. Ch., Powell, 1985-88, Unity Bapt. Ch., Powell, 1988—; fin. officer Martin Marietta Energy Systems, Oak Ridge, Tenn., 1976—. 2d class petty officer USN, 1965-69. Mem. Alpha Chi.

SHERLOCK, JOHN MICHAEL, bishop; b. Regina, Sask., Can., Jan. 20, 1926; s. Joseph and Catherine S. Student, St. Augustine's Sem., Toronto, Ont., Can., 1950; student canon law, Catholic U. Am., 1950-52; LLD (hon.), U. Windsor, 1986; DD (hon.), Huron Coll., London, Ont., 1986. Ordained priest Roman Catholic Ch., 1950, bishop, 1974; asst. pastor St. Eugene's, Hamilton, Ont., 1952-59, St. Augustine's, Dundas, Ont., 1959-63, Cathedral Christ the King, Hamilton, also, Guelph and Maryhill, Ont., 1950-52; pastor St. Charles Ch., Hamilton, 1963-74; aux. bishop London, Ont., 1974-78; bishop, 1978—; chaplain Univ. Newman Club, McMaster U., Hamilton, 1963-66; pres. Canadian Conf. Cath. Bishops, 1983-85, liaison with U. Chaplains Can. and Pres. Cath. Coll. and Univs.; chmn. social affairs com. commn. Ont. Conf. Cath. Bishops, edn. commn., family life com.; adv. judge for the Regional Marriage Truban, 1954-72. Mem. Wentworth County Roman Cath. Separate Sch. Bd., 1964-74, chmn., 1972-73. Address: 1070 Waterloo St, London, ON Canada N6A 3Y2

SHERMAN, CHARLES PHILIP, rabbi; b. Warren, Pa., Dec. 14, 1943; s. Samuel Louis and Ruth (Kovacs) S.; m. Nancy Rae Slone, Feb. 7, 1965; children: Aaron Reuben, Daniel Micah, Ruth Miriam. BA, U. Pitts., 1963; Bachelor of Hebrew Letters, Hebrew Union Coll., 1966, MA of Hebrew Letters, 1969. Ordained rabbi, 1969. Assoc. rabbi Temple Beth Israel, West Hartford, Conn., 1969-76; sr. rabbi Temple Israel, Tulsa, 1976—; pres. Tulsa Met. Ministry, 1985-87. Contbg. editor Tulsa Jewish Rev.; contbr. articles to profl. jours. Bd. dirs. Instl. Rev. Hillcrest Med. Ctr., Tulsa, 1980, Planned Parenthood, 1977-83, Okla. Religious Coalition for Abortion Rights; mem. Task Force to Study Religious Programs in Pub. Schs., Tulsa, 1979-80; bd. dirs. NCCJ, 1988—. Mem. Cen. Conf. Am. Rabbis (exec. bd. 1982-84), Tulsa Ministerial Alliance (pres. 1980-81), SW Assn. Reform Rabbis. Democrat. Office: Temple Israel 2004 E 22d Pl Tulsa OK 74114

SHERMAN, DOUGLAS RICHARD, religious organization administrator; b. Rantoul, Ill., July 29, 1950; s. Henry Richard and Mary Lee (Goff) S.; m. Janice Kay Blunt, Dec. 21, 1974; children: Jason, Matthew, Jennifer. BS in Engring. Mgmt., USAF Acad., 1972; ThM, Dallas Theol. Sem., 1984. Commd. 2d lt. USAF, 1972, advanced through grades to capt., 1977; resigned, 1977; dir. discipleship and evangelism Pantego Bible Ch., Arlington, Tex., 1981-83; pres. Career Impact Ministries, Little Rock, 1983—. Author: Your Work Matters to God, 1987, How To Balance Competing Time Demands, 1989, How To Succeed Where It Really Counts, 1989, Keeping Your Ethical Edge Sharp, 1990, Keeping Your Head Up When Your Job Has Got You Down, 1991; also pamphlets; monthly columnist New Eng. Christian; contbr. articles to various jours. Office: Career Impact Ministries 8201 Cantrell Rd Ste 240 Little Rock AR 72207

SHERMAN, HUNTER B., clergyman, educator; b. Long Beach, Calif., Aug. 30, 1943; s. Hunter B. and Mary Rawls (French) S.; B.A., Calif. State U., Long Beach, 1965; postgrad. Bapt. Bible Coll., 1965-66; M.Div., Talbot Theol. Sem., 1970; Ph.D., Calif. Grad. Sch. Theology, 1976; m. Louisa Ann Stahl, June 27, 1964; children—Whitnae Nicolle, Garrett Hunter. Prof., Bapt. Bible Coll., Springfield, Mo., 1970—, chmn. Bible dept., 1975-78, acad. dean, 1979-83; pastor Bellview Bapt. Ch., Springfield, 1983—. Mem. Soc. Bibl. Lit., Am. Assn. Collegiate Registrars, Am. Schs. Oriental Research, Israel Exploration Soc., Oriental Inst. U. Chgo. Author: Must Babylon Be Rebuilt, 1970; The Biblical Concept of Babylon, 1976. Recipient Audrey Talbot Meml. award Talbot Theol. Sem., 1970. Office: 628 E Kearney St Springfield MO 65802 *The only continuing contribution we can make to life is through other people. Our life must be invested in other lives if it is to produce fruit. This is why "God commended His love to us, in that while we were yet sinners, Christ died for us."*

SHERMAN, JOSEPH HOWARD, clergyman; b. Marion, S.C., June 14, 1923; s. Samuel and Alma (Cannon) S.; m. Daisy Lee Littles; children: Joseph Howard Jr., Beatrice Sherman Boone. D.D. (hon.), Trinity Hall Coll.; LL.D. (hon.), New Haven Theol. Appointed Jurisdictional Bishop of N.C., 2d Jurisdiction, 1963. Founder, pastor Pentecostal Temple Ch. of God in Christ, Charlotte, N.C.; pres. N.C. Youth Dept.; dist. supt. N.C. Jurisdiction, Wadesboro; chmn. Council of Bishops, Memphis, 1976—; pres. C. H. Mason System of Bible Colls., Charlotte, N.C., 1975; mem. Nat. Hymnal Com. Author: (book) Weapons of the Righteous; (phamplet) Witchcraft, The Work of the Devil; (album) Peace That Only Christ Can Give; editor The Mighty Voice That Crieth mag. pres., founder J. Howard Sherman Scholarship Fund, Charlotte, 1974—; bd. dirs. C. H. Mason Scholarship Found., Memphis, Saints Ctr.; mem. NAACP, Charlotte, Hiring of the Handicapped, Charlotte, 1984, Ch. of God in Christ Hosp. Fund; mem. grievance com. Housing Authority, Charlotte, 1983, 84; mem. steering com. Democratic Governorship, N.C., 1984. Named Knight of Queen City, Charlotte, 1976, hon. citizen City of Balt., 1981, hon. atty. gen. N.C., 1983; J.H. Sherman Day named in his honor, Charlotte, 1980-84. Mem. Ministerial Alliance (sec. Charlotte chpt. 1983—). Office: Pentecostal Temple Ch of God in Christ 1401 Parkwood Ave Charlotte NC 28205

SHERMAN, RAY SCOTT, consultant, minister, writer; b. Milw., June 4, 1939; s. Ray Elwin and Kathryn Elise (Hatch) S.; m. Judith Ann Schroeder, June 15, 1960 (div. Jan. 1987); children: David Scott, Douglas Clark. BA, Lawrence U., 1960; MA, U. Hawaii, 1968. Ordained to ministry Unity Ch., 1970. Sr. minister Unity Ch. Spokane, Wash., 1970-74; nat. outreach dir. Assn. Unity Chs., Chgo., 1974-76; field services dir. Assn. Unity Chs., Unity Village, Mo., 1976-78, support services dir., 1978-79, exec. dir., 1979-80; pres. Assn. Unity Chs., 1991—; sr. minister Unity Ch. Seattle, 1980-90, Unity Ch. San Francisco, 1990—; ptnr. Vision Quest Confs., 1991—; cons., bd. dirs. Therma-Tron-X Inc., Sturgeon Bay, Wis., 1983—. Author: Meditation and Prayer, 1973, Small Prayers, 1988; (poetry) Gifts, 1983, More Gifts, 1989; contbr. numerous articles to mags. Bd. dirs. Puget Sound Big Sisters, Seattle, 1983-89, Three Mountain Found., Lone Pine, Calif., 1986—, Unity Movement Adv. Coun., 1988—; trustee Charles and Myrtle Fillmore Found., Unity Village, 1973—. Capt. USAF, 1960-68. Club: Wash. Athletic. Lodge: Rotary. Avocations: sailing, skiing, tennis. Office: Unity Ch of San Francisco 65 Ninth St San Francisco CA 94103 *Personal philosophy: A clear personal vision and an open heart create success and inner power.*

SHERMAN, WALTER PHILIP, priest; b. Newark, Ohio, Sept. 2, 1952; s. Gail W. and Florence A. (Cunningham) S. BA, Muskingum Coll., 1974; licentiate in modern letters, Université De Nice, France, 1976; MDiv, Gen. Theol. Sem., 1982. Asst. restaurant mgr. Old Warehouse Restaurant, Coshocton, Ohio, 1974-75; mem. faculty St. Charles Prep. Sch., Columbus, Ohio, 1976-79; asst. to rector Episc. Ch. of Ascension & Holy Trinity, Cin., 1982-84; exec. dir. Friends of the Sch. for Creative and Performing Arts, Cin., 1984-85; mem. faculty Cin. Pub. Schs., 1985-86, Ind. Vocat. Tech. Coll., 1989-90; vicar Trinity Episc. Ch., Lawrenceburg, Ind., 1986—; chair pers. subcom. Standing Com. Diocese of Indpls., 1989-91—, pres. Standing Com., 1992—, music and liturgy commn., 1988—, AIDS ministry commn., 1987—. Author: (chpt. in book) Handbook for Persons with HIV Infection; copy editor: The Miracle of Bill, 1989. Mem. Greater Cin. AIDS Task Force, 1988-89; bd. dirs. Caracole Housing Project, Cin., 1988-89, Nat. Episcopal AIDS Coalition, 1989—; vice chair Ohio AIDS Coalition, 1988; pres. AIDS Vols. of Cin., 1986-89; mem. Lawrenceburg Task Force on Discrimination, 1991. Mem. Dearborn County Ministers Fellowship (v.p. 1989-91, pres. 1991-92). Home: 322 Milton St Cincinnati OH 45210

SHERO, JOHN PAUL, III, minister; b. Dallas, Nov. 23, 1947; s. John Paul Jr. and Jean (Thompson) S.; m. Patsy E. Jennings, June 15, 1968; children: Kimberly Lenerts, Jennifer Shero. Ordained to ministy Ch. of Christ. Min. Rangerville Ch. Christ, San Beneto, Tex., 1969; min. Ch. Christ, Mart, Tex., 1970-71, Madill, Okla., 1971-77; min. Southgate Ch. Christ, San Angelo, Tex., 1977—. Mem. Kiwanis Internat. (pres. San Angelo chpt. 1986). Home: 307 N Jackson San Angelo TX 76901 Office: Ch of Christ 528 Country Club Rd San Angelo TX 76904

SHERRY, DALE ALFRED, minister; b. Mishawaka, Ind., Oct. 13, 1930; s. Ralph Witwer and Margaret Ann (Schaffer) S.; m. Betty Charlene, June 6, 1952; children: Thomas Edward, Jon Witwer, Robert James. BA, Bethel coll., Mishawaaka, 1954; MDiv, Asbury Sem., 1960. Ordained to ministry Bapt. Ch. Pastor Pleasant Hill Missionary Ch., Bronson, Mich., 1954-57, Zion Missionary Ch., Elkhart, INd., 1960-65; assoc. pastor North Ch., Columbus, Ohio, 1966-69, Redeemer Bapt. Ch., Warren, Mich., 1969-72; pastor Deford (Mich.) Community Ch., 1972-77, Trinity Missionary Ch., Burton, Mich., 1977-80; assoc. pastor Aboite Missionary Ch., Fort Wayne, Ind., 1980-83, Gospel Ctr. Ch., South Bend, Ind., 1983-86; Bibl. dramatist The Missionary Ch., Granger, Ind., 1986—; chaplain Flint (Mich.) Police Dept., 1975-80 (cert. recognition 1980); mem. Mich. Bd. of Corrections Pastors Com., 1978-80. Mem. Optimists (Meritorious Achievement award 1965). Avocatons: woodworking, golf, electronics. Home and Office: 51963 Hedge Ln Granger IN 46530

SHERRY, PAUL HENRY, minister, religious organization administrator; b. Tamaqua, Pa., Dec. 25, 1933; s. Paul Edward and Mary Elizabeth (Stein) S.; m. Mary Louise Thornburg, June 4, 1957; children: Mary Elizabeth, Paul David. BA, Franklin and Marshall Coll., 1955; ThM, Union Theol. Sem., N.Y.C., 1958, PhD, 1969; hon. doctorate, Ursinus Coll., 1981, Elmhurst Coll., 1990, Defiance Coll., 1991, Lakeland Coll., Sheboygan, Wis., 1991. Ordained to ministry United Ch. of Christ. Pastor St. Matthew United Ch. of Christ, Kenhorst, Pa., 1958-61, Community United Ch. of Christ, Hasbrouck Heights, N.J., 1961-65; mem. staff United Ch. Bd. Homeland Ministry, N.Y.C., 1965-82; exec. dir. Community Renewal Soc., Chgo., 1983-89; pres. United Ch. of Christ, Cleve., 1989—; mem. gen. bd. Nat. Coun. Chs., N.Y.C., 1989—; mem. cen. com. World Coun. Chs., Geneva, 1991—, del. 7th Assembly, Canberra, Australia, 1991; bd. dirs. Ind. Sector, Washington, 1991—. Editor: The Riverside Preachers; editor Jour. Current Social Issues, 1968-80; contbr. numerous articles to religious jours.; host weekly radio programs local sta., 1974-78, 84-85. Mem. Soc. Christian Ethics. Democrat. Avocations: reading, hiking, cultural events. Home: 13400 Shaker Blvd Cleveland OH 44120 Office: United Ch of Christ 700 Prospect Ave E Cleveland OH 44115

SHERTZER, LEONARD EUGENE, minister; b. Pa., May 1, 1929; s. Charles Stephen and Charlotte (Etzweiler) S.; m. Evelyn Sowers McCarty, June 5, 1990; children: Debra, Barbara, Susan; children from previous marriage: Denise, David, Diane. AB, Elizabethtown Coll., 1953; BD, Gettysburg Sem., 1957, MST, 1975. Ordained to ministry Evang. Luth. Ch. in Am., 1957. Pastor 1st Luth. Ch., Portage, Pa., 1957-61, Augsburg Ch., Harrisburg, Pa., 1961-69, St. Mark's Ch., Harrisburg, 1970-79, Union Evang. Ch., York, Pa., 1979—; pres. Johnstown Pastoral Assn., 1959-60, dist. dean, 1972-74; mem. Mission and Ecumenicity Commn., Coun. Pastoral Svcs., 1982-88. Bd. dirs. Tressler Luth. Social Svc., 1970-78. Mem. Lions (chaplain Portage club), Optimists (chaplain York club). Republican. Home: 311 Pennsylvania Ave York PA 17404 *Life is exciting; exciting when fueled by prayer, exciting by caring for each other, exciting by having goals and seeing them fulfilled.*

SHERWIN, BYRON LEE, religion educator, college official; b. N.Y.C., Feb. 18, 1946; s. Sidney and Jean Sylvia (Rabinowitz) S.; m. Judith Rita Schwartz, Dec. 24, 1972; 1 child, Jason Samuel. BS, Columbia U., N.Y.C., 1966; B of Hebrew Lit., Jewish Theol. Sem. of Am., 1966, M of Hebrew Lit., 1968; MA, NYU, 1969; PhD, U. Chgo., 1978. Ordained rabbi, 1970. Prof. Jewish philosophy and mysticism Spertus Coll. Judaica, Chgo., 1970—, v.p. acad. affairs, 1984—. Author: Judaism, 1978, Encountering the Holocaust, 1979, Abraham Joshua Heschel, 1979, Garden of the Generations, 1981, Jerzy Kosinski: Literary Alarm Clock, 1981, Mystical Theology and Social Dissent, 1982, The Golem Legend, 1985, Contents and Contexts, 1987, Thank God, 1989, In Partnership with God: Contemporary Jewish Law and Ethics, 1990, No Religion Is an Island, 1991, Toward a Jewish Theology, 1991; also articles. Mem. Midwest Jewish Studies Assn. (pres.), Am. Philos. Assn., Assn. for Jewish Studies, Rabbinical Assembly, Am. Acad. Religion, Religious Ednl. Assn. Republican. Avocations: cooking, book collecting. Office: Spertus Coll Judaica 618 S Michigan Ave Chicago IL 60605

SHERWOOD, JOHN MARTIN, rabbi; b. N.Y.C., Apr. 15, 1936; s. Lew and Rosalind Stella (Eckstein) S.; m. Dolores G. Singer, Apr. 5, 1983; children: Bruce, June, Jay, Robert, Wendy. BA, Calif. State U., Northridge, 1963; BHL, Hebrew Union Coll., L.A., 1964; MAHL, Hebrew Union Coll., 1967. Ordained rabbi 1967. Founding rabbi Temple Sholom, Vancouver, B.C., 1967-69; rabbi Temple Beth Ohr, La Mirada, Calif., 1969-71, Temple Emet of Woodland Hills (Calif.), 1971—; adj. prof. St. John's Cath. Sem., Camarillo, Calif., 1987—; dir. Hillel Found., Vancouver, 1967-68; lectr. U. B.C., Religious Studies Dept., 1968-69; chaplain L.A. Police Dept., 1981—. Author: High Holy Day Prayers, 1986. Active in past various charitable orgns. With U.S. Army, 1957-59. Recipient Walter S. Hilborn award, Hebrew Union Coll. 1963. Mem. San Fernando Valley Interfaith Coun. (past pres.), W. San Fernando Valley Clergy Assn., Cen. Conf. Am. Rabbis, Bd. Rabbis of So. Calif., Masons. *Liberal religion does not require guilt as a motivation. Guilt is the toxic waste of the human spirit. The faith experience at its best gives each person a sense of self-worth and a positive approach to personal accountability.*

SHERWOOD, MADISEN, minister, writer; b. Elgin, Oreg., Aug. 29, 1917; d. Calloway Cecil and Nellie Ann (Hug) Howard; m. William Gene Bellm, Oct. 21, 1961; children by previous marriage—Loren, Carolee, Melodie, Kaydence; stepchildren—Stephen, Melanie, Colleen. Ph.D., Inst. Creative Thinking, 1951; Mh.D. (hon.), U. Metaphysics, 1982. Ordained to ministry Ch. Universal of Master in Oakland, 1952. Founder, pres., bishop Esoterian Soc. (inc. 1968), Seattle, 1951—; pres. Nu-Manh Corp., Seattle, 1976—; treas. Priority One Co., Coeur d'Alene, Idaho, 1978—; Author: Carolee in Candyland, 1945; Tempered in Flame, 1970; Basic Disciplines, 1975; Karma Through the Eyes of a Seer, 1977; editor The Esoterian, 1971—. Home: PO Box 1336 Coeur d'Alene ID 83814

SHERWOOD, TRENT RAY, minister; b. Miami, Okla., Sept. 27, 1966; s. Robert Ray and Ellen Marie (Raines) S.; m. Mary Nell Holt, May 28, 1988. AA, Northeastern Okla. A&M Coll., 1986; B in Music Edn., Okla. State U., 1989; MRE, Midwestern Bapt. Theol. Sem., Kansas City, Mo., 1991. Cert. tchr. music, Okla. Dir. music Countryside Bapt. Ch., Stillwater, Okla., 1988-89; min., dir. music and youth 1st Bapt. Ch., Odessa, Mo., 1989-91, New Haven Bapt. Ch., Raytown, Mo., 1991—. Home: 6009 Farley Ave Baytown MO 64133 Office: New Haven Bapt Ch 5501 Blue Ridge Cutoff Raytown MO 64133

SHETTLER, WALTER ROBERT, JR. (BOB SHETTLER), minister, administrator; b. Maysville, Ky., July 23, 1950; s. Walter Robert and Read (Crow) S.; m. Connie Davis, Jan. 12, 1950; children: Elizabeth Read, Kelly Lynn. BA, Georgetown (Ky.) Coll., 1972; MS, Ea. Ky. U., 1973; postgrad. studies in Divinity, New Orleans Bapt. Theol. Sem., 1985—. Ordained to Ministry Bapt. Ch., 1979. Assoc. pastor First Bapt. Ch., Longwood, Fla., 1973-76, Highlands Bapt. Ch., Ocala, Fla., 1976-81, Coll. Pk. Bapt. Ch., Orlando, Fla., 1981—. Mem. Orlando AAA, Nat. Assn. Ch. Bus. Adminstrs., Fla Bapt. Assn. Recreators (v.p. 1984-86). Home: 1434 Cumbie Ave Orlando FL 32804 Office: Coll Pk Bapt Ch 1914 Edgewater Dr Orlando FL 32804

SHIBATA, GEORGE EISHIN, minister; b. Fukuoka-ken, Japan, Apr. 13, 1938; came to U.S., 1939, naturalized, 1963; s. Tesshin and Haruko (Fukuyoshi) S.; m. Yasuko Kawasaki, Oct. 27, 1973. Student, U. Wash., 1957-62; BA, Ryukoku U., Japan, 1966; MA, Ryukoka U., Japan, 1969. Ordained to ministry Jodo Shinshu Honganji Sect Buddhist Chs. Am., 1964. Asst. min. Gardena (Calif.) Buddhist Ch., 1970-73; asst. dir. Bur. Buddhist Edn., Buddhist Chs. Am. Hdqrs., San Francisco, 1974; resident min. Reedley (Calif.) Buddhist Ch., 1975—; overseer min. Buddhist Ch. Parlier, 1987-89; mem. literary propagation com. Buddhist Chs. Am., 1975-81, exec. com. Sunday sch. dept., 1976-78, 81-85, recording sec., 1980-81, chmn. Sunday sch. dept., 1982-85, mem. ministerial affairs com., 1980—, mem. Buddhist edn. com., 1986-89, trustee dept. Buddhist edn., 1986-87, interim dir. dept. Buddhist edn., 1987-89. Author: Buddhist Holidays, 1974. Trustee Inst. Buddhist Studies, 1982-83. Mem. Buddhist Chs. of Am. Mins. Assn. (English lang. recording sec. 1981-83, 89-90, vice chmn. 1986-87), Cen. Calif. Buddhist Ministerial Assn. (treas. 1975-77, 83-86, 90—, chmn. 1978-80, 86-87, 89-90, vice chmn. 1981-82, 87-88, auditor 1988-89). Home: PO Box 24 1459 J St Reedley CA 93654 Office: 2035 15th St Reedley CA 93654

SHIELDS, DAVID LYLE LIGHT, religion educator; b. Hollywood, Calif., July 4, 1950; s. H. Charles and Sylvia Jean (Lane) S.; m. Brenda Jo Light Bredemeier, July 18, 1987; 1 child, Micah Light. BA, Calif. Luth. Coll., 1973; MDiv, Pacific Luth. Theol. Sem., 1986; PhD, Grad. Theol. Union, 1983. Minister of edn. Trinity Luth. Ch., Alameda, Calif., 1980-84; dir. moral edn. St. Elizabeth's Elem. Sch., Oakland, Calif., 1981-84; dir. Unitas Hunger Action Ctr., Berkeley, Calif., 1986—; lectr. U. Calif., Berkeley, 1986—. Author: Growing Beyond Prejudices, 1986; contbr. articles to profl. jours. Bd. dirs. Calif. Luth. Coll., Thousand Oaks, 1972-73. Layne Found. fellow, 1972-79. Mem. Am. Acad. Religion, Assn. Profs. & Researchers in Religion. Home: 3970 Stevens St Castro Valley CA 94546 Office: Unitas Campus Ministry 2700 Bancroft Way Berkeley CA 94704

SHIELDS, RICHARD LEE, clergyman, international evangelist; b. Clinton, Iowa, May 21, 1955; s. Lester Alvin and Virginia Louise (Hardison) S.; m. Sheila Jeanette Larson, Aug. 23, 1974; children: Travis Loren, Tara Jeanette. BA, North Cen. Bible Coll., Mpls., 1976; BS, Oral Roberts U., 1982. In profl. rels. Lufkin Med. Labs., Mpls., 1976-77; assoc. pastor Worthington (Minn.) Assemblies of God, 1977-79; ch. administr. Christian Chapel Assembly of God, Tulsa, 1983-90; pres., dir. Open Doors, Inc., Broken Arrow,

Okla., 1990—; adj. faculty Oral Roberts U., Tulsa, 1982-87. Mem. Okla. Dist. Coun. Assemblies of God. Republican. Mem Assemblies of God Ch. Avocations: travel, racquetball, computers, geology. Home: 1241 W Knoxville St Broken Arrow OK 74012

SHIELDS, TERRELL MICHAEL, minister; b. Gainesville, Ga., Apr. 25, 1954; s. Jack William and Dora Mae (Shields) Tate; m. Sylvia Francis Gresham, Nov. 7, 1981; children: Cherish V., Terrica A. AA, Selma U., Ala., 1976; BA, Selma U., 1978. Ordained to ministry Baptist Ch., 1975. Pastor Fortson Grove Bapt. Ch., Elberton, Ga., 1977-81, Greater Timber Ridge Bapt. Ch., Gainesville, Ga., 1978-83, Greater Mt. Calvary Bapt. Ch., Rome, Ga., 1984—; pres. State of Ga. Bapt. Youth Conv., 1976-78. Author: We Belong to God, 1989. Mem. Ga. State MLK Celebration Com., 1986—; chmn. Rome and Floyd County Feed the Needy at Thanksgiving, 1989. Named Man of the Yr., Greater Timber Ridge, 1980. Mem. Rome-Floyd County Ministers Union (pres. 1987-89), Congress of Christian Edn. of N.W. Ga. (pres. 1985-87, asst. dean 1979-83), NAACP (chmn. lifetime memberships 1988—), Gents Club (fin. sec. 1973-75). Democrat. Baptist. Avocations: hunting, fishing, writing. Home: 1 Luminosa Ter Rome GA 30161 Office: Greater Mt Calvary Bapt Ch 445 E 14th St Rome GA 30161

SHIMOFF, EPHRAIM, retired rabbi, educator; b. Wengrow, Poland, June 12, 1913; came to U.S., 1927; s. Aaron Jacob and Esther (Brotstein) S.; m. Shirley Mann, Dec. 29, 1940; children: Eliot, Barbara. BA, CCNY, 1936; MA, U. Richmond, 1946; PhD, Yeshiva U., 1959. Ordained rabbi, 1938. Rabbi North End Synagogue, Bridgeport, Conn., 1938-41, Temple Beth Israel, Richmond, Va., 1941-51, Congregation Beth El, Astonia, N.Y., 1951-69; dir. adult Jewish edn. Jewish Fedn., East Orange, N.J., 1969-89; retired, 1989; civilian chaplain Camp Lee, McGuire VA Hoep., 1948-51; lectr. in religious denominations Richmond Profl. Inst. Coll. William and Mary, 1948-50; Hillel counselor U. Richmond, 1947-50; student advisor Med. Coll. Va., 1947-50; mem. nat. exec. bd. Religious Zionists Am., 1971-79, pres. Greater N.Y. coun. Author: Rabbi Isaac Elchanan Spektor - Life and Letters, 1959. Mem. Mayor's Com. of Religious Leaders, N.Y.C. Recipient Chief Rabbi Herzog Gold medal Religious Zionist Orgn. Am., 1989. Mem. Educators Coun. Am. (exec. com., trustee 1986—), Rabbinical Coun. Am. (exec. 1963-66). Home: 549 Chilton St Elizabeth NJ 07208

SHINN, GARLAND RAY, minister; b. Grass Valley, Calif., Oct. 2, 1931; s. Archie Wilbur and Iola Leona (Eisley) S.; m. Roberta Bernice Kline, Aug. 4, 1956; children: Garland Jr., Rhoda, Nathan, Rachel. BA, Sacramento State U., 1953; postgrad., Talbot Sem., 1954-56; MDiv, Am. Bapt. Sem of the West, 1958. Ordained to ministry Bapt. Ch., 1958. Pastor Penn Valley (Calif.) Community Ch., 1958-59; missionary Am. Missionary Fellowship, Gold Hill, Oreg., 1959-71; pastor Onecho Bible Ch., Colfax, Wash., 1971-75, Faith Bible Ch., Reno, 1975-89, Ashland (Oreg.) Bible Ch., 1989—; field dir. N.W. Ind. Ch. Extension, Reno, 1975-89, bd. dirs., Ashland, 1989—. Republican. Mem. Ind. Fundemental Chs. Am. Office: Ashland Bible Ch 400 Dead Indian Rd Ashland OR 97520

SHINN, KEVIN W., religious organization administrator; b. Bartlesville, Okla., June 27, 1963; s. Jack W. and Junarita R. (May) S.; m. Karen Renee Hendrick, Apr. 14, 1990. BS in Phys. Edn., U. Okla., 1986; MDiv, Golden Gate Bapt. Sem., 1989. Assoc. dir. Bapt. Student Union, Berkeley, Calif., 1987-89, Bapt. Student Union, U. Nebr., Lincoln, 1990—; vol. Mission Svc. Corps, So. Bapt. Ch., 1987—. Named to Outstanding Young Men of Am., 1989. Office: Bapt Student Union PO Box 30038 Lincoln NE 68503 *Lord, use my life to affect the nations, but first use me to affect one man.*

SHINN, ROGER LINCOLN, minister, educator; b. Germantown, Ohio, Jan. 6, 1917; s. Henderson L.V. and Carrie Margaret (Buehler) S.; m. Katharine Cole, Nov. 6, 1943; children: Carol Katharine Shinn Wheeler, Marybeth. BA, Heidelberg Coll., 1938, DLitt (hon.), 1963; MDiv summa cum laude, Union Theol. Sem., 1941; PhD, Columbia U., 1951; DD (hon.), Mission House Theol. Sem., 1960, Franklin and Marshall Coll., 1963; LHD(hon.), Drury Coll., 1984; HHD (hon.), Blackburn U., 1985. Ordained to ministry United Ch. of Christ, 1946. Pvt. practice horticulture, 1932-37; student asst. 2d Presbyn Ch., N.Y.C., 1938-41; instr. Union Theol. Sem., N.Y.C., 1947-49; chmn. Depts. Philosophy and Religion Heidelberg Coll., Tiffin, Ohio, 1949-54; prof. theology Vanderbilt U. Div. Sch., Nashville, 1954-57, prof. Christian Ethics, 1957-59; William E. Dodge Jr. prof. Applied Christianity Union Theol. Sem., N.Y.C., 1960-70, Reinhold Niebuhr prof. Social Ethics, 1970-85, dean of instruction, 1963-70, acting pres., 1974-75, counselor to grad. students, 1975-85; adj. prof. religion and society, Columbia U., 1962-86; adj. prof. econs., NYU Grad. Sch. Bus. Adminstrn., 1979; vis. prof. Philosophies of Judaism, Jewish Theol. Sem. Am., 1982; lectr. Pacific Sch. Religion, 1957, Harvard U., 1960, Garrett Theol. Sem., 1967, Assn. Am. Colls., 1970, Princeton Theol. Sem., 1971, U.S. Army Chaplain Sch., 1974, Woodstock Coll., 1971-74; occasional lectures in over 250 schs., colls. and univs. in N.Am. and abroad. Author: Beyond This Darkness, 1946, Christianity and the Problem of History, 1953, Life, Death and Destiny, 1957, The Existentialist Posture, 1959, rev. edit., 1970, The Educational Mission of Our Church, 1962, Moments of Truth, 1962, Tangled World, 1965, We Believe, 1966, Man: The New Humanism, 1968, Wars and Rumors of Wars, 1972, Forced Options: Social Decisions for the 21st Century, 1982, 3rd edit. 1991; editor, co-author: The Search for Identity: Essays on the American Character, 1964, Restless Adventure, 1968, The Thought of Paul Tillich, 1985; contbr. articles to religious jours., chpts. to books; writer, narrator TV series Tangled World; assoc. editor Bull. Sci., Tech. and Soc.; contbg editor Christianity and Crisis; mem. editorial bdd. Jour. Religious Ethics. Served to maj. U.S. Army, 1941-45, ETO. Decorated Silver Star; recipient Excellence award Grad. Faculties Alumni, Columbia U., 1981; named to U.S. Army Inf. Sch., Hall of Fame, 1973. Mem. ADA, NAACP, Am. Theol. Soc.(pres. 1975-76), Soc. Christian Ethics (pres. 1974-75), Soc. for Values in Higher Edn. (Kent fellow 1946), Conf. on Sci., Philosophy and Religion (fellow 1966), Am. Vets Com., Am. Assn. for UN, League for Indsl. Democracy. Home: 288 Cowles Rd Woodbury CT 06798 Office: 501 W 123rd ST #6A New York NY 10027 also: Union Theol Sem 3041 Broadway New York NY 10027 *In this world of mystery, beauty, joy, laughter and pain, I find opportunities to respond to love and strive for justice.*

SHIPLEY, HOWARD EUGENE, minister, principal; b. Mohawk, Tenn., Feb. 21, 1944; s. Howard Edgar and Florence (Smith) S.; m. Linda Elaine Gregg, Nov. 21, 1970; children: Howard E. II, Brandee. BA, Bob Jones U., 1966; MA, East Tenn. State U., 1976. Ordained to ministry Presbyn. Ch., 1975. Pastor Pilot Knob Cumberland Presbyn. Ch., Bulls Gap, Tenn., 1962-75, Willoughby Cumberland Presbyn. Ch., Bulls Gap, 1962-75, Bethesda Cumberland Presbyn. Ch., Chuckey, Tenn., 1964-69, Pleasant Hill Cumberland Presbyn. Ch., Chuckey, 1964-69, Mohawk (Tenn.) Cumberland Presbyn. Ch., Tenn., 1969-75, Dover Cumberland Presbyn. Ch., Morristown, Tenn., 1975—; tchr. Judson S. Hill Sch., Morristown, 1969-75; tchr., prin. Lincoln Heights Learning Ctr., Morristown, 1975-89, asst. prin., 1989—. Pres. Greene County Ruritan Coun., Greeneville, Tex., 1973; dist. chmn. Hamblen County Rep. Party, Morristown, 1990. Mem. NEA, Tenn. Edn. Assn., Hamblen County Edn. Assn., Morristown Edn. Assn. (treas. 1976-77). Presbyterian. Home: 1550 Dover Rd Morristown TN 37813 Office: Lincoln Heights Learning Ctr 217 Lincoln Ave Morristown TN 37814

SHIPP, GLOVER HARVEY, religious publication editor; b. Yakima, Wash., Aug. 1, 1927; s. Charles Harvey and Nola Gladys (Banton) S.; m. Marjorie Mae Smith, Sept. 23, 1948; children: Gerald H., David W., R. Mark, Terrell J., Cynthia E., Sofia F. BA, Pepperdine U., Malibu, Calif., 1948, MA, 1967; MA, Fuller Sem., Pasadena, Calif., 1982, D Missiology, 1986. Staff artist, writer Good New Press, Dallas, 1949-54; min. Ch. of Christ, Dallas, 1951-54, Kerman and Fresno, Calif., 1954-59; deacon, edn. dir. Ch. of Christ, Richmond and L.A., Calif., 1960-62, 63-66; deacon, mission com. Ch. of Christ, Abilene, Tex., 1988-89; mission chmn., deacon Ch. of Christ, Edmond, Okla., 1990—; missionary Ch. of Christ, Belo Horizonte, Brazil, 1967-85; mng. editor Christian Chronicle, Oklahoma City, Okla., 1989—; task force Continent of Great Cities Ministry, 1985-90; missionary in residence Abilene Christian U., 1972, 86-89; co-founder McCaleb Inst. for Missions Edn., 1986-89. Author 7 books in Portuguese, 1976-87, 8 books in English, 1976-91; editor Volta a Biblia, 1969-87. Bd. dirs Internat. Sch. of Belo Horizonte, Brazil, 1970-72. Named Writer of Yr. 20th Century Christian Found., 1982, Outstanding Writer Christian Life Pub. Co., 1977. Mem. Assn. of Missions Educators, Brazilian-Am. Cultural Inst. (bd. dirs. 1975—). Republican. Home: 3808 NE 140th Terr Cir Edmond OK 73013

SHIPP, KERRY DONALD, minister; b. Birmingham, Ala., Nov. 14, 1963; s. Donald Max and Ruth (Hardman) S.; m. Sue Lynn McNess, Dec. 27, 1986; child: Laura Monique. B. Biblical Study, Luther Rice Sem., 1982; Assc. Music Ed., Wallace St. Community Coll., 1984. Min. music/youth Friendship Bapt. Ch., Cullman, Ala., 1983-86; min. youth Cedar Bay Bapt., Jacksonville, Fla., 1986-87; min. music/youth East 44th St. Bapt., Jacksonville, Fla., 1987-88; min. music/activities Jones Rd. Bapt., Jacksonville, Fla., 1988-89; assoc. pastor First Bapt. Ch., Carbon Hill, Ala., 1989-91; min. music and youth 1st Bapt. Ch., Parrish, Ala., 1991—. Mem. Youth Assc., Jasper, Ala. Southern Baptist. Home: PO Box 33 Parrish AL 35580

SHIPP, WILLIAM LEE, deacon; b. Lincoln, Ill., July 31, 1938; s. Floyd Lee and Mary C. (Murray) S.; m. Ann Yong Choe, Sept. 14, 1963; 1 child, Francis Joseph. BS in Math., St. Louis U., 1961; BS in Meteorology, Pa. State U., 1962; MEd, U. Ill., 1971, EdD, 1978. Ordained deacon, Roman Cath. Ch., 1979. Parish asst. St. Malachy, Rantoul, Ill., 1979-84; assoc. chaplain Randolph AFB Chapel, Tex., 1986—; tng. specialist HQ Air Tng. Command, Randolph AFB, 1984—; faculty Permanent Deacon Program, San Antonio, 1984—; trustee Permanent Deacon Bd. Dirs., 1986—. Contbr. articles to profl. jours. Pres. bd. trustees Randolph Ind. Sch. Dist., 1984—. Lt. col. USAF, 1961-89. Mem. Res. Officers Assn. (pres. 1978, editor newsletter 1976-80), Nat. Soc. for Performance and Instrn. (v.p. Air Force 1988-91), K.C. Home: 12015 O'Connor Rd San Antonio TX 78233 Office: HQ ATC/TTIP Randolph AFB Universal City TX 78150

SHIPPS, JAN, history and religious studies educator; b. Hueytown, Ala., Oct. 4, 1929; d. William McKinley and Thalia Jenkins (Bell) Barnett; m. Anthony W. Shipps, May 25, 1949; 1 child, Stephen Barnett. BS in History, Utah State U., 1961; MA in History, U. Colo., 1962, PhD in History, 1965. Asst. prof. Ind. U.-Purdue U. at Indpls., 1973-78, assoc. prof., 1979-84, prof., 1985—; mem. policy adv. bd. Ind. U. Ctr. on Philanthapy, Indpls., 1988—. Author: Mormonism: The Story of a New Religious Tradition, 1985 (Arrington award 1986); co-editor Religion and American Culture: A Journal of Interpretation, 1990—; mem. editorial bd. Dialogue, A Jour. of Mormon Thought, 1978—; contbr. articles, revs. to profl. publs. Grantee Lilly Endowment, Inc., 1984-87; Glenn W. Irwin Rsch. scholar, 1989-91. Mem. Mormon History Assn. (pres. 1980), Orgn. Am. Histories, Am. Acad. Religion, Am. Hist. Assn., Am. Soc. Ch. Hist. (mem. coun. 1984-87, 91—), Ind. Acad. Religion (pres. 1983). Democrat. Methodist. Home: 2249 N Mt Gilead Rd Bloomington IN 47408 Office: Ind U Purdue U 425 University Blvd Indianapolis IN 46202

SHIRA, BRUCE DOUGLAS, minister, wholesale distribution executive; b. Cowden, Ill., July 18, 1956; s. Robert Keith and Ruth Matilda (Welten) S.; m. Gina Lea Hughes, May 19, 1978; children: Nathan Daniel, Naomi Renee. AB in Bible Ministries, Manhattan (Kans.) Christian Coll., 1978; postgrad., Lincoln (Ill.) Christian Sem., 1978-80. Ordained to ministry Christian Ch. as deacon, 1980, as elder, 1990. Youth min. Glenn Pk. Christian Ch., Wichita, Kans., 1976-78; intern Cen. Christian Ch., Mesa, Ariz., 1980-81; assoc. min. Taylorville (Ill.) Christian Ch., 1981-82; min. 1st Ch. of Christ, Globe, Ariz., 1983-85; home Bible study leader Desert Community Christian Ch., Chandler, Ariz., 1985-88, adult Bible Sch. tchr., 1986-89, high sch. Bible Sch. tchr., 1990—, elder, 1990—; owner Ultra Bath of Ariz., Scottsdale, 1990—. Bd. dirs. La Questa Drug and Alcohol Abuse Counseling, Globe, 1984-85; mgr. ch. co-ed softball league, Valley of Ariz., 1989; asst. coach Dobson Soccer League, Mesa, Chandler, 1990-91; mgr. Dobson South Little League, 1991. Home: 1737 W Posada Ave Mesa AZ 85202 *When men and women examine life for purpose and meaning there are but two choices. They were born to die, or they were created to be God's representatives on this earth.*

SHIRAYANAGI, PETER SEIICHI, archbishop; b. Hachioji, Japan, June 17, 1928. D Canon Law, Universitas Urbaniana, Rome. Archbishop of Tokyo Tokyo Cath. Archdiocese, 1966—; pres. Japanese Cath. Bishops' Conf., 1983—. Home: 16-15 3 chome Sekiguchi, Bunkyo-ku, Tokyo 112, Japan Office: Archbishop's House, 3-16-15 Sekiguchi, Bunkyo-ku, Tokyo 112, Japan

SHIRK, DAVID W., minister; b. Twin Falls, Idaho, Mar. 9, 1955; s. Charles Wesley and Ruth Helene (Lokkesmoe) S.; m. Carol Trellis Schaar, Mar. 18, 1978; children: Timothy, Lisa, Carissa. BA, Faith Luth. Sem., 1981. Minister Word of Life Ministries, Yakima, Wash.; mem. exec. coun. Messenger Internat., Nashville, 1988—; founder Pacific Coast Tng. Ctr., Yakima, 1986—. Author periodical The House That Faces East, 1990—. Avocations: golf, fly fishing, reading, writing, football. Office: Word of Life Ministries 1701 W Nob Hill Blvd Yakima WA 98902

SHIRK, JOHN CURTIS, librarian; b. Reading, Pa., Aug. 27, 1932. BA, Cen. Bible Coll., Springfield, Mo., 1957; MA, NYU, 1964; BD, So. Meth. U., 1968; MSLS, Syracuse U., 1973; EdD, Tex. A&M, 1983. Ordained to ministry United Meth. Ch. Pastor Pacific N.W. Conf., Seattle, 1968-72; libr. dir. North Cen. Bible Coll., Mpls., 1987—. Contbr. articles to religious jours. Bd. dirs. UN Assn., Houston, 1974-79, Casa de Amigos, Houston, 1977-78, Tchr. Corps, Houston, 1978-79. With USN, 1958-65. Mott fellow, 1982-83; Kellogg grantee, 1988. Mem. ALA, Minn. Libr. Assn., Twin Cities Watercolor Soc. (v.p. 1989-90). Mem. Democratic Socialist Party. Office: North Cen Bible Coll 910 Elliot Ave S Minneapolis MN 55404

SHIRLEY, EDWARD LEE, religious studies educator; b. Kansas City, Mo., Dec. 25, 1953; s. Edward B. and Velva Joice (Crow) S.; m. Beverley Ruth Vale, Apr. 23, 1977; 1 child, Matthew Edward. AB with honors, U. Mo., 1976; cert. corp. ministry, St. Louis U., 1977, MA in Religious Studies, 1978; PhD in Theology, Fordham U., Bronx, N.Y., 1990. Cert. pastoral chaplain. Dir. Cath. Youth Community, Council Bluffs, Iowa, 1978-81; adj. dept. theology St. Peter's Coll., Jersey City, 1983-84, St. John's U., Queens, N.Y., 1984, U. Nebr., Omaha, 1985; asst. prof. religious studies St. Edward's U., Austin, Tex., 1985-91, assoc. prof., 1991—; pres., formation dir. Secular Franciscan Order, Sacred Heart Fraternity, Austin, 1988-90; min. formation Sacred Heart Province, 1991—; theol. peritus Synod Diocese of Austin, 1989—, mem. theol. commn., 1989—; pres. faculty collegium St. Edward's U., 1990-92. Contbr. articles to profl. jours. St. Edward's U. faculty devel. grantee, 1986-91. Mem. Am. Acad. Religion, Cath. Theol. Soc. Am., Soc. for Buddhist Christian Studies. Home: 3906 Balcones Woods Dr Austin TX 78759 Office: St Edwards U 3001 S Congress Ave Austin TX 78704

SHIRLEY, JUDITH ELLEN, religious education director; b. Washington, Mar. 2, 1942; d. Walter and Elizabeth Dorothy (Pinger) Gray; m. Patrick Shirley, Mar. 25, 1983. Student, Notre Dame of Md., 1968; postgrad., Loyola U., New Orleans, 1987. Lic. amateur radio operator. Student, catechist Mission Helpers, Balt., 1960-71; dir. religious edn. Sts. Cosmas & Damian, Punxsutawney, Pa., 1971-76, Queen of the Americas, Conneaut Lake, Pa., 1976-78, St. Theresa, Gonzales, La., 1978-79, various parishes, 1979-81; diocesan cons. Diocese of Lafayette, La., 1981-86; dir. religious edn. St. Columba, Caledonia, N.Y., 1987-89, St. Matthew, Tolland, Conn., 1990—. Pub. affairs officer Civil Air Patrol, Lafayette, 1982-87, moral leadership officer, 1982-87. Home: 63 Fitts Rd Ashford CT 06278 Office: Saint Matthew PO Box 100 Tolland CT 06084 *If each of us could even make one other person's life a little brighter, giving him or her self-worth and an understanding and appreciation of the purpose of life, then our sojourn in life would be worthwhile.*

SHIRYON, KINNERET LEVINE, rabbi; b. N.Y.C., Dec. 8, 1955; d. Aaron Jules and Marilyn (Goldman) Levine; m. Baruch Mordechai Shiryon, Aug. 31, 1980; children: Ayelet, Erez, Inbar, Amichai. BA, U. Calif., Berkeley, 1977; MA, Hebrew Union Coll.-Jewish Inst. Religion, N.Y.C., 1980. Ordained rabbi, 1981. Rabbi, dir. interreligious affairs Am. Jewish Com., L.A., 1981-83; rabbi Kehillat Ramat Aviv, Tel Aviv, 1984—; lectr. Diaspora Mus., Tel Aviv, 1983-91, Israel Armed Forces, 1984-91; Israel rep. Assn. Reform Zionists of Am., Tel Aviv, 1984-87; religious judge beit Din of Maram, 1984-91; comptr. Maram-Israel Coun. Progressive Rabbis, 1990-91. Mem. Clergy for Peace, Israel, 1988-91; adv. com. Rabbis for Human Rights, Israel, 1989-91. Mem. Cen. Conf. Am. Rabbis, Women's Rabbinical Network, Hebrew Union Coll.-Jewish Inst. Religion Alumni Assn. Home: Rechov Andersen 2, Tel Aviv 69107, Israel *Life is full of challenges and although I have not yet found all the answers, I think I am asking the right questions.*

SHISHIDO, MILES MOTOYUKI, religion educator; b. Paia, Hawaii, Mar. 2, 1921; s. Genzo and Saku (Abe) S.; m. Florence Michie Kuwasaki, June 24, 1943; children—Nathan Miles, Neil Samuel, Nolan Mark. A.B., U. Hawaii, 1947; A.M., Chgo. Theol. Sem., 1948; A.M., U. Chgo., 1963, Ph.D., 1967. Ordained to ministry United Ch. Christ, 1952. Pastor., Lihue Christian Ch., Kauai, 1952-59; pastor Rollo Congl. Ch., Earlville, Ill., 1959-63; prof. religion and philosophy Pacific U., Forest Grove, Oreg., 1963—, faculty athletic rep., 1968-78, 84-88, chmn. humanities div., 1972-81, Disting. prof. emeritus, 1988—; part time prof. Portland State U., 1966-69; vis. prof. Internat. Coll., Cayman Islands, 1974, Hiroshima Women's Coll., 1980-81; cons. in genetic engring. United Ch., 1984—. Conf. dir. Danforth fellows Pacific N.W., 1970. Author: Oregon Essays, 1982, (with others) Harakiri and the Japanese Character, 1986, Reflections on the Nature and Style of the Liberal Arts, 1989, Nihon no Rinri, Amerika no Rinri, 1989. Mem. Hawaii Statehood Commn., 1956; mem. Recreation Commn. Forest Grove, Oreg., 1978-81, Forest Grove Youth Ctr., 1981-84; trustee, Pacific U., 1979-82. Research fellow Doshisha U., Kyoto, Japan, 1981. Mem. Am. Acad. Religion, Phi Kappa Phi, Pi Gamma Mu. Democrat. Mem. United Ch. Christ. Home: 1414 Hawthorne St Forest Grove OR 97116 Office: Dept Religion Pacific U Forest Grove OR 97116 *Life is a gift and challenge. What finally matters is not what we are born with, but what we do with it.*

SHOBERT, DONALD LYNN, pastor; b. DuBois, Pa., Jan. 12, 1952; s. Ronald Reid and Oral Doris (Henley) S.; m. Joyce Lynn Thompson, June 19, 1971; children: Reneé Dean, Lori Dawn. BA, Campbellsville (Ky.) Coll., 1979. Ordained to ministry So. Bapt. Conv., 1978. Pastor Cave Spring Bapt. Ch., Horse Cave, Ky., 1978-80; pastor 1st Bapt. Ch., Vermilion, Ohio, 1980-85, Oak Hill, Fla., 1985—; bd. dirs. Fla. Bapt. Conv., Jacksonville, 1991—; mem. Halifax Bapt. Assn. Trustee Fish Meml. Hosp., New Smyrna Beach, Fla., 1990—; mem. adv. bd. Oak Hill Elem. Sch., 1990-91. Home: PO Box 935 Oak Hill FL 32759 Office: 1st Bapt Ch PO Box 89 Oak Hill FL 32759

SHOCK, FRANK, religious facility administrator; b. East St. Louis, Ill., July 31, 1954; s. Frank and Evelyn Joan (Reiman) S.; m. Barbara Russell, Aug. 7, 1957; children: Elizabeth Anne, Forrest Benjamin. BS in Recreation Adminstrn., So. Ill. U., 1976; MA in Religious Edn., Southwestern Theol. Sem., Ft. Worth, 1982. Ordained to ministry Bapt. Ch., 1986. Assoc. exec. Bi-County YMCA, Belleville, Ill., 1976-80; assoc. dir. Recreation/Aerobics Ctr. Southwestern Theol. Sem., Ft. Worth, 1980-82; mgr. conf. ctr. La. Bapt. Conv., Forest Hill, 1982—; seminar leader Christian Camping Internat., Wheaton, Ill., 1986, La. State Evangelical Conf., Alexandria, 1987; lectr. La. Coll., Pinesville, 1985, 86, 87. Dir. Sunday Sch. Calvary Bapt. Ch., Alexandria, 1986. Named one of Outstanding Young Men of Am., 1985. Mem. So. Bapt. Camp and Assembly Mgrs., Christian Camping Internat. (regional cons. founds. for excellence program of camp certification).

SHOCK, JAMES EUGENE, minister, accountant; b. Oklahoma City, Feb. 22, 1942; s. James William and Elva Evorene (Lacy) S.; m. Lauren Kay Hobbs, June 30, 1981; children: James William, Joel, Holly. BS in Acctg., Okla. State U., 1965; MBA, U. Tulsa, 1969; D Ministry summa cum laude, Oral Roberts U., 1990; MDiv cum laude, Phillips U. Grad. Sch., 1986. CPA, Okla. Acct. Pan-Am. Petroleum Corp., Tulsa, 1965-69; mgmt. systems analyst Phillips Petroleum Corp., Bartlesville, Okla., 1969-70; gen. acctg. mgr. CMI Corp., Oklahoma City, 1970-72; controller Jerry Hatley Homes, Inc., Oklahoma City, 1972-73; pres. Shock Henley & Botkin CPA's, Oklahoma City, 1973-83; assoc. pastor Putnam City United Meth. Ch., Oklahoma City, 1983-86; sr. pastor Prattville United Meth. Ch., Sand Springs, Okla., 1986-89, Mountain View, 1989-90, Wesley United Meth. Ch., Duncan, Okla., 1990—; instr. acctg. Okla. State U. Tech. Inst., Oklahoma City, 1979. Tchr. trainer Evangelism Explosion, Ft. Lauderdale, Fla., 1986. Served to staff sgt. Okla. Air Guard, 1966-69. Mem. AICPAs, Okla. Soc. CPAs. Republican. Avocations: fishing, sailing, gardening. Home and Office: 323 N First Duncan OK 73533

SHOEMAKER, MELVIN HUGH, religious educator; b. Bryant, Ind., Feb. 11, 1940; s. H. Vaughn S. and Thelora Shoemaker (Avey) Mason; m. Glenna Joan Cockrell, Dec. 29, 1961; children: David Wesley, Diana Marie, Daniel Luther. BA, Ind. Wesleyan U., 1962; MDiv with honors, Asburg Theol. Seminary, Wilmore, Ky., 1967; postgrad., U. Wis., 1966; MPhil, Drew U., 1988. Ordained to ministry Wesleyan Ch. as elder, 1964. Instr. Ind. Wesleyan U., Marion, 1966-67; prof. Bartlesville (Okla.) Wesleyan Coll., 1979-84; assoc. prof. New Testament Azusa (Calif.) Pacific U., 1986—; sr. min. Hillside Wesleyan Ch., Marion, Ind., 1967-70, Houghton (N.Y.) Coll. Wesleyan Ch., 1970-73, Dearborn (Mich.) Free Meth. Ch., 1973-79, Calvary Wesleyan Ch., Bartlesville, Okla., 1980-82, 84-86; interim sr. min. Brethren in Christ Ch., Upland, Calif., 1989; asst. dist. supt. Tri-State Dist. Wesleyan Ch., Ark., Mo., Okla., 1985-86; mem. N.T. adv. bd. Baker Book House, 1990—. Author: The Blind Singer, 1976, Eerdmans Bible Dictionary, 1987 (Gold medal 1988). Youth affairs commr. City of Dearborn, 1976-78; pres. Dearborn Area Clergy, 1975-76; min.'s adv. coun. Youth for Christ of Greater Detroit, 1974-79. Mem. Soc. Bibl. Lit., Rotary (youth chmn. 1974-79), Theta Phi. Home: 1255 Bonnieglen Ln San Dimas CA 91773 Office: Azusa Pacific U 901 E Alosta Ave Azusa CA 91702

SHOEMAKER, PATRICIA NUSS, minister; b. Tripoli, Libya, Sept. 29, 1960; d. Horace James and Ruby (Hyatt) Nuss; m. Carey Wade Shoemaker, Jan. 21, 1989. BA, U. Montevallo, 1982. Campus min. intern Ala. Bapt. State Bd. Missions, 1982-84; min. edn. and youth North Brewton (Ala.) Bapt. Ch., 1984-87, Dalraida Bapt. Ch., Montgomery, Ala., 1987—. Named Outstanding Young Woman Am., 1983, 87. Home: 7134 White Oak Ln Montgomery AL 36117 Office: Dalraida Bapt Ch 3838 Wares Ferry Rd Montgomery AL 36109

SHONER, PATRICIA ANN, church secretary; b. Ann Arbor, Mich., July 22, 1946; d. Perry W. and Thelma A. (Anthony) Banghart; m. Richard August Shoner, Aug. 22, 1964; children: Richard II, Andrew, Timothy. Student, Clery Coll., 1964-65. Sec. Chilson Hills Bapt. Ch., Brighton, Mich. Election chair Hamburg (Mich.) Twp., 1971-91; election worker Pinckney Community Schs., 1979-91; scout leader Boy Scouts Am., Hamburg, 1972-76; coach, bd. dirs. Little League, Hamburg, 1971-85. Recipient Merit of Honor Boy Scouts Am. Democrat. Office: Chilson Hills Ch 4440 Brighton Rd Howell MI 48843-9433

SHONKWILER, RICHARD WAYNE, II, minister; b. Champaign, Ill., Aug. 31, 1953; s. Richard W. and Barbara L. (Cooper) S.; m. Nancy J. Wallace, Aug. 24, 1974; children: Heidi J., Hannah R., Jeannette M., Grant R.W. BA, Wabash Coll., 1975; MDiv, Cin. Bible Sem., 1982. Ordained to ministry Ind. Christian Ch., 1978. Min. youth and edn. Rossville (Ill.) Ch. of Christ, 1975-79; min. youth Lockland Christian Ch., Cin., 1979-81; min. Christian edn. White Oak Christian Ch., Cin., 1981—. Co-author: You Can Teach Adults Successfully, 1984; also articles. Chmn. bd. dirs. Pregnancy Crisis Ctr., Inc., Cin., 1986—. Office: White Oak Christian Ch 3675 Blue Rock Rd Cincinnati OH 45247

SHOOK, DALE ALFORD, JR., minister; b. Wichita Falls, Tex., May 19, 1945; s. Dale Alford and Betty (Rushing) S.; m. Jane Bradley, July 17, 1970; children: Joy, Brad. BA in Religious Edn., Hardin-Simmons U., 1967; MDiv, Southwestern Bapt. Sem., Ft. Worth, 1970. Ordained to ministry So. Bapt. Conv., 1970. Youth min. 1st Bapt. Ch., Merkel, Tex., 1965-68, Mineral Wells, Tex., 1968-71; assoc. pastor 1st Bapt. Ch., Albuquerque, 1971-80; assoc. pastor, adminstr. Taylor Meml. Bapt. Ch., Hobbs, N.Mex., 1980—; vice chmn. exec. bd..Mex. Bapt. State Conv., 1983-85, chmn., 1986. Contbr. articles to profl. jours. Bd. dirs. Young Assocs. Hardin-Simmons U., 1970-80, pres. alumni, 1985; mem. Coun. on Aging, Hobbs, 1988-90. Fellow Nat. Assn. Bus. Adminstrn., So. Bapt. Adminstrn., So. Bapt. Religious Edn. Assn. (vice chmn. 1988, v.p. 1987-88, bd. dirs. 1990—), So. Bapt. Assn. (moderator 1988). Office: Taylor Meml Bapt Ch 1700 E Yeso Hobbs NM 88240

SHORES, STEPHEN DALE, religion educator, counselor; b. Bethesda, Md., Feb. 2, 1954; s. Robert Merritt and Hazel Eugenia (Dale) S.; m. Susan Renee Cook, Aug. 14, 1976; children: Katy, Jenny, Christy. BA cum laude, U. N.C., 1976; ThM magna cum laude, Dallas Theol. Sem., 1982; MA, Grace Theol. Sem., Winona Lake, Ind., 1987. Lic. profl. counselor, Tex. Founder, pastor Jacksonville (N.C.) Bible Ch., 1983-86; asst. prof. bibl. studies Grace Coll., Winona Lake, 1987-88; asst. prof., pastoral ministries Dallas Theol. Sem., 1988—, dir. counseling, 1988—; pvt. practice counseling, Mesquite, Tex., 1988—. Mng. editor IBC Perspective jour., 1987-88; contbr. articles to profl. jours. Mem. Phi Beta Kappa. Republican. Office: Dallas Theol Sem 3909 Swiss Ave Dallas TX 75204

SHORNEY, GEORGE HERBERT, publishing executive; b. Oak Park, Ill., Dec. 16, 1931; s. George Herbert and Mary (Wallace) S.; m. Nancy Leith, Aug. 27, 1955; children: Cynthia, Herbert, John, Scott. BA, Denison U., 1954. Office mgr. Hope Pub. Co., Carol Stream, Ill., 1958-61, v.p., 1961-70, pres., 1970—; bd. dirs. Gary-Wheaton (Ill.) Bank, 1986—. Contbr. New Grove Handbook of Music, 1989. Pres. West Suburban Choral Union, Wheaton, 1984—, Gen. DuPage Hosp. bd. govs., Winfield, Ill., 1985—; mem. governing com. Chgo. Symphony Orch., 1986—; chmn. Wheaton Fire and Police Commrs., 1974-81; bd. dirs. Healthcorp Affiliates, Naperville, Ill., 1982—; chmn. bd. trustees Westminster Choir Coll., Princeton, N.J. With USN, 1954-56. Mem. Ch. Music Pubs. Assn. (pres. 1986-87), Denison Univ. Alumni Soc. (pres. 1976-78), Univ. Club (Chgo.), Nat. Liberal Club (London). Democrat. Presbyterian. Home: 160 W Elm Wheaton IL 60187 Office: Hope Pub Co 380 S Main Pl Carol Stream IL 60188

SHORT, BARBARA ANN, minister; b. El Reno, Okla., Sept. 11, 1940; d. Henry Edward and Pearl Ada (Swank) Schroeder; m. Donald Louis Short, Mar. 11, 1972; children: Ryan Edward, Mary Martha. BA in Religion, Phillips U., 1962; MRE, Christian Theol. Sem., Indpls., 1968. Ordained to ministry Christian Ch. (Disciples of Christ), 1968. Dir. Christian edn. and youth 1st Christian Ch., Stillwater, Okla., 1962-65; min. student youth Cen. Christian Ch., Huntington, Ind., 1966-68; min. edn. 1st Christian Ch., Portland, Oreg., 1968-69, West Creighton Christian Ch., Fort Wayne, Ind., 1969-71; adminstrv. asst. First Christian Ch., Ft. Wayne, Ind., 1972-82; student chaplain Parkview Hosp., Ft. Wayne, 1980-82; chaplain St. Anthony Hosp., Oklahoma City, 1982-84; pastor First Christian Ch., Pleasanton, Kans., 1984-87, Ill. St. Christian Ch., Lewistown, Ill., 1987—; pres. New Hope Cluster Chs., Lewistown, 1989—; bd. dirs. Regional Bd. Christian Chs., Ill., Wis., 1989—; recorder Christian Women's Fellowship Cabinet, 1988—. Bd. dirs. Spoon River Towers, Lewistown, 1987—, Lewistown Community High Sch. Edn. Found., 1991, Citizens Against Drug Abuse, Lewistown, 1988-89; sec.-chaplain Spoon River Profl. Women, Lewistown, 1988—. Mem. Assn. Clin. Pastoral Edn., Coll. of Ministers Christian Ch. in Ill./Wis. Democrat. Office: Ill St Christian Ch 101 N Illinois Lewistown IL 61542 *A gift is not a gift until it has both been given and received. Our lives are gifts. It is up to us to receive that gift and give what we can to the world.*

SHORT, DAVID LEROY, pastor; b. Howell, Mich., Dec. 8, 1955; s. Jack Thomas and Marlyn Lyn (Reed) S.; m. Janet Elaine Oliver, Mar. 6, 1976; children: Matthew, Heather, Sarah, Rebekah, Joshua. BA, Maranatha Bapt. Bible Coll., Watertown, Wis., 1979. Ordained to ministry Ind. Bapt. Ch., 1979. Asst. pastor Cen. Bapt. Ch., Plymouth, Mich., 1979-82; assoc. pastor Faith Bapt. Ch., Milw., 1982-85; pastor Anchor Bapt. Ch., Woburn, Mass., 1985—. Home and Office: Anchor Bapt Ch 10 Skyview Ln Woburn MA 01801

SHORT, HEDLEY VICARS ROYCRAFT, retired bishop; b. Toronto, Ont., Can., Jan. 24, 1914; s. Hedley Vicars and Martha (Parke) S.; m. Elizabeth Frances Louise Shirley, Apr. 14, 1953; children: Martha Short Bowden, Elizabeth Short Rodgers, Janet Short DeGirolamo, Margaret Short Zulkoskey, Desmond. B.A., U. Toronto, 1941; L.Th., Trinity Coll., Toronto, 1943, B.D., 1945, D.D., 1964; D.D. (hon.), U. Emmanuel, St. Chad, 1985. Ordained deacon Anglican Ch. of Can., 1943 ordained priest Anglican Ch. of Can., 1944, consecrated bishop Anglican Ch. of Can., 1970. Asst. curate ch. Toronto, 1943-46; jr. chaplain St. Michael's Cathedral, Coventry, Eng., 1946-47; lectr., sr. tutor, dean of residence Trinity Coll., Toronto, 1947-51; rector Cochraine, Ont., 1951-56, St. Catharines Ch., Ont., 1956-63; canon Diocese of Niagara, 1963-70; dean, rector St. Alban's Cathedral, Prince Albert, Sask., Can., 1963-70; archdeacon of Prince Albert, 1966-70, bishop of Sask., 1970-85; pres. council Coll. Emmanuel, St. Chad; chancellor U. Emmanuel Coll., Saskatoon, chmn. doctrine and worship coms., 1971-83; vis. prof. Emmanuel Coll., St. Chad, 1982; mem. no. devel. adv. council Gov. of Sask., 1985-86. Chmn. high sch. bd., Cochrane, 1953-56, Prince Albert, 1970; chmn. bd. dirs. Prince Albert Community Coll., 1974-77; mem. No. Devel. Adv. Council, Govt. of Sask., Jubilee Com., 1980. Named hon. fellow Coll. Emmanuel and St. Chad, 1980.

SHORT, JOHN RICHARD, minister; b. Kingsville, Tex., Apr. 5, 1944; s. James Aldridge and Margaret (Sanderford) S.; m. Dianne Louise Rickoll, June 14, 1969; children: Jennifer Anne, Tracey Elizabeth, Brandon David. AB, Davidson Coll., 1966; BTh, U. Montpellier, France, 1971; MDiv, Union Theol. Sem. Va., Richmond, 1971; MST, Yale U., 1972; D Ministry, McCormick Theol. Sem., Chgo., 1979. Ordained to ministry Presbyn. Ch. (U.S.A.), 1972. Assoc. pastor Parkway Presbyn. Ch., Metairie, La., 1972-78, acting head of staff, 1978; organizing pastor New Ch. Devel., Mandeville, La., 1978-79; pastor New Covenant Presbyn. Ch., Mandeville, 1979—; vis. prof. Union Theol. Sem., Richmond, 1987, 89; moderator Presbytery South La., 1989; pres. Mandeville Ministerial Alliance, 1982, 86; dir. Family Conf., Montreat, N.C., 1984; mem., bd. dirs. Evergreen Presbyn. Ministries, Bossier City, La., 1972-78. Pres. Golden Shores Civic Assn., Mandeville, 1983; moderator, bd. dirs. Samaritan Ctr., Mandeville, 1989. Moses D. Hoge fellow Union Theol. Sem., 1971. Mem. Adult Growth and Parent Effectiveness (accredited leader), Assn. for Psychol. Type (cert. adminstr. Myers-Briggs Type Inventory), Ctr. for Applications of Psychol. Type, Gen. Soc. Mayflower Descendants, John Alden Kindred, Rotary (chaplain Mandeville club 1980-86). Democrat. Home: 240 Carole Dr Mandeville LA 70448-4623 Office: New Covenant Presbyn Ch 4375 Highway 22 Mandeville LA 70448

SHORT, MARK, JR., religious organization administrator; b. Ft. Worth, July 12, 1929; s. Mark William and Eloise Ann (Harding) S.; m. Margie Ann Horne, Dec. 24, 1950; children: Mark III, Marla Morley, Marty, Marvin, Marlon. BA, Columbia U.; MA, U. Okla.; ThD, New Orleans Bapt. Theol. Sem. Mgr. Glorieta Bapt. Conf. Ctr., Santa Fe, 1967-79; bus. adminstr. South Main Bapt. Ch., Houston, 1979-84; prof. New Orleans Bapt. Sem., 1985-87; ch. growth cons. La. Bapt. State Conv., Alexandria, 1984-85, exec. sec., 1987—. Author: The Bible and Business, Time Management and Ministers. Mem. Rotary. Office: La Bapt State Conv PO Box 311 Alexandria LA 71309

SHORT, RAY EVERETT, minister, sociology educator emeritus, author, lecturer; b. Coffeyville, Kans., Jan. 5, 1919; s. Franklin Marion and Jennie (Messersmith) S.; m. Jeannette Louise Stephens, June 12, 1954; children: Glenn Alan, Linda Louise, Kenneth Ray, Timothy Wesley, Karen Amy; 1 stepdau., Mary Jennings. A.B., Willamette U., 1944; postgrad., U. Chgo., 1946; B.D., Duke, 1948, Ph.D., 1961; postgrad., U. Ida., 1950-51. Ordained to ministry Meth. Ch., 1946. Dir. Westminster Found., Duke, 1944-46; co-pastor Interracial Meth. Ch., Durham, N.C., 1947; asst. prof. religion, dir. chapel programs Fla. So. Coll., Lakeland, 1947-48; exec. dir. Fla. br. United World Federalists, 1948-51; dir. Intermountain Region, 1953-54, Wesley Found., U. Idaho, 1950-51; exec. dir. Student YMCA-YWCA, U. Denver, 1951-53; pastor Fairmont Meth. Ch., Lockport, Ill., 1954-56; grad. asst. sociology Duke, 1956-57; asso. prof. religion, head div. religion and philosophy, chaplain Tenn. Wesleyan Coll., 1957-60; asso. prof. sociology and religion, head dept. sociology U. Dubuque, Iowa, 1960-65; acting chmn. div. social sci. U. Dubuque, 1962-65; asso. prof. sociology, head dept. sociology and anthropology U. Wis.-Platteville, 1965-70, prof. sociology, 1966-87, prof. emeritus, 1987—; prof. sociology and anthropology U. Wis. Copenhagen Study Center, Copenhagen, Spring 1974, nat. lectr., 1975—; vis. prof. sociology Adams State Coll., Alamosa, Colo., 1963; chmn. Peace and World Order div. North Iowa Meth. Conf., 1963-69; Rep. U.S. Jr. C. of C. in testimony before U.S. Senate Com. on Fgn. Relations, 1950; Midwest region rep. on Nat. Council World Federalist Assn., 1964-73, pres. Midwest region, 1967-69, chmn. nat. coun., 1971-72, nat. v.p., 1991—; mem. spl. Wis. Conf. called with Pres.'s Comm. for Observance 25th Anniversary of UN, 1970; vice chmn. Wis. gov. commn. on UN, 1970-87 ; mem. Wis. Methodist Bd. on Church and Society, 1973-80, chmn. World Peace div., mem. exec. com., 1975-80. Author: Sex, Love or Infatuation: How Can I Really Know?, 1978, on videocassette, 1987, 2d edit., 1990, Sex, Dating and Love: 77 Questions Most Often Asked, 1984; contbr. articles to profl. jours. Democratic Party candidate for Wis. 3d Dist. Congl. seat, 1970, 72; del. Dist. and State Convs., 1969-87, mem. state platform com., 1975-87 ; Bd. dirs. Dubuque Salvation Army, 1961-65; mem. nat. bd. Am. Freedom Assn.; nat. v.p. Campaign for UN Reform, 1983-87, 1st v.p., 1989—; dir., founder Wis. Ann. High Sch. World Peace Study Program, 1975-87. Recipient NSF grant Anthropology Inst., Fairmont State Coll., W.Va., 1962. Fellow Am. Sociol. Assn.; mem. AAUP, Nat. Coun. on Family Rels., Fedn. Am. Scientists, Nat. United Meth. Men (peace adv. task force 1990—). Home: 505 S Miller Ave Lafayette CO 80026 *Nuclear and chemical weapons, crises of environments. While my life has largely been spent helping others have a better future, I now know we have to help assure that they have a future at all.*

SHORT, WILLIAM J., academic administrator. Head Franciscan Sch. Theology, Berkeley, Calif. Office: Franciscan Sch Theology Office of Pres 1712 Euclid Ave Berkeley CA 94709*

SHOTWELL, BOB EDD, minister; b. Eddy, Tex., Jan. 30, 1932; s. Cullen Wesley and Mary Louise (Carter) S.; m. Lane Elizabeth Poston, June 14, 1957; children: Laurie Kriegel, Carter Shotwell, Robbie Walters. BA, Baylor U., 1954, postgrad., 1955; MRE, Southwestern Bapt. Theol. Sem., Ft. Worth, 1957. Min. music and edn. Coll. Ave. Bapt. Ch., McGregor, Tex., 1954-57, Emmanuel Bapt. Ch., Waco, Tex., 1957-59, North Temple Bapt. Ch., Dallas, 1959-63, Pioneer Dr. Bapt. Ch., Abilene, Tex., 1963-67; min. edn. and adminstrn. Hyde Pk. Bapt Ch., Austin, 1967—; trustee Bapt. Sunday Sch. Bd., Nashville, 1974-82; chmn. trustees Tex. Bapt. Children Home, Round Rock, Tex., 1974-85; 1st v.p. Bapt. Gen. Conv. Tex., Dallas, 1976. Author: Helping Churches Grow, 1986. Mem. So. Bapt. Religious Educators Assn. (pres. 1989-90), Metro Religious Educators Assn. (pres. 1980-81), S.W. Relgious Educators Assn. (v.p.). Republican.

SHOTWELL, JOHN RALPH, minister, administrator; b. Brookneal, Va., Sept. 30, 1926; s. John Henry and Ada Mildred (Puckett) S.; m. Virginia Lambeth, June 22, 1947; children: Donna Lynn, Jo Ann. BA, U. Richmond, 1946; BD, MDiv, Colgate Rochester Div. Sch., 1949; DD (hon.), Internat. Coll., 1991. Ordained to ministry Bapt. Ch. Pastor Union Ave Bapt. Ch., Paterson, N.J., 1949-52; dir. religious activities U. Richmond, Va., 1952-56; sr. pastor Greece Bapt. Ch., Rochester, N.Y., 1956-65, Cen. Bapt. Ch., Hartford, Conn., 1965-75, Flossmoor (Ill.) Community Ch., 1975-81; exec. dir. Internat. Council Community Chs., Palos Heights, Ill., 1981-91, pres., 1980-81; bd. dirs. U.S. Conf. World Council Chs., N.Y.C.; exec. com., bd. dirs. Nat. Council Chs., N.Y.C.; exec. com. mem. Consultation on Ch. Union, Princeton, 1981-91. Author: Unity Without Uniformity, 1984, Manual for Ministry, 1986, In Christian Love, 1991; co-author: Postscript, 1985; editor: Postdenominational Pulpit, 1987; contbr. articles to profl. jours. Pres. Family Service Soc., Rochester, 1960-65. Lodge: Rotary (pres. Rochester chpt. 1964-65).

SHOTWELL, WILLIS ALLEN, retired college administrator; b. Bloomington, Ind., Aug. 22, 1920; s. William Albert and Alta Clara (White) S.; m. Betty Jane Koch, Oct. 12, 1944; children: Willis Allen, Kevin Jay. AB, Marshall Coll., 1941; ThM, So. Bapt. Theol. Sem., 1944, ThD, 1949; PhD, U. Chgo., 1954. Pastor Chaplin (Ky.) Bapt. Ch., 1946-48; asst. pastor First Bapt. Ch., Oak Park, Ill., 1952-53; asst. prof. Bible Cumberland (Tenn.) U., 1949-50; pastor Bridgeview (Ill.) Bapt. Ch., 1953-55; prof. New Testament Berkeley (Calif.) Bapt. Divinity Sch., 1955-66; adminstr. U. Calif., Berkeley, 1966-85. Author: Biblical Exegesis of Justin Martyr, 1965. Lt., chaplain USNR, 1944-46, PTO. Fellow music and speech So. Bapt. Theol. Sem., 1943-44, 46-49, Louis J. Horowitz Christian fellow Hebrew Union Coll., Cin., 1950-51, New Testament fellow U. Chgo., 1951-52, W.F. Albright fellow A.S.O.R., Jerusalem, 1963. Mem. Soc. Bibl. Lit. Home: 505 Thistle Circle Martinez CA 94553

SHOULTA, WILLIAM EDWARD, minister; b. Paducah, Ky., Oct. 5, 1953; s. Bob E. and Bettye Jean (McBride) S.; m. Jill Ann Thompson, May 31, 1975; children: Jeremy Thompson and Joshua William (twins), Molly Ann. AA, Paducah Community Coll., 1973; BS, Murray (Ky.) State U., 1975; MDiv, So. Bapt. Theol. Sem., Louisville, 1978, DMin, 1983. Ordained to ministry So. Bapt. Conv., 1976. Assoc. pastor Rosebower Bapt. Ch., Paducah, 1972-75; pastor Freedom Bapt. Ch., N. Vernon, Ind., 1976-78, Long Rung Bapt. Ch., Louisville, 1978-83, 1st Bapt. Ch., Providence, Ky., 1983-91, Melbourne Heights Bapt. Ch., Louisville, 1991—; trustee Clear Creek Bapt. Bible Coll., Pineville, 1986—; exec. com. Ky. Bapt. Conv., Middletown, 1987-90, chmn. fin. com., 1989-90. Chmn. Providence Sesquicentennial Com., Providence, 1989-90; chaplain Eastwood Fire Dept., Louisville, 1980-83. Mem. Providence C. of C. (pres. 1989-90, Pres.'s award 1990), Providence Ministerial Assn. (pres. 1987-88), Ruritan Club (bd. dirs. 1985-89). Home: 3005 Gleeson Ln Louisville KY 40299 Office: Melbourne Hts Bapt Ch 3728 Taylorsville Rd Louisville KY 40220

SHOUSE, ALLEN LEE, minister, counselor; b. Owensboro, Ky., Feb. 11, 1947; s. Ferman Jason and Margaret Ida (Young) S.; m. Pamela June Grass, Aug. 13, 1971; children: Jeffrey, Jennifer. BA, Cumberland Coll., 1977; M in Religious Edn., New Orleans Bapt. Theol. Sem., 1979; D in Ministry and Counseling, Trinity Theol. Sem., 1988. Ordained to ministry Bapt. Ch., 1979. Assoc. pastor, min. edn. and youth Huber Heights First Bapt. Ch., Dayton, Ohio, 1979-82; pastor Providence Bapt. Ch., Fordsville, Ky., 1982-84, Eaton Meml. Bapt. Ch., Owensboro, 1984—. Sgt. USAF, 1966-70. Democrat. Baptist. Avocations: bowling, running, softball, tennis. Office: Eaton Meml Bapt Ch 1225 W 3rd St Owensboro KY 42301

SHOUSE, KENNETH L., minister; b. Louisville, Mar. 5, 1934; s. Earldon Lee and Ruth (Morris) S.; m. Verlie Evelyn Maddox, June 5, 1954; children: Bruce, Blake. AB in Christian Edn., Ky. Christian Coll., Grayson, 1958. Ordained to ministry Christian Ch., 1958. Student min. Ninevah Christian Ch., Lawrenceburg, Ky., 1954-60; min. Antioch Christian Ch., Mt. Sterling, Ky., 1960-68, Shelby Christian Ch., Shelbyville, Ky., 1968—; mem. steering com. Calvary Christian Assembly, Mackville, Ky., 1986—; bd. dirs. Teen Mission USA, Lexington, Ky., 1990—. Chmn. fund raising ARC, Shelbyville, 1971. Recipient Christian Hour TV Ministry award, Lexington Mins. Assn., 1968, Ky. Col. award, Ky. gov's office, Frankfurt, 1972, Chaplain's award, Old Mason's Home of Ky., Shelbyville, 1987, NACC award Jefferson County Judge's Office, Louisville, 1989. Home: P O Box 13 Shelbyville KY 40066-0013 Office: Shelby Christian Ch P O Box 13 Shelbyville KY 40066-0013 *I have found that happiness is when I endeavor to help others, usually those who have no way of ever repaying me in the future.*

SHOWALTER, DOUGLAS KEITH, minister; b. New London, Conn., Feb. 24, 1948; s. Edward William Jr. and Lucille (Mayfield) S.; m. Christine Marie Buchli, June 23, 1973; children: Cherie, Carl. BA, Bowdoin Coll., 1970; MDiv, Yale Divinity Sch., 1973. Ordained to ministry United Ch. of Christ, 1973. Min. Benson-Orwell Parish, Vt., 1973-76; min. The First Ch. in Belfast, Maine, 1976-87, The First Congl. Ch. of Falmouth, Mass., 1987—. James Bowdoin scholar, Woodrow Wilson fellow designate in philosophy, 1970, Maine State finalist for Rhodes scholarship. Mem. Falmouth Hosp. Chaplain's Adv. Com., 1988—, Falmouth Clergy Assn., New England Historic Genealogical Soc., Soc. Mayflower Descendants, Phi Beta Kappa. Home: 54 Main St Falmouth MA 02540 Office: First Congl Ch Falmouth 68 Main St Falmouth MA 02540

SHOWALTER, JUDY MARIE, Christian education director, educator; b. Telluride, Colo., July 20, 1944; d. William Louis and Audrey Inez (Ramsey) Nardin; m. Victor Francis Showalter, May 14, 1965 (dec. Nov. 1980); stepchildren: Sidney Roy, Jan Michael. BS in Elem. Edn., Northeastern U., 1976. Jr. choir dir. Union Presbyn. Ch., Powell, Wyo., 1975-85, organist, 1979—, christian edn. dir., 1988—; pvt. practice piano tchr., Powell, 1970—; deacon Union Presbyn. Ch., 1989—. Scouting coord. Cub Scout Pack 144, Powell, 1972—. Recipient Silver Beaver award Cen. Wyo. coun. Boy Scouts Am., 1982. Home: 470 E 8th Powell WY 82435 Office: Union Presbyn Ch 329 N Bent PO Box 906 Powell WY 82435

SHOWERS, HAROLD ROBERT, JR., lawyer, lay church worker; b. Canton, Ohio, May 16, 1955; s. H. Robert and Marguerite Y. (Froehlich) S.; m. Evelyn Jean Pruitt, Sept. 8, 1984. BA in History cum laude, Wake Forest U., 1977, JD, 1980. Assoc. Westmoreland, Sawyer & Miller, Winston-Salem, N.C., 1980-81; asst. U.S. Atty.'s Office, Raleigh, N.C., 1982-83, chief civil sect., 1983-86; spl. asst. N.C. Atty. Gen., Raleigh, 1985-86; spl. asst. to atty. gen. U.S. Atty. Gen. Office, Washington, 1986-87; spl. counsel to asst. atty. gen. U.S. Atty. Gen. Office, 1987-88, acting dep. asst. atty. gen., 1988, exec. dir. nat. child exploitation and obscenity sect., 1987-88; sr. assoc. Gammon & Grange, Washington, 1989—; chmn. N.C. LECC on Pornography, Organized Crime and Child Abuse, 1984-86; chief N.C. Pornography Task Force, 1986; mem. N.C. Sexual Violence Task Force; cons. in field. Contbr. articles to profl. jours. Commr. N.C. Gov.'s Commn. Child Victimization, 1985—; bd. dirs. North Carolinians Against Alcohol and Drug Abuse, 1983-85, Christian Conciliation Service, 1983—, N.C. Baptist Men, 1985-87, chmn. statewide com., 1985-87; trustee, exec. com. Bapt. Joint Com., 1989—; mem. pub. affairs com. So. Bapt. Conv., 1989—; chmn. bd. deacons 1st Bapt. Ch. Alexandria, 1990—; commr. Christian Life Commn., 1991—. Recipient Spl. Achievement awards Dept. Justice, 1982, 84, 86; Hankins scholar, Kirkpatrick-Howell scholar; named Outstanding Am. 1985. Mem. ABA, N.C. State Bar Assn., Wake County Bar Assn., Christian Legal Soc., N.C. Christian Legal Soc. (pres. 1984-86), Mortar Bd., Phi Alpha Theta, Omicron Delta. Republican. Avocations: golf, tennis, hiking, basketball, racquetball. Office: Gammon and Grange 1925 K St Ste 300 Washington DC 20006

SHPEEN, SCOTT LOUIS, rabbi; b. Phila., Mar. 20, 1957; s. Harold and Judith (Goodman) S.; m. Susan Balan, Aug. 27, 1978; children: Hilary Rachel, Adam Laurence. BA, U. Mich., 1979; MAHL, Hebrew Union Coll., Cin., 1983. Ordained rabbi, 1984. Rabbi Temple Beth David, Commack, N.Y., 1984-85; chaplain Parsons Family Ctr., Albany, N.Y., 1985—; rabbi Congregation beth Emeth, Albany, 1985—; bd. dirs. Interfaith Partnership for Homeless, Albany, St. Peter's Hosp. Community Cons. Commn., Albany Med. Ctr. Pastoral Adv. Com. Mem. Capital Dist. Bd. Rabbis (pres. 1990—), Cen. Conf. Am. Rabbis, New Eng. Region Cen. Conf. Am. Rabbis, Rotary, B[nai B'rith (pres. 1990-91). Office: Cong Beth Emeth 100 Academy Rd Albany NY 12208

SHREIBMAN, HENRY M., religion educator; b. Phila., Jan. 21, 1952; s. Oscar and S. June (Snyder) S.; m. Barbara Miller, Apr. 3, 1981; children: Jesse Oscar, David Benjamin. BA, Dickinson Coll., Carlisle, Pa., 1974; MA, Columbia U., N.Y.C., 1976, MPhil, 1978, PhD, 1988. Rabbi, 1981. Rabbi Congregation Am Haskalah, Allentown, Pa., 1978-83; instr. Gratz Coll., Phila., 1978-85; lectr. Hebrew U., Jerusalem, 1984-86; adj. asst. prof. Spertus Coll., Chgo., 1988—; dir. Bd. Jewish Edn. Met. Chgo., 1986—; lectr. Phila. Coll. Performing Arts, 1979-83, Limmud Conf., European Jewish Edn., Oxford, Eng., 1989—; bd. dirs. Broadcast Commn., chgo., 1988—; cons. Spertus Mus., 1987—, Field Mus. exhibits, Chgo., 1989-90. Creator, writer TV programs, Seacher/Arts Alive, 1988—; performer, writer pantomime Everyman, 1968—. Organizer, lectr. Am. Assn. Christians and Jews, 12th Conf., Chgo., 1990. Recipient Outstanding Svc. award, Theater for Children, Blvd. Arts Ctr., Chgo., 1990, Exemplary Teaching award, Kohl Internat. Found., 1987; fellow, Columbia U. Ctr. for Israel and Jewish Studies, 1977-78, 76, Jerusalem Fellows, 1983-86. Mem. Chgo. Bd. Rabbis, Midwest Jewish Studies Assn., Bible Soc. Chgo., Reconstructionist Rabbinical Assn. Office: Bd of Jewish Edn 618 S Michigan St Chicago IL 60605 *Religion can be a catalyst for human good or evil. God being the source of good and evil challenges us with the potential for change. The test for any religion is its teaching not about its own followers but its approach toward others who differ.*

SHRIVER, DONALD WOODS, JR., theology educator; b. Norfolk, Va., Dec. 20, 1927; s. Donald Woods and Gladys (Roberts) S.; m. Peggy Ann Leu, Aug. 9, 1953; children: Gregory Bruce, Margaret Ann, Timothy Donald. B.A., Davidson Coll., 1951; B.D., Union Theol. Sem. Va., 1955; S.T.M., Yale U., 1957; Ph.D. (Rockefeller Doctoral fellow), Harvard U., 1963; L.H.D. (hon.), Central Coll., 1970, Davidson Coll., 1984, Union Medal Jewish Theol. Sem. Am., 1991; D.D. (hon.), Wagner Coll., 1978, Southwestern Coll., Memphis, 1983; LHD (hon.), Jewish Theol. Sem., 1991. Ordained to ministry Presbyterian Ch., 1955; pastor Linwood Presbyn. Ch., Gastonia, N.C., 1956-59; u. minister, prof. religion N.C. State U., Raleigh, 1963-72; dir. u. program on sci. and soc. N.C. State U., 1968-72; prof. ethics and soc. Emory U., Atlanta, 1972-75; William E. Dodge prof. applied Christianity Union Theol. Sem., N.Y.C., 1975—, pres. faculty, 1975-91; adj. prof. bus. ethics Sch. Bus. Adminstrn., Columbia U.; lectr. Duke U., Va. State U., Ga. State U., numerous colls., univs. in, Canada, Kenya, India, Japan, Korea. Author: How Do You Do and Why: An Introduction of Christian Ethics for Young People, 1966, Rich Man Poor Man: Christian Ethics for Modern Man Series, 1972, (with Dean D. Knudsen and John R. Earle) Spindles and Spires: A Restudy of Religion and Social Change in Gastonia, 1976, (with Karl A. Ostrom) Is There Hope for the City?, 1977, The Social Ethics of the Lord's Prayer, 1980, The Gospel, The Church, and Social Change, 1980, The Lord's Prayer: A Way of Life, 1983; co-author: Redeeming the City, 1982, Beyond Success: Corporations and Their Critics in the Nineties, 1991; editor: The Unsilent South, 1965, Medicine and Religion: Strategies of Care, 1979. Dir. Urban Policy Study N.C. State U., 1971-73; precinct chmn. Democratic Party, Raleigh, N.C., del. to nat. conv., 1968; mem. Mayor's Com. on Human Relations, Raleigh, 1967-71; chmn. Urban Policy Seminar, Center for Theology and Public Policy, 1978-82. Served with Signal Corps U.S. Army, 1946-47. Recipient The Union medal, Union Theol. Sem., 1991; Kent fellow in religion, 1959. Mem. Am. Soc. Christian Ethics (pres. 1979-80), Soc. for Values in Higher Edn., Soc. for Health and Human Values, Soc. for Sci. Study of Religion, AAAS, Am. Sociol. Assn., Am. Soc. Engring. Edn. (chmn. liberal arts div. 1972-73), United Christian Youth Movement of Nat. Council of Chs. (nat. chmn. 1951-53), Council on Fgn. Relations. Home: 440 Riverside Dr Apt 58 Apt 4E New York NY 10027 Office: Union Theol Sem 3041 Broadway St New York NY 10027 *Modern people need to recover connections between memory and hope. The past we applaud pre-enacts the future we hope for, and the past we deplore forms our obligation, in the present, to make a different future. In a time when young people find it hard to envision a long human future, the connections of history and ethics are indispensable. The forging of such connections is my vocation as an educator.*

SHRIVER, PEGGY ANN LEU, lay administrator; b. Muscatine, Iowa, July 23, 1931; d. George Chester and Zelda Marguerita (Wunder) Leu; m. Donald Woods Shriver, Aug. 9, 1953; children: Gregory, Margaret Ann, Timothy. BA, Central Coll., 1953, HHD (hon.), 1979. Staff exec. office rev. and evaluation Gen. Assembly Presbyn. Ch. U.S.A., Atlanta, 1973-75; asst. gen. sec. office rsch. evaluation and planning Nat. Coun. Chs. of Christ, U.S.A., N.Y.C., 1976-89, staff assoc. profl. ch. leadership, 1989—; nat. sec. United Christian Youth Movement, 1951-53; bd. dirs. Christianity and Crisis, 1977-90, Ctr. for Theology and Pub. Policy, Washington, 1978—; del. to World Coun. Chs. Faith, Sci. and Future Consultation, 1979; mem. interreligious delegation to Romania, Appeal to Conscience Found., 1980. Author: The Bible Vote: Religion and the New Right, 1981, Having Gifts That Differ, 1989, Pinches of Salt (poetry book), 1990; contbr. articles to profl. jours. Organizer, chmn. bd. dirs. New Bern Ave. Day Care Ctr., 1968-72; state pres. N.C. Consumers Coun., 1969-72; bd. dirs. League Women Voters, Raleigh, 1963-72, Wake Opportunities, 1966-68, So. Regional Coun., Atlanta, 1974-75. Recipient Union medal Union Theol. Sem., 1991. Mem. Religious Rsch. Assn. (pres. elect 1992), Nat. Assn. Ecumenical Staff. Democrat. Home: 440 Riverside Dr Apt 58 New York NY 10027 Office: Nat Coun Chs of Christ USA 475 Riverside Dr New York NY 10115

SHROCK, MICHAEL E., pastor; b. Greenville, S.C., Jan. 8, 1956; s. Lee Wallace and Billie Marie (Baker) S.; m. Lori Jean Nestor, July 23, 1982. Student, Bob Jones U., 1979; MusM, Boston U., 1985; postgrad., Northland Bapt. Bible Coll., Dunbar, Wis. Ordained to ministry Bapt. Ch., 1989. Music dir. Oak Forest (Ill.) Bapt. Temple, 1979-80; youth and music dir. First Bapt. Ch., Dedham, Mass., 1982-85; youth and music pastor First Bapt. Ch., East Longmeadow, Mass., 1985-87, Calvary Bapt. Ch., Windsor Locks, Conn., 1987—; sacred music trumpeter; band dir. Hampton Park

Christian Sch., Greenville, S.C., 1980-82, Dublin (N.H.) Christian Acad., 1986; guest speaker for Christian schs. and youth groups, New Eng. Tchr. pub. sch. Bible study Granby High Sch., Conn.; chaplain Windsor (Conn.) Fire Dept.; mem. Greenville Symphony, 1981-82, Foothills Brass Quintet, Greenville, 1981-82. Mem. Internat. Trumpet Guild, Fundamental Bapt. Fellowship. Home: 94 Clubhouse Rd Windsor CT 06095 Office: Calvary Bapt Ch 470 Elm St Windsor Locks CT 06096

SHROUT, DAVID IRVIN, minister; b. Fresno, Calif., June 5, 1952; s. Irvin Ewell and Dorothy Violia (Edie) S.; m. Connie Jean Bruss, Aug. 10, 1975; children: Laura, Ryan, Rebecca. BA, Warner Pacific Coll., 1975, M of Religion, 1977. Ordained to ministry Ch. of God, 1980. Interim pastor Ch. of God, Washougal, Wash., 1977; assoc. pastor Lynchwood Ch. of God, Portland, Oreg., 1977-79, Ch. of God, Tucson, 1979-81; sr. pastor Ch. of God, Riverside, Calif., 1981-88, First Ch. of God, Albany, Oreg., 1988—; chmn. State Oreg. Bd. Ch. Extension, Salem, 1988—; bd. dirs. Bd. Ch. Extension & Home Missions, Anderson, Ind., 1986—. Author: Pathways to God, 1991. Home: 1800 39th Ave SE Albany OR 97321 Office: First Ch of God 1225 15th Ave SW Albany OR 97321

SHROUT, LARRY WAYNE, lay worker; b. Owensboro, Ky., July 26, 1953; s. Walter T. and Ann B. (Brown) S.; m. Tanya L. Redd, Nov. 15, 1986. AD, U. Ky., 1978. Asst. Sunday sch. tchr. Southside Wesleyan Ch., Owensboro, 1986-88, bd. mem. at large, 1987-88, trustee, 1988—, asst. Sunday sch. supt., 1988—, youth dir., 1989-90, pres. Wesleyan Men, 1990-91; fleet mgr. Eck Miller Transp. Inc., Rockport, Ind., 1985—. Republican. Home: RR 3 Box 520 Rockport IN 47635 *The world would be a better place to live in, if everyone would treat the other person like they would like to be treated. (The Golden Rule).*

SHRUMM, DONALD ARTHUR, minister; b. Seattle, June 22, 1959; s. Arthur Railton and Mildred Maud (Breadner) S.; m. Kelly Elizabeth Crim, Aug. 28, 1983; 1 child, Kathryn Crim. BA in Psychology, Whitworth Coll., 1981; MDiv, San Francisco Theol. Sem., 1987. Ordained to ministry Presbyn. Ch. (U.S.A.), 1987. Chaplain intern Marin Gen. Hosp., Greenbrae, Calif., 1986; intern pastor St. Andrew Presbyn. Ch., Marin City, Calif., 1986-87; assoc. pastor Cen. Presbyn. Ch., Summit, N.J., 1987—; chair youth ministries Elizabeth Presbytery, Plainfield, N.J., 1987—; mem. devel. com. San Francisco Theol. Sem., San Anselmo, Calif., 1986-87. Founder, mem. Summit Working All Together, 1989—; clergy rep. Mayor's Task Force on Substance Abuse, Summit, 1989-90. Mem. Summit Interfaith Clergy. Democrat. Home: 17 Lowell Ave Summit NJ 07901 Office: Cen Presbyn Ch 70 Maple St Summit NJ 07901 *The Church continually struggles between approaching culture and risking its own identity on one hand and on the other standing apart, maintaining tradition, and risking irrelevancy. We tend towards the latter. We can still address the spiritual needs of this Age, but it will mean taking a chance on where the Spirit might lead.*

SHRYOCK, CARL MICHAEL, minister; b. Newton, Ill., Aug. 29, 1952; s. Carl William and Anna L. (Linz) S. AS, Olney Cen. Coll., 1972; BA, Ky. Christian Coll., 1975, ThB, 1977; MDiv, Lincoln Christian Sem., 1981. Ordained to ministry, 1977. Youth minister Assumption (Ill.) Christian Ch., 1975-77, Clarks Hill (Ind.) Christian Ch., 1978-79; campus minister Christian Student Fellowship, U. Ky., Lexington, 1979-80; assoc. minister Univ. Ave. Christian Ch., Bakersfield, Calif., 1981-85, First Christian Ch., Naperville, Ill., 1985—; bd. dirs., sec. No. Ill. U. Christian Campus Ministry, DeKalb, 1989—; sec. to faculty com. Rock River Christian Camp, Polo, Ill., 1987-90. Contbr. to Population Studies of Church Growth, Vol. I, 1977. Leader Webelo den Boy Scouts Am., Bakersfield, 1983-84; vol. chaplaing Kern Med. ctr., Bakersfield, 1981-82; big brother, 1979—. Recipient James D. Strauss award, 1981, Fristz scholarship, 1973. Republican. Home: 212 Pier Ave Naperville IL 60565 Office: First Christian Ch 25W 530 75th St Naperville IL 60565

SHTULL, JACOB, rabbi; b. Montreal, Que., Can., Nov. 18, 1925; came to U.S., 1957; s. Kassul and Blima (Schwartz) S.; m. Rita Estrin, Dec. 25, 1951; children: Kiva, Simcha, Dina, Ora. BSc, Sir George Williams Coll., Montreal, 1946; M. Hebrew Letters, Jewish Theol. Sem., 1953, DD (hon.), 1980. Ordained rabbi, 1953. Rabbi Bnai Israel Congregation, London, Ont., Can., 1953-56, Beth Am Congregation, Toronto, Ont., 1956-57, Congregation Shaarey Tikvah, Beachwood, Ohio, 1957—. Author: Kristallnacht Reader, 1983. Chmn. Coun. on Aging, Mayfield Heights, Ohio, 1975. Mem. Greater Cleve. Bd. Rabbis (chmn., pres. 1973-75). Rabbinical Assembly of Am. Home: 2900 Medfield Rd Pepper Pike OH 44124-4628 Office: Congregation Shaarey Tikvah 26811 Fairmount Blvd Pepper Pike OH 44124

SHULL, MERLIN GROSH, religious organization administrator; b. Chgo., July 1, 1927; s. Merlin Curlee and Pearl Marie (Grosh) S.; m. Mary Grace White, Aug. 19, 1955; children: Mark Allen, Mary Elizabeth Shull Kreitz. AB, Manchester Coll., 1949; BD, Bethany Theol. Sem., Oak Brook, Ill., 1955; STM, Luth. Sem., Gettysburg, Pa., 1973. Ordained to ministry Ch. of the Brethren, 1947. Svc. worker Brethren Svc. Commn., Linz, Austria, 1950-53; pastor East Nimishillen Ch. of the Brethren, Hartville, Ohio, 1955-63, Marsh Creek Ch. of the Brethren, Gettysburg, 1963-75; missionary Ch. of the Brethren Gen. Bd., Quito, Ecuador, 1975-78; pastor Dayton (Va.) Ch. of the Brethren, 1978-85; dist. exec. Shenandoah Dist. Ch. of the Brethren, Dayton, 1985—; mem. Gen. Bd. Ch. of the Brethren, Elgin, Ill., 1974-75; moderator So. Pa. Dist. Ch. of the Brethren, 1971-72; bd. chair Shenandoah Dist. Ch. of the Brethren, Va., 1981-84. Author: In His Spirit, Part 2 Teachers' Guide, 1966. Mem. Coun. Dist. Execs. (sec. 1989-92). Home: 103 Hillcrest Dr Bridgewater VA 22812 Office: Shenandoah Dist Ch of the Brethren 206 Main St Dayton VA 22821

SHULLENBERGER, BONNIE LOWRY ALEXANDER, lay minister, religion writer; b. Dayton, Ohio, Aug. 28, 1948; d. Estel Andrew and Doris Mae (Menges) Lowry; m. Jay Randall Alexander, Aug. 25, 1969 (div. 1973); 1 child, Shannon Jennifer; m. William A. Shullenberger II, May 20, 1978; 1 child, Geoffrey Amadeus. BA summa cum laude, U. Mass., 1976; MFA, Goddard Coll., 1978; MDiv cum laude, Gen. Theol. Sem., N.Y.C., 1989. N.Y. corrd. The Living Ch., Milw., 1988—; dir. Chrisitan edn. Caroline Episcopal Ch., Setauket, N.Y., 1989—; chaplain St. Luke's Hosp., N.Y.C., 1988-89; dir. Parish Resource Ctr., Rocky Point, N.Y., 1989—. Contbr. poetry, fiction and commentary to various jours. Mem. Soc. Companions of Holy Cross, Assoc. Alumni Gen. Theol. Sem., Order of St. Luke. Home: 14 Spyglass Ln Setauket NY 11733 *When I saw the Himalayas, I learned about a God of Grandeur. When I saw the inside of a working human lung, I met God of infinite care. When I saw the platypus, I realized God's playful smile.*

SHULMAN, ALBERT MAIMON, rabbi; b. USSR, Mar. 21, 1902; came to U.S., 1904; s. Morris and Rachel (Nemirovsky) S.; m. Rose Rosenberg, June 15, 1924; children: Jeremy, Naomi. AB, U. So. Calif., 1926, MA, 1927; B. Hebrew Letters, Hebrew Union Coll., 1934, DD, 1959. Ordained rabbi, 1932. Rabbi Temple Beth El, South Bend, Ind., 1934-67, Temple Beth Israel, Longboat Key, Fla., 1979-85; rabbi emeritus Temple Beth El, Temple Beth Israel, 1985—; nat. chaplain Am. Legion, 1962-63; bd. govs. Jewish Inst. of Religion, Hebrew Union Coll., 1963—. Author: Gateway to Judaism, 1970, Religious Heritage of America, 1980. Former chmn., former bd. dirs Pub. Housing Authority, South Bend; former pres. B'nai B'rith, Nat. Assn. for the Prevention of Blindness; mem. Gov.'s Adv. Com. on Mental Health, 1970—. Lt. comdr., chaplain USNR, 1943-46. Recipient citation Ind. State, 1956, Brotherhood award NCCJ, 1957, Chapel of Four Chaplains award, 1963. Mem. Cen. Conf. Am. Rabbis, Urban Coalition, South Bend Round Table, Masons, Elk, Alpha Kappa Delta. Democrat. Home: 700 John Ringling Blvd E203 Sarasota FL 34236

SHULMAN, NISSON ELCHANAN, rabbi; b. N.Y.C., Dec. 12, 1931; s. Moses Isaac and Ruth Rose (Port) S.; m. Rywka Kossowsky, Nov. 27, 1958; children: Eliahu B., Naomi L., Chaim O., Moshe B. BA, Yeshiva U., 1952, MA, 1960, DHL, 1970. Ordained rabbi, 1955. Rabbi North End Synagogue, Bridgeport, Conn., 1958-62, Sons of Israel Congregation, Yonkers, N.Y., 1962-71, Shaarei Torah Syn, L.A., 1971-78, Fifth Ave. Synagogue, N.Y.C., 1978-85, Cen. Synagogue, Sydney, Australia, 1985-88, St. John's Wood Synagogue, London, England, 1988—; pres. Rabbinical Coun. Conn., 1960-61; dean Yavneh Hebrew Acad., L.A., 1971-77; mem., dir. med. ethics dept. of chief rabbi's Rabbinic Cabinet, London, 1989—. Author: Authority and Community 16th Century Polish Jewry, 1986; editor: Australian Medical Ethics Symp, 1987, The Jewish Holy Days, 1982. Chmn. rabbis adv. bd. Joint Israel Appeal, Sydney, 1986-88; co-chmn. com. med. ethics Fellowship Jewish Drs., N.S.W., Australia, 1986-88. Capt. USNR, 1956-87. Gottesman scholar Yeshiva U., 1952-55. Mem. Rabbinical Coun. Am. (v.p. 1983-84), Rabbinical Coun. Gt. Britain, Union Jewish Congregations (co-chmn. unity commn.), Fedn. Jewish Philantropies (ethics com. 1971-78, v.p. com. synagogue rels. 1984-85), Mil. Chaplains Assn., Rabbinical Alumni Assn. N.Y. Office: St Johns Wood Synagogue, 37-41 Grove End Rd, London NW8 9NA, England

SHULTE, FRANCIS, bishop. Bishop Roman Cath. Ch., Washington. Office: Roman Cath Ch 3211 4th St Washington DC 20017*

SHULTE, JOANN CHERYL, church youth worker, director of Christian education; b. Eugene, Oreg., Sept. 29, 1936; d. Bernald and Carol May (Chase) Holtan; m. Albert Philip Shulte, Aug. 12, 1956; children: Vickie Jo Shulte Armstrong, Sharon Alair. BS in Home Econs., Linfield Coll., 1959; MA in Counselling, Oakland U., 1981. Tchr. homemaking Vocat Edn. Sch., Amity, Oreg., 1959-60; tchr. sewing Ann Arbor (Mich.) Div. Vocat. Edn., 1964-67, Fabers Fabrics, Ann Arbor, 1965-67; ind. seamstress Ann Arbor, 1965-67; kitchen mgr. First Bapt. Ch., Ann Arbor, 1965-67; tchr. sewing Vocat. Edn. Waterford Twp., Pontiac, Mich., 1968-77; Christian edn. coord. Bethany Bapt. Ch., Pontiac, 1978-84; instr., parent trainer Waterford Youth Assistance, Pontiac, 1985—; dir. children's ministries 1st Presbyn. Ch., Pontiac, 1989—; vol. trainer, Lighthouse Caregivers, Pontiac, 1985—; chmn. bd. Christian edn., Am. Bapt. Chs. of Mich., Lansing, 1987—, chmn. Southeastern area bd., Detroit, 1988-89. Mem. Mich. Assn. Counseling Devel., Mich. Bishop Sewing Coun. (pres. 1968-69), Oakland U. Alumni Assn., Paint Creek Folklore Soc. (treas. 1986-87, pres. 1989-90). Republican. Home: 320 Exmoor St Waterford MI 48328

SHULTZ, JOSEPH RANDOLPH, university president; b. Berlin, Pa., May 9, 1927; s. Harry S. and Ruth (Musser) S.; m. Doris Hart, June, 1950; Children: Timothy, David, Joe, Jody. B.A., Ashland Coll., 1950; M.R.E., Ashland Theol. Sem., 1952; Ed.D., Southwestern Baptist Theol. Sem., 1954; postgrad., New Coll., U. Edinburgh, Scotland, 1962-63. Ordained to ministry Brethren Ch., 1948; pastor ch. Williamstown, Ohio, 1948-52; exec. dir. Bd. Christian Edn., Brethren Ch., Ashland, Ohio, 1954-56; pastor ch. Washington, 1956-62; v.p. Ashland Coll. for the Sem., 1963-80; pres. Ashland U. and Sem., 1980—; chmn. bd. dirs. Inst. Holy Land Studies in Chgo. and Jerusalem, 1974-79; bd. dirs. Emerge Counseling Ctr.; treas. Brethren Ency., Inc.; city dir. Huntington Nat. Bank. Author: Soul of Symbols, 1966, Brethren Camp Manual, 1955; contbg. editor: Baker's Dictionary of Christian Ethics, 1973. Mem. Ohio Coll. Assn. (exec. com.). Republican. Club: Rotary. Office: Ashland U 401 College Ave Ashland OH 44805

SHULTZ, RETHA MILLS, retired missionary; b. Anderson, Ind., Apr. 22, 1914; d. Raymond White and Mary Beulah (Yoder) Mills; m. Clair Wilson Shultz, Dec. 25, 1935; children: Carol Ann Shultz Lehner, David Clair. BA, Anderson U., 1937. Missionary, bookkeeper Ch. of God Mission, Trinidad, W.I., 1945-58, Jamaica, W.I., 1958-62, Kenya, East Africa, 1962-70, 85-86; co-founder, tchr. music, bookkeeping W.I. Bible Inst., Trinidad, 1950-58; mem. missionary bd. Ch. of God, Anderson, Ind., 1980-90; missionary speaker, various churches in U.S., W.I., East Africa. Republican. Avocations: sewing, piano, reading, travel. *I have found that life is best lived following the instructions of our creator: "Seek ye first the kingdom of God and his righteousness and all this will be added onto you." (Matthew 6:33).*

SHURIN, AARON BEN-ZION, rabbi, Judaic studies educator; b. Rieteve, Lithuania, Sept. 3, 1914; came to U.S., 1940; s. Moshe and Ruth (Davidowitz) S.; m. Ella Rivkin, July 2, 1944; children: Jacob, Joseph, David. Student, Rabbinical Coll. Telz and Ponvez, Lithuania, 1930-36, Rabbinical Coll. Hebron, Jerusalem, 1936-40, Rabbinical Coll. Lomze, Petach Tikvah, Israel, 1936-40, Yeshivah U., 1940-44. Ordained rabbi, 1939. Rabbi Congregation Anshe Slutzk, N.Y.C., 1942-46, Congregation Toras Moshe, Bklyn., 1946-48; prin. New Hebrew Sch., N.Y.C., 1949-56; instr. Judaic studies Stern Coll., Yeshiva Univ., 1941-42, 66—. Columnist (biweekly) Jewish Daily Forward, 1944—; author: Keshet Giborim, 1964, Bein Yehudai Arzot Habrit, 1981; assoc. editor: Edenu, 1942; contbr. numerous articles to various publs. Recipient State of Israel Bonds 25th Anniversary award, 1975, award Alumni Assn. of Lomze, 1975, Chief Rabbi Kook award Religious Zionists of Am., 1980, Ponivez Yeshivah award, 1985. Mem. Union of Orthodox Rabbis of U.S. and Can. (vice chmn. exec. com. 1960-80), Rabbinical Coun. Am. (exec. bd. 1985-89, award 1985), Rabbinical Bd. Flatbush, Yiddish Writers Union (v.p. 1970—). Home: 2176 New York Ave Brooklyn NY 11210 Office: Stern Coll/Yeshiva Univ 245 Lexington Ave New York NY 10016 *Why would anyone want to be bad if it is so good to be good?.*

SHUSSETT, STEVEN HAROLD, minister; b. Pitts., Apr. 26, 1963; s. Sam and Beverly Sondra (Rothenburg) S.; m. Alicia Suzanne White, Dec. 3, 1988. BA, U. Pitts., 1985, M Pub. and Internat. Affairs, 1987; postgrad., Pitts. Theol. Sem., 1990—. Peace enabler peacemaking task force Pitts. Presbytery, 1989-90; deacon 6th Presbyn. Ch., Pitts., 1989—, student asst. min., 1990—; mem. worship and theology com. Pitts. Presbytery, 1990—. Organizer, founder Pitts. Cares, 1988, Common Ground, Pitts., 1988. Owens fellow and fellow Grad. Sch. Pub. and Internat. Affairs, U Pitts., 1986. Democrat. Home: 6001 St Marie St Pittsburgh PA 15206 *Everyone has a choice in life: to contribute to the world in a positive manner, or stand by and let others to do the work. It is a blessing then, to know so many who are attempting to contribute so much.*

SHUSTER, MARGUERITE, minister; b. Oxnard, Calif., Sept. 10, 1947; d. Carroll Lloyd and Grace Margaret (Hornbeck) S. BA (great distinction), Stanford U., 1968; MDiv, Fuller Sem., Pasadena, Calif., 1975; PhD, Fuller Grad. Sch. Psychology, Pasadena, Calif., 1977. Ordained to ministry Presbyn. Ch. (U.S.A.), 1980. From asst. to assoc. pastor Arcadia (Calif.) Presbyn. Ch., 1980-86; pastor Knox Presbyn. Ch., Pasadena, Calif., 1987—; adjunct asst. prof. of preaching Fuller Sem., Pasadena, Calif., 1988—; del. Gen. Assembly Mission Consultation Planning Team, 1984-85, Inst. Ecumenical and Cultural Rsch., Collegeville, Minn., 1985, 86, Gen. Assembly (com. chair), 1988; editorial bd. mem. Theology, News and Notes, Pasadena, 1986—. Author: Power, Pathology, Paradox, 1987, numerous articles, sermons, and reviews in religious jours. and books.; editor and contbr. Perspectives on Christology, 1991. Named one of Outstanding Young Women in Am., 1979, 83. Mem. Presbytery of San Gabriel (chair, com. on ministry 1991—), Phi Beta Kappa. Home: 172 S Craig Ave Pasadena CA 91107 Office: Knox Presbyn Church 225 S Hill Ave Pasadena CA 91106 *A goal: so to trust in Jesus Christ, especially in times of sorrow and disappointment, that others might find it easier rather than more difficult to believe in a loving, omnipotent God.*

SHUTES, ROBERT STEVEN, minister, physical therapist; b. Flint, Mich., Apr. 7, 1949; s. Warren Guy and Sylvia (Kovacevich) S.; m. Patricia Ann Giackino, Oct. 6, 1973; children: Kevin, Jason, Nathan, Courtney, Jordan. Student, U. Mich., 1967-70; BA, Coll. St. Scholastica, Duluth, Minn., 1978, postgrad., 1991. Lic. to ministry United Pentecostal Ch. Internat.; lic. phys. therapist, Minn., Mich., Wis. Youth pastor Apostolic Gospel Ch., Duluth, 1978-83, dir. evangelism, 1985; pastor, founder Cloquet (Minn.) Apostolic Ch., 1984—; v.p. Great Northern Rehab, Bessemer, Mich., 1982—; dir. phys. therapy Douglas County Health Dept., Superior, Wis., 1985—; instr. Coll. St. Scholastica, Duluth, 1980-81. Author: Surveyor's Course of the Bible, 1986; inventor bed mobility device. Troop leader Sea Scouts, Duluth, 1975. Devel. grantee Greater Minn. Corp., 1991. Mem. Am. Phys. Therapy Assn., Rehab. Engring. Soc. N.Am., Lambda Chi Alpha. Independent. Home and Office: 115 6th St Cloquet MN 55720 *It seems to me that Jesus Christ is the light and beauty of life. As grand as a sunrise, as intimate as a walk in the evening. To know His will is purpose and to walk with Him, that is life.*

SHUTTERS, DANIEL MOYER, minister; b. Harrisburg, Pa., Oct. 17, 1942; s. Malcolm Dare and Janet Catherine (Moyer) S.; m. Jean Margaret Zobus, May 27, 1967; children: Christine, Jason. BA, North Park Coll., 1965; MDiv, Waterloo Theol. Sem., 1969. Ordained minister, 1969. Asst. pastor St. Paul Luth. Ch., Warren, Ohio, 1969-71; pastor St. John's Luth. Ch., Steelton, Pa., 1971-78, Zion Luth. Ch., Dauphin, Pa., 1978-88, St. Christopher Luth. Ch., Lykens, Pa., 1988—. Mem. adv. bd. Dauphin County Area Agy. Aging, 1984—; coord. Meals-on-Wheels, 1985-88; chmn. Dauphin Area Sr. Transit, 1987-88; mem. disaster action team ARC, Harrisburg, 1978—. Mem. Mem. Cen. Pa. Synod Luth. Ch. Am. (steering com. 1985-87), Dauphin Area Ministerium (pres. 1980-88), Soc. Am. Magicians (chpt. 112 pres. 1980). Republican. Lodge: Lions. Avocations: magic, computer programming, photography. Home: 413 Vesta Dr Dauphin PA 17018 Office: St Christopher Luth Ch 635 N Second St Lykens PA 17048

SHYPULEFSKI, JOHN, minister, small business owner; b. Nanticoke, Pa., July 7, 1942; s. John and Helen Shypulefski; m. Linda Fay Morris, June 26, 1965; children: Amy Beth Shypulefski Duty, John Brent. BS, Phila. Coll. Bible, Langhorne, Pa., 1965; MRE, Grace Theol. Sem., Winona Lake, Ind., 1967. Ordained to ministry Ind. Fundamental Chs. Am., 1968. Min. 1st Bapt. Ch., Blossburg, Pa., 1968—, Tioga, Pa., 1970—; owner The Small Mall/Shyp's Sporting Goods, Blossburg, 1976—. Mem. Tioga County Conservation Com., Wellsboro, Pa., 1988—, Tioga Grange, 1980—; chaplain Tioga Fire Dept., 1985—. Mem. Blossburg Ministerium, Tioga Ministerium, Tioga Bapt. Assn., Tioga Bapt. Assn. Ordination Coun. Home and Office: 116 Hannibal St Blossburg PA 16912

SIBLEY, GORDON WRIGHT, minister; b. Huntsville, Ala., Oct. 12, 1938; s. Gordon Eugene and Uneta (Ross) S.; m. Dale Anne Hickman, Jan. 8, 1966; children: David Alan, Joan Eileen. Student, Ga. Mil. Acad., College Park, 1957; BS, U. Ala., 1962; MDiv cum laude, Emory U., 1977. Ordained to ministry United Meth. Ch. as deacon, 1976, as elder, 1978. Min. Hayden (Ala.) United Meth. Ch., 1978-80, Killen (Ala.) United Meth. Ch., 1980-82; sr. assoc. min. Trinity United Meth. Ch., Birmingham, Ala., 1982-87; sr. min. Crumly Chapel United Meth. Ch., Birmingham, 1987—; pres. Birmingham-East Dist. Mins., 1986-87; dir. dist. missions Birmingham-West Dist., United Meth. Ch., 1987—, v.p. dist. mins., 1990-91, pres., 1991—; asst. dean No. Ala. Coop. Sch. Missions, Birmingham, 1990—. Bd. dirs. The Riley Ctr., Birmingham, 1987—. 1st lt. inf. U.S. Army, 1962-64. Recipient Outstanding Min. award Birmingham-West United Meth. Women, 1990. Home and Office: 336 Crumly Chapel Rd Birmingham AL 35214

SIBLEY, JOYCE GREGORY, lay worker, consultant; b. Oklahoma City, Okla., Feb. 23, 1934; d. Marshall Wiley Gregory and Lola May Nichols; m. William A. Sibley, Dec. 21, 1957; children: W. Timothy, Lauren Shawn Leonard, Stephen Marshall. BS, U. Okla., 1955; student, Southeastern Bapt. Theol. Sem., 1955-57; MS, U. Okla., 1960. Dir. religious edn. U. Heights Bapt. Ch., Stillwater, Okla., 1974-83, coll. student min., 1983-88; cons. Stillwater, Okla., 1988—; trainer, instr. Bi/Polar, Inc., Austin, Tex., 1983—. Author: Who Growls in Your Jungle, 1991; contbr. articles to profl. jours. Pres. City-wide PTA, Stillwater, 1973-74. Mem. Okla. State Soc. (nat. conf. del. 1990), U. Ala. at Birmingham Faculty Women's Club (sec. 1990-91, newcomer del. 1991—), Mortar Bd., Phi Beta Kappa, Sigma Xi, Omicron Nu. Democrat. Home: 422 Delcris Dr Birmingham AL 35226

SIDEBOTTOM, IRVIN ELDRED, minister; b. Mason City, Ill., Oct. 16, 1924; s. Irvin and Laura Fern (Schoonover) S.; m. Beverly Jane Petersen, May 27, 1950; children: Phyllis Jane Sidebottom Studebaker, Daniel Irvin, Linda Elaine Sidebottom Sackett, Ronald Keith. Dipl., Milw. Bible Inst., 1951. Ordained to ministry Grace Gospel Fellowship, 1951. Pastor Belmont (Mich.) Community Ch., 1951-54, Cope (Colo.) Community Ch., 1954-66, Eckley (Colo.) Community Ch., 1985—; dir. Things to Come Mission, Inc., Craig, Colo., 1958—; treas. Things to Come Mission, Inc., Cope, Colo., 1960-67, dir., 1963-91. Vol. fireman Cope Fire Dist., 1964-91. Mem. Prairie Golf Club (sec.-treas. 1982—). Republican. Home and Office: 45410 Washington Ave Cope CO 80812-0096

SIDER, E. MORRIS, minister; b. Cheapside, Ont., Can., Nov. 20, 1928; s. Earl Morris and Elsie (Sheffer) S.; m. Leone Dearing, Aug. 11, 1951; children: Karen Redfearn, Donna Gable. AB, Upland (Calif.) Coll., 1952, ThB, 1953; MA, U. Western Ont., London, 1955; PhD, SUNY, Buffalo, 1966. Ordained to ministry, Brethren in Christ Ch. Prin. Niagara Christian Coll., Ft. Erie, Ont., 1956-58; prof. history and English lit. Messiah Coll., Grantham, Pa., 1963—; mem. pubs. bd. Brethren in Christ Ch., 1958-61, Bd. Adminstrn., 1984-90, Bd. for Ministry and Doctrine, 1984—, asst. moderator, 1986-88, archivist, 1979—; com. mem. Ea. Mennonite Coll. and Sem., Harrisonburg, Va., 1990—. Editor Brethren in Ch. History and Life Jour., Grantham, Pa., 1978—; cons. editor Mennonite Quar. Rev., Goshen, Ind., 1986—; author: Messiah College: A History, 1984, The Brethren in Christ in Canada, 1988, Nine Portraits, 1978, A Vision for Service, 1976, others; contbr. articles to profl. jours. Recipient Excellence in Teaching award, Messiah Coll., 1987, Teaching Excellence and Campus Leadership award Sear-Roebuck, 1991; named Alumnus of the Yr., Niagara Christian Coll., 1983; Can. Coun. fellow, 1958-59. Mem. Can. Hist. Assn., Brit. Hist. Assn., Am. Hist. Assn. Office: Messiah Coll Grantham PA 17027

SIDER, HARVEY RAY, minister, church administrator; b. Cheapside, Ont., Can., June 20, 1930; s. Earl M. and Elsie (Sheffer) S.; m. Erma Jean Heise, July 20, 1957; children: Cheryl Sider Giles, Steven. BA, Western U., Ont., 1957; BD, Winona Lake Sch. Theology, Ind., 1962. Ordained to ministry Brethren in Christ Ch., 1953; cert. tchr., Ont. Pastor Brethren in Christ Ch., Toronto, Ont., 1957-61; missionary, adminstr. missions dept. Brethren in Christ Ch., Bihar, India, 1962-74; pastor Brethren in Christ Ch., Stayner, Ont., 1974-76; bishop Brethren in Christ Ch., Can., 1978-90; moderator Brethren in Christ Ch., N.Am., 1990—; pres. Niagara Christian Coll., Ft. Erie, Ont., 1976-78. Office: Brethren Christ Ch Can Conf, 1301 Niagara Pkwy, Fort Erie, ON Canada L2A 5M4

SIDES, SUSAN HATLEY, minister; b. Albemarle, N.C., July 17, 1943; d. Bruce Franklin and Lillian (Deaton) H.; m. Johnnie M. Poplin, 1962 (div. 1968); children, Robin, Reba; m. Lewis Everette Sides Jr., July 28, 1969; 1 child, Lewis Everette III. AA in Applied Sci., Rowan Tech. Sch., 1977; postgrad., Pfeiffer Coll., 1989—. Student pastor Antioch-Bethel Charge, Matthews, N.C., 1990—; Sunday sch. tchr. Tabernacle United Meth. Ch., Albemarle, 1979-89, also mem. choir; v.p. Albermarle chpt. Aglow Fellowship, 1978-81; pres. women's ministry First Assembly of God, 1981-82. Mem. Stanly County Chorale, 1978-85. Democrat. Home: 6534 Old Monroe Rd Matthews NC 28105-6213 *When a person knows the direction which he or she should go, it is a blessing to know that there are people who can help to make that way possible. People do what they really waant to do. God is our source through others.*

SIDORAK, STEPHEN JAMES, JR., clergyman; b. Cleve., Dec. 5, 1949; s. Stephen James and Anne (Hirus) S.; m. Alexis Carol Rascati, Dec. 18, 1976; children—Alissa Anne, Stephen Alexander, Kristin Carol. B.A., Baldwin Wallace Coll., 1971; M.Div., S.T.M., Yale U.; postgrad. San Francisco Theol. Sem. Ordained to ministry United Meth. Ch., 1975; assoc. minister 1st United Meth. Ch., Ft. Collins, Colo.; minister Centenary United Meth. Ch., Salt Lake City, 1st United Meth. Ch., Aurora, Colo.; exec. dir. Colo. Council Chs., Denver. Charter mem. nat. com. Nuclear Weapons Freeze Campaign. Mem. Nat. Assn. Ecumenical Staff. Contbr. articles to profl. jours. Office: Christian Conf 60 Lorraine St Hartford CT 06105

SIEBENALER, AGNES GERTRUDE, nun; b. Edon, Ohio, July 10, 1922; d. Herbert John and Clara Louise (Nye) Siebenaler. BA, Coll. St. Francis, Joliet, Ill., 1950; MEd, Marquette U., Milw., 1960. Joined Sisters of St. Francis, Roman Cath. Ch., 1939. Tchr. cath./pub. schs. Diocese of Toledo, Ohio, 1944-70, prin., 1962-70; pastoral assoc. Sister Parishes of St. Mary, Kirby & St. Peter, Upper Sandusky, Ohio, 1979-88; dir. religious edn. St. Mary Parish, Marion, Ohio, 1988—. Mem. Diocesan Assn. Religious Educators, League Women Voters. Democrat. Office: St Mary Parish 251 N Main St Marion OH 43302

SIEBENMORGEN, PAUL, physician, lay church worker; b. Terre Haute, Ind., Sept. 16, 1920; s. Louis and Ruby E. (Curtis) S.; m. Jane Maxine Waggoner, June 20, 1948; children: Paul Stephen, Elizabeth Ann Siebenmorgen Brentlinger, Susan Lynn Siebenmorgen Amos. BS in Edn., Ind. State Teacher's Coll., 1941; MD, Ind. U., 1944. Pvt. practice Terre Haute, 1947—; pres. med. and dental staff Terre Haute Regional Hosp., 1974-75, trustee, 1975-81; assoc. clin. faculty Sch. Medicine, Ind. U., Inpls.,

1975—; deacon Cen. Christian Ch., Terre Haute, 1947, elder, 1948—, trustee 1965-86, chmn. bd. 1957-59; mem. bd. Ind. Region Christian Ch. (Disciples of Christ), 1966-76, pres.-elect 1972-74, moderator, 1974-76, mem. program audit com., 1981-84, chmn. 1983; del. Internat. Conv. and Gen. Assembly, 1966-69, 71, 73, 75, 77, 79, 81, 83, 85, 89; mem. gen. bd. Christian Ch. USA, and Can., 1969-75, 77-80; mem. exec. com. Conf. Regional Mins., chmn. bd., 1974-76; chmn. bd. dirs. Physicians Ins. Co. of Ind. Pres. Vigo County Bd. Health, 1967-68, 71-75, 80-81, v.p. 1976-79; trustee Ind. State U., Terre Haute, 1975-83; mem. alumni coun. Ind. U. Sch. Medicine, 1989—; mem. U. So. Ind. Found. Bd., 1984-86; mem. Gov.'s Commn. for the United Way of Ind. Centennial Observance, 1986, pres. elect, 1991; sec. Vigo County Comprehensive Health Planning Coun.; bd. dirs. So. Ind. Health Systems Agy., 1975-78, Ind. Med. Polit. Action Com., 1988—; mem. exec. com. Ind. Statewide Health Coord. Coun., 1982-84; pres. Vigo County Heart Assn., 1965-66; hon. parade marshall Ind. State U. Homecoming, 1990; hon. mem. Ind. State U. Found. Bd., charter mem. pres.'s soc., 1990. Recipient Sustained Outstanding Svc. award Scottish Rite Valley of Terre Haute, 1972, Meritorious Svc. award Ind. State U. Alumni Assn., 1972, Hand Clasp award Kiwanis Club of Terre Haute, 1991. Fellow Am. Acad. Family Physicians (charter); mem. AMA, Ind. State Med. Assn. (chmn. bd. trustees 1981-84, pres., chmn. delegation to AMA Ho. of Dels. 1985), Vigo County Med. Soc. (pres. 1970), Ind. Acad. Family Physicians (dir. 1973-82, dist. pres. 1961, 71, pres. 1981, Lester Bibler award 1989), Aesculapian Soc. Wabash Valley, Terre Haute C. of C., Sigma Alpha Epsilon, Alpha Phi Omega, Kappa Delta Pi, Phi Rho Sigma. Home: 2515 N 7th St Terre Haute IN 47804 Office: 501 Hospital Ln Terre Haute IN 47802 *Though we have precious memories and lessons from the past, it is the future, a new frontier experienced by no one, that holds exciting new discoveries, challenges, opportunities, hope, and progress. Under God let us proceed with diligence and in confidence.*

SIEFERT, THOMAS PAUL, pastor; b. Seattle, May 2, 1950; s. Paul Richard and Arlene Ethel (Newman) S.; m. Wendy Gayle Vanzegeren, Aug. 18, 1972; children: Caleb John, Judah Paul, Rebekah Joy. BRE, Grand Rapids Bapt. Coll., 1972; MDiv, Grand Rapids Bapt. Theol. Sem., 1976. Ordained to ministry Bapt. Ch. Pastor Community Bapt. Ch., Anderson, Ind., 1976-80; sr. pastor Algoma Bapt. Ch., Rockford, Mich., 1980-88, Mona Shores Bapt. Ch., Muskegon, Mich., 1988—; trustee Mich. Bapt. Gen. Conf., 1984-88; overseer Bapt. Gen. Conf., 1988—. Sch. bd. Algoma Christian Sch., Rockford, 1981-86, chmn. sch. bd., 1983-86. Office: Mona Shores Bapt Ch 3800 Lake Harbor Rd Muskegon MI 49441

SIEFKEN, JOHN HENRY, minister; b. Moline, Ill., May 21, 1939; s. John Henry and Florence F. (Ekblad) S.; m. Mary Lou McGregor, July 21, 1973; children: Todd Alan, Heather Marie. BA, Augustana, 1961; MDiv., Augustana Seminary, 1965; DMin., LSTC, 1981. Ordained Clergy-ELCA. Bank teller State Bank of E. Moline, E. Moline, Ill., 1956-61; tennis coach City of E. Moline, E. Moline, Ill., 1963; debate coach Augustana Coll., Rock Island, Ill., 1961-65; asst. pastor Immanuel Lutheran Ch, Detroit, Mich.; speech instr. Prudue Univ., West Lafayette, Ind., 1968-69; sr. pastor Prince of Glory Lutheran Ch., Mich., 1969—; dir. Metro Detroit Ch. Communications Com., 1985. Author: Murphy, 1979, Jocamer Squirrel, 1982, contbr. numerous articles in Religious Periodicals, 1980-88. Middle Sch. Advisor, Clamson Bd. of Educ., 1981-82. Mem. Red Rum Golf Club. Avocations: tennis, woodworking. Home: 597 Wellesley Birmingham MI 48009 Office: Prince of Glory Luth Ch 1357 W 14 Mile Rd Madison Heights MI 48071

SIEFKES, PHILIP DEAN, clergyman; b. Austin, Minn., Aug. 29, 1959; s. Cecil Henry and Betty Joy (Anacker) S.; m. Connie Elaine Baker, June 12, 1980; children: Caleb Andrew, Anastasia Joy. BS, Pillsbury Bapt. Bible Coll., 1981; MDiv, Cen. Bapt. Theol. Sem., 1985; postgrad., Trinity Theol. Sem., 1990—. Lic. to ministry Bapt. Ch., 1986. Youth and music dir. Rockford (Minn.) Bapt. Ch., 1982-85; pastor Calvary Bapt. Ch., Sleepy Eye, Minn., 1985—; dir. Sioux Valley Bible Inst., Sleepy Eye, 1989-91. Composer various mus. compositions. Home: 420 4th Ave SE Sleepy Eye MN 56085

SIEGEL, MORTON KALLOS, religious organization administrator, educational administrator; b. N.Y.C., Dec. 5, 1924; s. Samuel William and Esther (Sackin) S.; m. Pearl Fox, June 28, 1949; children: Deborah Siegel Eisenstadt, Daniel, Deenah Siegel Speiser. BA summa cum laude, Yeshiva U., 1945; MA in Philosophy and History, Columbia U., 1946, PhD, 1952. Ednl. dir. Laurelton Jewish Ctr., Queens, N.Y., 1945-49; ednl. dir., dir. educator placement United Synagogue Am., N.Y.C., 1949-51, dir. youth activities, 1953-64, exec. dir., 1970-75, ednl. dir., 1964-88, dir. regional and extension activities, 1988—; adj. asst. prof. Sch. Edn., NYU, 1971-76; lectr. in field. Contbr. numerous articles on pedagogy to profl. jours. Home: 43 Cross Bow Ln Commack NY 11725 Office: 155 Fifth Ave New York NY 10010

SIEGEL, ROBERT HAROLD, English literature educator, writer; b. Aug. 18, 1939; married; 3 children. Student, Denison U., 1957-59; BA in English, Wheaton Coll., 1961; MA, Johns Hopkins U., 1962; PhD in English, Harvard U., 1968. Instr. Dartmouth Coll., 1967-68, asst. prof., 1968-75; vis. lectr. Princeton (N.J.) U., 1975-76; poet-in-residence, McManes vis. prof. Wheaton (Ill.) Coll., 1976; asst. prof. U. Wis., Milw., 1976-79, assoc. prof. English, 1979-83, prof., 1983—; poet on faculty Summer Writers' Inst., Wheaton Coll., 1980; vis. prof. J. W. v. Goethe U., Frankfurt, Fed. Republic Germany, 1985; lectr., reader various univs. Author: (fiction) Alpha Centauri, 1980, Whalesong, 1981, The Kingdom of Wundle, 1982, White Whale, 1991; (poetry) The Beasts and the Elders, 1973, In A Pig's Eye, 1980; contbr. poems to Atlantic Monthly, Sewanee Rev., other jours. Recipient Margaret O'Loughlin Foley award Am. mag., 1970, award Cliff Dwellers' Arts Found., 1974, Chgo. Poetry prize Soc. Midland Authors, 1974, Poetry prize Prairie Schooner, 1977, Jacob Glatsetin Meml. prize Poetry mag., 1977, award Imgram Merrill Found., 1979, Gold medallion ECPA, 1981, Book of Yr. award Campus Life mag., 1981, 1st Pl. prize for juvenile fiction Coun. for Wis. Writers, 1981, 1st Pl. prize Soc. Midland Authors, 1981, Matson award Friend of Lit., 1982, Golden Archer award Sch. Libr. Sci., U. Wis., Oshkosh, 1986; Gilman fellow Johns Hopkins U., 1961-62; fellow Harvard U., 1965-67, Dartmouth Coll., 1971, Transatlantic Rev., 1974, Yaddo Artists' Colony, 1974, 75, Nat. Endowment for Arts, 1980; grantee U. Wis., 1978, 84, 88-89. Office: U Wis Comparative Study Religion Program Milwaukee WI 53201

SIEGMAN, HENRY, association executive; b. Germany, Dec. 12, 1930; came to U.S., 1942, naturalized, 1948; s. Mendel and Sara (Scharf) S.; m. Selma Goldberger, Nov. 8, 1953 (div.); children: Bonnie, Debra, Alan; m. Miriam Cantor, Aug. 11., 1981. Rabbi, Torah Vodaath Sem., N.Y.C., 1951; B.A., New Sch. Social Research, 1961, postgrad., 1961-64. Nat. dir. community activities div. Union Orthodox Jewish Congregations Am., 1953-59; exec. sec. Am. Assn. Middle East Studies, 1959-64; dir. internat. affairs Nat. Community Relations Adv. Council, N.Y.C., 1964-65; exec. v.p. Synagogue Council Am., N.Y.C., 1965-78; exec. dir. Am. Jewish Congress, N.Y.C., 1978—; guest lectr. U. Ill., Columbia, Williams Coll.; an organizer White House Conf. Civil Rights, 1967; nat. vice chmn. Religion in Am. Life, 1966—; exec. com. Interreligious Com. on Peace, 1966—; chmn. Interreligious Com. Gen. Secs. (Nat. Council Chs.-U.S. Cath. Conf.-Synagogue Council Am.), 1973. Editor: Middle East Studies, 1959-64; Contbr. articles to profl. jours. Steering com., exec. com. Nat. Urban Coalition. Served to 1st lt., chaplain AUS, 1952-54. Decorated Bronze Star; designated Disting. Am. by Pres. U.S., 1970. Mem. AAUP, Council on Fgn. Relations, Nat. Conf. Jewish Communal Service, Assn. Jewish Community Relations Workers. Home: 685 W End Ave New York NY 10025 Office: Am Jewish Cong 15 E 84th St New York NY 10028

SIEMENS, TIMOTHY JAY, minister; b. Upland, Calif., Sept. 20, 1951; s. Howard William and Viola Arletta (Hull) S.; m. Stephanie Ann Jeffries, Sept. 9, 1978; children: Vanessa, Brian. BS in Math., U. Stanislaus, 1974; ThM, Dallas Theol. Seminary, 1985. Pastor to the family Grace Community Ch., Columbia, Md., 1985—; dir. Youth Workers Assn., Columbia, 1985—; com. mem. Howard County Coalition for Spirtual Renewal, Columbia, 1990-91.

SIERACKI, ALOYSIUS ALFRED, religious organization administrator; b. Chgo., Nov. 5, 1929; s. Peter Paul and Mary Ann (Kroll) S. BS in Chem. Engring., Ill. Inst. Tech., 1951; cert. in theology, Whitefriars Hall, Washington, 1960; MS in Math., U. Notre Dame, 1962. Ordained priest Roman Cath. Ch., 1959. Secondary sch. tchr. Mt. Carmel High Sch., Chgo., 1960-67; instr. chemistry and math. Mt. Carmel Coll., Niagara Falls, Ont., Can., 1967-68; instr. math. Marquette U., Milw., 1968-75; assoc. pastor St. Agnes Parish, Phoenix, 1975-81; provincial dir. lay Carmelites in U.S. and Can. Aylesford Carmelite Ctr., Darien, Ill., 1981—; chmn. Comm. on Laity in Carmel, 1987-91. Author: Songs for God, 1990; editor: Carmel's Call, 10th edit., 1991; contbr. articles to profl. jours. With U.S. Army, 1951-53. Democrat. Avocations: hiking, card playing. Office: Aylesford Carmelite Ctr 8501 Bailey Rd Darien IL 60559

SIEUNARINE, EVERSON TULADATH, minister, moderator; b. Chaguanas, Trinidad, Mar. 31, 1937; s. Irwin Capildeo and Cynthia (Rampyaree) S.; m. Jennifer Grace Mohan, Apr. 7, 1969; children: Adrian, Damien; 1 child from previous marriage, Rosalind. BA, Mt. Allison U., Sackville, N.S., Can., 1959; BD, Pine Hill Div. Hall, Halifax, N.S., 1961. Ordained to ministry Presbyn. Ch., 1961. Chmn. of Presbytery Presbyn. Ch., Trinidad and Tobago, 1966-69, clk. of synod, 1967-69, moderator of Synod, 1985-91; tutor St. Andrew's Theol. Co., 1985—; prison chaplain, 1984—; del. Caribbean Conf. Chs., Barbados, 1986, Caribbean African Am. Alliance of Reformed Chs., 1988, World Alliance of Reformed Chs., Seoul, Korea, 1989, World Mission Reformed Chs., San Antonio, 1989, World Coun. Chs., Canberra, Australia, 1991. Editor Trinidad Presbyn., 1986-91. Home: Palm Grove Manse, Princes Town Region, Edward St, Princes Town Trinidad and Tobago Office: Presbyn Ch, Paradise Hill POB 92, San Fernando Trinidad and Tobago

SIFRIT, LYNN CURTIS, minister; b. Eldora, Iowa, Aug. 4, 1955; s. Robert LaVerne and Mina Mae (Davis) S.; m. Gayle Ann Unruh, Dec. 17, 1977 (div. Aug. 1986); m. Kathy Lynn Johnson, Nov. 5, 1988; children: Stewart Thomas Snyder, Benjamin Wayne Snyder, Paige Leann Snyder, Terry Lynn. BA in Philosophy and Religion, McPherson Coll., 1977; MDiv, Bethany Theol. Sem., Oak Brook, Ill., 1982. Ordained to ministry Ch. of the Brethren, 1982. Interim pastor Newton (Kans.) Ch. of the Brethren, 1978; program dir. Camp Blue Diamond, Petersburg, Pa., 1979; chaplain resident Wesley Med. Ctr., Wichita, Kans., 1982-83; pastor Canton (Ill.) Ch. of the Brethren, 1983-88, Garden City (Kans.) Ch. of the Brethren, 1988—; treas. Garden City Area Ministerial Alliance, 1988-89, v.p., 1989-90, pres. 1990—; pres. Graham Hosp. Chaplain of the Day Assn., Canton. Researcher: (biographies) Brethren Ency., 1982. Coord. Spoon River Country Peace Fellowship, Canton, 1985; phone worker Paul Simon for U.S. Senate, Peoria, Ill., 1986; chair. Changing Rels. Project Multicultural Action Com., Garden City, 1990—. Mem. The Alban Inst., The Fellowship of Merry Christians, Renovaré. Democrat. Home: 1714 Old Manor Rd Garden City KS 67846 Office: Ch of the Brethren 505 N 8th St Garden City KS 67846

SIGGELKOW, PHILIP F., religious organization administrator, minister. Head Western Can. Ch. of God (Cleveland, Tenn.), Saskatchewan. Office: Ch God, 175 Rogers Rd, Regina, SK Canada S4R 6V1*

SIGHTLER, HAROLD BENNETT, minister; b. St. George, S.C., May 15, 1914; s. Horace C. and Pauline (Bennett) S.; m. Helene Grace Vaughn, Dec. 11, 1935; children: James Harold, Elizabeth Ann Sightler Carper. BA, Furman U., 1946; DD, Tenn. Temple U., 1960; LTD, Emmanuel Coll., 1971; LLD (hon.), Bob Jones U., 1990. Ordained to ministry Bapt. Ch., 1942. Pastor 1st Bapt. Ch., Mauldin, S.C., 1943-48, Pelham, S.C., 1943-52; pastor Tabernacle Bapt. Ch., Greenville, S.C., 1952—. Author: (commentaries) Revelation, 1983, Romans, 1984, Hebrews and James, 1984, John, Daniel, Genesis Vol. 1, Vol. 2, Acts, 1-2-3 Peter, 1-2-3 John and Jude; founder The Bright Spot Hour Gospel broadcast, 1943—. Co-founder Southwide Bapt. Fellowship, 1954; founder Tabernacle Children's Home, 1962; bd. dirs. Bapt. Internat. Missions; asst. to pres. Tabernacle Bapt. Coll., Greenville, 1963—. Office: Tabernacle Bapt Bible Coll 3931 White Horse Rd Greenville SC 29611

SIGMAN, PHILLIP JEFFREY, minister; b. Noblesville, Ind., May 5, 1955; s. Billie Joseph and Bernice (Brown) S.; m. Frances Kay Parten, Sept. 23, 1978; children: Sara Bernice, Sadie Marie. BA, Criswell Coll., 1983; ThM, Dallas Theol. Sem., 1987. Chaplain Juvenile Detention, Dallas, 1980-83; trustee Mountain Lake Bapt. Ch., Dallas, 1981-83; tchr. Lay Inst. Dallas Theol., Dallas, 1987, Dr. Edwin Johnson Bapt. Inst., Dallas, 1986-87; pastor Rock Prairie Bapt. Ch., North Zulch, Tex., 1987—. Mem. Soc. Bibl. Lit., Cath. Bibl. Soc., So. Bapt. Pastors Conf. Republican. Home: Rt 1 Box 77-P North Zulch TX 77872

SIGURBJORNSSON, EINAR, theology educator; b. Reykajavik, Iceland, May 6, 1944; s. Einarsson and Magnea (Thorkelsdottir) Sigurbjorn; m. Gudrun Edda Gunnarsdottir, Sept. 1, 1946; children: Sigurbjorn, Gudny, Magnea. Candidatus theologie, U. Iceland, 1969; ThD, U. Lund, 1974. Minister Ch. of Icleand, Olafsjordur, 1969-70, Hals, 1974-75, Reynivellir, 1975-78; lectr. Faculty of Theology, U. Iceland, Reykjavik, 1975-77; prof. Christian Doctrine Faculty of Theology, U. Iceland, 1978—; chmn. Liturgical Commn., Ch. of Iceland, Reykjavik, 1979—, mem. Faith and Order Commn., Geneva, 1985—. Author: Ministry within the People of God, 1974, Ordid og truin, 1976, Kirkjan jatar, 1980, 2d edit., 1991, Dogmatics, 1989. Fellow Den norske vitenskaps akademi; mem. Soc. for Study of Theology. Home: Bauganes 28, Reykjavik Iceland Office: Haskoli Islands, Reykjavik Iceland IS-101

SIINO, LAWRENCE J., broadcasting technician, layworker; b. Manhattan, N.Y., Aug. 9, 1963; s. Dominick and Leonor (Tristani) S. Grad. with high honor, Inst. Banca, Ponce, P.R., 1984. Lic. operator FCC. Communications officer Operation Movilization (Ship Logos), Fed. Republic Germany, 1985-87; technician Sta. WCGB, Juana Diaz, P.R., 1987—; chief engr. Sta. WBMF, San Juan, P.R., 1989—.

SIKKEMA, RANDAL CHARLES, youth leader, accountant; b. Morrison, Ill., Apr. 16, 1960; s. Arnold Charles and Susan Jane (Ramsay) S.; m. Tami Sue Malcolm, Sept. 4, 1982; children: Trenton Charles, Nicole Marie. BA, Cen. Coll., 1982. CPA. Ptnr. Schuring & Uitermarkt, Pella, Iowa, 1986—; sr. high youth leader Bapt. Youth Fellowship, Pella, Iowa, 1987-90; auditor 1st Bapt. Ch., Pella, 1985—. Bd. dirs. Bd. Christian Edn., Pella, 1987-90, pres. 1989-90. Mem. AICPA, Iowa Soc. CPA. Republican. Home: 1536 Elmwood Dr Pella IA 50219 Office: Schuring & Uitermarkt 102 E 15th St Pella IA 50219

SILAS, HIS EXCELLENCY METROPOLITAN See KOSKINAS, SILAS

SILBERMAN, JEFFERY MARTIN, rabbi; b. Cin., Jan. 1, 1952; s. Helmuth and Helga (Levy) S.; m. Linda P. Lerman, June 10, 1979; 1 child, Avi Chuchad. BA in Philosophy, U. Dayton, 1973; MA in Hebrew Lit., Hebrew Union Coll., Cin., 1978; D Ministry, Andover Newton Theol. Sem., 1983. Ordained rabbi, 1979; cert. chaplain; cert. clin. pastoral edn. supr. Asst. rabbi Temple Shalom, Newton, Mass., 1979-81; rabbi Congregation Humanistic Judaism, Westport, Conn., 1981-87; coord. pastoral edn. Lenox Hill Hosp., N.Y.C., 1985—91, co-dir. dept. pastoral care and edn., 1991—. Contbr. articles to profl. jours. Fellow Coll. Chaplains; mem. Assn. Clin. Pastoral Edn. (regional dir. ea. region 1990—), Assn. Mental Health Clergy (profl. mental health clergy), Nat. Assn. Jewish Chaplain (founding pres. 1990—). Office: Lenox Hill Hosp 100 E 77th St New York NY 10021

SILBERMAN, LOU HACKETT, literature educator emeritus, rabbi; b. San Francisco, June 23, 1914; s. Lou Harry and Myrtle (Mueller) S.; m. Helen Sue Epstein, June 14, 1942 (dec. 1979); children: Syrl Augusta, Deborah (Mrs. Alan Cohn). Student, U. Calif. at Los Angeles, 1931-33; A.B., U. Calif. at Berkeley, 1934, postgrad., 1935; B.H.L., Hebrew Union Coll., Cin., 1939, M.H.L., 1941, D.H.L., 1943; postgrad., U. Basel, 1959. Rabbi, 1941; instr. medieval Bibl. exegesis Hebrew Union Coll., 1941-43; asst. rabbi Temple Emanuel, Dallas, 1943-45; rabbi Temple Israel, Omaha, 1945-52; asso. prof. Jewish lit. and thought Vanderbilt U., 1952-55, Hillel prof. Jewish lit. and thought, 1955-80, emeritus, 1980—; dir. grad. studies Bibl. field, 1960-65, 67-69, acting chmn. grad. dept. religion, 1960-61, chmn. dept. religious studies, 1970-77; vis. prof. Oriental Inst., U. Vienna, 1965-66, Carleton Coll., 1972, Emory U., 1973; Rosenstiel fellow Notre Dame U., 1972; Touhy lectr. interreligious studies John Carroll U., 1973; vis. prof. U. Chgo. Divinity Sch., 1978; vis. scholar Postgrad. Center Hebrew Studies Oxford, 1978; vis. prof. Toronto Sch. Theology, 1980, Duke U., 1988; vis. prof. U. Ariz., 1981-85, adj. prof., 1985—. Editor: Semeia Studies, 1981-87; editorial adviser: Ency. Internat; contbr.: Ency. Judaica, Ency. Britannica; editorial adviser Dictionary Bibl. Interpretation; author studies dealing with Dead Sea Scrolls, rabbinic lit., contemporary theology. Chmn. community relations com. Nashville Jewish Community Council, 1956-61; vice chmn. Nat. Jewish Community Relations Adv. Council, 1964-70. Mem. Soc. Bibl. Lit. and Exegesis (pres. So. sect. 1959-60, pres.-elect 1981, pres. 1982), Am. Acad. Religion, Central Conf. Am. Rabbis, Am. Soc. Study Religion, Assn. for Jewish Studies, Am. Theol. Soc., Studiorum Novi Testamenti Societas. Club: Shamus (Nashville). Home: 3202 E Third St Tucson AZ 85715

SILEVEN, EVERETT GLEN, minister; b. Muse, Okla., Apr. 21, 1939; s. Everett Leon and May (Hullander) Ramsey; m. Tressie Mae Brown, May 18, 1957; children: Tresa, David, Michael (dec.). BA, So. Ill. U., 1967; ThM, Faith Bapt. Sem., 1971, ThD, 1977; DLitt (hon.), Freedom U., 1982. Pastor Good Hope Bapt. Ch., Mansfield, Mo., 1958-59, various sm. chs., Mo., 1959-63; home missions So. Bapt., Sioux Falls, S.D., 1967-70; pastor Walther's Park Bapt. Ch., DeSoto, Mo., 1963-67, Faith Bapt. Ch., Louisville, Nebr., 1976-88, Faith Bapt. Ch. and Evangelistic Ministeries, Houston, Mo., 1988—; pub. speaker in field. Author: Story of Americas First Padlocked Church, 1982, Jail Writings, 1982, Dear Legislator, 1982, From Sovereignty to Slavery, 1982, Christian and the Income Tax, 1986; pub. Am. Today mag.; contbr. numerous articles to jours. Mem. Nat. Covenant Renewal Fellowship (nat. chmn., co-chmn. Am. div.), Am. Coalition Not Registered Chs. Office: Faith Bapt Ministry PO Box 188 Houston MO 65483 *Christianity that does not confront evil in all areas of life is not true Christianity.*

SILK, ELEANA S., librarian; b. Detroit, Aug. 10, 1951; d. John and Helen (Kavenski) S. BS in Zoology, Mich. State U., 1972; BS in Geology, George Washington U., 1979; MDiv, St. Vladimir's Sem., 1986, MA in Religious Edn., 1988; MLS, Columbia U., 1989. Asst. libr. St. Vladimir's Sem., Crestwood, N.Y., 1985-90, libr., 1990—; mem. history and archives commn., bicentennial commn. Orthodox Ch. in Am., Syosset, N.Y., 1989—. Editor: The Legacy of St. Vladimir, 1989; contbr. articles to religious jours. Mem. ALA, N.Y. Area Theol. Libr. Assn., Oral History Assn., Fellowship Orthodox Stewards, Orthodox Theol. Soc. Am., Federated Russian Orthodox Clubs (chpt. pres. 1978-80, gov. 1981-82). Office: St Vladimir's Sem 575 Scarsdale Rd Crestwood NY 10707

SILLIK, DALE ALVIN, minister; b. Waukegan, Ill., June 3, 1950; s. Vance A. and Leona M. (Oberdiek) S.; m. Donna K. Schipull, June 17, 1973; children: Angelina M., Micah A. AA, St. John's Luth. Coll., 1970; BA in Philosophy, Concordia Sr. Coll., Ft. Wayne, Ind., 1972; MDiv, Christ Sem.-Seminex, St. Louis, 1976. Ordained to ministry Luth. Ch.-Mo. Synod, 1976, Luth. Ch. in Am., 1980. Pastor Redeemer Luth. Ch., Elizabethton, Tenn., 1976-80, Good Shepherd Luth. Ch., Morristown, Tenn., 1980-84; asst. to bishop Southeastern Synod, Luth. Ch. Am., Atlanta, 1984-87; sr. pastor Trinity Luth. Ch., Lilburn, Ga., 1987—. Chair Carter County Community Svcs., Elizabethton, 1979; bd. dirs. Carter County Boys Club, Elizabethton, 1978-79, Hamblen County Cen. Svcs., Morristown, 1983-84; chaplain ARC, Elizabethton, 1978-79; dir. Affirm Youth Camp, 1989-92. Recipient Outstanding Community Svc. award Henry St., Seventh-day Adventist, 1984. Mem. South Gwinnett Ministerial Assn. (convenor 1989-91). Democrat. Office: Trinity Luth Ch 1826 Killian Hill Rd Lilburn GA 30246

SILLIMAN, HOWARD JEFFREY, minister; b. Fruita, Colo., Aug. 14, 1944; s. Howard Eugene and Lucille Lenore (Anderson) Silliman; m. Naomi Ruth Constance, Aug. 19, 1966; children: Sara Beth, Amy Ruth. Student, Wheaton (Ill.) Coll., 1962-64; BA, U. Utah, 1966; MDiv, Fuller Theol. Sem., Pasadena, Calif., 1969. Ordained to ministry Presbyn. Ch., 1969. Pastor Valley Community Presbyn. Ch., Richfield, Utah, 1969-75, Mt. Olympus Presbyn. Ch., Salt Lake City, 1976—; mem. adv. bd. Presbyn. Ctr. for Mission Studies, Pasadena, Calif., 1974—; pres. bd. trustees Wasatch Acad., Mt. Pleasant, Utah, 1987—; moderator local arrangements com. for 202nd assembly of Presbyn. Ch., Salt Lake City, Utah, May 29, June 6, 1990. Co-author, editor: (booklet) A Presnt Day Look at the Latter-day Saints, 1990; contbr. book reviews to profl. jours. Mem. City Coun. Richfield, Utah, 1974-75. Mem. The Alban Inst., Bread for the World, Evangelicals for Social Action. Office: Mt Olympus Presbyn Ch 3280 E 3900 S Salt Lake City UT 84124

SILLINGS, WILLIAM H., minister; b. New Albany, Ind., July 4, 1953; s. R. Harrison and J. Fennettia (Minton) S.; m. Shirley J. Sillings, July 21, 1972; children: Jennifer Lynnette, Laura Anne, Erica Marie. BTh., Covenant Found. Coll., 1975; MDiv with distinction, Anderson Sch. Theol., 1986; postgrad., So. Nazarene U., 1989, Fuller Theol. Sem., 1990—. Ordained to ministry Ch. Bible Covenant, 1977. Pastor Ch. Bible Covenant, Lake Charles, La., 1976-81, New Castle, Ind., 1983-87, Oklahoma City, 1987—; v.p. fin. Covenant Found. Coll., Greenfield, Ind., 1986-87; editor in chief Internat. Fellowship Bible Chs., Greenfield, 1988—, com. chmn., 1989—. Contbr. articles to denominational and religious edn. jours. Mem. Internat. Coordinating Coun. (com. chmn. 1989—). Home: 6713 NW 30 Terr Bethany OK 73008 Office: Church of Bible Covenant 3513 N Geraldine Oklahoma City OK 73112 *Success can be considered success ONLY when and if in the process of achieving success, I also help other people be all they can become in God's will and with His approval.*

SILVA, HENRIQUEZ RAUL CARDINAL, former archbishop of Santiago de Chile; b. Talca, Chile, Sept. 27, 1907. LLD (hon.), U. Notre Dame. Ordained priest Roman Catholic Ch., 1938; ordained bishop of Valparaiso, 1959; elevated to cardinal, 1962, Archbishop of Santiago de Chile, 1961-83; titular ch., St. Bernard (Alle Terme). Recipient Latin Am. Jewish Conf. Human Rights prize, 1972, UN prize, 1978. Mem. Commn.: Revision of Code of Canon Law. Address: Palacio Arzobispal, Casilla 30-D, Santiago Chile

SILVA, KITTIM, minister, chaplain; b. Guayama, P.R., June 13, 1950; s. Luis D. and Georgina A. (Bermudez) S.; m. Rosa M. Quiles, Nov. 18, 1972; children: Janet, Aimee R. Diploma, Internat. Bible Inst., 1974; cert. in ministry, N.Y. Theol. Sem., 1978; BA in Humanities, Coll. of New Rochelle, 1980; M Profl. Studies in Ministry, N.Y. Theol. Sem., 1982. Ordained to ministry Ind. Assemblies of God, 1974. Pastor Pentecostal Ch. of Jesus Christ of Queens, N.Y., 1983—; sub-sec., bd. dirs. Radio Vision, Cristiana, N.J., 1985—; radio host Retorno Ministry, N.J., 1985—; pres. Internat. Coun. of Pentecostal Chs. of Jesus Christ, N.Y., 1986—; mem. adv. bd. Clergy Assn. for Justice, Bklyn., 1989—, Ecos Pub. News, Bklyn., 1988-89; speaker numerous polit. events, N.Y.; dir., prof. Internat. Bible Inst., 1974-90. Author: A Ministerial Dialogue, 1983, Pentecostal Experience, 1985, From Darkness to Light, 1984, Daniel, History and Prophecy, 1985, Revelation of Jesus Christ, 1985, Outlines for Preachers I, II, and III, 1985, The Seven Words, 1988, Preaching on the Song of Songs, 1988, Preaching on Jonas, 1990, Preaching on Women of Faith, 1990, Eclesiastes, 1990, Outlines for Preachers IV, 1991, Jonas the Exclusive Prophet, 1991, David, a Role for Leadership, 1991, An Ailing Society, 1988. Clergyman The Assembly State of N.Y., Dept. of Correctional Svcs. Recipient Citation Pres. Borough of Bklyn., 1989, Pres. Borough of Manhattan, 1989, Assembly State of N.Y., 1989, Achievement Recognition award U.S. Congressman 16th Dist. N.Y., 1990, Proclamation by Pres. of Coun. City of N.Y., 1990. Democrat. Office: Pentecostal Ch of Jesus Christ of Queens 128-05 Liberty Ave Richmond Hill NY 11419 *Those who know how to be under authority, can be in authority and will exercise a good authority.*

SILVA, MARY DELORES, principal; b. Balt., Sept. 11, 1932; d. John Llwelyn Harvey and Beatrice Lee Kennedy; m. Otto Antonio Silva, May 12, 1951; children: Antonio, Ricardo, Vicki, Mica, Chenata. BS, Coppin State Coll., Balt., 1955; MS, Morgan State U., Balt., 1971; postgrad., Johns Hopkins U., Loyola Coll., U. W. Indies, Am. U. Elementary tchr. Dept. Edn., Balt., 1956-68; demonstration tchr. Dept. Edn., 1958—, supervising tchr., 1963-68, sr. tchr., 1968-73, asst. prin., 1974-78, prin., 1978—. Mem. Lambda Kappa Mu, Phi Delta Kappa. Democrat. African Methodist Episcopal Ch. Avocations: reading, decorating. Home: 4610 Norfolk Ave Baltimore MD 21216 Office: Robert Poole Mid Sch 1300 W 36th St Baltimore MD 21211

SILVA-NETTO, BENONI REYES, pastoral care and counseling educator, clergyman; b. Bulacan, Philippines, Aug. 27, 1944; s. Edward O. and Evangeline (Ryes) Silvo-Netto; m. Marilyn Figueroa, Jan. 2, 1971; children: Angeline, Christine. BA magna cum laude, Philippine Christian U., Manila, 1963; BD cum laude, Union Theol. Sem., Manila, 1967; STM, Perkins Sch. Theology, Dallas, 1969; DMin., Christian Theol. Sem., Indpls., 1974; PhD, Northwestern U., Evanston, Ill., 1984. Asst. dir. dept. pastoral care Winona Meml. Hosp., Indpls., 1971-81; pastoral counselor Ctr. for Mental Health, Anderson, Ind., 1984-85; adminstrv. dir. Asian Am. Pastoral Counseling Ctr., Chgo., 1983-84; care-doctoral faculty Grad. Theol. Union, Berkeley, 1985—; assoc. prof. pastoral care and counseling Am. Bapt. Sem. of the West, Berkeley, 1985—; bd. dirs. Bay Area Pastoral Counseling Ctr., San Francisco, 1988—; minister pastoral care Pinole (Calif.) United Meth. Ch., 1990. Vice-chairperson Sci. and Tech. Adv. Coun. for Philippines, San Francisco br., 1990. Fellow Am. Assn. Pastoral Counselors (ethics com. chair Pacific region 1988-89), Coll. Chaplains APHA; mem. AAMFT, AAR. Home: 154 Columbia Pl Hercules CA 94547 Office: Am Bapt Sem of the West 2606 Dwight Way Berkeley CA 94704

SILVER, DAVID MITCHELL, foundation director; b. N.Y.C., Oct. 27, 1960; s. Gerald J. and Irene S. (Soshnik) S.; m. Hilary Wolpert, Sept. 13, 1987; 1 child, Shira. BA, Brandeis U., Waltham, Mass., 1982, MA, 1984. Hillel dir. B'nai B'rith Hillel Found., Storrs, Conn., 1990—. Contbr. articles to profl. jours. Active mem. Soc. for Protection Nature in Israel, TELEM-The Movement for Zionist Fulfillment, Israel Movement for Progressive Judaism, 1984-90. Mem. Assn. of Hillel and Jewish Campus Profls., Storrs Area Assn. Religious Communities. Home: 137 Seperatist Rd Storrs CT 06268 Office: U Conn Hillel Found 54 N Eagleville Rd Storrs CT 06268

SILVER, ERIC AARON, rabbi; b. Bklyn., Apr. 15, 1942; s. Sholom and Marion (Halpern) S.; m. Mary Jennifer Dolcort, Sept. 3, 1978; children: Micah Samuel Dolcort-Silver, Jonathan Baruch Dolcort-Silver, Nathaniel Ephraim Dolcort-Silver. AB in Math., U. Mo., 1963; MA, Hebrew Union Coll., Cin., 1973; MBA, U. Phoenix, 1986. Ordained rabbi, 1974. Rabbi Temple Shalom, Winnipeg, Man., Can., 1977-81, Congregation Kol Ami, Salt Lake City, 1981-86, Temple Israel, Great Neck, N.Y., 1987-90, Temple Beth David, Cheshire, Conn., 1990—. Mem. Utah com. U.S. Civil Rights Commn., 1982—; mem. Gov.'s Blue Ribbon Com. on Med. Rights, Utah, 1984—, Gov.'s Alert Commn. on Edn., Utah Law Enforcement Coordinating Com., 1982—; presdl. appointment to Fed. Judiciary Selection Commn.; trustee United Way Great Salt Lake, Utah, 1982—. Lt. comdr., chaplain USN, 1963-77. Decorated Bronze Star medal with combat V, Purple Heart. Mem. Cen. Conf. Am. Rabbis, Rabbinical Assembly, Kiwanis, Masons, Shriners. Home: 45 Willowbrook Dr Cheshire CT 06410-2607 Office: Temple Beth David 3 S Main St PO Box 274 Cheshire CT 06410

SILVER, MARC, editor; b. Balt., Dec. 26, 1951; s. Donald Leon and Shirley Elinor (Freeman); m. Marsha Lee Dale; children: Maya Dale. BA, U. Md., 1973. Assoc. editor Balt. Jewish Times, 1974-79; freelance writer Balt., 1979-80; editor B'nai B'rith Jewish Monthly, Washington, 1981—. Recipient Smolar award Council Jewish Fedns., 1984, 86. Mem. Am. Jewish Press Assn. Democrat. Office: B'nai Brith Internat Jewish Monthly 1640 Rhode Island Ave NW Washington DC 20036

SILVER, SAMUEL MANUEL, rabbi, author; b. Wilmington, Del., June 7, 1912; s. Adolph David and Adela (Hacker) S.; m. Elaine Shapiro, Feb. 9, 1953; children: Lee, Joshua, Barry, Noah, Daniel. B.A., U. Del., 1933; M.H.L., Hebrew Union Coll., 1940, D.D., 1965. Ordained rabbi, 1940; dir. Hillel Found., U. Md., 1940-42; asst. rabbi in Cleve., 1946-52; rabbi Temple Sinai, Stamford, Conn., 1959-77, Jewish Community Center of Lee County, Cape Coral, Fla., 1977-79, Temple Sinai of South Palm Beach County, Fla., 1979—; Sec. Temple of Understanding, Greenwich, Conn., 1969; v.p. Stamford-Darien Council of Chs. and Synagogues; exec. bd. Fellowship in Prayer, 1970—; pres. Rabbinical Assn. South Palm Beach County, 1980-82. Author: (with Rabbi M.M. Applebaum) Sermonettes for Young People, 1964, How To Enjoy This Moment, 1967, Explaining Judaism to Jews and Christians, 1971, When You Speak English You Often Speak Hebrew, 1973, Mixed Marriage Between Jew and Christian, 1977, Speak to the Children of Israel, 1977; Editor: Am. Judaism, 1952-59, The Quotable American Rabbis, 1967; columnist Nat. Jewish Post, 1955—. Served as chaplain AUS, 1942-46. Mem. Central Conf. Am. Rabbis (nat. exec. bd. 1954-56), Jewish War Vets (chaplain 1966-70), Assn. Jewish Chaplains U.S. (pres. 1959-62), Stamford-Darien Ministers League (pres. 1961-62), Zionist Orgn. Am. (pres. Southeast region 1984—), Alpha Epsilon Pi. Home and Office: 2475 W Atlantic Ave Delray Beach FL 33445 *The greatest of all miracles is that we need not be tomorrow what we are today but that we can improve if we make use of the potential implanted within us by God.*

SILVERMAN, HILLEL E., rabbi; b. Hartford, Conn., Feb. 24, 1924; s. Morris and Althea (Osber) S.; m. Devora Halaban, Jan. 8, 1951 (div. 1981); children: Gila Rutta, Sharon Pollock, Jonathan Silverman; m. Roberta Dee Sigoloff, Feb. 15, 1981. BA, Yale U., 1945; PhD, Jewish Theol. Sem., 1949; DD, U. Judaism, L.A., 1971. Ordained rabbi, 1949. Rabbi Shearith Israel, Dallas, 1954-64, Sinai Temple, L.A., 1964-80, Temple Sholom, Greenwich, Conn., 1981—; exec. coun. Rabbinical Assembly, 1988—; pres. Greenwich Clergy, 1989—; dir. Greenwich Jewish Fedn., 1981—. Author: Judaism Looks at Life, 1968, Judaism Meets the Challenge, 1973, From Week to Week, 1979, From Heart to Heart, 1981. Comdr. USNR, 1952-54. Recipient Prime Minister's medal, State of Israel, 1974, Israel Svc. medal, Hillcrest Country Club, 1978; named Man of the Yr., Home for Aged, L.A., 1980. Mem. Rabbinical Assembly, N.Y. Bd. Rabbis. Office: Temple Sholom 300 E Putnam Ave Greenwich CT 06836

SILVERMAN, MARTIN ISAAC, rabbi; b. Bklyn., Jan. 9, 1927; s. Edmund George and Anna Lucille (Dorn) S.; m. Phyllis Olshin, July 6, 1952; children: Sara Lee, Amy Cohen, Ethan David. BA, Yale U., 1948; MHL, Hebrew Union, Cin., 1953; DDiv, Hebrew Union Coll., N.Y.C., 1978. Ordained rabbi. Rabbi Levittown (N.Y.) Reform Congregation, 1953-55; asst. rabbi Temple Ahavath Sholom, Bklyn., 1955-60; rabbi Temple Israel, Monroe, La., 1960-64, Temple Mizpah, Chgo., 1964-72, Congregation Beth Emeth, Albany, N.Y., 1973—; exec. com. Cen. Conf. Am. Rabbis, N.Y.C., 1989-91; pres. Capital Dist. Bd. Rabbis, Albany, 1976-78m, N.E. Region Cen. Conf. Am. Rabbis, 1987-89. Pres. United Jewish Fedn. N.E. N.Y., latham, 1989-91; chmn. Human Rights Commn., Albany, 1985—; mem. Community-Police Rev. Bd., Albany, 1987—; v.p. Planned Parenthood, 1985-87. With U.S. Army, 1945-46. Recipient Carlyle Adams Ecumenical award, Capital Area Coun. Chs., 1959, DeWitt Clinton Masonic award, 1990. Mem. Cen. Conf. Am. Rabbis, N.Y. Bd. Rabbis (exec. com. 1988—). Home: 25 Colonial Ave Albany NY 12203 Office: Congregation Beth Emeth 100 Academy Rd Albany NY 12208

SILVERMAN, ROBERT MALCOLM REUVEN, rabbi, educator; b. Manchester, Eng., July 26, 1947; s. Alan and Terry (Posner) S.; m. Isobel Pearl Braidman, Oct. 26, 1975; children: Avishalom, Yossef, Rafael. BA, Leeds (Eng.) U., 1968; rabbinical diploma, Leo Baeck Coll., London, 1974; PhD, Manchester U. Ordained rabbi Assembly Rabbis Ref. Synagogues Gt. Britain, 1974. Rabbi Manchester Ref. Synagogue; chmn. Assembly Rabbis Ref. Synagogues Gt. Britain, 1991—; lectr. dept. Mid. Ea. studies Manchester U., 1984—. Office: Manchester Ref Synagogue, Jackson Row Albert Sq, Manchester M2 5WD, England

SILVERSTEIN, DAVID, cantor, educator; b. L.A., Apr. 29, 1955; s. Merrill Saunders and Edith Esther (Krentzman) S.; m. Barbara Jean Prather, Jan. 11, 1981; 1 child, Joshua Adam. BA, UCLA, 1977, JD, 1980; postgrad., U. Judaism, 1985-87, 90—. Cantor Temple Emanu El, Burbank, Calif., 1975-79, Temple Aliyah, Woodland Hills, Calif., 1979-85, Adat Ari El, North Hollywood, Calif., 1985—; mem. exec. coun. Cantors Assembly, N.Y.C., 1986—; chmn. Conv. of Cantor Assembly, N.Y.C., L.A., 1989-91; bd. dirs. SVF Fedn. Coun., L.A., 1982-84. Producer rec. Windows of the Soul, 1988. Vol. Jewish Homes for the Aging, L.A., 1988-91; mem. Guardians for the Jewish Homes, 1989—. Democrat. Avocations: biking, camping, organ, opera, computing. Office: Adat Ari El 12020 Burbank at Laurel North Hollywood CA 91607

SILVESTRINI, ACHILLE CARDINAL, cardinal, prefect; b. Brisighella, Italy, Oct. 25, 1923. Ordained priest Roman Cath. Ch., 1946. Elected titular archbishop of Novaliciana Mauritania, 1979; consecrated bishop, 1979; sec. Coun. for Pub. Affairs of the Ch., 1979; created cardinal, 1988; prefect Supremal Tribunal of the Apostolic Signatura, 1988, Congregation for Oriental Chs., 1991. Address: Palazzo del Bramante, Via della Conciliazione 34, 00193 Rome Italy

SIM, JOHN KIM-CHYE, minister; b. Singapore, Feb. 28, 1957; came to U.S., 1981; s. Hai Yong Sim and Ah Soon Quek; m. Ammelia Beng-Geok Tan, Sept. 4, 1978; 1 child, Samuel. Diploma in Bible with high distinction, Tung Ling Bible Sch., Singapore, 1980; AA in Practical Theology, Christ for the Nations, 1982; BA with high honors, Life Bible Coll., 1984; diploma in teaching, Evang. Teacher Tng. Assn., 1984; MDiv, Alliance Theol. Sem., 1990. Ordained to ministry Christian and Missionary Alliance, 1991. Asst. pastor Ch. of Our Savior (Anglican), Singapore, 1980-81, Chapel of the Resurrection (Anglican), Singapore, 1984-87; pastor Toledo Chinese Alliance Ch., 1990—. Home: 6022 Black Oak Dr Toledo OH 43615 Office: Toledo Chinese Alliance Ch 2500 W Central Ave Toledo OH 43606 *Though life is not easy, it is full of excitement and adventures. The decisions that we make in life will either make us or break us. Life should be a challenge—not a compromise!.*

SIMMONDS, DONALD LEE, minister; b. Detroit, Jan. 30, 1935; s. Lee Shelton and Nina Bernice (Cooper) S.; m. Joanne Margaret Magnolia, July 28, 1960; children: Beverly Allison Simmonds Miner, Christine Lee. BA, Stanford U., 1956; BD, San Francisco Theol. Sem., 1960, MA, 1971. Ordained to ministry Presbyn. Ch. (USA), 1960. Pastor Flathead Presbyn. Parish, Hot Springs, Mont., 1960-65; pastor 1st Presbyn. Ch., Dillon, Mont., 1965-70, Mason City, Iowa, 1972—; moderator Yellowstone Presbytery, Dillon, 1970, North Cen. Iowa Presbytery, Mason City, 1989. Mem. Human Rights Commn., Mason City, 1977-82. Recipient Dr. Martin Luther King Jr. excellence award Martin Luther King Day, Inc., 1991; parish ministers fellow Fund. for Theol. Edn. Fellow Am. Assn. Pastoral Counselors; mem. Rotary. Home: 137 Lakeview Dr Mason City IA 50401 Office: 1st Presbyn Ch 201 Willowbrook Dr Mason City IA 50401

SIMMONDS, RANDY JAMES, pastoral counselor; b. Memphis, July 27, 1951; s. William Daus Simmonds and Virginia (Magee) Bryan; m. Clare Burleson, Aug. 18, 1973; children: Whitney Magee and Jamie Burleson. BA, Memphis State U., 1973; MDiv, So. Bapt. Theol. Sem., 1977, ThM, 1982, PhD, 1986. Ordained to ministry Bapt. Ch., 1977; lic. profl. counselor, La. Minister to youth First Bapt. Ch., Shreveport, La., 1977-80; interim pastor Sparta (Ind.) Bapt. Ch., 1981; staff counselor Ninth and O Counseling Ctr., Louisville, 1983-84; youth minister Crescent Hill Bapt. Ch., Louisville, 1982-85; staff counselor Personal Counseling Service, Jeffersonville, Ind., 1984-86; exec. dir., pastoral counselor Samaritan Counseling Ctr., Shreveport, La., 1986—; field supr. ch. careers Centenary Coll., Shreveport, 1978-80, mem. adv. bd. ch. careers, 1978-80; supr. ministry experience So. Bapt. Theol. Sem., Louisville, 1980-85. Named one of Outstanding Young Men of Am., U.S. Jaycees, 1982; Garrett Teaching fellow So. Bapt. Theol. Sem., 1980-85. Mem. Am. Assn. Pastoral Counselers, Family Rels. Coun. of La. (bd. dirs., chmn. counseling com. 1989—), Am. Assn. for Marriage and Family Therapy (clin. mem.). Democrat. Avocations: skiing, running, swimming, golf, tennis. Office: Samaritan Counseling Ctr 1525 Stephens St Shreveport LA 71101

SIMMONS, CHRISTOPHER LANNY, minister; b. Washington, Jan. 7, 1963; s. George and Josephine (Diggs) S.; m. Janie Marie Boone, Aug. 3, 1985; children: Christopher Lanny Jr., Christina Lynette. BA, Washington Bible Coll., 1985; ThM, Dallas Theol. Sem., 1989; postgrad., Southwestern Bapt. Theol. Sem., 1989—. Ordained to ministry So. Bapt. Conv. Clk. VA, Washington, 1978-85; security guard Silver Shield Co., Garland, Tex., 1985-88; assoc. pastor Jericho Bapt. Ch., Bowie, Md., 1983-85; assoc. min. True Vine Bapt. Ch., Dallas, 1986-88; min. music and Christian edn. Cornerstone Bapt. Ch., Dallas, 1988-89, pastor, 1989—; dean D. Edwin Johnson Bapt. Inst., Dallas, 1988—. Home: 8431 LaPrada Dr E # 2069 Dallas TX 75228 Office: Cornerstone Bapt Ch 2815 S Ervay Dallas TX 75228

SIMMONS, DEVANE T., JR., minister; b. Monroe, La., July 12, 1956; s. Devane T. and Barbara C. Simmons; m. Audrey Y. Cleveland, June 27, 1981; children: Matthew, Sarah. BA in History cum laude, La. Tech. U., 1978; MDiv, Southwestern Bapt. Theol. Sem., 1983. Ordained to ministry Bapt. Ch. Dir. met. Bapt. student ministries Home Mission Bd. So. Bapt. Conv. and State Conv. Bapts. in Ohio, Akron, Ohio, 1984—; Ohio mission svc. corps spl. worker Bapt. Sunday Sch. Bd., Nashville, 1988—; coord. U. Akron campus ministries orgn., 1989—, sec.-treas. 1990-91. Royal Amb. chpt. named in his honor La. Bapt. Conv. Brotherhood Dept., Jena, 1989. Mem. Assn. So. Bapt. Campus Mins. Avocations: tennis, swimming, reading. Office: Met Bapt Student Ministries 333 S Main Ste 607 Akron OH 44308

SIMMONS, ERNEST LEE, JR., religion educator, minister; b. Ennis, Tex., Sept. 19, 1947; s. Ernest Lee Sr. and Anna Louise (Moseley) S.; m. Martha Jean Johnson, June 14, 1970; children: Scott Ernest, Leah Kathleen. BA, Colo. State U., 1970; MDiv, Luther Theol. Sem., St. Paul, 1973; PhD, Claremont Grad. Sch., 1981. Ordained to ministry Am. Luth. Ch., 1978. Intern pastor St. Paul's Luth. Parish, Butte, N.D., 1977-78; instr. Great Plains Inst. Theology, Bismarck, N.D., 1977-79; pastor Carpio (N.D.) Luth. Ch., 1978-79; instr. Charis Ecumenical Ctr., Moorhead, Minn., 1979—; assoc. prof. dept. religion Concordia Coll., Moorhead, 1979—; asst. dir. Ctr. for Process Studies, Claremont, Calif., 1973-77. Contbr. articles and book revs. to religious publs. Supporter Minn. Congl. Senatorial Dem. Campaigns, 1982-84; co-chmn. Hunger Task Force, Good Shepard Luth. Ch., Moorhead, 1991—, Theology and Sci. Group of Am. Acad. of Religion, 1990—; bd. dirs. Dorothy Day House, Moorhead. Luth. Brotherhood fellow, 1973-74, Am. Luth. Ch. fellow, 1973-77, Claremont Grad. Sch. fellow, 1973-76; Aid Assn. for Luths. scholar, 1970-73, Bush Found. scholar, 1988. Fellow Ctr. for Process Studies; mem. Am. Acad. Religion (sec. Upper Midwest region 1981-88), nat. bd. dirs. 1983-88), Luth Human Rels., Inst. Religion in Age of Sci. Home: 2714 S Rivershore Dr Moorhead MN 56560 Office: Concordia Coll 901 8th St Moorhead MN 56562

SIMMONS, JAMES MICHAEL, pastor; b. Leaksville, N.C., Feb. 22, 1947; s. Oscar James and Frances June (Bryant) S.; m. Sandra Kaye Jones, Aug. 3, 1969; children: Jeffrey Brian, Sarah Beth. BA in Religion, Carson-Newman Coll., 1970; MDiv, Southeastern Bapt. Theol. Sem., Wake Forest, N.C., 1973, D of Ministry, 1978. Ordained to ministry So. Bapt. Conv., 1969. Pastor Macon (N.C.) Bapt. Ch., 1970-72, Providence Bapt. Ch., Stoneville, N.C., 1973-79, First Bapt. Ch., Canton, N.C., 1979-82, Midwood Bapt. Ch., Charlotte, N.C., 1982-89, Crabtree Valley Bapt. Ch., Raleigh, N.C., 1989—; chmn. deacon tng. Raleigh Bapt. Assn. Leadership Commn., 1989—; facilitator for case study Southeastern Bapt. Theol. Sem., 1990—; v.p. Raleigh Bapt. Ministers' Conf., 1990—; chmn. leadership commn. Raleigh Bapt. Assn., 1991—. Author: The Deacon And His Ministry in the Providence Baptist Church, 1978. Chaplain Y's Men's Club, Canton, 1982; pres. United Way, Canton-Bethel-Clyde, N.C., 1981; vol. Boy Scouts of Am., Charlotte, Raleigh, N.C., 1984—; steering com. Parent-to-Parent, Wake County, Raleigh, 1991. Named Eagle Scout Boy Scouts of Am., 1965. Mem. Nat. Eagle Scout Assn. Democrat. Home: 5501 Fieldstone Dr Raleigh NC 27609 Office: Crabtree Valley Bapt Ch 4408 Lead Mine Rd PO Box 30954 Raleigh NC 27612 *A step of faith is a step forward to claiming the future with the assurance of victory.*

SIMMONS, JESSE DOYLE, minister, educator; b. South Boston, Va., Sept. 3, 1926; s. Heyward Benjamin and Elizabeth (Smith) S.; m. Lois Virginia Ingram, Oct. 12, 1947; children: Nova Lee Norman, Debra S. Sturkie, Virginia S. Miller, Jesse D. Jr. STB, Holmes Theol. Sem, Greenville, S.C., 1954, B Sacred Lit., 1977; DD (hon.), Holmes Theol. Sem., Greenville, S.C., 1970; EdB, Wade Hampton Coll., Florence, S.C., 1956. Ordained to ministry Internat. Pentecostal Holiness Ch., 1952. Evangelist Internat. Pentecostal Holiness Ch., Lake City, S.C., 1950-54; pastor Internat. Pentecostal Holiness Ch., Columbia, S.C., 1954-75; dir. world missions and evangelism Internat. Pentecostal Holiness Ch. of S.C. Conf., 1975-82; supt. S.C. Conf. Internat. Pentecostal Holiness Ch. of S.C. Conf., Lake City, 1982-85; asst. gen. supt., vice chmn., dir. evangelism, world missions, armed forces dept. Internat. Pentecostal Holiness Ch. of S.C. Conf., Oklahoma City, 1985—; chmn. bd. trustees Holmes Coll. of the Bible, 1979—; gen. exec. bd. Gen. Bd. Administrn. Internat. Pentecostal Holiness Ch., Oklahoma City, 1985—; mem. bd. adminstrn. Nat. Assn. Evangelicals, Wheaton, Ill., 1990—, Pentecostal Fellowship N.Am., 1990—. State constable, S.C., 1976; notary publ., S.C., 1982. With U.S. Army, 1944-46, PTO. Mem. Am. Legion. Republican. Home: 8117 Willow Creek Blvd Oklahoma City OK 73162 Office: Pentecostal Holiness Ch PO Box 12609 Oklahoma City OK 73157-2609 *While much of society place great emphasis on self, independence and personal fulfillment, we would do well to remember that a fulfilled life is a life lived out for others, interdependent and challenging others to fulfillment.*

SIMMONS, JOHN EDWARD, minister; b. Charleston, W.Va., Dec. 11, 1955; s. John Henry and Ruth Elisabeth (Lawrence) S.; m. Lisa Beth Gillian, May 20, 1978; children: Timothy Davin, Chelsea Gillian. AA in Recreation, W.Va. State Coll., 1978; BS in Acctg., Univ. Louisville, 1981; MDiv, So. Seminary, Louisville, 1984. Ordained to ministry Am. Bapt. Chs. U.S.A., 1984. Intern Hanover (Ind.) Bapt. Ch., 1984; pastor Calvary Bapt. Ch., Shelbyville, Ind., 1984-86; pastor 1st Bapt. Ch., Webster Springs, W.Va., 1986-91, Weston, W.Va., 1991—; mem. min.'s adv. coun. Alderson Broaddus Coll., Philippi, W.Va., 1989-91; moderator Nicholas/Webster Assn., W.Va., 1989-90; del. Am. Bapt. Chs. USA, Charleston, 1991; treas., v.p. Webster County Ministerial Assn., 1986-91. Steering com. Church and Aging Project W.Va. Univ. Morgantown, W.Va., 1991. Mem. W.Va. Minister's Counsel. Democrat. Home: 622 Locust Ave Weston WV 26452 Office: 1st Bapt Ch 132 E 2d St Weston WV 26452 *Ministry is helping people; helping them discover God's plan for their lives; helping them through crisis; helping them prepare for eternity. Ministers must always be aware of their calling to equip others for ministry.*

SIMMONS, PAUL DEWAYNE, minister, theology educator; b. Troy, Tenn., July 18, 1936; s. Dewey Benjamin and Jewell LaVerne (Brown) S.; m. Betty Jo Kinlaw, Dec. 15, 1962; children: Brent, Brian, Catherine. AA, S.W. Bapt. Coll., Bolivar, Mo., 1956; BA, Union U., 1958; BDiv, Southeastern Bapt. Theol. Sem., 1962, MTh, 1967; PhD, So. Bapt. Theol. Sem., 1970. Ordained to ministry Bapt. Ch., 1957. Pastor First Bapt. Ch., Liberty, N.C., 1961-66; prof. christian ethics So. Bapt. Theol. Sem., Louisville, 1970—; dir. Clarence Jordan Ctr., 1985—. Author: Growing Up with Sex, 1973, Birth and Death: Bioethical Decision Making, 1983, Personhood, The Bible and the Abortion Debate, 1990; contbg. author: Abortion Rights and Fetal Personhood, 1990, Abortion, Medicine and the Law, 4th edit., 1992; editor, contbr.: Issues in Christian Ethics, 1980. Bioethicist instl. rev. bd. Humana Hosp., Audubon, Ky., 1985—; bioethicist IVF ethics rev. bd. Norton Hosp., 1989—. Democrat. Home: 2006 Bainbridge Row Dr Louisville KY 40207 Office: So Bapt Theol Sem 2825 Lexington Rd Louisville KY 40280

SIMMONS, PERRY, JR., minister; b. Cairo, Ga., Dec. 12, 1947; s. Perry and Pinkie Simmons; m. Elaine Griffin, Aug. 4, 1973; children: Perry III, Latoya, Tamara, Orinthius Jermaine. BA, Morris Brown Coll., Atlanta, 1970; DD (hon.), Faith Coll. and Sem., Birmingham, Ala., 1977; MTh, Internat. Sem., Orlando, Fla., 1981. Lic. to ministry Nat. Bapt. Conv., U.S.A., 1966, ordained, 1973. Pastor Union Bapt. Ch., Moultrie, Ga., 1973-75, Macedonia lst Bapt. Ch., Valdosta, Ga., 1975-76, Mt. Pleasant Bapt. Ch., Waycros, Ga., 1976-82, Abyssinian Bapt. Ch., Newark, 1982—; chmn. com. to feed nameless Newark North Jersey Com. Black Churchmen, 1982—; dir. New Day, Newark, 1989—; pres. Simmons Scholarship & Community Svc. Corp., Newark, 1987—. Author: Have You Got Good Religion, 1988. Pres. Newark Bd. Edn., 1990—. Recipient Outstanding Leadership award Abyssinian Bapt. Ch., 1984, Religious Achievement award Morris Brown Coll., 1984; Oct. 27 proclaimed as Perry Simmons Day, Essex County, 1990. Mem. Masons, Omega Psi Phi (life). Home: 39 Girard Pl Newark NJ 07108 Office: Abyssinian Bapt Ch 224 W Kinney St Newark NJ 07103

SIMMONS, TEDD C., pastor, educator; b. Dayton, Ohio, Mar. 29, 1956; s. Theo Clifton and Mary (Bergendaht) S.; m. Susan Ann Simmons, Feb. 8, 1978; children: Adam Joel, Todd Matthew. BA, Anderson (Ind.) U., 1978; MDiv, Anderson Sch. of Theology, 1985, MA in Applied Theology, 1988; postgrad., Trinity Evang. Coll. Assoc. pastor East Side Ch. of God, Anderson, 1985-88, Community Ch. of Greenwood, Ind., 1988-89; seminar instr. Walk Thru the Bible Ministries, Atlanta, 1985—; pastor Christ Community Ch., Greenwood, 1989—; mem. adj. faculty Trinity Coll., Deerfield, Ill., 1988-90. Mem. adv. bd. Tucson Home for Unwed Mothers, 1982-84, Sr. Adult Ministries of Tucson, 1982-84; bd. dirs. Youth for Christ, Ohio, 1979-80. Mem. Nat. Assn. Evangs., Nat. Assn. Dirs. of Ch. Edn., Christian Ministry Mgmt. Assn. Office: Christ Community Ch 430 N Madison Ave Unit 2 Greenwood IN 46142

SIMMONS, WILLIAM WELLS, lay worker; b. Colorado Springs, Colo., Sept. 5, 1933; s. Thomas Gerowe and Margaret (Wells) S.; m. Barbara Wharton Brill, May 27, 1955; children: Marcus, Mylinda, Mindy, Marsden. Student, Brown U., 1951-53; BA, U. Colo., 1958, MD, 1959; MPH, U. Calif., Berkeley, 1967. Diplomate Am. Bd. Preventive Medicine. Commd. ensign USN, 1955, advanced through grades to capt., 1973, ret., 1982; intern Naval Hosp., Oakland, Calif., 1959-60; resident in medicine Naval Hosp., Portsmouth, Va., 1963-64; resident in preventive medicine U. Calif., Berkeley, 1966-67; resident in aerospace medicine Naval Aerospace Med. Inst., Pensacola, Fla., 1967-69; resident in psychiatry Nat. Naval Med. Ctr., Bethesda, Md., 1977-80; sr. med. officer USS Constellation, 1969-71; asst. dir. tng. Naval Aerospace Med. Inst., Pensacola, 1971-72, head tng. dept., 1972-74; head aerospace medicine ops. BUMED, Washington, 1974-77; staff psychiatrist Naval Regional Med. Ctr., Portsmouth, 1980-82; lay reader Diocese of San Joaquin, Episcopal Ch., Calif., 1965-66, Diocese of Calif., 1966-67, Diocese of Cen. Gulf Coast, Fla., 1973-74, Diocese of Washington, 1978-80, Diocese of Southern Va., 1983-88; lay eucharistic min. Diocese of S.W. Fla., 1988—; mem. staff Tidewater Pastoral Counseling Svcs., Inc., 1983-86; ret., 1986; mgr. Open Door Bookstore, St. Boniface Episcopal Ch., Sarasota, Fla., 1989—. Scoutmaster Boy Scouts Am., Pensacola, Fla., 1973-74. Recipient Julian E. Ward Meml. award Aerospace Med. Assn. , 1970. Fellow Am. Coll. Preventive Medicine; mem. Am. Psychiat. Assn., Retired Officer's Assn. Republican. Office: St Boniface Episcopal Ch 5615 Midnight Pass Rd Sarasota FL 34242 *The greatest amount of good for the human race and the planet will be done by those people who will take responsibility for what they have done, and make amends wherever possible.*

SIMMS, ALBERT EGERTON, minister, retirement communities consultant; b. Raleigh, N.C., Jan. 24, 1918; s. Robert Nirwana and Virginia Adelaide (Egerton) S.; m. Helen Frances Canaday, Jan. 1, 1941; children: Albert Egerton Jr., Mary Helen, David Ernest. BA, Wake Forest U., 1938; postgrad., So. Bapt. Theol. Sem., Louisville, 1939-40, Va. Poly. Inst. & State U., 1976. Lic. nursing home adminstr. Pastor Wendell Bapt. Ch., Wendell, N.C., 1937-39; pastor Bear Swamp Bapt. Ch., Littleton, N.C., 1941-46, Littleton Bapt. Ch., 1943-46, Calvary Bapt. Ch., Newport News, Va., 1946-60, Rivermont Ave Bapt. Ch., Lynchburg, Va., 1960-74; adminstr. Lakewood Manor Retirement Community, Richmond, Va., 1974-83; interim adminstr. Springmoor Retirement Community, Raleigh, 1985; ind. cons. to retirement communities Va., N.C., 1982—; bd. dirs. So. Bapt. Home Mission Bd., Atlanta. Contbr. articles in Religious Herald, Christian Herald. Mem. customer adv. coun., U.S. Postal Svc., Richmond; solicitor United way campaigns, Newport News, Lynchburg, Richmond. Mem. Va. Assn. Non-Profit Homes for Aging (sec. 1979-81, bd. dirs. 1976-81, hon. life mem.), Richmond Bapt. Assn. (exec. com. 1986-89), Exec. Club Newport News, Rotary, Kiwanis. Home and Office: 1514 Chauncey Ln Richmond VA 23233

SIMON, ARTHUR, minister; b. Eugene, Oreg., July 28, 1930; children: Peter, Nathan; m. Rosamund James; children: Richard, Leah. Student, Dana Coll.; BA, BD, MST, Concordia Sem.; PhD, Valparaiso U., 1983, Loyola U., Chgo., 1985. Ordained to ministry Lutheran Ch. Pres. Bread for the World, Washington, 1974—. Author: Bread for the World, 1975, 84 (Religious Book award 1976), Christian Faith & Public Policy, 1987, Harvesting Peace, 1990. Recipient Presdl. End Hunger award U.S. Aid, Washington, 1990. Home: 3907 Newton St Colmar Manor MD 20722 Office: Bread for the World 802 Rhode Island Ave NE Washington DC 20018

SIMON, MORDECAI, religious association administrator, clergyman; b. St. Louis, July 19, 1925; s. Abraham M. and Rose (Solomon) S.; m. Maxine R. Abrams, July 4, 1954; children: Ora, Eve, Avrom. BA, St. Louis U., 1947;

MA, Washington U., St. Louis, 1952; MHL, Rabbi, Jewish Theol. Sem. Am., N.Y.C., 1952, DD (hon.), 1977. Ordained rabbi, 1952; rabbi in Mpls., 1952-56, Waterloo, Iowa, 1956-63; exec. dir. Chgo. Bd. Rabbis, 1963-80, exec. v.p., 1980—; nat. chaplain Jewish War Vets., 1977-78. Host: weekly TV program What's Nu?, Sta. WGN-TV, 1973—. Mem. Jewish Community Rels. Coun., Jewish United Fund.; mem. nat. council Joint Distbn. Com., Religious Leaders Com. With AUS, 1943-46. Recipient citation Jewish War Vets., 1967, citation Boy Scouts Am., 1966, 74, 88, citation Chgo. chpt. Am. Jewish Congress, 1973, citation Chgo. Conf. Jewish Women's Orgns., 1973, citation Chgo. Bd. Rabbis, 1973, Rabbinical Service award of Appreciation Jewish Theol. Sem. Am., 1988, Raoul Wallenberg Humanitarian award, 1989. Mem. Rabbinical Assembly, Coun. Religious Leaders Met. Chgo. Home: 621 County Line Rd Highland Park IL 60035 Office: 1 S Franklin Chicago IL 60606

SIMON, RALPH, rabbi; b. Newark, Oct. 19, 1906; s. Isaac and Yetta (Biddleman) S.; m. Kelsey Hoffer, June 30, 1931; children—Matthew, Tamar (Mrs. Tamar Hoffs), Jonathan Carmi. B.A., Coll. City N.Y., 1927; M. in Hebrew Lit, Jewish Theol. Sem., 1931; M.A., Columbia, 1943; postgrad., Oriental Inst. U. Chgo., 1944-47; D.D., Jewish Theol Sem., 1964; D.H.L., Spertus Coll. Judaica, 1972. Ordained rabbi, 1931. Rabbi Congregation Rodef Sholom, Johnstown, Pa., 1931-36, Jewish Center, Jackson Heights, N.Y., 1937-43, Congregation Rodfei Zedek, Chgo., 1943—; dir. Jewish Fedn. Met. Chgo., 1949-61; founder Camp Ramah, Conover, Wis., 1947; Pres. Chgo. Bd. Rabbis, 1952-54, Chgo. Council Rabbinical Assembly, 1943-45, Council Hyde Park and Kenwood Churches and Synagogues, 1956; mem. Ill. Bd. Mental Health Commrs., 1957-67, Chgo. Commn. on Human Resources, 1958-71; gen. chmn. Combined Jewish Appeal Met. Chgo., 1967, Bonds for Israel Campaign Greater Chgo., 1965-66; v.p. Rabbinical Assembly Am., 1966-67, pres., 1968-69; v.p. Bur. for Careers in Jewish Service, 1969-70; bd. dirs. World Council Synagogues, 1974—. Author: Challenges and Responses-Messages for the High Holy Day Period, 1985. Editorial writer: Sentinal Mag, 1976—. Recipient Julius Rosenwald award Jewish Fedn. Met. Chgo., 1991; named Man of Yr., Israel Bonds, 1976; named to Sr. Citizens Hall of Fame, 1979; Jewish Theol. Sem. created professorship, Ralph Simon chair in Jewish Ethics and Mysticism, 1959. Clubs: Standard (Chgo.), Idlewild Country (Chgo.). Home: 5000 East End Ave Chicago IL 60615 Office: 5200 Hyde Park Blvd Chicago IL 60615

SIMONDS, MILFORD DALE, minister; b. St. Paul, May 29, 1944; s. Robert Alonzo and Mildred Esther (Sundsmo) S.; m. Celesta Ann Dunbar, Apr. 5, 1969; children: Mary Ann (dec.), Lori Ann, Pamela Kay. BA, MidAm. Nazarene Coll., 1973; diploma in vocat. rehab., U. Wis., Menomonie, 1975; cert. in counseling, Braham Mental Health, 1983. Ordained to ministry Assemblies of God, 1986. Pastor Ch. of the Nazarene, Arnold Nebr, Nebr., 1977-80; asst. pastor Ch. of the Nazarene, North St. Paul, 1980-82; pastor Ch. of the Nazarene, Mora, Minn., 1982-84, Assemblies of God, Palisade, Minn., 1984-87, The Victory Ch., Dodge Center, Minn., 1988—; pres. Ministerial Assn., Arnold, 1978-79; speaker Nat. Counseling and Resource Ctr., Rochester, Minn., 1990—. Author: It Is Outright Spiritual Warfare, 1990. Hosp. chaplain Mora, 1982-84; commr. Dodge Center Star City Commn., 1989-90; dir. Econ. Devel. Corp., 1989—; bd. dirs. Housing and Redevel. Authority, 1990—. Staff sgt. USAF, 1988-90, Vietnam. Decorated Bronze Star, Air medal. Mem. Dodge Center Ministerial Assn. (sec. 1991—), Am. Legion (chaplain local post 1991—). Republican. Office: The Victory Ch 102 N Central Ave Dodge Center MN 55927 *There are many persons living around us that are hurting in so many ways, and who needs to have someone in whom they can turn to who truly cares. I want to be that person. Just to be able to give a helping hand to someone who needs it, is reward.*

SIMONE, JOSEPH, clergyman, educator; b. Bridgeport, Conn., Jan. 13, 1924; s. Dominic and Anna (Mastrianni) S.; B.A., Elon Coll., 1958; M.A., Andover Newton Theol. Sch., 1968; m. Viola Ruskay, June 27, 1953; children—J. Scott, Zachary D., Claudia A. Ordained to ministry Congl. Ch., 1960; pastor Congl. Ch., Chicopee Falls, Mass., 1958-61, 1st Congl. Ch., Farmington, N.H., 1961-63, Hope Congl. Ch., East Providence, R.I., 1963-65, All Souls Ch., Lowell, Mass., 1965-69; tchr. English, also guidance counselor, 1969-87 . Chmn. ecumenical commn. Greater Lowell Council Chs., 1967-68; founder Ecumenical Dialogue with Clergymen and Laymen, Lowell, 1966, Radio Ministry on Ecumenism, Lowell, 1966-69; chaplain Roger Hall Sch. for Girls, Lowell, 1965-69. Bd. dirs. Jewish-Arab Ednl. Fund, Lowell Served with AUS, 1942-45. Mem. Andover Assn. Ministers United Ch. of Christ (adv. com. 1966-87), Assn. Clin. Pastoral Edn., Am., Mass. sch. counselors assns., N.E.A., Nat. Vocational Guidance Assn., Am. Personnel and Guidance Assn., Sigma Mu Sigma (v.p. 1957). Mason. Home: 117 Jenkins Rd Andover MA 01810

SIMONEAUX, MICHEL S., minister, music educator; b. New Orleans, May 6, 1939; s. John N. Simoneaux and Myrtle (Gustine) Wiest; m. Bonnie Jean Rushing, July 5, 1959; children: Stephen, Susan. B Music Edn. with distinction, Miss. Coll., 1965; M Ch. Music, Bapt. Theol Sem., New Orleans, 1967, EdD in Music, 1969. Music missionary to Japan So. Bapt. Ch. Fgn. Mission Bd., Richmond, Va., 1969-81; min. music So. Bapt. Ch. Fgn. Mission Bd., Pensacola, Fla., 1981-86; chmn. music dept. Palm Beach Atlantic Coll., West Palm Beach, Fla., 1986-88; interpreter, music asst. Billy Graham Evangelist Assn., Greenville, S.C., 1980; part-time music dir. local chs. Palm Beach County, 1986—. Contbr. articles to jours. in field. Bd. dirs. Young Audiences, West Palm Beach, 1989—; Fla. Bapt. Childrn's Homes, Jacksonville, 1989-90, Morikami Mus., Delray Beach, Fla., 1991. With USAF, 1957-61. Mem. Fla. Bapt. Ch. Music Conf., So. Bapt. Ch. Music Conf., Nat. Assn. Teachers Singing, Nat. Assn. Schs. Music. Repub lican. Avocations: yard work, travel, Japenese language. Home: 201 Linda Ln West Palm Beach FL 33405 Office: Palm Beach Atlantic Coll 901 S Flagler Dr West Palm Beach FL 33401

SIMONIS, ADRIANUS JOHANNES CARDINAL, archbishop; b. Lisse, Rotterdam, The Netherlands, Nov. 26, 1931. ordained priest Roman Cath. Ch., 1957. Consecrated bishop Rotterdam, 1971; archbishop Utrecht, 1983—; proclaimed cardinal, 1985. Address: Bishop's Conf, POB 13049, 3508 LA Utrecht The Netherlands also: Aartsbisdom, Maliebaan 40, POB 14019, 3509 SB Utrecht The Netherlands

SIMONSON, CHARLES HENRY, minister; b. N.Y.C., Mar. 27, 1940; s. Charles Emil and Catherine (Byers) S.; m. Leslie Stewart, Dec. 13, 1969; 1 child, Mary. BA, CCNY, 1963; MDiv, Union Theol. Sem., 1968. Ordained to ministry United Ch. Christ, 1968. Asst. pastor Barrington (R.I.) Congl. Ch., 1968-72; asst. warden The Abbey on Iona, Scotland, 1972-76; co-pastor Ridgeview Congl. Ch., White Plains, N.Y., 1976-82; pastor South Ch., Peabody, Mass., 1983-88, Westmore Community Ch., Browningtom Congl. Ch., Orleans, Vt., 1988—; chmn. Vt. Conf. Com. on Evangelism, 1986—; mem. The Iona Community, 1972—; sec. Iona New World Found., 1986—. Vol. U.S. Peace Corps, East Pakistan, Bangladesh, 1963-65. Mem. Border Area Clergy Assn.. Home and Office: Westmore and Browningtom Chs PO Box 214 Greensboro VT 05841

SIMPKINSON, CHARLES HOFFMAN, psychologist, magazine publisher; b. Cin., Nov. 3, 1934; s. Helen (Hoffman) Simpkinson; m. Anne Adamcewicz, Sept. 24, 1978. BA, Williams Coll., 1958; PhD, U. Tenn., 1972. Mem. staff NTL Inst., Washington, 1969-71; mem. faculty dept. psychiatry Johns Hopkins Med. Sch., Balt., 1970-72; mem. staff Montgomery County Dept. Health, Rockville, Md., 1972-85; pvt. practice Bethesda, Md., 1974—; pub., founder Family Therapy Networker Mag., Washington, 1975-85, Common Boundary Mag., Chevy Chase, Md., 1980—. Author: Synopsis of Family Therapy Practice, 1978, Alternative Psychotherapy Training Programs, 1990. Recipient Disting. Svc. award Md. Psychol. Assn., Columbia, 1978. Mem. APA (pres. div. II, Md. chpt. 1974—), Assn. Transpersonal Psychology. Democrat. Episcopalian. Home: 7005 Florida St Chevy Chase MD 20815 Office: Common Boundary Inc 4304 East-West Hwy Bethesda MD 20814 *Understanding the psychological aspects of spiritual development and the spiritual dimensions of psychological health are the great questions of our decade.*

SIMPSON, CHARLES EDWARD, minister; b. Little Rock, Feb. 11, 1948; s. Charles L. and Ruth M. (Greenwood) S.; m. Helen L. Jackson, Aug. 2, 1969 (dec.); children: Kelli Joe, Amanda Michel; m. Pam Wallace, Dec. 15, 1989. BA, Ouachita U., 1970; MDiv, Southwestern Bapt. Theol. Sem., 1973; postgrad., Midwestern Theol. Sem., Mo., 1982-87. Ordained to ministry So. Bapt. Conv., 1966. Pastor chs. in La., 1969-70, Tex., 1972-73, Ark., 1973-78; pastor Lonoke (Ark.) Bapt. Ch., 1978-91, lst Bapt. Ch., Sheridan, Ark., 1991—; mem. exec. bd. Ark. Bapt. Conv., 1975-77, mem. nominating com., 1982—; bd. dirs. Christian Civic Found., Little Rock, 1976-79. Author: History of the Baptists in Israel, 1973, From My Life to His, 1984. Maj. USAR, 1982—. Mem. Rotary, Kiwanis (pres. Lonoke 1980), Optimists (pres. Lonoke 1974-75). Home: Rte 2 Box 515 Sheridan AR 72150 Office: lst Bapt Ch Sheridan AR 72150

SIMPSON, DEANNA LYNN, Christian education director; b. Amarillo, Tex., May 26, 1956; d. Carl V. and Audean (Gray) S. BS in Interior Design, Stepen F. Austin State U., 1978; MA in Christian Edn., Asbury Theol. Sem., Wilmore, Ky., 1989. Salesperson Gabberts Furniture, Dallas, 1979-86; salesperson, asst. mgr. Wood Works Plus, Carrollton, Tex., 1986-87; Christian edn. dir. Washington Crossing (Pa.) United Meth. Ch., 1989—. Mem. Profl. Assn. Christian Educators. Republican. Office: Washington Crossing UMC 1895 Wrightstown Rd Washington Crossing PA 18977 *Who better to guide you in writing meaningful chapters of your life than the Author of life? God gives the inspiration for us to live our lives so that His kingdom is advanced.*

SIMPSON, GARY MARTIN, theology educator; b. Saginaw, Mich., Dec. 17, 1950; s. Charles Maurice and Rita Elizabeth (Klemm) S.; m. Sharon Kay Geiger, July 5, 1975; children: Lara Schoen, Elena Kay, Krista Ann. AA, Concordia Jr. Coll., Ann Arbor, Mich., 1970; BA, Concordia Sr. Coll., Ft. Wayne, Ind., 1972; MDiv, Christ Sem.-Seminex, St. Louis, 1976, ThD, 1983. Ordained to ministry Luth. Ch., 1977. Worker-priest Immanuel Luth. Ch., Alameda, Calif., 1976-83; minister St. Charles (Mo.) Christian Ch., 1980-83; pastor Resurrection Luth. Ch., Portland, Oreg., 1983-90; assoc. prof. Luther Northwestern Theol. Sem., St. Paul, 1990—; chair commn. Ecumenical Ministries of Oreg., Portland, 1984-89; moderator ch. community action program Snow Cap, Portland, 1984-89; chair Jewish-Christian Assn. Oreg., Portland, 1986-87. Contbr. articles to profl. publs. Chair Oreg. Task Force on Hunger, Salem, 1989-90; v.p. Oreg. Holocaust Resource Ctr., Portland, 1986-87. Fuerbringer Fellow, 1980-83; named Religious Leader of Yr., Mid-County Memo, 1988. Mem. Am. Acad. Religion. Home: 916 Wheelock Pkwy E Saint Paul MN 55106 Office: Luth Northwestern Theol Sem 2481 Como Ave Saint Paul MN 55108 *The promise of God in Christ represents a promise worth promoting.*

SIMPSON, GARY WILLIAM, minister; b. Cape Town, Republic of South Africa, May 24, 1965; came to U.S., 1986; s. Harry William and Bernice (Wentzel) S. Diploma of theology, So. Africa Bible Sch., 1985; BA in Bible, Lubbock (Tex.) Christian U., 1988; cert. grad. studies, Sunset Sch. Preaching, Lubbock, 1989; postgrad., Abilene Christian U. Part-time youth worker Ch. of Christ, Johannesburg, Republic of South Africa, 1984-85; youth min. Ch. of Christ, Shallowater, Tex., 1987—; with Sentinel Bookstores, Lubbock, 1989—; camp counselor Skyridge Christian Youth Camp, Carlsbad, N.Mex., 1987, 89; youth camp speaker Quartz Mountain Christian Camp, Altus, Okla., 1988, Durban (Republic of South Africa) Youth Campy, 1985; lectureship speaker Durban Ch. of Christ, 1985. Recipient Christian Worker award Quartz Mountain Christian Camp, 1988. Mem. Soc. Bibl. Lit., Kyodai Club (chaplain 1987-88) Mission Outreach Club (v.p. 1987-88). Home: 5504 21st St Lubbock TX 79407 *The Lord will accomplish His aims in my life. Whether or not His purposes serve mine is a matter that only I can decide.*

SIMPSON, H. KENT, religious organization administrator; b. Big Spring, Tex., Sept. 19, 1951; s. Harold K. and Winona (Lawson) S.; m. Andrea Lynn Simpson, May 19, 1991; 1 child, Jenny Lynn. AAS in Mgmt., Odessa Coll., 1975; ABA, U. Okla., 1981, OBA, 1982. Chmn. bd. deacons Christian Ch., Odessa, Tex., 1974-75; pres., chief exec. officer Rolling Hills Bank, Piedmont, Okla., 1984-87; elder, min., prophet Cornerstone Ch., Roanoke, Tex., 1987—; prophetic min. Found. Ministries, Azel, Tex., 1990—; founder, dir. Prophetic Ministries Today, Ft. Worth, 1990—; speaker Full Gospel Businessmen, Ft. Worth, 1987—. Office: Prophetic Ministries Today PO Box 820882 Fort Worth TX 76182-0882 *Revelation from our heavenly Father is the requirement for all successful direction in this life. Hearing the Spirit of God speaking in our spiritual ears carries the ordinances of success. Gracefully giving faith to walk boldly in unknown territories. For faith comes by hearing and hearing the word of God.*

SIMPSON, LINDA MARIE, lay worker; b. New Castle, Pa., May 3, 1962; d. Ronald Carl and Carol Jean (Wyza) Doak. BS, U. Pitts., 1984. Cert. kindergarten tchr., Pa. Dir. youth, staff asst. 1st Presbyn. Ch., New Castle, 1988—; adult del. Presbyn. Youth Triennium, Purdue, Ind., 1989. Home: 519 Gardner Center Rd New Castle PA 16101 Office: 1st Presbyn Ch 125 N Jefferson St New Castle PA 16101

SIMPSON, MARY MICHAEL, priest, psychotherapist; b. Evansville, Ind., Dec. 1; d. Link Wilson and Mary Garrett (Price) S. B.A., B.S., Tex. Women's U., 1946; grad. N.Y. Tng. Sch. for Deaconesses, 1949; grad., Westchester Inst. Tng. in Psychoanalysis and Psychotherapy, 1976; S.T.M., Gen. Theol. Sem., 1982. Missionary Holy Cross Mission, Bolahun, Liberia, 1950-52; acad. head Margaret Hall Sch., Versailles, Ky., 1958-61; pastoral counselor on staff Cathedral St. John the Divine, N.Y.C., 1974-87, canon residentiary, canon counselor, 1977-87, hon. canon, 1988—; ordained priest Episcopal Ch., 1977; cons. psychotherapist Union Theol. Sem., 1980-83; dir. Cathedral Counseling Service, 1975-87; priest-in-charge St. John's Ch. Wilmot, New Rochelle, N.Y., 1987-88; pvt. practice psycholanalyst, 1974—; Bd. dirs. Westchester Inst. Tng. in Psychoanalysis and Psychotherapy, 1982-84; trustee Council on Internat. and Pub. Affairs, 1983-87. Mem. Nat. Assn. Advancement of Psychoanalysis, N.Y. State Assn. Practicing Psychotherapists, N.Y. Soc. Clin. Psychologists. Author: The Ordination of Women in the American Episcopal Church: the Present Situation, 1981; contbg. author: Yes to Women Priests, 1978. Home and Office: 215 E 95th St #3J New York NY 10128

SIMPSON, ROBERT L., counseling and Christian education director; b. Corsica, Pa., Aug. 11, 1927; s. Alverdi and Harriot (Sherman) S.; m. Bridget Simpson, May 30, 1947; children: Susan R., David L. M in Ministry, Internat. Bible Inst. & Sem., 1985, D Ministry with honors, 1987, PhD, 1990. Dir. counseling and Christian edn. Cornerstone Christian Ministries Inc., Huntsville, Ala., tchr. Bible topics and Jewish history. With USMS, 1943-46. Mem. AACD, Am. Mental Health Counselors Assn., Am. Assn. Christian Counselors, Nat. Assn. Evangelicals. Home: 11412 Maplecrest Dr SE Huntsville AL 38503 Office: Cornerstone Christian Ministries 3801 Triana Blvd Ste 4 Huntsville AL 35805

SIMPSON, ROBERT LEATHAM, clergyman, retired church official; b. Salt Lake City, Aug. 8, 1915; s. Heber C. and Lillie Clarissa (Leatham) S.; m. Jelaire Kathryn Chandler, June 24, 1942; children: Steven Chandler, Jelaire Christine, Kathryn Marie, Robert Michael. A.A., Santa Monica City Coll., 1937; student, U. So. Calif., 1942, Yale U., 1944. Missionary Mormon Ch., N.Z., 1937-40; pres. N.Z. Mission, 1958-61; 1st counselor to Presiding Bishopric, Salt Lake City, 1961-72; asst. to Council of Twelve Apostles, 1972-76; mem. 1st Quorum of the Seventy, 1976—; mng. dir. dept. social service Mormon Ch., 1972-74; Ch. area supr. South Pacific, 1975-78; pres. Los Angeles Temple, LDS, 1980-82; adminstr. for SE Asia Mormon Ch., 1982-84, gen. authority emeritus, 1989—; former dir. Zion Securities Corp., ZCMI Dept. Stores, Heber J. Grant Ins. Co., Beneficial Life Ins. Co., Deseret Gymnasium. Served to capt. USAAF, 1943-46. Recipient Silver Beaver and Silver Antelope awards Boy Scouts Am. Home: 822 Grandridge Dr Salt Lake City UT 84103 Office: 50 E North Temple Salt Lake City UT 84150 *As a very young man, a Church call sent me to the South Pacific for three years to work closely with the Polynesians (Maoris of New Zealand). These loving, warm folks lived simple lives. They taught me that the most important thing in life is people and that caring about others brings the greatest fulfillment. My priorities changed dramatically as these wonderful new friends taught me to simplify my life style, to accept all people, to be forgiving, and indeed to follow the teachings of the Master. I had been sent 8,000 miles to teach, and I was taught.*

SIMPSON, WALTER ROBERT, JR., minister; b. Marrero, La., Jan. 29, 1926; s. Walter Robert and Isabelle July (Brissalara) S.; m. Doris Elsie Mehrtens, June 5, 1957; children: Sheryl Lynn, Walter III, Diane Elaine. Student, La. State U., 1948-50; BA, Simpson Coll., 1954; MMin, Eden Theol. Sem., 1958. Ordained to ministry United Ch. of Christ. Pastor Round Grove United Ch. of Christ, Lewisville, Tex., 1958-59, Zion United Ch. of Christ, Clifton, Tex., 1959-68, St. Paul United Ch. of Christ, Schulenburg, Tex., 1968-84, Dodge Meml. United Ch. of Christ, Council Bluffs, Iowa, 1984—; bd. dirs. South Cen. Conf. United Ch. of Christ, Tex., 1968-82; vice moderator Southwestern Assn., Iowa Conf. United Ch. of Christ, 1990—, chmn. planning and coord. team, 1990-92, bd. dirs., 1988-92. With U.S. Army, 1946-48. Home: 308 N 32nd Council Bluffs IA 51501 Office: Dodge Meml Congl United Ch of Christ 3200 Ave C Council Bluffs IA 51501

SIMPSON, WILLIAM A., religious organization administrator; b. Sioux Falls, S.D., Aug. 14, 1935; s. Robert Jacob and Lillian (Borgendale) S.; m. Beverly Joan Rund, Nov. 25, 1955; children: Valerie Ann Simpson Peters, Steven Alan. BA, Augustana Coll., 1957; MS, George Williams Coll., 1959. Exec. dir. YMCA, Worthington, Minn., 1968-85; bus. adminstr. First Luth. Ch., Sioux Falls, 1985—. Mem. Nat. Assn. Ch. Bus. Adminstrn. Office: First Lutheran Church 327 S Dakota Ave Sioux Falls SD 57102

SIMS, BENNETT JONES, clergyman, academic administrator; b. Greenfield, Mass., Aug. 9, 1920; s. Lewis Raymond and Sarah Cosette (Jones) S.; children: Laura (Mrs. John P. Boucher), Grayson, David. AB, Baker U., 1943, LHD (hon.), 1985; postgrad., Princeton Theol. Sem., 1946-47; B.D., Va. Theol. Sem., 1949, D.D., 1966; D.D., U. of South, 1972; Merrill fellow, Harvard U., 1964-65; postgrad., Cath. U., 1969-71. Ordained to ministry Episc. Ch. as deacon, 1949, priest, 1950. Rector Ch. of Redeemer, Balt., 1951-64; dir. continuing edn. Va. Theol. Sem., 1966-72; bishop of Atlanta, 1972-83; vis. prof. theology Emory U., Atlanta, 1980-88, pres. Inst. for Servant Leadership, 1988—; priest-in-charge St. Alban's Ch., Tokyo, 1962; spl. lectr. Diocesan Confs., U.S., overseas, 1969-90. Trustee U. of South. With USNR, 1943-46. Named Young Man of Yr. Balt. C. of C., 1953; Disting. Alumnus of Yr., Baker U., 1972. Office: Inst Servant Leadership Hendersonville NC 28793

SIMS, JOSEPH DARYL, minister; b. Mobile, Ala., June 24, 1959; s. William Rex and Barbara Ann (Elliott) S.; m. Cheryl Dawn Shelton, June 20, 1981; children: Kyle Joseph, Cory William. BS, U. Montevallo, 1982; MRE, New Orleans Bapt. Theol. Sem., 1985. Ordained to ministry So. Bapt. Conv., 1985. Min. youth 1st Bapt. Ch., Clanton, Ala., 1980-82, La Place, La., 1983-85, Monroe, La., 1985-89, McKinney, Tex., 1989-91, Windermere, Fla., 1991—. Home: PO Box 876 Windermere FL 34786-0876 Office: 1st Bapt Ch 300 Main St PO Box 250 Windermere FL 34786-0250

SIN, JAIME LACHICA CARDINAL, archbishop of Manila; b. New Washington, Aklan, The Philippines, Aug. 31, 1928; s. Juan C. and Maxima R. (Lachica) S.; B.S. in Edn., Immaculate Conception Coll., 1959; LL.D. (hon.), Adamson U., 1975, Angeles U., 1978; S.T.D. (hon.), U. Santo Tomas, 1977; L.H.D. (hon.), De La Salle U., 1975; LLD (hon.), Adamson U., 1975. Ordained priest Roman Cath. Ch.; missionary priest Diocese of Capiz, Philippines, 1954-57; first rector St. Pius X Sem., Roxas City, 1957-67; domestic prelate of Pope John XXIII, 1960; titular bishop of Obba, from 1967; aux. bishop of Jaro, from 1967; apostolic adminstr. Sede Plena, archdiocese of Jaro, from 1970; titular archbishop of Massa Lubrense; met. archbishop of Jaro, from 1972; met. archbishop of Manila, 1974—; elevated to Sacred Coll. of Cardinals, 1976; pres. Cath. Bishops' Conf. of the Philippines, 1977; mem. Sacred Congregation for Cath. Edn., 1978—, Sacred Congregation for the Evangelization of Peoples, 1978—; participant Conclave, The Vatican, 1978. Recipient numerous awards and citations, latest being: Real Academia de la Lengua Española award, 1978; Ayuntamiento de Palma de Mallorca, España, award, 1978; Disting. and Meritorious Service award Am. Legion Aux., 1979; Outstanding Citizen's award Manila, 1979. Mem. Synod of Bishops. Author: The Revolution of Love, 1972; The Church Above Political Systems, 1973; A Song of Salvation, 1974; Unity in Diversity, 1974; The Future of Catholicism in Asia, 1978; Christian Basis of Human Rights, 1978; Separation, Not Isolation, 1978; Slaughter of the Innocents, 1979. Home: Villa San Miguel Shaw Blvd, Mandaluyong Metro Manila, The Philippines

SINCLAIR, J. W., religious organization administrator. Pres. The Gospel Missionary Assn., Red Deer, Alta., Can. Office: Gospel Missionary Assoc, 3901-44th St, Red Deer, AB Canada T4N 1G7*

SINCLAIR, LAWRENCE ALBERT, religion educator; b. Chgo., Sept. 19, 1930; s. James Lawrence Sinclair and Helen Marie Thompson Owens; m. Jean Marie Rabehl, June 5, 1952 (div. 1980), children: Stephen, Andrew, Susan, Elizabeth; m. Donna Alberta Behnke, July 30, 1981. BA, Carroll Coll., 1952; BD, McCormick Sem., 1955; PhD, Johns Hopkins U., 1958. Ordained to ministry United Presbyn. Ch., 1955. From asst. prof. to assoc. prof. Carroll Coll., Waukesha, Wis., 1958-67, prof., chairperson Religion dept., 1967—; vis. lectr. Marquette U., Milw., 1971—; vice-moderator Milw. Presbyn., Milw., 1972, moderator, 1973, chairperson of coun., 1974; cons. Assn. Coll. and Rsch. Librs. of the ALA, 1967—. Editor: The Psalms and Other Studies on the Old Testament, 1990. Nettie F. McCormick Grad. Fellow, 1955-57, Johns Hopkins Grad. Scholar, 1955-58, Presbyn. Grad. Fellow, 1958. Mem. Soc. of Bibl. Lit. (sec. midwest chpt. 1962-66, pres. 1971), Cath. Bibl. Soc., Chgo. Soc. of Bibl. Rsch., Am. Schs. of Oriental Rsch., Bibl. Archeol. Soc. Milw. (bd. dirs. 1981—, pres. 1985-87). Office: Carroll Coll 100 N East Ave Waukesha WI 53186

SINCLAIR, WILLIAM DONALD, church official; b. L.A., Dec. 27, 1924; s. Arthur Livingston and Lillian May (Holt) S.; m. Barbara Jean Hughes, Aug. 9, 1952; children: Paul Scott, Victoria Sharon. BA cum laude, St. Martin's Coll., Olympia, Wash., 1975; postgrad. Emory U., 1978-79. Commd. 2d lt. USAAF, 1944, advanced through grades to col., USAF, 1970; served as pilot and navigator in Italy, Korea, Vietnam and Japan; ret., 1975; bus. adminstr. First United Methodist Ch., Colorado Springs, Colo., 1976-85; bus. adminstr. Village Seven Presbyn. Ch., 1985-87; bus. adminstr. Sunrise United Meth. Ch., 1987—; vice-chmn. council fin. and adminstrn. Rocky Mountain conf. United Meth. Ch., U.S.A., 1979-83. Bd. dirs. Chins-Up Colorado Springs, 1983—, Pikes Peak Performing Arts Ctr., 1985—; pres. Pioneers Mus. Found., 1985—. Decorated Legion of Merit with oak leaf cluster, D.F.C. with oak leaf cluster, Air medal with 6 oak leaf cluster, Dept. Def. Meritorious Service medal, Vietnam Cross of Gallantry with Palms. Fellow Nat. Assn. Ch. Bus. Adminstrs. (nat. dir., regional v.p., v.p. 1983-85, pres. 1985-87; Ch. Bus. Adminstr. of Yr. award 1983), Colo. Assn. Ch. Bus. Adminstrs. (past pres.), United Meth. Assn. Ch. Bus. Adminstrs. (nat. sec. 1978-81), Christian Ministries Mgmt. Assn. (dir. 1983-85), USAF Acad. Athletic Assn. Clubs: Colorado Springs Country, Plaza, Garden of the Gods. Lodge: Rotary (pres. Downtown Colorado Springs club 1985-86), Order of Daedalians. Home: 3007 Chelton Dr Colorado Springs CO 80909 Office: Sunrise United Meth Ch 2655 Briargate Blvd Colorado Springs CO 80920 *Ten words of two letters each, spoken by a black clergyman during the civil rights crusade of the 60s, are my guide to the future: "If it is to be, it is up to me." Only with this in mind can change occur.*

SINESSIOS, archbishop. Archbishop Greek Orthodox Ch., Nubia, Sudan. Office: Greek Orthodox Ch, Nubia Sudan*

SINGER, MERLE ELLIOT, rabbi; b. Duluth, Minn., May 11, 1939; s. Samuel and Brenda (Naymark) S.; m. Myra Golden, Aug. 29, 1965; children: Jonathan, Jeremy, Michael, Mark. AB, U. Cin., 1961; BHL, M.A.H.L., Hebrew Union Coll., Cin., 1966; DHL, DD (hon.), Gwynedd-Mercy Coll., 1978. Ordained rabbi. Rabbi Temple Sinai, Washington, 1966-71, Reform Congregation Beth Or, Phila., 1971-78; sr. rabbi Temple Beth El, Boca Raton, Fla., 1978—; adj. prof. history, Judaic studies Fla. Atlantic U., Boca Raton,1978-79; adj. prof. Judaic studies Gwynedd Mercy Coll., Phila., 1975-78; instr. I.M. Wise div. Gratz Coll., Phila., 1971-76; chaplain Boca Raton Police Dept.; rabbinic and com. Camp Coleman, Union Am. Hebrew Congregations, Cleveland, Ga., 1978—. Sponsor inter-faith and Holocaust seminars for the Sisters of Mercy, faculty and students of Gwynedd Mercy Coll., 1978; Jewish student affairs advisor Phila. Coll. of Textiles and Scis., 1976-77, Villanova U., 1976-77; Rabbinic bd. overseers Hebrew Union Coll.,

1985—; campaign v.p. United Way of South Palm Beach County, 1986-87, pres., 1987-88; adv. bd. Mae Volen Sr. Ctr., Boca Raton, 1981; clergy advisor Planned Parenthood of Palm Beach County, Inc., Bocat Raton; bd. dirs. Edn. Found. of Palm Beach County, Inc., 1986-88. Recipient nat. award for outstanding svc. Domestic Policy Assn./Nat. Issues Forum, 1985-86, Ben Gurion award for Israel bonds State of Israel, 1975, 85, Torch of Liberty Humanitarian award Anti-Defamation League, 1981. Mem. South Palm Beach Bd. of Rabbis, Palm Beach Bd. of Rabbis (past pres.), Union of Am. Hebrew Congregations (com. for winning the unaffiliated), Assn. Reform ionists of Am. (bd. dirs. 1983—), Southeast Cen. Conf. Am. Rabbis (treas.), Cen. Conf. Am. Rabbis (com. on relief, subvention and solicitation), Israel Bonds (nat. rabbinic cabinet), Hebrew Union Coll. Inst. of Religion (presidents alumni assn. 1984—), Nat. Bd. Govs. Synagogue Coun. Am. Office: Temple Beth El 333 SW 4th Ave Boca Raton FL 33432

SINGH, GARNISH BENEDICT, bishop; b. Lusignan, Demerana, Guyana, Dec. 2, 1927; s. Joseph Alexander and Matilda Amanda (Fredericks) S. Licentiate in Philosophy, Urban U., Rome, 1951, STD, 1957. Ordained priest Roman Cath. Ch., 1957, ordained bishop, 1972. Asst. parish priest Diocese of Georgetown, Guyana, 1957-58, parish priest, 1959-71; aux. bishop of Georgetown, 1971-72, bishop, 1972—; mem. exec. com. Antilles Bishops' Conf., 1991—. Address: Bishop's House, 27 Brickdam/PO Box 10720, Georgetown Guyana

SINGH, HARBANS, religious organization administrator. Chmn. Sikh Adv. Bd., Singapore. Office: Ministry Community Devel, Pearl's Hill Terrace, Singapore 0316, Singapore*

SINGLETARY, PATRICIA ANN, minister; b. N.Y.C., Mar. 3, 1948; d. George and Minnie Juanita (Williams) Nickens; m. Edward Franklin Singletary, Feb. 5, 1966 (div. Apr. 1973); children: Erik Franklin, Don Andre. BTh, New World Bible Inst. and Sem., 1984, MRE, 1986; AS, BS, SUNY, Empire State Coll., 1985-91; AA, MDiv, Va. Sem. and Coll., 1988, DD, Tenn. Bapt. Sch. of Religion, 1989; postdoctoral New Brunswick Theol. Sem., 1990—. Sr. reorgn. underwriter Depository Trust Co., N.Y.C., 1968-90, account coord. 1990—; former nat. corr. sec. Nat. Baptist Conv. U.S.A. Inc., 1984-87; vice chmn. Spiritual Life Comm. of Clergywomen, 1987—; assoc. minister Morning Star Missionary Bapt. Ch. of Jamaica, N.Y. Nat. editor: Ekklesia, 1986. Recipient Vol. Services award City of N.Y., 1980. Mem. Nat. Assn. Negro Bus. and Profl. Women, NAFE, Interdenominational Bd. Clergywomen (gen. sec. 1985—), Nat. Bapt. Women Ministers Conv. (bd. mgrs. 1983—), Ea. Bapt. Assn. (instr. 1981-83, v.p. evangelistic unit 1982-83, gen. dir. women's aux. 1988—), Nat. Coun. Women U.S., Internat. Platform Assn., Bronx Bapt. Ministers Evening Conf. Greater N.Y. and Vicinity. Office: Morning Star Missionary Bapt Ch 114-44 Merrick Blvd Jamaica NY 11434

SINGLETON, GREGORY ALAN, religion educator; b. San Antonio, Aug. 27, 1952; s. C.B. and Joanne (Kennedy) S.; m. Martha Marie McMullan, July 8, 1978; children: Anne Holland, Matthew Alan. BBA St. Mary's U. of San Antonio, 1973. Min. of youth Trinity Ch., San Antonio, 1975-80; founder, sr. pastor Faith Community Ch., Seguin, Tex., 1980-85; clinician Sportsquest Family Forum, San Antonio, 1985—; founder, exec. dir. Marketplace Ministries, San Antonio, 1986—; owner Recruiting Resources, San Antonio, 1988—. Editor Today's Marketplace, 1988—, Kickoff, 1984-86. San Antonio Assn. Pers. Cons. (bd. dirs. 1988, Excellence award 1988), Nat. Assn. Pers. Cons. (cert. 1986). Home: 3006 Desert Morning San Antonio TX 78251 Office: Marketplace Ministries 6326 Sovereign Ste 136 San Antonio TX 78229

SINGLETON, WOODARD L., JR. (WOODY SINGLETON), minister; b. Brandenburg, Ky., Dec. 14, 1942; s. Woodard L. Sr. and Maxine Dell (Pipes) S.; m. Effie Anne Janway, Dec. 26, 1961; children: Debra, Don, Brian, Angel. Student, Henderson State U., 1972-73, So. Bapt. Sem., 1973-75; BTh, Internat. Sem., 1990. Ordained to ministry Bapt. Ch. Pastor Acorn Bapt. Ch., Mena, Ark., 1972-77; interim pastor First Bapt. Ch., Grannis, Ark., 1979-80; pastor Salem Bapt. Ch., Mena, Ark., 1980-81, Ringgold (Tex.) Bapt. Ch., 1981-83, Live Oak Bapt. Ch., Jacksboro, Tex., 1983—; with Reynolds Williams Constrn., Little Rock, 1963-64; foreman U.S. Electric Motors, Mena, 1965-75; v.p. Teague Leather Goods, Mena, 1975-81; plant mgr. Justin Leather Goods, Nocona, Tex., 1981-82; prayer chmn., Jack Bapt. Assn., 1990—, area com. rep., 1984-90, assn. moderator, 1987-90, evangelism chmn., 1985-87; pres. Jack County Ministerial Assn., 1986-88; assn. stewardship chmn. Montague Bapt. Assn., 1982-83; area com. chmn. North Cen. Bapt. Area, 1983-90, budget com. chmn., 1985-87. Author: Helps for the New Member, 1990, God Still Moves, 1991. With USAF, 1960-62. Mem. Lions. Democrat. Home: 402 N 7th Jacksboro TX 76056

SIN HYOK, CHONG, religious organization administrator. Chmn. Korean Chundoist Assn., Puongyang, Dem. People's Republic of Korea. Office: Korean Chundoist Assn, Pyongyang Democratic People's Republic of Korea*

SINISHTA, GJON, pastoral associate; b. Titograd, Yugoslavia, Apr. 8, 1930; came to U.S., 1965; s. Prenk and Viktoria (Gjokaj) S.; m. Maria Theresa Amaya, Jan. 3, 1968; 1 child, Michael John. Degree in radio broadcasting-journalism, Journalist Broadcasting Sch., Belgrade, Yugoslavia, 1947; student, Colombiere Coll., Clarkston, Mich., 1966-67, John Carroll U., 1967-68, U. Santa Clara, 1973-74. Broadcaster, translator, writer Yugoslav Broadcasting Inst., Belgrade, 1947-56; imprisoned for anti-communist propaganda, 1956-61; acct. Zagreb (Yugoslavia) Textile Co., 1961-63; escaped from Yugoslavia, in refugee camps in Italy, 1963-64; assembler Ford Motor Co., Wixom, Mich., 1965-66; pressman GM, Cleve., 1967-68; asst. food mgr. U. Santa Clara, Calif., 1968-71, dir. Mission Ch., 1971-77; pastoral assoc. St. Ignatius Ch., U. San Francisco, 1977—; exec. sec. Albanian Cath. Info. Ctr., San Francisco, 1970-90; editor Albanian Cath. Bull., San Francisco, 1980—. Author: The Fulfilled Promise: A documentary account on religious persecution in Albania, 1976; co-author: (booklet) Sacrifice for Albania, 1966. Lt. Yugoslav Army, 1951-52. Mem. Amnesty Internat. Democrat. Roman Catholic. Avocations: swimming, writing. Home: 650 Parker Ave San Francisco CA 94118 Office: U San Francisco St Ignatius Ch 2300 Fulton St San Francisco CA 94117

SINK, HENRY R(AY), minister; b. Lexington, N.C., Jan. 6, 1934; s. John Raymond and Gurlah May (Michael) S.; m. Martha Joanne Frye, Aug. 3, 1956 (div. 1979); children: Martha Elizabeth, Sarah Catherine; m. Susan Brant Sadtler, Oct. 13, 1979. AB in English and Religious Edn., Lenoir-Rhyne Coll., 1956; MDiv, Luth. Theol. So. Sem., Columbia, S.C., 1959. Ordained to ministry Luth. Ch., 1959. Pastor St. David's Luth. Ch., Kannapolis, N.C., 1959-63, Christ the King Luth. Ch., Cary, N.C., 1964-68, Messiah Luth. Ch., Burlington, N.C., 1969-72, Mt. Pleasant Luth. Ch., Burlington, 1973-76, Shiloh Luth. Ch., Lewisville, N.C., 1979-82, United Luth. Ch., Lock Haven, Pa., 1982-88; mission developer Luth. Ch. in Am., Cary, 1963-64; pastor, developer Evang. Luth. Ch. in Am., Bartlett, Tenn., 1988—; mem. exec. bd. Cen. Pa. Synod, Luth. Ch. in Am., Harrisburg, Pa., 1987-88. Bd. dirs. Lock Haven Day Care, 1982-85, Clinton County Arts Coun., Lock Haven, 1984, Luth. Social Svcs. Memphis, 1991—, Luth. Village Coop., 1991—; mem. Millbrook Playhouse, Mill Hall, Pa., 1983-88; mem. adv. bd. Clinton County Children and Youth, Lock Haven, 1984-85. Recipient Community Svc. award Lock Haven Area Jaycees, 1987. Mem. Rotary (pres. Lock Haven club 1985-86, pres. elect Bartlett, Ind. club 1991-92). Democrat. Avocations: wood carving, acting, directing. Home and Office: St Mary's Luth Ch 3875 N Bluff Point Bartlett TN 38135

SINNEMA, DONALD WILFRED, religion educator; b. Lethbridge, Alta., Can., Jan. 14, 1947; s. Cornelius and Hilda (Willemsen) S.; m. Lois Kathleen Gerritsma; July 23, 1971; children: Heather, Ethan, Lauren. AB, Dordt Coll., 1969; MPhil, Inst. for Christian Studies, Toronto, Ont., Can., 1975; PhD, U. of St. Michael's Coll., Toronto, Ont., Can., 1985. Curriculum writer Joy in Learning Curriculum Devel. Ctr., Toronto, 1975-77; intern pastor Calvin Christian Reformed Ch, Ottawa, Ont., Can., 1985-86; campus min. U. N.B., Fredericton, 1986-87; prof. theology, chmn. theology dept. Trinity Christian Coll., Palos Heights, Ill., 1987—. Author: Reclaiming the Land: A Study of the Book of Joshua, 1977; contbr. articles to jours. and chpts. to books. Bd. Dirs. Dutch Heritage Ctr., Palos Heights, 1988—; elder Park Lane Christian Reformed Ch., Evergreen Park, Ill., 1990—. Can. Coun. grantee, 1980-81; Ctr. for Reformation Rsch. fellow, St. Louis, 1978, Meeter Ctr. for Calvin Studies fellow, Grand Rapids, Mich., 1984, 88. Mem. Sixteenth Century Studies Conf., Calvin Studies Soc. Home: 12847 S Maple Ave Blue Island IL 60406 Office: Trinity Christian Coll Theology Dept 6601 W College Dr Palos Heights IL 60463

SINNOTT, ANNELIESE, theology educator; b. Chgo., Nov. 20, 1937; d. William Anthony and Anna Louise (Haack) S. MusM, De Paul U., 1971; MA, U. Detroit, 1977; MDiv, Sts. Cyril and Methodius Sem., 1978; PhD, Katholieke Univ., Leuven, Belgium, 1987. Elem. tchr. St. Denis Sch., Chgo., 1961-66; music instr. St. Philip Neri Sch., Chgo., 1966-74; assoc. dean S.S. Cyril and Methodius Sem., Orchard Lake, Mich., 1978-82; asst. dir. pastoral ministry dept. Marygrove Coll., Detroit, 1984—; dir. coop. MDiv Program Ecumenical Theol. Ctr., Detroit, 1988—; treas. PM Unlimited, Detroit, 1987-91; dir. initial formation Adrian (Mich.) Dominican Sisters, 1985-87. Editor: Pastoral Ministry Newsletter; mem. editorial bd. Parish Ministries Bull., 1990-91. Mem. Detroit Cath. Pastoral Alliance, 1988—, West Detroit Interfaith Community Orgn., 1990-91. Mem. AAUP, Coll. Theology Soc., Cath. Theol. Soc. Am. (mem. organizing com. 1989-91). Roman Catholic. Avocations: lace maker, musician, construction. Office: Marygrove Coll 8425 W McNichols Detroit MI 48221

SINNOTT, JOSEPH JOHN, III (TRIP SINNOTT), religious organization executive; b. Clinton Corners, N.Y., Sept. 1, 1954; s. Joseph John Jr. and Sarah Bowne (Marsh) S. BA with honors, Trinity Coll., Conn., 1976; EdM, Harvard U., 1977. Cert. high sch. tchr. Coord., editor Servants of the Cross, Topsham, Maine, 1983—; dir. Servants of the Cross, Topsham, 1982—, Sky-Hy Sch., 1988-91; treas. Brunswick (Maine) Area Ch. Coun., 1985-87, 89-91, v.p., 1987-89. Author: Tea Island: A Perfect Little Gem, 1983; editor: (jour.) Cross Winds, 1980—; contbr. articles to jours. Recipient svc. award Billy Graham Ministries, Mpls., 1985, Freeport (Maine) Nursing Home, 1990; President's fellow Trinity Coll., 1975-76. Mem. Christian Action Coun., Alliance d'Amour, Friends Bowdoin Coll., Harvard Club Maine, Phi Beta Kappa. Home: PO Box 456 Topsham ME 04086 Office: Servants of the Cross 85A Meadow Rd Topsham ME 04086 *There surely was an Eden on this planet and, as J.R.R. Tolkien has noted, we all catch occasional glimpses of it. Our yearning for the Garden leads us ultimately to Calvary and the Empty Tomb.*

SINSTEAD, RONEL EDMUND, minister; b. Toronto, Ont., Can., Dec. 3, 1930; s. Albert and Kathleen (McInnis) S.; m. Cori Swarzentruber, May 25, 1957; children: Dale Andrew, Carmen Joy. D Metaphysics, Coll. Universal Truth, 1959. Ordained to ministry Unity Ch., 1979. Min. Unity Ch., Palm Springs, Calif., 1979-86, Muskegon, Mich., 1986—. Author: Child's Guide, 1969. Home: 3008 Dawes Rd Muskegon MI 49441 Office: Unity Ch 2052 Bourdon St Muskegon MI 49441

SIPES, TIMOTHY LANE, equipping minister; b. Franklin, Ind., Sept. 1, 1951; s. Lane Hunter and Martha Naomi (Morris) S.; m. Marilyn Rose Poynter, July 9, 1977; children: Gabriel Lane, Jared Thomas. BS, Johnson Bible Coll., Knoxville, Tenn., 1987. Preacher Edinburgh (Ind.) Christian Ch., 1987; equipping min. Farwell (Mich.) Ch. of Christ, 1987—; continuation com. mem. Mich. Christian Conv., Lansing, 1990—. Home: 2190 Pine Crescent Farwell MI 48622 Office: Farwell Church of Christ 700 E. Michigan Farwell MI 48622 *If all those who profess to be followers of Jesus Christ would return to using the Bible as the standard by which we all live, there would be no need for the division experienced today. And thus we would be more effective in our witness.*

SIPES, WILLIAM DONAL, JR., clergyman, broadcasting executive; b. Memphis, Dec. 17, 1958; s. William Donal and Marjorie Lorene (Davis) S.; m. Jamie Charlyene Ervin, Sept. 21, 1979; 1 child, William James. AS, Jackson State Community Coll., 1990. Ordained to ministry Bapt. Ch. as deacon, 1985. Minister of music First Bapt. Ch., Middleton, Tenn., 1986—; gen. sales mgr. Sta. WLRC Radio, Walnut, Miss., 1986—. Mem. Hardeman Bapt. Assn. (associational music dir. 1989—). Office: First Bapt Ch 525 N Main Middleton TN 38052

SIRAT, RENÉ-SAMUEL, rabbi, educator; b. Bône, Algeria, Nov. 13, 1930; s. Ichoua and Oureida (Attlan) S.; m. Colette Salamon, 1951 (div. 1973); children—Hé lè ne, Gabriel, Annie; m. Nicole Holzmann, 1978 Grad. Rabbinical Sem. France, 1952; Diplome, Ecole Nat. des Langues Orientales; Ph.D., U. Strasbourg (France) and Hebrew U. Jerusalem, 1965; Dr. (hon.), Yeshiva U., 1985. Ordained rabbi, 1952. Rabbi, Toulouse, 1952-55; head religious instrn. dept. Assn. Consistoriale Israelite de Paris, 1957-63; prof. Ecole Nat. des Langues Orientales-Sorbonne, Paris, from 1965; gen. insp. Hebrew instrn. French Ministry Edn., 1972-80; head Hebrew dept. Inst. Nat. des Langues et Civilisations Orientales; chief rabbi of France, 1981—. Contbr. articles to sci. revs.; participant in Ency. Universalis, Ency. Judaica and Pleiade Ency. Author, editor: Omer Hasikha, Jerusalem, 1973. Bd. govs. Hebrew U. Jerusalem, U. Bar-Ilan, Ramat-Gan. Decorated chevalier Ordre National du Mérite, chevalier Légion d'Honneur, officier des Palmes Academiques, comdr. des Arts et des Lettres (France); recipient Jerusalem prize for edn. Pres. State of Israel, 1981. Mem. Société des Etudes Juives en Sorbonne (past pres.), Centre Interuniversitaire des Hautes Etudes du Judaisme Contemporain (past pres.). Office: Ecole des Haute Etudes du Judaisme, 106 quai de Clichy, 92110 Clichy France

SIROTKO, THEODORE FRANCIS, priest, army officer; b. Muskegon, Mich., Oct. 5, 1936; s. Theodore Felix and Dorothy Mary (Bray) S.; m. Phyllis Anne Bourziel, May 5, 1962; children: Mary Anne, Kathleen, Stephen, Michael. BS, Ferris State U., 1958, MDiv, Nashotah House Theol. Sem., 1965; D in Ministry, San Francisco Theol. Sem., 1982; MSA, U. Notre Dame, 1982. Ordained to ministry Episcopal Ch., 1965. Vicar St. Matthew Ch., Sparta, Mich., 1965-68; rector St. Mark Parish, Howe, Ind., 1968-70; sr. chaplain Howe Mil. Sch., 1968-70; served with U.S. Army, 1959-61, advanced through grades to lt. col., 1985; chaplain U.S. Army, 1970—; chief parish/profl. devel. U.S. Army, Europe, 1982-85; chief pastoral ministry and counselling U.S. Army Chaplain Ctr. and Sch., Fort Monmouth, N.J., 1985-88, asst. dir. dept. mil. ministry, 1988-89, dir., 1989; chief Resource Mgmt. Br., Ft. Knox, Ky., 1989-91; chief adminstrn./ops br., Fort Knox, Ky, 1991—. Bd. dirs. LaGrange County Mental Health Assn., Ind., 1969-70, Sch. Opportunity, LaGrange, 1969-70. Decorated Bronze Star with 1 bronze oak leaf cluster, Air medal with 2 bronze oak leaf clusters, Meritorious Service medal with 2 bronze oak leaf clusters, Army Commendation medal with 1 oak leaf cluster, parachutist badge. Mem. Mil. Chaplains Assn., Evang. and Cath. Mission, Order St. Benedict. Mem. DAV (life), U.S. Army Chaplain Mus. Assn. (bd. dirs. 1986-88), Am. Soc. Mil Comptrollers. Home: 1427 4th Ave Fort Knox KY 40121 *God's great gift to us is that of relationship with Him and with each other.*

SISEL, ERIC DESBIENS, minister; b. Paris, July 12, 1932; arrived in Can., 1956; s. Antoine Jean and Térèse Sophie (Desbiens) S.; m. Mary Louise Pomeroy, Apr. 11, 1958; children: Kevin, Jennifer, Cindy Lou, Andrew. PhD, Sorbonne, France, 1953, U. Vienna, Austria, 1956; BD, U. Toronto, Can., 1969. Ordained to ministry United Ch. Can., 1969. Pastor Lake of Bays Pastoral Charge, Huntsville, Ont., Can., 1969-78, Lake of Bays Mission Ch., Huntsville, Ont., Can., 1978—. Host An Hour with Eric Sisel, weekly radio show, CKAR, Huntsville, 1969-77; editor: Encounter, 1972-76. Pres. Big Bros. Muskoka, Huntsville, 1972-73, Franklin Home and Sch. Assn., Dwight, Ont., 1975-78, Huntsville and Dist. Assn. for Mentally Retarded, 1980-86; bd. dirs. Huntsville Fair Bd., 1972-76. Mem. Huntsville Agri. Soc. (bd. dirs. 1971-75), Evang. Fellowship Can., Rotary (dist. gov. 1973-74), Masons (Shriner, chaplain 1973—). Address: Box 2461, Huntsville, ON Canada P0A 1K0 *God will preserve only two things from this world: His Word and people. Therefore I must spend my life building His Word into people.*

SISK, MARK SEAN, priest, seminary dean, religious educator; b. Takoma Park, Md., Aug. 18, 1942; s. Robert James and Alma Irene (Davis) S.; m. Karen Lynn Womack, Aug. 31, 1963; children: Michael A., Heather K., Bronwyn E. BS, U. Md., 1964; MDiv, Gen. Theolog. Sem., 1967, DD, 1985. Asst. Christ Ch., New Brunswick, N.J., 1967-70; assoc. Christ Ch., Bronxville, N.Y., 1970-73; rector St. John's Ch., Kingston, N.Y., 1973-77; archdeacon Diocese of N.Y., N.Y.C., 1977-84; dean, pres. Seabury-Western Theol. Sem., Evanston, Ill., 1984—; sec. Council Episcopal Sem. Deans, 1984-85; mem. task force for recruitemnt, tng. and deployment of black clergy, Coun. for Devel. Ministry, 1988—, exec. com., 1991. Pres. Anglican Theol. Review. Active Coun. for Devel. Ministry, 1988—, exec. com., 1991. Named Hon. Canon Cathedral of St. John the Divine, N.Y.C., 1977. Mem. Soc. Biblical Lit., Conf. Diocesan Execs., Assn. Chgo. Theol. Schs. (pres. 1990-91), Soc. St. Francis (third order). Home: 625 Garrett Pl Evanston IL 60201 Office: Seabury-Western Theol Sem 2122 Sheridan Rd Evanston IL 60201

SISSON, DONNA GAYLE, lay worker; b. Mt. Carmel, Ill., Aug. 20, 1962; d. Therne Noble and Hazel Lee (Gambill) Scott; m. Neal Lynn Sisson, June 27, 1981; 1 child, Kimberly Sheryle. Cert. in secretarial sci., Oakland City Coll., 1981. Clk. typist O'Leary Law Office, Oakland City, Ind., 1982-83; ch. sec. First Ch. of God, Princeton, 1984—; chairperson Christian edn. bd. 1st Ch. of God, Princeton, 1986-87, ch. treas., 1990—; sec. Women of Ch. of God, 1990—, state soc. mem. 1st Ch. of God, So. Ind., 1986-88, 1990—. Home: 603 W Walnut Princeton IN 47670 Office: First Ch of God 2005 Keystone Dr Princeton IN 47670 *The only answer on how to survive in this constantly demanding, changing world is Jesus Christ. He is my only hope. His loving arms hold me tight as I daily face life's pressures and today's high cost of living.*

SISSON, STEVEN LOUIS, minister; b. Russell, Kans., Mar. 26, 1949; s. Robert Leroy and Marjorie Lee (Miller) S.; m. Vicki Lynn Morrison, July 30, 1971; children: Paul, Peter, Lexi. AB, Mid-Am. Nazarene Coll., 1974; postgrad., Nazarene Theol. Sem., Kansas City, Mo., 1974-75. Ordained to ministry Nazarene Ch., 1977. Assoc. pastor 1st Ch. of the Nazarene, Pensacola, Fla., 1977-79; pastor Ch. of the Nazarene, Superior, Nebr., 1975-77, Scottsbluff, Nebr., 1979-82, Hollywood, Fla., 1982-90, Longmont, Colo., 1990—; pres. Nazarene Youth Internat., Nebr., 1979-82, So. Fla., 1984-86; dist. sec. So. Fla. Dist., 1986-90; bd. mem. Dist. Adv. Bd., 1988-90. Sec. Vietnam Vets. Am., Miami, Fla., 1989-90. With USMC, 1967-70, Vietnam. Decorated Bronze Star with V; Cross of Gallantry (Vietnam); recipient Medal of Valor, Kiwanis Internat., 1987. Mem. Lions. Republican. Home: 1302 Torreys Peak Dr Longmont CO 80501 Office: Longmont Ch of the Nazarene 2111 Mountian View Ave Longmont CO 80501

SIT, HONG CHAN, minister; b. St. Louis, Nov. 25, 1921; s. Gan and Ying Foon (Wong) S.; m. Amy Wang, June 16, 1949; children: David, Daniel, Estelle Joy, Mary. BS summa cum laude, U. Ill., 1943; BD, Faith Theol. Sem., 1950, STM, 1950; ThD, No. Bapt. Theol. Sem., 1957. Ordained to ministry Blue Ch., Springfield, Pa., 1950. Missionary China Inter-Varsity Fellowship, Shanghai, 1947; pastor Chinese Evang. Ch., N.Y.C., 1950-51. Chinese Bapt. Ch., Houston, 1953-56, Grace Chapel, 1956-90, missionary pastor, 1990—. Pres. Chinese Fgn. Missionary Union, 1974—, Chinese Full Gospel Fellowship Internat., Hong Kong, 1983—; mem. bd. govs. Network of Christian Ministries, 1990—. Author: Your Next Step With Jesus, 1977; contbr. articles to profl. jours. Mem. Phi Beta Kappa, Phi Lambda Upsilon. Office: Grace Chapel 1055 Bingle Rd Houston TX 77055

SITRUK, JOSEPH, rabbi; b. Tunis, Tunisia, Oct. 16, 1944; came to France, 1958; s. Jacques and Emma (Portugais) S.; m. Danielle Azoulay, Dec. 19, 1965; children: Rebecca, Yakou, Hanel, Eliaou, Sarah, Efrain, Isaac, Esther. Chief rabbi of France Paris. Office: Consistoire Cen, 17 rue St Georges, 75009 Paris France

SITTON, MARYIANN, minister; b. Tex., Jan. 3. BA in Christian Edn., Cen. Bible Coll. Ordained to ministry Christian Ch. Pres., founder Shiloh Christian Ministries Inc., Hamilton, Mont., 1973—; host (TV show) Shiloh Christian Retreat. Office: Shiloh Christian Ministries NW 60 Bowman Rd Hamilton MT 59840

SIU, DAVID PATRICK, minister; b. Inglewood, Calif., Dec. 23, 1957; s. James Y.C. and Helen H. (Shiroma) S.; m. Frances Zug, May 14, 1983; children: Grace Lalani, Gabriel Eric, Nicolas Andrew. AA, Golden West Coll., Huntington Beach, Calif., 1978; NSEE, Calif. Poly. State U., 1980. Lic. to ministry Baptist Ch. Lead engr. avionics text space shuttle div. Rockwell Internat., Palmdale, Calif., 1980-86, test engr. B-1B bomber div., 1986; lead engr. Computer Scis. Corp., Edwards AFB, Calif., 1986-88; asst. pastor Bethel Bapt. Ch., Lancaster, Calif., 1988—. Coach, umpire Little League Baseball, San Luis Obispo, Calif., 1978-80; basketball coach YMCA, Lancaster, 1981. Recipient Good Citizenship award Rockwell Internat., 1985. Republican. Avocations: hunting, fishing, bicycling, family activities. Home: 1117 W Dianron Rd Palmdale CA 93551 Office: Bethel Bapt Ch 3100 W Ave K Lancaster CA 93536

SIVIN, NATHAN, historian, educator; b. May 11, 1931; m. Carole Delmore. BS in Humanities and Sci., MIT, 1958; MA in History of Sci., Harvard U., 1960, PhD in History of Sci., 1966. Prof. Chinese history and history of sci., dept. history and sociology of sci. U. Pa., Phila., 1977—, acting chmn. dept., 1989; vis. lectr., Singapore U., 1962; vis. prof. Rsch. Inst. Humanistic Studies, Kyoto, Japan, 67-68, 71-72, 74, 79-80; vis. scientist Sinologisch Inst., Leiden, The Netherlands, Cambridge U., Eng., People's Republic China; vis. assoc., dir. Needham Rsch. Inst., Cambridge, 1987—; advisor Acad. Traditional Chinese Medicine, Beijing; numerous lectures and colloquia in Europe, Asia, N.Am. Author: (monograph) Chinese Alchemy: Preliminary Studies, 1968, Chinese trans. 1973, Cosmos and Computation in Early Chinese Mathematical Astronomy, 1969, Traditional Medicine in Contemporary China, 1987; author with others, editor or co-editor: Chinese Science, 1973, Science and Technology in East Asia, 1977, Astronomy in Contemporary China, 1979, Science and Civilisation in China, Vol.5, 1980, Science and Medicine in Twentieth-Century China, 1989, The Contemporary Atlas of China, 1989; also numerous articles for profl. jours., essays, prefaces to books, book revs.; editor, pub. Chinese Science, 1973—; mem. editorial bd. U. Pa. Press, 1980-83, numerous jours.; gen. editor: (monograph series) Science, Medicine and Technology in East Asia, 3 Vol. MIT E. Asian Sci. Series, 6 vol.; adv. editor Tech. and Culture, 1973—. Mem. adminstrv. bd. Chinese Cultural and Community Ctr., Phila., 1983-84. Guggenheim fellow, 1971-72; Japan Soc. Promotion of Sci. rsch. fellow, 1979-80; grantee NSF, 1968-70, 79-81, Ford Found., 1970, Nat. Libr. Medicine NIH, 1976, IBM Corp., 1985, Nat. Program Advanced Study and Rsch. China, Com. Scholarly Communication with People's Republic China, 1986-87. Fellow Am. Acad. Arts and Scis., Am. Soc. for Study of Religion (exec. com. 1982-83), Soc. for Studies Chinese Religion (bd. dirs., exec. coun. 1986-89), T'ang Studies Soc. (bd. dirs. 1986—), Chinese Acad. Scis. (hon. prof. 1989—), Franklin Inn Club (sec., bd. dirs. 1989-90), Acad. Internat. D'histoire des Scis. Home: 8125 Roanoke St Philadelphia PA 19118 Office: U Pa Dept History Sociology Sci Philadelphia PA 19104-6310

SJOBERG, DONALD, bishop. Formerly bishop Western Can. Synod Lutheran Ch. in Am.-Can.; pres. Evangel. Luth. Ch. in Can., Winnipeg, Man., 1986—, Can. Council of Churches, 1988—. Office: Evang Luth Ch, 1512 St James St, Winnipeg, MB Canada R3H 0L2

SKA, JEAN LOUIS, biblical scholar; b. Arlon, Belgium, Jan. 26, 1946; s. Alfred and Elisabeth (Chardome) S. Licenciate in Philosophy, Notre Dame de La Paix, 1969; Licenciate in Theology, Sankt Georgen, Frankfurt, W. Ger., 1977; Licenciate Exegesis, Pontificio Istituto Biblico, Rome, 1980, Doctorate Exegesis, 1983. Joined Soc. of Jesus, Roman Cath. Ch. Prof. exegesis Istituto Biblico, Rome, 1983—. Author: Exodus 14, 1986, Narrative Analysis, 1990; contbr. articles to profl. jours. Home: via della Pilotta 25, I-00187 Rome Italy Office: Pontificio Istituto Biblico, via della Pilotta 25, I-00187 Rome Italy

SKAGGS, FRED RANDALL, minister; b. Jonesville, Va., Nov. 16, 1933; s. Jesse Milton and Osalene (Spurrier) S.; m. Jane Brugos, Sept. 12, 1953; children: Debra Jane, Fred Randall, Angela Ruth, Cynthia Lou, John Milton. BA, U. Richmond, 1955; MDiv, Southwestern Bapt. Theol. Sem., Ft. Worth, 1963; MA, Southwestern Bapt. Theol. Sem., 1965; D of Ministry, Union Theol. Sem., 1974. Ordained to ministry Bapt. Ch., 1962. Pastor various chs., Va., Okla., 1952—, Skipwith Bapt. Ch., Richmond, 1966-73, Walnut Grove Bapt. Ch., Mechanicsville, Va., 1974—; instr. Sch. Christian Studies, U. Richmond. Co-author: The Sound of Falling Chains, Colors of the Mind; author: A Bridge Over Troubled Waters, The Symphony of Marriage. Pres. Laurel (Va.) Athletic Assn., 1969; founder, pres. Skipwith

Football Assn., 1971; chmn. bd. Met. Youth Football League, 1973; chmn. adv. bd. Lee-Davis Med. Ctr. Named Orator Of Yr., U. Richmond, 1951. Fellow Acad. Parish Clergy; mem. Am. Assn. Marriage and Family Therapists, Kiwanis (hon., past pres.). Office: PO Box 428 Mechanicsville VA 23111

SKANSE, JOHN EDWARD, minister, chaplain; b. Chattanooga, Aug. 2, 1950; s. Peter Irwin Robert and Ruth (Thompson) S.; m. Melody Ann DeZeeuw, Aug. 5, 1972. BA in Christian Edn., Wheaton (Ill.) Coll., 1972; MDiv, Bethel Sem., St. Paul, 1976. Ordained to ministry Bapt. Gen. Conf., 1976. Pastor Park View Bapt. Ch., Mokena, Ill., 1976-80, Riverdale (Ill.) Bapt. Ch., 1980-88, Deerwood Bapt. Ch., Brown Deer, Wis., 1988—; installation staff chaplain 126th Air Refueling Wing, Ill. Air N.G., Chgo., 1983—, staff chaplain state hdqrs., 1991—; camp pastor Camp Hickory, Round Lake, Ill., 1983-85; ch. del. Midwest Bapt. Conf., Ill., 1976—, vice moderator, 1991; ch. del. Bapt. Gen. Conf., Ill., 1976—. Contbg. author: Boys Brigade Leaders Manual, 1975. Maj. Ill. Air N.G. Mem. N.G. Assn. U.S., N.G. Assn. Ill. Home and Office: Deerwood Bapt Ch 5825 W Fountain Ave Milwaukee WI 53223

SKEETE, F. HERBERT, bishop; b. N.Y.C., Mar. 22, 1930; s. Ernest A. and Elma I. (Ramsey) S.; m. Shirley C. Hunte, Oct. 4, 1952; children—Michael H., Mark C. BA, Bklyn. Coll., 1959; MDiv, Drew U., 1962, D in Ministry, 1975; STM, N.Y. Theol. Sem., 1970; DHL(hon.), Philander Smith Coll., 1983, Jewish Theol. Sem. N.Y., 1986; DD, Ea. Bapt. Theol. Sem., 1986. Ordained to ministry United Meth. Ch., 1961; pastor Union United Meth. Ch., South Ozone Park, N.Y.C., 1960-67, N.Y.C. Mission Soc., 1967-68, Salem United Meth. Ch., Harlem, N.Y.C., 1968-80; bishop Phila. area United Meth. Ch., Valley Forge, Pa., 1980-88, Boston area, 1988—. Office: United Meth Ctr 566 Commonwealth Ave Boston MA 02115

SKELTON, HUGH BOLDING, world mission superintendent; b. Cornelia, Ga., Aug. 23, 1929; s. Clifford Turner and Bernice (Warwick) S.; m. Thelma Louise Skelton, Aug. 9, 1952; 1 child, Allen. BA, Mercer U., 1954; postgrad., Columbia (S.C.) Bible Coll., 1985-89. Ordained to ministry Congl. Holiness Ch., 1952. Pastor Congregational Holiness Ch., Macon, Ga., 1952-54; missionary Congregational Holiness Ch., Cuba, 1955-61; pastor Emmanuel Assembly, Tampa, Fla., 1961-62; missionary, supt. missions Congregational Holiness Ch., Mex., Cen. and S. Am., 1963-78; pastor Congregational Holiness Ch., Nicholson and Cleve., Ga., 1978-82; dir. Ctr. Internat. Christian Chs. Pentecostal Holiness Ch., London, 1982-87; supt. world missions Congregational Holiness Ch., Griffin, Ga., 1987-91; tchr. Beulah Heights Bible Coll., Atlanta, 1990, Ctr. Internat. Christian Ctr., London, 1991; founder, pres. Missionary Tng. Ctr., McAllen, Tex., 1964-73; bd. dirs. Sch. Christian Ministries, Emmanuel Coll., Franklin Springs, Ga., 1978-82, Beulah HeightsColl., Atlanta, 1978—. Scout master Boy Scouts Am. Emmanuel Coll., Franklin Springs, 1947-49; pres. Youth Temperance Coun. State of Ga., 1963. Aided in establishing over 453 churches in 10 countries. Home: 42 Mission Circle Griffin GA 30223 Office: Congregational Holiness Ch 3888 Fayetteville Hwy Griffin GA 30223 *Instead of viewing life as living on the edge of a crisis, I have chosen to view life as living on the edge of a miracle.*

SKIBBE, EUGENE MORITZ, religion educator, minister; b. Mpls., July 16, 1930; s. Frank Eugene and Helen (Moritz) S.; m. Margaret Froiland, Aug. 1, 1953; children: Katharine, Stephen, Susan, Jonathan. BA, St. Olaf Coll., 1952; B. Theology, MDiv, Luther Theol. Sem., 1956; ThD, U. Heidelberg, Fed. Republic Germany, 1962. Ordained to ministry, Luth. Ch., 1963. Instr. religion dept. Augustana Coll., Sioux Falls, S.D., 1956-58; pastor Burke Luth. Ch., Madison, Wis., 1963-64; prof. religion dept. Augsburg Coll., Mpls., 1964—. Author: Protestant Agreement on the Lord's Supper, 1968; editorial assoc. Una Sancta, 1969-72; contbr. theol. articles to profl. jours. Bd. dirs. Mpls. Blood Ctr., Mpls., 1980-87; steering com. Asian Arts Coun., Mpls. Inst. Arts, 1990—. Mem. AAUP, Am. Acad. Religion, Assn. for Study of Prints, Japanese Print Club (pres.). Office: Augsburg Coll 731 21st Ave S Minneapolis MN 55454

SKIDDELL, ELLIOT LEWIS, rabbi; b. Chelsea, Mass., Mar. 3, 1951; s. Jack and Evelyn (Starr) S.; m. Julie F. Goldberg, May 27, 1979; children: Sarit, Elanit. BA, U. Mass., 1974; MA, Temple U., 1979. Ordained rabbi, 1980. Rabbi Temple Beth El, Newark, Del., 1977-80; asst. rabbi Har Zion Temple, Penn Valley, Pa., 1980-82; rabbi Ramat Shalom Synogogue, Plantation, Fla., 1982—; placement dir. Reconstructionist Rabbinical Assn., Wyncote, Pa., 1985—; pres. Jewish Nat. Fund Broward and Palm Beach, 1987-89, North Broward Bd. Rabbis, Ft. Lauderdale, 1986-87, Reconstructionist Rabbinical Assn., 1980-82. Co-editor booklet: Mordecai Kaplan Centennial Resource Booklet, 1981. Bd. dirs. Jewish Fedn. Greater Ft. Lauderdale, 1986-89. Office: 11301 W Broward Blvd Plantation FL 33325 *I believe that the most important task facing us today is the creation of community and a sense of belonging to a community. For our own sake and for future generations, the sense of belonging to something larger than ourselves needs to be instilled.*

SKIFF, DAVID MICHAEL, minister; b. Union City, Pa., Apr. 15, 1957; s. George William and Sandra (Wrona) S.; m. Ester Tarasiuk, Aug. 18, 1979; children: Lauren, Morgan. BSW, Roberts Wesleyan Coll., 1979; MDiv, Asbury Theol. Seminary, Wilmore, Ky., 1983; MSW, U. Ky., 1984. Minister of outreach Northgate Free Meth. Ch., Batavia, N.Y., 1984-87; minister of counseling Brockport (N.Y.) Free Meth. Ch., 1987—; publicity chmn. Covenant Acres Comp and Retreat Ctr., Pike, N.Y., 1986-90. Republican. Office: Brockport Free Meth Church 6787 4th Section Rd Brockport NY 14420 *The resources of the wonderful Counselor, Jesus Christ, are being unleashed throughout the world, one heart at a time. That's the only way that the condition known as hard heartedness will ever disappear.*

SKILLRUD, HAROLD CLAYTON, bishop; b. St. Cloud, Minn., June 29, 1928; s. Harold and Amanda Skillrud; m. Lois Dickhart, June 8, 1951; children: David, Janet, John. BA magna cum laude, Gustavus Adolphus Coll., 1950; MDiv magna cum laude, Augustana Theol. Sem., Rock Island, Ill., 1954; STM, Luth. Sch. Theology, Chgo., 1969; DD (hon.), Augustana Coll., 1978, Newberry Coll., 1988. Ordained to ministry Evang. Luth. Ch. in Am., 1954. Supply pastor Saron Luth. Ch., Big Lake, Minn., 1950-51; mem. staff 1st Luth. Ch., Rock Island, Ill., 1951-53; sr. pastor St. John's Luth. Ch., Bloomington, Ill., 1954-79, Luth. Ch. of the Redeemer, Atlanta, 1979-87; bishop Southeastern Synod Evang. Luth. Ch. in Am., Atlanta, 1987—; intern, organizer new mission Faith Luth. Ch., Syosset, N.Y., 1952-53; del to various convs. Luth. Ch. in Am., mem. bd. publ., 1976-84, pastor-evangelist Evang. Outreach Emphasis program, 1977-79, mem. exec. bd. Ill. synod, 1977-79, pres. bd. publ., 1980-84, leader stewardship cluster Southeastern synod, 1983, mem. exec. bd. Southeastern synod, 1984-87, mem. exec. coun., 1984-87; mem. task force on new ch. design Commn. on New Luth. Ch., task force on ch. pub. house, 1985; del. constituting conv. Evang. Luth. Ch. in Am., 1987; mem. commn. on clergy confidentiality Luth. Coun. in USA, 1987; co-chair USA Luth.—Roman Cath. Dialogue; mem. Task Force on Theol. Edn. Author: LSTC: Decade of Decision, 1969; also articles and sermons to religious jours. Former bd. dirs. Augustana Theol. Sem.; bd. dirs. Augustana Coll., 1969-77, chmn. bd., 1976-77; bd. dirs. Kessler Reformation Collection, Luth. World Relief, Augsburg Fortress; chmn. bd. dirs. Luth. Sch. Theology, Chgo., 1962-69; mem. Leadership Atlanta, 1980-81, United Way, Atlanta, 1980-81; mem. Bishop's Commn. on Econ. Justice, 1985-86; pres. bd. dirs. Atlanta Samaritan House, 1986-87. Recipient Alumni award Luth. Sch. Theology, Chgo., 1976, award Leadership Atlanta, 1981. Mem. Luth. Sch. Theology Alumni Assn. (pres. 1975-77), Conf. of Bishops, Kiwanis (pres. Midtown chpt. 1984-85). Avocations: travel, photography. Home: 368 E Wesley Rd NE Atlanta GA 30305 Office: Evang Luth Ch in Am Southeastern Synod 756 W Peachtree St NW Atlanta GA 30308

SKINNER, ROBERT EUGENE, minister; b. San Antonio, Mar. 2, 1948; s. Paul Pendleton and Ethel Irene (Clark) S.; m. Linda Kay Chapman, Aug. 25, 1973; children: Beth Renee, Kevin Michael. AA, San Antonio Coll., 1968; BA, Our Lady of the Lake Coll., San Antonio, 1970; MDiv, Southwestern Bapt. Theol. Sem., Ft. Worth, 1978; MAT, S.W. Tex. State U., 1990; certificat, Université de Caen, France, 1990. Ordained to ministry, So. Bapt. Conv., 1979. Pastor First Bapt. Ch., LaVernia, Tex., 1979-84, Woodhaven Bapt. Ch., Houston, 1984-85, First Bapt. Ch., Stockdale, Tex., 1985-89; French tchr. Mary Carroll High Sch., Corpus Christi, Tex., 1989—; itinerant missionary Stockdale, 1989—; leader discipleship tng. 1st Bapt. ch., Rockport, Tex., 1990—; moderator Gambrell Bapt. Assn., 1987-88, missions survey com., 1988-89, mem. steering com., 1988-89. Recipient Le Prix d'Honneur, French Consulate, 1968. Mem. Tex. Fgn. Lang. Assn., Assn. of Tex. Profl. Educators, Am. Assn. Tchrs. French. Home: PO Box 1837 Fulton TX 78358

SKINNER, THOMAS DALE, developer, fundraiser; b. Kenmore, N.Y., May 25, 1954; s. Harry B. and Marion (Eastlick) S.; m. Margaret A. Fuerschbach, Aug. 16, 1975; children: Nathan Thomas, Drew Colin. BA, Houghton Coll., 1980; MS, SUNY, Buffalo, 1985. Trumpeter The 26th U.S. Army Band, N.Y.C., 1974-77; assoc. pastor The Wesleyan Ch. of Orchard Pk., N.Y., 1980-81; dir. ch. rels. Houghton (N.Y.) Coll., 1981-84, dir. ann. giving, 1984-86, dir. corp. and found. rels., 1986-89; v.p. for devel. Bibl. Theol. Sem., Hatfield, Pa., 1989—; cons. in field. Lay preacher United Meth. Ch., 1982—. Mem. The Council for Advancement and Support of Edn., The Nat. Soc. of Fund Raising Consultants. Democrat. Avocations: trumpeting, jogging, soccer, Little League coaching. Home: 447 Park Dr Harleysville PA 19438 Office: Biblical Theol Sem 200 N Main St Hatfield PA 19440

SKIRBALL, HENRY FRANC, rabbi, educator, religious organization administrator; b. Boston, Jan. 2, 1929; s. Louis I. and Miriam A. (Franc) S.; m. Sheba Fishbain, June 10, 1956; children: Rachel Leah Skirball Alani, Rebekah Miriam. AB, Harvard U., 1949; B in Hebrew Letters, Hebrew Union Coll.-Jewish Inst. Religion, Cin., 1954, MA in Hebrew Lit., 1957, DD (hon.), 1982; EdD, Columbia U., 1977. Ordained rabbi, 1957. Assoc. dir. B'nai B'rith Hillal Found., U. Chgo., 1959-60; mem. faculty, dir. Hillal Found. Northwestern U., Evanston, Ill., 1960-62; dir. Nat. Fedn. of Temple Youth, N.Y.C. and Jerusalem, 1962-87; head dept. edn. and culture Jewish Agy., World Zionist Orgn., Jerusalem, 1988—; mem. exec. com. Zionist Exec., Jerusalem, 1988—, Joint Authority for Zionist Jewish Edn., Jerusalem, 1991—; gov. Jewish Agy. for Israel, Jerusalem, 1988—; chmn. Assn. Nat. Jewish Youth Dirs., N.Y.C., 1967-71; chmn. bd. Interns for Peace, Jerusalem, 1975-78. Author: I.B. Berkson and Jewish Education, 1976; editor: The Jewish Youth Group, 1954; contbr. numerous articles to profl. jours. Treas., bd. dirs. Meditrans, Jerusalem, 1974-78; bd. dirs. Frankel Sch., Jerusalem, 1978-81, Haim Sch., Jerusalem, 1986-90; exec. bd. Citizens Rights Party, Tel Aviv, 1978-83, party candidate for Knesset and Jerusalem City Coun. 1st lt. U.S. Army, 1957-59. Mem. Coun. Progressive Rabbis, Cen. Conf. Am. Rabbis, Assn. Jewish Chaplains, Assn. Ams. and Cans. in Israel (nat. pres. 1982-84). Home: Nehogei Ha Pradot 22/10, Jerusalem 97890, Israel Office: World Zionist Orgn, PO Box 92, Jerusalem 91920, Israel

SKLBA, RICHARD J., bishop; b. Racine, Wis., Sept. 11, 1935. Student, Old St. Francis Minor Sem., Milw., Pontifica. Bibl. Inst., Rome. Ordained priest Roman Cath. Ch., 1959. Titular bishop of Castra, aux. bishop Milw., 1979—.

SKOPITZ, LAURENCE MARTIN, rabbi; b. Toronto, Ont., Can., Aug. 26, 1948; came to U.S., 1974; s. Oscar and Ida (Dietchman) S.; children: Shalom, Hyla. BA, York U., 1971; MA in Hebrew Letters, Hebrew Union Coll., 1977; postgrad., Colgate Rochester Div. Sch. Ordained rabbi, 1978. Rabbi Congregation Bnai Israel, Kalamazoo, Mich., 1974-77, Temple Shalom, Louisville, 1978, Temple Beth El, Geneva, N.Y., 1978-81, Temple Beth David, Rochester, N.Y., 1981—; chaplain Rochester Psychiat. Ctr., 1987—; rabbinic cons. Jewish Family Svc., Rochester, 1987—; instr. Bur. Jewish Edn., Rochester, 1981-91; asst. adj. prof. Alfred (N.Y.) U., 1985-86; bd. mem. Jewish Community Fedn., Rochester, 1986—; v.p. United Empire Region Rabbinic Assembly, 1988—; mem. adv. bd. Jewish Media Rels. Coun.; bd. dirs. Rochester Interfaith Jail Ministry, 1991—. Artist illuminated Jewish marriage contracts; author, illustrator children's books; composer children's music; contbr. articles to profl. jours. Adv. bd. Anti-Drug Coalition, Rochester, 1988—; vol. Vols. Am., Rochester, 1989—. With Can. Army, 1965-66. Recipient Lion of Judah award, Israel Bonds N.Am., 1988. Mem. Cen. Conf. Am. Rabbis, N.Y. State Jewish Chaplains Assn., West Irondequoit Ministerial Assn., Rochester Bd. Rabbis (pres. 1985-87). Office: Temple Beth David 3200 St Paul Blvd Rochester NY 14617

SKRYPNYK, MSTYSLAV STEPAN, archbishop; b. Poltava, Ukraine, Apr. 10, 1898; came to U.S., 1950; s. Ivan and Mariamna (Petlura) S.; m. Ivanna Witkovytsky, Jan. 8, 1921; children: Yaroslav, Tamara Yarovenko, Mariamna Suchoversky. M. Polit. Sci., Sch. Polit. Sci., Warsaw, Poland, 1930; Ph.D. (hon.), Ukrainian Free U., 1951. Acting bishop Pereyaslav, Ukraine, 1942-44; sec. to Council of Bishops in Exile, Offenbach, Germany, 1945-46; bishop Ukrainian Orthodox Ch. Western Europe, 1946-47; archbishop Can. Ukrainian Orthodox Ch., Winnipeg, Man., 1947-50; archbishop, pres. consistory U.S. South Bound Brook, N.J., 1950-71; met. archbishop in Diaspora, 1969—; met. archbishop Ch. U.S., 1971—; patriarch of Kiev and all Ukraine, 1990—; dir. Coop. Union, Halychyna, 1923-26. Dep. mayor Rivne, Volyn, Ukraine, 1930-31; mem. Polish (Seym) Parliament, sec. presidium, mem. fgn. affairs, budget commns., 1931-39, Orthodox Council Volyn, 1932-39. Lt. Russian Army, 1916-17, Ukrainian Nat. Army, 1917-22. Address: PO Box 445 South Bound Brook NJ 08880 *There exists no situation in life entirely devoid of an opportunity to do something of benefit to man and society.*

SKULASON, OLAFUR, bishop. Bishop Evang. Luth. Ch. of Iceland, Reykjavik. Office: Biskupsstofa, Sudurgata 22, 150 Reykjavik Iceland*

SKURLA, LAURUS See LAURUS, ARCHBISHOP

SKUTNIK, BOLESH, optics scientist, lay worker; b. Passaic, N.J., Aug. 19, 1941; s. Boleslaw Stanley and Helen Marie (Dzierzynska) S.; m. Phyllis Victoria Wojciechowski, Sept. 2, 1967 (div. July 1991); children: Pam, Janeen, Todd. BS, Seton Hall U., 1962; MS, Yale U., 1964, PhD, 1967. Chief scientist Ensign Bickford Coating Co., Simsbury, Conn., 1979-91; prin. B.J. Assocs., New Britain, Conn., 1991—; lector, mem. parish coun. St. Catherine of Siena, West Simsbury, Conn., 1980-85, St. Maurice, New Britain, Conn., 1985—; chmn., del. synod Archdioces of Hartford, Conn., 1990—; chmn. parish Holy Family Retreat League, New Britain, 1989—; pres. Enbic Employee's Credit Union, Simsbury, 1988-91, bd. dirs., 1980—. Patentees in field; contbr. articles to profl. jours. Interviewer Yale Alumni Schs. Com., L.I. and Hartford, Conn., 1969—. Mem. Soc. Photo-optical Engrs., Am. Ceramic Soc., (coord. symposium 1991—), Materials Rsch. Soc. (chair symposium 1987-89), Am. Chem. Soc. (coun. 1988—), Porsche Club Am. (various positions Conn. Valley region). Democrat. Roman Catholic. Home: 70 Kenwood Dr New Britain CT 06052 Office: BJ Associates 70 Kenwood Dr New Britain CT 06052 *The human spirit is stronger than anything that can happen to it.*

SKYLSTAD, WILLIAM S., bishop; b. Omak, Wash., Mar. 2, 1934; s. Stephen Martin and Reneldes Elizzbeth (Danzl) S. Student, Pontifical Coll., Josephinum, Worthington, Ohio; M.Ed., Gonzaga U. Ordained priest Roman Catholic Ch., 1960; asst. pastor Pullman, Wash., 1960-62; tchr. Mater Cleri Sem., 1961-68, rector, 1968-74; pastor Assumption Parish, Spokane, 1974-76; chancellor Diocese of Spokane, 1976-77; ordained bishop, 1977; bishop of Yakima, Wash., 1977-90, Spokane, Wash., 1990—. Office: Diocese of Spokane W 1023 Riverside Ave PO Box 1453 Spokane WA 99210

SLAATTE, HOWARD ALEXANDER, minister, philosophy educator; b. Evanston, Ill., Oct. 18, 1919; s. Iver T. and Esther (Larsen) S.; m. Mildred Gegenheimer, June 20, 1951; children: Elaine Slaatte Tran, Mark, Paul. A.A., Kendall Coll., 1940; B.A. cum laude, U. N.D., 1942; B.D. cum laude, Drew U., 1945, Ph.D., 1956; Drew fellow, Mansfield Coll., Oxford (Eng.) U., 1949-50. Ordained to ministry Meth. Ch. as elder, 1943. Pastor Detroit Conf. United Meth. Ch., 1950-56; assoc. prof. systematic theology Temple U., 1956-60; vis. prof., prof. philosophy and religion McMurry Coll., 1960-65; prof. dept. philosophy Marshall U., Huntington, W.Va., 1965—, chmn. dept., 1966-81, mem. grad. council, 1970-73, mem. research bd., 1974-76, mem. acad. standards and policy com., 1975-77, research grantee, 1976, 77; mem. bd. Campus Christian Center, 1973-75; lectr. Traverse City (Mich.) State Hosp., 1966-71, Am. Ontoanalytical Assn. internat. conf., Acapulco, Mex., 1970, World Congress Logotherapy, San Diego, 1980, other orgns.; mem. W.Va. Conf., United Meth. Ch., 1965-85. Baritone soloist. Author: Time and Its End, 1962, Fire in the Brand, 1963, The Pertinence of the Paradox, 1968, The Paradox of Existentialist Theology, 1971, Modern Science and The Human Condition, 1974, The Arminian Arm of Theology, 1977, The Dogma of Immaculate Perception, 1979, Discovering Your Real Self, 1980, The Seven Ecumenical Councils, 1980, The Creativity of Consciousness, 1983, Contemporary Philosophies of Religion, 1986, Time, Existence and Destiny, 1988, Critical Survey of Ethics, 1988; co-author: The Philosophy of Martin Heidegger, 1983, Religious Issues in Contemporary Philosophy, 1988; contbr.: Analecta Frankliana, 1981; gen. editor: (series) Contemporary Existentialism; contbr. to theol. and philos. jours. Mem. W.Va. Conf. United Meth. Ch., 1966—; bd. dirs. Inst. for Advanced Philos. Research, 1979-90; chmn. bd. dirs. Salvation Army of Huntington, W. Va. Recipient Outstanding Educator Am. award, 1975, Profl. Excellence award Faculty Merit Fedn., State of W.Va., 1986; named to Honorable Order of Ky. Colonels, W. Va. Ambassador of Good Will; NSF fellow, 1965; Benedum Found. rsch. grantee, 1970; NSF rsch.grantee, 1965, 71. Mem. W.Va. Philos. Assn. (pres., 1966-67, 83-84), Am. Philos. Assn., AAUP, Am. Acad. Religion. Home: 14123 Oak Knoll St Spring Hill FL 34609-3157 *Most knowledge is relative except for the divine Absolute encountered by faith in existence. The revealed principles opened up thereby, especially the ultimacy of sacrifical love (Agape) give basis and motivation for vital morality and a healthy culture.*

SLACK, JIM L., minister; b. Savanah, Ga., Apr. 12, 1958; s. Terrance David and LaVerne Ruth (Morris) S.; m. Dawn Renae Sandoz, Feb. 27, 1982; children: Caleb Michael, Joshua David. BA, Trinity Bible Coll., Ellendale, N.D., 1981. Ordained to ministry Assemblies of God Ch. Youth pastor Harlingen (Tex.) First Assembly of God Ch., 1984-85; pastor Leander (Tex.) Assembly of God Ch., 1985—. Home: 1906 Killarney Leander TX 78641 Office: Leander Assembly of God Ch P O Box 437 Leander TX 78641

SLADKEVICIUS, VINCENTAS CARDINAL, bishop; b. Kaisiadorys, USSR, Aug. 20, 1920. Ordained priest Roman Catholic Ch., 1944. Elected bishop of Abora, 1957, consecrated bishop,, 1957, created cardinal,, 1988; apostolic adminstr. Sanctae Sedis of Kaisiadorys. Address: Vatican City Vatican City also: R Carno 31, 234230 Kaisiadorys Lithuania

SLADOWSKY, YITZCHAK ALFRED, rabbi; b. Hamburg, Ger., Jan. 1, 1932; s. Jacob and Greta (Kanarek) S.; m. Frayda Sladowsky, Feb. 27, 1955; children: Esther Miriam Sladowsky Friedman, Rayla Sara Sladowsky Krupka, Saul, Eve T., Deborah Horowitz, Rachel Leah. BA, Yeshiva U., N.Y.C., 1954; MA, Columbia U., 1955. Ordained rabbi 1956. Rabbi Forest Park Jewish Ctr., N.Y.C., 1958—; instr. Yeshiva U., N.Y.C., 1961-73, Touro Coll., N.Y.C., 1973-75; exec. v.p. Rabbinical Assn. Queens, N.Y.C., 1973—; exec. dir. Histadruth of Am., N.Y.C., 1983-86. Advisor Ombud Service Program, N.Y. Found. for Sr. Citizens, N.Y.C., 1978—; mem. community Adv. com. Wyckoff Heights Med. Ctr. Mem. Rabbinical Coun. Am. (exec. com.), Rabbinical Alumni Assn. Yeshiva U. (chmn. bd. edn. Yeshiva of Central Queens chpt.). Home: 78 Dartmouth St Forest Hills NY 11375 Office: Forest Park Jewish Ctr 90-45 Myrtle Ave Glendale NY 11375

SLAP, CHARLES S., clergyman; b. N.Y.C., Oct. 6, 1933; s. Leonard and Elizabeth (Goodman) S.; m. Jacquelyn Anne Becker, June 14, 1970 (div. 1983); children: Andrew, Derek. BA, NYU, 1954; JD, Columbia U., 1959; postgrad., Harvard Div. Sch., 1965-66; DMin, Meadville Theol. Sch., Chgo., 1969. Bar: N.Y., D.C. Staff atty. office chief counsel U.S. Customs Svc., Dept. Treasury, Washington and N.Y.C., 1961-65; minister Unitarian Fellowship of Greater Lafayette, West Lafayette, Ind., 1969-71, Unitarian Ch. of Davis, Calif., 1971-76, First Unitarian Ch., Springfield, Mass., 1976-84, First Unitarian Soc., Schenectady, 1985—; trustee Unitarian Universalist Assn., Boston, 1981-84, mem. Gen. Asys. Planning Com., 1982-84, chmn. Melcher Book Awd. Com., 1988—. Contbr. articles to profl. jours. Bd. dirs. Law, Order and Justice Ctr., Schenectady, 1988-89. 1st lt. U.S. Army, 1954-56. Mem. Unitarian Universalist Ministers Assn. (bd. dirs. 1979-81), English Speaking Union U.S. (pres. Albany area br. 1989-90), Torch Club (sec. Schenectady 1989-90), Harvard Club, Harvard Faculty Club, Masons. Home: 973 Balltown Rd Schnectady NY 12309 Office: First Unitarian Soc 1221 Wendell Ave Schenectady NY 12308

SLATE, C. PHILIP, academic administrator; b. Louisville, Oct. 1, 1935; s. John and Sarah (Phillips) S.; m. Patricia Anne Slate; children: Karen, Carla, Carl. BA in Speech, David Lipscomb Coll., 1957; MA in Old Testament, Harding Grad. Sch. Religion, Memphis, 1961; D Missiology, Fuller Theol. Sem., 1976. Asst. prof. Harding Grad. Sch. Religion, Memphis, 1972-76, assoc. prof., 1976-82, prof., 1982—, now head of sch. Office: Harding U Grad Sch Religion 1000 Cherry Rd Memphis TN 28114*

SLATER, CHRISTOPHER PETER, priest, theology educator; b. Newcastle-upon Tyne, Eng., Mar. 24, 1934; s. Robert H. Lawson and Alys Lennox Graham (Simpson) S.; m. Helen Riley, July 22, 1958 (div. Feb. 1987); children: Lynne P., Ruth A., Claire E.; m. Joanne McWilliam, June 6, 1987. BA in Philosophy with honors, McGill U., 1954; BA in Theology with honors, Queens Coll., Cambridge, U.K., 1957, MA, 1961; PhD in Religion, Harvard U., 1964. Asst. prof. Haverford (Pa.) Coll., 1964-70; chair, assoc. prof. Sir George Williams U., Montreal, Que., Can., 1970-71; assoc. prof. to prof., chair dept. religion Carleton U., Ottawa, Can., 1971-82; prof. theology Wycliffe Coll., Toronto, Ont., Can., 1982-85; prof. theology Trinity Coll., Toronto, Ont., Can., 1985—, dean, 1985-90. Author: The Dynamics of Religion, 1979; editor: Religion and Culture in Canada, 1977; co-editor Traditions in Contact and Change, 1983, Toronto Jour. of Theology, 1985-90. Fellow Soc. for Values in Higher Edn.; mem. Am. Acad. Religion (regional pres. 1977), Can. Soc. for the Study of Religion (pres. 1978-80), Am. Soc. for Study of Religion, Am. Theol. Soc. Office: Trinity Coll, 6 Hoskin Ave, Toronto, ON Canada M5S 1H8

SLATER, OLIVER EUGENE, bishop; b. Sibley, La., Sept. 10, 1906; s. Oliver Thornwell and Mattie (Kennon) S.; m. Eva B Richardson, Nov. 25, 1931; children: Susan Slater Edenborough, Stewart Eugene. AB, So. Meth. U., 1930, BD, 1932, LLD (hon.), 1964; DD (hon.), McMurray Coll., 1951; LHD, Southwestern Coll., Winfield, Kans., 1961; LLD, Baker U., 1962. Ordained to ministry Meth. Ch., 1932. Pastor Rochelle, Tex., 1932-33, Menard, Tex., 1933-36, Ozona, Tex., 1936-42, San Antonio, 1942-44, Houston, 1944-50; pastor Polk St. Ch., Amarillo, Tex., 1950-60; consecrated bishop, 1960; bishop Kans. area Meth. Ch., 1960-64, Kans. area Meth. Ch., San Antonio-N.W. Tex. area, 1964-68, San Antonio area United Meth. Ch., 1968-76; bishop-in-residence Perkins Sch. Theology, So. Meth. U., 1976-80; Mem. jurisdictional confs. Meth. Ch., 1948, 56, 60, gen. confs., 1956, 60, pres. gen. bd. edn. (now of United Meth. Ch.), 1964-72; mem. commn. on archives and history United Meth. Ch., 1968-76, mem. interboard com. on enlistment for ch. occupations, 1968-72; pres. designate Council Bishops, 1971-72, pres., 1972-73. Author: (autobiography) Oliver's Travels, One Bishop's Journey, 1988. Chmn. Commn. on Archives, 1972-76; Trustee So. Meth. U., 1960-76, vice chmn. trustees, 1973-76; trustee Southwestern U.; mem. Bd. Global Ministries, 1972-76. Recipient Disting. Alumnus award So. Meth. U., 1975. Home: 7424-9 W Northwest Hwy Dallas TX 75225

SLATER, THOMAS BOWIE, minister, educator; b. Magnolia, Ark., July 28, 1952; s. Thomas Jefferson and Thelma Lee (Bowie) S.; m. Renea Denise Bush, Dec. 27, 1986. BA in Journalism with honors, Ark. Tech. U., 1974; ThM, So. Meth. U., 1978, D of Ministry in Christian Edn., 1981; postdoctoral studies, U. Va. Ordained to ministry United Meth. Ch. Assoc. pastor St. James A.M.E. Temple, Dallas, 1975-76; min.-in-tng. El Paso (Tex.) Wesley Found./St. James-Myrtle United Meth. Ch., 1976-77; assoc. pastor Greater Garth Chapel A.M.E. Ch., Dallas, 1978-79; campus min. Greater Dallas Commmunity of Chs., 1978-80; pastor Conner Chapel A.M.E. Ch., Little Rock, 1980-83; acad. dean Jackson Theol. Sem., North Little Rock, Ark., 1980-83; assoc. dir. John Wesley United Meth. Parish, Little Rock, 1983-84; pastor Haden's Chapel United Meth. Ch., Palmyra, Va., 1985-86; teaching asst. dept. religious studies U. Va., 1986-87; instr. dept. religion U. Ga., Athens, 1988—, undergrad. advisor, 1989-91; learning assoc. student devel. and programs dept. Mountain View Coll., Dallas, 1979-80; instr. Bible Perkins Sch. Theology, So. Meth. U., 1980-88. Contbr. articles to religious jours. Bd. dirs. Wesley Found., U. Va., 1985-88, U. Ga.,

1990—. Mem. Soc. Bibl. Lit., Alpha Phi Omega. Home: 330 Jefferson River Rd Athens GA 30607 Office: U Ga Dept Religion Peabody Hall Athens GA 30602

SLATTERY, SISTER MARGARET P., academic administrator. Head Incarnate Word Coll., San Antonio. Office: Incarnate Word Coll 4301 Broadway San Antonio TX 78209*

SLATTON, JAMES HOYT, minister; b. Ft. Worth, Jan. 15, 1933; s. Hoyt Sitton and Mary Sue (Rumph) S.; m. Elberta Lee Thornton, July 21, 1956; children: Stewart Price, David Sterling, Elizabeth Thornton. BA, Baylor U., 1954; BDiv, Southwestern Bapt. Theol. Sem., 1957, ThD, 1965; DD (hon.), U. Richmond, 1985. Ordained to ministry So. Bapt. Conv., 1951. Pastor Fate (Tex.) Bapt. Ch., 1951-55, South Lancaster Bapt. Ch., Dallas, 1955-60, 1st Bapt. Ch., Altavista, Va., 1960-67, Royal Ln. Bapt. Ch., Dallas, 1967-71; sr. min., pastor River Rd. Ch., Richmond, Va., 1971—; chmn. So. Bapt. Conv. Moderates, 1985-87, chmn., vice chmn. Bapts. Committed, So. Bapt. Conv., 1988—/. Contbr. articles to jours. in field and chpts. to books. Trustee Va. Bapt. Hosp., Lynchburg, 1959-60, Golden Gate Bapt. Theol. Sem., San Francisco, 1980-90, U. Richmond, 1986—; commr. Va.-Israel Commn., Commonwealth of Va., 1987-89. Named Hon. Virginian, Gov. Va., 1986. Mem. Am. Soc. Ch. History. Home: 1108 Swissvale Pl Richmond VA 23229 Office: River Rd Bapt Ch Richmond VA 23229

SLATTON, PAUL SANDERS, broadcasting executive, radio station owner; b. Tuscumbia, Ala., Apr. 16, 1937; s. Herman Kell and Vesta Lee (Sanders) S.; m. Joyce Mae Clemmons, May 19, 1956; children: Chris, Vic. Student, Dallas Radio Engring., 1956. Owner, adminstr. Sta. WBTG FM/AM Radio, Sheffield, Ala., 1978—. Home: 2021 Stoddard Dr Florence AL 35630 Office: Slatton & Assocs Broadcasters Inc 1605 Gospel Rd Sheffield AL 35660

SLAYTON, JOEL CHARLES, religion educator, college dean; b. Gurdon, Ark., July 25, 1948; s. Joe M. Slayton and Doris Kissinger; m. Dianne Kelly, July 31, 1970; children: Joel S., Amy R. BA, Ouachita Bapt. U., Arkadelphia, Ark., 1970; MDiv, Bapt. Missionary Assn. Sem., Jacksonville, Tex., 1973; ThD, Mid-Am. Bapt. Sem., Memphis, 1982. Mem. faculty Cen. Bapt. Coll., Conway, Ark., grad. dean, 1975—; assoc. prof., 1976-78; chmn. dept. religion Cen. Bapt. Coll., Conway, Ark., 1977-80, v.p., 1980-85; prof., 1978—. Author: The Significance of the Papyrus Discoveries, 1983; contbg. author: Anchor Bible Dictionary, 1990; contbr. articles to profl. jours. Mem. Am. Assn. Papyrologists, Assn. Internat. Papyrologues, Soc. Bibl. Lit., Evang. Theol. Soc. Home: 3 Rockwood W Conway AR 72032 Office: Cen Bapt Coll Conway AR 72032

SLEASMAN, WILLIAM JACOB, minister; b. Rockwood, Pa., July 12, 1927; s. John William and Ruth (Kimmel) S.; m. Della Virginia Conley, Feb. 24, 1989; children: William Eugene, Debra Sleasman Nauman. BA, Ky. Christian Coll., 1949; MDiv, Christian Theol. Sem., Indpls., 1964. Ordained to ministry Ch. of Christ. Min. Banquo Christian Ch., LaFontaine, Ind., 1949-53, New Castle (Va.) Christian Ch., 1953-62, Portsmouth (Va.) Christian Ch., 1962-70; min. 1st Christian Ch., Roanoke Rapids, N.C., 1970-78, Charlottesville, Va., 1978-88, Somerset, Pa., 1988—; chaplain Craig County Vol. Fire Dept., New Castle, Va., 1954-62, Portsmouth Sports Club, 1969-70; bd. dirs. Golden Age Christian Home, Portsmouth, 1969-70; mem. Coun. of Fifty Ky. Christian Coll., 1971-74; N.C. Bicentennial Venture in Evangelism, 1975-77. Campaign dir. Craig County March of Dimes, 1955-56, chmn. Craig County chpt., 1957-58; dist. dir. Va. Congress of Parents and Tchrs., 1960-62, chmn. character and spiritual edn., 1963-64, chmn. group rels., 1965-68; pres. John Tyler PTA, Portsmouth, 1969; active Roanoke Rapids Postmasters Community Coun., 1976-77; jury commr. City of Charlottesville, Va., 1988. Mem. Va. Evangelizing Fellowship (bd. dirs. 1955-56, 68-69, 79-80, sec. 1981-83, v.p. 1984-85, pres. 1965-66, 85-86), Fellowship of Assocs. of Med. Evangelism (assoc. dir. 1972-85), Health and Salvation to Every Nation (bd. dirs. 1985—), Somerset Ministerial Assn. (pres. 1990-91), Keystone Christian Mins. Assn. (pres. 1991), Alliance of Interfaith Ministries (bd. dirs. 1985-88). Home and Office: 1st Christian Ch 139 E Main St Somerset PA 15501-2007

SLEDGE, LARRY DALE, education minister; b. High Point, N.C., June 15, 1936; s. Roscoe Early and Leola Gertrude (Chappell) S.; m. Helen Louise Parker, June 4, 1955; children: Brian Dale, Tamela Michelle. Diploma in Edn. Ministries, Sem. Extension Inst., Nashville, 1975; student, Bapt. Coll., Charleston, S.C., 1977-79. Ordained to ministry Bapt. Ch., 1975. Transmitter engr. Sta. WHPE, High Point, 1954-56; br. mgr. sales service Lanier Bus. Products, Greensboro, N.C., 1956-67; minister edn. Bessemer Bapt. Ch., Greensboro, 1967-68, Midwood Bapt. Ch., Charlotte, 1968-74, Citadel Sq. Bapt. Ch., Charleston, 1974-80, Ft. Johnson Bapt. Ch., Charleston, 1980-86, Rosewood Bapt. Ch., Columbia, S.C., 1986—; chmn. local arrangements com. S.C. Bapt. State Conv., 1982. Contbr. articles to religious jours. Mem. Columbia Met. Religious Edn. Assn., S.C. Bapt. Religious Edn. Assn., Profl. Assn. Christian Educators, Eastern Bapt. Religious Edn. Assn., So. Bapt. Religious Edn. Assn., Charleston Bapt. Assn. (vice-moderator 1984-85, chmn. self-study com. 1983-84), Mecklenburg Bapt. Religious Edn. Assn. (pres. 1972). Avocations: genealogy, computers, reading, electronics, tropical plants. Home: 2213 Cardington Dr Columbia SC 29209 Office: Rosewood Bapt Ch 2901 Rosewood Dr Columbia SC 29205

SLEDGE, TERRY LYNN, minister; b. Ponca City, Okla., Jan. 6, 1951; s. Orville Eugene and Ophelia Ann (Tullis) S.; m. Patricia Louise Humble, May 25, 1972; children: Tara Lynn, Patrick Todd. A of Divinity, Southwestern Bapt. Theol. Sem., 1990. Ordained to ministry So. Bapt. Conv., 1972. Pastor 1st Bapt. Ch., Ripley, Okla., 1972-74; assoc. pastor Trinity Bapt. Ch., Seminole, Okla., 1974; pastor Longwood Bapt. Ch., Ponca City, Okla., 1974-76; 1st Bapt. Ch. Fittstown, Okla., 1976-81, Victory Park Bapt. Ch., McAlester, 1981—; trustee Okla. Bapt. U., Shawnee, Okla., 1985-88. Coord. McAlester News Capitol Religious Article, 1984—; adminstr. Victory Park soup Kitch, McAlester, 1987—; location supr. Operation Oasis of Bapt. Conv., McAlester, 1991; bd. dirs. Okla. Commn. on Children and Youth. Mem. Bapt. Gen. Conv. (mem. resolution com. 1987, credentials com. 1988). Republican. Home: 639 E Harrison McAlester OK 74501 Office: Victory Park Bapt Ch 601 E Harrison McAlester OK 74501

SLEPOY, EPHRAIM P., rabbi; b. Bklyn., May 10, 1958; s. Martin Jiles and Beatrice (Rosenbaum) S.; m. Rivki B. Elstein, Aug. 10, 1982; children: Yosaif, Moshe, Esther, Akiva. Student, Cantorial Tng. Inst., 1976-83; BA in Biology, Yeshiva U., 1981. Ordained rabbi, 1986; Yoreh Yoreh cert. Rabbi Congregation Agudath Shalom, Jersey City, 1982-87, B'nai Israel Congregation, Norfolk, Va., 1987-90, Beth Israel Synagogue, Longmeadow, Mass., 1990—; chaplain VA Hosp., Northampton, Mass., 1991—; dir. Norfolk chpt. Nat. Conf. Synagogue Youth, 1987-90; v.p., sec. Bergen Hebrew Free Loan Soc., Jersey City, N.J., 1982-87; sec. Tidewater Bd. Rabbis, Norfolk, 1988-90; mem. Nat. Rabbinic Cabinet State of Israel Bonds; co-founder Rabbinical Bd. Hudson County, Jersey City, 1985. Author: (Bible studies) The Jewish Standard, 1982-87; contbr. articles to profl. jours. Recipient Rabbinic Leadership award Israel Bonds, Norfolk, 1990. Mem. Rabbinical Coun. Am. (exec. bd. 1991—), Assn. Orthodox Jewish Scientists, Rabbinic Alumni-Rabbi Isaac Elchonon Theol. Sem., Rabbinical Coun. New Eng., World Jewish Congress (diplomat). Office: Beth Israel Congregation 1280 Williams St Longmeadow MA 01106 *In my career in general, and concerning specific programs or lectures, etc., I do not measure successes quantitatively, but rather qualitatively. If I can touch even one person, but deep down, to the soul, I feel as though I have accomplished a great deal.*

SLICE, PAUL OWENS, minister; b. Chapin, S.C., July 1, 1932; s. George Bailey and Emma Louise (Summer) S.; m. Karilyn Louise Slye, Sept. 13, 1957; children: Stephen Paul, Kristeen Elizabeth. BA, Newberry Coll., 1954; MDiv, Luth. Theol. So. Seminary, Columbia, S.C., 1957. Ordained to ministry Luth. Ch.-S.C. Synod, 1957. Pastor St. Luke's Luth. Ch., Mt. Ulla, N.C., 1957-59, Mt. Hermon Luth. Ch., West Columbia, S.C., 1959-67, Holy Trinity Luth. Ch., Anderson, S.C., 1967—; trustee Lowman Home for Aged and Infirmed, White Rock, S.C., 1962-84; del. convs. of Luth. Ch., Boston, Chgo., 1976, 78; chmn. stewardship and social ministry coms. of S.C. Synod of Luth. Ch. Am., dean Piedmont Dist.; pres. Anderson Meml. Hosp. Clergy Staff, Anderson Ministers Assn.; bd. dirs. Anderson Interfaith Ministries. Bd. dirs. Anderson County Literacy Assn. Home: 406 Long Forest Circle Anderson SC 29625 Office: Holy Trinity Lutheran Ch 209 Broad St Anderson SC 29621

SLIE, SAMUEL N., minister. Cord. The Downtown Coop. Ministry, New Haven, Conn. Office: Downtown Coop Ministry 57 Olive St New Haven CT 06511*

SLINGER, SISTER BRIGETTA, school system administrator. Supt. Cath. schs. Archdiocese of Santa Fe. Office: Cath Schs Office 4000 St Joseph's Pl NW Albuquerque NM 87120*

SLOAN, JAMES LLOYD, minister, publisher; b. Marengo, Ind., Jan. 2, 1934; s. Lloyd Clark and Gladys Virginia (Thompson) S.; m. Joy Laree Dvorak (div. Apr. 1987); children: Gregory J., Bradley R., Clark P., Douglas M., Scott S. AA, Graceland Coll., Lamoni, Iowa, 1953; student, Ind. U., Indpls., 1959-60, Purdue U., Indpls., 1961-63; BA in Philosophy and Psychology, U. Mo., Kansas City, 1970. Ordained to ministry Reorganized Ch. of Jesus Christ of Latter Day Sts., 1951. Tchr. Reorganized Ch. of Jesus Christ of Latter Day Sts., Indpls., 1951-63, Kansas City, 1963-67; editor, writer Christian Singles Internat., Indpls., then Cin., 1986—; pub., editor Christian Singles News, Harrison, Ohio, 1986—. Author: Movers, Shakers and Change Makers, 1987, Fifteen Ways to Find Your True Love, 1988, The Dirty Dozen 1, 1989; also articles. With U.S. Army, 1956-58. Office: Christian Singles Internat Box 100 Harrison OH 45030

SLOAN, JOHNNY WADE, clergyman, broadcasting company executive; b. Greeley, Colo., Nov. 9, 1949; s. Johnny Washington and Vila Lou (Brake) S.; m. Martha Dianne Essary, Nov. 9, 1969; children: Sean Wade, Martyn Vaughn. BTh, Internat. Bible Inst., Orlando, Fla., 1983, MTh, 1985; DD, LittD, Internat. Bible Inst., 1986. Evangelist, 1968-75; assoc. pastor West Side Pentecostal Ch., Hamilton, Ohio, 1970; pastor Broadway Assembly, Lorrain, Ohio, 1975-87, Hamilton Christian Ctr., 1987—; founder, editor Sonlight, Inc., youth publ., West Plain, Mo., 1973-80; dir. Sunset Hills Youth Camp, Granite City, Ill., 1973-78; pres., chief exec. officer Sta. WZLE-FM, Lorain, 1980—; chmn. bd. Missing Link, Inc., Cleve., 1985—; bd. dirs. Labor-Mgmt. Prayer Commn., Lorain County, 1985-87, Reconciliation Ministries, Inc., Lorain, 1986—, Butler County Children's Svcs. Bd., 1989—, Tri-County Christian Sch. Bd., 1988—; speaker Truth for Today, 1985—. Author: Where Is the Rainbow, 1984, also religious booklets and instrn. guides. Dist. coord. Freedom Coun., Lorain, 1984-86; mem. Elyria (Ohio) Christian Acad. Sch. Bd., 1984-85. Mem. Nat. Religious Broadcasters, Lorain C. of C. (Industry Improvement award 1985). Republican. Avocations: travel, hunting, fishing. Home and office: 1940 Millville Ave Hamilton OH 45013

SLOAN, ROBERT BRYAN, religion educator; b. Coleman, Tex., Feb. 7, 1949; s. Robert Bryan and Maggie (Simonton) S.; m. Melinda Sue Collier, Jan. 17, 1970; children: Charissa, Bryan, Eraina, Michael, Alathea, Sophia, Paul. BA cum laude, Baylor U., Waco, Tex., 1970; MDiv magna cum laude, Princeton U., 1973; postgrad., U. Bristol (Eng.), 1973-74; D.Theol. insigni cum laude, U. Basel, Switzerland, 1978. Ordained to ministry So. Bapt. Conv. Pastor Twin County Bapt. Ch., Kendall Park, N.J., 1970-73, First Bapt. Ch., Roscoe, Tex., 1977-80; instr. Hardin-Simmons U., Abilene, Tex., 1979-80, Southwestern Bapt. Theol. Sem., Fort Worth, 1980-83; assoc. prof. religion Baylor U., Waco, 1983—; trustee The Second Century Jour., Malibu, Calif., 1987—; mem. credentials com. Bapt. Gen. Conv. Tex., Lubbock, 1989, resolutions com. So. Bapt. Conv., New Orleans, 1990. Author: The Favorable Year of the Lord, 1977, Discovering I Corinthians, 1985, Romans, 1992; N.T. editor commentary series: The New American Commentary, 1991—; contbr. articles to Novum Testamentum, Evang. Quar. Trustee Lorena (Tex.) Ind. Sch. Dist., 1986—, v.p. bd. trustees, 1987-90, bd. pres., 1991—; coach Lorena Little League Assn., 1984-90. Baylor U. young investigator grantee, Waco, 1984-86. Mem. N.Am. Patristic Soc., Nat. Assn. Bapt. Profs. Religion, Southwest Seminar on Devel. Cath. Christianity (moderator 1987-88), Soc. Bibl. Lit. (pres. S.W. region 1988-89), Southwest Commn. on Religious Studies (v.p. 1990-91), Inst. Bibl. Rsch. (nat. exec. com. 1990-91). Home: Rt 1 Box 332 Bruceville TX 76630 Office: Baylor U PO Box 97294 Waco TX 76798

SLOCUM, CHARLES BRUCE, entertainment industry futurist; b. Mt. Holly, N.J., July 15, 1958; s. Bruce and Dorothy (McCarraher) S. BS in Communications, Syracuse U., 1980; MBA, U. Pa., 1985. Supr. audience research ABC, Los Angeles, 1980-83; mgr. broadcast practices NBC, Burbank, Calif., 1985; sr. fin. analyst Paramount Pictures Corp., Hollywood, Calif., 1986-87; dir. indsl. analysis Writers Guild Am. West, West Hollywood, Calif., 1987—. Deacon Bel Air Presbyn. Ch., 1989—. Mem. Internat. Inst. Communications, Acad. TV Arts and Scis., Hollywood Radio and TV Soc. Presbyterian. Home: 1208 N Olive Dr Apt 211 West Hollywood CA 90069 Office: Writers Guild Am West 8955 Beverly Blvd West Hollywood CA 90048 *Progress is usually defined as an illusion. Each person born starts at birth with the same personal journey as each other person. That journey is unchanged since 500 years ago, 2000 years ago, indeed, it is unchanged since creation.*

SLOCUM, STEPHEN E., JR., religious organization administrator. Chmn. Am. Tract Soc., Dallas. Office: Am Track Soc PO Box 462008 Garland TX 75046*

SLOOP, GREGORY TODD, clergyman; b. Kannapolis, N.C., Jan. 25, 1962; s. Guy Lorraine and Ava Geraldine (York) S.; m. Lisa Halleen Pait, Sept. 20, 1986; 1 child, Hannah Elizabeth. BS, Davidson Coll., 1984. Ordained to ministry Chs. of God, 1987. Minister music Lane St. Ch. of God, Kannapolis, N.C., 1982-86, youth pastor, 1987-89; intern Eastway Ch. of God, Charlotte, N.C., 1986-87; youth pastor/asst. prin. White Oak Ch. of God/Christian Acad., Newport, N.C., 1989-90; youth pastor Yorkwood Ch. of God, Gastonia, N.C., 1990-91; pastor Yadkinville (N.C.) Ch. of God, 1991—; dir. Gastonia Area Youth Leaders Assn., 1990-91. Editor Solid Rock Teen Newsletter, 1990-91. Mem. Nat. Youth Leader's Assn., Western N.C. Youth Leader's Assn. (adv. bd. 1990-91). Home and Office: PO Box 128 Yadkinville NC 27055 *Our greatest failure in life is misdirect focus. Let us turn our attention toward the eternally important: to deeply know God, to love our family, and to serve our church and our fellow man.*

SLOUGH, KENNETH D., JR., religious organization administrator. Moderator Schwenkfelder Ch., Norristown, Pa. Office: Schwenkfelder Ch 197 N Whitehall Rd Norristown PA 19403*

SLOYAN, GERARD STEPHEN, religious studies educator, priest; b. N.Y.C., Dec. 13, 1919; s. Jerome James and Marie (Kelley) S. A.B., Seton Hall U., 1940; S.T.L., Cath. U. Am., 1944, Ph.D., 1948. Ordained priest Roman Cath. Ch., 1944. Asst. pastor in Trenton, Maple Shade, N.J., 1947-50; mem. faculty Cath. U. Am., Washington, 1950-67, chmn. dept. religion, 1957-67; prof. N.T. studies Temple U., Phila., 1967—, chmn. dept. religion, 1970-74, 84-86. English editor: N.T., The New American Bible, 1970; author: Jesus on Trial: Development of the Passion Narratives, 1973, Commentary on the New Lectionary, 1975, Is Christ the End of the Law?, 1978, Jesus in Focus, 1983, Advent-Christmas, 1985, The Jesus Tradition, 1986, John: "Interpretation" Commentary, 1988, Holy Week, 1988, Jesus, Redeemer and Divine Word, 1989, What Are They Saying About John?, 1991. Recipient Pro Ecclesia et Pontifice medal, 1970; Johannes Quasten medal Cath U. Am., 1985. Mem. AAUP, Cath. Bibl. Assn., Soc. Bibl. Lit., Cath. Theol. Soc. Am. (John Courtney Murray award 1981, pres. elect 1992—), Coll. Theology Soc. (pres. 1964-66), Liturg. Conf. (pres. 1962-64, v.p. 1970-71, 75-88, chmn. bd. dirs. 1980-88), N. Am. Acad. Liturgy (Berakah award 1986). Democrat.

SLUBERSKI, THOMAS RICHARD, theologian, educator, minister; b. Jersey City, Dec. 7, 1939; s. Walter and Anna Louise (Gall) S. BA with honors, Concordia Coll., 1962; MDiv with high honors, Concordia Sem., 1966; postgrad., U. Vienna, Austria, 1966, U. Erlangen-Nuremberg, Fed. Republic Germany, 1966-68; MA in English Lit., Washington U., 1970; ThD with honors, U. Heidelberg, Fed. Republic Germany, 1973. Ordained to ministry Luth. Ch.-Mo. Synod, 1969. Vicar Zion Luth. Ch., Wausau, Wis., 1964-65; asst. to dean chapel., lectr. dept. theology Valparaiso (Ind.) U., 1969-70; assoc. prof. English, humanities ch. history, O.T., N.T. Concordia Coll., Bronxville, N.Y., 1972—; pastor St. Matthew's Luth. Ch., Hastings-on-Hudson, N.Y., 1977-87; exec. dir. Am. Luth. Publicity Bur., 1987-89; coord. 9th and 10th Inter-Luth. forums, 1988, 90; asst. dir. pub. rels. Atlantic Dist. Conv., Luth. Ch.-Mo. Synod, 1976; bd. dirs. Luth. Soc. Worship, Music and Arts, 1971-73. Asst. editor Seminarian jour., 1956-66; lit. survey editor, rsch. asst. Luth. World, 1968-69; contbr. articles to profl. jours. Juror Am. Film Festival, N.Y.C., 1976-87. Austrian State scholar, 1966, Bavarian State scholar, 1966-67; World Coun. Chs. fellow, 1967, Deutscher Akademischer Austauschdienst fellow, 1970-72, Ctr. for Creative Persons fellow, 1975; Aid Assn. for Luths. Faculty Study grantee, 1972. Fellow Christian Writers Inst. Home: 26 Dusenberry Rd Bronxville NY 10708 Office: Concordia Coll Bronxville NY 10708

SLUSSER, LESTER ROBERT, music minister; b. Detroit, Oct. 13, 1921; s. Lester John and Myrtle Eva (Hemenway) S.; m. Shirley Evelyn Nelson, Dec. 7, 1946; children—Catherine, Stephen, Marilyn. B.Music, Am. Conservatory, Chgo., 1942; B.A., San Jose U., 1949; M.Music, Northwestern U., 1954. Minister of music 1st Presbyn. Ch., San Jose, Calif., 1948-50, 1st Presbyn. Ch., Birmingham, Mich., 1950-68, La Jolla Presbyn. Ch., Calif., 1968—; pvt. music tchr. Named Tchr. of Yr., U. Mich., 1967. Mem. Am. Guild Organists (dean Detroit chpt. 1957-59, chmn. nat. convention 1960, clinician 1962, dean San Diego chpt. 1975-77, chmn. scholarship com. San Diego chpt. 1980—), La Jolla Profl. Men's Soc. Lodge: Kiwanis. Home: 6388 Castejon Dr La Jolla CA 92037 Office: La Jolla Presbyn Ch 7715 Draper Ave La Jolla CA 92037

SLUTZ, ANTHONY LEE, minister; b. Douds, Iowa, Nov. 19, 1942; s. Theodore R. and Margaret (Moore) S.; m. Ellen Martisha Beshears, Aug. 14, 1965; children: Sandra Diane, Martisha Ann, Theodore Marvin. BA, Bob Jones U., Greenville, S.C., 1965; MDiv, Cen. Bapt. Theol. Sem., Mpls., 1969; STM, Dallas Theol. Sem., 1971. Ordained to ministry, Bapt. Ch., 1965. Pastor Gideon Bapt. Ch., Wichita, Kans., 1971-76, Liberty Bapt. Ch., Newton, Kans., 1977-79, Thompson Rd. Bapt. Ch., Indpls., 1979—; exec. bd. Bapt. World Mission, Decatur, Ala., 1985—; bd. dirs. Bapt. Internat. Evang. Mission, Chgo., 1989—. Mem. Ind. Fund. Bapt. Fellowship (pres. 1985-87, 89—). Home: 4748 S Walcott Indianapolis IN 46227 Office: Thompson Rd Bapt Ch 1700 E Thompson Rd Indianapolis IN 46227

SLUTZKY, RICHARD OWEN, endowment administrator; b. Omaha, May 11, 1956; s. Ben and Charlotte (Nogg) L.; m. Alyson Wolens, June 14, 1981; children: Diane Rebecca, Bethany Michelle. AB in Urban Studies, Washington U., St. Louis, 1978; JD, Emory U., 1981. Dir. Jewish Community Found. of MetroWest, N.J., East Orange; bd. dirs. Congregation Oheb Shalom. NSF grantee, 1976; Sherman fellow, Brandeis U., 1990. Mem. Planned Giving Group of Greater N.Y., Assn. of Jewish Communal Profls., Coun. of Jewish Fedns. (endowment adv. coun.), Unity Club. Office: Jewish Community Found 60 Glenwood Ave East Orange NJ 07017

SMALL, JOSEPH DUNNELL, religious organization administrator; b. Phila., July 18, 1941; s. Joseph Dunnell Jr. and Ellen Van Dalen (Stoker) S.; m. Jean Kathryn Alexander, Aug. 14, 1965; children: Kathryn Dalen Small Rogers, Douglas Joseph. AB, Brown U., 1963; MDiv, Pitts. Theol. Sem., 1966; ThM, Princeton (N.J.) Theol. Sem., 1971; DMin, Louisville Theol. Sem., 1981. Assoc. minister Towson (Md.) Presbyn. Ch., 1966-68; dean of students Pitts. Theol. Sem., 1968-72, dir. ch. studies, 1972-75; minister First Presbyn. Ch., Westerville, Ohio, 1975-83, Twelve Corners Presbyn. Ch., Rochester, N.Y., 1983-88; assoc. dir. theology and worship unit Presbyn. Ch. (U.S.A.), Louisville, 1988—. Author: Is Christ Divided?, 1988; contbr. numerous articles to profl. jours. Mem. Oxmoor Golf and Steeplechase Club. Democrat. Home: 7903 Deronia Ave Louisville KY 40222 Office: Presbyn Ch USA 100 Witherspoon St Louisville KY 40202-1396

SMALL, KIMBERLEY ANN, parochial school educator; b. Beaver Falls, Pa., Feb. 20, 1950; d. Charles Melvin and Dorothy May (marx) Porter; m. Perry Martin Small, Feb. 21, 1970; children: Martin Christopher, Matthew Timothy. BRE, Trinity Coll. Bible, Newburgh, Ind., 1986. Tchr. Kailua (Hawaii) Ch. Christian Sch., 1978-79, Redemption Acad., Kailua, 1979-84; Sunday sch. supt. Kailua Assembly of God, 1984-88, missions dir., 1990—; tchr. Christian Acad., Honolulu, 1984—. Del. Rep. Cen. Com., Hawaii, 1987. Mem. Friends of Kailua High Sch. Home: 1337 Ulupii St Kailua HI 96734 Office: Christian Acad 3400 Moanalua Rd Honolulu HI 96819-1470

SMALLEY, LEROY DALE, minister; b. High Gate, Mo., July 31, 1952; s. Richard Dale and Mary Catherine (Snodgrass) S.; widowed; 1 child, Michael Kenneth Guy; m. Myriam Lartigue Perez, Sept. 26, 1976; children: Keith Dwaine Guy, Betsy Lynn, Natheniel Kenneth. BA in History/Secondary Edn., InterAm. U., Hato Rey, P.R., 1977; BS in World Affairs, World U., Hato Rey, P.R., 1982; MRE in Ch. History, N.Y. Theol. Sem., 1986; LittD (hon.), U. Life Ctr., Phoenix, 1990. Cert. seconday tchr., P.R., Ariz.; ordained to ministry Disciples of Christ. Pastor Wurzburg (Fed. Republic Germany) Christian Servicemen's Ctr., 1974-76; pastor, founder Minstry to the Mil., Inc., Catano, P.R., 1977-89; pres. Caribbean Christian U., Brisas Del Mar, Luquillo, P.R., 1977-89; pastor Beulah Ch. of Christ, Bronx, N.Y., 1982-83, Gospel Temple Ch. of Christ, N.Y.C., 1983-84, West Manhattan Ch. of Christ, N.Y.C., 1984-86; founder, pres. Valley of the Sun Theol. Sem., Phoenix, 1991—; pastor First Ch. of Christ, 1991—; gen. bishop Chs. of Christ, Disciples of Christ Internat., 1991—; high sch. history tchr. Glendale (Ariz.) Union High Sch., 1990—; mem. U. of Life Ctr., Phoenix, 1990—, Disciples of Christ Ministerial Conf., Phoenix, 1989—, N.Am. Christian Conv., Cin., 1978—, Nat. Missionary Conv., Copeland, Kans., 1978—, World Conf. of Chs. of Christ, Richardson, Tex., 1978—. Author: A Confession of Faith, 1986; editor: We Are One/Somos Unos, 1989. Staff mem. New Progressive Party, Santurce, P.R., 1977-82; mem. Friends of P.R. in Ariz., Glendale, 1989—. Decorated Navy Cross, Silver Star, Cross of Gallantry. Mem. Am. Ministerial Assn. (regional min. 1989—). Republican. Home: Apt 203 1725 E Cambridge Ave Phoenix AZ 85006 Office: Valley of Sun Theol Sem 748 E McDowell Rd Phoenix AZ 85006

SMALLEY, STEPHEN MARK, minister; b. Washington, Sept. 11, 1953; s. Robert Fields and Ruth Elizabeth (Seymour) S.; m. Kristin Dorothy Peterson, June 28, 1975; children: Kathryn Elizabeth, Patrick Stephen. BA, Western Md. Coll., 1975; MDiv, Garrett-Evang. Theol. Sem., 1978. Ordained to ministry United Meth. Ch., deacon, 1976, elder, 1980. Pastor South Fluvanna Charge/United Meth. Ch., Palmyra, Va., 1978-81; assoc. pastor 1st United Meth. Ch., Charlottesville, Va., 1981-83; Protestant chaplain 323 Air Base Wing, Mather AFB, Calif., 1983-85; sr. Protestant chaplain 26 Combat Support Group, Zweibruecken Air Base, Fed. Republic Germany, 1985-88, 6500 Air Base Wing, Edwards AFB, Calif., 1988—. Maj. USAF, 1983—. Home: 5354 Sage Ave Edwards AFB CA 93523 Office: 6500 Support Wing/HC Edwards AFB CA 93523

SMALLEY, WILLIAM EDWARD, bishop; b. New Brunswick, N.J., Apr. 8, 1940; s. August Harold and Emma May (Gleason) S.; m. Carole A. Kuhns, Sept. 12, 1964; children: Michelle Lynn, Jennifer Ann. BA in Sociology, Lehigh U., 1962; MDiv, Episcopal Theol. Sch., 1965; MeD, Temple U., 1970; D of Ministry, Wesley Theol. Sem., 1987. Ordained to ministry Episcopal Ch., 1965, bishop, 1989. Vicar St. Peter's Episcopal Ch., Plymouth, Pa., 1965-67, St. Martin-in-the-Fields Ch., Nuangola, Pa., 1965-67; rector All Saints' Episcopal Ch., Lehighton, Pa., 1967-75; fed. program adminstr. Lehighton Area Schs., 1970-72; rector Episcopal Ministry of Unity, Palmerton, Pa., 1975-80; bishop Episcopal Diocese Kans., Topeka, 1989—. Pres. Gaithersburg (Md.) Pastoral counseling Inc., 1986-89; bd. dirs. Washington Pastoral Counseling, 1988-89; chmn. Turner House Inc., Kansas City, Kans., 1989—, Episcopal Social Svcs., Wichita, Kans., 1989—; bd. dirs. Christ Ch. Hosp., Topeka, 1989—, Passport for Adventure, Atchison, Kans, 1989—. Mem. Omicron Delta Kappa. Democrat. Avocations: gardening, swimming, cross-stitching, reading. Address: Bethany Pl Topeka KS 66612

SMALLEY, WILLIAM RICHARD, priest; b. Bayonne, N.J., Mar. 26, 1928; s. Denis William and Margaret (Brown) S. AB, Seton Hall U., 1951; postgrad., Immaculate Conception Sem., 1955, MDiv, 1978; postgrad., Nat. Staff Coll., USAF/CAP, 1974. Ordained priest Roman Cath. Ch., 1955. 1st asst. pastor Immaculate Conception, Secaucus, N.J., 1955-62, Christ The King Ch., Hillside, N.J., 1962-79; pastor St. Paul the Apostle, Irvington, N.J., 1979—, sec.-treas., 1979; police and fire chaplain, Irvington, 1982—; sheriff's chaplain Essex County, 1984. Mem. nat. legis. com. USAF Aux-

CAP, Maxwell AFB, Ala., 1976—, legis. liaison N.J. Wing, McGuire AFB, 1973, N.J. Wing Chaplain, 1980-87, chief chaplains N.E. region, 1983-91, dir. N.E. region Chaplain Staff Coll., U.S. Army Chaplain Sch., Ft. Monmouth, N.J., 1985-91. Lt. col. N.Y. Guard-MNA. Mem. Mil. Chaplains U.S. (chaplain), Vets. Corps Arty., Army-Navy Club (Washington), Blizzard Club (chaplain 1955), Panther Valley Golf and Country Club, U.S. Golf Assn., Suburban Golf Club (Union, N.J.), KC (chaplain 1980). Home and Office: 954 Stuyvesant Ave Irvington NJ 07111 *The entire world must be conscious of the preservation of life, whether it be in war or peace, otherwise such a disregard of this preservation of life will bring about the complete moral destruction of each state and nation, nor should preservation of life be sacrificed for political alliances or political advantage.*

SMALLWOOD, E(DWARD) L(OUIS), community organizer; b. Bridgeport, Conn., Aug. 27, 1950; s. Charles Wesley Smallwood and Lou Bertha (Garrett) Eidson. AAS, Community Coll. USAF, Maxwell AFB, Ala., 1984; BA, Va. Union, 1988. Gen. cert. Am. Inst. Banking. Adminstrv. officer State Nat. Bank, Bridgeport, 1969-76; founder, pres. Love Mgmt., Stratford, Conn., 1976, Love Svcs., 1990—; interim pastor Gospel Worship Svc., Misawa AB, Japan, 1983; asst. to pastor Messiah Baptist Ch., Bridgeport, 1988—; loaned exec. United Way, Bridgeport, 1974; pres. Love Svcs., Bridgeport, 1990—. Christian edn. Messiah Bapt. Ch., 1989; VUU Inter Alum Va. Union U., Richmond, 1988—. With USAF, 1978-85, US/Japan. Recipient Human Goals award, USAF Misawa AB, Japan, 1983; named MLK Jr. Scholar, Va. Union U., 1985-88. Mem. D.C. Sociol. Assn., Coun. of Chs. Bridgeport, Am. Inst. Banking (bd. govs. Bridgeport 1975), Adminstrv. Mgmt. Soc. (pres. Bridgeport chpt. 1975-77), Kiwanis (bd. dirs. 1988-92). Baptist. Office: PO Box 5777 Bridgeport CT 06610-0777

SMART, (RODERICK) NINIAN, religion educator; b. Cambridge, Eng., May 6, 1927; w. William Marshall and Isabel MacQuarrie (Carswell) S.; m. Libushka Clementina Baruffaldi, July 19, 1954; children: Roderick, Luisabel, Caroline, Peregrine. BA, Oxford U., Eng., 1951, MA, 1984, BPhil, 1954; LHD (hon.), Loyola U., Chgo., 1978, Kelaniya U., Sri Lanka, 1986; DLitt (hon.), Glasgow U., Scotland, 1984; DUniv (hon.), Stirling U., Scotland, 1986. H.G. Wood prof. theology U. Birmingham, Eng., 1961-67; prof. religious studies U. Lancaster, Eng., 1967-88; J.F. Rowny prof. religious studies U. Calif., Santa Barbara, Calif., 1976—; mem. Archbishops' Commn. on Christian Doctrine, Ch. of Eng., 1968-71. Author 24 books, including: Reasons and Faiths, 1958, The Philosophy of Religion, 1965, The World's Religions, 1989, Christian Theology in Global Context, 1990; contbr. articles to jours. in field. Capt. Brit. Army, 1945-48. Mem. Brit. Assn. for Religious Studies (pres. 1981-85), Oxford Hist. Theology Soc. (pres. 1981-82), Am. Soc. for Study Religion (pres. 1984-87), Athenaeum Club (London). Anglican. Home: 975 West Campus Ln Goleta CA 93117 Office: U Calif Religious Studies Dept Santa Barbara CA 93106

SMART, TREY, minister; b. Ryan, Okla., Dec. 7, 1956; s. T.J. and Nell (Swilling) S.; m. Becky Brown, Aug. 17, 1990. BJ, Okla. State U., 1980. Ordained to ministry Bapt. Ch., 1984. Minister of music First Bapt. Ch., Ryan, 1974-75; sports writer Stillwater (Okla.) NewsPress, 1976-80; minister youth and edn. Emmanuel Bapt. Ch., Ardmore, Okla., 1980-82, First Bapt. Ch. East, Lawton, Okla., 1982—; cons. Bapt. Sunday Sch. Bd. Met. Clinic, Denver, 1984, Houston, 1985, Atlanta, 1989, Jackson, Miss., 1991. Author: The Pride of RHS, 1977. Mem. Okla. State Alumni Assn., Okla. Youth Minister's Assn. Democrat. Avocation: sports. Home: 403 SE Sungate Lawton OK 73501 Office: First Bapt Ch E SE 40th at Elmhurst Lawton OK 73501

SMATT, EDDIE GEORGE, minister; b. Bklyn., Apr. 5, 1951; s. William and Hypha (Bardowell) S.; m. Donna Lynn Throckmorton, May 14, 1977; children: Brian, Justin, Angela. AA, Coll. Orlando, Fla., 1971; BA, Union U., Jackson, Tenn., 1973; MDiv, Southwestern Bapt. Theol. Sem., Ft. Worth, 1977. Ordained to ministry So. Bapt. Conv., 1973. Evangelist Miami, Fla., 1975-79; pastor St. Helen Bapt. Ch., Mich., 1977-78; pastor First Bapt. Ch., Center Hill, 1979-81, Eagle Lake, 1981-89; pastor Gulf State Bapt. Ch., Sarasota, 1989—. Mem. S. W. Bapt. Assn., Student Ministries Dirs. Assn. (vice moderator), Ridge Bapt. Assn. (various past coms., Christian life commn. com., 1984—). Republican. Home: 2717 Silver King Way Sarasota FL 34231 Office: Gulf State Bapt Ch 6501 S Lockwood Ridge Rd Sarasota FL 34231 *The only thing in life that really matters is to know Jesus Christ as Savior and Lord, to live for Him daily and to help other people in life. I believe we need to get back to the basics as a nation, which is God, family, country and work. We need to strengthen them.*

SMEDBERG, BARRY, ecumenical agency administrator. Exec. dir. San Fernando Valley Interfaith Coun., Chatsworth, Calif. Office: San Fernando Valley Interfaith Coun #7 10824 Topanga Canyon Blvd Chatsworth CA 91311*

SMEETON, DONALD DEAN, clergyman, missionary, educator; b. Denver, May 3, 1946; s. Wilbur Rex and Anna (Sterk) S.; m. Dolores Marie Rosenkrans, June 1, 1967; children: Diane, David. BA, Cent. Bible Coll., Springfield, Mo., 1967; BS, Evang. Coll., Springfield, 1969; MA cum laude, Trinity Evang. Div. Sch., Deerfield, Ill., 1971; MA, Assemblies of God Theol. Sem., Springfield, 1977; PhD summa cum laude, Cath. U. Louvain, 1983. Ordained to ministry Assemblies of God Ch., 1971. Youth pastor N.W. Assembly of God, Mt. Prospect, Ill., 1969-71; adminstr. Teen Challenge, Brussels, 1971-72; tchr. Continental Bible Coll., Brussels, 1972-82; assoc. dean Internat. Corr. Inst., Brussels, 1982—; guest prof. Assemblies of God Theol. Sem., 1982-91; educator Cape Coll. of Theology, Bloubergrant, Republic of South Africa, 1991—. Author: Lollard Themes in the Reformation Theology of William Tyndale, 1986, English Reformation 1500-1540: a Bibliography, 1988; contbr. numerous articles on history, theology and missions to profl. jours. Mem. Ecclesiastical History Soc., European Pentecostal Theol. Assn. (editor jour. 1982-90, v.p. 1985-87). Avocations: reading, walking. Office: Cape Coll Theology, PO Box 11066, Bloubergrant 7443, Republic of South Africa

SMELSER, JOHN MARK, clergyman, religious program official; b. Magnolia, Ark., May 29, 1948; s. Daniel P. and Rosa (Thurman) S.; m. Rachel Rebecca Konopnicki, Aug. 9, 1969; 1 child, Tiffini. BA in Theology, Christian Life Coll., Stockton, Calif., 1970. Ordained to ministry United Pentecostal Ch., 1970. Assoc. pastor United Pentecostal Ch., Stockton, 1969-72, Houston, 1972-73, Flint, Mich., 1973-74, Napa, Calif., 1974-75; pastor United Pentecostal Ch., Pomona, Calif., 1975-80; dir. promotion Harvestime, Hazelwood, Mo., 1980—. Home: 1492 Colgate Dr Saint Charles MO 63303 Office: Harvestime 8855 Dunn Hazelwood MO 63042

SMELTZ, SISTER JUDITH ANNE, nun, religion education director; b. Kingston, N.Y., Oct. 28, 1942; d. Robert Arthur and Margaret Mary (Bracken) S. BA in Edn., Elms Coll., 1965; MA in Pastoral Ministry, Emmanuel Coll., 1976, advanced cert. in pastoral counciling, 1990. Joined Sisters of St. Joseph, Roman Cath. Ch., 1960. Tchr. Holy Family Sch., Springfield, Mass., 1965-70; dir. religious edn., pastoral min. Spanish Apostolate, Springfield, Holyoke, Mass., 1970-81, St. Matthews Parish, Indian Orchard, Mass., 1981-83; co-dir. of renew Diocese of Springfield Mass., 1983-86, dir. Jericho homes, 1986-87; dir. religious edn. and youth Our Lady of Hope Parish, Springfield, 1987—; vocat. edn. team Sisters of St. Joseph, Holyoke, 1989—, wellness com. chairperson, 1989—. Mem. Holyoke (Mass.) Model Cities Housing, 1973-76. Mem. Parish Religious Educators (diocese bd. 1989—, diocese youth bd. 1988—). Office: Our Lady of Hope Parish 577 Carew St Springfield MA 01104

SMELTZER, PHYLLIS, ecumenical agency administrator. Head Mahone Bay Inter-ch. Coun., N.S., Can. Office: Mahone Bay Inter-Ch Coun, RR#1, Mahone Bay, NS Canada B0J 2E0*

SMELTZER, ROBERT BERYL, minister; b. Escanaba, Mich., Mar. 3, 1941; s. Donald Camp and Katheryn (Turner) S.; m. Constance June White, Aug. 22, 1964; children: Robert John, Jennifer Lynn. AB, Asbury Coll., Wilmore, 1964; Postgrad., Asbury Seminary, Wilmore, 1967; DRE, Covington Sem. Ordained to ministry Meth. Ch., 1967. Pastor Centerburgh United Methodist Ch., Centerbury, 1967-69; minister edn. Grace United Meth. Ch., Coshocton, Ohio, 1969-71; pastor Brentwood Buena Vista, Steubeville, 1971-75, Dalton United Meth. Ch., Dalton, 1975-77, Bethany United Meth. Ch., Canton, 1977-85, Woodlawn United Meth. Ch., Bueyrus, Ohio, 1985-87, Scott United Meth. Ch., Cadiz, Ohio, 1987—; chmn. Tappan Lake Ministry, 1988-89; exec. dir. Harrison County Food Bank. Author weekly column in newspaper entitled "Steeple to Street". Mem. E. Ohio Conf. Camp Curriculum Com., St. Clairsville Com. on Nominations, chmn., 1989-90. Mem. Harrison County Assn. of Chs. (bd. dirs.), St. Clairsville Parsonage Fellowship of United Meth. Ch. (chmn. 1990-91), Cadiz Ministerial Assn. (chmn.). Republican. Home: 640 Kerr Ave Cadiz OH 43907 *Working in tandem with God is the greatest guarantee of spiritual success.*

SMEND, RUDOLF, theologian; b. Berlin, Oct. 17, 1932; s. Rudolf and Gisela (Hübner) S.; m. Dagmar Erlbruch, May 24, 1969. Student, U. Tübingen, Fed. Republic of Germany, 1951-52, Göttingen U., Fed. Republic of Germany, 1952-54, U. Basel, Switzerland, 1954-55; DTheol, 1958; DivD (hon.), Saint Andrews U., Scotland, 1979. Privat dozent U. Bonn, 1962-63; prof. theology Kirchliche Hochschule, Berlin, 1963-65, U. Münster, Fed. Republic of Germany, 1965-71, U. Göttingen, 1971—. Author: Die Entstehung des Alten Testaments, 1978, Die Mitte des Alten Testaments, 1986, Zur ältesten Geschichte Israels, 1987, Deutsche Alttestamentler in drei Jahrunderten, 1989, Die Epochen der Bibelkritik, 1991. Mem. Akademie der Wissenschaften, Soc. for Study of the Old Testament (hon.), Deutsche Forschungsgemeinschaft (v.p. 1986—). Home: 6 Thomas Dehler Weg, 3400 Göttingen Federal Republic of Germany Office: Theologicum, Platz der Göttinger Sieben 2, 3400 Göttingen Federal Republic of Germany

SMICK, ELMER BERNARD, minister, educator; b. Balt., July 10, 1921; s. Frank and Marie (Hagert) S.; m. Jane Harrison, Aug. 19, 1944; children: Peter, Karen, Theodore, Rebecca. BA, King's Coll., 1944; STM, Faith Theol. Sem., 1948; PhD, Dropsie Coll., 1951. Ordained to ministry Presbyn. Ch. in Am., 1947. Pastor Evang. Presbyn. Ch., Trenton, N.J., 1947-56; prof. Old Testament langs. Covenant Theol. Sem., St. Louis, 1956-71; prof. Old Testament Gordon Conwell Theol. Sem., South Hamilton, Mass., 1971-91, prof. emeritus, 1991—; vis. prof. Ref. Theol. Sem., Orlando, Fla., 1991—; moderator N.J. Presbytery, Ref. Presbyn. Ch., 1953-54, asst. clk. of synod, 1965; trustee Nat. Presbyn. Missions, 1948-68, World Presbyn. Missions, 1979-81. Author: Archaeology of the Jordan Valley, 1973; editor: The New International Version of the Bible, 1968-78. Named Alumnus of Yr., King's Coll., 1984. Fellow Inst. Bibl. Rsch.; mem. Nat. Assn. Profs. Hebrew, Evang. Theol. Soc. (pres. 1988), Am. Oriental Soc., Soc. Bibl. Lit. Home: 84 Old Cart Rd South Hamilton MA 01982 Office: Gordon Conwell Theol Sem South Hamilton MA 01982

SMILEY, ALBERT KEITH, lay church worker; b. Mohonk Lake, N.Y., May 13, 1910; s. Albert K. and Mable (Craven) S.; m. Ruth Happel, Apr. 30, 1939; children: Sandra, Albert K. AB, Haverford Coll., 1932. Clk. of ministry and counsel N.Y. Yearly Meeting Religious Soc. Friends, 1960-62, chmn. com. for study of faith and beliefs, 1959-63; mem. exec. com. Friends World Com., Sect. of Americas, 1962-82, clk. com. on right sharing of world's resources, 1973-82; mem. Task Force on Christian Peacemaking as Lifestyle New Call to Peacemaking, 1977-79; pres. Smiley Bros., Inc., Mohonk Mountain House, 1969-80, chmn., 1980-85; clk. bd. mgrs. Mohonk Cons., Inc., Mohonk Lake, New Paltz, N.Y., 1980—. Coord. New Paltz Area Common Cause, 1973-75; bd. advisers Earlham Sch. Religion, Richmond, Ind., 1972-85; mem. bd. mgrs. Oakwood Sch., Poughkeepsie, N.Y., 1958-67. Home and Office: Mohonk Lake New Paltz NY 12561 *In this last decade of the 20th century it is imperative that all world religions become more involved in nurturing the vision of a healthy, habitable and sustainable planet, our common home.*

SMISKO, RICHARD G. See NICHOLAS, BISHOP

SMITH, ADRIAN, archbishop. Archbishop of Honiara Roman Cath. Ch, Solomon Islands. Office: Cath Mission, POB 237, Honiara Solomon Islands*

SMITH, ANN HAMILL, retired religion educator; b. Lumberton, N.C., Oct. 12, 1929; d. Walter Franklin and Mabel Willey (Braswell) H.; divorced; children: Leslie Wade Smith Hodeen, Courtney Drake Smith. BSEE, Old Dominion U., 1973; Edn. for Ministry degree, U. South, 1986; postgrad., Loyola U., New Orleans, 1986-89. Sunday sch. tchr. Christ Ch., Poughkeepsie, N.Y., 1957-60; E.C.W. pres. Christ Ch., Poughkeepsie, 1958-59; asst. Christ Ch. Nursery, Poughkeepsie, 1959-60; asst. parish sec. Christ and St. Luke's Ch., Norfolk, Va., 1970; mgr. Picnic in the Yard St. Paul's Ch., Norfolk, 1982-83; min. Christian edn. St. Andrew's Ch., Newport News, Va., 1985-90; spiritual dir. Virginia Beach, Va., 1990—. Author: (meditations) Our Church Times, 1988-91. Bd. dirs. Christ Ch. Day Sch., Poughkeepsie, 1960-65. Democrat.

SMITH, ASTON CARPENTER, minister; b. Richmond, Va., Nov. 26, 1957; s. Ashton Vivian and Mary Louise (Carpenter) S.; m. Lori Jean McConaghy, June 15, 1985. BS, Va. Commonwealth U., 1980; MDiv, Southeastern Sem., 1985. Ordained to ministry So. Bapt. Conv., 1982. Youth dir. Pine St. Bapt. Ch., Richmond, Va., 1979; youth pastor Living Clay Bapt. Ch., Henderson, N.C., 1982; pastor Ashland (Va.) Bapt. Ch., 1983-84, Globe Landing Bapt. Ch., Laneview, Va., 1984-87, Bethel Bapt. Ch., Fredericksburg, Va., 1987—; sec.-treas. Mid-Tidewater Pastors' Conf., Laneview, 1985-86, pres. 1986-87. Carmel Bapt. Ch., Ruther Glen, Va. scholar, 1984. Mem. Fredericksburg Bapt. Mins.' Conf. (v.p. 1991—), Fredericksburg Bapt. Christian Life Com. Home: 1197 White Oak Rd Falmouth VA 22405 Office: Bethel Bapt Ch 1193 White Oak Rd Falmouth VA 22405

SMITH, BAILEY EUGENE, minister; b. Jan. 30, 1939; s. Bailey Ezell and Amber Frances (Lucky) S.; m. Sandra Lee Elliff, June 8, 1963; children: Scott, Steven, Josh. BA, Ouachita Bapt. U., 1962, DD (hon.), 1978; BD, Southwestern Bapt. Theol. Sem., 1966; D Bibl. Studies (hon.), Dallas Bapt. Coll., 1981. Ordained to ministry So. Bapt. Conv. Pastor Meml. Bapt. Ch., Waldo, Ark., 1st Bapt. Ch., Hobbs, N.Mex., 1st So. Bapt. Ch., Del City, Okla., 1973-85; evangelist Bailey Smith Ministries, Atlanta; pres. Pastor's Conf. So. Bapt. Conv., 1978, Okla. Bapt. Gen. Conv., Oklahoma City, 1980, So. Bapt. Conv., St. Louis, 1980, L.A., 1981, Pres. Conf. of So. Bapt. Evangelists, 1990. Author: Real Evangelism, 1978, Real Christianity, 1979, Real Evangelistic Preaching, 1981, Real Revival Preaching, 1982, Real Christian Excellence, 1987, Nothing But the Blood, 1987, The Grace Escape, 1991. Address: Bailey Smith Ministries PO Box 450649 Atlanta GA 30345

SMITH, BARBARA ANN, diocesan director; b. Portland, Maine, Oct. 1, 1941; d. Ralph L. and Mary E. (Kane) S. BA in Elem. Edn., BA in Theology, St. Joseph's Coll., 1969; MA in Theology, St. John's U., 1975. Cert. tchr., N.Y. Tchr. Parochial Sch. System, N.Y., 1961-71; elem. sch. prin. Parochial Sch. System, Harrisburg, Pa., 1971-73; formation pers. Daughters of Charity, Albany, N.Y., 1975-81; dir. religion edn. various parishes, Mass.,, Maine, 1981-89; diocesan dir. Diocese of Portland, Maine, 1989—. Mem. Nat. Cath. Edn. Assn. Home: 117 Summit Terr Apt 91 South Portland ME 04106 Office: Diocese of Portland 510 Ocean Ave Portland ME 04106

SMITH, BARDWELL LEITH, religion educator; b. Springfield, Mass., July 28, 1925; s. Winthrop Hiram Smith and Gertrude Florence (Ingram) Behanna; m. Charlotte McCorkindale, Aug. 19, 1961; children: Peter McKay, Susan McCorkindale Moeller, Laura Bardwell Goodwin, Brooks Campbell, Samuel Bardwell. BA magna cum laude, Yale U., 1950, BD magna cum laude, 1953, MA, 1957; PhD, 1964. Ordained to ministry Episcopal Ch. Minn. diocese as priest, 1954. Asst. minister Trinity Episcopal Ch., Higland Park, Ill., 1954-56; asst. chaplain Yale U., New Haven, Conn., 1957-60; asst. instr. Yale U., New Haven, 1958-60; asst. prof. Carleton Coll., Northfield, Minn., 1960-65; assoc. prof. Carleton Coll., Northfield, 1965-69, dean of coll., 1967-72, prof. religion, 1969—, prof. Asian studies (John W. Nason chair), 1972—. Co-editor and contbr. Numerous books on Religion and Asian studies including: Religion and the Legitimation of Power in Sri Lanka, 1978, Warlords, Artists and Commoners: Japan in the 16th Century, 1981, Essays on Gupta Culture, 1983, The City as a Sacred Center: Essays on Six Asian Contexts, 1987. Mem. Yale U. Coun. chmn. Com. on Yale Coll., 1969-74; bd. dirs. Gen. Svc. Found., St. Paul, Minn., 1971-77; bd. internat. advisors, Chinese U. Hong Kong, 1976—; trustee The Blake Schs., Mpls., 1980-83; del. to Dem. Farm Labor State Conv., 1968, '90. Recipient Nat. Def. Edn. Rsch. grant, 1964-65, Am. Coun. of Learned Socs. grant, 1972-73, Fulbright Commn. fellowship at Kyoto U., Japan, 1986-87; NEH rsch. grantee, 1991—. Mem. AAUP, Am. Acad. of Religion (bd. dirs 1969-72, many other offices and coms.), Assn. for Asian studies (nominations com. 1982-83, chmn. Sri Lanka studies com. 1979-82), Internat. Assn. for Buddhist Studies (bd. dirs. 1976-86, gen. sec. 1980-81), Can. Assn. for South Asian Studies (v.p. 1972-73), Phi Beta Kappa. Democrat. Home: 104 Maple St Northfield MN 55057 Office: Carleton Coll One N College St Northfield MN 55057

SMITH, BARRY KEITH, lay worker, corrections officer; b. Little Rock, Ark., May 26, 1960; s. Albert Jacob and Geneva Louise (Compton) S.; m. Laurie Ann Lunsford, Jan. 21, 1984; children: Alison Kay, Carol Stephanie. BA in Bible, Tenn. Temple U., 1984; MDiv, Temple Bapt. Theol. Sem., 1991. Tchr. adult singles Sunday sch. Duncan Park Bapt. Ch., Chattanooga, 1986—; corrections officer Hamilton County Sheriff's Dept., Chattanooga, 1988—, asst. chaplain, 1991—; mem. missions com. Duncan Park Bapt. Ch., Chattanooga, 1984-90, choir mem., 1984—; missionary to the South Pacific, Bibl. Ministries Worldwide, 1991. Mem. Fellowship Christian Police Officers. Home: 1310A Reeves Ave Chattanooga TN 37412

SMITH, BENNETT WALKER, minister; b. Florence, Ala., Apr. 7, 1933; s. Pearline Smith; m. Marilyn J. Donelson, Dec. 29, 1985; children from previous marriage: Debra T., Bennett Jr., Lydia R., Matthew T. BS, Tenn. State U., 1958; DD (hon.), Cin. Bapt. Theol. Sem., 1967; LHD (hon.), Medaille Coll., 1979. Ordained to ministry Progressive Nat. Bapt. Conv., 1962. Pastor 1st Bapt. Ch., Cin., 1963-65, Lincoln Heights Bapt. Ch., Cin., 1965-72, St. John Bapt. Ch., Buffalo, 1972—; instr. Congress Christian Edn., 1968-80; first v.p. Progressive Bapts., 1988—. Author: Tithing Handbook, 1980; contbg. editor missionary handbook. Bd. dirs. People United to Serve Humanity, Buffalo, 1974—; pres. Va./Mich. Housing Co., 1982—. Recipient Outstanding Leadership award 1490 Entreprise, Inc., 1982, Community Leadership award Black Elected Officials, 1982, Outstanding Clergy award Black Religious Broadcasters, 1983. Mem. NAACP (life, Medgar Evers award 1982), Ptnrs. in Ecumenism, Operation PUSH (nat. bd. dirs., chaplain), Masons (32d degree), Kappa Alpha Psi. Democrat. Home: 292 Red Oak Dr Williamsville NY 14221 Office: St John Bapt Ch 184 Goodell St Buffalo NY 14204

SMITH, BILLY KENNETH, religion educator; b. Spearsville, La., July 14, 1928; s. Harmon and Eva (Rogers) S.; m. Irlene Monroe, Oct. 17, 1947; children: Ken, David, Joyce, Philip, Debra. BS, La. Tech U., 1951; BD, New Orleans Bapt. Theol. Sem., 1956, ThD, 1963; postgrad., New Coll., Edinburgh, Scotland, 1982. Ordained to ministry So. Bapt. Conv., 1955. Pastor 5 chs., La., Miss., Tex., 1954-75; prof. O.T. and Hebrew, New Orleans Bapt. Theol. Sem., 1976—; chmn. div. Bibl. studies, 1988—. Author: Never Alone, 1978, Layman's Bible Commentary, Vol. 13, 1982, Word's Speak, 1984; also articles. Mem. Nat. Assn. Hebrew Profs. Democrat. Home: 352 Lumpkin Rd Carriere MS 39426 Office: New Orleans Bapt Theol Sem 3939 Gentilly Blvd New Orleans LA 70126 *The shortest route from the real to the ideal in life is for the idealist to start walking in the direction of the ideal and to start encouraging others to do the same.*

SMITH, BOBBY RAY, pastor; b. Corpus Christi, Tex., Dec. 8, 1953; s. Carrol Ray and Elsie Ruth (Schneider) S.; m. Vicky Elizabeth Williams, Mar. 6, 1976; children: Laura Elizabeth, Nathan Ray. BA, Howard Payne U., 1976; MDiv, Southwestern Bapt. Theol. Sem., Ft. Worth, 1980, D Ministry, 1989. Ordained to ministry So. Bapt. Conv. Summer missionary 1st Bapt. Ch., Albuquerque, 1974; pastor 1st Bapt. Ch., Pettit, Tex., 1976, Mullin, Tex., 1980-82; edn. min. 1st Bapt. Ch., Roanoke, Tex., 1978-80; pastor 1st Bapt. Ch., Mont Belvieu, Tex., 1982—; chmn. missions com. San Jacinto Bapt. Assn., Baytown, Tex., 1983-90, dir. pastoral ministries, 1988—. Trustee Howard Payne U., Brownwood, Tex., 1988—; bd. dirs. Bay Area Women's Ctr., Baytown, 1988—; bd. dirs. Barbers Hill Sports Assn., Mont Belvieu, 1990—, coord. girls basketball, 1990. Mem. W.C.C. C. of C. (bd. dirs. 1990—). Home: 12914 Cherry Point Dr PO Box 943 Mont Belvieu TX 77580 Office: 1st Bapt Ch 10110 Eagle Dr Mont Belvieu TX 77580

SMITH, BRADLEY JOEL, minister; b. La Crosse, Kans., June 16, 1959; s. James William and Coral (Jane) S.; m. Joy Lynn Krivohlavek, Aug. 18, 1978; children: Adam J., Amber R., Aimee J. Ordained to ministry Assemblies of God, 1987. Children's pastor Faith Assembly of God, Salina, Kans., 1983-84; sr. pastor First Assembly of God, Morland, Kans., 1984-87, Iola, Kans., 1987-91; sr. pastor Praise Temple Assembly of God, Burleson, Tex., 1991—; pres. Iola Ministerial Assn., 1990-91, sec.-treas., 1988-90; sectional youth rep. Kans. Dist. Coun. of Assembly of God, 1985-87. Com. mem. United Way, Iola, 1990, Community Action, Iola, 1990, Whitehead Estate, Iola, 1990. Republican. Home: 225 Betty L Ln Burleson TX 76028 Office: Praise Temple Assembly of God PO Box 291 Burleson TX 76028 *Most people base the philosophies of their lives on the opinions of people who are more confused than they are.*

SMITH, CAROL LOU STUBBS, minister; b. New Castle, Ind., May 22, 1944; d. Russell A. and Mildred (Pentecost) Stubbs; m. Gary Randall Smith, June 17, 1967; children: Kimberly Ann, Clayton Dean. BS, Manchester Coll., 1965; postgrad., Princeton Theol. Sem., 1984-85; MDiv cum laude, Nazarene Theol. Sem., Kansas City, Mo., 1988. Ordained to ministry Presbyn. Ch., 1989. Christian edn. coord. 2nd Presbyn. Ch., Kansas City, Mo., 1982-83; student pastor Greenwood (Mo.) Presbyn. Ch., 1984-86; chaplain/intern St. Luke's Hosp., Kansas City, Mo., 1986-87; pastor Raymore (Mo.) Presbyn. Ch., 1989—; Mem. coun. Mid Am. Synod, Overland Park, Kans., 1990—, planning and rev. com. Heartland Presbyn., Kansas City, 1989—, com. chair, 1991—, presbytery clergywomen, 1988—, vice-chmn. Happening Ecumenical, Kansas City area, 1987—. Adv. bd. Rosebrooks Ctr. for Battered Women, Kansas City, 1987—, K.C. Friends of Hospice, Kansas City, Mo., 1989—, Women's Fund, Kansas City, 1991—; trustee Univ. Mo. Kansas City Conservatory of Music, 1988; fellow Nelson-Atkins Art Mus., Kansas City, Mo., 1988. Mem. Presbytery Small ch. Network. Home: 5520 State Line Rd Mission Hills KS 66208

SMITH, CHESTER ALLEN, JR., minister, educator; b. West Haven, Conn., Sept. 25, 1932; s. Chester Allen and Dorothy (Fuller) S.; m. Ellen Mae Pritchett, Feb. 23, 1932; children: Chester III, Mark W., Susan A., David T., Rebecca L. AA, Nazarene Bible Coll., 1971; BA, So. U., Bethany, Okla., 1973; ThB, Internat. Sem., Plymouth, Fla., 1983, ThM, 1985; D in Ministry, Mid-Atlantic Sem., Rock Hill, S.C., 1986; ThD, Covington Theol. Sem., Roseville, Ga., 1987. Ordained to ministry Ch. of the Nazarene, 1971. Pastor Ch. of the Nazarene, Shippensburg, Pa., 1965-69, Denver, 1969-73, Hydro, Okla., 1973-76, Tampa, Fla., 1976-81, Meridian, Miss., 1981-84, Rock Hill, 1984—; prof. Mid-Atlantic Theol. Sem., Rock Hill, 1986—. Author: The Search for Torejon, 1975, The Man in the Pulpit, 1986. Counselor Neighborhood Clin. Counseling Ctr., Denver, 1971; vol. tchr. York County Literacy Assn., Rock Hill, 1986. Served with USN, 1951-55. Mem. Rock Hill Ministerial Assn. (pres. 1985—), York County Nazarene Ministerial Assn. (pres. 1986). Republican. Avocations: golf, camping. Home: 4004 Memorial Blvd Port Arthur TX 77642

SMITH, CHESTER JUNIOR, minister; b. Dexter, Mo., Mar. 23, 1942; s. Chester Colman and Rachel Emma (Williamson) S.; m. Barbara Anne Camp, June 3, 1966 (dec. Feb. 1989); children: Sandra Kaye, Sharon Leigh; m. Nancy Jill Markel, Oct. 12, 1990. BA in Religion, Ouchita Bapt. U., 1967; MDiv, Southeastern Sem., Wake Forest, N.C., 1970. Ordained to ministry Bapt. Ch., 1966. Pastor Bethlehem Bapt. Ch., Gurdon, Ark., 1965-67, Corinth Bapt. Ch., Chadbourn, N.C., 1967-69, Hall Rd. Bapt. Mission, Hampton, Va., 1970-76, Farmville (Va.) Bapt. Ch., 1976-80, Fairview Bapt. Ch., Fredericksburg, Va., 1980—; trustee Religious Herald, Richmond, Va.; mem.-at-large Va. Bapt. Gen. Bd., Richmond, 1983-87; chmn. Comm. for Va. Bapt., Richmond, 1986; v.p. Va. Bapt. Pastor's Conf., 1982. Writer Sunday sch. lessons Religious Herald, 1981. Counselor Hospice, Fredericksburg, Va., 1989—, Personal Counseling Svc., Fredericksburg, 1981-83; mem. Prince Edward Adult Edn. Com., Farmville, 1979-80, YMCA Bd., Fredericksburg, 1988. With U.S. Army, 1960-63. Home: 11207 Carriage House Ct Fredericksburg VA 22408 Office: Fairview Bapt Ch 900 Charlotte St Fredericksburg VA 22401

SMITH, CHRISTOPHER LEE, lay worker; b. Neurenburg, Bavaria, Fed. Republic Germany, May 3, 1970; came to U.S., 1970; s. Keith LeeRoy and Carolyn Jean (Reger) S. Internat. Baccalaureate, United World Coll., St. Donat's, Wales, 1988; BS, Beloit Coll., 1990; MS, Baden Powell U., George Williams, B.W.I., 1990. Dir. Vol. Connection, Beloit, Wis., 1988-90; mgr. Summer Tutoring Program, Beloit, 1989; youth placement coord. Vol. Action Ctr., Beloit, summer 1989; chaplain Camp Indian Trails, Janesville, Wis., 1990—; dir. local mission First Presbyn. Ch., Beloit, 1990—; dir., sec. bd. dirs. Vol. Action Ctr., Beloit, 1988—. Chmn. World Devel. Confs., St. Donat's, 1987, 88; commr., committeeman at large Arrowhead Dist. Boys Scouts Am., Beloit, Janesville, 1988—; elder 1st Presbyn. Ch., Beloit, 1990—. Recipient Tng. awards Boy Scouts Am., 1989-90, God and Svc. award, 1990; named Vol. of Month City of Beloit, 1989; Wingspread fellow Johnson Found., 1988, 91; scholar Beloit Coll., 1991, fellow, 1989. Mem. No. Ill. So. Wis. Assn. Vol. Adminstrs. (chmn. pub. rels. 1989—), Rock County Prevention Network, Wis. Prevention Network, Order of Arrow (lodge chair 1989-90, advisor 1990—, Brotherhood award 1990, Anniversary award 1990), Ops. Rsch. Soc. Am., Math. Assn. Am., Kiwanis. Achievements include classroom demonstrations of semiconductor properties. Home: 810 Emerson St Beloit WI 53512 Office: 1st Presbyn Ch 501 Prospect St Beloit WI 53511

SMITH, CLYDE CURRY, historian, educator; b. Hamilton, Ohio, Dec. 16, 1929; s. Charles Clyde and Mabel Ethel Ola (Curry) S.; m. Ellen Marie Gormsen, June 13, 1953; children: Harald Clyde, Karen Margaret Evans. BA in Physics cum laude and MS, Miami U., Oxford, Ohio, 1951; BDiv, U. Chgo., 1954, MA, 1961, PhD, 1968. Ordained to ministry Christian Ch. (Disciples of Christ), 1954. Exec. asst. to dean Disciples Div. House, Chgo., 1956-57; lectr. in O.T., Univ. Coll. U. Chgo., 1957; asst. prof. St. John's Coll. U. Manitoba, Winnipeg, Can., 1958-63; instr. Brandeis U., Waltham, Mass., 1963-65; prof. ancient history and religions U. Wis., River Falls, 1965-90, prof. emeritus, 1990—; vis. prof. religious studies Culver-Stockton Coll., Canton, Mo., 1990; vis. lectr. Div., Edge Hill Coll. of Edn., Ormskirk, Eng., 1970-71; postdoctoral fellow Johns Hopkin's U., Balt., summer 1977; NEH fellow in residence U. Calif., Santa Barbara, 1978-79; vis. rsch. fellow, lectr. religious studies U. Aberdeen, Scotland, 1980, 85-86. Mem. Pierce County Hist. Assn., River Falls, 1965—, Wis. Dems., 1965—, Dem. Nat. Com., 1983—; charter mem. Sci. Mus. of Minn., St. Paul, 1973—. Recipient Gov.'s Spl. award State of Wis., 1990, several grants. Mem. Assn. Ancient Historians, Can. Soc. Ch. History (founder, treas. 1960-63), N. Am. Patristic Soc., Can. Soc. for Mesopotamian Studies, Soc. for Promotion Roman Studies of London, Hellenic Soc. London, Brit. Sch. Archaeology in Iraq, Brit. Inst. Archaeology in Ankara, Phi Beta Kappa. Democrat. Avocations: space battleships, dinosaurs. Home: 939 W Maple St River Falls WI 54022 Office: U Wis Dept History River Falls WI 54022 *We can begin thought with the assumption that there is a world which knows neither origin nor end but which includes us; we can conclude with the affirmations that there was a "when" whatever is was not, and that whatever is will with time cease to be. Our concern then can be to enhance value and empower others, especially those who follow.*

SMITH, DANIEL ALBIN, broadcasting executive; b. Seattle, Aug. 18, 1956; s. Roy Arthur and Mary Alice (Phoenix) S.; m. Laura Mary Kathryn Hollingsworth, Sept. 7, 1974. BA in Communications, Wash. State U., 1979. Lay worker Fox Island Alliance, Fox Island, Wash., 1986-87; radio program dir. Sta. KICY, Arctic Broadcasting Assn., Evang. Covenant Ch., Nome, Alaska, 1987—. Home and Office: Sta KICY PO Box 820 Nome AK 99762-0820

SMITH, DANIEL HAROLD, academic administrator; b. St. Louis County, Mo., June 6, 1933; s. Harold Sturdy and Helen Julie (Vouga) S.; m. Martha Maria Carrera, Aug. 9, 1958; children: Grace Marie, Anita Mae, John Daniel. ThB, Midwest Bible Seminary, St. Louis, 1957; BA, Greenville Coll., 1959; MEd, U. Mo., 1962; postgrad., Loyola U., Chgo., 1987—. Instr. Emmaus Bible Coll., Oak Park, Ill., 1959-69, dean of edn., 1969-71, exec. v.p., 1971-75; pres. Emmaus Bible Coll., Dubuque, Iowa, 1975—; rep. conf. ministry, Emmaus Bible Coll., N. Am., 1959—. Author: How to Lead a Child to Christ, 1987, God's Blueprint For Your Marriage, 1989. Mem. Nat. Assn. Dirs. Christian Edn., Evang. Tng. Assn. (bd. dirs., chmn. 1974—). Mem. Christian Brethern. Avocations: woodworking, hunting, fishing. Office: Emmaus Bible Coll 2570 Asbury Rd Dubuque IA 52001

SMITH, DANNY LEE, minister; b. Liverpool, N.Y., Dec. 15, 1953; s. Walter L. and Elizabeth Smith; m. Nancy S. Bartell, June 21, 1974; children: Joshua, Travis, Matthew. Degree in theology, Bapt. Bible Coll., Springfield, Mo., 1975; DD (hon), Bapt. Bible Coll., Simcoe, Ont., Can., 1989. Min. Halstead (Kans.) Bapt. Ch., 1975-77, Great Lakes Bapt. Temple, Flint, Mich., 1977-79, Buckley Rd. Bapt. Ch., Liverpool, N.Y., 1979—; v.p. Bapt. Bible Fellowship, N.Y., 1987-89, chmn., 1989-90. Trustee Bapt. Bible Coll. East, Boston, 1986—. Home: 3 Juniper Ln Liverpool NY 13090

SMITH, DAVID ROYCE, lay worker, ophthalmologist, educator; b. Montreal, Que., Can., Oct. 8, 1939; s. Royce O. and Muriel E. (Harris) S.; m. Catharine, Aug. 17, 1963; children: Todd, Darron, Brett. BSC, McGill U., Montreal, Can., 1960, MD, 1964. Asst. prof. U. Toronto, 1976—; aux. bd. mem. Bahai Faith, Ont., 1974-88; continental counsellor Bahai Faith, 1988—. Contbr. articles to jours. in field. Mem. Am. Assn. Pediatric Ophthalmology, Internat. Strabismological Assn., Can. Ophthal. Soc., Am. Acad. Ophthalmology. Office: Baha'i Faith, 7200 Leslie St, Thornhill, ON Canada L3T 6L8

SMITH, DAVID WAYNE, youth minister; b. Indpls., Jan. 13, 1963; s. Wayne Eugene and Marlene June (Roe) S.; m. Julie Lynn Thompson, Feb. 4, 1989. BA in Psychology, Baylor U., 1986; MDiv, Southwestern Bapt. Theol. Sem., 1988. Ordained to ministry Bapt. Ch., 1989. Min. of youth and edn. Oak Knoll Bapt. Ch., Ft. Worth, 1986-88; min. of youth, edn. and activities First Bapt. Ch., Eastman, Ga., 1989—; pres. Dodge County Ministerial Alliance, Eastman, 1990, 91, sec., 1989; assoc. youth min. Dodge County Bapt. Assn., Eastman, 1990. Mem. com. Eastman War of Drugs, 1990-91; "McGruff" role player Dodge County Sch.System, Eastman, 1989-91. Mem. Ga. Bapt. Youth Ministries, Rotary (Eastman). Home: 508 N Pine St Eastman GA 31023 Office: First Bapt Ch 201 Oak St Eastman GA 31023

SMITH, DENNIS EDWIN, religion educator; b. Conroe, Tex., Dec. 1, 1944; m. Barbara Kay McBride, May 27, 1966; 1 child, Adam Christopher McBride-Smith. BA, Abilene Christian U., 1967, MA, 1969; MDiv, Princeton Theol. Sem., 1972; ThD, Harvard Divinity Sch., 1980. Assoc. prof. Phillips Grad. Sem., Enid, Okla., 1986—; deacon First Christian Ch., Stillwater, Okla., 1983-86, elder, 1990—. Author: (with others) Many Tables, 1990. Mem. Am. Schs. of Oriental Rsch. Assn. (trustee 1988-90), Soc. Bibl. Lit., Am. Acad. Religion, Westar Inst. (regent 1988-90). Home: 704 N Dryden Circle Stillwater OK 74075 Office: Phillips Grad Sem PO Box 2335 Univ Sta Enid OK 73702

SMITH, DENNIS JACK, broadcasting executive; b. Beckley, W.Va., Feb. 9, 1955; s. Jack and Lillian Bice (McDaniel) S.; m. Sandra Lynn Darby, Aug. 21, 1982; children: Lauren, Grace. BA, Marshall U., 1979. Account exec. Sta. WEMM-FM, Huntington, W.Va., 1985-87, asst. mgr., 1987; sales mgr. Sta. WCGW, Lexington, Ky., 1988-89, gen. mgr., 1989—. Office: Sta WCGW AM Country Gospel Box 24776 Lexington KY 40524

SMITH, DENNIS LEBRON, youth director; b. Chattanooga, Apr. 18, 1962; s. Harl Leon and Frankie Joyce (Fairbanks) S.; m. Peggy Jean Kessel, Aug. 29, 1981; children: Joshua Kessell, Brittani Rene. BS in Organizational Behavior, Covenant Coll., Lookout Mountain, Ga., 1990. From youth dir. to asst. youth dir. Hixson (Tenn.) Presbyn. Ch., 1980-90; youth dir. East Ridge (Tenn.) Presbyn., 1990—; admissions coun. Covenant Coll., Lookout Mountain, Ga., 1991—. Webelos leader Boy Scouts Am., Chattanooga, 1986-87. Recipient Golden Glove awards Golden Glove Assn., Chattanooga, 1972-77, So. Jr. Olympic gold medalist AAU, 1976. Republican. Home: 3902 Fairfax Cr Chattanooga TN 37415 Office: East Ridge Presbyn Church 4919 Court Dr Chattanooga TN 37412-2435

SMITH, DESMOND MILTON, bishop; b. San Ignacio, Cayo, Belize, Mar. 10, 1937; s. Samuel Smith and Almira Young; children: Estel, Victoria, Desmond, Dorothy, Owen, Henry. Student, St. John's Sem., Lusaka, Zambia, 1969-71, Coll. of the Resurrection, York, Eng., 1976-77; Diploma in Theology, Codrington Coll., Barbados, 1982. Joined Soc. St. Francis, Anglican Ch., 1963; ordained to ministry Anglican Episcopal Ch. as deacon, 1970, as priest, 1971, as bishop, 1989. Deacon Diocese of Zambia, 1970; priest Diocese Cen. Zambia, 1971; bishop Diocese of Belize, Belize City, 1989—. Mem. exec. com. Belize Scout Assn., Belize City, 1990; active Nat. Coun. for Edn., Belmopan, Belize, 1991. Fellow Nat. Geog. Soc. Office: 25, Southern Foreshore, Box 535, Belize City Belize

SMITH, DEUEL COILY, JR., deacon; b. Muskogee, Okla., Feb. 19, 1943; s. Deuel Coily and Jewell G. (Burkett) S.; m. Sharon Jean Mann, Dec. 3, 1960; 1 child, Rebekah. BA in Sociology, N.E. La. U., 1967, MA in Criminal Justice, 1981; MDiv, Episc. Theol. Sem. S.W., 1988. With Troop F, La. State Police, 1964-66; with Monroe (La.) Police Dept., 1966-69, Gov.'s Commn. on Law Enforcement, 1969-70; spl. agt. FBI, 1970-76; security cons. to bus. and industry, 1976-78; security mgr. Mid-Continent Wood Products Mfg. div. Ga.-Pacific Corp., Crossett, Ark., 1978-85; seminarian Episcopal Theol. Sem. of the S.W., Austin, Tex., 1985-88, deacon Episc. Ch., 1988—; lectr. corporate security mgmt. Ind. U., 1979-82. Vestryman, sr. warden, St. Mark's Episcopal Ch., Crossett, 1979-81. Served as M.P., U.S. Army, 1961-64. Mem. Am. Soc. Indsl. Security (charter mem. Ark.; cert. protection profl.), Republican. Lodges: Masons, Shriners (Monroe, La.). Home: 2202 Pompton Ln Austin TX 78758 Office: 606 Rathervue Pl PO Box 2247 Austin TX 78768

SMITH, DEWEY WAYNE, clergyman, counselor; b. Winterville, N.C., Aug. 29, 1953; s. Cleveland Wilson and Pearlene Smith; m. Nellie Mae Rountree, Aug. 29, 1976; children: Kewan, Takiyah, Tarik. BS, N.C. Arts and Tech. State U., 1975; MDiv, Gammon Sem., Atlanta, 1979; postgrad., U. N.C., Charlotte, 1987—. Ordained to ministry United Meth. Ch., 1979. Minister Red. Oak-LaMar Johnson United Meth. Ch., Stockbridge, Ga., 1978-79, St. Paul-Mt. Beulah Province, Newton and Catawba, Ga., 1979-83, St. Paul-Galilee United Meth. Ch., Kings Mountain, Ga., 1983—; counselor intern Kings Mountain Sr. High Sch., 1988; chaplain intern Presbyn. Hosp., Charlotte, 1989; treas. Ea. Catawba County Christian Ministries, Newton, 1980-83; vol. chaplain Yoke-Fellow Prison Ministries, Newton, 1980-83; adj. chaplain Gaston Meml. Hosp., Gastonia, N.C., 1985—. Chmn. Kings Mountain Community Adv. Coun., 1984; mem.-at-large Cleveland County Dist. Dem. Com., 1984; mem. calendar com. Kings Mountain Dist. Schs., 1988. Mem. Am. Assn. for Counseling and Devel., Kings Mountain Ministers Alliance (chmn. helping hands 1984-85), Nat. Honor Soc., Masons, Alpha Phi Alpha. Avocations: reading, singing, fishing, swimming, sight seeing. Home: 318 Somerset Dr Kings Mountain NC 28086 Office: Galilee-St Paul UM Ch Kings Mountain NC 28086

SMITH, DONALD ARCHIE, religion business executive, consultant; b. Dayton, Ohio, Feb. 23, 1934; s. Archie Ford and Catherine Rosella (Rabold) S.; m. Joan Sandra Speedie, May 18, 1955; children: Douglas Alan, Keith Cameron, Deirdre Lynn, Neal Ramsey. BA in Sci. and Math., Harvard U., 1956; cert. Indsl. Coll. of Armed Forces, 1971. Nuclear research and project engr. N.Am. Aviation Co., 1956-62; fin. software specialist Nat. Cash Register, 1962-63; mgr. systems engring. N.Am. Aviation, 1963-67; mgr. bus. planning, mktg. services and pub. relations N.Am. Rockwell, Columbus, Ohio, 1967-72, mgr. internat. sales and mktg., 1968-73; mgr. stratetic planning Rockwell Internat. Corp., Columbus, 1973-76, program mgr. Condor weapons system, 1976-77, dir. guided bomb programs, 1977-78, dir. bus. devel. and legis. liaison, 1978-80; v.p. fin. applied tech. group Arvin Industries, Columbus, Ind., 1980-84; v.p. fin. Calspan Corp., Columbus, 1980-82, v.p. fin. and adminstrn., 1982-84, chief fin. officer, treas., dir., 1983-84; bus. dir. Franklin United Meth. Home, 1984-86; dir. fin. and adminstrn. North Ind. Conf. of the U.S. Meth. Ch., 1986—; ops. rsch. cons., 1962-64; instr. math. Sinclair Coll., Dayton, Ohio, 1961-63; mem. U.S.-U.K. Bipartite Com. on Nuclear Weapons, 1958-61; industry chmn. Mil. Specifications and Standards Rev. Com., 1972-79; mgmt. cons., 1984—. Pres., trustee Columbus Arts Guild, 1980-83; treas., dir. Franklin United Methodist Home, 1982-84; auditor First United Meth. Ch., 1981-84; past pres., treas., trustee Players Theatre of Columbus, 1975-80; v.p. Ohio Assn. of U.S. Army, 1979-80; dist. commr. Boy Scouts Am., 1970-73, cubmaster, 1965-70; mem. audit and rev. com. Gen. Coun. on Fin. and Adminstrn., 1988—; mem. Denominational Health Task Force, Gen. Bd. Pensions, 1989—; dir. Indpls. Interch. Ctr., 1989—; squadron comdr. CAP, 1976; chmn. Commn. on Racism in Columbus Pub. Schs., 1972. Recipient Nat. award Jr. Achievement, Inc., 1954; Letters of Commendation govt. agys., Am. Def. Preparedness Assn., Boy Scouts Am., 1958-78; Leadership award Nat. Mgmt. Assn., 1979. Mem. AIAA (nat. chmn. soc. and aerospace tech. com. 1980-83, nat. pub. policy com.), SAR, NRA, Royal Inst. Nav., Nat. Mgmt. Assn. (v.p., trustee), Nat. Rifle Assn. (life mem.), Palatines to Am., Harvard Club (Ind.), Army and Navy Club, Masons, Shriners. Contbr. articles to profl. jours. Home: 3811 Penbrook Dr Marion IN 46952 Office: 1105 N Western Ave Marion IN 46952 *As we learn to celebrate and use for the benefit of all humankind the gifts we have been given, including technology and democracy, we must remember that when we try to leave God out of being good, we are left with nothing.*

SMITH, DONNA HACKER, minister; b. Lake Forest, Ill., Aug. 30, 1954; d. Donald Richard and Charlotte (Haas) Hacker; m. Lawrence A. Smith, J.r, NOv. 7, 1987; stepchildren: Lawrence III, Amy Soppe, Ann Peterson, Andrew, Sean, Alicia, Margaret. BA, Northeastern Ill. U., 1975; MDiv, Luth. Sch. Theology, 1983. Ordained to ministry Luth. Ch., 1983. Lay missionary Luth. Ch. in Am., Kumamoto, Japan, 1975-78; assoc. pastor Holy Trinity Luth. Ch., St. Louis, 1983-86; pastor Prince of Peace Luth. Ch., Freeport, Ill., 1986—; bd. govs. Luth. Soc. Svcs., Ill.-NW, Rockford, 1986-91; sec. No. Ill. Synod Outreach Com., Rockford, 1988-91; mem. No. Ill. Synod Pastoral and Profl. Leadership Com.; supr. horizon internship program Evang. Luth. Ch. in Am., Freeport, Ill. Author: Women Followers of Jesus, 1986; editor Devotional Periodical, 1986—; contbr. articles to Luth. Woman Today mag. Res. chaplain St. Louis County Police, 1983-86. Mem. Alban Inst. Office: Prince of Peace Luth Ch 2700 W Stephenson St Rd Freeport IL 61032

SMITH, SISTER DORIS HELEN, college president; b. Cleve., June 1, 1930; d. Harold Peter and Ellen Mary (Keane) S. B.S., Coll. of Mt. St. Vincent, 1952; M.A., NYU, 1957; postgrad. Fordham U., 1960-65; L.H.D., (hon.), Manhattan Coll., 1979. Joined Sisters of Charity (N.Y.), 1952. Mem. faculty Coll. of Mount St. Vincent, Bronx, N.Y., 1955-71, adminstrv. asst. to pres., 1971-72, exec. v.p., 1972-73, pres., 1973—; spl. asst. to pres. Chatham Coll., Pitts., 1970-71; dir. Hudson River Trust of Equitable Variable Life Ins., N.Y.C.; trustee Higher Edn. Service Corp., Albany, N.Y., 1980-85, Com. on Independent Colls. and Univs., Albany, 1980-83. Recipient Higher Edn. Leadership award Com. on Independent Colls. and Corning Glass Works, 1983, several interfaith and brotherhood awards; named Riverdalian of Yr. Riverdale Community Council, 1978; Am. Council Edn. fellow, 1970-71. Mem. Assn. Colls. and Univs. of State of N.Y. (trustee 1989—), Bronx C. of C. Roman Catholic. Office: Coll Mt St Vincent Office of Pres Riverdale Ave Bronx NY 10471

SMITH, DUANE ROBERT, clergyman; b. S.I., N.Y., Aug. 30, 1953; s. Hawley N. and Mary Ceceil (Engels) S.; m. Katrina Bishop (div. June 1984); children: Kelley Lynn, Kevin Duane. Diploma in specialized ministry, Berean Sch. of Bible, 1978, diploma in ministerial studies, 1985. Ordained to ministry Pentecostal Holiness Ch., 1991. Minister Christian edn. Southside Assembly of God, Jacksonville, Fla., 1979-83; children's pastor Brooksville (Fla.) Assembly of God, 1984-90; pastor Bell Chapel, Spring Hill, Fla., 1990—; div. comdr. Royal Rangers, Franklin Springs, Ga., 1990-91; pres. frontiersman camping fellowship Sunshine Conf. Pentecostal Holiness Royal Rangers. Recipient Bishop's award Pentecostal Holiness Ch., Oklahoma City, 1991. Office: Bell Chapel 10472 Northcliffe Blvd Spring Hill FL 34608

SMITH, EDGAR WRIGHT, JR., religious books editor, b. Corning, N.Y., July 20, 1939; s. Edgar Wright and Grace I. (Hill) S.; m. Cheryl Elizabeth Gould, Aug. 26, 1961; 1 child, Edgar III. BA, Maryville (Tenn.) Coll., 1960; BD, Louisville Presbyn. Sem., 1963; PhD, Claremont (Calif.) Grad. Sch., 1975. Asst. pastor First Presbyn. Ch., Sanford, Fla., 1963-65; sr. editor Eerdmans Pub. Co., Grand Rapids, Mich., 1974—. Editor: International Standard Bible Encyclopedia, 1979-88; contbr. articles to profl. jours. Rte. planner Grand Rapids (Mich.) Area Hunger Walk, 1986-91. Rockefeller Found. fellow, 1969. Mem. Chgo. Soc. Bibl. Rsch., Soc. Bibl. Lit. Democrat. Home: 1150 E Chippewa SE Grand Rapids MI 49506 Office: W Eerdmans Pub Co 255 Jefferson SE Grand Rapids MI 49503

SMITH, EDWARD O'DELL, minister, social sciences educator; b. Bristol, Tenn., Mar. 22, 1929; s. Haskell V. and Eva M. (O'Dell) S.; m. Patricia Spencer Rees, Sept. 1, 1955; children: Mimi, Mark, Josh, Sean, Carrie. AB, Emory and Henry Coll., 1951; M.Div., Union Theol. Sem., 1958. Ordained to ministry Presbyn. Ch. U.S.A., 1958. Missionary to Brazil, 1958-62; pastor 1st Presbyn. Ch., Jefferson City, Tenn., 1962-68; dean students Lees-McRae Coll., Banner Elk, N.C., 1968-80, chmn. div. social scis., 1980—. Chmn. Town Planning Bd., Banner Elk, 1978-80; trustee Cannon Meml. Hosp., Banner Elk, 1984—. Served with U.S. Army, 1951-54. Home: Box 296 Banner Elk NC 78604 Office: Dept Social Sci Lees-McRae Coll Banner Elk NC 28604

SMITH, EDWIN BALL, academic administrator; b. Milw., Aug. 17, 1937; s. Alanson Follansbee and Mary Lois (Ball) S.; m. Joan Williamson, Aug. 27, 1960; children: Julie Louise, Jonathon Edwin, Richard William. BS, Carroll Coll., Waukesha, Wis., 1961; MEd, Ind. U., 1961; PhD, Kent State U., 1965. Asst. dean of men Ill. State U., Normal, 1965-66, dean of men, 1966-68, dean of students, 1968-72; dean of students U. Wis., Oshkosh, 1972-74, asst. chancellor, 1974—. Asst. to rector Trinity Episcopal Ch., Oshkosh, 1983-85; asst. All Saints Episcopal Ch., Appleton, Wis., 1985—; youth coord. Diocese of Fond du Lac, Wis., 1983—; pres. Boys' Club of Oshkosh, 1979; v.p. Big Brothers/Big Sisters, Neenah, Wis., 1975. Recipient Outstanding Svc. award U. Wis. Oshkosh, 1988. Mem. Am. Assn. Higher Edn., Nat. Assn. Student Pers. Adminstrs. Avocation: reading. Home: 1060 Westhaven Dr Oshkosh WI 54904 Office: U Wis 800 Algoma Blvd Oshkosh WI 54901

SMITH, ELDRED GEE, church leader; b. Lehi, Utah, Jan. 9, 1907; s. Hyrum Gibbs and Martha E. (Gee) S.; m. Jeanne A. Ness, Aug. 17, 1932 (dec. June 13, 1977); children: Miriam Smith Skeen, Eldred Gary, Audrey Gay Smith Vance, Gordon Raynor, Sylvia Dawn Smith Isom; m. Hortense H. Child, May 18, 1978; stepchildren: Carol Jane Child Burdette, Thomas Robert Child. Employed with sales div. Bennett Glass & Paint Co., Salt Lake City, 6 years; mech. design engr. Remington Arms Co., 2 years; design engr., prodn. equipment design Eastman Corp., Oak Ridge, Tenn., 3 years; now presiding patriarch Ch. Jesus Christ of Latter-day Saints. Home: 2942 Devonshire Circle Salt Lake City UT 84108 Office: 47 E South Temple St Salt Lake City UT 84111

SMITH, FRANK DAVID, minister; b. Cory, Pa., Apr. 2, 1950; s. Frank Delbert and Faith Honora (Scripture) S.; m. Cherylbeth Hall, May, 25, 1974; 1 child, Marcia Faith. Student, Taylor U., 1968-69; BA in Pastoral Ministry, Toccoa Falls (Ga.) coll., 1974; postgrad., Am. Bapt. Sem. of the West, 1978-79. Ordained to ministry Christian and Missionary Alliance, 1979. Pastor youth Village Ch., Ft. Myers, Fla., 1976-77, 1st Bapt. Ch., Sacramento, 1977-78; asst. pastor Fairmede Neighborhood Ch., Richmond, Calif., 1978-80; pastor Edgewater (Fla.) Alliance Ch., 1980-82, Alliance Bible Ch., Waynesboro, Ga., 1982-85, Nicholasville (Ky.) Alliance Ch., 1985—; dean of men Toccoa Falls Coll., 1974-76; bd. dirs. Lake Swan Camp, Melrose, Fla., 1980-81, Camp Begomi, Jenkins, Ky., 1989—; mem. dist. exec. com. Ohio Valley Dist., Christian and Missionary Alliance, Ohio and Ky., 1989—. Contbr. articles to profl. jours. Named one of Oustanding Young Men in Am. Jaycees, 1978. Republican. Home: 310 Peachtree Nicholasville KY 40356 Office: Nicholasville Alliance Ch 100 Blueberry Ln Nicholasville KY 40356

SMITH, FRANK WINFRED, clergyman; b. Redding, Calif., May 2, 1909; s. Chester Otis and Lena C. (Whitmore) S.; m. F. Rose Jolly, June 22, 1930 (dec. Apr. 1944); children: Ronald, David; m. Marie C. Christensen, Aug. 15, 1945; children: Joyce, Janice, Jonathan. BTh, Life Bible Coll., Los Angeles, BA; postgrad., Drake U., Des Moines; LittD (hon.), Eugene Bible Coll., 1989. Ordained to ministry, Internat. Ch. Foursquare Gospel, 1930, Open Bible Standard Chs., 1934. Pastor Foursquare Ch., Hollywood, Calif., 1930-34, Open Bible Ch., Ft. Des Moines, Iowa, 1934-38; pastor 1st Ch. Open Bible, Des Moines, 1939-76, pastor emeritus, 1989—; chmn. Pentecostal Fellowship N. Am., Springfield, Mo., 1979-83; chmn. Open Bible Standard Chs., Des Moines, 1976-79, dir., 1983—; chmn. Pentecostal Fellowship N. Am., 1980-83; pres. Midwest Nat. Assn. Evangelicals, 1955-57. Author: Pentecostal Positive, 1975. Recipient Disting. Christian award Midwest region Nat. Assn. Evangelicals, 1966. Mem. Des Moines Council Chs. (chmn. 1940), Iowa Assn. Evangelicals (pres. 1945). Republican. Office: Open Bible Standard Chs 2020 Bell Ave Des Moines IA 50315

SMITH, G. KENT, music minister; b. Doniphan, Mo., Nov. 10, 1957; s. Wilbur Leon and Etta Mae (Keathley) S.; m. Deborah L. Sullins, Feb. 23, 1979; 1 child, Elizabeth L. Student, Tree Rivers Community Coll., Poplar Bluff, Mo., 1976, S.W. Bapt. U., 1977-78. Ordained to ministry So. Bapt. Conv. Evangelist, soloist Emmanuel Bapt. Ch., Doniphan, 1974-81, minister of music, deacon, 1981—; owner Smith Enterprises, Doniphan, 1976—. Office: Smith Enterprises 1405 Hillcrest Pla Doniphan MO 63935

SMITH, GALEN EUGENE, clergyman. BA, Wm. Penn Coll., Oskaloosa, Iowa, 1981; MDiv, U. Dubuque Theol. Sem., 1988. Tchr. Bennett (Iowa) Community Sch., 1981-85; pastor Bethel Presbyn. Ch., Waterloo, Iowa, 1988-89, 1st Presbyn. Ch., Greene, Iowa, 1989—. Home: PO Box 160 Greene IA 50636

SMITH, GARY SCOTT, sociology educator, clergyman; b. Franklin, Pa., Oct. 12, 1950; s. Roger Gary and Cary Arlene (Boardman) S.; m. Patricia Marie Jamison, May 27, 1972; children: Gregory Scott, Joel Andrew. BA, Grove City Coll., 1972; MDiv, Gordon-Conwell Theol. Sem., 1977; MA in History, Johns Hopkins U., 1979, PhD in History, 1981. Ordained to ministry Presbyn. Ch. (U.S.A.), 1982. Campus missioner Coalition for Christian Outreach, Edinboro (Pa.) State Coll., 1972-74; guest lectr. religion and philosophy Grove City (Pa.) Coll., 1978-80, instr. sociology, 1980-81, asst. prof., co-dir. Christian ministries program, 1981-85, assoc. prof., 1985-90, prof., 1990—; interim pastor Clen-Moore United Presbyn. Ch., New Castle, Pa., 1983. Author: The Seeds of Secularization: Calvinism, Culture and Pluralism in America, 1870-1915, 1985; editor: Building a Christian World View, Vol. 1, God, Man and Knowledge, 1986, Vol. 2, The Universe, Society and Ethics, 1988, God and Politics. Four Views on the Reformation of Civil Government, 1989; also articles. Mem. Christian Sociol. Soc. Republican. Home: 806 Tidball Ave Grove City PA 16127 Office: Grove City Coll Grove City PA 16127

SMITH, GARY W., pastor; b. Abingdon, Va., Mar. 1, 1954; s. Everett V. and Myrba (Phipps) S.; m. Teresa Lynn Smith, Dec. 27, 1973; 1 child, Heather Lynn. BA, Free Will Bapt. Bible Coll., 1984; M. Ministry, Covington Theol. Sem., 1989, DMin, 1990. Ordained to ministry Bapt. Ch.; lic. pastoral counselor. Pastor Decatur (Ga.) Free Will Bapt. Ch., 1984-86, 1st Free Will Bapt. Ch., Grand Prairie, Tex., 1986-88, Hammock Springs Free Will Bapt., Donalsonville, Ga., 1988—; substance abuse counselor State Bd. Pardons and Paroles, Cairo, Ga., 1990—. Mem. Seminole County Ministerial Assn., Ga. Addiction Counselors Assn. Home: Rte 3 Box 319 Donaldsonville GA 31745

SMITH, GINGER ELAINE, lay worker, youth director; b. Pasadena, Md., Jan. 11, 1957; d. Edmond Eli and Imogene (Bradford) Taylor; m. Chris Russell, Sept. 23, 1983; children: Robert William, Dona Gene. Youth dir., Sunday sch. tchr. Grace Bapt. Ch., Pasadena, Md., 1990—; home health aide, nursing asst., Upjohn Home Health, Severna Park, Md., 1987—. Democrat. Home: 7839 Americana Circle Apt 203 Glen Burnie MD 21060 Office: Upjohn Home Health 692 Ritchie Hwy Severna Park MD 21122

SMITH, GREGORY K., minister; b. Decatur, Ill., Feb. 8, 1949; s. John William and Lela Louise (Billerman) S.; m. Alayne D. York, Dec. 27, 1977; children: Philip J.W., Melinda A.E. AA, Concordia U., Milw., 1969; BA with high distinction, Concordia Sr. Coll., Ft. Wayne, Ind., 1971; MDiv, Concordia Sem., St. Louis, 1975. Adm. asst. to pres. Concordia Sem., St. Louis, 1976-77; pastor Christ Meml. Luth. Ch., St. Louis, 1977—; mem. bd. govs. Luth. Med. Ctr., St. Louis, 1984—. Bd. dirs. H&S Tool & Die,

Warrensburg, Ill., 1978—. Mem. Soc. Bibl. Lit., Norwood Hills Country Club. Republican. Home: 5614 Hillridge Ct St Louis MO 63128 Office: Christ Meml Luth Ch 9712 Tesson Ferry Rd St Louis MO 63123

SMITH, MONSIGNOR GREGORY MICHAEL, priest, adult education administrator; b. Danbury, Conn., May 25, 1941; s. Michael Paul and Helen Marie (McFarland) S. MA, Fairfield U., 1973; MDiv, St. Mary U., Balt., 1976; MS, Fordham U., 1976; EdD, NYU, 1982. Assoc. pastor St. Teresa Ch., Trumbull, Conn., 1967-69, St. Joseph Ch., Danbury, Conn., 1969-72; asst. dir. rel. edn. Diocese of Bridgeport, Conn., 1972-75, dir. rel. edn., 1975-83, chancellor, 1983-90, sec. edn., 1985-89; adminstr. Office for Catechesis, Bridgeport, 1990—; dir. Inst. for Religious Edn. and Pastoral Studies Sacred Heart U., Fairfield, Conn., 1990—; bd. dirs. Conn. Cath. Conf. Author: Pilgrims in Process, 1978, The Fire in Their Eyes, 1984, (with others) Priming the Pump, 1989; contbr. articles to profl. jours. Bd. dirs. Fairfield Found., Bridgeport, 1983—, Danbury Assn. to Aid Handicapped/Retarded, 1970-72, com. on edn. and morality NYU, 1990—; commr. Youth Coun. City of Danbury, 1970-72. Mem. Am. Assn. Adult and Continuing Edn., Nat. Conf. Diocesan Dirs. (bd. dirs. 1974-77), Nat. Catholic Ednl. Assn., Religious Edn. Assn., New England Conf. Diocesan Dirs. (pres. 1977-79), Nat. Assn. Ch. Pers. Adminstrs., Assn. Grad. Programs in Ministry. Roman Catholic. Avocations: gardening, interior design. Home: 163 Ortega Ave Bridgeport CT 06606-3053 Office: Sacred Heart U 5151 Park Ave Fairfield CT 06432-1000 *The process of growth in life is less rooted in reality than in the perception of reality. Wherein one makes choices one chooses a perception, an image as it were, to pursue. But that choice is never solely one's own—with or without one's awareness, an Other joins in the pursuit.*

SMITH, GREGORY STANLEY, minister; b. Westland, Mich., Mar. 27, 1964; s. Stanley Gray and Betty Lou (St. Charles) S.; m. Amy Ruth Merideth, Sept. 13, 1985. BS in Bible, Freed-Hardeman U., Henderson, Tenn., 1985; MS in Christian Edn., Abilene Christian U., 1991. Youth ministry intern Los Altos Ch. of Christ, Long Beach, Calif., 1983, Beltline Ch. of Christ, Decatur, Ala., 1984; youth minister Beattie Ch. of Christ, Albany, Ga., 1985-86; youth family minister Brooks Ave. Ch. of Christ, Raleigh, N.C., 1986-89; family minister Summerville (S.C.) Ch. of Christ, 1989—; bd. dirs. Palmetto Bible Camp, Greenville, 1989—. Republican. Office: Summerville Ch of Christ 413 Old Trolley Rd Summerville SC 29485 *Ultimately, all difficult decisions in life seem to come back to a simple question of which you will choose to trust—your own instincts, or the infinite mind of God.*

SMITH, HARMON LEE, JR., clergyman, moral theology educator; b. Ellisville, Miss., Aug. 23, 1930; s. Harmon Lee Sr. and Mary (O'Donnell) S.; children: Pamela Lee, Amy Joanna, Harmon Lee III. AB, Millsaps Coll., 1952; BD, Duke U., 1955, PhD, 1962. Ordain to priest Episcopal Ch., 1972. Asst. dean Duke U. Divinity Sch., Durham, N.C., 1959-65, asst. prof. Christian ethics, 1962-68, assoc. prof. moral theology, 1968-73, prof. moral theology, 1973—, prof. community and family medicine, 1974—; cons. med. ethics; vis. prof. U. N.C., 1964, 70, 72, U. Edinburgh, Scotland, 1969, U. Windsor, Ont., 1974. Author books med. ethics; sr. editor: Social Science and Medicine, 1973-89; Contbr.: articles on Christian ethics to various publs. Lilly Found. fellow, 1960; Gurney Harris Kearns Found. fellow, 1961; Nat. Humanities Ctr. fellow, 1982-83. Mem. Am. Assn. Theol. Schs., Am. Soc. Christian Ethics, Am. Acad. Religion, Soc. for Religion in Higher Edn., Soc. Health and Human Values. Home: 3510 Randolph Rd Durham NC 27705 Office: Duke U The Divinity Sch Durham NC 27706

SMITH, HAROLD PHILIP, rabbi; b. Chgo., Sept. 4, 1915; s. Samuel and Rose (Siegel) S.; m. Lillian Waid, Nov. 14, 1943. B.A., U. Tulsa, 1937; D.H.L., Hebrew Theol. Coll., 1960; grad. work, U. Chgo. Fed. Schs. Theology. Ordained rabbi, 1940. Dir. edn. B'nei Emunah Sch., Tulsa, 1937-39; dir. activities Garfield Community Center, Chgo., 1939- 41; rabbi Beth El Synagogue, Gary, Ind., 1941-44; exec. dir. Midwest region Religious Zionist Am., 1944-49; rabbi Congregation Agudath Achim South Shore, Chgo., 1949-69; v.p. Jewish U. Am., Hebrew Theol. Coll., Skokie, Ill., 1969—; lectr. practical rabbinics Hebrew Theol. Coll.; Chmn. nat. com. on edn. Rabbinical Council Am., 1947-52; mem. Rabbinical Council Am. (Israel commn.), 1976—, mem. publs. com., 1952—, v.p., 1958-60, mem. religious standards com., 1960—, co-chmn. nat. legis. com., 1976—; chmn. Rabbinical Council Am. (Midwest legis. com.), 1963-; editor Passover Bull., Chgo. Rabbinical Council, 1950-54, v.p., 1954-58, mem. publs. com., 1956, pres., 1958-60, chmn. exec. bd., 1960—, mem. religious standards com., chmn. legislative com., 1961—, mem. coll. relations com., 1965—; mem. exec. bd. Council Traditional Synagogues, 1956—; mem. Commn. Religion in Pub. Schs., 1956—; mem. exec. com. Chgo. Bd. Rabbis, 1962—, mem. broadcasting commn., chmn. legislative com., 1963—, chmn. Israel affairs com., 1965—, chmn., 1965-66, v.p., 1976-82, pres., 1982-84; mem. exec. com. Chgo. Hebrew Culture Council, 1965-66; ofcl. del. Nat. Conf. Religion and Race, 1963; mem. exec. bd. Chgo. div. Am. Jewish Congress, mem. conv. com., 1963; mem. mediating commn. United Vaad Hakashruth, 1963; mem. exec. United Kashruth Commn. Greater Chgo., 1963—; co-chmn. United Kashruth Commn. Greater Chgo. (So. Shore regional com.), 1963—; mem. conv. com. Midwest region Union Orthodox Jewish Congregations Am., 1963; mem. pub. affairs com. Jewish Fedn. Met. Chgo., 1978—, mem. Middle East subcoms., 1978—, co-chmn. interfaith relations subcom., 1978—, mem. pub. affairs com., 1982—; bd. govs. Assoc. Talmud Torahs of Chgo., 1982—. Author: A Treasure Hunt in Judaism, 1942, Meaningfulness in Prayer, 1963, Anthology on Sunday Law Legislations, 1963, At Thirteen--Religious Responsibilities, 1963, Kiddushin Means Sanctity; The Holiness of the Jewish Marriage Vow, 1964, Anthology of State Aid to Non- Public Schools, 1969; Editor: The Scroll, 1949—; Compiler, translator: Sidduri, 1940; Translator: History and Spirit of Jewish Homiletics; Contbr. periodicals. Mem. Speaker's Bur.; mem. Combined Jewish Appeal, Bonds for Israel, South Shore Commn. Juvenile Delinquency; rabbinic adv. council Combined Jewish Appeal, Chgo., 1961—; nat. rabbinic adv. council United Jewish Appeal, 1961—, also mem. publs. com. rabbinic adv. council.; Mem. Gary Mayor's Youth Commn., 1942-43; chmn. Kosher Law Enforcement Com., 1956—; mem. law enforcement com. South Shore, 1957—; mem. Ill. Com. Equal Job Opportunities, 1959—, Jewish Religious Ct. Chgo., 1963—; spl. emissary Ill. Legislature, 1963; Exec. Jewish Nat. Fund, 1956—; director, Nat. chmn. com. for alumni fund raising Hebrew Theol. Coll.; pres. Nat. Rabbinical Alumni Assn., 1964-65; mem. academic com. Jewish U. Am., 1959—; also trustee, mem. president's adv. com. gov. Akiba Jewish Day Sch., 1955—; bd. govs. Chgo. Jewish Acad. Recipient award Chicago Sun-Times, 1954; Clergyman of Year award Chgo. Tribune, 1955; Merit citation Hebrew Theol. Coll., 1956; Spl. Service citation Chgo. Rabbinical Council, 1963; Spl. Service award Jewish Fedn. Met. Chgo., 1963; Community Service award Assn. Torah Advancement, 1963; Jewish United Fund award, 1967; Religious Zionists Man of Year award, 1969; Bonds of Israel award, 1969. Mem. South Shore Ministerial Assn., Conf. Religion and Race (bd. govs.), Nat. Assn. Jewish Day Schs., League Religious Labor (nat. exec.), Nat. Council Adult Edn., Am. Zionist Council, Ill. Conf. Jewish Orgns., Am. Assn. Higher Edn., Nat. Social Sci. Honor Soc., Anselm Forum (hon.), Hebrew Theol. Coll. Alumni Assn., Internat. Platform Assn., Pi Gamma Mu. Office: 7135 N Carpenter Rd Skokie IL 60076

SMITH, HAROLD VICTOR, JR., minister; b. Ridgely, W.Va., Sept. 25, 1943; s. Harold Victor and Lena Irene (Rockwell) S.; m. Patricia Ann Galford, Aug. 7, 1963; children: Jodi Patricia, Stacee Ann, Aaron Victor. Assoc. Practical Bible Theology, Christ for the Nations Coll., 1981, Southwestern Assembly of God, 1987. Ordained to ministry Assembly of God, 1989. Assoc. pastor Calvary Temple, Glen Burnie, Md., 1974-75, World Revival, Newark, Del., 1975-79; sr. pastor Grafton (W.Va.) Assembly of God, 1981-83, Beth Shan Assembly of God, Cumberland, Md., 1984-86, Christian Faith Assembly, Wellsburg, W.Va., 1986—; sect. treas. western sect. Assembly of God, Wellsburg, 1988—, mem. decade of harvest com., 1990—. Contbr. sermons to jour. Bible Theology. Recipient Honor plaque Faith City Christian Sch., 1977. Home: 730 Commerce St Wellsburg WV 26070 Office: Christian Faith Assembly 2640 Pleasant Ave Wellsburg WV 26070 *It is the grace of God that appears to us to bring salvation. It is this Spirit of Grace that teaches us to fear God, hate evil, live a godly life, and look forward to eternity. Grace is God's way to wisdom. A wise man will not trample the Spirit of Grace.*

SMITH, HERSCHEL BRET, minister, psychotherapist; b. Corpus Christi, Tex., June 20, 1959; s. Herschel B. Smith and Erma L. (Crawford) Calhoun; m. Angelia Gay Glover, Sept. 19, 1981; children: Dustin, Cameron, Carlyse. BS, Tex. A&M U., 1981; BBS, Abilene (Tex.) Christian U., 1983; MEd, U. North Tex., 1989. Family life minister Pond Springs Ch. of Christ, Austin, Tex., 1982-83; campus minister Cen. Ch. of Christ, Valdosta, Ga., 1983-84; singles minister Saturn Rd. Ch. of Christ, Garland, Tex., 1984-89, North Atlanta Ch. of Christ, 1989-90; psychotherapist Scott and Assocs., Atlanta, 1990—; co-sponsor Nat. Singles Retreat, Dallas, 1985—; sponsor Nat. Singles Upreach, Atlanta, 1989—. Mem. Am. Assn. for Counseling and Devel., Am. Assn. Christian Counselors, Kappa Delta Phi. Avocations: amateur triathlete, backpacking, trekking. Home: 6640 Akers Mill Rd #38T4 Atlanta GA 30339 Office: 5555 Peachtree Dunwoody Rd Ste G99 Atlanta GA 30342

SMITH, HORACE EARL, II, minister, pediatrician; b. Chgo., Dec. 10, 1949; s. Albert and Shirley (Rhone) S.; m. Susan Davenport, Sept. 4, 1976; children: Lauren Annette, Rachel Marie, Emily Therese. BS, Chgo. State U., 1971; MD, U. Ill., Chgo., 1975. Ordained to ministry Pentecostal Assemblies of World, 1980; diplomate Am. Bd. Pediatrics. Pastor Apostolic Faith Ch., Chgo., 1980—; elder Ill. Dist. Coun., Pentecostal Assemblies of World, Chgo., 1983—, chmn., 1986-91; attending physician, dir. comprehensive sickle cell program Children's Meml. Hosp., Chgo., 1980—; cons. in pediatric hematology and oncology Columbus Hosp., Chgo., 1980—; bd. dirs. Aenon Bible Coll., Pentecostal Assemblies of World, Indpls., 1989—; mem. med. adv. bd. Hemophilia Found., 1988—. Writer Sunday sch. materials. Mem. Ill. State's Atty.'s Task Force on Death and Dying, Chgo., 1990—, Grand Blvd. Residents Encouraging Action Together, Chgo., 1990—. Named Man of Yr., Mahogany Found., 1991. Mem. AMA, Nat. Med. Assn., Pastors Allied Under the Lord (treas. 1991). Office: Apostolic Faith Ch 3823 S Indiana Ave Chicago IL 60653

SMITH, HUGH LANSDEN, minister, religious organization administrator; b. Livingston, Tenn., Nov. 10, 1940; s. James W. and Ruby A. (Hayes) S.; m. Miriam J. Goodwin, Aug. 10, 1962; children: Kimberly Carol Smith Schmidt, Carla Kay. BA, Trevecca Nazarene Coll., Nashville, 1963; BD, Nazarene Theol. Sem., Kansas City, Mo., 1966. Ordained to ministry Ch. of the Nazarene, 1964. Pastor Chs. of the Nazarene, 1960-85; dist. supt. Washington Pacific Chs. of the Nazarene, 1985—; youth pres. Kansas City Dist. Nazarene, 1969-72; rep. mid-Am. Nazarene zone Gen. Youth Soc., 1972-74, mem. exec. com., 1973-74; dir. Internat. Teen Bible Quiz, 1972-74; Arlington pres. Tex. Ministerial Alliance, 1977-78. Contbr. articles to mags. Regent N.W. Nazarene Coll., 1985—; trustee Nazarene Theol. Sem., 1989—; hon. chaplain Ho. of Reps., Austin, Tex., 1982. Home: 9119 185th Pl SW Edmonds WA 98026 Office: Washington Pacific Dist 180 W Dayton # 103 Edmonds WA 98020

SMITH, HUSTON, religion educator; b. Soochow, China, May 31, 1919; (parents Am. citizens); s. Wesley Moreland and Alice (Longden) S.; m. E. Kendra Wieman, Sept. 15, 1943; children: Karen, Gael, Kimberly. AB, Cen. Meth. Coll., Fayette, Mo., 1940; 7 hon. degrees; PhD, U. Chgo., 1945; hon. degree, Franklin Coll., 1964, Lake Forest Coll., 1965, Alaska Pacific U., 1983, Hamline U., 1988. Ordained to ministry United Meth. Ch., 1946. Prof. philos. and religious studies Washington U., St. Louis, 1947-58, MIT, 1958-73, Syracuse U., 1973-83, U. Calif., Berkeley, 1990—. Author: The Religions of Man, 1958, Forgotten Truth, 1976, Beyond the Post-Modern Mind, 1989, The World's Religions, 1991. Home: 130 Avenida Dr Berkeley CA 94708

SMITH, JAMES DERRILL, minister; b. Seneca, S.C., July 28, 1952; s. Hubert Arnold and Bertha (Dyar) S.; m. Cynthia Phillips, Oct. 13, 1973; children: Phillip Ryan, Caroline Elizabeth. AA, Anderson Coll., 1972; BA, Central Wesleyan Coll., 1974; MDiv, Southern Sem., 1978; DMin, Erskine Sem., 1989. Ordained to ministry Bapt. Ch., 1974. Pastor Pond Run Bapt. Ch., Echols, Ky., 1975-78; assoc. pastor College St. Bapt., Wahalla, S.C., 1978-80; pastor Return Bapt. Ch., Seneca, S.C., 1980-88, Grace Bapt. Ch., Asheville, N.C., 1988—; moderator Beaverdam Bapt. Assn., Seneca, 1986, family life chair, 1984-86; mem. rural/urban task force S.C. Bapt. Conv., 1985-87. Author: Seven Last Words, 1989. Vol. United Way, Oconee, S.C. 1987; chair Foster Care Rev. Bd., Oconee, 1986-88; bd. dirs. Oconee A.I.D., Walhalla, S.C., 1987-88; vol. West Asheville Recreation, Asheville, 1991. Recipient Am. Legion Sch. award, 1970. Mem. Buncombe Bapt. Assn. (program chair pastor's conf. 1990—). Office: Grace Bapt Ch 718 Haywood Rd Asheville NC 28806

SMITH, JAMES EVERETT, minister; b. Winnipeg, Mo., May 6, 1927; s. Clarence Everett and Myrtle Frances (Woody) S.; m. Virginia Juanita Jones, June 14, 1953; children: Karen, Melinda. BA, Tex. Christian U., 1962; MDiv, Brite Sch. Div., 1962, D Ministry, 1980. Ordained to ministry Christian Ch. (Disciples of Christ), 1961. Min. 1st Christian Ch., Howe, Tex., 1953-54, Cen. Christian Ch., Stamford, Tex., 1954-61, Urbandale Christian Ch., Dallas, 1962-71; sr. min. 1st Christian Ch., Duncan, Okla., 1972—; mem. nat. gen. bd. Christian Ch. (Disciples of Christ), 1980-84; mem. com. on ministry, Okla. Disciples of Christ, 1982-84, moderator, 1986-88, regional exec. com., 1988-90; tour condr. Faith Roots Tour of Middle East, 1972, 75, 78, 84, tour Far East, 1973; moderator dist. Author: Standing on Holy Ground: An Ecumenical Study of Significant Biblical Sites, 1980. Pres. Duncan Community Residence, 1975-77, Duncan Sr. Citizens, 1976, Stephens County Mental Health Assn., 1976; v.p. Duncan United Way, 1979. Recipient Liberty Bell award Stephens County Bar Assn., 1980. Mem. Duncan Ministerial Alliance (pres. 1976), Rotary (pres. Duncan club 1988-89). Home: 1201 Harville Rd Duncan OK 73533 Office: 1st Christian Ch 916 Walnut Duncan OK 73533 *The Persian Gulf Desert Storm war calls for accelerated dialogue between Christians, Jews and Muslims with greater appreciation for a common spiritual heritage and the wisdom to work through past inequities which continue to disrupt the larger ecumenical fellowship.*

SMITH, JAMES G., minister, educator; b. Rockwall, Tex., Aug. 11, 1937; s. Quayle D. and Hassie (Dee) S.; m. Grace Dianne Armistead, June 4, 1955; children: Tonna Chreyce Evans, James G. Jr. BA, Dallas Bapt. U., 1973; MA in Religious Edn., Southwestern Bapt. Theol. Sem., Fort Worth, 1974. Minister of Edn., Adminstrn. Pleasant Terr. Bapt. Ch., Dallas, 1970-74, First Bapt. Ch., Ft. Walton Beach, Fla., 1974-78, Wilshire Bapt. Ch., Dallas, 1978—. Contbr. articles to profl. jours. Named J.L. Ward Disting. Alumnus, Dallas Bapt. U., 1979. Fellow The Nat. Assn. of Ch. Bus. Adminstrn., The So. Bapt. Ch. Bus. Adminstr. Assn. Home: 1421 Lexington Garland TX 75041 Office: Wilshire Bapt Ch 4316 Abrams Rd Dallas TX 75214-2398

SMITH, JAMES LEE, minister; b. Bremen, Ohio, Jan. 20, 1940; s. Halley Newton and Mable Frances (Bilyeu) S.; m. Linda Frances Lorren, Jan. 1, 1963; children: Douglas, Lorré, Duane. Student, Faulkner U., 1962-63; BTh., Internat. Sem., 1987, ThM, 1988, PhD magna cum laude, 1990. Ordained to ministry Ch. of Christ, 1961. Min. Ethridge (Tenn.) Ch. of Christ, 1973-75, 80-83, min., 1987—; min. Ashwood Ch. of Christ, Nashville, 1975-78, Southside Ch. of Christ, St. Joseph, Tenn., 1983-87; owner Smith Publs., Lawrenceburg, Tenn., 1989—; founder, pres. Lawrence County Bible Sch., 1978-81; producer, speaker Today's Story radio programs, 1985—; founder, tchr. South Bend (Ind.) Sch. Personal Evangelism, 1969-70; lectr., 1961—. Author: One Nation Under God or Man?, 1989, He Arose, 1972. Pres. Lawrenceburg chpt. Am. Cancer Soc., 1987-88. Home: 518 Lafayette Ave Lawrenceburg TN 38464 Office: Ethridge Ch of Christ PO Box 8 Hwy 43 Ethridge TN 38456 *Life is a continuous interlink of blessings and cursings. The latter can be the precursor of the former if we will allow it.*

SMITH, JAMES RONALD, religious organization administrator; b. Miami, Okla., Dec. 13, 1952; s. Palmer Newton and Hildred Faye (Underwood) S.; m. Debra Kay DaVee, July 31, 1971; children: Jordan Wade, Allison DaVee. BA, Okla. Bapt. U., 1975; MEd, Phillips U., 1978; MA in Religious Edn., SW Bapt. Theol. Seminary, 1980. Assoc. pastor Calvary Bapt. Ch., Enid, Okla., 1975-77, Cedar Heights Bapt. Ch., Dallas, 1977-80; assoc. pastor, adminstr. Immanuel Bapt. Ch., Shawnee, Okla., 1980-83; pastor Knob Hill Bapt. Ch., Oklahoma City, 1983-85; v.p. The Bapt. Found. of Okla., Oklahoma City. Vol. Oklahoma City United Way, 1985, 86; chaplain Mayor's Council, Oklahoma City, 1985. Mem. Assn. Bapt. Found. Execs. (sec.-treas. 1985—), Bapt. Pub. Relations Assn., Nat. Soc. Fund Raising Execs., Nat. Inst. Devel. Officers and Found. Execs. Republican. Home: 10001 Casa Linda Oklahoma City OK 73139 Office: Baptist Found of Oklahoma 1141 N Robinson Oklahoma City OK 73103

SMITH, JERRY EUGENE, religion educator; b. York, Pa., Mar. 3, 1947; s. Jerry Junior and Dorothy June (Hickman) S.; m. Carolyn Mae Eveler, Sept. 30, 1966; children: Brian, Julie, Mindy. BA, Oral Roberts U., 1969; MA, Wheaton (Ill.) Grad. Sch. Ordained to ministry Evang. Ch., 1970; cert. tchr., N.J., supr. Pastor Assembly of God Ch., Pocohontas, Ill., 1970-71; tchr. Ridgeville (Ohio) Christian Sch., 1971-72, prin., 1972-73; headmaster Cumberland Christian Sch., Vineland, N.J., 1973—; treas. Mid-Atlantic Christian Sch. Assn., Media, Pa., 1973—; pres. N.J. Christian Sch. Assn., Vineland, 1980—. Contbr. articles to Christian Teacher mag. Dir. Support Our Activity Program Community Trash-a-thon, Vineland, 1980; mem. N.J. Non-pub. Edn. Com., Trenton, 1982—. Mem. Nat. Assn. Secondary Sch. rins. Home: 1170 W Sherman Ave Vineland NJ 08360 Office: Cumberland Christian Sch 1100 W Sherman Ave Vineland NJ 08360

SMITH, JOHN LEE, JR., minister, former association administrator; b. Fairfax, Ala., Dec. 11, 1920; s. John Lee and Mae Celia (Smith) S.; m. Vivian Herrington, Aug. 15, 1942; children—Vicky Smith Davis, Joan Smith Wimberly, Jennifer Lee Smith Ruscilli. A.B., Samford U., 1950; student, New Orleans Bapt. Theol. Sem., 1950-51, 53; D.D., Ohio Christian Coll., 1967, Birmingham Bapt. Bible Coll., 1979; postgrad., Auburn U., 1956, Baylor U., 1972-73; LL.D., Nat. Christian U., 1974. Owner Smith's Grocery Co., Montgomery, Ala., 1945-47; ordained minister Bapt. Ch., 1947; pastor Dolomite Bapt. Ch., Birmingham, Ala., 1947-50, Elim Bapt. Ch., Brewton, Ala., 1950-51; pastor 1st Bapt. Ch., Tallapoosa, Ga., 1951-52, Villa Rica, Ga., 1952-54, Fairfax, Ala., 1954-57; pastor West End Bapt. Ch., Birmingham, 1957-59, 88—, Dalraida Bapt. Ch., Montgomery, 1959-66, 83-86, 1st Bapt. Ch., Demopolis, Ala., 1966-69; assoc. exec. dir. Ala. Council Alcohol Problems, Birmingham, 1969-70, exec. dir., 1970-78; exec. dir. Am. Council Alcohol Problems, Washington, 1972-74, sec., 1974-79, v.p., 1979-87; pastor Benton (Ala.) Bapt. Ch., 1987-88; tchr., dir. Bessemer Bapt. Inst., 1978-83; exec. dir. missions Bessemer Bapt. Assn., 1978-83; tchr. Mercer U. extension, Carrollton, Ga., 1953-54; tchr. Extension div. Samford U., Fairfax, Ala., 1955-57, South Ala. area dir., 1986-87; mem. bd. ministerial edn. Bapt. Ch., 1958-59, Christian Life Commn., 1959-60; pres. Bessemer Ministers Alliance, 1979-81. Contbr. profl. jours. Chmn. Marengo County Cancer Soc., 1967-68, Good News Ala., Jefferson County, 1977-79, Gov.'s Commn. on Pornography, 1970-78, Nat. Temperance and Prohibition Council, 1973-80, Nat. Coordinating Council on Drug Edn., 1972-78, Alcohol Drug Problems Assn. Am., 1972-78; exec. dir. Temperance Edn., Inc., Washington, 1972-74; trustee Internat. Reform Fedn., 1973-74; adv. bd. JCCEO, 1975-82; bd. dirs. Bessemer Rescue Mission, 1978-83, 89—, Bessemer YMCA, 1978-83; mem. adv. bd. Bessemer Salvation Army, 1978-83. Served to capt. USAAF, 1942-45, ETO. Mem. C. of C., Trident, Phi Kappa Phi. Club: Mason. Home: PO Box 26407 608 Staffordshire Dr Birmingham AL 35226 Office: West End Baptist Church 1133 Tuscaloosa Ave Birmingham AL 35211

SMITH, JOHN M., bishop; b. Orange, N.J., June 23, 1935. Ed., Immaculate Conception Sem., Darlington, N.J., South Orange, N.J., Cath. U., Washington. Ordained priest Roman Cath. Ch., 1961. Titular bishop Tre Tavern, aux. bishop Newark Roman Cath. Ch., 1988-91; bishop of Pensacola-Tallahassee Roman Cath. Ch., Fla., 1991—. Office: Chancery Office 31 Mulberry St Newark NJ 07102*

SMITH, JUSTIN WILSON, religious organization administrator; b. Harvey, Ill., Aug. 3, 1934; s. Wilson Goodridge and Florence (Slater) S.; m. Anna Ruth Davis, Sept. 2, 1955; children: James Ronald, David Michael, Justin Wilson Jr. AAS, Community Coll. of Air Force, Maxwell AFB, Ala., 1983; BA, S.W. Tex. State U., 1985, MS, 1987. Adminstr. Valley-Hi Ch. of the Nazarene, San Antonio, 1987—. Mem. Nat. Assn. Ch. Bus. Adminstrs. (treas. local chpt. 1989-91, sec. 1991—), Air Force Assn., Aerospace Found., Air Force Sgts. Assn., Armed Forces Ret. Enlisted Assn., Assn. Old Crows, Am. Assn. Profl. Bookkeepers. Republican. Office: Valley-Hi Ch of Nazarene 5834 Ray Ellison Dr San Antonio TX 78242 *The world's concept of friendship is a casual relationship without depth of meaning. True friendship is a spiritual quality. A spiritual friend is someone with whom one can reveal their deepest fears and anxieties without having to filter them first.*

SMITH, KATHY JANE, minister, nurse; b. Tiffin, Ohio, Feb. 14, 1952; d. Joallen and Dorothy Alice (Mellott) Smith; m. Scott William Smith, Nov. 6, 1970; children: Brett William, Chad Christopher, Kristine Renee, Mindy Michelle. LPN, Bowling Green (Ohio) Area Sch. Practical Nursing, 1984. Lic. practical nurse, Ohio. Pastor youth Fostoria (Ohio) New Covenant Ch., 1990—, tchr. Sunday sch., 1987—, supt., 1988—, leader jr. high youth group, 1989, trustee, 1991—. Author plays for local chs. Home: 134 Rock St Fostoria OH 44830 Office: Fostoria New Covenant Ch 417 S Main St Fostoria OH 44830

SMITH, KELVIN WAYNE, music minister; b. Kediri, Indonesia, May 15, 1962; (parents Am. citizens). s. James Leslie and Edna Earl (Broadley) S.; m. Jetta Ann Jimerson, June 9, 1984; children: Andrew, Adam. MusB, Union U., Jackson, Tenn., 1984. Interim min. music West Paris (Tenn.) Bapt. Ch., 1984, min. music and youth, 1984-86; min. music and edn. 1st Bapt. Ch., McKenzie, Tenn., 1986—. Mem. Carroll Benton Bapt. Assn. (music dir. 1986—). Office: First Bapt Ch 219 Stonewall St McKenzie TN 38201

SMITH, KENNETH ARNINK, minister; b. Yonkers, N.Y., Nov. 12, 1947; s. Thomas Roy and Lucy (Kalata) S.; m. Carol Springer, Sept. 8, 1973; children: Nathan, Benjamin, Thomas, Mary. BA, The King's Coll., Briarcliff Manor, N.Y., 1969; MA, U. No. Colo., 1973; MDiv, Princeton U., 1978. Ordained to ministry Presbyn. Ch. Am., 1978. Family counselor 1st Christian Ch., Lubbock, Tex., 1973-75; min. Princeton (N.J.) Presbyn. Ch., 1978—; mem. permanent com. on ch. planting Presbyn. Ch. in Am. Host radio program From the Firm Found., 1979—, regional TV program A Firm Found., 1985, radio and TV program A Firm Found.; contbr. to Liberty mag., 1985. Bd. dirs. Alpha Pregnancy Ctr., Princeton, 1979—; founder Together for Life. Capt. USAF, 1970-73. Home: 28 Pierson Ave Princeton NJ 08540 Office: Princeton Presbyn Ch 545 Meadow Rd Princeton NJ 08540

SMITH, KENNETH BRYANT, seminary administrator; b. Montclair, N.J., Feb. 19, 1931; m. Gladys Moran; children: Kenneth Bryant Jr., Kourtney Beth, Kristen Bernard. BA, Va. Union U., 1953; postgrad., Drew U., 1953-54; BD, Bethany Theol. Sem., 1960; DD (hon.), Elmhurst Coll., Shaw U.; D Ps (hon.), Nat. Lewis U.; LittD (hon.), Chgo. State U. Ordained to ministry United Ch. of Christ, 1960. Assoc. min. Park Manor Congl. Ch., Chgo., 1957-61; min. Trinity United Ch. of Christ, Chgo., 1961-66; min. urban affairs The Community Renewal Soc., 1966-68; sr. min. Ch. of Good Shepherd, Chgo., 1968—; pres. Chgo. Theol. Sem., U. Chgo., 1984—. Mem. Met. Chgo. YMCA, 1954-57, Community Renewal Soc., 1966-68. Office: Chgo Theol Sem 5757 University Ave Chicago IL 60637

SMITH, KENNETH EDWARD, clergyman, pastoral psychotherapist; b. Columbia, S.C., July 5, 1949; s. Edward Dubose and Daphene (Shell) S.; m. Donna Lynn Morgan, June 10, 1972; children: Alison Elizabeth, Ashley Morgan. BA, Wofford Coll., Spartanburg, S.C., 1971; M.Div., Yale U., 1974; D.Min., Vanderbilt U., 1975; postdoctorial student Duke U., 1980. Ordained elder S.C. Conf. United Meth. Ch., 1976; assoc. minister Bethel United Meth. Ch., Spartanburg, 1976-77; minister Lake View Charge (S.C.), 1977-81; dir. Grand Strand Pastoral Counseling Svc., Myrtle Beach, S.C., 1981—; adj. prof. religion and philosophy St. Leo's Coll.; cons. in field. Bd. dirs. Myrtle Beach Family YMCA, 1983—, Leadership Grand Strand, 1983. Mem. Am. Assn. Pastoral Counselors, Am. Assn. Marriage and Family Therapists, Am. Assn. Sex. Educators, Counselors and Therapists. Democrat. Clubs: Dunes Golf and Tennis (Myrtle Beach), Grand Strand Sertoma, Chicora Rotary. Office: PO Box 2967 Myrtle Beach SC 29578

SMITH, KENYON RAY, minister; b. Jasper, Ala., Dec. 22, 1963; s. Joseph Edward and Bettye Sue (Cosby) S.; m. Veronica Lynne Burt, Mar. 25, 1989. BA, Samford U., 1987; MDiv, New Orleans Bapt. Theol., Seminary, 1991. Ordained to ministry So. Bapt. Conv., 1987. Summer missionary So. Bapt. Home Mission Bd., Atlanta, 1984-86; min. children and sr. adults Westside Bapt. Ch., Jasper, 1987-88; min. youth and children Goodyear

Bapt. Ch., Picayune, Miss., 1989-91; pastor Evergreen Bapt. Ch., Cobbtown, Ga., 1991—. Mem. Ministerial Assn., Samford U., 1982-87. Mem. Youth Ministers Assn. Republican. Home: Rte 1 Box 54 Cobbtown GA 30420 *I believe that the Scripture is the inspired word of God. The Scripture is infallible. I also believe that our total sufficiency is in Christ.*

SMITH, KEVIN LEYON, pastor, teacher; b. Charleston, Ill., Aug. 19, 1956; s. Paul Earl and Mary Etta (Cummins) S. Student, Eastern Ill. U., 1974-76; BA, Bob Jones U., 1979. Ordained to ministry Bapt. Ch., 1981. Minister of music Hearon Circle Freewill Bapt. Ch., Spartanburg, S.C., 1979-80; sr. pastor Rock Prairie Bapt. Ch., Tipton, Ind., 1980-87; minister of christian edn. Oakford Bapt. Ch., Oakford, Ind., 1987—; bd. dirs. No. Ind. Youth Activity Bd., 1982-88; substitute tchr. Tri-Cen. Schs., Sharpsville, Ind., 1981-86; social worker The Villages of Ind., 1987-88. Republican. Baptist. Home: 1036 S Purdum Kokomo IN 46902 Office: Oakford Ch State Rd 26 E Oakford IN 46965

SMITH, KEVIN NEIL, minister; b. Fairfax, Va., Jan. 19, 1964; s. Nelson Duane and Elizabeth Ann (Walters) S.; m. Cynthia Louise Beeman, Nov. 17, 1984; children: Jason Michael, Bethany Renee, Jacob Paul. BS, Ind. Wesleyan U., 1988. Ordained to ministry Wesleyan Ch., 1989. Asst. pastor Converse (Ind.) United Meth. Ch., 1985-88; pastor youth Delaware Run Wesleyan Ch., Watsontown, Pa., 1988, sr. pastor, 1988—; dist. youth treas. Penn-Jersey Dist. of Wesleyan Ch., Bethlehem, 1989-91. Home: RD 1 Box 212 Watsontown PA 17777

SMITH, LAADAN HART, administrator; b. Sylvia, Kans., Oct. 7, 1921; s. Verne Hazelton and Edith Geneva (Green) S.; m. Frances Josephine Hildyard, July 15, 1943; children: Angela Jo Gilchrist, Pamela Lane Sisk, Lacey Jean Caldwell. Student, Hutchinson Jr. Coll., 1939-41, Wichita U., 1941-42. Consecrated to diaconal ministry Meth. Ch., 1977. Bus. adminstr. 1st United Meth. Ch., Dallas, 1952-86. Bd. dirs. Dallas Coun. Chs., 1967-71. With U.S. Army, 1940-46. Fellow Nat. Assn. Ch. Bus. Adminstrs. (co-founder 1956, v.p. 1971-72, dir. 1981-82, pres. Dallas chpt. 1963); mem. United Meth. Assn. Ch. Bus. Adminstrs. (past pres.). Home: 7129 Haverford Dr Dallas TX 75214 Office: 1st United Meth Ch 1928 Ross Ave Dallas TX 75201

SMITH, LARRY DON, minister; b. Amherst, Tex., Dec. 27, 1947; s. Bill and Christene (Griffin) S.; m. Peggy Hamilton Smith, June 4, 1970; 1 child, Larry Jr. BA, Harding U., 1970; MBA, So. Meth. U., 1981. Ordained to ministry Ch. of Christ, 1967. Youth minister Midtown Ch. of Christ, Ft. Worth, 1970-74; deacon Lake Highlands Ch. of Christ, Dallas, 1979-84; exec. dir. Christian Svcs. of SW, 1987-89; minister Statesboro (Ga.) Ch. of Christ, 1989—; instr. Ga. Southern U., Statesboro, 1989—; chmn. bd. dirs. Christian Svcs. of SW, Dallas, 1977-89. Youth chmn. Lions Club, Ft. Worth, 1970-74. Mem. So. Mgtm. Assn. Office: Ch of Christ PO Box 2929 Statesboro GA 30458-2929 *Some people view religion as a tool, others prefer to be used by the Lord as an instrument dedicated to His cause. I want to know as many people as I can meet in that latter category.*

SMITH, LARRY EARL, youth pastor; b. Winfield, Kans., Sept. 26, 1949; s. Wayne O. and Evelynne L. (Wheeler) S.; m. Johnette E. Smith, Aug. 15, 1970; children: Joshua C., Jacob C., Lacey Leigh. BA, Calvary Bible Coll., 1972. Ordained to ministry Non-Denominational Ch., 1976; cert. tchr. of personal fathering profile. Youth worker Kansas City Youth for Christ, Shawnee Mission, 1968-70; youth pastor Community Bapt. Ch., Arvada, Colo., 1972-74; pastor Perry Park Chapel, Castle Rock, Colo., 1974-79; youth pastor Shawnee (Kans.) Bible Ch., 1979-88, Olathe (Kans.) Bible Ch., 1989—. Chaplain Douglas County Sheriff Dept., Castle Rock, 1974-79. Republican. Office: Olathe Bible Ch 14841 Blackbob Rd Olathe KS 66062

SMITH, LAURIE, pastor; b. Malone, N.Y., May 17, 1964; d. Raymond Clark and Jane (Wilson) S. BA, St. Lawrence U., 1985; MDiv, Boston U., 1988. Ordained to ministry United Meth. Ch. as elder, 1990. Intern Community United Meth. Ch., Brighton, Mass., 1986-88; pastor Raquette River and Hogansburg United Meth. Ch., Massena, N.Y., 1988—; part time faculty Mater Dei Coll., Ogdensburg, N.Y., 1991—; sec. Conf. Ethnic Local Ch. Com., Cicero, N.Y., 1990—; mem.-at-large Conf. Commn. on Religion & Race, Cicero, 1988—, Conf. Coun. on Ministries, 1988—, Conf. Bd. of Discipleship, Cicero, 1990—. Recipient Cert. Appreciation Akwesasne Community, 1990. Mem. Massena Clergy Asn. Democrat. Home and Office: Rte 2 Box 409 Massena NY 13662 *A vision of Shalom, peace which is just and which nurtures wholeness in life, is our hope.*

SMITH, LAWRENCE J., bishop. Pres., regionary bishop The Liberal Cath. Ch.-Province of the U.S.A., Evergreen Park, Ill. Office: Liberal Cath Ch 9740 S Avers Evergreen Park IL 60642*

SMITH, LEROY SPENCER, minister; b. Hendersonville, N.C., July 26, 1926; s. Aaron Allen and Pearl Lee (Spencer) S.; m. Anita Louise Walden, Dec. 19, 1955; children: Susan Lynette Smith Brashier, Stephen craig. BA in Psychology, U. Houston, 1951; MS in Edn., Baylor U., 1954; DDiv, Christian Coll. Am., Houston, 1988. Ordained to ministry So. Bapt. Conv. Minister of music, edn. and youth various chs., Atlanta, Houston, 1950-56; pastor Minetex Bapt. Ch., Houston, 1957-59, South Post Oak Bapt. Ch., Houston, 1959-67, Second Bapt. Ch. of Jacinto City, Houston, 1967-85, Calvary Bapt. Ch., Houston, 1985—; v.p., registrar So. Bible Coll., Atlanta, 1951-54; area com. coord. Inst. Basic Life Prins., Oak Brook, Ill., 1973—; pres. Union Assn. Ministers Conf., Houston, 1970-71; trustee So. Bapt. Conv. Fgn. Mission Bd., Richmond, Va., 1989—. Author: God's Chosen Women, 1979, Workshop in Protection, 1979. With USN, 1944-46. Republican. Home: 12719 Old Pine Ln Houston TX 77015 Office: Calvary Bapt Ch 6511 Uvalde Houston TX 77049

SMITH, LORA LEE, missionary; b. Cleve., June 14, 1953; d. Thomas Joseph and Loretta Marie (Lee) S.; m. Tomas Santiago Felix, Oct. 6, 1973 (div. May 1981); children: Tomas Alejandro, Michael James, Amanda Marie. AS in Bus., ICM Sch. of Bus., 1985; student, Cleve. State U., 1988—. Dir. weekday ministries, trustee Victory Bapt. Chapel, Cleve., 1985—; dir. benevolent ministries Greater Cleve. Bapt. Assn., 1986—, bd. dirs.; exec. bd. dirs. State Conv. Bapts., Columbus; instr. martial arts Itoshii Kan, Cleve., 1989—; chaplain Cuyahoga County Nursing Home, Cleve., 1985—, MetroHealth Med. Ctr., Cleve., 1987-88; vol. Mission Svc. Corps, So. Bapt. Conv., 1985—; pres. Diagaku Kempo Kaisho, Cleve. State U., 1989—. Advocate, instr. Cleve. Rape Crisis Ctr., 1986—; field supr. U.S. Census, Cleve., 1980; mem. budget counsel Cuyahoga County Coop. Extension, Cleve., 1987—. Recipient Good Neighbor awards Coun. of Neighborhood Ctrs., Cleve., 1980, 81. Mem. Am. Gerontol. Assn., Christian Martial Arts Assn. Democrat. Home: 3173 W 43rd St Cleveland OH 44109 Office: Victory Bapt Chapel 2045 W 47st St Cleveland OH 44102

SMITH, MARILYN VIOLA, metaphysician, minister; b. Astoria, L.I., N.Y., Aug. 25, 1934; d. Bernard P. and DeRetta (Williamson) S.; B.S., U. Tex., 1955; grad. Esoteric Philosophy Center, Houston, 1984. m. Charles Stoneberg, June 28, 1958 (dec. Apr. 1968); m. Jon E. Curtis, Mar. 28, 1969 (div. May 1975); m. Charles Marchand, Aug. 21, 1981 (div. Oct. 1983). Ordained Minister, 1982. Pharmacist, Med. Arts Pharmacy, San Antonio, 1955-56, Northside Drug, San Antonio, 1956-58; pharmacist Jones Apothecary, Houston, 1958-68, 73-83; pharmacist Madings Drugs, 1968-69, Phillips Pharmacy, 1968-70, Gloyer's Pharmacy, 1969-73, Fed-Mart Pharmacy, Pasadena, Tex., 1970-72, Walgreen's, Houston, 1983—; founder Ctr. Metaphys. Studies, 1983, head creative manifestation of soul power, lectr. Esoteric Philosophy Center; tchr. New Age Chs., other orgns. flight instr. Barstow Aviation, Houston, 1962, free lance, 1962-64, Consol. Aero, Houston, 1967-68; participant Powder Puff Derby, 1960, Internat. Air Race, 1962, All Women's Internat. Air Race, 1964, other races; mem. 1st Women's Nat. Pylon Racing Team, 1967-71. Mem. Tex. Aviation Assn. (sec.-treas. 1962-64), Petticoat Pilots (pres. 1964-65), 99's (pres. Houston 1966-68), Aircraft Owners and Pilots Assn., Nat. Assn. Flight Instrs., Houston Metaphys. Council, Animal Behavior Soc., NOW, Tex. and Harris County Womens Polit. Caucus. Home: 22414 Lakeway Dr Spring TX 77373 Office: 10826 North Freeway Houston TX 77037

SMITH, MARK ALLINGTON, minister; b. Bklyn., May 22, 1948; s. Richard Hugh and Jane (Allington) S.; m. Katherine Ann Hibbard, Dec. 27, 1970; children: Kristen Ann, Gregory Kyle. BS, Denison U., 1970; MDiv, S.W. Bapt. Theol. Seminary, Ft. Worth, 1979. Ordained to ministry Bapt. Ch., 1976. Minister of youth and edn. First Bapt. Ch., Justin, Tex., 1976-79; pastor North Park Bapt. Ch., Bridgeport, Conn., 1979—; 2nd v.p. Bapt. Conv. of New Eng., Northborough, Mass., 1983-85; bd. dirs., vice-chmn. Fairfield County Christian Singles; v.p. Greater Bridgeport Fellowship of Evangelicals, Trumbull, Conn., 1984-85. Mem. We. Conn. Bapt. Assn. (moderator 1985-87). Home: 5160 Park Ave Bridgeport CT 06604 Office: North Park Bapt Ch 5200 Park Ave Bridgeport CT 06604

SMITH, MARVIN LAVERNE, educator; b. Oskaloosa, Iowa, Dec. 5, 1952; s. Herschel LaVerne and Norma Jean (Ver Steegh) S.; m. Betty Louise Jorgensen, Aug. 5, 1972; 1 child, Jennifer Joy. BA in Bible Pastoral Studies, North Cen. Bible Coll., 1975; MA in Theol. Studies, Bethel Theol. Sem., 1977; MA in Libr. Sci., U. Minn., 1985. Ordained to ministry Assemblies of God Ch., 1979. Min. 1st Assembly of God, Bloomington, Minn., 1975-77, Elgin, Ill., 1977-81; libr. dir. North Cen. Bible Coll., Mpls., 1981-85; assoc. prof. Christian edn. North Cen. Bible Coll., 1985—. Author: Computer Programs for Education Professionals, 1989. Mem. Fellowship Christian Magicians. Home: 1581 Lancaster Ln Eagan MN 55122 Office: North Cen Bible Coll 910 Elliot Ave S Minneapolis MN 55404

SMITH, SISTER MAURA, nun; b. Buffalo, N.Y., July 14, 1926; d. Edwin Leo and Eleanor Catherine (Oehler) S. BA, Mercyhurst Coll., Erie, Pa., 1952; MS, Cath. U. Am., 1963; EdD, U. Fla., 1970. Tchr. Diocesan High Schs., Erie, Pitts., 1950-66; assoc. prof. Mercyhurst Coll., 1970-76; prin. Mercyhurst Prep. Sch., Erie, 1976-87; superior Sisters of Mercy of Erie, 1987—; chairperson Leadership Conf. Women Religious, 1990—; trustee Mercyhurst Coll., 1980—, DuBois (Pa.) Regional Med. Ctr., 1988—; adv. coun. Sisters of Mercy Ams., 1986 . Bd. dirs. Stairways, Inc., Erie, 1985—, Grass Roots Opportunities for Women, Erie, 1988—; corporator St. Vincent Hosp., Erie, 1986—. Mem. Mercy Secondary Edn. Assn. (exec. com. 1986-89). Democrat. Home: 501 E 38th St Erie PA 16546 Office: Sisters of Mercy of Erie 444 E Grandview Blvd Erie PA 16504

SMITH, MAYNARD DWIGHT, minister; b. Milo, Iowa, Feb. 22, 1921; s. Foster Clayton and Myrtle May (Nutting) S.; m. Betty Luella Vander Wal; children: Todd Allen, Timothy Ray. BA, Cen. Coll., Pella, Iowa, 1943; BD, McCormick Theol. Sem., Chgo., 1950; D of Ministry, McCormick Theol. Sem., 1976; MA, Wayne State U., 1966; ThM, San Francisco Theol. Sem., 1967. Ordained to ministry Presbyn. Ch., 1950. Pastor Douglas Ave. Presbyn. Ch., Des Moines, 1950-58, Highland Park Presbyn. Ch., Detroit, 1958-66, Deerhurst Presbyn. Ch., Kenmore, N.Y., 1967-71, St. John's Presbyn. Ch., Houston, 1971-86; tchr. world religions Sierra Nev. Coll., Incline Village, Nev., 1987—; clergy v.p. The Met. Orgn., Houston, 1979-85; moderator Gen. Coun. New Covenant Presbytery, Houston, 1983-85. Contbr. prayers and short story to periodicals. Pres. Human Rels. Coun., Highland Park, Mich., 1964-65; bd. dirs. ACLU, Western N.Y., 1968-71. 1st lt. USMC, 1943-46, PTO. Home and Office: 22011 Timber Cove Rd Jenner CA 95450

SMITH, MICHAEL ADGER, minister; b. Pickens, S.C., Sept. 26, 1957; s. Adger and Evelene (Collins) S. BA, BTh, Faith Bapt. Coll., 1981; M Christian Edn., Faith Bapt. Sem., 1986, MTh, 1988; DMin, Covington Theo. Sem., 1988. Ordained to ministry Bapt. Ch., 1984. Tchr. Faith Christian Sch., Lancaster, S.C., 1981-82, Oakwood Christian Sch., Anderson, S.C., 1982-91; exec. dir. Worldwide Tentmakers, Anderson, 1988—; pres. Faith Bapt. Coll. and Sem., Anderson, 1988—; pastor Cove Creek Bapt. Ch., Pickens, S.C., 1989—; bd. mem. Horizon U., Honolulu, 1989—. Author: Restoring the Fallen: Guidelines to Restoration, 1990. Republican. Home: 307-B Lewis St Anderson SC 29624 Office: Faith Bapt Sem PO Box 3005 Anderson SC 29624-3005 *Every person in this world is either a part of the problem or a part of the solution. As Christians we should strive to be a part of the solution to this world's problems. That solution comes through a clear presentation and acceptance of the claims of Jesus Christ and allowing him to change the life.*

SMITH, MICHAEL ATWOL, clergyman; b. Nashville, Sept. 1, 1954; s. Robert D. and Shirley Ann (Agee) S.; m. Grace M. Kassner, May 4, 1976; children: Kelly Marie, Christopher M. BA, Belmont Coll., 1976; MDiv, So. Bapt. Theol. Sem., 1979, PhD, 1982. Ordained to ministry So. Bapt. Conv., 1976. Pastor New Prospect Bapt. Ch., Hanover, Ind., 1979-83, Bellevue Bapt. Ch., Nashville, 1983-85; chief editor Broadman Press, Nashville, 1985-90; pastor Hew Hope Bapt. Ch., Hermitage, Tenn., 1990—. Author: Devotionally Yours, Philippians, 1980; gen. editor: (series) The New American Commentary, 1987-90; editor numerous books; contbr. numerous articles to profl. jours. Mem. Scholar's Press. Office: New Hope Bapt Ch 6010 New Hope Rd Hermitage TN 37076

SMITH, MICHAEL HENRY, minister; b. Goldsboro, N.C., Aug. 18, 1959; s. Henry Jordan and Betty Lou (Adams) Smith; m. Melissa Elaine Jones, June 26, 1982; 1 child, Meagan Emily. AA, West Coast Christian Coll., 1979; BME, Lee Coll., 1981; M in Christian Ministry, So. Bapt. Theol. Sem., 1988. Ordained to ministry So. Bapt. Conv. Min. music and youth So. Hills Ch. of God, Oklahoma City, 1981-82; min. music Stewart Rd. Ch. of God, Monroe, Mich., 1982-86, Bashford Manor Bapt. Ch., Louisville, 1986-89, Ninth and O Bapt. Ch., Louisville, 1989—. Mem. Hymn Soc. Am. Home: 9713 Somerford Rd Louisville KY 40241 Office: Ninth & O Bapt Ch 2921 Taylor Blvd Louisville KY 40208

SMITH, MICHAEL LEE, minister; b. Columbus, Nebr., Dec. 18, 1953; s. Charles E. and Jean M. (Livingston) S.; m. Beverley K. Bolt, Nov. 22, 1975; children: Jennifer C., Benjamin M. BA, Anderson U., 1976; MDiv, Anderson Sch. of Theology, 1979. Ordained to ministry Ch. of God, 1980. With direct sales dept. Vita Craft Inc., Lincoln, Nebr., 1973-74; security officer Anderson (Ind.) U., 1974-75; assoc. pastor Ch. of God at West Anderson, Anderson, 1975-79; pastor Mio (Mich.) Ch. of God, 1979-89; ch. planter Ch. of God of Minn., St. Paul, 1989—. Bd. dirs. Ch. of God, 1981-84, chmn. youth div., 1979-84; chmn., bd. dirs. Ch. Planting Task Force, 1984-89. Republican.

SMITH, MORTON HOWISON, religious organization administrator, educator; b. Roanoke, Va., Dec. 11, 1923; s. James Brookes and Margaret Morton (Howison) S.; m. Lois Virginia Knopf, July 7, 1925; children: Samuel Warfield, Susanne Rochet Margaret. BA, U. Mich., 1947; BD, Columbia Theol. Sem., 1953; ThM, ThD, Free U., Amsterdam, The Netherlands, 1962. Ordained to ministry Presbyn. Ch., 1954. Pastor Springfield-Roller Presbyn. Chs., Carroll County, Md., 1954; prof. bible Belhaven Coll., Jackson, Miss., 1954-63; guest lectr. Westminster Theol. Sem., Phila., 1963-64; prof. Reformed Theol. Sem., Jackson, 1964-79; stated clk. gen. assembly Presbyn. Ch. in Am., Decatur, Ga., 1973-88; prof. systematic theology, dean faculty Greenville Presbyn. Theol. Sem., 1987—; advisor to bd. dirs. Greenville (S.C.) Presbyn. Theol. Sem., 1986—; mem. bd. dirs. Presbyn. Jour., Asheville, N.C., 1965-87; lectr. on theology Republic of So. Africa, June-July, 1988, on missions, Republic of Korea, June-July, 1989. Author: Studies in Southern Presbyterian Theology, 1962, 2d edit. 1987, How Is the Gold Become Dim, 1973, (pamphlet) Reformed Evangelism, 1970, Testimony, 1986, Commentary on the Book of Church Order, 1990, Harmony of the Westminster Confession and Catechisms, 1990; contbr. articles to Reformed Theology in Am., 1985. Trustee Covenant Coll., Lookout Mountain, Tenn., 1982-90. 1st lt. USAAF, 1942-45. Fulbright fellow U.S. Govt., 1958. Mem. N.Am. Presbyn. and Reformed Coun. of Chs. (sec. 1977—). Avocations: flying, traveling, genealogy. Office: Greenville Presbyn Theol Sem PO Box 9279 Greenville NC 29604

SMITH, MYRL ELDEN, minister; b. Circleville, Ohio, Oct. 21, 1938; s. Meryl Elden and Helen Goldie (Valentine) S.; m. Patricia Evelyn McBride, June 16, 1962; children: Gregory, Gretchen, Amy, David. BS in Edn., Wittenberg U., 1960; MDiv, Episcopal Div. Sch., 1964. Ordained deacon Episcopal Ch., 1964, priest, 1964. Asst. St. Philip's Ch., Columbus, Ohio, 1964-66; vicar St. Matthew's Mission, Ashland, Ohio, 1966-72; rector St. Paul's Ch., Norwalk, Ohio, 1972-79, Trinity Ch., Findlay, Ohio, 1979—; instr. philosophy Ashland Coll., 1967-71; examining chaplain Diocese of Ohio, Cleve., 1967-72, 86—, mem. diocesan coun., 1976-80, mem. planning commn., 1982-84, mem. liturgical commn., 1984—, chmn. 1989-90, chmn. architecture commn., 1988—, chmn. AIDS ministry, 1989—. Author: Racism and Racial Justice: Implications for the Episcopal Church fro a White Perspective, The Race Race. Pres. Svcs. for Aging, Huron County, Norwalk, 1978-79, Alcohol Ctr. for Huron County, Norwalk, 1978-79; pres., trustee Hancock County unit Am. Cancer Soc., Findlay, 1982-84. Recipient Red Apple award Findlay Bd. Edn., 1983, Clergyman of Yr. award, Findlay Civitan Club, 1983; Honoree of Yr., Black Studies and Libr. Assn., 1991. Democrat. Home: 1200 Sixth St Findlay OH 45840 Office: Trinity Episcopal Ch 128 W Hardin St Findlay OH 45840

SMITH, PATRICIA ANN, religious organization administrator; b. Strong City, Kans., Oct. 27, 1939; d. Ernest Dale and Zelma Leota (Ziegler) Humbargar; m. David Clarence Smith, Aug. 24, 1958; children: Gregory Allan, Shannon Lynn Smith Baldwin. Student, Emporia State, 1957-58. Chmn. Christian Women's Club, Overland Park, Kans., 1972-74; chmn. women's ministry Bapt. Women, Overland Park, 1974-76; with Reach Ministry, 1984-86; dir. Second Chance Ministries, Overland Park, 1988—; owner-mgr. The Ark Christian Book Store, Overland Park, 1974-91. Office: Second Chance Ministries PO Box 12265 Overland Park KS 66282-2265 *Caring, sharing, loving, hurting, that's what life is all about. Learning to love as Jesus loves and walk where Jesus walks. Watching a life being set free to love their Heavenly Father.*

SMITH, PAUL EDWARD, minister; b. Birmingham, Ala., June 17, 1961; s. Rufus E. and Evelyn J. (Bailey) S.; m. Lara Louise Paschal, May 26, 1984. B Gen. Studies, Samford U., 1984; MDiv, New Orleans Bapt. Theol. Sem., 1987, postgrad., 1987—. Ordained to ministry So. Bapt. Conv., 1985. Min. music Grantswood Bapt. Ch., Birmingham, 1981-84; assoc. pastor 1st Bapt. Ch., Livingston, Ala., 1985-86; pastor Knoxo Bapt. Ch., Tylertown, Miss., 1986-91, Bethel Bapt. Ch., Monticello, Miss., 1991—; moderator Walthal Bapt. Assn., Tylertown, 1989-91, mem. Christian action com., 1989-90; mem. bd. Miss. Bapt. Conv., Jackson, 1990-91. Office: Bethel Bapt Ch Rte 2 Box 28 Monticello MS 39654

SMITH, PAUL RICHARD, minister; b. St. Louis, June 22, 1937; s. Paul Weston and Mildred Catherine (Utterback) S.; m. Karen Sue Hiserote, May 7, 1966; children: Elizabeth Ann, Montgomery Weston. BA, Washington U., St. Louis, 1959; MDiv, Midwestern Bapt. Theol. Sem., 1964. Ordained to ministry So. Bapt. Conv., 1960. Sr. pastor Broadway Bapt. Ch., Kansas City, Mo., 1964—; adj. prof. Midwestern Bapt. Sem., Kansas City, Mo., 1979; Staly lectr. William Jewell Coll., Liberty, Mo., 1989; creator, lectr., leader seminars on ch. renewal and worship, U.S. Author: Is Your God Too Masculine?, 1992; contbr. articles to religious publs. Office: Broadway Bapt Ch 3931 Washington Kansas City MO 64111 *Renewing the church is like remodeling your house—it takes longer than you thought, costs more than you planned and makes a bigger mess than you ever thought possible. The proof of the resurrection is not in the empty tomb but in the Spirit-filled fellowship.*

SMITH, PERRY ANDERSON, III, pastor; b. Mound Bayou, Miss., May 16, 1934; Perry Smith II and Elease Wilson; m. Maude Alice Lee, July 11, 1964 (dec. July 1976); m. Elliece Victoria Saundle, May 6, 1978. AB in Sociology and Econs., Howard U., 1955, MDiv, ThM, 1958. Ordained to ministry Bapt. Ch., 1955. Chaplain Black Ministries Program U. MD., Coll. Pk., 1975-82; pastor 1st Bapt. Ch. Inc., North Brentwood, Md., 1958—; founding pres. Prince George's County (Md.) Community Ministry; founder, former chmn. Genesis Ventures Inc., Prince George's County; treas. Progressive Nat. Bapt. Conv., 1974-76, auditor, 1978-80. Pres. Black Faculty and Staff Assn., U. Md. Recipient 1st M.L. King Jr. award Black Student Union, U. Md., 1976, Black Leader religion award, Phi Beta Sigma, 1978, Rockefeller Pub. Svc. award, 1980. Mem. NAACP (life, pres. 1960-64, Hester V. King Humanitarian award 1985), Concerned Clergy of Prince George's County, Prince George's County Bd. Edn. (chmn. interfaith adv. coun., mem. supt.'s com. on black male achievement), Alpha Phi Alpha. Republican. Office: 1st Bapt Ch Inc 4009 Wallace Rd North Brentwood MD 20722 *Life is beautiful. We fail to see its beauty only as we permit mediocrity to cloud our vision. Faith clears the vision to see all of the beauty in life that God intended. Keep the way clear and let nothing between.*

SMITH, PHILIP ALAN, clergyman; b. Albany, N.Y., Nov. 1, 1938; s. Donnal Vore and Aline Mabel (Planson) S.; m. Lynn Rea Seelbach, July 1, 1961; children: Jeffrey Donnal, Julie Ann, Jennifer Lynn. BA, Colgate U., 1960; BD, U. Chgo., 1964. Pastor Calvary United Ch. of Christ, Buffalo, 1964-67, St. Peter's United Ch. of Christ, Buffalo, 1967-74, New Covenant United Ch. of Christ, Buffalo, 1974-80, Pilgrim-St. Luke's United Ch. of Christ, Buffalo, 1980-88, Lakewood United Ch. of Christ, St. Petersburg, Fla., 1988—; exec. bd. Clergy Assn., St. Petersburg, 1990—, Fla. Conf. United Ch. of Christ, St. Petersburg, 1990—; mem. commn. on peace and justice Fla. Coun. of Chs., St. Petersburg, 1990—. Home: 5300 19th Way S Saint Petersburg FL 33712

SMITH, QUEON PAUL, minister; b. Loganville, Ga., July 27, 1935; s. Roy Rufus and Nancy Sue (Paul S.; m. Jacquelyn Wilson, July 31, 1955; children: Timothy Paul, Lisa Kay Smith Pike. AA, Young Harris (Ga.) Coll., 1955; BS in Edn., U. Ga., 1959; MDiv, Candler Sch. Theology, Atlanta, 1963; STM, Wesley Theol. Seminary, Washington, 1968. Cert. min. Christian Edn., 1967. Pastor various chs., 1954-65; assoc. pastor, dir. weekday kindergarten Olive Meth. Ch., Randallstown, Md., 1965-67; min. edn. Wilmington (Ohio) United Meth. Ch., 1967-68, Dalton (Ga.) 1st United Meth. Ch., 1970-74, LaGrange (Ga.) 1st United Meth. Ch., 1974-76; pastor 1st United Meth. Ch./Corinth United Meth. Ch., Hogansville, Ga., 1976-80, Manchester (Ga.) 1st United Meth. Ch., 1980—; adj. prof. Candler Sch. Theology. Contbr. articles to profl. jours.; columnist: Manchester Star-Mercury, 1986—. Active County Cancer Soc., Manchester, 1981, County Salvation Army Com., Manchester, 1980, chair, 1981-84. Mem. North Ga. Annual Conf. (elder 1961—), Tri-County Ministerial Alliance (treas. 1990—, pres. 1984-86), LaGrange Dist. Coun. Ministries (chairperson 1990—), North Ga. Conf. Coun. on Ministries, Atlanta, 1990—, Com. on Stewardship, Kiwanis (pres. Hogansville chpt. 1977-78). Democrat. Office: 1st United Meth Ch 206 Broad St PO Box 449 Manchester GA 31816

SMITH, RALPH MORGAN, minister; b. Hot Springs, Alaska, Mar. 19, 1931; s. John Morgan and Maggie Bell (Bolding) S.; m. Bess Noble, June 12, 1951; children: Charlene Diane Smith Love, Wallace Morgan, Peyton Noble. BA, Ouachita Bapt. U., 1952, DD (hon.), 1974; BD, Southwestern Bapt. Theol. Sem., Ft. Worth, 1956, ThD, 1960. Ordained to ministry So. Bapt. Conv., 1956. Pastor 1st Bapt. Ch., Rosenberg, Tex., 1956-60, Hyde Pk. Bapt. Ch., Austin, Tex., 1960—; chmn. bd. trustees Home Mission Bd., So. Bapt. Conv., Atlanta; chaplain Nat. Western Life Ins., Austin, 1966-76. Author: Living the Spirit—Filled Life, 1967, Let Me Explain, 1970, Helping Churches Grow, 1986, Facing Our Challenges with Confidence, 1989, Basic Bible Sermons on the Church, 1990. Trustee Baylor U., Waco, Tex.; founding mem., bd. dirs. Shoal Creek Hosp., Austin; bd. dirs. Citizens Ins. Co., Austin; mem. adv. bd. Austin Diagnostic Clinic, 1990—. Mem. Austin Bapt. Assn. (moderator), Austin Club, Headliners Club. Office: Hyde Pk Bapt Ch 3901 Speedway Austin TX 78751

SMITH, RANDAL FANE, minister; b. Albion, Nebr., Aug. 19, 1961; s. Paul Robert and Mary Lou (Vawter) S. BA, Hastings Coll., 1983; MDiv, Wesley Theol. Sem., 1986. Ordained deacon, 1986, elder, 1988. Pastor Wauneta (Nebr.) United Meth. Ch., 1986-89; assoc. pastor Grace United Meth. Ch., Hastings, Nebr., 1989—; youth coord. S.W. Dist. Nebr. Conf., McCook, 1986-89. Bd. dirs. Hastings Family Planning, 1990—; coord. Nebr. Youth Ann. Conf., 1987-90; youth coord. South Cen. dist. Nebr. Conf., Grand Island, 1990—. Mem. Adams County Ministerial Assn., Am. Mensa (editor Omaha chpt. 1990—), Kiwanis (bd. dirs. Hastings chpt. 1990—). Home: 718 N California Hastings NE 68901 Office: Grace United Meth Ch 1832 W 9th Hastings NE 68901

SMITH, RANDALL MORRIS, youth minister; b. Atlanta, Sept. 3, 1958; s. Leslie M. Smith and Joyce (Green) Cambre; m. Kathy Dawkins, June 5, 1982 (div. Mar. 1991). BA, Atlanta Christian Coll., 1951. Youth min. West Rome (Ga.) Christian Ch., 1980-82, 83-86, Tucker (Ga.) Christian Ch., 1982-

83, 1st Christian Ch., Cumming, Ga., 1986—. Home: 2045 Honeysuckle Dr Cumming GA 30130 Office: 1st Christian Ch Cumming GA 30130

SMITH, RAY, administrator; b. Houston, Sept. 13, 1962; s. Dudley R. and Pearly T. (Tomek) S.; m. Kay Lyn Kemp, Dec. 26, 1987; 1 child, Brittany Kay. BA, Baylor U., 1984; MA, Grace Sem., 1989. Ordained to ministry Bapt. Ch., 1990. Pastor Travis (Tex.) Bapt. Ch., 1983-84; tchr. Bay Area Christian Sch., League City, Tex., 1985-86; tchr. coach Riverside Christian Acad., River Ridge, La., 1986-89; adminstr. West Side Christian Sch., El Dorado, Ark., 1989—. Mem. Fellowship Christian Sch. Adminstrs. Republican. Home: 2615 Parnell Rd El Dorado AR 71730 Office: West Side Christian Sch 2400 W Hillsboro El Dorado AR 71730

SMITH, RAY WILLIAM, clergyman, counselor; b. Kirksville, Mo., Mar. 1, 1952; s. Norman George and Amber Lou (Fairley) S.; m. Kathryn Diane Marshall Siegrist, Dec. 28, 1974; children: Ashley Dianne Marshall, Travis William Sterling, Austin Andrew Bondurant. BS, Cen. Mo. State U., 1974; MDiv, Austin Presbyn. Theol. Sem., 1978, DMin, 1978;, EdD, Memphis State U., 1985. Lic. profl. counselor, Tex.; cert. counselor; ordained to ministry, Presbyn. Ch., 1978. Intern, First Presbyn. Ch. Galveston (Tex.), 1976-77; pastor Grace Presbyn. Ch., San Antonio, 1978-81, Shady Grove Presbyn. Ch., Memphis, 1981-85, 1st Presbyn. Ch., Spokane, 1986-90; speaker Children Today Conf., 1989; founder Christian Counseling Ctr. of Spokane; mem. ordination exam. com. Memphis Presbytery, 1981-82, Chinook Dist. Boy Scouts Am. Eagle Scout Bd. Rev. Com.; bd. dirs. San Antonio Urban Coun., 1980, Family Svc. Memphis, Hospice of Spokane, Dismas House Memphis, mem. Hospice Com., San Antonio, 1981. Mem. Memphis Ministers Assn., Memphis Jaycees (dir.), Met. Inter-Faith Assn., Sales and Mktg. Execs. of Memphis (chaplain), Nat. Eagle Scout Assn., Presbyn. Musicians Assn., Am. Assn. Counseling and Devel., Am. Assn. Christian Counselors, C, Nat. Hospice Orgn., Spokane Meml. Assn. (bd. dirs.), Christian Assn. Psychol. Studies, Assn. Mental Health Clergy, Presbyn. Inland Empire (com. on ministry), Conf. Contemporary Cosmology, Internat. Platform Speakers Assn., Assn. for Religious and Value Issues in Couns., Assn. Grief Counselors and Death Educators, Am. Assn. Family Counselors, Delta Upsilon Internat., Kappa Delta Pi. Lodges: Toastmasters, Masons. Author: How to Cope with Grief: A Series of Sermons, 1982, also book revs., articles, liturgical prayer collections; (manuscript and cassettes) Civil Religion in Texas, 1983; editor Newsletter for Pastoral Care Ministers of Large Churches; host (radio show) Straight Talk. Office: 510 E Francis Spokane WA 99207-1038

SMITH, RAYMOND EVERETT, religious organization administrator, minister; b. Kanawha, Iowa, Mar. 29, 1932; s. Earl Melanchthon (dec.) and Anna (Lehman) (dec.) S.; m. Helen Alice Norris, Aug. 28, 1952; children: Danene Rae, Stephen Alan. Diploma, Open Bible Coll., Des Moines, 1953; student, Ea. Mont. U., 1958. Pioneer pastor Open Bible Standard Chs., Inc., Billings, Mont., 1953-59; pastor Open Bible Standard Chs., Inc., Rapid City, S.D., 1959-67, S.D. Dist. supt., 1959-63, midwest div. supt., 1963-67; gen. supt. Open Bible Standard Chs., Inc., Des Moines, 1967-76; pastor, Lighthouse Temple Open Bible Standard Chs., Inc., Eugene, Oreg., 1976-79; gen. supt. Open Bible Standard Chs., Inc., Des Moines, 1979—; Iowa coord. Am. for Jesus, Des Moines, 1981; convener and steering com. chmn. Iowans Concerned About Pornography, 1984—. Contbr. articles to profl. jours. Active on local caucus, Polk County and Iowa Polit. Convs. Mem. Nat. Assn. Evangelicals (bd. of adminstrs. 1967-76, 79—), Pentecostal Fellowship North Am. (bd. of asminstrs. 1967-76, 79—). Republican. Avocations: racquetball, golf, building. Office: Open Bible Standard Chs Inc 2020 Bell Ave Des Moines IA 50315-1096

SMITH, REILLY RICHARD, minister, law enforcement professional; b. Garfield Heights, Ohio, Mar. 28, 1953; s. Robert Charles Smith and Jane Lois Doing Mariner; m. Cynthia Kay Hall, Mar. 31, 1973; children: Jofaya Ann, Kara Jane, Sean Patrick. AA, Cuyahoga Community Coll., 1974; BS in Bible, Valley Forge Christian Coll., 1981; MDiv, Ashland Theol. Sem., 1985. Ordained to ministry Brethren Ch., 1986. Min. visitation Evangel Assembly, Norristown, Pa., 1980, interim pastor, 1981; pastor 1st Brethren Ch., Williamstown, Ohio, 1985, Mulvane (Kans.) Brethren Ch., 1985—; police officer Mulvane Police Dept., 1986—; mem. missionary bd. Brethren Ch., Ashland, 1989—, mem. gen. conf., Ashland, 1990—, supervising elder Midwest dist., Mulvane, 1989—. Contbr. articles to The Brethren Evangelist publ. Ministerial liason Care and Share, Inc., Mulvane, 1986-88, bd. dirs., 1989-90; mem. early intervention drug team local dist. Mulvane Pub. Schs., 1990—. Mem. Mulvane Ministerial Alliance (sec.-treas. 1987—). Republican. Home: 503 Eastview Dr Mulvane KS 67110 Office: Mulvane Brethren Ch 310 S Central Mulvane KS 67110

SMITH, RICHARD GRAEME, minister; b. Portland, Oreg., Mar. 15, 1945; s. Graeme Conlee and Margaret Edith (Moote) S.; m. Gail Lynn Poag, July 25, 1970; children: Anastasia Grace, Christal Lynn, Josiah Daniel. BS, UCLA, 1967; MDiv, Southwestern Bapt. Theol., Seminary, Fort Worth, 1972. Ordained to ministry Bapt. Ch., 1972. Minister of recreation MacArthur Blvd. Bapt. Ch., Irving, Tex., 1970-72; youth pastor Evangel. Free Ch. of Felton, Calif., 1972-76; assoc. pastor of youth First Evangel. Free Ch., Moline, Ill., 1976—; bd. dirs., treas. Aslan Prodns., Inc., East Moline, Ill.; pres., treas. Christian Youth Workers Fellowship, Moline, 1986—; dir. of nat. writing festival, Evangel. Free Ch. of Am., Mpls., 1985-88; coun. mem. Dist. Student Ministries Coun., Ill., 1990—; regional coord. Sonlife Ministries. Presenter Quad-Cities Youth Conf., Augustana Coll., 1988, 90, 91. Home: 3546 3rd St B East Moline IL 61244 Office: First Evangelical Free Ch 3321 7th St Moline IL 61265

SMITH, RICHARD LAMAR, education and youth minister; b. LaGrange, Ga., Aug. 3, 1952; s. Olin and Novil (Adams) S. AB in History, Ga. So. U., Statesboro, 1974; MRE, S.W. Bapt. Theol. Sem., Ft. Worth, 1979. Ordained to ministry So. Bapt. Conv., 1985. Min. edn. youth First Bapt. Ch., LaFayette, Ga., 1980—; V.P. Ga. Bapt. Youth Min. Fellowship, Ga. Bapt. Conv., 1985-86 (sec. 1989-90) (pres. 1990-91); sec. S.W. Sem. Alumni Assn., 1989-90. Named outstanding young man of Am., 1972. Mem. LaFayette Kiwanis Club. Home: 515 N Main St LaFayette GA 30728 Office: First Baptist Church 201 N Main St La Fayette GA 30728

SMITH, RICHARD LYNN, minister; b. Phoenix, Apr. 29, 1951; s. Glenn Donald and Jean (Landis) S.; m. Pamela Anderson, Apr. 14, 1973; children: Aaron, Alison. AB, U. Redlands, Calif., 1973; MDiv, Pacific Sch. of Religion, 1976. Asst. minister The Ch. at Litchfield Park, Ariz., 1976-77; minister Tombstone (Ariz.) Community Ch., 1977-82, Los Altos United Ch. of Christ, Long Beach, Calif., 1982—; alt. del. United Ch. of Christ Gen. Synod, 1991. Bd. dirs. Tombstone Community Health Svcs., 1978-82. Mem. United Ministries in Higher Edn. (pres. L.A. chpt. 1985—), Orange County United Ch. of Christ (chair ch. and ministry com. Long Beach chpt. 1983-86), Lions (v.p. Tombstone chpt. 1979-81). Office: Los Altos United Ch Christ 5550 Atherton Long Beach CA 90815

SMITH, ROBERT DOYLE, theology educator; b. Little Rock, Aug. 27, 1952; s. Emmett Hudson and Estelle Marie (Wooley) S.; m. Marsha Lee Pierce, May 24, 1975; children: Scott Alan, Stephanie Elizabeth. AB in Religion, So. Nazarene U., 1974, MA in Theology, 1975; MDiv, Nazarene Theol. Sem., 1977; PhD in History of Christianity, Baylor U., 1981. Ordained to ministry Ch. of Nazarene, 1985. Pastor 1st Ch. of Nazarene, Cleveland, Okla., 1982; asst. prof. theology Olivet Nazarene U., Bourbonnais, Ill., 1982-86, assoc. prof., 1986—. Contbr. articles, abstracts to profl. publs., book. Mem. Am. Acad. Religion, Am. Soc. Ch. History, Wesleyan Theol. Soc., World Meth. Hist. Soc., Am. Theol. Soc., Nat. Assn. Evang. Chaplains Commn. (mem. resource be. 1990). Home: 156 S Stadium Bourbonnais IL 60914 Office: Olivet Nazarene U Theology Dept Box 6048 Bourbonnais IL 60914

SMITH, ROBERT EUGENE, minister; b. Shawnee, Okla., Feb. 28, 1931; s. William and Inez Elizabeth (Slagel) S.; m. Eulene Opal Smith, May 27, 1949 (div. Nov. 1976); children: Stanley Paul, Ronald Eugene, Terry Douglas, Brian Lee; m. Dolores Mae Kile, May 20, 1978. BA, William Jewell Coll., 1952; BD, So. Bapt. Sem., 1957, MDiv, 1973; D Ministry, Eden Sem., 1974. Ordained to ministry So. Bapt. Conv., 1946. Student pastor various chs., Mo., Ky., 1948-57; pastor Ballwin (Mo.) Bapt. Ch., 1957-60; missionary So. Bapt. Fgn. Mission Bd., Brazil, 1960-67; pastor Green Trails Bapt. Ch., Chesterfield, Mo., 1967-70, King Hill Bapt. Ch., St. Joseph, Mo., 1971-72; pastor First Bapt. Ch., Coral Springs, Fla., 1972-76, Nickerson, Kans., 1977-81; pastor Peace/Trinity United Ch. of Christ, Hudson, Kans., 1982-90, First Congl. United Ch. of Christ, Lebanon, Mo., 1991—; instr. in religion Broward County Community Coll., Pompano Beach, Fla., 1972-76; adj. prof. ch. history Midwestern Bapt. Sem., Kansas City, Mo., 1979-80; mem. faculty Sterling Coll., Sterling, Kans., 1980-83; moderator Cen. Bapt. Assn., 1981-83; pres. Western Assn. United Ch. Christ Kans., 1984-85; pres. Kans.-Okla. Conf. United Ch. Christ, 1987-89; mem. Adminstrn. Commn. Mo. Conf. United Ch. Christ, 1991—. Mem. Coral Springs Civic Assn., 1973-76, Hudson (Kans.) Community Club, 1983-90, Stafford County (Kans.) Mental Health Bd., 1984-90; mem. home health adv. bd. Breech Meml. Hosp., Lebanon; mem. Coun. for Prevention Family Violence, Laclede, Colo. Recipient Life Svc. award SW Bapt. Coll., 1965. Mem. Alban Inst. (profl.), Rotary. Office: 1st Congl United Ch Christ 150 Harwood Ave Lebanon MO 65536-3018 *It has been my experience that out of what seemed the worst the best has come, and that, in spite of everything, life is eminently worth living.*

SMITH, ROBERT HOUSTON, archeologist, religious studies educator; b. McAlester, Okla., Feb. 13, 1931; s. Vaughn Hubert and Bobbie Louise (Nelson) S.; m. Geraldine Warshaw, Jan. 26, 1969; 1 child, Vanessa Eleanor. BA, U. Tulsa, 1952; BD, Yale U., 1955, PhD, 1960. Instr. Coll. Wooster, Ohio, 1960-62, asst. prof., 1962-65, assoc. prof., 1965-70, prof., 1970-72, Fox prof. religious studies, 1972-91, chmn. dept., 1981-91, chmn. archaeology program, 1979—; Grosvenor lectr. Nat. Geographic Soc., Washington, 1985; dir. Coll. Wooster Archeol. Expdn. to Pella, Jordan, 1966—; part-time cons. on devel. codes of ethics. Author: Excavations at Khirbet Kufin, 1962, Pella of the Decapolis, vol. 1, 1973, vol. 2, 1989, Patches of Godlight: The Pattern of Thought of C.S. Lewis, 1986; co-author: Pella in Jordan, 1982; lectr. Digging Up the Past NBC-TV Edn. Exchange series, 1968; contbr. articles to profl. jours. Trustee Am. Ctr. Oriental Research, Amman, Jordan, 1979-85. NEH grantee, 1979-81, Nat. Geographic Soc. grantee, 1979-85; Yale U. fellow Am. Sch. Oriental Research, 1958-59. Mem. Am. Schs. Oriental Research, Soc. Profl. Archaeologists, Soc. Biblical Lit., Archaeological Inst. Am. Democrat. Presbyterian. Avocation: Am. local history. Home: 1117 Quinby Ave Wooster OH 44691 Office: Coll Wooster Dept Religious Studies Wooster OH 44691

SMITH, ROBERT JOHN, minister; b. Toronto, Ont., Can., Feb. 22, 1943; s. Campbell Bannerman and Beulah May (Argue) S.; m. Brenda Joyce Frank, Feb. 1, 1969; children: Paul Andrew, Douglas James. Diploma, Peterboro (Ont.) Tchrs. Coll., 1963, Ea. Pentecostal Bible Coll., Peterboro, 1968; BTh, N.Am. Bapt. Coll., Edmonton, Alta., Can., 1974. Ordained to ministry Pentecostal Assemblies of Can. Asst. pastor Cen. Pentecostal Tabernacle, Edmonton, 1968-75, Christian Life Ctr., Santa Rosa, Calif., 1975-79; pastor Bethel Temple, San Francisco, 1979-81; from pastor to sr. pastor London (Ont.) Gospel Temple, 1981—. Office: London Gospel Temple, 288 Commissioners Rd W, London, ON Canada N6J 1Y3

SMITH, ROBERT JOHNSON, II, minister, consultant; b. Abington, Pa., Mar. 3, 1960; s. Robert Johnson and Jennie Mae (Smith) S.; m. Janine Allen, June 10, 1989; 1 child, Robert III. BA, Morehouse Coll., 1984; MBA, Ea. Coll., 1990; MDiv, Ea. Bapt. Theol. Sem., 1990. Ordained to ministry Bapt. Ch., 1988. Adminstrv. asst. Ea. Sch. of Christian Ministry, Phila., 1986-87; pastoral intern Pinn Meml. Bapt. Ch., Phila., 1986-87; adminstrv. min. Bright Hope Bapt. Ch., Phila., 1987-91; co-pastor Salem Bapt. Ch., Jenkintown, Pa., 1991—; cons. R.J. Smith & Assocs., Phila., 1990—; youth mentor Temple U., Ctr. for Social Policy, Phila., 1987—. Bd. dirs. YMCA-Columbia North Br., Phila., 1990—. Mem. Black Clergy of Phila. (gen. sec. 1990—), Phila. Bapt. Assn. (com. mem. 1987—), Am. Bapt. Conv., Progressive Nat. Bapt. Conv. Democrat. Home: 2242 Brookview Pl Elkins Park PA 19117 Office: Salem Bapt Ch Jenkintown 610 Summit Ave Jenkintown PA 19046 *If God has blessed you in this life and you fail to help those who are less fortunate than yourself, then you are no better than a thief.*

SMITH, SHARBER WAYNE, minister; b. State Line, Miss., June 11, 1943; s. Chapman and Anna (James) S.; m. Sally Rhodes Rideout, Oct. 29, 1977; children: Sharber Wayne Jr., Christopher Wade, Ginger Ann. Student, Clark Coll., 1966-67; BA, William Carey, 1971; ThM, So. Bapt. Ctr. Bibl. Studies, 1987, D of Ministry, 1989. Ordained to the ministry So. Bapt. Ch., 1966; lic. in ministry, 1965. Part time pastor various churches, Ala., 1966-70; pastor Orange Grove (Miss.) Bapt. Ch., 1970-72, Piave (Miss.) Bapt. Ch., 1972-74, West Brattleboro (Vt.) Bapt. Ch., 1976-79; v.p. Open Ch. Found., Gloucester, Mass., 1980-85; pastor Shady Grove First Bapt. Ch., Heidelberg, Miss., 1985—; visual evangelist Gospel Illusionist, 1974—; tv cast Capt. Hook's Children, 1976; gospel clown Broadman Films, Nashville, 1974. Author: Sparky the Clown, 1974, Teaching with Objects, 1989. Chaplain Heidelberg Police Dept., 1987-88, Marketplace Ministries, Inc., Dallas. Mem. Fellowship of Christian Magicians. Republican. Home: Rte 3 Box 346A Heidelberg MS 39439

SMITH, SHELTON LEO, minister, school administrator; b. Paducah, Ky., Dec. 4, 1942; s. William Leo and Marianna (Cumbee) S.; m. Betty Elaine Womble, Dec. 26, 1961; children: Davina Laine, Marlon Wesley. BA, Union U., 1966; ThM, Luther Rice Sem., Jacksonville, Fla., 1972, D Ministry, 1976. Ordained to ministry Bapt. Ch., 1961. Pastor various chs., 1961-79, Ch. of the Open Door, Westminster, Md., 1979—; pres. Carroll Christian Schs., Westminster, 1979—; pres. Camp Nicodemus, Westminster, 1979—; regional v.p. Trinity Bapt. Coll., Jacksonville, 1988—; bd. dirs. Sword of the Lord, Murfreesboro, Tenn., 1990—. Author: The Tongues Tangle, 1979, The Open Door Story, 1985, The Game Plan, 1987, The Funeral Handbook, 1991. Office: Ch of the Open Door 550 Baltimore Blvd Westminster MD 21157

SMITH, STEPHEN W., pastor; b. Charlotte, N.C., July 20, 1954; s. Sonny and Rena (Broome) S.; m. Gwen Harding, Oct. 18, 1980; children: Blake, Jordan, Cameron, Leighton. BA, Lendir Rhyne Coll., 1976; MDiv, So. Bapt. Theol. Sem., 1979; postgrad., Trinity Evang. Div. Sch. Pastor Arlington Bapt. Ch., Charlotte, 1979-85, Trinity Bapt. Ch., Wassenaar, Mass., 1985-90, Homestead Heights Bapt. Ch., Durham, N.C., 1990—; vis. prof. Tyndale Theol. Sem., Badhovedorp, Netherlands, 1988. Mem. European Bapt. Conv. (missions com. 1985-90), Yates Bapt. Assn. (missions coun. 1990—). Republican. Home: 610 Flagstone Way Durham NC 27704

SMITH, STEVEN FREDERICK, minister; b. Attleboro, Mass., Jan. 15, 1954; s. Frederick Polydor and Patricia Ann (Stevens) S.; m. Cynthia Ann Dickinson, Nov. 13, 1981; children: Emily Jean, Daniel Steven. BS in English and History, Plymouth State Coll., 1977. Min. music Trinity Evangel. Ch., Peterborough, N.H., 1981—; editor, gen. mgr. The Peterborough Transcript, 1989—. Mem. N.H. Press Assn. (Editorial Writer of Yr. 1989-90). Republican. Home: 49 Lobacki Dr Peterborough NH 03458 Office: The Peterborough Transcript PO Box 419 Peterborough NH 03458

SMITH, TERRY L., music minister; b. Seneca, S.C., Mar. 26, 1955; s. Alvin Clarence and Daisy Ruth (Medlin) S.; m. Bonnie Lynn Benny, June 18, 1977; children: Aaron Christopher, Bethany Lynne, Cathryn Elizabeth. AA, Anderson (S.C.) Coll., 1975; BA, Gardner-Webb Coll., Boiling Springs, N.C., 1977; M Ch. Music, Southwestern Bapt. Theol. Sem., Ft. Worth, 1980. Ordained to ministry So. Bapt. Conv. Min. music Arrow Wood Bapt. Ch., Chesnee, S.C., 1976-78, Rehoboth Bapt. Ch., Mansfield, Tex., 1978-79; min. music and youth Lincolnton (Ga.) Bapt. Ch., 1980-83, Statesville Avenue Bapt. Ch., Charlotte, N.C., 1983-89; min. music Liberty Bapt. Ch., Riverdale, Ga., 1989—.

SMITH, TERRY RAY, minister; b. Lynchburg, Va., Feb. 4, 1960; s. Warren Thomas and Sybil Mae (Mawyer) S.; m. Cathy Lynn Fleshman, June 3, 1978; children: T. R. II, Justin Thomas, Travis Randall. AA, Liberty U., 1982; BTh., Christian Bible Coll., 1984; MRE, Faith Bible Sem., 1986, DD, 1986; PhD in Religion, Christian Sem., 1988. Ordained to ministry Bapt. Ch., 1982. Youth evangelist LeeWood Bapt. Ch., Lynchburg, 1975-78; copastor Open Door Bapt. Ch., Volens, Va., 1978-79; interim pastor Yates Thagard Bapt. Ch., Whispering Pines, N.C., 1979-80; evangelist Leesville Rd. Bapt. Ch., Lynchburg, 1981-82; pastor Fairhavens Bapt. Ch., Kinston, N.C., 1982-84, Greenbrier Valley Bapt. Ch., White Sulphur Springs, W.Va., 1984-87, Faith Bapt. Temple, Louisville, 1987—; bd. dirs. Global Bapt. Missions, Seneca, S.C. Author: A Look at Stewardship, 1988, A Look at Romans, 1988, A New Walk For A New Believer, 1990; editor: Watchman, 1990. Asst. dir. Moral Majority, Kinston, 1982-83; mem. Am. Coalition of Decency, Louisville, 1987-89, Right to Life, Louisville, 1987—. Republican. Home: 209 Militia Dr Louisville KY 40214 Office: Faith Bapt Temple Ministry 5627 New Cut Rd Louisville KY 40214

SMITH, THEODORE DEWITT, minister; b. Chgo., Jan. 19, 1947; s. Theodore DeWitt Sr. and Ernestine (Clay) S.; m. Aretta Armentha Smith; children: Darin, Derrick, Tonya, Tamara. BA, Judson Coll., 1978; MDiv, Ashland (Ohio) Theol. Sem., 1983, D of Ministry, 1985. Ordained to ministry Bapt. Ch., 1965; cert. touch ministry tng. facilitator. Pastor Progressive Bapt. Ch., Elgin, Ill., 1970-78, New Hope Bapt. Ch., Akron, Ohio, 1978—; chmn. Progressive Nat. Bapt. Conv. Bd. Edn. and Publ., Washington, 1985-87; pres. Ohio Progressive Bapt. State Conv. Inc., Akron, 1989—; dean Progressive Nat. Bapt. Conv. Inc. Congress of Christian Edn., Washington, 1989— (Marshal A. Talley award 1986). Author: Deacon in the Black Baptist Church, 1986 (PNBC Author Recognition award 1987), Putting Lay People to Work, 1991. Recipient certs. of award EMERGE Ministries Inc., 1984. Mem. Akron and Vicinity Bapt. Ministerial Conf., Phi Beta Sigma. Office: New Hope Bapt Ch 1334 Diagonal Rd Akron OH 44307 *The things that I cannot effectively change I have taken to God in prayer, knowing that it many not be in the Divine scheme of things to alter circumstances at that time. When one makes this internal adjustment, one finds that all things do "work together for good" (Romans 8:28).*

SMITH, THOMAS, religious educator; b. Trenton, N.J., Aug. 10, 1956; s. Kenneth Roche S. and Shirley Ann (Rhodes) Angevine; m. Colleen Bridget McEvoy, Mar. 17, 1979; children: Kelly, Natalie, Alexander. BA, U. Wash., 1978; MCS, Regent Coll., Vancouver, British Columbia, 1984; MA, U. Notre Dame, 1986, PhD, 1988. Asst. prof. Loyola U., New Orleans, 1988—. Author: De Gratia: Faustus of Riez's Treatise on Grace and Its Place in the History of Theology, 1990. Mem. Am. Acad. Religion, North Am. Patristic Soc. Episcopalian. Office: Loyola U Religious Studies 6363 Saint Charles Ave New Orleans LA 70118

SMITH, THOMAS WESLEY, clergyman; b. Lenoir, N.C., May 26, 1952; s. Paul Eugene and Irene (Mills) S.; m. Carol Davis, Dec. 28, 1975; children: Kristin Michelle, Kimberly Diane. BA in Religion, Gardner-Webb Coll., Boiling Springs, N.C., 1974; M in Divinity, Southwestern Bapt. Theol. Sem., Ft. Worth, 1977. Ordained to ministry Bapt. Ch. 1977. Asst. pastor Grandin Bapt. Ch., Lenoir, 1972; assoc. pastor, minister Union Grove Bapt. Ch., Lenoir, 1973-74, youth dir., 1975; pastor Fairview (N.C.) Baptist Ch., 1977-85, Inman (S.C.) Mills Bapt. Ch., 1985—; cons. So. Bapt. Radio-TV Commn., Ft. Worth, 1980—; mem. ministerial bd. Gardner-Webb Coll., chmn., 1989-90. Vol. Jesse Helms for Senate campaign, Asheville, N.C., 1984. Mem. North Spartan Bapt. Assn. (moderator 1989-90). Lodge: Rotary. Avocations: reading, travel, automobiles. Home: 24 B St Inman SC 29349 Office: Inman Mills Bapt Ch 22 B St Inman SC 29349

SMITH, TIMOTHY BALDERSON, minister; b. St. Louis, Dec. 29, 1958; s. Stuart Horton and MaryEllen (Mueller) S.; m. Cynthia Anne Balderson, Apr. 30, 1983; 1 child, Adrianne Pierce. BA, Belhaven Coll., 1979; MDiv, Princeton (N.J.) Theol. Sem., 1983. Ordained to ministry Presbyn. Ch. (U.S.A.), 1983. Asst. pastor Maryland Heights, Mizpah and Overland Presbyn. Chs., St. Louis, 1983-86; assoc. pastor Pk. Presbyn. Ch., Beaver, Pa., 1986—; instr. ancient Greek Geneva Coll., Beaver Falls, Pa., 1988—. Pres. Bridgewater (Pa.) Community Devel. Corp.; bd. mem. Mental Health and Mental Retardation Adv. Bd. of Beaver County, Pa. Republican. Home: 111 Market St WB Beaver PA 15009-3021 Office: Pk Presbyn Ch McIntosh Sq Beaver PA 15009-2622

SMITH, TIMOTHY DEAN, music minister; b. Seattle, July 25, 1952; s. Elwood S. and Dorothy L. (Wilde) S.; m. Mary L. Bowers, May 25, 1974; children: David, Anna, Amy, Michael. BA in Music Edn., N.W. Nazarene Coll., 1974; postgrad., Western Oreg. State Coll., 1978. Orchestra dir. 1st Ch. of Nazarene, Nampa, Idaho, 1973-74; music tchr. The Dalles Jr. High and High Sch., 1974-80, Ockley Green Middle Sch., 1981-82; music min. Bible Way Fellowship, The Dalles, Oreg., 1975-81, Bible Temple, Portland, Oreg., 1982-84; music tchr. Temple Christian Schs., 1982—; music adminstr. Portland Bible Coll., 1982—. Author: Piano in Worship, 1989; composer/arranger: Orchestrations of Praise, 1985; (with others) The Lamb, 1981, Battle Zones, 1986. Dir. His Tapestry Internat., Portland, 1985-91, PBC Chorale, Portland, 1990-91; Repub. precinct person Multnomah County, Portland, 1987-90. Home: 624 NE 79 Portland OR 97213 Office: Portland Bible Coll 9201 NE Fremont Portland OR 97220

SMITH, TIMOTHY JAMES, pastor; b. Reading, Pa., Dec. 4, 1957; s. James Lee and Florence Louise (Denninger) S.; m. Donna Maire Fassio, Aug. 22, 1981; children: Rebecca Marie, Matthew Timothy. BA, Millersville U., 1981; MDiv, United Theol. Sem., 1984. Ordained to ministry Meth. Ch., 1983; cert. clin. pastoral edn. Assoc. pastor Mt. Hope United Meth. Ch., Aston, Pa., 1984-86; pastor Simpson & Salem United Meth. Ch., Gordon, Pa., 1986-90, St. Peter's United Meth. Ch., Saylorsburg, Pa., 1990—; dist. sec. Commn. on Edn., Valley Forge, Pa., 1985-90; dist. rep. Conf. Sessions, Valley Forge, 1990—. Author: Dynamic Preaching, 1990; contbr. short stories to Lancaster Sunday News, 1988-89, sermons in field. Mem. Order of St. Luke (formation officer 1987-90, vice chair 1991—), Rotary. Democrat. Home: PO Box 323 Saylorsburg PA 18353 Office: St Peters United Meth Ch PO Box 323 Saylorsburg PA 18353

SMITH, TIMOTHY MARK, minister; b. Anderson, Ind., Oct. 13, 1952; s. Robert Norton and Marilyn (Harrison) S.; m. Linda Kay Scott, Aug. 5, 1972; children: Amy Jo, Aaron (dec.), Nathan. BA, Anderson U., 1974; postgrad., Earlham Sch. Religion, Richmond, Ind., 1989, Anderson (Ind.) Sch. Theol., 1990-91. Ordained to ministry Ch. of God, 1986; cert. tchr., 1974. Pastor intern 1st Ch. of God, Portageville, Mo., 1970; assoc. pastor Rose Hill Ch. of God, Paulding, Ohio, 1974-76, 1st Ch. of God, Defiance, Ohio, 1976-83, Westwood Ch. of God, Kalamazoo, Mich., 1983-86; min. music 1st Ch. of God, Ansonia, Ohio, 1986—; tchr., coach Paulding Exempted Village Schs., 1974-83. Contbg. editor Creator Mag., 1979-90. Home: 112 N Main St Greenville OH 45331 Office: 1st Ch of God 9940 State Rte 118 S Ansonia OH 45303

SMITH, TIMOTHY RANDOLPH, minister; b. Meridian, Miss., July 7, 1945; s. Otho R. and Emily B. (Krouse) S.; m. Emily Clark, Aug. 4, 1973; children: Jason K., Stephen C., Emily. BA, U. Miss., 1967, JD, 1969; MDiv, Seabury-Western U., 1985; postgrad., Fuller Theol. Sem., 1988—. Ordained to ministry, Episcopal Ch. Pastoral asst. St. Andrew's By-the-Sea Episcopal Ch., Destin, Fla., 1980-82; curate Ch. of the Nativity, Dothan, Ala., 1985-86; canon evangelist Cathedral Ch. of Advent, Birmingham, Ala., 1986-88; rector St. Joseph's On-the-Mountain Episcopal Ch., Mentone, Ala., 1988—; retreat leader nat. teaching/preaching missions, 1988—; chaplain Kanuga Retreat Ctr., Hendersonville, N.C., 1988. Editor program Reaching Others for the Christ, 1988; contbr. articles to profl. publs. Named Outstanding Young Leader in Miss., M.E.C., 1976. Mem. North DeKalb County Ministerial Assn. (pres. 1990—), Ft. Payne Area Ministerial Assn. (sec. 1990—). Home: River Woods Rte 1 Box 218S Mentone AL 35984 Office: St Joseph's On-the-Mountain Episcopal Ch PO Box 98 Mentone AL 35984

SMITH, TIMOTHY SCOTT, education minister; b. Mableton, Ga., Mar. 7, 1962; s. Harry Frank and Carolyn (Wade) S.; m. Cathy Ann Cowart, Dec. 17, 1983; 1 child, Therron Jacob. AA in Religious Studies, Truett-McConnell Jr. Coll., 1982; BS in Edn., West Ga. Coll., 1985; MDiv, SE Bapt. Theol. Sem., 1989. Min. edn. bowdon (Ga.) Bapt. Ch., 1983-86; min. edn. and youth Wake Cross Roads Bapt. Ch., Raleigh, N.C., 1986-88; min. edn. 1st Bapt. Ch., Dallas, 1988—; ch. growth cons. Ga. Bapt. Conv., Atlanta, 1988—; camp pastor N.C. Royal Ambassadors Camp, Cary, N.C., 1987-89. Mem. So. Bapt. Religious Edn. Assn., Ga. Bapt. Religious Edn. Assn., Ea. Bapt. Religious Edn. Assn., Nat. Assn. Ch. Bus. Adminstrn., So. Bapt. Assn. Ch. Bus. Adminstrn. Home: 9107 Cooper Ct Dallas GA 30132 Office: 1st Bapt Ch 401 Main St Dallas GA 30132

SMITH, VIRGINIA, religious education director; b. Billings, Mont., Mar. 28, 1931; d. Raymond A. and Emma A. (McGarvey) S. B.A. in Journalism,

U. Mont., 1953; M.A. in Religious Studies, Gonzaga U., 1978. Copywriter, Sta-KBMY, Billings, 1953-55; in various positions Sta.-KGHL-Radio-TV, Billings, 1956-69; copy chief Sta.-KTVQ-TV, Billings, 1969-82, promotion dir., 1983-85; dir. religious edn. Holy Rosary Parish; chmn. religion dept. Billings Cen. Cath. High Sch. Columnist Eastern Mont. Catholic Register, 1982-83, 85—; creator , co-presenter Scripture from Scratch Adult Study Program; contbr. articles to Living Words, Ultreya mag., God's World Today, Cath. Evangelization, Cath. Digest, to nat. Cursillo lit.; creator Scripture from Scratch (basic Bible program for adults). Active Cursillo Movement, including past mem. workshops, past nat. encounter positions; conv. del. Mont. Assn. Chs.; mem. communications com. Mont. Cath. Conf. Named TV Copywriter of Yr., Greater Mont. Found., 1975, 82; recipient First Place awards Mont. Ad Club, 1983.

SMITH, W. ALAN, religion and philosophy educator; b. Cleveland, Tenn., Jan. 24, 1949; s. Ward Haskell Smith and Evelyn Rosalie (Weaver) Gray; m. Dee Ann Stark, Mar. 27, 1971; children: Nathaniel Dean, Skye Noel. BA, Fla. State U., 1972; MDiv, Vanderbilt U., 1976, D in Ministry, 1983; PhD, Sch. of Theology, Claremont, Calif., 1991. Ordained to Christian ministry, 1975. Minister 1st Christian Ch., Greenville, Ky., 1976-79; assoc. minister 1st Christian Ch., Pomona, Calif., 1984-87; minister Fairhope (Ala.) Christian Ch., 1979-84; asst. prof. religion and philosophy Fla. So. Coll., Lakeland, 1987—; rsch. assoc. Search Inst., Inc., Mpls., 1987—; seminar mem. Youth Ministry and the Theol. Sch., Richmond, Va., 1988. Author: Children Belong in Worship, 1984. Mem. Am. Acad. Religion, Soc. Bibl. Lit., United Meth. Assn. Profs. Religious Edn., Assn. Profs. and Researchers in Religious Edn., Religious Edn. Assn., Assn. Christian Ch. Educators. Democrat. Office: Fla So Coll 111 Lake Hollingsworth Dr Lakeland FL 33801-5698

SMITH, WALLACE BUNNELL, physician, church official; b. Independence, Mo., July 29, 1929; s. William Wallace and Rosamond (Bunnell) S.; m. Anne M. McCullough, June 26, 1956; children—Carolyn, Julia, Laura. A.A., Graceland Coll., Lamoni, Iowa, 1948; B.A., U. Kans., 1950, M.D., 1954. Diplomate: Am. Bd. Ophthalmology. Intern Charity Hosp. of La., 1955; resident in medicine U. Kans. Med. Center, 1958, resident in ophthalmology, 1959-62; pvt. practice medicine specializing in ophthalmology, 1962-76; ordained to ministry Reorganized Ch. of Jesus Christ of Latter Day Saints, 1945; asso. pastor Walnut Park Congregation, Independence, Mo., 1966-70, Pleasant Heights Congregation, Independence, 1975-76; president-designate Reorganized Ch. of Jesus Christ of Latter Day Saints, 1976-78, pres., 1978—; clin. assoc. U. Kans. Med. Center, 1962-76; dir. Pacific Land Devel. Assn. Bd. dirs. Mo. State Hist. Soc., Am. Lung Assn. W. Mo.; chmn. Independence Regional Health Ctr. Corp. Served to lt. M.C. USNR, 1955-58. Fellow Am. Acad. Ophthalmology, A.C.S.; mem. AMA, Jackson County Med. Soc., Independence C. of C., Phi Beta Pi. Club: Rotary. Home: 337 Partridge Independence MO 64055 Office: Auditorium PO Box 1059 Independence MO 64051

SMITH, WARREN THOMAS, clergyman, educator; b. Knoxville, Tenn., Oct. 20, 1923; s. Warren T. and Lola May (Jones) S.; m. Barbara Ann Sullards, Dec. 27, 1949; 1 child, James Warren. Student Maryville Coll., 1942-43; B.A., Ohio Wesleyan U., 1945; B.D., Emory U., 1948, postgrad., 1974-75; Ph.D., Boston U., 1953; D.D., Lincoln Meml. U., 1958. Ordained deacon Methodist Ch., 1947, elder, 1949; full connection N. Ga. Ann. Conf., 1951. Pastor, Waldo Meth. Ch. (Ohio), 1944-45, Howard Ave. Meth. Ch., Dorchester, Mass., 1949-50; assoc. pastor Peachtree Rd. Meth. Ch., Atlanta, 1950-53; pastor Sharp Meml. Meth. Ch., dir. religious life, head dept. religion Young Harris Coll., 1953-57; pastor Trinity Meth. Ch., Atlanta, 1957-60; mem. staff Bd. edn. Meth. Ch., 1960-64; pastor Young Harris Meml. Ch., Athens, Ga., 1964-66, N. Decatur Meth. Ch., 1966-68; sr. pastor First United Meth. Ch., College Park, Ga., 1968-74; asst. prof. ch. history Interdenominational Theol. Ctr., Atlanta, 1974-79, assoc. prof., 1979-84, prof., chmn. dept., 1984—; interpreter for Meth. Bicentennial, N. Ga., 1980-84. Author: Thomas Coke, Foreign Minister of Methodism, 1959; Heralds of Christ, 1963; Selections form the Writings of Thomas Coke, 1966; At Christmas, 1969; Preludes: Georgia, Methodism, The American Revolution, 1976; And the Play Goes On: Characters in the Biblical Drama, 1980; Augustine: His Life and Thought, 1980; Harry Hosier: Circuit Rider, 1981; 1784 I Remember the Christmas Conference, 1983; Journey in Faith, 1984; John Wesley and Slavery, 1986; contbr. articles to religious jours. Nat. Endowment for Humanities grantee, 1969. Mem. Am. Soc. Ch. History, Wesley Hist. Soc. (Eng.), Am. Hist. Assn., Southeastern Jurisdiction Hist. Soc., North Ga. Hist. Soc., World Meth. Hist. Soc., Theta Phi, Omicron Delta Kappa, Delta Tau Delta. Office: 671 Beckwith St SW Atlanta GA 30314

SMITH, WAYNE HAROLD, minister; b. Bridgeport, Conn., July 2, 1950; m. Beverly Jane Smith, 1976; children: Peter, Jonathan. BA, So. Meth. U., 1972; MDiv, Drew Theol. Sem., 1975, D Ministry, 1977. Ordained to ministry United Meth. Ch., 1974. Assoc. pastor Rowayton (Conn.) and Westport United Meth. Ch., 1976-78; pastor Norwalk (Conn.) and Rowayton United Meth. Ch., 1978-80, Cornwall (N.Y.) United Meth. Ch., 1980-88, St. James United Meth. Ch., Lynbrook, N.Y., 1988—; vice chmn. Dist. Coun. on Ministries, Conn., 1976-78, chmn., N.Y., 1981-83, sec., mem. exec. com., 1989-90; mem. dist. bd. ordination mins. Hudson West dist. United Meth. Ch., 1984-88; chmn. social svcs., bd. dirs. L.I. Coun. Chs. Contbr. articles to religious publs. Recipient award Robert Schuller Assn., 1983. Mem. City Soc. United Meth. Ch., Masons, Lions. Home: 244 Earle Ave Lynbrook NY 11563 Office: St James United Meth Ch Forest Ave and St James Pl Lynbrook NY 11563

SMITH, WAYNE L., elder. Moderator Duck River (and Kindred) Assn. of Bapts., Lynchburg, Tenn. Office: Duck River Rte 1 Box 429 Lynchburg TN 37352*

SMITH, WENDELL EUGENE, minister, author; b. Tacoma, July 15, 1950; s. Elwood Sherman and Dorothy Louise (Wilde) S.; m. Virginia Renee Melton, Sept. 2, 1972; children: Wendy Yvonne, Judah Elwood. BA, N.W. Nazarene Coll., Nampa, Idaho, 1972. Ordained to ministry Bible Temple Inc., 1979. Min. youth and evangelism Bible Temple, Portland, Oreg., 1974—, founder Generation Ministries, 1986—. Author: The Roots of Character, 1976, Pastoring Youth in a New Generation, 1986, The Dragon Slayer, 1987. Mem. Mins. Fellowship Internat. (apostolic team 1987—). Republican. Office: Bible Temple 9200 NE Fremont Portland OR 97220

SMITH, WESLEY W., academic administrator. Head Valley Forge Christian Coll., Phoenixville, Pa. Office: Valley Forge Christian Coll Office of President Charlestown Phoenixville PA 19460*

SMITH, WILFRED CANTWELL, educator, writer; b. Toronto, Ont., Can., July 21, 1916; s. Victor Arnold and Sarah Cory (Cantwell) S.; m. Muriel McKenzie Struthers, Sept. 23, 1939; children—Arnold Gordon, Julian Struthers, Heather Patricia, Brian Cantwell, Rosemary Muriel. B.A., U. Toronto, 1938; postgrad. Westminster Coll., Cambridge, Eng., 1938-40, St. John's Coll., Cambridge U., 1938-40; M.A., Princeton U., 1947, Ph.D., 1948; 12 hon. degrees. Ordained to ministry United Ch. of North India, 1944, Presbyn. Ch. in Can., 1945, United Ch. Can., 1961. Lectr. Indian and Islamic history Forman Christian Coll., India, 1941-45; research assoc. Henry Martyn Sch. Islamic Studies, India, 1941-46; Birks prof. comparative religion McGill U., 1949-63, dir. Inst. Islamic Studies, 1951-63; prof. world religions, dir. Ctr. Study of World Religions of Harvard, 1964-73; McCulloch prof. religion, chmn. dept. religion Dalhousie U., Halifax, N.S., Can., 1973-78; prof. comparative history of religion, chmn. The Study of Religion, Harvard U., 1978-84. Author: Modern Islam in India, 1943, Islam in Modern History, 1957, Faith of Other Men, 1963, Meaning and End of Religion, 1963, Questions of Religious Truth, 1967, Religious Diversity, 1976, Belief and History, 1977; Faith and Belief, 1979; Towards a World Theology, 1981, On Understanding Islam, 1981; writings transl. into French, German, Swedish, Arabic, Turkish, Urdu, Indonesian, Chinese, Korean, and Japanese; adv. editor Middle East Jour., 1950-77, Muslim World, 1956-84, Religious Studies, 1964-84, Studies in Religion, 1970-83; consulting editor Ency. Brit., 1969-90. Recipient Chauveau medal Royal Soc. Can., 1974. Fellow AAAS, Royal Soc. Can. (pres. humanities and social scis. 1973); mem. Am. Acad. Religion (pres. 1982-83), Middle East Studies Assn. N.Am. (pres. 1977-78), Can. Theol. Soc. (pres. 1979-80), Am. Soc. Study of Religion (pres. 1966-69). Sr. Killam research fellow U. Toronto, 1984-86. Home: 476 Brunswick Ave, Toronto, ON Canada M5R 2Z5

SMITH, WILLIAM CLARKE, clergyman; b. Bend, Oreg., Jan. 22, 1926; s. Jay Harvey Smith and Amelia Grace (Starr) Poor; m. Veta Maxine Davidson; children—Carolyn Jean Aldama, Virginia Ann Bennett, Barbara Lynn Farstad, Rebecca Ruth Sickler, Donald Allen, Patricia Bea Weinbrenner, Dwight David. A.B. cum laude, Ouachita Baptist U., 1949; postgrad. Golden Gate Baptist Theol. Sem., 1951-53. Ordained to ministry So. Baptist Ch., 1948. Pastor Owensville Baptist Ch., Ark., 1949-50, Grace Bapt. Ch., Corning, Calif., 1951; assoc. pastor 1st So. Bapt. Ch., Richmond, Calif., 1951-53; pastor Montalvin Bapt. Ch., San Pablo, Calif., 1953-60, 1st So. Bapt. Ch., Clovis, Calif., 1961-85, Hillside Bapt. Ch., La Puente, Calif., 1985, Trinity Bapt. Ch. Modesto, Calif., 1986—; mem. exec. bd. So. Bapt. Conv. Calif., 1981-85, cons. stewardship dept., 1976—, parliamentarian, 1964, 69, 74, 78; pres. Calif. So. Bapt. Ministers Conf., 1979—, Clovis Ministerial Fellowship, 1963-65, 67-70, 75-77; mem. So. Bapt. Bd. Child Care, 1966-67, chmn., 1966, 67; moderator Mid-Valley So. Bapt. Assn., 1965-66, clk., 1969-78; moderator Fresno Bapt. Assn., 1962-64. Chmn. fin. com. Clovis Civic Improvement Bond Com., Calif., 1976; chmn. religion com. Clovis Bicentennial Com., 1975-76; active Clovis Parks Adv. Com., 1977-78. Served with U.S. Army, 1944-46. Republican. Home: 1817 Scott Ave Modesto CA 95350 Office: Trinity Bapt Ch 1346 Ronald Ave Modesto CA 95350

SMITH, WILLIAM CLAY, minister; b. Wauchula, Fla., Nov. 3, 1959; s. Harold Wilson Smith and Trieste Alene (Clemons) Prescott; m. Constance Gina Watson, Aug. 9, 1986; 1 child, Abram Wilson. BA, Samford U., 1981; M in Divinity, So. Bapt. Theol. Sem., 1986, postgrad., 1986—. Ordained to ministry Bapt. Ch., 1982. Pastoral intern First Bapt. Ch., Indian Rocks, Fla., 1977; minister music and youth First Bapt. Ch., Vincent, Ala., 1980-81; asst. to pastor New Hope Bapt. Ch., Wauchula, Fla., 1982; pastor Southside Bapt. Ch., Wauchula, 1982-83, Finchville (Ky.) Bapt. Ch., 1985-89; Southside Bapt. Ch., Louisville, 1989—. Named One of Outstanding Young Men of Am., 1985, 86. Mem. Am. Assn. for Clin. Pastoral Edn., Hardee County Ministerial Assn. (sec. 1983), Shelby County Ministerial Alliance (treas. 1986-88), Shelby Bapt. Assn. (govtl. affairs dir. 1986, chair Christian life com. 1987-88),. Democrat. Avocations: woodworking, gardening, reading. Home: 812 Camden Ave Louisville KY 40215 Office: Southside Bapt Ch 804 Camden Ave Louisville KY 40215

SMITH, WILLIAM HOPKINS, minister; b. Pensacola, Fla., Nov. 9, 1947; s. Octavius Hopkins and Frances Isabel (Gingles) S.; m. Susan Kay Drexler, June 20, 1969; children: William Calvin, Jeremy Hopkins, James Daniel, Philip Walton, Joel Rust. BA, U. W. Fla., 1969; MDiv, Ref. Theol. Sem., 1972. Ordained to ministry Presbyn. Ch. in Am., 1972. Pastor Gretna and Woodland Presbyn. Chs., Gretna, Fla., 1972-73, Firest Presbyn. Ch., Union, Miss., 1973-77; campus minister Ref. Univ. Ministries, U. So. Miss., Hattiesburg, 1977-84; pastor Covenant Presbyn. Ch., Louisville, 1984-88; assoc. pastor Wallace Meml. Presbyn. Ch., Hyattsville, Md., 1988—; chmn. credentials com. Potomac Presbytery, 1991—. Contbr. articles to profl. jours. Exec. com. Newton County Rep. Party, 1976-77; chaplain Community Choir, Louisville, Miss., 1984-87. Mem. Winston County Ministerial Assn. (pres.), U. So. Miss. Campus Ministers Assn. (past pres.), Rotary. Home: 9226 Limestone Pl College Park MD 20740 Office: Wallace Meml Presbyn Ch 7201 Sixteenth Pl Hyattsville MD 20783

SMITH, WILLIAM LAWRENCE, minister; b. Pensacola, Fla., July 25, 1946; s. Clemen Turner and Enid Harrison (Rich) S.; m. Luna Annette Livingston, June 9, 1967; children: Christy Annette, Matthew Lawrence. BA, La. Bapt. Coll., 1968; ThM, New Orleans Bapt. Theol. Sem., 1970. Ordained to ministry So. Bapt. Conv., 1967. Assoc. pastor, dir. music and youth Lee Heights Bapt. Ch., Pineville, La., 1964-65, 1st Bapt. Ch., Georgetown, La., 1965-66; pastor Zion Bapt. Ch., Georgetown, 1966-77, Lakeshore Bapt. Ch., Monroe, La., 1977—; mem. exec. bd. La. Bapt. Conv., 1976—; moderator Shady Grove Bapt. Assn., 1970, N.E. Bapt. Assn., 1981; trustee La. Bapt. Coll., 1982—. Named Outstanding Rural Pastor State of La., La. Bapt. Conv., 1974. Address: 104 McCoy St Monroe LA 71203

SMITH, WILLIAM LESLIE, minister; b. Hot Springs, Ark., Oct. 31, 1931; s. Felix Leslie and Lottie Virginia (Mixon) S.; m. Betty Jean Fowler, July 25, 1951; children: Debra Jean Marty, Sharon Deane James. BA, Ouachita Bapt. U., Arkadelphia, Ark., 1954; MDiv, Southwestern Sem., Ft. Worth, 1957. Ordained to ministry So. Bapt. Conv., 1951. Pastor Archview Bapt. Ch., Little Rock, 1957-58, First Bapt. Ch., Altheimer, Ark., 1958-61, Rosedale Bapt. Ch., Little Rock, 1961-66, First Bapt. Ch., Pecos, Tex., 1966-78, Parkhills Bapt. Ch., San Antonio, 1978—; moderator, editor Pecos Valley Bapt. Assn., 1969-71; pres. Ark. Bapt. State Conv. Pastor's Conf., 1966; trustee Howard Payne U., Brownwood, Tex., 1969-76, exec. bd. Bapt. Gen. Conv. Tex., Dallas, 1970-75. Author booklet: How To Study Your Bible, 1975. Office: Parkhills Bapt Ch 17747 San Pedro San Antonio TX 78232

SMITH, WILLIAM MILTON, bishop; b. Stockton, Ala., Dec. 18, 1918; s. George and Elizabeth Smith; m. Ida M. Anderson, Jan. 19, 1935; 1 dau., Eula C. Goode. Ed., Ala. State U., Tuskegee Inst., Livinstone Coll., Hool Sem., So. Meth. U., Perkins Sch. Theology. Ordained to ministry AME Zion Ch.; minister various chs.; bishop AME Zion Ch., Buffalo, from 1960; now sr. bishop Mobile, Ala. Trustee Ala. State U., 1980. Recipient award Ebony mag., 1980. Republican. Office: AME Zion Ch 3753 Springhill Ave Mobile AL 36608

SMITH, WILLIAM ROBERT, clergyman, writer; b. Evansville, Ind., June 3, 1935; s. William Claude and Mary Lee (Toombs) S.; m. Josephine Freudt; children: Mary William Robert, Raymond. BS with honors, East Tenn. State U., 1958; B.D., Southwestern Baptist Theol. Sem., Ft. Worth, 1966, M.Div., 1967; D.Min., Union Theol. Sem., Richmond, Va., 1975. Ordained to ministry So. Bapt. Ch., 1956. Pastor Thalia Lynn Bapt. Ch., Virginia Beach, Va., 1960-63, Morningside Bapt. Ch., Savannah, Ga., 1967-71, Chamberlayne Bapt. Ch., Richmond, Va., 1971-81, Terry Parker Bapt. Ch., Jacksonville, Fla., 1981-82, 1st Bapt. Ch., South Miami, Fla., 1982—; pres. Norfolk (Va.) Bapt. Pastor's Conf. 1961, Savannah Bapt. Pastor's Conf., 1970, Chatham Clergy Conf., Savannah, 1970; v.p. Miami Bapt. Pastor's Conf. (Fla.), 1983; moderator Miami Bapt. Assn., 1984. Author: Our Unfinished Revolution, 1976; contbr. numerous articles to denominational and other religious and secular publs. Mem. Community Health Planning Agy., Savannah, 1969-70; mem. Savannah Mayor's Com. on Drug Abuse, 1970; chmn. The Ctr., Savannah, 1970; bd. dirs. Jacksonville Blood Bank, 1981-82. Recipient Bicentennial Preaching award Va. Bapt. Bd., 1976, also numerous awards for civic work.

SMITH, WILLIAM STANLEY, JR., minister; b. Alma, Ga., June 27, 1942; s. William Stanley Sr. and Natalie Bunnell (Buttolph) S.; m. Cheryl Anne Jones Cum, June 11, 1966 (div. 1984); children: Kristi Natel, Karla Annali; m. Ann Terry Smith, Aug. 10, 1985. BA, Emory U., 1964; BD, Andover Newton Theol. Sch., Newton Center, Mass., 1968; D of Ministry, Drew U., 1984. Ordained to ministry Meth. Ch., 1970. Assoc. min. Univ. United Meth. Ch., Chapel Hill, N.C., 1968-72; pastor Providence United Meth. Ch., Goldsboro, S.C., 1972-76, Aldersgate United Meth. Ch., Chapel Hill, 1976-79, Louisburg (N.C.) United Meth. Ch., 1979-84, United Meth. Ch. Camp, Shallotte, N.C., 1984-88, Trinity United Meth. Ch., Troy, N.C., 1988—; mem. Bd. Ordained Mins. N.C. Conf., Raleigh, 1972-76; sec. Div. of Worship N.C. Com., Raleigh, 1976-79; spiritual dir. Cape Fear Emmaus, Raleigh, 1987, bd. dirs. 1987—; pres. Brunswick Ministerial Assn., Shallotte, 1986, Troy Ministerial Assn., 1990—. Author: (devotionals) Upper Room, 1976—; newspaper columnist: Brunswick Beacon, 1986-88, Montgomery Herald, 1988—. Pres. Orange County Mental Health Assn., Chapel Hill, 1970-72; chmn. Orange County Heart Fund, 1979; bd. dirs. Montgomery United Way, Troy, 1990—. Named Sertoman of Yr., Meridian Sertoma Club, Chapel Hill, 1971, Vol. of Yr., Franklin County, Louisburg, 1982, Brunswick County, Shallotte, 1986, Montgomery County, Troy, 1990. Mem. Rotary. Democrat. Home: 234 N Russell St Troy NC 27371 Office: Trinity United Meth Ch 239 N Russell St PO Box 502 Troy NC 27371

SMITH, WILLIAM WALLACE, clergyman; b. Lamoni, Iowa, Nov. 18, 1900; s. Joseph and Ada Rachel (Clark) S.; m. Rosamond Bunnell, Nov. 12, 1924; children—Rosalee (Mrs. Otto Helmut Elser), Wallace Bunnell. A.A., Graceland Coll., Lamoni, 1922, D.D. (hon.), 1970; A.B., U. Mo., 1924. Ordained to ministry Reorganized Ch. of Jesus Christ of Latter Day Saints, 1928; asso. pastor Stone Ch. Congregation, Independence, 1929-30; pastor First Ch., Portland, Oreg., 1945-46; mem. council Twelve Apostles, 1947-50; counsellor to pres. Reorganized Ch. Jesus Christ of Latter Day Saints, 1950-58, pres., 1958-78, pres. emeritus, 1978—; asst. editor in chief Saints' Herald, 1950-58, editor in chief, 1958-78, contbg. editor, 1979—; dir. Pacific Land Devel. Assn. Mem. bd. trustees Independence Sanitarium and Hosp.; Hon. fellow Harry Truman Library Inst. for Nat. and Internat. Affairs. Mem. Mo. Hist. Soc. (trustee), Jackson County Hist. Soc., C. of C., Delta Upsilon. Club: Rotarian. Home: 428 Bellevista Dr Independence MO 64055 Office: PO Box 1059 Auditorium Independence MO 64051

SMITH, WOODROW MICHAEL, religious organization administrator; b. Langdale, Ala., Oct. 10, 1946; s. Woodrow Wilson and Mildred (Chapman) S.; m. Joyce Lynn Keilman, June 24, 1967; children: Susan, Michael. BA, Milligan (Tenn.) Coll., 1968; MDiv, Emmanuel Sch. Religion, Johnson City, Tenn., 1971; postgrad., Fuller Theol. Sem., Pasadena, Calif., 1973, 87-89. Min. Boones Creek Christian Ch., Johnson City, 1966-71, 1st Christian Ch., Columbus, Ga., 1971-73; missionary to Ethiopia Christian Missionary Fellowship, Indpls., 1974-77, missionary to Indonesia, 1978-85, gen. dir., 1985—. Contbr. articles to books. Mem. Christian Mgmt. Assn., Theta Phi. Office: Christian Missionary Fellowship 5674 Caito Dr Indianapolis IN 46226

SMITH, YOLANDA YVETTE, minister; b. San Antonio, Oct. 1, 1957; d. Louis Andrew and Vera Gay (Hearns) S. BA, Ariz. State U., 1979, MEd, 1984; MDiv, Sch. Theology Va. Union U., Richmond, 1990. Tchr. Phoenix Union High Sch. Dist., 1979-83; new mins. facilitator First Instl. Baptist Ch., Phoenix, 1982-83, min. evangelism and discipleship, 1983-87; program asst. Baptist Gen. Conv., Richmond, Va., 1988-90; min. evangelism and discipleship First Instl. Bapt. Ch., Phoenix, 1990—. Bd. dirs. Rightway Children, Phoenix, 1986-87; active Victory Together: One Clear Choice, Phoenix, 1990—. Recipient Benjamin E. Mays Fellowship Ministry Fund Theol. Edn., N.Y.C., 1988, 89, 90, Adam Clayton Powell award Va. Union U., 1989-90; named one of Outstanding Young Women of Am., 1983, 87. Mem. NAACP, Nat. Rainbow Coalition, Nat. Coun. Negro Women, Religious Edn. Assn., Alpha Kappa Alpha. Democrat. Office: First Instl Bapt Ch 1141 E Jefferson St Phoenix AZ 85034

SMITHER, GERTRUDE JACKSON, minister; b. Dallas, Oct. 6, 1937; d. John Nelson and Sallie Bell (Gaston) Jackson; m. Robert Bush Smither Jr., Aug. 20, 1960; children: Robert, Sallie, John, Mary Kate. BA, U. Tex., 1959; MDiv, Episcopal Theol. Sem. S.W., Austin, 1985. Ordained to ministry, Episcopal Ch., 1990. Dir. religious edn. Trinity Episcopal Ch., Galveston, Tex., 1979-83; chaplain U. Tex. Med. Br., Galveston, 1985—; asst. St. Luke the Physician Episcopal Ch., Galveston, 1985—; chaplain William Temple Found., Galveston, 1985—; chaplain U. Tex. Med. Br., 1985—; pres. St. Vincent's Episcopal House, Galveston, 1987, 88, 91; chmn. Campus Mins., 1987-91; mem. Coun. Religious Ministry, UTMB, 1985—. Fellow Coll. of Chaplains of Am. Protestant Health Assn.; mem. Galveston Ministerial Assn. (pres. 1991). Home: 4806 Denver Dr Galveston TX 77551 Office: The William Temple Found 427 Market St Galveston TX 77551

SMITHSON, RICKY DON, minister; b. Amarillo, Tex., Jan. 11, 1957; s. C.L. and Hazel (Adams) S.; m. Cindy C. Kilgore, Dec. 28, 1977; children: Timothy, Kristy. Diploma in pastoral ministry, So. Bapt. Sem. Extension, Amarillo, 1980; BS in Occupational Edn. and Religion, Wayland Bapt. U., Plainview, Tex., 1983; MA in Religious Edn., Southwestern Bapt. Theol. Sem., Ft. Worth, 1988. Lic. to ministry So. Bapt. Conv., 1980, ordained, 1991. Min. youth and edn. Wichita Street Bapt. Ch., Ft. Worth, 1985, B.H. Carroll Bapt. Ch., Ft. Worth, 1985-88; min. youth 1st Bapt. Ch., Mesquite, Tex., 1988—; tchr. Southlawn Christian Sch., Amarillo, 1982; leader group counseling Mesquite Ind. Sch. Dist., 1988—; conf. leader Sunday sch. bd. So. Bapt. Conv., Nashville, 1989-90; mem. Youth Outreach Network, 1990—; coord. Mesquite Youth Mins. Network, 1990—. Office: 1st Bapt Ch Mesquite TX 75149 *Being involved in ministry to youth I have come to a realization that in a time of family dysfunction teens are not so concerned about the next church social as they are to finding answers to life's problems.*

SMOLINSKI, EDWARD ALBERT, holding company executive, lawyer, accountant, deacon; b. N.Y.C., Jan. 6, 1928; s. Albert John and Adele (Weber) S.; m. Joan E. Winslow, Nov. 12, 1955; children: Albert, Edward, Linda, Donna. B.S. in Acctg., L.I. U., 1948; M.B.A., NYU, 1950, J.D., 1956. Bar: N.Y. 1957; C.P.A., N.Y.; ordained deacon Roman Cath. Ch., 1977. Acct. various cert. pub. acctg. firms. N.Y.C., 1948-53; acctg. supr. Curtiss Wright Co., Woodridge, N.J., 1953-60; mem. treasury staff Sperry-Rand Corp., Great Neck, N.Y., 1960-62; corp. controller Fairchild Camera and Instrument Co., Syosset, N.Y., 1968-69; v.p., treas., chief fin. officer Grow Group, Inc., N.Y.C., 1969-89; asst. treas./sec. United Indsl. Corp., N.Y.C., 1989—; adj. asst. prof. Hunter Coll., 1989. Bd. dirs. Long Island U.-Bus. Game, N.Y.C., 1977-83, NYU Mgmt. Decision Lab., 1983-88; deacon Diocese of Bklyn., Roman Cath. Ch., 1977—. Mem. AICPA (com. on nat. def. 1963), N.Y. Bar, Fin. Execs. Inst. Roman Catholic. Lodge: Elks. Home: 70-19 June St Forest Hills NY 11375 Office: United Indsl Corp 18 E 48th St New York NY 10017

SMOOSE, LARRY VICTOR, minister; b. Pitts., Dec. 11, 1946; s. Victor Charles and Elizabeth Edna (Kirsop) S.; m. Laura Ann Cressman, Aug. 12, 1972; 1 child, Matthew Cressman. BA, Thiel Coll., 1968; MDiv, Luth. Theol. Sem., 1972, D in Ministry, 1987. Ordained to ministry Evang. Luth. Ch. in Am., 1972. Asst. pastor Holy Trinity Luth Ch., Abington, Pa., 1972-75; sr. pastor Luth. Ch. of God's Love, Newtown, Pa., 1975—; sec. S.E. Pa. synod Evang. Luth. Ch. in Am., Phila., 1987—, mem. coun., exec. bd., 1987—; pastor, evangelist, Chgo., 1986—; mem. governing bd. Acad. for Evangelists, Columbus, 1987—. Author monographs for Luth. Ch. in Am., 1985-86. Bd. dirs. Found. for Pastoral Counsel, Norristown, Pa., 1982-85; mem. governing bd. Chandler Hall Hospice, Newtown, 1982-90, Newtown Welfare Coun., 1984—, Luth. Retirement Homes, Phila., 1990—; founder, chmn. Bucks County World Food Day Com., 1989—. Recipient Community Svc. award St. Mark's AME Zion Ch., 1989. Mem. Newtown Ministerium (convenor 1977, 82), Acad. for Evangelists, Rotary (pres. Newtown club 1983). Office: Luth Ch of God's Love 791 Newtown-Yardley Rd PO Box 102 Newtown PA 18940

SMUCK, HAROLD VERNON, retired minister, religious organization administrator; b. Huntington, Ind., Oct. 12, 1920; s. Vaughn M. and Elsie J. (Whiteman) S.; m. Evelyn May Sutton, Aug. 27, 1944; children: Norman, Amelia, Vernon. BRE, Ind. Wesleyan U., 1943; BD, Christian Theol. Sch., 1946; MA, Earlham Coll., 1950. Ordained to ministry Friends United Meeting, 1940. Missionary, pastor, youth sec. Friends United Meeting, 1957-66; sec. World Ministries Commn. Friends United Meeting, Richmond, Ind., 1966-81, Ministry Team leader W. Richmond, 1982-86; clk. Friends World Com. (sect. of the Ams.), Phila., 1989—. Author: I Do Not Climb This Mountain Alone, 1986, Friends in East Africa, 1987; contbr. articles to jours. in field. Home: PO Box 1661 Richmond IN 47375

SMULAND, PHILIP LEE, clergyman, educator; b. Duluth, Minn., Oct. 22, 1951; s. Norman Hilmar and Mildred (Breedon) S.; m. Rhonda Ann Versher, Apr. 21, 1984. BA, U. Tex., Arlington, 1975; MA and MDiv, Westminster Theol. Sem., 1983. Ordained to ministry Presbyn. Ch., 1987. Tchr. 1st Presbyn. Ch., Manhattan Beach, Calif., 1984-85, assoc. pastor, 1985-87; pastor Covenant Presbyn. Ch., Bridgewater, Va., 1988—; adj. prof. Nat. U., 1982-87, Loyola-Marymount U., 1987—; asst. tchr. U. So. Calif.. 1984-86. Named one of Outstanding Young Men in Am., 1983. Mem. Phi Alpha Theta, Phi Delta Gamma. Republican. Office: PO Box 1477 Harrisburg VA 22801

SMURL, JAMES FREDERICK, religious studies educator; b. Wilkes-Barre, Pa., Aug. 20, 1934; s. James J. and Rita R. (Gildea) S.; m. Mary Hennigan, Sept. 12, 1967; children: Peter, Linda, Beth, Paul. BA in Philosophy, St. Mary's U., Balt., 1955; STL in Theology, Gregorian U., Rome, 1959; STD in Religious Ethics, Cath. U. Am., 1963. Prof. in moral theology St. Pius X Sem., Scranton, Pa., 1963-67; prof. religious studies Ind. U., Indpls., 1973—. Author: Religious Ethics, 1972 (award), A Primer in Ethics, 1985, The Burdens of Justice, 1991; contbr. articles to profl. publs.

Lilly Endowment fellow, 1981. Mem. Am. Acad. Religion, Soc. Christian Ethics, Hastings Ctr. Office: Ind U 425 University Blvd Indianapolis IN 46202 *Few are the human conversations more important than those which explore what social systems do to, as well for, their members and with what degree of member participation.*

SNAVELY, CYNTHIA ANN, pastor; b. Reading, Pa., Sept. 4, 1959; d. Jay Lester and Jeanne (Hower) S. MA, Lebanon Valley Coll., 1981; MDiv, Drew Theol. Sch., 1984. Ordained to ministry Meth. Ch., 1984. Pastor Weatherly-Beaver Meadows (Pa.) United Meth. Ch., 1984—. Sec. Shepherd House, Inc., Carbon County, 1985-89; pres. Carbon County Prison Chaplaincy Bd., 1987-88; big sister Big Brothers/Big Sisters, Luzerne County, 1985-89. Mem. Weatherly Ministerium (sec., treas. 1985-89), Greater Hazleton Ministerium (v.p. 1988). Democrat. Methodist. Avocations: baking, travel. Home: 618 Sarah St Stroudsburg PA 18360 Office: Stroudsburg United Meth Ch 547 Main St Stroudsburg PA 18360

SNAVELY, FRANK RICHARDSON, minister; b. Rock, W.Va., Dec. 10, 1920; s. Frank Richardson and Samantha Belle (Littral) S.; m. Ella Mae Buttram, June 19, 1943; children: David, Keith, Michal Elaine. BA, Union Coll., Barbourville, Ky., 9146; BD, Vanderbilt U., 1949. Ordained to ministry Meth. Ch., 1949. Minister Tenn. Conf. United Meth. Ch., 1949-65, Holston Conf. United Meth. Ch., 1965—, Friendsville (Tenn.) United Meth. Ch., 1986—; bd. dirs. Tenn. Conf. Camp United Meth. Ch., Crossville, 1953-55; adj. prof. Hiwassee Coll., Madisonville, Tenn., 1980-85. Author: These Found the Way, 1951, The Rim of East Asia, 1962; contbr. articles to publs. Scoutmaster Boy Scouts Am., Gainesboro, Tenn., 1950; chmn. Uplands-Cumberland Med. Bd., Crossville, 1962-64. With USCG, 1942-45, PTO. Mem. Masons. Home: 430 Vernie Lee Rd Friendsville TN 37737 *How can one fulfill the high values of being human, and living here on planet Earth? Knowledge obtained by exterior means certainly helps, but my experiece has been that the most meaningful insights come from within oneself.*

SNEED, DAN CALVIN, minister; b. L.A., Dec. 13, 1944; s. George Calvin and Celia May (Lewis) S.; m. Beverly Ruth Carlson, June 24, 1967; children: Ken, Robert, Russell, Rebecca, Debbie. BTh, Life Bible Coll., L.A., 1967; postgrad., Oral Roberts U., 1989-90. Ordained to ministry Foursquare Ch., 1969. Pastor Altadena (Calif.) Foursquare Ch., 1968-70; youth pastor Cen. Luth. Ch., Van Nuys, Calif., 1970-72; dir. L.A. Teen Challenge, 1972-75; pastor Foursquare Ch., Northridge, Calif., 1974-86; tchr. Youth with a Mission, Kailua Kona, Hawaii, 1986—; bd. dirs. Jesus West Coast, L.A.; non-resident faculty U. of the Nations, Kailua, Kona, Hawaii, 1986—; tchr. Mercy Ships, Lindale, Tex. Co-dir. 1984 Olympic Outreach, L.A, 1983-84; chmn. Internat. Praise Celebration, L.A., 1984. Office: PO Box 3717 Granada Hills CA 91394

SNEED, KEVIN A., minister; b. New Albany, Ind., Jan. 28, 1969; s. Lawrence Ray and Paula Marcel (Bartenan) S.; m. Angela Marie Ball, May 20, 1989. Student, Olivet Nazarene U., 1987-90. Ordained to ministry Ch. of the Nazarene. Min. youth First Ch. of the Nazarene, Shelbyville, Ill., 1989—; bd. dirs. ministry Olivet Nazarene U., Bourbonnais, Ill., 1987-90; del. youth congress Nazarene Youth Internat., Kansas City, Mo., 1991. Mem. Shelbyville Ministerial Assn. Republican. Home: 416 N Will Shelbyville IL 62565 Office: First Ch of the Nazarene 701 W N 3d St Shelbyville IL 62565

SNEED, SHERRIE LYNN, clergy, educator, psychotherapist; b. Knoxville, Tenn., Apr. 17, 1954; d. Charles Herbert and Ann Marie (Maloney) S. B.A., U. Tenn., 1975; postgrad. Hamma Sch. Theology, 1975-78; M.Div., Trinity Luth. Sem., 1979; D.Min. in Pastoral Care and Counseling, Luth. Sch. Theology, 1983. Ordained to ministry Lutheran Ch., 1979. Counselor, Clark County Mental Health Satellite, New Carlisle, Ohio, 1975-76; bookstore bibliographer Hamma Sch. Theology, Springfield, Ohio, 1976-77; asst. to pastor Wittenberg U., Springfield, Ohio, 1977-78; interim pastor Rocky Point Chapel, Springfield, 1978-79; pastor Robinson-Sulphur Luth. Parish, St. Paul Luth. Ch., North Robinson, Ohio, 1979-81, St. John Luth. Ch., Sulphur Springs, Ohio, 1979-81; vice-pastor First Luth. Ch., Galion, Ohio, 1980-81; tchr. Unity Cath. High Sch., Chgo., 1981-82; tchr., dept. head Acad. of our Lady, Chgo., 1982-84; interim pastor St. Thomas Luth. Ch., Chgo., 1983-84, pastor, 1984-86; marriage and family therapist West Suburban Counseling and Ednl. Service, Luth. Social Services Ill., Wheaton, 1984-86; mem. Ohio Synod Task Force on Women in the Ch., 1979-81, Ohio Synod Ednl. Ministry Team, 1980-81, Ill. Synod Ednl. Ministry Team, 1984—; retreat dir. various chs. in Ohio and Ill., 1981—; stewardship cons. Ohio Synod Stewardship Team, 1980-81; supply pastor Ill. Synod, Luth. Sch. Theology, 1981-83; marriage and family therapist. Cons., instr. Contact, 24-hour hotline, Bucyrus, Ohio, 1980-81; CPR instr., area coordinator Mid-Am. chpt. ARC, Chgo., 1983—; chaplain Rehab. Inst. Chgo., 1986—. Vol. dep. registrar Cook County Bd. Elections, 1984—. Mem. Am. Acad. Religion, Soc. Bibl. Lit., Bucyrus Area Ministerial Assn., South Shore Ministerial Assn., South Shore Council Chs. Democrat. Lutheran. Home: 1606 E Hyde Park Blvd Chicago IL 60615 Office: Rehabilitation Inst Chgo 345 E Superior Chicago IL 60611

SNEED, TOMMY LYNN, church music director; b. Chattanooga, Tenn., Oct. 23, 1947; s. Grady and Beulah May (Watson) S.; m. Cynthia Louise Keasler, June 15, 1968; children: David, Jason. BA, Tenn. Temple U., 1969; postgrad., Tenn. Temple Sem., 1970-71. Sunday sch. tchr. Mile Straight Bapt. Ch., Soddy-Daisy, Tenn., 1968—, music dir., 1970—, asst. camp dir., 1973-88, ednl. dir., 1982-90; sta. mgr. Radio Paradise, Hixson, Tenn., 1970—. Mem. Optimist (charter mem. Hixson club, Key Man award 1982-83, pres. 1987-88, editor 1985-86). Home: 918 Delores Dr Hixson TN 37343 Office: Mile Straight Bapt Ch 8448 Springfield Rd Soddy-Daisy TN 37379

SNELL, ALDEN HENRY, pastor; b. Rochester, N.Y., Mar. 1, 1953; s. Robert David and Reta Marjorie (Puls) S.; m. Linda Elizabeth Harner, June 14, 1975; children: Alden Henry II, Christopher Roy. AA, Monroe Community Coll., Rochester, N.Y., 1973; BA, Roberts Wesleyan Coll., 1975; MDiv, Ea. Bapt. Theol. Sem., 1978. Ordained to ministry Am. Bapt. Chs. in U.S.A., 1978. Pastor First Bapt. Ch. of Richford, Vt., 1978-81, Community Bapt. Ch. of Montgomery Ctr., Vt., 1978-81, First Bapt. Ch. of Carthage, N.Y., 1981-82, First Bapt. Ch. of Clarence, N.Y., 1982—; bd. dirs. Am. Bapt. Chs. Niagara Frontier, Buffalo, 1989—, mem. exec. com., 1989-90; sec.-treas. Clergy Assn. Clarence, 1983-86; mem. Mins. Coun., 1978—. League dir. Clarence Baseball Assn., 1990; referee Clarence Soccer League, 1985—. Republican. Office: First Bapt Ch of Clarence 10790 Hunts Corner Rd Clarence NY 14031-1099

SNELL, DANIEL CLAIR, history educator; b. Jackson, Mich., Oct. 1, 1947; s. Clair John and Iva Edith (Hawkins) S.; m. Katherine Lane Barwick, June 28, 1986. BA, Stanford U., 1971; PhD, Yale U., 1975. Instr. near Eastern languages U. Wash., Seattle, 1975-76; vis. asst. prof. near Eastern studies U. Mich., Ann Arbor, 1977; asst. prof. religious studies Conn. Coll., New London, 1977-78, Barnard Coll., N.Y.C., 1978-80; asst. prof. religion Gustavus Adolphus Coll., St. Peter, Minn., 1981-82; Fulbright researcher Nat. Mus. of Aleppo (Syria), 1982-83; from asst. to assoc. prof. history U. Okla., Norman, 1983—; epigrapher, site supr. Yale U. expedition to Tell-Leilan, Syria, al-Qahtaniyah, 1980, U. Melbourne expedition to Tell-el-Qitar, Syria, Yusuf Pasha, Abu Galgal,1984, 85, 87. Author: A Workbook of Cuneiform Signs, 1979, The E.A. Hoffman Collection, 1979, Ledgers and Prices, 1982. Vol. extended families Juvenile Services, Inc., Norman. Mellon Found. fellow, 1976-77, NEH fellow, 1980-81, Nat. Humanities Ctr. fellow, 1989-90, Humanities Rsch. Ctr. fellow, Australian Nat. U., 1990. Mem. Am. Oriental Soc. (life), Am. Hist. Assn., Soc. Bibl. Lit. Democrat. Avocation: squash. Home: 504 Miller Norman OK 73069 Office: U Okla History Dept 455 W Lindsey Norman OK 73019

SNELL, VERLYN REID, minister; b. Independence, Mo., Nov. 10, 1934; s. LuVern and Anna Mattie (Rasmussen) S.; m. Frances Sammie Fisher, Aug. 17, 1960; children: Anne E. Snell Heinrich, Alathea J. Snell Voss, Ardeth V. Snell Hornbaker. BA, U. Western Ont., London, Can., 1957; BDiv, Asbury Theol. Sem., 1962; D Ministry, Phillips Grad. Sem., 1976. Ordained to ministry Meth. Ch. as elder. Pastor Enid (Okla.) Free Meth. Ch., 1967-75, Norman (Okla.) North Free Meth. Ch., 1975-78, MacArthur Free Meth. Ch., Oklahoma City, 1978-83; chaplain Deaconess Hosp., Oklahoma City, 1983-85; pastor 1st United Meth. Ch., Nardin, Okla., 1985-87, Madill, Okla., 1987—; bd. dirs. ordained ministry United Meth. Conf., Okla., 1987—; chairperson Dist. Com. on Evangelism, Ardmore, Okla., 1989—. Member Madill Community Day Care, 1987—, Marshall County chpt. Am. Cancer Assn., Madill, 1989, Madill Ednl. Excellence, 1991. Recipient cert. of merit Cir. Rider, 1991. Mem. Madill Ministerial Alliance (pres. 1989—), Lake Texoma United Ministry (pres. 1991—), Rotary (chmn. meals on wheels Madill chpt. 1989—). Home: 116 Sunset Dr Madill OK 73446 Office: First United Meth Ch 301 W Taliaferro Madill OK 73446

SNELLER, PHILLIP PAUL, clergyman; b. Fremont, Mich., July 30, 1951; s. Alden J. and Edna Louise (Boeskool) S.; m. Faye Lorene Brouwer, Dec. 19, 1975; children: Kimberly Faye, Kelley Lorene. Assoc. Agr., Mich. State U., 1971; BA, Hope Coll., 1977; MDiv, We. Theol. Sem., 1981. Ordained to ministry Reformed Ch., 1981. Pastor Immanuel Reformed Ch., Fennville, Mich., 1981-88, Am. Reformed Ch., Hull, Iowa, 1988—; bd. pres. Hope Haven Inc., Rock Valley, Iowa, 1990—; corp. pres. Valley Residential, Inc., Rock Valley, 1991—; chmn. West Sioux Classis Jud. Bus. Com., Hull, Iowa, 1991—; com mem. West Sioux Classis Christian Edn., Sioux Center, Iowa, 1988—. Contbr. articles to newspapers. With U.S. Army, 1971-73, Vietnam. Mem. Kiwanis Internat. Home: 1108 Locust St Hull IA 51239-0365 Office: Am Reformed Ch 911 1st St Hull IA 51239-0365

SNELLING, LONIE EUGENE, JR., minister; b. Laurinburg, N.C., Apr. 5, 1937; s. Lonie Eugene Sr. and Doris (Stevens) S.; m. Sally Still, Apr. 14, 1965; children: Cynthia Lyn, David Eugene. BA cum laude, Southeastern Bible Coll., Birmingham, Ala., 1960, Th.B. cum laude, 1961; MEd magna cum laude, Boston U., 1974; PhD, Columbia Pacific U., San Rafael, Calif., 1984. Minister music So. Bapt. Chs., Birmingham, 1957-61; youth evangelist Youth for Christ, Atlanta, 1962-63; enlisted U.S. Army, 1963, advanced through grades to capt., 1982; served in Vietnam; chaplain adminstr. U.S. Army, 1963-74; behavioral scientist Med. Service Corps, U.S. Army, various locations, 1974-83; dir. Royal Palm Bibl. Counseling Ctrs., Ft. Myers, Fla., 1983-86; pres. Royal Palm Ministries, Inc., Ft. Myers, 1986—; cons. in psychology and counseling Gulf Shore Bapt. Grad. Sch., Ft. Myers, 1983—, head dept. psychology and counseling; sem. prof. So. Bapt. extension dept. Decorated Legion of Merit. Fellow Nat. Assn. Nouthetic Counselors; mem. Nat. Judo and Karate Assn. Am. Republican. Avocations: skiing, boating, golf, teaching karate, fishing. Home: 5367 Colony Ct Cape Coral FL 33904 Office: Royal Palm Ministries Inc 5235 Ramsey Way #13 Fort Myers FL 33907

SNIDER, ALLEN WESLEY, minister; b. Helena, Ark., Jan. 1, 1953; s. Harm Wesley and Frances Ardella (Strother) S.; m. Jamie Carol Ferguson Hassler, Oct. 3, 1973 (div. 1978); m. Judy Carol Francis, Apr. 7, 1979; children: Lisa Marie, Tomi Gwen, Eric Nevin. AA, Grayson County Coll., Denison, Tex., 1989; student, Austin Coll., Sherman, Tex., 1989—. Lay dir. youth ministry Lay Speakers to Juvenile Detention Ctr., Pottsboro, Tex., 1986-89; cert. lay speaker United Meth. Ch., Sherman-McKinney, Tex., 1985-91; youth and edn. dir. Whaley United Meth. Ch., Gainesville, Tex., 1989—; lay del. to ann. conf. N. Tex. Conf. United Meth. Ch., Sadler, 1986-89. Mem. Gainesville Ministerial Alliance, Austin Coll. English Club. Home: Rte 2 Box 414 Whitesboro TX 76273 Office: Whaley United Meth Ch PO Box 417 Gainesville TX 76240

SNIDER, DOROTHY ELIZABETH, minister; b. Deming, N.Mex., May 21, 1923; d. George Ernest and Rebecca (Usrey) Still; m. Hubert Wesley Parks, Jan. 1, 1943 (div. 1977); children: Sharon, Dorothy, Rebecca, Faith, Jonathan; m. Donald Ward Snider, Nov. 6, 1978. Student, Apostolic Bible Coll., 1955. Ordained to ministry United Pentecostal Ch., 1945. Co-pastor Harmony Chapel, Stockton, Calif., 1945-46; evangelist Ont., Can., 1946-47; co-pastor La Mesa, Tex., 1949-50; asst. pastor various chs., Morris, Okla., 1951-52; co-pastor various chs., Monahans, Tex., 1955-56; dir. child evangelism Christian Life Ctr., Stockton, 1977-78; dir. youth Life Tabernacle, Kansas City, Mo., 1979-82; evangelist United Pentecostal Ch., various locations, 1983-84, Vt., Ark., Tex., Que.., Calif., 1983-85, 89-90; pastor Apostolic Pentecostal Ch., Moberly, Mo., 1986-88; missionary Liberia, 1953-54, Japan, 1956-62; tchr. Loomis Christian Sch., Calif., 1971-72, Christian Life Coll., Stockton, 1977-78; speaker Christian Ladies Seminar, Columbia, S.C., Poplar Bluff, Mo., 1986, Poplar Bluff, 1987-90. Pres. Western Dist. Ladies Aux., 1973-77, Ariz. Ladies Aux., 1965-68. Republican. Home: 2900 Milford Pl Blue Springs MO 64015 Office: United Pentecostal Ch Hazelwood MO 63042

SNIDER, LOUIS BECKHAM, psychotherapist; b. Taylorsville, Ky., Mar. 13, 1902; s. Courtney Scott and Mary Ella (Hume) S.; m. Margaret Russell Childress, Aug. 22, 1932; children: Louis, Marylen, Ermit, Mary. BS, Georgetown Coll., Ky., 1927; ThM, So. Bapt. Sem., Louisville, 1930; PhD, So. Bapt. Sem., 1936; MAS, Case Western Res. U., 1947. Ordained to ministry Bapt. Ch., 1928; cert. social worker. Pastor various chs., Ky., 1930-36; with Louisville Bapt. Children's Home, 1936-45; exec. dir. Children's Home, Monticello, Ark., 1947-49, Children's Ctr., Lake Villa, Ill., 1949-57; counselor Leyden High Sch., Franklin Park, Ill., 1957-69; psychotherapist Hot Springs, Ark., 1969—. Author manual; contbr. articles to profl. jours. Active various orgns. relative to care of children. Ecumenist. Avocations: reading, writing, gardening. Address: 206 Bellaire Dr Hot Springs AR 71901 *My experience has taught me that broad learning in the fields of religion, art, music, literature, psychology, philosophy and history are basic to the good or enlightened life, and that love is the one great motive that moves one to deep study in these fields.*

SNIDER, P(HILIP) JOEL, minister; b. Fairmont, W.Va., Dec. 29, 1952; s. Aubrey J. and Louisa Belle (Baughman) S.; m. Cheryl Brown, Oct. 11, 1975; children: Rachel, Jordan. BA, Auburn U., 1975; MDiv, So. Bapt. Theol. Sem., 1980, PhD, 1984. Ordained to ministry So. Bapt. Conv., 1976. Assoc. pastor First Bapt. Ch., Auburn, Ala., 1975-77; pastor Thixton Ln. Bapt. Ch., Louisville, 1980-84; assoc. pastor Second Bapt. Ch., Memphis, 1984-87; pastor Crievewood Bapt. Ch., Nashville, 1987—; 2d v.p. Tenn. Bapt. Conv., 1990-91; bd. dirs. Bapt. Ctr. for Ethics, 1991—. Author: The Cotton Patch Gospel, 1985: (audiocassette) Acts: The Gospel for All, 1990; contbr.: Holman Bible Dictionary, 1991. Trustee Belmont Coll., Nashville, 1988—. Office: Crievewood Bapt Ch 480 Hogan Rd Nashville TN 37220

SNIDER, RONALD ALBERT, minister; b. Detroit Lakes, Minn., May 31, 1931; s. George Albert and Mabel Schmidt (Warren) S.; m. Ida Jane Mettling, June 8, 1950; children: Brian, Craig, Robin, Kevin. BA, North Cen. Coll., 1953; ThB, Internat. Sem., 1980, ThM, 1981, DDiv (hon.), 1981. Ordained to ministry Assemblies of God, 1952. Founding pastor Assembly of God Ch., Staples, Minn., 1952-55, West Covina, Calif., 1955-57; pastor Assembly of God Ch., Spring Valley, Minn., 1957-61, Baywood Park, Calif., 1961-69; pastor Fallbrook (Calif.) Assembly of God, 1969—; chaplain Calif. Dept. Corrections, Rainbow, 1970-82; youth dir. North Coast sect. Assembly of God, Baywood Park, 1965-70, chmn. ministerial ethics com. So. Calif. dist. coun., Cosa Mesa, 1982. Contbr. articles to religious jours.; speaker in field. Office: Fallbrook Assembly of God 2000 Reche Rd Fallbrook CA 92028 *Often the choice seems to be between seeing the hands of the Lord, i.e., "What He can do for us," and seeing the face of the Lord, i.e., "An intimacy of relationship." I have found that I must have both to be my best for man and God.*

SNIDER, RONALD LYNN, pastor; b. Amarillo, Tex., Oct. 18, 1950; s. Weldon Leo and Melba Janett (Isaacs) S.; m. Brenda Dee, Mar. 30, 1954; 1 child, Luke. BS in Natural Sci., Southwestern Okla. State U., 1974; MDiv, Southwestern Baptist Seminary, Ft. Worth, Tex., 1981; postgrad., Midwestern Baptist Seminary, Kansas City, Mo., 1988. Pastor First Baptist Cleo Springs, Mo., 1975-76; assoc. pastor First Baptist Carrollton, Tex., 1977-81; pastor Fairway Baptist Ch., Wichita Falls, Tex., 1981-85, Bellaire Baptist, Carrollton, Tex., 1985-87, First Baptist West, Lawton, Okla., 1987—; pres. Dallas Bapt. Assn. Singles, 1979-81, Pastors Conf. Wichita Bapt. Assn., Wichita Falls, Tex., 1984-88; tchr. Seminary Extension Classes, Southern Bapt. Conf., Lawton, Okla., 1987-88; mem. nominating and program coms. Bapt. Gen. Conv. Okla. Advisor Carrollton (Tex.) Bd. of Edn., 1985-87; advisor drug abuse Carrollton Police Dept., 1986; founder, pres. S.W. Oklamons for Life. Recipient Eagle award, Southern Baptist Sunday Sch. Bd., 1987, 88; Pace Setter award Baptist Gen. Conv. of Oklahoma. Mem. Comanche-Cotton Bapt. Assn. (pres. pastor's conference 1987-88, chmn. resolutions 1987-88, also moderator), Nat. Right to Life, Bapt. Gen. Conv. Tex. Evangelism (pace setter), Phi Delta Theta. Republican. Home and Office: 7302 Cache Lawton OK 73505

SNIPSTEAD, RICHARD, minister. Pres. The Assn. of Free Luth. Congregations, Mpls. Office: Free Luth Congregation 3110 E Medicine Lake Blvd Minneapolis MN 55441*

SNODGRASS, KLYNE RYLAND, seminary dean; b. Kingsport, Tenn., Dec. 28, 1944; s. Charles Sidney and Wanda Virginia (Lauderback) S.; m. Phyllis Parks, Aug. 28, 1966; children: Nathan, Valerie. BA, Columbia Bible Coll., 1966; MDiv magna cum laude, Trinity Evang. Div. Sch., 1969; PhD, St. Andrews U., 1973. Instr. N.T. Georgetown (Ky.) Coll., 1973-74; asst. prof. bibl. lit. North Park Sem., Chgo., 1974-78, assoc. prof., 1978-84, prof., 1984-89, Paul Brandel prof. N.T. studies, 1989—, dean of faculty, 1988—. Author: The Parable of the Wicked Tenants, 1983, Between Two Truths, 1990; contbr. articles to profl. jours. Assn. Theol. Schs. grantee, 1981. Fellow Inst. Bibl. Rsch. (exec. sec. 1989—); mem. Chgo. Soc. Bibl. Rsch. (pres. 1990-91), Soc. Bibl. Lit., Assn. Bapt. Profs. of Religion, Studiorum Novi Testamenti Societas. Office: North Park Theol Sem 3225 W Foster Chicago IL 60625

SNOW, ALAN ALBERT, humanist ministry administrator, insurance agent, publisher; b. Van Nuys, Calif., July 20, 1946; s. Perry William and Virginia (Show) S. BA, Pepperdine U., L.A., 1969; MA, Sch. of Theology, Claremont, Calif., 1974; Magister Operae Onerosae (hon.), Inst. Antiquity-Christianity, Claremont, 1972. Lic. fire, casualty, life and disability ins. agt., Calif. Dir., min Ind. Humanist Ministries, Newport Beach, Calif.; agt. Farmers Ins. Group of Cos., Fountain Valley, Calif.; owner, operator Cairo West Pub. Co., Santa Ana, Calif.; owner Radieux Music Pub. Co., Santa Ana; clin. ethicist Bioethical Consultation, Santa Ana.; marriage officiant Confidential Marriages, County of Orange. Contbr. articles to profl. jours. and newspapers. Dep. registrar of voters, Orange County, Calif.; mem. Mayor's Adv. Com. of L.A. Mem. Nat. Notary Assn. (ethics com., Cert. Accomplishment), Am. Soc. Notaries, SAR, Am. Humanist Assn., Orange County Bird Breeders, Am. Cocatiel Soc., Inc., South Coast Finch Soc., Ethical Cultural Soc. L.A., Ethical Cultural Soc. N.Y., Pekin Pekingese Club, Newport Beach Tennis Club. Libertarian. Home: 518 S Bay Front Balboa Island CA 92662 Office: Cairo West Pub Co 3500 W Moore St Ste G Santa Ana CA 92704-6818

SNOW, HAROLD EDWIN, minister; b. Jacksonville, Ill., Nov. 14, 1951; s. Herbert Anderson and Virginia Kathleen (Conover) S.; m. Katherine Joan Garver, June 19, 1971; children: Matthew Edwin, Kathleen Elizabeth. BA with honors, Northwestern U., 1973; M Div magna cum laude, Yale U., 1977; postgrad., Harvard U., 1979-80, U. Ill., 1984-85. Ordained to ministry Meth. Ch., 1978. Reporter Jour.-Courier Newspaper, Jacksonville, 1971; intern pastor United Meth. Ch., Canton, Ill., 1975-76, assoc. pastor, 1977-79, 80-84; law clk. Land Lincoln Legal Asst., Champaign, Ill., 1985; pastor Stronghurst (Ill.)-Carman United Meth. Ch's., 1985-89; chaplain The Baylor Sch., Chattanooga, 1989—; vice chairperson Com. Christian Unity & Interrel. Conv. Bloom, Ill., 1986-89; spiritual dir. Walk to Emmaus & Faith Hope Love Peoria, Ill., 1982-89; clergy del. Conf. Coun. Ministries, Bloom, 1987-89; mem. zen's adv. group Mental Health Ctr. and Graham Hosp., Canton, 1981-84; part time instr. Spoon River Coll., Canton, 1981-83. Cons. Fulton County Mental Health, Canton, 1977-79; co-chair professional div. United Way, Canton, 1981-84; v.p. Kamping & Recreational Experiences for Special Edn. Children, Canton, 1981-84; mem. extension coun. Human Resources , Stronghurst, 1987-89; bd. dirs. Henderson County Food Cellar, Stronghurst, 1988-89, Wesley Found. West Ill. Univ., Macomb, 1987-89. Mem. Ctr. Study World Religions, Am. Acad. Religion, Soc. for Bibl. Lit., Chattanooga Assn. Chs. (pres. 1991—), Cath. Social Svcs. (bd. dirs. 1991—), Yale Divinity Sch. Alumni/Alumnae Fund (class agt. 1986—), Kiwanis (co-citizen of Yr. 1984), Jaycees (Citizen of Yr. 1987). Avocations: Chinese language & culture, astronomy, basketball,traveling, humor. Office: The Baylor Sch PO Box 1337 Chattanooga TN 37401

SNOW, MARK EUGENE, evangelist; b. Mt. Vernon, Ohio, Dec. 31, 1955; s. Jack Wayne and Jean (Booth) S.; m. Stephannie Lynn Varner, May 29, 1977; children: Adam David Snow, Justin Mark Snow. BA, Ky. Christian Coll., 1986. Sr. min. Union City (Ky.) Christian Ch., 1985-87, Salineville (Ohio) Ch. of Christ, 1987-89, Victory Ch. of Christ, Mt. Vernon, Ohio, 1989—; counselor. Served with U.S. Navy, 1974-78. Home: 6 N Monroe Ave Mount Vernon OH 43050 Office: Victory Ch of Christ 12470 Up Fredericktown Rd Mount Vernon OH 43050

SNOWBERGER, CHARLOTTE ANN, educator, administrator; b. Flint, Mich., July 17, 1931; d. John McClure Owen and Opal Stoll Labo; m. John Robert Snowberger, Dec. 23, 1953; children: John Jr., Gay, Ann, Rene, Michele, Yvette. BA, Houghton (N.Y.) Coll., 1953; MRE, Grand Rapids Bapt. Sem., Mich., 1985. Dir. Light and Life Christian Presch., Phoenix, Camelback Bible Ch. Presch., Paradise Valley, Ariz., 1984-91; adj. prof. Ariz. Coll. of the Bible, Phoenix, 1991—. Bd. dirs. Camelback Girls Residence, Phoenix, 1965-75, pres. aux. Mem. Assn. Christian Schs. Internat., Internat. Fellowship of Christian Sch. Adminstrs. Republican. Office: Camelback Bible Presch 3900 E Stanford Dr Paradise Valley AZ 85253

SNOWDEN, JOHN SAMUEL PHILIP, bishop. LTh, Anglican Theol. Coll., Vancouver, B.C., 1951; BA, U. B.C., 1956. Ordained deacon The Anglican Ch. of Can., 1951, priest, 1952. Curate Kaslo-Kokane, 1951-53, Oak Bay, 1953-57, Nanaimo, 1957-60; with St. Timothy Parish, Vancouver, 1960-64; priest pastoral Christ Ch. Cathedral, Vancouver, 1964-66; rector St. Timothy, 1966-71; dean, rector St. Paul's Cathedral, Kamloops, B.C., 1971-73; bishop Diocese of Cariboo, Kamloops, B.C., 1974—. Office: Diocese of Cariboo, 465 Victoria St, Kamloops, BC Canada V2C 2A9

SNYDER, EUGENE HAROLD, minister; b. Reading, Pa., Feb. 1, 1929; s. Harvey Harrison and Grace Catherine (Richard) S.; m. Ruth Marie Haugh, Aug. 2, 1952; children: Susan Beth, Christina Hope, Kurt Alan. AB, Albright Coll., 1952; S.T.B., Westminster Theol., 1956; MDiv, Wesley Theol. Sem., 1971. Ordained to ministry United Ch. of Christ, 1956. Pastor St. Matthew's Evang. United Brethren Ch., Balt., 1956-59, Port Trevorton (Pa.) Charge, 1959-62, Emmanuel United Ch. of Christ, Penns Creek, Pa., 1962-64, Carlisle (Pa.) Rural Charge, 1964-71, St. Peter's United Ch. of Christ, Hilltown, Pa., 1971-85, United Ch. of Christ-East Goshen, West Chester, Pa., 1985—; chmn. div. evangelism/ch. extension Pa. SE Conf. United Ch. of Christ, Collegeville, 1991—, chmn. ch. extension com., 1990-91, mem. stewardship promotion div., 1985-91. Pres. pennridge C. of C., Perkasie, Pa., 1982; sec. Pa. Coun. on Alcohol Problems, Harrisburg, 1990—. Mem. C. of C. Greater West Chester (bd. dirs. 1987—), Loyal Order of Moose, Masons. Republican. Home: 544 Dorothy Ln West Chester PA 19380-4702 Office: United Ch of Christ East Goshen 1201 N Chester Rd West Chester PA 19380-6873 *Life can't be completely lived without commitment, whether it be to a person, cause or philosophy. The choice is made whether we consciously make it or not. Make your choice and serve it with your whole being.*

SNYDER, JEDIDIAH NEWELL, minister; b. Towanda, Pa., Sept. 22, 1944; s. Horace Newell and Alice Josephine (Summers) S.; m. Anna Elizabeth Cook, May 17, 1969; children: Timothy, Rebekah, Nathan. BS, Phila. Coll. of Bible, 1966; MEd, Temple U., 1967. Ordained to ministry non-denominational ch., 1967. Instr. in psychology Phila. Coll. of Bible, 1966-69; dir. Christian edn. Grace Bible Ch., Souderton, Pa., 1969-70; minister to youth North Syracuse (N.Y.) Bapt. Ch., 1970-75; pastor Community Bible Chapel, Brattleboro, Vt., 1975-80, Columbia (S.C.) Evang. Ch., 1980—; mem. sect. associated chaplains Lexington Med. Ctr., Columbia, 1991—; chmn. Servants Missionary Svc., Columbia, 1988-90; mem. president's adv. coun. Columbia Bible Coll., 1986—. Author Sunday sch. curriculum. Recipient Citizenship award Am. Legion, 1957. Mem. Pastor's Fellowship (chmn. 1980—). Republican. Office: Columbia Evang Ch 1015 Barnwell St Columbia SC 29201

SNYDER, JOHN JOSEPH, bishop; b. N.Y.C., Oct. 25, 1925; s. John Joseph and Katherine Marie (Walsh) S. Ordained priest Roman Cath. Ch., 1951; assoc. pastor St. Mel's Parish, Flushing, N.Y., 1951-57; sec. to bishops Diocese Bklyn., 1957-72; titular bishop of Forlimpopoli, vicar gen., aux.

bishop Diocese Bklyn., 1972-79; bishop of St. Augustine, Fla., 1979—. Office: Cath Ctr PO Box 24000 Jacksonville FL 32241-4000

SNYDER, ROBERT CARL, minister; b. Chgo., Dec. 26, 1937; s. Harold Homer and Gertrude Mary (Bischof) Snyder; m. Gwen Ardith Smith, Aug. 15, 1959; 1 child, Melisa Joy Snyder Izzo. BA, Western Mich. U., 1959; MDiv, Hartford Sem. Found., 1963. Ordained to ministry United Ch. of Christ, 1963. Pastor 1st Congl. Ch., Crystal, Mich., 1963-65, Trinity Congl. Ch., Grand Rapids, Mich., 1965-72, Park Congl. Ch., Toledo, 1972-78; pastor 1st Congl. Ch., Armada, Mich., 1980-83, South Haven, Mich., 1983—; moderator Grand Rapids Assn., United Ch. of Christ, 1971-72, N.W. Ohio Assn., Tiffin, 1978-79, S.W. Assn., Kalamazoo, Mich., 1988-89, Mich. Conf., United Ch. of Christ, 1990—. Mem. Kiwanis (sec. South Haven chpt. 1985-91). Office: 1st Congl Ch 651 Phoenix St South Haven MI 49090 *The strongest defense a nation possesses is the contentment and satisfaction of its own people, established in part by the religious establishment serving in the role of national conscience.*

SNYDER, ROBERT JAMES, deacon; b. St. Louis, July 22, 1936; s. John M. and Ann E. (Cochran) S.; m. Elaine K. Snyder, Oct. 3, 1958; children: John, Stephen, Daniel, Christopher. Student, Washington U., St. Louis, 1964. Ordained deacon Roman Cath. Ch., 1986. Adminstr. Kenrick Pastoral Ctr., Archdiocese St. Louis, 1987—; permanent deacon St. Elizabeth of Hungary Parish, Crestwood, Mo., 1985—. With USNR, 1954-66. Office: Kenrick Pastoral Ctr 7800 Kenrick Rd Saint Louis MO 63118

SNYDER, TIMOTHY DAVID, minister; b. Charleroi, Pa., Sept. 24, 1962; s. David John and Joanne Sue (Andrie) S.; m. Beth Snyder, Oct. 8, 1988. BA, Ky. Christian Coll., 1984. Assoc. minister Farmdale Ch. Christ, Barboursville, W.Va., 1983—; bd. dirs. Koinonia, Huntington. Mem. Ky. Christian Coll. Alumni Assn., Tri-State Ministerial Assn. of Christian Chs. (pres. 1988—). Republican. Home: 1761 Martha Rd Barboursville WV 25504 Office: Farmdale Ch Christ 6476 Farmdale Rd Barboursville WV 25504

SNYDER, WILLIAM RICHARD, lay worker, accountant; b. Osceola, Ind., Oct. 6, 1929; s. William Cleo and Mary Elizabeth (Suppes) S.; m. Eleanor Dolores Morehouse, Aug. 6, 1955; children: John, Thomas, Stewart, Eric. AA, San Bernardino Valley Coll., 1968. CPA, Calif. Acctg. dept. mgr. Grace Community Ch., Sun Valley, Calif., 1984-88, benefits adminstr., 1988—; pres. To His Glory, Panorama City, Calif., 1985—; bd. dirs. Atascadero (Calif.) Christian Home, 1981-82. Asst. treas. Calif. Rep. Party, Fresno, 1979-80, controller, Burbank, Calif., 1981-82. Sr. sgt. USMC, 1951-59. Mem. AICPA, Calif. Soc. CPAs.

SODANO, ANGELO CARDINAL, cardinal, Vatican official; b. 1927. Ordained priest Roman Cath. Ch., 1950. Bishop Roman Cath. Ch., consecrated archbishop, 1978; sec. of state Vatican City, 1990—; created cardinal Roman Cath. Ch., 1991—. Office: Secretariat of State, Palazzo Apostolico Vaticano, 00 120 Vatican City Vatican City

SOEKOTO, LEO, archbishop. Archbishop of Jakarta, Roman Cath. Ch., Indonesia. Office: Archbishop of Jakarta, Jalan Katedraal 7, Jakarta 10710, Indonesia*

SOENS, LAWRENCE D., bishop; b. Iowa City, Aug. 26, 1926. Student, Loras Coll., Dubuque, Iowa, St. Ambrose Coll., Davenport, Iowa, Kenrick Sem., St. Louis, U. Iowa. Ordained priest Roman Catholic Ch., 1950, consecrated bishop, 1983. Bishop of Sioux City Iowa, 1983—. Office: Chancery Office PO Box 3379 1821 Jackson St Sioux City IA 51102

SOKOBIN, ALAN MAYOR, rabbi; b. Newark, Mar. 8, 1926; s. Max and Pauline (Ferster) S.; m. Miriam Levy, May 19, 1957; children: Sharon, Jonathan. AB, Syracuse U., 1950; MAHL, Hebrew Union Coll., Cin., 1958; ThD, Burton Coll., 1962; DD, Hebrew Union Coll., Cin., 1980. Ordained rabbi, 1955. Rabbi Temple Beth El, Laurelton, N.Y., 1955-57, Temple Menorah, Bloomfield, N.J., 1958-60, Temple B'nai Israel, Elmont, N.Y., 1960-72; sr. rabbi Congregation Shomer Emunih, Sylvania, Ohio, 1972—; adj. prof. history U. Toledo, 1978—; rabbinic adv. bd. United Jewish Appeal, Jewish Nat. Fund. Contbr. articles to profl. jours. With USN, 1942-45. Mem. Cen. Conf. Am. Rabbis. Office: Congregation Shomer Emunih 6453 Sylvania Ave Sylvania OH 43560

SOKOL, FRANK CARL, priest; b. Sewickley, Pa., June 2, 1947; s. Anthony T. and Rose M. (Lucenti) S. BA, St. Francis Coll., Loretto, Pa., 1969; MA, U. Louvain, Belgium, 1972; PhD, Cath. U., 1983. Ordained priest Roman Cath. Ch., 1973. Deacon St. Mungo's Ch., Garthamlock, Scotland, summer 1972; asst. pastor St. Maurice Ch., Pitts., 1973-78; asst. diocesan dir. Diocese of Pitts., 1982-87, diocesan dir., 1987—; speaker, presenter at major confs., U.S., Europe, 1978—. Author: New Catholic Encyclopedia, 1989; editor: Issues in the Christian Initiation of Children, 1989; contbr. articles to religious jours. Mem. Grad. Coun. Duquesne U., 1987—. Mem. Cath. Theol. Soc. Am., Coll. Theology Soc., Religious Edn. Assn., Nat. Conf. Diocesan Dirs., N.Am. Forum (steering com.). Address: Diocese Pittsburgh 111 Boulevard of the Allies Pittsburgh PA 15222 *Our life together leads us more deeply into the mystery of existence. The closer we grow to each other, the closer we are to God.*

SOKOLOW, MOSHE, Jewish studies educator; b. N.Y.C., Dec. 13, 1947; s. Joseph and Hannah (Appel) S.; m. Judy Sussman, June 19, 1977; 1 child, Shalom. BA, Yeshiva Coll., 1969, MA, 1971, PhD, 1974. Asst. prof. Yeshiva U., N.Y.C., 1974-81, assoc. prof. Jewish studies, 1985—; vis. asst. prof. Jewish Theol. Sem., N.Y.C., 1974-76, Ben Gurion U., Beersheva, Israel, 1980-81; vis. assoc. prof. Bar Ilan U., Ramat Gan, Israel, 1982-85; ednl. cons. World Zionist Orgn., 1985—. Editor, translator: On Teaching Tanakh, 1986; editor, translator: On Teaching Jewish History, 1989; contbr. articles to profl. jours. Coord. Hatzalah, Vol. Ambulance Corps, N.Y.C., 1988—. Jerusalem fellow, World Zionist Orgn., 1982-85. Mem. Assn. Jewish Studies, Am. Acad. Jewish Rsch., Assn. for Supervision and Curriculum Devel.

SOLC, JOSEF, minister; b. Prague, Czechoslovakia, Aug. 6, 1943; came to U.S., 1970; s. Milos and Bohumila (Husakova) S.; m. Joy Cheryl Roeda, Nov. 25, 1978; children: Joy, Maria, Josef. BA, Oral Roberts Univ., 1972; MDiv, Southwest Bapt. Theol., Seminary, Ft. Worth, 1974, PhD, 1978. Ordained to ministry So. Bapt. Conv., 1974. Missionary Ill. Bapt. Conv., Chgo., 1974-75, Trans World Radio, Monte Carlo, Monaco, 1979-80; exec. bd. Tarrant Bapt. Assn., Ft. Worth, 1980; with Caree, N.Y.C., 1989; minister Hulen St. Bapt. Ch., Ft. Worth, 1980—; cons. Lausanne Com. World Evangelism/Pattaya, Thailand, 1980, participant, Manila, 1989. Contbr. articles to profl. jours. Home: 4800 Courtside Dr Fort Worth TX 76133 Office: Hulen Street Bapt Ch 7100 S Hulen St Fort Worth TX 76133 *Coming to America after living for 25 years in a Communistic country of Czechoslovakia taught me a lesson, not to take freedom for granted. Freedom provides an opportunity to be used to the fullest for the advancement of God's Kingdom and the betterment of men everywhere.*

SOLENDER, SANFORD, social worker; b. Pleasantville, N.Y., Aug. 23, 1914; s. Samuel and Catharine (Goldsmith) S.; m. Ethel Klonick, June 19, 1935; children: Stephen, Peter, Ellen, Susan. BS, NYU, 1935; MS, Columbia U., 1937. Dir. activities Neighborhood House, Bklyn., 1935-36; asst. headworker Bronx House, N.Y., 1936-39; headworker Madison House, N.Y.C., 1939-42; exec. dir. Coun. Ednl. Alliance, Cleve., 1942-48; dir. bur. pers. and tng., also dir. Jewish community ctr. div. Nat. Jewish Welfare Bd., N.Y.C., 1948-60, exec. v.p. bd., 1960-70; exec. v.p. Fedn. Jewish Philanthropies N.Y., 1970-81, exec. cons., 1982—; exec. v.p. United Jewish Appeal Fedn. Campaign, 1975-81; past pres. Nat. Conf. Jewish Communal Svc.; past chmn. planning com. Internat. Conf. Jewish Communal Svc.; chmn. Task Force on N.Y.C. Crisis, 1976-81. Contbr. articles to profl. jours., chpts. in books. Mem. Mt. Vernon Bd. Edn., 1953-58, pres., 1957-58, chmn. sec. HEW's ad hoc. com. to study fed. govt. social welfare programs, 1961; adv. coun. pub. welfare HEW, 1963-65; mem. Gov. Hugh Carey's Task Force on Human Svcs., N.Y. State, 1975; bd. dirs. Lavanburg Corner House, Herman Muehlstein Found.; adv. bd. Brandeis U., Hornstein Program in Jewish Communal Svc.; mem. Helsinki Watch, Md. East Watch, Am.'s Watch coms. bds., Nat. Found. for Jewish Culture, 1985—, Jewish Mus., 1982—, Welfare Rsch. Inc., 1985—; vice chmn. Nat. Jewish Ctr. for Learning and Leadership, 1984—. Named Most Disting. Citizen of Mt. Vernon, 1960; recipient Joseph E. Kappel award Nat. Conf. Jewish Communal Svc., 1968, Florence G. Heller award Nat. Jewish Welfare Bd., 1972. Mem. Nat. Assn. Jewish Ctr. Workers (past pres.), Nat. Assn. Social Workers (co-chmn. adv. com. Ctr. on Social Policy), Nat. Conf. Social Welfare (past pres.). Home: 1935 Gulf of Mexico Dr Seaplace G7-107 Longboat Key FL 34228 Office: 130 E 59th St New York NY 10022

SOLENDER, STEPHEN DAVID, philanthropic organization executive; b. N.Y.C., Feb. 25, 1938; s. Sanford L. and Ethel (Klonick) S.; m. Elsa Adelman, June 5, 1960; children: Michael, Daniel. BA, Columbia U., 1960, MS, 1962. Dir. community ctrs., community orgn. and fundraising Am. Jewish Joint Distbn. Com., Geneva, 1969-75, dir. svcs. Muslim and Arab countries, 1969-75; dir. social planning and budgeting Assoc. Jewish Charities and Welfare Fund, Balt., 1975-79, pres., 1979-86; exec. v.p. United Jewish Appeal-Fedn. Jewish Philanthropies N.Y. Inc., N.Y.C., 1986—; mem. profl. adv. com. Brandeis U. Hornstein Ctr., Boston, 1982—; mem. health policy forum United Hosp. Fund, N.Y.C., 1987—, mem. presdl. coun., 1989—; chmn. Human Svcs. Coun. of N.Y.C.; chmn.'s coun. Mut. of Am., N.Y.C., 1991—. Bd. dirs. Jill Fox Meml. Fund, Balt., 1979—; bd. govs. Wurzweiler Sch. Social Work, N.Y.C., 1987—. Office: UJA-Fedn NY 130 E 59th St New York NY 10022

SOLHEIM, JAMES EDWARD, church executive, journalist; b. Thief River Falls, Minn., May 16, 1939; s. Edward and Verna (Sagmoen) S. BA, St. Olaf Coll., 1961; MDiv, Luther Sem., 1968; MS in Journalism, Columbia U., 1975. Admissions counselor St. Olaf Coll., 1962-67; editor Am. Luth. Ch., Mpls., 1968-74; dir. communications St. Peter's Ch., N.Y.C., 1975-77; editor A.D. mag., N.Y.C., 1977-83, Luth. Ch. in Am., Phila., 1983-88; dir. communications Episcopal Diocese Mass., Boston, 1988-89; news dir. Episcopal Ch. in U.S.A., N.Y.C., 1989—. Bush Found. fellow, 1974. Mem. Assn. Ch. Press (v.p. 1987-89, Merit award 1969-89, Writing fellow 1969), Religious Pub. Rels. Coun. (v.p.), St. Olaf Alumni Assn. (pres.), Sigma Delta Chi. Democrat. Lutheran. Avocation: photography. Home: 168 W 100th St New York NY 10025 Office: Episcopal Ch in USA 815 2d St New York NY 10017

SOLIS, DANIEL GOMEZ, minister; b. Corpus Christi, Tex., Feb. 16, 1956; s. Eustaquio Muniz and Petra Trujillo (Gomez) S.; m. Cynthia Sue Allen, Dec. 19, 1976; children: Heather, David, Jonathan. BA in Theology, So. Coll., Chattanooga, 1976; MDiv, Andrews U., 1979; D of Ministry, Reformed Theol. Seminary, Jackson, Miss., 1988. Asst. pastor The Seventh Day Adventist Ch., Huntsville, Ala., 1978-79; pastor The Seventh Day Adventist Ch., Vicksburg, Miss., 1979-84, Bedford, Ind., 1984-89; assoc. pastor Glendale Seventh Day Adventist Ch., Indpls., 1989-91; community svcs. dir. Ind. Conf. Seventh Day Adventists, Carmel, 1990—; exec. com. Gulf States Conf. of Seventh Day Adventists, Montgomery, Ala., 1983-84. Bd. dirs. Total Health Found., Vicksburg, 1983-84, Ind. Voluntary Orgns. Active in Disaster, Indpls., 1990—; concert coord. Limestone Heritage Festival, Bedford, Ind., 1988-89. Recipient Svc. award Bloomington (Ind.) Hosp., 1985. Home: 10650 Hoosier Rd Fishers IN 46038-9768 Office: Ind Confs Seventh-day Adventists 15250 N Meridian PO Box 1950 Carmel IN 46032

SOLL, WILLIAM MICHAEL, philosophy and religion educator; b. N.Y.C., Jan. 29, 1953; s. Lloyd George and Eleanor Vivian (Ashe) S.; m. Sharon A. Kelts, May 12, 1979; children: Amy Elizabeth, Katherine Rehomah. BA in English, U. Rochester, 1974; M.C.S., Regent Coll., Vancouver, B.C., Can., 1977; PhD in Religion, Vanderbilt U., 1982. Assoc. prof. Coll. of Ozarks, Point Lookout, Mo., 1981-91; assoc. prof. bibl. studies Aquinas Inst. Theology, St. Louis, 1991—; host radio programs, 1988, 91. Author: Psalm 119: Matrix, Form and Setting, 1990; contbr. articles, revs., papers to profl. publs. Harold S. Vanderbilt scholar, 1977-81; Mo. Humanities Coun. grantee, 1988, 91. Democrat. Home: 809 Lynda Ct Kirkwood MO 63122 Office: Aquinas Inst Theology 3642 Lindell Blvd Saint Louis MO 63108

SOLNICA, HERSHEL, rabbi; b. N.Y.C., July 1, 1938; s. Samuel and Rose S.; m. Betty, Sept. 15, 1959; children: Rifka, Devorah, Shulamit, Shimon, Simcha. BS, CCNY, 1959; postgrad., Ferkauf Grad. Sch., N.Y.C., 1967; DD, Mes. Fia Tifereth, Jerusalem, 1959. Ordained rabbi, 1960. Rabbi Congregation B'nai Israel, Woodbourne, N.Y., 1961-63, Congregation Shaare Zedek, Providence, 1963-65, Young Israel of Rockaways, Queens, N.Y., 1965-74, Congregation Tifereth Israel, Queens, 1974—; prin. Yeshivat Mizrachi L'Banim, Bklyn., 1983—; chaplain Elmhurst City Hosp., Queens, 1974—; pres. Rabbinical Bd. Queens, 1982-84; founder Kehilla of Jackson Hts., 1974. Author Messenger, mo. newsletter, 1974—. Bd. dirs. Community Bd. #3, Queens, 1980-86. Mem. Rabbinical Coun. Am., Rabbinical Bd. Queens, others. Home: 30-39 86th St Jackson Heights NY 11369 Office: Yeshivat Mizrachi 2810 Nostrand Ave New York NY 11369

SOLOFF, MORDECAI ISAAC, retired rabbi; b. Igumen, Minsk, Russia, July 2, 1901; s. Louis and Rivko Esther (Goldberg) S.; widowed; children: Rav Asher, Tamar. BS, CUNY, 1923; MA, Tchr.'s Coll., N.Y.C., 1927; DD (hon.), Hebrew Union Coll., 1965. Ordained rabbi, 1940. Tchr., prin. various Jewish schs., 1920-24; mem. staff Bur. Jewish Edn., N.Y.C., 1924-27; supr. Jewish Schs. Chgo., 1927-29; instr. Hebrew Union Coll., Cin., 1937-40; rabbi Temple Akiba, Culver City, Calif., 1952-73, now rabbi emeritus, 1973—. Author: (textbooks) When the Jewish People Was Young, 1934, How the Jewish People Grew Up, 1936, How the Jewish People Live Today, 1940, 49, 52, The Covenant People, Vols. I-III, 1973, 74, 79, (with Soloff and Brower) Sacred Hebrew Series: Jewish Life, 1981, 90, Your Siddur, 1981, 91, Torataynu I, 1982, Torataynu II, 1983, The Faithful Jew, Vols. 1-6. Mem. Cen. Conf. Am. Rabbis (B'yad Chazakah award), Pacific Assn. Reform Rabbis, Nat. Assn. Ret. Reform Rabbis. Home: 6426 Firebrand St Los Angeles CA 90045 *God's greatest gift to humanity is free will. It encourages study to make wise choices. It creates a sense of responsibility for decisions and actions. It clothes us human creatures with the dignity of serving as God's partner's in improving our world.*

SOLOFF, RAV ASHER, rabbi; b. Bklyn., Jan. 4, 1927; s. Mordecai Isaac and Eve Lee (Miller) S.; m. Harriet Leibowitz, Jan. 27, 1952; children: Rebecca, Sharon, Michael. BA, U. Cin., 1947; MHL, Hebrew Union Coll., 1951, DD (hon.), 1976; PhD, Drew U., 1967. Ordained rabbi. Rabbi Temple Israel, Lafayette, Ind., 1951-52; chaplain U.S. Army, various cities, 1952-54; asst. rabbi Temple B'Nai Jeshurun, Newark, 1954-59; rabbi East End Temple, N.Y.C., 1959-70; co-rabbi Fairmount Temple, Cleve., 1970-76; rabbi Beth Sholom Congregation, Johnstown, Pa., 1976-92; contract chaplain Ebensburg Ctr., Somerset (Pa.) State Hosp., 1982—, Fed. Correctional Instn., Loretto, Pa., 1987—; vis. prof. Ind. U. of Pa., 1989, U. Pitts., Johnstown, 1990-91; instr. sch. edn. Hebrew Union Coll. Author: (with others) Sacred Hebrew: Jewish Life, Your Siddur, Torataynu A&B, 1981-83; contbr. numerous articles to scholarly and popular publs. State chmn. N.J. Com. for Human Rights, Newark, 1958; sec. East Midtown Conservation and Devel. Corp., N.Y.C., 1968-70; pres. Cleve. Zionist Fedn., 1973-74; chmn. Cambria County Mental Health Bd., Ebensburg, 1977-79; moderator Johnstowners for Nuclear Awareness, 1987-90. Recipient Israel Cummings award Fedn. Jewish Philanthropies N.Y., 1968. Mem. Cen. Conf. Am. Rabbis (organizer, leader post-convention study mission 1988, exec. com. and others 1951—), Greater Johnstown Clergy Assn. (v.p. 1977-79), Assn. for Humanistic Psychology, Acad. Polit. and Social Scis., B'nai Brith. Democrat. Avocation: fishing. Home: 1440 Mary Dr Johnstown PA 15905 Office: Beth Sholom Congregation 700 Indiana St Johnstown PA 15905

SOLOMON, DAN EUGENE, bishop; b. Matador, Tex., Dec. 15, 1936; s. Henry Monroe and Mabel Amy (Jenkins) S.; m. Joy Causseaux, May 30, 1957; children: Stuart, Paul, Julie Beth. BA summa cum laude, McMurry Coll., 1958; M Div with honors, Perkins Sch. Theology, 1961; D Ministry, United Theol. Sem., Dayton, 1973; DD (hon.), Oklahoma City U., 1989. Assoc. pastor First Meth. Ch., Plainview, Tex., 1961-62; sr. pastor St. Stephen United Meth. Ch., Amarillo, Tex., 1962-69, St. John's United Meth. Ch., Corpus Christi, Tex., 1969-76; supt. Kerrville (Tex.) Dist., 1976-77; sr. pastor Travis Park United Meth. Ch., San Antonio, 1977-83, First United Meth. Ch., Corpus Christi, 1983-88; bishop Okla. area, Okla. Ann. Conf., Okla. Indian Missionary Conf. United Meth. Ch., Oklahoma City, 1988—; mem. Gen. Conf. and Jurisdictional Conf., Gen. Bd. Ch. and Soc., Gen. Bd. Status and Role of Women. Author/creator simulation game Cabinet; contbr. articles to profl. pubs. Trustee Oklahoma City U.; bd. dirs. Suicide Prevention Group, Crimestoppers. Recipient Homiletics award Perkins Sch. Theology. Avocation: golf. Office: United Meth Ch 2420 N Blackwelder Oklahoma City OK 73106

SOLOMON, EMMETT WEBSTER, minister; b. Memphis, Tex., Jan. 2, 1936; s. Emmett W. and Velma (Upton) S.; m. Janet L. Goodman, Dec. 22, 1957; children: Matthew, Mark. BA, Bob Jones U., 1958; MDiv., N.Y. Theol., 1963; MA, Sam Houston State U., 1972. Ordained to ministry So. Bapt. Conv., 1964; cert. clin. pastoral educator. Pastor Reformed Ch. of Mamakating, Wurtsboro, N.Y., 1959-63; chaplain Tex. Dept. of Corrections, Huntsville, Tex., 1964-85; Tex. Dept. Criminal Justice, $D; asst. adminstr. of chaplains Tex. Dept. Criminal Justice, Huntsville, 1985-88, adminstr. chaplaincy programs, 1988—. Pres. bd. dirs. Houston County Hosp., Crockett, Tex., 1984. Mem. Am. Protestant Corrections Chaplains Assn. (pres. 1987-88, sec. 1991), Tex. Pub. Employees Assn. (pres. 1982-83, com. chair 1984-91). Democrat. Office: Tex Dept Criminal Justice PO Box 99 Huntsville TX 77342

SOLOMON, FRANK S., bishop. Bishop Ch. of Our Lord Jesus Christ of the Apostolic Faith Inc., N.Y.C. Office: Ch Our Lord Jesus Christ Apostolic Faith Inc 2081 Adam Clayton Powell Jr New York NY 10027*

SOLOMON, LON NEAL, minister; b. Portsmouth, Va., Aug. 24, 1948; s. Irving Benjamin and Hermoine Gilda (Levine) S.; m. Brenda Kay Lowry, June 28, 1974; children: Jamie, Justin, Jonathan. BS in Chemistry, U. N.C., 1971; ThM, Capital Bible Sem., Lanham, Md., 1975; MA in N. Ea. Studies, Johns Hopkins U., 1979. Ordained to ministry Barcroft Bible Ch., 1975. Asst. prof. Old Testament Capital Bible Sem., Lanham, 1975-80; sr. pastor McLean (Va.) Bible Ch., 1980—; coll. career pastor Riverdale Bapt. Ch., Largo, Md., 1977-80. Author: Brokenness. Bd. dirs. Jews for Jesus, San Francisco, 1988—. Named one of Outstanding Young Men Am., Jr. Jaycees, 1979. Office: McLean Bible Ch 850 Balls Hill Rd McLean VA 22101

SOLOMON, ROBERT ELLIOTT, cantor; b. Balt., Nov. 3, 1947; s. Marvin Bernard and Shirley (Potash) S.; m. Helen Lorraine Solomon, Nov. 26, 1977; children: Byron Thomas, Samuel Zachary. BA, Gettysburg (Pa.) Coll., 1968; postgrad., Hebrew Union Coll., Cin., 1968-69; Rubin Acad., Jerusalem, 1969-73. Cantor Temple Ner Tamid, Peabody, Mass., 1976-77, Temple Sinai, Sharon, Mass., 1977-91, Temple Ohabei Shalom, Brookline, Mass., 1991—. Singer/composer/arranger SAFAM, Newton, 1975—; pubr. Contemporary Jewish Mus. Pub., Sharon, 1990—; composer numerous songs. Mem. Cantors Assembly (reg. treas. 1988—), Am. Conf. Cantors, Jewish Ministers and Cantors of N.E. (pres. 1986-88). Home: 261 N Main St Sharon MA 02067 Office: Temple Ohabei Shalom 1187 Beacon St Brookline MA 02146

SOLOMON, RON, religious organization administrator. Pres. Ethical Culture Movement, N.Y.C. Office: Ethical Culture Movement 2 West 64th St New York NY 10023*

SOMAH, HARRISON, minister, educator; b. Bassa County, Liberia, Sept. 21, 1950; came to U.S., 1974; s. Frank Y. and Dobormah S.; m. Gwendolyn Bond, Oct. 10, 1980; children: Vivaca Jonel, Harrison Franklin. BA in Theology, Open Bible Coll., 1978; MDiv, Payne Theol. Sem., 1980; MA, Memphis Theol. Sem., 1981; postgrad., U. of the South, 1983—, Princeton Theol. Sem., summer 1991. Ordained to ministry Christian Ch., 1980. Pastor Mt. Sinai Christian Ch., Little Rock, Ark., 1982-86, United Christian Ch., Jackson, Miss., 1986-87; chaplain Jarvis Christian Coll., Hawkins, Tex., 1987-89, asst. prof. of religion, 1987—. Mem. Nat. Assn. Coll. and Univ. Chaplains, Assn. for Religion and Intellectual Life, Assn. of Profs. in Religious Edn. Home: 806 Sweetgum Lindale TX 75771 *Religion without prayer is the absence of the Higher Power.*

SOMERS, RONALD EUGENE, pastor; b. Odessa, Tex., Oct. 13, 1951; s. Marshall Warren and Opal Musette (Crawford) S.; m. Linda Kay Osborne, June 24, 1972; children: Jennifer Linda, Jaime Janette. BA, Wayland Bapt. U., 1974; M in Divinity, So. Bapt. Theol. Sem., 1982; postgrad., Southwestern Bapt. U. Ordained to ministry Bapt. Ch., 1973. Youth evangelist So. Bapt. Gen. Conv. of Calif., Fresno, 1974; pastor Vinson (Okla.) Bapt. Ch., 1973-74, First Bapt. Ch., Cloverdale, Calif., 1975-77, Indian Creek Bapt. Ch., Mineral Wells, Tex., 1979-82; interim pastor Trinity Bapt. Ch., Seminole, Tex., 1978-79; missions dir. Lakeland Bapt. Ch., Lewisville, Tex., 1982-86, asst. pastor, 1986-87; pastor Bellaire Bapt. Ch., Lewisville, 1987—; seminar leader ch. extension div. Bapt. Gen. Conv. of Tex., Dallas, 1982—, ch. extension sect. Home Mission Bd. So. Bapt. Conv., Atlanta, 1983-84; seminar leader Sunday sch. div. Bapt. Gen. Conv. of Tex., 1985. Contbr. articles to profl. jours. Named one of Outstanding Young Men Am., Nat. Jaycees, 1980, 81. Republican. Baptist. Avocations: softball, basketball, golf, racquetball, counseling behavior modification. Home: 862 Mulberry Lewisville TX 75067 Office: Bellaire Bapt Ch 1687 S Edmonds PO Box 732 Lewisville TX 75067

SOMERVILLE, ROBERT EUGENE, historian; b. New Kensington, Pa.; s. Andrew Eugene and Gladys (Hodel) S.; m. Beatrice Terrien, Dec. 22, 1987. BA, Case Western Res. U., 1964; MA, Yale U., 1965, PhD, 1968. Asst. prof. history Columbia U., N.Y.C., 1969-75, prof. religion and history, 1976—; assoc. prof. religion U. Pa., Phila., 1975-76. Author: Councils of Urban II, 1972, Pope Alexander III and the Council of Tours, 1977, Scotia Pontificia, 1982, Papacy, Councils and Canon Law in The 11th-12th Centuries, 1990. NEH fellow, 1979-80, Guggenheim fellow, 1974-75, 87-88. Fellow Medieval Acad. Am. (councillor 1985-88); mem. Am. Soc. Ch. History, Inst. for Advanced Study, Monumenta Germaniae Historica (corr. mem.). Office: Columbia U 615 Kent Hall New York NY 10027

SOMERVILLE, ROBERT STANLEY, minister, religious organization administrator; b. Bakerstown, Pa., Oct. 3, 1938; s. Arnold David and Hazel Columbine (Koch) S.; m. Darlene Faye Edge, Nov. 9, 1964; 1 child, Lezlie Annette. Student, Kent Coll., Cleveland, Tenn., 1960. Pastor Ch. of God, Greensburg, Pa., 1966-67; dir. youth Ch. of God, Cleveland, 1962-64, gen. supt., 1972-80; dir. Awareness Ministry, Huntsville, Ala., 1981—; nat. rep. Internat. Christian Embassy, Jerusalem, 1983-85. Author: The Seed of Abraham, 1987, The Lamp of God, 1988, Hours of Prayer, 1989, Present Truth on Middle East, 1990. With USAF, 1959-63. Republican. Home: 2105 Denham Dr Cleveland TN 37311 Office: Awareness Ministry PO Box 364 Huntsville AL 35804

SOMMER, ARMIN BREWSTER, JR., minister; b. Bronxville, N.Y., Oct. 1, 1952; s. Armin Brewster and Marjorie Alice (Jeckyll) S.; m. Nancy Mae Shults, June 19, 1976; children: Rachel, Kristin. BS in Music, Hartwick Coll., 1975; MDiv with honors, Denver Sem., 1980. Ordained to ministry Bapt. Ch., 1980. Assoc. pastor Manahawkin (N.J.) Bapt. Ch., 1979-84; sr. pastor Grace Ch. on the Mt., Metcong, N.J., 1984—; sec. Conservative Bapt. Assn. of N.J., 1989—. Contbr. articles to profl. jours. Bd. dirs., sec. Friendship Pregnancy Ctr., Morristown, N.J., 1988-89. Mem. Phi Mu Alpha (v.p. 1972-75). Republican. Office: Grace-The Ch on the Mt Box 35 Netcong NJ 07857 *The most pressing task for God's people is simply to be the church. If will be sure to be the church, Christ will be sure to build His church.*

SOMMERKAMP, THEO ENOCH, religious magazine editor; b. Tampa, Fla., Feb. 11, 1929; s. Theo E. and Mozelle (King) S.; m. Jean Childers, July 28, 1951; children: Bradley, Julia, Karl. BS, Okla. Bapt. U., 1951; MS, Fla. State U., 1954. Asst. dir. Bapt. Press, So. Bapt. Conv., 1955-65; dir. European Bapt. Press Svc., Ruschlikon, Switzerland, 1965-71; assoc. dir. pub. rels. Bapt. Annuity Bd., Dallas, 1971-76; editor Ohio Bapt. Messenger, Columbus, 1976—. Mem. Pub. Rels. Soc. Am., Bapt. Pub. Rels. Assn., Religious Pub. Rels. Coun. Home: 3000 Easthaven Ct S Columbus OH 43232 Office: Ohio Bapt Messenger 1680 E Broad St Columbus OH 43203

SOMMERS, GORDON L., religious organization administrator. Pres. Moravian Ch. in Am., Bethlehem, Pa. Office: Moravian Ch in Am 1021 Center St PO Box 1245 Bethlehem PA 18016*

SONG, BEN CHUNHO, minister, seminary executive; b. Choong Chung, Republic of Korea, Feb. 22, 1937; came to U.S., 1966; s. Jay Song and Moo Kim; m. Kyungho Kathy Lee, Oct. 11, 1960; children: John, Paul, Karen. BA, Seoul Bible Coll., Republic of Korea, 1962; MDiv, Korea Presbyn. Theol. Sem., Republic of Korea, 1965; ThM, Faith Luth. Sem., Tacoma, 1984; LHD (hon.), Linda Vista Bible Coll., Sem., El Cajon, Calif., 1974; postgrad., Concordia Theol. Sem., Ft. Wayne, Ind.; D Ministry, Faith Luth. Sem., 1990. Ordained to ministry Presbyn. Ch., 1976. Exec. dir. Teen Life Internat., Tacoma, 1966-76; dean Faith Luth. Sem., Tacoma, 1978-88; sr. min. Korean Mission Ch., Federal Way, Wash., 1977—; pres. All Asia Evangelistic Assn., Federal Way, 1961—; bd. dirs. ACTS U.S.A., Seoul, Korea. Author: No Longer an Orphan, 1966, Born Out of Conflict, 1970, Acts in China, 1986. Recipient hon. citizenship State of Calif., 1969; named pres. emeritus Faith Union Sem., Federal Way, 1988. Home: 220 S 329th Ln Federal Way WA 98003

SONSINO, RIFAT, rabbi; b. Ankara, Turkey, Sept. 4, 1938; came to U.S., 1961; s. Albert and Victoria Sonsino; m. Ines Sonsino, Feb. 9, 1967; children: Daniel, Deborah. LLB, Istanbul U., 1959; MA, Hebrew Union Coll., 1966; Premier Degré, Inst. Internat. Hebrew Studies, Paris, 1961; PhD, U. Pa., 1975; DD, Hebrew Union Coll., 1991. Ordained rabbi, 1966. Rabbi Temple Emanuel, Buenos Aires, 1966-69, Main Line Reform Temple, Phila., 1969-75, North Shore Congregation Israel, Glencoe, Ill., 1975-80, Temple Beth Shalom, Needham, Mass., 1980—. Author: Motive Clauses in Hebrew Law, 1980; co-author: Finding God-Ten Jewish Responses, 1986, What Happens After I Die? - Jewish Views, 1990. Mem. Soc. Bibl. Lit., Cen. Conf. Reform Rabbis (v.p. New Eng. region 1990—), Mass. Bd. Rabbis, Needham Clergy Assn. Office: Temple Beth Shalom Needham MA 02194

SONTGERATH, MARY, school system administrator. Head dept. Cath. schs. Archdiocese of Seattle. Office: Cath Schs Dept 910 Marion Seattle WA 98104*

SORBO, JOSEPHINE CUSATO, lay church worker, former school administrator; b. Butler, Pa., Aug. 19, 1921; d. Domenic and Josephine (Mediate) Cusato; m. John Charles Sorbo, Apr. 3, 1948 (dec. Oct. 1988). Grad. high sch., Ellwood City, Pa.; student, Dale Carnegie Mgmt. Seminar, 1981. Office mgr. A.A. Allen Tent Revivals, Inc., Miracle Valley, Ariz., 1958-61; registrar Miracle Valley Tng. Ctr., 1958-61; sec., treas., bookkeeper, organist Schambach Miracle Revivals Inc., 1965-71; office mgr., corp. sec. Schambach Miracle Revivals Inc., Ellwood City, 1971-82; v.p. East Tex. Bible Coll., Tyler, Tex., 1978-82. Republican. Pentecostal. Home: 508 Haig St Ellwood City PA 16117

SORENS, WILLIAM BRYAN, writer; b. Dallas, Mar. 29, 1955; s. William Bryan Fulfer and Norma Lee LaRue Fulfer Sorens; m. Patty Davis, July 2, 1976 (div. 1989); children: Jason, Neil, Andra, Joanna. BS, Oral Roberts U., 1977; MA, Grace Christian Coll., 1987; postgrad., U. Houston, 1987—. Freelance writer various publs. Rosharon, Tex., 1980—; columnist Christian News, 1989—; writer, producer Oral Roberts U., Tulsa, 1977-78. Editor Grace Newsletter, 1985-87, The Bryan Report, 1990—; contbr. articles to various jours. Campaign vol. Dick Armey for Congress, Dallas, 1983-84. Home: 23d Jud Dist RR 4 Box 1100 Rosharon TX 77583

SORENSEN, CHRISTINA MARIE, Christian education director; b. Ft. Campbell, Ky., June 26, 1968; d. Kenneth Christ and Annette Marie (Bowman) S. BS in Sacred Music, Southwestern U., Georgetown, Tex., 1989. Organist, choi dir. St. John's United Meth. Ch., Georgetown, 1988-89; dir. Christian edn. Asbury United Meth. Ch., El Paso, Tex., 1990—; youth counselor St. John's United Meth. Ch., 1988-89; children's music dir. Asbury United Meth. Ch., 1990—. Mem. Nat. Christian Educators Fellowship (chpt. treas.). Office: Asbury United Meth Ch 3501 Hueco El Paso TX 79903

SORENSEN, JOHN FREDERICK, minister; b. Cadillac, Mich., Apr. 4, 1923; s. Neil Thomas and Helga S. (Anderson) S.; m. D. Marieta Moore, Mar. 16, 1944; children: Jack, Keith, Robert. BA, Mich. State U., 1957; MDiv, Garrett Theol. Sem., 1962. Ordained to ministry United Meth. Ch. as deacon, 1960, as elder, 1962. Pastor Mulliken (Mich.) United Meth. Ch., 1951-55, Upton Ave. United Meth. Ch., Battle Creek, Mich., 1955-64, Haven United Meth. Ch., Jackson, Mich., 1964-67, Ithaca (Mich.) United Meth. Ch., 1967-72, 1st United Meth. Ch., Lansing, Mich., 1972-78; assoc. pastor Community United Meth. Ch., Holiday, Fla., 1985—; mem. various coms. for Conf. Dist., United Meth. Ch., 1962—; summer exch. pastor to Loughton, Eng., 1975. Contbr. columns to newspapers, 1967-72. Recipient Spl. Tribute Gov. Mich., 1985, Ionia Hospice award, 1986; named Rural Pastor of Yr., United Meth. Ch., Mich., 1955, Amb., Ionia C. of C., 1983-85. Fellow Designate Acad. Parish Clergy (edn. com. 1982-84), West Pasco Ministerial Assn., Shriners (past master 1972), Masons. Home: 4618 Weasel Dr New Port Richey FL 34653

SORENSEN, STEVEN LEONARD, minister; b. Mason City, Iowa, Sept. 28, 1949; s. Thorvald Leonard and Beverly Berniece (Bohl) S.; m. LaVonne Bea Oettchen, Aug. 1, 1970; children: Kristen, Yvette. BA, Barclay Coll., Haviland, Kans., 1972; MA, U. Kans., 1974; DMin, Luther Rice Sem., Jacksonville, Fla., 1976. Ordained to ministry, MidAmerica Yearly Mtg., 1975. Minister Hesper Friends Ch., Eudora, Kans., 1972-74; Minister Riverton (Kans.) Friends Ch., 1974-79, Mason City, Iowa, 1979-89; Minister Christian Parish of Charles City, Nora Springs, Iowa, 1989—; pres. Ecumenical Coun., Nora Springs, 1989—; mem. Floyd County Ministerium, Charles City, 1989—, N. Iowa Evang. Assn., 1979—; conv. chaplain Danish Brotherhood in Am., 1990-91. Bd. dirs. Meals on Wheels, Mason City, 1982-86; precinct chmn. dem. Party, Mason City/Plymouth, 1980-89; coach Little League, Plymouth, 1980-90; dist. trustee Danish Brotherhood in Am., 1989—; vol. trainer Hospice, Mason City/Charles City, 1987—. Recipient Religion award, Barclay Coll., 1972. Mem. Lions. Home: 801 Bison Dr Nora Springs IA 50458 Office: Christian Ch PO Box 601 Nora Springs IA 50458

SORENSON, CAROL JOHNSON, minister, pastoral counselor; b. Yakima, Wash., Dec. 28, 1953; d. Norman Burke and Eileen Winifred (Ricker) Johnson; m. Andrew Donald Sorenson Jr.; children: Sarah Ann (dec.), Andrew David, John Daniel. BA, Western Wash. U., Bellingham, 1976; postgrad., Scarritt Coll., Nashville, 1976-77; MA in Christian Edn., Garrett Evang. Theol. Sem., 1979, MDiv, 1980; postgrad., BroMenn Pastoral Inst., Bloomington, Ill., 1985-91. Ordained elder United Meth Ch. Pastor United Meth. Ch., Sadorus, Ill., 1979-80, Urbana, Ill., 1980-81, Henning, Ill., 1981-84, Danville, Ill., Morton, Ill., 1985-91; pastoral counselor Presbyn. Counseling Svc. North Puget Sound Presbytery, Snohomish, Wash., 1991—; chaplain resident Meth. Med. Ctr., Peoria, Ill., 1984-85; chair Clin. Pastoral Edn. Advanced Standing com., 1986-90, Morton (Ill.) Ministerial Assn., 1987-88; mem. Dist. Com. on Ministry, Peoria, 1988—; liturgical dancer, workshop leader. Author: Christian Ednl. material, 1979-80. Bd. mem., group therapy counselor, Shelter for Battered Wives and Children, Danville, Ill, 1982-84. Mem. AAUW, Am. Assn. Pastoral Counselors, Assn. for Death Edn. and Counseling. Avocations: golf, sewing. Home: 17624 182d Ave NE Woodinville WA 98072

SORKO-RAM, ARI, actor, company executive; b. Detroit, Oct. 30, 1941; s. J. Gordon Lindsay; m. Shira Lindsay, Feb. 11, 1977; 1 child, Ayal. V.p. Maoz, Inc., Dallas, 1976—. Jewish. Address: Maoz Box 763100 Dallas TX 75376-3100

SORKO-RAM, SHIRA, writer; b. Portland, Oreg., Oct. 13, 1940; d. J. Gordon and Freda (Schimp) Lindsay; m. Ari Sorko-Ram, Feb. 11, 1977; 1 child, Ayal. BA, So. Meth. U., Dallas, 1963. Freelance writer to various mags.; v.p. Maoz, Inc., Dallas, 1976—. Address: Maoz Inc Box 763100 Dallas TX 75376-3100

SOROKIN, STEPHAN S., religious organization head. Pastor Christian Community and Brotherhood of Reformed Doukhobors, Crescent Valley, B.C., Can. Office: Reformed Doukhobors Christian, Community/Site 8/ Comp 50, Crescent Valley, BC Canada V0G 1H0*

SOSIN, JUDITH LEIGHTMAN, religious organization administrator; b. Memphis, June 21, 1943; d. Herman and Bertha (Shankman) Leightman; m. Theodore M. Sosin, June 19, 1965; children: Rachel, Jeremy. BA, Ind. U., 1965. Asst. exec. dir. Jewish Community Ctr., Indpls., 1990—. Producer Nat. Commemorative Poster for Freedom Sun. March on Washington, 1987. Advocate for Soviet Jews, Jewish Community Rels. Coun., Indpls., 1986—, bd. dirs., 1986—. Mem. Assn. Jewish Ctr. Profls., Nat. Conf. on Soviet Jewry. Democrat. Office: Jewish Community Ctr 6701 Hoover Rd Indianapolis IN 46260

SOSTARICH, JOHN MARK, minister; b. San Antonio, Nov. 15, 1956; s. John F. and Ava Sue (Word) S.; m. Shery Lynn Fowlkes, Sept. 2, 1978; children: Carol Anne, John Matthew, David Kyle, Nathan Alan. BS, Howard Payne U., Brownwood, Tex., 1981. Ordained to ministry So. Bapt. Ch., 1989. Min. youth, music First Bapt., Lytle, Tex., 1973-75; min. youth St. Joe Bapt. Ch., De Leon, Tex., 1975-76; min. youth music, youth edn. Coggin Ave. Bapt. Ch., Brownwood, 1976-82; min. music, edn. First Bapt., Devine, Tex., 1982-89; min. praise and worship, adminstrn. Spring (Tex.) Meml. Bapt., 1989—; trustee Alto Frio Bapt. Encampment, Leakey, Tex.; associational youth min. Brown County, Brownwood; associational music min. Frio River, Pearsall, Tex. Mem. Nat. Ch. Bus. Adminstrs. Assn., Devine C. of C. (bd. dirs.). Home: 3030 Deer Valley Spring TX 77373 Office: Spring Meml Bapt Ch 24724 Aidine Westfield Spring TX 77373

SOTIRIOS OF TORONTO, BISHOP See ATHANASSOULAS, SOTIRIOS

SOUCEK, RAYMOND F., religious organization administrator; b. Chgo., June 3, 1945; s. Frank and Ann (Lakner) S. BA, Loras Coll., 1967; MA, Concordia U., 1984. Lic. counselor, Ill. Tchr. Holy Cross High Sch., River Grove, Ill., 1968-71; purchasing agt. HUD, Chgo., 1971-75; supr., addiction counselor Cath. Charities, Chgo., 1975-85; mktg. rep. Addiction Recovery of Chgo., Hoffman Estates, Ill., 1985-89; exec. dir. Chgo. Clergy Assn., 1989—; instr. Intervention Instruction, Inc., Chgo., 1983—; co-dir. Centre City Assoc., Palatine, Ill. Bd. dirs. Ill. Cert. Bd., Oak Park, Ill., 1987. Mem. Ill. Addiction Counselor Cert. Bd., Ill. Alcoholism and Drug Dependence ASsn. Office: Chgo Clergy Assn 120 N Sangamon Chicago IL 60607

SOU-HWAN, STEPHEN, archbishop. Archbishop of Seoul Roman Cath. Ch. Office: Archbishop's House, 1-ka 1, Myong-dong, Chung-ku, Seoul 100, Republic of Korea*

SOUKUP, ERWIN MYRON, retired priest; b. Oak Park, Ill., Mar. 1, 1921; s. Erwin R. and Libby V. (Hofreiter) S.; m. Janet McKay, June 3, 1944; children: Stephen M., Sarah. BA, North Cen. Coll., 1947; MDiv cum laude, Seabury-Western Sem., 1961, DD (hon.), 1980. Ordained to ministry Episcopal Ch. as deacon, 1961, as priest, 1962. Postulant, candidate Diocese of Chgo., Evanston, Ill., 1958-61; vicar St. Helena's Ch., Burr Ridge, Ill., 1961-67; priest-in-charge Grace Ch., Freeport, Ill., 1967-70; canon to ordinary Diocese of Chgo., 1970-86, archdeacon, 1978-86; ret., 1986; trustee Episcopal Charities, 1976-86; pres. Episc. Found. Chgo., 1967-86; sec. bd. trustees Seabury Western Theol. Sem., Evanston, 1975-86; convenor Epis. Communicators, Chgo., 1972-77. Editor Advance mag., 1971-86. Trustee Radio and TV Found., 1962-86. Maj. AUS, 1943-45. Home: 18056 San Carlos Blvd Apt 156 Fort Myers Beach FL 33931

SOUNG-SOO, SIMON KIM, bishop. Bishop of Seoul The Anglican Communion. Office: 3 Chong-dong, Chung-Ku, Seoul 100-120, Republic of Korea*

SOUTHARD, SAMUEL, religion educator; b. Lincolnton, N.C., Feb. 10, 1925; s. Samuel and Stella Miller Southard; m. Frances Allen, May 10, 1951 (dec. 1980); children: Pamela, Melanie; m. Donna Williams, Aug. 15, 1982. AB, George Washington U., 1948; BD, So. Bapt. Sem., 1951, PhD, 1954; MBA, Ga. State U., 1975. Ordained to ministry Bapt. Ch., 1950. Chaplain Cen. State Hosp., Lakeland, Ky., 1951-53; pastor Ft. Mitchell (Ky.) Bapt. Ch., 1953-55; prof. Inst. of Religion, Tex. Med. Ctr., Houston, 1955-58, So. Bapt. Sem., Louisville, 1959-66; dir. rsch. Presbyn. Ch. U.S., Atlanta, 1966-69; dir. profl. svcs. Ga. Mental Health Inst., 1969-75; pastor Isle of Hope Bapt. Ch., Svannah, Ga., 1976-79; prof. Fuller Theol. Sem., Pasadena, Calif., 1979-89; sr. prof. Fuller Theol. Sem., Pasadena, 1989—; dir. Hospice of Pasadena, 1979-80. With U.S. Army, 1944-46. Home: Box 884 2825 Lexington Rd Louisville KY 40280 Office: Fuller Theol Sem 135 N Oakland Ave Pasadena CA 91182

SOUTHERN, LONNIE STEVEN, minister; b. San Diego, Sept. 6, 1947; s. Henry Benjamin and Juanita Hilda (Fishburn-Bandy) S.; m. Vicki Leona Musgrave, Aug. 18, 1968; children: Katherine Michelle, Jesse Ryan. BTh, N.W. Christian Coll., Eugene, Oreg., 1970; D of Ministry, Sch. Theology, Claremont, Calif., 1977. Ordained to ministry Christian Ch., 1974. Min. to youth Hillsboro (Oreg.) Christian Ch., 1967-69; assoc. min. Lebanon (Oreg.) Christian Ch., 1969-70; min. in tng. 1st Christian Ch., Pomona, Calif., 1970-74; assoc. min., pastor Sullivan (Ill.)-Allenville Christian Chs., 1974-76; sr. pastor South Bay Christian Ch., Redondo Beach, Calif., 1976-80; pastor Allenville (Ill.) Christian Ch., 1980-86; sr. min. 1st Christian Ch., Selma, Calif., 1986-88, Bethany Park Christian Ch., Rantoul, Ill., 1988—; v.p. Sullivan Ministerial Assn., 1975, pres., 1982-83; chmn. Regional Christian Edn. Commn., Sullivan, 1975-76, Lakeland Cluster of Christian Chs., Sullivan, 1983-86, South San Joaquin Cluster of Christian Chs., Fresno, Calif., 1986-88; bd. dirs., mem. exec. com. So. Calif. Coun. of Chs., L.A., 1976-78; v.p., bd. dirs. All Peoples Community Ctr., L.A., 1977-79, Coll. Christian Profl. Mins., Ill., Wis., 1988-90; pres. South Bay Interfaith Coun., Redondo Beach, 1979-80, Selma (Calif.) Ministerial Assn., 1987-88; regional bd. dirs. Christian Chs. of Ill. and Wis., 1983-86; dean East Prairie Cluster, Rantoul, 1989—. Mem. Redondo Beach Coordinating Coun., 1976-79, Redondo Beach Mayor's Roundtable, 1977-80, Moultrie County Adult Youth Awareness Coun., Sullivan, 1981-86, Base Reuse and Devel. Exec. Com., Rantoul, 1990—; mem. exec. com. Save Chanute AFB, Rantoul, 1990. Capt. U.S. Army-Ill. N.G., 1983—. Decorated Army Achievement medal, Res. Officer Achievement medal, Army Commendation medal; named Best Sr. Officer, 1990. Mem. Rotary (Paul Harris fellow 1990). Avocations: photography, backpacking. Home: 1509 Locust Rantoul IL 61866 Office: Bethany Park Christian Ch 1401 E Grove Ave Rantoul IL 61866

SOUTHWORTH, BRUCE ALAN, minister; b. Balt., Nov. 15, 1951; s. James Larry and Lois Ellen (Gill) S.; m. Kay Sunday Xanthakos, Sept. 1, 1974; children: James Michael, Kayla Zoe. AB, Harvard U., 1973; MDiv, Union Theol. Sem., N.Y.C., 1976. Ordained to ministry Unitarian Universalist Assn., 1976. Min. Roanoke Valley Unitarian Ch., Roanoke, Va., 1976-79; min. Community Ch. N.Y., N.Y.C., 1979-82, sr. min., 1982—; chairperson youth-adult com. Unitarian Universalist Assn., Boston, 1978-84, mem. nominating com., 1989—; bd. dirs., exec. com. Unitarian Universalist UN Office, N.Y.C., 1988—; pres., exec. com. Manhattan div. N.Y.C. Coun. Chs., 1985-87. Author: This Day..., 1987; contbr. articles to profl. jours., book revs. Bd. dirs., mem. exec. com. RENA/COA Multi-Svc. Ctr., N.Y.C., 1980—; mem. exec. com. Religious Action Network of Am. Com. on Africa, N.Y.C., 1990—. Recipient Clarence R. Skinner Sermon award Unitarian Universalist Assn., 1988, 90; Union Theol. Sem. traveling fellow, 1976. Mem. Unitarian Universalist Mins. Assn. (nominating com. 1989-91), Greenfield Group (moderator 1985). Democrat. Office: The Community Ch 40 E 35th St New York NY 10016

SOWA, FRANK JOSEPH, deacon; b. Avoca, Pa., Mar. 5, 1914; s. Joseph Pater and Katerine (Gasior) S.; m. Helen Barbara Wisniewski, Nov. 12, 1938; children: Gerald Francis, Barbara Helen. Student, Trenton State Coll., Princeton Theol. Sem.; student Polish Lang., Mercer County Community Coll. Ordained deacon Roman Cath. Ch. Deacon St. Stanislaus, Trenton, N.J., 1978—; pressman, mill operator Rubber Factories; with Corrections, 1945-77, ret. capt., 1977; pastoral coun. St. Stanislaus Diocese Trenton, 1976—. Apostolate visitor Elderly Housing Facility, Forensic Psychiat. Hosp., Trenton State Hosp. Recipient Merit award, 1986. Mem. Holy Name Soc. (sec., v.p. 1977-81, secular Franciscan 1983—), Brackets-Golden Agers of St. Stan's (sec. 1976-78, pres. 1978-79, 82-83, 86-87, 90-91, treas. 1980-81, 84-89). Home: 230 Randall Ave Trenton NJ 08611-3116 *Life is based on the Golden Rule—if everyone lived it, the world would be second only to Paradise.*

SOWADA, ALPHONSE AUGUSTUS, bishop; b. Avon, Minn., June 23, 1933; s. Alphonse B. and Monica (Pierskalla) S. Student, Onamia (Minn.) Sem., 1947-53; grad., Crosier House of Studies, Ft. Wayne, Ind., 1959; M.A., Cath. U. Am., 1961. Ordained priest Roman Cath. Ch., 1958; arrived in Irian Jaya to work among Asmat, 1961, selected as mission superior, 1966; ordained bishop Diocese Agats-Asmat, 1969—. Contbr. to: Nat. Geog. Yearbook, 1968, other publs. Mem. Order of Alhambra, Crosier Order, Kappa Delta Gamma. Office: 3204 E 43d St Minneapolis MN 55406 also: Kantor Keuskupan Agats, Asmat Agats 99677, Irian Jaya Indonesia

SOWERS, JERRY ALLEN, music minister; b. High Point, N.C., May 17, 1950; s. Richard Thomas and Wilma Irene (Summey) S.; m. Jonnie Elizabeth Marshall, Aug. 12, 1979; children: P. Nathan, Phillip N. BM, Guilford Coll., 1977; M in Ch. Music, So. Theol. Sem., 1979. Ordained to ministry Bapt. Ch., 1980. Min. of music Temple Bapt. Ch., Newport News, Va., 1980-82, Langley Bapt. Ch., Hampton, Va., 1982-84, Calvary Bapt. Ch., Newport News, 1984—; chmn. Family and Spl. Ministry, Peninsula Assn., Newport News, 1989—. Composer: (anthems) God, Your Wondrous Life, 1980, Jesus Makes My Heart Rejoice, 1982, (handbell anthem) Simple Gifts, 1987. Dir. mus. activities Va. Bapt. Home, Newport News, 1980-89. With U.S. Army, 1970-73. Mem. Va. Bapt. Ch. Music Conf. (pres. elect 1989-90, pres. 1990-91), Va. Bapt. Male Chorale (treas. 1989-91). Office: Calvary Bapt Ch 4700 Huntington Ave Newport News VA 23607 *Selfishness is the most defeating mind set one could attain. Loving one's self can open any door given to man (or woman). To know the difference and live accordingly is true wisdom.*

SOWERS, SIDNEY GERALD, minister; b. Tacoma, Wash., Sept. 8, 1935; s. Sidney Gerald and Dorothy Margaret (Campbell) S.; m. Jacaline Kleinert, Feb. 10, 1979. AB, U. Puget Sound, 1957; BD, San Francisco Theol. Seminary, 1960; ThD, U. Basel, Switzerland, 1964. Ordained to ministry United Presbyn. Ch. in U.S.A., 1963. Pastor Mt. Baker Presbyn. Ch., Concrete, Wash., 1963-64; vis. asst. prof. religion U. Tulsa, 1964-65; asst. prof. religion Knoxville (Tenn.) Coll., 1965-68; vis. assoc. prof. religion Macalester Coll., St. Paul, 1968-70; pastor Coulee City (Wash.) Presbyn. Ch., 1970-74, Bethany United Protestant Ch., West Richland, Wash., 1974—; mderator Synod of Alaska Northwest, 1978-79; commr. gen. assembly Presbyn. Ch. USA, 1986. Author: Living Without a Magic Eight Ball, 1978, Hermeneutics of Philo and Hebrews, 1964; translator: Salvation in History, 1967. Mem. Soc. Bibl. Lit., Cen. Wash. Presbytery. Home: 710 S 41st Ave West Richland WA 99352 Office: Bethany United Protestant Ch Box 4106 West Richland WA 99352 *The world we live in is a dangerous place, and it is going to stay that way. Nothing you or I can do will change that fact. What we can do, however, is to reduce some of the risks.*

SPACH, JULE CHRISTIAN, church executive; b. Winston-Salem, N.C., Dec. 21, 1923; s. Jule Christian and Margaret Stockton (Coyner) S.; m. Nancy Clendenin, Sept. 18, 1948; children: Nancy Lynn Lane, Margaret Cunningham, Ann Thomerson, Cecelia Welborn, Robert. Student, Va. Mil. Inst., 1942-43; B.S. in Chem. Engring, Ga. Inst. Tech., 1949; postgrad., Union Theol. Sem., Richmond, Va., 1951-52, Duke U., 1955-56; M.A. in Ednl. Adminstrn, U. N.C. at Greensboro, 1976; L.H.D. (hon.), Stillman Coll., Tuscaloosa, Ala., 1977; Litt.D. (hon.), Belhaven Coll., Jackson, Miss., 1977; LL.D., King Coll., Bristol, Tenn., 1977. Salesman Mengle Corp. subs. Internat. Container Corp., Winston-Salem, 1950-52; prof. scis., athletic dir. Quinze de Novembro Coll., Garanhuns, Pernanbuco, Brazil, 1952-56; pres. Quinze de Novembro Coll., 1956-64; edn. dir. Cruzada ABC-Recife, Pernanbuco, 1965-70; pres. Cruzada ABC-Recife, 1969-70; exec. sec. Parliamentary Christian Leadership, Brasilia, Fed. Dist., Brazil, 1970-73; exec. dir. Presbyn. Mission in Brazil, Campinas, Sao Paulo, 1973-75; moderator Gen. Assembly of Presbyn. Ch. in U.S., Atlanta, 1976-77; exec. dir. Triad United Methodist Home, Inc., Winston-Salem, 1977—; dir. First Home Fed. Savs. and Loan. Bd. dirs. Instituto Gammon, Presbyn. Ch. U.S., Forsyth County Coun. on Aging Forsyth County Sr. Svcs. Forsyth County, Covenent Fellowship of Presbyns., William Black Lodge, Synod of N.C., Presbyn. Ch. U.S.A.; bd. visitors Lee's McRae Coll., Montreat Anderson Coll.; mem. cabinet United Way, 1987; chmn. Winston-Salem Forsyth County Coun. on Svcs. to Homeless; chmn. bd. dirs. Sr. Svcs., Inc., Winston-Salem. With USAAF, 1943-45, prisoner of war, Poland. Decorated Purple Heart. Republican. Clubs: Lions (Brazil); Rotary (Winston Salem). Home: Arbor Acres 1244 Arbor Rd #197 Winston-Salem NC 27104 Office: 1240 Arbor Rd Winston-Salem NC 27103 *The Christian faith teaches us that the greatest of all gifts is love. This gift comes from God, and it is ours through the presence of His spirit dwelling in us. This love gives man peace within and with his fellow man.*

SPADER, DANN LAVERNE, religious organization administrator; b. Mitchell, S.D., Jan. 10, 1951; s. John A. and Catherine M. (Reichling) S.; m. Charlene B. Blair, Nov. 17, 1979; children: Julie, Jamie, Christy. BA in Evangelism, Moody Bible Inst., Chgo., 1975; MRE, Trinity Sem., Deerfield, Ill., 1979, D Ministry, 1984. Youth pastor Carter Presbyn. Ch., Chgo., 1972-75; assoc. pastor Judson Bapt. Ch., Oak Park, Ill., 1975-80; exec. dir. Sonlife Ministries, Wheaton, Ill., 1980—. Author: Discipling Churches, 1991, (tng. manuals) Strategy Seminars, 1980-90, (videos) Youth Discipleship Instruction, 1980-90. Office: Sonlife Ministries 1119 Wheaton Oaks Ct Wheaton IL 60187

SPAIN, JOHN DAVID, clergyman; b. Rock Hill, S.C., June 18, 1948; s. Charles Raymond and Johnny Alma (Johnson) S.; m. Susan Farabee, Aug. 17, 1970 (dec. Jan. 1971); m. Darla Gail Newton, Dec. 18, 1971; children: Jonathan, Jeffery, Jared, Brooke, Gretchen. B Music Edn., Lee Coll., 1970; postgrad., Wittenberg U., 1973, U. Ga., 1978, Ariz. State U., 1985-86. Ordained to ministry Pentecostal Holiness Ch., 1990. Football coach high sch., Pompano Beach, Fla., 1976; minister music Faith Meml. Assemblies of God, Atlanta, 1977-79; choral dir., instr. Emmanuel Coll., Franklin Springs, Ga., 1978-80; minister music Valley Cathedral, Phoenix, 1980-85, Cathedral of the Valley, Phoenix, 1986, Christian Heritage Pentecostal Holiness Ch., Tallahassee, 1986—; mem. coun. outpost 10, Royal Rangers, Tallahassee, 1989—, conf. a.d.c., Fla., 1990—; mem. music com. Fla. Conf., Pentecostal Holiness Ch., 1986—; leader European tour high sch. choir, 1973; mem. tour Valley Cathedral Sanctuary Choir, Sweden, Fed. Republic Germany, The Netherlands, 1984. Producer, arranger: Just Keep Praisin', 1979; asst. editor: Vindaqua, 1970; arranger: In All of His Glory, 1991; arranger, creative dir: Overcomer: Through the Blood, 1990. Music dir. Fla. Right-to-Life, Leon County Civic Ctr., 1990. Named Tchr. of Yr., Pompano Beach Womens Club, 1976. Home: 2021 Shady Oaks Dr Tallahassee FL 32303 Office: Christian Heritage Ch 3881 N Monroe St Tallahassee FL 32303

SPAIN, RICHARD KENNETH, minister; b. Hartselle, Ala., Sept. 5, 1952; s. James Gordon and Opal Alline (Gibson) S.; m. Sandra Kay Kinney, Jan. 26, 1979. BA, Samford U., Birmingham, Ala., 1975; MDiv, Mid-Am. Bapt. Ch., Memphis, 1984, postgrad., 1990—. Ordained to ministry So. Bapt. Conv., 1972. Pastor Bellevue Bapt. Ch., Shelby, Miss., 1983-84; missionary Mission Svc. Corps, So. Bapt. Ch., Mich., 1984-90; pastor Evergreen Bapt. Ch., Cadillac, Mich., 1984-91, Hickory Grove Bapt. Ch., Conway, S.C., 1991—; mem. So. Bapt. Conv. exec. com., Nashville, 1988-91; exec. bd. Bapt. State Conv. Mich., 1989-90; bd. overseers Chriswell Coll., Dallas, 1991—; mem. So. Bapt. Com. on Bds., 1986-87; vice chmn. Instns. Work Group, So. Bapt. Exec. Com., 1989-90. Mem. Northland Bapt. Assn. (moderator 1989-91. Office: Hickory Grove Bapt Ch 2710 Hwy 905 Conway SC 29526

SPAIN, RICKY, minister; b. Virginia Beach, Va., Nov. 2, 1949; s. Luther and Florence (Small) S.; m. Annie Graves, Aug. 11, 1979; children: Titus, Amber, Ricky II. BA in Polit. Sci., N.C. Wesleyan Coll., 1975; MDiv, Wesley Theol. Sem., 1977; MS in Adult Edn., N.C. A&T State U., 1980, MS in Guiding and Counseling, 1986; DHL, Paul Quinn Coll., Dallas, 1990. Ordained to ministry A.M.E. Ch., 1976. Pastor Upper United Meth. Charge, Upper Hill, Md., 1976-77, Bethel AME Ch., Reedsville, N.C., 1977-80, St. James A.M.E. Ch., Asheville, N.C., 1980-82, Allen A.M.E. Ch., Balt., 1982-87, Mt. Olive A.M.E. Ch., Annapolis, Md., 1987—; additions counselor II Balt. City Health Dept., 1980-87; group leader Oak Hill Youth Ctr.,

Laurel, Md., 1989—; bd. dirs., chmn. fin. com. Buncombe InterChurch Credit Union. Mem. City Coun. of Reidsville, N.C., 1977-79; mem. Children at Risk, ethics com. City of Annapolis, nominating com. Anne Arundel County Sch. Bd., People Helping People Adv. Bd., Rockingham County Big Bros. and Bis Sis.; v.p. Black Polit. Forum, Annapolis; bd. dirs. Ann Arundel County ARC; mem. Anne Arundel County Sch. Guidance Adv. Coun., others in past; chaplain City of Annapolis Police Dept. With USMC, 1972-73. Mem. NAACP, Masons. Republican. Home: 1980 Valley Rd Annapolis MD 21401 Office: Mount Olive AME Ch 2 Hicks Ave Annapolis MD 21401-3921

SPAIN, ROBERT HITCHCOCK, bishop; b. Loretto, Tenn., Oct. 26, 1925; s. James Thomas and Grace (Hitchcock) S.; m. Syble Mink, May 14, 1948; children: Mollie Lou, John Philip. BA, Florence State Coll., 1950; BD, Vanderbilt U., 1954. On trial Tenn. Conf., 1951, ordained deacon United Meth. Ch., 1958, full connection, elder, 1960. Pastor 1st Meth. Ch., Livingston, Tenn., 1954-58, Lebanon, Tenn., from 1958; bishop Ky. Conf. 1st Meth. Ch., Louisville, 1988—. Youth dir., Tenn. Conf., 1953-54. Recipient George Washington award for sermons Freedom Found., 1964. Office: United Meth Ch 1115 S 4th St Louisville KY 40203

SPAINHOWER, JAMES IVAN, college president; b. Stanberry, Mo., Aug. 3, 1928; s. Elmer Enoch and Stella Irene (Cox) S.; m. Joanne Steanson, June 10, 1950; children: Janet Dovell, James Jeffrey. BA, Phillips U., Enid, Okla., 1950, LLD (hon.), 1967; BD, Lexington (Ky.) Theol. Sem., 1953; MA in Polit. Sci., U. Mo., Columbia, 1967, PhD, 1971; U. Ark., 1954; diploma, U. Pacific Sch. Religion, Berkeley, Calif., 1958; DPA (hon.), Culver-Stockton Coll., 1973; LL.D. (hon.), Maryville Coll., St. Louis, 1976; Litt.D. (hon.), Kirksville (Mo.) Coll. Osteo. Medicine, 1977; D.H.L. (hon.), Mo. Valley Coll., 1984. Ordained to ministry Christian Ch. (Disciples of Christ), 1950; pastor chs. in Ark. and Mo., 1953-70; mem. Mo. Ho. of Reps. from, Saline County, 1963-70; pres. Asso. Med. Schs. Mo., Jefferson City, 1970-72; part-time prof. polit. sci. Lincoln U., Jefferson City, 1970-72; treas. State of Mo., 1973-80; pres. Sch. of Ozarks, Point Lookout, Mo., 1981-82, Lindenwood Coll., St. Charles, Mo., 1983—; bd. dirs. Vanliner Ins. Co., Bank of St. Charles County. Author: Pulpit, Pew and Politics, 1979. Chmn. Mo. del. Democratic Nat. Conv., 1976; bd. dirs. Goodwill Industries Mo. Recipient Mental Health award Mo. Mental Health Assn., 1967, Meritorious Service award St. Louis Globe Dem., 1968, Harry S. Truman award Saline County Young Democrats, 1970, citation of merit Alumni Assn. U. Mo., 1975; named Mo. Lay Educator of Year Mo. chpt. Phi Delta Kappa, 1968. Home and Office: Lindenwood Coll Saint Charles MO 63301

SPALDING, ALMUT MARIANNE, minister; b. Heidelberg, Fed. Republic Germany, July 19, 1957; came to U.S., 1979;p; d. Heinz-Peter Georg Alexander and Helga Käthe Ruth (Könnecke) Grutzner; m. Paul Stuart Spalding, May 27, 1978; children: Peter James, Eckhart Arthur, Alex John. BA, U. Heidelberg, 1979; MDiv, McCormick Theol. Sem., 1984; MA, U. Iowa, 1985. Ordained to ministry Presbyn. Ch., 1984. Student chaplain U. Iowa Hosps., Iowa City, 1980-81; co-pastor Elba (N.Y.) Presbyn. Ch., 1984-88; with pulpit supply Perry (Ill.) Presbyn. Ch., 1989—; chaplain Ill. Coll., Jacksonville, 1990; instr. Ill. Coll., Jacksonville, 1988—. Translator ABC Club, Darmstadt, Fed. Republic Germany, 1987; mem. Jacksonville Symphony, 1990. Mem. AAUW (sec. 1989—), Planned Parenthood Fedn. Am., Nat. Assn. Presbyn. Clergywomen. Avocations: travel, hiking, music. Home: 926 W Douglas Ave Jacksonville IL 62650

SPALDING, JAMES COLWELL, minister, educator; b. Kansas City, Mo., Nov. 6, 1921; s. John W. and Helen Muriel (Kerr) S.; m. Virginia Esther Burford, Oct. 21, 1945; children: Paul Stuart, Helen Harriet, Peter Marshall, Mary Christine, Ann Louise. BA, U. Ill., 1942; BD, Hartford Theol. Sem., 1945; PhD, Columbia U., 1950. Ordained to ministry Presbyn. Ch. (U.S.A.). Asst. pastor Ft. Peck Larger Parish, Poplar, Mont., 1945-46; chaplain, prof. Mo. Valley Coll., Marshall, 1948-53; pastor 1st Presbyn. Ch., Slater, Mo., 1950-53; assoc. prof. religion Trinity U., San Antonio, 1953-56; prof. U. Iowa, Iowa City, 1956—; moderator Presbytery of Kansas City, Presbyn. Ch. (U.S.A.), 1953, Presbytery of Austin (Tex.), 1956, mem. theology and worship ministry unit, Louiseville, 1985—, mem. com. on theol. edn., Louisville, 1987—. Co-author: Piety, Politics, and Ethics, 1984; contbr. articles to profl. publs. Folger Shakespeare Libr. fellow, 1968. Fellow Swiss-Am. Soc. for Cultural Rels.; mem. Am. Soc. on Ch. History (chmn. program com. 1971), Coun. on Grad. Studies in Religion (sec./treas. 1968-81), Am. Acad. Religion, Presbyn. Hist. Soc., 16th Century Studies Conf. (pres. 1975-76, Leadership award 1977). Democrat. Home: 315 Ridgeview Ave Iowa City IA 52246

SPANGENBERG, CAROL ANNE, priest; b. Detroit, Mar. 24, 1941; d. William Audrey Thomas Harvey and Mary Alice (Lowe) Corner; m. David Cornelius Spangenberg, July 27, 1963; children: Tamara Anne, Christine Marymae, Matthew Anthony Strukel, David Warren. BA in Social Sci. Edn., Mich. State U., 1964, MA, 1978, EdS, 1980; D Ministry, Gen. Theol. Found., 1989. Ordained deacon, Episc. Ch., 1983, priest, 1990. Tchr. Lansing (Mich.) Sch. Dist., 1976-90; social worker State of Mich., Lansing, 1985-90; priest assoc. St. Paul's Episc. Ch., Lansing, 1990—. Mem. pastoral care dept., chaplain Sparrow Hosp., 1981—. Mem. Bus. and Profl. Women, Nat. Assn. Tchrs. of English. Office: St Paul's Episc Ch 218 W Ottawa Lansing MI 48933

SPANN, DAVID, bishop. Bishop of Greater Md. Ch. of God in Christ, Balt. Office: Ch of God in Christ 5023 Gwynn Oak Ave Baltimore MD 21207*

SPARER, MALCOLM MARTIN, rabbi; b. N.Y.C.; m. Erna Reichl (dec. Sept. 1990); children: Ruth, Arthur, Jennifer, Shoshana. AB, M in Hebrew Lit., Yeshiva U.; MA in Sociology, CCNY; cert. in pastoral counselling, Des Moines Coll. Osteopathic Medicine; PhD in Sociology, NYU. Ordained rabbi, 1953. Exec. dir. Rabbinical Coun. Calif., L.A., 1957-66; adminstr. Tchr's. Coll. of West Coast, Torah U. (later Yeshiva U.), 1957-66; rabbi Beth El Jacob, Des Moines, 1966-69, Chevra Thilim, San Francisco, 1969-72; liaison for Union of Orthodox Jewish Congregations Am., 1957-66, moderator radio series Lest We Forget, 1962, moderator TV specials on Jewish religion and holiday observances Sta. KNXT, L.A., 1964-65, Des Moines, 1967-69; instr. dept. philosophy Drake U., 1966-69; pres. San Francisco dist. Zionist Orgn. Am., 1969-82, also bd. dirs.; chmn., mem. nat. bd. San Francisco Bay Area Zionist Fedn., 1971-84; co-chmn. Jerusalem Fair, 25th Anniversary of State of Israel, 1973; chmn. Commn. on Soviet Jewry, Jewish Community Rels. Coun., 1974-81; bd. dirs. Jewish Community Fedn., 1982-84; cons. internat. leaders, founder Menorah Inst.; cons. Commn. on Christian-Jewish and Moslem Rels. to European Paliament Nations; cons. various govt. and non-govt. orgns.; writer, frequent lectr. colls., ch. groups on Judaica and world affairs.; pres. No. Calif. Bd. Rabbis; chmn. dept. world affairs/internat. politics Community Coll. San Francisco; chaplain Letterman Army VA Hosp., San Francisco Presidio; co-founder Black and Jewish Clergy; mem. San Francisco Coun. Chs. (bd. dirs. food bank program), United Jewish Appeal (chmn. rabbinic cabinet of western region); invited mem. del. bishops and ch. leaders various denominations conducting meml. svc. at Dachau, Fed. Republic Germany, 1988. Hon. chmn. Mayor's Commn. on Holocaust Meml., San Francisco; mem. Mayor's Task Force for Homeless; co-chmn. Gov.'s Family Task Force, San Francisco. With USN, World War II; Korean War. Address: PO Box 15055 San Francisco CA 94115

SPARGUR, ARLIE YON, minister; b. Wichita, Kans., Oct. 30, 1956; s. Eugene McCall and Rosalee Irene (Poovey) S.; m. Debra Sue Haun, Aug. 9, 1980;children: Vaughn, Charles, Matthew, Rosemarie, Sarah, John. BA in Bible, Tenn. Temple Coll., 1978; postgrad., Temple Bapt. Theol. Sem., 1978-82. Pastor Lakeside Bapt. Ch., Painesville, Ohio, 1985—. Republican. Home: 697 Liberty St Painesville OH 44077 Office: Lakeside Bapt Ch 314 Lake Rd Painesville OH 44077

SPARKS, BOBBY LEE, minister; b. Ft. Worth, Dec. 8, 1946; s. Aubrey Linwood and Margaret Oleta (Knight) S.; m. Cathyrn Rebecca Smith, June 29, 1968; children: Gregory Paul, Beckie Elaine, Brian Keith. B. English Bible, Tex. Bapt. Inst., 1969, BTh., 1972, ThM, 1975, ThD, 1987. Ordained to ministry Am. Bapt. Assn. Pastor various chs. in Tex., Mich., Ill. and Fla., 1966—, Emmanuel Bapt. Ch., Greenville, Tex., 1988—; v.p. West Fla. Bapt. Inst., Pensacola, 1985-88; moderator of missionary Bapt. Assn. Ill., 1983-84; chaplain Greenville Fire Dept., Greenville Police Dept., 1988—; mem. critical incident debriefing team Ft. Worth Fire Dept., 1989—; lectr. in field. Author: The Tabernacle of Israel, 1991; editor Eastern Bapt. Times, 1979-82. Mem. Toastmasters (Disting. Toastmaster 1980). Home: 6410 Chapman Dr Greenville TX 75401 Office: Emmanuel Bapt Ch 3103 Terrell Rd Greenville TX 75401

SPARKS, IRVING ALAN, biblical scholar, educator; b. Ft. Wayne, Ind., June 15, 1933; s. James Edwin and Isabelle Mildred S.; A.B., Davidson (N.C.) Coll., 1954; B.D., Union Theol. Sem., Richmond, Va., 1959; S.T.M., Lancaster (Pa.) Theol. Sem., 1970; Ph.D., Claremont (Calif.) Grad. Sch., 1970; m. Helen Daniels, Sept. 3, 1954; children—Lydia Isabelle Sparksworthy, Leslie Bishop, Robin Alan. Lectr. philosophy and religion LaVerne (Calif.) Coll., 1965-69; asst. prof. religion Claremont Grad. Sch., 1970-74, assoc. dir. Inst. Antiquity and Christianity, 1970-74; mem. faculty San Diego State U., 1974—, prof. religious studies, 1980—, chmn. dept. religious studies, 1983-90, assoc. dean grad. div. and research, 1974-83; adj. faculty Sch. Theol. Claremont, Calif., 1970-74, 89—; founder/pres. Inst. Bibl. Studies, 1983-85; cons. photog. archival conservation of Dead Sea Scrolls in Jerusalem, 1980; mem adv. bd. Inst. Antiquity and Christianity, 1974—. Trustee, Claremont Collegiate Sch., 1970-75, pres., 1972-74; trustee, mem. exec. com. Ancient Bibl. Manuscript Ctr., 1981—. Fellow Lilly Found., 1964-65, Layne Found., 1965-66; disting. vis. scholar James Madison U., 1982. Mem. Am. Soc. Papyrologists, Soc. Bibl. Lit., Phi Beta Delta. Author: The Pastoral Epistles: Introduction and Commentary, 1981, Exploring World Religions: A Reading and Writing Workbook, 1986, 4th edit., 1991; editor Studies and Documents, 1971-91; contbr. articles on papyrology and bibl. studies to scholarly jours. Office: San Diego State U San Diego CA 92182-0304

SPARKS, JAMES A., minister, educator; b. Mays Lick, Ky., May 31, 1933; s. Sherley Lee and Lillie Mae (Snyder) S.; m. Pauline Lenore Zahrte, Aug. 13, 1955; 1 child, Elizabeth Carole. BA, Transylvania Coll., 1955; MDiv, Pitts. Theol. Sem., 1958; MS, U. Wis., 1972. Ordained to ministry United Presbyn. Ch., 1958. Pastor Lisbon United Presbyn. Ch., Sussex, Wis., 1958-64, Dale Heights United Presbyn. Ch., Madison, Wis., 1964-73; prof. clergy continuing edn. U. Wis., Madison, 1973—. Author: Potshots at the Preacher, 1977, Friendship After Forty, 1980, Living the Bad Days, 1982, If This Pew Could Talk, 1985; columnist: Clergy Jour. monthly, 1983-87. Recipient Creativity award Nat. Univ. Extension Assn., 1979. Mem. Soc. Advancement Continuing Edn. for Ministry (bd. dirs. 1970-73, 79-81), Coun Wis. Writers (nonfiction Merit award, 1980), Nat. Com. Extension Continuing Edn. for Clergy and Laity. Office: U Wis Extension 610 Langdon St Madison WI 53703 *I've never been much for planning my life or career in advance. What's worked for me has been the "stumble-on theory". I've often stumbled on to people and events that have made a tremendous impact on my life. To make the stumble-on theory work, timing and a willingness to take risks is crucial.*

SPARKS, LOICE GREER, missionary; b. St. Maurice, La., Aug. 11, 1925; d. Robert Aubrey and Willie Ovelia (Melton) Greer; m. James William Sparks, May 23, 1947; children—David Aubrey, Kevin James. B.A., Coll. of Pentecost, 1981. Ordained to ministry, 1977. Evangelist, United Pentecostal Ch., Shreveport, La., 1953-64; pastor Haughton United Pentecostal Ch., La., 1964-77; evangelist United Pentecoastal Ch., Shreveport, 1977-81; pastor Holly Ridge, Waterproof, La., 1981-83; missionary United Pentecostal Ch., Tanzania, E. Africa, 1983—; ladies aux. pres. United Pentecostal Ch., Section 11, 1971-78; Sunday sch. dir., Monroe, La., 1982. Home: Rte 5 Box 245A Monroe LA 71203 Office: United Pentecostal Ch, PO Box 9527, Moshi Tanzania

SPARKS, RICKY LYNN, broadcasting educator; b. Atlanta, Jan. 23, 1954; s. Lewis Albert and Bertha Ophalene (Cannon) S.; m. Sandra Kay Hicks, July 16, 1976. BS, U. Tenn., 1976; M. Ch. Music, So. Bapt. Theol. Sem., 1983. Ordained minister in Bapt. Ch., 1989. Announcer Sta. WXLN, Louisville, 1980-83; minister of media First Bapt. Ch., Alcoa, Tenn., 1985-88; minister media/outreach Cen. Bapt. Ch., Chattanooga, 1988-89; prof. John Brown U., Siloam Springs, Ark., 1989—. Producer-dir. (TV documentary) Christy, 1986; producer spot message series for Cen. Bapt. Ch., 1989. Recipient Cert. of Appreciation, U.S. Jaycees, Vernon, Tex., 1985; named one of Outstanding Young Men of Am., 1980, 85. Mem. Gospel Music Assn., Jaycees. Office: John Brown U Siloam Springs AR 72761

SPARKS, WILLIAM SHERAL, librarian; b. Alden Bridge, La., Oct. 30, 1924; s. Fred DeWitt and Truda (Bradford) S.; m. Joy Eleanor Young, Aug. 7, 1947; children: David Frederick, Carol Eileen. AB, Phillips U., 1946; MDiv, Christian Theol. Sem., 1949; ThD, Iliff Sch. of Theology, 1957; MA, U. Denver, 1962. Pastor chs., 1950-60; asst. libr. Kans. Wesleyan U., Salina, 1962-66; dir. libr. and info. svcs. St. Paul Sch. of Theology, Kansas City, Mo., 1966—. Horowitz Found. fellow Hebrew Union Coll.-Jewish Inst. of Religion, 1949-52. Mem. Am. Theol. Libr. Assn. Home: 15401 E 36th St Terr Independence MO 64055-3610 Office: St Paul Sch Theol 5123 Truman Rd Kansas City MO 64127-2499

SPARROWK, CORA CATHERINE, lay church leader; b. Martin, Tenn., Aug. 23, 1917; d. Ernest Clark and Edna (Harris) C.; m. John Sparrowk, Jan. 19, 1937; children: Jack Ernest, Jill Ann. DD (hon.), Am. Bapt. Sem. West, 1978. Contbr. articles to profl. jours. Chmn. Commn. on Christian Ethics, Bapt. World Alliance, chmn. div. study and rsch., 1985-90, v.p., 1900—, also mem. exec. com. and gen. coun.; mem. internat. com. World Day of Prayer, 1982—; dep. v.p. Ch. Women United USA, N.Y.C., 1980-84; past trustee Am. Bapt. Sem. West; bd. dirs. Ea. Bapt. Sem. and Ea. Coll., 1981—; pres. Am. Bapt. Internat. Ministries, 1976-78, Am. Bapt. Chs. U.S.A., 1978-79. Named Layman of Yr., Berkeley Bapt. Div. Sch., 1959; recipient citation Cen. Bapt. Theol. Sem., 1978, Valiant Woman award Ch. Women United U.S.A., 1984. Mem. Round Hill Country Club. Democrat. Address: 3370 Camanche Pkwy N Ione CA 95640 *Only as the Lord rules in the hearts of Christian people will justice, hope and peace change the world scene.*

SPEAKS, RUBEN LEE, bishop; b. Lake Providence, La., Jan. 8, 1920; s. Benjamin and Jessie Bell (Nichols) S.; m. Janie Angeline Griffin, Aug. 31, 1947; children: Robert Bernard, Joan Cordelia, Faith Elizabeth. A.B., Drake U., 1946; M.Div., Drew Theol. Sem., 1949; S.T.M., Temple U., 1952; postgrad., Div. Sch., Duke U., 1961; D.D., Hood Theol. Sem., 1972. Ordained deacon Christian Ch., 1942; elder A.M.E. Zion Ch., 1947; minister St. Thomas A.M.E. Zion Ch., Somerville, N.J., 1947, Wallace Chapel A.M.E. Zion Ch., Summit, N.J., 1948-50, Varick A.M.E. Zion Ch., Phila., 1950-56, St. Mark A.M.E. Zion Ch., Durham, N.C., 1956-64, 1st A.M.E. Zion Ch., Bklyn., 1964-72; bishop 10th Episcopal Area, Roosevelt, N.Y., 1972-84, 8th Episcopal Area, Wilmington, N.C., 1984-88, 6th Episcopal Area, Salisbury, N.C., 1988—; ch. world service chmn. Overseas Mission Bd., A.M.E. Zion Ch. Author: Higher Catechism for Ministers and Laymen, 1966, The Minister and His Task, 1968, The Church and Black Liberation, 1972, God, In An Age of Scarcity, 1981, Prelude to Pentecost, A Theology of the Holy Spirit, 1985. Bd. dirs. Durham Com. on Negro Affairs, 1958-63, N.Y. Urban League, 1967-72; trustee Lincoln Hosp., Durham, Livingstone Coll., 1972—, U. N.C., Wilmington, 1984-88; chmn. exec. com. NAACP, 1958-63. Recipient Citizens award City of Durham, 1964, Meritorious Service award N.Y. Urban League, 1968, Chancellor's award for meritorious services as trustee U. N.C. at Wilmington, 1988. Mem. Nat. Acad. Sci. and Religion, World Methodist Coun. (exec. com.), Nat. Coun. Chs. U.S.A., World Coun. Chs. Home: 1238 Maxwell St PO Box 986 Salisbury NC 28144

SPEAR, HARRY BINGHAM, III, pastor; b. Portsmouth, Va., Aug. 15, 1942; s. Harry Bingham Jr. and Minnie Brooks (Parker) S.; m. Patricia Marie Wild, June 3, 1967; children: Patricia, Rebecca, Harry IV. BA in Philosophy, Randolph-Macon Coll., 1964; MDiv, Wesley Theol. Sem., 1968. Ordained to ministry Meth. Ch. as deacon, 1965, as elder, 1968. Pastor Galilee United Meth. Ch., Sterling, Va., 1967-72, St. Mark's United Meth. Ch., Daleville, Va., 1972-75, Trinity United Meth. Ch., Orange, Va., 1975-81, Huntington Ct. United Meth. Ch., Roanoke, Va., 1981-84; pastor First United Meth. Ch., Norfolk, Va., 1984-89, Hopewell, Va., 1989—; chmn. rural Va., Va. Coun. of Chs., Richmond, 1988—. Mem. Lions (pres. Norfolk chpt. 1980, tail-twister Orange chpt. 1978), Ruritan Club (pres. Daleville chpt. 1974-75), Grand Lodge of Va. (grand chaplain 1983-84). Home: 804 North Ave Hopewell VA 23860 Office: First United Meth Ch 6th and Broadway PO Box 636 Hopewell VA 23860 *Our life is really a gift from God who I am convinced loves us and helps us reach beyond our own strength. When we accept his love it shines in our relationships and even our darker days seem brighter.*

SPEAR, LARRY ROSS, minister; b. Indpls., Sept. 16, 1941; s. Horace Ross and Evelyn Alice (Lynn) S.; m. Brenda Eveline Sexton, June 22, 1963; children: Lynnelle, Michele. BS in Mil. Sci., U.S. Mil. Acad., 1963; MS in Systems Mgmt., Air Force Inst. Tech., 1974; MDiv., So. Bapt. Theol. Sem., 1983. Ordained to ministry So. Bapt. Ch., 1978. Commd. 2d lt. USAF, 1963, advanced through grades to maj., 1973, resigned, 1976; assoc. pastor First Bapt. Ch., Englewood, Ohio, 1976-77; min. of youth First Bapt. Ch. of Dent, Cin., 1977-78; pastor Calvary Bapt. Ch., Lebanon, Ill., 1978-90, First So. Bapt. Ch., Terre Haute, Ind., 1990—. Vol. emergency med. technician City of Lebanon, 1986-90; vol. fireman, treas. Lebanon Fire Dept.; mem. Lebanon Zoning Bd., 1986-87; alderman Lebanon City Coun., 1987-90. Recipient 1987 Community Builder's award Lebanon Masonic Lodge. Republican. Avocations: bowling, counted cross stitch, tennis. Home: 3814 Hulman St Terre Haute IN 47803 Office: First So Bapt Ch 2403 S 8th St Terre Haute IN 47802

SPEAR, PAUL WILBURN, church administrator; b. Crawfordsville, Ind., Feb. 13, 1926; s. Perry Wilburn and Lula Bell (Calder) Godbye; m. Lythia Paulean Flick, Feb. 13, 1944; children—Paula Jean Spear Reeves, Priscilla Sue. B.A., Olivet Nazarene Coll., 1954. Bookbinder, R. R. Donnelly & Sons, Crawfordsville, 1944-50; employment mgr. A.O. Smith Corp., Kankakee, Ill., 1954-68; dir. personnel and services Ch. of the Nazarene Internat. Hdqrs., Kansas City, Mo., 1968—; bd. dirs. Faith Village, Lenexa, Kans., 1981—, Southtown Council, Kansas City, Mo., 1982—. Contbg. author: Church Building Source Book, 1980. Bd. dirs. Southtown Council, Kansas City, Mo., 1982-83, 83-84. Served with USN, 1944-46; PTO. Fellow Nat. Assn. Ch. Bus. Adminstrs. (regional v.p. Dallas, 1982); mem. Am. Mgmt. Soc., Am. Soc. Personnel. Republican. Home: 700 E 90th St Kansas City MO 64131 Office: Ch of the Nazarene 6401 The Paseo Kansas City MO 64131

SPEAR, TIMOTHY GEORGE, minister; b. Daytona Beach, Fla., June 8, 1962; s. Russell Jordan and Carol Ann (Thomas) S.; m. Patricia Anne Townsend, Dec. 9, 1989; 1 child, Hannah Rebecca. BA, Samford U., 1984; MDiv, Southeastern Bapt. Theol. Sem., Wake Forest, N.C., 1988. Minister of children/youth Mt. Vernon Bapt. Ch., Raleigh, N.C., 1985—; assn. youth ministries coord. Raleigh Bapt. Assn., 1989, assn. Sunday Sch. improvement support team mem., 1987—, Sunday Sch. growth cons., 1991—; children's spl. worker N.C. Bapt. State Conv., Cary, 1989—. Charter mem. Young Reps., Birmingham, Ala., 1980. Mem. N.C. Bapt. Religious Educators Assn., N.C. Bapt. Youth Ministers Assn., So. Bapt. Religious Educators Assn., Raleigh Bapt. Religious Educators, Raleigh Bapt. Youth Ministers (chmn. 1989—). Office: Mount Vernon Baptist Church 7600 Falls of Neuse Rd Raleigh NC 27615 *We make many decisions in life, but the most important is what one does with Jesus Christ because on this single decision hinges all of life and eternity.*

SPEARMAN, WILLIAM GLENN, minister, religion educator; b. Oklahoma City, May 25, 1927; s. Crawford Henry and Freda Muriel (Stewart) S.; m. Sylvia Eileen Gibbs, June 14, 1957; children: Steven Glenn, Paul William, Susan Eileen, Sarah Gibbs. BS in Bus., U. Okla., 1948, MA in History, 1961; BD, Princeton Theol. Sem., 1956, D. Ministry, 1981. Ordained to ministry Presbyn. Ch. (U.S.A.), 1956. Asst. min. First Presbyn. Ch., Salem, Ohio, 1956-58; min. Coll. Presbyn. Ch., Murray, Ky., 1958-60; missionary United Ch. of Christ (Kyodan), Iwakuni, Japan, 1961-63; min. United Presbyn. Ch., Kent, Ohio, 1963-72, First Presbyn. Ch., La Junta, Colo., 1972-77, Trinity Presbyn. Ch., Denton, Tex., 1977-82; sr. staff supr. eastern div. Southwestern Bell Telephone Co., Tulsa, 1948-53; chaplain, asst. prof. religion Hastings (Nebr.) Coll., 1982—; moderator Pueblo (Colo.) Presbytery, United Presbyn. Ch., 1975-76, vice moderator Cleve. Presbytery, 1971-72; pres. United Campus Ministry, Denton, 1979-80. Chair CROP drive World Coun. Chs., Hastings and Adams County, 1985-88. With USn, 1945-46, 1st lt. U.S. Army, 1948-53, Korea. Mem. Am. Acad. Religion, Presbyn. Coll. Chaplains Assn., Lions, Kiwanis, Rotary, Beta Gamma Sigma, Omicron Delta Kappa. Home: Rte 1 Box 32 Hastings NE 68901 Office: Hastings Coll 7th and Turner Hastings NE 68901

SPEARS, ROBERT RAE, bishop; b. Rochester, N.Y., June 18, 1918; s. Robert Rae and Phebe (Wing) S.; A.B., Hobart Coll., 1940, D.D. (hon.), 1969; S.T.B., Gen. Theol. Sem., N.Y.C., 1943, S.T.D. (hon.), 1967; m. Charlotte Lee Luttrell, June 16, 1947; children—Robert Rae, Deborah Wing, Gregory Luttrell. Ordained priest Episcopal Ch., 1944; curate in Olean, N.Y., 1943-44; rector in Mayville, N.Y., 1944-48; canon St. Paul's Cathdral, Buffalo, 1948-50; rector in Auburn, N.Y., 1950-54; vicar Chapel of the Intercession, N.Y.C., 1954-60; rector Trinity Ch., Princeton, N.J., 1960-67; suffragan bishop Diocese West Mo., 1967-70; bishop of Rochester (N.Y.), 1970—. Pres. Met. Interch. Agy., Kansas City, Mo., 1968. Trustee Gen. Theol. Sem., 1955—. Home: 40 Douglas Rd Rochester NY 14610 Office: Episcopal Diocese of Rochester 935 East Ave Rochester NY 14607

SPECK, GREGORY OTIS, youth minister, educator; b. San Francisco, Apr. 23, 1951; s. Armand Major and Florence (Johnson) S.; m. Bonnie Lou Cupp, July 30, 1977; children: Justin Joseph, Julia Camille, Kelley Cameron, Garrett Gregory. BA, Bethel Coll., 1973. Ordained to ministry Bapt. Gen. Conf., 1980. Case worker Sunny Ridge Home, Wheaton, Ill., 1973-75; assoc. pastor Temple Bapt. Ch., Rockford, Ill., 1975-80; pres. Youth Ministries Internat., Rockford, 1980-85; youth specialist Moody Bible Inst., Chgo., 1985—; communicator Metal Fabrication Inst., Rockford, 1982-87; speaker Moody Bible Inst., 1980—; European missions leader Reign Ministries, Royal Servants Internat., 1981—. Author: Sex, It's Worth Waiting For, 1989 (quarter finalist Campus Life Book of Yr.), Living for Jesus When the Party's Over, 1991; (videotape series) It's Worth Waiting For, 1989; (audio-cassette series) Youth Issues for the '90s, 1985. Chaplain Rockford Police Dept., 1980—; deacon Temple Bapt. Ch., 1988-89. Recipient Gold Std. Achievement, Scottish Youth Coun., Glasgow, 1986. Mem. Nat. Network Youth Mins., Youth Mins. Rockford, Bethel Coll. Athletic Letterman's Club. Avocations: watching football, playing tennis, basketball, jogging, collecting sports cards. Office: Moody Bible Inst 820 N LaSalle Chicago IL 60610

SPEESE, JAMES STANLEY, minister; b. Harrisburg, Pa., Nov. 24, 1911; s. August Friar and Elizabeth Erna (Flora) S.; m. Mary Florence Giddings, June 14, 1941; children: Carolyn, James, Shelley. BA, Gordon Coll., Boston, 1940; MA, U. N.H., 1943; BD, Gordon-Conwell Div. Sem., 1946, MDiv, 1989; ThD, Burton Sem., Manitou Springs, Colo., 1960. Ordained to ministry Am. Bapt. Conv., 1943, United Presbyn. Ch. in USA, 1964. Pastor chs. in New Eng., Wis., Mich., Ohio and Ill., 1941-43, 47-50, 58-68; prof., head dept. history and polit. sci. Coll. Emporia, Kans., 1968-71; pastor Woodland Heights Presbyn. Ch., Springfield, Mo., 1971-76; assoc. pastor St. Paul's Presbyn. Ch., Orlando, Fla., 1976-78; adj. prof. history and religion Fla. So. Coll., Orlando, 1977—. Co-chmn. steering com. Springfield Area Key 73 Evangelism Effort. Chaplain USAAF, 1943-47, USAFR, 1947-50, 58-71, USAF, 1950-58, 58-71. Recipient Freedoms Found. awards, 1970-76, 79-80, 84, 89-90, Prin. awards, 1973, 75, Gold medal Alpine Motoring Contest, 1972; named Prof. of Yr. Coll. Emporia, 1971. Mem. VFW, Res. Officers Assn. (chaplain Cen. Fla. chpt. 1987—, state chaplain 1988—, Minute Man award nat. hdqrs. 1989), Air Force Assn. (chpt. chaplain 1984, 91), Mil. Order World Wars (chaplain Cen. Fla. chp. 1988—, region VI 1990—, dept. of North Fla. 1990—), Ret. Officers Assn. (chaplain Fla. chpt. 1987—, Hero award Cen. Fla. chpt. 1989), Mil. Chaplains Assn. (pres. Cen. Fla. chpt. 1989-90), Am. Legion, Smithsonian Instn., Phi Alpha Chi. Home: 900 Whitewater Altamonte Springs FL 32714 *Our prayer to God is to have the wisdom to face aggressive challenges, the courage to take decisive action as needed, the willingness to sacrifice to meet the tensions and crises of life. For I believe that for individuals and America, peace, prosperity and stability can only be assured by strength, by sacrifice and by continuous determination.*

SPEHEGER, STEVAN WALTER, radio station executive; b. Bluffton, Ind., Mar. 10, 1944; s. Walter Willard and Mary Leona (McAfee) S.; m. Monica Rae Sutton, June 11, 1967; children: Douglas Alan, Roger Kent. BSEE, Purdue U., 1968. Dir. of media ministries First Assembly of God, Lafayette, Ind., 1979—; gen. mgr. Sta. WCFY Radio, Lafayette, 1984—; deacon First Assembly of God, Lafayette, 1973-79. Inventor, patentee residual current checker, automatic transmitter controller; co-inventor, patentee solid state appliance controller. Bd. dirs. Right to Life Tippecanoe County, Lafayette, 1988-90; mem. adv. bd. Life Care Svcs., Lafayette, 1990. Mem. Soc. Broadcast Engrs., Ind. Assn. Bd. of Nat. Assn. Evangelicals. Mem. Assemblies of God. Office: Sta WCFY Radio 108 Beck Ln Lafayette IN 47905

SPELTZ, GEORGE HENRY, bishop; b. Altura, Minn., May 29, 1912; s. Henry and Josephine (Jung) S. BS, St. Mary's Coll., Winona, Minn., 1932, LLD, 1963; student theology, St. Paul Sem., 1936-40; MA, Cath. U. Am., 1942, PhD, 1944; DD, Holy See, Italy, 1963. Ordained priest Roman Cath. Ch., 1940. Vice chancellor Diocese Winona, 1944-47, supt. schs., 1946-49, aux. bishop, 1963-66; pastor St. Mary's Ch., Minneiska, Minn., 1946-47; tchr. St. Mary's Coll., 1947-63; rector Immaculate Heart of Mary Sem., Winona, 1948-63; co-adjutor bishop St. Cloud, Minn., 1966-68; bishop, 1968-87; pres. Nat. Cath. Rural Life Conf., 1970-72; mem. bishops' com. for pastoral on Cath. social thought and U.S. economy Nat. Coun. Cath. Bishops, 1981-86; cons. NCCB/USCC Task Force on Food and Agr. Chpt. Economy Pastoral, 1987-89.

SPENCE, DOUGLAS MORCOM, minister; b. Pasadena, Calif., June 23, 1928; s. Harold Gerald Spence and Robina Jean (Ellis) Stapleton; m. Diana Bond Prince, June 23, 1956; children: John Ellis, Paul Wright, Anne Moore Spence Perry. AB, Occidental Coll., 1956; MDiv, Ch. Div. Sch. of Pacific, Berkeley, Calif., 1959; postgrad., U. Pa., 1959-63. Ordained to ministry Episcopal Ch., 1959. Asst. Grace Ch., Mt. Airy Phila., 1959-63; rector St. Aidan's Ch., Cheltenham, Pa., 1963-69, Trinity Episcopal Ch., Highland Park, Ill., 1969—; pres. Nat. Network Episcopal Clergy Assns., 1977-80; bd. dirs. Coun. for Devel. Ministry, Episcopal Ch., N.Y.C., 1977--79; dean Waukegan Deanery, Diocese of Chgo., 1981-87, bd. dirs. Commn. on Ministry, 1982-87. Contbg. author: Winery, Defenses and Soundings at Gibeon, 1963. Mem. exec. com. Avenue of Righteous, Glencoe, Ill., 1986—; treas. Friends Highland Park Pub. Libr., 1989—; v.p. allocations United Way, Highland Park, 1989-90. Fellow Ch. Soc. for Coll. Work, 1959-62. Mem. Rotary (bd. dirs., treas. Highland Park 1990-92). Democrat. Office: Trinity Episcopal Ch 425 Laurel Ave Highland Park IL 60035 *Life is a gift which may easily be diminished in a selfish attempt to satisfy only our own needs and desires, or it can be given an opportunity for nurture and growth if shared and used to benefit all life. The more I share it, the more I find that my life is enriched.*

SPENCE, FRANCIS JOHN, archbishop; b. Perth, Ont., Can., June 3, 1926; s. William John and Rose Anna (Jordan) S. BA, St. Michael's Coll., Toronto, 1946; postgrad., St. Augustine's Sem., Toronto, 1946-50; JCD, St. Thomas U., Rome, 1955. Ordained to priest Roman Cath. Ch., 1950. Consecrated bishop, 1967; diocesan sec. Kingston, Ont., 1950-52; parish asst., 1955-61; mem. marriage Tribunal, 1961-66; diocesan dir. hosp. and charities, 1961-66; pastor Sacred Heart Ch., Marmora, Ont., 1966-67; aux. bishop Mil. Vicar Canadian Forces, 1967-70; bishop of Charlottetown P.E.I., 1970-82; archbishop of Kingston Ont., 1982—; mil. vicar of Can., 1982-88. Office: 390 Palace Rd, Kingston, ON Canada K7L 4T3

SPENCE, GLEN OSCAR, clergyman; b. Willow Springs, Mo., Jan. 20, 1927; s. John Oscar and Emma Adelia (Kentch) S.; m. Margaret Carolyn Hunter, Sept. 10, 1948; children: Rodney Glen, Randall Eugene. B.S. in Agr, U. Mo., 1950; B.A. in Bible, Oakland City (Ind.) Coll., 1957, D.Div. (hon.), 1982. Tchr. agr. Mountain View, Mo., 1950-55; instr. biology Oakland City Coll., 1955-57; ordained to ministry Gen. Bapt. Ch., 1954; pastor chs. in Evansville, Ind., 1958-65, 73-76; dir. denominational affairs Oakland City Coll., 1965-72; exec. dir. Gen. Assn. Gen. Bapts., Poplar Bluff, Mo., 1977—; moderator Gen. Assn. Gen. Bapts., 1961, pres. gen. bd., 1963-64. Served with USNR, 1945-46. Club: Kiwanis (pres. 1991-92). Office: 100 Stinson Dr Poplar Bluff MO 63901

SPENCE, HUBERT TALMADGE, II, school principal; b. Greenville, S.C., Oct. 18, 1948; s. Othniel Talmadge and Joye M. (Spinney) S.; m. Joy Kathryn Klepper, July 11, 1970; children: Othniel Talmadge II, Carrie Elizabeth, Jessica Kathryn. BTh, Holmes Theol. Sem., Greenville, S.C., 1970; BA, BD, Trinity Coll., Clearwater, Fla., 1971; MTh, Heritage Bible Coll., Dunn, N.C., 1974; MDiv, Founds. Grad. Sch., Dunn, 1978; ThD, Founds. Sem., 1984. Ordained to ministry, 1970. Pastor Plainview Ch., Clinton, N.C., 1971-73; tchr. theology Heritage Bible Coll., Dunn, 1971-74; head theology dept. Founds. Bible Coll., Dunn, 1974-79; assoc. pastor Founds. Bible Coll. Ch., Dunn, 1979—; v.p. Founds. Ministry, Dunn, 1979—; prin. Founds. Christian Acad., Dunn, 1983—; v.p. Christian Purities Fellowship, 1980-90; nat. lectr., authority on contemporary rock and gospel music, evangelist, tchr.; v.p. Christian Purities Fellowship, 1979—, Founds. World Missions Bd., 1986—. Editor Sunday Bible Pointer, 1980—; founding editor Timotheus Commitment, 1980—; author: A Preacher Am I, 1984; composer over 100 hymns; writer, dir. four major multi-medias, 10 major religious dramas. Recipient Conservatory Studies in Theology award Founds. Conservatory, Dunn, 1977. Mem. Christian Fundamentalists World Congress. Avocation: collector of old Bibles and religious books, travel. Home: 509 N Orange Ave Dunn NC 28334 Office: Founds Bible Ministries PO Box 1166 Dunn NC 28334

SPENCE, JOSEPH STEPHEN, minister; b. Huntington, W. Va., Feb. 1, 1949; s. John Quintin and Argyl Mae (Bostic) S.; m. Kathy Sue Jarrell; children: Jennifer Christin, Cara Michelle. BA in Edn., Marshall U., 1976; M in Religious Edn., Southern Baptist Theol. Seminary, 1978. Ordained to ministry Bapt. Ch. Pastor The Logan (W. Va.) Chapel, 1972; minister youth and children First Baptist Ch., Ceredo, W. Va., 1973-76; owner Soundcraft Co., Huntington, W. Va., 1973-76, Soundcraft Co., Louisville, Ky., 1976-79; assoc. TV producer 9th and O Baptist Ch., Louisville, 1978-79; assoc. pastor, minister of edn. W. Lonsdale Baptist Ch., Knoxville, Tenn., 1979-81; assoc. pastor, min. adminstrn. Thalia Lynn Bapt. Ch., Virginia Beach, Va., 1981-90; min. edn. King's Grant Bapt. Ch., Virginia Beach, Va., 1991—; co-owner Signs, Plaques & More, Virginia Beach, 1990—. Contbr. articles to Southern Baptist Mags. Served with U.S. Army, 1969-71. Republican. Avocations: model railroading, woodwork, electronics.

SPENCE, KENNETH FREDERICK, minister, district superintendent; b. Jersey City, Sept. 28, 1943; s. Kenneth McKenzie and Dorothy Rose (Schneitzer) S.; m. Joan Dorothy Stillwell, July 24, 1965; children: Michelle, Kenneth, Daniel, Christy. BS in Econs., Wagner Coll., 1965; ThM in Christian Edn., Dallas Theol. Sem., 1972. Ordained to ministry Evang. Free Ch. Am., 1976. Dir. Christian edn. No. Valley Evang. Free Ch., Cresskill, N.J., 1972-73; pastor Faith Chapel, Acton, Mass., 1973-79; sr. pastor Faith Evang. Free Ch., Trexlertown, Pa., 1979-85; dist. supt. Evan. Free Ch., Allentown, Pa., 1985—; vice-chmn. Dist. Supt. Coun., 1990—. Mem. Ministerial Assn. Evang. Free Ch., Eastern Dist. Assn. (bd. dirs. 1979-85). Home: RR2 Box 500 Breinigsville PA 18031 Office: Eastern Dist Assn Box 3451 Allentown PA 18106 *The value of today's efforts are greatest if they are an investment for eternity and not simply for today. The clearer my focus is on eternal things the more effective my accomplishments will be for today.*

SPENCER, ALAN LEE, minister; b. Biloxi, Miss., July 24, 1960; s. Melvin Lee and Brenda Gail (Lawrence) S.; m. Kimberly Lynn Falkenrath, Aug. 12, 1983; children: Matthew Alan Spencer, Rachel Lauren. MusB, Okla. Bapt. U., 1982; MusM, Southwestern Bapt. Theol. Sem., 1984. Ordained to ministry So. Bapt. Conv., 1989. Min. of music Agnew Ave. Bapt. Ch., Oklahoma City, 1980-82; min. of music/youth Friendship Bapt. Ch., Mansfield, Tex., 1982-84, 1st Bapt. Ch., Elgin, Okla., 1984-87; min. of music Bapt. Temple, Oklahoma City, 1987—. Dir. Rainbow Connection (city-wide choir for mentally handicapped), Oklahoma City, 1987—. Named Outstanding Soloist, Tri-State Music Festival, Enid, Okla., 1978. Mem. Am. Choral Dirs. Assn., Singing Churchmen Okla., Omega Chi Delta (pres. 1981-82), Kappa Kappa Psi (v.p. 1981-82). Republican. Avocations: tennis, golf, bowling, reading. Home: 1008 N Farra Dr Oklahoma City OK 73107 Office: Bapt Temple Ch 2433 NW 30th Oklahoma City OK 73112

SPENCER, FAITH M., state administrator, social worker; b. Brookfield, Ill., Mar. 6, 1937; d. Ralph D. and Florence M. Spencer. B.M.E., Ottawa (Kans.) U., 1959; MS, Emporia State U., 1963; MSW, U. Ill., 1971; MDiv, Cen. Bapt. Theol. Sem., Kansas City, Kans., 1985. Lic. master social worker, 1985. Social worker Franklin County Dept. Social Work, Ottawa, 1967-69; sch. prin., dir. music, tchr. Wellsville, Hartford, Colony Kincaid Schs., Kans., 1959-67; child care programs State of Kans. Social Welfare, Topeka, 1971-73; area dir. Junction City (Kans.) Social & Rehab. Svcs., 1974-78, Topeka Social & Rehab. Svcs., 1978-89; dir. community based svcs. State of Kans. Social & Rehab. Svcs., Topeka, 1989-90, dir. spl. projects, 1990—. Mem. cabinet, Christian edn. bd.; formerly mem. mission bd., pulpit supply bd. 1st bapt. Ch., Topeka. Mem. Am. Pub. Welfare Assn. (bd. dirs. 1980-84, Cert. of Appreciation 1985), Kans. Conf. on Social Welfare (bd. pres. 1982—), Interfaith Topeka (bd. pres. 1987-89), Let's Help (bd. v.p. 1989—). Avocations: reading, swimming, walking. Home: PO Box 4358 Topeka KS 66604-0358 Office: State of Kans Gen Svcs Docking State Office Bldg 10th & Harrison Topeka KS 66612-1570

SPENCER, HARRY CHADWICK, minister; b. Chgo., Apr. 10, 1905; s. John Carroll and Jessie Grace (Chadwick) S.; m. Mary Louise Wakefield, May 26, 1935; children: Mary Grace Spencer Lyman, Ralph Wakefield. B.A., Willamette U., 1925, D.D. (hon.), 1953; M.Div., Garrett Bibl. Inst., 1929; M.A., Harvard U., 1932. Ordained to ministry Meth. Ch., 1931; pastor Washington Heights Ch., Chgo., 1931-33, Portage Park Ch., Chgo., 1933-35; rec. sec. bd. missions Meth. Ch., 1935-40, asst. exec. sec., 1940-45, sec. dept. visual edn., 1945-52, exec. sec. radio and film commn., 1952-56, gen. sec. TV, radio and film commn., 1956-68, asso. gen. sec. program council div. TV, radio and film communication, 1968-72; asso. exec. sec. joint commn. on communications United Meth. Ch., 1972, ret., 1973; mem. exec. com. Nat. Council Chs. Broadcasting and Film Commn., 1952-73, chmn., 1960-63; mem. exec. com. Nat. Council Chs., 1960-63, mem. gen. bd., 1967-72, v.p. Cen. div. communications, 1969-72; chmn. constituting assembly World Assn. for Christian Broadcasting, 1963; mem. constituting assembly World Assn. Christian Communication, 1968, dir. assembly, 1975; mem. adminstrv. com. Ravemco, 1950-70, Intermedia, 1970-72; vis. prof. Garrett Evang. Theol. Sem., 1975; lectr. in field. Exec. producer: TV series Learning to Live; radio series Night Call; motion pictures John Wesley, etc.; Contbr. articles on films to ch. publs. Trustee Scarritt Coll., 1967-74, emeritus, 1974-88; bd. dirs. Outlook Nashville, 1977-83, sec., 1980; bd. dirs. Nashville chpt. UN Assn., 1976-83. Recipient award excellence art communications Claremont Sch. Theology, 1973, The Pioneer in Religious Communications award, 1989; inducted into United Meth. Communicators Hall of Fame, 1983. Mem. United Meth. Assn. Communicators, World Assn. Christian Communications. Clubs: Kiwanis (Woodmont); Harvard (Nashville). Home: PO Box 150063 Nashville TN 37215 *The most precious quality we know is human personality. Unfortunately, innumerable hazards constantly beset each individual even from the time of conception. Nevertheless, every person has inherited many priceless advantages. The ability to store up knowledge and the imagination to foresee future events, which make possible human communication, have enhanced the value of human personality and brightened our hope for the future—if human beings can now learn the secret of self-discipline and will use it to achieve long-range benefits for a world community.*

SPENCER, JEREMY LAWRENCE, minister; b. Warwick, R.I., Mar. 19, 1958; s. George Joseph and Ruth Louise (Palmiter) S. BA, William Jewell Coll., 1980; MDiv, Cen. Bapt. Theol. Sem., 1983. Ordained to ministry Am. Bapt. Chs. in U.S.A., 1988. Campus min. 1st Bapt. Ch., Iowa City, Iowa, 1984-86; pastor Corwith-Renwick (Iowa) Larger Bapt. Parish, 1987—; area V sec., treas. Mid-Am. Bapt. Chs., Iowa, Minn., 1987-90; area V v.p. Minister's Coun., Iowa, Minn., 1989—. Contbr. articles to profl. jours. Bd. dirs. Bobkiddies Preschool, Renwick, 1988—; mem. Humboldt (Iowa) County Hunger Task Force, 1989—. Mem. Am. Soc. Ch. History, Mins. Coun. of Am. Bapt. Chs. in U.S.A., Humboldt County Ministerial Assn. (treas. 1989—). Republican. *Human beings have faith in many things—faith in automobiles, government, family, insurance policies, and education, among others. But faith in Jesus Christ is, in the end, the only thing that really matters.*

SPENCER, LEWIS GRANT, III, music minister; b. Miami, May 19, 1952; s. Lewis Grant Jr. and Dorothy (Gibson) S.; m. Betsy Saunders, Apr. 26, 1975; 1 child, Jessica Grace. BA in Music Theory, Palm Beach Atlantic Coll.; M in Ch. Music, So. Bapt. Sem., 1980. Minister music and youth Euclid Ave Bapt. Ch., Bristol, Va., 1980-83, Western Br. Bapt. Ch., Portsmouth, Va., 1983-85; dir. sacred music Smithfield (Va.) Bapt.Ch., 1987-88; minister music Emmanuel Bapt. Ch., Farmington, N.Mex., 1988—; Mem. Ch. Music Adv. Bd., 1988; facilitator Master Life Conf., Eagle Eyrie, Va., 1984; guitar instr. U.S. Army Chaplains Ch. Music Conf., 1973. Mem. San Juan Symphony League, Farmington, 1989—; mem., past pres. Toastmasters Club 686, Norfolk, Va., 1984-88. Recipient Irene Wicker Music award Palm Beach Atlantic Coll., 1972, 75. Home: 200 Lynwood Dr Farmington NM 87401 Office: Emmanuel Bapt Ch 211 W 20th St Farmington NM 87401 *Success in ministry is the ability to love God, yourself and others as yourself. This love is expressed in managing to pray, study, build relationships and administrate efficiently.*

SPENCER, MARK WILLIAM, music minister, educator; b. Binghamtom, N.Y., Apr. 11, 1955; s. James Walter and Beulah Augusta (Wormuth) S.; m. Cathy Jean Tinkham, Aug. 1, 1981; children: Scott, Cheryl. AA, Broome Community Coll., 1975; BA, Judson Coll., 1981; MusM, Southwestern Sem., Ft. Worth, 1984. Announcer Sta. WNBF/WQYT, Binghamton, 1974-78, Sta. WSKG FM-TV, Binghamton, 1978-79; min. of music Trinity So. Bapt. Ch., Kaufman, Tex., 1982-84, St. Timothy Cumberland Presbyn. Ch., Bedford, Tex., 1984-86; instr. of music Golden Gate Bapt. Theol. Sem., Mill Valley, Calif., 1986-88; reader Christian Edn. for the Blind, Ft. Worth, 1988-89; asst. prof. Calif. Bapt. Coll., Riverside, 1989—; min. of music 1st Bapt. Ch., Riverside, 1989—; adj. prof. Golden Gate Sem., So. Calif. extension, Brea, 1990—. Soloist oratorios in Riverside/San Bernardino area, 1989—, Dodger Stadium, L.A., 1991, choral tours U.S. and abroad. Mem. Nat. Assn. Tchrs. Singing. Avocations: home video, classic film collection, swimming. Home: 4875 Merrill Ave Riverside CA 92506 Office: Calif Bapt Coll 8432 Magnolia Riverside CA 92504

SPENCER, PETER LEVALLEY, clergyman; b. Providence, Nov. 18, 1938; s. Lee Valley and Mary Josephine (Henry) S.; m. Eugenia Louise DiCostonzo-Bruno, May 4, 1961; children: Peter LeValley, David Louis, Mary Lee, Sarah Eugenia. BA, Brown U., 1960; ThM, Gen. Sem., 1965. Ordained to ministry Episcopal Ch. as priest, 1966. Curate St. Paul's Episcopal Ch., Pawtucket, R.I., 1965-67; curate St. Paul's Episcopal Ch., North Kingstown, R.I., 1967-71, rector, 1971—; canon Diocese of R.I., Providence, 1972—, spiritual dir., 1984—. Pres. Am. Cancer Soc., South County Div., Washington County, R.I., 1980. Lt. USN, 1960-62. Home: 14 Gold St North Kingstown RI 02852 Office: St Pauls Ch 5 S Main St North Kingstown RI 02852

SPENDER, ROBERT DON, religion educator; b. Waterbury, Conn., Nov. 17, 1945; s. Donald L. and Grace (Towle) S.; m. Aurie M. Austin, Aug. 8, 1970; children: David, Deborah, Joshua. BA, Barrington Coll., 1963; MA, Trinity Evang. Div. Sch., Deerfield, Ill., 1970; PhD, Dropsie U., 1976. Founder, prin. West Woods Christian Acad., Hamden, Conn., 1975-78; asst. prof. Bibl. studies Barrington (R.I.) Coll., 1978-85; assoc. prof., then prof. King's Coll., Briarcliff Manor, N.Y., 1985—, chair dept. religion. Author: Baker Encyclopedia of the Bible, 1988; also revs. Mem. sch. bd. Barrington Christian Acad., 1979-85, Hudson Valley Christian Acad., Carmel, N.Y., 1986—. Recipient Faculty of Yr. award Barrington Coll., 1982, Achievement award Barrington Coll. Alumni Assn., 1982, Faculty of Yr. award King's Coll., 1991. Mem. Soc. Bibl. Lit., Evang. Theol. Soc., Near East Archeol. Soc. Republican. Home: 35 Oriole St Lake Peekskill NY 10537 Office: The King's Coll Dept Religion & Philosophy Briarcliff Manor NY 10510

SPER, SHELDON, religious organization administrator. Pres. Jewish Immigrant Aid Svcs. Can., Montreal. Office: Jewish Immigrant Aid Svcs, 5151 Cote Ste Catherine Rd, Montreal, PQ Canada H3W 1M6*

SPERO, SHUBERT, rabbi, religion educator; b. N.Y.C., Sept. 23, 1923; s. Earl H. and Belle (Goldfarb) S.; m. Iris Sandra Mostofsky, Feb. 25, 1951; children: Moshe, Jonathan, Debra. BS, CCNY, 1946; MA, Case Western Res. U., 1960, PhD, 1971. Ordained rabbi, 1947. Rabbi Young Israel of Cleve., 1950-83; prof. Jewish thought Bar Ilan U., Ramat Gan, Israel, 1984—. Author: God in All Seasons, 1967, Morality, Halakha and the Jewish Tradition, 1983; editor: Religious Zionism, 1989. Mem. Rabbinical Coun. Am. Office: Bar Ilan U, Ramat Gan Israel

SPERRY, JOHN REGINALD, bishop; b. Leicester, Eng., May 2, 1924; s. William Reginald and Elsie Agnes (Priest) S.; m. Elizabeth Binnie Maclaren, Apr. 24, 1952; children: Angela Elizabeth Sperry Friesen, John. S.Th., King's Coll., Halifax, N.S., Can., 1956; D.D., Coll. Emmanuel-St. Chad, Saskatoon, Sask., Can., 1972, Wycliffe Coll., Toronto, 1979. Ordained to ministry Anglican Ch. of Canada, 1950; missionary Coppermine, N.W.T., Can., 1950-69; rector ch. Ft. Smith, N.W.T., 1969-73, Yellowknife, N.W.T., 1974; bishop of the Arctic Frobister Bay, Yellowknife, 1974-90, ret. Translator into Copper Eskimo: Canadian Prayerbook, 1962; Four Gospels and Acts, 1972. Served with Royal Brit. Navy, 1943-46. Recipient Can. Decoration. Home: 1 Dakota Ct, Yellowknife, NT Canada X1A 2A4 Office: 1055 Avenue Rd, Toronto, ON Canada M5N 2C8

SPEYRER, JUDE, bishop; b. Leonville, La., Apr. 14, 1929. Ed., St. Joseph Sem., Covington, La., Notre Dame Sem., New Orleans, Gregorian U., Rome. Ordained priest Roman Cath. Ch., 1953. Consecrated bishop Lake Charles, La., 1980—. Office: PO Box 3223 414 Iris St Lake Charles LA 70602

SPICER, CHARLES WALLING, JR., religious organization executive; b. Balt., Oct. 14, 1930; s. Charles Walling Sr. and Addie Augusta (Martin) S.; m. Phyllis Ann Schwartz, June 29, 1952; 1 child, Barbara Ann Spicer Graves. BA, Johns Hopkins U., 1951, BS, 1958; DD (hon.), Madras (India) Bible Sem., 1986. CLU. Dir. N.Am. Men for Mission Internat., Greenwood, Ind., 1967-70; dir. devel. OMS Internat., Greenwood, 1970-74, treas., 1974-75, v.p. devel., 1975-80; pres. Overseas Coun. Internat., Greenwood, 1978—; bd. dirs. Chinese Overseas Christian Mission, Fairfax, Va., 1970—. Author: Yours For the Asking, 1983. Pres. Stanita Found., Lima, Ohio, 1974-89. 1st lt. U.S. Army, 1951-55, Korea. Mem. Christian Stewardship Assn. (bd. dirs. 1982—), Rotary, Scabbard and Blade. Republican. Home: 810 Richart Greenwood IN 46142

SPIEGELMAN, RANDE LESTER, religious organization administrator; b. San Francisco, May 15, 1956; s. Lester and Ramona Ruth (Eberhardt) S.; m. Lillian Mary Mendoza, Aug. 22, 1980; children: Randall, Erika. Student, San Francisco State U. Legal asst. L. Bacci, San Francisco, 1976-79; mgr. World's Best Imports, San Francisco, 1979-85; chief adminstrv. officer, office mgr. Jews for Jesus, San Francisco, 1985—. Mem. Christian Ministries Mgmt. Assn. Republican. Baptist. Avocations: computers, gardening, reading, theatre. Office: Jew for Jesus 60 Haight St San Francisco CA 94102

SPILLMAN, EUGENE RAYMOND, JR., minister; b. Oklahoma City, Jan. 11, 1947; s. Eugene Raymond and Idena V. (Milliron) S.; m. Sallie Wade, Nov. 20, 1982; children: Tracy Lyn Mitchell, Stephen Scott. Student, Okla. State U., 1965-68; BA in Religion, Phillips U., 1970, MDiv, 1974. Ordained to ministry Christian Ch. (Disciples of Christ), 1974. Pastor 1st Christian Ch., Hominy, Okla., 1972-75; assoc. min. 1st Christian Ch., Edmond, Okla., 1975-79; sr. min. 1st Christian Ch., Cherokee, Okla., 1979-88, Cushing, Okla., 1989—; pres. Cushing Min.'s Fellowship, 1990-91; mem. Leadership Devel. for Mission and Ministry Commn., Christian Ch. (Disciples of Christ), Okla., 1990—. Guest editor columnist Sermon of Week, Cushing Daily Citizen, 1989-91. Mem. Cushing C. of C. (ambs. com. 1989-91), Rotary (pres. Cherokee 1981-82), Masons (chaplain 1990-91). Home: 1217 E 13th St Cushing OK 74023-5227 Office: 1st Christian Ch 300 E Moses PO Box 489 Cushing OK 74023-0489

SPINDLER, MARC ROBERT, theologian; b. Mulhouse, France, Aug. 25, 1930; s. Daniel and Suzanne (Herrenschneider) S.; m. Antoinette Theis, Apr. 9, 1956; children: Lorraine, Aldric, Aurore, Brieuc. Student, State U., Lyons, France, 1948-50, State U., Strasbourg, France, 1950-57; D degree, State U., Strasbourg, France, 1967; lic. letters, State U., Montpellier, France, 1974. Ordained to Min. Reformed Ch., 1959. Parish min. Reformed Ch. in Alsace and Lorraine, 1957-60; missionary Paris Evangel. Missionary Soc., Evangel. Ch. Madagascar, 1960-68, United Ch. of Jesus-Christ in Madagascar, 1968-73; assoc. prof. missiology and ecumenics U. Leiden (The Netherlands), 1974—; dir. dept. missiology, Interuniversity Inst. for Missiological and Ecumenical Rsch. Joint editor Exchange Jour. of Missiological and Ecumenical Rsch., 1975—. Served with French Army, 1954-57. Mem. Internat. Assn. for Mission Studies, Malagasy Acad., European Assn. of Mission History (pres.). Home: 25 van Diepenburchstraat, 2597 PR The Hague The Netherlands Office: 61 Rapenburg, 2311 GJ Leiden The Netherlands

SPINELLA, JOSEPH DOMINIC, theology educator; b. N.Y.C., Apr. 21, 1934; s. Joseph Peter and Anna (Giannattasio) S.; m. Freeda Fay Fichtner, Nov. 20, 1954; children: Steven Paul, Linda Fay Spinella Kemp, Sharon Joy Spinella Owen, Carolyn Ruth Spinella Drevets. BSEE, San Jose State U., 1957; ThM, Dallas Theol. Sem., 1967, ThD, 1981; cert., Spanish Lang. Inst., San Jose, Costa Rica, 1970. Diagnostic systems engr. Lawrence Radiation Lab., Livermore, Calif., 1957-62; cons. various engring. firms, Dallas, 1963-69, 73-76; prof. Las Delicias Bible Inst, Monagas, Venezuela, 1969-73, Associated Evangel. Sem., Maracay, Venezuela, 1976-80; cons. Team, Wheaton, Ill., 1980-83; prof. Washington Bible Coll., Lanham, Md., 1983-89; chmn. missions dept. Washington Bible Coll., 1984-89; prof. Capital Bible Sem., Lanham, 1985—. Inventor, neutron spectroscope borehole logger; contbr. articles to various publs. Mem. Evangel. Theol. Soc., Assn. Evangel. Profs. of Missions, IEEE. Office: Capital Bible Sem 6511 Princess Garden Lanham MD 20706

SPINKS, LEROY CULVER, pastor; b. Rockmart, Ga., Dec. 31, 1941; s. Arthur Ophard and Helen Lucille (Garner) S.; m. Annette Devaira Scoggins, Dec. 22, 1963; children: Leroy Kyle, Leigh Anne. BA, Wake Forest U., 1963; ThM, New Orleans Bapt. Theol. Sem., 1968, D Ministry, 1978. Ordained to ministry So. Bapt. Conv., 1965. Pastor 1st Bapt. Ch., Sunset, La., 1968-72, Apison (Tenn.) Bapt. Ch., 1972-76, 1st Bapt. Ch. Lakeview, Rossville, Ga., 1976—; moderator Coosa Bapt. Assn., Ft. Oglethorpe, Ga., 1978-80; mem. exec. com. Ga. Bapt. Conv., 1979-84, mem. com. on resolutions, 1991; v.p. Ga. Bapt. Pastors' Conf., 1991. Contbr. articles to religious publs. Home: 1609 Cannon Dr Fort Oglethorpe GA 30742 Office: 1st Bapt Ch Lakeview 901 Hudson St Rossville GA 30741

SPINKS, MARY C., administrator; b. Milw., Jan. 22, 1946; d. Gilbert Frank and Estelle (Shelenske) Herbert; m. Nick Spinks, Aug. 27, 1966; children: Tricia, Nichole, Kendal. BS, U. Houston. Tchr., religious edn. Stafford, Tex., 1971-73; tchr., 1978-83; parish adminstr. Christ Good Shepherd Ch., Spring, Tex., 1989—; adult sponsor, Cath. Youth Orgn., Stafford, 1971-73, sponsor, couple program, Spring, 1978—. Bd. dirs. Tex. State Bd. Dental Examiners, Austin, 1987—; pres. Spring Environ. Com., 1984-86, 1960 Area Republicans, 1989; chmn. legis. com. Tomball C. of C., 1988-89. Named Top Republican Vol. Republican Club, 1986. Mem. Nat. Assn. Ch. Bus. Adminstrs., Varity Club Am., Tex. Fedn. Republican Women, Houston Livestock Schow and Rodeo (speakers com. 1988—). Office: Christ Good Shepherd Ch 18511 Klein Ch Rd Spring TX 77379-4998

SPITTERS, MICHAEL JOHN, minister; b. St. Joseph, Mich., Oct. 9, 1961; s. Frank Jr. and Nancy Carol (Watterworth) S. BA in Religion, Hope Coll., 1984; MDiv, Tex. Christian U., 1989. Youth minister First United Meth. Ch., Ft. Worth, 1986-88; assoc. minister Cen. Christian Ch., Ft. Worth, 1988-89, First Christian Ch., San Angelo, Tex., 1990—; rep. Regional Task Force on Leadership Devel., S.W. region, 1990—; mem. christian edn. com. Cen. Area of Christian Ch., 1990—. Mem. clergy com. Am. Cancer Soc., Ft. Worth, 1988-89. Mem. SWACCE (steering com. 1990—), Ministerial Assn. of San Angelo. Office: 1st Christian Ch 29 N Oakes San Angelo TX 76903

SPITTLER, RUSSELL PAUL, seminary educator; b. Pitts., Aug. 6, 1931; s. Russell Paul and Helen Virginia (Maguire) S.; m. Roberta Jeane Watson, Aug. 13, 1955; children: Cheryl Ruth Spittler Azlin, Heidi Jeane Spittler

Morgan, Russell Watson. BA, Fla. So. Coll., 1954; MA, Wheaton Coll., 1957; BD, Gordon-Conwell Theol. Sem., 1958; PhD, Harvard U., 1971. Ordained to ministry Assemblies of God, 1961. Asst. prof. Bible Cen. Bible Coll., Springfield, Mo., 1958-62; acad. dean So. Calif. Coll., Costa Mesa, 1967-76; assoc. dean Fuller Theol. Sem., Pasadena, Calif., 1976-85, prof. of N.T., 1985—. Editor: Perspectives on the New Pentecostalism, 1976, others; contbr. articles to profl. jours. Served to capt. USNR, 1963-91. Mem. Soc. Pentecostal Studies (sec. 1983-88), Evang. Theol. Soc., Internat. Orgn. Septuagint and Cognate Studies. Home: 2075 Fox Ridge Dr Pasadena CA 91107 Office: Fuller Theol Sem 135 N Oakland Ave Pasadena CA 91101 *"Knowledge puffs up, but love builds up." (1 Corinthians 8:1).*

SPITZ, CHARLES THOMAS, JR., clergyman; b. Hazard, Nebr., May 26, 1921; s. Charles Thomas and Magdalene (Schneemann) S.; m. Dorothy O. Gross, June 11, 1944 (dec. 1982); children: Charles Thomas III, Gretchen Ann.; m. Karen Ankener Lucas, Aug. 25, 1983; 1 child, Garrett Richard. Grad., St. Paul's Coll., Concordia, Mo., 1939; A.B., Concordia Sem., St. Louis, 1944, D.D., 1965; D.D., Capital U., Columbus, Ohio, 1967, Muhlenberg Coll., 1967, Gettysburg Coll., 1970; L.H.D., Luther Coll., Decorah, Iowa, 1967. Ordained to ministry Lutheran Ch., 1944; pastor in Waterloo, Iowa, 1944-46, Marengo, Iowa, 1947-53; dir. broadcasting Luth. Laymen's League, St. Louis, 1953-66; gen. sec. Luth. Council U.S. 1966-73; pastor in Manhasset, L.I., N.Y., 1974-84; exec. assoc. Fuchs, Cuthrell & Co., 1984-85; sr. ptnr. Corp. Exec. Outplacement, 1986—; pres. Creative Energetics, 1985—; exec. asso. Evang. Lutheran in Mission, 1974-76; pres. Luth. Ch. in Mission, 1975-78; dir. Assn. Evang. Luth. Chs., 1976-83; mem. Commn. Luth. Unity, 1978-83; mem. commn. on faith and order Nat. Council Chs., 1977-83, vice chmn., 1979-82. Trustee Eger Luth. Home, 1987—. Home: 21 Deepdale Drive Manhasset NY 11030

SPITZ, ROBERT JOHN, lawyer; b. N.Y.C., May 26, 1947; s. Charles H. and Ola G. (Monroe) S.; m. Suzie Choi, Dec. 8, 1979; 1 child, Danory Michael Carleton. BS in Aero. Engring., Purdue U., 1969; JD, U. So. Calif., 1975. Bar: Calif. 1975, D.C. 1978, N.Y. 1979. Gen. counsel News World Communications, Inc., N.Y.C., 1978-87; exec. dir. Am. Constn. Com., Calif., 1987-88; dir. Am. Freedom Coalition, Ontario, Calif., 1988—; speaker Strategic Def. Assn. Calif. Editor: Legal Audits for Corporations, 1984. Project mgr. Victory '88, Calif. Reps., 1988. Recipient award, Kiwanis. Mem. ABA (gen. practice sect., chmn. corp. counsel com. 1986—, chmn. ann. meeting com. 1986—). Republican. Avocations: tennis, golf, swimming. Office: Am Freedom Coalition 650 S Spring St Ste 1230 Los Angeles CA 90014

SPITZER, LEE BARNETT, minister; b. Bklyn., Apr. 30, 1957; s. William and Norma (Landau) S.; m. Lois Nancy Yellin, Aug. 20, 1977; children: Joshua, Larisa. BA in Religion, King's Coll., Briarcliff Manor, N.Y., 1977; MDiv, Gordon-Conwell Theol. Sem., 1981, DMin, 1989. Ordained to ministry Am. Bapt. Chs. in U.S.A., 1981. Intern Bethlehem Presbyn. Ch., Buffalo, 1976; youth minister St. Mark's Episc. Ch., Glendale, Calif., 1977-79, Trinity Bapt. Ch., Lynnfield, Mass., 1979-80; pastor First Bapt. Ch. in East Providence, Rumford, R.I., 1981-86, Seaview Bapt. Ch., Linwood, N.J., 1986—; founding bd. mem. Caring Internat., Pleasantville, N.J., 1990—; U.S. del. Lausanne II Congress on World Evangelization, Manila, Philippines, 1989; del. Bapt. Peace Tour to USSR, Bapt. Peace Fellowship, 1983; speaker/lectr. on missions, 1983—, on peacemaking/nuclear issues, 1982-86. Author: (course-book) Bible Hi-Lites, 1990; editor: (devotional book) Peacemaking Throughout the Year, 1984. Bd. dirs. So. N.J. Health Systems Agy., 1989—, Caring Inc., Pleasantville, 1989—, Caring Fellowship Ctrs., Inc., Linwood, N.J., 1986—; founder, pres. Am. Bapt. Peacemakers R.I., 1983-86. Mem. Am. Bapt. Chs. N.J. (evangelism com. 1988—). Home: 1714 Woodlynne Blvd Linwood NJ 08221 Office: Seaview Bapt Ch 2025 Shore Rd Linwood NJ 08221 *I believe in searching for and celebrating God's presence in all spheres of life. I especially affirm the timeless themes of the Christian spiritual journey: reconciliation with God, union with Christ, and service in His name. Through such themes, the essence of life is manifest.*

SPITZER, S. BRIAN, clergyman; b. Chgo., July 17, 1953; s. Otto Allen and Virginia (Quinlan) S.; m. Barbara Ruth Fleming, Sept. 30, 1975; children: Bradley, Brenda. BS, Bradley U., 1975; ThM, Dallas Theol. Sem., 1982. Ordained to ministry Bapt. Ch., 1982. Asst. pastor Bethany Bapt. Ch., Moline, Ill., 1983-86; dir. camping and retreat ministries Midwest Bapt. Conf., Park Ridge, Ill., 1987-89; assoc. pastor Christian edn. Grandview Bapt. Ch., Davenport, IA, 1989—. Mem. Profl. Assn. Christian Educators. Office: Grandview Bapt Ch 4316 Ripley St Davenport IA 52806

SPIVEY, ED L., minister; b. Rusk, Tex., Oct. 12, 1933; s. Verner and Eddie (Sherman) S.; m. Ann Claudette Ray, May 26, 1956; children: Kevin, Sandra. Student Rice U., 1951-52; BA, Baylor U., 1955; MDiv, Southwestern Bapt. Theol. Sem., 1959. Ordained to ministry Baptist Ch., 1959. Pastor First Bapt. Ch., Flomot, Tex., 1959-61, First Bapt. Ch., Lefors, Tex., 1961-68, Eden Hills Bapt. Ch., Wichita Falls, Tex., 1968-71, First Bapt. Ch., Mexia, Tex., 1971-82, Quail Valley Bapt. Ch., Missouri City, Tex., 1982—; moderator Palo Duro Bapt. Assn., Pampa, Tex., 1965-67, Wichita Bapt. Assn., Wichita Falls, Tex., 1970-71, Bi-Stone Bapt. Assn., Mexia Tex., 1974-75, San Felipe Bapt. Assn., Rosenberg, Tex., 1987-88, Montague Bapt. Assn., 1989-91. Contbr. articles to profl. jours. Chaplain, City Council, Mexia, Tex., 1972-82, San Felipe Bapt. Assn., 1987—; commr. Planning and Zoning Commn., Missouri City, Tex., 1982—; trustee U. Mary Hardin Baylor, Belton, Tex., 1975—; bd. dirs. Ft. Bend Texans War on Drugs, 1983-89, Ft. Bend Am. Cancer Soc., 1984-86. Mem. Tri-Cities Ministers Fellowship (chmn. 1983-86). Lodge: Lions (tailtwister 1972-79, v.p.). Avocations: travel, sports, family activities. Office: Bethel Bapt Ch 310 7th St Nocona TX 76255

SPIVEY, WILLIAM LEE, minister; married; 5 children. Grad., Malone Coll., U. Akron, Grand Rapids Bapt. Coll. & Sem., Ashland Theol. Sem. Ordained to ministry Conservative Bapt. Assn. Am., 1981. Min. various chs. Ohio, Mich.; min. 1st Bapt. Ch., Gila Bend; sr. pastor West High Bapt. Ch., Phoenix, 1991—. Capt. USNG. Mem. S.W. Conservative Bapt. Pastors Assn. (treas.). Office: West High Bapt Ch 3301 N 19th Ave Phoenix AZ 85015-5799

SPIVEY, WILLIAM MICHAEL, minister; b. Piedmont, Ala., Jan. 6, 1956; s. William Elmer and Dorothy (Wilson) S.; m. Pamula Suzette Spillers, Dec. 20, 1985. BS, Jacksonville State, 1978; MDiv, Emory U., 1984. Ordained to ministry Meth. Ch., 1984. Youth minister 1st United Meth. Ch., Piedmont, Ala., 1978; Christian edn. asst. 1st United Meth. Ch., Talladega, Ala., 1978-85; chaplain United Meth. Children's Home, Selma, Ala., 1985—; chaplain Talladega High Football Team, 1980-83, Jaycees, Talladega, 1982-84. Jr. high camp dir. Camp Sumatanga, Gallant, Ala., 1978—; children's coord. Selma Dist., 1985—; staff mem. Team Walk Am., March of Dimes, Selma, 1991. Named Outstanding Young Religious Leader, Jaycees, 1980, as Most Achieved Since Graduation, Piedmont High Class of '74, 1984. Home: 2004 Broad St Selma AL 36701 *If "time waits for no man" and "no man is an island unto himself", then maybe our "time" on this "island" is short unless we do a better job of taking care of it.*

SPOFFORD, WILLIAM B., clergyman, administrator; b. Bklyn., Jan. 28, 1921; s. William B. and Dorothy Grace (Ibbotson) S.; m. Pauline Lindall Fawcett, Sept. 9, 1944; children—Timothy, Mark, Stephen, Andrew, Daniel. A.B., Antioch Coll, 1943; M.S.T., Episcopal Div. Sch., 1945; M.S.W., U. Mich., 1950; D.D. (hon.), Ch. Div. Sch. Pacific, Berkeley, 1968; D.S.T. (hon.), Coll. of Idaho, 1972. Ordained to ministry Episcopal Ch., 1945; asst. dir Div. Nat. Town-Country Ch. Inst. Western Extension, Weiser, Idaho, 1950-56; chief of chaplain Mass. Gen. Hosp., Boston, 1956-60; dean St. Michael's Cathedral, Boise, Idaho, 1960-68; bishop Diocese of Eastern Oreg., Bend, 1969-79; assoc. bishop-asst. bishop Diocese of Washington, D.C., 1980-85; chaplain, religious coordinator Mountain States Tumor Inst., Boise, Idaho, 1985-89; chaplain Elks Rehab. Hosp., Boise, 1986-89; supervisory chaplain ACPE, Boise, 1985-89. Editor: Crossroads, 1951-56, Idaho Messenger, 1951-56. Contbr. articles to Witness, Living Ch., Episc. Jour. of Pastoral Care, Christian Ministry. Mem. Assn. Clin. Pastoral Edn. (life), Pastoral Counsellors for Social Responsibility. Avocations: hiking; skiing; gardening; theater. Home: 3544 12th St SE Salem OR 97302

SPOMAR, JOHN PETER, JR., religion educator; b. Chgo., Jan. 7, 1945; s. John Peter and Dorothy Ida (Dubberka) S.; m. Lydia Marie Carroll, Aug. 20, 1966; children: Janet, John Jr., Eric. BS in Edn., Chgo. State U., 1965; MS in Acctg., Roosevelt U., Chgo., 1967; DBA in Bus., Pacific Western U., L.A., 1984; postgrad., Liberty U., Lynchburg, Va., 1989. Evangelist Secular Productive Mgmt. Coll., 1973—; tchr. Sun. sch. Faith Reformed Ch., South Holland, Ill., 1978-81, sch. supt., 1989—; pres. Norco Cleaners, Inc., Dolton, Ill., 1965—. Author coloring book: Fabric Care History, 1979; author newsletter Spiritual Fitness in Business, 1986-87. Pres. Laren Montessori Sch., South Holland, 1972-76; dir. Hospitality Mgmt. Progam, Roosevelt U., 1989—. Mem. S. Suburban Fabricare Assn. (pres. 1974-76), Ill. Fabricare Assn. (dir. 1974-76), Internat. Fabricare Assn., Fellowship of Cos. for Christ, Mennonite Econ. Devel. Assn. Home: 1003 E 173d St South Holland IL 60473 Office: Norco Cleaners Inc 1320 E Dolton Ave Dolton IL 60419 *Success in life depends on whether or not you are maturing in Christ.*

SPONG, JOHN SHELBY, bishop; b. Charlotte, N.C., June 16, 1931; s. John Shelby and Doolie Boyce (Griffith) S.; m. Joan Lydia Ketner, Sept. 5, 1952 (dec. 1988); children: Ellen Elizabeth, Mary Katharine, Jaquelin Ketner; m. Christine Mary Bridger, Jan. 1, 1990. A.B., U. N.C., 1952; M.Div., Va. Theol. Sem., 1955; D.D., St. Paul's Coll., 1976, Va. Theol. Sem., 1977. Ordained to ministry Episcopal Ch., 1955, bishop, 1976; rector St. Joseph's Ch., Durham, N.C., 1955-57, Calvary Ch., Tarboro, N.C., 1957-65, St. John's Ch., Lynchburg, Va., 1965-69, St. Paul's Ch., Richmond, Va., 1969-76; bishop Diocese of Newark, 1976—; mem. governing body Nat. Episc. Ch., 1973-76. Author: Honest Prayer, 1973, This Hebrew Lord, 1974, Dialogue—In Search of Jewish-Christian Understanding, 1975, Christpower, 1976, The Living Commandments, 1977, The Easter Moment, 1980, Into the Whirlwind: The Future of the Church, 1983, Beyond Moralism, 1986, Survival and Consciousness, 1987, Living in Sin? A Bishop Rethinks Human Sexuality, 1988, Rescuing the Bible from Fundamentalism—A Bishop Rethinks the Meaning of Scripture, 1991, Born of a Woman, 1992. Mem. Richmond Human Relations Commn. Club: Rotary. Home: 43 Ogden Pl Morristown NJ 07960 Office: 24 Rector St Newark NJ 07102

SPOOLSTRA, LINDA CAROL, minister, educator, religious organization administrator; b. Hillsdale, Mich., July 11, 1947; d. Jay Carroll and Carol Elsa (Linstrom) Lehmann; m. Gerald William Spoolstra, Feb. 17, 1973. BA, Bethel Coll., 1969; MA, Fla. State U., 1970; M of Div., McCormick Theol. Sem., Chgo., 1978; DD (hon.), Cen Bapt. Theol. Sem., Kansas City, Kans., 1988. Ordained Am. Bapt. Clergywoman. Tchr. Dade County Pub. Schs., Miami, Fla., 1970-71; ins. claims adjustor Safeco Ins. Co., Chgo., 1971-72; dir. of community outreach and edn. N. Shore Bapt. Ch., Chgo., 1972-78, assoc. pastor, 1978; pastor First Bapt. Ch., Swansea, Mass., 1978-84; exec. dir. commn. on the ministry Am. Bapt. Chs. U.S.A., Valley Forge, Pa., 1984-90; exec. minister Am. Bapt. Chs. Mass., Dedham, 1990—; mem. Nat. Coun. of Chs. Profl. Ch. Leadership, N.Y.C., 1984—; commn. on pastoral leadership Bapt. World Alliance, McClean, Va., 1986—; mem. gen. bd. Nat. Coun. Chs. of Christ, 1990—. Avocations: sailing, tennis, travel, classical music. Office: Am Bapt Chs Mass 20 Milton St Dedham MA 02026

SPOONER, BERNARD MYRICK, religious organization admininistrator; b. Pine Hill, Ala., Oct. 15, 1934; s. Earl William and Lomie (Vick) S.; m. Patricia Ann Spooner, June 8, 1957; children: Myra Joan Spooner Bush, Jane Ann Spooner Carlisle. BS, Miss. Coll., 1957; MA, Southwestern Bapt. Tehol. Sem., 1962, EdD, 1975. Min. edn. First Bapt. Ch., Ruston, La., 1962-65, Immanual Bapt. Ch., Tulsa, 1965-66; min. edn. and adminstrn. Travis Ave. Bapt. Ch., Ft. Worth, 1966-77; prof. adminstrn. New Orleans Bapt. Theol. Sem., 1977-79; dir. Sunday sch. discipleship div. Bapt. Gen. Conv. Tex., Dallas, 1979—; bd. dirs. The Sweet Shop, USA, Inc., Ft. Worth; ptnr. Center St. Properties, Ft. Worth, Tex., 1977—. Co-author: You Can Reach People Now, 1971, The People Challenge, 1985; contbr. articles to various publs. cons. ch. growth and adminstrn., 1975—. Capt. USMCR, 1957-60. Mem. So. Bapt. Religious Educators Assn. (v.p. 1975-76, chmn. bd. dirs. 1990—), Metro Bapt. Religious Educators Assn. (chmn. 1974), Tarrant Bapt. Religious Educators Assn. (pres. 1970), Southwestern Bapt. Religious Edn. Assn. (pres. 1976). Avocations: investing, gardening, traveling, reading. Home: 900 Glen Vista Irving TX 75061 Office: Bapt Gen Conv Tex 333 N Washington Dallas TX 75246-1798

SPRADLEY, HERSHALL WESLEY, II, religion educator, pastor; b. Ft. Worth, Sept. 14, 1945; s. Hershall Wesley and Dollie Blanche (Boren) S.; m. Donnie Ward McReynolds, Aug. 26, 1967; children: Leslie Robin, Jonathan Wesley, Daniel Scott. BA, U. Tex., Arlington, 1967; ThM, Dallas Sem., 1972. Youth pastor Blue Ridge Bible Ch., Kansas City, Mo., 1972-74; pastor Grace Bible Ch., Oklahoma City, 1974-78, Community Bible Ch., Austin, Tex., 1978-89; prof. Tex. Bible Coll., San Antonio, 1988—. Mem. Evang. Theol. Soc. Office: Tex Bible Coll 255 Savannah San Antonio TX 78213

SPRADLIN, BYRON LEE, minister; b. Richmond, Calif., Apr. 29, 1949; s. Richard L. and Meathel Spradlin; m. Pamela A. Spradlin, May 11, 1974; children: Sarah Ann, Nathan Lee. BA, U. Calif., Davis, 1971; M in Ch. Music, Western Conservative Bapt. Sem, 1977, MDiv, 1978. Youth minister 1st Bapt. Ch., Richmond, 1971-73; chmn. bd. Jews for Jesus, San Francisco, 1973—; founder, exec. dir. Artists in Christian Testimony, Cucamonga, Calif., 1976—; assoc. pastor Community Bapt. Ch., Alta Loma, Calif., 1981-86; founder, exec. dir. Ch. Planting Internat., Cucamonga, 1986—; founder, sr. pastor New Hope Community Ch., Cucamonga, 1986—; tour dir. Continental Singers, 1968-71; mem. staff music outreach ministries Western Conservative Bapt. Sem., Portland, Oreg., 1973-78, adj. faculty, 1978-80; mem. World Christian Curriculum Com., Devel. Third World Nations, 1982-84, Campus Crusade for Christ, U. Calif., Davis, 1968-71. Contbr. articles to profl. jours. Named to Athletic Hall of Fame, City of Sacramento, 1970, U. Calif., Davis, 1990. Mem. ASCAP, Nat. Acad. Recording Arts & Scis., Evang. Theol. Soc. Office: New Hope Community Ch 9521-A Business Ctr Dr Cucamonga CA 91730

SPRADLIN, ROGER LEE, minister; b. Elk City, Okla., Feb. 7, 1955; s. Donald Laverne and Elsie May (Bratcher) S.; m. Virginia Inez East, Aug. 25, 1976; children: Matthew, Andrew, Faith, Charity (dec.). BA, Okla. Bapt. U., 1977; MABS summa cum laude, Criswell Coll., 1983, DD, 1988. Ordained to ministry Bapt. Ch., 1978. Youth min. Canadian Heights Bapt. Ch., Yukon, Okla., 1974-77; student union dir. So. Bapt. Ch. of Calif., 1977; pastor Panama Bapt. Ch., Bakersfield, Calif., 1978-80, Abbott (Tex.) Bapt. Ch., 1981-83, Valley Bapt. Ch., Bakersfield, 1983—; com. on cons. So. Bapt. Conf., 1984, com. on order of bus. So. Bapt. Ch. of Calif., 1991—. Office: Valley Bapt Ch 800 Airport Dr Bakersfield CA 93308

SPRADLING, DONALD RAY, minister; b. Honubia, Okla., Aug. 7, 1943; s. Elbert Darrell and Edith (Walker) S.; m. Kay Carol Batchelor, Oct. 25, 1963; children: Gregory Jon, Stephanie Dawn. AA, Ea. Okla. State Coll., 1962; BS, East Cen. U., 1966, MA, 1967; postgrad., Berean Bible Sch., Springfield, Mo., 1967—. Ordained to ministry Assemblies of God. Pastor Assemblies of God, Elmore City, Okla., 1967-68; sr. pastor 1st Assembly of God, Antler's, Okla., 1968-70, Cushing, Okla., 1970-72; sr. pastor Christian Life Ctr., Ashland, Oreg., 1972074, Calvary Temple, Concord, Calif., 1974-86, Christian Life Ch., Long Beach, Calif., 1986-90; mem. Okla. Men's Ministry bd., 1970-72, Oreg. Christian Edn. bd., 1972-74, Calif. Fin. bd., 1977-86, So. Calif. Evangelism Com., 1989-90; councilman So. Calif. Dist. Coun. Assemblies of God. Producer TV program: Thy Kingdom Come (10 awards of excellence, 5 Angel award Angel Acad., Beverly Hills, Ca. 1987, 88, 89); contbr. articles to profl. jours. and mags. Councilman Light for the Lost (Pastor award 1986, 87, 88, 89). Mem. Light for the Lost (councilman, Pastor award 1986-89). Republican. Home: 16547 Tropez Ln Huntington Harbour CA 92649 Office: Christian Life Ch 3400 Pacific Ave Long Beach CA 90807

SPRAGUE, ASA WILLIAM, minister; b. Schuyler Lake, N.Y., June 10, 1935; s. Asa Wilson and Vivian (Fay) S.; m. Beverly K. Closson, Oct. 8, 1977. BS, U. State N.Y., Albany, 1981; BTh., McGill U., 1984; MDiv., United Theol. Sem., 1985. Ordained to ministry United Meth. Ch. as elder, 1985. Pastor The United Meth. Christian Community of Mooers, N.Y., 1979-83, The United Meth. Ch., Broadalbin, N.Y., 1983-85, Trinity United Meth. Ch., Montpelier, Vt., 1985-91; pres. BACK-UP Religious Edn. Corp., Montpelier, 1986-91; pastor Plantation (Fla.) United Meth. Ch., 1991—; bd. dirs. Cen. Vt. Hosp., Montpelier, Vt. Ethics Network, Waterbury; sec. trustees Vt. Recovering Profls., Montpelier, 1989—; ethics com. Cen. Vt. Hosp., Montpelier, 1988; mem. planning and rsch. com. Fla. Ann. Conf. United Meth. Ch., 1991. Composer various music, media programs; contbr. articles to profl. jours. Mem. Montpelier Clergy Assn. (treas. 1985—), Troy Annual Conf. (chmn. 1988-90), World Future Soc. (profl. mem.). Home: 4851 NW 1st St Plantation FL 33317 Office: Plantation United Meth Ch 1001 NW 70th Ave Plantation FL 33313

SPRAGUE, STUART RUSSELL, minister, educator; b. Dallas, Mar. 18, 1947; s. Russell Earl and Julia Margareit (Boswell) S.; m. Sarah Lee Cellar, Aug. 14, 1971; 1 child, Drew Stuart. BS, Duke U., 1969; MDiv, So. Bapt. Theol. Sem., Louisville, 1972, PhD, 1975. Ordained to ministry So. Bapt. Conv., 1977. Mem. faculty dept. religion Anderson (S.C.) Coll., 1977—; adj. instr. family medicine Med. U. S.C., Anderson Family Practice Ctr., 1983-90, adj. asst. prof., 1990—; deacon, chmn. Deacons Blvd. Bapt. Ch., Anderson, 1979-86. Trustee Montessori Sch., Anderson, 1982-84. Mem. Nat. Assn. Bapt. Profs. Religion (v.p. S.E. region 1986, pres. 1987), Am. Acad. Religion, Am. Philos. Assn., S.C. Acad. Religion (sec. 1984, v.p. 1985, pres. 1986), Soc. Health and Human Values. Home: 202 Holly Creek Dr Anderson SC 29621-2011 Office: Anderson Coll 316 Boulevard Anderson SC 29621

SPRAKER, CHARLES EDWARD, hospital administrator, minister, educator; b. Tazewell, Va., June 5, 1933; s. Stephen Marco and Cynthia Polly (Cook) S.; m. Martha Cecelia Harris, May 26, 1956; 1 child, Cynthia Marceil. BA, Roanoke Coll., 1955; BD, Luth. Theol. So. Sem., 1958, MDiv, 1972; MEd, U. Va., 1971. Ordained to ministry Luth. Ch. in Am., 1958. Pastor Our Savior Luth. Ch., Norge, Va., 1958-65, Faith Luth Ch., Staunton, Va., 1965-68; counselor, adminstr. Commonwealth of Va., Staunton, 1968—; dir. Shenandoah Geriatric Treatment Ctr., Staunton, 1981-89; adminstr. Western State Hosp., Staunton, 1989—; clin. asst. prof. behavioral medicine and psychiatry dept. medicine U. Va., Staunton, 1985—. Home: 107 Oxford Circle Staunton VA 24401 *The challenge for twenty-first century for our religious institutions involves committment to the main stream of society. Gods transformation of our world will occur in our culture; its communities, work places and homes. Our calling is to these cultural settings not the hierarchy or structure of our religious institutions. Religious leaders must go out to the poeple and work in their environment.*

SPRING, PAUL E., bishop. Bishop Northwestern Pa. Evang. Luth. Ch. in Am., Oil City. Office: Evang Luth Ch in Am 308 Seneca St Oil City PA 16301*

SPRINGER, KARL GOERGE, religious organization administrator; b. N.Y.C., Oct. 20, 1949; s. Gustave and Florence (Hacker) S.; m. Jane Anne Condon, June 10, 1978 (div. 1981). BA, Brandeis U., 1971; DD, Naropa Inst., 1977. Ordained to ministry, Vajradhatu Buddhist Assn., 1977. Dir. Karme Choling Retreat Str., Barnet, Vt., 1971-75; dir., chief exec. officer Naropa Inst., Boulder, Colo., 1975-77; v.p. Vajradhatu Internat., Boulder, 1977—; exec. dir. U.S. Com. UN Lumbini Project, Boulder, 1983—; founder, co-chmn. Am. Buddhist Congress, L.A., 1986—; bd. dirs. Karma Triyana Dharmachakra, Woodstock, N.Y., San Luis Valley Tibetan Project, Crestone, Colo., World Resources Com., Bangkok; regional dir. World Fellowship Buddhists, Bangkok. Compiler, dir. Asian Art Exhbn.. MIT, 1974; contbr. articles to mags. Del. UN Conf. on Disarmament and Devel., N.Y.C., 1987. Mem. UN Assn., UN Assn. in India, Acad. Polit. Sci. Democrat. Avocations: skiing, swimming, walking, travel, Asian art. Home: 431 S Padre Juan Ave Ojai CA 93023 Office: 323 E Matiuja Ste 112 Ojai CA 93023 *We live in a world in need of revolutionary change if we are to address the deep suffering of human beings. Such change can only take place in ourselves. There begins a revolution.*

SPRINGSTED, ERIC OSMON, minister, philosophy and religion educator; b. St. Paul, May 27, 1951; s. Osmon Rutherford and Elaine B. (Kirchhoff) S.; m. Brenda Margaret Lockhart, June 11, 1976; children: Simone Anne, Mary Leidy, Elspeth Elaine. BA, St. John's Coll., Santa Fe, N.Mex., 1973; MDiv, Princeton Theol. Sem., 1976, PhD, 1980. Ordained to ministry Presbyn. Ch., 1981. Supply pastor Calvary United Presbyn. Ch., Jersey City, 1976-77; interim pastor The Congregational Ch., Jacksonville, Ill., 1983-84, 88-89; chaplain, assoc. prof. philosophy and religion Ill. Coll., Jacksonville, 1981—; mem. com. on higher edn. Synod of Lincoln Trails, Indpls., 1982-88; del. Assn. Presbyn. Colls. and Univs., 1983-87. Author: Who Will Make Us Wise? How the Churches Are Failing Higher Education, 1988, Simone Weil and the Suffering of Love, 1986, Christus Mediator, 1983; contbr. articles to profl. jours. Pres. Friends of the Libr., Jacksonville, 1990-91; steering com. Clergy and Laymen Concerned About Vietnam, Santa Fe, 1971-73. Mem. Am. Weil Soc. (pres. 1981—), Ctr. Theol. Inquiry, Am. Acad. Religion, Am. Philos. Assn., Presbyn. Coll. Chaplains Assn. Democrat. Office: Ill Coll 1101 W College Jacksonville IL 62650

SPRINKLE, STEPHEN VENABLE, minister, educator; b. Elkin, N.C., Oct. 22, 1951; s. Thedford Guy and Hazel Annie (Martin) S. BA summa cum laude, Atlantic Christian Coll., 1974; MDiv, Yale U., 1977; postgrad., Duke U., 1984—. Ordained to ministry Christian Ch. (Disciples of Christ), 1977. Assoc. min. Thomas Chapel Ch. of Christ, New Haven, 1974-77; pastor Wendell (N.C.) Christian Ch., 1977-79; sr. min. 1st Christian Ch., Greensboro, N.C., 1979-83; assoc. prof. Atlantic Christian Coll. Wilson, Greensboro, N.C., 1983-90; hon. assoc. min. St. James Christian Ch., Fountain, N.C., 1986-90; sr. min. Pleasant Union Christian Ch., Newton Grove, N.C., 1990—; adj. prof. ch. polity Duke U. Div. Sch., Durham, N.C., 1983—; mem. gen. bd. Christian Ch. (Disciples of Christ), Indpls., 1985-91, mem. administrv. com., 1987-91, dir. div. homeland ministries, 1987—. Contbr. articles to religious jours., chpts. to book. County organizer Jimmy Carter for Pres., Surry County, N.C., 1976; mem. N.C. Com. of 100-Mondale for Pres., 1984. Recipient Best Faculty award Atlantic Christian Coll., 1986, Staff award, 1987. Mem. AAUP. Democrat. Avocations: saltwater fishing, Civil War buff, rearing English bulldogs. Home: Mt Olive Dr Newton Grove NC 28366 Office: Pleasant Union Christian Ch PO Box 1 Newton Grove NC 28366 *The summation of life is the final accounting of one's loyalties: the vows we make and keep, the friendships bonded, the causes and religion we espouse. To whom we belong makes all the difference.*

SPROTT, RODNEY MCDOWELL, religious organization administrator; b. Charlotte, N.C., July 7, 1953; s. James McDowell and Ruth (Hill) S. BA, Clemson U., 1975; JD, U. S.C., 1978. Spl. projects adminstr. Trinity United Meth. Ch., Sumter, S.C., 1986-88; ch. adminstr. Hollywood (Calif.) United Meth. Ch., 1988-90, Westwood United Meth. Ch., L.A., 1990—; treas. Wesley Found., UCLA, 1990—. Mem. Nat. Assn. Ch. Bus. Adminstrn., So. Calif. chpt. Nat. Assn. Ch. Bus. Adminstrn. Home: 2250 N Beachwood Dr # 105 Hollywood CA 90068 Office: Westwood United Meth Ch 10497 Wilshire Blvd Los Angeles CA 90024

SPRUILL, HOWARD VERNON, minister, college official; b. South Norfolk, Va., Dec. 27, 1919; s. Veron B. and Mabel E. (Kirby) S.; m. Daisy Lee Singleton, Dec. 11, 1943; 1 child, Ruth Elaine. BS, Valley Forge Christian Coll., 1977; MDiv, Luther Rice Sem., 1978, DMin, 1980. Ordained to ministry Assemblies of God, 1953. Auditor, U.S. Navy, Little Creek, Va., 1945-50; pastor Elk Garden, W.Va., 1950-52, Emporia, Va., 1952-57, Manassas, Va., 1957-69, dist. sec., treas., 1968-74; pastor, Silver Spring, Md., 1974-79; dist. supt. Potomac Dist. Council, Assemblies of God Ch., 1979—; pres. Valley Forge Christian Coll., 1982; chmn. bd. regents, 1968—; pres. Prince William County Ministerial Assn., 1966-68. Served with U.S. Army, 1937-45. Author: Deacon Servant to God and Man, 1980. Home: 5945 Windwood Dr Lakeland FL 33813

SPRUNGER, KEITH L., history educator; b. Berne, Ind., Mar. 16, 1935; s. Arley and Lillian (Mettler) S.; m. Aldine Mary Slagell, June 13, 1959; children: David, Mary, Philip. BA, Wheaton Coll., 1957; MA, U. Ill., 1958, PhD, 1963. Tchr. Berne (Ind.) High Sch., 1958-60; history prof. Bethel Coll., N. Newton, Kans., 1963—. Author: Dutch Puritanism, 1982, The Learned Doctor William Ames, 1972, Voices Against War, 1973, Auction Catalogue of The Library of William Ames, 1988. Recipient Harbison award for gifted teaching Danforth Found., 1972; Am. Coun. Learned Soc. fellow, 1976, Huntington Libr. fellow, 1990; grantee Am. Philos. Soc., 1983, The

Netherlands Orgn. for Advancement of Pure Rsch., 1983. Mem. AAUP, Oral History Assn., Am. Hist. Assn., Am. Soc. Ch. History (coun. 1974-76), Conf. on Faith and History. Mennonite. Avocation: book collecting. Home: 2412 College Ave N Newton KS 67117 Office: Bethel Coll 300 N 27th St E Newton KS 67117

SPRUNGER, MEREDITH JUSTIN, editor, minister; b. Woodburn, Ind., Apr. 16, 1915; s. Alvin A. and Sylvia (Lochner) S.; m. Irene L. Scherry, June 30, 1940; children: Ruth Irene, Grace Ellen. BA, Lakeland Coll., 1937; BD, United Theol. Sem., 1940; ThM, Princeton Theol. Sem., 1941; PhD, Purdue U., 1947. Ordained to ministry United Ch. of Christ, 1941. Minister Trinity United Ch. of Christ, Mulberry, Ind., 1941-50, Grace United Ch. of Christ, Culver, Ind., 1952-59; tchr. Elmhurst (Ill.) Coll., 1950-51; tchr., adminstr. Ind. Inst. Tech., Ft. Wayne, Ind., 1959-77; psychol. cons. Ft. Wayne, 1965-77; exec. dir. Christian Fellowship of Students of Urantia Book, 1979—; editor Spiritual Fellowship Jour., 1990—; bd. dirs. Greater Ft. Wayne Campus Ministry, 1985—; mem. Ind.-Ky. Conf. United Ch. of Christ. Author: Spiritual Psychology, 1990, The Origin of the Urantia Book, 1979. Pres. Ft. Wayne Urantia Soc., 1970-74, Urantia Brotherhood, Chgo., 1976-79. Purdue rsch. grantee, 1944; recipient Leadership Fellowship award Ft. Wayne YMCA, 1962. Mem. Am. Acad. Religion, Am. Philos. Assn., Soc. Sci. Study of Religion, Religious Futurists' Network, Ind. Psychol. Assn. Home: 4109 Plaza Dr Fort Wayne IN 46806 *The greatest challenge to contemporary humanity is to achieve better communication with the indwelling Spirit of God and actualize this guidance in living. Our society desperately needs enlarged and solid spiritual foundations with the visionary potential to give stability and direction to the new era which is struggling to be born.*

SPRUNGER, VIRGIL LEWIS, retired clergyman; b. Adams County, Ind., Dec. 29, 1921; s. Leo N. and Mary (Wanner) S.; m. Mary Anna Snuggs, June 10, 1944; 1 child, Linda Jeanne. BA, Olivet Nazarene U., 1944, ThB, 1945; postgrad., Garrett Theol. Sem., 1956-59, Northwestern U., 1956-59. Ordained to ministry, Ch. of Nazarene, 1944. Pastor Ch. of Nazarene, various cities, Ohio, 1944-56, Brookfield, Ill., 1956-58; chaplain Ill. Dept. Corrections, 1959-85; ret., 1985. Clk., Village of Elkhart, Ill., 1985—. Fellow Coll. of Chaplains; mem. Am. Correctional Assn., Ill. State Chaplains Assn. (pres. 1964-68), Nat. Chaplains Assn. for Youth (pres. 1967-68), Optimists. Avocations: woodworking, golf, genealogy. Home: 4 Chapel Rd Elkhart IL 62634

SPYKMAN, GORDON JOHN, religion educator; b. Holland, Mich., Mar. 25, 1926; s. Albert and Dena (Klompmaker) S.; m. Eleanor Bernice Hendriksen, July 18, 1952; children: Steven, Erik, Donald, Gary, EveLynn. AB, Calvin Coll., 1949; Thm, Calvin Theol. Sem., 1952; ThD, Free U. Amsterdam, The Netherlands, 1955. Ordained to ministry Christian Ref. Ch., 1955. Min. Christian Ref. Ch., Bendheim, Ont., Can., 1955-59; prof. religion and theology Calvin Coll., Grand Rapids, Mich., 1959—; guest lectr. Inst. for Christian Studies, Toronto, Ont., 1976, curator, 1980-86; guest lectr. Dordt Coll., Sioux City, Iowa, 1982, Potchefstrom (Republic of South Africa) U., 1983. Author: Council of Trent, 1955, Human Rights, 1987; co-author: Society, State, and Schools, 1980, Let My People Live, 1989. Bd. dirs. Assn. for Pub. Justice, Washington, 1972-77. Office: Calvin Coll Dept Religion and Theology Grand Rapids MI 49506

SQUIRE, ANNE MARGUERITE, religious leader; b. Amherstburg, Ont., Can., Oct. 17, 1920; d. Alexander Samuel and Coral Marguerite Park; m. William Robert Squire, June 24, 1943; children: Frances, Laura, Margaret. BA, Carleton U., Ottawa, 1972, BA with honors, 1974, MA, 1975; LLD (hon.), Carleton U., 1988; DD (hon.), United Theol. Coll., 1979, Queen's U., 1985. Cert. tchr., Ont. Adj. prof. Carleton U., 1975-82; sec. div. ministry personnel and edn. United Ch. Can., Toronto, 1982-85, moderator, 1986-88. Author curriculum materials, 1959—; contbr. articles to profl. jours. Mem. bd. mgmt. St. Andrew's Coll., Saskatoon, Sask., 1982, Queens Theol. Coll., Kingston, Ont., 1980-82. Recipient Senate medal Carleton U., 1972. Mem. Can. Research Inst. for Advancement Women, Delta Kappa Gamma (pres. 1978-79). Office: 731 Weston Dr, Ottawa, ON Canada K1G 1W1

SRAON, HARBANS SINGH, temple executive, geneticist; b. Ludhiana, Punjab, India, Jan. 15, 1941; came to U.S., 1970; s. S. Kehar Singh and Dhan K. Sraon; m. Surinder Kaur Thind, Apr. 3, 1966; children: Dilber S., Maninder K. BS, Punjab Agrl. U., Ludhiana, 1963, MS, 1965; PhD, S.D. State U., 1974; L.I. in Biology, Inst. Biology, London, 1969. Pres. MIC, Irvine, Calif., 1989—. Co-editor: Advanced Studies of Sikhism, 1989 (Community Excellence award); contbr. papers to profl. publs. Pres. Midwest Sikh Assn., Kansas City, Kans., 1985-86, Sikh Temple, Buena Park, Calif., 1988—; coord. Sikh Community of N.Am., Irvine, 1989; founder Sikh Community Found., Irvine, 1987; mem. S.O.S. Fellow Interfaith Coun. (civic svc. award 1981); mem. Am. Acad. Religion, Kiwanis (pres. 1985-86). Home: PO Box 16635 Irvine CA 92713 Office: Sikh Community Found 18021 Skypark Circle J Irvine CA 92714

SROUFE, CLINTON SCOTT, music minister; b. Bartlesville, Okla., Mar. 22, 1964; s. Clinton Wayne and Sally Ann (Kinsch) S.; m. Lorraine Jessie, Nov. 18, 1989. B Mus Edn, Ouachita Bapt U, Arkadelphia, 1987; postgrad., S.W. Bapt. Theol. Sem., Shawnee, Okla., 1988. Lic. to ministry So. Bapt. Conv., 1984. Music minister Twin Oaks Bapt. Ch., Wagoner, Okla., 1984; music/youth minister Lee Chapel Bapt. Ch., Pearcy, Ark., 1985, SouthSide Bapt. Ch., Damascus, Ark., 1985-88; music and youth minister Victory Park Bapt. Ch., McAlester, Okla., 1989—; associational music min. Pitts. Bapt. Assn., 1990—. Mem. Phi Mu Alpha. Home: 635 E Harrison Ave McAlester OK 74501 Office: Victory Park Bapt Ch 601 E Harrison Ave McAlester OK 74501 *Our youth today are so impressionable. How can we impress upon them the proper ideals of self and others when so much around us deals only with materialism and pursuit of wealth? We must learn to instill in ourselves and others the ideals of true worship.*

STABE, DONALD WAYNE, minister, composer, educator; b. Kansas City, Mo., Aug. 16, 1957; s. Russell Raymond and Ruth Mae (Jones) S.; m. Sheryl Lynn Weeks, June 23, 1979; 1 child, Marissa Donnell. Lic., Mt. Vernon Bible Coll.; student, U. Mo., Kansas City, Simpson Coll., Lamar U. Ordained to ministry Assemblies of God. Composer musical works include Ruth, 1985, Dear Dedushka, 1990, youth dramas Spots, 1990, S.S. Magnolias, 1990. Bd. dirs. S.E. Tex. Youth Symphony, Beaumont, 1980-81; mus. dir., del. Internat. Olympics Outreach Com., L.A., 1984; chmn. Mayor's Com. Citywide Thanksgiving and Patriotic Svcs., Beaumont, 1988, 89, 90, Mayor's Com. Sesquicentenial, 1987; asst. dir. music spls. Iowa PBS, Des. Moines, 1981, Christ is the Answer broadcast, N.Y.C., 1977-79. Office: Cathedral in the Pines 2350 Eastex Frwy Beaumont TX 77703

STACK, GEORGE SAMUEL, minister; b. Lexington, Ky., Dec. 19, 1961; s. George Alfred and Joyce Ann (Roland) S.; m. Sue Marie Foster, June 25, 1983; children: Steven Paul, Rebecca. B Music Edn., Georgetown (Ky.) Coll., 1985; M Ch. Music, So. Bapt. Theol. Sem., 1989. Ordained to ministry So. Bapt. Conv., 1988; cert. elem. and secondary music tchr., Ky. Pianist Bethel Bapt. Ch., Frankfort, Ky., 1982-83, min. music, 1983-85; min. music Pigeon Fork Bapt. Ch., Waddy, Ky., 1985-89; tchr. St. Lawrence Sch., Louisville, 1990; min. music, activities 1st Bapt. Ch., Folkston, Ga., 1990—; del. Ga. Bapt. Conv., 1990, 91, So. Bapt. Conv., 1991. Democrat. Home: 511 W Main St Folkston GA 31537 Office: 1st Bapt Ch 401 W Third St Folkston GA 31537 *Greatness in life can only be measured by the lasting good impression one makes on future generations.*

STACK, JOHN CHARLES, minister; b. St. Louis, May 21, 1962; s. Belvin Neal and Hildred Ione (Saxon) S.; m. Juliana Elizabeth Plummer, Apr. 25, 1987; 1 child, Brianna Joy. BA, Calvary Bible Coll., 1984; MA, Covenant Sem., 1990. Ordained to ministry, 1988. Youth pastor West Overland (Mo.) Bible Ch., 1984-87; assoc. pastor Hazelwood (Mo.) Bapt. Ch., 1987—; missionary, tchr. Internat. Missions, Kenya, East Africa, 1984-85. Office: Hazelwood Bapt Ch 6161 Howdershell Rd Hazelwood MO 63042

STACKHOUSE, MAX LYNN, Christian ethics educator; b. Ft. Wayne, Ind., July 29, 1935; s. C. Dale and Naomi Elizabeth (Graham) S.; m. N. Jean Hostetler, Aug. 19, 1959; children: Dale Emil, David Graham, Sara Elizabeth. BA, De Pauw U., 1957; cert., Nijehrode Sch., Breukelen, The Netherlands, 1958; BD, MDiv, Harvard U., 1961, PhD, 1965. Ordained to ministry United Ch. of Christ. Lectr. Harvard Divinity Sch., Cambridge, Mass., 1964-66; asst. prof. Andover-Newton (Mass.) Theol. Sch., 1966-69, assoc. prof., 1969-73, prof., 1973-78, Herbert Gezork prof., 1978—; vis. prof. United Theol. Coll., Bangalore, India, 1973, 76, 82, 87, Pacific Theol. Coll., Suva, Fiji, 1982, Das Sprackenkonvikt, East Berlin, 1983; pres. joint doctoral program Andover-Newton Theol. Sch., 1988-89, also chmn. Rels. and Soc. Dept., 1975—. Author: Creeds Society of Human Rights, 1984, Public Theology and Political Economy, 1987, Apologia, 1988 (Best Booklist Internat. Bull. Missiology 1988); author, editor 5 books; mem. ediorial bd. Jour. Religious Ethics, First Things, Christian Century; contbr. articles to religious jours. Mem. investigation team Am. Com. for Human Rights, Philippines, 1984; pres. James Luther Adams Found., 1987—; exec. sec. Am. Com. for Higher Edn. in India, 1986-91. Rsch. grantee Ctr. for Urban Studies, Harvard U., 1965-66, Assn. Theol. Schs., 1986-87, video grantee Lilly Endowment, Indpls., 1989, 91; recipient Outstanding Alumnus award DePauw U., 1988. Fellow Soc. for Sci. Study of Religion (bd. dirs. 1980-84), Soc. for Values in Higher Edn.; mem. NAACP, Amnesty Internat., Civil Liberties Union Mass., Soc. Christian Ethics (past pres., past exec. sec.), Stockbridge Club. Democrat. Office: Andover-Newton Theol Sch Herrick Rd Newton MA 02159

STACKHOUSE, REGINALD, priest, college professor; b. Toronto, Ont., Can., Apr. 30, 1925; s. Edward Ingram and Emma (McNeill) S.; m. Margaret Eleanor Allman, June 2, 1951; children: Mary, Elizabeth, Ruth, John. BA, U. Toronto, 1946, MA, 1951; LTh, Wycliffe Coll., Toronto, 1953, BD, 1954; DD (hon.), Wycliffe Coll.; PhD, Yale U., 1962; DD (hon.), Huron Coll., 1982. Ordained to ministry Anglican Ch. as deacon, 1949, as priest, 1950. Rector St. Matthew's Ch., Islington, Ont., 1946-56, St. John's Ch., Toronto, 1956-60; prof. theology Wycliffe Coll., Toronto, 1962—, prin., 1975-85; M.P. Parliament of Can., Ottawa, Ont., 1972-74, 84-88; trustee Wycliffe Coll.; hon. Canon St. James Cathedral, Toronto. Author: Christianity and Politics, 1964, The God Nobody Knows, 1985, How Can I Believe When I Live In A World Like This, 1990. Can. rep. to UN Gen. Assembly, 1986; mem. Can. Human Rights Commn., 1990—. Office: Wycliffe Coll, 5 Hoskin Ave, Toronto, ON Canada M5S 1H7

STACY, JOHN WILLIAM, evangelist; b. Columbus, Ohio, Feb. 5, 1942; s. John Troy and Eleanor Catherine (Smith) S.; m. Hilda Naomi Stacy, Aug. 6, 1965; 1 child, John Troy II. BA, Okla. Christian Coll., 1966; MA, Ala. Christian Coll., 1981; D Ministry, Internat. Bible Inst. & Sem., Orlando, Fla., 1982; LittD (hon.), Internat. Bible Inst. & Sem., 1981. Ordained to ministry Ch. of Christ, 1962. Minister Ch. of Christ, various locations, 1967—, Newbern, Tenn., 1984—; itinerant missionary, Ch. of Christ, Ghana, West Africa, India, Guyana, S.Am. and Caribbean, 1977-89; pres. adv. com. Freed-Hardeman Coll., Henderson, Tenn., 1977-78. Author religious books, sermons, evangelism works. Mem. Republican Nat. Com., 1987. With USN, 1959-63. Home: Rte 2 Box 53 Newbern TN 38059 Office: Glendale Ch of Christ Rte 2 Box 53 Newbern TN 38059

STADELMANN, RICHARD WILLIAM, clergyman, educator; b. Lynn, Mass., Dec. 16, 1932; s. William Louis and Olga Ann (Halbich) S.; BA, Earlham Coll., 1954; MDiv, Yale, 1958; postgrad. Tulane, 1960-65; m. Bonnie Sue Shelton, June 16, 1956 (div. Dec. 1972); children: Marcus Richard, Lowell Shelton, Mary Idell, Kristine Marie; m. 2d, Patricia Annette Perry, June 12, 1976; children: Olga Gertrude, Greta Katryn; stepchildren: Aimee Elizabeth, Lisa Annette. Ordained minister Christian Ch., 1954; minister Bethel Christian Ch., Fountain City, Ind., 1952-54, Perry (Ohio) Christian Ch., 1958-60; instr. Tulane, 1962-63, La. State U., New Orleans, 1963-67; asst. prof. philosophy Tex. A & M U., College Station, 1967—; minister Brenham (Tex.) Christian Ch., 1968-76, Smithville (Tex.) Christian Ch., 1978-80. County chmn. Burleson County Republican party, 1973-74, county vice-chmn. Brazos County, 1974-84. Served with USNR, 1958. Lindemuth scholar, 1950-54; Elk scholar, 1950-54; Am. Legion scholar, 1950-54; Yale U. scholar, 1957-58; Tulane scholar, 1960-65; recipient Downes award, 1958. Mem. AAUP (pres. 1971-72), Am. Philos. Assn., Metaphys. Soc. Am., Soc. Process Studies, Southwestern Philos. Soc., Am. Forensic Assn., Assocs. for Religion and Intellectual Life, Soc. Christian Philosophers, Tau Kappa Alpha. Home: Rte 5 Box 57 Brenham TX 77833 Office: Tex A&M Univ College Dept Philosophy Station TX 77843

STAFFORD, BERNICE, religion educator; b. Webbers Falls, Okla., Mar. 11, 1925; d. Mack and Lorean (Washington) Martin; m. Leo C. Stafford (dec.); children: Fleetless, Nathan. Student, Draughon's Bus. Sch., Tulsa, Tulsa Bus. Coll., Tulsa Jr. Coll. Tchr. of children St. John Bapt. Ch., Tulsa, 1971—; tchr. Nat. Congress Christian Edn. U.S.A. Inc., Tulsa, 1987—. Recipient Cert. Appreciation Dist. Congress, Tulsa. Home: 1802 N Troost Tulsa OK 74106

STAFFORD, GILBERT WAYNE, religion educator; b. Portageville, Mo., Dec. 30, 1938; s. Dawsey Calvin and Orell Elvesta (Smith) S.; m. Darlene Dawn Covert, Dec. 30, 1962; children: Matthew, Heather, Anne, Joshua. AB, Anderson Coll., 1961; MDiv, Andover Newton Theol. Sch., 1964; ThD, Boston U., 1973. Ordained to ministry Ch. of God, 1965. Pastor Malden (Mass.) Ch. of God, 1962-66; dir. Christian edn. First Congregational Ch. of Hyde Park, Boston, 1968-69; pastor East Ashman Ch. of God, Midland, Mich., 1969-76; faculty Anderson (Ind.) U. Sch. Theology, 1976—, assoc. dean, 1980-89, dean of chapel, 1984-89; speaker Christian Brotherhood Hour-English, Anderson, 1986—; chair commn. on Christian unity, Ch. of God, Anderson, 1985-90; commr. working group on faith and order NCCC in USA, N.Y.C., 1984—; mem. task force on governance and polity Ch. of God, Anderson, 1987—. Author: The Life of Salvation, 1979, Beliefs that Guide Us, 1977, The People of God, 1977, The Person and Work of the Holy Spirit, 1977, The 7 Doctrinal Leaders of the Church of God, 1977, Living as Redeemed People, 1976; author: (with others) Educating for Service, 1984, A Contemporary Wesleyan Theology, 1983, An Inquiry into Soteriology, 1981. Recipient Bethany Heritage award Bethany Ch. of God, Detroit, 1982, Disting. Ministry award Anderson U., 1991. Mem. Wesleyan Theol. Soc., Am. Acad. Religion. Home: 2424 Albert St Anderson IN 46012 Office: Anderson U Sch of Theology Anderson IN 46012

STAFFORD, J. FRANCIS, archbishop; b. Balt., July 26, 1932; s. F. Emmett and Mary Dorothy S. Student, Loyola Coll., Balt., 1950-52; B.A., St. Mary's Sem., Balt., 1954; S.T.B., S.T.L., Gregorian U., Rome, 1958; M.S.W., Catholic U., 1964; postgrad., Rutgers U., 1963, U. Wis.-Madison, 1969, St. Mary's Sem. and Univ., Balt., 1973-75. Spiritual moderator Ladies of Charity Ch., Balt., 1966-76; spiritual moderator Soc. St. Vincent de Paul, Balt., 1965-76; urban vicar Archdiocese of Balt., 1966-76, monsignor, 1970, vicar gen., auxiliary bishop, 1976-83; bishop Diocese of Memphis, 1983-86; archbishop Archdiocese of Denver, 1986—; dir. Assn. Cath. Charities, Balt., 1966-76; archdiocesan liaison to Md. Cath. Conf., Balt, 1975-78; Oriental Orthodox/Roman Cath. consultation Nat. Cath. Conf. Bishops, 1977-85, com. on doctrine, 1978-82, chmn. ecumenical and interreligious affairs com., 1987-90; co-chmn. bilateral dialogue Roman Cath./World Meth. Council, 1977-86; co-chmn. U.S. Roman Cath.-Luth. Dialogue, 1986—; chmn. Bishops' com. marriage and family life U.S. Cath. Conf., 1978-84; mem. gen. Synod Bishops, Vatican City, 1980. Contbr. articles to profl. jours. Trustee Good Samaritan Hosp., Balt., 1973-77, Cath. U. Am., 1990—, Blue Cross of Md., Inc., 1973-76, Balt. Urban Coalition, 1970-75; trustee, chmn., St. Thomas Theol. Sem., 1987—; bd. dirs. Sch. Social Work and Planning, U. Md., 1973-76. Recipient Father Kelly Alumni award Loyola High Sch., 1978; Alumni Laureate, Loyola Coll., 1979. Mem. World Meth. Conf. Roman Cath. Dialogue (co-chmn. 1977-86), Oriental Orthodox Roman Cath. Consultation (co-chmn. 1977-85), Nat. Conf. Cath. Bishops, Luth. Roman Cath. Dialogue, Congregation for Doctrine of Faith. Office: Archdiocese of Denver 200 Josephine St Denver CO 80206

STAFFORD, KENNETH VICTOR, SR., minister; b. Claremont, N.H., Dec. 30, 1926; s. Victor Ernest and Marion (Dodge) S.; m. Doreen Beverly Mossey, Apr. 12, 1947; children: Beverlee, Kenneth Jr., Marilee, Mark. Diploma in airframe/powerplant, Spartan Sch. Aeronautics, Tulsa, 1948, diploma in airport mgmt., 1949; B in Counseling, Valley Christian U., Fresno, Calif., 1981; M in Counseling, Valley Christian U., 1983. Ordained to ministry Christian Ch., 1978; cert. counselor, 1990. Pres. Jacob's Well, Tulsa, 1974-78; dir. spiritual life Christian Broadcasting Network, Virginia Beach, Va., 1978, assoc. dir. counseling, 1978-83, dir. counseling, 1984, counselor tng. dir., 1985-87; founder, pres. Bearers of Light Ministries, Chesapeake, Va., 1987—; elder Greenbrier Christian Fellowship, Chesapeake, 1990—. Author: Basic 8, 1982, Handbook for Helping Others, 1986. Staff sgt. U.S. Army, 1945-46, PTO; staff sgt. USAF, 1950-51. Recipient First Line Mgmt. award Am. Mgmt. Assn., 1981, Supervising People award Batten, 1984. Office: Bearers of Light Ministries PO Box 2672 Chesapeake VA 23327 *I have found that the Bible, the written word of God, contains the keys to victorious living.*

STAGAMAN, DAVID JOHN, priest, theology educator; b. Cin., July 29, 1935; s. Harry Terstage and Elinora (Willenbrink) S. A.B., Loyola U., Chgo., 1958; Ph.L., West Baden Coll., 1960; M.A., Loyola U., Chgo., 1967; S.T.L., Bellarmine Sch. Theology, 1967; Docteur en Théologie, Institut Catholique, Paris, 1975. Ordained priest Roman Catholic Ch., 1966. Tchr. math. St. Xavier High Sch., Cin., 1960-63; lectr. theology Loyola U., Chgo., 1968; asst. prof., assoc. prof. systematic theology Jesuit Sch. Theology, Berkeley, Calif., 1972—, dean, 1987—. Am. Theology Schs. fellow, 1978-79. Mem. Am. Acad. Religion, Cath. Theol. Soc. Am. (chair ecclesiology seminar 1983-84). Democrat. Roman Catholic. Office: Jesuit Sch Theology 1735 LeRoy St Berkeley CA 94709

STAGER, STEVEN FRANK, minister; b. Lima, Ohio, Sept. 20, 1952; s. William Francis and Pauline (Smith) S.; m. Sylvia Anne Reich, Aug. 13, 1983. BA in History cum laude, Wittenberg U., 1974; MDiv magna cum laude, Gordon Conwell Sem., 1978; postgrad., Fuller Theol. Sem. Ordained to ministry Presbyn. Ch., 1978. Asst. pastor First Presbyn. Ch., Ridgewood, N.J., 1978-81; pastor Eliot Presbyn. Ch., Lowell, Mass., 1981-88; sr. pastor First United Presbyn. Ch., Greeley, Colo., 1988—; trustee Presbytery of No. New England, Haverhill, Mass., 1982-88; del. Synod Ministries Agy., Synod of the N.E., Syracuse, N.Y., 1984-87; renewal assoc., Presbyns. for Renewal, 1990—. Author: (white paper) Affordable Housing in the Northeast, 1987. Chairperson Housing Rev. Bd., Lowell, 1987-88. Mem. Phi Eta Sigma. Office: First United Presbyn Ch 1321 9th Ave Greeley CO 80631 *The greatest challenge facing Christians at the end of Twentieth Century is to distinguish true spirituality from the many counterfeits that abound.*

STAHL, FRANKLIN PHILLIP, II, educator; b. Muncy, Pa., Aug. 10, 1956; s. Melvin LaRue and Pauline Mae (Hagerman) S.; m. Kay Ann Stackhouse, Sept. 10, 1978. As, Area Community Coll., Williamsport, Pa., 1977; BA in Theology, Walla Walla Coll., 1983. Elem. tchr. cert. with secondary religion endorsement; missionary credentials Seventh-day Adventists Ch. Student dean of boys Walla Walla Coll., College Place, Wash., 1981-83; pastor, asst. dean, tchr. Holbrook (Ariz.) Seventh-day Adventists Sch., 1983-85; prin., tchr. Zanesville (Ohio) Seventh-day Adventists Sch., 1985-86, Forestdale Seventh-day Adventists Sch., Bryant Pond, Maine, 1986—; dean's coun. Walla Walla Coll., 1981-83; bd. dirs., elder Holbrook Seventh-day Adventists Ch., 1983-85; sec. Forestdale Seventh-day Adventist Ch., Bryant Pond, 1986—; head elder Woodstock Seventh-day Adventist Ch., Bryant Pond, 1987—. Author-compilor: (histories) Williamsport SDA Church, 1988, Woodstock SDA Church, 1991, Forestdale SDA Elementary, 1991. Mem. Northumberland County Hist. Soc., Sunbury, Pa., 1989-90, Snyder County Hist. Soc., Middletown, Pa., 1989-90. Mem. Pathfinder, Bryant Pond. Home: RFD 2 Box 1160 Bryant Pond ME 04219 Office: Forestdale Seventh-day Adventists Elem Sch Bryant Pond ME 04219

STAHL, SAMUEL MORTON, rabbi; b. Sharon, Pa., Aug. 25, 1939; s. Harry and Pearl (Sherman) S.; m. Lynn Ann Cohodas, Aug. 28, 1966; children: Heather Sara, Alisa Michelle. BA, U. Pitts., 1961; B. Hebrew Letters, Hebrew Union Coll., 1963, MA, 1967, D. Hebrew Letters, 1975. Ordained rabbi, 1967. Chaplain U.S. Army, Ft. Belvoir, Va., 1967-68, Seoul, Republic of Korea, 1968-69; rabbi Temple B'nai Israel, Galveston, Tex., 1969-76; sr. rabbi Temple Beth-El, San Antonio, 1976—; pres. SW Assn. Reform Rabbis, 1984-86, Kallah of Tex. Rabbis, 1977-78; mem. pastoral adv. bd. Hospice San Antonio, 1990—. Editor Jour. Reform Judaism, 1984-90. Mem. institutional rev. com. St. Luke's Luth. Hosp., San Antonio, 1978-91; chmn. scholarship com. Martin Luther King Commn., 1990—. Recipient Brotherhood award NCCJ, San Antonio, 1989, Shalom award State of Israel Bonds, Galveston, Tex., 1971. Mem. Cen. Conf. Am. Rabbis (liturgy com.), Tex. Conf. Chs. (Jewish-Christian forum 1987—), State of Israel Bonds (rabbinic cabinet 1986—), B'nai Brith. Democrat. Home: 4218 Bluemel San Antonio TX 78240 Office: Temple Beth-El 211 Belknap San Antonio TX 78212

STAHLMAN, JOHN RICHARD, minister; b. Centralia, Ill., Dec. 30, 1937; s. Oscar Frederich and Helen Alisha (Dickey) S.; m. cArrol Lee Bryan, Feb. 2, 1957; children: Cornell Scott, Joni Lee. BS, U. Ill., 1959; MDiv, Louisville Presbyn. Theol. Sem., 1969. Ordained to ministry, Presbyn. Ch. (USA). Pastor Richmond, Ind., 1969-73; exec. dir. Yokefellow (Ind.) Ctr., 1973-77; columnist Suburban Newspapers, St. Louis, 1982-90; interim pastor S. Pk. Presbyn. Ch., Rock Island, Ill., 1990—. Author mag. articles; editor Fishing & Hunting Jour., 1989; author newspaper colums. Capt. U.S. Army, 1960-66. Decorated Bronze Star medal. Home: Route 3 Sparta IL 62286 Office: South Park Presbyn Ch 1501 30th St Rock Island IL 61201

STAHMER, HAROLD MARTIN, JR., former college dean; b. Bklyn., Aug. 7, 1929; s. Harold Martin and Ann Lillian (Truntz) S.; children—Sarah Anne, Jennifer Betsy, Hannah Mary; m. Paula Jessica Rosenstock Huessy, Sept. 21, 1985. B.A., Dartmouth Coll., 1951; vis. scholar, Benedictine Abbey of Maria Laach, 1951-52; B.D., Union Theol. Sem., 1955; Ph.D., Cambridge U., Eng., 1955-57; vis. scholar, Columbia U. Law Sch., 1965-66. Instr. religion Barnard Coll., 1957-60, acting dept. chmn., 1958-60, asst. prof., 1961-62; asso. prof. Barnard Coll. and Columbia U., 1962-67; chmn. dept. religion Barnard Coll., 1962-68; dir. undergrad. program in religion Columbia U., 1962-67, prof., 1967-69; dir. intensive summer studies program Harvard-Yale-Columbia, 1967-69; asso. dean U. Fla. Coll. Arts and Scis., Gainesville, 1969-79, assoc. dir., Center for Gerontol. Studies and Programs, prof. religion and philosophy; lectr. contemporary western religious trends CBS, 1966. Author: Speak That I May See Thee, 1968; Editor: Religion and Contemporary Society, 1963. Mem. standing com. ch. and state ACLU, 1960-69; coordinator Gov. Askew's Conf. Higher Edn. Disadvantaged, 1970; mem. Gov.'s Capital Punishment Commn., 1972. Recipient Community Service award B'nai B'rith Rockland County, 1966; E. Harris Harbison Distinguished Teaching prize, 1968. Fellow Am. Council Learned Socs., Soc. Human Values in Higher Edn.; mem. AAUP, Soc. Sci. Study Religion, Am. Acad. Religion, ACLU. Home: 4621 Clear Lake Dr Gainesville FL 32607

STAKE, BRENT DENNIS, minister; b. Chgo., Mar. 14, 1950; s. Robert Harry and Hilda Josephine (Soukkala) S.; m. Vickie Lynn Ball, Dec. 1, 1973; children: Jeffry Scott, Stephen Bradley, Joshua Brent. BA, North Park Coll., 1971; postgrad., Am. Conservatory of Music, 1971-72, Moody Bible Inst., 1971-72; ThM, Dallas Theol. Sem., 1976, postgrad., 1983—. Ordained to ministry Bapt. Ch., 1976. Dir. youth ministries Cuyler Covenant Ch., Chgo., 1969-71; youth worker Fairmeadows Bapt. Ch., Duncanville, Tex., 1972-76; pastor First Congl. Ch., Kinder, La., 1976-86, Oak Hill Evang. Free Ch., Evansville, Ind., 1987; sr. pastor Grace Bible Ch. & Grace Christian Acad., Jacksonville, Fla., 1988—; dir. Grace Christian Acad., Jacksonville, 1988—. Sponsor Soc. Disting. Am. High Sch. Students, Kinder, 1977-86; coach Kinder Dixie Youth Baseball League, 1982-86, Chandler (Ind.) Baseball League, 1987. North Park Coll. scholar, 1967, State of Ill. scholar, 1967-71. Mem. Bible Confs. and Missions Mins. Fellowship (v.p. 1979-81, pres. Reeves, La. chpt. 1981-83), Dallas Theol. Sem. Alumni Assn. (treas. local chpt. 1990—). Republican. Office: Grace Bible Ch 6118 Bowden Rd Jacksonville FL 32216

STALEY, JEFFREY LLOYD, theology educator; b. Kansas City, Mo., Dec. 22, 1951; s. Robert Trenary and Mary Elizabeth Jean (Sheldrake) S.; m. Barbara Lynn Wong, May 22, 1982; children: Benjamin Walter, Allison Jean. BA, Wheaton (Ill.) Coll., 1973; MA, Fuller Theol. Sem., Pasadena, Calif., 1979; PhD, Grad. Theol. Union, Berkeley, Calif., 1985. Asst. prof. theology U. Portland (Oreg.), 1985—. Author: The Print's First Kiss, 1988. Mem. AAUP, Soc. Bibl. Lit., Cath. Bibl. Assn., Westar Inst., Wilderness Soc., Amnesty Internat., Sierra Club. Democrat. Presbyterian. Office: U Portland 5000 N Willamette Blvd Portland OR 97203-5798

STALLINGS, MARK EDMOND, music educator; b. Tampa, Fla., Jan. 3, 1956; s. Kindle Edmond and Rozene (Carpenter) S.; m. Terry Stehle, Mar. 2, 1985. MusB in Music. Edn., U. Miami, Fla., 1978; DMA in Choral Music, U. Miami, 1984; EdM in Music Edn., Fla. Atlantic U., 1981. Soloist Allapattah United Meth. Ch., Miami, 1974-78; dir. music Wesley United Meth. Ch., Miami, 1975-78; co-dir. Sonrise, Miami, 1976-78; dir. music and youth ministries Trinity United Meth. Ch., Lighthouse Point, Fla., 1978-82, First Congl. Ch., Miami, 1982-84; dir. music ministries First United Meth. Ch. Winter Park, Fla., 1984-89; dir. ch. activities U. Cen. Fla., Orlando, 1989-90; min. music St. Stephen United Meth. Ch., Amarillo, Tex., 1989—; mgr. U. Miami Singers, Coral Gables, 1976-78, 81-83, dir. mixed chorus, 1982-84; music camp dir. Christ Congl. Ch., Miami, 1983; music clinician, adjudicator So. stes; baritone solist Mark and Mark Sacred Concerts, Miami, 1981—; music libr., mgr. Miami Civic Chorale, Coral Gables, 1974-84; camp dir., clinician, counselor, U. Miami, 1974-78, 82. Mem. Music Educators Nat. Conf., Am. Choral Dirs. Assn., Fla. Vocal Assn., Music Soc. (chairperson), Fellowship United Meths. in Worship, Music and Other Arts, Am. Guild Organists, Am. Guild Handbell Ringers, Chorister Guild (area chmn. 1990-91), Omicron Delta Kappa, Phi Kappa Lambda, Phi Kappa Phi. Office: St Stephen United Meth Ch 4600 S Western Ave Amarillo TX 79109

STAMBAUGH, CURVIN DONALD, minister, educator; b. South Mountain, Pa., May 21, 1939; s. Curvin Wilson and Lottie Ellen (Shaffer) S.; m. Darlene Ellen Goetz, Jan. 27, 1968; children—Lori Ellen, Curtis Nathan. B.A. in Bibl. Edn., Washington Bible Coll., 1964; postgrad. Christian Counseling and Ednl. Found., 1976; M.A. in Bibl. Studies, Antietam Bibl. Sem., 1983, D.Ministry, 1984. Ordained to ministry Independent Bible Ch., 1966. Asst. pastor Hagerstown Bible Ch. (Md.), 1964-69; instr. adult edn. program Washington Bible Coll., Lanham, Md., 1965-82; instr. music and Bible, Antietam Bible Coll., Hagerstown, Md., 1981—; dean pastoral studies Antietam Bibl. Semi, 1985—; pastor Locust Valley Bible Ch., Middletown, Md., 1969—; accompanist Washington Bible Coll. quartet on U.S. and Hawaii tour, 1959-63; instr. piano and organ, Middletown and Hagerstown, 1965-87; sacred concert artist for various churches; banquet and conf. speaker various orgns., 1965—; dean teen camp Camp Tohiglo, Mercersburg, Pa., 1977-84, other camps, 1968-75; tour host, Egypt, Israel, Jordan, 1982, 84, 87; concert artist sr. citizens groups, 1978—; judge music competition Regional Fine Arts Festival, Md. Assn. Christian Schs., Frederick and Hagerstown, Md., 1974-83. Author: Evaluating a Bible Church Teen Age Camp Program in the Perspective of it's Goal, 1984; composer gospel songs including; In Christ Victory, 1965, Ye Shall Know the Truth, 1965, Christ Above All, 1966. Co-inventor emulsification apparatus. Instr. hunter safety Md. Natural Resources Police, Clear Spring, 1970-75; bd. dirs. Frederick Christian Acad. (Md.), 1974-77, also co-founder. Mem. Assocs. for Bibl. Research, Fellowship Bible Chs. (pres. 1971-75, v.p. 1979-80). Republican. Home and Office: 1319 Marker Rd Middletown MD 21769

STAMEY, JUDY JOHNSON, church administrator; b. Hickory, N.C., Oct. 13, 1942; d. Jackson Julian and Virginia Inez (Martin) Johnson; m. Wade Stamey, Oct. 2, 1960; children: Lisa Anne, Kimberly, Anglea. BA, Gardner Webb Bapt., Boiling Springs, N.C., 1973; MRE, S.W. Bapt. Sem., Ft. Worth, 1975, EdD, 1980. Min. edn. Highland Bapt. Ch., Hickory, N.C., 1970-72; min. youth New Hope Bapt. Ch., Earl, N.C., 1972-73; min. outreach Univ. Bapt. Ch., Ft. Worth, 1976-81; min. edn. and adminstrn. Ridglea West Bapt. Ch., Ft. Worth, 1981—. Contbr. articles to Ch. Administrn. mag. Mem. Southwestern Bapt. Religious Educators Assn. (pres.' coun. 1988—, v.p. 1988-89), Nat. Assn. Ch. Bus. Adminstrs. (cert. coord.), South Bapt. Ch. Bus. Adminstrs. Assn. (cert. coord. 1988—), Tarrant Bapt. Religious Edn. Assn. (pres.), Tex. Min. Edn. (pres.), So. Bapt. Religious Edn. Assn. (asst. sec., trea.). Home: 2800 Larkin Fort Worth TX 76133 Office: Ridglea West Bapt Ch 3954 S W Blvd Fort Worth TX 76116

STAMPIGLIA, FAUSTO S., religious administrator; b. Rome, Italy, Oct. 7, 1935; came to U.S., 1964; s. Carlo and Antonio (Falciatori) S. Ph.B., Gregorian U., 1957, B.A., M.A., 1961; M.S. in Psychology, Fordham U., 1975; S.T.D., St. Thomas Aquinas U., Rome, 1979. Ordained priest Roman Catholic Ch., 1960. Pastor, St. Ann Ch., N.Y.C., 1972-75, Sacred Heart Ch., Cohoes, N.Y., 1975-77, St. Rita Ch., Cohoes, 1975-77, St. Joseph Ch., Port St. Joe, Fla., 1977-80; episcopal vicar Rural Vicariate, Chipley, Fla., 1980-82; instr. St. Leo Coll., Fla., 1979-85; dir. permanent diaconate Diocese of Pensacola, Fla., 1977-82, Diocese of St. Petersburg, Fla., 1982-85, Diocese of Venice, Fla., 1984-85, Diocese of Corpus Christi, Tex., 1985—. Author: Study of New York City Immigrant Parish, 1979. Contbr. articles to profl. jours. Bd. dirs. 1199 Housing Corp., N.Y.C., 1972-75. Decorated Order of Knights of Holy Sepulcher. Mem. Am. Assn. Counseling and Devel., Assn. for Religious Values in Counseling. Democrat. Lodge: K.C. Avocations: music composition; photography; camping; hunting; reading. Home: PO Box 1899 Corpus Christi TX 78403 Office: Permanent Diaconate Office 1200 Lantana Corpus Christi TX 78407

STANFILL, JEFFERY KENNETH, minister; b. Winnfield, La., Jan. 28, 1961; s. Kenneth Delmar and Barbara Elizabeth (Walker) S.; m. MariAnne Margaret Bowen. BA in Bible Studies, Cen. Bible Coll., Springfield, Mo., 1985. Ordained to ministry Assemblies of God Ch., 1987. Youth pastor First Assembly of God Ch., Fordyce, Ark., 1980-82; youth pastor Broadmoor Assembly of God Ch., Shreveport, La., 1985-87, assoc., Christian edn. dir., 1987—; area youth dir. Assemblies of God Ch., Fordyce, 1980-82, sectional youth rep., 1981-82, sectional Christian edn. rep., Shreveport, 1987—, asst. dist. dir., asst. to the presbyter, 1990—. Named one of Outstanding Young Men of Am., 1985, 87. Republican. Avocations: golf, racquetball, reading.

STANFORD, JOHN R., minister; b. Whitesboro, N.J., Apr. 20, 1916; s. Matthewu Dock and Marie (Simmons) S.; m. Rebecca J. McLean, Dec. 25, 1939. Student, Shaw U., 1939-42, DD (hon.), 1975. Pastor 1st Bapt. Ch., Chapel Hill, N.C., 1937-46, 2d Bapt Ch., Atlantic City, N.J., 1946-55, Zion Hill Bapt. Ch., Newark, 1955—; builder ch. edifice, Zion Hill Bapt. Ch., 1986; pres. Gen. State Conv., N.J., 1972-76, Chaplain of Police, Newark, 1970-75, Tchr. Young People's Assembly, N.J., 1950-60. Home: 43 Yates Ave Newark NJ 07112 Office: Zion Hill Bapt Ch 182 Osborne Terr Newark NJ 07112

STANG, SISTER JEANETTE TERESA, nun; b. Sandusky, Ohio, Aug. 6, 1928; d. Charles John and Bertha Mary (Dietrich) S. BA, St. Mary of the Springs, 1953; MA, Laval U., 1959; PhD, St. Mary's Coll., Notre Dame, Ind., 1967. Joined Dominican Sisters, Roman Cath. Ch., 1948. Elem. tchr. Cath. Schs., Steubenville and Columbus, Ohio, 1950-54; high sch. tchr. Cath. Schs., Steubenville and Ossining, N.Y., 1954-58; mem. formation program Dominican Sisters, Columbus, 1958-64; lectr. religious studies Ohio Dominican Coll., Columbus, 1967-76; assoc. dir. religious edn. Diocese of St. Petersburg (Fla.), 1977-82; dir. pastoral ministries St. James Ch., Port Richey, Fla., 1986—; assoc. dir. religious edn. Diocese of Columbus, 1967-77; dir. Summer Inst., Pastoral Ministry, Ohio Dominican Coll., Columbus, 1977. Bd. mem. Human Growth and Devel., New Port Richey, Fla., 1987-88, Cath. Social Svcs., New Port Richey, 1988-91; organizer Walk-A-Thon, St. Jude Hosp., Port Richey, 1988. Mem. N.Am. Forum Catechumenate. Office: St James the Apostle Ch 8400 Monarch Dr Port Richey FL 34668

STANG, SISTER MARY ASSUNTA, nun, religion organization administrator; b. Ft. Loramie, Ohio, Feb. 17, 1920; d. Bernard and Catherine (Hoying) S. BS, Coll. of Mt. St. Joseph, Cin., 1941, LHD (hon.), 1978. Joined Sisters of Charity of Cin., Roman Cath. Ch., 1941. Tchr. secondary edn. local schs., 1941-50; bus. mgr. St. Joseph Hosp., Albuquerque, 1950-53, adminstr., 1956-57; asst. adminstr. St. Vincent Hosp., Santa Fe, 1953-56; assoc. adminstr., then adminstr. Penrose Hosp., Colorado Springs, Colo., 1957-65; exec. treas. Srs. of Charity, 1965-71; pres. Sisters of Charity, Mt. St. Joseph, Ohio, 1971-79, cons. health care instns., 1979-81, exec. treas., 1983-87; missionary Diocese of Roraima, Boa Vista, Brazil, 1981-83; adminstr. Seton Enablement Fund, Mt. St. Joseph, 1987—; trustee, chmn. collaborative svcs. Sisters of Chrity Health Care Systems, Cin., 1986—; trustee St. Joseph Health Network, Mt. Clemens, Mich., 1987—, St. Joseph Healthcare System, Albuquerque, 1987—, Sisters of Charity Sr. Care Corp., Cin., 1989—. Contbr. articles to hosp. jours. Trustee Bethany House Svcs., Cin., 1988—. Named Hosp. Trustee of Yr., Modern Hosp., 1987. Fellow Am. Coll. Healthcare Execs. (life), Hosp. Fin. Mgmt. Assn. (life, Follmer award 1969), Am. Coll. Hosp. Adminstrs.; mem. Am. Assn. Hosp. Accts. (pres. Chgo. 1964-65). Home: 5770 Delhi Rd Cincinnati OH 45233-1605 Office: Seton Enablement Fund Mount Saint Joseph OH 45051

STANGER, RICHARD LEONARD, minister; b. Detroit, Nov. 11, 1935; s. Robert Christian and Juel Elizabeth (Wolf) S.; m. Joan P. Stanger, June 14, 1958; children: Allison, Karen, Robert. BA, Elmhurst (Ill.) Coll., 1958; MA, Northwestern U., 1964; BDiv, McCormick Sem., 1966; PhD, U. Mich., 1978. Program dir. St. Paul's Ch., Chgo., 1960-65; dean of men MacMurray Coll., Jacksonville, Ill., 1965-67, asst. prof. philosophy, 1967-74; sr. minister Plymouth Ch., Ft. Wayne, Ind., 1974-88, Plymouth Ch. of Pilgrims, Bklyn., 1988-91, Plymouth Congl. Ch., Miami, Fla., 1991—. Bd. dirs. Mental Health Ctr., Ft. Wayne, 1975-81, Parkview Hosp., Ft. Wayne, 1977-80; bd. trustees Defiance (Ohio) Coll., 1978-82. Danforth Found. fellow, 1972. Home: 3432 Devon Rd Miami FL 33133 Office: Plymouth Congl Ch Miami FL 33133

STANIECKI, BROTHER H. MARK, educational administrator; b. Bklyn., Dec. 4, 1959. BA, Iona Coll., 1981; MS, Fordham U., 1986. Joined Congregation Christian Bros., Roman Cath. Ch. Tchr. Rice High Sch., N.Y.C., 1981-83; dept. chmn. Bergen Cath. High Sch., Oradell, N.J., 1984-89, dean students, 1987-88, asst. prin., 1987-89; asst. headmaster Iona Prep. Sch., New Rochelle, N.Y., 1989—; co-dir. Christian Svc. Program, Ordaell, 1985-86, Student Activity Program, New Rochelle, 1991—. Mem. Nat. Cath. Edn. Assn., Cath. Sch. Adminstrs. Assn. N.Y., Cath. League for Religious and Civil Rights, Edmond Rice Soc. (bd. dirs. 1989—). Office: Iona Prep Sch Wilmot Rd New Rochelle NY 10804

STANLEY, CHARLES FRAZIER, minister; b. Dry Fork, Va., Sept. 25, 1932; s. Charles Frazier Stanley and Rebecca (Hardy) Hall; m. Anna Margaret Johnson; children: Andrew, Rebecca Stanley Broderson. BA, U. Richmond, 1954; ThM, Southwestern Bapt. Theol. Sem., 1957; ThD, Luther Rice Sem., 1970. Pastor Fruitland (N.C.) Bapt. Ch., 1957-59; prof. Fruitland Bible Coll., 1957-59; pastor First Bapt. Ch., Dearborn, Ohio, 1959-62, Miami, Fla., 1962-68, Bartow, Fla., 1968-69, Atlanta, 1969—; pres. Bapt. Pastors Conf., So. Bapt. Ch., 1983-84, So. Bapt. Conv., 1984-84, 85-86. Author: Confronting Casual Christianity, 1985, How to Listen to God, 1985, Forgiveness, 1987, Temptation, 1988, How to Handle Adversity, 1989, Eternal Security: Can You Be Sure, 1990. Recipient Freedom award Freedom Found., 1973, Father of Yr. award State of Georgia, 1984, Clergyman of Yr., Religious Heritage Am., 1989. Republican. Office: First Bapt Ch 754 Peachtree St NW Atlanta GA 30365

STANLEY, DARRYL SCOTT, minister; b. Houston, Apr. 19, 1966; s. Charles A. and Nancy (Craig) S. BS, Houston Bapt. U., 1989. Min. youth Garden Rd. Bapt. Ch., Pearland, Tex., 1985-87, Chocolate Bayon Bapt. Ch., Alvin, Tex., 1988-89, 1st Bapt. Ch., Galena Park, Tex., 1989—; salesman Stanley Sales Co., Inc., Houston, 1985—; pres. Bapt. Student Union-Alvin Community Coll., 1985-86. Office: 1st Bapt Ch 206 Woolfe Galena Park TX 77547 *The essence of life is truth. Faith is that gift of God which allows us to face truth without fear, to be at peace in the presence of truth.*

STANLEY, SUSIE CUNNINGHAM, religious educator, minister; b. Ashland, Ky., May 3, 1948; d. Clayton Allen and Jamie Sue (Rogers) C.; m. John Elias Stanley, Nov. 28, 1970; children: Michael David, Mandy Lynn. BA, Towson State U., 1976; MA, Iliff Sch. Theology, 1982; PhD, Iliff Sch. Theology and U. Denver, 1987. Prof. of ch. history women's studies Western Evang. Sem., Portland, 1983—, ecumenical minister, 1983—; coms. Ecumenical Ministries of Oreg., Portland, 1983—; conf. leaders, 1977—. Author: (with others) Women Authority and the Bible, 1986, Called to Ministry, 1989; contbr. articles to profl. jours. Sec. Women's Polit. Caucus, Portland, 1988—. Mem. Am. Acad. Religion, Wesleyan Theol. Soc., Am. Soc. Ch. History, N.W. Women's Studies Assn. Democrat. Home: 114 SE 63rd Ave Portland OR 97215 Office: Western Evang Sem 4200 SE Jennings Portland OR 97267

STANLEY, VAUGHAN, minister; b. Charleston, W.Va., Oct. 21, 1950; s. James Virgil Stanley and Lois Jean (Vaughan) Starbuck; m. Katheryne May Giles, June 12, 1976; children: Kara Suzanne, Kelly Amanda, Krista Elizabeth, Jonathan Vaughan. BA, Hampden-Sydney Coll., 1972; MDiv, Reformed Theol. Sem., 1979, M. Missiology, 1979; D. Ministry, Luther Rice Sem., 1982. Ordained to ministry Presbyn. Ch. Am. Assoc. minister Seacrest Blvd. Presbyn. Ch., Delray Beach, Fla., 1979-88; minister of evangelism Orangewood Presbyn. Ch., Maitland, Fla., 1988—; bd. dirs. Liberty Found., Ft. Lauderdale, Fla., 1986-88; chmn. candidates com. So. Fla. Presbytery, Delray Beach, 1986; chmn. minister and his work com. Cen. Fla. Presbytery, Orlando, 1990. Mem. Fla. Rep. Com., 1981. Mem. Nat. Right to Life. Home: 506 Astria Ct Altamonte Springs FL 32201 Office: Orangewood Presbyn Ch 1300 W Maitland Blvd Maitland FL 32751

STANLEY-SOULEN, MELANIE, pastor; b. Ft. Knox, Ky., June 2, 1959; d. William Hayes and Rosie (Reinbold) Stanley; m. Stephen Lewis Soulen, Jan. 7, 1984; children: David Lewis, Stanley Matthew. BA in Christian Edn. cum laude, Huntingdon Coll., 1980; MDiv, Emory U., 1983. Ordained to ministry Meth. Ch., 1989. Asst. pastor, youth minister Clarkdale (Ga.) United Meth. Ch., 1981-83; asst. pastor, youth minister First United Meth. Ch., Thomaston, Ga., 1983-84, Madison, Ga., 1984-86; assoc. pastor First United Meth. Ch., Temple, Tex., 1986-88; co-pastor First United Meth. Ch., Meridian, Tex., 1988—; co-coord. family ministries Cen. Tex. Conf., United Meth. Ch., Ft. Worth, 1990-92; mem. Clergy Couples, United Meth. Ch., Portsmouth, Va., 1989—. Bosque County coord. Food for Families Project, Meridian, Tex., 1990. Mem. Sigma Sigma Sigma, Chi Omega. Home: 410 N Main St Meridian TX 76665

STANO, LESTER PAUL, minister; b. St. Louis, Mar. 31, 1947; s. Paul and Anna (Dinga) S. BSBA, U. Mo., St. Louis, 1969; MDiv, Concordia Sem., 1973; MBA in Ch. Mgmt., Grad. Theol. Found., 1991. Ordained to ministry Luth. Ch.-Mo. Synod, 1974. Asst. pastor Immanual Luth. Ch., Balt., 1974-75; instr. of religion Balt. Luth. High Sch., Towson, Md., 1975-76; pastor 1st Luth. Ch., Towson, 1976—; chaplain VA Med. Ctr., Balt., 1976—; trustee Acts, Ministry, Inc., Towson, 1988—, Timothy House, Inc., Towson, 1989—; cir. counsel Southeastern Dist., 1982-91; bd. dirs. Luth. Mission Soc., 1976-90. Pres., treas. Towson Ministerial Assn., 1981; chmn. communication Towson Manor Village, 1991; bd. dirs. Balt. Luth. High Sch., Towson, 1976—. Mem. Coll. Chaplains, Assn. Clin. Pastoral Edn. Home: 29 Linden Terr Towson MD 21204 Office: 1st Luth Ch 40 E Burke Ave Towson MD 21204

STANTON, KATHLEEN SUSANNE, lay worker; b. Denver, June 22, 1962; d. James Francis and Elizabeth Anne (Kafonek) S. BA, Bethany Coll., Lindsborg, Kans., 1984. Cert. alcoholism counselor. Camp counselor Rainbow Trail Luth. Camp, Hillside, Colo., summers 1981-82, summer 1984; youth counselor Zion Luth. Ch., Farmington, N.Mex., 1985—; outpatient counselor Presbyn. Med. Svcs., Farmington, 1987-91; substance abuse dir. N.Mex. State Youth Authority, Farmington, 1991—; researcher-presenter in psychology field. Mem. La Nueva Civitans, Farmington, 1986-87. Recipient Most Respected Sr. award Bethany Coll., 1984. Mem. Nat. Assn. Alcoholism and Drug Abuse Counselors, Psi Chi. *Through all varieties of human experiences, the spirit of man connects with a power to continue growth and vitality. It is part of my choice to continue to help find that force which urges us on to positive and constructive choices.*

STANTON, TOM ARDEN, minister; b. Johnson City, Tenn., Nov. 29, 1957; s. Robert J. and Nellie Kate (Potter) S.; m. Deborah Dianne Watkins; children: Tenecia Dawn, Constance Beth, Katy Arlene. AS, Walter's State Community Coll., Morristown, Tenn., 1977; student, Carson-Newman Coll., 1978, Liberty U., 1989; ThB, Covington Theol. Sem., 1991; ThD (hon.), Am. Bible Inst., 1991. Ordained to ministry, So. Bapt. Conv., 1977. Assoc. pastor, minister of music Henard"s Chapel Bapt. Ch., Rogersville, Tenn., 1977-81, Persia Bapt. Ch., Rogersville, Tenn., 1981-82; pastor Chaptack Bapt. Ch., Rogersville, Tenn., 1982-85, East End Bapt. Ch., Marian, Va., 1985-88, Clark St. Bapt. Ch., Johnson City, Tenn., 1988—; dir. discipleship tng. Holston Bapt. Assn., Johnson City, 1988-89, chmn. exec. com., 1983-85; assoc. moderator Holston Valley Bapt. Assn, Rogersville, 1984. Arranger, instrumentalist religious recording: Stepping on the Clouds, 1973; writer, arranger recording: The Masters Payroll, 1975. Chaplain of the day Tenn. Ho. of Reps., Nashville, 1989; col., aide-de-damp Staff, Tenn. Gov., Nashville, 1989; vol. Johnson City Sr. Citizens Ctr., 1989 (Outstanding Vol. award 1989). Republican. Home: 805 W Hillcrest Dr Johnson City TN 37604 Office: Clark St Bapt Ch 200 Clark St Johnson City TN 37604

STAPERT, JOHN CHARLES, minister, chaplain, editor; b. Kalamazoo, Sept. 25, 1942; s. Elko M. and Martha Edith (Van Zee) S.; m. Barbara Sue Vander Linde, Aug. 17, 1963; children: Criag William, Terri Lynne. AB, Hope Coll., 1963; MDiv, Fuller Sem., 1966; MA, U. Ill., Urbana, 1968, PhD, 1969. Ordained to ministry Reformed Chs. Am.; lic. psychologist. Assoc. prof. psychology Northwestern Coll., Orange City, Iowa, 1969-72; exec. coord. Synod of the West Reformed Chs. in Am., Orange City, 1972-74; editor The Ch. Herald, Grand Rapids, Mich., 1974-91; mng. editor Perspectives, Grand Rapids, 1986—; exec. dir. Associated Ch. Press, Ada, Mich., 1990—; chaplain psychol./med. unit St. Mary's Hosp., Grand Rapids, 1991—. Mem. APA, Evang. Press Assn. (pres. 1987-89). Office: Associated Ch Press PO Box 162 Ada MI 49301

STAPLETON, JOHN MASON, clergyman; b. Union, S.C., Aug. 22, 1932; s. John Mason and Mary (Lee) S.; m. Cynthia Enos, June 6, 1956; children: Catherine, Mark, David. BA, Wofford Coll., 1953; MDiv, Union Sem., N.Y.C., 1956, MST, 1959, PhD, 1969. Ordained to ministry United Meth. Ch., 1956; notary pub., S.C. Instr. Boston U., 1961-63; minister United Meth. chs., S.C., 1956-76; prof. Emory U., Atlanta, 1976-85; minister Trinity United Meth. Ch., North Myrtle Beach, S.C., 1985—; chmn. Belin bd. trust United Meth. Ch., 1986—; coord. program in preaching Intentional Growth Ctr., Lake Junaluska, N.C., 1989—; Luccock visitor Yale Div. Sch., New Haven, 1970; vis. prof. Meth. Sem., Seoul, 1980, Evang. Sem., Mantanzas, Cuba, 1980. Author: Preaching in Demonstration of the Spirit and Power, 1988; contbr. articles and revs. to religious publs. Avocations: acting, running, tennis. Office: Trinity United Meth Ch PO Box 373 North Myrtle Beach SC 29597

STARK, JERRY KEITH, minister; b. Moran, Kans., Jan. 28, 1952; s. John Evertt and Wanda Louise (Hobart) S.; m. Kathy Lynne Del Bello, June 20, 1981; children: Jeremy Michael, Jonathan David. Student, Emporia State U.; A in Theology, Christ For The Nations, Dallas, 1981; Diploma, Worship Leaders Inst., Dallas, 1989. Asst. dir., worship leader Christ For The Nations, Dallas, 1980-82; asst. dir. Living Praise Choir, Dallas, 1979-81; voice instr. Christ For The Nations, Dallas, 1980-82; music dir. Faith Ministries Fellowship, Greeley, Colo., 1982-84; praise and worship tchr. U.S., Europe, Mexico, 1984—; assoc. pastor, worship leader Agape Fellowship, Green Mountain Falls, Colo., 1985-88, Liberty Lighthouse Ch., Ft. Worth, 1988-90; assoc. pastor Northwest Christian Ctr., Corpus Christi, Tex., 1990—. Home: 11325 I H 37 # 3001 Corpus Christi TX 78410 *Love is a journey, not a destination.*

STARKEY, ROBERT ERIC, minister; b. Dunbar, W.Va., July 16, 1939; s. Dorsey Remington and Edith Cora (Nichols) S.; m. Rebecca Joyce McDaniel, Aug. 19, 1960 (div. Oct. 1984); children: Cindy Alice, Lynda Carol; m. Margie Lorraine Farr, July 13, 1985. MusB, W.Va. State Coll., 1961; MEd, Trinity U., 1966; MA, U. Detroit, 1973; D of Ministry, Drew U., 1980. Ordained to ministry Ch. of God (Anderson, Ind.), 1967; lic. psychologist, Mich. Min. 1st Ch. of God, El Paso, 1966-70, Evanswood Ch. of God, Troy, Mich., 1970-83, 1st Congl. Ch., Port Huron, Mich., 1985—; chmn. gen. assembly Ch. of God, Lansing, Mich., 1980-82. Contbr. articles to mags. Adv. bd. Port Huron Area Sch. Dist., 1989; chmn. CROP WALK, Port Huron, 1989—. 1st lt. USAF, 1962-66. Home: 1919 Military St Port Huron MI 48060 Office: First Congl Ch 723 Court St Port Huron MI 48060 *Henry Drummond echoed the words of the Apostle Paul when he said that love is the greatest thing in the world. Jesus said love would be the identifying mark of His disciples. Ultimately, our love relationships with God and each other determine our success and happiness and our usefulness in God's kingdom.*

STARKS, CHARLES WILEY, minister; b. Bastian, Va., June 27, 1954; s. Clarence Eugene and Mattiline Mae (Compton) S. BA, Emory and Henry Coll., 1976; MDiv, Emory Univ., 1979, D of Ministry, 1988. Lic. to ministry United Meth. Ch., 1972, ordained as deacon, 1977, as elder, 1981. Personnel recruiter and trainer A Christian Ministry in the Nat. Parks, N.Y.C., 1979-80; minister Meadowview United Meth. Ch., Meadowview, Va., 1980-84, Pleasant View United Meth. Ch., Abingdon, Va., 1984—; adj. prof. of philosophy/religion, Va. Highlands Community Coll., Abingdon, 1986—; coord. Abingdon Dist. Youth, 1980-84; New Life Missioner, 1983—; apptd. counseling elder in Holston Conf., supervising pastor, other, 1985—; mem. Abingdon Dist. Com. on Superintendency, 1985—, Holston Conf. Bd. of Ordained Ministry Exec. Com., 1985—, chair Holston Conf. Psychol. Testing and Assessment Com., 1987—, mem. Holston Conf. Task Force on Conf. Strategy and Structure for Ministry and Mission, and Com. on Episcopacy, 1990—; mem. alumni exec. com. for Candler Sch. Theology, Emory U., Atlanta, 1991—. Vol. Big Bro., Washington County Big Bro./Big Sister Orgn., 1985-88; chmn. Washington County Office on Youth Svcs. Citizens Bd., 1988-90; mem. Washington County Commonwealth Alliance for Drug Rehab. and Edn., 1989-90, Washington County Multi-Discipline Bd., 1989-90, Washington County Fed. Emergency Mgmt. Authority Bd., 1987—; mem. ethics com. Johnston Meml. Hosp., 1991—. Named to Outstanding Young Men in Am., 1985; Chaplain of the Day U.S. Senate, Washington, 1989. Mem. United Meth. Assn. of Ch. Bus. Adminstrs., Kiwanis (religious affairs com. 1988), Mason, others. Home: Rte 11 Box 268 Abingdon VA 24210 Office: Pleasant View United Meth 3219 Lee Hwy Abingdon VA 24210 *Increasingly it seems, for individuals, families and nations, life becomes more complex and knotty to the point that people resign themselves to hopelessness. But, in giving ourselves to maturing relationships with God and others, based on trust, hopelessness can be uprooted. Confidence can flourish. Peace of mind and simplicity in living can be restored.*

STARKS, NORMAN LESTER, minister; b. Sycamore, Kans., Apr. 10, 1938; s. Sylvan F. and Florence P. (Miner) S.; m. Mary K. Clark, Oct. 19, 1957 (div. Jan. 1972); children: Trisha K., Deena J. Starks-Roberts; m. Phyllis J. Bishop, July 6, 1974; stepchildren: Larry Jukes, Russell Jukes, Jean Jukes-Martin. BA in Ministry, Midwest Christian Coll., 1961; BA, U. Evansville, 1968, MA, 1970. Ordained to ministry Christian Ch., 1960. Youth min. Blvd. Christian Ch., Muskogee, Okla., 1960-62; youth min. First Christian Ch., Evansville, Ind., 1962-72; music and worship min. First Christian Ch., Evansville, 1972-87, Cen. Christian Ch., Beloit, Wis., 1987—; program dir. Rock River Christian Camp, Polo, Ill., 1987—; ropeholder capt. Wis. Christian Missionary Assn., Wisconsin Rapids, 1990-91. Author/composer music and lyrics numerous songs for barbershop quartets including Little Girl, 1968, 1st place winner in internat. competition Sweet and Lovely, 1970, included in basic songs to be learned by 38,000 mems. Soc. Preservation Encouragement Barbershop Quartet Singing Am., 1970; contbr. articles Christian Standard mag.; correspondent Janesville Gazette, 1990—. Bell ringer Salvation Army, Beloit, 1989; dir. Compiled Christmas Choir, Beloit, 1990; mem. Beloit Kiwanis, 1988-89. Named Barbershopper of Yr. Evansville chpt. SPEBSQSA. 1969; recipient journalism scholarhip U. Okla., 1956-57. Mem. Christian Mins. Assn. Republican. Office: Cen Christian Ch 2460 Milwaukee Rd Beloit WI 53511 *The secret to a happy and contented life is to focus on what is right and good about your life, and to put your energies into improving those areas. Look upon your problems as marvelous learning experiences.*

STARLING, GEORGE EDWARD, radio broadcaster, director; b. Roebling, N.J., Dec. 28, 1927; s. James and Celia (Lotts) S. Student, Howard U., 1945, 59. Religious radio announcer WILD, Boston, KSAY, San Francisco, WFAB, Miami, Fla.; religious dir., announcer, sales WTTM, Trenton, N.J., 1981—; auto broker Nat. Auto Brokers, L.A., 1987—; owner print shop, 1945—; dir. Gospelite Mission, Trenton, 1981—; promoter radio evangelism Sta. WTNJ, Trenton, 1952—; sales profl. motor vehicles, 1969—; distbr. satellite TV, 1985—; participant evangelistic crusades, Tokyo and Seoul, Korea, 1987—; owner auto dealership, 1973—. Newspaper editor Internat. Corr. Mem. YMCA, Trenton, JCC, Trenton. Mem. Nat. Assn. Broadcasters, N.J. Broadcasters Assn., Internat. Religious Radio Broadcasters, Nat. Assn. Minority Ownership Broadcasters, Radio Assn. Broadcasters. Democrat. Home and Office: 77 Amboy Rd PO Box 9783 Trenton NJ 08650-1783 *Strive to enter the less traveled narrow gateway that leads to eternal life. Cultivate your relationship with God and be a witness for*

Christ. Reach out for the helpless and hurting. Share the good news of the love of God with compassion. Your peace and happiness are based directly on your daily commitment and consecration with unification.

STARR, CHARLES MARION, minister; b. Hickory, N.C., May 31, 1925; s. Charles Burton and Annie Iona (Abernethy) S.; m. Mary June Hollar Jan. 1948; children: Carol Ann, Charles Emery, Mary June. AB, Lenoir-Rhyne Coll., 1945, DD (hon.), 1973; MDiv, Luth. Theol. So. Sem., 1948. Ordained to ministry Luth. Ch., 1948. Pastor St. Paul Luth. Ch., Hamlet, N.C., 1948-52, Calvary Luth. Ch., Spencer, N.C., 1952-58, Redeemer Luth. ch., Charlotte, N.C., 1958-66, Kimball Meml. Luth Ch., Kannapolis, N.C., 1966-76, St. Paul Luth. Ch., Wilmington, N.C., 1976-83, St. Mark Luth. Ch., Asheville, N.C., 1983-90; conv. del. Luth. Ch. in Am., 1984. Trustee, sec. bd. Lenoir-Rhyne Coll., Hickory, N.C., 1980-89, Luth. Svcs. for Aging; bd. dirs. Western. N.C. Cerebral Palsy, Luth. Retirement Ctr., Arden, N.C.; vice chair allocations com. United Way. Home: 116 Kyfields Weaverville NC 28787 *I am deeply thankful for having had the years of service to a wide range of individuals who have served me more richly than I have ever served them.*

STARR, JAMES MILTON, clergyman; b. St. Johns, Mich., Dec. 29, 1961; s. James Leroy and Loretta Marie (Young) S.; m. Kristina Ulla Fredriksson, Aug. 6, 1988; 1 child, Jacob William. BA, U. Va., 1984; MDiv magna cum laude, Yale U., 1990. Ordained to ministry Am. Bapt. Chs., 1990. Regional dir. Operation Mobilization, Liege, Belgium, 1983, 84-86; youth dir. First Bapt. Ch., Laurel, Md., 1984, 86-87; asst. minister Trinity Evang. Free Ch., Woodbridge, Conn., 1988-89, First Bapt. Ch., Branford, Conn., 1989-90; minister First Bapt. Ch., North Stonington, Conn., 1990—; asst. project dir. Phi Beta Kappa, Washington, 1986-87. Mem. Yale Club Ea. Conn. Office: First Bapt Ch 793 Pendleton Hill Rd North Stonington CT 06359

STARR, RANDY JOE, minister; b. Wauseon, Ohio, Oct. 27, 1951; s. Lyle Edwin and Ada Virginia (Miser) S.; m. Shirley Marlene Zehr, Sept. 9, 1972; children: Christopher, Heidi, Marcia. BS in Edn., Bowling Green State U., 1973; MS in Edn. Adminstrn., Bob Jones U., 1980; postgrad., Detroit Bapt. Theol. Sem., 1988. Ordained to ministry Bapt. Ch., 1980. Assoc. pastor, prin., asst. pastor Harvest Temple, Clyde, Ohio, 1975-80, 81-90; pastor Mt. Zion Bapt. Ch., Brogue, Pa., 1990—; prof. Heritage Bapt. U., Akron, Ohio, 1979-80; acad. dean Ohio Bible Coll., Conneaut, 1980-81; radio sta. mgr. Sta. WHVT FM, Clyde, 1987—; state cons. Accelerated Christian Edn., Lewisville, Tex., 1981-89; tax cons. home bus., Clyde, 1973—; co-founder Harvest Temple Christian Acad., Clyde, 1975—, Sta. WHVT, Clyde, 1987—. Author: Research Paper Workbook, 1990, Health Manuals for Christian Schs., Vols. I-II. Home: RD 5 Box 259 Red Lion PA 17356 Office: Mt Zion Bapt Ch RD 1 Muddy Creek Forks Rd PO Box 16 Brogue PA 17309

STARRETT, STANLEY YOUNG, religious organization executive; b. Elmhurst, Ill., Jan. 28, 1936; s. C. Gordon and Gertrude L. (Holden) S.; m. Claudia J. Gruber, Jan. 14, 1956; children: Connie J., Edward S., Michael R., Patrick G. AA equivalent, N.Y. Inst. Criminology, 1959; postgrad., Coll. of DuPage, 1984. Loss prevention mgr. Shopper's World, Chgo., 1960-64, Community Discount Ctrs., Chgo., 1964-65; v.p. sales Western zone Tultex Corp., Martinsville, Va., 1966-84; pres. The Elm Dept. Store, Elmhurst, 1984-87; pres. Provision Principles Ministries, Bartlett, Ill., 1987—, bd. didrs.; bd. dirs. Podolak Metal Products Inc., Chgo. Author: Stewardship & Christian Financial Principles, 1988. Bd. dirs., vice chmn. Restoration Coll., Mt. Carroll, Ill., 1989-90; bd. dirs. Covenant Fin. Svcs. Inc., 1991—. With U.S. Army, 1955-58. Mem. Fellowship of Cos. for Christ (co-founder DuPage chpt. 1990). Avocations: tennis, fishing, traveling. Home and Office: 1548 Wood Creek Tr Bartlett IL 60103

STATON, CECIL POPE, JR., religious publisher; b. Greenville, S.C., Jan. 26, 1958; s. Cecil Pope and Shirley Ann (Hughes) .; m. Catherine Lynn Davidson, Aug. 23, 1986. BA, Furman U., 1980; MDiv, Southeastern Bapt. Theol. Sem., 1982, ThM, 1985; PhD, U. Oxford, 1988. Assoc. minister Washington Ave. Bapt. Ch., Greenville, S.C., 1977-79; pastor Maple Heights Bapt. Ch., Greenville, 1979-80, Trinity Bapt. Ch., Arcadia, N.C., 1983-85; prof. Christianity Brewton-Parker Coll., Mount Vernon, Ga., 1989-91; pub. Smyth & Helwys Pub., Greenville, 1990—; bd. dirs. Smyth & Helwys Pub., Greenville, 1990—. Editor: Interpreting Isaiah for Preaching and Teaching, 1991; contbr. articles to profl. jours. Recipient Am. scholarship Regent's Park Coll., 1986-87, G. Henton Davies Prize in Hebrew, 1985, R.T. Daniel award in Old Testament, 1983, Baggott award Furman U., 1980. Mem. Soc. Biblical Lit., Am. Acad. Religion, Nat. Assn. Bapt. Profs. Religion. Home: 116 Kathryn Ct Greenville SC 29602 Office: PO Box 72 Greenville SC 29602 *I dream of a church which recaptures the radical nature of the Gospel. I hope for a time when what people of faith say is what we do, when what we do in church becomes what we do in the world.*

STAUFFER, BRUCE W., minister; b. Sabina, Ohio, Mar. 3, 1963; s. Warren E. and Janet Lee (Fenner) S.; m. Teresa Ann Rogers, Nov. 18, 1988; 1 child, Jacob Ryan. Student, Miami U., 1981-82, Wright State U., 1982-83; BS, Cin. Bible Coll., 1987. Preaching min. Modest (Ohio) Christian Ch., 1987-90, Vanceburg (Ky.) Christian Ch., 1990—. Bd. dirs. Lewis County Adult Literacy, Vanceburg, 1991. Home and Office: Christian Ch 412 Front St Vanceburg KY 41179

STAYER, BENJAMIN CLAY, lay worker; b. Ephrata, Pa., Feb. 24, 1963; s. Oscar Wayne and Doris Marguerite (Gehman) S.; m. Lori Lynn Robinson, Nov. 13, 1982; children: Allison Lynn, Holly Ann, Amanda Joy. Grad. high sch., Denver, Pa.; student, Southeastern Bible Coll., 1991—. Tchr. Sunday sch. Grace Fellowship Ch., Ephrata, 1984-86, youth group leader, 1986-89, coll., career leader, 1989—; mechanic Wayne Stayer Truck Repair, Inc., Reinholds, Pa., 1987—. Group leader Rally for Life '90, Washington. Republican. Mem. Ind. Fundamental Chs. Am. Home: 110 Heritage Rd Ephrata PA 17522 *God's plan for our lives is so very basic: that is to get into His word and study to show ourselves approved, praying biblically while submitting to God's will for our lives.*

STEAD, (GEORGE) CHRISTOPHER, retired divinity educator; b. Wimbledon, Eng., Apr. 9, 1913; s. Francis Bernard and Rachel Elizabeth (Bell) S.; m. Doris Elizabeth Odom, Apr. 15, 1958; children: William John, Martin Patrick, Catherine Rachel. Student Marlborough Coll., 1926-31. BA, King's Coll., Cambridge, Eng., 1935, MA, 1938; LittD, 1978; BA, New Coll., Oxford, Eng., 1935, MA, 1949. Ordained priest Ch. of Eng., 1941. Curate St. John's Ch., Newcastle on Tyne, Eng., 1939; asst. master Eton Coll., 1941-44; fellow, lectr. in divinity King's Coll., Cambridge, 1938-40, 45-48; fellow, tutor, chaplain Keble Coll., Oxford, 1949-71; Ely prof. div. U. Cambridge, 1971-80, emeritus prof., 1980—; canon residentiary Ely Cathedral, 1971-80; professorial fellow King's Coll., 1971-80, fellow 80-85. Author: Divine Substance, 1977; Substance and Illusion in the Christian Fathers, 1985, Philosophie und Theologie I: Die Zeit der Alten Kirche, 1990; also numerous articles in English, German and Italian theol. jours. and dictionaries. Fellow Brit. Acad. Avocations: walking; sailing; music. Home: 13 Station Rd, Haddenham, Ely CB6 3XD, England

STEADMAN, J. P., bishop. Bd. apostles, bishop Ch. of Our Lord Jesus Christ of the Apostolic Faith Inc., N.Y.C. Office: Ch Our Lord Jesus Christ Apostolic Faith Inc 2081 Adam Clayton Powell Jr New York NY 10027*

STEAGALD, THOMAS RAY, minister; b. Nashville, Jan. 4, 1955; s. Ray Lassister and Sadie Frances (Nall) S.; m. Wanda Jo O'Neal, May 22, 1983; children: Bethany Hope, Jacob Christopher. BA, Belmont Coll., 1976; MDiv, So. Bapt. Theol. Sem., 1980; postgrad., Emory U., 1989—. Ordained to ministry So. Bapt. Conv., 1976; ordained elder United Meth. Ch., 1988. Editor Sunday Sch. Bd. So. Bapt. Conv., Nashville, 1981-82; tchr. Rutledge Coll., Winston-Salem, N.C., 1984-85; pastor Forsyth-Stokes United Meth. Ch., Walnut Cove, N.C., 1985-88, Highlands (N.C.) United Meth. Ch., 1988—; speaker Nat. Conf. on Preaching. Author: Devotionally Yours, Philippians, 1980, The Birth That Changed My Life, 1988; contbr.: Great Preaching, 1991; also articles and revs. to profl. jours. Bd. dirs. Macon County Hospice, Franklin, N.C., 1989—. Home and Office: Highland United Meth Ch PO Box 848 Highlands NC 28741 *If I am to be known for the company I keep, let me keep the company of saints. If I must be known by my enemies, let mine be those of Christ, and the Church, and the will of God in the world. If I must give my life for something, let me give it gladly as those whose deaths make the place of their falling like the Garden of the Lord.*

STEBINGER, PETER ARNOLD ROBICHAUD, rector; b. London, Oct. 14, 1954; came to U.S., 1956; s. Arnold and Jean (Ahlness) S.; m. Caron Sue Robichaud, June 5, 1976; children: Katharine Elizabeth, Ian Michael. BA, Bowdoin Coll., 1976; MDiv, Yale Div. Sch., 1980. Curate St. John's Ch., Waterbury, Conn., 1980-82; rector Christ Episcopal Ch., Bethany, Conn., 1982—; lectr. Yale Div. Sch., New Haven, Conn., 1990—; diocesan spiritual dir. Conn. Episcopal Cursillo, 1989—; cons. Diocese Conn., 1987—; mem. Diocesan Review Commn., Conn., 1987-89. Author: Faith, Focus & Leadership, 1990; contbr. articles to profl. jours. Publ. grantee Ch. Missions Publ. Co., Hartford, Conn., 1990, rsch. grantee Diocese of Conn., Hartford, 1988, Berkeley Div. Sch. at Yale, New Haven, 1988. Mem. Assn. for Creative Change. Republican.

STEC, ROBERT GERARD, school administrator, theologian, priest; b. Cleve., Oct. 8, 1961; s. Frank J. and Rita Jane (Penn) Stec. BA in Psychology, Borromeo Coll., 1983; M in Divinity, MA in Systematic Theology, St. Mary Sem., 1988. Ordained priest Roman Cath. Ch., 1988. Asst. devel. dir. Padua Franciscan High Sch., Parma, Ohio, 1983—, cons., 1984—; cons. Gerald Jindra Devel. Inc., Parma, 1985—; adminstrv. asst. St. Charles Ch., Parma, 1983-87. Author: Adolescent Chemical Dependency: A Diocesan Perspective, 1983, Christian Leadership: Raising a New Paradigm for Vocation Awareness, 1988. Named one of Outstanding Young Men of Am., 1985. Mem. Young Reps. for Reagan, Serra, Internat. Roman Catholic. Lodge: KC. Avocations: skiing, photography, football, classical music. Home: 6319 W Ridgewood Dr Parma OH 44129 Office: St Gabriel Church 9920 Johnnycake Ridge Rd Mentor OH 44060

STEED, ERNEST HORACE JOSEPH, minister; b. Bendigo, Victoria, Australia, Mar. 18, 1925; s. Edward Horace and Violet May (Gadsen) S.; m. Roda Joan Shaw, May 18, 1948; children: Lincoln, Leonie, Martin. Student, Avondale Coll., N.S.W., 1943; diploma in Salesmanship and Sales Mgmt., Internat. Corr. Schs., London, 1952; LLD (hon.), Grant Theol. Sem., 1976; PhD in Behavioral Sci., Pacific Western U., Los Angeles, 1986. Ordained to ministry Seventh-day Adventist Ch., 1960. Pub. sec. West Australia Conf., 1945-47; home missions, pub. relations dir. West Australia Sabbath Sch., 1947-52; youth pub. relations and temperance dir. Australian Div., 1959-66; assoc. dir. temperance dept. Gen. Conf., Washington, 1966-68, dir., 1968-80; spl. asst. to pres. gen. Conf. of Seventh-day Adventists, 1980-88; exec. dir. Real Life Inc., Takoma Park, Md., 1989—. Author: Impaled, 1970, Answer to Alcoholism, 1972, The Great Alternative, 1976, Two be One, 1978, Winds of Change, 1987; editor Alert mag., 1959-66; exec. dir. Listen mag., 1968-80; editor ICPA Quar., 1966-88. Exec. dir. Internat. Commn. for Prevention Alcoholism, 1966-88 (hon. pres., spl. cons. 1988—), Internat Temperance Assn., 1968-80, Am. Temperance Soc., 1968-80; v.p. Am. Council on Alcohol Problems, 1968—; dir. Inst. Sci. Studies for Prevention Alcoholism, Australia, 1960-66; exec. dir. Narcotics Edn., Inc., 1968-80, Non-Smokers Internat, 1968-80; chmn. Washington Council on Smoking and Health, 1971-72; UN rep. for Internat. Commn. for Prevention Alcoholism as Non Govt. Orgn., 1971—; v.p. Nat. Temperance Council (U.S.), 1972-74, pres. 1987—; ofcl corr. Olympic Games, 1956, 64. Recipient St. Ambrose medal City of Milan, 1968, Freedom of City, Medal Sao Paulo, Brazil, 1984. Mem. Pub. Relations Inst. Australia, Pub. Relations Soc. Am., Religious Pub. Relations Council, Internat. Narcotics Law Enforcement Officers Assn., Pub. Health Assn. of Seventh-day Adventist, Christian Writers Assn. N. Am., N.Y. Acad. Scis.. Club: U.S. Nat. Press. Home: 8013 Barron St Takoma Park MD 20912

STEED, TOM ALAN, minister; b. Memphis, Dec. 26, 1950; s. Thomas Adkins and Betty (Kennemore) S.; m. Linda Kay Colvett, Aug. 25, 1972; children: Zachary, Benjamin, Joshua. BA, Harding U., Searcy, Ark., 1972; MAR in Ch. Growth, Harding Grad. Sch. Religion, Memphis, 1984; postgrad., So. Ill. U., 1985—. Assoc. min. Nettleton Ch. of Christ, Jonesboro, Ark., 1975-80; min. Ch. of Christ, Monette, Ark., 1980-85, Carbondale, Ill., 1985—. Contbr. articles to profl. jours. Coach Little League, Carbondale, 1984-90; leader Citizens for a Better Community, Carbondale, 1991—. Mem. Lions (Pres. 1983, Lion of the Yr. 1983). Home: 1719 W Sycamore Carbondale IL 62901 Office: 1805 W Sycamore Carbondale IL 62901

STEEGER, WILLIAM PAUL, religion educator; b. Bklyn., June 26, 1945; s. William Elwood and Elizabeth Theresa (Damm) S.; m. Martha Susan Bowman, Dec. 23, 1968; children: William David, Heidi Elisabeth, Liesl Ruth, Gretchen Ann. BA with honors, U. Fla., 1967; MDiv with honors, So. Bapt. Theol. Sem., Louisville, 1970, PhD, 1983; MA with honors, U. Louisville, 1972. Ordained to ministry So. Bapt. Conv., 1967. Assoc. pastor First Christian Ch., Charlestown, Ind., 1968-70; instr. of history U. Louisville, 1969-73; pastor New Salem Bapt. Ch., Vine Grove, Ky., 1970-76; juvenille ct. liaison specialist Ky. Dept. Human Resources Bur. for Social Svcs., Elizabethtown, Ky., 1973-76; instr. of religion Carson Newman Coll., Jefferson City, Tenn., 1973; pastor Valley View Bapt. Ch., Vine Grove, 1981-84; prof. religion Oakland City (Ind.) Coll. Grad. Sch. of Theology, 1983-84; missionary educator Fgn. Mission Bd. So. Bapt. Conv., Ethiopia, Seychelles, South Africa, 1976-86; prof. religion, dir. Ctr. for Christian Ministry Ouachita Bapt. U., Arkadelphia, Ark., 1986—, chmn. dept. religion, div. religion philosophy, 1989—; dir. Ctr. for Christian Ministries Quachita Bapt. U., Arkadelphia, 1988—. Contbr. articles to profl. jours. Fellowship So. Bapt. Theol. Sem., 1969-73. Fellow Inst. for Bibl. Rsch.; mem. Soc. of Biblical Lit., Evang. Theol. Soc., Nat. Assn. Bapt. Profs. of Religion, Assn. Gen. and Liberal Studies, Phi Kappa Phi. Avocations: organ building, hiking, travel. Office: Ouachita Bapt U OBU Box 3720 Arkadelphia AR 71923

STEELE, JAMES ISAAC, JR., minister; b. Houston, Mar. 22, 1959; s. James Isaac Sr. and Johnnie Victor (McKee) S.; m. Gina Marlene Berry; 1 child, James Isaac III. BS in Bibl. Studies, Abilene Christian U., 1990. Ordained to ministry Ch. of Christ, 1983. Min. youth and family Oak Hills Ch. of Christ, San Antonio, 1984-88, Mayfair Ch. of Christ, Oklahoma City, 1990—; substitute teacher, speaker Chs. of Christ, Tex., Okla., 1981—; bd. dirs., treas. Christian Camps, San Antonio, 1985-88; founder South Tex. Youth Conf., 1987. Writer, puppeteer, performer local TV show Carpenter's Children, 1990—. clown ministry. Recipient Founding award South Tex. Youth Conf., South Tex. Youth Mins., 1991. Mem. Nat. Conf. on Youth Ministry, A Club. Republican. Avocations: reading, wilderness trek, collecting coke memorabilia. Home: 2417 NW 47th Oklahoma City OK 73112 Office: Mayfair Ch of Christ 2340 NW 50th Oklahoma City OK 73112

STEELE, MICHAEL LEO, priest; b. Lynn, Mass., Mar. 15, 1950; s. Ernest Leo Steele and Mary Theresa O'Shea. BA, Merrimack Coll., 1972; MDiv, St. John's Sem., Brighton, 1977, ThM, 1978; MRE, U. San Francisco, 1988. Ordained priest Roman Cath. Ch., 1977; lic., cert. social worker. Dir. religious edn. Blessed Sacrament Parish, Walpole, Mass., 1977-81; dir. religion edn. St. Susanna Parish, Archdiocesan Cath. Sch., 1982—; archdiocesan dir. religious edn. Cath. Schs., Boston, 1991—. Recipient Cardinal's Leadership award Archdiocese Boston, 1988. Mem. Nat. Cath. Edn. Assn., Chief Adminstrs. Cath. Educators. Office: Cath Sch Office 468 Beacon St Boston MA 02115

STEELE, PAUL EUGENE, pastor; b. South Bend, Ind., May 20, 1933; s. Floyd Calvin Steele and Bertha M. (Hildebrand) Steele-Keller; m. Diana M. Johnson, Sept. 8, 1961; children: Richard Paul, Jennifer Joanne Steele Guebard. BA, North Cen. Coll., Naperville, Ill., 1955; BD, Evang. Theol. Sem., Naperville, Ill., 1958, MDiv, 1972; D of Min., McCormick Theol. Sem., Chgo., 1987. Ordained to ministry Evang. United Brethren Ch., 1958. Pastor United Meth. Ch., various cities, Ind., 1958-60, Wanatah, Ind., 1960-64; pastor Parkview United Meth. Ch., Peru, Ind., 1964-72; pastor United Meth. Ch., Lydick, Ind., 1972-75, North Webster, Ind., 1975-78; pastor Calvary United Meth. Ch., Syracuse, Ind., 1978-82, Bethany United Meth. Ch., Ft. Wayne, Ind., 1982-89, North Manchester (Ind.) United Meth. Ch., 1989—; trustee United Meth. Ch. North Ind. Conf., Marion, 1968-76, 84-91, chmn. 1990-91; pres. Peru Ministerial Assn., 1968; exec. coun. St. Joseph County Ministerial Assn., South Bend, 1973-75; pres. Syracuse Ministerial Assn., 1981-82. Home: 110 College Ave North Manchester IN 46962 Office: North Manchester United Meth Ch 306 E Second North Manchester IN 46962

STEEN, MICHAEL BRADLEY, minister; b. Kannapolis, N.C., Aug. 12, 1948; s. Julius Bradley and Lucy Marie (Huie) S.; m. Sherry Ann Julian; children: George Michael, Richard Bradley. AA in Div., Southeastern Sem., 1984; BA in Religion, Mid-Atlantic Bible Coll., 1988, postgrad.; DD (hon.), Asia Bible Coll., 1990. Ordained to ministry So. Bapt. Conv., 1984. Pastor Olive Br. Bapt. Ch., Black Ridge, Va., 1983-84; pastor Thomasboro Bapt. Ch., Charlotte, N.C., 1984-88, Grace Bapt. Ch., Charlotte, 1988—; attended Grad. Sch. Consumer Banking, U. Va., 1979, Exec. Sch. for Bankers, U. Va., 1981, Nat. Compliance Sch. for Bankers, U. Okla., 1980. With USAF, 1966-68. Home: 6335 Teaneck Pl Charlotte NC 28215 Office: Grace Bapt Ch 5232 The Plaza Charlotte NC 28215 *The Bible contains inspiration, challenge and opportunity for all who read it. Let us become encouragers to others so they may find the same things in God's Word that we have found.*

STEEN, RONALD ARDIS, religious music director; b. Greenville, Tex., Sept. 12, 1954; s. Rush Ardis and Winnie Mae (Wright) S.; m. Cynthia Ann Mallory, May 1, 1983. MusB, Stephen F. Austin State U., 1977. Ordained to ministry Assemblies of God Ch., 1983. Minister fine arts, founder and dean sch. music Northland Cathedral, Kansas City, Mo., 1978—; clinician, workshop leader, guest conductor various chs., colls., performing groups. Producer religious music and drama presentations; piano soloist. Named one of Outstanding Young Men Am. U.S. Jaycees, 1981, 88. Mem. Internat. Platform Assn., Am. Choral Dirs. Assn., Choristers Guild. Republican. Avocations: fishing, hunting, racquetball. Home: 5104 N Olive Kansas City MO 64118 Office: Northland Cathedral 600 NE 46th St Kansas City MO 64116

STEFANCIN, JOSEPH FRANK, lay worker; b. Milw., Sept. 3, 1957; s. Joseph Albert and Deloris Francis (Fabry) S.; m. Audrey Ann Schauer, Oct. 10, 1987. Diploma in Printing and Pub., Milw. Area Tech. Coll., 1977, AA in Comml. Art, 1982; BA in Religious Studies, Cardinal Stritch Coll., 1984. Youth min. St. Benedict's Cath. Ch., Fontana, Wis., 1984-85, St. Robert Bellarmine Cath. Ch., Merrill, Wis., 1985-86, St. Aloysius Cath. Ch., West Allis, Wis., 1986-87; lay pastoral assoc. St. Joseph's Cath. Ch., Rhinelander, Wis., 1987—; lay presider Diocese of Superior, Wis., 1990—; lay dir., team worker Teens Encounter Christ, Rhinelander, Park Falls, Hurley, Wis., 1987—; team mem. Engaged Couples Day, Rhinelander, 1987—; bd. mem. Youth Ministry Office, Archdiocese Milw., 1985-86. Contbr. articles to newspapers. Chaplain Boy Scouts Am., Rhinelander, 1989—, summer camp staff, Milw., 1979-87. Mem. Rhinelander Ministerial Assn. (sec. 1988-91), KC (ch. rep. 1990). Office: St Josephs Cath Ch 1350 N Stevens St Rhinelander WI 54501

STEFANIAK, ALICE MARY, religious educator, adult education director; b. Chgo., June 15, 1948; d. Stanley Michael and Helen Marie (Skupien) S. AA, Felician Coll., 1969; BS in Elem. Edn., DePaul U., 1974; MA in Religious Studies, Villanova U., 1979; postgrad., U. Denver, 1989—. Tchr. St. Stanislaus's Elem. Sch., Posen, Ill., 1968-73, St. Hubert's Elem. Sch., Hoffman Estates, Ill., 1973-74; dir. religious edn. St. Hubert's Parish, Hoffman Estates, Ill., 1974-78, St. Mary's Parish, Centralia, Ill., 1979; home visitor for elderly Irvington Mental Health, Centralia, 1980; campus minister Newman Ctr., Ill., 1980-81; adminstrn. coord., tchr. permanent diaconate Diocese Belleville, Ill., 1980-82; dir. adult edn. Diocese Jefferson City, Mo., 1983-88, writer renewal program, 1983—; cons. NACARE Nat. Adult Edn. Group, Wash., 1985-88, writer video NACARE, 1987-88, retreat for women, Belleville, 1980-84. Author, editor: (series books) Crossroads of Faith, 1988, (video segment) Priming the Pump, 1988. Tchr. Laubach Lit. Course, Jefferson City, 1985-88; facilitator Non-violence course for prisoners, 1987. Mem. Nat. Diocesan Dirs. Religious Edn., Nat. Adv. Com. on Adult Religious Edn. Democrat. Roman Catholic. Avocations: nautilus tng., photography, computers, giving parties, travel.

STEFANKO, LEONA EVANS, minister; b. Chgo., Jan. 25, 1945; d. Hyman and Sophie Shapiro; m. D. George Stefanko; 1 child, Tony. BA in Religion, Ottawa U., 1985; MA in Religion, Park Coll., 1988. Ordained to ministry, Unity Ch., 1986. Instr. Unity Sch. Christianity, Unity Village, Mo., 1985-86, dept. chmn., 1986-89; min. Unity Ch. Christianity, Pensacola, Fla., 1989-90; minister Unity of Gulf Breeze, Fla., 1991—. Active theatre, U.S., Can., South Am., Asia, 1963-76. Avocations: reading, theatre, writing.

STEFFEN, LLOYD HOWARD, minister, religion educator; b. Racine, Wis., Nov. 27, 1951; s. Howard C. and Ruth L. (Rode) S.; m. Emmajane S. Finney, Feb. 14, 1981; children: Nathan, Samuel, William. BA, New Coll., 1973; MA, Andover Newton Theol. Sch., 1978; MDiv, Yale U., 1978; PhD, Brown U., 1984. Ordained to ministry United Ch. of Christ, 1983. Chaplain Northland Coll., Ashland, Wis., 1983—, assoc. prof., 1982-90; assoc. prof. Lehigh U., Bethlehem, Pa., 1990—, chaplain, 1990—; mem. theol. com. Wis. Conf. United Ch. of Christ, Madison, 1985-87, mem. div. ch. and ministry NW assn. Wis. Conf., Eau Claire, 1987-90. Author: Self-Deception and the Common Life, 1986; contbr. articles to profl. jours. Town supr. Town of La Pointe, Wis., 1984-87. Recipient NEH Inst. award Harvard U., 1988; univ. fellow Brown U., 1982; faculty devel. grantee Northland Coll., 1986, 90. Mem. Soc. Christian Ethics, Am. Acad. Religion, Assocs. for Religion and Intellectual Life, Assn. for Coordination of Univ. Religious Affairs. Home: 224 W Packer Ave Behtlehem PA 18015 Office: Lehigh U Johnson Hall 36 Bethlehem PA 18015

STEFFENSON, DAVID CONRAD, minister, religion educator; b. Moline, Ill., May 19, 1937; s. John Morris and Esther A. (Conrad) S.; m. Kathleen Davis, Sept. 9, 1959 (div. 1979); children: Mark David, Stacy Serene, Kevin Michael, Kyla Noel, Jeanne Doran, Jamie Doran; m. Jane Petersen, July 7, 1984. BA, U. Denver, 1959; MDiv with honors, Iliff Sch. Theology, 1962; MST, Yale U., 1963; PhD in Environ. Social Ethics, Union Inst., 1985. Ordained to ministry United Meth. Ch. Pastor Walsh (Colo.) and Two Buttes United Meth. Ch., 1963-65; youth minister Park Hill United Meth. Ch., Denver, 1965-67; campus minister U. Wyo., Laramie, 1967-71, U. Wis., Green Bay, 1971-87; pastor Wesley United Meth. Ch., Oshkosh, Wis., 1988—; adj. instr. Cardinal Stritch Coll., Milw., 1987—; mem. ch. and society bd. Wis. Conf. United Meth. Ch., 1987—. Editor conf. proceedings, 1973; contbr. articles to profl. jours. Mem. Winnebago County Literacy Coun., Oshkosh, 1988—. Elizabeth Iliff Warren fellow, 1962, Bishop James Baker fellow Nat. United Meth. Bd. Higher Edn., 1979. Mem. Am. Assn. Religion, Soc. Christian Ethics. Democrat. Office: Wesley United Meth Ch 761 Florida Ave Oshkosh WI 54901 *May our grandchildren thank us rather than curse us for the choices we are now making in our stewardship of God's Creation.*

STEGALL, JOEL RINGGOLD, university administrator; b. Hartford, N.C., Apr. 7, 1939; s. Joel Frank and Irma (Ringgold) S.; m. Ruth Ellen Sorrell (div. June 1974); children: Paul, Sharon, Diana; m. June Carol Langston; 1 child, Jeffrey Randall. BA, Wake Forest U., 1961; M of Music Edn., U. N. Tex., 1962; postgrad., La. State U., 1967-68; PhD, U. N.C., 1975. Tchr. vocal music Montgomery County Schs., Silver Spring, Md., 1964-65; instr. to assoc. prof., dept. chmn. Mars Hill (N.C.) Coll., 1968-76; dean sch. of music Ithaca (N.Y.) Coll., 1976-85; prof., chmn. dept. of music U. Fla., Gainesville, 1985-90; v.p. acad. affairs Shenandoah Univ., Winchester, VA, 1990—; conductor, clinician, adjudicator of 24 choral festivals; cons. higher edn. to numerous colls. and univs.; steward Am. Civilization Seminar, Gainesville, 1986—; discussion leader State of Fla. Univ. System Confs. on Acad. Leadership, 1967—; speaker profl. confs. Contbr. articles to profl. jours. and chpts. to books; reviewer of choral music. 1st lt. U.S. Army, 1962-64. Mem. Nat. Assn. Schs. of Music (vice-chmn. Region 7 1986-89), Fla. Assn. Schs. of Music (v.p. 1987-89), Am. Choral Dirs. Assn., Music Educators Nat. Conf., Phi Kappa Phi, Phi Mu Alpha, Phi Delta Kappa. Avocation: photography. Office: Shenandoah Univ Office of Acad Affairs Winchester VA 22601

STEGMAN, ROSE BERTHA, religion educator; b. Pitts., Jan. 22, 1946; d. Herman Joseph and Bertha Kathrine (Lebo) S. Student, Mt. Mercy Coll., Pitts., 1962, Cath. U. P.R., 1971; BA, La Roche Coll., 1972; MEd, Duquesne U., 1975. Cert. dir. religious edn. Preschool tchr. Concord Acad., 1975-76; elem. tchr. St. Mary Sch., Glenshaw, Pa., 1976-79, St. Joseph Sch., Pitts., 1979-80; parish sec., pastoral aid St. Mary Ch., Glenshaw, 1981-82, dir. religious edn., coord., 1982—; mem. Parish Coun., Sharpsburg, Pa., 1988—; del. Deanery Rep. to Diocese, Pitts., 1989—; chairperson Diocesan Coord. Planning Com., Pitts, 1989—; mem. Diocesan Task Force, Pitts, 1990—. Mem. De Nada (assoc.). Office: 2510 Middle Rd Glenshaw PA 15116

STEHR, JOHN WILLIAM, minister; b. Lake City, Minn., May 31, 1911; s. John William Stehr and Paulina Sprikes; m. Martha Ann Hass, June 22, 1937; children: Harriet Alice, Phyllis Ann, John William Jr., Richard Allen, Ronald Eugene. Student, Concordia Coll., St. Paul, 1925-31, Concordia Sem., St. Louis, 1931-35; BA in History, Valparaiso U., 1933. Missionary Blackduck Tenstrike (Minn.) Mission, 1936-40; pastor Red Lake Falls, Wylie Plummer, Minn., 1940-48, St. John Luth. Ch., Wood Lake, Minn., 1948-54, Trinity Luth. Ch., Waconia, Minn., 1954-81; part-time pastoral worker Trinity and neighboring congregations, 1981—; counsellor Carver County Cir., Minn. South Dist., 1968-74; Bible Class Leader Westview Retirement, Waconia, 1985—, Bible Study Leader Trinity Srs. for Christ, 1985—, cir. dir. Luth. Ch. Extension Fund, Minn. South Dist., 1985—. Founder Luth. High Sch., Mayer, Minn., 1962; zone chmn. Luth. Laymens League, 1970-87; Minnetonka rep. to Saints Alive; Growing Ever Serving, 1990; chmn. State Ret. Pastors and Tchrs. Conf., 1990; bd. dirs. Minn. South Dist. Named Outstanding Sr. Citizen Carver County, Minn., 1988. Republican. Home: 351 W 4th St Waconia MN 55387 *I am convinced that the most rewarding activity of my life has been to bring the comfort of the Gospel to young and old, to see them walking in the truth, and to hear an expression of gratitude for this blessing.*

STEIB, JAMES TERRY, bishop. Ordained priest Roman Cath. Ch., 1967. Titular bishop Fallaba, 1983; aux. bishop St. Louis, 1983; consecrated bishop, 1984. Address: Old Cathedral Rectory 209 Walnut St Saint Louis MO 63102

STEICKE, LANCE GRAHAM, church executive; b. Murray Bridge, Australia, Feb. 19, 1933; s. Ewald Rudolph and Olga Gertrude (Schutz) S.; m. Leah Gwenneth Briese, Dec. 13, 1955; children: Janet Ruth, Peter Andrew, Michael James, Liisa Kathryn. BTh., Concordia Sem., Australia, 1955; DD (hon.), Luth. Ch.-Mo. Synod, St. Louis, 1989. Sec. Evang. Luth. Ch. New Zealand, 1960-63, v.p., 1963-64, pres., 1964-79; bd. dirs. Bd. Radio & TV Luth. Ch. Australia, 1979-87, 2d v.p., 1981, pres., 1987. Office: Luth Ch House, 58 O'Connell St, North Adelaide SA 5067, Australia

STEIMLE, PAUL R., small business owner, pharmacist; b. Grand Rapids, Mich., May 26, 1930; s. Paul B. and Helen G. (Schofield) S.; m. Sylvia B. Harris, Aug. 9, 1952; children: Russell P., Judith L. Becker, Autumn J. Bosch. BS, Ferris State U., 1952. Registered pharmacist. Trustee Christian Counseling Svc., Holland, Mich., 1970-72, Good Samaritan Ctr., Holland, 1978-80, Echo Broadcasting, Inc., Zeeland, Mich., 1981-90; owner Niagara Therapy Dealership, Holland, Mich., 1986—; treas. Echo Broadcasting Inc., Zeeland, 1983-90. With U.S. Army, 1952-54, Korea. Mem. Mich. Pharmacist Assn. Baptist. Home: 57 W 21st St Holland MI 49423 Office: Echo Broadcasting Inc PO Box 40 Zeeland MI 49464

STEIMLING, FREDERICK RALPH, religious lay worker, broadcasting executive; b. New Brunswick, N.J., Dec. 5, 1961; s. Allen Warren and Shirley Mae (Applegate) S. Grad. high sch., Spotswood, N.J., 1980. Lay worker Gateway Community Ch., Freehold, N.J., 1981-85, New Life Assembly of God, Lancaster, Pa., 1985—; ops. mgr. Sta. WJTL, Joy Pub. Broadcasting, Lancaster, 1985—. Mem. YMCA, Lancaster, 1988—. Mem. Gospel Music Assn. Office: Sta WJTL 780 Eden Rd Lancaster PA 17601 *As mankind continues to endure tragic events it is with hope and prayer that those of who know the truth will cling unswervingly to His precepts and habits. The reality of all that Christ embodies is desperately needed regardless of convenience.*

STEIN, DAVID TIMOTHY, minister; b. Chillicothe, Mo., Apr. 25, 1936; s. Frederick Carl and Irene Edith (Kroggel) S.; m. Judith Ann Ritchhart, June 6, 1959; children: Laurie Beth, David Scott, Timothy Christian, Michelle Ann. BA in Humanities, Concordia Coll., St. Louis, 1958; diploma in theology, Concordia Sem., St. Louis, 1961; MA in Speech, St. Louis U., 1962, PhD in Higher Edn. Adminstrn., 1979. Ordained to ministry Luth. Ch.-Mo. Synod, 1962. Prof. Concordia U., River Forest, Ill., 1962-79, dean of students, asst. to pres., dir. pub. rels., dir. placement, 1962-79; dir. parish rels. and lay tng. Luth. Gen. Hosp., Park Ridge, Ill., 1979-85; exec. adminstr. Park Ridge Ctr. Luth. Gen. Health Care System, 1985-89; sr. pastor Evang. Luth. Ch. of the Apostles, Melrose Park, Ill., 1989-91, Evang. Ch. of the Holy Spirit, Elk Grove Village, Ill., 1991—; trustee Luth. Film Assocs., N.Y.C., 1968-80; mem. com. on campus life Luth. Ch.-Mo. Synod, Chgo., 1979-82; assoc. Hastings Inst., 1985—; pres. Ethics Mgmt. Cons. Svc., River Forest, 1988—. Author: A Circle of Love, 1967; editor Chronicle of Pastoral Care, 1980-88; producer film College With a Cause, 1964 (award San Francisco Film Festival). Co-chair coll. and sch. div. Community Chest, Oak Park/River Forest, Ill., 1964-65, coach, sponsor Little League Assn., River Forest, 1970-78; active Citizens Adv. Com., River Forest, 1975-78; bd. mgrs. Gen. PTA, River Forest, 1977-78; bd. dirs. Luth. Community Svcs. for the Aged, Arlington Heights, Ill., 1985—. Recipient citation N.Y. Graphic Arts Soc., 1967, Chgo. Graphic Arts Soc., 1968; Aid Assn. for Luths. fellow, 1973. Mem. Park Ridge Assocs., Oak Park/River Forest Clergy Assn., Religious Pub. Rels. Coun. Inc. (pres. Chgo. chpt., nat. gov. 1986-90, DeRose Hinkhouse award 1968-87). Home: 550 Clinton Pl River Forest IL 60305 Office: Evang Luth Ch of the Holy Spirit 666 Elk Grove Blvd Elk Grove Village IL 60007 *The most significant dilemma the religious communities and traditions face in a world of diminishing services is the allocation of resources, moral, spiritual, social, educational, economic, and their applications to the growth of artificial intelligence.*

STEIN, JOHN CHRISTOPHER, minister; b. Kansas City, Mo., July 13, 1961; s. Neil Leslie and Carolyn Faye (Cagle) S.; m. Anne Elizabeth Spencer, May 30, 1987; 1 child, Joshua Christopher. BA, Cen. Meth. Coll., 1983; MDiv, Candler Sch. Theology, 1986. Ordained to ministry United Meth. Ch. as elder, 1988. Minister to youth Linn Meml. United Meth. Ch., Fayette, Mo., 1980-81, Versailles (Mo.) United Meth. Ch., 1981-83, Griffin (Ga.) United Meth. Ch., 1983-86; pastor Clayton United Meth. Ch., St. Louis, 1986-89, Green Trails United Meth. Ch., Chesterfield, Mo., 1989-91, Bismarck United Meth. Ch., 1991—, Belgrade (Mo.) United Meth. Ch., 1991—; del. to jurisdictional conf. Mo. E. conf., United Meth. Ch., Little Rock, 1980, alt. del. to gen. conf., 1980, del. to World Meth. Evangelism Convocation, Singapore, 1991, World Meth. Conf., Singapore, 1991; mem. com. on parish and community devel. St. Louis North dist., 1989-91, mem. com. on ch. bldg. and location, 1988-91, new life missioner, key event herald gen. bd., Nashville, 1986—; coord. com. on parish and community devel. Cape-Girardau-Farmington dist., 1991—, mem. com. on evangelism, 1991—, coord. youth ministries, 1991—; cons. L.E.A.D. Cons., Columbus, Ohio, 1989—. Bd. dirs. Coop. Offender-Parish Enterprise, St. Louis, 1990. Avocations: photography, softball, backpacking, table tennis. Office: Belgrade United Meth Ch Hwy C Belgrade MO 63622

STEIN, KENNETH JAMES, minister, church history educator; b. Grand Forks, N.D., Dec. 22, 1929; s. Gustav and Anna Marie (Sommer) S.; m. Leatta Mae Bahr, July 12, 1953; children: Mary Beth, Paul Robert. BA, Westmar Coll., 1953, DD (hon.), 1974; BD, Evang. Theol. Sem., 1956; MST, Union Theol. Sem., N.Y.C., 1958, PhD, 1965. Ordained to ministry United Meth. Ch., 1956. Pastor Christ Evang. United Brethren Ch., Paterson, N.J., 1956-60; prof. ch. history Evang. Theol. Sem., Naperville, Ill., 1960-72, dean, 1972-73, pres., 1973-74; dean Garrett-Evang. Theol. Sem., Evanston, Ill., 1974-77, prof. ch. history, 1977—, dir. Inst. for Study Methodism and Related Movements, 1979—. Author: Philipp Jakob Spener: Pietist Patriarch, 1986, Great Devotional Classics Study Guide, 1989. Hartmann scholar Evang. Theol. Sem., 1955-56, Hartmann fellow, 1957-58; Faculty fellow Assn. Theol. Schs., 1970-71; Fulbright travel grantee, 1977-78. Mem. Am. Soc. Ch. History. Office: Garrett-Evang Theol Sem 2121 Sheridan Rd Evanston IL 60201

STEIN, ROBERT HARRY, educator; b. Jersey City, N.J., Mar. 13, 1935; s. William and Ella (Schiller) S.; m. Joan L. (Thatcher), July 28; children: Julie Joan, Keith Robert, Stephen William. BA, Rutgers U., 1956; BD, Fuller Theol. Sem., 1959; MST, Andover Newton Theol. Sem., 1966; PhD, Princeton Theol. Sem., 1968. Asst. prof. Bethel Coll., St. Paul, 1969-79; prof. Bethel Theol. Sem., St. Paul, 1980—. Author: The Method and Message of Jesus' Teachings, 1978, An Introduction to the Parables, 1981, The Synoptic Problem, 1987, Difficult Passages in the N.T., 1990. Fellow Inst. Biblical Rsch.; mem. Soc. Biblical Lit., Evang. Theol. Soc. Home: 417 Bear Ave S Vadnais Heights MN 55127 Office: Bethel Theol Sem 3949 Bethel Dr Saint Paul MN 55112

STEIN, STEPHEN JAY, cantor; b. Pitts., Dec. 20, 1952; s. Murray George and Frances Stein; m. Abbe G. Kaufman, July 31, 1977; children: Scott Michael, Deana Sheryl. BA, Duquesne U., 1974; diploma of Hazzan, Jewish Theol. Sem., 1978. Cantor Beth Jacob Congregation, Norwich, Conn., 1976-80, Beth El Congregation, Akron, Ohio, 1980—. Initiator recordings for pub. radio; contbr. articles on Jewish music to newspapers. Bd. dirs. Jerome Lippman Sch., Akron, 1989—. Mem. Am. Soc. Jewish Music, Cantors Inst. Alumni Orgn., Cantors Assembly (chmn. tri-state region 1987-89, internat. treas. 1989-91, internat. v.p. 1991), Jewish Community Profls. of Akron. Office: 464 S Hawkins Ave Akron OH 44320

STEINBACH, ALAN HENRY, church official; b. St. Louis, Aug. 5, 1930; s. John Emil and Erna (Gieselmann) S.; m. Ruth A. Wischmeier, June 28, 1953; children—Steven, Carol. B.S., Concordia Coll., 1952; M.A., San Diego State U., 1957; M.Sci. Teaching, U. Ariz., 1964; Ph.D., U. Tex., 1968; cert. in theology Concordia Seminary, St. Louis, 1987. Sch. prin., San Diego, 1952-61; prof. chemistry St. John's Coll., Winfield, Kans., 1961-70, acad. dean, 1970-78; v.p., acad. dean Bethany Coll., Lindsborg, Kans., 1979-85; dir. student Personnel Bd. Hgher Edn. Services, Luth. Ch.-Mo. Synod, 1985—. ednl. cons. Kans. Dist. Luth. Ch.-Mo. Synod, 1979-85. Mem. Total Community Devel., Winfield, 1970-72; bd. dirs. Kans. Dist., Lutheran Ch.-Mo. Synod, 1973-85; vice chmn. Cowley County chpt. Am. Cancer Soc., 1975-76; chmn. Kans. Corrections Ombudsman Bd., 1976-84. Named Winfield Citizen of Month, Optimist Club, 1978. Mem. Luth. Edn. Assn., Nat. Assn. Student Pers. Adminstrs., Am. Assn. Univ. Adminstrs., Rotary, Phi Delta Kappa. Contbr. chpts. to books, publs. in field. Home: 12868 Crab Thicket Ln Saint Louis MO 63131 Office: Internat Hdqrs Luth Ch-Mo Synod 1333 S Kirkwood Saint Louis MO 63122

STEINBOCK, JOHN T., bishop; b. Los Angeles, July 16, 1937. Student, Los Angeles Diocesan sems. Ordained priest Roman Cath. Ch., 1963. Aux. bishop Diocese of Orange, Calif., 1984-87; bishop Diocese of Santa Rosa, Calif., 1987—; titular bishop of Midila, 1984. Office: Diocese of Santa Rosa 547 B St PO Box 1297 Santa Rosa CA 95402

STEINBRUCK, JOHN FREDERICK, minister. BS, U. Pa., 1954; MDiv, Luth. Theol. Sem., Phila, 1959, DMin., 1979; student, Urban Tng. Ctr., Chgo., 1970. Ordained minister Luth. Ch., 1959. Asst. pastor St. John's Luth. Ch., Nazareth, Pa., 1959-60; pastor Zion Luth. Ch., Easton, Pa., 1960-62; indsl. engr. Standard Pressed Steel, Jenkintown, Pa., 1954-57; pastor St. John's Luth. Ch., Easton, 1962-1970, Luther Pl. Meml. Ch., Washington, 1970—; dean Easton dist. LCA's S.E. Pa. Synod, 1968-69; instr. Wshington Consortium of Sems. course. Bd. dirs. Luther Place N St. Village for Homeless. Capt. USNR, ret. Mem. Nat. Conf. Christians and Jews (bd. dirs.), Interfaith Conf. Met. Washington (bd. dirs.). Avocations: handball, jogging, travel to bible lands. Office: Luther Pl Meml Ch 1226 Vermont Ave NW Washington DC 20005

STEINER, KENNETH DONALD, bishop; b. David City, Nebr., Nov. 25, 1936; s. Lawrence Nicholas and Florine Marie (Pieters) S. B.A., Mt. Angel Sem., 1958; M.Div., St. Thomas Sem., 1962. Ordained priest Roman Catholic Ch., 1962, bishop, 1978; asso. pastor various parishes Portland and Coos Bay, Oreg., 1962-72; pastor Coquille Ch., Myrtle Point, Powers, Oreg., 1972-76, St. Francis Ch., Roy, Oreg., 1976-77; aux. bishop Diocese of Portland, Oreg., 1977—; vicar of worship and ministries and personnel dir. clergy personnel Portland Archdiocese. Democrat. Office: 2838 E Burnside St Portland OR 97214

STEINER, LUKE JOSEPH, priest; b. Mandan, N.D., Aug. 27, 1930; s. Joseph Nickolas Steiner and Helen Rose Landeis. BA, St. John's U., Collegeville, Minn., 1951; STL, Collegio de S Anselmo, Rome, 1957; SSL, Pontil Bibl. Inst., Rome, 1960. Ordained priest Roman Cath. Ch., 1956. Dean Sch. Theology St. John's U., Collegeville, Minn., 1965-68, prof. N.T. studies, 1960—, dir. Jerusalem studies program, 1978—. Mem. Cath. Bibl. Assn., Soc. Bibl. Lit. Home: St Johns Abbey Collegeville MN 56321

STEINHAUS, O. OTTO, minister; b. Bolivar, Mo., Aug. 26, 1929; s. Oliver Otto and Pearl Thelma (Linton) S.; m. Carolyn Joan Riehm, Dec. 28, 1953; children: Carol Lynn, Philip Alan, Charles Linton, Stephen Otto. BA, Cen. Meth. U., 1951; MDiv, Garrett Sem., 1954; MA, Northwestern U., 1960. Pastor Immanuel United Meth. Ch., Canton, Mo., 1962-68; dir. Wesley Found. Campus Ministry, Columbia, Mo., 1968-78; sr. pastor Court St. United Meth. Ch., Fulton, Mo., 1978-85, Concord Trinity United Meth. Ch., St. Louis, 1985-89, New McKendree United Meth. Ch., Jackson, Mo., 1989—; trustee Ozarks Meth. Manor, Marionville, Mo., 1989—; chair deaf ministry com. Mo. East Conf., 1986—; chmn. Wesley Found. Bd., Cape Girardeau, Mo., 1989—; conf. coord. United Meth. Ch. age-level coun. Mo. East Conf., 1988—. Pres. Kiwanis Internat., Fulton, 1983-84. Mem. Rotary. Democrat. Home: 605 Connie Jackson MO 63755 Office: New McKendree United Meth Ch 209 S High Jackson MO 63755

STEINKAMP, SISTER MARY KATHLEEN, religious organization administrator; b. Balt., May 21, 1935; d. Herman August and Catherine Eileen (Fogarty) S. BA in Math., Mt. St. Agnes, 1957; MAT in Math. Edn., Tulane U., 1969; BA in Legal Studies, U. Balt., 1982. Joined Sisters of Mercy, Roman Cath. Ch., 1957. Tchr., adminstr. Mercy High Sch., Mobile, Ala., 1962-67; tchr. Mt. De Sales High Sch., Macon, Ga., 1967-68; tchr., adminstr. St. Pius X High Sch., Atlanta, 1968-75; dir. fin. Sisters of Mercy, Balt., 1976-82; exec. dir. Nat. Assn. of Treas. of Religious Insts., Silver Spring, Md., 1982-88; project dir. Joint Retirement Project, Balt., 1988-91, chair maj. gifts, 1991—; del. Sisters of Mercy of Union, Silver Spring, 1976-88; mem. fin. com. Sisters of Mercy of Balt., 1980-90; chmn. bd. dirs. St. Joseph Hosp., Dahlonega, Ga. Trustee Mercy Health Service of the South, Atlanta, 1970—. Mem. Am. Soc. Assn. Execs., Am. Mgmt. Assn., Mensa, Kappa Gamma Pi, Sigma Phi Sigma. Democrat. Avocation: needlepoint. Office: 6806 Bellona Ave Baltimore MD 21212

STEINKE, PETER LOUIS, minister, counselor; b. Glen Cove, N.Y., June 18, 1938; s. Arthur Ferdinand and Marguerite (Frankel) S.; m. Carolyn Joyce Wagner, June 14, 1963; children: Rene, Timothy, Krista, Matthew. BA, Concordia Sr. Coll., Ft. Wayne, Ind., 1960; STM, Concordia Sem., St. Louis, 1964; MA, Presbyn. Sch. Christian Edn., Richmond, Va., 1968; D of Religion, Chgo. Theol. Sem., 1971. Ordained minister Luth. Ch.-Mo. Synod, 1964; lic. profl. counselor, Tex. Pastor Grace Luth. Ch., Chester, Va., 1964-68, Hope Luth. Ch., Friendswood, Tex., 1973-82; dir. clergy care Luth. Soc. Svcs. Tex., Austin, 1982—; bd., dirs. S.W. Career Devel. Ctr., Arlington, Tex.; lectr. workshops, seminars to clergy groups, confs. and convs. Author: Dealing With Your Discontent, 1988, Preaching the Theology of the Cross, 1983; contbr. numerous articles to religious jours. Mem. Am. Assn. Pastoral Counselors. Home: 11459 Rustic Rock Dr Austin TX 78750 Office: Luth Social Svc Tex 314 Highland Mall Blvd Ste 110 Austin TX 78752

STEINMANN, ANDREW ERWIN, religion educator, editor; b. Cin., May 29, 1954; s. Melvin Louis and Grace Marie (Masters) S.; m. Rebecca Ann Sizelove; children: Christopher, Jennifer. BS in Chem. Engring., U. Cin., 1977; MDiv, Concordia Theol. Seminary, Fort Wayne, Ind., 1981; PhD, U. Mich., 1990. Assoc. pastor St. John Luth. Ch., Fraser, Mich., 1981-86; asst. prof. Concordia Coll., Ann Arbor, Mich., 1986-91; supervising transl. editor new evang. transl. of Bible, God's Word to the Nations Bible Soc., Fairview Park, Ohio, 1991—. Contbr. articles to profl. jours. Mem. Soc. Bibl. Lit., Evang. Theol. Soc., Mich. Acad. Sci., Arts and Letters. Office: God's Word to the Nations Bible Soc 22050 Mastick Rd Fairview Park OH 44126

STEINWURZEL, DAVID MOSHE, rabbi; b. Vienna, Austria, Feb. 25, 1934; came to U.S., 1939; s. Lazar and Esther (Gutstein) S.; m. Rivke Nitzlich, June 9, 1954; children: Fraida, Isaac, Abraham, Chaya Miriam, Leah, Israel, Esther, Rachel, Dubbie, Ephraim, Mordechai, Sarah, Devorah, Naftali. Degree, Mesivta Torah Vodaat, 1954. Ordained rabbi, 1954. Head postgrad. dept. Mesivta Torah Vodaat, Bklyn., 1961-64; rosh yeshiva Mesivta Eitz Chaim of Bobov, 1965—; rabbi Bais Ephriam of Flatbush, Bklyn., 1970—; pres. Noam Shabbos Charity, Jerusalem, 1988—. Contbr. articles to religious mags. Fellow Igud Horabonim. Home: 2802 Ave J Brooklyn NY 11210 Office: Mesivta Eitz Chaim 1577 48th St Brooklyn NY 11210 *Life is meaningful only when one devotes it to the service of God and humanity.*

STELLING, NANCY JOAN, religious periodical editor; b. Oak Park, Ill., May 20, 1937; d. Raymond Harold and Ruth Marie (Edmunds) Corbett; m. Gary Dean Stelling, Sept. 1, 1973. BA, Valparaiso U., 1959; MA, Webster U., 1987. Editorial assoc. Luth. Witness Reporter, Luth. Ch.-Mo. Synod, St. Louis, 1964-66, editor Interaction mag., 1966-73; editorial assoc. World Encounter mag., Luth. Ch. in Am., Phila., 1975-80; sec. for program resources Luth. Ch. Women, Phila., 1980-87; editor Luth. Woman Today Women of the Evang. Luth. Ch. Am., Chgo., 1987—. Contbr. articles to religious publs. Vol. Cystic Fibrosis orgn., St. Louis, 1985-86; supporter, mem. Bread for the World, St. Louis, 1985-91. Mem. Religious Pub. Rels. Coun. (bd. govs. 1987-91, DeRose Hinkhouse award 1989, 90), Associated Ch. Press (profl. growth com. 1989-90, award of merit 1990). Home: 206 Kilmorack Dr Cary NC 27511-6350 Office: Luth Woman Today 8765 W Higgins Rd Chicago IL 60631

STELMACH, SISTER MARIE ANNA, nun, religious education director; b. Balt., July 10, 1945; d. John Julien and Jean Lillian (Kaczmarczyk) S. BA, Rosary Coll., River Forest, Ill., 1968; MDiv, Immaculate Conception Sem., 1983; MA in Systematic Theology, Seton Hall U., 1984; postgrad., St. Michael's Coll., Winooski, Vt., 1990—. Joined Sinsinawa Dominican Sisters, Roman Cath. Ch., 1963. Jr. high sch. tchr., 1967-74; pastoral min., missionary Santa Cruz, Bolivia, 1974-77; ministry Missionaries of Charity, Bronx, N.Y., 1978; parish dir. religion edn. Sacred Heart Parish, Washington, 1979-84; pastor, missionary Port of Spain, Trinidad, 1984-87; dir. Inst. Catechetics and Spirituality, New Orleans, 1987—, dir. Office Religious Edn., 1989—. Contbr. articles to profl. jours.; author tapes. Organizer U.S. Cath. Conf. for Cuban refugees, Ft. Camp McCoy, Wis. and Ft. Indian Town, Pa., 1980. Mem. N.Am. Forum on The Catechumenate (nat. presenter, lectr. 1987—). 1st women appointed by archbishop to serve as New Orleans archdiocesan dir. of religious edn., 1990. Home: 2824 Keith-Way Dr Harvey LA 70058 Office: Archdiocese New Orleans 7887 Walmsley Ave New Orleans LA 70125

STELMACHOWICZ, MICHAEL JOSEPH, religion educator; b. St. Louis, Sept. 18, 1927; s. Michael Joseph Sr. and Esther Fern (Boylan) S.; m. Betty Alma Rivers; children: Candyce Stelmachowicz Seider, Cheryl Stelmachowicz Wawrzyniak, Cary, Crystal Stelmachowicz Welter, Corrie Stelmachowicz Klatt. AA, St. John's Coll., Winfield, Kans., 1947; BS in Edn., Concordia Tchrs. Coll., Seward, Nebr., 1950; MEd, St. Louis U., 1954; BA, MDiv, Concordia Sem., St. Louis, 1957; PhD, U. Nebr., 1966. Cert. elem. tchr.; cert. secondary tchr.; cert. secondary sch. adminstr. Prin. Luth. High Sch., St. Louis, 1957-61; dean of students, placement dir. Concordia Tchrs. Coll., Seward, 1961-68, pres., 1978-84; supt. Luth. High Sch. Assn., Detroit, 1968-73; pres. St. John's Coll., Winfield, Kans., 1973-78; exec. dir. Bd. for Higher Edn. Svcs., Luth. Ch.-Mo. Synod, St. Louis, 1984—; mem., chair Bd. Youth Ministry, Luth. Ch.-Mo. Synod, St. Louis, 1965-77, Commn. on Theology and Ch. Rels., St. Louis, 1978-84; mem. div. theol. studies Luth. Coun.-USA, N.Y.C., 1982-87. Editor: Peace and the Just War Tradition, 1986; Issues in Christian Edn. jour., 1966-68. Active Mayor's Commn. on Human Resources, Detroit, 1969-70; mem. exec. bd. Quivera coun. Boy Scouts Am., Wichita, Kans., 1976-78. Recipient St. Paul's award St. Paul's Coll., 1989, Christus Primus award Concordia Coll., 1990. Mem. Luth. Edn. Assn., Am. Assn. Higher Edn., Assn. Luth. Secondary Schs. (hon. life), Execs. in Ch.-Related Higher Edn. Office: Luth Ch-Mo Synod 1333 S Kirkwood Saint Louis MO 63122

STEMBRIDGE, RUDY, JR., religious organization administrator, author; b. Miami, Fla., Oct. 26, 1956; s. Melvin R. Sr. and Dorothy M. (Adams) S.; m. Cynthia M. Smith, July 6, 1979; children: Steven Scott, Kevin Lee. BS, Tenn. Temple U., 1980. Music dir., trustee Tri-County Bapt. Temple, Rossville, Ga., 1980—; v.p., dir. adminstrn. and accounts. Word for the World Bapt. Ministries, Rossville, 1980—. Author: Personal Finances, 1991. Office: Word for World Bapt Mins PO box 849 Rossville GA 30741-0849 *Christians today have "robbed themselves" of so many blessings the Lord wants to give to them. The way most Christians miss these blessings is by their vision being blurred, or even blinded by money, or the "love of money". By getting their finances in proper Biblical order, they can begin to experience what the Bible calls "True Riches." (See Luke 16:10-11 KJV).*

STEMPER, WILLIAM HERMAN, JR., clergyman; s. William Herman Sr. and Mildred (Wells) S. BA in History with honors, Stetson U., 1969, Emory U., 1972; MDiv., Union Theol. Sem., 1974. Founder, coordinator, dir. Forum for Corp. Responsibility, Inc., N.Y.C., 1974-76; cons. com. on social responsibility in investments Episcopalian Ch. Exec. Council, N.Y.C., 1975-76; curate, asst. rector Episcopal Ch. of the Epiphany, N.Y.C., 1976-80; exec. sec. Grottoes of N.Am., Columbus, Ohio, 1980-83; chmn., dir. Stemper Realty, Inc., Fla., 1982-85; vicar for corp. affairs Episcopal Diocese of N.Y., 1981—; exec. dir. Corp. Forum of N.Y., Inc., N.Y.C., 1981—; originator, tchr. grad. sem. NYU, 1979—; lectr. in field; guest lectr. Columbia U., NYU, The Browning Sch., Gen. Theol. Sem., Auburn Sem./Union Theol. Sem., Bryant Coll., Shrewsbury Sch., King Edward VI Grammar Sch., Norwich, St. John's Coll. Sch., Cambridge, Eng.; assoc. The Ch. of the Resurrection, N.Y.C., 1982-85; cons. in Pub. Issues to Citibank, N.A., 1980-85, Avon Products, Inc.; organizer numerous religious consultations and seminars; chmn. Consultation on Ch. and Corp. Philanthropy, 1989; cons. in bus. and corp. outreach Christ Ch. (Episc.), Cin., 1989. Contbr. numerous articles in field. Mem. exec. com. Cranmer Soc.-Univ. Anglican Soc., Oxford U.; dir. consultation with Rev. Desmond Tutu and State Pres. of Republic of South Africa with U.S. corp. and religious leaders, 1990. Fellow Royal Soc. Arts, Medici Acad. (U.S. rector, senator Florence, Italy); mem. SAR, S.R., KT, KP, Pilgrims of U.S., Soc. Bus. Ethics Mil. Order Loyal Legion, Pub. Rels. Soc. (N.Y. chpt.), Mayflower Soc. (elder N.Y. State chpt.), Friends of St. George's (U.S. v.p.), Royal Soc. St. George (London; life), Windsor, Descendants of Knights of Garter, Internat. Soc. Fraternal Chief Execs. (pres. 1989-90), Soc. Descendants Colonial Clergy, The Netherlands Soc. (Phila.), Somerset chpt. Order of Magna Charta Barons, Baronial Order Magna Charta, Order of Crown of Charlemagne, Jr. Order United Am. Mechanics, Sons Union Vets., Keble Coll. Oxford U., Sion Coll. Club (London), Oxford U. Soc., United Oxford and Cambridge Univs. Club (London), Elks, Moose, Masons (32 degree, hon. imperial chaplain Shrine of N.Am., Anson Jones lectr. in history of freemasonry Waco, Tex., 1989, Royal Arch Masons Internat. gen. grand chaplain, Knight Comdr. Ct. Honour, Order Amaranth), Odd Fellows (past noble grand), Shriners (past noble grand), Order of DeMolay (hon., internat. supreme coun.), Pi Kappa Phi, Omicron Delta Kappa, Phi Alpha Theta. Home: 774 9th Ave Ste 3FN New York NY 10019 Office: 593 Park Ave New York NY 10021 also: Oxford U, Keble Coll, Oxford 0X1 3PG, England *Faith enables enhanced perception in day-to-day life, which discloses increased opportunity for service.*

STENBERG, RICHARD STEPHEN, deacon, tax analyst; b. South Bend, Ind., Aug. 24, 1937; s. Richard Roland and Margaret Elaine (Kertesz) S.; m. Margaret Christine Hudon, June 29, 1963; children: Kristin, Katherine, Stephen, Richard A. BS in Metall. Engring., Purdue U., 1959; MBA, U. Pitts., 1975. Tax analyst Union Carbide Corp., Danbury, Conn., 1959—; mem. pastoral coun. Diocese of Bridgeport, Conn., 1987-90, dir. permanent deacons, 1990—; deacon St. Pius X Roman Cath. Ch., Fairfield, 1985. With U.S. Army, 1960. Home: 355 Gilbert Hwy Fairfield CT 06430 Office: Union Carbide Corp Old Ridgebury Rd Danbury CT 06817-0001

STENDAHL, KRISTER, retired bishop; b. Stockholm, Sweden, Apr. 21, 1921; came to U.S., 1954, naturalized, 1967; s. Olof and Sigrid (Ljungquist) S.; m. Brita Johnsson, Sept. 7, 1946; children: John, Anna, Daniel. Teol. kand., U. Uppsala, Sweden, 1944, teol. lic., 1949, teol.dr., 1954; Litt. D. (hon.), Upsala Coll., 1963; D.D., St. Olaf Coll., 1971, Harvard U., 1985, St. Andrews U., 1987; LL.D., Susquehanna U., 1973; L.H.D. (hon.), Hebrew Union Coll./Jewish Inst. Religion, 1980, Brandeis U., 1981. Ordained priest

Ch. of Sweden, 1944; chaplain to students Uppsala U., 1948-50, instr. O.T., N.T. exegesis, 1951-54, docent, 1954; asst. prof. N.T. Harvard U. Div. Sch., 1954-56, asso. prof., 1956-58, John H. Morison prof. N.T. studies, 1958-63, Frothingham prof. Bibl. studies, 1963-68, dean, John Lord O'Brian prof. div., 1968-79, Andrew W. Mellon prof. div., 1981-84; pastor Luth. Ch. Am., 1968-84; bishop of Stockholm Ch. of Sweden, 1984-88; Robert and Myra Kraft and Jacob Hiatt Disting. prof. Christian studies Brandeis U., 1991—; moderator consultation on ch. and Jewish people World Council Chs., 1975-86. Author: The School of St. Matthew, 1954, 2d edit., 1968, The Bible and the Role of Women, 1966, Holy Week, 1974, Paul Among Jews and Gentiles, 1976, Meanings, 1984, Energy for Life, 1990. Recipient Disting. Service award Assn. Theol. Schs., 1988. Fellow Am. Acad. Arts and Scis.; mem. Nathan Soederblom Soc.

STENHOUSE, EVERETT RAY, clergy administrator; b. Minco, Okla., May 15, 1931; s. George E. and Jessie Loraine (Dean) S.; m. Alice Irene English, Aug. 22, 1948; children: Brenda Jones, Judy Lundberg, Stephen, Andrew. Student, U. Calif. Berkeley, U. Athens, 1969-71. Ordained to ministry Assemblies of God, 1955. Pastor Wayside Chapel, Bakersfield, Calif., 1955-59, Bethel Temple, Bakersfield, 1960-63; dist. dir. youth So. Calif. Dist. Assemblies of God, Costa Mesa, Calif., 1963-67; assoc. pastor 1st Assembly of God, San Diego, 1968-69; missionary Assemblies of God Fgn. Missions, Athens, Greece, 1969-73; pastor Bethany Ch., Alhambra, Calif., 1974-79; supt. So. Calif. Dist., Assemblies of God, Costa Mesa, 1979-85; asst. gen. supt. Gen. Coun. Assemblies of God, Springfield, Mo., 1986—; bd. adminstrn. Nat. Assn. Evangs., Wheaton, Ill., 1986—, Pentecostal Fellowship of No. Am., Ontario, Canada, 1986—; chmn., bd. dirs. Assemblies of God Theol. Sem., Springfield, 1991—, Ministers Benefit Assn., Springfield, 1986—. Contbr. articles to various mags. Home: 2952 S Brentmoor Springfield MO 65804 Office: Gen Coun Assemblies of God 1445 Boonville Ave Springfield MO 65802

STENNER, CHARLES EDWIN, minister; b. Detroit, Oct. 26, 1926; s. Alfred Jackson and Katherine Ann (Schwesinger) S.; m. Patricia Mae Smith, Sept. 2, 1949; children: Charles Edwin Jr., David Edward, Timothy Henry. BA, Wayne State U., 1950, MEd, 1957; ThM, Princeton Theol. Sem., 1964; D of Ministry, Meth. Theol. Sch., 1981. Ordained to ministry Presbyn. Ch. (U.S.A.), 1964. Student pastor Sykesville (N.J.) Presbyn. Ch., 1963-64; pastor Plain City (Ohio) Presbyn. Ch., 1964—; mem. Presbytery Bills and Overtures Com., Columbus, 1990—; chmn. Presbytery Staff Svcs., Columbus, 1990—. mem., past chmn. Faith Mission, Columbus, 1982—; chairperson ethics com. Johnny Appleseed Barbershop Singers, 1988—, Task Force on Village Charter Com., 1990, Mental Health Assn. Union County, Marysville, Ohio, 1990—; mem. Task Force on Zoning Reform, Plain City, 1990—. Recipient medal Freedoms Found. at Valley Forge, 1968, Community Svc. award Jonathan Alder Bd. Edn., 1984, Rodney B. Hurl award Charles Mills Ctr., 1988; named to Sr. Citizen Hall of Fame, Union County, 1989. Mem. Presbytery of Scioto Valley (stated clk. 1977-79, chmn. search com. 1985, chmn. coun. 1987-90), Princeton Theol. Sem. Alumni, Marysville Ministerial Assn., Plain City Ch. Fellowship (chmn. 1964—), Singing Buckeyes, Lions (pianist 1987—, bd. dirs. 1990—). Home: 395 S Chillicothe St Plain City OH 43064 *You can't improve on the Lord's timetable.*

STENSETHER, JOHN ELDON, minister; b. Mpls., Feb. 28, 1944; s. John H. and Gertie Marie (Stensaas) S.; m. Barbara L. Erickson, Sept. 3, 1966; children: Julie Lyn, Kevin John. BA, U. Minn., 1966; postgrad., Fuller Theol. Sem., Pasadena, 1966-69; PhD, Calif. Grad. Sch. Theology, Glendale, 1970. Ordained to ministry Evang. Free Ch. Am., 1972. Sr. pastor Del Rey Hills Evang. Free Ch., Playa del Rey, Calif., 1968-72, Calvary Evang. Free Ch., Essex Fells, N.J., 1972-76, Trinity Evang. Free Ch., South Bend, Ind., 1976-80, Evang. Free Ch., Turlock, Calif., 1980—; vis. prof. Northeastern Bible Coll., Essex Fells, N.J., 1973-75; staley disting. Christian scholar lectr. Trinity Coll., Deerfield, Ill., 1985; speaker various Colls., sems. and confs. Fellow Evang. Free Ch. of Am. Ministerial, Turlock Evang. Assn. of Ministers. Office: Evang Free Ch 1360 N Johnson Rd Turlock CA 95380 *The older I grow, the more I experience life, the greater is my confidence in, and reliance upon, the Sovereignty of God.*

STENSVAAG, SAUL GEORGE, minister; b. Mpls., Jan. 10, 1950; s. John Monrad and Hannah Ovidia (Mehus) S.; m. Mary Kay Johnson, Aug. 20, 1972; children—Maya Regina, Ken David, Emma Hannah. B.A., Augsburg Coll., 1972; M.Div., Luther Sem., 1979. Ordained to ministry Am. Luth. Ch., 1979. Missionary pastor Am. Luth. Ch., Hakodate-Shi, Japan, 1979-85, Sapporo, Japan, 1985—; mem. exec. com. Am. Luth. Ch., Japan Missionary Assoc., Tokyo, 1983—. Contbr. (sermon collection) Augsburg Sermons II, 1982. Recipient 4th prize Japanese Speech Contest for Foreigners, 1980. Mem. Shield Motorcycle Touring Club. Home and Office: North Church 1-8 Kita 31jo,, Nishi 4 Chome, Kita-Ku,, Sapporo 001, Japan

STENSVAD, ALLAN MAURICE, minister; b. Melstone, Mont., Mar. 27, 1934; s. Arthur Leonard and Mabel Violet (Rykken) S.; m. Margaret Lillian Fountain, Aug. 21, 1954; children: Sondra Louise, Joy Lynn, Jill Linda, Janiece Lorraine, Sharla Lee. BA in History, Cascade Coll., 1956; ThM, Dallas Theol. Sem., 1960. Ordained to ministry Conservative Bapt. Assn. Am., 1962. Interim pastor Trinity Bapt. Ch., Walla Walla, Wash., 1960-61; missionary to Brazil Unevangelized Fields Mission, Bala Cynwyd, Pa., 1962-71; min. of evangelism Bible Bapt. Ch., Auburn, Wash., 1972-75; pastor 1st Bapt. Ch., Dayton, Wash., 1975-80, Berean Bapt. Ch., Eugene, Oreg., 1980—; dir. No. Evang. Christian Sem., Sao Luis, Brazil, 1966-71; trustee Conservative Bapt. Assn. Wash., 1976-80, Conservative Bapt. Assn. Oreg., N.W. Conservative Bapt. Assn., 1985-91; mem. consolidation com. Conservative Bapt. Assn. Oreg./Wash., 1985, ann. meeting program chmn., 1986-91. Republican. Home: 1965 Fillmore St Eugene OR 97405 Office: Berean Bapt Ch 1210 Chambers St Eugene OR 97402

STEPHENS, JERRY CALDWELL, JR., church accountant; b. Mt. Clemens, Mich., Nov. 4, 1954; s. Jerry C. Stephens Sr. and Marian L. (Wilkinson) Whittle; m. Jeanie E. Coleman, Sept. 6, 1975; children: Jonathan, Kristina, Rebeccah, Hannah, Timothy. AA, Fla. Community Coll., Jacksonville, 1983; BS in Acctg., Franklin U., 1990. Youth min. Baldwin (Fla.) Assembly of God, 1977-80; founding pastor Maxville (Fla.) Assembly of God, 1980-82; pastor Corpus Christi Fellowship, Jacksonville, 1983-86; ch. bus. adminstr. Christian Assembly, Columbus, Ohio, 1988—; owner, founder Ch. Account-Ability, Columbus, 1989—. Author Church and Clergy Tax Issues, 1990. With USN, 1973-79. Mem. Nat. Assn. Ch. Bus. Adminstrs. (Cen. Ohio chpt. pres. 1991), Christian Mgmt. Assn., Christian Civil Liberties Union (dir., treas. 1991). Office: Christian Assembly 4099 Karl Rd Columbus OH 43224

STEPHENS, WILLIAM RICHARD, college president; b. Ashburn, MO., Jan. 2, 1932; s. George Lewis and Helen S.; m. Arlene Greer, June 28, 1952; children—Richard, Kendell, Kelli. B.S., Greenville Coll., Ill., 1953; M.Ed., U. Mo., 1958; Ed.D., Washington U., St. Louis, 1964. Tchr. Sturgeon High Sch., Mo., 1955-57; asst. prof. then assoc. prof. edn. Greenville Coll., 1957-61, dir. NCATE self-study, 1960-61; spl. instr. Washington U., St. Louis, 1961-64; mem. faculty Ind. State U., 1964-70; vis. prof. Ind. U., Bloomington, 1969-70; prof. history and philosophy of edn. Ind. U., 1970-71; v.p. acad. affairs, dean of faculty Greenville Coll., 1971-77, acting pres., 1977, pres., 1977—. Author: Social Reform and the Origins of Vocational Guidance, 1890-1925, 1970; Education of American Life (with William Van Til), 1972; also curriculum materials, reports; editor procs. ednl. meetings. Vice-chmn. Kingsbury Park Dist., Greenville, 1972-77; mem. edn. com. Bond County Mental Health Assn., 1974. Served with U.S. Army, 1953-55. Recipient Merit award Nat. Vocat. Guidance Assn., 1973. Mem. History of Edn. Soc. (chmn. nominating com. 1969), Midwest History of Edn. Soc. (pres. 1971-72), Philosophy of Edn. Soc., Ohio Valley Philosophy of Edn. Soc. (sec.-treas. 1967-70), Soc. Profs. Edn. (assoc. editor publs. 1968-70), Central States Faculty Colloquium (chmn. 1969—), John Dewey Soc. (pres.-elect 1978-80, pres. 1980-82, editor Insights 1973-78), North Central Assn., Assn. Free Methodist Ednl. Instns. (pres. 1980—). Office: Greenville Coll 315 E College St Greenville IL 62246

STEPHENSON, DEVIN GARRY, minister; b. Gadsden, Ala., Mar. 31, 1953; s. James Wesley and Etta (Lafayette) S.; m. Judy Annette Dodd, July 7, 1974; children: Jon Dodd, Julianne Grace. AS, Walker Coll., 1973; BA, Birmingham So. Coll., 1975. Minister of music Sumiton (Ala.) Ch. of God, 1978—; dean of students Walker State Tech. Coll., Sumiton, 1976—; mem. Internat. Ch. Music Com., Ch. of God, Cleveland, Tenn., 1984-88, Ala. State Music Com., Ch. of God, Birmingham, 1980-88. Composer numerous musical works. Chmn. East Walker Heart Fund Assn., Sumiton, 1980-82. Named to Outstanding Young men of Am., 1979, Outstanding Young Person, Roebuck/Ctr. Point Jaycees, Birmingham, 1988, Hon. Mem. Ala. Militia, Gov.'s Office, Montgomery, Ala., 1984, Outstanding Adminstrv. finalist Dept. Postsecondary Edn., Montgomery, 1987. Mem. Ala. Assn. Pub. Rels. Officers (pres.-elect 1990—), Deans of Students Assn., Ala. Assn. Sutdent Fin. Aid Aminstrs., So. Assn. Student Fin. Aid Adminstrs., Nat. Assn. Student Fin. Aid Adminstrs., Rotary (bd. dirs. East Walker chpt. 1991). Home: PO Box N Sullivan Rd Sumiton AL 35148

STEPP, WILLIAM RIGBY, minister; b. Tybee Island, Ga., May 10, 1943; s. William H. and Amy Stepp; m. Bettie Ann Smith, June 22, 1968; children: William Ruffin, Owen Raiford, John Daniel, Andrew Robert. BS, Belhaven Coll., 1965; BDiv, Columbia Theol. Sem., 1968, MDiv, 1971; postgrad., U. Ga., 1967; cert. in child care, U. N.C., 1982; D of Ministry, McCormick Theol. Sem., 1982. Ordained to ministry Presbyn. Ch. (U.S.A.), 1968. Pastor 1st Presbyn. Ch., Tallassee, Ala., 1968-72; sr. min. Golden Gate Presbyn. Ch., Naples, Fla., 1972-76; adminstr., pastor Thornwell Home and Sch. for Children, Clinton, S.C., 1976-82; sr. min. Meml. Presbyn. Ch., West Palm Beach, Fla., 1982—. Bd. dirs., chaplain Fellowship of Christian Athletes in S. Fla., 1984-90; bd. dirs. Rehab. Ctr. for Children and Adults, Palm Beach, 1990. Mem. Presbyns. for Renewal (bd. dirs. 1989—, co-dir. Christian Life Conf., Montreat, N.C. 1990-91), West Palm Beach C. of C., Kiwanis (chmn. spiritual aims 1983—, bd. dirs. Kiwanis Found. 1987-91). Office: Meml Presbyn Ch 1300 S Olive Ave West Palm Beach FL 33401

STERLING, JAMES A., minister; b. Phoenix, Aug. 13, 1942; s. Rothacker Loe and Ramona (May) S.; m. Joyce Ellen Lewis, May 31, 1968; children: Eric James, Joel Christopher. AB, Lincoln Christian Coll., 1964; MDiv, Vanderbilt Div. Sch., 1970, DMin, 1972; MA, Butler U., 1985. Ordained to ministry, Christian Ch. (Disciples of Christ). Chaplain St. Vincent Hosp., Indpls., 1973-87; chaplaincy dir. Scottsdale (Ariz.) Meml. Hosp., 1987—; guest lectr. Scottsdale Community Coll., 1988—; bd. dirs. United Christian Campus Ministry, Tempe, 1991—. Fellow Coll. Chaplains; mem. Am. Assn. of Pastoral Counselors (pastoral counseling in-tng.), Ariz. Chaplain's Assn. (pres. 1990-91). Avocation: 4th degree Black Belt Wado Ryu Karate-Do. Home: 1907 E Inglewood Mesa AZ 85203 Office: Scottsdale Meml Hosp 7400 E Osborn Rd Scottsdale AZ 85251

STERN, FRANK, rabbi; b. L.A., Dec. 13, 1936; m. Muriel Bernstein (div. 1989); children: Debra Susan Stern Simon, David Samuel. BA, UCLA, 1958; PhD, U. Calif., Riverside, 1983; MA in Hebrew Lit., Hebrew Union Coll.-Jewish Inst. Religion, Calif. Br., 1965, DD (hon.), 1990. Ordained rabbi, 1965. Rabbi Temple Sinai of Portsmouth (Va.), 1965-68, Temple Beth Shalom, Santa Ana, Calf., 1971—; asst. rabbi Fairmont Temple, Cleve., 1968-71; instr. Gilmore Acad., 1969-71, John Carroll U., 1970-71, U. Calif., Riverside, 1982-84, Calif. State U., Fullerton, 1985—; pres. Coll. Jewish Studies Orange County, 1989—, U. Judaism, L.A., 1989—; pres. Orange County Bd. Rabbis, 1976-79. V.p. United Way, Orange County, 1975-78; treas. Orange County Jewish Fedn., 1980-81; bd. dirs. Jewish Family Svc. Orange County, UCI Interfaith Coun., Anti-Defamation League Orange County, 1985—, Orange County Zoo, 1987—; mem. coord. coun. on drug edn. Orange County Dept. Edn., 1989—. Mem. Pacific Assn. Reform Rabbis (pres. 1986-87), Pacific Assn. Reform Rabbis (officer 1981-86), Cen. Conf. Am. Rabbis, Am. Assn. Religion. Office: Temple Beth Sholom 2625 N Tustin Santa Ana CA 92705

STERN, JAY BENJAMIN, religion educator; b. Bklyn., Feb. 17, 1929; s. Mena and Lillian (Grossman) S.; m. Suzanne Cutler, Aug. 13, 1950; children: Judith Avigail Stern Flax, Aviva Nehama Stern Groskin, Menahem David. BA, CUNY, 1951; BDiv, MRE, Jewish Theol. Sem., N.Y.C., 1956, DRE, 1963, D Pedagogy (hon.), 1984. Author: What's A Nice God Like You Doing in a Place Like This, 1987; editor: A Curriculum for the Jewish Afternoon School, 1978, A Curriculum for the Jewish Day School, 1989, Comparative Religious Literature, 1977. Mem. Jewish Educators Assembly (pres. 1976-78). Office: Jewish Edn Mgmt Assocs 10802 Cavalier Dr Silver Spring MD 20901

STERN, MALCOLM HENRY, rabbi, educator; b. Phila., Jan. 29, 1915; s. Arthur Kaufman and Henrietta (Berkowitz) S.; m. Louise Steinhart Bergman, May 25, 1941. BA, U. Pa., 1935; MA in Hebrew Letters, Hebrew Union Coll., Cin., 1941, DHL, 1957, DD, 1966. Ordained rabbi, 1941. Asst. rabbi Congregation Keneseth Israel, Phila., 1941-43, 46-47; rabbi Ohef Sholom Temple, Norfolk, Va., 1947-64; dir. Rabbinic Placement Commn., N.Y.C., 1964-80; student fieldwork counselor, adj. prof. Jewish history Hebrew Union Coll., N.Y.C., 1981—; chmn. admissions Cen. Conf. Am. Rabbis, N.Y.C., 1981-91, chmn. music com., 1949-83. Author genealogy: Americans of Jewish Descent, 1960, First American Jewish Families, 1977, rev. 1991; co-author: AA Guide to Jewish History in the Caribbean, 1975; editor hymnal: Union Songster, 1960. Mem. Local Govt. Records Advisory, Albany, 1986—; creator Nat. Archives Gift Fund, 1980—, Genealog. Coord. Com., 1980—. Capt. USAF, 1943-46. Fellow Am. Soc. Genealogists, Nat. Genealog. Soc.; mem. Am. Jewish Archives (genealogist), Fedn. Geneal. Socs. (v.p., bd. dirs. 1980-91, George Williams award 1988, Dvid Vogels award 1991). Democrat. Home: 300 E 71st St # 5R New York NY 10021 Office: Hebrew Union Coll 1 W 4th St New York NY 10012-1186

STERN, SEYMOUR (SHOLOM), retired rabbi; b. N.Y.C., Oct. 29, 1920; s. Harry and Frances (James) S. BA, CCNY, 1939; MA, Hebrew Union Coll.-Jewish Inst. Religion, 1943; postgrad., Grad. Sch. of Judaism, L.A., 1952-57, U. So. Calif., 1955-57, Jewish Theol. Sem. Am., 1962; DD (hon.), Jewish Theol. Sem. Am., 1984. Ordained rabbi, 1943. Rabbi congregations Bnai Abraham, Hagerstown, Md., 1942-43, East Liverpool, Ohio, 1943-44; rabbi Beth Israel Congregation, Waltham, Mass., 1944-47, Salinas, Ventura, Calif., 1948-56; chaplain Calif. State Dept. Mental Health, 1957-79; counselor Hillel Found. Brandeis U., 1944-45; chaplain Nat. Jewish Welfare Bd., San Francisco, 1947-48; officiated Pacific War Dead Repatriation Program. Chaplain surviving German Jews and Jewish Displaced Persons Occupied Germany, 1945-47; sec. Monterey County Jewish Community Coun., 1950-52; exec. dir. Ventura County Jewish Coun., 1953-56. Capt. U.S. Army, 1945-47, ETO. Recipient Presdl. Unit citation, 1949. Mem. The Rabbinical Assembly, Bd. Rabbis of So. Calif., Soc. Bibl. Lit., Jewish War Vets., Jewish Geneal. Soc. L.A. Home: 360 S Burnside Ave Los Angeles CA 90036 *Living "for bread only" is not the human way, our rabbi, Moses, maintained (Deut. 8:3). What, then, is one to do? Amos answered, If you want to live right, seek the Lord...seek the good. (Amos 5:6, 14). Three Hebrew words of the prophet Habakkuk (Hab. 2:4) are considered to be an epitome of Jewish religion: "Righteous living stems from steadfast faith". That grows as one lives, if one learns. (Talmud Tractate Makkot 24a).*

STERN, SHIRA, rabbi; b. N.Y.C., May 10, 1956; d. Isaac and Vera (Lindenblit) S.; m. Donald A. Weber, Mar. 6, 1983; children: Noah Stern Weber, Ariel Stern Weber, Eytan Stern Weber. BA in Religious Study, Brown U., 1978; MA in Hebrew Lit., Hebrew Union Coll., 1982. Ordained rabbi, 1983. Educator Temple Beth El, Huntington, N.Y., 1983-84; rabbi The Monroe Twp. Jewish Ctr., Spotswood, N.J., 1984—; bd. dirs. Hebrew Immigrant Aid Soc., N.Y.C.; policy chmn. Religious Coaltion For Abortion Rights, N.J., 1989-91; active Jewish Family Svc., Middlesex County N.J., 1989-90. Bd. dirs. Planned Parenthood, Huntington, 1983-84, Monmouth City, N.J., 1984-91; speaker Nat. Abortion Rights Action League, Washington, 1984-88; commn. mem. Human Rels. Coun., Middlesex County, 1990—. Fellow Cen. Conf. Am. Rabbis; mem. Women's Rabbinic Network (sec. 1991—). Home: 38 Longfellow Terrace Morganville NJ 07751 Office: The Monroe Twp Jewish Ctr PO Box 71 Spotswood NJ 08884 *I believe our charge is to comfort the disturbed, and disturb the comfortable. I live my life trying to balance my time between the two-no easy task, but necessary.*

STERNBERG, JOHN RICHARD, retired minister; b. Chgo., Feb. 12, 1920; s. Max Arthur and Bertha Heneritta (Pretzel) S.; m. Pearl Dorothy Wilshusen, Feb. 4, 1945; children: Richard Nolan, Rhoda Jane Sternberg Becker. AB, Concordia Coll., 1940; BD, Concordia Sem., 1945. Pastor Grace & Trinity Luth. Chs., Neligh and Elgin, Nebr., 1945-50, Meml. Luth. Ch., Vancouver, Wash., 1950-60; pastor St. Peter Luth. Ch., Schaumburg, Ill., 1960-90, ret., 1990; mem. religion dept. Concordia Coll., Portland, Oreg., 1957-58; chmn. Bd. Christian Edn., Chgo., 1963-90. Mem. Olde Schaumburg Commn., Schaumburg, 1978-90, Hist. Soc., Schaumburg, 1960-90. Mem. Cerge Coun. of Schaumburg, Rotary (Schaumburg chpt.). Home: 13209 SW 61st Ave Portland OR 97219 *Be grateful for your church, community and country in life of service. Whatever your hand finds to do, do with all your might for the welfare of your fellow man and the glory of God.*

STERNSTEIN, JOSEPH PHILIP, rabbi; b. Bklyn., Aug. 20, 1925; s. Charles and Bertha (Milman) S.; m. Geraldine S. Cohen, Dec. 21, 1947; children—Judith, Rachel, Gerson, Hillel. B.A., Bklyn. Coll., 1944; J.D., St. John's U., 1943; rabbi, Master Hebrew Letters, Jewish Theol. Sem., 1948; D.Hebrew Letters, 1961. Rabbi Temple Tifereth Israel, Glen Cove, L.I., 1948-51, Beth Abraham Synagogue, Dayton, Ohio, 1951-62; nat. dir. Jewish Nat. Fund Am., N.Y.C., 1962-64; rabbi Temple Ansche Chesed, N.Y.C., 1964-69, Temple Beth Sholom, Roslyn Heights, N.Y., 1969—; Dean Women's Inst., Jewish Theol. Sem. Am., 1965—; vice chmn. rabbinic cabinet Jewish Theol. Sem.; sec. N.Y. Bd. Rabbis, UN del. Synagogue Council Am.; chmn. Am. Zionist Youth Found. Author: Theology of the Hassidic Rabbi of Ger, 1961, American Zionism-Diagnosis and Prognosis, 1955, Comparative Studies of Secular and Rabbinic Laws of Inheritance, 1947; Contbr. articles to profl. publs. Chmn. Montgomery County Mental Health Assn., 1958; speakers bur. Greater Dayton Com., 1958-61; bd. dirs. Ohio Mental Health Assn., 1954-61, Ohio Civil Liberties Union, 1955-61; Charter fellow Herbert H. Lehman Inst. Talmudic Ethics.; nat. pres. Hista drut I vrit, Hebrew Lang. and Culture Movement; nat. chmn. Am. Council on Tourism to Israel; vice chmn. Nat. Conf. on Soviet Jewry; nat. pres. Jewish Nat. Fund Am., 1985-89; nat. chmn. Am. Zionist Youth Found., 1991—. Mem. Rabbinical Assembly Am. (exec. council), Zionist Orgn. Am. (past nat. pres. 1974-78), World Union Gen. Zionists (exec. com.), Am. Zionist Fedn. (past nat. pres.), World Zionist Council (presidium), World Zionist Orgn. (world exec.), Am. Jewish Hist. Soc., Jewish Nat. Fund Am. (nat. pres.), Soc. Bib. Lit., Conf. Jewish Social Studies. Home: 320 Locust Ln Roslyn Heights NY 11577 Office: Temple Beth Sholom Roslyn Rd Roslyn Heights NY 11577

STERZINSKY, GEORG MAXIMILIAN, bishop. Bishop of Berlin; pres. Bishops' Conf., Roman Cath. Ch., Bonn, Fed. Republic Germany. Office: Diocese of Roman Cath Ch, Kaiserstr. 163, 5300 Bonn Federal Republic of Germany*

STEVENS, DANIEL LOUIS, pastor; b. West Palm Beach, Fla., Jan. 21, 1961; s. William L. and Pamela A. (Rich) S.; m. Dawn Irene Morrison, July 23, 1983; children: Carolann R., Daniel Tyler, Seth William. BA, Spurgeon Coll., Mulberry, Fla., 1983. Lic. to preach Westgate Bapt. Ch., Plantation, Fla., 1984; ordained to ministry Bapt. Ch., 1989; cert. assoc. profl. Fla. Assn. Christian Schs. Youth pastor Westgate Bapt. Ch., 1981-86, 1st Portland Bapt. Ch., 1987—; tchr. Bible, Amb. Christian Acad., Plantation, 1983-86; instr. Moody Bible Inst., Ft. Lauderdale, Fla., spring 1986; chmn., treas. Bethany Youth Com., Brocton, 1988—. Mem. Impact, chem. dependency program Brocton Cen. Sch., 1988—. Republican. Home: 109 Lake Ave Brocton NY 14716 Office: 1st Portland Bapt Ch 35 W Main St Brocton NY 14716

STEVENS, DAVID ALLEN, minister; b. Camden, N.J., Dec. 6, 1957; s. Norman A. and Ruth (Wallace) S.; m. Carole D. Braddock, June 9, 1984; 1 child, Laura B. BA, Rutgers U., 1982; MDiv, Ea. Bapt. Sem., Phila., 1985; postgrad., Iliff Sch. Theology/U. Denver, 1991—. Ordained to ministry Bapt. Ch., 1985, Mennonite Ch., 1991. Pastor 1st Bapt. Ch., Salem, N.J., 1985-88; assoc. pastor 1st Mennonite Ch., Denver, 1988—. Mem. Soc. Bibl. Lit. Mem. Mennonite Ch. Office: 1st Mennonite Ch 430 W Ninth Ave Denver CO 80204

STEVENS, DEBORAH IRENE, lay worker; b. Lansdale, Pa., Mar. 4, 1959; d. Richard Russell and Madeliene May (Umstead) Clayton; m. Lawrence George Stevens, Sept. 20, 1981; children: Jennifer Ranee, Cristina Marie. Cert., Lansdale Sch. of Business, 1981; student, Christian Counseling and Ednl. Facility, Laverock, Pa., 1989, Christian Bible Coll., N.C., 1992—. Children's choir dir. Emmanuel Evangel. Congregational Ch., Hatfield, Pa., 1986—, youth dir., 1986—, bd. mem., 1989—, sec. Ladies Aide Soc., 1986-90, tchr. Sunday sch., 1987—, various other duties including choir and prayer/study groups, 1986—. V.p. Ladies Aux. Hatfield Fire Co., 1990-91; pres. The Laymen Playmen, Inc., Hatfield, 1989-90. Composer/soloist: (song) Jesus Is The Only Way, 1989. Mem. Hatfield C. of C. (corrs. sec. 1991—), Indian Valley C. of C.. Home: 221 1/2 W Broad St Hatfield PA 19440 Office: Lott Constructors Inc 272 Ruth Rd Harleysville PA 19438 *I have experienced many things in life but none surpass the honor of knowing our Lord and Savior, Jesus Christ. To Him belongs all the glory, honor and praise!.*

STEVENS, EARL PATRICK, minister; b. Vicksburg, Miss., Nov. 21, 1925; s. Elton Alva and Mary Elizabeth (Keathley) S.; m. Vonda Jean Tuttle, Aug. 7, 1949; children: Teresa Darlene, Deborah Lalene, Earl P. II, David Paul. BA, Abilene Christian U., 1949; BRE, Coll. of the Bible, 1966; MA, MRE, Nat. Christian U., 1968, ThM, 1969, PhD, ThD, 1969; DD (hon.), Ohio Christian Coll., 1968. Ordained to ministry Ch. of Christ, 1943; cert. neuropsychiat. technician. Minister Ch. of Christ, Olden, Tex., 1946-49, Barrackville, W.Va., 1949-62, Parkersburg, W.Va., 1962-66, St. Mary's, W.Va., 1966-77, Shinnston, W.Va., 1977-90, Fairmont, W.Va., 1990—, Mt. Nebo, W.Va., 1990—; instr. Ohio Valley Coll., Parkersburg, 1964-66; prof. Nat. Christian U., Ft. Worth, 1968-78. Author: The Glory of Christ, 1963, Doctrinal Study of I Timothy, 1987, 15 other books. Served with USN, 1944-46. Named to Eagle Scout, Boy Scouts Am., 1942; recipient Golden Record award Word Records, 1968, Colin Anderson award Colin Anderson Ctr., 1968. Mem. So. Assn. Marriage Counselors, Am. Numismatic Assn. Democrat. Lodge: Kiwanis. Avocations: writing, stamps, hunting and fishing, bowling. Home and Office: 204 Russell St Fairmont WV 26554 *Every life has value; the strong must protect the weak; men belong together; friendship is a two-way street; everyone must mould his heart, shape his life and enrich his mind. These are living guidelines for my life and all others, too. Neglect any or all and we are the poorer for it.*

STEVENS, EDWARD FRANKLIN, college president; b. Newcastle, Wyo., Sept. 7, 1940; s. Edward Downey and Esther Elizabeth (Watt) S.; m. Linda Elaine Loewenstein, June 3, 1962; children: Carla, Cathy. Student, U. Denver, 1959-60; BA in Edn. cum laude, Nebr. Wesleyan U., 1963; MA, U. Nebr., 1967; PhD, U. Minn., 1983. Tchr., head basketball coach Alvo-Eagle (Nebr.) High Sch., 1963-64, Madison (Nebr.) High Sch., 1964-65; asst. basketball coach U. Nebr., Lincoln, 1965-67; coach, asst. prof. edn. Augustana Coll., Sioux Falls, S.D., 1967-71; v.p., gen. mgr. tng. Iseman div. U.S. Ind., Sioux Falls, 1971-74; chief devel. officer Sioux Falls Coll., 1974-79, asst. prof. then prof., 1980-83; exec. v.p. Kearny (Nebr.) State Coll. Found., 1979-80; pres. George Fox Coll., Newberg, Oreg., 1983—. Chmn. campaign Yamhill County United Way, Newberg, 1988; bd. commrs. Newberg Community HOsp., 1988-91. NDEA fellow, 1965; recipient Young Alumni Achievement award, Nebr. Wesleyan U., 1973, Leadership Fellows award, Bush Found., St. Paul, 1976. Mem. Nat. Christian Coll. Cons. (chmn. 1987-88), Nat. Assn. Intercollegiate Athletics (exec. com. 1988-92, chmn. 1992), Oreg. Ind. Colls. Assn. (bd. dirs. 1983-92, chmn. 1986-87), Oreg. Ind. Colls. Found. (bd. dirs. 1983-92), Coun. of Ind. Colls. (bd. dirs. 1990), Rotary. Republican. Mem. Soc. Friends. Office: George Fox Coll Office of Pres 414 N Meridian Newberg OR 97132

STEVENS, ELLIOT LESLIE, clergyman; b. N.Y.C., Apr. 11, 1948; s. Stanley and Perry (Needleman) S.; m. Laura Orefice, Sept. 6, 1971; children: Sara Ida, Daniel Elvio. Student, Hebrew U. Jerusalem, 1968-69; B.A., SUNY, Oneonta, 1970; M.H.L., Hebrew Union Coll.-Jewish Inst. Religion, 1974. Ordained rabbi, 1975. Rabbinic intern Congregation Beth Elohim, Flushing, N.Y., 1973-74; adminstrv. sec., dir. publs. Central Conf. Am. Rabbis, N.Y.C., 1975—; rabbi Congregation Beth David, Amenia, N.Y., 1988—; trustee Transcontinental Music, 1982—; mem. Joint Bd. on Music Publs. of Reform Judaism, 1983-88; pres. Assn. Jewish Book Pubs., 1990—. Editor: Yearbook of Central Conf. of Am. Rabbis, 1973—; mng. editor: Jour. Reform Judaism, 1980—; editor: Rabbinic Authority, 1983—. Mem. Assn. Reform Zionists Am., Central Conf. Am. Rabbis, Assn. Jewish Book Pubs., Jewish Book Council, Nat. Assn. Parliamentarians, Interfaith Council on

Family Fin. Planning, N.Y. Assn. Reform Rabbis, Westchester Bd. Rabbis. Democrat.

STEVENS, GLENN DOUGLAS, minister; b. Roanoke, Va., Aug. 27, 1947; s. Walter Ezra and Elizabeth Mae (Holdren) S.; m. Ann Elizabeth Dunmire, Aug. 24, 1968 (div. 1982); children: Jason Randal, Melanie Ann; m. Patricia Gayle Dellis, Dec. 23, 1982. BS, McPherson (Kans.) Coll., 1972; MS, Ind. U., 1978; MA, Goshen Bibl. Sem., Elkhart, Ind., 1991. Ordained to ministry Ch. of the Brethren, 1991. Houseparent Luth. Social Svcs., Balt., 1972-73; counselor Camp Woodland, Harrisonburg, Va., 1970; adminstr. Elkhart (Ind.) Youth Svc. Bur., Inc., 1974—; bd. dirs. No. Ind. Dist. of Ch. of the Brethren, Nappanee, 1990—; adj. prof. Ball State U., Muncie, Ind., 1989—; field instr. Western Mich. U., Kalamazoo, 1986-87. Author: Our Most Beloved Poems, 1985; contbr. to quar. New Designs, 1985, Youth Guide, 1989, Our Most Beloved Poems. Bd. dirs. No. Ind. Job Alliance, Goshen, 1982-88, Ind. Juvenile Justice Task Force, Indpls., 1982-83. Named Ky. Col., 1987, Sagamore of the Wabash, 1989; recipient Liberty Bell award Elkhart City Bar Assn., 1988. Mem. Kiwanis. Home: 58654 Oxbow Ct Elkhart IN 46516 Office: Elkhart Youth Svcs Bur 222 Middlebury St Elkhart IN 46516

STEVENS, JERRY W., minister; b. Itawamba, Miss., Nov. 25, 1932; s. William Sidney and Ozelle Antham (Farrar) S.; m. Bonnie Alice Pierce, July 11, 1959; children: Sheri, Traci. AA, Itawamba Jr. Community Coll., 1953; diploma, Bob Bale Inst. Personal Devel., 1960, U. Richmond (Va.), 1965; BA, Blue Mountain (Miss.) Coll., 1972; M in Div., New Orleans Sem., 1975; D in Ministry, So. Bapt. Ctr., Jacksonville, Fla., 1983; diploma in banking, San Francisco Sem., 1979; postgrad., So. Bapt. Ctr. Bibl. Studies, Jacksonville, 1983. Banker Peoples Bank, Tupelo, Miss., 1954-58, Bank of Miss., Tupelo, 1958-70; pastor Midway Bapt. Ch., Pontatoc, Miss., 1970-72, First Bapt. Ch., Nicholson, Miss., 1973-75, Calvary Bapt. Ch., Columbus, Miss., 1975-80; dir. missions Winston Bapt. Assn., Louisville, Miss., 1980—; mem. home health care State Health Dept., Louisville, 1985—; fact finding com. Bue Mountain Coll., Louisville, 1986—; coun. on literacy job tng., Louisville, 1987—; cons. Miss. Bapt. Coop. Missions, 1978; advisor com. mem. Home Health Winston County Health Dept., 1985; mem. coun. on literacy, Winston County, Miss., 1987. Fin. chmn. Christian Friends Soc., Louisville, 1987—. Mem. Miss. Conf. Dir. Missions, So. Bapt. Conf. Dir. Missions, Blue Mountain Coll. Alumni (pres. 1978), Blue Mountain Coll. Ministers' Alumni Assn. (pres. 1977-78), Civitan Club (pres. 1969). Avocations: golf, gardening. Office: Winston Bapt Assn 1001 Columbus Louisville MS 39339

STEVENS, JOHN FLOURNOY, priest; b. Des Moines, June 19, 1914; s. Ralph Stoddard and Jeanne Flournoy (Thompson) S.; m. Ruth Elizabeth Brown, Jan. 19, 1945 (div. 1976); children: John Bruce, Michael Paul, James Andrew; m. Betty Louise Sinkola, June 2, 1976. BS with distinction, U.S. Naval Acad., 1938; MDiv, Va. Theol. Sem., 1948. Ordained to ministry as priest, 1949. Assoc. rector to rector Episcopal Chs., 1948-64; dir. dept. Christian social rels. Episcopal Diocese of Tex., Houston, 1964-66; mem. staff exec. coun. Episcopal Ch., 1966-74; assoc. coord. Joint Urban Prog., 1966-67, assoc. dir. gen. conv. spl. prog., 1967-69, asst. to dep. for prog., 1969-70, adminstrv. officer, also sec. exec. council, 1971-74, coord. Gen. Conv., 1972-73; bus. and circulation mgr. Episcopal Ch. Pub. Co., 1974-75, dir. Joint Strategy and Action Com., 1975-77; ret.; asst. to pastor Wheeler Ave. Bapt. Ch., Houston, 1978-80; non-stipendiary rector Ch. of Advent, Houston, 1980-86, non-stipendiary assoc. rector Ch. of Good Shepherd, Friendswood, 1987-89; interim exec. dir. Houston Met. Mins., 1981; non-stipendiary assoc. rector Ch. of Advent, Houston, 1991—. Author: To Tell the Story, 1963, No Place to Go, 1964. Bd. dirs. Houston Civil Liberties Union, 1963-66. Comdr. USN, 1938-46. Decorated Bronze Star medal. Mem. Episc. Soc. Cultural and Racial Unity, (sec. 1964-66), Washington Fedn. Chs. (dir. 1950-53, fin. com. 1953-56), NAACP (dir. Houston chpt. 1962-66). Democrat. Episcopalian. Avocations: music, photography, golf, tennis, hiking, cooking.

STEVENS, LARRY OTIS, minister; b. Lawton, Okla., Feb. 15, 1948; s. Otis L. and Alice Marie (Zimmerman) S.; m. F. Janice Nethery, Aug. 31, 1974; children: Zachery Scott, Allison Elizabeth. BA, Okla. Bapt. U., 1970; MDiv, Southwestern Bapt. Theol. Sem., 1974; MEd in Counseling, Okla. U., 1976; D of Ministry, Midwestern Bapt. Theol. Sem., 1990. Ordained to ministry So. Bapt. Conv., 1977. Assoc. min. N.W. Bapt. Ch., Ardmore, Okla., 1976-81; pastor Noble Ave. Bapt. Ch., Guthrie, Okla., 1981—. Mem. campaign com. United Way, Guthrie, 1989; v.p., bd. dirs. Logan County Youth and Family Svcs., Guthrie, 1984-85, Action Inc., Guthrie, 1986—. Mem. Guthrie Ministerial Alliance, Cen. Bapt. Assn. (mem. exec. bd. 1981—, dir. family ministry 1985-87).

STEVENS, LELAND ROBERT, minister; b. Mpls., July 1, 1929; s. Leland J. and Mathilda Marie (Cloeter) S.; m. Meta Adele Asendorf, June 15, 1952; children: Kathryn, David, Elizabeth, Jonathan. BA, Concordia Seminary, St. Louis, 1950; MA, Syracuse U., 1968; MDiv, Concordia Seminary, St. Louis, 1983; PhD, St. Louis U., 1987. Ordained to ministry Lutheran Ch., 1953. Mil. chaplain USAF, 1953-73, commd., 1953, advanced through grades to col., retired, 1973; pastor First Luth. Ch., Bowie, Md., 1970-76, Trinity Luth., Alamogordo, N.Mex., 1976-79; editor Luth. Witness, St. Louis, 1979-84; pastor Shepherd of the Hills, Ruidoso, N.Mex., 1984-90; religious editor, freelance Alamogordo, 1990—; instr. Park Coll., Chapman Coll., Holloman AFB, N.Mex., 1988—; commd. armed forces Luth. Ch./Mo. Synod, St. Louis, 1974-81; dir. of communications Rocky Mountain dist., Luth. Ch./Mo. Synod, Denver, 1989—. Republican. Avocations: gardening, hiking, photography. Home: 403 Sunglow Ave Alamogordo NM 88310

STEVENS, MARION EUGENE, minister; b. Hammond, Ind., Feb. 13, 1926; s. Charles Marion and Hazel Mae (Olds) S.; m. Ruth Alline Pickering, Sept. 7, 1945; children: Sharon Rose, Martha Jane, Norma Jean, Lora Lee. Student, Moody Bible Inst., Chgo., 1943-44, William Jennings Bryan Coll., 1949-55; BTh, ThM, ThD, Internat. Sem., 1980. Ordained to ministry Bapt. Ch., 1958. Pastor Highland Parkside Bapt. Ch., Joliet, Ill., 1946-49, Grace Bapt. Ch., Corwith, Iowa, 1949-53, Munster (Ind.) Bible Ch., 1953-57, First Bapt. Ch., Cedar Lake, Ind., 1957-63, Cen. Bapt. Ch., Salt Lake City, 1963-64, North Hill Bapt. Ch., Carlsbad, N.Mex., 1964-67, First Bapt. Ch., Lordsburg, N.Mex., 1967-70, Southside Bapt. Ch., Monahans, Tex., 1970—. Exec. com. Midland, Odessa, Pecos Valley Bapt. Area., Bapt. Gen. Conv. Tex.; asst. rec. sec. State Conv. Bapt. in Ind.; bd. dirs. Drug-free Youth in Tex., N.Mex. Area Mission; trustee Internat. Bapt. Bible Inst. El Paso; adv. bd. Christian Mission Ctr. U. Mary Hardin Baylor; active Better Breathing Club, Monahans, Tex. Mem. Pecos Valley Bapt. Assn. Tex., Southwestern Bapt. Assn. N.Mex., South Pecos Valley Bapt. Assn. N.Mex., Salt Lake Bapt. Assn., Lake Mich. Bapt. Assn. Ind., Kiwanis, Lions, Ward County C. of C., Monahans Masonic Lodge 952, Scottish Rite Bodies of Freemasonry. Republican. Home: 1205 S Bruce Monahans TX 79756 Office: Southside Bapt Ch 14th & Alice PO Box 2068 Monahans TX 79756

STEVENS, MICHAEL DALE, evangelist, clergyman; b. Pampa, Tex., Apr. 9, 1958; s. James Alvin Stevens and Jo Ann Stevens Keller; m. Tonya Beth Hurley, Dec. 3, 1983. BS, West Tex. State U., 1981. Lic. So. Bapt. minister; ordained minister Christian Ctr. Shreveport. Founder, evangelist, clergyman, pres., chief exec. officer Crucified Life Ministries, Shreveport, La., 1981—; staff minister evangelism Christian Ctr. Shreveport, 1983—. Author, editor, pub. World Changer newsletter, 1984—. Republican. Avocations: writing, researching subject of revival, skiing, golf. Office: Crucified Life Ministries PO Box 29128 Shreveport LA 71149-9128

STEVENS, ROBERT TINDALL, minister, consultant; b. Allentown, Pa., Dec. 27, 1951; s. Robert Tindall and Susan Elayne (Firing) S.; m. Carol Ann Silver, Sept. 11, 1976; children: Robert Jr., Joanna, Rebecca. BA in Philosophy, Pa. State U., State College, 1975; MDiv, Princeton Theol. Sem., 1978. Ordained to ministry United Ch. of Christ, 1978; accredited interim ministry specialist. Pastor Trinity United Ch. of Christ, Freemansburg, Pa., 1978-85; instr. Moravian Theol. Sem., Bethlehem, Pa., 1983—; interim ministry specialist United Ch. of Christ, Lehigh Valley, Pa., 1985—. Editor (newsletter) In-Between Times, 1989—; columnist Bethlehem Globe-Times, 1986-87; contbr. articles, sermons, hymns to religious jours. Mem. Acad. Parish Clergy, Interim Ministry Network (bd. dirs. 1989—). Democrat. Office: United Ch of Christ PO Box 175 Schnecksville PA 18078

STEVENS, ROBERT WILLIAM, church denomination administrator; b. Coquille, Oreg., Mar. 23, 1936; s. Stanton Frank and Eva R. (Mossholder) S.; m. Marilyn Ludlow, Sept. 10, 1957; children: Paul, Ruth. BA in Econs., Willamette U., 1958; postgrad., U. Wash., 1958-59. Treas. Pacific N.W. Ann. Conf., United Meth. Ch., Seattle, 1966—; del. Western Jurisdictional Conf., United Meth. Ch., 1968, 72, 76, 80, 84, 88, 92, Gen. Conf., 1976, 80, 84, 88, 92, mem. com. audit and rev. Gen. Coun. Fin. and Adminstrn., 1972-76, mem. Gen. Coun. Fin. and Adminstrn., 1976-84, mem. Gen. Bd. Pensions, 1984—, v.p., 1988-92; chairperson Denominational Health Care Task Force, United Meth. Ch., 1989-91. Trustee Seabeck Christian Conf. Camp, Wash., 1973-84, pres., 1982-84. Republican. Home: 13011 20th Ave NE Seattle WA 98125 Office: United Meth Ch NW Ann Conf 2112 3d Ave Ste 300 Seattle WA 98121

STEVENS, ROGER DALE, executive; b. Bristol, Va., Sept. 12, 1950; s. Homer Evert and Betty Sue (Mitchell) S.; m. Sandra Sue Eads, July 11, 1970; children: Brandon, Brock. A of Drafting, Va. Highlands Community Coll., 1972. Tchr., sunday sch. Bristol Bapt. Ch., Va., deacon, 1979-90, treas., 1983-90, choir dir., 1988-90; project engr. Tenn. Eastman Co., Kingsport, 1974-90. Home: 116 Campground Rd Bristol VA 24201

STEVENS, RONALD DAVID, religious organization executive; b. Kenosha, Wis., Jan. 5, 1953; s. Fred Byron and Esther Helen (Pedersen) S.; m. Betty Mae Schliesmann, July 14, 1977. Printer, advt. salesman, editor Union Coop. Pub. Co., Kenosha, 1971-85; exec. dir. Christian Youth Coun., Kenosha, 1985-88, 89—; home sec. to Congressman Les Aspin, Kenosha, 1988-89. Editor numerous newspaper articles, 1978-85. Mem. United Way of Kenosha County Bd., 1980-82, top vice chairperson, 1985, top group chairperson, 1985; charter mem. Kenosha Night at Brewers, Kenosha, 1980—; chair Community Support Task Force; alderman City of Kenosha, 1990-91, fin. com.. Recipient citation Senate of State of Wis., 1985, exec. proclamation Kenosha County Exec., 1988; Ron Stevens day proclaimed by Mayor of City of Kenosha, 1988. Mem. AFL-CIO (life), Wis. Pks. & Recreation Assn., Rotary (pres.-elect Kenosha-West club 1991—). Democrat. Lutheran. Avocations: volleyball, golf, fishing. Home: 8019 15th Ave Kenosha WI 53143 Office: Christian Youth Coun 1715-52nd St Kenosha WI 53140

STEVENS, SHIRLEY SUE, religion educator; b. New Orleans, Sept. 2, 1939; d. Samuel and Esther (Trudel) S. BS in Edn., Indiana (Pa.) U., 1961; MA in English, U. Pitts., 1965. Leader, co-founder First Word Christian Writers Group, Sewickley, Pa., 1981—; tchr. Quaker Valley Sch. Dist., Leetsdale, Pa., 1961—; pres. St. David's (Pa.) Christian Writers Conf. Ea. Coll., 1988-90; poetry tutor. Author: (poetry) Pronouncing What We Wish to Keep, 1990. Recipient Lois Henderson award, St. David's Christian Writers Conf., 1990. Mem. Western Pa. Coun. Tchrs. English (treas. 1983—). Home: 326 B Glaser Ave Pittsburgh PA 15202

STEVENS, WESLEY FOSTER, religious organization administrator, minister; b. Medina, Tex., Sept. 21, 1932; s. Thomas Foster and Vannie Molissia (Shuptrine) S.; m. Joyce Marilyn Andel, May 28, 1960; children: Joyce Carolyn, Van Wesley. BE, S.W. Tex. State U., 1954; BD, Perkins Sch. Theology, 1960, MST, 1962; D Ministry, St. Paul Sch. Theology, 1987. Ordained to ministry United Meth. Ch., 1960; lic. nursing home administr., Tex. Pastor United Meth. Chs., Tex., 1958-71; adminstr. Holly Hall Retirement Community, Houston, 1971—; interim pastor Parker Meml. United Meth. Ch., Houston, 1984-85; mem. Tex. Ann. Conf. United Meth. Ch., Houston, 1958—. Author: Grow Old Along with Me, 1991. Mem. Am. Soc. on Aging. Home and Office: 8304 Knight Rd Houston TX 77054 *Too often we find ourselves in the grip of complacency. The force of habit lays some terrible burdens upon us. The Gospel is liberating.*

STEVENS, WILLIAM LOUIS, bishop; b. Yuba City, Calif., Jan. 12, 1932; s. Ralph Fremont and Elsie Mae (Schultz) S.; B.A., San Francisco State Coll., 1953; M.Div. Gen. Theol. Sem., 1956. Ordained priest, Episcopal Ch.; curate St. Luke's Ch., San Francisco; sr. curate St. Savior's, London, Order of the Holy Cross, N.Y.; rector St. Benedict's Ch., Plantation, Fla. to 1980; bishop Episcopal Diocese of Fond du Lac (Wis.), 1980—. Trustee, Nashotah Ho. Sem.; bishop visitor Sisterhood of the Holy Nativity; mem. Nat. Right to Life Com. Office: Diocese of Fond du Lac Grafon Hall 39 N Sophia PO Box 149 Fond du Lac WI 54935

STEVENS, WOODIE JAMES, pastor; b. North Platte, Nebr., Oct. 15, 1951; s. Jerry Duwaye and Ada Loralee (Hisel) S.; m. Cheryl Anne Hancock, May 19, 1973; children: Michelle Danae, Geoffrey Kyle. BA, Mid-Am. Nazarene Coll., 1973; MDiv, Nazarene Theol. Sem., 1976; DMin, Trinity Evang. Div. Sch., 1982. Pastor Grace Ch. Nazarene, Vermillion, S.D., 1976-78; sr. pastor First Ch. Nazarene, Mundelein, Ill., 1978-87, Colo. Springs, 1987—. Author: How to Fill the Emptiness, 1986 (Chinese ed. 1990); contbr. editor Bread Mag., 1985—. Dist. youth pres. Chgo. Cen. Ch. Nazarene, 1980-83; regional youth pres. Cen. Region Ch. Nazarene, Kankakee, Ill., 1982-85; gen. internal youth pres., Internat. Ch. Nazarene, Kansas City, Mo., 1985-89 (bd. dirs.), v.chmn. Colo. dist. adv. bd. 1990-91; bd. regents NW Nazarene Coll. 1990-93. Home: 3018 Nevermind Ln Colorado Springs CO 80917 Office: First Ch of Nazarene 4120 Fountain Blvd Colorado Springs CO 80916

STEVENSON, BENJAMIN HOWARD, worship and music minister; b. Muskegon, Mich., Apr. 20, 1929; s. Benjamin Arthur and Dorothy Elva (Goodrich) S.; m. Marilyn Jane Danielson, Aug. 15, 1953; children: Bruce Alan, Suzanne Kay, Elizabeth Anne. BA, Westmont Coll., 1950; MA, U. Wash., 1960; DMA, U. So. Calif., L.A., 1970. Lic. to ministry Bapt. Ch., 1980. Min. of youth and music Tabernacle Bapt. Ch., Seattle, 1950-56; dir. music Multnomah Sch. of the Bible, Portland, Oreg., 1956-63; mem. faculty, chmn. music dept. Westmont Coll., Santa Barbara, Calif., 1963-80; min. of music and worship 1st Evang. Free Ch., Fullerton, Calif., 1980—; Staley lectr. We. Bapt. Sem., Portand, 1972, Multnomah Sch. of the Bible, 1978. Co-author: Mastering Worship, 1990. Mem. Choral Conductors Guild, Am. Choral Dirs. Assn. Republican. Avocations: sailing, flying, motorcycle touring, travel. Office: 1st Evang Free Ch 2801 N Brea Blvd Fullerton CA 92635

STEVENSON, JEFFERY SCOTT, minister; b. Cedar Rapids, Iowa, Nov. 1, 1956; s. Milton Whitt and Ruth Ellen (Alton) S.; m. Tonnie Leigh Osburn, May 21, 1977; children: Micah Leigh, Meghann Kay, Mallory Danielle. AA, Ohio Valley Coll., 1977; BA, Freed-Hardeman U., 1979; postgrad., Marshall U., 1982-85, U. Akron, 1991. Ordained to ministry Chs. of Christ, 1975. Min. Ceredo (W.Va.) Ch. of Christ, 1979-86, Uniontown (Pa.) Ch. of Christ, 1986-87, Norway Ave. Ch. of Christ, Huntington, W.Va., 1987-91, Louisville (Ohio) Ch. of Christ, 1991—; bd. dirs. Huntington Harvest Outreach Ministry, 39'ers Ministry to the Elderly, The Lord's Lap Children's Ministry. Author: The Heart of the Bible, 1989, Closer to Home, 1992. Home: 6166 Louisville St NE Louisville OH 44641 Office: Louisville Ch Christ 6140 Louisville St NE Louisville OH 44641

STEVENSON, JON WAYNE, elder, broadcast technician; b. Glendale, Calif., Nov. 2, 1946; s. Wayne J. and Charlotte A. (Ellis) S.; m. Marian E. Brown; children: Jeni, Jonathan, Judi, Jolene, Jeremy. BA in secondary edn., Dordt Coll., 1969. Ordained to ministry Orthodox Presbyn. Ch. as elder, 1974. Tch. Sunday sch. Grace Orthodox Presbyn. Ch., Vienna, Va., 1969-70; tchr. Fairfax (va.) Christian Sch., 1969-70; announcer Christian Missionary WIVV Radio, Vieques, P.R., 1970-73; engr. Christian Radio Sta. WRIO, Rio Grande, N.J., 1973-80, Christian Radio Sta. WRYO, Crystal River, Fla., 1976-78; dir. Boardwalk Chapel, Wildwood, N.J., 1978—; suspension monitor Wildwood High Sch., 1981—; elder Calvary Orthodox Presbyn. Ch., Wildwood, 1978—. Home: 2206 New Jersey Ave Wilwood NJ 08260 Office: The Boardwalk Chapel 4300 Boardwalk Box 602 Wildwood NJ 08260

STEWART, ALEXANDER DOIG, bishop; b. Boston, Jan. 27, 1926; s. Alexander Doig and Catherine Muir (Smith) S.; m. Laurel Gale, June 5, 1953. A.B. cum laude, Harvard U., 1948, M.B.A., 1961; M.Div. cum laude, Union Theol. Sem., N.Y.C., 1951; D.D. (hon.), Gen. Theol. Sem., N.Y.C. Ordained priest Episcopal Ch., 1951; asst. (Christ Ch.), Greenwich, Conn., 1950-52; priest-in-charge (St. Margaret's Parish), Bronx, N.Y., 1952-53; rector (St. Mark's Episc. Ch.), Riverside, R.I., 1953-70; bishop Episc. Diocese Western Mass., Springfield, 1970-83; exec. for adminstrn. Episcopal Ch., N.Y.C., 1983-86, exec. v.p., mgr. pension fund, 1987-91, part-time cons., 1992—; mem. faculty Barrington Coll., 1955-70; Mem. budget and program com. Episc. Ch. U.S.A.; bd. dirs. Ch. Ins. Co., Ch. Life Ins. Co., Ch. Hymnal Corp. Author: Science and Human Nature, 1960 (Wainwright House award), The Shock of Revelation, 1967; also articles. Chmn. Urban Renewal, E. Providence, R.I., 1967-70; vice chmn. United Fund Springfield, 1972; mem. schs. and scholarship com. R.I. chpt. Harvard Coll., 1960-70; A founder, 1959; since mem. bd. dirs., sec. corp. Health Havens, Inc., E. Providence; trustee Barrington Coll., 1971-76, Episcopal Radio-TV Found., 1980—, Providence Country Day Sch., 1964-70, Ch. Pension Fund, N.Y.C., 1976—; mem. corp. St. Elizabeth's Hosp., Providence, 1954-70, Springfield Hosp., 1970—. Mem. Religious Research Assn. Clubs: Union League (N.Y.C.); Harvard Western Mass.). Address: 75 Severn St Longmeadow MA 01106

STEWART, ALEXANDER RONALD, III, minister; b. Springfield, Mo., Sept. 15, 1945; s. Alexander Ronald, Jr. and Maxine Lola (Waid) S.; m. Donna Mauree Boylan; children: Scott Matthew, Jennie Mauree. BA, Drury Coll., 1967; MDiv, McCormick Seminary, Chgo., 1970, MST, 1981; D Ministry, McCormick Sem., Chgo., 1982. Ordained to ministry Presbyn. Ch., 1972. Assoc. min. Arcadia Ave. Presbyn. Ch., Peoria, Ill., 1972-80; min. Ellington Meml. Presbyn. Ch., Quincy, Ill., 1980-85, Westminster Presbyn. Ch., Springfield, 1985—; pres., bd. dirs. Springfield Presbyn. Manor Bd. Trustees; del. Synod Coun. of Synod of Mid-America, 1990—. Mem. Rotary, Omicron Kappa Delta. Office: Westminster Presbyn Church 1551 East Portland Springfield MO 65804

STEWART, BRUCE C., academic administrator. Head Reformed Presbyn. Theol. Sem., Pitts. Office: Reformed Presbyn Theol Sem 7418 Penn Ave Pittsburgh PA 15208*

STEWART, CHARLES F(RANKLIN), JR., clergyman; b. Evanston, Ill., Apr. 6, 1942; s. Charles Franklin and Constance (Brocker) S.; m. Nancy Jean Autio, Jan. 1, 1983. BA, Ariz. State U., 1967; MDiv, San Francisco Theol. Sem., 1970, DMin, 1973. Ordained to ministry, Presbyn. Ch., 1971. Pastor Fruitvale Presbyn. Ch., Oakland, Calif., 1973—, Immanuel Presbyn. Ch., San Jose, Calif., 1985, Christ Presbyn. Ch., San Leandro, Calif., 1987; stated clk. Presbytery of San Francisco, 1990—; cons. gerontolgoy, Alameda, Calif., 1986—; pension cons. Older Adult Svc. Agys. Contbr. articles on ch. mgmt., aging, to various publs. Chmn. bd. dirs. MM Fed. Credit Union, Berkeley, Calif., 1988-90, Fred Finch Youth Ctr., Berkeley, 1988-90; vice-chmn. Mental Health Svc. Dist.; hon. chmn. campaign com. County supr. election, Alameda County. Mem. Am. Assn. Aging. Republican. Office: Presbytery San Francisco 2024 Durant Ave Berkeley CA 94704

STEWART, CHARLES WESLEY, minister; b. Portsmouth, Ohio, Feb. 20, 1930; s. John Lynn and Grace Esther (Thornton) S.; m. Dorothy Jean Currier, July 15, 1950; children: Stephen, Paul, Miriam. BTh, Owosso Bible Coll., 1953; MA, Whitworth Coll., 1967; ThM, Princeton Theol. Sem., 1975; D of Ministry, Western Evang. Sem., 1984. Ordained to ministry, 1956. Pastor Wesleyan Ch., Hope, Mich., 1955-56, Twin Falls, Idaho, 1956-57, Post Falls, Idaho, 1957-61, Portland, Oreg., 1961-65; tchr. N.T. and pastoral ministries United Wesleyan Coll., Allentown, Pa., 1967-75; pastor Crown Hills Wesleyan Ch., Seattle, 1975-84, 87—, Eugene (Oreg.) Wesleyan Ch., 1984-87; lectr. in religion U.S. Postal Svc., Portland, 1962-65, Spokane, Wash., 1965-67, Seattle Pacific U., 1976-77; chaplain DIET, 1976-78, Decency in Environment-Entertainment Today, 1976-77. Contbr. articles to religious jours. Mem. Wash. State Assn. Evangs. (bd. dirs. 1977-80), Seattle Assn. Evangs. (v.p. (1976-80). Home: 9202 11 Ave N W Seattle WA 98117 Office: 9204 11th Ave N W Seattle WA 98117 *The key to a powerful life is single-mindedness. When that center of focus is Christ, a life filled with joy, love, and service follows.*

STEWART, DAVID TABB, minister; b. Arlington, Va., May 17, 1949; s. William Moseley and Elsie Lucille (Banks) S.; m. Cathleen Laurie Hill, July 6, 1969; 1 child, Sarah Hope. BS, U. Oreg., 1978; MA, U. Utah, 1990. Pastor Shiloh Youth Revival Ctrs., Dexter, Oreg., 1968-70, treas., v.p. fin., 1970-78; pastor Calvary Chapel Salt Lake City, 1978-88, Resurrection Fellowship, Salt Lake City, 1989—. Author, editor: (magazine) The Well, 1979; artistic dir.: (play) Job, 1974, (TV spl.) Psalms; dir., author: (play) The Ass' Colt, 1975. Pres. Assn. for Retarded Citizens Utah, Salt Lake City, 1989-90, Agape Ctr., Salt Lake City, 1978-83; bd. dirs. Legal Ctr. for Handicapped, Salt Lake City, 1989-90, ARC Utah, Salt Lake City, 1984-90, Utah Parent Ctr., Salt Lake City, 1984-87. Grantee Gov.'s Coun. for People With Disabilities, 1988-89, Bishop Episc. Ch., 1989; recipient Louis C. Zucker award U. Utah Middle East Ctr., 1985. Mem. Soc. for Scientific Study of Religion, Soc. Bibl. Lit., Nat. Hist. Communal Soc., Utah Inst. for Bibl. Studies (chmn. 1989-90, bd. dirs. 1984-87). Home: 819 E 900 S Salt Lake City UT 84105

STEWART, DWIGHT CALVERT, philosophy educator; b. Ionia, Mich., Oct. 10, 1930; s. Paul Lemuel and Brite Frances (Beal) S.; m. Jane Hale Howerton, Dec. 28, 1951; children—Carol Jane, Joseph Dwight, Paul Robert. B.A., Culver-Stockton Coll., 1952; M.Div., Drake U., 1955; A.M., Harvard U., 1960; Ph.D., Northwestern U., 1973. Asst. prof., then assoc. prof. religion and philosophy Culver-Stockton Coll., Canton, Mo., 1959-65; asst. prof. religion Boston U., 1968-73; assoc. prof. philosophy Union Coll., Barbourville, Ky., 1974-77, prof., 1977-84, dean undergrad. acad. affairs, 1978-79, dean of faculty, 1979-83, v.p. acad. affairs, 1983-84; dean acad. affairs Midway Coll., Ky., 1984-86, pres., Stewart Info. Services, Inc., 1986—. Danforth Found. grantee, 1966. Mem. AAUP, Am. Acad. Religion. Contbg. editor publs. in field. Home: 807 Pheasant Lane Versailles KY 40383 Office: 1628 Nicholasville Rd Lexington KY 40503

STEWART, GEORGE E., minister; b. Karnes City, Tex., Mar. 13, 1915; s. George E. and Willie (Campbell) S.; m. Mildred Eldise Moss, (wid. Nov. 1979); children: George, Elizabeth Ann; m. Carolyn Barrow. BA, Baylor U., 1938; MA, Southwest Tex. State, 1954; postgrad., Southwestern Baptist Seminary, Ft. Worth, 1939-42; DD, Howard Payne U., 1954. Pastor First Baptist Ch., Wellborn, Tex., 1938-40, Kennedy, Tex., 1942-44, San Marcos, Tex., 1944-50; pastor Harlandale Baptist Ch., San Antonio, 1950-55, Southern Ave. Baptist Ch., Memphis, Tenn., 1955-61; dir. of missions San Antonio Baptist Assn., San Antonio, 1961-80; retired, 1980; trustee San Marcos (Tex.) Acad., 1944-50, U. Corpus Christi (Tex.) 1952-55; mem. State Exec. Bd. BAGT, Dallas, 1952-55. Author: Manual For New Church Members, 1942, Giants In The Land, 1989. Republican. Avocations: oil painting, golf, cartooning. Home: 310 W Lynwood San Antonio TX 78212

STEWART, GLEN JAY, minister; b. Lorain, Ohio, Nov. 12, 1949; s. Charles Leonard and Connie Rae (Jellison) S.; m. Joyce Ellen Long, May 24, 1975; 1 child, John-Paul. BA, U. Toledo, 1971; MDiv, Vanderbilt U., 1974, D in Ministry, 1975. Ordained to ministry of Christian Ch. (Disciples of Christ), 1974. Pastor Matlock Meml. Christian Ch., Salem, Ky., 1972; pastor 1st Christian Ch., Madison, Tenn., 1974-75, Sidney, Ohio, 1975-80; sr. minister 2d Christian Ch., Warren, Ohio, 1980-85; assoc. regional minister Christian Ch. Greater Kansas City, Mo., 1986—; bd. dirs. Christian Ch. Elyria, Ohio, 1983-85. Co-founder, pres. Big Bros./Big Sisters Shelby County, Sidney, 1978, 80; chmn. Safety Task Force, Lenexa, Kans., 1986; trustee Battered Spouse Shelter, Warren, 1983-85. Named to Lenexa Vol. Hall of Fame. Mem. Amnesty Internat., Conf. Area and Assoc. Regional Mins. of the Christian Ch. (pres. D.C.)., Mensa. Democrat. Lodge: Rotary. Avocations: investments, sports, leading glass, geneology. Office: Christian Ch Greater Kansas City 5700 Broadmoor # 408 Mission MO 66202

STEWART, HAL ALDRIDGE, minister; b. Winterville, Ga., Nov. 2, 1937; s. Thomas R. and Zelma (Whitehead) S.; m. Lynette Railey, June 26, 1959; children: Thomas R., James A., J. Scott. Student, Columbus Coll., 1970-74. Ordained to ministry Assemblies of God, 1970. Min. of music, bus. adminstr. Evangel Temple, Columbus, Ga., 1967—; mem. nat. music com. Assemblies of God, Springfield, Mo., 1982-84, dist. music dir., Macon, Ga., 1985—. Office: Evangel Temple 5350 Beallwood Connector Columbus GA 31904

STEWART, JACQUES, religious organization administrator. Pres. Protestant Fedn. of France, Paris. Office: Fedn Protestante, 47 rue de Clichy, 75009 Paris France*

STEWART, JAMES CLIFTON, III, clergyman; b. Picayune, Miss., Jan. 1, 1957; s. James Clifton and Betty Lu (Coston) S. MPA in Acctg., La. Tech. U., 1981; MDiv, New Orleans Bapt. Theol. Sem., 1984. Ordained to ministry Bapt. Ch., 1984. Pastor Port Sulphur (La.) Bapt. Ch., 1984-86, First Bapt. Ch., Lockport, La., 1988-90; singles minister Calvary Bapt. Ch., Alexandria, La., 1990—; student summer missionary La. Bapt. Student Union, Alexandria, 1981; dir. singles Cen. La. and North Rapides Bapt. Assn., 1991—. Mem. So. Bapt. Assn. Ministers with Single Adults. Office: Calvary Bapt Ch 5011 Jackson St Alexandria LA 71303

STEWART, JAMES JOSEPH, minister, consultant; b. Long Beach, Calif., Nov. 1, 1944; s. Frank Walter and Florence Marie (Franz) S. AA, Long Beach City Coll., 1966; BA, Calif. State U., 1969; MDiv, Tex. Christian U., 1973, D of Ministry, 1976, cert. in pastoral counseling, 1976. Ordained to ministry Disciples of Christ, 1972. Min. edn. Torrey Pines Christian Ch., La Jolla, Calif., 1973-74; pastor 1st Christian Ch., Wheatland, Calif., 1977-79, Glendora, Calif., 1979-83, Oakland, Calif., 1983-86; pastor Mirror Lake Christian Ch., St. Petersburg, Fla., 1990—; part-time adj. cons. Nat. Evang. Assn., Lubbock, Tex., 1989—. Mem. Ministerial Assn., Glendora (treas. 1981-82), Lions, Theta Phi. Home: 9942 12 Way N # 101 Saint Petersburg FL 33716 *Perhaps the greatest discovery anyone can make is to realize that Jesus Christ is a clear picture window through whom one can see God. The closer one gets to that window, the more one sees of the Eternal One.*

STEWART, KIMBERLY CLARICE, religious educator; b. Ashland, Ky., Aug. 24, 1968; d. William L. and Ann (Herrell) Wheatley. Student, Fla. So. U., 1990—. Student asst. to v.p./athletic dir. Brevard Community Coll., Clearwater, Fla., 1987-89; student asst. to athletic dir. Asbury Coll., Wilmore, Ky., 1989, Fla. So. Coll., Lakeland, Fla., 1990—; dir. youth ministries First United Meth. Ch., Ft. Meade, Fla., 1990—; nat. youth del. for N.Y./Washington, First United Meth. Ch., 1987, counselor Music Wk., Camp Brandon, 1987, tchr. vacation bible sch., 1988-89; asst. lay dir. Teens Encounter Christ, 1989, youth coord. Lay Witness Missions; dir. youth ministries Ft. Meade United Meth. Ch., 1990-91, dist. lay rep. Children's Ministry. Recipient numerous athletic and academic scholarships. Mem. Theta Chi Beta, Sigma Rho. Democrat. Home: 811 Peachtree St Cocoa FL 32922

STEWART, LARRY WAYNE, minister; b. Corbin, Ky., Oct. 6, 1947; s. Raleigh O. and Edna Lorene (Cummins) S.; m. Marilyn Marie Smith, Dec. 30, 1972; children: Alison Marie, Lauren Renee. BS, Cumberland Coll., 1969; MDiv, So. Bapt. Theol. Sem., 1979. Ordained to ministry Am. Bapt. Chs. in U.S.A., 1967. Assoc. pastor Oakland Ave. Bapt. Ch., Covington, Ky., 1977-78; pastor First Bapt. Ch., Manchester, Ohio, 1978-79; min. of edn. First Bapt. Ch., Cin., 1980-83; area min. South Cen. Bapt. Assn., Columbus, Ind., 1983-89; pastor First Bapt. Ch., Hillsboro, Ohio, 1989—. Trustee chmn. Samaritan Outreach Svcs., Hillsboro, 1990—. Mem. Ohio Bapt. Mins., Clinto Bapt. Assn. (pres. mins. fellowship 1990—), Hillsboro Area Ministerial (treas. 1990—), Rotary Internat. Home: 125 S West St Hillsboro OH 45133 Office: First Bapt Ch 127 S West St Hillsboro OH 45133

STEWART, LELAND PERRY, minister, educator, administrator; b. Detroit, Mar. 4, 1928; s. Hoyt Clifford and Gladys (Woodward) S.; m. Elizabeth Elliot, June 13, 1953; children: Deanna Jennings, Dana, Lynn Murphy. BS in Math. and Mech. Engring., U. Mich., 1949; STB, Harvard Divinity Sch., 1953. Cert. secondary edn. tchr., Calif. Minister Universalist Ch. of Hollywood, Calif., 1959-60; tchr. Glendale (Calif.) Unified Sch. Dist., 1960-62, L.A. Unified Sch. Dist., 1962-72; cen. coord. Unity-and-Diversity World Coun., L.A., 1965—; founding minister Unity-and-Diversity Fellowship, L.A., 1974—; substitute tchr. L.A. Unified Sch. Dist., 1972-75; mem. faculty World U. in L.A., 1987—; mem. adv. bd. Emperor's Coll., Santa Monica, Calif., 1990—; bd. dirs. Interfaith Coun. for UN, L.A. Author: From Industrial Power to Lasting Peace, 1953. Recipient Community Svc. award UNICEF, 1986. Democrat. Avocations: writing, trumpet, swimming, travel. Office: Unity-and-Diversity World Coun 1010 S Flower St # 401 Los Angeles CA 90015-1428

STEWART, LEON OTTO, bishop, general superintendent; b. Pineville, Fla., Dec. 5, 1929; s. John Wesley and Susie Ann (Allen) S.; m. Donna Marie Dooley, Sept. 5, 1952; children: Dianne Marie, Karen Denise. STB, Holmes Bible Coll., 1952; grad., Famous Writers Sch., 1970. Ordained to ministry Pentecostal Holiness Ch. Inc., 1952. Christian edn. dir. Pentecostal Holiness Ch. Inc., Ala., 1952-53, 55-57; conf. supt. State of Ala. Pentecostal Holiness Ch. Inc., 1960-69, asst. gen. supt. for denom., Oklahoma City, 1969-77, dir. ch. loan fund, superannuation and publs., 1969-73, dir. evangelism, 1973-81, vice chmn. of denomination, 1977-81, gen. supt. congregation, bishop, 1981-89. Author: Too Late, 1956; editor in chief The Advocate, 1981-89; editor: Prep mag., 1960-71, Witness mag., 1974-81. Trustee Holmes Theol. Sem., Lion. Address: Pentecostal Holiness Ch 105 Fernway Dr Atmore AL 36502

STEWART, MICHAEL STEVEN, minister, educator; b. Balt., Sept. 25, 1956; s. Theodore Maine and Elizabeth (Walter) S.; m. Pamela Renée Boggs, Mar. 18, 1978; children: Justin, Michael, Joshua Maine. AA, Emmanuel Coll., 1977, BA, 1979; MA, Liberty U., 1989. Ordained to ministry, Pentecostal Ch. Assoc. pastor New Life Temple, Roanoke, Va., 1979; sr. pastor Christian Heritage Ch., Danville, Va., 1979-88; assoc. pastor Pentecostal Holiness Ch., Franklin Springs, Ga., 1988-90, First Assembly of God, Winston-Salem, N.C., 1990—; admistrv. dir. The Ctr. of Emmanuel Coll., Franklin Springs, Ga., 1989—. Chmn. bd. Social Svcs., Danville, Va., 1982-88; pres. Little Life, Danville, 1986-88. Recipient Benson Preaching award, Emmanuel Coll., 1979. Mem. Am. Assn. Counseling and Devel., Optimist Club (pres. Danville, Va. 1988). Republican. Mem. Assemblies of God Ch. Home: 339 Merrimont Dr Winston-Salem NC 27106 Office: First Assembly of God 3730 University Pkwy Winston-Salem NC 27106

STEWART, ROBERT CLARENCE, JR., minister; b. Alliance, Ohio, Oct. 28, 1936; s. Robert Clarence Sr. and Geraldine Jean (Palmer) S.; m. Nancy Pearl Payton, Mar. 17, 1956; children: Terry Lynn, Robin Renee, Tracy Lucretia. Grad. in evangelism, Malone Coll., 1987. Ordained to ministry A.M.E. Ch., 1985. Supr. Sunday sch. St. Luke A.M.E. Ch., Alliance, 1980-85; pastor Bethel A.M.E. Ch., Massillon, Ohio, 1985-90, Asbury Chapel A.M.E. Ch., Waynesburg, Ohio, 1990—; with Am. Steel Foundry, Alliance, 1956-87, ret., 1987; chaplain Alliance City Coun., 1985—. Bd. dirs. svc. rev. com. Alliance Community Hosp., 1987—; pres. bd. trustees Alliance Family Counseling Ctr., 1988—; trustee John Slimak Shelter Ctr., Alliance, 1989—, Alliance Are United Way, 1989—. Mem. NAACP, The Alliance of Chs. (pres. 1989—), Elks (exalted ruler Cantell club 1975-79). Home: 11809 Sioux Ave NE Alliance OH 44601 Office: Asbury Chapel AME Ch 8771 Greer St Waynesburg OH 44688

STEWART, ROBERT RAY, minister; b. Chandler, Ariz., Nov. 30, 1938; s. Eunice Alfred and Dona Belle (Weathers) S.; m. Violet Sue Ruth, May 27, 1957 (div. Feb. 1969); children: Terry Ray, Deborah Lynn; m. Gina Targosz, Feb. 12, 1990. Student, Bethany Coll., Santa Cruz, Calif., 1959-60. Ordained to ministry Assemblies of God, 1966. Evangelist Assemblies of God, Fremont, Calif., 1960-64; pastor 1st Assembly of God Ch., Coolidge, Ariz., 1964-65; founder, exec. dir. Teen Challenge Ariz., Inc., Phoenix, 1965-67; exec. dir. Teen Challenge, San Francisco, 1967-69; founder, exec. dir. City Harvest Ministry, Inc., Phoenix, 1990—; dist. mgr. Equitable Fin. Cos., Phoenix, 1970-90. Chmn. fund raiser ticket sales Palmer Drug Abuse Ctr., Phoenix, 1988-89; precinct committeeman Ariz. Rep. Com., Phoenix, 1989; bd. dirs. Teen Challenge Ariz., Inc., 1991—. With USN, 1956-59. Mem. Nat. Assn. Life Underwriters. Home: 1717 E Union Hills Apt 1088 Phoenix AZ 85024 Office: City Harvest Ministry Inc PO Box 26806 Phoenix AZ 85068 *The greatest thing in all the world is love. The greatest experience in life is to witness the transformation of misplaced humanity. That takes place when they experience the loving hand of compassion from their fellowmen.*

STEWART, THOMAS PENNEY, clergyman; b. Auburn, N.Y., May 24, 1927; s. Weir and Margaret (Penney) S.; m. Ann Maxwell Field, June 24, 1950 (div. 1986); children: Katherine, Elizabeth, Alison; m. Gaynor Studds, 1987. Grad., Hotchkiss Sch., Lakeville, Conn., 1945; A.B., Princeton U., 1951; M.Div., Union Theol. Sem., N.Y.C., 1954. Ordained to ministry Presbyn. Ch., 1954; pastor in Ballston Spa, N.Y., 1954-59; pastor Rosyln (N.Y.) Presbyn. Ch., 1959-71, Westminster Presbyn. Ch., Buffalo, 1971—; Chmn. Commn. on Religion and Race, Presbytery L.I., 1961-66; moderator Synod N.Y., 1968-69, Presbytery Western N.Y., 1982-83; pres. Religious Communities for Arts, 1980-84; treas. Artpark & Co., 1976-78. Bd. dirs. Union Theol. Sem., Buffalo Philharmonic Orch., 1978-86, Auburn Theol. Sem., N.Y.C., 1985—; bd. counselors Smith Coll., 1966-71; term trustee Princeton U., 1968-72; pres. Am. Friends of NesAmmim, Israel, 1981-86; chmn. bd. Auburn Theol. Sem., N.Y.C., 1991—. Mem. Alumni Assn. Union Theol. Sem. (pres. 1963-65). Home: 39 St George's Sq Buffalo NY 14222 Office: 724 Delaware Ave Buffalo NY 14209 *In a rapidly changing world one of the most important virtues is the ability and the willingness to be open to new truth.*

STEWART, VERNON EDWIN, music minister; b. Pampa, Tex., Sept. 5, 1938; s. Vernon Elias and Amy (Hancock) S.; m. Celia Ann Gomillion, Jan. 11, 1957; children: Timothy Edwin, Charmaine Louise Stewart Smith, Joy Beth Stewart Potts. Student, Frank Phillips Jr. Coll.; grad. sacred music, Bapt. Bible Coll., 1961; BS in Edn., S.W. Mo. State U., 1966; MusM, Pitts. State U., Kans., 1972. Minister music Cherry St. Bapt. Ch., Springfield, Mo., 1959-64, 67-71, Blueridge Bapt. Temple, Kansas City, Mo., 1965-66; prof. music Bapt. Bible Coll., Springfield, Mo., 1966-72, 75-79; headmaster Hollywood (Fla.) Christian Sch., 1972-75; rep., choral cons. Good Life Pub., Scottsdale, Ariz., 1979-86; pres. First Link of Atlanta, Morrow, Ga., 1986-89; minister of music Mt. Zion Bapt. Ch., Jonesboro, Ga., 1989—; music cons. Good Life Publs., Scottsdale, 1979-86; trainer Leadership Dynamics, Atlanta, 1984—; part-time minister of music Mt. Zion Bapt. Ch., 1982-88. Dep. Mounted Sheriff's Posse, Springfield, 1976-79; staff advisor overcomers outreach Susbstance Abuse Recovery Group, Jonesboro, 1989—. Republican. Baptist. Avocations: hunting, fishing, golf. Home: 6580 Charles Dr Morrow GA 30260 Office: Mt Zion Bapt Ch 7102 Mount Zion Blvd Jonesboro GA 30236

STEWART, WARREN HAMPTON, SR., pastor; b. Independence, Kans., Dec. 11, 1951; s. Jesse J. Stewart and Jessie Elizabeth (Washington) Jenkins; m. Serena Michele Wilson, June 18, 1977; children: Warren Hampton Jr., Matthew Christian, Jared Chamberlain, Justin Mitchell, Aaron Frederick Taylor. AA, Coffeyville Community Jr. Coll, 1971; BA, Bishop Coll., 1973; MDiv and MST, Union Theol. Sem., 1976, 77; D Ministry, Am. Bapt. Sem. of West, 1982. Lic. 1969, ordained to ministry Bapt. Ch. 1973. Assoc. min. 12th St. Bapt. Ch., Coffeyville, Kans., 1969-71, Bethlehem Bapt. Ch., Dallas, 1971-73, Cornerstone Bapt. Ch., Bklyn., 1973-77; pastor 1st Instl. Bapt. Ch., Phoenix, 1977—; past. pres. Am. Bapt. Chs. of Pacific Southwest, 1988-89, (Roy B. Anderson Evang. award 1986), Paradise M.B. State Congress Christian Edn., Ariz., Paradise State Conv. Ariz., founder Mins., Lay Persons Inst., Sandy F. Ray Inst., 1981. Author: Interpreting God's Word in Black Preaching, 1984. Chmn. Arizonans for Martin Luther King Jr. State Holiday, 1986-90; co-founder Clergy Against Drugs, Phoenix, 1988. Recipient Disting. Svc. award, Greater Phoenix Chpt. UN Assn., 1987. Mem. NAACP (Maricopa County chpt. Roy Wilkins Meml. Award).

STEWART, WILLIAM, religious organization administrator. Chmn. Ch. of the Nazarene, Moncton, N.B., Can. Office: Ch Nazarene, 14 Hollywood Dr, Moncton, NB Canada E1E 2R5*

STEWART, WILLIAM HIRAM, minister, educator; b. Washington, Dec. 27, 1935; s. George Moody Stewart and Jane (Halliwell) Biederman; m. Janila Lee Oertel, June 15, 1962; children: Lucinda Kay, Mark William. BA in Bible Studies cum laude, Northwestern Coll., Mpls., 1958; 1st class FCC lic. and diploma, Don Martin Sch. Radio and TV Arts and Sci., 1959; MA, Mennonite Brethren Bibl. Sem., 1978. Ordained to ministry Bapt. Ch., 1970. Minister Youth for Christ, Mpls., 1954-58; youth minister Grace Community Ch., Panorama City, Calif., 1958-59, adminstr., youth minister, 1965-68; minister Youth for Christ, Los Angeles, 1960-63, Oakland, Calif., 1963-65; minister youth edn. 1st Bapt. Ch., Modesto, Calif., 1968-90; assoc. prof., dean of students Western Sem. Phoenix, Scottsdale, Ariz., 1990—; mem. com. Youth for Christ Nat. Club, 1960's. Author: Wittenburg Door, 1970. Mem. Pub. Sch. Com., Modesto, 1970's; vice chmn. 15th Dist. Congl. Awards Com., 1985. Mem. Nat. Network Youth Ministries Bd., Am. Sci. Affiliation. Republican. Avocations: radio, TV, hunting. Office: Western Sem Phoenix 7601 E Shea Blvd Scottsdale AZ 85260

STICKLER, ALFONS MARIA CARDINAL, retired cardinal, librarian, archivist; b. Neunkirchen, Vienna, Austria, Aug. 23, 1910. ordained priest Roman Cath. Ch., 1937. Prefect Vatican Libr., Rome, 1971-84; pro-libr., pro-archivist Vatican Libr., 1984-90; Consecrated archbishop Titular See Volsinium, 1983; proclaimed cardinal, 1985-90; deacon S. Giorgio of Velabro, 1985-88; mem. various depts. Roman Curia, Supreme Ct. Signature Apostolica, Congregations of Canonisation, Religious Life, Coun. of Interpretation Canon Law, Communication Media, Patrimonial Adminstrn. Address: Città del Vaticano, Rome Italy

STIEMKE, FREDERICK ADOLF, chaplain; b. Balt., Feb. 20, 1929; s. Adolf John and Adele Myrtle Louise (Hoffmann) S.; m. D. Jean Wilton Dec. 5, 1953; children: John W., Mark F., David W. BA, Concordia Seminary, St. Louis, 1951, diploma in theology, 1955. Pastor Holy Trinity Luth. Ch., Rome, Ga., 1955-60, Messiah Luth. Ch., Valdosta, Ga., 1960-63, Bethlehem Luth. Ch., Richmond, Va., 1963-67; chaplain southeastern dist. Luth. Ch.-Mo. Synod, Raleigh, N.C., 1967-74; dir. chaplaincy svcs. Bethesda Luth. Home, Watertown, Wis., 1974-88, religious life adminstr., 1988—; sec., bd. dirs. southeastern dist. Luth. Ch.-Mo. Synod, Washington, 1971-74, chmn. com. on svcs. to devel. disabled persons, St. Louis, 1986—. Author, narrator tape Counseling and Pastoral Care With Persons Who Are Mentally Retarded and Their Families, 1990. Chmn. North Ga. Clinic for Crippled Children, Rome, 1952-55. Mem. Am. Assn. on Mental Retardation (religion div., chairperson Wis. chpt.), Am. Protestant Hosp. Assn., Coll. of Chaplains, Lions (pres. Watertown club 1987-88). Office: Bethesda Luth Home 700 Hoffmann Dr Watertown WI 53094-0294 *If we really get to know persons whom the world labels "mentally retarded", they have much to teach and give us.*

STIENSTRA, BRADLEY RICHARD, minister; b. Palo Alto, Calif., Sept. 27, 1949; s. Ralph Eugene and Dorothy Joan (Bradrick) S.; m. Carol Jean Nolting, June 7, 1975; children: Kaia Lynn, Johna Kristine. BA, U. Calif., Santa Barbara, 1971; MDiv, Luther Northwestern Theol. Sem., St. Paul, 1975. Ordained to ministry Evang. Luth. Ch. Am., 1975. Asst. pastor Christ Luth. Ch., Orange, Calif., 1975-78, pastor, 1978-89; pastor Trinity Luth. Ch., Riverside, Calif., 1989—; dir. Luth. High Sch., Orange, 1981-87. Office: Trinity Luth Ch 5969 Brockton Ave Riverside CA 92506

STIER, ROBERT GORDON, minister; b. Balt., Aug. 29, 1947; s. Gordon Leroy and Elizabeth Gertrude (Hansge) S.; m. Harmony Elaine Hill, Dec. 9, 1972; children: Amanda Janet, Timothy David. BA in Philosophy and Psychology, U. Del., 1969; MDiv., Gordon-Conwell Sem., 1972. Ordained to ministry Presbyn. Ch. (U.S.A.), 1973. Asst. pastor Bethany Presbyn. Ch., Loves Park, Ill., 1972-75, Presbyn. Ch., New Providence, N.J., 1975-78; pastor Forks of Brandywine Presbyn. Ch., Glenmore, Pa., 1978—; pres. Donegal chpt. Presbyn. Pro Life, 1991—. Author: Ideas Books, 1977-78. Mem. Phi Beta Kappa, Phi Kappa Phi. Office: Forks of Brandywine Presbyn Ch RD 2 Box 205 Glenmore PA 19343 *In our busy world, we need to learn to say "no" to people but always "yes" to God. Rather than oversimplification, we need balance and wholeness.*

STIFEL, FREDERICK BENTON, pastor, biochemist, nutritionist; b. St. Louis, Jan. 30, 1940; s. Carl Gottfried and Alma J. (Clark) S.; m. Gail Joane Stewart, Aug. 10, 1963; children: Tim, Faith, Seth, Elizabeth. BS, Iowa State U., 1962, PhD, 1967; MDiv., Melodyland Sch. Theol., Anaheim, Calif., 1979. Ordained to ministry Evang. Presbyn. Ch., 1981. Lab. supr., research chemist U.S. Army Med. Research and Nutrition Lab., Denver, 1968-74, Letterman Army Inst. Research, San Francisco, 1974-76; intern pastor Melodyland Christian Ctr., Anaheim, 1979-80; assoc. pastor Faith Presbyn. Ch., Aurora, Colo., 1980—; chmn. care of candidates com. Presbytery of West, Denver, 1985-88, 91—; bd. dirs., v.p. Love Inc. of Metro Denver, 1987-90; regional coord. Nat. Assn. Single Adult Leaders, 1987-90, coord. Denver area, 1990—. Contbr. clin. med. and nutritional articles to profl. jours. Del. Iowa State Rep. Conv., Des Moines, 1964, Colo. State Rep. Conv., Denver, 1984; mem. parent adv. council IMPACT drug intervention team Rangeview High Sch., Aurora, 1985-89, accountability com., 1989—; young life leader Hinkley High Sch., Aurora, 1968-74; vice chmn. Young Life Com., Marin County, Calif., 1974-76. Capt. U.S. Army Med. Svc. Corps, 1967-70. Recipient Sci. Achievement award U.S. Army Sci. Conf., West Point, N.Y., 1968, 70. Mem. Am. Inst. Nutrition, Am. Soc. Clin. Nutrition, Am. Sci. Affiliation, Evang. Theol. Soc., Phi Eta Sigma, Phi Kappa Phi, Alpha Zeta, Gamma Sigma Delta, Kappa Sigma, Sigma Xi. Avocations: reading, hiking, swimming, writing poetry, gardening. Home: 3492 S Blackhawk Way Aurora CO 80014 Office: Faith Presbyn Ch 11373 E Alameda Ave Aurora CO 80012

STIFFMAN, JEFFREY BARRY, rabbi; b. Balt., Apr. 28, 1939; s. George Josef and Ernestine (Lubarsky) S.; m. Arlene Ruth Rubin, June 26, 1960; children: Michael Nathan, Martha Lynne, Cheryl Beth. BS in Biology, Loyola Coll., Balt., 1960; B in Hebrew Letters, Hebrew Union Coll.-Jewish Inst. Religion, Cin., 1962, MA in Hebrew Lit., 1965, DD (hon.), 1990; PhD in Theology, St. Mary's U. Md., Balt., 1974. Ordained rabbi, 1965. Asst. rabbi Congregation Shaare Emeth, St. Louis, 1965-68, sr. rabbi, 1970—; assoc. rabbi Balt. Hebrew Congregation, 1968-70; mem. exec. com. Rabbinic Cabinet, United Jewish Appeal, N.Y.C., 1980—. Mem. Cen. Conf. Am. Rabbis (ethics com. 1979—), St. Louis Jewish Fedn. (bd. dirs. 1990—), Jewish Chautauqua Soc. (life), Am. Soc. for Technion (Einstein award 1990), Hebrew Union Coll.-Jewish Inst. Religion Alumni Assn. Home: 21 Ramsgate Dr Saint Louis MO 63132 Office: Congregation Shaare Emeth 11645 Ladue Rd Saint Louis MO 63141

STIGERS, HAROLD GENE, retired pastor; b. Spokane, Wash., June 5, 1917; s. Robert Orlen and Helen (Mosier) S.; m. Mary J. Olson, Jan. 4, 1943; children: Sarah Elizabeth, Rebecca Jean, Roberta Louise, Timothy Harold. BA, U. Calif., Berkeley, 1941; BD, Faith Theol. Sem., Wilmington, Del., 1945; MDiv with honors, Faith Theol. Sem., 1969; PhD, Dropsie Coll., 1953. Ordained to ministry Presbyn. Ch., 1953. Lectr. Semitic langs. Faith Sem., Elkins Park, Pa., 1953-55; lectr. Old Testament langs./archaeology Covenant Theol. Sem., St. Louis, 1955-57; with Washington U., St. Louis, 1964-66, Wheaton (Ill.) Coll., 1964-67; architect, expedition to Hebron, Israel, 1964, 66, Acco excavations, Israel, 1975; chief architect Abila excavations, Jordan, 1988, 90. Author: Commentary/Genesis, 1976; contbr. significant articles to profl. jours. Mem. Am. Soc. Oriental Rsch., Archaeol. Inst. Am., Evang. Theol. Soc., Near Eastern Archaeol. Soc. (bd. dirs.). Home: 24 Cheyenne Ct Saint Louis MO 63122 *One cannot think always of getting; he must give more than he gets to insure that his whole life is not merely getting.*

STILES, B. J., minister, coalition executive; b. Maypearl, Tex., Feb. 6, 1933; s. Cloyd F. and Ubah E. (Armstrong) S.; divorced; children: Katherine E., Allison Stiles Culver. BA, Tex. Wesleyan Coll., 1954; BD, So. Meth. U., Dallas, 1957. Assoc. dir. Bd. Higher Edn. Dept. Campus Ministry, Nashville, 1957-60; editor Motive mag. Bd. Higher Edn., Nashville, 1960-69; pres., chief exec. officer Nat. Leadership Coalition on AIDS, Washington, 1987—. Mem. staff Robert F. Kennedy for Pres., Washington, 1968; dir. Forum Inst., Washington, 1984-90. Recipient numerous awards Assn. Ch. Press, 1960-68, Nat. Leadership Award The Prudential Found., Newark, 1991, Stewart McKinney Found., Stamford, Conn., 1991. Founder Washington Book Publishers Soc. (chmn. 1971-72); mem. Nat. Orgn. Responding to AIDS. Democrat. Home: 2828 Connecticut Ave NW Apt 813 Washington DC 20008

STILES, MERVIN, clergyman; b. Cazadero, Calif., Oct. 27, 1917; s. Earl and Katherine (Ancel) S.; m. Beulah May Matteson, Aug. 3, 1943; children: Enid Ruth Bundy, Steven Eugene S., L. Margaret DeMers. BA, Simpson Bible Coll., San Francisco, 1959. Pastor Bapt. City Mission Soc., Portland, Oreg., 1947-51, First Christian Ch., Mansfield, Wash., 1951-52; tchr., mem. adv. bd. New Life Ctr., Santa Cruz, Calif., 1972-90; contbr. SBL Regional Meetings, 1973-90. Author, editor: Shofar, Vols. I to XX, 1973-90. Home: 213 Siesta Dr Aptos CA 95003 *The Hebrew records of the Holy Scriptures, only as they are presented in the original Hebrew, will stand the test of historical comparison and synchronization with the Assyrian and other contemporary historical records.*

STILLER, BRIAN CARL, writer, religious broadcaster; b. Naicam, Sask., Can., Aug. 10, 1942; s. Carl Hilmer and Mildred Ruth (Parsons) S.; m. Lily Muriel Rogers, Aug. 31, 1963; children: Murray, Muriel. BA, U. Toronto, Can., 1966, M of Religion, 1975; LHD (hon.), Briercrest Coll., Sask., 1987. Ordained to ministry Pentecostal Assemblies Can., 1968. Exec. dir. Youth for Christ, Montreal, Que., Can., 1967-71, Toronto, 1971-75; pres. Youth for Christ/Can., 1975-83; exec. dir. Evang. Fellowship Can., 1983—; chmn. younger leaders com. Lausanne Com. for World Evangelization, Charlotte, N.C., 1981-89. Author: A Generation Under Siege, 1983; co-author: LifeGifts, 1990, Critical Options for Evangelicals, 1991; editor in chief Faith Today mag., 1983—; host TV show The Stiller Report, 1989—. Bd. dirs. Child Care Internat., London, Ont., Can., 1971-83. Office: Evang Fellowship Can, Box 8800, Station B, Willowdale, ON Canada M2K 2R6

STILSON, DAVID CHARLES, minister; b. Alliance, Nebr., Mar. 30, 1933; s. David Lyman and Cloe Ellen (Regler) S.; m. Fay Iola Grammer, Dec. 31, 1959. BA, Tex. Christian U., 1960, MEd, 1978; MDiv, Southwestern Bapt. Theol. Sem., 1965; PhD, North Tex. State U., 1983. Ordained to ministry So. Bapt. Conv., 1955; lic. profl. counselor, Tex. Pastor Bethel Bapt. Ch., Ft. Worth, 1962—; pres. White Settlement Ministerial Alliance, 1982—; pvt. practice counseling, Ft. Worth, 1980—; instr. psychology Tarrant County Jr. Coll., 1984-86. Co-author: Crisis Intervention, 1983, Human Development Education, 1983, Holistic Education, 1984. Mem. White Settlement Mayor's Com. Community Devel., 1979. With USN, 1951-53, Korea. Mem. Am. Assn. Marriage and Family Therapists, Tarrant County Bapt. Assn. (exec. bd., moderator 1977, clk. 1978-81). Home: 801 Kate St Fort Worth TX 76108 Office: Bethel Bapt Ch 1208 S Grants Ln Fort Worth TX 76108 *Joy and peace can replace fear and shame for any person who trusts in Christ.*

STIMMEL, JOHN ROBERT, minister; b. Oxnard, Calif., Aug. 20, 1946; s. John Robert and Lorna Loree (Pfander) S.; m. Nancy Emma Bycroft, Aug. 22, 1969 (div. 1984); children: Robert Eric, Amy Marie; m. Billie Jo Black, Oct. 22, 1989. BA, Calif. State U., L.A., 1968; MA, Pepperdine U., L.A., 1981; Rel.D., Sch. Theology, Claremont, Calif., 1972. Ordained to ministry United Meth. Ch. as deacon, 1969, as elder, 1974. Pastor Bardsdale United Meth. Ch., Fillmore, Calif., 1972-74; Pastor First United Meth. Ch., Safford, Ariz., 1974-77, Highland, Calif., 1977-78, Palmdale, Calif., 1978-81; Pastor Grace United Meth. Ch., Riverside, Calif., 1981-85, Moreno Valley (Calif.) United Meth. Ch., 1985-86; asst. conf. treas. Calif. Pacific Ann. Conf., United Meth. Ch., Pasadena, 1986-90; pastor St. James United Meth. Ch., Pasadena, 1990—; conf. statistician Calif. Pacific ann. conf. United Meth. Ch., 1984—. Home: 1921 Polaris Dr Glendale CA 91208 Office: St James United Meth Ch 2033 E Washington Blvd Pasadena CA 91104

STIMSON, DELTON GERALD, JR., minister; b. Woodsville, N.H., July 28, 1949; s. Delton Gerald and Rita Mae (Chase) S.; m. Belinda Ann Fleming, Sept. 6, 1969; children: Todd, Troy, Tye, Travis, Trent, Tate, Christine, Torrey, Thane, Trever, Tad, Tal, Taylor. Diploma, Elohim Bible Inst., Castile, N.Y., 1981. Ordained to ministry Bapt. Ch., 1982. Pastor LaGrange (N.Y.) Bapt. Ch., 1981-82, Christian Fellowship Ch., Scotland, Conn., 1982—. EMT Scotland Fire Dept., 1990—. Sgt. U.S. Army, 1969-70, Vietnam. Home: 142 Pudding Hill Rd Scotland CT 06264

STINES, JAMES WILLIAM, religion educator; b. Asheville, N.C., Jan. 21, 1934; s. Ernest Zachariah and Thelma Doris (Searcy) S.; m. Joyce Arlene Peterson, Dec. 28, 1955; children: Stephanie, Tracy. BA, Wake Forest U., 1954; BDiv, So. Bapt. Theol. Sem., 1958; PhD, Duke U., 1970. Bapt. campus min. U. Fla., 1958-61; Bapt. campus min. Duke U., Durham, N.C., 1961-64, dir., co-founder Duke U. Project, Nicaragua, 1963-65, instr. in philosophy and religion, 1965-67; asst. prof. religion Campbell U., Buies Creek, N.C., 1967-68; from asst. to prof. philosophy and religion Appalachian State U., Boone, N.C., 1968—; chairperson dept. philosophy and religion Appalachian State U., 1972-74, dir. honors program, 1982-89, co-founder Watauga Coll. Contbr. articles to profl. jours. Chairperson Blowing Rock (N.C.) Planning and Zoning Bd. Duke U. scholar, 1965-67; HEW fellow Appalachian State U., 1971-72, grantee, 1986, 87, 89. Mem. Am. Acad. Religion, Am. Philos. Assn., Polanyi Soc., Inst. on Study Religion in Age of Sci., Kierkegaard Soc. Democrat. Avocations: running, tennis, golf, scuba diving. Office: Appalachian State U Dept Philosophy & Religion Boone NC 28608

STINNETTE, TIMOTHY EARL, minister; b. Lynchburg, Va., Sept. 29, 1956; s. Sherwood Earl and Barbara Ann (Wiley) S.; m. Jenifer D. Wills, June 5, 1982. BA in Religion, Carson-Newman Coll., 1978; MDiv, Southeastern Bapt. Theol. Sem., 1982; cert. in life basics, Mng. and Mktg. Inst., West Palm Beach, Fla., 1983. Ordained to ministry So. Bapt. Conv., 1984; lic. preacher. Edn. and youth min. Oak St. Bapt. Ch., Elizabethton, Tenn., 1978; youth min. Big Island (Va.) Bapt. Ch., 1979-80; missionary assoc., ch. planter apprentice Home Mission Bd., Atlanta, 1984-86; pastor Midway and Emmanuel Bapt. Chs., Amherst, Va., 1988—; sales mgr. Kirby Project North Industries, San Diego, 1986-88. Recipient R.B. Park Fun Raising award Los Rancheros Kiwanis, 1986, Master Life, Master Builder and Continuing Witness Tng. award Sunday Sch. Bd., Nashville, 1986. Mem. Piedmont Bapt. Assn. (convener population study group 1989, vice moderator 1990, moderator 1990—, chmn. office search com. 1990), Pedlar Ruritan Club (chaplain 1989—), Alpha Phi Omega (life, 1st v.p. 1977-78). Home and Office: Midway and Emmanuel Bapt Chs RR 1 Box 200 Amherst VA 24521

STITES, RAY DEAN, minister, college president; b. Herington, Kans., Oct. 13, 1946; s. George Darby and Edna Myrtle (Anderson) S.; m. Merelyn Kay Rich, Sept. 2, 1966; children: Ross Mitchell, Britain Darby. BA, Manhattan Christian Coll., Manhattan, Kans., 1968; MDiv, Emmanuel Sch. Religion, Johnson City, Tenn., 1974. Ordained to ministry Christian Ch., 1968. Min. Bozco (W.Va.) Christian Ch., 1968-72; min. Cen. Christian Ch., Richardson, Tex., 1972-78, First Christian Ch., Abilene, Kans., 1979-88, Newton (Kans.) Christian Ch., 1988-91; pres. Nebr. Christian Coll., Norfolk, 1991—; instr. Ch. History, Dallas Christian Coll., 1974-76; pres. North Tex. Evangelizing Assn., 1975-77, Manhattan Christian Coll. Alumni Assn., 1983-85, Christian Evangelizing Assn. of Kans., 1987-89, 91, Kans. Christian Conv., 1989. Bd. dirs. Abilene United Way, 1981-84; mem. Dickinson County Health Dept. Adv. Bd., 1983-88, Dickinson County Coun. on Aging, 1984-88; pres. Abilene Optimist Club, 1983-84. Office: Nebr Christian Ch 1800 Syracuse Norfolk NE 68701

STITH, FORREST C., bishop; b. Marshall, Tex., May 18, 1934; s. Forrest M. and Daisy (Haynes) S.; m. Josephine Mitchell, June 19, 1960; 1 child, Lori Crystal. BD, Drew U., 1948; BS in Edn., U. Nebr., 1955; DD, Western Md. Coll., 1979, Nebr. Wesleyan U., 1986. Pastor Douglas Meml. Ch. United Meth. Ch., Washington, from 1958; resident bishop N.Y. West Area United Meth. Ch., 19846—. Treas., Commr.'s Youth Coun., Area P Bd.; chaplain Pub. Interest Civic Assn.; trustee Syracuse U., Colgate Rochester Div. Sch. Recipient Grass Roots award D.C. Fedn. Civic Assns. for Vol. Svc. Address: 3049 E Genesee Stt Syracuse NY 13224

STITT, MARI LEIPPER, writer; b. Salem, Ohio, May 1, 1923; d. Robert and Myrtle (Cost) Leipper; m. Rodney Dean Stitt, Apr. 22, 1944; children: Dana Lovelace, Rodney D. Jr. BA in Music, San Diego State U., 1946; MA in Human Rels., Calif. Western U., 1966. Dir. religious edn. Cen. Congl. Ch., 1941-50; tchr. sociology San Diego Evening Coll., 1966-84; writer poetry, 1984—. Home: 16686 Iron Springs Rd Julian CA 92036 *Did we miss the point? Somehow the stories of the Garden of Eden, Cain and Abel, and the Tower of Babel seemed so simple—take only what you need, care for your brother, stay with your own kind. After all our pious ponderings, why don't we get it?.*

STITT, WALTER BOSTON, JR., minister; b. Marietta, Ohio, July 24, 1924; s. Walter Boston and Ada Ruth (Crickenberger) S.; m. Elizabeth Bailey, June 2, 1952; children: Robert, William (dec.), Beverly. Student, Marietta Coll., 1946-49; BA, Wittenberg U., 1963; MDiv, Hamma Sch. Theology, 1965. Ordained to ministry Evang. Luth. Ch., 1965. Pastor Messiah Luth. Ch., Louisville, 1965-77, Bethany Luth. Ch., South Bend, Ind., 1988—; asst. to bishop I-K Synod, Luth. Ch. Am., South Bend, 1977-87; chair evangelism I-K Synod, Luth. Ch. Am., Louisville, 1968-73; shared staff minister div. for congl. life Evang. Luth. Ch. Am., South Bend, 1988-89; chair adv. com. United Religious Com., South Bend, 1990—. Contbr. articles, devotional materials to profl. publs. Bd. dirs. Wittenberg U., Springfield, Ohio, 1976-87; nat. chaplain 3d Armored Div. Assn., Phoenix, 1989-90. Cpl. U.S. Army, 1943-45, ETO. Decorated Purple Heart with oak leaf cluster; recipient Disting. Svc. award Okolona Jaycees, 1966. Mem. Kiwanis (pres. Michiami club 1982-83, 87-88, lt. gov. Ind. dist. 1990-91), Elks. Republican. Home: 2915 Erskine Blvd South Bend IN 46614 Office: Bethany Luth Ch 5302 W Sample St South Bend IN 46619

STITZINGER, JAMES FRANKLIN, religion educator, library director; b. Abington, Pa., July 27, 1950; s. James Franklin and Elizabeth (Kocher) S.; m. Deborah Lynn Benner, July 22, 1972; children: Rachael, James, David, Jonathan. BA, Northwestern Coll., Roseville, Minn., 1975; MDiv, Central Sem., 1975; ThM, Grace Theol. Sem., 1977; MLS, Drexel U., 1978; postgrad., Westminster Theol. Sem., 1991—. Acquisition libr. Grace Theol. Sem., Winona Lake, Ind., 1975-77; libr., prof. ch. history Calvary Bapt. Sem., Lansdale, Pa., 1977-87; dir. libr. svcs., assoc. prof. hist. theology The Master's Sem., Sun Valley, Calif., 1987—; chief exec. officer Books for Libraries, Inc., North Hollywood, Calif., 1989—. Mem. Am. Theol. Libr. Assn., Am. Soc. Ch. History, Evang. Theol. Soc. Republican. Baptist. Office: The Masters Sem 13248 Roscoe Blvd Sun Valley CA 91352

STJERNHOLM, PAUL DAVID, minister; b. Pueblo, Colo., July 18, 1959; s. Thomas and Mary Elizabeth (Hoffmeister) S.; m. Julie Ann Lamb, June 20, 1981; children: Joel, Maren. BA, St. Olaf Coll., 1981; MDiv, Luther-Northwestern Sem., St. Paul, 1985. Ordained to Evangelical Luth. Ch., 1985. Pastor St. Paul Luth. Ch., Calhan, Colo., 1985—. Chmn. Sch. Accountability Com., Calhan, Colo., 1986-90. Mem. Lions Club (sec. Calhan 1986-87). Home and Office: St Paul Congregation Seventh & Colorado Canon City CO 80808

STOAKES, RICHMOND BRUCE, minister; b. Chgo., Sept. 3, 1940; s. Harold Ralph and Delores Valma (Richmond) S.; m. Susan Estelle Gates, Sept. 30, 1962; children: Glenn, Sheila, Heather, Matthew, Seth, Christopher. BS in Marine Engring., Calif. Maritime Acad., 1962; BA in Internat. Rels., MS in Pers. Mgmt., Naval PG Sch., 1971, 72; MS equivalent, Naval War Coll., 1973; MDiv, Iliff Sch. Theology, 1989. Ordained to ministry United Meth. Ch., 1990. Commd. ensign USN, 1963, advanced through ranks to capt., ret., 1987; lay leader Greeley Peaks Sub-Dist., Longmont, Colo., 1986-89; dir. visitation 1st United Meth. Ch., Longmont, 1987-89; pastor United Meth.-Presbyn. Ch., Rifle, Colo., 1989-91; assoc. pastor Phillips United Meth. Ch., Lakewood, Colo., 1991—; chaplain Clagett Meml. Hosp., Rifle, 1989-91; counselor Camp for Hanidcapped Persons, Grand Mesa, Colo., 1990—, Camp for Sr. High Sch. Youth, Grand Mesa, 1990—; mem. conf. coun. Retreats and Camps, Denver, 1990—, nominating com., 1991—. Bd. dirs. Lift-Up, Lifes Inter-Faith Team Against Unemployment and Poverty, Rifle, 1990-91; adv. bd. Colo. Mountain Coll., Rifle, 1990. Mem. U.S. Naval Inst. Home: 1470 S Pierce St Lakewood CO 80232 Office: Phillips United Meth Ch 1450 S Pierce St Lakewood CO 80232

STOBBE, LESLIE HAROLD, publishing executive; b. Kent, B.C., Can., June 7, 1930; s. Peter John and Marie E. (Harder) S.; m. Rita Laurine Langemann, Sept. 7, 1956; children: Carol June, Gerald Lane. BTh, Mennonite Brethren Bible Coll., 1955. Editor Mennonite Observer, Winnipeg, Can., 1955-59; tchr. Mennonite Ednl. Inst., Clearbrook, B.C., Can., 1959-60; selling fl. supr. Moody Bible Inst. Bookstore, Chgo., 1960-62; editor Christian Bookseller Mag., Chgo. and Wheaton, Ill., 1962-66; editorial dir. Cambridge Pubs., Winnipeg, 1966-70; editor-in-chief Moody Press, Chgo., 1970-78; v.p., editorial dir. Christian Herald Books & Book Clubs, Chappaqua, N.Y., 1978-82; editoral dir. Here's Life Pubs., Inc., San Bernardino, Calif., 1982-85, pres., 1985—; cons. Mennonite Brethren Bd. of Christian Lit., Fresno Calif., 1970-80; bd. dirs. Voice of Calvary Ministries, Jackson, Miss., Christian Svc. Brigade, Carol Stream, Ill. Author: Preteen Bible Exploration, 1980, (with others) Managing Your Emotions, 1981, When a Good Man Falls, 1985, Reconcilable Differences, 1985, Life After Divorce, 1991. Pres. San Bernardino City Grand Opera, 1984-85. Mem. Evang. Christian Pubs. Assn. Avocation: gardening. Office: Here's Life Pubs PO Box 1576 San Bernardino CA 92402

STOCK, BEN, religious organization consultant; b. N.Y.C., June 27, 1948. BA, CUNY, 1975. Chmn. Religious Orgns. Computing Group, N.Y.C., 1989—; co-dir. Non-Profit Computing Inc., N.Y.C., 1991—. Home: 277 Van Cortlandt Ave E Bronx NY 10467 Office: Non-Profit Computing Inc 40 Wall St Ste 2124 New York NY 10005

STOCKMAN, ROBERT HAROLD, religious organization administrator, educator; b. Meriden, Conn., Oct. 6, 1953; s. Harold Herman and Margery (Fothergill) S. BA in Geology and Archaeology, Wesleyan U., 1975; MSc in Geology, Brown U., 1977; MTS, Harvard U., 1984, ThD, 1990. Coord. rsch. office Baha'i Nat. Ctr., 1990—; grad. rsch. asst. geology dept., Brown U., Providence, 1975-77; instr. geology and oceanography, Community Coll. R.I., Lincoln, 1977-80; instr. geology, Boston State Coll., 1980-82, U. Lowell, Mass., 1983-84; instr. geology and astronomy and operator of Astronomy Observatory, Bentley Coll., Waltham, Mass., 1983-90; teaching asst. Harvard U., 1986-89; instr. religion, De Paul U., Chgo., 1990-91; speaker on Baha'i faith, 1984—. Author: The Baha'i Faith in America, Vol. 1, Origins, 1892-1900, 1985; mem. editorial bd. World Order, 1990—; contbr. articles to profl. jours. Mem. Am. Acad. Religion (mem. Baha'i studies unit 1984—, chairperson 1985-86, 89-90), Mid. East Studies Assn., Soc. Iranian Studies, Assn. Baha'i Studies (mem. exec. com. 1990—, chair study of religious sect. 1989—). Home: 610 Oakton St # 3 Evanston IL 60202 Office: Baha'i Nat Ctr Rsch Office Wilmette IL 60091

STOCKSTILL, MARIA MUTERSPAUGH, religion educator; b. Indpls., Nov. 7, 1963; d. Lloyd Eugene and Linda Lou (Wyatt) Muterspaugh; m. Luke Earl Stockstill, Feb. 3, 1990. BA, Oral Roberts Univ., 1987; MA in Religion, Oklahoma City Univ., 1991. Youth minister Epworth United Meth. Ch., Tulsa, 1983-87; dir. Christian edn. First United Meth. Ch., Weathorford, Okla., 1987-89; dir. children and youth First United Meth. Ch., Fairview, Okla., 1989-91; min. edn. St. Paul's United Meth. Ch., Shawnee, Okla., 1991—; dist. children's coord. United Meth. Ch., Fairview, 1990-91. Mem. Okla. Youth Ministers Network, Okla. Christian Educators Fellowship. Office: St Paul's United Meth Ch PO Box 3337 10th and Beard Shawnee OK 74802

STOCKTON, CARL R., history educator; b. Monett, Mo., Oct. 13, 1935; s. Ira James and Edith (Turner) S.; m. Gillian Winifred Adams, Dec. 30, 1972; children: Matthew Basil, Adam Francis. BS, Southwest Mo. State U., 1957; STB, Boston U., 1960; DPhil, Oxford U., Eng., 1970. Assoc. chief-of-party Internat. Vol. Services, Vietnam, 1963-65; asst. prof. history McKendree Coll., Lebanon, Ill., 1967-70; prof. history, chmn. social sci. div. Talladega (Ala.) Coll., 1970-82; prof. history, acad. dean. U. Indpls., 1982—; cons., evaluator N. Cen. Assn. Colls. and Schs., 1986—. Author: Christ Church in Indianapolis: A Selected Chronology, 1987; editor: KAIROS, 1959-60, The Origin and Development of Extra-Liturgical Worship in 18th Century Methodism, 1970; contbr. articles to profl. jours. Mem. Ind. Coun. World Affairs, 1984—; standing com. Diocese of Indpls.; judge Brain Game, Sta. WTHR-TV, Indpls., 1982—; sr. warden Christ Ch. Cathedral, Indpls.; chmn. Consortium for Urban Edn. Acad. Deans, 1985-88; v.p. gov. bd. Ind. Office Campus Ministries, 1988—, Danforth assoc., 1970-76. Mellon fellow, 1981, Lester So. fellow, 1974-75. Mem. Ecclesiastical Hist. Soc. Gt. Britain, Oxford Soc., Am. Soc. Ch. History, Ch. History Soc., AAUP, English Speaking Union, Ind. Assn. Historians, Oxford and Cambridge Club, Kiwanis (pres. Indpls. 1987-88), Alpha Sigma Lambda, Alpha Chi, Alpha Psi Omega, Phi Alpha Theta. Democrat. Episcopalian. Home: 1400 E Hanna Ave Indianapolis IN 46227 Office: U Indpls 1400 E Hanna Ave Indianapolis IN 46227

STOCKTON, THOMAS B., bishop; b. Winston-Salem, N.C., July 26, 1930; s. Norman V. and Emorie (Barber) S.; m. Jean Stevens, Aug. 22, 1953; children: Lisa S. Stockton Howell, Thomas B. Jr., Shannon Stockton Miller. BA, Davidson Coll., 1952; MDiv, Duke U., 1955; DD (hon.), Pfeiffer Coll., 1973. Ordained to ministry United Meth. Ch., 1956. Min. Thrift United Meth. Ch., Paw Creek, N.C., 1956-60, 1st United Meth. Ch., Reidsville, N.C., 1960-64, Dilworth United Meth. Ch., Charlotte, N.C., 1964-70, Cen. United Meth. Ch., Asheville, N.C., 1970-75, Myers Pk. United Meth. Ch., Charlotte, N.C., 1975-83, Wesley Meml. United Ch., High Point, N.C., 1983-88; bishop Va. Conf., United Meth. Ch., Richmond, 1988—. Trustee Duke U., Durham, N.C., 1981—, all United Meth. colls. and homes in Va. Ann. Conf., 1988—; mem. gen. bd. discipleship U. Meth. Ch., Nashville, 1988—. Home: 12923 Fox Meadow Dr Richmond VA 23233 Office: United Meth Ch Va Conf 4016 W Broad St Richmond VA 23230

STOEHR, RICHARD ALLEN, minister; b. Bridgeport, Conn., Nov. 7, 1932; s. Louis Joseph and Alice Elizabeth (Persiana) S.; m. Judith Anne Collins, June 11, 1966; children: Marna, Garen. BA, Middlebury Coll., 1958; BD, Andover Newton Theol. Sch., 1968. Ordained to United Ch. Christ Ministry, 1965. Dir. edn. Federated Ch., Orleans, Mass., 1962-64; asst. pastor Congl. Ch., South Dennis, Mass., 1964-65, pastor, 1965-90; copastor Rollstone Congl. Ch., Fitchburg, Mass., 1990—; gen. synod. del. United Ch. Christ, 1972-82; moderator Barnstable Assn. United Ch. Christ, Mass., 1971; bd. dirs. Mass. Conf. United Congl. Ch., Farmingham, 1975-79, Cape Cod Coun. Chs., Hyannis, 1968-72. Author: Organizational Restructuring, 1987, 88. founder, pres. Retocom Projects Inc., Monument Beach, Mass., 1968, Chapel Park Homes, South Dennis, 1971; organizer Help of Cape Cod, Hyannis, 1970; mem. exec. bd. Cape Cod and Islands Coun. Boy Scouts Am., Hyannis, 1987. Recipient Silver Beaver award Boy Scouts Am, 1988. Mem. Rotary Internat. Republican. Office: Rollstone Congl Ch Fitchburg MA 01420 *Each person is a horizon where heaven and earth meet; and each of us makes the choice daily as to whether to honor our higher of lower nature.*

STOESZ, WILLIS MILTON, religion educator; b. Mt. Lake, Minn., Nov. 20, 1930; s. Peter P. and Anna (Wall) S.; m. Dolores Donley, July 1, 1955; children: Sarah, Michael, David. BA, U. Minn., 1955; MDiv, Union Seminary, N.Y.C., 1958; PhD, Columbia U., 1964. Asst. prof. Dillard U., New Orleans, 1961-65, Western Coll. for Women, Oxford, Ohio, 1965-70; assoc. prof. Wright State U., Dayton, Ohio, 1970—, chmn. dept. religion, 1986—. Editor, author: Kurozumi Shinto, 1989; contbr. articles to profl. jours. Mem. Am. Acad. Religion, Assn. for Asian Studies, Soc. for Comparative Study of Civilizations, Internat. Assn. Buddhist Studies. Home: 1443 N Euclid Ave Dayton OH 45406 Office: Wright State U Dayton OH 45435 *It becomes ever more important to see life as constituted beyond the narrow limits of creed or clan; to live our separate lives from the point of view of the whole of things, however our various religions comprehend that whole.*

STOHLMAN, STEPHEN CHRISTIAN, minister; b. Norfolk, Nebr., Nov. 30, 1942; s. Paul F. and Pearl (Holtz) S.; m. Jeanette D. Zabel, Feb. 2, 1974; children: Naomi, Seth, Mary, Micah, Philip. BA, Concordia Sr. Coll., 1964; MDiv, Concordia Sem., 1968; MA, PhD, Brandeis U., 1971. Ordained to ministry Luth. Ch.-Mo. Synod, 1971. Parish pastor Zion and Immanuel Luth. Chs., Hampton and Polk, Nebr., 1971-76; asst. prof. Concordia Coll., St. Paul, 1976-81, assoc. prof. religion, 1981-88; prof., 1988—; coord. presem. studies Concordia Coll., St. Paul, 1979-86, 89—, acting dean of chapel, 1982-84; chmn. faculty planning com. Oswald Hoffman Sch. Christian Outreach, 1984—, acting dir. sch., 1984-88; coord. Hispanic summer intern prog., 1982-88. Author: Out of Egypt I Called My Son, 1984; contbr. articles to profl. jours. Mem. Soc. Bibl. Lit., Luth. Edn. Assn., Nat. Assn. Profs. of Hebrew. Office: Concordia Coll 275 N Syndicate Saint Paul MN 55104 *Jesus is Lord of my life and of my death. His Lordship gives meaning to life and identity to all who acknowledge Him. He is a shelter in every trouble and defense against all evil.*

STOJAK, RICHARD MICHAEL, deacon; b. Blue Island, Ill., Mar. 19, 1941; s. Michael I. and Emilie M. (Dzierwa) S.; m. Kathleen JoAnn Kasmirs, Aug. 22, 1964; children: Richard M., Mary B., Amy K., Andria JoAnn, Steven B. AB, Loyola U., 1963, M in Pastoral Studies, 1989. With Social Security Adminstrn., 1964—; claims rep. dist. office Social Security Adminstrn., Chgo., Harvey, Ill., 1964-71; field rep. dist. office Social Security Adminstrn., Decatur, Ill., 1970-71; staff officer regional office analysis and appraisal staff Social Security Adminstrn., Chgo., 1974-76; br. mgr. Social Security Adminstrn., Merrillville, Ind., 1976-80; asst. dist. mgr. Social Security Adminstrn., Madison, Ind., 1980; program analyst evaluation staff Social Security Adminstrn., FAO, Chgo., 1980-81, supr. social ins. claims examiner SSI Quality Br., 1981-85, program analyst social ins. program specialist, 1985-86; supr., quality rev. analyst Chgo. satellite office Social Security Adminstrn., FAO, 1986-87; sect. mgr. office of program and integrity rev. Social Security Adminstrn., Chgo., 1987—. Pastoral min. St. Jude parish Roman Cath. Ch., South Holland, Ill., 1985-90, area del. Permanent Diaconate Coun., Chgo., 1991—. Home: 17941 Davids Ln Orland Park IL 60462 Office: Social Security Adminstrn 600 W Madison St 10th Fl Chicago IL 60461

STOKER, CHRISTOPHER LEE, minister; b. Ft. Worth, May 8, 1956; s. Jack Harold and Ola Nell (Dewberry) S.; m. Kennetha Gail Hopkins, July 9, 1982; children: Candace Gail, Daniel Lee. Assoc. Degree Divinity, Southwestern Bapt. Theol. Sem., 1989. Ordained to ministry Bapt. Ch., 1989. Outreach dir. 1st Bapt. Briar, Azle, Tex., 1983-89; benevolence dir. Azle Ministerial Alliance, 1986-89; pasorolence dir. Wilderness Bapt. Ch., DuBois, Wyo., 1989—; exec. bd. Wyo. So. Bapt. Conv., Casper, 1990—. Contbr. articles to DuBois Frontier newspaper. Recipient Benevolent plaque Azle Pastors, 1989; named Bible Study Leader, Volkswagon of Am., Ft. Worth, 1986. Home: 405 Carson DuBois WY 82513 Office: Wilderness Bapt Ch 304 Hay DuBois WY 82513 *All people are striving for greatness, either in this world or the world to come. It can be lasting in God's kingdom or fleeting in this world. I'll choose to be great in His kingdom.*

STOKES, (GLADYS) ALLISON, minister, researcher, religion educator; b. Bridgeport, Conn., Aug. 17, 1942; d. Hugh Vincent and Mildred Roberta (Livengood) Allison; m. Jerome Walter Stokes, June 1, 1964 (div. 1977); children: Jonathan Jerome, Anne Jennings. BA, U. N.C., 1964; MPhil, Yale U., 1976, PhD, 1981, MDiv, 1981. Ordained to ministry United Ch. of Christ, 1981. Acting univ. min. Wesleyan U., Middletown, Conn., 1981; assoc. pastor Orange Congl. Ch., Conn., 1981-82; chaplain, asst. prof. religion Vassar Coll., Poughkeepsie, N.Y., 1982-85; assoc. univ. chaplain Yale U., New Haven, 1985-87; pastor Congl. Ch., West Stockbridge, Mass., 1987—; rsch. assoc. Hartford (Conn.) Sem., 1987—; bd. dirs. Dutchess Interfaith Coun., Pughkeepsie, 1984-85. Author: Ministry after Freud, 1985; contbr. articles to profl. jours. Mem. steering com. Dutchess County Citizens for Safer World, Pughkeepsie, 1982-85. AAUW fellow, 1978; travel grantee Kanzer Fund Psychoanalysis and Humanities, 1977. Mem. Am. Assn. Pastoral Counselors (hist. cons.), Assn. for Clin. Pastoral Edn. (hist. cons.), Religious Rsch. Assn., Kiwanis. Home: 22 Gilmore Ave Great Barrington MA 01230 Office: Congl Ch 45 Main St West Stockbridge MA 01266

STOKES, DAVID WESLEY, minister; b. Ashtabula, Ohio, Nov. 9, 1946; s. Wesley H. and Clara (Kinney) S.; m. Marilyn Elaine Villars, Aug. 17, 1968; children: Kimberly, Kristine (dec.), Karen, Kathleen. Student, Cuyahoga Community Coll., 1964-65; AB, Cinn. Bible Coll., 1969; MA in Religion, Cinn. Bible Sem., 1975; postgrad., Reformed Theol. Sem., 1990. Ordained to ministry Ch. of Christ, 1969. Interim minister Penn Line Ch. of Christ, Pierpont, Ohio, 1966; minister Plumville Ch. of Christ, Maysville, Ky., 1966-68; youth minister Westwood Cheviot Ch. of Christ, Cinn., 1968-70; minister Edon (Ohio) Ch. of Christ, 1970-74; sr. minister Bachelor Creek Ch. of Christ, Wabash, Ind., 1974-87, S.E. Christian Ch., Orlando, Fla., 1987—; trustee Cen. Brazil Mission, Goiania, Goias, Lake Aurora Christian Assembly, Lake Wales, Fla.; dir. Cen. Fla. New Ch. Evangelism, Kissimmee, Alexander Christian Found., Kissimmee. Author: Millennial Directions, 1975. Com. mem. Orange County Sch. Bd., Orlando, 1988-91. Mem. Fla. Christian Ministers Assn. (v.p. 1990, pres. 1991—). Office: SE Christian Ch 2413 S Goldenrod Rd Orlando FL 32822

STOKES, JOHN LEMACKS, II, clergyman, university administrator; b. Songdo, Korea, Aug. 23, 1908; s. Marion Boyd and Florence Pauline (Davis) S.; m. Alda Grey Beaman, June 20, 1933; children: John Lemacks III, Mary Anne (foster dau.). A.B., Asbury Coll., 1930; postgrad., Asbury Theol. Sem., 1930-31; M.Div., Duke U., 1932; Ph.D., Yale U., 1936; LL.D., Pfeiffer Coll., 1975. Ordained to ministry Meth. Ch., 1931. Pastor Meth. chs., Randleman, Franklin and Elkin, N.C., 1936-45, Rock Hill, St. John's, S.C., 1945-50; sec. religion higher edn., div. ednl. instns. Bd. Edn. Meth. Ch., Nashville, 1950-53; del. jurisdictional conf. Meth. Ch., 1952, 60, 68; pres. Pfeiffer Coll., Misenheimer, N.C., 1953-68; exec. sec. Quadrennial Emphasis, United Meth. Ch., 1968-69; asso. dir. N.C. Bd. Higher Edn., Raleigh, 1969-71; acting dir. N.C. Bd. Higher Edn., 1972; asso. v.p. U. N.C., Chapel Hill, 1972-75; spl. asst. in acad. affairs U. N.C., 1976—; dir. out-of-state programs in health professions, 1972—; mem. Gov.'s Commn. Citizens for Better Schs. N.C., 1956-60, N.C. Com. on Nursing and Patient Care, 1956-64, N.C. Higher Edn. Facilities Edn., 1964-68; chmn. N.C. adv. com. Farmers Home Adminstrn., 1967-69, Marine Sci. Council, 1969-72; mem. N.C. Com. on Drug Abuse, 1970-76 , N.C. Com. on Aero. Edn., 1971-86 ; dir. N.C. Inst. Undergrad. Curricular Reform, 1972-78; coordinator Fort Bragg-Pope Grad. Program, 1973-77; adv. com. Nat. Four-Year Servicemen's Opportunity Coll., 1973-78. Contbr. articles to religious publs. Bd. dirs. ARC, 1940-48, YMCA, 1946-50; vice chmn. Western N.C. Conf. Bd. Missions, 1960-64; trustee Asbury Coll., 1945-51. Recipient award of merit So. Coun. Optometrists, 1990. Mem. Aircraft Owners and Pilots Assn., U.S. Lawn Tennis Assn., Am. Assn. Higher Edn., So. Srs. Golf Assn., NEA, Nat. Christian Edn. Assn., So. Philos. Soc., Woman's Soc. Christian Service, Laurel Ridge Country Club, Sandpiper Country Club, Masons, Shriners, Rotary Civitan. Address: U NC PO Box 2688 Chapel Hill NC 27514

STOKES, KENNETH IRVING, religious organization administrator; b. Pasadena, Calif., Sept. 16, 1928; s. Willard Edward and Nelle Ruth (Clayberg) S.; m. Anne Dorothy Gates, June 30, 1951; children: Alan, Randall, Bradley, Harlan. BA, Pomona Coll., 1950; MDiv, Yale U., 1954; PhD, U. Chgo., 1965. Pastor Highland Park Congl. Ch., Miles City, Mont., 1954-58, Faith Congl. Ch., Glen Ellyn, Ill., 1958-63, Summerdale Community Ch., Chgo., 1963-65, United Ch. Gainesville (Fla.), 1965-73; cons. ch. edn. Synod Lakes & Prairies United Presbyn. Ch., Blommington, Minn., 1974-78; dir. rsch. Religious Edn. Assn., Blommington, Minn., 1979-87; exec. dir. Adult Faith Resources, Blommington, Minn., 1988—; adj. prof. edn. Sch. Divinity, U. St. Thomas. Author: Faith is a Verb, 1989; editor: Faith Development in the Adult Life, 1982. Avocations: running, skiing, light opera. Home and Office: 9709 Rich Rd Minneapolis MN 55437

STOKES, MACK (MARION) BOYD, bishop; b. Wonsan, Korea, Dec. 21, 1911; came to U.S., 1929; s. Marion Boyd and Florence Pauline (Davis) S.; m. Ada Rose Yow, June 19, 1942; children: Marion Boyd III, Arch Yow, Elsie Pauline. Student, Seoul Fgn. High Sch., Korea; A.B., Asbury Coll., 1932; B.D., Duke, 1935; postgrad., Boston U. Sch. Theol., 1935-37, Harvard, 1936-37; Ph.D., Boston U., 1940; LL.D., Lambuth Coll., Jackson, Tenn., 1963; D.D., Millsaps Coll., 1974. Resident fellow systematic theology Boston U., 1936-38, Bowne fellow in philosophy, 1938-39; ordained to ministry Meth. Ch., deacon, 1938, elder, 1940; vis. prof. philosophy and religion Ill. Wesleyan U., 1940-41; prof. Christian doctrine Candler Sch. Theology, Emory U., 1941-56, asso. dean, Parker prof. systematic theology, 1956-72, chmn. exec. com. div. of religion of grad. sch., 1956-72; acting dean Candler Sch. Theology, Emory U. (Candler Sch.), 1968-69; faculty mem. Inst. Theol. Studies, Oxford U., 1958; Del. Meth. Ecumenical Conf., 1947, 52, 61, 71, Holston, Gen. confs., S.E. Jurisdictional Conf., 1956, 60, 64, 68, 72; chmn. com. ministry Gen. Conf. Meth. Ch., 1960; nat. com. Nature Unity We Seek, 1956—; mem. gen. com. ecumenical affairs theol. study com. United Meth. Ch., 1968-72, com. on Cath.-Meth. relations, 1969—, bishop, 1972—. Author: Major Methodist Beliefs, 1956, rev. 15th edit., 1990, also Chinese transl., The Evangelism of Jesus, 1960, The Epic of Revelation, 1961, Our Methodist Heritage, 1963, Crencas Fundamentals Dos Methodistas, 1964, Study Guide on the Teachings of Jesus, 1970, The Bible and Modern Doubt, 1970, Major United Methodist Beliefs, 1971, Korean transl., 1977, rev. 15th edit., 1990, The Holy Spirit and Christian Experience, 1975, Korean transl., 1985, Twelve Dialogues on John's Gospel, 1975; Jesus, The Master-Evangel, 1978, Can God See the Inside of an Apple?, 1979, Questions Asked by United Methodists, Philippine transl., 1980; The Bible in the Wesleyan Heritage, 1981, Respuestas A Preguntas Que Hacen Los Metodistas Unidos, 1983, The Holy Spirit in the Wesleyan Heritage, 1985, Scriptural Holiness for the United Methodist Christian, 1988, Talking with

God: A Guide to Prayer, 1989. Trustee Emory U., Millsaps Coll., Rust Coll., Wood Jr. Coll. Mem. Am. Philos. Assn., Am. Acad. Religion, Metaphys. Soc. Am., Theta Phi (nat. sec.), Pi Gamma Mu. Home: 2940 Bakers Farm Rd Atlanta GA 30339 *Faith in God and basic trust in people. Knowing the direction in which to go, and moving toward it with persistence, resourcefulness, imagination and patience.*

STOKES, MICHAEL DAVID, minister; b. Fitzgerald, Ga., Aug. 1, 1953; s. Emory Lewis and Lottie Pearl (Huggins) S.; m. Teresa Davis, Sept. 5, 1972; children: Melodie Renee, Michelle Rose. AA, Brewton Parker Coll., Mt. Vernon, Ga., 1974; BS, Dallas Bapt. Coll., 1976. Ordained to ministry So. Bapt. Conf. Min. music Buckner Benevolence Home Bapt. Ch., Dallas, 1974-76, 1st Bapt. Ch., Cochran, Ga., 1979-81; min. music and youth 1st Bapt. Ch., McRae, Ga., 1976-79, Nashville, Ga., 1981-85; min. music and youth Beulah Bapt. Ch., Douglasville, Ga., 1985—; music dir. West Metro Bapt. Assn., Austell, Ga., 1988—. Office: Beulah Bapt Ch 4031 Bankhead Hwy Douglasville GA 30134

STOKES, THOMAS S., pastor; b. Lakeland, Fla., Jan. 12, 1946; s. Edwin B. and Melva (Douglas) S.; m. Virginia Lee Cooper, June 17, 1972; children: David, Debra. BA, Stetson U., 1968; MDiv, So. Bapt. Sem., Louisville, 1973, D of Ministry, 1978. Ordained to ministry So. Bapt. Conv. Pastor Enon Bapt. Ch., Salem, Ind., 1971-73, Wolf Creek Bapt. Ch., Battletown, Ky., 1973-75, Franklin Crossroads Bapt. Ch., Cecilia, Ky., 1975-80, Calhoun (Ky.) Bapt. Ch., 1980-85, 1st Bapt. Ch., Whitesburg, Ky., 1985—; mem. adminstrv. com. Ky. Bapt. Conv., Middletown, Ky., 1981-83, 87-88, mem. exec. bd., 1986-89. Mem. Three Forks Assn. (chmn. stewardship com. 1989—), Rotary. Democrat. Home: 404 Tennessee Ave Whitesburg KY 41858 Office: 1st Bapt Ch 317 Madison St Whitesburg KY 41858

STOLL, HARRY LLOYD, minister; b. East Chicago, Ind., Aug. 27, 1930; s. Lloyd and Doris Cora (Vaux) S.; m. Margaret Coe Hagans, July 23, 1960; 1 child, Brian Lloyd. BS in Bus. Admin., Ind. U., 1952; MDiv in Sacred Theology, Wesley Theol. Sem., 1961. Ordained to ministry United Meth. Ch. Asst. pastor St. Luke's United Meth. Ch., Washington, 1960-61; assoc. pastor United Meth. Chs., N.Y., 1961-66; pastor First United Meth. Chs., N.Y., 1966-74, United Third Meth. Ch., Sodus, N.Y., 1974-83, First United Meth. Ch., Chittenango, N.Y., 1983-85, Grace United Meth. Ch., Corning, N.Y., 1985-88, First United Meth. Ch., Ilion, N.Y., 1988—; registrar Mohawk Dist. Com. on Ordained Ministries, Utica, N.Y., 1988; chmn. North Cen. N.Y. Camping Ministries Com., United Meth. Ch., 1990—; mem. North Cen. N.Y. Conf. Coun. on Ministries, Cicero, N.Y., 1990—. Author: Best Loved Poems, 1979. Sgt. U.S. Army, 1953-55. Mem. Christian Educator's Fellowship, Oddfellows, Rotary, Am. Assn. Retired Persons. Home: RD 1 Box 396 Ilion NY 13357 Office: First United Meth Ch 36 Second St Ilion NY 13357

STOLL, JEFFREY WILLIAM, clergyman; b. Painesville, Ohio, July 22, 1957; s. George Herbert and Irene Norma (Kelbaugh) S. BS, Bowling Green State U., 1979; MDiv, Meth. Theol. Sch., Delaware, Ohio, 1990, MA in Christian Edn., 1991. Ordained to ministry United Meth. Ch., 1991. Cook LK Restaurants, Painesville, 1977, Holiday Inn, Bowling Green, Ohio, 1978-79; mgr. Ground Round Restaurants, Redford, Mich., 1979-81; area dir. Little Caesar's Pizza, Farmington Hills, Mich., 1981-84; mgr. LK Restaurants, Marion, Ohio, 1984-86; dir. food svc. Meth. Theol. Sch., Delaware, 1986-90; pastor Masury (Ohio) United Meth. Ch., 1990—; Christian clown workshop leader, 1988—. Mem. Alpha Tau Omega. Avocations: nature hiking, softball. Home: 1386 Broadway Ave Masury OH 44438

STOLPER, PINCHAS ARYEH, religious organization executive, rabbi; b. Bklyn., Oct. 22, 1931; s. David Bernard and Nettie (Rosch) S.; m. Elaine Liebman, Nov. 22, 1955; children: Akiva Psachia, Michal Hadassah Cohen, Malka Tova Kaweblum. B.A., Bklyn. Coll., 1952; M.A., New Sch. for Social Research, 1971. Rabbinical ordination Chaim Berlin-Gur Aryeh Rabbinical Acad., 1956; dir. L.I. Zionist Youth Commn., 1956-57; dir. public relations, adminstrv. dean, adviser to English-speaking students Ponevez Yeshiva, Bnai Brak, Israel, 1957-59; also prin.; instr. English and Talmud Gimnazia Bnei Akiva High Sch., 1959-77; nat. dir. youth div. Union Orthodox Jewish Congregations Am., Nat. Conf. Synagogue Youth, N.Y.C., 1959-76; founder NCSY, Torah Fund, Ben Zakai Honor Soc. Union Orthodox Jewish Congregations Am., Nat. Conf. Synagogue Youth, 1959-76; editor Jewish Youth Monthly, 1967—; exec. v.p. Union Orthodox Jewish Congregations Am., 1976—; adj. prof. Jewish studies Touro Coll., N.Y., 1975—; mem. publs., Israel, campus commns., staff mem. responsible for edn., Talmud Torah, day sch. commns. Union Orthodox Jewish Congregations Am., 1965—; del. White House Conf. on Children and Youth, 1961; cons. N. Am. Jewish Youth Conf., 1967—. Author: Tested Teen Age Activities, 1961, rev. edit., 1964, Day of Delight, 1961, Tefilah, Text and Source Book, 1963, Revelation, What Happened on Sinai, 1966, Prayer, The Proven Path, 1967, The Road to Responsible Jewish Adulthood, 1967, Jewish Alternatives in Love, Dating and Marriage, 1985; contbr. numerous articles, plays and revs. to Jewish publs. Bd. dirs. Chaim Berlin Torah Schs.-Mesivta Rabbi Chaim Berlin-Rabbinical Acad., 1965—. Recipient Alumi Amudim award Mesivta Rabbi Chaim Berlin-Gur Aryeh Inst., 1967, Alumnus of Yr. award Flatbush Yeshiva, 1989. Mem. Rabbinical Coun. Am., Nat. Assn. dir. Nat. Jewish Youth Orgns. Home: 954 E 7th St Brooklyn NY 11230 Office: Union Orthodox Jewish Congregations of Am 333 7th Ave New York NY 10001

STOLTZ, MARY ANN, religious education director, pastoral associate; b. Callon, Wis., May 2, 1937; d. Emil Matthew and Susan A. (Wanta) S. BS, St. Norbert, De Pere, Wis., 1969; MEd, Boston Coll., 1978. Pres. La Crosse (Wis.) Sisters Coun., 1972-74; v.p. Green Bay (Wis.) Sisters Coun., 1986-88; pastoral minister St. Patrick Ch., Elroy, Wis., 1991—; Chairperson La Crosse (Wis.) Area Prins., 1973-75; area rep. Green Bay (Wis.) Adminstrs., 1984-86. Home and Office: Saint Patrick 110 Spring St Elroy WI 53929

STOLTZFUS, MILTON LEROY, minister, charitable organization administrator; b. Lancaster, Pa., Apr. 8, 1961; s. Menno K. and Mildred B. (Smoker) S. BS, Lancaster Bible Coll., 1987. Lic. to ministry Lancaster Conf. Mennonite Ch., 1987, ordained, 1989. Pastor Landis Valley Mennonite Ch., Lancaster, 1987-90; program dir. Laurelville Mennonite Ch. Ctr., Mt. Pleasant, Pa., 1990-91; coord. Shared Living, Friendship Community, Lititz, Pa., 1991—. Home and Office: 282 Baumgardner Rd Willow Street PA 17584

STONE, ALTON LEVON, JR., minister; b. Walterboro, S.C., Sept. 1, 1953; s. Alton Levon Sr. and Mary M. (Craven) S.; m. Rebecca Sue Brigman, Feb. 13, 1972; 1 child, Shane Blake. Student, S.C. Bible Inst., 1970-72, Berean Coll., 1980-81. Ordained to ministry Pentecostal Ch., 1981. Evangelist S.C. Ch. of God, 1970-72; assoc. pastor Palmetto St. Ch. of God, Florence, S.C., 1972-74, Pine Valley Ch. of God, Wilmington, N.C., 1974-78; assoc. pastor Elm St. Ch. of God, Kappapolis, N.C., 1978, Gaffney, S.C., 1978-79; sr. assoc. pastor First Assembly of God, Lancaster, S.C., 1979-84, Rock Hill, S.C., 1984-87; sr. pastor Southside Assembly of God, Greenville, S.C., 1987—; regional youth dir. Ch. of God, Ea. S.C., 1972-74; state music com. Ch. of God, N.C., 1974-78; chaplain Lancaster County Nursing Home, 1979-84; sectional presbyter S.C. Assemblies of God, Lancaster and Rock Hill, 1981-85; co-host, host Nite Line TV Network, Greenville, 1987—. Named one of Outstanding Young Men in Am. Jaycees, 1978. Mem. Broadcast Music Inst., Pentecostal Fellowship of N.Am. (pres. Lancaster chpt. 1982-84). Office: Southside Assembly of God 3315 Anderson Rd Greenville SC 29642

STONE, ALVIN MARION, minister; b. Nashville, Apr. 6, 1919; s. Elbert Homer and Lavena (Crouch) S.; m. Margaret Risinger, June 26, 1943; 1 child, Janie Sue Stone Scroggins. BA, Howard Payne U., 1948; BDiv, Southwestern Bapt. Theol., Seminary, Ft. Worth, Tex., 1951. Minister Fair Park Bapt. Ch., Dallas, 1953-56, Meml. Bapt. Ch., Corsicana, Tex., 1956-60, North Waco (Tex.) Bapt. Ch., 1961-68, Fairbanks Bapt. Ch., Houston, 1968-84, Timber Grove Bapt. Ch., Houston, 1985—; sales rep. Meml. Guardian Plan, Houston, 1984—; moderator Corsicana Bapt. Assn., 1959-60, Waco Bapt. Assn., 1966-67, Union Bapt. Assn., Houston, 1977-78; pres. Houston Bapt. Pastors Conf., 1971. Mem. Meml. Guardian Plan, Pres.'s Cabinet, 1988. Sgt. U.S. Army, 1942-46. Mem. Kiwanis (sec. Northwest club/Houston 1981). Republican. Home: 8226 Celina Houston TX 77040 Office: Timber Grove Bapt Church 946 W 17th Houston TX 77008 *Although it is impossible to stop thinking, I thank God that it is possible to change our thinking.*

STONE, EARL STANLEY, retired rabbi; b. Chilos, Pa., July 2, 1914; s. Benjamin Louis and Bertye (Breakstone) S.; m. Judith W. Wilensky, June 4, 1942 (dec. May 1990); children: Theodore Jay, Jeremy Elliot. BA, Syracuse U., 1935; M. Hebrew Lit., Hebrew Umom Coll., 1939, DD (hon.), 1964. Ordained rabbi, 1939. Assoc. rabbi Temple Isaiah Israel, Chgo., 1940-41, Temple Soc. Concord, Syracuse, 1945-48, The Temple, Cleve., 1948-56; sr. rabbi Temple Emmanuel, Denver, 1956-81. Pres. Denver Rotary Club, 1971-72, Alumnae Assn. Hebrew Union Coll., Cin., 1978-79, Nat. Assn. Ret. Reform Rabbis, Cin., 1987-88, Rocky MOuntain Rabbinical Assembly, Denver, 1970-71. Maj. U.S. Army, 1941-45, ETO. Mem. Cen. Conf. Am. Rabbis, Nat. Assn. Res. Officers (nat. chaplain), Rotary. Home: 3400 E Dartmouth Ave Denver CO 80210

STONE, GEORGIA GOSSOM, minister; b. St. Louis, Feb. 27, 1939; d. Woodrow Wilson and Georgia Frances (Dalton) Gossom; m. James George Stone, Mar. 2, 1957; children: David Mark, Deana, Larry. BS in Adminstrn. Human Svcs., Met. State Coll., 1984. Sec. Wesley Meth. Ch., Wichita Falls, Tex., 1955-57; sec. St. James Presbyn. Ch., Littleton, Colo., 1974-78, ch. adminstr., 1978-85; ch. adminstr., pres. ministry mgmt. counseling Genesis Presbyn. Ch., Lakewood, Colo., 1985; dir. edn. and program Travis Park United Meth. Ch., 1986-89; pastor McKinley Ave. United Meth. Ch., San Antonio, 1989—. Contbr. articles to profl. jours. Capt. Jefferson County Dem. Com., 1974-76, com. mem., 1974-76, 82-84; pres. bd. dirs. Presa Community Svc. Ctr., 1991—. Named Woman of Yr., Columbine Ind. News, 1975. Mem. Nat. Assn. Ch. Bus. Adminstrs. (v.p. Colo. Mile High chpt. 1981-82, sec. 1983-84), United Meth. Assn. of Ch. Bus. Adminstrs. (pres. San Antonio chpt. 1986-88, nat. bd. dirs. 1987-89). Home: 1607 Hawks Ridge San Antonio TX 78248 Office: McKinley Ave United Meth Ch 2926 S Presa San Antonio TX 78210 *The purpose of life is to be so in relationship with God as to be in relationship with our fellow human beings working for a world filled with the spirit of love and peace. Having a positive attitude is the key ingredient, and that comes from God's spirit of hope.*

STONE, HERBERT LYNN, minister; b. St. Charles, Va., Feb. 4, 1941; s. Herbert Allen and Edna Eloise (Holmes) S.; m. Mary Ruth Morris, Sept. 1, 1961; children: Kenneth Alan, Timothy Lynn, David Neil, Jonathan Morris. AA, Lee Coll., 1961, BA, 1963; MDiv, Ch. of God Sch. Theology, 1985; D of Ministry, Fuller Theol. Sem., 1990. Ordained to ministry Ch. of God. Pastor, evangelist, 1961-67; state dir. youth and Christian edn. Ch. of God, Ala., Va., Ark., N.J., 1967-82; dir. devel. fin. Ch. of God Sch. Theology, Cleveland, Tenn., 1982-86; state overseer, bishop Chs. of God, Iowa and Nebr., 1986-88; coord. ministerial devel. Ch. of God, Cleveland, 1988—. Author: Sing a New Song, 1981; (resource notebooks) Church Administration, 1989, Marriage and the Family, 1989, Ministerial Development, 1990. Mem. Nat. Assn. Evangs. (commn. higher edn. 1988—), Am. Assn. Christian Counselors, Christian Assn. Psychol. Studies. Home: 1520 Rockland Ct Cleveland TN 37311 Office: Ch of God Internat Offices Keith at 25th St Cleveland TN 37311

STONE, JACK, religious organization administrator. Gen. sec. Ch. of the Nazarene, Kansas City, Mo. Office: Ch Nazarene 6401 The Paseo Kansas City MO 64131*

STONE, JERRY HURD, religion educator; b. St. Louis, Nov. 9, 1926; s. E.M. And Pauline (Hurd) S.; m. Judith L. Gibson, Aug. 20, 1955; children: Jeffrey, Douglas, Claire, Steven. LLB, U. Okla., 1951; MDiv, Garrett Theol. Sem., 1958; PhD, Northwestern U., 1964. Ordained to ministry Meth. Ch., 1958. Pastor Honor Heights Meth. Ch., Muskogee, Okla., 1963-64; prof. religion Ill. Wesleyan U., Bloomington, 1964—, Daisy L. McFee prof. religion, 1984—. Author: (with others) Encyclopedia of Religious Education, 1990; contbr. articles to profl. jours. Mem. Am. Acad. Religion, Phi Kappa Phi, Phi Delta Phi. Office: Ill Wesleyan U Bloomington IL 61702

STONE, JON ROBERT, educator; b. Fullerton, Calif., June 10, 1959; s. Robert H. and Bobbie Jean (Reed) S. BA in Theology, San Jose Christian Coll., 1981; MA in Pastoral Theology, Pacific Christian Coll., Fullerton, 1984; MA in Religious Studies, U. Calif., Santa Barbara, 1987, PhD in Religious Studies, 1990. Ordained to ministry Christian Ch. (Ind. Disciples of Christ), 1980, laicized, 1986. Asst. min. Oxnard (Calif.) Christian Ch., 1980-83; assoc. min. Ventura (Calif.) Christian Ch., 1983-85; music dir. Cathedral Oaks Christian Ch., Santa Barbara, 1985-87; vis. asst. prof. U. No. Iowa, Cedar Falls, 1990—. Founder, sec. Calif. Whig Party, 1983-90. Wang and Lee East Asian scholar Calif. Luth. Coll., 1985; rsch. grantee Lilly Found., 1987-89; fellow humanities U. Calif., Santa Barbara, 1989-90. Mem. Am. Acad. Religion, Am. Soc. Ch. History, Soc. for Sci. Study Religion, Religious Rsch. Assn. Office: U No Iowa Cedar Falls IA 50614

STONE, JUDSON IRWIN, minister; b. Rochester, N.Y., Mar. 15, 1952; s. Frederic Albert and Nella Grace (Kilbourn) S.; m. Janice Sue Wylie, June 30, 1979; children: Nathaniel, Aaron, Adam. BA, Maryville Coll., 1974; MDiv, Gordon-Conwell Theol. Sem., 1978. Ordained to ministry Am. Bapt. Chs. in U.S.A., 1981. Pastor Machias (Maine) Bapt. Ch., 1979-82; pastor First Bapt. Ch., Waldoboro, Maine, 1982-85, Dexter, Maine, 1985—. Mem. Chem. Health Adv. Team, Dexter, 1990—. Mem. Am. Bapt. Chs. of Maine Ministers Coun., Am. Bapt. Chs./USA Ministers Coun. (senate 1990-94). Home: 7 Free St Dexter ME 04930

STONE, SAMUEL EDWIN, religious publishing company editor, minister; b. Clovis, N.Mex., Oct. 12, 1936; s. Samuel Eli and Stella (Brown) S.; m. Gwen Gardner, June 6, 1958; children: Jeffrey Edwin, David Lee. BA, Ozark Christian Coll., Joplin, Mo., 1958; BTh, Cin. Bible Sem., 1966, MDiv, 1974; LittD (hon.), Ky. Christian Coll., 1978. Ordained to ministry Christian Chs. and Chs. of Christ, 1957. Preacher Christian chs., Mo., Ohio, 1955-74; dean Cin. Bible Sem., 1974-77; editor Christian Standard, Standard Pub., Cin., 1978—; pres. Christian Ch. Found. for Handicapped, Knoxville, Tenn., 1981-87; v.p. N.Am. Christian Conv., Cin., 1987. Author: Grounded Faith for Growing Christians, 1975, The Christian Minister, 1980, How To Be an Effective Church Leader, 1987. Mem. Evang. Press Assn. Office: Standard Pub 8121 Hamilton Ave Cincinnati OH 45231

STONE, STANLEY WARREN, minister; b. Charleston, S.C., July 7, 1953; s. Bobby R. and Syble M. (Davidson) S.; m. Nancy J. Fagerstrom, Aug. 14, 1982; 1 child, Peter Davidson. BA, Bapt. Coll., Charleston, 1975; MRE, So. Bapt. Theol. Sem., 1977. Ordained to ministry So. Bapt. Conv., 1978. Assoc. pastor, youth min. 1st Bapt. Ch., Mt. Pleasant, S.C., 1978-85; min. of youth and coll. Citadel Sq. Bapt. Ch., Charleston, 1985-88; min. of youth and singles 1st Bapt. Ch., Gallatin, Tenn., 1988—; chmn. Assn. Youth-Recreation Com., Charleston, 1980-88, Internat. Seamen's Ministry, Charleston, 1983-84; pres. S.C. Bapt. Youth and Recreation Mins. Assn., 1985-86. Author: (case study) The Great Train Robbery, 1977; (with others) Success in Southern Baptist Youth Ministry, 1987, More Successes in Southern Baptist Youth Ministry, 1991. Mem. Tenn. Bapt. Youth Mins. Assn. Office: 1st Bapt Ch 205 E Main St PO Box 369 Gallatin TN 37066

STONE, SUSAN BERMAN, rabbi; b. N.Y.C., July 7, 1957; d. Eugene and Marilyn Joan (Friedrich) Berman; m. John C. Stone, July 3, 1988. BA, Vassar Coll., 1978; MA in Hebrew Lit., Hebrew Union Coll., 1982. Ordained rabbi, 1983. Assoc. rabbi The Temple, Cleve., 1983-87; dir. religious activities Vassar Coll., Poughkeepsie, N.Y., 1987-88; rabbi Beth Israel-The West Temple, Cleve., 1988—. Author: The Twelve Steps and Jewish Tradition, 1988. Vice chair Alcohol and Drug Addiction Svcs. Bd. Cuyahoga County, 1989—. Mem. Womens Rabbinic Network (treas. 1985-88), Cleve. Bd. Rabbis (sec., v.p., then pres. 1988—), Am. Jewish Congress (chair task force for women's equality 1989-91), Women's Interfaith Clergy Network (convener 1983-87), Cen. Conf. Am. Rabbis. Democrat. Avocations: needlework, reading. Office: Beth Israel The West Temple 14308 Triskett Rd Cleveland OH 44111

STONE, WARREN GERALD, rabbi; b. Quincy, Mass., Mar. 2, 1950; s. Earl and Elaine Ruth (Friedman) S.; m. Elaine Carol Wintroub, Aug. 4, 1974; children: Naomi Shira, Lia Rebecca. BA, Brandeis U., 1972; MAHL, Hebrew Union Coll., 1976; D of Ministry, Andover Newton Theol., Seminary, Mass., 1979. Ordained rabbi, 1978; cert. marriage and family therapist. Rabbi Stephen S. Wise Temple, L.A., 1979-82, Temple Beth El, Corpus Christi, Tex., 1982-88, Temple Emanuel, Kensington, Md., 1988—; counselor Am. Inst. Family Rels., L.A., 1979-82; Eisendrath Social Justice intern, Religious Action Ctr., Washington, 1974, 78; commr. Religious Living Union of Am. Hebrew Congregations/Wash. Bd. Rabbis, 1988-91; co-chmn. religious living com. Union of Am. Hebrew Congregations, 1990-91. Contbr. articles to profl. jours. Bd. dirs. Creative Art Ctr., Corpus Christi, 1982-86, Planned Parenthood, Corpus Christi, 1982-86. Recipient Disting. Merit award Nat. Conf. Christians and Jews, 1988. Mem. Ministerial Alliance (pres. Corpus Christi assn. 1986-88). Office: Temple Emanuel 10101 Connecticut Ave Kensington MD 20895

STONE, WILLIAM LYNDON, retired minister; b. Detroit, Mar. 1, 1926; s. Paul Lyndon and Johnnie (Graham) S.; m. Gladys Helen Farley, Aug. 9, 1948; children: William Paul, John Wesley, Beth Ann. AB, Taylor U., 1948; MDiv., Garrett-Evang. Theol. Sem., 1957. Lic. local preacher, 1944; ordained deacon, 1952; ordained elder, 1957. Min. Meth. Ch., Napoleon, Mich., 1948-53, Am. Bapt. Ch., Norvell, Mich., 1948-52, Meth. Ch., Constantine, Mich., 1953-57, Court St. Meth. Ch., Flint, Mich., 1957-58; min. to students Wesley Found., Flint, 1958-60; min. Atherton Meth. Ch., Flint, 1958-63, 1st Meth. Ch., Mt. Morris, Mich., 1963-68, Met. Meth. Ch., Detroit, 1968-69, United Meth. Ch., Oscoda, Mich., 1969-76; supr. Oscoda Indian Mission, Oscoda, Mich., 1969-76; min. Wilber United Meth. Ch., East Tawas, Mich., 1980-83, United Meth. Ch., Harrisville and Lincoln, Mich., 1983-90; mem. Detroit conf. United Meth. Ch. Supr. Oscoda Indian Mission, 1969-76; trustee Charter Twp. of Oscoda, 1978, 80, 84, 88, planning commn., 1986—; chmn. planning commn. City of Mt. Morris, 1966-68, domestic action program Wurtsmith AFB, Mich., 1969-72; dir., founder Hotline of Oscoda, 1970—, Oscoda Area Non-Profit Housing Corp., 1970-75; former bd. dirs. Child and Family Svcs., Northeast Mich. Housing Corp., E. Cen. Mich. Housing Com., Au Sable Valley Community Mental Health Bd., Mich Assn. Community Mental Health Bds.; bd. dirs. Wurtsmith Re-Use Com., Charter Twp. Oscoda, 1978—; chaplain CAP, 1978—; mem. exec. com. Iosco County Rep. Com., precinct del., 1984—; chmn. Oscoda Twp. Dept. Pub. Works, Oscoda Twp. Roads and Grounds Commn.; life mem. Oscoda Safety Com.; initiated into Chippewa Tribe, 1975. Named to Honorable Order Ky. Cols., 1983; initiated into Chippewa Tribe, 1975; recipient Vandenberg award, 1983, Medal of Merit, 1983, 85, 87, Exceptional Svc. medal, 1990, Presdl. Citation award, 1991. Mem. Mich. Twps. Assn. (bd. dirs. 1989—), Air Force Assn. (life, pres. state chpt. 1986-91, Huron chpt. 1980-83, Traverse City chpt. 1990—, Medal of Merit 1983, 85, 87, exceptional svc. award 1990, Presdl. citation 1991), Mich. Air Force Assn. (Hoyt S. Vandenberg trophy 1983), Mich. Assn. Community Mental Health Bds., Iosco County Twps. Assn. (chmn. 1984-87), Aerospace Edn. Found. (life); charter mem. Mich. Aviation Hall of Fame. Republican. Avocations: music, singing, piano, organ, photography. Home: 7357 Lakewood Dr Oscoda MI 48750

STONER, JAMES LLOYD, retired foundation executive, clergyman; b. Point Marion, Pa., Apr. 23, 1920; s. Martin Clark and Bess (Hare) S.; m. Janice Faller Evans, Aug. 28, 1943; children: Thomas Clark, James Douglas and Geoffrey Lloyd (twins). B.S., Bethany Coll., 1941, D.D. (hon.), 1958; B.D., M.A., Yale U., 1944. Ordained to ministry Christian Ch., 1943; minister in Hamden, Conn., 1942-44; assoc. exec. sec. U. Tex., YMCA, 1944-45; dir. Student Christian Fellowship, Bowling Green State U., 1945-47, Univ. Christian Mission, Fed. Council Ch. and Nat. Council Chs., 1947-56; minister North Christian Ch., Columbus, Ind., 1956-66; asst. gen. sec. for exec. operations Nat. Council Chs., 1966-72; sr. minister Central Christian Ch., Austin, Tex., 1972-80; dep. exec. dir. Found. for Christian Living, Pawling, N.Y., 1980-83, exec. dir., 1983-87; Chmn. com. recommendations Internat. Conv. Christians Chs., 1962-65; bd. mgrs. United Christian Missionary Soc., 1956-63; mem. adv. bd. Am. Bible Soc., 1966-72; life mem. coun. Christian Unity, Christian Ch.; a founder, 1st pres. LINK Award, Ridgewood, N.J., 1966-72; mem. Austin Conf. Chs., pres., 1973-75; rep. Tex. Conf. Chs., 1976-80; mem. goals com. Austin Tomorrow; mem. adv. bd. 1st Comml. Bank of Lakeway, Austin, Tex., 1990—. Contbr. articles to profl. publs. A founder, bd. dirs. Fellowship Christian Athletes, Kansas City, Mo., 1956-68; trustee Tougaloo (Miss.) Coll., 1968-74; v.p., mem. exec. com. Ecumenical Center Continuing Edn., Yale, 1966-72; mem. exec. com. Boy Scouts Am., Austin, 1980, Dutchess County council, 1981-82; bd. mgrs. New Milford Hosp., 1983-88; bd. dirs. Holiday Hills YMCA, 1983-87; com. mem. Town of Pawling 200th Anniversary, 1985-88, Lakeway Ecumenical Ch. Mem. Pawling C. of C. (exec. com. 1984-87), Greater Austin Fellowship of Christian Athletes (adv. bd. 1989—), Masons (32 deg.), Rotary (pres. 1983-84, dist. gov.-elect 1991—), Paul Harris fellow), Shriners, Rotary (dist. gov. #5870 1992—), Alpha Psi Omega, Beta Theta Pi. Home: 1134 Challenger Austin TX 78734-3802 *Fill every day with rainbow colors, and punctuate life with a positive outlook... Even the Cross of Christ is a positive sign.*

STONER, LAURA MARIE, minister; b. Carywood, Ida., Dec. 3, 1938; d. Jesse Thomas and Luti Pearl (Kennedy) Jett; m. Charles K. Stoner, July 1, 1931; children: Charles Patrick, Paul Lenard, Della Rose. Student, Wesley Co., Jackson, Miss., 1988. Self-employed writer Marblehill, Mo., 1970—; clk. Knoll Crest Orchards, Burfordville, Mo., 1975-85; min. Congl. Meth. Ch., Marblehill, Mo., 1984—; clk. The Corner Store, Barfordville, Mo., until 1990; minister Nursing Home Ministry, Lutesville, Jackson, 1972-89. author, illusrator children's Bible coloring books. Home: RR 1 Box 296 Burfordville MO 63739 *There is nothing in the world greater than pure love.*

STONES, JOHN STANLEY, minister; b. Anderson, S.C., Dec. 31, 1957; s. John Robert and Frances Lois (Barrett) S.; m. Rhonda Jesemine Barefoot, Aug. 9, 1980; children: Jessica Erline, Joshua Robert, Adrienne Lawson. BA, Central (S.C.) Wesleyan Coll., 1980; MDiv in Religious Edn., Southeastern Bapt. Theol. Sem., Wake Forest, N.C., 1983; postgrad., Liberty U., 1990—. Ordained to ministry Bapt. Ch. Assoc. pastor Union View Bapt. Ch., Franklinton, N.C., 1980-83, Mount Bethel Bapt. Ch., Belton, S.C., 1982-83; pastor Pinecrest Bapt. Ch., Portsmouth, Va., 1983-86, Black Br. Bapt. Ch., Chase City, Va., 1986-90, Euhaw Bapt. Ch., Ridgeland, S.C., 1990—; sec.-treas. Portsmouth Bapt. Pastors' Conf., 1984-85, pres. 1985-86; pres. OliveBr. Coop. Christian Ministries, Portsmouth, 1984-86, West Mecklenburg Ministerial Assn., Chase City, Va., 1987-90; sec. Jasper County Ministerial Alliance, Ridgeland, 1990—. Area rep. Virginian's Against State Sponsored Gambling, Chase City, 1987-89. Mem. Savannah River Associational Pastor's Conf. Republican. Home and Office: Euhaw Bapt Ch PO Box 1361 Ridgeland SC 29936

STOOKEY, LAURENCE HULL, clergyman, theology educator; b. Belleville, Ill., Apr. 8, 1937; s. Loyd Leslie and Gladys E. (Hull) S.; m. Peggy Ann Reynolds, June 8, 1963 (div. 1990); children: Laura, Sarah. B.A., Swarthmore Coll., 1959; STB. magna cum laude, Wesley Theol. Sem., Washington, 1962; Th.D. with honors, Princeton Theol. Sem., 1971. Ordained to ministry United Meth. Ch., 1962. Pastor Peninsula Ann. Conf., United Meth. Ch., 1962-67, 71-73; instr. preaching and worship Princeton (N.J.) Theol. Sem., 1967-71; mem. faculty Wesley Theol. Sem., Washington, 1973—, Hugh Latimer Elderice prof., 1979—; guest lectr. Union Theol. Sem., Richmond, Va., McCormick Theol. Sem., Duke U. Div. Sch., Garrett-Evangel. Theol. Sem.; vis. prof. U. Auckland, New Zealand, U. Melbourne; mem. Nat. Lutheran-United Meth. Bi-Lateral Theol. Dialogue, 1977-80; bd. dirs. Ctr. for Art and Religion 1983-87, Liturgical Conf., 1983—; officer Hymnal Revision Com. United Meth. Ch., 1984-88; cons. in field. Author: Living in a New Age: Sermons for the Season of Easter, 1978, Baptism-Christ's Act in the Church, 1982; co-author: Handbook of the Christian Year, 1986; mem. editorial bd.: Homiletic, 1974-86; contbr. articles to profl. jours. Fellow Assn. Theol. Schs. in U.S. and Can., 1979-80. Fellow N. Am. Acad. Liturgy, Acad. Homiletics; mem. Fellowship United Methodists in Worship, Music and Other Arts (officer 1981-83). Home: 13500 Justice Rd Rockville MD 20853 Office: 4500 Massachusetts Ave NW Washington DC 20016 *The pursuit of happiness can be dangerous. To ask ourselves whether we are happy may only fasten our attention upon those demons of discontent and frustration that plague us all. The proper query is, "How best can we contribute to the welfare of others?" Individuals-and nations-do well to abandon both oppressive practices of dependency and the destructive illusion of absolute independence. True happiness comes only with the discovery that we are designed to be constructively interdependent.*

STOREY, ARTHUR WILLIAM, minister; b. Pitts., Dec. 4, 1945; s. Edmunt T. and Naomi Marie (Martin) S.; m. Carolyn Faye Witcher, June 21, 1966; children: Joye, Bill. Student, Sch. for Officer's Tng., San Francisco, 1974-76, Pasadena Nazarene Coll., 1964-67, Trevecca Nazarene Coll., Nashville, 1963-64. Ordained to ministry Salvation Army, 1975. Instr., staff mem. The Salvation Army, Rancho Palos Verdes, Calif., 1976-78; commanding officer The Salvation Army, Grand Junction, Colo., 1978-80, Denver, 1980-86, Cheyenne, Wyo., 1986—. Pres. Laramie County Sheriff's Dept., Cheyenne, Wyo., 1987—; pres. chaplain's corps Wyo. Vol. Orgn. Active in Disasters, 1987—; mem. Wyo. Critical Stress State Debriefing Team, 1990—. Named Masonic Citizen of Yr., 1990, Law Enforcement Officer of the Yr., Grand Junction Police Dept., 1982-83, Crimestopper Office of the Yr., Dallas, 1984. Mem. Kiwanis. Republican. Office: Salvation Army 3695 1st St Riverside CA 92501 *We must not be content with a perpetuation of mediocrity, we have been give an opportunity to provide a helping hand out of a situation rather than merely a handout in a situation.*

STORFJELL, JOHAN BJORNAR, archaeology educator, university program director; b. Ballangen, Norway, Mar. 9, 1944; came to U.S., 1962; s. Arthur Hagrup and Margit (Pedersen) S.; m. Judith Irene Lloyd, July 14, 1963; children: Troy Alan, Thor Leif Erik. BA, Walla Walla Coll., 1966; student, Portland State U., 1969; BD, Andrews U., 1969, PhD, 1983. French and German tchr. Auburn (Wash.) Acad., 1968-69; from instr. to asst. prof. biblical langs., archeology and ancient history Mid. East Coll., Beirut, 1970-73; contract tchr. Theol. Sem. Andrews U., Berrien Springs, Mich., 1977, 78, asst. curator Siegfried H. Horn Archaeol. Mus., 1980-84, editor Siegfried H. Horn Archaeol. Mus. newsletter, 1980-85, asst. prof. archaeology and History of Antiquity Seventh-day Adventist Theol. Sem., 1981-85, libr. Seventh-day Adventist Theol. Sem., 1984-85, acting dir. Inst. Archaeology, 1986-89, assoc. prof. Seventh-day Adventist Theol. Sem., 1985-89, prof., 1989—, dir. religion, 1987—; vol. Wymer Indian Site Excavation Andrews U., 1976; contbg. speaker various lectr. series and seminars on archaeology and religion, 1983-86; cons. Frankinsense and Myrrh exhibit Kresge Art Mus. Mich. State U., 1986; adminstrv. dir. Tell el-Umeiri Excavation, Jordan, 1987; vol. diver underwater archaeol. project South Haven Maritime Mus., 1987; ceramicist Mt. Carmel Project, Haifa, Israel, 1988-90; dir. Grove Park Archaeol. Project, Berrien Springs, 1988-91. Mem. Lake Michigan Maritime Mus., Berrien County Hist. Assn. Rsch. grantee Nat. Endowment for the Humanities, 1978. Mem. Nat. Assn. Profs. of Hebrew, Soc. of Biblical Lit., Biblical Archaeology Soc., Israel Exploration Soc., Am. Schs. Oriental Rsch., Andrews Soc. Religious Studies. Avocations: photography, sailing, skiing. Home: 4720-1 E Hillcrest Dr Berrien Springs MI 49103-9583 Office: Seventh Day Adventist Theol Sem Andrews U Berrien Springs MI 49104-1500

STORMER, JOHN ANTHONY, minister emeritus, author, publisher; b. Altoona, Pa., Feb. 9, 1928; s. Regis Walter and Mary Ann (Forr) S.; m. Elizabeth Ruth Lewis, July 2, 1951; 1 child, Holly. BS in Journalism, San Jose (Calif.) State U., 1954; DLitt (hon.), Manahath Sch. Theology, Hollidaysburg, Pa., 1965; LittD (hon.), Shelton Coll., 1976. Ordained to ministry Bapt. Ch., 1968. Pastor Heritage Bapt. Ch., Florissant, Mo., 1968-86; supt. Faith Christian Acad., Florissant, 1968—; owner Liberty Bell Press, Florissant, 1963-91; bd. dirs. Internat. Coun. Christian Chs., 1965-87; dir. I Chronicles 12:32 Ministry, Florissant, 1985-91. Author: None Dare Call It Treason, 1964, The Death of a Nation, 1968, Growing of God's Way, 1984, NDCIT—25 Years Later, 1990. Mem. com., state chmn. Mo. Young Reps., 1962-64, state del. Rep. Nat. Conv., San Francisco, 1964. With USAF, 1950-53. Mem. Coun. for Nat. Policy. Office: Faith Christian Acad 2300 Parker Rd Florissant MO 63033 *Through the resurrected life of the Lord Jesus Christ, individuals who have received Him have everything they need to be and do all that God the Father calls them to.*

STORMS, MARGARET LARUE, librarian; b. Armstrong County, Pa., Mar. 11, 1938; d. Oscar Henry and Ella Margaret (Titus) Fry; m. Roger Clair Storms, Aug. 24, 1963 (dec. 1980); children: Ethel Charis, Eric Malcolm. BA in Christian Edn., Eastern Coll., 1961; MSLS, Clarion U., 1991. Organist, pianist Lee Bapt. Ch., Maine, 1965-78; tchr. sewing Beth Eden Bapt. Sch., Wheatridge, Colo., 1978-81; organist, pianist Evang. Meth. Ch., Altoona, Pa., 1984-91; libr. Manahath Sch. Theol., Hollidaysburg, Pa., 1984-90; piano tchr. Altoona, Pa., 1986-90; cataloging libr. Lancaster (Pa.) Bible Coll., 1991—; music libr. Blair Concert Chorale, Altoona, 1987-90; choir dir. Bapt. Ch., New Bethlehem, Pa., 1990-91. Nat. sec. Nat. Temperance and Prohibition Coun., 1983-89, del., sec. Prohibition Nat. Com., Denver, 1979—. Mem. Am. Theol. Libr. Assn., Harmony Club (pres. 1977), Assn. Christian Librs., Lee Lit Club (community project chmn. 1976-77). Avocations: music, needlework, sewing, knitting, reading. *The building of today is not finished. Each day influences the next. Yesterday was the foundation that set the general outline for today's framework of living—built with solid materials of learning, experiences, relationships and memories. The life materials of today include a possibility of change and involvement with others as essential to our life building. Today's building influences the interior decorating of Tomorrow and its beauty to be revealed. Thus God's blueprint will be made visible.*

STORRIE, JAMES BRIEN, minister; b. Midland, Tex., Aug. 26, 1962; s. James Jennings and Patricia Gail (O'Brien) S.; m. Amy Elizabeth Bunting, Sept. 17, 1988; 1 child, Shelby Anne. BA, Howard Payne U., 1984; MA, Southwestern Sem., 1987. Youth and recreation assoc. 1st Bapt. Ch., Midland, 1980-81; min. of youth Greenwood Bapt., Midland, 1981, 1st Bapt. Ch., Brady, Tex., 1981-83, Gambrell St. Bapt., Ft. Worth, 1984-85, 1st Bapt. Ch., Big Spring, Tex., 1987-91, Shiloh Terr. Bapt. Ch., Dallas, 1991—; pres., trustee Circle 6 Ranch Camp, Stanton, Tex., 1988-91, camp dir., 1989; dir. Off Campus Ministries, Big Spring, 1988-91. Author: (with others) Disciple Now Manual, 1989. Mem. Big Spring Drug Task Force, 1989-91. Recipient Outstanding Youth award Rotary Club, Midland, 1980, Billy Graham award Midland Coll. Bapt. Student Union, 1981. Home: 2136 Birch Bend Mesquite TX 75181 Office: Shiloh Terr Bapt Ch 9810 La Prada Dallas TX 75228

STORY, BENJAMIN SPRAGUE, clergyman; b. Cleve., Apr. 24, 1924; s. Benjamin S. and Jean Dale (Marshall) S., Sr.; m. Cleo Josephine Davis, Jan. 7, 1944; children—Benjamin S., III, Willard E., Constance Ann. B.B.A., U. Minn., 1949; postgrad. Presbyn. Theol. Sem., 1975. Sales mgr. Town and Country Real Estate, Louisville, Ky., 1951-78; pres., owner Ben Story Apt. Rentals, Jeffersonville, Ind., 1967-79; priest Episcopalian Ch. Diocese of Indpls., 1978—; social minister Episcopal Ch., Daviess and Jackson Counties, Ind., 1978—. Served with AUS, 1943-46. Mem. Louisville Apt. Assn. (bd. dirs. 1972—, pres. 1974). Republican. Club: Seymour Country (Ind.). Lodge: Elks. Avocations: travel; reading; theater; radio control flying; swimming; scuba diving; boating. Home: 21 Bellewood Ct New Albany IN 47150-1843

STORY, CULLEN IK, retired religious educator; b. Osceola, Iowa, July 26, 1916; s. William Henry and Lenore Blanche (VanScoy) S.; m. Wilma Brundage Pentecost, Dec. 29, 1942; children: Edward Cullen, John Lyle, Donald James. ThM, Dallas Sem., 1940; MA, Johns Hopkins U., 1943; PhD, Princeton Sem., 1964. Ordained to ministry Presbyn. Ch. in U.S.A., 1940. Instr. Dallas Sem., 1943-45; nat. missions pastor Presbyn. Ch. in U.S.A., McIntosh, S.D., 1945-47, Weaverville, N.C., 1952-54; missionary Presbyn. Ch., Lebanon, 1947-52, 54-57; assoc. prof. religion Coll. of Ozarks, Clarksville, Ark., 1965-67; assoc. prof. N.T., Princeton (N.J.) Theol. Sem., 1960-65, 67-85, assoc. prof. emeritus, 1985—. Author: The Nature of Truth, 1971, (with John Lyle Story) Greek to Me, 1979; contbr. articles to profl. jours. Mem. Soc. Bibl. Lit., Bibl. Rsch. Soc. Home: 78 Edgemere Ave Plainsboro NJ 08536 Office: Princeton Theol Sem Mercer St Princeton NJ 08542 *Since our true selves are known to God, it is immaterial whether we are known or recognized for what we do or even if we are misunderstood by others. Hugo's Jean Valjean endured—on all sides—serius misunderstanding, but he made little or no attempt to clear himself, content as he was to reflect the light of Christ which the bishop had brought into his soul.*

STORY, W. W., clergyman; b. Tulsa, Dec. 20, 1934; s. W. W. Sr. and Hazel Mary (Miller) S.; m. Patsy Sue Story, June 4, 1954; 1 child, Larry Michael. BA, Bartlesville Wesleyan Coll., 1975. Ordained minister Meth. Ch., 1979. Pastor Verdigris United Meth. Ch., Garber, Okla.; pastor First United Meth. Ch., Garber, Skiatook, Okla.; sr. pastor First United Meth. Ch., Grove, Okla.; chaplain Okla. Ho. of Reps., 1981; dir. Grand Lake Ministries, Grove; founder World Svc. Evangelism Inc. Mem. Lay Speaking in United Meth. Chs. (bd. dirs.). Home: Rte 3 Box 1112 Grove OK 74344

STOTT, JOHN R. W., priest, religious organization administrator; b. 1921. BA, Cambridge (Eng.) U., 1944, Cambridge (Eng.) U., 1947; Lambeth DD, Cambridge (Eng.) U., 1983. Ordained priest Ch. of Eng., 1945. Asst. curate All Souls Ch., London, 1945-50, rector, 1950-75, rector emeritus, 1975—; apptd. chaplain to Queen of U.K., 1959-91, apptd. extra chaplain, 1991—; hon. gen.sec. Evang. Fellowship, Anglican Communion, pres., 1986-90; chmn. Evang. Coun., Ch. of Eng., 1967-84, Nat. Evang. Anglican Congress, 1967, 77, Evang. Lit. Trust, 1971—; exec., chmn. theology and edn. group Lausanne Continuation Com., 1974-81; missionary various univs., U.K., N.Am., Australia, New Zealand, Africa, Asia; speaker in field. Author: Men with a Message, 1954, Fundamentalism and Evangelism, 1956, Basic Christianity, 1958, rev. edit., 1971, Your Confirmation, 1958, rev. edit., 1991, What Christ Thinks of the Church, 1958, rev. edit., 1990, The Preacher's Portrait, 1961, Confess Your Sins, 1964, The Epistles of John, 1964, rev. edit., 1988, Baptism and Fullness, 1964, rev. edit., 1975, The Canticles and Selected Psalms, 1966, Men Made New, 1966, Our Guilty Silence, 1967, The Message of Galatians: Only One Way, 1968, One People, 1969, rev. edit., 1982, Christ the Controversialist, 1970, Understanding the Bible, 1972, Your Mind Matters, 1972, The Message of 2 Timothy: Guard the Gospel, 1973, Balanced Christianity, 1975, Christian Mission in the Modern World, 1975, The Lausanne Covenant, 1975, The Message of the Sermon on the Mount: Christian Counter-Culture, 1978, The Message of Ephesians: God's New Society, 1979, Focus on Christ, 1979, The Bible Book for Today, 1982, I Believe in Preaching, 1982, Issues Facing Christians Today, 1984, rev. edit., 1990, The Authentic Jesus, 1985, The Cross of Christ, 1986, Essentials, 1988, The Message of Acts: To the Ends of the Earth, 1990, The Message of Thessalonians: Preparing for the Coming King, 1991; columnist Christianity Today mag., 1977-81. Chmn. coun. mgmt. Care & Counsel, 1975-81; bd. dirs. London Inst. for contemporary Christianity, 1982—, pres., 1986—; pres. TEAR Fund, 1983—. Mem. Brit. Scripture Union (pres. 1965-74), Brit. Evang. Alliance (pres. 1973-74), Univs. and Colls. Christian Fellowship (pres. 1961-62, 71-72, 77-78, 81-82), United Bible Socs. (v.p. Europe region 1982-86). Avocations: birdwatching, photography. Office: 12 Weymouth St, London W1N 3FB, England

STOUFFER, AUSTIN HITCHINS, clergyman, marriage therapist; b. Dryden, Ont., Sept. 9, 1941; s. Ronald Edgar and May Lantrow (Hitchins) S.; m. Jean Eleanor Pearson, Sept. 26, 1964; children: Kirsten Joy, Heidi Elan. BA in Psychology and Sociology, Lakehead U., Thunder Bay, Ont., 1973; BTh, Winnipeg (Man.) Bible Coll., 1973; MDiv, Winnipeg Theol. Sem., 1975; D of Ministry, Fuller Theol. Sem., Pasadena, Calif., 1976. Dean of students Burrard Inlet Bible Inst., Vancouver, B.C., 1965-67; exec. sec. John Howard Soc., Thunder Bay, 1967-73; minister Emmanuel Evang. Free Ch., Steinbach, Man., 1973-75, 76-80, Cen. Evang. Free Ch., Thunder Bay, 1980-88; acad. dean Trinity Western Sem., Langley, B.C., 1988-90; dist. supt. Evang. Free Ch. of Can., Langley, 1988—; chmn. Thunder Bay Coun. of Clergy, 1987-88; counseling program advisor Associated Can. Theol. Schs., Langley, 1989—; chaplain Thunder Bay Police Dept., 1987-88. Mem. Am. Assn. for Marriage and Family Therapy (clin. mem.), B.C. Assn. Clin. Counselors (registered clin. counselor), Christian Assn. for Psychol. Studies (clin. mem.). Avocations: fishing, furniture refinishing. Home: 21110 91 A Ave, Langley, BC Canada V1M 2C3 Office: Trinity Western Univ, 7600 Glover Rd, Langley, BC Canada V3A 6H4

STOUFFER, RICHARD RAY, retired pilot, clergyman, photographer; b. Peoria, Ill., Feb. 12, 1923; s. Ernest Lawrence and Reba Ellene (Woods) S.; m. Marjorie Eileen Asplund, Apr. 23, 1944; children: James Craig, Kevin Richard, Michael Lawrence, Barbara Joanne. BS in Commerce, U. Ill., 1952; MDiv, McCormick Theol. Sem., Chgo., 1981. Ordained minister United Ch. of Christ, 1982. Photographer Stouffer's Photo Svc., Urbana, Ill., 1945—, Champaign-Urbana (Ill.) Evening Courier, 1950-52; pilot United Air Lines, Chgo., 1952-83; interim min. St. John's United Ch. of Christ, Waukegan and Lincoln, Ill., 1985-86, 1st Congl. Ch., United Ch. of Christ, Wyoming, Ill., 1986-87, 1st Congl. Ch., Beardstown, Ill., 1987-88, Christian Ch., Urbana, Ill., 1989—; pastor Disciples of Christ Community Ch., Urbana, 1989—; min. adult edn. St. Peter United Ch. of Christ, Lake Zurich, Ill., 1982-84. Contbg. columnist (weekly newspaper) Frontier Enterprise, 1985-86; author, photographer mag. articles. Bd. dirs. Lake Zurich Parent Tchrs. Club, 1964-65. Capt. USAAF, 1943-45, ETO, USAF, mem. USAFR ret. Mem. Exptl. Aircraft Assn. (photographer 1960-84, trustee Found. 1972-88, President's award 1970, 72), Acad. Model Aeros., Lake Zurich C. of C. (bd. dirs. 1954-57, pres. 1958). Republican. Avocations: photography, music, model aviation, railroading, audio and video recording. Home and Office: 1807A Glenwood Oaks Ct Urbana IL 61801 *I find most "churched" people have so little Bible understanding that my ministry is both prophetic and teaching as principal thrust and work.*

STOUGH, FURMAN CHARLES, bishop; b. Montgomery, Ala., July 11, 1928; s. Furman Charles and Martha Elizabeth (Turnipseed) S.; B.A., U. of South, 1951, B.D., 1955, D.D., 1971; m. Margaret Dargan McCaa, May 12, 1951; 2 children. Ordained priest Episcopal Ch., 1955, rector St. Andrew's Ch., Sylacauga, Ala., St. Mary's Ch., Childersburg, Ala., 1955-59, Grace Ch., Sheffield, Ala., 1959-65; priest in charge All Souls Ch., Machinato, Okinawa, 1965-68; missioner, Ala., 1968-70; rector St. John's Ch., Decatur, Ill., 1970-71; bishop Diocese of Ala., 1971-89. Office: 521 N 20th St Birmingham AL 35203

STOUT, ARTHUR PAUL, minister; b. Phoenix, Feb. 10, 1932; s. Floyd Hamilton and Lucille Catherine (Robinson) S.; m. Marilyn Sue Munsil, Aug. 15, 1953; children: Roger Paul, Kellie Joanne, Amanda Beth, Eric Revell. BA, Ariz. State U., 1953; STB, Boston U., 1956. Ordained to ministry, United Meth. Ch., 1956. Pastor Sunapee & Georges Mills (N.H.) Community Meth. Chs., 1958-60, Huachuca (Ariz.) Meth. Ch., 1960-65, St. Andrew Meth. Ch., Mesa, Ariz., 1972-76; assoc. pastor Christ United Meth. Ch., Tucson, 1976-82; pastor Ajo (Ariz.) Federated Ch., 1982-85, St. James United Meth. Ch., Tucson, 1985-91, White Mountain United Meth. Ch., Show Low, Ariz., 1991—; pres. Cochise County Coun. Chs., Bisbee, Ariz., 1963, Tucson Ministerial Assn., 1989; chaplain Squadron III, CAP, Tucson, 1990-91. Contbr. editorials to newspapers. Mem. Optimist (pres. 1967), Toastmasters (pres. 1981, 84, 87), Gifted and Talented Edn. Home: 1021 N 34th Dr Show Low AZ 85901 Office: White Mountain United Meth Ch 261 N 5th St Show Low AZ 95901

STOUT, GLENNA FAYE, lay worker; b. Whitesberg, Ky., June 1, 1947; d. Benjamin and Avie Lee (Ison) Taylor; m. Dale H. Stout, May 25, 1968; 1 child, Kelly James. A. Applied Bus., Terra Tech. Coll., Fremont, 1990. Treas. First Missionary Ch., Clyde, Ohio, 1984—, The Missionary Ch., E. Cen. Dist., Troy, Ohio, 1985—; owner Glenna Stout, E.A., Clyde, 1988—. Speaker/author Seminar Workbook. Mem. screening com. United Way, Fremont, 1990. Mem. Accreditation Coun. for Accountancy, Nat. Assn. Enrolled Agts., Ohio Soc. of Enrolled Agts., Nat. Soc. Pub. Accts., Pub. Accts. Soc. Ohio, Nat. Assn. Tax Practitioners, Christian Mgmt. Assn., Terra Tech. Coll. Alumni Assn., Phi Theta Kappa. Home: 324 E Forest St Clyde OH 43410 Office: 125 W McPherson Hwy Clyde OH 43410

STOUT, JON E., pastor, artist; b. Oskaloosa, Iowa, Jan. 7; s. Donald Dale and Shirley Irene (Ellsworth) S.; m. Kim Irene McCauley, May 7, 1977; children: Gretchen, Garrett. Student, William Penn, 1975-77; BTh, Olivet Nazarene U., 1980. Ordained to ministry Ch. of the Nazarene. Youth pastor Ch. of the Nazarene, Grand Haven, Mich., 1980-82, Auburn, Ind., 1985-87, Elkhart, Ind., 1987—; self-employed artist Stout-Hearted Graphics, Oskaloosa, 1982-84; sr. youth dir. N.E. Ind. Nazarene Youth Int., 1987-90. Commd. artist Main Street Inc., Oskaloosa, 1988. Home: 320 Maumee Ct Elkhart IN 46517 Office: First Ch of the Nazarene 2601 Benham Ave Elkhart IN 46517

STOUT, PHILLIP RAY, minister; b. Goshen, Ind., May 3, 1956; s. Tommy Howard and Ruby Darlene (Chapman) S.; m. Carol Jean Posey, May 28, 1977; children: Rebekah Lauren, Nathan Philip. AB in Bibl. Lit., Olivet Nazarene U., 1978; MDiv, Nazarene Theol. Sem., 1981; postgrad., Mennonite Bibl. Sem., 1984. Ordained to ministry Ch. of the Nazarene, 1985. Assoc. pastor First Ch. of the Nazarene, Elkhart, Ind., 1984-87; pastor First Ch. of the Nazarene, Jackson, Mich., 1987—; co-speaker religious radio broadcast Masterdesign, 1989—. Contbr. articles to radio, religious periodicals. Bd. dirs. Health and Human Svcs. Com., Jackson Sch. System, 1989— (mem. human sexuality subcom., 1990—). Democrat. Home: 708 S Higby St Jackson MI 49203 Office: First Ch of the Nazarene 706 S Higby St Jackson MI 49203

STOUT, WAYNE EVERETT, minister; b. Indpls., Sept. 1, 1930; s. Everett and Mable (Grove) S.; m. Patricia Ann Mauler, Sept. 2, 1948; children: Timothy, Cynthia. BTh, Berean Bible Coll., 1960. Ordained to ministry Ch. of God (Anderson, Ind.), 1960. Pastor 1st Ch. of God, Greenfield, Ind., 1960-72, Portageville, Mo., 1972-79, Norfolk, Va., 1979—; chmn. Mo. Assembly, Ch. of God, 1978-79, Va. Assembly, Wise, 1986-88, 89-90; chmn. adminstrv. com. Ch. of God Bd. Pensions, Anderson, 1979-90. Bd. dirs. Boys Club Am., Greenfield, 1969-72; mem. adv. bd. Lifenet, Virginia Beach, Va., 1990. Home: 106 Cap Ln Norfolk VA 23503 Office: 1st Ch of God 8600 Granby St Norfolk VA 23503

STOVALL, GERALD THOMAS, religious organization administrator; b. Dallas, Mar. 4, 1940; s. James Roy and Gladys Wilton (Moore) S.; m. Marcia Louise Hearn, May 27, 1967; children: Traci Lynn, Amy Reneé, Keith Roy. BS in Edn., N. Tex. State U., 1964; MRE, Southwestern Bapt. Theol. Sem., 1966. Min. of music and edn. Siloam Bapt. Ch., Marion, Ala., 1967-69; min. of youth N. Dallas Bapt. Ch., 1969-71; min. of music Emmanuel Bapt. Ch., Lafayette, La., 1971-75; dir. Bapt. Student Ctr., Thibodaux, La., 1975-79, New Orleans, 1979—; Bd. dirs. Morality in Media, New Orleans, 1989—, Bapt. Assn. Greater New Orleans, 1990-91, Fedn. Chs., New Orleans, 1991—. Mem. Assn. Bapt. Campus Ministers, La. Chaplain's Assn. Office: Bapt Student Ctr 2222 Lakeshore Dr New Orleans LA 70122

STOVER, FRANKLIN FREDRICK, minister; b. Rockwell, Iowa, Feb. 15, 1936; s. Henry P. and Esther Stover; m. Ruth Ann Keifer, July 1, 1960; children: Robert Murray, Holly Janell, David Franklin. BA, Bob Jones U., 1958, MA, 1960. Ordained to ministry Ind. Fundamental Chs. Am., 1970. Dir. Christian edn. and youth program Sequoia Bible Ch., Eureka, Calif., 1960-65; pastor Grace Bible Ch., Stockton, Calif., 1965-67; dir. Christian edn. and youth program Valley Bible Ch., Northridge, Calif., 1967-69; prin. Valley Christian Acad., Northridge, 1967-69; dir. Christian edn. Meadowview Bible Ch., Sacramento, 1969-70, 72-74; min. Christian edn. 4th Meml. Ch., Spokane, Wash., 1970-72; prin. Sacramento Christian Schs., 1972-74; headmaster Am. Heritage Christian Acad., Sacramento, 1974-90. Bd. dirs. Humboldt County Christian Youth Fellowship, 1962-64, No. Calif. Victors through Christ, 1966-67; bd. dirs., rep. No. Calif. dist. Western Assn. Christian Schs., 1975-77; chaplain CAP, 1984—; field rep. BJU Press, 1984-90; with Champion Student Systems, 1989—. Office: 9027 Calvine Rd Sacramento CA 95829 *Consider the significance of a simple U-turn: at any given point in life (today) you are neither a success nor a failure - only on the road to one or the other.*

STOVER, W. ROBERT, lay worker, temporary services executive; b. Phila., June 26, 1921; s. Robert William Stover and Jane Horton; m. Joan Cote; children: Stephen R., Susan J., Amy J. BS, Waynesburg Coll., 1942, LHD (hon.), 1991; postgrad., U. Ill., 1942-43, U. Pa., 1946. Founder, chief exec. officer Western Temporary Svcs., Walnut Creek, Calif., 1948—, also chmn. bd. dirs.; chmn., chief exec. officer Prebyn. Lay Com., Phila.; mem. Latin Am. Missions Gen. Coun., Miami, Fla., Luis Palau Adv. Com., Portland, Oreg.; past chmn. Oakland Billy Graham Crusade. Trustee, former chmn. Fuller Theol. Sem., Pasadena, Calif.; mem. adv. bd. San Francisco State Sch. Bus., African Enterprise, L.A.; mem. nat. bd. Internat. Students, Inc., Colorado Springs; mem. Calif. State Bd. Wage and Hour Com.; life mem., former nat. chmn. Young Life Campaign, Colorado Springs. Lt. USN, World War II. Office: Western Temporary Svcs Inc 301 Lennon Ln Walnut Creek CA 94598

STOWE, DAVID METZ, clergyman; b. Council Bluffs, Iowa, Mar. 30, 1919; s. Ernest Lewellyn and Florence Mae (Metz) S.; m. Virginia Ware, Nov. 25, 1943; children—Nancy F. (Mrs. Thomas Inui), Elizabeth A. (Mrs. Charles Hambrick-Stowe), Priscilla B. (Mrs. Thomas Nelson), David W. BA, UCLA, 1940; BD, Pacific Sch. Religion, 1943, ThD, 1953, DD (hon.), 1966; postgrad., Yale U., 1945-46. Ordained to ministry Congl. Ch., 1943; assoc. min. Congl. Ch., Berkeley, Calif., 1943-45, 51-53; missionary, univ. prof. Peking, China, 1947-50; chaplain, chmn. dept. religion Carleton Coll., 1953-56; ednl. sec. Am. Bd. Commnrs. and United Ch. Bd. World Ministries, 1956-62; prof. theology Beirut, 1962-63; exec. sec. div. fgn. missions Nat. Coun. Chs., 1963-64, assoc. gen. sec. overseas ministries, 1965-70; also bd. govs.; exec. v.p. United Ch. Bd. for World Ministries, 1970-85; cons. mission and religion China, 1985—; adj. prof. Andover Newton Theol. Sch., 1987—; del. 2nd, 3rd and 4th Assemblies of World Coun. of Chs.; mem. Div. of World Mission & Evangelism, 1963-75. Author: The Churches' Mission in the World, 1963, When Faith Meets Faith, 1963, Ecumenicity and Evangelism, 1970; also articles in religious books and periodicals. Mem. Am. Soc. Missiology (sec.-treas. Ea. fellowship 1986—), Internat. Assn. Mission Studies, Nat. Soc. Values in Higher Edn., Phi Beta Kappa, Pi Gamma Mu, Blue Key. Home: 54 Magnolia Ave Tenafly NJ 07670

STOWELL, DON A., minister; b. Niles, Mich., May 27, 1959; s. Donna Lee (Mathie) Fryatt; m. Sharlene May Trabert, May 30, 1981; children: Tammy Lee, Patricia Ann, Barbara Lynn. B Religious Edn., Great Lakes Bible Coll., 1981; M Ministry, Ky. Christian Coll., 1984; postgrad., Bethany Theol. Sem., 1990—. Ordained to ministry Ch. of Christ, 1981. Min. Ch. of Christ, Buckhannon, W.Va., 1981-83, Glenmont (Ohio) Ch. of Christ, 1983-89; sr. min. Grove Ch. of Christ, Gambier, Ohio, 1989-91; min. Calvary Christian Ch., Swartz Creek, Mich., 1991—; dir. Round Lake Christian Assembly, Lakeville, Ohio, 1984—; trustee Christian Childrens' Home, Wooster, Ohio, 1986—; mem. adv. bd. Holmes County Dept. Human Svcs., Millersburg, Ohio, 1986. Trustee Bd. Pub. Affairs, Glenmont, Ohio, 1987-89; mem. adv. bd. Holmes County Dept. Human Svcs., Millersburg, Ohio, 1986. Republican. Office: Calvary Christian Ch 7315 Corunna Rd Swartz Creek MI 48473

STOWELL, JOSEPH, III, academic administrator. Head Moody Bible Inst., Chgo. Office: Moody Bible Inst 820 N LaSalle Dr Chicago IL 60610*

STOWELL, KIMBERLY JEAN, minister; b. Phila., July 1, 1960; d. Paul Chesterfield Jr. and Jean Pearl (Kittinger) S. BA in Psychology, Religion, Carthage Coll., 1982; MDiv, Luth. Theol. Sem., 1986. Ordained to ministry Luth Ch., 1986. Min. St. Paul's Immanuel Luth. Chs., Baileys HArbor, Wis., 1986—; bd. dirs., Help of Door County Inc., Sturgeon Bay, Wis., 1987—; pres., North Door Clergy Assn., 1988-89; chmn. Luth. Soc. Svcs. Adv. bd., Green Bay, Wis., 1988—, Door County Vol. Chaplains, 1989—. Mem. Global Missions Com., Appleton. Wis., 1988-89, Door County Meml. Hosp. Ethics. Com., 1990—. Home: 3536 Hwy F Fish Creek WI 54212 Office: Immanuel Luth Ch PO Box 115 Baileys Harbor WI 54202 *We live in such a fast paced—quick fix society where we expect instant results from a behavior or a product that we are totally unable to handle the pregnant times of our lives—times when we have to wait—times when we don't know what is growing within us—times when we are uncomfortable and scared about where to go and what to do.*

STOWES, PATRICIA ANNE, minister; b. Alexander City, Ala., Aug. 21, 1948; d. Ned and Thelma Odell (Glenn) S. Student, Tenn. State U., 1965-66, Ky. State U., 1966-67, Sarah Thomas Sch. Beauty, Louisville, 1968-69. Lic. cosmetologist, Ala., Ky. Cosmetologist Exclusive Beauty Salon, Louisville, 1968-82, Deeper Life Beauty Salon, Alexander City, 1984-88; min. R.E. Jones United Meth. Ch., Louisville, 1988-91, minister, 1991—. Mem. NAFE. Avocations: reading, bowling, travel, church activities. Home: 2435 W Broadway # 1 Louisville KY 40211 *Many people are searching for peace. I believe that true peace comes only when one is in harmony with both God and man.*

STRADER, DOUGLAS J., minister; b. Pontiac, Mich., Feb. 9, 1957; s. Melvin Cleveland and Marion Ruby (Obrien) S.; m. Lisa Denise Strickland, Sept. 27, 1980; children: Matthew, Lindsey. BA in Bibl. Studies, Grace Coll., Winona Lake, Ind., 1979. Ordained to ministry Bapt. Ch. Assoc. pastor Grace Brethren Bible Ch., Ft. Myers, Fla., 1979-81; min. youth and music Highlawn Bapt. Ch., Hunington, W.Va., 1981-82; assoc. pastor, min. music and edn. Northside Bapt. Ch., Ft. Myers, 1982-89; assoc. pastor, min. music, edn. and youth Coral Bapt. Ch., Coral Springs, Fla., 1989—. Republican. Home: 992 NW 83d Dr Coral Springs FL 33071 Office: Coral Bapt Ch PO Box 9719 201 N University Dr Coral Springs FL 33075

STRADER, KARL DAVID, pastor; b. Homestead, Okla., June 16, 1929; s. Cloa Faithful Strader; m. Joyce Arlene Wead; children: Stephen, Danny, Karla, Dawn. BA, BD, Bob Jones U., 1954; DD (hon.), Oral Roberts U., 1985. Pastor Ind.; dean of men Southeastern Coll., Lakeland, Fla.; youth pres. Peninsular Fla. dist. Assemblies of God; pastor Carpenters Home Ch., Lakeland, sr. pastor. Author several books; contbr. articles to profl. jours. Active Civil Svc. Bd., Lakeland. Republican. Office: Carpenters Home Ch 777 Carpenters Way Lakeland FL 33809

STRADER, LAURIE ANN, religion educator; b. Northampton, Mass., Sept. 10, 1968; d. Dominic Frank and Dorothy Ruth (Aughtry) Labato; m. Eric Christopher Strader, June 2, 1990. Grad. high sch., Northampton, 1986; student, U. Mass., 1986-89. Nursery attendant Christ United Meth. Ch., Northampton, 1984-85, Sunday Sch. tchr., 1985-95, mem. choir, 1989-91, mem. pastor parish com., 1989-90, mem. Add Bd., 1990-91, trustee, 1990-91; teller, customer svc. Shawmut Nat. Corp., Hadley, Mass., 1990-91. Leader Camp Lewis Perkins, Girl Scouts Am., 1988-89; asst. leader Girl Scouts Am., Coun. 121, Western Mass., 1989-90. Home: 70 C N Whitney St Amherst MA 01002

STRAIN, JOHN DENNIS, minister; b. Ft. Worth, Oct. 21, 1946; s. Joseph Lusk and Annabelle (Cooper) S.; m. Barbara Anne Bright, Jan. 16, 1971; children: Theresa Dawn Strain McDougal, Randall Dale. BTh, Bapt. Bible Coll., 1968; MA, Wheaton Grad. Sch., 1987. Ordained to ministry in Bapt. Ch., 1967. Pastor Berean Bapt. Ch., Magnolia, N.J., 1976-83; dean students Bapt. Bible Coll. East, Boston, 1983-84; pastor Westfair Bapt. Ch., Jacksonville, Ill., 1984-85; dir. stewardship Columbia (S.C.) Bible Coll. and Sem., 1987—; trustee Bapt. Bible Coll. East, Boston, 1981-83; bd. dirs. Bapt. Bible Fellowship, Springfield, Mo., 1979-81; pres. N.J. Bapt. Bible Fellowship, 1978-79. Contbr. articles to publs. Republican. Office: Columbia Bible Coll & Sem PO Box 3122 Columbia SC 29230 *The "summum bonum," i.e., the highest good, in this life is to give glory to God. I have chosen to live my life for that quest!.*

STRAIT, CLIFFORD NEIL, religious organization administrator; b. New Lexington, Ohio, Nov. 10, 1934; s. Ira Clifford and Iva May (King) S.; m. Ina May Niccum, Sept. 2, 1958; children: David Milton, Philip Ryan, Jolyne Renee. AB, Olivet Nazarene U., Kankakee, Ill., 1958, ThB, 1959, DD, 1990; BD, Nazarene Theol. Seminary, Kansas City, Mo., 1969. Ordained to ministry Ch. of the Nazarene, 1963. Pastor Rosewood Heights Ch. of the Nazarene, East Alton, Ill., 1961-63, Carmi (Ill.) Ch. of the Nazarene, 1963-66, East Liberty Ch. of the Nazarene, Akron, Ohio, 1966-73, Taylor Ave. Ch. of the Nazarene, Racine, Wis., 1973-77, First Ch. of the Nazarene, Lansing, Mich., 1977-80; dist. supt. Mich. Dist. Ch. of the Nazarene, Grand Rapids, 1980—; chmn. book com. Ch. of the Nazarene, Kansas City, Mo., 1990—; trustee Olivet Nazarene Univ., Kankakee. Author five books; contbg. author six books; editor three books; contbr. more than 1200 articles to mags. Home and Office: 2754 Barfield Dr SE Grand Rapids MI 49546

STRALING, PHILLIP FRANCIS, bishop; b. San Bernardino, Calif., Apr. 25, 1933; s. Sylvester J. and Florence E. (Robinson) S. B.A., U. San Diego, 1963; M.S. in Child and Family Counseling, San Diego State U., 1971. Ordained priest Roman Catholic Ch., 1959, consecrated bishop, 1978. Mem. faculty St. John Acad., El Cajon, Calif., 1959-60, St. Therese Acad., San Diego, 1960-63; chaplain Newman Club, San Diego State U., 1960-72; mem. faculty St. Francis Sem., San Diego, 1972-76; pastor Holy Rosary Parish, San Bernardino, 1976-78; bishop Diocese of San Bernardino, 1978—; pub. Inland Catholic newspaper, 1979—; bd. dirs. Calif. Assn. Cath. Campus Ministers, 1960s; exec. sec. Diocesan Synod II, 1972-76; Episcopal vicar San Bernardino Deanery, 1976-78. Office: Diocesan Pastoral Ctr 1450 North D St San Bernardino CA 92405

STRAND, KENNETH ALBERT, minister, educator; b. Tacoma, Sept. 18, 1927; s. Jens Albright and Bertha Johanna (Odegaard) S.; m. Lois Marie Lutz, June 1, 1952. BA, Emmanuel Missionary Coll., 1952; MA, U. Mich., 1955, PhD, 1958. Ordained to ministry Seventh-day Adventist Ch., 1956. Pastoral svcs. Mich. Conf. of Seventh-day Adventists, Battle Creek, Ann Arbor, Monroe & Kalamazoo, 1952-59; assoc. prof. religion Emmanuel Missionary Coll., Berrien Springs, Mich., 1959-62; assoc. prof. ch. history Andrews U. Sem., Berrien Springs, Mich., 1962-66, prof., 1966—; dir. grad. religion program Andrews U. Sem., Berrien Springs, $, 1967-77. Author: Reformation Bibles in the Crossfire, 1961, German Bibles Before Luther, 1966, Early Low-German Bibles, 1967, Brief Introduction to the Ancient Near East, 1969, The Open Gates of Heaven; A Brief Introduction to Literary Analysis of the Book of Revelation, 1970-72, Interpreting the Book of Revelation, 1976, Catholic German Bibles of the Reformation Era, 1982; assoc. editor Andrews U. Sem. Studies, 1967-74, editor, 1974—; contbr. numerous articles on religion to scholarly jours. Mem. Am. Hist. Assn., Am. Soc. Ch. History, Am. Soc. for Reformation Rsch., Internat. Soc. Comparative Study of Civilizations, Soc. Bibl. Lit., Cheiron, Phi Beta Kappa. Home: 8856 George Berrien Springs MI 49103

STRANG, STEPHEN EDWARD, magazine editor, publisher; b. Springfield, Mo., Jan. 31, 1951; s. A. Edward and Amy Alice (Farley) S.; m. Joy Darlene Ferrell, Aug. 19, 1972; children: Cameron Edward, Chandler Stephen. B.S. in Journalism, U. Fla., Gainesville, 1973. Reporter Orlando Sentinel Star, Fla., 1973-76; editor Charisma mag. Calvary Assembly, Winter Park, Fla., 1976-81; pres. Strang Communications Co., Lake Mary, Fla., 1981—; owner Creation House Books, 1986, Christian Retailing mag., 1986, Inside Music mag., 1990. Founding editor Charisma mag., 1975, Ministries Today mag., 1983; founding pub. CharismaLife Learning Resources, 1990. Recipient First Place award Nat. Writing Championship, William Randolph Hearst Found., 1973. Mem. Internat. Pentecostal Press Assn., Christian Booksellers Assn., Fla. Mag. Assn. (pres. 1979-80), Evang. Christian Pubs. Assn., Evang. Press Assn. Republican. Mem. Assemblies of God. Avocation: Racquetball. Home: 627 Estates Place Longwood FL 32779 Office: Strang Communications Co 600 Rinehart Rd Lake Mary FL 32746

STRANGE, JAMES FRANCIS, religion educator; b. Pampa, Tex., Feb. 2, 1938; s. Jerry Donald and Buena (Frost) S.; m. L. Carolyn Midkiff, Aug. 19, 1960; children: Mary E., James R., Katherine A., Joanna C. BA, Rice U., 1959; MDiv, Yale U., 1964; PhD, Drew U., 1970. Asst. prof. religious studies U. South Fla., Tampa, 1972-75, assoc. prof., 1975-79, prof., 1980—, dean Coll. Arts & Letters, 1980-89, chmn. dept. religious studies, 1991—; assoc. dir. excavations at Khirbet Shema, Meiron, Israel, 1971-73, Meiron Excavation Project, 1973-80; lectr. bibl. archaeology U. Orange Free State, Bloemfontein, Republic of South Africa, 1979; dir. excavations, Sepphoris, Israel, 1983—. Co-author: Ancient Synagogue Excavations at Khirbet Shema, 1976, Merion, 1981, Archaeology, the Rabbis, and Early Christianity, 1981, Excavations at Gush Halav, 1990. Recipient Silver Medallion award NCCJ, 1987; Montgomery fellow Albright Inst. for Archeol. Rsch., 1970-71, NEH fellow, 1980; IBM grantee, 1974. Mem. Am. Schs. Oriental Rsch., Israel Exploration Soc., Nat. Assn. Bapt. Profs. Religion, World Assn. for Jewish Studies. Democrat. Baptist. Avocations: reading, walking. Home: 9712 Woodland Ridge Dr Tampa FL 33637 Office: U South Fla 4202 Fowler Ave Tampa FL 33620

STRANGE, WILLIAM BAZZLE, JR., lay minister, information systems specialist; b. Blue Island, Ill., Dec. 12, 1946; s. William Bazzle Sr. and Sylvia Gladys (Amato) S.; m. Earlene Winifred Newcomb, Dec. 10, 1966; children: James M., Trudei A., William B. III. Customer engr. IBM, Tallahassee, Fla., 1966—; asst. pastor St. Francis Roman Cath. Ch., Blourtstown, Fla., 1980-84, St. Thomas the Apostle Ch., Quincy, Fla., 1984—; chaplain River Junction Correctional Inst., Chattahoochie, Fla., 1980-85, Apalachee Correctional Inst., Sneads, Fla., 1980—. With U.S. Army, 1967-70. Mem. Am. Correctional Chaplains Assn., Am. Cath. Correctional Chaplains Assn., Nat. Deacons Assn., K.C. (sec. Tallahassee chpt. 1978-79). Democrat. Home: Rte 1 Box 286 Quincy FL 32351-9742 Office: IBM 101 N Monroe Tallahassee FL 32301

STRANGES, FRANK ERNEST, clergyman, scientific investigator, producer; b. Bklyn., Oct. 6, 1927; s. Natale Antonio and Catherine (Filardo) S. Cert. Eastern Bible Coll., 1945, Buluah Heights Bible Coll., 1946; diploma North Central Bible Sem., 1951; Ph.D., Th.D., D. in Psychology, B. in Internat. Law, D.D. (hon.), Tenn. Christian U., 1952-61; D.D. (hon.), Williams Coll., Berkeley, Calif., 1965; D. Internat. Law, Union U., 1983. Lic. psychologist, Calif. Pres. Internat. Evangelism, Van Nuys, Calif., 1959—, Nat. Investigators Com. Unidentified Flying Objects, Van Nuys, 1967—, Globe Internat. Pictures, Van Nuys, 1970—; Internat. Theol. Sem., Van Nuys, 1975—. Author: Saucerama, 1959; Stranger at the Pentagon, 1967; UFO Conspiracy, 1984. Producer TV films UFO Journal, Interstellar Connection, 1982-84. Named hon. atty. gen. State of La., 1968. Mem. United Sci. Fedn., Am. Police Fedn. (J. Edgar Hoover FBI award 1982, cert. honor 1982) Internat. Chaplain's Assn. (4 star gen. March AFB). Republican. Lodges: Royal Knights of Justice (knight comdr. 1982), Knights of Malta (knight comdr. 1981), Mystical Order of St. Peter (knight comdr. 1982). Home: PO Box 5 Van Nuys CA 91408

STRAPPELLO, RICHARD L., religious organization administrator; b. Meyersdale, Pa., Nov. 3, 1953; s. Alexander Anthony Strappello and Grace Elizabeth (Lindimen) Miller; m. Connie Elizabeth Miller, June 2, 1974; children: Jessica, Carina, Lee, Larissa. BA, Grace Coll., 1976. Asst. to program dir. YMCA of the Rockies, Estes Park, Colo., 1977; exec. dir. W. Pa. Dist. Grace Brethren Men Inc., Saxton, Pa., 1977—; instr. Nat. Wildlife Fedn., Washington, 1986-89; Sunday sch. supt. Martinsburg (Pa.) Grace Brethren Ch., 1984-85; elder Martinsburg Grace Brethren Ch., 1990—. Leader Martinsburg Boy's Club, 1986-89, club comdr., 1991—, dist. treas., 1980-89. Mem. Christian Camping Internat. Home and Office: Camp Mantowagan Box 95 Saxton PA 16678

STRATAS, JACK GEORGE, minister, editor; b. Starkville, Miss., Mar. 2, 1942; s. Michael Nicholas and Irene (Miaouls) S.; m. Jeanette Rogers, Mar. 1970. BS, U. So. Miss., 1964; postgrad., Duke U., 1988, High Point Coll., 1991. Lic. to ministry United Meth. Ch., 1988; cert. crisis counselor. Copy editor, reporter Bristol (Va.) Herald-Courier, 1964, Mobile (Ala.) Register, 1964-66; copy editor Comml. Appeal, Memphis, 1966-71; news editor Post-Herald, Birmingham, Ala., 1971-84; minister Meth. Ch., Denton, N.C., 1988—; assoc. editor Hometown News, Denton, 1988—; bd. dirs. A.P., N.C., 1984-88. Author: South Davidson Churches, 1989; author book of poetry. Bd. dirs., pres. Mental Health Assn., Asheboro, N.C., 1984—; bd. dirs., sec. ARC, Asheboro, 1984—; bd. dirs. Contact, Asheboro, 1984-86, Energy Adv. Commn., Ashboro, 1984-88, Emergency Preparedness, Asheboro, 1984-88; mem. dist. com. Rep. Party, Memphis, 1967-71. U.S. Navy, 1964-66. Recipient Pres.'s award Mental Health Assn. N.C., 1987, 88; Valley Forge award Freedoms Found., 1984; named Vol. of Yr., Interagy. Council, Asheboro, 1980-84. Mem. Ahepa (editor 1984), Civl War Soc., Am. History Soc., Lions, Kiwanis, Sigma Delta Chi, Alpha Phi Omega. Office: 1st Meth Ch Box 425 South Main Denton NC 27239

STRATON, GEORGE DOUGLAS, minister, religion educator; b. Norfolk, Va., Mar. 19, 1916; s. John Roach and Georgia Elizabeth (Hillyer) S.; m. Ruth Isabelle Riley, June 12, 1943; children: Kathryn Anne, David Skeen, Peter Riley, John Carter. AB, Harvard U., 1938; postgrad., Yale U., 1938-39; BD, Andover Newton Theol. Sch., 1941; PhD, Columbia U., 1950. Ordained to ministry Am. Bapts. in U.S.A., 1942, subsequently United Ch. of Christ. Prof. philosophy and religion Colby Jr. Coll., N.H., 1941-42; instr. religion Coll. of Wooster, Ohio, 1948-50; prof. philosophy Cen. Coll., Pella, Iowa, 1951-54; assoc. prof. religion Colo. Coll., Colorado Springs, 1954-59, dean chapel, 1954-58; prof. U. Oreg., Eugene, 1959—, chmn. dept. religious studies, 1959-73. Author: Theistic Faith for Our Time: An Introduction to the Process Philosophies of Royce and Whitehead, 1979, 2d edit., 1981; also articles. Chaplain AUS, 1942-46. Mem. Am. Acad. Religion. Home: 2243 Potter St Eugene OR 97405 Office: U Oreg Dept Religious Studies Eugene OR 97403 *Even amid the uncertainties and perils and pains of life, we know in our heart of hearts that it's better to be than not to have been, and this is our vision of the Everlasting Being, Goodness and Love of God.*

STRATTAN, ERIC JESSE, minister; b. Cleve., July 20, 1956; s. Robert Martin and Joanne Julia (Lovejoy) S.; m. Marcia Anne Frier, July 4, 1981; children: Arianne, Valerie, Alissa. BA in Religion, Grand Rapids (Mich.) Bapt. Coll., 1981; MA in Pastoral, Faith Bapt. Coll., 1983. Ordained to ministry Bapt. Ch., 1983. Assoc. pastor Calvary Bapt. Ch., Muskegon, Mich., 1983—. Author: (evangelism manual) L.E.A.D., 1983; also articles. Active steering com. Muskegon County Crisis Pregnancy Ctr., 1985. Avocations: gourmet cooking, model rocketry, music, computer programming and use. Office: Calvary Bapt Ch 1600 Clinton St Muskegon MI 49442

STRAUGHAN, GARY MARVIN, minister; b. Edmonton, Alberta, Can., Nov. 8, 1941; s. George Basil and Annie (Enns) S.; m. Phyllis Mary Regier, Dec. 21, 1963 (div. Mar. 1985); children: Kevin Bruce, Georgina Lynn Pierzchala, Todd Lyle. BA, Moravian Coll., 1963; MDiv, Moravian Theol. Seminary, Bethlehem, Pa., 1966. Ordained to ministry Moravian Ch., 1966. Minister Freedom Moravian Ch., Appleton, Wis., 1966-69, Moravian Ch., Sturgeon Bay, Wis., 1969-76; co-minister Moravian Ch., Rudolph, Wis., 1976-81; minister Moravian Ch., Wisconsin Rapids, Wis., 1976-87, Downey, Calif., 1987—; pres. Pacific Southwest Dist. Bd., Downey, 1990—; v.p. Western Dist. Exec. Bd., Madison, 1978-86. Recipient Disting. Community Svc. award Jaycees, Sturgeon Bay, 1975. Mem. Downey Ministerial Fellowship (treas.), Rotary. Home: 7349 Via Amorita Downey CA 90241 Office: Moravian Church 10337 Old River School Rd Downey CA 90241

STRAUS, DAVID EDWARD, rabbi; b. Newark, Jan. 6, 1957; s. Eric J. and Marlene R. (Roesberg) S.; m. Lynne G. Breslau, May 5, 1985; children: Max, Isaac. BA, Northwestern U., 1978; MAHL, Hebrew Union Coll., Jewish Inst. Religion, Cin., 1983. Ordained rabbi, 1983. Rabbi Washington Hebrew Congregation, 1983-86, Anshe Chesed Fairmount Temple, Cleve., 1986-88, Har Sinai Hebrew Congregation, Trenton, N.J., 1988—; trustee Blum Men Trust, Trenton, 1988—; pres. Del. Valley Bd. Rabbis, 1990—. Trustee WUPJ, N.Y.C., 1986—, Jewish Community Fedn. Mercer County, 1988—, Planned Parenthood, Trenton, 1991—. Mem. Cen. Conf. Am. Rabbis, Mazon Rabbinic Table, N.J. Am. Jewish Com. (exec. com.). Home: 2223 Stackhouse Dr Yardley PA 19067 Office: Har Sinai 491 Bellevue Ave Trenton NJ 08668

STRAUSER, CHARLES, religious organization administrator. Pres. Full Gospel Assemblies Internat., Parkesburg, Pa. Office: Full Gospel Assemblies Internat RD #2 Box 520 Parkesburg PA 19365*

STRAUSS, ROBERT LYNN, clergyman; b. Harrisburg, Pa., Aug. 20, 1959; s. Oliver Penrose and Dolores Dawn (Matinchek) S.; m. Laurie Jean Hopkins, Oct. 5, 1985; 1 child, Kimberly. BA, Moravian Coll., 1981; MDiv, Moravian Theol. Sem., 1984. Ordained to ministry Meth. Ch., 1983. Asst. to pastor First United Meth. Ch., Bangor, Pa., 1981-84; assoc. pastor Stroudsburg (Pa.) United Meth. Ch., 1984-87; pastor Salem United Meth. Ch., Shoemakersville, Pa., 1987—. Alumni fellow Moravian Coll., Bethlehem, Pa., 1981. Home and Office: Salem United Meth Ch 605 Main St Shoemakersville PA 19555

STRAVERS, DAVID EUGENE, minister; b. Oskaloosa, Iowa, May 10, 1949; s. Joe and Pearl H. (Booy) S.; m. Janet Ruth Driesens, Jan. 1, 1972; children: James J., Andrew J., Juliana M. BA, Calvin Coll., 1971, MDiv, 1976; MA, Fuller Theol., Pasadena, Calif., 1984, PhD, 1991. Ordained to ministry Christian Ref. Ch. N.Am., 1976. Missionary tchr. Christian Ref. World Missions, Republic of China, The Philippines, 1974-84; v.p. of ministry The Bible League, South Holland, Ill., 1986—. Contbr. articles to religious mags., 1971-90. Mem. Am. Soc. Missiology. Office: The Bible League 16801 Van Dam Rd South Holland IL 60473

STRAYER, GENE PAUL, lay worker, educator; b. York, Pa., Aug. 17, 1942; s. Paul Martin Henry and Hope Romaine (Asper) S. BA, Am. U., 1964; MA, U. Chgo., 1968; M in Sacred Music, Union Theol. Sem., 1972; PhD, U. Pa., 1991. Asst. prof. religious studies U. Colo., Boulder, 1972-78; lectr. in religious studies U. Pa., Phila., 1979-86; organist, choirmaster Trinity United Ch. of Christ, York, Pa., 1986—; sem. organist, adj. prof. ch. music and world religions Lancaster (Pa.) Theol. Sem., 1987—; mem. hymnal com. United Ch. Christ, 1990—. Author: The Theology of Beethoven's Masses, 1991. Recipient Dean's award for disting. teaching U. Pa., 1981, Woodrow Wilson teaching intership Woodrow Wilson Found., 1969, Woodrow Wilson fellowship, 1964. Mem. Am. Acad. Religion, Am. Guild of Organists (dean York chpt. 1990—), Am. Musicological Soc., Soc. Bibl. Lit., Hymn Soc. U.S. and Can. Democrat. Home: 2783 Carnegie Rd # 204 York PA 17402 Office: Lancaster Theol Sem 555 W James St Lancaster PA 17603

STRECKER, IGNATIUS J., archbishop; b. Spearville, Kans., Nov. 23, 1917; s. William J. and Mary B. (Knoeber) S. Student, St. Benedict's Coll., Atchison, Kans., 1931-37, Kenrick Sem., St. Louis, 1937-42, Cath. U. Am., 1944-45. Ordained priest Roman Cath. Ch., 1942; aux. chaplain USAAF, Great Bend, Kans., 1942-44; chancellor Diocese Wichita, 1948-62; bishop Diocese Springfield-Cape Girardeau, Mo., 1962-69; archbishop Archdiocese of Kansas City, Kans., 1969—. Office: Chancery Office PO Box 2328 2220 Central Ave Kansas City KS 66110

STREET, STEPHAN EDWARD, minister; b. Columbus, Miss., Aug. 23, 1960; s. Ed Leamon and Gail (Stratton) S.; m. Carla Ann Crenshaw, June 25, 1988. BA in Religion, Miss. Coll., 1982; MDiv, Southwestern Bapt. Theol. Sem., 1987. Minister to youth Fairview Bapt. Ch., Columbus, Miss., 1983-84; minister with single adults First Bapt. Ch., Charlotte, N.C., 1988-89, Broadmoor Bapt. Ch., Jackson, Miss., 1989—. Bd. dirs. Uptown Day Shelter for Homeless, Charlotte, N.C., 1989. Mem. Hinds/Madison Metro Religious Edn. Assn. (v.p. 1991). Office: Broadmoor Bapt Ch 787 E Northside Dr Jackson MS 39206

STREET, WOODROW W., broadcasting executive; b. Sycamore, Ill., Feb. 5, 1955; s. Woodrow W. and Myrtle M. (Littlejohn) S.; m. Peggy L. Robbins, Sept. 4, 1976; children: Darren M., Eric M., Rebecca L. AAS in Agr. Mktg., Parkland Coll., 1976; BA in Communication, Sangamon State U., 1980. Music dir. Sta. WIBI Radio, Carlinville, Ill., 1981-84, program/prodn. dir., 1984-88, ops. dir., 1988—; bd. dirs. Latter Rain Ministries, Litchfield, Ill., 1989—. Mem. Soc. of Broadcast Engrs., Christian Mothers Club (Brighton, Ill., bd. dirs. 1989—). Office: PO Box 126 Carlinville IL 62626

STREETER, JARVIS, VII, religion educator; b. Oakland, Calif., July 6, 1949; s. Jarvis VI and Marie Madelene (Sandquist) S.; m. Susan Haron Gresham, July 2, 1988; children: Kamaliah Nicole Smith, Megan Simone Smith. BA, U. So. Calif., L.A., 1971; MDiv, Luther Theol. Sem., St. Paul, 1978; STM, Yale Div. Sch., New Haven, 1981; PhD, So. Meth. U., Dallas, 1990. Ordained to ministry Evang. Luth. Ch. Am., 1978. Pastor Southwest Luth. Parish, Mpls., 1978-79; asst. prof., chmn. dept. religion Calif. Luth. U., Thousand Oaks, 1988—; del. Convocation Teaching Theologians, Evang. Luth. Ch. Am., 1990—. Bd. dirs. Alleluia Dance Theater, Moorpark, Calif., 1989—. Zion fellow Am. Schs. Oriental Rsch., 1976; Yale Div. Sch. rsch. fellow, 1982-83. Mem. Am. Acad. Religion, Amnesty Internat. Democrat. Home: 566 Timberwood Ave Thousand Oaks CA 91360 Office: Calif Luth U 60 Olsen Rd W Thousand Oaks CA 91360

STREETT, RICHARD ALAN, minister, theologian; b. Christiansburg, Va., July 11, 1946; m. Lynn Fenby, June 8, 1974; children: Aaron, Daniel, Andrew. BA, U. Balt., 1969; MDiv, Wesley Theol. Sem., 1972; PhD, Calif. Grad. Sch. Theology, 1982. Ordained to ministry United Meth. Ch., 1973. Pastor Meth. Chs., Balt., 1970-74; exec. dir. SMI, Balt., 1974-82; prof. The Criswell Coll., Dallas, 1982-88; sr. pastor Trinity Evang. Ch., Dallas, 1988—; adj. prof. Calif. Grad. Sch. Theology, Glendale, 1985—; curriculum advisor Mex. Theol. Sem., San Antonio, 1986-87; speaker SMI Syndicated Radio Program, U.S. and Caribbean, 1978-90; bd. dirs. Balt. Fellowship Found. Author: The Effective Invitation, 1984, The Cult Invasion, 1986; producer: (TV program) Behold, the Man!, 1988, (4-part video series) Sharing the Gospel with Cultists; contbr. articles to profl. publs. R. Alan Streett Day established in his honor Mayor of Balt., William Donald Schaefer, 1982. Mem. Am. Soc. Missiology, Nat. Assn. for Evangs., Nat. Religious Broadcasters, Evang. Theol. Soc., Acad. for Evangelism in Theol. Edn., Majority Text Soc. Office: Trinity Evang Ch PO Box 180804 Dallas TX 75218

STREGE, MERLE DENNIS, theology educator, minister; b. St. Paul, June 10, 1947; s. Ivan Elroy and Joyce June (Wiuff) S.; m. Frances Marie Schmidt, Aug. 23, 1969; children: Frederick Ivan, Peter Alfred. AB, Anderson U., 1969, MDiv., 1972; ThD, Grad. Theol. Union, 1982. Ordained to ministry Ch. of God (Anderson, Ind.), 1981. Prof. hist. theology Anderson U., 1980—; min. Ch. of God., Anderson, 1981—; historian Ch. of God, Anderson, 1985—. Author: A Look at the Church of God, 1989, Tell Me the Tale, 1991; editor: Baptism and Church, 1986. Theol. rsch. grantee Assn. Theol. Schs., 1987. Home: 4880 Berwick Way Anderson IN 46012 Office: Anderson U Anderson IN 46012 *Our lives flourish neither as an individual achievement nor as heroic mastery over circumstance, but as members of a beloved community which guides and sustains us through tragedy and joy.*

STREIKER, LOWELL DEAN, minister; b. Chgo., Mar. 14, 1939; s. Frederic Burton and Alice (Peller) S.; m. Lois Susanne Leff, Sept. 9, 1957 (div. Jan. 1974); children: Stephen Dean, Susan Lynn; m. Connie Lorraine Johnson, Aug. 1, 1975. BA, Temple U., 1962; MA, Princeton U., 1965, PhD, 1968. Ordained to ministry United Ch. of Christ, 1960. Pastor Kensington Congregational Ch., Phila., 1961-62; tchr. dept. religion Temple U., Phila., 1964-72; v.p. Microtech Computer Svcs., Burlingame, Calif., 1984-87; pastor Ladera Community Ch., Portola Valley, Calif., 1990—; exec. dir. Freedom Counseling Ctr., Burlingame, 1979-84, Mental Health Assn., San Mateo, Calif., 1976-79, Wilmington, Del., 1973-76. Author: New Age Comes to Main Street, 1990, Fathering-Old Game, New Rules, 1989, Family, Friends and Stranger, 1988, The Gospel Time Bomb, 1986; contbr. articles to profl. jours. Asst. dir. presdl. primary campaign for Wash. Senator Henry M. Jackson, Fla., Ohio, 1972. Mem. Spiritual Devel. Network (chmn. 1988—), Am. Acad. Religion, Soc. for Bibl. Lit. Democrat. Home: 886 Gull Ave Foster City CA 94404 Office: Ladera Community Church 3300 Alpine Rd Portola Valley CA 94028

STRELAN, JOHN GERHARD, clergyman, educator; b. Ungarie, New South Wales, Australia, Nov. 10, 1936; s. Peter Gerhard and Erica Clara (Appelt) S.; diploma in theology Concordia Sem., Adelaide, S. Australia, 1959; Th.D., Concordia Sem., St. Louis, 1973; m. Bronwyn Helene Burgess, Mar. 6, 1965; children—Peter Gerhard, John William, Kylie Louise, Luana Jane. Ordained to ministry Luth. Ch., 1960; pastor Wangaratta Victoria, Australia, 1960-62; circuit missionary Menyamya, Papua New Guinea, 1962-65; found. faculty mem., dean of studies, lectr. in N.T., Martin Luther Sem., Lae, Papua New Guinea, 1966-84, registrar, 1980-81; lectr. various seminars and workshops on religious movements in primal societies; guest lectr. U. Erlangen, Bavaria; lectr. Luther Sem., North Adelaide, Australia, 1986—; v.p. Luth. Ch. Australia, 1987—. Editor Luth. Theol. Jour., 1986—Bd. govs. Lae Internat. High Sch., 1980-83, chmn., 1983. Mem. Australian Assn. for Study of Religion. Composer hymn: Lord God our Guardian and our Guide; author: Search for Salvation, 1977; Glory be to Thee O Lord, 1979; Ephesians: A Commentary, 1981; The Letters of John: A Commentary, 1984; editor Bible Commentary series, 1982-84, Luth. Theol. Jour., 1986—. Home and Office: Luther Seminary, 104 Jeffcott St, North Adelaide 5006, Australia

STRELZER, MARTIN, religious organization administrator; b. N.Y.C., Oct. 17, 1925; s. Samuel Strelzer and Sadie Rothman; m. Florence Moskowitz, Jan. 30, 1947; children: Stuart, Amy. BBS, N.Y. Sch. Commerce, 1953. Pres. Harry D. Spielberg, Inc., N.Y.C., 1967-70, Amstrel Textiles, Inc., N.Y.C., 1970-83, Temple Beth-El, Closter, N.J., 1971-83; pres. N.J. West Hudson Valley region Union of Am. Hebrew Congregations, Paramus, N.J., 1976-80; trustee Union of Am. Hebrew Congregations, N.Y.C., 1976-83, mem. exec. com., 1982-83, chmn. new congregations com., 1979-83; N.Am. dir. World Union for Progressive Judaism, N.Y.C., 1984—; arbitrator Am. Arbitration Assn., N.Y.C., 1970-83. Chmn. Israel Bonds Campaign, Bergen County, N.J., 1971-72, United Jewish Appeal campaign, No. Valley, N.J., 1973-74, Community Rels. Com., Bergen County, 1980-81. Recipient Circle of Light Israel Bonds Testimonial Closter, N.J., 1980. Democrat. Office: World Union for Progressive Judaism 838 Fifth Ave New York NY 10021

STREMMING, DENNIS RAY, music and youth minister; b. Vincennes, Ind., Apr. 25, 1949; s. Raymond Lee and Juanita (Hogan) S.; m. Sandra Dale Nichols, July 24, 1971; children: Christy, Jonathan, David. BA, Tenn. Temple Coll., 1971. Minister music Hialeah (Fla.) Bapt. Temple, 1975-80, Shelton Beach Rd. Bapt., Saraland, Ala., 1980-84; minister music/youth Capitol City Bapt. Ch., Des Moines, 1984-87, East Side Bapt. Ch., Memphis, 1987—; youth and music dir. East Side Bapt. Ch., Memphis, 1987—. Songwriter in field. Republican. Home: 6266 Gillham Dr Memphis TN 38134 Office: East Side Bapt Ch 3232 Covington Pike Memphis TN 38128

STRENG, FREDERICK JOHN, religion educator; b. Seguin, Tex., Sept. 30, 1933; s. Adolph Carl Sr. and Elizabeth Marie (Hein) S.; m. Ruth Helen Billnitzer, June 6, 1955 (div. 1977); children: Elizabeth Ann, Mark Andrew; m. Bette Sue Blossom, May 23, 1981; stepchildren: Steven Deane, Lisa Deane Evans. BA, Tex. Luth. Coll., 1955; MA, So. Meth. U., 1956; BD, U. Chgo., 1960, PhD, 1963. Asst. prof. U. So. Calif., L.A., 1963-66; assoc. prof. So. Meth. U., Dallas, 1966-74, prof., 1974—; vis. prof. U. Calif., Berkeley, 1973, Harvard U., Cambridge, Mass., 1973, Kwansei Gakuin U., Nishinomiya, Japan, 1986-87; pres. North Tex. Assn. Unitarian Universalist Socs., Dallas, 1990—. Author: Emptiness—A Study in Religious Meaning, 1967, Understanding Religious Life, 3d edit., 1985; editor: (series) Religious Life of Man Series, 1969—; sr. editor: Ways of Being Religious, 1973; co-editor: Spoken and Unspoken Thanks, 1989; contbr. articles to profl. jours. Active various coms. 1st Unitarian Ch. Dallas, 1968—; advisory mem. religious communities task force Dallas Ind. Sch. Dist., 1975—. Recipient Outstanding Prof. award So. Meth. U., 1974, Disting. Alumni award Tex. Luth. Coll., 1988; Fulbright scholar, 1961-62; NEH grantee, 1979. Fellow Ctr. for World Thanksgiving; mem. Soc. for Asian and Comparative Philosophy (pres. 1970-72), Am. Soc. for Study of Religion (pres. 1987-90), Soc. for Buddhist-Christian Studies (v.p. 1989—), Am. Acad. Religion, Nat. Coun. on Religion and Pub. Edn., Dallas Civil Liberties Union. Office: So Meth U Dept Religious Studies Dallas TX 75275-0202

STRICKER, BARRY ARTHUR, religion educator; b. Lexington, Ky., Mar. 5, 1957; s. Jesse Clifford and Elva Ruth (Smith) S.; m. Julie Jan Jackson, June 20, 1981. BA, Harvard U., 1979; MDiv, Golden Gate Bapt. Theol. Sem., 1982, PhD, 1987. Asst. prof. theology and Christian philosophy Golden Gate Bapt. Theol. Sem., Mill Valley, Calif., 1987—, assoc. dean acad. affairs, 1991—. Contbr. articles, denominational curriculum to profl. publs. Mem. Am. Acad. Religion, Bapt. Assn. Philosophy Tchrs. Office: Golden Gate Bapt Theol Sem # 357 Mill Valley CA 94941

STRICKERT, FREDERICK M., religion educator; b. Chillecothe, Mo., May 21, 1948; s. Walter F. and Mary E. (Boyd) S.; m. Gloria Jean Naber, July 25, 1970; children: Angela, Benjamin, Rachel. BA, Concordia Sr. Coll., Ft. Wayne, Ind., 1970; MDiv, Christ Sem.-Seminex, St. Louis, 1974, STM, 1975; PhD, U. Iowa, 1988. Ordained minister Evangel. Luth. Ch. Am. Lectr. Timothy Luth. Sem., Papua, New Guinea, 1975-81; asst. prof. religion Wartburg Coll., Waverly, Iowa, 1986—, chmn. dept. religion, 1990—; participant archeol. excavation Caesarea, Israel, 1974; area supr. archeol. excavation Bethsaida, Israel, 1988—. Author 4 books on Bibl. studies, 1978-81; contbr. articles on religion, archeology to various publs. Mem. Soc. Bibl. Lit., Am. Schs. for Oriental Rsch., Assn. Luth. Coll. Faculties, Lions Club. Avocations: jogging, racquetball, gardening, travel. Home: 417 4th St NW Waverly IA 50677 Office: Wartburg Coll Box 1003 Waverly IA 50677

STRICKERT, WALTER FREDERICK, minister; b. Scott City, Kans., June 8, 1916; s. Henry John and Minna Laura (Rook) S.; m. Mary Elizabeth Boyd, Apr. 7, 1942; children: Richard, Frederick, Dorothea Dehne, Tamarah Humphreys, David. Student, Concordia Sem., St. Louis, 1936-41. Ordained to ministry Luth. Ch., 1942. Pastor Our Savior Luth. Ch., El Dorado, Ark., 1942-45, St. John's Luth. Ch., Chillicothe, Mo., 1945-48, St. Paul's Luth. Ch., Sedalia, Mo., 1948-68, King of Kings Luth. Ch., Chesterfield, Mo., 1968—; bd. dirs. Mo. dist. Luth. Ch.-Mo. Synod, 1970-78, 4th v.p., 1966-70, 2d v.p., 1978-82, 1st v.p., 1982—. Home and Office: 13172 Greenbough Dr Saint Louis MO 63146-3622

STRICKLAND, ANNIE RUTH, minister; b. Vossburg, Miss., Oct. 22, 1949; d. John D. and Ruth (Hales) Smith; m. Dairy Strickland, June 28, 1968; children: Tyrone, Dary Jr., Adarianne. AA, Mary Holms Coll., Moist Point, Miss., 1976. Asst. minister East Jerusalem Ch., Laurel, Miss., 1986—; owner Strickland Bible Bookstore, Quitman, Miss., 1988—; pres., founder Women and Men of God in Christ Jesus, Vossburg, Miss., 1985—; alumni pres. Living Word Coll., Hattiesburg, 1990—. Mem. C. of C. (membership com.). Office: East Jerusalem Ch 100 W Church St Quitman MS 39355-2133

STRICKLAND, JOHN ARTHUR VAN, minister; b. Detroit, Sept. 25, 1952; s. Maurice Alexander and Irma (Surovy) S.; m. Constance Fillmore, Dec. 24, 1976 (div. Aug. 1984); m. Brenda Cecile Bunch, Nov. 23, 1985. BA cum laude, Ga. State U., 1974; ministry program, Unity Ministerial Sch., 1974-76. Ordained to Assn. Unity Chs., 1976. Minister Unity Ch. Christianity, Santa Rosa, Calif., 1976-77, Jacksonville, Fla., 1978-79; v.p. prayer ministry Unity Sch. Christianity, Unity Village, Mo., 1979—, mem. task force, 1984-87; mem. adv. council Unity Sch. Christianity, Unity Village, 1987—; vol. chaplain, Jackson County Jail, Kansas City, 1974-75; coordinator internat. youth of unity Assn. Unity Chs., Unity Village, 1975-76. Contbr. articles to profl. jours. Trustee, Kans. Children's Mus.; vol. Unity Help Line, Unity Village, 1975-76. Named one of Outstanding Young Men Am., 1982. Mem. Rotary (youth svcs. com., chmn. invocation com. 1988-89, Paul Harris fellow). Republican. Avocations: running, physical fitness, golf, hiking, music. Home: 405 NE Stanton Ln Lee's Summit MO 64064 Office: Unity Sch Christianity Hwy 350 and Colbern Rd Unity Village MO 64062

STRICKLIN, KATHRINE KOMENAK, educator; b. Atlanta, Sept. 26, 1951; d. Albert Jay and Ruth (Morgan) Komenak; m. Paul Eugene Stricklin, May 14, 1977; 1 child, Charles Stough. AB, Converse Coll., 1973; M of Theol. Studies, Va. Sem., 1978. Dir. Christian edn. St. Stephen's Episc. Ch., Birmingham, Ala., 1982-84; Bishop's edn. staff Diocese Ala., Birmingham, 1982-84; dir. Christian edn. St. Peter's Episc. Ch., Oxford, Miss., 1984-86; lay asst. to rector St. Stephen's Episc. Ch., Charleston, S.C., 1987-89; asst. for edn. St. James Episc. Ch., Hendersonville, N.C., 1989—; freelance writer, Arden, N.C., 1987-89; mem. Christian Edn. Com., Diocese Ala., Miss., S.C., N.C., 1989—. Author/editor: Private Choices/Public Consequences, 1989, Diocesan Curriculum for Companion Dioceses, Alabama and South Carolina. Vol., com. mem. Am. Cancer Soc., Birmingham, 1980-84; bd. dirs. Birmingham Community Soup Kitchen, 1981-84; vol., coord. Crisis Ministry to Homeless, Charleston, 1987-89. Mem. Asheville Writers Workshop, Converse Coll. Alumnae Assn. (recipient Disting. Alumnae award, 1989, various com. positions, 1989—). Office: St James Episc Ch 766 N Main St Hendersonville NC 28792

STRITE, JACOB JAY MILLER, clergyman; b. Greencastle, Pa., Dec. 19, 1904; s. John Calvin and Daisy Belle (Miller) S.; Anna Irene Eckert Foltz, Aug. 9, 1929 (dec. 1953); children—Georgia Annabelle Strite Flock, Martha Eckert Strite Scull; m. Clara Belle Fleishman, Oct. 23, 1954 (dec. May 1987). AB, Lynchburg Coll., 1930; student Christian Theol. Sem., Indpls., 1933-37; BD Lexington Theol. Sem., 1958, ThM, 1959. Ordained to ministry Disciples of Christ Ch., 1933; minister North Eastwood Christian Ch., Indpls., 1933-35, Daleville (Ind.) Christian Ch., 1935-44, Corydon (Ind.) Christian Ch., 1945-50, Melrose Christian Ch., Roanoke, Va., 1950-57, Mt. Carmel Christian Ch., Winchester, Ky., 1957-60, Christian Coll. Ga., Athens, Ga., 1960-61 (also counselor, tchr.), Friendship Christian Ch., Athens, 1962-64, minister at large, 1964-69; assoc. Bethany Christian Ch., Roanoke, Va., 1969-87; mem. council on Christian Unity, Christian Ch. Named Tchr. of Yr., Bethany Christian Ch., 1983. Mem. Disciples of Christ Hist. Soc., Nat. Audubon Soc., Smithsonian Assocs., Postal Commemorative Soc., Am. Assn. Ret. Persons, Va. Christian Ministers Conf., Roanoke Valley Ministers Conf., Nat. Wildlife Fedn., Automobile Club Va. Republican. Club: Pioneer (Lynchburg Coll.) (dir.). Home: 1678 Springbrook Rd NW Roanoke VA 24017

STROBEL, SHIRLEY HOLCOMB, magazine editor, educator, non-profit organization writer; b. Hastings, Nebr., May 8, 1929; d. Dent Z. and Helen (Spriegel) Holcomb; m. Howard Austin Strobel, Aug. 26, 1953; children: Paul Austin, Gary Dent, Linda Susan Strobel Helgeson. BS, Northwestern U., 1951; MA, Duke U., 1953. Cert. counselor, N.C.; tchr., N.C. English tchr. Salem Acad., Winston-Salem, N.C., 1952-53; tchr. Durham city schs., N.C., 1954-55, Durham County schs., 1967-90; editor Ch. Tchrs. mag. Nat. Tchrs. Edn. Project, Durham, 1986-89; editor Ch. Tchrs., Harper Collins, San Francisco, 1990—; part-time instr. Program in Edn. Duke U., Durham, 1991—; part-time instr. Duke U., Durham, 1986—; chmn. dept. English Jordan High Sch., Durham, 1967-75; reader Nat. Coun. Tchrs. English, 1969-71; rsch. asst. CUNY, 1973-74; mem. accreditation team Duke U. Edn. Program, 1985; judge mag. competition for Episcopal Communicators Conf., 1992. Co-author: Advanced Placement English, 1983. Founder, pres. Threshold Clubhouse for Mentally Ill, Durham, 1985, chmn. capital campaign, 1988-91; active Area Bd. Mental Health, Durham, 1990—. Democrat. Baptist. Avocations: mountain climbing, reading. Home and Office: 1119 Woodburn Rd Durham NC 27705

STROHMER, CHARLES RICHARD, minister, writer; b. Detroit, July 14, 1949; s. Richard Henry and Lenore Rachael (Rapin) S.; m. Linda Elizabeth Misenheimer, Apr. 3, 1987. Cert., Billy Graham Sch. Evangelism, 1977, Christian Worldview Studies, Livonia, Mich., 1986, Decision Mag. Sch. Christian Writing, 1981. Lay worker Evangel Ministries, Detroit, 1977-78; radio broadcaster Shine Ministry, Detroit, 1977-82; missions worker Youth With A Mission, Paisley, Scotland, 1986-89; freelance writer, 1982—; Christian educator on the New Age movement to numerous univs., ch. orgns., 1986—. Author: What Your Horoscope Doesn't Tell You, 1988; contbr. articles to religious mags. Mem. Christian Writers of S.E. Mich. (founder 1983), Trinity Arts Group (rep. 1983—). Office: PO Box 4325 Sevierville TN 37864 *It is a sad irony that in the only generation we Christians really know—our own—our Christianity often winds up irrelevant to it. We're chronically anachronistic. Some relevancy without syncretism would raise up an apposite church, no longer alienated from the people we should have been equipped to help.*

STROJNY, MARIANO, clergyman; b. Bnin, Poland, Nov. 20, 1906; s. Mieczyslaw and Wloczewski (Boleslawa) S.; student U. Krakow, 1927-31; D.C.L., Lateran U., Rome, 1935. Ordained priest Roman Catholic Ch., 1931, monsignor, 1949; parish priest, Katowice, Chorzow, Poland, 1935, 37-38; dir. Pontifical Missions Works, 1937-39; notary Diocesan Tribunal Katowice, 1938-39; advocate Sacred Roman Rota, Rome, 1939-43; judge 1st Instance Tribunal Vicariate Rome, 1943-54, Tribunal Appeal Vicariate Rome, 1954-77; rector Pontifical Polish Coll., Rome, 1945-48, Pontifical Polish Inst., 1949-58; consultor Sacred Congregation for Oriental Ch., 1947-73; comm. and consultor Sacred Congregation for Sacraments, 1940—; consultor of commn. Preparatory for Eastern Ch. Vatican Council, 1961-62; advocate Sacred Congregation Holy Office, 1966-72; procurator Sacred Congregation Causes of Beatification and Canonization of Saints, 1954—; mem. Supreme Tribunal Signatura Apostolica, 1960-85, Commn. for Sacred Congregation Doctrine of the Faith, 1960—; canon Patriarchal Archbasilica St. John Lateran, 1963—. Apostolic Supernumerary Protonotary, 1963—; corr. mem. European Acad. Arts, Scis. and Humanities, Paris, 1987—. Editor: Pius XII: In Memoriam, 1984. Recipient Anno Mariano silver medal from Pope Pius XII, 1954; judge of Tribunal Vicariate Rome for the process of beatification of Pope Pius Xii; recipient Silver cup for sculpture Internat. Prize Arte Pro Arte Rome, 1972; Prix du Musée National at 13th internat. Grand Prix competition, Monte Carlo, 1978; decorated Order Polonia Restituta, 1963, 66. Sculptor Chopin, Rome, Marie Sklodowska Curie, Rome, Wolfgang Amadeus Mozart, Rome, 1991. Address: Casella Post, 9019 Aurelio, 00165 Rome Italy

STROKER, WILLIAM DETTWILLER, religion educator; b. Paris, Ky., May 23, 1938; s. Francis Marshall and Josephine Clendenen (Dettwiller) S.; m. Mary Ann McLellan, Nov. 11, 1967; 1 child, Mary Katherine. BA, Transylvania U., 1960; BD, Yale U., 1963, MA, 1966, PhD, 1970; postgrad., U. Basel, Switzerland, 1963-64. Lectr. Yale U., New Haven, 1965-69; acting dean of students Yale Div. Sch., New Haven, 1968-69; asst. prof. religion Drew U., Madison, N.J., 1969-76, assoc. prof., 1976-82, prof., 1982—. Author: Extracanonical Sayings of Jesus, 1989. Rotary fellow, 1963-64. Mem. AAUP, Soc. Bibl. Lit., Coun. on Grad. Studies in Religion (sec./treas. 1990—). Democrat. Episcopalian. Home: 20 Hoyt St Madison NJ 07940 Office: Drew U 36 Madison Ave Madison NJ 07940

STROM, EVERALD HANSON, church offical; b. Wahpeton, N.D., June 7, 1921; s. Erwin Martinius and Bertha Caroline (Hanson) S.; m. Sylvia Eunice Kilde, June 5, 1943; children: Edward Charles, David Everald. BA, Augsburg Coll., Mpls., 1942; MA, N.Y.U., 1948; BD, Northwestern Luth. Sem., 1956. Ordained to ministry Ch. of the Luth. Brethren of Am., 1944. Pastor Bethany Luth. Ch., Staten Island, N.Y., Ebenezer Luth Ch., Mpls., Faith Luth. Ch., Briarcliff Manor, N.Y., Triumph Luth. Ch., Moorhead, Minn.; pres. Ch. of the Luth. Brethern of Am., Fergus Falls, Minn., 1966-86, pres. emeritus, 1986—; exec. dir. Tuscarora Resource Ctr., Mt. Bethel, Pa., 1986-89; bd. dirs. Luth. Evangelistic Movement. Editor: Faith and Fellowship mag., 1955-67. Mem. Nat. Assn. Evangs., Kiwanis. Office: PO Box 655 Fergus Falls MN 56537

STROMBERG, MONICA NELL, elementary school educator; b. Crete, Nebr., Sept. 26, 1963; d. Paul Donald and Rose Arlene (Schroeder) Winkler; m. James Todd Stromberg, May 25, 1985. AA, Mid Plains Coll., 1984; BS, Bartlesville (Okla.) Wesleyan Coll., 1988. Cert. tchr., Nebr., Okla. Tchr. Grand Island (Nebr.) Christian Elem. Sch., 1988—, head tchr., 1989-91; youth vol., camp counselor, tchr. Sunday sch. 1st Wesleyan Ch., Bartlesville, 1985-87; camp counselor, children's ch. leader, tchr. Sunday sch. Wesleyan ch., Grand Island, Nebr., 1988-89; mem. youth staff, tchr. Sunday sch. Evang. Free Ch., Grand Island, 1990-91. Office: Grand Island Christian Elem Sch RR 2 Box 51A Grand Island NE 68803

STRONG, JOHN STIVEN, educator; b. Tunghsien, Hopei, Republic of China, Sept. 13, 1948; s. Robbins and Katherine (Stiven) S.; m. Sarah Mehlhop, Mar. 13, 1971; children: Anna, Aaron. BA, Oberlin Coll., 1969; MA, Hartford Sem., 1972; PhD, U. Chgo., 1977. Assoc. prof. philosophy and religion Bates Coll., Lewiston, Maine, 1978—. Author: Legend of King Asoka, 1983, (with others) Guide to Buddhist Religion, 1981. Mem. Am. Acad. Religion, Am. Soc. for the Study of Religion, Assn. for Asian Studies. Office: Bates Coll Lewiston ME 04240

STRONG, LESLIE THOMAS, III, minister; b. Nashville, May 20, 1961; s. Leslie Thomas II and Shirley Louise (Dixon) S.; m. Jana Kathryn Law, Dec. 22, 1984; 1 child, Kathryn Elizabeth. BA, Union U., 1983; MDiv, New Orleans Bapt. Theol. Sem., 1987, postgrad., 1987—. Ordained to ministry Bapt. Ch., 1990. Instr. religion William Carey Sch. Nursing, New Orleans, 1988-90; instr. religion, Greek New Orleans Bapt. Theol. Sem., 1989—; pastor Enon Bapt. Ch., Franklinton, La., 1989—; teaching fellow New Orleans Bapt. Theol. Sem., 1986-89. Mem. Soc. Bibl. Lit., Alpha Chi. Republican. Home: 15028 Hwy 16 Franklinton LA 70438 Office: Enon Bapt Ch 14049 Hwy 16 Franklinton LA 70438

STRONSTAD, ROGER JONATHAN, college administrator; b. Turner Valley, Alta., Can., Nov. 15, 1944; s. Melvin Theodore and Edith Cavelle (Bendiksen) S.; m. Laurel Marion Smith, July 10, 1971. Diploma in theology, Western Pentecostal Bible Coll., 1971; M in Christian Studies, Regent Coll., 1975. Orained to ministry Pentecostal Assemblies Can., 1975. Minister Pentecostal Assemblies Can., Clinton, B.C., Can., 1971-73; instr. Western Pentecostal Bible Coll., Clayburn, B.C., 1974, assoc. prof., 1985, dean of edn., 1985—; lectr. various colls. Author: Models for Christian Living: A Commentary on First Peter, 1983, The Charismatic Theology of St. Luke, 1984; co-editor (with Lawrence M. Van Kleek): The Holy Spirit in the Scriptures and the Church, 1987; contbr. articles to profl. jours. Mem. Soc. Pentecostal Studies. Office: Western Pentecostal Bible Coll, PO Box 1700, Abbotsford, BC Canada V2S 7E7

STROPE, KEVIN LIND, minister; b. Pekin, Ill., Feb. 7, 1957; s. Quentin Leroy and Gerda Magdalena (Steckmann) S.; m. Shellie Kay Mahr, May 31, 1980; children: Adam Mahr, Natalie Kay. BA, U. S. Fla., 1979; MDiv., Eden Theol. Sem., St. Louis, 1982. Ordained to ministry United Ch. of Christ, 1982. Assoc. minister The Community Ch., Vero Beach, Fla., 1982-83; pastor Union Congregational Ch., Holly Hill, Fla., 1983-86, Bethlehem United Ch. of Christ, Bridgeton, Mo., 1986—; youth minister Fla. Conf. United Ch. of Christ, 1982-86. Mem. Halifax Area Ministerial Assn. (pres. 1985-86). Democrat. Avocations: bicycling, reading. Office: Bethlehem United Ch of Christ 11625 Old St Charles Rd Bridgeton MO 63044

STROTHMAN, WENDY JO, book publisher; b. Pitts., July 29, 1950; d. Walter Richard and Mary Ann (Hodtum) S.; m. Mark Kavanaugh Metzger, Nov. 25, 1978; children: Andrew Richard, Margaret Ann. Student, U. Chgo., 1979-80; AB, Brown U., 1972. Copywriter, mktg. U. Chgo. Press, 1973-76, editor, 1977-80, gen. editor, 1980-83, asst. dir., 1983; dir. Beacon Press, Boston, 1983—; trustee Brown U., 1990—. Bd. editors Brown Alumni Monthly, 1983-89, chmn., 1986-89. Bd. dirs. Editorial Project for Edn., trustee, 1987—, treas., 1988-90. Mem. Renaissance Soc. (bd. dirs. 1980-83), Women's Media Group (N.Y.C.), Pubs. Lunch Club (N.Y.C.). Office: Beacon Press 25 Beacon St Boston MA 02108

STROUD, BILL AUBREY, youth minister; b. Shreveport, La., Aug. 2, 1963; s. Joe Richard and Dorothy Ann (Pannel) S.; m. Karen Sanders, July 19, 1985 (div. 1987). BA in Christian Ministries, East Tex. Bapt. U., 1986; MDiv in Pastoral Counseling, New Orleans Bapt. Theol. Sem., 1990. Summer youth missionary La Pryor (Tex.) Bapt. Ch., 1983; youth minister Park View Bapt. Ch., Marshall, Tex., 1983-84; interim pastor Fair Play (Tex.) Bapt. Ch., 1984-85; evangelism tchr. self-employed, Marshall, 1985-87; youth minister First Bapt. Ch., Waskom, Tex., 1987—; youth coord. Ministerial Alliance, Waskom, 1989—. Republican. Home: PO Box 1248 Waskom TX 75692

STROUD, DAVID ALLEN, minister; b. Houston, Sept. 17, 1952; s. Allen Josiah and Doris Annette (Ivy) S.; m. Sandra Jean Schalk, Aug. 23, 1975; children: Kristen Leigh, Jonathan Barrett. B Music Edn., Baylor U., 1975; M Ch. Music, Southwestern Bapt. Theol. Sem., Ft. Worth, 1977. Lic. to ministry So. Bapt. Conv., 1980, ordained, 1981. Min. music and youth Riverside Bapt. Ch., Stephenville, Tex., 1975-77, Retama Park Bapt. Ch., Kingsville, Tex., 1977-80; min. music and youth 1st Bapt. Ch., Wylie, Tex., 1980-89, min. music and edn., 1989—; mem. Christian helps com. Collin Bapt. Assn., McKinney, Tex., 1985—. Mem. Wylie Community-Sch. Task Force, 1985; dir. Wylie Community Choir, 1980—; mem. master plan com. City of Wylie, 1991; parent vol. Wylie Ind. Sch. Dist., 1991. Mem. Wylie Ministerial Alliance, Wylie C. of C. (chmn. Christmas activities 1990), Singing Men Tex., Baylor U. Alumni Assn., Collin County Baylor U. Alumni Assn. Office: 1st Bapt Ch 100 N 1st St Wylie TX 75098

STROUD, JOHN NATHAN, religious book shop owner, librarian; b. Waupaca, Wis., Nov. 9, 1948; s. Bronnie Ellis and Annabelle Frances (Dorman) S.; m. Linda May Meyer, Aug. 16, 1969 (div. Feb. 1985); 1 child, John Nathan II; m. Elizabeth Anne Daigle, Nov. 29, 1986; 1 child, Anne Lorecia Daigle. BA, Cen. Bible Coll., 1971; MLS, U. Ky., 1973. Reference libr. Bethan Bible Coll., Santa Cruz, Calif., 1974-75; antiquarian bookseller Stroud Booksellers, Williamsburg, W.Va., 1975—. Mem. Am. Theol. Libr. Assn. (assoc.), Antiquarian Booksellers Assn. Am. Home and Office: Star Rte Box 94 Williamsburg WV 24991

STROUD, WILLIAM JOSEPH, minister; b. Atkins, Ark., Mar. 26, 1937; s. Joe Bryan and Carrie Lee (Griffen) S.; m. Judith Ann Beck, Dec. 30, 1956; children: Annette Marie, Bruce William. BA, Calif. Western U., 1959; MDiv, Iliff Sch. Theology, 1963, ThD, 1970. Instr. religion U. Denver, 1965-66; asst. prof. philosophy Wesleyan Coll., Macon, Ga., 1966-70; assoc. prof. philosophy and religion Salem Coll., Salem, W.Va., 1970-75; minister Smithburg Charge, Smithburg, W.Va., 1978-80, Perryville (Ark.) United Meth. Ch., 1980-84, First United Meth. Ch., Brinkley, Ark., 1984-87, Sylvan Hills United Meth. Ch., Sherwood, Ark., 1987—. Author: Celebrate: Jesus is Born, 1985. Mem. Soc. for Bibl. Lit., Am. Sch. Oriental Rsch., Sherwood C. of C. (bd. dirs. 1989-90), Rotary (sec. 1987-89). Office: Sylvan Hill United Meth Ch 9921 Sylvan Hills Hwy Sherwood AR 72120

STROUP, HERBERT, sociology educator, retired. BD, Union Theol. Seminary, N.Y.C.; D in Sociology, New Sch. for Social Rsch. Retired prof. sociology Bklyn. Coll./CUNY; head study team to survey refugees in West Bengal, India for Ch. World Svc.; various social welfare projects nationwide; others. Author: Bureaucracy In Higher Education, 1966, Church and State in Confrontation, 1967, Four Religions of Asia, 1968, The Future of the Family (with others), 1969, Like a Great River: An Introduction to Hinduism, 1972, Social Welfare Pioneers, 1986, others; contbr. articles, book reviews to profl. jours. Trustee Ripon Coll.; active Dept. Higher Edn., Nat. Coun. Chs.; chmn. Div. Health and Welfare, United Ch. of Christ, numerous other denominational activities.

STROUP, JERRY DONALD, minister; b. Sapulpa, Okla., Aug. 5, 1939; s. David Ralph and Juanita Bessie (Gray) S.; m. Karen Sue Frazier, Aug. 24, 1958; children: Elizabeth, Deborah, Mark, Timothy, Matthew, Miriam. BA, Cen. Bible Coll., 1963; postgrad., Oral Roberts U. Ordained to ministry Assemblies of God, 1963. Pastor Assemblies of God, Kans., Okla., Ill., N.J. and Ark., 1959-83; pastor Ch. of the Rock, Tex., 1984-89, Grass Valley, Calif., 1990—. Mem. Nevada County Planning Com., 1991. Republican. Home: 11379 Goodridge Way Grass Valley CA 95949

STROUSE, THOMAS MORTON, religion educator; b. Indpls., Mar. 31, 1945; s. Thomas Morton Sr. and Wilma June (Hollowell) S.; m. Janis Kathleen Wood, Aug. 27, 1966; children: Brent, Aaron, Kristen, Kayla, Mark, Kerith, Joshua, Karis, Luke, Keren, Katie, Kiera, Ryan, Tyler. BS, Purdue U., 1967; MDiv, Maranatha Bapt., Watertown, Wis., 1974; PhD, Bob Jones U., 1978; ThD, Maranatha Bapt., 1988. Prof. Maranatha Bapt. Sem., Watertown, 1978-88; prof., chmn. Tabernacle Bapt. Theol. Sem., Virginia Beach, Va., 1988—; guest lectr. Somonauk (Ill.) Faith Bible Inst., 1985-88. Author: The Lord God Hath Spoken: A Guide to Bibliology, 1991; contbr. articles to profl. jours. Mem. Trinitarian Bible Soc. (exec. mem.), Fundamental Bapt. Fellowship, Soc. Bibl. Lit., Bibl. Archeology Soc., Iota Lambda Sigma. Home: 6251 Drew Dr Virginia Beach VA 23464 Office: Tabernacle Bapt Ch 717 N Whitehurst Landing Rd Virginia Beach VA 23464 *When the trials of life come, I attempt to ask the question: What is the lesson the Lord is trying to teach me?.*

STRUCKMEYER, ALAN DEAN, minister; b. Brenham, Tex., Dec. 24, 1959; s. Marvin Henry and Verna Mae (Borman) S.; m. Linda Rose Knapp, Nov. 29, 1985; children: Andrew Alan, Aaron Alan. AA, Concordia Luth. Coll., 1980, BA, 1982; MDiv., Concordia Sem., 1986. Pastor St. John Luth. Ch., Pryor, Okla., 1986-89; assoc. pastor Immanuel Luth. Ch., Temple, Tex., 1989—; cir. counselor Okla. dist. Luth. Ch. Mo. Synod, Pryor, 1988-89; assoc. pastoral advisor Tex. dist. Luth. Laymen's League, Temple, 1990—; pastoral advisor Cen. Tex. Luths. for Life, Temple, 1990—. Home: 820 Filly Temple TX 76504 Office: Immanuel Luth Ch 2109 W Avenue H Temple TX 76504

STRUGNELL, JOHN, theology educator; b. Barnet, Herts, Eng., May 25, 1930; s. James Archibald and Margaret Julia (MacConochie) S.; m. Cécile Pierlot, July 25, 1956; children—David H., Andrew M., Anne C., Mary Claire, Monique M. B.A., Jesus Coll. Oxford U., 1952, M.A., 1955. Epigraphist Palestine Archeol. Mus., Jerusalem, 1954-60; asst. prof. O.T. Duke U. Divinity Sch., Durham, N.C., 1960-66; prof. Christian origins Harvard U. Divinity Sch., Cambridge, Mass., 1966—. Editor in chief Discoveries in Judaean Desert, 1986-90. Am. Council Learned Socs. fellow, 1968-69, 75-76, NEH fellow Albright Inst. Jerusalem, 1981-82, Hebrew U. Inst. Advanced Studies fellow. Mem. Brit. Sch. Archeology in Jerusalem, Soc. Bibl. Lit. and Exegesis, Cath. Bibl. Assn. Roman Catholic. Office: Harvard U Div Sch 45 Francis Ave Cambridge MA 02138

STRYNKOWSKI, JOHN J., academic administrator. HEAD Sem. of the Immaculate Conception, Huntington, N.Y. Office: Sem Immaculate Conception Diocese Rockville Ctr 440 W Neck Rd Huntington NY 11743*

STUART, ALLAN REEVES, minister; b. Tampa, Fla., Jan. 24, 1929; s. Herbert John and Elizabeth Lucille (Reeves) S.; m. Rebecca Anne Hinton, Oct. 4, 1953; children: Rebecca Susan, John Russell. BA, U. Fla., 1950; BDiv, Emory U., Atlanta, 1953, MDiv, 1972; Dr.Laws, U. Sarasota (Fla.), 1987. Ordained to ministry. Pastor Meth. Ch., various locations, 1953-60, Alachua (Fla.) Meth. Ch., 1960-64; sr. pastor First United Meth. Ch., Stuart, Fla., 1964-72, Dunedin, Fla., 1972-82; founding pastor North Bay Community Ch., Clearwater, Fla., 1982—. Editor: Manual of Church Practices, 1989. Pastoral care bd. Morton Plant Hosp., Clearwater, Fla. Mem. Internat. Coun. Community Chs., Fla. Fellowship Community Chs., Acad. Parish Clergy, Fellowship of Merry Christians, Am. Assn. for Counseling and Devel., Coun. of Orgns. (pres. 1978), Kiwanis (pres. 1976-77). Democrat.

STUART, DAVID MICHAEL, minister; b. Murphy, N.C., Mar. 24, 1952; s. George Wilborn and Eva Lou (Chastain) S.; m. Helen Bernice Stuart; children: Benjamin David, Hannah Elizabeth. B of Ch. Music, Shorter Coll., 1974. Ordained to ministry Bapt. Ch., 1974. Minister of music 1st Bapt. Ch., Fairmont, Ga., 1970-71; minister of music and youth Gilmer Street Bapt. Ch., Cartersville, Ga., 1971-72; minister of music and youth 1st Bapt. Ch., Dallas, Ga., 1972-74, Jasper, Ga., 1974—. V.p. Tater Patch Players, Jasper, 1983, pres, 1984. Mem. Ga. Bapt. Ch. Music Conf. (regional dir. 1975-76, 88-90). Home: PO Box 103 Jasper GA 30143 Office: 1st Bapt Ch 553 Church St Jasper GA 30143

STUART, RICHARD THOMPSON, minister, counselor; b. Summerville, S.C., Feb. 2, 1943; s. Burton Baldwin and Katherine (Blakeslee) S. m. Ruth Emily Neubert, Dec. 27, 1969; 1 child, Elizabeth Anne. BA, Lawrence U., 1965; M in Div., Andover Newton Theol. Sch., Newton Center, Mass., 1970; MEd, U. N.H., 1973; D in Ministry, Andover-Newton Theol. Sch., 1982. Assoc. pastor United Ch. of Christ, N. Ch., Portsmouth, N.H., 1969-73; pastor Kogarah (Australia) Congl. Ch., 1973-77; assoc. pastor Congl. Ch. of Laconia (N.H.), 1977-85; jr. high sch. counselor Franklin (N.H.) Jr. Sr. High Sch., 1985-87; pvt. practice counselor Laconia, 1987—; program coordinator Geneva Pt. Conf. Ctr., Moultonboro, N.H., 1987—; bd. dirs. Lakes Region Family Services, Laconia, 1983-87, N.H. Habitat for Humanity, 1984-87; founder Kogarah Community Aid and Information Ctr., 1975, Seacoast Family Pastoral Counseling Ctr., 1976. Adv. bd. Lakes Region Domestic Violence Task Force and Shelter, Laconia, 1980; provider Emergency Foster Care. Mem. N.H. Assn. for Counseling and Devel., N.H. Assn. of United Ch. Educators (convenor 1983-84). Democrat. Avocations: wind-surfing, gardening, skiing, tennis, camping. Home: 131 Winter St Laconia NH 03246 Office: Pastoral Counselor 968 N Main St Laconia NH 03246

STUART, ROBERT FRANKLIN, priest; b. Ft. Collins, Colo., June 24, 1920. MBA, So. Meth. U., 1955; MRE, U. Dallas, 1977. Ordained priest Roman Cath. Ch. Pastoral asst. St. Francis Ch., Grapevine, Tex., 1977-85, St. Catherine's Ch., Carrollton, Tex., 1985-87, St. Phillips Ch., Lewisville, Tex., 1987-88, St. John's U., Valley View, Tex., 1988—; pres. State Tex. Deacon Assn., Ft. Worth, 1978-79. Precinct helper Rep. party, Lewisville. Maj. USAF, 1940-45. Mem. Tex. Assn. Alcohol Counselors, KC (chaplain). Home and Office: 930 Ashwood Dr Lewisville TX 75067

STUBBE, RAY WILLIAM, minister; b. Milw., Aug. 15, 1938; s. Clarence Arnold and Ruby Otillie (Mueller) S. BA, St. Olaf Coll., 1962; MDiv, Northwestern Luth. Theol. Sem., 1965; postgrad., U. Chgo., 1967. Ordained to ministry Evang. Luth. Ch. Am., 1965. Mission devel. bd. Am. missions Luth Ch. in Am., Oak Creek, Wis., 1965-66; pastor All Saints Luth Ch., Oak Creek, 1966-67; enlisted USN, 1955; commd. ensign USNR, 1963, advanced through grades to lt., comdr. chaplain corps, 1971; augmented to USN, 1971, ret., 1985; chaplain, 1967-85; ret. USN, 1985; asst. pastor Evang. Luth. Ch. of Redeemer, Milw., 1985—. Author: Inside Force Recon, 1989, Khe Sanh Chaplain, 1970, Paddles, Parachutes, Patrols, 1979, Type: Jung's Typology, 1984, Journalling, 1984, Aarugha, 1989, Valley of Decision, 1991. Chaplain Wis. Vietnam Vets., Milw., 1984—, 3d Marine Div. Assn., 1988; founder, pres. Khe Sanh Vets., Inc., 1988—. Decorated Bronze Star medal with combat V. Mem. Am. Assn. Religion, Wis. Acad. Scis., Arts and Letters, Soc. Bibl. Lit., Faith At Work. Home: 8766 Parkview Ct Wauwatosa WI 53226 Office: Redeemer Luth Church 631 N 19th St Milwaukee WI 53233 *The most powerful Words of God have always been communicated to me by the occasional people encountered in life's pathways. These are the quiet ones whose very being reflect possibilities of being the image of God we all are; living Words of God who make us know we are free, forgiven, loved, blessed with value and future; heroes, who at great risk and pain to themselves, transform negatives into positives; great, good people who empty themselves into servants and incarnate love into all human conditions. When the vision they offer becomes life's task of who to become, all of life becomes a gift of everdeepening wells which nourish everything living with the deep underground stream, which is God.*

STUBBLEFIELD, JERRY MASON, religious educator, minister; b. Paducah, Ky., May 15, 1936; s. Bobbie and Lorene (Fleming) S.; m. Joanne McCaffrey, June 28, 1957; children: Robert, Mason, Alice. BA, Belmont Coll., 1957; MA, Vanderbilt U., 1958; BD, So. Bapt. Theol. Sem., 1961, MRE, 1962, EdD, 1967. Ordained to ministry So. Bapt. Conv., 1955. Pastor Victory Bapt. Ch., Shepherdsville, Ky., 1958-65; spl. instr. religious edn. Southeastern Bapt. Sem., Wake Forest, N.C., 1965-66; prof. religion Norman Coll., Norman Park, Ga., 1966-70; min. edn. First Bapt. Ch., Greenville, S.C., 1970-75; dir. ch. community ministry Greenville Bapt. Assn., 1975-77; assoc. prof. religious edn. Golden Gate Bapt. Theol. Sem., Mill Valley, Calif., 1977-83, prof., 1983-88, J.M. Frost Sunday sch. bd. chair Christian edn., 1988—; mem. various acad. coms. Golden Gate Bapt. Theol. Sem., Mill Valley; min. edn. Tiburion (Calif.) Bapt. Ch., 1978-81; trustee Calif. Bapt. Coll., 1984-88. Editor, contbg. author: A Church Ministering to Adults, 1986; contbg. author: Christian Education Handbook, 1981; contbr. articles to religious jours. Mem. Western Bapt. Religious Edn. Assn. (pres. 1983-84), So. Bapt. Religious Edn. Assn. (pres. 1988-89), Am. Soc. Aging. Avocations: golf, running, reading, travel, sports. Home: 602 Seminary Dr Mill Valley CA 94941 Office: Golden Gate Bapt Theol Sem Strawberry Point Mill Valley CA 94941 *It is my desire to live each day at my best and enable those around to live life at their best. I hope that the world will be a better place because of the quality of life that I have lived.*

STUCKEY, DEAN VANCE, minister; b. Washington, Ind., Aug. 19, 1937; s. Russell Dean and Norma (Lydia Vance) S.; m. Sandra June Armes, Sept. 1, 1957; children: Gregory Dean, Gary Vance, Carrie Elizabeth. AB, Butler U., 1959; BD, MDiv, Garrett Theol. Sem., 1963. Ordained to ministry Meth. Ch., 1963. Pastor Grace United Meth. Ch., Gary, Ind., 1970-73, Christ United Meth. Ch., Wabash, Ind., 1973-78; sr. pastor First United Meth. Ch., Chesterton, Ind., 1978-82; dist. supt. Ft. Wayne (Ind.) Dist. United Meth. Ch., 1982-85; sr. pastor First Wayne St. United Meth. Ch., Ft. Wayne, 1985—; del. Jurisdictional Conf. United Meth. Ch., 1984, 88. Author: Think About It, 1987. Trustee De Pauw U., Greencastle, Ind., 1987—, Warren (Ind.) Meml. Home, 1991—; founding mem. YMCA, Portage, Ind., 1968. Recipient Disting. Svc. award Jaycees, Portage, 1969. Mem. Clergy United for Action. Office: First Wayne St United Meth Ch 300 E Wayne St Fort Wayne IN 46802

STUCKEY, JAMES EDWARD, lay worker; b. Burlington, Okla., Oct. 3, 1939; s. Edward Edmond and Ruth Velma (Frey) S.; m. Roberta Dunnington, Feb. 28, 1963; 1 child, Kimberly Dawn. BBA, U. Okla., 1962. Vol. treas. Ea. Heights Christian Ch., Ponca City, Okla., 1977-90; acct. Conoco Inc., Ponca City, 1965—. Bd. dirs. Camp Fire Inc., Ponca City, 1983-86, treas., 1986. Capt. USMCR, 1962-69. Home: 1612 Queens Ave Ponca City OK 74604

STUCZKO, RICHARD JULIAN, priest; b. Utica, N.Y., Apr. 22, 1929; s. John Charles and Isabelle Martha (Zdanowicz) S. Student, Niagara U.; AA, St. Andrew's Minor Sem., Rochester, N.Y., 1948; BA, St. Bernard's Major Sem., Rochester, 1950; grad., S.S. Cyril and Methodius Sem., Orchard Lake, Mich., 1954. Ordained priest Roman Catholic Ch., 1954. Chaplain N.Y. State Vets. Home, Oxford, 1969-74, Oneida County Correctional Facility, Oriskany, N.Y., 1975—; mem. priests' senate Roman Cath. Diocese Syracuse, N.Y.; bd. dirs. Clerical Fund Soc., Diocese of Syracuse; mem. Diocesan Commn. on Ecumenism. Mem. Am. Correctional Chaplains Assn., Am. Cath. Correctional Chaplains Assn., Oriskany Hist. Soc., Whitestown C. of C. (bd. dirs.). Address: 120 Dexter Ave Oriskany NY 13424

STUDEBAKER, ALDEN HENRY, minister; b. East Chicago, Ind., Feb. 19, 1957; s. Alden Henry and Cynthia Ann (Elster) S.; m. Donna Lynn Clink, May 18, 1980; children: Jennifer, Nathaniel. BA, Western Mich. U., 1980; Diploma, Unity Ministerial Sch., 1984. Ordained to ministry Assn. Unity Chs., 1984. Min. Unity Ch. of the Valley, Vacaville, Calif., 1984-85, La Crescenta, Calif., 1986—; min. Unity Ctr. El Paso, Tex., 1985-86; v.p. S.W. Unity Region, so. Calif., so. Nev., Ariz, 1988-91, exec. dir. layperson's retreat, 1988—; mem. min.'s assistance team Assn. Unity Chs., Lee's Summit, Mo., 1990—. Office: Unity Ch of the Valley 2817 Montrose Ave La Crescenta CA 91214 *The Bible reveals to us that we were all created in God's image and likeness. This is as true today as it was in the beginning. Our purpose in life is to return to an awareness of our divine origins, live lovingly, peaceably and positively, and to encourage others along the way.*

STUDER, GERALD CLYDE, minister; b. Smithville, Ohio, Jan. 31, 1927; s. Martin G. and Edna Lucille (Blough) S.; m. Marilyn Ruth Kreider, June 16, 1950; children: Jerri Lynn Studer Longacre, Maria Studer de Domenico. BA, Goshen Coll., 1947; BTh., Goshen Biblical Sem., 1949, BD, 1957, MDiv, 1971. Ordained to ministry Mennonite Ch., 1947. Pastor Smithville Mennonite Ch., 1947-61, Scottdale (Pa.) Mennonite Ch., 1961-73, Plains Mennonite Ch., Lansdale, Pa., 1973-90; conf. minister Atlantic Coast Mennonite Conf., 1990—; pres. Mennonite Youth Fellowship N.Am., 1947-50; mem. Mennonite Publ. Bd., Scottdale, 1956-59, 65-68; mem. Gen. Bd. Mennonite Ch., 1971-73. Author: Christopher Dock, 1967, After Death, What?, 1976. Mem. Hist. and Rsch. Com., Goshen, Ind., 1960-71. Mem. Internat. Soc. Bible Collectors (pres. 1988—). Home: 1260 Orchard Ln Lansdale PA 19446

STUDER, JIMMY JOE, lay worker; b. Hannibal, Mo., Aug. 20, 1941; s. Cecil Gilbert Studer; m. Rebecca Kathryn Bolin, May 24, 1964; children: Megan, Ahren. BA, Mo. Sch. Mines and Metallurgy, Rolla, 1963; MA, U. Mo., Rolla, 1970. Deacon Forest Hills (Pa.) Presbyn. Ch., 1984—; prin. engr. Westinghouse Electric Co., Pitts., 1973—. Mem. Am. Soc. for Metals. Office: Westinghouse Electric Co West Miffin PA 15122

STUDTMANN, ROBERT H., bishop. Bishop Ark.-Okla. region Evang. Luth. Ch. in am., Tulsa. Office: Evang Luth Ch in Am 4802 S Lewis Tulsa OK 74105*

STUEBBE, ROBERT, minister. V.p. Reformed Ch. in the U.S., Bakersfield, Calif. Office: Reformed Ch US 401 Cherry Hill Dr Bakersfield CA 93309*

STUEHRENBERG, PAUL FREDERICK, librarian; b. Breckenridge, Minn., Mar. 14, 1947; s. Henry Ernest Frederick and Marian Violet (Sandberg) S.; m. Suzanne Elaine Draper, June 14, 1969 (div. Apr. 1982); m. Carole Lee DeVore, Aug. 1, 1983. BA, Concordia Sr. Coll., 1968; MDiv, Concordia Sem., 1976; STM, Christ Sem., 1974; MA, U. Minn., 1978, PhD, 1988. Asst. libr. U. Minn., Mpls., 1974-82; monographs libr. Yale Divinity Libr., New Haven, 1982-91, interim div. libr., 1991—; asst. pastor Christ Meml. Luth. Ch., Plymouth, Minn., 1974-82; adj. pastor Bethesda Luth. Ch., New Haven, 1984—; sec. Luth. Student Found., Mpls., 1978-81. Contbr. articles to profl. jours. Sec. North Haven (Conn.) Libr. Bd., 1989—. Mem. Am. Theol. Libr. Assn., Soc. Bibl. Lit. Home: 280 Bayard Ave North Haven CT 06473 Office: Yale Div Libr 409 Prospect St New Haven CT 06510

STUHLMUELLER, CARROLL, Old Testament studies educator; b. Hamilton, Ohio, Apr. 2, 1923; s. William and Alma (Huesing) S. Licentiate in Sacred Theology, Cath. U., Washington, 1952; D Sacred Sci., Pontifical Bibl. Inst., Rome, 1968; DHL (hon.), St. Benedict Coll., 1969, Rosary Coll., 1987. Asst. prof. scripture Passionist Theologate, Chgo., 1954-65; assoc. prof. scripture St. Meinrad (Ind.) Sem., 1965-68; prof. Old Testament Cath. Theol. Union, Chgo., 1968—; prof. scripture St. John's U., N.Y., 1970-74. Author: Biblical Foundations for Mission, 1983, Psalms (2 vols.), 1983, Collegeville Bible Commentary Old Testament, vol. 5, 1986, Rebuilding with Hope, 1988, New Paths Through the Old Testament, 1989, Deutero-Isaiah, Trito-Isaiah, New Jerome Biblical Commentary, 1990; assoc. editor Cath. Study Bible NAB, 1987-90, Jour. Biblical Literature, 1987-92. Mem. Cath. Biblical Assn. (pres. 1978-79), Chgo. Soc. Biblical Rsch. (pres. 1982-83). Roman Catholic. Address: 5401 S Cornell Ave Chicago IL 60615 *My finest insights into biblical interpretation come from the challenges of world mission and culture as well as from sick and disabled persons. These people test the limits and force the orthodox expressions of religion to reach outwards.*

STUHR, WALTER M., seminary educator, clergyman; b. Mpls., June 4, 1932; s. Walter M. and Norma (Bodenschatz) S.; m. Barbara Jean Gordon, June 13, 1953; children—Deborah Jean, Rebecca Ann, Philip Martin. B.A., Yale U., 1954; B.D., Pacific Lutheran Sem., 1958; M.A., U. Chgo., 1965, Ph.D., 1970. Ordained to ministry United Lutheran Ch. Am. 1958. Pastor Luth. Ch. of our Redeemer, Sacramento, Calif., 1958-63; interim pastor various chs., Chgo., 1963-67; prof. ethics Pacific Luth. Theol. Sem., Berkeley, Calif., 1967—, pres., 1979-88. Mem. Richmond-Shimada Sister City Program, Calif., 1975—. Mem. Soc. Christian Ethics. Democrat. Office: Pacific Luth Theol Sem 2770 Marin Ave Berkeley CA 94708

STUMME, WAYNE CURTIS, religion educator; b. Northfield, Minn., June 28, 1929; s. Lawrence Albert and Esther Kathryn (Engelstad) S.; m. Carol D. Alden, Sept. 19, 1953; children: Mary, Ann, John, Peter, Sarah. BA in History, Wartburg Coll., 1951; BD, Wartburg Sem., Dubuque, Iowa, 1958; DD (hon.), Trinity Luth. Sem., Columbus, Ohio, 1982; STM, Wartburg Sem., Dubuque, Iowa, 1972. Ordained to ministry Evang. Luth. Ch. in Am., 1959. Pastor St. Paul's Luth. Ch., Corby, Eng., 1959-66, Waverly, Iowa, 1966-68; pastor 1st Luth. Ch., Waterloo, Iowa, 1968-70; dir. CHARIS Ecumenical Ctr., Moorhead, Minn., 1970-74; asst. dir. div. theol. edn. Am. Luth. Ch., Mpls., 1974-84; dir. Inst. for Mission in USA, Columbus, 1984—; assoc. prof. theology and mission Trinity Luth. Sem., Columbus, 1984—; chmn. United Luth. Synod Gt. Britain, 1963-66; mem. com. on studies Luth. World Ministries, 1973-84, convenor task force on Christianity and Marxism, 1980-83. Editor, author: Christians and Many Faces of Marxism, 1984, Bible and Mission, 1986, Women and Children Living in Poverty, 1989, The Experience of Hope, 1991; mem. editorial coun. Dialog, 1986—. Mem. adv. com. U.S. Civil Rights Commn., Iowa, 1969-70; chmn. religious affairs adv. bd. U. Minn., 1978-82; mem. Coalition for Justice in Maquiladora, 1991—. Grad. scholar Am. Luth. Ch., Scotland, 1958; fellow Bush Found., summer 1974. Mem. Am. Acad. Religion, Am. Soc. Missiology, Internat. Assn. for Mission Studies, Christians Assoc. for Rels. with Ea. Europe, Bread for World. Democrat. Home: 1190-F Stone Ridge Dr Columbus OH 42113 Office: Trinity Luth Sem 2199 E Main St Columbus OH 43209

STUMP, MIRIAM ELLEN, minister; b. Worcester, Mass., Nov. 16, 1928; d. Robert E. Marston and Irene Ellen (Prairie) Marston Dodd; m. Myron Eugene Stump, Aug. 6, 1949; children: Philip Alan, Paul Marston, Stephen Eugene, Timothy Jon, Lydia Ellen. BS, U. Mass., 1950; MDiv, Sch. of Theology, Claremont, 1982. Ordained deacon United Meth. Ch., 1982, elder, 1984. Chaplain David and Margaret Home, LaVerne, Calif., 1980; assoc. min. West Covina (Calif.) United Meth. Ch., 1982-84, East Whittier (Calif.) United Meth. Ch., 1984-86; min. Crescent Heights United Meth. Ch., West Hollywood, Calif., 1986-88, First United Meth. Ch., Brawley, Calif., 1988—; mem. rules com., Calif.-Pacific Conf., 1985—; mem. adv. bd. Camp Virginia, Julian, Calif., 1988—. Bd. dirs. Womanhaven, El Centro, Calif. (v.p. 1991); bd. dirs. Neighborhood House, Calexico, Calif., 1988—. Mem. Brawley Ministerial Assn. (pres. 1989—), Kiwanis. Home: 350 Willard Ave Brawley CA 92227 Office: First United Meth Ch 133 K St Brawley CA 92227

STURGEON, DAVID HAMILTON, minister; b. Columbia, S.C., June 23, 1953; s. Goodrich Raymond and Bernice Elizebeth Hamilton S. BS, Columbia Bible Coll., 1977; MDiv, Southwestern Bapt. Seminary, Ft. Worth, Tex., 1980; D of Ministry, Mid-Atlantic Seminary, Rock Hill, S.C., 1988. Mission pastor So. Bapt. Mission Bd., Roosevelt, Ariz., 1982-84; youth pastor Trinity Bapt. Ch., Globe, Ariz., 1984-85, Jackson Creek Bapt. Ch., Columbia, 1986—; chaplain S.C. Air Nat. Guard, Eastover, 1989—; youth cons. Cola (S.C.) Metro Bapt. Assn., 1991-93; single adult adv. com. S.C. Bapt. Conv., Cola, 1990—. Mem. Red Stocking Revue, Cola, 1988—; tutor Ariz. Adult Vols. in Edn., Roosevelt, 1984. Named Citizen of Yr., Town Coun., Roosevelt, 1984; recipient Achievement award Group Pubs., Charlotte, N.C., 1988. Mem. Columbia Christian Singles, Nat. Guard Assn., New Life Fitness Club. Home: 6300 Pine Hill Rd Columbia SC 29203 Office: Jackson Creek Baptist Ch 7778 Two Notch Rd Columbia SC 29203

STURGEON, KARLA SUE, lay worker; b. Marion, Ohio, May 13, 1961; d. James Neal and Ardith Louis (Montgomery) Shenefield; m. Michael Wayne Sturgeon, July 31, 1982. BA in Human Rels., Judson Coll., 1982. Youth leader United Meth. Ch., Elgin, Ill., 1980-81; organist, youth leader Am. Bapt. Ch., Westerville, Ohio, 1982-84; youth leader, dir. children's choir 1st Bapt. Ch., Sunbury, Ohio, 1987—; child care provider Sunbury, 1987—; advisor Marion Youth Assn., 1989—.

STURM, DOUGLAS EARL, religion and political science educator; b. Batavia, N.Y., Apr. 22, 1929; s. Fred William and Louise (Gillette) S.; m. Margie Jean Anderson, Sept. 13, 1953; children—Hans Martin, Rolf Anderson. A.B., Hiram Coll., 1950; D.B., U. Chgo., 1953, Ph.D., 1959; postgrad., Harvard, 1964-65. Exec. sec. Christian Action, N.Y.C., 1954-55; asst. prof. religion Bucknell U., Lewisburg, Pa., 1959-64; asso. prof. religion Bucknell U., 1964-67, asso. prof. religion and polit. sci., 1967-70, prof. religion and polit. sci., 1970—, Presdl. prof., 1974-80, dir. honors council, 1970-72; Vis. prof. Perkins Sch. Theology, summer 1963; vis. tutor Grad. Inst. in Liberal Edn., St. John's Coll., Santa Fe, summer 1972; vis. prof. social ethics Andover Newton Theol. Sch., Newton Centre, Mass., 1972-73; vis. prof. ethics and soc. U. Chgo., 1976-77. Author: Community and Alienation, 1988; cons. editor Bucknell Press, 1971-83; bd. cons. Jour. Religion, 1972-83; assoc. editor JRE Studies in Religious Ethics, 1974—; chmn. bd. dirs. Jour. Law and Religion, 1982-89; columnist Christianity and Crisis, 1983-85; contbr. articles to profl. jours., chpts. to books. Bd. dirs. Inst. Study of Human Values, 1966-67; bd. dirs. Susquehanna Valley Symphony Orch. Assn., 1977-82, pres., 1980-82. Recipient Lindback award for excellence in teaching, 1966; named Alumnus of Yr., U. Chgo. Div. Sch., 1988; fellow Am. Coun. Learned Socs., 1964-65, Soc. for Religion in Higher Edn., 1967-68, Inst. Advanced Study Religion, U. Chgo. Div. Sch., 1983-84. Mem. Am. Soc. Legal and Polit. Philosophy, Am. Polit. Sci. Assn., AAUP, Council on Religion and Law (bd. dirs. 1977—), Soc. Christian Ethics (dir. 1963-67, exec. sec. 1968-72, pres. 1980-81), Council Study Religion (exec. com. 1971-77, 80-81, vice chmn. 1974-76, chmn. 1976-77), Am. Acad. Religion, A.C.L.U., La Société Européenne de Culture. Home: 37 S Water St Lewisburg PA 17837

STURM, EPHRAIM H., rabbi; b. N.Y.C., May 5, 1924; m. Marion Schneck, Sept. 5, 1948; children: Ava, Ira, Jay, Joel. BA, Bklyn. Coll., 1944; MA, Columbia U., 1946. Ordained rabbi, 1947. Exec. v.p. Nat. Coun. of Young Israel, N.Y.C., 1948—; mem. Fedn. Ohel, Young Israel Far Rockaway, Mid-West Coun. of Young Israel. Author: (with others) The Sanctity of the Synagogue, 1959, Sunset at Midday, 1964. Trustee Meml. Found. for Jewish Culture, N.Y.C.; mem. N.Y. State Adv. Bd. for Consumer Protection, N.Y. State Kashruth Commn. Lt. col. U.S. Army; ret. Recipient Spl. award Fedn. of Jewish Philanthropies, 1985, Rabbin Club Am., 1985, Rabbinical Leadership award, 1986, also numerous citations and certs. of merit. Mem. Rabbinical Alliance, Coun. of Am., Coun. Young Israel Rabbis, Religion Adv. Coun., Commn. Human Rights, Phi Delta Kappa. Democrat. Home: 774 Empire Ave Far Rockaway NY 11691 Office: Nat Coun of Young Israel 3 W 16th St New York NY 10011

STUTTS, DAVID HUGH, religion educator, protective services official; b. Orlando, Fla., Oct. 28, 1949; s. Joseph Wayne and Mary Lee (Bayne) S.; m. Bobbie Joyce Pugh, June 20, 1976; children: Amanda Denise, Harrison Reid. BA, U. Ala., 1972; MDiv, New Orleans Bapt. Sem., 1985, ThD, 1989. Prof. N.T. and Greek Union Theol. Sem., New Orleans, 1986; probation and parole officer Bd. Pardons and Paroles, Birmingham, Ala., 1990—. Author: Introduction to Set Algebra, 1975, Introduction to Machine Logic, 1975, A Textual History of Matthew, 1989. CAP, 1973-75. Mem. Soc. Bibl. Lit., Am. Soc. Papyrologists, Assn. Internat. de Papyrologues, Fraternal Order Police. Home: 1737 Sixth Pl NW Birmingham AL 35215

STUTZMAN, ERVIN RAY, bishop; b. Kalona, Iowa, Apr. 27, 1953; s. Tobias J. and Emma L. (Nisly) S.; m. Bonita Lee Haldeman, Apr. 27, 1974; children: Emma Ruth, Daniel Tobias, Benjamin Lee. BA, Cin. Bible Coll., 1978; MA, U. Cin., 1979; postgrad., Temple U., 1991. Ordained to ministry Mennonite Ch., as bishop, 1984. Co-pastor Mennonite Christian Assembly, Cin., 1976-82; assoc. pastor Mt. Joy (Pa.) Mennonite Ch., 1983-84; assoc. dir. of home ministries Eastern Mennonite Bd. Missions, Salunga, Pa., 1982-89; bishop Landisville (Pa.) dist. Lancaster Mennonite Conf., 1984—, moderator, 1991—. Author: Welcome!, 1990; co-author: Creating Communities of the Kingdom, 1988. Home: 374 Donegal Springs Rd Mount Joy PA 17552 Office: Lancaster Mennonite Conf 2160 Lincoln Hwy E Lancaster PA 17602

STUTZMAN, L. LEE, pastor; b. Clinton, Okla., June 13, 1953; s. Clamens L. Stutzman and Viola Darlene (Waters) Bonn; m. Connie R. Stutzman, June 3, 1972; children: Elizabeth, Jonathan, Rebecca. With traveling ministry, 1972-78; founder Liberty Temple, Lima, Ohio, 1978-88, Liberty Christian Cathedral, 1988—; with nat. traveling ministry; apostle Liberty Network of Chs., Dayton, Ohio, 1986—; exec. officer Internat. Congress on the Local Ch., Washington, 1988—; Author: From the Ground Up, 1987; producer (TV show) Foundation for Faith, 1985—. Mem. Open Bible Standard Chs. Inc. Republican. Office: Liberty Christian Cathedral 1001 Beatrice Dr Dayton OH 45404 *The greatest key to Godly success: you've got to start where you're at to get where you're going.*

SUAREZ RIVERA, ADOLFO ANTONIO, archbishop; b. San Cristobal de las Casas, Mexico, Jan. 9, 1927. Ordained priest Roman Cath. Ch., 1952; bishop of Tepic, 1971-80, Tlalnepantla, 1980-83; archbishop of Monterrey, 1984—. Office: Porfirio Barba Jacob No 906,, Col Anahuac, San Nicolas L Garza,, Nuevo Leon Mexico CP 66450 also: Zuazua # 10o Sur con Ocampo, Apartado Postal 7, CP 64000 Monterrey Mexico

SUBLETT, MARVIN THOMAS, minister; b. Asheville, N.C., May 26, 1935; s. Marvin Timothy and Gladys Deliah (Poovey) S.; m. Elizabeth Beck Sink, Aug. 22, 1959; children: Katherine Elizabeth Sublett Minardi, Karol Elaine Sublett Hoffman. AB in Bus. Adminstrn., Lenoir-Rhyne Coll., Hickory, N.C., 1957; MDiv, Luth. Theol. So. Seminary, Columbia, S.C., 1960; D of Ministry, McCormick Seminary, Chgo., 1975. Ordained to ministry Evangel. Luth. Ch., 1960. Pastor Good Shepherd Luth. Ch., Hickory, 1960-64, St. Paul Luth. Ch., Tampa, Fla., 1964-71, Martin Luther Luth. Ch., Charleston, S.C., 1971-74, Trinity Luth. Ch., Jacksonville, Fla., 1974-88, Grace Luth. Ch., Ormond Beach, Fla., 1988—; exec. bd. Fla. Synod, Luth. Ch. in Am., Tampa, 1978-80, v.p. 1979-87, commn. mem. Div. for Ministry, 1988—, conf. chmn. Flagler-Volusia Country Conf., 1990—; del. to 5 nat. convs. Clergy chmn. United Way Appeal, Jacksonville, 1987; mem. Interfaith Coun., Jacksonville, 1983-88; trustee Lenoir-Rhyne Coll., 1988—, Luth. Theol. So. Seminary, 1966-69. Mem. Luth. Pastors' Assn., Halifax Area Mins. Assn. Democrat. Home: 19 Marjorie Trail Ormond Beach FL 32174 Office: Grace Lutheran Church 338 Ocean Shore Blvd Ormond Beach FL 32176 *The thought that finally led me to accept God's call to the ministry and that has sustained me all these years came from a statement made by E. Stanley Jones which stated that with God "what counts is not my ability, but my usability."*

SUDBERRY, JOHNNY RAY, pastor; b. Gadsden, Ala., Sept. 17, 1958; s. John Emment (dec.) and Kathryn (Henderson) S.; m. Remona Kay Sewell, Aug. 19, 1983. BS, Jacksonville State U., 1983; M of Divinity, New Orleans Bapt. Sem., 1986. Residential asst. The Bridge, Gadsden, Ala., 1980, drug therapist, 1980-82, asst. residential dir., 1982-84; asst. pastor Eastsied Bapt. Ch., Gadsden, 1981-84; pastor Hathorn Bapt. Ch., Columbia, Miss., 1985-86, Immanuel Bapt. Ch., Gadsden, 1987—. Bd. dirs. Christian Bros., Inc., Gadsden, 1981-82; bible sch. tchr. Eastside Bapt. Ch., Gadsden, 1980-83. Named one of Outstanding Men Am., 1985. Baptist. Avocations: tennis, basketball, reading. Home: Rt 5 Box 89W Gadsden AL 35903 Office: Immanuel Bapt Ch Rt 7 Box 690 Gadsden AL 35903

SUDBURY, JOHN DEAN, religious foundation executive, petroleum chemist; b. Natchitoches, La., July 29, 1925; s. Herbert J. and Mary Flora S.; m. Jean Elizabeth Jung, July 18, 1947; children: John Byron, James Vernon (dec.), Linda Gail. BS, U. Tex., Austin, 1943, MA, 1947, PhD, 1949. Registered profl. engr., Okla. With Conoco Inc., various locations, 1949-83; asst. to v.p. tech. Conoco Inc., N.Y.C., 1970-72; v.p. coal research Conoco Coal Devel. Co. subs. Conoco Inc., Pitts., 1972-83; pres. Eastern European Mission & Bible Found., Houston, 1983—. Author: Oil Well Corrosion, 1956; contbr. articles to profl. jours. Mem. Ponca City (Okla.) Sch. Bd., 1965-67; trustee Okla. Christian Coll., 1968—. Served with USN, 1943-45. Recipient Frank Newman Speller award Nat. Assn. Corrosion Engrs., 1967. Mem. Am. Chem. Soc., N.Y. Acad. Scis., AAAS, Sigma Xi. Republican. Mem. Ch. of Christ. Club: Woodlands Country (Tex.). Patentee in energy field. Home: 42 Cascade Springs Pl The Woodlands TX 77381 Office: PO Box 90755 Houston TX 77290

SUDDARTH, DEBORAH K., superintendent; b. Beech Grove, Ind., Jan. 18, 1951; d. William A. and Madelon M. (Kershner) S. BA, Coll. St. Francis, Joliet, Ill., 1976; MA, Ind. State U., 1984. Prin. St. Philip Neri, Indpls., 1984-87, St. Mary Sch., Park Forest, Ill., 1987-89, St. Charles Borromeo Sch., Ft. Wayne, Ind., 1989-91; assoc. supt. Cath. schs. Diocese of Ft. Wayne-South Bend, 1991—; mem. Franciscan Edn. Adv. Bd., Mokena, Ill., 1988—, chairperson, 1989-91. Mem. ASCD, Nat. Cath. Edn. Assn., Nat. Assn. Elem. Sch. Prins., Ind. Non-Pub. Schs. Assn., Allen County Non-Pub. Schs. Assn., Orton-Gillingham Assn., Diocesan Prins. Coun., Ft. Wayne Prin. Assn. (vice chairperson 1990-91). Avocation: music. Home: 4904 Trier Rd Fort Wayne IN 46815-6050 Office: Cathedral Ctr PO Box 390 Fort Wayne IN 46801

SUDOL, SISTER BARBARA, nun; b. Bklyn., Aug. 21, 1942; d. George Anthony and Angela Nellie (Ozustowicz) S. BA, Holy Family Coll., Phila., 1971; MA, So. Conn. State U., 1977, Fairfield U., 1989. Joined Holy Family of Nazareth, 1960; cert. tchr., adminstr., Conn. Prin. St. Jude Elem. Sch., Monroe, Conn., 1985-91. Contbr. articles to profl. jours. Mem. Nat. Cath. Edn. Assn. Home: 1428 Monroe Turnpike Monroe CT 06468 Office: St Jude Elem Sch 707 Monroe Turnpike Monroe CT 06468

SUELTENFUSS, SISTER ELIZABETH ANNE, university president; b. San Antonio, Apr. 14, 1921; d. Edward L. and Elizabeth (Amrein) S. B.A. in Botany and Zoology, Our Lady of Lake Coll., San Antonio, 1944; M.S. in Biology, U. Notre Dame, 1961, Ph.D., 1963. Joined Sisters of Divine Providence, Roman Catholic Ch., 1939; tchr. high schs. Okla. and La., 1942-49; mem. summer faculty Our Lady of Lake U. (formerly Coll.), 1941-49, mem. full-time faculty, 1949-59, chmn. biology dept., 1963-73, pres., 1978—; mem. adminstrv. staff to superior gen. Congregation Divine Providence, 1973-77. Author articles in field. Bd. dirs. Am. Cancer Soc., San Antonio, Avance, Mind Sci. Found., YWCA, Sta. KLRN Pub. TV, S.W. Rsch. Found., I Have a Dream Found., Inst. Ednl. Leadership, Trim and Swim, San Antonio Pub. Libr., Communities in Schs.; chmn. edn. com. Pvt. Sector United San Antonio; mem. bd. visitors Air Force Inst. Tech. Recipient Achievement and Leadership awards U. Notre Dame, 1979, Svc. to Community award, 1991, Headliner award Women in Communications, 1980, Good Neighbor award NCCJ, 1982, Today's Woman award San Antonio Light, 1982, Outstanding Women award San Antonio Express-News, 1983; named to San Antonio Women's Hall of Fame, 1985. Mem. AAAS, AAUP, AAUW, Am. Soc. Microbiology, Nat. Assn. Women Religious, Tex. Acad. Sci., San Antonio 100 and Tex. Women's Forum, Hispanic Assn. Colls. and Univs. (exec. com.), Greater San Antonio C. of C. (vice chmn.), San Antonio Coun. Pres. (pres.), Zonta. Home and Office: Our Lady of the Lake U 411 SW 24th St San Antonio TX 78207-4666

SUENENS, LEO JOSEPH CARDINAL, former archbishop; b. Brussels, Belgium, July 16, 1904; s. Jean and Jeanne Janssens; student Coll. Ste. Marie, Brussels, 1915-21; Ph.D., Gregorian U., Rome, 1924, B.C.L., 1927, S.T.D., 1929. Ordained priest Roman Cath. Ch., 1927; aux. bishop, vicar-gen. Archdiocese of Malines, 1945-61; consecrated bishop, 1945; archbishop of Malines-Brussels, primate Belgium, 1961-79, ret., 1979; elevated to cardinal, 1962; moderator Vatican Council, 1962-65; chancellor Louvain U.; pres. Belgian Bishops Conf., 1966—; mem. Pontifical Commn. for Revision Code of Canon Law. Recipient Templeton Found. prize in religion, 1976. Author: Theology of the Legion of Mary, 1954, The Right View of Moral Rearmament, 1954, The Gospel to Every Creature, 1957, Mary, the Mother of God, 1959, The Nun in the World, 1962, Love and Control, 1962, Christian Life Day by Day, 1964, Co-responsability in the Church, 1968, A New Pentacost?, 1975, Ecumenism and Charismatic Renewal and Social Action, 1979, Renewal and The Powers of Darkness, 1982, Nature and Grace in Vital Unity, 1986, A Controversial Phenomenon: Resting in Spirit, 1987, Spiritual Journey, 1990; (with Archbishop M. Ramsey) The Future of the Christian Church, 1970; (with D. H. Camara) Charismatic Renewal and Social Action, 1979. Address: Blvd de Smet de Nayer 570, 1020 Brussels Belgium

SUFFERN, EDWARD WILLIAM, minister; b. Ridgewood, N.J., Nov. 20, 1957; s. Richard Munn and Eugenia Maud (Gibson) S.; m. Lois Gail Kooistra, Aug. 10, 1985. BS, Grove City Coll., 1979; MDiv, New Brunswick (N.J.) Sem., 1987. Ordained to ministry Ref. Ch. in Am., 1987. Assoc. pastor 6th Ref. Ch., North Haledon, N.J., 1986—. Mem. attending clergy Wayne Gen. Hosp.; pres. bd. dirs. Dawn Treader Sch., Paterson, N.J., 1991—. Office: 6th Ref Ch 21 Pleasant View Dr North Haledon NJ 07508

SUFRIN, JODI LEE, cantor; b. N.Y.C., Mar. 14, 1955; d. Mel Harvy and Malcah (Goldenberg) S.; m. Roy Bennett Einhorn, Aug. 23, 1980; children: Laura, Jessica. BA in French and Italian, Univ. Toronto, 1976; BA in Sacred Music, Hebrew Union Coll., 1983. Cantor Temple Beth Elohim, Wellesley, Mass., 1983—. Office: Temple Beth Elohim 10 Bethel Rd Wellesley MA 02181

SUGDEN, RICHARD LEE, pastor; b. Compton, Calif., Apr. 13, 1959; s. L. Fred Sugden and Nancy Jane (Motherwell) Coulter; m. Rebecca Lynn Travis, June 1981; children: Richard Lee II, Ryan Leon, Rachel Lynn. BA, Pensacola (Fla.) Christian Coll., 1981. Ordained pastor, 1985. Assoc. pastor Chippewa Lake Bapt. Ch., Medina, Ohio, 1981-84; dir., evangelist Victory Acres Christian Camp, Warren, Ohio, 1985; asst. pastor Bible Bapt. Temple, Campbell, Ohio, 1985—; del. pastors' sch. 1st Bapt. Ch., Hammond, Ind., 1982—. Author: Philippians on Your Level, 1990, James on Your Level, 1991, I Timothy On Your Level, 1991. Mem. Christian Law Assn., Buckeye Ind. Bapt. Fellowship. Republican. Avocations: gardening, home improvements. Home: 3208 Powersway Youngstown OH 44502 Office: Bible Bapt Temple 230 Lettie Ave Campbell OH 44405 *Purpose is found in life when you are involved in the work of God. Jesus said, "This is the work of God, that ye believe on Him whom He hath sent." Trusting and following Jesus is what life is all about.*

SUGGS, MARION JACK, minister, college dean; b. Electra, Tex., June 5, 1924; s. Claude Frank and Lottie Maye (Gibson) S.; m. Ruth Barge, Nov. 13, 1943; children: Adena Ruth Suggs Beck, James Robert, David Nathan. BA, U. Tex., 1946; BD, Tex. Christian U., 1949; PhD, Duke U., 1954. Ordained to ministry Christian Ch. (Disciples of Christ), 1948. Min. First Christian Ch., Gladewater, Tex., 1948-50, Wendell Christian Ch., N.C., 1950-52; asst. prof. Brite Div. Sch. Tex. Christian U., Ft. Worth, 1952-54, assoc. prof., 1954-56, prof., 1956-89, dean Brite Div. Sch., 1977-89; emeritus dean and prof. Tex. Christian U., Fort Worth, 1989—, univ. lectr., 1961; mem. com. on ministry Christian Ch. in the Southwest, 1976-89; chmn. coun. on theol. edn. Div. Higher Edn., 1987-88; mem. ch. fin. coun., 1985-89, also bd. dirs.; mem. gen. bd. Christian Ch. (Disciples of Christ), 1986-87; lectr. Lexington Theol. Sem., 1966, S.W. Mo. State U., 1977; mem. Disciples-Roman Cath. Internat. Bilateral Conv., 1978-87. Author: The Layman Reads His Bible, 1957, The Gospel Story, 1960 (Adult Book of Yr. Christian Lit. Com. 1960), Wisdom, Christology and Law in Matthew's Gospel, 1970 (Christian Rsch. Found. award 1967); also articles ; co-editor: Studies in the History and Text of the New Testament, 1967, New English Bible: Oxford Study Edition, 1976 (Religious Book award 1977). Bd. dirs. Granville T. Walker Found. G.H. Kearns fellow, 1951, Am. Coun. Learned Socs. fellow, 1963-64, Assn. Theol. Schs. fellow, 1963-64; recipient Disting. Alumnus award Tex. Christian U., 1973. Mem. Soc. Bibl. Lit., Studiorum Novi Testamenti Societas, Internat. Greek N.T. Project, Ridglea Country Club, Phi Beta Kappa, Alpha Kappa Delta, Pi Gamma Mu, Theta Phi. Democrat. Home: 5605 Winifred Dr Fort Worth TX 76133

SUH, PAUL MANSOO, missionary, educator; b. Seoul, Korea, Apr. 5, 1939; s. Kwang-Ok and Sang-Ok, Seung) S.; married. BA, Dongkook U., Republic of Korea, 1962; MDiv, Chongshin Theology Seminary, Republic of Korea, 1967; MA, Dongkook U., 1970; PhD, Immanuel U., 1986. Ordained to ministry Presbyn. Ch., 1970. Mgr. Presbyn. Theol. Rev., Seoul, 1966-69; instr. Seoul Theol. Sem., 1966-69, G.P.A. Theol. Sem., Seoul, 1967-69; editor Christian Times, Seoul, 1968-69; exec. sec. G.P.A. Ch. in Korea, Seoul, 1969-70; dir. Dong-Ak Linguistic and Lit. Soc., Seoul, 1970—; pastor G.P.A. Ch. in Korea, Seoul, 1970—; missionary The 55th G.P.A. Ch. in Korea, Taegu, 1970; dir. Korea Mission in Indonesia, Jakarta, 1971—, supr. Korean Ch. Sch., Jakarta, 1974—; chmn. Hallelujah Inter-Service Inc., Jakarta, 1985—; coordinator Christian U. Indonesia, Ambon, 1987—. Editor: (book) Introduction to Korean Language and Literature, 1967; author: Study of Songs of Songgang, 1970, Christian Education of Indonesia, 1987. Recipient Presdl. medal Republic of Korea, 1977. Avocation: golf. Office: Korea Mission in Indonesia, PO Box 2355 Jkt, Jakarta 10001, Indonesia

SUHOR, MARY LOU, religious magazine editor, lay worker; b. New Orleans, July 11, 1929; d. Anthony Bernard and Marie Odette (Porte) S. BS in Edn. and Journalism, Loyola U., New Orleans, 1949; MA in Sociology, Cath. U. Am., 1961. Staff writer Cath. Action of South, New Orleans, 1949-52; instr. journalism and pub. rels. Loyola U., 1952-55; asst. editor North Cen. La. Register, Alexandria, 1956-58; staff editor The Queen's Work, Cath. Pub. House, St. Louis, 1960-63; staff asst. Fgn. Visitors Office, Nat. Cath. Welfare Conf., Washington, 1963-65; adminstrv. asst. Latin Am. div. U.S. Cath. Conf., Washington, 1966-73; coord. Cuba Resource Ctr., N.Y.C., 1973-76; mng. editor The Witness mag., Ambler, Pa., 1976-80, editor, 1981-91; ret., 1991. Co-editor: Struggling with the System Probing Alternatives, 1979; editor: (with others) Vol. I—Christian Commitment for the '80s: Must We Choose Sides, Vol. I, 1979, Vol. II— Which Side Are We On?, 1980; mem. editorial bd.: My Story's On: Ordinary Women Extraordinary Lives, 1985; contbr. articles to Ency. of Am. Left and numerous articles to profl. jours. Bd. dirs. Montgomery County Ctr. for Peace and Justice, Ambler, 1985-90; cons. nationwide women's com. Am. Friends Svc. Com., 1985-90; mem. info. com. Nat. Coun. Chs., 1987-90. Recipient Best Series in Pub. Interest award Cath. Press Assn., 1957, Best Feature Story award, 1958; Polly Bond awards Episcopal Communicators, 1985, 87, 88-91. Mem. Associated Ch. Press (Best Feature Story award 1985, 89, Best News Story award 1986), Women's Inst. for Freedom of Press, Latin Am. Studies Assn. Democrat. Home: 3443 Esplanade Apt 616 New Orleans LA 70119

SUITER, NORMA JEAN, church official; b. Houston County, Tenn., Oct. 17, 1936; d. Roy Pascal and Emma Pearl (Provo) Mobley; m. Lacy Edward Suiter, Mar. 15, 1958; 1 child, Melissa Elaine Suiter Gregory. Student U. Tenn., Tenn. State U., 1970-82. Ins. clk. Royal Globe Ins. Co., Nashville, 1955-57; sec. Interbd. Com. on Missionary Edn., The Methodist Ch., Nashville, 1957-66, adminstrv. asst. to gen. sec. Div. of the Local Ch., Bd. Edn., 1966-76, rec. sec. Bd. Discipleship, 1972-73, exec. dir. Gen. Bus. Services, Bd. Discipleship, 1976—, cons. affiliate mem. United Methodist Interagy. Task Force on Telecommunications Gen. Council on Fin. and Adminstrn. subcom. on Use of Personal Computer in Local Ch. Chairperson adminstrv. bd., mem. council on ministries fin. com. Donelson Heights United Meth. Ch. Mem. Am. Mgmt. Assn. Home: 2728 Pennington Bend Rd Nashville TN 37214 Office: United Meth Bd of Discipleship PO Box 840 Nashville TN 37202

SULKIN, HOWARD ALLEN, college president; b. Detroit, Aug. 19, 1941; s. Lewis and Vivian P. (Mandel) S.; m. Constance Annette Adler, Aug. 4, 1963; children—Seth R., Randall K. PhB, Wayne State U., 1963; MBA, U. Chgo., 1965, PhD, 1969; LHD (hon.), De Paul U., 1990. Dir. program rsch., indsl. rels. ctr. U. Chgo., 1964-72; dean Sch. for New Learning, De Paul U., Chgo., 1972-77; v.p. De Paul U., Chgo., 1977-84; pres. Spertus Coll. Judaica, Chgo., 1984—; St. Paul's vis. prof. Rikkyo U., Tokyo, 1970—; cons., evaluator North Central Assn., Chgo., 1975—. Contbr. articles to profl. jours. Sec.-treas. Grant Park Cultural and Ednl. Community, Chgo., 1984—; bd. dirs. Chgo. Sinai Congregation, 1972—, pres., 1980-83; bd. dirs. S.E. Chgo. Commn., 1980—, United Way, 1984—, Crusade of Mercy United Way, 1990—; bd. dirs., mem. exec. com. World Parliament of Religion, 1989—. Mem. Adult Edn. Assn. U.S.A., Acad. Internat. Bus. Club: Cliff Dwellers (Chgo.). Office: Spertus Coll Judaica 618 S Michigan Ave Chicago IL 60605

SULLENDER, RICHARD JOHN, pastor; b. Ventura, Calif., June 29, 1952; s. John L. and Melba Jean (Tucker) S.; m. Stephanie Marlene Wyrick, Dec. 13, 1980; children: Taylor, Deanna, Ethan. BA, Biola U., 1976; MDiv, Cen. Bapt. Theol. Sem., 1980. Ordained to ministry Am. Bapt. Chs. in U.S.A., 1980. Assoc. pastor Community Bapt. Ch., Frazier Park, Calif., 1980-81, Judson Bapt. Ch., San Bernardino, Calif., 1981-85; pastor 1st Bapt. Ch., Trinidad, Colo., 1985-88, Castleford, Idaho, 1988—. Natural helpers trainer Castleford High Sch., 1991. Mem. West End Ministerial Assn. (pres. 1991), Castleford Men's Club. Home and Office: PO Box 660 Castleford ID 83321

SULLINGER, WILLIAM STANCIL, religious administrator; b. Rockford, Ill., Nov. 12, 1954; s. William Arvil and Helen (Jenkins) S.; m. Kima Ann Markwell, June 21, 1980; children: Leeann Michelle, John Markwell. BA in Ch. Recreation, SW Bapt. U., Bolivar, Mo., 1976; MRE, Southwestern Theol. Sem, Ft. Worth, 1980. Asst. minister of recreation Briarlake Bapt. Ch., Decatur, Ga., 1976-78; minister of youth and recreation First Bapt. Ch., Bolivar, Mo., 1981-84; minister of recreation Memorial Bapt. Ch., Baytown, Tex., 1984—; trustee Buckner Benevolences, Bapt. Gen. Conv. Tex. Bd. dirs. Bay Area Rehab. Ctr. Fellow Christian Recreators (pres. 1981-83); mem. Tex. Recreation and Parks Soc., Fellowship of Christian Athletes. Lodge: Kiwanis. Avocations: jogging, swimming, tennis, biking. Home: 3505 Knight Ln Baytown TX 77521 Office: Meml Bapt Ch 600 W Sterling Baytown TX 77520

SULLIVAN, BRUCE M., religion educator; b. Tyler, Tex., Apr. 16, 1951; s. Bruce M. and Betty Stell Sullivan; m. Patricia Wong Hall, May 16, 1987. BA, Trinity U., San Antonio, 1973, MA, 1975; PhD, U. Chgo., 1984. Prof. No. Ariz. U., Flagstaff, 1986—. Author: Krsna Dvaipayana Vyasa and the Mahabharata, 1990; contbr. articles to profl. jours. Fellow Am. Inst. Indian Studies, Poona, India, 1979-80. Mem. Am. Acad. Religion, Am. Oriental Soc., Assn. for Asian Studies.. Office: No Ariz U Box 6031 Flagstaff AZ 86011

SULLIVAN, DONALD, college president; b. Bklyn., Oct. 22, 1930; s. John T. and Catherine (Lane) S. B.S., Fordham U.; M.A., N.Y. U.; Ph.D., St. John's U.; LittD, St. Francis Coll., 1979. Former asst. prof., dean students St. Francis Coll., Bklyn.; now pres. St. Francis Coll.; mem. Commn. Ind. Colls. and Univs.; bd. dirs. Ridgewood Savs. Bank. Trustee Helen Keller Svcs. for the Blind. Mem. C. of C. (dir.), Downtown Bklyn. Dirs. Assn. (bd. dirs.). Clubs: Brooklyn. Office: St Francis Coll 180 Remsen St Brooklyn NY 11201

SULLIVAN, HERBERT PATRICK, educator, dean; b. Detroit, May 27, 1932; s. Herbert Luke and Gertrude Lennie (Hosking) S.; m. Joyce Ann Robinson, June 24, 1960; children—Bridget Mary Magdalene, Siobhan Marie Clare. Student, Highland Park (Mich.) Coll., 1949-50, N.Mex. Highlands U., 1950-51; B.D., U. Chgo., 1956; Ph.D., U. Durham (Eng.), 1960; DD (hon.), U. Canterbury (Eng.), 1987; LittD (hon.), U. Bombay, 1989. Research asst. Indsl. Relations Center, U. Chgo., 1951-54; research scholar Sch. Oriental Studies, U. Durham, 1956-60; instr. religion Duke U., 1960-62, asst. prof., 1962-64, asso. prof., 1964-70; prof. Vassar Coll., 1970-89, dean coll., 1978-89. Contbr. to: Ency. Brit; contbr. chpts. to books and articles to profl. jours. Fulbright-Hays fellow, 1965-66. Fellow Royal Asiatic Soc.; mem. Am. Oriental Soc., Am. Soc. Study of Religion, Internat. Congress Orientalists, Internat. Assn. History of Religions. Home: 1400 Northwood Rd Austin TX 78703

SULLIVAN, JAMES E., religious center administrator, priest; b. N.Y.C., Aug. 10, 1920; s. Patrick J. and Mary G. (Coughlan) S. BA, Immaculate Conception Sem., Huntington, N.Y., 1942; MS, Iona Coll., 1966. Parish priest Our Lady of Angels Ch., Nativity Ch., St. Marks Ch., Bklyn., 1946-66; dir. Religious Consultation Ctr., Bayside, N.Y., 1966—. Author: My Meditation on the Gospel, 1962, My Meditation on St. Paul, 1967, Journey to Freedom-Path to Self Esteem, 1987. Named Counselor of Yr. Iona Coll., 1986. Mem. APA, AACD. Home: 14-51 143d St Whitestone NY 11357 Office: Religious Consultation Ctr 5301 206th St Bayside NY 11364

SULLIVAN, JAMES LENOX, clergyman; b. Silver Creek, Miss., Mar. 12, 1910; s. James Washington and Mary Ellen (Dampeer) S.; m. Velma Scott, Oct. 22, 1935; children: Mary Beth (Mrs. Bob R. Taylor), Martha Lynn (Mrs. James M. Porch, Jr.), James David. B.A., Miss. Coll., 1932, D.D., 1948; Th.M., So. Bapt. Theol. Sem., 1935. Ordained to ministry of Baptist Ch., 1930; pastor Baptist Ch., Boston, Ky., 1932-33, Beaver Dam, Ky., 1933-38, Ripley, Tenn., 1938-40, Clinton, Miss., 1940-42; pastor First Bapt. Ch., Brookhaven, Miss., 1942-46, Belmont Heights, Nashville, 1946-50, Abilene, Tex., 1950-53; exec. sec., treas. Bapt. Sunday Sch. Bd., Nashville, 1953-73; pres. Bapt. Sunday Sch. Bd., 1973-75; exec. sec. Broadman Press, 1953-75, Convention Press, 1955-75; pres. So. Bapt. Conv., 1977. Author: Your Life and Your Church, 1950, John's Witness of Jesus, Memos for Christian Living, Reach Out, Rope of Sand with Strength of Steel, God Is My Record, Baptist Polity As I See It, Southern Baptist Polity at Work in a Church; also articles and manuals. Trustee Union U., Cumberland U., So. Bapt. Theol. Sem., Hardin-Simmons U., Midstate (Tenn.) Bapt. Hosp., Hendrick Meml. Hosp., Tex. Recipient E.Y. Mullins Denominational Service award, 1973; named Miss. Bapt. Clergyman of Century. Mem. Baptist World Alliance (exec. com. 1953-80, v.p. 1975-80). Clubs: Rotary (Ripley, Tenn.); Lions (Brookhaven, Miss.); Kiwanis (Abilene, Tex.).

SULLIVAN, JAMES STEPHEN, bishop; b. Kalamazoo, July 23, 1929; s. Stephen James and Dorothy Marie (Bernier) S. Student, St. Joseph Sem.; BA, Sacred Heart Sem.; postgrad., St. John Provincial Sem. Ordained priest, Roman Cath. Ch., 1955, consecrated bishop, 1972. Assoc. pastor St. Luke Ch., Flint, Mich., 1955-58; assoc. pastor St. Mary Cathedral, Lansing, Mich., 1958-60, sec. to bishop, 1960-61; assoc. pastor St. Joseph (Mich.) Ch., 1961-65, sec. to bishop, 1965-69; assoc. pastor Lansing, 1965, vice chancellor, 1969-72; aux. bishop, vicar gen. Diocese of Lansing, 1972-85, diocesan consultor, 1971-85; bishop Fargo, N.D., 1985—. Mem. Nat. Conf. Cath. Bishops (bishop's liturgical commn.). Office: Bishop's House 608 Broadway PO Box 1750 Fargo ND 58107

SULLIVAN, JOHN JOSEPH, bishop; b. Horton, Kans., July 5, 1920; s. Walter P. and Mary (Berney) S. Student, Kenrick Sem., St. Louis, 1941-44. Ordained priest Roman Catholic Ch., 1944; parish priest Archdiocese of Oklahoma City, 1944-61; nat. dir. extension lay vols. Extension Soc., Chgo., 1961-68; parish priest Tulsa, 1968-72; bishop Diocese of Grand Island, Nebr., 1972-77, of Kansas City-St. Joseph, Mo., 1977—. Vice pres. Extension Soc., Chgo. Office: Chancery Office PO Box 419037 Kansas City MO 64141

SULLIVAN, JOSEPH M., bishop; b. Bklyn., Mar. 23, 1930. Ed. Immaculate Conception Sem., Huntington, N.Y., also, Fordham U. Ordained priest Roman Catholic Ch., 1956; consecrated titular bishop of Suliana and aux. bishop of Bklyn., 1980—. Office: Diocese of Bklyn 256 Clinton Ave Brooklyn NY 11205

SULLIVAN, JOSEPH R., school system administrator. Supt. schs. Diocese of Marquette, Mich. Office: Office Supt Schs PO Box 280 Marquette MI 49855*

SULLIVAN, SISTER KATHLEEN, academic administrator. Head Dominican Coll. of Blauvelt, Orangeburg, N.Y. Office: Dominican Coll Blauvelt Western Hwy Orangeburg NY 10962*

SULLIVAN, LEON HOWARD, clergyman; b. Charleston, W.Va., Oct. 16, 1922; m. Grace Banks, Aug. 1945; children—Howard, Julie, Hope. B.A., W.Va. State U., 1943, H.H.D. (hon.), 1956; student, Union Theol. Sem., N.Y.C., 1943-45; M.A. in Religion, Columbia U., 1947; D.D. (hon.), Va. Union U., 1956, Dartmouth Coll., 1968, Princeton U., 1969, Yale U., 1971; D.H.L. (hon.), Del. State Coll., 1966; D.Social Scis. (hon.), Villanova U., 1968; LL.D. (hon.), Beaver Coll., 1967, Swarthmore Coll., 1968, Bowdoin Coll., 1968, Denison U., 1968, Gannon Coll., 1969, Temple U., 1969; Ed.D. (hon.), Judson Coll., 1967. Ordained to ministry Bapt. Ch., 1941. Pastor Zion Bapt. Ch., Phila., 1950-88, now pastor emeritus; founder, chmn. bd. Zion Home for Ret., 1960—, Opportunities Industrialization Ctrs. Am., 1964—, Zion Investment Assocs., Inc., Progress Aerospace Inc.; dir. Girard Bank Phila., Gen. Motors Corp. Pres. Internat. Found. for Edn. and Self-Help, 1984—. Named One of Ten Outstanding Young Men Am., U.S. Jr. C. of C., 1955; One of 100 Outstanding Young Men Am., Life mag., 1963; recipient Freedom Found. award, 1960; Russwurm award Nat. Pubs. Assn., 1963; Edwin T. Dalhberg award Am. Bapt. Conv., 1968; Am. Exemplar medal, 1969; Phila. Book award; Phila. Fellowship Commn. award.

SULLIVAN, ROGER WILLIAM, minister; b. Baton Rouge, Oct. 1, 1947; s. Ezra L. Sullivan and Ada (Hughes) Chandler; m. Shirley Ann Gill, Aug. 29, 1970; children: Leslie, Ashley, Joy. BA, La. State U., 1970; BS, N.E. La. U., 1972; MDiv, New Orleans Bapt. Theol. Sem., 1980, ThD, 1986. Ordained to ministry So. Bapt. Conv., 1974. Youth dir. Vancleave (Miss.) Bapt. Ch., 1973-74; interim youth dir. Amite Bapt. Ch., Denham Springs, La., 1974; asst. pastor Porter Meml. Bapt. Ch., Lexington, Ky., 1975-78; interim pastor Thomas Bapt. Ch., Pine, La., 1980; pastor Bluff Creek Bapt. Ch., Clinton, La., 1980-91, East Leesville (La.) Bapt. Ch., 1991—; exec. bd. La. Bapt. Conv., Alexandria, La., 1988-91, chmn. oper. com., 1991. Adv. com. La. Moral & Civic Found., Baton Rouge, 1988—, coun. on aging, Clinton, La., 1990-91. Office: East Leesville Bapt Ch PO Box 1511 Leesville LA 71446

SULLIVAN, STEVE DWAYNE, music minister; b. Waco, Tex., Feb. 19, 1963; s. Dewey Dwayne and Carolyn Faye (Jones) S.; m. Karrie Leigh DePriest, May 31, 1985; 1 child, Larry Dwayne. B in Music Edn., Midwestern State U., 1985. Min. of music 1st Bapt. Ch., Knox City, Tex., 1985-86, Trinity Bapt. Ch., Wichita Falls, Tex., 1987-89; min. music, youth, sr. adults 1st Bapt. Ch., Coleman, Tex., 1989—; associational music dir. Coleman Assn., 1990—. Mem. Singing Men West Tex. Home: 1001 Commercial Coleman TX 76834 Office: 1st Bapt Ch 200 E College Coleman TX 76834

SULLIVAN, WALTER FRANCIS, bishop; b. Washington, June 10, 1928; s. Walter Francis and Catherine Jeanette (Vanderloo) S. B.A., St. Mary's Sem. U., Balt., 1947; S.T.L., St. Mary's Sem. U., 1953; J.C.L., Catholic U. Am., 1960. Ordained priest Roman Catholic Ch., 1953; asst. pastor St. Andrews Ch., Roanoke St. Mary's, Star of Sea, Ft. Monroe, 1956-58; sec. Diocesan Tribunal, 1960-65; chancellor Diocese of Richmond, Va., from 1965; rector Sacred Heart Cathedral, Richmond, from 1967; ordained aux. bishop of Richmond, 1970, bishop of Richmond, 1974—. Office: Chancery Office 811 Cathedral Pl Ste B Richmond VA 23220

SULLIVAN, WILLIAM JAMES, university president; b. Freeport, Ill., Dec. 20, 1930; s. Arlend Eugene and Bessie (Burton) S. B.A. in Philosophy, St. Louis U., 1954, M.A. in Philosophy, 1956, Ph.L., 1956; S.T.L., Faculté de Theologie, Lyons, France, 1962; M.A., Yale U., 1966, M.Phil. in Religious Studies, 1967, Ph.D. in Religious Studies, 1971; D.D. (hon.), Concordia Sem. in Exile, 1977. Joined S.J., Roman Cath. Ch. Tchr. classical lang. Creighton Prep. Sch., 1955-58; asst. prof. theology Marquette U., 1967-71; dean Sch. Div., St. Louis U., 1971-75; provost Seattle U., 1975-76, pres., 1976—; bd. dirs. Internat. Fedn. Catholic Univs., 1978-88, Maryville Coll., 1972-75, Am. Council Edn., 1978-81, U. San Francisco, 1976-84; founder, bd. dirs. Wash. Student Loan Guaranty Assn.; trustee Carnegie Found. Advancement of Teaching, 1985—; mem. Wash. State Higher Edn. Facilities Authority, 1984—, Wash. State Math. Coalition, co-chair with Gov. Gardner, 1990—, Wash. State Coalition for Student Svc., 1990—; bd. dirs. U.S. Bank of Wash. Contbr. articles on theology, edn. and cultural topics to profl. jours., popular publs. Bd. dirs. World Without War Council, Seattle, 1978-81; bd. dirs. Seattle United Way, 1979-81, Creighton U., 1982-86, Loyola U. Chgo., 1983-87; chmn. host com. 1990 Goodwill Games, 1986-90. Recipient Edmund Campion award Campion High Sch., 1970; Pope John XXIII award Viterbo Coll., 1979; Brotherhood award NCCJ, 1981; Torch of Liberty award Anti-Defamation League, B'nai Brith; named Seattle First Citizen, 1990. Mem. Assn. Cath. Colls. and Univs. (bd. dirs. 1986—), Nat. Assn. Ind. Colls. and Univs. (bd. dirs. 1983-86), Assn. Jesuit Colls. and

Univs. (bd. dirs. 1986—), Wash. Friends Higher Edn., Ind. Colls. Wash., Seattle C. of C. (dir. 1979-82, 88—). Catholic. Clubs: Rainier, Seattle Yacht, Columbia Tower (bd. dirs.), University (Seattle). Lodge: Rotary (Seattle). Home and Office: Seattle U Broadway and Madison Seattle WA 98122

SULYK, STEPHEN, archbishop; b. Balnycia, Western Ukraine, Oct. 2, 1924; s. Michael and Mary (Denys) S. Student, Ukrainian Cath. Sem. of Holy Spirit, Fed. Republic Germany, 1945-48, St. Josaphat's Sem., 1948-52; Licentia in Sacred Theology, Cath. U. Am., 1952. Ordained priest Ukrainian Cath. Ch., 1952. Assoc. pastor Omaha, 1952, Bklyn., 1953, Minersville, Pa., 1954, Youngstown, Ohio, 1955; pastor Ch. Sts. Peter and Paul, Phoenixville, Pa., 1955, St. Michael's Ch., Frackville, Pa., 1957-61, Assumption of Blessed Virgin Mary Ch., Perth Amboy, N.J., 1962-81; sec. Archeparchy Chancery, 1956-57; adminstr. St. Nicholas, Phila., 1961; archbishop Met. of Ukraine-Rite Catholics of Archeparchy, Phila., 1981—; vice chmn. Priests Senate, 1977-78; bd. dirs. Diocesan Adminstrn., 1972-79; pres. Ascension Manor, Inc.; archbishop Ukranian Rite Caths. Archeparchy Phila., Met. Ukranian-Rite Caths. U.S.A.; chmn. Priest's Senate; chmn. ad-hoc inter-rite com. Nat. Cath. Conf. Bishops/U.S. Cath. Conf., 1991. Mem. Providence Assn. Am. (Supreme Protector), Coll. Bishops of Roman Cath. Ch., Presidium of Synod of Ukranian Cath. Bishops (treas.). Office: 827 N Franklin St Philadelphia PA 19123

SULYOK, PETER ARPAD, minister; b. North Conway, N.H., May 23, 1955; s. Kalman Laszlo and Catherine (Hagerman) S.; m. Jeannine Marie Frenzel, June 6, 1987; 1 child, Jared Samuel Frenzel. BA, Rutgers U., 1977; MDiv, Princeton Theol. Sem., 1980, ThM, 1981, postgrad., 1988—. Ordained to ministry Presbyn. Ch. (U.S.A.), 1981. Campus chaplain Trenton (N.J.) Ecumenical Area Ministry, 1980-81; pastor Immanuel Presbyn. Ch., Binghamton, N.Y., 1981-88; interim pastor 1st Presbyn. Ch., Stockton, N.J., 1988-90, United 1st Presbyn. Ch. Amwell, Ringoes, N.J., 1991—. Mem. Soc. Christian Ethics, Am. Acad. Religion, Soc. Bibl. Lit. Home: 101 Farber Rd Apt 8B Princeton NJ 08540 Office: United 1st Presbyn Ch of Amwell PO Box 348 Ringoes NJ 08551 *In a world of violence—both natural and human—we can realize how we can care for ourselves while simultaneously caring for others.*

SUMMERLIN, PHILIP HARBIN, minister, clinical pastoral educator; b. Port Arthur, Tex., Mar. 10, 1940; s. Max Iverson and Dorothy (Merwin) S.; m. Sherryl Price, May 29, 1964 (div. July 1976); children: Joshua B., Daniel P., Reuben J.; m. Catherine Aline Fuselier, Sept. 15, 1978. BA, Abilene Christian U., 1962, MA, 1963; STB, Harvard U., 1967; D Ministry, Columbia Theol. Sem., Decatur, Ga., 1990. Ordained to ministry Christian Ch. (Disciples of Christ), 1979. Chaplain resident St. Luke's/Tex. Children's Hosps., Houston, 1976-77; supervisory resident chaplain Bapt. Med. Ctrs., Birmingham, Ala., 1977-79; clin. chaplain N.W. Ga. Regional Hosp., Rome, 1979-82; chaplain, clin. pastoral educator Ga. Retardation Ctr., Atlanta, 1982-85; clin. pastoral educator Erlanger Med. Ctr., Chattanooga, 1985—. Fellow Coll. Chaplains (state chmn. certs. 1990—); mem. Assn. for Clin. Pastoral Edn. (sec. 1981-87, supr. 1983—, treas. 1991—, rsch. award 1990). Home: 813 Ravine Rd Signal Mountain TN 37377 Office: Chattanooga Assn for Clin Pastoral Care/Erlanger Med Ctr 975 E 3d St Chattanooga TN 37403

SUMMERLIN, TRAVIS LAMAR, minister; b. Waco, Tex., Nov. 27, 1954; s. Travis Jerrell and Margaret Lucile (Adams) S. BA, Baylor U., 1976, PhD, 1984; MDiv, Southwestern Bapt. Theol. Sem., 1979. Ordained to ministry United Meth. Ch., 1976; elder 1989. Pastor Satin (Tex.) Bapt. Ch., 1975-77, Little River Bapt. Ch., Cameron, Tex., 1977-88; chaplain Meth. Home, Waco, 1988—; lectr. religious faculty Baylor U., Waco, 1984-87. Contbr. articles to profl. jours. Named one of Outstanding Young Men of Am., 1987. Mem. Waco Ministerial Alliance, United Meth. Hist. Soc., Baylor Alumni Assn. (life). Home and Office: Methodist Home 1111 Herring Ave Waco TX 76708 *The central fact of Christianity is that no person has to remain the way he or she is at present. There is always an opportunity for positive change and growth through God's grace.*

SUMMERS, THOMAS ABRAM, clergyman, clinical pastoral educator; b. Orangeburg, S.C., Oct. 29, 1934; s. Carroll Erwin and Anabel (Hill) S.; m. Marilyn Boyd, Aug. 31, 1962; children: Boyd Erwin, Mason Abram. BA, Wofford Coll., 1956; MDiv, Emory U., 1959; DMin, Luth. So. Sem., 1978. Ordained to ministry United Meth. Ch., 1962; lic. profl. counselor. Sr. clin. chaplain Cen. State Hosp., Milledgeville, Ga., 1962-65; supr. clin. pastoral edn. S.C. State Hosp., Columbia, 1965-66; chief chaplain Hall Psychiat. Inst., Columbia, 1966-83; dir. Acad. Pastoral Edn., Columbia, 1983—; bd. dirs. Pastoral Care Network Social Responsibility; adj. prof. Theology Sch., Drew U., 1981-89. Contbr. articles to profl. jours. and books. Bd. dirs. Wesley Found. U. S.C., 1968-72, State Employees Assn., Columbia, 1968; v.p. PTA, Columbia, 1976; mem. allocations panel United Way, Columbia, 1990. 2d lt. U.S. Army, 1959-60. Mem. Assn. Clin. Pastoral Edn. (cert. supr., regional chair 1979), Am. Psychiat. Assn. (com. chronically mentally ill 1988—), Assn. Mental Health Clergy (cert. chaplain, pres. 1985-86), Am. Assn. Pastoral Counselors. Avocations: gardening, hiking, photography, charcoal sketching, athletics. Home: 3017 Kilkee Circle Columbia SC 29223 Office: Office Pastoral Edn PO Box 119 Columbia SC 29202

SUMMEY, JAMES ALLEN, minister; b. Thomasville, N.C., Jan. 23, 1955; s. James Clayton and Frances Rebecca (Kinley) S.; m. Kathy Ann Freeman, May 26, 1979; children: Emily Dianne, Jennifer Leanne, John Brandon. AA, Davidson Community Coll., Lexington, N.C., 1977; BA, Gardner-Webb Coll., Boiling Springs, N.C., 1979; MDiv, Southeastern Bapt. Theol. Sem., Wake Forest, N.C., 1982; D Ministry, Columbia Theol. Sem., Decatur, Ga., 1991. Lic. min. 1976; ordained to ministry So. Bapt. Conv., 1979. Assoc. pastor North Lexington Bapt. Ch., 1978-79; min. youth and music Union Chapel Bapt. Ch., Zebulon, N.C., 1980; chaplain N.C. Alcoholic Rehab. Ctr., Butner, N.C., 1981-82; pastor Woodland Bapt. Ch., Wake Forest, 1983-86, Kerr Meml. Bapt. Ch., Concord, N.C., 1987—; instr. case studies Southeastern Bapt. Theol. Sem., 1983-86; instr. sem. extension dept. So. Bapt. Conv., Concord, 1987—. Mem. CAP (capt. 1989—). Home: 221 Union St N Concord NC 28025 Office: Kerr Meml Bapt Ch 25 Hwy 49 S Concord NC 28025 *With many decisions that we face in life, it appears to me that the most profound decisions are theological. Whether we approach life from the many disciplines that surround the sphere of academics, we eventually come down to the basics-being. I find great comfort that God in Christ gives life the ultimate meaning. The decision to follow God's vocation for living gives new hope that humanity can move toward our intended purpose: being in fellowship with God.*

SUMNER, ROBERT LESLIE, minister; b. Norwich, N.Y., Aug. 3, 1922; s. Clarence Larkin and Gladys Mae (Thompson) S. M. Orphina M. Mingori, Aug. 16, 1942; children: Richard Lee, Ralph Leslie, Ruth Lynn Sumner Purvis, Rita Louise Sumner Phipps, Ronald Lloyd. Grad., Bapt. Bible Sem., Johnson City, N.Y., 1943; DD (hon.), Bob Jones U., 1964; D Sacred Laws and Letters (hon.), Bethany Coll. and Sem., Dothan, Ala., 1985. Ordained to ministry Gen. Assn. Regular Bapt. Chs., 1944. Pastor Calvary Bapt. Ch., Pontiac, Ill., 1943-45; evangelist, 1945-47, 54-59, Calif. Heights Bapt. Ch., Long Beach, 1947-49, Morningside Bapt. Ch., Graham, Tex., 1949-54; dir. Bibl. Evangelism, Ingleside, Tex., 1959-62, 64-88, asst. dir., 1988—; pastor Temple Bapt. Ch., Portsmouth, Ohio, 1962-64; mem. coun. 14 Gen. Assn. Regular Bapt. Chs., Schaumburg, Ill., 1964-68. Author 32 books including: Man Sent From God, 1959, Hell is No Joke, 1959, Evangelism - The Church on Fire, 1960, Biblical Evangelism In Action!, 1966, Saved By Grace . . . For Service, 1979, Jesus Christ is God, 1983; founder, editor The Bibl. Evangelist, 1966-80, 82-89, editorial cons., 1989—; mng. editor The Sword of the Lord, 1980-82. Trustee Sword of the Lord Found., Murfreesboro, Tenn., 1954-82, Bibl. Evangelism, Ingleside, 1959—, Cedarville Coll., Ohio, 1962-87, trustee emeritus, 1987—; mem. cooperating bd. Bob Jones U., Greenville, S.C., 1962-77. Inducted into Fundamentalist Hall of Fame, San Francisco Theol. Sem., 1977. Home: 340 Lovers Ln Ingleside TX 78362 Office: Drawer 940 Ingleside TX 78362-0940 *Life is a series of decisions, each new one an expansion of the ones that have gone before. This is why each should be made prayerfully, seeking the leading of the Holy Spirit of God. Decisions determine destiny.*

SUMNEY, JERRY LEE, religion educator; b. LaGrange, Ind., July 7, 1955; s. Paul Gene and Alberta Mae (Cox) S.; m. Diane Furlong, June 18, 1978; children: Elizabeth, Victoria. BA, David Lipscomb U., 1978; MA in Religion, Harding U., 1982; PhD, So. Meth. U., 1987. Asst. prof. religion Ferrum (Va.) Coll., 1986-91, assoc. prof., 1991—. Author: Identifying Paul's Opponents, 1990; contbr. articles to profl. publs. James Still fellow Appalachian Coll. Program, Mellon Found., 1988, 90. Mem. Soc. Biblical Lit. Office: Ferrum Coll Ferrum VA 24088-9001

SUMRALL, LESTER FRANK, missionary, evangelist; b. Feb. 15, 1913; s. George William and Betty Elizabeth (Chandler) S.; m. Louise Margaret Layman, Sept. 30, 1944; children: Frank Lester Jr., Stephen Philip, Peter Andrew. DD, Berea Bible Co., 1964; LittD, Ind. Christian U., 1974; PhD in Religious Studies, Golden State U., 1983; DD (hon.), Oral Roberts U., 1983. Founder, chmn. LeSEA Ministries, South Bend, Ind., 1959—; founder, pastor Christian Ctr. Cathedral of Praise, South Bend, 1965—; founder, owner 9 TV stas., South Bend, 1972—, LeSea Brodcasting, South Bend, 1972—; founder, pres. World Harvest Bible Coll., South Bend, 1975—; pres. Ind. Christian U., South Bend, 1989—. Author numerous books; pub., founder World Harvest Mag., WHRI Short Wave Radio, 1988. Founder Feed the Hungry, 1987—. Named Hon. Citizen of Knoxville, Tenn., Mayor of Knoxville, 1984, Leader of Yr., Internat. Christian Bus. Leaders, 1988; recipient Congl. award U.S. Ho. of Reps., 1980, Honor Citation Nat. Religious Broadcasters, 1982, award of merit Nat. Religious Broadcasters, 1983, Meritorious Achievement award Internat. Assn. Christian Clin. Counselors, 1983, Meritorious Hoosier award Ind. Sec. State, 1983, Outstanding Community Svc. award FaithAm. Found, 1984.. Mem. Full Gospel Ch. Office: LeSea Broadcasting 530 E Ireland Rd South Bend IN 46614

SUNDERLAND, JAMES CORNELIUS, chaplain; b. kDenver, Dec. 25, 1924; s. James Cornelius and Anna Loretta (Solan) S. BA, St. Louis U., 1951, MA, 1953. Tchr. Campion High Sch., Prairie du Chen, Wis., 1952-55, Kapaun High Sch., Wichita, Kans., 1960-64; retreat master Paraclete Retreat House, Wichita, 1964-67; coll. chaplain Spokane U.-in-Florence, Italy, 1967-68; tchr. St. Louis U. High Sch., 1968-70; hosp. chaplain St. Louis U. Hosps., 1970-77, St. John's Hosp., Springfield, Mo., 1977-80, Cox Med. Ctr., Springfield, 1980-81, St. Joseph Hosp., Denver, 1981-83; jail chaplain Archdiocese of Denver, 1983—; campus minister S.W. Mo. U., Springfield, 1980-81. Pres. Colo. Coalition to Abolish the Death Penalty, 1984—. With U.S. Army, 1943-45. Democrat. Roman Catholic. Avocations: reading, walking, biking. Home: 2305 Gaylord Denver CO 80205 Office: Catholic Jail Ministry 2305 Gaylord Denver CO 80205

SUNDERLAND, RONALD HARRY, minister; b. Wangaratta, Victoria, Australia, Oct. 15, 1929; came to U.S., 1966; s. Harry and Ethel (Reid) S.; m. Noel Elizabeth Watson, Nov. 17, 1956; children: Dion J., Brent A., Quentin L., Granger K. BA, U. Melbourne, 1954; BD, Melbourne Coll. Divinity, 1966; MST, So. Meth. U., 1968; EdD, U. Houston, 1978. Cert. clin. pastoral educator, chaplain supr. Dir. pastoral care and edn. Harris County Hosp. Dist., Houston, 1968-76; dir. The Inst. of Religion, Houston, 1976-82, rsch. fellow, 1982-88; assoc. dir. Found. for Interfaith Rsch. and Ministry, Houston, 1988—; exec. dir. Equipping Laypeople for Ministry, Houston, 1980—; trustee Found. for Interfaith Rsch. and Ministry, 1988—; speaker in field. Author: AIDS: Personal Stories in Pastoral Perspective, 1986, AIDS: A Manual for Pastoral Care, 1987, AIDS and the Church, 1987, 2d edit., 1992, Handle with Care: A Handbook for Care Teams Serving People with AIDS, 1990, When Sorrows Come: Grief Ministry in the Congregation, 1992; contbr. articles to profl. jours.; editor: The College of Chaplains, The Jour. of Pastoral Care. Mem. Assn. for Clin. Pastoral Edn. (founding mem., chmn. found. com. 1980-87, del. 1990—), Coll. of Chaplains, Internat. AIDS Soc., Doctor's Club. Office: Equipping Laypeople for Ministry PO Box 20392 Houston TX 77225-0392

SUNIM, MU RYANG See BERALL, ERIK DUSTIN

SUPANCHECK, NORMAN ANTHONY, priest; b. Long Beach, Calif., June 9, 1942; s. Anthony Nicholas and Louise Alice (Bigelow) S. B.Philosophy, St. John's Coll., Camarillo, Calif., 1964; postgrad., St. John's Sem., Camarillo, Calif., 1968, Grad Theol. Union, Berkeley, Calif., 1980. Ordained priest Roman Catholic Ch., 1968. Assoc. pastor Santa Isabel Ch., E. Los Angeles, 1968-70, St. Joseph Ch., Placentia, Calif., 1970-75, Resurrection Ch., E. Los Angeles, 1975-80; western region chaplain Boy Scouts/Girl Scouts/Campfire, 1980-85; campus min. CSULA and ELAC, 1980-88; pastor St. Francis of Assisi Ch., Fillmore, Calif., 1988—; mem. youth ministry bd. Nat. Cath. Com., 1980-85; bd. dirs. Youth Encounter Spirit, L.A., 1970—; chaplain K.C., Fillmore, 1988-91; mem. team Marriage Encounter, L.A., 1970—. Chaplain Monterey Park (Calif.) Police, 1980-88, Ventura County Sheriff, 1989-91. Recipient Pelican award, Boy Scouts Cath. Com., L.A., 1987, St. George award, 1988, St. Anne award, 1988. Mem. Fillmore Ministerial Assn. (pres. 1990-91), Nat. Fedn. Priest Coun., Cath. Campus Ministry Assn., Jesus Caritas. Home and Office: St Francis of Assisi Ch PO Box 205 1048 W Ventura Fillmore CA 93016-0205 *Our God does not judge us by what we know or how much we succeed in life. Neither does he judge us by past failures. The God who is love looks in our heart to see if we image God's love, to see who we belong to.*

SUQUIA GOICOECHEA, ANGEL CARDINAL, archbishop; b. Zaldivia, San Sebastian, Spain, Oct. 2, 1916. ordained priest Roman Cath. Ch., 1940. Consecrated bishop Almeria, Spain, 1966, Malaga, 1969; archbishop Santiago de Compostela, Spain, 1973, Madrid, 1983—; proclaimed cardinal, 1985. Office: Arzobispado, Bailen 8, 28071 Madrid Spain

SURINACH CARRERAS, RICARDO ANTONIO, bishop; b. Mayaguez, P.R., Apr. 1, 1928; s. Ricardo and Esther (Carreras) S. Student, St. Bonaventure Coll., Olean, N.Y., 1947-48, Seminario San Ildefonso, 1948-50; BA in Philosophy, Seminario St. Tomas, Dominican Republic, 1953, STB in Theology, 1957; student, U.S. Army Chaplain Sch., Ft. Slocum, N.Y., 1962, U.S. Army Chaplain Sch., Ft. Hamilton, N.Y., 1965; BA, Cath. U. of P.R., Ponce, 1968, EdM, 1970; PhD candidate, Fordham U., 1970-72. Ordained priest Roman Catholic Ch., 1957. Asst. San Sebastian Parish Diocese of Ponce, 1957-58, pastor of Maunabo, 1958-66; lectr. in theology Cath. U. P.R., 1960-66, asst. exec. to pres., 1966-67, instr. social scis., 1966-67, v.p. devel., 1967-68; v.p. student affairs Cath. U. P.R., P.R., 1968-70, asst. prof. edn., 1970-73, dean arts and humanities and v.p. acad. affairs, 1974, bd. trustees and vice grand chancellor, 1975; diocesan consultor Diocese of Ponce, from 1967, aux. bishop, vicar gen., 1975, now bishop; pres. edn. commn. P.R. Bishop's Conf., 1976; mem. dept. religion Latin Am. Coun. Bishops, 1976-80, mem. dept. edn., 1983-90, coun. del., 1990; v.p. Episc. Conf. P.R., P.R. Bishop's Conf., 1982; del. ordinary Synod of Bishops, Rome, 1983. Ford Found. grantee. Mem. Am. Personnel and Guidance Assn., AAUP, Am. Assn. Higher Edn., Phi Delta Kappa, Phi Alpha Theta, Pi Gamma Mu. Address: PO Box 205 Sta 6 Ponce PR 00732

SURRETT, DAVID COFIELD, minister; b. Greensboro, N.C., Nov. 13, 1958; s. Forest Cofield and Davie Rose (Kelly) S.; m. Donna Lynn Mercer, Nov. 12, 1983; children: Myles David, Lydia Emily. BS in BA, U. S.C., 1980; MDiv, Duke U., 1983. Ordained to ministry United Meth. Ch., 1982. Asst. to ministers St. John's United Meth. Ch., Aiken, S.C., 1979-80; assoc. pastor Pleasant Grove United Meth. Ch., Thomasville, N.C., 1980-81; pastor McClellanville (S.C.) United Meth. Ch., 1983-85, St. Paul's Waccamaw United Meth. Ch., Pawleys Island, S.C., 1985-88, St. John's United Meth. Ch. and Lebanon United Meth. Ch., Norway, S.C., 1988—; sec. Marion Dist. Coun. on Ministries, 1985-88; vice chmn. Orangeburg (S.C.) Dist. Coun. on Ministries, 1990—; chmn. S.C. Conf. Career Planning Com., Columbia, 1990—; communications coord. Marion Dist. United Meth. Ch., 1987-88. Mem. exec. com. Carolina Low Country Girl Scouts U.S.A., Charleston, 1989-91, bd. dirs., 1987-91; bd. dirs. Georgetown County Mental Health Assn., 1986-88; scouting coord. Boy Scouts Am., Norway, 1988—. Recipient Torch award, S.C. Conf. United Meth. Ch., 1990, Nat. Disting. Svc. Award, Order of the Arrow, 1986. Mem. Rotary. Democrat. Home: St Johns Ave Norway SC 29113 Office: St Johns United Meth Ch PO Box 367 Norway SC 29113 *The Christian faith calls us to serve God and our neighbor. All the world's great religions have similar beliefs. Our world needs persons deeply committed to giving sacrifically of their time and talent. With such devotion, issues of the environment, hunger, poverty, social justice and education can be confronted.*

SUSSENBACH, WARD VIRGIL, minister; b. Highland, Ill., Nov. 6, 1944; s. Virgil Gustav and Sarah Edna (Ward) S.; m. Norma Alice Vought, May 24, 1969; children: Julie Dawn, Jill Naomi, Jeffrey Ward. BA, Greenville Coll., Ill., 1966; MS in Edn., So. Ill. U., 1976, EdS, 1980; DMin, Calif. Grad. Sch. Theology, Anaheim, 1987. Ordained to ministry Free Meth. Ch., 1979. Bi-vocat. pastor Free Meth. Ch., Sorento, Ill., 1976-81; pastor Free Meth. Ch., Adrian, Mich., 1981-85; sr. pastor Free Meth. Ch., Hillsdale, Mich., 1985—; sec. So. Mich. Conf., Spring Arbor, Mich., 1984—, Bd. Adminstrn., 1984—, Bd. Stewardship and Fin. of So. Mich. Conf., 1990—. Author: Dealing with the Memories - A Biblical Approach, 1987. Precinct del. Rep. Party, 1988-90; mem. Am. Family Assn., Hillsdale, 1988-91; chaplain ARC Mil. Support Group, Hillsdale, 1991. With USAF, 1969-70. Mem. Adrian Ministerial Assn., Hillsdale County Ministerial Assn. (pres. 1986, 91, hosp. chaplain 1987-90), Kiwanis. Republican. Home: 149 Union St Hillsdale MI 49242 Office: Free Meth Ch 150 Union St Hillsdale MI 49242 *The key to inner healing rests on the willingness to forgive others and to receive the forgiveness of God through faith in Jesus Christ. Life is too short to allow unforgiveness to destroy our relationship with mankind and God.*

SUSTAR, CHRISTOPHER DAVID, minister; b. Winfield, Kans., Jan. 26, 1966; s. Thomas David and Phyllis Marie (Gosnell) S.; m. Leah Talley Sustar, June 4, 1988. BS in Bibl. Studies, East Coast Bible Coll., 1988. Lic. min. Ch. of God, 1990. Minister youth Praise Cathedral Ch. of God, Greer, S.C., 1988—; youth camp speaker, youth rally speaker Ch. of God; youth seminar speaker Ch. of God-S.C. Youth Leaders Fellowship. Mem. S.C. Youth Leaders Fellowship (pres. 1991). Home: 420 Hwy 912 Travelers Rest SC 29690 Office: Praise Cathedral Ch of God Brushy Creek Rd Greer SC 29651

SUTER, DAVID WINSTON, religion educator, minister; b. Staunton, Va., Mar. 1, 1942; s. Beverly Wills and Sarah Frances (Anderson) S.; m. Kristine Ann Pearson, July 8, 1978; 1 child, Jessica Eden. BA, Davidson Coll., 1964; BD, U. Chgo., 1967, MA, 1970, PhD, 1977. Ordained to ministry Presbyn. Ch. (U.S.A.), 1967. Pastor Longbranch (Wash.) Community Ch., 1986-90; prof. St. Martin's Coll., Lacey, Wash., 1983—, dean of humanities, 1991—. Author: Tradition and Composition in the Parables of Enoch, 1979; contbr. articles to profl. publs. Mem. Soc. Biblical Lit. Democrat. Office: St Martin's Coll Lacey WA 98503

SUTHERLAND, MALCOLM READ, JR., clergyman, educator; b. Detroit, Nov. 11, 1916; s. Malcolm Read and Edith Ione (Osborne) S.; m. Mary Anne Beaumont, Dec. 23, 1943; children: Malcolm Read III, Maryanne B. AB, Miami (Ohio) U., 1938; MS, Western Res. U., 1941; BD, Fed. Theol. Faculty U. Chgo., 1945; LLD, Emerson Coll., 1963; LHD, Meadville-Lombard Theol. Sch., 1975. Ordained to ministry Unitarian Universalist Assn., 1945. Dir. boys work Goodrich Social Settlement, Cleve., 1938-40; housing mgr. Cleve. Met. Housing Authority, 1940-41; regional housing supr. Farm Security Adminstrn., 1941-42; housing mgmt. supr. FPHA, 1942-43; pastor in Ill., Va., Mass., 1944-60; exec. v.p. Am. Unitarian Assn., 1959-60; Robert Collier prof. ch. and soc., pres., dean faculty Meadville Theol. Sch. of Lombard Coll., Chgo., 1960-75; minister Harvard (Mass.) Unitarian Ch., 1975—; exec. dir. U.S. com. World Conf. on Religion and Peace, N.Y.C., 1980-83, internat. council, 1984—, also v.p. U.S. exec. council; former dir. Unitarian Universalist Service Com., Beacon Press; chmn. editorial adv. bd. Christian Register, 1955-60; field rep. Unitarian Service Com., Mexico, 1950-51; mem. sr. secretariat World Conf. Religion and Peace, Kyoto, 1970 and del. to Louvain, 1974, Princeton, 1979, Nairobi, 1984, Melbourne, Australia, 1989; lectr., del. Japan-U.S. consultation on peace Internat. Assn. for Religious Freedom, 1970; v.p., trustee Dana McLean Greeley Found. for Peace and Justice, 1986—; Thomas Minns lectr., Boston, 1955, Charlottesville, Va., 1978, Berry St., lectr., Boston, 1956; Harvard chair lectr. Warner Free Lectures, 1985; chmn. common council Chgo. Cluster of Theol. Schs., Inc., 1970-74; pres. Inst. on Religion in an Age of Sci., 1969, 75-77, hon. v.p., 1980—, acad. fellow, 1988; bd. dirs., sec. Ctr. for Advanced Study Religion and Sci., Chgo., 1965—. Author: Personal Faith, 1955, Creators of the Dawn, 1979; Co-chmn. publs. bd., editorial adv. bd.: jour. religion and sci. Zygon; Contbr. articles to publs. Bd. govs. Manchester Coll., Oxford, also hon. fellow, 1974—. Recipient Disting. Svc. award Charlottesville (Va.) Jr. C. of C., 1949, Disting. Svc. award Internat. Assn. Religious Freedom, 1975, Disting. Svc.award Konko Kyo Chs. Am., 1975. Mem. Unitarian Universalist Ministers Assn., Phi Delta Theta, Phi Mu Alpha, Alpha Kappa Delta, Omicron Delta Kappa. Club: Bucks Harbor Yacht (Maine) (commodore 1979-81). Home: 21 Woodside Rd Harvard MA 01451 Office: PO Box 217 Harvard MA 01451

SUTHERLAND, RAYMOND CARTER, clergyman, English educator emeritus; b. Horse Cave, Ky., Nov. 5, 1917; s. Raymond Carter and Nellie Ruth (Veluzat) S. A.B., U. Ky., 1939, M.A., 1950, Ph.D., 1953; grad., Gen. Theol. Sem., N.Y.C., 1942; postgrad., St. John's Theol. Sem., Camarillo, Calif., 1948, Gen. Theol. Sem., N.Y.C., 1979. Ordained priest Episcopal Ch., 1942, reactivated, 1985; curate St. Luke's Ch., Anchorage, Louisville, 1942-44; prof. English U. Tenn., Knoxville, 1953-57; mem. faculty Ga. State U., Atlanta, 1957-84; prof. English Ga. State U., 1965-84, dir. English grad. studies, 1978-84, prof. emeritus, 1985—; lectr. Oriental ceramics. Author: Medieval English Conceptions of Hell as Derived from Biblical, Patristic, and Native Germanic Sources, 1953, The Religious Background of Swift's Tale of a Tub, 1958, The Mechanics of Versification, 1963, 64; contbr. articles to profl. jours. Served as chaplain AUS, 1944-47. Omicron Delta Kappa disting. prof., 1979-80. Mem. Alumni Assn. Gen. Theol. Sem., Am. Assn. Advancement Humanities, Medieval Acad. Am., MLA, New Chaucer Soc., Heraldry Soc. Eng., Oriental Ceramics Soc. Eng., Ky. Hist. Soc., Hart County Hist. Soc., Phi Kappa Phi, Omicron Delta Kappa. Office: care Episcopal Diocese of Atlanta 2744 Peachtree Rd NW Atlanta GA 30363

SUTHERLAND, TERRY MICHAEL, minister; b. Covington, Va., Mar. 16, 1954; s. James Edmund Thomas and Veda Marie (Bratton) S. BA, Presbyn. Coll., 1976; MDiv, Union Theol. Sem. Va., 1979. Ordained to ministry Presbyn. Ch., 1979. Minister Warm Springs (Va.) Presbyn. Ch., 1979-82, Fayetteville (W.Va.) Presbyn. Ch., 1982-85, Poplar Hill Presbyn. Ch., Lexington, Va., 1985-91, Ben Salem Presbyn. Ch., Lexington, 1985-91, McCutchen Presbyn. Ch., Lexington, 1985-91, Clarkton (N.C.) Presbyn. Ch., 1991—. Mem. Bath County Spl. Edn. Com., Va., 1981-82, Fayette County Juvenile Probation Program Com., W.Va., 1985. Mem. Bath County Ministerial Assn. (sec. 1981-82), Fayetteville Ministerial Assn. (pres. 1983-85), Scottish Clan Sutherland Soc. of N. Am., Scottish Clan Buchanan Soc. of Am. Avocations: oil and acrylic painting, monitoring shortwave radio, photography. Home: N Singletary St Box 633 Clarkton NC 28433 Office: Clarkton Presbyn Ch College St Box 675 Clarkton NC 28433

SUTTERFIELD, JAMES KIRBY, minister; b. Amarillo, Tex., Aug. 13, 1957; s. Theo Burton and Beulah Imogene (Gist) S.; m. Cheryl Lynn Van Buren, Jan. 7, 1978; 1 child, Jason. BS, Howard Payne U., 1978; postgrad., Liberty U. Ordained to ministry So. Bapt. Conv., 1977. Min. music and youth 1st Bapt. Ch., Early, Tex., 1976-78; mental health clinician Psychiat. Inst. Ft. Worth, 1980-81; min. music and youth Bethel Bapt. Ch., 1978-80; min. music and ch. activities Forest Home Bapt. Ch., Kilgore, Tex., 1981-83; min. music and youth 1st Bapt. Ch., Queen City, Tex., 1983—; mem. assist team Bapt. Gen. Conv., Tex., 1989-91; associational youth min. Ewon Bapt. Assn., Linden, Tex., 1990-91. Dist. chaplain Queen City Ind. Sch. Dist., 1984-91. Home: 2011 Mary Ln Carrollton TX 75006 Office: Rosemeade Bapt Ch 1225 Rosemeade Pkwy Carrollton TX 75007

SUTTON, CLAUDIUS HENRY (MIKE SUTTON), minister; b. Loxley, Ala., Jan. 26, 1939; s. Percy Augusta and Mary Odessa (Huggins) S.; m. Anna Belle Smith, Aug. 8, 1964. BA, Tenn. Temple U., 1966; MTh with honors, New Orleans Bapt. Theol. Sem., 1969, MRE, 1970. Ordained to ministry So. Bapt. Conv., 1970. Pastor Carmel Bapt. Ch., Monticello, Miss., 1970-73; min. youth, assoc. pastor East McComb (Miss.) Bapt. Ch., 1973-81; min. youth and outreach 1st Bapt. Ch., Grenada, Miss., 1981-85; pastor Calvary Bapt. ch., Silver Creek, Miss., 1985—; assnl. min. youth activities Pike Bapt. Assn., McComb, 1975-89, Grenada Bapt. Assn., 1981-85; dir. family ministry Lawrence Bapt. Assn., Monticello, Miss., 1987—. With USAF, 1957-61. Home: PO Box 28 Silver Creek MS 39663

SUTTON, DAVID BRUCE, minister, journalist; b. Ft. Lewis, Wash., Feb. 27, 1949; s. Delbert Theodore and Lois Elma (Bremer) S.; m. Vickie Dawn

Clifford, May 8, 1971; children: Joshua, Emily, Hannah, Rachel. BA in Journalism, Ea. Wash. U., 1973; MRE, Southwestern Bapt. Theol. Sem., 1976. Ordained to ministry Bapt. Ch., 1977. Youth dir. Inland Empire Bapt. Assn., Spokane, Wash., 1972-73; chaplain Forrest Hills Nursing Home, Ft. Worth, 1973-76; sr. adult pastor Overland Bapt. Ch., St. Louis, 1976-80; pastor Valleyview Bapt. Ch., Spokane, 1980-85; sr. pastor 44th Ave. Bapt. Ch., Seattle, 1985—; religion editor Spokane Valley Herald, 1980-85; trustee Puget Sound Bapt. Assn., Seattle, 1989—; cons. N.W. Bapt. Found., Portland, Oreg., 1989—; bd. dirs. N.W. Bapt. Conv., Portland. Columnist Everett (Wash.) Herald, 1985—; feature writer ARC Excellence in Journalism (1st Pl. award 1984), Wash. Better Newspaper Assn. (2d Pl. award 1984). Chmn. Spokane County Storm Water Mgmt., 1983-85; founder, advisor Friend to Friend of Greater Spokane, 1980-85; vol. ARC, St. Louis, 1976-80; cons. 2d Congl. Dist. Com. on Aging, St. Louis, 1977-80. With U.S. Army, 1970-72. Mem. Nat. Assn. Sr. Adults, Bapt. Sr. Adults. Home: 17330 Meadowdale Dr Lynnwood WA 98037 Office: 21910 44th Ave W Mountlake Terrace WA 98043

SUTTON, JESSE NOEL, music minister; b. Gilmer, Tex., Jan. 18, 1926; s. Rufus Noel and Jessie Lola (Parnell) S.; m. Norma Dell Beard, Dec. 24, 1948; children: Rhonda Cheryl Sutton Stege, Lola Celeste Sutton Bailey, Andrea Gay Sutton Holcek. Student, Hardin-Simmons U., 1946-48; cert., So. Tech. Inst., Dallas, 1950; B Sacred Music, So. Bapt. Theol. Sem., Ft. Worth, 1957. Ordained to ministry So. Bapt. Conv., 1979. Min. music, edn. and youth Hilltop Drive Bapt. Ch., Irving, Tex., 1955-56; min. music, edn. and youth 1st Bapt. Ch., Ranger, Tex., 1957-58, Freeport, Tex., 1958-65, Canyon, Tex., 1965-67; min. music, edn. and youth Trinity Bapt. Ch., Amarillo, Tex., 1967-74; min. music and edn. 1st Bapt. Ch., Van Buren, Ark., 1974-78; min. music 1st Bapt. Ch., Delhi, La., 1978—; 2d v.p. Ark. Bapt. Religious Edn. Conf., 1975-76, 1st v.p., 1976-77, pres., 1977-78. Mem. Singing Men of Ark., 1974-78. With AUS, 1944-46, ETO, PTO. Mem. La. Singing Mins., Lions (pres. Delhi 1984-85). Republican. Office: 1st Bapt Ch Box 5 Delhi LA 71232 *An exciting life would include: discipline in your social, moral and spiritual life, giving of oneself to your fellowman, country and family. I find that music is a natural way of expressing all of these.*

SUTTON, JOSEPH CORNELIUS, chaplain; b. Chgo., Feb. 18, 1959; s. Cornelius and Saniah (Anderson) S. BS in Acctg., Fla. A&M U., 1983. Tchr. Sunday sch. Braeswood Assembly of God, Houston, 1984-88; mem. coun. Royal Rangers Assembly of God, Houston, 1986-88; youth pastor New Life Christian Ctr., Houston, 1988-91; mem. nat. adv. coun. Nat. Coalition of Urban Youth Ministries, 1990—; coord. Neighborhood Ministry, Houston, 1985-91; chaplain Burnett Bayland Home, 1987-91; coord. urban ministries Youth for Christ of Twin Cities, Plymouth, Minn., 1991—; mem. planning com. Youth for Christ/Youth Guidance, Denver, 1989-91; trustee Nat. Common Ground Coalition, Houston, 1991—. Home: 11718 Bowlan Ln Houston TX 77036 Office: Youth for Christ of Twin Cities 14375 23d Ave Plymouth MN 55447

SUTTON, LARRY ALLEN, minister; b. Uniontown, Pa., July 21, 1961; s. Howard Bruce and Patricia Ruth (Smith) S.; m. Janet Louise Pfab, Dec. 29, 1979; children: Brockton Corey, Annastasia. Student, Memphis Sch. Preaching, 1989—. Ordained to ministry Ch. of Christ. Min. East Laurel (Miss.) Ch. of Christ, 1987-89, Wilson (Ark.) Ch. of Christ, 1989—. Sgt. USAF, 1979-86.

SUTTON, MICHAEL ARNOLD, lay worker, special education educator, consultant; b. Ludington, Mich., Oct. 1, 1951; s. Arthur J. and Katherine Jane (Baltzer) S. m. Carol Graham (div. 1972); 1 child, Theresa; m. Polly Gale Pease, July 5, 1977; children: Rosanna, Matthew, Nathanial, David. BS in Spl. Edn., Western Mich. U., 1974, MA in Spl. Edn., 1978. Cert. tchr., Mich. deacon, chmn. Mason County Ref. Ch. Am., Scottville, Mich., 1982-84, elder, chmn. Christian edn., 1986-87, tchr. Sunday sch., 1986—, Bible study leader, 1988-91. Booth worker Mason County Right to Life, 1989-90. Tchr. of Yr. award Scottville Optimist Club, 1988. Republican. Home: 6306 E Hansen Rd Fountain MI 49410 Office: Mason Lake Intermediate Sch Dist 2130 W US 10 Ludington MI 49431

SUTTON, PETER ALFRED, archbishop; b. Chandler, Que., Can., Oct. 18, 1934. BA, U. Ottawa, 1960; MA in Religious Edn, Loyola U., Chgo., 1969. Ordained priest Roman Catholic Ch., 1960, bishop, 1974; oblate of Mary Immaculate; high sch. tchr. St. Patricks, Ottawa, Ont., 1961-63, London (Ont.) Cath. Cen. Sch., 1963-74; bishop of Labrador-Schefferville, Que., Can., 1974—; archbishop Missionary Diocese of Keewatin-Le Pas, Man., 1986, apptd. coadjustor archbishop, 1986—, archbishop, 1986—; mem. Can. Conf. Cath. Bishops, Western Cath. Conf. of No. Bishops, Man. Bishops; accompanying Bishop L'Arch Internat. (homes for mentally handicapped), 1983—. Contbr. religious articles to newspapers. Address: PO Box 270, 108 1st St W, The Pas, MB Canada R9A 1K4

SUTTON, RAY RONNY, minister; b. Louisville, Aug. 28, 1950; s. Ray Rodman Sutton and Joretta (Clary) Williams; m. Susan Jean Schaerdel, Dec. 19, 1971; children: Stephen, Seth, Sarah, Samuel, Esther, Evelyn. BFA, So. Meth. Coll., 1972; ThM, Dallas Theol. Seminary, 1976; ThD, Cen. Sch. of Religion, Worchester, Eng., 1988. Pastor Presbyn. Ch. in Am., Tyler, Tex., 1977-80, Assn. of Reformation Chs., Tyler, 1980-87; rector Am. Episcoal Ch., Tyler, 1987-88, Reformed Episcopal Ch., Tyler, 1988—; del. Athanasian Soc., Tyler, 1990-91; bd. dirs. Christian Action Coun., Tyler. Author: That You May Prosper, 1987, Who Owns the Family, 1987, Second Chance, 1988; assoc. editor: Christianity and Civilization jour., 1982-87; contbr. articles to profl. jours. Chaplain Boy Scouts of Am., Tyler, 1989-91. Fellow Inst. for Christian Econs.; mem. Rep. Club. Home: 625 Windsor Tyler TX 75701 Office: Good Shepherd Reformed Episcopal Church 708 Hamvasy Tyler TX 75701

SUTTON, RICHARD RUEL, pastor; b. Mason City, Iowa, Jan. 20, 1934; s. Reuben Reul and Florence Irene (Schultz) S.; m. Florence Alice Sage, Sept. 15, 1951; children: Steven Lee, John Allen, Richard Dean, James Milton, Sharon Beth, Karen Ann. Grad. high sch., Mason City, 1952. Ordained to ministry Seventh Day Adventist Ch., 1986. Printer Arrow Printing Co., Mason City, 1951-60, M.C. Blue Print, Mason City, 1960-63; postal clk. Mason City Post Office, 1963-77; publ. mgr. Allied Purchasing, Mason City, 1980—; pastor Seventh Day Remnant Advent Ch., Nora Springs, Iowa, 1986—; pres. Am. Postal Workers Union, 1965-77. Republican. Home: 330 9th St NE PO Box 1628 Mason City IA 50401

SUTTON, STANLEY R., clergyman; b. Logansport, Ind., July 28, 1949; s. Charles and Rosemary (Ehrman) S.; m. Janis Ann Hoffer, Aug. 18, 1972; children: Angela M., Gregory N. BS, Ball State U., Muncie, Ind., 1971; MA, Cin. Bible Coll and Sem., 1982. Ordained to ministry Christian Ch., 1976. Youth min. Macedonia Christian Ch., Kokomo, Ind., 1969-71; assoc. campus min. Christian Student Found., Muncie, 1971-72; youth min. Kokomo (Ind.) Main St Ch. of Christ, 1972-74, Faith Ch. of Christ, Burlington, Ind., 1974-77; min. Refuge Christian Ch., Noblesville, Ind., 1977—; bd. dirs. Christian Counseling Svcs., Inc., Muncie, former bd. chmn., and vice bd. chmn. vis. chaplain Riverview Hosp., Noblesville, 1977—, mem. instl. rev. com., 1987—; vis. chaplain Harbor Manor Health Care Ctr., Noblesville, 1989—. Mem. Fellowship Christian Mins., Hamilton County Christian Ch. Mins. Assn., Cin. Bible Coll. and Sem. Alumni Assn. Republican. Office: Refuge Christian Ch 11772 E 196th St Noblesville IN 46060

SUTTON, WALTER C., clergyman, editor, educator; b. East McKeesport, Pa., Apr. 23, 1927; s. Harold E. and Zora (Harvison) S.; m. Edith McMillan, June 8, 1956; children—Harold M., Stephanie J. B.A., Muskingum Coll., 1950; B.D., Louisville Presbyterian Theol. Sem., 1957, Th.M., 1963. Ordained to ministry Presbyn. Ch. U.S., 1957. Pastor 1st Presbyn. Ch., Elizabethtown, Ky., 1964-76, Eminence, Ky., 1957-63; instr. journalism and communications U. Ky. Elizabethtown Community Coll., 1968-76; dir. pub. relations Louisville Presbyn. Theol. Sem., 1976-79; pastor 1st Presbyn. Ch., Maysville, Ky., 1979-80; pub., editor Presbyn. Survey mag., 1980-83; editorial dir. John Knox Press, Atlanta, 1982—. Mem. Am. Acad. Religion, Soc. for Bibl. Lit. Office: John Knox Press 341 Ponce de Leon Ave NE Atlanta GA 30365

SUTTON, WILLIAM BLAYLOCK, pastor; b. Little Rock, Aug. 10, 1942; s. Richard Otto and Bettye (Blaylock) S.; m. Martha Davis, Apr. 19, 1968; children: Blake, Bryan, Stephen. BBA, Baylor U., 1964; BD, Southwestern Bapt. Theol. Sem., Ft. Worth, 1967; ThM, Internat. Theol. Sem., Orlando, Fla., 1982, DD, 1984. Ordained to ministry So. Bapt. Conv., 1965. Pastor North Hopkins Bapt. Ch., Sulphur Springs, Tex., 1965-67, 1st Bapt. Ch. Pine Hills, Orlando, 1969-77, Windsor Park Bapt. Ch., Ft. Smith, Ark., 1977-86; assoc. pastor Dauphin Way Bapt. Ch., Mobile, Ala., 1968-69; pastor 1st Bapt. Ch., McAllen, Tex., 1986—; v.p. Fla. Bapt. Pastors Conf., Orlando, 1973; pres. Ark. Bapt. Pastors Conf., Ft. Smith, 1983; trustee fgn. mission bd. So. Bapt. Conv., Richmond, Va., 1990—. Bd. visitors Criswell Coll., Dallas, 1991. Office: 1st Bapt Ch 1200 Beech McAllen TX 78501

SUZUKI, NORIHISA, history of religion educator; b. Aichi, Japan, Jan. 7, 1935; s. Kazuichi and Tsune (Ohiwa) S.; m. Misako Shibata, May 5, 1960; 2 children. MA, Tokyo U., 1960. Librarian Japanese Soc. Ethnology, Tokyo, 1972-73; prof. Rikkyo U., Tokyo, 1974—. Author: Religious Thoughts in Meiji Ear, 1979, Uchimura Kanzo, 1984, Modern Mind and Buddhism, 1986. Named Hon. Citizen, Koda-Town, 1985. Mem. Japanese Assn. Religious Studies (award 1972).

SVIHEL, RILEY LENARD, clergyman, educator; b. Hutchinson, Minn., Apr. 13, 1934; s. Albin Emil and Emily (Zastera) S.; m. Beverly Ann Kaiser, Oct. 11, 1935; 1 child, Mark. BA, Northwestern Coll., Mpls., 1960; MDiv, Cen. Bapt. Sem., 1964. Pastor Faith Bapt. Ch., Silver Lake, Minn., 1959-80; instr. Jesus People Inst., Mpls.-St. Paul, 1979-85; sr. pastor Zion Christian Ctr., North St. Paul, Minn., 1985-87; founding pastor Victorious Life Ministries Ch., Oakdale, Minn., 1987-90; assoc. pastor, dir. sch. ministry Ch. on Mt. Zion, St. Paul, 1990—; bd. dirs., sec. Missionary Revival Crusade, Laredo, Tex., 1959—; adviser Full Gospel Businessmen's chpt., Hutchinson, 1976-78, Minn. Prayer Watch, Mpls.-St. Paul, 1988—, Paraclete Ministries, Mpls., 1990—. Troop com. chmn. Boy Scouts Am., Silver Lake, Minn., 1972-76. Republican. Avocations: photography, camping, hiking, crafts, gardening.

SWACHA, STANLEY JOSEPH, priest; b. Oil City, Pa., May 27, 1953; s. Frank Raymond and Anna Marie (DeLucia) S. BA, Gannon U., Erie, Pa., 1975; MDiv, Mt. St. Mary's Sem., Emmitsburg, Md., 1979. Ordained priest Roman Cath. Ch., 1979. Parochial vicar St. Leo Magnus Ch., Ridgway, Pa., 1979-82, Queen of the Americas Ch., Conneaut Lake, Pa., 1982, St. Michael Ch., Greenville, Pa., 1982-89; adminstr. St. Bernard Ch., Falls Creek, Pa., 1989—; chaplain Western sect. Cen. Caucus of the Pa. State Coun., K.C., Clarion, 1988—. Co-founder, v.p. Greenville (Pa.) Literacy Coun., 1986-89; com. mem. Seneca dist., Bucktail coun. Boy Scouts Am., DuBois, Pa., 1990—. Democrat. Home: 205 Taylor Ave Falls Creek PA 15840 Office: Saint Bernard Ch 205 Taylor Ave Falls Creek PA 15840 *Everything else is secondary to being a disciple of Jesus Christ.*

SWADENER, MARK WILLIAM, religious organization executive; b. Mishawaka, Ind., Aug. 25, 1954. BS in Bus. Adminstrn., Ind. U., 1976. CPA, Okla. Acct. Coopers & Lybrand, Tulsa and Ft. Wayne, Ind., 1977-84; v.p., chief fin. officer Oral Roberts Ministries, Tulsa, 1984—; chief fin. officer Oral Roberts U., Tulsa, 1984—; bd. dirs. Mark Roberts Motors, Inc., Bank of Commerce, Tulsa; bd. dirs., v.p. fin. 8181 Mgmt. Co.; pres. Abundant Life Ins. Co., Bethany Real Estate, Prism Enterprises Ltd., Sycamore Co., The Stork's Nest; pres. S & P Leasing; chmn. The HMO Okla.; treas. TV-Radio Advt. Co. Bd. dirs. Early Learning Ctr.; treas. City of Faith Hosp. Mem. Ind. Soc. CPA's, Okla. Soc. CPA's, Am. Mgmt. Assn., Health Care Fin. Mgmt. Assn., Tulsa Jr. Philharm. Republican. Avocations: music, sports. Office: Oral Roberts Ministries 8181 S Lewis Tulsa OK 74137

SWADLEY, J. PAUL, pastor; b. Springfield, Mo., Aug. 23, 1928; s. Lynn V. and Martha Jestina Ruth (Little) S.; m. Elizabeth Susan Youngblood, June 1, 1947; children: John Paul, Mark, Suzan A. BS in History, S.W. Mo. State U., 1958; MDiv, Midwestern Bapt. Theol. Sem., 1961; DD, S.W. Bapt. U., 1983. Ordained to ministry Bapt. Ch., 1953. Pastor Chestnutridge (Mo.) Bapt. Ch., 1953-56; pastor First Bapt. Ch., Rogersville, Mo., 1956-62, Richland, Mo., 1962-70; pastor South Haven Bapt. Ch., Springfield, 1970—; pres. bd. dirs. Mo. Bapt. Children's Home; mem. exec. bd. Mo. Bapt. Conv., pres., 1977-78. Home: 720 W LaSalle Springfield MO 65807 Office: South Haven Bapt Ch 2353 S Campbell Springfield MO 65807

SWAFFIELD, WILLIAM ROBERT, music minister; b. Nipawin, Sask., Can., Feb. 22, 1934; s. William Robert and Mabel (Millar) S.; m. Phyllis Nora Grafham, Sept. 5, 1955; children: Wendy May, Cindy Lee. BA, U. Sask., 1956; BE, U. Alta., Can., 1959; MusM, U. Mont., 1967; PhD, U. Wash., 1972. Lic. to ministry Assembly of God Ch., 1970. Music min. Danforth Ch., Toronto, Ont., Can., 1959-60, Capitor Hill Ch., Calgary, Alta., Can., 1960-62, Eighty Ave. Ch., Calgary, 1962-69, Univ. Pl. Assembly of God Ch., Calgary, 1970-71, Neighborhood Ch., Bellevue, Wash., 1973-88, Renton Assembly of God Ch., Kirkland, Wash., 1989—; music coord. Northwest Coll., Kirkland, 1972—. Mem. Music Educators Nat. Conf. Republican. Home: 5514 106th Ave N E Kirkland WA 98033 Office: Northwest Coll Box 579 Kirkland WA 98033

SWAGGART, JIMMY LEE, evangelist, gospel singer; b. Ferriday, La., Mar. 15, 1935; s. W. L. and Minnie Bell S.; married; 1 child. Began preaching on street corners Mangham, La., 1955; traveled throughout U.S. preaching at revival meetings, recording and marketing gospel songs, 1960's, preacher on TV and radio broadcasts; min., pastor Jimmy Swaggart Ministries, Baton Rouge. Gospel albums include This Is Just What Heaven Means To Me, 1971, There Is A River, 1972; author: (with Robert Paul Lamb) To Cross A River, 1977. Office: 8919 World Ministry Ave Baton Rouge LA 70810

SWAIKO, JOSEPH (BISHOP HERMAN OF PHILADELPHIA), bishop. Bishop of Phila. The Orthodox Ch. in Am. Office: Orthodox Church in Am Saint Tikhon's Monastery South Canaan PA 18459*

SWAIM, JEFFREY LYNN, minister; b. Eugene, Oreg., Aug. 14, 1956; s. Laurence Erven and Winifred Marie (Hansen) S.; m. Kathy Lyn Crow, Aug. 13, 1977; children: Stephanie Ann, Lyndsey Elain Marie. BA in Bible, Cen. Bible Coll., 1978. Ordained minister Assemblies of God Ch., 1981. Youth minister First Assembly, Medford, Oreg., 1978-81, Albany, Oreg., 1981—; lectr. South Albany High Sch., 1982-89; mem. state youth senate Assemblies of God, Salem, Oreg., 1981-85, youth rep., Medford, 1978-81, Albany, 1984-85; named Youth Rep. of Yr., 1980, 81. Author (booklet) Questions for New Teen Christians, 1985; editor (booklets) Youth Leaders Training Manual, 1983, Camp Counselor Manual, 1984. Bd. dirs. Juvenile Svcs. Commn., Linn County, Oreg., 1981-82. Republican. Avocations: big game hunting, jogging.

SWAN, ALLAN HOLLISTER, minister; b. Ridgewood, N.J., Oct. 29, 1929; s. Merriam Hollister and Irene Louise (Ferres) S.; m. Janet Louise Peterson, June 6, 1958; children: Jennifer, David, Kimberly, Rebecca. BA, Lafayette Coll., 1951; MDiv, Princeton Sem., 1954; D of Min., San Francisco Theol. Sem., 1975. Ordained to ministry Presbyn. Ch., 1954. Pastor Valmont and Nederland Presbyn. Chs., Boulder, Colo., 1954-57; assoc. pastor 1st Presbyn. Ch., Boulder, 1958-62; pastor Westminster Presbyn. Ch., Ft. Collins, Colo., 1963-70, Lincoln Presbyn. Ch., Stockton, Calif., 1970-80, Covenant Presbyn Ch., Boise, 1981-90; interim pastor Whitworth Presbyn Ch., Spokane, 1990-91; bd. dirs. Coun. Evangelism, N.Y.C., 1967-69; bd. dirs., exec. com. Vocation Agy., N.Y.C., 1979-86. Mem. orgn. bd. Larimer County Youth Home, Ft. Collins, 1966-70; bd. dirs. Rotary, Stockton, Calif. and Boise, 1970-90. Mem. Psi Chi, Pi Gamma Mu. Avocations: photography, gardening, bicycling. Home: 15520 N Meadowglen Ct Spokane WA 99208

SWANN, SAMUEL DOUGLAS, minister; b. Mildenhaul, Eng., May 21, 1963; came to U.S., 1963; s. William Lee and Missy (Olshaskie) S.; m. Brenda Kay Young, July 28, 1984; children: Stephenie Rae, Randi LaNell. BS in Religion, Ea. N.Mex. U., 1986. Lic. to ministry So. Bapt. Conv., 1984. Min. youth and music 1st Bapt. Ch., Dora, N.Mex., 1984-86, Silver City, N.Mex., 1986-89; min. youth 1st Bapt. Ch., Carlsbad, N.Mex., 1990—. Mem. Singing Churchmen N.Mex., Bapt. Student Union Alumni (pres. 1989—). Home: 1606 Lamont Pl Carlsbad NM 88220 Office: 1st Bapt Ch Box 489 Carlsbad NM 88220

SWANN, WILLIAM SHIRLEY, clergyman, theology educator, academic administrator; b. Rome, N.Y., Jan. 7, 1947; s. William S. and Virginia (Norton) S. B.A., St. Joseph Sem., 1970; M.Div., Notre Dame Sem., New Orleans, 1974, S.T.M., 1976; S.T.D., Catholic U., 1981. Ordained priest Roman Catholic Ch., 1974. Tchr. religion St. John Vianney Prep Sch., New Orleans, 1974-75; assoc. pastor St. Matthias Parish, New Orleans, 1975-76; prof. theology Notre Dame Sem., New Orleans, 1979-80, acad. dean., 1980—; prof. Loyola U., New Orleans, 1982-83; adj. prof. Spring Hill Coll., Mobil, Ala., 1981—. Mem. Am. Acad. of Religion, Coll. Theology Soc., Catholic Theology Soc. Am., N.Am. Patristic Soc. Democratic. Avocations: jogging; handball. Home: 2901 S Carrollton Ave New Orleans LA 70118 Office: Notre Dame Sem 2901 S Carrollton Ave New Orleans LA 70118

SWANSON, ALLEN JOHN, religious educator; b. Duluth, Minn., June 22, 1934; s. Arvid John and Ada Jane (Haugen) S.; m. Jean Marie Gilleland, June 9, 1956; children—Cindy, Jeffrey, Michael, Julianne, Stephen. B.A., Augsburg Coll., 1956; M. Div., Augustana Sem., 1961; Th.M., Fuller Sem., 1968; D.Min., Luther Northwestern, 1986. Ordained to ministry Lutheran Church in America, 1961. Missionary, pastor Taiwan Luth. Ch., Taichung, 1964-74; assoc. prof. China Evang. Sem., Taipei, Taiwan, 1975-83, 85—; vice chmn. Taiwan Ch. Growth Soc., Taichung, 1971-79, founder, dir., 1971-83; co-founder, mem. Ctr. Ch. Renewal Devel. and Research, Taipei, 1982—; field edn. dir. China Evang. Sem., Taipei, 1978-83. Author: Taiwan: Mainline vs. Independent Church Growth, 1970; The Church in Taiwan: Profile 1980, 1981; Mending the Nets: A Mid-1980s Review of the Church in Taiwan, 1986. Author and editor: I Will Build My Church, 1975. Contbr. articles to profl. jours. Del. Taiwan Good-Will Del., Taipei, 1979. Mem. Am. Soc. Missiology, Lodge: Kiwanis. Home: 215 S Kipling Apt 250 Saint Paul MN 55119 Office: China Evang Sem, 707 Ting Chou St, Taipei 107, Republic of China

SWANSON, BYRON RALPH, religion educator; b. Omaha, Apr. 22, 1930; s. Ralph William and May Alice (Anderson) S.; m. Kathryn Ann Segerhammar, Oct. 26, 1956; children: Kimberly Kathryn, Timothy William, Todd Sterling, Bradley Krister. BA, Augustana Coll., 1952; MDiv summa cum laude, Luth. Sch. Theology, Chgo., 1956; STM, Yale U., 1961; PhD, Princeton Theol. Sem., 1970. Ordained to ministry Evang. Luth. Ch. Am., 1956. Parish pastor St. Timothy Luth. Ch., Gladstone, Mo., 1956-60, Old Saybrook, Conn., 1960-61; campus pastor Ariz. State U., Tempe, 1961-62; prof. Midland Luth. Coll., Fremont, Nebr., 1968-79, Calif. Luth. U., Thousand Oaks, 1979—; del. NEH summer seminar U. Calif., Santa Barbara, 1976; mem. NEH Curriculum Projects, Calif. Luth. U., 1982-88. Author numerous book revs., 1969—. mem. Am. Acad. Religion, Am. Soc. Ch. History, Luth. Hist. Conf., Augustana Hist. Soc., N.Am. Acad. Ecumenists. Democrat. Home: 2887 N Keats Thousand Oaks CA 91360-1714 Office: Calif Luth U 60 W Olsen Rd Thousand Oaks CA 91360-2787

SWANSON, PAUL REGINALD, marriage and family therapist; b. Moline, Ill., June 10, 1928; s. Herbert Carl Morton and Regina Alfreda Naomi (Rosenberg) S.; m. Cordelia Kathleen Morrison, May 25, 1957; children: Jonathan, Rosanne. AB, Augustana Coll., 1950; MDiv, Augustana Theol. Sem., 1955; STM, Andover Newton Theol. Sch., 1958; PhD, Boston U., 1962. Registered clin. psychologist, Ill. Pastor Bethesda Luth. Ch., Page City, Kans., 1955-56; chaplain Mass. Gen. Hosp., Boston, 1957-62; prof. of pastoral care Luth. Sch. Theology, Chgo., 1962-90; family therapist Marriage and Family Therapy Ctr., Orland Park, Ill., 1983—; pastor Evang. Luth. Ch. in Am. Mem. Mass. Coun. of Chs., Boston, 1957-62; pres. Coun. of Chs. of Rock Island, Scott County, 1966-67; chmn. bd. Rock Island County Coun. on Alcoholism, 1966-67. Augustanta Centennial scholarship, 1956; Judge Baker Guidance Ctr. fellowship NIMH, 1957, marriage counseling fellowship, 1969; Danielsen fellowship Boston U., 1959. Fellow Coll. Chaplains, Am. Protestant Hosp. Assn.; mem. Psychol. Assn., Assn. for Clin. Pastoral Edn. (supr.), Am. Assn. of Pastoral Counselors, Am. Assn. for Marriage and Family Therapy (supr.). Lutheran. Avocations: skiing, bicycling, motorcycling, boating, golf. Home: 41 Aspen Rd Box 1230 Portage IN 46368

SWANSON, REUBEN THEODORE, clergyman, church administrator; b. Bertrand, Nebr., Sept. 22, 1922; s. Theodore C. and Minnie S. (Malm) S.; m. Darlene Marie Carlson, Aug. 8, 1948; children: Conrad Theodore, Joyce Marie. Student, Luther Coll., 1941-43, Doane Coll., 1943-44; B.A., Augustana Coll., Ill., 1947; M.Div., Augustana Theol. Sem., Ill., 1951; D.D. (hon.), Midland Lutheran Coll., 1964; LL.D. (hon.), Susquehanna U., 1981. Ordained to ministry Lutheran Ch. Am., 1951; pastor St. Andrew's Luth. Ch., West Hempstead, N.Y., 1951-55, Augustana Luth. Ch., Omaha, 1955-64; pres. Nebr. Synod, Luth. Ch. Am., Omaha, 1964-78; sec. Luth. Ch. Am., N.Y.C., 1978-87; also mem. exec. council, mem. bd. parish edn., mem. div. world mission and ecumenism Luth. Ch. Am.; pres. Luth. Council in, U.S.A.; commr. Luth. World Ministries; mem. Commn. for New Luth. Ch. Mem. Omaha Public Sch. Citizens Adv. Com., Bd. of Pensions; bd. dirs. Omaha Douglas County chpt. ARC; trustee Immanuel Med. Center, Tabitha Home, Luth. Sch. Theology, Midland Luth. Coll., Bethpage Mission, Luth. Family and Social Services, Nebr. Luth. Outdoor Ministry, Gettysburg Coll.; bd. dirs. Urban League Nebr., Religion in Am. Life, Interch. Ctr., N.Y.C. Served with USN, 1943-46. Club: Union League (N.Y.C.). Lodge: Rotary. Office: Luth Ch Am 231 Madison Ave New York NY 10016

SWANSON, RONALD, religious organization administrator. Pres. Evang. Free Ch. of Can., Langley, B.C. Office: Evang Free Ch Can, #4/10008-29A Ave, Edmonton, AB Canada T6N 1A8*

SWARTLEY, WILLARD MYERS, theologian, educator; b. Doylestown, Pa., Aug. 6, 1936; s. William Henry and Ida (Myers) S.; m. Mary Louise Lapp, Aug. 16, 1958; children: Louisa Renee Swartley Oyer, Kenton Eugene. BA, Ea. Mennonite Coll., 1959; BD, Goshen Bibl. Sem., Elkhart, Ind., 1962; PhD, Princeton Theol. Sem., 1973. Ordained to ministry Mennonite Ch., 1961. Instr. Ea. Mennonite Coll., Harrisonburg, Va., 1965-68, prof., 1971-78; teaching fellow Princeton (N.J.) Theol. Sem., 1969-70; prof. N.T. Associated Mennonite Bibl. Sems., Elkhart, 1978—; vis. prof. Conrad Grebel Coll., Waterloo, Ont., Can., 1975-76; dir. Inst. Mennonite Studies, Elkhart, 1979-88. Author: Mark: The Way for All..., 1979, Slavery, Sabbath, War..., 1983; editor: Essays on Biblical Interpretation, 1984; editor Occasional Papers 1-4, 7-12, 1981-88, Annotated Bibliography of Mennonite Writings on War and Peace, 1930-80, 1987; N.T. editor Believers Ch. Bible Commentary, 1989—; co-editor Studies on Peace and Scripture Series, Westminster/John Knox, 1990—. Mem. Soc. Bibl. Lit., Chgo. Soc. Bibl. Rsch., Network Bibl. Storytellers. Home: 307 E Lusher Elkhart IN 46517 Office: Associated Mennonite Bibl Sems 3003 Benham Ave Elkhart IN 46517-1999

SWARTZ, ELIZABETH ANNE, principal; b. Washington, July 15, 1943; d. Newell Major Swartz and Harriet Anne (Potts) Cunningham. Student, Sch. Sisters of Notre Dame, 1962; BA in Elem. Edn., Coll. Notre Dame of Md., 1972; MA in Teaching, Trinity Coll., 1975; cert. adminstrn. and supervision, Tex. Woman's U., 1981. Cert. tchr., adminstrn. and supervision. Tchr. St. Patrick's Sch., Cumberland, Md., 1965-71, Our Lady of Perpetual Help, Washington, 1971-75, Coolidge (Ariz.) Intermediate Sch., 1975-78, St. Elizabeth, Dallas, 1978-80; prin. Holy Rosary, San Antonio, 1980-89, Our Lady of Perpetual Help Sch., Glendale, Ariz., 1989—; tchr., coord. Our Lady of Perpetual Help Tutorial Program, Washington, 1972-75. Mem. Nat. Cath. Edn. Assn., ASCD, SSND (chair Dallas province peace and justice com. 1988—, mem. interprovincial peace and justice com. 1988—). Democrat. Roman Catholic. Office: Our Lady Perpetual Help Sch 7521 N 57th Ave Glendale AZ 85301

SWARTZ, PAUL FREDERICK, clergyman; b. New Philadelphia, Ohio, Mar. 2, 1943; s. Luther Franklin and Dorothy Mae (Keppler) S.; m. Betty Lou Lacina, Apr. 24, 1965; children: Aaron Joel, Lynnea Renee. Student, Bowling Green State U., 1963-64; BA, Wittenberg U., 1965; BD, Trinity Luth. Sem., 1968, MDiv, 1976. Ordained to ministry Luth. Ch. in Am., 1968. Pastor Trinity Luth. Ch., Sebring, Ohio, 1968-72; mission developer Christ the Redeemer Luth. Ch., Brecksville, Ohio, 1972-73, pastor, 1973-75; asst. to bishop, mem. exec. bd. Ohio Synod, Luth. Ch. in Am., Columbus,

Ohio, 1975-88; sr. pastor St. Matthew's Luth. Ch., Urbana, Ill., 1989—; cons. Profl. Leadership, Columbus, 1981-87; treas., bd. dirs. Midwest Career Devel. Svcs., Columbus and Chgo., 1981-87; del. Luth. Ch. in Am. Conf., Toronto, Ont., Can., 1984, mem. Cen. So. Ill. Synod, 1989—; dean E. Cen. Conf. Cen./So. Ill. Synod Coun., Evang. Luth. Ch. Am., 1990; news corr. The Luth., 1970-75. Contbr. articles to religious publs., chpt. to book. Vice pres. Community Action Ctr., Sebring, 1969-72; bd. dirs. Luth. Children's Aid and Family Svcs., Cleve., 1973-75, Luth. Social Svcs. N.E. Ohio, 1980-84, Luth. Metro Ministries, Cleve., 1980-85; mem. Goals for Greater Akron (Ohio), 1982; cons. Greater Cleve. East Strategy, 1984-87, Greater Akron Strategy, 1985-87. Bowling Green State U. President's scholar, 1962-64; Nat. Luth. Coun. European study grantee, 1963. Avocations: U.S. stamps, Luther and Reformation stamps, model railroading, sailing, 1933 Plymouth. Office: St Matthew Luth Ch 2200 S Philo Rd Urbana IL 61801 *To accomplish great things one must not only act, but also dream; not only plan, but also believe!.*

SWATOS, WILLIAM HENRY, JR., priest; b. Paterson, N.J., Sept. 25, 1946; s. William H. Sr. and Lucille (MacNab) S.; m. Priscilla Lampman, June 16, 1969; children: Giles S., Eric B. AB, Transylvania U., 1966; MDiv, Episc. Theol. Sem., Lexington, Ky., 1969; MA, U. Ky., 1969, PhD, 1973. Ordained to ministry Episcopal Ch., 1970. Mem. sociology faculty King Coll., Bristol, Tenn., 1973-80; vicar St. Mark's Episc. Ch., Silvis, Ill., 1980—; chair dept. edn. Diocese of Quincy, 1988-90; mem. faculty Black Hawk and Scott Community Coll., Moline, Ill., Bettendorf, Iowa, 1988—. Editor: Time, Place and Circumstance, 1990, Religious Politics in Global and Comparative Perspective, 1989, Religious Sociology, 1987; editor Sociol. Analysis: A Jour. in the Sociology of Religion, 1989—; contbr. articles to profl. jours. Full grantee World Soc. Found., Zurich, Switzerland, 1987, grantee NEH, 1974, 79, 85, 89, rsch. grantee Soc. for the Sci. Study of Religion, 1984-85, 91-92; named Disting. Alumnus Dept. of Sociology, U. Ky., Lexington, 1990. Mem. Assn. for the Sociology of Religion (editor 1989-94, book rev. editor 1986-88, exec. coun. 1984-86), Religious Rsch. Assn. (sec. 1990-91, bd. dirs. 1986-89). Republican. Home and Office: 1500 7th Ave Silvis IL 61282-2611

SWAUGER, PAUL LANDIS, SR., religious organization administrator, consultant; b. Titusville, Pa., Feb. 4, 1930; s. John Robert and Lois Arlene (Cogan) S.; m. Nancy Lee Philippe, Aug. 8, 1952; children: Paul Landis Jr., Reba Dawn, Sharon Lynn, Nancy Arlene. BA, Houghton (N.Y.) Coll., 1954; MA, Ball State U., 1979. Ordained to ministry Wesleyan Ch., 1955. Pastor Wesleyan Chs., 1954-63; dist. officer South Ga. Dist. Wesleyan Ch., 1956-63; missionary Wesleyan Ch., Colombia, S. Am., 1963-66; dir. various depts. Wes World Missions, Ind., 1967—; editor Wesleyan World Mag., 1970-84; dir. Metro Move for Wes World Missions, internationally, 1979—; participant World Congress on Evangelization Lausanne, Switzerland, and Manila, 1974, 89. Author, editor: A Church Planting Manual, 1986; contbr. various articles to profl. jours. Mem., advisor Meshangomeshia Boy Scouts Am. coun., Marion, Ind., 1971-72. Mem. Nat. Assn. Evangs., Dept. World Missions (mem. adminstrv. cabinet 1986—). Republican. Avocations: home and auto maintenance. Home: 8760 Wintergreen Way Indianapolis IN 46256 Office: Wesleyan Ch Corp 6060 Castleway W Dr 50434 Indianapolis IN 46256

SWEARENGIN, GARY LEE, minister; b. Springfield, Mo., Oct. 10, 1957; s. Virgil and Mary Esther S.; m. Jennifer Dee Goss, June 27, 1976; children: Michael Cody, Nathan Shawn, Larissa Lanae. Grad. high sch., Ava, Mo.; home study ministry course (4 yrs.). Ordained, Aug., 1987. Pastor Halltown (Mo.) Ch. of the Nazarene, 1978-80, Banner Ch. of the Nazarene, Anderson, Mo., 1980-86, Nixa (Mo.) Ch. of the Nazarene, 1986—; pres. Joplin Dist. Nazarene Youth Internat., 1988—; mem. Joplin Dist. Nazarene Youth Coun., 1979-88. Mem. Nixa Project 2000, 1989—; coach Mighty Mite Football, Nixa, 1987-90, YMCA 7th grade basketball, 1987-88. Mem. Nixa Ministerial Alliance (pres. 1986—), Nixa Optimist Club (v.p. 1988—). Republican. Avocations: singing, softball, basketball. Office: Nixa Ch of the Nazarene 306 Northview Rd Nixa MO 65714

SWEARER, DONALD KEENEY, Asian religions educator, writer; b. Wichita, Kans., Aug. 2, 1934; s. Edward Mays and Eloise Catherine (Keeney) S.; m. Nancy Chester; children: Susan Marie, Stephen Edward. AB, Princeton U., 1956, MA, 1965, PhD, 1967; BD, Yale U., 1962, STM, 1963. Instr. English dept. Bangkok Christian Coll., 1957-60; adminstrv. asst. Edward W. Hazen Found., New Haven, 1961-63; instr., then asst. prof. Oberlin (Ohio) Coll., 1965-70; assoc. prof. Swarthmore (Pa.) Coll., 1970-75, prof. Asian religions, 1975—, Eugene M. Lang Rsch. prof., 1987—, chair dept. religion, 1986-91; adj. prof. U. Pa., Phila., 1979—; film cons. ABC, 1972; lectr. Smithsonian Instn., 1982—, Asia Soc. N.Y., 1982—. Author: Wat Haripunjaya, 1976, Dialogue. The Key to Understanding Other Religions, 1977, Buddhism and Society in Southeast Asia, 1981; co-author: For the Sake of the World. The Spirit of Buddhist and Christian Monasticism, 1989; co-editor: Ethics, Wealth and Salvation. A Study in Buddhist Social Ethics, 1989, Me-and-Mine. Selected Essays of Bhikkhu Buddhadasa, 1989; mem. editorial bd. Jour. Religious Ethics, 1978—; book rev. editor S.E. Asia Religious Studies Rev., 1985—; contbr. articles various pubs. Chair adult edn. Swarthmore Presbyn. Ch., 1985-87. Asian religions study fellow Soc. Religion in Higher Edn., Sri Lanka, Thailand, Japan, 1967-68; NEH sr. fellow Thailand, 1972-73, rsch. fellow, 1990-91; Rockefeller Found. humanities fellow, Thailand, 1985-86; sr. rsch. scholar Fulbright Found., 1989-90; NEH Transl. grantee, 1990-91. Mem. AAUP, Assn. Asian Studies (bd. dirs. 1977-80), Am. Acad. Religion (v.p. mid-Atlantic region 1971-72), Am. Soc. Study of Religion (editorial bd. Jour. Religious Ethics 1978—), Soc. Buddhist-Christian Studies. Democrat. Home: 109 Columbia Ave Swarthmore PA 19081 Office: Swarthmore Coll Dept of Religion Swarthmore PA 19081

SWEARINGEN, BERT CHARLES, minister; b. Jacksonville, Fla., June 13, 1936; s. Stephen Burton and Mary Thelma (Neustadtl) S.; m. Barbara Lee Heckroth, Dec. 22, 1962; children: Stephen Adam, David Lee. BA, Jacksonville U., 1962; BD, Columbia Theol. Sem., 1965. Ordained to ministry Presbyn. Ch., 1966. Pastor First Presbyn. Ch., Leakesville, Miss., 1965-68, 1st Presbyn. Ch., Chipley, Fla., 1968-75; organizing pastor Sunny Hills (Fla.) Community Ch., 1972-74; pastor Vidalia (Ga.) Presbyn. Ch., 1975-87, First Presbyn. Ch., Hernando, Miss., 1987-89, Ch. on the Bayou Presbyn., Tarpon Springs, Fla., 1989—; mgr. Dogwood Acres Camp, 1970-75; commr. Gen. Assembly, Presbyn. Ch. U.S.A., 1974; moderator Savannah (Ga.) Presbytery, 1977-78; mem. coun. Synod of S.E., 1982-87; sec. Ga. Christian Coun., Macon, 1983; pres. adv. bd. Brewton Parker Coll., Mt. Vernon, Ga., 1984-87. Commr. Chipley Housing Authority, 1971-75; sec. Mental Health Assn., Chipley, 1973. Sgt. USAF, 1954-60. Recipient Servant Leadership award Savannah Presbytery, 1978, Pub. Svc. award Vidalia C. of C., 1987. Mem. Acad. Parish Clergy, Optimists (bd. dirs. Hernando chpt. 1987-89), Kiwanis (editor Vidalia chpt. 1982-87). Office: Ch on the Bayou 409 Whitcomb Blvd Tarpon Springs FL 34689

SWEARINGEN, JEFFREY REA, minister; b. West Union, Ohio, July 9, 1964; s. Daryl R. and Joyce (Wilson) S.; m. Peggy M. Miranda, Sept. 22, 1990. BA, Cin. Bible Coll., 1986. Ordained to ministry Ch. of Christ, 1986. Children's min. 1st Christian Ch., Ft. Myers, Fla., 1986-90; sr. min. Delaware (Ohio) Christian Ch., 1990—; trustee Alexander Christian Found. of Fla., Kissimmee, Fla., 1989-90; del. Fla. Christian Youth Conv. Planning, Orlando, 1988-90. Mem. Fellowship Christian Mins., Kiwanis. Office: Delaware Christian Ch 2280 Maryville Rd Delaware OH 43015

SWEEM, BILLY DON, minister; b. Bartlesville, Okla., Aug. 7, 1942; s. Verl D. and Viola (Benner) S.; m. Roberta Marie Hawthorn, Dec. 26, 1990; children: Mark A. Bradburn. Dipl., Internat. Bible Inst. & Sem., Portsmount, Fla. Ordained to ministry Gospel Mins. and Chs. Internat., 1991, Ind. Assemblies Fellowship, 1991. Evangelist Lighthouse Temple, Colorado Springs, Colo., 1977-80, Tulsa, 1980-85; youth pastor Echoes of Faith, Las Vegas, Nev., 1985-89; exec. dir. Billy Sweem Gospel Ministries, Tulsa, 1990—; evangelist United Meth. Coop. Ministries, Tulsa, 1990—. Home: 715 N Quaker Tulsa OK 74106-5421 Office: Billy Sweem Gospel Ministry PO Box 2716 Tulsa OK 74101-2716

SWEENEY, DOROTHY LOVE, minister, nurse; b. Worcester, Mass., May 22, 1922; d. Joseph Wilfred and Lillian Mary (Fagga) Fournier; children: Helen F. Hunter, Joseph Wayne Jodrey; m. John L. Sweeney, Mar. 15, 1986; stepchildren: Susan, Florence Moreno, Cathleen Bunn, John L., James, Thomas, Robert. Diploma in nursing, St. Mary's Hosp., 1963; ministerial diploma Religious Sci. Internat., 1973, DD, 1982, DD, United Ch. of Religious Sci., 1988. RN, Ga.; ordained to ministry Ch. of Religious Sci., 1980. Dir., Southeast States region VIII, United Ch. of Religious Sci., Beverly Hills, Calif., 1980 (internat. bd. trustees); staff min. World Ministry of Prayer, United Ch. of Religious Sci., Los Angeles, 1980-81, dir., v.p., Los Angeles, 1983-85 ; min., dir. Golden Circle Ch. of Religious Sci., Santa Ana, Calif., 1981-83; staff min. Redondo Beach Ch. Religious Sci.; ministerial staff cons. alcohol recovery services Tustin Community Hosp. (Calif.), Villa Recovery Home for Women, Santa Ana. Author: A Time for Healing, 1975; TV ministry: The Hour of New Thought, 1983. Mem. Southeast Clergy of Religious Sci. (sec., v.p., pres. 1974-77). Club: Toastmaster (treas., sec., v.p., pres. 1971-72). Home: 635 Paseo Dela Playa # 303 Redondo Beach CA 90277-6547 Office: 907 Knob Hill Ave Redondo Beach CA 90277 *In my journey thru life, I have found I am a participant but more than that, I want to be a contributor to life. My work is the vehicle to that end.*

SWEENEY, MARK OWEN, publisher; b. Cherryvale, Kans., Dec. 27, 1942; s. Paul Eldon and Clelia Eugenia (Bosette) S.; m. Janet Lynn Turner, July 24, 1964; children—Douglas, Jonathan. Grad., Moody Bible Inst., 1963; B.A., Pacific Coll., 1965; M.A., Wheaton Coll., Ill., 1967. Instr. history Cascade Coll., Portland, Oreg., 1967-70; editor Moody Bible Inst., Chgo., 1970-72; exec. producer Moody Corr. Sch., Moody Bible Inst. (Radio div.), 1972-74; dir. public relations Moody Bible Inst. (dir. Moody Lit. Ministries), 1974-77, mgr. publ. div., 1977-81; dir. Victor Books, Scripture Press Publs., 1981-83, v.p., 1983—. Mem. Christian Booksellers Assn., Evang. Christian Publs. Assn., Nat. Assn. Evangelicals. Home: 1067 Wexford Ct Wheaton IL 60187 Office: Victor Books 1825 College Ave Wheaton IL 60187

SWEENEY, MARVIN A., religious studies educator; b. Springfield, Ill., July 4, 1953; s. Jack H. and Leonore R. (Dorman) S.; m. Jodi Magness, May 5, 1988. AB, U. Ill., 1975; MA, Claremont Grad. Sch., 1981, PhD, 1983. Head cataloguer Ancient Bibl. Manuscript Ctr., Claremont, Calif., 1979-83; asst. prof. U. Miami, Coral Gables, Fla., 1983-89; coord. pre-law advising U. Miami, Coral Gables, 1987—, assoc. prof. religious studies, 1989—. Author: Isaiah 1-4 and the Post-Exilic Understanding of the Isaianic Tradition. Bd. dirs. Hillel Jewish Student Orgn., Coral Gables, 1983—. Postdoctoral fellow Yad Hanadiv Barecha Found., Hebrew U. Jerusalem, 1989-90. Mem. Soc. Bibl. Lit., Am. Acad. Religion, Assn. Jewish Studies, Am. Schs. Oriental Rsch., Nat. Assn. Profs. Hebrew, Am. Oriental Soc., So. Assn. Pre-Law Advisers, Phi Kappa Phi. Jewish. Office: U Miami Dept Religious Studies PO Box 248264 Coral Gables FL 33124

SWEENEY, MARY DEVOTA, nun; b. Wichita Falls, Tex., Aug. 27, 1921; d. Clarence Francis and Sarah Haz (Walsh) S. BS, Our Lady of the Lake Coll., San Antonio, 1967. Rchr. St. Ann's Sch., Beaumont, Tex., 1941-46, Our Lady of Victory Acad., Ft. Worth, Tex., 1946-48, St. Mary's Convent, Lowestoft, Eng., 1955-58; provincial superior Sisters of St. Mary of Namur, Ft. Worth, Tex., 1958-64; tchr., assoc. adminstr. Corpus Christi (Tex.) Acad., 1986—. Mem. Nat. Cath. Edn. Assn. Democrat. Home and Office: Corpus Christi Acad 3036 Saratoga Blvd Corpus Christi TX 78415-5715

SWEET, MALCOLM STUART, clergyman; b. Canandaigua, N.Y., Sept. 16, 1905; s. Louis Matthews and Margaret (Stuart) S.; A.B. summa cum laude, Hobart Coll., 1933; B.D., McCormick Theol. Sem., 1936, Bernadine Orme Smith fellow, 1936-37; m. Mildred Emily Wood, Sept. 6, 1934; children—Martha Lee, Bonnie Jean, Mildred Emily, Mary Margaret. Asso. Halsey, Stuart & Co., 1924-29; ordained Presbyn. minister, 1936; minister 1st Presbyn. Ch., Carbondale, Pa., 1949-53, No. Light Presbyn. Ch., Juneau, Alaska, 1953—; broadcaster Religion in the News program, Juneau, Alaska; dir. KSEW The Voice of Sheldon Jackson (Sitka, Alaska); chaplain of senate Alaska, 1955-63; pastor Shepherd of the Hills United Presbyn. Ch., Lakewood, Colo., 1963—. Organizing minister Bd. Nat. Missions, United Presbyn. Ch. U.S., Snyod Colo.; chmn. Dept. on Care of Candidates, Presbytery of Denver; chmn. adv. council Alaska Employment Security Commn. Mem. permanent commn. on inter-ch. relations Gen. Assembly Presbyn. Ch. U.S. Dir. Alaska Crippled Childrens Assn.; mem. Committee of 100 for Lackawanna Indsl. Fund Enterprise and co-chmn. Upper Lackawanna Valley; chmn. 1953 Community Chest Campaign and Permanent Com. on Planning. Mem. Mayor's Com. Indsl. Rehab.; adv. com. Sheldon Jackson Jr. Coll. Served as chaplain AUS, regimental chaplain 363d Regt., 91st Inf. Div., Rome-Arno-North Apennines campaigns, 1943-46. Mem. Presbytery of Alaska, moderator 1956, pres. trustees, chmn. stewardship and promotion com., mem. council; mem. stewardship and promotion com. Synod Wash.-Alaska. Scranton Ministerium; chmn. dept. communications Synod Colo., mem. gen. council; mem. communications commn. Colo. Council of Churches; chaplain Colo. Senate, 1969—. Mem. Am. Legion (local chaplain), Officers Res. Corps, Res. Officers Assn., Mil. Order World Wars, Juneau C. of C. (vice pres. 1961, dir.), Juneau Ministers Assn. (pres. 1958), Founders and Patriots Am., V.F.W., Mil. Chaplains Assn., Ill. Hist. Soc., Sons Union Vets. Civil War (chaplain Colo.), S.A.R. (chaplain Colo.), Sons Am. Colonists, Internat. Platform Assn., Phi Beta Kappa. Mason. Clubs: Rotary, Exchange. Author: The Pastoral Ministry in Our Time (with Louis Matthews Sweet), 1948; Unto Everlasting Life, 1954. Home: 7653 Lee Dr Arvada CO 80002 Office: 11500 W 20th Ave Lakewood CO 80215

SWEETEN, GARY RAY, religious counseling educator; b. Ina, Ill., May 5, 1938; s. Thomas Jefferson and Leota Leone (Taylor) S.; m. Karen J. Sweeten, Nov. 21, 1961; children: Julie Rae, Timothy Andrew. AA, Rend Lake Coll., 1960; BS, So. Ill. U., 1965, MS, 1967; EdD, U. Cin., 1975. Tchr., coach pub. schs. Ina, Bellerive and Mt. Vernon, Ill., 1960-65; asst. dean U. Cin., 1967-69, asst. to univ. provost, 1969-73; minister of Christian edn. Coll. Hill Presbyn. Ch., Cin., 1973-76, minister of counseling and growth, 1973-89; chief exec. officer, pres. Lifeway Counseling Ctr., Cin., 1989—; founder, chairperson Equipping Mins. Internat., Cin., 1978—; cons., founder Sweeten Creative Cons., Cin., 1970—; founder, pres. Christian Info. Com., Cin., 1978—; pres., bd dirs. Presbyn. Renewal Ministry, Oklahoma City, 1980-85. Author numerous articles, monographs, tng. manuals. Bd. dirs. Citizens Against Substance Abuse. Named Outstanding Alumni Rend Lake Coll., Ina, 1986. Mem. Ohio Assn. Counselor Devel., Christian Assn. Psychol. Studies. Avocations: travel, basketball. Home: 11863 Tennyson Ct Cincinnati OH 45241 Office: Lifeway Counseling Ctr 4015 Executive Park Dr Cincinnati OH 45241

SWEETING, GEORGE, clergyman, educational institution administrator; b. Haledon, N.J., Oct. 1, 1924; s. William and Mary Roger (Irving) S.; m. Margaret Hilda Schnell, June 14, 1947; children: George David, James Douglas, Donald William, Robert Bruce. Pastors course diploma, Moody Bible Inst., Chgo., 1945; B.A., Gordon Coll., Wenham, Mass., 1948; D.D. (hon.), Gordon-Conwell Theol. Sem., South Hamilton, Mass., 1970; H.H.D. (hon.), Azusa (Cal.) Pacific Coll., 1971; LL.D. (hon.), Tenn. Temple Coll., Chattanooga, 1971; D.Litt. (hon.), John Brown U., Siloam Springs, Ark., 1983. Pastor Grace Ch., Clifton, N.J., 1948-50; world-wide evangelist, 1951-61; pastor Madison Ave. Bapt. Ch., Paterson, N.J., 1961-66, Moody Ch., Chgo., 1966-71; pres. Moody Bible Inst., Chgo., 1971-87, chancellor, 1987—; pres. Moody Inst. Sci., 1971-87, Moody Press, 1971-87; editor Moody Monthly mag., 1971-87. Author: How to Discover the Will of God, 1975, How to Begin the Christian Life, 1975, How to Witness Successfully, 1978, Talking It Over, 1979, Faith that Works, 1983, Catch the Spirit of Love, 1983, Special Sermons, 1985, Great Quotes and Illustrations, 1986, Psalms of the Heart, 1988, (with Donald W. Sweeting) The Acts of God, 1987, Lessons From the Life of Moody, 1989, Secrets of Excellence, 1990. Club: Union League (Chgo.).

SWEIGART, JOHN ANDREW, pastor; b. Dayton, Ohio, Apr. 16, 1954; s. Donald Raymond and Rita Germaine (Lang) S.; m. Susan Rae Berkshire, Aug. 12, 1979; children: Nathan Andrew, Michael John. BA in English, U. Cin., 1977, BS in Secondary Edn., 1977; MDiv, Andrews U., 1986. Ordained to ministry Adventist Ch., 1989. Pastor S.E. Ohio Dist., Athens, Ohio, 1985-88, Mount Vernon (Ohio) Dist. Seventh-day Adventists, 1988—; Mem. Ohio Conf. (constn. and by-laws com. 1987-90). Precinct judge Dem. Party, Cin., 1975-77, Lions, Mt. Vernon, 1990-91. Mem. Cen. Ohio Seventh Day Adventists Ministerial Assn. (pres. 1990, sec. 1991), Ohio Conf. Assn. (bd. dirs., trustee 1990-91). Democrat. Home: 419 Wooster Rd Mount Vernon OH 43050 Office: Mt Vernon City Ch 425 S Edgewood Rd Mount Vernon OH 43050 *Each individual is created in God's image, mentally, physically and spiritually. Each person who comes to Him by faith in Jesus is being transformed into His likeness more each day. Through each of us so transformed He is reaching out to all people that all may be like Him.*

SWEITZER, HARRY PHILLIPS, minister, consultant; b. Youngstown, Ohio, July 30, 1916; s. Benjamin Henry and Agnes Letittia S.; m. Margaret Crosbie Reed, Aug. 9, 1941; children—Paul, Mary Jean. B.A., Muskingum Coll., 1938, diploma in speech, 1938; M.Div., McCormick Theol. Sem., Chgo., 1941; D.D. (hon.), Muskingum Coll., 1972, LittD (hon.), Westminster Coll. of Salt Lake City, 1991. Ordained to ministry Presbyn. Ch., 1941. Sr. pastor First Presbyn. Ch., Kingfisher, Okla., 1941-42, Chickasha, Okla., 1942-45; asst. pastor Westminster Presbyn. Ch., Minneapolis, 1945-51; sr. pastor First Presbyn. Ch., Grand Forks, N.D., 1951-58, Central Presbyn. Ch., St. Paul, 1958-73, First Presbyn. Ch., Salt Lake City, 1973-82, pastor emeritus, 1983—; interim pastor 1st Bapt. Ch., Bountiful, Utah, 1985-87, 88-89, Ch. of Christ Congl., Ogden, Utah, 1989-90; moderator Presbytery of Pembina, Grand Forks, N.D., 1962-63, Presbytery of St. Paul, 1969, Synod of N.D., Grand Forks, 1963-64. Sec.-treas. Westminster Coll., Salt Lake City, 1979—; bd. dirs. Utah Alcohol Found., Salt Lake City, 1978—, Bush Found., St. Paul, 1970-89, YMCA, 1975-81. Democrat. Mem. Kiwanis (pres. 1955-56, 84-85), Masons, Shriners. Home: 15803 N 6th Dr Phoenix AZ 85023

SWENSEN, OSCAR WARREN, priest; b. Stoneham, Mass., Oct. 24, 1931; s. O. Walter and Gunhild J. (Munnick) S.; m. Constance E. Speedie, June 27, 1958; children—Kristin, Bara, Sonje. A.B., Harvard U., 1953; M.Div., Episcopal Theol. Sch., 1959. Ordained priest Episcopal Ch., 1959. Vicar, rector Ch. of the Transfiguration, Derry, N.H., 1959-68; rector Calvary Ch., Danvers, Mass., 1968—. Mem. Council on Aging, Danvers, 1975-81. Served with U.S. Army, 1952-54. Mem. Phillips Brooks Clericus (past pres.), Mass. Episcopal Clergy Assn. Lodge: Kiwanis (dir. 1982-85). Avocations: piano; skiing; water-skiing; carpentry; gardening. Home: 44 Cherry St Danvers MA 01923

SWENSON, BRUCE HENRY, minister; b. N.Y.C., June 13, 1932; s. Carl Henry and Alva W. (Valley) S.; m. Sondra Elaine Hennessy; children: Erik J., Laurel J. BEE, Poly. Inst. Bklyn., 1954; M of Div., Princeton (N.J.) Theol. Sem., 1961; postgrad., Grad. Sch. Pub. and Internat. Affairs, Pitts., 1968-69. Ordained to ministry Presbyn. Ch., 1962. Elec. engr. Westinghouse Electric Co., Pitts., 1954-58; pastor First United Presbyn. Ch., Pitts., 1961-65; dir. div. care and tng. United Oakland Ministry, Pitts., 1965-68; assoc. exec. dir. research and planning Christian Assocs. S.W. Pa., Pitts., 1972-86, assoc. exec. dir., 1987—; mem. Commn. on Religion in Appalachia, Nashville, 1972—; chair consistory Community Reconciliation, Pitts., 1981-83; sec. bd. dirs. Ecumenical Urban Ministry, 1980-87. Election judge 30th Dist. 14th Ward, Pitts., 1970. Served with U.S. Army, 1956. Recipient cert. Recognition Nat. Assn. Ecumenical Staff, 1987. Mem. Religious Research Assn., North Am. Acad. Ecumenists. Democrat. Avocations: walking, tennis, reading. Office: Christian Assocs SW Pa 1817 Investment Bldg Pittsburgh PA 15222

SWENSON, DANIEL LEE, bishop; b. Oklahoma City, Feb. 2, 1928; s. Daniel and Lillian (Twedt) S.; m. Sally Mason, June 9, 1951; children: Martha Mason, Sara Swenson Shuford, Daniel Gerald. BA, U. Minn., 1950; DD (hon.), Seabury-Western Theol Sem., Evanston, Ill., 1987. Pvt. practice bus. mgmt. St. Martin's by the Lake, Alexandria, Minn., 1952-58; asst. min. St. Martin's By the Lake, Minnetonka Beach, Minn., 1959-62; vicar St. Edward's Mission, Wayzata, Minn., 1962-65; rector St. Paul's Ch., Virginia, Minn., 1965-75; dean Cathedral of Our Merciful Saviour, Faribault, Minn., 1975-78; rector St. John in the Wilderness, White Bear Lake, Minn., 1978-86; bishop Episc. Diocese Vt., Burlington, 1986—; dean Region II, Diocese of Minn., 1972-75; chmn., Diocesan Commn. on Ministry, Minn., 1976-83; examining chaplain Diocese of Minn., 1974-86; trustee Seabury-Western Theol. Sem., Evanston, Ill., 1978-89. Vice chmn. City Human Rights Commn., Virginia, Minn., 1972-75; dist. chmn. N.E. Minn. Boy Scouts Am., 1970-73; coun. mem. Indianhead and Green Mountain Boy Scouts Am., 1975-89. With U.S. Army, 1946-48. Office: Diocesan Ctr Rock Point Burlington VT 05401

SWENSON, STEPHEN DOUGLAS, minister; b. Watertown, S.D., May 16, 1949; s. Elden William and Jean Eleanor (Uhrich) S.; m. Lois Joy Gabel, June 6, 1971; children: Timothy, Karissa. BA, Augustana Coll., Sioux Falls, S.D., 1971; MDiv, Luther Theol. Sem., 1975; MA, U. Notre Dame, 1982. Ordained to ministry Evangelical Luth. Ch. Am. Pastor Orient and Our Savior Luth. Ch., Faulkton, S.D., 1975-78, Trinity Luth. Ch., Edgemont, S.D., 1978-81, 1st English Luth. Ch., Mishawaka, Ind., 1981—; ecumenical officer Ind.-Ky. Synod Evangelical Luth. Ch. Am., Indpls., 1988—, mem. coun., exec. bd., 1989—, liaison Luth. Ecumenical Network, Chgo., 1989—. Author: With This Bread and Cup, 1985, Holy Communion and Daily Life, 1988. Mem. St. Joseph County Cult Awareness Task Force, South Bend, Ind.; pres. Faulkton Ministerial Assn., 1977, Edgemont Ministerial Assn., 1980. Lt. (j.g.) USNR, 1971-75. Fellow N.Am. Acad. Liturgy, Nat. Workshop Christian Unity, Liturgical Conf.; mem. Lions (Lion tamer 1982—, pres. Faulkton chpt. 1977-78). Democrat. Home: 1542 Kensington Pl Mishawaka IN 46544 Office: 1st English Luth Ch 16495 Ireland Rd Mishawaka IN 46544

SWETMON, BILLY ROBERT, minister; b. Bowling Green, Ky., Mar. 9, 1943; s. Shelby Viven and Monica Jeraldine (Richards) S.; m. Linda Kaye Houchens, Dec. 17, 1963; children: Melanie Diane, Jennifer Kaye. Cert., Nashville Sch. Preaching, 1970; BA, Washington Internat. Coll., 1979; MS, Emmanuel Bapt. U., 1990. Ordained to ministry Ch. of Christ. Minister Ch. of Christ, Bowling Green, 1970-73; min. Ch. of Christ, Lubbock, Tex., 1973-79, Plano, Tex., 1979—; staff writer The World Evangelist jour., Florence, Ala., 1974—, Christian Family Mag., Dallas, 1980—, Power for Today, Nashville, 1982—; bible tchr. Lubbock (Tex.) Christian Coll., 1974-76, bd. dirs. Family Life Ctr., 1978-79, pres. adv. coun., 1983—; chaplain Tex. Tech. Teaching Hosp., Lubbock, 1977-78; mem. adv. bd. Lubbock (Tex.) Children's Home, 1977-78. Author: Christian Apologetics, 1974 (with others) Great Moments With Christ, 1974, Great Personalities With Christ, 1975, That Ye May Believe, 1976, Exploring God's Mysteries, 1985, Unlocking Mysteries of God's Word, 1989, Your Friendship Potential, 1989, A Giving Heart, 1987; editor: spl. edit. 1983 World Fair, Christian Family Mag., 1983; contbr. articles to profl. jours. Named to Honorable Order of Ky. Colonels, 1966, Outstanding Young Man Am., Nat. Jaycees, 1978. Mem. United Assn. Christian Counselors, Rotary. Avocations: photography, physical fitness. Home: 2005 Midcrest Plano TX 75075 Office: Fellowship in Christ 1615 Dorchester Ste 108 Plano TX 75075 *To live life with the full assurance that what you are doing, where you are living, and the direction you are going are pleasing and acceptable to God is to have found success in the fullest meaning of that word.*

SWETNAM, JAMES HUBBARD, priest, educator; b. St. Louis, Mar. 18, 1928; s. Henry Hubbard and Helen Mary (Luth) S. PhM, St. Louis U., 1953; MTh, St. Mary's (Kans.) Coll., 1960; M of Sacred Scripture, Pontifical Biblical Inst., Rome, 1962; PhD, U. Oxford, Eng., 1981. Joined S.J., 1945; ordained priest Roman Cath. Ch., 1958. Editor Pontifical Biblical Inst., Rome, 1962-75, 78—, instr., 1963-75, 78-84, prof., 1984—, vice rector, 1984—, dean biblical faculty, 1986-89, registrar, dean of students, sec., 1991—. Author: Jesus and Isaac, 1981; contbr. articles to profl. jours. Mem. Soc. Jesus, Cath. Biblical Assn. Am., Soc. New Testament Studies. Avocation: touring Rome. Home and Office: Pontifical Biblical Inst, Via della Pilotta 25, 00187 Rome Italy

SWEZEY, CHARLES MASON, Christian ethics educator, administrator; b. Charlottesville, Va., May 16, 1935; s. Fenton Hendy and Catherine Jane (Mason) S.; m. Mary Evelyn Knight, June 16, 1960; children: Christopher Stephen, Margaret Fenton, Mary Mason. BA, Washington and Lee U., 1957; BD, Union Theol. Sem., 1961; STM, Yale U., 1962; MA, PhD, Vanderbilt U., 1974, 78. Ordained to ministry, Presbyterian Ch., 1962. Asst. minister Lexington (Va.) Presbyn. Ch., 1962-70; stated clk. Lexington Presbytery, 1967-68; vis. lectr. Mary Baldwin Coll., Staunton, Va., 1966-67, 68; asst. prof. Union Theol. Sem., Richmond, Va., 1974-80, assoc. prof., 1980-83, prof. Christian ethics, 1983—, dean of faculty, 1990—; mem. coop. com. on examination for candidates, Presbyn. Ch. U.S.A., 1978-88. Editorial bd. Interpretation, Richmond, 1981—; co-editor: James Gustafson's Theocentric Ethics, 1988; contbr. articles to theol. publs. Bd. dirs. Richmond Met. Blood Svc., 1987—; mem. Human Fetal Tissue Transplantation panel NIH, Bethesda, Md., 1988. Grantee Danforth Found., 1968-69; Woodrow Wilson Found. fellow, 1970-71. Mem. Soc. Christian Ethics. Office: Union Theol Sem 3401 Brook Rd Richmond VA 23227

SWICHKOW, LOUIS JUDAH, rabbi; b. Chgo., July 13, 1912; s. Joseph Swichkow and Dora Shafran; m. Gertrude Astrachan, Feb. 11, 1936; children: Rashalee, Morton C., Daniel M., Deborah. BS, DePaul U., 1934; MA, Marquette U., 1943, PhD, 1973; DHL, Jewish Theol. Sem., 1953. Ordained rabbi, 1935. Rabbi Beth El Ner Tamid Synagogue, Milw., 1937-85, rabbi emeritus, 1985—. Author: (with Lloyd P. Gartner) History of the Jews of Milwaukee, 1963; Invocations, 1964, Counting Our Blessings, 1990. Mem. law com. Wis. Legis. Coun., Milw., 1957-59; mem. Milw. Com. on Community Rels., 1961-65; mem. Milw. County Family Ct. Adv. Com., 1963-67; vice-chmn. Milw. County Juv. Ct. Adv. Com., 1967-69. Recipient award Milw. County Hist. Soc., 1959. Mem. Rabbinical Assembly Am. Home: 11305 N Mulberry Dr Mequon WI 53092 Office: Beth El Ner Tamid Synagogue 2909 W Mequon Rd Milwaukee WI 53092

SWILLEY, BARBARA JOYCE, church business administrator; b. Poplarville, Miss., Mar. 3, 1950; d. Oscar Doyle and Bernice Joyce (Owen) Entrekin; m. Don R. Swilley, Oct. 14, 1966; children: Karen Renee, Donna Lisa. Grad. high sch., Lumberton, Miss. Officer mgr. Temple Bapt. Ch., Hattiesburg, Miss., 1985—. Mem. Miss. Bapt. Secs. Assn. (area rep. 1990-91), Hattiesburg Racquet Club (sec. 1983—). Office: Temple Bapt Ch 1508 Hardy St Hattiesburg MS 39401

SWINDALL, MARSHALL GUY, minister; b. Clearwater, Fla., Feb. 19, 1951; s. Oscar and Nora (Pitts) S.; m. Alayne Sealey, Feb. 16, 1951; children: Ryan Joshua, Lindsey Rachel. AA in Bus. Adminstrn., St. Petersburg Jr. Coll., 1971; minister's cert., Bear Valley Sch. Bibl. Studies, Denver, 1975. Ordained to ministry Ch. of Christ, 1975. Assoc. minister Northside Ch. of Christ, St. Petersburg, Fla., 1975-76; missionary preacher Limon Ch. of Chris, Colo., 1976-78; pulpit minister Suncoast Ch. of Christ, 1978—. Contbr. numerous articles to religious publs. Motivational spkr. Mothers Against Drunk Drivers, West Palm Beach, Fla., 1980-81, Palm Beach County Schs. (Fla.), 1984—. Mem. Nat. Spkr.'s Assn. Democrat. Club: Toastmasters. Avocations: photography, jogging. Office: Suncoast Ch of Christ 5561 Hypoluxo Rd Lake Worth FL 33463-7301

SWINEY, WILLIE LEE, minister, educator; b. Bennestsville, S.C., July 16, 1948; s. Willie and Julia Mae (Monroe) S.; m. Cora Bell Suggs, Aug. 29, 1972 (div. July 1991); 1 child, Willie Terrell. BA, Livingstone Coll., 1970; MDiv, Hood Theol. Sem., 1973; postgrad., So. Calif. Grad. Sch. Theology, 1991. Lic. to ministry A.M.E. Zion Ch., 1966, ordained as deacon, 1971, as elder, 1973. Pastor St. Frances AME Zion Ch., Portchester, N.Y., 1973-74; assoc. min. Naomi AME Zion Ch., Bklyn., 1974-77, 82-85; pastor Sojourner Truth AME Zion Ch., St. Albans, N.Y., 1977-82; min., pastor Community Centralized, Bklyn., 1985-87; pastor, pres. Universal House of Prayer, Bklyn., 1987—; vol. chaplain N.Y.C. Police Dept., 1986—, N.Y.C. Housing Authority Police Dept., 1986—, Sea Gate Police Dept., Bklyn., 1988—, N.Y.C. Transit Police Dept., Bklyn., 1990—. Tchr. N.Y.C. Bd. Ed., Bklyn., 1986-87; office aide Dept. Social Svcs., N.Y.C., 1977-86; supr. Neighborhood Youth Corps, N.Y.C., summers 1970-75; aide summer work U.S. Naval Applied Sci. Lab., Bklyn., 1967; mem. Rep. Presdl. Task Force, 1989-91, Rep. Nat. Com. Named Outstanding Community Leader Consol. Edison Co., Bklyn., 1988; recipient cert. merit Rep. Nat. Com., 1990, Presdl. Order Merit Nat. Rep. Senatorial Com., 1991, cert. recognition Pres. and Vice-Pres. U.S., 1991. Mem. United Fedn. Tchrs., U.S. Senatorial Club, Masons, Phi Beta Sigma. Home and Office: 2749 W 33d St # 6-A Brooklyn NY 11224-1638 *The secret of my success is also what I strongly believe in. It can be found summed up in the Bible. Ecclesiastes 12:12, "Let us hear the conclusion of the whole matter: Fear God, and keep his commandments: for this is the whole duty of man." (King James version).*

SWINFORD, MAURICE LYSLE, religious association administrator; b. Charleston, Ill., Mar. 17, 1928; s. George Albert and Bessie Josephine (Murphy) S.; m. Charlotte Fender, June 20, 1948; children: Valorie Jean, Debra Lynn, Laurel Ann. BE, Ea. Ill. U., 1950; MDiv, So. Bapt. Theol. Sem., 1955; DD, Judson Coll., 1989. Pastor Union Bapt. Ch., Charleston, 1948-49, Enon Bapt. Ch., Ashmore, Ill., 1949-52, Bethel Bapt. Ch., Scottsburg, Ind., 1952-55; pastor First Bapt. Ch., Casey, Ill., 1955-58, Pinckneyville, Ill., 1958-68, Herrin, Ill., 1968-78; ch. devel. div. dir. Ill. Bapt. State Assn., Springfield, 1978-88, exec. dir., 1988—. Mem. Ill. Bapt. State Assn. (v.p. 1963-64, pres. 1965-66), SBC Christian Life Comm., Westfield Bapt. Assn. Avocations: reading, biking, golf. Office: Ill Bapt State Assn 3085 Stevenson Dr Springfield IL 62794-9247

SWING, WILLIAM EDWIN, bishop; b. Huntington, W.Va., Aug. 26, 1936; s. William Lee and Elsie Bell (Holliday) S.; M. Mary Willis Taylor, Oct. 7, 1961; children—Alice Marshall, William Edwin. B.A., Kenyon Coll., Ohio, 1954-58; D.Div. (hon.), Kenyon Coll., 1980; M.A., Va. Theol. Sem., 1958-61, D.Div., 1980. Ordained priest Episcopal Ch. Asst. St. Matthews Ch., Wheeling, W.Va., 1961-63; vicar St. Matthews Ch., Chester, W.Va., 1963-69, St. Thomas Ch., Weirton, W.Va., 1963-69; rector St. Columbias Episcopal Ch., Washington, 1969-79; bishop Episcopal Ch. Calif., San Francisco, 1980—; chmn. bd. Ch. Div. Sch. of the Pacific, 1983-84; founder, chmn. Episcopal Found. for Drama, 1976—. Republican. Home: 2006 Lyon St San Francisco CA 94115 Office: Episcopal Ch Diocesan Office 1055 Taylor St San Francisco CA 94108

SWINK, DAVID WESLEY, minister; b. High Point, N.C., Apr. 16, 1948; s. Lloyd Webster and Ruth Elizabeth (Daves) S.; m. Grace James Talton, July 3, 1970; children: Grace Elizabeth, Margaret Lillian. BA, Furman U., 1970; MDiv, Duke U., 1973; D Ministry in Spiritual Care and Counseling, Ecumenical Theol. Ctr., Detroit, 1987. Ordained to ministry Am. Bapt. Chs. in U.S.A., 1973. Asst. min. St. Michael's Ch., Dumfries, Scotland, 1973-74; assoc. pastor 1st Bapt. Ch., Birmingham, Mich., 1974-79; pastor Chilson Hills Bapt. Ch., Brighton, Mich., 1979—; chmn. Am. Bapt. Div. Christian Edn., Detroit, 1977-79; counselor youth Leader Core Mich., 1979-80; mem. Cen. Area Div. Evang. and New Ch. Devel., 1981—. Trustee Inst. for Advanced Pastoral Studies, Detroit, 1981-86; bd. dirs. Livingston Area Coun. Against Spouse Abuse, 1982—, Livingston Sr. Citizen Housing Commn., Brighton, 1982—; mem. Brighton Community Edn. Adv. Com., 1982-84, Livingston Internal Sch. Gifted Students Com., 1982-84; chmn. Brighton Sch. Planning for Growth Com., 1986; exec. bd. mem. Ecumenical Theol. Ctr. Detroit, 1986-90, treas., 1989-90; mem. Am. Bapt. Mich. Leadership Devel. Task Force, 1988-89; founding mem. Brighton Community Leadership Com., 1988-90. Honors scholar Duke U., 1970-73. Mem. Mins. Coun. of Am. Bapt. Chs., Mich. Bapt. Mins. Coun. (v.p. 1988-89), Brighton Mins. Fellowship (sec. 1988-90), Internat. Platform Assn., Royal Soc. Arts, Manufacture and Commerce of London, Blue Key, Optimist Club (bd. dirs. 1980-83), Rotary. Democrat. Avocations: swimming, sailing, reading, travel. Home: 969 Lakeside Dr Brighton MI 48116 Office: Chilson Hills Bapt Ch 4440 Brighton Rd Brighton MI 48116

SWOPE, GEORGE WENDELL, minister, educator; b. Norfolk, Va., Feb. 2, 1916; s. Dr. George W. and Nellie (Guthrie) S.; student Drexel U., 1940-41, U. Pa., 1941-42, Marshall U., 1960-63; AB, Eastern Coll., 1945; ThB, Eastern Bapt. Theol. Sem., 1945, DD, 1958, M. in Divinity, 1972; STB, Temple U., 1946; m. Winifred A. Devlin, June 26, 1940; children: George Wendell, Gregory Willard, Winifred Ruth. Ordained to ministry Bapt. Ch., 1945; pastor, Essington, Pa., 1940-43, Camden, N.J., 1943-46; dir. evangelism, Christian edn. Am. Bapt. Conv., 1946-54; pastor East Orange, N.J., 1954-58, Kenova, W.Va., 1958-63, Port Chester, N.Y., 1963-70; registrar Westchester Community Coll., 1970-74, asst. dir. guidance services, 1975-84; founder, owner Maplecroft Realty Ltd., 1988-90; pastor, Sutton, N.H., 1989-90. Pres. Nat. Alumni Assn., Ea. Bapt. Theol. Sem., 1956-58; pres. N.J. Bapt. Ministers Council, 1955-57, East Orange Protestant Council, 1955-56; mem. pastor's adv. com. Am. Bapt. Publs., 1957-62; vice chmn. press relation com. Am. Bapt. Conv., 1958-62, chmn. nominations com., 1962; chmn. commn. on Christian unity W.Va. Council Chs., 1958-60; pres. Port Chester Council Chs., 1969-70; mem. dept. evangelism Fed. Council of Chs., Nat. Council Chs. Chaplain East Orange His. Soc., 1957-58, mem. moderator council ordination Met. N.Y. Bapt. City Soc., also v.p.; chmn. ministers div. Planned Parenthood Assn. So. Westchester County; mem. Port Chester Anti-Poverty Commn.; chmn. mayor's commn. on community improvement Port Chester; chmn. Nat. Com. Engaged in Freeing Minds, 1976-79; exec. dir. Am. Family Found., 1979-81; minister-at-large Am. Bapt. Ch., 1985—; chmn. Diaconate in Bradford Bicentennial Meml. Day Program, Bradford Bapt. Ch.; hospice vol., 1986—; chmn. Bradford Bicentennial Meml. Day; mem. Rep. Presdl. Citizens Adv. Commn. Mem. SAR, Sunapee Region Bd. Realtors, Nat. Assn. Realtors, Religious Liberty Coun. (charter 1990—), New London Country Squires, Plantation Golf And Country Club, Masons (past master), Rotary (past pres.). Home: High St RFD 1 Box 49 Bradford NH 03221 also: 772 Harrington Lake Dr N Venice FL 34293 *I have observed that in these turbulent times, those people who ride through the stormy nights and sunny days most successfully and happily have a cluster of characteristics: viable religious faith, positive philosophy of life, healthy psyche, loving support by important others and altruistic goals and activities.*

SWOPE, STEVEN EDWARD, minister; b. Bangor, Me., Jan. 12, 1957; s. Glenn Edward and Carole Mae (Tempest) S.; m. Rebecca Ann Goodin, Dec. 15, 1979; children: Benjamin David, Sarah Ellen, Hannah Rose, Rachel Ann. BA, Heidelberg Coll., Tiffin, Ohio, 1979; MDiv, Harvard U., 1983. Ordained to ministry United Ch. of Christ, 1983; cert. clin. pastoral educator. Pastor Fairview United Ch. of Christ, Georgetown, Ohio, 1983-86, Russellville (Ohio) United Ch. of Christ, 1984-86, 2d Congl. United Ch. of Christ, Ashtabula, Ohio, 1986—; coord. Brown County Hosp. chaplains, Georgetown, 1985-86; sec. Ch. and Edn. Dept. Western Res. Assn., Cleve., 1989-91; bd. dirs. Home Health Care, Georgetown, 1985-86; pres. Interfaith Mins. Assn., Ashtabula, 1989-90. Actor, dir., vol. Ashtabula Arts Ctr., 1987—. Mem. Ashtabula County HIV/AIDS Task Force, 1990—; mem. reorganization steering com. Ashtabula Area City Schs., 1991; vol. chaplain Ashtabula County Med. Ctr., 1986-91. Avocations: community theater, reading, music, softball, volleyball. Office: 2d Congl United Ch Christ 319 Lake Ave Ashtabula OH 44004

SYBESMA, KENNETH L., pastoral musician, liturgical music consultant; b. San Bernardino, Calif., July 16, 1961; s. Marion J. and Nelvina (Van Essen) S. Student, Westminster Choir Coll., 1979-82; MusB in Ch. Music, Mt. St. Mary's Coll., L.A., 1987; postgrad., U. Redlands, 1988-90. Dir. music ministry Ch. St. Catherine of Alexandria, Riverside, Calif., 1983-88; interim musician Sacred Heart Ch., Redlands, Calif., 1988-90; dir. music ministry Ch. of St. Joseph-on-the-Brandywine, Wilmington, Del., 1990—; liturgist, musician Campus Ministry, Mt. St. Mary's Coll., 1983-87; asst. to univ. organist U. Redlands, Calif., 1988-90; mem. ad hoc com. on music Liturgy Commn., Diocese of Wilmington, 1991—; cons. parishes, 1980—. Commd. composer: Brandywine Acclamations, 1990; commd. composer, arranger: Mass of St. Joseph the Worker, 1991; composer psalmody settings. Recipient 1st pl. awards in organ performance Walker Competition, 1977-79. Mem. ACLU, Nat. Assn. Pastoral Musicians, Am. Guild Organists, Hymn Soc. Am., Royal Sch. Ch. Music, Pax Christi USA, Quixote Ctr. Republican. Roman Catholic. Avocations: cooking, foreign films, theatre, photography, travel. Office: Ch St Joseph-on-the-Brandywine Ten Old Church Rd Greenville Wilmington DE 19807-3096

SYLLA, MAODO, religious leader. Grand imam Islamic Faith, Senegal. Office: Grand Imam, Dakar Senegal*

SYME, DANIEL BAILEY, rabbi, institution executive; b. Sharon, Pa., Feb. 6, 1946; s. Monte Robert and Sonia (Hendin) S.; m. Deborah Shayne, Mar. 28, 1977; 1 child: Joshua B.A., U. Mich., Ann Arbor, 1967; B.H.L., M.A.H.L., Hebrew Union Coll.-Jewish Inst. Religion, Cin., 1972; M.Ed., Columbia U., 1977, Ed.D., 1980. Ordained rabbi, 1972. Rabbi, Stamford Fellowship for Jewish Learning, Stamford, Conn., 1973-77; asst. dir. Nat. Fedn. Temple Youth, 1972-73; asst. nat. dir. edn. Union of Am. Hebrew Congregations, N.Y.C., 1973-77, dir., 1977—; asst. dir. Commn. Jewish Edn. for Reform Movement, N.Y.C., 1973-77, dir., 1977—; dir. Union Am. Hebrew Congregations TV Inst., N.Y.C., 1982-83, exec. asst. to pres., 1983-85, v.p., 1985-91, sr. v.p., 1991—; chmn. Coalition for Alternatives in Jewish Edn., N.Y.C., 1978-80; mem. Nat. Assn. Temple Educators, 1972-91, Commn. on Teaching of Israel and Zionism, World Zionist Orgn., 1980-84; dir. at large Jewish Nat. Fund; dir. at large internat. bd. Meml. Found. for Jewish Culture. Author: Finding God, My Body Is Something Special, Prayer Is Reaching, I'm Growing, I Learn about God, Books Are Treasures, Jewish Home, What Happens After I Die?, Why I Am a Reform Jew, Drugs, Sex and Integrity, The Jewish Wedding Book; exec. producer TV programs A Conversation with Menachem Begin, 1981, Choosing Judaism, 1981, To See the World through Jewish Eyes, 1983, A Conversation with Yitzchak Navon, 1983, You Can Go Home Again, Jewish Youth and Cults, 1984; contbr. articles to religious publs. Mem. Rabbinic Adv. Council, United Jewish Appeal, Nat. Religious Edn. Assn. (exec. bd.), Nat. Council for Jewish Edn. (exec. bd.). Office: Union Am Hebrew Congregations 838 Fifth Ave New York NY 10021

SYMONETTE, JEROME ALPHONZA, minister; b. Nassau, New Providence, The Bahamas, Mar. 15, 1961; came to U.S., 1973; s. John Alfred and Elfreda Deloise (Collie) S.; m. Marcia Louise Barge, Aug. 16, 1986; children: Jwan Anthoni, Jasmine Alexandria. B in Music Edn., U. Louisville, 1984; M in Ch. Music, So. Bapt. Theol. Sem., Louisville, 1988. Lic. to ministry Bapt. Ch., 1986; ordained, 1990. Min. music Greater Tabernacle Bapt. Ch., Louisville, 1980-88, Mt. Olive Bapt. Ch., Ft. Lauderdale, Fla., 1988—; tchr. music, cantor Christ the King Cath. Sch., Louisville, 1986-87; instr. State Congress Christian Edn., Tallahassee, 1989—, Greater Christ Bapt. Ch., Detroit, 1990, Ch. Music Inst., Jehovah Bapt. Ch., Sumter, S.C., 1990-91; youth evangelist Elevated Bapt. Ch., Nassau, The Bahamas, 1990. Judge Acad., Cultural, Tech., Sci. Olympics (NAACP), Ft. Lauderdale, 1990-91. Mem. Am. Choral Dirs. Assn., Am. Guild Organists. Office: Mt Olive Bapt Ch 400 NW 9th Ave Fort Lauderdale FL 33311

SYMONS, J. KEITH, bishop; b. Champion, Mich., Oct. 14, 1932. Student, St. Thomas Sem., Bloomfield, Conn., St. Mary Sem., Balt. Ordained priest Roman Catholic Ch., 1958, consecrated bishop, 1981. Titular bishop of Siguritanus and aux. bishop of St. Petersburg Fla., 1981-83, bishop of Pensacola-Tallahassee, 1983-90, bishop of Palm Beach, 1990—. Office: 9995 N Military Trail Palm Beach Gardens FL 33410

SYNAN, EDWARD ALOYSIUS, JR., clergyman, former institute president; b. Fall River, Mass., Apr. 13, 1918; s. Edward Aloysius and Mary F. (McDermott) S. AB, Seton Hall Coll., 1938; student, U. Louvain, Belgium, 1938-40, Immaculate Conception Sem., Darlington, N.J., 1940-41; STL, Cath. U. Am., 1942; LMS, Pontifical Inst. Medieval Studies, Toronto, 1951; MA, PhD, U. Toronto, 1952. Ordained priest Roman Cath. Ch., 1942. Curate Immaculate Conception Ch., Montclair, N.J., 1942-44; prof. philosophy, chmn. dept. Seton Hall U., South Orange, N.J., 1952-59; prof. history of mediaeval philosophy Pontifical Inst. Mediaeval Studies, U. Toronto, 1959, pres., 1973-79, acting pres., 1989-90. Author: The Popes and The Jews in the Middle Ages, 1965, The Works of Richard of Campsall, Vol. I, 1968, Vol. II, 1982; assoc. editor, contbr.: The Bridge, Yearbook of Judaeo-Christian Studies, 1955-62; adv. bd.: Speculum, 1971-74; contbr. chpts. to books, articles and revs. to publs. Served as capt. (chaplain) USAF, 1944-48. Fellow Royal Soc. Can.; mem. Am. Cath. Philos. Assn. (Aquinas medal 1991), Mediaeval Acad. Am., Renaissance Soc. Am., Am. Soc. Polit. and Legal Philosophy. Address: 59 Queen's Park, Toronto, ON Canada M5S 2C4

SYNAN, HAROLD VINSON, minister; b. Hopewell, Va., Dec. 1, 1934; s. Joseph and Minnis Evelyn (Perdue) S.; m. Carol Lee Fuqua, Aug. 13, 1960; children: Mary Carol, Virginia Lee, Vinson Jr., Joseph. BA, U. Richmond, 1958; MA, U. Ga., 1964, PhD, 1967. Ordained to ministry Pentecostal Holiness Ch., 1957. Pastor Pentecostal Holiness Ch., Va., Ga., 1958-75; tchr. Emmanuel Coll., Ga., 1960-75; gen. sec. Pentecostal Holiness Ch., Oklahoma City, 1973-77, asst. gen. supt., 1977-85; chmn. N.Am. Renewal Svc. Com., Oklahoma City, 1984—; tchr. Oral Roberts U., 1991—. Author: Holiness-Pentecostal Movement, 1971, Emmanuel College: The First Fifty Years, 1968, Old Time Power, 1973, Charismatic Bridges, 1974, Azusa Street, 1976, In the Latter Days, 1984, Twentieth-Century Pentecostal Explosion, 1987, Launching the Decade, 1990; editor: Aspects of Pentecostal-Charismatic Origins, 1975; contbr. articles to profl. jours. Mem. Soc. Pentecostal Studies (pres. 1974). Republican. Home: 7412 N Ann Arbor Oklahoma City OK 73132 Office: PO Box 23445 Oklahoma City OK 73123 *I have but one goal in life; to see the power of the Holy Spirit so released in the Church and the world that every person on earth can have an opportunity to know Jesus Christ as personal Savior and Lord.*

SZOKA, EDMUND CASIMIR CARDINAL, cardinal; b. Grand Rapids, Mich., Sept. 14, 1927; s. Casimir and Mary (Wolgat) S. B.A., Sacred Heart Sem., 1950; J.C.B., Pontifical Lateran U., 1958, J.C.L., 1959. Ordained priest Roman Catholic Ch., 1954; asst. pastor St. Francis Parish, Manistique, Mich., 1954-55; sec. to bishop Marquette, Mich., 1955-57, 59-62; chaplain St. Mary's Hosp., Marquette, 1955-57; tribunal, notary, defender of bond Marquette, 1960-71; asst. chancellor Diocese of Marquette, 1962-69, chancellor, 1970-71; pastor St. Pius X Ch., Ishpeming, Mich., 1962-63, St. Christopher Ch., Marquette, 1963-71; bishop Diocese of Gaylord, Mich., 1971-81; archbishop of Detroit, 1981-90; elevated to cardinal, 1988; sec.-treas. Mich. Cath. Conf., Lansing, 1972-77; chmn. region VI Nat. Conf. Cath. Bishops, 1972-77, treas., 1981-84; mem. adminstrv. bd. and adminstrv. com., budget and fin. com. Nat. Conf. Cath. Bishops/U.S. Cath. Conf., 1981-84; trustee, mem. exec. com., chmn. com. for univ. relations Cath. U. Am., 1981-90; trustee Nat. Shrine of the Immaculate Conception, Washington, 1981-90; chmn. bd. trustees Cath. Telecommunications Network Am., 1984-90; pres. Prefecture for Econ. Affairs of the Holy See, 1990. Mem. Congregation Religious and Secular Insts., Congregation for Clergy, Congregation for Causes of Saints. Address: Prefecture for Econ Affairs, 00120 Vatican City Vatican City

SZTO, MARY CHRISTINE, lay worker, lawyer; b. N.Y.C., Oct. 12, 1960; d. Paul Chu-Hsuen and Clarice Mui-jung (Huang) S. BA in English, Wellesley Coll., 1981; postgrad., Chinese U., Hong Kong, 1981-82; MA in Religion, Westminster Sem., 1983; JD, Columbia U., 1986. Bar: N.Y. 1987. Atty. Citibank, N.A., N.Y.C., 1989—; chmn. Jubilee Legal Svcs., N.Y.C., 1990—; mem. synodical com. race rels. Christian Ref. Ch., dir., 1986—. Adminstrv. dir. Briarwood Summerfest, Jamaica, N.Y., 1989-90. Rotary fellow Chinese U., 1981-82. Mem. Christian Legal Soc. (pres., dir. N.Y. chpt. 1989—), Assn. for Pub. Justice (dir. 1988—). Home: 143 55 84 Dr Jamaica NY 11435 Office: Citibank NA One Court Sq 41st Fl Long Island City NY 11120 *Trust in the Lord with all your heart and lean not on your own understanding; in all your ways acknowledge him, and he will make your paths straight. (Proverbs 3, 5, 6).*

SZYMANSKI RAMÍREZ, ARTURO, archbishop; b. Tampico, Mex., Jan. 17, 1922; s. Julio Szymanski Castello and Cristina Ramírez Campos. Ed., Seminario Conciliar de San Luís Potosí, Montezuma Sem., N.Mex. Ordained priest Roman Catholic Ch., 1947; rector Seminario de Tampico; consecrated bishop, 1960, bishop of San Andrés Tuxtla, 1965, bishop of Tampico, 1968-87; bishop of San Luis Potosí Mex., 1987-89, archbishop of San Luis Potosí, 1989—. Author: Cuadernos de Pastoral. Office: Francisco I Madero 300, San Luis Potosí 78000, Mexico

TABER, CHARLES RUSSELL, theology educator; b. Neuilly, France, Nov. 1, 1928; came to U.S., 1936; s. Floyd William and Ada Dolores (Zellner) T.; m. Betty Joyce Hanna, Aug. 24, 1951; children: Christine Anne, Diana Ruth, Kathleen Lois, Charles Stephen, Patricia Doris. BA magna cum laude, Bryan Coll., 1951; postgrad. Grace Theol. Sem., 1951-52; MA, Hartford Sem. Found., 1964, PhD, 1966. Missionary educator Fgn. Missionary Soc. Brethren Ch., Central African Republic, 1952-60; pastor Community Grace Brethren Ch., Warsaw, Ind., 1960-62; translation cons. United Bible Socs. Hamden, Conn., also West Africa, 1966-73; assoc. prof. Milligan Coll., Johnson City, Tenn., 1973-79; prof. world mission Emmanuel Sch. Religion, Johnson City, 1979—. Author: (with others) Theory and Practice of Translation, 1969, La Traduction: Théorie et Méthode, 1971; The World Is Too Much with Us: Culture in Modern Protestant Missions, 1991; editor: (with others) Christopaganism or Indigenous Christianity?, 1975; The Church in Africa, 1978. Bd. dirs. Pioneer Bible Translators, Duncanville, Tex., 1976-80, 82— . Fellow Am. Anthrop. Assn.; mem. Assn. Profs. Missions (pres. 1982), Am. Soc. Missiology (1st v.p. 1984, pres. 1985), Internat. Assn. for Mission Studies. Democrat. Home: 906 Huffine Rd Johnson City TN 37604 Office: Emmanuel Sch Religion One Walker Dr Johnson City TN 37601

TABOR, JAMES DANIEL, ancient religions educator; b. Gorman, Tex., Mar. 2, 1946; s. Elgie Lincoln and Hazel Mae (Woods) T.; m. Linda Kay Langford, Dec. 27, 1966 (div. 1981); children: David Shannon, Daniel Ted, James Nathan; m. Lori Lee Woodall, July 13, 1983; children: Eve Ashley, Seth Alexander. BA, Abilene Christian U., 1966; MA, Pepperdine U., 1971; MA, PhD, U. Chgo., 1981. Asst. prof. U. Notre Dame, Ind., 1981-85; vis. prof. Coll. William and Mary, Williamsburg, Va., 1985-89; assoc. prof. ancient Christianity and Judaism U. N.C., Charlotte, 1989—; pres. Genesis 2000, Charlotte, 1987—; lectr., presenter scholarly papers at profl. confs. Author: Things Unutterable, 1986, A Noble Death, 1991; contbr. articles and essays to theol. publs., chpts. to books. Grantee NEH, 1982, 85, 87. Mem. Phi Beta Kappa. Democrat. Avocations: archaeology, Judaica. Office: U NC Dept Religious Studies Charlotte NC 28223

TABURIMAI, KOAE, minister; b. Buota Village, Tabiteuea, Republic of Kiribati, Apr. 30, 1936; s. Taburimai Tiitiu and Teangiua Temeeti; m. Ua E. Taburimai, Dec. 13, 1975; children: Tetuare, Tuata, Kaewanib'a. Cert., Tanginiebu Theol. Coll., Republic of Kiribati, 1965; diploma in theology, Pacific Theol. Coll., Fiji, 1969. Ordained to ministry Kiribati Protestant Ch. Village pastor Kiribati Protestant Ch., Arorae, 1970-71; gen. sec. Kiribati Protestant Ch., Tarawa, 1972-80; dist. bishop Kiribati Protestant Ch., Christmas, Line Islands, 1985-88; moderator Kiribati Protestant Ch., 1988—; with ch. adminstrn. tng. sect. Coun. for World Mission, London, 1971-72; chaplain U. South Pacific, Suva, Fiji, 1981-82; commr. Pub. Svc. Commn., Republic of Kiribati, Tarawa, 1988—. Office: Kiribati Protestant Ch, Antebuka Tarawa, Central Kiribati, Republic of Kiribati

TACHÉ, ALEXANDRE, priest, educator; b. Hull, Que., Can., June 13, 1926; s. Alexandre and Berthe (Laflamme) T. BA, U. Ottawa, Can., 1946, Licentiate in Philosophy, 1947; Licentiate in Theology, Gregorian U., Rome, 1951, ThD, 1960; Licentiate in Canon Law, St. Paul U., 1980. Ordained priest Roman Cath. Ch., 1951. Prof. philosophy U. Ottawa, Ont., 1951-53; mem. staff Oblate Internat. Sem., Rome, 1953-63, 65-72; prof. Oblate Sem., Santiago, Chile, 1963-65; prof. canon law St. Paul U., Ottawa, 1975—, acad. vice rector, 1983-88; mem. Christian Coun. Capital Area, Ottawa, 1974—; eccles. judge Regional Tribunal, Ottawa, 1983—; asst. sec. Ont. Conf. Cath. Bishops, Toronto, Can., 1982-88; gen. sec. Can. Conf. Cath. Bishops, 1988—. Mem. Mayor's Consultative Com. on Religious Affairs, Ottawa, 1981-85. Mem. Can. Canon Law Soc., Internat. Canon Law Soc., N.Am. Acad. Ecumenists. Home: 249 Main St, Ottawa, ON Canada K1S 1C5 Office: 90 Parent Ave, Ottawa, ON Canada K1N 7B1

TAFEL, RICHARD H., religious organization administrator. Pres. Gen. Conv. of the Swedenborgian Ch., Newton, Mass. Office: Gen Conv The Swedenborgian Ch 101 Williams Dr Goldsboro NC 27530*

TAFOYA, ARTHUR N., bishop; b. Alameda, N.Mex., Mar. 2, 1933; s. Nicholas and Rosita Tafoya. Ed., St. Thomas Sem., Denver, Conception (Mo.) Sem. Ordained priest Roman Cath. Ch., 1962. Asst. pastor Holy Rosary Parish, Albuquerque, 1962-65; pastor Northern N.Mex., from 1965, San Jose Parish, Albuquerque; rector Immaculate Heart of Mary Sem., Santa Fe; ordained bishop of Pueblo Colo., 1980—. Office: 1001 Grand Ave Pueblo CO 81003

TAFT, ADON CALVIN, newspaper editor, lay worker; b. Pittsburg, Kans., Aug. 31, 1925; s. Raymond Albert and and Marie (Hartley) T.; m. Alfrieda Joyce Ford, Aug. 8, 1954; children: Joyce Marie, Johanna Ruth. Student, George Washington U., 1943, Am. U., Biarritz, France, 1945, U. Denver, 1948; BA in Journalism, U. Ariz., 1949; MA, U. Miami, 1960; postgrad., Fla. State U., 1963-66. Ordained to ministry So. Bapt. Conv. as deacon, 1953. Religion editor Miami (Fla.) Herald, 1953—; instr. social sci. Miami-Dade Community Coll.; instr. journalism Fla. Bible Coll.; mem. faculty, trustee Miami Christian Coll. Contbg. editor Christian Life mag., 1971-74; contbr. chpts. to Florida from Indian Trial to Space Age, 1965. Mem. exec.

com. Miami Bapt. Assn., 1956-57; mem. pub. rels. com. Fla. Bapt. Conv., 1959-60, mem. state bd. missions adminstrv. com., 1974-77; mem. host com. Bapt. World Alliance, 1965; chmn. bd. deacons 1st Bapt. Ch. South Miami, Fla., 1974; bd. dirs. home mission bd. So. Bapt. Conv., 1977-84; chmn. interfaith tutoring program Lee Elem. Sch., 1965-66; mem. ad hoc com. for religion exhibit Bicentennial 3d Century Celebration, 1974; bd. dirs. Miami Christiian Sch., Greater Miami Youth for Christ, Dade County Youth Coun., Commn. Concern. With inf. AUS, 1944-46. Decorated Bronze Star, Purple Heart; recipient Supple Meml. award, 1957, award Religious Pub. Coun., 1960, Disting. Svc. award Greater Miami Coun. Chs., 1960, award of merit United Fund, 1962, award Women of Hillel, 1973, Faith and Freedom award Religious Heritage of Am., 1975, Pioneer Women, 1977, journalism award Fla. Religion Newswriters Assn., 1989, Salvation Army, Golden award Internat. Fellowship Youth for Christ. Mem. Religion Newswriters Assn. (v.p. 1958), Fla. Hist. Assn., Am. Guild Organists (hon.), Soc. Profl. Journalists, Omicron Delta Kappa, Phi Alpha Theta. Office: Miami Herald Pub Co 1 Herald Pla Miami FL 33132

TAFT, CHARLES JOHN, clergyman; b. Shelby, Mont., Sept. 7, 1938; s. Charles Ludwig and Margaret Ida (Schrader) T.; m. Susan Ernestine Kapaun, June 14, 1969; children: Charles Howard, Rachel Susan. Student, U. Denver, 1956-58; BA, U. Colo., 1961; postgrad., Luth. Theol. Sem., St. Paul, 1969-72. Ordained to ministry Luth. Ch., 1972. Self-employed Boulder, Colo., 1963-65, Watkins, Colo., 1965-69; pastor First and Bethany Luth. Chs., Rhame, N.D., 1972-77, Grace and West Scandia Luth. Chs., McClusky, N.D., 1977-85, Greater Kenmare (N.D.) Area Luth. Parish, 1985-90; self-employed Minot, N.D., 1991—. Contbg author: Augsburg Sermons 2 Gospel Series, 1984, The Passion of the Land, 1979. With U.S. Army, 1961-63. Avocations: computers, outdoor activities. Office: 1608 1st Ave SE Minot ND 58701

TAKEUCHI, SHOKOH AKIRA, religious studies educator; b. Amagasaki, Hyogo, Japan, Dec. 17, 1920; s. Shoko and Sue Takeuchi; m. Asako T. Harada, Apr. 2, 1944; children: Shisako Tokunaga, Tsuguhito. BA, Ryukoku U., 1943, postgrad., 1947. From lectr. to prof. Ryukoku U., Kyoto, 1950-89, dir. library, 1972-75, dir. Inst. Buddhist Cultural Studies, 1976-82, dean grad. sch., 1983-87, councilor of juristic person, 1981-85, dir. juristic person, 1983-85, prof. emeritus, 1989—; lectr. Tenri U., Nara, 1977-79, Osaka U., 1977-79, Hanazono U., Kyoto, 1980-81. Author: Construction and Contents of Mahayana-sangraha, 1952, Study on Yogacara-Vijnaptimatrata, 1979, Buddha and His World, 1981, Pratityasamutpada and Karma, 1988. Dir. Japan Soc. for Promotion of Buddhist Studies, Tokyo, 1967—, Rsch. Assn. for Chinese Tri-pitaka, Kyoto, 1958-83, chief dir., 1983—; standing dir. Conf. on Religion and Modern Soc., Kyoto, 1985—. Mem. Japanese Assn. for Religious Studies (dir. 1979—), Japanese Assn. of Indian and Buddhist Studies (dir. 1987-89), Japanese Assn. Buddhist Studies (dir. 1982-88). Buddhist. Home: 2-59 Hamadacho, Amagasaki Hyogo 660, Japan Office: Ctr for Shin Buddhist Studies, Aburanokoji-Shomen Kado, Kyoto 600, Japan

TALBERT, CHARLES H., religion educator; b. Jackson, Miss., Mar. 19, 1934; s. Carl E. and Audrey (Hale) T.; m. Betty O'Neal Weaver, June 30, 1961; children: Caroline O'Neil, Charles Richard. BA, Samford U., 1956, LittD (hon.), 1990; BD, So. Bapt. Theol. Sem., Louisville, 1959; PhD, Vanderbilt U., 1963. Asst. prof. Wake Forest U., Winston-Salem, N.C., 1963-68, assoc. prof., 1968-74, prof., 1974-89, Wake Forest prof., 1989—. Author: Reading Luke, 1982, Reading Corinthians, 1987, Learning Through Suffering, 1991. Postdoctoral fellow U. N.C., 1968-69, Soc. for Values in Higher Edn., 1971-72. Mem. Soc. Bibl. Lit. (editor jour. 1984-89), Cath. Bibl. Assn. (assoc. edn. Cath. Bibl. Quar. 1990—), Nat. Assn. Bapt. Profs. Religion (pres. 1985), Studiorum Novi Testamenti Societas. Democrat. Baptist. Home: 3091 Prytania Rd Winston-Salem NC 27106 Office: Wake Forest U Dept Religion Box 7212 Winston-Salem NC 27109

TALBERT, MELVIN GEORGE, bishop; b. Clinton, La., June 14, 1934; s. Nettles and Florence (George) T.; m. Ethlelou Douglas, June 3, 1961; 1 child, Evangeline. BA, So. U., 1959; MDiv, Interdenominational Theol. Ctr., Gammon Theol. Sem., Atlanta, 1962; DD hon., Huston Tillotson Coll., Austin, 1972; LLD (hon.), U. Puget Sound, Tacoma, 1987. Ordained deacon, Meth. Ch., 1960 , elder, 1962, elected to episcopacy, United Meth. Ch., 1980. Pastor Boyd Chapel, Jefferson City, Tenn., 1960-61, Rising Sun, Sunrise, Tenn., 1960-61, St. John's Ch., L.A., 1961-62, Wesley Ch., L.A., 1962-64, Hamilton Ch., L.A., 1964-67; mem. staff So. Calif.-Ariz. Conf. United Meth. Ch., L.A., 1967-68; dist. supr. Long Beach dist. So. Calif.-Ariz. Conf. United Meth. Ch., 1968-73; gen. sec. Gen. Bd. Discipleship, Nashville, 1973-80; resident bishop Seattle area Pacific N.W. conf. United Meth. Ch., 1980-88, resident bishop San Francisco area Calif.-Nev. Conf., 1988—, sec. coun. bishops, 1988—; mem. exec. com. World Meth. Coun., 1976-81, 84—; mem. governing bd. Nat. Coun. Chs., 1980—; v.p., chmn. funding com. Gen. Commn. on Religion and Race, 1980-84, pres., 1984-88; chmn. Missional Priority Coordinating com. Gen. Coun. Ministries, 1980-84; mem. Gen. Commn. on Christian Unity and Interreligious Concerns, 1984—, African Ch. Growth and Devel. Com., 1981-84. Mem. steering com. Student Non-Violent Coordinating com. Atlanta U. Ctr., 1960-61; trustee Gammon Theol. Sem., Atlanta, 1976—, U. Puget Sound, Tacoma, 1980-88 , Sch. Theology at Claremont, Calif., 1981-88, Pacific Sch. Religion, 1988—; bd. dirs. Glide Found., 1988—. Recipient award of merit for outstanding svc. in Christian edn. Gen. Bd. Edn., 1971; recipient Spl. achievement award Nat. Assn. Black Bus. Women, 1971; Nat. Meth. scholar, 1960; Crusade scholar, 1961. Mem. Theta Phi. Democrat. Home: 13816 Campus Dr Oakland CA 94605

TALBOT, FREDERICK HILBORN, bishop, former Guyanese diplomat; b. Mahaicony, East Coast Demerara, Guyana, Oct. 13, 1927; m. Sylvia Ross. Student, Allen U., Yale U., Pacific Sch. Religion. Pastor St. Peter's A.M.E. Ch., Georgetown, 1961-71; permanent rep. UN, 1971-73; Guyanese ambassador to U.S., 1973-75, high commr. to Can., 1973-74, high commr. to Jamaica, 1975-82; bishop, formerly pres. gen. bd. 6th Dist. A.M.E. Ch., Atlanta, 1987—. Office: 208 Auburn Ave NE Atlanta GA 30303 also: PO Box 684 Frederiksted Saint Croix VI 00840-0684

TALBOT, MARY LEE, minister; b. Cleve., Apr. 18, 1953; d. Richard William and Mary Helen (Jacobs) T. BA, Coll. Wooster, 1975; MDiv, Andover-Newton Theol. Sch., 1979; MPhil, Tchrs. Coll. Columbia U., 1990. Ordained to ministry Presbyterian Ch. (U.S.A.), 1981. Asst. in ministry Grace Congl. Ch., Framingham, Mass., 1975-78; resources coord. Women's Theol. Coalition, Boston, 1977-79; assoc. editor Youth Mag., Phila., 1979-80; co-dir. youth and young adult program Presbyn. Ch. U.S.A., N.Y.C., 1981-88; cons. in religious edn. N.Y.C., 1988-90; dir. continuing edn. Pitts. Theol. Sem., 1990—; bd. dirs. Christian Assn., U. Pa.; mem. religion com. Chautauqua Inst., 1988-91. Author, editor: (program resource) Suicide and Youth, 1981, (newsletter) Trackings, 1986-88; editor: Racism and Anti-Racism, 1982, One Fantastic Book, 1982, My Identity: A Gift from God, 1987, A Guidebook for Presbyterian Youth Ministry, 1988, God's Gift of Sexuality, 1989, Celebrate Bible Study, 1990; contbr. articles to Youth Mag., Alert, Chautauquan Daily. Recipient English award Bus. and Profl. Women, 1971. Mem. Assn. Presbyn. Ch. Educators, Assn. Presbyn. Clergywomen, Religious Edn. Assn. (bd. dirs. 1986-91), History of Edn. Soc., Kappa Delta Pi. Democrat. Office: 616 N Highland Ave Pittsburgh PA 15206

TALIAFERRO, GARY DAY, minister; b. Ft. Worth, Aug. 8, 1940; s. Arthur and Wilma (Day) T.; m. Kay Allen, June 22, 1962; children: Anthony, Steven, Justin. BS, Abilene Christian U., 1962, MA, 1974; DMin, Drew U., 1987. Life ins. agt., real estate sales rep. Ft. Worth, 1963-66; minister Lueders (Tex.) Ch. of Christ, 1967-68, Friendswood (Tex.) Ch. of Christ, 1968—; assoc. counselor Samaritan Counseling Ctr., Houston, 1990; program asst. Baywood Psychiat. Hosp., Houston, 1987-90; spiritual dir. Brookwood Recovery Ctr., Houston, 1985; resident Samaritan Counseling Ctr., Houston, 1988-90. Columnist Friendswood Jour., 1983-85. Bd. dirs. Friendswood Ind. Sch. Dist., 1982-88; mem. devel. bd. Abilene Christian U., 1975—; adv. bd. Tex. Commerce Bank, Friendswood, 1983; mem. regional alcohol and drug abuse adv. com., 1985. Reciepient Outstanding Vol. award City of Friendswood, 1985. Mem. Acad. of Parish Clergy, Am. Assn. of Pastoral Counselors (clin.), Guild of Clergy Counselors, Am. Assn. Christian Counselors. Mem. Ch. of Christ. Avocations: golf, reading. Office: 301 Leisure Ln P O Box 616 Friendswood TX 77546

TALLAKSEN, TURNER E., minister; b. Orange, N.J., June 3, 1928; s. Isaac and Clara (Conrad) T.; m. Doris Pedersen; children: Sylvia Tallaksen Swanson, Sonja Tallaksen Keller, Todd. BTh, Trinity Evang. Divinity Sch., Deerfield, Ill., 1950; postgrad., U. Va., U. Nebr., U. Minn. Sr. pastor Nat. Evang. Free Ch., Washington, 1950-65, Buckeye Evang. Free Ch., Madison, Wis., 1965-68, Westbrook Evang. Free Ch., Omaha, 1968-73, Grace Evang. Free Ch., Mpls., 1973-86, Zion Evang. Free Ch., Weatherford, Okla., 1987-90; interim pastor Siloam Springs, Ark., 1990—; moderator Mid-South Dist. Conf. Evang. Free Ch. Am., 1989-90, Mid-West Dist., 1971-72; chmn. Christian Counseling Ctr. Bd., Mpls., 1985-86. Mem. Rotary. Republican.

TALLEY, CLARENCE HOLLIS, minister; b. Winters, Tex., Oct. 28, 1945; s. William Clarence and Mattie Lucille (Hoover) T.; m. Kathleen Louise Bahlman, Dec. 29, 1967; children: William Thomas, Holly Dorinda, Mary Anna, Tiffany Renee. Ordained to ministry Ch. of Christ, 1967. Missionary Ch. of Christ, Battle Creek, Mich., 1967-68; minister Ch. of Christ, L.A., 1968-73, Abilene, Tex., 1973—; adv. bd. John Abraham Meml. Christian Relief, Amarillo, Tex., 1974—, Berean Family Home, Albany, La., 1981—, San Angelo (Tex.) Bible Inst., 1985—, India Missions, El Dorado, Ark., 1990—. Mem. adv. coun. Mental Health Mental Retardation, Abilene, Tex., 1975-77; mem. parents adv. coun. Wylie Ind. Sch. Dist., Abilene, 1989—. Office: Ch of Christ 602 Palm Abilene TX 79602

TALLEY, JIM ALLEN, minister, counselor; b. Swink, Okla., Dec. 20, 1942; s. Hubert Lee and Dora Murdice (Robirds) T.; m. C. Joyce Burr, Dec. 22, 1961; children: Renee Talley Jenckes, Paul, Kent. AA, Bakersfield (Calif.) Jr. Coll., 1962; BA, Calif. State U., Turlock, 1971; MA, Mennonite Sem., Fresno, Calif., 1978; PhD, Columbia Pacific U., San Rafael, Calif., 1991. Ordained to ministry Am. Bapt. Chs. in U.S.A., 1971; cert. gen. bldg. contractor, Calif. Elder Ch. in the Pk., Modesto, Calif., 1970-76; min. single adults 1st Bapt. Ch., Modesto, 1976-91; pvt. practice counseling Oklahoma City, 1991—; dir. west coast Nat. Community Marriage Policy, Modesto, 1988—. Author: Relationship Instruction, 1984, Reconciliation Instruction, 1988; co-author: Too Close Too Soon, 1981, Reconcilable Differences, 1985, True Colors, 1991, Life After Divorce, 1991. Mem. Nat. Assn. Single Adults, Greater Modesto Ministerial Assn. (bd. mem. 1990—). Republican. Office: PO Box 720522 Oklahoma City OK 73172-0522 *Integrity is the ability to ware a helmet around all day that prints out our thought life on a screen for everyone to read.*

TALLEY, JOHN D., academic administrator. Head Southeastern Bible Coll., Birmingham, Ala. Office: Southeastern Bible Coll Office of President 3001 Hwy 280 E Birmingham AL 35243*

TALLEY, PAUL, youth minister; b. Odessa, Tex., Jan. 6, 1949; s. Bill C. and Ozella (Lenard) T.; m. Linda Bruton, Nov. 28, 1968; children: Stephanie, Paul. BBA, West Tex. State U., 1971; postgrad., Abilene Christian U., 1990—. Asst. youth min. Cen. Ch. of Christ, Amerillo, Tex., 1974-76; youth min. Crestview Ch. of Christ, Waco, Tex., 1976—. Author: Talking With Your Kids About the Birds and the Bees, 1990. Trustee Iron Springs Christian Camp, Whitney, Tex., 1980—, chmn. bd., 1988-89; pres. Midway High Sch. PTA, 1987. Democrat. Mem. Churches of Christ. Home: 528 Fairway Waco TX 76712 Office: Crestview Ch of Christ 7129 Delhi Waco TX 76712

TALLEY, ROBERT LAVERNE, minister; b. Cookeville, Tenn., May 1, 1959; s. Robert Laverne and Doris (Knott) T.; m. Jennifer Lynn Byard, July 21, 1984. BA in Psychology, N.C. State U., 1982; MDiv, Southeastern Bapt. Theol. Sem., Wake Forest, N.C., 1986. Ordained to ministry So. Bapt. Conv., 1985. Summer missionary So. Bapt. Conv. and N.C. Bapt. Conv., Raleigh, N.C., 1978-82; campus ministry intern N.C. Bapt. Conv., Raleigh, N.C., 1982; youth minister Temple Bapt. Ch., Durham, N.C., 1983-86; minister youth and activities Swope Park Bapt. Ch., Kansas City, Mo., 1986-88; min. youth 1st Bapt. Ch., Burlington, N.C., 1988—; Bapt. campus minister Elon (N.C.) Coll., 1989—. Mem. N.C. Bapt. Youth Ministers Assn. Democrat. Office: 1st Bapt Ch 400 S Broad St Burlington NC 27215

TALTON, CHESTER LOVELLE, bishop; b. El Dorado, Ark., Sept. 22, 1941; s. Chester Talton and Mae Ola (Shells) Henry; m. Karen Louise Warren, Aug. 25, 1963; children: Kathy Louise, Linda Karen, Frederick Douglass, Benjamin Albert. BS, Calif. State U., Hayward, 1967; MDiv, Ch. Divinity Sch. of Pacific, 1970. Ordained to ministry Episcopal Ch., as deacon, 1970, as priest, 1971, as bishop, 1991. Vicar Good Shepherd Episc. Ch., Berkeley, Calif., 1970-71, St. Mathias Mission, Seaside, Calif., 1971-73, Ch. of the Holy Cross, Chgo., 1973-76; curate All Sts. Episc. Ch., Carmel, Calif., 1971-73; rector St. Philips Episc. Ch., St. Paul, 1976-81, St. Philips Ch., N.Y.C., 1985-90; mission officer Parish of Trinity Ch., N.Y.C., 1981-85; suffragan bishop Diocese of L.A., Episc. Ch., 1990—. Pres. Community Svc. Coun. Greater Harlem, N.Y.C., 1985-90, Upper Manhattan Child Devel. Ctr., N.Y.C., 1985-90, Peter Williams Jr. Housing Corp., N.Y.C., 1988-90. Mem. Union of Black Episcopalians. Office: Episc Diocese LA PO Box 90051 1220 W 4th St Los Angeles CA 90051

TALVE, SUSAN ANDREA, rabbi; b. N.Y.C., Dec. 18, 1952; d. Mark and Marilyn (Gochman) T.; m. James Stone Goodman, June 29, 1980; children: Jacob Moses Talve-Goodman, Sarika Stone Talve-Goodman, Adina Chaya. BA, St. Lawrence U., 1974; MA in Hebrew Lit., Hebrew Union Coll.-Jewish Inst. Religion, 1981. Ordained rabbi, 1981. Rabbi Shaare Emeth Temple, St. Louis, 1981-84, Cen. Reform Congregation, St. Louis, 1985—; prof. St. Louis U., 1984-86; founder, exec. dir. Jewish Early Learning Coop., Cin, 1979-81; mem. Joint Community Ministries Bd., St. Louis. Bd. dirs. S.H.A.R.E. Breast Cancer Support Group, St. Louis, 1988-91, Parenting for Peacead Justice, St. Louis; mem. adv. bd. Delta Mental Health, St. Louis; founder, leader Heart to Heart Support Group, Children's Hosp. St. Louis, 1989-91. Mem. Women Rabbinical Assn., Cen. Conf. Am. Rabbis, St. Louis Rabbinical Assn. (treas., v.p.). Office: Cen Reform Congregation 77 Maryland Pla Saint Louis MO 63108

TAMBASCO, ANTHONY JOSEPH, theology educator; b. Bklyn., May 23, 1939; s. Montana Joseph and Filomena Josephine (Nofi) T.; m. Joan Elizabeth McNeil, Aug. 9, 1980. STL magna cum laude, Catholic Inst., France, 1968; SSB magna cum laude, Bibl. Inst., Italy, 1969, SSL magna cum laude, 1970; PhD, Union Theol. Sem., 1981. Asst. prof. theology St. Louis U., 1970-73, Maryknoll (N.Y.) Sch., 1975-79; assoc. prof. theology Georgetown U., Washington, 1979—. Author: The Bible for Ethics, 1981, In the Days of Jesus, 1983, What Are They Saying about Mary, 1984, Theology of Atonement and Paul's Vision of Christianity, 1991; Contbg. author: Christian Biblical Ethics, 1984, The Deeper Meaning of Economic Life, 1986, also editor: Blesed Are the Peacemakers, 1989. Vol. stewardship to profl. jours. Mem. Am. Acad. Religion, Cath. Bibl. Assn., Soc. Bibl. Lit., Coll. Theology Soc. Office: Georgetown U Theology Dept Washington DC 20057-0998

TAMMINEN, KALEVI REINO, religion educator, researcher; b. Maaria, Finland, Apr. 5, 1928; s. Artturi Reino and Sylvi Dagmar (Honkaniemi) T.;m. Lea Annikki Viljakainen, Mar. 25, 1961; 1 child, Kaisa. PhD, ThD, U. Helsinki, Finland, 1967. Lectr. Tchr. Tng. Coll., Savonlinna, 1952-54, Tchrs. Coll., Helsinki, 1961-62; gen. sec. edn. Evang.-Luth. Ch. of Finland, 1955-63; asst. in practical theology U. Helsinki, 1958-68, docent in pedagogy, 1967-70, prof. religious edn., 1970—; dean faculty theology U. Helsinki, 1984-87. Editor: Kristillinen Kasvatus Jour., 1955-67, Religious Development in Childhood and Youth, 1991; several other studies and publs. mainly in the field of religious devel. and religious edn. Pres. Finnish Theol. Lit. Soc., 1978-83, Christian Soc. Tchrs., 1966-84; pres. commn. on edn. Evang.-Luth. Ch. of Finland, 1986-89. Mem. Soc. of the Sci. Study of Religion, Assn. Profs. and Researchers in Religious Edn. Home: Gunillankuja 5 A 3, SF-00870 Helsinki Finland Office: U Helsinki Faculty Theology, Neitsytpolku 1 B, 00140 Helsinki Finland

TAMPKINS, ERMA, religion educator; b. Oklahoma City, Apr. 11, 1938; d. Chester Anthony and Erma (Campbell) Walker; m. Leonard Tampkins, Nov. 30, 1956; children: Leonard, Diana, Teresa, Justina. AS, Rose State Coll., 1974; BS in Health, U. Okla., 1976; BSN, Cen. State U., Edmond, Okla., 1977; Diploma in Ministry, Berean Coll., Springfield, Mo., 1991. RN; lic. minister Assembly of God Ch., 1991. Sunday Sch. and Bible tchr. Faith Meml. Ch., Oklahoma City, 1979; Sunday Sch. tchr. Faith Tabernacle Assembly of God, Oklahoma City, 1989—. Home: 421 NE a5 Oklahoma City OK 73104 Office: Faith Tabernacle I-40 at Portland Ave Oklahoma City OK 73108

TANENBAUM, MARC HERMAN, clergyman; b. Balt., Oct. 13, 1925; s. Abraham and Sadie (Siger) T.; m. Helga Weiss, May 22, 1955 (div. Sept. 1977); children: Adena, Michael, Susan; m. Georgette F. Bennett, June 6, 1982. B.A., Yeshiva U., 1945; M in Hebrew Lit, Jewish Theol. Sem. Am., 1950, DDiv, 1975. Rabbi, 1950; exec. dir. Synagogue Council Am. (nat. coordinating agy. Orthodox, Conservative and Reform rabbinic and congl. bodies of Judaism U.S.), 1954-60; dir. dept. interreligious affairs Am. Jewish Com., 1961-83, dir. dept. internat. relations, 1983-89; Editor, pub. relations counselor Abelard Schuman (pub.), 1956, Henry Schuman, Farrar, Straus & Giroux; staffer Eternal Light radio program; corr., columnist Jewish Telegraphic Agy.; TV writer and panelist WMAR-TV, Balt.; writer, narrator, dir. religious films; editor Interreligious Newsletter, Trend of Events (news weekly.). Editor: Judaism: Orthodox, Conservative and Reform; Author, co-author 7 books; contbr. articles to religious publs. Mem. exec. com. White House Conf. on Children and Youth, 1960; nat. adv. council White House Conf. on Aging, 1961; nat. vice chmn. ARC; v.p., dir. Religion in Am. Life; dir. Clergymen's Econ. Inst.; mem. council trustees United Seamen's Service; mem. religious adv. com. U.S. Com. for UN; mem. U.S. nat. commn. for UNESCO, Com. Internat. Econ. Growth; bd. dirs. Internat. Rescue Com., Am. Jewish World Svc., Nat. Peace Bd.; chmn. emeritus Internat. Jewish Com. for Interreligious Consultations with the Vatican, Covenant House Bd. Recipient Internat. Interfaith Achievement award Internat. Conf. Christians and Jews; 15 hon. doctorates. Mem. Nat. Conf. Christians and Jews, Rabbinical Assembly Am. Home: 45 E 89th St Apt 18F New York NY 10128

TANIS, JAMES ROBERT, history educator, clergyman; b. Phillipsburg, N.J., June 26, 1928; s. John Christian and Bertha Marie (Tobiasson) T.; m. Florence Borgmann, June 26, 1963; children—Marjorie Martha, James Tobiasson. B.A., Yale, 1951; B.D., Union Theol. Sem., N.Y.C., 1954; Dr. Theol., U. Utrecht, Netherlands, 1967. Ordained to ministry Presbyn. Ch., 1954. Co-pastor Greystone Presbyn. Ch., Elizabeth, N.J., 1954-55; librarian, mem. faculty Harvard Div. Sch., 1956-65; univ. librarian Yale, 1965-68; mem. faculty Yale Div. Sch., 1968-69; dir. libraries, prof. history Bryn Mawr (Pa.) Coll., 1969—. Author: Calvinistic Pietism in the Middle Colonies, 1967; co-author: Bookbinding in America, 1983. Home: 111 Deep Dene Rd Villanova PA 19085 Office: Bryn Mawr College Canaday Libr Bryn Mawr PA 19010

TANNENBAUM, ARTHUR, religious educational administrator; b. N.Y.C., June 15, 1931; arrived in Can., 1974; s. Herman and Fannie (Pearlman) T.; m. Beatrice Milstone, Oct. 15, 1955; children: Eliot Barry, Marc Steven. BA, CCNY, 1961. Organizer, 1st pres. Traditional Synagogue Rochdale Village, N.Y., 1964-66; exec. dir. Temple Adath Yeshurun, Syracuse, N.Y., 1969-74, Congregation Beth El, Cherry Hill, N.J., 1971-74; office mgr. Yeshiva U., N.Y.C.; exec. v.p. Assoc. Hebrew Schs., Toronto, Ont., Can., 1974—. Author: Bar Mitzvah Handbook, 1971, The Proper Functioning Synagogue, 1973, To Serve the Jewish Community, 1974, (plays) Trial and Error, 1983, Equal Justice for All, 1985. Founder Syracuse Jewish Cemeteries Assn.; active Syracuse Urban Renewal Commn., Boy Scouts Am., United Jewish Appeal, Israel Bonds, North York Condominimum Com., North York Environment Com. Mem. Jewish War Vets., Nat. Assn. Synagogue Adminstrs., Orthodox Synagogue Adminstrs. Assn., Hebrew Day Schs. Adminstrs., Assn. Jewish Ctr. Workers, Ont. Assn. Edn. Adminstrv. Ofcls. Home: 100 Antibes Dr Apt 2101, Willowdale, ON Canada M2R 3N1 Office: 3630 Bathurst St, Toronto, ON Canada M6A 2E3

TANNENBAUM, BERNICE SALPETER, association executive; b. N.Y.C.; d. Isidore and May Franklin; B.A., Bklyn. Coll.; 1 child, Richard Salpeter. Mem. exec. bd. Nat. Conf. Soviet Jewry; chmn. Commn. on the Status of Women of the World Jewish Congress; mem. exec. bd. Am. sect. World Jewish Congress, chmn. internat. affairs com.; mem. Zionist Gen. Council; chmn. Am. sect. World Zionist Orgn.; bd. govs., mem. gen. assembly Jewish Agy.; bd. dirs., v.p. United Israel Appeal, Jewish Nat. Fund; mem. exec. com. Am. Zionist Fedn.; mem. Conf. of Pres. of Maj. Jewish Orgns.; nat. pres. Hadassah, N.Y.C., 1976-80, immediate past pres., 1980—; nat. chmn. Hadassah Med. Relief Assn.; mem. Jewish Telegraphic Agy.; bd. govs. Hebrew U. Office: WZO-AS 110 E 59th St Rm 4030 New York NY 10019 also: Hadassah 50 W 58th St New York NY 10019

TANNER, DENIS ALAN, education and youth minister; b. Mobile, Ala., June 17, 1961; s. Calvin C. and Elmiria Francis (Shumock) T.; m. Patricia Lynn Usack, Feb. 16, 1960; children: Andrew, Jenna Leigh. BS in Bus. and Math., Mobile Coll., 1983; MRE, Southwestern Theol. Sem., 1988. Ordained to ministry Bapt. Ch., 1991. Min. of youth Daphne (Ala.) Bapt. Ch., 1983-85; min. of edn. and youth intern Travis Ave. Bapt. Ch., Ft. Worth, 1985-87; min. of edn. and youth Inspiration Point Bapt. Ch., Ft. Worth, 1987-88, Davis Chapel Bapt. Ch., Austell, Ga., 1988—; youth specialist Associated Sunday Sch. Improvement Support Team, Austell, 1989-91; children, youth conf. leader assoc. Vacation Bible Sch., 1989-91. Mem. So. Bapt. Religion and Edn. Assn. Home: 1556 Virginia Pl Austell GA 30001 Office: Davis Chapel Bapt ch 5717 S Gordon Rd Austell GA 30001

TANNER, JAMES CLARK, JR., minister; b. Ripley, Tenn., May 20, 1960; s. James Clark Sr. and Martha Faye (Baskin) T.; m. Carole Lynn Cobb, Nov. 9, 1985; 1 child, Jill Marie. BA, Union U., Jackson, Tenn., 1981; MDiv, Southwestern Bapt. Theol. Sem., Ft. Worth, 1984; D of Ministry, Southwestern Bapt. Theol. Sem., 1990. Ordained to ministry Bapt. Ch., 1978. Pastor Cotton Grove Bapt. Ch., Jackson, Tenn., 1978-81; ch. planter Denton (Tex.) Bapt. Assn., 1982-84; pastor Southwood Bapt. Ch., Iuka, Miss., 1984-85, Emmanuel Bapt. Ch., Coeur d'Alene, Idaho, 1985-86, First Bapt. Ch., Pearsall, Tex., 1986—. Chapt. advisor Boy Scouts Am. Order of the Arrow, Ft. Worth, 1982-84, asst. scout master, Iuka, 1984-85, com. chmn. troop 213, Pearsall, 1990—; mem. Rep. Presdl. Task Force, 1984—; pres. bd. dirs. Brush County Coun. on Alcohol and Drug Abuse Inc., 1991—. Mem. Pi Gamma Mu, Phi Alpha Theta. Home: 623 E San Marcos Pearsall TX 78061 Office: First Bapt Ch 204 S Walnut Pearsall TX 78061 *The most important facts in my life are that Jesus Christ died to give me eternal life and He called me to equip others to share their faith as I share mine.*

TANNER, REBECCA J., minister; b. Susquehanna, Pa., June 13, 1949; d. Cleon Rial and Florence Irene (Pettit) T. BS in Elem. Edn., Mansfield U. Pa., 1972; MDiv, Pitts. Theol. Sem., 1982. Ordained to ministry Presbyn. Ch.; cert. elem. tchr., Pa. Pastor Silver Lake Presbyn. Ch., Brackney, Pa., 1983-87, Hyde Pk. Presbyn. Ch., Scranton, Pa., 1987—; pres. Westside Ministerium, Scranton, 1990—; mem. Scranton Presbytery. Bus. Profl. Women grantee, 1978. Mem. Order Ea. Star (dist. dep.). Republican. Home: 107 Yale Blvd Clarks Green PA 18411 Office: Hyde Pk Presbyn Ch 1126 Washbarn St Scranton PA 18504

TANQUARY, OLIVER LEO, minister; b. Springfield, Ill., Nov. 18, 1918; s. Lawrence Henry and Minnie (Potter) T.; m. Winifred Lillian Keen, June 24, 1939; children: Sylvia June, Lowell Emerson. BA, U. Pacific, 1933; MA, Boston U., 1940, STB, 1941; EdD, Fla. State Christian Coll., 1972; postgrad., Walden U., 1977-79. Ordained to ministry United Meth. Ch., 1941; cert. tchr., pub. sch. adminstr., Calif. Min. Hughes Meml. Meth. Ch., Edmonds, Wash., 1941-44; dir. guidance and rsch. County of Humboldt, Calif., 1948-52; min. Union Congl. Ch., Braintree, Mass., 1952-58, Paradise Hills Congl. Ch., San Diego, 1958-62; dir. guidance and counseling Paso Robles (Calif.) City Schs., 1962-68; dir. guidance and vocat. counseling County of Inyo, Calif., 1968-72; min. 1st Congl. Ch., Big Timber, Mont., 1972-77, 1st Meth. Ch., Big Pine, Calif., 1979-84, United Ch. of Christ, Quartz Hill, Calif., 1984—; chaplain Mayflower Gardens Retirement Community, Quartz Hill, 1986—; dir. vocat. counseling YMCA, San Diego, 1958-68; del. So. Calif. Conf., United Ch. of Christ, Pasadena, Calif., 1984—, moderator Kern Assn., Calif., 1990—; pres. Big Timber Ministerial Assn., 1967. Author: Choosing My Vocation, 1968, (booklets) At Home in the Universe, 1944, Providential Guidance, 1954; contbr. articles to denominational publs. Mem. Inter-County Libr. Bd. So. Calif., 1982, Inyo County

Schs. Adv. Bd., 1982-83, Inyo County Grand Jury, 1983-84. 1st lt., chaplain USAAF, 1944-48. Recipient svc. award Kiwanis Club, Paso Robles, Calif., 1965. Mem. Masons. Home: 42126 67th St W Apt 45-A Lancaster CA 93536 Office: Quartz Hill United Ch of Christ 6570 W Ave L-12 Lancaster CA 93536

TANTAWI, MUHAMMAD SAYED ATTIYAH, religious leader. Grand mufti of Egypt Islamic Faith. Office: Grand Mufti of Egypt, Cairo Arab Republic of Egypt*

TAO, YOUNG, minister; b. Xiengkhouang, Laos, Sept. 12, 1940; came to U.S., 1976; s. Khou Pao and Mai (Vang) T.; married; children: Mana, Enosey, Daniel, Jedidiah, Sinai, Mosicrown, Misilina. Diploma, Xiengkhouang Sch., 1973, The Lamp of Thai, Chiang Mai, Thailand, 1975. Ordained to ministry Hmong Christian Ch. of God, 1984. Pastor Hmong Christian and Missionary Alliance, Indpls. and Mpls., 1978-83, Hmong Christian Ch. of God, Mpls., 1984-86, 90—, Hmong Meml. Assembly of God, Mpls., 1986-90; various positions Hmong Christian Ch. of God. Bd. mem. Twin Cities Urban Prayer, Mpls.-St. Paul, 1985-90; del. Assn. Ch. Ministry Com. Prayer Watch, Mpls.-St. Paul, 1986-90. Home: 4120 17th Ave S Minneapolis MN 55407 *Many preachers said a Minister must know the Ten Commandments and keep. But I say we have to know all God's Commandments and keep them with a practical 2d. Among the hundred of thousands people from Laos they do not know what they should do. But I have done my 14th Celebration and thanks God.*

TAOFINU'U, PIO CARDINAL, archbishop; b. Falealupo, Western Samoa, Dec. 9, 1923. Ordained priest Roman Catholic Ch., 1954, joined Soc. of Mary, 1955, consecrated bishop, 1968. Bishop of Apia Samoa and Tokelau, 1968-73; elected to Coll. Cardinals, 1973, archbishop of Samoa-Apia and Tokelau, 1982—. Mem. Congregation Causes of Saints. Address: Archdiocese of Samoa-Apia, POB 532, Apia Western Samoa

TAPPAN, CINDY BEARD, pastor, nurse; b. Appling, Ga., May 15, 1930; d. Levi and Mary Lue (Frails) Beard; m. Marion Joseph Tappan, Oct. 14, 1951; children: Marcus Stephen, Susan Tappan Rucker. BSN, Kent (Ohio) State U., 1973, MA, 1979; MDiv, Meth. Theol. Sch., Del., Ohio, 1988. RN, Ohio; cert. gerontological nurse; ordained to ministry United Meth. Ch. as deacon, 1988, as elder, 1990.. Pastor St. Paul United Meth. Ch., Ashland, Ohio, 1987-88; assoc. pastor Windermere United Meth. Ch., East Cleveland, Ohio, 1988-90; pastor Asbury United Meth. Ch., Elyria, Ohio, 1990—; trustee Copeland Oaks Med. Ctr., Sebring, Ohio, 1989-90; mem. Nat. Bd. Peace/Justice, Washington, 1990—; spl. observer World Meth. Coun., Nairobi, Kenya, 1986; mem. exec. coun. World Meth. Coun., Singapore, 1991. Mem. Mayor's Crime Task Force City of Cleve., 1976, Interchurch Coun. Task Force on Domestic Violence, Cleve., 1989. Mem. United Meth. Clergywomen Assn. East Ohio (treas. 1989-90), Black Meth. for Ch. Renewal, Delta Sigma Theta. Democrat. Home: 1425 Forest Hills Blvd Cleveland Heights OH 44118 Office: Asbury United Meth Ch 1611 Middle Ave Elyria OH 44035 *People are uniquely endowed to be a source for self and a resource for others. We have a choice in the outcome of life. My choice is to be all that I can be to the glory of God and the good for humankind.*

TARAZI, PAUL NADIM, priest; b. Jaffa, Palestine, Oct. 2, 1943; came to U.S., 1976; s. Jamal Bshara and Widad Jurji (Dides) T.; m. Imkje Mathilde de Jongh, Sept. 9, 1972; children: Jalal, Reem, Bassam. Baccalaureate, Christian Bros. Sch., Beirut, 1960; MDiv, Theol. Inst., Bucharest, Romania, 1969, MTR, 1972, TrD, 1975. Ordained priest Antiochian Orthodox Christian Archdiocese, 1976. Pastor St. John The Bapt. Ch., Uniondale, N.Y., 1981—; prof. St. Vladimir's Seminary, Crestwood, N.Y., 1977—. Author: I Thessalonians: A Commentary, 1982, Old Testament Introduction, 1991, Galatians: A Commentary, 1991; contbr. articles to profl. jours. Mem. Orthodox Theol. Soc. Am. Home: 5 Judith Dr Danbury CT 06811 Office: St Vladimirs Theol Sem 575 Scarsdale Rd Crestwood NY 10707

TARLOW, PETER EVERETT, rabbi; b. N.Y.C., May 4, 1946; s. Irving and Marlene (Kass) T.; children: Nathaniel, Lysander. BS, George Washington U., 1968; M.Hebrew, Hebrew U., N.Y.C., 1973; PhD, Tex. A & M U., 1990. Ordained rabbi, 1974. Asst. rabbi Temple Emanuel, Worcester, Mass., 1973-77; rabbi Bayonne, N.J., 1977-80, Santiago, Chile, 1980-83; rabbi B'nai B'rith Hillel, College Station, Tex., 1983—; prof. counseling Tex. A & M U., 1984—; chaplain Fed. Prison, Bryan, Tex., 1990—, Police, Fire of College Station, 1990—. Mem. Am. Statis. Assn. (treas. SE Tex. chpt.), Travel and Tourism Rsch. Assn. (co-pres. Tex. chpt.). Home: 1218 Merry Oaks College Station TX 77820 Office: Hillel at Tex A&M 800 George Bush Dr College Station TX 77870

TARPLEY, MARGARET JOHNSON, librarian, writer; b. Dickson, Tenn., Aug. 23, 1944; d. James Moses and Margaret Emily (Richardson) Johnson; m. John Leeman Tarpley, Mar. 26, 1966; children: James, John, Leeman. BA, Vanderbilt U., 1965, MLS, 1966. Libr. Nigerian Bapt. Theol. Sem., Ogbomoso, 1978—. Author: Paper Writing Guide, 1988; editorial asst. Ogbomoso Jour. Theology, 1987—; contbr. articles to Nigerian library jours. Democrat. Baptist. Home and Office: Nigerian Bapt Theol Sem, Box 30, Ogbomosho Oyo, Nigeria

TATE, DARRYL ALLEN, minister; b. New Iberia, La., Feb. 15, 1961; s. Clarence W. and Lela Mae (Cox) T.; m. Carolyn Vaughn, Mar. 1, 1987; children: Misti R., Emilie Mae. MDiv, Perkins Sch. Theology, So. Meth. U., 1989; BS in New Testament, Fairfex U., 1990. Min. United Meth. Ch., New Roard, La., 1982-83, Grand River and Donaldsville, La., 1983-87, Kinder, Oberlia and Basile, La., 1987-91, Kinder-Squires, La., 1991—; trustee Uskichitto Retreat Ctr., LeBlanc, La., 1987-91; com. mem. Rural (Town & Country) Com., 1990-94. Pres. G.C. Meaux Lifeline Bd.; bd. dirs. Kinderfest, 1990-91; Webelo leader Boy Scouts of Am., 1989-91. Mem Kinder C. of C. (bd. dirs.), Order of St. Luke, Rotary, Order of Ea. Star, Masons. Republican. Home: 1017 13th St PO Box 297 Kinder LA 70648-0297 Office: 1st United Meth Ch 1002 5th St PO Box 297 Kinder LA 70648-0297

TATE, DENNIS RAY, minister, social worker; b. Washington, Oct. 16, 1943; s. Harry Lee and Gladys-Opal (Neher) T.; m. Carolyn Ann Pyzner, Aug. 18, 1966; children: Denise, Deanna, Shari, Brian, Justin, Jared. BA, East Cen. U., Ada, Okla., 1976. Ordained to ministry So. Bapt. Conv., 1969. Pastor Roff (Okla.) Bapt. Ch., 1969-71, Ahloso Bapt. Ch., Ada, 1971-74, Francis Bapt. Ch., Ada, 1974, Virginia Ave. Bapt. Ch., Anadarko, Okla., 1974-75, Homer Bapt. Ch., Ada, 1976—; social worker Dept. Human Svcs., Wewoka, Okla., 1990-91; chaplain McCall's Chapel for Mentally Retarded, Ada, 1990—. Chaplain Vol. Chaplains for Hosp., Ada, 1989-90. With USNG, 1964-69. Home: Rte 3 Box 169 Ada OK 74820 Office: Homer Bapt Ch Rte 7 Box 258 Ada OK 74820 *I read a bumper sticker once that said, "Ones life will soon be passed, only what's done for Christ will last." My motivation in life is to only please him.*

TATE, GEORGE LAWRENCE, minister; b. Greenville, S.C., Nov. 30, 1948; s. Jack Murry and Cleo Early (Turner) T.; m. Wanda Faye Rowland, Dec. 30, 1972; children: Laura Jean, Timothy Lawrence. A. Bus., Tri-County Tech., Pendleton, S.C., 1977; AA, N. Greenville Coll., Tigerville, S.C., 1980. Ordained to ministry, So. Bapt. Conv. Pastor Slabtown Bapt. Ch., Easley, S.C., 1980—. With USAF. Decorated Air Force Commendation medal. Mem. Piedmont Bapt. Assn. (pres. ministers conf. 1988-89, moderator, 1990-91). Home: 1810 Arial St Easley SC 29657 Office: Slabtown Bapt Ch PO Box 1025 Easley SC 29641

TATHAGATANANDA, SWAMI, religious organization head. Leader Vedanta Soc., N.Y.C. Office: Vedanta Society 34 W 71st St New York NY 10023*

TATUM, COLIN CURTISS, pastor; b. Elizabethtown, N.C., June 16, 1935; s. William Geddie and Annie (Davis) T.; m. Violet Hall, Sept. 25, 1960. BTh, William Carter Coll., Goldsboro, N.C., 1958; MA in Bibl. Edn., Evang. Theol. Sem., Goldsboro, 1959. Ordained to ministry Pentecostal Free Will Bapt. Ch., 1957. Pastor Pine Level (N.C.) Pentecostal Free Will Bapt. Ch., 1962-72, Congl. Pentecostal Free Will Bapt. Ch., Chesapeake, Va., 1972-75, St. Delight Pentecostal Free Will Bapt. Ch., Angier, N.C., 1976-85, Hodges Chapel Pentecostal Free Will Bapt. Ch., Benson, N.C., 1985—; mgr. Blessings Book Store, Dunn, N.C., 1976—. Home: 403 E Hill St Benson NC 27504

TATUM, LYNN WAYNE, religion educator; b. Brownfield, Tex., Jan. 19, 1954; s. Delton Francis and Freddie Jaunita (Riley) T.; m. Marilyn Ruth Gordon, Dec. 18, 1982. BA, Baylor U., 1975; postgrad., Claremont (Calif.) Grad. Sch., 1976-78; PhD, Duke U., 1988. Lectr. Baylor U., Waco, Tex., 1986—. Chair Dem. Party McLennan G. Resolutions, Waco, 1990; steering com. Waco Peace Alliance, 1989-90; exec. com. Tex. Coun. on U.S. Arab Rels., Tex., 1989. Malone fellowship Nat. Coun. U.S.-Arab Rels., 1989; hon. rsch. fellowship Am. Schs. Oriental Rsch., 1984-85; rsch. award Duke U., 1983; rsch. scholarship Zion Rsch. Found., 1980. Mem. Am. Schs. of Oriental Rsch. (v.p. S.W. region 1990), Soc. Bibl. Lit., Tex. Assn. of Middle East Scholars, Am. Sch. of Oriental Rsch., Tex. Coun. on U.S. Arab Rels. Democrat. Home: 1317 Dove Waco TX 76706 Office: Baylor U Dept Religion PO Box 97294 Waco TX 76798-7294

TAUBENFELD, HARRY SAMUEL, lawyer; b. Bklyn., June 27, 1929; s. Marcus Isaac and Anna (Engelhard) T.; m. Florence Spatz, June 17, 1956; children: Anne Gail Weisbrod, Stephen Marshall. BA, Bklyn. Coll., 1951; JD, Columbia U., 1954. Bar: N.Y. 1955, U.S. Supreme Ct. 1965, U.S. Dist. Ct. (so. and ea. dists.) N.Y. 1976. Assoc. Benjamin H. Schor, Bklyn., 1955-58; ptnr. Zuckerbrod & Taubenfeld, Cedarhurst (N.Y.), N.Y.C., 1958—; village atty. Village of Cedarhurst, 1977-88, trustee, 1989—; legis. chmn., counsel Nassau County Village Ofcls., 1979-86, v.p., 1991—, mem. exec. com., 1989; mem. legis. com. N.Y. State Conf. Mayors, 1979-87; arbitrator Dist. Ct. Nassau County, 1980—, Assessment Rev. Bd. Supreme Ct. Nassau County, 1981—; mem. Constl. Bicentennial Com., 1987-89. Assoc. chmn. Am. Zionist Fedn., 1985-87; pres. Herut Zionists Am., 1977-79; v.p. Hartman YMHA,, 1983-87; del. World Zionist Congress, 1977, 82, 87, mem. Zionist Gen. coun., 1977-83; bd. govs. Jewish Agy, 1983—; mem. exec. com. World Zionist Orgn., 1983—; trustee United Jewish Appeal, 1986—; bd. dirs. United Israel Appeal; hon. vice chmn., bd. dirs. Jewish Nat. Fund, Am. for a Safe Israel; hon. pres. Heirut Zionist Am., World Coun. Herut Hatzoa, Jerusalem. With USAR, 1948-56. Recipient Centennial award Jabotinsky Found., 1981, Betar Youth award World Betar 1982, award Internat. League for Repatriation of Russian Jews, Youth Towns of Israel Leadership award Israel Bonds Leadership award Life Time Achievement award Israel Bonds, 1991, Defender of Jerusalem award, 1991. Mem. ABA, Nassau County Bar Assn. (mcpl. com. 1987, real property com. 1987), Internat. Assn. Jewish Lawyers and Jurists, B'nai B'rith, Nordau Circle Club, Cong. Beth Shalom (Lawrence, N.Y.). Home: 288 Leroy Ave Cedarhurst NY 11516 Office: 575 Chestnut St PO Box 488 Cedarhurst NY 11516

TAVENNER, HERBERT GALE, clergyman; b. Dixon, Ill., Nov. 5, 1928; s. Albion Joseph and Mildred (Gale) T.; m. Anna Elaine Casner, Aug. 23, 1953 (dec. 1978); children: Mark, David, John, Sharon, Paul; m. Mary Kathryn Hanna, Mar. 16, 1980; m. D'Aun Weaver, Dec. 26, 1989. BA, Ill. Wesleyan U., 1950; MDiv, Garrett Evang. Theol. Sem., 1956; MA, Northwestern U., 1961. Ordained to ministry United Meth. Ch., 1953. Social worker, tchr. math. Bd. Missions, Santiago, Chile, 1950-53; prof. N.T. studies Evang. Theol. Sem., Matanzas, Cuba, 1957-58; dir., prof. Meth. Tng. Sch., Alajuela, Costa Rica, 1958-68; missionary pastor 1st United Meth. Ch., San Jose, Costa Rica, 1964-68; pastor 1st United Meth. Ch., Panhandle, Tex., 1982-83; mem. Bd. Ordained Ministry, Lubbock, Tex., 1972-84; pastor Asbury United Meth. Ch., Lubbock, 1985—; mem. Dist. Coun. on Ministries, Amarillo, Tex., 1981-84, dist. mission sec., 1981-83. Mem. Blue Key, Lions. Home: 3019 42d St Lubbock TX 79413 Office: Asbury United Meth Ch 2005 Ave T Lubbock TX 79411 *Life is not always fair. We may not understand the mystery of why life is not always fair, but we can and do understand that the Lord of life is with us throughout all life's circumstances, and for that we can be truly thankful.*

TAWIL, JOSEPH E., retired archbishop; b. Damascus, Syria, Dec. 25, 1913. Ordained priest Greek Catholic Ch., 1936. Consecrated archbishop of Myra in Lycia, 1960; patriarchal vicar Damascus, Syria, 1960-70; exarch for Melkites in U.S., 1970-76, exarch of Melkite Diocese of Newton, 1976-90, ret., 1990. Address: 19 Dartmouth St West Newton MA 02165

TAY, MOSES LENG KONG, bishop. Bishop of Singapore The Anglican Communion. Office: Bishopsbourne, 4 Bishopsgate, Singapore 1025, Singapore*

TAYLOR, ALBERT SPENCER, minister; b. Phila., Nov. 15, 1917; s. Albert Theodore and Florence (Dunkelberger) T.; grad. Banks Bus. Coll., 1939, Phila. Coll. Bible, 1941; A.B., Eastern Bapt. Theol. Sem., 1945, Th.B., 1946; D.D. (hon.), Internat. Coll. and Grad. Sch. Theology, Honolulu, 1990; m. Esther Faith Margerum, Oct. 5, 1940; children—Albert Lee, Carey W. Ordained to ministry Bapt. Ch., 1946; pastor Grace Baptist Ch., Williamsport, Pa., 1969-72, Central Bapt. Ch., Trenton, N.J., 1982—; founder, pres. Hearthstone Publs. Inc.; employed Yardley (Pa.) Nat. Bank, 1935-36; employed Joseph K. Davison Sons, Phila., 1936-37; bookkeeper, clk. Automatic Electric Co., Phila., 1937-41; secretarial-sales Jackson Bapt. Ch., Benton, Pa., 1939-46, Moreland Bapt. Ch., Muncy, Pa., 1941-48, First Bapt. Ch., Hughesville, Pa., 1946-48; eastern dir., editor Conservative Bapt. Assn. Am., Chgo., 1948-55; eastern dir. Nat. Assn. Evangelicals, Wheaton, Ill., 1956-64; pres. Audio Bible Soc. Am., Inc., Williamsport, Pa., 1954—; mem. bd. adminstrn., pres. Hearthstone Publs. Inc., 1969-77; with eastern div. Lee Bernard & Co., Palm Springs, Calif., 1977—. Bd. dirs. Evang. Child & Family Welfare Service, N.Y., 1961—; bd. dirs. Evang. Family Service, Phila., 1962—. Owner, dir. Ashurst Manor Conf. Center, Muncy, Pa., 1963-70. Mem. Nat. Assn. Evangelicals, Conservative Bapt. Assn. Am. Author: The Meaning of Baptist Church Membership. Home: 1449 Dolington Rd Yardley PA 19067 Office: 14 Grieb Ave Levittown PA 19057

TAYLOR, DAVID NEIL, minister; b. Tampa, Fla., Feb. 15, 1954; s. O.L. Zack and Bessie Nell (Miley) T.; m. Laura Nanette Thompson, Oct. 29, 1977; children: Jonathan, Stephen, Christina. Student, U. So. Miss., 1972-75. Ordained to ministry Bapt. Ch., 1973. Youth pastor Ridgecrest Bapt. Ch., Hattiesburg, Miss., 1969-70; assoc. minister Big Level Bapt. Ch., Wiggins, Miss., 1971-74, Glendale United Meth. Ch., Hattiesburg, 1975; sr. pastor New Christian Fellowship, Port Gibson, Miss., 1976-83, Word of Life Ch., Auburn, 1983, The Storehouse Ch., Hattiesburg, 1984—; founder Youth Leadership Camps, 1979—, Nat. Intercessors Congress, 1981—; officer, exec. coun. Internat. Congress Local Chs., Washington, 1990—. Editor in chief: Harvest Report. Pastor's coun. Ams. for Robertson, Miss. Chpt., 1987-88; state rep. Christian Coalition, 1991. Named to Outstanding Young Men of Am., 1986. Home: Rte 3 Box 831 Sumrall MS 39482 Office: The Storehouse Ch 6837 US Hwy 98 Hattiesburg MS 39402 *Yesterday, regardless of how good or bad, will always influence Today. Many will dread Tomorrow because of the memory of Yesterday. The glory of life, however, is that the success of Tomorrow is determined by the choices made Today. Never allow Tomorrow to be like Yesterday. Choose wisely and live.*

TAYLOR, DAVID WYATT AIKEN, clergyman; b. Tsingkiangpu, Kiangsu, China, Dec. 13, 1925; s. Hugh Kerr and Fanny Bland (Graham) T.; m. Lillian Ross McCulloch, Aug. 25, 1951; children: Frances Bland, David Wyatt. B.A., Vanderbilt U., 1949; B.D. cum laude, Union Theol. Sem. Va., 1952; Th.M., Princeton Theol. Sem., 1953; D.D. (hon.), King Coll., Bristol, Tenn., 1959. Ordained to ministry Presbyn. Ch. U.S., 1952. Pastor chs. Elkton, Va., 1953-55, Bristol, Va., 1955-62; ednl. sec. bd. world missions Presbyn. Ch. U.S., 1962-68, program div. dir., 1968-73; ecumenical officer gen. assembly mission bd. Presbyn. Ch. U.S., Atlanta, 1973-82; pastor Orange Park Presbyn. Ch., Orange Park, Fla., 1982-86; gen. sec. for strategy and interpretation Consultation on Ch. Union, Princeton, N.J., 1986-88, gen. sec., 1988—; instr. Bible Presbyn. Jr. Coll., Maxton, N.C., 1951; mem. program bd., div. Christian edn. Nat. Council Chs., 1965-69, bd. mgrs., dept. edn. for mission, 1962-68, mem. program bd., div. overseas ministries, 1968-78, mem. governing bd., 1976-80, chmn. governing bd. credentials com., 1978; chmn. Church World Service, Inc., 1973-75; mem. adminstrn. and fin. com. Nat. Council Chs., 1973-75, mem. commn. on faith and order, 1978-83; mem. commn. on interchurch aid World Council Chs., 1973-75; mem. 5th Assembly, 1975; rep. Presbyn. Ch. U.S. to World Alliance Ref. Chs., 1976-82; bd. dirs. Presbyn. Survey mag., 1963-68; mem. Consultation on Ch. Union, 1974—; chmn. Nat. Ecumenical Officers Assn., 1978-81. Bd. dirs. Abingdon Presbytery's Children's Home, Wytheville, Va., 1958-62. Served with AUS, 1944-46, PTO. Mem. Sigma Chi. Home: 66 Probasco Rd East Windsor NJ 08520 Office: Consultation on Ch Union 151 Wall St Princeton NJ 08540

TAYLOR, DELBERT HARRY, JR., minister; b. Tulia, Tex., Feb. 9, 1934; s. Delbert Harry Sr. and Pauline (Swepton) T.; m. Celia Sue Taylor; children: Wallace B., Kenneth E. BS, Tex. Wesleyan U., 1956; BD, Tex. Christian U., 1959. Minister 1st United Meth. Ch., Olney, Tex. Lodges: Lions (pres. Cleburne club 1970-71, pres. Alvarado club 1978-79), Masons. Office: First United Meth Ch Box 305 Olney TX 76374

TAYLOR, DONALD LEON, minister; b. Omaha, Apr. 12, 1938; s. Orvia N. and Viola E. (Niemann) T.; m. LaVona M. Knehans, Aug. 13, 1966; children: Terri Lynn Taylor Bentz, Tom Donald, Todd Allen. AA, St. John's Jr. Coll., 1958; BA, Concordia Sr. Coll., 1960; MDiv., Concordia Sem., 1964. Ordained to ministry Luth. Ch.-Mo. Synod, 1964. Vicar Zion Luth. Ch., Omaha, summer 1961, St. Andrew/Redeemer Luth. Ch., Detroit, summer 1962, Trinity Luth. Ch., Waconia, Minn., 1962-63; min. Bethlehem Luth. Ch., Clements, Minn., 1964-66, Trinity Luth. Ch., Sanborn, Minn., 1964-66, Beautiful Savior Luth. Ch., San Antonio, 1966-72, St. Paul Luth. Ch., Watertown, Minn., 1972-85; interim pastor Christ Luth. Ch., Shakopee, Minn., 1991—; asst. to pres. Minn. South Dist. Social Ministry and Ministerial Health, Burnsville, 1985—; active Minn. South Dist. Conv., 1980, chmn. edn. flr. com., 1982—; bd. govs. Luth. Counseling and Family Svc., Mpls., 1990—; visitation pastor Bexar County Hosp. for Mental Health, San Antonio, 1967-71; mem. adult edn. adv. bd. Watertown-Mayer Pub. Sch. Dist. 111, 1974-85; mem. Carver County Rural Families Task Force, Waconia, 1984-88; chmn., bd. dirs. Luth. High Sch., Mayer, Minn., 1980-82, others. Contbr. articles to profl. jours. Judge speech contest Dist. Future Farmers Am., Watertown, 1975-83; vol. chaplaincy steering com. Waconia Ridgeview Hosp., 1978-80; chem. dependency resource person Carver County, 1979-85; vol. chaplain Carver County Sheriff's patrol, 1980-83. Named to Outstanding Young Men of Am., 1971. Republican. Office: Minn S Dist Luth Ch Mo Synod 14301 Grand Ave S Burnsville MN 55337

TAYLOR, GEORGE BLANEY, III, minister; b. New Britain, Conn., Oct. 17, 1946; s. George Blaney Jr. and Alice Arnold (Chase) T.; m. Viola Seilonen, Aug. 26, 1967; children: Alison Chase, Jeffrey Charles, Andrew David. BA, Yale U., 1968, MDiv, 1971. Ordained to ministry Congl. Ch., 1971. Assoc. min. 1st Congl. Ch., Kalamazoo, Mich., 1971-73; sr. min. 1st Congl. Ch., Ravenna, Ohio, 1978-83; min. 1st Congl. Ch., Rochester, Mass., 1985—, Congrl. Ch. Wilmington, Mass., 1973-78; min. to young adults and singles Holden (Mass.) Chapel, 1983-84; pastoral counselor Lighthouse Hospice Assn., Wareham, Mass., 1987—. Author: Out of the Mainline, 1990. Home: 33 Abels Way Marion MA 02738 Office: 1st Congl Ch Rounseville Rd Rochester MA 02770

TAYLOR, GREGORY BLACKWELL, priest, lawyer; b. Cleve., Aug. 13, 1930; s. S. Blackwell and Helen (Gregory) T.; m. Anne Barbour Doak, Sept. 8, 1956; children: Sarah Taylor Swearer, Jonathan P. BA, Yale U., 1952; JD, Harvard U., 1957; MDiv, Va. Theol. Sem., 1963; MA in LS, Georgetown U., 1991. Bar: Ohio 1957; ordained to ministry Episcopal Ch. as priest, 1963. Univ. chaplain Episcopal Diocese of Ohio, Cleve., 1963-67, non-stipendiary priest, 1967-80; non-stipendiary priest Episcopal Diocese of Va., Alexandria, 1980—; Sunday asst. St. Anne's Ch., Reston, Va., 1989—; supervising atty. U.S. Dept. Labor, Washington, 1980—. Mem. Lawyers Alliance for World Security, Washington, 1984—. Capt. USAF, 1952-54. Mem. Common Cause, Assn. for Religion and Intellectual Life, Phi Beta Kappa. Home: 106 W Rosemont Ave Alexandria VA 22301 Office: US Dept Labor 200 Constitution Ave NW Washington DC 20210

TAYLOR, JIM DANIEL, minister; b. Ruidoso, N.Mex., Jan. 19, 1954; s. Claude William Taylor and Katherine Lucille (Boyer) Estes; m. Renee Duvene Harwood, May 24, 1975; children: Laura, Michael, Daniel. BA in Ch. Music, Pacific Coast Bapt. Bible Coll, 1975. Ordained to ministry Bapt. Ch., 1977. Minister music Temple Bapt. Ch., Las Cruces, N.Mex., 1975-76, Inland Empire Bapt. Temple, Spokane, Wash., 1976-80; youth pastor, music minister Bible Bapt. Ch., Bowie, Tex., 1980-88; assoc. pastor Ryan Rd. Bapt. Ch., Warren, Mich., 1988-89, Central Bapt. Ch., Tyler, Tex., 1989—; activities dir. East Tex. Christian Action Coun., Tyler, 1991—. Bd. dirs. Bowie (Tex.) Sports Assn. (Church), 1987. Named Outstanding Alumni Pacific Coast Bapt. Bible Coll. Alumni Assn., San Dimas, Calif., 1985. Republican. Home: Rte 15 Box 732 Tyler TX 75707 Office: Central Bapt Ch 6153 Copeland Rd Tyler TX 75703 *No man is ready to live until he is ready to die. To know Jesus Christ as personal Saviour is the greatest privilege afforded mortal man. To spend a lifetime in the pursuit of sharing His love is joy indeed.*

TAYLOR, JOHN EARL, minister; b. New Orleans, Oct. 13, 1935; s. Earl Tobias and Clarice (Hines) T.; m. Sarah Viginia Carter, July 31, 1956; children: Kathryn, Gordon Douglas. BA, Tex. Tech U., 1957; ThM, So. Meth. U., 1960. Ordained to ministry Meth. Ch., 1958. Assoc. pastor Floral Heights United Meth. Ch., Wichita Falls, Tex., 1960-63; pastor Wilmer (Tex.) United Meth. Ch., 1963-65; pastor 1st United Meth. Ch., Breckenridge, Tex., 1967-71, Grapevine, Tex., 1971-72; pastor University United Meth. Ch., Wichita Falls, 1972-75, Plymouth Pk. United Meth. Ch., Irving, Tex., 1975-79, Arapaho United Meth. Ch., Richardson, Tex., 1979-81; pastor 1st United Meth. Ch., Mesquite, Tex., 1981-85, Sherman, Tex., 1985-90, Decatur, Tex., 1990—; mem. Bd. Ordained Ministry, North Tex. Conf., 1972-80, 88—; sec. Wesley Village Bd., Denison, Tex., 1985-90. Mem. Grayson County Rehab. Soc., Sherman, 1985-90, Child Protective Svcs. Bd., Sherman, 1987-90; sec. Red River Hist. Mus. Bd., Sherman, 1986-90. Mem. Rotary (bd. dirs. community svc. com. Sherman chpt. 1987-88). Avocations: bridge, reading, photography, travel. Office: PO Box 302 Decatur TX 76234

TAYLOR, JOHN LEE, clergyman; b. Crystal Springs, Miss., Apr. 30, 1933; s. Shelby John and Jewel (Myers) T.; m. Dolores Slay, June 27, 1954; children: Melanie, Michael, Mark. BA, Miss. Coll., 1955; BD, So. Bapt. Theol. Sem., 1959, MD, 1969; DD (hon.), William Carey Coll., 1969. Ordained to ministry So. Bapt. Ch., 1952. Pastor Concord Bapt. Ch., Bentonia, Miss., 1952-56, South Fork Bapt. Ch., Hodgenville, Ky., 1957-59, Drew (Miss.) Bapt. Ch., 1959-64; pastor First Bapt. Ch., Canton, 1964-68, McComb, 1968-73, Grenada, 1973-79; pastor West Jackson (Tenn.) Bapt. Ch., 1979-87, First Bapt. Ch., Gainesville, Ga., 1987—; exec. bd., Tenn. Bapt. Conv., Brentwood, 1985-88; coord. 1990 simultaneous revivals, Ga. Bapt. Conv., Atlanta, 1988—. Trustee William Carey Coll., Hattiesburg, Miss., 1954-64; chmn. McComb United Givers Fund, 1970, Jackson City Beautiful Commn., 1984-86; chmn. bd. dirs., mem. exec. com. Jackson Crime Stoppers, 1985-86. Office: First Bapt Ch 751 Green St Gainesville GA 30501

TAYLOR, JULANE HART, minister, educator, counselor; b. Anadarko, Okla., July 28, 1953; d. Ira D. and Wilma Etta (McBride) Hart; m. V. Micheal Taylor, Aug. 11, 1972; children: Scott Micheal, John Bradley, Tiffany Dawn. A in Edn., Tulsa Jr. Coll., 1988; BS, Northwestern Okla. State U., 1990, MEd, 1992. Cert. tchr., Okla.; cert. guidance counselor, Okla. Min. youth Foursquare Gospel Chs., Okla. Conf., 1981-83; pastor youth Owasso (Okla.) Christian Fellowship, 1984-86, United Meth. Chs., Okla. Conf., 1986-91, United Meth. Ch., Helena, Okla., 1988—; tchr. Helena-Goltry Pub. Schs., 1990—; mem. at large com. on children and youth ministries United Meth. Ch., Okla. Conf., 1990—. Dir., facilitator The Teen Ctr., Helena, 1988—. Mem. AACD, NEA, Sports for Children Assn. (sec. 1983-88), Helena-Goltry Edn. Assn. (legis. rep. 1991—), Phi Theta Kappa (sec. 1986-88). Republican. Office: PO Box 146 Helena OK 73741

TAYLOR, JUNE RUTH, minister; b. Annapolis, Md., June 27, 1932; d. Benjamin and Naomi Medora (Dill) Michaelson; m. Thomas Wayne Taylor, Mar. 20, 1954; children: Rebecca Susan Taylor DeLameter, Michael Steven. AB, Goucher Coll., 1952; MRE, Presbyn. Sch. of Christian Edn., Richmond, Va., 1954; MDiv., McCormick Theol. Sem., 1978. Ordained to ministry Presbyn. Ch. (U.S.A.), 1976. Min. Christian Edn. Congl. United Ch. of Christ, Arlington Heights, Ill., 1974-79; dir. pastoral svcs. Presbyn. U. Hosp., Pitts., 1979-89; dir. chaplaincy svcs. Ephrata (Pa.) Community Hosp., 1991—; chaplain Rush-Presbyn. St. Luke's Med. Ctr., Chgo., 1976-78; chair exec. com., pres. Assn. Specialized Pastoral Ministries, Louisville, 1987-89. Book reviewer in field. Fellow Coll. Chaplains (sec. exec. com. 1985-87);

mem. Soc. Chaplains, Assn. Mental Health Clergy, Hosp. Assn. Pa. (pres. Camp Hill chpt. 1983), Assn. for Clin. Pastoral Edn. (clin.), Rotary (liaison to Boys and Girls Clubs S.W. Pa. Pitts. chpt. 190-91), Gamma Phi Beta Alumnae Club (pres. 1989-91).

TAYLOR, LARRY LEE, minister; b. Jacksonville, Ill., Dec. 5, 1949; s. Basil L. and Madeline L. (Smith) T.; m. Phyllis J. Coultas, Oct. 23, 1971; children: Jerusha, Aaron, Ivy. BA, Roberts Wesleyan Coll., 1978; MA cum laude, Trinity Div. Sch., 1980. Ordained to ministry Neo-Pentecostal Ch., 1981. Assoc. pastor Christian Life Ch., Mt. Prospect, Ill., 1980-84; pastor Ecclesia Christian Fellowship, Boulder, Colo., 1984-89; founder, pastor New Life Christian Fellowship, Lafayette, Colo., 1989—; academic dean Christian Life Coll., Mt. Prospect, 1980-84; adj. prof. Regis U., Denver, 1991—; para-profl. Centaurus High Sch., Lafayette, 1991—. Author: Vital Signs, 1991. Co-founder Evangs. for Social Action, Boulder, 1989-90; founder, coach Centaurus Ironworkers Assn., Lafayette, 1990—. With U.S. Army, 1969-71, Vietnam. Mem. Nat. Strength and Conditioning Assn., Son City Youth Ministries (founder, dir. 1987—), Kappa Gamma Sigma. Home: 1605 Centaur Circle Lafayette CO 80026 Office: New Life Christian Fellowship PO Box 703 Lafayette CO 80026

TAYLOR, LISA MONET, religious organization administrator; b. Pasadena, Tex., Nov. 5, 1961; d. James Lewis and Anita Ann (Adkins) Brown; m. D. Edgar Taylor, June 25, 1988. BA, Tex. A&M U., 1983; MA, Ohio State U., 1986. Worker Dalts Restaurant, Hurst, Tex., 1987-89, Internat. Claim Svc. Corp., Richardson, Tex., 1989-90; dir. sponsorship devel. So. Bapt. Refugee Resettlement, Atlanta, 1990—. Republican. Baptist. Home and Office: 8601 Mystic Tr Fort Worth TX 76118

TAYLOR, SISTER MARIE DE PORRES, religious organization administrator; b. Los Angeles, May 27, 1947; d. James Sam Taylor and Isabel (McCoy) Clark. BA, Marylhurst (Oreg.) Coll. for Lifelong Learning, 1970; MA, San Francisco State U., 1976; MPA, Hayward (Calif.) State U., 1986. Cert. secondary tchr., Calif. Tchr., counselor Holy Names High Sch., Oakland, Calif., 1970-79; assoc. pastor St. Benedict Ch., Oakland, 1979-83; dir. Black Caths. Diocese of Oakland, 1982—; exec. dir. Nat. Black Sisters Conf., Oakland, 1982—; dir. displaced worker program Oakland Pvt. Industry Coun., 1989—; coordinator conf. Joint Conf. of Black Priests, Sisters and Bros., Oakland, 1982-87; facilitator Nat. Black Cath. Congress, Balt., 1986-87; conf. designer, cons. Denver Black Caths., 1986; cons. Sacramento Black Caths., 1986; preacher in ch. Author: Lenten Reflections, 1987; editor (book) Tell It Like It Is, 1987. Bd. dirs. Holy Names Coll., Oakland, 1987—; 1st vice chmn. bd. dirs. Police Activities League, Oakland, 1987—; chmn. bd. dirs. Bay Area Black United Fund, Oakland, 1987—; chmn. bd. dirs. com. for urban renewal Oakland Citizens, 1987—. Recipient Rose Casanave award Black Cath. Vicariate, 1982, Outstanding Community Service award, United East Oakland Clergy, 1983, Outstanding Community Leader award Bay Area Links, 1984, Ella Hill Hutch award Black Women Organized for Polit. Action, 1990; named Woman of Yr., YWCA, 1987. Mem. Am. Home Econs. Assn., United East Oakland Clergy (pres. 1980-84), Nat. Assn. of Black Cath. Adminstrs., Nat. Black Sisters Conf., Nat. Assn. of Female Execs. Democrat. Roman Catholic. Club: Ladies of Peter Claver (Oakland) (chaplain 1984-85). Avocations: stringing beads, knitting, gardening, travel, reading. Office: Nat Office Nat Black Sisters Conf 3014 Lakeshore Ave Oakland CA 94610 also: Oakland Pvt Industry Coun 540 16th St Oakland CA 94612

TAYLOR, MARK COOPER, religion educator; b. Plainfield, N.J., Dec. 13, 1945; s. Noel Alexander and Thelma Kathryn (Cooper) T.; m. Mary-Dinnis Stearns, June 22, 1968; children—Aaron Stearns, Kirsten Jennie. B.A., Wesleyan U., 1968; Ph.D., Harvard U., 1973; Doktorgrad., U. Copenhagen, 1971-72, 78-79. Instr. religion Harvard U., Cambridge, Mass., 1972-73; prof. religion Williams Coll., Williamstown, Mass., 1973-86, William R. Kenan, Jr. prof. religion, 1986—, dir. Ctr. for Humanities and Social Scis., 1987-89; trustee Scholars Press, Chico, Calif., 1979-82. Author: Kierkegaard's Pseudonymous Authorship, 1975, Journeys to Selfhood, 1980, Deconstructing Theology, 1982, Erring: A Postmodern A/theology, 1984, Deconstruction in Context, 1986, Altarity, 1987, Teras, 1990, Double Negative, 1991. Fellow Deutscher Akademischer Austauschdienst, 1975, 78, Guggenheim Found., 1978-79, Nat. Humanities Ctr., 1982-83, Fulbright Found., 1983. Mem. Am Acad. Religion (chmn. research and publs. com. 1979-82), Hegel Soc. Am., Soc. for Values in Higher Edn. Home: 235 Stone Hill Rd Williamstown MA 01267 Office: Williams Coll Stetson Hall Williamstown MA 01267

TAYLOR, MARK LLOYD, religion educator; b. Lawrence, Kans., Dec. 3, 1953; s. William Lloyd and Elizabeth Ann (Jones) T.; m. Deborah Ruth Hysong, Aug. 4, 1973; children: Rachel Maywood, Rebekah Elisabeth. BA, Ea. Nazarene Coll., 1975; M Theol. Studies, Emory U., 1977; PhD, So. Meth. U., 1982. Asst. prof. Ea. Nazarene Coll., Quincy, Mass., 1982-88; vis. asst. prof. Vassar Coll., Poughkeepsie, N.Y., 1988-89; assoc. prof. Seattle Pacific U., 1989—. Author: God is Love: A Study in the Theology of Karl Rahner, 1986; co-author: (with Carmen Berry) Loving Yourself as Your Neighbor, 1990; contbr. articles to profl. jours. Art docent Quincy Pub. Schs., 1983-85. Study grantee Deutscher Akademischer Austauschdienst, Munich, 1980-81; grad. fellow Danforth Found., 1980-82. Mem. Am. Acad. Religion. Mem. United Ch. of Christ. Office: Seattle Pacific U Sch of Religion Seattle WA 98119

TAYLOR, PHYLLIS JOHNSTONE, minister; b. Hopkins, Minn., Apr. 20, 1933; d. William Wycoff Jr. and Arna Leona (Yahn) Johnstone; m. Richard Bartlett Taylor, June 16, 1956; children: Beverly Taylor Sher, Richard, William and Virginia (twins), Margaret. BA, U. Minn., 1956; MDiv., Iliff Sch. Theology, 1979; PhD, Grad. Theol. Union, 1987. Ordained to ministry United Ch. of Christ, 1979. Assoc. minister Wheat Ridge (Colo.) Congregation Unite Ch. of Christ, 1977, Applewood Valley United Meth. Ch., Golden, Colo., 1977; assoc. pastor Lakewood (Colo.) United Ch. of Christ, 1978-79; pastor 7th Ave Congregational Ch., Denver, 1980-84, 1st Congregational Ch., United Ch. of Christ, Anoka, Minn., 1987-90; com. mem. annual meeting Minn. conf. United Ch. of Christ, 1989, 91; convener spiritual life task force United Ch. of Christ, Minn., 1988—; mem. Ministerial Alliance, Anoka, Minn., 1987—; chaplain Am. Guild of Organists, Denver, 1980-82. Contbr. articles to profl. jours. Mem. Women's Club (Philolectians), Anoka, 1988—, LWV, Anoka, 1988—. Recipient Nat. String Players prize Sigma Alpha Iota, 1981. Mem. Am. Acad. Religion, Soc. Bibl. Lit., The Hymn Soc. Am., Phi Beta Kappa. Democrat.

TAYLOR, RAYNOR DUNHAM, retired clergyman; b. Pasadena, Calif., Dec. 7, 1908; s. John Raynor Chadwick and Edna (Lewis) T.; m. Martha Virgina Bebee, June 28, 1936. Student, Occidental Coll., Los Angeles, 1927-30; A.B., Redlands (Calif.) U., 1935; L.Th., Northwestern and Seabury-Western Theol. Sem., 1934, D.D., 1964. Ordained to diaconate of Episcopal Ch., 1934, to priesthood, 1935; vicar St. Stephen's Ch., Beaumont-Banning, Calif., 1934-37; rector St. Mathew's Ch., National City, Calif., 1937-42, St. Mary's Ch., Laguna Beach, Calif., 1942-43; asst. rector St. Mark's Ch., San Antonio, 1943-45; dean Saint Mark's Cathedral, Salt Lake City, 1945-51; rector Meml. Ch. of the Good Shepherd, Phila., 1951-73, St. Cuthberts Chapel, MacMahan Island, Maine, summer 1958, St. Augustine's Coll., Canterbury, Kent, Eng., summer 1959, St. Mary's Ch., Anchorage, St. Peter's Ch., Sitka, Alaska, summer 1962; now ret.; hon. asso. St. George's Ch., Laguna Hills, 1973—; exam. chaplain to Bishop of Utah; also sec. Corp. of Missionary Dist. Utah; chmn. dept. Christian Edn., mem. Bishop and exec. council, 1945-51. Author articles in field. Mem. Newcomen Soc., Ch. Soc. Coll. Work, Ch. Hist. Soc., Alpha Tau Omega. Republican. Clubs: Masons (32 deg.), K.T, Shrine (pres. Leisure World 1979), Rotary (pres. 1950), Exchange (pres. 1982), Univ, Salt Lake Country, Canterbury; Union League (Phila.), Franklin Inst. (Phila.), Cricket (Phila.), Racquet (Phila.). Address: 3298 Via Carrizo Apt N Laguna Hills CA 92653

TAYLOR, RICHARD ANDREW, biblical studies educator; b. Sikeston, Mo., Mar. 25, 1944; s. William Andrew and Lena (Eaton) T.; m. L. Diane Palmer, May 30, 1969; children: Alison Michele, William Alan. BA, Bob Jones U., 1966, MA, 1968, PhD, 1973; MA, Cath. U. Am., 1985, PhD, 1990. Prof. Old Testament lit. and exegesis Capital Bible Sem., Lanham, Md., 1976-89; prof. Old Testament studies Dallas Theol. Sem., 1989—. Contbr. articles to profl. jours. Mem. Am. Schs. Oriental Rsch., Am. Oriental Soc., Cath. Bibl. Assn., Evang. Theol. Soc., Internat. Assn. for Coptic Studies, Internat. Orgn. Septuagint and Cognate Studies, Nat. Assn. Profs. Hebrew, Soc. Bibl. Lit., N.Am. Patristics Soc. Home: 7109 Don Gomez Ln Garland TX 75043 Office: Dallas Theol Sem Dept Old Testament Studies 3909 Swiss Ave Dallas TX 75204

TAYLOR, RICHARD HENRY, minister; b. Paterson, N.J., Oct. 6, 1943; s. John Henry and Dorothy (Hutton) T. BA, Marietta Coll., 1965; MDiv, Andover-Newton Theol. Sch., 1969. Ordained to ministry United Ch. of Christ, 1969. Pastor St. Luke's United Ch. of Christ, Kittanning, Pa., 1968-72, 1st Congl. Ch., Hinsdale, Mass., 1972-80, Congl. Ch., Middlefield, Mass., 1972-80, 1st Congl. Ch., Andover, Conn., 1980-87, 1st Congl. Ch. Benton Harbor, 1987—; v.p. Congl. Christian Hist. Soc., Boston, 1981—; hist. cons. Census Project, United Ch. Bd. for Homeland Ministries, N.Y.C., 1983; convenor Task Force on Small Chs., United Ch. of Christ, Framingham, Mass., 1978-80; sec. Hist. Commn., United Ch. of Christ, N.Y.C., 1974-75; mem. exec. com dept. mission and stewardship Conn. Conf., United Ch. of Christ, 1983-87; mem. Hist. Coun. United Ch. of Christ, 1991—. Author: Building a Community of Faith, 1974, Historical Directory of the Berkshire Association, 1979, The Churches of Christ of the Congregational Way in New England, 1989; contbr. articles to profl. jours. Pres. Hop River Homes for Elderly, Andover, 1981-87; chmn. Hist. Commn., Hinsdale, 1977-80; founder Armstrong County Hist. Mus., Kittanning, 1971-72. Mem. Assn. Statisticians Am. Religious Bodies, Omicron Delta Kappa. Address: 1211 Seneca Rd Benton Harbor MI 49022

TAYLOR, ROBERT EDWARD, religion educator; b. Shreveport, La., July 16, 1931; s. Robert Gray and Mary Elizabeth (Currie) T.; m. Norma Sue Shackelford, Dec. 18, 1954; children: Robert Marshall, Kathryn Elizabeth Taylor Burkhalter. BA, Centenary Coll., 1952; MDiv, So. Meth. U., 1955, MST, 1970; DMin, Austin Presbyn. Theol. Sem., 1989. Ordained to ministry United Meth. Ch., 1955. Assoc. pastor 1st United Meth. Ch., Baton Rouge, 1955-57; pastor 1st United Meth. Ch., Zachary, La., 1957-61; chaplain, prof. religion Centenary Coll., Shreveport, 1961—, T.L. James prof. religion, 1989—; acting dean Centary Coll., Shreveport, 1977-78, asst. to the pres., 1977-81, dir. church rels., 1967-70; dean pastors' sch. La. Ann. Conf., 1965-69. Contbr. Ch. Sch. Lit. Bibl. Studies, 1983-84. Chmn. bd. dirs. Open Ear crisis line, Shreveport, 1971-72; mem. Amnesty Internat., Shreveport, 1988—, N.W. Mental Health Assn., Shreveport, 1968-70, ACLU, 1988—, Commn. on the Status and Role of Women. Mem. AAUP, Soc. Bibl. Lit., Ecumenical Lecture Series (bd. dirs.). Democrat. Office: Centenary Coll Dept Religion PO Box 41188 Shreveport LA 71134

TAYLOR, ROBERT M, minister; b. Englewood, N.J., Mar. 5, 1932; s. Robert M. and Irene Maude (Benner) T.; widowed; children: Robert M., William Harrison, Joanne Elizabeth, Susan Ruth. BA cum laude, Lafayette Coll., 1953; MDiv, Princeton Seminary, 1956. Ordained to ministry Presbyn. Ch., 1956. Pastor Mahoning Presbyn. Ch., Danville, Pa., 1956-59; asst. pastor Harundale Presbyn. Ch., Glen Burnie, Md., 1959-62; pastor Cen. Presbyn. Ch., Downingtown, Pa., 1962-69; sr. pastor The Presbyn. Ch., New Brunswick, N.J., 1969-75, Rosedale Gardens Presbyn. Ch., Livonia, Mich., 1975-79, Immanuel Presbyn. Ch., Albuquerque, 1979-85; interim pastor Community Presbyn. Ch., Mountainside, N.J., 1985-86; interim sr. pastor First Presbyn. Ch., Matawan, N.J., 1986-88; pastor Christ Ch. on Quaker Hill, Pawling, N.Y., 1988—; commr. Gen. Assembly/Presbyn. Ch., Mpls., 1968; supr. Princeton Seminary Teaching Ch., New Brunswick, N.J., 1969-75; v.p. Inter-Church Coalition on Mission in the Southwest, Phoenix, 1984; mem. Hudson River Presbytery, Presbytery Mission Study Project; mem. ethics com. Harlem Valley Psychiat. Ctr.; mem. Interfaith Clergy Coun.; bd. dirs., pres. Community Resource Ctr. Mem. United Fund Bd. Govs., Downingtown, 1969, Citizen's Adv. Com., 1969, Mayor's Youth Adv. Com., East Brunswick, 1973; sec. Coll. Scholarship Found., 1975. Fellow in Pastoral Leadership Devel., Princeton Theol. Seminary, 1973. Mem. Rotary, Alpha Chi Rho (pres. 1952-53). Home: One Church Rd Pawling NY 12564 Office: Christ Church Quaker Hill One Church Rd Pawling NY 12564 *Life is a marvelous journey of caring and sharing with continual opportunities for growth. The challenge is to remain open to God's leading, even when the necessary hurdles are many.*

TAYLOR, RONALD ERIC, minister; b. San Diego, Aug. 19, 1950; s. Edna Maxine (McWhorten) T.; m. Cheryl Ann Ford, Feb. 12, 1977; children: Luke, Andrew, Daniel. BA, Biola U., 1974; MA, Fuller Sem., Pasadena, Calif., 1979. Camp dir. Sea and Summit, Inc., Santa Barbara, Calif., 1973-77, Nautico, Lodi, Calif., 1982-83; tchr. Foothill Christian Sch., Milpitas, Calif., 1980-82; assoc. pastor The Calvary Congregation, Stockton, Calif., 1983—. Democrat. Home: 219 Leslie Ave Stockton CA 95207

TAYLOR, SAMUEL MILES, minister; b. Vincennes, Ind., Nov. 24, 1929; s. Samuel Anson and Bertha May (Ravelette) T.; m. Lois Aileen (Barekman), Apr. 8, 1950; children: Rebecca Ruth, Rachel LeAnn. Theol. cert., Olivet Nazarene U., 1953; MRE, Covington Theol. Sem., 1983, DRE, 1984. Ordained to ministry Ch. of Nazarene, 1955. Pastor S.W. Ind. Ch. of Nazarene, Roachdale and Winslow, 1953-60; missionary Bd. of World Missions-Ch. of Nazarene, Guyana, Trinidad, Barbados, St. Lucia, and Bahamas, 1960-79, dist. supt., 1965-79; pastor S.W. Ind. Ch. of Nazarene, Bloomington and Vincennes, 1979-88, 1st Ch. of Nazarene, Columbus, Ind., 1988—; clergy mem. adv. bd. S.W. Ind. Dist. Ch. of Nazarene, 1981—. Contbr. articles to profl. jours. Recipient Great Commn. Leaders award S.W. Ind. Dist. Ch. of Nazarene, 1985, 88. Mem. Civitan (chaplain 1985-88, Civitan Clergy Week award 1986).

TAYLOR, SARAH MCFERRIN, minister; b. Nashville, Sept. 23, 1957; d. Fred Taylor and Anne Adele Jarman; m. Randall States, June 20, 1981 (div. June 1990); 1 child, Campbell States. AB, Guilford Coll., 1979; MDiv, Yale U., 1990. Chaplain Conn. Mental Health Ctr., New Haven, 1989—, Hosp. of St. Raphael, New Haven, 1990-91. Helena Rubenstein fellow Whitney Mus., N.Y.C., 1981. Mem. Coll. of Chaplains, Assn. for Clin. Pastoral Edn. Home: 79 Foster St New Haven CT 06511

TAYLOR, SCOTT HENRY, youth minister; b. Orlando, Fla., Jan. 29, 1960; s. Terrance Norwood and Kathleen Muriel (Rush) T.; m. Carolyn Jean Carpenter, May 18, 1985. MusB, Hardin Simmons U., 1984. Ordained minister, Bapt. Ch. Dir. children's choir 1st Cen. Presbyn. Ch., Abilene, Tex., 1983-84; minister of music 1st Bapt. Ch., Rule, Tex., 1984-85; minister of youth 1st Bapt. Ch., Perryton, Tex., 1985-87; minister of edn., youth 1st Bapt. Ch., Spearman, Tex., 1987—; associational youth minister Can. Bapt. Assn., Pampa, Tex., 1986-87, exec. bd. dirs., 1986-87; sec. Perryton & Vicinity Ministerial Alliance, 1986-87. Music dir., condr. Perryton Community Choir, 1986; student dir. Billy Graham Crusade, Perryton, 1987. Recipient cert. of merit Boy Scouts of Am., Abilene, 1982, Andy J. Patterson award Phi Mu Alpha-Theta Lambda chpt., Hardin Simmons U., 1984. Republican. Home: 727 Wilbanks Spearman TX 79081 Office: 1st Bapt Ch PO Box 275 Spearman TX 79081

TAYLOR, THOMAS FULLER, religious society administrator; b. Evanston, Ill., May 7, 1937; s. Lewis Archer and Margaret Fox (Nicholson) T.; m. Nancy Louise Emmons, June 16, 1963; children: Jennifer Louise, Clarke Bentley. BA in Physics, Earlham Coll., 1959; MusM, Northwestern U., 1962, PhD in Musicology, 1967. Instr. Oakwood Sch., Poughkeepsie, N.Y., 1959-61, Earlham Coll., Richmond, Ind., 1962-64; lectr. Northwestern U., Evanston, 1964-66, Ind. U., Bloomington, 1966-67; assoc. prof. U. Mich., Ann Arbor, 1967-87; assoc. sec. Friends World Com. Consultation, London, 1986-91, gen. sec., 1992—. Author: The Catalog of Works of Jeremiah Clarke, 1973; editor Soc. of Friends publs. Clk., chmn. Ann Arbor Friends Meeting, 1974-78. Avocations: walking, musicology and performance, travel. Office: Friends World Com, 4 Byng Pl, London WC1E 7JH, England

TAYLOR, TIMOTHY PAUL, music educator; b. Parsons, Kans., Feb. 20, 1962; s. Jerry Lavern and Judith Anne (Divine) T.; m. Tamara Lynette Brown, Oct. 13, 1984; children: Lucas Paul, Leslie Nicole. MusB, Oral Roberts U., 1989. Tchr., minister music Good Shepherd Ch. and Sch., Owensboro, Ky., 1984-87; minister music Cen. Assembly of God, Muskogee, Okla., 1987-88, Westside Assembly of God, Davenport, Iowa, 1989, Englewood Assembly of God, Independence, Mo., 1989—. Mem. Mo. Music Educators Assn. Republican. Mem. Assembly of God. Avocations: piano, reading, volleyball, bowling. Home: 605 38th St N Independence MO 64050 Office: Englewood Assembly of God 10628 Winner Rd Independence MO 64052

TAYLOR, VINCENT LOPEZ, pastor; b. Detroit, Dec. 26, 1930; s. Clarence Genca Sr. and Edna Pauline (Bell) T. Exec. sec. Mich. State Congress Met. Spiritual Chs. of Christ, Kansas City, Mo., 1961-64, pres. youth dept. nat. hdqrs., 1964-65; pastor The Ch. of the New Commandment, Atlanta, 1987—. Office: The Ch of New Commandment PO Box 4605 Atlanta GA 30302

TAYLOR, WALTER FREDERICK, JR., minister, educator; b. Omaha, Dec. 15, 1946; s. Walter Frederick and Natalie Ann (Nimmo) T.; m. Dyann Adele Gottula, Aug. 10, 1969; children: Frederick Louis, Jennifer Adele. BA, Midland Luth. Coll., 1969; student, Yale Div. Sch., 1969-70; MDiv, Luth. Theol. Sem., 1973; PhD, Claremont Grad. Sch., 1981. Ordained to ministry Luth. Ch. in Am., 1978. Instr. Sch. Theology, Claremont, Calif., 1973-76; interim pastor Mt. Olive Luth. Ch., LaCrescenta, Calif., 1976-77; assoc. pastor 1st Luth. Ch., Lincoln, Nebr., 1978-81; asst. prof. N.T. Trinity Luth Sem., Columbus, Ohio, 1981-83; assoc. prof. Trinity Luth Sem., 1983-91; prof. 1st Luth. Ch., 1991—; Word and Witness instr. Luth. Ch. in Am., 1980-88; conv., conf. and continuing edn. speaker; Bible study leader Lakeside, Ohio, 1984, 87, 90, Acad. for Evangelists, 1990, 91. Author: Ephesians, 1985; contbg. author: Mission 90: Bible Study Witness Course, 1991; various taped presentations; editor: Trinity Sem. Rev., 1982-91; contbr. articles, revs. to religious jours. Chaplain Police Dept., Lincoln, 1979-81. Recipient Assn. Theol. Schs. scholarship and rsch. award, 1988-89; Fulbright prof. U. Heidelberg, Fed. Republic Germany, 1988-89; Women's Aux. scholar Luth. Theol. Sem., 1970-73; Luth. Brotherhood Grad. Sch. fellow, 1973; Grad. Sch. fellow Claremont Grad. Sch., 1973-76. Mem. Soc. Bibl. Lit., Soc. for Antiquity and Christianity. Office: Trinity Luth Sem 2199 E Main St Columbus OH 43209

TAYLOR, WILLIAM AL, church administrator; b. Danville, Va., Sept. 26, 1938; s. P.F. and Helen Elizabeth (Doss) T.; m. Brenda F. Owen, June 4, 1961; children: Fawnia Rae, Albert Todd, Athena Dawn. A.A., Lee Coll., 1957; student Ann. and Deferred Gifts Inst., 1977, Inst. Advanced Studies in Personal Fin. Planning, 1980; Br. mgr. Ency. Brit., Greensboro, N.C., 1960-62, div. trainer, Mpls., 1963, dist. mgr., Omaha, 1964-72; adminstrv. asst. Forward in Faith Internat. Broadcast, Cleveland, Tenn., 1972-80; gen. mgr. Sta. WQNE, Cleveland, 1980; dir. stewardship Ch. of God Gen. Offices, Cleveland, 1980—; chmn. NAE Stewardship Commn., 1985-89, bd. adminstrs., 1985—; bd. dirs. Christian Stewardship Assn., 1988—. Pres., Clean Water Soc., Gastonia, N.C., 1974-75, Pathway Credit Union, 1985—; exec. dir. Vision Found., 1979-80, pres., 1985—; speaker Citizens Against Legalized Liquor, 1973, cons., 1975; adv. Mothers on March, 1976; mem. Com. for Nat. Conf. on Drug Abuse, 1978; master ceremonies Nat. Religious Leaders Conf. on Alcohol & Drug Abuse, 1979; chmn. Internat. Commn. on Prayer, 1986—. Recipient named master of sales award Ency. Britannica, 1960, top dist. mgr. award, 1967, Million Dollar Dist. award, 1968; Mass Communications award Forward in Faith, 1980, Stephen award 1990. Mem. Nat. Religious Broadcasters. Contbr. articles to profl. jours. Home: 3600 Hillside Dr NE Cleveland TN 37312 Office: Keith at 25th St Cleveland TN 37311 *We are all spending the precious gift of life, and we have been given the privilege to decide upon what we shall spend it. I have found the most worthy and fulfilling investment of life is God's stated purpose, "that we be conformed to the image of His son Jesus Christ."*

TCHILINGIRIAN, HRATCH, clergyman; b. Beirut, Lebanon, Dec. 16, 1962; came to U.S., 1981; s. Garabed and Marie (Satchian) T. Cert., Armenian Sem., Jerusalem, 1981; BA, Concordia Coll., N.Y., 1984; MDiv, St. Vladimir's Sem., Scarsdale, N.Y., 1987; M of Pub. Adminstrn., Calif. State U., Northridge, 1991. Ordained to ministry Armenian Orthodox Ch., 1979. Spiritual adminstr. Armenian Ch., North Westchester, N.Y., 1984-86; asst. pastor St. Peter Armenian Ch., Van Nuys, Calif., 1987-91; rector St. Nersess Armenian Sem., New Rochelle, N.Y., 1991—; bd. dirs. Christian Theol. Students Assn., N.Y., 1986-87, Am. Friends Dormition Abbey, Jerusalem, 1987-88; instr. Armenian Gen. Benevolent Union Manoogian Sch., Canoga Park, Calif., 1989-90; co-founder Armenian Ch. Rsch. and Analysis Group, Reseda, Calif., 1989. Co-editor Window Mag., 1989—. Vol. Westchester County Dept. Community Mental Health, N.Y., 1983-85. Mem. Nat. Assn. Armenian Studies and Rsch., Assn. Sci. Study Religion, St. Nersess Alumni Assn. (chmn. 1989-90). Home: 150 Stratton Rd New Rochelle NY 10804

TEAFF, RODGER LYNN, youth minister; b. Abilene, Tex., Sept. 24, 1963; s. Harold Bryan and Gertie (Wilson) T.; m. Ginger Leigh Cleckler, May 27, 1989. BBA, Angelo State U., 1986; MRE, Southwestern Bapt. Sem., Ft. Worth, 1988. Summer youth min. 1st Bapt. Ch., Eden, Tex., 1984; asst. youth min. 1st Bapt. Ch., San Angelo, Tex., 1984-86; summer youth min. 1st Bapt. Ch., Coleman, Tex., 1987; youth min. Allen Heights Bapt. Ch., Allen, Tex., 1988-89, Island View Bapt. Ch., Orange Park, Fla., 1989—. Office: Island View Bapt Ch 900 Park Ave Orange Park FL 32073

TEAGUE, BARRY DOUGLAS, minister; b. Lumberton, N.C., Oct. 6, 1955; s. Jack Dempsey and Helen Elizabeth (Mahaffee) T.; m. Kimberly Stuart Buffaloe, Aug. 2, 1980; children: Corban David, Bethany Christina. BA in Psychology, East Carolina U., 1977; ThM in Semitic Studies, Dallas Theol. Sem., 1982; postgrad., Hebrew U., Jerusalem, 1979-80. Ordained to ministry Ind. Bible Ch., 1983,. Pastor Brices Creek Bible Ch., New Bern, N.C., 1983—. Author: Making Your Faith Make A Difference, 1990. Republican. Home: 1302 Hunter's Rd New Bern NC 28562 Office: Brices Creek Bible Ch PO Box 3081 New Bern NC 28560 *If I want to reap eternal results, I must sow with eternal seed.*

TEAGUE, BENJAMIN CLATON, minister; b. Jacksfork, Mo., Oct. 5, 1952; s. Carl Washington and Armenda Jane (Fears) T.; m. Sherry Ellen Dixon, Nov. 26, 1968; children: Robert Dwayne, William David, Tammy Dawn. BA in Bible, Mo. Bapt. Coll., 1983, BA in Behavioral Sci., 1983; MDiv, Midwestern Bapt. Theol. Sem., 1987; postgrad., Trinity Theol. Sem., Newbergh, Ind., 1990—. Ordained to ministry So. Bapt. Convention Ch., 1980. Youth pastor Tabernacle Bapt. Ch., St. Louis, 1980-82; assoc. pastor Overland (Mo.) Bapt. Ch., 1982-85; pastor Osborn (Mo.) Bapt. Ch., 1985-87, 1st Bapt. Ch., Marshall, Mo., 1987—; dir. evangelism Clinton County Assn., Osborn, 1985-87; mem. Grand Oaks Bd., Marshall, 1987-90; trustee Mo. Bapt. Coll., St. Louis, 1989—. Chaplain Overland Police Dept., 1984, Am. Legion, Osborn, 1985-87, Marshall Police Dept., 1989; chaplain, capt. CAP, Marshall, 1987-88. Staff sgt. USAF, 1971-80. Fellow Charles Haddon Spurgeon Soc. of William Jewell Coll.; m. Saline Bapt. Assn. (dir. evangelism 1989—). Home: PO Box 362 Marshall MO 65340

TEAGUE, C(HARLES) STEVEN, minister; b. Hickory, N.C., Apr. 20, 1950; s. C. Vandiver and Adelaide (Shuford) T.; m. Karen Wolfe; children: Benjamin, Stephanie. BA, U. N.C., 1972; M in Divinity, So. Bapt. Theol. Sem., 1975; cert. in mgmt., Wake Forest U., 1982; D in Ministry, Southeastern Bapt. Theol. Sem., 1983; DD, Hampden-Sydney (Va.) Coll., 1986. Ordained to ministry Bapt. Ch., 1973. Disc-jockey, newsman Sta. WSPF Radio, Hickory, 1965-71; asst. minister Cen. Christian Ch., New Albany, Ind., 1973-75; assoc. minister U. Bapt. Ch., Chapel Hill, N.C., 1975-81; sr. minister Farmville (Va.) Bapt. Ch., 1981-86, Calvary Bapt. Ch., Roanoke, Va., 1986—; speaker, lectr. Jaycees, colls. and sems., Hampden-Sydney and Longwood, N.C., U. N.C., 1981-86; baccalaureate speaker Hampden-Sydney, 1986; mem. mins. adv. coun. Averett Coll., Danville, Va., 1986—. Mem. pres's. coun. Hampden-Sydney Coll., 1982-86; mem. athletic fund raising Longwood Coll., Farmville, 1983-84; mem. citizens adv. bd. Southside Hosp., Farmville, 1985-86; coord. Bread for the World, N.C., 1976-80; bd. dirs. Widowed Persons Svcs., Farmville, 1984-85; chmn. town and country ch. com. Va. Bapt. Gen. Assn., 1985-87; pres. Prince Edward unit Am. Heart Assn., Farmville, 1985-86; trustee Fork Union (Va.) Mil. Acad., 1987—; pres. New Humanity, Inc., 1991; mem. Regional Housing Network, Roanoke, Advanced Med. Directives Task Force, Roanoke; v.p. Roanoke Valley Ministerial Conf., 1991—. Named one of Outstanding Young Men in Am., 1978, Order of Ky. Cols., 1985. Mem. Acad. Parish Clergy, Roanoke Valley Ministerial Assn., Farmville Area Ministerial Assn. (pres. 1983-84), So. Bapt. Alliance, Jaycees (Jaycee of Quarter award 1983, Spark Plug award 1984), Lions, Elks. Democrat. Avocations: running, reading, music. Office: Calvary Bapt Ch 608 Campbell Ave SW Roanoke VA 24016

TEAGUE, JANE LORENE, lay worker; b. Brainerd, Miss., May 27, 1918; d. Willis Ernest and Ellenora Christine (Yde) Lively; m. Jasper Uriah Teague, Nov. 26, 1939; children: Jack, James, Janet. Grad., high sch. Pres. Women's Aux., L.A. Bapt. City Mission Soc., 1968-69; leadership devel. chairperson Am. Bapt. Women, 1969-70, conf. chairperson, 1971-75, v.p., program chmn., 1975-77, pres. Pacific S.W. region, 1980-83, pres. local ch., 1983-85; pres. Am. Bapt. Chs. of Pacific S.W., 1973, bd. mgrs., exec. com., chmn. bd. edn., 1975-76, also mem. nominating and camping coms., reps. from L.A. Bapt. Assn.; mem. gen. bd. Am. Bapt. Chs. in U.S.A., 1974—; moderator L.A. Assn., 1974—, bd. nat. ministries, mem. standing rules com., 1976-79; mem. com. local arrangements, women's dept. Bapt. World Alliance, 1983-85; chairperson bd. chs. edn. 1st Bapt. Ch., North Hollywood, Calif., 1985-90; mem. Prayer Task Force Am. Bapt. Chs. of Pacific S.W., 1990—, bd. mgrs., 1990—; program chairperson Children's Bapt. Home Aux., 1968-69; bd. dirs. Atherton Bapt. Homes, Am. Bapt. Homes of West, Children's Bapt. Home, Inglewood, Calif. Address: 1030 E Valencia Ave Burbank CA 91501 *If we seek to have others respect us, we must first show a pattern of living that is worthy of respect.*

TEAGUE, PETER WESLEY, superintendent; b. Gary, Ind., Jan. 15, 1952; s. Robert Wesley and Gladys Eve (Dunlop) T.; m. Paulette Joan Neymeyer, June 23, 1973; children: Robert, Angela, Jessica, Nicole. BS in Bus. Adminstrn./Psychology, Sterling Coll., 1973; MA in Christian Edn., Luther Rice Sem., 1987. Mgmt. trainee Skaggs Drug Co., Denver, 1973-74; spl. asst. to dir. Grace & Truth Evangelistic Assn., York, Pa., 1974-75; dir. devel. Christian Sch. of York, Pa., 1975-79; supt. Christian Sch. of York, 1979—; elder York (Pa.) Gospel Ctr., 1977-86, 89-90, chmn. bd., 1984-86, 89-90, adult s.s. tchr., 1977—, mem. Christian edn. com., 1977-86; workshop presenter for various convs. Contbg. author: Handbook for Christian Living, 1991; co-editor: Manual for Christian Sch. Adminstrs., 1988. Mem. Corp. Bd. Lancaster (Pa.) Bible Coll., 1989—. Mem. Assn. Christian Schs. Internat. (regional coun. 1983-91), Mid-Atlantic Christian Schs. Assn. (conv. dir.), Nat. Assn. Secondary Prins. Home: 4 Crestlyn Dr York PA 17402 *I am amazed how important encouragement is to a person. A word fitly spoken can change the outlook of a person for the day.*

TEAGUE, THOMAS WILL, minister; b. Memphis, June 22, 1953; s. William G. and Dorothy (Hill) T.; m. Rita Ann Groth, June 4, 1977; children: Jonathan Andrew, Julie Kathleen, Joy Elizabeth. BBA, Memphis State U., 1976; MRE, Southwestern Bapt. Theol. Sem., 1979; postgrad., New Orleans Theol. Sem., 1991. Ordained to ministry So. Bapt. Conv., 1981. Min. youth Hickory Hills Bapt. Ch., Memphis, 1975-77; min. edn. Calvary Bapt. Ch., Irving, Tex., 1977-79, Edmundson Rd. Bapt. Ch., St. Louis, 1979-84, Hunters' Glen Bapt. Ch., Plano, Tex., 1984-89; exec. pastor Bell Shoals Bapt. Ch., Brandon, Fla., 1989—; featured speaker Ridgecrest Bapt. Conf. Ctr., 1992. Author: Policies/Procedures, 1990. Mut. assistance family Mo. Bapt. Children's Home, St. Louis, 1980-81. Recipient Fastest Growing Bible Study award Collin County Bapt. Assn., 1984-86. Mem. Fla. Bapt. Religious Edn. Assn. (featured speaker 1991, pres. 1992—), So. Bapt. Religious Edn. Assn. (facilitator 1991), Fla. Bapt. Educators Roundtable (pres. 1992—), Nat. Assn. Ch. Bus. Adminstrs. Home: 2817 Fairway View Dr Valrico FL 33594 Office: Bell Shoals Bapt Ch 2102 Bell Shoals Rd Brandon FL 33511-6606 *Through my pilgrimmage I have confronted a reality that never fades away...One must live with the consequences of that which they tolerate. Therefore, one must daily serve for excellence within the boundaries of the will of God.*

TEAGUE, WILLIAM J., university president; b. Olney, Tex., July 12, 1927; s. D.T. and Susan (Crain) T; m. Margaret Louise Newlen, June 4, 1948; children: Thomas Richard, Susan Amelia (Mrs. Phillip David Reid), Helen Louise (Mrs. Brian Eliot Wildman). BA, Abilene Christian U., 1952; MA, Columbia U., 1959; EdD, UCLA, 1965. Exec. asst. to pres. Abilene (Tex.) Christian U., 1952-57; v.p. Harding Coll., 1957-59, Pepperdine U., 1959-70; prin. William J. Teague Assocs., 1964-70; adminstrv. v.p. Purex Corp., 1970-78, Kerr-McGee Corp., 1978-81; pres. Abilene Christian U., 1981—. Dir. Met. Water Dist. of So. Calif., 1969-72; mem. Los Angeles County Spl. Rev. Com. on Air Pollution Control, Los Angeles Town Hall, March of Dimes, United Way; chmn. Cen. Okla. United Savings Bond Campaign; bd. dirs. Abilene C. of C., Ind. Colls. and Univs. of Tex., Tex. Ind. Coll. Fund, Western Interstate Commn. for Higher Edn., Southern Regional Edn. exec. com. With USN, 1945-49. Recipient George Washington Honor Medals (3) Freedom's Found. at Valley Forge, Indsl. Was Coll. award, Abilene Christian U. Alumni Citation award, 1973; named 20th Century Christian Mag. Christian Educator of Yr., 1985. Mem. Am. Heart Assn. (affiliate bd. dirs. Okla.), Am. Coll. Pub. Relations Assn., Boy Scouts Am., Better Bus. Bur. (bd. dirs.), Calif. Council of Product Design and Mkgt., Calif. State C. of C., Oklahomans for Energy and Jobs Inc, Kiwanis. Republican. Avocation: tennis. Office: Abilene Christian U PO Box 8000 Abilene TX 79699-8000

TEASDALE, PAUL JAMES, missionary; b. Kijabe, Kenya, Dec. 20, 1935; s. Charles William and Mae Alice (Vonasek) T.; m. Betty Lou Pierson, Aug. 1, 1934; children: James Lee, Bobbi Lou, Daniel Richard. BS, Wheaton (Ill.) Coll., 1959. Pioneer missionary Africa Inland Mission, Kenya, 1959-79; pres. The Master's Mission, Robbinsville, N.C., 1979—; bd. dirs. The Master's Coll., Newhall, Calif., The Master's Fellowship, Newhall; pastor Little Snowbird Ch., Robbinsville, 1985—. Home: Box 1148 Mission Rd Robbinsville NC 28771 Office: The Master's Mission PO Box 547 Robbinsville NC 28771

TEAT, FRANKLIN ALVIN, JR., minister; b. Selma, Ala., May 9, 1956; s. Franklin Alvin Sr. and Joyce (Mays) T.; m. Carol Beth Patrick, Aug. 14, 1976; children: Sara Danielle, Jonathan Samuel. BS, La. Tech., 1978; MEd, McNeese State U., 1984. Ordained to ministry So. Bapt. Conv., 1988. Lay youth leader Cook Bapt. Ch., Ruston, La., 1978-79, 2nd Bapt. Ch., Pasadena, Tex., 1979-81; lay youth leader North Orange Bapt. Ch., Orange, Tex., 1981-87, youth min., 1888—; v.p. Golden Triangle Youth Ministry, Beaumont, Tex., 1988-89, 89-90; faculty So. Bapt. Con. Recreation, Glorieta, N.Mex., 1988. Author Bible Studies, 1989, 90. Coord. Jump Rope for Heart, Am. Heart Assn., Mauriceville, Tex., 1981-88; bd. dirs. Little Dribblers, Orange, 1990. Mem. Nat. Network Youth Ministries, Tex. Bapt. Assn. Recreation. Democrat. Home: 15 Stradford Orange TX 77630 Office: North Orange Bapt Ch 4775 Hwy 87 N Orange TX 77630 *The time we have here on this earth, called our "life", is not really our own. It has been given to us by the Author and Finisher of our faith—Jesus Christ. It is our responsibility to allow the Creator to mold our every heartbeat into life worth living.*

TEATS, MARK BATES, minister; b. Portland, Oreg., Dec. 11, 1945; s. Fred A. and Agnes H. (Helland) T.; m. Patricia A. Dehn, Dec. 16, 1968; children: Krista L., Korri L. BA, San Jose Bible Coll., 1968. Ordained to ministry Christian Ch., 1968. Youth min. First Christian Ch., Inglewood, Calif., 1968-70; min. Rockwood Christian Ch., Portland, 1970-78, Mountainview Christian Ch., Gresham, Oreg., 1988—; seminar leader Single Adult Ministries, 1989—. Contbr. articles to profl. jours. Office: Mountainview Christian Ch 1890 NE Cleveland Gresham OR 97030

TEDESCO, RICHARD ALBERT, minister; b. Phila., Sept. 14, 1942; s. Vito and Esther (Iannelli) T.; m. Joyce Lea Morando, Aug. 1, 1964; children: Lisa Renee, Stephanie Ruth. Grad., N.E. Bible Inst., 1964; BS in Bible, Valley Forge Christian Coll., 1976; M of Bible in Theology, Internat. Bible Inst. & Sem., Orlando, Fla., 1985; PhD in Theology, Honolulu U., 1988; DD (hon.), Clarksville Sch. Theology, 1985. Ordained to ministry Christian Ch. N.Am., 1967, Covenant Ministries Internat. Inc., 1988. Pastor Christian Assembly Ch., Uhrichsville, Ohio, 1967-69, Follansbee, W.Va., 1969-73; bus. mgr., sec./treas. dept. missions Gen. Coun. Christian Ch. N.Am., 1973-80, gen. sec.-treas. Gen. Coun., 1975-82, exec. dir. dept. home and fgn. missions, 1981-85, asst. gen. overseer for fgn. concerns, 1981-85; staff min., dir. dept. missions and world outreach Faith Fellowship Ministries World Outreach Ctr., Edison, N.J., 1988—; founding trustee, exec. adminstrv. sec. Covenant Ministries Internat., Edison, 1988—. Recipient cert. of honor Pentecostal Christian Ch. Argentina, 1984. Fellow Internat. Acad. Edn. Office: Covenant Ministries Internat 2177 Oak Tree Rd Edison NJ 08820 *Let me quote the song writer: "If I've gained any praise, let it go to Calvary," for I am what I am and do what I do by the strength and enablement of our Lord, Jesus Christ.*

TEEGARDEN, KENNETH LEROY, clergyman; b. Cushing, Okla., Dec. 22, 1921; s. Roy Albert and Eva B. (Swiggart) T.; m. Wanda Jean Strong, May 28, 1944; children: David Kent, Marshall Kirk. Student, Okla. State U., 1938-40; A.B., Phillips U., 1942, M.A., 1945, D.D., 1963; B.D., Tex. Christian U., 1949, D.D., 1976; D.D., Bethany Coll., 1974; LL.D., Lynchburg Coll., 1975; L.H.D., Culver-Stockton Coll., 1975. Ordained to ministry Christian Ch. (Disciples of Christ), 1940; pastor in Chandler, Okla., 1944-47, Texas City, Tex., 1947-48, Healdton, Okla., 1948-49, Vernon, Tex., 1949-55, Fort Smith, Ark., 1955-58; exec. minister Christian Ch. in Ark., 1958-65; asst. to pres. Christian Ch. in U.S. and Can., Indpls., 1965-69; exec. minister Christian Ch. in Tex., 1969-73; gen. minister, pres. Christian Ch. in U.S. and Can., 1973-85; faculty Brite Div. Sch., Tex. Christian U., 1985-89; mem. governing bd. Nat. Council Chs., 1973-85; del. 5th Assembly of World Council Chs., Nairobi, Kenya, 1975, 6th Assembly, Vancouver, B.C., Can, 1983; rep. Nat. Council Chs. in Exchange of Ch. Leadership with Soviet Union, 1974. Author: We Call Ourselves Disciples, 1975. Named Disting. Alumnus Tex. Christian U., 1973, Phillips U., 1975; Outstanding Citizen Vernon, Tex., 1954. Home: 7013 Serrano Dr Fort Worth TX 76126

TEETERS, DENNIS MONROE, minister; b. Lamesa, Tex., Dec. 5, 1951; s. Lucian Monroe and Snowie Mae (Bratcher) T.; m. Kimberly Sue Mayes, June 30, 1979; children: Caleb Austin, Summer Dawn, Nathan Dennis. BA, U. Tex., Odessa, 1979; MDiv, Southwestern Bapt. Theol. Sem., 1985. Ordained to ministry So. Bapt. Conv., 1977. Music, youth minister Airport Bapt. Ch., Big Spring, Tex., 1975; youth minister Colonial Hill Bapt. Ch., Snyder, Tex., 1975-77; pastor Knapp Bapt. Ch., 1977-81, Possum Kingdom Bapt. Ch., Graford, Tex., 1981-82, 1st Bapt. Ch., Jayton, Tex., 1982-86, First Bapt. Ch., Abernathy, Tex., 1986—; tchr. Borden County Ind. Sch. Dist., Gail, Tex., 1979-81; chmn. com. Bapt. Student Union, Tex. Tech U., Lubbock, 1987—, Ch. Achievement Com., Lubbock, 1990—, mem. sem. studies com. Lubbock Bapt. Assn., 1990—; moderator West Cen. Bapt. Assn., 1985. Author mo. newspaper religious col., 1986. Mem. com. Susquicentennial Com., Jayton, 1985; coach Little Dribblers Basketball Team, Snyder, 1976; umpire Little League Baseball, Snyder, 1976; asst. to election judge Precinct 45 Abernathy, 1990. Mem. Lubbock Bapt. Assn., Abernathy Ministerial Assn. (pres. 1987), Bible. Archaeology Soc., C. of C., Lions (pres. 1989). Home: 1112 2nd St Abernathy TX 79311 Office: First Bapt Ch 411 7th St Abernathy TX 79311

TEIS, ROBERT WILLIAM, JR., minister; b. Canton, Ohio, Dec. 11, 1944; s. Robert William Teis and Anna Mae (Pergrum) Montgomery; m. Barbara Sue Wolford, Auf. 9, 1963; children: Robert John, Tammi Lynn, Shari Ann. BA, Calvary Bible Coll., 1968. Ordained to ministry Gen. Assn. Regular Bapt. Chs. Tchr. Muncie Bapt. Sch., Kansas City, Kans., 1968-69; min. edn., youth Wheelersburg (Ohio) Bapt. Ch., 1969-73; youth pastor Grace Bapt. Ch., Canton, 1973-74; tchr. Massilon (Ohio) Christian Sch., 1973-75, Elyria (Ohio) Christian Acad., 1975-78, Grand Rapids (Mich.) Coll. and Sem., 1978—; mem. State youth com. Ohio Assn. Regular Bapt. Chs., 1971-73; gen. chmn. Life Action Crusade, Canton, 1974. Office: Grand Rapids Bapt Coll and Sem 1001 E Beltline NE Grand Rapids MI 49505

TEISSIER, HENRI, archbishop; b. Lyon, France, July 21, 1929; s. Henri and Marie-Claire (Richard) T. Licence de lettres, U. de Rabat, Morocco, 1948; Licence de philosophie, U. Paris, 1950; Licence de théologie, Cath. Inst., Paris, 1955. Ordained priest Roman Cath. Ch., 1955, bishop, 1973, archbishop, 1981. Dir. Study Centre of Ch. in Algiers, Algeria, 1966-73; bishop of Oran West Algeria, 1973-81; archbishop of Algiers, 1981—; pres. Bishop Conf. of North Africa, Algiers, 1981; mem. Vatican Sec. for Interreligious Dialogue, 1978-81, coun. Synod of Bishops, Vatican City, 1983-87, v.p. Caritas Internat., 1981-87. Author: Eglise en Islam, 1984, La Mission de l'Eglise, 1985; coord.: Histoire des chrétiens d'Afrique du Nord, 1991. Address: 13 rue Khalifa Boukhalfa, 16000 Algergare Algeria

TELESMANIK, JUDITH J., lay minister, nurse; b. New Britain, Conn., Sept. 29, 1949; d. John G. and Helen (Rossal) Jackie; m. Robert J. Telesmanick, Sept. 9, 1972: children: Mark, Steven, Joyce. RN, Hartford (Conn.) Hosp. Sch. Nursing, 1970; BSN cum laude, Western Conn. State Coll., 1977. Tchr. Immaculate Conception ch., Southington, Conn., 1986—, dir. religious edn., 1987—; staff nurse Bradley Meml. Hosp., Southington, 1988—. Editor children's newspaper, 1986—. Mem. PTO, Plantsville, Conn.; com. mem. Plantsville Nature Ctr.

TELLONI, JOHN LOUIS, clergyman; b. Lorain, Ohio, Mar. 7, 1950; s. Dominic Louis and Mildred Suzanne (Mihok) T.; m. Mary Susan Cutka, Aug. 12, 1979; children—John Michael, Stephen Andrew. B.S. Ed., Bowling Green State U., 1972; M. Div., Concordia Theol. Sem., Ft. Wayne, Ind., 1977; postgrad. Concordia Sem., St. Louis, 1972-73, Lutheran Sch. Theology, Chgo., 1983. Ordained to ministry Luth. Ch., 1977; pastor St. Paul Evang. Luth. Ch. of Whiting (Ind.), 1977; interim pastor Martin Luther Ch. of Gary (Ind.), 1979-80, St. John Luth. Ch. of Whiting, 1981-83; dir. Luth. Retirement Village, Crown Point, Ind.; sec. student welfare bd., mem. youth bd. St. Paul Evang. Luth. Ch. dist. Luth. Ch.-Mo. Synod, chmn. gen. pastoral conf., 1983; dir. action group, forward in remembrance spl. appeal Luth. Ch.-Mo. Synod, 1980-81; lay youth del. to Luth. Ch.-Mo. Synod Conv., 1975; pres. central dist. Internat. Luther League, dist. Luth. Ch.-Mo. Synod, 1969-74, mission dir., 1974-75, v.p., 1975-81. Trustee, Luth. Haven, Oviedo, Fla. Democrat. Columnist Wheat & Chaff mag., 1969-70; editor The Courier, 1983; newsletter The Herald, 1979. Home: 8155 Walter St NW Massillon OH 44646 Office: St Paul Evang Luth Ch 1801 Atchison Ave Whiting IN 46394

TEMME, JON MARK, pastor; b. Omaha, Oct. 8, 1954; s. Norman Louis and Marian Elizabeth (Laible) T.; m. Heidi Anne Diamond, July 31, 1976; children: Gretchen, Krister. AA, Concordia Coll., Bronxville, N.Y., 1973; BA, Concordia Sr. Coll., Ft. Wayne, Ind., 1975; MDiv, Trinity Luth Sem., Columbus, Ohio, 1980; postgrad., U. Regensburg, Fed. Republic Germany, 1981-82. Ordained to ministry Evang. Luth. Ch. Can., 1980. Pastor Trinity Luth. Ch., Red Deer, Alta., Can., 1980-81, Peace Luth. Ch., Ft. St. John, B.C., Can., 1982-85, Ascension Luth. Ch., Edmonton, Alta., Can., 1985—; pres. Peace River Conf. Evang. Luth. Ch. Can., 1982—; mem. bd. communication 1984—, planning com. B.C. Synod, Evang. Luth. Ch. Can., 1984—; chmn. Div. Can. Mission, 1988—, Good Samaritan Soc., 1990—. Contbr. articles to religious publs. Grad. asst. Pa. State U., 1975, Trinity Luth. Sem., 1978, 80, U. Regensburg, 1981. Office: Ascension Luth Ch, 8405 83rd St, Edmonton, AB Canada T6C 2Z2 *It is time to bring a sense of wonder, mystery and awe back to our civilization of technocratic deceit. God's purposes continue to be revealed in many and various, wonderful ways.*

TEMPLE, NICHOLAS LAWRENCE, minister; b. Louisville, Feb. 14, 1946; s. Robert Lawlrence and Katheryn (Hertle) T.; m. Janel Marie Troidl, Mar. 21, 1970; children: Nicholas Lawrence III, Robert Lawrence II. BE, U. Ky., 1969, MSW, 1977; MDiv, Eden Theol. Sem., 1987. Ordained to ministry United Ch. Christ. Pastor St. John United Ch. Christ, Cannelton, Ind., 1987—; bd. dirs. Ind.-Ky. Conf., United Ch. Christ, Indpls., 1990—. Bd. dirs. Ress Care Group Homes, Troy, Ind., 1989; mem. Perry County Drug Abuse Task Force, Tell City, Ind., 1990. With U.S. Army, 1969-72. Named to Honorable Order of Ky. Colonels. Mem. Perry County Clergy Assn. (v.p. 1988-89, pres. 1989—, chairperson youthful ministries div., 1990—). Home: 620 Taylor St Cannelton IN 47520 Office: St John United Ch Christ 7th and Taylor Sts Cannelton IN 47520

TEMPLETON, ELIZABETH LINDSAY, minister, ministry director; b. Greenville, S.C., Nov. 28, 1948; d. George Denton and Dorcas P. (Barnett) Lindsay; m. David Samuel Templeton Jr., May 31, 1969; children: David III, Matthew L. BA, Presbyn. Coll., Clinton, S.C., 1969; MDiv, Erskine Theol. Sem., Due West, S.C., 1982. Ordained to ministry Presbyn. Ch. (U.S.A.), 1982. Supply pastor Foothills Presbytery, Presbyn. Ch. (U.S.A.), Greenville, 1982—; exec. dir. United Ministries, Greenville, 1983—; workshop leader Foothills Presbytery and S.C. United Meth. Conf., 1982—; chaplain Furman U., Greenville, 1982—; commr. Synod South Atlantic, Panama City, Fla., 1990. V.p. Brockwood Housing Project, Greenville, 1984-88; bd. dirs. Emergency Food and Shelter Bd., 1984—; advisor Greenville Free Med. Clinic, 1986-88; pres. Greenville Area Dirs. Social and Health Agys., 1986, 87, 91; v.p. Nat. Urban Ministry Acad. Bd., Nashville, 1988—; active Com. for Continuing Edn., Greenville, 1989—; founder Greenville Homeless Coalition, 1989—. Recipient Disting. Svc. award Greenville Lions, 1988, Disting. Svc. award Greenville Jaycees, 1989; named Outstanding Young Religious Leader, Greenville Jaycees, 1985. Mem. Coun. United Way Execs., Greenville Jr. League (mem. adv. bd. 1990—). Democrat. Office: United Ministries 606 Pendleton St Greenville SC 29601

TEMPLETON, WILLIAM MILTON, minister; b. Lynchburg, Va., Apr. 11, 1951; s. Jesse Milton and Miriam Klair (Orndorff) T.; m. Bonita Arlene Irby, May 12, 1979; children: Amie, Michael, Allison, Jeffrey. Student, Va. Poly. Inst. and State U., 1972, Liberty U., Lynchburg, Va., 1972-73. Ordained to ministry So. Bapt. Conv., 1975. Pastor Charlotte Bapt. Ch., Charlotte Court House, Va., 1973-78; assoc. pastor Northside Bapt. Ch., Charlottesville, Va., 1982-84, 1984—; founder, chmn. bd. dirs. Northside Christian Schs., Inc., Charlottesville, 1987—; bd. overseers Criswell Coll., Dallas; bd. dirs. Bapt. Banner, Inc., 1990—; pres., mem. coun. Good News Mission, Charlottesville, 1984—. Republican. Office: Northside Bapt Ch 1325 Rio Rd E Charlottesville VA 22901

TENG, PHILIP CHIN HUEI, religion educator; b. Tsingtao, Shantung, China, Jan. 15, 1922; came to U.S., 1987; m. Lily Chang Oi Foo, Feb. 7, 1953. BA, Northwestern U. China, 1946; BD, Edinburgh (Scotland) U., 1950; LLD (hon.), Nyack Coll., 1970. Pres. China Grad. Sch. Theology, Hong Kong, 1974-87, Chinese Chs. Assn., Christian and Missionary Alliance in U.S.A., 1987—; dir. Chinese bi-cultural and pastoral program Alliance Theol. Sem., Nyack, N.Y., 1987—; Bible expositor Asian Congress on Evangelism, Singapore, 1966, Thailand Congress on Evangelism, 1969, 88, Japan Congress on Evangelism, 1982; mem. Urbana (Ill.) Student Conv., 1973; mem. exec. com. Lausanne Movement, 1974-75; chmn. Chinese Ctr. for World Evangelization, 1976—; pres. Asian Missions Assn., 1973-86, Alliance World Fellowship, 1982-87. Author 14 books. Home and Office: Alliance Theol Sem Nyack NY 10960

TENGBOM, LUVERNE CHARLES, religion educator; b. Poskin, Wis., May 30, 1919; s. Carl John and Ida Carolina (Carlson) T.; m. Mildred Helena Hasselquist, May 23, 1953; children: Daniel, Judith, Janet, David. BA, Gustavus Adolphus Coll., 1943; MDiv, Augustana Sem., 1946; ThM, Luther Sem., St. Paul, 1962; PhD, Hartford Sem. Found., 1977. Ordained to ministry Luth. Ch. in Am., 1946. Pastor 1st Luth. Ch., Calgary, Alta., Can., 1946-56; missionary, mem. bd. world missions Augustana Luth. Ch., Tanzania, 1956-67; prof. Luth. Bible Inst., Anaheim, Calif., 1967-85, acad. dean, 1976-85, prof., 1987-91; sec. Can. Conf., Augustana Luth. Ch., 1950-56; mem. commn. on world mission Pacific S.W. Synod, Luth. Ch. in Am., 1981—, bd. world missions, 1985-87; prof. Trinity Theol. Coll., Singapore, Singapore Bible Coll., 1985-87. Author: Fill My Cup, Lord, 1978, Bible Readings for Families, 1981. sec. Luth. Bible Inst., Camrose, Alta, 1946-56; dean Luth. Bible Sch., Moshi, Tanzania, 1960-61. Home: 789 Cambridge Way Claremont CA 91711 *My purpose and prayer in life has been to have a greater commitment to the Lord Jesus, to proclaim the good news with greater conviction, and to have a greater concern for others.*

TENINTY, BILLY L., religious organization administrator; b. San Francisco, Jan. 29, 1946; m. Edna C. Teninty; children: Lilia Jeanette, Edwin Vincent. Mgr. ops. REAP Internat., Upland, Calif., 1980-84, dir. ops., 1984-86, v.p., 1986-90, pres., 1990—. Staff sgt. USAF, 1966-69. Mem. Assn. for the Advancement of Med. Instrumentation (cert. biomed. equipment technician). Office: REAP Internat 972 W 9th St Upland CA 91786

TENNENBAUM, LLOYD, retired rabbi; b. Rochester, N.Y., Sept. 3, 1925; s. Ben and Leah (Kovinsky) T.; divorced; children: Jeremy, David, Raphael. AB cum laude, Yeshiva U., 1946; M.H.L., Jewish Theol. Sem. Am., N.Y.C., 1950, DD (hon.), 1975. Ordained rabbi, 1950. Rabbi Agudath Shalom, Lynchburg, Va., 1951-58, Huntington (N.Y.) Jewish Ctr., 1959-69; rabbi, founder Kehillath Shalom, Cold Spring Harbor, N.Y., 1969-76; chaplain Bronx (N.Y.) Psychiat. Ctr., 1964-80; psychotherapist; mem. exec. bd. Clergy Concerned about Vietnam, N.Y.C., 1965-72. Organizer Consultative Conf. on Desegregation, Va., 1955; participant Prayer Vigil and Imprisonment in Albany (Ga.), 1962, March on Washington, 1963. Named Honoree, LI Salute to Human Rights, Garden City, N.Y., 1965. Democrat. Home: 175 W 12th St New York NY 10011

TENNER, MELITTA JOHANNA, physician, lay worker; b. Proesen, Germany, Oct. 4, 1933; d. Tenner Hermann and Hulda Sophie (Reiche) T. MD, Humboldt U., Berlin, 1970. Physician hosp. and polyclinic Riesa, Gröditz, German Dem. Republic, 1969-79; pvt. practice Proesen, 1979—; various positions United Meth. Ch., Fed. Republic Germany, 1973—; pres. World Meth. Coun., 1986-91. Contbr. articles to religious jours. Leader Free German Assn. Trade Union, 1970-74, 79-89. Recipient numerous medals. Home: Eichbusch 4, 7909 Proesen Federal Republic of Germany Office: Artzpraxis, Riesaer Strasse 122, 7909 Proesen Federal Republic of Germany

TENNEY, TOM FRED, bishop; b. DeRidder, La., Dec. 6, 1933; s. Fred and Jenny Veve (Nichols) T.; m. Thetus Pearl Caughron, Dec. 27, 1952; children: Tom Gregory, Teri Denise Tenney Spears. Student, Apostolic Bible Inst., St. Paul, 1952. Ordained to ministry United Pentecostal Ch., 1954. Pastor United Pentecostal Ch., Monroe, La., 1953-56, DeRidder, 1976-78; youth pres. La. dist. United Pentecostal Ch., 1953-60; dist. supt. for La. United Pentecostal Ch., Tioga, 1978—; youth pres. United Pentecostal Ch., Internat., St. Louis, 1960-69, dir. fgn. missions, mem. exec. bd., 1969-76, mem. gen. bd., 1978—; internat. radio speaker Harvestime, St. Louis, 1976-78. Author: Pentecost: What is That?, 1975, The Flame Still Burns, 1989. Trustee Tupelo (Miss.) Children's Mansion, Spirit of Freedom, Metairie, La., Lighthouse Ranch for Boys, Hammond, La. Democrat. Home and Office: PO Box 248 Tioga LA 71477

TENNIES, ARTHUR CORNELIUS, minister; b. Boston, Apr. 15, 1931; s. Raymond Ara and Frances Eden (Fiske) T.; m. Stella Janet Trowbridge, Sept. 7, 1959 (div. Dec. 1980); children: Diane, Linda, Susan, Philip. BS in Commerce, Grove City (Pa.) Coll., 1953; BD, Louisville Presbyn. Theol. Sem., 1956; MS in Ch. Rsch. and Planning, Christian Theol. Sem., Indpls., 1968. Ordained to ministry Presbyn. Ch. (U.S.A.), 1956. Pastor various chs., 1956-66, United Ch., Mt. Morris, N.Y., 1976-81, Bloomingdale (Ohio) Presbyn. Ch., 1982-87, Trinity United Presbyn. Ch., New Washington, Ind., 1987—; mem. staff N.Y. State Coun. Chs., 1967-73, United Presbyn. Program Agy., N.Y.C., 1973-76. Author: A Church for Sinners, Seekers, and Sundry Non-Saints, 1973, (short stories) The Promise and the Power, 1990, (novel) The Star Still Shines, 1991. Home and Office: Trinity United Presbyn Ch PO Box 219 New Washington IN 47162 *Life is a journey, and no matter how difficult the journey, one can walk in sunlight if his heart is open to God's love.*

TENNIS, CALVIN CABELL, bishop. Bishop Episcopal Ch., Wilmington, Del., 1986—. Office: Diocesan Office 2020 Tatnall St Wilmington DE 19802

TENZIN GYATSO See **DALAI LAMA**

TERAN, SISTER MARY INEZ, nun, educator; b. Austin, Tex., Nov. 15, 1924; d. Jose Julian and Petra (Meza) T. BA, Our Lady of the Lake U., 1960; MDE, Cath. U. Am., 1965. Joined Congregation Sisters of Divine Providence, Roman Cath. Ch., 1941. Coord. religious edn. Archdiocese San Antonio, 1966-71; dir. religious edn. Dolores Ch., Austin, 1971-74, St. Henry's Ch., San Antonio, 1974-78, St. Margaret Mary Ch., San Antonio, 1978-82, St. John Berchmans Ch., San Antonio, 1982-84, St. Cyril and Methodius Ch., Granger, Tex., 1986-88, Sacred Heart Ch., Von Ormy, Tex., 1988—. Mex.-Am. Cultural Ctr. scholar, San Antonio, 1985-86. Home: 515 SW 24th St San Antonio TX 78207 *Life for me is a journey that slowly, sometimes gently, at other times not so gently, but gradually, leads me to my eternal goal, which is heaven. The beauty is that I do not go alone!.*

TERANDO, JUDY RAE, religion educator; b. Peoria, Ill., Oct. 12, 1943; d. William and Betty Marie (Gavin) Maholland; m. Mark Terando, Dec. 16, 1972 (div. Jan. 1981); children: Heath, Brandon. BS in Phys. Edn., Ill. State U., 1965, MS in Phys. Edn., 1970. CCD coord. Immaculate Conception, Mt. Palatine, 1982—; phys. edn., health tchr. Lasalle (Ill.)-Peru High Sch.,

1970—. Roman Catholic. Home: 803 27th St Peru IL 61354 Office: Lasalle-Peru High Sch 531 Chartres Lasalle IL 61301

TERBUSH, JAY MURRAY, IV, minister, psychotherapist; b. Owosso, Mich., Sept. 6, 1952; s. Jay Murray and Geraldine Wesla (Porterfield) T.; m. Marlene Elizabeth Patterson, Nov. 8, 1975; children: Katharine Rose, Carolyn Jeanne, Jessica Anne, Jonathan David Christian. BA, U. Mich., 1974; MA, Trinity Evang. Divinity Sch., Deefield, Ill., 1979; MDiv, Trinity Evang. Divinity Sch., 1980; PhD in Counseling Psychology, Mich. State U., 1989. Psychotherapist Concern Counseling Ctr., Waukegan, Ill., 1979-80; teaching asst. Mich. State U., E. Lansing, 1980-84; psychotherapist Counseling Ctr. for Health Psychology, Okemos, Mich., 1982-83; youth dir. Plymouth Congl. Ch., Lansing, Mich., 1983-85; psychotherapist Okemos Psychol. Svcs., Okemos, Mich., 1983-85, Grand Ledge Counseling Ctr., Grand Ledge, Mich., 1985—; sr. minister 1st Congl. Ch., St. Johns, Mich., 1985—; treas., mem. youth commn. Mich. Congl. Christian Chs., 1981-86; co-dir. Heritage of Pilgrim Endeavor Congl. Christian Chs., 1985-89; bd. dirs. Congl. Found Theol. Studies, 1991—; cons. Rivendell Adolescent Psychiat. Hosp., 1991—. Mem. Sex Edn. Adv. Com., St. Johns, 1986-87. Butler Meml. scholar Coll. Edn. Mich. State U., 1983; Kinnick fellow Congl. Found. for Theological Studies, 1978-80, doctoral fellow Coll. Edn. Mich. State U., .• 80-81. Mem. Am. Psychol. Assn. (assoc.), Mich. Psychol. Assn. (assoc.), Christian Assn. Psychol. Studies (assoc.), Cen. Mich. Assn. Congl. Christian Chs. (moderator, chair nominating com., 1989-91). Office: First Congl Church 100 Maple Ave Saint Johns MI 48879 *What gives life meaning for me is to encourage the growth of others in "shalom", that is a sense of inner peace and love, integrity and balance, wholeness and holiness, and emotional, relational and spiritual health, which is grounded in and nurtured by God's grace.*

TERESA, MOTHER (AGNES GONXHA BOJAXHIU), nun, missionary; b. Skopje, Yugoslavia, Aug. 27, 1910. D.D. (hon.), U. Cambridge, 1977; Dr. med. (hon.), Cath. U. of Sacred Heart, Rome, 1981, Cath. U. Louvain, Belgium, 1982. Joined Sisters of Loreto, Roman Cath. Ch., 1928. Came to India; founder, head Missionaries of Charity, Calcutta, India, 1950-90, re-elected, 1990—; opened Nirmal Hriday Home for Dying Destitutes, 1952; started leper colony, West Bengal, 1964; founder Missionary Bros. of Charity, 1963, Internat. Assn. Co-workers of Mother Teresa and Contemplative Sisters and Brothers, 1976. Recipient Pope John XXIII Peace prize, 1971, Templeton Found. prize, 1973, Nobel Peace prize, 1979, Bharat Ratna (Star of India), 1980, U.S. Presdl. medal of Freedom, 1985; named hon. citizen of Assisi 1982, Woman of Yr. award, 1989. Address: Missionaries of Charity, 54-A A J C Bose Rd, Calcutta 700 016 W B, India

TERHO, MATTI ILMARI, minister, chaplain; b. Karstula, Finland, Mar. 14, 1944; came to Can., 1965; naturalized, 1972; s. Veikko Ilmari and Helmi (Kauppala) T. Matriculated, Toolon Yhteislyseo, Finland, 1963, Helsinki U., Alkututkinto, 1965; MDiv, Waterloo Luth. U., 1969; postgrad., Helsinki U., 1985-86. Ordained to ministry Evang. Luth. Ch. in Can., 1969. Pastor St. Michael's Finnish Evang. Luth Ch., Montreal, Que., Can., 1969-75; vice pastor Our Saviour Luth Ch., Lachine, Que., Can., 1970-71; part-time chaplain Sir George Williams U., Montreal, 1971-73; univ. chaplain Concordia U., 1974—. Olympic chaplain (agt. oecumenique), 1976; chmn. organizing com. for XXXVII Finnish-Can. Grand (cultural) Festival, Montreal, 1976; dir. Dept. Pastoral Svcs. to Winter Olympics, Lake Placid, N.Y., 1980; vice pastor Good Shepherd Luth Ch., St. Lambert, Que., 1984-85; spl. cons. to Chs. Com. on Migrant Workers in Europe, 1985-86; vice pastor Internat. Evang. Ch., Helsinki, 1986. Mem. Can. Friends of Finland (chmn. 1987—). Home: 3780 LaSalle Blvd, Apt 4, Verdun, PQ Canada H4G 3H9 Office: 1455 de Maisonneuve Blvd W, Montreal, PQ Canada H3G 1M8 *Life would be so much easier and happier if more people would put sharing before having or owning.*

TERRELL, GAIL E., clergyman, educator; b. Dayton, Ohio, Dec. 25, 1943; s. Seymore F. and Doris L. (Thompson) T.; m. Carolyn L. Ervin, July 29, 1967; children: Shelley Terrell Woodby, Deborah Terrell Hall, Gail E., Matthew A. BS in Chem. Engring., U. Cin., 1967, MBA, 1968, MEd, 1980, PhD, 1981; MDiv, Cin. Bapt. Coll., 1972, ThD, 1973; D Christian Svc. (hon.), Temple Bapt. Coll., 1982, postgrad. studies, 1982-85. Ordained to ministry Bapt. Ch., 1975. Chem. technician Monsanto Chem. Co., Inc., Miamisburg, Ohio, 1962-67; chem. engr. Emery Industries, Inc., Cin., 1967-72; pres. Temple Bapt. Coll., Cin., 1972-85; broker/owner G.E. Terrell Realty, Cin., 1968—; tchr. sci. Landmark Christian Sch., Cin., 1985—; pastor Grace Bapt. Ch., Hamilton, Ohio, 1986—; mgr. Grace Bookstore, Hamilton, 1986—; coll. tchr. Cin. Bapt. Coll., 1968-72; seminar speaker nat. and regional ednl. and religious confs., 1972—; chemist AEC, Miamisburg, 1967-72. Author, editor: Systematic Theology Outlines, 1990, New Testament Outlines, 1991; contbr. articles to profl. jours. Cons. Republican Election Com., Dillsboro, Ind., 1990. Recipient Carsey award Cin. Engring. Soc., 1967; U. Cin. grad. scholar, 1967-81. Mem. Creation Rsch. Soc., Bible Sci. Assn., Dean Burgeon Soc., Cin. Bd. Realtors, Hamilton-Fairfield Bd. Realtors, Nat. Asns. Realtors. Baptist. Avocations: camping, piano. Home: 3291 Greenwich Dr Fairfield OH 45014 Office: Grace Bapt Ch 2630 Hamilton-Mason Rd Hamilton OH 45011

TERRELL, JERRY D., church organization administrator; b. McComb, Miss., May 3, 1944; s. William Newton and Thelma (Day) T.; m. Mary Ethel Dykes, June 9, 1963; children: Rex Edward, Jeffery Newton, Timothy Alan. BS, U. So. Miss., 1963; MRE, Southwestern Bapt. Theol. Sem., Ft. Worth, 1968. Ordained to ministry Bapt. Ch. Assoc. pastor Valley Bapt. Ch., Longview, Wash., 1963-64, South Hills Bapt. Ch., Ft. Worth, 1964-68, Van Winkle Bapt. Ch., Jackson, Miss., 1968-72, Plymouth Park Bapt. Ch., Irving, Tex., 1972-77; mgr. Bapt. Sunday Sch. Bd., Nashville, 1977-80; pres. Ch. Svcs. Assocs., Orlando, Fla., 1982—. Author: Basic Preschool Work, 1980, Preschool Teacher Development, 1981, also curriclum materials for children. Mem. Rep. Presdl. Task Force, Washington, 1988—; mem. Orlando Better Bus. Bur. Mem. Christian Edn. Assn. Internat., Nat. Assn. Ch. Bus. Adminstrs., Orlando C. of C., Platform Speakers Assn. Office: Ch Svcs Assocs 3114 Corrine Dr Orlando FL 32803

TERRELL, JOSEPH WILLIAM, pastor; b. Sullivan, Ind., July 31, 1946; s. Lavergne Franklin and Mary Ruth (Humphrey) T.; m. Beverly Sue Lapham, July 16, 1972; children: Larry Lavergne, Daniel Aaran. BA in Religion, Community Bapt. Coll., Indianola, Iowa, 1983; cert. edn. in western rite orthodoxy, Duarte Costa Sch. Religion, Altoona, Pa., 1989. Ordained orthodox sub-deacon, Western Orthodox Ch. in Am., 1978; ordained to ministry Ind. Bapt. Chs. in USA, 1984. Youth coord. Christus Victor Luth. Ch., Terre Haute, Ind., 1979-80; pastor St. Luke's Bapt. Ch., Terre Haute, Ind., 1981-83, Friendship Bapt. Ch., Terre Haute, 1986-90; asst. pastor Beacon Bapt. Ch., Marshall, Ill., 1983-84; deacon 8th Avenue Bapt. Ch., Terre Haute, 1985-86; pastor Fairview Immanuel Bapt. Ch., Youngstown, Ohio, 1990—; puppet ministry coord. bus. ministry Calvary-Tabernacle Bapt. Ch., Terre Haute, 1970-78; pres. Vigo County Clergy Assn., 1986; mem. pastoral care com. Union Hosp., Terre Haute, 1987-89; coord. TV, Greater Terre Haute Ch. Fedn., 1985-90; mem. Am. Bapt. Mins. Coun., 1990—. With U.S. Army, 1966-69, Vietnam. Recipient award for outstanding ministry Evangistic Biog. Assn., 1980, Ch. of Yr. award Am. Bapt. Ch. Ind., 1989. Mem. Nat. Chaplains Assn. Democrat. Home: 670 Poland Ave Struthers OH 44471 Office: Fairview Immanuel Bapt Ch 4220 Youngstown-Poland Rd Youngstown OH 44514

TERRIEN, LAWRENCE B., academic administrator. Head Cath. U. Am. (Theol. Coll.), Washington. Office: Cath U Am 401 Michigan Ave NE Washington DC 20017*

TERRINONI, DAVID MICHAEL, minister; b. Cleve., Mar. 17, 1957; s. William Peter and Sally Ann (Smith) T.; m. Victoria Lynn Malo, Oct. 2, 1982; children: Marissa, Alanna. AA, William R. Harper Coll., Palatine, Ill., 1978; BS, Western Ill. U., 1981; MDiv, McCormick Theol. Sem., Chgo., 1990; grad., USAF Chaplain Sch., 1991. Ordained to ministry Presbyn. Ch. (USA), 1990. Sem. asst. pastor Presbyn. Ch., Palatine, Ill., 1987-88; intern minister Third Presbyn. Ch., Rockford, Ill., 1988-89; vol. night chaplain Rockford (Ill.) Meml. Hosp., 1988-90; interim assoc. pastor First Presbyn. Ch., Sterling, Ill., 1990—; mem. Middle East task force Blackhawk Presbytery, Oregon, Ill., 1991—; mem. Sem. Governance Reorgn. Task Force, Chgo., 1987-88; M.Div. rep. Sem. Common Coun., Chgo., 1988-89. Contbr. articles to profl. jours. Unit commr. Boy Scouts Am., N.W. Suburban Coun., Ill., 1981—; bd. dirs. Presbyn. Nursery Sch., Sterling, 1990—. Chaplain USAFR, 1991—. Recipient James W. Angell award for preaching McCormick Theol. Sem., 1988, Samuel Robinson award, 1988, Outstanding Chaplain Candidate award USAFR, 1990. Mem. Mil. Chaplains Assn., Sterling Rock Falls Clery Assn., Nat. Eagle Scout Assn., Kiwanis. Office: First Presbyn Ch 410 Second Ave PO Box 441 Sterling IL 61081 *For anyone who cares, this is my perspective on life. "We never know when God will call us home. It could be today, it could be years from now. The point is, we are given the gift of life. The gift to touch the lives of other people and to enjoy the miracles of God's creation. To waste this precious gift of time is a sin. It is ignoring God's gift to us by worrying about something beyond our control."*

TERRY, DENNIS EDWARD, minister; b. Pensacola, Fla., Mar. 14, 1957; s. James Edward and Martha Lee (Fant) T.; m. Penny LuAnn Brown, Sept. 1, 1984; children: Mandy, Dennis Jr., Joshua. Assoc. Divinity, New Orleans Bapt. Sem., 1983. Ordained to ministry Bapt. Ch., 1987. Pastor North Shore Bapt., Avinger, Tex., 1986-90, First Bapt. Swan, Tyler, Tex., 1990—; resort ministry dir. North Shore Bapt., Avinger, Tex., 1987-90; fire chaplain Mims Fire Dept., Avinger, 1989-90. Mem. Smith Bapt. Assn. (Bapt. standard rep. 1990-91, named for Sunday Sch. Growth 1990), Enon Bapt. Assn. (ministry support team 1988-89, named for Most Baptisms 1989). Republican. Home: PO Box 1747 Lindale TX 75771 Office: First Bapt Swan Rte 5 Box 104 Tyler TX 75706

TERRY, MIRIAM JANICE, minister; b. Aliceville, Ala., May 4, 1956; d. Ernest Lee Jr. and Nolie (Lee) T. Student, U. Tex., Arlington, 1974-75, Am. Banking Sch., Tampa, Fla., 1978; BA in Bibl. Studies, Living Word Coll. and Sem., St. Louis, 1991. Ordained to ministry Life Anew Missionary Fellowship, 1987. Children's pastor Brandonville (Fla.) Christian Ch., 1975, Oxford (Ala.) Ch. of God, 1980-81; dir. children's ministries Newark Heights Ch. of God, Newark, Ohio, 1982-83, Life Christian Ctr., Madisonville, Ky., 1984—; dir. promotions Life Anew Ministries, Inc./Sta. WLCN-TV, Madisonville, 1984—; dir. edn. Life Christian Acad., Madisonville, 1990—; dir. day care Life Ctr. Day Care Plus, Madisonville, 1991—. Vol. Regional Med. Ctr., Madisonville, 1984—, mem. laughter therapy com., 1990-91; vol. St. Jude's Children's Hosp., 1991—. Recipient Outstanding Svc. award Regional Med. Ctr., 1986. Republican. Office: Life Anew Ministries Inc 721 Princeton Pike PO Box 1087 Madisonville KY 42431-1087 *The teaching of Jesus declares that life does not consist in the abundance of things which one possesses. This I have experienced to be true. The essence of life is not in things of material value but in the ideals and aspirations of the human spirit being in harmony with all of mankind and the world.*

TERRY, ROGER HAROLD, minister, musician, composer, author, editor; b. Salisbury, N.C., Feb. 3, 1925; s. Roger Harold and Marie (Kneeburg) T.; m. Martha Frye, June 30, 1948 (div. July 1973); children: Barbara (dec.), Ruth, Julia, Glenn; m. Kathryn Wagoner, Nov. 22, 1973. AB, Lenoir-Rhyne Coll., Hickory, N.C., 1945, D Sacred Music (hon.), 1973; BD, Lutheran Theological Southern Seminary, Columbia, S.C., 1948; MS in Theology, Union Theological Seminary, 1955. Asst. pastor St. John Luth. Ch., Salisbury, N.C., 1948-50; pastor Emanuel Luth. Ch., Ridgefield Park, N.J., 1950-53, St. Mark Luth. Ch., China Grove, N.C., 1953-59; worship/music editor Bd. Parish Edn., 1959-62; worship/music editor div. for parish services United Luth. Ch. in Am., Phila., 1963-77; pastor Peace Luth. Ch., Gibsonville, N.C., 1977-83, Macedonia Luth. Ch., Burlington, N.C., 1983-84, Nazareth Luth. Ch., Rural Hall, N.C., 1985-87; program dir. Lutheridge Sch. Music, Arden, N.C., 1956-72; pres. Council of Chs., Ridgefield Park, N.J., 1952-53; chaplain Internat. Order of St. Luke Physician, 1978—. Author Church School Hymnal for Children, 1964, Young Children Sing, 1967, Music Resource Book, 1967, Music in Christian Education, 1969, Sing! Hymnal for Youth and Adults, 1970, Children Sing, Books 1-3, 1972-77, Celebrate, 1974-77, (with others) Hymnal Companion to the Lutheran Book of Worship, 1981; editor, author of numerous Luth. curriculum resources; contbr. articles to religious pubs. Sec., bd. trustees Lowman Home for Aged, White Rock, S.C., 1957-59; vol. relief worker, fund raiser Hurricane Hugo victims, 1989-90. Mem. Forsyth Luth. Council. (pres. 1986-87), Am. Guild Organists (exec. com. 1985-86), Hymn Soc. Am. (pres. Phila. chpt. 1970-72). Republican. Club: Rotary. Avocations: organic gardening, small scale tree farming. Home and Office: 1951 Gibsonville-Ossipee Rd Elon College NC 27244 *The love of power, the addiction of dictators, dehumanizes and destroys. The power of love, which Jesus revealed, creates willing hands and servant hearts to heal brokenness and bring good out of evil. Our destiny depends upon how we choose.*

TESELLE, EUGENE ARTHUR, JR., religion educator; b. Ames, Iowa, Aug. 8, 1931; . Eugene Arthur and Hildegarde (Flynn) TeS.; m. Sallie McFague, Ssept. 12, 1959 (div. Oct. 1976); children: Elizabeth, John; m. Penelope Saunders, Mar. 4, 1978; children: William, James, Thomas. BA, U. Colo., 1952; BD, Princeton Theol. Sem., 1955; MA, Yale U., 1960, PhD, 1963. issues analyst Witherspoon Soc., 1987—; chmn. global missions com. Presbytery Middle Tenn., 1989—. Author: Augustine, the Theologian, 1970, Augustine's Strategy as an Apologist, 1974, Christ in Context, 1975. Incorporator Belmont-Hillsboro Neighbors, Nashville, 1971, Consumer Coalition for Health, Nashville, 1980, Nashville Local, Dem. Socialists Am., 1983, Cen. Am. Solidarity Assn., Nashville, 1986. Presbyn. Grad. fellow, 1958, Rockefeller doctoral fellow, 1960, Kent fellow, 1961. Mem. Am. Acad. Religion, Am. Soc. Ch. History, Soc. for Values in Higher Edn., Workgroup on Constructive Christian Theology, Phi Beta Kappa. Home: 2007 Linden Ave Nashville TN 37212 Office: Vanderbilt U Div Sch Nashville TN 37240

TETLIE, HAROLD, priest; b. Madison, Minn., Aug. 24, 1926; s. H. Ben and Anna (Mauland) T. BA cum laude, St. Olaf Coll., Northfield, Minn., 1951; MBA, U. Denver, 1956; postgrad., Cornell U., 1959-60; BST, Luther Theol. Sem., St. Paul, 1965. Ordained to ministry Am. Luth. Ch., 1965. Pastor Christ the King Chs. (Evang. Cath. Ch.), Alice, Tex., 1965—, congregation supr., 1969—; cir. parish priest, Nuevo Leon, Tamaulipas, Hidalgo, San Luis Potosi, Mex. Coord. Joint Action in Community Svc., Inc., Alice, 1970—. Sgt. U.S. Army, 1945-46, PTO. Recipient Svc. to Mankind award Sertoma Club, Corpus Christi, Tex., Regional Vol. of Yr. award Joint Action in Community Svc., Inc., 1991. Mem. NEA (life), VFW, Am. Legion, 40 et 8, Family Motor Coach Assn., Sons of Norway, Internat. Platform Assn., Thousand Trails. Home and Office: Christ the King Chs Box 1607 Alice TX 78333-1607 *The grace of our Lord Jesus Christ is ours for the receiving and He tells us in John 13:34: "Love one another, even as I loved you."*

TETLOW, ELISABETH MEIER, writer, researcher, scholar; b. Cin., Mar. 26, 1942; d. Carl L. and Margaret (Hersey) Meier; m. L. Mulry Tetlow, July 5, 1970; children: Tania C., Maria A., Sonia M., Sarah A. BA, Columbia U., 1964; MA, Fordham U., 1967, Fordham U., 1970; STM, Woodstock Coll., 1974; MDiv, Jesuit Sch. Theology, Berkeley, 1979; JD, Loyola U., New Orleans, 1984. Bar: La. 1984. Instr. Coll. Mary and St. Vincent, Riverdale, N.Y., 1968-68, Fordham U., 1970, Loyola U., New Orleans, 1979-82; law clk. La. Supreme Ct., New Orleans, 1984-85; staff atty. U.S. Ct. Appeals (5th cir.), New Orleans, 1985-87; rsch. atty. Kierr, Gainsburgh, Benjamin, New Orleans, 1988; law clk. La. Ct. Appeals (4th cir.), 1989-91. Author: Women and Ministry in the New Testament, 1980, 2d edit., 1984, Partners in Service, 1983, The Spiritual Exercises of St. Ignatius Loyola, 1987; contbr. articles to profl. jours. Active Amnesty Internat., Bread for the World, Pax Christi, Women's Ordination Conf. Recipient U.S. Gold Medal USA Karate Fedn. Nat. Championships, 1989. Mem. ABA, Cath. Bibl. Assn. Am., Am. Acad. Religion, Soc. Bibl. Lit., Coll. Theology Soc., La. Bar Assn., La. Karate Assn., USA Karate Fedn., Internat. Shotokan Karate Fedn., New Orleans Symphony Chorus. Democrat. Roman Catholic. Avocations: shotokan karate, swimming, piano, choral music, hiking. Home and Office: 16 Fontainebleau Dr New Orleans LA 70125

TETRO, FRANK LUVERNE, JR., minister, educator; b. L.A., Jan. 8, 1919; s. Frank L. and Daisy Olive (Daniels) T.; m. Margaret Marie Reed, June 1, 1944; children: Darlene R. Pritchard, Frank L. III, Daisy L. Whaley, Dolores Y. Klemm, John C. Student, Biola U., LaMirada, Calif., 1947; BA and BRE, Calif. Bapt. Theol. Coll./Sem., 1949; MRE, Western Bapt. Theol. Sem., Portland, Oreg., 1964; PhD, Calif. Grad. Sch. Theology, Glendale, 1977. Ordained to ministry. Founder, tchr./adminstr. Blackler Meml. Bible Sch., Tachikawa, Japan; missionary to Japan Calvary Bapt. Ch., Los Gatos, Calif.; pastor/tchr. Spurgeon Meml. Bapt. Ch., Riggins, Idaho; v.p. Ind. Fundamental Chs. of Am., Western Idaho region. Contbr. articles to profl. jours. With U.S. Army, 1941-45. Home: HC 69 Box 130 Riggins ID 83549

TEUBAL, SAVINA J., religion educator; b. Manchester, Eng., July 25, 1926; came to U.S., 1959; d. Nissim and Violet Rebekah (Mansour) T.; m. Alan Tabbush, Dec. 20, 1953 (div.). MA, U. Without Walls, 1974; PhD in Ancient Near Ea. Studies, Internat. Coll., 1977. affiliated scholar U. So. Calif., 1985—. Author: Sarah the Priestess, 1984, Hagar the Egyptian, 1990; author: (with others, anthology) Fields of Offering, 1983. Mem. Am. Acad. Religion, Soc. Bibl. Lit. Jewish. Home: 541 Stassi Ln Santa Monica CA 90402

TEUTSCH, DAVID ALAN, rabbi, college administrator; b. Salt Lake City, Mar. 7, 1950; s. Eric F. and Hilda A. (Wormser) T.; m. Betsy P. Platkin, Dec. 27, 1973; children: Zachary, Nomi. BA, Harvard U., 1972; MA, Hebrew Union Coll., 1975, M Hebrew Letters, 1977; PhD, U. Pa., 1991. Ordained rabbi, 1977. Dir. program adminstrn. Ctr. for Learning and Leadership, N.Y.C., 1978-80; asst. dir. Fedn. of Reconstructionist Congregations, N.Y.C., 1980-82, exec. dir., 1982-86; dean of admissions Reconstructionist Rabbinical Coll., Wyncote, Pa., 1986-90, exec. v.p., 1990—; mem. editorial bd. Reconstructionist Mag., 1980—; mem. adv. bd. trustees Nat. Havurah Com., N.Y.C., 1979—; mem. edn. adv. bd. Hadassah, N.Y.C., 1979-84. Editor-in-chief: (prayerbook series) Kol Haneshamah, Vol. I, 1989, Vol. II, 1991; contbr. articles to profl. publs. Mem. Reconstructionist Rabbinical Assn. (Prayerbook commn. 1981—), Cen. Conf. Am. Rabbis, Rabbinical Assembly, Conf. Jewish Communal Svc. Democrat. Office: Reconstructionist Rabbinical Coll Church Rd and Greenwood Ave Wyncote PA 19119

TEWES, MARK S., pastor; b. Spokane, Wash., Sept. 29, 1957; s. Wilbur G. and June (Bader) T.; m. Debora Ann Tewes, Aug. 9, 1980; children: Thaddaeus Wilbur, Jessica Jane. BA, Concordia Tchrs. Coll., Seward, Nebr., 1980, BS, 1980; MDiv, Concordia Sem., St. Louis, 1989. Ordained to ministry Luth. Ch.-Mo. Synod. Dir. Christian edn. Christ Luth. Ch., Brea, Calif., 1981-85; pastor Praise Luth. Ch., Eagan, Minn., 1989—; program team coord. Luth. Ch.-Mo. Synod. Nat. Youth Gathering Com., St. Louis, 1990—. Contbr. articles to profl. jours. Republican. Office: Praise Luth Ch 670 Diffley Rd Eagan MN 55123

THADEN, STEVEN ARTHUR, lay worker; b. Cresco, Iowa, Apr. 22, 1957; s. Clifford A. and Mildred M. (Conklin) T.; m. Camela F. Gebhard, May 25, 1975; children: Joshua, Courtney, Whitney. Elder Presbyn. Ch., Winfield, Kans., 1979-81; youth leader United Meth. Ch., Agra, Kans., 1988—, trustee, 1989—; postmaster U.S. Postal Svc., Agra, 1984—. Mem. Nat. Assn. Postmasters (dist. pres. 1989-90, sec./treas. 1987-88). Home: 420 North Main St PO Box 15 Agra KS 67621 *In working with the youth of today, it is quite obvious to me that they are "hungry" for the direction Christianity provides.*

THAMES, MARK RANDALL, minister; b. Charleston, S.C., Aug. 26, 1961; s. Hugh Lloyd and Mary Ruth (Harwell) T.; m. Judy Renee Hodge, Jan. 14, 1984; children: Mark Randall Jr., Jacob Daniel, Andrew Franklin, Charles Matthew. Student, Coll. of Charleston, 1979-81. Dir. Christian edn. Mt. Olivet Pentecostal Holiness Ch., Awendaw, S.C., Wnado Pentecostal Holiness Ch., Huger, S.C., Tidewater Dist. Pentecostal Holiness Ch., 1990—; pastor Rhems (S.C.) Pentecostal Holiness Ch., 1987-88, St. Andrews Pentecostal Holiness Ch., Charleston, 1988—; nuclear marine machinist Charleston Naval Shipyard, North Charleston, S.C., 1983—. Home: 9 Tovey Rd Charleston SC 29407

THARP, DONALD ANDREW, minister; b. Havre de Grace, Md., Mar. 20, 1958; s. Donald Monroe and Betty Marie (Cunningham) T.; m. Cindy Lee Mohnen, Feb. 5, 1976; children: Amber Dawn, Donald Joseph. B, U. Indpls., 1981; MD, Christian Theol. Sem., 1985. Ordained to ministry Christian Ch., 1985. Youth min. Olive Br. Christian Ch., Indpls., 1978-81; adminstrv. asst. Discipledata, Inc., Indpls., 1981-84; assoc. min. Martinsville (Ind.) Christian Ch., 1984-90; sr. min. Mackinaw (Ill.) Christian Ch., 1991—; chmn. Salvation Army Unit, Martinsville, 1987-90; mgr. Osco Drug, Indpls., 1977-80. Organizer Citizens for Cultural Enhancement, Martinsville, 1985-90; pres., founder Concert for Christ, Inc., Martinsville, 1987-90; asst. treas. Community Svc. Ctr. Morgan County, Martinsville, 1988-90; organizer Morgan County Habitat for Humanity, Martinsville, 1990; chair Family Community Leadership Team, Martinsville, 1990. Recipient Community Leadership award Ind. U. Com. on Human Understanding, Bloomington, 1990. Mem. Martinsville Ministerial Assn. (pres. 1990), Rotary (v.p., sec. 1988-90, Paul Harris fellow 1990), Oddfellows. Office: Mackinaw Christian Ch 201 E Orchard PO 259 Mackinaw IL 61755

THARP, DONALD M., minister, stockbroker; b. Paxinos, Pa., May 15, 1930; s. Donald H. and Mary Louise (Yourdy) T.; m. Doris Elaine Hanks, Aug. 25, 1953 (dec.); children: Daniel, Robin; m. Betty Marie Cunningham, July 20, 1959; children: Donald, Marie, Stephen. BS, Johnson Bible Coll., Knoxville, Tenn., 1952; MA, Butler Sch. Religion, Indpls., 1958; MDiv, Christian Theol. Sem., Indpls., 1960. Min. Havre de Grace (Md.) Christian Ch., 1959-60; min. Christian Ch., Frankton, Ind., 1960-63, Bedford, Ind., 1963-72; adminstr. Altenheim Home, Indpls., 1972-73, Barton Stone Christian Home, Jacksonville, Ill., 1973-74, Hillsboro (Ill.) Nursing Home, 1974-76, Monticello Nursing Home, Mt. Carmel, Ill., 1977-82; stockbroker W.H. Schafer, Inc., Mt. Carmel, 1982—. Pres. Am. Heart Assn. chpt. County of Wabash, Ind., 1978-89. Named Rural Min. of Yr. Disciples of Christ, Ind., 1963. Mem. Lions, Kiwanis. Republican. Home and Office: 1031 Cherry Mount Carmel IL 62863

THATCHER, DAVID ALLAN, religious organization administrator; b. Duluth, Minn., May 2, 1945; s. Charles Drummond and Ruth Elizabeth (Dahl) T.; m. Barbara Gayle Dahlin, June 28, 1969; children: Anna Elizabeth, Amy Alison. BA, U. Minn., Duluth, 1968. Fin. analyst UNIVAC Fed. Systems div., Eagan, Minn., 1968-71; asst. bus. adminstr. Cen. Luth. Ch., Mpls., 1971-72; parish adminstr. Bethlehem Luth. Ch., Mpls., 1972-76; bus. mgr. Calvary Luth Ch., Golden Valley, Minn., 1976—; vice chmn. adminstrv. div. Greater Mpls. Coun. of Chs., 1976-77, chmn., 1977-78. mgr. Ecumenical Folk Group of St. Paul, 1971-72; chmn. Luth. Voice Children's Choir of Taiwan Concert Tour, Mpls., 1976; mem. design team staff Start-Up Project Study, The Am. Luth. Ch., Mpls., 1976-77. Mem. Christian Ministries Mgmt. Assn., Assn. Luth. Devel. Execs., Nat. Assn. Ch. Bus. Adminstrs., N. Cen. chpt. Nat. Assn. Ch. Bus. Adminstrs, Kiwanis (bd. dirs. S.W. Mpls. chpt. 1974-76, editor weekly newsletter 1973-75). Home: 2071 Rosewood Ln S Roseville MN 55113 Office: Calvary Luth Ch 7520 Golden Valley Rd Golden Valley MN 55427

THAYER, JAMES M., architect, lay worker; b. Deckerville, Mich., Feb. 25, 1941; s. Milton Butler and Frances Marquerite (Pritchard) T.; m. Lotta Jean Furness; children: Thane, Timothy, Tracy. Grad. high sch., Deckerville, 1969. V.p. architectural co., El Toro, Calif., 1976-79; owner, pres. Timeless Architecture, Laguna Hills, Calif., 1979—; elder Mission Hills Bapt. Ch., Mission Viejo, Calif., 1983-89. Designer over 100 chs. Office: Timeless Architecture 23276 Southpointe Dr Laguna Hills CA 92653

THAYER, MARCIA LYNN, lay worker; b. Sidney, Ohio, Mar. 27, 1948; d. John Luther and Lois Mae (Deemer-Nichols) Adams; m. Lyman Keith Thayer, Aug. 1, 1970. AA, Concordia Luth. Coll., Ann Arbor, Mich., 1968; BS in Edn., Concordia Tchrs. Coll., Seward, Nebr., 1970. Tchr. 3d grade Zion Luth. Sch., Akron, Ohio, 1970-71; acting dir. parish music, organist Peace Luth. Ch., Slidell, La., 1986-88; organist Concordia Luth. Ch., Wooster, Ohio, 1971-74, Redeemer Luth. Ch., Jackson, Mich., 1974-77, Abiding Savior Luth. Ch., Anderson, S.C., 1983-85, Messiah of the Mountains Luth. Ch., Burnsville, N.C., 1988-89, St. James Luth. Ch., New Haven, Ind., 1990—; coord. numerous worship svcs., 1986—. Home: 620 Broadway New Haven IN 46774

THEE, FRANCIS CHARLES RUDOLPH, religion educator; b. Lexington, Mo., Mar. 8, 1936; s. Paul Rudolph and Yetta Mary (Willer) T.; m. Mary

Ellen Bartlett, Jan. 24, 1959; 1 child, Paul Leslie. BA, Cen. Bible Coll., 1957, MA in Religion, 1959; MA, Wheaton Coll., 1963; PhD, U. Chgo., 1980; postgrad., Inst. of Holy Land Studies, Jerusalem, 1983. Ordained to ministry Assemblies of God, 1967. Pastor's asst. Woodmere Gardens Tabernacle, Grand Rapids, Mich., 1959-61; assoc. prof. religion N.W. Coll. of the Assemblies of God, Kirkland, Wash., 1963-86, prof., 1986—. Author: Julius Africanus and the Early Christian View of Magic, 1984; contbr. articles to religious jours. Recipient Bible Lands Study Grant N.W. Coll., 1983, Pope Meml. Grant N.W. Coll., 1985. Mem. Am. Acad. Religion, Soc. Pentecostal Studies. Avocations: reading, traveling, hiking, computer program patching. Home: 5829 112th Pl NE Kirkland WA 98033 Office: NW Coll PO Box 579 Kirkland WA 98083-0579

THEIMER, AXEL KNUT, music educator; b. St. Johann, Tirol, Austria, Mar. 10, 1946; came to U.S., 1969; s. Otto and Iris M. (Zerzawy) T.; m. Lois A. Worms, July 3, 1976; children: Kira, Natalia, Stefan. BA, St. John's U., Collegeville, Minn., 1971; MFA in Choral Conducting, U. Minn., 1974, D Music Arts in Voice Performance, 1984. Condr. Chorus Viennensis, Vienna, Austria, 1967-69; instr. St. John's U., 1969-75, asst. prof., 1975-81, assoc. prof., 1981-87, prof., 1987—; asst. dir. Voice Care Network, Mpls., 1986—, pres. bd. dirs. 1990—, pres., exec. dir., 1991—; dir, Kantorei, Mpls., 1988—; vocal and choral clinician throughout U.S., 1988—; bd. dirs. Intercollegiate Men's Chorus, 1988—. Vocal soloist and recitalist throughout midwest. Recipient Burlington No. Faculty Achievement award St. John's U., 1989. Mem. Nat. Assn. Tchrs. Singing (bd. govs. Minn. 1984-88), Am. Choral Dirs. Assn. (chmn. repertoire and standards com. North Cen. div. 1985—), Music. Educators Nat. Conf., Music Tchrs. Nat. Assn. Roman Catholic. Avocations: stamp collecting, model trains, tennis, skiing, table tennis. Office: St John's U Dept Music Collegeville MN 56321

THEISEN, MICHAEL JOURDAN, religion educator, minister; b. Norfolk, Va., Mar. 4, 1961; s. Richard Roy and Barbara (Jourdan) T.; m. Mary Louise Robinson, Aug. 10, 1984; children: Christopher Michael, David Jourdan. BSW, Va. Commonwealth U., 1982, MSW, 1983; M Religious Edn., Loyola Univ., New Orleans, 1990. Pastoral social worker Ch. of the Epiphany, Richmond, Va., 1984-88, youth minister, 1984-91, dir. religious edn., 1991—; sec./co-dir. Region 7 Youth Coun., Richmond, 1985-88; team leader Region 7 Marriage Formation, Richmond, 1984—; speaker Diocesan Youth Conv., Richmond, 1987-91; dir. Signs and Cymbols Drama Group, Richmond, 1990—; chmn. Diocesan Retreat Ctr. Bd., 1990—. Active Big Bros. Richmond, 1983-85, Freedom House, Richmond, 1986, Refugee Resettlement, Richmond, 1986—; donor Richmond Metro Blood Svc., 1989—. Home: 11530 Leiden Lane Midlothian VA 23112 Office: Church of the Epiphany 11000 Smoketree Dr Richmond VA 23236

THEODOSIUS, HIS BEATITUDE METROPOLITAN See LAZOR, THEODOSIUS

THERIOT, LEO JUDE, minister; b. New Orleans, Mar. 2, 1956; s. Leo Joseph and Floy (Williams) T.; m. Myra Ann Badeaux, Jan. 7, 1978; children: Rachel Janell, Holly Michelle. Diploma, Draughn Bus. Sch., New Orleans, 1975; BA, Cen. Bible Coll., 1987; MDiv, Assemblies of God Theol. Sem., 1990. Ordained to ministry Assemblies of God Ch., 1991. Pastor 1st Assembly of God, Dulac, La., 1982-83; Christian edn. dir. Fair Grove (Mo.) Christian Ctr., 1986-88; Christian edn. dir., children's pastor Calvary Assembly of God, Fayetteville, N.C., 1990—. Sgt. USAR, 1986-90. Republican. Office: Calvary Assembly of God 2512 Ft Bragg Rd Fayetteville NC 28303 *God has chosen to let us live in today's world because He knows we can meet its challenges. Let us follow Him and be worthy of His confidence.*

THERRIEN, EILEEN MARIE, youth minister; b. St. Petersburg, Fla., Oct. 5, 1956; d. Joseph Clark and Elsie Faye (Sargent) Cornwell; m. Frederic Howard Therrien, Nov. 27, 1981; children: Rachel Jean, Alexander Joseph. BA, Barry U., 1978. Religion tchr. Madonna Acad. for Girls, Hollywood, Fla., 1978-79; assoc. youth dir. Diocese of St. Petersburg, 1979-82; youth minister St. Paul's Cath. Ch., Tampa, Fla., 1982—; speaker Nat. Cath. Young Adult Ministry S.E. Regional Conf., Norfolk, Va., 1986; cons. Diocese os St. Petersburg Youth Office, 1982-87. Mem. Nat. Assn. Female Execs. Democrat. Roman Catholic.

THESING, KENNETH FRANCIS, priest; b. Winona, Minn., May 9, 1942; s. Theodore John and Evelyn Regina (Ries) T. BA in Philosophy, Maryknoll Sem., 1964, BD, 1968, MA, 1969. Joined Maryknoll Fathers and Bros. Order, 1962; ordained priest Roman Cath. Ch., 1969. Asst. regional superior Maryknoll Fathers & Brothers, Tanzania, East Africa, 1975-84; asst. gen. Maryknoll Fathers & Brothers, Maryknoll, N.Y., 1984-90; superior gen. Maryknoll Fathers & Brothers, Maryknoll, 1990—; chmn. Bd. Trustees Maryknoll Sch. Theology, 1990—. Home and Office: Maryknoll Fathers & Bros Maryknoll NY 10545

THEUNER, DOUGLAS EDWIN, bishop; b. N.Y.C., Nov. 15, 1938; s. Alfred Edwin Kipp and Grace Elizabeth (MacKean) T.; m. Jane Lois Szuhany, May 16, 1959; children: Elizabeth Susan, Nicholas Frederick Kipp. BA, Coll. of Wooster, 1960; BD, Kenyon Coll., 1962; MA, U. Conn., 1968. Ordained to ministry Episcopal Ch. as deacon, then priest, 1962. Curate St. Peter's Episcopal Ch., Ashtabula, Ohio, 1962-65; vicar St. George's Episcopal Ch., Bolton, Conn., 1965-68; rector St. Paul's Episcopal Ch., Wllimantic, Conn., 1968-74, St. John's Episcopal Ch., Stamford, Conn., 1974-86; bishop Diocese of N.H., Concord, 1986—. Chmn. Community Housing Coalition, Stamford, Conn., 1975-86, Instituto Pastoral Hispano, N.Y.C., 1979-86; pres. Holderness (N.H.) Sch., 1987—, White Mountain Sch., Littleton, N.H., 1987—. Mem. N.H. Coun. Chs. (v.p.). Avocations: photography, cooking, hiking, skiing. Office: Concord Diocese Diocesan Office 63 Green St Concord NH 03301

THEWES, MARK ALLAN, music director; b. Canton, Ohio, May 26, 1954; s. Donald Anthony and Elizabeth J. (Campagnoli) T. MusB, U. Akron, 1985; cert. in ch. music, Baldwin Wallace Coll., 1988. Organist St. Clement ch., Navarre, Ohio, 1965-73, First Meth. Ch., Massillon, Ohio, 1974-75, Mt. Tabor Ch., East Canton, Ohio, 1975-77; dir. music Westbrook Park United Meth. Ch., Canton, Ohio, 1977—; dist. salesman Moller Pipe Organ Co., Hagerstown, Md., 1990—; sec. United Meth. Musicians, Canton, 1982-84; reader cons. United Meth. Hymnal, Nashville, 1989; hymnal trainer United Meth. Ch., Nashville, 1989-90. Dean Canton chpt. Am. Guild Organists, 1986-88. Mem. Tri County Trail Assn. (sec. 1973-74). Democrat. Home: 944 Wales Rd NE Massillon OH 44646 Office: Westbrook Pk United Meth Ch 2521 12th St NW Canton OH 44708

THEWS, DANIEL PAUL, minister; b. Appleton, Wis., Feb. 5, 1963; s. Donald Edward and Bonita Mae (Hinkens) T.; m. Kelly Michelle Hurt, July 11, 1987. BA in Edn., Concordia U., 1985; MDiv, Concordia Sem., 1989. Assoc. pastor St. Paul Luth., Leavenworth, Kans., 1989—; dir. evangelism and youth St. Paul Luth., Leavenworth. Bd. dirs. fundraising com. United Way, Leavenworth, 1989—, H.E.L.P.; mem. City Housing Bd. Mem. Leavenworth Lions. Home: 1003 S 2d St Leavenworth KS 66048 Office: St Paul Luth 301 N 7th Leavenworth KS 66048

THIANDOUM, HYACINTHE CARDINAL, archbishop of Dakar; b. Poponguine, Senegal, Feb. 2, 1921; s. François Fari and Anne Ndiémé (Sene) T.; student Sem. Dakar, 1936-49; B.A. in Dogmatics and Social Scis., U. Propaganda, Gregorian U., Rome, 1955. Ordained priest Roman Catholic Ch., 1949; parish vicar, dir. works, Dakar, 1955-60; curate-dean cathedral, gen. vicar Dakar, 1960-62; archbishop of Dakar, 1962—; elevated to Sacred Coll. Cardinals, 1976; mem. Congregation of the Doctrine of the Faith, Rome, 5 yrs.; pres.-del. Synod of Bishops, 1977; pres. Conf. Bishops of Senegal and Mauritamia, Symposium of Bishops Conf. Africa and Madagascar; mem. permanent com. Conf. Francophone West African Bishops; mem. Bishops Commn. Mass Media, Papal Commn. Social Communications Media, Congregation Religious and Secular Insts.; mem. council Gen. Secretariat of Roman Synod Bishops. Decorated grand cross Nat. Order Lion, 1976; comdr. Ordre National Français de la Légion d'Honneur, 1980; hon. chaplain Monastic Grand Cross Sovereign Order Malta, 1972. Office: de l'Archevêché, BP 1908, Dakar Senegal

THIEDE, MICHAEL ERNEST, deacon, business manager; b. Detroit, Nov. 15, 1947; s. Harold F. and Helen C. (Hill) T.; m. Patty Mae Oaks, June 15, 1985 (dec. July 1991); children: Sherry, Christopher, Matthew. Student, Liberty Coll., Lynchberg, Va., 1990-91. Supt. Sunday sch. Kirby Free Will Bapt. Ch., Taylor, Mich., 1983-84, asst. clk., 1985-87; clk. Met. Assn. of Free Will Bapt. Ch., 1986-88; deacon New Faith Chapel, Romulus, Mich., 1991; bus. mgr. Spritwind Prodns., Dearborn, Mich., 1991—; exptl. technician Ford Motor Co., Dearborn, 1973-91; del. Nat. Assn. of Free Will Bapt. Ch., Nashville, 1987-88. Contbr. articles to So. Gospel News. Pherisis donor ACR, Detroit, 1986—. With USAF, 1967-70. Home: 6710 Caribou Westland MI 48185 Office: Spiritwind Prodns 25121 Doxtator Dearborn MI 48128

THIEL, JOHN E., religious studies educator; b. St. Albans, N.Y., July 28, 1951; s. Arthur Edwin and Louise Anita (Alagia) T.; m. Dorothea Cook; children: David, Benjamin. AB, Fairfield U., 1973; MA, McMaster U., Can., 1974, PhD, 1978. Prof. religious studies Fairfield (Conn.) U., 1977—. Author: Imagination and Authority: Theological Authorship in the Modern Tradition, 1991. Mem. AAUP, Am. Acad. Religion, Cath. Theol. Soc. Am. Home: 375 Westfield Ave Bridgeport CT 06606 Office: Fairfield U N Benson Rd Fairfield CT 06430

THIEL, WINFRIED WERNER, theology educator; b. Cottbus, June 29, 1940; s. Werner Thiel and Ruth (Elsner) Schwärzel; m. Elfriede Schmidt; children: Elisabeth, Franziska, Katharina. Maturity, 1. Oberschule, Cottbus, 1958; ThD, Humboldt U., Berlin, 1970, Dr. Sc. Theology, 1977. Asst. Humboldt U., Berlin, German Dem. Republic, 1970-78, sr. asst., 1979-82; prof. Philipps U., Marburg, Fed. Republic Germany, 1982—. Author: Die deuteronomistische Redaktion von Jeremia 1-25, 1973. Home: Tilsiter Str 8, D-3550 Marburg Federal Republic of Germany Office: Philipps U/FB 05, Lahntor 3, D-3550 Marburg Federal Republic of Germany

THIELEN, THORALF THEODORE, priest; b. St. Donatus, Iowa, May 23, 1921; s. Peter Joseph and Loretta (Bushman) T. BA, Pontifical Coll. Josephinum, 1943, MDiv, 1970; STL, Pontifical Gregorian U., Rome, 1949, STD, 1950. Ordained priest Roman Cath. Ch., 1947, named monsignor, 1958. Asst. prof. theology Pontifical Coll. Josephinum, Columbus, Ohio, 1950-61, prof. systematic theology, 1962-67, dean of theology, 1967-70, prof. pastoral theology, 1971-86; founder, dir. Pastoralia, Bellevue, Iowa, 1987—; nat. chaplain Nat. Marriage Encounter, St. Paul, 1979-82. Author: Eucharist in Works of F.W. Faber, 1956, What is an Ecumenical Council, 1961 (Papal commendation). Capt., chaplain USAF, 1961-62; maj. gen., chaplain Res., 1978-81. Decorated Legion of Merit, 1981. Mem. Cath. Theol. Soc. Am., Am. Legion (dept. chaplain 1983-84), Air Force Assn., Mil. Chaplains Assn., K.C., Tri-State German Am. Club. Democrat. Avocations: aeronautics, travel. Office: Pastoralia 4721 Saint Catherine Rd Bellevue IA 52031-9507

THIEMAN, THEODORE EUGENE, minister; b. Lockwood, Mo., Feb. 19, 1930; s. Theodore Roosevelt and Nola Celia (Wright) T.; m. Mary Frances Strawhand, Sept. 24, 1951; children: Warren, Linda, Theodore Jr., Deborah, David, Cheryl. Cert. theology, Southeastern Bapt. Theol. Sem., Wake Lake Forest, N.C., 1976; ThD, Fredericksburg Bible Inst., 1978; STB, MRE, D Ministry, Luther Rice Sem., 1976. Student, lay ministries So. Bapt., Va., N.C., 1972-76; pastor Poolesville (Md.) Bapt. Ch., 1976-79; interim pastor Zoar Bapt. Ch., Rhoadesville, Va., 1979-80, Geneva Bapt. Ch., Camden, N.C., 1980; pastor Knotts Island (N.C.) Bapt. Ch., 1980-86; real estate agt. Pungo Reality, Virginia Beach, Va., 1988—; pastor Nanjemoy (Md.) Ch., 1988—; numerous ch. coms. Chaplain Knotts Island Ruritans, 1980-85, Jr. Order Am. Mechanics, Kempsville, Va., 1975-88; explorer leader Boy Scouts Am., Creeds, Va., 1955-57; game warden Va. Game and Fish Commn., Creeds, 1953-57. With USN, 1948-52. Mem. Norfolk Bapt. Assn., Airline Pilots Assn., Montgomery Bapt. Ministerial Assn., West Chowan Bapt. Ministerial Assn., Potomal Bapt. Ministerial Assn. Avocations: fishing, boating, reading, flying, bowling. Home: 1428 Campbells Landing Rd Virginia Beach VA 23457 *Life, to the fullest degree, cannot be ours until we are at peace with God. Then we shall be at peace with our world and our fellow man.*

THIEMANN, RONALD FRANK, dean, religion educator; b. St. Louis, Oct. 4, 1946; s. Frank Joseph and Marie Magdalene (Graeser) T.; m. Beth Arlene Barkow, June 15, 1968; children: Sarah Elizabeth, Laura Kristen. B.A. magna cum laude, Concordia Sr. Coll., Fort Wayne, Ind., 1968; M.Div., Concordia Sem., St. Louis, 1972; M.A., Yale U., 1973, M.Philosophy, 1974, Ph.D., 1976; postgrad., Eberhard-Karls Universitat, Tubingen, W.Ger., 1974-75. Asst. prof. dept. religion Haverford Coll., Pa., 1976-82, assoc. prof. dept. religion, 1982-85, prof. dept. religion, 1985-86, acting provost, 1985, acting pres., 1986; dean Div. Sch. Harvard U., Cambridge, Mass., 1986—; John Lord O'Brian prof. divinity Harvard U., Cambridge, 1986—; vis. prof. honors program Villanova U., 1981; vis. asst. prof. Luth. Theol. Sem., Phila., 1977; mem. Ctr. Theol. Inquiry, Princeton, N.J., 1982-83; mem. consultation on Christianity and Marxism, U.S.A. Nat. Com., Lutheran World Fedn., 1979-83, mem. consultation on civil religion, 1983-86, mem. consultation on problem of common good, 1985-88; bd. dirs. Trinity Press Internat. Author: Revelation and Theology, 1985, Constructing a Public Theology: The Church in a Pluralistic Culture, 1991; editor: The Legacy of H. Richard Niebuhr, 1991; mem. editorial bd. Dialog, 1987—; contbr. numerous articles to profl. jours. Mem. bd. trustees Buckingham Browne & Nichols Schs., 1988-90; mem. task force on theol. education, Evang. Luth. Ch. in Am., 1989-91, task force on Luth.-Reformed Conversations, Evang. Luth. Ch. Am., 1988—. Recipient Disting. Teaching award Lindback Found., 1982; Mellon Found. fellow, 1982-83; Deutscher Akademischer Austauschdienst fellow, 1974-75. Mem. Am. Acad. Religion, (chmn. narrative interpretation and theology group 1982-86). Avocations: tennis; squash; piano. Home: 44 Francis Ave Cambridge MA 02138 Office: Harvard Div Sch 45 Francis Ave Cambridge MA 02138

THIERET, MARK LYNN, minister; b. Parma, Ohio, Oct. 16, 1962; s. Eugene George and Mary Jane (Tucker) T.; m. Wendy Lee Ronk, June 13, 1987. BS, Bapt. Bible Coll., Clarks Summit, Pa., 1985; MDiv, Grace Sem., Winona Lake, Ind., 1989, ThM, 1990. Lic. to ministry Gen. Assn. Regular Bapt. Chs., 1991. Dir. youth and music Faith Bapt. Ch., North Manchester, Ind., 1987—; computer mgr. Ins. 1 Svcs., Akron, Ind., 1991—. Mem. Evang. Theol. Soc. Office: Greencastle Bible Ch 350 W Madison T Greencastle PA 17225

THIERFELDER, PAUL EDWARD, minister; b. Milw., Mar. 5, 1956; s. Frederick Edward and Ananda (Sandsmark) T.; m. Susan Lynn Thusius, Apr. 24, 1981; children: Matthew, Mark, Sara. BA, Northwestern Coll., 1978; MA, MDiv, Wis. Luth. Sem., 1982. Ordained to ministry Wis. Evang. Luth. Synod Ch., 1982. Pastor Our Savior Luth. Ch., Burlington, Iowa, 1982-88, Wis. Evang. Luth. Synod and Ch. Planter, Green Bay, Wis., 1988-, Beautiful Savior Luth. Ch., Green Bay, 1990—; dist. cir. pastor WELS, State of Iowa, 1984-88. Author: Devotions, 1988-91; contbr. articles to profl. jours. Community rep. Ashwaubenon Sch. Bd., Green Bay, Wis., 1991; bd. dirs. Regional Planning Authority, Green Bay, 1990-91. Mem. Optimist Club (bd. dirs. 1989-91), Profl. Businessmen's Assn. Home: 2372 Key Way Green Bay WI 54313 Office: Beautiful Savior Luth Ch 2640 West Point Rd Green Bay WI 54304

THIGPEN, CHARLES ALLEN, religious educator; b. Olanta, S.C., Sept. 26, 1926; s. Jesse Allen and Mabel Irene (Thomas) T.; m. Laura Jane Coker, June 20, 1947; children: Jonathan Noel, Laura Jane, Ann Marie, Ruth Irene. BA, Bob Jones U., Greenville, S.C., 1947; MA, Winona Lake Sch. Theology, Ind., 1953; MEd, Middle Tenn. State U., 1970, DA, 1975. Dean men and registrar Free Will Bapt. Bible Coll., Nashville, 1948-53; acad. dean Free Will Bapt. Bible Coll., 1957-79, pres., 1979-90, chancellor, 1990—. Mem. Nat. Assn. Free Will Baptists (moderator 1954-60), Am. Assn. Bible Colls. (pres. 1984-86), Tenn. Coll. Assn. (pres. 1990-91). Free Will Baptist. Office: Free Will Bapt Bible 3606 West End Ave Nashville TN 37205

THOEN, SISTER ROBERTA, nun; b. Buffalo, Mar. 1, 1944; d. Richard Girard Thoen and Maureen Winifred (O'Hara) Golden. BS in Edn., Trinity Coll., Washington, 1967; MS in Adminstrn., Boston Coll., 1987. Cert adminstr. Supervising prin. Lockport (N.Y.) Cath. Sch., 1987—; mem. prins. coun. Diocese Buffalo, 1987—; mem. steering com. Erie I. Boces - Drug Free Consortium for Non Pub. Schs., 1988-92. Mem. Mayor's Com. for Drug Free Am., Lockport, 1989-91; bd. dirs. Health Assn. Niagara County, Inc., Niagara Falls, N.Y., 1990—. Mem. Cath. Sch. Adminstrs. Assn. N.Y. (exec. bd. 1991—), Region 12 Prins. (chairperson 1987-93). Office: Lockport Cath Sch 160 Chestnut St Lockport NY 14094

THOM, DRUMMOND ROBERT, minister, educator; b. Landsdown, South Africa, Oct. 29, 1936; came to U.S., 1957; s. Robert Anderson and Joyce Madgeline (O'Conner) T.; m. Charlotte Tonette Zabel, Nov. 22, 1958; 1 child, Jennifer Joy Antonia. Student, Capetown Tech. Coll., 1953-56, Zion Bible Inst., East Providence, R.I., 1957-58; BA, Breadloaf Bible Coll., Burlington, N.C., 1981, DD, 1982. Founder, pres. World Wide Native Evangelism, Inc., Louisville, 1961—; pastor Deeper Life Christian Ctr., Louisville, 1973—. Author: The Heart Cry of the Apostle Paul, 1967, foundation and advanced Bible courses; editor mag. The Victorious and Deeper Life, 1965-75. Named Ky. Col., State of Ky., 1986. Republican. Avocations: swimming, racquetbell, golf. Home: 8308 Shepherdsville Rd Louisville KY 40219 Office: World Wide Native Evangelism 8300 Shepherdsville Rd Louisville KY 40219

THOMA, KURT MICHAEL, religious healing practitioner; b. Boston, Aug. 9, 1946; s. Kurt Richard and Janet (Holdsworth) T.; divorced; children by previous marriage: Heather Anne, Heidi. Student U. N.H., 1968. Clk., supr., asst. div. EDP coord., EDP coord., mut. funds div. 1st Nat. Bank Boston, 1968-69; v.p. cen. N.H. bldg. corp. Barry Dashner, Inc., 1969-72; field rep. Acorn Structures, Inc., 1972-75; v.p., treas. Design Structures Group, Inc., 1975-76; pres. Witthom Assocs., Inc., 1976-79; v.p. Confetti, Inc., 1978-89; pres., treas., propr. dessin batir, Newport, R.I., 1979-89; Christian Sci. practitioner, 1990—. Served with U.S. Army N.G., 1966-72. Republican. Avocations: writing, tennis, skiing, residential and furniture design, photography. Home and Office: RFD #2 Box 1585 Warner NH 03278 *"Prior" to the Knowledge or Science of Christ, I was an atheist. In King James Bible demonstrations, I Kings 17, II Kings 4, Daniel 3, Matthew, Mark, Luke, John, Acts 9, 14 and 20 all express the Christ Fact that there is no "death." In medical science "near death experience" is unfolding the same truth, which converges as One. "Death" is only in the "eye of the beholder." You will never see "death" for yourself.*

THOMAS, ANDREW L(YNN), minister; b. Hoopeston, Ill., Oct. 10, 1963; s. Larry Lynn and Ruth Ellen (Bell) T. BS, Cin. Bible Coll., 1986. Ordained to ministry Ch. of Christ, 1987. Youth minister Rossville (Ill.) Ch. of Christ, summer 1982, Ruddles Mills (Ky.) Christian Ch., summer 1983, Milford (Ill.) Ch. of Christ, summer 1984; youth minister and tchr. Goshen (Ohio) Christian Acad., 1986-88; youth minister Havana (Ill.) Ch. of Christ, 1988—; substitute tchr. Havana (Ill.) Schs., 1989—; exec. bd. Lake Springfield Christian Assembly, Chatham, Ill., 1989—; youth coun. mem. Coop. Extension Svc., Havana, 1990—; local arrangements vice chmn. Ill. Christian Teen Conv., Springfield, 1990-91. Home: 220 S High Havana IL 62644 Office: Ch of Christ 350 S Broadway Havana IL 62644

THOMAS, AUBREY DAMON, minister; b. Timpson, Tex., Jan. 23, 1931; s. Ernest J. and Alma (Sapp) T.; m. Lois Mae Cox, Feb. 27, 1956 (dec. May 1971); m. Helen Mae Crain, May 6, 1972; 1 child, Bradley Damon. Student, East Tex. Bapt. Coll., 1950-55. Ordained to ministry So. Bapt. Conv. Pastor 1st Bapt. Ch., Connerville, Okla., 1955-56, Mill Creek, Okla., 1956-57, Milburn, Okla., 1957-59; pastor Trinity Bapt. Ch., Durant, Okla., 1959-63, 1st Bapt. Ch., Colbert, Okla., 1963-65, Cen. Bapt. Ch., Longview, Tex., 1968-71, 1st Bapt. Ch., Crocker, Mo., 1971-74, Halltown (Mo.) Bapt. Ch., 1974-77; assoc. pastor, dir. edn. Thomas Avenue Bapt. Ch., Pasadena, Tex., 1965-68; pastor Immanuel Bapt. Ch., Springfield, Mo., 1977—. Home: 1921 W Nichols Springfield MO 65802 Office: Immanuel Bapt Ch 1931 W Nichols Springfield MO 65802

THOMAS, CALDWELL, pastor; b. Racford, N.J., Mar. 27, 1932; s. William and Lillie (Ingrim) T.; m. Emily H. Lovett, Nov. 22, 1950 (div. 1988); children: Patricia, Deborah, Carwell, John, Estella, Kevin. DD, Am. Bible Coll., 1969; LittD (hon.), U. Wis., 1976. Ordained minister. Gen. bishop Unified Free Will Denomination, Newark, 1965-78; nat. bishop Nat. Holiness Chs., Newark, 1978—; bd. dirs. Miracle Temple Ministeries, Newark, 1978—. Editor Free Will Herald, 1979-78, Miracle Messenger of Faith, 1979; author: My Heavely Vision, 1979, Renewal of the Mind, 1979. Scoutmaster Boy Scouts Am., N.J., 1957; officer Potica Reserve, N.J., 1955, Policeman and Fireman, Edison, N.J., 1951. Democrat. Home: 208 Cheryl Dr Iselin NJ 08830 Office: Miracle Temple Nat Holiness Chs 786-794 S 20th St Newark NJ 07103

THOMAS, CLYDE PICKNEY, JR., minister; b. Gaffney, S.C., Aug. 7, 1953; s. Clyde Pickney and Evelyn Mae (Vinesett) T.; m. Joanne Cash, Jan. 14, 1979; children: Clyde Preston, James Grady. BA, Limestone Coll., Gaffney, 1975; MDiv, Southeastern Sem., Wake Forest, N.C., 1978, D of Ministry, 1986. Supply pastor Cherokee Ave. Bapt. Ch. Mission, Gaffney, 1976; asst. activities dir. Cherokee Ave. Bapt Ch., Gaffney, 1974-75, min. edn. and family life ministries, 1979—; dir. youth and activities Draytonville Bapt. Ch., Gaffney, 1977-78; pastor Oakdale Bapt. Ch., Gaffney, 1978-79; pres. Greater Gaffney Mins. Fellowship, 1989-90; ministerial bd. dirs. Gardner-Webb Coll., Boiling Springs, N.C., 1988-91. Mem. Appalachian State Coun. of Govts. Adv. to Pub. Safety Bd.; bd. dirs. Cherokee County Boys Club, Gaffney. Home: 886 Cherokee National Hwy Gaffney SC 29340 Office: Cherokee Ave Bapt Ch 805 Cherokee Ave Gaffney SC 29340

THOMAS, DAVID MALCOM, music and services minister; b. Allendale, S.C., Dec. 24, 1953; s. David Thomas III and Evelyn Gladys (Benton) Schafer; m. Theresa Ann Adair, Ar. 5, 1975; children: Melita Ellen, Nathan Aaron. MusB, Cumberland Coll., 1975; M of Ch. Music, So. Bapt. Theol. Sem., 1977. Ordained to ministry So. Bapt. Conv., 1986. Min. of music First Bapt. Ch., Lenoir, N.C., 1978-80; min. of music and svcs. First Bapt. Ch., Asheboro, N.C., 1981—; regional dir. N.C. Bapt. Conv., Cary, 1982-85, instrumental specialist, 1987—; festival coord. N.C. Bapt. Intrumental Festival, Cary, 1983—; dir. Older Children's Choir Camp, Mars Hill, N.C., 1990-91. Composer and arranger musical pieces for handbells and woodwinds. Mem. Community Schs. Adv. Coun., Asheboro, 1990—; pres. Loftin Sch. PTA, Asheboro, 1990—. Named Outstanding Young Man in Am., Outstanding Young Men in Am., 1982. Mem. The Centrymen, Am. Guild of English Handbell Ringers, Christian Instrumental Dirs. Assn., The Singing Churchmen, N.C. Bapt. Brass and Winds. Republican. Home: 2211 Lambert Dr Asheboro NC 27203 Office: First Bapt Ch 133 N Church St Asheboro NC 27203

THOMAS, DOMINIC, religious organization administrator. Pres. Ch. of Jesus Christ, Dearborn, Mich. Office: Ch of Jesus Christ 6010 Barrie Dearborn MI 48126*

THOMAS, DONNA STANLEY, lay organization official; b. Tulsa, Jan. 18, 1928; d. Charles Roy and Sarah Hazel (Bynum) Stanley; m. Charles Franklin Thomas, June 12, 1947; children: Charles Mark, Paul Stanley, John David. BA, Anderson Coll., Ind., 1949; postgrad., Wichita State U., Kans. Dir. Corinthian Nursery Sch., Wichita, 1961-78; v.p. Project Ptnr. with Christ, Inc., Middletown, Ohio, 1968-84; pres., chief exec. officer Project Ptnr. with Christ, Inc., Middletown, 1984—; Christian edn. specialist Nat. Sun. Sch. Assn., Wichita; co-pastor Pawnee Ave. Ch. of God, Wichita, 1961-77. Editor Onward newsletter, 1971-74, 78-86. Bd. dirs. Terrace Gardens Nursing Ctr., Starnet, Airtrac Aviation Svcs. Mem. World Evang. Fellowship, Evang. Agy. CEO's. Mem. Ch. of God. Office: Project Ptnr with Christ 6432 Hendrickson Rd Middletown OH 45044

THOMAS, ERNEST, minister; b. Raeford, N.C., Apr. 30, 1938; s. John Foster and Kattie (Gales) T.; m. Maggie Lloyd, Dec. 31, 1939; children: Cynthia, Carolyn, Ernest, Garrett. Student, Hawthorne (N.J.) Bible, 1980. Ordained to ministry Meth. Ch., 1988. Local preacher, 1980-86; minister Westside African Meth. Episcopal Zion Ch., Paterson, N.J., 1986—.

THOMAS, GEORGE, theologian; b. Vakathanam, Kerala, India, Feb. 16, 1941; s. Wattachanackal Cherian and Enchakattu (Joseph) T.; m. Yin Ling Lee, Apr. 9, 1980; children: Anandh, Joseph, Anna. BDiv, United Theol. Coll., India, 1969, ThM, 1972; ThD, U. Hamburg, Ger., 1979. Faculty Tamilnadu Theol. Sem., Madurai, India, 1979-80; pastor Evangelische

Studentingemeinde, Karlsruhe, Fed. Republic Germany, 1981-84; dir. Markham (Ill.) Peace Ministry, 1985-88; asst. prof. Calumet Coll. St. Joseph, Whiting, Ind., 1988-90; peace educator and dir. Midwest Peace & Justice Inst., Markham, Ill., 1988—; Author: Christian Indians and Indian Nationalism 1885-1950, 1979. Mem. Consortium on Peace Rsch., Edn. and Devel., Luth. Peace Fellowship (nat. bd. dirs. 1989—). Office: Midwest Peace & Justice Ins 3548 W 161st St Markham IL 60426 *A new economic system that can mediate justice for all nations and a serious commitment of all nations to peaceful conflict management techniques are prerequisites for letting the developing nations reach a more full life.*

THOMAS, HERBERT TALMADGE, minister; b. Coal Valley, Ala., Dec. 18, 1939; s. William Talmadge and Ethel Annie (Knight) T.; m. Virginia Ruth Cornwell, Aug. 14, 1959; children: Cynthia Ann Thomas Kearney, Herbert Darren. AS, Walker Coll., 1969; BS, Luther Rice Sem., 1978, MDiv, 1982, D of Ministry, 1983. Ordained to ministry So. Bapt. Conv., 1965. Pastor Sayre (Ala.) 1st Bapt. Ch., 1965-70, Lookout Valley Bapt. Ch., Chattanooga, 1970-79, Circlewood Bapt. Ch., Tuscaloosa, Ala., 1979—; mem. bd. missions Ala. Bapt. Conv., Montgomery, 1990—. 1st lt. U.S. Army, 1963-69. Named Min. of Yr., Tuscaloosa Bapt. Assn., 1989. Republican. Home: 33 Summerfield Tuscaloosa AL 35404 Office: Circlewood Bapt Ch 2201 Loop Rd Tuscaloosa AL 35405

THOMAS, HOWE OCTAVIUS, JR. (TOM THOMAS), minister; b. Richmond, Va., Aug. 13, 1950; s. Howe Octavius and Elizabeth Stuart (Pettyjohn) T.; m. Pamela Jo Snavley, Sept. 4, 1976; 1 child, Karissa Grace. BA, Ariz. State U., 1972; MDiv, Asbury Theol. Sem., 1976; MA, U. Bristol (Eng.), 1984, PhD, 1990. Ordained to ministry United Meth. Ch., 1978. Assoc. minister Grace United Meth. Ch., Long Beach, Calif., 1976-78; minister First United Meth. Ch., Seal Beach, Calif., 1978-82, Weston Meth. Ch., Bath, Eng., 1983-84, Trona (Calif.) Community (United Meth.) Ch., 1987-90, Christ United Meth. Ch., San Diego, 1990—; mem. dist. bd. of ordained ministry United Meth. Ch., 1980-82, 91—, dist. bd. of evangelism Pasadena dist. Calif.-Pacific Conf., 1988-89; vis. lectr. Sch. Theology, Claremont Coll. Contbr. articles to religious jours. Mem. svc. com. Salvation Army, Orange County, Calif., 1980-82; mem. sch. attendance rev. bd. Trona Unified Sch. Dist., 1987-90; sec. bd. dirs. Trona Community Svcs. Coun., 1990; pres. North Park Christian Svc. Agy., 1991. John Wesley Rsch. fellow Wesley Coll., Bristol, 1984, 85. Mem. Oxford Inst. of Meth. Theol. Studies, Am. Acad. Religion, Brit. Soc. for 18th-Century Studies. Home: 3283 Meade Ave San Diego CA 92116 Office: Christ United Meth Ch 3295 Meade Ave San Diego CA 92116 *A reknown hymnist's verse encapsulates my life's motto "Jesus, confirm my heart's desire to work, and speak, and think for Thee".*

THOMAS, J. MARK, research fellow; b. Ft. Worth, Dec. 20, 1947; s. Jacob Gillespie and Eleanor Rose (Geivett) T.; m. Jacquelyn Higby, Sept. 2, 1978; children: Megan Lane, Drew Martin. BA, Tex. Christian U., 1971, MDiv, 1974; PhD, U. Chgo., 1983. Asst. prof. philosophy and religion, chaplain Drury Coll., Springfield, Mo., 1983-85; adj. asst. prof. religion, chaplain Ripon (Wis.) Coll., 1985-87; vis. asst. prof. philosophy and religion Beloit (Wis.) Coll., 1987-89; sr. rsch. fellow Au Sable Inst. Environ. Studies, Mancelona, Mich., 1989—. Author: Ethics and Technoculture, 1987, (with others) Being and Doing, 1987, Philosophy and Technology, Vol. 10, 1990; editor: Paul Tillich, The Spiritual Situation in Our Technical Society, 1988, God and Capitalism, 1991. Chmn. planning com. Congress of Sci., Tech. and Religion for the Parliament of World Religion, 1993. Mem. Soc. Christian Ethics, Am. Acad. Religion. Democrat. Mem. United Ch. of Christ. Home: 816 Lincoln St Madison WI 53711

THOMAS, JACK SYDNEY, lay leader, camp director; b. Kansas City, Kans., Sept. 12, 1926; s. Alexander Small and Myrtle Lydia (White) T.; m. Lucille Mae Hester, Sept. 14, 1951; children: Scott Sidney, Diane Lucille Thomas Himes, Catherine Renee Thomas Felt. BS in Archtl. Engring., Iowa State U., 1952. Registered architect; cert. camp dir. Architect The Salvation Army, Chgo., 1965-70; exec. dir. Wonderland Camp-Conf. Ctr. The Salvation Army, Camp Lake, Wis., 1976—; bd. dirs. Chgo. Bible Soc., 1970-76; mem. Salvation Army Divisional Layman's Adv.Coun., Chgo., 1972-73, Salvation Army Nat. Soldiers' Commn., Chgo., 1976-78. With U.S. Army, 1945-47, PTO. Mem. Christian Camping Internat., Am. Camping Assn. (pres. Ill. sec. 1984-88). Home: 9241 Camp Lake Rd P O Box 222 Camp Lake WI 53109-0222 Office: Salvation Army Wonderland Camp P O Box 222 Camp Lake WI 53109-0222

THOMAS, JAMES SAMUEL, bishop; b. Orangeburg, S.C., Apr. 8, 1919; s. James and Dessie Veronica (Mark) T.; m. Ruth Naomi Wilson, July 7, 1945; children: Claudia Thomas Williamson, Gloria Jean Thomas Randle, Margaret Yvonne Thomas Glaze, Patricia Elaine. AB, Clafin Coll., Orangeburg, 1939, DD (hon.), 1953; BD, Gammon Theol. Sem., Atlanta, 1943; MA, Drew U., 1944, LHD (hon.), 1986; PhD, Cornell U., 1953; LLD (hon.), Bethune Cookman Coll., 1963, Simpson Coll., 1965, Morningside Coll., 1966, Iowa Wesleyan Coll., Coe Coll., 1968, Westmar Coll., 1970, W.Va. Wesleyan Coll., 1980; LHD (hon.), Cornell Coll., 1965, Ohio Weslyan U., 1967, DePauw U., 1969; HHD (hon.), St. Ambrose Coll., 1970; STD (hon.), Parsons Coll., 1972, Baldwin-Wallace Coll., 1977; DH (hon.), Rust Coll., 1975; DD (hon.), Allegheny Coll., 1979, Wofford Coll., 1972, Ohio No. U., 1983, Asbury Theol. Sem., 1983, Emory U., 1985; LittD (hon.), Mt. Union Coll., 1979; LHD, Drew U., 1986. Ordained to ministry Meth. Ch., 1944; pastor Orangeburg Circuit, 1942-43, York, S.C., 1946-48; chaplain S.C. State Coll., 1944-46; prof. Gammon Theol. Sem., 1948-53; asso. sec. Meth. Bd. Edn., 1953-64; bishop Iowa area Meth. Ch., 1964-76; bishop Ohio East area United Meth. Ch., 1976-89; pres. Gen. Council on Ministries; dir. Equitable of Iowa; vis. prof. Perkins Sch. Theology, So. Meth. U., summer 1958, Duke U. Div. Sch., fall 1978. Trustee Baldwin-Wallace Coll., Meth. Theol. Sch. in Ohio, Mt. Union Coll., Ohio Wesleyan U., Otterbein Coll., Copeland Oaks, Elyria Home, Berea Children's Home, St. Luke's Hosp. Address: 4037 Colgate St Dallas TX 75225

THOMAS, JOHN RUSSELL, minister; b. Montgomery, Ala., June 17, 1955; s. Raymond Harold and Frances Jean (Browning) T.; m. Cynthia Kay Auchey, Apr. 5, 1975; children: Adam John, Krystal Ann. BRE, Bapt. Bible Inst., Graceville, Fla., 1988; postgrad., New Orleans Theol. Sem. Ordained to ministry So. Bapt. Conv., 1988. Youth min. Hodgesville Bapt. Ch., Dothan, Ala., 1984; assoc. pastor for edn. Rehobeth Bapt. Ch., Dothan, 1985-89; min. for edn., Outreach Heritage Bapt. Ch., Dothan, 1989—; marriage enrichment counselor, 1987—; associational Sunday sch. dir. Columbia Bapt. Assn., Dothan, 1988—; spl. worker Ala. State Conv., Montgomery, 1990—. Home: 200 Sunset Rd Dothan AL 36301 Office: Heritage Bapt Ch 1905 Westgate Pkwy Dothan AL 36303

THOMAS, JONATHAN GRIFFEN, JR., minister; b. Jefferson, Miss., Jan. 6, 1928; s. Jonathan Griffen and Ida (Beck) T.; m. Elizabeth Hill Johnson, Oct. 9, 1952; children: Danny Ray, Rita Jean. Grad. high sch. Ordained to ministry, So. Bapt. Conv., 1980. Music dir. Holcomb (Miss.) Bapt. Ch., 1958-69, pastor, 1970; pastor Friendship E. Bapt. Ch., Charlston, Miss., 1970-74, Leflore (Miss.) Bapt. Ch., 1974-75, Friendship E. Bapt. Ch., Charleston, Miss., 1975—. With U.S. Army, 1950-52. Home: Route 2 Box 222 Oakland MS 38948 Office: Friendship E Bapt Ch Box 134 Charleston MS 38921

THOMAS, MALAYILMELATHETHIL, English educator; b. Chengannur, Kerala, India, Jan. 26, 1932; came to U.S. 1959; s. Malayilmelathethil Thomas and Rachel (Thomas) Koruthu. BA, Kerala U., 1952; BD, Serampore U., Calcutta, 1956; MTh, Princeton Theol. Sem., 1960; MA, Morehead State U., 1961; EdD, U. Tulsa, 1964. Prin. St. George Mid. Sch., Kizharalloor, Kerala, India, 1952-53; tchr. Catholicate High Sch., Pathanamthitta, Kerala, 1956-59; asst. prof. English Morehead (Ky.) State U., 1964-65, assoc. prof. English, 1965-67, prof. English, 1967—. Mem. MLA, Ky. Philol. Soc., Coll. Composition and Communication, Nat. Coun. Tchrs. English, Phi Kappa Phi, Phi Delta Kappa, Kappa Delta Pi. Democrat. Mem. Indian Orthodox Ch. Avocations: travel, cooking, gardening. Home: 310 W Sun St Morehead KY 40351 Office: Morehead State U UPO 884 Morehead KY 40351

THOMAS, MARGARET JEAN, clergywoman, religious research consultant; b. Detroit, Dec. 24, 1943; d. Robert Elcana and Purcella Margaret (Hartness) T. BS, Mich. State U., 1964; MDiv, Union Theol. Sem., Va., 1971; DMin, San Francisco Theol. Sem., 1991. Ordained to ministry United Presbyn. Ch., 1971. Dir. rsch. bd. Christian edn. Presbyn. Ch. U.S., Richmond, Va., 1965-71; dir. rsch. gen. coun. Presbyn. Ch. U.S., Atlanta, 1972-73; mng. dir. rsch. div. support agy. United Presbyn. Ch. U.S.A., N.Y.C., 1974-76; dep. exec. dir. gen. assembly mission coun. United Presbyn. Ch. U.S.A., 1977-83; dir. N.Y. coordination Presbyn. Ch. (U.S.A.), 1983-85; exec. dir. Minn. Coun. Chs., Mpls., 1985—; mem. permanent jud. commn. Presbyn. Ch., 1985-91, moderator, 1989-91; sec. com. on ministry Twin Cities Area Presbytery, Mpls., 1985-91, dir. joint religious legis. coalition, 1985—; bd. dirs. Franklin Nat. Bank, Mpls. Contbr. articles to profl. jours. Adv. panel crime and victim svcs. Hennepin County Atty.'s Office, Mpls., 1985-86, Police and Community Rels. task force, St. Paul, 1986, Hennepin County Crime Victim Coun., Mpls., 1990—, chair, 1991—; bd. dirs. Minn. Foodshare, Mpls., 1985—, Minn. Coalition on Health, St. Paul, 1986—, Minn. Black-on-Black Crime task force, 1988, Twin Cities Coalition Affordable Health Care, 1986-87; co-chair Minn. Interreligious Com., 1988-91; bd. dirs. Abbott Northwestern Pastoral Counseling Ctr., 1988-91, chair, 1990-91. Recipient Human Rels. award Jewish Community Rels. Coun./Anti-Defamation League, 1989. Mem. Nat. Assn. Ecumenical Staff, Religious Edn. Assn. (sec. 1974-76), People for the Am. Way, NOW (Outstanding Woman of Minn. 1986), Amnesty Internat. Democratic Farm Laborer. Avocation: archaeology. Office: Minn Coun of Chs 122 W Franklin Ave Ste 100 Minneapolis MN 55404

THOMAS, MARY FRANCISCA, religion educator; b. Pawling, N.Y., Apr. 8, 1919; d. Frank Joseph and Kathryn Teresa (Flanigan) T. BA, Good Counsel Coll., 1945. Joined Sisters of the Divine Compassion, Roman Cath. Ch., 1942; cert. tchr., N.Y. Tchr. Good Counsel Acad. High Sch., White Plains, N.Y., 1944—, libr., 1985—. Mem. Music Educators Nat. Conf., Cath. Libr. Assn. Greater N.Y., Westchester Libr. Assn. Roman Catholic. Avocations: reading, walking, piano. Home: 52 N Broadway White Plains NY 10603 Office: Good Counsel Acad 52 N Broadway White Plains NY 10603

THOMAS, NATHANIEL CHARLES, clergyman; b. Jonesboro, Ark., June 24, 1929; s. Willie James and Linnie (Elias) T.; B.A., Miss. Indsl. Coll., Holly Springs, 1951; B.D., Lincoln U., 1954, M.Div., 1974; student Lancaster (Pa.) Theol. Sem., 1952-53; D.Div., Tex. Coll., Tyler, 1981; m. Juanita Fanny Jefferson, May 20, 1961 (dec. 1970); children—Gina Charlise, Nathaniel Charles, Keith Antony; m. 2d, Mary Elizabeth Partee, June 8, 1971. Ordained to ministry Christian Meth. Episcopal Ch., 1954; dir. Christian edn. 8th dist. Christian Meth. Episc. Ch., 1954-58; pastor in Waterford, Miss., 1949-51, Wrightville, Ark., 1955-57, Hot Springs, Ark., 1957-60, Little Rock, 1960-62, Mt. Pisgah Christian Meth. Episc. Ch., Memphis, 1966-67, Greenwood Christian Meth. Episc. Ch., Memphis, 1980-81; dir. Christian edn., adminstrv. asst. to Bishop B. Julian Smith, Christian Meth. Episc. Ch., Memphis, 1954-74, presiding elder South Memphis dist., 1971-74, sec. gen. conf. of ch., 1970-82, gen. sec. gen. bd. personnel services, 1978—, also mem. gen. connectional bd., program adminstr. ministerial salary supplement program, 1974—, asst. to sec. gen. Gen. Bd. Pensions, gen. sec. personnel services Gen. Bd., 1974-78; plan mgr. CME Ch. Group Fire & Casualty Ins. Plan, 1978—; sec. Ministerial Assn. Little Rock, 1960-62; v.p. youth work sect., div. Christian edn. Nat. Council Chs., del. World Council Chs. Conf., Upsalla Sweden, 1968. Dir. Haygood-Neal Garden Apts., Inc., Eldorado, Ark., 1969—, Smith-Keys Village Apts., Inc., Texarkana, Ark., 1968—, East Gate Village Apts., Inc., Union City, Tenn., 1971—; trustee Collins Chapel Health Care Center, Memphis, 1974—, Tex. Coll., 1981—; bd. dirs. Family Service Memphis, 1972-73; chmn. bd. dirs. Memphis Opportunities Indsl. Ctr., 1976-78. Mem. NAACP, Urban League, Community on Move for Equality, Memphis Interdenomminational Ministers Alliance, Memphis Ministers Assn., Tenn. Assn. Chs., Ark. Council Chs., Ark. Council Human Relations, Tenn. Council Human Relations, Family Service Memphis, A.B. Hill PTA. Author: Christian Youth Fellow Guide, 8th Episcopal District, 1959; Living Up to My Obligations of the Christian Methodist Episcopal Church, 1956; Steps Toward Developing an Effective Program of Christian Education, 1972; co-author: Worship in the Local Church, 1966; co-author, editor: Coming to Grips with the Teaching Work of the Church, 1966. Co-editor: Developing Black Families, 1975; compiling editor: Dedicated . . . Committed-Autobiography of Bishop B. Julian Smith, 1978—. Home: PO Box 9 Memphis TN 38101 Office: PO Box 74 Memphis TN 38101

THOMAS, NORMAN ERNEST, theology educator; b. Manchester, N.H., Mar. 29, 1932; s. George Ernest and Mildred Winslow (Klein) T.; m. Winifred Ellen Williams, Sept. 9, 1955; children: Paul Norman, Mary Ellen, Bruce Alan, Jean Elizabeth. AB, Yale U., 1953, MDiv, 1956; PhD, Boston U., 1968. Ordained to ministry United Meth. Ch. Pastor Errol Heights Meth. Ch., Portland, Oreg., 1956-59; nat. dir. Christian Edn., youth work United Meth. Ch., so. Rhodesia, 1962-66; urban sec. Christian Council of Rhodesia, 1967-70; sr. lectr., dean students United Theol. Coll., Salisbury, Rhodesia, 1970-72; dean studies and assoc. dir. Mindolo Ecumenical Found., Kitwe, Zambia, 1973-76; staff assoc. Africa Task Force Bd. Global Ministries, United Meth. Ch., N.Y.C., 1976-78; dir. mission and evangelism prog. and lectr. Boston U., 1978-83; Vera B. Blinn prof. world Christianity United Theol. Sem., Dayton, Ohio, 1983—, trustee; vis. lectr. Pacific Sch. Religion and Grad. Theol. Union, Berkeley, Calif., 1972; vis. lectr. missions Div. Sch., Yale U., New Haven, 1976-78; vis. prof. humanities and internat. studies Va. Poly. Inst. and State U., Blacksburg, 1978; mem. exec. com. New Eng. Graham Crusade, 1981-83; Growth Plus cons. Bd. Discipleship, United Meth Ch., 1987—; core mission interpreter Bd. Global Ministries, United Meth. Ch., 1980—; chmn. bd. global ministries N.H. Conf., United Meth. Ch., 1982-83). Gen. editor Internat. Bibliography on Missiology, 1985—; editor: Missiology: An International Review, 1985—, Rise Up and Walk: An Autobiography by Abel T. Muzorewa, 1978; contbr. articles to profl. jours. Fulbright fellow, 1984. Mem. Internat. Assn. Mission Studies (exec. com. 1988—, chmn. documentation, archives and bibliography working group 1988—), Am. Soc. Missiology (bd. dirs. 1981-84), Assn. Profs. of Mission, N. Am. Acad. Ecumenists (exec. com. 1986-88), Am. Case Study Inst. (bd. dirs. 1985-88), Acad. for Evangelism in Theol. Edn., Soc. Christian Ethics, Soc. for Sci. Study of Religion. Democrat. United Methodist. Avocations: music, running. Home: 1326 Ruskin Rd Dayton OH 45406 Office: United Theol Sem 1810 Harvard Blvd Dayton OH 45406

THOMAS, OOMMEN KULANGARAMADHOM, minister; b. Kerela, India, Oct. 4, 1940; m. Leela Mathew, Apr. 27, 1967; children: Anil, Indu, Udaya. MSW, U. Pitts., 1977; MDiv, Theol. Sem., Pitts., 1978, postgrad. Ordained to ministry Presbyn. Ch. (U.S.A.), 1979. Pastor Yellow Creek (Ohio) United Presbyn. Ch., 1978-89; with transitional svc. WPIC Family Therapy Clinic, Pitts., 1976-77; with preaching assn. Pitts. Theol. Sem., 1975-77; student pastor univ. and city ministries U.A.C.M., 1975-76; pastor St. Andrew's Presbyn. Ch., Olmsted Falls, Ohio, 1989—; commr. Gen. Assembly Presbyn. Ch. (U.S.A.); moderator Upper Ohio Valley Presbytery, Wheeling, W.Va., 1985; moderator justice and social issues Gen. Assembly, Balt. Presbyn. Ch. (U.S.A.), 1991. Recipient Keys to the City of Berea, Mayor of Berea, 1989. Home: 19758 Braeamar Way Oval Strongsville OH 44138 Office: St Andrews Presbyn Ch 23114 W Rd Olmsted Falls OH 44138

THOMAS, OWEN CLARK, clergyman, educator; b. N.Y.C., Oct. 11, 1922; s. Harrison Cook and Frances (Arnold) T.; m. Margaret Ruth Miles, June 6, 1981; children: Aaron Beecher, Addison Lippitt, Owen Clark Jr. A.B., Hamilton Coll., 1944, D.D., 1970; grad. student physics, Cornell U., 1943-44; B.D., Episcopal Theol. Sch., Cambridge, Mass., 1949; Ph.D., Columbia U., 1956. Ordained to ministry Episcopal Ch., 1949. Dir. coll. work Episcopal Diocese, N.Y., 1951-52; chaplain to Episcopal students Sarah Lawrence Coll., 1950-52; mem. faculty Episcopal Divinity Sch. (formerly Episcopal Theol. Sch.), Cambridge, Mass., 1952—, prof. theology, 1965—; chmn. dept. coll. work Episcopal Diocese Mass., 1956-59; vis. prof. Pontifical Gregorian U., 1973-74, N. Am. Coll., Rome, 1982-83. Author: William Temple's Philosophy of Religion, 1961, Science Challenges Faith, 1967, Attitudes Toward Other Religions, 1969, rev. edit., 1986, Introduction To Theology, 1973, rev. edit., 1983, God's Activity in the World, 1983, Theological Questions: Analysis and Argument, 1983; contbr. chpts. to books. Mem. Cambridge Democratic City Com., 1966-80, 88—. Served to ensign USNR, 1944-45. Elihu Root fellow Hamilton Coll., 1943; Univ. fellow Columbia U., 1949-50; scholar in residence Rockefeller Found. Study and Conf. Ctr., Bellagio, Italy, 1991. Fellow Soc. Values in Higher Edn.; mem. Am. Theol. Soc., Phi Beta Kappa. Home: 9 Phillips Place Cambridge MA 02138

THOMAS, PAGE ALLISON, minister, librarian; b. Leslie, Ark., July 2, 1936; s. Page Hatchett and Lou (Hollabaugh) T.; m. Wenda Sue Johnson, Aug. 17, 1958 (div. 1977); 1 child, Benjamin Randall; m. Caryetta M. Grissom, June 5, 1978. Student, U. Ark., 1954-55; BA, Hendrix Coll., 1958; ThM, Perkins Sch. Theology, Dallas, 1961. Ordained to ministry United Meth. Ch., 1962. Pastor Commerce (Tex.) Larger Parish, 1958-59, Hugo (Okla.) Meth. Ch., 1959-60; assoc. libr. Bridwell Libr., So. Meth. U., Dallas, 1961—. Joint editor: The Synoptic Problem: A Bibliography, 1716-1988, 1988. Mem. Am. Theol. Libr. Assn. Home: 1231 Camino Real McKinney TX 75069 Office: So Meth U Bridwell Libr Dallas TX 75275

THOMAS, RANDALL CRAIG, clergyman; b. Wichita, Kans., June 7, 1956; s. Ralph Cullen and Mary Lou (Walker) T.; m. Kathy Lee Williams, July 7, 1956; children: Grant, Natalie, Chase. BA in Bible, Okla. Christian Coll., 1977; postgrad., Harding Grad. Sch. Religion, 1980-83. Ordained to ministry Ch. of Christ, 1977. Youth minister Pleasant Ridge Ch. of Christ, Arlington, Tex., 1977-80; youth minister/involvement minister Macon Rd. Ch. of Christ, Memphis, 1980-83; religious edn. minister Meml. Ch. of Christ, Houston, 1983-86; singles minister Montgomery Ch. of Christ, Albuquerque, 1988—. Office: Montgomery Blvd Ch Christ 7201 Montgomery Blvd NE Albuquerque NM 87109

THOMAS, RAYMOND, academic administrator. Head Manna Bible Inst., Phila. Office: Manna Bible Inst 700 E Church Ln Philadelphia PA 19144*

THOMAS, REGINALD HARRY, minister; b. Wilkes-Barre, Pa., Aug. 1, 1954; s. Warren Leroy and Nancy Carol (Roche) T.; m. Linda Lee Fine, May 31, 1975; children: Reginald H., Jamie Lynn. BA, Messiah Coll., Grantham, Pa., 1976. Ordained to ministry Primitive Meth. Ch. in the USA, 1981. Minister Boone (Iowa) Primitive Meth. Ch., 1976-77, Shamokin (Pa.) Primitive Meth. Ch., 1977-78, 2nd Primitive Meth. Ch., Pitts., 1978-80, Maitland Meml. Primitive Meth. Ch., New Castle, Pa., 1980-82, Messiah Primitive Meth. Ch., Wilkes-Barre, Pa., 1982—; sec. bd. trustees Primitive Meth. Ch. Conf., 1982-89, conf. gen. sec., 1989—. Republican. Home: 110 Pittston Blvd Wilkes-Barre PA 18702-9607 Office: Messiah Primitive Meth Ch 100 Pittston Blvd Wilkes-Barre PA 18702

THOMAS, RICHARD SYLVESTER, minister, substance abuse services counselor; b. Greensboro, N.C., Mar. 26, 1953; s. Richard Jr. and Dorothy Mae (Flowers) T.; m. Patricia Gail Walker, June 30, 1973; children: Richard Sylvester Jr., Bojuana Joyette. Student, N.C. Agr. and Tech. State U., Shaw Div. Sch., 1980; MDiv, Greensboro Bible Inst., 1990. Ordained to ministry Bapt. Ch., 1976; cert. substance abuse counselor, N.C.; cert. reality therapist, N.C.; registered practicing counselor, N.C.; nat. cert. addiction counselor. Sr. instr. Praise Bible Study, Greensboro, 1974-82; sr. min. Locust Grove Bapt. Ch., Brown Summit, N.C., 1982—; with Psychiat. Hosp., Greensboro, 1990—; pastor campus ch. N.C. Agr. and Tech. State U., Greensboro, 1975-76. Mem. Nat. Bapt. Conv., Gen. Bapt. State Conv. N.C., N.C. Chaplains Assn. (assoc.), High Point Ednl. and Missionary Bapt. Assn. N.C., Pulpit Forum Greensboro, Am. Assn. Counseling and Devel., Christian Assn. for Psychol. Studies, N.C. Psychol. Assn. (affiliate), Inst. for Reality Therapy, Nat. Assn. Alcoholism and Drug Abuse Counselors. Home: PO Box 13327 Greensboro NC 27415 Office: Locust Grove Bapt Ch PO Box 13327 Greensboro NC 27415-3327 *Throught the life span of mankind there is the goal of wellness in the area of the Emotional, Occupational, Intellectual, Physical, Social and yes—even the Spiritual self. It is because of my understanding of these areas that I preach Jesus, the one who meets our every need.*

THOMAS, SAMUEL, JR., pastor, consultant; b. Nashville, June 7, 1957; s. Samuel Sr. and Laura (Hubbard) T.; m. Karen Elaine Jones, May 26, 1985. BA in Religion and Bus. Adminstrn., Oakwood Coll., 1980; MDiv, Andrews U., 1984. Christian youth motivational speaker; ch. fin. cons. Mgmt. assoc. Banksouth, N.A., Atlanta, 1981; operating mgr. Security Pacific, Riverside, Calif., 1982; pastor Lake Region Conf. Seventh Day Adventists, Peoria, Ill., 1985-86, East St. Louis, Ill., 1986-89, Flint and Saginaw, Mich., 1989-91, Benton Harbor, Mich., 1991—. Contbr. articles to profl. jours. Cons. Urban League, Peoria, Ill., 1986-89, Saginaw, Mich., 1989-91, Benton Harbor, Mich., 1991—, Ministerial Alliance Drug Prevention Task Force, Saginaw, Mich., 1990—. Mem. Saginaw Alliance for Community Improvement, Detroit-Moto City Fedn. Seventh-day Adventist Mins. Avocations: reading, fishing, tennis, golf. Home: 6005 Westknoll Dr Apt 630 Grand Blanc MI 48439 Office: Lake Region Conf Seventh Day Adventists 8517 S State St Chicago IL 60619

THOMAS, T. VARUGHESE, evangelism educator; b. Malacca, Malaysia, Mar. 14, 1948; arrived in Can., 1971, naturalized 1973; s. T. Thomas and Chinnamah (Thomas) Varughese; m. Mary George, Apr. 17, 1982. BS, Nagpur U., India, 1970, BA, 1971; MDiv, Can. Theol. Sem., Regina, Sask., 1974; D of Ministry, Luther Rice Sem., 1978. Ordained to ministry Christian and Missionary Alliance, 1977. Nat. evangelist Christian and Missionary Alliance, Nyack, N.Y., 1974-80, Willowdale, Ont., Can., 1980-83; asst. prof. Can. Bible Coll., Can. Theol. Sem., Regina, 1978-84, prof. evangelism, Murray Downey chair. evangelism, 1984—, dir. ctr. for evangelism, 1984—. Contbr. articles to religious publs. Office: Can Bible Coll, 4400 4th Ave, Regina, SK Canada S4T 0H8 *The only place "success" comes before "work" is in the dictionary. Work is both profitable and therapeutic.*

THOMAS, TED, SR., minister; b. Raeford, N.C., Oct. 19, 1935; s. Simuel and Nancy Anna (McPhatter) T.; m. Charletta Virginia Clifton, May 30, 1957; children: Ted, Christopher, Marc, Charles, Jonathan, Reuben. BS, Norfolk State Coll., 1959; MA in Math., Edn. and Secondary Edn., Hampton Inst., 1972. Ordained to ministry Ch. of God in Christ Inc., 1957. Pastor New Community Ch. of God in Christ, Churchland, Portsmouth, Va., 1967—; State project dir. Chs. of God in Christ, Va. Jurisdiction 1, 1965—; supt. cen. dist. Chs. of God in Christ, Va., 1964—; asst. prin. Ruffner Jr. High Sch., Norfolk, Va., 1983-84; past pres. young people Willing Works, 1962-66; Sunday sch. supt., 1970-73; asst. bishop 1st jurisdiction Chs. of God in Christ Inc. of Va., 1977-84, State Bishop, 1984—. Mem. NEA, Va. Edn. Assn., Edn. Assn. Norfolk. Home: 4145 Sunkist Rd Chesapeake VA 23321 Office: Ch of God in Christ 3615 Tyre Neck Rd Portsmouth VA 23703

THOMAS, TERRY CLIFFORD, minister; b. Bellingham, Wash., Apr. 24, 1942; s. Clifford George T. and Norma LaVern (Toler) Bruget; m. Janice Marie Teeter, Oct. 12, 1971; children: Karen, Matthew, Rebecca, Mark. MDiv, Luther Northwestern Seminary, St. Paul, 1979; PhD, Marquette U., 1985. Pastor Eagle Lake Luth. Ch., Willmar, Minn., 1977-81, Williams Bay (Wis.) Luth. Ch., 1981-89; sr. pastor Faith Luth. Ch., Redmond, Wash., 1989—; lectr. in theology Marquette U., 1986-89. Author: The St. Paul-Luther Relationship, 1986, At Least We Were Married, 1969; co-author: Annotated Bibliography of Luther Studies 1984-89; contbr. articles to profl. jours. Chair eyebank Lions Internat., Willmar, 1979-81. Fellow Soc. Bibl. Lit., 16th Century Studies, Am. Acad. Religion, Internationalen Luther Forshungen. Home: 9041 166th Ave NE Redmond WA 98052 *To the agonizing question of suffering, pain, evil, I find participation in the death and resurrection of Jesus Christ as the only satisfying response.*

THOMAS, TONY, pastor, basketball coach; b. Miami, Okla., Apr. 5, 1954; s. Reginald Gregg and Alice Nanette (Beville) T.; m. Christie Kay Cramer, Dec. 22, 1973; children: Angela S., Ashley K., Abigail E. BS in Eng. bible, Cin. Christian Coll., 1976; studied, Ind. U., 1980-82, Pacific Christian Coll., 1984-86, Cin. Christian Sem., 1987. Youth min. Harrison Ch. of Christ, Harrison, Oh., 1973-77; sr. min. St. Joseph Ch. of Christ, St. Joseph, Ill., 1978-79, Harrison Ch. of Christ, Harrison, Oh., 1980-83; sr. pastor East Hills Christian Ch., Bakersfield, Calif., 1984-87, Lakota Christian Ch., West Chester, Oh., 1988—; evangelist Revival Fives 1967-72, White Fields Overseas Evangelism 1973-75, Joplin, Mo. Author various articles. Coach, Pisgah Youth Orgn., West Chester, Oh. Mem. Optimist Club, West Chester, Oh. Christian Church. Home: 7125 Inverness Ct West Chester OH 45069 Office: Lakota Christian Ch PO Box 575 West Chester OH 45071-0575

THOMAS JIRAUCH, SISTER MARY, nun; b. St. Louis, Sept. 26, 1928; d. Milton B. and Margaret M. (Thomas) Jirauch. B.Nursing, St. Louis U., 1958, M.Hosp. Adminstrn., 1960. Joined Sisters of Divine Providence, 1946. Provincial counsellor, St. Louis, 1970-80; pres. St. Elizabeth Med. Ctr., Granite City, Ill., 1960-84, chmn. bd., 1984—. Contbr. articles to profl. jours. Recipient Woman of Achievement award St.Louis Globe-Dem. 1985, Citizen of Achievement award C. of C., 1988. Fellow Am. Coll. Hosp. Adminstrs.; mem. Am. Hosp. Assn., Cath. Health Assn., Ill. Hosp. Assn. (bd. mem.), Ill. Cath. Hosp. Assn. (bd. dirs.). Home: 2100 Madison Ave Granite City IL 62040 Office: St Elizabeth Med Ctr 2100 Madison Ave Granite City IL 62040

THOMASMA, DAVID CHARLES, humanities educator, academic administrator; b. Evergreen Park, Ill., Oct. 31, 1939; s. Charles W. and Rosemary (Olma) T.; divorced; children: Pieter Jon, Elizabeth (Lisa) Rose. BS, Aquinas Coll., Grand Rapids, 1961; BA, Aquinas Inst., 1963; MA, Ph.L., 1964; STB, Dominican House of Studies, 1965, Sacrae Theol. Licentiate, 1968; PhD, Cath. U. Am., 1972. Instr. Cath. U. of Am., Washington D.C., 1967-69; asst. prof. Christian Bros. Coll., 1969-73; dir. med. humanities U. Tenn. Ctr. Health Sci., 1973-81; prof., dir. med. humanities Loyola U. Chgo. Med. Ctr., 1981—; pres. Chgo. Clin. Ethics Programs, 1988-89. Author 15 pub. books; contbr. numerous articles to profl. jours. Bd. dirs. Hospice of Memphis, Inc., 1979-81, Soc. of the right to Die, N.Y., 1987-90; mem. ethics adv. com. Am. Hosp. Assn., Chgo., 1986-90, Theology and Ethics adv. com. Cath. Health Assn., St. Louis, 1986-91. Sr. Fulbright fellow, 1984, Woodrow Wilson fellow, 1986—. Mem. Soc. for Health and Human Values Coun., Am. Acad. of Religion, Am. Philos. Assn., Am. Cath. Philos. Assn., Am. Geriatics Soc., Soc. for Bioethics Cons., Inst. of Medicine of Chgo. Democrat. Avocations: classical music, woodworking, swimming, hi-fidelity. Office: Loyola U Med Ctr 2160 S 1st Ave Maywood IL 60153

THOMASON, DANA ANDREW, chaplain; b. Memphis, Jan. 4, 1954; s. Elmo Andrew and Irma Audry (Bookout) T.; m. Ctherine Margurite Pierce, June 12, 1976; 1 child, Jonathan. BA, Hendrix Coll., Conway, Ark., 1976; MTh, So. Meth. U., Dallas, 1979; PhD, U. Denver, 1987. Pastor Tyronza (Ark.) United Meth. Ch., 1982-85, Centerview United Meth. Ch., Payneway, Ark., 1982-85; assoc. pastor First United Meth. Ch., Benton, Ark., 1985-88; asst. counselor, chaplain Hendrix Coll., Conway, 1988—. Mem. Soc. Bibl. Lit. Methodist. Office: Hendrix Coll Conway AR 72032

THOMASON, DON ALBERT, minister; b. Clinton, Okla., Aug. 23, 1958; s. Lindel Leroy and Judith Anora (Eakins) T.; m. Deborah Kay Smith, May 19, 1979; children: Sonya, Katrina, Dana, Alicia. BA, Midwest Christian Coll., 1980; MA, Cin. Bible Sem., 1990, MRE, 1991; postgrad., Phillips Grad. Sem., 1990-91. Ordained to ministry Christian Ch. Youth min. 1st Christian Ch., Hydro, Okla., 1978-80; assoc. min. Pershing Ave. Christian Ch., Liberal, Kans., 1980-81; grad. asst. Cin. Bible Coll., 1981-84; assoc. min. Rising Sun (Ind.) Ch. of Christ, 1982-89; assoc. min., dir. Davis Park Christian Ch., Enid, Okla., 1989—. Sponsor Students Against Drunk Driving, Rising Sun, 1987-89. Home: 2720 E Cherokee Enid OK 73701 Office: Davis Park Christian Ch 749 N 11st St Enid OK 73701

THOMASON, RONNY DALE, minister; b. Amarillo, Tex., Oct. 24, 1950; s. Seth and Irene Pearl (King) T.; m. Norma Joyce Pratt, Mar. 26, 1970; children: Heather Fawn, Aaron Lee. BS, West Tex. State U., 1972. Ordained to ministry Assemblies of God; cert. secondary tchr., Tex. Evangelist Gen. Coun. Assemblies of God, Tex., 1968-72; pastor Assembly of God, White Deer, Tex., 1972-74, First Assembly of God, Rockwall, Tex., 1974-84; adminstr., assoc. pastor Victory Acad. & Victory Ch., Amarillo, Tex., 1984-89; sr. pastor Christian Life Ctr., Broken Bow, Nebr., 1989—; pres. Rockwall Ministerial Assn., 1976-77, v.p. 1978-79; day care dir. Amarillo Christian Ctr., 1984-87; adminstr., prin. Victory Acad., Amarillo, 1984-89. Author newspaper column, 1972-74; pub., editor ch. newsletters, 1977-80; editor sch. yearbooks, 1981-89. Del. Rep. Party County Conv., Rockwall, 1980, Rep. Party Precinct, Amarillo, 1988. Mem. Full Gospel Bus. Men's Fellowship Internat., Charismatic Bible Ministries, Broken Bow Ministerial Assn. Home: 911 S 3rd Ave Broken Bow NE 68822 Office: Christian Life Ctr 204 N 5th Ave Broken Bow TX 68822

THOMFORDE, CHRISTOPHER MEREDITH, minister; b. Cleve., Jan. 25, 1947; s. Fredrich Henry and Marie (Meredith) T.; m. Christine Elizabeth Stone Huber, June 10, 1972; children: Christopher, Rebecca, Sarah, Jonathan. BA, Princeton U., 1969; MDiv, Yale U., 1974. Ordained to ministry Luth. Ch. in Am., 1976. Asst. chaplain Colgate U., Hamilton, N.Y., 1974-78; pastor St. Paul's Luth. Ch., Dansville, N.Y., 1978-86; chaplain Susquehanna U., Selinsgrove, Pa., 1986—; pres. Dansville Ministerim, 1979-81. Sec. ARC, Danville, 1983-86. Named Citizen of Yr., Dansville, 1986. Home: 413 University Ave Selinsgrove PA 17870 Office: Susquehanna U Chaplain's Office Selinsgrove PA 17870

THOMPSON, BETTY ANNE, lay worker; b. Atlanta, Feb. 4, 1926; d. Joseph Rodgers and Anna Mary (Jamerson) T. AB cum laude, Wesleyan Coll., Macon, Ga., 1947. Info. dir. World Coun. of Chs., Geneva, 1955-56; publ. dir. World Coun. of Chs., N.Y.C., 1957-65; asst. gen. sec. United Meth. Bd. Global Ministries, N.Y.C., 1965-74, assoc. gen. sec., 1974-87, pub. rels. dir., 1987—; mem. World Coun. Chs. Assemblies, New Delhi, 1961, Uppsala, Sweden, 1968, Nairobi, Kenya, 1975, Vancouver, Can., 1983, Canberra, Australia, 1991; vice chmn. World Coun. Chs. Communictions Com., Geneva, 1968-83; chmn. news and info. com. Nat. Coun. Chs., N.Y.C., 1975-79. Author: Turning World, 1960, The Healing Fountain, 1973, A Chance to Change, 1983; editor at large The Christian Century, 1962—; mem. editorial adv. com. Christianity and Crisis, 1990—. Recipient Distinguished Svc. award Wesleyan Coll., 1970. Mem. Nat. Religious Pub. Rels. Coun. (v.p. 1991), Thomas Wolfe Soc., World Assn. Christian Communication (cen. com. mem. 1990—). Democrat. Home: 14 Fifth Ave New York NY 10011 Office: United Meth Bd Global Ministries 475 Riverside Dr New York NY 10115

THOMPSON, CHARLES ALFRED, editor; b. Atlanta, June 25, 1957; s. Charles Everett and Joan (Garrett) T.; m. Sheila Virginia Eubanks, Jan. 24, 1981; children: Hannah Leah, Nathaniel David. AS in Journalism, Gainesville Coll., 1978; BS in Social Scis., North Ga. Coll., 1980. Editor Christian Fin. Concepts, Gainesville, Ga., 1988—. Editor: (newsletter) How to Manage Your Money, 1989, 90, 91. Recipient third pl. Way Cry News Contest, The Salvation Army, 1984, first pl., 1986, third pl. Ga. Newspaper Contest, Ga. Press Assn., 1985, writing award Biola U., 1991. Home: 6380 Concord Rd Cumming GA 30130 Office: Christian Fin Concepts 601 Broad St SE Gainesville GA 30501 *Far too many of life's tragedies, from addiction to divorce, are the result of well-intentioned but misinformed choices in humanity's ongoing search for happiness. The key to happiness is God and when His people put this principle into action, the rest of humanity takes notice.*

THOMPSON, CYNTHIA L., religious press editor; b. Buffalo, June 3, 1943; d. Thomas K. and Elsie (Press) T. BA, Wellesley Coll., 1966; MA, Yale U., 1968, PhD, 1973. Editor religious books Westminster Press, Phila., 1980-89; assoc. editorial dir. acad. and reference books Westminster/John Knox Press, Louisville, 1989—; lectr. in field. Contbr. articles to religious jours. Recipient grant-in-aid Am. Coun., Learned Socs., 1991. Mem. Soc. Bibl. Lit., Am. Philol. Assn. Democrat. Office: Westminster/John Knox Press 100 Witherspoon St Louisville KY 40202

THOMPSON, DAVID POLLOCK, minister; b. Monaghan, Ireland, July 24, 1920; came to U.S., 1921; s. Frederick William and Jeanne Elizabeth (Pollock) T.; m. Jananne Larson, June 22, 1946; children: Thomas James, Marcia Ann, Jananne Elizabeth. BA, Coe Coll., 1948; MDiv, McCormick Theol. Sem., 1951. Ordained to ministry United Presbyn. Ch. in the U.S.A. Pastor United Presbyn. Ch., Russellville, Ark., 1951-55, Marysville, Ohio, 1955-64; pastor Am. Protestant Ch. of the Hague, Netherlands, 1964-68, Oak Ln. Presbyn. Ch., Phila., 1968-84; pastor emeritus, 1984—. Home: 4747 N Rd 33 Box 167 Lakeland FL 33805 *The longer I live, the more aware I become of the similarity of the people of God: individually striving to do what we think God desires of us, failing in that striving, and coming back to try again to be like our divine example.*

THOMPSON, DEBORAH KAYE, minister; b. Camden, Ark., Dec. 22, 1965; d. James Daniel and Patsie Louise (Barnhart) T. BS in Christian Edn., B in Sacred Music, Southwestern Assemblies of God Coll., 1989. Lic. to ministry Assemblies of God, 1989. Tchr. Cloverdale Christian Acad., Little Rock, 1989; asst. pastor, min. youth and music Owasso (Okla.) Assembly of God, 1989—. Mem. Delta Epsilon Chi. Office: Owasso Assembly of God PO Box 49 106 N Main Owasso OK 74055 *My heavenly father is the source of true life. Anyone denying his need of a relationship with Almighty God is witholding from his immortal soul the privilege of eternal communion with its Maker.*

THOMPSON, EDWARD ARTHUR, minister; b. Chgo., Sept. 5, 1947; s. Harold Louis and Mary Edna (Wesper) T.; m. Faye Alice Barton, Oct. 17, 1970; children: Rebeccah Anne, Elizabeth Ann. Student, Thornton Jr. Coll., Harvey, Ill., 1964-66, Lancaster Sch. of Bible, Lancaster, Pa., 1971-72. Ordained to ministry, Ind. Bapt. Ch., 1980. Deacon Bible Bapt. Ch., Romeoville, Ill., 1977-78, asst. pastor, 1978-80; pastor Stewartville (Minn.) First Bapt. Ch., 1980-82, Silvis Hts. (Ill.) Bapt. Ch., 1982-87; sr. pastor Griswold St. Bapt. Ch., Port Huron, Mich., 1988—; resolutions chmn. Coun. of Ten, Ill. and Mo. Assn. of Reg. Bapt. Chs., 1983-89; bd. dirs. Chs. Unltd., Inc., Grand Rapids, Mich., 1990—. With USN, 1967-70. Mem. Black Hawk Area Regular Bapt. Pastors Fellowship (chmn. 1983-87), Shepherds and Servants Pastors Fellowship (chmn. 1990—). Republican. Home: 1617 Court St Port Huron MI 48060 Office: Griswold St Bapt Ch 1232 Griswold St Port Huron MI 48060

THOMPSON, ELIZABETH, minister; b. North Conway, N.H., May 2, 1962; d. George Edward and Frances May (Cooper) T. BA in Classics, U. N.Mex., 1985; MDiv, Princeton Theol. Sem., 1989. Ordained to ministry, United Ch. of Christ, 1991. Chaplain resident Hartford (Conn.) Hosp., 1989-90; minister First Congl. Ch., Canterbury, Conn., 1990—; bd. dirs. Quinebaug Valley Pastoral Counseling Ctr., Danielson, Conn., 1991—; mem. com. on ecumenical and interreligious concerns, Conn. Conf. United Ch. of Christ. Bd. dirs. Conn. AIDS Residence Coalition, Hartford, 1991—; mem. Conn. AIDS Com. of United Ch. of Christ, Hartford, 1991—. Democrat. Office: First Congl Ch 6 S Canterbury Rd Canterbury CT 06331

THOMPSON, EMERSON MCLEAN, JR., clergyman; b. Raleigh, N.C., Dec. 3, 1931; s. Emerson McLean and Grace (Neathery) T.; m. Catherine Traynham, June 9, 1956; children: Catherine Elizabeth, Emerson III, David Stuart. AB in English, Duke U., 1954; BD, Duke Divinity Sch., 1958. Ordained to ministry Meth. Ch. as deacon, 1956, as elder, 1958. Pastor Stantonsburg (N.C.) Meth. Ch., 1958-64, Scotland Neck (N.C.) Meth. Ch., 1964-70, McMannen United Meth. Ch., Durham, N.C., 1970-75, Grace United Meth. Ch., Wilmington, N.C., 1975-80, 1st United Meth. Ch., Roanoke Rapids, N.C., 1980-84; sr. minister 1st United Meth. Ch., Elizabeth City, N.C., 1984-90; dist. supt. Greenville (N.C.) Dist. United Meth. Ch., 1990—; trustee Meth. Coll., Fayetteville, N.C., 1977-85, Meth. Retirement Homes, Inc., 1986—. Mem., chmn. bd. dirs. Migrant and Seasonal Farmworkers, Inc., Raleigh, N.C., 1977-83; mem. Rotary Internat., Wilmington, 1975-80, Roanoke Rapids, 1980-84, Elizabeth City, 1984-90. Home and Office: Greenville Dist United Meth Ch 101 Martinsborough Rd Greenville NC 27858

THOMPSON, FRANCIS W. B., bishop. Bishop of Accra, Anglican Communion, Ghana. Office: Bishop Ct, POB 8, Accra Ghana*

THOMPSON, FRED PRIESTLY, JR., educator, minister; b. Lawton, Kans., Nov. 15, 1917; s. Fred Priestly and Mattie (Leonard) T.; m. Dorothy Louise Williams, Sept. 29, 1940; Janet Thompson McClain, David Michael, Donald Gordon, Dennis Fred. BA, Pacific Christian Coll., 1939, George Pepperdine Coll., 1948; MA, George Pepperdine Coll., 1950; BD, Christian Theol. Sem., 1956; STD (hon.), Milligan Coll., 1970. Ordained to ministry Christian Ch., 1938. Min. Cen. Christian Ch., Medford, Oreg., 1940-41, Ch. of Christ, Elsinore, Calif., 1941-42, Alvarado Christian Ch., L.A., 1943-50; min. First Christian Ch., Greenwood, Ind., 1950-53, Chgo., 1953-68, Kingsport, Tenn., 1968-69; pres., prof. Christian doctrine Emmanuel Sch. Religion, Johnson City, Tenn., 1969-84, prof.-at-large, 1984—. Author: Biblical Prophecies, 1966, The Holy Spirit: Teacher, Comforter, Guide, 1978, What the Bible Teaches About Heaven and Hell, 1982; contbg. editor: Christianity Today, 1971—; columnist: Action, 1965-83, Christian Standard, 1973-82. Mem. European Evang. Soc., Karl Barth Soc. N. Am., Am. Acad. Religion, Chgo. Bible Soc. (bd. dirs.), Nat. Assn. Evangs. (bd. amministrn. 1960—), Theta Phi, Eta Beta Rho. Office: Emmanuel Sch Religion Box 6 Johnson City TN 37601

THOMPSON, FRED WELDON, clergyman, administrator; b. Durant, Okla., Aug. 1, 1932; s. Fredrick Weldon and Mary Mauvolyn (Barnes) T.; m. Lois Bell Reedy, Apr. 25, 1954; children—Alicia Ann, Penny Sue. B.A., Ottawa U., 1954, D.D. (hon.), 1984; B.D., Central Bapt. Theol. Sem., 1958, Th.M., 1959. Ordained to ministry Am. Bapt. Chs. U.S.A., 1956; pastor South Broadway Bapt. Ch., Pittsburg, Kans., 1961-66; campus minister Bapt. Student Union, Pittsburg, 1962-66; area minister Am. Bapt. Ch. Central Region, Topeka, Kans., 1966-77, assoc. exec. minister, exec. minister, 1982—; assoc. gen. sec. Am. Bapt. Chs., Valley Forge, Pa., from 1982. Bd. dirs. Central Bapt. Theol. Sem., Kansas City, Kans., 1982—, Ottawa U., Kans., 1980—, Bacone Coll., Muskogee, Okla., 1974-82; bd. dirs. United Sch. Dist. 503 Sch. Bd., Parsons, Kans., 1971-77, pres., 1973-76. Recipient Ch. and Community award for Outstanding Alumni, Ottawa U., 1979. Mem. Ottawa U. Alumni Assn. (pres. 1977), Central Bapt. Sem. Alumni Assn. (pres. 1964).

THOMPSON, GARY DEWAYNE, minister; b. Philadelphia, Miss., Dec. 23, 1948; s. Robert Murphy and Bertha Alice (Skipper) T.; children: Aletheia Ann, Stephanie Elizabeth, Mark Alan; m. Robin Jane Beverly, June 26, 1982; 1 child, Kimberly Alice. Ordained to ministry United Meth. Ch. as deacon, 1984, as elder, 1986. Pastor Hinds Chapel-Eudora (Miss.) United Meth. Ch., 1983-86; assoc. pastor 1st United Meth. Ch., Columbus, Miss., 1986-89; pastor St. Luke United Meth. Ch., Cleveland, Miss., 1989-91, Capitol St. United Meth. Ch., Jackson, Miss., 1991—; chmn. task force on hunger and human needs Miss. Conf., United Meth. Ch., 1985-88, chmn. missions com. North Miss. Conf., 1988-90, coord. missions Cleveland Dist., 1989-91. Organizer, chmn. bd. Helping Hands of Columbus, 1988-89, Helping Hands of Cleveland, 1990-91. Recipient Leadership award Helping Hands of Columbus, 1990, Helping Hands of Cleveland, 1991. Home: 110 Swanlake Cove Jackson MS 39212 Office: Capitol St United Meth Ch 531 W Capitol Jackson MS 39203

THOMPSON, GEORGE RALPH, church denomination administrator; b. Barbados, Mar. 20, 1929; s. George Gilbert and Edna (Griffith) T.; m. Imogene Clotilde Barker, July 19, 1959; children: Carol Jean, Linda Mae, Gerald Randolph. BA, Atlantic Union Coll., 1956; MA, Andrews U., 1958, BD, 1962, DD (hon.), 1983. Ordained to ministry Seventh-day Adventists, 1959. Evangelist South Caribbean conf. Seventh-day Adventists, Trinidad and Tobago, 1950-53; tchr., ch. pastor, chmn. dept. theology Caribbean Union Coll., Trinidad and Tobago, 1953-54, 59-64; pres. East Caribbean conf. Seventh-day Adventists, Barbados, 1964-70; pres. Caribbean Union conf. Seventh-day Adventists, Trinidad and Tobago, 1970-75; v.p. Gen. Conf. Seventh-day Adventists, Washington, 1975-80; sec. Gen. Conf. Seventh-day Adventists, Silver Spring, Md., 1980—; host radio shows, Barbados. Office: Gen Conf Seventh-day Adventist Ch 12501 Old Columbia Pike Silver Spring MD 20904-6600

THOMPSON, GEORGE WALTER MURRY, JR., minister; b. Richmond, Va., Oct. 12, 1931; s. George Walter Murry Sr. and Inez Arnessa (Arrington) T.; m. Sarah E. Thompson, June 2, 1955 (dec. Sept. 1986); 1 child, Sarita T. Lockley. BA, Va. Union U., 1954; MDiv, So. Bapt. Theol. Sem., 1957; MA, U. Chgo., 1962, PhD, 1974. Ordained to ministry Bapt. Ch. Prof. Bluefield (W.Va.) State Coll., 1962-63; prof., coord. Ctr. Theol. Studies, Dayton, Ohio, 1963-72; vis. prof. Harvard U., Cambridge, Mass., 1975-77, Luth. Theol. Sem., Phila., 1981—; pastor New Horizon Bapt. Ch. and Oak Ln. United Ch. Christ, Phila., 1981—; prof. philosophy and religious studies East Stroudsburg (Pa.) U., 1972—; Wesley Found. honor lectr. U. Mo., Rolla, 1989; lectr. Mexico, Australia, Africa, Carribean, Nicaragua, Eng., USSR. Author: Technology and Human Fulfillment, 1985. Mem. Germantown Cen. Coun., Phila., 1981—; mem. Coord. Com. Community Orgns., Chgo., 1965-66, Pa. Prison Soc., Phila., 1990—. Mem. NAACP, Am. Assn. Higher Edn., Soc. for Study Black Religion, Am. Bapt. Chs. Soc. for Study Social Philosophy, Soc. Study Creativity. Home: PO Box 925 Glenside PA 19038 Office: East Stroudsburg U Box 112 East Stroudsburg PA 18301

THOMPSON, GUS HOWARD, minister; b. Orange, Tex., Aug. 19, 1956; s. George and Lenette (Sikes) T.; m. Marla Sue Nash, May 19, 1979; children: Cara Diane, Austin Nash. BBA, Sam Houston State U., 1977, MBA, 1979; ThD, St Georges Anglican Sch., 1990. CPCU; cert. in gen. ins. Vicar Ch. of Resurrection (Am. Episcopal Ch.) Anglican Ch. in Am., 1988-90; pres. Continuing Ch. Found., Richmond, Tex., 1991—; sr. underwriter Rnger Ins. Co., Houston, 1987—; adv. bd. mem. KSBJ Edn. Found., Houston, 1991—; bd. trustees Continuing Ch. Found., Houston, 1991—. Exec. bd. Citizens for Excellence in Edn., Rosenberg, Tex., 1990—. Capt. U.S. Army, 1979-85. Recipient Army Commendation medal, 1990, Meritorious Svc. medal, 1985. Mem. Phi Chi Theta, Forrest Lodge AF&AM. Republican. Home: 6603 Harpers Dr Richmond TX 77469 Office: Ranger Ins Co PO Box 2807 Houston TX 77252

THOMPSON, H. B., JR., academic administrator. Head West Coast Christian Coll., Fresno, Calif. Office: W Coast Christian Coll Office of the President 6901 N Maple Ave Fresno CA 93710*

THOMPSON, HENRY ORRIN, minister, archaeologist. B.S., Iowa State U., 1953; M.Div., Drew U., 1958, Ph.D., 1964; M.S. in Edn., Syracuse U., 1971; M.A. in Ednl. Psychology, Jersey City State Coll., 1975, diploma in sch. psychology, 1976; postgrad. in cognitive psychology Rutgers U., 1978-80. Ordained to ministry United Methodist Ch., 1956. Pastor, Neshanic Station, Centerville and Mt. Zion, N.J., 1956-59; pastor Jersey City United Meth. Ch., 1959-61; lectr. Upsala Coll., 1961-62; instr. Colgate Rochester Div. Sch., 1962-63; lectr. Syracuse U. (N.Y.), 1963-64, asst. prof., 1964-67; assoc. prof. N.Y. Theol. Sem., 1967-69, prof., 1969-70, 1970-74; pastor Bayonne United Meth. Ch. (N.J.), 1969-70; adj. prof. U. Jordan, 1971-72; pastor Fairfield United Meth. Ch. (N.J.), 1974-81; pastoral counselor Inst. for Personal and Family Relations, Boonton, N.J., 1974-81; adj. prof. Jersey City State Coll., 1975-76; adj. asst. prof. Unification Theol. Sem., 1977-79, assoc. prof., 1979-87, prof., 1987—; vis. assoc. prof. Oberlin Coll. (Ohio), 1980; sr. fellow Sch. Nursing, U. Pa., 1981-87, adj. prof. ethics, 1987—; vis. faculty Eastern Coll., Pa., 1985. Author: Approaches to the Bible, 1967, Mekal: The God of Beth-shan, 1970, Archaeology and Archaeologists, 1972, Hidden and Revealed, 1973, (with Joyce Elaine Beebe Thompson) Ethics in Nursing, 1981, Bioethical Decision Making for Nurses, 1985, Biblical Archaeology, 1987, World Religions in War and Peace, 1987, Archaeology in Jordan, 1989, Case Study in Antisemitism, 1990, Jerusalem, 1990, New Perspectives, 1990; editor: The Global Congress of the World's Religions, 1982, The Implications of Carl Michalson's Theological Method for Christian Education, 1983, Unity in Diversity, 1984, The Answer Lies Below, 1984, Put Your Future in Ruins, 1985, Global Outreach, 1987; co-editor: (with E.J. Wynne) Prayer for Today's People: Sermons on Prayer by Carl Michalson (1915-1965), 1982, The Wisdom of Faith, 1989, What is Truth, 1989, The Contributions of Carl Michalson to Modern Theology, 1991; (with K.L.S. Rao) World Problems and Human Responsibility: Gandhian Perspectives, 1988, (with Roa and others) GCWR in South Asia, 1988, (with Arthur Berger) Religion and Parapsychology, 1989, (with Padmasiri De Silva) Man's Search for Meaning in a Fragmental Universe: A Buddist Dialogue, 1989, (with Joyce E. Thompson) Professional Ethics in Nursing, 1990, (with Sulayman Nyang) The Relevance of Islam, 1991; author filmstrips, also film Shechem: The Biography of a Bibilical City, 1973; contbr. articles to profl. jours. Served with USAF, 1953-55. Recipient Mayor's Proclamation, Fairfield, N.J., 1981; Drew U. grantee, 1959; U.S. State Dept. grantee, 1972-73. Am. Schs. Oriental Research, Archaeol. Inst. Am., Conf. Faith and History, Global Congress World's Religions, Carl Michalson Soc. of Drew U. (pres. 1979-81, bd. dirs. 1977—), Profs. World Peace Acad., Internat. Assn. for Gandhi Studies, Univ. Mus. (Phila.). Address: 2942 Valley View Dr Doylestown PA 18901

THOMPSON, HERBERT, JR., bishop; b. N.Y.C.; m. Ruselle Cross, 1968; children: Herbert, Owen, Kyrie. Grad. cum laude, Lincoln U., 1962; MDiv, Gen. Theol. Seminary, N.Y.C., 1965; postgrad., Stony Brook U., Ch. Divinity Sch. of Pacific. Ordained to ministry Episcopal Ch. as deacon, 1965, then as priest. Chaplain Chester County, Pa.; vicar St. Gabriel's Ch., Bklyn.; rector Christ Ch., Bellport, N.Y., 1971-77, Grace Ch., Jamaica, 1977-88; bishop coadjutor Diocese of Southern Ohio, 1988—; exec. dir. Interfaith Svcs., Bklyn.; colloquium moderator Gen. Theol. Seminary; instr., lectr. Mercer Sch. Theology; bd. dirs. Jamaica Devel. Corp. Reader Gen. Ordination Examinations; mem. Presiding Bishop's Commn. on Black Ministries, Coalition for Human Needs, joint standing com. on planning for Gen. Conv., coun. of advice to thr Pres. of the House of Deps.; bd. dirs. Cen. Queens YMCA, Queens Fedn. of Chs., St. Christopher-Ottilie Home. Served with USAF. Named Hon. Canon Cathedral of the Incarnation Diocese of Long Island, 1985. Mem. Jamaica C. of C. (bd. dirs). Address: 412 Sycamore St Cincinnati OH 45202

THOMPSON, JAMES B., retired minister; b. Cooke County, Tex., Jan. 25, 1929; s. John Burton and Tennie Belle (Germany) T.; m. Betty Jeanne Clark, June 11, 1950; 1 child, Karla Kay. BA, Baylor U., 1950, D in Divinity, 1988; MDiv, S.W. Bapt. Theol. Sem., 1953. Pastor Rural Student Pastorates, Mexia, Tex., 1950-51, Calvary Bapt. Ch., Brownsboro, Tex., 1951-53, Tabernacle Bapt. Ch., Pickton, Tex., 1953-56; pastor First Bapt. Ch., Robstown, Tex., 1956-58, Mineola, Tex., 1958-77; pastor Calvary Bapt. Ch., Beaumont, Tex., 1967-77; with stewardship dept. Bapt. Gen. Convent of Tex., Dallas, 1977-83, dir. stewardship, 1983-91. Author: Creative Stewardship for Texas Baptist Churches, 1991; contbr. articles to profl. jours. Mem. Beaumont C.A.P. Program, 1974, Jefferson County Coun. on Alcoholism, Beaumont, 1969-71; pres. Mineola Community Chest, 1966; trustee S.E. Tex. Bapt. Hosp. (trustee 1972-77), San Marcos Bapt. Acad. (trustee 1970-73). Named Man of the Yr., Mineola C. of C., 1965. Mem. Rotary (pres. 1964). Republican. Baptist. Avocations: antique cut glass, fly fishing, hunting. Home: Rte Box 2290 Mineola TX 75773 Office: Bapt Gen Conv of Tex 333 Washington Dallas TX 75246

THOMPSON, JAMES MARTIN, minister, protective services official; b. LaGrange, Ga., Aug. 13, 1943; s. James D. Thompson and Zora B. Hyatt Wheelus; m. Janet L. Thompson, Aug. 8, 1988; children: James M. Jr., Charles J., Barbaretta P. AA in Edn., Clayton State Coll., 1972; AA in Bible, Immanuel Bible Coll., 1987; BMin, MMin, Bethany Bible Coll., 1990; D of Ministry, Bethany Theol. Sem., 1991. Ordained to ministry Bapt. Ch., 1960. Pastor numerous chs. including Antioch Bapt. Ch. Rex, Ga., 1961—; police officer Clayton County Police Dept., Jonesboro, Ga., 1970—. Named Outstanding Law Enforcement Officer Clayton County Jaycees, 1976. Mem. Ga. Assn. Police Community Rels. Officers (pres. 1974). Home: 6042 Katherine Rd Rex GA 30273 *Man's ability is not the major thing God looks for in our service; it is our availability to God that is a deciding factor in our success or failure rate.*

THOMPSON, JAMES WALKER, III, minister; b. Bennettsville, S.C., June 24, 1952; s. James Walker Thompson Jr. and Clara Coleen (Hayes) Poole; m. Donna Stack, Dec. 30, 1978; children: James Walker IV, Daniel. BS, U. S.C., 1975; MDiv, Southwestern Bapt. Theol. Sem., Ft. Worth, 1979. Ordained to ministry So. Bapt. Conf., 1978; cert. master life trainer. Assoc. pastor Pleasant Glade Bapt. Ch., Colleyville, Tex., 1975-80; pastor Beulah Bapt. Ch., Hopkins, S.C., 1980—. Home: 509 Horrell Hill Rd Hopkins SC 29061 Office: Beulah Bapt Ch 9487 Garner's Ferry Rd Hopkins SC 29061 *When Christ becomes more than a word to us, we begin a life of discovery. It is an unending pilgrimage which carries us into His presence finally.*

THOMPSON, JEFFERY ELDERS, health care administrator, minister; b. Bremen, Ga., Feb. 21, 1951; s. Jack Elders and Jewell Dean (Hutto) T.; m. Pamela Jennette Watson, Aug. 26, 1972; children: Rebecca Lynn, Joshua Elders. Ordained to ministry So. Bapt. Conv., 1977. Youth min. Calder Bapt. Ch., Beaumont, Tex., 1977-79, First Bapt. Ch., Florence, S.C., 1979-82; chaplain Ga. Regional Hosp., Augusta, Ga., 1982-84; dir. pastoral care East Ala. Med. Ctr., Opelika, 1984—. Pres. Hospice of Lee County, Opelika, 1986-87, bd. dirs. 1987—; bd. dirs. Widowed Person Svc., Opelika; mem. Leadership Lee County, 1991. Fellow Coll. Chaplains; mem. Lions (chaplain Opelika club 1985, named Outstanding Lion 1986). Office: East

Ala Med Ctr 2000 Pepperell Pkwy Opelika AL 36802-3201 *I spent the first part of my life attempting to find answers to all the questions of life. I am now beginning not to be so concerned about life's answers. I am now more willing simply to live with it's questions.*

THOMPSON, JOHN LESTER, bishop; b. Youngstown, Ohio, May 11, 1926; s. John Lester and Irene (Brown) T.; m. Shirley Amanda Scott, Aug. 1, 1951; children: Amanda, Ian. B.A., Youngstown Coll., 1948; S.T.B., Episcopal Theol. Sch., Cambridge, Mass., 1951. Ordained priest Episcopal Ch., 1951; curate, then rector chs. Ohio, Oreg. and Calif., 1951-78; bishop Episcopal Diocese No. Calif., Sacramento, 1978—; trustee Ch. Divinity Sch. Pacific, Berkeley, Calif. Pres., Oreg. Shakespeare Festival, 1955-56, chmn. bldg. com. for outdoor theatre, 1957-58. Served with USNR, 1943-46. Office: PO Box 161268 Sacramento CA 95816

THOMPSON, JOHN ROSS, minister; b. Union City, Pa., Oct. 31, 1943; s. Lawrence Elmer and Agnes Alberta (Applebee) T.; children: Ross, Jean, Lynn. BA, Pa. State U., University Park, 1965; MDiv, Drew U., 1968; D in Ministry, Pitts. Theol. Sem., 1984. Pastor Grace United Meth. Ch., Ridgebury, N.Y., 1966-68, Center United Meth. Ch., Natrona Heights, Pa., 1968-80, St. Paul's United Meth. Ch., Allison Park, Pa., 1980-90; coun. dir. Western Pa. Conf., Mars, 1990—; chairperson Ch. Devel. Task Force, 1987-88; tchr., rep. Bethel Series; ch. cons. Growth Plus. Recipient Denman award for Excellence in Evangelism, 1987. Mem. Western Pa. Conf. (chmn. vital congregations emphasis 1988-90), Bd. of Ordained Ministry (chairperson 1984-87). Home: 214 Dombey Dr Pittsburgh PA 15237 Office: Western Pa Conf 1204 Freedom Rd Mars PA 16046 *With George Bernard Shaw and Robert Kennedy, I believe that while many see what happens in the world and say "why?", the greater vision is to look at the world and say "why not?". I find my challenge is to open doors for others.*

THOMPSON, KENNETH POPE, minister; b. Quincy, Fla., May 26, 1956; s. Hal Warren and Christine Annette (Poppell) T.; m. Patricia Carol Crotty, July 2, 1977; children: Patrick Kent, Kendall Kirby. AA, N. Fla. Jr. Coll., 1978; BS, Fla. State U., 1981; MDiv, Duke U., 1985; cert. in clin. pastoral edn., John Umstead Hosp., Butner, N.C., 1984; postgrad., Luth. Theol. So. Sem., 1987-88. Ordained to ministry as deacon United Meth. Ch., 1984, to ministry Evang. Luth. Ch. Am., 1988. Pastor Chaires United Meth. Ch., Tallahassee, 1980-82; assoc. pastor Brookland United Meth. Ch., Roxboro, N.C., 1982-85, 1st United Meth. Ch., Deltona, Fla., 1985-87; intern pastor St. Matthew's Luth. Ch., Jacksonville, Fla., 1987-88; pastor Hope Luth. Ch., Port St. Lucie, Fla., 1988—; coord. Church World Svc. CROP WALK, Port St. Lucie, 1991; mem. Luth. Liturgical Renewal, Lehigh Valley, Pa., 1990—. Contbr. poems to poetry jours. Quincy Rotary scholar, 1974. Mem. Port St. Lucie Ministerial Assn. (sec.-treas. 1989—0, Space Coast Luth. Pastors Assn., The Liturgical Conf., Fellowship Merry Christians.

THOMPSON, LARRY BRUCE, minister; b. Raleigh, N.C., May 14, 1954; s. Bruce Hoover and Bernice (York) T.; m. P. Pamela Prescott, Dec. 18, 1976; children: Christin Hart, Lauren Elizabeth. AA, Anderson (S.C.) Coll., 1974; BA, Furman U., Greenville, S.C., 1976; MDiv, New Orleans Bapt. Theol. Sem., 1979. Ordained to Gospel Ministry, So. Bapt. Conv., 1980. Min. youth Calvary Bapt. Ch., New Orleans, 1976-79; pastor Hillcrest Bapt. Ch., North Charleston, S.C., 1980-83; mission pastor Harbison Bapt. Mission, Columbia, S.C., 1983-84; pastor First Bapt. Ch., Englewood, Tenn., 1985-87, Loganville (Ga.) Bapt. Ch., 1987-91, Retta Bapt. Ch., Burleson, Tex., 1991—; seminar leader evangelism Home Mission Bd., Atlanta, 1987-91, ch. growth, revival preparation, 1985-91; chmn. mission com. Charleston Bapt. Assn., 1982-83; pres. Campus Ministries, Anderson Coll., 1972-74; prayer seminar leader Assn. Pastors Confs.; author of Ga. Bapt. Conv.'s Resolution on Encouraging Laws Regulating Abortion, 1989. Author: Prayer: Acts of Joy, 1986; composer folk opera: The Earth is Ours, 1971. Bd. dirs. United Tenn. League, Nashville, 1986; pastor advisor Bapt. Student Union, Med. U. S.C., 1981-83; corp. Bible study tchr. BellSouth Advt. & Pub. Corp., Atlanta, 1988-91; karate instr. Harbison Community Ctr., Columbia, S.C., 1983-84. Mem. Gwinnett Metro Bapt. Ministers Conf. (pres. 1990-91), Messenger-Gwinnett Metro Bapt. Assn. (evangelism coun. 1989-91, Sun. Sch. Growth award 1989, Tarrant Bapt. Assn. ch. extension com.), Denmark Soc., Phi Theta Kappa. Home: 13045 Rendon Rd Burleson TX 76028 Office: Retta Bapt Ch 13201 Rendon Rd Burleson TX 76028 *Everything I ever wanted out of life, I have found in Christ. Everything I ever wanted to learn about life, I have found in His Word. Every purpose I ever wanted in my life, I have found in serving His Church.*

THOMPSON, LEONARD LEROY, theology educator; b. LaFontaine, Ind., Sept. 24, 1934; s. Russell Charles and Ruth Alice (Dyson) T. BA, DePauw U., 1956; B.D., Drew U., 1960; MA, U. Chgo., 1963, PhD, 1968. Instr. Lawrence U., Appleton, Wis., 1965-66; Wright State U., Dayton, Ohio, 1966-68; prof. religion Lawrence U., 1968—, dean faculty, 1988-91. Author: Introducing Biblical Literature, 1978, The Book of Revelation, 1990; contbr. articles to theol. publs. Nat. Endowment for Humanities fellow, 1981-82. Mem. Soc. Bibl. Lit., Am. Acad. Religion, Chgo. Soc. Bibl. Research. Home: 346 Winnebago Ave Menasha WI 54952 Office: Lawrence U Religious Studies Appleton WI 54912

THOMPSON, MALCOLM CALDWELL, minister; b. Pitts., Mar. 7, 1919; s. Harry Byron and Sara Thelma (Caldwell) T.; m. Catherine Elisabeth Mayer, June 23, 1952; children: Mark Roy, Glen Gordon. AB, Maryville (Tenn.) Coll., 1944; BDiv, McCormick Theol. Sem., 1947; PhD, U. Edinburgh, Scotland, 1949. Pastor First Presbyn. Ch., New Carlisle, Ohio, 1949-54, Sidney, Ohio, 1954-71; pastor Oak Hill Presbyn. Ch., St. Louis, 1971-88, pastor emeritus, 1988—; founder Jefferson Acad. of History, 1976; moderator Synod of Ohio-Presbyn. Ch., Columbus, 1964-65, Synod of Mid-Am., Mo. and Kans., 1991—; chmn. Grand-Oak Hill Ministerial Alliance, St. Louis, 1979—, Coun. of Synod Mid-Am., Mo. and Kans., 1980-86. Graduate CORO Reinvest (Pub. Svc. Tng.), St. Louis, 1989; v.p. Tower Grove South Housing Corp., St. Louis; bd. dirs. Grand Oak Hill Community Corp., St. Louis. McCormick Theol. Sem. fellow, 1947, scholar, 1944-47. Mem. Presbytery of Giddings-Lovejoy, Coun. of South Side Presbyn. Chs. United, Sch. for Christian Faith (bd. dirs.), Mo. Numismatic Soc. (bd. dirs. St. Louis chpt.). Republican. Home: 5207 Tholozen Ave Saint Louis MO 63109

THOMPSON, MICHAEL DON, theology educator, pastor; b. Ponca City, Okla., Sept. 12, 1950; s. Kenneth Eugene and Bonnell (Williams) T.; m. Deborah Kathleen Spicer, May 19, 1973; children: Melissa Diane, Mary Elizabeth. BS, U. Okla., 1972; MDiv, Southwestern Bapt. Theol. Sem., 1980; PhD, Golden Gate Bapt. Theol. Sem., 1989. Univ. minister First So. Bapt. Ch., Del City, Okla., 1973-77; assoc. pastor Fielder Road Bapt. Ch., Arlington, Tex., 1977-82; spiritual formation cons. Golden Gate Bapt. Theol. Sem., Mill Valley, Calif., 1982-89, v.p. student affairs, prof. spiritual formation, 1989—; guest faculty fgn. mission bd. So. Bapt. Conv. Missionary Learning Ctr., Richmond, Va., 1986-90; guest lectr. Pastors Tng. Conf., Calcutta, India, 1987. Pres.'s scholar U. Okla., 1968. Baptist. Avocations: sports, music. Office: Golden Gate Bapt Theo Sem Strawberry Point Mill Valley CA 94941

THOMPSON, MICHAEL NEAL, minister; b. Logan, W.Va., Sept. 4, 1963; s. Neal Baxter and Iva Elaine (Flannery) T.; m. Cynthia LaRee Huxford, July 1, 1989. BA in Christian Ministry, Atlanta Christian Coll., 1985. Ordained to ministry Christian Ch., 1990. Assoc. min. 1st Christian Ch., Carrollton, Ga., 1985-87, Moncks Corner, S.C., 1987—; leader Berkeley High Sch. Fellowship Christian Athletes, Moncks Corner, 1990-91. Basketball coach Lord Berkeley Acad., Moncks Corner, 1987-91. Named Outstanding Young Man of Am., 1989. Office: 1st Christian Ch Rte 5 Box 859 Moncks Corner SC 29461

THOMPSON, MILO, JR., academic administrator. Head Bapt. Bible Coll. and Sem., Clarks Summit, Pa. Office: Bapt Bible Coll & Sem 538 Venard Rd Clarks Summit PA 18411*

THOMPSON, PATRICIA (SISTER), religious education administrator; b. Oak Park, Ill., May 28, 1942; d. Robert Thompson and Jane (Smith) Broomfield. BA, St. Ambrose U., 1978; MA in Religious Edn., St. Scholastica U., 1978. Dir. religious edn. St. Ambrose Parish, Roman Cath. Ch., Milan, Ill., 1967-75, Christ the King Parish, Moline, Ill., 1974-75, St. Joseph Parish, Downers Grove, Ill., 1978-83, Holy Trinity Parish, Westmont, Ill., 1983-87, St. Elizabeth Seton Parish, Naperville, Ill., 1987—; cons. Silver Burdett & Ginn Pubs., Morristown, N.J., 1988—. Author guideline book: Correlation Total Religious Content for Joliet Diocese, 1982-83 (Honor award 1983). Treas. Safe Place, Naperville, 1990—. Ill. Parish Coords. and Dirs. of Religious Edn. (state sec. 1985-89, founding mem.), Diocese of Joliet Cluster of Religious Edn. (sec. 1982-87, 90, chair 1988). Home: 1333 Lorraine Rd Wheaton IL 60187 Office: St Elizabeth Seton Parish 2220 Lisson Rd Naperville IL 60565-5234

THOMPSON, PETER BOYD, pastor; b. Newton, Mass., Dec. 26, 1955; s. Chauncey Boardman II and Mary Ann (Woodard) T.; m. Lynne Marie Frederiksen, Aug. 12, 1978; 1 child, Jesse Boyd. BS, Coe Coll., 1978; MDiv, Princeton Theol. Sem., 1981. Ordained to ministry Presbyn. Ch., 1981. Student pastor Woodside Presbyn. Ch., Yardley, Pa., 1979-81; asst. pastor Grace Presbyn. Ch., Jenkintown, Pa., 1985-86; organizing pastor West Pasco County New Ch. Devel., New Port Richey, Fla., 1985-86; pastor Presbyn. Ch. of Seven Springs, New Port Richey, 1986—; vice chmn. exec. search com. Tampa Bay Presbytery, St. Petersburg, Fla., 1990-91, chmn. profession support com., 1990; commr. Gen. Assembly Presbyn. Ch. (U.S.A.), Phila., 1989, Synod of Fla., Orlando, 1988. Bd. dirs. Big Brother, Big Sister, Pasco County, Fla., 1986-87. Mem. Am. Guild Organists (chaplain West Pasco chpt. 1991—), The Alban Inst. Republican. Office: Presbyn Ch of Seven Springs 4651 Little Rd New Port Richey FL 34655 *When I began my ministry I believed one of the tasks of a pastor and the church was to help "fix" people and their relationships. Now I realize that if people get healthier or more whole it is because they worked at it with God's help. God is the changing agent, my role is to be with and for people in the struggles of life.*

THOMPSON, PRINCE EUSTACE SHOKEHU, bishop. Bishop of Freetown The Anglican Communion, Sierra Leone. Office: Bishopcourt, Fourah Bay Rd, POB 128, Freetown Sierra Leone*

THOMPSON, RICHARD RICHARDO, minister; b. Detroit, June 26, 1955; s. Richard and Juanita Nellie (Hall) T.; m. Regina Denise Davis, Jan. 21, 1978 (div. July 1979); m. Carol Corene Scott, Oct. 21, 1989. BA, Morehouse Coll., 1977. Ordained to ministry Bapt. Ch., 1978. Asst. pastor Russel St. Bapt. Ch., Detroit, 1977-81, Greater Concord Bapt. Ch., Detroit, 1981-84; sr. pastor Union Bapt. Ch., Deresen, Ont., 1984-91, 2d Corinthian Bapt. Ch., Detroit, 1991—; asst. v.p. First of Am. Bank, Detroit, 1983—; loan rev. com. Clergy United for Leadership, Detroit, 1988—; mem. Detroit Pastor's Coun., 1978—; chaplain Black Republican Coun., Detroit, 1989, Detroit Police Dept., 1990. Commr. Detroit Hist. Commn., 1989; bd. dirs., treas. Todd Phillip's Devel. Ctr., 1986. Mem. NAACP (life), Urban Bankers Forum, Detroit Bd. Realtors, Detroit Real Estate Brokers (bd. dirs. 1989), Mich. Housing Coalition (bd. dirs. 1989), Mich. Housing Trust Fund (bd. dirs. 1989), Masons, Kappa Alpha Psi (life). Republican. Home: 18068 Washburn Ave Detroit MI 48221 *Education will open most doors of opportunity. Hard work, loyalty and integrity will keep doors open.*

THOMPSON, ROBERT JAYE, minister; b. Coffeyville, Kans., Nov. 4, 1951; s. Julis Levi and Verna Belle (Hardrick) T.; m. Carolyn Robinson, Aug. 23, 1971; children: Montie Shannon, Monica Shea, Marquis Shane, Marissa Seana. AA in History, Coffeyville Community Jr. Coll, 1971; BA in History, Pittsburg (Kans.) State U., 1973; MDiv cum laude, Memphis Theol. Sem., 1991. Ordained to ministry Bapt. Ch., 1983. Pastor Sweet Home Bapt. Ch., Dardanelle, Ark., 1983-88; assoc. pastor Springdale Bapt. Ch., Memphis, 1988—; instr. Tenn. Sch. of Religion, Memphis, 1989—; chaplain intern Federal Correctional Institution, Memphis, 1990; pastor Greenfield Presbyn. Ch., Waterford, Miss., 1990—; sgt. Guardsmark, Inc., Memphis, 1989—; treas. Antioch Dist. Assn., Ft. Smith, Ark., 1987-88, youth minister, 1987-89; sec. Ft. Smith Interdenominational Assn., 1984-88. Block worker Am. Heart Assn., Memphis, 1991; student body pres. Memphis Theol. Seminary, 1990-91. Capt. U.S. Army, 1973-80, Europe. Recipient Benjamin E. Mays fellowship Fund for Theol. Edn., N.Y.C., 1990-91, Disting. Mil. Grad. Pittsburg State U., 1973. Mem. Memphis Bapt. Ministers Assn. Democrat. Home: 3518 Wilshire Rd Memphis TN 38111-5612 *It is a good thing that God gives us only one day at a time because it is hard enough to organize that one so that we still look forward to the next with joy.*

THOMPSON, RON EVERETT, minister; b. Hopewell, Va., Feb. 4, 1935; s. Samuel Griffith and Ruth Rebecca (Oliver) T.; m. Thelma Doris Nichols, Apr. 23, 1957; children: Evangeline Leigh, Melody Lynne. AB, Bridgewater Coll., 1957; MDiv, Grace Theol. Sem., 1963. Ordained to Christian ministry, 1964. Pastor STone Ch. of the Brethren, Buena Vista, Va., 1957-59, Omega Ch., Akron, ind., 1961-63; staff evangelist Brethren Bd. Evangelism, Winona Lake, Ind., 1961, 63-67; pastor Patterson Meml. Grace Brethren Ch., Roanoke, Va., 1967-73, 78-89; exec. dir. Brethren Evang. Ministries, Roanoke, 1989—; mem. Bd. of Evanglism, Winona Lake, 1978-89. Home and Office: 3580 Robin Hood Circle Roanoke VA 24019

THOMPSON, RONALD CHARLES, evangelist; b. Que Que, Zimbabwe, Feb. 8, 1932; came to U.S., 1978; s. Charles Edward and Iris Maud (Wright) T.; m. Dawn Averil Ansley, Jan. 9, 1956; children: Glynn Mark, Lester Daron R. Diploma in Arts and Theology, Helderberg Coll., West South Africa, 1955; MA in History, Andrews U., 1968; PhD in Ecclesiastical History, Rhodes U., South Africa, 1979, diploma in Theology, 1979. Ordained to ministry Seventh-day Adventists, 1965. Mission dir. East African Union of Seventh Day Adventists, Musoma, 1956; tchr. Bugema Missionary Coll., Kampala, Uganda, 1957-60; pastor Seventh Day Adventist Ch., various, South Africa, 1961-69; conf. evangelist, union evangelist South Africa, 1970-74; pastor, evangelist various, 1975—; faculty mem. various colls. and univs.; mem. The Union for Experimenting Faculty, 1985. Contbr. articles to religious periodicals. Mem. Johnson County (Tex.) Amateur Radio Club. Home: 1223 Stone Lake Dr Cleburne TX 76031

THOMPSON, SHEILAH, religious organization administrator. Trustee-at-large Unitarian Universalist Assn., North Vancouver, B.C., Can. Office: Unitarian Universal Assoc, 930 Whitchurch St, North Vancouver, BC Canada V7L 2A6*

THOMPSON, SUSAN LYNNE, minister; b. Flint, Mich., Apr. 30, 1950; d. John Seth and Doris Adelia (Almeling) T. BS in Edn., Cen. Mich. U., 1971; MFA, Eastern Mich. U., 1974; diploma in art, Universita Per Straneri, Perugia, Italy, 1972; postgrad., Princeton Theol. Sem., 1987-90. Ordained to ministry, Presbyn., 1990. Art tchr. Lapeer (Mich.) Pub. Sch. System, 1974-75; beauty advisor Estée Lauder, Inc., Chgo., 1975-77; acct. coord. Estée Lauder, Inc., Peoria, Ill., 1977-78; acct. exec. Estée Lauder, Inc., St. Louis, 1978-81; regional mktg. mgr. Estée Lauder, Inc., Oklahoma City, 1981-86; regional acct. mgr. Estée Lauder, Inc., St. Louis, 1986-87; pastor 1st Presbyn. Ch., Charleston, Ill., 1990; instr. art therapy Oak Theraputic Sch., Chgo., 1975-76. Recipient 1st Place award Flint Inst. Art, 1972, 5th Place award Detroit Inst. Art, 1972; named one of Outstanding Young Women Am., 1983, one of 2000 Notable Am. Women, 1989. Republican. Presbyterian. Home: 606 Greenbriar Ct Charleston IL 61920

THOMPSON, THEODORE WARREN, SR., retired religion educator; b. Oklahoma City, Aug. 18, 1923; s. Leslie Paul and Helen Louise (Parker) T.; m. Dora Jean Britt, Apr. 15, 1949; children: Theodore W. Jr., Susan, William, James (dec.). BA, John Brown U., 1948; MDiv., Southwestern Bapt., 1951; ThM, Cen. Bapt. Sem., 1955, ThD, 1959. Ordained to ministry Bapt. Ch., 1954. Prof. religion/philosophy Butler Coll., Tyler, Tex., 1951-53; min. of music/edn. Maywood Bapt. Ch., Independence, Mo., 1953-55; pastor Utica (Mo.) Bapt. Ch., 1955-57; dir. Bapt. Fellowship Ctr., Mobile, Ala., 1957-61; prof. religion/philosophy Bishop Coll., Dallas, 1961-83; adj. instr., philosophy Brookhaven Coll., Farmers Branch, Tex., 1983—. Mem. Mobile (Ala.) Inter-Racial Assn., 1958-61, Jewish-Christian Task Force, Dallas, 1982-86. With U.S. Army, 1943-46. Recipient Humanitarian award AF&M Masonic Lodge, Dallas, 1973, Alumni Achievement award Cen. Bapt. Sem., Kansas City, Kans., 1974. Mem. North Tex. Philos. Assn. (pres. 1971), Southwestern Philos. Assn., Am. Theatre Organ Soc. (Dallas, v.p. 1979), Dallas Organ Soc. Home: 11628 Sonnet Dr Dallas TX 75229

THOMPSON, THOMAS HENRY, academic dean, philosophy educator; b. Sioux City, Iowa, Jan. 10, 1924; s. Elmer Edwin and Ruth Alma (Baker) T.; m. Diane Sargent, Nov. 23, 1955; children: Brenda, Alicia, Mark, Rosemary. B.A., U. Iowa, 1948, M.A., 1950, Ph.D., 1952. Asst., instr. U. Iowa, Iowa City, 1948-52; mem. faculty U. No. Iowa, Cedar Falls, 1952—; prof. philosophy U. No. Iowa, 1969—, head dept., 1969-81, acting dean Coll. Humanities and Fine Arts, 1981-82, dean Coll. Humanities and Fine Arts, 1982-90. Mem. Sigmund Freud Gesellschaft (Vienna), Am. Philosophy Assn. Home: 2122 California St Cedar Falls IA 50613 Office: U No Iowa Communication Arts Ctr 269 1222 W 27th St Cedar Falls IA 50614

THOMPSON, TYLER, minister, philosophy educator; b. Corona, Calif., Oct. 18, 1915; s. Francis Forbes and Sadie Cassandra (Tyler) T.; m. Phyllis Elizabeth Oechsli, June 19, 1937; children: Francia, Wendy, Heidi, Becky, Peter. B.S., Calif. Inst. Tech., 1936; S.T.B., Boston U., 1939, Ph.D., 1950. Ordained to ministry Meth. Ch., 1938. Exec. sec. Calif. Inst. Tech. YMCA, 1935-36; asst. pastor Epworth Meth. Ch., Cambridge, Mass., 1936-37; pastor Barre (Mass.) Meth. Ch., 1937-39; Meth. missionary Singapore, 1939-46; pastor Weston (Mass.) Meth. Ch., 1946-49; asst. prof. religion and philosophy Allegheny Coll., 1949-51, chaplain, 1950-51; assoc. prof. philosophy of religion Garrett-Evangelical Theol. Sem., 1951-56, prof., 1956-78, dir. summer sessions, 1959-72; Vis. prof. philosophy Northwestern U., 1952-58; vis. prof. philosophy of religion McCormick Theol. Sem., 1963-65; adj. prof. Fuller Theol. Sem., 1981-84. Author: Freedom in Internment: Under Japanese Rule in Singapore, 1942-45, 1990. Pres. Evanston (Ill.) Human Relations Council, 1952-54, Evanston Democratic Club, 1956-58; Dem. nominee for Congress 13th Dist. in Ill., 1960; mem. Cook County (Ill.) Central Com. Dem. Party, 1966-68; pres. Dem. Party Evanston, 1970-72; Bd. dirs. Ill. div. ACLU, 1953-68, pres., 1959-64. Am. Assn. Theol. Schs. Faculty fellow, 1965. Mem. Am. Theol. Soc. (pres. div. 1965-66), Am. Philos. Assn., AAUP, Am. Acad. Religion, Tau Beta Pi. Home: 415 Oaklawn Ave South Pasadena CA 91030 Office: Garrett-Evangelical Theol Sem Evanston IL 60201 *Useful life depends on hope, but every object of hope is subject to some uncertainty. The more important the object, the less possibility of proof. Risk is needed: we live by faith. To reflect and act on what it means to love one's enemies is to probe the deepest dimensions of faith.*

THOMPSON, WILLIAM DAVID, minister, homiletics educator; b. Chgo., Jan. 11, 1929; s. Robert Ayre and Mary Elizabeth (McDowell) T.; m. Linda Brady Stevenson, Nov. 2, 1968; children—Tammy, Kirk, Lisa, Rebecca, Gwyneth. A.B., Wheaton Coll., Ill., 1950; B.D., No. Baptist Sem., 1954; M.A., Northwestern U., 1955, Ph.D., 1960. Ordained to ministry Am. Baptist Ch., 1954. Instr. speech Wheaton Coll., 1952-55; pastor Raymond Baptist Ch., Chgo., 1956-58; assoc. prof. homiletics No. Bapt. Sem., Chgo., 1958-62; mem. faculty Eastern Bapt. Sem., Phila., 1962-87, prof. preaching, 1969-87; minister 1st Bapt. Ch., Phila., 1983-90; pres. Speaker Svcs., Inc., 1987—. Author: A Listener's Guide to Preaching, 1966, Recent Homiletical Thought, 1967, Dialogue Preaching, 1969, Preaching Biblically, 1981, Listening on Sunday for Sharing on Monday, 1983, Philadelphia's First Baptists, 1989. Mem., Phila. Hist. Commn., 1984—. Mem. Acad. Homiletics (pres. 1973), Religious Speech Communication Assn. (v.p. 1983, pres. 1984), Internat. Platform Assn., Union League Club. Republican. Home: 765 Ormond Ave Drexel Hill PA 19026

THOMPSON, WILLIAM GILBERT, minister; b. Houston, Mar. 9, 1945; s. Vincent Dill and Dorothy Odessa (Burton) T.; m. Patricia Irene Hirsch, Jan. 23, 1965; children: Michelle Renee, John Michael. BBA, Sam Houston state U., 1969; MDiv, Concordia Theol. Sem., 1973; D Ministry, Hartford (Conn.) Sem., 1982. Ordained to ministry Luth. Ch.-Mo. Synod, 1973; cert. social worker. Pastor Mt. Calvary Luth. Ch., Galesburg, Ill., 1973-77; sr. pastor Immanuel Luth. Ch., Bristol, Conn., 1977-81, Trinity Luth. Ch., Utica, Mich., 1981—; pres. bd. dirs. Luth. Friends of the Deaf, Mill Neck, N.Y., Brazil Mission Soc., Utica, Mich. Trustee Mill Neck Found., 1981—; bd. dirs. Valparaiso U. Recipient Servus Ecclesiae Christi Concordia Theol. Sem., 1982. Office: Trinity Luth Ch 45160 Van Dyke Utica MI 48317

THOMPSON, YAAKOV, rabbi; b. St. Mary's, Ohio, Dec. 2, 1954; s. Herbert and Carolyn Jean (Gallimore) T.; m. Sarah Jeffery, Dec. 30, 1982; children: Adina Michal, Benjamin Asher. BA, Ohio State U., 1977; MA, Jewish Theol. Sem. Am., 1983, DHL, 1988. Ordained rabbi, 1983. Asst. rabbi Jewish Ctr. Kew Gardens Hills, Flushing, N.Y., 1980-82; rabbi Uniondale Jewish Ctr., N.Y., 1982-84, Suburban Park Jewish Ctr., East Meadow, N.Y., 1984-88, Congregation Benai Israel of Fair Lawn, N.J., 1988—; bd. govs. L.I. Bd. Rabbis, 1985—; lectr. Jewish Welfare Bd. Lecture Bur., N.Y.C., 1986—; asst. prof. Bible Jewish Theol. Sem. Am., 1988—, Rabbinical Assembly, Nassau, Suffolk, L.I., N.Y., 1983—, com. chmn. 1986—; bd. dirs. Fair Lawn Mental Health Ctr. Contbr. articles to profl. jours. Bd. dirs. Fair Lawn Mental Health Ctr. Mem. East Meadow Interfaith Clergy Assn., N.Y. Bd. Rabbis, Soc. Bibl. Lit., Am. Acad. Religion, Assn. for Jewish Studies, Union for Traditional Conservative Judaism, Rotary Internat. Avocations: music, reading, sports. Home: 28-02 Berkshire Rd Fair Lawn NJ 07410 Office: Congregation Benai Israel of Fair Lawn 30th St and Pine Ave Fair Lawn NJ 07410 *Life is most meaningful when lived with a sense of being a part of that which is greater than any individual. Let us make the task of religion the construction of new paths to the Holy One and to each other. Such paths can lead all of us to a better world.*

THOMSEN, DARRELL EVERETT, JR., minister; b. Portsmouth, Va., Apr. 9, 1958; s. Darrell Everett Thomsen Sr. and Patricia Faye (Thompson) Reynolds; m. Kitty Charleen Miller, July 18, 1980; 1 child, Melissa Jean. BA, Bluefield Coll., 1983; MDiv, Southeastern Bapt. Theol. Sem., 1985. Sales and service Norfolk County Feed and Seed, Portsmouth, 1979-81; minister Cleveland (Va.) Bapt. Ch., 1981-83, Grove Park Bapt. Ch., Portsmouth, 1983—; chaplain City of Portsmouth Police Dept., 1987—. Vol. chaplain Portsmouth Gen. Hosp., 1987—. Served with U.S. Army, 1976-79. Mem. Portsmouth Bapt. Ministers Assn. (chmn. ordination examination com. 1986—, pres. 1986), Portsmouth Area Resource Coalition, Inc. (bd. dirs. 1987—). Avocations: golf, boating, fishing, hunting, woodworking. Home and Study: 2300 Oregon Ave Portsmouth VA 23701

THOMSEN, HALVARD JESSEN, minister; b. Tulsa, Jan. 7, 1917; s. Hans Jessen and Ninni (Hansen) T.; m. Hester Ida Bryan, Sept. 15, 1940; children: Joyce Elaine, Halvard Bryan. BTh, Walla Walla Coll., 1938. Ordained to mininstry Seventh-day Adventist Ch., 1944. Lit. evangelist Mont. Conf., Culbertson, 1938, minister, 1939-47; pastor Humboldt Park Seventh-day Adventist Ch., Chgo., 1947-53, Wash. Conf. Seventh-day Adventists, 1953-64, Bklyn. Seventh-day Adventist Ch., 1967-76, Babylon (N.Y.) Seventh-day Adventist Ch., 1976-86; exec. dir. Soc. Issachar's Offspring, Milton-Freewater, Oreg., 1986—; exec. producer films Bibl. archaeology, 1960-66, including The Marks of Man series, 1962; pub. info. officer Dogubayazit Expdn. to Turkey (search for Noah's ark), 1962, writer, producer, performer radio programs, 1944-62; pres. Griffon Graphics. Co-author: Ahmed, Boy of Jerusalem, 1965; contbr. articles to religious jours. Mem. exec. com. Greater N.Y. Conf. Seventh-day Adventists, Greater N.Y. Acad.; mem. bd. Council Concerned Citizens, Manhattan; founder, pres. Ch. Aid Found.; chmn. bd Bklyn. Seventh-day Adventist Sch. Address: Rt 3 Box 147F-1 Milton-Freewater OR 97862

THOMSON, DAVID, bishop. Bishop The Old Cath. Ch. of Can., Midland, Ont. Office: Old Cath Ch Can, RR 1, Midland, ON Canada L4R 4K3*

THOMSON, JOANNE, minister; b. Malden, Mass., Sept. 9, 1953; d. Edward Joseph and Natalie (Haines) T.; m. Donald Bruce Hausch, June 28, 1986. BA summa cum laude, Tufts U., 1975; MDiv cum laude, Harvard U., 1981. Ordained to ministry United Ch. of Christ, 1981. Pastor Prospect Congl. Ch., Cambridge, Mass., 1981-84; assoc. pastor North Congl. Ch., Cambridge, 1981-84; min. First Congl. Ch., Madison, Wis., 1984-89; pastor Middleton (Wis.) Community Ch., 1989—. Mem. United Ch. Bd. for World Ministries (corp.), Phi Beta Kappa.

THORN, FRED EARL, pastor; b. Brilliant, Ohio, Apr. 13, 1937; s. Joshua Levingston Thorn and Mary Catherine (Hudson) Long; m. Norma Lou Parsons, June 15, 1958; children: Robert Eugene, Mary Rebecca. BA in Philosophy, Ohio U., 1959; MDiv, Wesley Sem., Washington, 1963; MA in Evangelism, Scarritt Coll., 1974. Ordained minister in Meth. Ch., 1961.

Pastor Wabasso (Fla.) United Meth. Ch., 1968-73, Redland United Meth. Ch., Homestead, Fla., 1973-76, Springhead United Meth. Ch., Plant City, Fla., 1976-80, Hilliard (Fla.) Meth. Ch., 1980-85, First United Meth. Ch., Immokalee, Fla., 1985-91, Golden Gate Meth. ch., Naples, Fla., 1991—; mem. ch. and soc. bd. Fla. Annual Conf., 1986—; mem. Immokalee Neighborhood Svcs. Bd., 1985—. Mem. Rotary (Immokalee chpt., sec. 1990-91, head polio plus drive 1987-88). Republican. Home: 4215 23d Pl SW Naples FL 33999 Office: Golden Gate Meth Ch Naples FL 33999

THORNDIKE, NICHOLAS STURGIS, layworker, librarian; b. Alma, Mich., June 28, 1962; s. Samuel Lothrop and Sarah R. (Simons) T. AB magna cum laude, Bowdoin Coll., 1984; postgrad., Harvard Divinity Sch., 1985-86, Western Theol. Sem., 1987-88; MLS, U. Mich., 1991. Ministerial asst. Harvard Meml. Ch., Cambridge, Mass., 1986, Community Reformed Ch., Zeeland, Mich., 1987-88; mem. Peace Task Force, Ann Arbor, Mich., 1989—; asst. libr. U. Mich., Ann Arbor, 1988—; resident Ecumenical Campus Ctr., Ann Arbor, 1990-91; co-founder Campus Adult Ministry, Ann Arbor, 1990—. Author: (with others) The God Pumpers, 1987; author poetry. Campaign asst. senator Carl Levin, Ferndale, Mich., 1990—; campaign asst. L.D. Hollenbeck, Ithaca, Mich., 1987. Wilmot scholar Bowdoin Coll., 1985. Mem. ALA, Am. Theol. Libr. Assn., Mich. Libr. Assn., Mich. Acad. Arts and Scis., Internat. Forum (assoc.). Democrat. Home: 1058 N Glenwood Apt 1B Griffith IN 46319 Office: 426 Thompson Ann Arbor MI 48103

THORNHILL, WILLIAM GREGORY, SR., minister; b. Greenville, S.C., Dec. 3, 1946; s. William Ira and Virginia Rommell (Fowler) T.; m. Linda Joyce Garabedian, June 18, 1966; 1 child, William Gregory Jr. Diploma, Greenville TEC Coll., 1966. Ordained to ministry So. Bapt. Conv., 1983. Mgr. retail stores, 1966-83; pastor Westwood Bapt. Ch., Easley, S.C., 1983—; trustee Marietta (S.C.) Bapt. Camp, 1991—, chmn. properties com., 1991—; mem. resolutions com. S.C. Bapt. Conv., 1989-90. Pres. PTA, Berea Middle Sch., Greenville, 1987-88, chmn. adv. bd., 1988-89. With S.C. NG, 1966-73. Mem. Greenville Bapt. Assn. (time/place/preacher com. 1986-87, moderator 1988-89). Republican. Home: 230 Champlain Dr Greenville SC 29611 Office: Westwood Bapt Ch 3821 Saluda Dam Rd Easley SC 29640 *In this day of fast pace and constant change, I believe that people need more than ever the love of Jesus, who will never change.*

THORNLEY, JEFFREY MARK, minister; b. Fairbanks, Alaska, May 10, 1955; s. James Flemon and Olga Marie (Simpson) T.; m. Cynthia Ann Holt, Dec. 30, 1977; children: John, Paul, Luke. BS in Life Scis., U. Md., 1976; MDiv, Grace Theol. Sem., 1979. Ordained to ministry, 1986. Ch. planter, asst. pastor Grace Brethren Ch., Temple Hills, Md., 1979-81; sr. pastor, headmaster Grace Brethren Ch. and Sch., Waldorf, Md., 1981—. Named to Outstanding Young Men of Am., 1982. Republican. Home: 378H Leman Ln Waldorf MD 20601 Office: Grace Brethren Ch Hwy 5 Box 283-1 Waldorf MD 20601

THORNTON, ARVIE GORDON, minister, missions administrator; b. Screven, Ga., Oct. 24, 1928; s. Romie G. and Lula (Thompson) T.; m. Doris Anita Reddish, Dec. 1, 1950; children: Judy Elaine, Mark Arvie. Grad., Brewton-Parker Jr. Coll., 1950; AB, Mercer U., 1953; MDiv, So. Bapt. Theol. Sem., 1958. Ordained to ministry, So. Bapt. Ch., 1948. Pastor various Bapt. chs. Alston, Ga., 1948-50, Glennville, Ga., 1949-50, Lumber City, Ga., 1950-52, Oglethorpe, Ga., 1953-55; pastor Canmer (Ky.) Bapt. Ch., 1955-58, Whitewater, Ga., 1958-59; pastor 1st Bapt. Ch., Marshallville, Ga., 1959-76, LaBelle Heights Bapt. Ch., Marietta, Ga., 1959-76; dir. missions Fairburn Bapt. Assn., College Park, Ga., 1976—; vice-moderator Noonday Bapt. Assn., 1965-67, chmn. evangelism com., 1975-76, moderator, 1968-69, chmn. nominating com., 1974-75, pres. Bapt. Minister's Conf., 1974; mem. exec. com. Ga. Bapt. Conv., 1967-72; chmn. bd. dirs. Christian Index; v.p. Cobb County Ministerial Assn., 1974-75. Mem. Kennestone Hosp. Chaplain Assn., Urban Med. Ctr. Chaplain Assn., Cobb County C. of C. Home: 145 White Oak Ct Fayetteville GA 30214 Office: PO Box 549 Union City GA 30291

THORNTON, BARRY STANLEY, evangelist; b. Pearisburg, Va., Mar. 28, 1956; s. Clarence Stanley Thornton and Barbara Carol (Mann) Holtmann; m. Janet Denise Riley, July 28, 1978. BS, Cin. Bible Coll., 1978; postgrad., Cin. Christian Sem., 1985-92. Evangelist Marion (Ind.) Ch. of Christ, 1978-80, Montezuma (Ohio) Ch. of Christ, 1980-85; sr. evangelist Chesterton (Ind.) 1st Christian Ch., 1985—; trustee Lake Region Christian Assembly, Crown Point, Ind., 1986—. Bd. dirs. Duneland YMCA, Chesterton, 1990—. Mem. Duneland Rotary (v.p. 1990-91, sec. 1989-90, bd. dirs. 1987-89, Outstanding Rotarian 1990). Republican. Home: 1303 Jefferson Ave Chesterton IN 46304 Office: 1st Christian Ch 1110 Porter Ave Chesterton IN 46304 *The three most important words to every human being are still the most profound: JESUS LOVES ME!.*

THORNTON, JAMES WILLIAM, III, priest; b. Palo Alto, Calif., Jan. 18, 1937; s. James William Jr. and Cyrilla Mary (Dolan) T. BA, BS, U. Notre Dame, 1959; STB, Pontiff Gregorian U., Rome, 1961, Sacrae Theologiae Licentiatus, 1963; PhD, U. Oreg., 1981. Ordained priest Roman Cath. Ch., 1964. Tchr. Notre Dame High Sch., Niles, Ill., 1963-66; spiritual dir. Moreau Sem., South Bend, Ind., 1971-72; assoc. dean students U. Portland, Oreg., 1972-79, asst. acad. v.p., 1981-82; counselor on alcoholism Portland Med. Ctr. Hosp., 1982-83; counselor on alcoholism De Paul Ctr. Inc., Portland, 1983-86, dir. adult treatment svcs., pres., chief exec. officer, 1986-89; chief exec. officer Our Primary Purpose, Des Moines, 1989-90, pres., chief exec. officer, 1990—. Bd. dirs. Oreg. Inst. Alcoholism Studies, Waldport, 1983—, vice chmn., 1988— Alcohol and Drug Counselor Cert. Bd. Oreg., 1986—; chmn. Shared Housing, Portland, 1984-86. Mem. Assn. Alcohol and Drug Counselors of Oreg. (bd. dirs. 1986—). Democrat. Avocations: computers, reading.

THORNTON, SYBIL ANNE, East Asian religions and history educator; b. Munich, Fed. Republic Germany, Dec. 18, 1950; d. Howard Lee and Irmgard Ottilie (Weber) T. BA, U. Calif., Berkeley, 1973; MA, San Fransisco State U., 1978, U. Cambridge (Eng.), 1984; PhD, U. Cambridge (Eng.), 1990. Vis. asst. prof. U. Mo., Columbia, 1990—. Contbr. articles to profl. publs. Grantee Asian Cultural Coun., 1985, Toyota Found., 1984-85. Mem. Am. Acad. Religion, Assn. for Asian Studies, Soc. for Study of Japanese Religions. Democrat. Office: U Mo Columbia Dept Hist 101 Read Hall Columbia MO 65211

THORNTON, THOMAS JAY, minister; b. Pitts., Aug. 28, 1951; s. James Thomas and Grace Lucille (Ferguson) T.; m. Denise A. Hricik, June 10, 1972; children: Bethani, Alyson, Emily, Ian. BA, Carnegie-Mellon U., 1973; MDiv, Princeton Theol. Sem., 1976. Ordained to ministry Presbyn. Ch. (USA), 1976. Assoc. pastor 1st Presbyn. Ch., Irwin, Pa., 1976-81; organizing pastor Beaver-Butler Presbytery, Mars, Pa., 1981-83; pastor Cranberry Community United Presbyn. Ch., Mars, 1983—; del. Synod of the Trinity, 1984; chairperson Presbytery Evangelism Com., 1989-90; mem. Presbytery New Ch. Devel. Task Force, 1990—. Mem. organizing com. Cranberry Crime Watch Program, Pa., 1985-86; commr. Cranberry Twp. Planning Commn., Pa., 1986—, sec., 1989, chairperson, 1991; mem. exec. com. Cranberry Eating Disorder Alliance, Pa., 1989—. Home: 101 Briarwood Ln Mars PA 16046 Office: Cranberry Community United Presbyn Ch 2662 Rochester Rd Mars PA 16046-9119

THORP, CHARLES PHILIP, minister; b. San Francisco, Nov. 27, 1949; s. Robert Jay and Natalie Ann (Lotti) T. Student, San Francisco State U., 1970-71, Diablo Valley Jr. Coll., 1983-84; PhD (hon.), Siberian Inst. Devel. Resources, USSR, 1979. Ordained minister The Church For Unity And Service, 1978. Cons. EST, San Francisco, 1973-75; counsellor SDSI, San Francisco, 1976-78; founder, minister The Church For Unity And Service, San Francisco, 1979—; cons. Rivendell Sch., San Francisco, 1976-78; host Radio Free Religion, Sta. KWUN, Concord, Calif., 1985. Author: Quotes from the Inner Door, Vol. 1-3, 1980-88. Mem. Child Abuse Coun. of Contra Costa County. Mem. Am. Humanist Assn. (counselor 1974-83), COAST User Group (pres. 1986-88, 90), San Francisco State GLF (founder, chmn. 1970-71), East Bay Macintosh User Group, Berkeley Macintosh User Group, Diablo Valley Apple User Group (contbr, mem. nat. claosed captions assn. 1991—), Am. Biog. Inst. (bd. govs.). Democrat. Mem. Progressive Charismatic. Avocations: computers, writing, watercolors, desktop pub., acting. Home and Office: 1015 Esther Dr Ste A Pleasant Hill CA 94523-4301

THORP, GLEN ALAN, minister; b. Santa Rosa, Calif., Oct. 28, 1944; s. Robert Clarendon and Bernice Augusta (Anderson) T.; m. Eugenia Eleanor Stewart, June 16, 1967. BA, Whitworth Coll., 1967; MDiv, Bethel Sem., St. Paul, 1971; D Ministry, San Francisco Theol. Sem., 1982. Ordained to ministry Presbyn. Ch. (U.S.A.), 1971. Pastor Bethany Presbyn. Ch., Mpls., 1971-77; assoc. pastor St. John's Presbyn. Ch., L.A., 1978-83; pastor North Presbyn. Ch., Denver, 1983-89; organizing pastor Santa Clarita (Calif.) Presbyn. Ch., 1989-91, pastor, 1991—; moderator radio program Minn. Coun. Chs., Mpls., 1972-73; pres. Westside Ecumenical Coun., Santa Monica, Calif., 1981-83; del. Gen. Assembly, Presbyn. Ch. (U.S.A.), Atlanta, 1983. Del. Rep. Party, Mpls., 1976, Denver, 1988; bd. dirs. New Horizons for Teenagers, Denver, 1987-89. Recipient cert. appreciation Westside Ecumenical Conf., 1983. Mem. Interfaith Coun., Presbytery of San Fernando, Alpha Psi Omega. Office: Santa Clarita Presbyn Ch PO Box 801507 Santa Clarita CA 91380-1507 *The short lives of our sons, Matthew Stewart and Jonathan David, taught us that "It is not what we do for God, rather what God has done for us (God's unconditional and transforming love) that gives us value as human beings."*

THORSEN, DONALD ARTHUR, theology educator; b. Turlock, Calif., Jan. 16, 1955; s. Rodney J.B. and Esther M. (Wells) T.; m. Cynthia Beth Drechsel, Oct. 5, 1985; children: Liesl Hope, Heidi Rose. BA, Stanford U., 1977; MDiv, Asbury Theol. Sem., 1980; ThM, Princeton Theol. Sem., 1982; MPhil, PhD, Drew U., 1984, 88. Adj. prof. Montclair State Coll., Upper Montclair, N.J., 1984-85; instr. in theology Asbury Theol. Sem., Wilmore, Ky., 1986-87; assoc. prof. Azusa (Calif.) Pacific U., 1988—; asst. dir. John Wesley Sem. Found., Azusa, 1988—; campus dir. John Wesley Inst., Azusa, 1988—; warden Bicentennial Consultation on Methodism and Ministry, Madison, N.J., 1982-83. Author: Theological Method in John Wesley, 1988, The Wesleyan Quadrilateral, 1990. Goethe Inst. grantee, 1982. Mem. Am. Acad. Religion, Am. Philos. Assn., Wesleyan Theol. Soc., Polanyi Soc., Theta Phi. Democrat. Free Methodist. Office: Azusa Pacific U PO Box A PU Azusa CA 91702-7000 *In seeking truth, empathy, in keeping justice, patience, in meeting judgement, mercy.*

THOTTUMKAL, THOMAS JOSEPH, priest; b. Kerala, India, Dec. 31, 1934; came to U.S., 1987; s. Joseph Chacko and Elizabeth Thomas (Thayil) T. BA, St. Paul Sem., India, 1966; STL, St. Paul U., 1968; ThM, U. Ottawa, Ont., Can., 1968; MA, McMaster U., 1970; ThD, U. Paris, 1971. Ordained priest Roman Catholic Ch., 1958. Prof. liturgy St. Paul Sem., Trichy, India, 1956-58; parish priest, superior Sophia Ashram and St. Joseph Ch., Kuttiadi, Kozhikode, India, 1959-62; novice master, counsellor Congregation Blessed Sacrament, Kerala, 1962-66; chaplain St. Joseph's Mother House, Hamilton, Ont., 1968-71; prof. theology Toronto (Ont.) Sch. Theology, 1971-86; dir. vocations Archdiocese of Toronto, 1975-80; vice rector St. Augustine's Sem., Toronto, 1976-86; pres. Wadhams Hall Sem.-Coll., Ogdensburg, N.Y., 1987—. Author: Nirchalukal, Palai, 1958, Virunnu, Mannanam, 1958, Priesthood and Apostleship, 1973, Ministry, 1982, People's Spirituality, 1983; mem. editorial bd. Jeevadhara, Aleppy, India. Mem. Coll. Theology Soc., Cath. Theol. Soc. Am. Home and Office: Wadhams Hall Sem-Coll RR 4 Box 80 Ogdensburg NY 13669 *My life is a day by day unfolding of myself to opportunities—like a flower bud opening up to sunlight, breeze, beauty, birds, bees-environments for progress and perpetuity.*

THRAILKILL, FRANCIS MARIE, college president; b. San Antonio, Sept. 21, 1937; d. Franklin E. and Myrtle M. (Huggins) T. B.A. cum laude, Coll. New Rochelle, N.Y., 1961; M.A., Marquette U., Milw., 1969; Ed.D., Nova U., Ft. Lauderdale, Fla., 1975. Joined Ursuline Order of Sisters, Roman Catholic Ch., 1955; tchr. Ursuline Acad., Dallas, 1961-64; prin. Ursuline Acad., 1970-77; vice prin. Ursuline Acad., New Orleans, 1965-70; pres. Springfield (Ill.) Coll., 1978-87, Coll. of Mt. St. Joseph, Ohio, 1987—. Trustee Community, Found. Ind. Colls., Little Miami Inc.; mem. Leadership Cin.; mem. edn. com. Cin. At Mus.; bd. dirs. Dan Beard Coun., Ursuline Acad., Cin. Assn. for Blind, Coun. Ind. Colls., Summit Country Day, Joy Outdoor Edn. Ctr., Community Mut. Blue Cross/Blue Shield. Mem. Assn. Cath. Colls. and Univs., Assn. Governing Bds. of Colls. and Univs., Assn. Ind. Colls. and Univs., Greater Cin. Corsortium Colls., Nat. Assn. Ind. Colls. and Univs., Ohio Bd. Regents, Council Ind. Colls. Office: Coll of Mt St Joseph Mount Saint Joseph OH 45051

THREADCRAFT, HAL LAW, III, counselor, pastor; b. Birmingham, Feb. 10, 1952; s. Hal L. Jr. and Helen Barbara (Foster) T.; m. Marion Lee Haygood, Aug. 18, 1973; children: Joshua, John Caleb, Anna. BSCE, U. Ala., 1975; ThM, Dallas Theol. Sem., 1979; MA, U. Ala., 1990, postgrad., 1991—. Lic. profl. counselor. Minister Young Life, Dallas, 1975-79; prof. Evangelische Theologische Facultait, Heverlee, Belgium, 1979-83; preacher at large Christian Brethren, Alberta, Can., 1983-85; sr. pastor Grace Chapel, Halifax, N.S., Can., 1985-88; counselor Christian Brethren, Tuscaloosa, Ala., 1989—; cons. Christian Brethren, Halifax, 1985-89, Edmonton, Alta., 1983-85, Ghent, Belgium, 1979-83; rep. student/faculty advisory behavioral studies U. Ala., 1989-90. Author: Apostle Paul's Principles of Church Growth, 1980. Mem. AACD, Internat. Assn. Marriage and Family Counselors, U. Ala. Counseling and Devel. Assn. (pres. 1989-90), Kappa Delta Pi, Phi Kappa Phi, Chi Sigma Iota. Home: 1213 King's Mountain Rd Tuscaloosa AL 35406

THREADGILL, CECIL RAYMOND, minister, counselor; b. Mt. Vernon, Ala., June 15, 1925; s. Daniel George and Addie Gertrude (Oliver) T.; m. Bonnie Jeanne Wise, June 2, 1946; children: Gloria Jeanne, Gay Dean. AA, Jacksonville Coll., 1949; BA, Baylor U., 1951; postgrad., Tex. Christian U., 1957, U. North Tex., 1960-61, U. Md., 1967-68; MDiv, Southwestern Bapt. Theol. Sem., 1973; postgrad., San Francisco Theol Sem., 1978-79; DEd, New Orleans Bapt. Theol. Sem., 1983; postgrad., U. of Sci. and Arts of Okla., 1987-88, Tex. Women's U., 1991. Ordained to ministry So. Bapt. Conv., 1946; lic. profl. counselor, Okla., Tex. Pastor Bapt. chs., Tex., 1947-54, Plainview Bapt. Ch., Krum, Tex., 1958-59, Calvary Bapt. Ch., Pilot Point, Tex., 1959-61; lt. (j.g.), chaplain USN, 1961, advanced through grades to lt. comdr.; ret., 1982; dir. student affairs and ch.-min. rels. New Orleans Bapt. Sem., 1982-83; dir. Counseling-Edn. Ctr., Grady Bapt. Assn., Chickasha, Okla., 1984-88; pastor Michigan Avenue Bapt. Ch., Chickasha, 1988-90, Antioch Bapt. Ch., Aubrey, Tex., 1990—; mem. Christian life com. Denton (Tex.) Bapt. Assn., 1990-91. With USMCR, 1944-46, PTO. Decorated Purple Heart. Mem. Am. Assn. for Marriage and Family Therapy (clin.). Republican. Home and Office: 308 E Main St PO Box 1236 Pilot Point TX 76258 *I am deeply grateful to God for the privilege of being a part of His creation that challenges me to keep reaching beyond my grasp as I grow in His likeness in love for and service to others.*

THROCKMORTON, HAMILTON COE, minister; b. Bangor, Maine, Jan. 15, 1955; s. Burton Hamilton and Ansley (Coe) T.; m. Mary M. Senechal, July 5, 1987; children: Alexander, Taylor. BA, Williams Coll., 1977; MDiv, Bangor Theol. Sem., 1987. Ordained to ministry United Ch. of Christ, 1988. Pastor Old Brick Ch., Old Meeting House, East Montpelier, Vt., 1987—. Bd. dirs. Habibat for Humanity, Cen. Vt., Montpelier, 1989—. Office: The Old Brick Ch and The Old Meeting House PO Box 38 East Montpelier VT 05651

THROENER, MARY ELLA, religious education director; b. Norfolk, Nebr., July 18, 1949; d. Gerald Edward and Mable Geneva (Robbins) Clinch; m. Lawrence Herman Throener, July 6, 1968; children: Lori, Loretta, Kathy, MaryMae, LaDonna, Christina. Dipl. Ministry, U. Coll. Creighton, Omaha, 1990. Sec. religious end. Sacred Heart Parish, Norfolk, Nebr., 1985-86, dir. religious edn., 1986—; coord. Rainbows for All of God's Children, Norfolk, 1991—; mem. Catechist Cert. Bd., Omaha, 1990—; team presentor Cath. Engaged Encounter, Norfolk, 1979—; Norfolk site coord. U. Coll. Creighton. Home: RR 2 Box 020 Norfolk NE 68701 Office: Sacred Heart Parish 204 S 5th St Norfolk NE 68701 *The value and appreciation one has for life is exemplified in their creative and productive responses to each moment.*

THROOP, JOHN ROBERT, minister; b. Evanston, Ill., June 10, 1956; s. Robert Smith Jr. and Catherine Ann (Nelson) T.; divorced; children: Sarah, Emilie. Student, U. Redlands, 1973-74; BA, U. Chgo., 1978; MDiv, U. of the South, 1981. Ordained to ministry Episcopal Ch. as deacon, 1981, as priest, 1981. Curate St. Simon's Episcopal Ch., Arlington Heights, Ill., 1981-83; rector Ch. The Mediator, Chgo., 1983-85; assoc. rector Christ Episcopal Ch., Shaker Heights, Ohio, 1985-87; exec. dir. Episcopalians United, Shaker Heights, 1987-89; vicar St. Francis Episcopal Ch., Chillicothe, Ill., 1989—; chmn. evangelism commn. Diocese of Quincy, Peoria, Ill., 1989—, alt. dep. gen. conv., 1991; spiritual dir. Encounter with Christ, Springfield, Ill., 1989—; scholar in residence Community of Cross of Nails, Coventry (Eng.) Cathedral, 1980. Author: Shaping Up from the Inside Out, 1986, Dealing with Suicide, 1988; contbr. articles to profl. jours. Roothbert fellow, 1978-81. Mem. Illinois Valley Ministerial Assn. (convener 1990-91), Rotary (pres. Chillicothe club 1991—). Republican. Home: 303 S Hollybrook Dr Chillicothe IL 61523 Office: St Francis Episcopal Ch 616 Wilmot St Chillicothe IL 61523

THROWER, GREGORY MICHAEL (MIKE THROWER), minister; b. Columbus, Miss., Jan. 17, 1950; s. Thomas Clyde and Mary Lou (Stimpson) T.; m. Ettie Frances Markel, Sept. 24, 1970; children: Bethany Ann, Danielle Elaine. BA, Miss. Coll., 1972; MDiv, New Orleans Bapt. Theol. Sem., 1974. Ordained to ministry So. Bapt. Conv., 1974. Pastor Thomastown (Miss.) Bapt. Ch., 1974-77, Sunflower (Miss.) Bapt. Ch., 1977-81, Brunswick (Tenn.) Bapt. Ch., 1981—. Contbr. articles to profl. jours. Pres. Arlington (Tenn.) Elem. Sch. PTA, 1990—. Mem. Tenn. Bapt. Conv. (exec. bd. 1990—), Pastors Conf. (program chmn. fall 1985), Shelby Bapt. Assn. (chmn. various coms. 1981—). Home: PO Box 96 Brunswick TN 38014-0096 Office: Brunswick Bapt Ch 5079 Brunswick Rd Brunswick TN 38014-0098

THULLBERY, MARION FRANCIS, minister; b. Lake Wales, Fla., Nov. 22, 1954; s. Alfred Charles and Betty Frances Thullbery. BA, Erskine Coll., 1976; MDiv, Trinity Sem., Ambridge, Pa., 1984. Curate St. Richards Episcopal Ch., Winter Park, Fla., 1984-87; vicar Hope Episcopal Ch., Melbourne, Fla., 1987-90; asst. rector All Sts. Episcopal Ch., Enterprise, Fla., 1990—. Office: All Saints Episcopal Ch 155 Clark St Enterprise FL 32725

THUNDER, SUZANNE JEANNETTE, radio news director; b. Kansas City, Mo., Jan. 5, 1958; d. Eugene Earl Harvey and Edwina Betty ann (Swanson) Strickland; m. Scott Kevin Thunder, May 23, 1987; 1 child, Seth Kyle. BA in Communication, Western Wash. U., 1980. News anchor Sta. KCIS/KCMS Radio, CRISTA Broadcast, Seattle, 1985-87, news. dir., talk show host, producer, 1987—.

THURSBY, GENE ROBERT, religion educator, consultant; b. Akron, Ohio, May 8, 1939; s. Gene Faye Thursby and Mariella (Icenhower) Newman; m. Linda E. Olds, May 16, 1988. AB, Oberlin Coll., 1961, MDiv, 1964; PhD, Duke U., 1972; postgrad., Grad. Theol. Union, 1987, Yale U., 1991. Ordained to ministry United Ch. of Christ, 1964. Instr. Duke U., Durham, N.C., 1967-68; asst. prof. religion U. Fla., Gainesville, 1970-75, assoc. prof., 1976—. Author: Hindu-Muslim Relations, 1975, The Sikhs, 1991; editor: Zen und Die Wiederentdeckung des Offensichtlichen, 1986; contbr. articles to profl. jours. Fulbright fellow, 1968-69; grantee NEH, 1985, 87, 89, 91, So. Regional Edn. Bd., 1989. Fellow Royal Asiatic Soc. (life), Buddhist Soc. (life), Internat. Assn. for Asian Studies; mem. Soc. for Sci. Study Religion (rsch. award 1989-90), Am. Acad. Religion (rsch. award 1988-89), Assn. for Asian Studies. Avocations: bicycling, hiking. Office: U Fla 125 Dauer Hall Gainesville FL 32611-2005

THURSTON, BONNIE BOWMAN, religion educator, minister; b. Bluefield, W.Va., Oct. 5, 1952; d. Ernest Venoy and Eleanor Sabina (King) Bowman; m. Burton Bradford Thurston, May 29, 1980 (dec. Nov. 1990). BA summa cum laude, Bethany Coll., 1974; MA, U. Va., 1975, PhD, 1979; postgrad. Eberhard Karls U., Fed. Republic Germany, 1983-84. Ordained to ministry Disciples of Christ Ch., 1984. Instr., asst. dean U. Va., Charlottesville, 1979-80; adj. prof. Wheeling Coll. (name now Wheeling Jesuit Coll.), W.Va. 1980-81, asoc. prof., chair dept. theology, 1985—; asst. prof. Bethany Coll., W.Va., 1981-83; vis. scholar Harvard U. Div. Sch., Cambridge, 1983; tutor Inst. Study of Christian Origins, Tübingen, Fed. Republic Germany, 1983-85; co-pastor Knoxville Ch., Pitts., 1982-83, Taylorstown Christian Ch., 1985-88; lectr. Sch. Religion, Council of Chs., Wheeling, 1980-81, 85-90. Author: The Widows, 1989, Wait Here and Watch., 1989; contbr. articles to profl. jours. Mem. Fellowship of Reconciliation. Dupont fellow 1975-76. Mem. Cath. Bibl. Assn. , Soc. Bibl. Lit. (chmn. sect. 1984), Internat. Thomas Merton Soc. (pres.), Soc. for Buddhist-Christian Studies (bd. dirs.), Disciples Hist. Soc. Republican. Avocations: gardening, music, cooking. Home: 260 GC and P Rd Wheeling WV 26003 Office: Wheeling Jesuit Coll Dept Theology Wheeling WV 26003

THURSTON, ELWYN ODELL, minister; b. Sperry, Okla., Aug. 4, 1922; s. Clarence Ralph and Bessie Loren (Parish) T.; m. Betty L. Fant, June 4, 1972; children: Mary Elaine, Robert E., Rickey L. Student, Okla. State U., 1940-41; AB, Southern Meth. U., 1944; BD, Perkins Sch. Theology, Dallas, 1947; DD (hon.), Oklahoma City U., 1980. Pastor United Meth. Ch. of Okla., 1946-76; dist. supt. Woodward (Okla.) Dist. United Meth. Ch., 1976-81; exec. dir. Okla. United Meth. Found., Oklahoma City, 1981—. Trustee, Oklahoma City U., 1976—.. Home: 14901 N Pennsylvania # 315 Oklahoma City OK 73134 Office: Okla United Meth Found 2420 N Blackwelder Oklahoma City OK 79112

THURSTON, STEPHEN JOHN, pastor; b. Chgo., July 20, 1952; s. John Lee and Ruth (Hall) T.; m. Joyce DeVonne Hand, June 18, 1977; children: Stephen John II, Nicole D'Vaugh, Teniece Rael, Christian Avery Elijah. BA in Religion, Bishop Coll., 1975; Hon. degree, Chgo. Baptist Inst., 1986. Copastor New Covenant Missionary Bapt. Ch., Chgo., 1975-79, pastor, 1979—; corr. sec. Nat. Bapt. Conv. Am., mem. exec. com. Christian Edn. Congress; exec. v.p. Ill. Nat. Bapt. State Conv.; mem. Northwood River Dist. Bapt. Assn.; lectr. various orgns.; instr. New Covenant Bapt. Ch., Fellowship Bapt. Ch. Mng. editor The Crier (Nat. Bapt. Conv. Am. Evangelical Bd. quarterly pub.). Co-chmn. religious affairs div. Operation People United to Save Humanity (PUSH); bd. dirs. nat. alumni assn. Bishop Coll.; active NAACP; trustee, fin. chmn. Chgo. Bapt. Inst.; mem. Campus Crusade for Christ, Here's Life Black Am. Mem. Broadcast Ministers Alliance, Bapt. Ministers Conf. Chgo. (Ministerial Pioneer award). Club: Bishop Coll. (Chgo.). Office: New Covenant Missionary Bapt Ch 740 E 77th St Chicago IL 60619

THURSTON, THOMAS MICHAEL, writer; b. Ft. Wayne, Ind., June 25, 1951; s. William Harley and Rosemary Elizabeth (Risk) T. BA, Christian Bros. Coll., 1973; MA, St. Louis U., 1977; PhD, Grad. Theol. Union, Berkeley, Calif., 1989. Tchr. religion Roncalli High Sch., Omaha, 1973-76; tchr. religion, chmn. dept. Bishop Kelley High Sch., Tulsa, 1976-79; asst. prof. theology De La Salle U., Manila, Philippines, 1979-82; subdir. scholastics Christian Bros. Scholasticate, Manila, 1980-81; freelance writer San Francisco, 1989—; adj. prof. St. Mary's Coll., Moraga, Calif., 1990—. Author: Chosen People/Promised Land, 1981, I Have Seen the Lord, 1982; mem. editorial bd. Jour. Homosexuality, 1990—. Vol. Refugee Resettlement Program, Memphis, 1983; del. Archdiocesean Pastoral Coun., Roman Cath. Ch., Omaha, 1973-74; theologian, mem. task force for gay/lesbian outreach Cath. Diocese Oakland (Calif.), 1990—. Mem. Am. Acad. Religion (mem. steering com. group on gay men's issues in religion 1989—), Cath. Theol. Soc. Am., Com. Gay and Lesbian History. Democrat. Home and Office: 165 Divisadero St San Francisco CA 94117

TICE, TERRENCE NELSON, philosopher, educator; b. Beloit, Kans., Dec. 1, 1931; s. William Nelson and Georgia Catherine (Buck) T.; divorced; children: Karin, Jonathan. BA, U. Ariz., 1953; MDiv, Princeton Theol. Sem., 1957, ThD, 1961; PhD in Philosophy, U. Mich., 1970. Theol. sec. World Alliance of Reformed Chs., Geneva, 1962-65; prof. philosophy and religion Ctr. Coll. of Ky., Danville, 1961-62; prof. philosophy Sch. of Edn. U. Mich., Ann Arbor, 1970—; affiliate faculty mem. doctoral program in urban, tech., and environ. planning U. Mich., Ann Arbor, 1970—. Author: Research Guide to Philosophy, 1983 (Outstanding Acad. Book award 1983, ALA Reference Book award 1983), also over 35 other books; editor, translator: On Religion (by Friedrich Schleiermacher), 1969 (Outstanding Acad. Book award 1969); contbr. numerous articles to profl. jours. Bd. dirs. Ecumenical Campus Ctr., Ann Arbor, 1966—. Mem. Am. Acad. Religion, Internat. Schleiermacher Assn. (chair 1990—), Schleiermacher Soc. Am. (chair 1989—). Presbyterian. Home: 2040 Columbia Ann Arbor MI 48104

TICE, WILLIAM FLEET, JR., pastor; b. Rockford, Ill., Aug. 20, 1942; s. William Fleet and June Edna (Clark) T.; m. Martha Elizabeth Robertson, June 8, 1963; children: Elizabeth Ann, Belinda Sue, William Fleet III. BA in Religion, Ind. Wesleyan U., 1964; postgrad., Loyola U., New Orleans, 1989—. Ordained to ministry Wesleyan Ch., 1966. Minister Sims (Ind.) Meth. Ch., 1963-64; asst. pastor 1st Wesleyan Ch., Waterloo, Iowa, 1964-66; minister, chaplain Oak Hills Wesleyan Ch./Mayo Clinic, Rochester, Minn., 1966-70; sr. pastor Wheaton (Ill.) Wesleyan Ch., 1970-73, 1st Wesleyan Ch., Bossier City, La., 1973—; prs. Rochester Ministerial Alliance, 1968-70, Bossier City Ministerial Alliance, 1975-78; dist. bd. advisors Delta Dist. Wesleyan Ch., Jackson, Miss., 1983—, dist. sec., 1987—. Pres. Bossier City Kiwanis Club, 1976, Bossier City Clean City Com., 1987; trustee Bossier Med. Ctr., Bossier City, 1980; mem. human concerns com. Priorities for the Future, La., 1978. Mem. Kiwanis (founder South Bossier club 1982). Republican. Home: 125 Oaklawn Dr Bossier City LA 71112 Office: 1st Wesleyan Ch 3200 Schuler Dr Bossier City LA 71112 *A personal, freely chosen, responsible faith; a faith continually formed from sources in the experience of life and of God, is the ultimate experience of life and of God.*

TIDIANE TRAORE, AHMED, religious organization administrator. Sec. gen. Islamic League, Conakry, Guinea. Office: Islamic League, Conakry Guinea*

TIDWELL, HAROLD RODNEY, minister; b. Alexander, Ala., July 22, 1957; s. George Harold and Mary Frances (Baker) T. m. Deborah Ann Smith, Aug. 18, 1974; children: Christopher Aaron, Benjamin Isaac. AA, Ala. Christian Coll., 1980; postgrad., Faulkner U., 1981-83, Ala. Christian Sch. Religion, 1985-86, 91. Ordained to ministry Ch. of Christ, 1979. Youth assoc. minister Alexander City Ch. of Christ, 1978-80; pulpit minister Dadeville (Ala.) Ch. of Christ, 1980-82; youth minister Alexander City Ch. of Christ, 1982-83, Tallassee (Ala.) Ch. of Christ, 1983-85; pulpit minister Hamilton Crossroads Ch. of Christ, Brundidge, Ala., 1987—; bd. dirs. Wiregrass Christian Youth Camp, Enterprise, Ala., 1984—, Collegedale Christiana Sch., Troy, 1988—; mem. adv. bd. Sta. WLBF Christian Radio, Montgomery, Ala., 1985-87. PTO pres. Pike County Elem. Sch., Brundidge, 1989-91. Mem. Pike County Ministerial Assn. Republican. Home: Rte 2 Box 311-A Brundidge AL 36010 Office: Hamilton Crossroads Ch of Christ Rte 2 Box 311-AA Brundidge AL 36010

TIDWELL, LLOYD DAVID, minister, editor; b. Ft Smith, Ark., Mar. 4, 1939; s. Benjamin Harrison and Eula Pearl (Thompson) T.; m. Barbara Jean Wesson, Dec. 18, 1958; children: Benjamin Louie, Rejeana Jo. Student, U. So. Ark., Magnolia, 1960-62, Cen. Bapt. Coll., Conway, Ark., 1957-60. Ordained to ministry Bapt. Missionary Assn., 1956. Pastor County Line Bapt. Ch., Nashville, Ark., 1957-60, Brister Bapt. Ch., Emerson, Ark., 1960-62, Sky Lake Bapt. Ch., Memphis, 1962-69; editor, mgr. Bapt. Trumpet, Little Rock, 1969—; trustee Cen. Bapt. Coll., Conway, Bapt. Pub. Com., Texarkana, Ark.; clk. Bapt. Missionary Assn. of Ark. Office: Baptist Trumpet 10712 Interstate # 30 Little Rock AR 72219-2209

TIEDE, DAVID L., minister, seminary administrator; b. St. Peter, Minn., June 29, 1940; s. John and Vivan (Ulvestad) T.; m. Martha Tiede; children: Peter, Kathryn. Grad., St. Olaf Coll., 1962; BD, Luther Sem., 1966; PhD, Harvard U., 1971; postgrad., Claremont Grad. Sch., Yale Div. Sch. Asst. prof. Scripps Coll., 1970-71, Claremont Grad. Sch., 1970-71; pres., prof. Luther Northwestern Theol. Sem., St. Paul, 1971—; vis. prof. Claremont Grad. Sch., 1978-79. Rockefeller fellow, Danforth fellow. Fellow Am. Theol. Soc.; mem. Soc. Bibl. Lit., Cath. Bibl. Assn., Studiorum Novi Testamenti Societas. Office: Luther Northwestern Theol Sem 2481 Como Ave Saint Paul MN 55108*

TIEMSTRA, JOHN PETER, economics educator; b. Chgo., July 15, 1950; s. Peter John and Margaret (Lamont) T.; m. Suzanne Spicer, Dec. 28, 1985; 1 stepchild: Remi Spicer. AB, Oberlin Coll., 1971; PhD, MIT, 1975. Asst. prof. econs. Calvin Coll., Grand Rapids, Mich., 1975-81, assoc. prof., 1981-85, prof., 1985—. Editor, co-author: Reforming Economics, 1990; contbr. articles to profl. jours. Dean Grand Rapids Am. Guild of Organists, 1990-91; pres. West Mich. Irish Heritage Soc., Grand Rapids, 1988-91, Forest Hills Condo Assn., Cascade, Mich., 1988-91. Mem. Assn. for Social Econs., Assn. of Christian Economists, Am. Econ. Assn. Christian Reformed. Avocation: folk music. Office: Calvin Coll 3201 Burton St SE Grand Rapids MI 49546 *Simple competence or skill is usually easy to find or at least to develop. What is much harder is to find a basis in shared values that can lead to a powerful relationship.*

TIERNAN, LINDA KAY, radio station executive, educator; b. Belleville, Ill., Aug. 15, 1947; d. Robert Barrow and Mary Elizabeth (Harding) O'Neal; m. Robert Tiernan, Aug. 7, 1971 (div. Apr. 1978); children: Erin Elizabeth, Jessie Colene. BS in Edn., So. Ill. U., 1969; postgrad. in psychology, Fielding Inst., Santa Barbara, Calif., 1980-81. Tchr. various elem. schs., St. Clair County, Ill., 1969-73; tng. coord. May Co. Dept. Stores, St. Louis, 1973-75; family counselor Miami County Juvenile Ct., Shelby, Ohio, 1975-78; therapist Shiloha Ctr. for Human Growth, Dayton, Ohio, 1978-80; saleswoman, sales mgr. Sta. WCBW-FM, St. Louis, 1981-82, gen. mgr., v.p., 1982—; mem. adv. bd. Lewis and Clark Community Coll., Alton, Ill., 1982-88; mem. adj. faculty Mo. Bapt. Coll., St. Louis, 1988—, bd. dirs. Living Praise Ministries, 1984-89; sec. bd. dirs. New Image Ministries, St. Louis, 1988—; mem. steering com. Nat. Christian Radio Seminar, 1986—; condr. workshop Women in Christian Media Conv., 1989. Vice pres. bd. dirs. Metro Christian Sch. Parent Tchrs. Fedn., St. Louis, 1987. Mem. Gospel Music Assn. (dove week com. 1988-89), Nat. Religious Broadcasters Assn., Nat. Assn. Evangs. (Ill. bd. dirs. 1990—). Pentecostal. Avocations: painting, reading, skiing, cooking. Office: Sta WCBW-FM 4121 Union Rd Ste 201 Saint Louis MO 63129

TIERNEY, PATRICIA A., school system administrator. Supt. schs. Diocese of St. Augustine, Jacksonville, Fla. Office: Office Supt Schs Po Box 24000 Jacksonville FL 32241*

TIGAY, ALAN MERRILL, editor; b. Detroit, June 23, 1947; s. Leonard and Ethel (Cooper) T.; m. Lois Kathryn Carlson, Dec. 27, 1970; 1 child, Rafael Leonard. B.A. in Sociology, U. Mich., 1969; M.S. in Journalism, Columbia U., 1976. Feature writer United Feature Syndicate, N.Y.C., 1976-78; editor-in-chief Near East Report, Washington, 1978-80; exec. editor Hadassah Mag., N.Y.C., 1980—; judge Nat. Mag. Awards, 1981—, Nat. Jewish Book Awards, 1988—; adminstr. Harold U. Ribalow prize, 1983—. Editor: The Jewish Traveler, 1987, Myths and Facts: A Concise Record of the Arab-Israeli Conflict, 1978, 2d edit., 1980; free-lance writer various N.Y. and nat. newspapers, mags., 1972—. Pres., vol. Owners Corp., N.Y.C., 1982-86; vol. Partnership for Homeless Rodeph Sholom Winter Shelter Program, N.Y.C., 1983-85, Interfaith Hospitality Network, Montclair, N.J., 1988—. Mem. Am. Soc. Mag. Editors, Am. Jewish Press Assn. Avocation: collecting newspapers. Office: Hadassah Mag 50 W 58th St New York NY 10019

TILLARD, JEAN MARIE ROGER, theology educator, ecumenist; b. St. Pierre, France, Sept. 2, 1927; came to Can., 1959; s. Ferdinand and Madeleine (Ferron) T. Ph.D., Angelicum, Rome, 1953; Ph.D., Le Saulchoir, Paris, 1958; Magisterium in Div., Rome, 1963; Ph.D. in Div., Trinity Coll., Toronto, 1980; Ph.D. in Theology, St. Michael's U., Toronto, 1983. Prof. div. Dominican Faculty of Theology, Ottawa, Ont., Can., 1959—; invited prof. Oxford U., Fribourg, Quebec, Nottingham, Geneva; cons. to Vatican's Secretariate for Christian Unity, 1968—; prof. theology Dominican U., Ottawa, 1959—; mem. Internat. Roman Catholic and Anglican Commn., Internat. Roman Catholic and Orthodox Commn., v.p. Faith and Order. Author: L'Eucharistie Paque de L'Eglise, 1965; The Bishop of Rome, 1982, Eglise d'Eglises, 1987. Home: 96 Empress, Ottawa, ON Canada K1R 7G3 Office: Faculty of Theology, 96 Empress, Ottawa, ON Canada K1R 7G3 *I am more and more convinced that our societies are suffering from the crisis of truth. On very basic issues it becomes impossible to know where the truth is!.*

TILLER, CARL WILLIAM, lecturer, retired church official and government executive; b. Battle Lake, Minn., Sept. 25, 1915; s. Carl J(ohn) and Edith (Wells) T.; m. Olive M. Foerster, June 21, 1940; children: Robert W., Jeanne L. (Mrs. John E. Peterson). BA summa cum laude, Concordia Coll., Moorhead, Minn., 1935, LLD, 1966; MA in Pub. Adminstrn., U. Minn., 1940. Budget sec., examiner Minn., 1936-41; exec. asst. to dir. Mcpl. Fin. Officers Assn., 1941-42; with U.S. Office of Mgmt. and Budget, 1942-72, spl. adviser budgetary devel., 1967-72; adj. prof. Am. U., 1952-70; assoc. sec. Bapt. World Alliance, Washington, 1972-78; dir. Interchurch Ctr., N.Y.C., 1978-80, pres. and exec. dir., 1980-86; dir. of libr. Am. Bapt. Hist. Soc., Rochester, N.Y., 1987-88; free lance writer, lectr., 1988-91; v/p. Twin City Bapt. Union, 1937-41; moderator Twin City Bapt. Assn., 1939-41; mem. gen. bd. Nat. Coun. Chs., 1964-75, treas., 1970-75; mem. gen. coun. Am. Bapt. Conv., 1946-53, 54-60, 63-68, pres., 1966-67; Western treas. Bapt. World Alliance, 1956-72, assoc. sec., 1972-78, rep. to UN, 1981-89; sec. N.Am. Bapt. Fellowship, 1972-78, pres. D.C. Bapt. Conv., 1969-70; v.p. CARE Inc., 1972-78; mem. gen. bd. Am. Bapt. Chs. U.S.A., 1982-85, mem. com. on Christian unity, 1982-85, mem. bd. ednl. ministries, 1982-85. Author: The Twentieth Century Baptist, 1980; contbr. articles to profl. jours. Active Am. Cancer Soc.; bd. dirs. Luther Rice Coll., 1971-77, chmn., 1973-76; bd. dirs. Japan Internat. Christian U. Found., treas., 1982-85; bd. dirs. Nat. Interreligious Svc. Bd. for Conscientious Objectors, 1983-91, treas., 1988-91. Recipient Dahlberg Peace award Am. Bapt. Chs. U.S.A., 1991. Mem. Am. Polit. Sci. Assn., Am. Soc. Pub. Adminstrn., Am. Acctg. Assn., Am. Bapt. Hist. Soc. (pres. 1982-85), Assn. Govt. Accts. Avocations: philately, genealogy, baseball statistics. Home: 100 Norman Dr Apt 217 Mars PA 16046

TILLER, ROBERT WELLS, minister, government relations specialist; b. St. Paul, July 20, 1941; s. Carl William and Olive Marie (Foerster) T.; m. Dora Elaine Cremer, Sept. 5, 1964; children: Nathan, Caleb. BA, Ottawa U., 1962; MDiv, Yale U., 1966, M in Urban Studies, 1967. Ordained to ministry Am. Bapt. Chs. in U.S.A., 1967. Pastor Mariners' Temple Bapt. Ch., N.Y.C., 1967-72; dep. dist. mgr. Office Neighborhood Govt., Mayor's Office, N.Y.C., 1972-74, dist. mgr., 1974-77; sr. planner Dept. of City Planning, N.Y.C., 1977-78; housing dir. Prospect Heights Neighborhood Corp., Bklyn., 1978-79; policy adv. Office of Govtl. Rels., Am. Bapt. Chs. in U.S.A., Washington, 1979-82, dir., 1982—; bd. dirs. Bapt. Joint Com. on Pub. Affairs, Washington, 1982—, Chs. Ctr. for Theology and Pub. Policy, Washington, 1990—; lectr. Cen. Bapt. Sem., Kansas City, Kans., 1991. Contbr. articles to religious jours. Mem. Am. Bapt. Mins. Coun. Avocation: golf. Home: 208 E Indian Spring Dr Silver Spring MD 20901 Office: Am Bapt Chs USA 110 Maryland Ave NE Washington DC 20002

TILLEY, DORIS RUTH BELK, lay worker, retired army office secretary; b. Lancaster, Pa., July 7, 1924; d. Reece Griffin and Ruth Domer (Grim) Belk; m. Preston Roland Tilley, Feb. 22, 1947; children: Clifford Roland, Doris Anne Tilley Hair. Student, King's Bus. Coll., Charlotte, N.C., 1941-42, Duke U., 1974-76. Mem. ch. women St. Paul's Luth. Ch., Durham, N.C., 1950—, circle chmn., 1988, tch. Sunday sch., 1959-69, sec., treas., 1955-59, historian, 1973—, chmn. various coms., 1976—, sec. meml. garden bd., 1991—; sec. U.S. Army Rsch. Office, Durham, N.C., 1956-72, ret., 1972; sec. communications com. N.C. synod Luth. Ch. in Am., Salisbury, 1977-85; staff mem. Synod Conv. Press, Radio and TV Office, Hickory, N.C., 1979-85. Author: Sixty Years with the People of St. Paul's Lutheran Church, Durham, N.C. (1923-83), 1983; also articles. Treas. Holt Sch. PTA, Durham, 1963-64, No. High Sch. Band Boosters, Durham, 1965-66; trustee No. High Sch. Meml. Fund for Band Dir., 1966-67; mem. Hist. Preservation Soc., Durham, 1975—, chmn. old cemeteries com., 1978-85. Bartlett Durham award Hist. Preservation Soc. Durham, 1987. Mem. Nat. Assn. Ret. Fed. Employees (chmn. pub. com. 1976-79). Democrat. Home: 4620 Guess Rd Durham NC 27712 *I believe, and I have found, that individuals must find their peace with God, and convey this peace to all with whom they come in contact. This is the beginning of healing and peace for individuals, communities and nations.*

TILLEY, MARCUS RANDALL, minister; b. Durham, N.C., Nov. 14, 1960; s. Dolphus Ebert and Nancy Elizabeth (Thomas) T.; m. Candis Elaine Kimrey, Aug. 4, 1984; 1 child, Kathryn Elizabeth. BS in Mech. Engrin., N.C. State U., 1983; MDiv magna cum laude, Mid-Am. Bapt. Theol. Sem., 1986. Ordained to ministry Bapt. Ch., 1986. Assoc. pastor Longcrest Bapt. Ch., Memphis, 1984-86; pastor Huggins Meml. Bapt. Ch., Harkers Island, N.C., 1987-88, Union Hope Bapt. Ch., Zebulon, N.C., 1988—. Recipient Durham Engrs. Club award, 1979. Republican. Home and Office: Rte 1 Box 115-A Zebulon NC 27597

TILLEY, TERRENCE WILLIAM, religion educator; b. Milw., Apr. 19, 1947; s. John C. and Audrey A. (Kau) T.; m. Maureen Antonia Molloy, Dec. 27, 1969; children: Elena, Christine. AB, U. San Francisco, 1970; PhD, Grad. Theol. Union, 1976. Asst. prof. theology Georgetown U., Washington, 1976-79; from asst. to assoc. prof. religious studies St. Michael's Coll., Winooski, Vt., 1979-89; from assoc. prof. to full prof. religion Fla. State U., Tallahassee, 1989—; dir. seminars NEH, 1987, 90. Author: Talking of God, 1978, Story Theology, 1985 (Book of Yr., Coll. Theology Soc. 1986), The Evils of Theodicy, 1991. NEH fellow, 1987-88. Mem. AAUP, Am. Acad. Religion, Coll. Theology Soc. (conv. dir. 1988—), Cath. Theol. Soc. Am., Soc. Christian Philosophers, Soc. for Philosophy of Religion. Roman Catholic. Office: Fla State U Religion Dept Tallahassee FL 32306

TILLY, LOIS AMELIA, music minister; b. Chgo., Jan. 27; d. Andrew Thomas and Leona (Arsheal) T. BS, So. U., Baton Rouge, 1969; MA, Xavier U., New Orleans, 1979. Organist, dir. Mt. Zion Missionary Bapt. Ch., New Orleans, 1955—; min. music Cen. Missionary Bapt. Ch., New Orleans, 1961—; itinerant vocal music tchr. Orleans Parish Sch. Bd., New Orleans, 1979—; asst. organist Ideal Bapt. Chorus, Edn. Assn. Chorus, 1988—, Nat. Bapt. Conv. U.S.A. Inc. Musical, New Orleans, 1978, 88, 90; clinician ch. music workshops, 1980—; organist for inceptional meeting of the SCLC. Author: Guidelines for a Church-Music Workshop, 1983, Teaching Piano and Beginner Theory in Elementary School, 1990, A Survival Kit for Quick Learning for the Elementary School, 1990, A Quick Way to Play Piano, 1990. Recipient Pioneer award Gospel Music Workshop, 1986, Recognition award New Orleans City Coun., 1989, Trailblazer award New Orleans Gospel and Jazz Heritage Found., 1991; Lois A. Tilly Day proclaimed by New Orleans City Coun., 1987. Mem. Am. Choral Dir. Assn., Music Educators Nat. Conf., Music Tchrs. Nat. Assn., Choirister's Guild, Nat. Bapt. Conf. Am., U.S.A. Inc. Woman's Conv., Ideal Miis Bapt. and Edn. Assn. Woman's Aux. Democrat. Home: PO Box 3442 New Orleans LA 70177

TILMAN, DAVID FRANK, cantor; b. Albany, N.Y., Sept. 14, 1944; s. Alexander Robert and Hannah (Brucker) T.; m. Ellen Ann Rosenberg, Apr. 13, 1981; children: Avrum Michael, Howard Jonah, Alana Miriam. BA, Columbia U., 1966; B in Sacred Music, diploma of Hazzan, Jewish Theol. Sem., 1971; MusM, Juilliard Sch., 1975. Asst. cantor Park Ave Synagogue, N.Y.C., 1969-75; cantor, music dir. Beth Sholom Congregation, Elkins Park, Pa., 1975—; instr. of Jewish music edn. Cantors' Inst., Jewish Theol. Sem., N.Y.C., 1974-85; instr. of Jewish music Reconstructionist Rabbinical Coll., Wyncote, Pa., 1984—; instr. of synagogue skills and Jewish music Solomon Schechter Day Sch., Melrose Park, Pa., 1985—; summer music dir. Brandeis-Bardin Inst., Simi Valley, Calif., 1976-78, 83-89; condr., music dir. concerts Beth Sholom Youth Chorale, Beth Sholom Adult Chorale; guest condr. Philly Pops Symphony Orch., 1985, 86, 88. Condr. for classical recs. Recipient Solomon Schechter award United Synagogue Am., 1977, 83, 87. Mem. Cantors' Assembly of Am., Cantors' Assembly of Delaware Valley (pres. 1980-81, music dir., condr. 1979—). Home: 1096 Sparrow Rd Jenkintown PA 19046 Office: Beth Sholom Congregation Old York & Foxcroft Rds Elkins Park PA 19117

TILMAN, ELLEN ROSENBERG, religious school educator; b. N.Y.C., May 26, 1949; d. Sidney S. and Theda (Portnow) Rosenberg; m. David Frank Tilman, Apr. 13, 1981; children: Avrum Michael, Howard Jonah, Alana Miriam. AB, Goucher Coll., 1971; MSW, Bryn Mawr Coll., 1973; MBA, Northwestern U., 1978. Children's worker Rogers Park Jewish Community Ctr., Chgo., 1973-75; tchr. Jewish Reconstructionist Congregation, Evanston, Ill., 1973-75, Keneseth Israel, Elkins Park, Pa., 1982—; owner, chief exec. officer Raanan Enterprises, Jenkintown, Pa., 1982—. Editor: Beginnings and Endings, 1989. Vol. Nat. Coun. Jewish Women, Elkins Park, 1978—, Hadassah, Phila., 1970—, Forman Ctr. PTA, Melrose Park, Pa., 1987—. Mem. Assn. Jewish Community Orgn. Profls.

TIMERDING, ERIC FRANCIS, music and youth minister; b. Cin., Sept. 29, 1960; s. Edward Kenneth and Nora Iva (Carander) T.; m. Rebecca Gail King, June 18, 1982; 1 child, Eric Nathanael. B of Music Edn., No. Ky. U., 1981; postgrad., The So. Bapt. Sem., 1987-88. Choir dir. children's handbell Hyde Park Bethlehem United Meth. Ch., Cin., 1979-83; children's music coord. First Bapt. Ch., Walton, Ky., 1983-84; minister music Bullittsburg Bapt. Ch., Burlington, Ky., 1984-88; minister music and youth First Bapt. Ch., Barbourville, Ky., 1988—; music dir. Cedarmore Bapt. Assembly, Bagdad, Ky., 1989. Composer in field. Mem. Ministerial Assn., Barbourville, 1988—, Barbourville Community Chorus, 1988; dir. music Youth for Christ Crusade, Knox County, 1990; handbell dir. Chorus/Chamber Orch., Cin., 1983. Recipient Presdl. scholarship No. Ky. U., 1978. Mem. Ky. Bapt. Chorale, North Concord Bapt. Assn. (minister music 1988—, assoc. exec. bd. 1988—). Home: Hwy Contract 73 Box 35 Barbourville KY 40906

TIMLIN, JAMES CLIFFORD, priest; b. Scranton, Pa., Aug. 5, 1927; s. James C. and Helen E. (Norton) T. A.B., St. Mary's Sem., Balt., 1948; S.T.B., Gregorian U., Rome, Italy, 1950. Ordained priest Roman Catholic Ch., 1951; asst. pastor St. John the Evangelist Ch., Pittston, Pa., 1952-53, St. Peter's Cathedral, Scranton, Pa., 1953-66; asst. chancellor, sec. Diocese of Scranton, 1966-71, chancellor, 1971-77; aux. bishop, vicar gen. Diocese of Scranton, Scranton, 1976-84; pastor Ch. of Nativity, Scranton, 1979-84; bishop of Scranton, 1984—. Address: 300 Wyoming Ave Scranton PA 18503

TIMLIN, ROBERT CHRISTOPHER, SR., pastor; b. Phila., Aug. 31, 1963; s. John David and Evelyn Denise (Fischer) T.; m. Debra Lynn Smith, Nov. 11, 1989; 1 child, Robert Christopher Jr. BA in Music Edn., Temple U., 1985; MD, Asbury Theol. Sem., 1988; postgrad., Princeton Theol. Sem. Cert. tchr., Pa.; ordained to ministry United Meth. Ch. as elder, 1990. Assoc. pastor Wash. Crossing (Pa.) United Meth. Ch., 1988-89; pastor Christian edn. Wayne (Pa.) United Meth. Ch., 1989—. Mem. Aldergate Fellowship, Good News Alliance, Wesley Theol. Soc., Chapel of the Four Chaplains. Home: 100 Runnymede Ave Wayne PA 19087 Office: Wayne United Meth Ch 210 S Wayne Ave Wayne PA 19087 *Each life has its moments on the stage of Salvation history. May every act of our lives foreshadow the great finale; when "Every knee shall bow and every tongue confess that Jesus Christ is Lord, to the glory of God the Father." (Phil 2:10, 11).*

TIMM, JEFFREY THOMAS, chaplain, air force officer; b. Denver, Mar. 22, 1949; s. Paul A. and Louise (White) T.; m. Donna Faye Blanks, Sept. 7, 1974. BA, Tex. Christian U., 1971; M Div, Duke U., 1974; postgrad., U. Ark., 1974-76; PhD, Columbia Pacific U., 1980. Ordained to ministry Christian Church (Disciples of Christ), 1973. Commd. capt. USAF, 1974, advanced through grades to lt. col., 1983; chaplain Osan AB, Korea, 1976-77, Eglin AFB, Ft. Walton Beach, Fla., 1977-80, Luke AFB, Phoenix, 1980-82, Italy, 1982-85; sr. protestant chaplain Dover AFB, Del., 1985—. Author: A Potpourri of Worship Resources, 1976, A Title, A Talk, and A Tool for Pastoral Pre-Marital Counselors, 1981, Living With Stress, 1985. Mem. Adlerian Soc., Sigma Phi Epsilon. Home: 10 Freedom Dr Dover DE 19901 Address: 384 CSF/HC Mc Connell AFB KS 67221-5000

TIMM, ROGER EDWIN, college pastor; b. Neenah, Wis., Apr. 2, 1945; s. Edwin August and Paula (Rathjen) T.; m. Marilyn Louise Rodenbeck, June 18, 1967; children: Sarah Christine, Anne Louise. BA, Concordia Sr. Coll., 1966; MDiv, Concordia Sem., 1970; MA, Washington U., St. Louis, 1970; PhD, Columbia U., Union Theol. Sem., 1975. Ordained to ministry Luth. Ch., 1971. Pastor St. John, Concordia Luth Ch., Bronx, 1970-73; asst. prof. philosophy Concordia Coll., Bronxville, N.Y., 1973-74; campus pastor UCLA, U. Luth Chapel, L.A., 1975-80; asst. chaplain Muhlenberg Coll., Allentown, Pa., 1980-85, asst. prof. religion, 1980-88; coll. pastor, assoc. prof. religion Carthage Coll., Kenosha, Wis., 1989—; coord. profl. continuing edn. Northeastern Pa. Synod., Allentown, 1985-88; dialogue team leader Luth.-Episcopal Dialogue, Kenosha, Racine, 1990—. Author: (with others) Cosmos as Creation, 1989; contbr. articles to profl. jours. Bd. dirs. Shalom Interfaith Ctr., Kenosha, 1990—; founder, mem. Campus Action Groups Amnesty Internat. Muhlenberg Coll., Allentown, 1980-88, Carthage Coll, 1989—. Faculty Rsch. grantee, Muhlenberg Coll., 1982, 85, 88. Mem. Am. Acad. Religion (mem. exec. com. Mid-Atlantic region 1986-88), Luth. Campus Ministry Assn., Bread for World, Omicron Delta Kappa. Democrat. Office: Carthage Coll 2001 Alford Park Dr Kenosha WI 53140-1994

TIMMER, DAVID ERNEST, religion educator; b. Lafayette, Ind., Sept. 10, 1951; s. Harold Nelson Timmer and Rosemary Carole Buenting; m. Mary Beth Spoelman, Aug. 16, 1975; children: Rebecca, Miriam, Nicholas. AB, Calvin Coll., 1973; PhD in Theology, U. Notre Dame, 1983. Instr. Calvin Coll., Grand Rapids, Mich., 1979-80; prof. religion Cen. Coll., Pella, Iowa, 1980—, chmn. dept. philosophy and religion, 1985—; moderator Theol. Commn. of the Reformed Ch. in Am., 1991. Contbr. articles to profl. jours. Jr. fellow Ecumenical Inst. for Theol. Rsch., Jerusalem, 1978-79. Democrat. Home: 712 Huber St Pella IA 50219 Office: Central Coll Pella IA 50219

TIMMERMAN, JOAN HYACINTH, theology and sexuality educator; b. Dickeyville, Wis., Nov. 14, 1938; d. John Joseph and Lillian Frances (Chase) T. BA, Marquette U., 1961, MA, 1968, PhD, 1974. Mem. theology faculty Coll. of St. Catherine, St. Paul, 1968—, instr., 1968-74, asst. prof., 1974-78, assoc. prof., 1978-85, now prof. systematic and philosophical theology, 1985—. Author: Not Yet My Season, 1969, The Mardi Gras Syndrome, 1984, Sexuality and Spiritual Growth, 1991; (audio) Thank God It's Tuesday. Mem. Urban Affairs Commn., 1978. Named Schmitt Fellow, 1972, DAAD Fellow, 1974. Mem. Am. Acad. Religion, Cath. Theol. Soc. Am., Coll. Theology Soc., Am. Assn. Sex Educators, Counselors and Therapists. Avocations: reading, travel, horses. Office: Coll of St Catherine 2004 Randolph St Saint Paul MN 55105

TIMOTHY, BISHOP See NEGREPONTIS, MICHAEL

TINDALL, THERON WAYNE, lay worker; b. Houston, Oct. 8, 1962; s. Joel Wayne and Louise Francis (Smith) T.; m. Kelly Jean Beyl, Mar. 30, 1985; 1 child, Priscilla. BS in Mech. Engring., U.S. Mil. Acad., 1984, postgrad., 1989—. Operation rescue participant, tchr. Sunday Sch. Full Gospel Ch., Missouri City, Tex., 1989-91; ops. mgr. Toffejorg Inc., Pasadena, Tex., 1990—. Alt. del. to State Rep. Conv., Houston, 1988-90; del. Dist. Rep. Conv., Houston, 1988-90; bd. dirs. Repub. Mens Club, Sugar Land, Tex., 1989. 1st lt. U.S. Army, 1984-88. Home: 1606 Middlesbrough Missouri City TX 77459

TINDELL, RICHARD WAYNE, minister; b. Wachula, Fla., Mar. 7, 1952; s. Houston Edward T. Sr. and Alicia Beatrice (Lord) Pierce; m. Marjorie Ruth Beachers, Feb. 19, 1972; children: Valerie June, Gretchen Holly, Richard Charles, Constance Elaine. BS in Mgmt., Troy State U., 1985, M of Counseling, 1988; PhD, Emmanuel Bapt. Coll., 1990. Ordained to ministry Charismatic Ch. as deacon, 1976, as min. 1988; lic. temperment therapist, 1991. Deacon Abundant Life Ch., Ft. Walton Beach, Fla., 1976-88; v.p. Full Gospel Businessmens Fellowship Internat., Ft. Walton Beach, 1978-79; min. Nat. Christian Counselors Assn. Northwest, Ft. Walton Beach, 1988—; founder, Nat. Christian Counselors Assn. Northwest, 1988. Sgt. USAF, 1971-79. Republican. Home: 25 Walnut Ave Shalimar FL 32579 Office: Nat Christian Counselors 362 Beal Pkwy NW #204 Fort Walton Beach FL 32548

TINDER, DONALD GEORGE, theology educator, lecturer; b. Miami, Fla., July 23, 1938; s. George Beckham and Lucille (Brown) T.; m. Edith Charlotte Johnson, Aug. 21, 1965; children: Derek, Craig. BA, Yale U., 1960, PhD, 1969; postgrad., Dallas Theol. Sem., 1960-62; MDiv, Fuller Theol. Sem., 1964. Commended to ministry Plymouth Brethren, 1969. Asst. editor, then assoc. editor Christianity Today, 1969-79; assoc. prof. ch. history New Coll., Berkeley, Calif., 1979-85; vis. prof. theology Biola U., La Mirada, Calif., 1985-86; adj. prof. Tyndale Theol. Sem., Amsterdam, The Netherlands, 1987—, Evang. Theol. Faculty, Leuven, Belgium, 1989—; adj. lectr. hist. theology Capital Bible Sem., Lanham, Md., 1970-77, Wheaton (Ill.) Coll., Trinity Evang. Div. Sch., Deerfield, Ill., 1977-79. Contbr. articles to religious jours. and ref. books. Office: Tyndale Theol Sem PO Box 242 Wheaton IL 60189 also: Christian Missions In Many Lands PO Box 13 Spring Lake NJ 07762

TINGELHOFF, MARTIN DENNY, minister; b. Hampton, Va., Nov. 11, 1954; s. Benjamin Meredith and Mercedes Annette (Denny) T.; m. Donna Ellen Crowe, Mar. 5, 1977; children: Shannon, Marty II. Student, East Tenn. State U., 1973-77; diploma, RHEMA Bible Tng. Ctr., 1978; BA, Golden State U., 1982; PhD (hon.), Immaculate Theol. Sem., Nairobi, Kenya, 1985. Ordained to ministry, 1978. Evangelist various locations, 1977; min. Prison Ministries/Intercessory Prayer Group, Pryor, Okla., 1977-78; founding pastor Abundant Living Christian Fellowship, Kingsport, Tenn., 1978—; motivational speaker, 1980—; state dir. Freedom Coun./Christian Broadcasting Network, 1983-86. Active Nat. Right to Life, Concerned Women Am. Named one of Ten Outstanding Pastors in Area, Kingsport Times News, 1982. Mem. RHEMA Ministerial Assn. Office: Abundant Living Ch 260 Victory Ln Kingsport TN 37664

TINNIN, ALBERT BRADLEY, education minister; b. New Bern, N.C., Aug. 24, 1956; s. Ernest Bradley and Hazel Gertrude (Parsons) T.; m. Mischia Ann Hendrick, Aug. 13, 1978; children: Charity Elizabeth, Faith Michelle. BA, Gardner Webb Coll., 1978; MRE, Southwestern Bapt. Theol. Sem., 1981. Ordained to ministry So. Bapt. Ch. Assoc. pastor 1st Bapt. Ch., Hamlet, N.C., 1981-86; min. of edn. Derita Bapt. Ch., Charlotte, N.C., 1986—. Mem. N.C. Bapt. Religious Educators Assn. Democrat. Office: Derita Bapt Ch 2835 W Sugar Creek Rd Charlotte NC 28262

TINOKO, JOSE MARIA BALUIS, clergyman, university official; b. Daraga, Albay, Philippines, Apr. 20, 1936; s. Juan Morato Tinoko and Cristeta Marcellaña Baluis; Licentiate in Philosophy, U. Santo Tomas, Manila, 1965; B.A., 1969; D.C.L., Angelicum, Rome, 1973. Ordained priest Roman Catholic Ch., 1967; procurator U. Santo Tomas Central Sem., Manila, 1968-70, vice rector, 1973-75; regent Coll. Architecture and Fine Arts, U. Santo Tomas, 1970-72, treas., 1976-82; vice rector U. Santo Tomas; mem. bd. consultors in canon law Diocese of Manila, 1977-80, dean faculty of canon law, 1986—; mem. econ. council Philippine Dominican Province. Trustee, U. Santo Tomas; chmn. governing bd. U. Santo Tomas Hosp. Mem. Assn. Cath. Univs. of The Philippines (sec. gen. 1989—), Clubs: Philippine Columbian Assn., Strata, Financiers, KC. Editor: Boletin Ecclesastico de Filipinas, 1969-71. Home: Univ Santo Tomas, Espana St, Manila 2806, The Philippines

TINSTMAN, MARC RICHARD, minister; b. Mt. Vernon, Ohio, Mar. 17, 1951; s. Charles Richard and Letha May (Snare) T.; m. Terri Gail Laird, Aug. 6, 1977; 1 child, Nathan Richard. BS, Northwest Christian Coll., Eugene, Oreg., 1973; MDiv, Tex. Christian U., 1980. Ordained, 1980. Student asst. Univ. Christian Ch., San Diego, 1970; student youth min. 1st Christian Ch., St. Helens, Oreg., 1971-72; student pastor 1st Christian Ch., Dublin, Tex., 1975-80; sr. pastor 1st Christian Ch., Luling, Tex., 1980-84; assoc. min. Cen. Christian Ch., Ft. Worth, 1984-87, 1st Christian Ch., Lubbock, Tex., 1987-90; sr. pastor 1st Christian Ch., Mineral Wells, Tex., 1990—; summer ministerial student Peachtree Christian Ch., Atlanta, 1972, 73; asst. pastor North Hill Christian Ch., Spokane, Wash., 1973-75; interim pastor Spangle (Wash.) Community Christian Ch., 1975; exec. dir. Project Frontline, Mineral Wells, 1986—; del. Mineral Wells Ministerial Alliance, 1990, pres., 1991-92; pres. Mineral Wells Area Youth Com., 1991—. Author, editor: (tng. manuals) Project Frontline Training Manual, 1990, Project Frontline Training Manual on Native Americans and the Yakima Indian Christian Mission, 1989, Youth Hunger Mission Project: Hunger and the Kokokahi Tropical Hunger Mission, 1986. Recipient Disting. Svc. award Luling Jaycees, 1983, Letters of Disting. Svc. and Appreciation Kokokahi Tropical Hunger Mission, 1986, Westaid, 1987, Yakima INdian Christian Mission, 1989. Mem. Assn. Christian Ch. Educators, Bread for the World, Nat. Network Youth Ministries, Rotary, Kiwanis. Republican. Office: 1st Christian Ch 302 NW 6th St Mineral Wells TX 76067

TIPPIT, JEAN DEANN, lay worker; b. Mobile, Ala., Mar. 16, 1963; d. Walter Devan and Melba Daniel (Hobbs) Milne; m. Bryan Keith Tippit, Oct. 15, 1988. BA, U. S. Ala., 1986. Dir. youth Christ United Meth. Ch., Mobile, 1987—; sec. youth ministry Fellowship Ala./W. Fla. Conf., 1990—. Rape crisis counselor Mobile Mental Health, 1987-88; bd. dirs. Girl Scouts, Mobile, 1988-89. Republican. Office: Christ United Meth Ch 6101 Grelot Rd Mobile AL 36609

TIRYAKIAN, EDWARD ASHOD, educator; b. Bronxville, N.Y., Aug. 6, 1929; s. Ashod Haroutioun and Keghinee (Agathon) T.; m. Josefina Cintron, Sept. 5, 1953; children: Edmund Carlos, Edwyn Ashod. BA summa cum laude, Princeton U., 1952; MA, Harvard U., 1954, PhD, 1956; PhD (hon.), U. Rene Descartes, Paris, 1987. Instr. Princeton U., 1956-57, asst. prof., 1957-62; lectr. Harvard U., 1962-65; assoc. prof. Duke U., Durham, N.C., 1965-67, prof., 1967—, chmn. dept. sociology and anthropology, 1969-72, dir. internat. studies, 1988—; vis. lectr. U. Philippines, 1954-55, Bryn Mawr Coll., 1957-59; vis. scientist program Am. Socl. Assn., 1967-70; vis. prof. Laval U., Quebec, Que., Can., 1978; summer seminar dir. Nat. Endowment for Humanities, 1978, 80, 83, 89, 91; lectr. Kyoto Am. Studies Summer Seminar, 1985. Author: Sociologism and Existentialism, 1962; Editor: Sociological Theory, Values and Sociocultural Change: Essays in Honor of P.A. Sorokin, 1963, The Phenomenon of Sociology, 1971, On the Margin of the Visible: Sociology, the Esoteric, and the Occult, 1974, The Global Crisis: Sociological Analyses and Responses, 1984; co-editor: Theoretical Sociology: Perspectives and Developments, 1970; New Nationalisms of the Developed West, 1985. Recipient Fulbright Research award, 1954-55; Ford Faculty Research fellow, 1971-72. Mem. Am. Sociol. Assn., African Studies Assn., Am. Soc. for Study Religion (council 1975-78, pres. 1981-84), Assn. Internationale des Sociologues de Langue Française (v.p. 1985-88, pres. 1988—), Soc. for Phenomenology and Existential Philosophy, Phi Beta Kappa. Clubs: Princeton, Century Assn. (N.Y.C.). Home: 16 Pascal Way Durham NC 27705 *As a sociological researcher, I have sought to understand on a comparative basis the dynamics of social consciousness in the process of historical change. As a teacher, I have sought to encourage in students—undergraduates, graduates, and postgraduates— a gusto for intellectual curiosity in exploring the myriad of linkages that make up social reality, our human patrimony.*

TITUS, LONNIE ELLIS, minister; b. Minot, N.D., Jan. 1, 1950; s. George Lester and Eunice Mable (Lundgren) T.; m. Bonnie Mae Johnson, May 26, 1972; children: Jonathan, Alicia, Nathan. AAS, N.D. State U., Bottineau, 1970; Diploma in Bible, Trinity Bible Coll., Ellendale, N.D., 1973, postgrad., 1991—; postgrad., U. N.D., Williston, 1989. Ordained to ministry Assemblies of God, 1977. Sectional presbyter Assemblies of God, Bismarck, N.D., 1980-88, state men's dir., 1983-89, state vice dir. youth dept., 1985-88, dist. sec.-treas., 1989-90; exec. sec., treas. Trinity Bible Coll., Ellendale, 1985-89. Bd. dirs. Eckert Youth Home, Williston, 1988-91; probation officer Fed. Ct. and Dept. Corrections and Rehab., Bismarck, 1990—; chmn. Williston Community Corrections Bd., 1991; chaplain CAP, 1991—. Recipient appreciation S.W. Sect. Mins. Assn., 1989. Mem. Delta Epsilon Chi. Republican. Home: 313 W 13th St Williston ND 58801 Office: Assemblies of God 1905 26th St W Williston ND 58801

TITUS, WILLIAM RAY, minister; b. Tampa, Fla., Oct. 2, 1950; s. Jay D. and Martha Ann (Shepherd) T.; m. Beverly Jo Monroe, Aug. 16, 1975; children: John, James, Jeremy, Jeffry, Jessica. BA, Ottawa (Kans.) U., 1983; MDiv, St. Paul Sch. Theology, Kansas City, Kans., 1983; postgrad., Emory U., 1988-89. Ordained to ministry United Meth. Ch. Pastor Happy (Tex.)-Wayside United Meth. Chs., 1977-80, McBee Cir. United Meth. Chs., Breckenridge, Mo., 1980-83, Wesley United Meth. Ch., Amarillo, Tex., 1983-87; 0administr. St. Paul United Meth. Ch., Amarillo, 1987—; chmn. rsch. NW Tex. Conv., United Meth. Ch., Lubbock, 1985—; v.p. City Bd. Missions, Amarillo, 1985-91. Bd. dirs. Amarillo Montessori Acad., 1985-91, pres., 1990-91; bd. dirs. Amarillo Aquatic Club, 1986-89. Mem. United Meth. Assn. Ch. Bus. Adminstrs. Office: St Paul United Meth Ch 4317 I 40 W Amarillo TX 79106

TOAFF, ELIO, rabbi. Chief rabbi of Rome. Office: Union Italian Jewish Community, Lungotevere Sanzio 9, 00153 Rome Italy*

TOALE, THOMAS EDWARD, school system administrator, priest; b. Independence, Iowa, Aug. 30, 1953; s. Francis Mark and Clara R. (DePaepe) T. BS in Biology, Loras Coll., 1975, MA in Ednl. Adminstrn., 1986; MA in Theology, St. Paul Sem., 1980; PhD in Ednl. Adminstrn., U. Iowa, 1988. Ordained priest Roman Cath. Ch., 1981; cert. tchr., prin., supt., Iowa. Tchr. St. Joseph Key West, Dubuque, Iowa, 1975-77; tchr. Marquette High Sch., Bellevue, Iowa, 1981-84, prin., 1984-86; assoc. supt. Archdiocese of Dubuque, 1986-87, supt. schs., 1987—; assoc. pastor St. Joseph Ch., Bellevue, 1981-84; pastor Sts. Peter and Paul Ch., Springbrook, Iowa, 1984-86, St. Peter, Temple Hill, Cascade, Iowa, 1986—. Mem. Nat. Cath. Edn. Assn. Office: Archdiocese of Dubuque 1229 Mount Loretta Ave Dubuque IA 52001

TOBET, WILLIAM CLINTON, III, lay church worker; b. Nutley, N.J., Apr. 16, 1933; s. William Clinton Jr. and Nancy Eleanor (Dunkinson) T.; m. Peggy Joyce Roberts, July 1, 1956 (div.); children: John C., James Lee, Lula Mae, Franklin E.; m. Sheila Ann Conners, Sept. 22, 1976 (div. Feb. 1991). Student, Blanton's Bus. Coll., Asheville, N.C., 1959-60. Missionary, officer The King's Army, Rosewood, Ohio; usher, Sunday sch. tchr. Living Word Ministries, West Haven, Conn.; sch. bus. driver Winkle Bus Co., Orange, Conn., 1984—. Vol. Compassion Internat., 1991—. With USN, 1950-54, U.S. Army, 1954-57. Mem. Albert Schweitzer Internat. Soc. (regional rep. Guatemala div.), Am. Legion, Tiyospaye Club, Order Sigum Fidei (hon.). Episcopalian. Home: 786 Derby-Milford Rd Orange CT 06477

TOBIAN, JOHN, clergyman; b. Shelbyville, Ind., June 24, 1944; s. Morris and Helen (McLane) T.; m. Lydia Ross, Dec. 30, 1967; children: Anne, Aaron. AB, Hanover Coll., 1966; BD, MDiv, Princeton Sem., 1970; DMin, McCormick Theol. Sem., 1982. Ordained to ministry, Presbyn. Ch. 1970. Instr. U. Tehran (Iran), 1968-69; pastor Presbyn. Ch. USA, Grand Rapids, Mich., 1970—; ch. cons. Presbyn. chs., Ind., Ill., Mich., 1970-90; bd. dirs. Milroy (Ind.) Canning Co., 1980—. Mem. Alma (Mich.) Coll. Coun., 1989—. Recipient Disting. Svc. award Am. Cancer Soc., 1973. Mem. Presbytery of Lake Michigan, Alban Inst., Masons (Easter speaker). Avocations: tennis, reading, physical fitness, traveling. Home: 1016 San Lucia SE Grand Rapids MI 49506 Office: Eastminster Presbyn Ch 1700 Woodward SE Grand Rapids MI 49506

TOBIAS, CHARLES EDWARD, pastor; b. Akron, Ohio, Apr. 24, 1957; s. Thurman Edward and Alice Pauline (Etling) T.; m. Diane Elaine Prelac, Aug. 4, 1979; children: Sarah Rebecca, Andrew John. BA, Hiram Coll., 1979; MDiv, Vanderbilt U., 1982. Ordained to ministry Meth. Ch. as deacon, 1981, as elder, 1984. Pastor Belmont (Ohio) United Meth. Ch., 1982-86, Strasburg (Ohio) Meth. Ch., 1986-90, New Hope United Meth. Ch., Richfield, Ohio, 1990—; v.p. Bethesda (Ohio) Learning Ctr. Steering Com., 1982-90; chairperson Leadership Devel. Task Group, North Canton, Ohio, 1987-88. V.p. Rotary Club, Bethesda, 1986. Mem. Acad. for Preaching, Kiwanis. Democrat. Home: 3131 Overdale Dr Richfield OH 44286 Office: New Hope United Meth Ch PO Box 256 Richfield OH 44286

TOBIN, THOMAS HERBERT, priest, religion educator; b. Chgo., Nov. 8, 1945; s. Thomas David and Irene Elizabeth (Sheehan) T. LittB, Xavier U., 1967; AM, Loyola U., Chgo., 1973; student, Hebrew U., Jerusalem, 1976-77; PhD, Harvard U., 1980. Joined S.J., Roman Cath. Ch., 1964, ordained priest, 1973. Assoc. prof. Loyola U., Chgo., 1980—. Author: The Creation of Man, 1983, The Spirituality of Paul, 1987; author, editor: Timaeus of Locri, 1985, Of Scribes and Scrolls, 1990; assoc. editor: Catholic Bible Quarterly, 1989—. Democrat. Office: Loyola Univ of Chgo 6525 N Sheridan Rd Chicago IL 60626

TOBY, DENNIS MICHAEL, minister; b. Ada, Okla., Feb. 18; s. C.M. and Helen Pauline (Johnson) T.; m. Jackie Kay Compton, Aug. 19, 1967; children: Joshua David, Scott Michael. Student, Houston Bapt. U., 1965-67; BA, Sam Houston State U., 1969; postgrad., New Orleans Bapt. Sem., 1969-70; MDiv, Southwestern Bapt. Sem., 1974. Ordained to ministry So. Bapt. Conv., 1967. Assoc. pastor Wayside Bapt. Ch., Miami, Fla., 1971-72, 2d Bapt. Ch., Little Rock, 1972; pastor Pleasant Grove Bapt. Ch., Texarkana, Tex., 1973-77, 1st Bapt. Ch. Woodway, Waco, Tex., 1977—. Author: Share Jesus Now, 1989. Bd. dirs. Spl. Wish Found., Waco, 1985-89, Boys Club, Woodway, 1979-81, Human Welare Coordinating Bd., Dallas, 1982-87, Bapt. Meml. Geriatric Ctr., San Angelo, Tex., 1990—. Mem. Bapt. Gen. Conv. Tex. (bd. dirs. 1988—), WACO Bapt. Assn. (moderator 1988-89), Rotary (pres. Hewitt-Woodway club). Home: Rte 12 Box 176 Waco TX 76712 Office: 1st Bapt Ch Woodway 401 Estates Waco TX 76712

TODD, VIRGIL HOLCOMB, clergyman, religion educator; b. Jordonia, Tenn., June 22, 1921; s. George Thurman and Nellie Mai (Dutton) T.; m. Irene Rolman, Sept. 21, 1941; 1 child, Donald Edwin. BA, Bethel Coll., 1945; BD, Cumberland Presbyn. Sem., 1947; MA, Scarritt Coll., 1948; PhD, Vanderbilt U., 1956. Ordained to ministry Presbyn. Ch., 1944. Minister Cumberland Presbyn. Chs., Tenn. and Ky., 1943-52; assoc. prof. Bethel Coll., McKenzie, Tenn., 1952-54; prof. of Old Testament Memphis Theol. Sem., 1954—; interim minister Presbyn. chs. in Tenn., Ky. and Miss., 1952—; vice-moderator Gen. Assembly Cumberland Presbyn. Ch., 1984-85, moderator, 1985-86. Author: Prophet Without Portfolio (2d Isaiah), 1972, A New Look at an Old Prophet (Ezekiel), 1977, Biblical Eschatology, 1985. Active Shelby (County) United Neighbors, Memphis, 1973-74, United Way of Greater Memphis, 1974-82. Mem. Soc. Bibl. Lit., Memphis Ministers' Assn. Democrat. Lodge: Civitan (chaplain, bd. dirs. local chpt.). Avocations: travel, golf. Office: Memphis Theol Sem 168 E Parkway S Memphis TN 38104

TODEA, ALEXANDRU CARDINAL, cardinal; b. Teleac, Romania, June 5, 1912. Ordained priest Roman Cath. Ch., 1939. Ordained bishop (secret appointment), 1950, arrested, sentenced to life imprisonment, 1951, amnesty granted, 1964, archbishop of Faguras and Alba Julia, 1990, elevated to the Sacred Coll. of Cardinals, 1991; with titular ch. St. Athanasius. Office: Archdiocese Roman Cath Ch, Apalinei 34, 4225 Reghin Romania*

TOH, JOSEPH CHIN SOO, minister, educator; b. Seoul, July 12, 1938; came to U.S., 1976; s. Chang Hyun Toh and Jung Az Yoo; m. Nancy Sung Woo, June 13, 1967; children: Linda, Samuel. BA, Soong Sil Univ., Seoul, 1963; STM, N.Y. Theol. Sem., 1980; ThD, Trinity Theol. Sem., Newburg, Ind., 1983; DD (hon.), Internat. Theol. Sem., 1981; PhD (hon.), Calif. Missionary Sem., 1984, Evang. Christian U., 1991; ThD (hon.), Trinity Internat. U., 1991. With Christian Missionary Alliance, N.Y.C., 1975—; chmn. Korean Minister's Assn. of Greater N.Y., 1985; pres. N.Y. United Theol. Seminary, Sunnyside, N.Y., 1980—; pres. World Omega Mission, N.Y.C., 1978—. Author translations of religious publs., 1984. Named Lt. Gen., Internat. Chaplains Assn., Springfield, Mo. Mem. SBL, Religious Acad. Home: 4 Bryant Crescent 1-N White Plains NY 10605 Office: New York United Theology 45-09 Greenpoint Ave Sunnyside NY 11104

TOHT, DAVID WARREN, publisher; b. Chgo., Jan. 15, 1949; s. Arthur Edward and Arlene Mae (Limkeman) T.; m. Rebecca Ruth JonMichaels, June 22, 1971; children: Adam, Betony, Ben. BA in English, Trinity Coll., Deerfield, Ill., 1973; MA in English, No. Ill. U., 1978. Assoc. editor David C. Cook, Elgin, Ill., 1983-84; pub. Lion Pub. Corp., Batavia, Ill., 1989—. Author: Seasons of Parenthood, 1992; producer: (video) Famous Fathers, 1984. Episcopalian. Office: Lion Pub Corp 1705 Hubbard Ave Batavia IL 60510

TOKAYER, MARVIN, rabbi; b. Bklyn., Sept. 4, 1936; s. Louis and Fanny (Rosenberger) T.; m. Mazal Ovadia, June 11, 1967; children: Shira T., Amiel Y., Naama M., Dan B. AB, Yeshiva U., 1958, B Religious Edn., 1960; M Hebrew Letters, Jewish Theol. Sem., 1960, DD (hon.), 1988. Ordained rabbi, 1962. Rabbi Hillcrest Jewish Ctr., Flushing, N.Y., 1964-68, Jewish Community of Japan, Tokyo, 1968-79; prin. Temple Israel, Great Neck, N.Y., 1979-81; dir. North Shore Hebrew Acad., Great Neck, 1981—; lectr. Am. Program Bur., Boston, 1980—; v.p. Jewish Culture Ctr., Tokyo, 1989—. Author: The Fugu Plan, 1979, Yudaya Gosen Nen No Chie, 1972, also numerous other books in Japanese on Judaism and Japan; contbr. articles to Encyclopedia Judaica, 1968. Capt. USAF, 1962-64. Recipient Achievement award Japan-Israel Friendship Assn., 1969. Mem. Rabbinical Assembly, Asiatic Soc. Home: 9 Stony Run Rd Great Neck NY 11023

TOLEDANO, JOSEPH C., religion educator; b. San Fernando, Luzon, The Philippines, Mar. 17, 1934; s. Cir C. and Rose C. (Cuellar) T.; m. Hazel E. Harrison, July 22, 1960; children: Susan, David, Jonathan. AA, U. St. Thomas, 1953, D in Medicine, 1958; BA, Cen. Bible Coll., 1971; MA, Covenant Theol. Sem., 1972. Ordained to ministries of Assemblies of God Ch. Instr. Bethel Bible Coll., Manila, 1973-83; pastor Assembly of God Ch., San Fernando, 1976-79; health counselor Meditrim Health Svcs., San Bernardino, Calif., 1990—. Author: Biblical Preaching, 1977. Mem. Soc. of Bibl. Lit., AMA, Lion's Club (sec. 1985-86). Home: 23399 Rolanda Dr Morena Valley CA 92388

TOLER, DESMOND BURTON, religion educator; b. Mobile, Ala., Jan. 25, 1941; s. Ardie Desmond and Goldie Marie (Fisher) T.; m. Betty Ann Bankston, Aug. 29, 1964; children: John, Elizabeth, Peter. BA, La. State U., 1963; JD, U. Ala., 1966; M in Religious Edn., New Orleans Bapt. Theol. Sem., 1982. Bar: Ala. Children's dir. Sage Ave. Bapt. Ch., Mobile, Ala., 1975-81; bus. ministry dir. Sage Ave. Bapt. Ch., Mobile, 1981-82; edn. dir. Westlawn Bapt. Ch., Mobile, 1982-84; minister edn. Travis Rd. Bapt. Ch., Mobile, 1984—; atty. Desmond B. Toler, Mobile, 1967—; Mem. Christian Life Commn. Ala. Bapt. Conv., Montgomery, Ala., 1990—; chmn. Christian Life Com. Mobile Bapt. Assn., 1986—; bd. dirs. Mobile Rescue Mission, 1970-79; vol. missionary Home Mission Bd., Seattle, 1973. Pres. South Ala. Safety Coun., Mobile, 1973-75, Phillips Prep. Sch. PTSA, Mobile, 1988-90, Westlawn Elem. Sch. PTSA, Mobile, 1975-76; pres., founder HELPline, Inc., Mobile, 1970. Mem. Ala. Bar Assn., Mobile Bar Assn. Home: 6 Maury Dr Mobile AL 36606 Office: Desmond B Toler Atty 203 B Government St Mobile AL 36602

TOLLEFSON, ROBERT JOHN, philosophy and religion educator; b. Frederic, Wis., Apr. 6, 1927; s. Herbert T. and Karn I. (Hatleli) T.; m. Barbara J. Phillips; children: Rebecca, Elizabeth, Priscilla, Jeff. BS in EE, Mich. Tech. U., Houghton, 1950; BD, Princeton Theol. Sem., 1954, ThM, 1956; PhD, U. Iowa, 1963. Ordained to ministry Presbyn. Ch., 1954. Pastor Presbyn. Chs., Vesta and Milroy, Minn., 1955-58; mem. faculty Buena Vista Coll., Storm Lake, Iowa, 1960—, prof. philosophy and religion, 1967—; moderator N.W. Iowa Presbytery, 1970, Synod of Lakes and Prairies, Bloomington, Minn., 1976-77. Organizing pres. Storm Lake Arts Coun., 1975—; trustee Buena Vista County Hosp., Storm Lake, 1988—. With USN, 1944-46, 50-51. Vis. scholar U. Cambridge (Eng.), 1978-79. Mem. Am. Soc. Ch. History, Am. Acad. Religion, Soc. History of Tech., inst. Soc., Ethics and Life Scis., Humanities and Tech. Assn., Nat. Assn. Sci., Tech. and Soc. Democrat. Home: 1305 Shoreway Storm Lake IA 50588 Office: Buena Vista Coll Storm Lake IA 50588 *A servant style of living is crucial, especially for white males. Enabling others to be their best, losing oneself in simple assistance to others and working to influence structures that will provide for the vulnerable are the noblest of goals.*

TOLLISON, ROBERT LEE, minister; b. Borger, Tex., Feb. 24, 1959; s. Robert E. and JoAnn (McWhorter) T.; m. Susan Camille Schultz, Aug. 8, 1981. BS, Tex. Tech U., 1981; MDiv, Southwestern Bapt. Theol. Sem., 1985; D of Ministry, New Orleans Bapt. Theol. Sem., 1990. Ordained to ministry Bapt. Ch., 1986. Assoc. pastor First Bapt. Ch., Wolfforth, Tex., 1981-82, Northrich Bapt. Ch., Richardson, Tex., 1983-86; pastor First Bapt. Ch., Bloomington, Tex., 1986-91, Bethany Bapt. Ch., Dallas, 1991—; moderator Guadalupe Bapt. Assn., Victoria, Tex., 1990-91; instr. Sem. Extension Dept., Victoria, 1987-89; pastoral advisor Bapt. Student Union, Victoria, 1989-91. Adult supr. Bobcats Against Drugs, Bloomington, 1990; organizer Community Thanksgiving Svc., Bloomington, 1987-90. Republican. Home and Office: Bethany Bapt Ch 5836 Emrose Terr Dallas TX 75227 *People only live their life one time, so they should strive to live that life to the fullest. I believe that starts with a life that glorifies Jesus Christ, and also helps meets the needs of other people. This is real living.*

TOLLIVER, NILA MOZINGO, pastoral care educator, chaplain; b. Charleston, W. Va., Aug. 7, 1928; d. Samuel Franklin and Lulu Myrtle (Foster) Mozingo; m. Robert Fulton Tolliver, July 29, 1944; children—Trulafaye, Samuel Robert, Dorothy Charlene. Cert. clin. pastoral educator, chaplain; ordained minister Ch. of God, 1972. A.A., Gulf-Coast Bible Coll., Houston, 1969; B.A., Houston Baptist U., 1971; M.A., Anderson (Ind.) Sch. Theology, 1978, LHD Houston Grad. Sch. Theology. Adminstr. Houston Christian Mission, 1967-70; adminstr. group home Roanoke City Welfare Dept. (Va.), 1971-73; tchr. Nicholas County Schs., Summersville, W.Va., 1973-76; adminstr. Group Home, Hillcrest Girls Home, Anderson, Ind., 1976-78; instr. Gulf-Coast Bible Coll., Houston, 1979-83; prof., Houston Baptist Grad. Sch. Theology, 1983—; cons. chaplaincy Harris County (Tex.) Hosp. Dist., Houston, 1979—; chaplain Tex. Inst. Rehab. Research, 1979—part time, Ben Taub Gen. Hosp., 1978—, San Jacinto Bus. and Profl. Women, 1979-82 (all Houston); chairperson SETEX Bd. Christian Edn., Ch. of God, Seoul, 1987; dir. chaplain interns AMI Park Plaza Hosp., Houston, AMI Heights Hosp. Contbr. articles to religious publs. Mem. state com. Am. Cancer Soc., 1983. Named Tchr. of Yr., Bay Ridge Christian Coll., Kendalton, Tex., 1980. Mem. Assn. Clin. Pastoral Edn., Coll. Chaplains (nominating com. 1983), SE Texa Assn. Chaplains (sec.-treas. 1982, pres. 1984), Christian Assn. Psychol. Studies, Hosp. Christian Fellowship. Clubs: Women of Ch. of God (sec. 1964-66) (Anderson). Office: Houston Grad Sch Theology 1129 Wilkins St Suite 200 Houston TX 77030

TOLO, PAUL GUDVIN, minister; b. Noonan, N.D., June 23, 1925; s. Gudvin Walther and Hilma Elfreida (Mickelson) T.; m. Lillian Carolyn Isenberg, Aug. 17, 1946; children: Carolyn Tolo Houck, Janet Tolo Gutierrez, Peter. BA, Luther Coll., 1949; Candidate in Theology, Luth. Sem., 1952. Ordained to ministry Evang. Luth. Ch., 1952. Pastor various Luth. chs., Iowa, Minn., 1952-75; bishop's asst. SW Minn. dist. Am. Luth Ch., Willmar, 1975-79; pastor Redeemer Luth. Home Missions, Woodstock, Ill., 1979-83, St. Johhn Luth. Ch., Peoria, Ill., 1983—; chmn. Bible camps, Graettingger, Iowa, Twin Valley, Minn., 1953-61; chmn. Indian evangelism and dist. ednl. com. No. Minn. dist. Am. Luth. Ch., Twin Valley, 1958-61, chmn. Crookston Conf., 1958-60, chmn. world mission com. SW Minn. dist., 1963-66, former chmn. West Cen. Conf.; dean North Cen. Conf., Evang. Luth. Ch. in Am., mem. Cen. So. Ill. Synod coun., mem. synod liaison with global mission com.; bd. dirs. Luth. Social Svc. Ill., 1988—. Rep. candidate for Minn. Ho. of Reps., Willmar, 1977. With USN, 1943-46. Mem. Lions, Kiwanis (pres. Limestone club 1990-91). Home: 426 Long Bow Dr Peoria IL 61604-4212 Office: St John Luth Ch 6614 W Smithville Rd Peoria IL 61607

TOLZMANN, ARLYN L., clergyman; b. Amery, Wis., Apr. 12, 1943; s. Leonard Charles and Irene Bernice (Hendrickson) T.; m. Jeanne Ann Mingus, July 1, 1967; children: Nathan, Matthew. BA, Gustavus Adolphus Coll., 1965; MDiv, Northwestern Theol. Sem., 1969. Ordained to ministry Luth. Ch., 1969. Pastor St. Paul's Luth. Ch., Marion, Ohio, 1969-73; pastor, developer Div. for Mission in N.Am., Plano, Tex., 1973-74; pastor Resurrection Luth. Ch., Plano, 1975—; Dean Dallas Synodical Area, 1981-83; mem. synod consulting com. on women, 1984-85, synod council, 1985-87; chmn. One in Mission Appeal, 1985-86. Author: Life is a Gift, 1976. Chmn. mission appeal follow-up com. Collin County Women's Shelter, 1987—; chmn. Bethpage Human Rights and Research Com., Dallas, 1987; cofounder Luth. Assn. Scouters, Circle 10, Dallas, 1982. Named one of Outstanding Young Men of Am., Jaycees, 1975. Mem. Sprignhill Retreat Ctr., Plano Ministerial Alliance. Avocations: writing poetry, photography. Office: Resurrection Luth Ch 1919 Independence Pkwy Plano TX 75075

TOM, JAMES LEROY, minister; b. South Bend, Ind., May 28, 1945; s. Evert Boyd and Florence Ann (Phillippi) T.; m. Tamara Ann Kern, July 29, 1967; children: Tanya, Travis. BA, U. Calif., Riverside, 1967; MDiv, United Theol. Sem., 1970; PhD, Claremont Grad. Sch., 1984. Lic. to ministry Evang. United Brethren Ch., 1967; ordained to ministry United Meth. Ch. as elder, 1970. Pastor Christ United Meth. Ch., Norwalk, Calif., 1971-73; assoc. minister First United Meth. Ch., Santa Ana, Calif., 1974-77; pastor Murrieta (Calif.) Community United Meth. Ch., 1977-84, Colton (Calif.) United Meth. Ch., 1984-88, Wesley United Meth. Ch., Riverside, 1988—; prof. San Bernardino Valley Coll., 1985-88, Crafton Hills Coll., Yucaipa, Calif., 1988—; pres. Riverside Dist. Union, 1989—; v.p. United Campus Ministry Bd., Riverside, 1990—; sec. Riverside Interfaith Fellowship, 1990—. Grad. fellow Claremont Grad. Sch., 1973-75. Mem. Am. Acad. Religion, Am. Hist. Assn., Am. Soc. Ch. History, Alban Inst. Democrat.

Home: 6951 Malibu St Riverside CA 92504 Office: Wesley United Meth Ch 5770 Arlington Ave Riverside CA 92504

TOMASEK, FRANTISEK CARDINAL, archbishop of Prague; b. Studenka, Czechoslovakia, June 30, 1899; s. Frantisek and Zdenka (Vavreckova) T. DD, Faculty Theology, Olomouc, 1938. Ordained priest Roman Cath. Ch., 1922, consecrated bishop, 1949. Tchr. religion, 1922-34; asst. Pedagogik-Catechetik, Theol. Faculty SS Cyril and Methodius, Olomouc, 1934-40; sch. insp. religion, 1940-46; lectr., then prof. pegadogics and catechetik Faculty of Theology, Olomouc, 1945-50; arrested, 1951-54; pastor parish Moravská Huzová, 1954-65; consecrated aux. bishop of Olomouc, 1949; apostolic adminstr. Archdiocese Prague, 1965-77; archbishop of Prague, primate of Bohemia, 1977-91; elevated to Sacred Coll. Cardinals, 1977. Author monographs, articles; editor: Letters on Education, 1934-47.

TOMBAUGH, RICHARD FRANKLIN, religious organization administrator; b. Syracuse, N.Y., Aug. 18, 1932; s. John Richard and Mary Louise (Scranton) T.; m. Sandra Phillips Clarke, Jan. 31, 1959; children: Geoffrey, Philip, Julia. AB, Princeton U., 1954; MA, Columbua U., 1956; STB, Gen. Theol. Sem., 1958, ThD, 1964. Ordained as priest Episcopal Ch., 1958. Chaplain various colls. and univs., St. Louis, 1964-73; priest-in-charge Trinity Ch., St. Louis, 1967-80; developer of small congregations Episc. Ch., St. Louis, 1980-86; exec. dir. Episc. Ednl. Ctr., St. Louis, 1984-86; Canon to the Ordinary Diocese of Conn., Hartford, 1986—; pres. Resources Mgmt., Inc., Hartford, 1970—; cons. Coalition-14, N.Y.C., 1987-90; mem. staff Leadership Acad., New Directions, N.Y.C., 1974-89. Bd. dirs. Greater Hartford Arts Coun., 1989—, Community Sch., St. Louis, 1972-78, New City Sch., St. Louis, 1967-72, St. Louis U. Divinity Sch., 1969-72. Mem. Princeton Club Con Conn.(pres. 1990—), Phi Beta Kappa, Sigma Xi. Office: Diocese of Conn 1335 Asylum Ave Hartford CT 06105

TOMBERLIN, CHARLES E., youth pastor; b. Alma, Ga., Aug. 22, 1966; s. William E. and Joyce W. (Rain Water) T.; m. LaDonna M. Green, Mar. 29, 1986; children: Amanda Nicole, Jareb Stephen. Assoc. youth pastor Baxley (Ga.) Ch. of God, 1984-86; youth/music pastor Buckingham Pl. Ch. of God, Brunswick, Ga., 1986-88; youth, music, assoc. pastor Monroe (Ga.) Ch. of God, 1988—; bd. dirs. South Ga. Youth Leaders Assoc., Tifton, Ga., 1986-88. Creator (youth ministries program) High Voltage, 1989. Chaplain Youth Alive, Brunswick, 1987-88; bd. dirs. L.A.P.C. Drug Awareness, Monroe, Ga., 1989—. Recipient Ministerial Intern Cert. Ch. of God, 1987, Exhorter Cert., 1988. Mem. North Ga. Youth Leaders Assn., Nat. Youth Leaders Assn. Home: 601 Alcovy St Monroe GA 30655 Office: Monroe Ch of God 1204 Church St Monroe GA 30655

TOMKO, JOZEF CARDINAL, ecclesiastic; b. Udavské, Kosice, Czechoslovakia, Mar. 11, 1924. ThD, Lateran U., Rome, 1951, JCD, 1962; D Social Sci., Gregorian U., Rome, 1955. Ordained priest Roman Cath. Ch., 1949. Consecrated archbishop Titular See Doclea, 1979; proclaimed cardinal, 1985; sec. gen. Synod Bishops; prefect Congregation for Evangelization of Peoples. Address: Villa Betania, Via Urbano VIII 16, 00165 Rome Italy

TOMLINSON, MILTON AMBROSE, clergyman; b. Cleveland, Tenn., Oct. 19, 1906; s. Ambrose Jessup and Mary Jane (Taylor) T.; m. Ina Mae Turner, Sept. 18, 1928; children: Wanda Jean (Mrs. Hugh Ralph Edwards), Carolyn Joy (Mrs. Verlin Dean Thornton). Ed., Tenn. pub. schs. Printer, Herald Printing Co., Cleveland, ten years; pastor ch. Henderson, Ky., 1 yr.; gen. overseer Ch. of God of Prophecy, Cleveland, 1943—; editor and pub. The White Wing Messengers; pres. Bible Tng. Inst., chmn. trustees. Author: Basic Bible Beliefs. Pres., Tomlinson Home for Children. Office: Bible Pl PO Box 2910 Cleveland TN 37320

TOMLINSON, WILLIAM LEE, minister; b. Portsmouth, Va., Mar. 9, 1939; s. Raymond Walter and Nellie (Overman) T.; m. Jane Gracey, Jan. 23, 1965. BA, U. Richmond, 1966; MDiv, Southeastern Bapt. Sem., 1970; DMin, Luther Rice Sem., Jacksonville, Fla., 1980. Ordained to ministry, So. Bapt. Conv., 1959. Pastor Pine St. Bapt. Ch., Richmond, Va., 1971-76, First Bapt. Ch., Newport News, 1976-86, Main St. Bapt. Ch., Emporia, Va., 1986-88, Arlington Bapt. Ch., Rocky Mount, N.C., 1988—; trustee Hargrave Mil. ACad., Chatham, Va., 1982-86. Mem. Hospice Adv. Bd., Nash Hosp., Rocky Mount, 1989-90, mem. pastoral care adv. bd., 1991—; bd. dirs. Internat. Seamen's Friends House, Newport News, 1980-82; pres. bd. United Campus Ministries, Newport News, 1986. Mem. Southeastern Sem. Alumni Assn. (nat. pres. 1976), Lions (past pres., host Newport News club). Home: 3113 Amherst Rd Rocky Mount NC 27804 Office: Arlington Bapt Ch 1500 Bethlehem Rd Rocky Mount NC 27803 *The measure of my life is not to be found in how much of it I possess. Rather, it is found in my willingness to invest it in others for the sake of the One who gave it to me.*

TOMLONSON, JOHN DEAN, minister, church executive; b. Middlebury, Ind., May 5, 1929; s. Guy Eugene Tomlonson and Ethel Sadie (Sherck) Rupel; m. Veva May Crumrine, Aug. 20, 1950; children: Mark Eugene, Janet Rae. BS, Manchester Coll., 1951; BD, Bethany Theol. Sem., Oak Brook, Ill., 1954. Ordained to ministry Ch. of the Brethren, 1950. Pastor Fairview Ch. of the Brethren, 1954-57, Stony Creek Ch. of the Brethren, Bellfontaine, Ohio, 1957-62, Skyridge Ch. of the Brethren, Kalamazoo, Mich., 1962-83; dist. exec. Mich. Dist. Ch. of the Brethren, Kalamazoo, 1968-83, McPherson, Kans., 1983—. Trustee McPherson Coll., 1983—, Cedars Retirement Community, McPherson, 1983—. Mem. Coun. Dist. Execs. (chair 1989—). Office: Western Plains Dist PO Box 394 Mc Pherson KS 67460

TON, JOSEF, minister; b. Aiud, Romania, Sept. 30, 1934; came to U.S., 1981; s. Ioan and Irina (Cocut) T.; m. Elisabeta, Sept. 7, 1959; 1 child, Dorothy. BA in Lit., U. Cluj, Romania, 1955; BA and Ma in Theology, Oxford U., Eng., 1972, 80; DD, Gordon Conwell Seminary, Boston, 1985; LLD, Wheaton Coll., 1991. Ordained to ministry Bapt. Ch., 1974. Tchr. State Schs., Romania, 1959-68; prof. Bapt. Seminary, Bucharest, 1973-74; pastor Peoiesti and Oradea, Bucharest, 1974-81; pres. Romanian Missionary Soc., Wheaton, Ill., 1981—; chancelor Oradea Bible Inst., Romania, 1991—; pastor 2nd Bapt. Ch. of Oradea, Romania, 1990—. Author: The Christian Manifesto, 1974, Religious Persecution in Romania, 1985, The True Faith, 1988. Home: 1415 Hill Ave Wheaton IL 60187 Office: Romanian Missionary Soc PO Box 527 Wheaton IL 60189

TONE, L. GENE, minister; b. Monahans, Tex., Aug. 6, 1934; s. Waldo Emerson and Myrtle Lucille (McCleskey) T.; m. Billie Lou Mitchell, July 24, 1954; children: Candy Ann Tone Powell, Melody Elaine Tone Bamburg, Chere Michelle, Timothy Andrew. BA, Hardin-Simmons U., 1955; BD, Southwestern Bapt. Theol. Sem., Ft. Worth, 1967. Ordained to ministry So. Bapt. Conv., 1953; cert. rehab. counselor, Tex. Pastor Amity Bapt. Ch., Merkel, Tex., 1951-53; with Sid Richardson Oil Co., Monahans, Tex., 1955-57; athletic coach, tchr. Monahans-Wickett Ind. Sch. Dist., Monahans, 1957-59; pastor Calvary Bapt. Ch., Crane, Tex., 1959-61, Union Bapt. Ch., Brownfield, Tex., 1961-63; preacher Asian New Life Crusade, 1963; pastor First Bapt. Ch., Morgan, Tex., 1963-65, Trinity Bapt. Ch., Corsicana, Tex., 1965-69, Lake View Bapt. Ch., San Angelo, Tex., 1969-71, Trinity Bapt. Ch., San Angelo, 1971-78; counselor Tex. Rehab. Comm., San Angelo and Odessa, Tex., 1971-81; pastor Frio Bapt. Ch., Hereford, Tex., 1981-83; pastor First Bapt. Ch., Corrigan, Tex., 1983-87, Seagraves, Tex., 1987—. Mem. Seagraves Ministerial Alliance (pres. 1987-90). Home: 1212 Ave G PO Box 1316 Seagraves TX 79359 Office: 1st Bapt Ch Box 7 Seagraves TX 79359 *I have seen and known the hand of God guiding and providing all the days of my life. He is the overriding and controlling factor and person in my life.*

TONEY, CREOLA SARAH, minister; b. Darlington, S.C., Mar. 29, 1920; d. Lonnie John and Mary Rosella (Marsh) Staton; m. Calvin William Toney, Jr., May 16, 1937 (dec. 1985); children: Calvis Loretta, Donald Wallace, Johnnie, Joyce, Paula, Anthony, Creola, Mildred, Luwanna, Philip. AA, Wayne Community Coll., Detroit, 1986; BSW, Wayne State U., Detroit, 1992. Lic. social worker, Mich. With Chartered Greyhound Bus Svcs., 1964-80; pastor Faith Temple Ch. of God in Christ, Detroit, 1984—; tchr. Sleepy Hollow Schs., Detroit, 1986-87; local, dist. and state pres., nat. rep., prayer and Bible band aux. Ch. of God in Christ Inc., S.W. Mich., 1960-83. Vol. Wayne County Dept. Social Svcs., Detroit; founder, organizer Vols. for Christ Visitation Group; state sec. examining bd. Women's Dept., Ch. of God in Christ, Mich., 1974-86; active Met. Jail Ministry, 1964—; notary pub. Wayne County, State of Mich., 1973-82. Recipient cert. of recognition and letter Wayne County Sherrif's Dept., 1988, 89, cert. of recognition Wayne County Execs., 1990, Mich. Gov. William Milliken, 1977, 78, 82, Spirit of Detroit award and cert. of recognition Detroit City Coun., 1991. Mem. DAV Aux. (comdr. 1986-89, legis. chmn. 1975—, legislation award plaques 1985, 86, 87). Avocations: sewing, interior decorating, baseball, bicycling, horse shoes. Home: PO Box 04310 Detroit MI 48204

TONEY, GLENDALL RALPH, lay worker; b. Christopher, Ill., Nov. 20, 1951; s. Ralph W. and Aretia Fae (Riley) T.; m. Janet Lee Boldt, June 14, 1974; children: Chad Michael, Gretchen Michelle. AA, Rend Lake Coll., 1971; BA, Letourneau Coll., 1973. Campus minister Am. Bapt. Campus Ministry, Carbondale, Ill., 1973-76; commended worker Cape Bible Chapel, Cape Girardeau, Mo., 1979—; supported elder Neighborhood Bible Fellowship, Carbondale, 1978—; ins. salesman Old Am. Ins., Kansas City, Mo., 1976-78; radio disc jockey WXAN Christian Radio, Ava, Ill., 1983-89; co-dir. teen camp, Mid-South Bible Conf., Dickson, Tenn., 1976-90; camp Bible tchr. Los Timber Bible Camp, Chandler, Minn., 1980—; discipling Student Bible Fellowship, So. Ill. U., Carbondale, 1977—; instr. seminar Principles of N.T. Ch., 1981; mem. bd. Covenant Christian Sch., 1989—. Home: 602 W Owens Carbondale IL 62901 Office: Neighborhood Bible Fellowship 2605 Striegel Rd Carbondale IL 62903 *The more I learn of the meaning of the first part of my chosen life verse, "For to me to live is Christ," I am absolutely convinced the last part is also true, "and to die is gain." (Philippians I:21), and what a joy to be on that comma!.*

TONEY, MARK ANTHONY, minister; b. Cin., June 25, 1959; s. Thomas James and Rosemary (Jackson) T.; m. Carandal Kay Dubose, Sept. 27, 1981; children: Mark A. II, Michael Angelo. Cert. of Evangelism, Temple Bible Coll., Cin., 1974-76, dipl., 1987. Ordained to ministry, Bapt. Ch. Minister New Unity Bapt. Ch., Cin., 1974-80, pastor, 1980—; radio minister and gospel announcer WTSJ, Cin., 1989—. Home: 2126 Burnet Ave Cincinnati OH 45219 Office: New Unity Bapt Ch 2124 Burnet Ave Cincinnati OH 45219-3112 *I believe in the power of prayer. But it is very important that our morality is in keeping with God's word. I am rich! Not because I have material gain but because I know the joy of living by prayer and the word of God.*

TONEY, THOMAS CLIFFORD, minister, entrepreneur; b. Dallas, Feb. 17, 1958; s. Almon Gene and Flora Ruth (Hill) T. AA, So. Bapt. Coll., 1980; BA in Psychology, Ouachita Bapt. U., 1982; MA in Religious Edn., Southwestern Bapt. Theol. Sem., 1987, MDiv, 1989. Itinerate ch. musician, 1979—, itinerate preacher, 1979—; customer svc. asst. Sears Roebuck & Co., Ft. Worth, 1982, salesperson, 1982-85; salesperson Sears Roebuck & Co., Jonesboro, Ark., 1986-87; direct merchandiser United Merchandising Enterprises, Ft. Worth and Jonesboro, 1986—; automotive trade cons. Auto Pro Motors, Ft. Worth, 1985—; property mgr. Hill Properties, Jonesboro, 1986—; crusade dir. Jay Strack Evangelistic Assn., Dallas; minister of music First Bapt. Ch., Tioga, Tex., 1984-85, minister of youth and music, Tyronza, Ark., 1979-80. Mem. Assn. Collegiate Entrepreneurs, So. Bapt. Religious Edn. Assn., Craighead County Hist. Soc. (life), Nat. Geographic Soc. Avocations: trumpet, racquetball, softball. Home: 418 W Matthews Ave Jonesboro AR 72401

TONG, FAR-DUNG, minister; b. Kudat, Sabah, Malaysia, Sept. 20, 1946; s. Moo-Shing and Kuen-Jen (Lee) T.; m. Ming Ming L. Tong, May 23, 1976; children: Rachel, Irene, Rebecca. BTh., Trinity Theol. Coll., Singapore, 1973; MST, Christ Sem.-Seminex, St. Louis, 1981, ThD, 1983. Ordained to ministry Luth. Ch. Chaplain DCS Hostel, Kudat, 1973-75; parish in-charge Kudat-N. Parish, Protestant Ch. in Sabah, 1975-77, Sekuati Parish, 1977-79; pastor Truth Luth. Ch., Naperville, Ill., 1983—; tchr. Tinagol Bible Sch., Kudat, 1977-79; mem. credential com. Met. Chgo. Synod, Evang. Luth. Ch. Am., 1988-89, mem. multicultural com., 1988—. Chaplain, v.p. Naperville Police Dept., 1984—. Mem. Assn. Evang. Luth. Chs. (nominating com. 1986-87). Home: 908 Hidden Lake Rd Naperville IL 60565 Office: Truth Luth Ch 3S 460 Curtis Ave Warrenville IL 60555

TONGDONMUAN, ARUN, minister; b. Nakornphatom, Thailand, June 14, 1938; s. Chuntra and Ngeab Tondonmuan; m. Ura, June 9, 1967; 1 child, Narongchai. BTh, Thailand Theol. Sem., Chiangmai, 1966. Ordained to ministry Ch. of Christ. Chaplain McKormic Hosp., Chiangmai, 1966-67, moderator, 1991—; co-pastor The First Ch., Chiangmai, 1967-74, pastor, 1975-82; moderator The Ch. of Christ in Thailand, Bangkok, 1983-90; dir. Pastoral Care Unit, Chiangmai, 1991—. Home: 147 Kawe na wa rat, Chiangmai 50000, Thailand Office: Pastoral Care Unit, PO Box 37, Chiangmai 50000, Thailand

TONGUE, JAMES MELVIN, minister; b. New Market, Va., May 2, 1946; s. Wrightson Samuel and Elizabeth Mae (Modisher) T.; m. Judith Farnum Abbott, June 17, 1967; children: Sarah Rebecca, Elizabeth Ann, James Matthew. BA, U. Va., 1968; MDiv., Yale Div. Sch., 1971. Ordained deacon United Meth. Ch., 1969; elder, 1972. Min. Sherando (Va.)-Lyndhurst United Meth. Charge, 1966-68, Monterey (Va.) United Meth. Charge, 1971-78, Wakefield (Va.) United Meth. Charge, 1978-84, Lane Meml. United Meth. Ch., Altavista, Va., 1984—; coord. Highland Larger Parish, Monterey, 1971-78; mem. bd. Discipleship Va. Conf., Richmond, 1972-80; co-dean Pastor's Convocation, Va. Conf., Blackstone, Va., 1973-76; mem. supervisory bd. Soc. of St. Andrew, Big Island, Va., 1985—, chmn. 1989-90. Editor: (worship periodical) Resource, 1977-80; author: (book) The Gospel in Glass, 1989. Bd. dirs. YMCA, Altavista, 1986-91. Named Rural Min. of the Yr., Va. Annual Conf., 1974-75. Mem. Lions Club (Monterey pres. 1974-75), Ruritan Club (Wakefield chaplain 1978-84). Home: 319 Myrtle Ln Altavista VA 24517 Office: Lane Meml United Meth Ch 1201 Bedford Ave Altavista VA 24517

TONNOS, ANTHONY, bishop; b. Port Colborne, Ont., Can., Aug. 1, 1935. Ordained priest Roman Cath. Ch., 1961. Bishop Archdiocese of Hamilton, Ont., Can., 1984—. Office: 700 King St, West Hamilton, ON Canada L8P 1C7

TONSING, CECILIA ANN DEGNAN, lay worker, foundation administrator; b. Washington, Apr. 20, 1943; d. Peter David and Elizabeth (Corcoran) Degnan; m. Michael John Tonsing, Jan. 29, 1966; children: Catherine Michele, Michael John Jr. BA, Holy Names Coll., Oakland, Calif., 1965; MPA, Calif. State U., Hayward, 1976. Tchr. Our Lady of Angels Cath. Ch., Claremont, Calif., 1966; instr. confirmation St. Perpetua's Cath. Ch., Lafayette, Calif., 1970-72; educator youth and family liturgy Corpus Christi Cath. Ch., Piedmont, Calif., 1981-83, eucharistic min., 1983—, reader, lector, 1985—; pres., chief exec. officer Providence Hosp. Found., Oakland, 1984-87, St. Luke's Hosp. Found., San Francisco, 1987—; mem. devel. com. Corpus Christi Sch., Piedmont, 1981-90; mem. fund raising com. Episc. Charities Appeal, San Francisco, 1989-91. Chmn. Calif. Heritage Preservation Commn., Sacramento, 1984—; trustee Calif. State Archives Found., Sacramento, 1986—; vol., trainer Girl Scouts U.S., N.Y.C., 1989—. Fellow Nat. Assn. Hosp. Devel.; mem. Nat. Soc. Fund Raising Execs. (cert.), Nat. Com. on Planned Giving, No. Calif. Planned Giving Coun., Claremont Country Club, Women's Athletic Club, Lakeview Club. Republican. Roman Catholic. Home: 911 Longridge Rd Oakland CA 94610 Office: St Lukes Hosp Found 3555 Army St San Francisco CA 94110 *Each of us has an immense potential for spiritual, emotional, and intellectual growth. Perhaps the greatest growth comes when realistically reviewing what didn't happen the way we planned it.*

TOOHEY, JEROME VINCENT, deacon; b. St. Louis, July 20, 1914; s. Joseph Michael and Theresa Ann (Sauerhage) T.; m. Marion Weaver, Sept. 8, 1937; children: Daniel W., Michael W., Kathleen Gunn. Cert., Alex. Hamilton Bus. Coll., N.Y.C., 1957. Ordained deacon Roman Cath. Ch., 1977. Deacon Incarnate Word Ch., Chesterfield, Mo., 1977—; dean Permant Deaconate St. Louis Archdiocese, 1965—. Home: 13555H Coliseum Dr Chesterfield MO 63017 Office: Incarnate Word Ch 13416 Olive St Chesterfield MO 63017

TOOLAN, DAVID STUART, priest, editor; b. Portland, Maine, Aug. 11, 1935; s. John Edward and Gertrude (Maher) T. BA, Georgetown U., 1957; MA, Fordham U., 1964; STB, Woodstock Coll., 1967; PhD, So. Meth. U., 1974. Joined S.J., Roman Cath. Ch., 1958; ordained priest, 1967. Consultor N.Y. province S.J., N.Y.C., 1970-72; asst. prof. Canisius Coll., Buffalo, 1970-79; assoc. editor Commonweal mag., N.Y.C., 1979-89; dir. Merton Community, N.Y.C., 1981-88; superior West Side Jesuit Community, N.Y.C., 1986-92; assoc. editor Am. mag., N.Y.C., 1989—; bd. dirs Children of War task force, N.Y.C. Author: Facing West from California's Shores, 1987; mem. editorial bd. Seminar on Jesuit Spirituality, 1988-91; assoc. editor: The Way, 1990—. Coord. Harrisburg Def. Com., Buffalo, 1971-73, Fair Jury Project, Attica Def. Com., Buffalo, 1973-74. So. Meth. U. fellow, 1967-70, 72; Agnes L. Schneider Found. grantee, 1975; recipient award for best book rev. sect. Nat. Cath. Press Assn., 1980-85, 88. Mem. Cath. Theol. Soc. Am., Am. Acad. Religion, Nat. Book Critics Circle (bd. dirs. 1983-84). Office: America mag 106 W 56th St New York NY 10019 *Spirit is like the wind; you never know where it is coming from or when. Strictly speaking, you can do nothing about it, except to prepare a vessel and let it happen.*

TOOLE, CHARLES JULIAN, IV, minister; b. Macon, Ga., Nov. 30, 1956; s. Charles Julian III and Ruth Irene (Sockwell) T.; m. Deborah Kaye Wilcox, June 25, 1977; children: Angela Kaye, Charles Caleb. BA, Mercer U., 1977; MDiv, Southeastern Bapt. Theol. Sem., 1983; postgrad., Ref. Theol. Sem., 1991—. Ordained to ministry So. Bapt. Conv., 1986. Min. Log Cabin Bapt. Ch., Macon, 1979-80; min., vol. 1st Bapt. Ch., Pickerington, Ohio, 1980-81; min. Wake Cross Rds. Bapt. Ch., Raleigh, N.C., 1981-84, Fairfield Highlands Bapt. Ch., Birmingham, Ala., 1984-87; min., pastor 1st Bapt. Ch., Russellville, Ala., 1987—; facilitator seminars Ala. So. Bapt. Conv. Bd. dirs. A Baby Crisis Pregnancy Ctr., Russellville; facilitator City Sponsored Seminars for Family Enrichment, Russellville. Recipient Outstanding Young Man of Am. award U.S. Jaycees, 1989. Mem. Franklin County Bapt. Assn. (dir. family ministries 1987-88, moderator 1991—). Office: 1st Bapt Ch Russellville AL 35653

TOOLEY, R. ERIC, minister; b. Dallas, Oct. 22, 1962; s. Richard Lee and Jane (Jackson) T.; m. Laura June Ely, Aug. 28, 1982; 1 child, Sara. BS in Youth Ministry, Okla. Christian, 1984. Ordained to ministry Ch. of Christ, 1982. Intern min. Richardson (Tex.) East Ch. of Christ, 1982; youth min. North MacArthur Ch. of Christ, Oklahoma City, 1983-84, Antlers (Okla.) Ch. of Christ, 1985-86, DeGaulle Ch. of Christ, New Orleans, 1986-89; min. Webb Chapel Ch. of Christ, Dallas, 1989—; bd. dirs. Webb Chapel Christian Camp, Lake Texoma, Okla., Crescent City Christian Camp, New Orleans, 1988, 91; coord. Wilderness Trek Christian Camp, Buena Vista, Colo., 1989—, bd. dirs., 1991—. Editor (newsletter) Plugged in Parents, 1987—. Mem. Christian Edn. Assn., Youth Outreach Network. Republican. Home: 13229 Glenside Dallas TX 75234 Office: Webb Chapel Ch of Christ 13425 Webb Chapel Rd Dallas TX 75234 *Teenagers are the church's greatest unused resource. They are willing to attempt new things and have tremendous contact with unchurched people through the schools. While society constantly criticizes its young people, the church can change the world by inspiring them.*

TOON, CATHY JEAN, physical education consultant; b. Beaufort, S.C., Sept. 27, 1957; d. John Elbert and Cynthia Jane (Taylor) T. BA in Edn., Ea. Wash. U., 1979, BA, 1980, MS, 1982; PhD, Tex. Woman's U., 1991. Tchr., coach Cusick (Wash.) Sch. Dist., 1979-80; grad. asst. Ea. Wash. U., Cheney, 1980-82; project mgr. U. Idaho, Moscow, 1982-83; adapted phys. edn. specialist Shelton (Wash.) Sch. Dist., 1983-86; grad. asst. Tex. Woman's U., Denton, 1986-87; adapted phys. edn. cons. Duncanville (Tex.)-Cedar Hill Spl. Edn. Coop., 1987-89, Azle (Tex.) Ind. Sch. Dist., 1988-91, Parker County Coop. Spl. Svcs., Weatherford, Tex., 1989-91; adapted phys. edn. specialist Cen. Valley Sch. Dist., Greenacres, Wash., 1991—; presenter in field. Contbr. articles to profl. publs. Mem. Denton Humane Soc., 1989—, People for Ethical Treatment Animals, 1991—. Mem. Assn. for Retarded Citizens, Coun. for Exceptional Children, Am. Alliance for Health, Phys. Edn., Recreation and Dance, Assn. for Rsch., Adminstrn., Profl. Couns. and Socs., Nat. Assn. Sport and Phys. Edn. Avocations: racquetball, cycling, golf, camping.

TOON, RONALD LYNN, minister; b. Ft. Smith, Ark., Feb. 4, 1962; s. Richard Lee and Esther Earlene (Ross) T.; m. Cheryl Reneé Box, July 2, 1983; children: Brittney Rashae, Taylor Nicole. BA, So. Bapt. Coll., Walnut Ridge, Ark., 1987; postgrad., Mid-Am. Bapt. Theol. Sem., Memphis, 1991—. Lic. to ministry So. Bapt. Conv., 1984; ordained, 1985. Pastor Egypt (Ark.) Bapt. Ch., 1984-85; pastor 1st Bapt. Ch., Tupelo, Ark., 1985-89, Luxora, Ark., 1989—; mem. evangelism com. Mt. Zion Bapt. Assn., Jonesboro, Ark., 1984-85, camp com. Calvary Bapt. Assn., Searcy, Ark., 1985-89; associational dir. youth Miss. County Bapt. Assn., Blytheville, Ark., 1989-90. Republican. Home: 1115 Calhoun PO Box E Luxora AR 72358 Office: 1st Bapt Ch 105 Calhoun St Luxora AR 72358

TOOTHMAN, TAMARA ANNE, youth director; b. Fairmont, W.Va., Dec. 21, 1962; d. Burl Eugene and Linda Diane (Thorne) T. BA in Edn., Fairmont State Coll., 1985; MA in Christian Edn., Meth. Theol. Sch. in Ohio, 1991, postgrad., 1991—. Youth dir., coord. Bellpoint United Meth. Ch., Delaware, Ohio, 1989—. Democrat. Home: 3081 Columbus Pike Delaware OH 43015 Office: Bellpoint United Meth Ch Delaware OH 43015

TOOTIKIAN, VAHAN H., minister; b. Kessab, Syria, June 22, 1935; came to U.S., 1965; s. Hagop Avedis and Keghanoush (Arakel) T.; m. Juliette Nazarian, Aug. 18, 1959 (dec. May 1985); children: Ann Zartarian, Alice and Jacqueline (twins). BA, Am. U. of Beirut, 1959; BDiv, Near East Sch. of Theology, Beirut, 1959; MDiv, Hartford (Conn.) Sem. Found., 1966; MST, Andover-Newton (Mass.) Theol., 1970, D of Ministry, 1973. Minister, prin. Am. Evang. Ch. & Sch., Damascus, Syrian Arab Republic, 1959-60; minister Armenian Evang. Congl. Ch., Cairo, 1960-65, Armenian Meml. Ch., Watertown, Mass., 1965-75, Armenian Congl. Ch., Southfield, Mich., 1975—; lectr. Lawrence Tech. U., Southfield, 1975—, U. Mich., Dearborn, 1985—. Author: Reflections of an Armenian, 1980, The Armenian Evangelical Church, 1982, Armenian Congretaionalism, 1985, From A Minister's Desk, 1986, Perspectives, 1987, A Survey of the Hebrew Bible, 1990. Chaplain Belmont (Wash.) Masons, 1967-75, Armenian Post Masters Assn., Boston, 1970-75. Mem. Armenian Evang. Union of N.Am. (moderator 1974-76, 86-88), Armenian Evang. World Coun. (pres. Detroit chpt. 1986—), Armenian Missionary Assn. (exec. bd. Paramus, N.J. chpt. 1966—). Home: 3922 Yorba Linda Royal Oak MI 48073 Office: Armenian Congl Ch of Christ PO Box 531 Southfield MI 48075

TOPEL, L(OUIS) JOHN, priest, educator; b. Seattle, Aug. 9, 1934; s. Louis John and Helen Marie (Giersch) T. BA in Classical Langs., Gonzaga U., 1958, MA in Philosophy magna cum laude, 1959; MST in Dogmatic Theology summa cum laude, Santa Clara U., 1966; Licentiate of Sacred Scripture magna cum laude, Pontifical Bibl. Inst., Rome, 1969; PhD in Religious Studies magna cum laude, Marquette U., 1973. Joined S.J., Roman Cath. Ch., 1952, ordained priest, 1965. Asst. prof. theology Seattle U., 1973-76, assoc. prof., 1976-83, prof. theology, 1989—, rector Jesuit Community, 1975-78; novice dir. Oreg. Province S.J., Portland, 1983-85; vis. prof. Pontifiical Bibl. Inst., Rome, 1978, 81, Sophia U., Tokyo, 1979. Author: The Way to Peace, 1979; contbr. articles to profl. jours. Trustee Seattle U., 1979-81, 90—, Marquette U., 1985—. Named Outstanding Tchr. Seattle U., 1982; Jesuit Coun. on Theol. Reflection grantee, 1974-75. Mem. Cath. Bibl. Assn., Soc. Bibl. Lit. Home: Seattle U C-900 Seattle WA 98122 Office: Seattle U CSY 209 Broadway and Madison Seattle WA 98122

TOPPING, EVA CATAFYGIOTU, writer; b. Fredericksburg, Va., Aug. 23, 1920; d. Themistocles John and Katherine (Polizou) Catafygiotu; m. Peter Topping, June 20, 1951; 1 child, John T. BA, Mary Washington Coll., 1941; MA, Radcliffe U., 1943; postgrad., U. Athens, 1950-51. trustee Greek Orthodox Ch. of Fredericksburg, 1990—; bd. dirs. Orthodox Christian Laity, Chgo., 1988—; exec. coun. Ch. Women United, N.Y.C., 1981-85. Author: Sacred Stories from Byzantium, 1977, Holy Mothers of Orthodoxy, 1987, Saints and Sisterhood, 1990; contbr. articles to profl. jours. Exec. bd. Greek Am. Women's Network, N.Y.C., 1990—; adv. com. Athenaeum Univ. Club, Washington, 1982—, Helen Z. Papanikolas Trust, Salt Lake City, 1989—. Fulbright scholar U.S. Ednl. Found., N.Y.C., 1950. Mem. Philoptochos Women's Soc., Women's Ordination Conf., Orthodox Christian Assn. of Medicine, Psychology and Religion, Women's Alliance for Theology, Ethics and Ritual, Phi Beta Kappa. Democrat. Home: 1823 Rupert St McLean VA 22101 *Given the ambiguities, uncertainties and complexities of life today,* *in our search for peace and justice most of us need inspiration and reasons for hope. These I find in the spirituality and Christian humanism of the Eastern Orthodox Church (into which I was born). It is good to have the support of Orthodoxy's long experience and ancient traditions.*

TORBETT, JEANNE ALOMA, lay church worker; b. Sellersville, Pa., Nov. 23, 1952; d. Richard Earl and Aloma Joyce (Krieder) Henry; m. Elvin Lige Torbett, Aug. 3, 1971; children: Thomas Elvin, Timothy Lige, Teena Ann. Grad., Pennridge High Sch., Perkasie, Pa., 1970. Sec.-treas. Faith Full Gospel Ch., St. Albans, Vt., 1978-84; asst. founder, asst. adminstr., tchr. Green Mountain Christian Acad., St. Albans, Vt., 1978-84, Sonshine Christian Acad., Callahan, Fla., 1985-87; owner, tchr. Little Giggles Christian Kindergarten, Callahan, Fla., 1987-88; sec.-treas. Oceanway Assembly of God, Jacksonville, Fla., 1988—. Recipient plaque, Ch. Bd., Sonshine Christian Acad., 1987, Green Mountain Christian Acad., 1983. Home: 4909 Lannie Rd Jacksonville FL 32218 *We can do many worthwhile things in this life, but the one thing that will last an eternity is when we lead someone to Christ! "Only things done for Christ will last!".*

TORGERSEN, SISTER SUE, nun, youth ministry director; b. Chgo., Oct. 7, 1944; d. Ralph Morse and Marie (O'Beirne) T. BA in Econs., Rosary Coll., 1967; MS in Edn., Northern Ill. U., 1974; M in Pastoral Studies, Loyola U., Chgo., 1982. Cert. advanced studies in youth ministry. Tchr., elem. sch. Archdiocese Chgo., 1967-77; faith formation and retreats cons. Archdiocese Chgo., Religious Edn. Office, Cath. Youth Office, 1977-87; parish dir. youth ministry St. Isaacs Parish, Niles, Ill., 1987-89; dir. youth ministry Diocese Joliet, Ill., 1989—; exec. com., sec., v.p., pres. Nat. TEC Conf., Omaha, 1983-87. Office: Religious Edn Office 430 N Center St Joliet IL 60435

TORIZ COBIAN, ALFONSO, bishop; b. Juchitlan, Mexico, Aug. 12, 1913. Ordained priest Roman Cath. Ch., 1939; named titular bishop of Avissa, 1954, bishop of Chilapa, 1956-58; bishop of Queretaro Mexico, 1958—. Office: Obispado Apartado 49, CP 76000 Queretaro Mexico Queretaro

TORJESEN, KAREN JO, religion educator; b. San Francisco, Oct. 10, 1945; d. Charles William and Mildred (Pedersen) Hall; m. Leif P. Torjesen, June 3, 1967. BS, Wheaton (Ill.) Coll., 1967; M Religion, Sch. Theology, Claremont, Calif., 1972; PhD, Claremont Grad. Sch., 1982. Asst. prof. Georg August U., Goettingen, West Germany, 1978-82, Mary Washington Coll., Fredericksburg, Va., 1982-84, Fuller Theol. Sem., Pasadena, Calif., 1985-87; Margo L. Goldsmith prof. women's studies in religion Claremont Grad. Sch., 1987—; chairperson regional bd. Evang. Women's Caucus, L.A., 1985-88; convener Women Ch., Pomona, Calif., 1988—. Author: Hermeneutical Procedure and Theological Structure in Origen's Exegesis, 1986, Sex, Sin and Woman, 1992. Am. Coun. Learned Soc. fellow, 1987. Mem. Am. Acad. Religion (pres. western region 1990-91, collaborative projects grant 1988), N.Am. Patristics Soc., Nat. Women's Studies Assn., Soc. for Culture and Religion of Ancient Mediterranean. Office: Claremont Grad Sch 831 N Dartmouth Claremont CA 91711

TORNFELT, JOHN VINCENT, minister; b. Kearny, N.J., Feb. 22, 1952; s. Vincent Herman and Barbara Ellen (Harris) T.; m. Deborah Ellen Parsons, July 13, 1974; children: Leslie, Eric. BS, Davidson (N.C.) Coll., 1974; MDiv, Denver Conservative Bapt. Sem., 1978; EdD, Trinity Evang. Div. Sch., Deerfield, Ill., 1990. Ordained to ministry Conservative Bapt. Assn., 1982. Lectr. ECWA Theol. Sem., Igbaja, Nigeria, 1979-81; pastor, ch. planter Galilee Bapt. Ch., Freehold, N.J., 1981-86; assoc. pastor Libertyville (Ill.) Evang. Free Ch., 1986-90; sr. pastor First Bapt. Ch., Ashland, Oreg., 1990—. Mem. Nat. Assn. Profs. of Christian Edn. Home: 1680 Greenmeadows Way Ashland OR 97520 Office: 2004 Siskiyou Blvd Ashland OR 97520

TORREBLANCA REYES, MAGIN, bishop; b. Huajuapan de Leon, Mexico, Aug. 19, 1929. Ordained priest Roman Cath. Ch., 1953; named titular bishop of Assava, 1973; bishop of Texcoco Mexico, 1978—. Office: Apartado Postal 35, CP 56100 Texcoco Mexico

TORRENCE, BILLY HUBERT, minister; b. Lynchburg, Va., Aug. 29, 1949; s. Charles Hubert and Mabel (Pillow) T.; m. Linda P. Pool, Apr. 1, 1972; children: Joseph Scott, Susan Marie. Student, Cen. Va. Coll., Wesley Sem., Washington, 1990—. Local pastor New Hope/Trinity United Meth. chs., Lynchburg, 1990—; bookkeeper Va. Dept. Hwys., 1972—; foreman, crew leader Va. Dept. Transp., Lynchburg, 1987-90. With U.S. Army, 1968-72, Vietnam. Mem. Ruritan (zone gov. Peaks of Otter chpt. 1983, lt. dist. 1984-86, dist. gov. 1985, 87, Ruritan of the Yr. 1984). Home: Rte 2 Box 73 Lynchburg VA 24501 *I have found that a person is never to old to learn the ways of God for their life. Seek God in the morning, evening and all day long for continuing guidance.*

TORRES, NOE, lay worker; b. Edinburg, Tex., Dec. 9, 1956; s. Eusebio and Maria De Jesus (Acosta) T.; m. Robin Leah Bartz, Oct. 7, 1984; 1 child, Sarah Christina. BA with hons., U. Tex., 1979, M Lib. and Info. Sci., 1991. Cert. secondary edn. tchr. English, Spanish, learning resources, Tex.; lic. FCC radio telephone operator. Pub. rels. sec. Seventh Day Adventist Ch., Edinburg, 1984—, elder, 1986—, personal ministries dir., 1986-90, head elder, 1989—; libr. Edinburg Cons. Ind. Sch. Dist., 1988—; del. Tex. Lay Adv. Com., Alvarado, 1989—. Contbr. articles to newspapers/jours. Recipient Pilot Project Teaching award Edinburg Cons. Ind. Sch. Dist, 1990, scholarship Marie Peckinpaugh Fund, Austin, 1978. Mem. Tex. Libr. Assn., Tex. Assn. Sch. Librs. Home: Rte 1 PO Box 330-A Mission TX 78572

TORRES, RALPH CHON, minister; b. San José, Calif., Oct. 18, 1948; s. Chon Poncé and Dora (Grijalva) T.; m. Pamela Ellen Hansen, Mar. 6, 1971; children: Chon, Brita, Samuel, Sarah. BTh, L.I.F.E. Bible Coll., L.A., 1970. Ordained to ministry Internat. Ch. of the Foursquare Gospel, 1981. Missionary asst. Internat. Ch. of Foursquare Gospel, Mexicali, Mex., 1970; youth pastor Internat. Ch. of Foursquare Gospel, Redondo Beach, Calif., 1971-72, Pueblo, Colo., 1972-74; sr. pastor Internat. Ch. of Foursquare Gospel., Pasadena, Calif., 1984—; youth pastor Ch. on the Way, Van Nuys, Calif., 1975-84; asst., dir. children's camps, Jr. and Sr. High camps for So. Calif. Dist. Foursquare Chs., 1978—; tchr. L.I.F.E. Bible Coll., L.A., 1979-86; bd. dirs. Holy Ghost Repair Svc., Hollywood, Calif., Centrum of Hollywood, Christians in Govt., L.A., Camp Cedar Crest, Running Springs, Calif.; bd. dirs., speaker Mainstream Inc., Tacoma, 1978-83. Composer: Kids of the Kingdom, 1976. Mem. Prop. 98 Sch. Report Card Com., Pasadena, 1989-90; adv. com. Marshall Fundamental Sch., Pasadena, 1989-90, Pasadena Unified Sch. Dist., 1990—. Recipient commendation for svc. Mayor of Pasadena, 1990. Office: Pasadena Foursquare Ch 174 N Harkness Ave Pasadena CA 91106

TORRES OLIVER, JUAN FREMIOT, bishop; b. San German, P.R., Oct. 28, 1925. Ordained priest Roman Cath. Ch., 1950. Bishop of Ponce P.R., 1964—. Office: Cath U Obispado Apartado 205 Sta 6 Ponce PR 00732

TORRES-REAVES, CARMEN NELLIE, religious worker; b. Bklyn., Jan. 5, 1954; d. Ferdinand and Felicita (Castro) Torres; m. Robert McKinley Reaves Jr., Feb. 14, 1976; 1 child, Robert McKinley Reaves 3rd. AAS, Bronx Community Coll., 1982; cert. ministry, N.Y. Theol. Sem., 1987; BA in Religious Studies, Coll. New Rochelle, 1989; MDiv, Harvard U., 1989. Lay speaker United Meth. Ch., Bronx, N.Y., 1987-89; staff asst., bilingual tchr. Coll. New Rochelle (N.Y.), 1988-89; workshop leader Bonds of Difference Conf., Cambridge, Mass., 1990; pastoral counselor Windsor House, Cambridge; youth counselor Hispanic Coun. Inc., Cambridge. Active N.Y. ann. conf. United Meth. Ch., 1989—. Recipient Hopkins award Harvard Div. Sch., 1991; United Meth. Ch. Bd. Higher Edn. scholar, 1989—; Hispanic fellow Fund for Theol. Edn., 1989—. Mem. Phi Theta Kappa. Democrat. Methodist. Office: Harvard Divinity Sch 45 Francis Ave Cambridge MA 02138

TORRES ROMERO, ALFREDO, bishop; b. Puruandiro, Michoacan, Mex., Aug. 8, 1922; s. Crescencio Torres Cortes and Maria Ines Romero Cardiel. Ed., Seminario de Morelia y Montezuma. Ordained priest Roman Cath. Ch., 1945; bishop Diocese of Toluca, Mex., 1968—. Office: Apartado 82, Toluca Mexico 50000

TORTORELLI, KEVIN MICHAEL, priest, friar, theology educator; b. Boston, Sept. 5, 1947; s. Vincent Joseph and Mary Agnes (Jennings) T. BA in Philosophy, Immaculate Conception Sem., 1970; MA in Theology, Washington Theol. Union, 1973; MA in Classics, St. Bonaventure U., 1975; MA in Theol., Boston Coll., 1986. Joined Franciscan Order, 1965, ordained priest Roman Cath. Ch., 1973. Priest St. Francis Ch., N.Y.C., 1973-75; asst. dir. Franciscan Formation Program Siena Coll., Loudonville, N.Y., 1975-76, lectr. in theology, 1975-76, 82—, chaplain to Rugby team, 1984—, lectr. classics dept., 1987—; priest to 7 parishes Diocese of Albany, N.Y., 1982—; vis. scholar St. Edmund's House, Cambridge U., Eng., 1979-80; mem. diocesan ad hoc com. on World Coun. Chs. Lima Documents, 1982-90. Translator from Latin: Plan for Franciscan Living, 1974, rev. edit., 1987. Mem. Internat. Conf. on Patristic Studies. Democrat. Home: The Friary Siena Coll Loudonville NY 12211

TOSATO, ANGELO, biblical scholar; b. Venice, Italy, Dec. 29, 1938; s. Egidio and Cecilia (Valmarana) T. Lic. in Philisophy, Gregorian U., 1960, PhD in Theology, 1972; PhD in Scripture, Bibl. Inst., Rome, 1982. Prof. Lateran U., Rome, 1975—, Gregorian U., Rome, 1984-86, Bibl. Inst., Rome, 1985—; cons. Commn. for Relations with Jews, Vatican, 1981-89. Author: Il Matrimonio Israel, 1982; contbr. papers on bibl. matters to numerous publs. Mem. Italian Bibl. Assn. (sec. 1987-89). Roman Catholic. Home: Via della Scrofa 70, 00186 Lazio Rome, Italy

TOTTY-KUBLAWI, MARY KAY, minister; b. Hartselle, Ala., Dec. 27, 1963; d. Charles Ray and Mary Emogene (Weems) Totty; m. Robert Munir Kublawi, May 19, 1990. BA, La. State U., 1985; MDiv, Tex. Christian U., 1989. Ordained to ministry United Meth. Ch., 1989. Pastor Amherst and Faith United Meth. Chs., Kearney, Nebr., 1989-91, William's Meml. United Meth. Ch., Shenandoah Junction, W.Va., 1991—; liaison gen. com. on status and role of women United Meth. Ch., Evanston, Ill., 1988-92, dir. gen. com. Christian unity and interreligious concerns, N.Y.C., 1988-92; steward Consultation on Ch. Union Plenary, New Orleans, 1988, Gathering of Christians, Nat. Coun. Chs., Arlington, Tex., 1988. Mem. Nebraskans for Peace, 1990—. *All we do, say, pray or think impacts our world because of the radical interrelatedness of the whole of creation. Profound realization of this necessitates our response of love, justice, and peace.*

TOUCHTON, BOBBY JAY, minister; b. Burlington, N.C., Dec. 9, 1962; s. Charles E. Jr. and Linda L. (Burke) T.; m. Trina D. Beach, June 22, 1985. BA, Wake Forest U., 1985; MDiv, So. Bapt. Theol. Sem., 1988, postgrad., 1991—. Lic. to ministry So. Bapt. Conv., 1987, ordained, 1987. Min. youth, sr. adults Southside Bapt. Ch., Winston-Salem, N.C., 1983-85; min. youth and edn. Chapel Park Bapt. Ch., Louisville, 1985-87; pastor Covington Bapt. Ch., Westport, Ky., 1988-89, 1st Bapt. Ch., Big Stone Gap, Va., 1989—; mem. exec. com. Wise (Va.) Bapt. Assn., 1989—, ASSISTeam for Pilot Mountain Bapt. Assn., Winston-Salem, 1984-85. Contbg. author: American Voices, 1987; contbr. articles to profl. jours. Vol. Big Brothers/Big Sisters, Winston-Salem, 1982-83, ARC, 1979. Named one of Outstanding Young Men of Am., 1988. Mem. Big Stone Gap Ministerial Assn. Republican. Home: 5 East First St N Big Stone Gap VA 24219 Office: First Bapt Ch Wood Ave & E First St Big Stone Gap VA 24219 *It is my fear that Christ as we know him may no longer exist in the whited sepulchers of the church with their golden crosses and diamond encrusted chalices; instead, I believe we will find him among the homeless, the indigent, and the oppressed of our society.*

TOUCHTON, JAMES WESLEY, minister; b. St.Augustine, Fla., Sept. 23, 1952; s. Ollie Eugene and Susie Mae (Lewis) T.; m. Constance Marie Millberg, June 9, 1979; children: Alexis Gabrielle, John William, Timothy James. B of Ch. Music, Stetson U., 1974; postgrad., So. Sem., Louisville, 1976, Conservatory Music, Frankfurt, Fed. Republic Germany, 1976-77. Ordained to ministry So. Bapt. Conv., 1983. Minister youth and music various chs., Fla., 1971-73; minister music, youth,outreach 1st Bapt. Ch, Lehigh Acres, Fla., 1981-82; minister music and youth 1st Bapt. Ch, Apopka, Fla., 1982—; dir. music State Youth Vocat. Guidance Conf. ,Fla. Bapt. Conv, 1979, 83, music dir. ann. State Youth Assembly, 1983-84; organizer Fellowship Christian Athletes Bikathon, 1984; mem. Camp Joy com. Greater Orlando Bapt. Assn., Fla., 1984-85; guest speaker and singer various Rotary lodges, 1977-84; bass soloist various choirs 1975,79, 84. Christian solo artist civic events Apopoka High Sch., 1983-84. Bd. dirs. Anthony House Ctr. for Homeless, 198-90, pres., 1990-91. Named one of Outstanding Young Men Am., U.S. Jaycees, 1984; Paul Harris fellow Rotary Internat., Frankfurt Conservatory Music, 1976-77. Mem. Greater Orlando Bapt. Associational Music (bd. dirs. 1986, 87, 88). Republican. Avocations: tennis, softball, basketball. Home: 409 Hickory Rd Apopka FL 32703 Office: 1st Bapt Ch Apopka 441 S Highland Ave Apopka FL 32703

TOULOUSE, MARK G., religious educator; b. Des Moines, Feb. 1, 1952; s. O.J. and Joan (VanDeventer) T.; m. Jeffica L. Smith, July 31, 1976; children: Joshua Aaron, Marcie Joann, Cara Lynn. BA, Howard Payne U., 1974; MDiv, Southwestern Bapt. Theol. Sem., 1977; PhD, U. Chgo., 1984. Instr. Ill. Benedictine Coll., Lisle, 1980-82, asst. prof., 1982-84; asst. prof. Grad. Sem., Phillips U., Enid, Okla., 1984-86; assoc. prof., assoc. dean Brite Divinity Sch., Tex. Christian U., Ft. Worth, 1986—. Author: The Transformation of John Foster Dulles, 1985, Our Past and Present Faith, 1991; contbr. articles to religious jours. Theol. scholar, rsch. award Assn. Theol. Schs., 1990-91. Mem. Am. Acad. Religion (jr. scholar S.W. region 1990-91), Am. Soc. Ch. History. Office: Tex Christian U Brite Divinity Sch Fort Worth TX 76129 Home: 4129 Alava Dr Fort Worth TX 76133

TOURNAS, METHODIOS (BISHOP METHODIOS OF BOSTON), bishop, academic administrator; b. N.Y.C., Nov. 19, 1946; s. Vasilios and Stavroula (Stavropoulos) T. B.A., Hellenic Coll., Brookline, Mass., 1968; M.Div., Coll. of Holy Cross, 1971; S.T.M., Boston U., 1972, D.D. (hon.), 1985. Ordained priest Greek Orthodox Ch., 1979. Archdeacon Greek Orthodox Archdiocese, N.Y.C., 1973-79, aux. bishop, 1982-84; priest St. Spyridon Ch., N.Y.C., 1980-82; bishop Greek Orthodox Diocese of Boston, 1984—; pres. Hellenic Coll., Holy Cross Greek Orthodox Sch. Theology, Brookline, Mass., 1989—. Trustee Hellenic Coll. Inc. Mem. Nat. Coun. Chs. Office: Greek Orthodox Diocese Boston 162 Goddard Ave Brookline MA 02146 also: Hellenic Coll S Goddard Ave Brookline MA 02146

TOV, EMANUEL, theology educator; b. Amsterdam, The Netherlands, Sept. 15, 1941; s. Juda and Toos (Neeter) Toff; m. Lika Aa, Dec. 3, 1964; children: Ophirah, Ariel, Amitai. BA, Hebrew U., Jerusalem, 1964, MA, 1967, PhD, 1973. Prof. of bibl. studies Hebrew U., 1980—, chmn. bibl. dept., 1982-84; vis. prof. U. Pa., Phila., 1980-81, 1985-86; Grinfield lectr. on Septuagint Oxford (Eng.) U., 1982—; bd. dirs. Computer Assisted Tools Septuagint Studies, Jerusalem/Phila. Editor Hebrew U. Bible Project, 1981—. Jewish. Avocation: photography. Office: Hebrew U, Dept of Bible, Jerusalem Israel

TOWLER, JOEL CURTIS, former lay worker, poet, writer; b. Raleigh, N.C., Aug. 2, 1938; s. Ernest Clarence and Mabel Elizabeth (Smith) T.; m. Lynda Jo Underwood, Mar. 5, 1960 (div. 1974); children: Lori Ann, Steven Curtis, Eric Joel. Usher, lay reader, pres. youth fellowship, pres. Meth. men's orgn. L.A., 1952-60; mem. choir, jr. and sr. high sch. Sunday tchr., chmn. building fund Lennox, Calif., 1960-63; usher, sec. fin. jr. and sr. Sunday sch. tchr. Huntington Beach, Calif., 1964-73; freelance writer Orange, Calif., 1989—. Contbr. author: (poetry) American Poetry Anthology, 1990, Selected Works of Our World's Best Poets/World of Poetry, 1991, Great Poems of Our Time/World of Poetry, 1991; lyricist works include Teach Me Lord, 1990 (Writer of Month award 1990), He Died for Me, 1991. With Calif. Army N.G., 1956-62. Mem. Internat. Soc. Poets, World of Poetry (Golden Poet award 1991). Democrat. Home: 446 S Tustin Ave Space 52 Orange CA 92666 *A great idea is only great when tried. God, in His Greatness, has seen fit to speak throught the pens of his children. There are no higher ideals or greater ideas than those of God.*

TOWNE, EDGAR ARTHUR, theologian, educator; b. Albany, N.Y., Feb. 27, 1928; s. Arthur Bethuel and Margaret (Shug) T.; m. Sara Jean Wright, June 14, 1952 (div. 1961); children: Mary Michal, Jonathan Wright, Nathan Arthur; m. Marian Kleinsasser, Dec. 18, 1961; 1 child, Stephen Edgar. BA, Coll. Wooster, 1949; BD, Pitts. Theol. Sem., 1952; MA, U. Chgo., 1962, PhD, 1967. Ordained to ministry Presbyn. Ch. (USA), 1952. Assoc. prof. systematic theology Winebrenner Theol. Sem., Findlay, Ohio, 1962-67; prof. philosophy and religion Findlay Coll., 1967-70; min. Hyde Park Union Ch., Chgo., 1971-75; prof. theology Christian Theol. Sem., Indpls., 1975—; vis. prof. theology Christian Theol. Sem., Indpls., 1970-71; vis. scholar Grad. Theol. Union, Berkeley, Calif., 1981-82, Pitts. Theol. Sem., 1988-89; co-moderator com. on pub. ministry Synod of Lincoln Trails, Ind., Ill., 1986-88. Mem. ethics com. Meth. Hosp. Ind., Indpls., 1985-90. Mem. Am. Theol. Soc. (pres. Midwest div. 1986-87), Am. Acad. Religion, Soc. Christian Ethics, Highlands Inst. for Am. Religious Thought. Democrat. Home: 5129 N Illinois St Indianapolis IN 46208 Office: Christian Theol Sem 1000 W 42d St Indianapolis IN 46208

TOWNER, PHILIP HAINES, religious educator; b. St. Paul, Jan. 20, 1953; s. Earl Carlton and Martha Elizabeth (Nyquist) T.; m. Anne Louise Dahlen, Dec. 29, 1978; children: Rebekah Elizabeth, Erin Marie. BA, Northwestern Coll., Roseville, Minn., 1979; MA, Trinity Evang. Divinity Sch., Deerfield, Ill., 1981; PhD, U. Aberdeen, Scotland, 1984. Asst. min. Bethesda Ch., Mpls., 1978-79; asst. prof. N.T. China Evang. Sem., Taipei, Taiwan, 1985—; missionary Overseas Missionary Fellowship, Robesonia, Pa., 1987—; adj. prof. N.T. Covenant Theol. Sem., St. Louis, 1990-91. Sgt. USAF, 1972-76. Grantee Tyndale Fellowship for Bibl. Rsch., 1983-84. Mem. Soc. Bibl. Lit. Mem. Evang. Free Ch. Home: 5528 26th Ave S Minneapolis MN 55417 Office: Overseas Missionary Fellowship, PO Box 30-254, Taipei 10098, Republic of China

TOWNS, ELMER LEON, university dean, minister; b. Savannah, Ga., Oct. 21, 1932; s. Elmer Leon and Erin (McFaddin) T.; m. Ruth Jean Forbes, Aug. 21, 1953; children: Deborah, Stephen, Polly. BA, Northwestern Coll., 1954; MA, So. Meth. U., 1958; ThM, Dallas Theol. Sem., 1958; MRE, Garrett Theol. Sem., 1970; D Ministry, Fuller Theol. Sem., 1970; DLitt (hon.), Calif. Grad. Sch. Theology, 1972; DMin, Fuller Theol. Sem., 1958. Ordained to ministry Ind. Bapt. Ch., 1956. Prof. Christian edn. Midwest Bible Coll., St. Louis, 1958-61, Trinity Evang. Div. Sch., Deerfield, Ill., 1965-71; pres. Winnipeg (Man., Can.) Bible Coll., 1961-65; dean Sch. Religion, Liberty U. (formerly Liberty Bapt. Coll.), Lynchburg, Va., 1971—; pres. Can. Conf. Christian Edn., 1963. Contbr. articles to profl. jours. Home: 103 Fox Run Dr Lynchburg VA 24503 Office: Liberty U Lynchburg VA 24506

TOWNSEND, BRUCE WALTER, pastor; b. Nelsonville, Ohio, July 28, 1953; s. Dallas Dale and Virginia Kay (Potts) T.; m. Sarah Lynn Rosine, Feb. 6, 1982; 1 child, Sean Patrick. Student, Kalamazoo Valley Community, 1978-79, Bethany Bible Sch., 1987-88; grad., Supernatural Ministries Tng., Midland, Mich., 1990. Ordained to ministry Ind. Assemblies of God, 1979, Christian Internat. Network Prophetic Ministries, 1988. Sr. pastor Conquering Faith Fellowship, Kalamazoo, Mich., 1980—; pres. Bruce W. Townsend Ministries, Portage, Mich., 1990—; area dir. Internat. Conf. Faith Ministries, Little Rock, 1985—. Author: Stirring Up the Supernatural, 1990; contbg. editor newsletter. Dir. Concerned Citizens for Decency, Kalamazoo, 1984-87; Rep. party precinct and state delegate, 1984-88; caucus leader for Mich. Com. for Freedom, 1986-88. Office: Conquering Faith Fellowship PO Box 1450 Portage MI 49002 *The number one question in the universe is: "Who is going to rule?" All the failings of society hinge on the authority question, and it will never be settled completely until "every knee bows and every tongue confesses that Jesus Christ is Lord."*

TOWNSEND, JIM A., Bible editor; b. Memphis, Oct. 12, 1943; s. Arthur H. and Mary (Stockton) T.; m. Lucy Mellicant Forsyth, Jan. 1, 1972. BA, Bryan Coll., 1966; ThM, Dallas Theol. Sem., 1970; PhD, Fuller Theol. Sem., 1979. Instr. Mid-South Bible Coll., Memphis, 1970-74; pastor Grace Gospel Chapel, Memphis, 1970-73; asst. to pastor Temple Bapt. Ch., L.A., 1975-79; bible editor David C. Cook Pub. Co., Elgin, Ill., 1979—; conf. speaker David C. Cook Pub. Co., Elgin, Ill., 1987—. Author: The Bible Master Series, 1986-90. Recipient F.R. Rogers Bible award Bryan Coll., 1966, Henry Thiessen award Dallas Sem., 1970. Mem. Soc. Bibl. Lit., Evang. Theol. Soc. Home: 675 Linden Ave Elgin IL 60120 Office: David C Cook Pub Co 850 N Grove Ave Elgin IL 60120

TOWNSEND, JOHN TOLSON, clergyman, religion educator; b. Halifax, N.S., Can., July 25, 1927; came to U.S., 1927; s. William Thomas and Olley Haystead (Tolson) T.; m. Mary VanZandt Rust, June 13, 1956; children: William Thomas III, Stephen John. AB, Brown U., 1949; Lic. Theology, U. Toronto, 1952; STM, Harvard U., 1953, ThD, 1959. Instr. Phila. Div. Sch., 1960-63, asst. prof., 1963-66, assoc. prof., 1966-74; prof. Episcopal Div. Sch., Cambridge, Mass., 1974—; co-chairperson Phila. Seminar on Christian Origins, 1972-73. Author: A Liturgical Interpretation in Narrative Form of the Passion of Jesus Christ, 2d edit., 1984, Midrash Tanhuma, 1989. Mem. Conf. Anglican Theologians, Assn. Jewish Studies, Soc. Bibl. Lit., Christian Study Group on Judaism (chairperson 1983-85). Home: 40 Washington St Newton MA 02158-2220 Office: Episcopal Div Sch 99 Brattle St Cambridge MA 01238

TOWNSEND, KENNETH ROSS, priest; b. Holly Grove, Ala., Oct. 31, 1927; s. James Ernest and Mary H. (Jordan) T.; m. Irene Fogleman, Mar. 18, 1951; children; Marietta, Martha, Kenneth Ross, Elizabeth. AB, Birmingham South Coll., 1956; postgrad., Union Theol. Sem., 1960-63; MDiv, Va. Theol. Sem., 1964. Ordained priest Episcopal Ch., 1965. Pastor meth. chs. N.C. and Va. Confs., 1954-63; priest Bath Priest Parish, Dinwiddie, Va., 1964-69, St. Paul's Ch., Vanceboro, N.C., 1969—; lectr. philosophy Richard Bland Coll. of Coll. William and Mary, Williamsburg, Va., 1966-68; del. to synod Province IV, 1973; mem. liturgical com. Episcopal Diocese of East Carolina, Wilmington, N.C., 1971-82, mem. prison commn., 1984. Mem. Delta Sigma Phi. Address: 2521 Paxton St Lake Ridge Woodbridge VA 22192 *Yearning for self fulfillment in a better world is the 'mother of the will' to be and to accomplish. By this will we define ourselves. This will identifies our goals in work and relationships. Such a self concept informs our minds as to what is right and correct. The yearning, the will, the goals and accomplishment are thinkable and obtainable. The world awaits our resolve.*

TOWNSLEY, MARSHALL WAYNE, religious organization administrator; b. Abilene, Tex., July 8, 1954; s. Arthur Douglas and Anna Isabel (Keys) T.; m. Cindi Ann Pace, Apr. 13, 1973; children: Hannah Beth, Jordan Rochelle. Grad. high sch., Mesquite, Tex., 1972. Student elec. engr. Tex. Power & Light, Mesquite, 1972-73; assoc. min. Andrew Wommack Ministries, Mesquite, 1973-75; pastor Ch. at Sylvester, Hamlin, Tex., 1975-77; assoc. dir. Bible Tng. Ctr., Albuquerque, 1977-80; founder, pres., pastor Churchbuilder Ministries, Inc., Albuquerque, 1980—; bd. dirs. New Creation Ch., Glennwood Springs, Colo.; cons. Conciliation Svcs. N.Mex., Albuquerque, 1987-88. Author: Culmination of the Ages, 1990. Recipient Cert. Appreciation Word of Faith Leadership and Bible Inst., 1987-89. Mem. ICFM (state dir. 1986-88). Republican. Avocations: golf, snow skiing, fishing, basketball. Office: Believers Ctr Albuquerque 4800 Lomas NE Albuquerque NM 87110

TRACY, DANIEL LEROY, minister of music; b. Monterey, Calif., Dec. 16, 1946; s. Albert LeRoy and Alene Inez (Selman) T.; m. Donna Francine Fillman, June 6, 1967; children: Danny, Deborah. MusB, Okla. Baptist Univ., 1968; MA, Cen. Mo. State Univ., 1980. Minister music/youth First Bapt. Ch., Davis, Okla., 1965-67; minister music/youth Calvary Bapt. Ch., Sulphur, Okla., 1967-68, Enid, Okla., 1968-70; minister music/youth First Bapt. Ch., Broken Arrow, Okla., 1970-74, Macedonia Bapt. Ch., Springfield, Mo., 1974-75; minister music First Bapt. Ch., Warrensburg, Mo., 1975-84, Canyon, Tex., 1984—; leadership trainer Mo. Bapt. Conv., 1976-84; music dir. Johnson County Bapt. Assn., 1975-84; choir dir. Bapt. Student Union, W. Tex. State U., 1988. Mem. Singing Men of W. Tex., 1985—; bd. dirs. Greater Southwest Music Festival, Amarillo, Tex., 1988—; announcer Canyon High Sch. Varsity Eagles, 1985—; mem. Lady Buff Club W. Tex. State U., Canyon, 1988—; music dir. Canyon Sr. Citizens Ctr., 1987—. Mem. Tex. Choral Director's Assn., Tex. Music Educators Assn., So. Bapt. Ch. Music Conf., Am. Guild Handbell Ringers. Avocations: golf, traveling, gardening, reading. Home: 1717 Third Ave Canyon TX 79015 Office: First Baptist Church 1717 Fourth Ave Canyon TX 79015

TRACY, DAVID, theology educator; b. Yonkers, N.Y., Jan. 6, 1939. Licentiate in Theology, Gregorian U., Rome, 1964, Doctorate in Theology, 1969; hon. doctorate, U. of the South, 1982, Cath. Theol. Union, 1990. Instr. theology Cath. U. Am., Washington, 1967-69; prof. theology Divinity Sch., U. Chgo., 1969—, prof. com. analysis of ideas and methods, 1981—, Disting. Svc. prof., 1985, Andrew Thomas Greeley and Grace McNichols Greeley Disting. Svc. prof. Cath. studies, 1987, prof. com. social thought, 1990—; lectr. Beijing Inst. Sci. Study of Religion, Trinity Coll., Dublin, Gregorian U., Rome, World Coun. Chs., Geneva, Cath. U., Leuven, Belgium, Union Theol. Sem., Princeton Theol. Sem., numerous U.S. univs. including Harvard, Yale, Fordham, Notre Dame, Vanderbilt, So. Meth., Xavier, Marquette. Author: The Achievement of Bernard Lonergan, 1970, Blessed Rage for Order: The New Pluralism in Theology, 1975, The Analogical Imagination: Christian Theology and the Context of Pluralism, 1981, Plurality and Ambiguity: Hermeneutics, Religion and Hope, 1987, Religion and the Public Realm, 1987; co-author: (with John Cobb) Talking About God, 1983, (with Stephen Happel) The Catholic Vision, 1983, (with Robert M. Grant) A Short History of the Interpretation of the Bible, 1984; co-editor: (with Hans Küng and Johann Baptist Metz) Towards Vatican III: The Work That Needs to be Done, (with H. Küng) Theologie-Wohin?. German edit., 1983, English edit., 1985, (with Hans Küng) Paradigm Change in Theology, 1989; editor or co-editor various spl. vols. for Jour. Religion, Concilium jour.; co-editor Jour. Religion, Religious Studies Rev., Commonweal; past mem. editorial bd. Jour. Am. Acad. Religion, Theol. Studies jour.; current editorial bd. Theology Today, Jour. Pastoral Psychology; contbr. articles to scholarly and popular jours. including Jour. Religion, Theology Today, Critical Inquiry, Daedalus, Jour. Am. Acad. Religion, New Republic, N.Y. Times Book Rev., Christian Century. Mem. Am. Acad. Arts and Scis., Am. Acad. Religion, Am. Theol. Soc., Cath. Theol. Soc. Am. (pres. 1977-78). Office: U Chgo The Divinity Sch 1025 E 58th St Chicago IL 60637

TRACY, DENISE DIANE, clergywoman; b. Hartford, Conn., Aug. 8, 1950; d. Robert Clark and Theresa (Bolduc) T.; m. William Herman Decker III, Jan. 16, 1982; 1 child, Clarke L. Decker. BA cum laude, U. Hartford, 1971; MDiv with honors, Andover Newton Theol. Sch., Newton, Mass., 1974; cert. therapy, Avanta Inst., Calif., 1981. Ordained fellow Unitarian Universalist Assn., 1979. Campus minister Greater Hartford (Conn.) Campus Ministry, 1974-75, Univ. Christian Movement, Cambridge, Mass., 1975-76; parish minister Unitarian Universalist Ch. of Greater Lansing, Mich., 1976-84; dist. exec. central midwest dist. Unitarian Universalist Assn., Chgo., 1984—; founder Ministerial Sisterhood Unitarian Universalist Assn., Boston, 1976, Nat. Coun. of Chs. Commn. on Women in Ministry, N.Y.C., 1974; convenor Womanquest com., Unitarian Universalist Assn., 1987—; mem. CMD/Meadville Lombard Continuing Edn. Com., 1987—. Author: Stream of Living Souls, Vols. I, II and III, 1986-88, Myths of Time and History, 1988. Vice-pres. Drug Counseling Ctr. East Lansing (Mich.), 1978-80; gov.'s rep. State Bd. on Mortuary Sci., Lansing, 1979-83. Mem. Coun. Religion Leaders Chgo., Unitarian Universalist Ministers Assn. (v.p. 1982-84, chmn. continuing edn. com. 1982-83), Zonta Club (v.p. 1983). Avocations: T'ai chi, skiing, saving, cooking, clothes designing. Home: 421 Clinton Ave Oak Park IL 60302

TRACY, JAMES WAYNE, pastor, educator; b. Tulsa, Nov. 17, 1945; s. James Kenneth and Margaret Eunice (Pickett) T.; m. Carolyn Marie Haugan, Aug. 7, 1976; children: Keith Scott, Tonya Raylene; m. Judith Ann Cornwall, Sept. 12, 1967 (div. 1972); 1 child, James Robert. BA, So. Calif. Coll., Costa Mesa, 1970; MA, Calif. Grad. Sch. of Theol., Glendale, 1985. Cert. sch. adminstr. Assn. Christian Schs. Internat. Assoc. pastor 1st Assembly of God, Grants Pass, Oreg., 1967-68; christian sch. tchr. Wilmington (Calif.) Christian Sch., 1968-70, 72-75; assoc. pastor 1st Assembly of God, Salem, Oreg., 1970-72, New Life Christian Ctr., Fresno, Calif., 1976-81, Assembly of God, Hawthorne, Calif., 1981; pastor Calvary Chapel, Los Alamos, N.Mex., 1982—. Author: Divorce Re Marriage: The Letter of the Law vs. The Spirit if the Law, 1985. Active mem. United Way Funding Com., Los Alamos, N.Mex., 1987. Mem. Assn. Christian Schs., Internat., Assn. Christian Schs. Internat. Admnistrs. Fellowship. Republican. Office: Calvary Chapel 580 N Mesa Rd Los Alamos NM 87544

TRACY, MARK LUTHER, minister; b. Portsmouth, Ohio, May 24, 1943; s. W. Luther and Margaret Virginia (Davis) T.; m. Barbara Allen Thompson, July 27, 1969. BA, Ohio U., 1965; MDiv, Andover Newton Theol. Sch., Newton Centre, Mass., 1969; MBA, George Mason U., 1980. Cert. ch. adminstr. Assoc. minister Nat. Bapt. Meml. Ch., Washington, 1969-75; bus. mgr. Bapt. Home of D.C., Washington, 1975-78, Bapt. Home for Children, Bethesda, Md., 1978-81; exec. officer New York Ave. Presbyn. Ch., Washington, 1982-87; bus. mgr. retirement home Culpepper Garden, Arlington, Va., 1987-90; field rep. Am. Bapt. Extension Corp., Valley Forge, Pa., 1990—. Contbr. articles to profl. newsletter. Mem. Ch. Mgmt. Alumni Assn. (pres. Am. Univ. chpt. 1975), Soc. for Religious Orgn. Mgmt. (bd. dirs. 1976-79), Nat. Assn. Ch. Bus. Adminstrn. (nat. conf. chmn. 1988-90), Interfaith Forum on Religion, Art and Architecture. Home: 618 General Scott Rd King of Prussia PA 19406 Office: American Baptist Ext Corp PO Box 851 Valley Forge PA 19482

TRAER, ROBERT A., minister, educator; b. Kalamazoo, Mich., Jan. 12, 1943; s. James K. and Effie (Bosker) T.; m. Nancy L. Staab, June 9, 1968; children: Kim, Anh, Elie, Emily, James. BA, Carleton Coll., 1965; D of Ministry, U. Chgo., 1969; JD, U. Calif., Davis, 1976; PhD, Grad. Theol. Union, 1988. Mem. faculty Coll. of St. Francis, Joliet, Ill., 1976-85, St. Mary's Coll. of Calif., Moraga, 1987-90, U. San Francisco, 1988-90; gen. sec. Internat. Assn. for Religious Freedom, Frankfurt, Fed. Republic of Germany, 1990—. Author: Faith in Human Rights, 1991; contbr. articles to profl. jours. Pres. Colorado Springs (Colo.) Bd. of Edn., 1982-84. Rockefeller Found. fellow. Mem. Am. Acad. Religion, Phi Beta Kappa. Home: Hasenpfad 125, 6000 Frankfurt 70, Federal Republic of Germany Office: Internat Assn, for Religious Freedom, Oreieichstrasse 59, 6000 Frankfurt 70, Federal Republic of Germany

TRAN, ANTHONY DOAN, priest; b. Ninh Binh, Vietnam, June 20, 1950; came to U.S., 1980; MDiv, Notre Dame Sem. Grad. Sch. Theology, 1988. Ordained to ministry Roman Cath. Ch., 1988. Assoc. pastor Sacred Heart Ch., D'Iberville, Miss., 1988—. Author: Tieng Noi Con Tim, 1990; Linh-Muc-Nguoi-La-Ai, 1991. Home and Office: 10446 LeMoyne Blvd D'Iberville Biloxi MS 39532

TRANEL, JAMES MICHAEL, priest, principal; b. Hazal Green, Wis., Mar. 17, 1951; s. Albert Herman and Mary Agnes (Plear) T. BA in Philosophy, Loras Coll., 1973; STB, Pontifical Gregorian U., Rome, 1976, MA, 1977; MA in Ednl. Adminstrn., No. Ill. U., 1986. Ordained priest Roman Cath. Ch., 1977; cert. tchr., Ill. Assoc. pastor St. Patrick Ch., Dixon, Ill., 1977-81, St. Mary Ch., Woodstock, Ill., 1981-82, Holy Family Ch., Rockford, Ill., 1982-83; pastor St. Mary Cath. Ch., Tampico, Ill., 1987—; prin. Newman High Sch./Middle Sch., Sterling, Ill., 1987—; mem. Rockford Diocesan Bd. Edn., 1981—. Active Clergy Relief Soc., Rockford, 1987—; mem. personnel bd. Diocese of Rockford, 1988—. Mem. Nat. Cath. Edn. Assn. Avocations: camping, racquetball, gardening. Office: Newman High Sch/Middle Sch 1101 St Mary Rd Sterling IL 61081

TRAPANI, ROBERT DON, minister; b. N.Y.C., May 4, 1939; s. Dominic and Elsie (Magloosky) T.; m. Hilda Berniece Latta, Oct. 4, 1958; children: Geoffrey, Anthony, Nathan, David, Julia, Andrea. Student, U. Ind., 1956-57, Apostolic Bible Inst., St. Paul, 1957-59, U. Minn., 1958-61, U. Akron, 1968-71; BTh, Ohio Bible Coll., Cuyahoga Falls, 1973, BRE (hon.), 1974. Ordained to ministry United Pentecostal Ch. Internat. Pastor Christchurch Apostolic/New Life, Richfield, Ohio, 1966-91; pres. Ohio Bible Coll., Northampton, 1975-78; dir. New Life Ministries, Akron, 1980—; pastor New Life Ch., Akron, 1980—; mem. steering com. Christian Leadership Alliance, Cleve., 1987-89; mem. camp ground com. Ohio Dist. United Pentecostal Ch. Internat., Millersport, 1989-90; presbyter United Pentecostal Ch. Northeastern Ohio, 1989-91. Author: In His Image, 1990, Preparing the Ministry, 1991; contbr. Brother Theophilus, 1980-88; editor Ohio Dist. Mins.' Manual, 1989-90. Trustee, bd. drs. Brinkhaven Children's Home, Lawrence, Ohio, k1989—, mem. bldg. com., 1990-91. Fellow Nat. Assn. Pastoral Counselors; mem. Mensa, Intertel. Home: 89 Conger Ave Akron OH 44303 Office: New Life Counseling Office 1240 Weathervane Ln A Akron OH 44313

TRAPP, THOMAS HARVEY, religion educator; b. Detroit, May 4, 1946; s. Harvey Edward and Eleanore Christina (Kerstein) T.; m. Kathleen Susan Hoelzel, Aug. 15, 1970; children: Matthew, Joanna, Daniel. BA, Concordia Sr. Coll., 1967; MDiv, Concordia Sem., 1971; DTh, U. Heidelberg, West Germany, 1980. Parish pastor Emmanuel Luth. Ch., Britton, Mich., 1973-82; prof. Concordia Coll., St. Paul, 1982—. Translator in field. Fulbright grant U.S. Govt., 1971-73. Mem. Soc. Bibl. Lit., Cath. Bibl. Assn., Am. Philos. Assn. Home: 1698 Hubbard Ave Saint Paul MN 55104-1130 Office: Concordia Coll 275 N Syndicate Saint Paul MN 55104-5494

TRAUB, GEORGE MICHAEL, pastor, counselor; b. Richmond, Va., Apr. 8, 1958; s. Milton Michael and Marjorie Ellen (Deaton) T.; m. Charlotte Elizabeth Pryor, June 20, 1981; 1 child, Ryan Michael. BA, Bryan Coll., 1980; ThM, Grace Sem., 1984. Ins. investigator Equifax, Richmond, 1977-79; maintenance supr. Grace Schs., Winona Lake, Ind., 1980-84; pastoral intern Winona Lake Grace Brethren Ch., 1982-83; counselor Inst. Bibl. Counseling, Winona Lake, summer 1984; pastor Washington Heights Grace Brethren Ch., Roanoke, Va., 1984—; pvt. practice counseling, Roanoke, 1984—, Harrisonburg, Va., 1988-89, Blacksburg, Va., 1988—; seminar tchr. Brethren Evangelistic Ministries, Roanoke, 1988—. Bd. dirs. Crisis Pregnancy Ctr., Roanoke, 1989—. Mem. Am. Assn. for Counseling and Devel. Republican. Avocations: golf, basketball, reading. Home: 8325 Willow Ridge Rd Roanoke VA 24019 Office: Washington Heights Ch 3833 Michigan Ave NW Roanoke VA 24017

TRAUTMAN, DALE CHARLES, minister; b. Bridgeville, Pa., Aug. 13, 1941; s. George J. and Mercedes L. (Gallagher) T.; m. Nancy Ellen Hast, June 12, 1965; children: Todd, Dawn. BA, Capital U., 1964; MDiv, Trinity Sem., Columbus, Ohio, 1968. Ordained to ministry Evang. Luth. Ch. Am., 1968. Pastor Christ the King Luth. Ch., Columbus, 1968-72; sr. pastor Faith Luth. Ch., Massillon, Ohio, 1972-80, Olivet Luth. Ch., Fargo, N.D., 1986—; dir. evangelism Am. Luth. Ch., Mpls., 1980-86; bd. dirs. Trinity Luth. Sem., 1976-81, Acad. Parish Evangelist, Columbus, 1985—. Contbr. articles to profl. publs. Office: Olivet Luth Ch 1330 S University Dr Fargo ND 58103

TRAUTMAN, DONALD W., bishop; b. Buffalo, June 24, 1936. Ed., Our Lady of Angels Sem., Niagara Falls, N.Y., Theology Faculty, Innsbruck, Austria, Pontifical Biblical Inst., Rome, Cath. U., St. Thomas Aquinas U., Rome. Ordained priest, Roman Cath. Ch., Apr. 1962. Ordained titular bishop of Sassura and aux. bishop Diocese of Buffalo, 1985; bishop of Erie, Pa., 1990—; Episc. moderator Diocesan Fiscal Mgmt. Conf.; mem. com. on doctrine and communications, Nat. Conf. Cath. Bishops. Address: St Mark's Center PO Box 10397 Erie PA 16514

TRAVELL, JOHN CHARLES, minister; b. Gloucester, Gloucestershire, Eng., Apr. 4, 1930; s. George Edward and Winifred Mary (Cook) T.; m. Annette Patricia Fare, Sept. 14, 1957; children: Richard John, Diana Rosemary. BD with honors, New Coll., London, 1965; ThM, Kings Coll., London, 1969. Ordained to ministry Congl. Ch., 1966. Assoc. min. Christ Ch. and Upton Chapel Lambeth, London, 1966-68; min. Penge Congl. Ch., London, 1969-89; co-chmn. Internat. Congl. Fellowship, Dorchester, Eng., 1989—; officer world mission Coun. for World Mission, 1973-86; pres. Congl. Fedn., 1982-83; mem. trust and libr. com. Congl. Meml. Hall Trust, London, 1974—. Contbr. articles to profl. jours. Chmn. Penge Forum, S.E. London, 1972-79. Fellow Royal Soc. Arts; mem. Inst. Religion and Medicine, United Ref. Ch. History Soc., Wesley Hist. Soc. Home and Office: Internat Congl Fellowship, 44 Cornwall Rd, Dorchester DT1 1RY, England

TRAVERS, DAVID OWENS, chaplain; b. Lynn, Mass., June 27, 1934; s. Daniel Otis and Helena (Owens) T. BA, Boston Coll., 1961, MDiv, 1969; MEd, Tufts U., 1969. Ordained priest Roman Cath. Ch., 1968. Retreat dir. Jesuit Ctr., Boston, 1969-74; chaplain Boston City Hosp., 1974-76; commd. 2d lt. USN, 1970, advanced through grades to commdr., 1982, chaplain, 1976—. Mem. Jesuits of New England. Home: 490 Aulima Loop Kailua HI 96734 Office: Chaplains Office Marine Corps Air Station Kaneohe Bay HI 96863-5001

TRAVIS, ADRIAN PAUL, minister; b. Nhatrang, Vietnam, Apr. 7, 1931; s. Chester Earl and Mary (Hall) T.; m. Ruth Marie Travis, Sept. 6, 1952; children: Robin, Leslie. BA, Simpson Coll., Redding, Calif., 1952; MA, Berkeley Div. Sem., 1955. Ordained to ministry Christian and Missionary Alliance, 1959. Minister Christian Missionary Alliance Ch., San Jose, 1954-56, Cathedral of Tomorrow, Oakland, Calif., 1957-63, Ch. in the Round, L.A., 1964-66, Pinewood Alliance LeTourneau Coll., Longview, Tex., 1966-71, Cathedral at the Crossroads, Castro Valley, Calif., 1971-80; prof. Chabot Coll., Hayward, Calif., 1976-79; minister Village Ch., Hayward, Calif., 1981-85, Calif. Community Ch., Pleasanton, 1985-90, Walnut Creek Ch. of the Nazarene, Walnut Creek, Calif., 1990—; ch. planting cons. Christian Missionary Alliance, Foster City, 1984-87, Ch. of the Nazarene, Walnut Creek, 1990—. Contbr. articles to profl. jours. Mem. Commonwealth Club (San Francisco). Republican. Avocations: water skiing, biking, travel. Home: 2324 Mallard Dr Walnut Creek CA 94596 Office: Walnut Creek Nazarene Ch 1755 Sunnyvale Ave Walnut Creek CA 94596

TRAVIS, JAMES LESLIE, religion educator; b. Carlisle, Pa., Nov. 2, 1923; s. James Leslie and Fleta Marie (Shaeffer) T.; m. Lucille Evangeline Wall, June 18, 1950; children: James Leslie III, Philip, LuAnne, John. BA, Okla. Bapt. U., 1949; BD, New Orleans Bapt. Theol. Sem., 1952, ThD, 1960. Ordained to ministry So. Bapt. Conv., 1948. Pastor various chs. La., Miss., Okla., 1950-60; prof. Blue Mountain (Miss.) Coll.; Miss. rep. Chistian Life Commn., So. Bapt. Conv., Nashville, 1966-74; pres. ministerial bd. edn. Miss. Bapt. Conv. Bd., Jackson, 1973-77. Co-author: Introduction to Baptist Work, 1962; contbr. to: Wycliffe Bible Encyclopedia, 1975, Holman Bible Dictionary, 1991; author bibl. commentaries; contbr. articles to religious jours. Named Tchr. of Yr., Blue Mountain Coll., 1980, Alumnus of Yr., Miss. chpt. New Orleans Bapt. Theol. Sem., 1989. Republican. Avocations: golf, jogging, gardening. Home: Box 237 College Blue Mountain MS 38610 Office: Blue Mountain Coll Blue Mountain MS 38610

TRAVIS, MURRAY WILLIAM, clergyman; b. Chgo., Aug. 6, 1931; s. Frank Douglas and Laura Jessie (Gunter) T.; m. Jane Ella Brooks, Sept. 2, 1952; children: Douglas B., Jan Marie Travis Evans, Drew G., Kara K. Travis Wells, Karl B. BA, Trinity U., San Antonio, 1953; MDiv, McCormick Theol. Sem., 1957, DMin, 1979. Ordained to ministry, Presbyterian Church, 1957. Pastor Trinity Presbyn. Ch., Oak Lawn, Ill., 1956-60, Northminster Presbyn. Ch., Amarillo, Tex., 1960-67, First Presbyn. Ch., Tulia, Tex., 1967-81, Sinton (Tex.) Presbyn. Ch., 1981-86, Westminster Presbyn. Ch., Abilene, Tex., 1986—; moderator, Plains Presbytery, Tex. Panhandle, 1967; chmn. numerous coms., Palo Duro Presbytery, Tex. Panhandle, 1972—. Pres. Tulia Day Nursery, 1971-73; chmn. United Fund Campaign, Tulia, 1975, Community Concerns, Sinton, 1984-85. Mem. Tulia Rotary. Democrat. Office: Westminster Presbyn Ch 4515 S 14th St Abilene TX 79605

TRAW, STEVEN PAUL, minister; b. Emporia, Kans., Apr. 7, 1947; s. Paul Richard and L. Doris (Williamson) T.; m. Susan Doree Wittmer, Sept. 1, 1968; children: Michael Steven, Judi Marie, Rebecca Sue. BS in Edn., Emporia State U., 1969; MTh, Dallas Theol. Sem., 1982. Ordained to ministry Christian Ch. (Disciples of Christ), 1982. Assoc. min. Pleasant Grove Christian Ch., Dallas, 1979-82; min. 1st Christian Ch., Post, Tex., 1982-87, Iola, Kans., 1987—; pres. Christian Ch. SE Dist. Kans., Iola, 1991—. Author: Pilgrim's Progress Illustrated, 1982, Disciples Character, 1986; weekly pastor's columnist Dispatch-Post, Tex., 1984-85. Mem. endowment bd. Allen County Coll., 1989—. Capt. USAF, 1971-77. Recipient Excellence in Evangelism award Nat. Evangelistic Assn., 1989. Mem. Emporia State U. Alumni Assn., Dallas Theol. Sem. Alumni Assn., Rotary (pres. 1986-87). Home: 1011 E Buchanan Iola KS 66749 Office: 1st Christian Ch 301 East St Iola KS 66749

TRAYLOR, CHARLES HAROLD, minister; b. Atlanta, Nov. 14, 1955; s. George Harold and Frances (Howard) T.; m. Ronda Christine Long, June 11, 1977; children: Lethia Brooke, Jared Ezekiel, Micah Shane. MusB, Ga. State U., 1978; M in Ch. Music, Southwestern Bapt. Theol. Sem., Fort Worth, 1980. Minister of music Calvary Bapt. Ch., Marietta, Ga., 1976-77; minister of music Zion Bapt. Ch., Covington, Ga., 1977-78, assoc. pastor, 1978; minister of music First Bapt. Ch. Forest Hill, Ft. Worth, 1978-80; minister of music, edn. Highland Bapt. Ch., Laurel, Miss., 1981-83, minister of music, sr. adults, 1983-86; minister of music First Bapt. Ch., Winter Haven, Fla., 1986—. Mem. So. Bapt. Ch. Music Conf., Blue Key, Phi Eta Sigma (freshman honor soc. 1974). Republican. Avocation: woodworking. Home: 455 Broward Ter Winter Haven FL 33880 Office: First Bapt Ch 198 W Central Ave Winter Haven FL 33884

TRAYLOR, JOHN HARDIE, minister; b. Columbia, La., Jan. 11, 1928; s. John hardie and Bernice Inez (Bogan) T.; m. Bettye Virginia Colvin, Jan. 25, 1950; children: Kathryn Elizabeth Traylor Johnson, Angela Kay Traylor Mann. BSME, La. Tech. U., 1951; BDiv, New Orleans Bapt. Theol. Sem., 1954, ThD, 1963. Ordained to ministry, So. Bapt. Conv. Pastor Kelly (La.) Bapt. Ch., 1953-54, Fla. Ave. Bapt. Mission, New Orleans, 1954-56, Seven Hill Bapt. Ch., Mobile, Ala., 1956-59, Coll. Hts. Bapt. Ch., Plainview, Tex., 1959-66, Calvary Bapt. Ch., Tupelo, Miss., 1966-69; Pastor First Bapt. Ch., Gulfport, Miss., 1969-76, Monroe, La., 1976—; trustee Wayland Bapt. Coll., Plainview, 1959-66, Midwestern Bapt. Theol. Sem., Kansas City, Kans., 1968-76; mem. Miss. Bapt. Ednl. Commn., 1968-76; trustee La. Coll., 1978-84; mem. La. Bapt. Conv. Exec. Bd., Alexandria, 1986—, pres. exec. bd., 1991—. Author: Bible Book Series for Adult Teachers, 1970—, Bible Book Commentary, 1982; contbr. articles to profl. jours. With U.S. Army, 1946-48. Home: 18 Winchester Cir Monroe LA 71203 Office: First Bapt Ch 201 St John Monroe LA 71201

TREACY, SISTER JOAN, religious order executive, nun; b. Kilkenny, Ireland, May 23, 1944; came to U.S., 1961; d. Thomas and Mary (Hoyne) Treacy. B.A., Marymount Coll., 1967; M.A., St. Mary's Coll., Moraga, Calif., 1979; postgrad., St. Mary's Sem. and U., Balt. Joined Sisters Religious of Sacred Heart of Mary. Tchr. St. Francis de Sales Parish, Sherman Oaks, Calif., 1964-67; tchr., adminstr. Marymount Sch., Santa Barbara, Calif., 1967-71; dir. religious edn. St. Barbara's Parish, Santa Barbara, Calif., 1972-76, St. Jane Frances Parish, North Hollywood, Calif., 1976-78; dir. formation Religious of Sacred Heart of Mary, Western Am. Province, Los Angeles, 1978-80, provincial superior, 1985—; dir. spiritual devel. program Loyola Marymount U., Los Angeles, 1980-85; provost Loyola Marymount U., 1981-85; mem. Nat. Religious Formation Conf., Los Angeles Religious Formation Conf.; mem. adv. bd. religious edn. Archdiocese of Los Angeles; condr. retreats, Santa Barbara and Los Angeles counties, organized, dir. adult spiritual renewal programs for religious and lay people, spiritual counsellor for youths and adults; provincial team mem. Religious of the Sacred Heart of Mary, provincial council mem., del. to 1980 and 1985 gen. chpt., chmn. province formation team, provincial chpt. steering com., 1979-80, mem. internat. constns. commn., mem. province spiritual life com. Mem. Calif. Women in Higher Edn., AAUW, Assn. Governing Bds. of Univs. and Colls. Office: 8008 Loyola Blvd Los Angeles CA 90045

TREADGOLD, DONALD WARREN, educator, historian; b. Silverton, Oreg., Nov. 24, 1922; s. Frederic Vere and Mina Belle (Hubbs) T.; m. Alva Adele Granquist, Aug. 24, 1947; children—Warren Templeton, Laura Margaret, Catherine Mina. B.A., U. Oreg., 1943; M.A., Harvard U., 1947; D.Phil. (Rhodes scholar 1947), U. Oxford, Eng., 1950. Mem. faculty U. Wash., Seattle, 1949—; prof. history U. Wash., 1959—, chmn. dept., 1972-82, chmn. Russian and East European program, Sch. Internat. Studies, 1983-86, annual faculty lectr., 1980; vis. prof. Nat. Taiwan U., Taipei, 1959; vis. research prof. USSR Acad. Scis., Moscow, 1965, 82, Toyo Bunko, Tokyo, 1968; scholar-in-residence Villa Serbelloni, Bellagio, Italy, 1982; John A. Burns Disting. vis. prof. history U. Hawaii, Manoa, 1986-87; chmn. Far Western Slavic Conf., 1961-62, Conf. on Slavic and East European History of Am. Hist. Assn., 1965, mem. council, 1960-63; chmn. joint com. Slavic studies Social Sci. Research Council and Am. Council Learned Socs., 1962-64; chmn. organizing com. XIV Internat. Congress Hist. Scis., San Francisco, 1975; chmn. program com. III World Congress Soviet and East European Studies, Washington, 1985; mem. acad. council Kennan Inst. for Advanced Russian Studies, 1977-81, chmn., 1986—; trustee Nat. Council Soviet and East European Research, 1977-84. Author: Lenin and His Rivals, 1955, reprint, 1976, Spanish transl., 1958, The Great Siberian Migration, 1957, reprint, 1976, Twentieth Century Russia, 7th edit, 1990, Malay transl., 1986, The West in Russia and China, 2 vols, 1973, 85, A History of Christianity, 1979, Freedom: A History, 1990; also articles; editor: The Development of the USSR, 1964, Spanish transl., 1969, Soviet and Chinese Communism, 1967, Slavic Review, 1961-65, 68-75, (with P.F. Sugar) A History of East Central Europe, Vols. V, VII-IX, 1974-77, Vol. VI, 1984, (with Lawrence Lerner) Gorbachev and the Soviet Future, 1989. Trustee Bush Sch., 1973-76. Served to capt. AUS, 1943-46. Decorated Bronze Star; recipient E. Harris Harbison award, 1968, Saionjii Fgn. Area Studies profl. award, 1991; Ford fellow, 1954-55; Rockefeller grantee, 1959, 61; Guggenheim fellow, 1964-65; Phi Beta Kappa vis. scholar, 1974-75. Fellow Am. Acad. Arts and Scis.; mem. Am. Hist. Assn. (mem. council 1970-73, v.p. Pacific Coast br. 1977-78, pres. 1978-79), Am. Assn. Advancement Slavic Studies (dir. 1968-75, Distinguished Service award 1975, pres. 1977-78, Disting. Contbr. to Slavic Studies award 1988), Am. Assn. Rhodes Scholars, Internat. House of Japan, Phi Beta Kappa (council nominating com. 1973-78, chmn. 1977-78), Sigma Delta Pi. Club: United Oxford and Cambridge U. Home: 900 University St Seattle WA 98101

TREADWELL, FREDRICK CARLTON, pastor; b. Bonifay, Fla., Feb. 16, 1956; s. H. Carlton and Kathryn Mary (Zappolo) T.; m. Barbara Amy Haye, June 10, 1978; children: Amanda Kathryn, Aimee Rebekah, Andrew Carlton. BA cum laude, Samford U., 1977; MDiv. with distinction, Southeastern Bapt. Theol. Sem., 1981, postgrad., 1984—. Assoc. pastor Haw River (N.C.) Christian Ch., 1977-83; pastor First Cross Rds. Bapt. Ch., Turbeville, Va., 1983-84; min. of youth and sr. adults First Bapt. Ch., Sebring, Fla., 1984-88; pastor Glen Hope Bapt. Ch., Burlington, N.C., 1988—; spl. worker Sunday sch. Fla. Bapt. State Conv., Jacksonville, Fla., 1986-88; dir. Vacation Bible Sch. Orange Blossom Assn., Avon Park, Fla., 1987-88. Mem. Mt. Zion Bapt. Assn. (pastors conf. 1988—, missions com. 1991—, chmn. evangelism com. 1991—, assn. discipleship tng. worker 1991—), Phi Theta Kappa. Republican. Home: 605 Ridgeway Dr Burlington NC 27217 Office: Glen Hope Bapt Ch 911 North Ave Burlington NC 27217 *I live life as a debtor. I owe God and His people redemption, acceptance, love and an enormous investment of time. I can only repay the debt as I invest in the lives of others.*

TREESE, DONALD HOWARD, minister, religious organization executive; b. Mines, Pa., Sept. 11, 1930; s. Watson Irvin and Bessie (Hughes) T.; m. Lois Audrey Ward; children: Joel Donald, Laura Grace, Hope Anne. BA, Juniata Coll., 1952; MDiv, Chgo. Theol. Sem., 1955; DD (hon.), Lebanon Valley Coll., 1976; LHD (hon.), Lycoming Coll., 1983. Ordained to ministry United Meth. Ch., 1957. Pastor United Meth. Ch., Gettysburg, Pa., 1961-65, Williamsport, Pa., 1965-69, Altoona, Pa., 1969-73, Carlisle, Pa., 1973-79; assoc. gen. sec. Bd. Higher Edn., Nashville, 1979—; dir. Wesley Works Project, Nashville, 1979—; cons. World Meth. Coun., Lake Junaluska, N.C., 1981—. Contbg. author: Whom Shall We Send, 1991. Bd. dirs. Crisis Intervention Svc., Altoona, 1969-73; trustee Altoona Hosp., 1970-73, Evang. Sem. P.R., San Juan, 1984—, Fund for Theol. Edn., N.Y.C., 1989—; mem. Community Health Coun., Carlisle, 1976-79, Community Hunger Program, Nashville, 1989—. Mem. Kiwanis. Democrat. Office: Bd Higher Edn PO Box 871 Nashville TN 37202

TREFSGAR, THEODORE WEBSTER, JR. (), pastor; b. Phila., June 17, 1961; s. Theodore W. and Joyce C. (Messick) T.; m. Sheryl Anne Duffy, Sept. 17, 1988. BS, Pa. State U., 1984; MDiv, Reformed Episcopal Sem., Phila., 1988. Cert. tchr. Spl. educator Devereaux Sch., Devon, Pa., 1984-85; dir. youth and Christian edn. Southwestern Presbyn. Ch., Phila., 1985-88; spl. educator Melmark Home, Inc., Berwyn, Pa., 1988-89; assoc. pastor Grace Ch. of Harmony, Pa., 1990—. Republican. Presbyterian. Avocations: sports, reading, hiking, photography. Home: 212 Mercer St Harmony PA 16037

TREFZGER, JOHN DENNIS, retired clergyman; b. Peoria, Ill., Sept. 4, 1923; s. Charles Joseph and Dorothy Angelica (Trockur) T.; m. Marilyn Lestilie Wilson, June 9, 1946; children—Richard C., James E., Robert T. Student Bradley U., 1941-43; B.A., Eureka Coll. (Ill.), 1948; M.D., Lexington Theol. Sem. (Ky.), 1951; D. Ministry, Christian Theol. Sem., Indpls., 1978; D.D. (hon.), Eureka Coll., 1965. Ordained to ministry Christian Ch., 1948. Sr. pastor First Christian Ch., Waukegan, Ill., 1951-57, Bloomington, Ill., 1957-73, South Bend, Ind., 1973-80, Bloomington, Ind., 1980-83; regional minister Christian Ch. Ill./Wis., Bloomington, 1984-88; ret., 1988. Trustee Eureka Coll., 1951-77, pres. 1964-70; chmn. ecumenical concerns commn., Christian Ch. Ind., 1978-82; vice moderator Christian Ch. Ind., 1982-84. Author: Reading the Bible With Understanding, 1978. Contbr. articles to profl. publs. Chmn. United Way Fund Drive, Bloomington, 1972. Served to sgt. USAAC, 1942-46; CBI. Paul Harris fellow, 1983. Mem. Disciples of Christ Hist. Soc., Council on Christian Unity of Christian Ch. (Disciples), Coll. Profl. Christian Ministers Ill., Cursillo, Theta Phi. Lodges: Masons, Rotary. Avocations: Astronomy, athletics camping, fishing, travel.

TREINEN, SYLVESTER WILLIAM, bishop; b. Donnelly, Minn., Nov. 19, 1917; s. William John and Kathryn (Krausert) T. Student, Crosier Sem., Onamia, Minn., 1935-41; B.A., St. Paul's Sem., 1943. Ordained priest Roman Cath. Ch., 1946; asst. pastor Dickinson, N.D., 1946-50; sec. to bishops Ryan and Hoch, 1950-53; asst. pastor Cathedral Holy Spirit, Bismarck, N.D., 1950-57; chancellor Diocese Bismarck, 1953-59; asst. pastor St. Anne's Ch., Bismarck, 1957-59; pastor St. Joseph's Ch., Mandan, N.D., 1959-62; bishop Boise, Idaho, 1962—. Address: 420 Idaho St PO Box 769 Boise ID 83701 also: PO Box 161 Arco ID 83212

TREIT, ELROY MALCOLM, clergyman; b. Wilkie, Sask., Can., Mar. 6, 1933; s. Henry and Hilda (Rosnau) T.; m. Carol Jean Schneider, Jan. 29, 1960; children—Jonathan, Matthew, Marla Jean. AA, Concordia Coll., 1953, BA, 1954; BD, Concordia Sem., 1959; MS in Sociology, Simon Fraser U.; DD, Concordia Sem., Edmonton, Alta., 1989; LLD, Brock U., 1989. Ordained to ministry Luth. Ch., 1959. Pastor Parish Killarney Park Luth. Ch., Vancouver, B.C., Can., 1959—; 2d v.p. Alta.-B.C. Dist. Luth. Ch. of Can., 1970-88, dir. fund raising, 1971-86; family life dir. Alta.-B.C. Dist. Luth. Ch. of Can. (Western Region), 1972-76; pres. Luth. Ch. of Can., 1977-88, now hon. pres.; mem. Fed. Family Life Bd.; counsellor ABC Dist. for women's orgns.; lectr. in seminars on human sexuality. Researcher, author publs. in philately. Bd. dirs Vancouver YMCA, 1961-76; adv. B.C. Human Resources Dept., 1976-79. Mem. Profl. Counsellors Assn. of Province B.C., Luth. Laymen's League, Luth. Women's Missionary League (counsellor). Conservative. Home: 3871 Hurst St, Burnaby, BC Canada V5J 1M4 Office: 3022 E 49th St, Vancouver, BC Canada V5J 1K9

TRELEASE, RICHARD MITCHELL, JR., bishop; b. Berkeley, Calif., Apr. 16, 1921; s. Richard Mitchell and Ruth (Walker) T.; m. Jean Ronayne, July 2, 1943; children: Richard Mitchell III, Christopher, Phyllis Hope. B.A., U. Mo., 1943; B.D., Ch. Div. Sch. Pacific, 1945, D.D., 1966; D.S., U. of South, 1972. Ordained priest Episcopal Ch., 1945; curate St. Andrew's Cathedral, Honolulu, 1945; vicar, rector St. Christopher's Ch., Kailua, St. John's-by-the-Sea, Keneohe, 1947-50; rector St. Andrew's Cathedral, Honolulu, 1950-54, dean, 1954; dean St. Andrew's, Wilmington, Del., 1954-61, St. Paul's Episcopal Ch., Akron, Ohio, 1962-71; bishop Diocese of Rio Grande, New Mexico and S.W. Tex., 1971-89; Pres. Akron Ministerial Alliance; pres. Inpost, Akron, 1966-68, Goodwill Industries Akron, 1965-68; chmn. Kent State Chaplaincy Com., 1963; adv. com. United Community Council, Akron, 1968-70, Poverty Program, Akron, 1968-70, Eye Bank, Akron, 1965-71; pres. N.Mex. Inter-Ch. Agy., 1974—; mem. Nat. Coalition for Ordination Women, Episcopal Ch., 1975—, Nat. Commn. Regional and Local Ecumenism Nat. Council Chs., 1975—, N.M. Humanities Council, 1974—. Bd. dirs. Tb Soc., Multiple Sclerosis Soc., Planned Parenthood Soc., Youth Service Advisory; v.p. Newcastle County Council Chs.; pres. People's Settlement; trustee Ch. Div. Sch. Chs.; pres. People's Settlement; trustee Ch. Div. Sch. Pacific, 1969-75, Episcopal Radio TV Found.; mem. adv. bd. Bataan Hosp. and, and Lovelace Clinic; bd. dirs. Santa Fe Opera Guild, 1973-74; adv. bd. Episcopal Theol. Sem. of Southwest. Mem. Aloha Tau Omega, Psi Chi. Club: Rotarian (asso. mem.; trustee 1961-71). Address: 4304 Carlisle NE Albuquerque NM 87107

TREMBLAY, GERARD, bishop; b. Montreal, Que., Can., Oct. 27, 1918; s. Francois Tremblay and Rose-Anna (Fortin); B.A., Univ. of Montreal, B. Th., Montreal U. Ordained Priest Roman Catholic Ch., 1946; consecrated titular bishop of Trisipa and aux. bishop of Montreal (Que.), May 22, 1981. Office: Archdiocese of Montreal, 2000 Sherbrooke St, West Montreal, PQ Canada H3H 1G4

TREMBLEY, DAVID ALAN, pastor; b. Berwick, Pa., Nov. 5, 1942; s. Harold Maxwell and Laura Jean (DeHaba) T.; m. Mary Caroloyn Cunningham, Dec. 11, 1964 (div. Feb. 1972); m. Lo-Ann Zhora Fuller, June 13, 1978; 1 child, Matthew. BS in Edn., Ind. U., 1966; MDiv, Chgo. Theol. Sem., 1977. Assoc. pastor Am. Bapt. Ch., Munster, Ind., 1976-77; pastor Juda (Wis.) Bapt. Ch., 1977-80, Faith Bapt. Ch., Germantown, Wis., 1983—; writer Milw., 1978—; mem. bd. mgrs. ABC of Wis., Elm Grove, 1984-85. Author: Confession in the 3rd Degree, 1982; contbr. articles to profl. jours. Bd. dirs. Wash. County Family Orgn., West Bend, 1990, Citizen Advocacy of Washington County, West Bend, 1986-88. Fellowship Chgo. Theol. Sem., 1976-77; scholarship Inland Steel Co., 1961-65. Democrat. Home: 5526 N 34th St Milwaukee WI 53209 Office: Faith Bapt Ch Box 102 Germantown WI 53022

TREMMEL, WILLIAM CALLOLEY, minister, theology educator; b. Denver, June 11, 1918; s. William Anthony and Eva Ruth (Calloley) T.; m. Opal LaVerne, June 22, 1944; children: William Michael, James Harold, Susan Tremmel Young. AB, U. Denver, 1940; ThM, Iliff Sch. Theology, 1944, ThD, 1950. Ordained to ministry United Meth. Ch., 1943. Min. United Meth. Ch., Colo., Kans., 1943-84; prof., chmn. dept. religious studies U. South Fla., Tampa, 1969—. Mem. Highlands Inst. Am. Theology. Home: 11503 Carrollwood Dr Tampa FL 33618 Office: U South Fla Dept Religious Studies Tampa FL 33620

TRENCHARD, WARREN CHARLES, academic administrator, religion educator; b. St. John's, Nfld., Can., July 16, 1944; s. Charles Edward and Violet Frances (Noseworthy) T.; m. Marilyn Joyce Beaumont, Aug. 20, 1967; children: Mark Edward, David Wayne, Kevin Scott. BA, Andrews U., 1966, MA, BD, 1968; PhD, U. Chgo., 1981. Ordained to ministry Seventh-day Adventists, 1982. Instr. religion Andrews U., Berrien Springs, Mich., 1968; pastor Seventh-day Adventist Ch., Lancaster, Mass., 1968-69, Attleboro, Mass., 1969-70; prof. religious studies, v.p. acad. adminstrn. Can. Union Coll., College Heights, Alta., 1975—; mem. Pvt. Colls. Accreditation Bd., Edmonton, Alta., 1987—. Author: Ben Sira's View of Women, 1982; contbr. articles to religious publs. Fellow Inst. Bibl. Rsch.; mem. Andrews Soc. Religious Studies (v.p. 1990—), Cath. Bibl. Assn. Am., Internat. Orgn. Septuagint and Cognate Studies, Soc. Bibl. Lit., Am. Assn. Higher Edn. Home: Box 458, College Heights, AB Canada T0C 0Z0 Office: Can Union Coll, Box 430, College Heights, AB Canada T0C 0Z0 *If everyone had to face others as individuals, we might get nations and other groups to stop doing to each other what one individual would never think of doing to another.*

TRENT, GEORGE CURTIS, minister; b. Lynch, Ky., Nov. 20, 1958; s. George Washington and Glenda Fae (Broaddus) T.; m. Rosemary Jane Hardin, June 4, 1983; children: Michael Curtis, Bethany Diane. BS in Phys. Edn., East Tenn. State U., 1982; MDiv, Emory U., 1986. Ordained to ministry United Meth. Ch. as deacon, 1984, as elder, 1988. Min. St. Andrews United Meth. Ch., Chattanooga, 1983-85, Evensville (Tenn.)-New Bethel United. Meth. Ch., 1985-89; min. youth Broad St. United Meth. Ch., Cleveland, Tenn., 1989—; spiritual dir. Chrysalis Community, Cleveland, 1989—. Bd. dirs. Teen Ctr. Cleveland, 1990, Wesley Found., U. Tenn., Chattanooga, 1990—. Mem. Cleveland Dist. Mins. (v.p. 1988-90, pres. 1990-91), Dayton Ministerial Assn. (pres. 1988-89), Fellowship Christian Athletes. Republican. Home: 433 Centenary Ave Cleveland TN 37311 Office: Broad St United Meth Ch 253 Broad St Cleveland TN 37364

TREPP, LEO, rabbi; b. Mainz, Germany, Mar. 4, 1913; s. Maier and Selma (Hirschberger) T.; m. Miriam de Haas, Apr. 26, 1938; 1 child, Susan Trepp Lachtman. PhD, U. Wurzburg, Ger., 1935; Dr.Phil, U. Oldenburg, Ger., 1989; DD, Hebrew Union Coll., 1985; postgrad., Harvard U., 1944-45. Ordained rabbi, 1936. Rabbi various temples, various locations, 1940-51; part-time rabbi Santa Rosa, Calif., 1951-61, Eureka, Calif., 1961-90; Jewish chaplain Vets. Home of Calif., Yountville, Calif., 1954—; prof. Judaic studies U. Mainz, 1983—. Author: Eternal Faith, Eternal People - A Journey into Judaism, 1962, Judaism, Development and Life, 1966, 2d edit. 1984, A History of the Jewish Experience, 1974, The Complete Book of Jewish Observance, 1980, Judaism and the Religions of Humanity, 1985, What if Shylock were a Marrano, 1985, The Controversy between Samson Raphael Hirsch and Seligmann Baer Bamberger—Halakhical and Societal Implications, 1991, Yamim Nora'im: The Traditional Liturgy and "Gates of Repentance", 1991; author numerous books in other langs.; major works include Die Juden, 1982, Der jüdischen Gottesdienst—Form und Entfaltung, 1991, Die Amerikamischen Juden—Profil einer Gerneinschaft, 1991; contbr. articles to profl. jours. Mem. Napa Planning Commn., 1964-69. Recipient Great Seal, City of Oldenburg, 1971, George Washington Honor medal, Freedoms Found., 1979; hon. freeman City of Oldenburg, 1990. Mem. Cen. Conf. Am. Rabbis, Rabbinical Assembly, Am. Philos. Assn., Am. Acad. Religion, No. Calif. Bd. Rabbis, Silverado Club. Home: 295 Montecito Blvd Napa CA 94559

TRESSLER, CHARLES THOMAS, minister; b. Newport, Pa., May 21, 1943; s. Thomas William and Marion Louise (Lenig) T.; m. Susan Elaine Gribler, May 25, 1969; children: Paul Jacob, Jeremy Chase, Brandon Lee. BA in Acctg., Grove City Coll., 1965; MDiv, United Theol. Sem., 1969. Ordained to ministry United Meth. Ch.,1969. Youth min. Corinth Blvd. Presbyn. Ch., 1966-67, Brandt (Ohio) United Meth. Ch., 1968-69; pastor Linden United Meth. Charge, Salladasburg, Pa., 1969-72, Cocolamus (Pa.) United Meth. Charge, 1972-76; assoc. pastor 1st United Meth. Ch., Hershey, Pa., 1976-79; pastor Christ United Meth. Ch., Tower City, Pa., 1979-81, Millville-Greenwood United Meth. Parish, Millville, Pa., 1981-86, St. Paul's Emmanuel United Meth. Ch., Danville, Pa., 1986—; cluster leader Danville Cluster United Meth. Ch., 1987-90, Millville Cluster, 1983-86; mem. structure com. Cen. Pa. Conf. United Meth. Ch., 1989-90. Bd. dirs. Habitat in Bloom, Bloomsburg, Pa., 1987-88. Mem. Danville-Riverside Area Ministerial Assn. (com. mem. 1987-90, pres. 1988-89), Lewisburg Dist. Mins.-United Meth. Ch., Preachers' Aid Soc., N.E. Jurisdictional Town and Country Assn., Oliver Grange #1069, Phi Tau Alpha (founding pres. 1965). Office: St Paul's Emmanuel United Meth Ch PO Box 271 Danville PA 17821

TREVER, JOHN CECIL, religion educator; b. Milw., Nov. 26, 1915; s. John Henry and Hilda Amanda (Carpenter) T.; m. Elizabeth Signe Burman, Aug. 29, 1937; children: John Paul, James Edgar. AB magna cum laude, U. So. Calif., 1937; BD, Yale Div. Sch., 1940; PhD, Yale U., 1943. Ordained to ministry United Meth. Ch., 1943. Assoc. min. 1st Meth. Ch., Santa Monica, Calif., 1942-44; assoc. prof. Drake U., Des Moines, 1944-47; exec. dir. dept. English Bible Nat. Coun. Chs., 1948-53; prof. religion Morris Harvey Coll., Charleston, W.Va., 1953-59, Baldwin-Wallace Coll., Berea, Ohio, 1960-75; prof. Sch. Theology at Claremont, Calif., 1975-80, dir. Dead Sea Scrolls Project, 1975—. Author: The Cradle of Our Faith, 1954, The Untold Story of Qumran, 1965, Scrolls from Qumrân Cave I, 1972, The Dead Sea Scrolls: A Personal Account, 1977. Two Bros. fellow Yale U., 1940. Mem. Phi Beta Kappa.

TREXLER, EDGAR RAY, minister, editor; b. Salisbury, N.C., Sept. 17, 1937; s. Edgar Ray and Eula Belle (Farmer) T.; m. Emily Louise Kees, Aug. 21, 1960; children—David Ray, Mark Raymond, Karen Emily. AB, Lenoir-Rhyne Coll., 1959, LittD, 1978; MDiv, Luth. Theol. So. Sem., 1962; MA, Syracuse U., 1964; postgrad., Boston U., 1960, Luth. World Fedn. Study Project, Geneva, 1977, 81; LittD (hon.), Midland Coll., 1990. Ordained to ministry United Luth. Ch. Am., 1962; pastor St. John's Luth. Ch., Lyons, N.Y., 1962-65; features editor Luth. Mag., Phila., 1965-72, assoc. editor, 1972-78, editor, 1978-87; editor Luth. Mag., Chgo., 1988—; sec. Commn. Ch. Papers, Luth. Ch. Am., 1971-72, mem. staff team communications, 1972-78; chmn. Interch. Features, 1971-76; chmn. postal affairs com. Assoc. Ch. Press, 1983-90, Work Group on New Ch. Periodical, 1985-86; Evangelical Luth. Ch. Am. Cabinet of Execs., 1988—. Author: Ways to Wake Up Your Church, 1969, Creative Congregations, 1972, The New Face of Missions, 1973, Mission in a New World, 1977, LWF/6, 1978, Anatomy of a Merger, 1991. Pres. Lyons Council Chs., 1964; trustee Lenoir Rhyne Coll., 1975-84. Recipient Disting. Alumnus award Lenoir-Rhyne Coll., 1991; named for Best Articles in Mission Mags. Assoc. Ch. Press, 1974. Mem. Nat. Luth. Editors Assn. (pres. 1975-77). Home: 1401 Sequoia Rd Naperville IL 60540 Office: Luth Mag 8765 W Higgins Rd Chicago IL 60631

TREXLER, MICHAEL ERIC, lay worker; b. Columbus, Ohio, Oct. 19, 1967; s. Charles Dechant and Sandra Sue (Petry) T. Dir. youth St. George Episcopal Ch., San Antonio, 1989-91; coord. Bishop's Happening Movement, San Antonio, 1987-88; del. Diocese Youth Conv., San Antonio, 1986, Bishop's Consultation on Mission Edn., Washington, 1990. Author: (poetry) Yea God, 1986, Friends, 1987, Family, 1987. Asst. commr. Apt. League Baseball, Austin, Tex., 1990—. Office: 2030 E Oltort # 106 Austin TX 78741 *An eye observes the colors of the earth. An ear hears all that music sings. A hand touches the shapes of magical things. Life is living and loving is enough to sparkle an eye, mesmorize an ear and warm a hand.*

TRICKETT, DAVID GEORGE, theological educator, administrator; b. Shreveport, La., Sept. 16, 1949; s. James Albert and Elizabeth Gordon (Sample) T.; m. Susan Mary Bell, July 8, 1978; children: Beatrice, Gillian, Piers. BA magna cum laude, La. State U., 1971; ThM with honors, Perkins Sch. Theol., Dallas, 1975; PhD, So. Meth. U., 1982. Ordained to ministry United Meth. Ch., 1972. Teaching fellow Perkins Sch. Theol., Dallas, 1978-81; pastor United Meth. Ch., New Orleans, 1981-84; chaplain, faculty mem. Tulane U., New Orleans, 1984-88; exec. dir. The Washington Theol. Consortium, 1988—; del., cons. World Coun. Chs., U.S.A., Switzerland, Brazil, etc., 1978-89; observer gen. conv. Episcopal Ch. U.S.A., New Orleans, 1982; mem. World Meth. Coun., U.S.A., Kenya, Singapore, 1986—; mem., del. Oxford Inst. Meth. Theol. St. Oxford, United Kingdom, 1987—. Author: Toward a Christian Theology of Nature, 1982; author, editor: The Challenge of Genetic Science, 1990; editor: Faith, Hope, and Reason . . ., 1980; contbr. articles and revs. to publs., 1976—. Vice-chair North Tex. Articulation Coun., Dallas, 1980-81; chair U.S. Com. UNICEF Southeastern Region steering com., 1984-86; mem. Instl. Rev. Bd. Tulane U., New Orleans, 1986-88; dist. co-chair Fairfax County Pub. Schs. Citizens Referendum Leadership Com., 1990. Recipient Phi Beta Kappa Recognition award La. State U.; named John Moore fellow So. Meth. U. Mem. N.Am. Acad. Ecumenists, Am. Acad. Religion (regional chair 1984-85), Am. Soc. Ch. History, History of Sci. Soc., Soc. Christian Ethics. Democrat. Office: Washington Theol Consortium 487 Michigan Ave NE Washington DC 20017

TRIGILIO, FATHER JOHN PATRICIO, priest, parochial vicar; b. Erie, Pa., Mar. 31, 1962; s. John Eugene and Elizabeth Louise (Lagner) T. BA, Gannon U., 1983; MDiv, Mary Immaculate Coll., 1988. Ordained priest Roman Cath. Ch., 1988. Deacon St. Gregory the Great Ch., Lebanon, Pa., 1987-88; parochial vicar St. Joseph Ch., Mechanicsburg, Pa., 1988—. Contbr. articles to profl. jours. Chaplain Cath. War Vets., Mechanicsburg, 1989-91. Mem. Cath. Conservative Clergy (pres. 1991—), St. Gregory Latin Liturgy Assn., Canon Law Soc. Am., Confraternity of Cath. Clergy, Sons of Italy (chaplain 1991), KC (chaplain 1990-91). Republican. Home: 200 S Filbert PO Box 2012 Mechanicsburg PA 17055 Office: St Joseph Roman Cath Ch 200 S Filbert St Mechanicsburg PA 17055

TRINKLEIN, MICHAEL CHARLES, lay organization official, clergyman; b. Lethbridge, Alta., Can., Sept. 7, 1930; (parents Am. citizens); s. Alfred Walter and Emma Mary (Salomon) T.; m. Janice Lous Asche, June 24, 1955; children: Gary Michael, Jennifer Lauri, Andrea Jan, Jeffrey Martin. BA, Concordia Sem., 1952, MDiv, 1955; MA, Wichita State U., 1967. Ordained to ministry Luth. Ch.-Mo. Synod, 1955. Missionary Luth. Ch.-Mo. Synod, Taiwan, 1955-61, Hong Kong, 1967-70; pastor Savior Luth. Ch., Bedford, Mass., 1961-64, Reedemer Luth. Ch., Wichita, Kans., 1964-67, Zion Luth. Ch., Pittsburg, Kans., 1970-77, Immanuel Luth. Ch., Boonville, Mo., 1977-83; coord. stewardship emphasis Mo. dist. Luth. Ch.-Mo. Synod, St. Louis, 1984-85; exec. producer radio Internat. Luth. Laymen's League, St. Louis, 1986—. Contbr. articles to religious publs. Pres. Boonville Arts Com., 1978. Mem. Rotary (pres. Boonville club 1982). Home: 1968 Meadowtree Ln # 7 Kirkwood MO 63122 Office: Internat Luth Laymen's League 2185 Hampton Ave Saint Louis MO 63139

TRIPOLE, MARTIN RALPH, religion educator, priest; b. Penn Yan, N.Y., June 14, 1935; s. James and Mary T. BA, Fordham U., 1957, MPhil, 1963; postgrad., Syracuse U., 1957-58; ThM, Woodstock Coll., 1968; STD, Inst. Catholique de Paris, 1972. Joined S.J., Roman Cath. Ch., 1958, ordained priest, 1967. Instr. Bellarmine Coll., Plattsburg, N.Y., 1957-58, Le Moyne Coll., Syracuse, N.Y., 1962-64; asst. prof. Marquette U., Milw., 1974-75; assoc. prof. St. Joseph's U., Phila., 1972—; instr. St. Agnes Coll., Balt., 1967. Author: Jesus Event and Our Response, 1980; contbr. articles to profl. jours. Mem. Am. Acad. Religion, Cath. Theol. Soc. Am., Coll. Theol. Soc. Roman Catholic. Home: 5600 City Ave Philadelphia PA 19131 Office: St Josephs Univ 5600 City Line Ave Philadelphia PA 19131

TRIPP, KEVIN FRANCIS, priest; b. New Bedford, Mass., May 17, 1942; s. Philip Francis and Helen Catherine (FitzGerald) T. BA, St. John's Sem., Brighton, Mass., 1964, MDiv., 1968; postgrad., Notre Dame U., 1965-68. Ordained priest Roman Cath. Ch., 1968. Parish priest Diocese of Fall River (Mass.), 1968-74; dir. religious ministries St. Luke's Hosp., New Bedford, Mass., 1974-83; dir. clin. pastoral edn. Our Lady of the Lake Roman Cath. Ch., Baton Rouge, La., 1983-87; dir. chaplain svcs. St. Mary's Hosp. and Med. Ctr., San Francisco, 1987—. Contbr. articles to profl. jours. Recipient Disting. Svc. award Mass. Jaycees, Fall River, 1970. Mem. Nat. Assn. Cath. Chaplains (Disting. Svc. award 1987, pres. elect 1991). Avocations: sailing, reading, playing piano, listening to classical music. Home: 97 Prospect Dr San Rafael CA 94901-1957 Office: St Marys Hosp & Med Ctr 450 Stanyan St San Francisco CA 94117

TRISCO, ROBERT FREDERICK, church historian, educator; b. Chgo., Nov. 11, 1929; s. Richard E. and Harriet Rose (Hardt) T. B.A., St. Mary of Lake Sem., Mundelein, Ill., 1951; S.T.L., Pontifical Gregorian U., Rome, 1955, Hist. Eccl.D., 1962. Ordained priest Roman Catholic Ch., 1954. Mem. faculty Cath. U. Am., Washington, 1959—; prof. ch. history Cath. U. Am., 1975—; editor Cath. Hist. Rev., 1963—; exec. sec. Am. Cath. Hist. Assn., 1961—, sec., treas., 1983—; expert 2d Vatican Coun., 1962-65; pres. Am. subcom. Internat. Commn. Comparative Ch. History, 1978-80; mem. subcoms. Nat. Conf. Cath. Bishops, 1966-76, 87—; assesseur (mem. bur.) Internat. Commn. for Comparative Ch. History, 1980—; mem. Pontifical Com. Hist. Scis., 1982—; hon. mem. Accademia di San Carlo (Milan), 1986—. Author: The Holy See and Nascent Church in the Middle Western U.S., 1826-1850, 1962, Bishops and Their Priests in the United States, 1988; co-author: A Guide to American Catholic History, 2d edit., 1982; editor: Catholics in Am., 1976; co-editor, contbr.: Studies in Catholic History in Honor of John Tracy Ellis, 1985; contbr. numerous articles to profl. publs. Mem. Am. Soc. Ch. History (council 1980-82). Office: Cath U Am Mullen Libr Rm 318 Washington DC 20064

TROEGER, THOMAS HENRY, religion educator; b. Suffern, N.Y., Jan. 30, 1945; s. Henry and Lorena (McDonald) T.; m. Merle Marie Butler, June 25, 1967. BA in English cum laude, Yale U., 1967; BD, Colgate Rochester Div. Sch., 1970. Ordained to ministry United Presbyn. Ch., U.S.A., 1970. Assoc. pastor New Hartford (N.Y.) Presbyn. Ch., 1970-77; assoc. prof. preaching and parish ministry Colgate Rochester (N.Y.) Div. Sch., Bexley Hall, Crozer Theol. Sem., 1977-86, prof., 1986-91; Ralph E. and Norma E. Peck prof. preaching and communication Iliff Sch. Theology, Denver, 1991—; editor preaching series Abingdon Press, 1990—; lectr., preacher, seminar leader; condr. workshops in field. Author: Meditation: Escape to Reality, 1977, Rage! Reflect! Rejoice!, 1977, Creating Fresh Images in the Pulpit: New Rungs for Jacob's Ladder (One of 10 Most Important Books award Acad. Parish Clergy 1983), (with Carol Doran) Open to Glory: Renewing Worship in the Congregation, 1983, New Hymns for the Lectionary: To Glorify the Maker's Name, 1985, Imagining a Sermon, 1990; contbr. numerous articles to religions jours., chpts. to books; art and media editor Homiletic, 1985—; mem. editorial bd. Worship, 1990; also hymns. Trustee Utica (N.Y.) Family Svc., 1972-77, Rochester Planned Parenthood, 1977-83; trustee pub. broadcasting sta., Rochester, 1984—. Scholar Scriven Found., 1963-67, ecumenical scholar Colgate Rochester Div. Sch., 1967-68. Mem. Acad. Homiletics (pres. 1987), N.Am. Acad. Liturgy, Hymn Soc. in U.S. and Can. Office: Iliff Sch Theology 2201 S University Blvd Denver CO 80210

TROGLIN, EARL THOMAS, chaplain, counselor; b. Atlanta, Feb. 16, 1936; s. James Luther and Mattie (Thomas) T.; m. Sharon Glenda Pike, Nov. 23, 1962; children: Tammy Judith, Kristi Lane Troglin Cradit. AB, Mercer U., 1962; MDiv, So. Bapt. Theol. Sem., 1966. Intern in clin. pastoral edn. Ga. Bapt. Med. Ctr., Atlanta, 1966-67, resident in clin. pastoral edn., 1972-73; dir. dept. pastoral svcs. Valley Bapt. Med. Ctr., Harlingen, Tex., 1973-90; dir. pastoral care Self Meml. Hosp., Greenwood, S.C., 1990—; cons. deacon intern program Cath. Diocese of Brownsville, Harlingen, 1975-90; instr. Mary Hardin Baylor U., Harlingen, 1985-90; facilitator Presbyn. and Meth. Mins. Group, Harlingen, 1976-89. Bd. dirs. Midway House, alcoholic rehab., Harlingen, 1974-90, Am. Cancer Soc., Harlingen, 1978-90. With U.S. Army, 1957-59. Fellow Coll. of Chaplains, Inc.; mem. Assn. for Clin. Pastoral Edn. (cert.), Am. Assn. for Marriage and Family Therapy (clin.). Baptist. Avocations: travel, fishing, golf, bicycling, comedies. Office: Self Meml Hosp 1325 Spring St Greenwood SC 29646

TROIA, ROBERT PAUL, deacon, computer programmer; b. Providence, R.I., June 7, 1943; s. Angelo and Rose (Cannata) T.; m. Arlene Barbara Bianchi, Oct. 2, 1965; children: Lisa Ann, Julie Anne. Grad. high sch., Providence. IBM systems programmer R.I. Blue Cross, Providence, 1967—; chaplain Aged/Campus, Providence. Mem. K.C., Holy Name Club (pres. 1989-90). Roman Catholic. Home: 233 Stony Acre Dr Cranston RI 02920

TROMBLEY, CHARLES C., religion educator; b. Littleton, N.H., Aug. 24, 1928; s. Carroll Cyprian and Beulah Ashell (Bradshaw) T.; m. Gladys Olivine Allen, Jan. 27, 1951; children: David Earl, Darlene Dale, Deborah Faith, Deanna Lisa. BA in Theology, Immaneul Bapt., 1984; MA in Bib. Lit., Luther Rice Sem., 1989; DD (hon.), Kingsway Theol. Sem., 1987. Ordained to ministry Assemblies of God, 1957. Founder, pastor Assemblies of God Tabernacle, Bellows Falls, Vt., 1956-59; pastor Christian Fellowship Ch., Sarasota, Fla., 1960-62; exec. sec. Gospel Crusade, Sarasota, 1960-63, evangelist, 1962-69; dir. Gospel Light Telecast, Ottumwa, Iowa, 1970-72; pastor Sheridan Assembly, Tulsa, 1972-73; dir. Charismatic Teaching Ministries, Tulsa, 1973—, CTM Pubs., Broken Arrow, Okla., 1972—; supr. Mfulu Za Yehova Mission, Blantyre, Malawi, 1976-89; dir. Victory Bible Inst., Tulsa, 1989-90; trustee Fayetteville (Ark.) Christian Ctr., 1989—. Author: Visitation-Key to Church Growth, 1970, Kicked Out of the Kingdom, 1974, Bible Answer for Jehova Witness, 1975, Praise-Faith at Work, 1976, Guilty as Charged, 1976, Released to Reign, 1979, Who Said Women Can't Teach?; editor The Expositor Pubs., Sarasota, 1966—, Sword of the Spirit, 1974; editorial com. Logos Mag., Plainfield, N.J., 1979—; contbr. articles to profl. jours. Mem. World Ministry Fellowship (cen. ordination coun. 1985-90), Victory Fellowship Ministries. Home: 293 W Ithica Broken Arrow OK 74012 Office: 500 N Elm Pl Broken Arrow OK 74012

TROMBLEY, FITTERER See ST. ANDREWS, BARBARA

TROOP, H. GRANT, missionary; b. Lancaster, Pa., Aug. 4, 1951; s. Hiram George and Claire Marie (McFalls) T. BS, Pa. State U., 1973; postgrad., Moody Bible Inst., 1981; Cert. in Teaching, Pa. State U., 1985. Cert. educator in agriculture and sci. Pres. Lancaster (Pa.) County Youth for Christ Alumni Club, 1979-80; campground minister Millbridge Village, Ronks, Pa., 1981-83; assoc. missionary Campsite Evangelism Inc., Hudson, Fla., 1984—; mem. Calvary Monuments Bible Ch., Paradise, Pa., 1970—; farmer self-employed, Quarryville, Pa., 1973—; tchr. Atglen, Pa., 1985—. Bd. dirs. So. Lancaster County Community Fair, Quarryville, 1981—, pub. rels. chmn., 1985-89; county commr. Lancaster County Agrl. Stabilization and Conservation Svc. Office USDA, 1984-89; sustaining mem. Nat. Right to Life Com., Washington, 1985—; official Pa. Interscholastic Athletic Assn., 1991—. Recipient Svc. award Lancaster County Conservation Dist., 1984, cert. of Appreciation Octorara Area Future Farmers of Am., 1985, Philip & Clara D. Calhoun scholarship Pa. State U., 1972. Mem. Pa. Pro Life Fedn., Lancaster Christian Action Coun., Lancaster County Action, Am. Family Assn., Concerned Women for Am., Pa. Forage and Grassland Coun., Nat. Corn Growers Assn. (Pa. master, dir. 1987, 91—), Pa. Young Farmers Assn.

(Solanco chpt., Octorara chpt.), The Rutherford Inst., Phi Sigma. Home and Office: 286 Furnace Rd Quarryville PA 17566-9423 *Purpose in life is found in knowing God, our Creator, and in making Him known to a lost and dying world. In Christ alone is release from sin and death, love, joy and peace today and abundant life everlasting.*

TROTTER, F(REDERICK) THOMAS, university president; b. Los Angeles, Apr. 17, 1926; s. Fred B. and Hazel (Thomas) T.; m. Gania Demaree, June 27, 1953; children—Ruth Elizabeth, Paula Anne (dec.), Tania, Mary. AB, Occidental Coll., 1950, DD, 1968; STB, Boston U., 1953, PhD, 1958; LHD, Ill. Wesleyan U., 1974, Cornell Coll., 1985, Westmar Coll., 1987; LLD, U. Pacific, 1978, Wesleyan Coll., 1981; EdD, Columbia Coll., 1984;, LittD, Alaska Pacific U., 1987. Exec. sec. Boston U. Student Christian Assn., 1951-54; ordained elder Calif.-Pacific, Methodist Ch., 1953; pastor Montclair (Calif.) Meth. Ch., 1956-59; lectr. So. Calif. Sch. Theology at Claremont, 1957-59, instr., 1959-60, asst. prof., 1960-63, assoc. prof., 1963-66, prof., 1966, dean, 1961; prof. religion and arts, dean Sch. Theology Claremont, 1961-73; mem. Bd. Higher Edn. and Ministry, United Meth. Ch., 1972-73, gen. sec., 1973-87; pres. Alaska Pacific U., Anchorage, 1988—; dir. Third Nat. Bank, Nashville, Inst. for Antiquity and Christianity at Claremont. Author: Jesus and the Historian, 1968, Loving God with One's Mind, 1987, weekly column local newspapers; editor-at-large: Christian Century, 1969-84. Trustee Dillard U. Served with USAAF, 1944-46. Kent fellow Soc. for Values in Higher Edn., 1954; Dempster fellow Meth. Ch., 1954. Mem. Rotary Internat. (Anchorage Downtown), Commonwealth North. Office: Alaska Pacific U Office Pres 4101 University Dr Anchorage AK 99508

TROTTER, JAMES MICHAEL, minister; b. St. Louis, Mar. 26, 1958; s. James Hughes and Alma Jean (Shipley) T.; m. Kathryn Elizabeth Gordon, Dec. 30, 1979; children: Joshua Alan, Jennifer Elaine. BA in Christian Edn., Oakland City Coll., 1981. Ordained to ministry Assn. Gen. Bapt. Chs., 1978. Mgr. Christian Book Ctr., Evansville, Ind., 1981-82; pastor Mt. Olive Gen. Bapt. Ch., Dale, Ind., 1979-82, Bethany Gen. Bapt. Ch., Campbell, Mo., 1982-86, South Poplar Bluff (Mo.) Gen. Bapt. Ch., 1986—; adv. bd. mem. Camp Allen Youth Camp, Greenville, Mo., 1991-94; bd. rep. Gen. Bapt. Evangelism Coun., 1987-92; treas. Gen. Bapt. Min.'s Conf. Com., 1988-91. Trustee Oakland City (Ind.) Coll., 1985-92; mem. Foodbank, Sikeston, Mo., 1987—. Mem. Gen. Bapt. Brotherhood, Poplar Bluff Area Assn. Gen. Bapt. Chs. (co-founder 1988, moderator 1989-90), Poplar Bluff Area Presbytery. Home: 812 Arthur St Poplar Bluff MO 63901 Office: South Poplar Bluff Ch 817 Arthur St Poplar Bluff MO 63901

TROTTER, RICHARD DONALD, psychologist, clergyman, consultant; b. Grand Island, Nebr., June 9, 1932; s. P. Dean and Ethel Dell (Masters) T.; m. Kathleen Marie Tyler, Apr. 10, 1966; children—Terri Marie, Nancy Lee, Laurel Lynn. Student U. Wis.-Madison, 1950; B.S., U. Nebr., 1968; M.Div., Iliff Sch. Theology, Denver, 1970; Ph.D., Southwest U., Phoenix, 1974; D.H.L. (hon.), London Inst., 1973. Ordained to ministry United Meth. Ch., 1971. Sr. pastor, 1st United Meth. Ch., Miller, S.D., 1970-73; pvt. practice counseling and therapy, Rapid City, S.D., 1974-78; sr. pastor Canyon Lake United Meth. Ch., Rapid City, 1978-80; theologian in residence Collins Ctr., Portland, Oreg., 1981-83; counselor, therapist Wellspring Inc., Marion, Inc., 1983—, also dir. Author: 40,000 Pounds of Feathers, 1970; 'Til Divorce Do Us Part, 1982. Mem. council City of West Lincoln, Nebr., 1960-61, mayor, 1962; mem. Rapid City Bd. Edn., 1977-80, pres., 1979-80; bd. dirs. Marion Civic Theatre, 1984—. Served with USAF, 1949-52. Named hon. col. Cody Scouts of North Platte, 1965; recipient Service award Rapid City Bd. Edn., 1980. Mem. Nat. Council Family Relations, Sex Info. and Edn. Council, Assn. for Humanistic Psychology, Am. Assn. Marriage and Family Therapists, Nat. Assn. Social Workers, Assn. for Transpersonal Psychology, U. Nebr. Alumni Assn. Democrat. Avocations: philately, sports officiating, acting. Home: 3320 Wildwood Dr Marion IN 46952-1218

TROTTI, JOHN BOONE, librarian, educator; b. Asheville, N.C., Dec. 11, 1935; s. Clarence Trotti and Janice Trotti Lyon; m. Joan Thompson, June 12, 1957; children: Elizabeth, Margaret, Michael. BA, Davidson Coll., 1957; BD cum laude, Union Theol. Sem. Va., 1960; MA, Yale U., 1961, PhD, 1964; MLS, U. N.C., 1964. Ordained to ministry Presbyn. Ch. in the U.S., 1964; instr. O.T. Yale Div. Sch., 1961-62; minister ch. Altavista, Va., 1964-68; asst. prof. religion Randolph Macon Woman's Coll., Lynchburg, Va., 1965-68; asst. librarian, asst. prof. Union Theol. Sem. Va., 1968-70, librarian, 1970—, assoc. prof. bibliography, 1972-80, prof. bibliography, 1980—; mem. library adv. com., Va.; mem. Va. State Networking Users Adv. Council, 1983-88; pres. Altavista Area Ministerial Assn., 1967. Author: Lesser Festivals 2, 1980; editor: Aids to a Theological Library, 1977; editor: Scholar's Choice, Building a Pastor's Library, 1991; contbr. articles to religious and profl. jours., ch. sch. curriculum. Trustee Stillman Coll., 1969-78; bd. dirs. Hist. Found. Presbyn. and Ref. Chs., 1979-86. Mem. Am. Theol. Library Assn. (exec. com. 1971-74, 78-79, pres. 1977-78), Va. Library Assn., Presbyterian Library Assn. (pres. 1973), Soc. Bibl. Lit., Beta Phi Mu. Home: 1222 Rennie Ave Richmond VA 23227 Office: 3401 Brook Rd Richmond VA 23227 *Life is a gift from God to be expended with zest, joy, and a concern for others. In our free society achieving an education appropriate for one's vocation involves seizing opportunities when they come and much hard work. An effective education puts one more, not less, in touch with our common humanity.*

TROUP, RONALD EUGENE, minister; b. Bloomsburg, Pa., July 17, 1952; s. Clarence Harry and Ethelene (Swank) T.; m. Leila Christine Nyberg, June 21, 1979. BA, Wheaton (Ill.) Coll., 1974; MDiv, Gordon-Conwell Theol. Sem., 1979. Ordained to ministry Am. Bapt. Chs. USA, 1979. Pastor Montowese Bapt. Ch., North Haven, Conn., 1979-86, First Bapt. Ch., Ulysses and Gold Church, Pa., 1986—; moderator North Haven (Conn.) Clergy Assn., 1980-84; alt. rep. gen. bd. Am. Bapt. Chs. USA, 1989-91; pres. Ulysses Area Ministerium, 1988—. Bd. dirs. Human Resources, North Haven, 1983-85. Home and Office: 605 Main St PO Box Ulysses PA 16948 *Life consists not in avoiding pain but in reaching for joy.*

TROUTMAN, GERALD STEVENSON, religious organization administrator; b. Andrews, N.C., Dec. 16, 1933; s. Edwin Flavious and Estelle (Brown) T.; m. Marihope Shirey, Aug. 19, 1959; children: Steven, Lee Frances. AB, Lenoir Rhyne Coll., 1956; MDiv, Luth. Theol. So. Sem., 1960; DD, Newberry Coll., 1976; Dr Ministry, Emory U., 1986. Ordained to ministry Luth. Ch. in Am., 1960; bishop, 1975-89. Pastor Reformation Luth. Ch., Greeneville, Tenn., 1960-63, St. John's Luth. Ch., Atlanta, 1963-69; sec. Southeastern Synod. Luth. Ch. in Am., Atlanta, 1969-75, pres. Southeastern Synod., 1975-89, Southeastern synodical bishop, 1980-87; regional min. div. ministry and conf. of bishops Evang. Luth Ch. in Am., 1987—; chaplain Greenville Fire Dept., 1960-63. Bd. dirs. Druid Hills Civic Assn., 1965-68, Lutheridge Assembly, Arden, N.C., 1962-69; trustee Luth. Theol. So. Sem., Newberry Coll., Williams-Henson Luth. Home for Children, Luthridge Assembly, 1975-87; mem. Lenois Rhyne Coll. Bd., 1989— . Mem. Ga. Interch. Assn. (dir. 1972—), Atlanta Luth. Ministerial Assn. (pres. 1967-68). Office: Evang Luth Church in Am 756 W Peachtree St NW Atlanta GA 30308

TROVALL, CARL CURTIS, minister; b. St. Cloud, Minn., July 2, 1961; s. Jack Robert and Darlene Carol (Mix) T.; m. Carol Diane Swanson, July 6, 1985; 1 child, Elizabeth Christine. BA, Concordia Coll., St. Paul, Minn., 1983; MDiv, Concordia Seminary, St. Louis, 1987. Ordained to ministry Luth. Ch., 1987. Pastor Faith Luth. Ch., Laredo, Tex., 1987—. Mem. Assn. Laredo Ministers, Rotary. Republican. Home: 1010 Laurel Dr Laredo TX 78041 Office: Faith Lutheran Church 2419 Seymour Laredo TX 78040

TROY, J. EDWARD, bishop; b. Chatham, N.B., Can., Sept. 2, 1931; s. J. Thomas and Lilian Mary (Barry) T. BA, St. Francis Xavier U., Antigonish, N.S., 1951; lic. philosophy, Louvain (Belgium) U., 1953, PhD, 1962; BD, Holy Heart Sem., Halifax, N.S., 1959; LLD (hons), St. Thomas U., Fredericton, N.B., 1985. Ordained priest Roman Cath. Ch., 1959. Prof. philosophy St. Thomas U., Chatham, N.B., 1959-63; commd. Canadian Armed Forces, 1963, advanced through grades to col., 1979, ret., 1984, chaplain, 1963-84; dir. personnel adminstrn. Can. Forces Chaplaincy, Ottowa, Ont., 1981-84; bishop Roman Cath. Ch., St. John, N.B., 1984—; episcopal promoter Apostleship of the Sea, Can., 1985—. Columnist New Freeman newpaper, 1984—. Chancellor St. Thomas U., 1986—. Mem. Canadian Conf. Cath. Bishops, Anglican/Roman Cath. Dialogue. Avocations: reading, bird watching. Office: Diocese St John, 1 Bayard Dr, Saint John, NB Canada E2L 3L5

TROY, KEITH ALAN, minister; b. Toledo, Oct. 20, 1953; s. Leon Lee and Berniece Pauline (Jordan) T.; m. Brenda Faye Patterson, June 14, 1975; children: Myeshia Danae, Tiffane Charisse, Andre Ramone, Kendall Cole. BA, Morehouse Coll., 76; MDiv, Colgate Rochester, 1979; postgrad., United Theol. Seminary, Dayton, Ohio, 1990—. Student intern Second Bapt. Ch., Mumford, N.Y., 1976-79; assoc. pastor Second Bapt. Ch., Columbus, Ohio, 1979-83; pastor New Salem Bapt. Ch., Columbus, 1983—; chmn. New Salem Devel. Corp., 1989—; coord. Columbus Bapt. Pastor's Conf., 1989—. Coord. One Church, One Child Prog., Ohio, 1990—; chmn. United Negro Coll. Fund, Columbus; bd. dirs. Pastoral Counseling, Columbus, 1987-90. Recipient Outstanding Community Svc. award Ohio Black Expo, Columbus, 1990, Martin L. King Internat. Bd. Preachers, Morehouse Coll., Atlanta, 1991. Office: New Salem Baptist Ch 2956 Cleveland Ave Columbus OH 43224

TRUBY, WILLIAM F., education minister; b. Cleve., Jan. 10, 1949; s. William Irwin and Margaret (Savel) T.; m. Kathy Bower, June 21, 1974 (div. Oct. 1976); m. Sherry Ann Jones, Dec. 14, 1979; children: Steven, Holly. BS in Edn., Kent State U., 1971, MEd, 1984, postgrad., 1991; DRE, Internat. Bible Inst., 1986. Adminstr. Valley Christian Acad., Aurora, Ohio, 1979-85, New Covenant Christian Acad., Bedford Hts., Ohio, 1985—; min. edn. Faith Fellowship Ch., Bedford Hts., 1988—. Author: In Pursuit of Christ-Centered Schools, 1986. Bowman fellow finalist Kent State U., 1988, 90. Mem. Assn. Supervision and Curriculum Devel., Assn. Christian Schs. Internat., Phi Delta Kappa. Office: New Covenant Christian Acad 23600 Columbus Rd Bedford Heights OH 44146

TRUEHILL, MARSHALL, JR., minister; b. New Orleans, Sept. 5, 1948; s. Marshall Truehill and Inez Gary Williams; adopted s. Elizabeth (May) T.; m. Mary Ola Williams, Dec. 20, 1969 (div. 1972); m. Valli Maria Dobard, July 22, 1972; children: Briana Traci, Marshall III, Jessica, Quentin. B in Music Edn., Xavier U., 1973; BTh, Christian Bible Coll., 1979; MDiv, Orleans Bapt. Theol. Sem., 1986; D Ministry, New Orleans Bapt. Theol. Seminary, 1990. Ordained to ministry Bapt. Ch., 1980; cert. tchr., La. Tchr. Orleans Parish Sch. Bd., New Orleans, 1973-78, Delgado Community Coll., New Orleans, 1975-78; pastor Faith in Action Bapt. Ch., New Orleans, 1982—; founder, dir. Faith in Action Evangel. Team, New Orleans, 1977—; lectr. Nat. Bapt. Conv. on Congl. Evangelism, New Orleans, 1977-79; cons. So. Bapt. Conv. Home Mission Bd., La., 1986—. Bd. dirs. Project New Orleans, 1983—. Democrat. Avocations: computers, aquariums, interior decorating, aerobics. Office: Faith in Action Evang Team 2544 Onzaga St New Orleans LA 70119 *The greatest investment one can make in this life is an investment in the life of another person. That is the only investment with eternal value.*

TRUEMPER, DAVID GEORGE, theology educator, computer company executive; b. Aurora, Ill., Feb. 1, 1939; s. George Carl and Erna Hildegarde (Stallman) T.; m. Joanna Ruth Mitschke, June 29, 1963; children: Pamela Jo, Rebekah Ruth. BA, Concordia Sr. Coll., 1961; MDiv, Concordia Sem., 1965, STM, 1969; STD, Luth. Sch. of Theology, 1974; postgrad., U. Chgo., 1984-85. With Valparaiso (Ind.) U., 1967—, prof. theology, 1985—; pastor St. John Luth. Ch., LaCrosse, Ind., 1979-85; asst. dir. programming The Luth. Hour, St. Louis, 1966-67; vis. lectr. Fachhochschule, Reutlingen, Fed. Republic of Germany, 1974-76; pres. Three Pro Computer Systems, Inc., Valparaiso, 1985—; dir. Inst. Liturgical Studies, Valparaiso; vis. scholar Herzog August Bibliothek, Wolfenbuttel, Fed. Republic of Germany, 1984. Author: Keeping the Faith, 1981; editor: Institute of Liturgical Studies Occasional Papers, 1986—, Proceedings of the North American Academy of Liturgy, 1989—. Inst. Advanced Study Religion, U. Chgo. fellow, 1984-85. Mem. Am. Soc. Reformation Rsch., Am. Acad. Religion, Coun. Socs. for the Study of Religion (exec. com. 1987—), N.Am. Acad. Liturgy (sec. 1983—), Societas Liturgica. Lutheran. Avocations: golf, tennis. Office: Valparaiso U Dept Theology Valparaiso IN 46383

TRUESDELL, WALTER GEORGE, minister, librarian; b. N.Y.C., Oct. 22, 1919; s. George Anson and Hattie (Evans) T.; m. Mary Schurok, June 10, 1944; children: Walter George, Susan Hattie. AB, Columbia U., 1941, MA, 1975; MDiv, Theol. Sem. Ref. Episcopal Ch., 1944; BLS, Pratt Inst., 1950. Ordained to ministry Ref. Episcopal Ch., 1944. Asst. min. 1st Ref. Episcopal Ch., N.Y.C., 1944-54; lectr. apologetics and English Bible Theol. Sem. Ref. Episcopal Ch., Phila., 1945-48, libr., 1964—; libr. Shelton Coll., 1951-69; rector Ch. of the Redemption, Bklyn., 1956—; chmn. com. on state of ch. Ref. Episcopal Ch., 1960-87, mem. gen. com., 1978—, mem. com. on state of ch., 1987—. Editor Episcopal Recorder, 1980—. Mem. ALA (life), Pa. Libr. Assn., Assn. Statisticians Am. Religious Bodies. Home: 306 E 90th St New York NY 10128 Office: Ref Episcopal Sem 4225 Chestnut St Philadelphia PA 19104 *Out of the privilege of a broad educational background and living in the astonishing technology of the 20th century, and yet to be in the turbulence of war, crime, starvation, and distress of mind and spirit, I am convicted anew of the need to know Christ, who said, "I am the way, the truth, and the life."*

TRUEX, EARLE MELVIN, minister; b. Circleville, Ohio, Sept. 29, 1937; s. C. Melvin and Mary Lee (Grimes) T.; m. Sally Ann Welker, June 25, 1966; children: Wendy, Jon, Marci, Luke. ThB, Circleville Bible Coll., 1959; BA, Malone Coll., 1963; MEd, Kent State U., 1971. Ordained to ministry Chs. of Christ in Christian Union, 1959. Pastor Little Country Ch., Waynesburg, Ohio, 1962-87; sr. pastor Faith Meml. Ch., Lancaster, Ohio, 1987—; pres. Hollow Rock Camp Meeting Assn., Toronto, Ohio, 1977—; trustee Circleville Bible Coll., 1987—; bd. dirs. World Gospel Mission, 1983—. Named Pastor of Yr. World Gospel Mission, 1985, Alumnus of Yr. Circleville Bible Coll., 1972; recipient Christian Svc. award Malone Coll., 1987. Mem. Wesleyan Theol. Sem. Home: 2668 W Fair Ave Lancaster OH 43130 Office: Faith Meml Ch 2610 W Fair Ave Lancaster OH 43130-9502

TRULOVE, HARRY DAVID, religious organization administrator; b. Rome, Ga., Jan. 13, 1927; s. Robert Don and Vida Nelson (Harris) T.; m. Carolyn Cecelia Goss, Jan. 16, 1949; children: Teresa Trulove Walker, James David, Timothy Goss. BA, Mercer U., 1948; BD, Southwestern Bapt. Theol. Sem., Ft. Worth, 1957. Ordained to Bapt. ministry, 1955. Asst. dept. mgr. J. C. Penney Co., Macon, Ga., 1948-49; dept. mgr. J. C. Penney Co., Dublin, Ga., 1949-50; ins. agt. Met. Life Ins., Macon, 1950-52; machinist Am. Mfg. Co., Ft. Worth, 19554, Chgo. Pneumatic Tool Co., Ft. Worth, 1955-57; pastor Leon Bapt. Ch., Okla., 1955-56, various chs., Tex., 1957-68; exec. dir. estate stewardship dept. Bapt. Gen. Conv. of Tex., Dallas, 1968-74; pres. Ark. Bapt. Found., Little Rock, 1974—; bd. dirs. Ark. State Coun. Econ. Edn., Little Rock, Christian Civic Found., Little Rock. Author: Financial Planning Workbook - A Better Tomorrow, 1970, 6th edit., 1982; contbr. articles to Home Life mag., Bapt. Program mag., Ch. Adminstrn. mag., weekly devotionals. Bd. dirs. Bapt. Gen. Conv. Texas, Dallas, 1963-68, Bapt. Meml. Geriatric Hosp., San Angelo, 1966-68. With USN, 1944-46. Mem. Assn. of So. Bapt. Found. Exec. (sec., treas. 1975, pres. 1985). Avocations: water skiing, reading, landscaping. Home: 2308 Gunpowder Little Rock AR 72207 Office: Ark Bapt Found Superior Fed Bank 500 W Broadway Ste 402 Little Rock AR 72201

TRUSCOTT, JUDITH FARREN, religious education administrator; b. Parkersburg, W.Va., Mar. 20, 1939; d. Oran Bearl and Marjorie Elizabeth (Bergen) Farren; m. Frederick G. Truscott Jr., Aug. 25, 1961; children: Lisa Kay Truscott Wiggins, Tina Diane Truscott Strautman, Lynne Noelle. BA, Marietta Coll., 1961; MA, U. West Fla., 1981. Ordained to ministry Presbyn. Ch. as elder, 1976; cert. Christian educator, 1989. Dir. Christian edn. Grace Presbyn. Ch., Lakewood, Ohio, 1973-76, elder, 1976—; dir. Christian edn. 1st Presbyn. Ch., Pensacola, Fla., 1977-83, John Knox Presbyn. Kirk, Kansas City, Mo., 1983-91, Westover Hills Presbyn. Ch., Little Rock, 1991—; moderator, mem., Ecumenical Ch. Resource Ctr., Kansas City, 1986-91; cert. advisor, Heartland Presbytery, Kansas City, 1989-91, edn. cons., 1984—; mem. Christian edn. com. Presbytery of Cleve. Mem., treas. Preschool PTA, Lakewood, 1966-70; mem., sec. PTA, Lakewood, 1970-76; mem. Ch. Women United Speaker's Bur., Cleve., 1970-76; mem. PTO, Pensacola, 1976-83, Girls Volleyball, Basketball Boosters, Shawnee, Kans., 1989-91. Mem. Mid-Cen. Assn. Presbyn. Ch. Educators (cabinet 1990—), Heartland Presbyn. Assn. Christian Educators (steering com. 1984-88, cert. advocate 1989-91, Heartland Presbytery certification advisor), Assn. Presbyn. Ch. Educators, Chi Omega Alumni Assn. Republican. Office: Westover Hills Presbyn Ch Little Rock AR 72207 *I believe in a personal God who is present in every aspect of my life. John 17:3, Romans 8:28 and Matthew 17:206 are Biblical passages from which I receive much inspiration.*

TSAI, PETER YING-SHIH, minister; b. TaiChung, Taiwan, Taiwanese, Jan. 7, 1923; s. James Yu and Chien-Ju (Lee) T.; m. Mary Su-Chin Chiang, July 22, 1949; children: Geoge Hsin-Tao, Hsin-Cheng, Hsin-Sheng, Hsin-Mei. Grad., Tokyo Theol. Sem., 1987; M of Missions, Kyoritsu Christian Inst., 1988. Elec. engr. Taiwan Power Co., 1949-79; com. mem. Gen. Assembly Presbyn. Ch., Taiwan, 1977-80; chief fin. dept. Presbyn. Ch., Taiwan, 1978-80; minister, 1983—; dir. Fund of Taiwanese Religious Edn. in Am., L.A., 1991—. Home and Office: 3711 Cogswell Rd #302 El Monte CA 91732 *There is nothing more important than religious education in modern society. Churches should have the responsibility for carring out the plan. That is the solution to prevent our society from expanding juvenile delinquency and all other serious immorality.*

TSCHANNEN-MORAN, ROBERT KEITH, minister; b. Cleve., Dec. 7, 1954; s. Robert Albert and June Ann (Uhlir) Tschannen; m. Megan Moran, Aug. 21, 1976; children: Bryn Mari, Evan Joseph. B, Northwestern U., 1975; postgrad., Garrett-Evang. Theol. Sem., 1976-78; M of Div., Yale U., 1979. Ordained to ministry United Meth. Ch. as deacon, 1976, as minister United Ch. Christ, 1980. Student pastor Middlefield (Conn.) Federated Ch., 1975-76, First Spanish United Ch. Christ, Chgo., 1976-78; organizing pastor Good News Community Ch., Chgo., 1979—; tri-dir. Interfaith Clergy, Rogers Park, Chgo., 1981—. Chmn. Peoples Housing, Chgo., 1979—, Congregations for Career Devel., Chgo., 1982-87; treas. Triangle Park Corp., Chgo., 1985—. Home: 7643 N Greenview Ave Chicago IL 60626-1208 Office: Good News Community Ch 7649 N Paulina St Chicago IL 60626

TSCHOEPE, THOMAS, bishop; b. Pilot Point, Tex., Dec. 17, 1915; s. Louis and Catherine (Sloan) T. Student, St. Thomas Sch. Pilot Point, 1930, Pontifical Coll. Josephinum, Worthington, Ohio, 1943. Ordained priest Roman Cath. Ch., 1943; asst. pastor in Ft. Worth, 1943-46, Sherman, Tex., 1946-48, Dallas, 1948-53; adminstr. St. Patrick Ch., Dallas, 1953-56; pastor St. Augustine Ch., Dallas, 1956-62, Sacred Heart Cathedral, Dallas, 1962-65; bishop San Angelo, Tex., 1966-69; bishop Dallas, 1969-90, ret. bishop, 1990; asst. pastor St. Joseph Parish, Waxahachie, Tex., 1990—. Home and Office: St Joseph Ch 504 E Marvin Box 190 Waxahachie TX 75165

TSE, JOHN C. M., religious organization administrator. Pres. Evang. Luth. Ch., Kowloon, Hong Kong. Office: Evang Luth Ch, 50a Waterloo Rd, Kowloon Hong Kong*

TSOHANTARIDIS, TIMOTHEOS, minister, religion educator; b. Katerini, Greece, Feb. 7, 1954; came to U.S., 1967; s. Ioannis and Parthena (Karipidis) T.; m. Valerie Ann Hoffman, July 11, 1977; children: Demetrius, Thaddeus. BA, Barrington Coll., 1977; MDiv, Gordon-Conwell, 1980; MA, Ashland Theol. Sem., 1985. Ordained to ministry Evang. Friends Ch., 1986. Ch. planter Ea. region Evang. Friends Ch., North Ridgeville, Ohio, 1980-85; prof. religion, Greek, dir. Christian life, soccer coach George Fox Coll., Newberg, Oreg., 1985—; bd. didrs. Greek Evang. Camps, 1989—. Author: (in Greek) Greek Evangelicals: Pontus to Katerini, 1985. Mem. Am. Acad. Religion, Soc. Bibl. Lit., Nat. Soccer Coaches Athletic Assn. (soccer coach, Nat. Coach of Yr. 1989). Home: 2018 Villa Rd Newberg OR 97132 Office: George Fox Coll 414 N Meridian St Newberg OR 97132

TSUKADA, (DAVID) OSAMU, theology educator, priest; b. Joetsu, Niigata, Japan, Dec. 31, 1929; s. Kensaku and Tsuneko (Sekiguchi) T.; m. Alice Gilgen, Jan. 2, 1965; 1 child, Andreas Shinichi. BA, Rikkyo U., Tokyo, 1952; BD, Cen. Theol. Coll., Tokyo, 1956; DPhil, Oxford U., 1962. Ordained priest Anglican Ch. Japan, 1959. Co-dir. Student Ctr., Nagoya, Japan, 1957-58; tutor Cen. Theol. Coll., 1958-59, asst. prof., 1963-68, adj. prof., 1968—; asst. prof. theology Rikkyo U., 1968-70, prof., 1970—, dean Coll. Arts, 1974-78, 91—, dir. Presdl. Office, 1983-86, trustee, 1983-87, 91—; vis. prof. Gen. Theol. Sem., N.Y.C., 1988, Ch. Div. Sch. Pacific, Berkeley, Calif., 1989, dean Coll. Arts, 1975-79, 90. Author: The Idea of Revelation, 1965, History of the Anglican Church, 1975, Church under the Emperor System, 1978, The New Imperial System and Christianity, 1990. Mem. Assn. Christian Studies (trustee 1989—), Assn. Brit. Philos. Studies, Internat. House. Avocations: tennis, skiing, hiking, gardening. Home: Higashi-Ohizumi, 3-4-8-202, Nerima-ku, Tokyo 178, Japan Office: Rikkyo U, Nishi-Ikebukuro 3, Tokyo 171, Japan

TUCHMAN, LOUIS M., rabbi; b. N.Y.C., Jan. 24, 1924; s. Alter Moshe and Anna Breindel (Klarman) T.; m. Ruth R. Lieberman, June 18, 1946; children: Asher Yaakov (dec.), Nachum Yehudah, Anne Bryna. BA magna cum laude, Yeshiva U., N.Y.C., 1944; MA, NYU, 1947. Ordained rabbi, 1947. Rabbi Congregation Beth Israel, Charleston, S.C., 1948-53, Congregation Beth El, Durham, N.C., 1953-58; dir. field activities Yeshiva U., N.Y.C., 1967-74; rabbi Congregation Shaaray Tzedek, Calgary, Alta., Can., 1974-79, Skokie (Ill.) Valley Traditional Synagogue, 1985—; chmn. Rabbi Action Com., Chgo. Jewish Fedn., 1989—, State of Israel Bonds, Chgo., 1988—. Asst. editor Traditional mag., 1953-65; contbr. article to Jewish Life mag., 1961. Honored, State of Israel Bonds, San Francisco, 1965, recipient Jerusalem medal, 1977, Shofar award, Boy Scouts Am., 1981. Mem. Rabbinical Coun. Am. (exec. bd.), Chgo. Bd. Rabbis (v.p. 1989-91, pres. 1991—), Chgo. Rabbinical Coun. (v.p. 1988—), No. Calif. Bd. Rabbis (pres. 1965-67). Office: Skokie Valley Synagogue 8825 E Prairie Rd Skokie IL 60076 *Effective remembrance is not a momentary or passing fancy. It must be a continuous process of recall and an application of the ideals bequeathed to us in order to bring about a more glorious tomorrow. It is this spirit of remembrance that should grow with us.*

TUCHMAN, MAURICE SIMON, library director; b. Bklyn., Sept. 14, 1936; s. William and Rose (Luria) T.; m. Helene Lillian Bodner, Aug. 30, 1959; children: Joel Aron, Miriam Auri. BA, CUNY, 1958; MLS, Columbia U., 1959; B Hebrew Lit., Jewish Theol. Sem., N.Y.C., 1964; D of Arts in LS, Simmons Coll., 1979. Cataloger. svcs. Buffalo and Erie County, 1959-60; asst. libr. N.Y. State Maritime Coll., Ft. Schuyler, 1962-64; libr. cons. Mid-Hudson Librs., Poughkeepsie, N.Y., 1964-66; libr. dir. Hebrew Coll., Brookline, Mass., 1966—; book appraiser, Auburndale, Mass., 1980—; book reviewer Libr. Jour., 1970—. With U.S. Army, 1960-62. N.Y. Regents scholar, 1959. Mem. ALA, Assn. Jewish Librs., Coun. Archives and Rsch. Librs. Jewish Studies, Ch. and Synagogue Libr. Assn. (pres. 1974-75), Fenway Libr. Consortium (coord. 1980-82, treas. 1990—). Home: 16 Duffield Rd Auburndale MA 02166 Office: Hebrew Coll 43 Hawes St Brookline MA 02146 *It is our most difficult task and our greatest accomplishment to reach our potential as a thinking and ethical human being.*

TUCK, DONALD RICHARD, religious educator; b. Albany, N.Y., Apr. 24, 1935; s. Raymond and Beulah (Schermerhorn) T.; m. Ann Lee Livermon, June 29, 1957; children: Karen Lee Tuck Druzak, Carolyn Thelma Tuck Phillips. BS cum laude, Nyack (N.Y.) Coll., 1957; MA magna cum laude, Wheaton (Ill.) Coll., 1965; PhD, U. Iowa, 1970. Minister United Presbyn. Ch., River Forest, Ill., 1963-65, Congl. United Ch. Christ, Hartwick, Iowa, 1968-69; instr. Western Ky. U., Bowling Green, 1969; asst. prof. religion Western Ky. U., 1970-73, assoc. prof. religion, 1973-78, prof. religion, 1978—; critical reviewer NEH, 1978-84; cons. in field. Editorial reviewer S.E. Conf. Assn. Asian Studies, 1982; author: Buddhist Churches of America, 1987, The Concept of Maya, 1986. Faculty Excellence, Western Ky. U., 1981, 82; Tenney award for excellence, Wheaton Coll., 1965. Mem. Am. Acad. Religion, Assn. Asian Studies, Bengal Studies Conf., Religion in South India, Tenn. Consortium for Asian Studies. Methodist. Avocations: travel, gardening, woodwork, furniture building. Office: Western Kentucky U Dept Philosophy/Religion Bowling Green KY 42101

TUCK, WILLIAM POWELL, minister; b. Lynchburg, Va., Oct. 30, 1934; s. Hillard Witt and Elsie Mae (Scott) T.; m. Emily Sue Campbell, June 4, 1960; children: Catherine, William Powell III. BA, U. Richmond, 1957, DD (hon.), 1977; BD, Southeastern Bapt. Theol. Sem., 1960, ThM, 1961; ThD, New Orleans Bapt. Theol. Sem., 1965. Ordained to ministry So. Bapt. Conv., 1956. Pastor Good Hope Bapt. Ch., Radiant, Va., 1955-60, Calvary

Bapt. Ch., Slidell, La., 1963-66, Harrisonburg (Va.) Bapt. Ch., 1966-69, First Bapt. Ch., Bristol, Va., 1969-78; prof. preaching So. Bapt. Theol. Sem., Louisville, 1978-83; pastor St. Matthews Bapt. Ch., Louisville, 1983—; chmn. commn. on Christian unity Ky. Coun. Chs., 1987—; moderator forum of congregations Kentuckiana Interfaith Community, Louisville, 1986—; mem. Bapt. joint com. Long Run Assn., Louisville, 1987—; bd. dirs. Acad. Parish Clergy, 1990—; pres. Augusta Bapt. Pastor's Conf., Harrisonburg, 1968; trustee Va. Intermont Coll., 1973-83; adj. prof. religion and philosophy Va. Intermont Coll., Bristol, 1972-78; adj. prof. Christian preaching So. Bapt. Theol. Sem., Louisville, 1983-86, 90. Author: Facing Grief and Death, 1975, Knowing God: Religious Knowledge in the Theology of John Ballie, 1978, The Way For All Seasons, 1987; editor, contbg. author: The Struggle for Meaning, 1977; Ministry: An Ecumenical Challenge, 1988; book rev. editor Sharing the Practice jour., 1988—; contbr. articles to collections, various jours. Mem. Louisville and Jefferson County AIDS Task Force, 1987-89; bd. dirs. Bristol YMCA, 1976-78, Bristol Boys' Club, 1971-78, v.p., 1972-73, pres., 1973-74; mem. dist. com. Sequoyah coun. Boy Scouts Am., 1971-73, Bristol, 1971-73; mem. drug and sex edn. com. Bristol Pub. Schs., 1975-78; mem. community rels. coun. Job Corps, Bristol, 1972-73; chmn. Interracial and Interdenominational Washington St. Sch. Project, 1971-73; chmn. Manssanutten dist. Protestant Com. on Scouting, 1968-69; mem. gov.'s spl. edn. rsch. com. Harrisonburg Sch. System, 1968. Walter Pope Binns fellow William Jewell Coll., 1983; recipient Man and Boy award Bristol Boys' Club, 1974. Mem. Ky. Bapt. Conv. (exec. bd. 1990—, nominating com. 1990—), Ky. Coun. Chs. (exec. bd. dirs. 1991—), La. Bapt. Conv. (mem. state exec. bd. 1964-66), La. Protestant Ministerial Assn. (pres. 1965), Bapt. Gen. Assn. Va. (chmn. com. om coms. and bds. 1977-78), Am. Acad. Religion, Acad. Homiletics, Acad. Parish Clergy, So. Bapt. Hist. Soc., Acad. Preachers, Rotary (bd. dirs. Bristol club 1971-78), Kappa Delta Pi, Phi Theta Kappa. Democrat. Home: 2322 Thornhill Rd Louisville KY 40222 Office: St Matthews Bapt Ch 3515 Grandview Ave Louisville KY 40207

TUCKER, BOBBY GLENN, minister; b. Grand Saline, Tex., Sept. 11, 1954; s. Glen Burton and Edna LaFaye (Phillips) T. BS, Tex. A&M U., 1979; student, Southwestern Bapt. Theol., Seminary, Ft. Worth, 1980-83. Minister of music and youth First Missionary Bapt. Ch., Terrell, Tex., 1980; minister of youth Farley St. Bapt. Ch., Waxahachie, Tex., 1980-83; assoc. pastor First Bapt. Ch., Magnolia, Ark., 1983-86; youth ministry cons. Dept. Ch. Ministries Bapt. Missionary Assn. of Am., Waxahachie, 1986-87; exec. dir. Nat. Youth Dept. Bapt. Missionary Assn. of Am., Texarkana, Tex., 1987—; dir. Nat. Christian Youth Leadership Conf., Washington, 1984-87; trustee Found. for Christian Youth Leadership, 1983—; cons. to denominational curriculum com., 1987—. Named Outstanding Young Religious Leader, Jaycees, Magnolia, 1986, Outstanding Young Man of Am., 1976. Republican. Home: PO Box 1253 Texarkana AR 75504 Office: National Youth Dept PO Box 3376 Texarkana TX 75504

TUCKER, GENE MILTON, religion educator, minister; b. Albany, Tex., Jan. 8, 1935; s. Charlene Marye Williams, July 27, 1957; children: Teresa Lynne, Rebecca Michelle. BA cum laude, McMurry Coll., 1957; BD, Yale U., 1960, MA, 1961, PhD, 1963. Ordained to ministry United Meth. Ch., 1959, 66. Asst. prof. U. S.C. Grad. Sch. Religion, 1963-66; asst. prof., assoc. prof. Duke U. Div. Sch., Durham, N.C., 1966-70; assoc. prof. O.T., Emory U Candler Sch. Theology, Atlanta, 1970-77, prof., 1977—, assoc. dean, 1978-83; bd. advisors Ring Lake Ranch Retreat Ctr., Dubois, Wyo., 1981—, bd. dirs., 1983—; mem. com. New Rev. Standard Version translation, 1981—. Author: Form Criticism of the Old Testament, 1971, (with J. Maxwell Miller) Joshua, 1974, (with F.B. Craddock, J.H. Hayes and C.R. Holladay) Preaching the New Common Lectionary: Year B: Lent, Holy Week, Easter, 1984, Preaching the New Common Lectionary: Year B: After Pentecost, 1985; The Minor Prophets, Student Book and Teacher Book, 1984; editor: (with D.A. Knight) Humanizing America's Iconic Book, 1982, The Hebrew Bible and Its Modern Interpreters, 1985, (with David L. Petersen and Robert R. Wilson) Canon, Theology and Old Testament Interpretation, 1988; contbr. articles to jours., chpts. to books. Rsch. grantee Emory U., 1972-73, 76-77; fellow Assn. Theol. Schs., 1980-81. Mem. Soc. Bibl. Lit. (chmn. rsch. and publs., 1985-90), Internat. Orgn. for Study O.T., Inst. for Antiquity and Christianity, Colloquium for Old Testament Rsch. (pres. 1973-74). Democrat. Home: 2852 Ponderosa Circle Decatur GA 30033 Office: Emory U Candler Sch Theol 102 Bishops Hall Atlanta GA 30322

TUCKER, TRACY L., clergyman; b. Sarasota, Fla., Aug. 24, 1959; s. Jay H. and Joanne E. (Santrock) T.; m. Anna Denise Young, Dec. 12, 1981. BA, Trevecca Nazarene Coll., 1981; MDiv, Nazarene Theol. Sem., 1986. Ordained to ministry. Pastor Englewood (Fla.) Ch. of the Nazarene, 1986-89; assoc. pastor Leesburg (Fla.) Ch. of the Nazarene, 1989—; sr. high dir. North Fla. Dist. Nazarene Youth Internat., Leesburg, 1990-91, fall retreat dir., 1990-91; youth camp dir. So. Fla. Dist. Nazarene Youth Internat., Englewood, 1988-89; local coord. Lake County Schs. Ptnrs. for Success, Leesburg, 1989-90. V.p. Helping Hand Community Emergency Assistance, Englewood, 1986-89. Recipient Golden Apple award, 1990. Office: Leesburg Ch of the Nazarene 1111 Pamela St Leesburg VA 34748

TUDESCO, JAMES PATRICK, minister; b. Hartford, Conn., Mar. 17, 1946; s. James Peter and Olive (McClean) T.; m. Sherrie Jane Stockwell; children: Sarah Jenny, James Peter, Andrew Robert. BA, Oberlin (Ohio) Coll., 1968; MDiv, Yale Div. Sch., 1972; MA, U. Conn., 1974, PhD, 1980. Ordained to ministry United Ch. of Christ, 1973. Lectr. U. Conn., Storrs, 1977-80; asst. minister Storrs Congl. Ch., 1972-79; assoc. minister Second Congl. Ch., Attleboro, Mass., 1980-84; sr. minister Dane Street Congl. Ch., Beverly, Mass., 1984—; registrar Essex Assn. United Ch. Christ, 1988—, bd. dirs., 1985-88. Contbr. articles to profl. jours., author book revs. Bd. dirs. Beverly Reg. YMCA, 1988—, fin. com., 1991. Fulbright fellow, 1978; grantee Richard D. Irwin Found., 1979-80. Mem. Phi Beta Kappa, Phi Kappa Phi. Office: Dane Street Congl Ch 10 Dane St Beverly MA 01915

TUELL, JACK MARVIN, bishop; b. Tacoma, Nov. 14, 1923; s. Frank Harry and Anne Helen (Bertelson) T.; m. Marjorie Ida Beadles, June 17, 1946; children—Jacqueline, Cynthia, James. B.S., U. Wash., 1947, LL.B., 1948; S.T.B., Boston U., 1955; M.A., U. Puget Sound, 1961; D.D., Pacific Sch. Religion, 1966; LLD, Alaska Pacific U., 1980. Bar: Wash. 1948; ordained to ministry Meth. Ch., 1955. Practice law with firm Holte & Tuell, Edmonds, Wash., 1948-50; pastor Grace Meth. Ch., Everett, Wash., 1950-52, South Tewksbury Meth. Ch., Tewksbury, Mass., 1952-55, Lakewood Meth. Ch., Tacoma, 1955-61; dist. supt. Puget Sound dist. Meth. Ch., Everett, 1961-67; pastor 1st United Meth. Ch., Vancouver, Wash., 1967-72; bishop United Meth. Ch., Portland, Oreg., 1972—, Calif.-Pacific Conf., United Meth. Ch., L.A., 1980—; Mem. gen. conf. United Meth. Ch., 1964, 66, 68, 70, 72; pres. coun. of Bishops United Meth. Ch., 1989-90. Author: The Organization of the United Methodist Church, 1970. Pres. Tacoma U.S.O., 1959-61, Vancouver YMCA, 1968; v.p. Ft. Vancouver Seamens Cnt., 1969-72; vice chmn. Vancouver Human Rels. Commn., 1970-72; pres. Oreg. Coun. Alcohol Problems, 1972-76; Trustee U. Puget Sound, 1961-73, Vancouver Meml. Hosp., 1967-72, Alaska Meth. U., Anchorage, 1972-80, Willamette U., Salem, Oreg., 1972-80, Willamette View Manor, Portland, 1972-80, Rogue Valley Manor, Medford, Oreg., 1972-76; pres. nat. div. bd. global ministries United Meth. Ch., 1972-76, pres. ecumenical and interreligious concerns div., 1976-80, Commn. on Christian Unity and interreligious concerns, 1980-84, Gen. Bd. of Pensions 1984—, Calif. Coun. Alcohol Problems, 1985-88. Jacob Sleeper fellow, 1955. Club: Rotarian. Office: The United Meth Ch 110 S Euclid PO Box 6006 Pasadena CA 91102

TUGGY, ARTHUR LEONARD, religious organization administrator; b. Port of Spain, Trinidad and Tobago, July 9, 1929; came to U.S., 1932; s. Arthur William and Roe Olive (Williams) T.; m. Jeannette Lenora Stokes, Jan. 24, 1953; children: Stephen, Michael, Lynette. BA, UCLA, 1953; MDiv, Fuller Theol. Sem., 1956; D of Missiology, Sch. of World Mission, 1974; ThM, SWM, Fuller, 1968. Ordained to ministry Conservative Bapt. Ch., 1957. Missionary Conservative Bapt. Fgn. Mission Soc., Philippines, 1956-74; dir. Asia ministries Conservative Bapt. Fgn. Mission Soc., Wheaton, Ill., 1974—; chmn. Cooperating Home Bds. of Union Biblical Sem. (India), Wheaton, 1990-91. Author: The Philippine Church, 1971, Iglesia ni Cristo, 1976, The Gospel of John: An Inductive Study, 1986; co-author: Seeing the Church in the Philippines, 1972. Mem. Am. Soc. Missiology. Republican. Office: Conservative Bapt Fgn Mission Soc PO Box 5 Wheaton IL 60189

TUITE, JOSEPH PATRICK, clergyman, educator; b. Newark, July 31, 1914; s. Patrick J. and Ann (Sheridan) T. B.A., Seton Hall Coll., 1937; grad., Immaculate Conception Sem., 1941; Ph.D., St. John U., 1954. Ordained priest Roman Cath. Ch., 1941; tchr. classical langs. Seton Hall Prep. Sch., 1941-42, 46-59; comptroller Seton Hall Coll., 1942-43; mem. Archdiocesan Ednl. Commn., Newark, 1954-59; supt. schs. Archdiocese of, Newark, 1959-72; episcopal vicar/sec. edn. Archdiocese Newark, 1972-76; prof. Seton Hall U. Sch. Edn., South Orange, N.J., 1972—; dir. budget Seton Hall U. Sch. Edn., 1973—; mem. Archdiocese Newark Bd. Edn., 1972-76. Served to capt. Chaplain Corps AUS, 1943-46. Office: Seton Hall U South Orange NJ 07079

TULLIS, EDWARD LEWIS, retired bishop; b. Cin., Mar. 9, 1917; s. Ashar Spence and Priscilla (Daugherty) T.; m. Mary Jane Talley, Sept. 25, 1937; children: Frank Loyd, Jane Allen (Mrs. William Nelson Offutt IV). AB, Ky. Wesleyan Coll., 1939, LHD, 1975; BD, Louisville Presbyn. Theol. Sem., 1947; DD, Union Coll., Barbourville, Ky., 1954, Wofford Coll., 1976; LHD, Claflin Coll., 1976, Lambuth Coll., 1984. Ordained to ministry Methodist Ch., 1941; service in chs. Frenchburg, Ky., 1937-39, Lawrenceburg, Ky., 1939-44; asso. pastor 4th Ave. Meth. Ch., Louisville, 1944-47, Irvine, Ky., 1947-49; asso. sec. ch. extension sect. Bd. Missions, Meth. Ch., Louisville, 1949-52; pastor First Meth. Ch., Frankfort, Ky., 1952-61, Ashland, Ky., 1961-72; resident bishop United Meth. Ch., Columbia, S.C., 1972-80, Nashville area, 1980-84; ret. United Meth. Ch., 1984; instr. Bible Ky. Wesleyan Coll., 1947-48; instr. Louisville Presbyn. Theol. Sem., 1949-52; mem. Meth. Gen. Conf., 1956, 60, 64, 66, 68, 70, 72, Southeastern Jurisdictional Conf., 1952, 56, 60, 64, 68, 72, 84, 80, bd. mgrs. Bd. Missions, 1962-72, mem. bd. discipleship, 1972-80, v.p. Gen. Council on Fin. and Adminstrn., 1980-84; Chaplain Ky. Gen. Assembly, 1952-61; chmn. Frankfort Com. Human Rights, 1956-61, Mayor's Advisory Com. Human Relations, Ashland, 1968-72. Author: Shaping the Church from the Mind of Christ, 1984. Contbr. articles to religious jours. Sec., bd. dirs. Magee Christian Edn. Found.; trustee Emory U., 1973-80, Alaska Meth. U., 1965-70, Ky. Wesleyan Coll., Martin Coll., Lambuth Coll., McKendree Manor, Meth. Hosps., Memphis, Lake Junaluska Assembly, 1966-88. Recipient Outstanding Citizen award Frankfort VFW, 1961, Mayor's award for outstanding service. Ashland, 1971. Club: Kiwanis. Home: PO Box 754 Lake Junaluska NC 28745

TULLOCH, EDWIN FRED, minister, chaplain, psychotherapist; b. Belton, Tex., Aug. 19, 1937; s. Robert Euclid and Clara Laura (Muehlhause) T.; m. Marianne Brevard, Sept. 19, 1959; children: Melanie Ruth, Valerie Anne. BA, Baylor U., 1959; MDiv, Austin Presbyn. Theolog. Sem., 1962, THM, 1969; DMin, So. Meth. U., 1978; PhD, East Tex. State U., 1985, MS, 1987. Lic. profl. counselor, Tex. Pastor Highland Presbyn. Ch., Hot Springs, Ark., 1962-66, First Prebyn. Ch., Dickinson, Tex., 1966-69; assoc. pastor First Prebyn. Ch., Dallas, 1969-87; chaplain Presbyn. Hosp. Dallas, 1988—; psychotherapist Pastoral Counseling and Edn. Ctr., Dallas, 1988—. Adv. bd. editor (book) Kerygma: Bible Study in Depth, 1984. Recipient Eastern Star Religious award, Belton, Tex, 1960. '61; named Outstanding Alumni East Tex. State U., Commerce, 1987. Mem. Am. Assn. for Marriage and Family Therapy (clin.), Am. Assn. Pastoral Counselors (cert.). Avocations: tennis, hiking. Home: 326 Robin Hill Ln Duncanville TX 75137 Office: Pastoral Counseling and Edn Ctr 4525 Lemmon Ave Ste 200 Dallas TX 75219

TULLY, WALTON JEANES, pastor; b. Phila., May 16, 1931; s. Walton Jeanes and Laura Grace (Woolcock) T.; m. Marjorie Jean Sellick, Aug. 20, 1954; children: Bruce Eric, Sheryl Ann Krocek, Linda Kay. Grad., Ohio Peace Officer Tng. Acad., Knox County, Ohio, 1978. Ordained to ministry Meth. Ch., 1967. Pastor Bellville (Ohio) United Meth. Ch., 1964-71; assoc. pastor Central United Meth. Ch., Mansfield, Ohio, 1971-73; pastor Homer (Ohio) Charge, 1973-78, Orwell (Ohio)-Windsor United Meth. Chs., 1978-85, Faith United Meth. Ch., Cambridge, Ohio, 1985-88, Scio (Ohio) United Meth. Ch., 1988—; comml. underwriting supr. Kemper Ins., Mansfield, 1965-73. 50th ward committeeman Republican Party, Phila., 1956-58; chaplain Knox County Sheriff's Dept., 1977-78, Ashtabula County Sheriff's Dept., 1978-85, Cambridge Police Dept., 1985-88, Harrison County Sheriff's Dept., 1988—. Staff sgt. U.S. Army, 1950-52, Korea. Named Dep. of Yr., Ashtabula County Sheriff's Dept., Jefferson, Ohio, 1984. Mem. Internat. Conf. Police Chaplains (cert. sr. chaplain, bd. dirs. East Great Lakes region 1988—), Nat. Sheriffs Assn. Home: 206 W Main St PO Box 554 Scio OH 43988-0554

TULOWITZKY, MAX WILLIAM, music director; b. Alexandria, Ind., June 30, 1935; s. Eric Walter and Leota (Goins) T.; m. Mary Imogene, May 17, 1957; children: Ty Alan, Tara Lynn Gooding. Grad. high sch., Alexandria, 1953. Dir. music Alexandria Nazarene Church, Alexandria, Ind., 1963-81, Goodwin Nazarene Church, Anderson, Ind., 1981-85; dir. sound Alexandria Nazarene Church, Alexandria, Ind., 1985-86; dir. music Goodwin Nazarene Church, Anderson, Ind., 1986--. Active Little League (pres., commr., secy.), Boy Scouts, Alexandria Band Boosters (v.p., pres.); chmn. Alexandria 150th Birthday; co-chmn. United Fund; Caravan dir.; elected to Twp. Adv. Recepient County Scout award, Scout Citizen award, Civic award, Youth Assistanceaward and Citizen-of-Year award Alexandria Chamber of Commerce, Outstanding Service award General Motors, 1980. Mem. U.S. Advisory Bd., Alexandria Nazarene Ch. Bd., Alexandria Weekday Religion bd. Nazarene. Home: RR #3 Box 209 Alexandria IN 46001 Office: Goodwin Nazarene 3615 Raible Ave Anderson IN 46011

TUMBLIN, RANDALL S., seminary admissions director; b. Birmingham, Ala., July 30, 1957; s. Clayburn Sparks and Myrtice Rachael (Wood) T.; m. Carroll Jean Kledzik, Jan. 10, 1981; children: Hannah Elizabeth, Jonathan Randall. BA, Olivet Nazarene U., 1980. Dir. campus life Youth for Christ, Valparaiso, Ind., 1981-82; youth pastor Nazarene Ch., Grand Rapids, Mich., 1982-84; admission counselor North Park Coll., Chgo., 1984-86, asst. dir. admissions, 1987-89, dir. admissions, 1989—. Worship leader, guitarist, singer Irving Pk. Free Meth. Ch., Chgo., 1985-91. Mem. Christian Higher Edn. Pers. Serving Internat. Students. Office: North Park Coll 3225 W Foster Chicago IL 60625

TUMBLIN, THOMAS FREDERICK, religious organization administrator, clergyman; b. Columbus, Ohio, June 23, 1958; s. Eldred Eugene and Wilma Lee (Williams) T.; m. Sophia Yvonne Crabtree, Apr. 13, 1985; 1 child, Hope Marie. BA, Asbury Coll., 1980; MDiv, Asbury Sem., 1984; MA in Edn., U. Mich., 1989, postgrad., 1989—. Ordained to ministry United Meth. Ch. as deacon, 1982, as elder, 1986. Pastor Edenton Charge United Meth. Ch., Blanchester, Ohio, 1980-84; chmn. Ichthus Ministries, Wilmore, Ky., 1982-83; adminstrv. asst. Asbury Sem., Wilmore, 1983-84; pastor Burlington United Meth. Ch., South Point, Ohio, 1984-87; adminstr. Ginghamsburg United Meth. Ch., Tipp City, Ohio, 1989—; supply pastor Milan (Mich.) Free Meth. Ch., 1989. Trustee Lancaster, Ohio camp ground, 1985-87; co-founder Community Mission Outreach, Chesapeake, Ohio, 1985-87; coord. Lawrence County, Ohio Info. Referral, 1985-87; participant Leadership '88, Washington, 1988,. Fellow Soc. for Values in Higher Edn.; mem. Wesleyan Theol. Soc., Nat. Assn. Ch. Bus. Adminstrs., Soc. for Christian Ethics (student), Christian Mgmt. Assn. Republican. Office: Ginghamsburg United Meth Ch 7695 S County Rd 25A Tipp City OH 45371

TUMI, CHRISTIAN WIYGHAN CARDINAL, bishop; b. Kikaikelaki, Cameroon, Oct. 15, 1930. Ordained priest Roman Cath. Ch., 1966. Elected to Yagoua, 1979, consecrated bishop,, 1980, coadjutor bishop,, 1982, diocesan bishop,, 1984, created cardinal,, 1988. Address: Archvêché, BP 272, Garoua Cameroon

TUNE, MICHAEL THOMAS, minister; b. Nashville, May 22, 1953; s. Myles Thomas and Charlene Lowe (Porch) T.; m. Monica Denise Thompson, Mar. 22, 1975; children: Michael, Adam, Clayton. BS, Muray State U., 1974; MA in Religion, Harding U., 1985. Min. Harrisburg (Ill.) Ch. of Christ, 1974-77; min. East Wood Ch. Christ, Paris, Tenn., 1977-78, edn. dir., 1978-86; min. Univ. Ch. of Christ, Monroe, La., 1986—; staff writer Gospel Advocate Pub. Co., Nashville, 1984—; developer tchr. tng. program, 1984—. Author: Studies in Minor Prophets, 1978, Studies in Major Prophets, 1980. Reader Jack Hayes Elem. Sch., Monroe, La., 1987—. Mem. Soc. Bibl. Lit. Office: Univ Ch of Christ 3605 Desiard PO Box 4272 Monroe LA 71203

TUNNELL, CAROLYN JOYCE, youth ministries director; b. Dallas, Feb. 4, 1947; d. George Marvin and Joyce Jo (Johnson) Hodges; m. Leonard Hartford Tunnell Jr., Feb. 13, 1971; children: Aaron, Brock, Benjamin, Brianna. BA in English, Ind. Wesleyan U., 1969; postgrad., S.W. Tex. State U., 1971, U. Tex., San Antonio, 1974, San Antonio Coll., 1983. Info. dir. San Antonio Youth for Christ, 1970-71, mem. inner city, troubled teen ministry, 1980-85; youth worker Youth for Christ, S.W. Mo. (Campus Life), Joplin, 1985—; dir. youth ministry 1st United Meth. Ch., Joplin, 1987—; regional women's min. coord. Youth for Christ/USA, Mid Plains Region, 1986—, tng. com., 1986—; counselor Crisis Pregnancy Ctr., Joplin, 1990-91; advisor Dist. Youth Coun., Joplin Area, 1991—. Editor: (monthly) In Touch, 1980-84. Precinct chmn. Rep. Orgn., San Antonio, 1982. Recipient Appreciation award Alazan-Apache Cts., San Antonio, 1984, Girlsville, San Antonio, 1984, Pres. award Youth for Christ/USA, Denver, 1990. Home: 411 Sergeant Joplin MO 64801 Office: 1st Meth Ch 501 W 4th Joplin MO 64801

TUNSTALL, FRANKLIN GEORGE, religion educator; b. Lake City, S.C., Aug. 3, 1943; s. Henry C. and Ida Belle (Floyd) T.; m. Lula Mae Flowers, Mar. 30, 1964; children: Claudena Marie, Franklin George Jr., Derek Allen. AA, Emmanuel Coll., Franklin Springs, Ga., 1963; BA, Meth. Coll., Fayetteville, N.C., 1966; MA, U. Tulsa, 1969; MDiv, Oral Roberts U., 1969; DMin, Phillips U., 1972. Campus pastor Southwestern Coll., Oklahoma City, Okla., 1969-71; dean sch. religion Southwestern Coll., Oklahoma City, 1971-73; editor chief publs. Pentecostal Holiness Ch., Inc., Oklahoma City, 1973-80; pastor NW Christian Ctr., Oklahoma City, 1980-83, 89—; pres. Southwestern Coll., Oklahoma City, 1983-89, prof. Bible, 1989—. Author: Dinah Went Out on the Town, 1974, Walking the Romans Road, 1990, So Much Better: A Study Guide to the Book of Hebrews, 1990, An Introduction to Bible Theology, 1991. Republican. Avocations: basketball, fishing. Home: 7312 NW 113 TR Oklahoma City OK 73162 Office: Southwestern Coll PO Box 340 Bethany OK 73008 *I consider it the greatest discovery of my life. It came the day the reality dawned in my consciousness that truth is not to be found in any philosophical system, but in the person—Jesus Christ. He is the personification of the sum total of truth.*

TURBEVILLE, CAROLL DALE, pastor; b. Baton Rouge, Mar. 28, 1957; s. Cunliffe Adam and Nellie (Feazel) T.; m. Christy Jo Bradstreet, Jan. 19, 1980; children: Carrie Elizabeth, Adam Dale, Joseph Aaron. BTh summa cum laude, Bapt. Bible Coll., 1977, BS summa cum laude, 1978; MRE summa cum laude, Temple Bapt. Theol. Sem., 1980. Ordained to ministry Bapt. Ch., 1980. Prof. bible Bapt. Bible Coll., Springfield, Mo., 1980-82; assoc. pastor Berea Bapt. Ch., Adrian, Mich., 1982-84; sr. pastor Manitou Rd. Bapt. Ch., Manitou Beach, Mich., 1984—; adminstr. Manitou Rd. Bapt. Acad., Manitou Beach, 1984—. Home: 207 Manitou Rd Manitou Beach MI 49253 Office: Manitou Rd Bapt Ch 175 Manitou Rd Manitou Beach MI 49253

TURCOTTE, JEAN-CLAUDE, archbishop; b. Montreal, Que., Can., June 26, 1936; s. Paul-Emile and Rita (Gravel) T. Ordained priest Roman Catholic Ch., consecrated bishop. Aux. bishop Diocese of Montreal, Que., Can., 1982-90, archbishop, 1990—. Home: 1071 de la Cathedrale St, Montreal, PQ Canada H3B 2V4 Office: Diocese de Montreal, 2000 Sherbrooke ouest, Montreal, PQ Canada H3H 1G4

TURLEY, MARION E., minister; b. Winchester, Ky., June 16, 1938; s. Everett Linwood and Edith (Everman) T.; m. Carolyn Clarke Couchman, Aug. 19, 1961; children: Rhoda, Stephen. Cert., Clear Creek Bapt. Coll., Pineville, Ky., 1970. Ordained to ministry Bapt. Ch., 1968. Pastor Bapt. chs., St. Charles, Va., 1969-71, Winchester, Ky., 1971-75; pastor Broadway Bapt. Ch., Richmond, Ky., 1975-79, Blue Lick Bapt. Ch., Berea, Ky., 1985-88; interim pastor, mem. exec. bd. Gilead Bapt. Ch., Richmond, Ky., 1989—; outreach dir. Unity Bapt. Ch., 1988-89; moderator Boonescreek Bapt. Assn., Winchester, 1974; water treatment specialist Richmond Utilities, 1985—; mem. credentials com. Tates Creek Bapt. Assn., Richmond, 1986-89. With USAF, 1956-60. Mem. Woodmen of World. Republican. Home: 526 Meadowbrook Rd Richmond KY 40475

TURNBAUGH, RONALD NEAL, minister; b. Nebo, Ill., Sept. 25, 1935; s. Marvin Rudyard and Vera Maudin (Scranton) T.; m. Dorothy J. Pearson, Feb. 14, 1955; children: Ronald N. Jr., Deborah A., Jeanette L. AA, Hannibal Lagrange Coll., 1967; AB, William Jewell Coll., 1971; M in Div., Midwestern Bapt. Sem., 1974; D in Ministry, Luther Rice Sem., 1980. Enlisted USAF, 1954, advanced through ranks to staff sgt., 1960, resigned, 1963; pastor Curryville (Mo.) Bapt. Ch., 1967-70, Utica (Mo.) Bapt. Ch., 1970-74, Temple Bapt. Ch., Poplar Bluff, Mo., 1974-76; dir. missions N.W. Bapt. Mission Group, Maryville, Mo., 1976-1984; minister edn., adminstrn. Plaza Heights Bapt. Ch., Blue Springs, Mo., 1984—. Mem. Nat. Assn. Bus. Adminstrn. Avocations: golf, hunting, fishing. Address: 904 Wein Blue Springs MO 64015-2258

TURNBEAUGH, TERRY DEAN, minister; b. Litchfield, Ill., Dec. 8, 1954; s. John R. and Joyce (Thomas) T.; m. Linda K. Swinney, Dec. 20, 1973; children: Aaron, Adam. BA in Theology, Clarksville (Tenn.) Bapt. Coll., 1977. Ordained to ministry Bapt. Ch., 1977. Pastor Gethsemane Bapt. Ch., Marengo, Ohio, 1977-78; assoc. pastor New Hope Bapt. Ch., Dearborn Heights, Mich., 1978-79; music minister Northside Bapt. Ch., Madison Heights, Mich., 1980-81; deckhand Valley Lines Co., St. Louis, 1981-83; pastor First Bapt. Ch., Pineville, Mo., 1983-86, Armour Heights Bapt. Ch., Kansas City, Mo., 1986—; conf. leader Mole St. Nicolas, Republic of Haiti, 1985; evangelism dir. Shoal Creek Baptist Assn., 1983-86; mem. evangelism com. Blue River/Kansas City Baptist Assn. Contbr. column to BMW Owners mag., 1985—. Organizer Home Aid Motorcycle Rally Charity event, Crosses, Ark., 1986; bd. dirs. Samll Victories, Inc., Powell, Mo., 1986. Mem. BMW Motorcycle Owners Am. Avocations: motorcycling, golf, music, hunting, photography. Office: Armour Heights Bapt Ch 7900 Jarboe Kansas City MO 64114

TURNBOLE, KATHLEEN MCCOMBE, minister; b. N.Y.C., Oct. 2, 1951; d. John Harold and Dorothy Mae (Skove) McCombe; m. David Paul Turnbole; children: Samantha, John, Katherine, Heath. BA, Baldwin-Wallace Coll., Berea, Ohio, 1974; MDiv, Princeton Theol. Sem., 1977. Minister Nicholville (N.Y.) Parish, 1977-79, First United Meth. Ch., Little Falls, N.Y., 1979-81, Four Steeples Parish, Belleville, N.Y., 1981-82, Summerfield United Meth. Ch., Staten Island, 1983-86, First United Meth. Ch., E. Hampton, N.Y., 1986-90; chaplain, pastoral care, dir. bereavement Hospice of Jefferson County, Inc., Watertown, N.Y., 1990—. Author poetry, Sojourner, 1982; lyricist, We Are One..., 1972. Pres. E. Hampton Town Clericus, 1988-89; bd. dirs. Bd. Ethics, Town of E. Hampton, 1988-89; soloist, chorister Choral Soc. of the Hamptons, 1987-89. Mem. AAUW, NAFE, Am. Guild Organists. Avocation: music.

TURNBULL, THOMAS KENT, priest; b. Lancaster, Ohio, Aug. 3, 1934; s. Donald Curtis and Lucy Gordon (Taylor) T.; m. Ingrid Johanne Moeller, Apr. 15, 1967; children: Michael David, John Christopher, Rachael Maria. BA in Theatre Arts, Denison U., 1959; BDiv., Episcopal Theol. Sch., 1965. Ordained to ministry Episcopal Ch. as deacon, 1965, as priest, 1966. Rector Christ Ch., Ironton, Ohio, 1967-71; vicar Ch. of the Holy Spirit, Cin., 1971-74; assoc. rector Christ Ch., Denver, 1974-75; vicar St. George's Ch., Leadville, Colo., 1975-78; rector Ch. of the Transfiguration, Vail, Colo., 1975-85; on sabbatical in England and Colo., 1985-86; interim rector Ch. of Holy Comforter, Broomfield, Colo., 1986-87; rector St. Andrew's Episc. Ch., Chelan, Washington, 1987—; pres. standing com. Diocese of Colo., 1984-85, mem. examining chaplains, 1980-87; leader numerous workshops and retreats, 1967—; alt. gen. conv. The Episcopal Ch., 1985; Diocese of So. Ohio del. to Mutual Responsibility and Interdependance Conf. on Prayer, 1972; vis. fellow The Episcopal Theol. Sem. of Southwest, Austin, Tex., 1987; mem. bishop search com. Diocese of Spokane, 1989-90; assoc. St. Gregory's Benedictine Abbey, Three Rivers, Mich.; Evang. Sisters of Mary, Darmstadt, Fed. Republic Germany. Contbr. articles, numerous poems; exhibiting photographer. Chaplain Vail Valley Med. Ctr., 1980-85, Vail Police Dept., 1982-85. Served as sgt. USMC, 1953-56. Mem. The Anglican Soc. Avocation: photography. Office: St Andrew's Episcopal Ch 120 Woodin Ave PO Box 1226 Chelan WA 98816

TURNER, DENNIS EDWARD, music and youth minister; b. Gainesville, Ga., Sept. 14, 1960; s. Thomas E. and Ophelia R. Turner. AA, Truett-McConnell Coll., 1982; BA, North Ga. Coll., 1985. Min. of youth First Bapt. Ch., Cleve., Ga., 1980-86, min. of youth and music, 1986—; mem. scholarship com. White County Bapt. Assn., Cleve., Ga., 1990—, exec. com., 1988—; adv. bd. mem. Truett-McConnell Coll., Cleve., Ga., 1988—; mem. Sons of Jubal Ga. Bapt. Conv., Atlanta, 1990—. Mem. pub. rels. com. Am. Heart Assn., White County, 1988. Home: PO Box 1602 Cleveland GA 30528 Office: PO Box 250 North Main St Cleveland GA 30528

TURNER, FLOYD RAY, minister; b. Tifton, Ga., Apr. 8, 1951; s. Floyd B. and Lula Mavis (Goff) T.; m. Kay F. Holton, May 29, 1971; children: Monica Lisa, Floyd Ray, Jr. BS in Mktg., Abraham Baldwin Coll., Tifton, 1971; student, Valdosta (Ga.) State Coll., 1976-77; BTh., Luther Rice Seminary, Jacksonville, Fla., 1979. Div. mgr. Belk-Hudson Co., Tifton, 1969-72; mgr. Belk Budget Fair, Tifton, 1972, Tift-Town Clothing Ctr., Tifton, 1972-73; prodn. control mgr. Tifton Aluminum Co., 1973-78; salesman Jim Tatum Fashion Showroom, Jacksonville, 1979; pastor Live Oak Bapt. Ch., Callahan, Fla., 1978-82, 1st Bapt. Ch., Pinetta, Fla., 1981-82, 1st Bapt. Ch. of Garden City, Jacksonville, 1983-87, Vision Baptist Ch., Jacksonville, 1987-86; trustee Jacksonville Bapt. Childrens' Home, 1985—, annuity bd. So. Bapt. Conv., 1986—; cons. Fla. Bapt. Brotherhood, Jacksonville, 1983-86. Coach San Mateo Little League, Jacksonville, 1985, mgr., 1986; bd. dirs. Madison (Fla.) County Council on Aging, 1981. Recipient Callaway Leadership award Ida Cason Callaway Found., Pine Mountain, Ga., 1969; named Outstanding Young Man of Yr., 1985. Mem. Duval County Cattleman's Assn. Democrat. Avocation: private pilot. Home: 11337 Duval Rd Jacksonville FL 32218 Office: Vision Baptist Ch 11749-B US 1 N Jacksonville FL 32219

TURNER, FRANCES BERNADETTE, minister, lecturer, author; b. Superior, Wis., June 28, 1903; d. Fyler Bedell and Eleanor Dolores (Donaly) Rainsford; m. Delos Ashley Turner, Dec. 8, 1936. BS in Edn., U. Minn., 1926; MA in Sociology, Northwestern U., 1938; postgrad. social service adminstrn., U. Chgo., 1941-44; PhD in Sociology and Social Work, Washington U., St. Louis, 1948. Ordained to ministry Episcopal Ch. as deacon, 1986, as priest, 1990. Tchr. high sch. Bessemer, Mich., 1924-28; field rep. nat. staff ARC, 1929-36, chpt. exec. sec. Kans., Wash., Nev., 1929-36; psychiat. social worker Chgo. State Hosp. and Ill. Inst. Research, 1938-41; chief social service Dixon (Ill.) State Hosp., 1945; assoc. prof. sociology and social work Ariz. State Coll., Tempe, 1946-56; student counselor nursing schs. Good Samaritan Meml. Hosps., Phoenix, 1946-56; ordained minister Divine Sci. Ch., 1965; founder Divine Sci. Ctr., Evanston, Ill., 1965; pastor Divine Sci. Ch., Roanoke and Evanston, Ill., 1971-72; conducted chapel service Carrillo Hotel, Santa Barbara, Calif., 1979-80; resident counselor Retirement Home, Wichita, Kans., 1974-76; instr. div. continuing edn. Marquette U., 1976, 81-82, Calif. State U., 1976; chaplain Hillcrest Retirement Home, Boise, Idaho, 1986-87, North Shore Retirement Hotel, Evanston, Ill., 1987-88; min. St. John's Episcopal Ch., Roanoke, Va., 1989-90; chaplain, lectr. Park Shore Retirement Home, Roanoke, Va., 1990-91; host radio program Pages from My Notebook, Sta. KTAR, Phoenix, Sta. KYND, Tempe, Ariz., Stas. WEAW and WRSV, Chgo. area, Sta. WFIR, Roanoke, Sta. KICT, Wichita, Kans., Stas. WTMJ and WYMS, Milw., Sta. KSUL, Long Beach, Calif., Sta. KRUZ, Santa Barbara, Calif., radio program Growing Older Graciously, Sta. WRIS, Roanoke, 1990-91; mem. St. Michael's Cathedral, Boise, Idaho. Author: Happy Is the Man, 1965, God-centered Therapy, 1968, Faith of Little Creatures, 1972, Prosperity and the Healing Power of Prayer, 1984; contbr. articles and poetry to newspapers and mags. Bd. dirs. Maricopa council Campfire Girls, Phoenix, 1955-61. Fellow Am. Sociol. Assn.; mem. Nat. Assn. Social Workers, Assn. Cert. Social Workers, Am. Assn. Marriage Counselors, Internat. Assn. Women Ministers, Am. Assn. Pastoral Counselors (affiliate), Nat. League Am. Pen Women, Kans. Authors Club, World Poetry Soc., Internat. New Thought Alliance, Ret. Officers Assn. (aux.), St. Hilda's Guild, Channel City Women's Forum, Santa Barbara, Calif., Daus. of Nile. Home: 924 E Juneau Ave Apt 404 Milwaukee WI 53202 *Knowing God through consistent daily prayer gives us the necessary assurance to take whatever the risks maybe in our decision-making, confident that God is our direction.*

TURNER, FRANKLIN DELTON, bishop; b. Norwood, N.C., July 19, 1933; s. James T. and Dora (Streeter) T.; m. Barbara Dickerson, July 6, 1963; children: Jennifer, Kimberly, Franklin. AB, Livingstone Coll., 1956, LHD (hon.), 1991; MDiv, Yale U., 1965; DD (hon.), Berkeley Div. Sch., Yale U., 1977. Ordained to ministry Episcopal Ch. as deacon, 1965, as priest, 1965. Vicar Epighany Ch., Diocese of Dallas, 1965-66; rector St. George's Ch., Diocese of Washington, 1966-72; officer nat. staff Episcopal Ch. Ctr., N.Y.C., 1972-83; mem. bishop's staff for congl. devel. Episcopal Diocese of Pa., Phila., 1983-86, suffragan bishop, 1988—. Author: Black Leaders in the Episcopal Church, 1975. 1st lt. U.S. Army, 1966-72. Office: Diocese of Pa 240 S 4th St Philadelphia PA 19106

TURNER, GEORGE ALLEN, minister, educator; b. Willsboro, N.Y., Aug. 28, 1908; s. Charles Doyle and Bertha Eunice (Hayes) T.; m. Lucile Marjorie McIntosh, Oct. 8, 1938; children: Allen Charles, Carol Jean Turner Swanson. AB, Greenville Coll., 1932, BD, 1934, LLD (hon.), 1964; STB, Bibl. Sem. N.Y., 1935, STM, 1936; PhD, Harvard U., 1946. Ordained to ministry Free Meth. Ch. N.Am., 1940. Prof. Bible and religion Wessington Springs (S.D.) Jr. Coll., 1936-42; pastor ch. Gregory, S.D., 1938-39, Wessington Springs, 1939-42; prof. Bibl. lit. Asbury Theol. Sem., 1945-79; vis. lectr. Natal, Republic of South Africa, 1983-84, Aldersgate Coll., Can., 1984-85; tchr. Taiwan, The Philippines, 1975. Author: The More Excellent Way, 1952, The Vision Which Transforms, 1968, Portals to Bible Books, 1972, Historical Geography of the Holy Land, 1973, The True and Living Way, 1974, Christian Holiness, 1977, Witnesses of the Way, 1978, Paul, Apostle for Today, 1981; (with J.R. Mantley) The Gospel of John, 1968, others. Supt. Ky.-Tenn. Conf. Free Meth. Ch., 1956-58. Postdoctoral rsch. fellow Yale U., 1967-68, U. Toronto, 1971. Mem. Soc. Bibl. Lit., Evang. Theol. Soc., Wesley Theol. Soc., Theta Phi. Address: 608 Kinlaw Dr Wilmore KY 40390 *"Seek first The Kingdom of God and His Righteousness" Matthew 6:33.*

TURNER, JACQUELINE PAULA, minister; b. New Orleans, Apr. 5, 1964; d. Rufus Paul and Jacqueline Irene (Culley) T. Grad., Min.'s Tng. Inst., Baton Rouge, 1988, Calvary Lang. Sch., El Carmen, Mex., 1989. Ordained to ministry New Roads Ch., 1988. Tchr. children's ch. New Roads (La.) Ch., 1982-85, min. children's ch. coord., adminstrv. asst., missions dir., bd. dirs., educator, outreach coord., 1990—; sound coord. Min.'s Tng. Inst., 1986-88; missionary apprentice Calvary Lang. Sch., El Carmen, Neuvo Leon, Mex., 1988-89; coord. Gulf State Mission Agy., Reserve, La., 1989; sec.-treas. Abundant Life Ministries, New Roads, 1991—. Home and Office: PO Box 867 New Roads LA 70760-0867

TURNER, JAMES BENION, JR., minister; b. Macon, Ga., Sept. 18, 1949; s. James Benion and Lora June (Ethridge) T.; m. Brenda Faye Carter, Dec. 4, 1970; children: Heather Paige, James Benion III. MusB cum laude, Valdosta (Ga.) State Coll., 1980; MRE, New Orleans Bapt. Theol. Sem., 1982; postgrad., Southwestern Bapt. Theol. Sem., Ft. Worth, 1985-87. Ordained to ministry So. Bapt. Conv., 1982. Min. edn. Lake Carroll Bapt. Ch., Tampa, Fla., 1986—; adult leader Associational Sunday Sch. Improvement Support Team Tampa Bay Bapt. Assn., 1986—, dir. discipleship tng., 1988-90; cons. ch. growth Ark. and Fla. Bapt. convs., 1983—, Great Commn. Breakthrough, So. Bapt. Conv., 1990—; conf. leader Fla. Bapt. Conv., 1986—; sec.-treas. Jonesboro (Ark.) Evang. Ministerial Fellowship, 1983-85, v.p., 1985-86. Chmn. Vocat. Ednl. Assessment Com., Jonesboro, 1985-86. Mem. ASTD, Nat. Assn. Ch. Bus. Adminstrs., So. Bapt. Religious Edn. Assn., Fla. Bapt. Religious Edn. Assn., Tampa Bay Bapt. Assn. (dir. associational Sunday sch. improvement support team 1991—). Home: 16107 Country Crossing Dr Tampa FL 33624 Office: Lake Carroll Bapt Ch 12012 N Rome Tampa FL 33612

TURNER, KENDALL ALLEN, minister; b. Gaffney, S.C., Nov. 6, 1962; s. Harry Lee and Mary (Dover) T.; m. Jennifer Lou Norman, Aug. 29, 1987; 1 child, Bethany Leigh. BA, Pensacola Christian Coll., 1987. Ordained to ministry Bapt. Ch., 1990. Youth worker Campus Ch., Pensacola, Fla., 1982-83, Fundamental Bapt. Ch., Pensacola, 1984-87; youth min. Met. Bapt. Ch., Madison, Tenn., 1987-89, Community Bapt. Ch., South Bend, Ind., 1989—. Home: 1503 E Ewing Ave South Bend IN 46613 *Those who seem to make a difference in this world are those who have a definite purpose and specific goals. I know of no greater purpose than to seek to glorify God in every endeavor.*

TURNER, LELAND SMITH, JR. (LEE TURNER), composer, musician; b. Jacksonville, Fla., Nov. 22, 1936; s. Leland Smith and Dorothy Cora (Blackburn) T.; m. Murrhee Dianne Gross, Aug. 31, 1956; children: Leland Smith III, Kelly Randall, Gavin Shawn. BS in Advt., U. Fla., 1959; B in Sacred Music, So. Baptist Theol. Sem., 1961. Pianist, arranger The Dream Weavers, Gainesville, Fla., 1954-56; minister of music Calvary Baptist Ch., Clearwater, Fla., 1962-65, Main St. Baptist Ch., Jacksonville, Fla., 1965-70, First Baptist Ch., Jacksonville Beach, Fla., 1970-74; freelance musician Nashville, 1974-76; minister of music San Jose Baptist Ch., Jacksonville, 1976—; co-owner (with Dianne Turner) TurnerSong music pub. Composer, arranger (popular song) Into The Night, 1956, five musicals, over 100 pub. songs and arrangements. Recipient Composer award ASCAP, 1974-91. Democrat. Baptist. Avocations: running, reading, movies, writing, the ocean. Home: 4263 San Jose Blvd Jacksonville FL 32207

TURNER, MARTA DAWN, youth program specialist; b. Morgantown, W.V., Oct. 7, 1954; d. Trubie Lemard and Dorothy Genevieve (Helmick) T.; m. David Michael Dunning, Mar. 1, 1980. Student, Royal Acad. Dramatic Art, London, 1975; BA with honors, Chatham Coll., 1976; grad. cert. in arts adminstrn., Adelphi U., 1982; MA Devel. Drama, Hunter Coll., 1988. Cert. video prodn. specialist. Asst. dir. Riverside Communications, N.Y.C., 1985-88; dir. drama, video youth environ. group Water Proof, Cornell Coop. Extension, 1989—. Exec. producer video projects including Hispanic City Sounds, Time for Peace, Home, Home In Inwood, 1985—; asst. dir./dir. video series Riverside at Worship, 1985-88. Bd. dirs. Trinity Presbyn. Ch., N.Y.C, 1980—; mem. Am. Diabetes Assn. Mem. Am. Assn. Theatre Edn., W.Va. Soc. N.Y.C. (bd. dirs. 1986-87). Avocations: golf, swimming, Scrabble, karate, Marilyn Monroe fan/memorabilia collector. Home: 316 Center St Bangor ME 04401 Office: Pilgrim Presbyn Ch 375 Mt Hope Bangor ME 04401

TURNER, MEIR, cantor; b. Jerusalem, Dec. 8, 1948; s. Elisha and Bracha T. BA in History, Queens Coll. of CUNY, 1968; BSM, Jewish Theol. Sem., N.Y.C., 1982; student, Juilliard Sch. Cantor Temple Beth Shalom, Mahopac, N.Y., 1982—; Hebrew interpreter, translator. Researcher, editor: The Chaim Weizmann Letters and Papers, 1971-72; mng. editor The Patent and Trademark Rev., 1974-75. Recipient Yiddish Folk Song award Workman's Cir./WEVD Radio, 1985.

TURNER, REVIS EUGENE, minister; b. Vandalia, Ill., Sept. 15, 1947; s. Edgar Revis and Rheba Lea (Doyle) T.; m. Denise Dunn Watkins, Dec. 22, 1967; children: Rebecca Jill, Stephen Robert. BS, So. Ill. U., 1969; MA in Christian Edn., So. Bapt. Theol. Sem., Louisville, 1971; postgrad., McCormick Theol. Sem., Chgo., 1990—. Ordained to ministry Bapt. Ch., 1972. Youth dir. Deer Park Bapt. Ch., Louisville, 1970-72; minister Christian edn. 1st Bapt. Ch., Lima, Ohio, 1972-78, Middletown, Ohi, 1978-87; assoc. pastor 1st Bapt. Ch., Twin Falls, Idaho, 1988—; curriculum cons. Am. Bapt. Chs./USA, Valley Forge, Pa., 1989-90; pastoral chaplain Magic Valley Regional Med. Ctr., Twin Falls, Idaho, 1989—. Contbr. devotional articles to publs. Bd. dirs. Fed. Emergency Med. Agy., Butler County, Ohio, 1982-87; advisor Intermountain ABYouth, Twin Falls, 1988—; trustee Intermountain Cabinet, Twin Falls, 1988—; mem. Jaycees, Lima, Ohio, 1973-78. Mem. Am. Bapt. Ministers Coun., Kiwanis (spiritual aims Twin Falls chpt. 1989-91). Home: 1880 Falls Ave E Twin Falls ID 83301

TURNER, REX A., JR., academic administrator. Head Ala. Christian Sch. of Religion, Montgomery. Office: Ala Christian Sch Religion 7500 Taylor Rd Montgomery AL 36117*

TURNER, THOMAS WAYNE, minister; b. Marion, S.C., Jan. 17, 1949; s. John Henry and Jennie Emma (Carter) T.; m. Catherine Virginia Waters, July 6, 1974; children: Jennifer Catherine, Wilson Wayne. AA, N. Greenville Jr. Coll., Tigerville, S.C., 1969; BA, Campbell U., Buies Creek, N.C., 1971; MDiv, So. Bapt. Theol. Sem., Louisville, 1974, DMin, 1986. Ordained to ministry, Am. Bapt. Chs. USA, 1974. Campus life supr. Bapt. Home for Children, Bethesda, Md., 1975-77; pastor Commiskey (Ind.) Bapt. Ch., 1978-83, First Bapt. Ch., Sullivan, Ill., 1983—; chmn. Area 4 World Mission Com., Great Rivers Region, 1985-90; bd. dirs. Hudelson Bapt. Children's Home, Centralia, Ill., 1987—; moderator Area 4, Great Rivers REgion, Am. Bapt. Chs., 1991—. Author: Family Enrichment Through Bible Study, 1986. Rep. Moultrie County Interagy. Coun., Sullivan, Ill., 1984—; vol. coord. Meals on Wheels, Sullivan, 1988—; vol. night chaplain St. Mary's Hosp., Decatur, Ill., 1989—. Mem. Sullivan Ministerial Assn. (pres. 1986-88). Democrat. Home: 407 E Louis Sullivan IL 61951 Office: First Bapt Ch 215 E Harrison Sullivan IL 61951 *I am a mere speck in time, but I can be a speck that enriches time as I open my life to the Eternal.*

TURSKY, ANNE BARBARA, lay worker; b. Brookline, Mass., June 13, 1960; d. Norman and Gertrude (Edith) Gralnick) T. BS, U. Mass., 1982; MA, Brandeis U., 1985. Advisor United Synagogue Youth, Brookline, Mass., 1983; liaison Jewish Young Adult Ctr., Brookline, Mass., 1984; unit leader B'nai Brith Perlman Camp, Starlight, Pa., summer 1984; teen worker Leventhal-Sidman Jewish Community Ctr., Newton, Mass., 1985; asst. reg. dir. B'nai Brith Youth Orgn., Dallas, 1985-88; asst. dir. N.J. YM-YWHA Camps, Fairfield, N.J., 1988—. Richard Klutznik scholar, 1985. Mem. Conf. Jewish Communal Svc., Assn. Jewish Communal Profls., Am. Camping Assn. Office: New Jersey YM-YWHA Camps 21 Plymouth St Fairfield NJ 07004

TUTTLE, ELSIE ELEANOR, religious organization executive; b. Springfield, Ill., Feb. 15; 1927; d. Percy Bayard and Anna Gertrude (Veail) Smith; m. Daniel Webster Tuttle, Jr., June 28, 1947; children: Kay Tuttle Hancock, Daniel Webster III, David Bayard Hampton. A.B., Ill. Coll., 1948; postgrad. U. Minn., 1948; M.A., U. Wyo., 1950. Prof. Spanish, Honolulu Christian Coll., 1953-60; lectr. Spanish, U. Hawaii, part-time, 1960-62; interim exec. dir. Women's Bd. of Missions for Pacific Islands, United Ch. of Christ, Honolulu, 1984—; pres. Woman's Bd. of Missions, Honolulu, 1982-84; bd. dirs. Oahu Assn. United Ch. of Christ, 1980-86, Hawaii Conf. United Ch. of Christ, 1980-86. Editor Morning Star newsletter, 1984—. V.p. YWCA of Oahu, 1968-72; bd. dirs. PTA, Honolulu, 1968-70, Laryngectomee Assn., 1960-64; sec. Friends of Library of Hawaii, 1974-80; trustee Central Union Ch., Honolulu, 1976-80, vice moderator, moderator gen., 1987-89; panel mem. Aloha United Way, 1980-85; dist. chmn. Am. Cancer Soc., 1983-85; bd. dirs. Kalihi-Palama Immigrant Svc. Ctr., 1990—. Mem. Phi Kappa Phi, Psi Chi, Phi Sigma Iota. Home: 14 Akilolo St Honolulu HI 96821 Office: Woman's Bd of Missions for Pacific Islands United Ch of Christ Hawaii Conf 15 Cragiside Pl Honolulu HI 96817

TUTU, DESMOND MPILO, South African ecclesiastic; b. Klerksdorp, Republic of South Africa, Oct. 7, 1931; m. Leah Nomalizo Shenxane; children: Trevor Thamsanqa, Theresa Thandeka, Naomi Nontombi, Mpho Andrea. Diploma in teaching, Pretoria (Republic of South Africa) Bantu Normal Coll., 1953; BA, U. South Africa, 1954; licentiate in theology, St. Peter's Theol. Coll., Republic of South Africa, 1960; postgrad, King's Coll., U. London; DD (hon.), Gen. Theol. Sem., N.Y., 1978, Aberdeen U., Scotland, 1984, Trinity Luth. Sem., 1985, Trinity Coll., Hartford, Conn., 1986, Chgo. Theol. Sem., 1986, U. West Indies, Trinidad and Tobago, 1986, Oberlin Coll., 1986, U. of the South, 1988, Emory U., 1988, Wesleyan U., 1990, Lincoln U., Pa., 1990, Oxford U., Eng., 1990; DCL (hon.), Kent (Eng.) U., 1978; LLD (hon.), Harvard U., 1979, Claremont Grad. Sch., 1984, Temple U., 1985, 86, Mt. Allison U., Sackville, N.B., Can., 1988, Northeastern U., 1988; ThD (hon.), Ruhr U., 1981; STD (hon.), Columbia U., 1982, Dickinson Coll., 1984; LHD (hon.), St. Paul's Coll., 1984, Howard U., 1984, Morehouse Coll., 1986, Cen. U., 1986, CUNY, 1986; HHD (hon.), Wilberforce U., 1985; PhD (hon.), U. Rio, Rio de Janiero, 1986; hon. doctorate, U. Strasbourg, France, 1988, Wesleyan U., 1990, Lincoln U., 1990, U. Mo., 1990, U. New Rochelle, 1990, 1990, Brown U., 1990, Seton Hall U., 1990, U. P.R., 1990, others. Ordained priest Anglican Ch., 1961. Schoolmaster, 1954-57, parish priest, 1960—; lectr. Fed. Theol. Sem., 1967-69, UBLS Roma, Lesotho, 1970-72; assoc. dir. theol. edn. fund World Coun. Chs., Bromley, Kent, Eng., 1972-75; dean of Johannesburg Republic of South Africa, 1975-76; bishop of Lesotho, 1976-78, bishop of Johannesburg, 1985-86; archbishop of Cape Town Republic of South Africa, 1986—; sec.-gen. South African Council Chs., 1978-85; vis. prof. Anglican Studies, N.Y. Gen. Theol. Sem., 1984; pres. All Africa Conf. of Chs., 1987—; chancellor U. Western Cape, Republic of South Africa, 1988—. Author: Crying in the Wilderness, 1982, Hope and Suffering, 1983 (both collections of sermons and addresses). Vice chmn. Internat. Alert, 1986; mem. disbursements adv. com. Fund for Edn. in South Africa, N.Y.C., 1988; mem. com. of honor for meml. to Imre Nagy and companions Hungarian Human Rights League, 1988; mem. hon. com. Spl. Fund for Health in Africa, 1990. Recipient Prix d'Athene Onassis Found., 1980, Family of Man gold medallion, 1983, Martin Luther King Jr. Humanitarian award Ann. Black Am. Hero and Heroines Day, 1984; Nobel prize for peace, 1984, Martin Luther King Jr. Peace award, 1986, Internat. Integrity award John-Roger Found., 1986, Pres. award Glassboro State Coll., 1986, World Pub. Forum award City of San Rafael, Calif., 1986, Order of So. Cross Govt. of Brazil, 1987, Order of Merit Govt. of Brazil, 1987, Pacem in Terris award Quad Cities, 1987, Albert Schweitzer Humanitarian award Emmanuel Coll., 1988, Freedom of the City Florence, Italy, 1985, Methyr Tydfil, U.K., 1986, Durham, Eng., 1987, Hull, Eng., 1988, Disting. Peace Leadership award Nuclear Age Peace Found., 1990, Pres.'s medal Claremont Grad. Sch., U.S., 1990, Freedom of the Borough of Lewisham, U.K., 1990, Freedom of the City of Kinshasa, 1990; co-recipient Third World prize, 1989; King's Coll. fellow, 1978. Mem. NAACP (life), World Council Global Co-operation. Address: Bishop's Ct, Claremont, Cape Town 7700, Republic of South Africa also: S African Coun Chs, 42 De Villiers St, PO Box 4921, Johannesburg Republic of South Africa

TUYN, WILLIAM ROBERT, priest; b. Buffalo, Aug. 21, 1937; s. William H. and Dorothy E. (Duquette) T. BA, St. Bonaventure U., 1959; STB, Gregorian U., Italy, 1961, Licentiate in Sacred Theology, 1963. Ordained priest Roman Cath. Ch., 1962. Campus min. Alfred U., SUNY, 1963-66; prof., libr. St. John Vianney Sem., Christ the King Sem., East Aurora, N.Y., 1969-76; parish adminstr. Diocese of Buffalo, 1977-78; pastor St. John Ch., Jamestown, N.Y., 1979-91, St. Vincent de Paul Ch., North Evans, N.Y., 1991—; rep. to Jamestown Ecumenical Ministries, pres., 1984-88; participant religious radio programs. Contbr. articles to profl. jours. Mem. Cath. Theol. Soc. Am., Jamestown Area Ministerial Assn. (sec. 1980-82, pres. 1982-83). Address: 2050 S Creek Rd North Evans NY 14112

TWOMEY, BURT CHRISTIAN (NICK TWOMEY), minister; b. Detroit, Aug. 23, 1958; s. James Francis and Irene Betty (Tillman) T.; m. Rose Marie Mascorro, Aug. 10, 1979; children: Stephen James, Kristen Rose. AA in Sociology, John Wesley Coll., 1978; AB in Religion, Hope Coll., 1981; MDiv, Western Theol. Sem., 1985. Ordained to ministry Reformed Ch. Am. Assoc. pastor Faith Reformed Ch., Traverse City, Mich., 1985—; bd. dirs. Love Inc., Traverse City, 1984—, Youth for Christ, Traverse City, 1985-89, Good Samaritan Emergency Lodge, Traverse City, 1988-89; pres. Grand Traverse Ministerial Assn., Traverse City, 1989. Mem. adv. bd. Grand Traverse Families in Action, Traverse City, 1989-90. Mem. Nat. Right to Life. Home: 1121 Anderson Rd Traverse City MI 49684 Office: Faith Reformed Ch 1139 E Front St Traverse City MI 49684

TWORUSCHKA, UDO, religious historian; b. Seesen, Fed. Republic Germany, Feb. 12, 1949; s. Alfred and Charlotte (Köppe) T.; m. Monika Funke, Dec. 23, 1975; children: Miriam, Christopher, Sarah, Ronja. Dr. phil., Bonn U., 1972. Instr. comparative religion, U. Cologne, W. Ger., prof., 1984—; dir. Interdisciplinary Inst. History of Religions, Bad Münstereifel, 1982; mem. steering group internat. project Islam in Textbooks, 1989—. Author: Die Einsamkeit, 1974; Methodische Zugänge zu den Weltreligionen, 1982; Die vielen Namen Gottes, 1985; Analyse der evangelischen Religionsbücher zum Thema Islam, 1986; (with Monika Tworuschka) Vorlesebuch Fremde Religionen, 2 vols., 1988; Sucher, Pilger, Himmelsstürmer, 1991, (with A. Falaturi) Islam im Unterricht, 1991. Pres. Bund für Freies Christentum, 1986. Mem. Deutsche Gesellschaft für Missionswissenschaft, Internat. Assn. History of Religions, Deutsche Vereinigung für Religionsgeschichte, Wissenschaftliche Gesellschaft für Theologie. Avocations: swimming, film, activity in mass media. Office: Univ Cologne, Klarenbachstrasse 4, D-5000 Cologne 41, Federal Republic of Germany

TYLER, DANIEL JAMES, minister; b. Orlando, Fla., Nov. 27, 1953; s. Glenn Emerson and Rebecca Mae (Smith) T.; m. Dawn Renee Sparks, Apr. 21, 1979; children: Cynthia Renee, Andrea Danielle. BS, Rollins Coll., Winter Park, Fla., 1980; BRE, Internat. Sem., Orlando, Fla., 1979; MA, Liberty Christian Coll., Pensacola, Fla., 1986; DMin, N. Fla. Bapt. Sem., 1989. Ordained to ministry Internat. Christian Ch., 1972. Vice pres. Tyler Crusades, Inc., Internat. Sem., Orlando, 1966-88; pres. Tyler Crusades, Inc., Plymouth, Fla., 1988—; pres. Internat. Sem., Plymouth, 1988—; chaplain Apopka (Fla.) Police Dept., 1990—; ecclesiastical endorsing agt. Internat. Christian Ch., Plymouth, 1989—. Author 20 gospel songs; vocalist 5 gospel albums. Maj. USAF Aux., 1988. Recipient Key to City of Apopka, 1988; recipient Order of St. Gregory Merit, Am. Orthodox Ch., 1989. Mem. Fla. Fedn. Christian Colls. (bd. dirs. 1990—), Nat. Conf. on Ministry to Armed Forces, Mil. Chaplains Assn. USA, Internat. Conf. Police Chaplains, Sertoma. Office: Internat Sem 3927 Hwy 441 N Box 1208 Plymouth FL 32768-1208

TYNER, JOHN C., music minister, school administrator; b. Detroit, Sept. 8, 1947; s. Robert C. and Shirley R. (Trealor) T.; m. Catherine E. McRae, Jan. 16, 1971; children: Matthew J., Sara E. MusB, Wayne St. U., 1976; M. of Sch. Adminstrn., Eastern Mich. U., 1981. cert. secondary sch. adminstrn. Sch. adminstr. Monroe Public Sch., Monroe, Mich., 1976—. Ensign USN, 1968-72. Named State Honors Choir Dir., Mich. Sch. Vocal Assn., 1985, Music Tchr. of Yr., 1989. Mem. Am. Choral Dirs. Assn. (exec. bd. 1984-86), Mich. Sch. Vocal Assn. (exec. bd. 1988-89, 91—), Am. Soc. for Curriculum Devel. United Methodist. Office: St Paul's United Meth Ch 12 E 2nd St Monroe MI 48161-2216

TYNER, MAX RAYMOND, minister; b. Kokomo, Ind., Nov. 21, 1925; s. Paul Raymond and Dora May (Schroeder) T.; m. Marjorie Jane Tobias, Dec. 30, 1949; children: Renita (Mrs. Lee Miller), Shawnee Marthel (Mrs. James Overstreet). Student Ind. U. extension, 1946; B. Liberal Studies, U. Okla.; postgrad. Calif. State U.; Gen. mgr. Becraft Motor Express, Inc., Kokomo, 1946-58; owner Tyner Realty & Ins., McAllen, Tex., 1959-72; buyer Summer Inst. Linguistics, Mexico City, 1972-73; ordained to ministry Methodist Ch., 1968; pastor 1st United Meth. Ch., George West, Tex., 1973-77, First United Meth. Hosp., Port Isabel, Tex., 1985-88; pastor Dakota-Rock Grove Charge, Dakota, Ill., 1990—. Author: The Tyner Family and Some Other Relatives. Bd. dirs., sec. Rio Grand Children's Home, Mission, Tex., 1968-72; bd. dirs. Alliance Village Nursing Home, McAllen, 1970-72, Salvation Army, 1965-69. Served with USNR, 1944-45. Named hon. citizen Guadalajara, Mexico, 1964, Xalapa, Mexico, 1963; named outstanding mem. Kokomo Jr. C. of C., 1956. Mem. Am. Assn. Christian Counselors, Internat. Platform Assn., Am. Legion, Wycliffe Assocs., Christian Writers Guild, Christian Motorcyclists Assn., Circuit Riders. Republican. Home: 133 Wyler Dr Dakota IL 61018 Office: PO Box 224 Dakota IL 61018-0224

TYÖRINOJA, REIJO JUHANI, theology educator; b. Tampere, Finland, Aug. 26, 1948; s. Aarne Oskari and Toini Tellervo (Lehtinen) T.; m. Pirjo Helena Kurikka, Dec. 31, 1971; children: Anu, Samuli, Tuomas. D in Theology, U. Helsinki, Finland, 1984, docent in theol. ethics and philosophy of religion, 1986. Asst. U. Helsinki, 1983-85, asst. prof., 1986-87, chief asst., 1987—; Author: The Grammar of Faith, 1984; contbr. articles to profl. jours. Mem. Soc. Internat. pour L'Etude de la Philosophie Médiévale. Lutheran. Home: Myllykallionrinne 2 C 23, 00200 Helsinki 20 Finland Office: Univ Helsinki, Neitsytpolku 1b, SF-00140 Helsinki Finland

TYREE, ALAN DEAN, clergyman; b. Kansas City, Mo., Dec. 14, 1929; s. Clarence Tillman and Avis Ora (Gross) T.; m. Gladys Louise Omohundro, Nov. 23, 1951; children: Lawrence Wayne, Jonathan Tama, Sharon Avis. B.A., U. Iowa, 1950; postgrad., U. Mo.-Columbia, 1956-58, U. Mo.-Kansas City, 1961-62. Ordained minister Reorganized Ch. of Jesus Christ of Latter-day Saints, 1947; appointee minister Lawrence, Kans., 1950-52; mission adminstr. (Mission Sanito), French Polynesia, 1953-64; regional adminstr. Denver, 1964-66; mem. Council Twelve Apostles, Independence,

Mo., 1966-82; sec. Council Twelve Apostles, 1980-82, mem. First Presidency, 1982—; also mem. Joint Council and Bd. Appropriations; originator music appreciation broadcasts Radio Tahiti, 1962-64, Mission Sanito radio ministry, 1960-64. Editor: Cantiques des Saints French-Tahitian hymnal, 1965; mem. editing com.: Hymns of the Saints, 1981. Bd. dirs. Outreach Internat. Found., 1979-82, mem. corporate body, 1982—; Mem. corporate body Independence Regional Health Ctr., 1982—, v.p., 1983—, bd. dirs., 1984—; mem. bd. publ. Herald House, 1984—; mem. corp. body Restoration Trail Found., 1982—. Recipient Elbert A. Smith Meml. award for publ. articles, 1968, 72. Mem. Phi Beta Kappa, Phi Eta Sigma. Club: Lion. Home: 18804 RD Mize Rd Independence MO 64057 Office: Box 1059 Independence MO 64051

TYREE, MARGARET ELIZABETH, minister; b. Lynchburg, Va., May 28, 1951; d. Aubrey Nathaniel and Audrey (Riley) T. BA, Averett Coll., 1978; MDiv, Southeastern Bapt. Theol. Sem., Wake Forest, N.C., 1981. Ordained to ministry So. Bapt. Conv., 1982. Min. youth Moffett Meml. Bapt. Ch., Danville, Va., 1976-78, West Main Bapt. Ch., Danville, 1979-81; min. edn. and youth North Run Bapt. Ch., Richmond, Va., 1981-84; min. edn., youth and adminstrn. Grandin Ct. Bapt. Ch., Roanoke, Va., 1984—. Contbr. articles to profl. jours. Devotional officer Jr. Women's Club, Madison Heights, Va., 1971-75; alumni rep. Averett Coll., Danville, 1984—, mem. mins. adv. com., 1991; usher Mill Mountain Theater, Roanoke, Va., 1990—. Mem. Religious Edn. Assn. of U.S. and Can. (bd. dirs. 1991), Va. Bapt. Gen. Assn. (gen. bd. 1989—), Va. Bapt. Religious Edn. Assn. (pres. 1989), So. Bapt. Religious Edn. Assn., Roanoke Area Religious Edn. Assn. (pres. 1991). Home: 2440 Lofton Rd SW Roanoke VA 24015 Office: Grandin Ct Bapt Ch 2660 Brambleton Ave SW Roanoke VA 24015 *Make the most of every movement of your life. It is given to you by God to be enjoyed and lived to the fullest.*

TYSON, ALBERT DILLARD, JR., minister; b. Selma, Ala., Jan. 2, 1927; s. Albert Dillard Sr. and Beulah V. (Foster) T.; m. Marion Winifred Hughes, Aug. 1, 1947; children: Albert III, Margaret, Fredrick, Mark. MS, Wilberforce U., 1948, Rutgers U., 1950; MDiv, Princeton Theol. Sem., 1963; LHD (hon.), Monrovia Coll., Liberia; LLD (hon.), Edward Waters Coll. Ordained to ministry A.M.E. Pastor Mt. Pisgah A.M.E. Ch., Princeton, N.J., 1961-66, Jersey City, 1972-83; pastor St. Luck A.M.E. C., Newark, 1966-72, Union Chapel, Newark, 1983-89, Macedonia A.M.E. Ch., Flushing, N.Y., 1989—; del. Gen. Conf. A.M.E., Dallas, Atlanta, Ft. Worth, 1972-76, 88, World Conf. on Methodism, Singapore, 1991; bd. dirs. Self Help, Inc., Phila.; adv. bd. Bank of N.Y., Flushing, 1990—. Contbr. articles to profl. jours. Founder, head master Mt. Pisgah Sch., Jersey City, 1976-83; budget dir., chmn. polit. action Black Clergy, Newark, 1983-89; chmn. bd. Coalition for Planned Flushing, 1990—. Recipient plague Flushing Businessmen's Assn., 1990, Queens Dem. Club, 1990. Mem. A.M.E. Ministerial Inst. (bd. examiners), A.M.E. Mins. Alliance (chmn. polit. action 1990—), Queens Fedn. Chs. (bd. dirs.), Kappa Alpha Psi. Home: 8556 Chelsea St Jamaica NY 11432 Office: Macedonia AME Ch 37-22 Union St Flushing NY 11354

TYSON, JOHN RODGER, theology educator; b. Pitts., June 9, 1952; s. John J. and Betty A. (Nicholas) T.; m. Beth Milner, May 31, 1975; 1 child, Loralee Milner. BA in History and Religion, Grove City Coll., 1974; MDiv, Asbury Theol. Sem., 1977; MPhil, Drew U., 1981, PhD, 1983. Ordained deacon United Meth. Ch., 1975. Assoc. pastor Cocoa (Fla.) United Meth. Ch., 1976; spl. appointment Houghton Coll., Houghton, N.Y., 1981-85, prof. theology, 1979—; del. World Meth. Coun. on Meth. Theol., U. Oxford, Eng., 1987. Author: Charles Wesley: On Sanctification, 1987, Charles Wesley: A Reader, 1989; contbr. articles to jours. in field. Trustee Filmore, N.Y. United Meth. Ch., 1985—. John Wesley fellow A Found. for Theol. Edn., Marshall, Tex., 1977-80; NEH rsch. grantee, 1990. Mem. Am. Acad. Religion, Soc. Bibl. Lit., Wesleyan Theol. Soc., Am. Soc. Ch. Historians, Charles Wesley Soc. (bd. dirs. 1989—). Office: Houghton Coll Box 420 Houghton NY 14744

TYSON, JOSEPH BLAKE, religion educator; b. Charlotte, N.C., Aug. 30, 1928; s. Joseph B. and Lucy (Lewis) T.; m. Margaret H. Helms, June 12, 1954; 1 child, Linda S. BA, Duke U., 1950, BD, 1953; STM, Union Theol. Sem., 1955, PhD, 1959. Prof. religious studies So. Meth. U., Dallas, 1958—. Author: The New Testament and Early Christianity, 1984, The Death of Jesus in Luke-Acts, 1986; editor: Luke-Acts and the Jewish People, 1988. Mem. Soc. Bibl. Lit., Am. Acad. Religion, Cath. Bibl. Assn., Soc. for N.T. Studies. Methodist. Office: So Meth U Dept Religious Studies Dallas TX 75275-0202

TZADUA, PAULOS CARDINAL, archbishop of Addis Ababa; b. Addifinni, Ethiopia, Aug. 25, 1921; s. Tzadua and Tensaye (Hailu) Asgeda. Dr. Polit. Sci., Cath. U. Milan, 1957, Dr. Law, 1958. Ordained priest Roman Cath. Ch., 1944. Elected bishop, 1973; appointed archbishop of Addis Ababa, Ethiopia, 1977; elevated to Sacred Coll. of Cardinals, 1985. Translator: The Fetha Nagast (The Law of the Kings). Contbr. articles to profl. jours.

UDOD, HRYHORY, priest, church official; b. Kharkiw, Ukraine, Jan. 30, 1925; s. Ivan and Vera (Pisarewsky) U.; m. Alice Levchenko, July 20, 1957; children: Taras, Greg. BD, St. Andrews Coll., Winnipeg, Man., Can., 1958, BA with honors, BE, 1972; MA, U. Sask., 1974; PhD, Ukrainian Free U., Munich, 1975. Ordained priest Ukrainian Greek Orthodox Ch. Can., 1958. Parish priest various parishes New Westminster, B.C., Westlock, Alta., Ft. Frances, Ont., Sheho, Sask., Kamsack, Sask.; parish priest Ukrainian Orthodox Cathedral, Saskatoon, Sask., Can., 1966-80; chmn. presidium Ukrainian Orthodox Ch. Can., Winnipeg, Man., 1980-85; parish priest Canora, Sask., 1991—. Author books; contbr. articles to profl.jours.; radio broadcaster. Office: Box 425, Canora, SK Canada S0A 0L0

UEMURA, JOSEPH NORIO, philosophy educator, clergyman; b. Portland, Oreg., July 3, 1926; s. Seijiro and Hana (Morishita) U.; m. Maye Mitsuye Oye, Sept. 10, 1949; children: Wesley Makoto, Charissa Keiko. BA, U. Denver, 1946; ThM, Iliff Sch. Theology, 1949; PhD, Columbia U., 1958. Ordained to ministry United Meth. Ch., 1949. Sec. Colo. Conf. Bd. Edn., United Meth. Ch., Denver, 1946-50; asst. prof., assoc. prof. philosophy and religion Westminster Coll., Salt Lake City, 1953-59, Sheldon Jackson prof., 1958-59; prof. philosophy, chmn. dept. Morningside Coll., Sioux City, Iowa, 1959-66; prof. philosophy, chmn. dept. Hamline U., St. Paul, 1966—, Paul and Jean Hanna prof., 1987—. Author: Seven Dialogues on Goodness, 1986, Six Dialogues of Plato: An Interpretation, 1990; also articles. Recipient Merrill Burgess Excellence in Teaching award Hamline U., 1969, R.P. Bailey Excellence in Writing award, 1980; Elizabeth Iliff Warren fellow, John Hay Whitney fellow, Carnegie philos. studies fellow U. Calif., Irvine, 1969, fellow NEH Brown U., 1974; Danforth assoc., 1961—. Mem. AAUP, ACLU, Am. Philos. Assn., Phi Beta Kappa, Omicron Delta Kappa. Home: 1641 Stanbridge Ave Saint Paul MN 55113 Office: Hamline U 1536 Hewitt Ave Saint Paul MN 55104

UGENT, GEOFFREY RAYMOND, religious organization administrator; b. Milw., June 1, 1956; s. Irving Manuel and Nancy (Coppage) U.; m. Joann Vinci Lass, Jan. 3, 1976; 1 child, Timothy David. AA, N.W. Coll. Assemblies of God, 1981, BA, diploma in Christian Edn., 1982. Ordained to ministry Assemblies of God Ch., 1986. Assoc. youth pastor 1st Assembly of God Ch., Aberdeen, Wash., 1977-78, Cedar Park Assembly of God Ch., Kirkland, Wash., 1978-80; intern in pastoral ministry Christ Ch. of Bellevue, Wash., 1981-82; dir. campus life club Youth for Christ U.S.A., Mount Prospect, Ill., 1983—; producer community TV Cablenet, Inc., Mount Prospect, 1983—; area del. 1985 Youth Congress Youth for Christ U.S.A., Washington, 1984—. Served with USN, 1974-78. Mem. Evang. Tchr. Tng. Assn. (cert., tchr. 1982—), Ill. Dist. Council Assemblies of God, Guild Am. Luthiers. Lodge: Kiwanis (dir. high sch. activities Elk Grove club 1984—). Avocations: cycling, rock climbing, canoeing and canoe building, instrument building. Office: Youth for Christ USA North Division Campus Life 530 W Northwest Hwy Mount Prospect IL 60048

UHLEIN, GABRIELE, education administrator; b. Klingenberg, Federal Republic of Germany, Apr. 25, 1952; came to U.S., 1954; BS in Clin. Psychology, Ind. State U., 1979; MA in Spirituality/Religious Studies, Mundelein Coll., 1982. Mem. preaching staff Mount St. Francis (Ind.) Retreat Ctr., 1975-77; mental health worker DuPage Health Dept., Wheaton, Ill., 1979-81; regional coordinator Cath. Charities, Chgo., 1982-83; dir. Edn. Mission Services-Wheaton Franciscan Services, 1983-86, v.p., 1986—; cons. to parishes and religious orgns. in Midwest, 1982—; cons., trustee Hospice of DuPage, Lisle, Ill., 1980-86; trustee, mem. adv. bd. Christine Ctr. for Meditation, Willard, Wis., 1981—; trustee Francis Heights/Clare Gardens, Denver, 1983—; presenter workshops Cosmology for Peace, 1984—, Bereavement, Death and Dying, 1981—; mem. adv. bd. Advent Ctr. for Spiritual Devel., 1987—. Author: Meditation with Hildegard of Bingen. Active DuPage Pledge of Resistance Affinity Group, Ill., 1985; networker Action Linkage. Mem. Cath. Health Assn. Wis., Friends of Creation Spirituality. Office: Wheaton Franciscan Services Inc PO Box 667 Wheaton IL 60189

UITTI, ROGER WILLIAM, religion educator; b. Chgo., Oct. 29, 1934; s. William Leopold and Julia Margaretta (Lund) U.; m. Janet Elizabeth Drews, June 6, 1959; children: Ryan, Brent, Grant, Ann. BA, Northwestern Coll., Watertown, Wis., 1956; BD, Wis. Evang. Luth. Sem., 1959; MTh, Luth. Sem., St. Paul, 1964; STD, Luth. Sch. Theology, Chgo., 1973. Ordained to ministry Evang. Luth. Ch., 1959. Pastor Immanuel Luth. Ch., Plum City, Wis., 1959-62; instr. theology Concordia Coll., River Forest, Ill., 1962-66, asst. prof., 1966-80; prof. O.T., Luth. Theol. Sem., Saskatoon, Sask., Can., 1980—; lectr. dept. Greek-Roman studies, ancient Nr. Ea. studies U. Sask., Saskatoon, 1980—; adj. asst. prof. religious studies Rosary Coll., River Forest, 1977-79; vis. asst. prof. Mundelein Coll., Chgo., 1979; field asst. Concordia-Am. Schs. Oriental Rsch. Expdn., Tell-Ta'annek, 1968. Editor: Old Testament Synopticon, 1979; contbr. articles, book revs. and sermon studies to religious publs. Mem. Soc. Bibl. Lit. Home: 74 O'Neil Crescent, Saskatoon, SK Canada S7N 1W8 Office: Luth Theol Sem, 114 Seminary Crescent, Saskatoon, SK Canada S7N 0X3 *We live in a world in which the model of a defiant servant has emerged as the ideal. To the contrary, I believe that the patience, sharing, and self-giving of a "suffering servant" will triumph as more effective and powerful in the long run.*

UKPONG, JUSTIN SAMPSON, priest, educator, religious institute dean; b. Etinan, Cross River, Nigeria, Dec. 26, 1940; s. Sampson Akpan and Elizabeth Eshiet (Ekwere) U. BA in Philsophy, Bigard Sem., Enugu, Nigeria, 1963, BD, 1968; MA in Bibl. Theology, Pontifical Urban U., Rome, 1978, PhD in Bibl. Theology, 1980. Ordained priest Roman Cath. Ch., 1967; diploma in social adminstrn. and journalism. Asst. priest Cath. Cathedral, Calabar, Nigeria, 1968-69; adminstr. Cath. Cathedral, Calabar, 1974-76; lectr. U. Calabar, 1980-81; lectr./prof. Cath. Inst. West Africa, Port Harcourt, Nigeria, 1981—; acting rector, 1985-86, faculty dean, 1986—. Author: African Theologies New, 1984, Sacrifice: African and Biblical, 1987, Introduction to African Theology, 1988; editor Bible and Life mag. 1984—, Incarnation Monograph Series, 1986—; contbr. articles to profl. jours. Misereor study fellow, Can., 1969; Missio research grantee, Nigeria, 1982. Fellow Cath. Bibl. Assn. Am.; mem. West African Assn. Theol. Insts. (sec. 1987—), Nigerian Assn. Bibl. Studies, Cath. Theol. Assn. Nigeria, Port Harcourt Music Soc. Avocations: music, swimming, lawn tennis, aviation. Home: PO Box 270, Etinan Nigeria Office: Cath Inst West Africa, PO Box 499, Port Harcourt Nigeria

ULDERICH, THOMAS EARL, minister; b. Ravenna, Ohio, Mar. 22, 1955; s. Edwin Dean and Virginia Catherine (Rose) U.; m. Mary Margaret Whitesides; children: Jonathan Randall, Emily Anne. BS in Acctg., Freed-Hardemann Coll., 1982. Min. Cherry Grove Ch. of Christ, Weir, Ky., 1983-86, Trezevant (Tenn.) Ch. of Christ, 1986-88, Cedar Grove Ch. of Christ, Big Sandy, Tenn., 1990—; minister gospel meetings Ch. Christ, Deer Lodge, Mont., Whitlock, Tenn. Mem. Nat. Rifle Assn. Republican. Avocations: fishing, reading. Home: PO Box 325 Hollow Rock TN 38342 Office: Cedar Grove Ch of Christ Big Sandy TN 38258

ULMER, RONALD JOSEPH, deacon; b. Beverly, N.J., July 14, 1929; s. Joseph James and Harriet (Schooley) U.; m. Alfreda Olga Fortini, Sept. 24, 1949; children: Joanne Carol, Alfred Joseph. AS, Burlington County Coll., 1978. Deacon St. Joseph's Ch., Beverly, N.J., 1988—; tech. assoc. David Sarnoff Rsch. Ctr., Princeton, N.J., 1962—. Officer, mem. Beverly Fire Co. #1, 1946—, Beverly Emergency Squad, 1947—, Beverly City Bd. Health, 1981-85. With USN, 1951-55, Korea. Recipient Eagle Scout award Boy Scouts Am., 1946; named Commdr. of the Yr., 1964-65. Democrat. Home: 610 Wheatley Ave Beverly NJ 08010

ULRICH, ARTHUR RAYMOND, JR., minister, city official; b. Newcomerstown, Ohio, Aug. 7, 1946; s. Arthur Raymond and Mary Nell (Shafer) U.; m. Jade Ann Mason, Dec. 3, 1966; children: Chella Marie, Abby Renee, Amanda Rae, Lance Raymond. Grad. high sch., Dover, Ohio. Ordained to ministry Good News Christian Fellowship, 1989. Pastor Good News Christian Fellowship, Dover, 1989—; crew leader Dover Parks, 1980—. Mgr. Dover Little League, 1971-73. With U.S. Army, 1966-68, Vietnam. Democrat.

ULRICH, CHRISTIAN ROY, chaplain, counselor; b. Harrisburg, Pa., Dec. 23, 1953; s. Melchior Joseph and Mary Jane (Brill) U. AA, Pinebrook Jr. Coll., 1978; BA, Taylor U., 1980; MDiv, Asbury Theol. Sem., 1988. Counselor New Horizons Ministries, Jarabacoa, Dominican Republic, 1980-82; counselor, dean of men, camp dir. New Horizons Ministry, Marion, Ind., 1982-84, 88—; dean men, camp dir. Missanabie (Ont., Can.) Woods Survival Acad., 1983-84; youth pastor Stonewall Wesleyan Ch., Lexington, Ky., 1987; co-founder, bd. dirs. HAND Food Bank, Wilmore, Ky., 1986-88. Mem. Wilmore Fire Dept., 1985-88; recovery officer Jessamine County Rescue Squad, Nicholasville, Ky., 1986, tng. officer, 1987-88. With USAF, 1972-76. Mem. Grant County Ministerial Assn., Loons of Missanabie Woods Survival Acad., Lions. Avocations: hiking, camping, exploring, athletics, travel. Home and Office: 114 N Broadway # 1 Gas City IN 46933

ULRICH, REINHARD, educator, clergyman; b. Treysa, Germany, July 1, 1929; came to U.S., 1949, naturalized, 1959; s. Karl and Martha (Hubach) U.; m. Helen E. Neuhaus, June 10, 1952; children—Martin K., Joan M., Karl R. B.A., Lakeland Coll., 1951, LL.D. (hon.), 1984; B.D., Mission House Theol. Sem., 1953; S.T.M., Luth. Sch. Theology, 1960, S.T.D., 1963. Ordained minister United Ch. Christ. Instr., Lakeland Coll., Sheboygan, Wis., 1951-53, prof., 1964—, chmn. dept. philosophy and religion, 1964—, chmn. div. humanities, 1973—; pastor Saron United Ch., Sheboygan, 1953-56, Eden United Ch., Chgo., 1953-64; interim pastor United Ch. of Christ; lectr. in field. Author: (with W. Jaberg et al) A History of Mission House/Lakeland, 1962; transl. Church as Dialogue, 1968; Theology of Play, 1972; also articles. Bd. dirs. Howards Grove Bd. Edn., Wis., 1974—, pres., 1979—. Mem. Wis. Assn. Sch. Bds. (bd. dirs. 1982—, v.p. 1983-84, pres. 1985), AAUP, Am. Philos. Assn. Office: Lakeland Coll Box 359 Sheboygan WI 53081

ULSETH, HAROLD ALLYN, minister, retired educator; b. Mpls., July 19, 1928; s. Harold A. and Helen Dorothy (Allyn) U.; m. Marilyn June Johnson, June 25, 1960; children—Linda Marie, Pamela June. B.A., U. Minn., 1954, B.S., 1965, M.A., 1973; B.D., Chgo. Theol. Sem. and U. Chgo., 1958. Ordained to ministry Congregational Ch. (now United Ch. of Christ), 1959. Min. Eden Prairie Methodist Ch., Minn., 1955-57, Minnewashta United Ch. Christ, Excelsior, Minn., 1958-62; tchr. sci. Mpls. Pub. Schs., 1965-89, ret. 1989. Author numerous children's stories. Min., counselor Alcohol Anonymous, Mpls., 1959-62; mem. Augsburg Coll. Parents Bd., Mpls.; bd. dirs. Minn. Am. Swedish Council, Mpls. Served with USN 1952-54. Mem. Twin Cities East Assn. (Minn. conf.), Minn. Fedn. Tchrs. Innovator in sci. edn. Home: 5704 Colfax Ave S Minneapolis MN 55419 *God's specific love is creative within each of us, and all. Our task in this place is to make others aware of God's Love in them through our message, our ethics, our morality, our stewardship of God's many gifts revealed to us in the Gospel of Jesus Christ.*

UMBEHAGEN, MARK DEAN, youth and education minister; b. New Orleans, Sept. 15, 1960; s. Elmer Joseph Sr. and Rose M. (Montelero) U. BS, U. New Orleans, 1982; MDiv., New Orleans Bapt. Theol. Sem., 1985. Pastor Alluvial City Bapt. Ch., Yscloskey, La., 1985-87; min. youth edn. First Bapt. Ch., Oliver Springs, Tenn., 1987-90, South Harriman (Tenn.) Bapt. Ch., 1990—. Exec. bd. Aid to Distress Families of Anderson County, Oak Ridge, Tenn., 1988-90, bd. dirs., 1988-90; com. mem. Boy Scouts of Am. Pack 425, Oliver Springs, 1988-90. Mem. Tenn. Bapt. Religious Educators Assn., Clinton Bapt. Assn. (associational youth dir. 1987-90, exec. bd. 1987-90), Big Emory Bapt. Assn. (exec. com. 1990—, discipleship dir. 1991—). Home: 318 Ray St Kingston TN 37763 Office: South Harriman Bapt Ch Rt 6 Box 136 Harriman TN 37748-0136

UMBEHOCKER, KENNETH SHELDON, priest; b. Mpls., Sept. 23, 1934; s. Kenneth and Mildred Adeline (Johnson) U. BA, Vanderbilt U., 1956; Licentiate in Theology, Seabury-Western, Evanston, Ill., 1959; M in Mgmt., U. Ga., 1974. Ordained to ministry Episcopal Ch., 1959. Priest-in-charge St. John's Ch., Hallock, Minn., 1959-62; rector St. Paul's Ch., Virginia, Minn., 1962-67; priest-in-charge Emmanuel Ch., Rushford, Minn., 1968-74; asst. to dean Gethsemane Cathedral, Fargo, N.D., 1974-86; priest-in-charge St. Peter's Ch., Warroad, Minn., 1986-90; rector Ch. of the Good Shepherd, Windom, Minn., 1990—, St. John's by the Lake, Worthington, Minn., 1990—, Holy Trinity, Luverne, Minn., 1990—; community developer, 1968—; trustee Episcopal Diocese of Minn., Mpls., 1987—, coun. mem., 1980—. Field rep. Am. Cancer Soc., Mpls., 1965-67; dept. mgr. Rochester (Minn.) Area C. of C., 1967-74; exec. dir. Fargo Parking Authority and Downtown Assn., 1974-86. Seabury fellow Seabury-Western Sem., 1980; named Young Man of Yr. Rochester Jaycees, 1970; recipient Order of Purple Cross, York Rite Coll. North Am., 1988. Mem. Am. Acad. Parish Clergy, Am. C. of C. Execs., Nat. Parking Assn. (v.p. 1983-86, Disting. Svc. award 1985), Knights Templar (grand comdr. N.D. club 1985-86), Masons (grand chaplain N.D. club 1990-91). Home: 1830 N Red Leaf Ct PO Box 69 Windom MN 56101 *Working in the secular world as well as in the sacred makes a person more attuned to the needs and wants of the people in the pew and I find that that has enhanced my life tremendously.*

UMMEL, J. WESLEY, pastor; b. Elkhart, Ind., Jan. 23, 1942; s. Paul and Phoebe Mae (Brenneman) U.; m. Joan Martin Fuller, June 22, 1963; children: Heather, James. BA, Bethel Coll., Ind., 1963; MDiv, Asbury Theol. Sem., 1967. Ordained as United Meth. Elder, 1971. Pastor United Missionary Ch., Marshall, Mich., 1967-69; assoc. pastor Grace United Meth. Ch., Springfield, Mo., 1969-74; pastor New Hope United Meth. Ch., Arnold, Mo., 1974-76, Kimberling City (Mo.) United Meth. Ch., 1976-82, Ashland United Meth. Ch., St. Joseph, Mo., 1982-87; dist. supt. S.W. dist. Mo. West Conf. United Meth., Joplin, 1987-91; pastor Wesley United Meth. Ch., Springfield, 1991—; chmn. bd. Ozarks Meth. Manor, Marionville, Mo.; bd. curators Cen. Meth. Coll., Fayette, Mo. Mem. Lions (officer), Rotary (officer). Avocations: sport fishing, horticulture. Office: 922 W Republic Rd Springfield MO 65807

UNDERWOOD, BERNARD EDWARD, religious organization administrator; b. Bluefield, W.Va., Oct. 26, 1925; s. W. B. and Annie Theresa (Bain) U.; m. Esther Parramore, Dec. 22, 1947; children: Paul, Karen, Pam. BA, Emmanuel Coll., Franklin Springs, Ga., 1947; MA, Marshall U., 1954. Lic. to ministry Pentecostal Holiness Ch., 1942; ordained, 1944. Mem. Pentecostal Holiness Youth Soc. bd. Va. conf. Pentecostal Holiness Ch., Kingsport, Tenn., 1946-53; Christian edn. dir. Pentecostal Holiness Ch., Va. Conf., 1951-60, asst. supt., 1958-64; supt. Va. conf. Pentecostal Holiness Ch., Roanoke, 1964-69, 74-78; exec. dir. world missions Pentecostal Holiness Ch., Oklahoma City, 1969-73, 77-89, vice chmn., 1981-89, gen. supt., 1989—. Author: Gifts of the Spirit, 1967, Spiritual Gifts: Ministries and Manifestations, 1984, 16 New Testament Principles for World Evangelization, 1988; contbr. numerous articles to profl. jours. Phi Alpha Theta scholar, 1954. Mem. Nat. Assn. Evangelicals (mem. exec. com. 1989—), Pentecostal Fellowship N.Am. (pres. 1991—), Pentecostal Renewal Svcs. (chmn. 1987—), Evang. Fgn. Missions Assn. (bd. adminstrn. 1981—). Republican. Avocation: reading. Office: Internat Pentecostal Holiness Ch PO Box 12609 Oklahoma City OK 73157

UNDERWOOD, CHARLES DAVID, minister; b. Durham, N.C., July 17, 1957; s. Richard Eugene and Annie Ruth (Harward) U.; m. Teresa Donnel Moore, July 1, 1978; children; Jennifer Nicole, Matthew David, Jesse McKinley. BA in Bible, Theology, Toccoa Falls Coll., 1986; tchr. diploma, Evang. Tchr. Tng. Assn., 1986. Asst. pastor Dorseyville Alliance Ch., Pitts., 1986-91; pastor Hillcrest Christian and Missionary Alliance Ch., Lower Burrell, Pa., 1991—; dir. Dist. Sr. High Retreat, Western Pa., 1989-91. Republican. Office: Hillcrest Christian and Missionary Alliance Ch 232 Hillcrest Dr Lower Burrell PA 15068 *In light of the fact that there is so much hypocrisy and living under a facade, I have come to relize the importance of being genuine. I want to present to mankind the person I really am.*

UNDERWOOD, EARL FREDERICK, JR., clergyman; b. Ft. Smith, Ark., Aug. 31, 1943; s. Earl Fredrick and Pearl Lucille (Kukuk) U.; m. Laura Ruth Anderson, July 23, 1967; 1 child, Ray Charles. B.A., Huron Coll., 1968; M.Div., Louisville Presbyterian Sem., 1971. Ordained to ministry Presbyn. Ch., 1971. Pastor, Faith Pres. Ch., Brandon, S.D., 1971-76, Riverside Presbyn. Ch., Sioux Falls, S.D., 1971-76, Akron Plymouth Presbyn. Ch., Iowa, 1976-79, Meml. Presbyn. Ch., Marysville, Kans., 1979—. Author (booklets) Family Budgeting, 1984, Your Money: Make It Do More, 1985, Marshall County Kans.: 1540-1880, 1986, 125 Years of Presbyterianism in Marysville, Kansas, 1988; (genealogy) From Vilson Germany to Linn Kansas, 1980; editor (geneology) Reedy Family Assn., 1980-84. Treas. Pride Marysville Kans., 1982-84. Mem. Iowa Genealogy Soc. (Outstanding Genealogist award 1975), Blue Valley Genealogy Soc. (pres. 1980-82, v.p. 1983-84). Avocation: Bridge; geneology. Home: 809 N 12th St Marysville KS 66508 Office: Meml Presbyn Ch 200 N 10th St Marysville KS 66508

UNDERWOOD, (ORRIE) FREDERICK, priest; b. Evansville, Ind., July 23, 1923; s. Orrie Clinton and Clara Josephine (Pirnat) U. BA, U. Notre Dame, 1952, Holy Cross Coll., 1956. Ordained priest Roman Cath. Ch., 1956. Co-founder, dir. Vol. Tchr. Svc. and Cath. Lay Mission Corps, Killeen, Tex., 1960-64; pastor Dolores Ch., Austin, Tex., 1962-76; vocat. dir. Holy Cross Congregation, New Orleans, 1976-82; pastor San Jose Ch., Austin, 1982—; evangelist Austin, 1982—; cons. U. Tex., 1965-68; co-founder, dir. asst. provincial So. Province Holy Cross, Austin, 1970-76; vicat for Tex., 1970-76. Exec. dir. Montopolis Community Ctr., Austin, 1964; project dir. Austin Neighborhood Youth Corps, 1965, Poverty Island Transp., 1965, Country Club Gardens Housing, 1968; chmn. Community Action Com., Austin, 1972-73; mem. Austin Child Guidance Ctr. Bd., 1973-75; chmn. sub-com. on housing City of Austin, 1974-75; mem. adv. bd. Travis County Juvenile Ct., Tex., 1974-75. Recipient Coronat award St. Edward's U., 1971. Home and Office: 2425 Oak Crest St Austin TX 78704 *To know and experience Jesus, the Risen Christ, in a personal relationship, is the ultimate experience in this life; a foretaste of heaven; and the goal of evangelization; and my purpose in life—to lead as many as possible into this personal relationship with Jesus, our Brother and very Best Friend.*

UNFRIED, DONA LEE, clergywoman, realtor; b. Los Angeles, Oct. 11, 1928; d. Howard Peter and Helyn Grace (Howson) Wraith; student Santa Monica State Coll., 1948; grad. Unity Sem., 1973, D.D., 1981; diploma in hypnotherapy Ft. Worth Inst., 1970; m. Sept. 1, 1950 (div. 1969); children—Robert F., Teri Lynn. Mgmt. personnel Pacific Telephone, Sacramento, 1947-68; mgr. Match-O-Mates, Ft. Worth, 1968-70; ordained to ministry Unity Ch., 1973; minister Unity Village Chapel, Kansas City, Mo., 1972-75; sr. minister Unity Ch., Overland Park, Kans., 1975-76; sr. minister, chmn. bd. Unity Ch. of Light, Longview, Tex., 1976-83; realty mgr. Realty World, Longview, 1976-83; v.p. Century C-21, 1982; owner employment agy., La Jolla, Calif., 1984-87; field rep. U.S. Gov. Dept Commerce, Kansas City, Kans., 1987—; tchr. in field; condr. workshops; counselor. Mem. Indsl. rels. com., public rels. com. Longview C. of C., 1981; bd. dirs. Gateway Found., Sacramento. Recipient 4 Gold medals, 2 Silver medals Sr. Olympics, 1990. Mem. Internat. New Thought Alliance, Nat. Assn. Realtors, Tex. Assn. Realtors, Million Dollar Club, Nat. Assn. Female Execs., Assn. Unity Chs., Longview Assn. Realtors, Longview Bd. Realtors (chmn. edn. com. 1982). Club: Toastmistresses (pres. Limerick club 1967; numerous speaking awards 1966-72. Home: 2600 Hub Dr Independence MO 64055 *God is good, and I am a part of this goodness! We are here to empower one another, each expressing his uniqueness!.*

UNGER, ELIZABETH BETTY, hospital chaplain; b. Manitoba, Can., Mar. 4, 1936; came to U.S. 1962; d. Johann Cornelius and Ottillie (Hirsch) U. BA, Andrews U., 1967, MA in Teaching, 1972. Office clk. Overland Express, St. Catherines, Ont., Can., 1954-55; bookkeeper G.A. Moggridge Printing Co., St. Catherines, Ont., Can., 1955-56; sec., receptionist, asst. to cost acct. Anthes-Imperial, St. Catherines, Ont., Can., 1956-60; ins. claims dir. North York Branson Hosp., Ontario, Toronto, Can., 1960-62; teacher, registrar Mt. Pisgah Acad., Chandler, N.C., 1967-69; spiritual counselor, chaplain Portland (Oreg.) Adventist Med. Ctr., 1971-83; chaplain Hinsdale (Ill.) Hosp., 1984-90, Porter Hospice, Denver, 1991—. Fellow Coll. of Chaplains. Seventh-day Adventist. Avocations: designing and building a house, decorating, cooking, painting. Home: 2570 S Downing St Denver CO 80210 Office: Porter Meml Hospice 2465 S Downing St Denver CO 80210

UNSWORTH, RICHARD PRESTON, minister, school administrator; b. Vineland, N.J., Feb. 7, 1927; s. Joseph Lewis and Laura (MacMillan) U.; m. Joy Merritt, Aug. 20, 1949; children: Sarah, John, Mary, Lucy. BA, Princeton U., 1948; BD, Yale U., 1954; ThM, Harvard U., 1963; STD, Dickinson Coll., 1971; LHD, Washington and Jefferson Coll., 1971. Ordained to ministry Presbyn. Ch., 1953. Tchr. Bible and English Mt. Hermon Sch., 1948-50; asst. chaplain Yale U., New Haven, Conn., 1950-54; chaplain, assoc. prof. Smith Coll., Northampton, Mass., 1954-64, chaplain, prof. religion, 1967-80; dean William Jewett Tucker Found. and prof. religion Dartmouth (N.H.) Coll., 1963-67; headmaster Northfield (Mass.) Mt. Hermon Sch., 1980-88, pres., 1989-91; headmaster Berkshire Sch., Sheffield, Mass., 1991—; pres. Critical Langs. and Area Studies Consortium, 1987—; bd. dirs. Bank of New Eng.-West, 1984-90; cons. Ednl. Assocs., Inc., 1967-69, U.S. Office Edn., 1969-77. Author: Sexuality and the Human Community, 1970, Dignity and Exploitation: Christian Reflections on Images of Sex in the 1970s, 1974, A Century of Religion at Smith College, 1975, (with Arnold Kenseth) Prayers for Worship Leaders, 1978; contbg. author; Sex Edn. and the Schs., 1967. Leader Operation Crossroads Africa unit, Nigeria, 1961, mem. adv. bd., 1961-66; mem. adminstrv. com. Student Christian Movement New Eng., 1964; mem. Mass. unit So. Christian Leadership Conf., 1968; trustee Conf. on Religion in Ind. Schs., 1961-63; pres. Am. Friends of Coll. Cevenol, France, 1957-63, 90—, Am. rep., 1958-82; trustee Mt. Holyoke Coll., 1982-89, chair, 1984-89, chmn. emeritus, 1989—, Am. Sch. Tangier, Morocco, 1982-87; bd. dirs. Family Planning Coun. Western Mass., 1972-81. Mem. AAUP, Nat. Assn. Coll. and Univ. Chaplains, Am. Acad. Religion. Home and Office: Berkshire Sch Sheffield MA 01257

UNTENER, KENNETH E., bishop; b. Detroit, Aug. 3, 1937. Ed., Sacred Heart Sem., Detroit, St. John's Provincial Sem., Plymouth, Mich., Gregorian U., Rome. Ordained priest Roman Cath. Ch., 1963; ordained bishop of Saginaw Mich., 1980—. Office: Chancery Office 5800 Weiss St Saginaw MI 48603

UNTERKOEFLER, ERNEST L., bishop; b. Phila., Aug. 17, 1917; s. Ernest L. and Anna Rose (Chambers) U. A.B. summa cum laude, Catholic U. Am., 1940, S.T.L., 1944, J.C.D., 1950. Ordained priest Roman Cath. Ch., 1944; asst. pastor in Richmond, Va., 1944-47, 50-54, Arlington, Va., 1947-50; sec. Richmond Diocesan Tribunal, 1954-60; moderator Council Cath. Women and Council Cath. Nurses, 1956-61; sec. Diocesan bd. Consultors, 1960-64; founder Cath. Physicians Guild, Richmond, 1957-64; chancellor Richmond Diocese, 1960-64; papal chamberlain, 1961; aux. bishop Richmond; titular bishop Latapolis; vicar gen. Richmond Diocese, 1962-64; bishop of Charleston, S.C., 1964—; promoter IV Synod Diocese Richmond, 1962-64; sec. Nat. Conf. U.S. Bishops, 1966-70, chmn. permanent diaconate com., 1968-71, 74—; chmn. Region IV, 1972-74, mem. adminstrv. com., 1974—; sec. adminstrv. bd. Nat. Cath. Conf., 1966-70; mem. Bishops' Com. on Ecumenical and Inter-religious Affairs, 1965-78, chmn., 1978—; mem. Bishops' Com. on Pastoral Plans and Programs, 2d Vatican Council, 1962-65, Anglican-Roman Catholic subcommns. theology of marriage and mixed marriage; co-chmn. Anglican/Roman Cath. Commn. Theology of Marriage; chmn. Roman Cath.-Presbyn./Reformed Consultation; mem. com. social devel. and world peace U.S. Council Chs., 1971-74; mem. adminstrv. com. and bd. NCCB-USCC, 1978—; mem. Ad Hoc Com. Women in Ch. and Soc., 1971—; co-chmn. Charleston Bicentennial Commn. on Religious Liberty; host bishop for visit of Pope John Paul II to U.S., 1987. Bd. dirs. CARA, 1969—, pres., 1972—; mem. alumni bd. govs. Cath. U. Am. Recipient Pax Christi award St. John's U., Collegeville, Minn., 1970; medal of U. Santa Maria La Antiqua, Panama, 1976; Pacem In Terris award, 1980; decorated grand cross Republic of Panama, 1976. Address: 119 Broad St PO Box 818 Charleston SC 29402 *Where would I be without the love and care of God, our Father? Answers to that question I ponder. Indeed I am among people who share their gifts and strength; I live with them joyfully in their response to me in friendship and common care. Life continues to be an adventure for the curious.*

UPTHEGROVE, FRANKLIN JOHN, clergyman; b. Lima, Ohio, Dec. 18, 1921; s. George F. and Mary E. (Thomas) U.; BS in Edn., Ohio U., 1958; BD, Crozer Theol. Sem., 1961, M Div, 1972; postgrad. Conwell Sch. Theology, 1963-65, Hartford Sem., 1964; DD (hon.), Eastern Neb. Christian Coll., 1970; m. Margaret children—Sylvia M. Gable, Barbara J. Richardson, Rita J.; stepchildren—Robert H. Reid, Milton Reid, Joseph Reid. Ordained to ministry United Ch. of Christ, 1961; pastor Mt. Zion Baptist Ch., Athens, Ohio, 1954-58, 1st Bapt. Ch., Rutland, Ohio, 1954-58, St. Paul's Bapt. Ch., Utica, N.Y., 1966-82; ret., 1982; organizer Antioch United Ch. of Christ, Phila., 1961, pastor, 1961-66; substitute tchr. secondary edn., Phila., 1960-66, Utica, 1966—. Mem. youth com. North br. Phila. YMCA, 1964-66; spl. examiner personnel dept. Civil Service, Phila., 1965-66; mem. Selective Service System, N.Y.C., 1983—; chmn. housing com. Utica Community Action Commn., 1966—; chmn. bd. Utica Community Action, Inc.; mem. Mohawk Valley Regional Econ. Devel. Council, N.Y. State; pres., bd. dirs. Mid-Utica Neighborhood Preservation Corp., 1975—; exec. dir. Commn. Human Relations City of Utica; gen. counsel Mohawk Valley Community Coll; mem. Selective Service Bd., 1983—, Gov's. Econ. Devel. Commn. N.Y. State; pres. Black Ministerial Alliance, Utica-Rome, 1980-85, Mid-Utica Neighborhood Preservation Corp., 1979—. Bd. dirs. Cosmopolitan Center, Utica, Utica Found. Served with USNR, 1943-46. Recipient citation Chapel of Four Chaplains, 1965. Mem. N. Central Ministerium (Phila. pres. 1966), Inter-Ch. Child Care Soc. Phila. (bd. dirs.). Office: 219 Leah St Utica NY 13502 *I do not know what the future holds, but I know who holds the future.*

URBAN, CARL ANTHONY, priest, educator; b. Schenectady, N.Y., Sept. 16, 1939; s. Anthony and Clara Helen (Turski) U. AA, Mater Christi, 1959; BA, U. Ottawa, 1961, B in Philosophy, 1961, MTh, 1966; STL, St. Paul U., 1966. Ordained priest Roman Cath. Ch., 1966. Jr. lectr. theology U. Ottawa, Ont., Can., 1964-65; instr. religion Vincentian Inst., Albany, N.Y., 1966-67, Cardinal McCloskey Inst., Albany, 1967-74; pastor Ch. of St. Adalbert, Schenectady, 1974—; bd. dirs. Cath. Family and Community Svcs., Schenectady, 1978-87; asst. nat. chaplain Polish Union Am., Buffalo, 1974-90; mem. ecumenical commn. Roman Cath. Diocese of Albany, 1973-79, Polish Am. Congress, Schenectady, 1974—. Mem. adv. bd. County Office for Aging, Schenectady, 1979-88, Ellis Hosp., 1984—; chmn. Crane St. Revitalization Com., Schenectady, 1977; mem. Mt. Pleasant Neighborhood Com., Schenectady, 1977—. Mem. Polish Roman Cath. Union, Polish Nat. Alliance, Polish Union Am. Club, Univ. Club. Home and Office: Ch of St Adalbert 550 Lansing St Schenectady NY 12303

URBROCK, WILLIAM JOSEPH, religion educator; b. Chgo., Sept. 14, 1938; s. Ernest August and Emma Caroline (Kollaritsch) U.; m. Barbara Jean Wrege, June 9, 1962; children: Stephen Paul, Rebecca Marie. BA, Concordia Sr. Coll., 1960; MDiv, Concordia Theol. Sem., 1964; PhD, Harvard U., 1975. Prof. Religious Studies U. Wis., Oshkosh, 1972—; asst. prof. Religion Lycoming Coll., Williamsport, Pa., 1969-71; assoc. dean of Humanities U. Wis., Oshkosh, 1985—. Contbr. articles to profl. jours. Active program com. The Clearing Sch. of the Arts, Nature, and Humanities, Ellison Bay, Wis. Mem. Soc. Bibl. Lit. (chair upper midwest region 1977-78, 86-87), Cath. Bibl. Assn., Am. Acad. of Religion, Chgo. Soc. Bibl. Rsch. (v.p. 1991-92), Wis. Acad. Scis. Arts and Letters (v.p. letters 1989—). Office: U Wis Dept Religious Studies Oshkosh WI 54901

URIS, LEON, author; b. Balt., Aug. 3, 1924; s. Wolf William and Anna (Blumberg) U.; m. Betty Katherine Beck, Jan. 5, 1945 (div. 1968); children: Karen Lynn, Mark Jay, Michael Cady; m. Margery Edwards, 1968 (dec. 1969); m. Jill Peabody, Feb. 15, 1971. Ed., Balt. City Coll.; hon. doctorate, Lincoln Coll., 1985. Author: Battle Cry, 1953, The Angry Hills, 1955, Exodus, 1957, Exodus Revisited, 1959, Mila 18, 1961, Armageddon, 1964, Topaz, 1967, QB VII, 1970, Trinity, 1976, Jerusalem, Song of Songs, 1981, (with Jill Uris) Ireland: A Terrible Beauty, 1975, The Haj, 1984, Mitla Pass, 1988; (screenplays) Battle Cry, 1955, Gunfight at the O.K. Corral, 1957. Served with USMCR, 1942-46. Nat. Inst. Arts and Letters grantee, 1959. Office: care Doubleday & Co 245 Park Ave New York NY 10017

URSACHE, VICTORIN (HIS EMINENCE THE MOST REVEREND ARCHBISHOP VICTORIN), archbishop; b. Manastioara-Siret, Dist. of Suceava, Romania, 1912. Grad., State Lyceum of Siret; L.Th., U. Cernauti, Romania; postgrad., Bibl. Inst. Jerusalem. Ordained deacon Romanian Orthodox Ch., 1937, ordained priest, 1937. Consecrated bishop Romanian Orthodox Ch., 1966, elevated to archbishop, 1973; prof. religion Orthodox Lyceum of the Romanian Orthodox Metropolis of Cernautsi, 1936-37; prof. theology Seminary of Neamtzu Monastery, 1937-46, asst. dir. sem., 1937-40, dir. sem., superior of monastery, 1940-44; rep. Romanian Orthodox Ch. at Holy Places in, Jerusalem, 1946-56; bishop Romanian Orthodox Missionary Episcopate in Am., 1966-73; archbishop Romanian Orthodox Archdiocese in Am., 1973—; Mem. Holy Synod, Romanian Orthodox Ch. of Romania; bd. dirs. U.S. Conf., World Council Chs.; mem. central com.; mem. Standing Conf. Canonical Orthodox Bishops in, Ams. Editor: Locurile Sfinte. Address: Romanian Orthodox Ch in Am 19959 Riopelle St Detroit MI 48203

URSHAN, NATHANIEL A., minister, church administrator; b. St. Paul, Aug. 29, 1920; s. Andrew David and Mildred (Hammergren) U.; m. Jean Louise Habig, Oct. 1, 1941; children: Sharon, Annette, Nathaniel, Andrew. Student, Columbia U., 1936-39; DTh (hon.), Gateway Coll. Evangelism, 1976. Ordained to ministry United Pentecostal Ch. Internat. Evangelist, 1941-44; assoc. pastor Royal Oak, Mich., 1944-46, N.Y.C., 1947-48, Indpls., 1948-49; pastor Calvary Tabernacle, Indpls., 1949-78; presbyter Ind. Dist. United Pentecostal Chs., 1950-77; asst. gen. supt. United Pentecostal Ch. Internat., 1971-77; gen. supt. United Pentecostal Ch. Internat., Hazelwood, Mo., 1977—; host radio show Harvestime, 1961-78; chaplain Ind. Ho. of Reps., 1972. Author: Consider Him, 1962, These Men Are Not Drunk, 1964, Book of Sermons of the Baptism of the Holy Spirit, 1968, Major Bible Prophecy, 1971. Mem. internat. com. YMCA, 1958-79, bd. dirs. Indpls. chpt. 1961-79, world service chmn. Region L., 1969-71; chmn. Heart Fund Campaign, 1968-69; mem. screening com. Marion County Reps., Ind., 1973-74; chmn. Ministerial Com. of Richard Lugar for May of Indpls., 1968, William Hudnut for Mayor, 1975; bd. dirs. Little Red Door, Cancer Soc. Indpls., 1974-77. Recipient gold and brass medallion Heart Fund., Indpls., 1968-69; Nathaniel A. Urshan Day named in his honor, Nov. 3, 1979, Mayor Hudnut, Indpls. Mem. Indpls. Ministerial Assn. Office: United Pentecostal Ch Internat 8855 Dunn Rd Hazelwood MO 63042

URSI, CORRADO CARDINAL, archbishop of Naples; b. Andria, Italy, July 26, 1908; s. Riccardo and Apollonia (Sterlicchio) U.; ed. Seminario Regionale di Molfetta, Bari, Italy. Ordained priest Roman Catholic Ch., 1931; with Pontifical Regional Seminary of Molfetta, vice rector, later rector, 1931-51; mem. Congregation Cath. Edn.; bishop Nardò (Italy), 1951; archbishop of Acorensa, 1961; archbishop of Naples, 1966-87; elevated to Sacred Coll. Cardinals, 1967. Address: Largo Donnaregina 23, 80134 Naples Italy

URSICH, DONALD WEAVER, clergyman, marriage and family counselor, drug and alcohol counselor; b. Morgantown, W.Va., Mar. 24, 1939; s. Charles and Freda Marie (Weaver) U.; m. Barbara Christina Neeser, Sept. 22, 1962; children: Christine, Sarena. BA, Southeastern Coll., 1968; MDiv, Interdenominational Theol. Ctr., 1971; MEd, Boston U., 1979; MA in Edn., East Carolina U., 1980. Cert. alcoholism counselor, N.C.; cert. marriage and family therapist, N.C.; registered practicing counselor, N.C. Ordained to ministry United Ch. of Christ, 1981; officer Salvation Army, 1958-81; pvt. practice marriage and family counselor, Fayetteville, N.C., 1979—; drug and alcohol counselor U.S. Army, Ft. Bragg, N.C., 1981—; lectr. and cons. in field. Bd. dirs. Mental Health Assn. Cumberland County (N.C.); asst. dist. commr. Occoneechee council Boy Scouts Am. Served as chaplain U.S. Army, 1971-79. Decorated Commendation medal. Mem. Nat. Alliance for Family Life, Am. Assn. Marriage and Family Therapy, Am. Assn. Counseling and Devel., Nat. Acad. Counselors and Therapists, Am. Group Psychotherapy Assn. Republican. Lodges: Masons, Shriners.

USHER, JUAN OSCAR, rector, priest; b. Asunción, Paraguay, June 12, 1928; s. Fernando and Evelina (Tapponier) U. BA in Theology, Pontifical Sem. of Theology, Buenos Aires; PhD in Canonical Law, Pontifical U. Salaman, Salamanca, Spain. Parish priest Mercedes Parish, Asunción; adviser Cath. Action, Asunción; sec. gen. Paraguayan Bishop Conf., Asunción; dir. Catechesis Dept. Conf., Asunción; defender Marriege entail Tribunal, Asunción; pro-sec. chancellor Archbishopric Asunción, administr. gen.; dir. Catechistical Office, Asunción; rector Cath. U., Asunción, 1971-80, 86—; exec. sec. Latin Am. Faith Edn. Latin Am. Bishop Coun.; mem. exec. coun. Union of Latin Am. Univs., first v.p., 1986, pres., 1989; v.p. Program U. Integration and TV Edn., 1979-80; expert II Latin Am. Bishop Conf., Medellín, Colombia; coord. gen. Worls Congress, MedeLín, Columbia. Author: Church legislation on Catechesis, Course on Canonical Law; editor: (mag.) Latin American Catechesis. Office: Universidad Católica, CC 1718, Asunción Paraguay

USHER-KERR, MARVA DIANNE, corporate records administrator; b. Henderson, N.C., Feb. 24, 1955; d. Millie Lucille (Usher) Johnson. BA, SUNY, Stony Brook, 1977; postgrad., N.Y. Inst. Tech., 1989—. With customer svc. dept. F.W. Woolworth's, N.Y.C., 1977-82; with Gen. Bd. Global Ministries, N.Y.C., 1983—, records supr., 1985-87, corp. records mgr., 1987-91. Founder Nat. Network of Minority Info. Profls., N.Y., 1988-91; youth organizer L.I. West Dist. United Meth. Ch., Jamaica, N.Y., 1988-91. Mem. Assn. Records Mgrs. and Adminstrs. (v.p. info. and resources N.Y.C. chpt. 1989—, program com. 1989—), Assn. Image and Info. Mgmt. Democrat. Avocations: photography, reading. Home: 91-35 193rd St New York NY 11423 Office: Gen Bd Global Ministries 475 Riverside Dr New York NY 10115 *God loves all of our family, the human family, especially our youth. We each need to go out of self and show them God's love at its fullest.*

USSERY, CALVIN CLIFFORD, minister; b. Denison, Tex., July 17, 1920; s. Garland Hayes and Nellie Lou (Westbrook) U.; m. Juanita Hazel Seabourn, Jan. 21, 1938; children: Joyc Brady, Ronald Wayne. BA, Ouachita Bapt. U., 1948; postgrad., Southwestern Bapt. Theol. Sem. Ordained to ministry Bapt. Ch., 1942. Pastor various chs. Ark., 1947-54, Okla., 1954-89; pastor chs. Sherman, Garland, McKinney, Tex., 1991—; moderator Hope Assn., Texarkana, 1951—; clk. Frisco Assn., Idabel, Okla., 1956; speaker Bapt. Gen. Conv., Okla., 1956; speaker evangelism conf., Okla., 1966. Pres. Ministerial City Assn., Idabel, 1955-56, Bristow, Okla., 1973. Home: 140 Dale Dr McKinney TX 75069

USSERY, DAN KENNETH, minister; b. El Paso, Tex., Aug. 14, 1948; s. Lewis Kenneth and Margaret Edna (Olsen) U.; m. Priscilla Johnson, June 13, 1991; children: Aaron Daniel, Whitney Lisa-Marie. BTh, Life Bible Coll., 1970; postgrad., Azusa Pacific Coll., 1970-72, L.A. City Coll., 1970. Youth pastor Colorado Springs (Colo.) First Foursquare Ch., 1972-73; dist. youth dir. Midwest Dist. Foursquare Chs., Denver, 1973-75; asst. to supr. Midwest Dist. Foursquare Chs., Colorado Springs, 1979-84; nat. youth dir. Internat. Ch. of the Foursquare Gospel, L.A., 1975-78, dir. communication, 1978-79; sr. pastor First Foursquare Ch., Longmont, Colo., 1984-86, New Horizons Foursquare Ch., Grand Junction, Colo., 1987—; bd. dirs. Colo. Task Force on Religious Freedom, Grand Junction, 1988—; cabinet rep. Internat. Foursquare Ch., L.A., 1988-91; supt. western slope div. Midwest Foursquare Chs., 1987—. Editor Action Mag. for Youth Ministry, 1976-78; co-editor: Teaching Moments, 1976. Bd. dirs. Midwest Children's Home, Longmont, 1984-87. Republican. Avocations: volleyball, tennis, photography, videography. Office: New Horizons Foursquare Ch 641 Horizon Dr Grand Junction CO 81506

U THAN AUNG, ALPHONSE, archbishop. Archbishop of Mandalay Roman Cath. Ch., Myanmar. Office: Cath Bishops', Conf Myanmar, 292 Pyi Rd, Sanchaung PO, Yangon Myanmar*

UTKE, ROBERT AHRENS, minister; b. Milw., Mar. 15, 1933; s. Gustave Peter and Beth E. (Ahrens) U.; m. Doris Lucille Gissenaas, Sept. 17, 1960; children: Robert John, William Gissenaas, Richard David. BA, Elmhurst Coll., 1955; BD, Eden Theol. Sem., 1959. Ordained to ministry United Ch. of Christ, 1959. Min. Zion-St. John United Ch. of Christ, Waterloo and Fults, Ill., 1957-59, Immanuel United Ch. of Christ, Milw., 1959-64; min., initiator, adminstr. Fellowship Community Ch., Milw., 1965-67; initiator, coord. Milw. Assocs. In Urban Ministries, 1967-69; adminstr., property mgr. Lenore St. Garden Homes, Robert's Park Apts., Nashville, 1969-90; min. St. Peter's and St. John's United Ch. of Christ, Stone Church and Johannisburg, Ill., 1982—; v.p., treas. United Campus Christian Fellowship, Milw., 1959-64; dir. lab. sch. Wis. Conf. United Ch. of Christ, Green Lake, 1962, Urban Seminar for Wis. Coun. Chs., 1964-67. Editor, contbr.: A Guide to Prayer, 1965; columnist Living Your Life, 1965-67; contbr. articles to profl. jours. Chaplain Cosmopolitan Internat. convs. in U.S., Mex., Can., 1955-67; mem. steering com. Am. Friends Svc. Com. Weekend Workcamp, Milw., 1959-64; chmn. Milw. Planned Parenthood Clergy Com., Milw., 1963-64; pres. Met. Milw. Civic Alliance, 1966. Recipient Presdl. citation Cosmopolitan Internat., 1965, citation for youth work Senate of State of Wis., 1965; named Mr. Cosmopolitan Internat. Editor Cosmo Topics mag., 1963, Clergyman of Yr. Milw. Sentinal newspaper, 1966. Mem. Washington County Ministerial Alliance. Home and Office: St Peter's Ch Rte 1 Box 49 Stone Church Addieville IL 62214 *Accomplishments fade. Life's meaning comes from being a worthy servant of Christ, reaching out to those in need, remembering that I am simply a servant among servants. Life for all and all of life is to minister.*

VAAGENES, MORRIS GEORGE CORNELL, minister; b. Eau Claire, Wis., Sept. 30, 1929; s. Morris George Carlson and Hanna (Boure) V.; m. Bonnie Kay Bieri, Dec. 27, 1953; children: Lois Ziolkowski, Paul Luther, Timothy Jon, Mark G.C. AB, Augsburg Coll., 1951; BTh., Augsburg Seminary, Mpls., 1954; MTh., Luther Seminary, St. Paul, 1970, D of Ministry, 1979. Ordained to ministry Luth. Ch., 1954. Missionary to Madagascar Luth. B. of Missions, Mpls., 1954-57; pastor Christiania Trondhjem Chs., Farmington, Minn., 1957-61; sr. pastor North Heights Luth. Ch., St. Paul, 1961—; chmn. Internat. Luth. Conf. on Holy Spirit, Mpls., 1972-83; bd. dirs. Internat. Luth. Renewal Ctr., St. Paul. Office: North Heights Luth Ch 2701 Rice St Roseville MN 55113

VACHÉ, CLAUDE CHARLES, retired bishop; b. New Bern, N.C., Aug. 4, 1926; s. Jean Andre and Edith Virginia (Fitzwilson) V. B.A., U. N.C., 1949; M.Div., Seabury-Western Theol. Sem., Evanston, Ill., 1952, D.D. (hon.), 1976; D.D. (hon.), Va. Theol. Sem., 1977, St. Paul's Coll., Lawrenceville, Va., 1977. Ordained to ministry Episcopal Ch. as deacon, 1952, as priest, 1953. Min.-in-charge St. Michael's Ch., Bon Air, Va., 1952-54, rector, 1955-57; chaplain St. Christopher's Sch., Richmond, Va., 1953-56; rector Trinity Ch., Portsmouth, Va., 1957-76; bishop coadjutor Diocese of So. Va., Norfolk, 1976-78, bishop, 1978-91, chmn. ch. deployment bd., 1984-91; mem. com. on pastoral devel., 1976—, mem. standing commn. on ecumenical relations, 1982-85, mem. standing commn. on constns. and canons, 1986-91; chaplain St. George's Coll., Jerusalem, 1992.

VACHER-MORRIS, ELIZABETH MICHELE, lay worker; b. Morgantown, W.Va., July 2, 1963; d. John Michael Vacher and Carole Jean (Doughton) Vacher-Mayberry. BA in Communications, Carson-Newman Coll., 1986; postgrad., Div. Sch., Duke U., 1990—. Intern Sta. WBIR-TV, Knoxville, Tenn., 1986; camera operator Media Svcs. Ctr., Jefferson City, Tenn., 1986, 87; advt. account exec. Sta. WKJQ-WJFC-AM-FM, Jefferson City, 1986-87; reporter Sta. WKPT-TV, Kingsport, Tenn., 1986, 87; prodn. specialist Sta. WTVK-TV, Knoxville, 1987-88; electronic graphics producer Sta. WATE-TV, Knoxville, 1988-90. Vol. Blount Meml. Hosp., Maryville, Tenn., 1981, Contact Teleministries, Knoxville, 1982; mem. choir, pres. Sunday sch., adminstrv. bd. coun. on ministries, worship coord. Cokesbury United Meth. Ch., Knoxville, 1987—, sponsor mission family, 1988—, dir. singles, 1990—; pres. 1st yr. grad. class Duke Divinity Sch. Mem. Alpha Xi Delta. Republican. Avocations: travel, singing, photography. Home: 2752 Middleton Ave #31E Durham NC 27705

VACHON, LOUIS-ALBERT CARDINAL, archbishop; b. St. Frederic, Que., Can., Feb. 4, 1912; s. Napoleon and Alexandrine (Gilbert) V. D.Ph., Laval U., 1947, hon. degree, 1982; D.Th., St. Thomas Aquinas U., Rome, 1949; hon. degrees, U. Montreal, McGill and Victoria, 1964, Guelph U., 1966, Moncton U., 1967, Bishop's, Queen's and Strasbourg U., 1968, U. Notre Dame, 1971, Carleton U., 1972, Laval U., 1982. Superior Grand Seminaire Québec, 1955-59; superior gen. Le Séminaire de Qué., 1960-77; prof. philosophy Laval U., 1941-47, prof. theology, 1949-55, vice-rector, 1959-60, rector, 1960-72; protonotary apostolic, 1963-77, aux. bishop of Que., 1977-81, archbishop of Que. and primate of Can., 1981-90, apptd. Cardinal with title St. Paul of the Cross, 1985; Past pres. Corp. Laval U. Med. Centre; mem. Sacred Congregation for Clergy, Vatican, 1986—; adminstrv. bd. Nat. Order of Qué., 1985—, Can. Conf. Cath. Bishops, 1981—. Author: Espérance et Présomption, 1958, Verité et Liberte, 1962, Unité de l'universite, 1962, Apostolat de l'universitaire catholique, 1963, Memorial, 1963, Communauté universitaire, 1963, Progres de l'universite et consentement populaire, 1964, Responsabilite collective des universitaires, 1964, Les humanites aujourd'hui, 1966, Excellence et loyauté des universitaires, 1969, Pastoral Letters, 1981—. Hon. pres. La Société des etudes grecques et latines du Québec; assoc. mem. bd. Quebec Symphony Orch.; bd. govs. Laval U. Found. Decorated officier de l'Ordre de la Fidelité française, companion Order of Can., du Conseil de langue française, Ordre nat. du Qué., officier de la Légion d'honneur, France. Fellow Royal Soc. Can.; mem. Canadian Assn. French Lang. Educators (pres. 1970-72), Assn. Univs. and Colls. Can. (pres. 1965-66), Conf. Rectors and Prins. Que. Univs. (pres. 1965-68), Internat. Assn. Univs. (dep. mem. adminstrv. bd. 1965-70), Assn. des universites partiellement ou entierement de langue française (adminstrv. bd. 1961-69), Internat. Fedn. Cath. Univs. (adminstrv. bd. 1963-70), Ordre des francophones d'Amérique. Office: l'Universite Laval, 1073 Blvd St-Cyrille E, Sillery, Quebec, PQ Canada G1S 4R5

VAGGIONE, RICHARD PAUL, priest, monk; b. San Jose, Calif., Jan. 19, 1945; s. Roger Cesar Guilbert and Evelyn Howell (Compton) V. BA, U. Santa Clara, 1966; STM, STB, Gen. Theol. Sem., 1970; lic. philologie biblique, U. Louvain, Belgium, 1969; PhD, Oxford (Eng.) U., 1976. Priest-in-charge St. David's Episcopal Ch., East Greenbush, N.Y., 1983-85; rsch. assoc. Trinity Coll., Toronto, Ont., Can., 1985-89; incumbent St. Matthias' Anglican Ch., Toronto, Ont., Can., 1985-89; monk Order of the Holy Cross, 1980—; adj. prof. Ch. Div. Sch. of the Pacific, Berkeley, Calif., 1989—; spiritual dir. Trinity Coll., Toronto, 1986-89, retreat dir., 1980—. Editor: The Extant Works Eunomius of Cyzicus, 1987; contbr. articles to profl. jours. Mem. Soc. Bibl. Lit., Assn. Internat. Etudes Patristiques, N.Am. Patristics Soc., Conf. of Anglican Theologians. Home: Incarnation Priory 1601 Oxford St Berkeley CA 94709 Office: Ch Div Sch of the Pacific 2451 Ridge Rd Berkeley CA 94709-1211 *If "now" is the only time when grace is available, joy felt, or sorrow endured, then to construct a calm center in a chaotic world, "now" is when we must live.*

VAIVODS, JULIJANS CARDINAL, Latvian ecclesiastic; b. Vorkova, Latvia, Aug. 18, 1895. Ordained priest Roman Cath. Ch., 1918. Chaplain various schs., 1918-23; vicar gen., Liepaja, Latvia, from 1944; apostolic activity curtailed by polit. situation, in exile, 1958-60; vical gen., Riga, Latvia, 1962-64; attended Vatican II, 1964; consecrated titular bishop of Macriana Maior, apostolic adminstr. diocese of Riga and diocese of Liepaja, 1964; elevated to Sacred Coll. of Cardinals, 1983. Author catechetical books and theatrical works for youth. Address: Pils Iela 2, 226047 Riga Latvia

VALADEZ, MARK ALAN, minister; b. Upland, Calif., Feb. 3, 1960; s. Raul Favela and Winifred Irene (Alber) V.; m. Rebecca Ruth Ralston, June 27, 1981. AA in Telecommunications, Cuesta Jr. Coll., San Luis Obispo, Calif., 1981; AA in Bibl. Studies, Nazarene Bible Coll., 1984. Ordained to ministry Ch. of the Nazarene, 1988. Youth pastor Colorado Springs Ch. of Nazarene, 1982-84, Las Cruces (N.Mex.) Ch. of Nazarene, 1984-85, Pismo Beach (Calif.) Ch. of Nazarene, 1985-88; sr. pastor Ojai (Calif.) Ch. of Nazarene, 1988—; activities dir. L.A. Dist. Ch. of Nazarene, 1986-89. dir. jr. high boys basketball Ojui Recreation Dept., 1989-90, coach 5th and 6th grade boys basketball, 1990; bd. dirs. Youth Employment Svc., Ojai, 1990—. Named Alumnus of Yr. for L.A. dist. Ch. of the Nazarene, 1990-91. Home and Office: 603 Lion St Ojai CA 93023

VALDES, OTHONIEL AURELIO, missionary; b. Havana, Cuba, Dec. 19, 1956; came to U.S., 1968; s. Benjamin and Carmen (Gonzalez) V.; m. Maria

Carmen Lopez, Aug. 7, 1982; children: Othoniel Jr., Benjamin. BA, Mercer U., 1981; MDiv, New Orleans Bapt. Theol. Sem., 1984, MRE, 1986. Ordained to ministry So. Bapt. Conv., 1982. Mission pastor Calvary Bapt. Ch., New Orleans, 1982-87; dir. Lang. Mission, Birmingham (Ala.) Bapt. Assn., 1987-89; regional missionary Fla. Bapt. Conv., Tampa, 1989—. Republican. Home: 4605 Farmhouse Dr Tampa FL 33624

VALENTINE, FOY DAN, clergyman; b. Edgewood, Tex., July 3, 1923; s. John Hardy and Josie (Johnson) V.; m. Mary Louise Valentine, May 6, 1947; children: Mary Jean, Carol Elizabeth, Susan Foy. B.A., Baylor U., 1944, LL.D. (hon.), 1979; Th.M., Southwestern Baptist Theol. Sem., 1947, Th.D., 1949; D.D., William Jewell Coll., 1966, Louisiana Coll., 1989. Ordained to ministry Bapt. Ch., 1942. Dir. Bapt. student activities colls. in Houston, 1949-50; pastor First Bapt. Ch., Gonzales, Tex., 1950-53; dir. Christian life commn. Bapt. Gen. Conv. Tex., 1953-60; exec. dir., treas. Christian life commn. So. Bapt. Conv., 1960-87, exec. officer for devel., 1987-88; chmn. So. Bapt. inter-agy. council, 1965-67; Willson lectr. applied Christianity Wayland Bapt. Coll., 1963; Christian ethics lectr. Bapt. Theol. Sem., Ruschlikon-Zurich, Switzerland, 1966; Layne lectr. New Orleans Bapt. Theol. Sem., 1974; Jones lectr. Union U., 1976; Staley Disting. Christian scholar/lectr. La. Coll., 1981; Simpson lectr. Acadia Divinity Coll., Nova Scotia, 1982; H.I. Hester lectr. on preaching Midwestern Bapt. Theol. Sem., 1984; Belote lectr. on Christian ethics Hong Kong Bapt. Theol. Sem., 1990; co-chmn. commn. religious liberty and human rights Bapt. World Alliance, 1966-75; chmn. commn. Christian ethics, 1976-80, mem. gen. council, 1976-80; mem. Nashville Met. Human Relations Commn., 1966-78, Pres.'s Commn. for Nat. Agenda for the Eighties, 1980; guest columnist USA Today; lectr. on Christian ethics Bible Inst. for Evangelism and Missions, St. Petersburg, USSR, 1991; pres. Ctr. for Christian Ethics, 1990—. Author: Believe and Behave, 1964, Citizenship for Christians, 1965, The Cross in the Marketplace, 1966, Where the Action Is, 1969, A Historical Study of Southern Baptists and Race Relations 1917-1947, 1980, What Do You Do After You Say Amen?, 1980, Hebrews, James, 1 and 2 Peter: Layman's Bible Book Commentary, 1981; editor: Christian Faith in Action, 1956, Peace, Peace, 1967; contbr. to numerous anthologies; also author articles. Trustee Ams. United for Separation of Church and State, 1960—, pres. 1989—; bd. dirs. Bapt. Joint Com. Pub. Affairs, 1960-87, Chs. Center Theology and Pub. Policy, 1976-87; bd. fellows Interpreter's House, 1967-78, Ctr. for Dialogue and Devel., 1987—. Recipient Disting. Alumnus award Southwestern Bapt. Theol. Sem., 1970, Brooks Hays Meml. Christian Citizenship award, 1983, Disting. Alumni award Baylor U., 1987. Mem. Am. Soc. Christian Ethics. Democrat. Home and Office: 12527 Matisse Ln Dallas TX 75230

VALENTINE, FRANK MICHAEL, minister; b. Jackson, Mich., Sept. 18, 1951; s. Gerard Clyde and Phyllis Elaine (Martin) V.; m. Joan Barbara Galioto, July 6, 1980; 1 child, Cassandra Elaine. AB, Anderson U., 1973, MA in Religion, 1975, MDiv, 1976. Ordained to ministry Ch. of God, 1979. Youth minister Hazelwood Christian Ch., Muncie, Ind., 1975-78; pastor 1st Ch. of God, Portage, Pa., 1978-80, Crystal, Mich., 1980-83; pastor 1st Christian Ch., Ionia, Mich., 1983—; chaplain Ionia Pub. Safety, 1989—. Bd. dirs. Ionia YMCA, 1989—. Mem. Acad. Parish Clergy, Alban Inst., Rotary. Home: 122 E Washington St Ionia MI 48846 Office: 1st Christian Ch 130 E Washington St Ionia MI 48846

VALENTINE, ROBERT JEROME, priest, family therapist; b. Bronx, N.Y., June 11, 1943; s. Thomas and Katherine Mary (Collopy) V.; B.S. in Edn., Seton Hall U., 1969; M.Div., Immaculate Conception Sem., 1969; M.A., Columbia U., 1971, M.Ed., 1972. Ordained priest Roman Catholic Ch., 1969; sch. community counselor Haverstraw-Stony Point Schs., 1972-75; staff therapist, clinician trainer, supr. Center for Family Learning, New Rochelle, N.Y., 1972—; family therapy supr. Cath. Charities, Bridgeport, Conn., 1975—. Mem. Am. Personnel and Guidance Assn., Am. Family Therapy Assn., Am. Assn. Marriage and Family Therapy, Am. Orthopsychiat. Assn. Home: 914 Newfield Ave Stamford CT 06905 Office: 400 Stillson Rd Fairfield CT 06430

VALERO, RENÉ ARNOLD, clergyman; b. N.Y.C., Aug. 15, 1930; s. Caesar J. and Maria Luisa (Cordova) Valero; B.A. in Liberal Arts, Immaculate Conception-Cathedral Coll., 1952; M.S.W., Fordham U., 1962. Ordained to ministry Roman Cath. Ch., 1956; asso. pastor St. Michael-St. Edward, Bklyn., 1956-57, St. Agatha, Bklyn., 1957-60; dir. Bklyn. Cath. Charities Family Service, 1960-69; dir. Bklyn. Diocesan Office for Aging, 1969-74; coordinator Bklyn. Diocesan Hispanic Apostolate, 1974-79; pastor Blessed Sacrament, Jackson Heights, N.Y., 1979—; aux. bishop Diocese of Bklyn., 1980—; vicar for immigrants and refugees Diocese of Bklyn., 1983—. Home: 34-43 93rd St Jackson Heights NY 11372

VALOIS, CHARLES, bishop; b. Montreal, Apr. 24, 1924. Ordained priest Roman Cath. Ch., 1950; ordained bishop St. Jerome, Que., Can., 1977—. Office: 355 St George St, Saint Jerome, PQ Canada J7Z 5V3

VALVERDE, ERADIO, JR., minister; b. Kingsville, Tex., Oct. 25, 1952; s. Eradio and Maria del Jesus (Jimenez) V.; m. Maria Nellie Rosales, Feb. 25, 1978; children: Nellie Maria, Sarai, Carli Ilsa, Caitlin Demi. AA, Lon Morris Coll., 1973; BA in Sociology, Southwestern U., 1975; MTh, So. Meth. U., 1979. Ordained to ministry Meth. Ch. Pastor Latin Am. United Meth. Ch., Waco, Tex., 1978-79, First United Meth. Ch., Rio Grande City, Tex., 1979-80; campus minister Pan Am. U., Edinburg, Tex., 1980-86; coun. dir. Rio Grande Conf. United Meth. Ch., San Antonio, 1986-87; pastor El Mesias United Meth. Ch., Mission, Tex., 1987—; pres. Mission Ministerial Alliance, 1989—; dir. United Meth. Campus Ministry Bd., Edinburg, 1989—; v.p. Bd. of Discipleship, San Antonio, 1988—; pres. Hymnal Revision Com., San Antonio, 1990—. Author: Lecciones Cristianas, 1990. Pres. Youth Emphasis Com.-Rotary, Mission, 1990; bd. dirs. Reach Our Children, Mission, 1991; mem. Complete Count Com. Census '90, Mission, 1990; mem. bioethics com. Rio Grande Regional Hosp., McAllen, Tex., 1991—. Recipient Outstanding Svc. to Ch. and Community award, 1984. Democrat. Office: El Mesias United Meth Ch PO Box 1787 Mission TX 78572-1787

VAN ALLEN, RODGER, theology educator; b. Phila., Apr. 13, 1938; s. John F. and Helen T. (McAnany) V.A.; m. Judith Ann McGrath, Aug. 17, 1963; children: Rodger, Kathryn, Thomas, Paul, Peter. BS in Econs., Villanova U., 1959, MA in Theology, 1965; PhD in Religion, Temple U., 1973. Prof. Villanova (Pa.) U., 1964—. Author: The Commonweal and American Catholicism, 1974; co-author: Catholic America, 1986; editor: American Religious Vales and the Future of America, 1978; founding co-editor Horizons jour. 1974. Recipient Lindbach Teaching award Villanova U., 1986, Outstanding Scholar award, 1988. Mem. Coll. Theology Soc. (pres. 1982-84), Cath. Theol. Soc. Am., Am. Cath. Hist. Soc. Roman Catholic. Home: 106 Maple Ave Bala-Cynwyd PA 19004 Office: Villanova U Dept Religious Studies Villanova PA 19085

VAN APPLEDORN, E(LIZABETH) RUTH, writer; b. Holland, Mich., Dec. 19, 1918; d. John and Elizabeth (Rinck) van A. B of Music, Oberlin Coll., 1940; M of Music, Mich. State U., 1942. Prof. emeritus U. Minn., Duluth, 1946-82; lectr. in field, 1955-70; substitute Ch. organist, 1950-70. Contbr. prose poetry to religious publs. Recipient U. Svc. award, U. Minn., 1983. Mem. Mu Phi Epsilon (life). Home: 5120 Norwood St Duluth MN 55804 *Life offers meaning and fulfillment when the spiritual self awakens to its inward need for God's grace, redemptive healing, and guidance, inducing loving gratitude, dependence, selfless service, and equanimity.*

VAN ARSDALE, HERMAN WESLEY, minister; b. Geneseo, Kans., Jan. 23, 1925; s. Louis Wesley and Dorothea Wilhelmina (Schroeder) Van A.; m. Ruth Louise Ekstrom, Aug. 6, 1949; children: Deborah Ruth (dec.), Paul Wesley. BA, Sterling (Kans.) Coll., 1955; BDiv, Bethel Theol. Sem., 1959; D Ministry, San Francisco Theol. Sem., 1980. Ordained to ministry Am. Bapt. Chs. in U.S.A., 1951. Pastor 1st Bapt. Ch., Dell Rapids, S.D., 1960-64, Fort Scott, Kans., 1965-71, Salina, Kans., 1971-80; dir. ch. rels. Ottawa (Kans.) U., 1980-83; pastor Cen. Bapt. Ch., Great Bend, Kans., 1983-90; part-time min. 1st Bapt. Ch., Sterling, 1990—; trustee Kans. Bapt. Conv., Topeka, 1968-79, pres., 1978. City clk., Raymond, Kans., 1953-56; chmn. Salvation Army Com., Fort Scott and Salina, 1969-70, 74, 76, Salina County Commn. on Aging, 1974-79; trustee Ottawa U., 1974-80; bd. dirs. Am. Bapt. Chs. in U.S.A., Valley Forge, Pa., 1975-80. With USMCR, 1943-46, PTO. Recipient Disting. Svc. award N.E. Area Agy. on Aging, Manhattan, Kans., 1978, S.W. Area Agy. on Aging, Dodge City, Kans., 1990. Mem. Mins. Coun. Am. Bapt. Chs. in U.S.A. (pres. 1957-59), Kiwanis (pres. Fort Scott chpt. 1963-64, pres. Salina chpt. 1974-75). Home: 2536 Forest St Great Bend KS 67530

VAN BEECK, BROTHER FRANS JOZEF, priest; b. Helmond, The Netherlands, June 11, 1930; came to U.S., 1968; s. Lambertus Wilhelmus Maria and Johanna Hendrica (Mennen) van B. Lic. Phil., Berchmanianum, Nijmegen, The Netherlands, 1954; PhD, U. Amsterdam (The Netherlands), 1961; Licentiate in Sacred Theology, Canisianum, Maastricht, The Netherlands, 1964. Joined S.J., Roman Cath. Ch., ordained priest, 1963. Province dir. of studies Dutch Jesuit Province, the Hague, the Netherlands, 1965-68; from asst. prof. to prof. Boston Coll., Chestnut Hill, Mass., 1968-85; John Cardinal Cody prof. sacred theology Loyola U., Chgo., 1985—. Author: Christ Proclaimed, 1979, Grounded in Love, 1981, Catholic Identity After Vatican II, 1985, God Encountered, 1989, Loving the Torah More than God?, 1989. Mem. North Am. Acad. Ecumenists, Cath. Theol. Soc. Am., Am. Theol. Soc. (program chair 1986-87, v.p. 1990-91, pres. 1991-92). Address: 6525 N Sheridan Rd Chicago IL 60626

VAN BINH, PAUL NGUYEN, archbishop. Archbishop of Ho Chi Minh City Roman Cath. Ch., Vietnam. Office: Archeveche, BP 2371, 180 Nguyen Dinh Chieu, Ho Chi Minh City Socialist Republic of Vietnam*

VAN BROEKHOVEN, HAROLD, religious organization adminstrator; b. Rutherford, N.J., Feb. 10, 1913; s. Adrian and Wilhelmina V.; m. Lois Mary Loraine Chafer, Sept. 20, 1938; children: Rollin Adrian, Cornelia Louise, Harold Jr., Lois Loraine. BA, Wheaton Coll., 1935; ThM, Dallas Theol. Sem., 1939, postgrad., 1939-41; DD (hon.), Trinity Evang. Divinity Sch., 1987. Missionary Cen. Am. Mission, Nicaragua, 1941-43; prof. C.A. Bible Inst., Guatemala, 1943-56; found., dir. Sta. TGNA, Guatemala, 1950-56; asst. to pres. W.R.M.F., Inc., Europe, 1957-64; founder, dir. Outreach, Inc., Grand Rapids, Mich., 1966—, Inst. Theol. Studies, Grand Rapids, 1967—; bd. reference Braille Circulating Library, Richmond, Va., 1973—, Internat. Aid., Spring Lake, Mich., 1981-91; bd. trustees So. Bible Inst., Dallas, 1981—, W.R.M.F., USA, Inc., Miami, 1980-90; founder, dir. Outreach, Inc., Grand Rapids, 1956—; bd. dirs. China Ministries Internat., Pasadena, Calif. Author: The Spirit-Filled Life, 1967. Mem. Evangelical Theol. Soc. Club: Peninsular (Grand Rapids). Avocations: philatelics. Home: 841 Knapp St NE Grand Rapids MI 49505 Office: Outreach Inc 1553 Plainfield NE Grand Rapids MI 49501

VAN BUREN, PAUL MATTHEWS, theology educator; b. Norfolk, Va., Apr. 20, 1924; s. Harold Sheffield and Charlotte (Matthews) van B.; m. Anne Hagopian, Feb. 7, 1948; children: Alice, Ariane, Philip, Thomas. B.A., Harvard U., 1948; B.D., Episcopal Theol. Sch., Cambridge, Mass., 1951; D. Theol., U. Basel, Switzerland, 1957. Ordained to ministry Episcopal Ch., 1951. Minister in Detroit, 1954-57; asst., then assoc. prof. theology Episcopal Sem. S.W., Austin, Tex., 1957-64; assoc. prof. Temple U., Phila., 1964-66; prof. religion Temple U., 1966-86, prof. emeritus, 1986—, chmn. dept. religion, 1974-76; vis. prof. theology Harvard Divinity Sch., 1981, Union Theol. Sem., 1984; dir. Ctr. for Religious Pluralism Shalom Hartman Inst. Judaic Studies, Jerusalem, 1983—; hon. prof. U. Heidelberg, Fed. Republic Germany, 1987—. Author: Christ in Our Place, 1957, The Secular Meaning of the Gospel, 1963, Theological Explorations, 1968, The Edges of Language, 1972, The Burden of Freedom, 1976, A Theology of the Jewish-Christian Reality: Part 1, Discerning the Way, 1980, Part 2, A Christian Theology of the People Israel, 1983, Part 3, Christ in Context, 1988. Served with USCGR, 1942-43; Served with USNR, 1943-45. Fellow Am. Assn. Theol. Schs., 1962-63; Fulbright sr. lectr. Oxford (Eng.) U., 1967-68; Guggenheim fellow, 1967-68; NEH sr. fellow, 1982-83. Fellow Soc. Values in Higher Edn.; mem. Am. Acad. Religion, AAUP, ACLU, Am. Theol. Soc., Consultation on the Ch. and the Jewish People of World Council Chs., Presiding Bishop's Com. on Christian-Jewish Rels. (Sir Sigmund Sternberg award 1989). Home: RD Box 322 Little Deer Isle ME 04650

VANCE, BUZZ DWANE, minister; b. Park Rapids, Minn., July 20, 1954; s. Arthur Dwane and Kathryn Blanche (Fraser) V.; m. Joanne Marrie Schmelz, Aug. 7, 1982; children: Anthony Daniel, Jeremiah Matthew. BS, U. Nebr., 1976, MS, 1983. Ordained to ministry, 1986. Assoc. pastor Oak Lake Bible Ch., Lincoln, Nebr., 1986—. instr. Brite Lites, Lincoln, 1988-90; sponsor 4-H, Lincoln, 1990-91. Republican. Home: 3225 Orchard Lincoln NE 68503 Office: Oak Lake Bible Ch 3630 N First Lincoln NE 68521

VANCE, CHARLES RANDALL, minister; b. Huntington, W.Va., May 28, 1953; s. Tony and Rinda Gertrude (Caserta) V.; m. Patricia Ann Armstrong, Oct. 29, 1971; children: Charles Stephen, Cynthia Denise. DD (hon.), Internat. Sem., Plymouth, Fla., 1991. Lic. to ministry Ch. of God, 1990. Min. music Ch. of God, Barboursville, W.Va., 1983—, asst. pastor, 1986—, assoc. pastor, 1990—; owner, v.p. Simpson-Vance Constrn., Inc., Barboursville, 1981—; pres. Spirit of Victory Ministries, Barboursville, 1986—. Co-host, producer Spirit of Victory TV, Radio. Republican. Home: 4756 Route 10 Barboursville WV 25504 Office: Spirit of Victory 4751 Route 10 Barboursville WV 25504 *If we will apply Biblical principles to our life on a consistent basis, then we will have the results of those applied principles coming to fruition with the same consistency.*

VANCE, DONALD RICHARD, religion educator, lay worker; b. Mobile, Ala., July 18, 1957; s. Joseph Robert Jr. and Denise (Pratt) V.; m. Mary Anne Watson, Mar. 21, 1987. BA, Oral Roberts U., 1980; MA, Inst. of Holy Land Studies, Jerusalem, 1982; postgrad., Oriental Inst., U. Chgo., 1982-85, Iliff Sch. Theology, 1985—. With NIV cross reference project Zondervan Pub. House, Jerusalem, Tulsa, 1981-82; instr. Hebrew U. Denver, 1990; owner, pres. Vancefonts, Denver, 1989—; adj. faculty Oral Roberts U., Tulsa, 1986-87, Iliff Sch. Theology, Denver, 1989—; minister of discipleship Praise Temple Assembly of God, Chgo., 1984; tchr. in adult sch. of the Bible, Aurora (Colo.) First Assembly of God, 1989. Inventor computer fonts for Ancient Nr. East and Bibl. studies, 1989—. Mem. Soc. Bibl. Lit. Republican. Home: 2068 S Vaughn Way 101 Aurora CO 80014-1358 Office: Iliff Sch Theology 2201 S University Denver CO 80210 *Diligence is a relentless but faithful taskmaster. She drives hard but rewards well.*

VANCE, KEVIN MARK, minister; b. Xenia, Ohio, Mar. 3, 1966; s. Roy Lee and Helene Lucille (Rust) V. BS in Edn., Ohio U., 1989; postgrad., Atheneaum of Ohio, 1989-91. Campus min. Ohio U. Campus Ministry, Athens, 1987-88; Philmont scout chaplain Boy Scouts Am., Cimarron, N.Mex., 1990; min. youth St. Veronica Cath. Ch., Cin., 1989-91; pastoral assoc. for youth Good Shepherd Cath. Ch., Cin., 1991—. Bd. dirs. Diabetic Assn. Cin., 1989—; asst. camp dir. Am. Diabetic Assn., 1991—. Mem. Cath. Youth Mins. Assn. (steering com. 1991—). Home: 4446 Mt Carmel Tobasco Rd Cincinnati OH 45244 Office: Good Shepherd Cath Ch 8815 E Kemper Rd Cincinnati OH 45249 *In my life I have found that there is a tip in the scales of life. The scales tip in favor of our God and Creator. It is the acceptance of this fact that brings peace to my life.*

VANCE-WELSH, MARY CATHERINE, minister; b. Hammond, Ind., Jan. 26, 1957; d. Raymond Stanley and Edna Mae (Cornwell) V.; m. Brady Thomas Welsh, Aug. 18, 1979; children: Emily Lark, Philip Raymond. BA, Valparaiso U., 1979; MDiv, Luth. Sch. Theology, 1984, ThM, 1991—, postgrad., 1989—. Ordained to minister Luth. Ch., 1984. Assoc. pastor Bethlehem Luth. Ch., Chgo., 1984-88; adj. faculty mem. Luth. Sch. Theology, Chgo., 1989-91; mem. Luth./Roman Cath. Covenant Commn., Chgo., 1988-91; speaker in field; mem. Met. Chgo. Synod, Evang. Luth. Ch. Am.; mem. adv. coun. Inst. Liturgical Studies, 1991—. Mem. editorial bd. Currents in Theology and Mission, 1987—; contbr. articles to religious jours. Home: 29 Queens Ct Racine WI 53402

VAN CULIN, SAMUEL, religious organization administrator; b. Honolulu, Sept. 30, 1930; s. Samuel and Susie (Mossman) Van C. A.B., Princeton U., 1952; B.D., Va. Theol. Sem., 1955, D.D. (hon.), 1955. Curate St. Andrew's Cathedral, Honolulu, 1955-56; Canon precentor, rector Hawaiian Congregation, Honolulu, 1956-58; asst. rector St. John's Ch., Washington, 1958-60; gen. sec. Lyman Internat., Washington, 1960-61; asst. sec. overseas Exec. Council of Episcopal Ch., N.Y.C., 1962-68, sec. for Africa, Middle East, 1968-76; exec. for world mission Episcopal Ch. U.S.A., N.Y.C., 1976-83; sec. gen. Anglican Consultative Council Eng., London, 1983—. Named Hon. Canon Canterbury, 1983, Jerusalem, 1983, Ibadan, 1984, Ch. Province of So. Africa, 1989. Clubs: Atheneum (London); Princeton (N.Y.). Avocations: Music; travelling. Home: 94 Ebury Mews, London England SWI Office: Anglican Consultative Coun, Ptnrship House, 157 Waterloo, London SE1 8UT, England

VANDALE, ROBERT LEROY, religion educator, minister; b. Milw., Nov. 28, 1935; s. LeRoy and Lavonna Gertrude (Singbush) VanD.; m. Carla Jean Kuhn, Oct. 16, 1959; children: Laura Beth, Heather Lynn. BA cum laude, Lawrence Coll., 1957; MDiv cum laude, Pitts. Theol. Sem., 1960; PhD, U. Iowa, 1968. Ordained to ministry United Presbyn. Ch. (USA), 1960. Pastor United Presbyn. Ch. (USA), Freeport, Ohio, 1959-62; vol. missionary United Presbyn. Ch. (USA), Ethiopia, 1962-64, fraternal worker, 1968-72; prof. religion Westminster Coll., New Wilmington, Pa., 1972—; mem. gen. bd. Pa. Coun. Chs., Harrisburg, 1991; mem. com. theol. consultation Pa. Conf. on Interch. Coop., Harrisburg, 1982—. Editor Religion and Pub. Edn., 1987—; contbr. articles to religious jours. Active Assn. for Pub. Justice, Bread for the World. Fellow Inst. for Ecumenical and Cultural Rsch., 1982—; fellow in residence Princeton U., 1977. Mem. Nat. Coun. Religion and Pub. Edn. (bd. dirs. 1988—), Soc. for the Sci. Study of Religion, Peace Studies Assn. Home: 224 Francis St New Wilmington PA 16142 Office: Westminster Coll Dept Religion & Philosophy New Wilmington PA 16172

VANDAME, CHARLES, archbishop. Archbishop of N'Djamena, Roman Cath. Ch., Chad. Office: BP 456, N'Djamena Chad*

VAN DE BEEK, ABRAHAM, theologian, educator; b. Lunteren, Gelderland, The Netherlands, Oct. 9, 1946; s. Cornelis and Fopkje (van den Top) van de B.; m. Neeltje Lydia de Bruijn; children: Fopkje Ruchama, Willem Johan Timotheus, Cornelis Zacharja. Theol. exam., Rijksuniversiteit, Utrecht, 1970; D in Theology, Rijksuniversiteit, Leiden, 1980; D in Botany, Rijksuniversiteit, Utrecht, 1974. Pastor Dutch Reformed Ch. (Nederlandse Hervormde Kerk), Lexmond, 1970-74, Vriezenveen, 1974-79, Raamsdonk, 1979-81; prof. dogmatics and bibl. theology Rijksuniversiteit, Leiden, 1981—. Author: Die Brombeeren des geldrischen Distriktes, 1974, De menselijke persoon van Christus, 1980, Waarom? Over lijden schuld en God, 1984, De Adem van God, 1987, Wonderen en wonderverhalen, 1991; contbr. articles to profl. jours. Avocation: biology. Home: Hoofdstraat 32, 2235 CH Valkenburg The Netherlands Office: U Leiden Theol Inst, Matthias de Vrieshof 1, 2300RA Leiden The Netherlands

VANDE BERG, JAMES L., minister; b. Sioux Center, Iowa, Feb. 28, 1939; s. Lawrence W. and Johanna (Punt) V.; m. Kathleen Joan Redeker, June 11, 1960; children: Jocelyn Kay, Kirsten Jane. BA, Cen. Coll., Pella, Iowa, 1960; BD, Union Theol. Sem., Richmond, Va., 1965; MST summa cum laude, Union Theol. Sem., N.Y.C., 1967; D Ministry, McCormick Theol. Sem., Chgo., 1984. Ordained to ministry Presbyn. Ch. (U.S.A.), 1965. Assoc. min. Ponds Reformed Ch., Oakland, N.J., 1966-69; campus min. Va. Poly. Inst. and State U., Blacksburg, 1969-76; exec. Highlands Presbytery, Presbyn. Ch. (U.S.A.), 1976-79; dir. Office Ch. Devel. Office Ch. Devel., Presbyn. Ch. (U.S.A.), Atlanta, 1979-83; co-min. Presbyn. Ch., Atlanta, 1983-88; exec. presbyter Presbytery of Hudson River, Pleasantville, N.Y., 1988—; trustee Union Theol. Sem., Richmond, 1974-83; v.p. Joint Strategy and Action Com., N.Y.C., 1981-83; chair of collegium Synod of N.E., Syracuse, N.Y., 1990—; adj. prof. McCormick Theol. Sem., 1988—; mem., chief adminstrv. officer Presbytery of Hudson River. Co-author handbook: Developing Faithful and Vital Congregations, 1986; editor notebook: Basics in Small Church Development, 1981. Organizer, chair Crisis Ctr., Blacksburg, 1969-76; chair New River Community Devel. Orgn., Christiansburg, Va., 1972-74, New River ACLU, Radford, Va., 1973-75. Danforth Found. intern, 1962-63. Mem. Alban Inst., Assn. Exec. Presbyters, Presbyn. Ch. (U.S.A.), Kiwanis. Office: Presbytery of Hudson River 410 Bedford Rd Pleasantville NY 10570

VANDE KEMP, HENDRIKA, psychology educator; b. Voorthuizen, Gelderland, the Netherlands, Dec. 13, 1948; d. Hendrik and Petronella (Van Peursem) van de Kemp. BA, Hope Coll., 1971; MS, U. Mass., 1974, PhD, 1977. Lic. psychologist, Calif. Instr. psychology Fuller Theol. Sem., Pasadena, Calif., 1976-77, asst. prof., 1977-81, assoc. prof., 1981-91, prof., 1991—. Author: Psychology and Theology in Western Thought 1672-65, 1984; series co-editor: (book series) Christian Explorations in Psychology; contbr. articles to profl. jours. Mem., speaker So. Calif. C.S. Lewis Soc., Pasadena, 1979—; mem. com. on preparation for ministry Presbyn. Ch. USA, 1984-89; program chair Western Assn. of Christians for Psychol. Studies, Malibu, Calif., 1978. Christian Worker's Found. scholar Hope Coll., 1970-71. Fellow Am. Psychol. Assn. (sec.-treas. Psychologists Interested in Religious Issues div. 36 1985-88, pres. Psychologists Interested in Religious Issues div. 36 1988-89, William Bier award 1990), Psychology Grad. Union/Fuller Theol. Sem. (Community Bldg. award 1990). Democrat. Home: 219 N Primrose Ave Monrovia CA 91016 Office: Fuller Theol Sem 180 N Oakland Ave Pasadena CA 91101

VANDEN BERG, MICHAEL STEWART, minister; b. Kalamazoo, Jan. 2, 1954; s. Richard Stewart and Louise Joyce (Tarnow) Vanden B.; m. Nancy Jo VanHeest, Aug. 16, 1975; children: Christopher Michael, Joshua Stewart. AB, Hope Coll., Holland, Mich., 1976; MDiv, Western Theol. Sem., Holland, Mich., 1979. Ordained to ministry Ref. Ch. in Am., 1979. Pastor Bethany Community Ref. Ch., Flint, Mich., 1979-84; dir., founder Love Inc., Genesee County Chs., Flint, Mich., 1982-84; pastor First Ref. Ch., Lafayette, Ind., 1984—; founder Ch. Clearinghouse, 1981-84; co-developer, trainer Vol. Chaplins, Hurley Hosp., 1982. Bd. dirs. Boys and Girls Club, Lafayette, 1987-90, Am. Cancer Soc., Lafayette, 1989-90. Mem. Christian Educators Ref. Ch. (treas. 1991—). Home: 1628 N 15th St Lafayette IN 47904 Office: First Ref Ch 1718 N 15th St Lafayette IN 47904-1325

VANDER AARDE, ROBERT LEON, minister; b. Orange City, Iowa, Aug. 20, 1936; s. Bernard John and Christina (Luchtenburg) Vander A.; m. Marjorie Ielleen Hartog, June 18, 1960; children: Tamela Joy Vander Aarde-Scholten, Liesl Renee. AA, Northwestern Coll., Orange City, 1956; BA, Hope Coll., 1958; MDiv, Western Theol. Sem., Holland, Mich., 1961; postgrad., Luther Theol. Sem., St. Paul, 1968-70, Univ. Hosp., Ann Arbor, Mich., 1962, Luth. Deaconess Hosp., Mpls., 1969. Ordained to ministry Reformed Ch. Am., 1961. Missionary Bd. World Ministries Reformed Ch. Am., Kuwait, 1961-70; pastor Christ's Ch. on the Hill, Great Falls, Mont., 1970—; mem. exec. com. Arabian Mission, Kuwait, 1964-67; bd. dirs. Words of Hope (Temple Time Radio Broadcast), 1971-77, sec. Christians United for Forgiveness, Great Falls, 1984-85; trustee Northwestern Coll., 1979-83. Bd. dirs. Great Falls Crisis and Info. Ctr., 1971-85, pres. 1974; bd. dirs. Opportunities Inc., Great Falls, 1971-72; founding mem., bd. dirs. Great Falls Mercy Home for Battered Women, 1977-90, pres., 1982; bd. dirs. Big Sky chpt. ARC 1982—, 2nd v.p., 1983-85, chmn. 1985-88; mem. mil. families and vets. com., ARC, 1977-85, 88—, chmn. 1981-85; mem. Lang. Bank ARC, 1977—, chmn., 1989—; chmn. past chmn.'s coun., ARC, 1988—, mem. nat. resolution com., 1990; bd. dirs. Am. Heart Assn., Mont. affiliate, 1979-86, 87—, chmn. 1984-85, N.W./Rocky Mountain Regional Heart Com., 1984-86, treas. Mont. affiliate 1989—; mem. Cascade County Human Svc. Coord. Coun., Mont., 1984-86; bd. dirs. Alliance for Youth, Inc., 1989—, pres., 1990—. Recipient Silver medallion Great Falls Crisis Ctr., 1980, Vol. Merit award Big Sky chpt. ARC, 1985, Vol. award Am. Heart Assn., Mont. affiliate, 1985. Mem. Am. Soc. Missiology, Internat. Assn. Mission Studies, Great Falls Ministerial Assn. (pres. 1984-85), Great Falls Area Ch. Assn. (treas. 1986—), Great Falls Evang. Assn., Great Falls Counselor's Assn. (pres. 1982-83, Counselor of Yr. award 1986), Bread for the World, Mid. East Peacemakers. Home: 2100 5th St NW Great Falls MT 59404 Office: Christ's Ch on the Hill 809 Smelter Ave NW Great Falls MT 59404 *Life is a commitment to relationships, a relationship to one's self—to those around us and to our Creator-God.*

VANDERGRIFF, KENNETH LYNN, minister; b. Knoxville, Tenn., Nov. 12, 1954; s. Kenneth Charles and Dorothy Jean (Frazier) V.; m. Beth Foster, Aug. 6, 1976; children: Kenny, Jeananne. BS in English Edn., Fla. State U., 1976; MDiv, Southwestern Bapt. Seminary, Ft. Worth, 1981, PhD in Old Testament, 1988. Teaching fellow Southwestern Bapt. Theol. Seminary, 1984-87, adj. instr., 1989; min. of edn. Northwest Hills Bapt. Ch., San

Antonio, 1989—; instr. Inst. Christian Studies, Ft. Worth, 1983, 86, Wayland Bapt. U., San Antonio, 1988—. Recipient Stella Ross award in Old Testament studies Southwestern Bapt. Theol. Seminary, 1981. Mem. Soc. Bibl. Lit. Democrat. Home: 8215 Meadow Forest San Antonio TX 78251 Office: Northwest Hills Bapt Ch 6585 Heath Rd San Antonio TX 78250 *Integrity in relationships and the pursuit of excellence in endeavors—these I have found yield a life of satisfaction and joy.*

VANDERHAAR, GERARD ANTHONY, religion educator; b. Louisville, Aug. 15, 1931; s. Gerhard August and Margaret (Hammerstein) V.; m. Janice Marie Searles, Dec. 22, 1969. BA, Providence Coll., 1954; STB, Pontifical Faculty Theology, Dominican House of Studies, 1956, Licentiate in Sacred Theology, 1958; STD, U. St. Thomas, Rome, 1965. Ordained priest Roman Cath. Ch., 1957. Instr. philosophy and theology Christian Bros. Coll., Tenn., 1958-61; instr., chair dept. philosophy Spalding Coll., Ky., 1961-62; asst. prof. theology St. John's U., N.Y.C., 1964-65; assoc. prof. Providence Coll., 1965-68; vis. asst. prof. Wesleyan U., Conn., 1968-69; laicized, 1969; vis. asst. prof. U. Wis., Oshkosh, 1969-70, Ripon Coll., Wis., 1969-70; assoc. prof. Siena Coll., Memphis, 1970-71; prof. Christian Bros. U., Memphis, 1971—, chair dept., 1973-76, 88-91, active in found. of M. K. Gandhi Inst. for Study of Nonviolence, 1991. Author: Christians and Nonviolence in the Nuclear Age, 1982, Enemies and How to Love Them, 1985, Active Nonviolence: A Way of Personal Peace, 1990 (Book award Cath. Press Assn. 1991); also booklets and articles; (with Francis Loring and David Thomasma) A New Vision and a New Will for Memphis, 1974; co-editor: (with Mary Lou Kownacki) Way to Peace: A Guide to Nonviolence, 1987. Co-dir. Greater Memphis Consortium, 1970-71; active Pax Christi—USA, 1973-75, mem. nat. coun., 1975-79, 82-85, chmn. nat. coun., 1978-79, 83-85, coord. Tenn. region, 1981-82, coord. Memphis chpt., 1986-87; active founding of Mid-South Peace and Justice Ctr., Memphis, 1982, chmn. bd., 1991-92; chmn. bd. trustees M. K. Gandhi Found. NEH grantee, 1979. Mem. AAUP, NCCJ, Am. Acad. Religion, Consortium on Peace Rsch., Edn., and Devel., Fellowship of Reconciliation, War Resisters League. Home: 3554 Boxdale Apt 3 Memphis TN 38118 Office: Christian Bros U 650 E Parkway S Memphis TN 38104

VANDER HOEK, GERALD WAYNE, minister, theology and classical languages educator; b. Monroe, Iowa, Oct. 26, 1955; s. William Carl and MIldred Elsie (Branderhorst) Vander H.; m. Mary Lois Huyser, Aug. 13, 1976; children: Natalia, Carrie, Jonathan. MDiv, Calvin Theol. Sem., Grand Rapids, Mich., 1981, ThM, 1982; MA in Religion, Claremont (Calif.) Grad. Sch., 1986, PhD in Religion, 1988. Prof. Calvin Theol. Sem., Grand Rapids, 1987-88; prof. theology and classical langs. Dordt Coll., Sioux Center, Iowa, 1988-91; asst. pastor Covenant Christian Reformed Ch., Sioux Center, 1989—. Calvin Sem. grad. fellow, Grand Rapids, 1982. Mem. Soc. Bibl. Lit., Inst. Bibl. Rsch. Office: 328 2d St NE Sioux Center IA 51250

VANDERKAM, JAMES CLAIR, religion educator; b. Cadillac, Mich., Feb. 15, 1946; s. Henry and Elaine Ruth (Dekker) Vander Kam; m. Mary Ann Vander Molen, Aug. 24, 1967; children: Jeffrey, Laura, Daniel. AB, Calvin Coll., 1968; BD, Calvin Theol. Sem., 1971; PhD, Harvard U., 1976. Prof. Old Testament U. Notre Dame, Ind., 1991—. Author: Textual and Historical Studies, 1977, Enoch, 1984, The Book of Jubilees, 1989. Fulbright scholar, 1971-72; NEH grantee, 1982-83; NEH fellow, 1989-90. Mem. Soc. Bibl. Lit., Cath. Bibl. Assn., Am. Schs. Oriental Rsch. Presbyterian. Office: U Notre Dame Dept Theology Notre Dame IN 46556

VANDERMARCK, WILLIAM HENRY, religion educator; b. Zwolle, The Netherlands, Mar. 21, 1929; came to U.S., 1967; s. Jacobus Johannes and Maria Elizabeth (Glas) van der Marck; m. Mary Cecile Carpentier, Apr. 2, 1969; children: Paul William, Monique Mary. MA in Philosophy, Aquinas Inst., The Netherlands, 1950, MA in Theology, 1954; PhD, U. Fribourg, Switzerland, 1958. Prof. theology Aquinas Inst., Nijmegen, The Netherlands, 1960-68; assoc. prof. DePaul U., Chgo., 1970-76, prof. dept. religious studies, 1976—; vis. prof. theology U. Nijmegen, 1964-65, U. Notre Dame, 1967-68. Author: Statuta pro Missionibus, 1958, Love and Fertility, 1965, Toward a Christian Ethic, 1967; also articles: co-editor: Theological Encyclopedia, 1956-58. Mem. Am. Acad. Religion, Cath. Theol. Soc. Am., Am. Theol. Soc. Home: 3125 Sprucewood Ln Wilmette IL 60091 Office: 2323 N Seminary Ave Chicago IL 60614

VANDERMEY, HERMAN RONALD, dean, religion educator; b. Buffalo, Sept. 28, 1952; s. Robert Benjamin and Marion Isabel (Reed) V.; m. Denise Bonta Tart, June 5, 1982. BA, Masters Coll., 1974; MDiv, Biola U., 1977, ThM, 1980; EdD, Faith Sem., 1988; LittD (hon.), Faith-Los Angeles Sch. of Theology, 1989. Cert. secondary edn. tchr., Calif. Youth min. Bethany Bible Presbyn. Ch., Glendale, Calif., 1973—; dir. Verdugo Christian Day Camps, Glendale, 1973—; dean, prof. ch. history Cohen Theol Sem, L.A., 1988—; tchr. Glendale Unified Schs., 1985—; vice chmn. India Nat. Inland Mission, Glendale, 1988—; moderator S.W. Presbyn., L.A., 1985—; vice moderator Bible Presbyn. Synod, Cape May, N.J., 1986—. Author: Hosea/Amos, 1981. Mem. Curtis Hutson Assocs. for Evangelistic Work. Republican. Home: 400 N Louise Apt #108 Glendale CA 91206-2255 Office: Bethany Bible Presbyn Ch 3229 N Verdugo Rd Glendale CA 91208 *The secret of success is sacrifice. We can achieve those goals for which we are willing to sacrifice all the pleasures and allurements that would prevent the realization of these goals. Even the Lord Jesus Christ could succeed in his mission only through sacrificing his life for our sins.*

VANDERPOOL, C(RAWFORD) DANIEL, minister; b. Spokane, Wash., Sept. 2, 1944; s. Crawford T. and Mildred E. (McDowell) V.; m. Jennie Lou Wilson, Nov. 29, 1968. BA, N.W. Nazarene Coll., 1966; MDiv, Nazarene Theol. Sem., 1970. Ordained to ministry Ch. of Nazarene, 1972. Min. Christian edn., youth 1st Ch. of Nazarene, Moscow, Idaho, 1970-72; assoc. pastor, Christian edn. Biltmore Ch. of Nazarene, Phoenix, 1972-78; assoc. pastor College Ch. of Nazarene, Olathe, Kans., 1978—; bd. dirs. Kansas City (Mo.) Sunday Sch. Ministries; pres. Nazarene Multiple Staff Assn., 1985—, SW Christian Edn. Conv., Phoenix, 1976-77; mem. alumni coun. Nazarene Theol. Sem., 1985—. Mem. Drug Free Adv. Coun.-Sch. Dist., Olathe, 1990-91. Mem. Olathe Ministerial Assn. (pres. 1987). Home: 33 Holly Dr Olathe KS 66062 Office: Coll Ch of the Nazarene 2020 E Sheridan Olathe KS 66062

VANDER STELT, NATHAN JOHN, minister, former sales executive; b. Amsterdam, The Netherlands, Sept. 24, 1963; came to U.S., 1964; s. John Cornelius and Sandra Mae (De Jong) Vander S. BA in Polit. Sci., Dordt Coll., 186. Chmn. Leadership Network, Grandville, Mich., 1987-88; advisor Prism-Single Adult Ministry, Grandville, 1987-89; account mgr. Sta. WJQ Radio, Holland, Mich., 1988-90; bd. mem. Crossfire-Singles Ministry, Hudsonville, Mich., 1989—; youth pastor 1st Allendale (Mich.) Christian Reformed Ch., 1989—. Mem. Lions. Office: 1st Allendale Christian Ref Ch 5710 Country View Dr Allendale MI 49401

VANDER VORST, DARLENE M., lay worker; b. Glendive, Mont., Aug. 8, 1937; d. Harold George and Evelyn Martha (Clemmons) Larsen; m. G.K. Cooper, Aug. 15, 1959 (dec. Oct. 1967); 1 child, John T.; m. H.G. Vander Vorst, Feb. 14, 1974; 1 child, Diana Westberg. BA, Cascade Coll., 1959. With World Vision Inc., Portland, Oreg., 1955-59; vol. chair Evangelism dept. United Meth. Ch., Mandan, N.D., 1970-76, pastor parish rels., 1976-86, supt. Sunday sch., 1986-88, choir dir., 1983—; broadcast assoc. Sta. KNDR-FM, Mandan, 1977—, soloist, mem. quartet, 1980-90. Precinct chair Rep. Party, Mandan, 1983—; bd. dirs. crusade Am. Cancer Soc., Mandan, 1978, co-chair jail and bail com., 1985. Recipient Harry Denham Evangelism award, 1989. Mem. Mandan C. of C., P.E.O. Home: Box 342 Mandan ND 58554 Office: Sta KNDR-FM Box 516 Mandan ND 58554

VANDERVORT, DARRELL LYNN, minister; b. Geneva, Ohio, Nov. 1, 1956; s. William Braden and Laurel Jean (Unsinger) V.; m. Marsha Sue Owens, May 31, 1980; children: Elisabeth, Sarah, Thomas, Lauren. BA, Bethany Coll., W.Va., 1979; MDiv, Lexington (Ky.) Theol. Sem., 1983. Ordained to ministry Christian Ch. (Disciples of Christ), 1982. Student pastor Mill Creek Christian Ch., Mayslick, Ky., 1979-80; student youth assoc. First Christian Ch., Shelbyville, Ky., 198-82; pastor Firestone Pk. Christian Ch., Akron, Ohio, 1982-86, First Christian Ch., Paulding, Ohio, 1986-88, LaGrange (Ky.) Christian Ch., 1988—; sec.-treas. Christian Ch., Dist. 9 in Ky., 1988-90, pres. Dist. 5 in Ohio, 1987-88. Mem. Citizens Task Force for Bd. of Edn., Oldham County, Ky., 1991; counselor Religious Coalition for Abortion Rights, 1990—; treas. Human Svcs. Coun., Paulding, 1988. Mem. Nat Conf. Christians and Jews, Greater LaGrange Ministerial Assn. (pres. 1989—), Kiwanis. Democrat. Home: 407 N 5th Ave LaGrange KY 40031 Office: La Grange Christian Ch 214 N First Ave La Grange KY 40031

VANDERWERFF, LYLE LLOYD, religious educator, minister; b. Stickney, S.D., July 12, 1934; s. Evert and Mabel (Krutsch) VanderW.; m. Phyllis J. Lovins, Aug. 22, 1958; children: David, Kathryn, Kristyn. AA, Northwestern Coll., 1954; BA, Hope Coll., 1956; MDiv, Western Theol. Sem., 1959; MTh, Princeton (N.J.) Theol Sem., 1961; PhD, U. Edinburgh, Scotland, 1968. Pastor Cloverhill Reformed Ch., Flemington, N.J., 1959-61; missionary minister Internat. Congregation, Kuwait, 1961-64; prof. religion Northwestern Coll., Orange City, Iowa, 1967—; dir. internat. programs Northwestern Coll., 1985—. Author: Christian Mission to Muslims, 1977, Countering the Cults, 1981, Towards a Biblical World View, 1990; (with others) Muslims and Christians on the Emmaus Road, 1989. Mem. Am. Acad. Religion, Am. Soc. Missiology, Am. Schs. Oriental Rsch. Home: 506 Zuider Zee Dr Orange City IA 51041 Office: Northwestern Coll Orange City IA 51041

VANDER WIELE, DEAN KENNETH, minister; b. North Haledon, N.J., June 21, 1958; s. Kenneth Eugene and Esther Marie (Kruzinga) Vander W.; m. Kathy Ann Bundy, June 7, 1980; children: Kari Michelle, Kiel Lewis, Kaleb Andrew. Diploma, Word of Life Bible Inst., Pottersville, N.Y., 1977; BS in Bible, Lancaster (Pa.) Bible Coll., 1980; MA in Religion, Liberty Bapt. Theol. Sem., Lynchburg, Va., 1989; MA, Liberty U., 1991. Ordained to ministry Bible Ch., 1987. Pastor Bethel-Greenville-Rockton Ch. of the Brethren, Dubois, Pa., 1981-83, Lewisburg (Pa.) Bible Ch., 1984—; counseling intern Bethesda Day Treatment Ctr., West Milton, Pa., 1991; involvement chmn. Susquhanna Valley Celebration, Lewisburg, 1990—; pres. Kenneth E. Vander Wiele Ministries, Inc., Lewisburg, 1989—. Bd. dirs. Jefferson/Clearfield Drug and Alcohol Commn., Dubois, 1982-83. Named to Outstanding Young Men of Am., 1987; recipient Outstanding Christian Leadership award Dublin (N.H.) Christian Acad. Mem. Am. Assn. Counseling and Devel. Home: 317 Hospital Drive Lewisburg PA 17837 Office: Lewisburg Bible Church 311 Hospital Drive Lewisburg PA 17837

VANDERWYDEN, P. WILLIAM, III, minister, consultant, religious organization official; b. Cleve., May 24, 1947; s. Peter William and Frieda Luise (Tuller) V.; m. Renee Christine Shearey, June 19, 1971; children: Peter William IV, Annalisa Shearey, Christine Ellen, Melissa Susan. BA, Kent State U., 1969, MA, 1971; teaching. cert., Cleve. State U., 1970; MDiv, Chgo. Theol. Sem., 1973. Ordained to ministry, 1973. Mem. rsch. staff Greater Cleve. Growth Assn., 1969; tchr. Cleve. Pub. Schs., 1970-71; asst. minister Christ Ch. of Chgo., 1971-72, 1st Presbyn. Ch., Chgo., 1972-73; assoc. minister Woodside Interdenom. Ch., Flint, Mich., 1973-75; sr. pastor Congl. United Ch. Christ, Amherst, Ohio, 1975-87; ch. fin. advisor United Ch. Christ, N.Y.C., 1987—; mem. ministerial staff Crystal Cathedral, Garden Grove, Calif., 1981; cons. Nat. Fundraising Adv. Svcs., 1987—; speaker in fields of fundraising and children's issues. Author: Butterflies: Talking with Childen about Death and Life Eternal, 1991. Mem. Leadership Flint (hon. 1975); councilman City of Amherst, 1985-87; campaign cons., chmn. levy com. Amherst Pub. Libr., 1989, co-chair com. for issue 2 pub. schs., 1990; bd. dirs. United Way, Lorain, Ohio, 1985-87, County Econ. Devel. Com., Lorain County, 1983-85; dist. coord. Common Cause, Ohio, 1978-80; 13th dist. candidate for U.S. Congress, 1980; pres. Community Devel. League, Amherst, 1983-84; mem. Amherst Youth Soccer Assn. Mem. Amherst Area Ministerial Assn. (pres. 1976-78), Firelands Dist. Clergy (dean 1985-87), Ohio-Western Res. Assn. (clergy 1975—, conf. com., coun.), Nat. Soc. Fundraising Execs., Blue Key (hon.), Sigma Chi, Psi Chi. Avocations: writing, public speaking, soccer coaching politics, children. Home: 118 Westchester Dr Amherst OH 44001 Office: United Ch Christ 700 Prospect Ave Cleveland OH 44115 also: United Ch Bd Homeland Ministries 475 Riverside Dr New York NY 10115

VAN DEVENTER, PIETER GABRIEL, minister, economic consultant; b. Johannesburg, Transvaal, Republic of South Africa, Apr. 19, 1945; s. Pieter Gabriel Sr. and Johanna Cornelia (Van Goeverden) Van D.; m. Charmain Olivier; children: Pieter Gabriel, Riaan, Juan Petrus. Diploma in Div. cum laude, Berea Theol. Coll., Republic of South Africa, 1971; BS, Lee Coll., 1990; D of Human Sci. (hon.), Calif. Grad. Sch. Theology. Ordained to ministry Full Gospel Ch. of God. Pastor Full Gospel Ch. of God, Westonaria, 1971—; overseer Full Gospel Ch. of God, Namibia, 1972-91; exec. dir. for Africa Nat. Religious Broadcasters; chmn. dist. youth bd., mem. ch. exec. coun., other bds., sgt.-at-arms Gen. Assembly, Full Gospel Ch. of God; mem. various religious, ecumenical, diplomatic dels.; advisor Reformed Ind. Chs. Africa; econ. adviser various nat. govts., Africa. Vice chmn., then chmn. bd. govs. Westonaria Afrikaans Primary Sch.; active in establishment Ch. Alliance South Africa, All-African Congress. Recipient spl. award Gov. Chung Mo/Republic of Korea, citation of honour Nat. Religious Broadcasters, Disting Svc. award, Brotherhood award Am. Forum for Jewish-Christian Cooperation, Scholars award Pacific States U.; named an hon. Indian chief; received key to City of Tuskegee, Ala. Mem. Pub. Rels. Inst. South Africa, Soweto Black Pastors Assn. Home: PO Box 97, Irene Pretoria Transvaal 1675, Republic of South Africa Office: Full Gospel Ch of God, 8 Ian Smuts Ave, Irene 1675, Republic of South Africa

VAN DE VYVER, SISTER MARY FRANCILENE, academic administrator; b. Detroit, Sept. 6, 1941; d. Hector Joseph and Irene Cecilia (Zygailo) V. BA, Madonna Coll., 1965; MEd, Wayne State U., 1970, PhD, 1977. Joined Sisters of St. Felix of Cantalice, Roman Cath. Ch., 1967. Tchr. Ladywood High Sch., 1965-74; adminstrv. asst. to pres. Madonna Coll., Livonia, Mich., 1974-75, acad. dean, 1975-76, now pres. Office: Madonna Coll Office of Pres 36600 Schoolcraft Rd Livonia MI 48150-1173*

VAN DE WORKEEN, M. C., minister, philanthropy consultant; b. Worcester, Mass., Nov. 3, 1927; s. Ivan Boris and Elizabeth L. (Shaw) Van de W.; m. Joan Minot Wetherbee, June 28, 1952 (div. 1973); children—Brian Cole, Scott Minot; m. Priscilla Townsend, Oct. 27, 1973. B.A. in Physics, Clark U., 1947; M.Div., Tufts U., 1951; S.T.M., Harvard U., 1952, postgrad. Boston U., 1951-53. Ordained to ministry Unitarian Universalist Assn., 1951. Math. tchr. Williston Acad., Easthampton, Mass., 1948-49; pastor First Parish Ch., Taunton, Mass., 1951-53; exec. officer Mass. and Conn. Universalist convs., Boston, 1953-60; asst. to chief exec. officer Universalist Ch. Am., Boston, 1960-62; pastor Community Ch. N.Y., N.Y.C., 1962-66; pres. Nat. Charities Info. Bur., Inc., N.Y.C., 1966-84, Philanthropy Counsellors, Inc., N.Y.C., 1984-88; chief exec. officer, chief oper. officer Vernalwood Conceptual Enhancements, Dudley, Mass., 1991—; pres. Nat. Ctr. Charitable Stats., Washington, 1982-84; mem. accreditation commn. Nat. Accreditation Council for Agys. Serving Blind and Visually Handicapped, 1980-86; mem. nonbus. task force Fin. Acctg. Standards Bd., 1981-87; mem. pvt. sector adv. group solicitations law project Nat. Assn. Attys. Gen., 1983-86. Bd. dirs. Unitarian Universalist UN Office, 1962-88; minister/mem. Unitarian Universalist Humanist Fellowship Greater N.Y., 1969—. Recipient Silver Bell award Advt. Council, 1977. Mem. Unitarian Universalist Ministers Assn., Am. Assn. Retired Persons (state coord., citizens rep. program Mass. chpt.). Democrat. Avocations: gardening; fishing; woodcarving. Home: Vernalwood RR 3 Box 375 Dudley MA 01571

VAN DINE, HOWARD ARTHUR, JR., priest; b. Mineola, N.Y., Feb. 25, 1921; s. Howard Arthur and Anna (Janson) Van D.; m. Margaret Ardella Ryan, Aug. 28, 1948; children: Kristen Lynne, Howard Arthur, Kathrina-Ellen, Pieter James. BSEE, Bucknell U., 1949; postgrad., U. Vt., 1958-63. Ordained deacon Episcopal Ch., 1963, priest, 1965; registered profl. engr. Asst. St. Paul's Ch., Burlington, Vt., 1963-71; missioner Calvary Ch., Underhill, Vt., 1971-74; canon residentiary Cathedral Ch. of St. Paul, Burlington, 1974-81; rector St. Paul's Ch., Vergennes, Vt., 1981-89, interim min., 1989—; mem. diocesan deployment com., canon to the ordinary Diocese of Vt., Burlington, 1977-89; min. Cathedral Ministry of Arts.; quality control engr. GE, Burlington, 1949-81. Author: Jesus Stories for Matthew, 1974; contbr. articles to profl. jours., poetry to anthologies. Mem. Prudential Com., South Burlington, 1956-59. 1st lt. USAAF, 1942-45, ETO, MTO. Mem. Vt. Soc. Profl. Engrs., Poetry Soc. Vt. Home: 6 Park St Vergennes VT 05401 Office: Diocesan Ctr Rock Point Burlington VT 05401

VAN DINE, PAUL EDWIN, clergyman; b. Bluffton, Ind., June 19, 1939; s. Charles W. and Nellie Ruth (Maupin) Van D.; m. Carolyn Ann Shimp, June 12, 1960; children: Vicki Linn, Mark David, Karen Joan. BA magna cum laude, U. Miami, 1960; MDiv cum laude, Drew U., 1964. Ordained to ministry Meth. Ch., 1961. Student pastor Stockholm (N.J.) Meth. Ch., 1961-64; pastor Sylvan Abbey Meth. Ch., Clearwater, Fla., 1964-67, Union Park United Meth. Ch., Orlando, Fla., 1967-69, Port Orange (Fla.) United Meth. Ch., 1969-75, Cypress Lake United Meth. Ch., Ft. Myers, Fla., 1980—; assoc. pastor Pasadena Community Ch., St. Petersburg, Fla., 1975-80; sec. bd. missions and ch. extension Fla. Conf. United Meth. Ch., 1972-75, chmn. com. on communications, 1980-84; chmn. St. Petersburg Dist. Council on Ministries, 1977-80; bd. dirs., mem. exec. com. United Meth. Reporter newspaper, 1980-86. Contbr. prayers and sermons to religious publs. Democrat. Home: 879 Deep Lagoon Ln SW Fort Myers FL 33919 Office: Cypress Lake United Meth Ch 8570 Cypress Lake Dr Fort Myers FL 33919

VAN DUSEN, ERIC LAUREN, mission executive; b. Albany, N.Y., Nov. 20, 1946; s. John Allison and Emilie Katherine (Buchaca) Van D.; m. Barbara Jean Brooks, June 24, 1972; children: Kristina, Katherine, Karen, David. BA in Psychology, Calif. State U., L.A., 1975; EdM in Counseling, Ga. State U., 1977; cert., Psychol. Studies Inst., Atlanta, 1977. Counselor, adminstr. Capital Area Christian Counseling Ctr., Delmar, N.Y., 1977-79; ch. rels. rep. Frontier Fellowship, U.S. Ctr. for World Mission, Pasadena, Calif., 1983-84; maintenance worker William Carey Internat. U., Pasadena, 1984; mgr. warehouse Christian Pilots Assn., Arcadia, Calif., 1984-85; chief exec. officer 2500 Translations, mission agy., Pasadena, 1984—. Contbr. articles to profl. jours. Vol., officer Ravena (N.Y.) Fire Dept., 1977-82; unit pres. Longfellow Sch. PTA, Pasadena, 1989-90. Sgt. USAF, 1964-68. Home and Office: PO Box 40725 Pasadena CA 91114

VAN DUZER, ALBERT WIENCKE, clergyman; b. Newburgh, N.Y., July 15, 1917; s. Albert Barton and Clara Helen (Wiencke) Van D.; m. Marion R. Lippincott, Apr. 31, 1939; children: Daryl (Mrs. Henry Gorczycki), Margaret Lynn (Mrs. Donald Muller), Marianne Gayle (Mrs. Joseph M. Carson). AB, Trinity Coll., Hartford, Conn., 1940; BTh, Gen. Theol. Sem., 1945, STD, 1966; BD, Phila. Div. Sch., 1954, DD, 1967. Ordained to ministry Episcopal Ch., 1946; curate Grace Ch., Merchantville, N.J., 1946-47; rector Grace Ch., 1949-66, Ch. of Advent, Cape May, N.J., 1947-49; suffragan bishop N.J. Diocese, 1966-72; bishop coadjutor of N.J., 1972-73, bishop of N.J., 1973-82; Past youth dir., past pres. Youth Cons. Service N.J. Diocese; Camden (N.J.) County rep. White House Conf. Aging, 1957; mem. Bd. Examining Chaplains N.J., 1957-66; past chaplain Merchantville Fire Co.; mem. exec. council Episcopal Ch. Trustee Evergreen's Home Aged, Camden County Children's Shelter, Camden County council Girl Scouts Am., Cooper Hosp. and Univ. Med. Ctr., Camden, Cooper Found. Named Man of Year Merchantville Fire Co.; recipient Medal of Honor Diocese N.J., 1962, Boyle award citizenship and community service Camden County Bar Assn., 1965; Nat. Alumni Achievement award Trinity Coll., Hartford, 1976; named hon. canon Trinity Cathedral, Trenton, N.J., 1957. Mem. Camden County Health and Welfare Assn. (mem. bd.), Nat. Assn. Social Service. Clubs: Mason (33 deg.; past grand chaplain N.J.), Kiwanian, Lion.

VAN DYK, A. S., clergy member, priest. Moderator Dutch Reformed Ch., Harare, Zimbabwe. Office: Dutch Reformed Ch, 35 Samora Machel, POB 967, Harare Zimbabwe*

VAN ECK, ARTHUR ORVILLE, religious organization administrator, consultant; b. Denver, June 6, 1925; s. Arthur S. and Bessie (De Voogd) Van E.; m. Aug. 24, 1949; children: Barbara, Arthur, Mary, Timothy. BA, Hope Coll., 1948; MDiv, Western Theol. Sem., 1951; EdD, Columbia U., 1969. Pastor Calvary Community Ch., Southgate, Mich., 1951-63; dir. adult and family edn. Bd. Edn. Reformed Ch. in Am., N.Y.C., 1963-69; sec. ch. life, witness Reformed Ch. in Am., N.Y.C., 1969-74, sec. Met. region, 1974-82; exec. dir. Edn. for Christian Life & Mission, N.Y.C., 1982-86; assoc. gen. sec. div. edn. and ministry Nat. Coun. of Chs., N.Y.C., 1986-90, dir. NRSV project, 1991—. Chairperson Citizen's Adv. Coun., Waldwick, N.J., 1978. 1st lt. USMCR, 1946054. Named Outstanding Educator of the Yr., Reformed Ch. Am., 1982. Mem. Assn. for Presbyn. Ch. Educators (Eductor of Yr. award 1990), Assn. for Creative Change, Assn. for Supervision and Curriculum Devel., Assn. Couples in Marriage Enrichment. Democrat. Avocations: racquetball, tennis, hiking, video taping. Office: Nat Coun Chs 475 Riverside Dr New York NY 10115-0050

VAN EK, LYNN CAROL, minister; b. Passaic, N.J., Nov. 5, 1947; d. Warren Frederick and Eleanor Jean (Van Hook) Mierop m. Edwin William Van Ek, Apr. 3, 1971; children: Jared Douglas, Jeremy Scott, Jonathan Kyle. AA in Nursing, Fairleigh Dickinson U., Rutherford, N.J., 1969; AB in Religion, Thomas A. Edison Coll., 1987; MDiv, New Brunswick Theol. Sem., 1989. Ordained to ministry Ref. Ch. in Am., 1990. Asst. pastor Second Ref. Ch., Wyckoff, N.J., 1990—. Recipient awards, in N.T., O.T., Pastoral Care and Ch. History, New Brunswick Theol. Sem., 1986, 88, 89. Office: Second Reformed Ch 475 Lafayette Ave Wyckoff NJ 07481

VAN ENS, JACK RONALD, minister, church growth consultant; b. Grand Rapids, Mich., Dec. 31, 1946; s. Meinard and Winnifred Van Ens; m. Sandra Jo Broene, June 25, 1969; children: Craig Michael, Megan Kristine, Christopher Gene. AB, Calvin Coll., Grand Rapids, 1969; MDiv, Princeton Theol. Sem., 1972, ThM, 1976, D Ministry, 1984. Ordained to ministry Presbyn. Ch. (U.S.A.), 1972. Pastor, head of staff 1st Presbyn. Ch., Mt. Pleasant, N.J., 1972-76; sr. pastor, head of staff 1st Presbyn. Ch., Pitman, N.J., 1976-81, Arvada (Colo.) Presbyn. Ch., 1981-88; pres., chief exec. officer Creative Growth Assocs., Arvada, 1987—; exec. dir. Wheat Ridge (Colo.) C. of C., 1989-90; spl. asst. to pres. West C. of C., Denver, 1991—; chmn. com. Denver Presbytery, 1988. Writer, dir., co-producer Window on the World, weekly radio and cable TV show, 1978-81; author, editor bi-weekly column Bus. at Its Best. Leader motivational tng. workshops Jefferson County Schs. PTA's, 1987; alumni fund raising liaison Princeton Theol. Sem., 1981-89. Named Man of Yr., City of Wheat Ridge, 1990. Mem. Arvada-North Jeffco C. of C. (bd. dirs., program chmnn. 1985-89, exec. bd. 1986-89, treas. 1989-90, pres.-elect 1990, Key Man award 1989), Colo. Calvin Coll. Alumni Assn. (chpt. pres. 1983-85). Home and Office: 9745 W 77th Dr Arvada CO 80005 *The winning dynamics of effective advertising may be applied to motivational preaching. Start a fire—be enthusiastic rather than dull. Build a bridge—be concrete rather than esoteric. Deliver the goods—be convictional rather than merely informative. Appeal for action—be expectant that listeners will respond rather than lethargically open-ended.*

VANGEMEREN, WILLEM ARIE, theology educator; b. Boskoop, The Netherlands, Apr. 7, 1943; came to U.S., 1962; s. Jacobus Johannes and Sarah Cornelia (Langeveld) Van G.; m. Evona Leslie Adkins; children: Nurit, Tamara, Shoshanna. Diploma, Moody Bible Inst., Chgo., 1966; BA, U. Ill., Chgo., 1968; postgrad., Hebrew U., Jerusalem, 1969-70; BD, Westminster Theol. Sem., 1971; MA, U. Wis., 1972, PhD, 1974. Ordained to ministry Presbyn. Ch. Am., 1976. Asst. prof. Geneva Coll., Beaver Falls, Pa., 1974-78; prof. Old Testament, chmn. dept. Ref. Theol. Sem., Jackson, Miss., 1978-90; commr. examinations Presbytery of Mississippi Valley, 1984-91. Author: The Progress of Redemption, 1988, Interpreting the Prophetic Word, 1990, Expositor's Bible Commentary: Psalms, 1991; editor: New International Dictionary of Old Testament Theology; Issues in Old Testament Biblical Theology; contbg. author Bible Almanac of the Old Testament, 1980, Nelson's Expository Dictionary, 1980, Continuity and Discontinuity, 1988, Evangelical Dictionary of Theology, 1989; also articles. Recipient Sam A. Baskind Meml. Found. award, 1977. Fellow Am. Coll. Bibl. Theologians; mem. Evang. Theol. Soc., Inst. Bibl. Rsch., Soc. Bibl. Lit. Office: Ref Theol Sem 5422 Clinton Blvd Jackson MS 39209 *The greatest challenge of Moses, the prophets, Jesus Christ, and the apostles is the shift of focus from human mythologies and religious structures to God as the Holy One. They call for a shift in focus from the many sacred objects, places, times and rituals to God as the one center. They call for the radical change of leaving the false orbit around human definitions of the sacred to orbiting around the Holy Triune God.*

VAN GORP, GARY WAYNE, clergyman; b. Reasnor, Iowa, July 16, 1953; s. Laverne Leroy Sr. and Emma Jean (Meyers) Van G.; m. Marietta Louise Burns, Dec. 29, 1972; children: Caleb Aaron, Kari Beth, Micah Alan, Faith Elise. Diploma in Pastoral Studies, Bible and Doctrine, Berean Coll., 1975;

BS in Pastoral Studies, Religious Edn., North Cen. Bible Coll., Mpls., 1978; Diploma in profl. office mgmt., Alexandria (Minn.) Tech. Sch., 1984. Ordained to ministry Assembly of God Ch., 1981. Pastor Verndale (Minn.) Assembly of God Ch., 1979-82; asst. mgr., caretaker Lake Geneva Bible Camp, Alexandria, 1982-83; Christian edn. and outreach pastor Alexandria Assembly of God Ch., 1983-84; pastor, adminstrv. asst. Allison Park (Pa.) Assembly of God Ch., 1984-90; vice prin. Faith Acad. Christian Sch., 1980-83; book store mgr. Gospel Supply Ctr., Minn., 1981-82; pastor Elbow Lake (Minn.) Assembly of God, 1983-84. Bd. dirs., treas., mem. adv. bd. The DoorWay, Inc., Pitts., 1988—. Sgt. Air NG, 1971-77. Mem. Nat. Assn. Ch. Bus. Adminstrs. (pres. Pitts. chpt. 1987-90). Home and Office: PO Box 75 Reasnor IA 50232

VAN HEERDEN, LAWRENCE, minister, ecumenical agency administrator. Exec. min. Inter-Ch. Coun. Greater New Bedford, Mass. Office: Inter-Ch Coun Greater New Bedford 412 County St New Bedford MA 02740*

VAN HOUSE, MARK A., minister; b. Austin, Minn., Feb. 11, 1961; s. John P. and Doris (Lukes) VanH.; m. Rhonda Rae Eidsness, Sept. 24, 1988. BA, St. Olaf, 1983; MDiv., LNTS, 1987. Pastor Luth. chs. of Reserve Homestead, Medicine Lake, Mont., 1987-88, Am. Luth. Parish, Harlem, Mont., 1988-91; assoc. pastor Holy Shepherd Luth. Ch., Lakewood, Colo., 1991—; del. Flathead Lake Luth. Camp, Kalispen, Mont., 1987-91, Sky Ranch Luth. Camp, Fort Collins, Colo., 1991—; pres. Harlem (Mont.) Ministerial Assn., 1988-91; sole clergy rep. Mont. March of Dimes, 1989-91. Author: (plays) The Trial of Christ, 1985, Pilate, 1988, Who is Advent?, 1989, (manual) Critical Stress De-Briefing, 1990. Team leader critical incidence de-briefer North Cen. C.I.S.D. Team, Blaine, Phillips and Hill Counties, Mont., 1989-91. Recipient Svc. Recognition award Harlem (Mont.) Fire Dept., 1989. Mem. Nat. Alzheimers Assn. (clergy), Mont. State Alzheimers Rsch. (clergy), YMCA fundraiser 1991—), Lions Club (Harlem 1990-91, Lakewood 1991—). Office: Holy Shepherd Luth Ch 920 Kipling St Lakewood CO 80215

VAN HOUSE, ROBERT WENDELL, minister; b. Cordell, Okla., Feb. 22, 1932; s. Wendell Earnest and Lorene (Cunningham) Van H.; m. Waltraud Saile, Dec. 22, 1956; children: Robert W. Jr., Katharina. BA, Okla. City U., 1954; BD, So. Meth. U., Dallas, 1962; D of Ministry, Philips U., 1974; postgrad., Augsburg Coll., Mpls., 1978. Ordained to ministry United Meth. Ch., 1964. Assoc. min. First United Meth. Ch., Ponca City, Okla., 1962-64, min., 1985-91; min. So. Hill. United Meth. Ch., Oklahoma City, 1964-70, Aldersgate United Meth. Ch., Tulsa, 1970-72, First United Meth. Ch., Cushing, Okla., 1972-76, East Cross United Meth. Ch., Bartlesville, Okla., 1981-85, 1st United Meth. Ch., Ponca City, Okla., 1985-91, First United Meth. Ch., Edmond, Okla., 1991—; mem. Conf. Coun. Fin. and Adminstrn., Oklahoma City, 1990—, Conf. Com. for Disasters, Oklahoma City, 1986—; mem. Dist. Bd. Trustees, Stillwater, Okla., 1985-91. Mem. Rotary Internat. (Paul Harris fellow 1988), C. of C., Ministerial Alliance. Democrat. Home: 2516 Stamford Ct Edmond OK 73034

VAN HOUTEN, RICHARD LEE, religious organization administrator; b. Grand Rapids, Mich., July 4, 1946; s. Herman and Rose (Vennema) van H.; m. Christiana DeGroot, May 28, 1972; children: Rosemarie, Nicholas, Adrianna, Katrine. BS, Calvin Coll., Grand Rapids, 1968; MA, U. Chgo., 1974; PhD, U. British Columbia, 1981. Instr. religion Calvin Coll., 1979, U. Notre Dame, South Bend, Ind., 1980, Hope Coll., Holland, Mich., 1981; missionary Chinese Ch. Rsch. Ctr., Hong Kong, 1982-87; gen. sec. Reformed Ecumenical Coun., Grand Rapids, 1987—. Editor: Wise as Serpents, Gentle as Doves, 1988; editor monthly newsletter; contbr. articles to mags. With U.S. Army, 1968-70, Vietnam. Office: Reformed Ecumenical Coun 2017 Eastern Ave SE Rm 201 Grand Rapids MI 49507

VAN HUDSON, MARK VALENTINES, religion educator; b. Pitts., Aug. 26, 1949; s. Paul Franklin van Hudson. BS in Engring., U. N.Mex., 1971; MS, Cogate Rochester Sem., 1985; PhD, Georgetown U., 1990. Asst. prof. Georgetown U., Washington, 1989—; chmn. Asian Theol. Congress, Singapore, 1983-84; chmn. Hist. Lit. Symposium, 1988; del. Congress Bibl. Archeologists, 1990; chmn. S.W. Spiritual and Theol. Conf, 1991. Author: Ballal and Christ, 1982, Urban Christianity in the 1st Century, 1989, Berashith and Minor Prophets, 1990; editor: the Mimetic Jesus, 1985; editor Agama-Apoliti, Jakarta, Indonesia, 1978-82, Asian Religious Lit. Jour. Singapore, 1982-84, Am. Theologian, 1986-89; contbg. editor S.W. Spirituality, 1991—. Del. U.S. Bicentennial Commn., Washington, 1987-90. Mem. Am. Congress Bibl. Lit. (sec. gen. 1991), Soc. Bib. Lit., Am. Acad. Religion (assoc.), Assn. Am. Hebrew Scholars (pres. 1990-91), Md. Hist. Restoration Soc. (pres. 1987). Home: PO Box 873 Tijeras NM 87059

VAN IERSEL, BASTIAAN MARTINUS, theology educator; b. Heerlen, Limburg, The Netherlands, Sept. 27, 1924. PhD in Theology, Cath. U. Nymegen, 1953, Dr. Theology, 1961. Joined Montfort Fathers, 1944; ordained priest Roman Cath. Ch., 1950. Asst. Faculty of Theology, Cath. U. Nymegen, 1960-66, lectr., 1966-71, full prof. theology, 1971-90, dean faculty theology, 1969-70, 72-73, bd. dirs., 1974-76, rector magnificus, 1987-90; bd. dirs. Katholieke Bybelstichting, The Netherlands, 1965—, Concilium; chmn. bd. Stegon, 1986-92. Author: Reading Mark; editor Concilium Jour., 1965—, Schrift Jour., 1969—, also others. Chmn. bd. Found. Prof. Mr. W.P.J. Pompe Clinic, Nymegen, 1977-80, Inst. for the Blind "Theofaan", 1982—. Grantee Netherlands Orgn. for Advancement Pure Rsch., 1970-75. Mem. Studiorum Novi Testamenti Societas. Home: Mgr Suyslaan 4, 6564 BV Heiligland Stichting The Netherlands

VAN KLEEK, LAURENCE MCKEE (LAURIE VAN KLEEK), minister, librarian, educator; b. Vancouver, B.C., Can., Dec. 14, 1944; m. Darlene H. Van Kleek, May 11, 1974; children: Lineke E., Kyle L., Benjamin C. ThB diploma, Western Pentecostal Bible Coll., 1969; BA, Wilfrid Laurier U., 1971; MDiv, Waterloo Luth. Sem., 1972; MA, Assemblies of God Theol. Sem., 1977; libr. technician diploma, Fraser Valley Coll., 1984; MLS, U. B.C., 1988. Ordained to ministry Pentecostal Assemblies Can., 1975. Lectr. Western Pentecostal Assemblies Can., 1975; lectr. Western Pentecostal Bible Coll., Clayburn, B.C., 1972-76, libr., asst. prof., 1978—; supply chaplain Regional Psychiat. Centre, Abbotsford, B.C., 1978—. Vol. in prison ministry Regional Psychiat. Centre, 1975-77. Gale-Beitel Meml. scholar, 1965. Mem. Assn. Christian Librs., B.C. Libr. Assn., Can. Libr. Assn., Northwest Assn. Christian Librs. Home: 32216 Mouat Dr, Abbotsford (Clearbrook), BC Canada V2T 4H9 Office: Western Pentecostal Bible Coll, 35235 Straiton Rd, Clayburn, BC Canada V0X 1E0 also: PO Box 1700, Abbotsford, BC Canada V2S 7E7 *To God I am so grateful for my wife, children and vocation. I enjoy immensely serving as a librarian and wish that more people could be as contented with vocation as I am.*

VANLANINGHAM, TODD ALAN, minister; b. Winfield, Kans., July 9, 1956; s. E.L. and Lois (Zehnder) VanL. BA, Calif. State U., 1983; MDiv, Pacific Luth. Theol. Sem., 1986. Ordained minister in Luth. Ch. Intern pastor Prince of Peace Luth. Ch., Saratoga, Calif., 1984-85; pastor Luth. Ch. of Our Redeemer, Sacramento, 1986—; Luth. rep. No. Calif. Ecumenical Commn., Sacramento, 1986-90. Author: (with others) Protocol for Care of HIV-ARC-AIDS in Northern California, 1989. Mem. pub. affairs com. Planned Parenthood Fedn. of Sacramento Valley, Sacramento, 1987-89. Democrat. Office: Luth Ch of Our Redeemer 4641 Marconi Ave Sacramento CA 95821

VAN LEEUWEN, CORNELIS, religion educator; b. Amsterdam, Mar. 11, 1924; s. Wijnand and Antonia Hendrika (Boon) van L.; m. Adriana Valk. PhD, State U. Utrecht, The Netherlands, 1949, U. Amsterdam, 1954. Minister Dutch Reformed Ch., Maarn-Maarsbergen, The Netherlands, 1948-56, Elst, The Netherlands, 1956-64; minister Psychiatric Hosp., Ermelo, The Netherlands, 1964-70; Old Testament scholar State U. Utrecht, The Netherlands, 1966-76, prof. Old Testament, 1977-91. Author: Le Développement du Sens Social en Israël, 1954, Commentary on Hosea, 1968, Commentary on Amos, 1985; co-author: (with A. R. Hulst) Liberation in the Old Testament, 1986 (in Dutch).

VAN LEEUWEN, RAYMOND CORNELIUS, religion and theology educator; b. Artesia, Calif., Oct. 2, 1948; s. Cornelis and Greta (Kruithof) Van L.; m. V. Mary Stewart, May 31, 1975; children: Kenneth Dirk, D. S. Neil. BA, Calvin Coll., 1971; MA, St. Michael's Coll., Toronto, Ont., Can., 1975, PhD, 1984; BD, Calvin Theol. Sem., 1976. Ordained to ministry Christian Reformed Ch., 1986. Vis. instr. Calvin Theol. Sem., Grand Rapids, Mich., 1981-82; instr., asst. prof. Calvin Coll., Grand Rapids, 1982-85; asst. to assoc. prof. old testament Calvin Theol. Sem., Grand Rapids, Mich., 1985-90; prof. religion and theology Calvin Coll., Grand Rapids, 1990—; assoc. minister 1st Christian Reformed Ch., 1986-90. Author: Context and Meaning in Proverbs 25-27, 1988; contbr. articles to profl. jours. Fellowship Ont. Govt., Toronto, 1979-81, Social Scis. and Human Rsch. Coun. Can., 1980-81; Calvin Alumni Faculty Rsch. grant, 1986, Faculty Enrichment grant U. Mich., 1990. Mem. Soc. Bibl. Lit. (v.p. Midwest region 1990, sec. 1986-90, nat. coun. 1989—, editorial com.), Chgo. Soc. Bibl. Rsch., Inst. for Bibl. Rsch., Nat. Assn. Profs. Hebrew. Home: 1924 Lenawee SE Grand Rapids MI 49506 Office: Calvin Coll Grand Rapids MI 49546 *To tell the truth is hard. To live it is both hard and easy. For the truth is we live by dying.*

VAN LIERE, CARMA PARKHURST, retired English language educator, writer; b. Garrett, Ind., Sept. 23, 1918; d. Frank and Albertine (Johnson) Parkhurst; m. Donald W. Van Liere, Sept. 19, 1941; children: Jean, Mark, Pat, Judy, Eric, Christopher. AB with hons., Ind. U., 1940, MA, 1946. Instr. English Western Mich U., Kalamazoo, 1954, 56, 66-71, 75-80. Author: Hallowed Fire, 1991; contbr. articles to religious jours. Mem. AAUW, YWCA (bd. dirs. Kalamazoo chpt. 1970), Evang. Women's Caucus, Phi Beta Kappa. Mem. Reformed Ch. in Am. Home: 2011 Timberlane Kalamazoo MI 49008 *Christian women need to know what the Bible really tells us and what our history as women in religion has been. Then we can be empowered to active discipleship.*

VAN METER, JAMES GORDON, missionary; b. San Diego, May 13, 1944; s. Burt Gordon and Elaine (Remple) Van M.; m. Leta June Copeland, June 3, 1967; children: John Mark, Joy Lynette. BA, San Diego State U., 1966; ThM, Dallas Theol. Sem., 1970. Missionary to Indonesia Overseas Crusades Inc., 1972-82, Indonesian field dir., 1980-82, missionary to Philippines, 1983-89, north team dir. Philippine Crusades, 1986-89, attrition survey coord., 1990-91; dir. tng. Overseas Crusades Internat., Milpitas, Calif., 1991—; lectr. Asian Ctr. for Missionary Edn., Manila, 1983-86; cons. Shalomita Missions Inc., Jakarta, Indonesia, 1976-78; adj. prof. Indonesian Evang. Inst., Batu Malang, Indonesia, 1980-82, E. Java Bible Inst. of Assemblies of God, Karanglo, Indonesia, 1980-82, coord. Philippine Nat. Missions Com., Manila, 1986-89. Coord. Nat. Missions Cons. 1986; mem. sch. bd. Bogor Expatriate Sch., Indonesia, 1974-75, Wesley Internat. Sch., Indonesia, 1980-82; pres. Faith Acad. Assn., Phillipines, 1985-87; mem. South Hills Community Ch., San Jose, Calif. Avocations: tennis, piano, singing. Office: O C Internat 25 Corning Ave Milpitas CA 95035

VAN OOSTENBURG, GORDON L., pastor; b. Grand Rapids, Mich., Sept. 2, 1921; s. William and Lena (Huyser) Van O.; m. Mildred Elizabeth Timmer, June 13, 1946; children: Mark Gordon, Mavis Elizabeth, Paul Gary, Philip John. Student, Western Theol. Sem., 1949. Pastor New Era (Mich.) Reformed Ch., 1949-52, First Reformed Ch., Midland Park, N.J., 1952-56, Bethany Reformed Ch., Grand Rapids, 1956-62; pastor Trinity Reformed Ch., Holland, Mich., 1962-78, Lynden, Wash., 1978-85; pastor Richmond Reformed Ch., Grand Rapids, 1985-89; pres. gen. synod Reformed Ch. in Am., N.Y.C., 1964-65; mem. exec. com. Words of Hope Radio Broadcast, Grand Rapids, 1986—; bd. dirs. Reformed Bible Coll., Grand Rapids. Lt. (j.g.) USN, 1943-46, PTO. Home: 153 Katherine NE Grand Rapids MI 49505

VANORSOW, ALICE MARIE, lay worker; b. Willow City, N.D., Mar. 11, 1931; d. Emil Wilhelm and Laura Elizabeth (Pick) Nilson; m. J. Lynn Pearson, July 9, 1952 (div. 1962); children: Victoria Lynne Ohm, Kristine Anne Wilson, Mark Steven. Student, Luth. Bible Inst., 1951, Swedish Hosp. Sch. Nursing, 1951-52; BA, Rocky Mt. Synod ELCA, 1990. Cert. assoc. ministry Evang. Luth. Ch. in Am., 1990. Christian edn. dir. King of Glory Luth. Ch., Loveland, Colo., 1987-90; Christian edn. dir./youth ministry Grace Evang. Luth. Ch., Lakeland, Fla., 1991—; del. Rocky Mt. Synod Luth. Ch. Women, Englewood, Colo., 1983, Rocky Mt. Synod Luth. Ch. of Am., Cheyenne, Wyo., 1985; no. Colo. dist. assembly chairperson Luth. Ch. Women, Loveland, 1985-87. Bd. mem. PTA, Annandale, Minn., 1964-66; bd. mem. Luth. Women of Loveland, 1980-82; br. sec., vol. Luth. Brotherhood Br. 8693, Loveland, 1987-89; charter mem. Hospice Aux., Loveland, 1986. Mem. Assocs. in Ministry Evang. Luth. Ch. Am. (rostered), Lake Conf. Clergy & Assoc. in Ministry, Fla. Synod Clergy & Assocs. in Ministry. Office: Grace Evang Luth Ch 745 S Ingraham Ave Box 2526 Lakeland FL 33806

VAN PAY, RANDY JOHN, pastor; b. Green Bay, Wis., July 17, 1949; s. Donald Henry Van Pay and Betty (Werner) Copley; m. Mary Kathryn Sellers, Nov. 28, 1970; children: John Mark, Shara Lee, Ricky Morgan. BS, Southwestern Assemblies of God Coll., 1972. Ordained to ministry Assemblies of God. Evangelist Assemblies of God, U.S.A., 1972-74; sr. pastor Calvary Assembly of God, Monroe, Wis., 1974-78, Magnolia Christian Ctr., Port Neches, Tex., 1978-84, Grace Assembly of God, Salem, N.H., 1984-88, Victory Assembly of God, Universal City, Tex., 1988—; built 1st three chs. as sr. pastor, 1974-87; contact chaplain RAFB Assemblies of God, Universal City, 1988—; committeeman Assemblies of God San Antonio Sect., 1990—. Home: 4819 Wedgewood Cibolo TX 78108

VAN PELT, W(ESLEY) AUSTIN, clergyman, educator; b. Rahway, N.J., Aug. 24, 1930; s. Charles Wesley and Grace Elizabeth (DeHart) Van P.; m. Elenor Kramer, June 11, 1952; children: Mary, Anne, Peter, David. BA, Maryville Coll., 1952; MDiv, Louisville Presbyn. Sem., 1955; MA, U. Denver, 1964, PhD, 1970. Ordained to ministry Presbyn. Ch. U.S.A., mem. faculty Maryville (Tenn.) Coll., 1954-57, Sheldon Jackson Jr. Coll., Sitka, Alaska, 1957-59; gen. mgr. Sta. KSEW, 1959-61; pastor, New Castle, Pa., 1961-63; asst. prof. sociology Peru State Coll., 1964-68; dean Arapahoe Community Coll., Littleton, Colo., 1969-75, instr. sociology, 1976-87; pastor 1st Presbyn. Ch., Leadville, Colo., 1987—; interim pastor chs., Colo., Alaska, Utah, Wyo., 1984—; Synod of Rocky Mountains, chair advocacy com., moderator com. on boundries; adj. prof. U. Denver, 1976, McCormick Theol. Sem., Chgo., 1979-81, Colo. Mountain Coll. Mem. NEA, Colo. Edn. Assn., Presbytery of Denver. Office: 1st Presbyn Ch PO Box 498 Leadville CO 80461

VANSANDT, VAN HENRY, evangelist; b. Okinawa, Japan, Aug. 14, 1961; came to U.S., 1962; s. James Ira and Bonita Marie (Henry) V.; m. Maryanne Adcock, May 15, 1982; 1 child, Van Henry Jr. BS, Freed Hardeman Coll., 1984. Minister Fairbury (Ill.) Ch. of Christ, 1979; assoc. minister Hwy. Ch. of Christ, Sullivan, Ill., 1980, Refuge Ch. of Christ, Bethel Springs, Tenn., 1980-82, Independence Ch. of Christ, Lexington, Tenn., 1982-83; evangelist Lakeview Ch. of Christ, Samburg, Tenn., 1983-84; assoc. minister Humboldt (Tenn.) Ch. of Christ, 1984-87; evangelist Adamsville Ch. of Christ, 1988—; co-planner Annual Reelfoot Youth Rally, Hornbeak, 1985-87. Editor Ch. Bulletin, 1987. Named one of Outstanding Young Men Am., 1985. Mem. Ch. of Christ. Club: Preachers (Henderson, Tenn.) (v.p. 1981-82, pres. 1982-83). Avocations: sports, guitar, singing. Home: 210 Baptist St PO Box 838 Adamsville TN 38310 Office: Adamsville Ch of Christ Adamsville TN 38310

VANSELOW, DUANE ROBERT, pastor; b. Milw., May 19, 1949; s. Duane Orlando and Melba Ruth (Schallock) V.; m. Janis Robin Horvath, June 12, 1976; children: Andrew, Matthew, Sarah. BA, Northwestern Coll., Watertown, Wis., 1974; MDiv, Wis. Luth. Sem., Mequon, 1978. Ordained to ministry Luth. Ch., 1978. Pastor Beautiful Savior Evang. Luth. Ch., Corvallis, Oreg., 1978—; cir. pastor Oreg.-Idaho Cir. of the Pacific N.W. Dist., Wis. Evang. Luth. Synod, 1988—. With U.S. Army, 1970-72, Vietnam. Republican. Home: 2685 NW 13th St Corvallis OR 97330 Office: Beautiful Savior Evang Luth Ch 2605 NW 13th St Corvallis OR 97330

VAN SETERS, JOHN, biblical literature educator; b. Hamilton, Ont., Can., May 2, 1935; s. Hugo and Anne (Hubert) Van S.; m. Elizabeth Marie Malmberg, June 11, 1960; children: Peter John, Deborah Elizabeth. B.A., U. Toronto, 1958; M.A., Yale U., 1959, Ph.D., 1965; B.D., Princeton Theol. Sem., 1962. Asst. prof. dept. Near Eastern studies Waterloo Luth. U., 1965-67; asso. prof. Old Testament Andover Newton Theol. Sch., 1967-70; asso. prof. dept. Near Eastern studies U. Toronto, 1970-76, prof., 1976-77; James A. Gray prof. Bibl. lit., dept. religion U. N.C., Chapel Hill, 1977—; chmn. dept. religious studies U. N.C., 1980-88. Author: The Hyksos: A New Investigation, 1966, Abraham in History and Tradition, 1975, In Search of History, 1983, Der Jahwist als Historiker, 1987. Recipient James Henry Breasted prize Am. Hist. Assn., 1985, Book award Am. Acad. Religion, 1986; Woodrow Wilson fellow, 1958; J.J. Obermann fellow, 1962-64; Guggenheim fellow, 1979-80; NEH fellow, 1985-86, ACLS fellow, 1991—. Mem. Soc. Bibl. Lit., Am. Schs. Oriental Research, Soc. Study of Egyptian Antiquities, AAUP, Am. Oriental Soc. Mem. United Ch. of Christ. Home: 104 Mullin Ct Chapel Hill NC 27514 Office: 101 Saunders Hall Univ of NC Chapel Hill NC 27599

VAN STONE, RAYMOND JAMES, minister; b. Bklyn., Jan. 11, 1928; s. Albert Edward Van Stone and Pauline Friedman; m. Elizabeth Tamblyn Hicks, Jan. 11, 1968. BA, Maryville (Tenn.) Coll., 1956; STB, N.Y. Theol. Sem, 1961, MST, 1961; LHD (hon.), Windsor Locks, Conn., 1985. Ordained to ministry Presbyn. Ch. (U.S.A.), 1961. Pastor Presbyn. Ch., Wyo., Wash., N.Y., 1961-91; mem. Wyo. Ann. Conf., United Meth. Ch., Equinunk, Pa., Charge and Camptown, Pa., 1972-79. With USN, 1945-52; with U.S. Army 1962-63,. Mem. VFW. Republican. Home and Office: PO Box 127 Maple Ave Tioga Center NY 13845-0127

VAN TIL, ALYSSA BARBARA, religious educator; b. Phila., Jan. 3, 1936; d. Henry R. and Elizabeth (Zandstra) Van T.; 1 child, Edward James. BA in English, Calvin Coll., Grand Rapids, Mich., 1957; MA in Lit., U. Mich., 1968; MA, Western Mich. U., 1978; ordained, Unity Sch., Unity Village, Mo., 1990. High sch. English tchr. various schs., 1957-71; adult edn. tchr. Grand Rapids, 1971-78; Bible interpretation tchr. Unity Sch., 1985—. Mem. AAUW, Am. Acad. Religion, Soc. Bibl. Lit., Holy Women (leader 1986—). Mem. Assn. Unity Chs. Office: Unity Sch for Religious Studies Unity Village MO 64065

VANTINE, DONALD ARTHUR, lay worker; b. Nehawka, Nebr., Sept. 26, 1919; s. Harry Elmer and Hanna (Hansen) V.; m. Alice Loriene Pothast, Feb. 26, 1947 (wid. July 1979); children: Don, Scot; m. Dorothy Andrea Harmes, Aug. 15, 1981; stepchildren: Michael A. Innis, Mary Elizabeth Innis Garber, Susan Innis Collins. Grad. high sch., Tecumseh, Nebr. Commd. U.S. Army, advanced through grades to col., retired, 1970; lay leader Alexandria (Va.) dist. United Meth. Ch., 1974-84; sec. Va. Conf. Coun. on Ministries, Richmond, 1976-84; treas. ST. John's United Meth. Ch., Springfield, Va., 1975-84, Duncan Meml. United Meth. Ch., Berryville, Va., 1985—; chmn. Commn. on Equitable Salaries, Richmond, 1984—; del. Va. Annual Conf., various cities, 1971—, Southeastern Jurisdiction Conf., Lake Junaluska, N.C., 1976, 84, 88; first res. del. Gen. Conf., Balt., 1984. Pres. Clarke Unit, Am. Cancer Soc., Berryville, Va., 1989-91. Decorated Legion of Merit. Mem. Lions. Home and Office: Rte 2 Box 107A5 Boyce VA 22620

VAN TINE, JOHN WILLIAM, minister; b. Phila., Nov. 3, 1946; s. Karldon Kynett and Ruth (Cherry) Van T.; m. Virginia Roosa, July 18, 1970; children: Peter, Lynne. AA, Wesley Coll., Dovr, Del., 1967; BA, Greensboro (N.C.) Coll., 1969; MDiv, Wesley Theol. Sem., Washington, 1973. Ordained to ministry United Meth. Ch., 1970. Pastor St. James Charge United Meth. Ch., Worton, Md., 1970-73, Cheswold (Del.) Charge United Meth. Ch., 1973-77, Queen Anne (Md.) Charge United Meth. Ch., 1977-83, Oxford (Md.) Charge United Meth. Ch., 1983-89; pastor of pastoral care Aldersgate Charge, Wilmington, Del., 1989—; chmn. progam com.-ethnic local ch. com., Dover, Del., 1990—, Inclusive Lang. Sect., Racial Incl. Com., Dover, 1990—; pres. Talbot County Ecumenical Assn., Easton, 1987-88; chmn. program com. Camp Pecometh, Centreville, Md., 1986-88; chaplain Oxford (Md.) Fire Co., 1985-89, Easton Meml. Hosp., 1978-89. Mem. Nat. Assn. Christians and Jews, Ruritan (chaplain 1983-89). Office: Aldersgate United Meth Ch 2313 Concord Pike Wilmington DE 19803 *God's gift of grace through Jesus Christ is offered to all people regardless of their race, sex, or economic situation. I believe that this is the purpose of the Church and its ministry to extend that grace.*

VAN VALIN, CLYDE EMORY, bishop; b. Windham, N.Y., Nov. 24, 1929; s. Ernest Clyde and Josephine Louise (Howard) Van V.; m. Beatrice Mae Roushey, Aug. 25, 1950; children: Carolyn, Wendell, Martha, Luella, Loretta. A.B., Roberts Wesleyan Coll., North Chili, N.Y., 1951; B.D., Asbury Theol. Sem., Wilmore, Ky., 1954, D.D. (hon.), 1972. Ordained deacon Free Meth. Ch. N.Am., 1954, elder, 1955, consecrated bishop, 1976. Pastor Free Meth. Ch., Allentown, Pa., 1954-58; Eastern regional dir. Free Meth. youth, Winona Lake, Ind., 1958-60; dir., chaplain John Wesley Sem. Found., Wilmore, 1960-74, asst. dir., 1974-76; pastor Wilmore Free Meth. Ch., 1961-76; bishop Free Meth. Ch. N.Am., Winona Lake, 1976-91; internat. quizmaster Free Meth. Youth, 1958-60; chmn. bd. dirs. Nat. Coalition Against Pornography, 1988-91; pres., bd. dirs. Free Meth. Ch., 1985-91, pres. bd. adminstrn., 1985-89; pres. Free Meth. World Fellowship, 1985-89; chmn. constl. counsel Free Meth. Ch., 1985—, pres. bd. adminstrn., 1985, 89; chmn. Free Meth. Bd. of Bishops, 1989-90; chmn. study commn. on doctrine, Free Meth. Ch., 1979-85, 90—. Author: Transforming Grace and Tithing, God's Plan for the Church, 1990; editor: Pastor's Handbook Free Methodist Church of North America, 1982. Trustee Asbury Theol. Sem., 1982-91. Named Today's Young Leader, Roberts Wesleyan Coll., 1959; recipient Disting. Service award Asbury Theol. Sem., 1973. Mem. Christian Holiness Assn. (dir.), Theta Phi. Republican. Club: Nicholasville Rotary (Ky.) (hon. life).

VAN VALKENBURG, WILLIAM LEE, minister; b. Hudson, Mich., June 23, 1951; s. William Gene and Hazel Betty (Biddix) Van V.; m. Rosalyn Ann Chroninger, June 10, 1978; children: William, Andrew, Timothy. B in Ministry summa cum laude, Bethany Bible Coll., 1988; M in Ministry summa cum laude, Bethany Theol. Sem., 1991; postgrad., Ea. Mich. U., 1990—. Ordained to ministry Bapt. Ch., 1975. Home missionary RBM Ministries, Plainwell, Mich., 1972-75; interim pastor 1st Bapt. Ch., Morenci, Mich., 1975-76; sr. pastor Olive Br. Christian Union Ch., Fayette, Ohio, 1977-79, Seneca (Mich.) Community Ch., 1983—; speaker in field on behalf of elderly population. Mem. exec. bd. Lenawee Widowed Person's Svc. Mem. Gerontol. Soc. Am., Lenawee County Hist. Soc. Office: Seneca Community Ch 8547 Seneca Hwy Seneca MI 49280

VAN VLIET, DAVID R., minister; b. Lincoln, Nebr., Oct. 4, 1957; s. John Edward and Myrna Jean (Johnson) Van V.; m. Fay Ellen Persons, June 13, 1981; children: Ginger Renae, Emily Michelle, Anna Marjorie. Student, Moody Bible Inst., 1975-77, 78; B in Bibl. Sci., Western Bible Coll., 1980; ThM, Dallas Theol. Sem., 1987. Ordained to ministry Midlothian Bible Ch., 1987. Pastor Burr Oak Ch., Eddyville, Nebr., 1987-90, Woodland Community Ch., Westboro, Wis., 1990—.

VAN ZANDT, RICHARD LOUIS, broadcasting executive; b. Elmhurst, Ill., Sept. 27, 1948; s. Richard and Rosalie Van Zandt; m. Patricia Pedtke, Aug. 8, 1970; children: Jacqueline, Carolyn, Noah. Student, Elgin Community Coll., No. Ill. U. Cert. 1st class FCC. Engr. Sta. WEMI Radio, Menasha, Wis., 1979-82; pres. Cornerstone Radio, New Smyrna Beach, Fla., 1983—; mgr. Sta. WLUJ Radio, Petersburg, Ill., 1985—, Sta. WJLU Radio, New Smyrna Beach, 1988—. Mem. Soc. Broadcast Engrs. Office: Sta WJLU Radio 2596 State Rd 44 New Smyrna Beach FL 32168

VARGAS, DANIEL GOMEZ, youth leader; b. Watsonville, Calif., Feb. 19, 1955; s. Jesse Jimenez Vargas and Mary (Gomez) Torres; m. June 15, 1981 (div. Oct. 1990); children: Carlos Rodriguez, Danny Alexis Jr., Delilah Raquel. Student, Patten Coll., 1991—. Sunday sch. worker Christian Cathedral, Oakland, Calif., 1989—, jr. high sch. youth leader, 1990—. With U.S. Army, 1972-75. Democrat. Christian Evangelical. Home: 2350 Coolidge Ave C Oakland CA 94601 Office: Patten Coll Christian Cathedral 2433 Coolidge Ave Oakland CA 94601 *We must reach our youth for Christ now. Youth are not the church of tomorrow but of today. We should minister to them with fervor, as time is running out and many souls are being lost.*

VARGAS, MANUEL JOHN, clinical psychologist, consultant; b. Ft. Worth, Aug. 30, 1919; s. Hermenegildo and Macedonia (Toledo) V.; m.

Judith Wells, Oct. 4, 1975 (div. May 1986); children: Philip, Richard, Veronica; m. Elizabeth A. Brown, Feb. 4, 1989. BA, U. Chgo., 1943, MA, 1944, PhD, 1952. Lic. psychologist, Ill., Ind. Asst. prof. psychology Auburn (Ala.) U., 1952-55; chief psychologist Beatty Meml. State Hosp., Westville, Ind., 1958-63, Adult Psychiatric Ctr., Ft. Wayne, Ind., 1963-64, Lake County Mental Health Clinic, Gary, Ind., 1964-75; psychologist Psychol. Svcs., Merrillville, Ind., 1975—; cons. Lake County Juvenile Ct., Gary, 1964-75, Southlake Care Ctr., Merrillville, 1982-86, Wildwood Manor, Gary, 1975-84; lectr. in psychology Ind. U. Northwest, Gary, 1972-75. Mem. 1st violin sect. N.W. Ind. Symphony Orchestra, 1965-84. Office: Psychol Svcs 1000 E 80th Pl Merrillville IN 46410 *The Creator has given each one a part of Itself and also sent great teachers in ongoing revelations of the universal reality. We are to seek the One Life in God and the Brotherhood of All. Let us seek the kingdom within.*

VARGO, EDWARD PAUL, priest, English and literature educator; b. Lorain, Ohio, Aug. 10, 1935; s. Joseph and Julia (Dobos) V. A.A., Divine Word Coll., Conesus, N.Y., 1955; A.B., Divine Word Sem., Techny, Ill., 1957; A.M., U. Chgo., 1964, Ph.D., 1968. Ordained priest, Roman Catholic Ch., 1963. Instr. Divine Word Coll., Epworth, Iowa, 1965-66, assoc. prof., 1966-73, chmn. dept. English, 1966-73; assoc. prof. Fu Jen U., Taipei, Taiwan, 1974—, dean Coll. Fgn. Langs., 1984-90, trustee, 1981-84, trustee Middle Sch., 1986—; dir. overseas tng. program Soc. Divine Word, Taipei, 1980-84, provincial consultor, 1981-87; vis. scholar Harvard U., 1990-92. Author: Rainstorms and Fire, 1973; editor Jour. Fu Jen Studies, 1974—; contbr. articles to profl. publs. U. Chgo. fellow, 1964, 66; Ford Found. fellow, 1967; recipient Nat. Sci. Council Research awards Republic China, 1985, 86, 87, 88, 89. Mem. MLA, Nat. Council Tchrs. English. Democrat. Roman Catholic. Avocation: hiking. Home and Office: Fu Jen U, 24205 Hsinchuang, Taiwan Republic of China also: 184 Beacon St Boston MA 02116

VARNER, IVORY LEON, clergyman; b. Liberty, Tex., Nov. 25, 1948; s. Leo Varner and Lillie Pearl (Redman) Grandney; m. Mary Virginia Polk, Nov. 4, 1971; children: Catina Nicole, Ivory Lemont. BS, Prairie View A&M U., 1970; postgrad., Dallas Theol. Sem. Ordained to ministry Bapt. Ch. Asst. pastor New Jerusalem Bapt. Ch., Dickinson, Tex., 1978; sr. pastor Bible Way Fellowship Bapt. Ch., Houston, 1979—; mem. adv. com. Urban Alternative, Houston, 1990. Address: Bible Way Fellowship Bapt Ch 9000 Frey Rd Houston TX 77034

VARSBERGS, VILIS, minister, religious organization administrator; b. Prauliena, Latvia, June 1, 1929; s. Viktors and Marta (Barbans) V.; m. Biruta Grinbergs, July 2, 1960; children: Anita Valda, Krista Maija, Victor Andrew. BA magna cum laude, Midland Coll., 1954; MDiv, Luth. Sch. Theology, Chgo., 1957. Ordained to ministry United Luth. Ch., 1957. Mission developer, pastor Grace Luth. Ch., Albion, Mich., 1957-63; pastor Messiah Luth. Ch., Constantine, Mich., 1963-69; adminstr., dir. Latvian Ctr. Garezers, Inc., Three Rivers, Mich., 1969-72; pastor Zion Latvian Luth. Ch., Chgo., 1973—; pres. Latvian Evang. Luth. Ch. in Am., 1984—; assembly del. Luth. World Fedn., Budapest, Hungary, 1984, Curitiba, Brazil, 1990. Sec. Helsinki Monitoring Com., Chgo., 1983-85; mem. adv. bd. Ill. Ethnic Cons., Chgo., 1986; bd. dirs. Luth. Immigration & Refugee Svc., N.Y.C., 1988—. Office: Zion Latvian Luth Ch 6551 W Montrose Ave Chicago IL 60634

VASEY, WILLIAM LESLIE, minister; b. Dodgeville, Wis., Oct. 19, 1943; s. William and Norine Virginia (Ashcraft) V.; m. Rachel Ann Huss, Oct. 23, 1964; children: Amy Lynn, Nathan David. BS, Wheaton (Ill.) Coll., 1965; postgrad., Prim. Meth. Sch. Theo., Wilkes-Barre, Pa., 1971, U. Tex., 1974. Pastor Primitive Meth. Ch., Hyde Park, N.Y., 1965-68; missionary Internat. Mission Bd., Guatemala, 1968-84, field dir., 1978-84; gen. dir. Internat. Mission Bd., Youngstown, Ohio, 1985; pastor Glenwood Primitive Meth. Ch., Youngstown, Ohio, 1984—. Builder reconstruction after earthquake in Guatemala, 1976-78; translator El Nuevo Testamento en Quiche de Joyabaj, 1983. Mem. Rotary. Republican. Avocations: golf, hunting. Home: 155 Rockland Dr Youngstown OH 44512 Office: Glenwood Primitive Meth Ch 7872 Glenwood Ave Youngstown OH 44512

VASQUEZ, EDMUNDO EUSEBIO, religious organization administrator; b. Chacon, N.Mex., May 14, 1932; s. Eusebio and Dora (Ortiz) V.; B.A., N.Mex. Highlands U., 1953; postgrad. U. Colo., 1958, Brigham Young U., 1959; M.A., Stanford U., 1961; postgrad. U. Costa Rica, 1966; m. Carol Vallendar, June 16, 1957 (div. Aug. 1978); children—Amarante, Daniel, Amalio; m. Jane Atkins, Nov. 1983. With Sta. KFUN, 1949-53; dean Wasatch Acad., Mt. Pleasant, Utah, 1955-65; dean Colegio Americano, Ibagué, Colombia, 1966-71; pres. Menaul Sch., (Albuquerque, 1971-78; agt. Nat. Life of Vt. and Northwestern Mut. Life, Albuquerque, 1978-81; dir. So. Calif. Found., 1981—; rep. United Presbyn. Found., 1981—; cons. in field; lectr., cons. Hispanic affairs; cons. multicultural edn. Bd. dirs. United Presbyn. Health, Edn. and Welfare Assn., 1975-78, March of Dimes, 1976-79, ARC, 1979-82; trustee San Francisco Theol. Sem., San Anselmo, Calif., 1982—; fundraiser charitable and polit. orgns. Served with USAF, 1953-55. Mem. Assn. Supervision and Curriculum Devel., Nat. Assn. Life Underwriters. Clubs: Rotary, Lions, Masons. Office: So Calif Found 1501 Wilshire Blvd Los Angeles CA 90017

VASQUEZ ELIZALDE, SERAFIN, bishop; b. St. Martin Xaltocan, Mexico, Sept. 13, 1922. Ordained priest Roman Cath. Ch., 1948. Named bishop, 1968; bishop of Ciudad Guzman Jalisco, Mexico, 1978—. Office: Ramon Corona, 26 Apartado 86, Ciudad Guzman Jalisco, Mexico

VASSAR, MILAS ROBERT, pastor; b. Huntsville, Ala., May 5, 1953; s. Milas Robert Sr. and Mary Martha (Roberson) V.; m. Lisa Renee Johnson, Jan. 13, 1965; 1 child, Mary Elizabeth. BA, Samford U., 1975; MDiv, Southern Baptist Theol. Seminary, 1980. Ordained to Baptist Ch., 1980. Youth dir. Lincoln Meml. Baptist Ch., Huntsville, Ala., 1974; minister of youth Ruhama Baptist Ch., Birmingham, Ala., 1974-76; minister of youth First Baptist Ch., Shelbyville, Ky., 1977-80, assoc. pastor, 1980-83, pastor, 1983—. Mem. Juvenile Justice Commn., Ky.; exec. bd. Ky. Bapt. Conv., 1985-88. Named one of Outstanding Young Men of Am., 1984. Mem. Shelby County Ministerial Alliance (v.p. 1982-83). Democrat. Baptist. Avocations: photography, sports. Home: 152 Cheyenne Rd Shelbyville KY 40065 Office: First Baptist Ch 1516 W Main St Shelbyville KY 40065

VASSILAQUI, ALEJANDRO, international religious organization administrator. Pres. World Alliance of YMCA, Geneva. Office: World Alliance of YMCA, 37 Quai Wilson, 1201 Geneva Switzerland*

VAUGHAN, AUSTIN BERNARD, bishop; b. N.Y.C., Sept. 27, 1927; s. Austin Bernard and Delia (Considine) V. A.B., St. Joseph's Sem., 1948; S.T.D., Gregorian U., 1954. Ordained priest Roman Catholic Ch., 1951; tchr. modern langs. Cathedral Coll., N.Y.C., 1955-56; prof. theology St. Joseph's Sem., Yonkers, N.Y., 1956-73; rector St. Joseph's Sem., Yonkers, 1973-79; aux. bishop of N.Y., 1977—; vicar for Orange County, 1979—; chmn. Nat. Conf. Cath. Bishops Com. on Human Values, from 1977; U.S. del. World Synod of Bishops, 1983. Mem. Cath. Theol. Soc. Am. (pres. 1968-69), Mariological Soc. Am. (pres. 1971-73), Coll. Theology Soc. Office: St Patrick's Ch 55 Grand St Newburgh NY 12550

VAUGHAN, JOHN NOLEN, minister; b. Memphis, Nov. 23, 1941; s. Nolen L. and Montez (Cannon) V.; m. Joanne Wooten, Jan. 26, 1962; children: Johnna, John. Student, Union U., 1959-61; BA in Sociology and History, Memphis State U., 1964; MDiv, Southwestern Bapt. Theol. Sem., 1967; D of Ministry, Fuller Theol. Sem., 1984. Ordained to ministry Bapt. Ch., 1962. Assoc. pastor Westridge Bapt. Ch., Euless, Tex., 1964-67; asst. pastor Hunter St. Bapt. Ch., Birmingham, Ala., 1967-69; pastor U. Bapt. Ch., Iowa City, 1969-73; asst. pastor Trinity Bapt. Ch., Memphis, 1973-77, Briarcrest Bapt. Ch., Memphis, 1977-85; asst. prof. ch. growth and chmn. ch. growth S.W. Bapt. U., Bolivar, Mo., 1985—. Author: The World's 20 Largest Churches, 1984, The Large Church, 1985, Absolutely Double, 1990; co-author: The Complete Book of Church Growth, 1980, Church Growth-State of the Art, 1988; editor: North American Society for Church Growth. Founder, dir. Internat. Mega-Ch. Rsch. Ctr., Bolivar. Recipient Cert. of Merit Cambridge, Eng., 1985. Mem. Assn. of Statiticians of Am. Religious Bodies, N.Am. Soc. for Ch. Growth, So. Baptist Rsch. Fellowship.

VAUGHAN, PAUL IRVINE, minister; b. Toronto, Ont., Can., Sept. 11, 1937; came to U.S., 1987; s. Irvine John and Doris Bernice (Price) V.; married Nov. 8, 1958; children: Steven, Bryan, Grayden. BA, Can. Christian Coll., 1982, BTh, 1982, MA, 1983, D of Ministry, 1984. Ordained to ministry Christian Ch., 1975. Pastoral counselor Toronto, 1975—; chaplain CAP, Calif., 1975—; missionary to East Africa Kenya, 1985; pastor Yours for Life Ministries Inc., Santa Ana, Calif. Past leader Boy Scouts of Can., Toronto; active St. John Ambulance/Red Cross, Dominon of Can. Office: Yours For Life Ministries PO Box 27023 Santa Ana CA 92799-7023

VAUGHN, GORDON E., bishop. Bishop of Western Pa. Ch. of God in Christ, Pitts. Office: Ch of God in Christ 6437 Stanton Ave Pittsburgh PA 15206*

VAUGHN, JIMMY FREDRICK, minister; b. Parkursburg, W.Va., Aug. 8, 1965; s. Jimmy Fredrick and Lorian (McGary) V.; m. Sharon Elizabeth Sampson, Feb. 20, 1988; 1 child, Lindsey Annette. Student, Richland Coll., 1984-86, Eastfield Coll., 1990-91. Lic. to ministry Bapt. Ch., 1987, ordained, 1989. Youth pastor Merit (Tex.) Bapt. Ch., 1987; interim youth pastor Park St. Bapt. Ch., Greenville, Tex., 1988; youth pastor Ardis Heights Bapt., Greenville, 1988-91; asst. pastor, min. youth Dixon Bapt. Ch., Greenville, Tex., 1991—; asst. supr. Hunt County Juvenile Detention Ctr., Greenville, 1988—; mem. Hunt Bapt. Exec. Bd., Greenville, 1988—; mem. mission to Belize, 1990. Home: PO Box 1983 Greenville TX 75403-1983 Office: Dixon Bapt Ch Rte 5 Box 172 Greenville TX 75401

VAWTER, JAMES KEITH, minister; b. St. Louis, Sept. 12, 1953; s. William Oliver and Elsie Alene (Goodman) V.; m. Debra May, July 3, 1971; 1 child, Bonnie Jean. AA, So. Bapt., Walnut Ridge, Ark., 1973; BS, Southwest Bapt. Univ., Bolivar, Mo., 1985; postgrad., Mo. Bapt. Coll., St. Louis, 1974, 82. Minister Daly Bapt. Ch., St. Clair, Mo., 1973-77, New Friendship Bapt., Gerald, Mo., 1977-80; assoc. pastor Union (Mo.) First Bapt., 1980-82; minister First Bapt. Ch., Birch Tree, Mo., 1987—; moderator Shannon County Bapt. Assn., Alton, Mo., 1987-90, Birch Tree Ministerial Alliance, 1986-90; youth and music dir. Shannon County and Laclede County Assn. Office Future Farmers Am., Hardy, Ark., 1967-71, star farmer, 1971. With Air Nat. Guard. Home: PO Box 68 Birch Tree MO 65438 Office: First Baptist Church Birch Tree MO 65438

VAYDA, JEFFREY GEORGE, minister; b. Pitts., May 28, 1953; s. George Edward and Olga Anna (Pavlik) V.; m. Anna Jogun, Dec. 9, 1989; 1 child, Ryan Joseph. BA, Susquehanna U., 1975; MDiv, Luth. Theol. Sem., Gettysburg, Pa., 1979; MBA, Robert Morris Coll., 1984. Ordained to ministry Evang. Luth. Ch. in Am., 1979. Intern Luth. Ch. of Good Shepherd, Cin., 1977-78; asst. to pastor St. Paul's Luth. Ch., Carlisle, Pa., 1978-79; pastor Faith luth. Ch., Oklahoma Boro, Pa., 1979-83, 1st Luth. Ch., Greensburg, Pa., 1983-91, Christ Luth. Ch., Gettysburg, Pa., 1991—; chaplain on call Westmoreland Hosp., 1984-91; mem. youth com. West Pa.-W.Va. Synod, Pitts., 1979-80, social ministry com., 1980-85; bd. dirs., synod rep. Luth. Svc. Soc., Pitts., 1980-86; bd. dirs. Luth. Coalition Pub. Policy, Harrisburg, Pa., 1980-86; mem. Bishop's Task Force on Econ. Stress, 1985; chairperson Intersynodical Com. on Econ. Justice, 1986-90. Author: The System and Self-Image: Aged in America, 1979. Mem. Am. Mgmt. Assn., Assn. MBA Execs., Alban Inst., Gettysburg Ministerium. Office: Christ Luth Ch 44 Chambersburg St Gettysburg PA 17325 *The person who has come to know a life of peacefulness, contentment, joy and fulfillment begins each new day by praying: Father, not my will, but thy will be done.*

VAYHINGER, JOHN MONROE, psychotherapist, minister; b. Upland, Ind., Jan. 27, 1916; s. Paul Johnson and Hariet Estelle (Palmer) V.; m. Ruth Imler, Sept. 19, 1939; children: John Earl, Karen Lynn Vayhinger Kuper. AB, Taylor U., 1937; grad., Asbury Theol. Sem., Wilmore, Ky., 1937-39; BD, MA, Drew U., 1940, 51; MA, PhD, Columbia U., 1948, 56. Diplomate Am. Bd. Psychology; ordained Meth. Ch. as pastor. Pastor United Meth. Ch., Conn., Ind., N.Y., Colo., 1938-68, ret.68; assoc. prof., head dept. W.Va. Wesleyan U., Buckhannon, 1949-51; chief clin. psychologist Mental Health Clin., South Bend, Ind., 1951-58; prof. psychology Garrett Theol. Sem. Northwestern U., Evanston, Ill., 1958-64; prof. psychology Iliff Sch. Theol. U. Denver, 1964-67; prof. psychology and pastoral counseling Anderson (Ind.) U. Sch. Theology, 1968-81, Asbury Theol. Sem., Wilmore, Ky., 1981-84, ret.84; pvt. practice Ky., Ind., 1958-84, Colorado Springs, Colo., 1984—; dir. inst. ministries Ind. Coun. Chs., Indpls., 1968-81; chairperson Pastoral Counseling Inst., Atlanta, 1985—. Author: Before Divorce, 1972, (with Norman Cryer) Casebook of Pastoral Counseling. Tchr. police schs., South Bend, Ind., Anderson, Denver. Capt. AUS, 1944-47, PTO. Fellow Am. Orthopsychiatric Assn., Am. Assn. Sci. Study of Religion, Christian Assn. Psychol. Studies; mem. Am. Assn. Pastoral Counselors (diplomate), Soc. Psychol. in Pvt. Practice, Am. Psychol. Assn., AAUP, AAAS, Colo. Psychol. Assn., Ind. Psychol. Assn., Am. Assn. Marital and Family Therapists (clin.), Religious Rsch. Assn., Am. Assn. Sex Educators, Counselors and Therapists, Nat. Coun. Family Relations, Assn. Clin. Pastoral Edn., Nat. Congress Parents and Tchrs. (life), USN Inst., and more. Republican. Home: 119 Illini Dr Woodland Park CO 80863-8802 Office: 420 N Nevada Ave Colorado Springs CO 80903

VEAL, BILLY ROBERT, clergyman; b. Ft. Worth, Dec. 13, 1961; s. James Robert and Laura Betty (Enloe) V.; m. Cheryl Denice Cox, July 25, 1981; children: Stephanie Lyn, Tiffany Rae, Bethany Paige. BA in Communication, U. North Tex., 1984; MA in Religious Edn., Southwestern Bapt. Theol. Sem., 1989. Minister music Gribble Springs Bapt. Ch., Denton, Tex., 1981-83; choir dir. Colony Park Bapt. Ch., The Colony, Tex., 1983-84; minister music Northview Bapt. Ch., Lewisville, Tex., 1984-87; minister music/edn./outreach First Bapt. Ch., Watauga, Tex., 1987-89; minister music/edn. First Bapt. Ch., Sweetwater, Tex., 1989—; growth cons. Sunday Sch. Bd./So. Bapt. Conv., Nashville, 1990—; guest dir. Sunday Sch. Bd., Bapt. Gen. Conv. Tex., Nashville, Dallas, 1989—; asst. dir. Sweetwater Bapt. Assn., 1989—; guest musician So. Bapt. Chs. throughout Tex., 1978—. Compiler: ORPGC Policies Manual, 1984. Dir. Sch. and Civic Talent Show, Sweetwater, 1990, 91, SNAP Community Sr. Adult Choir, Sweetwater, 1990, 91; organizer Christmas Feeding of Needy Families, Sweetwater, 1990, 91; guest reader Readers are Leaders Program, Sweetwater, 1991. Named Kiwanian of Yr., Kiwanis Civic Club, Sweetwater, 1989-90. Mem. So. Bapt. Religious Edn. Assn., Tex. Bapt. Religious Edn. Assn., Singing Men of West Tex., Kiwanis (v.p. 1990-91), Goodfellows Club. Home: 1710 Woodruff Sweetwater TX 79556 Office: First Bapt Ch 3d and Elm Sts Sweetwater TX 79556

VEAL, KENNETH WAYNE, minister, church organization administrator; b. Portland, Oreg., Aug. 9, 1943; s. Claude Henry and Ruth Elizabeth (Schmid) V.; m. June Louise Ledbetter, June 13, 1965; children: Tamera Lynn, Timothy Lee, Thomas Lyle. BA, Walla Walla Coll., 1967; MDiv, Andrews U., 1969. Ordained to ministry Seventh-day Adventists, 1969. Pastor No. Calif. Conf. Seventh-day Adventists, 1969-73; youth dir. Fla. Conf. Seventh-day Adventists, Orlando, 1973-75; dir. youth and family life Cen. Calif. Conf. Seventh-day Adventists, San Jose, 1975-80; family life cons., San Jose, 1980-82; pastor, coll. instr. Cleburne (Tex.) Seventh-day Adventist Ch., 1982-85; pastor Hutchinson (Minn.) Seventh-day Adventist Ch., 1985-88; dir. youth and family life Ill. Conf. Seventh-day Adventists, Brookfield, Ill., 1988—; mem. N.Am. resource com. Seventh-day Adventists, 1973-79; pres. Salt Mine Resources, San Jose, 1979-84; dir., speakere Success Seminars, Minn. and Ill., 1985—, Creative Assocs., San Jose, 1982-85. Author: How To Start a Pathfinder Club, 1989; also articles. Mem. Hutchinson Mayor's Com. on Youth, 1987, Creative Edn. Found. and Camping Orgns., 1988—, Christian Camping Internat., 1977—. Home: 78 Saratoga Batavia IL 60510 Office: Ill Conf Seventh-day Adventists 3721 Prairie Ave Brookfield IL 60513 *Success is not what we were, or are, or shall be; success is rather what others become because of what we were, and are, and shall be. Biblical success is always relational, never positional, and certainly conditional. It is measured in the development of people, not by accumulations of achievement. To seek any other form of success is to chase a delusion.*

VEALE, ALAN KEITH, minister; b. L.A., Aug. 2, 1950. A in Bibl. Studies, Nazarene Bible Coll., 1989. Ordained to ministry Wesleyan Ch., 1990. Youth dir. Hope Wesleyan Ch., Escondido, Calif., 1982-85; youth pastor First Wesleyan Ch., Colorado Springs, Colo., 1985-87; asst. pastor Life Spring Wesleyan Ch., Colorado Springs, 1987-89; pastor Scottsdale (Ariz.) Wesleyan Ch., 1989—; dist. sec. world missions Ariz.-N.Mex. Dist. of Wesleyan ch., 1989—, auditing com., 1990-91. Asst. soccer coach N. County Youth Soccer Assn., Escondido, 1981-85; soccer coach Chargers Soccer Club, Colorado Springs, 1985-87, Colo. Springs Soccer Club, 1987-89. With USAF, 1969-71. Named Outstanding Young Man of Am., Outstanding Young Men of Am., 1986. Mem. Delta Epsilon Chi. Republican. Home: 8532 E Pasadena Ave Scottsdale AZ 85250 Office: Scottsdale Wesleyan Ch 4640 N Granite Reef Rd Scottsdale AZ 85251 *God's great gift of life is meant to be shared. It is not only sharing the life of His son with others but also the sharing of our lives together. I endeavor to do both with all my heart.*

VEASEL, WALTER, minister; b. Balt., Apr. 11, 1925; s. William Edward Veasel and Mary Lula (Boyd) Ebert; m. Helen Ilene Gank; children: William, Holly, Bradley, Heide. ThB, Holmes Coll. of the Bible, 1947; BS in Elem. Edn., Towson State U., 1970; M in Ministries, Zion Sem., 1986. Ordained to ministry Christian Ch., 1947; cert. tchr., Md. Pastor Mid Atlantic Conf. Pentecostal Holiness Ch., 1948-54, St. Catharines and London, Ont., Can., 1955-59; pastor Mid Atlantic Conf. Pentecostal Holiness Ch., Georgetown, D.C. and Daniels, Md., 1960-70; founder, pastor Community Ch., 1970-90; pastor emeritus Woodbridge Valley Ch. of God, 1990—; prin. Tabernacle Christian Sch., Balt. Vol. nursing homes, reform schs. and prisons, 1948—. Recipient Vols. Cert., House of Correction, 1975-90. Mem. Ministerial Assn. Republican. Home: 5025 Montgomery Rd Ellicott City MD 21043 Office: Tabernacle Christian Sch 8855 Belair Rd Baltimore MD 21236

VEAZEY, JIMMY L., minister; b. Birmingham, Ala., Sept. 17, 1960; s. Robert L. and Dorothy J. (Douglass) V.; m. Cindy Michelle Taylor, June 11, 1983; children: Joshua Mark, Caleb Andrew. BS, U. Ala., 1984; M of Religious Edn., New Orleans Bapt. Sem., 1991. Minister music Flatwoods Bapt. Ch., Northport, Ala., 1980-82, Catoma Bapt. Ch., Montgomery, Ala., 1984-87; minister music and youth Mt. Hebron West Bapt. Ch., Elmore, Ala., 1987—. Mem. Elmore Bapt. Assn. (youth dir. 1990-91, nominating com. 1989-91, del. 1988, 90). Office: Mt Hebron W Bapt Ch PO Box 86 Hwy 143 Elmore AL 36025

VEENKER, RONALD ALLEN, religion educator, research scholar; b. L.A., May 13, 1937; s. Albert George and Lillian Wanda (Allen) V.; m. Lola Lee Kix, Aug. 28, 1960 (div. 1981); 1 child, Jonathan Allen; m. Beverly D. Long, Mar. 11, 1983. BA, Bethel Coll., 1959; BDiv, Bethel Sem., 1963; PhD, Hebrew Union Coll., 1967. Asst. prof. U. Miami, 1967-68; prof. O.T. and Judaism, Western Ky. U., Bowling Green, 1968—. Contbr. articles profl. jours. Bd. dirs. Bowling Green Western Symphony, pres.-elect, 1989; trustee, mem. coun. Episcopal Diocese of Ky., Louisville, 1988—. Recipient post-doctoral fellowship Hebrew Union Coll., 1977. Mem. Am. Oriental Soc. (Midwest sect. 1971-76), Soc. Bibl. Lit. (Midwest sec. 1982), Cath. Bibl. Soc., Delta Tau Delta (chpt. advisor 1985—). Democrat. Avocation: early music (recorders, viols). Home: 562 E Main Ave B3 Bowling Green KY 42101 Office: Western Ky U College Heights Bowling Green KY 42101

VEENKER, RUSSELL RALPH, minister, counselor; b. L.A., Mar. 18, 1953; s. Louis Frederick and Josephine (Verplank) V.; m. Kandace Rebecca Stilwell, Dec. 30, 1978; children: Jeremy, Jason. BA in Communication Theory, Calif. State U. Northridge, 1977; MA, Dallas Theol. Sem., 1982. Ordained to ministry, 1985. Minister Calvary Ch., Pacific Palisades, Calif., 1971-77; founding pastor Mountain Bible Fellowship Ch., June Lake, Calif., 1986-89; founder, exec. dir. Mountain Learning Ctr., June Lake, 1982—. Pres., leader June Lake Mountain Rescue, 1984—. Recipient Medal of Valor Mond County Suprs., 1990, State of Calif. Mem. Mountain Rescue Assn. Republican. Home: POB 625 June Lake CA 93529 Office: Mountain Learning Ctr POB 625 June Lake CA 93529

VEENSTRA, A. PAUL, minister; b. Moline, Mich., Feb. 12, 1931; s. Henry and Lyda (Buist) V.; m. Kathryn Mae Soetenga, Nov. 1, 1952; children: Dawn Juanita Van Essen, Randall Paul, Nancy Kay Wissing, Daniel Kent. BA, Calvin Coll., 1952; BTh, Calvin Sem., 1955. Ordained to ministry Christian Ref. Ch., 1955. Pastor Hamilton (Mich.) Christian Ref. Ch., 1955-60; founding pastor and sr. pastor Chula Vista (Calif.) Community Ch., 1960—. Author: Sun. Sch. Tchrs. Guide, 1960, 68. Long range planning com. mem. City of Chula Vista, 1965-68; bd. dirs. Adult Protective Svcs., San Diego. Mem. Christian Reformed Bd. Fgn. Missions (sec. 1956-60); Christian Reformed Bd. Home Missions (evangelist 1969-72), Rotary Chula Vista (treas. 1991-92). Republican. Home: 823 Lori Ln Chula Vista CA 91910 Office: Chula Vista Community Ch 271 East J St Chula Vista CA 91910

VEIT, FREDERICK CHARLES OTTO, lawyer, lay worker; b. Summit, N.J., Nov. 22, 1960; s. Frederick Decker and Lois Ellen (Ritchel) V. Student, Lehigh U., 1979-80; BS summa cum laude, The King's Coll., 1983; JD, Pace U., 1986. Bar: N.Y., N.J., Conn., D.C. Legal asst. Paul Feiner Westchester County Bd. Legislators, White Plains, N.Y., 1984-86; dir. adminstrn. Entre Ven, Inc., Montclair, N.J., 1987-89; pvt. practice law Briarcliff Manor, N.Y., 1987—; cons., lectr. ch. law, taxation, fin. planning The Christian and Missionary Alliance, North Plainfield, N.J., 1987—; adjunct prof. The King's Coll., Briarcliff Manor, N.Y., 1988—; dir. personal fin. planning and planned giving The King's Coll., Briarcliff Manor, 1989-91; cert. N.Y. state peace officer, 1988—, instr., 1990—; tax cons. in charge Deloitte, Haskins & Sells, Stamford, 1987-89. Mem. Aux. Police, Mamaroneck, N.Y.; deacon Grace Alliance Ch., Ossining, N.Y. Mem. ABA, N.Y. State Bar Assn., N.J. Bar Assn., Conn. Bar Assn., D.C. Bar Assn., Christian Legal Soc. Home and Office: 21 Gordon Ave Briarcliff Manor NY 10510

VEITCH, D. PHILIP, navy chaplain; b. Toronto, Ont., Can., Apr. 17, 1953; s. Donald Lyman and June Alicia (Tonkin) V.; m. Sharon Ruth Battishill, June 17, 1978; children: Robert Montgomery, Alison Elizabeth, David Hamilton, Brittany. BA, Wayne State U., Detroit, 1978; MAR, Westminster Theol. Sem., Phila., 1981; MDiv, Phila. Theol. Sem., 1987. Ordained to ministry, Reformed Episcopal Ch. Pulpit supply Grace Episcopal Ch., Phila., 1985-87; chaplain USN Submarine SQD10, Groton, Conn., 1987-90, USS Kalamazoo, Norfolk, Va., 1990—. Bd. dirs. Southeastern Conn. chpt. ARC, 1988-90, Letter of Appreciation, 1989; adv. bd. Navy Family Svc. Ctr., 1987-90; founder Covenant Renewal Ministries, 1990—. Lt. USN, 1987—, 90-91, Persian Gulf. Decorated Navy Commendation medal. Republican. Home: 1220 Renoir Ct Virginia Beach VA 23454 Office: USS Kalamazoo (AOR-6) FPO AE NY 09576-3028

VELÁZQUEZ DE CANCEL, LOURDES, religion educator, interpreter, translator, writer; b. Santurce, P.R., Jan. 28, 1941; d. Manuel Velázquez-Conde and Ramonita Torres-Marrero; m. Eduardo Cancel-Rodriguez, June 3, 1961; children: Lourdes Isabel, Eduardo Juan, Daniel Eduardo. Student, U. P.R., Rio Piedras. Translator, writer, 1961—; 1st soprano Fuente de Aqua Viva Choir, Carolina, P.R., 1984-89; psalmist, preacher Fuente de Aqua, Misicn Cristiana, Carolina, 1984-89; psalmist, preacher, tchr. Seventh-day Adventist Ch., Rio Piedras, P.R., 1989—; pres., founder Ralvec Ministries, Carolina, 1991—. Author: A Crisis of Faith, 1986, Does Anyone Care? 1991, My Secret Garden, 1991, On Love and Power, 1991, On a Daily Basis, 1991, A Question of Integrity, 1991, Amidst Deep Waters, 1991; author numerous hymns, psalms, poems and short stories; editor Resurrection Life Mag., 1991. Translator ARC, San Juan, P.R., 1989-90. Mem. Soc. Tech. Writers, Women's Aglow P.R. Office: Ralvec Ministries PO Box 9466 Plaza Carolina Sta Carolina PR 00628

VENCER, AGUSTIN BALDONASA, JR., religious organization administrator; b. Barotac Viejo, Iloilo, The Philippines, Feb. 11, 1946; s. Agustin Sr. and Candelaria (Baldonasa) V.; m. Annabella Castillo; children: Andrew John, Alystaire Ann, Alcoe Philip, Augustine Paul. BS, Cen. Philippines U., Iloilo City, 1968; BA in Literature, BS in Gen. Sci., So. Island Colls., 1970; LLB, Univ. of East, Manila, 1972; LittD (hon.), Toccoa Falls Coll., 1990. With bus. legal office Christian & Missionary Alliances of Philippines, Zamboanga, 1974-77; office adminstr. Metro Manila Billy Graham Crusade, 1977; gen. sec. Philippine Coun. Evang. Chs., Quezon City, 1978—; chmn., pres. Philippine Alliance Coll. Theology, Quezon City, 1990—; chmn. prodn.

Philippine Bible Soc., Manila, 1974-75; assoc. dir. ch. rels. World Vision Philippines, Manila, 1979-80; country dir. Compassion Philippines, 1981-88; gen. dir. Philippine Relief & Devel. Svcs., Quezon City, 1980-; chmn. Philippine Congress on World Evangelization, 1989—; country dir. World Relief Philippines, 1980-; spl. asst. Asian rels. World Relief Internat.; sec. Nat. Ecumenical Consultative Com.; exec. chmn. Say Yes to Christ with Luis Palan, 1991. Author: (booklets) Towards an Evangelical Response to the Current Ideological Unrest: A Study Paper, 1984, A Biblical Framework Towards an Evangelical Participation in Elections, 1984; contbr. articles to profl. jours. Pulpit min. Alliance Fellowship Ch., Quezon City, 1984-. Recipient Recognition of Devel. award Olangapo News, The Philippines, 1979. Mem. Overseas Missionary Fellowship Philippines Home Council, World Evang. Fellowship (exec. com. 1980—, internat. bd. dirs. designate 1992), Discipling A Whole Nation Philippines (chmn. 1983—), Lausaunne Congress World Evangelization (alt.), Evang. Fellowship of Asia (founding chmn. exec. com. 1983), Asia Mission Congress (chmn. 1990), John Knox Fellowship, Inter-Ch. Relief and Devel. Alliance (founding chmn. 1980), Quezon City Sports Club. Avocations: bowling, tennis, basketball, swimming. Home: 34 Ferdinand II, Kingsville Subd Mayamot, Antipolo Rizal The Philippines Office: Philippine Coun Evang Chs, 62 Molave, Quezon City 1102, The Philippines

VENDELIN, ROBIN RAE WOODS, minister; b. Martinez, Calif., Aug. 23, 1951; d. Duane Eugene and Evelyn Theresa (Heflin) Woods; m. John Sulo Vendelin, June 29, 1969; children: Benjamin David, Sara Anne, Abigail Rebecca. BA in Bibl. Lit., NW Coll., Kirkland, Wash., 1987. Ordained to ministry Assemblies of God, 1987. Coord. social svcs. and recreation New Horizons Ministries, Seattle, 1987—. Contbr. articles to religious publs. Mem. Homeless Youth and Young Adult Coalition. Mem. Delta Epsilon Chi. Office: New Horizons Ministries PO Box 2801 Seattle WA 98111 *Following Jesus Christ in service to the poor, the needy and the destitute of this world is a privilege that is available to all men and women of faith. To share in God's love for them is an unmerited opportunity. It's a pity more people don't avail themselves of this joy.*

VENEMA, CORNELIS PAUL, religion educator; b. Grand Rapids, Mich., Apr. 25, 1954; s. Richard James and Carrie (Van Surksum) V.; m. Nancy Beth Van Gorp, Aug. 27, 1974; children: Joseph, Charissa, Rachel, Carolyn. AB, Dordt Coll., 1975; BD, Calvin Sem., 1978; PhD magna cum laude, Princeton Sem., 1985. Ordained minister in Christian Reformed Ch., 1982. Minister Ontario (Calif.) Christian Reformed Ch., 1982-88; prof. doctrinal studies Mid-Am. Reformed Sem., Orange City, Iowa, 1988—. Contbg. editor The Outlook, 1990—; contbr. articles to profl. jours. Talen scholar Calvin Sem., 1978; doctoral teaching fellow Princeton Theol. Sem., 1979-81. Mem. Am. Acad. Religion, Calvin Studies Soc., The Sixteenth Century Studies Soc., Evang. Theol. Soc. Home: 703 1st St NW Orange City IA 51041 Office: Mid Am Reformed Sem PO Box 163 Orange City IA 51041

VENTO, JOHANN MARIE, lay minister; b. Pitts., Dec. 4, 1965; d. Arthur Vincent and Julia Virginia (Colizza) V. BA in English and German, U. Md., 1987; MA in Theology, Washington Theol. Union, 1990. Co-dir. RCIA, College Park, Md., 1987-89; instr. in adult edn. St. Pius X Parish, Bowie, Md., fall 1988; dir. religious edn. and youth ministry Ascension Parish, Balt., 1989—; participant NCCJ-Seminarians Interacting, N.Y.C., 1989-90; del. Women's Intersem. Conf., Kansas City, Mo., 1989. Vol. Mary PIRG, U. Md., 1984; canvasser Young Dems., 1984. U. Md. scholar, 1983-87, grantee, 1985-86. Mem. Assn. Profl. Youth Ministers of Balt. Home: 1190 W Northern Pkwy #316 Baltimore MD 21210 Office: Ch of the Ascension 4603 Poplar Ave Baltimore MD 21227 *We live in a century rockes by religious wars and in a country where fear of "the other" permeates all levels of society. It seems increasingly necessary that religious people of good will advocate dialogue and cooperation between various religious groups. My hope is that we can begin to see pluralism as a catalyst for growth rather as an excuse for strife.*

VERBRUGGE, VERLYN DAVID, minister, theological editor; b. Grand Haven, Mich., Sept. 4, 1942; s. John Cornelius and Marie (Sinkey) V.; m. Maria M. VanderSteen, June 11, 1966 (div. June 1986); children: John V., Dorothy J., Theodore J., Maria J.; m. Lori Janine Crum, Dec. 30, 1988. AB, Calvin Coll., Grand Rapids, Mich., 1964; BD, Calvin Sem., Grand Rapids, 1968, ThM, 1979; PhD, U. Notre Dame, 1988. Ordained to ministry Christian Reformed Ch. in N. Am., 1968. Pastor Leighton (Iowa) Christian Reformed Ch., 1968-72, So. Height Christian Reformed Ch., Kalamazoo, 1972-84; part-time pastor Woodland Drive-In Ch., Grand Rapids, 1984—; theol. editor Zondervan Corp., Grand Rapids, 1986—. Contbr. to Bibles pub. by Zondervan Pub. House; also articles. Mem. Soc. Bibl. Lit., Cath. Bibl. Assn. Home: 1235 Hope SE Grand Rapids MI 49506 Office: Zondervan Bible Pubs 1415 Lake Dr SE Grand Rapids MI 49506

VERDESI, ELIZABETH HOWELL, religious association educator, historian; b. Elmira, N.Y., Feb. 5, 1922; d. Everts Howe and Gladys Mae (Shaw) Howell; m. Alan G. Gripe, 1951 (div.); children: Stephen Howell, David Alan; m. Ariel E. Verdesi. BA magna cum laude, Elmira Coll., 1944; MA, Union Theol. Sem., Tchrs. Coll., Columbia U., N.Y.C., 1952, EdD, 1975. Traveling fellow Bd. Christian Edn. Presbyterian Ch. U.S.; sec. youth work Bd. Nat. Missions, 1946-51; dir. Christian edn. 1st Presbyn. Ch., Westfield, N.Y., 1962-64; cons. Crisis in Nation Project United Presbyn. Ch. U.S., N.Y.C., 1968; assoc. Council on Women and Ch., N.Y.C., 1977—; dir. cultivation Ch. Women United in U.S., 1971-77; ruling elder 1st Presbyn. Ch., Congers, N.Y.; mem. ministerial relations com. Hudson River Presbytery. Author: In But Still Out: Women in the Church, 1976; (play) Straight Furrow (with Hilda Benson), 1948; contbr. articles to mags. Pres., Westfield PTA, 1960-62; organizer, bd. dirs. Westfield Counseling Service, 1963-64; treas. Women's Club, West Point, N.Y., 1954-55; pres. Div. Dames Western N.Y. Presbytery, 1960; organizer, dir. Choral Speaking Group, West Point and Westfield, 1953-64. Mem. AAUW, Phi Beta Kappa. Democrat. Office: 475 Riverside Dr New York NY 10115

VERHALEN, PHILIP A., theologian, philosopher of religion, educator; b. Milw., Apr. 2, 1934; s. Andrew Nicholas and Amanda E. (Rose) V.; m. M. Kathleen Quinn, July 25, 1981. BA, St. Francis Coll., Milw., 1956; STB, Gregorian U., Rome, 1958, STL, 1960, PhD, 1969. Ordained priest Roman Cath. Ch., 1959; cert. tchr., Wash. Tchr., adminstr. Marycliff High Sch., Spokane, 1962-66; tchr., dean Bishop White Sem., 1960-62, 68-69; tchr. Seattle U., 1969-71, St. Patrickk's Sem., Menlo Park, Calif., 1971-73, Coll. of Great Falls (Mont.), 1973-75; vis. scholar Claremont (Calif.) Sch. Religion, 1975-76; instr., cons., exec. sec. dept. edn. Pierce County Cath. Edn. Bd., Archdiocese of Seattle, 1977-79; instr. Bellarmine Prep. Sch., Tacoma, 1980-86; adj. prof. Pacific Luth. U., U. Puget Sound, Tacoma, 1980—, Seattle U., 1980—; local dir. summer sch. Christian Apostolate, Spokane, 1965, 66. Author: Faith in a Secularized World, 1976, Religion is a Personal Matter, 1990; contbr. articles to profl. publs. Mem. planning commn. City of Tukwila (Wash.), 1988-89, mem. bd. archtl. rev., 1988-89. Mem. Am. Acad. Religion, Soc. Biblical Lit., Elks. Home: 619 S 31st Renton WA 98055

VERHEY, ALLEN DALE, religion educator, minister; b. Grand Rapids, Mich., May 14, 1945; s. Richard and Catherine (Kass) V.; m. Phyllis Jean DeKruyter, Sept. 2, 1965; children: Timothy, Elisabeth, Kathryn. BA, Calvin Coll., 1966; BD, Calvin Sem., 1969; PhD, Yale U., 1975. Ordained to ministry Christian Ref. Ch., 1975. Guest lectr. Calvin Sem., Grand Rapids, 1972-75; asst. prof. dept. religion Hope Coll., Holland, Mich., 1975-78, assoc. prof., 1978-86, prof., 1986—; assoc. pastor Neland Avenue Christian Ref. Ch., Grand Rapids, 1975-78, 14th Street Christian Ref. Ch., Holland, 1978—. Author: The Great Reversal: Ethics in the New Testament, 1984, Living the Heidelberg: The Catechism and the Church's Moral Life, 1984; co-author: Christian Faith, Health, and Medical Practice, 1989; co-editor: On Moral Medicine: Theological Perspectives on Medical Ethics, 1987; contbr. articles to profl. jours. Fellow NEH, 1981-82. Mem. Soc. Christian Ethics, Hastings Ctr., Soc. Bibl. Lit. Home: 93 W 14th St Holland MI 49423 Office: Hope Coll Dept Religion Holland MI 49423

VERHEYDEN, JACK CLYDE, theology educator; b. Wichita, Kans., July 5, 1934; s. Clyde J. and Ruby Elizabeth (Wilson) V.; m. Sue Carroll Brugier, Sept. 6, 1958; 1 child, Jack C. III. BA, Rice U., 1956; STB, Harvard U., 1961, PhD, 1968. Prof. theology Sch. Theology, Claremont, Calif., 1965—. Editor: Schleiermacher's Life of Jesus, 1975. Lt. (j.g.) USN, 1956-58. Mem. Am. Acad. Religion. Democrat. Office: Sch Theology 1325 N College Claremont CA 91711

VERIGIN, JOHN J., religious organization head. Hon. chmn. exec. com. Union of Spiritual Communities of Christ (Orthodox Daukhobors in Can.), Grand Forks, B.C. Office: Union Spiritual Communities, Christ, Box 760, Grand Forks, BC Canada V0H 1H0*

VER LEE, RONALD F., clergyman; b. Ft. Wayne, Ind., Dec. 6, 1948; s. Franklin George and Frances (Esther) Ver L.; m. Lorelei Beth Johnson, June 6, 1970; children: Sean-Paul, Vanessa. BA, Marion Coll., 1971; MDiv, United Theol. Sem., 1975; DMin, McCormick Theol. Sem., 1987. Ordained to ministry Meth. Ch. Home: 11415 Trails N Fort Wayne IN 46845 Office: United Meth Ch of the Covenant 10001 Coldwater Rd Fort Wayne IN 46825

VERMES, GEZA, religious studies educator; b. Mako, Hungary, June 22, 1924; arrived in Eng., 1957, naturalized, 1962; s. Ernö and Terezia (Riesz) V.; m. Pamela Hobson, May 12, 1958. Lic. Oriental philology and history, Louvain U., Belgium, 1952, ThD, 1953; MA, Oxford (Eng.) U., 1965, LiH, 1988; DD (hon.) Edinburgh U., 1989, Durham U., 1990. Researcher Ctr. Nat. Recherche Scientifique, Paris, 1954-57; lectr. in religious studies U. Newcastle, Tyne, Eng., 1957-64, sr. lectr., 1964-65; reader in Jewish studies Oxford U., 1965-89, prof. Jewish studies, 1989-91, prof. emeritus, 1991—, gov. Ctr. for Hebrew Studies, 1972, dir. publs., 1987-91; dir. Oxford Forum for Qumran Rsch., 1991—. Author: Scripture and Tradition in Judaism, 1961, The Dead Sea Scrolls in English, 1962, 3d edit., 1987, Jesus the Jew, 1973, Jesus and the World of Judaism, 1983, others; editor: Jour. Jewish Studies, 1971. Fellow Brit. Acad.; mem. Soc. for Old Testament Study, European Assn. for Jewish Studies (pres. 1981-84), Brit. Assn. for Jewish Studies (pres. 1975-88). Mem. Liberal Party. Avocation: studying wildlife. Home: West Wood Cottage, Foxcombe Ln, Boars Hill, Oxford OX1 5DH, England

VERNON, JOHN L(EROY), JR., lay church worker, real estate professional; b. Charlotte, N.C., Apr. 22, 1959; s. J. Leroy and Lois Laverne (Seawell) V.; m. Kimberly Dawn Brendle, Aug. 15, 1981; children: John Travis, Robert Kyle. Lay youth worker Providence Wesleyan Ch., High Point, N.C., 1983-85; lay youth worker 1st Wesleyan Ch., High Point, 1986—, mem. adminstrv. bd., 1991—; property mgr. Maxwell Assocs., Greensboro, N.C., 1987—. Mem. Christian Bus. Men's Com. (chmn. outreach com. 1990-91), Nat. Assn. Realtors, N.C. Assn. Realtors, Greater Greensboro Bd. Realtors. Republican. Home: 311 Skeet Club Rd High Point NC 27265

VERNON, WALTER NEWTON, JR., minister, historian; b. Verden, Okla., Mar. 24, 1907; s. Walter Newton and Fannie Hawling (Dodd) V.; m. Ruth Mason, Dec. 27, 1931; children: Walter Newton III, Kathleen Frances Vernon Clark. BA, So. Meth. U., 1928, BD, 1931, MA, 1934; LittD, W.Va. Wesleyan U., 1963. Ordained to ministry United Meth. Ch., 1929. Pastor, Lakewood Meth. Ch., Dallas, 1931-38; assoc. editor Ch. Sch. Publs., 1938-72. Author: Methodism Moves Across North Texas, 1967; Methodism in Arkansas, 1976. Mem. N. Tex. conf. United Meth. Ch., 1929—, conf. historian, 1967—; mem. div. Christian edn. Nat. Council Chs., 1944-72; mem. A-V Team, Africa, 1953; del. World Sunday Sch. Assn., Tokyo, 1958; Fair lectr. Southwestern U., Georgetown, Tex., 1962. Editor The Ch. Sch., 1944-72, Daily Christian Adv., 1940-72; assoc. editor Ency. World Methodism, 1974. Editor, co-author: The Methodist Excitement in Texas, 1984. Author: Becoming One People, History of Louisiana Methodism, 1987, The United Methodist Publishing House, A History Vol. II, 1989; contbr. articles to ch. jours. Weekly columnist Christian Adv., 1948-53; spl. corr. Dallas News, Dallas Times Herald, others. Named to United Meth. Communicators Hall of Fame, 1983. Mem. Sigma Delta Chi, Tau Kappa Alpha. Home: 4835 W Lawther Dr Apt 802 Dallas TX 75214

VERSCHUREN, PAUL M., bishop. Bishop of Helsinki, Roman Cath. Ch., Finland. Office: Katolinen Kirkko Suomessa, Rehbinderintie 21, 00150 Helsinki Finland*

VEST, FRANK HARRIS, JR., bishop; b. Salem, Va., Jan. 5, 1936; s. Frank Harris and Viola Gray (Woodson) V.; m. Ann Jarvis, June 14, 1961; children: Nina Woodson, Frank Harris III, Robert Alexander. BA, Roanoke Coll., 1959; MDiv, Va. Theol. Sem., 1962, DD, 1985; DD (hon.), U. of South, 1987. Ordained to ministry Episcopal Ch. as deacon, 1962, as priest 1963. Curate St. John's Episcopal Ch., Roanoke, Va., 1962-64; rector Grace Episcopal Ch., Radford, Va., 1964-68; rector Christ Episcopal Ch., Roanoke, 1968-73, Charlotte, N.C., 1973-85; suffragan bishop Diocese of N.C., Raleigh, 1985-89; bishop coadjutor Diocese of So. Va., Norfolk, 1989—. Chmn. exec. com. Thompsons Children's Home, Charlotte, 1976-79; pres. Crisis Assistance Ministry, Charlotte, 1983-85; trustee Va. Theol. Sem., Alexandria, 1968-73, 91—, U. of South, Sewanee, Tenn., 1985-89, Episc. Radio TV Found., Atlanta, 1976-82, Appalachian People's Svcs., Blacksburg, Va., 1985-89. Democrat. Avocations: tennis, reading, walking, golf, fly-fishing. Office: Diocese of So Va 600 Talbot Hall Rd Norfolk VA 23505

VEST, JAY HANSFORD CHARLES, Native American religious leader and educator; b. Lexington, Va., Nov. 7, 1951; s. Hansford Charles and Loraine (Turner) V. BS, U. Wash., 1978; MA in Philosophy, U. Mont., 1984, M.I.S. in Religious Studies, 1984, PhD in Philosophy/Religion, 1987. Traditionalist Occaneechi-Monacan, Buena Vista, Va., 1951-68; traditional leader Monacan ceremony sacred to the sun, 1989—; asst. prof. U. Wash., Tacoma, 1990—. Editor Jour. for the Soc. for the Study of Native Am. Religious Traditions; contbr. articles to profl. jours. Coor. sec., newsletter editor exec. bd. Missoula County Dem. Party, Missoula, Mont., 1983-84. Named Miisinssk'tokaan (Badger Head) by Blackfoot elder Joseph Crowshoe, Sr., Peigan Band, Brocket, Alberta, 1989. Mem. Am. Acad. Religion (William C. Shepard Meml. award Pacific Northwest region 1987), Western Lit. Assn., Soc. for Environ. History. Office: U Wash. 1103 A St Perkins Bldg Tacoma WA 98402

VIBERTI, VICTOR LAWRENCE, priest; b. Alba, Italy, Aug. 6, 1913; came to U.S., 1938, naturalized, 1945; s. John Joseph and Rosa (Scavino) V. Student, Minor and Maj. Sem. Soc., St. Paul, Alba, 1926-38. Joined Soc. of St. Paul, Roman Cath. Ch., 1926, ordained priest, 1938. Superior St. Paul Monastery, Canfield, Ohio, 1949-52; dir. St. Paul Publs., Staten Island, N.Y., 1952-60; founder, editor Cath. Home Messenger mag., 1946-52, Pastoral Life mag., 1953-64, 70-80; superior Soc. St. Paul; editor Voice of the People, Dearborn, Mich., 1964-70; superior St. Paul Monastery, 1974-80; provincial of Soc. St. Paul in U.S., 1980-84. Acquisition editor Alba House Pubs., 1985—; contbr. articles to profl. jours. Home: 2187 Victory Blvd Staten Island NY 10314

VICK, JEFFREY HOWARD, minister; b. Livingston County, Ky., May 15, 1962; s. Winfred Davis and Jean Alma (Kirkham) V.; m. Carol Jean Blankenship, Jan. 4, 1986. B in Music Edn., Cen. Mo. State U., 1985; M of Ch. Music, Midwestern Bapt. Theol. Sem., 1991. Missionary 1st Bapt. Ch., Farmington, Mo., summer 1982; youth intern Manor Bapt. Ch., Mobile, Ala., summer 1985; min. music and coll. 38th Ave. Bapt. Ch., Hattiesburg, Miss., 1985-87; min. youth Country Estates Bapt. Ch., Midwest City, Okla., 1987-89; min. music and youth 1st Bapt. Ch., Greenwood, Mo., 1989—; band instr. Lee's Summit (Mo.) Schs., 1990; tng. assoc. Blue-River K.C. Assn., Kansas City, 1990; mem. Mo. Musicmen, trombone player Mo. Brass Players, 1989-90; pres. Midwestern Singers, Kansas City, 1990—. Regents scholar Cen. Mo. State U., 1981, scholar Midwestern Sem., 1991. Mem. Am. Choral Dirs. Assn., Music Educators Nat. Conv., Nat. Assn. Youth Mins., Hymm Soc. Am., Phi Mu Alpha Sinfonia (alumnus mem.). Home: 1228 NE Country Ln Lee's Summit MO 64063 Office: 1st Bapt Ch 1601 W Main Greenwood MO 64034

VICTORIA, ROGER DALE, minister; b. Cuba, Kans., Aug. 8, 1959; s. Victor Vernon and Mabel Irena (Nash) V. BA in Religious Studies, Macalester Coll., St. Paul, 1981; MDiv, San Francisco Theol. Sem., 1988. Ordained to ministry Presbyn. Ch. (USA), 1989. Vol. in mission Coun. of Chs. of Santa Clara County, San Jose, 1982-84; intern pastor Orick (Calif.) Community Presbyn. Ch., 1986-87; minister of word and sacrament First Presbyn. Ch., St. Paul, Nebr., 1989—; mem. Coun. of Synod of Lakes & Praries, 1991—; chmn. peacemaking com. Cen. N.E. presbytery, Nebr., 1990—. Trustee St. Paul Pub. Libr., 1990—. Mem. Howard County Ministerial Assn., Grand Island City Singers, Rotary. Office: First Presbyn Ch 816 Indian St Saint Paul NE 68873

VICTORIN, HIS EMINENCE THE MOST REVEREND ARCHBISHOP See URSACHE, VICTORIN

VIDAL, RICARDO CARDINAL, archbishop of Cebu; b. Mogpoc, Lucena, Philippines, Feb. 6, 1931; s. Fructuoso and Natividad (Jamin) V. ordained priest Roman Cath. Ch., 1956. Consecrated bishop Titular Ch. Claterna, 1971; archbishop Lipa, Philippines, 1973-81, Cebu, Philippines, 1982—; proclaimed cardinal, 1985. Office: Chancery, PO Box 52, 6401 Cebu City The Philippines

VIDES, ALEXIS, religious organization administrator. Pres. Bapt. Conv. of Honduras, Tegucigalpa. Office: Bapt Conv, Apdo 868, Tegucigalpa Honduras*

VIEGLAIS, NIKOLAJS, clergyman; b. Dundaga, Latvia, Mar. 31, 1907; s. Andrew P. and Eugenia (Jakobson) V.; grad. Theol. Sem., Latvia, 1928, Music Sch., 1932; baccalaureate Theol. Faculty, U. Latvia, 1940; m. Natalija Calders, Oct. 18, 1931; children: Natalija, Marina (Mrs. Alfredo Alva), Alexis, Olga (Mrs. J. Kuhlman), Tatjana (Mrs. C. Tressler); came to U.S., 1949, naturalized, 1955. Ch. choir dir., Cesis, Latvia, 1928-34; deacon cathedral, Riga, Latvia, 1934-37; ordained priest Eastern Orthodox Ch., Latvia, 1937; priest, Riga, 1937-44; priest refugee camps, Germany, 1944-49; apptd. priest Orthodox Ch. in Am., 1949; priest, Lykens, Pa., 1949-51, Berkeley, Calif., 1952—. Editor, pub. ch. books and music, Latvia, 1935-40, 41-44, Germany, 1946-49, U.S.A., 1950-79; dean No. Calif., Orthodox Ch. in Am., 1955-74, 75-76; sec. Exarchate for Baltic States, 1942-44; sec. San Francisco Diocese, 1960-72, mem. council, 1952-76; spiritual adviser local chpt. Federated Russian Orthodox Clubs, 1964-70, Pacific-Alaska Dist., 1967-68. Home: 1908 Essex St Berkeley CA 94703 Office: 1900 Essex St Berkeley CA 94703

VIEHE, CARL ARMIN, minister; b. Cin., May 29, 1917; s. Albert E. and Martha E. (Wulfman) V.; m. Mary Louise Spratt, Sept. 18, 1954; children: Carolyn E. Voss, Stephen R. AB, U. Mich., 1939; MDiv, Yale Div. Sch., 1948; postgrad., Mansfield Coll., Oxford, Eng., 1966, 74, 80; D of Ministry, Drew U., 1979. Ordained to ministry, 1948. Pastor First Congl. Ch., Aberdeen, Wash., 1948-50, Woodmont Union Chapel, Milford, Conn., 1951-54, First Plymouth Congl. Ch., Lincoln, Nebr., 1954-56, Park Congl. Ch., Phila., 1956-59; pastor St. Stephens-Bethlehem United Ch. Christ, Buffalo, 1959-82, min. emeritus, 1982—; bd. dirs. Conn. Coun. Chs., 1953-54, N.Y. Conf. United Ch. Christ, 1969-71, Cen. for Justice, 1985-91, Niagara Frontier Radio Reading Svc., 1987-91; sec. New Haven (Conn.) Coun. Chs., 1953-54, Buffalo and Erie County (N.Y.) Coun. Chs., 1968-70; moderator Western Assn. (N.Y.) United Ch. Christ, 1970-71; co-chmn. Disciples of Christ, United Ch. of Christ task force on unity, 1972-80; book critic Buffalo Courier Express, 1961-82; host religious news program, WWKB Buffalo, 1982-91. Author: Experiment in Holland, 1954; composer: Come, Ye Shepherds, 1974, We Thy Children Come Rejoicing, 1974, Hail We Our King, 1974, Come Ye Children of Our Lord, 1974. Corp. mem. Bd. World Ministries, United Ch., 1973-79; mem. Religion Com. Chautauqua Instn., 1981-87; pres. Western N.Y. chapt. Ams. for Dem. Action, 1983-88, Amherst Museum Presdl. Soc., 1990-91; v.p. Buffalo-Tver (USSR) Sister Cities, Inc., 1989-91. Mem. Amherst Clergy Assn. (pres. 1972-73), Cheektowaga Ministerial Assn., Chautauqua Soc. for Peace (v.p. 1988—), North American Alumni Soc. Mansfield Coll., Oxford, Eng. (sec. 1974—). Avocation: world traveler. Home: 100 Bay Colony Ct Chapel Hill NC 27514 *Bishop John Heyl Vincent, founder of Chautauqua, once said you are never too old to learn. You can begin at any age and continue in heaven.*

VIERA, RODOLFO ELIAS, minister; b. Roswell, N.Mex., Feb. 6, 1948; s. Adnres Basterrechea and Raquel (Armenclariz) V.; m. Isabel Louise Márquez, June 9, 1972; children: Joseph Andrew, Jeremy Rudolfo, Jennifer Rachelle. BA, U. N.Mex., 1970; MDiv, Golden Gate Bapt. Theol. Sem., 1974. Ordained to ministry So. Bapt. Ch. Pastor Meml. Bapt. Mission, Las Cruces, N.Mex., 1974-77; pastor 1st Spanish Bapt. Ch., Douglas, Ariz., 1977-78, Escondido, Calif., 1978-80; commd. ens. USN, 1980, advanced through grades to lt. comdr., chaplain, 1980-88, retired, 1988; sr. pastor Denver Temple Bapt. Ch., 1988—. With USNR, 1988—. Mem. Denver Assn. So. Bapts. (mem. constitution com. 1990—). Republican.

VIKSTRÖM, JOHN EDWIN, archbishop; b. Kronoby, Finland, Oct. 1, 1931; s. Edwin and Hilma Elisabet (Lindström) V.; m. Märta Ulla Birgitta Hellberg, Aug. 24, 1957; children: Ulf, Monika, Björn. Theol. Candidate, U. Helsinki, Finland, 1956; Theol. Licentiate, Abo Acad., Turku, Finland, 1962, ThD, 1966; Dr. honoris causa, Leningrad (USSR) Theol. Sem., 1986, Budapest (Hungary) Luth. Theol. Sem., 1988. Ordained to ministry Evang. Luth. Ch. Finland, 1956. Pastor Espoo Swedish-speaking Congregation, 1956, Diocese of Borgå, 1957-61; rsch. asst. systematical theology, then instr. theol. faculty Åbo Acad., 1963-70, assoc. prof. ethics and philosophy religion, 1970; bishop Borgå Diocese, 1970-82; archbishop Turku and Finland, 1982—; participant theol. negotiations Evang. Luth. Ch. of Finland/Russian Orthodox Ch., 1977—, also between Evang. Luth. Ch. of Finland and Anglican Ch.; mem. doctrinal discussions Luth. World Fedn./Roman Cath. Ch., 1978-81; del. Gen. Assemblies, World Coun. Chs., Uppsala, Finland, 1968, Vancouver, Can., 1983, Canberra, Australia, 1991; mem. cen. com. World Coun. Chs., 1983-91; rep. Ch. of Finland, Luth. World Fedn. Assembly in Budapest, 1984; chmn. Finnish Missionary Soc., 1980-84; mem. Ecumenical Coun. Finland, 1969—, chmn., 1984-90; chmn. coun. Pori Deacony Inst., 1991—. Author: Religion och kultur. Grundproblemet i G. G. Rosenqvists religiösa tänkande, 1966, Religionssociologin i Finland, 1967, Kyrka och revolution, 1968, Kyrkan och kuturradikalismen, 1968, Effekten av religiös fostran, 1970, Fråa biskopen om tro, 1980, Ihmisen usko, 1982, Herdestaven, 1982, Uusi rohkeus elää, 1985, (with Eero Silvasti) Kirjeen Kääntöpiiri, 1987; Suuntaviittoja, 1988, also textbooks on religion. Decorated comdr. Grand Cross of Order of White Rose (Finland); comdr. Grand Cross (Fed. Republic Germany); comdr. 1st class Order of Holy Lamb; recipient Hallberg award 1967, Swenska Kulturfonden award, 1981, Isländska Falk Orden award, 1984; World Coun. Chs. scholar U. Tübingen, Fed. Republic Germany, 1956-57. Avocation: sports. Address: Office of Archbishop, PO Box 60, 20501 Turku Finland

VILLALOBOS PADILLA, FRANCISCO, bishop; b. Guadalajara, Mexico, Feb. 1, 1921. Ordained priest Roman Cath. Ch., 1949; named titular bishop of Colonnata, 1971; now bishop of Saltillo Mexico, 1975—. Office: Bishop's Residence, Obispado Apartado 25, Saltillo Coahuila, Mexico also: Hidalgo Sur 166, Apartado 25, CP 25000, Saltillo Mexico Coahuila

VILLEGAS, ROLANDO VILLENA, bishop. Bishop Evang. Meth. Ch. in Bolivia, La Paz. Office: Iglesia Evangelica, Metodista, Casila 356, La Paz Bolivia*

VINCENT, JOHN JAMES, minister, theologian, urban mission administrator; b. Sunderland, Eng., Dec. 29, 1929; s. David and Ethel Beatrice (Gadd) V.; m. Grace Johnston Stafford, Dec. 4, 1958; children: Christopher John, Helen Faith, James Stafford. BD, London U., 1954; STM summa cum laude, Drew U., 1955; ThD insigni cum laude, Basel U., Switzerland, 1960. Ordained to ministry Meth. Ch., 1956. Min. Manchester and Salford Mission, U.K., 1956-62; supt. min. Rochdale Mission, U.K., 1962-69, Sheffield Inner City Ecumenical Mission, England, 1970—; dir. Urban Theology Unit, Sheffield, 1970—; vis. prof. theology Boston U., 1969, Drew U., Madison, N.J., 1977; vis. prof. N.Y. Theol. Sem., 1970, adj. prof., 1979-88; extra-mural lectr. Manchester, Leeds, Birmingham univs., 1966-78; lectr. Oxford (Eng.) Congresses on N.T., 1957, 61, 65, 72; vis. lectr. St. Paul Sch. Theology, Kansas City, 1968, Claremont (Calif.) Sch. Theology, 1976; Harris Franklin Rall lectr. Garrett Theol. Sem., Evanston, Ill., 1969; hon. lectr. dept. bibl. studies Sheffield U., 1990—; pres. Meth. Ch. Gt. Britain, 1989-90; founding mem., leader Ashram Community Trust, 1967—; chair, trustee Savs. Bank Depositors Assn., 1986; dir. British Liberation Theology Project, 1984—. Author: Christ in a Nuclear World, 1962, Christ and Our Stewardship, 1963,

Christian Nuclear Perspective, 1964, Christ and Methodism: Towards a New Christianity for a New Age, 1965, Secular Christ: A Contemporary Interpretation of Jesus, 1968, Here I Stand: The Faith of a Radical, 1967, The Working Christ: Christ's Ministries through His Church in the New Testament and in the Modern City, 1968, The Race Race, 1970, The Jesus Thing, 1973, Alternative Church, 1976, Disciple and Lord: Discipleship in the Synoptic Gospels, 1976, Starting All Over Again, 1981, Into the City, 1982, OK Let's Be Methodists, 1984, Radical Jesus, 1986, Britain in the 90's, 1989, Discipleship in the 90's, 1991; co-author: (with J.D. Davies) Mark at Work, 1986; translator: Man in the New Testament (W.G. Kümmel), 1963; editor, contbr.: Stirrings: Essays Christian and Radical, 1976, also booklets and pamphlets; editor New City, 1971—. Mem. Studiorum Novi Testamenti Societas, 1961—, Christian Orgns. for Social, Polit. and Econ. Change (coun. 1981-89), Assn. Centres of Adult Theol. Edn. (exec. 1984-90), Urban Mission Tng. Assn. Gt. Britain (chmn. 1976-77, 84-90). Office: Urban Theology Unit, 210 Abbeyfield Rd, Sheffield S4 7AZ, England Home: 178 Abbeyfield Rd, Sheffield S4 7AY, England

VINCENT, MARK LAVON, minister; b. Elkhart, Ind., May 7, 1963; s. Keith LaVon and Charlene Fay (Shaum) V.; m. Lorie Lynn Sonnentag, May 13, 1984; children: Autumn Christyne, Zachary LaVon. BA, Summit Christian Coll., 1985; postgrad., Assoc. Mennonite Bibl. Sem., 1990, Moody Grad. Sch., Chgo. Ordained to ministry Mennonite Ch., 1987. Actor His Co. Drama Troupe, Ft. Wayne, Ind., 1982-83; youth pastor First Mennonite Ch., Ft. Wayne, 1983-84, assoc. pastor, 1985, sr. pastor, 1986—; sec. Ft. Wayne Area Mennonite Mins., 1987—; sec. Justice Peace and Svc. Commn. for Ind.-Mich. Mennonite Conf., Goshen, 1986-88; chairperson Justice, Peace to Svc. Commn., Goshen, 1989—, grante com. 1991; del. Ind.-Mich. Mennonite Conf., Goshen, 1985—; del. Mennonite Cen. Com. Great Lakes Region, Kidron, Ohio, 1991. Mem. YWCA, Ft. Wayne. New Ministries Edn. grant New Ministries Project, 1990. Mem. Associated Chs. of Ft. Wayne, Summit Christian Coll. Alumni (adv. bd.). Office: First Mennonite Ch 1213 Saint Marys Ave Fort Wayne IN 46808 *One of the life's greatest lessons is to learn from the mistakes of others and thus avoid making them yourself.*

VINCENT, MICHAEL ALLEN, clergyman; b. Lawrence, Kans., Aug. 10, 1961; s. James Warren and Elizabeth Ann (Allen) V.; m. Kathryn Anne Rankin, Aug. 16, 1986; 1 child, Abigail Elizabeth. BS in Bus. Adminstrn., U. Kans., 1983; MDiv, Trinity Evang. Div. Sch., 1988, ThM, 1989. Lic. to ministry Evang. Free Ch., 1990. Youth dir. First Presbyn. Ch., Brewton, Ala., 1983-85; pastoral intern St. John's Ch. of Eng., Clacton-on-Sea, 1987; pastor Trinity Evang. Free Ch., Lee's Summit, Mo., 1989—; pres. Evang. Pastors Fellowship, Lee's Summit, 1991. Home: 516A SE Morningside Dr Lee's Summit MO 64063 Office: Trinity Evang Free Ch 101 SW Market Lee's Summit MO 64063 *If Jesus Christ, who was unworthy of death, willingly gave His life to save us, should we not walk in humble obedience to Him down the path of life as His crucified servants.*

VINCENT, ROBERT BENN, minister; b. Bennettsville, S.C., May 16, 1947; s. William Wyman and Janet Rose (Benn) V.; m. Sandra Jean Price; Lydia Price, Amy Rose, Virginia Ruth, Robert Benn Jr., Andrew William. BA, Presbyn. Coll., 1969; diploma, Reformed Presbyn. Theol. Sem., 1973. Ordained to ministry Presbyn. Ch., 1973. Pastor Park City Reformed Presbyn. Ch., Wichita, Kans., 1973-75, Jackson St. Presbyn. Ch., Alexandria, La., 1975—; stated clk. La. Presbytery, 1990—; pres. Cen. La. Ministerial Alliance, Alexandria, 1979-80. Mem. Rotary (sec. Alexandria 1980-81). Office: Jackson St Presbyn Ch 4900 Jackson St Alexandria LA 71303-2509

VINES, CHARLES JERRY, minister; b. Carroll County, Ga., Sept. 22, 1937; s. Charles Clarence and Ruby Johnson V.; m. Janet Denney, Dec. 17, 1960; children: Joy Vines Williams, Jim, Jodi, Jon. BA, Mercer U., 1959; BD, New Orleans Bapt. Sem., 1966; ThD, Luther Rice Sem., Jacksonville, Fla., 1974; DD (hon.), Criswell Coll., 1991, Liberty U., 1991. Pastor West Rome Bapt. Ch., Rome, Ga., 1968-74, 79-81, Dauphin Way Bapt. Ch., Mebrite, Ga., 1974-79, 1st Bapt. ch., Jacksonville, Fla., 1981—. Author: Practical Guide to Sermon Preparation, An Effective Guide to Sermon Delivery, Great Events in the Life of Christ, I Shall Return—Jesus, Family Fellowship, Great Interviews of Jesus, God Speaks Today. Office: First Bapt Ch 124 W Ashley St Jacksonville FL 32206

VINEYARD, HARRIETT ANDERSON, chaplain; b. Oklahoma City, Dec. 18, 1932; d. William Douglas and Harriett Ellen (Long) Anderson; m. John Pendelton Vineyard, Dec. 27, 1952 (div. Sept. 1987); children: John Pendelton III, David Douglas, Harriett Elizabeth, Catherine Jane. BS in Edn., So. Meth. U., 1954; MAR, Episcopal Theol. Sem. SW, Austin, 1989, postgrad., 1989—. Cert. tchr., Tex. Med. sec. Beverly Hills Sanitarium, Dallas, 1955-56; elem. tchr. Dallas Ind. Sch. Dist., 1954-55, Highland Park Ind. Sch. Dist., Dallas, 1955-56; lay chaplain St. David's Community Hosp., Austin, Tex., 1986-88; emergency disaster team chaplain St. David's Community Hosp., Austin, 1986—; asst. chaplain Healthcare Rehab. Ctr., Austin, 1990—; reader gen. ordination examination Episcopalian Ch., 1980—. Dirs. coun. St. Andrew's Episcopal Sch. Mem. Assn. Clin. Pastoral Edn., The Nature Conservancy, The Smithsonian Assocs., Amnesty Internat., Austin Lyric Opera Guild, Greenpeace. Republican. Avocations: sailing, investments, music, art, needlework. Office: Healthcare Rehab Ctr 1106 W Dittmar Rd Austin TX 78745

VINSON, WILLIAM CHARLES, minister; b. Louisville, Oct. 6, 1949; s. William C. Vinson and Norma Lee (Carrier) Higdon; m. Cynthia L. Perkins, Mar. 5, 1971; children: Michelle Marie, Stephenie Loraine. BTh, Faith Bible Coll., Louisville, 1990. Ordained to ministry So. Bapt. Conv., 1986. Min. bus evangelism 9th & O Bapt. Ch., Louisville, 1978-85, Whitesburg Bapt. Ch., Huntsville, Ala., 1985—; speaker Nationwide Bring them in Bus Conf., 1990—. Contbr. articles to mags. in field. Home: 2116 Cecille Dr Huntsville AL 35803

VINTON, SAMUEL R., JR., academic administrator. Head Grace Bible Coll., Grand Rapids, Mich. Office: Grace Bible Coll 1011 Aldon St SW Grand Rapids MI 49509*

VINZ, WARREN LANG, history educator; b. Washington, Iowa, Dec. 4, 1932; s. Arthur Athens and Catherine (Lang) V.; m. Amy R. Wik, Sept. 16, 1960 (div. July 1978); 1 child, Scott; m. Ruth Hahn, Aug. 29, 1978; children: Tracy, Jason, Katherine Elizabeth. BA, Sioux Falls (S.D.) Coll., 1954; BD, MDiv, Berkeley (Calif.) Bapt. Div., 1957; MA, U. Utah, 1966, PhD, 1968. Ordained to ministry Am. Bapt. Assn., 1957. Assoc. min. 1st Bapt. Ch., Salt Lake City, 1957-61; min. 1st Bapt. Ch., Blackfoot, Idaho, 1961-65; prof. history, chair dept. Boise (Idaho) State U., 1968—. Mem. Am. Soc. Ch. History, Am. Acad. Religion, Am. Hist. Assn., Soc. for Sci. Study Religion. Home: 712 Warm Springs Ave Boise ID 83712 Office: Boise State U 1910 University Dr Boise ID 83725

VINZANT, DAVID GENE, minister; b. Sao Paulo, Brazil, May 28, 1963; s. Don Eugene and Carol Jean (Mitchell) V.; m. Rebecca Susan Yeakley, Apr. 28, 1984; 1 child, Sarah Anne. BA in Bible, Okla. Christian Univ., 1984; MDiv, Abilene Christian U., 1987. Ordained to ministry Ch. of Christ, 1988. Minister of involvement and edn. Austin St. Ch. of Christ, Garland, Tex., 1988—. Co-author: The Discipling Dilemma, 1988; contbr. articles to newspaper. Mem. Christian Edn. Assn. Home: 1509 Reisen Garland TX 75040 Office: Austin Street Ch of Christ 800 Austin St Garland TX 75040

VIOLETTE, BETTY, minister; b. Laurel, Miss., Aug. 30, 1928; d. William L. and Reilly (Rogers) Hutto. Grad. High Sch., Indpls., Ind. Staff position Chgo. Teen Challenge, 1965-68; evangelist Assemblies of God Ch., various cities across the nation, 1956-65; dir. Indpls. Teen Challenge, 1968-80; minister Calvary Ministries Internat., Ft. Wayne, Ind., 1980—; pres. Third Phase, Inc., Noblesville, 1980—. mem. Nat. Teen Challenge Com. Pres. Lovenet, Noblesville, 1988; mem. mayor's task force "People Helping People", Noblesville. Republican. Speaks to colls., high schs., chs., clubs, and prisons. Avocation: fishing. Home and Office: 15755 Allisonville Rd Noblesville IN 46060

VISCARDI, CHRISTOPHER JAMES, theology educator; b. Austin, Tex., May 25, 1946; s. Andrew H. and Josephine R. (Perrone) V. BA in Humanities, U. Tex., 1967; MA in Theology, St. Louis U., 1971; STD, Gregorian U., Rome, 1979. Instr. Jesuit High Sch., New Orleans, 1971-73; rsrch. fellow Yale U. Div. Sch., New Haven, 1977; prof. theology Spring Hill Coll., Mobile, Ala., 1979—; vicar Hispanic ministry Archdiocese of Mobile, 1981—; province consultor S.J., New Orleans, 1986—; trustee Spring Hill Coll., 1982—, chmn. theology, 1983—, rector Jesuit community, 1989—. Author, editor: Encyclopedic Dictionary of Jesuit History, 1991; contbg. author Spanish newsletter El Hispano, 1985—. Trustee Loyola U., New Orleans, 1986—; founder, bd. dirs. Christus Theol. Inst., Mobile, 1988—, Hispanic Folkfest, Mobile, 1985—. Mem. Coll. Theology Soc., Am. Soc. Ch. History. Home: 4000 Dauphin St Mobile AL 36608 Office: Spring Hill Coll 4000 Dauphin St Mobile AL 36608

VISSER, RICHARD EDGAR, minister; b. South Weymouth, Mass., Apr. 28, 1937; s. Edgar and Marjorie (McPhee) V.; m. Carol Naomi Edwards, June 21, 1958; children: Andrew, Thomas, Peter. AB, Gordon Coll., 1958, BS, 1959; BD, Gordon Div. Sch., 1962, MRE, 1965; D Ministry, Asbury Theol. Sem., 1983. Ordained to ministry Am. Bapt. Chs. in U.S.A., 1962. Pastor Acton-Milton Mills Bapt. Ch., Milton Mills, N.H., 1962-65; First Bapt. Ch., Derry, N.H., 1966-69; min. edn. Peters Creek Bapt. Ch., Library, Pa., 1969-73; pastor 1st Bapt. Ch., Warren, Pa., 1973-79; min. ch. edn. and music 1st Bapt. Ch., St. Albans, W.Va., 1980-83; pastor 1st Bapt. Ch., Waynesburg, Pa., 1983—; pres. Clergymen's Assn. of Derry, 1967-69; founder, chmn. Pitts. Ch. Edn. Conv., 1972-73; clk. Pitts. Bapt. Assn., 1971-73; pres. Ministerial Assn., Warren, 1975-76, St. Albans, 1982-83, Waynesburg, 1988-90; moderator Ten Mile Assn. Waynesburg, 1985-87; co-founder, vice chmn. Ten Mile and Monogahela Assns. Lic. Lay Pastor Tng. Program, 1988-90; pres. Am. Bapt. Chs. of Pa. and Del., 1991—, chmn. Sunday Sch. Team, 1987-90. Founder, chmn. Warren (Pa.) Community Chorus, 1974-78; pres. Warren County Health and Welfare Coun., 1975-77; chmn. Forest-Warren Counties Human Svcs. Adv. Commn., 1978-79; co chmn. Greene County Human Svcs. Adv. Commn., Pa., 1988—; chmn. Greene County chpt. ARC, 1989-91; bd. dirs. Greene County Meml. Hosp., 1989—. Mem. Am. Bapt. Mins. Coun. (v.p. Pa. and Del. chpt. 1978-79), Rotary (v.p. Waynesburg club 1990-91). Avocations: jogging, reading, singing. Home: 711 Second Ave Waynesburg PA 15370 Office: 1st Bapt Ch High and West Sts Waynesburg PA 15370 *I feel that sometimes people avoid leadership roles because they can be costly. I do not seek leadership roles, but when I see needs and suggest possible solutions, these roles often seem to find me. I have found that an open, ordinary person such as I can make a difference and enjoy some rich rewards.*

VITALE, A. PERRY, deacon; b. Bklyn., Sept. 25, 1940; s. Americo M. and Josephine (Farnese) V.; m. Rosalie Drudi, Sept. 2, 1961; children: Patricia Ann, Lisa Marie, Perry, Mary Jo. BA, St. Thomas U., 1987, MS, 1990; postgrad., Pecos Monestary, 1987. Ordained deacon Roman Cath. Ch., 1984. Dir. family ministry St. Boniface Ch., Pembroke Pines, Fla., 1975-79, dir. pastoral ministries, 1976-81, parish adminstr., 1979—, dir. parish cell system, parish adminstr., 1981—. Co-author: Cell System Leadership Training Manual, 1989. With U.S. Army, 1962-67. Mem. ASCD, Am. Assn. Marriage and Family Therapists, Kiwanis (pres. 1976). Home: 601 NW 96th Terr Pembroke Pines FL 33024

VITHAVONG, JEAN KHAMSE, bishop. Vicar apostolic of Vientiane, titular bishop of Moglaena Roman Cath. Ch., Laos. Office: Vicar Apostolic, Ctr, Catholique, BP 113, Vientiane Lao People's Democratic Republic*

VITOSKY, F. RON, pastor; b. Welch, W.Va., Nov. 29, 1948; s. Frank and Anna Louise (Nunley) V.; m. Bonnie Sue Byrd, May 31, 1960; children: Jennifer, Stephen, John, Heather. Cert., Bob Jones U., 1975. Ordained to ministry Bapt. Ch., 1978. Pastor Emmanuel Bapt. Ch., Kearney, Neb., 1975-79, Liberty Bapt. Ch., Newton, Kans., 1979-89, Bay City (Tex.) Bapt. Ch., 1989—; organizer, dir. Camp Sonshine Summer Youth Camp, 1986-88. Mgr. Boys Baseball Team, Newton, 1986. Sgt. USAF, 1967-71. Mem. Bob Jones U. Alumni Assn.

VIVAS, DAVID L., minister, evangelist; b. Delano, Calif., July 22, 1967; s. David Soria and Adelaida Silva (Lara) V. Lic. to ministry United Pentecostal Ch. Internat., 1988; ordained with Global Christian Ministries. Credit collector McMahan's Furniture Stores, Delano, 1986—; min. United Pentecostal Ch. Internat., St. Louis, 1988—. Prison chaplain Wackenhut RTC Facility, McFarland, Calif., 1989—.

VLADIMIROFF, SISTER CHRISTINE, school system administrator. Supt. diocesan schs. Diocese of Cleve. Office: Dept Diocesan Edn Cath Ctr 1031 Superior Ave Cleveland OH 44114*

VLAZNY, JOHN GEORGE, bishop; b. Chgo., Feb. 22, 1937; s. John George and Marie Hattie (Brezina) V. BA, St. Mary of the Lake Coll., Mundelein, Ill., 1958; STL, Pontifical Gregorian U., Rome, 1962; MA in Classics, U. Mich., 1967; MEd, Loyola U., 1972. Ordained priest Roman Catholic Church, 1961, consecrated bishop, 1983. Assoc. pastor St. Paul of the Cross Ch., Park Ridge, Ill., 1962-63; assoc. pastor St. Clement Ch., Chgo., 1963-68; assoc. pastor St. Aloysius Ch., Chgo., 1968-72, pastor, 1979-81; assoc. pastor St. Sylvester Ch., Chgo., 1972-74, Precious Blood Ch., Chgo., 1974-79; faculty Quigley Prep., North Chgo., 1963-79; dean of studies Quigley Prep., 1969-79; rector Niles Coll., Chgo., 1981-83; aux. bishop Archdiocese of Chgo., 1983-87; Episcopal vicar Vicariate I, Chgo., 1983-87; bishop Episc. Ch., Winona, Minn., 1987—; pres. Presbyteral Senate, Chgo., 1976-77; mem. Diocesan Clergy Personnel Bd., Chgo., 1981-84, chmn., 1983-84. Bd. dirs. NED, Latino Tng. Ctr., Chgo., 1980-81, Sacred Heart Sch. Theology, Hales Corners, Wis., 1986—, St. Mary's Coll., Winona, 1987—. Mem. Nat. Communications Found. (bd. dirs. 1990—), Nat. Conf. Cath. Bishops (various coms. 1983—). Roman Catholic. Avocations: music; running. Office: Chancery Office 55 W Sanborn PO Box 588 Winona MN 55987

VOELKEL, JANE EMMA, minister; b. Bloomington, Ind., Dec. 19, 1960; d. Ralph Henry and Drusilla Marie (Overbeck) V. BS in Acctg., Ind. U., 1982, MBA in Finance, 1983; MDiv in Theology, So. Meth. U., 1989. Ordained to ministry United Meth. Ch., 1987; CPA, Ind. Assoc. pastor St. John's United Meth., Lubbock, Tex., 1987-88; chaplain intern Terrell State Hosp., Dallas, 1989-90; assoc. pastor Carmel (Ind.) United Meth. Ch., 1990—. Mem. Assn. for Pastoral Edn., Alban Inst. Office: Carmel United Meth Ch 621 S Range Line Rd Carmel IN 46032 *The key to contentment and health is finding adequate balance in all aspects of life.*

VOELKER, CHARLES ROBERT, archbishop, academic dean; b. Cleve., June 12, 1944; s. Charles Christ and Bertha Elizabeth (Zak) V. BA, Nat. Coll. Edn., 1968; STL, Holy Trinity Sem., 1989; PhD, Internat. Sem., 1989. Ordained to ministry Orthodox Ch. as priest, 1974, as bishop, 1984. Parish priest Am. Orthodox Ch., Cleve., 1974-84; bishop Am. Orthodox Ch., Deltona, Fla., 1984—; tchr., adminstr. Ashtubula County Schs., 1971-76; acad. dean Internat. Sem., Plymouth, Fla., 1990—; pres., rector Holy Trinity Sem., Deltona, 1985—; dir. human svcs. New London (Ohio) Hosp., 1981-84; pres. Eagles Fitness Ctr., Middleburg Heights, Ohio, 1979-84; tchr. Polaris Vocat. Ctr., Middleburg Heights, 1981-83. Bd. dirs. PA, Cen. Fla., 1987-89. Mem. Order of St. Gregory the Illuminator (comdr. 1989—), Order of St. George (comdr. 1989—). Home: 1088 Eastbrook Deltona FL 32738 Office: Internat Sem PO Box 1208 Plymouth FL 32768 *To feed God's people you must first feed yourself.*

VOGEL, ARTHUR ANTON, clergyman; b. Milw., Feb. 24, 1924; s. Arthur Louis and Gladys Eirene (Larson) V.; m. Katharine Louise Nunn, Dec. 29, 1947; children: John Nunn, Arthur Anton, Katharine Ann. Student, U. of South, 1942-43, Carroll Coll., 1943-44; B.D., Nashotah House Theol. Sem., 1946; M.A., U. Chgo., 1948; Ph.D., Harvard, 1952; S.T.D., Gen. Theol. Sem., 1969; D.C.L., Nashotah House, 1969; D.D., U. of South, 1971. Ordained deacon Episcopal Ch., 1946, priest, 1948; teaching asst. philosophy Harvard, Cambridge, Mass., 1949-50; instr. Trinity Coll., Hartford, Conn., 1950-52; mem. faculty Nashotah House Theol. Sem., Nashotah, Wis., 1952-71; asso. prof. Nashotah House Theol. Sem., 1954-56, William Adams prof. philosophical and systematic theology, 1956-71, sub-dean Sem., 1964-71; bishop coadjutor Diocese of West Mo., Kansas City, 1971-72; bishop Diocese of West Mo., 1972-89; rector Ch. St. John Chrysostom, Delafield, Wis., 1952-56; dir. Anglican Theol. Rev., Evanston, Ill., 1964-69; mem. Internat. Anglican-Roman Cath. Consultation, 1970-90; mem. Nat. Anglican-Roman Catholic Consultation, 1965-84, Anglican chmn., 1973-84; mem. Standing Commn. on Ecumenical Relations of Episcopal Ch., 1957-79; mem. gen. bd. examining chaplains Episcopal Ch., 1971-72; del. Episcopal Ch., 4th Assembly World Council Chruches, Uppsala, Sweden, 1968, and others. Author: Reality, Reason and Religion, 1957, The Gift of Grace, 1958, The Christian Person, 1963, The Next Christian Epoch, 1966, Is the Last Supper Finished?, 1968, Body Theology, 1973, The Power of His Resurrection, 1976, Proclamation 2: Easter, 1980, The Jesus Prayer for Today, 1982, I Know God Better Than I Know Myself, 1989; editor: Theology in Anglicanism, 1985; contbr. to profl. jours. Vice chmn. bd. dirs. St. Luke's Hosp., Kansas City, Mo., 1971, chmn., 1973-89. Research fellow Harvard, 1950. Mem. Am. Philos. Assn., Metaphys. Soc. Am., Soc. Existential and Phenomenological Philosophy, Catholic Theol. Soc. Am. Home: 524 W 119th Terr Kansas City MO 64145

VOGEL, EUGENIA JACKSON, lay worker; b. Nashville, Nov. 15, 1932; d. Keener Harrison and Martha Virginia (McPherson) Jackson; m. George William Vogel Jr., Aug. 6, 1953 (dec. Mar. 1984); children: Virginia V. Hjalmarson, Dorothy V. France, Leslie Argueta-Vogel, Paul W., James P. BA, Maryville (Tenn.) Coll., 1954. Ordained elder Presbyn. Ch. (U.S.A.), 1987. Pastor's wife Presbyn. Ch. (U.S.A.), Tenn., Ariz., Nebr., 1953-84; dir. Phoenix Sanctuary Def. Fund, 1985; adminstrv. asst. Chs. Opposed to Undercover Govtl. Activities in Religion, Phoenix, 1985-91; dir. Clergy Spouse Ministry, Phoenix, 1986—; adminstrv. asst. Cen. Ariz. Refugee Ecumenical Svc., Phoenix, 1988—; ex officio Presbyn. Women's Ministries Com., Phoenix, 1986—; bd. dirs. Valley Religious Task Force, Phoenix, 1987—. Mem. Gen. Fedn. Women's Clubs (sec. Winslow chpt. 1966-67, chmn. pub. affairs Bellevue, Nebr. chpt. 1981-82). Home: 1006 E Cheryl Dr Phoenix AZ 85020 Office: Presbytery Grand Canyon 4423 N 24th St Ste 200 Phoenix AZ 85016 *Might does not make right, nor will it maintain peace. I pray for the day when all nations will fortify justice for all peoples, for then and only then will the world be successful in its quest for peace!.*

VOGEL, JOHN H., broadcasting executive; b. Dec. 5, 1944; m. Nelda B. Vogel. BS, Montevallo U., 1966. Program dir. Sta. WYEA Christian Radio, Sycacauga, Ala., 1983—.

VOGEL, MANFRED HENRY, philosophy educator; b. Tel-Aviv, Sept. 15, 1930; came to U.S., 1947, naturalized, 1954; s. Henry and Rachel (Fellman) V.; m. Susan A. Sugarman, Apr. 15, 1962; children: Evan James, Henry Michael. BA, Wayne State U., 1953; MA, Columbia U., 1955, PhD, 1964; M Hebrew Lit., Jewish Theol. Sem., 1957. Hillel dir., adj. lectr. philosophy Brandeis U., Waltham, Mass., 1958-62; Hillel dir. Northwestern U., Evanston, Ill., 1962-65, asst. prof. religion, 1965-67, assoc. prof., 1967-71, prof., 1971—, chmn. dept., 1972-75, 84-87. Author: A Quest for a Theology of Judaism, 1987; translator: Philosophy of the Future (L. Feuerbach), 1988; contbr. articles to profl. jours.; contbg. editor Christian Century, 1970-74. Mem. Am. Theol. Soc., Am. Acad. Religion. Jewish. Home: 2517 Greenwood St Wilmette IL 60091 Office: Northwestern U Dept Religion 1940 Sheridan Rd Evanston IL 60201

VOGEL, THOMAS TIMOTHY, surgeon, lay church worker, health care consultant; b. Columbus, Ohio, Feb. 1, 1934; s. Thomas A. and Charlotte A. (Hogan) V.; m. M.M. Darina Kelleher, May 29, 1965; children: Thomas T., Catherine D., Mark P., Nicola M. AB, Coll. of Holy Cross, 1955; MS, Ohio State U., 1960, PhD, 1962; MD, Georgetown U., 1965. Pvt. practice surgery Columbus, 1971—; chmn. liturgy com., pres. parish coun. St. Catharine Parish, Columbus, 1971-73; chmn. diocesan adminstrn. com. Diocesan Pastoral Coun., Columbus, 1972-73, chmn., 1973-75; vice prefect Sodality of Holy Cross, 1953-55; mem. Ohio Bishop's Adv. Coun., Columbus, 1976-79; clin. asst. prof. surgery Ohio State U., Columbus, 1974—; mem. med. adv. com. Comed Mgmt., Dublin, Ohio; trustee Peer Rev. Systems, Inc. Contbr. articles to profl. jours. Bd. dirs. St. Vincent's Children's Ctr., 1975-83, chmn., 1981-82; past chmn. bd. trustees St. Joseph Montessori Sch. Recipient Layman's award Columbus Ea. Kiwanis, 1972. Mem. Am. Coll. Surgeons, Am. Physiol. Soc., Assn. for Acad. Surgery, Ohio Med. Assn., Columbus Acad. Medicine, Sigma Xi, Delta Epsilon Sigma. Roman Catholic. Home: 247 S Ardmore Rd Columbus OH 43209 Office: 621 S Cassingham Rd Columbus OH 43209

VOGELS, WALTER ALFONS, theology educator; b. Berchem, Antwerp, Belgium, Oct. 14, 1932; came to Can., 1960; s. Jozef and Maria (Bats) V. S.T.L., Gregorian U., Rome, 1958; S.S.L., Biblical Inst., Rome, 1960; Ph.D., Ottawa U., 1968; S.T.D., St. Paul U., Ottawa, 1970; élève titulaire, Ecole Pratique des Hautes Etudes, Paris, 1976. Prof. Theol. Sch. White Fathers, Ottawa, Ont., Can., 1960-68; prof. Faculty of Theology, St. Paul U., Ottawa, 1966—, vice dean Faculty of Theology, 1976-82; mem. Ottawa Univ. Senate, 1982-85; vis. lectr. numerous colls. and univs. Author: La Promesse royale de Yahweh, 1970; Le prophète, un homme de Dieu, 1973; God's Universal Covenant, 1979, 2d edit., 1986; Bijbel Lezen Nu, 1982; The Prophet, A Man of God, 1982; En Hij ontsloot de Schriften, 1985; Reading and Preaching the Bible, 1986; La Bible Entre Nos Mains, 1988; Becoming Fully Human, 1988; Vivre Selon la Bible; 1988; Job, 1989; Les Prophètes, 1990. Mem. Soc. Biblical Lit., Cath. Biblical Assn. Am., Association catholique de la Bible au Canada, Société Catholique de la Bible, Atelier sémiotique du texte religieux. Home: 252 Argyle Ave, Ottawa, ON Canada K2P 1B9 Office: St Paul U, 223 Main St, Ottawa, ON Canada K1S 1C4 *If we accept ourself as we are, with our gifts and our limits, our dreams can become reality and we can make reality a dream.*

VOGT, HERMANN JOSEF, theology educator; b. Saarbrucken, Saarland, Federal Republic of Germany, July 1, 1932; s. Joseph and Klara (Walbach) V. Lic. Theology, Gregoriana, 1959; D in Theology, U. Bonn, 1968, habil., 1971. Chaplain Diocese of Trier, Bad Kreuznach, 1959-62; univ. asst. U. Bonn, 1963-69; prof. theology U. Tübingen, 1971—. Author: The Church in Novatian, 1968, The Church in Origen, 1975, Origens Commentary on the Gospel of Matthew, Vol. I, 1983, Vol. II, 1990. Mem. Commn. for Cath. Orthodox Dialogue. Home: Danzigerstr 7, D7400 Tübingen Federal Republic of Germany Office: U Tubingen, Dept Theology, Liebermeisterstr 12, D7400 Tübingen Federal Republic of Germany

VOGT, HUGH FREDERICK, minister, college administrator; b. Aberdeen, Sask., Can., Mar. 30, 1916; came to U.S., 1938; s. Harry F. and Queena Elva (Morrison) V.; divorced; children: Heather, Keren, Barbara; m. Kathleen Josephine D'Angelo, Oct. 21, 1983; children: Gregg, Steven, Scott, Michael. BA, Pasadena Coll., 1944; MA, U. Calif., L.A., 1958; DD (hon.), Ernest Holmes Coll., L.A., 1980; D of Religious Sci. (hon.), Ernest Holmes Coll., 1985. Ordained to ministry Ch. of the Nazarene, 1945. Min. Ch. of the Nazarene, Oroville, Calif., 1944-45, Pomeroy, Wash., 1945-48, Richland, Wash., 1948-51, Vancouver, Wash., 1951-56; min. Mile Hi Ch. of Religious Sci., Denver, 1966—; tchr. homiletics and ch. adminstrn. Ernest Holmes Coll., Denver, 1988—; mem. United Ch. Religious Sci., L.A. (trustee 1975-80, pres. 1982-88; Min. of Yr. 1978, Pres. award 1982); dir. Ernest Holmes Coll., Denver, 1988—. Author: Up Your Bracket, 1980, Keys to Life, 1986; host TV program New Design For Living (Angel award, 1989). Mem. United Clergy Religious Sci., Assn. Counselors and Therapists, Lakewood C. of C. (trail boss 1982-84), Rolling Hills Country Club. Republican. Office: Mile Hi Ch 9277 W Alameda Lakewood CO 80226 *To me, it is important that I frequently check as to the quality of the life I am living. I don't want to wonder at the end, in the words of the song, "Did I ever really live?".*

VOGÜÉ, ADALBERT DE, monk, researcher; b. Paris, Dec. 4, 1924; Melchior and Geneviève (Brincard) de V. ThD, Cath. Inst., Paris, 1959. Joined Benedictine Order, 1944. Prof. theology Coll. St. Anselmo, Rome, 1966-75, 88—; researcher in monastic history, dir. western monasticism sect. Dizionario Degli Istituti Di Perfezione, Rome, 1970—. Author: La Règle de S. Benoît, 1971, Vol. 7, 1977, Les Règles des Saints Pères, 1982, Le Maître, Eugippe et S. Benoît, 1984, Aux Sources du Monachisme Colombanien, 1988, Vol. 2, 1989, Histoire Littéraire du Mouvement Monastique dans l'Antiquité, 1991; mem. editorial bd. Studia Monastica, Montserrat, Spain, Monastic Studies, Montreal, Que., Can., 1983—; contbr. articles to profl. jours. Home and Office: Abbaye de la Pierre-qui-Vire, 89630 Saint Léger Vauban France

VOLKMAR, LLOYD BAKER, financial planner, minister, author; b. Westerville, Ohio, Mar. 6, 1925; s. John Frederick and Rosa Evalena (Baker) V.; m. Jeanne Faye Kemmerling, June 9, 1950; children: Kimber Leigh Volkmar Orlidge, Timothy Paul. Student, U. Chattanooga, 1943-44, U. Wis., 1945; BA, Capital U., 1949; BD, Evang. Luth. Theol. Sem., Columbus, Ohio, 1952, postgrad., 1963-65; ThM, Tex. Christian U., 1972; PhD (hon.), U.S. U. Am., 1975. Ordained to ministry Evang. Luth. Ch. Am., 1952. Instr. Conservatory of Music Capital U., 1949-51; intern Broad St. Presbyn. Ch., Columbus, 1950-51; pastor St. Peter Luth. Ch., New Haven, Mich., 1952-54; founding pastor Christ Luth. Ch., Willoughby, Ohio, 1954-60; pastor St. Luke Am. Luth. Ch., Zanesville, Ohio, 1960-65, Luth. Ch. of Our Savior, Ft. Worth, 1969-82, St. John's Luth. Ch., Dallas, 1986-88, Prince of Peace Luth. Ch., Arlington, Tex., 1988; pres. Profl. Rsch. Assocs., Ft. Worth, 1988—; instr. ethics Luth. Student Assn., Case Western Res. U., 1957; vice chmn. evangelism com. Ohio dist. Evang. Luth. Ch. Am., Columbus, 1957-58, dir. area stewardship Ohio dist., Cleve., 1958-59; fin. planner United Svcs. Planning Assn., Ft. Worth, 1965-69; instr. religion Tex. Christian U., 1973-77; pres. Tarrant Area Community of Chs., Ft. Worth, 1980-81; trustee S.E. Area Chs., Ft. Worth, 1980-81; chmn. for social action Dallas—Ft. Worth conf. Am. Luth. Ch., 1980-81, com. on social issues so. dist., 1982. Author: High Potency Thought Pills, 1971, Inject a Little Humor, 1971, Luther's Two Kingdom Doctrine from the Perspective of the Peasants' Revolt, 1972, Luther's Response to Violence, 1974, Let the Light Shine Through, 1989, Bound with Chains of Gold, 1991; also articles, essays, and poetry. Dir. Community Programs and Svcs., 1971-75, mem. com. on child abuse, 1981-82; mem. planning group Allied Communities Tarrant, Ft. Worth, 1979-82. Staff sgt. USAF, 1943-45. Decorated D.F.C., Air medals, Presdl. citation; recipient 25 Yrs. Svc. award Am. Luth. Ch., 1977, Disting. Svc. to Chs. and Community plaque Tarrant Area Community of Chs., 1981, plaque S.E. Area Chs., 1981. Mem. Rotary. Democrat. Home and Office: 3205 Reno Rd Fort Worth TX 76116-4924 *The only enduring life that is eminently worthwhile is that which is lived in Jesus Christ and lived in the world, serving the needs of those who need our help, especially the poor and the oppressed.*

VOLKWIJN, KAY-ROBERT, minister; b. Republic South Africa, June 24, 1938; s. Philip Cornelis and Mildred Gwendoline (Kay) V.; m. Desiré Eileen Lyners, Oct. 1, 1964; children: Lynne-Corinne, Donita. MA in Religion, Pitts. Theol. Sem., 1976; D Ministry with honors, McCormick Theol. Sem., Chgo., 1980. Ordained to ministry Calvin Protestant Ch. South Africa, 1961, Presbyn. Ch. South Africa, 1969. Asst. pastor Athlone Calvin Protestant Ch., Cape Town, Republic South Africa, 1961-62; pastor Retreat Calvin Protestant Ch., Cape Town, 1962-68, various chs. on Cape Flats, Cape Town, 1969-74, Timothy Darling Presbyn. Ch., Oxford, N.C., 1976-84; staff assoc. for spl. ministries, hunger action enabler Orange Presbytery, Durham, N.C., 1984-88; mem. interim staff Salem and New Hope Presbyteries, Clemmons and Rocky Mount, N.C., 1989-90; interim staff assoc. for witness and society Salem Presbytery, Clemmons, 1990; assoc. synod exec. Synod of Mid-Am., Overland Park, Kans., 1990—; commr. to Gen. Assembly, 1981, 82; moderator Cape Fear Presbytery, 1983; mem. planning com. Presbyn. Peacemaking Conf., Montreat, N.C., 1984, 89-90; vis. fellow Duke U. Div. Sch., Durham, N.C., 1990. Chmn. bd. dirs. Ctr. for Peace Edn., Chapel Hill, N.C.; founding mem. South African Med. Aid Project, Durham. Christian Trust fellow, 1972; Presbyn. Ch. (U.S.A.) scholar, 1974. Mem. Presbyn. Health, Edn. and Welfare Assn. Office: Synod of Mid-Am 6400 Glenwood Ste 111 Overland Park KS 66202 *My ministry will continue, and my hope will always be for a world where peace and justice will embrace.*

VOLL, DONALD CASPER, minister; b. Louisville, Oct. 23, 1935; s. Frederick William and Emma Emilia (Wagner) V.; m. Corita Margaret Aleff, Aug. 24, 1957; children: Randall William, Robert Todd, Daniel Scott, Jeffrey Dean, Donna Jean. BA, Lakeland Coll., Sheboygan, Wis., 1957; MDiv, United Theol. Sem., Mpls., 1960. Cert. counselor, Minn. Sr. pastor United Ch. of Christ, Wis., Ill., 1959-67; exec. dir. Boy Scouts Am., Ill., Wis., W.Va., 1967-85; ch. adminstr. Assembly of God Ch., Bloomington, Minn., 1986-87; pres. Shepherds of Peace Ministries, Burnsville, Minn., 1988—; vol. pastor Antioch Christian Fellowship, Eden Prairie, Minn., 1989—; TV producer Love Lines, Inc., Mpls., 1989—; chaplain Mpls. Police Dept., 1987—, Burnsville Police Dept., 1989—. Mem. Am. Assn. Christian Counselors, Internat. Conf. Police Chaplains, Antioch Ministerial Assn. Office: Shepherds of Peace Ministries 1708 Raleigh Dr Burnsville MN 55337

VOLP, RAINER WILHELM, theology educator, researcher; b. Worms, Germany, Oct. 11, 1931; s. Carl and Anna (Storck) V.; m. Hildegard Starke, Apr. 2, 1964; children—Annette, Hans-Henrich, Clemens-Ulrich. Student U. Heidelberg,, U. Marburg, Fed. Republic Germany, 1950-55; Exam Reverend grad. U. Marburg, Fed. Republic Germany, 1955, D. Theology, 1964. Ordained to ministry Lutheran Ch., 1960. Lectr. U. Paris, 1956-57; pastor chs., Dillenburg and Mainz, Fed. Republic Germany, 1960-68; German Research Found. scholar, Marburg, 1968-70; univ. prof. theology U. Marburg, 1970-75; ordinary prof. Coll. of Ch., Berlin, 1975-79; ordinary prof. theology U. Mainz, 1979—; dir. Institut fur Kirchenbau und kirchliche Kunst der Gegenwart der Evang. Kirche in Deutschland, Marburg, 1972-75, dean dept. theology, 1983-85. Author books including: Kunstwerk als Symbol, 1966, Liturgik, 2 vols., 1992; author and pub. books including: Zeichen—Semiotik in Theologie und Gottesdienst, 1983. Editor jour. Kunst und Kirche. Pres. Evangelischer Kirchbautag, Berlin, 1971—. Recipient grand prize Assn. German Architects, 1975. Mem. Deutscher Werkbund, Wissenschaftliche Gesellschaft. Office: Johannes Gutenberg-Univ Mainz, Saarstrasse 21, D-6500 Mainz Federal Republic of Germany

VOLZ, ARTHUR WILLIAM, clergyman; b. Washington, May 13, 1942; s. Frederick Emil and Mabel Grace (Fulk) V.; m. Arlene Catherine Grow, July 10, 1965; children: Jonathan Frederick, Julee Catherine. BCE, U. Wash., 1965; ThM, Dallas Sem., 1970. Ordained to ministry non-denominational community ch., 1970. Dir. edn. and youth Calvary Bible Ch., Wenatchee, Wash., 1970-74; dir. edn. and youth West Park Baptist Ch., Bakersfield, Calif., 1974-77; adminstr. Community Christian Acad., Cave Junction, Oreg., 1978-81; minister edn. Lacey (Wash.) Bapt. Chapel, 1981—; seminar instr. Walk Thru Bible Ministries, Atlanta, 1987-90. Asst. athletic coach Evergreen Christian Sch., Olympia, Wash., 1981-82; mem. human relations coun. North Thurston High Sch., Olympia, 1988—. Mem. Profl. Assn. Christian Educators. Avocations: sports, gardening. Home: 7910 Shasta Ct SE Olympia WA 98503 Office: Lacey Bapt Chapel 6646 Pacific Ave SE Lacey WA 98503

VOLZ, CARL ANDREW, religious educator; b. Fairbault, Minn., Oct. 7, 1933; s. Oswald Samuel and Louise Marie (Werling) V.; m. Lydia Anna Rittmann, Aug. 17, 1958; children: Carol, Martin, Stephen, Katherine, Michael. MDiv, Concordia Sem., 1958; MA, Wash. U., 1961; STM, Concordia Sem., 1959; PhD, Fordham U., 1966. Asst. prof. Concordia Coll., Bronxville, N.Y., 1959-64; pastor Christ Luth. Ch., Yonkers, N.Y., 1961-64; prof. Concordia Sem., St. Louis, 1964-74, Luther N.W. Theol. Sem., St. Paul, 1974—; chmn. dept. ch. history, Luther Sem., St. Paul, 1985—. Editor: Teaching the Faith, 1967; author: The Church in the Middle Ages, 1970, Faith & Practice in The Early Church, 1983, Pastoral Life and Practice in the Early Church, 1989; contbr. articles to numerous publs. Bd. dirs. Luth. Social Svcs., St. Louis, 1964-74, Ecumenical Inst., Collegeville, Minn., 1974—. Named John W. Behnken fellow, Aid Assn. for Luths., Appleton, Wis., 1971, Luth. Brotherhood scholar, Luth. Brotherhood, Mpls., 1987. Fellow N.Am. Acad. Liturgy, N.Am. Patristics Assn.; mem. Am. Soc. Ch. History, Medieval Acad. Am., Concordia Hist. Inst., Phi Beta Kappa. Lutheran. Home and Office: 2481 Como Ave Saint Paul MN 55108

VON BEHREN, RONALD CRAIG, educator, administrator; b. Detroit, July 12, 1946; s. Ovian Walter and Bettie Jane (Cox) Von B.; m. Deborah Lois Davidson, May 25, 1969; children: Kerry Jodi, Jason. BA, Fla. Bible Coll., 1968, ThB, 1976, DD, 1990; MDiv, Biblical Theol. Sem., Hatfield, Pa., 1976; AA, Broward Community Coll., Ft. Lauderdale, Fla., 1978; BA, U. Cen. Fla., 1985, MA, 1992. Ordained to ministry Bapt. Ch., 1968. Youth dir. Davisville Bapt. Ch., Southampton, Pa., 1969-74; instr. Fla. Bible Coll., Kissimmee, 1976-79, acad. dean, 1983-86, pres., 1986-91, mem. full time faculty, 1991—; tchr. Carolina Christian Sch., Charlotte, N.C., 1979-80, Lehigh Christian Acad., Allentown, Pa., 1980-81; tchr., prin. Salem Christian Sch., Macungie, Pa., 1981-83; adj. prof. Valencia Community Coll., Kissimmee, 1985—; cons., Kissimmee, 1987—. Named Alumnus of Yr. Fla. Bible Coll. Mem. Creation Social Sci. and Humanities Soc. Republican. Avocations: tennis, softball. Home and Office: Fla Bible Coll 1701 N Poinciana Blvd Kissimmee FL 32758

VON CRAIGH, BERTHA THERESA, minister; b. Buffalo, Sept. 8, 1939; d. Francis McKinley and Gertrude (Kaczorowski) von C. BA in Religion, Wittenburg U., 1967; MA in Religion, Luth. Sch. Theol., 1969, MDiv, 1974. Ordained to ministry Luth. Ch., 1974. Deaconess Manheim (Pa.) Luth. ch., 1970-74; assoc. dir. div. profl. leadership Phila., 1981; asst. to bishop Cen. Pa. Synod Luth Ch. Am., Harrisburg, 1984-87; pastor Zion Luth. Ch., Manheim, 1974-75, St. Mark's Luth. Ch., West Fairview, Pa., 1977-80; acct., product sales mgr. Hemlock Girl Scout Council, Harrisburg, Pa., 1982-84; specialist for region and synod relationships Evang. Luth. Ch. in Am., 1988—, Ministry in Daily Life, 1988—. Author poems. Mem. fin. mgmt. com. Hemlock Girl Scout Coun., Harrisburg, 1984-89, life mem. Girl Scouts U.S. Mem. Acad. Preachers, Acad. Evangelists. Democrat. Avocations: photography, writing, reading, gardening, angling for trout and bass. Home: 880 Piketown Rd Harrisburg PA 17112 Office: 8765 W Higgins Rd Chicago IL 60631

VON DOHLEN, WILLIAM AUGUST, II, minister; b. Charleston, S.C., June 5, 1954; s. William August and Dorothy Mae (Wheeling) Von D. BS, Coll. of Charleston, 1976; MDiv, Southern Sem., 1980, DMin, 1991. Ordained to ministry Bapt. Ch., 1978. Min. youth Rutledge Ave Bapt. Ch., Charleston, 1974-76; chaplain Bapt. Hosp., Little Rock, 1980-81, St. Elisabeths Hosp., Washington, 1981-82, U. Va. Med. Ctr., Charlottesville, Va., 1982-85; staff chaplain St. Thomas Hosp., Nashville, 1985—; pres. bd. dirs. St. Thomas Credit Union, Nashville, 1986—. Mem. Coll. of Chaplains, Spiritual Companioning Svcs. (bd. dirs.), Masons, Rotary. Republican. Home: 229 Patterson St Dickson TN 37055-9701 Office: St Thomas Hosp 4220 Harding Rd Nashville TN 37205

VON GONTEN, KEVIN PAUL, priest, liturgist, theologian; b. Bklyn., Mar. 21, 1949; s. Joseph William and Marion (Loughran) Von G.; m. Lauranne Marie Coxon, May 20, 1984. BA in Religious Studies, St. Francis Coll., Bklyn., 1979; AM in Hist. Theology, Fordham U., 1982; STM, Gen. Theol. Sem., N.Y.C, 1987. Ordained to ministry Episcopal Ch. as deacon, 1987, as priest, 1987. Prof. St. Francis Coll., Bklyn., 1982-87; asst. pastor St. Gregory's Ch., Parsippany, N.J., 1985-87; assoc. rector St. Stephen's Ch., Port Washington, N.Y., 1987-89; vicar All Souls Ch., Stony Brook, N.Y., 1989—; prof. George Mercer Sch. Theology, Garden City, N.Y.; chmn. Diocesan Commn. on Liturgy; dir. exploration of ministry program Diocese of L.I., 1987—. Mem. Am. Acad. Religion, N.Am. Acad. Liturgy, Coll. Theology Soc., Theta Alpha Kappa. Office: All Souls Ch 10 Mill Pond Rd Stony Brook NY 11790

VON STIETENCRON, HEINRICH H., educator; b. Ronco, Switzerland, June 18, 1933; s. Georg Eduard von S. Dr.phil., U. Munich, 1965; Dr.habil., U. Heidelberg, 1970. Asst. prof. South Asia Inst., Heidelberg, 1970-73; prof., head Seminar für Indologie u. Vgl. Religionswiss, U. Tubingen, W.Ger., 1973—, dean Fakultät für Kulturwissenschaften, 1981-82; vis. prof. Temple U., Phila., 1983, Universita La Sapientia, Rome, 1989. Author: Indische Sonnenpriester, 1966; Ganga und Yamuna, 1972; co-author: The Cult of Jagannath and the Regional Tradition of Orissa, 1978; Christentum und Weltreligionen, 1984,Das Alte Indien, 1990; editor: Der Name Gottes, 1975; Angst und Gewalt, 1979; Dämonen und Gegengötter, 1984; Theologen und Theologien in verschiedenen Kulturkreisen, 1986,Krieg und Kultur, 1986; Purana Research Publs., Tübingen, Vol. I: Sanskrit Indices and Text of the Brahma Purana, 1987, Vol. II: Brahma Purana: Summary of Contents with Index of Names and Motifs, 1989, Vol. III: Annotated Bibliography of Epics and Puranas, Part I: Bibliography, Part II: Indexes, 1991; Angst und Religion, 1991; translator: Sitakant Mahapatra, Hahnenkampf, poems from the Oriya, 1991; contbr. articles to profl. jours. Mem. Deutsche Morgenländische Gesellschaft, Deutsche Vereinigung für Religionsgeschichte (pres. 1980-88), Deutsche Gesellschaft für Asienkunde (exec. com. 1982—), Wiss Gesellschaft für Theologie (hon.), South Asian Religious Art Studies (adv. bd.), Inst. für Historische Anthropologie (chmn. 1984-91). Office: U Tübingen, Seminar für Indologie, Münzgasse 30, D-7400 Tübingen Federal Republic of Germany

VON WAHLDE, URBAN CAMILLUS, religion educator; b. Covington, Ky., Oct. 28, 1941; s. Urban Bernard and Louise Catherine (Reeves) von W.; m. Carol Anne Dvorak, May 13, 1973; children: Michael David, Lisa Maureen. BA in Philosophy, Loyola U., Chgo., 1965, MA in Classics, 1966; PhD in Religious Studies, Marquette U., 1975. Asst. prof. theology St. Mary of the Plains Coll., Dodge City, Kans., 1974-76; assoc. prof. theology, chairperson U. Scranton, Pa., 1976-81; assoc. prof. Loyola U., 1981-90, prof., 1990—, chairperson dept. theology, 1987—. Author: The Earliest Version of John's Gospel, 1989, The Johannine Commandments: 1 John and the Struggle for the Johannine Tradition, 1990; editor: Catholic Biblical Quarterly, 1988—. Rsch. fellow Yale Divinity Sch., 1979. Mem. Cath. Bibl. Assn. Am., Soc. Bibl. Lit., Chgo. Soc. Bibl. Rsch. Office: Loyola U Chgo Dept Theology 6525 N Sheridan Rd Chicago IL 60626

VON WEIZSÄCKER, ERNST ULRICH, environmental scientist; b. Zürich, Switzerland, June 25, 1939; s. Carl Friedrich and Gundalena (Wille) Von W.; m. Christine Radtke; children: Jakob, Paula, Adam, Franz, Maria. Diploma in Physics, U. Hamburg, Fed. Republic of Germany, 1965; PhD in Biology, U. Freiburg, Fed. Republic of Germany, 1969. Fellow Protestant Interdisc Rsch. Inst., Heidelberg, Fed. Republic of Germany, 1969-72; prof. Biology U. Essen, Fed. Republic of Germany, 1972-75; pres. U. Kassel, Fed. Republic of Germany, 1975-80; dir. UN Ctr. for Sci. and Tech., N.Y.C., 1981-84, Inst. for European Environ. Policy, Bonn, 1984-91; pres. for climate, environ. and energy Wuppertal (Fed. Republic Germany) Inst., 1991—. Author, editor: Offene Syteme I, 1974, Erdpolitik, 1989. Recipient Pfaff prize Pfaff Found., 1977, Premio de Natura award, 1989. Mem. AAAS, German Zool. Soc., Club of Rome. Mem. Social Dem. Party. Lutheran. Avocation: chess. Office: Wuppertal Inst, Doeppersberg 19, 5600 Wuppertal Federal Republic of Germany

VOORHEES, RAYMOND CARL, minister; b. Granite City, Ill., June 13, 1947; s. Gerald Lee and Beulah Ruth (Hoffman) V.; m. Shirley Annette Simmons, Aug. 25, 1967; children: Matthew, Michele, Stephanie, Rebecca, Joshua. BA in Music Edn. and Voice Performance, So. Ill. U., 1969. Cert. tchr., Ill., Mo. Min. music 1st Bapt. Ch., Deridder, La., 1971-75; assoc. pastor 1st Bapt. Ch., Tijeras, N.Mex., 1980-85; with evangelistic ministry God's Love in Action, Switzerland, 1975-77; min. music Chambers Rd. Bapt., Aurora, Colo., 1977-80; assoc. pastor South Kansas City (Mo.) Bapt., 1985—. Home: 6812 E 127th Terr Grandview MO 64030 Office: South Kansas City Bapt Ch 10200 James A Reed Rd Kansas City MO 64134

VOSS, CARL HERMANN, clergyman, humanities educator, author; b. Pitts., Dec. 8, 1910; s. Carl August and Lucy (Wilms) V.; m. Dorothy Katherine Grote, Nov. 25, 1940 (div. 1957); 1 dau., Carlyn Grote (Mrs. Harold Iuzzolino); m. Phyllis MacKenzie Gierlotka, May 9, 1959; 1 dau., Christina Elisabeth Gierlotka (Mrs. Russell P. Wynings Jr.). AB, U. Pitts., 1931, PhD, 1942; student, Internat. People's Coll., Elsinore, Denmark, U. Geneva, Switzerland, 1931, Chgo. Theol. Sem., 1931-32; M.Div., Union Theol. Sem., 1935; postgrad., Yale Div. Sch., 1938-40; postgrad. in Hebrew studies, Oxford U., 1977-79; postgrad., Ecumenical Inst. Bossey, World Council Chs., Geneva, 1980-81; L.H.D., Hebrew Union Coll.-Jewish Inst. Religion, N.Y.C., 1981. Minister United Ch. (Congl.-Christian-Friends), Raleigh, N.C., 1935-38; chaplain Cheshire (Conn.) Acad., 1938-40; assoc. minister Smithfield United Ch., Pitts., 1940-43; extension sec. Ch. Peace Union and World Alliance for Internat. Friendship Through the Chs., 1943-49; editor World Alliance News Letter, 1944-49; exec. sec. Christian Council on Palestine, 1943-46; chmn. exec. council Am. Christian Palestine Com., 1946-57; minister Flatbush Unitarian Ch., Bklyn., 1953-57, N.E. Congl. Ch., Saratoga Springs, N.Y., 1957-64; Merrill research asso. Brandeis U., 1965-67; lectr. New Sch. for Soc. Research, 1948-56; lectr. dept. philosophy and religion Skidmore College, Saratoga Springs, 1960-61, 65-66; vis. prof. theology and history religions Theol. Sch. St. Lawrence U., Canton, N.Y., 1964-65; prof. humanities Edward Waters Coll., Jacksonville, Fla., 1973-76; chmn. humanities div. Edward Waters Coll., 1974-76; NCCJ ecumenical-scholar-in-residence; resident scholar Ecumenical Inst. Advanced Theol. Studies, Tantur, Jerusalem, 1976-77; Centre Postgrad. Hebrew Studies Oxford U., 1977, 79; conducted European tours, 1930, 31, 35, (Arab countries and Israel), 1949, 51, 53, 55, 58, 63, 66, 70, 73, 75, 79; (lectr. tour), Rhodesia, South Africa under auspices Good Will Council S.Africa, 1947. Author: The Palestine Problem Today, 1953, (with Theodore Huebner) This Is Israel, 1956, Rabbi and Minister: The Friendship of Stephen S. Wise and John Haynes Holmes, 1964, In Search of Meaning: Living Religions of the World, 1968, Stephen S. Wise: Servant of The People-Selected Letters, 1969, A Summons unto Men: An Anthology of the Writings of John Haynes Holmes, 1971, Living Religions of the World: Our Search for Meaning, 1977, (with David A. Rausch) Protestantism: Its Modern Meaning, 1987; editor: The Universal God: An Interfaith Anthology, 1953, Excalibur Books, 1964—, Quotations of Courage and Vision: A Source Book for Speaking, Writing and Meditation, 1972, (with David A. Rausch) World Religions: Our Quest for Meaning, 1989; contbr. to mags. and religious jours. Recipient Nat. Brotherhood award NCCJ, 1978; hon. fellow Hebrew U., Jerusalem, 1979; Carl Hermann Voss scholarship named in honor by Ctr. for Hebrew Studies Oxford U., Eng., 1990. Mem. Sigma Alpha Epsilon, Theta Alpha Phi, Druids. Unitarian Universalist. Home: 7783 Point Vicente Ct Baymeadows Jacksonville FL 32256

VOSS, KATHRYN ANN, church program administrator; b. Salida, Colo., Dec. 13, 1933; d. Edgar William and Helen Faye (Robertson) Lujan; m. Donald Paul Voss, June 15, 1957; children: Martin, Gregory, Annette, Rita, Theresa, Margaret, Cathy, Mary, Joanie, Jennifer. BA in Math., Immaculate Heart Coll., Los Angeles, 1955. Dance tchr. Louis DaPron Studio, Hollywood, Calif., 1945-52; prin. Westchester Sch. of Dance, Los Angeles, 1953-57; aero. engr. N.Am. Aviation, Los Angeles, 1955-59; dir. office of family life Roman Cath. Diocese, Phoenix, 1981—. Contbr. articles to profl jours.; performed with USO, 1950-57; free lance choreographer, Los Angeles, Phoenix, 1953-57; choreographer Washington Dist. Project Potential Choir, Phoenix, 1979-83; speaker on marriage and family topics, Phoenix, 1968—. Mem. resource com. State Task Force on Marriage and Family, Phoenix, 1977; mem. adv. bd. County Youth Service Bur., Maricopa County, Ariz., 1978-81; chmn. family affairs Phoenix Diocesan Council of Cath. Women, 1975-81. Mem. Nat. Assn. Cath. Diocesan Family Life Ministers (bd. dirs. 1983—, nat. treas. 1985—). Avocations: choreography, music, sports. Home: 347 W Pine Valley Dr Phoenix AZ 85023 Office: Cath Diocese of Phoenix 400 E Monroe Phoenix AZ 85004

VOSS, MARCUS JOSEPH, priest; b. Cullman, Ala., Aug. 29, 1943; s. Joseph William and Catherine (Clark) V. BA, St. Bernard Coll., Cullman, 1966; MDiv, St. Louis U., 1970; M of Spirituality, Creighton U., 1981. Joined Order of St. Benedict, 1963, ordained priest Roman Cath. Ch., 1971. Retreat dir. St. Bernard Ctr., Cullman, 1972—; choirmaster St. Bernard Abbey, Cullman, 1973-86, master of novices, 1979-81, bus. mgr., 1981-82, formation dir., 1982-86; headmaster St. Bernard Prep. Sch., Cullman, 1986—. Editor: Office of the Hours, 1985. Mem. Cath. Boarding Schs. Am. Home and Office: St Bernard Prep Sch 101 St Bernard Dr SE Cullman AL 35055

VOSS, RICHARD WILLIAM, pastoral counseling educator, psychotherapist; b. Phila., Aug. 27, 1950; s. Aaron H.G. and Sophie (Kuras) V.; m. Patricia Ann Blastic, June 3, 1977,. BA, St. Fidelis Coll., 1973; MSW, Fordham U., 1977; MTS, Washington Theol. Union, 1986; D Pastoral Counseling, Loyola Coll., 1989. Cert. social worker; lic. social worker, Pa. Staff counselor Catholic Social Svcs., West Chester, Pa., 1977-78, clin. supr., 1978-86; clin. supr. Chester County Children & Youth, West Chester, Pa., 1986-89, dir. program, 1988-89; pvt. practice West Chester, Pa., 1986—; asst. prof. grad. program Neumann Coll., Aston, Pa., 1989—. Contbr. articles to profl. jours. Recipient Messenger John O'Grady award Nat. Conf. Catholic Charities, 1984. Fellow Am. Assn. Orthopsychiatry; mem. NASW, Am. Assn. Pastoral Counselors (profl. affiliate). Home: RD 2 Box 449 Glenmoore PA 19343 Office: 1501 Mc Daniel Dr West Chester PA 19343

VOTARY, R. E., minister. Gen. supt. Independent Holiness Ch., Sydenham, Ont., Can. Office: Independent Holiness Ch, Sydenham, ON Canada K0H 2T0*

VOUGA, FRANCOIS, theologian, educator; b. Neuchâtel, Switzerland, Oct. 25, 1948; s. Paul-Henri and Jacqueline (Rochat) V.; m. Anne Fontaine Downs, June 6, 1983; children: Paul Etienne, Maren Elisabeth, Alexandre Gérard. ThD, U. Genève, 1985. Asst. N.T. U. Lausanne, Switzerland, 1973-74; pastor Eglise Nat. Protestant, Genève, 1975-82; maître-asst. Faculté libre de théologie, Montpellier, France, 1982-85, prof. N.T., 1985-86, assoc. prof., 1986-88; prof. N.T. Kirchliche Hochschule Bethel, Bielefeld, Fed. Republic Germany, 1986—. Author: Le cadre historique et l'intention théologique de Jean, 1977, L'épître de Jacques, 1984, Jésus et la Loi selon la tradition synoptique, 1988, Die Johannesbriefe, 1990; contbr. articles to profl. jours. Mem. Conseil Communal, Morges, Switzerland, 1969-70. Mem. Studiorum Novi Testamenti Societas, Wissenschaftliche Gesellschaft für Theologie. Mem. Socialist Party. Home: An der Rehwiese 42, D4800 Bielefeld 13, Federal Republic of Germany Office: Kirchliche Hochschule Bethel, Remterweg 45, D4800 Bielefeld 13, Federal Republic of Germany

VOUGHT, JOHN MARK, JR., minister; b. Danville, Pa., Nov. 7, 1937; s. John Mark and Florence Elizabeth (Anderson) V.; m. Joyce Marie Burrell, Sept. 1, 1956; children: Joseph M., Joy Michelle. BA, Susquehanna U., Selinsgrove, Pa., 1964; MDiv, Gettysburg (Pa.) Sem., 1968; AA, Harrisburg Area Community Coll., 1973. Ordained to ministry Evang. Luth. Ch. Police officer Boro of Lewisburg (Pa.), 1961-62; night watch and radio operator Penn Dot, Gettysburg, Pa., 1962-68; pastor Union Deopsit Parish, Hershey, Pa., 1968-73; pastor-spl. call Brickerville Luth. Chs., Lititz, Pa., 1973-77; pastor Luther Meml. Evang. Luth. Ch., York, Pa., 1977—; instr. police adminstrn. Harrisburg Area Community Coll., 1974-76; v.p. C.P. Luth. Credit Union, York, 1978-82; chair C.P. Synod Compensation and Benefits Com., Harrisburg, 1980—; coord., leader pre-retirement seminars, Harrisburg, York, 1980—, clergy tax/fin/negotiation seminars, Gettysburg, York, 1984—. Flood rescue and housing coord. South Hanover Twp. Schs., Hershey, Pa., 1972. Mem. Sertoma (chaplain 1980-90). Office: Luther Meml Evang Luth Ch 1907 Hollywood Dr York PA 17403

VOWELL, LARRY KAY, clergyman; b. Ft. Worth, Aug. 25, 1944; s. William Burks and Glenna Belle (Higgins) V.; m. Brenda Mary Colyer, June 25, 1965; children: Laura Michelle, Julie Kay. BA, Tex. Wesleyan U., 1967; MRE, Southwestern Bapt. Theol. Sem., Ft. Worth, 1969. Ordained to ministry Bapt. Ch., 1967. Minister music and edn. Southside Bapt. Ch., Irving, Tex., 1966-68; minister edn. and youth Calvary Bapt. Ch., Irving, 1968-69, East Temple Bapt. Ch., Dallas, 1969-70, 1st Bapt. Ch., Dickinson, Tex., 1970-71; minister edn. Northway Bapt. Ch., Dallas, 1971-75, Mobberly Bapt. Ch., Longview, Tex., 1975-77, 79-83; dir. ch. svcs. Waco (Tex.) Bapt. Assn., 1977-79; minister edn. and adminstrn. Columbus Avenue Bapt. Ch., Waco, 1983—; former conf. leader Dallas Bapt. Assn.; former conf. leader Gregg Bapt. Assn., moderator, 1981-83; cons. Bapt. Gen. Conv. Tex., Dallas, 1980—; conf. leader So. Bapt. Sunday Sch. Bd., Nashville. Mem. City of Woodway Planning and Zoning Commn., Waco, 1989—. Mem. Nat. Assn. Ch. Bus. Adminstrn., So. Bapt. Religious Edn. Assn., Southwestern Bapt. Religious Edn. Assn. (com. chmn. 1969—), So. Bapt. Ch. Bus. Adminstrn. Assn., Met. Religious Edn. Assn., Tex. Bapt. Ministers Edn. Assn. (pres. 1987-88), Waco Bapt. Assn. (conf. leader, moderator 1985-86), Waco C. of C., Dr. Pepper Collectors (editor 1990—). Republican. Avocations: golf, snow skiing, camping. Home: 210 Whitehall Waco TX 76712 Office: Columbus Avenue Bapt Ch 1300 Columbus Ave Waco TX 76703

VOYTKO, SISTER M. MERCEDES, nun; b. Hazleton, Pa., June 2, 1931; d. Michael and Anna (Vantuch) V. B.A., Marywood Coll., 1961, M.S., 1974; postgrad. Scranton U., 1976-77; postgrad. in pastoral ministry, LaSalle U., 1982—. Joined Sisters of Sts. Cyril and Methodius. Elem. tchr. Cath. schs., 1952-70; high sch. tchr. Cath. schs., Kingston and Dunmore, Pa., 1976-78; prin. St. Joseph's Sch., Nanticoke, Pa., 1976-78; pastoral asst. St. Joseph's Ch., Danville, Pa., 1982—, health care minister, 1980—, spl. eucharistic minister, 1980—; CCD dir. Cath. schs., 1979—. Mem. St. Vincent De Paul Soc., Danville-Riverside Ministerium, Phi Alpha Theta. Avocations: secretarial work, visiting the sick, computers. Home: 9 Bloom St Danville PA 17821 Office: St Josephs Ch 18 E Center St Danville PA 17821 *We are begotten of love. Love gives life and meaning to our everyday actions. God is love! Hence our contribution to humanity will parallel our personal relationship and love of God.*

VREUGDENHIL, RALPH LYLE, minister; b. Venus, Nebr., Feb. 21, 1940; s. Harmen and Eunice Rachel (Bennett) V.; m. Velera Faye Downer, Apr. 3, 1964; children: John Alan, Timothy James. BA in Religion, Miltonvale (Kans.) Wesleyan Coll., 1961; MEd, U. Portland, 1975. Ordained to ministry Wesleyan Ch., 1970. Tchr. Dakota Mission to the Philippines, Luzon, The Philippines, 1961-62; pastor Guymon (Okla.) Wesleyan Ch., 1967-69; counselor Youth Outreach Inc., Vancouver, Wash., 1968-77; dir. men's div. Tacoma Rescue Mission, 1982-89; adminstrv. pastor Puyallup (Wash.) Ch. of the Nazarene, 1989—; elder Wash./Pacific Dist. Nazarene Ch., 1981-91. Developed New Life Program, 1982. Mem. Christian Mgmt. Assn., Wash. Ch. Adminstrs., Kiwanis, Rotary. Office: Puyallup Ch of the Nazarene 1026 7th Ave SW Puyallup WA 98371 *True "life" is a series of decisions to obey God.*

VSEVOLOD, bishop. Primate Ukrainian Orthodox Ch. in Am., Jamaica, N.Y. Office: Ukranian Orthodox Ch in Am 90-34 139th St Jamaica NY 11435*

VUNDERINK, RALPH WILLIAM, lay minister; b. Amsterdam, The Netherlands, Jan. 7, 1939; s. Rudolf M. Vunderink and Wietske Vunderink Stienstra; m. Tena Harkema, May 24, 1963; children: Randolph M., Phillip J. BA, Calvin Coll., 1960; BD, Calvin Sem., 1963; MA, U. Chgo., 1965, PhD, 1969. Ordained to ministry Christian Reformed Ch., 1986. Lay minister Classis Lake Erie, ea. Mich. and Ohio, 1968-75, 83-85; prof. of religion Hope Coll., Holland, Mich., 1975-79, Winebrenner Sem., Findlay, Ohio, 1983-87; pastor Bloom Ctr. Ch. of God, Cygnet, Ohio, 1985-87; freelance writer, editor Jenison, Mich., 1987—. Editorial asst.: The International Standard Bible Encyclopedia, vol. 1, 1979, vol. 2, 1982; co-translator, co-editor: Eerdmans Bible Dictionary, 1987; translator: (H. Bultema) A Brief Commentary on Zechariah, 1987. Mem. Am. Philos. Assn., Am. Acad. Religion, Calvinistic Philos. Soc. Republican. Home: 899 Village Lane Jenison MI 49428 *A faithful Savior Christ will never let go those loved, even if momentarily the facts seem to point contrariwise.*

WACHS, SAUL PHILIP, Jewish education educator; b. Phila., Dec. 24, 1931; s. Abraham and Annette (Schaller) W.; m. Barbara Ruth Eidelman, Jan. 27, 1957; children: Sharona Rachel, Hillel Eliezer, Devorah Leah, Aviva Marcia. BS in Edn., Temple U., 1953; BRE, Jewish Theol. Sem., 1956, B in Sacred Music, 1959, D Pedagogy (hon.), 1989; MA, Ohio State U., 1966, PhD, 1970. Dir. edn. Congregation Tifereth Israel, Columbus, Ohio, 1960-70, Park Ave Synagogue, N.Y.C., 1970-72; asst. prof., dir. Jewish edn. program Brandeis U., Waltham, Mass., 1972-75; dean Gratz Coll., Phila., 1975-80, Rosaline B. Feinstein prof. of Jewish edn., chair dept. 1980—; bd. dirs. Jewish Edn. Assembly, N.Y.C., 1965-70, Akiba, Merion, Pa., 1975—, Beth Hillel-Beth El, Wynnewood, Pa., 1984-88, Coun. for Jewish Edn., N.Y.C., 1970-74; vis. lectr. Hebrew U., 1986-89, tutor, 1988-89, vis. researcher, 1985; vis. professorial lectr. Am. U.-George Washington U.; vis. prof. Jewish Theol. Sem. Am.; vis. instr. Coll. of Jewish Studies, Cleve., 1965-69. Co-author texts: Judaism, 1979, Jewish Education, 1991, also curriculum materials; contbr. articles to religious publs. Mem. Soviet Jewry com. Phila Jewish Community Rels. Coun.; bd. dirs. Akiba Hebrew Acad. Recipient Aaron Zacks award Am. Assn. for Jewish Edn., 1969. Mem. Coalition for Jewish Edn., ASCD, Phi Delta Kappa. Home: 107 Maple Ave Bala Cynwyd PA 19006 Office: Gratz Coll Melrose Ave and Old York Rd Melrose Park PA 19126 *"Happiness consists of the fulfillment of the need to be needed." (Abraham Joshua Heschel). Teaching can make a person happy because a teacher is needed.*

WADDELL, R. EUGENE, minister; b. Wayne County, N.C., Feb. 7, 1932; s. Robert Lee and Rena (Holland) W.; m. Elva Leah Nichols, July 22, 1954 (dec. Apr. 1962); children: Rhonda Waddell Sagraves, Robert, Paul, Marcia Waddell Thompson; m. Genevieve Johnson, July 4, 1963; children: Michael, John. BA, Free Will Bapt. Bible Coll., Nashville, 1954; MA, Columbia (S.C.) Bibl. Sem., 1966. Ordained to ministry Free Will Bapt. Ch., 1952. Pastor Bay Branch Free Will Bapt. Ch., Timmonsville, S.C., 1954-56, 1st Free Will Bapt. Ch., Portsmouth, Va., 1956-60, Garner (N.C.) Free Will Bapt. Ch., 1960-64, Cofer's Chapel Free Will Bapt. Ch., Nashville, 1964-81; assoc. dir. Free Will Bapt. Fgn. Missions Dept., Nashville, 1981-86, gen. dir., 1986—; bd. dirs. Free Will Bapt. Fgn. Missions, Nashville, 1959-78, bd. sec., 1971-78; founder, editor Free Will Bapt. Witness, Garner, 1962-63. Mem. Bd. United Tenn. League, Nashville, 1969—. Office: Free Will Bapt Fgn Missions 5233 Mt View Rd Antioch TN 37013-2306

WADDELL, RICHARD LORD, JR., minister; b. L.A., Oct. 14, 1936; s. Richard Lord Sr. and Margaret Preston (Grotthouse) W.; m. Shirley Mae Ginther, Aug. 24, 1957; 1 child, Christopher Lord. BA, Vanderbilt U., 1958, BD, 1962, MDiv, 1976, D Ministry, 1986. Ordained to ministry United Presbyn. Ch. (U.S.A.), 1962. Dir. Student Christian Assn. Vanderbilt U., Nashville, 1962-66; radio announcer Sta. WPLN-FM Pub. Libr. of Nashville and Davidson County, Tenn., 1966-68; assoc. minister First Ch. of Christ, New Haven, 1968-80; minister First Congl. Ch. United Ch. of Christ, Farmington, Maine, 1980—; pres. Downtown Coop. Ministry, New Haven, 1979-80; pres. bd. chaplains Franklin Meml. Hosp., Farmington; chmn. com. on ministry Franklin Assn. Maine Conf. United Ch. of Christ, 1986—. Author: Stewardship: A Response to the Gift of Creation, 1986. Bd. dirs. Franklin County Children's Task Force, Farmington, 1990—. Danforth Found. sem. intern, 1960-61. Democrat. Home: 8 Highland Ave Farmington ME 04938 Office: First Congl Ch United Ch of Christ PO Box 509 Farmington ME 04938

WADDLE, DAVID BOURNE, minister; b. Lexington, Ky., Dec. 26, 1945; s. Cornelius Bourne and Crystal (Girdler) W.; m. Lynn Ann Boggess, Jan. 31, 1970; children: Wesley David, Anne Bourne, Andrew Boggess. BA, U. Louisville, 1983; MDiv, So. Bapt. Theol. Seminary, Louisville, 1986. Pastor Bethel United Meth. Ch., Brandenburg, Ky., 1984-86; assoc. minister Meml. United Meth. Ch., Elizabethtown, Ky., 1986-89; pastor Grace Heartland Ch., Elizabethtown, 1989—. Home: 406 Smith Ave Elizabethtown KY 42701 Office: Grace Heartland Church 617 N Mulberry Elizabethtown KY 42701

WADDY, LAWRENCE HEBER, religious writer; b. Sydney, Australia, Oct. 5, 1914; came to U.S., 1963; s. Percival Stacy and Etheldred (Spittal) W.; m. Laurie Hancock, July 10, 1972. BA, Oxford (Eng.) U., 1937, MA, 1945. Asst. master Winchester Coll. Eng., 1938-42; headmaster Tombridge Coll., Eng., 1949-62; edn. officer BBC, Eng., 1962-63; chaplain The Bishop's Sch., La Jolla, Calif., 1963-67; lectr. in Greek and Latin lit. U. Calif., San Diego, 1969-80; vicar Ch. of Good Samaritan, University City, Calif., 1970-74; hon. asst. St. James By The Sea Episcopal Ch., La Jolla, 1975—. Author: Pax Romana & World Peace, 1950, The Bible as Drama, 1975, Drama in Worship, 1978, Symphony, 1976, A Parish By the Sea, 1988. Chaplain Royal Navy of Eng., 1942-46. Recipient Drama 1st prize BBC, 1964. Republican. Home: 5910 Camino De La Costa La Jolla CA 92037

WADE, ANDREW THOMAS, pastor; b. Orlando, Fla., July 27, 1954; s. Andrew Thomas Sr. and Anna (Wells) W.; m. Candye Finley, Nov. 13, 1976; children: Traci Renee, Nathanael Thomas, Amy Christina, Andrea Clarece. BA, U. Fla., 1976; postgrad., United Bible Coll., 1979-81. Cert. civil defence, CPR. Corrections officer Dept. Rehab., Correctional Inst., Raiford, Fla., 1976-79; adminstrv. asst. Park Fed. Savings, Winter Park, Fla., 1979-80; employement dir. Urban LEague, Orlando, Fla., 1980-83; community svc. officer Orlando Police Dept., Fla., 1983-84, police officer, 1984-90; assoc. pastor El Bethel Temple, Orlando, 1990—; bd. dirs. Met. Orlando Urban League, 1989—, Nat. Coalition Christians and Jews, Orlando, 1990, Interdenominational Ministrial Alliance, Orlando, 1990; pres., exec. dir. Onesimus Substance Abuse Ctr., Orlando, 1988—. Bd. dirs. Cen. Fla. Police Athletic League, Orlando, 1986—, Southwest Orlando Youth Task Force, 1990. Athletic scholar, U. Fla.

WADE, DAVID CARLTON, minister; b. Burlington, N.C., June 23, 1957; s. William Calvin Sr. and Ann (Wilbourne) W.; m. Cynthia Garnet Keener, Aug. 5, 1978; children: Zebulun Heath, Cornelius-Jörn Malachi, David William Jesse (dec.). AA, Brevard Coll., 1977; BA, Meth. Coll., 1979; MDiv, Duke U., 1983. Ordained to ministry Meth. Ch. as deacon, 1980, as elder, 1984. Sec. Conf. Budget Com., Raleigh, N.C., 1986-91; v.p. dist. com. on ministry Sanford (N.C.) Dist., 1989-90, chair dist. higher edn., 1990-91, chair dist. com. on ministries, 1990—; mem. Conf. Coun. on Ministry, Raleigh, 1991—; chair adult and family coord. Sanford Dist., 1988-90, mem. bd. missions, 1990-91. Mem. Mont. County Nursing Home Bd., Troy, N.C., 1989-91; charter mem. Chatham County-Hospice, Siler City, N.C., 1987-91; vol. Candor (N.C.) Elem. Sch., 1987-91; deliverer Meals on Wheels, Candor, 1989-91; town chair Am. Cancer Soc., Troy, 1988-91. Mem. Masons. Democrat. Home: Randolph St Candor NC 27229

WADE, LARRY EDWARD, minister, academic administrator; b. Tallahassee, Fla., June 2, 1948; s. Lawrence Edward and Kathleen Louise (White) W.; m. Angela Ruth Davis, Oct. 22, 1966; children: Rebecca Suzanne, Jessica Ruth. AA in Religion, Gulf Coast Community Coll., 1971; BA in Religion, Trinity Coll., 1976; MA in Religion, Gulf Coast Sem., Panama City, Fla., 1977, DRE, 1978; MDiv, Temple Bapt. Sem., 1986. Tchr. Pinellas Christian Sch., Largo, Fla., 1974-76, Panama City Christian Sch., 1976-78; dir. edn. 1st Bapt. Ch., Lynn Haven, Fla., 1985-86; pastor Brannonville Bapt. Ch., Panama City, 1978-81, Bayou George Bapt. Ch., Panama City, 1981-84, Westview Bapt Ch., Panama City, 1989—; pres. Gulf Coast Sem., Panama City, 1990—; lectr. Outreach Tours Internat., Panama City, 1980—; speaker at colls. and civic clubs; gospel magician. Chmn. Cystic Fibrosis, 1977. With USN, 1966-71, Vietnam. Recipient citation of excellence U.S. Hosp., 1970; named Religious Leader of the Yr., Jaycees, 1984; Sara Brown McCellan scholar Temple Bapt. Sem., 1986. Democrat. Home: 4600 Tropical Dr Panama City FL 32404 Office: Westview Bapt Ch 4101 W 21st St Panama City FL 32405 *Life may only be filled with real purpose when one empties his or herself of personal desires. My life has been filled with the encouragment of others, for which I thank God, above all.*

WADE, MARY LOUISE POWELL, minister; b. Springfield, Ohio, Sept. 25, 1932; d. Gamaliel Wyatte Holmes and Lucy Maxwell (Sloan) Powell; m. Walter B. Wade, Aug. 25, 1956 (div. July 1980); children: Susan Sloan Wade Massey, Holly Bibb Wade Crane, Walter Wyatte. AA Meridian Jr. Coll., 1951; B.A., U. So. Miss., 1953, M.A., 1954; counselor cert. U. So. Ala., 1979; student Columbia Theol. Sem., Decatur, Ga., 1984-85; grad. St. Paul Theol. Sem., Kansas City, Mo., 1987. Ordained to ministry Presbyn. Ch., 1987. Speech therapist Moultrie Ga. Speech Clinic, 1954-55, U. Tenn. Speech and Hearing Center, 1955-56, Jackson County Exceptional Sch., 1957-58; vending machine sales Morrisons Co., Pascagoula, 1974; newspaper dealer, Clarion Ledger, Jackson, Miss., 1974-75; audiologist, hearing aid salesman Beltone Co., Hattiesburg, Miss., 1975-77; receptionist Singing River Mental Health Services, Pascagoula, 1977; youth services counselor Jackson County Youth Ct., Miss. Dept. Youth Services, Pascagoula, 1977-84, also chief counselor, probation officer; night mgr. N.E.W.S. Shelter for Battered Women, 1985-87; youth minister Grace Presbyn. Ch., Kansas City, 1985-86; stated supply pastor Argentine Presbyn. and John Calvin Presbyn. chs., Kansas City, Kans., 1987-91, pastor, 1989—. Neighborhood chmn. Girl Scouts, 1958-68; trombonist Gulf Coast Symphony, 1981-84; asst. coach Aquatic Club swim team, 1960-70; dir. youth choir 1st Presbyn. Ch., Pascagoula; instr. water safety ARC; rape crisis counselor Gulfcoast Women's Center, Biloxi, Miss.; mem. Pas-Point Singers; sec. Urban Ministry Network Bd., Kansas City, Mo., 1987-89; bd. dirs. Franklin Community Ctr., Kansas City, Kans., 1989, Interfaith Ministry-Indian Springs Mall, Kansas City; clergy Argentine Ministerial Alliance, Kansas City. Mem. Miss. Assn. Clin. Counselors, State Employees Assn. Miss. Democrat. Home: 233 Edgewood Ave Apt A-3 Pittsburgh PA 15218

WADEWITZ, NATHAN RODOLFO, minister; b. Porto Alegre, Rio Grande de Sul, Brazil, Dec. 16, 1939; came to U.S., 1959; s. Werner Karl and Ella Victoria (Wasemiller) W.; m. Betty Mae Haake, Aug. 21, 1971; 1 child, Adrianne. BA, Concordia Sr. Coll., Ft. Wayne, Ind., 1971; MDiv, Concordia Theol. Seminary, Springfield, Ill., 1973; D of Ministry, Christ Seminary-Seminex, St. Louis, 1986. Pastor Zion Luth./Trinity Luth. Ch., Herkimer and Waterville, Kans., 1963-67; assoc. pastor Trinity Luth. Ch., Mission, Kans., 1967-74; sr. pastor Pacific Hills Luth. Ch., Omaha, 1974-88, First Evangel. Luth. Ch., North Platte, Nebr., 1988—; coord. Luth. World Relief, Greater Kansas City Area, 1972-74; v.p. Met. Luth. Ministries, Kansas City, Mo., 1972-74; pres. Greater Omaha Clergy Assn., 1986-87; chmn. High Plains Conf./Nebr., North Platte, 1990—. Chaplain Civil Air Patrol, Overland Park, Kans., 1972. Recipient Outstanding Svc. award Met. Luth. Ministries, 1973, Families for Christ award Kans. Dist. Luth. Ch./Mo. Synod, Waterville, 1965. Mem. Kiwanis, Rotary. Office: First Evangel Luth Church 305 West 5th St North Platte NE 69101

WADSWORTH, LONNIE ADREN, minister; b. Birmingham, Ala., Nov. 19, 1946; m. Mary Ball; children: Michael Vincent, Timothy Alvan, Emily Elizabeth. BA in Bibl. Studies, William Carey Coll., 1975; postgrad., New Orleans Bapt. Theol. Sem., 1975-76; MEd in Curriculum and Instrn., U. New Orleans, 1980. Ordained to ministry Christian Ch. (Disciples of Christ), 1984. Various religious positions various chs., 1963-89; minister at 3 orphanages Saigon, Republic of Vietnam, 1967-68; various religious positions Fed. Republic Germany, 1972-73; pastor 1st Christian Ch., Maysville, Mo., 1989-91, Nevada, Mo., 1991—; instrument and electrical supply driver Brown and Root Constrn. Co., Luling, La., 1976-77; job placement counselor and interviewer for mil. vets. La. State Employment Svc., New Orleans, 1977-78; letter carrier U.S. Postal Svc., New Orleans, 1982-89; v.p. acad. affairs bd. dirs. Christian Edn. Ministries Internat.; mem. evangelism com. NW Mo. Area Disciples of Christ; rep. for DeKalb County Ministerial Alliance for Econ. Opportunity Corp., Maysville, Mo., St. Joseph, Mo. Sgt. U.S. Army, 1966-73. Decorated Purple Heart, Good Conduct medals (2), Vietnam Svc. and Campaign medal, Nat. Def. Svc. medal, Unit Meritorious citation, Republic of Vietnam Gallantry Cross with Palm Unit citation. Mem. DAV (life), Theta Kappa Sigma. Home: Box 397 Maysville MO 64469

WAETJEN, HERMAN CHARLES, theologian, educator; b. Bremen, Germany, June 16, 1929; Arrived in U.S., Sept., 1931.; s. Henry and Anna (Ruschmeyer) W.; m. Mary Suzanne Struyk, July 15, 1960; children: Thomas (dec.), Thembisa, Lois, David. BA, Concordia Sem., St. Louis, 1950, BD, 1953; Dr. Theol., Tuebingen U., Fed. Republic Germany, 1958; postgrad., Hebrew U., Jerusalem, 1955. Instr. Concordia Sem., 1957; asst. prof. U. So. Calif., L.A., 1959-62; assoc. prof. San Francisco Theol. Sem., San Anselmo, Calif., 1962-70, prof., 1970-74, Robert S. Dollar prof. of New Testament, 1974—; vis. prof. U. Nairobi, Kenya, 1973-74, Fed. Theol. Sem., Republic South Africa, 1979-80, U. Zimbabwe, 1986-87. Author: Origin and Destiny of Humanness, 1976, 78, A Reordering of Power, 1989. mem. Soc. Biblical Lit., Pacific Coast Theol. Soc., Pacific Coast Theol. Soc. Democrat. Presbyterian. Avocations: backpacking, photography, travel. Home: 83 Jordan Ave San Anselmo CA 94960 Office: San Francisco Theol Sem 2 Kensington Rd San Anselmo CA 94960

WAGERS, LEONARD GORDON, minister; b. Dayton, Ohio, Sept. 30, 1959; s. James Gordon and Laura Frances (Marquette) W.; m. Ann Gail Ayres; children: Daniel Gene, Lucas Cleveland. Student, Stetson U., 1977-79; BS, Miami U., 1981; MA in Religious Edn., Southwestern Bapt. Theol. Sem., Ft. Worth, Tex., 1985. Ordained to ministry Bapt. Ch., 1987. Acct. Bee-Gee Shoe Corp., Dayton, 1982-83; minister edn. and youth Smoke Rise Bapt. Ch., Warrior, Ala., 1985-87, Connell Bapt. Ch., Ft. Worth, 1987-88; min. edn. and youth Zion Baptist Ch., Henderson, Ky., 1989-90; internal auditor Citizens Bank, Evansville, Ind., 1991—; Mem. adv. council Bapt. Telecommunications Network, Nashville, Tenn., 1986-87; assist team mem. Friendship Bapt. Assn. Ala., 1986-87, Youth Com., 1986-87; minister youth First Bapt. Ch. Brookville (Ohio), 1981-83; instrnl. asst. Tarrant County Jr. Coll., Ft. Worth, 1983-85. Contbg. author: Youth Ministry Planbook 4, 1989. Mem. Phi Alpha Theta. Avocations: softball, other sports, collecting baseball cards. Home: 927 First St Henderson KY 42420 Office: Citizens Bank PO Box 778 Evansville IN 47705

WAGGENER, CRAIG STEVEN, pastor; b. St. Louis, Mar. 13, 1956; s. Amos G. and Ruth (Graham) W.; m. Shirley Ann Mogensen, July 12, 1975; children: Zachary Steven, Andrea Marie. BA in Bus. Mgmt., Webster U., 1984; BTh, Oreg. Bible Coll., 1986. Ordained to ministry Ch. God. Pastor Troy (Ohio) View Ch. of God, 1986—. Home: 2773 De Weese Rd Troy OH 45373 Office: Troy View Ch of God 1879 Staunton Rd Troy OH 45373

WAGGONER, G. THOMAS, minister; b. Atlanta, Sept. 15, 1953; s. George Thomas Sr. and Mary Frances (Ivey) W.; m. Linda Gail Kuhn, Aug. 25, 1979; children: Kelly Marie, Lauren Hope, Thomas Kuhn. BS in Edn., Ga. State U., 1976; MRE, Southwestern Bapt. Theol. Sem., Ft. Worth, 1978. Activities asst. Park Cities Bapt. Ch., Dallas, 1976-77, Broadway Bapt. Ch., Ft. Worth, 1977-78; minister of activities First Bapt. Ch., Arlington, Tex., 1978-81; activities asst. Wieuca Rd. Bapt. Ch., Atlanta, 1974-76; minister activities Wieuca Rd. Bapt. Ch., 1981-89; founder, pastor North Gwinnet Bapt. Ch., Sugar Hill, Ga., 1989—; pres. Bapt. and North Atlanta Ch. Recreation League, 1985-89. Mem. sr. adult adv. com. Dekalb County, 1987; bd. dirs. Ch. Youth Softball League, Arlington, 1978-81, North Atlanta Sr. Svc., 1984-86; adv. coun. Renaissance on Peachtree Sr. Adult Home, 1987. Named on of Outstanding Young Men Am., 1980, 85. Mem. AAHPERD, Ga. Bapt. Recreators Assn. (pres.), Bapt. Student Union (pres.), North Gwinnett Mins. Assn. (pres. 1991), Kiwanis. Home: 381 Clarion Rd Lawrenceville GA 30243 Office: North Gwinnet Bapt Ch 5608 Suwanee Dam Rd Sugar Hill GA 30518

WAGNER, ANDREW JAMES, meteorologist, elder, educator; b. Greenwich, Conn., Apr. 12, 1934; s. Andrew and Ruth (Machette) W.; m. Betty Christina Ritenour, Aug. 9, 1969; children: Jonathan, Nathaniel. BA, Wesleyan U., 1956; MS, MIT, 1958. Ordained elder Congl. Ch., 1968. Meteorologist Nat. Weather Svc., NOAA, 1965—, sr. forecaster, 1990—; elder, tchr. Sunday sch. Garden Meml. Presbyn. Ch., Washington, 1966-68; elder Ch. No. Va., Oakton, 1969—, treas., 1969-75, tchr. adult Sunday sch., 1990—; adj. prof. N.T. Greek, Whole Word Sem., Oakton, 1981-82. Pres. Beverly Forest Civic Assn., Springfield, Va., 1976-77, v.p., 1977-78. Fellow Washington Acad. Scis. (del. bd. govs. 1981-84, 1989—); mem. Am. Meteorol. Soc., Am. Geophys. Union, Royal Meteorol. Soc., Am. Sci. Affiliation. Republican. Avocations: photography, music. Home: 7568 Cloud Ct Springfield VA 22153 Office: NOAA Nat Weather Svc Rm 604 World Weather Bldg Washington DC 20233 *As a scientist and Christian layman, I see increasing evidence that scientific advances alone can better life in only a limited way. Only when we individually and as a nation return to the "faith of our fathers" and put Jesus Christ in His rightful position as Lord of all, will we find true meaning and purpose in life.*

WAGNER, BLAKE DOUGLAS, clergyman; b. Akron, Ohio, Oct. 27, 1931; s. John Ernest and Ruth Etta (Daniel) W.; m. Gere Caryl Fulmer, Aug. 6, 1954; children—Lynn Ann Wagner Wood, Blake Douglas, Jr. B.A., U. Akron, 1953; M.Div., Oberlin Grad. Sch. Theology, 1957; D.Ministry, Vanderbilt U., 1974. Ordained to ministry Meth. Ch., 1957. Pastor Zion Evang. United Brethren, Cuyahoga Falls, Ohio, 1951-53, Montrose Zion Evang. United Brethren Ch., Akron, 1953-59, The Emmanuel Ch., Evang. United Brethren, Lorain, Ohio, 1959-67, The Master's Ch., United Meth. Ch., Euclid, Ohio, 1967-74; sr. pastor Main St. United Meth. Ch., Mansfield, Ohio, 1974—; field rep. The Robert H. Schuller Inst. for Successful Church Leadership, Garden Grove, Calif., 1980—. Mem. adv. bd. Mansfield Gen.Hosp. Hospice, adv. bd. Richland County Human Svcs., exec. bd. Johnny Appleseed council Boy Scouts Am., Mansfield, 1983—; participant Ohio State U. Commn. on interprofl. edn. and practice, Columbus. Named life mem. Ohio Pastor's Convocation Ohio Council of Chs., 1973; recipient Dean Thomas Graham award Oberlin Coll. Grad. Sch., Theology, 1957, St. Martin DePorres award Lorain County Cath. Council, 1966, Founders award Ohio Wesleyan U., 1980; Pixley scholar U. Akron, 1952-53. Mem. Inter-Church Council (pres. 1984-85), The Mansfield Ministerial Assn., (pres. 1978-79), East Ohio Conf. United Meth. Ch. (bd. ministry 1984—), Mansfield Dist. Com. on Ministry (chmn. 1983—), Dist. Council on Ministries. Republican. Lodges: Optimist (pres. 1978-79), Masons. Avocations: travel, camping, photography. Home: 516 Fairoaks Blvd Mansfield OH 44907 Office: 230 S Main St Mansfield OH 44903

WAGNER, C. PETER, theology educator, author; b. N.Y.C., Aug. 15, 1930; s. C. Graham Wagner and Mary Lewis; m. Doris Mueller, Oct. 15, 1950; children: Karen Potter, Ruth Irons, Rebecca. BS, Rutgers U., 1952; MDiv, Fuller Theol. Sem., 1955, MA in Missiology, 1968; ThM, Princeton (N.J.) Theol. Sem., 1963; PhD, U. So. Calif., 1977. Ordained to ministry, 1955. Missionary South Am. Mission, San Jose, Bolivia, 1956-61, SIM Internat., Cochabamba, Bolivia, 1963-71; sr. cons. Charles E. Fuller Inst., Pasadena, Calif., 1971—; prof. ch. growth Fuller Theol. Sem., Pasadena, 1971—; charter mem. Lausanne Com. for World Evangelization, London, 1974-89; coord. Spiritual Warfare Network, Pasadena, 1990—. Author over 30 books including: Your Church Can Grow, Your Spiritual Gift, Leading Your Church to Growth, Engaging the Enemy; contbr. articles to profl. jours. Mem. Evang. Missiological Soc., Am. Soc. Missiology, N.Am. Soc. for Ch. Growth, Soc. for the Sci. Study of Religion. Office: Fuller Theol Sem 135 N Oakland Ave Pasadena CA 91182

WAGNER, CAROL ANNE, lay worker; b. Louisville, Oct. 9, 1942; d. John Andrew and Helen Marguerite (Herzog) Hammond; m. John Philip Wagner, June 14,1969; children: John J., Timothy A. BA, St. Josephs Coll., 1964. Rschr. Nat. Security Adminstrn., Ft. Meade, Md., 1964-65; tchr. Balt. (Md.) City Sch. System, 1965-71; staff St. Thomas Aquinas Ch., College Sta., Tex., 1987—. Mem. Coll. Sta. (Tex.) Parent Teacher Orgn., City Coun., Parents Supporting Students Tchrs.; candidate Coll. Sta. Ind. Sch. Dist. Bd. Trustees. Recipient Leadership Brazos, Coll. Sta. C. of C., 1988-89. Mem. AAUW (various coms.), Tex. A&M Women's Social Club, Mothers Club, C. of C., Supporters of Excellence Edn. Roman Catholic. Avocations: needlework, gourmet cooking, advocate for excellence in public edn. Home: 203 Ember Glow Circle College Station TX 77840

WAGNER, DONALD EDWARD, minister; b. Medina, N.Y., Sept. 3, 1942; s. Donald E. and Thelma C. (Nelson) W.; m. Drew McAllister, June 23, 1979; children: Jay Douglas, Matthew, Anna. BA, Westminster Coll., 1964; MA, Princeton Sem., 1967; ThM, Princeton Theol. Sem., 1969; DMin, McCormick Sem., 1984. Ordained to ministry Presbyn. Ch., 1968. Asst. to dean Princeton (N.J.) Sem., 1965-67; assoc. minister Elmwood Presbyn. Ch., East Orange, N.J., 1967-69, West Side Presbyn. Ch., Ridgewood, N.J., 1970-73, 1st Presbyn. Ch., Evanston, Ill., 1973-80; nat. dir. Palestine Human Rights Campaign, Chgo., 1980-90; dir. Middle East program Mercy Corps Internat., Chgo., 1990—; campus min. Northwestern U., Evanston, 1978-80; spl. cons. Mid. East Coun. Chs., Limassol, Cyprus, 1987-88; Mid. East task force Chgo. Presbytery, 1978—, chair, 1979-81; adv. bd. New Outlook, Tel Aviv, 1987—. Author: All in the Name of the Bible, 1987, Anxious for Armageddon, 1992; editor: Israeli Settler Violence, 1986. Active Drug Prevention and Edn., East Orange, 1969-70, Youth Adv. Coun., Ridgewood, 1971-73. Recipient Arab Am. U. Grads. award, 1982, Disting. Svc. award United Holy Land Fund, 1991. Avocations: travel, running, reading. Office: Mercy Corps Internat 175 W Jackson Blvd Ste 1800 Chicago IL 60604

WAGNER, DOROTHY CAROLINE, retired church organization official; b. St. Louis, Dec. 5, 1917; d. Elmer Henry and Susie Wagner. BA, Washington U., St. Louis, 1938, MA, 1939; postgrad., Yale U., 1944-46. Missionary Presbyn. Ch. (U.S.A.), People's Republic China, 1947-50; mem. nat. staff Presbyn. Ch. (U.S.A.), N.Y.C., 1951-73, Ch. Women United, N.Y.C., 1974-86; adminstrv. sec. internat. com. World Day of Prayer, N.Y.C., 1974-86; elder, moderator Presbyn. Women, Ch. of Master, N.Y.C., 1988—; enabler Presbyn. Women, Presbytery of N.Y.C., 1988—. Contbr. numerous articles to ch. publs. Vol. program for disabled persons Lincoln Ctr., N.Y.C. Mem. Phi Beta Kappa. Democrat.

WAGNER, E. GLENN, pastor; b. Trenton, N.J., May 15, 1953; s. Elwood Wilson and Dorothy Lucy (Esposti) W.; m. Susan Louise Cleninger, June 7, 1975; children: Haven J., Justin S. Student, Fla. Bible Coll., 1974-76; BA, S.W. Inst. Biblical Studies, 1978; MA, Grace Grad. Sch., 1982; PhD, Oxford Grad. Sch., 1984. Asst. pastor Sylvania Heights Bapt. Ch., Miami, 1977-78; sr. pastor First Bapt. Ch., Morrisville, Pa., 1980-83, Clayton, N.J., 1983-90; sr. pastor Galilee Bapt. Ch., Denver, 1990—; instr. in field; founder, chmn. bd. Compassion Ministries, Inc., Clayton, 1986-90; trustee Seminary of the East, Dresher, Pa., 1986—; founder, pres. Aletheia Bible Inst., Clayton, 1985-86; bd. dirs. Mile High Ministries, Denver, 1991—. Fellow Oxford Soc. Scholars; mem. Grace Evang. Soc., Evang. Theol. Soc. Home: 11597 E Adriatic Pl Aurora CO 80014 Office: Galilee Bapt Ch 1091 S Parker Rd Denver CO 80231

WAGNER, GLENN MARIS, pastor; b. Elmhurst, Ill., Oct. 18, 1953; s. David Prugh and Doris Ray (Rhodes) W.; m. Nancy Beth Oosting, Aug. 30, 1975; children: Michael David, Bethany Maris. BA cum laude, Hope Coll.,

1975; postgrad., Am. U. Beirut, 1973-74; MDiv, Yale Divinity Sch., 1978; DMin, Garrett-Evang. Theol. Sem., Evanston, Ill., 1986. Ordained to ministry Meth. Ch. Tchr. Bible, English Presbyn. Ch. of Taiwan, Kaoshiung, Republic of China, 1975; student pastor 1st United Meth. Ch., Meriden, Conn., 1976-77; chaplain resident Pine Rest Christian Hosp., Grand Rapids, Mich., 1978-79; asoc. pastor Faith United Meth. Ch., Freeport, Ill., 1979-86; sr. pastor 1st United Meth. Ch., Harvard, Ill., 1986—; pres. Stephenson County Clergy Assn., Freeport, Ill., 1973-75; supervising pastor Elgin Dist. Com. on Ministry, 1988—; convener Western Cluster Elgin Dist. United Meth. Ch., 1986—; elder No. Ill. Conf. United Meth. Ch. Bd. dirs. Student Assistance Program, Harvard, 1988—, Freeport Rotary Club, 1983-86; pres. Harvard Rotary Club, 1989-90; mem. young execs. coun. State Bank of Freeport, 1986; clergy team leader Stephenson County United Way, Freeport, 1983-86. Mem. Harvard Clergy Assn. (pres.), Rotary (bd. dirs. Freeport club 1983-86, Harvard club 1987—). Office: 1st United Meth Ch 1100 N Division St PO 339 Harvard IL 60033

WAGNER, JAMES RICHARD, minister; b. Pitts., Mar. 4, 1946; s. Frank Orland and Evelyn Marie (Wright) W.; m. Karen Ann Brown, Aug. 26, 1967; children: Jennifer Lynn, Brett Christian, Mark Edward. BA, W.Va. Wesleyan U., 1968; MDiv., MRE, Meth. Theol. Sch. of Ohio, 1972. Ordained min. United Meth. Ch., 1973; cert. min. of edn. Student asst. Marysville (Ohio) Presbyn. Ch., 1969-72; min. St. Mary's (Pa.) United Meth. Ch., 1972-76; min. of edn., assoc. min. Monroeville (Pa.) United Meth. Ch., 1976-82; min. Ctr. United Meth. Ch., Natrona Heights, Pa., 1982—; musical therapist St. Peter's Child Devel. Ctr., Monroeville, 1977-83; pres., chaplains Allegheny Valley Hosp., Natrona Heights, 1988—. Artist 17th Century paper cutting, Scherenschnitte, 1980. Adv. bd. Allegheny Valley Hosp. Mental Health, Natrona Heights, 1988—; bd. dirs. Allegheny Valley Mental Health/Mental Retardation Program, New Kensington, Pa., 1991. Mem. Assn. of Chs. (v.p. Natrona Heights 1990—), Kiwanis Club (Tarentum, Pa., pres. 1987-89). Republican.

WAGNER, JOHN EDWARD, II, youth minister; b. St. Louis, Sept. 18, 1966; s. John Elmar and Corinne Marie (Shontz) W.; m. Marisa Elaine Morris, Nov. 22, 1986. BA in Ministry, St. Louis Christian Coll., Florissant, Mo., 1988. Ordained to ministry Christian Ch., 1988. Youth min. 1st Christian Ch., Sullivan, Mo., 1985-87, Wood River, Ill., 1987—. Mem. St. Louis Christian Coll. Alumni Assn. (v.p. 1990, pres. 1991), St. Louis Area Youth Mins. (pres. 1990, v.p. 1991). Republican. Home: 906 Willow St Wood River IL 62095 *I honestly believe that if we can turn the lives of children on to Jesus Christ they will be able to set the world on fire for Him.*

WAGNER, LANNY MARK, minister; b. Frederick, Okla., June 21, 1956; s. Jack William and Peggy Rhea (Hawkins) W.; m. Cynthia Jean Robbins, Oct. 16, 1981; children: Nikki Lynn, Nathan William. BA, Mt. Vernon Nazarene Coll., 1991. Lic. to ministry Wesleyan Ch., 1990. Youth pastor Calvary Assembly of God Ch., Victoria, Tex., 1983-84; Sunday sch. tchr. 1st Ch. of the Nazarene, Victoria, 1984-86, First Ch. of the Nazarene, Bryan, Tex., 1986-88; local preacher Evang. Ch. of the Nazarene, Mt. Vernon, Ohio, 1988; pastor 1st Wesleyan Ch., Mt. Vernon, 1988—; elem. tchr. Christian Star Acad., Mt. Vernon, 1988-90; v.p. Assn. Married Students, Mt. Vernon Nazarene Coll., 1989-90. With USN, 1975-78. Mem. Ministerial Assn. (Mt. Vernon). Home: 120 Cassil St Mount Vernon OH 43050 Office: First Wesleyan Ch 103 Madison St Mount Vernon OH 43050

WAGNER, MARY ANTHONY, student advisor; b. Miesvillle, Minn., Dec. 5, 1916; d. Anton M. and Marie (Wagner) W. BA, St. Louis U., 1945; MA, Cath. U. Am., 1948; PhD, St. Mary's Notre Dame, 1957. Joined Benedictine Sisters, Roman Cath. Ch., 1936. Elem. sch. tchr. various schs., Buckman, Minn., 1936-39, Famington, Minn., 1939-43; tchr. St. Benedict's High Sch., St. Joseph, Minn., 1945-48, high sch. prin., 1950-54; tchr. Coll. of St. Benedict, St. Joseph, 1948-91; prof. emerita Coll. St. Benedict, St. Joseph, 1986—; dean grad. sch. and asst. dean St. John's U., Collegeville, Minn., 1957-78; editor The Liturgical Press, Sisters Today, Collegeville, 1979—; retreat dir. Religious women and priests in midwest; lecturer at various parishes for men, women, and youth groups, 1960—. Contbr. articles to profl. jours. Fellow Danforth Found. Democrat. Avocations: writing, reading, needlework, music. Home: St Benedicts Convent Saint Joseph MN 56374 Office: Sisters Today Liturgical Press Collegeville MN 56321

WAGNER, RON JAY, biblical studies educator, minister; b. Denver, Apr. 21, 1926; s. James and Mae E. (Krutzer) W.; m. Paulette Farris, Feb. 20, 1960 (div. 1971); 1 child, Otis B.; m. Mary L. Osborne, Dec. 9, 1972. DD (hon.), Ch. Salvation, Bowlegs, Okla., 1980. Ordained to ministry Ch. of Salvation, 1980. Tchr. Old Testament Ch. of Salvation, Bowlegs, 1988-91, Yes'Hivah Sch., Bowlegs, 1991—. Author: School Help on Old Testament, 1991. With U.S. Army, 1952-53. Democrat. Office: Yes'Hivah Sch P O Box 325 Bowlegs OK 74830-0325

WAGNER, STANLEY M., rabbi; b. N.Y.C., Jan. 4, 1932; s. Albert and Stella (Ludmer) W.; chidren from previous marriage: Frady, Chaya; m. Renee G. Rabinowitz, Nov. 25, 1990. Diploma in Hebrew Teaching, Yeshiva U., 1952, BA magna cum laude, 1953, BRE, 1954, MHL, 1955, DHL, 1964. Ordained rabbi, 1956. Rabbi Congregation Ohavay Zion, Lexington, Ky., 1957-61, Baldwin (L.I.) Jewish Ctr., 1961-70; nat. exec. v.p. Religious Zionists Am., N.Y.C., 1970-72; rabbi Congregation Beth Hamedrosh Hagadol, Denver, 1972—; prof. Judaic studies, dir. Ctr. for Judaic Studies, U. Denver, 1972—; pres. L.I. Commn. Rabbis, 1966-68, Nassau-Suffolk County Assn. Rabbis, 1968-69, Rocky Mountain Rabbinical Coun.; chaplain Holly Patterson Home for the Aged, Uniondale, N.Y., 1962-69, Denver Police Dept., 1972—, Colo. State Senate, 1980—; dir. Col. Mizel Mus. Judaica, 1982—. Contbg. author: A Piece of My Mind, 1979; editor: Traditions of the American Jew, 1978; co-editor: Great Confrontations in Jewish History, 1977, Great Schisms in Jewish History; gen. editor 6 vol. series Traditions in Christianity and Judaism, 1980-89. Alumni award for outstanding svc. U. Denver, 1983, Mowshowitz award for disting. community svc. N.Y. Bd. Rabbis, 1990. Mem. Rabbinical Coun. Am., Am. Zionist Orgn., Conf. Pres. Maj. Jewish Orgns., Am. Conf. Soviet Jewry, Nat. Assn. Jewish Studies. Home: 6660 E Exposition Denver CO 80224 Office: Congregation Beth Hamedrosh Hagadol 560 S Monaco Pkwy Denver CO 80224

WAGNER, WALTER HERMANN, chaplain, educator; b. Frankfurt, Germany, Nov. 21, 1935; came to U.S., 1936, naturalized, 1944; s. Ludwig Anton and Karolina Wilhelmina (Hann) W.; m. Deborah Marianne Kus, Aug. 24, 1958; 1 child, Nathan Samuel. AB, Gettysburg Coll., 1957; MDiv, Luth. Sem., Phila., 1960; PhD, Drew U., 1968; MA, Princeton Sem., 1988. Ordained to ministry Luth. Ch., 1960. Co-pastor Calvary Luth. Ch., Cranford, N.J., 1959-63; asst. prof. Calif. Luth. Coll., Thousands Oaks, 1963-65; assoc. prof. Upsala Coll., East Orange, N.J., 1965-73; pastor Epiphany Luth. Ch., Warren, N.J., 1973-77; dir. theol. edn. Luth. Ch. in Am., Phila., 1977-84; assoc. prof. religion Muhlenberg Coll., Allentown, Pa., 1984—; chmn. N.Y. Patristics Seminar, 1968-77; adj. faculty Luth. Theol. Sem., Phila., 1970, 85; mem. N.J. Bicentennial Com. on Religion, 1974-76; bd. dirs. N.J. Coun. Chs., 1972-77; cons. Luth. Coun. in U.S.A., 1977-84, First Korean Meth. Ch., Cherry Hill, N.J., 1981-84. Contbr. articles to religious jours. Luth. Ch. in Am. grantee, 1961-63; faculty fellow Upsala Coll., 1968; Anti-Defamation League postgrad. fellow, 1970; recipient Lindback Teaching award, Upsala Coll., 1969. Mem. AAUP (pres. N.J. coun. 1970-73), Am. Soc. Ch. History, Soc. Religious Edn. Home: 1802 Snyder St Bethlehem PA 18017 Office: Muhlenberg Coll Allentown PA 18104

WAGNER, WILLIAM LYLE, engineer, missionary; b. Albuquerque, Jan. 23, 1936; s. William Chauncy and Opal (Strayer) W.; m. Sally Ann Crook, Nov. 21, 1956; children—Candice, Mark. B.S., U. N.Mex., 1957; M.Divinity, Southwestern Sem., Fort Worth, 1961; D. Missiology, Fuller Sem., Pasadena, Calif., 1976. Registered profl. engr., N.Mex. Engr. Albuquerque Testing Lab., Inc., 1957—, pres. bd. dirs., 1977-85; pastor Herman Bapt. Ch., Albuquerque, 1961-65; missionary fgn. mission bd. Southern Bapt. Conv., Richmond, Va., 1965-80, cons. for evangelism for Europe and Middle East, 1980-85; interim exec. sec. European Bapt. Conv., 1982-83; prof. missions Free Evangelical Sem., Leuvan, Belgium, 1983—. Author: New Move Forward in Europe, 1977; Nehemiah-The Man and The Task, 1985. Mem. ASCE, N.Mex. Soc. Profl. Engrs. (dir. 1965—), Consulting Engrs. Council, Internat. Assn. Mission Studies, Sigma Alpha Epsilon. Republican. Lodge: Rotary. Office: Fgn Mission Bd, Rue du Try Bara 19, 1328 Ohain Belgium

WAGONER, RICHARD CALVIN, music minister; b. Salisbury, N.C., Apr. 5, 1956; s. Adam Calvin Wagoner and Norma Jean (Baker) Boger; m. Karen Ann Crawford, July 8, 1978; children: Timothy Adam, James Owen. BA in Music, U. Cen. Fla., 1980; MDiv, Southwestern Bapt. Theol. Sem., 1986. Ordained to ministry So. Bapt. Conv., 1989. Music and youth min. First Bapt. Ch., Covington, Tex., 1983-86; min. of worship First Bapt. Ch., Lake Alfred, Fla., 1986-89; min. of music N. Park Bapt. Ch., Orlando, Fla., 1989—; youth dir. Ridge Bapt. Assn., Winter Haven, Fla., 1988-89; music dir. Great Orlando Bapt. Assn., 1990—; host Lake Alfred Ministerial Assn., 1987-88. Host Lake Alfred Round Table, 1987-88; program coord. various pub. observances, Lake Alfred, 1987—. Mem. Fla. Bapt. Singing Men. Republican. Office: N Park Bapt Ch 741 N Mills Ave Orlando FL 32803 *Truth and love exist only in dependence upon each other.*

WAHL, JOSEPH ANTHONY, priest; b. Jersey City, N.J., May 31, 1929; s. Maurice Anthony and Mary (Morrin) W. D of Sacred Theol., Cath. U., 1958. Provost (pres.) The Oratory, Rock Hill, S.C., 1966-77, 1989-91; sem. prof. Cardinal Newman Coll., Rock Hill, S.C. 1958-63, diocesan dir. Cammpaign Human Devel., Charleston, S.C.. Mem. Knights of Columbus, Rock Hill, S.C. Democrat. Roman Catholic. Home: 434 Charlotte Ave Rock Hill SC 29730 Office: The Oratory PO Box 11586 Rock Hill SC 29731

WAHL, THOMAS PETER, priest, monk, educator; b. Saint Cloud, Minn., Nov. 23, 1931; s. Arthur Lewis and Romana (Seberger) W. BA, St. John's U., Collegeville, Minn., 1954; licentiate in theology, Cath. U. Am., 1959; licentiate in Scripture, Pontifical Bibl. Inst., Rome, 1967; PhD, Union Theol. Sem., 1976. Joined O.S.B., Roman Cath. Ch., ordained priest, 1958. Monk St. John's Abbey, Collegeville, Minn., 1952—; asst. pastor St. Bernard's Ch., St. Paul, 1959-61, St. Boniface Ch., Mpls., 1961-64; assoc. prof. theology St. John's U., Collegeville, Minn., 1967—; founding dir. Jerusalem Program of St. John's U., 1974—. Author: How Jesus Came, 1962, Esther and Judith, 1971; also articles. Mem. Cath. Bibl. Assn., Soc. Bibl. Lit. Home: St John's Abbey Collegeville MN 56321 Office: St John's U Collegeville MN 56321 *Reflection on vocation to ministry. If you see someone drowning you ask if you can swim, if you dare to risk your life, not whether you will find it personally gratifying. Still, few things are more gratifying than saving a life.*

WAHLBERG, PHILIP LAWRENCE, former bishop, legislative liaison; b. Houston, Jan. 18, 1924; s. Philip Lawrence and Ella Alieda (Swenson) W.; m. Rachel Conrad, June 1, 1946; children: David, Christopher, Pauli, Sharon. AA, Tex. Luth. Coll., 1942, DD (hon.), 1963; BA, Lenoir Rhyne Coll., Hickory, N.C., 1944; MDiv, Luth. Theol. Sem., Columbia, S.C., 1946. Ordained to ministry United Luth. Ch. in Am., 1946. Pastor St. Luke Luth. Ch., Thunderbolt, Ga., 1946-50, Redeemer Luth. Ch., Wilmington Island, Ga., 1946-50, St. Mark Luth. Ch., Corpus Christi, Tex., 1950-59; pres. Tex.-La. Synod, United Luth. Ch. Am., Austin, Tex., 1959-62; bishop Tex.-La. Synod, Luth. Ch. Am., Austin, 1963-87; acting dir. devel. Lutheran Outdoor and Retreat Ministries Southwest, 1987-88; legis. liaison Tex. Impact, Austin, 1989-91; interim coord. Regional Ctr. for Mission Evang. Luth. Ch. in Am., Dallas, 1991—; mem. com. on appeals, also chmn. Evang. Luth. Ch. in Am., 1988—; also mem. exec. coun. Luth. Ch. in Am., N.Y.C., 1980-87, chmn. com. on legal matters, 1984-87; mem. mgmt. com. Div. for Mission in N.Am., N.Y.C., 1972-80, chmn., 1972-76; bd. dirs. Bd. Am. Missions, N.Y.C., 1963-72, chmn., 1968-72; bd. dirs. Luth. Sch. Theology, Chgo., 1967-87. Author articles in religious jours., sermons; author theol. cassette, 1973. Named Disting. churchman Tex. Luth. Coll., 1978; Disting. Alumnus, Lenoir Rhyne Coll., 1962; named Man of Year, Thunderbolt, Ga. C. of C., 1950. Mem. Impact, Interreligious Coalition for Central Am., Christian Urgent Action Network for El Salvador. Democrat. Lutheran. Avocations: winemaking, golf, fishing, bridge, choral singing. Office: 5804 Cary Dr Austin TX 78757

WAHLSTROM, LINDA NETTIE, minister, elementary school educator; b. Alexandria, Minn., Apr. 15, 1948; d. Lorrin Joseph and Dorothy Eleanor (Ramstedt) Munson; m. Richard John Wahlstrom, July 10, 1971 (div. Feb. 1987); children: Jason, Shannon. BA, Augsburg Coll., 1970; MDiv, Luther Northwestern Sem., 1990. Ordained to ministry Evang. Luth. Ch. in Am., 1990; cert. elem. tchr., Minn., N.D. Christian edn. dir. St. Stephens Luth Ch., White Bear, Minn., 1973-76; pastor Marion/Trinity Luth. Chs., Marion, N.D., 1990—. Home: Marion ND 58466 Office: Marion Luth Ch Box 127 Marion ND 58466-0127

WAIARU, AMOS STANLEY, archbishop; b. Nafinuatog, Makira, Solomon Islands, Apr. 19, 1944; s. Stanley and Emma (Kaifo) Bwagora; m. Mary Marjorie Mwele, Mar 12, 1976; children: Stanley Edgell, Emma Lansley, Rose Musiro, Elizabeth Mary. Diploma in theology, Bishop Patteson Theol. Ctr., Kohimarama, Solomon Islands, 1972, Pacific Theol. Coll., Suva, Fiji, 1975. Ordained priest Anglican Ch., 1976. Tchr., chaplain Vureas High Sch., Vanuatu, 1977-78, headmaster, 1979-80; bishop Diocese of Temotu Anglican Ch., Solomon Islands, 1981-87, archbishop Melanesia, bishop Diocese Cen. Melanesia, 1988—. Office: POB 19, Honiara Solomon Islands

WAINWRIGHT, ARTHUR WILLIAM, minister, religion educator; b. Leeds, Eng., Oct. 14, 1925; came to U.S., 1965; s. Alfred Harforth and Doris Hannah (Shires) W.; m. Betty Ward, July 4, 1959; children: Martin, Philip. BA, MA, Corpus Christi Coll., Oxford, Eng., 1949, BD, 1963; BA, Wesley House and Fitzwilliam Coll., Cambridge, Eng., 1952, MA, 1955. Ordained to ministry Brit. Meth. Ch., 1955. Min. Meth. Ch., Yeovil, Eng., 1952-53, Oxford Hall Meth. Ch., Manchester, Eng., 1957-62, All Sts. Meth. Ch., Abingdon, Eng., 1962-65; asst. prof. N.T. Candler Sch. Theology, Emory U., Atlanta, 1965-69, assoc. prof., 1969-87, prof., 1987—; asst. tutor Handsworth Coll., Birmingham, Eng., 1953-57. Author: The Trinity in the New Testament, 1962, A Guide to the New Testament, 1965, Beyond Biblical Criticism, 1982; editor: John Locke's Paraphrase and Notes on the Epistles of St. Paul, 2 vols., 1987; contbr. articles to profl. jours. Mem. Soc. Bibl. Lit., Soc. N.T. Studies. Home: 2728 Shetland Dr Decatur GA 30033 Office: Emory U Candler Sch Theology Atlanta GA 30322

WAITS, JIM L., academic administrator. Head Chandler Sch. Theology, Emory U., Atlanta. Office: Emory U Chandler Sch Theology Atlanta GA 30322*

WAKEFIELD, JOHN CONRAD, minister; b. Lincoln, Ill., Feb. 7, 1947; s. Albert Merl and Alice Louise (Conrad) W.; m. Vicki Louise Bell, June 26, 1971; children: Scott Conrad, David Jensen. BA, MacMurray Coll., 1969; MM, Northwestern U., 1971. Min. music Cen. Holston Christian Ch., Bristol, Tenn., 1975-77, First Christian Ch., Johnson City, Tenn., 1977-80; assoc. min. Westwood Hills Christian Ch., L.A., 1980-85; min. worship Clovernook Christian Ch., Cin.; asst. prof., dir. choral activities Milligan Coll., Johnson City, 1973-80. Contbg. editor Music Ministry Jour.; contbr. articles to profl. jours. Bd. govs. B. Carroll Reece Mus. of Art, Johnson City, 1976-80. Am. Choral Found. grantee Yale U., 1976. Mem. Assn. Christian Coll. Music Educators (founder), Nat. Ch. Music Conf. (speaker), N.Am. Christian Conv. (speaker), SAR. Republican. Home: 1010 Eastgate Dr Cincinnati OH 45231

WAKEFIELD, WESLEY HALPENNY, church official; b. Vancouver, B.C., Can., Aug. 22, 1929; s. William James Elijah and Jane Mitchell (Halpenny) W.; m. Mildred June Shouldice, Oct. 24,1959. Ed. pub. schs., 1936-45, student tech. inst., 1945-47, student theology, 1947-51. Ordained to ministry The Bible Holiness Movement, 1951. Pastor Penticton, B.C., 1949-56; itinerant evangelist, 1956-59; internat. leader, bishop-gen. The Bible Holiness Movement, Vancouver, 1949—; mission to native Indians in Alta., Can., 1960-65, to Nigeria and Liberia, 1966, to drug culture youth in Pacific N.W., 1969—, among alcoholics, 1956-59, 64-66, 73; guest speaker, dir. Bible Broadcast, 1952-56, Freedom Broadcast, 1984-85; sec.-treas. Penticton Ministerial Assn., 1956; mgr. Evang. Book Svc., 1964—, Liberty Press, 1964—; presented opening prayer Fall legis. session, B.C., 1972; pres. Cumo Resources ltd.; sec. NP Energy Corp.; pres., founder Double-Dial Lock Co., Manual Offset Printing Press Co.; bd. dirs. Agarwal Resources Ltd. Author: Bible Doctrine, 1951, Bible Basis of Christian Security, 1956, Jesus Is Lord, 1976, How to Incorporate a Nonprofit Society, 1976, Foundations of Freedom, 1978, Fire from Heaven, 1987, Bringing Back the Ark, 1987, John Wesley: The Burning Heart, 1988, Like Lightning, 1990, Antinomianism: The Curse of the Ages, 1990; legis. rsch. submissions: Effects of Marijuana and Youth, 1969, Labour Legislation Clauses, 1973, Religious Liberty in the Constitution, 1978, Alternatives to Electro-shock Therapy, 1988, 90, Present Day Slavery, 1973, 90; editor Hallelujah mag. (formerly Truth on Fire!), 1949—, Christian Social Vanguard, 196-61, Canadian Church and State, 1977-90, Hallelujah Songbook, 1981-83, Wesleyan Annotated Edition of the Bible, 1980—, Miniature Railways (quar.), 1988—. Chmn. Christians Concerned for Racial Equality, 1975—; v.p. Can. United for Separation of Ch. and State, 1977-90; chmn. Religious Freedom Coun. of Christian Minorities, 1978—; rsch. dir. United Citizens for Integrity, 1979—; v.p. Can. Coun. Japan Evang. Band, 1988—; chmn. Religious Info. Ctr., 1978—; Western Can. rep. Can. for the Protection of Religious Liberty, 1979—. Recipient Internat. Community Svc. award Gt. Britain, 1976, 79, Religious Liberty Advocacy award Religious Freedom Crusade, 1986, 87. Mem. NAACP, Anti-Slavery Soc., Can. Bible Soc., Bible Sci. Assn., Christian Holiness Assn. (com. mem.), Nat. Black Evang. Assn. (denomination rep. 1980-86), Wesley Study Bible (reference com. 1988-90), Evangs. for Social Action, Internat. Platform Assn., Salvation Army Hist. Soc. Avocation: miniature railways. Office: Bible Holiness Movement, PO Box 223 Postal Sta A, Vancouver, BC Canada V6C 2M3 *The real Christian is one who has exchanged the love of life for a life of love and desires the whole will of God—nothing else, nothing less, and nothing more. This consistency of service is the jewel of life and holiness its crowning glory.*

WAKO, GABRIEL ZUBIER, archbishop. Archbishop of Khartoum Roman Cath. Ch., Sudan. Office: Cath Ch, POB 49, Khartoum Sudan*

WALCK, ALFRED WILLIAM, clergyman; b. St. Paul, June 26, 1921; s. Alfred William Alexander and Amanda (Milleville) W.; m. Marion Dolores Garbisch, Feb. 6, 1947: children: Leslie W., John A., Kenneth J., Daniel P. BA, Wartburg Coll., 1942; BD, Wartburg Sem., 1945; BS in Edn., U. Minn., Mpls., 1954, MA in Edn. Psychology, 1967. Ordained to ministry Luth. Ch., 1945. Missionary Am. Luth. Ch., Papua, New Gueinea, 1946-72; pastor Trinity Luth. Ch., Linn Grove, Iowa, 1973-80, St. Peter and St. Paul Luth. Ch., Brunsville & Merrill, Iowa, 1980-85; chaplain Sunrise Manor, Sioux City, Iowa, 1985—. Editor ch. paper New Guinea Luth., 1964-72. Mem. Dist. Adv. Com., Madang, Papua, New Guinea, 1949-72; mem. St. Luke's Nursing Home Bd., Spencer, Iowa, 1976-80. Avocations: photography, collecting crosses, wood-working. Home: 3434 Douglas St Sioux City IA 51104

WALDEN, ALVIN EARL, minister; b. Morgantown, W.Va., Sept. 10, 1948; s. Benjamin Fred and Freda Mae (Blosser) W.; m. Linda Elaine Martin, Dec. 31, 1969; 1 child, Daniel John. Bible diploma, Liberty Coll., 1983; BTh, John Wesley Coll., 1989. Ordained to ministry Evang. Friends Ch., 1988. Min. Evang. Friends Ch., Danville, Va., 1983-86, Evang. Meth. Ch., Burlington, N.C., 1986-90. Sgt. USMC, 1967-71, Vietnam. Home: Rte 9 16 Kings Rd Morgantown WV 26505

WALDENFELS, HANS, theologian; b. Essen, W. Ger., Oct. 20, 1931; s. Bernhard and Therese (Schröder) W. Lic. Phil., Berchmanskolleg, München, 1956; Lic. Theol., Sophia U., Tokyo, 1964; Dr. Theol., Gregorian U., Rome, 1968; Dr. Theol. habil., U. Würzburg, 1976. Joined Soc. of Jesus, 1951; ordained priest Roman Catholic Ch., 1963. Prof. fundamental theology, theol. non-Christian religions, philosophy of religion U. Bonn, Fed. Republic Germany, 1977—, dean, 1979-80, 88-90. Author: Offenbarung, 1969; Absolute Nothingness, 3d edit., 1980; Faszination des Buddhismus, 1982; Kontextuelle Fundamentaltheologie, 2d edit., 1988, An der Grenze des Denkbaren. Meditation—Ost und West, 1988, Begegnung der Religionen. Theologische Versuche I, 1990; editor: FS Glazik/Willeke, 1978; FS Dolch, 1982; FS Dumoulin, 1985; Lexikon der Religionen, 2d edit., 1988. Mem. Internat. Assn. Mission Studies, Internat. Inst. Studies of Missions (chmn. 1978—), German Soc. Theol. Missiology, Assn. History Religion. Lodge: Rotary. Home: Grenzweg 2, D-4000 Düsseldorf 31, Federal Republic of Germany Office: Faculty RC Theology, Univ Bonn, D-5300 Bonn Federal Republic of Germany *People yearn for peace. What is the use of religions, if they do not contribute to the achievement of peace? How can they contribute to peace, if they do not find peace among each other? The encounter of religions is one of the most important ways which lead to a deeper understanding and to peace between people of various creeds, races and nations in the world.*

WALDKOENIG, GILSON CHRISTIAN, minister; b. Pitts., May 5, 1928; s. Arthur Christian and Carolyn Ellen (Metcalfe) W.; m. Lois Virginia Arentz, July 11, 1952; children: Martha Ann Waldkoenig Clementson, Virginia Lee Waldkoenig Blackwell, Gilson Arthur Christian. AB, Gettysburg Coll., 1949; BD, Luth. Theol. Sem., Gettysburg, 1952; MA, W.Va. U., 1964. Ordained to ministry Luth. Ch. in Am., 1952. Assoc. pastor Luther Meml. Ch., Erie, Pa., 1952-54; pastor St. Paul Luth. Ch., Uniontown, Pa., 1954—. Contbr. articles to profl. jours. Mem. Uniontown Area Chs. Assn., Alpha Kappa Alpha. Republican. Home: 120 Bierer Ln Uniontown PA 15401 Office: St Paul Luth Ch 71 N Gallatin Ave Uniontown PA 15401

WALDROP, JOHN MICHAEL, pastor, interpreter; b. Ft. Worth, May 9, 1956; s. John Gaylen and Anita May (Grimes) W.; m. Cindy Lee Terry; children: Joshua Mark, Caleb Michael. BA, Trinity U., 1980. Cert. spl. edn. tchr.; ordained to ministry Bapt. Ch. Sign lang. interpreter San Antonio Coll., 1976-80; tchr. Balcones Regional Day Sch. for Deaf, Uvalde, Tex., 1980-82; pastor North Irving (Tex.) Bapt. Mission of the Deaf, 1982-84, Austin (Tex.) Bapt. Mission of the Deaf, 1984—; bd. dirs. Tex. Bapt. Deaf Youth Camp, Dallas; program dir. Tex. Lions Camp for Crippled Children, Kerrville, summers 1975-82, staff mem. 1975-81; leader, worship dir. Tex. Bapt. Conf. of Deaf, Waco, Tex., 1986; revival preacher various deaf chs. in Tex., 1985—; tchr. sign lang. Uvalde Continuing Edn. Dept., 1982, North Irving Bapt. Ch., 1984; interim pastor Congress Ave. Bapt. Ch. Spokesman, liaison Religious Reps. of Deaf Chs., Austin, 1987—. Named one of Outstanding Young Men Am., 1986; recipient Devotion to Youth award Tex. Lions Camp for Crippled Children, 1977, Plaque Appreciation, 1982. Mem. So. Baptist Ministers to the Deaf Fellowship, Austin Bapt. Assn. (evangelism com. 1985—). Replican. Club: Austin Area Racing Pigeon. Home: 7306 Buttonbush Austin TX 78744 Office: Austin Bapt Mission of Deaf 1700 S 1st St Austin TX 78704-4208

WALDSCHMIDT, PAUL EDWARD, clergyman; b. Evansville, Ind., Jan. 7, 1920; s. Edward Benjamin and Olga Marie (Moers) W. B.A., U. Notre Dame, 1942; student, Holy Cross Coll., Washington, 1942-45; S.T.L., Laval U., Que., Can., 1947; S.T.D., Angelicum U., Rome, Italy, 1948. Ordained priest Roman Catholic Ch., 1946; prof. apologetics and dogmatic theology Holy Cross Coll., 1949-55; v.p. U. Portland, 1955-62, dean faculties, 1956-60, pres., 1962-78; aux. bishop of Portland, 1978-90. Mem. Cath. Theol. Soc. Am. (v.p. 1954-55), NEA, Delta Epsilon Sigma. Club: K.C. (4 deg.). Address: 5402 N Strong St Portland OR 97203

WALFISH, BINYAMIN H., clergyman, synagogue official; b. Nov. 13, 1925; s. Abraham and Minnie (Kurtz) W.; m. Hinda L. Goldklang, June 26, 1949; children—Avie, Tova, Joshua. B.B.A. cum laude, CCNY Sch. Bus., 1948; postgrad., BRGS Yeshiva U. Ordained rabbi, 1949. Rabbi Congregation Knesset Israel, Mpls., 1951-53; rabbi Quebec City, Que., Can., 1953-57, Congregation Ahavath Torah, Englewood, N.J., 1957-59; dir. new communities Yeshiva U., N.Y.C., 1959-66; pres. Olam Travel Network, N.Y.C., 1966-79; assoc. dir. Rabbinical Council Am., N.Y.C., 1979-80, exec. v.p., 1980—; bd. dirs. Synagogue Council Am., N.Y.C., 1980—; mem. exec. com. N.Y. Bd. Rabbis, 1980—, Commn. on Synagogue Relations, N.Y.C., 1980—; mem. of scope and membership coms. Conf. of Presidents of Major Jewish Orgns., N.Y.C., 1982—. Contbr. articles to profl. publs. Pres., bd. dirs. Assn. Retarded Citizens, Bergen Passaic Unit, N.J., 1958—; mem. bd. dir. edn. Yavneh Acad., Paterson, N.J., 1957-70; bd. dirs. Central Yeshiva Rav Kook, Jerusalem, 1973—; mem. Spl. Edn. Bd., Bergen County, N.J., 1966-71; nat. v.p. Assn. Parents Am. Israelis, N.Y.C., 1977-81. Recipient Louis Greenbaum Meml. award CCNY, 1948; recipient awards Yeshiva U., Lubavitch Campus and Youth Orgn., Rabbinic Alumni Yeshiva U., Bnai B'rith, Israel Bonds, Assn. Retarded Citizens, Bergen County Freeholders. Mem. Rabbinical Council Am., N.Y. Bd. Rabbis, Rabbinic Alumni Yeshiva U., Congregation Bnai Yeshurun, Religious Zionists Am. Home: 258

Maitland Ave Teaneck NJ 07666 Office: Rabbinical Coun Am 275 7th Ave New York NY 10001

WALHOF, FREDERICK JAMES, minister; b. Edgerton, Minn., Nov. 30, 1938; s. Henry and Jennie (VandenBosch) W.; m. Christine Posthuma, Aug. 17, 1960; children: Tamela Kay, James LeRay. AA, Dordt Coll., Sioux Center, Iowa, 1958; BA, Calvin Coll., 1960; BD, Calvin Theol. Sem., Grand Rapids, Mich., 1963. Ordained to ministry Christian Ref. Ch. in N.Am., 1963. Pastor Community Christian Ref. Ch., Saginaw, Mich., 1963-68; missionary pastor Univ. Christian Ref. Ch., Ames, Iowa, 1968-81; campus pastor, dir. Ref. Campus Ministries, Ames, Iowa, 1981-86; evangelistic pastor Hope Community Ch., Flagstaff, Ariz., 1986—; assoc. prof. No. Ariz. U., Flagstaff, 1988-89; pres. Evang. Mins. Assn., Saginaw, 1966-67, Campus Mins. Assn., Ames, 1972-73. Contbr. articles to Ref. Worship mag. Mem. Saginaw Area Religious Coun. on Human Rels., 1961-68; founder, bd. dirs. Birthright of Ames, Inc., 1971-81; mem. Teen Pregnancy Prevention Task Force, Flagstaff, 1989—, Eastside Community Alliance, Flagstaff, 1990—; bd. dirs. Citizens Against Substance Abuse, Flagstaff, 1991—. Mem. Ariz. Assn. Evangs. (bd. dirs. 1988—), Flagstaff Ministerial Assn. (pres. 1988). Democrat. Office: Hope Community Ch 3700 N Fanning Dr Flagstaff AZ 86004 *The Devil can and often does, use the best intentions of people in devious ways. But, God can and usually does, use the devious intentions of people in positive ways.*

WALKER, ALAN, minister; b. Sydney, Australia, June 4, 1911; s. Alfred Edgar and Violet Louise (Lavis) W.; MA, U. Sydney, 1943; DD (hon.) Bethany Bibl. Sem., Chgo., 1956; m. Winifred Garrard Channon, Mar. 26, 1938; children: Lynette, Bruce, David, Christopher. Ordained to ministry Meth. Ch., 1935; minister, Cessnock, New South Wales, 1939-44; supt. Waverley Meth. Mission, 1944-53; leader mission to nation, Australia, 1953-56; supt. Cen. Meth. Mission, Sydney, 1958-78; dir. world evangelism World Meth. Coun., 1978-87; prin. Pacific Coll. for Evangelism, 1988—; vis. prof. evangelism Boston Sch. Theology, 1957. Chmn. Australian Nat. Goals and Directions Movement, 1981—. Author: Coaltown: A Sociological Survey of Cessnock, 1945, The Whole Gospel for the World, 1957, The Many Sided Cross of Jesus, 1965, Break-Through, 1969, God, The Distributor, 1973, Life Begins At Christ, 1980, Standing Up to Preach, 1983, Life in the Holy Spirit, 1986, Try God, 1990. Decorated knight bachelor, 1981, officer Order Brit. Empire, 1954: recipent Inst. De La Vie award, Paris, 1978, World Meth. Peace award (with wife), 1986. Home: 14 Owen Stanley Ave, Beacon Hill 2100 Australia Office: 1 Angel Pl, Sydney 2000, Australia

WALKER, ARTHUR LONZO, religious organization administrator; b. Birmingham, Ala., Apr. 10, 1926; s. Arthur Lonzo and Nannie Agnes (Bynum) W.; m. Gladys Evelyn Walker, Aug. 4, 1949; children: Marcia Lea Hamby, Gregory Arthur. BA, Samford U., 1949; MDiv, So. Bapt. Theol. Sem., 1952; ThD, New Orleans Bapt. Theol. Sem., 1956; LHD (hon.), Campbell U., 1984; HHD (hon.), Houston Bapt. U., 1985. Prof. theology Samford U., Birmingham, 1956-76, v.p. student affairs, 1965-68, v.p. adminstrv. affairs, 1968-73; v.p. student affairs So. Bapt. Theol. Sem., Louisville, 1976-78; exec. dir. edn. commn. So. Bapt. Conv., Nashville, 1978—; sec., treas. So. Bapt. Commn. Am. Bapt. Theol. Sem., Nashville, 1978—; mem. adv. bd. Ctr. for Constl. Studies, Macon, Ga., 1978-90; mem. nat. adv. coun. J.M. Dawson Inst. of Ch. State Studies, Waco, Tex., 1990—. Author: By Their Fruits, 1982; editor: Educating For Christian Missions, 1981, Directory of Southern Baptist Colleges, 1986; (jour.) The Southern Baptist Educator, 1978—. Pres. Birmingham Council of Christian Edn., 1970-71. Served as sgt. U.S. Army, 1944-46, PTO. Mem. Nat. Assn. Ind. Colls. and Univs. (bd. dirs. 1987-91). Office: Assn So Baptist Colls 901 Commerce Ste 600 Nashville TN 37203

WALKER, BILLY CUMMINS, minister, evangelist; b. Detroit, Dec. 28, 1937; s. William Burgess and Pearl Marie (Cummins) W.; m. Sharon Anne Harris, Sept. 26, 1958; children: Billy Harris, Craig David. BA, Wayne State U., 1964. Ordained to ministry Bapt. Ch., 1959. Evangelist Billy Walker Evangelistic Assn., Southgate, Mich., 1955—; camp dir. Hiawatha Youth Camp, Eckerman, Mich., 1964—; pastor Calvary Bapt. Ch., Southgate, 1974—; dir. Billy Walker Presents, weekly TV program. Author: Billy Walker Talks with Teens, 1967; contbr. articles to religious jour. Mem. Southgate Schs.. Adv. Com., Southgate Compensation Commn., Southgate Nativity Scene Com. Recipient Peace Oratory award Wayne State U., 1958, Community Svc. award City of Southgate; grantee Kresge Found., 1973. Mem. Detroit Econ. Club. Avocations: yard, sports, ping pong, collecting books. Office: Box 1456 Southgate MI 48195

WALKER, CARL KINGSLEY, minister; b. Hays, Kans., Aug. 3, 1959; s. Carl S. and Eunice M. (Duncombe) W.; m. Glenda Lavonne Lovins, June 4, 1983; children: Kourtney, Kolby, Kameron. BS, Evangel Coll., Springfield, Mo., 1984. Ordained to ministry Assemblies of God, 1988. Min. youth Colonial Heights Assembly of God Ch., Wichita, Kans., 1948-88; min. youth and worship lst Assembly of God Ch., St. Charles, Mo., 1988—; sectional rep. Kans. dist. coun. Assemblies of God, Wichita, 1986-88, chmn. spl. events, 1987, sectional rep. No. Mo. dist. coun., Excelsior Springs, 1989—; dir., pastor Rock Solid Youth Ministries, St. Charles, 1988—; pastor T.A.S.K. Force Youth and Young Adult Ministries, St. Charles, 19990—. Composer, lyricist song You Are My God, 1989. Home: 2509 Charann Saint Charles MO 63301 Office: lst Assenbly of God Ch 2429 Charwood Saint Charles MO 63301

WALKER, CONSTANCE MAE, library director, librarian; b. Providence, July 22, 1928; d. Bayden Powell and Mae Eliza (Hobson) Taylor; m. Billy Jack Walker, Nov. 16, 1956. BA, U. Tex., 1954, MLS, 1956. Asst. libr. U. Houston, 1960-67, libr. dir., 1967-76; libr. dir. U. St. Thomas, Houston, 1978-80, libr. dir. Sch. of Theology, 1980—. Contbg. author: (reference book) Magazines for Libraries, 1978. Mem. Am. Theol. Libr. Assn., Cath. Libr. Assn., Phi Beta Kappa, Beta Phi Mu. Home: 8117 Albacore Dr Houston TX 77074 Office: U St Thomas Sch Theology 9845 Memorial Dr Houston TX 77024

WALKER, DAVID ALLEN, pastoral counselor; b. Indpls., Feb. 26, 1942; s. Samuel Arno and Mildred E. (Bassett) W.; children from previous marriage: Jon Douglas, Mariabeth, Wendell Scott; m. Diana L. Wells, Nov. 23, 1988; children: Julie Lynn, Haylea Jo, Alissa Beth. BA, So. Ill. U., 1966; MDiv, McCormick Theol. Sem., 1975; D Min., Pitts. Theol. Sem., 1986. Cert. pastoral counselor; ordained as pastor Presbyn. Ch., 1975. Youth dir. YMCA, Granite City, Ill., 1963-66; asst. dir. Madison County Econ. Opportunities Commn., Edwardsville, Ill., 1966-68; dep. exec. dir. Cuyahoga County Econ. Opportunities Commn., Cleve., 1968-71; trainer, cons. Control Systems Rsch., Arlington, Va., 1971-75; pastor Paris (Pa.) Presbyn. Ch., 1975-78; dir. Washington (Pa.) Acad., 1978-80; pastor, head staff Ctr. Presbyn. Ch., McMurray, Pa., 1980-87; exec. dir. Westmont Family Ministries, Johnstown, Pa., 1988—; sexual abuse therapist Cambria County Mental Health Mental Retardation, Johnstown, 19881. Author: Rainbow Around My Neck, 1990; (manual) Getting It Together, 1970; author and editor jour. Familytalk, 1990—. Mem. AACD, Am. Assn. Pastoral Counselors, Laurel Mountains Psychol. Assn., Pitts. Cleric, Fortnightly Speakers Forum (pres. 1983), Greater Johnstown Clergy Assn. (treas.), Johnstown C. of C., Jaycees (officer 1966-68). Avocations: vocal music, acting, writing. Office: Westmont Family Ministries 639 Luzerne St Johnstown PA 15905

WALKER, DAVID DEAN, minister, headmaster; b. Ft. Wayne, Ind., Oct. 4, 1937; s. Gilbert Alva and Eleanora (Lee) W.; m. Dorla Jean White, Nov. 21, 1964; children: Susan, Mike, Barry, Mark, Christopher, Scott. BA, St. Francis Coll., Ft. Wayne, 1963, BS, 1966. Ordained to ministry Ch. of God., 1980. Assoc. pastor White Chapel Ch. of God, South Daytona, Fla., 1976-79; pastor Lighthouse Christian Ctr., DeLeon Springs, Fla., 1979—; founder, headmaster Lighthouse Christian Acad., DeLand, Fla., 1980—. Fellow Ball State U., 1970-71. Mem. Fla. State Ch. of God Ministerial Assn. (pres. 1985), Greater DeLand Area Ministerial Assn. (pres. 1985-87). Republican. Home: 1116 S Pearl St DeLand FL 32720 Office: Lighthouse Christian Ctr 4390 Grand Ave DeLeon Springs FL 32130

WALKER, DAVID ELLIOTT, minister; b. Yakima, Wash., Feb. 19, 1947; s. Frank Manly and Franka Allene (Burnham) W.; m. Catherine Ann Ybarrola, Apr. 5, 1970; children: Mercedes, John, Jordan. Grad. high sch., San Lorenzo, Calif. Ordained to ministry Christian Ch., 1972. Assoc. pastor Prayer Chapel, San Leandro, Calif., 1972-75; pastor New Covenant Fellowship, Las Vegas, 1976-79; assoc. pastor Christian Life Community, Las Vegas, 1980-86, sr. pastor, 1987—; bd. dirs. Clark County Christian Sch., Las Vegas; clergy adv. bd. Charter Mental Health Hosp., Las Vegas. Editor Directions mag., 1980-85; author: Deacons Handbook, 1984, Handbook for Leaders, 1989. Sgt. U.S. Army, 1966-68, Vietnam. Republican. Office: Christian Life Community 800 E Karen Ave Las Vegas NV 89107

WALKER, DAVID GLENN, pastor; b. Monticello, Iowa, Apr. 16, 1927; s. Abram Frank and Ethel Mary (Hutton) W.; m. Shirley Ann Rollings, May 29, 1954; 1 child, Jeffrey William. BS, Iowa State U., 1949; postgrad., Princeton Theol. Sem., 1949-51; MDiv, Andover Newton Theol. Sem., 1953; DD (hon.), Dubuque U., 1970. Ordained to ministry Presbyn. Ch., 1952; cert. tchr. Tchr. VA, Coggon, Iowa, 1949; pastor Webster (N.H.) Congl. Ch., 1951-52; asst. pastor 1st Presbyn. Ch., Muncie, Ind., 1952-56; pastor Natrona Heights (Pa.) Presbyn. Ch., 1956-62; exch. pastor St. Andrew's and West Kirk, Auchterarder, Scotland, 1960; sr. pastor Roseland Presbyn. Ch., Chgo., 1962-69, Village Presbyn. Ch., Northbrook, Ill., 1969-80; exchange pastor Magara Presbyn. Ch., Derry, Ireland, 1966; sr. pastor, head staff 1st Presbyn. Ch., Wichita, Kans., 1980—; chmn. Evang. pastoral care Chgo. Presbyn. Synod, Lincoln Trails, 1969-79, div. Synod Ministries Kans. and Mo., 1980-87; moderator coun. Presbytery South Kans., 1984-88; trustee Presbyn. Manors Mid-Am., 1985—, chmn. bd. trustees, 1987-89. Editor, participant TV spls., One Life for Us All, 1985, Jesus of Nazareth - His Story, 1990. Bd. dirs. Prison Ministries, Wichita, 1990—; chmn. Global Learning Ctr., Wichita, 1988—. Mem. Downtown Clergy Fellow, Rotary Club (various coms.). Republican. Avocations: travel, gardening, woodworking, photography, hiking. Office: 1st Presbyn Ch 525 N Broadway Wichita KS 67214

WALKER, DONALD MURRAY, minister; b. Lansing, Mich., Oct. 10, 1938; s. Paul H. and Margaret V. (Holloway) W.; m. Jacquelyn Touchstone, June 7, 1958; children: Donalyn Renee Scoggins, S. Denise Walker. BS, Lee Coll., 1977; MA, Ashland Univ., 1978; MDiv, Sch. of Theology, 1980; EdD, Nova Univ., 1983. Ordained to ministry Ch. of God, 1968. Evangelist Ch. of God, Minot, N.D., 1958-60; state dir. youth and Christian edn. Ch. of God, Indpls., 1960-64; pastor Ch. of God, S.C., 1964-70; state dir. youth and Christian edn. Ch. of God, Mich., 1970-74, Ohio, 1974-78, Tenn., 1978-82; pres. Northwest Bible Coll., Minot, 1982-86; state overseer Ch. of God, N.D., S.D., 1984-86; asst. dir. gen. edn. dept. Ch. of God, Cleveland, Tenn., 1986-88; state overseer Ch. of God, Ind., 1988—; chmn. Ch. of God Chaplains Commn., Cleveland, 1990—. Home: 315 Love Ave Greenwood IN 46142 Office: Ch of God State Exec Office 311 State Rd 135 South Greenwood IN 46142 *While there are many issues and crises in life that we often do not understand our attitude toward our faith in God and His mercy can never be dictated by our circumstances.*

WALKER, DONALD ROBERT, JR., minister; b. Leavenworth, Kans., Oct. 24, 1955; s. Donald Robert and Norma Elizabeth (Wagner) W.; m. June Marie Chinn, Jan. 1, 1976; children: Heather Renee, Eric David, Michelle Renee. Student, Kans. City Kans. Community Coll., 1973-75, Full Faith Bible Coll., 1977-79. Ordained minister, 1979. Sr. pastor Abundant Life Fellowship, Leavenworth, 1978-82; assoc. pastor Full Faith Ch. of Love, Shawnee, Kans., 1982-84; sr. pastor Full Faith Ch. of Love East, Kans. City, Mo., 1984—; exec. coun. Nat. Leadership Conf., Montreat, N.C., 1988-90, bd. dirs., 1990—; mem. adv. bd. World Indigenous Missions, New Braunfels, Tex., 1990—. Pres. Found. for the Family, Overland Park, Kans., 1989—. Mem. Internat. Churchill Soc. Republican.

WALKER, DONNA LOU, religion and English educator; b. Denton, Tex., Mar. 8, 1953; d. Donnie C. and Virtie Verlyn (Joiner) W. BA, Tarleton State U., 1974; MA, U. Nebr., 1976; EdD, East Tex. State U., 1979. Instr. Ranger (Tex.) Jr. Coll., 1980-83; asst. prof. U. Mary Hardin-Baylor, Belton, Tex., 1983-84, assoc. prof., 1989—; legal asst. Vial, Hamilton, Koch & Knox, Dallas, 1985-87; instr. Tex. State Tech. Inst., Waco, 1987-89. Contbr. poem, short story to collections. Mem. Nat. Coun. Tchrs. of English, Modern Lang. Assn., Tex. Assn. Creative Writing Tchrs., Tex. Faculty Assn. Home: 6901 Bosque Waco TX 76710 Office: U Mary Hardin-Baylor Belton TX 76513

WALKER, DOROTHY KEISTER, minister; b. Lock Haven, Pa., Sept. 24, 1920; d. Charles Lester and Eva Derr (Schuyler) K.; m. Dean E. Walker, May 28, 1962 (dec. 1988). BS in Elem. Edn., Lock Haven U., 1942; BD in Ch. History, MS in Religious Edn., Butler U., 1949; DD (hon.), Milligan Coll., 1962. Ordained to ministry Ch. of Christ, 1949. Asst. min. Fleming Garden Christian Ch., Indpls., 1946-49; with Jones-Keister Evang. Team, nat., 1949-59; dir., lectr. Mission to Women, nat., 1959—; elder Hopwood Christian Ch., Milligan Coll., Tenn., 1985—; co-founder Emmanuel Sch. of Religion, Johnson City, Tenn.; asst. bd. mem. N.Am. Christian Conv., 1985-87; trustee Appalachian Christian Village, Johnson City, 1986—, European Evang. Soc., Tubingen, Germany, 1989—. Contbr. articles to religious jours. Mem. Phi Kappa, Theta Phi, Kappa Delta Pi. Home and Office: PO Box 449 Milligan College TN 37682 *A well rounded education included studies in the humanities, the sciences and in revelation.*

WALKER, EDWARD M., minister; b. Rose Hill, N.C., June 8, 1935; m. Jane Brown; children: Eddie, Pam Smith, Gordon. Degree, Holmes Bible Coll. Pres. Pitt-Greenville C. of C., Greenville, N.C., 1976-91; pastor Grace Ch., Greenville, 1984—. Mem. Travel Coun. N.C. (pres. 1991-92). Democrat. Baptist. Avocations: reading, woodworking. Office: Grace Ch Rte 13 Box 60 Greenville NC 27858

WALKER, EDWIN STUART, III, missionary organization executive; b. Cumberland, Va., Sept. 12, 1928; s. Edwin Stuart Jr. and Thea Boyd (Womack) W.; m. Mary Lee Fry, Sept. 11, 1953; children: Stuart, Mary Anne, David, Thomas, Sara. BA, Columbia (S.C.) Bible Coll., 1951; postgrad., Wheaton (Ill.) Coll., 1951, 53, U. Haiti, Port-au-Prince, 1972, Columbia Bibl. Sem., 1982. Ordained to ministry Fellowship Ind. Evang. Chs., 1951. Pastor Grace Presbyn. Ch., Lexington, Va., 1952-56; tchr. Inst. Biblique Lumière, Cayes, Haiti, 1957-64; chief exec. officer Radio Lumière, Port-au-Prince, 1965-79; min. missions Worldteam, Norfolk, Va., 1980-84; pres., chief exec. officer, bd. dirs. Worldteam USA, Miami, Fla., 1985—; chmn. Communications Commn., Concile des Eglise Evangelique, Haiti, 1965-79; bd. dirs. Worldteam Internation, Inc., Atlanta, 1985—, Worldteam Assocs., Inc., Morton, Ill., 1989—. Author: (booklets) La Trinite, 1960, Church/Mission Partnership, 1982, Philosophy of Resource Development, 1991; contbr. article to ency. Mem. cen. com. Haitian Red Cross, Port-au-prince, 1974-79; mem. curriculum com. Haiti Dept. Agr., 1970-75; pres. Pedodontic Found., Port-au-Prince, 1972-75; cons. on radio edn. Haiti Presdl. Cabinet, 1978-79. Recipient Disting. Lectureship in Communications award Wheaton Coll. Grad. Sch., 1976. Mem. Christian Mgmt. Assn. Office: Worldteam USA 1607 Ponce de Leon Blvd Coral Gables FL 33134

WALKER, GEORGE GARY, minister, psychologist; b. Boston, Sept. 14, 1948; s. Richard Earl and Helen Elaine (Hinds) W.; m. Julia Kathleen Walton, May 22, 1971; children: Joel, Benjamin, Micah. BA, Harding U., 1970; MS, U. Cen. Ark., 1971; PhD, Bangalore U., India, 1978; diploma (hon.), Lubbock Christian U., 1983. Ordained to ministry Ch. of Christ, 1968. Dir. Univ. Ctr. Ch. of Christ, Magnolia, Ark., 1971-73; missionary to India Ch. of Christ, Bangalore, 1973-78; faculty Sunset Sch. Preaching Ch. of Christ, Lubbock, Tex., 1979—, dir. India City Evangelism, 1979—, family therapist, 1979—; vis. prof. Harding U., Searcy, Ark., 1978-79. Home: 5203 28th St Lubbock TX 79407 Office: Sunset Church of Christ 3723 34th St Lubbock TX 79410

WALKER, GORDON ALFRED, minister; b. Toronto, Ont., Can., July 27, 1924; s. Alfred and Flora (May) W.; m. Mary Jean Melick, July 7, 1951. BA, McMaster U., 1952, BD, 1956. Ordained to ministry Bapt. Conv., 1956. Pastor Caledonia (Ont.) Bapt. Ch., 1955-60, 1st Bapt. Ch., Barrie, Ont., 1960-66; asst. sec. Dept. Can. Missions Bapt. Conv. Ont. and Que., 1966-71, mem. social concerns com., 1971-81, chmn., 1976-79, mem. coun., mem. div. pastoral resources, mem. credentials com., chair credentials com., 1988-91; mem. coun. Evang. Fellowship Can., 1968-70; gen. sec. The Lord's Day Alliance of Can., Toronto, 1971-81; pastor Thornhill Bapt. Ch., 1984-89; chmn. Nat. Inter-Faith Immigration Com., 1972-76. Bd. dirs. Royal Victoria Hosp., Barrie, 1962-65, Provincial Uniform Store Hours Assn., 1974-76. Home: 3 Massey Sq, Ste 3504, Toronto, ON Canada M4C 5L5

WALKER, HAROLD BLAKE, minister; b. Denver, May 7, 1904; s. Herbert R. and Ethel G. (Blake) W.; m. Mary Alice Corder, Feb. 1, 1930; children—Herbert Elwood, Howard Deane, Timothy Blake. AB, U. Denver, 1925, DD, 1952; AM, Boston U., 1927; BD, McCormick Theol. Sem., 1932; postgrad., U. Chgo., 1933-34; DD, Emporia Coll., 1944, Hamilton Coll., 1949, U. Denver, 1952, Rocky Mountain Coll., 1971; LHD, Lake Forest U., 1959, Nat. Coll. Edn., 1970; STD, Northwestern U., 1970. Editor, writer A.P., Kansas City, 1927-30; ordained to ministry Presbyn. Ch., 1932; minister Fullerton-Covenant Ch., Chgo., 1932-36; minister First Ch., Utica, N.Y., 1936-42, Oklahoma City, 1942-47; minister 1st Presbyn. Ch., Evanston, Ill., 1947-69; columnist Splty. Salesman mag., 1954-67, Chgo. Tribune-N.Y. News syndicated columnist, 1954-81; lectr. homiletics McCormick Theol. Sem.; lectr., bd. dirs. Harold Blake Walker chair pastoral theology; cons. W. Clement Stone Enterprises, 1970-74; sem. v.p. Bd. Fgn. Missions Presbyn. Ch. U.S.A.; Nat. Commn. Evangelism, 1946-47; dir. Presbyn. Tribune, 1943-55; mem. Presbyn. Commn. on Consolidation, 1957-58, Commn. on Ecumenical Mission Relations, 1958-61. Author: Going God's Way, 1946, Ladder of Light, 1951, Upper Room on Main Street, 1954, Power to Manage Yourself, 1955, (with wife) Venture of Faith, 1959, Heart of the Christian Year, 1962, Faith for Times of Tension, 1963, Thoughts to Live By, 1965, To Conquer Loneliness, 1966, Prayers to Live By, 1966, Memories to Live By, 1968, Inspirational Thoughts for Everyday, 1970, Days Demanding Courage, 1978, History of St. John's of Red Cross of Constantine, 1985, Caring Community, 1986; contbr. to religious publs. Bd. dirs. Nat. Presbyn. Ch. and Ctr., Washington; bd. dirs. McCormick Theol. Sem., pres., 1953-55, 57-71; bd. dirs. Ill. Masonic Med. Center, Chgo., Lake Forest Coll.; trustee Maryville Coll. Recipient DeMolay Legion of Honor; Freedoms Found. sermon prize, 1950, 55, 77; citations Protestant Fund. Greater Chgo., 1970; Chgo. Inst. Medicine Citizens fellow, 1987; citations Chgo. Friends of Lit., 1971, 79; Disting. Alumnus award McCormick Theol. Sem., 1979. Mem. Utica Council Chs. (pres. 1940), Am. Theol. Soc. Chgo. Cleric, Pi Kappa Alpha. Clubs: Univ. (Chgo.). Lodge: Masons (Chgo., Evanston) (Shriner, 33 deg., grand chaplain N.Y. 1940-41). Home: 422 Davis St Evanston IL 60201

WALKER, HARRIETTE KATHERINE, religious administrator; b. Cad, Ga., Jan. 7, 1929; d. James Wilden and Eugie Arleen (Harton) Pack; m. William Daniel Walker, June 4, 1960. AA, Tenn. Wesleyan Coll., 1948; BA, U. Tenn., Chattanooga, 1953. Edn. dir. 1st United Meth. Ch., Copperhill, Tenn., 1953-55, Morristown, Tenn., 1955-57, Alcoa, Tenn., 1957-59; field exec. Citrus Coun. Girl Scouts, Inc., Orlando, Fla., 1968-85; program dir. United Meth. Ch., Satellite Beach, Fla., 1985-87; del. Fla. Annual Conf., Lakeland, 1978-90; mem. Exec. Bd. Haitian Refugee Ministry, Ft. Pierce, Fla., 1988-90; United Meth. rep. Fla. Coun. Chs., Orlando, 1990— ; del. Meth. World Conf., Nairobi, 1986, Singapore, 1991; mem. Meth. World Coun., 1991—. Mem. Girl Scouts U.S. Recipient Conf. Laity Christian Svc. award United Meth. Ch. Fla. Conf., 1988, Thanks Badge Citrus Coun. Girl Scouts U.S., 1988. Mem. AAUW, Nat. Assn. United Meth. Scouters Ministry, Missile, Space and Range Pioneers, Inc. (life), Fla. So. Coll. Pres. Coun., Pi Beta Phi. Home: 145 Allan Ln Melbourne Beach FL 32951 *The church is not an organization that has an educational program, it is an educational program.*

WALKER, HIRAM H., minister; b. Thomaston, Ga., Feb. 2, 1920; s. David M. and Viola (Robinson) W.; 1 child, Capree Walker. AA, Campbell Coll., 1942; BTh., Lampton Theol. Sem., 1948; DD, Moody Bible Inst., 1976. Ordained to ministry African Methodist Episcopal Ch. Pastor Calumet (Ind.) Mission African Meth. Episcopal Ch., Scott's Chapel African Meth. Episcopal Ch., Chg., Mt. Zion African Meth. Episcopal Ch.; pastor St. James African Meth. Episcopal Ch., Elgin, Ill., Elkhart, Ind.; pastor St. Paul African Meth. Episcopal Ch., Chgo., Bethal African Meth. Episcopal Ch., Champaign, Ill.; ward chapel African Meth. Episcopal Ch., Peoria, Ill. Mem. Peoria Urban League, Peoria Community Action Agy. Recipient Humanitarian award Carver Ctr., Pastor of Yr. award Southside Pastor's Assn., Mayor's Proclamation, Martin Luther King Jr. Drum Major award. Mem. Champaign Ministerial Assn., NAACP (exec. bd.), Masons, Kiwanis. Democrat. Address: 405 E Park St Champaign IL 61820

WALKER, JAMES ALVIN, retired minister; b. Greensburg, Ky., May 3, 1925; s. John Alvin W. and Mattie Lee (Paxton) Walker-Wayne; m. Beatrice Dalene Chaudion, Aug. 2, 1943; children: Ernest Edward, Maurice Ray, Audry Kay, James Frederick. AB, Ky. Wesleyan U., 1951; ThM, Emory U., 1953; PhD in Psychology, U. So. Miss., 1973. Ordained to ministry United Meth. Ch., 1953; lic. profl. counselor. Min. United Meth. Ch., Ky., Miss., 1951-87; ret. United Meth. Ch., 1987; owner, mgr. Christian Life Bookstore, Jackson, Miss., 1979—. Vol. Hinds Mental Health Assn., Jackson, 1978, The Stew Pot, Goodwill, Salvation Army, 1980—. Democrat. Home: 3449 Shannondale Dr Jackson MS 39212 Office: Christian Life Bookstore 1335 Ellis Ave Pla Jackson MS 39212

WALKER, JAMES LYNWOOD, seminary group executive. B.A., N.Carolina Central U., 1963; M.Div., Pacific Sch. Religion, 1967; Ph.D. Grad. Theol. Union/U. Calif.-Berkeley, 1970. Assoc. prof., asst. dean Grad. Theol. Union, 1970-73; exec. dir. Pastoral Inst. of Wash./Ida., 1973-78; pastor Magnolia Presbyn. Ch., Seattle, 1979-81; interim pastor Newport Presbyn. Ch., Bellevue, Wash., 1981-82; pres. Northwest Theol. Union, Seattle, 1984—; cons., therapist, 1982-84. Author: Body and Soul: Gestalt Therapy and Religious Experience, 1971; editor: Agendas for Black Churches, 1985. Office: Northwest Theol Union 914 E Jefferson St Seattle WA 98122*

WALKER, JAMES SILAS, college president; b. LaFollette, Tenn., Aug. 21, 1933; s. John Charles and Ruth Constance (Yeagle) W.; m. Nadine Leas Mortenson, May 28, 1954; children—Steven J., David K., Bradley P., Scott C. B.A., U. Ariz., 1954; B.Div., McCormick Theol. Sem., 1956; postgrad. U. Basel, Switzerland, 1956-57; Ph.D., Claremont Coll., 1963. Ordained to ministry Presbyterian Ch., 1956. Asst. pastor Central Presbyn. Ch., Denver, 1957-60; prof. Huron Coll., S.D., 1963-66; prof. Hastings (Nebr.) Coll., 1966-75, dir. devel., 1975-79, dean, 1979-83; pres. Jamestown Coll., N.D., 1983—; adj. faculty mem. Luther Northwestern Theol. Sem., St. Paul, 1984—; bd. dirs. Synod of Lakes and Prairies Coun. Author: Theology of Karl Barth, 1963. Bd. dirs. Salvation Army, Jamestown, Nat. Ghost Ranch Found. Rotary Internat. Found. fellow, 1956-57; Nat. Def. Title IV grantee, 1960-63. Mem. Assn. Presbyn. Colls. and Univs., Presbytery of No. Plains (coun. Synod of Lakes and Prairies), Jamestown C. of C. (bd. dirs.), Rotary (dist. 563 gov. 1978-79). Republican. Avocations: travel, hunting, photography. Office: Jamestown Coll Office of the Pres Box 6080 Jamestown ND 58401

WALKER, JESSE MARSHALL, church organization official, clergyman; b. Enfield, N.C., July 21, 1917; s. Jesse Makton and Marie (Crawley) W.; m. Anne Lashley Thompson; children: Jesse Marshall Jr., William T., Martha Marie, Frances Ann; stepchildren: Glenn, Michael, David, Gregory Thompson. AB, Elon Coll., 1938; ThM, So. Bapt. Theol. Sem., 1941, D Ministry, 1979. Ordained to ministry So. Bapt. Conv., 1938. Pastor Bethel and Dabney Bapt. chs., Holton, Ind., 1938-41, Stovall (N.C.) Bapt. Ch., 1941-46, Liberty Bapt. Ch., Appomattox, Va., 1946-50, Braggtown Bapt. Ch., Durham, N.C., 1950-56, Southside Bapt. Ch., Miami, Fla., 1956-60, Bedford (Va.) Bapt. Ch., 1960-73; dir. missions East River and Highlands Bapt. assns., Dublin, Va., 1973—. Mem. Ga. Assn. Virginia Bapts., So. Bapt. Assn. Dirs. Missions. Home: Rte 1 Box 3 Staff Village Dublin VA 24084 Office: Box 965 Dublin VA 24084 *The Christian community has credibility when the things that bind us together are stronger than the things which divide us.*

WALKER, JEWETT LYNIUS, clergyman, church official; b. Beaumont, Tex., Apr. 7, 1930; s. Elijah Harvey and Ella Jane (Wilson) W.; BA, Calif. Western U., 1957; MA, Kingdom Bible Inst., 1960; B.R.E., St. Stephens Coll., 1966, D.D., 1968; LLD, Union Bapt. Sem., 1971; grad. Nat. Planned Giving Inst., 1981, St. Paul Sch. Theology, 1979, Philanthropy Tax Inst., 1982; m. Dorothy Mae Croom, Apr. 11, 1965; children: Cassandra Lynn, Jewett L., Kevin, Michael, Ella, Betty Renne, Kent, Elijah H. Ordained to ministry A.M.E. Zion Ch., 1957; pastor Shiloh A.M.E. Zion Ch., Monrovia,

Calif., 1961-64, Martin Temple A.M.E. Zion Ch., Los Angeles, 1964-65, 1st A.M.E. Zion Ch., Compton, Calif., 1965-66, Met. A.M.E. Zion Ch., Los Angeles, 1966-73, Logan Temple A.M.E. Zion Ch., San Diego, 1973-74, Rock Hill A.M.E. Zion Ch., Indian Trail, N.C., 1974-79, Bennettsville A.M.E. Zion Ch., Norwood, N.C., 1979-86, Price Meml. A.M.E. Zion Ch., Concord, N.C., 1986-89, Mt. Zion A.M.E. Zion Ch., Hickory Grove, S.C., 1989—; sec. dept. home missions, brotherhood pensions and relief A.M.E. Zion Ch., Charlotte, N.C., 1974; mem. exec. bd. Prophetic Justice Unit Com. Nat. Coun. Chs., co-chairperson pers. com.; mem. World Meth. Coun., del. 14th World Conf. Trustee, Clinton Coll., Rock Hill, Lomax-Hannon Coll., Greenville, Ala., Union Bapt. Theol. Sem., Birmingham, Ala.; bd. mgrs. McCrorey br. YMCA; pres. Am. Ch. Fin. Service Corp., Carolina Home Health Service Inc., Methodist Life Ins. Soc. Inc., bd. trustees State N.C. Coll. Found., Inc., 1987, del. Presbyn. Partners in Ecumenism Nat. Council Chs. Christ, 1986, pres., 1988—; del. Presbyn. Ch. U.S. Gen. Assembly, 1985. Fellow Nat. Assn. Ch. Bus. Adminstrs., Ch. Bus. Adminstrn., Presbyn. Ch. Bus. Adinstrn. Assn.; mem. NAACP (life), Nat. Soc. Fund Raising Execs., Christian Ministries Mgmt. Assn. Clubs: Shriners, Masons (33 deg.). Republican. Author articles. Home: 910 Bridle Path Ln Charlotte NC 27211 Office: 4501 Walker Rd Charlotte NC 28211

WALKER, JOHN E., priest; b. N.Y.C., Mar. 16, 1948; s. Edward G. and Jane E. (Fitzgerald) W.; m. Judith E. Walker, May 6, 1978; 1 child, Meaghan Kelly. AA, Queensborough Community Coll., 1969; BA, Hunter Coll., 1971; MDiv, Nashotah (Wis.) House, 1974. Cert. bereavement, drug, alcohol counselor. Asst. pastor Holy Apostles Ch., Oneida, Wis., 1974-75; curate Transfiguration Ch., Freeport, N.Y., 1977-78; asst. St. Mark's Ch., Islip, N.Y., 1978-80; rector Holy Trinity Ch., Greenport, N.Y., 1980—; dean Peconic Deanery, Diocese L.I., 1985—; mem. nominating coun. for bishop coadjutor, 1987, Diocesan Coun. L.I., 1988-90. Chaplain Boy Scout Troop #51, Greenport, 1980; mem. Drug and Alcohol Abuse Com., Greenport, 1986—; pres. Greenport Ecumenical Ministries, 1988; mem. bd. mgrs. Episcopal Health Svcs., 1988. Mem. Rotary (pres. Greenport club 1983-84, Rotarian of Yr. 1983). Home: 768 Main St Greenport NY 11944 Office: Holy Trinity Ch 768 Main St Greenport NY 11944

WALKER, JOSEPH WILLIAM, minister; b. Greenville, S.C., Aug. 23, 1930; s. Joseph Gabriel and Olive (Jones) W.; m. Betty Jo McCormick, June 29, 1955; children: Deborah Jo, Jeanette Elizabeth, Jennifer Anne. BA, Davidson Coll., 1951; BD, Union Theol. Sem., 1954, D. Ministry, 1976; ThM, U. Edinburg (Scotland), 1959. Ordained to ministry Presbyn. Ch. (U.S.A.), 1954. Pastor Selma (N.C.) and Belleview Presbyn. Chs., 1954-56; pastor 1st Presbyn. Ch., Maxton, N.C., 1957-61, Decatur, Ala., 1961-79; pastor Whitehaven Presbyn. Ch., Memphis, 1979-85, 1st Presbyn. Ch., Fayetteville, N.C., 1985—; commr. gen. assembly Presbyn. Ch. (U.S.A.), moderator Synod of Middle South, 1976, Fayetteville Presbytery, 1988. Mem. bio-ethics com. High Smith Rainey Hosp., Fayetteville, 1987—. Mem. Ministerial Assn., Kiwanis. Home: 2454 Vandemere Ave Fayetteville NC 28304 Office: 1st Presbyn Ch Box 569 Bow and Ann Sts Fayetteville NC 28302

WALKER, L. T., bishop. Bishop of Ark. ch. of God in Christ, Little Rock. Office: Ch of God in Christ 2315 Chester St Little Rock AR 72206*

WALKER, LARRY LEE, religious organization administrator, consultant; b. Modesto, Calif., Dec. 4, 1948; s. Oliver Andrew and Betty Jean (Carter) W.; m. Kathleen Gale Lynch, Sept. 13, 1969; children: Jennifer, Lori, Pamela, Angela. BA in History, Calif. State U., Turlock, 1971; ThM, Dallas Theol. Sem., 1976. Ordained to ministry, Fellowship Bible Ch., 1976. Missionary CAM Internat. (formerly C.Am. Mission), Costa Rica and Guatemala, 1977-81; assoc. pastor Fellowship Bible Ch., Dallas, 1981-83, missions pastor, 1983-89; dir. SW region ACMC, Inc. (formerly Assn. Ch. Missions Coms.), Escondido, Calif., 1989—. Home: 1960 S Citrus Ave Escondido CA 92027 Office: ACMC Inc 1523 E Valley Pkwy Ste 202E Escondido CA 92027

WALKER, ROBERT EUGENE, minister; b. Memphis, June 20, 1936; s. Sterling Granville and Jessie Eugenia (Darling) W.; m. Elizabeth Ann Lyle, June 1, 1957; children: Suzanne Rene, Paul Timothy, Stephen Lyle, Robert Andrew, Mark Sterling. Student, Union U., 1955-58; BA, Blue Mountain Coll., 1964; postgrad., New Orleans Bapt. Theol. Sem., 1964-65, U. Miss., 1970. Ordained to ministry Bapt. Ch., 1954. Pastor Temple Bapt. Ch., Myrtle, Miss., 1957-60, Springdale Bapt. Ch., Ripley, Miss., 1960-64, First Bapt. Ch., White Castle, La., 1964-67, Concord Bapt. Ch., Booneville, Miss., 1967-79, Sunrise Bapt. Ch., Carthage, Miss., 1979-83, Antioch Bapt. Ch., Florence, Miss., 1983-86, Northside Bapt. Ch., Vicksburg, Miss., 1986-91, Mountain Creek Bapt. Ch., Florence, Miss., 1991—; substitute tchr. Warren County Pub. Schs., Vicksburg; tchr. Prentiss County Pub. Schs., Booneville, Miss., 1967-68; prin. Gray Acad. Grammar Sch., Ashland, Miss., 1969. Author: History of Antioch Bapt. Ch., 1985. Mem. Fairfield S.C. Genealogy Soc., Warren County Pastor's Conf. Republican. Home: Rte 7 Box 443 Florence MS 39073 *Looking back across almost four decades of ministry I know my greatest discovery was finding God's will for my life as a very young man. God has added the blessing of a devoted and supportive wife and family. Looking ahead my greatest hope is to hear God's affirmation: "Well done."*

WALKER, ROBERT GLENN, minister, church official; b. Norfolk, Va., June 25, 1929; s. Robert Glenn and Randi Lillian (Mathisen) W.; m. Cecelia Mary Cone, June 23, 1951; children: Kathryn Marie, Victoria Elizabeth (dec.). BA, Lenoir-Rhyne Coll., 1951, DD (hon.), 1985; MDiv, Luth. Sch. Theology, Chgo., 1954; MS, Fla. State U., 1964. Ordained to ministry Luth. Ch. in Am., 1954. Pastor Christ Luth. Ch., St. Petersburg, Fla., 1954-57, St. Stephen Luth. Ch., Tallahassee, 1957-61; chaplain Lenoir-Rhyne Coll., Hickory, N.C., 1961-66; dir. so. and Ohio region Nat. Luth. Campus Ministry, Chapel Hill, N.C., 1966-87, deployed dir. for campus ministry, 1988—; mem. N.C. Synod Task Force on Family Life, 1972-74; chmn. examining com. sr. seminarians N.C. Synod, 1984—. Trustee Luth. Theol. So. Sem., 1970-73, 76-77, 80—, bd. chairperson, 1986—. Danforth Found. grantee, 1969. Mem. Nat. Coun. Family Rels., Southeastern Coun. on Family Rels. Home: 409 Thornwood Rd Chapel Hill NC 27514 Office: 1301 E Franklin St Ste 206 Chapel Hill NC 27514

WALKER, RONALD LEE, minister, librarian; b. St. Joseph, Mo., Nov. 1, 1934; s. Arthur Francis and Hilma Dell (Atwood) W.; m. Patricia Ann Walker, May 15, 1954; children—Mitchell Scott, Matthew Craig, Martin Wayne. B.A., Biola Coll., 1963; M.A., Talbot Theol. Sem., 1976; M.A. in Library Sci., U. Mo., 1983. Ordained to ministry Baptist Ch., 1967; asst. pastor Central Bapt. Ch., Anaheim, Calif., 1963-65; adminstr. Springfield (Mo.) Christian Schs., 1966-72; asst. pastor N.T. Bapt. Ch., Springfield, 1966-72; dir. Faith of Our Fathers Radio Broadcast, Springfield, 1967-71; dir. Sheltering Heights Bible Camp, Springfield, 1967-71; pastor Quint City Bapt. Temple, Davenport, Iowa, 1972-75; prof. Bibl. studies Bapt. Bible Coll., Springfield, 1976-86, librarian, 1981-86; pastor Heritage Bapt. Temple, Little Rock, Ark., 1986—. Pres., Iowa Bapt. Fellowship, 1973-74, state rep., 1973-74. Author: King James Controversy, 1980; editor: The Baptist Church, 1981. Served as sgt. USMC, 1954-57. Mem. ALA. Republican. Office: Heritage Bapt Temple 4910 Stagecoach Rd Little Rock AR 72204

WALKER, STEVEN EUGENE, minister; b. Terre Haute, Ind., Jan. 4, 1960; s. Richard Eugene Walker and Phyllis M. (Dispennette) Fugate; m. Jennifer Jean Eder, Aug. 21, 1981; 1 child, Calvin Andrew. BS in Physics, Ind. State U., 1982; MA in Religion, Olivet Nazarene U., 1984; MDiv, Christian Theol. Sem., 1988. Ordained to ministry United Meth. Ch., 1990. Pastor Rosedale (Ind.)/Bridgeton United Meth. Chs., 1984-88, Wilkinson (Ind.) United Meth. Ch., 1988—. Dir. Boy Scouts of Am., Wilkinson, 1990—. Home: RR 1 Box 28A Wilkinson IN 46186 Office: Wilkinson United Meth Ch 310 S Main Wilkinson IN 46186

WALKER, VICKI RENEE, religious education professional; b. Madisonville, Ky., Sept. 24, 1959; d. Aubrey Calvin and Evelyn Marie (Hoskins) Walker; m. John Leo Eshelman III, June 4, 1983. BA in Communications, U. Ky., 1981; MA in Religion, Asbury Theol. Sem., 1983. Diaconal min. Christian edn. First United Meth. Ch., Newark, Ohio, 1984-88; diaconal min. programming First United Meth. Ch., Wapakoneta, Ohio, 1988-89, dist. program assoc., 1989—; edn. cons., West Ohio Conf. United Meth. Ch., 1986—; edn. chair, children's chair, Newark and Lima dist. United Meth. Ch., 1986—; sec. Conf. Bd. Diaconal Ministry, Columbus, Ohio, 1988—; del. N. Cen. Jurisdictional Conf., 1988, 91; alt. Gen. Conf., 1988, 91. Co-editor, contbr. Framework of Our Faith, 1983; contbg. author: The Heritage of Hopkins County, Kentucky, 1988, If I Grew Up with John Wesley, 1989. Chair Battered Women's Adv. Com., Newark, 1986-88; bd. dirs., Newark Family Counseling Agy., 1986-88, Wapakoneta Children's Learning Ctr., 1988; del. West Ohio Conf. to Pax World Found. Study tour of Cen. Am., Nicaragua, Guatemala, and Honduras, 1990, North Cen. Jurisdictional Conf., 1988, 91; gen. conf. alt. del., 1988, 91; founding pres., bd. dirs. Hope House; HIV/AIDS instr. ARC. Recipient Findlay Bus. and Profl. Women's award, 1990. Mem. Nat. Christian Educators Fellowship, West Ohio Christian Educators Fellowship. Democrat. Avocations: music, sports, reading, theatre, needlework. Home: 1705 Fostoria Ave Apt F Findlay OH 45840 Office: Findlay Dist Office United Meth Ch 1215 Tiffin Ave Findlay OH 45840

WALKER, WILLIAM OLIVER, JR., religion educator; b. Sweetwater, Tex., Dec. 6, 1930; s. William Oliver and Frances Baker (White) W.; m. Mary Scott Daugherty, Dec. 22, 1955 (div. Dec. 1978); children: William Scott, Mary Evan, Michael Neal. BA, Austin Coll., 1953; MDiv, Austin Presbyterian Sem., 1957; MA, U. Tex., 1958; PhD, Duke U., 1962. Instr. religion Austin Coll., Sherman, Tex., 1954-55, Duke U., 1960-62; from asst. to prof. religion Trinity U., San Antonio, 1962—, chmn. dept., 1980-88, acting dean div. Humanities and Arts, 1988-89, dean, 1989—. Contbr. articles and book reviews to profl. jours. Editor: The Relationships, 1978, Harper's Bible Pronunciation Guide, 1989; assoc. editor Harper's Bible Dictionary, 1985. Mem. Studiorum Novi Testamenti Soc., Soc. Bibl. Lit. (regional sec.-treas. 1980-86), Am. Acad. Religion (regional pres. 1966-67), Soc. Sci. Study Religion, Cath. Bibl. Assn. Am., Coll. Theology Soc. Democrat. Presbyterian. Avocations: tennis, traveling, photography. Home: 315 Cloverleaf Ave San Antonio TX 78209 Office: Trinity U Dept Humanities and Arts 715 Stadium Dr San Antonio TX 78212

WALKER-SMITH, ANGELIQUE KETURAH, minister, religious organization administrator; b. Cleve., Aug. 18, 1958; d. Roosevelt Victoreold and Geneva (Willis) Walker; m. R. Drew Smith. BA, Kent State U., 1980; MDiv, Yale U., 1983; postgrad., Princeton U., 1987—. Prodn. asst. Sta. WFSB-TV, Hartford, Conn., 1980-81; assoc. min. Convent Ave. Bapt. Ch., N.Y.C., 1981-82, Horace Bushnell United Ch. Christ, Hartford, 1981, 83; overseas leader Operation Crossroads Africa, N.Y.C., 1983-86; assoc. pastor Cen. Bapt. Ch., Hartford, 1983-86; exec. dir. Trenton (N.J) Ecumenical Area Ministry, 1986-90; ecumenical liaison Nat. Bapt. Conv. USA, Inc., Bloomington, Ind., 1990—; co-mem. team seminars on continuing edn. Princeton U. Theol. Sem.; mem. cen. com. World Coun. Chs.; project dir., TV host Ch. Fedn. Greater Indpls., Am. Bapt. Conv.; mem. cen. com., commr. unit IV World Coun. Chs., 1990—. Contbr. articles to profl. jours. Pub. rels. coordinator Urban League, Cleve., 1979-80, staff mem., 1979, 81-83; subcom. chmn. Mayor's Task Force on Hunger/Homelessness, Trenton, 1986—; mem., minister Hartford Action Plan on Infant Health, 1984-86; mem. NAACP, Hartford, 1981-85. Recipient Mercer County recognition Mercer County Exec., 1987, recognition State of N.Y. Senate, 1990, City of Trenton, 1990. Mem. Ptnrs. in Ecumenism (officer for internat. affairs 1986—), Nat. Assn. Ecumenical Staff (sec. 1987—), Women in Communications, Commn. on Local and Regional Ecumenism, Black Women in Ministry (founder, coordinator Hartford chpt. 1984-86), Nat. Bapt. Conv. U.S.A. Inc. (ecumenical liaison), Am. Bapt. Chs., Ch. Fedn. Greater Indpls. (project dir., TV host), ABC: Impact Ind., global Exch. Study Assn, World Coun. chs. (cen. com.), Blue Key. Avocations: tennis, travel, reading. Office: Nat Bapt Conv USA Inc PO Box 6295 Bloomington IN 47407

WALL, ARTHUR EDWARD PATRICK, editor; b. Jamestown, N.Y., Mar. 12, 1925; s. George Herbert and Doris (Olmstead) W.; student pub. schs.; m. Marcella Joan Petrine, Nov. 5, 1954; children—John Wright, Marie Ann, David Arthur Edward. Copy editor Worcester (Mass.) Telegram, 1958; Sunday editor Hawaii Island Corr., Honolulu Star-Bull., 1958-60; editor Hilo (Hawaii) Tribune-Herald, 1960-63; Sunday editor Honolulu Advertiser, 1963-65, mng. editor, 1971-72; mng. editor Cath. Rev., 1965-66, editor, 1966-71; editor-in-chief Nat. Cath. News Service, Washington, 1972-76; editor, gen. mgr. The New World (name changed to Chgo. Catholic 1977), Chgo., 1976-86, pres., 1979-86; pres. New World Pub. Co., 1977-86; communications officer Diocese of Cen. Fla., Orlando, 1988—; editor Cen. Fla. Episcopalian, Orlando, 1989—; dir. Noll Printing Co., Inc., Huntington, Ind. Dir. bur. info. Archdiocese Balt., 1965-66; mem. fin. com. Archdiocese Chgo., 1979-82; mem. council Internat. Cath. Union of Press, Geneva, 1972—, v.p., 1974-77. Chmn., Gov.'s Com. Ednl. TV, Honolulu, 1964-65; regent Chaminade Coll., Honolulu, 1959-65, chmn., 1963-65; trustee St. Mary's Sem. and Univ., Balt., 1975-76; bd. dirs. Cath. Journalism Scholarship Fund, 1976—, Our Sunday Visitor, Inc., Huntington, Ind., 1977—; mem. spiritual renewal and devel. com. 41st Internat. Eucharistic Congress, Phila., 1975-76. Named Young Man of Year, Hilo, Hawaii, 1960, Fla. Writer of Yr., 1988; recipient St. Francis de Sales award Cath. Press Assn., 1977; Father of Year, Honolulu C. of C., 1964; Spl. award U.S. Cath. Conf., 1980. Mem. Internat. Fedn. Cath. Press Agys. (pres. 1974-77), Internat. Fedn. Cath. Journalists (pres. 1977-80, v.p. 1981-83), Cath. Press Assn. U.S. and Can. (bd. dirs. 1978-86), Sigma Delta Chi (past chpt. pres.), Internat. Order St. Luke the Physician (religious pub. rels. coun.). Roman Catholic. Clubs: Nat. Press (Washington); Overseas Press (N.Y.C.); Chgo. Press. Author: The Big Wave, 1960, The Mind of Cardinal Bernardin, 1983, The Spirit of Cardinal Bernardin, 1988, If I Were Pope, 1989; editor: Origins and Catholic Trends, 1972-76; contbr. articles to mags. Home: 1684 Hull Cir Orlando FL 32806 Office: Diocese Cen Fla 1017 E Robinson St Orlando FL 32801 *Most of my life has consciously involved words; almost everyone is a captive of words (fatso, nigger, turncoat, byu-now-pay-later, stupid, I love you) that trigger moods and actions almost in themselves. I guess it is the power of words, and especially the power of what most Christians call the Word, that has influenced me since a fortunate childhood in a literate household. I learned from my grandfather that a loud word limps (although I forget that once in a while), that decibel doesn't equal impact. I sometimes forget something else he taught me, that kinky four-letter words are weak and express a weakness inside. There are stronger words of the same size, such as soul and love, life and holy, good and idea, hear and talk. One who listens for those words hears something special; or to put it in a different vocabulary, God guides, and following that Guide leads to the only success there is.*

WALL, JAMES MCKENDREE, minister, editor; b. Monroe, Ga., Oct. 27, 1928; s. Louie David and Lida (Day) W.; m. Mary Eleanor Kidder, Sept. 11, 1953; children: David McKendree, Robert Kidder, Richard James. Student, Ga. Inst. Tech., 1945-47; BA, Emory U., 1949, BD, 1955, LHD (hon.), 1985; MA, U. Chgo., 1960; LittD (hon.), Ohio No. U., 1969; DHL (hon.), Willamette Coll., 1978; DD (hon.), MacMurray, 1981; DHL (hon.), Coe Coll., 1987. Ordained to ministry United Meth. Ch., 1954. Staff writer, sports dept. Atlanta Jour., 1948-50; asst. minister East Lake Meth. Ch., Atlanta, 1953; asst. to dean students Emory U., Atlanta, 1954-55; pastor North Ga. Conf. Moreland, Luthersville Meth. Chs., Ga., 1955-57, Bethel United Meth. Ch., Chgo., 1957-59; mng. editor Christian Adv. mag., Park Ridge, Ill., 1959-63, editor, 1963-72; editor Christian Century mag., Chgo., 1972—. Author: Church and Cinema, 1971, Three European Directors, 1973, Winning the War, Losing Our Soul, 1991; author, editor: Theologians in Transition, 1981, A Century of the Century, 1987, How My Mind Has Changed, 1991. Del. Dem. Nat. Conv., 1972, 76, 80; mem. Dem. Nat. Com., 1976-80, Dem. State Cen. Com., 1974-86, Pres. Commn. White House Fellowships, 1976-80. Served to 1st lt. USAF, 1950-52. Mem. Alpha Tau Omega, Omicron Delta Kappa, Sigma Delta Chi. Home: 451 S Kenilworth Elmhurst IL 60126 Office: Christian Century 407 S Dearborn St Ste 1405 Chicago IL 60605

WALL, JOE LAYTON, university president; b. Dallas, Jan. 11, 1939; s. Charles and Frances Wall; m. Linda Gay Galbraith, 1960; children: Scot Daniel, Christopher Layton. BA, Baylor U., 1961; M of Theology, Dallas Theol Sem., 1965, D of Theology, 1978. Ordained to ministry Bible Ch., 1974. Youth dir. Richmond Pla. Bapt. Ch., Houston, 1956-57; dir. student outreach Edgefield Bapt. Ch., Waco, Tex., 1958-59; pastor Travis (Tex.) Bapt. Ch., 1960-61, Fate (Tex.) Union Ch., 1962-65, Grace Bible Ch., Bryan, Tex., 1965-67, Spring Br. Community Ch., Houston, 1967-74; dean acad. affairs Dallas Bible Ch., 1974-76; co-founder Houston Bible Inst., 1978-83; radio speaker Sta. KWBI Radio, Morrison, Colo., 1984—, Sta. KJOL Radio, Grand Junction, Colo., 1985—; pres. Western Bible Coll., Morrison, 1984-85; pres. Colo. Christian U., Lakewood, Colo., 1985-91, chancellor, dean of Grad. Sch. of Ministry, 1991—; assoc. pastor Foothills Bible Ch., Littleton, Colo., 1991—; youth dir. Magnolia Park Bapt. Ch., Houston, summer 1959. Author: Bob Thieme's Teachings on Christian Living, 1978, Going for the Gold, 1991. Mem. Alpha Chi. Home: 16105 E Belleview Ave Morrison CO 80465 Office: Colo Christian U 180 S Garrison Lakewood CO 80226

WALLACE, BETTY JEAN, educator, lay minister; b. Denison, Tex., Dec. 5, 1927; d. Claude Herman and Pearl Victoria (Freels) Moore; m. Billy Dean McKneely, Sept. 2, 1950 (div. Nov. 1964); children: Rebecca Lynn, Paul King, David Freels, John Walker, Philip Andrew McKneely. Student, Tulane U., 1947; BA, Baylor U., 1949; postgrad., U. Houston, 1949-50, 74, 81, Rocky Mountain Bible Inst., 1959, U. Colo., 1969-70, U. No. Colo., 1965, 68, 72, Rocky Mountain Bible Inst., 1959; MEd, Houston Bapt. U., 1985. Cert. life profl. elem., high sch., life profl. reading specialist, Tex. Tchr. Galena Park (Tex.) Ind. Sch. Dist., 1949-50, 52-53, 72—, Corpus Christi (Tex.) Independent Sch. Dist., 1950-51, Denver Pub. Schs., 1953-54, 63-72. Author: The Holy Spirit Today, 1989, Our God of Infinite Variety, 1991, God Speaks in a Variety of Ways, 1991. Sun. sch. tchr. So. Bapt. Conv. chs., Tex., 1946-50, Denver, 1952-56; tchr. kindergarten Emmanuel Bapt. Ch., Denver, 1956-59; missionary, Queretaro, Mex., 1977,78; mem. Rep. Senatorial Inner Circle, Washington, 1989-91, Round Table for Ronald Reagan, Washington, 1989-90; tchr. Kindergarten Ch., Denver, 1960-63; helper Feed the Poor, Houston, 1983-85; active Suicide Prevention, Houston, 1973-76, Literacy, Houston, 1978-81; rep. NEA, Denver, 1966-72; mem. Retirement Com., Denver, 1970-72. Grantee NSF, 1969-70. Mem. Tex. Classroom Tchrs. Assn. (officer rep., pres. Galena Park chpt. 1988-91), Delta Alpha Pi (pres. Waco chpt. 1948-49), Alpha Epsilon Delta. Republican. Avocations: writing, archeology, gardening, reading, gem/jewelry collecting and designing. Home: 14831 Anoka Dr Channelview TX 77530 Office: North Shore Elem Sch 14310 Duncannon Dr Houston TX 77015 *The love of God is spread abroad through us. We need to let our lights shine before men so they will glorify the Father.*

WALLACE, CHARLES ISAAC, JR., religion educator; b. Balt., Sept. 28, 1943; s. Charles I. Sr. and Miriam Ann (Shroyer) W.; m. Mary Elizabeth Sargent, July 10, 1971; children: Hannah Margaret, Mary Shroyer. AB, Bowdoin Coll., 1965; BD, Yale U., 1968; PhD, Duke U., 1975. Ordained to ministry United Meth. Ch., 1975. Minister Mt. Zion United Meth. Ch., Finksburg, Md., 1973-79; campus minister, adj. prof. Western Md. Coll., Westminster, 1975-85; vis. lectr. Wesley Theol. Sem., Washington, 1975-85; univ. chaplain, assoc. prof. religion Willamette U., Salem, Oreg., 1985—. Contbr. articles to scholarly jours. Mem. Am. Acad. Religion, Am. Soc. Ch. History, Assn. for Religion and Intellectual Life, Nat. Assn. Coll. and Univ. Chaplains, Wesley Hist. Soc. Democrat. Office: Willamette U 900 State St D-219 Salem OR 97301

WALLACE, C(LYDE) HOWARD, minister, educator; b. Wellington, Kans., Jan. 6, 1924; s. Adlai Grover and Charlene (Duggan) W.; m. Margaret McHenry, June 10, 1946 (div.); children: David, Susan, Martha, Mark; m. Nancy Lee Davis, Nov. 17, 1973; children: Andrew, Matthew. BA, Park Coll., 1945; BD, McCormick Sem., 1948; ThD, U. Basel, Switzerland, 1961. Ordained to ministry Presbyn. Ch. (USA), 1948. Interim pastor Community Presbyn. Ch., East Gary, Ind., 1948-49; Presbyn. univ. pastor Harvard U., Cambridge, Mass., 1951-59; prof. Bibl. theology U. Dubuque, Iowa, 1959—; pres. Presbyn. Alcohol Network, 1983-86; moderator John Knox Presbytery, 1977-78, chmn. gen. coun., 1978-79. Author: Biblical Archaeology Reader, 1961; contbr. articles to profl. jours. Pres. Dubuque Community Sch. Bd., 1968, S.W. Neighborhood Assn., Dubuque, 1983-84. Mem. Soc. Bibl. Lit., Am. Acad. Religion, Men's Garden Club. Democrat. Office: Dubuque U Theol Sem 2000 University Ave Dubuque IA 52001

WALLACE, DANIEL BAIRD, religion educator; b. Pasadena, Calif., June 5, 1952; s. Vard Beecher and Nayda (Baird) W.; m. Patricia Kathryn O'Brien, June 8, 1974; children: Noah, Benjamin, Andrew, Zachary. BA, Biola U., La Mirada, Calif., 1975; ThM, Dallas Sem., 1979, postgrad., 1990—. Ordained to ministry Bapt. Ch., 1986. Asst. pastor Coll. Park Ch., Fullerton, Calif., 1973-75; instr. New Testament Dallas Seminary, 1979-81, asst. prof. New Testament, 1988—; instr. New Testament Grace Seminary, Winona Lake, Ind., 1981-83; rsch. assoc. Probe Ministries, Dallas, 1984-88. Contbr. articles to profl. jours. Mem. Soc. Bibl. Lit., Evang. Theol. Soc. (sec.-treas. southwestern region sect. 1989—), Internat. Orgn. Septuagint and Cognate Studies, Majority Text Soc., BMW Car Club Am. Mem. Ind. Bible Ch. Home: 3117 High Plateau Garland TX 75044 Office: Dallas Seminary 3909 Swiss Ave Dallas TX 75204 *It seems to me that those who are outstanding in a given field are not supermen or superwomen. They do not do all things well. They even intentionally do some things poorly or minimally. They succeed because they know that half of wisdom is learning when to settle for limited objectives.*

WALLACE, DEWEY D., JR., educator; b. Chgo., Jan. 8, 1936; s. Dewey D. and Junietta D. (Jeremy) W.; B.A., Whitworth Coll., 1957; B.D., Princeton Sem.; 1960; M.A., Princeton U., 1962, Ph.D., 1965; m. Marion Elizabeth Allen, Sept. 16, 1956; children—Mark, Paul. Asst. prof. religion George Washington U., Washington, 1963-66, asso. prof., 1966-74, prof., 1974—. Author: The Pilgrims, 1977, Puritans and Predestination, 1982, The Spirituality of the Later English Puritans, 1988. Rockefeller Bros. fellow, 1962-63. Mem. Am. Soc. Ch. History, Am. Acad. Religion, Presbyn. Hist. Soc. Democrat. Office: 2106 G St Washington DC 20052

WALLACE, JOEL KEITH, hospital chaplain; b. San Bernardino, Calif., Nov. 3, 1933; s. Perry A. and Margaret S. (McCuen) W.; m. Winifred Lynne Capps, June 17, 1961; children: David Mark, Susanne Lynne Wallace Trumble, Jason Glenn. BA, Bob Jones U., 1958; BD, Talbot Theol. Sem., 1961, MDiv, 1970; DMin, Luther Rice Sem., 1977. Ordained to ministry Ind. Fundamental Chs. Am., 1961. Commd. 2d lt. U.S. Army, 1962, advanced through grades to lt. col., 1985, chaplain, various locations including Vietnam, 1962-72; ret. USAR, 1986; pastor Amarillo (Tex.) Bible Ch., 1972-76; ins. agt. Prudential Ins. Co., Amarillo, 1976-80; intermittent chaplain VA Med. Ctr., Amarillo, 1975-80; staff chaplain VA Med. Ctr., Dayton, Ohio, 1980-87; chief chaplain svc. VA Med. Ctr., Boise, Idaho, 1987—; instr., Regional Med. Edn. Ctr., Salt Lake City, 1988—. Police dept. chaplain, City of West Carrollton, Ohio, 1986-87; mem. City Beautiful Commn., 1987; loaned exec. United Way/Combined Fed. Campaign, 1989. Decorated Bronze Star from Vietnam. Mem. Ind. Fundamental Chs. Am. (regional pres. 1989—), Idaho Assn. Pastoral Care (pres., treas. Valley chpt. 1990-91), Coll. Chaplains (state rep. 1989—), Res. Officers Assn. (pres. Idaho 1989-92), VFW (chaplain), Mil. Order World Wars (chaplain 1989-92, sr. vice comdr. 1991-92), Mini Le Bois, Dayton Miniature Soc., Kiwanis. Democrat. Avocations: miniatures, woodworking, bowling, foreign languages. Office: VA Med Ctr 500 W Fort St Boise ID 83702-4598

WALLACE, LAWRENCE EUGENE, minister; b. Independence, Mo., July 6, 1940; s. Joe Thomas Patterson and Virginia Lee Kinnemer Rasmuson; m. Mary Ellen Wesson, Oct. 11, 1957; children: Larry Edward, Rhonda Kaye, Rodeny Alan. AA, Tulsa Jr. Coll., 1981; BA, Northeastern State U., 1983; postgrad., Dallas Bapt. U., 1968-69. Ordained to ministry So. Bapt. Conv., 1974. Min. youth 3 So. Bapt. chs. Tehlequah, Okla. and Tulsa area, 1969-77; pastor 3 So. Bapt. chs. Tulsa area, 1978-88, 83-88; min. edn. White City Bapt. Ch., Tulsa, 1980-83; pastor First Bapt. Olive Ch., Drumright, Okla., 1983-88, First Bapt. Ch., Pawhuska, Okla., 1988—; past bd. dirs. Bapt. Conv. Okla., Oklahoma City, 1985-89; regional sales mgr. fountain sales div. Nat. Dr. Pepper Co., Dallas, 1963-68; sales rep. Andrew Jergens Co., Cin., 1973-74; speaker in field. With U.S. Army, 1957-60. Avocations: fishing, hunting. Home: 521 Prudom St Pawhuska OK 74056 Office: First Bapt Ch 302 E 6th Pawhuska OK 74056

WALLACE, LEIGH ALLEN, JR., bishop; b. Norman, Okla., Feb. 5, 1927; s. Leigh Allen Sr. and Nellie Elizabeth (Whittemore) W.; m. Alvira Kinney, Sept. 2, 1949; children: Jenny Leigh, Richard Kinney, William Paul. BA, U. Mont., 1950; M in Divinity, Va. Theol. Sem., 1962, DD, 1979. Ordained priest Episcopal Ch.; vicar chs., Sheridan, Virginia City, Jeffers, Mont., 1962-65; rector St. Luke's Ch., Billings, Mont., 1965-71, Holy Spirit Parish, Missoula, Mont., 1971-78; bishop of Spokane, 1979—. Served with USNR, 1945-46. Address: 245 E 13th Ave Spokane WA 99202

WALLACE, MARK HARRIS, minister; b. Albany, Ga., Sept. 14, 1955; s. Lawrence Theodore and Grace (Justice) W.; m. Kelly Sue Noe, Mar. 3, 1979; children: Justin, Andrew, Brittany Hope, Marcie Faith. BS in Psychology, Ga. State U., 1978; MS in Clin. Psychology, Augusta Coll., 1985; M of Ministry, Internat. Bible Inst., Plymouth, Fla., 1983, D of Ministry, 1985. Ordained to ministry Faith Christian Fellowship Internat., 1988 ; lic. to ministry Ch. of God, 1989. Assoc. pastor Riverdale (Ga.) Ch. of God, 1977-82; youth pastor Maranatha Fellowship, Augusta, 1982-84; sr. pastor, founder New Hope Christian Ctr., Augusta, 1984-89; resident pastor New Hope Ch. of God, Augusta, 1989-90, world missions pastor, 1990-91; elder, co-pastor Living Word Christian Ctr., Augusta, 1991—; co-elder minister Oneln Spirit Ministries, Augusta, 1986—; praise team musician and singer A Great Love Ministries, Toccoa, Ga., 1987—; pres., founder Wallace Ministries Internat. Augusta, 1989—; minister Internat. Conv. Faith Ministries, Tulsa, 1988—. Author 10 books including: The Servant's Heart, The Christian's Call to War, Grace: God's Greatest Gift; songwriter gospel music; contbr. articles to profl. jours. Co-founder, co-dir. Augusta Thanksgivine Dinner of Love Outreach, 1986—, Augusta Christmas Food/Toy Baskets Outreach, 1986—. Mem. Ga. State U. Alumni Assn., Augusta Coll. Alumni Assn., Golden Key, Psi Chi. Office: Wallace Mins Internat PO Box 211256 Augusta GA 30917-1256 *If a person will give Jesus Christ their past, He in turn will give them a future.*

WALLACE, MARK I., religion educator; b. Covina, Calif., June 26, 1956; s. H. Homer and Shirley (Hastings) W.; m. Ellen Marie Ross, Sept. 11, 1983. BA, U. Calif., Santa Barbara, 1978; MDiv, Princeton Theol. Sem., 1982; PhD, U. Chgo., 1986. Ordained to ministry Presbyn. Ch., 1990. Asst. prof. Ga. State U., 1987-89, Swarthmore (Pa.) Coll., 1989—. Author: The Second Naiveté. Summer grantee Nat. Endowment for the Humanities, 1989. Fellow Soc. for Values in Higher Edn.; mem. Am. Acad. Religion. Democrat. Home: 318 N Chester Rd Swarthmore PA 19081 Office: Swarthmore Coll Religion Swarthmore PA 19081

WALLACE, ROBERT BRUCE, minister; b. Phoenix, Aug. 28, 1933; s. Samuel S. and Mildred (Butterbaugh) W.; m. Donna J. Sutton, June 28, 1957 (div. May 1980); m. Peggy Ruth Riggins, June 19, 1981; children: Lynn, Bonnie, David, Richard. BA, U. Redlands, 1955; MDiv, Am. Bapt. Seminary, Berkeley, Calif., 1958; STD, San Francisco Theol. Seminary, 1978. Ordained to ministry Bapt. Ch., 1958. Assoc. min. 1st Bapt. Ch., L.A., 1958-61; campus min. Ariz. State U., Tempe, 1961-65; min., univ. pastor University Bapt., State College, Pa., 1965-73; sr. min. 1st Bapt. Ch., Redlands, Calif., 1973-83, Ann Arbor, Mich., 1984-91, Melrose, Mass., 1991—; chmn. Interfaith Counseling Svc., Ann Arbor, 1985-90, East Valley Area Health Coun., Redlands, 1980-82, Div. Christian Higher Edn., East Lansing, Mich., 1985-90; bd. dirs. North Am. Bapt. Peace Fellowship. Chmn. Housing Commn., Redland, 1982-83, Shelter Assn., Ann Arbor, 1988; mem. Housing Policy Bd., Ann Arbor, 1990-91. Recipient Citizen of Yr. award Social Workers Assn., Ann Arbor, 1987. Mem. Am. Bapt. Mins. Coun., Bapt. Joint Com. on Pub. Affairs, Am. Bapt. Campus Ministry Assn., Rotary. Democrat. Home: 108 Youle Melrose MA 02176

WALLACE, RONNIE LEE, minister; b. Miami, Fla., June 29, 1958; s. Michael Duane Wallace and Mary Sue (Parker) Humm; m. Denise Ana Ortiz, Aug. 27, 1983; 1 child, Jesse Lee. BS in Religious Edn., Evang. Bible Coll., 1985; BS in Bibl. Studies and Human Resource Mgmt., Miami Christian Coll., 1991, postgrad., 1991—. Ordained to ministry Bapt. Ch., 1988. Pastor youth Tamiami Bapt. Ch., Miami, 1984-85; assoc. pastor Pembroke Lakes Community Ch., Pembroke Pines, Fla., 1985-86; worship leader Gladeview Bapt. Ch., Miami, 1986-87; youth pastor Pembroke Rd. Bapt. Ch., Miramar, Fla., 1987-90; pastor Jubilee Fellowship Ch., Pembroke Pines, 1990—; pres. Jubilee Fellowship Inc., Pembroke Pines, 1990—. Recipient 1st place male vocalist Masters Staff Talent Inc., Ft. Lauderdale, Fla., 1985. Home: 110 NW 207th Way Pembroke Pines FL 33029 Office: Jubilee Fellowship PO Box 9221 Pembroke Pines FL 33084 *In this life a call has been given. This call is to follow Jesus. To follow Jesus is to accept Him as Lord and Savior. When one accepts Him and His atoning sacrifice for their sins...we have responded to His call...and life truly begins.*

WALLACE-PADGETT, DEBRA KAYE, minister; b. Ashland, Ky., June 15, 1958; d. Joseh F.W. and Lena Idella (Walters) Wallace; m. Ivan Lee Padgett, Jr., Sept. 19, 1981. BA in Phys. Edn., Berea (Ky.) Coll., 1979; MA in Christian Edn., Scarritt Coll., Nashville, 1981; MDiv, Lexington Theol. Sem., 1990. Consecrated to ministry United Meth. Ch. as diaconal min., 1983. Dir. Christian Edn. Epworth United Meth. Ch., Lexington, Ky., 1981-83; dir. leadership devel. First United Meth. Ch., Lexington, 1984—; conf. chmn. edn. Ky. Conf. Coun. on Ministries, Lexington, 1988—. Mem. Nat. Christian Educators Fellowship, Ky Christian Educators Fellowship. Democrat. Home: Star Rt 1 Box 55 Ravenna KY 40472 Office: First United Meth Ch 214 W High St Lexington KY 40507

WALLACH, BENNO M., retired rabbi; b. Vienna, Austria, Sept. 27, 1923; came to U.S., 1936; naturalized; s. Mark and Lena Wallach; m. Madeline Harris, Dec. 21, 1947; children: Naomi Wallach Schwartz, Joshua D. BA, Western Res. U., 1945; B. Hebrew Letters, Hebrew Union Coll., 1948, M. Hebrew Letters, 1950; DD (hon.), William Carter Bible Coll., 1959; DD, Hebrew Union Coll., 1975. Ordained rabbi. Rabbi Temple Emanuel, Roanoke, Va., 1950-53, Ref. Jewish Congregation Merrick, L.I., N.Y., 1953-57, Temple Sinai, Miami, Fla., 1957-63, Congregation of Liberal Judaism, Orlando, Fla., 1963-70, Temple Emanuel, Beaumont, Tex., 1970-77; retired, 1977; adj. prof. Lamar State U., Beaumont, 1973-74; pres. Beaumont Ministers Assn., 1975-76, Ministers Assn., Winter Park, Fla., 1968. Author: David Einhorn's Sinai, 1856-62, 1950. Brotherhood Through Freedom, 1954. Bd. dirs. United Appeal, ARC, Family Svc., United Jewish Appeal, many other civic orgns. Mem. Cen. Conf. Am. Rabbis. Home: PO Box 246 Crosby TX 77532

WALLEN, RAEBURN GLENN, religion educator; b. Leadwood, Mo., Dec. 17, 1931; s. Ray Bryan and Fanny Pearl (McGee) W.; m. Marcelene M. Owens; children: Tamra M. Wallen Kluckman, Ronald, Michael. AB, Findlay Coll., 1956; BD, MDiv magna cum laude, Winebrenner Theol. Sem., 1959; MRE, Oberlin Theol. Sem., 1961; MA in Religion, Case Western Res. U., 1975. Ordained to ministry Chs. of God. (Gen. Conf.), 1953. Pastor numerous chs.; prof. religion U. Findlay, Ohio, 1959—; adj. prof. Defiance Coll., Ohio, 1990—; cons. world religions at confs. and seminars; participant Cin. Coun. World Affairs seminars. Author: Life and Death in the Old Testament, A Guide to the Holy Land, Zoroastrianism; other books and manuals. Trustee Winebrenner Theol. Sem., mem. and chmn. exec. com.; trustee Winebrenner Haven Extended Care for Elderly, Findlay; mem. adminstrv. coun. Chs. of God, Gen. Conf., chmn. Commn. on Ordination and Ministerial Rels.; mem. Faith and Order Commn. of Ohio Couns. Chs.; mem. Mayor's Civil Svc. Commns.; others. Regional Coun. Internat. Edn. grantee, 1968-73, Danforth grantee, 1971, World Festival of Islam grantee, 1976. Mem. Am. Schs. Oriental Rsch., Am. Acad. Religion, Nat. Assn. for Fgn. Student Affairs, Religious Edn. Assn., Toledo Internat. Inst. (life), Findlay Country Club, Kiwanis (past dist. rep. for Circle K clubs in No. Ohio, chmn. Circle K and Key club coms.), Phi Beta Delta (editor newsletter 1991—). Home: 607 Winterhaven Dr Findlay OH 45840

WALLER, GARY LEE, minister; b. Bertha, Minn., Apr. 24, 1950; s. Ray Lee and Eleanor Ann (Perkins) W; m. Ann Rose Blacklock, July 15, 1972; children: Mark, Sarah. BA, N.W. Nazarene Coll., 1972; MDiv, Nazarene Sem., 1977; D Ministry, San Francisco Sem., 1989. Ordained to ministry Ch. of the Nazarene, 1977. Pastor Rocky Butte Ch. of the Nazarene, Brewster, Wash., 1977-81, Quincy (Wash.) Ch. of the Nazarene, 1981-83; assoc. pastor Kent (Wash.) Ch. of the Nazarene, 1983—; chmn. N.W. Christian Singles, Ken, 1979—; dir. singles Wash. Pacific Dist., Edmonds, 1983—, adult dir., 1983-86; chmn. bd. ministerial studies Wash. Pacific Dist. Ch. of the Nazarene, 1985—. Author: Leadership Boot Camp, 1986, Life of A.M. Hills, 1989, Divorce Recovery Manual, 1989. Mem. Wesleyan Theol. Soc., Christian Marriage Enrichment (instr.), Single Speakers' Bur., N.W. Christian Singles. Office: Ch of the Nazarene 930 E James Kent WA 98031

WALLER, KEITH G., lay worker, protective services official; b. Detroit, Feb. 5, 1957; s. Alan Eugene and Beverly Jean (Kidder) W.; m. Kim Allison Humphrey, June 12, 1976; children: Kelly Marie, Danielle Louise, Keith Alan. AA, Macomb Community Coll., 1982; BS, Wayne State U., 1986. Patrolman City of Roseville, Mich., 1979—; sec. Hope Luth. Ch, Warren, Mich., 1988-90, chmn. steering com., 1990—. With U.S. Army, 1975-78. Mem. Police Officers Assn., Roseville, Mich. (pres. 1991—, 3 citations). Office: Roseville Police Dept 29753 Gratiot Ave Roseville MI 48066

WALLICK, CHARLES C., minister; b. Red Lion, Pa., Sept. 6, 1916; s. Charles C. and Minnie B. (Smith) W.; m. Elizabeth Griswold, Aug. 22, 1942 (div. Sept. 1954); m. Nancy Cole, Oct. 30, 1954; children: Stephen W., David M. BA, Ursinus Coll., 1938; MDiv, Yale U., 1941; PhD, U. Edinburgh, Scotland, 1950; postgrad., U. Pa., 1951-52. CLU. Chaplain USN, 1942-46; asst. prof. Ursinus Coll., Collegeville, Pa., 1946-49; lectr. U. Conn., Storrs, 1955-56; bd. dirs. Rocky Mt. Conf., United Ch. Christ, Denver, 1989—; mem. Christian bd. RSVP, Garfield County, Glenwood, Colo., 1989—. Contbr. articles to newspaper. Lt. comdr. USN, 1942-46. Recipient 3d Life award Cleve. Life Underwriters, 1966. Mem. Am. Legion (chaplain 1989-90), Lions (chaplain 1975-76). Home: PO Box 56 Molina CO 81646

WALLING, ALBERT CLINTON, II, clergyman; b. Ft. Lauderdale, Fla., Sept. 24, 1925; s. Jacob Biffle and Nora Maurine (Stone) W.; m. Carroll Langlois Wicher, Dec. 26, 1964; children: Maurine Carroll, Elizabeth Hancock. BA, Trinity U., 1948; M in Div., Episcopal Div. Sch., 1953; D in Ministry, U. of the South, 1977; postgrad., Harvard U., 1961, 63. Ordained priest Episcopal. Ch., 1954. Vicar, asst. rector various chs., Tex., 1953-66; rector Ch. of Good Shepherd, Terrell, Tex., 1966-71, Ch. of Ascension, Dallas, 1971-73; assoc. rector St. Mark's Episcopal Ch., Houston, 1974-77; rector St. Alban's Episcopal Ch., Houston, 1977-82; diocesan supply priest Episcopal Diocese Tex., Houston, 1982-86; ins. agt., broker Mass. Mut. Ins. Co., Houston, 1982-86; ind. ins. broker San Antonio, 1986-90, diocesan supply clergy, 1986—; Episcopal chaplain Terrell State Hosp., 1966-71. Trustee U. of the South, 1971-74. Named hon. Ky. Col., 1973. Fellow Tex. State Geneol. Soc. (life); life mem. Soc. of the Lees of Va.; mem. San Antonio Assn. Life Underwriters (chaplain 1987), Nat. Soc. Ams. of Royal Descent (chaplain gen. 1980—), Jamestowne Soc. (gov. 1st Tex. Co. Houston 1985-89), San Jacinto Descendants (founder), Order of First Families Va., Tex. State Gen. Soc. (1st v.p. 1977-80), Harvard Club (Houston chpt.). Republican. Avocations: genealogy, gardening, swimming, travel, cooking. Home: 7011 Spring Briar St San Antonio TX 78209

WALLIS, JOE D., minister; b. Pampa, Tex., Apr. 5, 1958; s. Joe Leeman and Bobbie Jean (Brewer) W.; m. Cynthia Diane Thrower, July 8, 1989. BA cum laude, Okla. Bapt. U., Shawnee, 1980; MA in Religious Edn., Southwestern Bapt. Theol. Sem., 1984. Lic. to ministry, So. Bapt. Conv., 1978. Minister edn. and adminstrn. Riverside Bapt. Ch., Miami, Fla., 1984-87; minister youth, edn. and music Southside Bapt. Ch., Bowie, Tex., 1987-90; minister students, outreach and recreation Easthaven Bapt. Ch., Houston, 1990-91; minister music and youth 1st Bapt. Ch., Englewood, Fla., 1991—; bd. dirs. Camp Copass Bapt. Encampment, Denton, Tex., 1989-90. Nat. newsletter co-editor Baptists Committed, Houston, 1990—. Adv. bd. Montague County Outreach Ctr., Bowie, 1988-90. Mem. Houston Area Bapt Students United, Omicron Delta Kappa. Republican. Home: 325 Cowles Englewood FL 34223

WALLS, ANDREW FINLAY, missiologist and religious research administrator; b. Apr. 21, 1928; s. Andrew Finlay Walls and Florence Johnson; m. Doreen Mary Harden, Apr. 4, 1953; children: Christine, Andrew. BA in Theology with honors, U. Oxford, Eng., 1948, MA, 1952, LittB, 1954. Librarian Tyndale House, Cambridge, Eng., 1952-57; lectr. theology Fourah Bay Coll., Sierra Leone, 1957-62; head religion dept. U. Nigeria, Nsukka, 1962-65; sr. lectr. church history U. Aberdeen, Scotland, 1966-70, head religious studies dept., 1970-85; dir. Ctr. Study Christianity in Non-Western World U. Aberdeen, U. Edinburgh, Scotland, 1982—; vis. prof. various univs., sec. Scottish Inst. Missionary Studies, 1967—. Editor: Jour. Religion Africa, 1967-86, Bull. Scottish Inst. Missionary Studies, 1967—, Quar. bibliography World Mission, 1972—; contbr. articles to profl. jours. Councillor Aberdeen, 1974-80; chmn. Council Mus. Galleries Scotland, 1977-81, Disablement Income Group, Scotland, 1977-81; trustee Nat. Mus. Scotland, 1985-87. Served with RAF, 1948-50. Decorated officer Order of Brit. Empire. Fellow Soc. Antiquaries Scotland; mem. Brit. Assn. History Religions (pres. 1976-79), Internat. Assn. Mission Studies (gen. sec. 1974-76), African Studies Assn. U.K., Deutsche Gesellschaft für Missionswissenschaft, British and Irish Assn. for Mission Studies. Mem. Labour Party. Methodist. Avocations: writing verse, plays, sketches. Home: 58 Stanley St, Aberdeen AB1 6UR, Scotland Office: Univ Edinburgh Ctr Study, Christianity Non-Western World, New Coll, Mound Pl, Edinburgh EH1 2LU, Scotland

WALLS, DAVID ROBERT, minister; b. London, Ont., Can., May 25, 1953; s. Robert Wesley and Doris E. (Saunders) W.; m. Patrcia Anne McNeill, Aug. 23, 1975; children: Jeremy David, Robert Kent. BS, U. Waterloo, Ont., 1974; MDiv, Talbot Theol Sem., 1977; D Ministry, Trinity Evang. Div. Sch., Deerfield, Ill., 1983. Ordained to ministry Assn. Gospel Chs. Can., 1980. Asst. pastor Met. Bible Ch., Paramount, Calif., 1976-77; pastor Victory Bapt. Ch., Newmarket, Ont., 1977-80; sr. pastor Brant Bible Ch., Burlington, Ont., 1980-84, Bethany Bible Ch., Phoenix, 1984-89, Ch. of the Open Door, Elyria, Ohio, 1989—; tchr. Ont. Bible Coll., Toronto, 1977-80; bd. dirs. Internat. Ministries to Israel, Wheaton, Ill.; speaker in field. Author: Ordinary Heroes, 1991. Republican. Office: Ch of the Open Door 43275 Telegraph Rd Elyria OH 44035

WALLS, JAMES DOUGLAS, minister; b. Washington, Aug. 1, 1931; s. George Washington and Emma (Benson) W.; m. Donna Marie Payne, June 16, 1962; children: Quentin Douglas, Janice Marie. Student, Washington Bible Inst., 1957-61; DD, Faith Evangelistic Christian Coll., Detroit, 1990, So. Calif. Sch. Ministry, Inglewood, 1991; HHD (hon.), Faith Evang. Christian Schs., Detroit, 1991. Ordained to ministry Ch. of God, 1960. Pastor Ch. of God, Xenia, Ohio, 1968—; mem. program and planning com., nominating com. Nat. Assn. Ch. of God, West Middlesex, Pa., 1983-89, coord. nat. preachers clinic, 1984—, mem. mass communication bd., 1988—, mem. ch. rels. bd., 1989—; chair. bd. dirs. Women's Abuse of Substance Intervention Tactics, 1989—. Editor Words of Truth, 1972-84, Xenia Herald, 1988—. Mem. Cumberland Ridge Civic Assn., Columbus, Ohio, 1971—. With U.S. Army, 1952-54. Mem. Urban Christian Leadership Assn. Home: 3032 Pine Valley Rd Columbus OH 43219

WALMSLEY, ARTHUR EDWARD, bishop; b. New Bedford, Mass., May 4, 1928; s. Harry Barlow and Elizabeth Doris (Clegg) W.; m. Roberta Brownell Chapin, Dec. 29, 1954; children: Elizabeth Trent, John Barlow. B.A., Trinity Coll., Hartford, Conn., 1948; D.D. (hon.), Trinity Coll., 1982; M.Div., Episcopal Theol. Sch., Cambridge, Mass., 1951; Hum.D. (hon.), New Eng. Sch. Law, Boston, 1970; D.D. (hon.), Berkeley Div. Sch., New Haven, 1980. Ordained to ministry Episcopal Ch., 1952, consecrated bishop, 1979. Asst., then rector Ch. of Holy Apostles, St. Louis, 1951-53; rector Trinity Ch., St. Louis, 1953-58; staff office exec. council Episcopal Ch., N.Y.C., 1958-68; dir. Mass. Council Chs., Boston, 1969-72; dep. to rector Trinity Ch., N.Y.C., 1972-73; rector St. Paul's Ch., New Haven, 1974-79; bishop Diocese of Conn., Hartford, 1979—. Editor: The Church in a Society of Abundance, 1963. Trustee Berkeley Div. Sch., 1979—, Trinity Coll., 1982—. Sr. fellow Am. Leadership Forum; mem. Phi Beta Kappa, Pi Gamma Mu. Home: 134 Oxford St Hartford CT 06105 Office: Conn Episcopal Diocese 1335 Asylum Ave Hartford CT 06105

WALRATH, HARRY RIENZI, minister; b. Alameda, Calif., Mar. 7, 1926; s. Frank Rienzi and Cathren (Michlar) W.; A.A., City Coll. San Francisco, 1950; B.A., U. Calif. at Berkeley, 1952; M.Div., Ch. Div. Sch. of Pacific, 1959; m. Dorothy M. Baxter, June 24, 1961; 1 son, Gregory Rienzi. Dist. exec. San Mateo area council Boy Scouts Am., 1952-55; ordained deacon Episcopal Ch., 1959, priest, 1960; curate All Souls Parish, Berkeley, Calif., 1959-61; vicar St. Luke's, Atascadero, Calif., 1961-63, St. Andrew's, Garberville, Calif., 1963-64; asso. rector St. Luke's Ch., Los Gatos, 1964-65, Holy Spirit Parish, Missoula, Mont., 1965-67; vicar St. Peter's Ch., also headmaster St. Peter's Schs., Litchfield Park, Ariz., 1967-69; chaplain U. Mont., 1965-67; asst. rector Trinity Parish, Reno, 1969-72; coordinator counciling services Washoe County Council Alcoholism, Reno, 1972-74; adminstr. Cons. Assistance Services, Inc., Reno, 1974-76; pastoral counselor, contract chaplain Nev. Mental Health Inst., 1976-78; contract mental health chaplain VA Hosp., Reno, 1976-78; mental health chaplain VA Med. Ctr., 1978-83, staff chaplain, 1983-85, chief, chaplain service, 1985-91, also triage coord. for mental health, ret., 1991; dir. youth Paso Robles Presbytery; chmn. Diocesan Commn. on Alcoholism; cons. teen-age problems Berkeley Presbytery; mem. clergy team Episcopal Marriage Encounter, 1979-85, also Episc. Engaged Encounter. Mem. at large Washoe dist. Nev. area council Boy Scouts Am., scoutmaster troop 73, 1976, troop 585, 1979-82, asst. scoutmaster troop 35, 1982—, assoc. adviser area 3 Western region, 1987-89, regional com. Western Region, 1989—; lodge adviser Tannu Lodge 346, Order of Arrow, 1982-87; South Humboldt County chmn. Am. Cancer Soc. Trustee Community Youth Ctr., Reno. Served with USNR, 1944-46. Decorated Pacific Theater medal with star, Am. Theater medal, Victory medal, Fleet Unit Commendation medal; recipient dist. award of merit Boy Scouts Am., St. George award Episc. Ch.-Boy Scouts Am., Silver Beaver award Boy Scouts Am., 1986, Founders' award Order of the Arrow, Boy Scouts Am., 1985; performance awards VA-VA Med. Ctr., 1983, 84; named Arrowman of Yr., Order of Arrow, Boy Scouts Am. Cert. substance abuse counselor, Nev. Mem. Ch. Hist. Soc., U. Calif. Alumni Assn., Nat. Model R.R. Assn. (life), Sierra Club Calif., Missoula Council Chs. (pres.), Alpha Phi Omega. Democrat. Club: Rotary. Home: 580 Huffaker Ln E Reno NV 89511 *The study of history has taught me one thing: that human nature has not changed, only the means of its execution. This same study has also taught me that human nature reveals the glory of God in our quest for our future.*

WALSH, BARBARA MARY, religion educator; b. Fall River, Mass., May 24, 1932; d. Thomas Henry and Jessie (Hyson) W. BA, Anna Maria, 1965; MusM, Boston U., 1970. Tchr. Parish St. William of York, Balt., 1951-60, Parish Holy Name, Fall River, Mass., 1960-69; prin. Parish Holy Name, Fall River, 1969-81; assoc. pastor, coord. Literacy Inter-Generational Program St. Peter's, Monticello, Ky., 1982—; dir. religious studies St. Peter's, Monticello, 1982—; coord. Sch. on Wheels Literacy Program, Monticello, 1986—. Contbr. articles to profl. jours. Singer, Community Chorus, Monticello, 1985-90. Mem. AARP, NRVC. Roman Catholic. Office: School on Wheels PO Box 669 Monticello KY 42633

WALSH, BROTHER BRIAN, school system administrator. Supt. schs. Diocese of Rochester, N.Y. Office: Office Supt Cath Schs 1150 Buffalo Rd Rochester NY 14624*

WALSH, DANIEL FRANCIS, bishop; b. San Francisco, Oct. 2, 1937. Grad., St. Joseph Sem., St. Patrick Sem., Catholic U. Am. Ordained priest, Roman Catholic Ch., 1963. Ordained titular bishop of Tigia, 1981; aux. bishop of San Francisco, 1981-87, bishop of Reno-Las Vegas, 1987—. Office: 515 Court St Reno NV 89501 also: Diocese of Reno-Las Vegas Office of Bishop PO Box 18316 Las Vegas NV 89114

WALSH, JANE DORA WEST, religion educator; b. Allentown, Pa., Oct. 31, 1952; d. Howard and Rose Bonnie (Forstater) West; m. Ariel Walsh, Aug. 12, 1990; stepchildren: Micah, Matthew, Benjamin. BA, Boston U., 1974; MA, Hebrew Union Coll., 1985. Cert. Reform Jewish educator. Edn. intern Skirball Mus., L.A., 1983-84; dir. edn. Temple Israel, Omaha, 1985-87; congregational sch. cons. Bd. Jewish Edn., Balt., 1987—; instr. Balt. Hebrew U., 1988—. Hebrew U. Sr. Educators Program fellow, 1991-92. Mem. Nat. Assn. Temple Educators (bd. dirs. 1990—, co-chair cons. 1990—, del. Nat. Conf. 1991), ASCD, Coalition for Alternatives in Jewish Edn. Office: Bd Jewish Edn 5800 Park Heights Ave Baltimore MD 21215

WALSH, THOMAS GERALD, administrator, educator; b. Lousiville, Nov. 8, 1949; s. William J. and Edna B. (Bottoms) W.; m. Lynn Stambaugh Robinson, July 1, 1982. BA in English, Western Ky. U., 1971; MA in Theology, Vanderbilt U., 1981, PhD in Theology, 1986. Acting dir. Internat. Conf. on the Unity of Scis., N.Y.C., 1984-88; prof. Iowa State U., Ames, 1986; exec. dir. Internat. Religious Found., N.Y.C., 1988—; adj. prof. philosophy Maris Coll., Poughkeepsie, N.Y., 1987-88, N.Y. Inst. Tech., N.Y.C., 1987-88, Seton Hall U., South Orange, N.J., 1989—; adj. prof. bus. ethics Caldwell Coll., 1990; adj. prof ethics Coll. of Mt. St. Vincent, 1990-91. Assoc. editor: Dialogue Alliance Jour., 1988—; contbr. articles to profl. jours. Mem. Am. Acad. Religion, Soc. for Christian Ethics, Am. Philosophical Assn. Avocations: sailing, tennis. Office: Internat Religious Found JAF Box 2347 New York NY 10116

WALTER, GERRY HENRY, rabbi; b. Chgo., Sept. 12, 1947; s. Leon and Annette (Siglin) W.; m. Carenjean Simon, Apr. 15, 1973; children: Stacy, Adam. BA, Knox Coll., 1969; B in Hebrew Letters, Hebrew Union Coll., 1972, MA in Hebrew Letters, 1974. Ordained rabbi, 1974. Rabbi Temple Emanuel, Roanoke, Va., 1974-84, Temple Sholom, Cin., 1984—; instr. practical rabbinics Hebrew Union Coll.-Jewish Inst. Religion, 1985—, mem. admissions com., 1986—; adj. prof. No. Ky. U., Highland Heights, 1987—; pres. Cin. Bd. Rabbis, 1988-89; mem. Cen. Conf. of Am. Rabbis, Commn. on Religious Living/Cen. Conf. Am. Rabbis-Union Am. Hebrew Congregations. Recipient Brotherhood award Nat. Conf. of Christians and Jews, Roanoke, 1981. Office: Temple Sholom 3100 Longmeadow Lane Cincinnati OH 45236 *What greater joy can there be than to devote one's life to teaching Torah, celebrating Judaism and serving God?.*

WALTER, HOLLIS CLIFFORD, JR., religion educator; b. Buffalo, W. Va., May 5, 1941; s. Hollis Clifford and Geraldine (Lambert) W.; m. Mary Jo Cheatham, May 26, 1963; 1 child, Holly. BA, Lexington Bapt. Coll., 1963, ThB, 1964. Ordained to ministry Bapt. Ch., 1969. Mem. faculty Teays Valley Bapt. Coll., Hurricane, W.Va., 1967—, dean, 1968—; clk. Emmanuel Bapt. Ch., Hurricane, 1967-83, treas. mission fund, 1978-84; salesman Zondervan, Huntington, W.Va., 1981—; book reviewer. Home: 9 Nilan Dr Hurricane WV 25526 Office: Teays Valley Bapt Coll 3655 Teays Valley Rd Hurricane WV 25526 *We have been blessed by having many truths given to us by others. Now it is our task to pass these on to others.*

WALTER, PAUL RYDER, religious organization administrator; b. Ordway, Colo., July 22, 1937; s. Victor Edson and Mable (Skogsberg) W.; m. Susan Adele Goddard, Feb. 3, 1962; children: Carolyn Victoria, Matthew Twentyman, Peter Behzad. BA, Yale U., 1959; MA Theol., Oxford U., Eng., 1978; DMiss, Trinity Evang. Div. Sch., Deerfield, Ill., 1988. Lending officer Irving Trust Co., N.Y.C., 1959-66; v.p., asst. to chmn. Great Western United Corp., Denver, 1966-69; pvt. practice investments Boulder, Colo., 1969-71; sr. v.p. Project Devel. Corp., Tehran, Iran, 1971-74; ptnr. PBG & W, Tehran, 1974-76; exec. dir. So. Am. Missionary Soc. of Episcopal Ch., Union Mills, N.C., 1978-82; exec. dir., trustee Episcopal World Mission, Forest City, N.C., 1982—; bd. dirs. Pewsaction, N.Y.C. Democrat. Home: 107 River Hills Dr Forest City NC 28043 Office: Episcopal World Mission PO Box 490 Forest City NC 28043

WALTERMIRE, DONALD EUGENE, JR., minister; b. Lexington, Ky., Nov. 15, 1957; s. Donald E. and Betty Roger (Stone) W. BA, Campbellsville Coll., 1980; MDiv, So. Bapt. Theol. Sem., 1983, PhD, 1990. Summer missionary Ky. Bapt. Conv., Middletown, 1982; assoc. pastor Immanuel Bapt. Ch., Louisville, 1982-86; coord. social svcs. St. John Ctr. for Homeless, Louisville, 1987—. Coord. St. John Ctr.'s vol. lawyer program, 1989—. Named Ky. Amb. Good Will, State of Ky., 1980. Mem. Louisville Coalition for the Homeless. Office: St John Ctr 700 E Muhammad Ali Blvd Louisville KY 40202-1643

WALTERS, FOWLER MCCOY, JR., minister; b. Aberdeen, Miss., July 7, 1951; s. Fowler McCoy and Olga (Coleman) W.; m. Susan Elizabeth Perkins, Dec. 22, 1972; children: Trey, Amy, Ty. AA, Itawamba Jr. Coll., 1971; 3rd Year Bible Degree, Freed-Hardeman Coll., 1972; BA, Harding U., 1974; MA, Harding Grad. Sch., 1981. Min. Welcome Hill Ch. of Christ, Mammoth Spring, Ark., 1972-76; youth min. Levy Ch. of Christ, N. Little Rock, Ark., 1976-77; missionary Levy Ch. of Christ, Campinas, Sao Paulo, Brazil, 1977-89; pulpit min. Levy Ch. of Christ, N. Little Rock, Ark., 1989-91; missions instr. Harding U., Seary, Ark., 1985-86. Recipient Award for Achievement Dale Carnegie & Assocs., Inc., 1991. Office: Ch of Christ 4311 Oak Hill Rd Evansville IN 47711 *To know Christ is to know God, the Creator of the universe. To commune with our maker is the only way to understand life and ourselves. Jesus is the way to God. Jesus is truth. He is life. I want to know Christ and to commune with God.*

WALTERS, JAMES WILLIAM, Christian ethics educator; b. Orlando, Fla., Nov. 1, 1945; s. Chester Herbert and Mildred Lynn Walters; m. Priscilla Philips, Aug. 23, 1970; children: Wendy Michelle, Christina Joy. BA, So. Coll., 1968; MDiv, Andrews U., 1970; MA, Claremont Grad. Sch., 1978, PhD, 1979. Ordained to ministry Seventh-day Adventist Ch., 1977. Pastor Seventh-Day Adventist ch., Ellijay, Ga., 1971-73, Claremont, Calif., 1976-80; mem. staff So. Coll., Collegedale, Tenn., 1973-74; prof. Loma Linda (Calif.) U., 1980—; co-founder Ctr. for Christian Bioethics, Loma Linda, 1984. Editor: Bioethics Today: A New Ethical Vision, 1988, War No More? Options in Nuclear Ethics, 1989; author: Living is Loving: Relationships Matter Most, 1985; contbr. articles to profl. publs. NEH fellow, 1986, NEH grantee, 1990. Mem. Soc. Christian Ethics (pres. Pacific sect. 1987), Am. Acad. Religion, Soc. Bioethics Consultation. Democrat. Home: 4053 Olive Point Pl Claremont CA 91711 Office: Loma Linda U Griggs Hall Loma Linda CA 92350

WALTERS, JEANETTE WEST, ministries director; b. Lumberton, N.C., Aug. 27, 1953; d. Herman Manley and Aileen (Lovette) West; m. Larry Wayne Walters, Sept. 6, 1975; children: Michael Wayne, Matthew Lee. AA, Southeastern Community Coll., 1973; BA, Campbell U., 1975; M of Religious Edn., Southeastern Bapt. Theol. Sem., 1981. Pres. Wayne Ministerial Assn., Goldsboro, N.C., 1989-90; dir. ch. and community ministries Neuse Bapt. Assn., Goldsboro, 1988—; home missionary So. Bapt. Conv., 1988—; bd. dirs. So. Bapt. Conv., Atlanta. Mem. Vol. Emergency Families for Children (sec. 1990—), Lenoir Community Coll. Program Adv. Com. Home: 405 Bryan Blvd Goldsboro NC 27530 Office: Neuse Bapt Assn PO Box 10136 Goldsboro NC 27532

WALTERS, STANLEY DAVID, religion educator, clergyman; b. Lawrence, Kans., July 30, 1931; s. Orville S. and Geneva Fern (Faley) W.; m. Adrienne Ruth Swallow, Aug. 13, 1955; children: David Stewart, Constance Ruth. ThM, Princeton Sem., 1960; BA, Greenville Coll., 1952; BD, Asbury Theol. Sem., 1955; PhD, Yale U., 1962. Ordained to ministry Free Meth. Ch., 1955. Prof. Greenville (Ill.) Coll., 1961-68; prof., head dept. Cen. Mich. U., Mt. Pleasant, 1970-76; prof. O.T., Knox Coll., U. Toronto, Ont., Can., 1976—. Author: Water for Larsa, 1971; also articles. Fellow Inst. for Advanced Christian Studies, 1968-70, Nat. Humanities Inst., 1976-77. Fellow Bibl. Colloquium; mem. Soc. Bibl. Lit. Home: 3787 Tooley's Rd, Courtice, ON Canada L1E 2G8 Office: U Toronto Knox Coll, 59 St George St, Toronto, ON Canada M5S 2E6

WALTERS, WILLIAM RAYMOND, lay worker, locksmith; b. Portsmouth, Ohio, Oct. 28, 1934; s. Emory Heyward Walters and Juanita Marie Grisselle Kuperovich; m. Virginia Raub, Sept. 10, 1960 (dec. Apr. 1976); children: Cynthia, Lee Ellen (dec.), William 2d, Steven, Glenn. Dir., counselor Singles for Christ Ministries, Ocean Grove, N.J., 1989—; elder counselor Kings Highway Faith Fellowship, Atlantic Highlands, N.J., 1991—; locksmith Ted Hall Security, Red Bank, N.J., 1990—. Vol. Am. Heart Assn., Ocean Grove, 1991. Staff sgt. USAF, 1952-59, Korea. Mem. Inst. Christian Living, Am. Assn. Christian Counselors, Nat. Christian Counselors Assn. (assoc.). Republican. Home and Office: Singles for Christ Ministries 13 Broadway Ste 4 Ocean Grove NJ 07756-1303

WALTHOUR, BRUCE SHUEY, minister; b. Jeannette, Pa., Jan. 7, 1949; s. Murry Caldwell and Alice Jean (Shuey) W.; m. Joanna Darlene Patrick, Aug. 15, 1982; children: Bruce Elliott, Heather Marie. BA, Catawba Coll., 1970; M Div., Lancaster (Pa.) Seminary, 1973. Ordained to ministry United Ch. of Christ, 1973. Correctional specialist Md. State Dept. Corrections, Balt., 1974-78; minister 1st United Ch. Christ, Warren, Ohio, 1978-81; minister edn. 2d Christian Ch., Warren, Ohio, 1982-85; minister First Congregational Ch., Pontiac, Mich., 1985—; cons. First Congl. Ch., Pontiac, 1987—. dist. exec. Clinton Valley Council Boy Scouts of Am., Pontiac, 1987—. Mem. Pontiac Clergy Assn., Warren Area Clergy Assn. Republican. Home: 5240 Clarkston Rd Clarkston MI 48016-9121 Office: 1st Congl Ch PO Box 3012 Pontiac MI 40859

WALTHOUR, FRED ALLEN, minister; b. Greensburg, Pa., Mar. 28, 1943; s. Willis Lester and Juliette Margaret (Peterson) W.; m. Carol Louise Soles, Aug. 13, 1966; children: Heidi Lynn, Brian Allen. BA, Taylor U., 1965; BD, Lancaster Theol. Sem., 1968. Min. Trinity United Ch. Christ, Dorseyville, Pa., 1968-80, Salem United Ch. Christ, Jacobus, Pa., 1980—; pres. York Assn. United Ch. Christ, Pa., 1983-85; bd. dirs. Pa. Cen. Conf. United Ch. Christ, Harrisburg, 1986-89. founder, pres. Spring Happening Arts & Crafts Festival, Lake Redman, Pa., 1988-90. Mem. York Assn. United Ch. Christ Ministerium (pres. 1989-90), Community Ch. Witness Coun. Office: Salem United Ch Christ 24 Franklin St Jacobus PA 17407

WALTON, JON MAXWELL, minister; b. Oklahoma City, Aug. 14, 1947; s. Clarence Donald and Camille (Holland) W. BA, Macalester Coll., 1969; MDiv, Union Theol. Sem., 1972; D. Ministry, San Francisco Theol. Sem., 1985. Ordained to ministry Presbyn. Ch. (U.S.A.), 1972. Asst. pastor 1st Presbyn. Ch., New Canaan, Conn., 1972-78; pastor, head of staff Setauket (N.Y.) Presbyn. Ch., 1978-85, Westminster Presbyn. Ch., Wilmington, Del., 1985—; vis. lectr. in homiletics Union Theol. Sem., N.Y.C., 1976, bd. dirs. 1972-78; bd. dirs. Auburn Theol. Sem., N.Y.C., 1982-85; mem. adv. bd. Del. Hospice, Wilmington, 1990—; mem. adv. bd. Word and Witness mag. Contbr. articles to profl. publs. Recipient award in preaching Christian Sermon Soc., 1977; named Man of Yr. in Religion, The Village Times, Setauket, 1984. Home: 1900 Marsh Rd Wilmington DE 19810 Office: Westminster Presbyn Ch 1504 W 13th St Wilmington DE 19806

WALTON, MEREDITH, religious organization administrator; b. Media, Pa., June 30, 1936; d. Aymar Allison and Alice Walton; divorced; children: Douglas, Dean, Scott, Julie. BA, Earlham Coll., 1958. Customer svc. mgr. MPI Label Systems, Sebring, Ohio, 1978-83, asst. gen. mgr., 1984-85; gen. sec., head Friends Gen. Conf., Phila., 1985—. Mem. Soc. of Friends. Office: Friends Gen Conf 1216 Arch St 2B Philadelphia PA 19107

WALTON, PHILLIP VERNAL, lay minister; b. Spot Bay, Cayman Islands, Feb. 27, 1963; came to U.S., 1977; s. Levi Harrison Walton and Angelita (Cecila) Bodden; m. Donna Ann Durichek, July 29, 1984; children: Patricia Violet, Donita Angela. BS in Biology, Southwestern Adventist Coll., 1985. Supt. Seventh-day Adventist Ch., Cayman Islands, 1976-77; Sunday sch. tchr. Seventh-day Adventist Ch., Dayton, Tenn., 1978-80, ch. elder, 1980-81, 85-87; lay minister Seventh-day Adventist Ch., Waco, Tex., 1988—; computer operator Lacy Autos, Waco, 1989—; del. Seventh-day Adventist World Conv., Indpls., 1991; dir. bldg. com. Seventh-day Adventist Ch., Waco, 1990—, elder, 1981—; mem. ch. exec. bd. Seventh-day Adventist Ch., 1987—. Contbr. World Vision, 1990; sports dir., cons. Cayman Islands Elem. Sch., 1984. Home: Rte 2 Box 284-F Valley Mills TX 76689 Office: Waco Seventh-day Adventist Ch 800 W Hwy 6 Waco TX 76712

WALTON, ROBERT CUTLER, theology educator; b. Jersey City, Dec. 18, 1932; s. Donald James and Elizabeth (Reed) W.; m. Charlotte Wilhelmine Kollegger, Mar. 25, 1966; children: Alexander, Deborah, Christina. BA, Swarthmore Coll., 1954; BDiv, U. Harvard, 1958; MA, PhD, Yale U., 1961; cert., Göttingen U., 1957. Instr. Duke U., Durham, N.C., 1961-64; from asst. to assoc. prof. U. B.C., Vancouver, Can., 1964-71; prof. Wayne State U., Detroit, 1971-78; prof., dir. Westfälische-Wilhelms U. Münster, Fed. Republic Germany, 1978—; dean of faculty Westfälische-Wilhelms U. Münster, 1987-90, assoc. dean of faculty, 1990—; v.p. Ctr. for Theol. Exploration; mem. adv. bd. The Religion and Soc. Report, Rockford Inst. Ctr. for Religion and Soc.; pres. Verein für die Erforschung der Kirchen-und Theologiegeschichte der deutschen Freikirchen. Author: Zwingli's Theocracy, 1967, European View of the Americans 1914-1918, 1972; editor: Studies in the Reformation, 1978. Mem. Detroit Com. on Fgn. Relations, 1974-78; mem. The Knights of the Hosp. of St. John at Jeruselem, Münster, 1983—. Mem. Am. Soc. for Reformation Rsch. (v.p. 1977-78, pres. 1978-79, co-editor editorial bd. 1978—), Pan-European Union (steering com. 1979-83), German-Am. Soc., Kiwanis (Springe), Harvard Club Rhine-Ruhr, Harvard Club (N.Y.C.). Avocations: hiking, handloading, late Roman history. Home: Kapellenkamp 3, D4412 Ostbevern Federal Republic of Germany Office: U Münster Dept Theology, Universitatsstr 13-17, D-4400 Münster Federal Republic of Germany

WALTZ, ALAN KENT, clergyman, denominational executive; b. Normal, Ill., Oct. 10, 1931; s. James Edwin Sr. and Ethel Leona (Hawkins) W.; m. Mary Joyce Horton, June 5, 1966; children: Sharon Kay, Reid Alan. BA, Ill. Wesleyan U., 1953; MDiv, Garrett Theol. Sem., Evanston, Ill., 1957; MA, Northwestern U., 1958, PhD, 1961. Ordained to ministry United Methodist Ch., 1957. Pastor Braceville Meth. Ch., Ill., 1954-56; denominational exec. United Meth. Ch., 1960—, asst. dir. Bd. Missions, Phila., 1960-64, asst. gen. sec. Council on Fin., Evanston, 1964-68, assoc. gen. sec. Gen. Council on Ministries, Dayton, Ohio, 1969-84; assoc. gen. sec. Gen. Bd. Discipleship, Nashville, 1984—. Author: Images of the Future, 1980, To Proclaim the Faith, 1983, Facts and Possibilities, 1987, A Dictionary for United Methodists, 1991; editor book series Into Our Third Century, 1981-84. Trustee Ill. Wesleyan U., Bloomington, 1984—. Mem. Am. Sociol. Soc., Soc. Sci. Study Religion, Religious Research Assn., World Future Soc. Office: Gen Bd Discipleship United Meth Ch PO Box 840 Nashville TN 37202

WALVOORD, JOHN FLIPSE, seminary president, chancellor, theologian; b. Sheboygan, Wis., May 1, 1910; s. John Garrett and Mary (Flipse) W.; m. Geraldine Lundgren, June 28, 1939; children: John Edward, James Randall, Timothy, Paul. A.B., Wheaton Coll., 1931, D.D., 1960; B.Th., Dallas Theol. Sem., 1934, M.Th., 1934, D.Th., 1936; A.M., Tex. Christian U., 1945; D.Litt. (hon.), Liberty Bapt. Sem. Registrar Dallas Theol. Sem., 1935-45, asso. prof. systematic theology, 1936-52, prof., 1952-85, regent, 1940-86, asst. to pres., 1945-52, pres., 1952-86; editor Sem. Bull., 1940-53; pastor Ft. Worth, 1935-50; editor Bibliotheca Sacra, 1952-85. Author: The Doctrine of the Holy Spirit, 1943, The Holy Spirit, 1954, The Return of the Lord, 1955, The Thessalonian Epistles, 1956, The Rapture Question, 1957, The Millennial Kingdom, 1959, To Live Is Christ, 1961, Israel in Prophecy, 1962, The Church in Prophecy, 1964, The Revelation of Jesus Christ, 1966, The Nations in Prophecy, 1967, Jesus Christ Our Lord, 1969, Philippians, 1971, Daniel, 1971, The Holy Spirit at Work Today, 1973, Major Bible Themes, 1974, Armageddon, Oil and the Middle East Crisis, 1974, 2d edit., 1990, Matthew: Thy Kingdom Come, 1975, The Blessed Hope and the Tribulation, 1976, Prophecy Knowledge Handbook, 1990, What We Believe: Discovering the Truths of Scripture, 1990, Major Bible Prophecies, 1991; contbr. to: Four Views of Hell, 1991; editor: Inspiration and Interpretation, 1957, Truth for Today, 1963; co-editor: The Bib Sac Reader, 1983, The Bible Knowledge Commentary, N.T. edit., 1983, Old Testament edit., 1985; editor: Lewis Sperry Chafer Systematic Theology, abridged edit., 1988. Named Alumnus of Yr. Wheaton Coll., 1981. Mem. Evang. Theol. Soc., Wheaton Coll. Scholastic Honor Soc. Home: 1302 El Patio Dr Dallas TX 75218

WALZER, WILLIAM CHARLES, church official, interdenominational religious publishing agency executive; b. Rochester, N.Y., July 20, 1912; s. William Frederick and Mable Beatrice (McElroy) W.; m. Dorothy Mae Kramer, Aug. 28, 1938; children—Carolyn Walzer Dennis, Lorraine Walzer Harbaugh, William T. B.A., U. Rochester, 1935; M.A., 1937; B.D., Colgate-Rochester Div. Sch., 1941; Ph.D., U. Chgo., 1944; postgrad., Syracuse U. Sch. Journalism, 1951. Ordained to ministry United Meth. Ch., 1941, United Ch. of Christ, 1985, Christian Ch. (Disciples of Christ), 1986. Tchr. high sch., 1935-38; pastor Stafford (N.Y.) Meth. Ch., 1938-41; asst. pastor Hyde Park Meth. Ch., Chgo., 1941-43; asst. prof. Garrett Theol. Sem., Evanston, Ill., 1943-45; prof. Scarritt Coll. for Christian Workers and Vanderbilt U. Div. Sch., Nashville, 1945-51; mem. staff Bd. Missions, Presbyn. Ch. in U.S.A., N.Y.C., 1951-54; exec. dir. dept. edn. for mission Nat. Council Chs., N.Y.C., 1954-77; exec. dir. Friendship Press, N.Y.C., 1954-77; interim pastor Westminster Presbyn. Ch., N.Y.C., 1955-59, 66-68, 75-77; minister Community Ch. of Great Neck, N.Y., 1979-85; treas. Eastern Ecumenical Conf. Christian World Mission, 1985—; interim minister Fairfax (Va.) Christian Ch., 1987-88; cons. div. world mission and ecumenism Luth. Ch. in Am., N.Y.C., 1978-79; chmn. Eastern Ecumenical Conf. on World Mission, Silver Bay, N.Y., 1978-80; pres. Religious Pub. Relations Council, 1959-61; bd. dirs. Religion in Am. Life, 1965-68; del. World Council Christian Edn., Tokyo, 1958, Lima, Peru, 1971; cons. Pacific Council of Chs., Suva, Fiji, Joint Bd. Christian Edn., Australia and N.Z., 1972; staff World Council Chs. Assembly, New Delhi, 1961, Uppsala, Sweden, 1968. Author: American Denominations, 1953, Your World, Your Mission, 1963, Great Protestant Leaders, 1965. Mem. U.S. Nat. Commn. for Unesco, 1972-78. Mem. Am. Soc. Ch. History, Internat. Soc. Missiology, Gray Panthers, Phi Beta Kappa, Phi Sigma Iota. Home: 1901-A Villa Ridge Dr Reston VA 22091-4820 *I am committed to educating people for interracial, intercultural and international understanding and concern. To that end a major goal has been a better educated church and community, leading to social justice, world peace and human mutual helpfulness, all of which I feel are demands of my religious heritage.*

WAMESTER, BLAKE HANSON, clergyman, therapist; b. Middletown, Conn., Aug. 28, 1945; s. Walter Kneiling and Alide Evleyn (Hanson) W.; m. Pamela Ann Ricci, Nov. 24, 1979; 1 child, Leah Abby. BA, Augusta Coll., Rock Island, Ill., 1967; MDiv, Luth. Sch. Theology, Chgo., 1971. Ordained to ministry Luth. Ch. Assoc. pastor Immanuel Luth. Ch., Holden, Mass., 1971-72; dist. exec. Boy Scouts Am., Lowell, Mass., 1972-74; pastor Luth. Ch. of Good Shepherd, Kingston, R.I., 1974-84, Bethany Luth. Ch., Cranston, R.I., 1984—; exec. dir. Chronic Fatigue Immune Deficiency Syndrome Assn. R.I., Warwick, 1989—; dean R.I. Luth. Chs., 1974-80, area coord., 1980-85; intern supr. Luth. Sch. Theology, Phila., 1987-88; cons. Chronic Fatigue Immune Deficiency Syndrome/Fibromyalgia Assn. R.I., Warwick, 1989—. Author: I Can Cope, 1989. Mem. Cranston Community Action Program, 1986-89. Recipient Civic award Cranston Community Action Program, 1987. Mem. Nat. Assn. Children of Alcoholics, Am. Psychiat. Assn., Augustana Alumni Assn. Lutheran. Avocations: astronomy, wine-tasting, phys. fitness, bowling, video tape prodn. Office: Bethany Luth Ch 116 Rolfe St Cranston RI 02910

WANG, JOSEPH SHOU-JEN, religion educator; b. Tainan, Taiwan, Republic of China, Dec. 17, 1933; came to U.S., 1960; s. John Chin-Yuan and Ping (Huang) W.; m. Esther Ching-Huey Lin, Aug. 22, 1964; 1 child, David Hong-En. BS, Nat. Taiwan U., Taipei, 1957; BD, Asbury Theol. Sem., Wilmore, Ky., 1963; ThM, Princeton Theol. Sem., 1964; PhD, Emory U., 1970. Ordained to ministry Free Meth. Ch. N.Am., as deacon, 1971, as elder, 1973. Prof. N.T. Asbury Theol. Sem., Wilmore, Ky., 1970—. Contbg. author: An Inquiry into Soteriology, 1981, The Wesley Bible, 1990; contbr. book chpts., articles to profl. jours. Recipient Outstanding Educator of Am. award Nat. Com., 1975. Fellow Inst. for Bibl. Rsch.; mem. Soc. Bibl. Lit., Evang. Theol. Soc., Wesleyan Theol. Soc. Home: 216 S Lexington Ave Wilmore KY 40390 Office: Asbury Theol Sem 204 N Lexington Ave Wilmore KY 40390

WANG, L. EDWIN, church official; b. Medford, Oreg., Nov. 2, 1919; s. Lorang Edwin and Laura (Thomas) W.; m. Astrid H. Wikander, Sept. 4, 1942; children: David M., Linnea M., Judith L. Extension student, U. Calif., 1947-48, U. Minn., 1956-65; LHD, Midland Luth. Coll., 1970. CLU. Field underwriter, then asst. mgr. Mut. of N.Y., 1943-51; mgr. Standard Ins. Co., Oakland, Calif., 1951-56; exec. sec. Augustana Pension & Aid Fund, Mpls., 1956-62; pres. bd. pensions Luth Ch. Am., 1962-87; acting ins. commr., Minn., 1967; part-time ins. instr. Oakland Jr. Coll., Contra Costa Jr. Coll., 1954-56; pres. Oakland-East Bay Life Underwriters Assn., 1951, Oakland Mgrs. and Gen. Agts. Assn., 1955; pres. Ch. Pensions Conf., 1967; mem. pension research council U. Pa. Wharton Sch. Fin., 1971—; bd. dirs. Mut. of Am. Life Ins. Co. Bd. dirs. Nat. Found. for Philanthropy, 1981—; pres. Lewis and Clark Trail Heritage Found. Inc., 1985-86; pres. Luth. Ch. Libr. Assn., 1988-90, bd. dirs., 1988—. Recipient Outstanding Service award Gov. Minn. Mem. Am. Risk and Ins. Assn., Am. Soc. CLU's (bd. dirs. 1980-84), Mpls. Chpt. CLU's (pres. 1973-74). Home: 6013 St Johns Ave Minneapolis MN 55424

WANG, PAUL H., minister; b. Taichung, Taiwan, Feb. 17, 1954; s. Maw Shiv and Su Fei (Lin) W.; m. Man Yuk Winnie Chan, June 28, 1979; children: Grace Christine, Nathan Philip. BS in psychology, S.E. Mo. State U., 1975; MTS in Pastoral Counseling, Gordon-Conwell Theol. Sem., 1980; MDiv in Theology, Fuller Theol. Sem., 1984; PhD in Clin. Psychology, Fuller Grad. Sch. Psychology, 1983. Ordained to ministry Presbyn. Ch.; lic. psychologist, Mo. Calif. Psychol. asst. Lee E. Travis Psychol. Group, Pasadena, 1980-84; post-doctoral fellow Occupational Health Svcs., L.A. County, 1982-83; asst. prof. Am. Inst. Family Rels., Hollywood, Calif., 1982-84; assoc. prof. Calif. Christian Inst., Orange, Calif., 1983-84; chaplain USN U.S. Naval Mobil Constrn. Battalion Five, Port Hueneme, Calif., 1984-86, Naval Air Sta., Point Mugu, Calif., 1986-87; dir. Cen. Christian Counseling Ctr., St. Louis, 1987-90; pres. Christian Counseling & Consultation Ctr., St. Louis, 1990—; vis. prof. Columbia (S.C.) Bibl. Sem., 1989—; proctor and quality assurance cons. Alpha Counseling Corp., Laguna Mills, Calif., 1990; chaplian USNR, St. Louis, 1979—; exec. officer Marine Amphibious Religious Support, St. Louis, 1990—. Mem. Internat. Children's Advocate, Seattle, 1987—. Recipient Plaque of Appreciation VX-4, 1987, Plaque of Appreciation NAAIRER, 1987; named Outstanding Personal Contbn. 1987, Outstanding Young Men Am., 1987. Mem. St. Louis Psychol. Assn. (pres. 1990-91, Outstanding Svc. award 1991, pres. elect 1990), Christian Assn. for Psychol. Studies (bd. dirs. mid-west 1989-91). Presbyterian. Avocation: swimming. Home: 15671 Sugarridge Ct Chesterfield MO 63017 Office: Christian Counseling Ctr 7700 Clayton Rd Ste 101A Saint Louis MO 63117

WANKE, GUNTHER, theology educator; b. Salzburg, Austria, Aug. 9, 1939; s. Adalbert Vinzenz and Ilse Barbara (Lehn) W.; m. Ulrike Katharina Fliegenschnee, Oct. 29, 1962; children: Michael, Daniel, Susanna. ThM, U. Vienna, 1962, ThD, 1964. Prof. U. Erlangen-Nürnberg, Fed. Republic Germany, 1976—, v.p., 1979-86. Author: Untersuchungen zur Sog Baruchschrift, 1971; editor: Zeitschrift für die Alttestamental Wissenschaft. Mem. Wissenschaftl Gesellschaft fur Theol. Lutheran. Home: Am Rothelheim 58, D8520 Erlangen Federal Republic of Germany Office: Univ Erlangen-Nurnberg, Kochstr 6, D8520 Erlangen Federal Republic of Germany

WANNEBO, ODE, religious organization executive, opera-concert singer, educator; b. Namsos, Trondelag, Norway, Mar. 11, 1932; came to U.S., 1963; s. Odin Mayer and Johanne (Alvhilde) W. Pres., min. music, concert singer, coord.-condr. vocal master class seminar tng. Odewind Prodns., North Hollywood, Calif., 1972—; founder, pres., counselor drugs addiction and alcoholics Victor's Circle, Van Nuys, Calif., 1982—; comml. artist Art & Handcraft Sch., Oslo, 1957-58; opera-concert singer, composer, songwriter Acad. Music and Performing Arts, Vienna, Austria, 1958-63. Composer music and lyrics for numerous sacred-secular songs; composer, producer Classical-Folk Cantata, 1974; appeared in movie A Day at Dandelions Sea, 1981; also several recs. including one with London Symphony. Cpl. Norway Army, 1958-59. Recipient Hon. Westerner award Can. Govt., 1967, Gold medal Norwegian Swimming Assn., 1973; Norwegian Govt. scholar, 1959-63. Mem. ASCAP, Sons of Norway. Office: Odewind Prodns PO Box 5316 North Hollywood CA 91616-5316

WANSTEN, DANIEL JOSEPH, minister; b. Grand Rapids, Mich., Mar. 16, 1959; s. Harry Joseph and Marilyn Jean (Eckinburg) W.; m. Rebecca Sharon Foster, July 10, 1981; children: Christine Sharon, Michelle Sharon. BS, North Cen. Bible Coll., Mpls., 1984; MRE, Grand Rapids Bapt. Sem., 1991. Lic. to ministry Assemblies of God, 1985, ordained, 1988. Deacon Northside Assembly of God, Mpls., 1982-84; sr. pastor North County Assembly of God, San Diego, 1984-88, Lowell Assembly of God, Grand Rapids, 1988—; del. Assemblies of God Gen. Coun., Springfield, Mo., 1988—; chmn. West Mich. Decade of Harvest Task Force, Grand Rapids, 1990—; com. mem. higher edn. com. Assemblies of God, Dearborn, Mich., 1990—, com. mem. supervised bd. West Cen. Dist., Grand Rapids, 1990; bd. dirs. Western Mich. Concert of Prayer, Grand Rapids, 1991—. Author: Spirtual Leadership Training, 1990. Bd. dirs. YMCA, Grand Rapids, 1989—. Office: Lowell Assembly of God 3050 Alden Nash Ave S Lowell MI 49331 *Lord Jesus Christ, I acknowledge that I have gone my own way in thought, word and deed. I believe you died bearing my sins in your body. I open myself for cleansing and yield to your control forever more.*

WANTLAND, WILLIAM CHARLES, bishop, lawyer; b. Edmond, Okla., Apr. 14, 1934; s. William Lindsay and Edna Louise (Yost) W. BA, U. Hawaii, 1957; JD, Okla. City U., 1967; D in Religion, Geneva Theol. Coll., Knoxville, Tenn., 1976; DD (hon.), Nashotah House, Wis., 1983, Seabury-Western Sem., Evanston, Ill., 1983. With FBI, various locations, 1954-59, Ins. Co. of N.Am., Oklahoma City, 1960-62; law clk.-atty. Bishop & Wantland, Seminole, Okla., 1962-77; vicar St. Mark's Ch., Seminole, 1963-77, St. Paul's Ch., Holdenville, Okla., 1974-77; presiding judge Seminole Mcpl. Ct., 1970-77; atty. gen. Seminole Nation of Okla., 1969-72, 75-77; exec. dir. Okla. Indian Rights Assn., Norman, 1972-73; rector St. John's Ch., Oklahoma City, 1977-80; bishop Episcopal Diocese of Eau Claire, Wis., 1980—; adj. prof. Law Sch. U. Okla., Norman, 1970-78; instr. canon law Nashotah House, 1983—; mem. nat. coun. Evang. & Cath. Mission, Chgo., 1977-90; co-chmn. Luth.-Anglican Roman Cath. Commn. of Wis., 1987—; mem. Episcopal Commn. on Racism, 1990—, Episcopal Coun. Indian Ministries, 1990—. Author: Foundations of the Faith, 1983, Canon Law of the Episcopal Church, 1984; co-author: Okla. Probate Forms, 1971; contbr. articles to profl. jours. Pres. Okla. Conf. Mcpl. Judges, 1973; v.p. South African Ch. Union, 1985—; trustee Nashotah House, Wis., 1981—; bd. dirs. SPEAK, Eureka Springs, Ark., 1983-89; mem. Wis. adv. com. U.S. Civil Rights Commn., 1990; mem. support com. Native Am. Rights Fund, 1990—. Recipient Most Outstanding Contbn. to Law and Order award Okla. Supreme Ct., 1975, Outstanding Alumnus award Okla. City U., 1980, Wis. Equal Rights Coun. award, 1986, Manitou Ikwe award Indian Alcoholism Coun., 1988. Mem. Okla. Bar Assn., Living Ch. Found., Oklahoma City Law Sch. Alumni Assn. (pres. 1968), Wis. Conf. Chs. (pres. 1985-86). Democrat. Episcopalian. Avocations: canoeing, skin-diving, cross-country skiing. Home: 145 Marston Ave Eau Claire WI 54701 Office: Diocese of Eau Claire 510 S Farwell St Eau Claire WI 54701 *If we truly believe that God reigns, we will so order our lives that such a belief is clearly reflected in all that we do and say; further, such a belief will shape our relations, not only with all other people, but all of God's created order.*

WARD, ALLEN RICHARD, evangelist; b. Portsmouth, N.D., Feb. 4, 1959; s. Disk E. and Lois Ruth (Davis) W.; m. Joy Miller Davine, Nov. 24, 1984; children: Richard A., Fox C., Alea Joy. BSBA, Northern State Coll., 1981; MS in Counseling, Northern State U., 1983; DD, Harvard Sch. Theology, 1987; LittD (hon.), Northern State Coll., 1990. Ordained to ministry, 1984. Evangelist Overseas Crusader, San Jose, Calif., 1981-83; dir. at large Campus Crusade for Christ, Colorado Springs, Colo., 1983-87; dir. NE region Fellowship Christian Athletes, Sioux Falls, S.D., 1987-89; world dir. Outreach Unltd., Aberdeen, S.D., 1989—; owner DVC Internat., Aberdeen, 1986—; del., World Meth. Coun., Nashville, 1986-90. Author: The Funeral of Religion, 1989, Best Seller, 1990. Mayor City of Aberdeen, 1988. Col. USAF, 1984-89. Mem. Elks (treas. 1989—), Moose (exalted ruler 1983-84). Republican. Home: 512 S Kline Aberdeen SD 57401 Office: DVC Internat 715 6th Ave SE Aberdeen SD 57401 *The ability to fail and fail boldly is an art not to be shunned but to be admired, for without failing, success is not, nor can be.*

WARD, ANTHONY HAINES, minister; b. Duncan, Okla., Dec. 19, 1949; s. Granville Odel and Louise (Haines) W.; m. Pamela Jo Stallings, Aug. 14, 1971; children: Natalie, Grant. B in Music Edn., Southwestern Okla. State U., 1974. Min. music 1st Bapt. Ch., Tonkawa, Okla., 1974-75, Clinton, Okla., 1975-77, Pryor, Okla., 1977-79; min. music Immanuel Bapt. Ch., Shawnee, Okla., 1979—; guest lectr. Okla. Bapt. U., Shawnee, 1980—, field supr. intern program, 1979—; dir. music Pott-Lincoln Bapt. Assn., Shawnee, 1985-89. Mem. Bicentennial Com., Clinton, 1976; musician City of Shawnee, 1985—. Mem. Am. Guild English Handbell Ringers, So. Bapt. Ch. Music Conf., Oklahoma City Metro Conf., Singing Churchmen Okla., Phi Mu Alpha Sinfonia. Avocations: snow skiing, collecting model trains, racquetball. Office: Immanuel Bapt Ch 1101 E Main Shawnee OK 74801

WARD, CHARLES HAMILTON, minister; b. Burlington, N.C., Feb. 15, 1952; s. Frank Lee and Nancy Marie (Hamilton) W.; m. Dawn Alane Peters, May 6, 1956; children: Christopher, Matthew. BA, U. N.C., 1974; M in Religious Edn., Southwestern Bapt. Theol. Sem., 1977. Ordained to ministry Bapt. Ch., 1989. Minister of youth First Bapt. Ch., Roanoke, Va., 1978-84; assoc. pastor First Bapt. Ch., Roanoke, 1984—. Mem. enrichment com. Mental Health Services, City of Roanoke, 1980, Mayor's Com. on Physically Handicapped, 1986. Named one of Outstanding Young Men Am., 1985. Mem. Roanoke Valley Bapt. Assn. (chmn. campus ministries com. 1984-85). Lodge: Rotary (Roanoke Valley) (bd. dirs. 1986—). Avocations: racquetball, golf, jogging, gardening. Office: First Bapt Ch PO Box 2799 515 3d St Roanoke VA 24001

WARD, DANIEL, bishop. Bishop Free Meth. Ch. of N.Am., Indpls. Office: Free Meth Ch N Am PO Box 535002 Indianapolis IN 46253-5002*

WARD, DEEANN ELLEN, minister; b. Arkansas City, Kans., Apr. 16, 1946; d. Carl and Iyla Mason; m. Don Ward, July 11, 1965; children: Courtney Shaffer, Jamee Harris. BA, Southwestern Coll., Winfield, Kans. Lic. to ministry Pentecostal Holiness Ch., 1991. V.p. Destiny Ministries, Arkansas City, 1984—. Office: 126 Random Rd Arkansas City KS 67005

WARD, DONALD BUTLER, minister; b. Boston, June 15, 1919; s. Donald Butler and Emma (Lyons) W.; m. Vera Barbara Bantz, June 10, 1944; children: Vera Margaret Ward McCarty, Laura Ann Ward Mollet, Christopher Donald. Student, Yankton Coll., 1937-39; BS, Northwestern U., 1942; MDiv, U. Chgo., 1959; DD, Lakeland Coll., 1964, Yankton Coll., 1981; LLD, Morningside Coll., 1964. Television account exec. Blair TV Assos., Chgo., 1951-54; mgr. Blair TV Assos., 1954-56; ordained to ministry Congl. Ch., 1959; minister First Congl. Ch. of Ravenswood, Chgo., 1958-60, Kirk of Bonnie Brae, Denver, 1960-62, First Congl. Ch., Evanston, Ill., 1970-79; v.p. Alaska Pacific U., Anchorage, 1979-80; sr. minister First Congl. Ch. of Los Angeles, 1980-86, minister emeritus, 1986—; commentator Viewpoint (daily radio program), 1978-79. Radio performer-producer, 1942-49, TV performer-producer, 1949-51; author: Not The Scabbard But the Blade, 1965, The Underground Church Is Nonsense, 1969, Master Sermon Series, 1973, Pray Then Like This, 1985, Great Preaching, 1990, William Brewster, My Pilgrim Ancestor, 1990; contbg. editor The Congregationalist; composer: The Bell in the Tower, 1965, Alaska Pacific U. Alma Mater, 1979. Pres. Yankton (S.D.) Coll., 1962-70; past pres. Tri-State Conf., S.D. Found Pvt. Colls.; chmn. bd. Colls. of Mid-Am., Consortium of Ten Colls.; co-chmn. Internat. Congl. Fellowship, 1989—; bd. dirs. Chgo. Theol. Sem., Sch. Theology, Claremont, Calif., Mental Health Assn. Named Man of Year First Congl. Ch. Evanston, 1956. Fellow Am. Congl. Ctr.; mem. Evanston Hist. Soc., Aircraft Owners and Pilots Assn., Nat. Speakers Assn., Acad. Magical Arts, L.A. Pianists Club, Westmoreland Country Club, University Club (Chgo.), Kiwanis, Masons (32 degree), Shriners, Sigma Chi (gov., Grand Tribune, Constantine award). Home: 999 E Valley Blvd Apt 56 Alhambra CA 91801

WARD, DOUGLAS SCOTT, minister; b. Indpls., Nov. 8, 1964; s. Roger Ray Ward and Edith May (McWherter) Kelly; m. Michelle Dawn Gardziella, Dec. 20, 1986; children: Adam Douglas, Sarah Christine. BS in Religion, Olivet Nazarene U., Kankakee, Ill., 1986. Ordained to ministry Ch. of Nazarene, 1990. Assoc. pastor Ch. of Nazarene, Middletown, Ohio, 1987-89, Newton, Kans., 1989-90; sr. pastor 1st Ch. of Nazarene, Marshall, Tex., 1990—; vol. Youth for Christ, Kankakee, 1984-86; chaplain Marshall Meml. Hosp., 1990—; cap dir. Dallas dist. Ch. of Nazarene, Richardson, Tex., 1991—. Mem. Kiwanis. Home and Office: 907 Pocono St Marshall TX 75670

WARD, HARRY LEE, minister; b. Portsmouth, Ohio, Sept. 27, 1945; s. Roy and Mae Marie (Gotherman) W.; m. Beatrice Shillito Hackstedde, Aug. 1, 1968; children: Alyssa, Anne, Adam, Andrew. Student, Ohio U., 1963-64; BS, Bob Jones U., 1968; postgrad., U. Mich., 1969. Ordained to ministry Bapt. Ch., 1987; cert. travel counselor. Mem. faculty Bob Jones U., Greenville, S.C., 1969-71, exec. asst., 1971-76; v.p. ops. Unusual Tours, Greenville, 1977-83; field rep. The Wilds, Greenville, 1983-86; adminstrv. pastor Grace Bapt. Ch., Chattanooga, 1987—. Contbr. artices to profl. jours. Del. Rep. State Conv., S.C., 1980, 84. Mem. Nat. Assn. Ch. Bus. Adminstrn., Midsouth Ind. Schs. Bus. Officers. Office: Grace Bapt Ch 7815 Shallowford Rd Chattanooga TN 37421

WARD, HOUSTON, bishop. Presiding bishop Apostolic Faith Mission Ch. of God, Birmingham, Ala. Office: Apostolic Faith Mission Ch of God 3344 Pearl Ave N Birmingham AL 36101*

WARD, JAMES EDWIN, minister; b. Brownwood, Tex., Oct. 29, 1933; s. Henry Sircy and Edith Estella (Fults) Ward; m. Ruth Arlene McRoberts, June 11, 1955; children: Kay, David, Julia Beth, Roger. Diploma, Moody Bible Inst., 1955; BA, Baylor U., 1960; MDiv, Southwestern Bapt. Theol. Sem., 1967. Ordained to ministry So. Bapt. Conv., 1956. Pastor Travis (Tex.) Bapt. Ch., 1956-60, Verhalen (Tex.) Bapt. Ch., 1961-64; assoc. pastor Retta (Tex.) Bapt. Ch., 1964-67; pastor Temple Bapt. Ch., York, Pa., 1967—; moderator Keystone Bapt. Assn., Mechanicsburg, Pa., 1975-77; pres. Bapt. Conv., Pa., N.J., Harrisburg, 1979-81; mem. Northeastern Theol. Task Team, So. Bapt. Conv., 1984—; bd. dirs. Home Mission Bd. So. Bapt. Conv., Atlanta, 1986—. Recipient Missions and Ministry award Westside Bapt. Ch., Omaha, 1986. Mem. York Evangelistic Assn., York County Ministerium. Home: 2709 Whitney Dr York PA 17402 Office: Temple Bapt Ch 2550 Pine Grove Rd York PA 17403

WARD, JOHN J., bishop; b. Los Angeles, 1920. Student, St. John's Sem., Camarillo, Calif., Catholic U. Am. Ordained priest, Roman Catholic Ch., 1946. Ordained titular bishop of Bria, aux. bishop Diocese of Los Angels Roman Cath. Ch., 1963; now vicar gen. Roman Cath. Ch., Los Angeles. Office: 10425 W Pico Blvd Los Angeles CA 90064

WARD, KAY K., religion educator; b. Madison, Wis., Apr. 17, 1942; m. Aden A. Ward, Dec. 17, 1963; children: Jennifer, Melissa, Benjamin, Jason. BA, Carroll Coll., 1964; MDiv magna cum laude, Moravian Theol. Sem., 1980. Ordained to ministry Moravian Ch., 1979. Pastor Haverford/Bethany Moravian Ch., Indpls., 1979-84, Good Shepherd Moravian Ch., Yorba Linda, Calif., 1984-89; dir. continuing edn. Moravian Theol. Sem., Bethlehem, Pa., 1989—, instr., 1990—; apptd. mem. publ. div. Moravian Ch., Bethlehem, 1982-90, faith and order commn., 1986—; instr. Claremont (Calif.) Sch. Theology, 1988-90. Mem. Soc. for Advancement Continuing Edn. in Ministry. Office: Moravian Theol Sem 60 W Locust St Bethlehem PA 18018

WARD, R. J., bishop. Bishop of Ea. Md. Ch. of God in Christ, St. Louis. Office: Ch of God in Christ 4724 Palm Ave Saint Louis MO 63115*

WARD, TED WARREN, international studies dean; b. Punxsutawney, Pa., Dec. 15, 1930; s. Ted Johnston and Thelma Grace (Hill) W.; m. Margaret Hockett, June 12, 1951; children: David, Daniel, Timothy, Sarah, Stephen. BA in Music Edn., Wheaton Coll., 1951; MEd, U. of Fla., 1954, EdD, 1956. Tchr. Wheaton Coll. Acad., Ill., 1950-52; choral dir. Univ. of Miami, Coral Gables, Fla., 1952-55; instr. and asst. prof. Univ. of Fla., Gainesville, 1954-56; prof. edn. Mich. State U., East Lansing, 1956-85, prof. emeritus, 1985—; dir. doctoral edn. and mission programs Trinity Evang. Div. Sch., Deerfield, Ill., 1985; dir. Inst. for Human Learning Research MSU, 1964-70; cons. USAID, Ford Found.; tng. cons. World Vision. Author: Living Overseas, 1984, Values Begin At Home, 1979 and 1989. Pres. Pontiac Symphony Orchestra Assn., 1958-60. Mem. Natl. Assn. of Professors of Christian Educ., Am. Soc. of Missiologists, Natl. Soc. for the Study of Educ. Evangelical Free Ch. of Am. Avocations: music, photography, woodworking. Office: Trinity Evang Div Sch 2065 Half Day Rd Deerfield IL 60015

WARD, TERRY GRANVILLE, music minister; b. Duncan, Okla., Jan. 15, 1941; s. Granville O. and Louise (Haines) W.; m. Karen Louise Raish, Feb. 1, 1964; 1 child, Jeffrey. MusB, Okla. Bapt. U., 1963; M. Religious Edn., S.W. Bapt. Theol. Sem., 1967; M.A.B.S., Dallas Theol. Sem., 1976. Ordained to ministry So. Bapt. Conv., 1970. Assoc. youth pastor Lakeside Bapt. Ch., 1963-65; minister of music, youth pastor MacArthur Blvd. Bapt. Ch., Irving, Tex., 1965-69; minister of music Green Acres Bapt. Ch., Tyler, Tex., 1969-76; assoc. pastor Allandale Bapt. Ch., Austin, Tex., 1976-81; min. music, adminstr. 1st Bapt. Ch., Brenham, Tex., 1982-84; min. music 1st Bapt. Ch., Midwest City, Okla., 1984—. Composer, arranger several songs. Mem. Centurymen, 1971-77, student recruitment com. alumni bd. Okla. Bapt. U., Shawnee, 1988—; soloist Singing Churchman of Okla., 1984—. Mem. Capital Bapt. Assn. (chmn. music com. 1986, 88, 90), Rotary (pianist 1988—), Lions (song leader, soloist 1960—). Home: 11784 Woodland Hill Choctaw OK 73020 Office: 1st Bapt Ch 705 E Rickenbacker Midwest City OK 73110

WARDEN, IVAN LEIGH, clergyman, educator; b. N.Y.C., Aug. 18, 1943; s. Charles Lee and Miriam (Burgess) W.; m. Jean Scantlebury, Feb. 17, 1968; children—Ariel Jeanine, Angela Jeanice. B.A. in Theolory, Oakwood Coll., 1967; M.R.E., N.Y. Theol. Sem., 1970, M.S.T., 1974; postgrad. Princeton U. Theol. Sem., 1974—. Ordained to ministry Seventh-day Adventist Ch., 1972. Asst. minister Bethel Seventh-day Adventist Ch., Bklyn., 1967-70; minister S.I. (N.Y.) Seventh-day Adventist Ch., 1970-73, Beth-El Seventh-day Adventist Ch., Jersey City, 1973-75; asst. prof. urban ministries Andrews U., Berrien Springs, Mich., 1976-81, adj. prof., 1981—; dir. urban ministries and community services So. Calif. Conf. Seventh-day Adventists, Glendale, 1981—. Former mem. adv. bd. Vols. in Probation of 5th Dist. Ct., State of Mich., 1977-81. Recipient award Concerned Citizens Alliance, Jersey City, 1975; faculty award Andrews U., 1979.

WARFIELD, CURTIS H., lay worker, logistics data program manager; b. Battle Creek, Mich., Jan. 2, 1960; s. Daniel Webster Sr. and Esther Estelle (Johnson) W.; m. Sharon Denise Moore, Oct. 12, 1985; children: Curtice Micalle Larweance, Bryen David Adam, Alexandria DeNiece Reaneé. BS in Pub. Adminstrn., Cen. Mich. U., 1982. Dist. sect. leader Wolverine State Bapt. Conv., Battle Creek, Mich., 1982; asst. to min. of music Second Missionary Bapt. Ch., Battle Creek, 1982-89, pres. adult choir, 1986-88, chmn. 138th ch. anniversary, 1989; logistics program mgr. Def. Logistics Svcs., Battle Creek, 1985—. Fed. campaign worker United Way, Battle Creek, 1988, 89. Named Outstanding Young Man of Am., Outstanding Young Ams. Inc., 1984. Mem. Internat. Tng. and Communications. Mem. Light of the World Christian Ch. *Not until man is able to accept man for who he is, what he stands for and why he is here will he ever understand his purpose in life.*

WARFIELD, JAMES MONHOLLEN, JR., minister; b. Highland, Ky., Oct. 12, 1918; s. James Warfield Sr. and Sarah Emily (Reed) W.; m. Ruth Pauline Vanteger, Apr. 21, 1948; children: David, Nancy, Paul. BS, Wayne State U., 1951. Ordained to ministry Christian Ch., 1941. Min. Christian Ch., Wyandotte, Mich., 1940-90; pres. Mich. Christian Conv., Lansing, 1984; mem. Continuation Com., N.Am. Christian Conv., St. Louis, 1975-78. Mem. Ministerial Assn. Greater Detroit (pres. 1954, 63, 71, 83), Kiwanis (pres. Southgate chpt. 1981-82, 86-87), Masons. Home: 12814 Sycamore Southgate MI 48195 *It is not WHAT you know, but what you DO with what you know that destroys or builds character.*

WARFORD, MALCOLM LYLE, seminary president, dean, theology educator; b. Lexington, Ky., June 18, 1942; m. Pamela Anne Neal; children: Mark Kellison, Wendy Kathryn. BA with honors, Transylvania Coll., 1964; BD with honors, Andover Newton Theol. Sch., 1967; EdD, Columbia U., 1973; post doctoral, McGill U., 1967-68. Ordained to ministry United Ch. Christ, 1967. Cons. Lilly Endowment Inc., Bd. Homeland Ministries, various theol. schs. Author: The Necessary Illusion: Church Culture and Educational Change, 1976, The Education of the Public, 1980, OUr Several Callings, 1990; co-editor: Good Stewardship: A Handbook for Seminary Trustees, 1991; contbr. articles to profl. jours. Mem. adv. com. Margaret Chase Smith Libr.; bd. dirs. Bangor Edn. Found., SALT Inc. Office: Bangor Theol Sem Office Pres 300 Union St Bangor ME 04401

WARFORD, WILLIAM SMITH, chaplain, church official; b. Springfield, Mo., May 13, 1921; s. Harold LeRoy and Pearl Julia (Bouldin) W.; m. Twila Darlene Gooding, Feb. 28,1954; 1 child Robin Ray. Student, Carthage Coll.; BS in Edn., Western Ill. U., 1956; postgrad., Augustana Sem., 1960, Quincy (Ill.) Coll., 1962. Ordained to ministry Am. Bapt. Ch., 1962. Protestant chaplain Ill. Vets. Home, Quincy, 1962—; pres. Quincy Coun. Chs., 1972-74. Contbr. hist. articles to scholarly jours. Mem. staff Am. Theatre, St. Louis, 1948-53; sec. Ill. State Tollway Adv. Commn., 1961-65; founder, pres. Western Ill. Coun. on Alcoholism, 1968-75; chmn. Water Commn., Quincy, 1968-78; mem. Quincy Pub. Works Commn., 1971-78, chmn., 1978; vice chmn. West Cen. Ill. Coun. on Aging, 1974, pres. 1975-76; bd. dirs. ARC, 1970-78, Salvation Army, 1972—, v.p., 1975, chmn., 1976-80; mem. West Cen. Mental Health Authority Bd., Quincy, 1973; mem. Ill. State Coun. on Aging, 1976—; bd. dirs. Hospice of Quincy and Adams Counties, 1983, 89; del. White House Conf. on Aging, 1981, 90; mem. Adams County, Ill. AIDS Task Force, 1988—. Recipient Disting. Svc. award Am. Heart Assn., 1965, Best Actor award Quincy Community Little Theatre, 1972, Disting. Alumni award Western Ill. U., 1975, Ill. Gov.'s award for unique achievement in aging field, 1986, VIP award Arthritis Found. Telethon, 1991. Mem. Ill. Hist. Soc. (life), Kans. Hist. Soc. (life), Quincy Ministerial Assn. (pres. 1969-73, award 1973), Ill. Assn. Chaplains (treas. 1973-75), Ill. Protestant Chaplains Assn. (vice chmn. 1968-70), Ill. State Assn. Chaplains (pres. 1978-82, award 1982), Ill. Assn. Agys. Aging (v.p. 1974-76). Home: 2140 Hampshire St Quincy IL 62301 Office: Ill Vets Home Protestant Chaplains Office Quincy IL 62301

WARING, EDWARD GRAHAM, JR., religious studies educator; b. Kansas City, Mo., Feb. 27, 1924; s. Edward Graham and Flora (Basye) W.; m. Carobeth Elaine McIntire, June 8, 1945; children—Judith Elizabeth, Linda Louise, Christopher Andrew. B.A., So. Meth. U., 1943; B.D., U. Chgo., 1946, Ph.D., 1950. Ordained to ministry Conglist. Ch., 1946; minister Pecatonica, Ill., 1946-48, West Chicago, Ill., 1948-50; acting chaplain Asso. Colls. Claremont, Calif., 1950-51; faculty Lawrence U., 1951—, chmn. dept. religion, 1953-68, 75-82, prof. religion, 1962-87, prof. emeritus, 1987—, asso. dean faculty, 1969-75; vis. prof. Dartmouth, summer 1967; dir. Lawrence U. German Study Center, Bonningheim, Germany, 1968-69. Editor, author: introduction On Religion, 1955, (Feuerbach), Essence of Christianity, 1957, Deism and Natural Religion, 1967; author 5 biog. essays on 17th and 18th century deists in Ency. of Unbelief, 1985. Mem. Am. Acad. Religion, Phi Beta Kappa. Home: 2900 S Carpenter St Appleton WI 54915

WARKE, GUY DONALD, minister; b. Detroit, Aug. 3, 1935; s. Lawrence Diffin and Violet Amanda (McDonald) W.; m. Helen Gertrude Jarosch, June 24, 1961; children: Kathleen Warke Stefans, Amy Lynn Gundersen, Christopher Lawrence. AA, St. John's Coll., Winfield, Kans., 1956; BA, Concordia Sem., St. Louis, 1961, degree in theology, 1961; D Ministry, Grad. Theol. Found. Ind., 1986. Ordained to ministry Luth. Ch.-Mo. Synod, 1961. Pastor Grace Luth. Ch., Bradford, Pa., 1961-64, North Park Luth. Ch., Buffalo, 1964-73, Our Savior Luth. Ch., Bradley, Ill., 1973—; night chaplain Riverside Med. Ctr., Kankakee, Ill., 1980—; cir. counselor N. Buffalo cir. Mo. Synod, Luth. Ch., 1970-72; dean Chgo./Milw. Conf. Mo. Conf. Assn. Luth. Chs., Chgo., 1980-86; mem. transition team Cen./So. Synod Evang. Luth. Ch. Am., 1988. Mem. Greater Kankakee Ministerial Assn. Home: 975 Brookmont Blvd Bradley IL 60915 Office: Our Savior Luth Ch 975 Brookmont Blvd Bradley IL 60915 *There are many joys and disappointments in life. To make certain the joys outweight the disappointments is to live a life in faith with one's eyes open to those things which really count, such as love, which never ends.*

WARNER, BENNIE D., minister; b. Monrovia, Libera, Apr. 30, 1935; came to U.S. 1980; m. Anna Harmon, Aug. 3, 1963; children: Mardea, Kaymah, Bennie Jr., Philip Warner. BSc, Cuttington U. Coll., Suacoco, Liberia, 1960; MSc, Syracuse U., 1962; ThM, Boston U., 1971; DD, U. Liberia, 1975. Ordained to ministry, United Meth. Ch., 1964. Pastor Ch. of All Nations, Boston, 1969-71, Quayle United Meth. Ch., Oklahoma City, 1982-87, Faith United Meth. Ch., Syracuse, N.Y., 1987-89, St. Paul/Mark's Chapel, Little Rock, 1990—; bishop United Meth. Ch., 1973-80; chmn. bd. trustees Coll. W. Africa, 1973-80; mission interpreter Okla. Ann. Conf. Bd. Global Ministries, Oklahoma City, 1981; adj. faculty Oklahoma City U., 1981-87, other positions in Liberia. Chmn. Rural Devel. Task Force, Republic of Liberia, 1978-80, v.p., 1977-80; chmn. bd. mgrs. Booker T. Washington Inst., Liberia, 1977-80; chmn. bd. trustees Coll. W. Africa, 1973-80. Named Disting Alumni/NEA awardee, Boston U. Sch. Theology, 1985. Mem. Syracuse Area Interreligious Coun. (sec. 1987-89), Interdenominational Ministerial Alliance, Black Ministerial Alliance, NAACP, Oak Springs Club. Home: 9721 Pinnacle Valley Rd Little Rock AR 72212 Office: St Paul United Meth Ch 9721 Pinnacle Valley Rd Little Rock AR 72212-9791

WARNER, HAROLD WALTON, JR., minister; b. Hatboro, Pa., Nov. 15, 1929; s. Harold Walton and Marian (Hollowell) W.; m. Eleanor Mae Washington, Nov. 19, 1949; children: Philip Harold, John Keith. Student, Phila. Sch. Bible, 1948, Ref. Episcopal Sem., Phila., 1949-51; DD, Trinity Coll., Dunedin, Fla., 1967. Ordained to ministry So. Bapt. Conv., 1950. Pastor chs., Wellsboro, Pa., 1952-55; evangelist N.Am., W.I., Eng., 1955-60, 65-70; pastor Palm Ave. Bapt. Ch., Tampa, Fla., 1960-65, West End Bapt. Ch, Mobile, Ala., 1970-75, 1st Bapt. Ch. Citrus Park, Tampa, 1980—; assoc. dir. Bay Islands Bapt. Bible Inst., Honduras, 1982—. Author: When the World's on Fire, 1965, Dear Hunting, 1968, The American Home and Its Needs, 1968. Mem. exec. bd. Tyoga Youth Ranch, Wellsboro, Pa., 1968-75. Republican. Home: 14308 Ravenwood Ln Tampa FL 33618 Office: 1st Bapt Ch Citrus Park 7705 Gunn Hwy Tampa FL 33625

WARNER, JAMES DANIEL, clergyman; b. Sheridan, Wyo., May 1, 1924; s. Stephan Daniel and Grace Margaret (Caple) W.; m. Barbara A. Wallgren, Sept. 6, 1952 (dec. 1957); m. Marcy Walk Swan, Feb. 8, 1960; children—Stephen, David, Cheryl, Mark, Kathryn, James, Tammy. BS, Northwestern U., 1950; M in Divinity, Seabury Western Theol. Sem., 1953, DD, 1977. Vicar St. James Ch., Mosinee, Wis., 1953-56; rector St. Paul's Ch., Marmette, Wis., 1956-60; asst. chaplain St. James Ch., U. Wichita, Kans., 1960-62; rector St. Stephen's Ch., Wichita, 1962-70, Trinity Ch., Oshkosh, Wis., 1970-77; bishop Diocese of Nebr., Omaha, 1977—; pres. St. Com., Diocese of Kans., 1966-68. Pres. Community Planning Council, Wichita, 1965-66, police chaplain several community social agencies. Served in USN, 1942-46, PTO. Episcopalian. Home: 64 Ginger Cove Valley NE 68064 Office: Diocese of Nebr 200 N 62nd St Omaha NE 68132

WARNER, SISTER SHIRLEY ANN, nun, religious education director; b. Cleve., Jan. 10, 1936; d. Louis Edwin and Winifred Margaret (Kilkenny) W. BS in Edn., St. John Coll., 1963; postgrad., John Carroll U., 1965-70, Meinrad Sem., 1989—. Cert. tchr., Ohio; joined Ursuline Nuns of Cleve., 1953. Primary tchr. Cleve. (Ohio) Cath. Diocese, 1955-65, jr. high tchr., 1965-90, asst. prin., 1967-77; dir. religious edn. St. Charles Parish, Parma, Ohio, 1990; dir. sacramental programs various parishes Cleve. (Ohio) Cath. Diocese, 1957—; dir. chem. abuse prevention Urban Community Sch., Cleve., 1987-90; organizer Chem. Abuse Awareness Program, 1987; coord. Confirmation Program, 1980. Mem. Nat. Cath. Edn. Assn., Ohio Dirs. Religious Edn., Cleve. Orgn. Religious Edn. Dirs. Democrat. Home: 6902 Charles Ave Parma OH 44129 Office: St Charles Parish 7107 Wilber Ave Parma OH 44129

WARNER, VANDER, JR., pastor; b. Georgetown, S.C., Apr. 24, 1930; s. Vander Sr. and Marrie Mae (MaCray) W.; m. Jane Carol Coggin, June 21, 1952; children: Sherri Leed, Vanda Jane. AA, Pfeiffer Coll., 1950; student, Wake Forest U., 1951-52; BS, Va. Commonwealth U., 1971; DD (hon.), Brown Theol. Sem., 1983. Ordained to ministry Bapt. Ch., 1952. Pastor 1st Bapt. Ch., Pocomoke City, Md., 1954-58, Oak Grove Bapt. Ch., Bel Air, Md., 1958-65, Grove Ave. Bapt. Ch., Richmond, Va., 1965—; pres. So. Bapts. Conv. Pastors USA, 1973, v.p., 1965, pres. Md., 1965. Author: The Cardinals and the Glass Wall, 1990. Mem. Welfare bd. County of Harford, Md., 1963. Home: Rt 2 Box 930 Rockville VA 23146 Office: Grove Ave Bapt Ch 8701 Ridge Rd Richmond VA 23229

WARNER, WAYNE MARSHALL, minister; b. South Haven, Mich., May 24, 1927; s. Lyle Wesley and Ruthe Adelia (Knapp) W.; m. Tommie Leora Stiles, Mar. 20, 1926; children: Meredith Lyn, Donald Scott. BTh, Warner Pacific Coll., 1951; MRE, Southwestern Bapt. Theol. Sem., Ft. Worth, 1969. Ordained to ministry Ch. of God (Anderson, Ind.), 1952. Pastor various chs., 1951-62, Ridglea Ch. of God, Ft. Worth, 1962-70; pastor, sch. adminstr. lst Ch. of God, Vallejo, Caif., 1970-73; pastor Capital Avenue Ch. of Gd., Battle Creek, Mich., 1973-77, lst Ch. of God, Three Rivers, Mich., 1979—; mem. ch. planting task force Mich. Ch. of God, 1986—; ch. bd. dirs. Warner Meml. Conf. and Retreat Ctr., 1989—. Contbr. articles to profl. jourss. Mem. St. Joe County Victim-Offender Reconciliation Program, St. Joe County Substance Abuse Coun. With USAAF, 1946-47. Home: 43 New England Ave Battle Creek MI 49017 Office: lst Ch of God 1111 S Main St Three Rivers MI 49093 *I experience life as dividing into two kinds of people. Some are mostly takers from life, but there are some who regardless of what life hands them, choose to be givers. I choose to act out of my beliefs, to be a gracious giver and never simply a reactor to life's circumstances.*

WARPULA, CALVIN WAYNE, minister; b. Oak Ridge, Tenn., June 30, 1944; s. Edwin William and Ota Vee (Tesney) W.; m. Judith Ann Hammitt, Dec. 21, 1965; children: Melissa, Timothy, Erick, Tiana. BA, Abilene Christian U., Abilene, Tex., 1967, MA, 1974; MA, W. Tex. State U., 1977; DMin, Fuller Theol. Sem., Pasadena, 1983. Ordained to ministry Ch. of Christ, 1960. Minister S.W. Ch. of Christ, Amarillo, Tex., 1972-78, Pleasant Valley Ch. of Christ, Mobile, Ala., 1978-80, White's Ferry Rd. Ch. of Christ, West Monroe, La., 1980-82, Eldridge Rd. Ch. of Christ, Sugar Land, Tex., 1982-87, Stillwater (Okla.) Ch. of Christ, 1987—; radio speaker World Radio Broadcasting, W. Monroe, La., 1980—; campaign dir. Jamaica Crusades for Chs. of Christ, 1980-88; lectr. Abilene Christian U., 1991. Contbr. articles to profl. jours. Republican. Home: 3101 N Lincoln Stillwater OK 74075 Office: Church of Christ 821 N Duck Stillwater OK 74075

WARREN, EDDIE LEE, clergyman; b. Baldwyn, Miss., Sept. 30, 1955; s. Eddie Lee and Arleather Warren; m. Ella Pearl Rockingham, June 25, 1978; children: Valecia, Malessa, Roderick. Cert., Bailey Tech. Sch., 1974; student, St. Louis U., 1977, St. Louis Christian Coll., 1978. Ordained to ministry Bapt. Ch., 1979. Salesman Mike Meyer Sales, St. Louis, 1973-78, Electronic Co., St. Louis, 1978-79, Calgon Corp., St. Louis, 1979-83; pastor Cathedral of Worship, Quincy, Ill., 1980—. Author: Fasting God's Way, 1986, Positioning Your Faith, 1989, Healing A Different Perspective, 1990. Bd. dirs. United Way, Adams County, 1986, Great Commn. Broadcasting, Adams County, 1988, Family Svc. Agy. Recipient Top Religious Leader award Quincy Jaycees, 1983. Mem. Full Gospel Ch. Home: 2001 S Sheridan St Quincy IL 62301 Office: Cathedral of Worship 25th and Vermont Quincy IL 62301

WARREN, JUDI DELL, minister; b. L.A., Feb. 25, 1940; d. Raymond Oliver Perry and Maria Luz (Wistler) Tumilty; m. Charles Robert Deemer (div.); 1 child, Christine Nel Deemer-Fonseca; m. Paul Blaisdell Warren, Aug. 22, 1981. Student, San Jose State U., 1959-62; BA in Edn., Calif. State U., L.A., 1964. Ordained to ministry Ch. of Inner Light, 1977, Ch. of Truth, 1985. Sr. pastor Ch. of Truth, Pasadena, Calif., 1978-89; founder, dean Albert Grier Sch. Religious Studies, Pasadena, 1982-84, instr., 1982—; founder, pres. Internat. Alliance of Chs. of Truth, Pasadena, 1987—; min. emeritus Ch. of Truth, Pasadena, 1989—; dir. Soc. for the Study of Metaphysical Religion, Santa Barbara, Calif., 1988—. Life mem. Internat. New Thought Alliance. Office: Internat Alliance Chs Truth 690 E Orange Grove Blvd Pasadena CA 91104 *All life is an expression of the Spirit. Every man's experience of life is an epic poem, a journey toward the fulfillment of his spiritual potential. Each person he meets is a reflection of his consciousness, offering him the opportunity to adjust his thoughts and heart and steer a more certain course.*

WARREN, LARRY MICHAEL, clergyman; b. Bonne Terre, Mo., Nov. 25, 1946; s. Orson Wesley and Ruth Margaret (Stine) W.; m. Bonnie Jean Monk Chandler, Apr. 9, 1983; children: Samantha Chandler, John, Abigail Chandler, Anne, Meredith. BA cum laude, Lincoln U., 1969; MDiv with honors, St. Paul Sch. Theology, Kansas City, Mo., 1976; D of Ministry, San Francisco Theol. Sem., 1987. Ordained elder United Meth. Ch., 1978. Pastor Cainsville (Mo.) United Meth. Ch., 1975-76, Lakelands Parish, Rathdrum, Idaho, 1976-78; assoc. pastor Audubon Park United Meth. Ch., Spokane, Wash., 1978-83; pastor Faith United Meth. Ch., Everett, Wash., 1983-90, Tacoma First United Meth. Ch., 1990—; adviser Kairos Prison Ministry Wash., Monroe, 1984—; conf. rep. grad. bd. St. Paul Sch. Theology, Kansas City, 1984. Contbr. to col. Dialogue Everett Herald, 1984-88. Adviser DeMolay, Spokane, 1979-81; team mem. Night-Walk, inner-city ministry, Spokane, 1979-82; coord. Ch. Relief Overseas Project Hunger Walk, Spokane and Everett, 1981, 85; vol. chaplain Gen. Hosp. Everett, 1983-90; trustee Deaconess Children's Svcs., Everett, 1983-88. Recipient Legion of Honor DeMolay Internat., 1982. Mem. Fellowship of Reconciliation, North Snohomish County Assn. Chs. (v.p. 1985-89), Pacific N.W. Ann. Conf. Bd. Global Ministries (sec. 1988—). Democrat. Avocations: reading, traveling, stamps and coins. Home: 3312 N 19th Tacoma WA 98406 Office: Tacoma 1st United Meth Ch 423 South K St Tacoma WA 98405 *Personal philosophy: To seek peace and reconciliation among all people and nations, and with the creation given to us as stewards.*

WARREN, RANDALL FULTON, clergyman; b. Longview, Tex., July 4, 1949; s. Ollie Woodrow and Vera Belle (Richardson) W.; m. Carol Sue Oefinger, Aug. 7, 1976; children: Mark, David, Laura Kristin. BS, Stephen F. Austin State U., 1971; postgrad. Emory U., 1971-72; Th.M., So. Meth. U., 1975. Ordained elder United Meth. Ch., 1976. Pastor, Walter Fair United Meth. Ch., Tyler, Tex., 1975-77, First Meth. Ch., Malakoff, Tex., 1977-81; campus minister Wesley Found., coord. dept. Bible Stephen F. Austin State U., Nacogdoches, Tex., 1981-85; pastor, First Meth. Ch., Trinity, Tex., 1985—; mem. com. on protection of human subjects, 1983-85; dir. edn. Nacogdoches Dist. United Meth. Ch., 1981-85; dir. ch. summer camp, Pal.-Nacogdoches Dist., Tex. Ann. Conf., United Meth. Ch., 1977—, also mem. commn. on the role and status of women. City fire marshall City of Malakoff, Tex., 1977-81; mem. Child Welfare Bd., Henderson, Tex., 1978-79, Child Welfare Bd. Trinity County, 1986— . Recipient Copeland award Tex. Conf. United Meth. Ch., 1979. Mem. Nat. Com. on Adoption, Nat. Com. Campus Ministry. Democrat. Lodge: Toastmasters (Nacogdoches, Tex.). Avocations: reading; snow skiing, fishing, travel, historical studies. Office: Trinity United Meth Ch Drawer 31 Trinity TX 75862

WARREN, RICK DUANE, minister; b. San Jose, Calif., Jan. 28, 1954; s. James Russell and Dorothy Nell (Armstrong) W.; m. Elizabeth Kay Lewis, June 21, 1975; children: Amy Rebecca, Joshua James, Matthew David. BA, Calif. Bapt. Coll., 1977; MDiv, Southwestern Bapt. Theol. Sem., 1979; DMin, Fuller Theol. Sem., 1989. Youth evangelist Calif. So. Bapt. Convention, Fresno, 1970-74; assoc. pastor First Bapt. Ch., Norwalk, Calif., 1974-76; asst. to pres. Internat. Evangelism Assn., Fort Worth, 1977-79; founding pastor Saddleback Valley Community Ch., Mission Viejo, Calif., 1980—; lectr. Saddleback Ch. Growth Seminars. Author: Dynamic Bible Study Methods, 1981, Answers to Life's Difficult Questions, 1985. Named Outstanding Preacher of 1977, McGregor Found. Mem. No. Am. Soc. for Ch. Growth. Baptist. Office: Saddleback Valley Comm Ch 24194 Alicia Pkwy Ste M Mission Viejo CA 92691

WARREN, RONALD BARRY, minister; b. Sandusky, Ohio, Nov. 22, 1944; s. Kenneth Henry and Evelyn Lucille (Hirt) W.; m. Neva Arlene Klepzig, June 8, 1968; children: Heather Lynn, Jeremy Todd. BA, Capital U., 1966; M in Divinity, Trinity Luth. Sem., Columbus, Ohio, 1970; Dr. of Ministry with distinction, Luth. Sch. Theology, Chgo., 1983. Ordained to ministry, Am. Luth. Ch., 1970. Pastor St. John Luth. Ch., Avoca, Wis., 1970-73; assoc. pastor 1st Luth. Ch., Janesville, Wis., 1973-76; pastor House of Paryer Luth. Ch., Franklin, Wis., 1976-83; sr. pastor Ascension Luth. Ch., Memphis, 1983-88; asst. to bishop Southeastern Synod Evang. Luth. Ch. in Am., Atlanta, 1988—; pres. Christian Ednl. Media Inc., Burnsville, Minn., 1980-83, edn. cons. and workshop instr., 1976-83. Firefighter, mem. rescue team, chaplain Franklin Fire Dept., 1976-83; pres. Memphis State U. Cluster Pastors, 1985; bd. dirs. Luth. Social Services Tenn., Memphis, 1985-87, Episcopal Samaritan Counseling Ctr., Memphis, 1987. Mem. Luth. Mins. Ga. (bishop's rep. on bd. dirs. 1989—), Luth. Soc. Mins. Tenn. (bishop's rep. on bd. dirs. 1988—), Luth. Mins. Ala. (bishop's rep. on bd. dirs. 1990—), Luth. Soc. Mins. Miss. (bishop's rep. on bd. dirs. 1991—), Met. Interfaith Assn. (bd. dirs. 1985-87), Tenn. Assn. of Chs. (bd. dirs. 1988—), Nat. Eagle Scout Assn. Club: Memphis Crosscut (v.p. 1987-88). Avocation: jogging, golf. Home: 616 Grecken Green Peachtree City GA 30269 Office: ELCA Southeastern Synod 756 W Peachtree St NW Atlanta GA 30308

WARREN, THOMAS BRATTON, evangelist, theology and philosophy educator; b. Carrizo Springs, Tex., Aug. 1, 1920; s. Thomas Clayton and Emma Mae (Russell) W.; m. Faye Cecilia Brauer, Oct. 3, 1941; children: Karen Faye, Jan Cecile, Lindsey Davis. Student, Abilene Christian U., 1947; MA in Religion, U. Houston, 1960; MA in Philosophy, Vanderbilt U., 1967, PhD in Philosophy, 1969. Evangelist, minister Chs. of Christ, Liberty, Tex., 1947-50, Ft. Worth, 1950-51, 53-64, Houston, 1951-53, Tenn., 1964-84; writer, editor, 1984—. Editor, writer 70 books, 1953-89. 2d lt. USAF, 1942-45. Mem. Soc. Bibl. Lit., Am. Acad. Religion, Southwestern Philos. Soc., Evang. Philos. Soc., Soc. Christian Philosophies. Republican. Home and Office: PO Box 937 Seagoville TX 75159

WARREN, VIRGIL, theology educator; b. Cin., Sept. 25, 1942; s. Ervin and Elanora Warren; m. Ruth Ann Warren, June 7, 1963; children: David, Steven, Tara, Michelle. AB, Cin. Bible Sem., 1967, ThB, 1968; MDiv, Wheaton (Ill.) Coll., 1971, MA, 1973; PhD, So. Bapt. Sem., Louisville, 1977. Ordained to ministry Chs. of Christ. Assoc. prof. Cin. Bible Sem., 1971-74; prof. theology Manhattan (Kans.) Christian Coll., 1977—. Author: What the Bible Says About Salvation, 1982. Mem. Am. Acad. Religion, Soc. Bibl. Lit., Evang. Theol. Soc., Evang. Philos. Soc. Avocation: music (guitar). Home: 1600 Stewart Ct Manhattan KS 66502 Office: Manhattan Christian Coll 1415 Anderson Ave Manhattan KS 66502

WARREN, WILLIAM FRAMPTON, JR., religion educator; b. Shelbyville, Tenn., Nov. 16, 1954; s. William Frampton Sr. and Miriam (O'Quinn) W.; m. Katie Cutrer, Dec. 22, 1979; children: William Frampton III, Benjamin Isaac. AA, Okaloosa Walton Jr. Coll., 1974; BS, Miss. Coll., 1976; MDiv, New Orleans Bapt. Theol. Sem., 1979, ThD, 1983. Asst. pastor Istrouma Bapt. Ch., Baton Rouge, 1978-80; pastor Plank Road Bapt. Ch., Slaughter, La., 1980-83; missionary prof. Seminario Teologico Bautista Internat., Cali, Colombia, 1983-89; asst. prof. N.T. New Orleans Bapt. Theol. Sem., 1990—; coord., advisor, missionary Buenaventura, Colombia, 1985-89, coord. hunger relief program, 1987-89; coordinating com. pres. grad. program Sem. Teologica Bautista, Cali, 1988-89; mem. exec. com. Colombian Bapt. Mission Bogota, Colombia, 1988-89. Editor: La Teologia De La Liberacion: Una Respuesta Evangelica, 1990; contbr. articles to profl. jours. Mem. Am. Acad. Religion, Soc. Bibl. Lit. Democrat. Office: New Orleans Bapt Theol Sem 3939 Gentilly Blvd Box 60 New Orleans LA 70126 *The context for doing theology consists of the doing of the will of God in the midst of a hurting world. One cannot claim to know God while at the same time refusing to participate in what God is doing in this world.*

WARTH, DONALD EUGENE, minister; b. New London, Iowa, June 9, 1932; s. Albert Edward and Martha Louise (Douglass) W.; m. Joyce Kaebnick, Aug. 20, 1955 (dec. 1988); children: Paul, Mark, Matthew; m. Darlene Rose Hornak Skiby, June 9, 1990; stepchildren: Laura Skiby, Jeffrey Skiby. AB, Coe Coll., Cedar Rapids, Iowa, 1953; BD in Pastoral Care, McCormick Sem., Chgo., 1956; D Ministry in Community and Communications, Eden Sem., Webster Groves, Mo., 1973. Ordained to ministry Presbyn. Ch. (U.S.A.), 1956. Asst. pastor Washington Ave. presbyn. Ch., Evansville, Ind., 1956-59; pastor First Presbyn. Ch., Union, Mo., 1959-64; assoc. pastor First Presbyn. Ch., Ferguson, Mo., 1964-75; pastor Cen. Presbyn. Ch., Zanesville, Ohio, 1975-91, 1st Presbyn. Ch., Dresden, Ohio, 1991—, Madison Presbyn. Ch., Adams Mills, Ohio, 1991—; commr. Gen. Assembly, Presbyn. Ch., 1958, 69, 84; sec. Assn. of Presbyn. Ch. Educators, 1970-74. Organizer, pres. Zanesville Habitat for Humanity, 1985-91, exec. dir., 1991—; pres. Samaritan Counseling Ctr., Zanesville, 1984, Muskingum Area Cath. Social Svc., Zanesville, 1978-79; chmn. Interfaith Com., Boy Scouts Am., Zanesville, 1976-80. Named Clergy of the Yr., Muskingum County Ministerial Assn. Republican. Home: 5130 Manchester Dr Zanesville OH 43701

WARTLUFT, DAVID JONATHAN, librarian, clergyman; b. Stouchsburg, Pa., Sept. 22, 1938; s. Cleaver Milvard and Dorothy (Stump) W.; m. Joyce Claudia Dittmer, June 15, 1963 (div. Sept. 1988); children: Elizabeth Marie, Deborah Joy, Rebecca Janet, Andrew Jonathan. A.B. (Trexler scholar), Muhlenberg Coll., 1960; Div.M. (Danforth scholar), Lutheran Theol. Sem., Phila., 1964; A.M. (scholar), U. Pa., 1964; M.S. (Lily Found. scholar), Drexel U., 1968. Asst. chaplain, instr. religion Springfield (Mass.) Coll., 1962-63; ordained minister Luth. Ch., 1964; pastor Jerusalem Luth. Ch., Allentown, Pa., 1964-66; cataloger, reference librarian Luth. Sem. Phila., 1966-68, asst. librarian, 1968-77, dir. library and archives, 1977—, chaplain, 1978-79, dir. 1st yr. field edn., 1979-81, 82-83, faculty sec., 1985—; exec. sec. Am. Theol. Libr. Assn., Phila., 1971-81, bd. dirs., 1991—; also editor procs. Am. Theol. Library Assn., Phila.; archivist Northeastern Pa. Synod, Luth. Ch. Am., 1970-87, mem. communications com., 1967-78, sec., 1975-78, mem. conv. com., 1976; archivist Northeastern Pa. Synod, Evang. Luth. Ch. Am., 1988-91; v.p. Luth. Archives Ctr. at Phila., 1979-85, bd. dirs., 1979—; libr. cons. Gurkul Luth. Coll., Madras, India, 1989, Huria Kristen Batak Protestant Sem., Pematang Siantar, Sumatra, Indonesia, 1989. Editor: Teamwork, 1970-84, The Periodical, 1979-84, Luth. Hist. Soc. Eastern Pa.; author: (index) Luther in Mid-Career (H. Bornkamm), 1983, Theodicy in the Old Testament (J. Crenshaw), 1983, The Roots of Anti-Semitism (H. Obermann), 1984, The Book of Revelation: Justice and Judgment (E.S. Fiorenza), 1985, Rediscovering Paul (N.R. Peterson), 1985, The Opponents of Paul in Second Corinthians (D. Georgi), 1986, Psychological Aspects of Pauline Theology (G. Theissen), 1986, Ethics of the New Testament (W. Schragg), 1987, Israel's Praise (W. Brueggemann), 1987, Commitment to Unity (W.K. Gilbert), 1988, Paul and His Letters (L. Keck), 2d rev. edit., 1988, Finally Comes the Poet (W. Bruggemann), 1989, Community and Commitment (G. Rupp), 1989, Protest and Praise (J.M. Spenser), 1990, After the Absolute (L. Swidler), 1990, Greeks, Romans and Christians, 1990, The New Era in Religious Education (P. Babin), A Commentary on the Book of Amos (S.M. Paul); contbr. articles to profl. jours. Active Boy Scouts Am., 1964-66. Mem. ALA, Am. Theol. Libr. Assn. (bd. dirs. 1991—), Southeastern Pa. Theol. Librarians Assn. (sec. 1970-73, chair 1982-85, chair planning com. 1986-89), Coun. Nat. Libr. and Info. Assns. (counselor 1978-81), Coun. on Study Religion (liaison) com. 1974-77, 81-82, nominating com. 1978-80), Luth Hist. Conf. (com. on scholarly rsch. and pub. 1981—, constl. revision com. 1984-86, bd. dirs. 1988—, treas. 1988—), Assn. Theol. Schs. in U.S. and Can. (selection panel for libr. grants), Paradise Falls Luth. Assn. (bd. dirs. 1985-87, chmn. religious activities 1985-86), Middle States Assn. (accreditation visitor), Luth. Hist. Soc. Eastern Pa. (life), Drexel U. Grad. Sch. Libr. and Info. Sci. Alumni Assn. (bd. dirs. 1978-80), Eta Sigma Phi, Phi Sigma Tau, Beta Phi Mu. Democrat. Home: 7238 Boyer St Philadelphia PA 19119 Office: Luth Theol Sem 7301 Germantown Ave Philadelphia PA 19119 *By God's grace I am freed to live a life of joyful service in gratitude.*

WASCOM, LONNIE LOUIS, minister; b. Baton Rouge, La., Sept. 2, 1948; s. Lonnie Louis and Patsy Ruth W.; m. Linda Faye LaCoste, May 16, 1970; children: Laura Lynette, Lane LaCoste. BA, Southeastern La. Univ., 1970; MDiv, Golden Gate Bapt. Theol., Seminary, Mill Valley, Calif., 1973, D of Ministry, 1990; MA, San Francisco State U., 1976. MasterLife discipleship tng., MasterBuilder discipleship tng., witness tng./evangelism tng. Assoc. pastor Northside Bapt. Ch., Denham Springs, La., 1969-70, Clinton Ave. Bapt. Ch., Richmond, Calif., 1970-75, First So. Bapt. Ch., Redding, Calif., 1975-78, Trinity Heights Bapt. Ch., Shreveport, La., 1978-90; sr. pastor Immanuel Bapt. Ch., Hammond, La., 1990—. Vice-pres. student govt., Golden Gate Bapt. Theol. Seminary, Mill Valley, 1971-73. Named to Outstanding Young Men of Am., 1975, 79. Mem. Chappapeela Bapt. Pastor's Conf., La. Bapt. Conv. Edn. Assn., Northwest La. Bapt. Religions Edn. Assn. (pres. 1986-87), Northwest La. Pastor-Staff Conf. (v.p. 1988), Northwest La. Bapt. Assn. (bd. dirs. 1978-90), others. Republican. Office: Immanuel Bapt Church 1503 Pecan St Hammond LA 70401 *To be properly related to others and to think rightly about oneself begins in relationship with God. This relationship is based on the greatest challenge facing everyone: to love.*

WASHBURN, ALPHONSO VICTOR, JR., religious organization administrator; b. Cleveland County, N.C., Aug. 4, 1912; s. Alphonso Victor and Mary Edith (Greene) W.; m. Ethel Kate Allison, Dec. 16, 1933; children: Ann Allison, James Kent, Mary Janet. BA, Wake Forest U., 1933; postgrad., So. Bapt. Theol. Sem., 1934-48; MA, George Peabody Coll., 1951; postgrad., Southwestern Bapt. Theol. Sem., 1955-57; LittD (hon.), Gergetown Coll., 1956. Summer field worker N.C. Bapt. Conv., 1929-32; supt. young people's Sunday Sch. work Sunday Sch. Bd., So. Bapt. Conv., Nashville, 1933-43; sec. teaching and tng. Sunday Sch. Bd., Soc. Bapt. Conv., Nashville, 1946-57, dir. Sunday sch. dept., 1958-77, ret., 1977; mem. coordinating com. inter-agy. coun. So. Bapt. Conv., 1958-77; mem. commn. on Christian teaching and tng. Bapt. World Alliance, 1965-75, sec. commn., 1970-75, mem. coordinating com. div. evangelism and edn., 1976—. Author: Young People in the Sunday School, 1955, Outreach for the Unreached, 1960, Administering the Bible Teaching Program, 1969, also numerous tracts; editor The Sunday Sch. Builder, 1958-70. Lt. (j.g.) USNR, 1943-45. Mem. Ea., Southwestern, So. Bapt. religious edn. assns. Home: 6420 Jocelyn Hollow Rd Nashville TN 37205

WASHBURN, JAMES THOMAS, II, minister; b. Midland, Tex., Dec. 22, 1958; s. Almas Preston and Mary Wynola (Waters) W.; m. Julie Ellen Eakin, Dec. 27, 1983; 1 child, James Thomas III. BA in Bible, Lubbock Christian Coll., 1983. Ordained to ministry Ch. of Christ, 1979. Intern Broadway Ch. of Christ, Lubbock, Tex., 1979-82; youth minister Ft. Worth and Jax Ch. of Christ (now Fairmont Park Ch. of Christ), Midland, 1981-84, 3d and Kilgore Ch. of Christ, Portales, N.Mex., 1984—; adventure leader Adventures in Christian Living, 1985. Basketball official, 1984—, Football official, 1985—. Named one of Outstanding Young Men of Am., 1983. Mem. N.Mex. Activities Assn., N.Mex. Officials Assn. Republican. Avocations: backpacking, reading, golfing. Home: 1028 E 3rd Portales NM 88130 Office: 3d and Kilgore Ch of Christ Box 450 Portales NM 88130

WASHBURN-OSBORN, DAISY MARIE, missionary foundation executive; b. Merced, Calif., Sept. 23, 1925; d. Christopher Columbus and Clara Irene (Otis) Washburn; m. T. L. Osborn, Apr. 5, 1942; children—Marie LaVon (dec.), T.L. (dec.), LaDonna Carol Osborn-Nickerson, Mary Elizabeth (dec.). Student pub. schs., Los Banos; LHD, Bethel Christian Coll., 1983; DD, (hon.), Zoe Coll., 1983. Co-founder, chairperson bd. OSFO Internat. (internat. missionary ch. orgn.), Tulsa, 1948, exec. adminstr., dir. overseas projects, Tulsa, 1948—; author 3 books, numerous mini-books; editor Faith Digest mag., 1956—; radio min., internat. speaker confs., convs., seminars, mass crusades. Internat. advisor and lifetime patron Christian Women's Fellowship Internat.; bd. regents Bethel Christian Coll. Office: PO Box 7572 Tulsa OK 74170

WASHINGTON, LINDA ANN, minister; b. Galveston, Tex., Mar. 25, 1949; d. Charlie James and Berta (Hawk) Allums; m. Freddie L. Washington, Aug. 1981 (div. Jan. 1990); children: Jon L. Vaughn, TaShana L. McGinty. Student, Alvin (Tex.) Jr. Coll., 1967-68, Galveston (Tex.) Community, Coll., 1968-69, Southwest Community Coll., Los Angeles, Tex., 1969-70, Coll. of the Mainland, Texas City, Tex., 1975-76. Assoc. minister Full Gospel Deliverance Ch., Hitchcock, Tex., 1983-86, Hedge and Hwy. Revival Ctr., Texas City, 1989—; founder Youth in Action, Texas City, 1989—; founder, chmn. Women in Ministry Fellowship, Texas City and Galveston, 1989—; sec. Univ. of Tex. Med. Br., Galveston, 1978—; a A Day Like Pentecost Crusades, Houston, 1984—, Soul Winners 1000, Dallas, 1989—; min. to elderly College Park Care Center, Texas City, 1991—. Contbr. articles to Love Banner News mag., 1983-84. Home: 6517 Memorial Dr # 3 Texas City TX 77591 Office: Women in Ministry Fellowsh 6517 Memorial Drive #3 Texas City TX 77591 Address: PO Box 129 Lamarque TX 77568 *Always put God first, esteem others higher than yourself, love with the God kind of love and the world will be a better place to love.*

WASHINGTON, SAUNDRA L., minister; b. Highland Park, Mich., July 14; d. Andrew and Reatha (Gardner) Smith. BSW, Marygrove Coll., Detroit, 1978; MA in Counseling Edn., Wayne State U., Detroit, 1981; MA in Theol. Studies, Ashland Theol. Sem., Ohio, 1986; D Ministry (hon.), Tenn. Sch. Religion, 1991. Lic. to ministry A.M.E. Ch., 1971, ordained as deacon, 1975, as elder, 1977. Assoc. minister St. Stephens AME Ch., Detroit, 1971-73; youth pastor St. Paul AME Ch., Detroit, 1973-75; pastor Brown Chapel AME Ch., Detroit, 1975-78; asst. pastor New St. James AME Ch., Detroit, 1978-86, pastor, 1986—; dir. pastoral bereavement and vol. svcs. Hospice of Southeastern Mich., Southfield, 1990—. Recipient Plaque for Svc., Eastwood Clinics, 1986; Ashland Sem. scholar, 1983, 84. Mem. Ministerial Alliance of Detroit, Women Ministers Coun. Home: 20520 Prevost # C2 Detroit MI 48235-2165 Office: New St James AME Ch 9321 Rosa Parks Blvd Detroit MI 48206 *God in His eternal wisdom determined that man should be gifted with freedom of personal choice. Therefore, it seems to me that man to a large extent is responsible for his own quality of life, which results inevitably from the decisions he makes.*

WASKOW, ARTHUR OCEAN, theologian, educator; b. Balt., Oct. 12, 1933; s. Henry B. and Hannah (Osnowitz) W.; m. Irene Elkin, 1956 (div. 1978); children: David, Shoshana; m. Phyllis Ocean Berman, 1986. B.A., Johns Hopkins, 1954; M.A., U. Wis., 1956, Ph.D., 1963. Legis. asst. Ho. of Reps., Washington, 1959-61; sr. staff mem. Peace Rsch. Inst., Washington, 1961-63; fellow Inst. Policy Studies, Washington, 1963-77; colleague Pub. Resource Ctr., Washington, 1977-82; faculty Reconstructionist Rabbinical Coll., Phila., 1982-89; dir. Shalom Ctr., 1983—; fellow Inst. for Jewish Renewal, 1990—; mem. adv. bd. Temple of Understanding. Author: The Limits of Defense, 1962, (with Stanley L. Newman) America in Hiding, 1962, Worried Man's Guide to World Peace, 1963, From Race Riot to Sit-In, 1966, The Freedom Seder, 1969, Running Riot, 1970, The Bush Is Burning, 1971, Godwrestling, 1978, Seasons of Our Joy, 1982, These Holy Sparks, 1983, (with David and Shoshana Waskow) Before There Was A Before, 1984; editor: Debate Over Thermonuclear Strategy, 1965, Menorah Jour, 1979—; screenwriter: In Every Generation, 1988; mem. editorial bd. Tikkun, Reconstructionist. Alt. del. Democratic nat. conv., 1968. Mem. Nat. Writers Union, Fabrangen, New Jewish Agenda, Nat. Havurah Com. (bd. dirs. 1979-80, 83-87), P'nai Or (bd. dirs. 1984—), Interat. Coordinating Com. on Religion and Earth (steering com.), Phi Beta Kappa. Address: 6711 Lincoln Dr Philadelphia PA 19119 *For about 500 years the human race has made no "Sabbath" from ceaseless working, making, producing, doing and it therefore has raced to the brink of destroying itself and much of life on the planet. Just as individuals need rhytmic rest, so do societies—a spiritual truth that we should again learn from Torah. Time to be!.*

WASMUS, ROBERT THEODORE, minister; b. Columbus, Ohio, Oct. 3, 1933; s. Robert Brannon and Jean McMath (Rust) W.; m. Patricia Annette McCleany, May 25, 1962; children: William, Richard, Francis, Victoria and Vincent (twins). Student, Drake Bus. Coll., 1957-59. Ordained to ministry Ch. of Living Savior. Minister Ch. of the Living Savior, Grove City, Ohio, 1973—; active TV ministry, Columbus, Ohio, 1973—. Active Columbus Reps. Served as sgt. USAF, 1953-57. Republican. Avoations: boating, camping, swimming, skiing. Home and Office: 1586 Dyer Rd Grove City OH 43132

WASSON, (ARNOLD) DOUGLAS, retired clergyman; b. Minot, N.D., Aug. 21, 1927; s. Robert Lawrence and Jenny Marguarite (Clark) W.; m. Mary Jo Peacock, June 2, 1958. BA, Case Western Res. U., 1950; M in Divinity, Oberlin (Ohio) Grad. Sch. of Theology, 1953; M in Edn., Auburn (Ala.) U., 1961. Ordained to ministry United Ch. of Christ, 1953. Adminstrv. asst. Pittman Community Ctr., Sevierville, Tenn., 1954-55; instr., pub. relations dir. So. Union Coll., Wadley, Ala., 1955-56, acting pres., 1956-58; asst. to pres. Snead Jr. Coll., Boaz, Ala., 1958-60; pastor First Congl. Ch., Rock Springs, Wyo., 1961-68, Colorado Springs, Colo., 1968-72; coordinator religious activities Woodmoor Corp., Monument, Colo., 1972-74; pastor The Ch. at Woodmoor, Monument, Colo., 1972-90, pastor emeritus, 1990—; moderator Wyo. Assn. United Ch. Christ, 1963, Southeastern United Ch. Christ, 1970; mem. mission and stewardship com. Rocky Mountain Conf. United Ch. of Christ, 1991—, coord. hunger action, 1991—. Chmn. Sweetwater County Outdoor Recreation Bd., Rock Springs, 1966-68, Pikes Peak Area Com. for Heifer Project Internat., 1989—; adv. mem. Wyo. Land and Water Conservation Com., Cheyenne, 1966-68; founder, coord. Pikes Peak Advocates for San Luis Valley, 1990—; coord. Pikes Peak Area 10K Hunger Hike, 1990; coord. Fast for the Hungry of the World, 1975—. Recipient Citation for Service award Circle K Internat., 1979, Citation for Leadership award Heifer Project Internat., 1986, Citation for Fund Raising award Ch. World Svc., 1985; named Young Men of Yr. Rock Springs Jaycees, 1963. Mem. San Luis Valley Christian Community Services (Alamosa, Colo. bd. dirs. 1975—), Christian Ministry in Nat. Parks (nat. bd. dirs. 1965—), Kiwanis (pres. 1958, 61, lt. gov. 1963, gov. Rocky Mountain dist. 1968, internat. trustee 1974-78). Democrat. Mem. United Ch. of Christ. Home: 1677 Shrider Rd Colorado Springs CO 80920-3375

WATERMAN, BYRON OLNEY, minister; b. Johnston, R.I., Nov. 23, 1909; s. Walter Day and Fannie May (Sweet) W.; m. Marion Palmer Eddy, Aug. 24, 1934; children: byron Eddy, Holden Tozer. AB, Brown U., 1932; BD, Andover-Newton Theol. Sch., 1934, MDiv, 1973. Ordained to ministry Am. Bapt. Chs., United Ch. of Christ. Asst. min. 1st Calvary Bapt. Ch., Lawrence, Mass., 1935-41; min. 1st Bapt. Ch., Plaistow, N.H., 1941-50, M. Vernon Larger Parish, Greene, R.I., 1950—; vis. chaplain R.I. Med. Ctr. Inst. Mental Health, 1953—. Active Griswold (Conn.) Conservation Commn., 1971—; violinist Conn. Coll. Orch., New London, 1967—, Ea. Conn. Symphony Orch., New London, 1968—, Nat. Sr. Symphony, Mystic (Conn.) and New London, 1989—; vol. chaplain R.I. Hosp., Providence, 1986—. Recipient citations R.I. Ho. of Reps., 1975, 90, citation R.I. Senate, 1990, Community Citizen award The Grange, 1990. Mem. Assn. Mental Health Chaplains, Am. Fedn. Musicians, Archeol. Soc. Am., Brown Faculty Club. Home: Rte 3 Norwich CT 06360 Office: PO Box 5055 Greene RI 02827-0055 *Sharing in this world is one of the most important contributions to living.*

WATERS, BRENT PHILIP, university chaplain; b. Delano, Calif., Feb. 20, 1953; s. Charles Fred and Donna Leona (Kelley) W.; m. Diana Louise Lieberg, July 21, 1975; 1 child, Erin Elizabeth. BA, U. of the Redlands, 1975; MDiv, Claremont Sch. Theology, 1979, D. Ministry, 1984. Ordained in Bapt. Ch. Campus minister United Ministries in Higher Edn., Ames, Iowa, 1979-84; Omer E. Robbins chaplain to the univ. Univ. of the Redlands, Redlands, Calif., 1984—; chair exploratory com. on sci., tech. and the Christian faith United Ministries in Edn., 1984-89; senator Am. Bapt. Ministers Coun., 1982-84; del. Biotech. Conf., Italy, 1989. Contbr. articles to profl. jours. Program chair Soc. for Christian Ethics-Pacific Region; participant Genetics, Ethics, and Religion Project, Houston; mem. Loma Linda (Calif.) U. Institutional Rev. Bd. for Human Studies, 1985-87. Mem. Nat. Assn. Coll. and Univ. Chaplains (exec. com.), Am. Acad. Religion, Nat. Assn. Sci., Tech., and Soc., Am. Bapt. Campus Ministers Editor Assn. Office: U of the Redlands Redlands CA 92373-0999

WATERS, CURTIS JEFFERSON, minister; b. Spartanburg, S.C., Apr. 8, 1929; s. Leroy Belton and Lillian Isola (Tucker) W.; m. Nancy Carol Taylor, Oct. 25, 1947; children: Curtis Michael, Ronald Stephen, Gloria Lynn. BA, North Greenville Coll., Tigerville, S.C., 1953; BD, Luther Rice Sem., Jacksonville, Fla., 1973; DD (hon.), North Fla. Bapt. Theol. Sem., 1988, ThD, 1991. Ordained to ministry So. Bapt. Conv., 1950; lic. real estate broker, N.C. Pastor Gap Creek Bapt. Ch., Marietta, S.C., 1950-51, Fairmont (S.C.) Bapt. Ch., 1951-55, Francis Bapt. Ch., Palatka, Fla., 1955-60, Double Springs Bapt. Ch., Greer, S.C., 1960-63, Churchwell Avenue Bapt. Ch., Knoxville, Tenn., 1963-71, Tuxedo (N.C.) 1st Bapt. Ch., 1971-75; pastor City View 1st Bapt. Ch., Greenville, S.C., 1975—, chmn. bd. dirs. Champions for Christ Found., 1987—; dir. E.J. Daniels Crusade, Palatka, Fla.; evangelist 9 states and Jamaica; sem. commencement speaker North Fla. Bapt. Theol. Sem., 1989-90, 90-91; speaker Bible confs. Republican. Home: 5 Colgate Ave Greenville SC 29611 Office: City View 1st Bapt Ch 2300 W Blue Ridge Dr Greenville SC 29611 *The rewards of life are incredible when one gives himself completely to the will of God. Sharing life with others and ministering to their needs brings invaluable satisfaction.*

WATERS, JOHN W, minister, educator; b. Atlanta, Feb. 5, 1936; s. Henry and Mary Annie (Randall) W. Cert., U. Geneva, Switzerland, 1962; BA, Fisk U., 1957; STB, Boston U., 1967, PhD, 1970. Ordained to ministry Bapt. Ch., 1967. Min. religious edn. Ebenezer Bapt. Ch., Boston, 1965-67, assoc. min., 1967-69; min. Myrtle Bapt. Ch., West Newton, Mass., 1969, Greater Solid Rock Bapt. Ch., Atlanta, 1981—; prof. Interdenominational Theol. Ctr., Atlanta, 1976-86, trustee, 1980—; prof. Interdenominational Theol. Ctr., Atlanta, 1976-86, trustee, 1980-83; bd. dirs. Habitat for Humanities, Atlanta, 1984—; chmn. S. Atlanta Joint Urban Ministries, 1983—. Contbr. articles to profl. jours. Mem. Va. Highlands Neighborhood Assn., Atlanta, 1977-87, Butler St. YMCA, 1980-86, South Atlanta Civic League, 1983, others; treas. Prison Ministries with Women Inc. Served with U.S. Army, 1960-63. Fund for Theol. Edn. fellow, 1965-67, Nat. Fellowship Fund fellow, 1968-70, Rockefeller doctoral fellow, 1969. Mem. AAUP (chpt. pres. 1971-72), Am. Acad. Religion, Soc. Bibl. Lit., Blacks in Bibl. Studies, New Era Missionary Bapt. Conv. Ga. Democrat. Home: 1516 Niskey Lake Trail SW Atlanta GA 30331 Office: The Greater Solid Rock Bapt Ch 6280 Camp Rd Riverdale GA 30296 *In life, each of us faces a variety of choices. The choices made determine our destiny, fate. When more of us assume responsibility and accountability for the choices made, the world in which we live will be decisively better.*

WATERSTON, WILLIAM KING, minister, educator, academic administrator; b. Elizabeth, N.J., Feb. 12, 1937; s. John Robert and Sylvia (Eadie) W.; m. Judith Jane Schramm, Aug. 29, 1959; children: John Scott, Gregory Glenn, Robert Ormsby; m. Kathryn Larsen, Dec. 17, 1983; 1 child, Chad. AB, Bates Coll., 1959; BD, Eastern Bapt. Sem., 1962, M.Div., 1973.

Ordained to ministry Am. Bapt. Chs. USA, 1962. Bus. mgr., editorial asst. Missions Mag., 1962-66, Crusader Mag., 1964-66; assoc. dir. radio and TV Am. Bapt. Chs. USA, 1966-69, dir. electronic media, 1969-72; host Dialogue TV Show, Phila., 1969-85; assoc. dir. communications div. Am. Bapt. Chs. USA, 1972-73; Parker Ford Bapt. Ch., 1973-81; dir. group homes ch. rels. devel. Bapt. Children's Svcs., Phila., 1981—; instr. Eastern Bapt. Coll., 1973-85, Eastern Bapt. Sem., 1970-85. Editor Mediathink, 1973. Lodge: Rotary (pres. Cen. Perkiomen 1968). Home: 528 Wilson St Pottstown PA 19464 Office: Bapt Children's Svcs Freedom Business Ctr 610 Ste 110 King of Prussia PA 19406

WATKINS, CHARLES MORGAN, lawyer; b. Newport News, Va., Sept. 12, 1954; s. Walter Edmond and Joanne Kathryn (Halla) W.; m. Margie Elizabeth Valentine, July 16, 1983; children: Kathryn Grace, Mark Emerson. AB, Franklin & Marshall Coll., 1976; JD, Dickinson Sch. of Law, 1981. Bar: D.C. 1981, U.S. Ct. Claims 1983, U.S.Ct. Appeals (Fed. cir.) 1987, U.S. Tax Ct. 1987. Atty. office of chief counsel IRS, Washington, 1981-85; assoc. Webster, Chamberlain & Bean, Washington, 1986—; instr. in tax law, ch. law and tax report; ruling elder McLean Pesbyn. Ch. Author: Nondiscrimination Rules for Employee Benefit Plans, 1988, (with others) Issues for Exempt Organizations: A Guide for State Associations, 1987; contbr. articles to profl. jours. Mem. ABA, Christian Legal Soc., Christian Mgmt. Assn. Republican. Presbyterian. Avocations: camping, canoeing, hiking, tennis. Office: Webster Chamberlain & Bean 1747 Pennsylvania Ave NW Ste 1000 Washington DC 20006 *Churches and other religious organizations must carry out their worship and other charitable work in a manner that is morally and ethically correct, wise in its accumulation and distribution of resources, and sensitive to the true needs of their beneficiaries.*

WATKINS, HAROLD R., religious organization administrator. Pres. World Conv. of chs. of Christ, Indpls. Office: World Conv Chs Christ 100 N Central Expwy Ste 804 Richardson TX 75080*

WATKINS, HAROLD ROBERT, minister; b. Wauseon, Ohio, July 30, 1928; s. Orra Lynn and Florence Margaret (Bruner) W.; m. Evelyn Norma Earlywine, June 18, 1950; children: Mark Edwin, Nancy Jo Watkins Boyd. AB, Bethany Coll., 1950; BD, Lexington Theol. Sem., 1953; DD, Phillips U., 1985. Ordained minister Disciples of Christ, 1950. Min. Park Ave. Christian Ch., Tucson, 1953-56, First Christian Ch., Tuscaloosa, Ala., 1956-57; gen. ch. adminstr. Bd. Ch. Extension of Disciples of Christ, Indpls., 1958—, pres., 1980—; trustee Bethany (W.Va.) Coll., 1976—; chmn. bd. Discipledata, Inc., Indpls., 1980—; bd. dirs. Ecumenical Ch. Loan Fund, Geneva, Switzerland; pres. World Conv. of Chs. of Christ, Richardson, Tex., 1988—; trustee Nat. City Christian Ch. Corp., Washington, 1981—. Recipient Outstanding Alumnus award Bethany Coll., 1975. Mem. Interfaith Forum on Religion, Art and Architecture (dir. officer 1979—, pres. 1981-82, Elbert M. Conover award 1989), Indpls. Athletic Club. Home: 1342 N Graham Indianapolis IN 46219 Office: Bd Ch Ext Disciples Christ 110 S Downey Ave Indianapolis IN 46219

WATKINS, JONATHAN LEE, deacon; b. Morristown, N.J., Apr. 10; s. Robert Harper and Mary Alice Watkins; m. Kelly Michelle Hendrickson, Aug. 16, 1988; children: Bianca Michelle, Lajon Lee and Lajean Louise (twins). Student, Drew U., 1982, County Coll. Morris, 1991—. Ordained to ministry Bapt. Ch. as deacon, 1984. Deacon 1st Bapt. Ch., Madison, N.J., 1984—, treas., 1989—; computer ops. supr. Phys. Security Group, Parsippany, N.J., 1990—. Mem. Morristown ambulance squad, 1979-86; counselor Community Corrections Coun., Morristown, 1988-89. Mem. Am. Mgmt. Assn., Am. Soc. Notaries. Home: 7 Linden St Morristown NJ 07960 Office: Phys Security Group 2 Campus Dr Parsippany NJ 07054 *Always keep your left hand in God's hand and the right hand reaching down to lift up someone less fortunate than you and show him the way.*

WATKINS, WILLIAM WALLACE, minister; b. Queen City, Tex., Nov. 28, 1939; s. James Weldon and Elsie Mae (Thomas) W.; m. Martha Sue Bull, Mar. 7, 1970; children: Jefferey Scott, David Glen. BA, East Tex. Bapt. U., 1963; MDiv, Southwestern Bapt. Theol. Sem., 1967; D Ministry, Ea. Bapt. Theol. Sem., 1988. Ordained to ministry So. Bapt. Conv., 1961. Pastor First Bapt. Ch., Hitchcock, Tex., 1970-72; assoc. pastor First Bapt. Ch., Texarkana, Tex., 1972-77; sr. pastor Cen. Bapt. Ch., Marshall, Tex., 1977—; trustee, bd. dirs. Bapt. Gene. Conv. Tex., 1978-87; trustee East Tex. Bapt. U., Marshall, 1979-88, chmn., 1986-88. Author (weekly column) Marshall News Messenger, 1977-81; contbr. articles to profl. jours. Pres., founder Marshall Vol. Chaplains Assn., 1983; bd. dirs. Interfaith Counseling Svc., Kilgore, Tex. Mem. Am. Assn. Marriage and Family Counselors, Assn. Couples for Marriage Enrichment (registrar 1991), Marshall Ministerial Alliance (pres. 1990-91). Office: Cen Bapt Ch 300 S Washington Marshall TX 75670

WATSON, ANITA LOUISE, minister; b. Wilmington, Del., Oct. 17, 1953; d. Mildred Louise (Houghton) Miller; m. Thomas Wilson Watson, May 5, 1972; children: Thomas Norman, Sara Day. BA, Lourdes Coll., 1989; postgrad., Meth. Sch. Ohio. Pastor Risingsun (Ohio) Charge, United Meth. Ch., 1991—, dir., 1989—; workshop advisor Cath. Social Svcs., Toledo, 1988; cluster facilitator Toledo dist. United Meth., 1990—. Scholar Med. Coll. Ohio, 1986, Honors scholar Meth. Sch. Ohio, 1989-90, Bradenbury scholar United Meth. Ch. West Ohio Conf., 1989, 90, 91. Mem. Theta Alpha Kappa.

WATSON, CLETUS CLAUDE, priest; b. Phila., Nov. 3, 1938; s. Ernest Samuel Jr. and Claudie B. (Bridges) W. BA in Sch. Philosophy, St. Francis Coll., Loretto, Pa., 1962; MA in Religious Edn., La Salle U., 1974; MDiv, St. Charles Sem., 1976. Joined Franciscan order, 1955, ordained priest Roman Cath. Ch., 1966. Theology tchr. Bishop Egan High Sch., Fairless Hills, Pa., 1966-69, chmn. theology dept., 1969-75; assoc. pastor, theology tchr. Holy Faith Parish, Gainesville, Fla., 1976-77; chmn. theology dept. St. Francis Prep. Sch., Spring Grove, Pa., 1977-81, dean students, 1979-81; assoc. pastor Holy Faith Parish, Gainesville, 1981-85, San Jose Cath. Ch., Jacksonville, Fla., 1985-88; chmn. theology dept. St. Joseph Acad., St. Augustine, Fla., 1986-89; pastor Ch. of the Crucifixion, Jacksonville, 1988—; lectr. U. Fla., Gainesville, 1981-85; co-chmn. Afro-Am. Office, Jacksonville, 1987—; mem. Nat. Black Cath. Congress, Balt., 1987—; presbyteral coun. Diocese of St. Augustine, Jacksonville, 1989-91, mem. Cath. Charities, 1991—, mem. office of ministry, 1991—. Author: The Morality of the Suburban Teenager, The Seraphic Troubadour, 1973, The Concept of God and the American Black Man, The Seraphic Troubadour, 1974. Mem. adv. bd. Health and Rehab. Svcs.: One Ch./One Child Programs, Jacksonville, 1987—. Recipient Black History Month award Jacksonville Naval Air Sta., 1989, Alumni award St. Francis Coll., Loretto, Pa., 1991. Home and Office: 6079 Bagley Rd Jacksonville FL 32209 *Half my life is spent and I have not built a lofty parapet to accomplish all that the Author of Life, the Lord of Life, has called me to fulfill. The fulfillment of Life is sacred for all of us.*

WATSON, JOHN ALLAN, clergyman; b. Detroit, June 26, 1938; s. Roy Allan and Charlotte Luella (Piper) W.; m. Mary Louise Strawbridge, June 25, 1960; children: Paul Allan, Stephen John, Mark Andrew, Philip Scott. BA, Wheaton (Ill.) Coll., 1960; BD, Princeton Sem., 1964; MTh, U. Aberdeen, Scotland, 1971. Ordained minister Presbyn. Ch., 1964. Minister 1st Presbyn. Ch., Kentland, Ind., 1964-68, Bethel Presbyn. Ch., Columbus, Ohio, 1970—; dean Anselm Inst., Columbus, 1986—. Mem. Presbytery Scioto Valley (chmn. minister rels. 1982-85, jud. commn. 1987—), Internat. Brotherhood Magicians. Democrat. Home: 46 Winthrop Rd Columbus OH 43214 Office: Bethel Presbyn Ch 1735 Bethel Rd Columbus OH 43220 *One of the great mistakes of our time is live by a philosophy which has amended the great affirmation that "our chief end is to glorify God and enjoy Him forever" to "our chief end is to enjoy."*

WATSON, JOHN DUDLEY, minister; b. Denver, Jan. 21, 1930; s. Hugh Doane and Blessing E. (Maag) W.; m. Diane Alice McClintock, Aug. 24, 1954; children: Hugh D., William J., Kathryn Watson McAllen. BA, Oberlin Coll., 1952; BD, Yale U., 1955; D Ministry, McCormick Theol. Sem., 1982. Ordained to ministry Presbyn. Ch. (U.S.A.), 1955. Pastor Mt. Ida Presbyn. Ch., Troy, N.Y., 1955-57; asst. pastor Westminster Presbyn. Ch., Springfield, 1957-64; pastor 1st Presbyn. Ch., Glandale, Ohio, 1964-70, St. Joseph, Mo., 1970—; moderator Kansas City Union Presbytery, 1976; pres. Interfaith Community Svcs., St. Joseph, 1972-75. Pres. Social Welfare Bd., St. Joseph, 1978; bd. dirs. Heartland Hosp., St. Joseph, 1987—, Samaritan Counseling Ctr., St. Joseph, 1986—; sec. United Way, St. Joseph, 1988. Mem. Rotary. Home: 10 Lindenwood Ln Saint Joseph MO 64505

WATSON, LANCE DEAN, minister; b. Detroit, Jan. 5, 1959; s. Rosemond and Doreather (Whitley) W.; m. Rosemary Katherine Wilder, Apr. 30, 1977; children: Lance II, Rachel, Damon. BA, BS, Wayne State U., 1982, MA, 1983; MDiv, Va. Union U., 1986; MA, Presbyn. Sch. Christian Edn., 1986. Ordained to ministry Nat. Bapt. Conv. U.S.A., Inc., 1983. Min. youth New St. Paul's Bapt. Ch., Detroit, 1972-79; dir. edn. Tabernacle Bapt. Ch., Detroit, 1979-83; pastor St. Paul's Bapt. Ch., Richmond, Va., 1985—. Office: St Paul's Bapt Ch 2600 E Marshall St Richmond VA 23223

WATSON, MARGERY JEANETTE, religious organization financial administrator; b. Mt. Clemens, Mich., Aug. 11, 1943; d. Samuel Livingston and Estella Virginia (Porter) Thompson; m. Leroy Watson, July 29, 1961 (dec. Dec. 1980).; children: Wendy Darnel, Leroy. Grad. high sch., Mt. Clemens, 1961. Fin. adminstr. Deliverance Ctrs. of Am., Atlanta, 1985-87; gen. mgr., pres. Sta. WXLL Radio, Decatur, Ga., 1985—; fin. adminstr. Cathedral Ch. of God in Christ, Decatur, 1987—; trustee Calvary Bapt. Ch., Mt. Clemens, 1980-85. Mem. NAACP, Atlanta, 1986— (life mem., Outstanding Svc. 1987). Mem. Order of Ea. Star (matron Mt. Clemens chpt. 1984-85). Home and Office: Sta WXLL Radio 3333 Covington Dr Decatur GA 30032

WATSON, STANLEY ELLIS, clergyman; b. New Orleans, July 25, 1957; s. Joseph and Dorothy (Jones) W.. EdB, Jarvis Christian Coll., Hawkins, TX., 1977; MRE, T.C.U. Brite Divinity Sch., Ft. Worth, 1979; special edn., So. U. A&M, Baton Rouge, 1986; grad., U.S. Acad. Pvt. Investigation, 1991. Tchr. Asst. min. Jarvis Christian Coll., Hawkins, TX., 1974-77; tchr. pub. sch., Daingerfield, TX., 1977-78; asst. min. Park Manor Christian Ch., Chgo., 1980-81; asst. mgr. K Mart, Shreveport, LA., 1981-82; min. United Christian Ch., Jackson, Miss., 1982-83; tchr. pub. sch., Napoleonville, LA., 1986-87, Zachary, LA., 1987-88; min. Vermont Christian Ch., Flint, MI., 1988-90; sr. pastor, 1990—. Mem. NAACP, NEA. Christian Womens fellow, 1975-77, St. Louis Bd. of Edn. fellow, 1977-79, scholarship TCU Brite Divinity Sch., 1977. Mem. Aircraft Owners and Pilots Assn. Coun. for Exceptional Children, Forgotten Man Ministries, Jarvis Christian Coll. Alumni Assn. (v.p.), NAACP, Urban League of Flint, Urban Coalition of Greater Flint, Flint C. of C., Internat. Reading Assn., NEA, others. Dem. Avocations: bee keeping. Home: 4910 Walnut Sq Flint MI 48532 Office: Vermont Christian Church PO Box 310736 Flint MI 48531

WATSON, THOMAS ANDREW, II, minister; b. Kenosha, Wis., Sept. 6, 1953; s. Thomas Andrew and Margaret (Rothermel) W.; m. Debra May Starling, Nov. 28, 1981. BA, U. Wis., Eau Claire, 1976n; MDiv, Emory U., 1982. Ordained to ministry United Meth. Ch. as deacon, 1980, as elder, 1984. Pastor Ceres (Va.) United Meth. Ch., 1982-85; co-pastor Cen.-Mary's Chapel-Rutledge, Bean Station, Tenn., 1985-87; pastor Clinchport (Va.) United Meth. Ch., 1987-90, Emory-Centenary United Meth. Ch., Kingsport, 1990, Emory United Meth. Ch., Kingsport, 1991, Campground United Meth. Charge, Church Hill, Tenn., 1991—. Mem. Kingsport Ministerial Assn. (v.p. 1990-91, pres. 1991—), Rotary (bd. dirs. 1989-90), Sigma Tau Gamma. Home and Office: Rte 9 Box 10 Church Hill TN 37642-9038 *I pray that every day in every way I am getting better and better.*

WATSON, W. H., bishop. Bishop of N.W. Tex. Ch. of God in Christ, Lubbock. Office: Ch of God in Christ 1301 47th St Lubbock TX 80412*

WATT, PAUL BROOKS, religion educator; b. Youngstown, Ohio, Aug. 30, 1946; s. Charles Foster and Margaret (Wilson) W.; m. Yasuko Ito, Dec. 21, 1968. BA, Internat. Christian U., Tokyo, 1969; MA, Columbia U., 1975, M. Philosophy, 1976, PhD, 1982. Assoc. prof. and dir. Asian studies DePauw U., Greencastle, Ind., 1989—. Contbr. articles to profl. jours. Japan Found. Profl. grantee, 1984. Mem. Soc. for the Study of Japanese Religions (pres. 1987-93), Am. Acad. Religion, Assn. for Asian Studies (N.E. Asia Coun. grantee 1988), Soc. for the Study of Chinese Religions. Office: DePauw U 215 Asbury Hall Greencastle IN 46135

WATTERSON, DONALD HODGES, religious organization administrator; b. Decatur, Ala., Nov. 13, 1929; s. Charles Floyd and Mae Sue (Hodges) W.; m. Margaret Joan Cook, Sept. 2, 1950; children: Susan Joan, Melanie Carol, Leisa Ellen, Starla Dawn. BA, Samford U., Birmingham, Ala., 1952, DD (hon.), 1974; MDiv, Southwestern Bapt. Theol. Sem., Ft. Worth, 1956. Ordained to ministry So. Bapt. Conv., 1951. Pastor Sowers Bapt. Ch., Irving, Tex., 1954-57, First Bapt. Ch., Headland, Ala., 1957-59, Grace Temple Bapt. Ch., Denton, Tex., 1959-61; pastor First Bapt. Ch., Durant, Okla., 1961, Atmore, Ala., 1961-63; pastor Cottage Hill Bapt. Ch., Mobile, Ala., 1963-71; assoc. exec. Ala. Bapt. Conv., Montgomery, 1971—. Avocations: reading, golf, cooking. Home: 8348 Longneedle Dr Montgomery AL 36117 Office: Ala Bapt Conv Box 11870 Montgomery AL 36109

WATTERSON, GENE LEE, clergyman; b. Decatur, Ala., Dec. 10, 1929; s. Aulton Douglas and Eva Rose (Couch) W.; m. Yvonne Caudle, Aug. 7, 1954; children: Pamela Yvonne Watterson Runyans, Gene L. Jr., Lisa Dawn. Student, Samford U., 1948-51; BA, Jones U., 1952; MA, Coll. William and Mary, 1956; MDiv, Southeastern Bapt. Theol. Sem., 1960; DD (hon.), Gardner-Webb Coll., 1974. Ordained to ministry So. Bapt. Conv., 1952; cert. clin. counselor, Va., Fla., N.C. Pastor Woodlawn Bapt. Ch., Colonial Heights, Va., 1953-60, 1st Bapt. Ch., Crestview, Fla., 1960-67; sr. min. Murray Hill Bapt. Ch., Jacksonville, Fla., 1967-69, 1st Bapt. Ch., Shelby, N.C., 1969—; mem. exec. com. N.C. Bapt. State Conv., Carey, 1969-74, pres. coun. on Christian higher edn., 1971-74, 1st v.p., 1988-89, pres., 1990-91; officer exec. com. So. Bapt. Conv., Nashville, 1975-83. Author: (with others) Evangelism Today, 1966; also articles. Chmn. Commn. on Housing and Urban Devel., Shelby, 1969-74; mem. Commn. on Human Rels., Shelby, 1969-74; bd. dirs. Coun. on Abuse Prevention, Shelby, 1978-82; mem. N.C. Legislature Study Commn. on Youth Suicide, Raleigh, 1987-89. With USN, 1945-48, ETO, Asia. Recipient citation for excellence in Christian ministry Gardner-Webb Coll., 1972, citation for outstanding svc. So. Bapt. Conv., 1983. Mem. Friends of Missions, Religious Liberty Coun. Home: 617 Peach St Shelby NC 28150 Office: 1st Bapt Ch 120 N Lafayette St Shelby NC 28150 *The pleasure of fame, position, power and prominence is elusive and like the taste of cotton candy, soon gone. To live with integrity is to gather memories that last a lifetime.*

WATTS, RICHARD EUGENE, minister, educator; b. Texas City, Tex., July 21, 1956; s. Robert Andrew and Lois Pauline (Brown) W.; m. Cheryl Marie Kramer, Aug. 8, 1981. B in Music Edn., Sam Houston State U., 1980; MA, Southwestern Bapt. Theol. Sem., 1987; postgrad., U. North Tex., 1987—. Teaching fellow U. North Tex., Denton, 1991—; counselor Collin Bapt. Assn., McKinney, Tex., 1989—. Contbr. articles to profl. jours. Counselor Collin Country Crisis Ctr., Plano, Tex., 1988. Sam Houston State U. scholar, 1976. Mem. AACD, Assn. for Counselor Edn. and Supervision, Assn. for Regligious and Value Issues in Counseling, Internat. Assn. Marriage and Family Counselors, Phi Delta Kappa. Baptist. Avocations: reading, writing, composing music, basketball. Home: 202 W Graham McKinney TX 75069 Office: U North Tex Dept Counselor Edn PO Box 13857 Denton TX 76203-3857

WAUN, GEORGE GLEN, minister; b. Snover, Mich., Mar. 8, 1927; s. George Leonard and Bessie May (Flannigan) W.; m. Alison Mabel Learn, Sept. 11, 1948; children: Stephen Dale, William George, Deborah Anne. AB, Asbury Coll., 1948; MA, U. Mich., 1961; ThD, Trinity Theol. Sem., Newburgh, Ind., 1986. Ordained to ministry, 1953. Pastor various chs., Mich., 1948-65, Brenneman Meml. Ch., Goshen, Ind., 1965-79; dist. supt. over 60 chs., 1979—; bd. dirs. Bethel Coll., Christian Holiness Assn.; dir. Ind. United Missionary Loans and Investments, Inc., 1979—, Mich. U.M. Loans and Investments, Inc., 1959-62; bd. Nat. Assn. Evangs. Ind. Assn., 1991—; dir. Sunday schs., 1960-63; vice dist. supt. Mich. dist., 1963-65, North Cen. Dist., 1969-75, 77-79; denom. sec., 1965-68, 71-73. Author: The Christian Sabbath, 1986; editor jours. 1958-68, 71-73. Home: 23626 Creek Park Dr Elkhart IN 46517 Office: Missionary Ch 28042 CR 24 W Elkhart IN 46517 *The greatest decision one can make in life is to accept Jesus Christ as Lord and Savior and to put God first in everything. That is my personal testimony.*

WAUN, WILLIAM GEORGE, clergyman, naval officer; b. Petoskey, Mich., June 2, 1953; s. George Glen and Alison Mabel (Learn) W.; m. Cynthia Jo Frederick, Aug. 14, 1976; children: Nicholas George Frederick, Jillian ARlene Alison. BS, Oral Roberts U., 1976; MDiv, Asbury Theol. Sem., 1978; ThM, Princeton Theol. Sem., 1979; postgrad., Garret-Evang. Theol. Sem., 1980, United Theol. Sem., 1981, Trinity Evang. Divinity Sch., 1982, Faith Evang. Luth Sem., 1991—. Ordained deacon United Meth. Ch., 1981; ordained presbyter Missionary Ch., 1982. Pastor Grace United Meth. Ch., Royal Center, Ind., 1979-81, New Carlisle (Ohio) Missionary Ch., 1981-82; commd. lt. USN, 1983, advanced through grades to lt. comdr., 1991; staff chaplain, comdr. amphibious squadron 6 USN, Norfolk, Va., 1983; staff chaplain, comdr. amphibious squadron 4 USN, Norfolk, 1983-85; Protestant chaplain USMC base USN, Camp Lejeune, N.C., 1986-87; sr. Protestant chaplain naval air sta. USN, Sigonella, Sicily, Italy, 1987-91; protestant chaplain naval submarine base New London USN, Groton, Conn., 1991—. Mem. Wesleyan Theol. Soc., Evang. Theol. Soc., Brotherhood of St. Andrew, Order of St. Luke. Address: Office of Chaplain NAVSUBASE NLON Groton CT 06349

WAY, SCOTT WENDELL, lay worker; b. Canton, Ohio, Dec. 21, 1960; s. Wendell Lee and Donna Jean (Poling) W. BA in Bibl. Studies, The Criswell Coll., Dallas, 1986; postgrad., Dallas Theol. Sem., 1986—. Lay staff person Chi Delta Coll. Fellowship of Marsh Ln. Bapt. Ch., Dallas, 1983-85; pres. student congress Woodcrest Coll., Van, Tex., 1985; tchr., leader Omega Alpha Coll. Class of Countryside Bible Ch., Southlake, Tex., 1986-87, The Master's Class of Mountainview Bapt. Ch., Marietta, Ga., 1988-89; short-term missionary Belgian Evang. Mission, Brussels, 1990-91. *There is only one way I know to face the multitude of joys, trials, temptations, pains, successes and difficulties that life brings and that is to face them in utter, humble dependence on Almighty God.*

WAYMAN, DENNIS LYNN, minister; b. Alva, Okla., May 25, 1951; s. Hugh Delynn and Betty Jean (Shields) W.; m. Cheryl Lynne Hawkins, Mar. 30, 1972; children: Benjamin David, Timothy Joseph. BA, Greenville Coll., 1973; MDiv, Asbury Theol. Sem., Wilmore, Ky., 1976. Ordained to ministry Free Meth. Ch. N.Am., 1976. Pastor Free Meth. Ch., Santa Barbara, Calif., 1976—; exec. dir. Cliff Dr. Care Ctr., Santa Barbara, 1976—, asst. supt., 1988—; sec. Bd. Ministerial Edn., Azusa, Calif., 1978—; chmn. Free Meth. Social Action Coun., 1987—. Author: Church as a Redeeming Community, 1976. Bd. dirs. Mesa Improvement Assn., Santa Barbara, 1984-88; bd. dirs., trustee Western Evang. Sem., Portland, Oreg., 1986-88. Home: 266 Coleman Ave Santa Barbara CA 93109 Office: 1435 Cliff Dr Santa Barbara CA 93109

WAYMOUTH, CHARITY, retired cell biologist, editor; b. Blackheath, Eng., Apr. 29, 1915; came to U.S., 1953; d. Charles Sydney Herbert and Ada Curror (Scott Dalgleish) W. BSc, Bedford Coll., U. London, 1936; PhD, U. Aberdeen, Scotland, 1944; DD (hon.), Gen. Theol. Sem., N.Y.C., 1979; ScD (hon.), Bowdoin Coll., 1982. Biochemist City of Manchester Hosps., Eng., 1937-44; head tissue culture dept. Chester Beatty Research Inst., London, 1947-52; staff scientist Jackson Lab., Bar Harbor, Maine, 1953-63, sr. staff scientist, 1963-81, assoc. dir., 1977-80, interim dir., 1980-81, sr. staff scientist emeritus, 1981—; Rose Morgan vis. prof. U. Kans., Lawrence, 1971; bd. dirs. W. Alton Jones Cell Sci. Ctr., Lake Placid, N.Y., 1980-82. Editor symposium proc. and research monographs. Contbr. articles to tech. jours., chpts. to books. Dep. triennial gen. convs. Episcopal Ch., 1970-88. Recipient achievement award AAUW, 1962, Deborah Morton award Westbrook Coll., 1981; fellow Beit Meml. Found., Copenhagen and London, 1944-46, Am. Cancer Soc., 1952-53. Fellow AAAS; mem. N.Y. Acad. Scis., Tissue Culture Assn. (pres. 1960-62, editor-in-chief 1968-75, editor Decennial Rev. Conf. 1984-87). Avocations: reading, gardening, bread making. Home: 16 Atlantic Ave Bar Harbor ME 04609

WAZIR, TADAR JIHAD, chaplain, small business owner; b. Kansas City, Mo., Dec. 28, 1944; s. Roosevelt and Osceola (Moore) Byers; m. Kay Frances Kyle-Byers, May 17, 1969; children: Tarik, Ibrahim; 1 adopted child, Ajamu. AA in Adminstrn. of Justice, Penn Valley Community Coll., Kansas City, 1977. Ins. salesperson Western & So. Life Ins. Co., Kansas City, 1968-69, N.Y. Life Ins. Co., Kansas City, 1969; supr. check transit dept. First Nat. Bank, Kansas City, 1969-70, methods analyst, 1971-72; paramedic St. Joseph's Hosp., Kansas City, 1974-77; owner W. K. Enterprises, Kansas City, 1977-79; ins. salesperson Roosevelt Nat. Life, Independence, Mo., 1978-79; pvt. mcht., Kansas City, 1980-81, Marshall, Mo., 1989—; real estate salesperson Mid-Western Realty, Kansas City, 1980-86; chaplain Mo. Dept. of Corrections, Jefferson City, 1982—; speaker, cons. Masjid Omar, Inc., Kansas City, 1977—; contract chaplain, cons. U.S. Med. Ctr. Fed. Prison, Springfield, Mo., 1979—; co-chmn. report the drug pusher Ad-Hoc Group Against Crime, Kanas City, 1978-82. Chaplain chpt. 393, Vietnam Vets. Assn., Jefferson City, 1991. With USMC, 1962-66; mem. U.S. affiliate Islamic African Relief Agy. Mem. Am. Corrections Assn., Mo. Corrections Assn., Mo. Assn. Social Welfare, Nat. Assn. Muslim Chaplains, NACCP (pres. Marshall-Saline chpt. 1989-90, v.p., 1990-91), Mid-Am. Coun. Imams, Islamic Soc. N.Am., Optimists (chaplain Marshall 1990-91, chmn. community svcs. 1991—, co-organizer ROTC program Ark. AM&N Coll.). Avocations: reading, horseback riding, swimming, selling. Home: 456 W Porter St Marshall MO 65340 Office: Mo Dept of Corrections 2729 Plaza Dr Jefferson City MO 65102

WEAKLAND, REMBERT G., archbishop; b. Patton, Pa., Apr. 2, 1927; s. Basil and Mary (Kane) W. AB, St. Vincent Coll., Latrobe, Pa., 1948, DD (hon.), 1963, LHD (hon.), 1987; MS in Piano, Juilliard Sch. Music, 1954; grad. studies sch. music, Columbia U., 1954-56; LHD (hon.), Duquesne U., 1964, Belmont Coll., 1964, Cath. U. Am., 1975, St. Vincent Coll., Latrobe, 1987, Xavier U., Cin., 1988, DePaul U., 1989, Loyola U., New Orleans, 1986, 91; HHD (hon.), St. Ambrose U., Davenport, 1990; LLD (hon.), Cardinal Stritch Coll., Milw., 1978, Marquette U., 1981, U. Notre Dame, 1987, Mt. Mary Coll., Milw., 1989; D of Sacred Music (hon.), St. Joseph's Coll., Rensselaer, Ind., 1979; DST (hon.), Jesuit Sch. Theology, 1989, St. John's U., Collegeville, Minn., 1991, Santa Clara U., 1991; DD (hon.), Vincent Coll., 1983, Lakeland Coll., Sheboygan, 1991. Joined Benedictines, Roman Cath. Ch., 1945, ordained priest, 1951. Mem. faculty music dept. St. Vincent Coll., 1957-63, chmn., 1961-63, chancellor chmn. of bd. of Coll., 1963-67; elected co-adjutor archabbot, 1963; abbot primate Benedictine Confederation, 1967-77; archbishop of Milw., 1977—. Mem. Ch. Music Assn. Am. (pres. 1964-66), Am. Guild Organists. Office: PO Box 07912 Milwaukee WI 53207-0912

WEAN, RONALD HARRY, minister; b. Youngstown, Ohio, Apr. 30, 1953; s. John Edward and Ruth Virginia (Kreitzburg) W.; m. Kay Frances Roeder, Aug. 23, 1975; children: Kandis Elaine, Megan Kimberly. BS, U. Cin., 1975; MDiv, Trinity Luth. Sem., Columbus, Ohio, 1979; postgrad in clin. pastoral edn., Luth. Gen. Hosp., 1986-87. Ordained to ministry Luth. Ch., 1979. Pastor Peace Luth. Ch., Arapahoe, Nebr., 1979-82; assoc. pastor St. John Luth. Ch., Celina, Ohio, 1982-86; visitation pastor Christ Luth. Ch., Palatine, Ill., 1986-89; interim pastor Redeemer Luth. Ch., Chgo., 1989-90; pastor, counselor Parkside Lodge Mundelein (Ill.) Youth Addiction Treatment Ctr., 1987-91; pastoral counselor Miami Valley Hosp., Dayton, Ohio, 1991—. Author: (drama) One Must Die, 1986. Del. Ill. Assembly on Prevention of Alcohol and Drug Abuse, Springfield, 1990; bd. dirs. Mercer County Bd. Alcoholism, Celina, 1983-86. Home: 649 Eisenhower Palatine IL 60067 Office: Miami Valley Hosp Employee Care 1126 S Main Dayton OH 45409

WEARY, DOLPHUS D., minister, religious organization administrator; b. Sandy Hooks, Miss., Aug. 7, 1946; s. Albert Weary and Lucille (Grandberson) Craft; m. Rosie Marie Camper, Aug. 15, 1970; children: Danita Ronique, Reginald Demond, Ryan Donche. AA, Piney Woods (Miss.) Jr. Coll., 1967; BA in Biology, L.A. Bapt. Coll., Newhall, Calif., 1969; MRE in Christian Edn., L.A. Bapt. Sem., Newhall, Calif., 1971; MEd in Ednl. Adminstrn., U. So. Miss., 1978. Ordained to ministry Christian Ch., 1973. Asst. varisty coach L.A. Bapt. Coll., Newhall, 1969-71; coord. Christian edn. Piney Woods Sch., 1975-84; dir. summer leadership devel. Mendenhall (Miss.) Ministries, 1968-70, pastor ch. fellowship, 1971-74, dir. ministry, 1971-78, exec. dir., 1979-86, pres., 1986—. Co-founder Mendenhall Flood

Prevention Fund; mem. Miss. Flood Disaster Fund, John M. Perkins Scholarship Fund, Simpson County Econ. Devel. Found., NAACP. Recipient Miss. Religious Leadership Conf. award, 1985, Humanitarian award Cen. Miss. Legal Svcs., 1985; named Outstanding Citizen of the Yr., Civic Circle Club of Simpson County, 1981. Mem. Christian Community Devel. Assn., Christian Community Health Fellowship, Christian Ministries Mgmt. Assn., Nat. Assn. Evangs., Nat. Black Evang. Assn., Mendenhall C. of C. Office: Mendenhall Ministries Inc PO Box 368 Mendenhall MS 39114

WEATHERSBY, JOSEPH BREWSTER, civil rights administration executive; b. Cin., Nov. 23, 1925; s. Albert and Gertrude (Renfro) W.; m. Louberta Gray, Oct. 28, 1950 (div. Oct. 13, 1980). BBA, Salmon P. Chase Coll., 1950; MDiv., Berkley Div. Sch., 1960. Ordained priest Episcopal Ch. Rector St. Mary's Episcopal Ch., Detroit, 1961-68, St. Clement's Episcopal Ch., Inkster, Mich., 1973-74; dir. Saginaw Urban Ministry, Mich., 1969-72, 74-75; dist. exec. Mich. Dept. Civil Rights, Saginaw, 1976-83; exec. recipient rights Mich. Dept. Mental Health, 1986—. Served with USMC, 1944-46, PTO. Mem. Alpha Phi Alpha. Democrat. Home: 48641-1-94 Service Dr Apt 310 Bldg 44 Belleville MI 48111

WEAVER, CLYDE EUGENE, minister, international relations consultant; b. East Petersburg, Pa., Sept. 26, 1924; s. Clyde and Emma Weaver; m. Katherine Anne Linscheid, June 24, 1951; children: John Clyde, Mark Eugene, Rebecca Jean. BA, Elizabethtown (Pa.) Coll., 1949; ThM, Bethany Theol. Sem., Chgo., 1953. Ordained to ministry Ch. of the Brethren, 1942. Chaplain Bethany Hosp., Chgo., 1952-55; prof. Bapt. Tng. Sch., Chgo., 1954-56; chaplain Chgo. Parental Sch., 1955-57; assoc. exec. social welfare dept. Ch. Fedn. Chgo., 1957-59; auto dealer Weaver-Young Dodge, Elmhurst, Ill., 1960-69; dir. mktg. Brethren Press, Elgin, Ill., 1969-86; U.S.-USSR relations cons., prin. New Call to Peacemaking, Elgin, Ill., 1987—; chaplain Fox Valley Hospice, Elgin, 1986—; pres. Chicagoland Dodge Dealers Assn., 1969. Author: Plumbline, 1980; contbg. author: What About The Russians, 1984, My Sister Tatiana, My Brother Ivan, 1988; contbr. articles to mags. Bd. dirs., trustee Ecker Mental Health Ctr., Elgin, 1977-83, sec., 1985-89; arbitrator Chgo. Better Bus. Bur., 1983—; trustee Elgin Pub. Libr. Mem. Kiwanis. Home and Office: 38 W 691 Ridgewood Ln Elgin IL 60123 *Messages need messengers that live comfortably together in the same person. Otherwise words lose their meaning and people lose their integrity.*

WEAVER, E(LVIN) PAUL, minister; b. Everett, Pa., Oct. 13, 1912; s. Mahlon J. and Fanny S. (Ritchey) W.; m. Zalma Faw, Aug. 6, 1936 (dec. 1966); children: Nelda Weaver Sollenberger, Bruce H.; m. Eleanor Snare Carter, June 21, 1968. AB, Elizabethtown (Pa.) Coll., 1937; BD, Bethany Sem., Chgo., 1945; postgrad., Kennedy Sch. Missions, Hartford, Conn., 1939. Ordained to ministry, Ch. of the Brethren. Missionary Ch. of the Brethren, Nigeria, 1940-44; pastor Ch. of the Brethren, Huntington County, Ind., 1945-51, Mexico (Ind.) Ch., 1951-59; dist. exec. Mid Dist. of Ind., North Manchester, Ind., 1959-71, Nappanee, Ind., 1971-80; pastor SS Valley & Cherry Ln., Everett, Pa., 1981-88; ret.; pres. Ind. State Pastor Conf., Indpls., 1955; bd. dirs. Ind. Coun. Chs., Indpls., 1948-78; del. Nat. Coun. Chs., Detroit, Dallas; accredited visitor World Coun. Chs. Assemblies II, VI, VII; legis. counsel Ind. Coun. Chs., 1948-78, Ind. Christian Endeavor, 1948-78; rep. Ch. of Brethren at SSD III UN Disarmament, UN, 1988. Recipient Ecumenical award Ind. Coun. Chs./Pa. Coun. Chs., 1988. Home: Rte 1 Box 155 Everett PA 15537 *As I begin my second sixty years in ministry, my life is dedicated to seeking to know and do God's will. I find many opportunities to work for Justice and Peace to Preserve all Creation.*

WEAVER, G(AIL) NORMAN, minister, religion educator; b. Enon, Mo., Nov. 30, 1921; s. Gail James and Mary Lieurania (Enloe) W.; m. Garnet Elizabeth Newton, Oct. 1, 1942; children: Elizabeth Weaver Kronk, Marcia Sue Weaver Wood, David Norman. AE, SW Bapt. Coll., 1941; BS, SW Mo. State Coll., 1947; MEd, U. Mo., 1950; postgrad., Cen. Bapt. Theol. Sem., 1955-56. Ordained to ministry So. Bapt. Conv., 1959; cert. secondary tchr., Mo. Instr. SW Bapt. Coll., Bolivar, Mo., 1950-57; teaching fellow Southwestern Bapt. Sem., Ft. Worth, 1957-59; min. edn. 1st Bapt. Ch., Lake Worth, Tex., 1957-60; mem. faculty Hardin-Simmons U., Abilene, Tex., 1960—; interim pastor Elmdale Bapt. Ch., Abilene, 1969-72, min. edn. Wylie Bapt. Ch., Abilene, part-time 1972-75; asst. pastor 1st Bapt. Ch., Clyde, Tex., 1975-79, Immanuel Bapt.Ch., Abilene, 1980-83; aux. missionary tchr. Ghana Bapt. Sem., Abuaka, 1983-84; vol. tchr., leader ch. programs, Mo. and Tex., 1944-90; moderator, dir. Sunday sch. and ch. tng. Bapt. Assn., MO., Tex., 1955-70; tchr. So. Bapt. Leadership Tng. Ctrs., N.Mex., N.C., 1964-65; vol. missionary tchr. English Thailand Bapt. Mission, Bangkok, 1991. Contbr. articles to So. Bapt. Educator, Ch. Tng. mag., also others. Scoutmaster, com. mem. Ozarks and Chisholm Trail couns. Boy Scouts Am., 1955-88; sec., pres. Community Action Program, Abilene, 1980-88; sec. adv. coun. on aging West Cen. Tex. Coun. Govts., Abilene, 1981—; chmn. edn. cluster Abilene Coordinating Coun., 1978-80; precinct chmn. Taylor County Dem. Com., 1982-84. With USAAF, 1942-46. Mem. AAUP, Southwestern Bapt. Religious Edn. Assn. (v.p. 1962-64), Assn. Profs. and Researchers in Religious Edn., So. Bapt. Religious Edn. Assn., Kiwanis, Phi Delta Kappa (pres. local chpt. 1973-74). Home: 2302 Clinton St Abilene TX 79603 Office: Hardin-Simmons U PO Box 1136 Abilene TX 79698 *When I realize the magnitude of the needs of the world and the limits of my potential to meet these needs there may be a feeling of defeatism. Then I am strengthened by the realization that the only thing God requires of me is to take hold of the near edge of a great need and do my best.*

WEAVER, GRACE MARGARET, minister; b. Phila., Sept. 4, 1909; d. James Henry and Beulah Grace (Davis) W. BA, Morningside Coll., 1947; ThM, Iliff Sch. Theology, 1955. Tchr. elem. West Berlin, N.J., 1929-44, Clementon, N.J., 1944-45; missionary worker United Meth. Ch., Utah, 1948-51; min. Emmett, Glenns Ferry and American Falls, Idaho and Ketchikan, Alaska, 1954-76; ret., 1976. Recipient 4 Golden Poet awards, 1989. Avocation: pianist, bell ringer. Home: 1551 Center St NE Salem OR 97301

WEAVER, J. DENNY, religious educator; b. Kansas City, Kans., Mar. 20, 1941; s. J. Alvin and Velma Ferne (Beyler) W.; m. Mary Lois Wenger, June 7, 1965; children: Sonia Katharina, Lisa Denise, Michelle Therese. BA, Goshen (Ind.) Coll., 1963; postgrad., Kirchliche Hochschule Bethel, Bielefeld, Fed. Republic of Germany, 1968-69; MDiv, Goshen Bib. Sem., 1970; PhD, Duke U., 1975. Tchr. English Lsée Es-Salem, Al-Asnam, Algeria, 1966-68; prof. religion Goshen Coll., 1974-75; prof. religion Bluffton (Ohio) Coll., 1975-83, tenured prof. religion, 1983—; vis. prof. Can. Mennonite Bible Coll., Winnipeg, Man., Can., 1990-91; cons. editor Mennonite Quar. Rev., 1987—. Author: Becoming Anabaptist, 1987; contbr. articles to profl. jours. Mem. Am. Assn. Ch. History, Am. Acad. of Religion, Soc. for Reformation Rsch., Mennonite Hist. Soc., Conf. on Faith and History, Sixteenth-Century Soc. Office: Bluffton Coll Bluffton OH 45817

WEAVER, JAMES PAUL, minister; b. Rocky Mount, N.C., Dec. 6, 1933; s. William David and Betty (Langley) W.; m. Mary Helen Pridgen, Oct. 20, 1956; children: Paula, Jamie, Kim. Student, So. Bapt. Sem. Extension Dept., 1960-69. Ordained to ministry So. Bapt. Conv., 1962. Pastor Aenon Bapt. Ch., Elm City, N.C., 1962-64, Elm Grove and Wakelon Bapt. Chs., Colerain, N.C., 1964-69, Cedar Branch Bapt. Ch., Jamesville, N.C., 1969—. Mem. South Roanoke Bapt. Assn. (chm. fin. com., pres. pastors, vice moderator 1979-80, moderator and exec. chmn. 1981-82). Home and Office: Rte 1 Box 552 Jamesville NC 27846

WEAVER, KENNETH LAMAR, pastoral counselor; b. Locke Township, Ind., Apr. 26, 1950; s. Isaac G. and Pauline E. (Brendle) W.; m. Janet Carol, Mar. 14, 1981; children: Kristofer N. Frieden, Juliana J. Cert., Hiatt Inst., Jerusalem, 1971; BS, Purdue U., 1972; BA, Goshen Coll., 1977; MDiv, Goshen Bibl. Sem., 1977; MA, Adler Inst., 1986. Ordained to ministry Mennonite Ch., 1983. Psychiat. aid Southwood Hosp., Chula Vista, 1973; psychiat. tech. Elkhart (Ind.) Gen. Hosp., 1973-76; child welfare caseworker Dept. Pub. Welfare, Wabash and Valparaiso, Ind., 1977-80; mental health therapist Swanson Ctr., Michigan City, Ind., 1980-82, clin. dir., 1983-85; area dir. Northea. Ctr., Kendallville, Ind., 1985-89, dir. outpatient svc., 1989—; pvt. practice Ft. Wayne, Ind., 1987—; mem. Com. for Prevention Child Abuse, 1989—, Drug-Free Ind. Regional Bd., Ind., 1990—. Mem. Assn. Mental Health Clergy, East Noble Ministerial Assn. (pres. 1989-91), Community Action N.E. Ind. (bd. v.p. 1989—), Psi Chi. Mennonite. Avocations: reading, farming, sports, Middle Ea. studies. Office: Northea Ctr Inc 220 S Main St PO Box 817 Kendallville IN 46755

WEAVER, LEE JACKIE, music minister; b. Atlanta, Jan. 31, 1956; s. Lee J. and Juanita Mangum (Hughes) W. Min. music 1st United Meth. Ch., Chatsworth, Ga., 1978-80, Trinity United Meth. Ch., Dalton, Ga., 1980—; co-owner English Ave. Rec. Studio, 1984-91; owner Lite Bite Restaurant, Dalton, 1991—. Universal Acad. Music grantee, 1974, 75. Home: 4058 Jimmy Rocky Face GA 30740 Office: Trinity United Meth Ch 901 Fields Ave Dalton GA 30720

WEAVER, MACARTHUR, clergyman; b. Scottsboro, Ala., June 2, 1942; s. Otis and Nancy (Dobbs) W.; m. Judy Kay Dennis, Aug. 29, 1964; children: Joel Arthur, Jennifer Kay, John Andrew. AS, Walker Jr. Coll., Jasper, Ala., 1964; BA, McNeese State Coll., Lake Charles, La., 1967, MEd, 1968; MRE, So. Bapt. Theol. Sem., Louisville, 1971. Ordained to ministry So. Bapt. Conv., 1977. Dir. youth and recreation lst Bapt. Ch., Jasper, 1962-64, Buechel Park Bapt. Ch., Louisville, 1968-69; dir. recreation lst Bapt. Ch., Lake Charles, 1964-68; min. edn. Bethany Bapt. Ch., Louisville, 1970-71, lst Bapt. Ch., Valdosta, Ga., 1971—; pastor-advisor Bapt. Student Union, Valdosta State Coll.; vice moderator Valdosta Bapt. Assn.; chmn. membership com. Valdosta Area Ministerial Assn., 1975—. Coach Midget Football League, Valdosta Boys Club, 1974—, Cadet Basketball League, 1976—. Recipient Walk for Mankind award, 1974, 75, 76; named alt. Mr. Walker Coll., 1964. Mem. Valdosta Bapt. Ministerial Assn., Lowndes Adult Edn. Coun., Assn. Couples for Marriage Enrichment, Kiwanis (v.p. Azalea City 1975-76, pres. 1977-78). Home: 416 Lake Laurie Dr Valdosta GA 31602 Office: PO Box 670 Valdosta GA 31601

WEAVER, R(ICHARD) DONALD, clergyman; b. St. Louis, Mar. 25, 1926; s. Robert Raymond and Ada Viola (Holz) W. B.S.C., St. Louis U., 1949; M.Div., Garrett Theol. Sem., 1952; postgrad. U. Chgo., 1951-53; M.A., Scarritt Coll., 1979. Ordained to ministry United Methodist Ch., 1951; pastor, Lizton and Salem (Ind.) Meth. Chs., 1951-53, Centenary Meth. Ch., Veedersburg, Ind., 1953-58, Indiana Harbor United Meth. Ch., East Chicago, Ind., 1958-73, 1st United Meth. Ch., Hobart, Ind., 1973-80, 1st United Meth. Ch., Crown Point, Ind., 1980-84, Angola United Meth. Ch. (Ind.), 1984-87, St. Matthew United Meth. Ch. (Ind.), 1987—; lectr. Calumet Coll., Whiting, Ind., 1967-84. Pres., United Way, 1974, Twin City Community Svcs., 1970, Lake County Mental Health Assn., 1963, 64; v.p. Referral and Emergency Svcs., 1977-78, Steuben County United Way; bd. dirs. No. Ind. Health Systems Agy., 1976-78, Vis. Nurse Assn. N.W. Ind.; pres. Ind. United Meth. Children's Home, 1980-82; mem. East Chicago Housing Commn., 1965. Served with AUS, 1944-46; ETO. Recipient Community Leadership award Twin City Community Svcs., 1971. Mem. Am. Soc. Ch. History, Assn. Sociology of Religion, Hymn Soc. Am., Religious Edn. Assn. U.S. and Can., Religious Rsch. Assn., Soc. Sci. Study Religion, Clinton County Ministerial Assn., Rotary. Home: 1555 N Main St Frankfort IN 46041 Office: 1951 Wilshire Dr Frankfort IN 46041

WEAVER, WESLEY JAMES (JIMMY WEAVER), church administrator; b. Pensacola, Fla., Mar. 25, 1944; guardians James William and Martha Louise (Gray) Brock; m. Marie Nancelene Malone, Sept. 2, 1967; children: Daniel Wesley, Elizabeth Marie, Michael Todd, David Scott. BTh., Liberty Christian Coll., Pensacola, 1971; BS, U. West Fla., 1975. Elder, sec.-treas. Liberty Ch. Westside, Pensacola, 1978—; compt. Liberty Ministries, Pensacola, 1989—. Sec.-treas. bd. dirs. Liberty Christian Coll., Pensacola, 1987—. With USAF, 1963-67. Recipient award Fla. Dept. Revenue, 1980. Mem. Pensacola Athletic Ctr. Republican. Office: Liberty Ministries 8600 Hwy 98 West Pensacola FL 32506

WEBB, AARON WAYNE, minister; b. Hendrsonville, N.C., Aug. 28, 1953; m. Denise L. Raymond, Aug. 3, 1973; children: Amber, Aaron, Adam. BS, Tenn. Temple U., Chattanooga, 1976; MDiv, Grace Theol. Sem., Winona Lake, Ind., 1984. Ordained to ministry Conservative Bapt. Assn. Am., 1980. Youth pastor Sugar Grove Ch., Goshen, Ind., 1976-77; preacher, tchr. Wayside Bapt. Ch., Warsaw, Ind., 1977-80; pastor Mottville Bible Ch., White Pigeon, Mich., 1980-84; sr. pastor Battle Creek (Mich.) Bible Ch., 1984-89, Alpine Bapt. Ch., Comstock Park, Mich., 1989—; del., com. chmn. Ind. Fundamental Chs. Am., Grandville, Mich., 1988, mem. credentials com., 1987-89; mem. Grand Rapids (Mich.) Bapt. Acad. Sch. Bd., 1990—. Vol. Com. To Elect Jack Horton to Mich. Ho. of Reps., 1990; mem. parent steering com. Constintine (Mich.) Schs., 1983-84. Mem. Ind. Fundamental Chs. Am., Grand Rapids C. of C.

WEBB, ANDREW HOWARD, minister; b. Monterey Park, Calif., Dec. 28, 1945; s. Samuel Gorden and Jeannie (Stewart) W.; m. Marjorie Jean Pattison, June 20, 1970; children: Karen Jean, James Patrick. AB, San Diego State U., 1968, MA, 1975; postgrad., Mennonite Brethren Bibl. Sem., 1982—. Ordained deacon, 1983, ordained to ministry Free Meth. Ch., 1983. Min. Christian edn. and outreach Modesto (Calif.) Free Meth. Ch., 1981-85; pastor Oak Ave Free Meth. Ch., Orangevale, Calif., 1985—; dir. children's ministry Calif. Conf., 1978-83, bd. adminstrn., 1983—, chair bd. Christian edn., 1983—. V.p. Inter-Faith Ministries, Modesto, 1985; pres. Lemon Grove (Calif.) Tchrs. Assn., 1972-74, Imperial Valley coun. Internat. Reading Assn., El Centro, Calif., 1969; bd. dirs. Empire Union Sch. Dist., Calif., 1979-83; pres. Twin Lakes Food Bank, 1988—. Mem. Nat. Assn. Evangelists (pres. Sacramento County chpt. 1989—), Twin Lake Ministerial Assn. (pres. 1986-88), Wesleyan Theol. Soc., Alpha Phi Omega, Alpha Delta. Home: 8205 Crossoak Way Orangevale CA 95662 Office: 8790 Oak Ave Orangevale CA 95662 *As we approach the turn of the century, it is time for our nation to turn back to the Lord.*

WEBB, E. N., bishop. Bishop of Nev. Ch. of God in Christ, Las Vegas. Office: Ch of God in Christ 1941 Goldhill Las Vegas NV 89106*

WEBB, EUGENE, English language educator; b. Santa Monica, Calif., Nov. 10, 1938; s. Eugene and Marguerite (Rufi) W.; m. Marilyn Teruko Domoto, June 4, 1964; children—Alexandra Mariko, Christina Sachiko. B.A., U. Calif., Los Angeles, 1960; M.A., Columbia U., 1962, Ph.D., 1965. Asst. prof. English Simon Fraser U., 1965-66; asst. prof. U. Wash., Seattle, 1966-70, assoc. prof., 1970-75, prof. comparative lit. and comparative religion, 1975—. Author: Samuel Beckett: A Study of His Novels, 1970, The Plays of Samuel Beckett, 1972, The Dark Dove: The Sacred and Secular in Modern Literature, 1975, Eric Voegelin: Philosopher of History, 1981, Philosophers of Consciousness: Polanyi, Lonergan, Voegelin, Ricoeur, Girard, Kierkegaard, 1988. Mem. Am. Acad. Religion, Phi Beta Kappa. Episcopalian. Home: 6911 57th Ave NE Seattle WA 98115 Office: U Wash Thomson Hall DR05 Seattle WA 98195

WEBB, HENRY EMILE, church history educator, minister; b. Detroit, June 11, 1922; s. Hubert and Mabel Lavina (Postiff) W.; m. Emerald Mae Stevenson, Aug. 24, 1943; children: Karen, Mark, Wendy. AB, Cin. Bible Sem., 1943; PhB, Xavier U., 1944; BD, So. Bapt. Theol. Sem., 1947, Ph.D., 1954. Ordained to ministry Christian Ch./Ch. Christ, 1943. Minister Clifton Christian Ch., Louisville, Ky., 1944-49, First Christian Ch., Erwin, Tenn., 1950-63; prof. ch. history Milligan Coll., Tenn., 1950-90. Author: In Search of Christian Unity; contbr. articles to religious publs. Mem. Am. Soc. Ch. History, Disciples of Christ Hist. Soc., Theta Phi. Democrat. Lodge: Civitan (pres. 1979-80). Home: 1601 Idlewild Dr Johnson City TN 37601 Office: Milligan Coll Milligan College TN 37682

WEBB, JAMES CALVIN, minister; b. Washington, Ga., Dec. 16, 1947; s. Mack Clifton and Thelma (Walker) W.; m. Lynda Sue Gravely, Mar. 18, 1967; children: Wendell Lewis, Christopher Andrew. BA, Mercer U., Atlanta, 1977; MDiv, Southwestern Bapt. Theol. Sem., Ft. Worth, Tex., 1980, DMin, 1987. Ordained to ministry So. Bapt. Conv., 1980. Pastor Abbott (Tex.) Bapt. Ch., 1978-81, Bethesda Bapt. Ch., Burleson, Tex., 1981-84, White Oak Bapt. Ch., Lilburn, Ga., 1985—. Contbr. articles to profl. jours. With Army N.G. 1967-73. Home: 3083 Fireside Dr Snellville GA 30278 Office: White Oak Bapt Ch 1352 Martin Nash Rd Lilburn GA 30247

WEBB, JOHN BECK, minister; b. Memphis, June 6, 1951; s. Robert Daniel and Olive (Crumby) W.; m. Elisa Kay Broyles, June 12, 1976; children: Rachel, Daniel, Sarah. BA, Memphis State U., 1973; MDiv, Md-Am. Bapt. Theol. Sem., Memphis, 1978, DMin, 1990. Ordained to ministry, So. Bapt. Conv., 1976. Assoc. pastor Oakville Meml. Bapt. Ch., Memphis, 1975-77; pastor Mineral Wells (Miss.) Bapt. Ch., 1977-79, Faith Bapt. Ch., Atoka, Tenn., 1979-84, Pleasant Grove Bapt. Ch., Texarkana, Tex., 1984—; mem. pres.'s adv. coun. Mid-Am. Bapt. Theol. Sem., Memphis, 1979—. Author: The Selection and Hiring of Church Staff, 1990. Mem. Nat. Alumni Assn. Md-Am. Bapt. Theol. Sem. (pres. 1990). Republican. Home: Rt 3 Box 246 AB Texarkana TX 75503 Office: Pleasant Grove Bapt Ch 6601 Jones Ln Texarkana TX 75501

WEBB, JOHN WEBER, JR., minister; b. Memphis, Oct. 18, 1962; s. John Weber and Virginia (Thompson) W. BA, Memphis State U., 1986; MDiv, Ref. Theol. Sem., Jackson, Miss., 1989. Summer intern Commnity Presbyn. Ch., Live Oak, Fla., 1987, First Presbyn. Ch., West Point, Miss., 1988; dir. youth ministries Fifth St. Presbyn. Ch., Tyler, Tex., 1989—; pres. Tyler Area Youth Ministries Network, 1990—; current dir. Robert E. Lee chpt. Soldiers for Jesus, Tyler, 1990—; bd. dirs. Tyler Area Youth Ctr., 1990—. Author/contbr. PCA Bull., 1990. Republican. Home: 1526 S Mahon Ave Tyler TX 75701 Office: Fifth St Presbyn Ch 1616 E Fifth St Tyler TX 75701 *The task of the church is to perceive young people in a different way, not as the church of tomorrow, but as the church of today. Our goal is to train them for service, not simply entertain them. Our young people are capable of much more than we give them credit for.*

WEBB, LANCE, bishop; b. Boaz, N.Mex., Dec. 10, 1909; s. John Newton Shields and Delia (Lance) W.; m. Mary Elizabeth Hunt, June 30, 1933 (dec. Mar. 1990); children—Gloria Jeanne (Mrs. David B. Davis), Mary M. (Mrs. Lee Edlund), Ruth Elizabeth (Mrs. Allan Lindstrom). B.A. with highest honors, McMurry Coll., 1931, D.D., 1948; B.D., So. Meth. U., 1934, M.A., 1934; summer student, Union Theol. Sem., 1939, 47; D.D., Ohio Wesleyan, U., 1960, MacMurray Coll., 1967, McKendree Coll., 1970; Litt.D., Morningside Coll., 1977; H.H.D., Ill. Wesleyan U., 1966; LL.D., So. Meth. U., 1966; Litt.D., Simpson Coll., 1979; Litt.D. (hon.), Wiley Coll., 1986. Ordained to ministry Meth. Ch., 1935; pastor McCullough-Harrah Meth. Chs., Pampa, Tex., 1934-37; chaplain prof. religion McMurry Coll., Abilene, Tex., 1937-38; pastor Shamrock, Tex., 1938-40, Eastland, Tex., 1940-41; pastor University Park Meth. Ch., Dallas, 1941-52, North Broadway Meth. Ch., Columbus, Ohio, 1953-64; bishop Meth. Ch., 1964-80; resident bishop Meth. Ch., Ill. area, 1964-76, Iowa area, 1976-80; retired Meth. Ch.; Ann. Endowed Lance Webb lectr. on spiritual formation Cen. Ill. Conf., 1976—, cons. on spiritual formation for the upper rm., Nashville, 1980—; chmn. com. on worship Meth. Ch., 1964-72, mem. gen. and jurisdictional confs., 1956, 60, 64, co-chmn. world Meth. com. worship and liturgy, 1966-71; mem. World Meth. Council, 1966-71, sec., vice chmn. com. worship and liturgy, 1971-76 , chmn. com., 1976-81; mem. gen. bd. higher edn. United Meth. Ch., 1972-80; pres. north central jurisdiction Coll. of Bishops, 1979-80; conducted goodwill tours Middle East and Round the World, 1961, 63; Nat. Council Chs. interchange preacher Britain, 1959; chancellor Disciplined Order of Christ, 1964-89, chancellor emeritus, 1989—. Author: Conquering the Seven Deadly Sins, 1955, Discovering Love, 1959, Point of Glad Return, 1960, Art of Personal Prayer, 1962, On the Edge of the Absurd, 1965, When God Comes Alive, 1968, Disciplines for Life in the Age of Aquarius, 1971, God's Surprises, 1976, Onesimus, 1980, Making Love Grow, 1983, How Bad Are Your Sins, 1983, How Good Are Your Virtues, 1983, Disciplines for Life, 1986, Onesimus-Rebel and Saint, 1988; Sin and the Human Predicament, When Virtues Become Sins, Vol. I, God's Love and Human Transformation, Vol. II, 1988; A Traveller in the Company of God's Friends, 1991, Escape from Ephesus: A Novel of the First Century, 1991. Mem. Mayor's Com. on Human Relations, Columbus, 1953-64; chaplain Ohio Senate, 1963; internat. chaplain Civitain Internat., 1951; trustee Meth. Sch. Theology in Ohio, Garrett Evang. Theol. Sch., Evanston, Ill., McKendree Coll., Lebanon, Ill., Ill. Wesleyan U., MacMurray Coll., 1964-76; trustee Wiley Coll., 1972-87, emeritus, 1987—; chmn. bd. Wesley Found., U. Ill., 1964-76, Morningside Coll., Simpson Coll., Cornell Coll., Iowa Wesleyan Coll., Westmar Coll., 1976-80, Rust Coll., 1976-80. Clubs: Masons (Scottish Rite) (33 deg.), Torch (Columbus). Home: 10321 Van Dyke Rd Dallas TX 75218 also: Arlington VT 05250 *My life has been one continuous series of surprises in which the worst that has happened to me has turned out for the best. Since the age of 18 I have consciously lived by the faith that the Spirit creating, sustaining, and ruling our universe is like the spirit that was seen in Jesus. Whenever I have given myself to love and to serve upon this living faith, I have found my darkest nights turn into brightest dawns.*

WEBB, LILLIAN FRIER, minister, psychotherapist, writer; b. N.Y.C., July 13, 1926; d. Richard and Lillian (Manning) Frier; children from previous marriage: Leslie Frier, Jo-An Leslie Owings, Kathryn Louise. BA, CUNY, 1949; postgrad., NYU, 1959; MSW, Adelphi U., 1971. Ordained to ministry A.M.E. Ch., 1962; lic. clin. social worker, N.Y. Dir. Christian edn. Bridge St. A.M.E. Ch., Bklyn., 1962-65; assoc. pastor Bethel A.M.E. Ch., Freeport, N.Y., 1967-85; pastor Mt. Olive A.M.E. Ch., Port Washington, N.Y., 1985—; dir. Therapy Et Al, West Hempstead, N.Y., 1976—; adminstrv. asst. N.Y. Correctional Ctr., N.Y.C., 1967, chaplain, East Meadow, N.Y., 1982—; pres. Commn. on Women in Ministry, 1988—. Co-editor: AME/WIM Journals, 1990; columnist Essence mag., 1982. Mem. County Exec.'s Commn., Mineola, N.Y., 1991. Recipient Sojourner Truth award Black Business and Profl. Women, 1989. Mem. AME Women in Ministry (nat. pres. 1988—), World Coun. Chs. (chair worship Decade for Women program 1989—), Assect. Home and Office: 432 Scaneateles Ave West Hempstead NY 11552

WEBB, M. RODNEY, religious organization administrator; b. Leesburg, Fla., Sept. 26, 1944; s. Malcolm Rodney and Susie Pearl (Lawrence) W.; m. Suzanne Chaffin, June 10, 1967; children: Ellen Suzanne, Philip Rodney, Stephen Lawrence. BA, Carson-Newman Coll., Jefferson City, Tenn., 1966; MDiv, Southwestern Bapt. Theol. Sem., Ft. Worth, 1969. Missionary to deaf N.E. Home Mission Bd., New City, N.Y., 1969-75; lang. missions cons. Miss. Bapt. Conv., Jackson, 1975-78; asst. dir. lang. missions Home Mission Bd., So. Bapt. Conv., Atlanta, 1978-80, 80-82, asst. dir. ethnic ch. growth lang. missions div., 1982-870-82, dir. ethnic ch. growth dept. lang. missions div., 1987-89, dir. lang. ch. starting dept. lang. missions div., 1989—; chmn. credit com. Home Mission Bd. Credit Union, Atlanta, bd. dirs. Editor: Manual for Work with Deaf, 1983; compiler director: Directory of Southern Baptist Churches Ministering to Deaf, 1981. Adv. Miss. Adv. Com. to Vocat. Rehab., Jackson, 1976-77, Miss. Sch. for Deaf, 1976-77; active PTA, Lilburn, Ga., 1978-90. Recipient Ministry award, Vietnamese Bapt. Fellowship, 1989, Service award, Lang. Chs. in Calif., 1990. Mem. So. Bapt. Rsch. Orgn., So. Bapt. New Wk. Fellowship. Home: 5842 Trailwoods Ct Stone Mountain GA 30087 Office: Home Mission Bd So Bapt Con 1350 Spring St NW Atlanta GA 30367

WEBB, PERRY FLYNT, JR., clergyman; b. Malvern, Ark., Feb. 9, 1925; s. Perry Flynt and Thelma Fern (Stall) W.; m. Virginia Louise Powell, Oct. 3, 1949; children: Deborah Webb Smith, Perry F. III. BA, Baylor U., 1946; MDiv, So. Bapt. Theol. Sem., 1949. Ordained to ministry Baptist Ch., 1946. Pastor, Bapt. chs., Poteet, Tex., 1949-52, Natchitoches, La., 1952-64; Albany, Ga., 1964-75; First Bapt. Ch., Baton Rouge, 1975-88; past pres. and former pres. exec. bd. Dist. Eight Bapt. conv.; past mem. and officer La. Bapt. Exec. Bd.; past state pastor advisor Bapt. Student Union; past me. exec. com. Ga. Bapt. Con.; past mem. radio and TV commn. So. Bapt. Conv.; mem. program coordination com. La. Bapt. Conv. Woman's Missionary Union; guest speaker Bapt. Sem. of East Africa, Kenya, 1983; pres. La. Bapt. Conv., 1981-83, also mem. and pres. exec. bd. Contbr. articles to religious publs. Past mem. ad.v bd. Swega Youth Home; past mem. hosp. commn. Ga. Bapt. Hosp.; mem. adv. bd. Baton Rouge Gen. Hosp.; mem. Dist. Atty.'s Crime Commn.; past mem. bd. dirs. ARC; past trustee La. Bapt. Coll., Tift Coll.; chmn. bd. trustees So. Bapt. Theol. Sem., La. Moral and Civic Found. Republican. Avocations: woodworking, golf. Home: 476 Regency Blvd Shreveport LA 71106

WEBB, PHILLIP ALLEN, minister; b. Birmingham, Ala., Mar. 17, 1943; s. Robert Durrence and Catherine Violet (Brand) W.; m. Marcia Ruth Robbins, Aug. 3, 1969; 1 child, Phillip Robbins. AB, U. Ga., 1965; MDiv, Union Theol. Sem., 1968; DMin, Grad. Theol. Found., 1988. Ordained to ministry Presbyn. Ch., 1968. Pastor Westminster Presbyn. Ch., Norfolk, Va., 1968-74, Gracewood Presbyn. Ch., Memphis, 1974-78; sr. pastor Nelson Presbyn. Ch., St. Louis, Mo., 1979-84, First Presbyn. Ch., Alexandria, La.,

1984—; chmn. Faith and Order Commn., La. Interfaith Conf., Baton Rouge, 1988—, Presbytery Bus. Com., 1988—; deputy Ecumenical Affairs Presbytery, 1988; bd. dirs. Shepherd Ctr., Alexandria, La. Author: (monograph) Zebra Principle, 1980. Active Coun. So. La. Presbytery, Baton Rouge, 1988—; organizer Cen. La. Aids Support Svcs., Alexandria, 1988. Mem. North American Acad. Ecumenists, North American Patristic Soc., Religious Futures Netowrk, Acad. Parish Clergy. Republican. Office: First Presbyn Church 357 Windermere Blvd Alexandria LA 71303 *If we are to love life, one must find silence in themselves so that one may listen to others and see that life is so much better than they thought.*

WEBB, THOMAS HARLAN, minister; b. Springfield, Ohio, Mar. 31, 1944; s. Eugene Mumpher and Mary Marvalee (Powell) W.; m. Linda Suue Moore, June 6, 1964; children: Lori Ann, Jennifer Christine, Thomas Patrick. Student, St. Louis Christian Coll., 1982-83, Cin. Bible Coll., 1978-81. Pub. relation rep. CWBA, St. Louis, 1979-83; minister Marion Christian Ch., West Salem, 1983-85, Pleasant Christian Ch., Murphys Boro, Ill., 1985—. Served with USAF, 1963-67. Lodge: Masons. Avocations: fishing, woodworking. Home: Rte 4 Murphysboro IL 62966 Office: Pleasant Hill Christian Ch Rte 4 Murphysboro IL 62966

WEBB, WALTER WOODROW, minister; b. Marion, Ill., June 18, 1963; s. Woodrow and Delores Jean (Whittington) W.; m. Julie Marie Potter, July 30, 1988. BA in Religion, Olivet Nazarene U., Kankakee, Ill., 1986, MA in Religion, 1988. Lic. to ministry Ch. of the Nazarene, 1985. Minister Olivet Nazarene U., Kankakee, Ill., 1988—; admissions coun. Olivet Nazarene U., Kankakee, 1988—. Co-Coord. CROP orgn. ch. world svc., Kankakee, 1984—; ministry coord. Ill. Youth Ctr. Correctional Facility, 1986. Recipient Recognition award VA Hosp., Marion, Ill., 1980-82, Ill. Youth Ctr., 1983-86; named one of Outstanding Young Men of Am., 1987. Mem. Ind. Assn. Coll. Counselors., Nat. Assn. Christian Coll. Admissions Pers. Office: Olivet Nazarene University Box 6005 Kankakee IL 60901 *Our opportunities to succeed are so great we simply have to choose.*

WEBB, WILLIAM BRITTON, minister; b. Union, Miss., May 10, 1932; s. James Doris Sr. and Ola Mae (Adams) W.; m. Senita W. Webb, Aug. 26, 1955; children: Twila Michelle Massingale, Risa Cherise. BA, Baylor U., 1954; MDiv, So. Bapt. Theol. Sem., Louisville, 1957. Ordained to ministry So. Bapt. Conv., 1952. Pastor Monterey (Ky.) Bapt. Ch., 1954-60, Medway (Ohio) Bapt. Ch., 1960-66, Midway Bapt. Ch., Meridian, Miss., 1966—; chaplain Riley Meml. Hosp., Meridian, Miss., 1980—; mem. exec. bd. So. Bapt. Theol. Sem., Louisville, 1966-67; bd. dirs. Miss. Bapt. Conv. Bd., Jackson, Miss., 1977-82, exec. com. 1977-78. Office: Midway Bapt Ch Rte 9 Box 629 Meridian MS 39305

WEBB, WILLIAM CLEMENT, clergyman; b. Aransas Pass, Tex., Aug. 14, 1963; s. William Vernon and Maxine (Jordan) W.; B.A., Belmont Coll., 1968; M.Div., Midwestern Baptist Theol. Sem., 1971; M.A., U. No. Colo., 1976; m. Debra Ann Keenan, Dec. 15, 1972; children—Melinda Joy, Kristi Lin, William Robert. Dir. transp. Kemmerer (Wyo.) Sch. Dist. 1, 1973-74; ordained to ministry So. Bapt. Ch., 1964; pastor First Bapt. Ch., Kemmerer, 1973-74, First Bapt. Ch., Bamberg, W.Ger., 1974, Meml. Bapt. Ch., Wheatland, Wyo., 1975-76; social worker Platte County Dept. Social Services, Wheatland, 1975-76; counselor, chaplain Union Mission Settlement, Charleston, W.Va., 1976-77; dir. Nome (Alaska) Bapt. Ministries, 1977-83; clin. services dir. Alaska Bapt. Family Service Ctr., Anchorage, 1983-86; pastor, dir. Friendship Bapt. Mission, Fairbanks, Alaska, 1986—; mem. So. Bapt. conv. home mission bd.; publicity chmn. Wyo. Human Resouces Confedn., 1975-76; bd. dirs. Nome chpt. ARC, 1978; pres. Alaska Assn. Homes for Children. Mem. Am. Personnel and Guidance Assn., Am. Assn. Rehab. Counselors, Assn. Counselor Edn. and Supervision, Am. Assn. Specialists in Group Work, Am. Council on Alcohol Problems, Mental Health Counselor Assn., Assn. for Religious Issues and Values in Counseling. Democrat. Clubs: Rotary, Masons. Home: 1501 Lacey Fairbanks AK 99701

WEBBER, M. L., clergyman; b. Webbers Falls, Okla., June 15, 1938; s. Malcolm and Bessie (DeMeyer) W. DD, Faith Bible Sem., Ft. Lauderdale, Fla., 1964; cert. bus. mgmt., Lincoln Extension Inst., Cleve., 1967; DD, Christian Coll., Mobile, Ala., 1965, Holy Faith Sem., Bay City, Mich., 1984. Internat. pres. Congl. Bible Holiness Ch., Abilene, Kans.; Grand Council Head Chief Itxa Anasazi Kiowah Indian Nation, New Bern, 1969—; v.p. Ministerial Alliance of New Bern, 1985-86; mem. minister Interdenominational Evangelism Team, New Bern, 1987-88. Bd. dirs. Human Rights Assn. Am. Minorities, Chgo., 1989—; mem. New Bern Voters League, 1987-88; nat. chmn. Am. Indean Def. of the Ams., 1964-88, asst. treas., mem. planning com. United Black Communities Assn., Craven County, N.C., 1987-88. Served with U.S. Army, 1956-64. Recipient Clergy Appreciation Honor Craven County, 1984, 85. Mem. NAACP (chmn. lifetime memberships for Craven County), Pan-Am. Indian Assn., Am. Indian Medicine Soc. Republican. Office: Congl Bible Chs Internat PO Box 573 Abilene KS 67410

WEBBER, ROBERT EUGENE, theology educator; b. Stouchburg, Pa., Nov. 27, 1933; s. Chester R. and Harriet B. (Russell) W.; m. Dawn McCollum, June 21, 1964 (div. Apr. 1977); children: John, Alexandra, Stephanie; m. Joanne Lindsell, May 4, 1978. BA, Bob Jones U., 1956; BD, Reformed Episcopal Sem., Phila., 1959; ThM, Covenant Theol. Sem., St. Louis, 1960; ThD, Concordia Theol. Sem., St. Louis, 1968. Prof. Wheaton (Ill.) Coll.; founder, pres. Inst. Worship Studies, 1991. Author: Common Roots, 1978, The Secular Saint, 1980, The Moral Majority, 1980, Worship Old and New, 1982, The Church in the World, 1985, The Majestic Tapestry, 1985, The Book of Family Prayer, 1985, Celebrating Our Faith, 1986, People of the Truth, 1988, Evangelicals on the Canterbury Trail, 1989, What Christians Believe, 1990, Worship Is a Verb, 1991, Signs of Wonder, 1991. Mem. N.Am. Acad. Liturgy. Episcopalian. Home: 219 W Franklin Wheaton IL 60187 Office: Wheaton Coll 500 College Wheaton IL 60187

WEBBER, WILLIAM DIDERICHSEN, clergyman; b. St. Charles, Ill., July 1, 1930; s. Leroy Dewey and Freda Franklina (Diderichsen) W.; m. Marilynn Joyce Carlson, June 15, 1952; children: Sharon Linnea Webber Scott, Stephen William. BA with honors, Wheaton (Ill.) Coll., 1952; MDiv, No. Bapt. Theol. Sem., 1955; D Ministry, Midwestern Theol. Sem., 1975. Ordained to ministry Am. Bapt. Chs., 1955. Sr. pastor First Bapt. Ch., Park Forest, Ill., 1960-66, University Heights Bapt. Ch., Springfield, Mo., 1966-77, Seattle First Bapt. Ch., 1977-79, First Bapt. Ch., Stockton, Calif., 1979-86; adminstr. Mt. Rubidoux Manor Retirement Community, Riverside, Calif., 1986—; pres. Am. Bapt. Chs. Ill. and Mo., 1974-75; exec. com. Am. Bapt. Chs. U.S.A., Valley Forge, Pa., 1980-86, Bapt. Internat. Ministries, Valley Forge, 1980-86; bd. dirs. Am. Bapt. Chs. of Pacific S.W. Calif., Hawaii, Ariz., 1989-90. Author plays: Is It I, Lord, 1987, Robrt Rackes, Isaac Bachus. Mem. Downtown Adv. Com., Riverside, 1990—. Named Pastor of Yr., Coun. Am. Bapt. Men, Chgo., 1960. Mem. Am. Assn. Homes for the Aging, Am. Bapt. Homes and Hosps., Calif. Assn. Homes for the Aging. Home: 275 Celeste Dr Riverside CA 92507 Office: Mt Rubidoux Manor 3993 10th St Riverside CA 92501

WEBB-MITCHELL, BRETT PARKER, minister, educator; b. Bklyn., July 1, 1955; s. Donald Porter and Elizabeth Wilson (Ferguson) Mitchell; m. Pamela Jane Webb, Dec. 31, 1978; 1 child, Adrianne Dawn. B in Music Therapy, U. Kans., 1978; MDiv, Princeton Sem., 1983; ThM, Harvard U., 1985; PhD, U. N.C., Chapel Hill, 1988. Ordained to ministry Presbyn. Ch., 1983. Asst. pastor 1st Presbyn. Ch. of East Boston, 1983-85; religion educator Community Ch., Chapel Hill, 1988; youth leader Westminster Presbyn. Ch., Durham, N.C., 1988-89; cons. on religious life Devereux Hosp., Melbourne, Fla., 1990-91, dir. of religious life, 1991—; asst. prof. Whitworth Coll., Spokane, Wash., 1989-91; bd. dirs. L'Arche Spokane; rep. Nat. Coun.chs. Christ Task Force on Devel. Disabilities, N.Y.C., 1983-87; book reviewer The New Oxford Rev., Berkeley, Calif., 1990—. Contbr. articles to profl. jours. Min. Nightwalk Ministry in Spokane, 1990-91; bd. dirs. Covenant Ctr., Western Carolina Ctr., Morganton, N.C., 1987-88. Grantee Valley Community Presbyn. Ch., 1986, World Coun. Chs., 1988. Mem. Am. Assn. Mental Retardation, Am. Ednl. Studies Assn., Assn. Profs. and Researchers in Religious Edn., Religious Edn. Assn., Phi Kappa Phi, Pi Kappa Lambda. Office: Devereux Hosp and Children's Ctr 8000 Devereux Dr Melbourne FL 32940

WEBER, DONALD A., rabbi; b. Jamaica, N.Y., June 13, 1953; s. Sol B. and Naomi Plapinger (Sills) W.; m. Shira Stern, Mar. 6, 1983; children: Noah, Ariel, Eytan. BA, Brandeis U., 1975; MA, Hebrew Union Coll., 1980. Ordained rabbi, 1981. Rabbi Temple Beth David, Commack, N.Y., 1981-84, Temple Rodeph Torah of Western Monmouth, Marlboro, N.J., 1984—. Mem. EMT team Morganville (N.J.) 1st Aid and Rescue Squad, 1985—, capt., 1991—; speaker N.J. Religious Coalition for Abortion Rights, 1987—. Mem. Cen. Conf. Am. Rabbis (chmn. com. on computers 1988—, mem. com. on ch. and state 1986-88), N.J. Assn. Reform Rabbis (sec. 1989—), Shore Area Bd. Rabbis. Democrat. Office: Temple Rodeph Torah of Western Monmouth PO Box 125 Mohawk Dr Marlboro NJ 07746 *My rabbi taught me to hold two goals for my rabbinate: to comfort the disturbed and to disturb the comfortable.*

WEBER, DOUGLAS D., rabbi; b. N.Y.C., Feb. 26, 1954; s. Stanley L. and Renee (Harrison) W.; m. Jessica Brodsky, Nov. 22, 1975; children: Zachariah, Taliah, Eliezer. BA, SUNY, Albany, 1976; MA in Hebrew Lit., Hebrew Union Coll.-Jewish Inst. Religion, N.Y.C., Jerusalem, 1980. Ordained rabbi, 1982; cert. pastoral psychologist. Rabbi Beth El Congregation, Harrisonburg, Va., 1982-84, Temple B'nai Abraham, Elyria, Ohio, 1984-91, Temple Shalom, Auburn, Maine, 1991—; regional coord. Rabbinic Network for Ethiopian Jews, Pasadena, Calif., 1986—; mem. exec. bd. Greater Cleve. Bd. Rabbis, 1989-91; Jewish chaplain Grafton (Ohio) Correctional Inst., 1989-91. Author: Jewish Baby Handbook, 1990; contbr. articles to profl. jours. Bd. dirs. Family Planning, Lorain County, Ohio, 1984-90; pres. Family Svc. Assn., Lorain County, 1990-91. Recipient Svc. award United Way, 1988, Family Svc. Assn., 1989. Mem. Cen. Conf. Am. Rabbis. Democrat. Home: 78 Houghton St Auburn ME 04210 Office: Temple Shalom 74 Bradman St Auburn ME 04210

WEBER, GARY RICHARD, minister; b. Carbondale, Ill., Sept. 6, 1950; s. Leslie Richard and Donna Marie (Gibson) W.; m. Valerie Jo Wheeler, Mar. 15, 1973 (div. June 1978); m. Elizabeth Love Smith, Aug. 4, 1979; children: Katherine Marie, Scott Gordon. BS in Secondary Edn., Russian, So. Ill. U., 1972; MDiv, Eden Theol. Sem., Webster Groves, Mo., 1975. Ordained minister in United Ch. of Christ, 1975; cert. tchr. Minister Bethany United Ch. of Christ, Tioga, Ill., 1972-81, Parkview Ch. United Ch. of Christ, Peoria, Ill., 1981—; chmn. assn. coun. cen. assn. Ill. Conf. United Ch. of Christ, 1986, chmn. stewardship com. cen. assn., 1981. Mem. editorial bd. Referee mag. Mem. Cornstock Theatre, Peoria; mem., chmn. Peoria Area Friends of Internat. Students, Bradley U. Mem. Nat. Assn. Sports Officials, Ill. High Sch. Assn., Nat. Fedn. Interscholastic Officials Assn. Office: Parkview Ch United Ch of Christ 2221 N Gale Ave Peoria IL 61604

WEBER, JAMES MITCHELL, missionary, religious organization administrator, photographer; b. Newark, Mar. 30, 1927; s. Harry J. and Barbara Keith (Mitchell) W.; m. Dorothy F. Tyler, June 15, 1948; children: James N., Barbara Burrage, Deborah Millard, Kathy Daumer. BA in Sociology, Rockmont Coll., 1951; postgrad., Denver Sem., 1951-52. Ordained to ministry Conservative Bapt. Assn. Am., 1951. Pastor 1st Bapt. Ch., Elizabeth, Colo., 1949-52; missionary, ch. planter Conservative Bapt. Fgn. Mission, Japan, 1952-78; conf. speaker Ministering in Missions, Ft. Collins, Colo., 1979-91; dir. mission Christian Chiropractic Assn., Ft. Collins, 1991—; developer, dir. Kinshuko Bible Camp, Iwate Ken, Japan, 1965-78; organizer Bapt. Chs., Japan, 1955-78; owner, photographer Weber Photo Prodns., Ft. Collins, 1980-91. Author: Let's Quit Kidding Ourselves About Missions, 1979. With USN, 1944-46. Mem. Wilderness Ranch Conf. Assn. (chmn. 1989-91), Estes Park C. of C. Republican. Office: Ministering in Missions PO Box 1929 Fort Collins CO 80522 *He who plans for the future and ignores eternity will be wise for a moment and a fool forever. (Amon.).*

WEBER, JAMES ROBERT, minister; b. Brownwood, Tex., Sept. 10, 1961; s. Robert Donald Weber and Patricia Anne (Brashear) Gill; m. Sheri Lynn Turner, May 27, 1983; children: Caleb Dean, Logan Royce, Kenneth Robert. Student, Hardin-Simmons U., 1987-90, Luther Rice Sem., Atlanta, 1991. Lic. to ministry So. Bapt. Conv., 1987, ordained, 1989. Pastor 1st Bapt. Ch., Trent, Tex., 1989-91, Lemmon (S.D.) Bapt. Ch., 1989—, Hettinger (N.D.) Bapt. Ch., 1989—; mem. exec. bd. Sweetwater (Tex.) Bapt. Assn., 1989-91, nominating com., 1991; assoc. dir. Vacation Bible Sch., mem. exec. bd. Western N.D. Bapt. Assn., Bismarck, 1991—. Vol. Selected Polit. Candidates and Issues orgn., 1970-80. Mem. Hettinger Ministerial Assn. (treas. 1991—), Ministerial Group of Harding-Simmons U. Avocations: reading. Home: 104 N 4th St PO Box 1230 Hettinger ND 58639 Office: Hettinger Bapt Ch S 8th St and S 4th Ave Hettinger ND 58639

WEBER, KAREN JEANNE, ministry administrator; b. Englewood, N.J., Sept. 24, 1960; d. Richard Remmel and Joanne Frances (McHenry) Rutter; m. Mark Wesley Weber, July 5, 1986. BA, U. Pacific, 1982; MEd, Boston Coll., 1983. Cert. elem. tchr., early childhood/spl. edn. tchr. Dir. early childhood edn. King's Schs., CRISTA Ministries, Seattle, 1986—; endorsed trainer High/Scope Ednl. Rsch. Found., Ypsilanti, Mich., 1989—; pvt. cons. Mem. Nat. Assn. Edn. Young Children, Western Washington Christian Childcare Assn. (pres. bd. dirs. 1988—), High/Scope Registry, Kappa Alpha Theta. Republican. Office: Kings Early Childhood Edn CRISTA Ministries 19303 Fremont Ave N Seattle WA 98133 *Christ calls us to excellence in all things. For those in the growing field of childcare, that means providing the Very Best quality care for the little ones entrusted to us. Every child deserves nothing less than an environment of love, security, developmentally appropriate activities—to help them become all God intended them to be.*

WEBER, SISTER MARY AQUINAS, nun, academic administrator; b. Kingsley, Mich., May 2, 1923; d. Jacob John and Anna Helka (Zenner) W. MA, U. Mich., 1974. Cert. tchr., Mich.; joined Dominical Sisters, 1943. Tchr. St. Stephen Elem. Sch., Grand Rapids, Mich., 1947-55; prin. St. Mary Sch., New Salem, Mich., 1955-56, St. Boniface Sch., Bay City, Mich., 1956-60, St. Alfred Sch., Taylor, Mich., 1957-63; directress Marywood Ho. of Studies, Grand Rapids, 1963-66; prioress Marywood Dominican Sisters, Grand Rapids, 1966-72; dir. neighborhood project Aquinas Coll., Grand Rapids, 1974-76, chancellor, trustee, trustee, 1966—; treas. Marywood Dominican Sisters. Bd. dirs. YMCA, Grand Rapids, 1984—, St. John's Home, Grand Rapids, 1985—, Gleanders, Grand Rapids, 1986—, Porter Hills Presbyn. Retirement Village, 1990. Recipient Outstanding Svc. award Aquinas Coll. Alumni Assn., 1977, award of yr. U. Notre Dame, 1990. Mem. Assn. Governing Bds. Colls. and Univs. (Disting. Svc. in trusteeship award 1985). Avocations: reading, aerobics, cooking, walking. Office: Aquinas Coll 1607 Robinson Rd SE Grand Rapids MI 49506

WEBER, ROBERT DONALD, minister, psychotherapist; b. Apache, Okla., June 12, 1935; s. Henry G. and Tressa Arlyn (Windsor) W.; m. Patricia Anne Brashear, Apr. 9, 1957; children: Patricia Gayle, James Robert, Paul Kevin. BS, Howard Payne U., 1966; ThM, New Orleans Bapt. Theol. Sem., 1969. Ordained to ministry So. Baptist Ch., 1961; pastor Trinity Bapt. Ch., Oakdale, La., 1969-71, First Bapt. Ch., LeCompte, La., 1971-74, Southside Bapt. Ch., Carthage, Tex., 1974-75; chaplain Lufkin State Sch. (Tex.), 1975-77; pastor First Bapt. Ch., Anthony, N.M., 1977-78; pastoral psychotherapist, adminstrv. asst. Pastoral Care and Counseling Ctr., Abilene, Tex., 1981—; pastor Rochelle Bapt. Ch., 1982—; assoc. pastor of counseling Harris Ave. Bapt. Ch., San Angelo, Tex., 1982—. Bd. dirs. Mothers Against Drunk Drivers, 1982—. Served with USAF, 1954-60. Mem. Am. Assn. for Marriage and Family Therapy (clin.), Am. Assn. Pastoral Counselors, Tex. Bapt. Family Minister Assn. Lodges: Rotary. Home: 2102 Westview Abilene TX 79603 Office: 751 Hickory St Abilene TX 79601

WEBER, STEPHEN CLARK, minister; b. Kansas City, Mo., Oct. 14, 1954; s. Eugene Clark and Georgia Mae (Steincross) W.; m. R. Brooksyne Sherril, May 8, 1976. BA in Bible, Cen. Bible Coll., Springfield, Mo., 1977. Ordained to ministry Assemblies of God, 1979. Pastor Sunnyvale Assembly of God Ch., Fair Grove, Mo., 1976-77, AGAPE' Assembly of God Ch., St. Marys, Pa., 1977—; mem. fgn. missions com. Pa.-Del. dist. Assemblies of God, Camp Hill, Pa., 1981—, mem. western screening com., 1989—. Chaplain CAP, St. Marys, 1989—. Mem. Kiwanis (treas. St. Marys 1988—). Home: 643 Center St Saint Marys PA 15857 Office: AGAPE' Assembly of God Ch 1000 Earth Rd Saint Marys PA 15857

WEBER, THOMAS SCOTT, clergyman; b. Mechanicsburg, Pa., Jan. 15, 1955; s. Richard Henry and Patricia Miller (Spaid) W.; m. Karen Ruby Cook, May 7, 1977; children: Jeremy Scott, Jami Leigh. B Religious Edn., Bapt. Bible Coll., 1979; postgrad., Bethany Coll., 1981, Trinity Sem., 1990—. Ordained to ministry Bapt. Ch., 1979. Pastor, tchr. Calvary Bapt. Ch., Richland, N.Y., 1979-81, Phoenix (N.Y.) Bapt. Ch., 1981-85, Community Bapt. Ch., Carlisle, Pa., 1985—; pres. Life Saver Ministry Pa., Carlisle, 1990—; mem. adv. coun. Camp of Nations, South Gibson, Pa., 1982—. Mem. Demolay (jr. counselor 1972-73). Home: 251 Old Stonehouse Rd Mechanicsburg PA 17055

WEBER, TIMOTHY PRESTON, seminary educator, minister; b. L.A., May 25, 1947; s. Jack Brown and Ruth Marie (McNutt) W.; m. Linda Lee Gryde, July 20, 1968; children: Jonathan Mark, Michael David. BA, UCLA, 1969; MDiv, Fuller Theol. Sem., 1972; MA, U. Chgo., 1974, PhD, 1976. Ordained to ministry Bapt. Ch., 1976. Asst. prof. church history Denver Sem., 1976-81, assoc. prof. church history, 1981-87; pastor Heritage Bapt. Ch., Aurora, Colo., 1983-87; prof. Denver Sem., 1987—; bd. dirs. Evang. Concern, Denver, 1980-83; pres. bd. dirs. Christian Conciliation Svc., Denver, 1982-85; cons. Inst. Ch. Devel., Denver, 1987—. Author: Living in the Shadow of the Second Coming, 1979 (One of the Best Evang. Books of 1979, Eternity Mag.); author: (with others) Dictionary of Christianity in America, 1990, Encyclopedia of Religion, 1987, Evangelical Dictionary of Theology, 1984. Mem. Am. Soc. Ch. History, Conf. on Faith & History, Am. Bapt. Hist. Soc., Am. Acad. Religion, Am. Hist. Assn. Home: 7498 E Davies Pl Englewood CO 80112 Office: Denver Sem Box 10000 Denver CO 80210

WEBERMAN, PHINEAS (PINCHAS A. WEBERMAN), rabbi; b. N.Y.C., July 22, 1930; s. Ben Zion and Julia (Horowitz) W.; m. Gladys Green, Sept. 3, 1952; children: Sara, Eli, David, Shaya, Brachah, Shoshanah, Miriam, Zalman, Hannah, Shlomo, Brendy, Ben Zion, Beth, Israel, Judith. Grad., Nesevos Olum Sem., Bklyn., 1952. Ordained rabbi, 1952. Rabbi Congregation Anshe Sfard, Arverene, N.Y., 1957-60, Yeshiva B Eer Shmuel, Bklyn., 1957-60, Ohev Shalom Congregation, Miami Beach, Fla., 1960—; sec. Orthodox Rabbinical Coun. Fla., 1975-82, pres., 1982—; chaplain Talmudic U., Miami Beach, 1972—, Miami Beach Police Dept., 1980—; med. examiner Dade County, Fla., 1980—. Author: Rabbi's Message, 1975. Chmn. Dade County Right to Life, 1969-73; mem. adv. bd. Fla. State Right to Life, 1973—; vice chmn. Human Rels. Com., Miami Beach, 1985—. Recipient dedication and achievement awards Jewish Fedn., 1982-83, 86, Moral Leadership award Fla. Conservative Union, 1983, award Inst. Criminal Justice, South Fla., 1984, Outstanding Svc. award Am. Legion, 1987. Mem. Internat. Conf. Police Chaplains. Office: Ohev Shalom Congregation 7055 Bonita Dr Miami Beach FL 33141

WEBORG, JOHN, theology educator; b. Omaha, Jan. 20, 1937; s. Reuben Leonard and Pearl Teresa (Olson) W.; m. Lois Elaine Johnson, June 7, 1958; children: Clement, Catherine. BA, U. Nebr., 1958; BD, North Park Theol. Sem., Chgo., 1961; ThM, Princeton U., 1970; PhD, Northwestern U., 1983. Ordained to ministry Evang. Covenant Ch., 1961. Pastor 1st Covenant Ch., Peoria, Ill., 1961-66, Springhouse (Pa.) Covenant Ch., 1966-70, Evang. Covenant Ch., Princeton, Ill., 1970-75; assoc. prof. theology North Park Theol. Sem., 1975-86, prof., 1986—; exch. prof. Teologiska Seminariet, Lidingo, Sweden; bd. dirs. Inst. for Spiritual Companionship, Chgo., 1989—; bd. cons. editors Ency. Worship Resources. Author: Where Is It Written, 1979, Alive In Christ, Alert to Life, 1985; columnist The Covenant Companion; contbr. numerous articles to religious jours. Mem. Am. Soc. for Ch. History, Am. Acad. Religion, Am. Theol. Soc. (sec.-treas. Midwest sect.).

WEBSTER, BRUCE RONALD, minister; b. Huntsville, Ala., Mar. 7, 1946; m. Roy E. and Eldiva (Patterson) W.; m. Carolyn Upchurch, Apr. 11, 1969 (div. 1987); children: Phillip Jason, Jared Stephen, Shawn Tyson. BA, Internat. Bible Coll., Florence, Ala., 1978. Ordained to ministry Ch. of Christ. Minister Ch. of Christ, Cuba, Mo., 1974-75, Flintville, Tenn., 1976-84, Huntsville, 1984-86, Jefferson, Iowa, 1987—. Co-author: Hansen-Webster Debate, 1976. Adv. bd. Hospice/Respite, Jefferson, 1990—. With U.S. Army, 1966-68. Home: 500 E Park St Jefferson IA 50129 *The true purpose of life is not found in possessions, power, pleasure, popularity, or position; but in obedience to the will of God.*

WEBSTER, GORDON VISSCHER, JR., minister; b. Huntington, N.Y., Oct. 2, 1947; s. Gordon Visscher and Marion Beatrice (French) W.; m. Gloria Marie Farwagi, May 31, 1975; children: David Gordon, Daniel Farwagi, Diana Alexandra. AB, Hamilton Coll., 1969; postgrad., St. Andrews Divinity Sch., 1970-71, McCormick Theol. Sem., 1982-87; MDiv, Union Theol. Sem., 1973. Ordained to ministry Presbyn. Ch. (USA), 1973. Staff assoc. Met. Ch. Bd., Syracuse, N.Y., 1973-75; assoc. pastor 1st Presbyn. Ch., Syracuse, 1975-83; missionary Middle East Coun. of Chs., Limassol, Cyprus, 1983-84; missionary-in-residence Presbyn. Ch. (USA), Stony Point Center, N.Y., 1984-86; interim pastor 1st Presbyn. Ch., Oneida, N.Y., 1988-89, United Presbyn. Ch., Cortland, N.Y., 1989-91; pastor Ogden Presbyn. Ch., Spencerport, N.Y., 1991—; exec. dir. Am. Coalition for Middle East Dialogue, Jamesville, N.Y., 1986-88, bd. dirs., Syracuse, 1989—; mem. coun. Susquehanna Valley Presbytery, Bainbridge, N.Y., 1990-91; mem. peace and justice group Synod of N.E., Syracuse, 1989—; leader workshops on Middle East; moderator Syracuse Middle East Dialogue Group, 1981-83; com. chmn. Presbytery of Utica, 1988-89. Chaplain Internat. Mgmt. Assn., Liverpool, N.Y., 1982-83, Svc. Club-Oneidas Tribe, 1988-89. Grantee George Gund Found., 1987, Presbyn. Women's Opportunity Giving, 1987. Mem. Witherspoon Soc. (steering com. 1974-76), Presbyn. Peace Fellowship (bd. advisors, nat. com. 1972-83). Democrat. Office: Ogden Presbyn Ch 2400 S Union St Spencerport NY 14559 *Can you marry someone from another culture and together still raise children with a similarity of mind? Yes. Unless, of course, you both let your cultural differences distort the love that created your family in the beginning.*

WEBSTER, MICHAEL LEE, academic administrator; b. Fulton, N.Y., Sept. 2, 1949; s. Fred Smith and Ida Josephine (Stewart) W.; m. Donna Eileen Turk, Aug. 16, 1969; children: Andrew Michael, Bethany Sarah. BS, Clarkson U., 1971; MDiv, Trinity Evangelical Div. Sch., 1974, DMin, 1981; student, Skyline Coll., San Bruno, Calif., 1981. Ordained to ministry, 1975. Grad. asst. Trinity Evangelical Divinity Sch., Deerfield, Ill., 1971-74; pastor Koinonia Ch., Potsdam, N.Y., 1974-78; faculty Melodyland Sch. Theology, Anaheim, Calif., 1978; pastor Coastside Christian Ctr., Pacifica, Calif., 1979-82; instr. Elim Bible Inst., Lima, N.Y., 1982-84, acad. dean, 1984-88, pres., 1988—; bd. adminstrn. Elim Fellowship, Lima, 1984—; assoc. staff Mobilized to Serve, Lima, 1982—; mem. NAE Commn. on Higher Edn., Network Christian Ministries; v.p. Crossroads Coun.; speaker in field. Bd. dirs. Ctr. for Theol. Studies, Newport Beach, Calif., 1978-81. Mem. Eta Kappa Nu, Tau Beta Pi. Republican. Avocations: amateur radio, music, electronics, chess, fishing. Home and Office: Elim Bible Inst 7245 College St Lima NY 14485 *We all have the resources to effectively serve our needy world: our value as a human being in the image of God, our destiny as a person in the purposes of God and our woundedness as an individual forming a conduit for the Grace of God.*

WEBSTER, ROY EDWARD, II, clergyman; b. Henderson, Ky., June 26, 1933; s. Roy E. and Mary (Reid) W.; m. Patricia Sleamaker, Oct. 2, 1954; children: Mary Patrice Hancock, Robert Wesley, Roy E. III. BA, Ky. Wesleyan Coll., Owensboro, 1955; MDiv, Presbyn. Sem., Louisville, 1958; DD (hon.), Union Coll., Barbourville, Ky., 1973. Ordained to ministry United Meth. Ch., 1955. Pastor West Broadway United Meth. Ch., Louisville, 1962-65, Jeffersontown United Meth. Ch., Louisville, 1965-74, St. Matthews United Meth. Ch., Louisville, 1974-81, Meml. United Meth. Ch., Elizabethtown, Ky., 1981-89; dist. supt. United Meth. Ch., Louisville, 1989—; mem. Gen. Conf. United Meth. Ch., 1984, 88. Trustee Union Coll., Barbourville, Ky., 1970-78, Ky. United Meth Found., Lexington, 1978-86, Ky. Wesleyan Coll., Owensboro, 1983—. Home: 301 Kinnaird Ln Louisville KY 40243-1220 Office: 1115 S 4th St Louisville KY 40203

WEBSTER, WILLIAM OSCEOLA, JR., minister; b. Plainfield, N.J., July 24, 1955; s. William Osceola and Margaret Mary (Mangione) W.; m. Linda Jean Jones, Feb. 21, 1981; children: Sarah, Rachel, Matthew. AA in Urban Studies, Union Coll., 1977; BA in English, Kean Coll., 1980; MDiv, Pitts. Theol. Seminary, 1984. Cert. counseling pastor Presbyn. Ch., 1981. Vol. in mission Presbyn. Ch., Tuba City, Ariz., 1977-79; asst. hosp. chaplain Presbyn. Univ., Pitts., 1981-84; youth leader 2nd United Presbyn. Ch.,

Wilkinsburg, Pa., 1981-84, asst. pastor, 1984-87; pastor Grace United Presbyn. Ch., Martins Ferry, Ohio, 1987—; founder, pres. Interfaith Com. on Housing, Inc., Pitts., 1985-87; founder./dir. Prisoners Against Drugs, Moundsville, W.Va., 1990—; chmn. Worship Com., Presbytery of the Upper Ohio Valley, 1989—; sec., treas. Martins Ferry Ministerial Assn., 1987-90, pres., 1990—. Author: Strategies for Youth, 1980. Adminstr. Boy Scouts Upper Ohio Valley, Martins Ferry, 1991—; founder, organizer Those Who Wait (organ transplant program), 1983; bd. dirs. Community Devel. Com., Martins Ferry, 1991. Named to Outstanding Young Men of Am., 1980. Mem. Kiwanis (v.p. 1986-87). Home: 21 South 10th St Martins Ferry OH 43935 Office: Grace United Presbyn Ch 7 North 4th St Martins Ferry OH 43935 *I believe that our life's attitude determines our altitude in life. If our attitude is right, then there are no barriers too high to stop us, no dream too extreme, no goal unobtainable.*

WECKERLY, WILLIAM CLARENCE, minister; b. Butler, Pa., Apr. 9, 1937; s. Albert K. Sr. and Helen Marjorie (Kepple) W.; m. Sheila Faye Saxman, May 26, 1962; children: William S., Eric S., Erin B., Brian T. BS in Edn., Indiana U. of Pa., 1959; MDiv, Pitts. Sem., 1967; D. Ministry, Christian Theol. Sem., 1987. Ordained to ministry Presbyn. Ch. (U.S.A.), 1967; cert. secondary tchr., Pa. Assoc. pastor 1st Presbyn. Ch., Batavia, N.Y., 1967-72; pastor Eastminster Presbyn. Ch., Cin., 1972-76, 1st Presbyn. Ch., Monticello, Ind., 1976-90, Graham (N.C.) Presbyn. Ch., 1990—; commr. Presbytery of Salem, Clemmons, N.C., 1990—. Author: Conflict in the Church: A Case Study, 1987. Chaplain Graham Police Dept., 1990. Recipient Civic Svc. award Batavia City Coun., 1972, Brotherhood award NCCJ, 1976. Mem. Graham Ministerial Alliance (pres. 1991), Alban Inst., Alamance Ministerial Assn., Rotary, United Comml. Travelers. Home: 1045 Camelot Ln Graham NM 27253 Office: Graham Presbyn Ch 216 W Harden St Graham NC 27253

WECKMAN, GEORGE A., philosophy educator; b. Phila., Mar. 20, 1939; s. George A. and Florence Mae (Colebaugh) W. BA, Muhlenberg Coll., 1960; BD, Luth. Sem., Phila., 1963; MA, U. Chgo., 1965, PhD, 1969. Assoc. prof. Ohio U., Athens, 1968—. Musician Salem Luth. Ch., Chgo., 1963-68, Christ Luth. Ch., Athens, 1968—. Mem. Am. Acad. Religion, Ohio Acad. Religion (pres. 1989-90). Home: 19 Park Pl Athens OH 45701 Office: Ohio U Dept Philosophy Gordy Hall Athens OH 45701

WEDDERBURN, ALEXANDER JOHN MACLAGAN, theology educator; b. Edinburgh, Scotland, Apr. 30, 1942; s. Thomas Maclagan and Margaret Marshall (Scott) W.; m. Brigitte Felber, July 17, 1971; children: Fiona, Martin. BA, Oxford U., 1964, MA, 1967; BD, U. Edinburgh, 1967; PhD, Cambridge U., 1971; postgrad., U. Göttingen, Fed. Republic of Germany, 1971-72. Ordained minister, 1975. Tutorial asst. U. St. Andrews, Scotland, 1972-74, lectr., 1974-89; lectr. U. Durham, Eng., 1990-91, sr. lectr., 1991—. Author: Baptism and Resurrection, 1987, The Reasons for Romans, 1988; co-author and editor: Paul and Jesus, 1989; editor New Testament Studies, 1991—; co-editor: The New Testament and Gnosis, 1983; contbr. articles to profl. jours.; dir. Scottish Jour. Theology, 1974-85, cons. editor 1985-76—. Mem. Soc. Biblical Lit., Studiorum Novi Testamenti Societas, Royal Soc. for the Protection of Birds. Avocations: walking, music, ornithology. Home: 30 Baliol Sq, Merryoaks, Durham DH1 3QH, England Office: U Durham Dept Theology, Abbey House, Palace Green, Durham DH1 3RS, England

WEDEKING, RALPH WEINBERG, minister, educator; b. Waverly, Iowa, Feb. 5, 1934; s. Martin and Edna (Weinberg) W. BA, U. No. Iowa, 1956, MA, 1971; MDiv, Eden Sem., 1959. Ordained to ministry United Ch. of Christ, 1959. Pastor St. Paul United Ch. of Christ, Washington, Iowa, 1959-62, Peace United Ch. of Christ, Waverly, 1962-66; assoc. pastor First Pleasant Valley Ch., Clarksville, Iowa, 1966-67; interim pastor St. Paul United Ch. Christ, Denver, Iowa, 1968-69; pastor 1st Congl. Ch., United Ch. Crist, Nashua, Iowa, 1969-89; interim pastor Little Brown Ch. in Vale, Nashua, 1969, 77-88, 87-88, 88-89; prof. Iowa Cen. Community Coll., Fort Dodge, Iowa, 1971—, speakers bur., 1971—, mem. faculty rels. com., 1978—, developer courses in marriage and family relationships and religion in culture, 1981, 78; part-time instr. sociology Wartburg Coll., Waverly, 1967-71. Organizer, dir. Waverly Sr. Citizens, 1966-71; active Fort Dodge Pre-Sch., 1974-77, Fort Dodge United Fund Com., 1976-78. Mem. Iowa Sociol. Soc. Democrat. Home: 606 S 14th St Fort Dodge IA 50501 Office: Iowa Cen Community Coll 330 Ave M Fort Dodge IA 50501 *By God's Grace I have come this far, by God's Grace I look to whatever the future holds. To be loved and to love are God's great gifts. In this is peace beyond human understanding.*

WEDELL, ROGER WILLIAM, campus minister; b. Burbank, Calif., Mar. 15, 1948; s. Jack A. and Rosetta Maxine (Davis) W. BA, Tex. Christian U., 1970; MDiv, Brite Div. Sch., 1974; PhD, Grad. Theol. Union, 1982. Assoc. minister First Christian Ch., Longview, Tex., 1974-76; adminstrv. asst. Thanks-Giving Sq. Found., Dallas, 1980-82, exec. dir., 1982-86; dean Sch. Theology for the Laity, Dallas, 1986-89; dir. Arlington (Tex.) Ministries in Higher Edn., 1989—; prof. religion studies Tex. Christian U., Ft. Worth, 1983—; mem. gen. bd. Christian Ch., U.S., Can., 1972-76; mem. awards jury Art Competition for Gen. Synod of U.C.C., Fort Worth, 1989; mem. exec. com., bd. dirs. Greater Dallas Community of Chs., Dallas, 1989. Contbr. articles to profl. jours. Founding trustee Children's Assn. of Gregg County, Longview, Tex., 1975-76. Mem. Am. Acad. Religion, Soc. for the Arts, Religion and Contemporary Culture, Arlington Ministerial Assn. (1st v.p. 1990). Democrat. Office: Arlington Ministries 304 S College St #1 Arlington TX 76010

WEEKES, MICHAEL MANNING, clergyman, lawyer; b. Leon, Iowa, July 12, 1938; s. Pearl Wilson and Marie Arvilla (Manning) W. B.S., Drake U., 1960, J.D., 1963; M.Div., Fuller Theol. Sem., 1979. Bar: Iowa 1963, Calif. 1964, U.S. Dist. Ct. 1964, U.S. Ct. Appeals 1966, U.S. Supreme Ct. 1973. Practiced law Los Angeles, 1964-76; assoc. Dillavou & Cox (later Dillavou, Cox, Castle & Nicholson), Los Angeles, 1964-68, Cox, Castle & Nicholson, Los Angeles, 1968-71; ptnr. Cox, Castle, Nicholson & Weekes, Los Angeles, 1972-76; asst. pastor Immanuel Presbyn. Ch., Los Angeles, 1980-86; pastor Culver City United Presbyn. Ch., Calif., 1986—; lectr. Christian Legal Soc., 1977-78, Oral Roberts U., 1978. Author: Manual for Application of Uniform Commercial Code for Surety Industry, 1964; co-editor: Words to Live By, 1969, Bible Riches, 1970; author: Christian Mediation, 1977. Bd. dirs. Hollywood Presbyn. Med. Center, Los Angeles, 1976—, Wilshire Community Involvement Assn., 1980-86, v.p. goals and objectives, 1985-86. Recipient award Los Angeles Human Relations Commn., 1983. Mem. Calif. Bar Assn., Iowa Bar Assn., Beta Gamma Sigma, Delta Theta Phi. Presbyterian (chmn. evangelism com. Presbytery of the Pacific 1983-85). Lodge: Rotary. Home: 10119 Lakeview Dr Rancho Mirage CA 92270-1424 Office: 11269 Washington Blvd Culver City CA 90230 *Success is a word of measurement. The true criterion is how we have been able to serve God and man, according to God's will. I have found that, whatever be the field of endeavor, no power to achieve can truly be effective, apart from Christ and the Holy Spirit.*

WEEKLEY, DEWITT TALMAGE, lay worker, farmer; b. Blackwater, Mo., Sept. 24, 1911; s. Thomas Alexander and Mary Jane (Hill) W.; m. Eunice Lee Mollet, Mar. 28, 1938; 1 child, Douglas David. Lay leader Ch. of Christ, Blackwater, 1928-64, elder, 1964—; farmer and farm owner, Blackwater, 1930—. Chmn. County Extension Coun., Boonville, Mo., 1944-54; mem. County Sch. Bd., Boonville, 1948-57; bd. dirs. Mo. Farmers Assn., Colombia, Mo., 1949-79; candidate for senator State of Mo., 1960. Republican. Home: Rte 1 Box 64 Blackwater MO 65322

WEEKS, HOWARD BENJAMIN, retired publisher; b. Tempe, Ariz., Jan. 6, 1924; s. Jesse Floyd and Edith Fannie (Mattison) W.; m. Dorothy Mae White, Dec. 12, 1946; children—John Howard, Douglas Alan, Carolyn Marie, Donna Louise. B.A., Loma Linda U., 1946; M.A., Am. U., 1963; Ph.D., Michigan State U., 1966. Journalist with Beverly Hills Bulletin, Calif., 1946-50; dir. pub. relations Okla. Conf. Seventh-Day Adventists, Oklahoma City, 1948-50, bur. dir. Gen. Conf., Washington, D.C., 1950-62; v.p. pub. relations and devel. Loma Linda Univ., Calif., 1964-71; pres. Woodbridge Press Pub. Co., Santa Barbara, Calif., 1971-86. Author: Adventist Evangelism in the Twentieth Century, 1969; Breakthrough: A Public Relations Guidebook for Your Church, 1983. Mem. Pub. Relations Soc. Am. (accredited, nat. grievance bd. mem. 1968-71), AAUP. *It may be true that one's spirit will, in a way that only faith knows, endure forever, but it is certain that the effect of one's present life will do so—in its influence on the lives of others down the chain of human generations. It is possible, therefore, that what we think, say or do may be both presently and eternally beneficial.*

WEEKS, JOHN STAFFORD, religious studies educator; b. Hanover, Pa., Sept. 27, 1920; s. John Barnhart and Erma Anna Jane (Leese) W.; m. Winifred Ann English, June 21, 1946; children: Pamela, Cynthia, Wendy. BA, Juniata Coll., Huntingdon, Pa., 1942; MDiv, United Theol. Sem., Dayton, Ohio, 1945; PhD, U. Chgo., 1962. Pastor Fayetteville (Pa.) Evang. United Brethren Ch., 1944-48, Norwood Park Evang. United Brethren Ch., Chgo., 1948-53; prof. religion and sociology Huron (S.D.) Coll., 1953-59; prof. religious studies Monmouth (Ill.) Coll., 1959-90, dean, 1974-78. Sec. Monmouth (Ill.) Sch. Bd., 1962-74. Ford postdoctoral fellow Asian studies, U. Wis., 1965; Ford Found. travel grantee, Tokyo, 1967. Mem. Am. Acad. Religious Studies, Rotary. Republican. Presbyterian. Avocations: music, swimming, travel, reading. Home: 114 S 10th St Monmouth IL 61462 Office: Monmouth Coll Monmouth IL 61462

WEEKS, THOMAS WESLEY, bishop; b. Boston, July 14, 1945; s. Thomas J. and Susan Weeks; m. Leona Brown, Sept. 3, 1966; children: Thomas Wesley Jr., Abdullah Azeez. B in Applied Sci., Boston U., 1969, M in Urban Affairs, 1974; MDiv, Luther Rice Sem., Jacksonville, Fla., 1990; DD (hon.), Aenon Bible Coll., 1984. Ordained to ministry Pentecostal Assemblies of the World, Inc. Asst. site mgr. rsch. ops. Rand Corp., South Bend, Ind., 1974-76, site mgr., 1974-80; pastor Greater Bethel Apostolic Temple, Wilmington, Del., 1980—; pastor, bishop Pentecostal Assemblies of the World, Inc., 1987—; pres. Aenon Bible Coll., Indpls., 1984—; pres. Mass. State Young People, 1960-67, Internat. Pentecostal Young People's Union, 1976-82, Interdenominational Mins. Coun. Del., 1986—; mem. com. Planning for Internat. Ministerial Conf., 1990—. Author: Pagan Holidays, 1983; editor Reachout jour. and newsletter. With USAR, 1963-71. Recipient Outstanding award Internat. Pentecostal Young People's Union, 1982, Betterment of Community award City of Indpls., 1982, commendations U.S. Senate, State of Del., Wilmington City Coun., 1984-87. Mem. NAACP (Disting. Svc. award Del. chpt. 1989). Home: PO Box 527 Wilmington DE 19899 Office: Greater Bethel Apostolic Temple 2900 N Van Buren St Wilmington DE 19802

WEEMS, MARION LEE, minister; b. Memphis, Nov. 25, 1948; s. John Wylie and Thelma Virginia (Robertson) W.; m. Karen Ann Beckloff, Aug. 4, 1972; children: Cari, Nathan. BA, Southwestern Okla. U., 1970; MRE, Southwestern Sem., Ft. Worth, 1974; D Ministry, Midwestern Sem., Kansas City, Mo., 1986. Ordained to ministry So. Bapt. Conv., 1978. Missionary FMB, Vietnam, 1970-72; min. edn. and youth Stevens Meml. Bapt. Ch., Newport News, Va., 1974-78, Deer Park Bapt. Ch., Newport News, 1978-80; assoc. min. edn. Englewood Bapt. Ch., Kansas City, Mo., 1980-86; assoc. pastor/edn. Emmanuel Bapt. Ch., Alexandria, La., 1986—; trustee Bapt. Mission Ctr., Pineville, La., 1989—; treas. Shepherd Ministries Inc., Alexandria, 1987-88, pres., 1988-91; v.p. Friendship House, 1991—. Fellow Nat. Assn. Ch. Bus. Adminstrs., So. Bapt. Ch. Bus.Adminstrs. Home: 705 Pearce Rd Pineville LA 71360 Office: Emmanuel Bapt Ch 430 Jackson Alexandria LA 71301 *Called to follow and chosen to share, go prepared among the people, go out in power and serve.*

WEEMS, RODGER CARY, minister; b. Temple, Tex., July 22, 1952; s. James Barton and Ruby Lee (Wright) W.; m. Jaki Lorraine Campbell, Sept. 29, 1973; children: Scott Campbell, Jay Tyler, Leigh Ann. AA, Temple Jr. Coll., 1972; BA in English/speech, U. Mary Hardin-Baylor, Belton, Tex., 1974; MS in Bible, Abilene Christian U., 1976. Minister Heidenheimer (Tex.) Ch. of Christ, 1968-72; assoc. minister Belton Ch. of Christ, 1972-74, Grape St. Ch. of Christ, Abilene, 1974-75; grad. teaching asst. Abilene Christian U., 1974-75; minister Cen. Ch. of Christ, Victoria, Tex., 1975-80, Jefferson St. Ch. of Christ, Hobbs, N.Mex., 1980-86; speech and English tchr. Killeen (Tex.) Ind. Sch. Dist., 1986-91; min. Troy (Tex.) Ch. of Christ, 1986-91, Graham Street Ch. of Christ, Stephenville, Tex., 1991—; chaplain Lea Reg. Hosp., Hobbs, N.Mex., 1980-82, Harris Hosp., Stephenville, 1991—; curriculum writer Killeen Ind. Sch. Dist., 1989; mem. devel. bd. Sherwood and Myrtie Foster Home for Children, Stephenville, 1991—; lectr. in field. Mem. at-risk student com. Killeen Ind. Sch. Dist., 1988, devel. bd. Sherwood and Myrtie Foster Home for Children, Stephenville, 1991—. Assn. Tex. Profl. Educators scholar, 1988. Mem. Assn. Tex. Profl. Educators, Lions. Home: 103 Lee Trevino Stephenville TX 76401 Office: Graham Street Ch of Christ 312 N Graham St Stephenville TX 76401

WEENER, JAY R., religion educator; b. Holland, Mich., Dec. 6, 1927; s. Frank and Martha (Wagenveld) W.; m. Jean M. Wiersma, July 1, 1949; children: Donald, James, Mary, Susan. BA, Hope Coll., 1949; MDiv, Western Theol. Sem., 1952; DD (hon.), Hope Coll., 1978. Ordained to ministry Ref. Ch., 1952. Pastor Beaverdam Reformed Ch., Zeeland, Mich., 1952-55, 3d Reformed Ch., Grand Rapids, Mich., 1955-60, Parkview Reformed Ch., Santa Ana, Calif., 1960-66, 2d Reformed Ch., Kalamazoo, Mich., 1967-84, 5th Reformed Ch., Grand Rapids, 1984-89; prof. preaching Western Theol. Sem., Holland, 1989—; trustee Hope Coll., Holland, 1981-91; exec. com. Gen. Program Coun. Reformed Ch. in Am., 1971-77; minister Night Ministry, Kalamazoo, 1967-68; bd. dirs. Released Time Christian Edn. Program, Santa Ana, 1962-66, Grand Rapids Area Ctr. for Ecumenism, Grand Rapids, 1985-86. Editorial coun. The Ch. Herald, Grand Rapids, 1964-69; contbr. articles to publs. Chpt. chmn. ARC, Kalamazoo, 1983-84. Mem. Acad. of Homiletics. Home: 1230 Beach Dr Holland MI 49423 Office: Western Theol Sem 86 E 12th St Holland MI 49423

WEESE, AMY JOANNE, former Christian radio worker; b. Kansas City, Mo., Oct. 8, 1968; d. Rex Eugene and Susan Darlene (Thomas) W. BA in Communication, William Jewell Coll., 1990. Bd. operator Sta. KNHN Radio, Kansas City, 1989-91. Campaign worker Mary Margaret Rafferty, Liberty, Mo., 1989; participant Habitat for Humanity, Liberty, 1988-89. Named Assoc. of Yr., Sta. KWJC Radio, 1989. Mem. Alpha Delta Pi. Republican. Baptist.

WEEZORAK, DENNIS ROBERT, priest; b. Punxsutawney, Pa., Mar. 16, 1953; s. Robert John and Pauline (Potochick) W. BS, Pa. State U., 1975; MDiv., St. John's Sem., Boston, 1986; Cert. Philos. Competency, Wadhams Hall Sem., Ogdensburg, N.Y., 1982. Ordained priest Roman Cath. Ch., 1986. Mgr. food services Clarkson U. Saga Corp., Potsdam, N.Y., 1975-76, Bloomsburg (Pa.) State U. Saga Corp., 1976-77; dir. food services Trinity Pawling Sch. Saga Corp., N.Y., 1977-78; mgr. food services Ohio No. U. Saga Corp., Ada, 1978, Cleve. State U. Saga Corp., 1978-79, St. Luke's Hosp Saga Corp., Newburg, N.Y., 1979-81; parochial vicar St. Patrick's Ch., Watertown, N.Y., 1986-89, St. Peter's Ch., Lowville, N.Y., 1989—, St. Mary's Ch., Glenfield, N.Y., 1989—, St. Thomas Ch., Grieg, N.Y., 1989—. Bd. dirs. Jefferson County Youth Bur., Watertown, 1987-88; coordinator ministry to separated and divorced Diocese of Ogdensburg, N.Y. Served to 2d lt. USAF, 1983-86. Fellow N.Am. Forum on Catechumenate; mem. Alpha Kappa Lambda, Sigma Phi Alpha. Roman Catholic. Lodge: KC, Rotary. Avocations: bicycling, photography, travel. Home and Office: St Patrick's Ch 123 S Massey St Watertown NY 13601-3275 Office: St Peter's Ch 5441 Shady Ave Lowville NY 13367-1696

WEGER, JEFFREY KIM, music minister; b. St. Petersburg, Fla., Apr. 15, 1961; s. James Harding and Martina Joyce (Woodworth) W.; m. Jennifer La Von Killian, June 11, 1982; children: Jordan Kyle, Joshua Kirk, Jarrod Keith. B in Music Edn., East Tex. State U., 1984; MRE, Southwestern Bapt. Theol. Sem., 1989. Asst. youth min. Northside Bapt. Ch., Weatherford, Tex., 1980-81; min. of music Highland Terrace Bapt. Ch., Greenville, Tex., 1981—; music evangelist Jaime Mayorga Evangelistic Assn., Spruce Pine, N.C., 1989-90. Mem. Singing Men. of Tex., Hunt Meml. Hosp. Chaplains Assn. Home: 2506 Paul St Greenville TX 75401 Office: Highland Terrace Bapt Ch 3939 Joe Ramsey Blvd Greenville TX 75401 *While the world still fails to acknowledge our Creator, I will never take a breath that I can't thank God for His creation and for loving me enough to send His Son in order that I (and the world) could have eternal life.*

WEGERMANN, RODNEY EDWIN, lay person; b. Cedar Rapids, Iowa, Mar. 18, 1941; s. Edwin Henry Wegermann and Harriet Anne (Stafford) Scheer; m. Martha Ann Kiesz, May 24, 1963 (div. Sept. 1976); m. Peggy Ann Stoehr, Dec. 22, 1984; children: Matthew, Andrew, David. BS in Secondary Edn., N.W. Mo. State Coll., Maryville, 1963; MA, Mich. State U., 1967; postgrad., Midwest Bible Coll., Stanberry, Mo., 1975-76. Cert. secondary tchr., Mo. Deacon Hallelujah House Ministries, St. Louis, 1988—; ref. asst. Olin Libr. Washington U., St. Louis, 1977—. Home: 4900 N Hanley Rd Saint Louis MO 63134

WEGNER, CARL FREDRICK, lay worker, purchasing agent; b. Ft. Lauderdale, Fla., Aug. 28, 1964; s. Edward James and Patsy (Rooney) H. Grad. high sch., Abington, Pa., 1983. Supt. Sunday sch. Abington United Meth. Ch., 1988—, dir. youth group, 1989—, asst. lay leader, 1990—; purchasing agt. Ajax Electric Co., Huntington Valley, Pa., 1990—. Mem. Young Reps. Montgomery County, Pa., 1984-89. With USAR, 1983-89. Home: 776 Tyson Ave Ardsley PA 19038

WEGNER, PAUL DEAN, religious educator; b. Charles City, Iowa, Mar. 31, 1956; s. Arthur C. Jr. and Darlene (DuShane) W.; m. Catherine L. Cutler, July 12, 1982; children: Matthew, Scott. BA, Moody Bible Inst., 1978; MDiv, ThM summa cum laude, Trinity Evang. Div. Sch., Deerfield, Ill., 1985; PhD, U. London, 1990. Instr. Moody Bible Inst., Chgo., 1988—. Overseas rsch. scholar U. London, 1986-87, 87-88. Mem. Soc. Biblical Lit., Evang. Theol. Soc. Home: 6061 N Newburg Chicago IL 60631 Office: Moody Bible Inst 820 N LaSalle Dr Chicago IL 60610

WEHR, POLLY JEANNE, religious school educator; b. Lansing, Mich., Dec. 10, 1962; d. Maxon Paul and Dorothy (Wildeman) W. BA in Edn., Concordia Luth. Coll., Ann Arbor, Mich., 1985. 3d and 4th grade tchr. Calvary Luth. Sch., Havertown, Pa., 1985-86; 5th grade tchr. St. John Luth. Sch., Stuttgart, Ark., 1987-90; 5th and 6th grade tchr. Trinity Luth. Sch., Reed City, Mich., 1990—. Office: Trinity Luth Sch 139 W Church Ave Reed City MI 49677

WEHRHEIM, CAROL ANN, writer, editor; b. Red Bud, Ill., Dec. 18, 1940; d. Elbert Elles and Fern Agnes (Gregson) W.; m. Harrison Henry Bender, Dec. 28, 1969 (div. 1976); m. Charles Daniel Kuehner Sr., June 6, 1982. BA, So. Ill. U., 1962; MA in Religious Edn., McCormick Theol. Seminary, Chgo., 1964. Cert. ch. educator United Ch. of Christ. Dir. Christian edn. Woods Meml. Presby. Ch., Severna Park, Md., 1964-69, Hammond St. Congl. Ch., Bangor, Maine, 1971-72, St. John's United Ch. of Christ, Catonsville, Md., 1972-74; tchr. Union 90, Alton, Maine, 1970-71; dir. Woods Meml. Child Devel. Ctr., Severna Park, Md., 1974-76; sec. early childhood edn. United Ch. Bd. Homeland Ministries, N.Y.C., 1976-79; asst. dir. dr. ministry program McCormick Theol. Seminary, Chgo., 1979-82; writer, editor Princeton, N.J., 1982—. Author: Planning Your Educational Ministry, 1988, The Journey Ahead, 1990; editor: Caregiver's Guide for Bible Discovery, 1987—, Growing Together Series, 1989—. Mem. AAUW (Outstanding Young Women Am. 1968), Assn. United Ch. Educators, Assn. Presbyn. Ch. Educators, Religious Edn. Assn. Home and Office: 40 Mountain Ave Princeton NJ 08540 *I cannot adequately express my gratitude for the persons and community of faith that has surrounded me from birth. Thus, the place of children and families in the faith community is of primary concern to me.*

WEHRLI, EUGENE S., academic administrator. Head Eden Theol. Sem., St. Louis. Office: Eden Theol Sem 475 E Lockwood Ave Webster Groves MO 63119*

WEIDLER, RONALD WALTER, pastor; b. Chgo., July 25, 1950; s. Henry and Anna Marie (Kalchbrenner) W.; m. Jean Gail Oelrich, June 11, 1972; children: Jonathan, Christa, Mark. AA, Concordia Coll., Ann Arbor, Mich., 1970; BA, Concordia Sr. Coll., Ft. Wayne, Ind., 1972; MDiv, Concordia Theol. Sem., Springfield, Ill., 1976. Pastor Holy Cross Luth. Ch., Carlisle, Iowa, 1976-80, Holy Trinity Luth. Ch., Tampa, Fla., 1980—; pastoral advisor Luths. for Life, Tampa Bay, Fla., 1989—. Contbr. articles sermons to religious publs.; counselor Luth. Ch.-Mo. Synod, Tampa cir., 1988—. Mem. Luth. Edn. Assn., Luth. Laymen's League, Optimists (pres. Tampa chpt. 1989—). Republican. Home: 3705 Kensington Ave Tampa FL 33629 Office: Holy Trinity Luth Ch 3712 El Prado Blvd Tampa FL 33629 *In a day when man would still be God, the Christian Gospel continues to affirm that God has become man. Therein is found not only an affirmation of human worth and dignity but especially the hope of salvation and immortality.*

WEIER, GARY WILBERT, minister; b. Shreveport, La., Dec. 10, 1943; s. Wilbert Louis and Esther (Bellhorn) W.; m. Evelyn Kay Nortrup, Sept. 30, 1967; children: Michael, David. BA, Concordia Sr. Coll., Ft. Wayne, Ind., 1965; MDiv, Concordia Sem., St. Louis, 1969; MA in Christian Edn., Presbyn. Sch. Christian Edn., 1970. Ordained to ministry Luth. Ch.-Mo. Synod, 1970. Vicar St. Mark's Luth. Ch., Cleve., 1967-68; pastor Bethlehem Luth. Ch., Pleasant Dale, Nebr., 1970-77, St. Paul's Luth. Ch., Malcolm, Nebr., 1970-77, Pilgrim Luth. Ch., Bellevue, Nebr., 1977—; community chaplain Meth. Hosp. Midtown, Omaha, 1981-83. Bd. dirs. Ctr. for Indian Ministries, Seward, Nebr., 1976-85, Luth. Met. Ministries, Omaha, 1977—, Luth. Med. Ctr., Omaha, 1986—; chmn. Bellevue CROP walk, 1980—; co-chmn. Effort Against Video Lottery, Bellevue, 1984. Republican. Home: 817 N 4th St Bellevue NE 68005 Office: Pilgrim Luth Ch 2401 Jackson St Bellevue NE 68005 *There may never be a better place on earth to serve the Lord than where you are right now.*

WEIGAND, WILLIAM KEITH, bishop; b. Bend, Oreg., May 23, 1937. Ed., Mt. Angel Sem., St. Benedict, Oreg., St. Edward's Sem. and St. Thomas Sem., Kenmore, Wash. Ordained bishop of Salt Lake City, 1980; Ordained priest Roman Cath. Ch., 1963. Office: Pastoral Ctr 27 C St Salt Lake City UT 84103

WEIGELT, HORST ERICH, theology educator; b. Liegnitz, Silesia, Fed. Republic Germany, Apr. 27, 1934; s. Erich and Margarete (Müller) W.; m. Eva-Elisabeth, Begrich, Dec. 27, 1961; children: Dorothea, Micheal. 1st and 2nd Exam in Theology, U. Erlangen, Fed. Republic Germany, 1958, 61, Promotion in church history, 1961, Habilitation, 1969. Lectr. U. Erlangen, 1973-75; prof. of protestant theology U. Bamberg, Fed. Republic Germany, 1975—. Author: Pietismus-Studien, 1965, Erweckungsbewegung u. konfess. Luthertum, 1968, Franck u.d. lutherische Reformation, 1971, Spiritualistische Tradition im Protestantismus, 1973, Castell u. Zinzendorf. Geschichte d.Herrnh. Pietismus, 1984, The Schwenkfelders in Silesia, 1985, Lavater und die Stillen im Lande - Distanz und Nähe, 1988, J. K. Lavater-Leben, Werk U. Wirkung, 1991. Mem. Verein bayerische Kirchengeschichte (2nd chmn. 1978), Historische Kommission Erforschung Pietismus, Wissenschaftliche Gesellschaft Theologie. Home: HennebergerstraBe 7, D-8600 Bamberg Federal Republic of Germany Office: Univ Bamberg, Markusplatz 3, D-8600 Bamberg Federal Republic of Germany

WEIGELT, MORRIS ALMOR, religious educator; b. Bremen, N.D., Oct. 18, 1934; s. Henry F. and Pauline E. (Sprenger) W.; m. Patricia Somerville, Aug. 26, 1955 (dec. 1962); children: Marva, Faye Anne; m. Eula-Adine Weigelt, June 23, 1963; children: LaDeana, Gerhard. MA in Religion, Northwest Nazarene Coll., Nampa, Idaho, 1957; BD in New Testament, Nazarene Theol. Seminary, Kans. City, Mo., 1959; ThM in New Testament, Princeton Theol. Seminary, 1960, PhD in New Testament, 1969. Min. Ch. of Nazarene, Danbury, Conn., 1960-63; prof. Northwest Nazarene Coll., 1965-75, Nazarene Theol. Seminary, 1975—. Editor: Epistle to Hebrews, 1984; contbr. articles to profl. jours. Mem. Soc. Bibl. Lit., Wesleyan Theol. Soc., Assn. for Psychol. Type. Office: Nazarene Theol Seminary 1700 E Meyer Blvd Kansas City MO 64131 *The only fears which manipulate our lives are those which have not yet been unmasked in the presence of the Risen Christ.*

WEINBERG, MICHAEL ALLEN, rabbi; b. Chgo., May 12, 1953; s. Norman and Eva Henrietta (Sichel) W.; m. Jo Ellen Zacher, Sept. 8, 1974; children: Joshua, Daniel, Sarah. BA, U. Chgo., 1976; MA in Hebrew Letters, Hebrew Union Coll., 1979. Ordained rabbi, 1980. Asst. rabbi, dir. edn. Emanuel Congregation, Chgo., 1980-85; rabbi Sinai Temple, Michigan City, Ind., 1985-87, Temple Beth Israel, Skokie, Ill., 1987—; mem. faculty Olin-Sang-Ruby Union Inst., Oconomowoc, Wis., 1980—. Mem. Coalition for the Advancement Jewish Edn. (pres. 1990—), Chgo. Bd. Rabbis, Cen. Conf.

Am. Rabbis, Religious Edn. Assn. Office: Temple Beth Israel 3601 Dempster Skokie IL 60076

WEINBERGER, LEON JUDAH, religion educator; b. Przemysl, Poland, Aug. 23, 1926; came to U.S., 1935; s. Jacob Aaron and Rachel (Wallach) W.; m. Estelle Greenberg, Feb. 7, 1954 (dec. 1978); children: Gary, David, Lisa Weinberger Veldran; m. Martha L. Bernatz, Aug. 20, 1983. Rabbinical studies, Torah Vodaath, Bklyn., 1956; BA, Clark U., 1957; MA, Brandeis U., 1959, PhD, 1963; M of Hebrew Lit., Jewish Theol. Sem. Am., 1964. Ordained rabbi, 1956. Rabbi Milford (Conn.) Jewish Ctr., 1959-63; asst. prof. U. Ala., Tuscaloosa, 1964-66, assoc. prof., 1966-72, prof. religious studies, 1972-84, Univ. rsch. prof., 1984—; vis. prof. sch. law U. Ala., 1988—; dir. Hillel Found., Tuscaloosa, 1964-66; assoc. Danforth Found., 1973—; mem. rsch. div. panel on Mid. East NEH, 1990; gen. editor Judaic Studies series U. Ala. Press. Author: Jewish Prince in Moslem Spain, 1973 (award AAUP), 8 others; also articles; editorial advisor Hebrew Studies; contbg. editor Menorah Rev. Mem. acad. coun. Hebrew U., Jerusalem, 1984—. Recipient Outstanding Prof. award Zeta Beta Tau, 1971-72, Algernon Sydney Sullivan award U. Ala., 1978; grantee NEH, 1971-73, 90—, Am. Acad. for Jewish Rsch., 1975, 78, 83, 90. Mem. AAUP (pres. U. Ala. chpt. 1971-72, Pres.'s Coun.), Assn. for Jewish Studies (bd. dirs. 1983—), Rabbinical Assembly Am., Am. Acad. Religion. Home: 2053 Idlewood Dr Tuscaloosa AL 35405 Office: U Ala Dept Religious Studies PO Box 870264 Tuscaloosa AL 35487-0264

WEINBLATT, STUART GARY, rabbi; b. Balt., Dec. 10, 1952; s. Sam and Toby (Angster) W.; m. Symcha Gabbay, Dec. 28, 1974; children: Ezra Zev, Margalit Alexandra, Micha Lev, Noam Benjamin. BA, U. Md., 1974; MA, Hebrew Union Coll.-Jewish Religion Inst., Cin., 1978. Ordained rabbi, 1979. Rabbi Temple Beth Am, Miami, Fla., 1979-81, Temple Solel, Bowie, Md., 1981-88, Congregation B'nai Tzedek, Potomac, Md., 1988—; pres. Washington Bd. Rabbis, 1989-91. Author: NFTY Energy Packet for the 80's, 1977; author, creator: (teaching game) The Great American Jewish Organization Fair, 1980. Bd. dirs. Jewish Community Coun., Washington, 1987-90, U.I.A. Fedn. Greater Washington, 1988—. Recipient Rabbinic Leadership award Coun. Jewish Fedns., 1987. Mem. U.I.A. Nat. Rabbinic Cabinet. Home: 11710 Rosalinda Dr Potomac MD 20854 Office: Congregation B'nai Tzedek PO Box 1477 West Bethesda MD 20827

WEINER, DEBORAH JANE, church organization administrator; b. New Haven, Nov. 9, 1951; d. Oscar Daniel and Vera (Racine) W. BA, Russell Sage Coll., 1973; MA, Emerson Coll., 1976. Dir. pub. info. Unitarian Universalist Assn., Boston, 1989—; exec. dir. Dept. Cultural Affairs, New Haven, 1981-86; mem. devel. com. and pers. com. Star Island Corp., Boston, 1990—. Contbr. articles to religious publs. Office: Unitarian Universalist Assn 25 Beacon St Boston MA 02108

WEINHAUER, CARLIN EUGENE, clergyman, college administrator, consultant; b. Wellsville, N.Y., Oct. 31, 1939; s. Henry Frank and Thelma Ethel (Campbell) W.; m. Marcia Arlene Watne, Aug. 11, 1962; children—Cheri, Lynda, Becky. B.A. in Bibl. Edn., Columbia Bible Coll., S.C., 1964; M.A. in Practical Theology, Chgo. Grad. Sch. Theology, 1971; M.A. in Christian Edn., Trinity Evang. Div. Sch., Deerfield, Ill., 1974; Ph.D. in Ednl. Adminstrn., U. Alta., Can., 1979. Ordained to ministry, 1964. Sr. pastor Mt. Olivet Bapt. Ch., Camden, S.C., 1963, 66; missionary Am. Mission Fellowship, Gt. Falls, Mont., 1966-67; minister edn. and youth Bethel Community Ch., Chgo., 1967-68; faculty Briercrest Bible Coll., Caronport, Sask., Can., 1969-79, v.p. pub. ministries, 1979-84; assoc. pastor leadership devel. Willingdon Ch., Burnaby, B.C., 1984-85; sr. pastor, 1986—; tchr. devel. sem. cons. Scripture Press, Whitby, Ont., Can., 1975—; mem. pub. relations commn. Am. Assn. Bible Colls., 1981-84. Grantee U. Alta., 1978; recipient service award Briercrest Bible Coll., 1984. Mem. Delta Epsilon Chi. Mem. Mennonite Brethren Ch. Home: 6818 Acacia Ave, Burnaby, BC Canada V5E 3J7 Office: Willingdon Ch, 4812 Willingdon Ave, Burnaby, BC Canada V5G 3H6

WEINHAUER, WILLIAM GILLETTE, retired bishop; b. N.Y.C., Dec. 3, 1924; s. Nicholas Alfred and Florence Anastacia (Davis) W.; m. Jean Roberta Shanks, Mar. 20, 1948; children: Roberta Lynn, Cynthia Anne, Doris Jean. BS, Trinity Coll., Hartford, Conn., 1948; MDiv, Gen. Theol. Sem., 1951, STM, 1956, ThD, 1970. Ordained to ministry Episcopal Ch., 1951. Pastor Episcopal parishes Diocese N.Y., 1951-56; prof. N.T. St. Andrews Theol. Sem., Manila, Philippines, 1956-60; asst. prof. N.T. Gen. Theol. Sem., 1961-71; rector Christ Ch., Poughkeepsie, N.Y., 1971-73; bishop Episcopal Diocese of Western N.C., Black Mountain, 1973-90, ret., 1990; chaplain to mil. bases, colls. hosps. Served with USN, 1943-46. Mem. Soc. Bibl. Lit. Office: PO Box 368 Black Mountain NC 28711

WEINSBERG, EDGAR JAMES, rabbi, consultant, lecturer; b. N.Y.C., Feb. 15, 1944; s. Egon Weinsberg and Lilli (Matzdorff) Singer; m. Yvonne Ruth Glogauer, Sept. 3, 1972; children: Daniel, Elana. BA, UCLA, 1966; M in Hebrew Lit., Jewish Theol. Sem., N.Y.C., 1970; EdD, Columbia U., 1974. Ordained rabbi, 1972; lic. tchr., N.Y. Rabbi Temple Beth El, Utica, N.Y., 1974-82, Swampscott, Mass., 1985—; lectr. SUNY, 1977-81; lectr. Judaica, lectr., coord. ednl. gerontology program Beit Berl Tchrs. Coll., Judaica and Kfar Sava, Israel, 1982-85; chaplain Jewish Home and Hosp. for Aged, N.Y.C., 1967-72, Utica Psychiatric Ctr., 1974-82; pres. Empire State Rabbinical Assembly, Albany, N.Y., 1978-80, Hospice Care, Inc., Utica, 1980-81; cons. Jewish Rehab. Ctr., Swampscott, 1989—. Contbr. articles to profl. jours. Chmn. Swampscott Com. on Elder Housing, 1988; coord. Greater Boston Clergy Walk in Behalf of Persons with AIDS/HIV, Lynn/Swampscott, 1990, North Shore Rally in support Israel and U.S. troops in Persian Gulf, Swampscott, 1991; bd. dirs. North Shore Community Hebrew High Sch. Meml. Fedn. for Jewish Culture grantee, 1968, Adminstrn. on Aging grantee, 1971-74; Am. Friends Hebrew U./Hillel Found. fellow, 1964-65. Mem. Jewish Fedn. of North Shore, North Shore Rabbinical Assn. (pres. 1989—), New Eng. Rabbinical Assembly (v.p. 1989—), Swampscott Ministerium (chmn. 1987-89). Office: Temple Beth El 55 Atlantic Ave Swampscott MA 01907 *Aging is a lifelong process that begins at conception and ends at death. No matter what point we have reached in the life span, there are innumerable opportunities for further development and growth.*

WEINSTEIN, STANLEY, Buddhist studies educator; b. Bklyn., Nov. 13, 1929; s. Louis Arthur and Ruth (Appleson) W.; m. Lucie Ruth Krebs, Sept. 23, 1951; 1 son, David Eli. BA, Komazawa U., Tokyo, 1954-58; MA, U. Tokyo, 1960; PhD, Harvard U., 1966; MAH (hon.), Yale U., 1974. Lectr. Sch. Oriental and African Studies, London, 1962-68; assoc. prof. Buddhist studies Yale U., New Haven, 1968-74, prof., 1974—, chmn. council East Asian studies, 1982-85. Author: Buddhism under T'ang, 1987. Served with U.S. Army, 1952-54. Ford Found. fgn. area fellow, 1958-62; NEH sr. fellow, 1974-75. Mem. Am. Oriental Soc., Assn. Asian Studies. Home: 270 Ridgewood Ave Hamden CT 06517 Office: Yale U Hall Grad Studies New Haven CT 06520

WEINTRAUB, SIMKHA YITZKHAK, social worker, therapist, rabbi; b. Charleston, S.C., Oct. 22, 1953; s. Lewis Aryeh and Fannie I. (Goldberg) W. BA summa cum laude, Brandeis U., 1975; Rabbi, Jewish Theol. Sem. Am., 1982; MS in Social Work, Columbia U., 1983; cert. in family and couples therapy, Postgrad. Ctr. Mental Health, N.Y.C., 1988. Tchr. Soc. for Advancement Judaism, N.Y.C., 1975-79, ednl. dir., 1979-81; instr., coord. and cons. Project CONNECT edn. dept. 92d Street YM-WYHA, N.Y.C., 1981-83; coord. grad. programs B'nai Brith Hillel-Jewish Assn. for Coll. Youth, N.Y.C., 1983-84; leader Jewish culture group Youth Residence Ctr., Jewish Child Care Assn., N.Y.C., 1984-85; coord. Melton adult mini-sch. program Hebrew U., Jerusalem, 1984-85, instr., 1986; tchr., mental health cons. Abraham Joshua Heschel Sch., N.Y.C., 1985-87; dir. pub. affairs New Israel Fund, N.Y.C., 1987—; caseworker Madeleine Borg Clinic, Jewish Bd. Family and Children's Svcs., N.Y.C., 1978-79; chaplain Mt. Sinai Med. Ctr., N.Y.C., summer 1979; psychiat. caseworker emergency rm. North Cen. Bronx (N.Y.) Hosp., summer 1982, Psychiat. Clinic, Jewish Child Care Assn., N.Y.C., 1982-83; pvt. practice family and couples therapy, Bklyn., 1988—. Home and Office: 325 Smith St Brooklyn NY 11231

WEIS, EARL AUGUST, priest, educator; b. Toledo, May 5, 1923; s. Sylvester Ignatius and Louise Marie (Lammers) W. Student, Xavier U., 1941-45; AB, Loyola U., Chgo., 1946; AM, Loyola U., 1948; PhL, W. Baden Coll., 1948; STD, Pontifical Gregorian Univ., Rome, 1958. Joined Soc. of Jesus, 1941, ordained priest Roman Cath. Ch., 1954. Prof. theology W. Baden Coll., 1958-66; assoc. prof. religious studies Univ. Detroit, 1970-71; prof., chmn. dept. theology Loyola Univ., Chgo., 1971—. Staff editor dogmatic theology New Cath. Ency., 1963-66; editorial bd. Cath. Theol. Ency., 1966-70; book review editor Review for Religious, 1958-63. Mem. Cath. Theol. Soc. Am., Cath. Bibl. Assn., Soc. Bibl. Lit., Coll. Theology Soc., Fellowship of Cath. Scholars (pres. 1983-85). Office: Loyola U 6525 N Sheridan Rd Chicago IL 60626

WEISS, CHARLES KARL, rabbi; b. McKeesport, Pa., June 1, 1933; s. Phillip and Ethel (Weiss) W.; m. Miriam Weiss, Feb. 15, 1955; children: Shimon, Sheina, Yehudah, Golda. Rabbi, 1955. Rabbi Young Israel of Pitts., 1961—; exec. dir. Yeshiva Sch., Pitts., 1961-85; adminstr. Congregation Poale Zedeck, Pitts., 1985—. Mem. Rabbinical Coun. Am., RAbbinical Coun. Pa. Home: 5604 Forbes Ave Pittsburgh PA 15217 Office: Young Israel of Pitts 5751 Bartlett Pittsburgh PA 15217

WEISS, DAVID, religion educator; b. Sighet, Romania, Dec. 21, 1928; came to U.S., 1947, naturalized, 1953; s. Callel and Fanny (Weiss) Wiederman; m. Tzipora Hager, Dec. 9, 1953; children—Baruch, Ephraim, Isaiah. B.A., Bklyn. Coll., 1953; M.A., N.Y.U., 1956; M.H.L., Jewish Theol. Sem., 1957, D.H.L., 1958. Instr. religion and Talmud Jewish Theol. Sem., 1957-62, asst. prof. Talmud, 1962-68, assoc. prof., 1968-86, prof. Rabbinics, 1970-86; lectr. religion Columbia U., N.Y.C., 1961-63, adj. asst. prof., 1963-65, adj. assoc. prof., 1965-68, adj. prof., 1968-86, prof., 1986—; vis. prof. Talmud Bar-Ilan U., Israel, 1974; Lady Davis vis. prof. Talmud Hebrew U., Israel, 1984. Author (under name Halivni): Sources and Traditions: A Source Ciritical Commentary on The Talmud, Vol. I on Seder Nashim, 1968; author Vol. II on Seder Moed, 1975, Vol. III on Tractate Shabbath, 1983, Vol. IV on Tractate Erubin and Pesahim, 1983, Midrash, Mishnah and Gemara, 1986, Peshat and Derash, 1991. Recipient Blalik prize City of Tel-Aviv, Israel, 1984; grantee Council Research Humanities Columbia, 1964; Guggenheim fellow, 1970-71; recipient L. Ginzberg award Jewish Theol. Sem., 1971-72; Nat. Endowment for Humanities fellow, 1980; fellow Inst. for Advanced Studies Hebrew U., Jerusalem, Israel, 1981. Mem. Am. Acad. Jewish Research (pres.). Home: 435 Riverside Dr New York NY 10025

WEISS, KENNETH JAY, rabbi; b. L.A., May 12, 1941; s. George Jerome and Charlotte Marie (Coffman) W.; m. Susan Gail Levy, July 3, 1966; children: Jennifer R., Amy R., Daniel A. BA, UCLA, 1962; MA Hebrew Letters, Hebrew Union Coll., 1968, D. Hebrew Letters, 1980. Ordained rabbi, 1968. Rabbi Temple Sinai, Glendale, Calif., 1971-79, Temple Mt. Sinai, El Paso, Tex., 1980—. Contbr. articles to profl. jours. Vice chair Life Mgmt. Ctr. Mental Health Mental Retardation/Tex., El Paso, 1991; bd. dirs., mem. editorial bd. Sta. KDBC-TV, El Paso, 1991; mem. instl. rev. com. Sierra Hosp., El Paso, 1985—, El Paso Inst. for Med. R & D, 1989—; bd. dirs. MADD, El Paso, 1984—. Lt. USN, 1968-71. Mem. Cen. Conf. Am. Rabbis, Pacific Assn. Reform Rabbis (pres. 1991), NCCJ. Office: Temple Mt Sinai 4408 N Stanton St El Paso TX 79902

WEISS, SAM, cantor; b. N.Y.C., Mar. 1, 1950; s. Ferenc and Lili (Weiss) W.; m. Roslyn Kestenbaum; children: Miriam, Dena. BA, Bklyn. Coll., 1971; student, Yeshiva U., 1972-74, U. Conn., 1974-76. Ordained cantor. Cantor, religious sch. prin. Bros. of Joseph Congregation, Norwich, Conn., 1974-76; cantor, youth dir. Adas Kodesh Shel Emeth Congregation, Wilmington, Del., 1976-79; cantor Ner Tamid Congregation, Balt., 1979—; faculty mem. Balt. Hebrew U., 1986—; conductor Ner Tamid Choral Group. Contbr. articles to profl. jours.; producer Heritage Trio Vocal Group.. Mem. Cantorial Council of Am., Md. Art League, Md. Art Guild, Jewish Folk Arts Soc., Am. Soc. Jewish Music, Jewish Community Ctr. Cultural Arts Com., Black Jewish Forum, Balt. Jewish Council. Democrat. Jewish. Avocations: trumpet playing, music composition, arranging, linguistic studies, photography. Home: 2510 Steele Rd Baltimore MD 21209 Office: Ner Tamid Congregation 6214 Pimlico Rd Baltimore MD 21209

WEISS, SAMSON RAPHAEL, clergyman, Jewish history educator; b. Emden, Germany, Mar. 9, 1910; came to U.S., 1938, naturalized, 1944; s. Aron and Judith (Schweiger) W.; m. Helene Carlebach, Dec. 27, 1936; children—Yetta (Mrs. Chaim Zelikowitz), Miriam (Mrs. Jonas J. Dissen), Israel Meyer, Devora (Mrs. Chaim Ezriel Kitevitz). Student, Breslau (Germany) U., 1928, Berlin (Germany) U., 1929, Zurich (Switzerland) U., 1933, Prague (Czechoslovakia) U., 1934, Yeshiva Mir, Poland, 1934; Ph.D. summa cum laude, U. Dorpat, Estonia, 1938. Ordained rabbi, 1934; dean Hebrew dept. Jewish Tchrs. Coll., Wuerzburg, Germany, 1934-38; prof. codes Ner Israel Rabbinical Coll., Balt., 1938-40; dean Beth Yehuda Talmudical Acad., Detroit, 1940-44; co-founder, nat. dir. Torah Umesorah, Nat. Soc. Hebrew Day Schs., N.Y.C., 1944-45; founder, dean Young Israel Inst. Jewish Studies, N.Y.C., 1945-56; nat. dir. Nat. Council Young Israel, 1947-56; exec. v.p. Union Orthodox Jewish Congregations Am., N.Y.C., 1956-72; prof. of philosophy, chmn. dept. Judaic studies Touro Coll., N.Y.C., 1971-75; founder, vis. dean Torah U., Los Angeles, 1961-62; lectr. Jewish Philosophy, Jewish history and contemporary Judaism, U.S., Can., Israel; exec. mem. Jerusalem Inst. for Talmudic Research; chmn. Am. Friends Mirrer Yeshiva in Jerusalem. Contbr. articles, poetry Jewish mags. Recipient Schiller prize City of Breslau, 1928. Mem. Rabbinical Council Am. Home: 1362 E 3d St Brooklyn NY 11230 also: 13 Even Hazel St, Jerusalem Israel

WEISSBARD, DAVID RAYMOND, minister; b. Albany, N.Y., July 10, 1940; s. Alfred Henry and E. Ramona (Van Wie) W.; m. Mary Linda Roberts, Mar. 31, 1963 (dec. May 1987); children: Melissa Anne, Michele Lee Weissbard Burns, Andrew Van Wie (dec.), Meredith Lynn; m. Karen Wells, Sept. 1, 1990. BA, St. Lawrence U., 1962, BD, 1965; diploma in applied social studies, U. Southampton, Eng., 1973. Ordained to ministry Unitarian Universalist Assn., 1965; cert. social worker, Eng. Student min. 1st Universalist Ch., Dexter, N.Y., 1963-65, Henderson, N.Y., 1963-65; min. 1st Parish in Bedford (Mass.) Unitarian Universalist Ch., 1965-74; sr. min. Fairfax Unitarian Ch., Oakton, Va., 1974-79, The Unitarian Ch., Rockford, Ill., 1979—; v.p. Cen. Midwest Dist. Unitarian Universalist Assn., 1989—; mem. editorial bd. WROK. Producer, host weekly TV program Fusion, WIFR-TV, 1980—. Mem. religious policy com. Rockford Sch. Dist., 1991. Recipient Skinner award Unitarian Universalist Assn., 1979; named One of Rockford's 15 Most Interesting People, 1990. Mem. ACLU (No. Ill. steering com.), Greater Rockford Clergy Assn., Unitarian Universalist Mins. Assn. (treas. 1976-78), Soc. for Profls. in Dispute Resolution. Democrat. Home: 5545 Inverness Dr Rockford IL 61107 Office: The Unitarian Ch 4848 Turner St Rockford IL 61107

WEISSBERG, VICTOR HOWARD, rabbi; b. Highland Park, Mich., June 26, 1927; s. Isadore and Ruth-Helen (Friedman) W.; m. Tamar Libovsky, Feb. 12, 1952; children: Amyra, Ariel, Alona. PhB, U. Chgo., 1948; B. Hebrew Letters, Hebrew Union Coll., 1950, M. Hebrew Letters, 1954, DHL, 1970. Ordained rabbi, 1953. Ednl. dir. Temple Isaiah-Israel, Chgo., 1953-54; rabbi Temple Beth-El, Chgo., 1954—; mem. Nat. Rabbinic Cabinet-U.S.A., Northbrook, Ill.; bd. dirs. Jewish Fedn. Metro Chgo. Author: Jerusalem in Biblical Eschatology, 1953, History of Jews in 17th Century Turkey, 1970, Psalma and Psychotherapy, 1980. Bd. dirs. Am.-Israel Pub. Affairs Com., Washington; exec. dir. To Protect Our Heritage PAC, Chgo. Mem. Cen. Conf. Am. Rabbis, Chgo. Bd. Rabbis (sec.), Northbrook Clergy Assn. (pres.), Northwotn Assn. of Clergy (v.p.), Rotary. Office: Temple Beth-El of Chgo 3050 W Touhy Chicago IL 60645-2989

WEISSENBUEHLER, WAYNE, bishop. Bishop of Rocky Mountain Evang. Luth. Ch. in Am., Denver. Office: Rocky Mountain Synod ABS Bldg #101 7000 Broadway Denver CO 80211*

WEISSER, WILLIAM JAMES, music minister, educator; b. Columbia, Pa., Feb. 7, 1948; s. Joseph Bartholemew and Mary Elizabeth (Baldwin) W.; m. Anne Clendenin Ferree, Oct. 1, 1977; 1 child, Chadwick Ferree. MusB, Westminster Choir Coll., 1970; postgrad., Ind. U. Minister of music 1st Presbyn. Ch., Joliet, Ill., 1970-74, White Meml. Presbyn., Raleigh, N.C., 1974-76; diaconal minister Edenton St. United Meth., Raleigh, 1976—; mem. bd. edn., bd. diaconal ministry, bd. worship N.C. United Meth. Conf., Raleigh, 1976—; mem. faculty Louisburg Coll., 1991-92. Mem. Am. Guild Organists (dean 1971-84), Nat. Assn. Tchrs. Singing, Fellowship United Meth. Worship Music and Other Arts (bd. dirs., rep. 1985—, nat. v.p. 1989—, interim exec. sec.-treas. 1990—, nat. pres.-elect 1991-93), Am. Choral Dirs. Assn., Am. Guild English Handbell Ringers, Choristers Guild, Nats, Masons. Republican. Avocations: records, tapes, compact discs, running, walking. Home: 1214 Currituck Dr Raleigh NC 27609 Office: Edenton St United Meth Ch 228 W Edenton St Raleigh NC 27603

WEISSHAAR, MILTON LEON, minister; b. Chgo., Dec. 14, 1921; s. Samuel and Elizabeth (Herr) W.; m. Jean Garnet Edwards, June 1950 (div. 1973); children: Barbara Pino, Janet Brigham, James Weisshaar; m. Eleanor Louise Bell, May 26, 1973. AB, U. Chgo., 1949; MA, Northwestern U., Evanston, 1952; BD, Garrett Sem., 1952. Ordained to ministry United Meth. Ch., 1953. Min. Wesley Meth. Ch., Wausau, Wis., 1952-58, First Meth. Ch., Oconomowoc, Wis., 1958-64, Pacific Beach United Meth. Ch., San Diego, 1966-71; asst. min. First United Meth. Ch., Santa Monica, Calif., 1972-78; min. North Long Beach (Calif.) United Meth. Ch., 1979-83, Crescenta Valley United Meth. Ch., Montrose, Calif., 1983-88, Los Altos United Meth. Ch., Long Beach, Calif., 1988—. Author: Prayers for Worship, 1977. Republican. Home: 9830 Belmont St #340 Bellflower CA 90706 Office: Los Altos United Meth Ch 5950 E Willow St Long Beach CA 90815

WEISZ, JAMES MILTON, minister; b. Pitts., May 11, 1945; s. Howard LeRoy and Ruth Carrie (Eisley) W.; m. Candice Jean Ramsay, Dec. 19, 1970; children: Eric James, Ryan Ramsay. BA, Otterbein Coll., 1967; MDiv, United Theol. Seminary, Dayton, Ohio, 1976. Ordained to ministry United Meth. Ch., 1977. Pastor Western Pa. Conf. of the United Meth. Ch., 1975-91; dir. pastoral care Beechwood/Bloche Community, Getzville, N.Y., 1991—; chaplain Christian Assocs., Sharon, Pa., 1987-91, Stairways, Inc., Erie, Pa., 1983-87, Braddock (Pa.) Gen. Hosp., 1979-82, Uniontown (Pa.) Hosp., 1976-79. Chaplaincy chmn. Assn. of Churches, Uniontown, 1979. Mem. Christian Assocs. Republican. Home: 368 Teakwood Williamsville NY 14221 Office: Beechwood/Blocher Community 2235 Millersport Hwy Getzville NY 14068-0123

WEITZ, DAVID L., pastor; b. St. Johns, Mich., Nov. 12, 1956; s. Darrell E. and Ruth E. (Van Ornum) W.; m. Kathy L. Stout, Aug. 6, 1977; 1 child, Adam D. AB, Olivet Nazarene U., Kankakee, Ill., 1978, MA, 1982; MDiv, Nazarene Theol. Sem., Kansas City, Mo., 1982. Ordained to ministry Ch. of Nazarene. Assoc. pastor Calvary Ch. of Nazarene, Crestwood, Ill., 1978-80, sr. pastor, 1982-86; sr. pastor Hillcrest Community Ch. of Nazarene, Vallejo, Calif., 1986-88; assoc. pastor 1st Ch. of Nazarene, Elkhart, Ind., 1988—; coun. mem. Chgo. cen. dist. Nazarene Youth Internat., Kankakee, 1983-85; sec.-treas. Greater Chgo. Nazarene Ministerial Assn., 1985-86. Mem. Wesleyan Theol. Soc. Office: 1st Ch of Nazarene 2601 Benham Ave Elkhart IN 46517

WEITZ, MARTIN MISHLI, minister, religious studies educator; b. Denver, Aug. 2, 1907; s. Joseph and Rachel (Kauffman) W.; m. Margaret Kalach, Aug. 5, 1934; children: Mimi, Jonathan David. Student, Colo. State Coll., 1925-27; BA, U. Cin., 1932; PhD, Hebrew Union Coll., 1959, DD (hon.), 1959; DD (hon.), Lincoln U., 1967; DHL (hon), Colo. No. U., 1964. Diplomate: ordained rabbi. Dir. Hillel Found., Northwestern U., Evanston, Ill., 1934-37, Temple Sholom Religious Sch., Chgo., 1935-37; rabbi Beth Hillel Temple, Kenosha, Wis., 1937-43, B'nai Jeshurun Temple, Des Moines, 1945-48; prof. Drake U., Des Moines, 1946-47; rabbi House of Israel, Hot Springs, Ark., 1949-51, Beth Israel Temple, Atlantic City, N.J., 1951-63, North Shore Synagogue, Syosset, N.Y., 1963-65; dir., prof. Ctr. Interfaith Studies, Lincoln U., Oxford, Pa., 1967-73; rabbi Temple of Israel, Wilmington, N.C., 1974-76; faculty Nat. U., San Diego, Irvine, Mission Viejo, Vista, Anaheim Centers, 1976-91, Saddleback Coll., Mission Viejo, Calif., 1978—; co-adj. lectr. Rutgers State U., N.J., 1955-61; founder, chmn. bd. Atlantic Community Coll., 1956-63; chmn. subventions com. Central Conf. Am. Rabbis, N.Y.C., 1954-60; part-time chaplain Heritage Pointe, Mission Viejo, Calif., 1991. Author over 100 books, including: Timberline, 1934, Wind Whispers, 1934, (demography) Jewish Community-Studies, 1936, Tercentenary Manual, 1936, Wind-Whispers, 1950, Ten Commandments Today, 1952, Year Without Fear, 1955, Life Without Strife, 1958, Decalogues for Our Day, 1962, Mission to Berlin, 1963, Campus-on-a-Compass, 1969, Mexican Odyssey, 1979; also articles; editor: Hebrew Union Coll. Monthly, 1930-32, Manuals, World Union for Progressive Judaism, 1952-56, The Hour-Glass Mag. Lincoln U., 1968-73. Chmn. Bicentennial Heritage Com., Wilmington, N.C., 1976; mem. Com. on Justice and Peace of Central Conf. Am. Rabbis, N.Y.C., 1951-52; mem. exec. bd. Central Conf., 1951-53; founder, pres. NCCJ, Atlantic City, 1956-61; chmn. Dr. Albert Schweitzer Festival of Culture, San Diego, 1986, Palm Springs, Calif., 1986, 88; chmn. dedication program Chamberlain Hall, Nat. U., San Diego, 1986, Bicentennial of Constn. Celebrity Series, Nat. U., 1987-88; vice chmn. emeritus Inst. Saddleback Community Coll., Mission Viejo, Calif., 1986—; chairperson U.S. Marine Band, Gym of Saddleback Coll., 1989. Capt. U.S. Army, 1943-46. Recipient citation Tchr. of the Yr. Saddleback Coll., 1982; recipient outstanding faculty award Nat. U., 1983, citation in recognition of help in 100th Anniversary of Orange County, Calif.; dedicated large sect. of Penrose Library to Weitz Library, U. Denver, 1987. Mem. Conf. of Sci. and Ethics (dir. 1977-80), Academians Soc. (pres. 1981-82), Leisure Worlder of Month 1985, Student and Alumni Assn. Hebrew Union Coll. (trustee 1951-55). Lodge: Rotary. Home: 394 C Ave Castilla Laguna Hills CA 92653 *What ever happens may happen for the best...if we make the best of whatever happens.*

WEITZ, RALPH WILLIAM, minister; b. Sellersville, Pa., Aug. 1, 1947; s. Ralph William Jr. and Edna Marion (Crist) W.; children: Brooke, Abby. A in Forest Tech., Pa. State U., 1968; BS in Forest Mgmt., Austin State U., 1970; Diploma in Bibl. Studies, Internat. Sch. of Theology, San Bernardino, Calif., 1974. Staff Campus Crusade for Christ, San Bernardino, 1970-72; campus dir. Campus Crusade for Christ, Little Rock, 1972-76; area adminstr. Campus Crusade for Christ, Richmond, Va., 1976-82; regional adminstr. Campus Crusade for Christ, Washington, 1982-89; stewardship pastor Immanuel Bible Ch., Springfield, Va., 1989—. Mem. Christian Ministries Mgmt. Assn. (chpt. pres. 1990-91), Nat. Assn. Evangelicals. Home: 8009 W Rockglen Ct Springfield VA 22152 Office: Immanuel Bible Church 5211 Backlick Rd Springfield VA 22151

WEITZEL, JOHN QUINN, bishop; b. Chgo., May 10, 1928; s. Carl Joseph and Patricia (Quinn) W. BA, Maryknoll (N.Y.) Sem., 1951, M of Religious Edn., 1953; PMD, Harvard U. Ordained priest Roman Cath. Ch., 1955. With ednl. devel. Cath. Fgn. Mission Soc. of Am., Maryknoll, 1955-63, nat. dir. vocations for Maryknoll, dir. devel. dept. and info. services, 1963-72, mem. gen. council, 1972-78; asst. parish priest Cath. Ch., Western Samoa, 1979-81, pastor, vicar gen., 1981-86; consecrated bishop, 1986; bishop Cath. Ch., Am. Samoa, 1986—. Office: Diocese of Samoa-Pago Pago Fatuoaiga PO Box 596 Pago Pago AS 96799

WELBORN, JEREMY RAY, youth minister; b. Lawton, Okla., Mar. 20, 1970; s. George Ray and Diana Kay (Fisher) W. BB, Cameron U., 1989, postgrad., 1990—; postgrad., Okla. Bapt. U., 1989-90. Lic. Min., Okla. Asst. youth min. Cen. Bapt. Ch., Lawton, 1988-89; youth min. 1st Bapt. Ch. West, Lawton, 1989—. Mem. Associational Youth Com., Associational Music Com., Bapt. Student Union (exec. coun., discipleship chmn.), Bus. Club, Phi Kappa Phi. Republican. Office: 1st Bapt Ch W 7302 Cache Rd Lawton OK 73505 *God has brought to my attention that the harder I try to do what He commands, the harder I fall. But when I become "He in me" success is all I see.*

WELCH, CARLOS HARLAN, lay minister; b. Brotherton, Tenn., Sept. 7, 1939; s. Henry Norris and Cornelia (Dishman) W.; m. Phillis Elaine Dement, May 27, 1967; 1 child, Kellie. BA in Edn., Harding U., 1965. Cert. elem. and secondary tchr., Mo. Elem. tchr. Bunker (Mo.) R-3 Sch., 1979—; lay min. Centerville (Mo.) Ch. of Christ, 1982—; song dir. Harmony Ch. of Christ, Searcy, Ark., 1961-65. Democrat. Home: HCR 1 Box 139 Centerville MO 63633 *Success in life is not dependent upon money or earthly possessions, but whether we have served the Lord and have been found faithful by Him.*

WELCH, CLAUDE (RAYMOND), theology educator; b. Genoa City, Wis., Mar. 10, 1922; s. Virgil Cleon and Deone West (Grenelle) W.; m. Eloise Janette Turner, May 31, 1942 (div. 1970); children—Eric, Thomas, Claudia;

m. Theodosia Montigel Blewett, Oct. 5, 1970 (dec. 1978); m. Joy Neuman, Oct. 30, 1982. BA summa cum laude, Upper Iowa U., 1942; postgrad., Garrett Theol. Sem., 1942-43; BD cum laude, Yale U., 1945, PhD, 1950; DD (hon.), Ch. Div. Sch. of Pacific, 1972, Jesuit Sch. Theology, 1982; LHD (hon.), U. Judaism, 1976. Ordained to ministry Meth. Ch., 1947. Instr. religion Princeton (N.J.) U., 1947-50, asst. prof., 1950-51, vis. prof., 1962; asst. prof. theology Yale U. Div. Sch., New Haven, 1951-54, assoc. prof., 1954-60; Berg prof. religious thought, chmn. dept. U. Pa., Phila., 1960-71, assoc. dean Coll. Arts and Scis., 1964-68, acting chmn. dept. philosophy, 1965-66; prof. hist. theology Grad. Theol. Union, Berkeley, Calif., 1971—, dean, 1971-87, pres., 1972-82; vis. prof. Garrett Theol. Sem., 1951, Pacific Sch. Religion, 1958, Hartford Sem. Found., 1958-59, Princeton Theol. Sem., 1962-63, U. Va., 1987; Fulbright sr. lectr. U. Mainz, Germany, 1968; Sprunt lectr. Union Theol. Sem., Richmond, Va., 1958; dir. study of grad. edn. in religion Am. Council Learned Socs., 1969-71; del. World Conf. on Faith and Order, 1963. Author: In This Name: the Doctrine of the Trinity in Contemporary Theology, 1952, (with John Dillenberger) Protestant Christianity, interpreted through its Development, 1954, 2d rev. edit., 1988, The Reality of the Church, 1958, Graduate Education in Religion: A Critical Appraisal, 1971, Religion in the Undergraduate Curriculum, 1972, Protestant Thought in the 19th Century, vol. 1, 1799-1870, 1972, vol. 2, 1870-1914, 1985; Editor, translator: God and Incarnation in Mid-19th Century German Theology (Thomasius, Dorner and Biedermann), 1965; Contbr. to publs. in field. Recipient decennial prize Bross Found., 1970; Guggenheim fellow, 1976; NEH research fellow, 1984, Fulbright research fellow, 1956-57. Mem. Am. Acad. Religion (pres. 1969-70), Council on Study of Religion (chmn. 1969-74, 1985-90), Soc. for Values in Higher Edn. (pres. 1967-71), Am. Soc. Ch. History, Am. Theol. Soc., Phi Beta Kappa. Home: 123 Fairlawn Dr Berkeley CA 94708

WELCH, DON MEREDITH, pastor, accountant; b. Detroit, Dec. 18, 1946; s. Willie L. and Willa M. (Smith) W.; m. Linda Jean Dozier, July 18, 1970; children: LaShawn, Andrè, Darnell. AA, Wayne County Community Coll., Detroit, 1976; student, U. Detroit, 1981. Ordained to ministry A.M.E. Ch. as deacon, 1983, as elder, 1985. Staff asst. Oak Grove A.M.E. Ch., Detroit, 1981-85, asst. to pastor, 1986-87; founder pastor Christ Temple A.M.E. Ch., Detroit, 1986—; v.p. mktg. Welch Bros. Paper, Inc., Detroit, 1991—; mem. women in ministry com. Mich. Ann. Conf., A.M.E. Ch., 1985-88, mem. meml. com., 1986—, mem. fin. com. so. dist., 1986—, mem. advance com., 1986—. Chmn. bd. dirs. Regal Group Home, Detroit, 1975-78; asst. coord. Detroit Mayor's Emergency Food Drive, 1983-84; bd. dirs. northwestern br. YMCA, Detroit, 1989-91, chmn. Christian effectiveness com., 1990—. Sgt. USAF, 1966-69. Recipient letter of commendation fin. dept. City of Detroit, 1983, resolution Wayne County Bd. Commrs., 1986; Spirit of Detroit award Detroit City Coun., 1988, testimonial resolution, 1991. Mem. A.M.E. Mins. Fellowship, Meth. Mins. Fellowship. Home: 2926 Beatrice Detroit MI 48217 Office: Christ Temple AME Ch 18920 Stoepel St Detroit MI 48221 *I have found that in life the true measure of success is not quantitative, but qualitative. It's what you give to life that speaks to your success in life—not what you take out of it.*

WELCH, HERBERT ALDEN, minister; b. Camden, N.J., Nov. 29, 1935; s. Herbert R. Jr. and Yvonne (Miller) W.; m. Dorothy Joyce Sherman, Sept. 7, 1957; children: Amelia Wallace, Herbert A. JR., Adam S. BA, Colgate U., 1958; MDiv, Garrett Theol. Sem., 1962; D in Ministry, Drew Theol. Sch., 1976. Asst. minister Grace Meth. Ch., Joliet, Ill., 1959-62; minister Belle Vista Meth. Ch., Clifton, N.J., 1963-67, Clinton (N.J.) United Meth. Ch., 1967-73, Wesley United Meth. Ch., South Plainfield, N.J., 1973-78; sr. minister First United Meth. Ch., Newton, N.J., 1978—; mem. No. N.J. Bd. Pensions, Madison, 1989—; bd. dirs. United Meth. Homes of N.J., Neptune. Mem. Sussex County Honors, Franklin, N.J., 1986—; bd. dirs. Newton Meml. Hosp., 1989—. Gustavus Swift fellow Am. U., 1962. Mem. World Meth. Coun., Newton Area Clergy Assn. (pres. 1989—), Newton Country Club, Rotary (scholarship com. Newton chpt. 1978—). Office: First United Meth Ch 111 Ryerson Ave Newton NJ 07860

WELCH, JAMES SCOTT, minister, religious organization administrator; b. Tulsa, Aug. 14, 1939; s. William Howard Taft and Mary Virginia (Jordan) W.; m. Nancy Jane Schaub, Sept. 11, 1982; 1 child, Kyle Samuel. BS, U. Okla., 1962; MDiv, Princeton Theol. Sem., 1965. Ordained to ministry Presbyn. Ch. (USA), 1965. Asst. min. 1st Presbyn. Ch., Darby, Pa., 1964-65; assoc. min. Elmwood Presbyn. Ch., Syracuse, N.Y., 1965-69, Fox Chapel Presbyn. Ch., Pitts., 1969-73; assoc. dir. Coalition for Christian Outreach, Pitts., 1973—; pres., exec. dir. Summer's Best Two Weeks, Christian Camps of Pitts., Inc., Boswell, Pa., 1969—. Mem. Christian Camping Internat. Home and Office: Summers Best Two Weeks RD 2 Box 299 Boswell PA 15531

WELCH, LOUISE BANNER, minister; b. McKinney, Tex., Aug. 6, 1926; d. Beverley Barrett and Ella Lorraine (Bost) Banner; children: John Goodloe, Mary Louise Dykes. MA in Econs., Western Ill. U., 1971; MA in Polit. Sci., Tex. A&M U., 1979; MA in Theol. Study, So. Meth. U., 1982. Minister United Meth. Ch., Ladonia, Tex., 1979-89, Ladonia-Pecan Gap, Tex., 1989—. Bd. dirs. Hunt County Mus., Greenville, Tex., 1986. Mem. K.P. (mgr. guest house retirement facility Greenville chpt. 1980-83), AAUW (pres. Greenville chpt. 1985-87). Republican. Avocation: structural analysis of Gospel of Luke. Home: 303 W Bonham Ladonia TX 75449 Office: Ladonia-Pecan Gap Meth Ch Pecan Gap TX 75401

WELD, ROGER BOWEN, clergyman; b. Greenfield, Mass., Dec. 1, 1953; s. Wayland Mauney and Luvycie (Bowen) W.; m. Patricia Ann Kaminski, June 7, 1978 (div. 1979). Grad., Sacred Acad. Jamilian U. of the Ordained, Reno, 1976-77, Seminary, 1978-82; student, U. Nev., 1983-85; postgrad., Sacred Coll. Jamilian Theology, 1988-90. Ordained to ministry, Internat. Community of Christ Ch. of Second Advent, 1977. Adminstrv. staff Internat. Community of Christ Ch. of Second Advent, Reno, 1977—, exec. officer dept. canon law, 1985—, exec. officer advocates for religious rights and freedoms, 1985—, exec. officer speakers bur., 1985—, exec. officer office pub. info., 1986—, mgr. Jamilian Univ. Press, 1987—, dir. advt. prodns., 1988—. Author: Twelve Generations of the Family of Weld: Edmund to Wayland Mauney, 1986. Staff sgt. USAF, 1971-75. Named Life Mem., Sacred Oversee, 1991. Mem. Nev. Clergyman's Assn., Andean Explorers Found. and Ocean Sailing Club (exec. sec. 1988—). Republican. Avocations: photography, cinematography, videography, print media. Office: Internat Community Christ 643 Ralston St Reno NV 89503 *In the volatile arena of international politics, mankind's hope rests upon the acceptance of its spiritual destiny, not dwelling on its material past.*

WELDER, SISTER THOMAS, academic administrator; b. Linton, N.D., Apr. 27, 1940; d. Sebastian Welder and Mary Ann Kuhn. BA in Music, Coll. St. Scholastica, 1963; MusM, Northwestern U., 1968; cert., Harvard Inst. Ednl. Mgmt. Joined Annunciation Priory, Benedictine Community of Religious Women, 1961. Asst. prof. music Mary Coll, Univ. of Mary, Bismarck, N.D., 1963-76, dir. deferred giving and ch. relations, 1976-78; pres. U. Mary, Bismarck, 1978—; bd. dirs. Provident Life Ins. Co., Bismarck, MDU Resources Group Inc., Bismarck. V.p. bd. dirs. St. Alexius Med. Ctr., Bismarck, 1984—, Health Care United, Inc., Bismarck, 1986—; charter mem. Theodore Roosevelt Medora Found.; mem. N.D. 2000 Com. Bush Found. fellow, Mpls., 1987. Mem. Coun. Ind. Colls., Am. Coun. Edn. Nat. Identification Program, N. Cen. Assn. Colls. & Schs. (cons., evaluator, accreditation rev. coun. mem.). Avocations: reading, swimming, concerts, art, community events. Office: U Mary 7500 University Dr Bismarck ND 58504

WELDING, SISTER MINNETTE SUSAN, nun, religious administrator; b. Pitts., Aug. 25, 1960; d. John Ronald and Mary Ann (Evans) W. BA, Marywood Coll., 1982; postgrad., Fordham U., 1988—. Coord. religious edn. St. Gabriel of the Sorrowful Virgin, Pitts., 1982-83; high sch. religion tchr. Bishop Guilfoyle High Sch., Altoona, Pa., 1986-89, dept. chairperson of religion, 1987-89; coord. youth ministries Blessed Sacrament Ch., Staten Island, N.Y., 1989—; cons. high sch. religion edn. Office for Parish High Sch. Religion Edn. Archdiocese of N.Y.-Catechetical, Staten Island; parish coun. mem., liturgy/musician com., Christian svc. com. Blessed Sacrament Parish, Staten Island, 1989—. Youth organizer Blood Dr.-Parish, Staten Island, 1989—; parish rep. Pro-Life Com., Staten Island, 1989—; youth organizer and server Project Hospitality Soup Kitchen, Outreach Ctr., Staten Island, 1990—; vol. worker/youth organizer Caritas Mission-Young People Who Care, Frenchville, Pa., 1990, 91. Office: Ch of the Blessed Sacrament 30 Manor Rd Staten Island NY 10310

WELDON, ANN BLAIN, religion writer; b. Roanoke, Va., June 12, 1911; d. Samuel Stuart and Jean Maurice (Vaughan) Blain; student Nat. Bus. Coll. 1931, U. Va. Extension, 1932-36; m. Jack Weldon, Sept. 11, 1937; children—Ann Stuart, John Blain. Mem. secretarial, writing staffs Roanoke (Va.) Times and World News newspapers, 1933-41, also Sta. WDBJ-AM; corr. Times Publ. Co., St. Petersburg, Fla., 1965-70; religion writer St. Petersburg Evening Ind., 1970-85; free-lance writer on religious events, other subjects, 1969-89; speaker women's groups. Author: Twenty Years as a Religion Writer, 1988. Bible tchr. Sunday Sch. Presbyn. Ch., 1928-64; bd. dirs. Aid to Refugees, 1983-87. Mem. DAR, Religion Newswriters Assn., Fla. Press Women, (sec. 1981-83, 1st and 2d Place awards 1982, 1st Place award 1983), PEO, Sigma Delta Chi. Democrat. Clubs: garden, womens. Home: 5025 39th St S Saint Petersburg FL 33711

WELDON, DAVID JOSEPH, JR., physician; b. Amityville, N.Y., Aug. 31, 1953; s. David Joseph and Anna (Mallardi) W.; m. Nancy Sourbeck, Nov. 26, 1956; 1 child, Kathryn. BS, SUNY, Stony Brook, 1978; MD, SUNY, Buffalo, 1981. Elder Zion Christian Fellowship, Palm Bay, Fla., 1991—; pvt. practice, Melbourne, Fla., 1987—; pres. Space Coast Family Forum, Melbourne, 1988-91. Maj. USAR, 1981—. Mem. AMA, Am. Coll. Physicians, Fla. Med. Assn. Home: 1602 Willard Rd Palm Bay FL 32907 Office: Melbourne Internal Medicine 200 E Sheridan Rd Melbourne FL 32907

WELLER, WENDY FOSSGREEN, minister; b. Lodi, Calif., July 19, 1958; d. Robert Donald and Doris Bernice (Moore) Fossgreen; m. Mark Edward Weller, Oct. 20, 1990. BA, Chico State U., 1981; MDiv, Chgo. Theol. Sem., 1984. Ordained to ministry United Meth. Ch., 1990. Assoc. pastor 1st United Meth. Ch., San Leandro, Calif., 1984-88; pastor Ione (Calif.) Community United Meth. Ch., 1988—; bd. dirs. Sierra Svc. Project, Calif., 1985—; chairperson Ann. Conf. Worship Task Force, United Meth. Ch., Calif.-Nev., 1990. Executed worship visuals for Calif.-Nev. Ann. Conf., 1989-90. Mem. Sch. Attendance Rev. Bd., San Leandro, 1984-88, Sexuality/Family Life Curriculum Com., Amador County United Sch. Dist., 1989—, Mental Health Adv. Bd., Amador County, 1990—. Pres.'s Prize fellow Chgo. Theol. Sem., 1981, Albert Newman fellow Chgo. Theol. Sem., 1982-83. Mem. AAUW, Am. Acad. Religion. Home: PO Box 1046 Ione CA 95640 Office: Ione Community United Meth Ch PO Box 1046 Ione CA 95640

WELLS, AUBREY (BRUCE), minister; b. Louisville, June 25, 1954; s. Kenneth William and Zelda Ruth (Banks) Seubold; m. Marsha Jo Lodgerwood, June 7, 1980; children: Joel, Nathan, David. Grad. high sch., Louisville. Min. Louisville Problem Pregnancy Ctr., 1984-86, Beautiful Feet Missions, Louisville, 1982—; owner Am. Discount Office Supply, Morganfield, Ky., 1990—; deacon, Trinity Chapel Assembly of God, Louisville, 1980-83; elder, Jacob's Well Ch, Louisville, 1986-88; bd. dirs., Beautiful Feet Missions, Louisville, 1982—. Author tape series, Easy Evangelsim, 1985. Office: Buautiful Feet Missions Inc 107 W Main ST PO Box 509 Morganfield KY 42437

WELLS, BARBARA, minister; b. Ft. Belvoir, Va., May 1, 1960; s. John Murrell and Rollene (Sumner) W.; m. Jaco ten Hove, Oct. 7, 1990. BA, George Mason U., 1981; MDiv, Meadville/Lombard U., 1985; MA, U. Chgo., 1985. Ordained to ministry Unitarian Universalist Ch., 1985. Intern minister Rockford (Ill.) Unitarian Ch., 1984-85; assoc. minister East Shore Unitarian Ch., Bellevue, Wash., 1985-91; minister Woodinville (Wash.) Unitarian Universalist Ch., 1991—; facilitator Peace Task Torce Ch. Coun. of Greater Seattle, 1986—; chair Young Adult Ministries Working Group Unitarian Universalist Assn., Boston, 1988—; mem. exec. com., bd. dirs. Ch. Coun. of Greater Seattle, 1988-90. Contbr. articles to profl. jour. Mem. Unitarian Universalist Ministers Assn. (nominating com. 1991—), Humptulips Study Group (scribe 1988-90), Unitarian Universalist Women's Fedn., Alban Inst. Democrat. Office: PO Box 111 Woodinville WA 98072

WELLS, BRIAN JEFFREY, minister; b. Indpls., Jan. 15, 1960; s. James Spencer and Grace Alma (Terry) Wells; m. Barbara Ann Jenkins, Dec. 18, 1982; children: Ryan, Briana. BS, Ind. Bapt. Coll., Indpls., 1982; M in Theol. Studies, Grand Rapids Bapt. Sem., 1987. Ordained to ministry, Bapt. Ch., 1980. Assoc. minister Zion Hope Bapt. Ch., Indpls., 1975-85, Community Bapt. Bible Ch., Grand Rapids, 1985-87; pastor Zion Hope Bapt. Ch., Indpls., 1987—; chmn. religion Martin U., Indpls., 1989—, prof. religion, 1988—; asst. dir. Inst. Urban Ministry, Indpls., 1989—. Author poetry: Tomorrow, 1978. Pres. Zion Hope Christian Sch., Indpls., 1987—. Office: Zion Hope Bapt Ch 5950 E 46th St Indianapolis IN 46226

WELLS, DONALD AUSTIN, minister; b. Brookline, Mass., June 25, 1937; s. Moses L. and Mary (Parsons) W.; m. Elizabeth Ann Granlund, June 27, 1939; children: Jeremy, Pamela. BS, Boston U., 1959; MDiv, Gordon-Conwell Theol. Sem., 1962; PhD, Boston U., 1972. Ordained to ministry United Ch. of Christ, 1964. Pastor Pilgrim Congl. Ch., Cambridge, Mass., 1964-69; co-mgr. Internat. Fellowship House, Boston, 1969-71, also bd. dirs.; pastor Trinity Covenant Ch., Lexington, Mass., 1971-79; sr. min. First Congl. Ch., Melrose, Mass., 1979-88; exec. dir. Mass. Bible Soc., Boston, 1988—; bd. dirs. Mass. Coun. of Chs., Boston, 1989—; mem. Mass. Commn. on Christian Unity, 1988—; mem. long lange planning com. City Mission Soc., Boston, 1988-90. Contbr. articles to profl. jours. Mem. Am. Soc. Ch. History, Am. Acad. Religion. Home: 54 Birch Rd Andover MA 01810 Office: Mass Bible Soc 41 Bromfield St Boston MA 02108

WELLS, GEORGE HENRY, minister; b. Durant, Okla., May 14, 1940; s. Philip Yancy and Delta Iona (Harlin) W.; m. Deborah Lynn Lehman, Mar. 21, 1984. BAEd, U. Okla., 1961; BD, St. Andrews U., Scotland, 1964; MDiv, San Francisco Theol. Sem., 1980, DMin, 1984. Ordained to ministry So. Bapt. Conv., 1962, United Presbyn. Ch. USA, 1980. Pastor Francis (Okla.) Bapt. Ch., 1960-61; min. evangelism and youth First Bapt. Ch., Ada, Okla., 1961-63; dir. crusades Haggai Evang. Assn. Atlanta, 1965-69; pastor adminstrn. First Presbyn. Ch., Bakersfield, Calif., 1969-76; assoc. pastor Fair Oaks (Calif.) Presbyn. Ch., 1976-83, co-pastor, 1983-84, pastor, 1985—; Bd. dirs. HIS Farm, Inc., Sacramento. Author: Electronic Church Awareness Guide, 1983. Chmn. Greater Sacramento Concert of Prayer, 1989-90; bd. dirs. Law Enforcement Chaplaincy, 1988-90; chaplain NBA Sacramento Kings, 1985—. Named one of Outstanding Young Men in Am. U.S. Jaycees, 1974; Rotary Found. fellow St. Andrews U., 1964. Mem. Nat. Assn. Christian Bus. Adminstrs., Nat. Assn. Evangs., Alpha Chi. Republican. Home: 4592 Minnesota Ave Fair Oaks CA 95628 Office: Fair Okas Presbyn Ch 11427 Fair Oaks Blvd Fair Oaks CA 95628 *The fact God loves me and provides for my salvation renders me speechless.*

WELLS, JERE' LEVERETTE, minister; b. Broken Bow, Nebr., Oct. 24, 1939; s. William Henry and Lucille Edna (Roberts) W.; m. Beverly Jeanne Moore, Aug. 17, 1963 (div. Sept. 1978); children: Jeffrey Lyn, Jason Jere', Jeremy Wayne, Joshua William; m. Patricia May Brown, Dec. 28, 1984; children: Patricia Michele Blakley, Mandy Camille Blakley. BA, BTh., Nebr. Christian Coll., 1964; MDiv, Phillips U., 1969; D in Ministry, McCormick Theol. Sem., 1979. Ordained to ministry Christian Ch., 1963. Min. Christian Ch., Orchard, Nebr., 1959-63, Akron, Iowa, 1963-64, Davenport, Okla., 1964-66, Billings, Okla., 1966-69, Pauls Valley, Okla., 1969-76; min. First Christian Ch., Guymon, Okla., 1976—; moderator S.W. region Hi-Plains Area Christian Ch., Amarillo, Tex., 1987-90, pers. com. S.W. region, Ft. Worth, 1989-90, regional coun. S.W. region, 1987-90; pres. Guymon Ministerial Alliance, Guymon, 1983-84. Contbr. articles to local newspaper. Chmn. Spiritual Aims Com., Pancake Day Com; pres. Panhandle Treatment Ctr., 1987. Mem. Tex. County Arts & Humanities Coun. (pres. 1979), Kiwanis, Masons. Democrat. Office: First Christian Church PO Box 409 Guymon OK 73942

WELLS, KEITH PHILIP, minister, librarian; b. Pitts., Mar. 4, 1955; s. Paul Lambert and Esther Marie (Herdle) W. BA, Westminster Coll., 1977; MDiv, Trinity Evang. Divinity Sch., 1980; MLS, U. Pitts., 1985. Intern pastor Grace United Meth. Ch., Prairieview, Ill., 1978-80; assoc. pastor Grace United Meth. Ch., Indiana, Pa., 1980-83; pastor 4th St. United Meth. Ch., North Braddock, Pa., 1983-84; theol. cataloger Drew U., Madison, N.J., 1985-86; reference libr. Trinity Evang. Divinity Sch., Deerfield, Ill., 1986—. Recipient God and Country award Boy Scouts Am., 1968. Mem. Intervarsity Urbana Conf. (del. 1976), Pa. Ministerial Assn., Indiana Ministerial Assn. (pres. chpt. 1982-83), West Pa. Conf. United Meth. Ch. (chmn. bd. child care 1981-82). Office: Trinity Evang Divinity Sch 2065 Half Day Rd Deerfield IL 60015 *It is not what happens to us that determines the quality of our lives. It is how we respond that makes the real difference.*

WELLS, LYNN ANNETTE, lay worker; b. Birmingham, Ala., Aug. 19, 1950; d. Ray Ernest Wells and Imogene Taylor; m. E. Gene Hall, May 12, 1985; children: Vincent, Erich. AS in Secretarial Studies, U. Palm Beach, 1969; BS, U. Tex., El Paso, 1980. Adminstr. Palm Lake Bapt. Assn., West Palm Beach, Fla., 1989-90; adminstrv. asst., dir. WMU and dir. presch. dept. Palm Springs (Fla.) Bapt. Ch., 1990—; cons. Palm Beach Atlantic Coll., West Palm Beach, 1989—; cons., computer program trainer Palm Beach County; dir. Woman's Missionary Union, Haverhill Bapt. Ch., West Palm Beach, 1988-89. Editor (newsletter) Gleam, 1989, Echo, 1990—; asst. editor (newsletter) Tng. Assistance Program, 1986-88. Mem. com. to elect Don Hazelton, West Palm Beach, 1972; chair com. to elect Gene Hall, Las Vegas, Nev., 1986. Lt. USAR, 1975-81. Networks cert. 3M and IBM, Novell, 1986. Mem. NAFE, ASTD (sec. 1987-88), Palm Lake Bapt. Assn.-Woman's Missionary Union (asst. dir. 1989—, dir. Mission Friends 1989-90). Republican. Home: 1702 Wharf Lna Ct Greenacres FL 33463 Office: Palm Springs Bapt Ch 3300 10th Ave N Palm Springs FL 33461 *I am reminded constantly of the influence of knowing Christ. He permeates each and every thing I do and say. My relationships with friends, family and others are enriched by this knowledge.*

WELLS, ROBERT LOUIS, priest; b. Alexandria, La., Mar. 18, 1939; s. Charles Alexander Jr. and Elouise (Hinton) W.; m. Michal Ann McCubbin, Mar. 12, 1966 (div. Oct. 1982); children: Steve, David (dec.), Melissa; m. Carol Hunter, Apr. 3, 1983; 1 child, Matthew. BA, La. State U., 1961; MDiv, Golden Gate Bapt. Theol. Sem., 1965. Pastor Second Bapt. Ch., Lubbock, Tex., 1966-78; exec. dir. CONTACT Lubbock, Inc., 1979-91; religion tchr. All Saints Episcopal Sch., Lubbock, 1988-91, dir. counseling, 1988-91; pvt. practice pastoral counselor Lubbock, 1982-91; asst. rector St. Paul's Episcopal Ch., Waco, Tex., 1991—; chaplain Canterbury Assn. Baylor U., Waco, 1991—; mem., chmn. bd. dirs. CONTACT USA, Inc., Harrisburg, Pa., 1971-82; mem., treas. secretariat Life Line Internat., Harrisburg, 1979-87; bd. dirs. Nat. Assn. Contact Dirs., Harrisburg, 1984-85. Editor (NASCOD jour.) Chiasma, 1984. Mem., chmn. Community Planning Coun., Lubbock, 1976-79; bd. dirs. United Way of Lubbock, Inc., 1977-78; mem. City-County Child Welfare Bd., Lubbock, 1968-71, South Plains Info. and Referral Bd., Lubbock, 1981, Nat. Assn. Eagle Scouts, Boy Scouts Am., 1979—. Parish Minister's fellow The Fund for Theol. Edn., Inc., 1975-76; named Citizen of the Yr., Lubbock unit Tex. chpt. NASW, 1980. Mem. Am. Assn. Pastoral Counselors, Assn. for Psychol. Type, Masons, Lambda Chi Alpha. Democrat. Episcopalian. Avocations: scuba diving, swimming, photography, travel. Home: 2823 Sanger Ave Waco TX 76707 Office: St Pauls Episcopal Ch 515 Columbus Ave Waco TX 76701

WELLS, WILLIAM LEROY, clergyman; s. Bion Orville and Pauline (Brashler) W.; m. Mary Jesse Apolinar, June 5, 1965; children: Jeffrey Grant, William LeRoy, Mark Andrew. B.A., Seattle Pacific Coll., 1956; M.Div., Berkeley Bapt. Div. Sch., 1959; D.Min., Pitts. Theol. Sem., 1978. Ordained to ministry, Baptist Ch., 1959; pastor First Bapt. Ch., Hay, Wash., 1959-62, Delta Community Bapt. Ch., Everett, Wash., 1962-66; minister Leadership Devel. program Pitts. Bapt. Assn., 1973-80; exec. minister Wis. Bapt. State Conv., 1980—. Served with AUS, 1966-73. Decorated Bronze Star medal. Democrat. Club: Milwaukee Athletic. Author: Planning for Evangelism in the Local Church, 1978.

WELLS, WILLIAM THOMAS, minister; b. London, Ont., Can., Aug. 3, 1938; s. Earnest Stanley and Winnifred Agnes (Staerck) W.; m. Judith Ann Green, Sept. 25, 1965; children: Gregory, Robert. BA, U. Western Ont., 1962; BDiv, Queen's U., 1965; DMin, Drew U., 1989. Ordained to ministry United Ch. Can., 1965. Min. Plumas-Lakeshore Pastoral Charge, Man., Can., 1965-67, 1st Westminster Ch., London, 1967-71; sr. min. Northminster Ch., Peterborough, Ont., 1971-90; min. The Donway Ch., Toronto, Ont., Can., 1990—; chmn. Peterborough Presbytery, 1981-83; pres. Bay of Quinte Conf., Kingston, Ont., 1984-85. Founding mem. Telecare, Peterborough, 1977. Capt. RCAF. Home: 26 Royal Doulton Dr, Don Mills, ON Canada M3A 1N5 Office: The Donway Ch, 230 The Donway W, Don Mills, ON Canada M3B 2V8 *The great discoveries and events of our times only reinforce that faith, hope and love are still the best passport to a better tomorrow.*

WELSH, LAWRENCE H., bishop; b. Winton, Wyo., Feb. 1, 1935. Ed., U. Wyo., St. John's Sem., Minn., Cath. U. Am. Ordained priest Roman Cath. Ch., 1962. Bishop Diocese of Spokane, Wash., 1978-90. Office: Spokane Diocese 1023 W Riverside Ave PO Box 1453 Spokane WA 99210

WELSH, THOMAS J., bishop; b. Weatherly, Pa., Dec. 20, 1921. Grad., St. Charles Borromeo Sem., Phila., Cath. U. Am. Ordained priest Roman Cath. Ch., 1946. Ordained titular bishop of Scattery Island and aux. bishop of Phila., 1970-74; 1st bishop of Arlington Va., 1974-83; bishop of Allentown Pa., 1983—. Office: Chancery Office 202 N 17th St PO Box F Allentown PA 18105

WELSH, WILLIAM CURTIS, consultant; b. Wichita, Kans., Dec. 28, 1952; s. William Spencer Welsh and Hazel (Talley) Pratt; m. Bonnie J. Wissink, June 4, 1971; children: Kimberly D., Angela L., Christina L. BA, Drake U., 1985; MA in Theol. Studies, No. Bapt. Sem., Lombard, Ill., 1988. Dir. Christian edn. South Ch., Mt. Prospect, Ill., 1985-87; dir. Mission Ctr. No. Bapt. Sem., Lombard, 1987-88; dir. pub. edn. Ams. United for Life, Chgo., 1988-91; cons. Covenant Ptnrs., 1991—. Pres. Fairfield (Iowa) Jaycees, 1977, Fairfield Area Community Theater, 1979. Recipient Outstanding Young Man in Am. award Fairfield Jaycees, 1978. Mem. Christian Mgmt. Assn. Republican. Home: 1010 Taft Ave Wheaton IL 60187

WELTMAN, SHELDON J., rabbi; b. Cleve., May 18, 1936; s. Ben W. and Sadie (Glassman) Lesnick. MHL, Jewish Theol. Seminary, N.Y.C., 1960; MPhil, Drew U., Madison, N.J., 1980, PhD, 1990; DD, U. Judaism, L.A., 1988. Ordained, 1962. Asst. rabbi Rodeph Shalom, Bridgeport, Conn., 1962-65; rabbi Morristown (N.J.) Jewish Ctr., 1967-81, Bnai Hayim, L.A., 1983—; cons. Groman Mortuary, L.A., 1987—; chaplain various prisons, nursing homes, and hosps., L.A., 1982—. Capt. U.S. Army, 1965-67. Mem. Rabbinical Assembly. Office: Temple Bnai Hayim 4302 Van Nuys Blvd Sherman Oaks CA 91403

WENCK, GUY ADDISON, minister; b. Balt., Nov. 9, 1943; s. Millard Fillmore III and Doris (Addison) W.; m. Martha Long, June 13, 1964; children: Guy Allen, Lori Jane. AB in Religion, Philosophy and History, Catawba Coll., Salisbury, N.C., 1965; BD, M in Divinity, Lancaster (Pa.) Theol. Sem. of United Ch. Christ, 1968; postgrad., Johns Hopkins U., 1969-85. Ordained to ministry United Ch. Christ, 1968. Pastor First and St. Stephen's United Ch. of Christ, Balt., 1975-87; account supr. Lewis Advt., Balt., 1988; mktg. dir. Art Comp and Design, Lutherville, Md., 1987; v.p. sales Pub. Corp. Am., 1986, also mktg. rep. and indsl. chaplain; dir. Loch-York Ecumenical Assn., Balt., 1983-86. Trustee Matthew 25:35 Assn., 1983—, bd. dirs., 1983—; coordinator York-Register Coalition, Balt., 1976-87; co-founder NE Cluster United Ch. of Christ Chs., 1980; chaplain Balt. County Fire Dept., 1985—. Named one of Baltimore's Best City of Balt.; recipient Silver award City of Balt.; recipient Outstanding Community Achievement award WCAO Radio, 1988. Mem. Chesapeake Assn. of United Ch. Christ Ministerium (sec. 1975-76). Democrat.

WENDOLOSKI, ANTHONY JOSEPH, JR., deacon; b. Providence, May 25, 1945; s. Anthony Joseph and Yvonne Virginia (Pichette) W.; m. Jo-Ann Giorgio, Nov. 19, 1966; children: Marie Elaine, Kimberly Ann, Gayle Ann. Student, Johnson and Wales Jr. Coll., Diocese of Providence. Ordained deacon Roman Cath. Ch., 1982. Asst. to pastor Our Lady of Lourdes Parish, Providence, 1982—; operator diamond cutter machine Park

Lane Assocs., Providence, 1987—. Deacon, chaplain R.I. Tng. Sch., Cranston, 1982—. Mem. KC, Cath. Order Foresters (fin. sec. 1960, chief ranger 1960-79). Democrat. Home: 62 General St Apt 3B Providence RI 02904

WENGEL, JOHN R., religion educator; b. Orange, Calif., Aug. 24, 1966; s. Norman O. and Claudia (Heinberg) W.; m. Cindy L. Bunker, Apr. 8, 1989. BA, Christ Coll., Irvine, Calif., 1988. Dir. Christian Edn. Trinity Luth. Ch., Alamogordo, N.Mex., 1988-89, Christ Luth. Ch., Brea, Calif., 1989—. Republican. Office: Christ Luth Ch 820 W Imperial Hwy Brea CA 92621

WENGER, JAMES CARL, pastor; b. Toledo, June 23, 1958; s. Victor Romain and Dorothy (Krieger) W.; m. Nancy Ann Howell, Dec. 29, 1984; 1 child, Erin LeAnn. BA, Wartburg Coll., 1980; MDiv, Wartburg Sem., 1985. Pastor Feast of Victory Luth. Ch., Acme, Mich., 1985-88, St. Paul Luth. Ch., Dearborn, Mich., 1988—; mem. com. div. for svc. and mission Mich. Synod, 1985-88; co-chair synod com. for youth ministry S.E. Mich. Synod, 1988—; chair bd. dirs. Dearborn Pastoral Counseling Ctr., 1989—. Treas. Acme Civic Assn., 1985-88; chair community involvement com. Kiwanis Internat., Traverse City, Mich., 1985-88. Office: St Paul Luth Ch 21915 Beech St Dearborn MI 48124

WENGERTSMAN, CAROL ANN, lay worker; b. Bridgeport, Conn., Feb. 9, 1951; d. Stephen Michael and Mary (Palacino) Swetz; m. John Francis Wengertsman, June 3, 1972; children: David, Nancy, Peter, Matthew, Timothy. BS, Cen. Conn. State U., 1972, postgrad., 1991—. Cert. tchr. English, Conn. Tutor in English Manchester (Conn.) Bd. Edn., 1985—; coord. religious edn. St. Bridget Ch., Manchester, 1988-90, dir. religious edn., 1990—. Co-pres. Waddell Sch. PTA, Manchester, 1986-88. Recipient 10-Yr. Svc. award Hartford Archdiocese Office Religious Edn., 1989. Mem. Hartford Dirs. Religious Edn. Deanery, Nat. Coun. Tchrs. English. Office: St Bridget Ch 80 Main St Manchester CT 06040

WENNES, HOWARD E., bishop. Bishop of Grand Canyon region Evang. Luth. Ch. in Am., Phoenix. Office: Synod of Ariz-So Nev 4423 N 24th St Ste 400 Phoenix AZ 85016*

WENSKI, THOMAS GERARD, priest; b. West Palm Beach, Fla., Oct. 18, 1950; s. Chester Stephen and Louise Mary (Zawacka) W. AA, St. John Vianney Sem., Miami, Fla., 1970; BA, St. Vincent De Paul U., Boynton Beach, Fla., 1972, MDiv, 1975; MA, Fordham U. Ordained priest Roman Cath. Ch., 1976. Assoc. pastor Corpus Christi Cath. Ch., Miami, 1976-79; assoc. dir. Haitian Cath. Ctr., Miami, 1979-84, dir., 1984—; pastor Notre Dame d'Haiti Roman Cath. Ch., Miami, 1984—; Episcopal vicar to cultural groups, Miami, 1990—; mem. Archdioces of Miami Presbyterial Coun., 1988—; host Cath. Focus, Religious TV, Miami, 1989-91. Editor Lavwa Katolik - Creole Lang., 1981—. Mem. Dade County Community Rels. Bd., Miami, 1989—; chmn. Greater Miami United Krome Liaison Com., 1982. Recipient St. Vincent de Paul award, St. Vincent Sem., 1987. Home: 110 NE 62nd St Miami FL 33138 Office: Pierre Toussaint Haitian Ct 110 NE 62nd St Miami FL 33138

WERB, HILLEL DAVID, rabbi; b. Glen Ridge, N.J., Apr. 15, 1941; s. Morris and Helen (Beiber) W.; m. Linda Iris Gershkowitz, Aug. 9, 1964; children: Rachel, Shira, Ari, Ezra. BA, Yeshiva U., N.Y.C., 1963; MHL, Jewish Theol. Sem., N.Y.C., 1965. Ordained rabbi, 1967. Rabbi Congregation Ahavath Achim, Belleville, N.J., 1965-67, Beth Israel Synagogue, Roanoke, Va., 1967-71, Temple Beth Emunah, Brockton, Mass., 1971—; bd. dirs. Jewish Community Ctr. Central Bd., Boston, 1984-88; prin. Temple Beth Emunah Religious Sch., Brockton, 1971—. Founder, bd. dirs. Brockton Interfaith Community, 1988; founder, exec. bd. Solomon Schechter Hebrew Day Sch., 1988. Mem. Rabbinical Assy. of Am., Mass. Bd. Rabbis (pres. 1984-86), New Eng. Reg. Rabbinical Assy. (pres. 1986-88), Brockton Interfaith Clergy Assn. Home: Temple Beth Emunah Pearl and Torrey Sts Brockton MA 02401 *It would be better if man had been born old and gotten progressively younger so that he could enjoy life before he became too ill or infirm to appreciate it. Since this is not possible, we must enjoy life now, to its' fullest while we have the opportunity.*

WERGER, PAUL MYRON, bishop; b. Greenville, Pa., June 13, 1931; s. Jacob Paul and Laura Annetta (Greenwalt) W.; m. Diane Mae Ellison, July 26, 1957; children: Paul Myron, Jonathan David, Matthew James, Mary Dianne. BA, Thiel Coll., 1954; MDiv, Northwestern Theol. Sem., Mpls., 1957, DD (hon.), 1976; LHD (hon.), Grand View Coll., 1985. Ordained to ministry, Luth. Ch. Am., 1957. Pastor Apostles Luth. Ch., St. Paul, 1957-61, St. Luke's Luth. Ch., Bloomington, Minn., 1961-78; bishop Iowa Synod Luth. Ch. Am., Des Moines, 1978-88, S.E. Iowa Synod, Iowa City, 1987—; chmn. Conf. Bishops Evang. Luth. Ch. Am. 1987-91, mem. ch. coun. 1988-91, bishop adv. mem., 1988, stewardship and evangelism com. NW Synod, 1959-62; mem. bd. social ministry Minn. Synod, 1963-70, mem. exec. bd., dean south suburban dist.; pres., bd. dirs. Luth. Social Services in Minn.; mem. mgmt. com. dir. mission N.Am. Luth. Ch. Am., 1983—; del. Luth. Ch. Am. convs.; pastor evangelist Evang. Outreach; corp. bd. dirs. Fairvi. Contbr. articles to profl. jours. Mem. Bloomington Human Rights Commn.; mem. citizens adv. com. Bloomington Sch. Dist. 271; bd. dirs. Luther Northwestern, 1976, Luth. Sch. Theology, Chgo., 1978-88, Luth. Ch. Am. Found., Grandview Coll., 1978, GrandView Coll., 1978-92, Iowa Luth. Hosp., 1978—, Luth. Soc. Svc. Iowa, 1978—, Fairview Corp., 1985— ; bd. fellows Sch. Religion, U. Iowa; Luth. Ch. in Am. observer Wartburg Theol. Sem., 1986-88. Recipient Thiel Coll. Alumni award for profl. achievement, 1979. Mem. Assn. Bloomington Clergy, Conf. of Luth./Roman Cath. Bishops. Avocations: travel, photography, golf, fishing, sports. Office: SE Iowa Synod Hdqrs 2635 Northgate Dr Iowa City IA 52240

WERK, ALLEN ARTHUR, minister; b. Milw., Jan. 12, 1956; s. Allen Elmer and Rose Mary (Picchiottino) W.; m. Ann Marie Meyer, June 21, 1980; children: Philip Allen, Samuel Walter. AA, Concordia Coll., Milw., 1976; BA, Concordia Coll., Ann Arbor, Mich., 1978; MDiv, Concordia Sem., St. Louis, 1982. Ordained to ministry Luth. Ch.-Mo. Synod., 1982. Vicar Ea. Height Luth. Ch., St. Paul, 1980-81; pastor St. Martins Luth. Ch., Anamoose, N.D., 1982-86, Zion Luth. Ch., Ashtabula, Ohio, 1986—; pub. rels. advisor N.D. Fedn. Luths. for Life, Anamoose, 1983-85, pres., 1985-86; zone pastoral counselor Luth. Women's Missionary League, Anamoose, 1984-86, Ashtabula, 1988—. Mem. Community Chem. Dependency Task Force, Anamoose, 1984-85. Mem. Luth. Laymen's League, Luths. for Life. Office: Zion Luth Ch 2310 W 9th St Ashtabula OH 44004

WERKSTROM, BERTIL, archbishop. Archbishop of Uppsala Ch. of Swedeb. Office: Archbishop of Uppsala, POB 640, 75127 Uppsala Sweden*

WERNER, JAMES EDWARD, minister; b. Elgin, Ill., Apr. 6, 1951; s. Edward Henry and Henrietta (Lichthardt) W.; m. Nancy Jo Lilly, Sept. 15, 1979; children: Megan Elizabeth, Mary Catherine, Melissa Anne, Melanie Amanda. BA, Elmhurst Coll., 1973; MDiv, Lancaster Theol. Sem., 1976. Ordained to ministry United Ch. of Christ, 1976. Assoc. pastor St. Paul United Ch. of Christ, 1976-82; pastor 1st Congl. Ch., Rock Falls, Ill., 1982—; rec. sec. Ministerial Assn., Sterling-Rock Falls, 1983-84, pres. 1984—; dean United Ch. Mission Coun., Sterling-Rock Falls, 1983-84; mem. spiritual growth com. No. Ill. Assn. United Ch. Christ, 1983-87, sec. 1990-91. Mem. sch. bd. Dist. 12, Ill. Home: 907 Dixon Ave Rock Falls IL 61071 Office: 1st Congl United Ch of Christ 905 Dixon Ave Rock Falls IL 61071

WERNING, WALDO JOHN, minister; b. Newhall, Iowa, May 1, 1921; s. George Conrad and Paula (Dornseif) W.; m. Ruth Charlotte Kienow, July 28, 1945; children: Sharon Ann, Daniel John, Charlotte Ruth, Jonathan Paul, James Mark. BA, Concordia Sem., St. Louis, 1945; DD (hon.), Concordia Sem., Porto Allegre, Brazil, 1970. Ordained to ministry Luth. Ch.-Mo. Synod, 1945. Pastor Zion Luth. Ch., Lockwood, Mo., 1945-48, Emmanuel Luth. Ch., Broken Arrow, Okla., 1948-52; asst. stewardship counselor Luth. Ch.-Mo. Synod, St. Louis, 1952-56; stewardship and mission counselor So. Nebr. dist. Luth. Ch.-Mo. Synod, Lincoln, Nebr., 1956-66; stewardship counselor South Wis. dist. Luth. Ch.-Mo. Synod, Milw., 1966-76; dir. devel. Concordia Theol. Sem., Ft. Wayne, Ind., 1976-88, adj. prof., 1976—; dir., cons. Discipling/Stewardship Ctr., Ft. Wayne, 1982—; editor topic Internat. Luth. Women Missionary League, 1959-69; speaker U.S. Congress on Ch. Growth, Garden Grove, Calif., 1975; sectional speaker Lausanne II Congress on World Evangelization, Manila, 1989; bd. dirs., sec. All Nations Missions, Pasadena, Calif., 1986—; condr. numerous seminars and workshops. Author: The Radical Nature of Christianity, 1975, Christian Stewards—Confronted and Committed, 1982, Vision and Strategy for Church Growth, 1983, Supply-Side Stewardship, 1986, Renewal for the 21st Century Church, 1988. Mem. Nat. Assn. Evang. Stewardship Commn., NET Bible Soc. (sec., bd. dirs. 1987—), Luth. Bible Transls. (chmn., vice chmn. 1965-85), Haiti Mission Soc. (bd. dirs. 1990—), Toastmasters (sec., treas.). Home: 1914 Wendmere Ln Fort Wayne IN 46825 Office: Discipling/Stewardship Ctr 5729 St Joe Rd Fort Wayne IN 46835

WERRY, ARTHUR EUGENE, minister; b. Weisbaden, Fed. Republic Germany, Apr. 28, 1960; came to U.S., 1962; s. Marshall Eugene and Delores June (Trobough) W.; m. Barbara Sue Elkins, June 16, 1979; children: Shonda Sue, Ashley Renee. BA, Trinity Coll., 1983; MDiv, So. Sem., Louisville, 1988. Ordained to ministry So. Bapt. Conv., 1989. Asst. pastor First Bapt. Ch., McHenry, Ill., 1985-86; youth min. intern St. Matthews Bapt., Louisville, 1987-88; ch. planter, pastor New Life Ch., Fraser, Mich., 1989—. Mem. Macomb Bapt. Assn. (dir. sem. extension, 1989—). Home: 25851 Carl St Roseville MI 48066 Office: New Life Ch 17301 Thirteen Mile Fraser MI 48026

WERST, KEVIN SCOTT, clergyman; b. Dayton, Ohio, Aug. 4, 1958; s. Jack Roger and Shirley Anne (Fitzgerald) W.; m. Patricia Perrello, May 7, 1983; children: Jocelyn, Sara, Matthew. BA, Miami U., Oxford, Ohio, 1980; MDiv, Trinity Evangel. Divinity Sem., 1990. Staff mem. Campus Crusade for Christ/U. Mich., Ann Arbor, 1980-82; v.p. Here's Life Black Am., Atlanta, 1983-87; sem. staff Campus Crusade for Christ, Deerfield, Ill., 1987-90; pastoral intern Rock Evangel. Free Ch., Chgo., 1989-90; campus minister, cons. Campus Crusade for Christ, Cin., 1990—. Mem. Assn. Believers Black Am. (sec. 1988-90). Avocations: theological study, golf, carpentry, basketball. Home: 245 E Shorewood Ct Vernon Hills IL 60061 Office: Campus Crusade for Christ 2065 Half Day Rd Deerfield IL 60015

WESBERRY, JAMES PICKETT, religious organization administrator; b. Bishopville, S.C., Apr. 16, 1906; s. William McLeod and Lillian Ione (Galloway) W.; m. Ruby Lee Perry, Sept. 5, 1929 (dec. Dec. 1941); 1 child, James Pickett; m. Mary Sue Latimer, June 1, 1943 (dec. Sept. 7, 1982); m. Alice Margaret Spratlin, Oct. 15, 1983. AB, Mercer U., 1929, MA, 1930, DD, 1957; BD, Newton Theol. Inst., 1931; M of Sacred Theology, Andover Newton Theol. Inst., 1934; postgrad., Harvard U., 1931, Union Theol. Sem., N.Y.C., 1935, 65, Yale U., 1946, So. Bapt. Theol. Sem., 1957, Princeton U., 1958, Oxford U., 1979; LLD, Atlanta Law Sch., 1946; LHD, LaGrange Coll., 1962; LittD, Bolen-Draughan Coll., 1967. Ordained to ministry Bapt. Ch., 1926; pastor Soperton, Ga., 1928-30, Medford, Mass., 1930-31, Kingstree, S.C., 1931-33, Bamberg, S.C., 1933-44; pastor Morningside Bapt. Ch., Atlanta, 1944-75; pastor emeritus Morningside Bapt. Ch., 1975—; engaged in evangelism, counseling, editing, publishing and chaplaincies, 1975—; mem. exec. com. So. Bapt. Conv., 1959-65, 74-86, mem. chaplains commn., 1973-79, chmn. adminstrv. com., 1974-79; pres. Ga. Bapt. Conv., 1956-57, 57-58, rec. sec., 1970—; prof. Mercer U. extension, Atlanta, 1944-53; pres. Highview Nursing Home, Atlanta, 1947-60, chaplain, 1975—; pres. Nat. Youth Courtesy Found., 1971—; staff corr. Christian Century, 1951-58; editor column The People's Pulpit; columnist Atlanta Times, 1964-65; chaplain Yaarab Temple, 20 yrs.; chaplain Grand Lodge of Ga. Author: Prayers in Congress, 1949, Every Citizen Has A Right to Know, 1954, The Georgian Literature Commission, 1957, Baptists in South Carolina Before the War Between the States, 1966, Rainbow Over Russia, 1962, Meditations for Happy Christians, 1973, Evangelistic Sermons, 1974, When Hell Trembles, 1974, The Morningside Man (Wesberry's biography by James C. Bryant), 1975, Bread in a Barren Land, 1982, The Lord's Day, 1986; editor: Sunday Mag., 1975—; editor: Basharet, 1976-77; asst. editor, 1977—, editor emeritus, 1978—. Chmn. Ga. Lit. Commn., 1953-74; acting chaplain U.S. Ho. Reps., July-Aug., 1949; mem. Gov.'s Citizens Penal Reform Commn., 1968, Fulton County Draft Bd., 1968-71; bd. dirs. Atlanta Fund Rev. Bd., 1964-70, Grady Met. Girls Club, 1969-72, hon. bd. dirs., Atlanta Union Mission, 1972—, Dogwood Assn. Festival, 1970-71; trustee Mercer U., 1944-49, 54-57, 72-74, mem. pres.'s coun., 1974-91, also mem. adv. com. Sch. Pharmacy; trustee Atlanta Bapt. Coll., 1964-72, Truett McConnell Coll., Cleveland, Ga., 1960-65; mem. pres.'s council Tift Coll., Forsyth, Ga., 1976—; bd. mgrs. Lord's Day Alliance U.S., 1971—, exec. dir., 1975—. Elected Man of the South Dixie Bus. mag., 1972; named to South's Hall of Fame, 1972. Mem. Atlanta Area Mil. Chaplains Assn. (hon.), SAR (state chaplain 1981), Royal Order Scotland. Clubs: Atlanta Harvard, Atlanta Athletic, Atlanta Amateur Movie, Half Century of Mercer U. (past pres.). Lodges: Kiwanis, Masons (Shriner), Lions. Home: 1715 Merton Rd NE Atlanta GA 30306 Office: Bapt Ctr 2930 Flowers Rd S Ste 107 Atlanta GA 30341 *Life's supreme joy is found in the service of God. Life becomes sublimely beautiful when it is dedicated to something far greater than ourselves. My greatest ambition is to magnify Christ and to serve the people. I am forever grateful for the privilege of sharing with Christ in making this a better world in which to live for others.*

WESELOH, MELVIN LESLIE, minister; b. Dickinson, N.D., Dec. 29, 1932; s. Henry John and Edith (Oehler) W.; m. Karen H. Miller, June 9, 1957; children: David, Debra, Diane, Daryl. AA, Concordia Coll., St. Paul, 1952; BA, Concordia Sem., St. Louis, 1954, MDiv, 1957. Ordained to ministry Luth. Ch., 1957. Asst. pastor St. Luke's Luth. Ch., N.Y.C., 1957-58; pastor parishes in Minn., 1958-74; pastor Trinity Luth. Ch., Coal Valley, Ill., 1974-77; missionary at large Luth. Ch. Mo.-Synod, Dunlap, Ill., 1977-80; pastor St. Paul's Luth. ch., Havana, Ill., 1980-87, Mt. Calvary Luth., Decatur, Ill., 1987—; counselor Decatur Cir., 1990-91; dist. counselor Luth. Laymen's League, Central, Ill., 1984-88, Luth. Women's Missionary, Central, 1990—; bd. dirs. Cen. Ill. Dist. Luth. Ch.-Mo. Synod, 1991—; camp advisor Camp Cilca, Central, 1975-84. Treas. Community Action, Mora, Minn., 1971-74; bd. dirs. Havana (Ill.) C. of C., 1986-87, Commn. on Aging, Hanava, 1983-84; adult leader Boy Scouts Am., 1955-87. Mem. Luth. Sch. Assn. (advisor 1989—), Confessional Luth. Forum (chmn. 1988—), Lions. Home: 109 Fenway Dr Decatur IL 62521 Office: Mt Calvary Luth Ch 2055 S Franklin St Rd Decatur IL 62521

WESLEY, JOHN PHILLIP, minister; b. Harrodsburg, Ky., Sept. 17, 1950; s. Rex and Margeret (Miller) W.; m. Susan Campbell, Dec. 29, 1979; children from previous marriage: Suzanne, Robert. BA, Cumberland Coll., 1972; M of Divinity, So. Bapt. Sem., Louisville, 1976; D of Ministry, Lexington Theol. Sem., 1983. Ordained to ministry Christian Ch., 1970. Pastor Irvington (Ky.) Bapt. Ch., 1976-77, Felts Chapel United Meth. Ch., Corbin, Ky., 1978-81; assoc. pastor 1st Christian Ch. Disciples of Christ, Corbin, 1983-84; pastor 1st Christian Ch. Disciples of Christ, London, Ky., 1984—. Chairperson Laurel County Foster Care Review Bd., London, 1985—; bd. dirs. State Foster Care Review Bd., Frankfort, Ky., 1985—, chairperson, 1988-89; bd. dirs. United Way of Laurel County, 1986—, chairperson, 1991-92; chairperson Come-Unity Coop. Care, 1989-91. Republican. Lodge: Rotary. Avocations: golf, dancing. Home: 721 Allf Lane London KY 40741

WESLEY, YVONNE EDITH, minister; b. South Woodslee, Ont., Can., July 2, 1936; came to U.S., 1955; d. Achille Lachapelle and Regina (Thibert) Katzenburger; divorced; 1 child, Edward Alvin Wesley. BS in Mental Health, Gannon U., 1980, MS in Community Counseling, 1983; MDiv, Trinity Luth. Sem., Columbus, Ohio, 1988. Ordained to ministry Evang. Luth Ch. in Am., 1988. Sales rep. in indsl. tools and electronics, 1967-77; employment counselor The Women's Ctr., Erie, Pa., 1977-79; counselor, dir. Summer Commonwealth Acad. Achievement Program Gannon U., 1980-84; pastoral intern 1st Luth ch., Xenia, Ohio, 1987-88; pastor Christ Luth. Ch., Mt. Wolf, Pa., 1988—. Mem. Pi Gamma Mu. Office: Christ Luth Ch RD 1 Mount Wolf PA 17347

WESLOH, FERDINAND JOSEPH, priest; b. St. Louis, Dec. 23, 1938; s. Ferdinand Joseph and Theresa Katherine (Wohlschlaeger) W. BA, Cardinal Glennon Coll., St. Louis, 1960; MEd, St. Louis U., 1967. Ordained priest Roman Cath. Ch., 1964; cert. prin., counselor, Mo. Assoc. pastor St. Peter Ch., St. Charles, Mo., 1964-74, St. Clement Ch., St. Louis, 1974-77; pastor St. Ann Ch., Clover Bottom, Mo., 1982-85; assoc. pastor St. John the Bapt. Ch., St. Louis, 1977-82, pastor, 1985—; adminstr. St. John the Bapt. High Sch., 1977-81; adminstr., founder St. Franics Borgia Regional High Sch., Washington, Mo., 1981-85; dean, South St. Louis Deanery of the Archdiocese of St. Louis, 1988—. Mem. KC (chaplain Mo. coun. 1972-74). Home and Office: St John the Bapt Ch 4200 Delor St Saint Louis MO 63116

WESOLOWSKI, KURT SCOTT, minister; b. Chgo., Mar. 9, 1962; s. Walter Charles Wesolowski and Margaret Dorothy (Ross) Hemalato; m. Patricia Ann Hoffman, June 23, 1984. AA, Chaffey Community Coll., Alta Loma, Calif., 1981; BA, Calif. State U., Fullerton, 1984; MDiv, New Orleans Bapt. Theol. Sem., 1990. Min. evangelism, discipleship Lakeside Bapt. Ch., Metairie, La., 1988-89; pastor First Bapt. Ch., Waveland, Miss., 1989-91, Trinity Bapt. Ch., Waterloo, Iowa, 1991—. Home: 1198 Lindner Dr Waterloo IA 50702 Office: Trinity Bapt Ch 3040 Hammond Ave Waterloo IA 50702

WESSEL, JONATHAN ANDREW, clergyman; b. Fairmont, Minn., July 5, 1962; s. Reinhardt Adolph Otto and Kathleen Marie (Klein) W. BA, Concordia Coll., 1984; MDiv, Concordia Theol. Sem., 1988. Ordained to ministry Luth. Ch. Asst. pastor St. Martin's Evang. Luth. Ch., Winona, Minn., 1988—; campus pastor Winona (Minn.) State U., 1988—; sec. Winona Area Ministerium, 1989—; advisor region 4 Luth. Student Fellowship, St. Louis, 1990—. Mem. student athlete assistance program core com. Winona State U., 1989—. Mem. Luth. Edn. Assn., Assn. Luth. Ch. Musicians. Republican. Office: St Martins Evang Luth Ch 328 E Broadway Winona MN 55987

WESSEL, ROGER D., educator; b. Rapid City, S.D., May 22, 1957; s. Alvin E. and Estelle N. (Van Deventer) W.; m. Rita L. Wyrick, May 31, 1980; children: Lindsey De Ann, Lauren Alicia. AA, Tomlinson Coll., 1977; BS, Lee Coll., 1979; MS in Edn., So. Ill. U., Carbondale, 1988, PhD, 1991. Youth pastor Ch. of God of Prophecy, Columbus, Ga., 1979-80; pastor North Pekin (Ill.) Ch. of God of Prophecy, 1983-85, Corinth (Ill.) Christian Fellowship, 1985-90; Sun. sch. sec. Ch. of God of Prophecy, Ill., 1990—; asst. dir. career svcs. Ball State U., Muncie, Ind., 1991—; dir. admissions Tomlinson Coll., Cleveland, Tenn., 1980-83; trustee Tomlinson Coll. Bd. Trustees, Cleveland, Tenn., 1990—; youth camp coord. Ch. of God of Prophecy in Ill., 1985-89. Named to Outstanding Young Man of Am., 1987. Mem. Phi Theta Kappa Nat. Honor Frat., Pi Delta Omricon Honor Soc., Alpha Chi Honor Soc., Phi Kappa Phi Honor Soc., Post-Doctoral Acad. Higher Edn. Home: 504 N Parkwood Dr Muncie IN 47304 *In his heart a man plans his course, but the Lord determines his steps. (Proverbs 16:9).*

WESSELS, DAVID JOSEPH, priest, political scientist; b. St. Louis, Mar. 22, 1945; arrived in Japan, 1970; s. Bernard Henry and Frances Bernadine (Krampe) W. AB in Philosophy, St. Louis U., 1968; MA in Govt., Georgetown U., 1970; Sacrae Theologiae Licentiatus, Sophia U., Tokyo, 1976; PhD in Polit. Sci., Yale U., 1981. Ordained priest Roman Catholic Ch., 1976. Instr. Internat. Coll. Sophia U., Tokyo, 1972-73, 75, assoc. prof., 1985—, asst. faculty fgn. studies, 1972-81, lectr. faculty fgn. studies, 1981-85; lectr. Yale Coll., New Haven, 1978; cons. UN Univ., Tokyo, 1981-82, 84, 86; vis. researcher Georgetown U., Washington, 1987; vis. scholar Ctr. Study Human Rights, Columbia U., 1987. Author: Human Rights and Contemporary World Politics, 1981, The International Politics of Peace, 1986, Faces of the International Political Economy, 1989; mem. editorial bd. Jour. Internat. Studies, 1981—; contbr. articles to profl. jours. Mem. Internat. Polit. Sci. Assn., Japan Assn. Internat. Relations, Peace Studies Assn. Japan, Internat. Studies Assn., Am. Polit. Sci. Assn. Roman Catholic. Office: Sophia U, 7-1 Kioicho, Chiyoda-ku, Tokyo 102, Japan

WESSELS, LAURA KAY, clergywoman; b. Waupun, Wis., Aug. 6, 1965; d. Harold and Gertrude (DeJager) Mulder; m. Timothy J. Wessels, Mar. 17, 1990. BA, Calvin Coll., 1987. Ordained to ministry Christian Reformed Ch. Outreach coord. Hayward (Calif.) Christian Reformed Ch., 1987-88; dir. outreach and edn. Park Lane Christian Reformed Ch., Evergreen Park, Ill., 1988—. Mem. Youth Commn., Evergreen Park, 1989—. Office: Park Ln Christian Ref Ch 3450 W Maple Ave Evergreen Park IL 60642

WESSELSCHMIDT, QUENTIN FREDERICK, minister, educator; b. Washington, Mo., Feb. 3, 1937; s. Raenhard Henry and Thelma Corinne (Hartge) W.; m. Susan Elizabeth Susanka, Nov. 16, 1963. Diploma, St. Paul's Jr. Coll., 1957; BA, Concordia Sr. Coll., Ft. Wayne, Ind., 1959; BD, MDiv, Concordia Sem., St. Louis, 1963; MA, Marquette U., 1969; PhD, U. Iowa, 1979. Ordained to ministry, Luth. Ch., 1963. Pastor Our Savior Luch. Ch., Hillsboro, Ill., 1963-65; asst. prof. Concordia Coll., Milw., 1965-71; lectr. in classics U. Wis., Milw., 1973-75; adminstrv. asst., instr. religion Luth. High Sch. Assn. Greater Milw., 1974-77; prof. hist. theology, dept. chmn. Concordia Sem., St. Louis, 1977—, editor Concordia Jour., 1982—; vacancy pastor St. Peter's Luth. Ch., Spanish Lake, Mo., 1989-91. Mem. Am. Philol. Assn., Classical Assn. Mid. West and South, Concordia Hist. Inst., N.Am. Patristics Soc. Home: 444 Eatherton Valley Rd Chesterfield MO 63005 Office: Concordia Sem 801 DeMun Ave Saint Louis MO 63105

WEST, BURL DWIGHT, minister; b. Hattiesburg, Miss., June 10, 1954; s. Bennie Dorman and Hazel Montele (Lambert) W.; m. Rebecca Jo Coy, July 29, 1973; children: Benjamin, Jodi, Sarah, Rachel. BA, Mobile (Ala.) Coll., 1983. Lic. to ministry So. Bapt. Conv., 1978; ordained, 1979. Pastor Smithtown Bapt. Ch., Mobile, 1982-90, Lawn Haven Bapt. Ch., Laurel, Miss., 1990—. Candidate Mobile County Pub. Sch. Bd., 1986. Republican. Home and Office: Rt 2 Box 1191 Laurel MS 39440 *I interpret my discontent with "the way things are" as being God's way of prodding me to be and to do the best I can. Through my desire to effect change, He has taught me patience.*

WEST, CAROL ANN, minister; b. Greeley, Colo., Nov. 24, 1938; d. William Carl and Merle Maurine (Hervey) N.; m. James Earle West, June 3, 1959; children: David C., Susan M. BA, Temple Buell Coll., Denver, 1969; postgrad., Pacific Luth. Theol. Sem., Berkeley, Calif., 1984-85; MDiv, Iliff Sch. Theol., Denver, 1983. Ordained to ministry Luth. Ch., 1985. Interim pastor Atonement Luth. Ch., Salt Lake City, 1983-84; pastor Mount Tabor Luth. Ch., Salt Lake City, 1985-91; interim pastor Ascension Luth. Ch., Ogden, Utah, 1991—; elected mem. synod coun., Rocky Mountain Synod Evang. Luth. Ch. Am., Denver, 1988—, candidacy com., 1988—; bd. dirs. Pastoral Care, Univ. Hosp. Salt Lake City; advisor Luth. Campus Ministry Coun., U. Utah, 1985—. Mem. Cen. Salt Lake City Counc. Chs. (sec. 1986-88), Salt Lake City Ministerial Assn. (sec. 1986-87). Office: Mt Tabor Luth Ch 175 S 700 E Salt Lake City UT 84102 *There are parts of ourselves we regard as beyond hope and change. We all have places where we draw the line. The gifts and call of God invite us to step over the lines we have drawn for ourselves and enter unlimited life, which is a gift of God.*

WEST, DANIEL C., lay worker, dentist; b. Trenton, N.J., July 23, 1955; s. Harry E. and Alma R. (Washburn) W.; m. Deborah L. Scott, May 28, 1977; children: Lauren Elizabeth, Colin Jeffrey. BS, Ea. Nazarene Coll., 1977; DMD, U. Pitts., 1982. Min. youth/music South Hills Ch. of the Nazarene, Bethel Park, Pa., 1977-82; pvt. practice specializing in family dentistry Terre Hill, Pa., 1982—; mem. Internat. Gen. Bd., Ch. of the Nazarene, Kansas City, Mo., 1989—, lay mem. dist. adv. bd. Phila. dist., Frazer, Pa., 1985—, coord. work and witness program, 1988-90, dir. compassionate ministries, 1990—; dir. Phila. dist. IMPACT, 1982-89; trustee Ea. Nazarene Coll., Wollaston, Mass., 1984—. Contbr. articles to jours. Lt. USPHS, 1982-85. Fellow Am. Acad. Gen. Dentistry; mem. ADA, Pa. Dental Assn., Lancaster County Dental Soc. Republican. Home: 1442 Hayfield Dr East Earl PA 17519 Office: 238 E Main St Terre Hill PA 17581 *The greatest joy I have is in serving others through ministry in the church, my dental practice, and especially in my home.*

WEST, EARL IRVIN, history educator; b. Indpls., May 18, 1920; s. James I. and Tena (Elliott) W.; m. Lois Louise Hinds, July 5, 1942 (dec. 1980); children: Robert Earl, Timothy Eugene; m. Dorothy Mae Carrel, Jan. 10, 1985. BA, Peprerdine U., 1943; MA, BD, Butler U., 1945, 1948, ThM, 1953; PhD, Ind. U., 1968. Preacher Irvington Ch. of Christ, Indpls., 1943-53, Franklin Rd. Ch of Christ, Indpls., 1957-85; tchr. Freed-Hardeman Coll., Henderson, Tenn., 1953-55; tchr. Harding U., Memphis, 1966-89, semi-ret., 1989; lect. in field. Auhtor: The Search For The Ancient Order, 1948, 2d vol., 1960, 3d vol., 1975, 4th vol., 1987, Biography David Lirscomb, 1950,

Biography of Elder Ben Franklin, 1984. Recipient Disting. Christian award Ala. Christian Sch. Religion, 1982. Mem. Ch. of Christ. Home and Office: 3011 Woodshore Ct Carmel IN 46302

WEST, ERICK CLAY, religious organization administrator; b. Wheaton, Md., July 23, 1962; s. Rex Channing and Melba Anne (Jackson) W. BA in Computer Sci., Asbury Coll., 1987; cert. in edn., Hood Coll., 1989. Mem. staff Campus Life, Damascus, Md., 1983—; tchr. math Montgomery County Pub. Schs., Rockville, Md., 1989—; treas. bd. dirs. Youth for Christ/ Campus Life, Damascus, 1991—. Wesleyan. Home: 3107 Pheasant Run Ijamsville MD 21754

WEST, JAMES C., bishop. Bishop Reformed Episcopal Ch., Charleston, S.C. Office: Reformed Episcopal Ch 91 Anson St Charleston SC 29401*

WEST, JOHN H(ENRY), III, clergyman, educator; b. Moorestown, N.J., 1954; s. John Henry Jr. and Gwendolyn (Clark) W.; m. Patricia Lynn Murray. BA in History, Lincoln (Pa.) U., 1976; MDiv, Pitts. Theol. Sem., 1979. Assoc. pastor Martin Luther King Jr. Meml. Bapt. Ch., Pitts., 1977-78, Cornerstone Bapt. Ch., Pitts., 1978-79; chaplain, intern John J. Kane Hosp., Pitts., 1978-79; chaplain Lincoln U., 1979—, instr. religion, 1981-84, asst. prof., 1984—, chair dept. religion, 1984—; pres. West Inspirational Network, Lincoln Univ., 1988—. Bd. dirs. Downtown (Pa.) Indsl. and Agrl. Sch., 1989; bd. dirs., v.p. Lincoln Community Assn. Mem. Am. Bapt. Chs., U.S.A., Nat. Bapt. Chs., U.S.A., Inc., Oxford Area Ministerium, Ministeries to Blacks in Higher Edn., Soc. Bibl. Lit., So. Chester County NAACP. Democrat. Avocations: computers, sports, music, travel, reading. Home: PO Box 59 Lincoln University PA 19352 Office: Lincoln U Campus Box 44 Lincoln University PA 19352

WEST, LEANDER, minister; b. Kinston, N.C., July 30, 1954; s. Leander West and Mary Leach Pate; m. Kaymani Daniels; children: Brian Leander, Bianca Kaymani. AS, Columbia (S.C.) Bible Coll., 1980; Dipl., Midlands Tech. Coll., Columbia, 1981, Moody Bible Coll., Chgo., 1977. Pastor Jerusalem Branch Bapt. Ch., Salley, S.C., 1985—; psychiatric nurse S.C. Dept. Mental Health, Columbia, 1979—; vice moderator Cedar Branch Assn., Wagner, S.C., 1988—; mem. S.C. Bapt. and Edn. Conv., Columbia, 1985—, nat. Bapt. Conv., Baton Rouge, 1985—. Author poetry pub. in Bapt. Informer, Coll. Poetry Rev. With USN, 1973-77. Mem. Columbia Ministerial Alliance. Democrat. Home and Office: Jerusalem Branch Bapt Ch 4703 Mistyvale Ln Columbia SC 29210

WEST, PETER LAWRENCE, minister; b. Williamston, N.C., Nov. 5, 1965; s. William Thomas and Susan Bernell (Stokley) W.; m. Tammy Michele Huffman, May 20, 1989; 1 child, Thomas David. BA, Lenoir Rhyne Coll., 1991. Ordained to gospel ministry, So. Bapt. Ch., 1989. Summer intern Pritchard Meml. Bapt., Charlotte, N.C., 1986; youth minister Independence Hill Bapt., Charlotte, 1986-87; summer intern University Hills Bapt., Charlotte, 1988; assoc. pastor Oxford Bapt. Ch., Conover, N.C., 1989-91; pastor Covenant Bapt. Ch., Conover, N.C., 1991—; dir. Vacation Bible Sch., Theron-Rankin Bapt. Assn., Hickory, N.C., 1990—; spl. youth worker State Sunday Sch. Dept. Cary, N.C., 1990—. Vol. Cooperative Christian Ministry, Hickory, 1989—, Salvation Army, Hickory, 1989—, Rep. Men's Forum, Hickory, 1990—. Mem. N.C. Bapt. Religious Educator's Assn. Office: Covenant Bapt Ch PO Box 1133 Conover NC 28613

WESTBLADE, DONALD JAMES, religion educator; b. Denver, Mar. 11, 1953; s. Maynard S. and H. Elaine (Zook) W.; m. Joni J. Eilers, July 3, 1983; children: Lucas R., Julia G. BA, Williams Coll., 1974; MDiv, Fuller Sem., 1978; MA, Yale U., 1983, postgrad., 1987—. Teaching fellow Yale U., New Haven, 1985; instr. Albertus Magnus Coll., New Haven, 1985; asst. prof. Hillsdale (Mich.) Coll., 1988—; minister of youth Evang. Covenant Ch., Simi Valley, Calif., 1974-76; instr. Christian Study Ctr., New Haven, 1984-87. Contbr. articles, revs. to profl. publs.; developer computer software. Mem. Mich. Right To Life, 1990; elder Evang. Free Ch., Branford, Conn., 1984-87; bd. Christian edn. Coll. Bapt. Ch., Hillsdale, 1990—. Gates Found. scholar, 1970-74. Mem. Soc. Biblical Lit., Am. Acad. Religion, Inst. Biblical Rsch. Libertarian. Office: Hillsdale Coll 33 E College Hillsdale MI 49242 *The more I try to approximate a God's-eye perspective on life, the more I am prompted to live it differently, more intensely.*

WESTBROOK, CHARLEY ERWIN, JR., minister; b. Ft. Worth, Sept. 27, 1957; s. Charley Erwin and Darlene Mae (Gursky) W.; m. Susan Jeanette Carr, May 17, 1980; 1 child, Charley Elijah. Ordained to ministry So. Bapt. Ch. Youth minister, dir. evangelism 1st Bapt. Ch., Bethany, Okla., 1980-82; pastor Little City Bapt. Ch., Madill, Okla., 1984-86, 1st Bapt. Ch., Lake Alfred, Fla., 1988—. Mem. Desert Storm Support Group, Lake Alfred, 1991. Home: 210 E Pierce Lake Alfred FL 33850 Office: 1st Bapt Ch 280 E Pierce Lake Alfred FL 33850

WESTBROOK, DON ARLEN, minister; b. Clinton, N.C., June 2, 1941; s. Ennis and Geneva (Gainey) W.; m. Carrol Ann Holder, Sept. 15, 1963; children: Felisha Ann, Neal Vance. Student, Logos Bible Coll./Grad. Sch., 1989, Duke Univ. Ordained to ministry Full Gospel Fellowship Chs. and Mins. Internat., 1965. Pastor Bethel Christian Ctr., Durham, N.C., 1969—; v.p. Full Gospel Fellowship Chs. and Mins. Internat., Dallas, 1982—; missionary to India, Nicaragua and Haiti, 1990. Chmn. Concerned Citizens for Moral Govt., Durham, 1989. Home: 4434 Talcott Dr Durham NC 27705 Office: Bethel Christian Ctr 3518 Rose of Sharon Rd Durham NC 27712

WESTBROOK, JEAN ANN, religious education director; b. Hot Springs, S.D., Dec. 31, 1948; d. John E. and Nancy Jean (Mullen) Bryant; m. James Everrett Westbrook, May 25, 1968; children: Jessie Erickson, Sandra, Ann, Nancy. Tutor Laubach Sign Lang., Eveleth Vocat. Sch., Minn., 1989. Religious educator Queen of Peace Ch., Hoyt Lakes, Minn., 1970-72, 74-88, dir. religious edn., 1988—; del. nat. conv. Coun. Cath. Women, Hoyt Lakes, 1989, family affairs chmn., 1989—; pastoral coun. mem. Coun. of Queen of Peace Ch., 1989—. Del. Community Forum, Hoyt Lakes, 1990—; pres. Am. Field Svcs., 1991; del. Interch. Ministries, 1989—. Mem. Rainbows for All God's Children (dir. 1990—), VFW Aux. (past pres.). Home: 223 Kent Rd Hoyt Lakes MN 55750

WESTBROOK, PAUL WAYNE, pastor; b. Dallas, July 10, 1964; s. Benjamen Wayne and Bobbie Geraldine (Boyer) W.; m. Sandra Kay Doss, Aug. 6, 1988. BA in Religion, Dallas Bapt. U., 1990; postgrad., Southwestern Bapt. Theol. Sem., Ft. Worth, 1990—. Ordained to ministry So. Bapt. Conv., 1987. Youth min. Wynnwood Bapt. Ch., Dallas, 1984, Harvest Bapt. Ch., Dallas, 1986-87, 2d Bapt. Ch., College Station, Tex., 1987; pastor Pecan Heights Bapt. Ch., Dallas, 1988—. Mem. Dallas Bapt. Assn. (Buckner com. 1990). Home: 410 Goodyear Irving TX 75062 Office: Pecan Heights Bapt Ch 4166 Lawnview Ave Dallas TX 75227-3022

WESTBROOK, T. L., bishop. Bishop of Wash. Ch. of God in Christ, Spanaway. Office: Ch of God in Christ 1256 176th St Spanaway WA 98402*

WESTBROOK, WALTER WINFIELD, minister; b. Chattanooga, Sept. 15, 1955; s. Robert Stanley and Ruth Louise (Fisher) W.; m. Betty Joan Blevins, June 3, 1978; 1 child, Cassandra Noel. BA, Emory (Va.) and Henry Coll., 1977; MDiv, Drew U., 1980. Ordained to ministry United Meth. Ch., 1980. Min. Dahlgren (Va.) United Meth. Ch., 1980-87, Highland Springs (Va.) United Meth. Ch., 1987—; dir. health and welfare ministries Ashland dist. United Meth. Ch., Va., 1989-90, dir. spiritual formation, 1990—, mem. bd. communication Va. Conf., 1990, mem. bd. discipleship div. spiritual formation, 1991—. Creator, host, producer weekly radio program Tell Me Why, 1987—; religion columnist The King George Jour., weekly newspaper, 1986-87; contbr. adult Sunday sch. lessons to Va. Adv., 1990. Bd. dirs. The Haven, battered women shelter, Fredericksburg, Va., 1983-86, The Bethlehem Ctr., Richmond, Va., 1989-90, Richmond Hill, Christian retreat ctr., Richmond, 1990—; mem. coordinating coun. Interfaith Svcs. Henrico County, Richmond, 1987-89; mem. Habitat for Humanity, 1986-90, Bread for World, 1986-90; vol. reader for Virginia Voice, 1989-90, 1989—. Co-recipient Couple of Yr. award Rappahannock Big Bros.-Big Sisters, 1985. Mem. Disciplined Order of Christ, Fellowship Merry Christians, Internat. Jugglers Assn., Renovaré, United Meth. Vols. in Mission (mission trip to Haiti 1977, to Charleston, N.C. 1989). Home: 510 N Daisy Ave Highland Springs VA 23075 Office: Highland Springs United Meth Ch 22 N Holly Ave Highland Springs VA 23075 *The healing of our troubled world will begin when people of every religion discover the way to take their spiritual journey more seriously while, at the same time, taking themselves less seriously.*

WESTBY, CARL MARTIN, JR., minister, educator; b. Aberdeen, S.D., Jan. 24, 1928; s. Carl Martin and Ruth Gudrun (Lundly) W.; m. Elaine Ruth Solomonson, Aug. 22, 1959; children: Joel Carl, Rebekah Kay, Nathan Andrew, Deborah Ann. BA, St. Olaf Coll., Northfield, Minn., 1951; MA, U. Mont., Missoula, 1954; BD, Luther Theol. Sem., St. Paul, 1961, D Ministry, 1991. Cert. tchr., Mont.; ordained to ministry Am. Lutheran Ch., 1961. Tchr. high sch., Red Lodge, Mont., 1954-55; mem. adminstrv. staff U. Mont., Missoula, 1955-58; youth worker Our Saviour's Luth. Ch., Mpls., 1958-61; pastor Fujieda Luth. Ch., Fujieda, Shizuoka-Ken, Japan, 1963-66; student worker Ichigaya Luth. Student Ctr., Tokyo, 1967-69; pastor St. Paul Internat. Lutheran Ch., Tokyo, 1969—; historian Exec. Com. of the Japan Luth. Mission of the Am. Lutheran Ch., 1964-66, vice chmn., 1968-70; chmn. bd., supr., worker Tokyo English Life Line, 1971—; chmn., treas. Tokyo Ecumenical Counsel, 1980—; membership com., exec. com. Nojiri Lake Assn., 1989-90; mem. refugee com. Japan Evan. Luth. Ch., 1988—. Active Boy Scouts Am., U.S. and Japan, 1950-73; trustee Am. Sch. Japan, Tokyo, 1975-84, bd. dirs., 1986-89. With U.S. Army, 1946-47. Mem. Internat. House of Japan, Am. C. of C. in Japan, Phi Alpha Theta, Alpha Phi Omega. Republican. Home: Homat Kojimachi 401, 1-12-2 Kojimachi, Tokyo 102, Japan Office: Saint Paul Internat Luth Ch, 1-2-32 Fujimi, Chiyoda-ku, Tokyo 102, Japan *The basic goal that never changes is to help our people to grow spiritually, to have a better sense of their own life of faith, and to live out that faith as they share what has been received, in the name of Jesus Christ.*

WESTCOTT, EDWARD AUGUST, JR., retired minister, church official; b. Selma, Ala., Oct. 18, 1922; s. Edward August and Louise Wilhemina (Hagemann) W.; m. Sylvia Jean Hyduk, Oct. 9, 1948; children: Rebecca Westcott Virden, Deborah Westcott-Callahan, Mark, Timothy, Elizabeth Westcott Rushlo. Student, Concordia Coll., 1939, Concordia Theol. Sem., 1947; DD (hon.), Concordia Theol. Sem., 1974. Ordained to ministry Luth. Ch.-Mo. Synod, 1948. Missionary Nigeria, 1948-55; pastor local ch. Milan, Mich., 1955-57, Detroit, 1957-71; pastor local ch. Ch. of the Holy Cross, Scottsdale, Ariz., 1971-78; exec. dir. bd. for mission svcs. Luth Ch.-Mo. Synod, St. Louis, 1978-89, ret., 1989; mem. mission svcs. Luth. Ch.-Mo. Synod, Ann Arbor, Mich., 1960-68, v.p. 1968-71, mem. mission study commn., St. Louis, 1974-75, mem. commn. on theology and ch. rels., 1975-77, bd. dirs., 1977-78; mem. bd. control Christ Coll., Irvine, Calif., 1973—; bd. dirs. Luth. Bible Translators, Orange, Calif., 1972—. Recipient Servus Ecclesiae Christi award Concordia Theol. Sem., 1971, St. Martin of Tours medal, 1989. Home: 11237 110th Dr Sun City AZ 85351

WESTER, DONALD GRAY, religion educator; b. Petersburg, Tex., Mar. 30, 1931; s. Jack D. and Rosanelle (Gray) W.; m. Martha Jane Martin; children: Donald G. Jr., James E., J. Mike, Thomas D. BA, Baylor U., 1952; BD, Southwestern Bapt. Theol. Sem., Ft. Worth, 1957; MA, U. Okla., 1968, PhD, 1979. Ordained to ministry So. Bapt. Conv., 1950. Pastor 1st So. Bapt. Ch., Rush Springs, Okla., 1959-64, Parkland Bapt. Ch., Tulsa, 1964-66, Tecumseh (Okla.) 1st Bapt. Ch., 1966—. Pub. Jour. Religion, 1970, Okla. Bapt. Chronicles, 1972. Recipient Outstanding Tchr. award Sears, Roebuck & Co.; NEH grantee. Mem. Am. Philos. Soc., Am. Acad. Religion, Hume Soc. Democrat. Office: Okla Bapt U 500 University Dr Shawnee OK 74801

WESTERFIELD, NANCY GILLESPIE, lay church worker; b. Cin., Dec. 24, 1925; d. Charles Herman and Lilian Elizabeth (Appleton) G.; m. Hargis Westerfield, Aug. 31, 1950. BA, U. Cin., 1947; MA, Ind. U., 1951. Exec. coun. Diocese of Nebr., 1974-79, 80—, sec. dept. missions, 1975—, dep. to gen. conv. Episcopal Ch., 1982, 85, 88, 91. Author: (poetry) Welded Women, 1983; (play) The Morning of the Marys, 1986; contbr. articles to profl. jours. Recipient award in poetry Nat. Cath. Press Assn., 1979, 90; Nat. Endowment for the Arts fellow, 1975, Yaddo fellow in poetry, 1979, 81. Mem. Phi Beta Kappa, Delta Zeta. Democrat. Office: St Luke's Ch PO Box 2285 2304 2d Ave Kearney NE 68848

WESTERLUND, PAUL LAWRENCE, minister; b. Mpls., Sept. 16, 1938; s. Lawrence Hilding Westerlund and Sophia Hilda (Soine) Cole. BA, U. Minn., 1960, MA, 1962; MDiv, Pacific Luth. Sem., 1972; diploma, Concordia Sem., 1976. Ordained to ministry Luth. Ch., 1976. Asst. pastor Mt. Olive Luth. Ch., Sebastopol, Calif., 1975-76; sr. pastor Zion Luth. Ch., Flagler, Colo., Immanuel Luth. Ch., Arriba, Colo., 1976-77; supply preacher at large Calif.-Nev. Dist. Luth. Ch., 1978-84; interim and supply pastor Minn.-South Dist. Luth. Ch., 1984—. Vol. various orgns. Lt. (j.g.) USN, 1962-67, Vietnam. Decorated Nat. Def. Svc. medal, Vietnam War Svc. medal. Republican. Home and Office: 5724 Drew Ave S Edina MN 55410 *Life is better when you're thankful and content.*

WESTERMEYER, PAUL HENRY, religion educator; b. Cin., Mar. 28, 1940; s. Paul Henry and Ruth Caroline (Hackstedt) W.; m. Sally Ann Young, June 22, 1963; children: Christopher, Timothy, Rachel, Rebecca. BA, Elmhurst Coll., 1962; BD, Lancaster Sem., 1965; M in Sacred Music, Union Theol. Sem., 1966; MA in Ch. History, U. Chgo., 1974, PhD in Ch. History, 1978. Ordained to ministry Evang. Luth. Ch. Am., 1986. Choirmaster, organist various chs. in Ill., Pa., Md., 1958-71; choirmaster Grace Luth. Ch., Villa Park, Ill., 1971-82; cantor Ascension Luth. Ch., Riverside, Ill., 1982-90, asst. pastor, 1986-90; successively instr., asst. prof., assoc. prof., prof. music Elmhurst (Ill.) Coll., 1968-90, dir. coll. choir and Elmhurst Choral Union-Pk. Dist. Chorus, 1973-90, coll. organist, 1968-90, chmn. music dept. and preparatory music dept., 1978-90; prof. ch. music Luther Northwestern Theol. Sem., St. Paul, 1990—; vis. prof. ch. music Inst. Sacred Music, Yale U., fall 1989. Author: The Church Musician, 1988; editor The Hymn, 1985-90; cons. to Book of Worship, United Church of Christ, 1986; contbr. numerous articles, revs. to profl. jours. Recipient Pres.'s Excellence in Teaching award Elmhurst Coll., 1988-89, Sears-Roebuck Found. award for teaching excellence, 1990. Mem. Am. Choral Dirs. Assn., Am. Guild Organists (dean Valley chpt. 1982-84, nat. chaplain 1991—), Am. Soc. Ch. History, Evang. and Reformed Hist. Soc., Hymn Soc. Am., Assn. Luth. Ch. Musicians (editor paper series 1988—), Internat. Arbeitsgemeinschaft für Hymnologie, Liturgical Conf., Mercersburg Soc., N.Am. Acad. Liturgy, Alpha Mu Gamma (hon.), Phi Kappa Phi, Omicron Delta Kappa. Avocations: tennis, cycling, bridge, automobile driving. Home: 1240 W Belmont Ln Roseville MN 55113 Office: Luther Northwestern Sem 2481 Como Ave Saint Paul MN 55108

WESTHOFF, FRANK DOMINIC, priest; b. Charleston, Ill., Sept. 13, 1933; s. Clarence Anthony and Emily Marie (Pendergast) W. Student, St. John's Home Missions Sem., 1953-61; BS, U. Little Rock, 1954; MA, U. Notre Dame, 1975; MDiv, St. Joh's Sem., 1960. Ordained priest Roman Cath. Ch., 1961. Asst. pastor St. Patrick's Parish, Alton, Ill., 1961-64, Decatur, Ill., 1964-68; asst. pastor Blessed Sacrament Ch., Springfield, Ill., 1968-72, St. James Parish, Decatur, 1972-75; pastor St. Mary's, Pittsfield, Ill., 1976-84, Holy Family, Greggsville, Ill., 1976-84, Holy Redeemer, Barry, Ill., 1976-84; adminstr. St. Margaret Mary, Granite City, Ill., 1984; admissions counselor Crosier Monastery and Sem., Onamia, Minn., 1986-87; cons. office social concerns Diocese of Jefferson City, Mo., 1987—; staff Census of Shumway, Ill., 1958; student counselor, dir. swimming instrn. Cath. Youth Orgn., 1960; chaplain St. Joseph's Hosp., Alton, Western Military Acad, Montecello Girl's Finishing Sch., Godfrey, Ill.; mem. Alton Human Rels. Commn., chmn. 1963-64; bd. dirs. Progress Sch. for Exceptional Children, Decatur, Ill., chmn. 1967-68; mem. Ill. interfaith housing program Ill. Conf. Chs., voting mem. Ill. consortium for social action, 1968-75, priest's senate mem., 1972-75. Contbr. articles to profl. jours.; speaker in field. Founder Coalition Against Discrimination, Wash., Calif., Fla., N.J., Mass., 1970; steering com. We Care Springfield Citizens Group; exec. sec. Springfield Interfaith Clergy Union, 1972. Mem. Beer Can Collectors Am., KC (chaplain 1968-75). Home and Office: St Peter Church 216 Broadway St Jefferson City MO 65101

WESTING, HAROLD JAY, religion educator; b. Grand Rapids, Mich., Oct. 24, 1929; s. Theodore J. and Florence (Muller) W.; m. Betty Jean Wakeman, Aug. 17, 1951; children: Deborah Sue Martin, Thomas Dean, Cindy Lou. Diploma, Moody Bible Inst., 1951; BA, Grace Coll., 1954; MDiv, Western Conservative Bapt. Sem, 1965, DD (hon.), 1982. Youth pastor and Christian edn. dir. First Bapt. Ch., Corvallis, Oreg., 1958-62, Montavilla Bapt. Ch., Portland, Oreg., 1962-64; Christian edn. dir. Conservative Bapt. Assn. of Oreg., Salem, 1964-72, Conservative Bapt. Assn. Am., Wheaton, Ill., 1972-76; assoc. prof., dean of students Christian edn. Pastoral Ministry, Denver, 1976—. Author: Evaluate and Grow, 1976, The Super Superintendent, 1980, Multiple Church Staff Handbook, 1985; compiled book on missions I'd Love to Tell the World, 1977; contbr. articles to profl. jours. Active Nat. Christian Camping Orgn., 1965. Mem. N.Am. Soc. for Ch. Growth, Profs. of Christian Edn. (bd. dirs.). Republican. Office: Denver Sem PO Box 10000 Denver CO 80210

WESTLING, LESTER LEON, JR., priest; b. Oakland, Calif., Oct. 19, 1930; s. Lester Leon and June Minerva (Holmes) W.; m. Marjorie Clark, Nov. 1, 1958; children: Karla Nancy Westling Bakke, Lester Leon III, Karen June. BA, U. of the Pacific, 1952; MDiv, Ch. Divinity Sch. of Pacific, 1955; MA in Psychology, San Francisco Theol. Sem., 1973, DMin, 1974. Ordained to ministry Episcopal Ch., as deacon, 1955, as priest, 1956. Curate St. Peter's Episcopal Ch., Redwood City, Calif., 1955-56; vicar Good Shepherd Episc. Ch., West Berkeley, Calif., 1956-60; missionary Epiphany Mission Outstations & Schs., Mountain Province, Philippines, 1960; chaplain St. Stephen's (Chinese) High Sch., Manila, Philippines, 1960-66; commd. lt. (j.g.) USNR, 1966; advanced through grades to capt. USN, 1983, chaplain, 1966-87, retired, 1987; rector All Saints' Episcopal Ch., Redding, Calif., 1987—; vol. chaplain Redding Police Dept., 1987—. Decorated Bronze Star, Purple Heart, Navy Commendation medal, Navy Achievement medal, Viet Nam Svc. medal, Nat. Def. Svc. medal, Viet Nam Campaign medal; recipient Presdl. unit citation (2), Vietnam Presdl. unit citation, Navy Unit citation (3), Vietnam Meritorious unit citation, others mil. awards; recipient Jubilee award Presiding Bishop of Episcopal Ch., 1985. Mem. Calif. Assn. Marriage and Family Therapists (clin.), Internat. Conf. Police Chaplains (sr. cert. chaplain), Ret. Officers' Assn. (chaplain-bd. dirs. Shasta County chpt. 1989—), DAV (life), VFW, Am. Legion. Office: All Saints Episcopal Ch PO Box 523 Redding CA 96099 *In this world there are doers and there are complainers. The Doers do not complain much, and the Complainers do not do much.*

WESTMAN, STEVEN RONALD, rabbi; b. Chgo., Sept. 16, 1945; s. Kurt S. and Hilda (Schmoller) W.; m. Sherri, Nov. 30, 1980; children: Rachel Dara, Emily Nicole, Molly Sarah Levin. BA, U. Ill., 1967; B of Hebrew Letters, Hebrew Union Coll., 1969, MA in Hebrew Letters, 1972. Ordained rabbi, 1972. Asst. rabbi Congregation Rodeph Shalom, Phila., 1972-75; rabbi Temple Israel, Stroudsburg, Pa., 1975-83, Temple Beth Torah, Wellington, Fla., 1983—; commr. Commn. for Jewish Edn., West Palm Beach, Fla., 1990—; bd. dirs. Jewish Community Day Sch., West Palm Beach, 1988—, Jewish Community Ctr., 1987—; pres. Palm Beach County Bd. Rabbis, 1989—. Bd. dirs. Palms West Hosp., Loxahatchee, Fla., 1986-91, Pocono Hosp., East Stroudsburg, Pa., 1979-83; found. bd. dirs. Hospice of Monroe County, East Stroudsburg, 1978-83; bd. dirs. Palm Beach Liturgical Culture Soc., West Palm Beach, 1986—. Recipient Tower of David award State of Israel Bonds, 1988, Leadership award Jewish Fedn. of Palm Beach County, 1985. Mem. Cen. Conf. of Am. Rabbis, Rotary. Home: 13587 Jonquil Place Wellington FL 33414 Office: Temple Beth Torah 900 Big Blue Trace Wellington FL 33414 *The theme and spirit of my rabbinate are found in the words of Pirkey Avot, the ethics of the fathers: "Be of the disciples of Aaron, loving peace and pursuing peace, loving your fellow creatures and bringing them close to the Torah." (Avot 1:12).*

WESTPHAL, ARNOLD CARL, religious publishing company executive, minister; b. Michigan City, Ind., June 23, 1897; s. Henry H. and Friederika (Laborn) W.; m. Esther Helen Dysard, Sept. 21, 1918 (dec. Dec. 1954); children: Rex, Juanita, Arlo; m. Addie Dysard, May 10, 1957 (dec. 1980); stepchildren: John, Wilbert, Marjory, Phyllis, Warren. Grad., Valparaiso U., 1922, Moody Bible Inst., Chgo., 1924, No. Bapt. Sem., Chgo., 1926, Harvard Mil. Chaplain's Sch., 1944. Lic. to ministry Bapt. Ch., 1918, ordained, 1922. Pastor 1st Bapt. Ch., Royal Ctr., Ind., 1922-23, Epiphany Bapt. Ch., Chgo., 1923-26, Eastside Bapt. Ch., Evansville, Ind., 1926-28; sr. pastor 1st Bapt. Ch., Salem, Ohio, 1928-37, Greensburg, Ind., 1937-40, Michigan City, 1940-44, Valparaiso, Ind., 1955-61; pres. Visual Evangels Pubs., Michigan City, 1922—. Author 29 visual aid books. With U.S. Army, 1918, capt. chaplain, 1944-46, ETO. Home and Office: Visual Evangels Pubs 1401 Ohio St Michigan City IN 46360-4341 *"The eyes of the ignorant are more learned than their ears." Shakespeare said it and I have tried to prove it. Street kids come in four assortments. Some are all mouth. For them we used choruses. Some were all ears and for them we told stories. Others were all hands and feet. For them we used games. The prevailing group were all eyes and the eyes had it. For them we visualized with magic, chemicals, surprise word plays, trick paper tearing, and mysteries, all with gospel and character building application. I urge—"visualize to evangelize."*

WETHINGTON, NORBERT ANTHONY, college administrator; b. Dayton, Ohio, Sept. 14, 1943; s. Norbert and Sophie Lillian W.; m. Martha M. Vannice, Aug. 13, 1966; children: Paula, Mark, Eric, Kristen, Rebecca, Lisa, Bethany. BA, U. Dayton, 1965; MA, John Carroll U., 1967; postgrad. Baldwin Wallace Coll., 1968-70, U. Toledo, 1990—. Grad. asst., teaching assoc. John Carroll U., Cleve., 1965-67; English tchr. Padua Franciscan High Sch., Parma, Ohio, 1967-70; instr., chmn. dept. tech. writing and speech N. Central Tech. Coll., Mansfield, Ohio, 1970-74; dir. evening div. Terra Tech. Coll., Fremont, Ohio, 1974-80, dir. public and community service technologies, 1980—; cons. several profl. assns. and non-profit groups. Vice pres. Sandusky County Bd. Health, 1979-80. Mem. Am. Vocat. Assn., Ohio Vocat. Assn. (pres. tech. edn. div. 1985-86, Disting. Svc. award 1987), Nat. Council Tchrs. English. Democrat. Roman Catholic. Contbr. articles to profl. jours. Home: 1036 Hazel St Fremont OH 43420 Office: Terra Tech Coll 2830 Napoleon Rd Fremont OH 43420

WETTA, SISTER THERESE CATHERINE, religious organization administrator; b. Andale, Kans., Oct. 1, 1941; d. George Joseph and Delphine D. (Thome) W. BS, Kans. Newman coll., 1964; MS, Kans. State U., 1972; PhD, Boston Coll., 1990. Joined Adorers of the Blood of Christ, 1961. Asst. dir. devel. St. Mary Coll., Leavenworth, Kans., 1988-90; provincial coord. Wichita ASC province, 1990—; del. Gen. Assembly, ASC, Rome, 1991. Bd. dirs. Kans. Newman Coll., 1988-90, Cath. Charities, Wichita, 1991—; vol. Bethany prison ministry, Leavenworth, 1989—, St. Dismas jail ministry, Wichita, 1990—, Connect-Care AIDS, Wichita, 1991. Mem. Leadership Conf. Women Religious, C. of C. Office: Adorers of the Blood of Christ 1400 S Sheridan Wichita KS 67213 *In today's challenging world of poverty amidst plenty, we are called to enter into partnership and collaborative efforts to insure that each person has a positive experience of his/her dignity as a child of God.*

WETTER, FRIEDRICH CARDINAL, archbishop of Munich and Freising; b. Landau, Speyer, Germany, Feb. 20, 1928. ordained priest Roman Cath. Ch., 1953. Consecrated bishop Speyer, 1968; archbishop Munich and Freising, Fed. Republic Germany, 1982—; proclaimed cardinal, 1985. Address: Kardinal-Faulhaber-str 7, D-8000 Munich 2, Federal Republic of Germany

WETZEL, GALE THOMAS, evangelist; b. Owensboro, Ky., Sept. 29, 1937; s. Carter Thomas and Dorothy Glidden (Bennett) W.; m. Nancy Duessa Gumm, June 3, 1962; children: Dorothy Pauline, Owen Thomas. Ordained to ministry United Meth. Ch. as deacon, 1964, as elder, 1967. Pastor Fordsville (Ky.) Circuit, 1962, New Springs-Fincastle Chs., Beattyville, Ky., 1963-65, Shiloh United Meth. Ch., Stanton, Ky., 1965-67, Bonnieville (Ky.) United Meth. Ch., 1967, Wesley-Baird St. Mission, Louisville, 1968-70; pastor Summit Heights Ch., Louisville, 1970-72, approved evangelist, 1972—; short-term missionary, prison worker, mem. bd. evangelism Louisville Conf., 1962-72, Louisville continuing com. on memls., 1976—. Author: A Guide to Reading the Bible in One Year, A Year With the Bible--Guide for Young Christians, booklets; contbr. to Born of the Spirit. Mem. Nat. Assn. United Meth. Evangelists, Louisville Conf. Bd. Global Ministries. Home and Office: 2476 Hack Brown Rd Franklin KY 42134

WEXLER, DOROTHY FRANKEL, religious education professional; b. Chgo., May 1, 1926; d. Samuel and Manya (Shklair) Frankel; m. Herman Wexler, June 23, 1956; children: David, Judith, Naomi. B Jewish Studies, Spertus Coll., 1986; PhB, U. Chgo., 1945; MSW, U. Ill., 1948. Caseworker ARC, Chgo., 1950-54, Michael Reese Hosp., Chgo., 1954-56; therapist, counselor Family Svcs. or Orange (N.J.) and Maplewood, 1956-58; prin. Congregation Bnai Torah, Highland Park, Ill., 1967-74; dir. edn. Congregation Solel, Highland Park, 1974-81; dir. edn., dir. adult edn. North Suburban Synagogue Beth El, Highland Park, 1981—. Recipient Dushkin Disting. Educator award Bd. Jewish Edn. Met. Chgo., 1989. Mem. Acad. Cert. Social Workers, Nat. Assn. Temple Educators, Jewish Educators Assembly (exec. bd. 1989-91), Coalition Advancement Jewish Edn. Office: North Suburban Congregation Beth El 1175 Sheridan St Highland Park IL 60035

WEXLER, STEVEN MARK, minister; b. Los Angeles, Sept. 3, 1955; s. Allan Irving and Gloria (Gingold) W.; m. Lois Ann Krause, June 17, 1988; children: David Aaron, Daniel Adam. BA in Lit., Psychology, Azusa Pacific U., 1978, ministries diploma, 1978; MDiv., Western Evangelical Seminary, Portland, Oreg., 1984. Chaplain intern UCLA Med. Ctr., Los Angeles, 1976-77; asst. chaplain Inter-Community Hosp., West Covina, Calif., 1977-78; tchr., counselor Portland Christian Schs., 1980-84; pastor Portland Foursquare Ch., 1984-88; talk show host Sta. KPDQ Radio, Portland, 1987—; pvt. practice as counselor, Portland, 1987—. Tchr. ARC, Portland, 1980-85; active Heritage Christian Schs. Bd., Portland, 1984-88. Served as lt. USAF, 1982-84, chaplain USAFR, 1982—. Stamps Found. grantee, 1976-77. Mem. Am. Assn. Marriage and Family Therapists (assoc.), Greater Portland Assn. Evangelists. Republican. Avocations: music, backpacking, racquetball, weightlifting, reading. Office: Sta KPDQ Radio 5110 SE Stark St Portland OR 97215

WHALEY, ZACHARY, minister, consultant, counselor; b. N.Y.C., Apr. 8, 1932; s. William Elliott and Katherine (Harris) W.; m. Elizabeth Helga Mueller, Jan. 12, 1957 (div. May 1972); m. Janice Lorraine Larson, Mar. 21, 1981; children: Jay Matthew De Bont, Katherine Lorraine, Jonathan Zachary. BA, Norwich U., 1953; postgrad., U. Del., 1960-61; MA, U. No. Colo., 1976. Cert. counselor Colo., Ariz. Program dir. Alcohol/Drug Control Program, Ft. Carson, Colo., 1971-73; counselor Pulpit Rock Ch., Colorado Springs, Colo., 1975-81, dir. counseling, 1981-88; chief exec. officer, counseling supr. Inst. for Alcohol Awareness, Colorado Springs, Colo., 1979-85; minister pastoral care and counseling Bethany Community Ch., Tempe, Ariz., 1988—; chief exec. officer, CHF trainer Inst. for Profl. Devel., Colorado Springs, 1980—; pres. Whaley Corp., Colorado Springs, 1979—; cons. Arthur D. Little, Inc., Cambridge, Mass., 1974-75, Nat. Coun. on Alcoholism, N.Y.C., 1975; cons., trainer Colo. Dept. Health, Alcohol and Drug Abuse Div., Denver, 1977-86. Author, trainer in field. Mem. Gov.'s Adv. Com., Denver, 1977-80; v.p. Pikes Peak Coun. on Alcoholism, Colorado Springs, Colo., 1973; pres. Colo. Alcholol and Drug Abuse Assn., Denver, 1974, Alcoholism Coun. of Colo., Denver, 1974-76, 81-82. Lt. col. U.S. Army, 1953-73. Mem. Christian Ch. Avocations: bicycling, skiing, swimming, racquetball. Home: 1920 E Calle de Caballos Tempe AZ 85284 Office: Bethany Community Ch 6240 S Price Rd Tempe AZ 85283

WHALING, FRANK, religious studies educator, clergyman; b. Pontefract, Yorkshire, Eng., Feb. 5, 1934; s. Frederick and Ida (Johnson) W.; m. Patricia Hill, Aug. 6, 1960; children: John Prem Francis, Ruth Shanti Patricia. BA in History, Christ's Coll., Cambridge U., 1957, BA in Theology, Wesley House, Cambridge U., 1959, MA, Cambridge U., 1961, PhD, 1990; ThD in Comparative Religion, Harvard U., 1973. Ordained to ministry, Methodist Ch. Minister, Methodist Ch., Birmingham, Eng., 1960-62; minister, coll. mgr. Methodist Ch., Faizabad and Banaras, India, 1962-66; minister Methodist Ch., Eastbourne, Eng., 1966-69; teaching fellow Harvard U., Cambridge, Mass., 1971-72, vis. prof., 1979; spl. tchr. to sr. lectr. in religious studies Edinburgh (Scotland) U., 1973—; spl. lectr., vis. prof. U. Ind., 1975, Dartmouth Coll., 1982, Peking U., 1982, 87, Witwatersrand U., S. Africa, 1984, Calcutta U., 1985; dir. Edinburgh-Farmington Project, Edinburgh and Oxford, 1977-81; cons. Radio Scotland, Glasgow, 1980—; dir. Edinburgh-Cook Project, Edinburgh and Gloucester, 1981-83. Author: An Approach to Dialogue: Hinduism & Christianity, 1966, The Rise of the Religious Significance of Rāma, 1980, John and Charles Wesley: Selected Writings, 1981, Religions of the World, 1985, Christian Theology and World Religions: A Global Approach, 1986, The World's Religious Traditions: Current Perspectives in Religious Studies, 1984, Contemporary Approaches to the Study of Religion: The Humanities, 1984, Contemporary Approaches to the Study of Religion: The Social Sciences, 1985, Religion in Today's World, 1987, Compassion Through Understanding, 1990; contbr. articles and revs. to profl. jours.; cons. 26 vol. series World Spirituality, 1981—. Mem. council Shap Working Party, London, 1973—; mem. Internat. Ctr. Integrative Studies, N.Y.C., 1974—; chmn. to pres. Scottish Working Party on Religion in Edn., Edinburgh, 1975—; mem. council Christian Edn. Movement in Scotland, Dunblane, 1979—; chmn. Scottish Churches China Group, 1986—, Scottish Inter-Faith Symposium, 1988—, Edinburgh Inter-Faith Assn., 1987—; dir. Edinburgh Cancer Help Ctr., 1988—. Recipient Theyer Honor award, Harvard U., 1971; Maitland fellow, Cambridge U., 1969, Fulbright fellow, Harvard U., 1981; Brit. Acad. to Chinese Acad. Social Scis. Exchange fellow, 1982, 87; Brit. Council grantee, Moray grantee, Commonwealth Inst. grantee, Carnegie grantee, Farmington grantee, Cook grantee. Fellow Royal Asiatic Soc., World Lit. Acad.; mem. Brit. Assn. History Religions (com. officer 1980-84), Theology Soc., Indian Religions Soc., Internat. Biog. Assn., Am. Biog. Inst., Internat. Hall of Leaders, World Inst. Achievement, World Lit. Acad., Internat. Assn. Buddhist Studies, Religion and Theology Soc., Brit. Fulbright Soc., Farmington Council, Soc. Authors. Home: 29 Ormidale Terr, Murrayfield, Edinburgh EH12 6EA, Scotland Office: U Edinburgh New Coll, The Mound, Edinburgh EH1, Scotland *Our greatest challenge in our developing global world is to think, and pray globally and integrally under God for human with the earth.*

WHAN, NORMAN WENDELL, minister; b. Aurora, Ill., Jan. 13, 1943; s. Lawrence Donald and Evelyn Irene (Nash) W.; m. Judith Ann Williams, Feb. 23, 1963; children: Jeffrey, Victoria, Tamara, Scott. Grad., Peoria, Ill., 1961. Dir. ch. planning Friends S.W. Yearly Meeting, Whittier, Calif., 1985-88; pres., founder Ch. Growth Devel. Internat., Brea, Calif., 1988—; bd. dirs. Missions Internat., Nashville, 1987—, Internat. Light & Life Network, Pasadena, Calif., 1988—, Ch. Growth Devel. Internat., Brea, 1988—; bd. advisors Ch. Planting Ctr., Orlando, Fla., 1990—. Author: (book kit) The Phone's for You, 1985; co-author: Keeping in Touch, 1989; editor newsletter Hook, Line, & Sinker, 1988. Mem. N.Am. Soc. Ch. Growth. Republican. Office: Ch Growth Devel Internat 420 W Lambert Ste E Brea CA 92621

WHARTON, ALBERT BENJAMIN, minister, eduator; b. Chesapeake City, Md., Jan. 9, 1938; s. James Raymond and Mary (Newton) W.; m. Cheri Lynn, Albert B. Jr. BA in History, Tenn. Temple U., 1968; MRE, Internat. U., 1978, DRE, 1979. bd. dirs. Senatorial Ednl. Com., Richmond, Va., 1979. Del. Rep. Cen. Com., Virginia Beach, Va., 1978. With U.S. Army, 1957-60. Mem. Old Dominion Assn. Schs., Nat. Scientific Rsch. Found., Nat. Curricuum Devel. Agy., Alpha Epsilon Theta. Home: PO Box 804 Warsaw VA 22572 Office: Old Richmond Rd W #2 Warsaw VA 22572

WHARTON, CHARLES, II, minister; b. Huntington, W.Va., May 25, 1936; s. Charles and Marguerite (Brooks) W.; m. Elaine Schurmann, June 2, 1958; children: Charles III, Karla Kim Williams, Robert Lee (dec.). AA, Fla. Christian, Tampa, 1957; BA, Abilene (Tex.) Christian, 1959. Ordained to ministry Ch. of Christ, 1959. Minister Churches of Christ, various locations, 1959-89; chaplain, Ft. Pierce (Fla.) Police Dept., 1986-89. Active in St. Lucie County Drug Task Force, 1987-89. Mem. Internat. Conf. Police Chaplains (regional dir. 1988-89). Democrat. Avocations: running. Home: 3096 W Midway Rd Fort Pierce FL 34981 Office: Midway Rd Ch of Christ 3040 W Midway Rd Fort Pierce FL 34981

WHEELER, BONNIE G., author; b. Charleston, W.Va., July 12, 1943; d. Earnest A. and Virginia F. (Barker) Lindner; m. Dennis R. Wheeler, June 14, 1961; children—Julie Lynn, Timothy Dennis, Robert Grant; adopted children—Rebecca Anne, Benjamin Joel. Student pub. schs., Ft. Lauderdale, Fla. Free-lance writer, 1977—; tchr. and workshop leader Writers' Workshops and Confs.; co-founder No. Calif. Christian Writers Ann. Workshop; co-founder and pres. Sutter-Buttes Christian Writers Fellowship. Mem. Colusa County Children's Health Adv. Bd., 1980—; chmn. Colusa County Spl. Edn. Adv. Bd., 1981-83; mem. Williams Sch. Site Council, 1981-83, Colusa County Mother and Child Adv. Commn., 1983—; dir. Hurrier I Go...Time Workshops; mem. Nat. Right to Life Com.; cons. editor The Caring Congregation; task force del. Christian and Missionary Alliance. Recipient Inspiration award Mt. Hermon Christian Writers Conf., 1982. Mem. Christian Writers Guild. Republican. Author: Of Braces and Blessings, 1980; Challenged Parenting, 1983; Meet the Overcomers, 1984; The Hurrier I Go, 1985; contbr.: Chosen Children, 1978; Wondrous Power, Wondrous Love, 1984; contbr. articles to religious publs. Home: 2470 Medallion Dr Union City CA 94587

WHEELER, DAVID LEE, theology educator; b. Louisville, Dec. 8, 1946; s. Robert Lee and Maureen Reid (Mosby) W.; m. Betty Davis, Feb. 2, 1974 (div. July 1988); children: Clare, Micah; m. Carol A. Allen, Oct. 12, 1990. BA, Georgetown Coll., 1968; MDiv, Yale Divinity Sch., 1971; ThD, Grad. Theol. Union, 1984. Ordained to ministry Bapt. Ch., 1971. Youth dir. Leitchfield (Ky.) Bapt. Ch., 1967-68; pastor Utopia Pkwy. Bapt. Chapel, Flushing, N.Y., 1971-73, Portola Bapt.Ch., San Francisco, 1978-82, Central Bapt. Ch., Elizabeth, N.J., 1984-85; assoc. prof. theology Central Bapt. Theol. Sem., Kansas City, Kans., 1985—; adj. prof. philosophy St. Mary Coll., Leavenworth, Kans., 1990—; faculty rep. Central Bapt. Sem., Kans. City Assn. Theol. Schs., Kansas City, Kans./Mo., 1987—. Author: A Relational View of the Atonement, 1989; contbr. articles to profl. jours. Bd. dirs. Kansas City Hispanic Ministries, 1985—; bd. dirs., sec. Kaw Valley Habitat for Humanity, Kansas City, Kans., 1988—; bd. dirs., edn. com. chair Kansas City Interfaith Peace Alliance, Kansas City, Mo., 1989—. Luther Wesley Smith citation Christian Higher Edn. Bd. Ednl. Ministries, Am. Bapt. Chs. in the USA, 1989. Mem. Am. Acad. Religion, Assn. Christian Philosophers, Bapt. Assn. Philosophy Tchrs. Democrat. Office: Central Bapt Theol Sem 741 N 31 St Kansas City KS 66102 *The Christian drama of creation and redemption suggests that self-giving love is at the root of reality.*

WHEELER, FRANK EARL, religion educator; b. Sidney, Nebr., Sept. 24, 1952; s. Lloyd E. and June (Fish) W.; m. Kathleen Baker, Aug. 19, 1973; 1 child, Frank E. Jr. AS, York (Nebr.) Coll., 1972; BA, Harding U., Searcy, Ark., 1974; MA, MTh, Harding Grad. Sch. Religion, Memphis, 1977, 78; PhD, Baylor U., Waco, Tex., 1985. Ordained to ministry Ch. of Christ, 1978. Minister Ch. of Christ, Glenwood, Minn., 1978-80, Moody, Tex., 1980-84; tchr., campus minister Eastern N.Mex. U., Portales, 1986-88; assoc. prof. Bible, chmn. dept. Bible York (Nebr.) Coll., 1988—. Mem. Soc. Bibl. Lit. Home: 702 Hutchins York NE 68467 Office: York Coll 10th and Kiplinger York NE 68467

WHEELER, GERALD WILLIAM, editor; b. Niles, Mich., Sept. 16, 1943; s. Elmer and Melva Louise (Tabb) W.; m. Penny Ann Estes, June 18, 1967; children: Robin, Noelle, Bronwen, James. BA, Andrews U., 1966, MA, 1981; MA, U. Mich., 1967. Cert. Seventh-day Adventists, 1973. Asst. copy editor So. Pub. Assn., Nashville, 1967, asst. book editor, 1968-74, assoc. book editor, 1974-80; assoc. book editor Rev. and Herald Pub. Assn., Hagerstown, Md., 1980-90, coord. advt., 1990; editor Winner mag., Hagerstown, 1990—. Author: The Two-Taled Dinosaur, 1975, Who Put the Worm in the Apple?, 1975, Is God a Committee?, 1975, God's Catalog of Gifts, 1976, Deluge, 1978, Footsteps of God, 1987; contbr. articles and religious study lessons to religious publs. Grad. scholar U. Mich., 1966-67. Mem. Andrews Soc. Religious Studies, Hist. Sci. Soc., Soc. Bibl. Lit. Home: 9937 Old National Pike Hagerstown MD 21740 Office: Rev and Herald Pub Assn 55 W Oak Ridge Dr Hagerstown MD 21740 *Each one of us is a small facet of the image of God in humanity, and if we destroy another person's individuality, we are forever defacing the image of God in His creation, and the world suffers an eternal loss.*

WHEELER, JEFFREY MORSE, minister; b. Pasadena, Calif., Dec. 6, 1960; s. John Theodore and Marcelene Faith (Palmer) W.; m. Shirlene Beth McDugald, July 25, 1981; children: Shannon, Heather, Jonathan. BA in Communication, Azusa Pacific U., 1982. Pastor Faith Community Ch., Covina, Calif., 1983-89, Hacienda Heights, Calif., 1989—. Republican. Office: Faith Community Ch 15658 E Gale Ste C Hacienda Heights CA 91745

WHEELER, JERRY BARTH, religious organization administrator; b. Muskegon, Mich., Oct. 22, 1951; s. Gerald Barth and Clarissa Wenting (Stegink) W.; m. Andrea Ruth Wendell, June 5, 1976. BA in Sociology, Trinity Coll., Deerfield, Ill., 1974. Assoc. dir. Center Lake Bible Camp, Tustin, Mich., 1974-77; exec. dir. Cadillac (Mich.) Area Youth for Christ, 1977—; northern Mich. area dir. Eastern Great Lakes Region Youth for Christ, Lansing, 1985—, tng. dir., 1986—; mem. exec. coun. Youth For Christ U.S.A., Denver, 1990—. Mem. Rotary. Republican. Office: Box 361 Cadillac MI 49601

WHEELER, JOHN HENRY, religious musician, music historian, composer, Hebraist; b. Toledo, July 8, 1959; s. Floyd James and Mary Madeline (Stephens) W. BA, Ambassador Coll., Pasadena, Calif., 1981. Dir. King David's Harp, Inc., San Francisco, 1987—. Editor: The Music of the Bible Revealed, 1991; author: (video) The Biblical Musical Signs: A New Interpretation, 1988; songwriter; contbr. articles to profl. jours. Mem. Fondation Roi David, Soc. Bibl. Lit., Am. Oriental Soc., Internat. Soc. Folk Harpers and Craftsmen. Mem. Worldwide Ch. of God. Home and Office: King David's Harp Inc 795 44th Ave San Francisco CA 94121-3305

WHEELER, MARK ALFRED, minister; b. Denver, Feb. 15, 1961; s. Russell Francis and Helen Louise (Duntze) W.; m. Jennifer Joy Jones, Jan. 5, 1985; children: Caitlin Elizabeth, Brianna Marie. BA in Religious Studies, Calif. State U., Fullerton, 1984; postgrad., Fuller Theol. Sem., Pasadena, 1985-86; MDiv, San Francisco Theol. Sem., San Anselmo, Calif., 1989. Ordained to ministry Presbyn. Ch. (U.S.A.), 1989. Summer program dir. Placentia (Calif.) Presbyn. Ch., 1980-86; pastor's asst. St. Andrew Presbyn. Ch., Marin City, Calif., 1987-89; chaplain's asst. Marin Gen. Hosp., Greenbrae, Calif., 1988; assoc. pastor Skyline Presbyn. Ch., Tacoma, Wash., 1989—. Home: 5722 N 12th St Tacoma WA 98406 Office: Skyline Presbyn Ch 6301 Westgate Blvd Tacoma WA 98406 *While the Bible teaches us what faith is, and great Christians of church history show us faith in action, it is the lives of the saints I minister with that educate me on how faith works.*

WHEELER, MARTY L., musician; b. Houston, Apr. 6, 1961; s. James C. and Gwendolyn (Lewis) W. MusB (summa cum laude), Rice U., 1988, MusM, 1988. Organist, choir dir. St. Paul Presbyn. Ch., Houston, 1979-83; asst. organist St. Luke's United Meth. Ch., Houston, 1983-84; organist, choirmaster St. Patrick's Episcopal Ch., Houston, 1984-85; dir. music, organist St. Peter's By-the-Sea Episcopal Ch., Gulfport, Miss., 1987-91; music instr. self-employed, Gulfport, 1987—; mem. Commn. on Ch. Music and Liturgy, Diocese of Miss., 1987—; staff accompanist Miss. Conf. on Ch. Music and Liturgy, Vicksburg, Miss., 1987—. Named Am. Mensa Scholarship winner, 1982-83; Bd. Gov.'s Durbin scholar Rice U., 1984-88. Mem. Am. Guild Organists, Choristers Guild, Am. Choral Dirs. Assn., Am. Guild English Handbell Ringers, Houston Chpt. Choristers Guild (treas. 1982-85), Music Tchrs. Nat. Assn. (nat. cert.), Miss. Music Tchrs. Assn., Omicron Delta Kappa, Alpha Chi. Home and Office: PO Box 1956 Gulfport MS 39502-1956

WHEELOCK, ROBERT DEAN, priest, director; b. Cherokee, Iowa, Sept. 27, 1936; s. Leslie Cyril and Cecilia Mary (Meyers) W. AB, St. Mary Sem., 1960; MA, St. Anthony Sem., 1965; D in Ministry, Aguinas Inst. Theol., 1976; MS in Edn., U. Wis., Oshkosh, 1987. Chaplain Archdiocese of Detroit, 1966-69, St. Mary Hosp., Marquette, Mich., 1969-71; dir. pastoral care services Cath. Hosp. Assn. USA, St. Louis, 1971-77; asst. prof. medicine and religion St. Louis U., 1977-79; dir. counseling St. Lawrence Sem., Mt. Calvary, Wis., 1981—. Author/editor 5 books; contbr. articles to profl. jours. Mem. com. rehab. Am. Cancer Soc., N.Y.C., 1975-79; moderator Pax Christi of St. Lawrence, Mt. Calvary, 1986—, Right to Life Club, Mt. Calvary, 1986—. Mem. Am. Assn. Counseling and Devel., Educators for Socail Responsibility, nat. Assn. Cath. Chaplains (pres. 1978-79, Prestigious award 1978), Kappa Delta Pi. Lodge: Kiwanis. Avocations: photography, classical music. Home and Office: St Lawrence Sem 301 Church St Mount Calvary WI 53057-0500

WHELAN, JOHN DAVID, lawyer; b. Eau Claire, Wis., Mar. 29, 1943; s. John Veale and Eleanor Josephine (Tandvig) W.; m. Amy Olette Moy, June 18, 1965; children: Sean, Mark. BA, U. Wash., 1965; JD cum laude, U. Wis., 1973. Lay supply preacher N.W. Synod of Wis. Evang. Luth. Ch. Am., 1977—; v.p. N.W. Synod of Wis. Evang. Luth. Ch. Am., Rice Lake, Wis., 1987—; pres. Am. Luth. Homes, Inc., Menomonie, Wis.; also bd. dirs. Am. Luth. Homes, Inc., Menomonie; sec. Cen. Luth. Ch. Trust Fund, Mondovi, 1988—; pvt. practice, Mondovi, Wis., 1973—. Sec. Act I, Inc.; atty. City of Mondovi, 1975—; family ct. commr. Buffalo County Wis., Alma, 1989—. Lt. USN, 1965-70. Mem. ABA, Tri County Bar Assn. (pres. 1990-91), Wis. Family Ct. Commrs. Assn., Lions (past pres. Mondovi club). Home: 471 Jefferson St Mondovi WI 54755 Office: 224 W Main St Mondovi WI 54755-0130

WHETSTONE, JAMES DEWITT, minister; b. Columbia, S.C., Nov. 27, 1935; s. Dewitt and Thelma (Jackson) W.; m. Sally Ann Rodwell, July 11, 1961; children: James D., David Rodwell. AA, Mars Hill Coll., 1955; BA, Wake Forest U., 1957; MDiv., Southeastern Sem., 1961, DMin., 1978. Youth minster First Bapt. Ch., Decatur, Ga., 1961-62; pastor Dudley Bapt. Ch., Pageland, S.C., 1963-65, First Bapt. Ch., Pamplico, S.C., 1965-72; assoc. pastor First Bapt. Ch., Columbia, 1972-76; pastor West Gannt FIrst Bapt. Ch., Greenville, S.C., 1976-82, Temple Bapt. Ch., Wilmington, N.C., 1982—; Trustee S.C. Ministries to Aging, 1972-76; chmn. S.C. Baptist Conv. Christian Life and Pub. Affairs Com., Columbia, 1975-80; bd. dirs. N.C. Bapts., Cary, Lower Cape Fear Hospice, Inc. Author: Baptist Courier, 1981. Bd. dirs. New Hanover Crimestoppers Inc., Wilmington, 1982—. Democrat. Club: Wilmington Execs. Lodge: Rotary (chmn. youth com. Wilmington club 1982). Home: 2222 Market Wilmington NC 28403 Office: Temple Bapt Ch 1801 Market Wilmington NC 28403

WHIDDEN, WOODROW WILSON, II, minister, theologian; b. Orlando, Fla., Oct. 15, 1944; s. Woodrow Wilson and Helen Belle (Wilson) W.; m. Margaret Jeaneette Gibbs, Oct. 26, 1969; children: Jamison G., Jonathan Thomas, Laura J. BA, So. Coll. 7th Day Adventists, 1967; BD, Andrews U., 1969; MPh, Drew U., 1987, PhD, 1989. Pastor Ga.-Cumberland Conf. of Seventh Day Adventists, Ga. & Tenn., 1969-74, Chesapeake Conf. of Seventh Day Adventists, Md., 1974-76, N.J. Conf. of Seventh Day Adventists, Wayne, 1976-79, N.Y. Conf. of Seventh Day Adventists, Elmira, 1979-85, Mich. Conf. of Seventh Day Adventists, Grand Rapids, 1988-90; assoc. prof. of religion Andrews Univ., Berrien Springs, Mich., 1990—; dist. supt. Mich. Conf. of Seventh Day Adventists, Grand Rapids, 1988-90. Sec. Grad. Student Assn., Drew Univ., Madison, N.J., 1987-88. Mem. Andrews Soc. for Religious Study, Am. Acad. of Religions. Republican. Home: Andrews U 208 Griggs Hall Berrien Springs MI 49104

WHIDDON, PAUL MICHAEL, minister, religious organization administrator; b. Jacksonville, Fla., June 27, 1952; s. Vannah Nolan and Gladys (Osborne) W.; m. Myrna Lynn Thornton, June 23, 1972; children: Rebecca Lynn, Paula Michelle. BTh, Zoe Bible Coll., Jacksonville, 1983. Asst. pastor, music dir. Middleburg (Fla.) Assembly of God, 1973-75; sr. pastor 1st Assembly of God, Middleburg, 1982-87; children's pastor Faith Temple Assembly of God, Jacksonville, 1976-78, 1st Pentecostal Holiness, Jacksonville, 1978-79; child evangelist Assemblies of God, Fla., Ga., 1976-80; missionary div. fgn. missions Assemblies of God, 1988-89; asst. pastor, adminstr. Calvary Assembly of God, Port St. Lucie, Fla., 1989-91; founder, pres. Profl. Planners and Data Tech., Springhill, Fla., 1991—; lobbyist Accelerated Christian Edn., Washington, 1986, 90, Tallahassee, 1986. Lobbiest Accelerated Christian Edn., Washington, 1986, 90, Tallahassee, 1986. Mem. Christian Ministries Mgmt. Assn., Port St. Lucie C. of C. Republican. Home: 930 Lake Asbury Dr Green Cove Springs FL 32043 Office: Profl Planners and Data Tech 8488 Northcliffe Blvd Spring Hill FL 34606 *The road to true success is paved with Godly character and can withstand the judgement of time.*

WHIPPLE, ELEANOR BLANCHE, educational administrator, social worker; b. Bellingham, Wash., June 7, 1916; d. Charles William and Susan Blanche (Campbell) W.; m. Robert Auld Fowler (div. 1947); children: Lawrence William, Jeanice Marie Fowler Roosevelt. BA in Sociology, U. Wash., 1938, MSW, 1949; PhD, U. Santa Barbara, 1983. Lic. clin. social worker. Founder, dir. Camp Cloud's End, Deception Pass, Wash., 1939-42; therapist Family Counseling Svc., Seattle, 1949-58; pvt. practice, Burbank, Calif., 1958-60; social svc. dir. Hollygrove Children's Residential Treatment Center, Hollywood, Calif., 1960-66, exec. dir., 1966-81; dean grad. sch. Calif. Christian Inst., Orange, 1981-85, pres., 1985—; adj. faculty Biola U., La Mirada, Calif., 1972-80; exec. dir. Hotline Help Ctr., Anaheim, Calif., 1988—; active Christian Fellowship for the Blind; deaconess So. Pasadena Christian Ch. (Disciples of Christ). Mem. Nat. Assn. Social Workers (chartered), Assn. Christian Therapists, Acad. Cert. Social Workers, N.Am. Assn. Christians in Social Work (former bd. dirs., disting. svc. award). Contbr. articles in field to profl. publs. Home: 1105 Mound Ave Apt 9 South Pasadena CA 91030 Office: Calif Christian Inst 1744 W Katella Ave Orange CA 92667

WHISNANT, PATRICK N., minister; b. Houston, Oct. 17, 1955; s. Jackson Runyon and Gretchen Elizabeth (Van Trease) W.; m. Judy Gail Jackson; 1 child, Jackson Drew; 1 step child, Sean Owen. Student, Furman U., 1973-77, East Tenn. State U., 1977-78, So. Calif. Sch. Evangelism, Buena Park, 1990—. Minister Hollywood Ch. of Christ, L.A., 1988—. Songwriter: (movie) Soldier's Fortune, 1991. Mem. Kiwanis. Office: Church of Christ 600 N Rossmore Los Angeles CA 90104

WHITAKER, O'KELLEY, bishop; b. Durham, N.C., Dec. 26, 1926; s. Faison Young and Margaret L. (O'Kelley) W.; m. Betty Frances Abernethy, Aug. 16, 1955; children: William F., Margaret V., John Andrew. B.A., Duke U., 1949; M.Div., Seabury-Western Theol. Sem., Evanston, Ill., 1952; D.D. hon., Seabury-Western Theol. Sem., 1981. Rector St. Andrew's Ch., Charlotte, N.C., 1952-57, St. Luke's Ch., Salisbury, N.C., 1957-69, Emmanuel Ch., Orlando, Fla., 1969-73; dean St. Luke's Cathedral, Orlando, 1973-81; bishop coadjutor Diocese of Central N.Y., Syracuse, 1981-83, bishop, 1983—; mem. standing liturgical commn. Episcopal Ch., 1982—; mem. operational cabinet N.Y. State Council Chs., 1983—. Author: Sister Death, 1974; hymn texts. Trustee Bexley Hall, Rochester, N.Y., 1982—; Served with USNR, 1944*46. Mem. Phi Beta Kappa. Democrat. Home: 7593 Glencliffe Rd Manlius NY 13104 *My life has been molded by many people who have nurtured me and shaped my life through their own. The major influences, though, have been just a few people whose lives have intersected my own at significant transition times. They have given me the freedom and strength to make the important decisions. It is my sense that they are for me the power and presence of God in Christ.*

WHITAKER, RICK D., minister; b. Pawnee, Okla., Mar. 18, 1951; s. Norma Wadlow W.; m. Catherine Jane Taylor, Sept. 3, 1971; children: Robert Kyle, Richard Kelly, Kathryn Kay. AS, Northeastern A&M Jr. Coll., Miami, Okla., 1971; BS, U. Tulsa, 1973; MA, Southwestern Bapt. Theol. Sem., Fort Worth, 1984. Minister of edn., adminstrn. First Bapt. Ch., Harrison, Ark., 1984-88, Duncan, Okla., 1988—. Home: 112 Pine Duncan OK 73533 Office: First Bapt Ch 901 Ash Duncan OK 73533

WHITCOMB, DONALD DOOLEY, pastor; b. Orlando, Fla., Jan. 19, 1946; s. Morris Glenn and Kathleen (Cleckley) W.; m. Jean Tschudy, Whitcomb, Jan. 7, 1971. BA in Religion, Eckerd Coll., 1968; MDiv, Andover Newton (Mass.) Theol. Sch., 1971. Co-minister East End Meeting House, Falmouth, Mass., 1970-72; pastor First Congl. Ch., Paxton, Mass., 1972—; supervising chaplain Treasure Valley Boy Scouts Am. Camps, Paxton, 1972-85. Coord. Salvation Army, Paxton, 1985-90; bd. overseers Holden (Mass.) Dist. Hosp., 1987-89. Mem. Worcester (Mass.) County Ecumenical Coun. (pres. 1989—), Worcester Area Missionary Soc. (v.p. 1990—). Republican. Home: 232 Grove St Paxton MA 01612-1145 Office: First Congl Ch 1 Church St Paxton MA 01612-1162

WHITCOMB, JOHN CLEMENT, JR., theology educator; b. Washington, June 22, 1924; s. John Clement and Salome Josephine (Fuller) W.; m. Edisene Marjorie Hanson, June 7, 1953; children: David, Donald, Constance, Robert; m. Norma Aileen Pritchett, Jan. 1, 1971; children: Daniel, Timothy. BA, Princeton U., 1948; BD, Grace Theol Sem., Winona Lake, Ind., 1951; ThM, Grace Theol Sem., 1953; ThD, Grace Theol. Sem., 1957.

Prof. theology and Old Testament Grace Theol. Sem., 1951-90, chmn. dept. theology, 1968-85; chmn. bd. Grace Brethren Fgn. Missions, Winona Lake, 1972-79; pres. bd. Spanish World Gospel Mission, 1962-90. Editor: Grace Thol. Jour., 1980-89. Adv. coun. Inst. for Creation Rsch., Santee, Calif., 1970—, Child Evangelism Ministries, Warsaw, Ind., 1988; pres. bd. dirs. Conservative Grace Brethren Assn., 1990—. Mem. Evangelical Theol. Soc. Republican. Avocations: photography, golf. Home: PO Box 277 Winona Lake IN 46590

WHITE, ALFRED E., bishop. Bishop 10th Episcopal dist. A.M.E. Zion Ch., Glastonbury, Conn. Office: AME Zion Ch 10 Hardin Ln Glastonbury CT 06033*

WHITE, ANDREW JOHN, III (JACK WHITE), theology educator; b. Columbus, Ohio, May 24, 1932; s. Andrew John Jr. and Dorothy Mildred (Veach) W.; m. Miriam Eileen Recker, May 30, 1953; children: Mary Sue White Burns, Daniel Allen, John Andrew, James Dirken. AB, Wittenberg U., 1954; MDiv, Trinity Luth. Sem., Columbus, 1957; ThM, Christian Theol. Sem., Indpls., 1960; PhD, Case Western Res. U., 1969. Ordained to ministry United Luth. Ch. in Am., 1956. Pastor Bethel Evang. Luth. Ch., Cicero, Ind., 1956-59, Calvary Evang. Luth. Ch., East Cleveland, Ohio, 1959-65; Hagan prof. practical theology Luth. Theol. Sem. at Phila., 1967—; del. to conv. Luth. Ch. Am., Pitts., 1964, chmn. unified edn. fund, 1974-79, acting adminstr. unified edn. fund, 1978; v.p. EMAN Group Homes Inc., Phila., 1971-78. Author: Metropolitan Mission: A Para-Political Problem for the Churches, 1969, Supervision: An Invitation to Dialogue, 1983; also articles; (with others) Renewal in the Pulpit, 1966, The Pastor's Role in Educational Ministry; editor Parish Practice Notebook. Chair Human Rels. Com., East Cleveland, 1962-65; local Dem. committeeperson, Phila., 1972-88; chmn. bd. Luth. Retirement Homes, Inc., Phila., 1977-88; sec. Mt. Airy Village Devel. Corp., Phila., 1981—; bd. dirs. Matrix Rsch. Inst., Phila., 1990—. Recipient Disting. Alumnus award Trinity Luth. Sem., 1986; Mather fellow Case Western Res. U., 1965-66, Fox fellow Case Western Res. U., 1966-67, U. Pa. fellow, 1982-83. Mem. Assn. for Clin. Pastoral Edn. (bd. representatives 1987—), Am. Assn. Religion, Soc. for Sci. Study of Religion, Assn. for Dr. of Ministry Edn. Democrat. Home: 518 E Durham St Philadelphia PA 19119-1224 Office: Luth Theol Sem at Phila 7301 Germantown Ave Philadelphia PA 19119-1794

WHITE, ANDREW PETER, church administrator; b. Lewiston, Maine, June 3, 1944; s. Wallace H. and Claire (Greenleaf) W.; m. Anita M. Miller, Dec. 30, 1967 (div. Apr. 1989); children: Caroline G., Tobin F., Christopher K. AB, Bowdoin Coll., 1966; MDiv., Bangor Theol. Sem., 1987. Dir. stewardship, mission interpretation, fin. Maine conf. United Ch. of Christ, Yarmouth, 1987—; gen. bd. mem. Nat. Coun. Chs., N.Y., 1986—; bd. dirs. United Ch. Bd. World Ministries, N.Y., 1987—.

WHITE, C. DALE, bishop; b. Sac City, Iowa, Jan. 20, 1925; s. Daniel Columbus and Anna Frances (Hollady) White; m. Gwendolyn Ruth Horton, Aug. 25, 1946; children: Hazel, Jerry, Rebecca, David, Teresa, Lisa. BA, Morningside Coll., 1949, D in Ministry; STB, Boston U., 1951, PhD, 1961. Assoc. gen. sec. Gen. Bd., Ch. and Society, Washington, 1961-68; pastor United Meth. Ch., East Greenwich, R.I., 1968-71; dist. supt. United Meth. Ch., S. New Eng. Conf., Providence, R.I., 1971-76; bishop United Meth. Ch., N.J. area, Pennington, 1976-84, N.Y. area, White Plains, 1984—. Author: Dialogue in Medicine and Theology, 1967; contbr. articles to profl. jours. Named Disting. sch. theol. Alumnus, Boston U., 1970, grad. sch. Alumni of Boston U., 1987. Methodist. Office: Bishop's Office 252 Bryant Ave White Plains NY 10605

WHITE, C. NOEL, retirement home administrator, minister; b. Dec. 18, 1938; m. Betty Jane Duff, June 18, 1961; children: John Noel, Mary Jane. BA, Union Coll., Barbourville, Ky., 1960; MDiv, Wesley Theol. Sem., 1965; DMin, Lexington Theol. Sem., 1976. Ordained to ministry United Meth. Ch. as deacon, 1963, as elder, 1965. Program dir. Kettering YMCA, Dayton, Ohio, 1961-62; youth minister Washington St. United Meth. Ch., Alexandria, Va., 1962-64; student pastor Accotink-Silver Brook Charge, Va., 1964-65; pastor Lawrenceburg (Ky.) United Meth. Ch., 1965-67, Trinity United Meth. Ch., Winchester, Ky., 1967-70, Trinity Hill United Meth. Ch., Lexington, Ky., 1970-84, Shiloh Congregational Ch., United Ch. of Christ, Dayton, Ohio, 1984-89; adminstr. Penney Retirement Community, Penney Farms, Fla., 1989—; past chmn. Louisville Area Campus Ministry Com., United Meth. Ch.; past bd. trustees Meth. Home of Ky.; past chmn. Ky. Conf. Evangelism Com., United Meth. Ch., Bd. of United Meth. Campus Ministry, U. Ky.; del. gen. synod United Ch. of Christ, 1987; mem. SW Ohio Bd. of Ch. Devel.; vice-chairperson Dayton Met. Chs. United. Bd. trustees Union Coll., Barbourville, 1980—; past bd. trustees Lindsey Wilson Coll., Columbia, Ky.; past mem. met. bd. Dayton YMCA; past mem. Shrine Chanter's Choir. Avocations: tennis, gardening, collecting comic strips related to theology, singing, piano. Home: PO Box 837 Studio Rd Penney Farms FL 32079 *All persons are seeking to find meaning in life. It can be found in Jesus' statement, "If you save your life for yourself, you will lose it, but if you lose your life in serving others, you will save it." That statement is the meaning to life for me.*

WHITE, CECIL RAY, librarian, consultant; b. Hammond, Ind., Oct. 15, 1937; s. Cecil Valentine and Vesta Ivern (Bradley) W.; m. Frances Ann Gee, Dec. 23, 1960 (div. 1987); children—Timothy Wayne, Stephen Patrick. B.S. in Edn., So. Ill. U., 1959; cert. in Czech., Syracuse, U., 1961; M. Div., Southwestern Bapt. Sem., 1964; M.L.S., N. Tex. State U., 1970, Ph.D., 1984. Librarian, Herrin High Sch. (Ill.), 1964-66; acting reference librarian Southwestern Sem., Ft. Worth, 1968-70, asst. librarian, 1970-80; head librarian Golden Gate Bapt. Sem., Mill Valley, Calif., 1980-88; head librarian West Oahu Coll., Pearl City, Hawaii, 1988-89; dir. spl. projects North State Coop. Library System, Yreka, Calif., 1989-90; dir. library St. Patrick's Sem., Menlo Park, Calif., 1990—; library cons. Hist. Commn., So. Bapt. Conv., Nashville, 1983-84, mem. Thesaurus Com., 1974-84. Bd. dirs. Hope and Help Ctr., 1986-88, vice chmn. 1987-88. With USAF, 1960-64. Lilly Found. grantee Am. Theol. Library Assn., 1969. Mem. Am. Theol. Library Assn. (coord. consultation svc. 1973-78, program planning com. 1985-88, chmn., 1986-88), Nat. Assn. Profs. Hebrew (archivist 1985—), ALA, Calif. Library Assn., Assn. Coll. and Rsch. Librarian, Phi Kappa Phi, Beta Phi Mu. Democrat. Baptist. Home: 920 Peninsula Ave San Mateo CA 94401 Office: St Patricks Sem 320 Middlefield Rd Menlo Park CA 94025 *Personal philosophy: Except for the gift of life and faith, the best gift that has been given to me, and which I can give, is the unique gift of oneself in friendship. No one else can give it, and it cannot be bought at any price.*

WHITE, CECILE HOLMES, religion editor; b. Columbia, S.C., Jan. 6, 1955; d. James Gadsden and Anne Keene (Searson) Holmes; m. Kenneth Herchel White, Apr. 21, 1979. BA in Journalism magna cum laude, U. S.C., 1977; postgrad., U. N.C., Greensboro, 1979-83, U. N.C., Chapel Hill, 1982. Writer sect. religion Greensboro News and Record, 1984-87; writer sect. religion Houston Chronicle, 1987-89, sect. editor, 1989—; faculty Houston Chronicle Summer Journalism Workshop, 1988-91; co-dir. News and Record Minority Journalism Workshop, 1988. Author: Witnesses to the Horror: North Carolinians Remember the Holocaust, 1988; contbr. articles, book revs. to profl. jours. Mem. N.C. Episcopal Diocese Hunger Commn., 1980s; vol. Greensboro Urban Ministry, 1983-86; moderator NCCJ Forum, 1985, Ethics of Humane Care, Greensboro, 1986; mentor Edn. for Miruzhu, Houston, 1989—; advisor United Way Campaign for Homeless, Houston, 1991. Recipient award Piedmont Bapt. Assn., 1984, Community Journalism award N.C. A&T State U., 1984, Pub. Svc. award N.C. Press Assn., 1985, others; U. N.C. fellow, 1982. Mem. Soc. Profl. Journalists (chpt. pres. and v.p., coord. registration nat. conv. 1989), Religion Newswriters Assn. (2d pl. award ann. contest 1989, treas. 1990—), Houston Press Club, Beta Sigma Phi (past v.p. Greensboro chpt., Woman of Yr. award in 1980s), Kappa Tau Alpha, Omicron Delta Kappa. Avocations: gardening, photography, reading, antiques. Office: Houston Chronicle 801 Texas St Houston TX 77002

WHITE, C(HARLES) EDWARD, minister; b. Alfred, Ohio, Apr. 20, 1920; s. Clyde E. and Mary L. (Stout) W.; m. Evelyn Juanita Garloch, June 30, 1942; children: R. Wayne, Charles O., Donald E., James L. BA, Marshall U., 1959, MA, 1961. Ordained to ministry Ch. of Christ, 1940. Min. Ch. of Christ, New Martinsville, W.Va., 1944-46, Athens, Ohio, 1946-51, Canton, Ohio, 1951-55, Huntington, W.Va., 1955-61; elder Ch. of Christ, Searcy, Ark., 1983—; assoc. prof. Harding U., Searcy, 1969-90; sales assoc. Town and Country Properties, 1978—. Co-author corr. course, 1956; contbr. articles, tracts to profl. publs. Co-chmn. White County ARC, Searcy, 1983—; bd. dirs. White County Govt. Employees Credit Union, 1983—. Mem. MLA (Southcentral region), Conf. Christianity and Lit., Optimists (pres. 1977-78, dist. lt. gov. 1980-81). Home: 122 Apache Dr Searcy AR 72143 Office: Harding U PO Box 828 Searcy AR 72143 *I am disturbed by the general trend to depart from Biblical teachings. We need to "get back to basics"—back to Biblical morals, back to fundamental truths taught in the Bible.*

WHITE, CHARLES RICHARD, religious organization administrator, minister; b. Fresno, Calif., July 15, 1937; s. Admiral Dewey and Maretta May (Wiley) W.; m. Elizabeth Hill, Dec. 20, 1958; children: Teresa Lynne White Alldredge, Richard E. AA, Allan Hancock Coll., 1963; BA, Calif. State U., L.A., 1965; BD, McCormick Theol. Sem., Chgo., 1968, D of Ministry, 1989. Ordained to ministry Presbyn. Ch. (USA), 1968. Exec. dir. Cleland House Neighborly Svc., L.A., 1968-70; pastor Community Presbyn. Ch., Onalaska, Wash., 1970-72, Utkeagvik Presbyn. Ch., Barrow, Alaska, 1972-74; mem. staff Ecumenical Met. Ministry, Seattle, 1974-80; exec. dir. Buffalo Area Met. Ministries, 1981—; pres. Multifaith Resources, Buffalo, 1991—; cons. Inuit Circumpolar Conf., Barrow, 1974-80; pres. Intersect, Inc., Buffalo, 1978—; accredited visitor World Coun. Chs., Vancouver, B.C., Can., 1983, Canberra, Australia, 1991. Founding chairperson Planning Commn., North Slope Borough, Barrow, Alaska, 1972-74; founding mem. Erie County Commn. on Status of Women, 1988; chairperson Common Coun. Drug Task Force, Buffalo, 1989—; co-chairperson N.Am. Interfaith Network, Buffalo, 1990—; bd. dirs. western N.Y. sect. United Cerebal Palsy Assn., Buffalo, 1991. Recipient Brotherhood/Sisterhood award Western N.Y. region NCCJ, 1992. Mem. Presbytery Western N.Y. Office: Buffalo Area Met Ministries 775 Main St Ste 405 Buffalo NY 14203-1310

WHITE, DARLENE MARY, religious studies educator; b. Chgo., Nov. 2, 1945; d. Joseph John and Josephine Mary (Wachter) Fischer; m. James Douglas White, Jan. 29, 1966; 1 child, Jeanne Ann. BA, Rosary Coll., 1989; MTS, Garrett-Evang. Theol. Sem., Evanston, Ill., 1991. Eucharistic min. Divine Providence Ch., Westchester, Ill., 1989—; instr. religious studies Joliet (Ill.) Cath. Acad., 1991—. Merit scholarship Garrett-Evang. Theol. Sem., 1989-90. Mem. Am. Acad. of Religion (student), Soc. Biblical Lit. (student). Home: 11318 W Alexandria Ln Westchester IL 60154

WHITE, E(ARL) CRAIG, minister; b. Indpls., July 9, 1960; s. Wilbur Earl and Wilma Katheryn (Stepro) W.; m. Rachelle Lynn Viar, June 16, 1984. BA, Cen. Bible Coll., 1982. Ordained to ministry Assemblies of God, 1987. Youth, music min. 1st Assembly of God, Terre Haute, Ind., 1982-84, Maranatha Assembly of God, Decatur, Ill., 1984-86; pastor One Way Christian Ch., Lebanon, Ind., 1986-87; pastor, founder Calvary Assembly, Munster, Ind., 1988—; fgn. mission rep., Section One Assemblies of God, Ind., 1990—, min. sponsor JOY Fellowship N.W. Ind., 1989—. Home: 1821 Redwood Ct Crown Point IN 46307 Office: Calvary Assembly PO Box 3093 Munster IN 46321 *The faith that we give to others is the greatest gift we can give. For with that gift any mountain can be climbed and river can be crossed.*

WHITE, ERSKINE NORMAN, III, minister; b. Providence, Mar. 16, 1951; s. Erskine Norman Jr. and Eileen (Lutz) W.; m. Caroline Grace Blackwell, June 20, 1980; children: Daniel Franklin, Joshua Leeland, Jordan Christa. BA cum laude, Middlebury Coll., 1973; MDiv, Yale Divinity Sch., New Haven, 1977. Ordained to ministry United Ch. of Christ, 1977. Community organizer Assn. Religious Communities, Danbury, Conn., 1975-80; issues analyst U.S. Cath. Conf. Bishops, Washington, 1980-84; minister Friedens United Ch. of Christ, Milw.; sr. minister 1st Congl. Ch., Melrose, Mass., 1988—; pres. Coop. Urban Ministry Ctr., Washington, 1982-84. Author: Together in Christ, 1990, The Victory of the Cross, 1991, Some Assembly Required, 1989; contbr. articles to profl. jours. Founder Melrose Human Rights Coalition, 1990—; v.p. Congress for a Working Am., Milw., 1985-86. Office: 1st Congl Ch 121 W Foster St Melrose MA 02176

WHITE, EUGENE, minister; b. Princeton, W.Va., Oct. 12, 1930; s. Clarence W. and Ruby Doris (Johnson) W.; m. Evelyn Louise Barrett, June 1, 1953; children: Steven Eugene, Sharon Louise, Jonathan Paul. Student, Wesleyan Coll., Frankfort, Ind., 1966-67; BTh, Fundamental Sem., Thornton, Colo., 1981; M Ministry, Bethany Sem., Dothan, Ala., 1986; D Ministry, Emanuel Sem., Rossville, Ga., 1987. Ordained to ministry Wesleyan Ch., 1963. Pastor Wesleyan chs., W.Va., 1959-66, Wesleyan Ch., Oneonta, N.Y., 1968-69, 70-76; asst. dist. supt. Wesleyan Ch., W.Va., 1973-76; pastor Bible Fellowship Ch., Monroe, Mich., 1976—; pres. Southeastern Mich. Holiness Assn., Monroe, 1978—. Contbr. articles to religious publs. Vol. chaplain Mercy-Meml. Hosp., Monroe, 1984—. With USN, 1948-52, Korea. Recipient chaplaincy recognition Mercy-Meml. Hosp., 1984, Monroe County Youth Ctr., 1989. Republican. Home: 14375 S Telegraph Rd Monroe MI 48161 Office: Bible Fellowship Ch 14395 Telegraph Rd Monroe MI 48161

WHITE, GARRETT MARQUET, minister, lawyer; b. Denver, Aug. 27, 1953; s. Alan McLain and Melanie Eloise (Marquet) W.; m. Taeko Miyamoto, May 14, 1983; children: Ashley H., Jeffrey K. BS, Colo. State U., 1976; JD, U. Colo., 1979; postgrad., Unification Theol. Sem., Barrytown, N.Y., 1983-85. Bar: Colo. 1979, N.Y. 1986, Tex. 1990; ordained to ministry Unification Ch., 1985. Lay missionary Unification Ch., Denver, 1981-82; city dir. Unification Ch., New Brunswick, N.J., 1985-88; regional coord. region 8 Unification Ch., Dallas, 1988-89; state dir. Unification Ch., Houston, 1989-91; atty. Unification Ch., N.J., Tex., 1986—; dir. Unification Ch., Houston, 1991—. Republican. Home: 16160 Kieth Harrow Blvd # 901 Houston TX 77084 Office: 10514 Lady Bug Dr Houston TX 77064 *If, as I believe, a tearful God agonizes over the sorrows of humanity, then it is our uniquely human responsibility to relieve God's suffering through loving and God-affirming action.*

WHITE, GEORGE HAL, minister; b. Clovis, N.Mex., July 18, 1946; s. Albin Buford and Mildred Ione (Hutton) W.; m. Evelynn Marie Wade, June 9, 1965; children: Tracy Marie, Jason Wade. BS, Southwestern Bible Coll., Phoenix, 1976. Ordained to ministry Conservative Bapt. Assn., 1975. Adminstr. Sangre De Cristo Hospice, Pueblo, Colo., 1984-86; pastor 1st Bapt. Ch., Superior, Ariz., 1975-79, Prairie Ave. Bapt. Ch., Pueblo, 1979-84, Calvary Bapt. Ch., Pueblo, 1986—; chmn. bd. dirs. Loving Homes Adoption Agy, Pueblo, 1989—; bd. mem. Child Evangelism Fellowship, Pueblo, 1984-86, Fellowship Christian Athletes, Pueblo, 1986-88; founder, adminstr. Sangre De Cristo Hospice, Pueblo, 1986; seminar instr. Singles Experiencing New Tomorrow, Pueblo, 1987-89. Leader, founder grief support group Sr. Resource Devel. Agy., Pueblo, 1985; fund raiser United Way Agy., Pueblo, 1989. Sgt. USAR, 1963-69. Mem. Am. Bapt. Min.'s Coun. Republican. Home: 2135 Elmwood Ln Pueblo CO 81005 Office: Calvary Bapt Ch 5 Tulane Pueblo CO 81005 *This life will pass very quickly. Only those things we have done for the sake of Christ will have eternal value.*

WHITE, HARRY CLIFFORD, minister; b. Hickory Grove, S.C., July 21, 1930; s. James Dale and Mary Jo (Allison) W.; m. June 1, 1957; children: Martha, Harry C. Jr. AB, Erskine Coll., 1951; MDiv, Erskine Sem., 1959, postgrad., 1989—. Min. Assoc. Reformed Presbyn. Ch., Bessemer City, N.C., 1959-60, First A. R. P. Ch., Charlotte, N.C., 1960-64, Rogers Meml. A. R. P. Ch., Rock Hill, S.C., 1964-68, First Spartanburg (S.C.) A.R.P. Ch., 1968—; chaplain U.S. Army Res., Greensboro, N.C., 1986—. Contbr. articles to mag. Mem. Rock Hill Ministerial Assn., 1964-68; dir. camporee Boy Scouts Am., Spartanburg, 1973, Rock Hill, 1964-68. Mem. Spartanburg Ministerial Assn., Second Presbytery, Res. Officers Assn. U.S., S.C. Army N.G. Assn., Mil. Chaplain Assn. Democrat. Presbyterian. Avocations: music, creative writing, hiking. Home: 271 Winfield Dr Spartanburg SC 29302 Office: 1801 Skylyn Dr Spartanburg SC 29302

WHITE, HUGH CLAYTON, religion educator; b. Columbus, Ga., Dec. 2, 1936; s. Otis Clayton and Marjorie Louise (Hines) W.; m. Ann McDonnel Shepard, Dec. 28, 1960; children: Lisa Mathews, Jessica Hines. AB, Asbury Coll., 1958; BD, Candler Sch. Theology, Atlanta, 1961; PhD, Drew U., 1967. Prof. religion Rutgers U., Camden, N.J., 1970—. Author: Narration and Discussion in the Book of Genesis, 1991. Mem. Zoning Bd. Adjustment, City of Haddonfield, 1988—. Mem. Soc. Bibl. Lit. (sect. co-chair 1989—), Am. Acad. Religion. Methodist. Home: 47 Trueman Ave Haddonfield NJ 08033 Office: Rutgers U Camden Coll 5th and Pennsylvania Camden NJ 08102

WHITE, JAMES F., theology educator; b. Boston, Jan. 23, 1932; s. Edwin Turner and Madeline (Rinker) W.; m. Marilyn Atkinson, Aug. 23, 1959 (div. 1982); children: Louise, Robert, Ellen, Laura, Martin; m. Susan Jan White, Oct. 28, 1982. Grad., Phillips Acad., Andover, Mass., 1949; AB, Harvard U., 1953; BD, Union Theol. Sem., 1956; PhD, Duke U., 1960. Ordained to ministry United Meth. Ch., 1955. Instr. Ohio Wesleyan U., Delaware, 1959-61, Meth. Theol. Sch. in Ohio, Delaware, 1960-61; prof. Perkins Sch. Theology, So. Meth. U., Dallas, 1961-83, U. Notre Dame, 1983—. Author: Cambridge Movement, 1962, New Forms of Worship, 1971, Introduction to Christian Worship, 1980, Protestant Worship, 1989, others; mem. editorial bd. Religious Book Club, 1980—. Named one of 100 most Influential People in Am. Religion, Christian Century mag., 1982. Mem. N.Am. Acad. Liturgy (pres. 1979, Berakah award 1983), Am. Soc. Ch. History, Liturgical Conf., Societas Liturgica, United Meth. Soc. for Worship. Avocations: hiking, travel, book and antiques collecting. Office: U Notre Dame Dept Theology Notre Dame IN 46556

WHITE, JAMES ROBERT, minister; b. Crescent, Okla., Aug. 31, 1936; s. James Franklin and Nellie Verona (Moffitt) W.; m. Willa June Mason, June 3, 1960; children: Jeri Lynn, James Robert Jr. BA, Okla. Bapt. U., 1959; MDiv, Southwestern Bapt. Theol. Sem., Ft. Worth, 1963. Ordained to ministry So. Bapt. Conv., 1960. Pastor Beaty Bapt. Ch., Pauls Valley, Okla., 1961-62, 1st Bapt. Ch., Stratford, Okla., 1962-65; pastor 1st Bapt. Ch., Ft. Cobb, Okla., 1965-67, Stroud, Okla., 1968-70; dir. students and missions and Bapt. Student Union, Kay Assn., Tonkawa, Okla., 1966-68; assoc. pastor Trinity Bapt. Ch., Oklahoma City, 1970-73; pastor Capitol Hill Bapt. Ch., Oklahoma City, 1973—; chmn., initiator Southside Crusade, Oklahoma City, 1975-79; trustee Okla. Bapt. U., Shawnee, 1978-81; mem. exec. bd. Capitol Bapt. Assn., 1973—, Union Bapt. Assn., 1989—. Contbg. author: Christian Life Bible, 1985. Pres. Olde Capitol Hill Coun., Oklahoma City, 1985-89; bd. dirs. Andrews Square Steering Com., Oklahoma City, 1980-91; mem. Oklahoma City Mayor's Adv. Com., 1987. Recipient svc. award Salvation Army, 1986-90. Office: Capitol Hill Bapt Ch 301 SW 25th St Oklahoma City OK 73109 *The most astounding thing about God (apart from His grace to us through Jesus) is that He would choose to redeem our world using mankind as help and energy.*

WHITE, J(OB) BENTON, religion educator; b. Birmingham, Ala., Sept. 3, 1931; s. Edith Branch (Benton) White; m. Mary Lou White, July 19, 1958; children: Thomas Raymond, Matthew Louis. BS, U. Ala., 1953; BD, Emory U., 1956; MTh, Pacific Luth. Theol. Sem., 1969. Ordained to ministry United Meth. Ch., as deacon, 1954, as elder, 1956. Assoc. dir. Wesley Found., U. Nebr., Lincoln, 1959-61; dir. Wesley Found. San Jose (Calif.) State U., 1961-67, dir. United Campus Christian Ministry, 1968-69, assoc. prof., 1968-69, asst. to pres., 1969-70, prof. religious studies, 1970—, ombudsman, 1967-68. Author: From Adam to Armageddon: A Survey of the Bible, 1986, 2d edit., 1990; contbr. articles to profl. jours., mags. Capt. USAF, 1956-59. Mem. Am. Acad. Religion (v.p., pres. western region). Democrat. Home: 2503 Briarwood Dr San Jose CA 95125 Office: San Jose State U Religious Studies Program San Jose CA 95192

WHITE, J(OHN) TIMOTHY, minister, educator; b. Gary, Ind., Jan. 6, 1951; s. Lester Carlton and Betty Ann (McCubbin) W.; m. Kathryn Diane Reinking, Aug. 19, 1972; children: David, Elizabeth. BA, So. Nazarene U., 1973, MA, 1978; MRE cum laude, Nazarene Theol. Sem., Kansas City, Mo., 1980; postgrad., U. Kans., 1984—. Min. religious edn. Ch. Nazarene, Woodward, Okla., 1980-81; gen. dir. Christian schs. and spl. edn. Nazarene Internat. Hdqrs., Kansas City, Mo., 1982-83; min. religious edn. Rainbow Blvd. Ch. Nazarene, Kansas City, Kans., 1986-87; instr. English Platt Coll., Overland Pk., Kans., 1987-88; assoc. staff person Nall Ave. Ch. Nazarene, Prairie Village, Kans., 1988-89; pastor Ch. Nazarene, Severy, Kans., 1989—; mem. Middler Curriculum Rev. com., Nazarene Internat. Hdqrs., 1987-88, Children's Ministries Coun., Kans. Dist., Ch. Nazarene, 1990—. Author: Paul, 1985, contbr. articles to mags. Parent vol. Kans. Spl. Olympics, 1985-87. Recipient Broadhurst scholarship, So. Nazarene U., 1971-73. Mem. Adv. com. Kans. U. Med. Ctr. Traumatic Brain Injury Re-entry project. Avocations: tennis, photography. Office: Ch Nazarene PO Box 157 Severy KS 67137

WHITE, JONATHAN BRUCE, minister; b. Greenville, Mich., Aug. 7, 1956; s. Robert Bruce and Patricia Ann (Bunker) W.; m. Linda Sue Reeves, Sept. 18, 1982; children: Jonathan Aaron, Joshua Eric. BS, Ind. Wesleyan U., 1978. Ordained to ministry Wesleyan Ch., 1985. Asst. pastor Brown St. Wesleyan Ch., Flint, Mich., 1979-82; pastor Monument Chapel Wesleyan Ch., Andrews, Ind., 1982-85; sr. pastor Grant (Mich.) Wesleyan Ch., 1985—; dist. Sunday sch. sec. North Mich. Dist., Wesleyan Ch., 1988—. Editor (newsletter) The Challenger, 1988—; author: Embrace the Cross, 1991. Republican. Home: 122 Arthur St Box 136 Grant MI 49327 Office: Grant Wesleyan Ch 688 112th St Grant MI 49327

WHITE, KEVIN JOHN, minister; b. Rockville, Conn., Nov. 21, 1956; s. John Edward and Joyce Katheryn (Prentiss) W.; m. Lynn Ann Felix, Sept. 15, 1979; children: Joanna Leigh, David Michael, Matthew Stephen. Dipl., Berean Sch., Springfield, Mo., 1978. Ordained to ministry Fellowship of Covenant Mins. and Chs., 1980. Pastor Ch. of the Second Advent, New Britain, Conn., 1980-87; chaplain Truth for Youth, Scotland, Conn., 1985-87; pastor Abundant Life Community Ch., Willimantic, Conn., 1987—; ednl. cons. Sys. Group, Glastonbury, Conn., 1989—. Contbr. articles to profl. jours. Mem. Students at Risk Com., Windham Pub. Schs., Willimantic, 1990—. Mem. Fellowship of Covenant Ministers & Chs., Burning Bush Fellowship (pres. 1985—), Windham Area Pastors Alliance. Office: Abundant Life Community Ch 8 Mountain St Box 108 Willimantic CT 06226

WHITE, LELAND JENNINGS, priest, theologian; b. Charleston, S.C., July 25, 1940; s. Leland S. and Rose Winifred (Budds) W. BA, St. Mary's Sem., Balt., 1962; STB, STL, Gregorian U., Rome, 1966; MA, U. Mich., 1972; PhD, Duke U., 1974. Ordained priest Roman Cath. Ch., 1965. Instr. theology St. Thomas Sem., Kenmore, Wash., 1968-69, St. John's Sem., Plymouth, Mich., 1969-70; asst. prof. religious studies Nazareth Coll., Kalamazoo, Mich., 1974-76, Siena Coll., Loudonville, N.Y., 1976-82; assoc. prof. theology St. John's U., N.Y.C., 1982-89, prof. theology and culture, 1989—; mem. editoral bd. Biblical Theology Bulletin, 1979-82. Author: Act in Theology, 1974, Christ and the Christian Movement, 1985, Jesus the Christ, 1988; asst. editor: Biblical Theology Bulletin, 1982-84, editor 1984—. Mem. ACLU, ABA, Am. Acad. Religion, N.J. Assn. Trial Lawyers of Am., Cath. Theol. Soc. Am., Coll. Theology Soc. Democrat. Office: St John's U Dept Theology Jamaica NY 11439 *The religious significance of life—our lives—is built on the actual stuff of our lives. What else is there? If our religious tradition begins with epics and law and culminates in an incarnation, we have no choice but to admit no separate domain apart from ordinary human affairs that is religious.*

WHITE, LERRILL JAMES, clinical pastoral educator; b. Lafayette, Ind., Mar. 13, 1948; s. Joe Lloyd and Wanita Irene (Robertson) W.; m. Deborah June Brown, Dec. 27, 1969; children: Krister Colin Brant, Kourtney Cassidy Benay. BA, Abilene Christian U., 1970, MS, 1973; MDiv, Princeton Theol. Sem., 1975; postgrad., Pa. State U., 1980-89. Ordained to ministry Ch. of Christ, 1975. Clin. chaplain Ft. Logan Mental Health Ctr., Denver, 1975-76, Meml. Med. Ctr., Corpus Christi, Tex., 1976-78; sr. pastor Centre Community Ch. of Christ, State Coll., Pa., 1978-87; assoc. dir. pastoral care Geisinger Med. Ctr., Danville, Pa., 1983-87; dir. pastoral care Yuma (Ariz.) Regional Med. Ctr., 1987—; author, presenter tng. courses, 1987—. Contbr. articles to profl. jours.; creator interview instrument P.C. Ranking Instrument, 1981. Bd. dirs. Behavioral Health Svcs., Yuma, 1991—; mem. Crane PTO, 1987—; mem., coach Yuma Youth Soccer Assn., 1987—. Fellow Coll. Chaplains; m. Assn. Clin. Pastoral Edn. (supr. 1983—, regional coun. Pacific region 1988-90), Ariz. Chaplain's Assn. (exec. com. 1988—, pres. 1989-90), Greater Yuma Ministerium. Office: Yuma Regional Med Ctr 2400 Ave A Yuma AZ 85364 *Making choices about how we live our lives in a responsible* *and meaningful way is ultimately what life is about and becomes our legacy for generations to come.*

WHITE, LLOYD MICHAEL, religion educator; b. Dallas, May 3, 1949; s. Lloyd Jr. and Marian Virginia (Bray) W.; m. Gloria A. Amstutz, Dec. 22, 1970; children: Jessica Alice, Travis Wesley Lloyd. BA, Abilene Christian U., 1971, MA, 1973; MDiv, Yale U., 1975, PhD, 1982. Instr. Yale U., New Haven, 1979-80, Ind. U., Bloomington, 1980-81; prof. Oberlin (Ohio) Coll., 1981—; bd. dirs. Tell el-Hesi (Israel) Archaeolog. Expedition, 1981—. Author: The Tabula of Cebes, 1983, Building God's House in the Roman World, 1989, The Domus Ecclesiae in its Environment, 1989; mem. editorial bd. Biblical Archaeologist; contbr. articles to profl. publs. H.H. Powers grantee, 1983, 88; fellow Andrew W. Mellon Found., 1985, NEH, 1986. Mem. Soc. Biblical Literature (chmn. social history rsch. group 1983—), Am. Schs. Oriental Rsch., Assn. Sociology of Religion, Archaeol. Inst. Am. Avocations: skiing, scuba diving, distance running, boating. Office: Oberlin Coll Dept Religion Rice Hall Oberlin OH 44074

WHITE, LYNN ALLEN, minister; b. Oklahoma City, Feb. 25, 1950; s. O'Dell and Rocena Elizabeth (McGill) W.; m. Alita Mae Van Dolah, Dec. 14, 1968; children: Clinton Michael, Alicia Dawn, Anthony Nathaniel. BA, Northwestern Coll. Assemblies of God, Kirkland, Wash., 1977; MA, Assemblies of God Theol. Sem., Springfield, Mo., 1990. Lic. to ministry Assemblies of God, 1973, ordained, 1980. Pastor Abundent Life Assembly of God, Tacoma, 1977-84, Highline New Life Ctr., Seattle, 1984—; police chaplain King County (Wash.) Police, 1987—. With U.S. Army, 1969-71, Vietnam. Republican. Office: Highland New Life Ctr 15434 10th Ave SW Seattle WA 98166

WHITE, MARK THOMAS, minister; b. Rutherfordton, N.C., Mar. 8, 1955; s. Harold Mitchell and Sue (Minton) W.; m. Dianne Lawrence, Aug. 2, 1981. BA, U. N.C., 1977; MDiv, Southeastern Bapt. Theol. Sem., Wake Forest, N.C., 1981, DMin, 1985. Ordained to ministry So. Bapt. Conv., 1977. Pastor Thanksgiving Bapt. Ch., Selma, N.C., 1977-83, Pleasant Grove Bapt. Ch., Willow Springs, N.C., 1983-86; sr. minister Coats (N.C.) Bapt. Ch., 1986-90; assoc. dir. N.C. Bapt. Men, Bapt. State Conv. N.C., Cary, 1990—; bd. ministers Campbell U., Buies Creek, N.C., 1989-90. Co-author: The Coat Lady and Other Worship Stories for Children, 1990; editor: The Windowsill of Heaven. Bd. dirs. Harnett Prodn. Ent., Dunn, N.C., 1987-90. Mem. Assn. Clin. Pastoral Edn. Democrat. Home: 1137 Turner Farms Rd Garner NC 27529 Office: Bapt State Conv of NC 205 Convention Dr Cary NC 27512

WHITE, POLLY SEARS, religious organization administrator; b. Phila., Jan. 29, 1931; d. W. Heyward and Emily P. (Welsh) Myers; m. Peter White, June 13, 1953; children: Katharine, Peter, Jennifer, Jeffrey. AB, Smith Coll., 1953. Adminstrv. aide Inst. Local and State Govt., U. Pa., Phila., 1953-55; parish sec. St. Mary's Episcopal Ch., Wayne, Pa., 1977-85; program dir. Metro Toledo Chs. United, 1987—. Sec., treas. Friends of Radnor Twp. Meml. Libr., Wayne, 1978-80; pres. Presbyn. Hosp. Med. Aux., Phila., 1983-85; bd. dirs. Wood County Planned Parenthood Coun., Bowling Green, Ohio, 1985-86, Perrysburg (Ohio) LWV, 1986-88; operating com. First Call for Help of United Way of Toledo; mem. St. Timothy's Episc. Ch. Altar Guild, Flower Guild; trustee Hist. Perrysburg., 1990, bd. dirs. 1990—. Democrat. Avocations: tennis, knitting, bird watching, gardening. Home: 525 E 6th St Perrysburg OH 43551 Office: Metro Toledo Chs United 444 Floyd St Toledo OH 43620

WHITE, QUENTIN JEROME, minister; b. Cleve., Nov. 18, 1952; s. Modest and Lillie Mae (Tarrence) W.; m. Pamela Small, July 6, 1985; 1 child, Cherise. BA, Wilberforce Univ., 1980; MDiv, Duke Univ., 1983; postgrad., Univ. Va., 1988-89. Ordained to ministry A.M.E. Ch., 1983. Pastor Bethel A.M.E. Ch., Roanoke, Va., 1986-90; chaplain VA Med. Ctr., Salem, Va., 1990—; pastor St. Paul AME Ch., Blacksburg, Va., 1990—; Bd. examiners Va. Conf. AME Ch., Norfolk, 1987—, conf. statistician, 1988—. Bd. dirs. Literacy Vols. of Am., Roanoke Valley,m Va., 1989-91. Lt. USN, 1984-86. Recipient minority grant State of Va., U. Va., 1988. Home: 3110 Linwood Rd Roanoke VA 24017

WHITE, RAYMOND, orthodontist; b. N.Y.C., Feb. 8, 1945; s. Arthur James and Zabel (Encababian) W.; m. Linda Marlene Netzer, June 28, 1974; children: Jonathan Raymond, Jennilyn Rebecca. BS, CUNY, 1966; DMD, U. Pa., 1970; MS, St. Louis U., 1977. Commd. lt. USN, 1970, advanced through grades to comdr., comdr. dental corps, 1975-88, ret., 1988; pvt. practice Oakbrook Terrace, Ill., 1988—. Mem. ADA, Am. Assn. Orthodontics (ethics com. 1988—), Midwestern Soc. Orthodontists (membership chmn. 1987—), Ill. Soc. Orthondontists (pres. 1987—), Ill. State Dental Soc., Chgo. Dental Soc. Avocations: photography, art, tennis, swimming. Office: 1 S 132 Summit Ave Oakbrook Terrace IL 60521

WHITE, REBECCA, religious educator; b. Columbus, Ind., Oct. 4, 1948; d. James Edward and Jacquelyn Kerr (Stevens) H.; m. Dennis Robert White, June 3, 1967; children: Eric Matthew, Benjamin Logan. Grad., Columbus (Ind.) High Sch., 1966. Office mgr. Hope Mission Tours, Hope, Ind., 1983—; girls gospel group leader E. Columbus (Ind.) United Meth. Ch., 1964-66, youth fellowship leader, 1967-71; Bible sch. music dir. Mt. Olive United Meth. Ch., Columbus, summer 1988, youth fellowship leader, 1991—, choir dir., 1986—; musician, singer Hope Trio, 1989—; mem. Haiti Missions, Hope Mission Tours, 1983—. Singer recording cassette tapes, 1985, 87, 89. Co-founder White Wood Sch. of Hope, Haiti, W.I., 1984; bd. dirs. Mission of Hope Compound, Haiti, 1989—; adminstrv. asst. Bartholomew County CETA Program, Columbus, 1978-79. Home: 15665 E 400 N Hope IN 47246 Office: Hope Mission Tours Inc PO Box 62 Hope IN 47246

WHITE, RICHARD ALLEN, minister; b. Damariscotta, Maine, Aug. 6, 1948; s. Fred Alonzo and Mary Lucille (Winslow) W.; m. Nancy Elizabeth Boyd, Oct. 18, 1985; children: Matthew Richard, Benjamin Sarad. Assoc. degree, Grahm Jr. Coll., Boston, 1968; BA, Curry Coll., 1970; MDiv, Andover Newton, 1980. Ordained to ministry United Ch. of Christ, 1981. Youth minister 1st Congregational Ch., Hampton, N.H., 1977-78; minister to youth Allin Congregational Ch., Dedham, Mass., 1978-80; pastor Topsham (Vt.) United Presbyn. Ch., 1980-89, East Corinth (Vt.) Congregational Ch., 1980-89, Brandon (Vt.) Congregational Ch., 1989—; Vt. del. Gen. Synod United Ch. of Christ, Cleve., 1989, Norfolk, Va., 1991; bd. dirs. bd. dirs. Vt. Conf. United Ch. of Christ, Burlington, 1983-89, pres., 1987, 89; chairperson Atkinson Retreat Ctr., Newbury, Vt., 1981-91. Coord. St. Jude Bike-a-Thon, Brandon, 1990, 91, Ch. World Svc. Walk-a-Thon, Bradford, Vt., 1988, 89; chairperson Sch. Dist. Union #36, East Corinth, 1986-89. Fellow Rotary (treas. Brandon club 1989—, bd. dirs. Brandon club 1990—, Paul Harris fellow); mem. Christian Counselors Assn. Republican. Home: 74 Park St Brandon VT 05733 Office: Brandon Congl Ch PO Box 97 Brandon VT 05733 *I have found in life that love of everyone is the most important Christian character trait, and it is the least understood.*

WHITE, ROBERT ARNOLD, religious organization administrator; b. Chgo., Apr. 24, 1944; s. Lester Charles and A. Lorraine (Erion) W.; m. JoAnne Kemink, Jan. 21, 1967; children: Erik Ethan, Kristina Michelle. BA, Hope Coll., 1966; MDiv, Western Theol. Sem., 1969; DD (hon.), Central Coll., 1986. Minister Clover Hill Reformed Ch., Flemington, N.J., 1970-75, Pitcher Hill Community Ch., North Syracuse, N.Y., 1975-80; ch. exec. Reformed Ch. in Am., N.Y.C., 1981-85; pres. New Brunswick (N.J.) Theol. Sem., 1985—. Co-author: Christ is Our Peace, 1982. Seminar leader Nat. Coun. Chs., Soviet Union, 1984-88; U.S. rep. Christian Peace Conf., Prague, Czechoslovakia, 1986; adv. bd. Bd. Higher Edn., N.J., 1989—. Avocations: reading, wilderness camping, antique collecting.

WHITE, RONALD LYNN, clergyman; b. Santa Ana, Calif., Feb. 24, 1944; s. John L. and Zanelli J. (Morton) W.; m. Janis Lee Seamon, June 10, 1967; children: Kimberly Jo, Tonya Lyn, Jeremy Lee. BA, Calif. Luth. U., 1965; MDiv, Wartburg Theol. Sem., 1969. Pastor of youth, parish edn. and evangelism Newport Harbor Luth. Ch., Newport Beach, Calif., 1969-71; pastor of youth and parish edn. Shepherd of the Valley Luth. Ch., Canoga Park, Calif., 1972-73; pastor Lord of Life Luth. Ch., Spring Valley, Calif., 1973-1981, Am. Luth. Ch., Burbank, Calif., 1981—; chmn. So. Calif. (West) Synod Commn. for Fin. Support, 1988—. Mem. Burbank Ministerial Assn. (v.p. 1988—). Office: Am Luth Ch 755 N Whitnall Hwy Burbank CA 91505

WHITE, RUTH BRYANT, counselor, communications specialist, minister; b. Denver, May 6, 1955; d. Volleny Bryant Sr. and Ruth Ada (Washington) Smith; m. Steven Alan White, Nov. 21, 1980; children: Pershaun R., LeJeune B., LaVonda M. Ed. high sch., Denver. Ordained to ministry Christian Ch. With acctg. sect. U.S. Govt., Denver and L.A., 1972-81; remittance processor Auto Club So. Calif., L.A., 1981-84; with acctg. dept. various agys. L.A., 1984-91; sr. adminstrv. support specialist Infonet, L.A., 1991—. Author: Free Indeed: The Autobiography of an Interracial Couple, 1989. Founder A Place for Us Ministry, Gardena, Calif., 1984—. Mem. Assn. Multiethnic Ams. (charter mem., regional v.p. western U.S. 1991—). Avocation: research on prejudice, racism, and interracial issues, public speaking. Office: A Place for Us PO Box 357 Gardena CA 90248-7857

WHITE, STEVEN D., music and worship minister; b. Pensacola, Fla., Nov. 5, 1950; s. William Gerald and Lillian Carzie (Merritt) W.; m. Cinde L. Stack, Jan. 3, 1976; children: Kristen Melodie, Benjamin Michael. MusB, La. State U., 1972, MusM, 1974; DD, So. Calif. Theol. Sem., 1990. Ordained to ministry, 1982; lic. pvt. pilot, 1979. Min. of music and worship Airport Blvd. Bapt. Ch., Mobile, Ala., 1975-76, Green Acres Bapt. Ch., Warner Robins, Ga., 1976-81, Kirby Woods Bapt. Ch., Memphis, 1981-86, Sherwood Bapt. Ch., Albany, Ga., 1986-88, First Bapt. Ch., Merritt Island, Fla., 1988—; tchr., trainer Evangelism Explosion Internat., Merritt Island, 1989—. Voice scholar Pensacola Jr. Coll., 1968, La. State U., 1971. Mem. Phi Mu Alpha Sinfonia. Republican. Office: First Bapt Ch 140 Magnolia Ave Merritt Island FL 32952 *When I consider and think about life, I am amazed and thrilled at what I do each week. What a privilege it is to lead people in praise and worship in a free land. The ministry I am called to perform is eternal as praise will continue in Heaven throughout all eternity.*

WHITE, STEVEN DOUGLAS, clergyman; b. Commerce, Tex., Sept. 18, 1953; s. Ralph Denton and Lois (Vaughan) W.; m. Teresa Ann DeLuna, Aug. 18, 1984; 1 child, Vanessa Ann. BS, North Tex. State U., 1976; MRE, Southwestern Bapt. Theol. Sem., Ft. Worth, 1982. Ordained to ministry Bapt. Ch., 1982. Youth minister lst Bapt. Ch., College Station, Tex., 1982-83; pastor Olive Branch Bapt. Ch., Axtell, Tex., 1984-86, Grove Haven Bapt. Ch., Dallas, 1986—. Recipient Scouter's Key, Longhorn coun. Boy Scouts Am., 1981; named one of Outstanding Young Men of Am., 1985. Mem. John Birch Soc. (chpt. leader 1988-89). Republican. Home: 7324 Vallejo Dallas TX 75227 Office: Grove Haven Bapt Ch 1115 Ridgewood Dallas TX 75217

WHITE, TERENCE D., pastor, church administrator; b. Kittanning, Pa., Dec. 3, 1942; s. Elzie M. and Helen (Hooks) w.; m. Sharon Auxt, Apr. 16, 1965; children: Jamie Lynn, Jonathan Andrew. BME, Grace Coll., 1964; MME, Ind. U., 1967; postgrad., U. Iowa, 1969-72. Band tchr. Goshen (Ind.) Pub. Schs., 1965-66; dir. pub. relations Grace Schs., Winona Lake, Ind., 1966-69; self-study coordinator Grace Coll. and Sem., Winona Lake, 1971-72; assoc. prof. journalism Grace Coll., Winona Lake, 1972-77, St. Paul Bible Coll., Mpls., 1977-81; assoc. pastor of adminstr. and music Wooddale Ch., Eden Prairie, Minn., 1981—. Photo editor Today's Handbook of Bible Times and Customs, 1985; founder Twin Cities Christian Newspaper; co-founder, editor Business Life Mag. Sec. Winona Lake Planning Commn., 1975; Rep. del. conv., precinct leader. Mem. Nat. Assn. Ch. Bus. Adminstrn. (pres. no. cen. chpt. 1985-86), Evang. Press Assn. (gen. conv. chmn. 1983, chmn. nominating com. 85-86), Minn. Christian Writers Guild (pres. 1985-86, founding editor Christian Communicator mag. 1988). Avocations: photography, free-lance writing, publishing consultant, music. Home: 6812 Sugar Hill Circle Eden Prairie MN 55346 Office: Wooddale Ch 6630 Shady Oak Rd Eden Prairie MN 55344

WHITE, THOMAS HARRINGTON, priest, counselor; b. Ft. Worth, Nov. 11, 1931; s. Harrington Hooper and Lida Geneva (Stovall) W.; m. Patsy Jo LaRue, Oct. 18, 1958; children: Harrington Hooper II, Lawrence Kenneth. BS, U. Houston, 1954; Licentiate in Theology, U. of the South, 1964; MSW, Our Lady of the Lake U., 1973. Lic. cert. social worker. Assoc. rector St. Mark's Episcopal Ch., San Antonio, 1964-68; vicar St. Mark's Episcopal Ch., Austin, Tex., 1968-71, St. Timothy's Episcopal Ch., Cotulla, Tex., 1972-74; assoc. rector St. Luke's Episcopal Ch., San Antonio, 1974-76; rector St. Helena's Episcopal Ch., Boerne, Tex., 1976-84; vicar St. James the Fisherman Episcopal Ch., Kodiak, Alaska, 1984-85; priest assoc. Holy Comforter Episcopal Ch., Gadsden, Ala., 1986-87; interim rector St. John's Episcopal Ch., Birmingham, 1987-88; rector St. Stephen's Episcopal Ch., Eutaw, Ala., 1988—; pvt. practice in counseling. Mem. Greene County Child Abuse Treatment Team, 1988—; trustee U. South, 1968. 1st lt. U.S. Army, 1954-56. Cited by Tex. Dept. of Human Resources for outstanding and significant personal svc. Mem. Nat. Assn. Social Workers. Democrat. Avocation: photography. Home and Office: St Stephens Episcopal Ch PO Box 839 Eutaw AL 35462

WHITEAKER, LINDA JOYCE, minister, educational administrator; b. Cookeville, Tenn., May 4, 1942; d. Beecher and Thelma Lee (Roberson) W. Student U. Hawaii, 1965, Hancock Jr. Coll., 1970—; Th.B., Clarksville Sch. Theology, 1980, M.Th., 1983; grad. Calif. Assn. Realtors, 1968. Lic. to ministry Ch. of God, 1960. Pastor, Ch. of God, Lahaina, Hawaii, 1962-64; dir. youth and Christian edn. Ch. of God, Hawaii, 1964-65; pastor Santa Maria Ch. of God, Calif., 1965—; owner/broker Lin*Etta Realty, Santa Maria, 1972—; builder. Founder, pastor, adminstr. Accelerated Christian Sch., 1976—; founder, pres. Lady Ministers Fellowship Internat., 1981—; mem. Santa Maria/Orcutt Gen. Plan Adv. Com., 1979-84; mem. Santa Maria Planning Commn., 1984-89, chmn., 1988-89; mem. congl. task force com. U.S. Ho. of Reps., 1983. Mem. Santa Maria Bd. Realtors (pres. 1978-79, legis. chmn. 1980), Calif. Assn. Realtors (bd. dirs. 1977-81), Nat. Assn. Realtors (bd. dirs. 1978-81), Santa Maria C. of C. (speakers club). Republican. Avocations: walking; collecting Bibles; travel; photography Home: PO Box 1342 Santa Maria CA 93454 Office: PO Box 1342 Santa Maria CA 93454 *God is concerned about concerns His children.*

WHITEHEAD, MICHAEL KENNETH, lawyer, religious organization counsel; b. Independence, Mo., Feb. 14, 1950; s. James Roddie and Dorothy Jean (Coada) W.; m. Janet Lynn, Apr. 24, 1976; children: Jonathan, Holly, Hannah. BA in Polit. Sci., U. Mo., 1972, JD, 1975. Bar: Mo.1975, U.S. Supreme Ct. 1981. Mem. Crews, Smart, Whitehead, Kansas City, Mo., 1978—; gen. counsel So. Bapt. Christian Life Commn., Washington, 1990—. Capt. U.S. Army, 1975-78. Office: Crews Smart Whitehead Brownlee & Waits 401 W 89th Kansas City MO 64114

WHITEHILL, JAMES DONALD, religion educator; b. Manchester, Conn., Jan. 4, 1942; s. William James and Virginia (Greene) W.; m. Patricia Little, Dec. 28, 1963 (div. Mar. 1985); children: Rebecca, Ethan; m. Hiroko Somers, Aug. 2, 1991. BA, Trinity Coll., 1963; MA, Columbia U., 1965; PhD, Drew U., 1970. Assoc. prof. Stephens Coll., Columbia, Mo., 1968—; dir. Columbia Zen Ctr., 1980—; Fulbright-Hays lectr. Kyushu U., Rukuoka, Japan, 1991—. Author: Enter The Quiet, 1980; contbr. articles to profl. jours. Mem. Am. Acad. Religion, Assn. for Asian Studies, Soc. for Buddhist-Christian Studies. Zen-Buddhist. Office: Stephens Coll Columbia CO 65215

WHITEMAN, DARRELL L., anthropology educator; b. Lexington, Ky., Jan. 3, 1947; s. Geo. Edgar Whiteman and Kathleen (Gaddis) Hicks; m. Laurie Whiteman, Aug. 7, 1971; children: Geofrrey, Julia. BA, Seattle Pacific U., 1970; PhD, So. Ill. U., 1980. Prof. cultural anthropology Asbury Theol. Sem., Wilmore, Ky., 1984—. Author: Melanesians and Missionaries, 1983 (named Outstanding Book Internat. Bull. Missionary Rsch. 1984); editor Missiology, 1988—. Fellow Soc. for Applied Anthropology, Am. Soc. Missiology, Assn. Profs. of Mission (pres. 1987); mem. Am. Anthrop. Assn., Am. Bible Soc. (trustee 1988—). Methodist. Home: 104 Hunter Cir Wilmore KY 40390 Office: Asbury Theol Sem Wilmore KY 40390

WHITENECK, JOHN SAMUEL, JR., clergyman, secretary; b. Aline, Okla., Mar. 14, 1905; s. John Samuel Sr. and Cora Lee (Beard) W.; m. Arlene Saylor, June 10, 1929 (dec. Dec. 1930); m. Lois Miriam Heckman, Aug. 26, 1933; 1 child, Gwen Lee. AB, McPherson (Kans.) Coll., 1928; BD, Bethany Theol. Sem., 1935; ThD, Iliff sch. Theology, 1941. Pastoral minister Ch. of the Brethen/United Ch. of Christ, 1934-72; asst. to v.p. Law Sch. Lewis & Clark Coll., Portland, Oreg., 1972-81; clergyman Generations for Peace, Portland, 1981—; marital counselor Alcoholics Anonymous. Mem. Masons, Rotary. Democrat. Avocation: golf. Home: 14205 SW Jenkins Rd Beaverton OR 97005 Office: Generations for Peace 1315 SW Park Portland OR 97201

WHITESIDE, BEVERLY LOIS, lay worker; b. Port Shepstone, Natal, Republic of South Africa, Sept. 10, 1955; came to U.S., 1977; d. Harry Lewis and Virginia Elizabeth (Devereaux) Wood; m. Richard Daniel Shepperson, Feb. 13, 1977 (div. Sept. 1985); children: Lisa Desiree, Danielle Lynn; m. Charles Walker Whiteside, Aug. 3, 1990. Student, Grays Hosp. Sch. Nursing, Pietermaritzburg, Republic of South Africa, 1974-76, Grand Rapids Bapt. Coll., 1977-79; AA, Lansing (Mich.) Community Coll., 1990. Sec. youth group Pietermaritzburg Cen. Bapt. Ch., 1970-74; sec. advt. dept. S. Bapt. Ch., Lansing, 1979—; Yearbook editor Colulmbia (S.C.) Bible Coll., 1983-84. Founder-dir. Div. Recovery Workshop, Lansing, 1987-89. Office: S Bapt Ch 1518 S Washington Lansing MI 48910 *Life brings us great heartache and many sorrows—in ourselves, in those we love, and in people we see in the street and around the world. But through it all we can have everlasting joy in Jesus. (Peter 1:8, John 1:1-4, Isaiah 51:11).*

WHITLOCK, CHARLES WAYNE, minister; b. Ft. Worth, Mar. 3, 1937; s. William Ray and Bonnie Luzell (Buck) W.; m. Sudie Bob Moore, Aug. 31, 1956; children: Richard Charles, Robert Lane, Randy Wayne, Russell Ray. Student, Tex. Wesleyan U., 1958-64; BA, Hardin-Simmons U., 1970. Ordained to ministry So. Bapt. Conv., 1966. Pastor Knapp Bapt. Ch., Snyder, Tex., 1965-66; pastor First Bapt. Ch., Lueders, Tex., 1966-70, Roby, Tex., 1970-74; pastor First So. Bapt. Ch., Fairmont, W.Va., 1974-82, Fellowship Bapt. Ch., Charleston, W.Va., 1982-84; dir. assoc. missions Summit Bapt. Assn., Akron, Ohio, 1984—; chmn. youth/evangelism/missions West Cen. Assn., Tex., 1965-74; moderator Monongahela Bapt. Assn., W.Va., 1978-80; pres. W.Va. State Conv. Bapts., 1980-82, ch. planter, dir. state missions, 1982-84. Mem. Lions. Home: 896 Carnegie Ave Akron OH 44314-1132 Office: Summit Bapt Assn 333 S Main St Ste 607 Akron OH 44308

WHITLOCK, LUDER GRADICK, JR., seminary president; b. Jacksonville, Fla., June 20, 1940; s. Luder G. and Juanita O. (Nessmith) W.; m. Mary Louise Patton, Aug. 29, 1959; children: Frank Christopher, Alissa Ann, Beth LaVerne. BA, U. Fla., 1962; MDiv, Westminster Theol. Sem., 1966; D of Ministry, Vanderbilt U., 1973. Ordained to ministry Presbyn. Ch. in Am., 1966. Pastor Sharon Presbyn. Ch., Hialeah, Fla., 1966-69, West Hills Presbyn. Ch., Harriman, Tenn., 1969-75; prof. Reformed Theol. Sem., Jackson, Miss., 1975—, acting pres., 1978-79, pres., 1979—; bd. dirs. Ligonier Ministries, Orlando, Fla. Trustee Westminster Theol. Sem., Phila., 1973-76, Covenant Coll., Chattanooga, 1973-80; bd. dirs. Internat. Grad. Sch. Theology, Seoul, Republic of Korea, 1987—. Mem. Evang. Theol. Soc., Evang. Sem. Pres. (exec. com. 1990), Country Club of Jackson. Republican. Office: Reformed Theol Sem 5422 Clinton Blvd Jackson MS 39209

WHITLOW, WILLIAM LA FOND, minister, theology school planter; b. Mpls., Oct. 20, 1932; s. George Lester and Wanona Nadine (Ridgeway) W.; m. Donna Mae Magnuson, June 13, 1953; children: Debra, Cathleen, Lisa Mae. Ministerial diploma, Eugene (Oreg.) Bible Coll., 1953; postgrad., Seattle Pacific U., 1961; BTh, ThM, Internat. Sem., Orlando, Fla., 1981, ThD summa cum laude, 1986, DD (hon.), 1984. Ordained to ministry Open Bible Standard Chs., 1954, Biltmore Bible Ch., 1988. Asst. and pastor Oreg. chs., 1949-55; dean pers. Calif. Open Bible Inst., Pasadena, 1957-58; pres., island supt. Bible Inst., Montego Bay, Jamaica, 1958-59, San Fernando, Trinidad, 1960-65; sr. pastor Biltmore Bible Ch., Phoenix, 1967—; pres. Biltmore Bible Sch. Theology, Phoenix, 1982-86; extension sch. rep. Internat. Sem., Orlando, 1984-91; adj. faculty mem. Evang. Theol. Sem., Dixon, Mo., 1989-91; affiliate prof. Vision Christian U., Ramona, Calif., 1991. Author, compiler: Basic Bible School Builder, 1986-91; also numerous Bible tng. courses. Recipient Outstanding Acad. Achievement award Internat. Sem., 1987. Office: Biltmore Bible Ch 3330 E Camelback Rd Phoenix AZ 85018

WHITNEY, BARRY LYN, religious studies educator; b. Cornwall, Ont., Can., Dec. 10, 1947; s. Earl Stanley Whitney and Gwendolyn Grace (Meldrum) Goddard. BA with honors, Carleton U., 1971; PhD in Religious Studies, McMaster U., Hamilton, Ont., 1977. Prof. religious studies U. Windsor, Ont., Can., 1976—; lectr. pastoral edn. Southwestern Regional Ctr., Cedar Springs, Ont., 1977-79; mem. Anglican commn. Canterbury Coll., London and Windsor, 1977-79, tutor of admissions, Windsor, 1979-82, fellow, 1979-82; regional coord. Ctr. for Process Studies, 1979—. Author: Evil and the Process God, 1985, What Are They Saying About God and Evil?, 1989, Theodicy, 1991; contbr. articles to profl. jours. Scholar Carleton U., 1967-71, McMaster U., 1971-76; Can. Coun. scholar McMaster U., 1972-75. Mem. Soc. for Study Process Philosophies, Coll. Theology Soc., Am. Acad. Religion, Coun. for Study Religion. Home: RR 1, Amherstburg, ON Canada N9V 2Y7 Office: U Windsor, Dept Religious Studies, Sunset Ave, Windsor, ON Canada N9B 3P4 *I am committed to the process vision of reality (Whitehead, Hartshorne) as a viable vision of God and a major advance in dealing with the terrible agony of suffering and injustice.*

WHITNEY, J. MARVIN, minister; b. Loma Linda, Calif., Oct. 1, 1948; s. Judson Homer and Alma Whitney; m. Corrie Joy Saulsbury, Sept. 6, 1970; children: Lonna, Carrie. BA, Pacific Union Coll., 1971; MA, Andrews U., 1991. Ordained to ministry Seventh-day Adventist Ch., 1977. Pastor Seventh-day Adventist Ch. Gulf States Conf., 1972-82; chaplain resident Kettering (Ohio) Med. Ctr., 1982-83; chaplain Parkview Meml. Hosp., Brunswick, Ohio, 1983-87; pastor Seventh-day Adventist Ch., Bemidji, Minn., 1987-90, Harlington, Tex., 1990—; valley parish coord. Tex. Conf. Seventh-day Adventist Ch., Alvarado, 1990—. Mem. Assn. for Clin. Pastoral Edn., Amateur Radio Club. Home: PO Box 3539 Harlington TX 78551

WHITNEY, LARRY KEITH, minister, business educator, lawyer; b. Marion County, Ill., Jan. 8, 1946; s. Charles Wayne and Doris R. (Mulvaney) W.; m. Karen Lynn Whitney, Feb. 6, 1971; children: Kirsten, Kari. MBA, Eastern Ill. U., 1972; JD, Tex. Tech. U., 1977. Bar: Ill. 1977. Tax acct. Arthur Andersen & Co., St. Louis, 1977-78; sole practice, Olney, Ill., 1978-81; atty. city of Olney, 1978-81; chmn. dept. bus. Freed-Hardeman Coll., Henderson, Tenn., 1981-83; assoc. prof. bus. law and fin. Pepperdine U., Malibu, Calif., 1983-86; sr. minister Northside Ch. of Christ, Santa Ana, Calif., 1986—. Author: Declaring the Dawn. Served with USAF, 1966-69. Decorated Air medal. Recipient Wall St. Jour. award. Mem. ABA, Ill. Bar Assn., Phi Delta Phi. Mem. Ch. of Christ.

WHITNEY-WISE, PATRICIA HELEN, religious organization executive, food program specialist; b. Salem, Oreg., Mar. 28, 1953; d. Loyal Aaron Whitney and Verena Louise (Fisch) Whitney-Nosbisch; m. Stephen Dale Whitney-Wise, Dec. 18, 1983; 1 child, Joshua Aaron. BA in Sociology and Communication Arts, U. San Francisco, 1975; postgrad., Grad. Theol. Union, Berkeley, Calif., 1980-84. Rsch. asst. Nat. Office for Social Responsibility, San Francisco, 1976; specialist Child Care Food Program, Oakland, 1976-77; nutrition adv., team supr. Children's Rights Group Child Care Food Program, San Francisco, 1977-80; cons. Office of Child Nutrition Svcs., Calif. State Dept. Edn., Sacramento, 1980; food program specialist Food Law Ctr., Calif. Rural Legal Assistance, San Francisco, 1980-84; food policy adv. Calif. Coun. Chs., Sacramento, 1984-88, exec. dir., 1990—; keynote speaker Nat. Hunger Conf., Washington, 1987. Mem. organizing team Senator Kennedy's Hearing on Hunger in San Francisco, 1983; apptd. mem. Mayor Feinstein's Task Force on Food and Hunger, San Francisco, 1984, steering com. Nat. Child Care Food Program Sponsors Forum, 1984, Hands Across Am. Funding Com. for Calif., 1986; mem., chairperson Sacramento Hunger Study Group, 1987; mem. vestry Trinity Cathedral, Episcopal Ch., 1987; bd. dirs. Child Care Law Ctr., 1988-90; mem. adv. com. Luth. Social Svcs., 1989—. Recipient Best in Hunger award U.S. Conf. of Mayors, 1989; Govt. grantee, Salem Referral Ctr., 1974. Office: Calif Coun Chs 1300 N St Sacramento CA 95814

WHITSITT, WILLIAM ALLEN, minister; b. Natchez, Miss., Nov. 30, 1943; s. Charles Dalton and Dorothea (Dickerson) W.; m. Rita K. Black, June 13, 1964; children: Bryant, Mark, Jeremy, Kayla. Student, U. Okla.,

1962-63, Apostolic Bible Inst., 1969-70. Ordained to ministry United Pentecostal Ch. Internat., 1973. Pastor Granby (Conn.) Pentecostal Tabernacle, 1972—; dist. supt. Conn. dist. United Pentecostal Ch. Internat., 1984—. With U.S. Army, 1967-69. Republican. Office: Granby Pentecostal Ch 23 Griffin Rd Granby CT 06035

WHITT, RICHARD KEITH, minister; b. Paintsville, Ky., Mar. 9, 1954; s. Herman and Wanda Lou (Marshall) W.; m. Teresa Sue Reynolds, July 2, 1976; 1 cild, Charissa Sue. BA in Bibl. Edn., Lee Coll., Cleveland, Tenn., 1981; postgrad., Ch. of God Sch. Theology, Cleveland, Tenn., 1989—. Ordained to ministry Ch. of God, 1984. Evangelist Ch. of God, Cleveland, 1978-81; pastor Wellsburg (W.Va.) Ch. of God, 1981, Weston (W.Va.) Ch. of God, 1981-84, Parkersburg (W.Va.) Ch. of God, 1984-90, Mill Creek Ch. of God, Pecks Mill, W.Va., 1990-91; Huntington (W.Va.) Ch. of God, 1991—; edn. bd. Ch. of God, W. Va., Beckley, 1983-86, youth and Christian Edn. bd. mem., 1984-88.

WHITTAKER, BILL DOUGLAS, minister; b. Bowling Green, Ky., June 14, 1943; s. Ewing A. and Lois (Jenkins) W.; m. Rebecca Kaye Howard, June 18, 1966; children: John, Karen, Mary. BA, Western Ky. U., 1965; MDiv, So. Bapt. Theol. Sem., Louisville, 1969, D of Ministry, 1974. Ordained to ministry So. Bapt. Conv., 1964. Pastor 1st Bapt. Ch., Sturgis, Ky., 1969-76, Murray, Ky., 1976-82; missionary Fgn. Mission Bd., So. Bapt. Conv., The Philippines, 1983-86; pastor Downtown Bapt. Ch., Orlando, Fla., 1986-88; pres. Clear Creek Bapt. Bible Coll., Pineville, Ky., 1988—. Author: Preparing to Preach, 1986; columnist Western Recorder newspaper, 1988—. Bd. dirs. Coalition for the Homeless, Cen. Fla. YMCA, Orlando, 1986-88. Mem. Am. Assn. Higher Edn., Am. Assn. Bible Colls. (del. 1988—), Assn. So. Bapt. Colls. and Schs. (del. 1988—), Ky. Bapt. Hist. Soc., Kiwanis (bd. dirs. Sturgis chpt. 1974-75), Ky. Bapt. Conv. (pres. 1980). Home and Office: 300 Clear Creek Rd Pineville KY 40977

WHITTAKER, DAVID JAY, Mormon archives curator; b. Lakeview, Oreg., Oct. 20, 1945; s. Douglas John and Althea (Harlow) W.; m. Linda Struhs, Sept. 10, 1966; children: Julie Ann, Jennifer Lyn, Kristen Kay, Stephen David. BA, Brigham Young U., 1967, PhD in Am. History, 1982; MA, Calif. State U., Northridge, 1973. Inst. instr., area dir. LDS Ch. ednl. system L.A. City Coll., 1970-72, U. So. Calif., 1972-73, Golden West Coll., 1973-76; instr. dept. ch. history and doctrine, Coll. Religion Brigham Young U., Provo, Utah, 1976-80, 85-87, part-time instr., then asst. prof., dept. history, 1976-82, assoc. prof., 1987—, univ. archivist, curator archives of Mormon experience, Harold B. Lee Libr., 1982-86, assoc. libr., curator, 1986—. Co-editor: Views on Man and God: Collected Essays of George T. Boyd, 1979, Supporting Saints: Life Stories of Nineteenth Century Mormons, 1985; asst. editor Dialogue, A Jour. of Mormon Thought, 1971-75, guest editor, 1982, 85; book rev. editor Brigham Young U. Studies, 1980-87, assoc. editor, 1987—, guest editor, 1989; also contbr. numerous articles, monographs and book chpts. Vis. fellow Yale U. Libr., 1990. Mem. Am. Acad. Religion, Mormon History Assn. (Grace Arrington award 1987), Am. Soc. Ch. History, Western Hist. Assn., Phi Kappa Phi. Mem. LDS Ch. Home: 1786 S 340 E Orem UT 84058 Office: Brigham Young U 5072 Harold B Lee Libr Provo UT 84602

WHITTEN, HUBERT FULTON, III, minister; b. Bartow, Fla., Apr. 13, 1955; s. Hubert Fulton Jr. and Betty (Mims) W.; m. Sheila Jo McMahan, June 14, 1980; children: Hubert Fulton IV, Christopher, Michael. AA, Polk Community Coll., Winter Haven, Fla., 1974; BA, Carson-Newman Coll., 1977; MDiv and M in Religious Edn., Southwestern Bapt. Coll. Theol, 1981. Youth dir. Pine Lake (Ga.) Bapt. Ch., 1978; minister of end. Wynnton Bapt. Ch., Columbus, Ga., 1982-84; assoc. pastor First Bapt. Ch., Avondale Estates, Ga., 1984-87, Southside Bapt. Ch., Savannah, Ga., 1987—; guest prof. New Orleans Bapt. Theol. Sem. Extension Ctr., Marietta, Ga., 1985. Mem. Nat. Assn. Ch. Bus. Adminstrs. Republican. Avocations: sports, reading, astronomy. Home: 67 Jameswood Ave Savannah GA 31406 Office: Southside Bapt Ch 5502 Skidaway Rd Savannah GA 31406

WHITTLE, DOUGLAS ALEXANDER, minister; b. Elizabeth, N.J., Apr. 18, 1947; s. Edward Douglas and Christina MacDonald (Stewart) W.; m. Katherine Yeaworth, June 10, 1946; 1 child, Alisa Stewart. BA in Art, West Chester State U., 1977; MDiv, Ea. Bapt. Sem., 1980, DM, 1989. Ordained to ministry Baptist Ch. 1980. Ins. cons. Met. Life Ins., Pottstown, Pa., 1071-72; ins. investigator Nat. Home Life Ins., Valley Forge, Pa., 1972-74; asst. dir. Valley Forge Films, Paoli, Pa., 1974-77; asst. minister Belmont Baptist Ch., Broomall, Pa., 1977-80; sr. minister Calvary Bapt. Ch., Belmar, N.J., 1980-87, First Bapt. Ch., Predicktown, N.J., 1987—; dir. youth missions Am. Baptist Ch. N.J., East Orange, 1987—. Pres. Citizens Adv. Bd. to Commrs., 1985; judge Juvenile Conf. Com., Monmouth Coutny; 1982-87 dir. Belmar (N.J.) Five Mile Run, 1984-87; supv. Salem County Probation Dept. Worksite, Pedricktown, N.J., 1988—. Sgt. USAF, 1967-71. Mem. Eastern Sem. Alumni Assn., Kiwanis (pres. 1986-87). Democratic. Avocations: art, photography, bicycling. Home: 90 W Mill St RD 1 Box 2 Predicktown NJ 08067 Office: First Bapt Ch W Mill St Predicktown NJ 08067

WHITTUM, NORMAN REX, lay worker, elementary school educator; b. Kaleva, Mich., June 20, 1939; s. Lawrence and Mamie Josephine (Soper) W.; m. Donna Lee Evens, July 14, 1962; children: Todd Allen, Lori Lee. BS, Ind. Wesleyan U., 1963; MA, Mich. State U., 1971. Cert. elem. tchr. and adminstr., Mich. Sunday sch. supt. Cadillac (Mich.) Wesleyan Ch., 1966-83; elem. tchr. Jenison (Mich.) Pub. Sch., 1963-65; vice-chmn. of bd. Cadillac (Mich.) Wesleyan Ch., 1966-91, music dir., 1966-88, ch. treas., 1979—; elem. tchr., Cadillac Area Pub. Schs., 1965—; mem. dist. bd. ministerial standing North Mich. Dist. of The Wesleyan Ch., Mt. Pleasant, Mich., 1970—, sec., 1978—, dist. bd. adminstrn., 1989—. Mem. NEA, Mich. Edn. Assn., Cadillac Edn. Assn., Gideons Internat. Home: 5581 E 46 Rd Cadillac MI 49601 Office: 1700 W Chestnut Cadillac MI 49601

WHITWORTH, ROBERT FRANCIS, pastor; b. Washington, Mo., Nov. 24, 1961; s. F. Robert and A. Jean (Ringkamp) W.; m. Julie Ann Waite, Aug. 3, 1985; childern: Alyssa Joan, Robert Francis Jr. BA in Religion, SW Bapt. U., Bolivar, Mo., 1983; MDiv, So. Bapt. Theol. Sem., Louisville, 1987. Ordained to ministry So. Bapt. Conv., 1986. Assoc. pastor 1st Bapt. Ch. Palatine, Ill., 1984, Hillcrest Bapt. Ch., Country Club Hills, Ill., 1985; pastor East Frankfort (Ky.) Bapt. Ch., 1986—; registrar Ky. Bapt. Conv., Frankfort, 1989; chmn. nominations com. Franklin County Bapt. Assn., Frankfort, 1990-91, chmn. Bapt. Student Union com., 1990-91. Bd. dirs. Franklin County chpt. ARC, 1990-91. Mem. Franklin County Ministerial Assn. Home: 160 Jackson St Frankfort KY 40601 Office: East Frankfort Bapt Ch 457 Versailles Rd Frankfort KY 40601

WHYTE, JAMES MCLAURIN (PAT WHYTE), minister; b. Kansas City, Mo., Feb. 6, 1933; s. James McLaurin and Harriet Marion (Mills) Whyte (Can. parents); stepfather Ronald O. Ekholm; m. Harriet Lodge Edwards, July 1, 1961 (div. 1987); children: Martin Edwards, Matthew Ekholm; m. Judith Carol Bechtold, July 1, 1989; stepchildren: Laura, Heather, Andrew. BA, Ill. Coll., Jacksonville, 1957; BD, Hartford Theol. Sem., 1961; certs. in clin. pastoral edn., Andover Newton Theol. Sch., 1968, 70, MST in Pastoral Care, 1970; postgrad., San Francisco Theol. Sem., 1990—. Ordained to ministry United Ch. of Christ, 1962, admitted into ministry United Ch. Can., 1979. Min. Congl. Chs., Bridport and Shoreham, Vt., 1961-67, Union Congl. Ch., Amesbury, Mass., 1968-70, Federated Ch., Ayer, Mass., 1970-77, Live-in Community of Jesus, Inc., 1977-78, Central Lanark (Ont., Can.) Pastoral Charge, 1978-86, Community Ch., Deep River, Ont., 1986—; active Renfrew Presbytery, supr. Theol. Interns for United Ch. Can. Address: Box 2050, Deep River, ON Canada K0J 1P0 *I was able to overcome severe stuttering by the grace of God and the help of many people. If we strive to do a good thing others will join us in the battle. The journey is more important than the destination, and anything worthwhile is always costly.*

WIATT, SUE BOSWELL, religious association executive; b. Manning, S.C., Dec. 19, 1921; d. Frank Dargan and Sarah (Snyder) Boswell; m. Stephen Knight Wiatt, Apr. 8, 1942; children: Stephen Knight Jr., Sarah Wiatt Smith, Wayne Davis, Thomas Julian. BA, Columbia (S.C.) Coll., 1942; postgrad., Fla. State U., 1963; U. S.C., 1949-50. Tchr. high sch. English pub. schs., Georgetown, S.C., 1945-48, Madison, Fla., 1964-69; Bible tchr. various chs., Valdosta, Ga., 1968-76, There is More Ministries, Inc., Valdosta, 1976-80; pres. There is More Ministries, Inc. at Living Waters, Balsam Grove, N.C., 1980—. Author: Early Morning Poems, 1968, Beloved in His Kingdom Love and Mine, 1989. Recipient Fla. Star award, 1965. Mem. Delta Kappa Gamma. Methodist. Home: Living Waters Balsam Grove NC 28708 Office: There is More Ministries Living Waters Balsam Grove NC 28708

WIAZOWSKI, KONSTANTY, religious organization administrator. Pres. Bapt. Ch., Warsaw. Office: Bapt Ch, ul Walicow 25, 00-865 Warsaw Poland*

WICE, DAVID HERSCHEL, rabbi; b. Petersburg, Va., Feb. 1, 1908; s. Henry and Rose (Cooper) W.; A.B., Washington and Lee U., 1927, M.A., 1928, D.D., 1948; Rabbi, Hebrew Union Coll., 1933, D.H.L., 1954; D.H.L., Gratz Coll., 1983; m. Sophie Salzer, Feb. 22, 1934; children—Carol Ruth Wice Gross, David Henry. Rabbi, Temple Israel, Omaha, 1933-41, Temple B'nai Jeshurun, Newark, 1941-47, Congregation Rodeph Shalom, Phila., 1947-81, emeritus, 1981—. Am. dir. World Union for Progressive Judaism, 1945-55, governing bd., exec. com., 1946, later chmn. exec. com., pres., 1973-80; mem. com. Central Conf. Am. Rabbis, 1945-47, 71-72, chmn. com. on structure and orgn., 1956-63, chmn. com. world Jewry, 1965, chmn. com. family, 1967—; pres. Phila. Bd. Rabbis, 1954-56; charter pres. Jewish Community Chaplaincy Service; pres. Marriage Council, 1961-64, also Planned Parenthood; co-chmn. com. on merger Family Service Assn. Am.-Child Welfare League Am., Nat. Conf. Christians and Jews, Phila.; mem. nat. bd. Council Religion Indep. Schs.; mem. forum 15, White House Conf. Children and Youth, 1970. Bd. dirs. Family Service Assn. Am., 1959—, v.p., 1963-65, pres., 1965-67; bd. dirs. Union Am. Hebrew Congregations New Ams., Council Jewish Edn., Fedn. Jewish Agys., Jewish Community Relations Council (all Phila.); co-chmn. bd. overseers Hebrew Union Coll.-Jewish Inst. Religion. Home: 135 S 19th St Apt 1510 Philadelphia PA 19103 Office: 615 N Broad St Philadelphia PA 19123 *Nothing in life is either good or bad except the way we use it, abuse it, or strive to improve it.*

WICHER, CHRIS CHARLES, minister; b. Buffalo, July 25, 1956; s. Daniel Paul Sr. and Joan Marie (Swannie) W.; m. Beverly Jane Aul, Aug. 12, 1978; children: Timothy John, Benjamin William, Gregory Alexander. BA, Concordia Coll., Bronxville, N.Y., 1978; MDiv, Concordia Sem., St. Louis, 1982, STM, 1983. Ordained to ministry Luth. Ch.-Mo. Synod, 1983. Min. Berea-by-the-Water Luth. Ch., Goderich, Ont., Can., 1983-85, Faith Luth. Ch., Newfane, N.Y., 1985—. Bd. dirs. Inter-Luth. Campus Commn. Western N.Y., Buffalo, 1988—. Mem. Newfane Clergy Assn. (pres. 1989—). Home: 6078 Exchange St Newfane NY 14108 Office: Faith Luth Ch 2730 Transit Rd Newfane NY 14108

WICK, SISTER MARGARET, college president; b. Sibley, Iowa, June 30, 1942. BA in Sociology, Briar Cliff Coll., 1965; MA in Sociology, Loyola U., Chgo., 1971; PhD in Higher Edn., U. Denver, 1976. Instr. sociology Briar Cliff Coll., Sioux City, Iowa, 1966-71, dir. academic advising, 1971-72, v.p., acad. dean, 1972-74, 76-84, pres., 1987—; pres. Colls. of Mid-Am., 1985-87; bd. dirs. 1st Interstate Bank Sioux City. Bd. dirs. Mary J. Treglia Community House, 1976-84, Marian Health Ctr., 1987—, Iowa Pub. TV, 1987. Mem. North Cen. Edn. Assn. (cons.-evaluator for accrediting teams 1980-84, 89—), Sioux City C. of C. (bd. dirs.), Quota Internat., Rotary. Home: 4216 Perry Way Sioux City IA 51104 Office: Briar Cliff Coll 3303 Rebecca Sioux City IA 51104

WICK, NORMAN G., bishop. Bishop of Mont. Evang. Luth. Ch. in Am., Great Falls. Office: Synod of Mont 2415 13th Ave S Great Falls MT 59405*

WICKARD, SAMUEL EUGENE, minister, school administrator; b. Albion, Mich., Dec. 8, 1950; s. Glenn Eugene and Barbara Ruth (Stephenson) W.; m. Dawn Joy Seiple, July 26, 1969; children: Chad Eugene, Wesley Andrew, Nathan Scott. BTh, Clarksville Sch. Theology, 1976, ThM, 1980; ThD, Internat. Bible Sem., 1981, DD (hon.), 1981; PhD, Bapt. U., 1984; D Ministry, Christian Bible Coll., 1991. Ordained to ministry Bible Meth. Ch., 1974. Pastor Wesleyan Missionary Ch., Fayette, Ohio, 1970-73, pastor, sch. adminstr., 1976-82; pastor Bible Meth. Ch., Anniston, Ala., 1973-76; pastor, sch. adminstr. Wesleyan Meth. Ch., Titusville, Pa., 1982-84, Fayette (Ohio) Bible Ch., 1984—. Mem. United Assn. Christian Counselors (cert. counselor, 1983, life), Am. Assn. Christian Counselors, U.S. Chaplaincy Assn., Nat. Christian Counselors Assn. (cert., lic. temperment therapist 1989). Home and Office: 305 S Maple St PO Box 249 Fayette OH 43521

WICKENHAUSER, GERALD MARTIN, priest; b. Alton, Ill., Nov. 16, 1934; s. Joseph John and Margaret Gertrude (Dixon) W. BA, Maryknoll Sem., Glen Ellyn, Ill., 1957; MRE, Maryknoll Sem., Ossining, N.Y., 1962; MA, St. Louis U., 1975; Licentiate in Sacred Theology, Gregorian U., Rome, 1979. Joined Maryknoll Fathers and Bros. Soc., Roman Cath. Ch.; ordained priest. Pastor Cath. parishes, The Philippines, 1962-77, Indonesia, 1980-83; dir. Maryknoll Edn. Ctr., Houston, 1986—. Democrat. Home and Office: Maryknoll Edn Ctr 2360 Rice Blvd Houston TX 77005

WICKER, JAMES ROBERT, minister; b. Corpus Christi, Tex., Sept. 30, 1954; s. David Elzy III and Carolyn (Reed) W.; m. Dana Abernathy, Dec. 22, 1978; children: Jessica Helen, Matthew Robert, Stephen Paul. BA in Oral Communications, Baylor U., 1977; MDiv., Southwestern Bapt. Theol. Sem., 1980, PhD in N.T., 1985. Lic. to ministry So. Bapt. Conv., 1973, ordained, 1981. Sunday Sch. cons. Mo. Bapt. Conv., Jefferson City, 1978; asst. dir. Youth Evangelism Schs. Evangelism div. Bapt. Gen. Conv. Tex., Dallas, 1979-81, dir., 1982-85; pastor 1st Bapt. Ch., Lavon, Tex., 1981-84; teaching fellow Southwestern Bapt. Theol. Sem., Ft. Worth, 1982-83; pastor 1st Bapt. Ch., Farmersville, Tex., 1984-91, 1st Bapt. ch., Frisco, Tex., 1991—; magician, 1974—; moderator Collin Bapt. Assn., 1989-91, evangelism com., 1982-85, Dallas Bapt. U. com., 1985-87, prayer com., 1986-89, exec. com., 1988-91; adj. prof. Old and N.T., Dallas Bapt. U., 1988—; missions advance team Bapt. Gen. Conv. Tex., 1989-90. Mem. Communications Network, Farmersville Ind. Sch. Dist., 1989-91; mem. Farmersville Alliance, 1984-91, pres., 1985, 87. Recipient awards talent shows, tng. award for religious leadership Order Ea. Star, Lavon, 1983. Mem. Farmersville C. of C. (bd. dirs. 1985-91, v.p. 1986, pres. 1987), Tex. Assn. Magicians (awards in comedy magic 1977, 79), Internat. Brotherhood of Magicians, Fellowship of Christian Magicians, Rotary (pres. elect 1986-87, pres. 1987-88), Kappa Omega Tau. Home: 5100 Ashland Belle Frisco TX 75034 Office: 1st Bapt Ch PO Box 307 Frisco TX 75034

WICKERT, VICTOR RAY, minister; b. Des Moines, June 7, 1956; s. Virgil and Ethel L. (Dahlgren) W. Diploma, Moody Bible Inst., 1978, BA in Pastoral Studies, 1980; BS in Secondary Edn., Drake U., 1980; MA in Marriage and Family Ministries, Talbot Sch. Theology, La Mirada, Calif., 1986. Lic. to ministry Evang. Free Ch. Am., 1983. Asst. pastor Ind. Heights Evang. Free Ch., Des Moines, 1978-84; coll. dir. Grace Community Ch., Los Alamitos, Calif., 1985-86; assoc. pastor Hope Evang. Free Ch., Dubuque, Iowa, 1989—; singles chmn. Cen. Dist. Evang. Free Ch., Iowa, 1982-84; sec. Counseling Resources Ministry Coun., 1989—. Mem. Nat. Right to Life, 1978—. Republican. Office: Hope Evang Free Ch 4935 JFK Dubuque IA 52001

WICKES, THOMAS LEE, minister; b. Indpls., Jan. 30, 1947; s. Homer Wilbert and Dorthy Elizabeth (Jeffries) W.; m. Mary Elizabeth Tompkins, June 1, 1948; children: James Daniel, Jeffrey Thomas. BS, Grand Canyon Coll., 1968; M of Ch. Music., Southwest Bapt. Theol. Sem., 1975. Ordained to ministry Bapt. Ch., 1975. Minister of music First Bapt. Ch., Alpharetta, Ga., 1975-79, Enterprise, Ala., 1979-84, Orange Park, Fla., 1984-85, Cleveland, Tenn., 1985—. Capt. USMC, 1968-72. Named to Outstanding Young Men in Am., 1976. Mem. So. Bapt. Ch. Music. Conf., Tenn. Ch. Music. Conf., Choirster's Guild. Avocations: golf, tennis. Home: 3730 Hillside Dr Cleveland TN 37312 Office: First Bapt Ch 340 Church St Cleveland TN 37312

WICKLIFFE, VERNE ALLEN, minister; b. Velleijo, Calif., July 12, 1955; s. Vernon C. and P. Fern (Elliott) W.; m. Vicki P. Parnell, Aug. 5, 1978; children: Kara Michelle, Troy Clinton. BA, Ouacita Bapt. U., 1978; MDiv, So. Bapt. Theol. Sem., 1981; D of Ministry, Midwestern Bapt. Theol. Sem., 1989. Ordained to ministry So. Bapt. Conv., 1978. Pastor Alton and Pleasant Ridge Bapt. Chs., Leavenworth, Ind., 1979-81; chaplain intern Bapt. Med. Ctr., Little Rock, 1981-82; pastor Pine Grove Bapt. Ch., Sweet Home, Ark., 1982-87, 1st Bapt. Ch., Des Arc, Ark., 1987—. Contbr. articles to jours. in field. Mem. Christian Civic Found., Little Rock, 1986, 87, 90, 91; bd. dirs. Prairie County Health Dept., Des Arc, 1990; county chmn. Citizens Against Legalized Lottery, Little Rock, 1990. Name one of Outstanding Young Men Am., U.S. Jaycees, 1983, 85. Mem. Pulaski Bapt. Assn. (mem. exec. bd. 1982-87, dir. summer camp 1984-86), Des Arc C. of C., Carolina Bapt. Assn. (mem. exec. bd. 1987—, vol. missions coord. 1991). Office: 1st Bapt Ch Des Arc AR 72040 *Courage is the means by which one overcomes fears, timidity and inadequacy. Life is full of the need for courage. God supplies our need.*

WIDEMAN, THOMAS WAYNE, minister; b. St. Louis, June 10, 1958; s. Donald Vivian and Marian Elizabeth (Kiepe) W.; m. Sally Ann Burnidge, Dec. 27, 1980; children: Jolee Ann, Andrew Thomas. BS, William Jewell Coll., 1980; MusM, Southwestern Bapt. Sem., 1984. Ordained to ministry Bapt. Ch., 1987. Minister of music Manchester (Mo.) Heights Bapt. Ch., 1981-82, Riverside Bapt. Ch., Ft. Worth, 1982-84, Second Bapt. Ch., Little Rock, 1984—. Mem. Centurymen So. Bapt. Choir, 1988—. Named one of Outstanding Young Men of Am., 1985, 86. Mem. So. Bapt. Ch. Music Conf., Pulaski Bapt. Assn. (music dir. 1986-89). Home: 21 Coachlight Little Rock AR 72207

WIDENER, RICHARD L., minister; b. Cleve., Mar. 21, 1948; s. L. Eugene Jr. and Joanne (Skivington) W.; m. Joanne Sklenka, Aug. 16, 1974; children: Mark A., Rachel L. BS in Edn., Cleve. State U., 1970; MA in Religious Studies, Ashland (Ohio) Theol. Sem., 1986. Ordained to ministry Alliance for Renewal Chs., 1982. Tchr. St. Richard's Sch., North Olmsted, Ohio, 1969-74; pastoral asst., youth min. St. Ladislas Ch., Westlake, Ohio, 1974-77; founding pastor Harvest Christian Ch. (Christians in Growth), Elyria, Ohio, 1980—; trustee Alliance for Renewal Chs., Mansfield, Ohio, 1990—. Office: Harvest Christian Ch 1245 East Ave #1 Elyria OH 44035

WIDMER, FREDERICK WILLIAM, religion educator; b. Canastota, N.Y., Nov. 19, 1915; s. Frederick Ernest and Pearl Agnes (Jaquin) W.; m. Frances Irene Waid, Apr. 18, 1945; 1 child, Frederick David. AB, Wheaton Coll., 1939; BD, MDiv, Columbia Theol. Sem., 1944, 71; ThM, Louisville Presbyn. Sem., 1948; ThD, Union Theol. Sem., 1958. Chaplain U. Fla., Gainesville, 1944-46; pastor Presbyn. Ch., Oakland, Fla., 1946-48, Sebring, Fla., 1950-54; dir. family edn. Bd. Christian Edn. Presbyn. U.S., 1954-60; assoc. pastor First Presbyn., Atlanta, 1960-70; pastoral asst. Ind. Presbyn., Birmingham, Ala., 1983—; prof. Beeson Div. Sch./Samford U., Birmingham, 1988—; trustee Presbyn. Sch. C.E., Richmond, Va., 1960-68; chmn. Presbytery Coun., Birmingham, 1984-85. Author: Living Together in Christian Homes, 1956, Christian Family Education, 1957, Home and Church Working Together, 1958; contbr. articles to religious paper. Pres. Lions Club, Winter Garden, Fla., 1946, chaplain, Tampa, Fla., 1970-74. Democrat. Home: 3511 Vicksburg Dr Birmingham AL 35213 Office: Samford U Beeson Div Sch Birmingham AL 35229 *The family is the most important of all groups. There nurture and growth begins its developmental task.*

WIECER, STEPHANIE BERNADETTE, lay worker; b. Jamaica, N.Y., Apr. 25, 1952; d. John F. and Adelle R. (Dubitsky) W. BS in Acctg., Wilkes Coll., 1975; postgrad., Widener U., 1988-89. CPA, Pa., N.J. Lector St. John's Ch., Lower Makefield, Pa., 1989—, coord. RCIA Team, 1990-91, agenda officer Parish Coun., 1990—, coord. eucharistic min., 1991—; tchr. religion St. John's (Pa.) Ch., 1989—. Mem. AICPA, N.J. Soc. CPAs, Pa. Inst. CPAs, Secular Franciscan, St. Bonaventure Fraternity. Home: PO Box 197 Morrisville PA 19067 Office: Manuel S Newman & Co 810 Bear Tavern Rd Ste 305 Trenton NJ 08628 *There are many events in our lives which are difficult for us to understand. Know always that above all else God is love and He wants us happy and we must place our trust and hearts with Him alone.*

WIECHMANN, HELMUT HENRY, minister; b. Lacrescent, Minn., Aug. 5, 1909; s. Frederick August and Bertha Ann (Stuemke) W.; m. Ruth Louise Krahn, Oct. 4, 1931 (dec. 1979); children: Gerald H., Ralph E., Ruthmary North. BD, Concordia Sem., Springfield, Ill., 1930. Ordained to ministry, Luth. Ch.-Mo. Synod. Missoin developer Killitas County, Ellensburg, Wash., 1930-43; pastor edn. St. Paul Luth. Ch., Olive, Calif., 1943-49; pastor Trinity Luth. Ch., Mequon, Wis., 1949-60, Faith Luth. Ch., Hialeah, Fla., 1960-73; assoc. pastor Prince of Peace Luth. Ch., Springfield, Va., 1973—; chmn. estate planning S.E. Dist. Luth. Ch.-Mo. Synod, 1974-80, others in past. Recipient Servus Ecclesiae Christi award, Concordia Sem, Ft. Wayne, 1978, Award of Achievement, 1980. Mem. Exchange Club (bull. editor). Republican. Home: 6302 Julian St Springfield VA 22150 Office: Prince of Peace Luth Ch 8304 Old Keene Mill Rd Springfield VA 22152

WIEDERAENDERS, ROBERT CHARLES, retired archivist; b. Clinton, Iowa, June 23, 1922; s. Martin Frederick and Olivia (Mix) W.; m. Wauneta Ione Gorrell, June 15, 1951; children: Paul, Catherine, Claudia, Carl. BA, Wartburg Coll., 1943; STM, Luth. Sch. Theol., 1959. Ordained to ministry Am. Luth. Ch., 1952. Pastor Our Savior Ch., Burbank, Ill., 1952-56, Kankakee, Ill., 1956-64; pastor Grace Luth. Ch., St. Anne, Ill., 1956-63; archivist Am. Luth. Ch., 1964-87, Region 5, Evang. Luth. Ch. Am., 1988—. Editor: Microfilm Corpus of American Lutheranism, 1952-60; author: (with W. G. Tillmanns) The Synods of American Lutheranism, 1968; assoc. editor: Biographical Directory of Clergymen of the American Lutheran Church, 1972. With U.S. Army, 1943-46. Mem. Soc. Am. Archivists, Luth. Hist. Conf. (past pres.), Midwest Archives Conf., Lions. Democrat. Home: 1255 N Booth St Dubuque IA 52001 Office: Wartburg Theol Sem 333 Wartburg Pl Dubuque IA 52002

WIEGERT, RAYMOND PAUL, minister; b. Danvers, Ill., Aug. 19, 1935. AA, Concordia Coll., St. Paul, 1955; MDiv, Concordia Sem., Springfield, Ill., 1959. Pastor Immanuel Luth. ch., Osceola, Iowa, 1959-64, St. John Luth. Ch. & Sch., Roselle, Ill., 1964-75; dist. missions chmn. Luth. Ch.-Mo. Synod, Missoula, 1978-88; cir. counselor, 1991—. Recipient Servus Ecclesiae Christi Concordia Sem., 1981. Mem. Rotary. Avocations: computer, electronics, mechanics. Home: 4007 Lincoln Rd Missoula MT 59802 Office: Messiah Luth Ch 3718 Rattlesnake Dr Missoula MT 59802

WIEMER, LOYAL HULBERT, minister; b. Syracuse, N.Y., Oct. 28, 1914; s. Bernhard A. and Bertha A. (Hulbert) W.; m. Lola Myrtle Horton, May 28, 1938; children: Douglas Loyal, Carol Jane. AB, Wheaton Coll., Ill., 1937; BD, Ea. Bapt. Theol. Sem., Phila., 1941. Ordained to ministry Am. Bapt. Chs. in U.S.A., 1941. Pastor various chs. N.Y., 1941-43, 48-53; dir. USO, Mass., Maine, R.I., 1943-47; dir. camping Detroit, 1954-59, Mass. Bapt. Conv., Groton, Mass., 1959-62; pastor Clarklake (Mich.) Community Ch., 1963-79; min. at large Am. Bapt. Chs. in U.S.A., 1979—; exec. dir. Jackson County Interfaith Coun., 1974—; bd. dirs. exec. com. Mich. Bapt. Chs., 1978-90, del. constn. revision com., 1968; pres. Mich. sect. Am. Camping Assn., 1964-68, chmn. standards com. Mich. sect/. 1963-73; chaplain Internat. Order Foresters-Rebekah Homes, 1963-79; chmn. caring ministries Mich.-Am. Bapts. Chs., 1984-90. Author: Flight of the Snow Goose, 1947. Bd. dirs., chmn. budget com. United Way Jackson County, 1969-79; bd. dirs. Jackson Osteo. Hosp., 1969—, United Way Mich., 1973-87, Land O'Lakes coun. Boy Scouts Am.; mem. Jackson Bd. Commrs., 1981-87, vice chmn., 1985—; chair Jackson Transit Authority, 1985. Mem. Am. Bapt. Chs., U.S.A. Mins. Assn., Mich Bapt. Mins. Address: 425 Oakwood Dr PO Box 156 Clarklake MI 49234 *Enjoying the marrying of 800 couples in the last 20 years, I tell them, as I do funeral attendants, "So live that the angels of heaven will count it a joy to live in your company all down through eternity." It is an electric prod for daily living up to the best lights we each have.*

WIENER, MARVIN S., rabbi, editor, executive; b. N.Y.C., Mar. 16, 1925; s. Max and Rebecca (Dodell) W.; m. Sylvia Bodek, Mar. 2, 1952; children: David Hillel, Judith Rachel. B.S., CCNY, 1944, M.S., 1945; B.H.L., Jewish Theol. Sem. Am., 1947, M.H.L., Rabbi, 1951, D.D. (hon.), 1977. Registrar, sec. faculty Rabbinical Sch., Jewish Theol. Sem. Am., 1951-57; cons. Frontiers of Faith TV Series, NBC, 1951-57; dir., instr. liturgy Cantors Inst.-Sem. Coll. Jewish Music, Jewish Theol. Sem. Am., 1954-58; faculty coordinator Sem. Sch. and Women's Inst., 1958-64; dir. Nat. Acad. for Adult

Jewish Studies, United Synagogue Am., N.Y.C., 1958-78; editor Burning Bush Press, 1958-78, United Synagogue Rev., 1978-86; dir. com. congrl. standards United Synagogue Am., 1976-86, cons. community relations and social action, 1981-82, mem. profl. staff Joint Retirement Bd., 1986—; mem. Joint Commn. on Rabbinic Placement, 1951-57, Joint Prayer Book Commn., 1957-62; mem. exec. coun. Rabbinical Assembly, 1958-86; editorial cons. N.Y. Bd. Rabbis, 1987-89; trustee joint retirement bd. Jewish Theol. Sem. Am., Rabbinical Assembly and United Synagogue Am., 1959-86, sec., 1968-76, 84-85, vice chmn., 1976-82, 85-86, chmn., 1982, treas., 1983-84; co-chmn. Jewish Bible Assn., 1960-64; chmn. bd. rev. Nat. Coun. Jewish Audio-Visual Materials, 1968-69; mem. exec. com. Nat. Coun. Adult Jewish Edn., 1966—; mem. exec. bd., editorial adv. bd., v.p. Jewish Book Coun.; chmn. Internat. Conf. Adult Jewish Edn., Jerusalem, 1972. Editor: Nat. Acad. Adult Jewish Studies Bull., 1958-78, Past and Present: Selected Essays (Israel Friedlaender), 1961, Jewish Tract Series, 1964-78 (15 titles), Adult Jewish Edn., 1958-78, Talmudic Law and the Modern State (Moshe Silberg), 1973. Mem. Am. Acad. Jewish Research, Assn. Jewish Studies, N.Y. Bd. Rabbis, Rabbinical Assembly. Home: 67-66 108th St Apt D-46 Forest Hills NY 11375 Office: Joint Retirement Bd 11 Penn Pla Ste 2224 New York NY 10001

WIENER, THEODORE, rabbi; b. Stettin, Ger., Sept. 28, 1918; s. Max and Toni (Hamburger) W. BA, U. Cin., 1940; MHL, Hebrew Union Coll., Cin., 1943; DD, Hebrew Union Coll., N.Y.C., 1990. Ordained rabbi, 1943. Rabbi Sinai Temple, Sioux City, Iowa, 1943-44, Temple Rodef Shalom, Port Arthur, Tex., 1944-47, Temple Beth Israel, Corsicana, Tex., 1947-48; Hebrew cataloger, later head cataloger Hebrew Union Coll. Libr., Cin., 1950-64; chaplain Home for Jewish Aged, Cin., 1958-64; sr. cataloger in Judaica, Libr. of Congress, Washington, 1964—; dir. govt. div. United Jewish Appeal, Washington, 1966—; del. Holocaust com. Jewish Community Coun., Washington, 1975—. Contbr. articles to profl. jours. Recipient Claude G. Montefiore Prize, Hebrew Union Coll., Cin., 1941. Mem. Cen. Conf. Am. Rabbis, Assn. Jewish Librs. (life, v.p. 1970-72), Nat. Libr. and Info. Assn. (chmn. coun. 1978-79, 88-89). Home: 1701 N Kent St Arlington VA 22209 Office: Library of Congress 1st and Independence Ave SE Washington DC 20540

WIER, PAUL BENJAMIN, minister; b. Peoria, Ill., Oct. 25, 1959; s. Ralph Roland and A. Delight (Bobilya) W.; m. Nancy Ellen Johnson, Dec. 15, 1979; children: Ellen Marie, Mary Elizabeth, Benjamin Charles, Matthew Carl. BS, Ill. State U., 1981; MDiv, Garrett-Evang. Theol. Sem., 1986. Ordained to ministry United Meth. Ch. as deacon, 1985, as elder, 1988. Local pastor Mt. Vernon United Meth. Ch., Champaign, Ill., 1982-84; local pastor Woodland/Crescent City (Ill.) United Meth. Chs., 1984-85, pastor, deacon, probationary mem., 1985-86; pastor, deacon, probationary mem. Broadlands (Ill.)-Longview Parish, 1986-88, pastor, elder, 1988—. Mem. coun. Mashall-Putnam 4-H Youth Coun., Henry, Ill., 1977-81. Mem. United Meth. Men of Broadlands-Longview, United Meth. Rural Fellowship, Champaign Dist. Coun. on Ministries United Meth. Ch., Champaign Dist. Rural Ch. Com. United Meth. Ch. (rep. 1988—), Cen. Ill. Conf. Rural Ch. and Community Com. (dist. rep. 1988—). Republican. Home: 302 S Lincoln Broadlands IL 61816 Office: Broadlands-Longview Parish 300 S Lincoln Broadlands IL 61816

WIERSBE, WARREN WENDELL, clergyman, author, lecturer; b. East Chicago, Ind., May 16, 1929; s. Fred and Gladys Anna (Forsberg) W.; m. Betty Lorraine Warren, June 20, 1953; children: David, Carolyn, Robert, Judy. B.Th., No. Baptist Sem., 1953; D.D. (hon.), Temple Sem., Chattanooga, 1965, Trinity Ev-Div. Sch., 1986; LittD (hon.), Cedarville Coll., 1987. Ordained to ministry Bapt. Ch., 1951; pastor Central Bapt. Ch., East Chicago, 1951-57; editorial dir. Youth for Christ Internat., Wheaton, Ill., 1957-61; pastor Calvary Bapt. Ch., Covington, Ky., 1961-71; sr. minister Moody Ch., Chgo., 1971-78; bd. dirs. Slavic Gospel Assn., Wheaton, 1973-87; columnist Moody Monthly, Chgo., 1971-77; author, conf. minister, 1978-80; vis. instr. pastoral theology Trinity Div. Sch., Deerfield, Ill.; gen. dir. Back to the Bible Radio Ministries, Lincoln, Nebr., 1984-89. Author: over 100 books including William Culbertson, A Man of God, 1974, Live Like a King, 1976, Walking with the Giants, 1976, Be Right, 1977, (with David Wiersbe) Making Sense of the Ministry, 1983, Why Us? Why Bad Things Happen to God's People, 1984, Real Worship: It Can Transform Your Life, 1986, Be Compassionate, 1988, The Integrity Crisis, 1988, Be What You Are, 1988, The New Pilgrim's Progress, 1989, Be Courageous, 1989. Home and Office: 441 Lakewood Dr Lincoln NE 68510

WIESE, JAMES LORENZ, religion educator, educational administrator, minister; b. Lafayette, Ind., Oct. 22, 1936; s. Lorenz Henry and Effie (James) W.; m. Rita Lois Bulmahn, June 18, 1960; children: Julie Lois, David James, Mark Lorenz, Jonathan Paul, Deborah Lynn, Joel Philip. BA, Concordia, St. Louis, 1958; MDiv, 1961; MA, Stanford U., 1969. Ordained to ministry Luth. Ch.-Mo. Synod, 1962. Intern, Zion Luth. Ch., Schenectady, N.Y., 1959-60; asst. pastor St. Paul Luth. Ch., St. Louis, 1961-62; ednl. missionary Luth. Ch. Mo. Synod, Saitama-Pref, Japan, 1962-76; sch. prin. Holy Hope Luth. Sch., Saitama Pref., 1969-77, chmn. bd. dirs., 1977-81, advisor, 1981-85; aux. chaplain Luth Council U.S.A., Yokota Air Base, Tokyo, 1976-90, Luth. Contact Pastors Iwakuni Marine Bd., 1990—; dir. office sch. advancement Am. Sch. Japan, Tokyo, 1977-90; headmaster Osaka (Japan) Internat. Sch., 1990—; exec. couple Tokyo Ecumenical Marriage Encounter, 1977—; council advisors Calif. Luth. Coll., Thousand Oaks, 1984—; pres. Fellowship Christian Missionaries Japan, Tokyo, 1983-84. Contbr. articles to profl. jours. Mem. Nat. Assn. Secondary Sch. Prins., Assn. Fgn. Tchrs., Council Advancement and Support Edn., Internat. House, Am. C. of C. Japan, Rotary (pres. Tokyo club 1989-90), Phi Delta Kappa. Republican. Home: 2-12 Onohara-Nishi, 4-Chome, Mino-shi, Osaka 562, Japan Office: Osaka Internat Sch, 4-12 Onohara-Nishi, 4-Chome, Mino-Shi, Osaka Fu 562, Japan

WIESEL, ELIE, writer, educator; b. Sighet, Transylvania, Sept. 30, 1928; came to U.S., 1956, naturalized, 1963; s. Shlomo and Sarah (Feig) W.; m. Marion Erster Rose, 1969; 1 child, Shlomo Elisha. Student, The Sorbonne, Paris, 1948-51; LittD (hon.), Jewish Theol. Sem., N.Y.C., 1967, Marquette U., 1975, Simmons Coll., 1976, Anna Maria Coll., 1980, Yale U., 1981, Wake Forest U., 1985, Haverford Coll., 1985, Capital U., 1986, L.I. U., 1986, U. Paris, 1987, U. Conn., 1988, U. Cen. Fla., 1988, Wittenberg U., 1989, Wheeling Jesuit Coll., 1989; LHD (hon.), Hebrew Union Coll., 1968, Manhattanville Coll., 1972, Yeshiva U., 1973, Boston U., 1974, Coll. of St. Scholastica, 1978, Wesleyan U., 1979, Brandeis U., 1980, Kenyon Coll., 1982, Hobart/William Smith Coll., 1982, Emory U., 1983, Fla. Internat. U., 1983, Siena Heights Coll., 1983, Fairfield U., 1983, Dropsie Coll., 1983, Moravian Coll., 1983, Colgate U., 1984, SUNY, Binghamton, 1985, Lehigh U., 1985, Coll. of New Rochelle, 1986, Tufts U., 1986, Georgetown U., 1986, Hamilton Coll., 1986, Rockford Coll., 1986, Villanova U., 1987, Coll. of St. Thomas, 1987, U. Denver, 1987, Walsh Coll., 1987, Loyola Coll., 1987, Ohio U., 1988, Concordia Coll., 1990, N.Y.U., 1990, Fordham U., 1990, Conn. Coll., 1990, Upsala Coll., 1991, Duquesne U., 1991, Roosevelt U., 1991; PhD (hon.), Bar-Ilan U., 1973, U. Haifa, 1986, Ben Gurion U., 1988; LLD (hon.), Hofstra U., 1975, Talmudic U. Fla., 1979, U. Notre Dame, 1980, La Salle U., 1988; HHD (hon.), U. Hartford, 1985, Lycoming Coll., 1987, U. Miami, 1988, Brigham Young U., 1989; D of Hebrew Letters, Spertus Coll. Judaica, 1973; DSc (hon.), U. Health Scis./Chgo. Med. Sch., 1989; ThD, U. Åbo Akadem, 1990. Disting. prof. Judaic studies CCNY, 1972-76; Andrew Mellon prof. humanities Boston U., 1976—; Henry Luce vis. scholar in Humanities and Social Thought, Whitney Humanities Ctr., Yale U., 1982-83; Disting. vis. prof. Lit. and Philosophy, Fla. Internat. U., 1982; chmn. U.S. Pres.'s Commn. on the Holocaust, 1979-80, U.S. Holocaust Meml. Council, 1980-86; hon. chmn. Nat. Jewish Resource Ctr., U.S. Com. to Free Vladimir Slepak, N.Y.C. Holocaust Meml. Commn., Am. Friends of Ghetto Fighter's House; hon. pres. Am. Gathering of Jewish Holocaust Survivors; bd. dirs. Nat. Com. on Am. Fgn. Policy, 1983—, Hebrew Arts Sch., HUMANITAS, Am. Assocs. Ben-Gurion U. of the Negev, Mut. of Am., France Libertés; v.p. Internat. Rescue Com., 1985—; bd. govs. Oxford Ctr. for Postgrad. Hebrew studies, Haifa U., Tel-Aviv U.; bd. trustees Yeshiva U., 1977—; colleague Cathedral St. John the Divine, 1975—; mem. adv. bd. Boston U. Inst. for Philosophy & Religion, Nat. Inst. Against Prejudice & Violence, Internat. Ctr. in N.Y., Friends of Akim USA, Friends of LeChambon; mem. jury Neustadt Internat. Prize Lit., 1984; lectr. Andrew W. Mellon Ann. Lecture Series Boston U., 92d St. YMHA, YWHA Ann. Lectr. Series, ann. radio broadcast series Eternal Light for Jewish Theol. Sem. Am. Author: Night, 1960, Dawn, 1961, The Accident, 1962, The Town Beyond the Wall, 1964, The Gates of the Forest, 1966, The Jews of Silence, 1966, Legends of Our Time, 1968, A Beggar in Jerusalem, 1970, One Generation After, 1971, Souls on Fire, 1972, The Oath, 1973, Ani Maamin, 1973, Zalmen, or the Madness of God, 1975, Messengers of God, 1976, A Jew Today, 1978, Four Hasidic Masters, 1978, The Trial of God, 1979, Le Testament D'Un Poète Juif Assassiné (France's Prix Livre-Inter 1980, Bourse Goncourt, 1980, Prix des Bibliothécaires, 1981), 1985, Images from the Bible, 1980, Five Biblical Portraits, 1981, Somewhere A Master, 1982, Paroles d'Étranger, 1982, The Golem, 1983, The Fifth Son (Grand Prix de la Littérature, City of Paris), 1985, Signes d'Exode, 1985, Against Silence (3 vols., ed. Irving Abrahamson), 1985, Job ou Dieu dans la Tempête, 1986, A Song for Hope, 1987, The Nobel Address, 1987 Tempete Twilight, 1988; (essays) Silences et Mémoire d'hommes, 1989, L'Oublié, 1989, From the Kingdom of Memory, 1990, Elie Weisel in London, 1991, Sages and Dreamers, 1991, (with John Cardinal O'Connor) A Journey of Faith, 1990, (with Albert Friedlander) The Six Days of Destruction, 1988, (dialogues with Philippe-Michaël Saint-Cheron) Evil and Exile, 1990; editorial and adv. bds. Midstream, Religion and Lit. (U. Notre Dame), Sh'ma: Jour. of Responsibility, Forthcoming: Jewish Imaginative Writing, Hadassah Mag., Acad. of the Air for Jewish Studies, Holocaust and Genocide Studies: An Internat. Jour.; subject of 17 books. Chmn. adv. bd. World Union Jewish Students, 1985—; comité d'Honneur Ligue Internationale Contre le Racisme et l'Antisemitisme, 1985—; founder Nat. Jewish Ctr. Learning and Leadership; mem. adv. bd. Andrei Sakharov Inst.; mem. soc. fellows Ctr. Judaic Studies, U. Denver; bd. overseer Bar-Ilan U., 1970—. Recipient Prix Rivarol, 1963, Jewish Heritage award, Haifa U., 1975, Remembrance award, 1965, Prix du Souvenir, 1965, Nat. Jewish Book Council award, 1965, 73, Prix Médicis, 1968, Prix Bordin French Acad., 1972, Eleanor Roosevelt Meml. award, N.Y. United Jewish Appeal, 1972, Am. Liberties medallion Am. Jewish Com., 1972, Martin Luther King Jr. medallion, CCNY, 1973, Annual award for Disting. Service to Am. Jewry, Nat. Fedn. of Jewish Men's Clubs, 1973, Faculty Disting. Scholar award Hofstra U., 1974, Rambam award Am. Mizrachi Women, 1974, Meml. award N.Y. Soc. Clin. Psychologists, 1975, First Spertus Internat. award, 1976, Myrtle Wreath award Hadassah, 1977, King Solomon award, 1977, Liberty award HIAS, 1977, Jewish Heritage award, B'nai B'rith, 1966, Avoda award, Jewish Tchrs. Assn., 1972, Humanitarian award, B'rith Sholom, 1978, Joseph Prize for Human Rights, Anti-Defamation League, 1978, Zalman Shazar award State of Israel, 1979, Presdl. Citation, NYU, 1979, Inaugural award for Lit., Israel Bonds Prime Minister's Com., 1979, Jabotinsky medal, State of Israel, 1980, Rabbanit Sarah Herzog award Emunah Women of Am., 1981, Le Grand Prix Littéraire du Festival Internat. Deauville, 1983, Internat. Lit. prize for Peace, Royal Acad. Belgium, 1983, Lit. Lions award N.Y. Pub. Library, 1983, Jordan Davidson Humanitarian award Fla. Internat. U., 1983, Anatoly Scharansky Humanitarian award, 1983, Commandeur de la Légion d'Honneur award, 1984, elected to Grand Officer, 1990, Congressional gold medal, 1984, Voice of Conscience award Am. Jewish Congress, 1985, Remembrance award, Israel Bonds, 1985, Anne Frank award, 1985, Freedom of Worship medal FDR 4 Freedoms Found., 1985, Medal of Liberty award Statue of Liberty Presentation, 1986, Nobel Peace Prize, 1986, First Herzl Lit. award, First David Ben-Gurion award, Nat. UJA, Gov.'s award, Shaarei Tzedek, Internat. Kaplun Found. award Hebrew U. Jerusalem, Scopus award, 1974, Am.-Israeli Friendship award, Disting. Writers award Lincolnwood Library, 1984, First Chancellor Joseph H. Lookstein award Bar-Ilan U., 1984, Sam Levenson Meml. award Jewish Community Relations Council, 1985, Comenius award Moravian Coll., 1985, Henrietta Szold award Hadassah, 1985, Disting. Community Service award Mut. Am., 1985, Covenant Peace award Synagogue Council Am., 1985, Jacob Pat award World Congress Jewish Culture, 1985, Humanitarian award Internat. League Human Rights, 1985, Disting. Foreign-Born Am. award Internat. Ctr. N.Y., Inc., 1986, Freedom Cup award Women's League Israel, 1986, First Jacob Javits Humanitarian award UJA Young Leadership, 1986, Freedom award Internat. Rescue Com., 1987, Achievement award Artist and Writers for Peace in the Middle East, 1987, La Grande Médaille de Vermeil de la Ville de Paris, 1987, La Médaille de la Chancellerie de l'Université de Paris, 1987, La Médaille de l'Université de Paris, 1987, First Eitinger Prize, U. Oslo, 1987, Lifetime Achievment award Present Tense mag., 1987, Spl. Christopher award The Christophers, 1987, Achievement award State Israel, 1987, Sem. medal Jewish Theol. Sem. Am., 1987, Metcalf Cup and Prize for Excellence in Teaching, Boston U., 1987, Spl. award Nat. Com. on Am. Fgn. Policy, 1987, Grã-Cruz da Ordem Nacional do Cruzeiro do Sul, Brazil's highest distinction, 1987, Profiles of Courage award B'nai B'rith, 1987, Centennial medal U. Scranton, 1987, Citation from Religious Edn. Assn., 1987, Golda Meir Sr. Humanitarian award, 1987, Presdl. medal Hofstra U., 1988, Human Rights Law award Internat. Human Rights Law Group, 1988, Bicentennial medal Georgetown U., 1988, Janus Korczak Humanitarian award NAHE, Kent State U., 1989, Count Sforza award in Philanthropy Interphil, 1989, Lily Edelman award for Excellence in Continuing Jewish Edn. B'nai B'rith Internat., 1989, George Washington award Am. Hungarian Found., 1989, Bicentennial medal N.Y.U., 1989, Internat. Brotherhood award C.O.R.E., 1990, Frank Weil award for Disting. Contbn. to Adv. of N.Am. Jewish Culture Jewish Community Ctrs. Assn. N.Am., 1990, 1st Raoul Wallenberg medal U. Mich., 1990; Beth Hatefutsoth hon. fellow, 1988; honors established in his name: Elie Wiesel award for Holocaust Rsch., U. Haifa, Elie Wiesel Chair in Holocaust Studies, Bar-Ilan U., Elie Wiesel Endowment Fund for Jewish Culture, U. Denver, 1987, Elie Wiesel Disting. Svc. award, U. Fla., 1988, Elie Wiesel awards for Jewish Arts and Culture B'nai B'rith Hillel Founds., 1988, Elie Wiesel Chair in Judaic Studies Conn. Coll., 1990. Fellow Jewish Acad. Arts and Scis., Am. Acad. Arts & Scis., Timothy Dwight Coll., Yale U.; mem. Fgn. Press Assn. (hon. life), Amnesty Internat., PEN, Writers & Artists for Peace in Middle East, Writers Guild of Am. East, The Author's Guild, Royal Norwegian Soc. Scis. and Letters, Phi Beta Kappa. Office: Boston U Dept Religion 745 Commonwealth Ave Boston MA 02215

WIEWEL, BRADFORD GERALD, lawyer; b. Quincy, Ill., Oct. 1, 1952; s. Gerald Anthony and Betty (Schwartz) W.; m. Cindy Sparks, Mar. 11, 1989; 1 child, Samuel Bradford. BA, U. Ill., 1974; JD, St. Mary's Univ., 1978. Bar: Tex. 1978. Pres. Austin (Tex.) House of Hope, 1985—; v.p. Christian Reconciliation Ctr., Austin, 1990—; pres. His Kids Adoptions, Austin, 1991—; pvt. practice lawyer Austin, 1987—; co-chmn. Law for Clergy Com./Tex. Young Lawyers, Austin, 1986-87; elder Westlake Bible Ch., Austin, 1990—; pres. Austin (Tex.) Young Lawyers Assn., 1984-85. Founder Dispute Resolution Ctr., Austin, 1984; candidate Tex. House of Reps., Austin, 1984. Mem. State Bar of Tex., Travis County Bar Assn. (dir. 1984-85), Christian Legal Soc. (Tex. membership dir. 1989—). Office: 1411 West Ave Ste 200 Austin TX 78701 *Christ and serving others should be the Who's Who and What's What of our lives.*

WIGGINS, DANIEL BRAXTON, JR., minister, retail company executive; b. Mobile, Ala., Jan. 16, 1952; s. Daniel Braxton Sr. and Christine Lovie (Dobbs) W.; m. Margaret Anne Stephens, Mar. 3, 1972; children: Karl Daniel, Matthew Braxton, Jacquelyn Christine. Student, U. Ala., Tuscaloosa, 1971-72, Home Study Inst. Sem. Extension, Nashville, 1980-81. Ordain minister Southern Bapt., 1978. Mgr. stock room W.T. Grants Co., Tuscaloosa, Ala., 1971-72; sales clk. Spillers Farm & Garden Store, Tuscaloosa, 1972; sales clk. Sears Roebuck & Co., Tuscaloosa, 1972-73, dept. mgr., 1973-74, mgr. auto ctr., 1974-75; sales agt. Ala. Farm Bur. Ins. Co., Northport, 1975; dept. mgr. Jarman Retail Depts. div. Gayfer's Merc. Stores, Inc., Tuscaloosa, Ala. and Columbus, Ga., 1975-77; asst. dept. mgr. Gayfers Merc. Stores, Inc. #75, Tuscaloosa, 1977-78; dept. mgr. Gayfer's Merc. Stores Co. #38, Auburn, Ala., 1978—; pastor Catherine (Ala.) Bapt. Ch., 1978-81, River Rd. Bapt. Ch., Tallassee, Ala., 1981—; mem. exec. com. Tuskegee Lee Bapt. Assn., Auburn, 1981-87; mem. clergy dept. East Ala. Med. Ctr., Opelika, 1986—. Active Tallassee PTA, 1981—; pres. Gayfer's Charity Com., Auburn, 1984-85. Mem. Tuskegee-Lee Assn., Greater Tallassee Ministerial Alliance. Democrat. Avocations: fishing, microcomputers.

WIGGINS, JAMES BRYAN, religion educator; b. Mexia, Tex., Aug. 24, 1935; m. Kay Wiggins, Aug. 15, 1956; children: Bryan, Karis. BA, Tex. Wesleyan U., 1957; BD, So. Meth. U., 1959; PhD, Drew U., 1963; postgrad., Tübingen U., Fed. Republic Germany, 1968-69. Ordained to ministry Meth. Ch., 1959. Instr. humanities Union Jr. Coll., Cranford, N.J., 1960-63; asst. prof. religion Syracuse (N.Y.) U., 1963-69, assoc. prof., 1969-75, prof., 1975—, dept. chair, 1980—; exec. dir. Am. Acad. Religion, 1983—, dir., 1973-75, 83-91; cons. in field. Author: The Embattled Saint, 1966, Foundations of Christianity, 1970; editor: Religion as Story, 1975, Christianity: A Cultural Perspective, 1987; contbr. articles to profl. jours. Trustee Scholars Press, Atlanta, 1983—, chmn., 1986—. Fellow Rockfeller Found., 1962-63. Fellow Soc. for Arts (bd. dirs. 1976—), Religion and Culture; mem. AAUP, Am. Acad. Religion, Am. Soc. Ch. History, Am. Hist. Assn. Democrat. Avocations: golf, tennis, music, reading, travel. Home: 308 Kimber Rd Syracuse NY 13224 Office: Syracuse U Dept Religion 501 Hall of Langs Syracuse NY 13244

WIGGINS, TODD KEITH, youth minister; b. Melbourne, Fla., Sept. 18, 1967; s. Charles Mark Sr. and Vivie Lewis (Johnson) W. BS in Christian Edn., Ky. Christian Coll., 1989. Ordained to ministry Christian Ch., 1989. Min. youth 1st Christian Ch., Clermont, Fla., 1989—; camp counselor Lake James Christian Assembly, Angola, Ind., 1987, Bluegrass Christian Svc. Camp, Levington, Ky., 1988, Lake Aurora Christian Assembly, Lake Wales, Fla., 1990; song leader Fla. Christian Children's Conv., Orlando, Fla., 1989. Vol. Campus Life, Youth for Christ, Clermont, 1990—, YMCA, Clermont, 1991. Office: 1st Christian Ch 796 Hook St Clermont FL 34711

WIKE, STEPHEN MICHAEL, publisher; b. North Hollywood, Calif., June 1, 1949; s. Franklin Everett and Dorothy Camella (Bennett) W.; m. Michele Marie Wike, Oct. 7, 1967; children: Daniel Stephen, Joseph Matthew, David Jonathan. Bus. mgr. Christianity Today, Washington, 1972-78; pub. Nat. and Internat. Religion Report, 1979—. Office: Media Mgmt PO Box 21433 Roanoke VA 24018

WIKER, EDGAR GUY, minister; b. Phila., July 26, 1932; s. Edgar Maine and Lillian Kandle (Honeker) W.; m. Irene Haines Rae, July 12, 1958; children: Mona, Christine. BA in Econs., Gettysburg Coll., 1954; MDiv, Luth. Theol. Sem., 1963. Ordained to ministry Luth. Ch. in Am., 1963. Pastor Lebanon Luth. Ch., DuBois, Pa., 1963-67; dir. camping svcs. Luth. Soc. Svcs., Bklyn, 1967-69; pastor Emanuel Luth. Ch., Friesburg, N.J., 1969—; bd. dirs. Faith Farm, Inc., Bridgeton, N.J., 1972—, supr. counselors, drug rehab. counselor, 1988—; bd. dirs. Habitat for Humanity, Salem County, N.J., 1988—. With U.S. Army, 1955-57. Home and Office: RR 3 Box 252 Elmer NJ 08318 *What a treasure life is to we who know Jesus Christ and what a privilege it is to serve Him.*

WIKLER, YOSEF, seminary dean; b. N.Y.C., Jan. 12, 1945; s. Samuel Jacob and Dorothy (Strogoff) W.; m. Sarah Yudin, May 18, 1973; children: Yeshaya, Devorah, Rachel, Alexander, Chaya, Miriam, Yochered, Chana, Moshe. B. Hebrew Letters, BA, Yeshiva U., 1962, MS in Jewish Edn., 1970. Ordained rabbi, 1974. Educator Regozin Yeshiva High Sch., Jersey City, 1973-76; educator, guidance counselor Jezra Acad. Queens (N.Y.), 1976-79; dean Yeshiva Birkas Reuven, Bklyn., 1980—; editor Kashrus Mag., Bklyn., 1980—; mem. kosher com. Agudath Israel of Am., N.Y.C., 1986—. Author: The Foods We Eat, 1980; contbr. articles to newspapers. Office: Yeshiva Birkas Reuven PO Box 204 Brooklyn NY 11204

WILBANKS, MARK OLIVER, minister; b. Tampa, Fla., July 14, 1951; s. Oliver Cleveland and Betty (Howell) W.; m. Kimberly Ann Perrin, Apr. 28, 1979; children: Andrew Mark, Jordan Perrin. BS in Edn., U. Ga., 1973; MRE, So. Bapt. Theol. Sem., 1975. Ordained to ministry So. Bapt. Conv., 1975. Minister edn./youth Kenwood Bapt. Ch., Louisville, 1974-75; minister youth activities College Park Bapt. Ch., Orlando, Fla., 1975-76; assoc. pastor First Bapt. Ch., Tallahassee, 1976-85; pastor Southside Bapt. Ch., Jacksonville, Fla., 1985—; v.p. Challenge Ministries, Inc., Jacksonville, 1981—; bd. dirs. Fellowship Christian Athletes, Tallahassee, 1983-85. Mem. instl. rev. com. Bapt. Med. Ctr., Jacksonville, 1985—. Mem. Jacksonville C. of C. Democrat. Office: Southside Bapt Ch 1435 Atlantic Blvd Jacksonville FL 32257 *The will of God will never take me where the grace of God cannot keep me.*

WILBER, DONALD BLAINE, medical psychotherapist, clergyman; b. Albuquerque, Oct. 5, 1952; s. M. Blaine and S. June (Warren) W.; m. Janet Marie Scott, Sept. 14, 1973; children—Eric, Casey, Ty, Daniel. B.A. in Religion, N.W. Nazarene Coll., 1976; M.A. in Gen. Counseling, Coll. Idaho, 1980; Ph.D. in Counseling Psychology, Columbia Pacific U., 1982. Ordained to ministry Ch. of the Nazarene, 1978; cert. Nat. Bd. Med. Psychotherapists. Pastor marriage and family counselor Ch. of the Nazarene, Harper, Oreg., 1976-79; intern, behavior health counselor, Mountain State Tumor Inst., Boise, 1980; dir., therapist Treasure Valley Counseling, Ontario, Oreg., 1980-82; pastor Ch. of the Nazarene, Prosser, Wash., 1983—. bd. dirs. Lower Valley Pregnancy Ctr.; adv. bd. Prosser Schs.; cons. Valley Family Medicine and Valley Family Dental Clinics; zone chmn., advisor to Chrisitian Action Standing Com., Ch. Nazarene; dir. Concerned Pastors for Traditional Values. Mem. Prosser Ministerial Assn. (pres.). Contbr. articles to profl. jours. Office: Ch of the Nazarene 1937 Highland Dr Prosser WA 99350

WILBERT, BRIAN KURT, clergyman; b. Elyria, Ohio, May 2, 1960; s. Richard Paul and Linda Lee (Sheldon) W. BA, Kenyon Coll., 1982; MDiv, Bexley Hall, 1985. Ordained to ministry Episocpal Ch. as deacon, 1985, as priest, 1986. Sem. asst. Calvary/St. Andrew's, Rochester, N.Y., 1983-85; curate St. Michael's in the Hills, Toldeo, 1985-88; rector Grace Episcopal Ch., Ravenna, Ohio, 1988—; bd. dirs. United Campus Ministries Kent State U., 1989—; mem. of the diocesan Christian Edn. Dept. Ohio, 1985—, Youth Council Ohio, 1986—; pres. Bexley Soc., Rochester, 1984-85. Named one of Outstanding Young Men of Am., 1985, 1987. Mem. Bexley Alumni Assn. (v.p. 1986—), Kenyon Toledo Alumni Admissions Program (chmn. 1985-88), Ravenna Rotary Club. Democrat. Home: 264 W Cedar Ave Ravenna OH 44266 Office: Grace Episcopal Ch 250 W Cedar Ave Ravenna OH 44266

WILBUR, MARVIN CUMMINGS, clergyman; b. Sprague, Wash., July 12, 1914; s. George Henry and Harriet Starr (Nutter) W.; B.S. with honors, Oreg. State U., 1936; postgrad. George Washington U., 1937-38; B.D., Union Theol. Sem., 1943; D.D., Alma Coll., 1956; m. G. Marie Lacy, Nov. 1, 1945; children—Judy Marie, George Marvin, John Cummings. Ordained to ministry Presbyterian Ch., 1943; Presbyn. chaplain Yale U., 1946-49; dir. public info. Union Theol. Sem., 1949-51; sec. program materials United Presbyn. Ch. U.S.A., N.Y.C., 1951-64; asst. v.p. U.P. Found., N.Y.C., 1964-87. Bd. dirs. Religion in Am. Life, Inc., 1951-87; bd. dirs., sec. Presbyn. Homes of N.J., Inc. Served as lt. comdr., chaplain, USNR, 1943-46. Recipient Outstanding Achievement award Nat. Visual Presentation Assn., 1954; Faith and Freedom award Religious Heritage Am., 1979. Mem. Religious Public Relations Council (pres. 1955-57, 1st exec. sec. 1959-86, 50th Anniversary citation 1979), Public Relations Soc. Am., Sigma Delta Chi, Phi Kappa Phi, Delta Phi Epsilon, Pi Kappa Phi. Editorial adv. bd. Public Relations News. Home: 32 Windsor Rd Tenafly NJ 07670

WILBURN, HOWARD LEE, college president; b. Daniels, W.Va., Sept. 25, 1945; s. Blanch Iva (Meador) W.; m. Judy Ann Ellison, June 2, 1972; children: John Howard, Michael Lee. BTh, Piedmont Bible Coll., 1973; MEd, U. N.C., Greensboro, 1983, postgrad. Ordained to ministry Bapt. Ch., 1973. Pastor Daniels Missionary Bapt. Ch., 1970-75; coord. alumni Piedmont Bible Coll., Winston-Salem, N.C., 1975-78, pres., 1988—; pastor Foot of Ten Bible Ch., Duncansville, Pa., 1978-82, Swan Creek Bapt. Ch., Jonesville, N.C., 1982-88. Airman 1st class, USAF, 1963-67, Vietnam. Republican. Office: Piedmont Bible Coll 716 Franklin St Winston-Salem NC 27101

WILBURN, RAYMOND ALLEN, minister; b. Newnan, Ga., July 29, 1947; s. Howard Raymond and Martha Lee (Davis) W.; m. Judy Diane Bell, Nov. 9, 1990. BRE, Messianic Sch. Theology, Powder Spring, Ga., 1975; BA, West Ga. Coll., 1969, MA, 1972, EDS, 1989. Ordained to ministry So. Bapt. Conv., 1973. Sr. pastor Bethel Bapt. Ch., Bremen, Ga., 1973-78; pastor Tallapoosa E. Bapt. Ch., Buchanan, 1980-89; interim pastor Providence Bapt. Ch., Tallapoosa, Ga., 1990-91; min. edn., assoc. pastor 1st Bapt. Ch., Buchanan, 1990—; chr. Haralson County Bd. Edn., Buchanan, 1969—; del. So. Bapt. Conv., 1980-87. uthor: Teaching Social Studies in Haralson County, 1991. amed Haralson County Tchr. of the Yr., 1990, Gordon Watson awardee, W. Ga. Coll., 1969, Waco Sch. Tchr. of the Yr., 1989. em. NEA, Ga. Assn. Educators, Phi Kappa Phi. Home: PO Box 132 Buchanan GA 30113

WILBURN, STEPHEN SALLIS, publishing company executive; b. West Point, Miss., Aug. 6, 1947; s. William and Mary Jane (Smith) W. B.A., Belhaven Coll., Jackson, Miss., 1969; M.Div., Fuller Theol. Sem., Pasadena, Calif., 1973. Asst. sales mgr. Oxford U. Press, N.Y.C., 1977-79, editor Bibles, 1979-83; editorial dir. Morehouse-Barlow Co., Inc., Wilton, Conn., 1984-87; dir. religious books Macmillan Publishing Co., N.Y.C., 1987—; dir. Religion Pub. Group. N.Y.C., 1980-82, 87-88, pres., 1988-89. Office: Macmillan Pub Co 866 Third Ave New York NY 10022

WILCOX, BRIAN WILLIAM, minister; b. South Bend, Ind., Sept. 9, 1964; s. John William and Cecilia Ann (Tanner) W.; m. Jeana Lyn Crain, Sept. 13, 1986; children: Seth, Jael. B in Religious Edn., Great Lakes Bible Coll., 1987. Ordained to minister Ch. of Christ, 1986. Youth min. Christian Ch. of Milford, Ind., 1987-91; min. Cedar Lake Ch. of Christ, Waterloo, Ind., 1991—; bd. dirs. Alexander Christian Found., Indpls., Lake James Christian Assmbly, Angola, Ind. Ambulance driver Milford (Ind.) Emergency Med. Svc., 1988-91. Home and Office: 1492 CR 27 Waterloo IN 46793

WILCOX, GEORGE FRANKLIN, priest; b. Camden, N.J., July 11, 1937; s. George F. and Dorothy (Dutton) W.; m. Mary M. Barr, Dec. 26, 1973. S.T.L., St. Francis Theol. Sem., 1967; PhD, Duquesne U., 1967; DD (hon.), Royal London Inst., 1972. Ordained priest, 1967. Dean Sullins Coll., Bristol, Va., 1972-76; pastoral assoc. St. John's Parish, Ft. Smith, Ark., 1976-78; pastor Grace Parish, Galesburg, Ill., 1978-88, St. Matthew's Parish, Bloomington, Ill., 1988—; pres. standing com. Diocese of Quincy, Peoria, Ill., 1981-85; chmn. Commn. on Ministry, 1983-88. Author: Liturgy and Church, 1969; editor: Campus Ministry Works, 1970. Bd. dirs. Gov.'s Sch. for Gifted, Commonwealth of Va., Bristol, 1976; chaplain Va. Poly. Inst. and State U., Blacksburg, Va., 1968. With USN, 1956-60, USAF, 1968-70. Mem. Kiwanis. Avocations: water sports, travel, model trains. Home: 20 Kenfield Circle Bloomington IL 61704 Office: St Matthew's Ch 1920 E Oakland Ave Bloomington IL 61701

WILCOX, JACKSON BURTON, religious writer; b. Altadena, Calif., June 16, 1918; s. Philip Burton and Ethel Ruth (Jackson) W.; m. Marjorie Viola Robbins, Sept. 8, 1940; children: Judith Karen, John Mark, Deborah Ellen, Carol Elisabeth. BA, U. Redlands, 1940; student, Am. Bapt. Sem. West, 1940; BD, Colgate Rochester Div. Sch., 1944; DD, Ea. Bapt. Coll., 1972. Ordained to ministry Bapt. Ch., 1943. Pastor First Bapt. Ch., Santa Cruz, Calif., 1960-65; pastor First Bapt. Ch., Lindsay, Calif., 1965-69; sr. pastor First Bapt. Ch., Hollywood, Calif., 1969-73, Panorama Bapt. Ch., Pacoima, Calif., 1973-88; editor Silver Wings Publs., Pearblossom, Calif., 1983—; editor Poetry on Wings, Pearblossom, 1983—; min. of communication Lancaster (Calif.) Presbyn. Ch., 1989—. Cartoonist (collection pub. 1972); author: poetry, 1983—. Pres. Pacoima Community Coordinating Coun., 1980-82. Recipient commendation resolutions L.A. City Coun., 1988, Calif. State Senate, 1982, Calif. State Assembly, 1980, L.A. Bapt. City Mission, 1988. Mem. L.A. Bapt. Mins. Assn., Am. Bapt. Mins. at Large, Sierra Club, Nat. Wildlife Fedn. Republican. Office: Poetry on Wings Inc PO Box 1000 Pearblossom CA 93553 *If a man or woman can live humbly with a pure heart, walking uprighty, working righteousness and speaking the truth in love, the years will wear well.*

WILCOX, MARY MARKS, Christian education consultant, educator; b. Madison, Wis., Apr. 23, 1921; d. Roy and Mary Celia (Leary) Marks; m. Ray Everett Wilcox, Nov. 28, 1942; children: Peter, Anne, Susan, Steven. BA, U. Wis., 1942; MRE, Iliff Sch. Theology, Denver, 1968. Cert. Christian educator. Cons. local chs., Lakewood, Littleton, Wheat Ridge, Colo., 1963-74; instr., leader numerous seminars throughout U.S. and Can., 1963—; interim parish cons. 1st Presbyn. Ch., Lakewood, 1988-90; adj. prof. Iliff Sch. Theology, 1970—. Author: Developmental Journey, 1979; contbr. articles to various publs., chpts. to books. Former vol. instr., life guard YMCA, Lakewood; trustee, mem. exec. bd. Nat. Ghost Ranch Found., Abiquiu, N.Mex., 1982—. Recipient award Iliff Alumni Assn., 1989. Mem. Assn. Profs. and Researchers in Religious Edn. (presentr), United Meth. Assn. Profs. Christian Edn., Religious Edn. Assn., Assn. Presbyn. Christian Educators (past mem. exec. bd.), Moral Edn. Assn. Democrat. Presbyterian. Home: 3590 Estes St Wheat Ridge CO 80033

WILCOX, RONALD WAYNE, minister; b. Hazlehurst, Ga., Mar. 15, 1941; s. Odis C. and Audrey Margelene (Schell) W.; m. Leita Euree Johnson, Aug. 26, 1960; children: Rhonda Ruth, Leree Denise, Karen Leann. BA, Luther Rice Bible Coll., Jacksonville, Fla., 1983; MDiv, Luther Rice Sem., Jacksonville, Fla., 1985, D Ministry, 1987. Ordained to ministry So. Bapt. Conv., 1978. Interim pastor Sardis Bapt. Ch., Alamo, Ga., 1976, Lumber City (Ga.) Bapt. Ch., 1976-77; pastor First Bapt. Ch., Screven, Ga., 1977—; tchr. Ga. Bapt. Edn. Extension Ctr., Jesup, Ga., 1989—; del. Ga. Bapt. Exec. Com., Atlanta, 1988-91. Guest columnist The Press-Sentinel, 1978—; pianist Gospel Quartet, 1968-78. Chmn. Heart Fund, Hazlehurst, 1976, St. Jude's Children's Hosp., Screven, 1981, Sex Edn. Adv. Com., Jesup, 1990—, Vocat. Edn. Adv. Coun., Jesup, 1984—. Mem. Luther Rice Alumni Assn. (sec.-treas.), Wayne County Ministerial Assn. (pres. 1983-84), Altamana Bapt. Assn. (moderator, 1983-85, trustee 1989—), Exchange Club (pres. 1976-78). Democrat. Home: 301 Grace St Screven GA 31560 Office: First Bapt Ch Church and School Sts Screven GA 31560 *The saddest commentary on American culture is the failure to adhere to God's standard for morals, ethics, and values; exchanging the truth of God for a lie (Romans 1:25).*

WILD, ROBERT ANTHONY, religious organization administrator; b. Chgo., Mar. 30, 1940; s. John Hopkins and Mary Dorothy (Colnon) W. BA in Latin, Loyola U. Chgo., 1962, MA in Classical Lang., 1967; STL, Jesuit Sch. Theology, Chgo., 1970; PhD in Study of Religion, Harvard U., 1977. Joined S.J., Roman Cath. Ch., 1957, ordained priest, 1970. From asst. to assoc. prof. Marquette U., Milw., 1975-83; vis. prof. Pont. Istituto Biblico, Rome, 1983-84; dir. Jesuit philosophate program Loyola U. Chgo., 1984-85, assoc. prof. theology, 1985—; provincial superior Chgo. Province S.J., Chgo., 1985—; trustee Jesuit Sch. Theology, Berkeley, Calif., 1985-90, Weston Sch. Theology, Cambridge, Mass., 1985—, Marquette U., 1990—. Author: Water in the Cultic Worship of Isis and Sarapis, 1981; co-editor: Sentences of Sextus, 1981; contbr. articles to profl. jours. Mem. Soc. Bibl. Lit., Cath. Bibl. Soc., Chgo. Soc. for Bibl. Rsch. Office: Chicago Province Soc Jesus 2050 N Clark St Chicago IL 60614

WILDER, GENE, pastor; b. Balt., Dec. 5, 1950; s. Mack Henry and Lucille Winifred (Martin) W.; m. Patricia Claire Childers, June 6, 1971; children: Jeffrey Jonathan, Ginger Joy. BA in Music Edn., Carson-Newman Coll., 1973; MDiv, Southwestern Bapt. Theol. Sem., Ft. Worth, 1977; D Ministry, So. Bapt. Theol. Sem., Louisville, 1989. Ordained to ministry So. Bapt. Conv., 1972. Pastor Zion Bapt. Ch., Fairview, Va., 1970-71, 1st Bapt. Ch. Brooklyn., Balt., 1977-83; min. music and youth Valley Brook Bapt. Ch., Decatur, Ga., 1972-74, 1st Bapt. Ch., Roanoke, Tex., 1974-77; pastor West Highland Bapt. Ch., Macon, Ga., 1984—; pres. Brooklyn-Curtis Bay Ministerial Assn., Balt., 1982-83, Macon Bapt. Mins. Conf., Macon, 1985-86, Macon Bapt. Am. Christian TV System, Macon, 1987—; moderator Macon Bapt. Assn., 1989—. Contbg. author: In Support of the Family, 1986; also articles to religious mags. Recipient Golden Pen award Macon News and Telegraph, 1990; named Pastor of Yr., Macon Bapt. Assn., 1988. Home: 3064 Willowstone Dr Lizella GA 31052 Office: West Highland Bapt Ch 4505 Mercer University Dr Macon GA 31210 *No personal asset is greater than the ability to relate to others. Those who possess this gift need nothing more to succeed. Those who lack this skill will seldom find the key to success elsewhere.*

WILDER, THOMAS HENRY, minister; b. Camp Atterbury, Ind., June 14, 1952; s. Cecil Orie and Sybil Grace (Posey) W.; m. Judy Dianne Rooks, Aug. 20, 1971; children: Thomas Christopher, Corey Everett, Karyn Elizabeth. BA in Sociology, Aurburn U., 1980; postgrad., Southwestern Bapt. Theol. Sem., 1987—. Ordained to ministry So. Bapt. Conv. Min. music, edn. and youth Woodley E. Bapt. Ch., Montgomery, Ala., 1975-81; min. music and youth Summerville Bapt. Ch., Phenix City, Ala., 1982-87; min. music Lakeland Bapt. Ch., Lewisville, Tex., 1988—; mem. faculty Ala. Bapt. Ch. Tng. Confs., Shocco Springs, 1882-86; associational music dir. Russell Bapt. Assn., Phenix City, 1985-87. With USAF, 1972-76. Decorated Air medal, Commendation medal. Home: 841 Creekside Dr Lewisville TX 75067 Office: Lakeland Bapt Ch 397 S Stemmons Lewisville TX 75067

WILDER, WILLIAM BRUCE, JR., minister; b. Charlotte, N.C., Oct. 8, 1957; s. William Bruce and Linda Grey (Belcher) W.; m. Kirsten Faye Braaten; children: Jessica, Emily, Meredith, Melinda. BA, Luther Coll., Decorah, Iowa, 1979; MDiv, Luther Theol. Seminary, St. Paul, Minn., 1984. Ordained to ministry Luth. Ch., 1984. Dir. of youth Our Savior's Luth. Ch., Pequot Lakes, Minn., 1979-80; pastor Christ the King Luth. Ch., Richmond, Va., 1984-89; sr. pastor Zion Luth. Ch., Warroad, Minn., 1989—; clergy mem. Transition Team for the new Va. Synod, Richmond, 1986-87; chmn. nominating com. Constituting Conv., Va. Synod, 1987; mem. Luth.-Anglican-Roman Cath. Coalition, Va., 1985-88; mem. Synod Congregational Life com., Moorhead, Minn., 1990—. Author: Christ in Our Home, 1985, 89. Bd. dirs. Freedom House: Homeless Shelter, Richmond, 1986, Warroad Chem. Awareness com., 1990—, Roseau (Minn.) County HIV/AIDS Task Force, 1990—; vol. chaplain Johnston-Willis Hosp., Richmond, 1986-89. Recipient Skattum Meml. scholarship Luther Coll., Decorah, 1979, Vol. Svc. award Richmond Area Blood Svc., 1986. Mem. Warroad Ministerial Assn., Lions. Home: 708 Mackenzie Ave Warroad MN 56763-2321 Office: Zion Lutheran Ch ELCA Virginia St Warroad MN 56763

WILDEY, WILLIAM EDWARD, religious organization adminstrator; b. Paterson, N.J., Nov. 10, 1952; s. Herbert Cornelius and Joan Kay (Kimble) W.; m. Maureen A. Branon, Nov. 9, 1991. BA in Communications, William Paterson Coll., 1981. Asst. regional dir. Church World Svc., Rocky Hill, N.J., 1973-76; regional dir. Nat. Coun. Chs. of Christ Church World Svc., Ludlow, Mass., 1983—; exec. dir. World Hunger Yr. of N.J., Fairlawn, N.J., 1976-80; mgr. Chris' Camera Ctr., Pompton Lakes, N.J., 1980-83; v.p. Coun. Chs. of Greater Springfield, Mass., 1985-86, pres., 1986-88, bd. dirs., v.p., 1989—; mem. adv. bd. Regional Ecumenical Network Mass. Coun. Chs., Boston, 1989-90; mem. allocations com. Food for All Western Mass., 1991—; mem. Greater Springfield CROP Walk Com., 1985—. Co-editor: Toward a Dynamic State Food Policy, 1979. Past mem. N.E. Task Force on Food and Farm Policy, Coalition for the Rights of N.J. Farmworkers, Community Action Coun. of Passaic County, N.J. State CROP Com.; mem. steering com. refugee resettlement program United Ch. of Christ, 1990. Mem. Interfaith Coun. of Western Mass. Democrat. United Ch. of Christ. Avocations: fishing, reading, photography. Home: 149 Barrett St Northampton MA 01060 Office: Ch World Svc 200 Center St 17B Ludlow MA 01056

WILDRICK, KENYON JONES, minister; b. Rahway, N.J., June 14, 1933; s. Stanley B. and Adele (Jones) W.; BA, Trinity Coll., Hartford, Conn., 1955, BD, Princeton U., 1958, ThM, 1962, DD, Trinity Coll., Conn., 1985; m. Nancy Ruth Mersfelder, Aug. 23, 1958; children—Catherine Ruth, Margaret Jeanne, Kenyon Douglas. Ordained to ministry Presbyterian Ch., 1958; asst. minister Community Congregational Ch., Short Hills, N.J., 1958-61, asso. minister, 1961-67, sr. minister, 1967—; campus ministry Middle Atlantic Conf., 1962-65. Bd. dirs. Milburn-Short Hills chpt. ARC, 1963-64; ch. and ministry com. N.J. Assn., 1965—; trustee Ctr. Theol. Inquiry, Princeton, N.J., 1985—; pres. bd. trustees Overlook Protestant Chaplaincy Program, 1973—; trustee Presbyn. Homes N.J., 1981—. Mem. Millburn Clergy Assn. (chmn. 1987—), Delta Phi. Club: Rotary (dir. Milburn Club 1973). Home: 79 Addison Dr Short Hills NJ 07078 Office: 200 Hartshorn Dr Short Hills NJ 07078

WILES, MARI ELENA, minister; b. Gardiner, Maine, Feb. 24, 1962; d. Everett Guy and Linda Foy (Lennon) W. BA in Psychology, Mars Hill (N.C.) Coll., 1984; MDiv, Southeastern Bapt. Theol. Sem., Wake Forest, N.C., 1988. Ordained to ministry, So. Bapt. Conv., 1989. Summer missionary So. Bapt. Ch., Maine, 1983, Spain, 1984; interim youth pastor Millbrook Bapt. Ch., Raleigh, N.C., 1986-87; minister youth, edn. First Bapt. Ch., Pageland, S.C., 1988; assoc. minister First Bapt. Ch., Fayetteville, N.C., 1989—. Fund raiser, chmn. Cystic Fibrosis Found. Wilson, N.C., 1990, 91; active Adopt-A-Hwy., N.C. Transp., Fayetteville, 1989—. Mem. N.C. Women in Ministry (bd. dirs. 1990—), So. Bapt. Women in Ministry. Office: First Bapt Ch 201 Anderson St Fayetteville NC 28301

WILFONG, JOHN FRANKLIN, religious organization administrator; b. Sugar Grove, W.Va., Aug. 20, 1951; s. Clarence Judy and Mary (Nelsen) W.; m. Wilma Marie Drake, May 20, 1970; children: Joy, Joshua. BTh, Piedmont Bible Coll., Winston Salem, N.C., 1975; MDiv, Grand Rapids Bapt. Seminary, 1978, MRE, 1991; postgrad., Liberty U., Lynchburg, Va. Ordained to ministry N.Am. Bapt. Ch., 1983. Asst. adminstr. E.M. Christian Schs., Stockton, Calif., 1979-83; ednl. missionary North Am. Bapts., Nigeria, 1983-86; pastor Willow Rancho Bapt. Ch., Sacramento, 1986-87; sr. adminstr. Barstow (Calif.) Christian Sch., 1987—; dist. Christian edn. dir. Evangel. Methodists Calif., 1981-83; com. Life and Light Sch., Calif., 1988-91. Mem. ASCD. Office: Barstow Christian Sch 800 Yucca Ave Barstow CA 92311

WILHITE, F. DOUGLAS, church music minister; b. Indpls., Apr. 25, 1953; s. Hartsel Charles and Regina (Charpie) W.; m. Sherry Lynn Huber, July 20, 1974; children: Douglas II, Trisha, Kristen, Zachary, Cassie. BA in Polit. Sci., Ga. State U., 1990. Sta. mgr. Sta. WNTS Christian Radio, Indpls., 1978-81; pres. Wings Communications Inc., Atlanta, 1981—, Sta. WELE Christian Radio, Daytona, Fla., 1990—, Sta. WSSA Christian Radio, Atlanta, 1981—; minister of music Riverdale (Ga.) Presbyn. Ch., 1989—; elder Riverdale Presbyn. Ch., 1987—, Sunday sch. tchr., 1984—; choir dir., organist Kessler Krest Bapt. Ch., Indpls., 1970-81; host radio talk show, 1984, TV show, 1985. Mem. Nat. Religious Broadcasters, Ga. Assn. Broadcasters, Am. Guild Organists, Presbyn. Assn. Musicians. Office: Sta WSSA Radio 2424 Old Rex Morrow Rd Morrow GA 30260

WILHOIT, MELVIN ROSS, music minister, music educator; b. Fort Wayne, Ind., May 26, 1948; s. Bert Harvey and Vivian C. (Hitchcock) W.; m. Susan Beth Cassidy, May 27, 1970; children: Robert Christian, Christina Elizabeth, Angela Noel. BS in Music Edn., Bob Jones U., 1971; MusM in Music History and Lit., Mankato State U., 1976; MusD, So. Bapt. Theol. Sem., 1982. Prof. music Pillsbury Bapt. Coll., Owatonna, Minn., 1971-76, Boyce Bible Sch., Louisville, 1977-80; min. music Oak Park Bapt. Ch., Jeffersonville, Ind., 1977-80; prof. music, chmn. Div. Fine Arts Bryan Coll., Dayton, Tenn., 1980—; min. music Oak St. Bapt. Ch., Soddy-Daisy, Tenn., 1982-85, Middle Valley Bapt. Ch., Hixson, Tenn., 1985—. Contbr. articles to religious and scholarly jours. Grantee NEH, 1984, 89, Pew Charitable Trust, 1989, Wesleyan Holiness Project Christian Coll. Coalition, 1985, 89. Mem. Music Educators Nat. Conf., Hymn Soc. Am., Internat. Trumpet Guild, Tenn. Music Educators, Sonneck Soc. for Am. Music, Christian Instrumental Dirs. Assn. Home: Rte 6 Box 517 Dayton TN 37321 Office: Bryan Coll Box 7000 Dayton TN 37321

WILKE, CARL EDWARD, retired priest; b. Milw., Apr. 1, 1920; s. Carl August and Edith (Bauer) W.; widower; children: Joan Frances, Carl Edward, Anne Mary, Peter Killian. BSBA, Marquette U., 1941; S.T.B., Gen. Sem., N.Y.C., 1944; S.T.M., Nashotah (Wis.) House, 1956. Ordained priest Episcopal Ch., 1944. Asst. St. Mark;s Episc. Ch., Milw., 1944-46; chaplain St. Mary's Hosp., N.Y.C., 1946-47; rector Calvary Episc. Ch., Richmond, Tex., 1947-51, St. Matthew's Episc. Ch., Bellaire, Tex., 1951-53; asst. Trinity Episc. Ch., Wauwatosa, Wis., 1953-57; rector All Saints Ch., Appleton, Wis., 1957-70, Christ Episc. Ch., Springfield, Mo., 1970-85. Avocations: swimming, sailing, reading, walking. Home: 2511 E Edgewood St Springfield MO 65804-3905

WILKE, WAYNE WILLIAM, religion educator; b. Sheboygan, Wis., June 26, 1948; s. William Martin and Ruth Esther (Oldenburg) W.; m. Grace Marie Klement, Aug. 1, 1970; children: Sarah Lynn, Nathan Aaron. BA, Concordia Sr. Coll., 1970; MDiv, Concordia Sem., 1974, MST, 1984; PhD, U. Mich., 1990. Pastor Prince of Peace and Shepherd of Hills Luth. Ch., Martinsville, Nashville, Ind., 1974-77; dir., instr. Concordia Coll., Ann Arbor, Mich., 1977-81, asst. prof., 1981-87, assoc. prof., 1987—; dean student svcs. Concordia Coll., 1984-88, dir. pre-sem. program, 1990—, chmn. div. religion and philosophy, 1990—. Chaplain Ind. State Police, Indpls., 1975-77; mem. Washtenaw County Task Force on Youth Drinking and Driving, Ann Arbor, 1986, Mich. Dist. Youth Bd., Ann Arbor, 1982-88. Named Outstanding Young Am., Jaycees, 1983. Mem. Am. Studies Assn., Concordia Hist. Inst. Home: 443 Pine Brae Ann Arbor MI 48105 Office: Concordia Coll 4090 Geddes Rd Ann Arbor MI 48105 *Religious education should make student aware of their spiritual and moral heritage so that they might be equipped and empowered to be agents for positive change in the society in which they live.*

WILKEN, ROBERT LOUIS, historian, theologian; b. New Orleans, Oct. 20, 1936; s. Louis Frederick and Mabel (Rayl) W.; m. Carol Weinhold, June 4, 1960; children: Gregory, Jonathan. BA, Concordia Sem., 1957, BD, 1960; MA, U. Chgo., 1961, PhD, 1963. Asst. prof. Luth. Theol. Sem., Gettysburg, Pa., 1964-67, Fordham U., N.Y.C., 1967-72; from assoc. prof. to prof. U. Notre Dame, Ind., 1972-85; William R. Kenan prof. of history of Christianity, U. Va., Charlottesville, 1985—; Lady Davis prof. Hebrew U., 1982. Author: The Christians as the Romans Saw Them, John Chrysostom & The Jews, The Myth of Christian Beginnings, Judaism and The Early Christian Mind. NEH research grantee, 1981-82. Mem. Am. Soc. Ch. History, Am. Acad. Religion (v.p. 1986-87, pres. 1988-89, Am. Hist. Assn., N.Am. Patristics Soc. (pres. 1985-86). Lutheran. Home: 1630 Brandywine Dr Charlottesville VA 22901 Office: U Va Locke Hall Dept Religious Studies Charlottesville VA 22903

WILKENS, THOMAS G., religion educator; b. Chgo., Aug. 22, 1936; s. Frank and Imogene Hildegard (Heald) W.; m. Betty Eileen Molde, Sept. 8, 1962; children: Kimberly Sue, Nicholas Todd. BA, Luther Coll., Decorah, Iowa, 1958; BD, Luther Theol. Sem., St. Paul, 1961; PhD, U. Aberdeen, Scotland, 1968. Ordained to ministry Evang. Luth. Ch. in Am. Pastor St. John's Luth. Ch., Avoca, Wis., 1963-66, 1st Luth. Ch., Lone Rock, Wis., 1963-66; prof. Tex. Luth. Coll., Seguin, 1968—. Contbr. articles to religious jours. Am. Luth. Ch. fellow, 1976-77; grantee NSF, 1980, NEH, 1983, Evang. Luth. Ch. in Am., 1986. Mem. Am. Acad. Religion. Democrat. Office: Tex Luth Coll 100 W Court Seguin TX 78155

WILKERSON, ROOSEVELT, JR., minister; b. Hollandale, Miss., Aug. 28, 1952; s. Roosevelt and Earlean (Gunn) W.; m. Christoria Ann Woods; children: LaTonya, Rodney. BA, Paine Coll., 1976; MDiv, Duke U., 1979; MA, N.C. Agrl. & Tech. State U., 1981. Sr. min. Cokesbury Meth. Ch., Raleigh, N.C., 1976-80, Erwin Temple Ch., Charlotte, N.C., 1980-83, St. Joseph Ch., Chapel Hill, N.C., 1983-89, New Covenant Christian United Ch. of Christ, Chapel Hill, 1989—. Bd. dirs. Chapel Hill YMCA, 1985-90, Orange County Habitat for Humanity, 1987-90, Triangle Housing Partnership, 1990-93; coun. mem. Town of Chapel Hill, 1987-91. Recipient Community Svc. award Prince Hall Masonic Lodge, Chapel Hill, 1987, Delta Sigma Theta, Chapel Hill, 1988, Marin Luther King, Jr. Community Svc. award South Orange black Caucus, Chapel Hill, 1989. Mem. Rotary (internat. fellow 1986). Democart. Avocations: coin collecting, stock market analysis, fishing. Office: Town of Chapel Hill 306 N Columbia St Chapel Hill NC 27516

WILKES, PETER, pastor; b. Manchester, Eng., Aug. 12, 1937; came to U.S., 1974; s. William A. Wilkes and Edith E. (Robinson) Gill; m. Norah A. Hobson, Sept. 6, 1958; children: Simon J., Elisabeth A., Jonathan M. MS, U. Manchester, 1962, PhD, 1967. Ordained to ministry, 1980. Lectr. U. Manchester, 1963-73; prof. U. Wis., Madison, 1974-80; assoc. pastor Elmbrook Ch., Waukesha, Wis., 1980-82; pastor South Hills Community Ch., San Jose, Calif., 1982—; assoc. evangelist Inter-Varsity Fellowship, Madison, 1984—. Author: Soild State Theory in Metallurgy, 1972; author/editor: Christianity Challenges the University, 1981. Avocations: racquetball, gardening. Home: 6846 Bret Harte Dr San Jose CA 95120 Office: South Hills Community Ch 6601 Camden Ave San Jose CA 95120

WILKEY, CYNTHIA DENISE, lay worker; b. Wichita, Kans., July 16, 1961; d. Don DeWayne and Mary Ellen (Voss) Arteberry; m. Curtis Wilkey, Aug. 16, 1980; children: Sarah Ruth, Blaine Curtis. BS in Edn., E. Cen. U., Ada, Okla., 1983, MEd, 1985. Sun. sch. tchr. First Bapt. Ch., Newalla, Okla., 1983-84; VBS worker Country Estates Bapt. Ch., Midwest City, Okla., 1986; children's choir dir. First United Meth. Ch., Mexia, Tex., 1987-89, VBS leader/worker, 1987-89, Sun. sch. tchr., 1987—; tchr. Mexia Ind. Sch. Dist., 1986—; sponsor Youth for Christ, Nicoma Park, Okla., 1985-86. Mem. Family Resource and Planning Com., Prairie View A&M, 1990—, Limestone County War on Drugs, Mexia, 1988. Mem. Assn. of Tex. Profl. Educators (sec. 1989, publicity chmn. 1990). Home: Rte 3 Box 254A Mexia TX 76667 Office: Mexia Ind Sch Dist 1010 N Ross Mexia TX 76667

WILKIN, JOHN MARTIN, minister; b. Flushing, N.Y., Dec. 24, 1949; s. John Frederick and Mary Gerda (Bledy) W.; m. Luanna Marie McGraw, June 15, 1973; children: Joshua James, Danae Alisa. BA in Math. cum laude, UCLA, 1973; Diploma in Ministry, LIFE Bible Coll., 1976; postgrad., UCLA, 1973-74, Fuller Theol. Sem., 1992. Ordained to ministry Presbyn. Ch., 1979. Youth dir. First Presbyn. Ch., Sherman Oaks, Calif., 1973; asst. pastor First Foursquare Ch., Van Nuys, Calif., 1976—; chmn. vol. ministries Church on the Way Ministry Coun., Van Nuys, 1987—, supr. maintenance/custodial ops., food svcs. ministry, spl. asst. to pastor, overseeing New Men, Inc., Love L.A., Citywide Bible Studies; dir. Love L.A. Prayer Gatherings, Hollywood, Calif., 1989—. Mem. Christian Ministry Mgmt. Assn. (del. 1980—). Republican. Office: The Church On The Way 14300 Sherman Way Van Nuys CA 91405

WILKINS, BRYAN JAMES, religious organization administrator; b. Fairbury, Nebr., Apr. 22, 1961; s. James Duane and Verna Mae (Kisser) W. BA in Bus. Adminstrn., Evangel Coll., 1983. House framer Horner Constrn., Grand Island, Nebr., 1976-78; with Chief Industries, Grand Island, 1979; salesman Davey's Locker Sportfishing, Newport Beach, Calif., 1980-82; valet mgr. Antonello Ristorante, Santa Ana, Calif., 1983-84; bus. mgr., treas. Colonial Bible Ch., Tustin, Calif., 1984—, athletic dir., 1985—; salesman Omega C.G. Ltd., Chgo., 1986. Recipient Gold Key Art award Nebr. Scholastic Art Soc., 1976; Basic Ednl. Opportunity Grants, 1979-81. Mem. Christian Ministries Mgmt. Assn. Clubs: Chess, Lettermen's (Grand Island) (sec. 1978-79). Avocations: bicycling, running, racquetball, music, drawing. Home: 258 Flower Apt C Costa Mesa CA 92627 Office: Colonial Bible Ch 13601 Browning Ave Tustin CA 92680

WILKINS, HOWELL OSCAR, minister; b. Wilmington, Del., Nov. 15, 1922; s. Howell Oscar Sr. and Lenora (Lee) W.; m. Dorothy Elizabeth Litz, Dec. 29, 1959; 1 child, Howell Oscar Jr. BA in English, Dickinson Coll., 1944; MDiv, Drew U., 1947; MST, Temple U., 1956. Ordained to ministry United Meth. Ch., 1945. Pastor St. John's Ch., Lewisville, Pa., 1945-46, Whatcoat Ch., Camden, Del., 1947-49, Middletown, Del., 1950-55, Hillcrest Ch., Wilmington, 1956-60, St. John's Ch., Seaford, Del., 1961-67; supt. Wilmington Dist., 1968-72, Delmarva Ecumenical Agy., 1970, Asbury Ch., Salisbury, Md., 1973-78; conf. coun. dir., 1979-81; supt. Easton Dist., 1981-86; pastor Richardson Park United Meth. Ch., Wilmington, 1987—. Mem. Christian Peace Conf. Continuation Com., Christians Associated for Rels. with Ea. Europe, N.Y. and Prague, Czechoslovakia, 1973—, Common Cause; chair strategic planning com. Wesley Coll., Dover, Del., 1985—; mem. Europe/USSR com. Nat. Coun. Chs., 1986; bd. dirs. Drayton Retreat Ctr., Worton, Md.; chair Peninsula Conf. Urban Com., 1988—; pres. Community Action Program, Richardson Park, Wilmington, 1990. Mem. World Meth. Coun. Democrat. Office: Richardson Park United Meth Ch 11 N Maryland Ave Wilmington DE 19804

WILKINS, KEITH EDWARD, minister; b. Springfield, Ohio, Dec. 30, 1952; s. David Eugene and Clara Jean (Sanders) W.; m. Nora Lee Miller, Aug. 5, 1972; children: Jamie Edward, Sheree Annette. BA, Warner So. Coll., 1984. Ordained to ministry Ch. of God, 1984. Assoc. pastor South Lake Wales (Fla.) Ch. of God, 1982-84; sr. pastor 1st Ch. of God, London, Ohio, 1984-88, New Castle, Pa., 1988—; coord. mission work camp various missions orgns., 1983, 88—; mem. exec. coun. Ch. of God in Western Pa., 1991—. Contbr. articles to profl. jours. Mem. Inst. for Servant Leadership. Home: 2 W Euclid Ave New Castle PA 16105-2814 Office: 1st Ch of God 12 W Euclid Ave New Castle PA 16105-2814 *In my world of abundance and over indulgence, my eyes have been open to see that most of the world still lives in object poverty. I can therefore no longer allow my cry for self-gratification to drown out the cries of those living in utter destitution. With the help of God, I must do more!.*

WILKINS, MERLIN JAMES, minister, religion educator; b. Nevinville, Iowa, May 1, 1928; s. James and Beulah (Chilcote) W.; m. Margaret Elaine Hirschy, June 26, 1953; children: Michael James, Marla Jo, Marcella Jayne,

Michelle Janine. BA, Taylor U., 1949; MA, N.W. Mo. State U., 1976. Ordained to ministry Christian Ch., 1954. Min. Meth. Ch., Shannon City, Iowa, 1952-63, Disciples Ch., Tingley, Iowa, 1963—; prof. humanities Southwestern Community Coll., Creston, Iowa, 1983—. Mem. NEA, Iowa State Edn. Assn. Home: Rte 1 Tingley IA 50863 Office: Southwestern Community Coll 1501 Townline Creston IA 50801

WILKINS, MICHAEL JAMES, biblical language and literature educator; b. Glendale, Calif., Aug. 7, 1949; s. William Lloyd Wilkins and Barbara Jean (Peale) Campbell; m. Lynne Allison Melia, Dec. 18, 1971; children: Michelle Lynne, Wendy Colleen. AA, Cuesta Coll., 1972; BA, Biola U., 1974; MDiv, Talbot Sch. of Theology, 1977; PhD, Fuller Theol. Sem., 1986. Pastor Carlsbad (Calif.) Evang. Free Ch., 1977-80, Cayucos (Calif.) Community Evang. Free Ch., 1980-83; prof. N.T. lang. and lit. Talbot Sch. of Theology, LaMirada, Calif., 1983—; pastoral scholar in residence San Clemente (Calif.) Presbyn. Ch., 1985—. Author: Concept of Disciple in Matthew, 1988, Following the Master, 1992; editor: Worship, Theology and Ministry in Early Church, 1992; columnist newspaper Herald Examiner, 1986-90. Mem. pub. rels. com. U.S. Surfing Fedn., San Clemente, 1989. Staff sgt. U.S. Army, 1967-70, Vietnam. Biola U. grantee, 1990. Fellow Inst. for Bibl. Rsch., Evang. Theol. Soc.; mem. Am. Acad. Religion, Soc. Bibl. Lit., Cath. Bibl. Assn., Biola Surf Club (faculty advisor La Mirada chpt. 1984—). Office: Biola U Talbot Sch Theology 13800 Biola Ave La Mirada CA 90639

WILKINS, THOMAS WAYNE, minister; b. Houston, Aug. 1, 1958; s Curtis Wayne and Jean Ann (Mills) W.; m. Gayle Lynn Gayden, Aug. 8, 1981; children: Jennifer Lia, Robert Wayne. B.Mus.Edn., Baylor U., 1980; MMus, Southwestern Bapt. Theol. Sem., Ft. Worth, 1985, postgrad., 1990—. Ordained to ministry So. Bapt. Conv., 1986. Minister music and youth First Bapt. Ch., Mart, Tex., 1979; music dir. First Bapt. Ch., Goliad, Tex., 1982; minister music Crestview Bapt. Ch., Dallas, 1983-85; minister music and youth First Bapt. Ch., Smithville, Tex., 1985-88; minister music and edn. Grace Temple Bapt. Ch., Waco, Tex., 1988—; youth orch. dir. Travis Ave. Bapt. Ch., Ft. Worth, 1982-83; prin. hornist Wind Ensemble, Southwestern Bapt. Theol. Sem. Arranger horn duets for Ch. Musician mag., 1988, 89. Vol. Am. Cancer Soc., 1987-88. Mem. Waco Bapt. Assn. (youth dir. 1989-90), Gonzales Bapt. Assn. (music dir. 1986-88, youth dir. 1985, 87-88), Singing Men of Tex., Tex. Music Educators Assn., Phi Mu Alpha. Republican. Home: 3729 Ethel Waco TX 76707 Office: Grace Temple Bapt Ch 3825 Bosque Waco TX 76710

WILKINSON, BRUCE HERBERT, religious publisher, educator; b. Kearny, N.J., Sept. 4, 1947; s. James S. and Joan M. (Heddy) W.; m. Darlene Marie Gahres, Aug. 23, 1969; children: David Bruce, Jennifer Sue, Jessica Joy. BA, Northeastern Bible Coll., N.J., 1969, ThB, 1970; ThM, Dallas Theol. Sem., 1974; DD, Western Conservative Bapt. Sem., 1988. Lic. to ministry Baptist Ch., 1969; editorial asst. Dallas Theol. Sem., mem. faculty, public relations dir. Dallas Theol. Sem. Lay Inst., 1972-74; prof. Bible, Multnomah Sch. Bible, Portland, Oreg., 1974-77; pres., founder Walk Thru the Bible Ministries, Atlanta, 1972—; pres. Nat. Inst. Bibl. Studies, 1980-84, chmn. bd. dirs., 1980-84; mem. adj. faculty Columbia Bible Coll., 1980—; seminar leader, 1972—; bd. dirs. Fellowship of Cos. for Christ, 1979-88; mem. Internat. Council Bibl. Inerrancy, 1978—, exec. rev. com. on new King James bible, 1979-81, mem. com. on Bible Expn., 1982—; chmn. Bible reading and study emphasis Yr. of Bible, 1983. Recipient Faith and Freedom award Religious Heritage of Am., 1986; named Alumnus of Year, Northeastern Bible Coll., 1976. Mem. Am. Mgmt. Assn., Pres. Assn. Author: (with others) Talk Thru the Old Testament, 1983; Talk Thru the New Testament, 1983; Talk Thru the Bible, 1983, Talk Thru Bible Personalities, 1983, The 7 Laws of the Learner, 1991, Almost Every Answer for Practically Any Teacher, 1991, How to Teach Almost Anything to Practically Anyone, 1991, Your Daily Walk: 365 Daily Devotions to Read Through the Bible in a Year, 1991, Family Walk: Love, Anger, Courage, and 49 Other Weekly Readings for Your Family Devotions, 1991, Youthwalk: Sex, Parents, Popularity, and Other Topics for Teen Survival, 1991; pub., exec. editor monthly mag. Daily Walk, 1978—, Closer Walk, 1980—, Family Walk, 1983—, Year of the Bible Devotional Guide, 1983, Youth Walk, 1987—, Lifewalk, 1990; author: Dynamic Bible Teaching, 1982, Book Introductions and Bible Outlines, The Open Bible, 1984; exec. editor: The Daily Walk Bible, 1987, Closer Walk New Testament. Office: Walk Thru the Bible Ministries 61 Perimeter Park Atlanta GA 30341

WILKINSON, KATHIE STEVENS, music minister; b. Raleigh, N.C., Jan. 5, 1952; d. Sherrill Gardner and Marguerite (Godwin) Stevens; m. Fred M. Blackwood, Jan. 23, 1971 (div. 1981); children: Jennifer, Melissa; m. Charles Timothy Wilkinson, Dec. 31, 1983; children: Andrew, Aaron. Student, Meredith Coll., 1979-70; BA, U. N.C., 1972. Min. music Rolesville (N.C.) Bapt. Ch., 1970-71, Calvary Bapt. Ch., Durham, N.C., 1971-73; min. music 1st Bapt. Ch., Garner, N.C., 1974-80, Butner, N.C., 1981-86; min. music Carrboro (N.C.) Bapt. Ch., 1986—; music dir. Yates Bapt. Assn., Durham, N.C., 1990—. Mem. Singing Church Women of N.C. Democrat. Home: 303 Cheryl Ave Durham NC 27712 Office: Carrboro Bapt Ch PO Box 156 Carrboro NC 27510

WILKINSON, LARRY DALE, minister; b. Charlotte, N.C., Sept. 27, 1936; s. Paul B. and Edna (Todd) W.; m. Blevin Ann Gillis, July 20, 1957; children: Eric Eugene, Cynthia Sue, Dale Ann. AB, High Point Coll., 1958; MDiv, Duke U. Div. Sch., 1961; MA in Edn., Wake Forest U., 1972; EdD, U. N.C.-Greensboro, 1976; attended numerous religious seminars. Ordained to ministry United Meth. Ch., 1959. Pastor Woodmont United Meth. Ch., Reidsville, N.C., 1961-66, First United Meth. Ch., Valdese, N.C., 1966-69, Maple Springs United Meth. Ch., Winston-Salem, N.C., 1969-72, Christ United Meth. Ch., High Point, N.C., 1972-76, First United Meth. Ch., Waynesville, N.C., 1976-79, Providence United Meth. Ch., Charlotte, N.C., 1984—; dist. supt. The North Wilkesboro Dist., N.C., 1979-80, The Marion Dist., N.C., 1980-84; vis. prof. psychology dept. High Point Coll., 1974-76; bd. mgrs. The Pastors' Sch. Duke Div. Sch., 1977-80, 88—; mem. exec. com. The Regional Commn. on Campus Ministry, 1979-80, Bd. Higher Edn. and Campus Ministry, The Western N.C. Ann. Conf., 1979-84, The State Commn. on Campus Ministry, 1980-84; mem. Bd. Ordained Ministry Western N.C. Ann. Conf., 1975-79, 1984—; chmn. psychol. guidance com. Western N.C. Ann. Conf., 1976-79; charter mem., bd. mgrs. The Western N.C. Conf. Learning Ctr., Winston-Salem, 1980-84, chairperson, 1980-81; del. to Jurisdictional Conf. of United Meth. Ch., 1980, Gen. and Jurisdictional Confs., 1984, 88. Contbr. articles to profl. jours. Mem. exec. com., bd. dirs. Greater Winston-Salem Wesley Found., 1969-72, Appalachian State U. Wesley Found., 1979-80; mem. exec. com. High Point Coll. Alumni Assn., 1974-76; bd. mgrs., exec. com. Givens Estates Meth. Retirement Community, 1976-84; trustee High Point Coll., 1983—; bd. dirs. High Point Youth Service Bur., High Point Urban Ministries; bd. dirs. High Point chpt. Am. Cancer Soc.; bd. dirs. Mecklenbgburg chpt. Am. Cancer Soc., 1986—, Rookie of Yr. award 1986-87; pres. Reidsville Ministerial Assn., The Valdese Ministerial Assn. Named Boss of Yr., Furniture Capital chpt. Am. Bus. Women's Assn., 1976. Mem. Am. Psychol. Assn., The Am. Assn. Pastoral Counselors, Pfafftown Jaycees (named top Jaycee Club in U.S. 1971). Lodges: Lions, Rotary, Kiwanis. Avocations: aquatic sports; golf; walking; gardening. Office: Providence United Meth Ch 2810 Providence Rd Charlotte NC 28211

WILL, JAMES EDWARD, theology educator; b. Palatine, Ill., Jan. 18, 1928; s. Albert John and Sylvia Violet (Schultz) W.; m. Lois Adelaide Weiss, Aug. 13, 1949 (div. 1982); children: Kristen, Laurie, Michael, Eric, Kevin. BA with high honors, North Cen. Coll., 1949; BD, Evang. Theol. Sem., Naperville, Ill., 1952; PhD, Columbia U., 1962. Ordained to ministry United Meth. Ch., 1952. Youth dir. 1st Evang. United Brethren Ch., Aurora, Ill., 1949-52; pastor Christ Evang. United Brethren Ch., Paterson, N.J., 1952-55; asst. prof., chmn. dept. religion North Cen. Coll., Naperville, 1955-59; successively asst. prof., assoc. prof., prof. philos. theology Evang. Theol. Sem., Naperville, 1959-73; Henry Pfeiffer prof. systematic theology Garrett-Evang. Theol. Sem., Evanston, Ill., 1973—, dir. Peace and Justice Ctr., 1975-85; mem. bd. ministry No. Ill. conf. United Meth. Ch., 1964-74, bd. dirs. Bd. Global Ministries, 1976-80, vice-chairperson com. on coordination; mem. Commn. on Faith and Order, Nat. Coun. Chs., 1970-78, chair panel, 1976-78; vis. prof., lectr. Southwestern Coll., Winfield, Kans., 1978, North Pk. Coll., Chgo., 1979, Cath. U. Lublin, Poland, 1980, Am. U., Washington, 1982, Coun. West Suburban Colls., Lisle, Ill., 1984, Wash. State U., Pullman, 1985, Inter-Faith Acad. Peace, Tantur, Israel, 1986, U. Zimbabwe, 1989, Nyadire Tchrs. Coll., Zimbabwe, 1989; mem. World Meth. Coun., 1986—. Author: Must Walls Divide? The Creative Witness of the Churches in Europe, 1981, A Christology of Peace, 1989; (with others) This We Believe, 1964, Varieties of Christian-Marxist Dialogue, 1978, Process Philosophy and Social Thought, 1981, Three Worlds of Marxist-Christian Encounters, 1985, Theology, Politics and Peace, 1989; editor, author (with others): The Moral Rejection of Nuclear Deterrence, 1985; editor Sem. Rev., 1959-67; mem. editorial bd. explor, 1975-78, Occasional Papers on Religion and Ea. Europe, 1980—; contbr. articles to religious jours. Mem. Bd. Edn. 78, Naperville, 1971-73; pres. Ill. and Greater Chgo. div. UN Assn., 1978-80; chairperson Christians Associated for Relationships with Ea. Europe, 1978-83, mem. exec. com. 1988—; bd. dirs. Inst. for Peace and Understanding, Inst. for Internat. Amity. Named Seminarian Preacher of Yr., Christian Century mag./Chgo. Sunday Evening Club, 1951; Hartmann scholar Evang. Theol. Sem., 1950-51; Assn. Theol. Schs. fellow, 1967-68, 81-82. Mem. Am. Soc. Christian Ethics, Am. Theol. Soc. (v.p. Midwest region 1983, pres. region 1984), Am. Acad. Religion. Office: Garrett-Evang Theol Sem 2121 Sheridan Rd Evanston IL 60201

WILLANS, JEAN STONE, religious organization executive; b. Hillsboro, Ohio, Oct. 3, 1924; d. Homer and Ella (Keys) Hammond; student San Diego Jr. Coll.; m. Richard James Willans, Mar. 28, 1966; 1 dau., Suzanne Jeanne. Asst. to v.p. Family Loan Co., Miami, Fla., 1946-49; civilian supr. USAF, Washington, 1953-55; founder, dir. Blessed Trinity Soc., editor Trinity mag., Los Angeles, 1960-66; co-founder, exec. v.p., dir. Soc. of Stephen, Altadena, Calif., 1967—, exec. dir., Hong Kong, 1975-81; lectr. in field. Republican. Episcopalian. Author: The Acts of the Green Apples, 1974; co-editor: Charisma in Hong Kong, 1970; Spiritual Songs, 1970; The People Who Walked in Darkness, 1977. Address: 1077 Alta Pine Altadena CA 91001 *I am interested in telling as many people as possible about the experience with the Holy Spirit which brings a language unknown to the speaker. I believe this experience is the source of the power of the early church and that anyone who appropriates it receives the power to change many things, not the least of these being himself.*

WILLEBRANDS, JOHANNES GERARDUS MARIA CARDINAL, former archbishop of Utrecht; b. Bovenkarspel, Netherlands, Sept. 4, 1909; s. Herman and Aafje (Kok) W. PhD, U. Rome, 1937; DLitt (hon.), St. Louis U., 1968; D of Rights (hon.), U. Notre Dame, 1970; ThD (hon.), Cath. U, Louvain, Belgium, 1971, Theol. Acad. Leningrad, USSR, 1973; D of Rights (hon.) Cath. U. Am., 1974; DLitt (hon.), St. Olaf Coll., 1976, Coll. St. Thomas, St. Paul, 1979; ThD (hon.), Assumption Coll., 1980, Hellenic Coll., 1985; hon. doctorate, Cath. U., Poland, 1985; ThD (hon.), U. Oxford, Eng., 1987, Cath. U. Munich, 1987; LHD (hon.), Bellarmine Coll., 1987, Seton Hall U., 1987; ThD (hon.), Holy Cross Greek Orthodox Sch. Theology, Brookline, Mass., 1989; DD, St. Michael's Coll., Toronto, Can., 1990. Ordained priest, Roman Cath. Ch., 1934, bishop, 1964, cardinal, 1969; chaplain, Amsterdam, Netherlands, 1937-40; prof. philosophy Filosoficum of diocese Haarlem (Netherlands), 1940-60, dir. Filosoficum, 1945-60; sec. Secretariat for Promoting Christian Unity, Rome, 1960, pres., 1969-89, pres. emeritus of Pontifical Coun. for Promoting Christian Unity, 1989; archbishop of Utrecht (Netherlands), 1975-83. Address: Via dell'Erba 1, 00193 Rome Italy

WILLEMS, ELIZABETH LEODENA, theology educator; b. Cologne, Minn., May 22, 1937; d. John P. and Leodena A. (Siegle) W. BS, Mt. Mary Coll., 1969; MA, Mundelein Coll., 1976, U. Chgo., 1981; PhD, Marquette U., 1986. Tchr. religion Grace High Sch., Mpls., 1969-76; assoc. dir Newman Ctr., Fargo, N.D., 1976-79; lectr. religion N.D. State U., Fargo, 1976-79, Concordia Coll., Moorhead, Minn., 1979; prof. moral theology Notre Dame Sem., New Orleans, 1985—; dir. pastoral field edn. Notre Dame Sem., New Orleans, 1986-90; com. on homosexuality Baton Rouge Diocese, 1985—; speaker on ch. and ethics, 1984—. Author: Adult Commitment, 1990; book reviewer Theol. Studies and Jour. of Am. Acad. Religion. Mem. Women's Group, New Orleans, 1988—; pres. Women's Caucus, Chgo., 1980. Tuition scholar U. Chgo., 1980-81; rsch. grantee Assn. Theol. Schs., New Orleans, 1990-91. Mem. Cath. Theol. Soc. Am., Coll. Theology Soc., Am. Acad. Religion, Soc. Christian Ethics. Democrat. Office: Notre Dame Sem 2901 S Carrollton Ave New Orleans LA 70118

WILLETTS, JEFFORY DEAN, lay worker; b. Berea, Ohio, Oct. 9, 1959; s. John Daniel and Carol (Jean) W.; m. Cathy Helen Swaney, Dec. 26, 1981; children: Jeremy Dean, Joshua David, Justin Daniel. BA in Bible, Cedarville Coll., 1982. Min. of youth Calvary Bapt. Ch., Quincy, Ill., 1982-86; min. of youth First Bapt. Ch., Rochester Hills, Mich., 1986—. Bd. dirs. Women's and Teens' Pregnancy Ctr., Pontiac, Mich., 1991—. Mem. Metro Detroit Bapt. Youth Assn. (sec.-treas. 1989—), Mich. Assn. of Regular Baptist Chs. State Youth Com. Home: 6373 Orion Rd Rochester Hills MI 48306 Office: First Bapt Ch 6377 Orion Rd Rochester Hills MI 48306

WILLHOIT, JIM, minister; b. Springfield, Ill., June 25, 1943; s. Richard and Virginia (Hampton) W.; m. Karen Huddleston, June 19, 1966; children: Amy Lynn, Todd Christopher. BA, Lincoln Christian Coll., 1969; MDiv., Lincoln Christian Sem., 1974, MA, 1975. Ordained to ministry Ch. of Christ, 1971. Minister Salisbury (Ill.) Christian Ch., 1964-72, Walnut Grove Christian Ch., Arcola, Ill., 1972-81; sr. minister First Ch. Christ, Highland, Ind., 1981—; mem. site com. Project 300, Lincoln, Ill., 1979-81; bd. dirs. Onesimus Ministries, 1978-81; chaplain Lake County Police Dept., Crown Point, Ind., 1982-83, Glenwood (Ill.) Police Dept., 1986—. Mem. sch. bd. Unit Dist. 306, Arcola, 1978-81. Mem. Soc. Bibl. Lit., Am. Sci. Affiliation (assoc.), Chgo. Dist. Minister's Assn. (sec.-treas. 1982—). Home: 8936 Schneider Dr Highland IN 46322 Office: First Ch Christ 2420 Lincoln St Highland IN 46322

WILLIAM, SISTER MARIAN, academic administrator. Head Immaculata Coll., Pa. Office: Immaculata Coll Office of Pres Immaculata PA 19345-0901*

WILLIAMS, A. L., bishop; b. Birmingham, Ala., Feb. 6, 1917; s. Willie and Lucile (Sims) W.; m. Katie Floyd; children—Cornelius, Benjamin, Glory, Lynne. Student Miles Coll., U. Ala., Interdenominational Theol. Ctr.; D.Div., Trinity Hall Sem., Louisville, 1980. Ordained to ministry Ch. of Kingdom of God in Christ, 1929, lic. minister, 1931; ordained pastor, 1942. Mem. pub. relations staff U.S. Steel, Birmingham, Ala.; minister Triumph the Ch. and Kingdom of God in Christ, Birmingham, Ala., chief bishop, 1980—; cons., lectr. in field. Address: PO Box 77056 Birmingham AL 35228

WILLIAMS, ALAN, clergyman; b. Montgomery, Ala., June 19, 1952; s. Archie C. and Sybil J. (Glass) W.; m. Terri C. Williams, Jan. 16, 1980; children: Heather, Esther, Christina. Student, U. Tenn., 1977-78, So. Coll., 1980-82; BA in Theology summa cum laude, Oakwood Coll., 1985. Ordained to ministry, Seventh-day Adventist Ch., 1989. Pastor Gulf States Conf. Seventh-day Adventists, Olive Branch, Miss., 1984-87, Ga.-Cumberland Conf. Seventh-day Adventists, Baxley, Ga., 1987-89, Ga.-Cumberland Conf. Seventh-day Adventist Ch., Greeneville, Tenn., 1989; instr. parenting and grief recovery seminars. Guest columnist, Baxley News-Banner, Alma (Ga.) Statesman, 1987-89. Pub. rels. officer Baxley unit Am. Cancer Soc., 1988; instr. Breath Free Smoking Cessation Clinic. Mem. Appling County Ministerial Assn., Internat. Platform Assn. Home: 1705 22d St Lake Charles LA 70601 Office: LC 7th-day Adventist Ch 1537 Country Club Rd Lake Charles LA 70605

WILLIAMS, SISTER BARBARA, academic administrator. Head Georgian Ct. Coll., Lakewood, N.J. Office: Georgian Ct Coll Lakewood NJ 08701*

WILLIAMS, CARL CARNELIUS, JR., minister; b. Jefferson City, Mo., June 29, 1926; s. Carl C. and Stella (Shikles) W. ThB, Anderson Theol. Sem., 1949; BA, Anderson Coll., 1950. Ordained to ministry Ch. of God (Anderson, Ind.), 1952. Pastor in Nebr., 1951-55; sec., treas. Nebr. Ch. of God Campgrounds, 1954-55; pastor Ch. of God, Lawrence, Kans., 1955-57; assoc. min. and sec. Ch. of God, Oklahoma City, 1959-62; pastor S. Agnew Ch., Oklahoma City, 1962-71; pastor Nowata (Okla.) Ch. of God, 1971-74, supr. constrn. of ch. plants, 1970-74; mem. bd. religious edn. Ch. of God Okla., 1971-73; supply pastor Independence (Kans.) Ch. of God, 1974-75. Composer: (words and music) Songbook of 52 Songs, 1974, Songs of Real Joy, 1980, Songs of Real Love, 1986; composer (with Carl C. Williams, Sr.) over 50 hymns, 1944-58; contbr. articles to religious publs. Mem. Nowata Ministerial Assn. (sec. 1972-74). Home: 718 S Delaware St Bartlesville OK 74003 *Life has taught me a valuable lesson; and that is, regardless how dark the world or circumstances around us may be, behind the clouds, God is still there, making intercession for us; and if we keep our eyes on Him, He will give us a victorious life with a sunny disposition, and we shall enjoy an eternity someday with Him forever.*

WILLIAMS, CHARLES D., bishop. Bishop of Alaska Ch. of God in Christ, Anchorage. Office: Ch of God in Christ 2212 Vanderbilt Cir Anchorage AK 99504*

WILLIAMS, DAVID, retired religious organization administrator; b. White Plains, N.Y., Oct. 30, 1904; s. David Louis and Alice Boyd (Johnston) W.; B.S., Princeton U., 1926; M.B.A., Harvard U., 1928; m. Parthenia D. Davis, June 12, 1928; children—Morton D., David L., R. Richardson. Syndicate dept. Kidder Peabody & Co., N.Y.C., 1928-31; security analyst Grayson M-P. Murphy & Co., N.Y.C., 1932-36; merchandiser Lord & Taylor, N.Y.C., 1936-47; divisional mgr. Cheney Bros., N.Y.C., 1947-53; mgmt. cons., N.Y.C., 1954-57; spl. asst. in mktg. Columbia U. Grad. Sch. Bus. Adminstrn., N.Y.C., 1957; prof. bus. adminstrn. Bates Coll., Lewiston, Maine, 1958-74, acting dean of men, 1968-70; acting adminstr. Episcopal Diocese of Maine, 1975-76, mem. Commn. on Ministry, 1976-82, chmn. Loring Program and Fund, 1976-82; v.p. Trustees of Diocesan Funds. Incorporator, Central Maine Gen. Hosp.; treas., chmn. fin. com. Hendrick Hudson council Boy Scouts Am., 1945-47. Mem. Am. Acctg. Assn., Am. Mktg. Assn., Am. Acad. Polit. and Social Scis. Episcopalian (sr. warden, vestryman 1944—). Clubs: Sleepy Hollow County (Scarborough, N.Y.); Martindale (Auburn, Maine). Home: 18 Mountain Ave Lewiston ME 04240

WILLIAMS, DAVID NEWELL, religion educator; b. Tulsa, Sept. 24, 1950; s. David Voorhees Williams and Mary Louise (Newell) Rose; m. Mary Susan McDougal, May 30, 1981; children: David McDougal, Richard Coert. BA, U. Tulsa, 1971; MA, Vanderbilt U., 1975, PhD, 1979. Instr. in religion Colby Coll., Waterville, Maine, 1977-78; asst. dean Brite Divinity Sch., Tex. Christian U., Ft. Worth, 1978-83, assoc. dean, 1983-84; assoc. prof. Christian Theol. Sem., Indpls., 1984—. Author: Ministry Among Disciples, 1985; editor: Case Study of Mainstream Protestantism, 1991; contbr. articles, book revs. to profl. publs. Bd. dirs. Heritage Place, Indpls., 1985—. Mem. Am. Acad. Religion, Am. Soc. Ch. History, Disciples of Christ Hist. Soc. (trustee 1988—), Indpls. Athletic Club. Office: Christian Theol Sem 1000 W 42d St Indianapolis IN 46208

WILLIAMS, DAVID STIDUM, II, minister; b. West Palm Beach, Fla., Feb. 5, 1960; s. David Stidum Sr. and Odessa (McCray) W. Student, Palm Beach Community Coll., 1977; BA, Bethune Cookman Coll., 1981; MDiv, Gammon Theol. Sem., 1985; D. Ministry, Columbia Theol. Sem., 1989. Ordained to ministry United Meth. Ch., 1987. Pastor St. Paul United Meth. Ch., New Smyrna Beach, Fla., 1978-81, Hawthorne (Fla.) Parish, 1985-87, St. Joseph Parish, Jacksonville, Fla., 1987—, Mt. Zion United Meth. Ch., Jacksonville, 1987—; Fla. state pres. Black Meth. for Ch. Renewal, 1990—. Mem. Local Sch. Adv. Coun., Jacksonville, 1988—; mem. State Atty. Learning Enhancement, Jacksonville, 1988—; mem. Mayor's Task Force "Say No to Drugs" campaign, Jacksonville, 1988—; mem. Fla. Community Coll. Adv. Bd., 1989—. Recipient Clergy award Jacksonville Sheriff's Dept., 1988, Outstanding Contbn. award Jacksonville Urban League, 1989, Mental Health Assn., 1989. Mem. Nat. Bus. League, Interdenominational Ministerial Alliance (sec. 1987—), SCLC, Christian Fellowship (v.p. 1989-91), NAACP, Jacksonville Campus Ministry Bd. (treas. 1987—), Omega Psi Phi (v.p. Tau chpt. 1983-85). Democrat. Home and Office: 6050 Glenn Rose Dr Jacksonville FL 32211-3417

WILLIAMS, DELORES J., lay worker; b. Altus, Okla., Apr. 12, 1929; d. Oliver Livingston and Lillie Mae (Edwards) Gardner; m. Robert G. Simpson, June 14, 1954 (div. 1960); 1 child, Russell L. Simpson; m. Sherwood Williams, Nov. 11, 1965; 1 child Dorsey R. BA, World Inst., 1982, MA, 1983, PhD, 1985. Tng. dir.. Corinth Bapt. Ch., Alamogordo, N.Mex., 1961—; pres. Mt. Olive State Conv. Usher, Alamogordo, 1964—; youth dir. New Hope Dist. Assn., 1968—; ch. treas. Corinth Bapt. Assn., Alamogordo, 1985—; v.p. Nat. Bapt. Ushers, Alamogordo, 1990—; supply technician U.S. Army Systems Command, Whitesands, N.Mex., 1974—; instr.-usher New Hope Dist., 1965—; instr. Corinth Bapt. Ch., Alamogordo, 1962—, Congress Christian Edn., 1975—; mem. finance Nat. Bapt. Ushers, 1979-90. County chmn. ARC, Alamogordo, 1973-77; vol. Hosp. Aux., Alamogordo, 1975, Women Who Care, Alamogordo, 1975. Mem. Prince Hall Grand Chpt. (assoc. grand matron 1984), Daus. of Isis (high priest 1982), Order Ea. Star (worthy matron 1979-83, 90-91). Democrat. Home: 511 Panorama Blvd Alamogordo NM 88310

WILLIAMS, DENNIS LEE, church administrator; b. Merced, Calif., June 19, 1958; s. James Kent and Ruby Mae (Zweimiller) W.; m. Vonda Jaine Nieves, April 16, 1983. AA, Centralia (Wash.) Coll., 1978; BA, Western Wash. U., 1981; postgrad., Berean Sch., 1983—. Supr. Payless Northwest, Lacey, Wash., 1981-83; minister Evergreen Christian Ctr., Olympia, Wash., 1983-84; bus. adminstr. Christian Life Assembly, Federal Way, Wash., 1985—. Mem. Am. Mgmt. Assn., Assembly of God Musicians Fellowship. Republican. Avocations: music, theater, sports, camping. Home: 2731 SW 332d Ct Federal Way WA 98023 Office: Christian Life Assembly 629 356th St Federal Way WA 98003-8611

WILLIAMS, DENNY, minister, administrator; b. Lansing, Mich., Nov. 9, 1949; s. Wayne Anson amd Bea (Phillips) W.; m. Judy Marie Hammar, Sept. 11, 1971; children: Leina Jo, Lance Joseph. AA, Lansing Community Coll., 1978; BBA, Northwood Inst., 1979; MBA, Bombay (India) Inst. Mgmt., 1980; DBA, Internat. U., Kansas City, Mo., 1982. Exec. dir. YOU Inc., Ft. Wayne, Ind., 1975-79, Leadership Lifestyle Inst., Kansas City, 1979-83; comptr. Christian Heritage Coll., San Diego, 1984-86; sr. pastor Bethel Ch., Roseville, Mich., 1987-89; adminstr. Coral Ch., Coral Springs, Fla., 1989—; cons. Life Mgmt. Inst., Pompano Beach, Fla., 1989—; chmn. rsch. project Boran Oil Co., Detroit, 1978. Author: Leadership Lifestyle, 1983 (award 1983); contbr. articles to mags. Advisor Secs. Assn. Greater Kansas City, 1980-82; cons. Bapt. Sunday Sch. bd., Nashville, 1981; mem. adv. bd. Wellspring Mission Found., Kansas City, Kans., 1985—. Mem. Christian Ministry Mgmt. Assn., Nat. Assn. Ch. Bus. Adminstrs. Home: 2605 NW 123d Ave Coral Springs FL 33065 *In our fast-passed, complex society, only the honest 'servant' will develop a sense of direction in leading others into the 21st century with God's blessing!.*

WILLIAMS, DONALD EUGENE, religious organization administrator, minister; b. DeLand, Fla., Jan. 4, 1929; s. John and Willie Bertha (Kenner) W., m. Leah Keturah Pollard, Sept. 11, 1954; children: Donald E., Celeste J., Michele A. Student, Shelton Coll., 1951-54. Ordained to ministry Ch. of God (Anderson, Ind.), 1962. Pastor Epworth United Meth. Ch., N.Y.C., 1955-58; assoc. pastor First Ch. of God, Far Rockway, N.Y., 1958-62; pastor North Main Ch. of God, Jamestown, N.Y., 1962-69, United Meth. Ch., East Randolph, N.Y., 1966-68, Ch. of God of Detroit, 1969-76; assoc. exec. sec., Missionary Bd. Ch. of God, Anderson, Ind., 1976-87, dir. Cross-Cultural Edn., World Svc. Exec. Coun., 1987—; chaplain Detroit Police Dept., 1971-76; Ind. State Police chaplain, 1990—. Author: Kenya Literacy Safari, 1966; contbr. articles to ch. publs.; editor: Missions, Messenger & Safari, 1981-87. V.p. Chautauqua County Literacy Coun., 1964-69; mem. Mayor's Commn. Human Rels., Anderson, 1987-89. Recipient Dedicated Svc. award Girls Clubs Am., Jamestown, 1969, Boy's Clubs Detroit, 1975, Outstanding Commitment award Anderson U., 1987. Home: 406 Stuart Circle Anderson IN 46012 Office: 1303 E 5th St Anderson IN 46012 *As I have traveled across the world I have discovered that the greatest riches are to be found not in silver or gold or diamonds or material treasures of any kind, but in the hearts of people.*

WILLIAMS, DONNELL SIL DORSEY, minister, counselor; b. Greenwood, Miss., Sept. 8, 1960; s. McKinley C. and Farris A. Williams. BS, U. Ala., 1984, MA, 1987. Bldg. inspector U. Ala., Tuscaloosa, 1980-85, admissions counselor, 1985-87; pastor, minister AME Zion Ch. of Am., Tuscaloosa, 1984—; psychotherapist Indian Rivers Mental Health Ctr., Tuscaloosa, 1986-87; instr. psychology Stillman Coll., Tuscaloosa, 1987—; research asst. U. Ala., 1984-85, Stillman Coll., 1984—; grad. asst. Minority Affairs U. Ala., 1985-87; academic and career counselor Shelton State Jr. Coll., Tuscaloosa, 1987—. Cons. Tuscaloosa City Schs., 1986-87; probation officer Tuscaloosa Youth Emergency Services, 1983-86; mem. bd. Crescent East Youth Enrichment, Tuscaloosa, 1985—. Named one of Outstanding Young Men of Am., 1986. Mem. Am. Assn. Counseling and Devel., Chi Sigma Iota, Phi Beta Sigma (sec. Tuscaloosa chpt. 1983—), Alpha Phi Omega (dean 1979—). Lodge: Ruth. Home: 3507 8th St Tuscaloosa AL 35402 Office: U Ala PO Box 4354 Tuscaloosa AL 35486

WILLIAMS, EDWARD, bishop. Gen. sec. Bible Way Ch. of Our Lord Jesus Christ World Wide Inc., Bklyn. Office: Bible Way Ch Our Lord Jesus Christ World Wide Inc 5118 Clarendon Rd Brooklyn NY 11226*

WILLIAMS, ERVIN EUGENE, religious organization administrator; b. Corning, N.Y., Feb. 25, 1923; s. Douglas Lewis and Mina P. (Barnes) W.; m. Ruth Evelyn Snyder, June 12, 1945; children: Roger Eugene, Virginia Ruth. Student, Toccoa Falls (Ga.) Bible Coll., 1939, Cornell U., 1942; BA, Pa. State U., 1949; MA, Mich. State U., 1961, PhD in Communications, 1971. Ordained to ministry Ind. Bapt. Ch., 1950. Acad. dean Greensburg (Pa.) Bible Inst., 1949-51; min. Bapt. Ch., New Kensington, Pa., 1951-53; instr. Pa. State U., 1953-55; sr. min. East Lansing (Mich.) Trinity Ch., 1955-71; vis. prof. Trinity Evang. Div. Sch., Deerfield, Ill., 1968-71, prof. communication and practical theology, 1971-77, dir. D Ministry program, 1975-76; gen. dir. Am. Missionary Fellowship, Villanova, Pa., 1977—; chaplain Mich. State U., East Lansing, 1955-71; cons. Evangelism Internat., Inc., Atlanta, 1969-75; lectr. Calvary Bible Coll., Kansas City, Mo., 1962, Haggai Inst. Third World Leaders, Singapore, 1970—; Staley lectr. Robert Wesleyan Coll., North Chili, N.Y., 1973, Judson Coll., Elgin, Ill., 1977—; cons. to mission bds., 1967-76; assoc. dir. Camp of Woods, Speculator, N.Y., 1971-77. Contbr. numerous articles to religious periodicals, also monographs. Trustee Dorothy H. Theis Meml. Found., Sierra Vista, Ariz., 1987—; mem. bd. trustees Gospel Vols., Speculator, N.Y., 1963—; mem. bd. regents Owosso (Mich.) Coll., 1971-73. Pilot USAAF, 1942-45, prisoner of war, ETO, 1945. Mem. Nat. Sunday Sch. Assn., Christian Assn. Psychol. Studies, Mich. Acad. Arts and Scis., Aircraft Owners and Pilots Assn., Phi Beta Kappa, Pi Gamma Mu, Phi Kappa Phi, Alpha Kappa Delta. Home: 19 Moores Rd Malvern PA 19355 Office: Am Missionary Fellowship Box 368 672 Conestoga Rd Villanova PA 19085 *It is much more difficult to conceal ignorance and prejudice than it is to acquire knowledge and fairness.*

WILLIAMS, ETHEL FRANCES (CHINA WILLIAMS), minister, radio personality; b. Shanghai, Republic of China, Sept. 16, 1928; (parents Am. citizens); d. James M. Smith and Mary Edith (Steinwachs) Smith; m. Robert Gayle Williams, Dec. 2, 1950; children: Susan Marie, Joan Diane. BE, U. Hawaii, 1950; DD (hon.), Am. Fellowship, Monterey, Calif., 1981, Coll. D Metaphysics, Glendora, Calif., 1990. Cert. secondary tchr., Calif.; ordained to ministry Am. Fellowship, 1981, College Divine Metaphysics, 1989; grad., lic. tchr., counselor Unity Sch. of Practical Christianity. Tchr. Ontario (Calif.) Sch. Dist., 1956-61, La Mesa-Spring Valley (Calif.) Sch Dist., 1962-83; founding min., pres. Ch. Living Christianity, Spring Valley, 1983—. Bd. dirs. women's com. Rep. Women's Cub, 1983-84, exec. bd. dirs., 1989; bd. dirs. San Diego Youth Symphony, 1981; mem. bd. Spring Valley Youth and Family Svc.; chairperson Communications Com. INTA, 1990. Recipient Outstanding Svc. award La Mesa Tchrs. Assn., 1983, Outstanding Am. Svc. award Le Mesa C. of C., Bi-Centennial, Outstanding Spanish Rels. award Community Spanish Club, San Diego, 1984; named Spark Plug Toastmasters, La Mesa, 1981. Mem. NEA, AAUW, Calif. Retired Tchrs. Assn., Internat. New Thought Alliance (speaker 1989), Internat. Clergy Assn., Assn. Unity Chs., La Mesa Concert Assn. (sec., bd. dirs. 1975-77), Network of San Diego, Nat. Assn. TV Arts and Scis., Heartland Creative Community Assn., Murdock Cultural Found. Office: Ch of Living Christianity 10435 Campo Rd Spring Valley CA 92077

WILLIAMS, GARRY DEE, minister; b. Mobile, Ala., Sept. 25, 1948; s. Dee and Mary Hildred (Shirley) W.; m. Cathy Smith, Dec. 27, 1969 (div. Nov. 1976); children: Stephen Douglas, Scott Allen; m. Alice Luker, Aug. 19, 1978. BS, Mobile Coll., 1971; MDiv, Emory U., 1974; D of Ministry, Trinity Sem., 1986. Ordained to ministry United Meth. Ch. as deacon, 1972, as elder 1981. Min. Rockland United Meth. Ch., Ala., 1971-73, Thorsby United Meth. Ch., 1973-75, Mt. Nebo United Meth. Ch., 1975-79, Uniontown United Meth. Ch., 1979-83, Autaugaville (Ala.) United Meth. Ch., 1983-87, Robertsdale United Meth. Ch., 1987-90, Ebenezer United Meth. Ch., Wagarville, Ala., 1990—. Active Lions Club, Autaugaville, 1983-87. Office: Ebenezer United Meth Church HC65 Box 162-A Wagarville AL 36585 *The greatest challenge facing the church today is to remain true to its mission to witness to the lost about the redemption provided by the Lord Jesus Christ through the power of the Holy Spirit.*

WILLIAMS, GEORGE MASAYASU, religious organization administrator, editor; b. Seoul, Korea, June 16, 1930; came to U.S., 1957; naturalized, 1973; s. Masao and Yae (Yoshimoto) Sadanaga; m. Virginia K. Sueta, Mar. 17, 1961; children: Andrew, Monica, David. BA in Law, Meiji U., Tokyo, 1954, Phd in Polit. Sci., 1988; MA in Polit. Sci., U. Md., 1962. Organizer, gen. dir. Nichiren Shoshu Soka Gakkai of Am., Santa Monica, Calif., 1960—; v.p. Soka Gakkai Internat., 1980—; founding editor, pub. World Tribune, newspaper, 1964—; editor, pub. Seikyo Times mag., 1981—; condr. Buddhist seminars at 80 univs.; hon. exec. dir. Soka U., L.A., 1984—. Author: An Introduction to True Buddhism, Freedom and Influence: The Role of Religion in America. Named Disting. Alumnus U. Md., 1974; fellow Soka U., Tokyo, 1975—. Office: Nichiren Shoshu Soka Gakkai Am 525 Wilshire Blvd Santa Monica CA 90406

WILLIAMS, GWENDOLYN ANN, minister; b. Knoxville, Tenn., May 6, 1945; d. Cleo Steele Hudgens and Lemuel (Stephens) Butler; m. Herbert F. Williams, Jr., Nov. 4, 1967 (div. 1989); children: Vonetra, Sharmean. BBA, Baruch Coll., 1975; student, New Brunswick Theol. Seminary, N.J., 1988—. Asst. minister Fellowship Missionary Bapt., Hempstead, N.Y., 1988-90; minister Church-in-the-Garden, Garden City, N.Y., 1990—; chief fin. officer Econ. Opportunity Coun. of Suffolk, Inc., Coram, N.Y.; choir supr. Shiloh Bapt., Rockville Centre, N.Y., 1985-88, Sunday Sch. tchr., 1985-88; with Fellowship Missionary Bapt. Ch., 1988-91; church choir Church of the Garden, Shiloh Fellowship and Conf., editor ch. newspaper, Garden City, 1990—. Mem. Lions, NAACP, ABC Ministers Coun., ABC Women in Ministry. Home: 1158 Ossipee Rd West Hempstead NY 11552 Office: Economic Opportunity Coun 356 Middle County Rd Coram NY 11727

WILLIAMS, HARRY GEORGE, minister; b. Kokomo, Ind., Aug. 9, 1925; s. Thomas Ralph and Marguerite Ann (Bergman) W.; m. Mary Virginia Carroll, Aug. 25, 1952 (dec. 1972); children: Barbara, Thomas, Kathleen, Mary Beth, Harry, Timothy; m. Trudy Anne Sly, June 17, 1980. BFA in Broadcast Edn., Cin. Coll. Music, 1949; MDiv, Gen. Theol. Sem., N.Y.C., 1978. Ordained priest Episcopal Ch., 1979. Canon residentiary St. Peter's Cathedral, St. Petersburg, Fla., 1978-80; rector/vicar St. Luke's Ch./Our Savior Ch., Lincolnton, N.C., 1980-83; founding rector St. Anne of Grace Ch., Seminole, Fla., 1983—; founding legis. del. Episcopal Synod of Am., Ft. Worth, 1989—; mem. Soc. Holy Cross. With USN, 1943-45. Mem. Evang. and Cath. Mission, Nat. Orgn. Episcopalians for Life. Democrat. Home: 8021 Bayhaven Dr Seminole FL 34646

WILLIAMS, HENRY LAWRENCE, clergyman, librarian; b. Boone, Colo., Apr. 23, 1923; s. John L. and Margaret Evelyn (McKee) W. Student, U. N.Mex., 1941-42; BA, Moravian Coll., 1948; MDiv, Moravian Theol. Sem., Bethlehem, Pa., 1951; MLS, Rutgers U., 1962. Ordained to ministry Moravian Ch., 1952. Pastor Fifth Moravian Ch., Phila., 1952-58; instr. Moravian Coll., Bethlehem, 1955-57, libr., 1958-84; ret., pastor of visitation Nazareth Moravian Ch., 1986—. Author: Bethlehem, A Reflection, 1979, Nazareth 1740, 1986; contbr. articles to profl. jours. Pres. Moravian Hist. Soc., 1973-83; bd. dirs. Sun Inn Preservation Soc., Bethlehem, 1973-75, Moravian Music Found., 1973-87. With U.S. Army, 1942-45, PTO. Recipient Moramus award Moravian Music Found., 1990. Mem. Am. Theol. Libr. Assn., Hymn Soc. Am. (exec. bd. 1973-75), Western History Assn., Western Lit. Assn., Bronte Soc., Rotary. Home: 1609 Chelsea Ave Bethlehem PA 18018

WILLIAMS, HERBERT J., bishop. Bishop of N. Cen. Mich. Ch. of God in Christ, Saginaw. Office: Ch of God in Christ 1600 Cedar St Saginaw MI 48601*

WILLIAMS, HUNTINGTON, JR., bishop suffragan; b. Albany, N.Y., Oct. 27, 1925; s. Huntington and Mary Camilla (McKim) W.; m. Mary Comer Britton, June 18, 1949; children: Sarah Britton, Huntington III, S. Wells, Thomas C. AB, Harvard Coll., 1949; MDiv, Va. Theol. Sem., Alexandria, 1952, DD (hon.), 1991. Ordained to ministry Episcopal Ch. as deacon, 1952, as priest, 1953, as bishop, 1990. Curate St. Thomas Episcopal Ch., Owings Mills, Md., 1952-54; asst. St. George's Episcopal Ch., N.Y.C., 1954-56; rector St. Timothy's Episcopal Ch., Winston-Salem, N.C., 1956-63, St. Peter's Episcopal Ch., Charlotte, N.C., 1963-90; bishop suffragan Diocese of N.C., Raleigh, 1990—; dep. Gen. Conv., 1988; bishop House of Bishops, 1990—; chmn. Constitution and Canons Com., 1977-91; cons. organizational devel., 1973-90. Bd. chair Planned Parenthood, Charlotte, 1976; bd. mem. Hospice, Charlotte, 1976-89. Sgt. U.S. Army, 1943-46. Named Pub. Citizen of Yr., NASW, 1974; Va. Theol. Sem. fellow, 1969. Fellow Coll. Preachers. Democrat. Home: 3412 Coleridge Dr Raleigh NC 27609 Office: Episcopal Diocese of NC PO Box 17025 Raleigh NC 27619

WILLIAMS, JAMES FRANCIS, JR., religious organization administrator; b. Coffeyville, Kans., June 20, 1938; s. James Francis and Sarah Kathryn (Tavenner) W.; m. Alice Carol Williams, June 1, 1963; children: James F. III, Todd Alexander, Leslie. BA, So. Meth. U., 1960; ThM, Dallas Theol. Sem., 1964. Campus dir. Campus Crusade for Christ, Dallas, 1961-64; area dir. Campus Crusade for Christ, various North Tex. locations, 1964-68; regional dir. Campus Crusade for Christ, Southwestern U.S., 1968-71; nat. dir. tng. Campus Crusade for Christ, U.S., 1971-72; founder, pres. Probe Ministries, Internat., Dallas, 1973—; dir. music Campus Crusade for Christ, Arrowhead, Calif., 1967-71. soloist, chorus Dallas Opera, 1982-84. Named one of Outstanding Young Men in Am. Dallas Jaycees, 1965. Evangelical Christian. Office: Probe Ministries 1900 Firman Ste 100 Richardson TX 75081

WILLIAMS, JAMES KENDRICK, bishop. Ed., St. Mary's Coll., St. Mary's, Ky., St. Maur's Sch. Theology, South Union, Ky. Ordained priest Roman Catholic Ch., 1963; ordained titular bishop Catula and aux. bishop of Covington, 1984; ordained first bishop of Lexington, Ky., installed 1988. Office: 1310 Leestown Rd PO Box 12350 Lexington KY 40582-2350 also: PO Box 12350 Erlanger KY 41018

WILLIAMS, JAMES MELVIN, youth minister; b. Clermont, Fla., June 20, 1958; s. James Cherry and Bobbie (Sullins) W. Cert. in real estate, Bert Rogers Sch., 1980; student, Berean Bible Coll., 1987-91. Youth pastor Clermont Assembly of God, 1982—; mgr. Williams Transmission, Clermont, 1976—; del. Peninsular Fla. Dist. Coun., Assemblies of God, Tampa, 1988, Winter Haven, 1989, Winter Park, 1990, Jacksonville, 1991; del. gen. coun. 75th Assembly of God, Indpls., 1989. Active Rep. Party, 1976—. Home: PO Box 120394 Clermont FL 34712-0394 Office: Clermont Assembly of God PO Box 12181 Clermont FL 34712

WILLIAMS, JAMYE COLEMAN, editor, educator; b. Louisville, Dec. 15, 1918; d. Frederick Douglass and Jamye (Harris) Coleman; m. McDonald Williams, Dec. 28, 1943; 1 child, Donna Margaret Williams Selby. BA, Wilberforce U., 1938; MA, Fisk U., 1939; PhD, Ohio State U., 1959. Instr. English Edward Waters Coll., Jacksonville, Fla., 1939-40, Shorter Coll., North Little Rock, Ark., 1940-42; asst. prof. Wilberforce (Ohio) U., 1942-56; assoc. prof. Morris Brown Coll., Atlanta, 1956-58; prof. Tenn. State U., Nashville, 1958-87; editor The A.M.E. Ch. Rev., Nashville, 1984—; alt. mem. Jud. Coun., A.M.E. Ch., 1976-84, pres. 13th dist. lay orgn., 1977-84, sec. bd. incorporators, 1980-92; mem. governing bd. Nat. Coun. Chs., 1979—. Co-editor: The Negro Speaks: The Rhetoric of Contemporary Black Leaders, 1970. Mem. exec. com. Nashville br. NAACP, 1961—; bd. dirs. Nashville chpt. NCCJ, 1988—, Nashville area sect. ARC, 1989—; apptd. by Gov. of Tenn. to Registry of Election Fin., Nashville, 1990—; trustee Wilberforce U., 1990—. Recipient Sarah Allen award Women's Missionary Soc., A.M.E. Ch., 1986, Salute to Black Women award Howard U., 1986; named Tchr. of Yr., Tenn. State U., 1968, 76, Outstanding Connectional Lay Person, A.M.E. Ch., 1983. Home: 2011 Jordan Dr Nashville TN 37218 Office: The AME Rev 500 8th Ave S Ste 211 Nashville TN 37203

WILLIAMS, JAY GOMER, religion educator; b. Rome, N.Y., Dec. 18, 1932; s. Jay Gomer Williams and Mary Christine (Craig) Williams Olson; m. Hermine H. Weigel, Sept. 9, 1956; children: Jay, Lynn, Daryl, Ruth. AB, Hamilton Coll., 1954; BD, Union Theol. Sem., 1957; PhD, Columbia U., 1964. Ordained to ministry Presbyn. Ch. Assoc. dir. Ministry in Nat. Parks, N.Y.C., 1958-60; from instr. to prof. religion Hamilton Coll., Clinton, N.Y., 1960—. Author: Ten Words of Freedom, 1970, Understanding the Old Testament, 1972, Yeshua Buddha, 1978, Judaism, 1980, The Riddle of the Sphinx, 1990, Along the Silk Route, 1991. Mem. Am. Acad. Religion, Hermetic Soc., Am. Theosophical Soc., Soc. for Buddhist-Christian Studies, Soc. for the Study of Chinese Religion. Democrat.

WILLIAMS, JEREMIAH GALLOWAY, minister; b. Sumter, S.C., Nov. 20, 1941; s. Rufus and Annie Mae (Williams) Galloway; m. Delores Wilson, Apr. 25, 1964 (div. 1980); children: Yvette, Denita, Bonita; m. Fannie Mae Gibson, May 20, 1990. BS, Coppins Coll., 1981; MDiv, Howard U., 1985. Ordained to ministry United Meth. Ch. Assoc. pastor Strawbridge United Meth. Ch., Balt., 1980-84, sr. pastor, 1984-87; sr. pastor Garrison Blvd. United Meth. Ch., Balt., 1987—; leader youth Apostolic Chs. Am., Wilson, N.C., 1970-80, chmn. bd. trustees youth conf., 1972-79. Mem. Howard Pk. Community Assn., Balt., 1975, NAACP, Balt., 1979; pres. Citizens for Fairplay Assn., Balt., 1977. With U.S. Army, 1964-66; Vietnam. Mem. Acad. Parish Clergy, Interdenominational Ministerial Assn., Balt. and Annopolis Mission Soc. (exec. bd. 1984—), VFW, Metro-Democrat Club Balt. (bd. dirs.),Operation Outreach Club (bd. dirs.), Alpha Kappa Mu. Home: 3407 Milford Ave Baltimore MD 21207 Office: Garrison Blvd United Meth Ch 2506-08 Garrison Blvd Baltimore MD 21216

WILLIAMS, JERRE STOCKTON, JR., priest; b. Austin, Tex., Sept. 9, 1951; s. Jerre Stockton and Mary Pearl (Hall) W.; m. Leslie Winfield Miller, Dec. 30, 1978; children: Jerre Stockton III, Caroline Winfield. BA cum laude, Amherst Coll., 1973; JD with honors, U. Tex., 1976; MDiv cum laude, Va. Theol Sem., Alexandria, 1986. Briefing atty. U.S. Ct. Appeals (5th cir.), Austin, 1976-77; assoc. Stubbeman, McRae, Sealy, Laughlin & Browder, Austin, 1977-83; asst. rector St. Paul's Episcopal Ch., Waco, Tex., 1986-89; vicar St. Mary's Episc. Ch., Cypress, Tex., 1989—; diocesan clergy pastoral care com., 1987—, diocesan com. on ecumenical rels., 1989—, diocesan com. on constns. and canons, 1987—. Sec., chmn. community Devel. Commn., Austin, 1979-81; sect. chmn. United Way, Waco, 1987-89; active Leadership Austin, 1979-80, Leadership Waco Alumni Assn., 1986-89; bd. dirs. Am. Cancer Soc., Waco, 1987-89, Evangelia Settlement, Waco, 1986-89, sec., 1988-89, Episcopal Youth Waco, 1986-89. Mem. Evang. Edn. Soc., Associated Parishes for Liturgy and Mission, Episcopalians United, Rotary. Democrat. Home: 10515 Laneview Dr Houston TX 77070 Office: St Mary's Episc Ch 15415 N Eldridge Pkwy Cypress TX 77429

WILLIAMS, JESSIE WILLMON, lay worker, retired librarian; b. Boynton, Okla., Feb. 23, 1907; d. Thomas Woodard and Eliza Jane (Adams) Willmon, m. Thomas Washington Williams, Dec. 12, 1946 (dec.). BA, East Tex. State U., 1930, MA, 1944. cert. English and Spanish tchr., Tex. Libr. Gladewater (Tex.) Pub. Libr., 1935-46; med. libr. VA Hosp., North Little Rock, Ark., 1946-58; base libr. Little Rock AFB, 1958-68; ret., 1968; lay worker 1st Bapt. Ch., Pecan Gap, Tex., 1988—. Mem. Delta Kappa Gamma, Phi Beta Kappa. Democrat. Mem. So. Bapt. Conv. Home: PO Box 43 Pecan Gap TX 75469 *Proverbs 30: 8-9 summarizes the good life for me! "Remove far from me vanity and lies; give me neither poverty nor riches; feed me with food convenient for me; lest I be full and deny thee and say 'Who is the Lord?' or lest I be poor and steal, and take the name of my God in vain.*

WILLIAMS, JOHN ALDEN, humanities educator; b. Ft. Smith, Ark., Sept. 6, 1928; s. Ray Edwin and Elizabeth Alden (Blair) W.; m. Caroline Hoffmann, June 5, 1967; children: Emily, Hilary, Felicity. BA, U. Ark., 1953; MA, Princeton U., 1957, PhD, 1958. Assoc. dir. Am. Rsch. Ctr. in Egypt, 1957-59; from asst. prof. to assoc. prof. McGill Inst. Islamic Studies, Montreal, Can., 1959-66; dir., prof. Ctr. for Arab Studies, Am. U., Cairo, Arab Republic of Egypt, 1966-72; prof. Am. U. in Cairo, 1972-84, U. Tex., Austin, 1972-88; William R. Kenan Jr. prof. of humanities Coll. of William and Mary, Williamsburg, Va., 1988—. Editor: Islam, 1961, Themes of Islamic Civilization, 1971; translator: The Abbasī Revolution, 1985, The Early Abbasī Empire, Vol. 1, 1988, Vol. 2, 1989. With U.S. Army, 1946-48. Mem. Am. Soc. for Study of Religion, Middle East Studies Assn. Office: Coll of William and Mary Dept Religion Williamsburg VA 23185 *The Muslim World is deeply challenged today to understand how profoundly human society has been altered by technology. In this, it is like the rest of us.*

WILLIAMS, JOHN RODMAN, theologian, educator; b. Clyde, N.C., Aug. 21, 1918; s. John Rodman and Odessa Lee (Medford) W.; m. Johanna SerVaas, Aug. 6, 1949; children: John, Lucinda Lee, David Bert. AB, Davidson Coll., 1939; BD, Union Theol. Sem., 1943, ThM, 1944; PhD, Columbia U., 1954. Ordained to ministry Presbyn. Ch., 1943. Chaplain USNR, 1944-46; chaplain, assoc. prof. philosophy Beloit Coll., 1949-52; pastor First Presbyn. Ch., Rockford, Ill., 1952-59; prof. systematic theology and philosophy of religion Austin Presbyn. Theol. Sem., 1959-72; prof. Christian doctrine, pres. Melodyland Sch. Theology, Anaheim, Calif., 1972-82; prof. Christian theology Regent U., Virginia Beach, Va., 1982—. Author: Contemporary Existentialism and Christian Faith, 1965; The Era of the Spirit, 1971; The Pentecostal Reality, 1972; Ten Teachings, 1974; The Gift of the Holy Spirit Today, 1980; Renewal Theology, Vol. 1, 1988, Vol. 2, 1990; God, the World and Redemption, 1988; Salvation, the Holy Spirit, and Christian Living, 1990. Home: 4105 Ace Ct Virginia Beach VA 23462 Office: Regent U Virginia Beach VA 23464 *There is only one ultimate "Who", Jesus of Nazareth, in whose light all the rest of us are but dimly burning candles.*

WILLIAMS, KEITH WILBUR, educator, minister; b. Los Angeles, Aug. 31, 1928; s. Walter Oliver and Helen (Jarvis) W.; m. Carmella Nacci, July 22, 1950; children: Timothy Keith, David Walter. BA, Wayne State U., 1950; MDiv, Fuller Theol. Sem., 1953; MA, La. State U., 1964; postgrad. Fla. State U., U. Miami, San Jose State U., Stetson U., Northwestern U., Loyola U., Chgo. Ordained to ministry, Baptist Ch., 1953. Home missionary CBHMS, Penobscot Indians, Maine, 1954; minister West Cannon Bapt. Ch., Grand Rapids, Mich., 1955-57, Berean Bapt. Ch., South Holland, Ill., 1957-58; asst. pastor Marquette Manor Bapt. Ch., Chgo., 1958-60; tchr. math. North Miami Sr. High Sch. (Fla.), 1960-64; prof. math Miami Dade Community Coll. North Campus, 1964—; mem. St. Andrews Presbyn. Ch. Mem. Nat. Council Tchrs. Math., Fla. Tchrs. Math., Math. Assn. Am., United Faculty of Fla. (past pres.), Two Year Coll. Council of Tchrs. Math in Fla. (past pres.), Nat. Model R.R. Assn., South Fla. Soc. Model Engrs., Rwy. and Locomotive Hist. Soc., Humane Soc. Broward County, Gold Coast R.R. and Mus. Mem. Gideons Internat. Author: Arithmetic: A Semi Programmed Text, 1970; (with others) Introduction to College Mathematics, 1972. Home: 611 SW 68th Ave Pembroke Pines FL 33023 Office: 11380 NW 27th Ave Miami FL 33167

WILLIAMS, KENNETH DANIEL, religious organization administrator; b. Leesburg, Fla., Dec. 10, 1963; s. James Daniel and Beatrice Geneva (Crawford) W.; m. Shawna Lou Letcher, Oct. 27, 1990. B in Music Edn., Fla. State U., 1985; MA, Southwestern Seminary, Fort Worth, 1987. Min. edn., adminstrn. 1st Bapt. Ch., Leesburg, Fla., 1987—. Republican. Office: 1st Bapt Ch Leesburg 220 N 13th St Leesburg FL 34748

WILLIAMS, KEVIN ERROLL, minister; b. Detroit, Nov. 11, 1957; s. Thomas Elder and Lois Theresa W.; m. Frieda Gail Davis, July 28, 1979; children: Micah Jo-El, Isaiah Luke. BA, Grand Rapids Bapt. Coll., 1986; MA in Christian Edn., So. Bapt. Theol. Sem., 1990. Ordained to ministry Bapt. Ch. Assoc. min. Temple of Faith Bapt. Ch., Detroit, 1974-83, mission pastor, 1989—; youth min. Messiah Missionary Bapt. Ch., Grand Rapids, Mich., 1983-87; tchr. Evang. Tchr. Tng. Assn., Detroit, 1976-90. Home: 22171 Cloverlawn Oak Park MI 48237

WILLIAMS, KIM ERIC, minister; b. West Chester, Pa., Nov. 1, 1943; s. Paul Ellsworth and Marjorie Elizabeth (Talley) W.; m. Jeannette Louise Tobing, Aug. 26, 1972; children: Lovisa Aurora, Pia Katarina, Justin Eskil. AB, Muhlenberg Coll., 1965; MDiv, Luth. Theol. Sem., Gettysburg, Pa., 1969; D Ministry, Grad. Theol. Found., 1986; postgrad., Uppsala U., 1972-73. Ordained to ministry Luth. Ch., 1969. Pastor Bethany Luth. Ch., North bergen, N.J., 1969-72, Täby Parish, Stockholm Diocese, Ch. of Sweden, 1972-73, Good Shepherd Luth. Ch., Lindenwold, N.J., 1973-79, St. Mark's Luth. Ch., Bridgeport, Conn., 1982-87; enabler So. Caribbean Project, Luth. Ch. Am., Port-of-Spain, Trinidad and Tobago, 1979-80; sr. pastor Concordia Luth. Ch., Manchester, Conn., 1987—; ecumenical officer State of Conn., New Eng. Synod Evang. Luth. Ch. Am., 1988—; bd. dirs. Christian Conf. Conn., Hartford, 1988—, chair Faith and Order Commn., 1991—; bd. dirs., chmn. worship com. Manchester Area Conf. Chs., 1987—; rep. New Eng. Synod Luth. Archives Ctr., Luth. Sem., Phila., 1990—. Vol. Samaritan Shelter, Manchester, 1987—; mem. Bread for the World, Washington, 1989—, Wadsworth Atheneum, Hartford, 1990—, Manchester Interracial Coun., 1987—. Me. New Eng. Luth. Hist. Soc. (pres. 1986-89, editor jour. 1989—, bd. dirs. 1984—), New Eng. Luth. Episcopal Dialogue, Luth./Anglican Soc., Liturgical Conf., Nature Conservancy. Home: 434 Foster St South Windsor CT 06040 Office: Concordia Luth Ch 40 Pitkin St Manchester CT 06040

WILLIAMS, LOUISE ANITA, advertising consultant, missionary; b. Portland, Oreg., Mar. 31, 1942; d. Homer Bruce and Ora Ellen (Diehl) W.; student public schs., Beaverton, Oreg.; 1 dau., Tiffany Joy Wlecial. Med. asst., physicians' practice, 1963-64; adminstrv. asst. St. Vincent's Hosp., 1964-70; salesman, sales mgr., nat. sales mgr. Indsl. Systems, 1970; regional sales mgr. Peel O'Matique, 1971; bus. devel. rep. Imperial Bank, 1971-72; pvt. practice fin. cons., Los Angeles, 1972-73; sales rep. Printing Services, Granada Hills, Calif., 1976; partner Art, Love, Time & Money, Marina City, Calif., 1978-79; pres., sole stock holder Corporate Creative Services, Sherman Oaks, Calif., 1979-85; advt. cons., Orange, Calif., 1985—; founder, exec. dir. C.H.R.I.S.T., El Toro, Calif., 1989—. Commr. Status of Women, Orange County, 1986-89; mem. Rep. Presdl. Task Force. Served with Hosp. Corps, USN, 1960-63. Named Angel of Yr. Childhelp USA, Los Angeles, 1984. Mem. Nat. Assn. Female Execs., Los Angeles Ad Club, Women in Bus., Nat. Assn. Women Bus. Owners, Western Los Angeles C. of C., Sales and Mktg. Execs., Med. Mktg. Assn., Sherman Oaks C. of C. Republican. Mem. Metro Church. Clubs: Buckley Parents Assn., Mid Town Exec. (Los Angeles). Home: 24331 Muirlands Blvd 4-331 El Toro CA 92630

WILLIAMS, LOWELL D., minister; b. Casey, Ill., June 25, 1931; s. Bryan Daniel and Gladys (Chapman) W.; widowed; children Kimberly Williams Wiston, Dan Williams, Dena Williams Nieman. BA, Abilene Christian U., 1956, MA, 1958. Ordained to ministry Ch. of Christ, 1954. Min. Ch. of Christ, Rochelle, Tex., 1954-56, Las Vegas, 1956-57, Trent, Tex., 1957-58, Beaverton, Oreg., 1958-60; min., elder Ch. of Christ, Kirkland, Wash., 1960—; dir. Kirkland Bible Sch., 1961-91; speaker Ch. of Christ, U.S. and The Philippines, 1961-91; speaker radio program Ask Your Preacher. Contbr. articles to religious papers; speaker bible on video and audio cassette. Sgt. USAF, 1950-54, Korea. Republican. Home: 506 W Main St Monroe WA 98272 Office: Ch of Christ 10421 NE 140th St Kirkland WA 98034

WILLIAMS, MARK ALAN, minister; b. St. Louis, Mar. 15, 1955; s. Claude Aaron and Barbara Harriet (Updyke) W.; m. M. Carolyn Fox, Aug. 4, 1979; children: Gabriel, Daniel, Benjamin. Diploma, Moody Bible Inst., Chgo., 1976; BA, Biola U., 1978; MDiv, Talbot Sem., La Mirada, Calif., 1981; D Ministry, Fuller Sem., Pasadena, Calif., 1990. Lic. to ministry Conservative Bapt. Assn. Am., 1981. Asst. producer Sta. WMBI Christian Radio, Chgo., 1974-76; travel asst. Josh McDowell Ministry, Dallas, 1978-79; ch. planting missionary Conservative Bapt. Home Missions Soc., Wheaton, Ill., 1981-84; sr. pastor Emmanuel Bapt. Ch., Vista, Calif., 1984—; area coord. Conservative Bapts. of So. Calif., Anaheim, 1987—. Participant Operation Rescue, San Diego, 1989; mem. bd. dirs. Lawson YMCA, Chgo., 1975-76. Republican. Home: 5844 Spur Ave Oceanside CA 92057 Office: Emmanuel Bapt Ch 342 Eucalyptus Ave Vista CA 92084

WILLIAMS, MARK ANTHONY, minister; b. Morristown, Tenn., Jan. 5, 1957; s. Robert Burl Williams and Betty Lois (Pinkston) W.; m. Deborah Ann Walker, Dec. 27, 1980; children: Brett Anthony, Kasey Ann. BS, Carson Newman Coll., 1979; MDiv, Southwestern Bapt. Theol. Sem., 1983; postgrad., Luther Rice Sem., 1991—. Ordained to ministry So. Bapt. Conv., 1982. Pastor Happy Hills Bapt. Ch., Alvarado, Tex., 1982-85, Blue Springs Bapt. Ch., Rutledge, Tenn., 1985-88, New Hopewell Bapt. Ch., Knoxville, Tenn., 1988—. Office: New Hopewell Bapt Ch 943 Kimberlin Heights Rd Knoxville TN 37920

WILLIAMS, MARY CAROL, minister; b. Greensboro, N.C., Dec. 24, 1953; d. Kenneth and Marth (Harwell) W.; m. Thomas J. Kowalski, May 19, 1979 (div. Apr. 1984); m. George N. Gilbert, Oct. 17, 1987; 1 child, Caroline Pennington. BA in Religion, Catawba Coll., 1976; MA, Duke U., 1979. Ordained to ministry Meth. Ch., 1977. Assoc. minister Cen. United Meth. Ch., Asheboro, N.C., 1979-81, Trinity United Meth. Ch., Tallahassee, 1981-82; minister Calvary United Meth. Ch., Tallahassee, 1982-86, Hickory Grove/Sedgefield Lakes United Meth. Chs., Greensboro, 1986—; chaplain Jr. Women's Club, Tallahassee, 1982-85; chaplain Moses Cane Hosp., Greensboro, 1986—. Mem. Am. Assn. Pastoral Counselors (student), Bd. Ordained Ministry, Greensboro Meth. Ministers (pres.). Democrat. Avocations: tennis, gardening. Home: 1228 Guilford Coll Rd Jamestown NC 27282 Office: Hickory Grove United Meth Ch 5959 Hickory Grove Rd Greensboro NC 27410

WILLIAMS, MICHAEL ALLEN, religion educator; b. Paducah, Ky., Aug. 30, 1946; s. Gerald Leon and Mary Sue (Walker) W.; m. Mary Louise Rodriguez, May 21, 1968; children: Melissa Ann, Mary Elizabeth. BA, Abilene Christian U., 1968; MA, Miami U., Oxford, Ohio, 1970; PhD, Harvard U., 1977. Asst. prof. religion U. Wash., Seattle, 1976-83, assoc. prof., 1983—, chmn. comparative religion program, 1985—, prof. liberal arts, 1990-91; com. mem. Christian Century Lectureship N.W., Seattle, 1983-87; adj. faculty mem. N.W. Theol. Union, Seattle, 1985—; prof.-chercheur invité Projet Nag Hammadi, U. Laval, Que., Can., 1991. Author: The Immovable Race, 1985; editor: Charisma and Sacred Biography, 1982; co-editor Innovation in Religious Traditions, 1991; translator: Martin Dibelius' Commentary on the Epistle of James, 1976; contbr. numerous articles to profl. jours. and essays collections. Research grantee U. Wash., Seattle, 1979, Am. Research Ctr., 1987. Mem. Am. Acad. Religion, Soc. Bibl. Lit. (editorial bd. jour. 1990—), Assn. Coptic Studies, Am. Rsch. Ctr. Egypt. Mem. Christian Ch. Office: U Wash Comparative Religion Program DR-05 Seattle WA 98195

WILLIAMS, MILTON A., bishop. Bishop 12th Episcopal dist. A.M.E. Zion Ch., Greensboro, N.C. Office: AME Zion Ch 1706 Lewellyn Dr Greensboro NC 27408*

WILLIAMS, PETER WILLIAM, religion educator; b. Hollywood, Fla., Aug. 8, 1944; s. William John and Harriet Elizabeth (Stacey) W.; m. Ruth Ann Alban, June 1, 1980; children: Jonathan A. Schneider, Dana A. Schneider. AB, Harvard U., 1965; MA, Yale U., 1967, M. Philosophy, 1968, PhD, 1970. Prof. religion Miami U., Oxford, Ohio, 1970—. Author: America's Religions, 1990, Popular Religion in America, 1980; editor: Encyclopedia of the American Religious Experience, 1988; editorial bd. Anglican and Episcopal History, 1990—. Lay reader Episc. Ch. of So. Ohio. Mem. Am. Soc. Ch. History (coun. mem. 1989-91), Am. Acad. Religion, Cath. Hist. Assn. Democrat. Episcopalian. Home: 206 Oak Hill Dr Oxford OH 45056 Office: Miami U Dept Religion The Old Manse Oxford OH 45056

WILLIAMS, RAYMOND ALAN, music minister; b. Muskegon, Mich., Oct. 10, 1945; s. David Harold and Virginia Pearl (Nelson) W.; m. Barbara Ann Ross, Jan. 9, 1971; children: Chad David, Bradley Dale, Misty Rae. Diploma, Moody Bible Inst., 1967. Min. music and youth Temple Bapt. Ch., Portsmouth, Ohio, 1970-74, Grace Bapt. Ch., Lorain, Ohio, 1974-76; min. music First Bapt. Ch., New Philadelphia, Ohio, 1976—; dir. Super Sixties (sr. citizen program), New Philadelphia, 1980—. With U.S. Army, 1968-69, Vietnam. Decorated Bronze Star. Home: Rte 7 Box 7500 New Philadelphia OH 44663 Office: First Bapt Church 878 Commercial Ave SW New Philadelphia OH 44663

WILLIAMS, RAYMOND BRADY, humanities educator; b. Bluefield, W.Va., Nov. 6, 1935; s. James Madison and Virginia (Brookey) W.; m. Lois Raye Baldwin, June 5, 1956; children: Kevin Michael, Thayer Lynn Kramer, Brian Scott. AB, Johnson Bible Coll., 1957, Phillips U., 1960; B.D., Phillips U., 1960; MA, PhD, U. Chgo., 1966. LaFollette Disting. prof. in the humanities Wabash Coll., Crawfordsville, Ind., 1965—; bd. trustees, sec. Disciples Divinity House, U. Chgo., 1986-91. Author: A New Face of Hinduism, 1984, Religions of Immigrants from India and Pakistan, 1988 (Disciples Book award 1990). Smithsonian Rsch. grantee Smithsonian Inst., 1990, Rockefeller Found., 1985-87. Mem. Am. Acad. Religion (bd. dirs., exec. com. 1989-92), Midwest Am. Acad. Religion (sec.-treas. 1989-92). Mem. Christian Ch. Home: 10 Locust Hill Crawfordsville IN 47933 Office: Wabash Coll Dept Philosophy & Religion Crawfordsville IN 47933

WILLIAMS, RHYS, minister; b. San Francisco, Feb. 27, 1929; s. Albert Rhys and Lucita (Squier) W.; m. Eleanor Hoyle Barnhart, Sept. 22, 1956; children: Rhys Hoyle, Eleanor Pierce. AB, St. Lawrence U., 1951, BD, 1953, DD (hon.), 1966; postgrad., Union Sem., summer 1956; LLD (hon.), Emerson Coll., 1962. Ordained to ministry Unitarian Ch., 1954. Min. Unitarian Ch., Charleston, S.C., 1953-60, 1st and 2d Ch., Boston, 1960—; mem. faculty, field edn. supr. Harvard U., 1969—; Russell lectr. Tufts U., 1965, Minns lectr., 1986. Pres. Edward Everett Hale House, 1987—, Soc. Cin., State N.H., 1986-89; v.p. Benevolent Fraternity Unitarian Universalist Chs., 1982—, Franklin Inst., 1981—; sec. bd. trustees Emerson Coll., 1962—; chaplain General Soc. Cin., Washington, 1977—, New Eng. coun. Navy League, 1980—; chmn. Festival Fund, Inc., Am.-Soviet Cultural Exch., 1989—; trustee Opera Co. Boston, 1970—; trustee Meadville Lombard Theol. Sch., Chgo., 1971-77, ministerial fellowship com., 1961-69, chmn., 1968-69; fin. chmn. Ch. Larger Fellowship, 1968-86; mem. Semetic Mus. Harvard U. Mem. Unitarian Universalist Mins. Assn. (pres. 1968-70), Unitarian Hist. Soc. (pres. 1960-75), Evang. Missionary Soc. (pres. 1965-80, v.p. 1980—), Soc. for Propagation Gospel Among Indians and Others in N.Am. (v.p. 1975—), Unitarian Svc. Pension Soc. (pres. 1973—), Soc. Ministerial Relief (mem. com. for ch. staff fin., pres. 1975—), Colonial Soc. Mass., Beta Theta Pi (pres. New Eng. 1964-66). Office: 1st and 2d Church in Boston 66 Marlborough St Boston MA 02116

WILLIAMS, ROBERT CARL, SR., academic administrator; b. Cin., Oct. 11, 1941; s. Eddie and Iona (Scott) W.; m. Joyce D. Odems, Dec. 9, 1967; children: Robert Jr., Sheri, Roderic, Margaret Iona. BTh, Bay Ridge Christian Coll., 1970; MEd, U. So. Miss., 1976, EdD, 1982. Pastor Ch. of God, Anderson, Ind., 1970-81; tchr. spl. edn. Concordia Parish Sch. System, Vidalia, La., 1973-83, assessment tchr., 1983-86; pres. Bay Ridge Christian Coll., Kendleton, Tex., 1987—; coord. curriculum guide Concordia Parish, 1984; mem. Gen. Assembly Ch. of God, Anderson. Coord. Regional Very Spl. Arts Festival, Concordia Parish, 1982-83; mem. Commn. on Christian Higher Edn., Anderson, 1991. With USN. Mem. Am. Assn. for Counseling and Devel., Phi Delta Kappa. Home: PO Box 865 East Bernard TX 77435

WILLIAMS, ROBERT DALE, JR., minister; b. Ames, Iowa, Sept. 29, 1950; s. Robert Dale and Peggy Ann (Cochrane) W.; m. Nora Elizabeth Heflin, June 9, 1973; children: Felder, John, Benjamin. BS, MIT, 1972; MDiv, Gordon-Conwell Theol. Sem., 1976; D Ministry, Columbia Theol. Sem., 1987; postgrad., Union Theol. Sem., 1987—. Ordained to ministry Presbyn. Ch. (U.S.A.), 1976. Pastor Heritage Presbyn. Ch., Memphis, 1976-85; assoc. minister Marble Collegiate Ch., N.Y.C., 1985—. Home: 208 Steilen Ave Ridgewood NJ 07450 Office: Marble Collegiate Ch 1 W 29th St New York NY 10001

WILLIAMS, ROBERT LEO, minister; b. Meridian, Miss., Aug. 20, 1949; s. Percy Lafayette and Bertha Ross (Ledbetter) W.; m. Karen Patricia Brown, June 21, 1969; children: Stephanie Kay, Robert L. II. Diploma in pastoral studies, Moody Bible Inst., Chgo., 1971. Ordained to ministry So. Bapt. Conv., 1991. Youth min. Bethal Bapt. Ch., Cleveland Heights, Ohio, 1972-72; dir. mission world Billy Graham Evangelistic Assn., Mpls., 1972—; bd. mem. Youth for Christ, Mpls., 1990—. Contbr. articles to mags. Republican. Office: Billy Graham Evangelistic Assn 1300 Harmon Pl Minneapolis MN 55403 *In my opinion, character is the most important determinant of a person's success, achievement, ability to handle adversity and create change.*

WILLIAMS, RONALD DEAN, minister, educator, editor; b. Decatur, Ill., Oct. 23, 1940; s. Henry Lawrence and Ella Loudica (Williams) W.; m. Carole Jeanette Lane, June 16, 1962; children: Scott Allan, Mark Lawrence, Derek James. ThB, LIFE Bible Coll., 1965; postgrad., Fuller Sem., 1988—. Ordained to ministry Internat. Ch. of the Foursquare Gospel, 1967. Pastor, ch. planter, mem. Bible Coll. faculty Internat. Ch. of the Foursquare Gospel, Vancouver, B.C., Can., 1965-69; missionary, mission adminstr. Internat. Ch. of the Foursquare Gospel, Hong Kong and China, 1969-85; denomination exec., editor, prof. Internat. Ch. of the Foursquare Gospel, L.A., 1985—, also bd. dirs. Editor Foursquare World Advance, 1985—; host radio program Foursquare Missions Update, 1985-90; contbr. articles to coll. curriculum. With USAF, 1958-61. Mem. Evang. Press Assn., Internat. Pentecostal Press Assn. (vice chmn. 1988—). Office: Internat Ch of the Foursquare Gospel 1910 Sunset Blvd Ste 200 Los Angeles CA 90026

WILLIAMS, RONALD EUGENE, minister, evangelist; b. Sioux Falls, S.D., Dec. 9, 1942; s. Donald Arthur and Marjorie Jane (Cook) W.; m. Patricia Ann Simms, Aug. 10, 1963; children: Donald, Heather, Daniel, Aaron, Joel, Naomi, Benjamin, Seth, Jesse. BA, Augustana Coll., Sioux Falls, 1964; MDiv, Grace Sem., Winona Lake, Ind., 1979; DD (hon.), Great Plains Bapt. Coll., Sioux Falls, 1987. Ordained to ministry Bapt. Ch., 1972. Dir. Hephzibah House, Winona Lake, 1971—; pastor, founder Believers Bapt. Ch., Warsaw, Ind., 1975—; evangelist U.S.A., Can., 1975—. Author: Man in Charge, 1976, Correction and Salvation of Children, 1976; contbr. articles to profl. jours. With USMCR, 1960-66. Named Fighting Fundamentalist of Yr., Fairhaven Bapt. Coll., 1989. Republican. Office: Hephzibah House 508 School St Winona Lake IN 46590 *If one looks at the alarming erosion of moral values in our land, one could became discouraged in the ministry. However, Biblical Christianity has always been a faith exemplified by a remnant.*

WILLIAMS, STEVEN MARK, worship and music minister; b. Harrisburg, Pa., Nov. 14, 1959; s. Richard Bailey and Virginia (Thomas) W. MusB, Syracuse (N.Y.) U., 1981; M in Sacred Music, Boston U., 1985. Music dir. St. Joseph Parish, Belmont, Mass., 1983-85; worship and music minister St. Francis de Sales Ch., Houston, 1987-91; dir. music Plymouth Congl. Ch., Seattle, 1991—. Mem. Am. Guild Organists, Societas Liturgica, Choristers Guild. Office: Plymouth Congl Ch 1217 Sixth Ave Seattle WA 98101

WILLIAMS, THOMAS STAFFORD CARDINAL, archbishop of Wellington; b. Wellington, N.Z., Mar. 20, 1930; s. Thomas Stafford and Lillian Maude (Kelly) W. S.T.L., Pontifical U. de Propaganda Fide, Rome, 1960; B. Soc. Sc., Nat. U. of Ireland (Dublin), 1962; ordained priest Roman Catholic Ch., 1959; Archbishop of Wellington, 1979—; elevated to Sacred Coll. Cardinals, 1983.

WILLIAMS, THORNTON, JR., deacon; b. Chgo., Mar. 7, 1942; s. Thornton Sr. and Gertrude (White) W.; m. Savada Rhoden, Dec. 31, 1977; 1 child, Curtis T. BS in Pub. Video, Columbia Coll., 1991; postgrad., Logos Christian Coll., 1990—. Ordained to ministry Christian Ch. as deacon, 1981. Libr. New Christian Union Ch., Chgo., 1986-87, pub. affairs, deacon, 1987-88; safety man Deluxe Check Printer Co., Chgo., 1971-83; bd. dirs. mission and Christian Coll. campus, Christian Ch., 1991; bd. dir. Love and Faith Outreach Ctr., 1987, Love and Faith Museum, Chgo., 1988-89; pres., owner Dot Transp., Chgo., 1982-84. Author: (video) Gospel in Our Lives, 1989. Mem. So. Bapt. Assn. Brotherhood (bd. dirs.), Video Graphy (events and documentry cameraman). Home: 7555 S Hermitage Chicago IL 60620 Office: Peter DeBartolo Found 410 S Michigan Rm 613 Chicago IL 60605 *I do believe that special people, young or old, do have a part to play in our great country.*

WILLIAMS, WESLEY KEITH, religious educator, consultant; b. DuQuoin, Ill., Aug. 7, 1953; s. Benjamin Wesley and Jessica Lovedith (Newman) W.; m. Carol Lynn Wise, June 13, 1975; 1 child, Allison Suzanne. BS, Union U., Jackson, Tenn., 1975; M.R.E., Southwestern Bapt. Theol. Sem., 1977. Minister of edn. First Bapt. Ch., Wills Point, Tex., 1978-80, Englewood Bapt. Ch., Jackson, Tenn., 1980-83; adult cons. Miss. Bapt. Conv., Jackson, 1984—. Mem. Am. Soc. Tng. and Devel., Southwestern Bapt. Religious Edn. Assn., Miss. Bapt. Religious Edn. Assn. Avocation: running. Home: 124 Spanish Moss Dr Clinton MS 39056 Office: Miss Bapt Conv PO Box 530 515 Mississippi St Jackson MS 39205

WILLIAMS, WILLIAM COREY, Old Testament educator, consultant; b. Wilkes-Barre, Pa., July 12, 1937; s. Edward Douglas and Elizabeth Irene (Schooley) W.; m. Alma Simmenroth Williams, June 27, 1959; 1 child, Linda. Diploma in Ministerial Studies, NE Bible Inst., 1962; BA in Bibl. Studies, Cen. Bible Coll., 1963, MA in Religion, 1964; MA in Hebrew and Near Ea. Studies, NYU, 1966, PhD in Hebrew Lang. and Lit., 1975. Ref. libr. Hebraic section Libr. of Congress, Washington, 1967-69; prof. Old Testament So. Calif. Coll., Costa Mesa, 1969—; adj. prof. Old Testament Melodyland Sch. Theology, Anaheim, Calif., 1975-77; vis. prof. Old Testament Fuller Theol. Sem., Pasadena, Caif., 1978-81, 84, Asian Theol. Ctr. for Evangelism and Missions, Singapore and Sabah, E. Malaysia, 1985, Continental Bible Coll., Saint Pieters-Leeuw, Belgium, 1985, Mattersey Bible Coll., Eng., 1985, Inst. Holy Land Studies, Jerusalem, 1986; transl. cons. and reviser New Am. Standard Bible, 1969—; transl. cons. The New Internat. Version; transl. cons. and editor Internat. Children's Version, 1985-86. Author: (book, tapes) Hebrew I: A Study Guide, 1986, Hebrew II: A Study Guide, 1986; translation editor: Everyday Bible, 1990; contbr. articles to profl. jours.; contbr. notes to King's Study Bible, NAS Study Bible. Nat. Def. Foreign Lang. fellow NYU, 1964-67; Alummi scholar N.E. Bible Inst., 1960-61. Mem. Soc. Bibl. Lit., Am. Oriental Soc., Evang. Theol. Soc. (exec. office 1974-77), Am. Acad. Religion, Nat. Assn. Profs. of Hebrew, Inst. Bibl. Rsch., The Lockman Found. (editorial bd. 1974—). Home: 1817 Peninsula Pl Costa Mesa CA 92627 Office: So Calif Coll 55 Fair Dr Costa Mesa CA 92626

WILLIAMS, WILLIAM STEPHEN, minister, educator; b. Brownsville, Tenn., Oct. 23, 1953; s. William A. and Barbara (Brantley) W.; m. C. Janine Bailey, June 5, 1976; children: William Nathan, Joanna Joy. BA, Union U., 1977; MDiv, Midwestern Bapt. Theol., 1980; cert. residency clin. pastoral edn., Vets. Hosp., Kansas City, Mo., 1985. Ordained to ministry So. Bapt. Conv., 1976. Pastor Stanton (Tenn.) Bapt. Ch., 1976-78, Jameson (Mo.) First Bapt. Ch., 1978-80, Pleasant Ridge Bapt. Ch., Harrisonville, Mo., 1980-85, Fairview Bapt. Ch., Newbern, Tenn., 1986-90, Holly Grove Bapt. Ch., Cooter, Mo., 1990—; adj. instr. speech and philosophy Dyersburg (Tenn.) State Community Coll., 1989—; field edn. supr. sem. program Midwestern Bapt. Theol. Sem., Kansas City, 1982-83, 85, vice chmn. solicitation com. Child Care and Family Life Ctr., 1979-80; assoc. interfaith dept. Home Mission Bd., So. Bapt. Conv., 1980-83.

WILLIAMS, WILMER DEMPSEY, minister; b. Evergreen, Ala., Sept. 3, 1937; s. Dempsey and Estelle (Murphy) W.; m. Marion Hobbs, Sept. 20, 1959; children: Dereke, Bettye, Beverly Katrina, Phrancia Lekaye, Tammy Lynn, Anjanette. Student, Washington Jr. Coll., Pensacola, Fla., 1957; MDiv, Pentecostal Coll., Pensacola, Fla., 1986. With Hewitt Soap Factory, Dayton, Ohio, 1961-69; salesman Harvey's Men's Clothing, Dayton, 1973-74, Price's Store, Dayton, 1969-72, Sears & Roebuck, New Orleans, 1970-71; minister A.O.H. Ch. of God, Inc., New Orleans, 1970-72; ramp clk. Eastern Airlines, Columbus, Ga., 1988-89; minister/pastor, nat. bd. official, nat. fgn. bd. A.O.H. Ch. of God, Inc., Pensacola, Fla., 1974—; choir dir. AOH Nat. Choir, Birmingham, 1985-86. Active in past various community orgns. Recipient Christian Family award, Ch. in the Home, 1975. Mem. Urban League. Democrat. Home: 4051 Dogwood Dr Columbus GA 31907 Office: Grace Temple 2403 Gusseta Rd Columbus GA 31903

WILLIAMSON, CLARK MURRAY, theology educator; b. Memphis, Nov. 3, 1935; s. Paul Godwin and Clarissa Van Horn (Taylor) W.; m. Barbara Emily Unger, June 11, 1966; 1 child, Scott Taylor. BA, Transylvania U., 1957; BD, U. Chgo., 1961, MA, 1963, PhD, 1969. Ordained to ministry Christian Ch. (Disciples of Christ), 1961. Minister Univ. Ch., Chgo., 1965-66; asst. dean Disciples Divinity House, Chgo., 1965-66; prof. Christian Theol. Sem., Indpls., 1966—, Indiana prof. Christian thought, 1991; vis. prof. Sch. Theology, Claremont, Grad. Sch. Ecumenical Inst., Switzerland; mem. ch. rels. com. U.S. Holocaust Meml. Coun. Author: God is Never Absent, 1977, Has God Rejected His People?, 1982, Interpreting Difficult Texts, 1989, When Jews and Christians Meet, 1989, The Teaching Minister, 1991, A Credible and Timely Word, 1991; editor, advisor: Systematic Theology (Paul Tillich); contbr. articles to profl. publs., chpts. to books. Named Disting. Disciple Scholar, Disciple Theol. Digest, 1990. Mem. Am. Acad. Religion, Am. Theol. Soc., Assn. Disciples for Theol. Discussion (pres. 1987). Democrat. Home: 5261 Boulevard Pl Indianapolis IN 46208 Office: Christian Theol Soc 1000 W 42d St Indianapolis IN 46208

WILLIAMSON, DAVID LOUIS, minister, counselor; b. Mpls., Nov. 27, 1937; s. Louis Wiliam and Hazel Irene (Johnson) W.; m. Anne Louise Schelke, Dec. 21, 1963; children: Mark D., Suzanne R., Sara E. BSB, U. Minn., 1959; M.Div., Fuller Theol. Sem., 1965; MTh, Luther Theol. Sem., 1973, DMin., 1978. Ordained to ministry United Ch. Christ, 1973; lic. marriage and family therapist, Minn. Youth dir. Colonial Ch. of Edina (Minn.), 1965-73, min. pastoral counseling, 1973-91; pastor of care and counseling First Presbyn. Ch. of Hollywood, Calif., 1991—. Author: Group Power, 1982, Opening Doors to Job Market, 1983. Bd. dirs. Human Rels. Commn., Edina, 1972-78, Sabathaani Community Ctr., Mpls., 1974-78, YMCA Camp Warren, Mpls., 1976-80, Minn. Youth Leadership, Mpls., 1990—. Mem. Am. Assn. Pastoral Counselors (clin. mem.), Am. Assn. for Marriage and Family Therapy (clin. mem.), Christian Assn. for Psychol. Studies. Avocations: alpine skiing, handball, traveling, gardening, canoeing. Office: First Presbyn Ch Hollywood 1760 N Gower Hollywood CA 90028

WILLIAMSON, EDWARD HENRY, chaplain, army officer; b. Jackson, Miss., Dec. 9, 1957; s. Oliver Frank and Edith Elise (Berch) W.; m. Jeanne Marie Lazio, May 28, 1988. B History, Miss. Coll., 1983; MDiv, Golden Gate Sem., 1988. Ordained to ministry So. Bapt. Ch., 1988. Commd. capt. U.S. Army, 1990; chaplain Letterman Army Med. Ctr. USAR, San Francisco, 1988-90; post chaplain U.S. Army, Camp Parks, Calif., 1990; chaplain U.S. Army, Ft. Rucker, Ala., 1990—. Mem. Army Aviator Assn. Am., Pi Gamma Mu, Phi Alpha Theta. Republican. Avocations: chess, model aircraft, computer programming, hiking, swimming. Home: PO Box 620046 Fort Rucker AL 36362

WILLIAMSON, JOHN ARTHUR, minister; b. Binghamton, N.Y., June 10, 1947; s. Marion A. and Bernice B. (Decker) W.; m. Linda S. Zobel, Aug. 1, 1970; children: Amy Sue, Karen Joy. ThG, Empire State Bapt. Sem., 1977; diploma, Christian Counseling Ctr., 1979; postgrad., Trinity Bible Coll. and Sem., 1991—. Ordained to ministry Bapt. Ch., 1977. Instr. Empire State Bapt. Sem., Syracuse, N.Y., 1980-86; pastor Southwood Bapt. Ch., Jamesville, N.Y., 1976-82, Calvary Bapt. Ch., Harford, N.Y., 1982-88, New Boston (N.H.) Bapt. ch., 1988—; program dir. Mars Hill Broadcasting Co. (Sta. WMHR), Syracuse, 1970-76; bd. dirs. Camp Ba-You-Ca, Marathon, N.Y., 1980-82, Empire Bapt. State Sem., Syracuse, 1980-86; moderator ESBS Assn. Chs., Syracuse, 1980-82. Author: Watchtower-Field White, 1988, Sin in the Assembly, 1990; editor: (jour.) Light From the Corner, 1991—; contbr. articles to profl. publs. Mem. Nat. Stuttering Project, San Francisco, 1988. Sgt. U.S. Army, 1966-69. Recipient Outstanding Spokesman for Freedom award VFW, 1964. Office: New Boston Bapt Ch 184 Mont Vernon Rd New Boston NH 03070

WILLIAMSON, LAMAR, JR., retired religion educator, writer; b. Monticello, Ark., July 24, 1926; s. Lamar and Lillian (Phillips) W.; m. Ruthmary Bliss, Sept. 1, 1949; children: Frederick T., Martha, Ruth, Allen. AB, Davidson Coll., 1947; BD, Union Theol. Sem., Richmond, Va., 1951; BTh., Faculte de Theologie Protestante de Montpellier, 1952; PhD in Religion, Yale U., 1963. Ordained to ministry Presbyn. Ch. (U.S.A.), 1951. Pastor Harveyton and Hull Meml. Presbyn. chs., 1952-56; prof. N.T. Inst. Superieur de Theologie, Kananga, Zaire, 1957-66; vis. prof. Union Theol. Sem., Richmond, 1966-68; mem. faculty, then Martin Ryerson Turnbull prof. Bibl. studies Presbyn. Sch. Christian Edn., 1968-91. Author: God's Work of Art: Images of the Church in Ephesians, 1971; (with Madeline H. Beck) Mastering New Testament Facts, 4 vols., 1973, Mastering Old Testament Facts, 4 vols., 1981, Mark in Gospel of Interpretation: A Bible Commentary for Teaching and Preaching, 1983; also articles. Active All Souls Presbyn. Ch., Richmond, 1966—; with div. mission and svc. Hanover Presbytery, Presbyn. Ch. (U.S.A.), 1982-88, mem. social justice com. Synod of Mid-Atlantic, 1988-90, mem. presbyteries' coop. com. on exams. for candidates, 1989—. With U.S. Army Air Corps, 1945. Democrat. Avocations: fishing, housebuilding, music, art, literature. Home: 3406 Gloucester Rd Richmond VA 23227

WILLICH, MICHAEL VON, youth minister; b. Topeka, July 7, 1969; s. Gene E. and Sharon L. (Thompson) W.; m. Cynthia Ann Yoder, Aug. 11, 1990. BA in Banking and Fin., Kans. State U.; BS in Christian Edn., Manhattan Christian Coll. Youth min. Ch. of Christ-Christian, Council Grove, Kans., 1989—; with Midwest Acoustics and Drywall, Manhatan, 1987—. Office: Ch of Christ-Christian 106 E Main Council Grove KS 66846

WILLIE, CLAUDE EDWARD, III, minister, educator; b. New Bern, N.C., Sept. 12, 1952; s. Claude Edward and Louise (Jones) W.; m. Linda Diane Shipman, May 22, 1972; children: Andre, Tawanna, Devita and Alcestis. BA, St. Augustine's Coll., Raleigh, 1974; MA, N.C. Cen. U., 1976. Mem. state steering com. N.C. State Dept. Pub. Instrn., Raleigh, 1987—; chaplain GArner Rd. YMCA. Mem. Nat. Assn. Elem. Sch. Prins., Am. Assn. Sch. Adminstrs., Alpha Kappa Mu, Masons. Avocation: photography. Home: 2904 Snowberry Dr Raleigh NC 27610 Office: LaGrange Elementary Sch 402 W Railroad St LaGrange NC 28551

WILLIMON, WILLIAM HENRY, minister; b. Greenville, S.C., May 15, 1946; s. Robert Charles and Ruby (Steer) W.; m. Patricia Parker, June 7, 1969; children: William Parker, Harriet Patricia. BA, Wofford Coll., 1968; MDiv, Yale U., 1970; STD, Emory U., 1972; DD (hon.), Westminster Coll., New Wilmington, Pa., 1990. Ordained to ministry United Meth. Ch., 1972. Pastor Level Creek/Trinity United Meth. Chs., Buford, Ga., 1970-71; assoc. pastor Broad St. United Meth. Ch., Clinton, S.C., 1971-73; pastor Trinity United Meth. Ch., North Myrtle Beach, S.C., 1973-76; assoc. prof. Duke Divinity Sch., Durham, N.C., 1976-80; pastor Northside United Meth. Ch., Greenville, S.C., 1980-84; minister to univ., prof. Duke U., Durham, 1984-89, dean of chapel, prof., 1989—. Author: Why I Am a United Methodist, 1990, Clergy and Laity Burnout, 1988, Acts of the Apostles, Interpretation, A Commentary for Teaching and Preaching, 1988, The Promise of Marriage, 1988, Preaching About Conflict in the Local Church, 1987, Rekindling the Flame, 1987, With Glad and Generous Hearts, 1986, The Laugh Shall Be First, 1986, Sighing for Eden, 1985, What's Right With the Church, 1984, Handbook on Preaching and Worship, 1984, On A Wild and Windy Mountain, 1984, many other books. 1st lt. U.S. Army, 1969-70. Fellow N.Am. Acad. of Liturgy; mem. Phi Beta Kappa. Home: 3104 Doubleday Pl Durham NC 27705 Office: Duke U Dean Chapel Durham NC 27706

WILLING, ROBERT NELSON, archdeacon; b. N.Y.C., June 15, 1934; s. Robert Nelson and Anne (Steinmetz) W.; divorced 1987; children: Theresa, Robert III, Catherine, Laura. BA in Philosophy, Hobart Coll., 1957; MDiv, Nashotah House, 1960; postgrad., NYU, 1962-68. Ordained to ministry Episcopal Ch. as deacon and priest, 1960. Curate St. Margaret's Ch., Bronx, N.Y., 1960-63; rector Trinity Ch., Mt. Vernon, N.Y., 1963-70, St. John's and St. Clement's, Mt. Vernon, 1967-70; vicar St. Paul's, Eastchester, N.Y., 1967-70; bd. dirs. Hudson Area Housing Authority, Tarrytown, N.Y., Mid-Hudson Rural Migrant Com., New Paltz, N.Y.; dep. Gen. Conv., Episcopal Ch., 1973—; del. N.Y. State Coun. Chs., Syracuse, 1978-88; adj. prof. Union Theol. Sem., N.Y.C., 1984—. Editor regional newsletter; contbr. articles to profl. jours. Mem. adv. com. to Supt. Schs. on race, religion, teaching history, Mt. Vernon, 1965-66, Mayor's Commn. on Housing, Mt. Vernon, 1967-69, Upward Bound, Sarah Lawrence Coll., 1968-70. Recipient Key to City of Mt. Vernon City Legislature, 1970, Bishop N.Y. Cross Right Rev. Paul Moore Jr., 1985. Mem. Am. Mgmt. Assn., Alban Inst., Episcopal Peace Fellowship, Order of Holy Cross, Am. Philatelic Soc., Kappa Alpha. Home and Office: Upper Boiceville Rd Boiceville NY 12412

WILLINGHAM, EDWARD BACON, JR., ecumenical minister, administrator; b. St. Louis, July 27, 1934; s. Edward and Harriet (Sharon) W.; m. Angeline Walton Pettit, June 14, 1957; children: Katie, Carol. BS in Physics, U. Richmond, 1956; postgrad., U. Rochester, 1958-59; MDiv., Colgate Rochester Div. Sch., 1960. Ordained to ministry Am. Bapt. Ch., 1960. Min. Christian edn. Delaware Ave. Bapt. Ch., Buffalo, N.Y., 1960-62; dir. radio and TV Met. Detroit Coun. Chs., 1962-75; exec. dir. Christian Communication Coun. Met. Detroit Chs., 1976—; broadcast cons. Mich. Coun. Chs., 1965-75; guest cons. religious broadcasting, Fed. Republic Germany, 1968; mem. coord. com. Mich. Ecumenical Forum, 1986, 90—, chair, 1991—. Bd. mgrs. Broadcasting and Film Commn., Nat. Coun. Chs., 1965-73. Recipient Gabriel award Cath. Broadcaster Assn., 1972. Mem. Assn. Regional Religious Communicators (pres. 1969-71), World Assn. Christian Communications (cen. com. 1973-78, bus. mgr. N.Am. broadcasting sect. 1970—), Phi Gamma Delta, Sigma Pi Sigma. Office: NAm Broadcast Sec/World Assn Christian Communication 1300 Mutual Bldg Detroit MI 48226

WILLIS, AVERY THOMAS, JR., discipleship training administrator; b. Lepanto, Ark., Feb. 21, 1934; s. Avery Thomas and Grace (Carver) W.; m. Shirley Morris, Dec. 17, 1955; children: Randal Kean, Sherrie Dennette, Wade Avery, Krista Dawn, Brett Lane. BA, Okla. Bapt. U., Shawnee, 1956; BD, Southwestern Bapt. Theol. Sem., Ft. Worth, 1961, MDiv, 1973, ThD, 1974; DST hon., Southwest Bapt. U., Bolivar, Mo., 1986. Ordained to ministry Bapt. Ch., 1954. Pastor Ctr. Point Bapt. Ch., Wilberton, Okla., 1954-56, Sunset Hts. Bapt. Ch., Ft. Worth, 1957-60, Inglewood Bapt. Ch., Grand Prairie, Tex., 1960-64; missionary, sem. pres. fgn. mission bd. So. Bapt. Conv., Indonesia, 1964-78; mgr. adult discipleship tng. Bapt. Sunday Sch. Bd., Nashville, 1978—. Author: Indonesian Revival: Why Two Million Came to Christ, 1978, Biblical Basis of Missions, 1979, MasterLife: Discipleship Training for Leaders, 1980 (transl. over 50 langs.), MasterBuilder: Multiplying Leaders, 1984, LifeGuide to Discipleship and Doctrine, 1989, and several books in Indonesian; host, writer over 100 video tng. tapes. Recipient 3d place award Indonesian Nat. Film Festival. Mem. Am. Soc. Bapt. Religion, Nat. Soc. Pastors, YMCA, Am. Soc. Tng. and Devel.,Nat. Soc. Performance Inst., Admirals Club. Republican. Home: 204 Rosehill Dr Goodlettsville TN 37072 Office: Bapt Sunday Sch Bd 127 9th Ave N MSN 150 A Nashville TN 37234

WILLIS, C. PAUL, minister; b. Harkers Island, N.C., Dec. 14, 1932; s. Cleveland Paul and Bertha Gray (Lewis) W.; m. Mary Jane Roberts, June 1, 1951; children: Deborah, Tamalie, Dennis. BA, Campbell U., 1966; Clin. Pastoral Edn. degree, Bowman Gray Sch. Medicine, Winston Salem, N.C., 1969; MDiv, Southeastern Bapt. Sem., Wake Forest, N.C., 1970; DMin, Oral Roberts U., 1989. Pastor Northside Bapt. Ch., Greensboro, N.C., 1970-73; pres. Christian Word Ministries, Greensboro, 1973-82; sr. pastor Cathedral of His Glory, Greensboro, 1982—; pres. Ministerio de Su Gloria, Antigua, Guatemala, 1990—; bd. dirs. Saint Ministries Internat., Cordoba, Argentina, 1985—. Author: Bells and Pomegranates, 1991; (booklets) Abiding Power, 1976, Visions of the Victory, 1976. Mem. Charismatic Bible Minitries, Congl. Club. Republican. Office: Cathedral of His Glory 4501 Lake Jeanette Rd Greensboro NC 27408 *A life of hope and joy is built on the possibility of a miracle. I have staked everything on my belief in the miracle of the resurrection of Jesus Christ. The miracle of His resurrection gives hope for a present miracle. It is upon this truth that Christianity stands or falls!.*

WILLIS, CHARLES DUBOIS, neuropsychiatrist, writer; b. N.Y.C., Dec. 30, 1925; s. William Charles and Alma Anna (Lazear) W.; m. Shirley Mae Clarke, Jan. 28, 1951; children: Carol, Nancy, John, Sarah, James. BA in Religion, Atlantic Union Coll., 1949; MD, Loma Linda U., 1955. Diplomate Am. Bd. Psychiatry and Neurology. Intern Orange (Calif.) County Hosp.; resident in psychiatry Met. State Hosp., Norwalk, Calif., 1956, 57-60; resident in neurology U. Calif. Med. Ctr., San Francisco, 1966-68; pres. Ancient World Found., Pinedale, Calif., 1990—; staff psychiatrist Dept. Corrections, Corcoran, Calif., 1983—; leader Mt. Ararat Expdns., 1983, 84, 86, 88. Author: End of Days=1971-2001, 1973. Capt. U.S. Army Med. Corps, 1957-60. Republican. Office: Ancient World Found PO Box 3118 Pinedale CA 93650

WILLIS, DARYL BRENT, minister; b. Ft. Worth, July 12, 1957; s. Ira Park and Cebela (Johnson) W.; m. Teresa Darlene Butts, Aug. 16, 1980; 1 child, Brittany Alyse. AA, Whites Ferry Rd. Sch. Bibl., Studies, West Monroe, La.; BA, Am. Christian Bible Coll., West Monroe, 1981. Youth minister Ch. of Christ, Lyons, Kans., 1977-78; assoc. youth minister Ch. of Christ, Monroe, La., 1979-81; youth/edn. minister Ch. of Christ, Little Rock, 1981-84; youth minister Ch. of Christ, Memphis, Tenn., 1984-90, Fayetteville, Tenn., 1990—. Author: Mountain Top Journal, 1990; co-author: Never The Same, 1991; contbr. articles, poetry to trade/profl. jours. Co-founder, teller Storytellers Guild, Fayetteville, 1990; storyteller Lincoln County Schs., Fayetteville, 1990. Mem. Nat. Assn. for the Preservation and Perpetuation of Storytelling. Republican. Home: PO Box 324 Fayetteville TN 37334-0324 Office: Church of Christ 209 E Washington St Fayetteville TN 37334

WILLIS, DAVID JACKSON, JR., minister; b. Weatherford, Tex., Apr. 12, 1956; s. David Jackson and Flora Grace (McGon) W.; m. Karen Lynn Hunter, May 25, 1990. BS, Dallas Bapt. U., 1980; MARE, Southwestern Bapt. Theol. Sem., 1986. Min. youth Walnut Springs Bapt., Walnut Springs, Tex., 1977-79; min. music Western Park Bapt., Dallas, Tex., 1980-85; assc. pastor First Bapt. Ch., Grants, N.Mex., 1986-87, Blue Ridge Bapt., Wetumpka, Ala., 1987-89; min. music/youth First Bapt. Ch., Eclectic, Ala., 1989--; assc. youth leader, Elmore Bapt. Assc., Wetumpka, Ala. Republican. Southern Baptist. Home: PO Box 89 Eclectic AL 36024 Office: First Baptist Church PO Box 400 Eclectic AL 36024

WILLIS, LEVY, bishop. Bishop Ch. of God in Christ, Norfolk, Va. Office: Ch of God in Christ 645 Church St Ste 400 Norfolk VA 23510*

WILLIS, STEPHEN MICHAEL, preacher, editor; b. Camden, Tex., July 22, 1947; s. Onan J. and Wilhelmina Elizabeth (Thompson) W.; m. Sandra Carol Parson, June 18, 1966; children: Jennifer Lynette, Corey Michael. AA, Fla. Coll., 1967; BA, Butler U., 1972; MA, Christian Theol. Sem., 1975. Preacher Ch. of Christ, various cities, Ind., Ky., Ohio, 1967—; nat. coun. mem. Fla. Coll., Temple Terrace, 1978—. Author: Commentary on 1 Corinthians, 1979; editor: Guardian of Truth, 1977—. Office: Guardian of Truth PO Box 9670 Bowling Green KY 46102

WILLIS, WESLEY ROBERT, college administrator; b. Rahway, N.J., Mar. 16, 1941; s. Meachen William and Mildred (Sisco) W.; m. Elaine Stanislaw, May 22, 1965; children: Mark, Kevin, Nathan. BS, Phila. Coll. Bible, 1963; ThM, Dallas Theol. Sem., 1967; EdD, Ind. U., 1978. Prof., dept. chmn. Washington Bible Coll., 1967-70; minister edn. Forcey Meml. Ch., Washington, 1967-71; prof., acad. v.p. Ft. Wayne (Ind.) Bible Coll., 1971-78; exec. v.p. Scripture Press Ministries, Wheaton, Ill., 1978-80; sr. v.p. Scripture Press Publs., Inc., Wheaton, 1980-90; v.p. acad. affairs Phila. Coll. Bible, Langhorne, Pa., 1990—; bd. dirs. Scripture Press Publs., Ltd., Whitby, Ont., Can.; bd. dirs., chmn. bd. Christian Svc. Brigade, Wheaton, 1972-88. Author: 200 Years and Still Counting, 1981, Make Your Teaching Count, 1984, Developing the Teacher in You, 1990, also 6 others; ocntbr. over 150 articles to religious publs. Sunday sch. tchr., elder Coll. Ch., Wheaton; bd. regents Dallas Theol. Sem., 1987—. Recipient Disting. Edn. Alumnus award Phila. Coll. Bible, 1988. Mem. Nat. Assn. Profs. Christian Edn., Nat. Assn. Dirs. Christian Edn., Evang. Press assn. Office: Phila Coll Bible 200 Manor Ave Langhorne PA 19047

WILLITS, BRUCE ALBERT, lay worker; b. Moline, Ill., Feb. 18, 1951; s. James Corwin and Helyn Athlene (Lum) W. AA in Art, Black Hawk Coll., 1972; BFA in Graphic Design, Mpls. Coll. Art and Design, 1975; MA in Christian Edn., Bethel Theol. Sem., 1988. Asst. mgr. Logos Coffee House, Mpls., 1980-81; exec. coun. mem. Singles Leaership Network Chs., Mpls., 1983-84; lay tchr., pastor to single adults Wooddale Ch., Eden Prairie, Minn., 1986-87; pres. career bridge Minnetonka (Minn.) Bapt. Ch., 1982-86, pastoral intern to single adults, 1987-88, mem. advt. com., 1989, lay leader to single adults, 1989-90; chaplain North Meml. Hosp., 1985; world evangelism week com. Wooddale Ch., 1987, tchr., pastor, gen. coord. One By One Congregation, 1986-87; graphic designer Design Ctr., Mpls., 1976-81; prin., graphic designer Bruce Willits Design, 1981—. Mem. Evang. Tchr. Tng. Assn. Home and Office: 1807 2d Ave S Apt 21 Minneapolis MN 55403

WILLKE, JOHN CHARLES, physician; b. Maria Stein, Ohio, Apr. 5, 1925; s. Gerard Thomas and Marie Margaret (Wuennemann) W.; m. Barbara Hiltz, June 5, 1948; children: Marie, Theresa, Charles, Joseph, Anne, Timothy. MD, U. Cin., 1948; Legum Dr. (hon.), U. Notre Dame, 1983; LHD (hon.), Thomas More Coll., Ky., 1978. Diplomate Am. Bd. Family Practice. Med. resident Good Samaitan Hosp., Cin., 1948-50; pvt. practice Cin., until 1988; sr. attending staff Providence & Good Samaritan Hosps., Cin.; co-chair Cin. Right to Life, 1970-87; pres. Ohio Right to Life, 1975-80, Nat. Right to Life Com., Washington, 1980-83, 84-91, Internat. Right to Life Fedn., Switzerland, 1985-91, Life Issues Inst., Cin., 1991—. Guest participant on radio & TV including Phil Donahue Show, 60 Minutes, Good Morning Am., The Today Show, Crossfire, Larry King, Voice of Am., 700 Club, Geraldo Rivera, and more; author: The Wonder of Sex, 1964, Sex Should We Wait, 1969, Sex Education: The How to for Teachers, 1970, Marriage, 1971, Handbook on Abortion, 1971, rev. edits., 1975, 79, How To Teach the Pro-Life Story, 1973, Sex Education, In the Classroom?, 1978, Abortion & Slavery, 1984, Abortion Questions & Answers, 1985, rev., 1991, Sex & Love, 1991; contbr. to books and articles to profl. jours. Mem. numerous bds. of social action orgns. Capt. USAF, 1952-54. Fellow Am. Bd. Family Physicians; mem. Ohio Acad. Family Physicians, Cin. Acad. Med., Ohio Med. Soc., Am. Assn. Sex Educators, Nat. Alliance for Family Life, Family Life Educators. Office: 1802 W Galbraith Rd Cincinnati OH 45239 *Each human life begins as a single cell. That is a scientific fact. Legal abortion is fatal discrimination against an entire class of living humans on the basis of place of residence—still living in the womb. It is a civil rights outrage.*

WILLMAN, SISTER VINCENT MARIE, nun; b. Cin., Sept. 29, 1932; d. Vincent Leo and Bertha Cecelia (Werle) W. BS in Elem. Edn., Mount St. Joseph Coll., 1962; MA in Religion, Aquinas Coll., 1970; MA in Religious Studies, St. Charles Sem., Phila., 1987. Joined Sisters of Charity, Roman Cath. Ch., 1950. Dir. religion St. Michael's Ch., Findlay, Ohio, 1970-77, St. Gabriel Parish, Glendale, Ohio, 1979—. Avocations: classical music, walking, gardening. *We are living in a time of challenge, change and indifference to God. In every possible way, we need to see and respond to the Will of God in our personal lives and challenge others to do likewise.*

WILLOUGHBY, JIMMY RAY, minister; b. San Antonio, Sept. 27, 1953; s. Jack Henry and Mildred Lucille (Moree) W.; m. Ireta June Owen, Aug. 28, 1976; children: Vielka Renee, Jamie Rae Ann. Student, Berean Sch. Bible, Springfield, Mo., 1980. Ordained to ministry Echos of Faith Revivals Inc., 1974, Assemblies of God, 1980. Assoc. pastor Echos of Faith Ch., Ontario, Calif., 1974-79; evangelist Jim Willoughby Ministries, Montclair, Calif., 1979-81; sr. pastor Echos of Faith Christian Ctr., Ontario, 1981—; del. Traditional Values Coalition, Anaheim, Calif., 1985—; dir. Agape Outreach, Ontario, 1986—; area dir. Internat. Conv. Faith Ministries, Little Rock, 1990—; mem. adv. bd. Athletics Internat. Ministries, Phoenix, 1991—. Author: Trick or Treat, Satan's Game, 1991; editor Faith Tabloid mag., 1986-89; host radio show The Uncompromising Word, 1984—. Organizer July 4th Freedom Celebration, Chino, Calif., 1984—; mem. Police Task Force on Satanic Crimes, Chino, 1990. Republican. Office: Echos of Faith 11255 Central Ave PO Box 3100 Ontario CA 91761 *There are two types of people who cross your path each day. Those who will charge your battery, those who will drain your battery. Who you associate with is your choice.*

WILLOUGHBY, WILLIAM GEORGE, minister; b. Elizabethtown, Pa., Sept. 26, 1917; s. William Almer and Lilian (Falkenstein) W.; m. Lena Buterbaugh, Aug. 30, 1941; children: Susan, James, Nancy, Thomas. BA, Elizabethtown Coll., 1941; B.D., Bethany Theol. Sem., 1944; PhD, Boston U., 1951. Ordained to ministry Ch. of the Brethren, 1944. Pastor Ch. of the Brethren, Olympia, Wash., 1944-48; prof. philosophy and religion Bridgewater (Va.) Coll., 1950-70; dir. Jr. Yr. Abroad Program, Marburg, Fed. Republic Germany, 1962-63, Brethren Svc. programs in Europe and North Africa, Geneva, 1963-66; prof. religion, chair humanities div. U. La Verne, Calif., 1970-80; chaplain Hillcrest Homes, La Verne, 1984-88; instr. in religion Pasadena City Coll., 1990—. Author: Counting the Cost, 1979. Mem. Friends of La Verne, 1988-90; pres. Pomona Valley Housing Corp., Pomona, Calif., 1978; bd. dirs. Nat. Coun. Chs., N.Y.C., 1966-69; trustee Bethany Theol. Sem., 1970-73; pres. Va. Philos. Assn., Bridgewater, Va., 1968. Mem. Am. Acad. Religion. Home: 2711 B St La Verne CA 91750

WILLS, DAVID WOOD, minister, educator; b. Portland, Ind., Jan. 25, 1942; s. Theodore Oscar Mitchell and Elizabeth Lochore (Wood) W.; m. Carolyn Reynolds Montgomery, Aug. 22, 1964; children: John Brookings, Theodore Worcester, Thomas Churchill. B.A., Yale U., 1962; B.D., Princeton Theol. Sem., 1966; Ph.D., Harvard U., 1975. Ordained to ministry Presbyn. Ch., 1970. Asst. prof. Sch. of Religion, U. So. Calif., 1970-72; asst. prof. dept. of religion Amherst Coll., Mass., 1972-78, assoc. prof., 1978-83, prof., 1983-90, prof. religion and Black studies, 1990—, also dir. Luce Program in Comparative Religious Ethics 1978-88. Editor (with Richard Newman) Black Apostles at Home and Abroad, 1982. Kent fellow Danforth Found., 1966-70, 75, Ford Found. fellow, 1972, Inst. for Ecumenical and Cultural Rsch. fellow, 1972, Nat. Humanities Ctr. fellow, 1980-81, NEH fellow for Coll. Tchrs., 1988-89, W. E. B. DuBois Inst. for Afro-Am. Rsch. fellow, 1989-91. Mem. Am. Acad. Religion (chair Afro-Am. religious history group 1975-78), Am. Hist. Assn., Am. Soc. Ch. History, Am. Studies Assn., Orgn. Am. Historians, Soc. Christian Ethics, So. Hist. Assn., Phi Beta Kappa. Home: 100 Woodside Amherst MA 01002 Office: Amherst Coll Dept Religion Amherst MA 01002

WILLS, GARRY, journalist, educator; b. Atlanta, May 22, 1934; s. John and Mayno (Collins) W.; m. Natalie Cavallo, May 30, 1959; children: John, Garry, Lydia. BA, St. Louis U., 1957; MA, Xavier U., Cin., 1958, Yale U., 1959; PhD, Yale U., 1961; LittD (hon.), Coll. Holy Cross, 1982, Columbia Coll., 1982, Beloit Coll., 1988. Fellow Center Hellenic Studies, 1961-62; assoc. prof. classics Johns Hopkins U., 1962-67, adj. prof., 1968-80; Henry R. Luce prof. Am. culture and public policy Northwestern U., 1980-88, adj. prof., 1988—; newspaper columnist Universal Press Syndicate, 1970—. Author: Chesterton, 1961, Politics and Catholic Freedom, 1964, Roman Culture, 1966, Jack Ruby, 1967, Second Civil War, 1968, Nixon Agonistes, 1970, Bare Ruined Choirs, 1972, Inventing America, 1978, At Button's, 1979, Confessions of a Conservative, 1979, Explaining America, 1980, The Kennedy Imprisonment, 1982, Lead Time, 1983, Cincinnatus, 1984, Reagan's America, 1987, Under God, 1990. Recipient Merle Curti award Orgn. Am. Historians, Nat. Book Critics Circle award, John D. Rockefeller III award Bicentennial Council., Wilbur Cross medal Yale U., Peabody award. Roman Catholic. Office: Northwestern U Dept History Evanston IL 60201

WILLS, KEITH CAMERON, archivist, librarian; b. McCleary, Wash., Aug. 11, 1917; s. Lee Allen and Frances (Mommsen) W.; m. Olin Florine Taylor, Sept. 28, 1944 (dec. July 1979); 1 child, Keith Cameron Jr.; m. Ruth Naomi Voirin, Aug. 2, 1980. BA, U. Wash., Seattle, 1940; BDiv, Southwestern Bapt. Sem., 1950, ThD, 1958; MLS, U. Denver, 1966; MDiv, Southwestern Bapt. Sem., 1973. Circulation libr. Southwestern Bapt. Sem., Ft. Worth, 1953-57, reference libr., 1957-58, libr. dir., 66-84, archivist, 1988—; libr. dir. Midwestern Bapt. Sem., Kansas City, Mo., 1966-84, 1958-66; acting libr. Can. So. Bapt. Sem., Cochrane, Alta., Can., 1986-88. Contbr. articles to profl. jours. Chaplain Civitan, Ft. Worth, 1976-84. Mem. ALA, Tex. Libr. Assn., So. Bapt. Hist. Soc. (bd. dirs. 1967-73), Tex. Bapt. Hist. Soc. (sec., treas. 1976-84). Home: 6133 Wrigley Way Fort Worth TX 76133 Office: Southwestern Bapt Sem Roberts Library Box 22, 000 Fort Worth TX 76133-2490

WILLS, OLAN KENNYON, clergyman; b. Sylvester, Ga., July 16, 1936; s. Kennyon Jefferson and Gladys Iola (Langdale) W.; m. Dorothy Jane Jones, May 2, 1958; children: Donna Elizabeth Wills McClam, Melinda Gail, Kimberly Jane Bodiford. Grad., John Gupton Sch. Mortuary Sci., 1959; ThD, Immanuel Bapt. Coll., 1970. Ordained to ministry Bapt. Ch., 1969. Pastor South College Park (Calif.) Bapt. Ch., 1969-70, Sharon Bapt. Ch., McDonough, Ga., 1970-71, New Bethel Bapt. Ch., Thomaston, Ga., 1974-81, Athena Bapt. Ch., Perry, Fla., 1981-84, Springhead Bapt. Ch., Plant City, Fla., 1984—; chaplain Sheriff Upson County, Thomaston, Ga., 1975-81; chaplain Taylor County, Perry, Fla., 1981-84, rep. nat. bd., 1981-84; chaplain Fla. Hwy. Patrol, Tampa, 1985-88; dir. Home Mission Bd., So. Bapt. Conv., 1987-95. Advisor Mental Health Bd. Plant City, 1985—. With USAF, 1954-58. Home: 3505 Medulla Rd Plant City FL 33566

WILMER, RICHARD HOOKER, JR., retired religion educator, priest; b. Ancon, C.Z., Panama, Apr. 13, 1918; (parents Am. citizens); s. Richard Hooker and Margaret Van Dyke (Grant) W.; m. Elisabeth F. Green, June 6, 1942; children: Richard, Margaret, Stephen, Natalie, Rebecca (dec.), Christine; m. Sarah King, Aug. 2, 1969. BA, Yale U., 1939; MDiv, Gen. Theol. Sem., N.Y.C., 1942, STD (hon.), 1958; DPhil, Oxford (Eng.) U., 1948; D.D. (hon.), Berkeley Div. Sch., New Haven, 1970. Ordained deacon and priest Episcopal Ch., 1942. Deacon-in-charge, vicar, rector St. John's Ch., Mt. Rainier, Md., 1942-45; chaplain, prof. English Bible, U. of South, Sewanee, Tenn., 1948-53; min. to Episcopal students Yale U., New Haven, 1953-57; prof. theology, dean Berkeley Div. Sch., 1957-69; vis. prof. religious studies U. Pitts., 1970-72, prof., 1972-83, chmn. dept., 1975-80, prof. emeritus, 1983—. Author: The Doctrine of the Church in the English Reformation, 1952. Chaplain USNR, 1945-46. Mem. Am. Soc. Ch. History, Am. Soc. for Reformation Rsch., Phi Beta Kappa. Home: 1128 Heberton St Pittsburgh PA 15206

WILMORE, GAYRAUD STEPHEN, retired religion educator; b. Phila., Dec. 20, 1921; s. Gayraud Stephen and Patricia (Gardner) W.; m. Lee Wilson, May 26, 1944; children: Stephen, Jacques, Roberta, David. BA, Lincoln U., Pa., 1947; BD, Lincoln Theol. Sem., 1950; STM, Temple U., 1952, Lincoln Coll., Ill., 1958, Tusculum Coll., 1960, Gen. Theol. Sem., 1988, Payne Theol. Sem., 1989; DD (hon.), Trinity Luth. Theol. Sem., 1991. Ordained to ministry Presbyn. Ch. (U.S.A.), 1950. Pastor 2d Presbyn. Ch., West Chester, Pa., 1950-53; regional sec. mid. Atlantic region Student Christian Movement, Phila, 1952-57; asst. prof. social ethics Pitts. Theol. Sem., 1960-63; exec. dir. Commn. on Religion and Race, United Presbyn. Ch., N.Y.C., 1963-72; M.L. King prof. social ethics Boston U. Sch. Theology, 1972-74; King prof. black ch. studies Colgate-Rochester (N.Y.) Div. Sch., 1974-83; prof. of African Am. Religious Studies, dean N.Y. Theol. Sem., 1983-86; prof. Ch. History Interdenom. Theology Ctr., Atlanta, 1986-90;mem. Faith and Order Commn., World Coun. Chs., 1983-91; chmn. closer cooperation com. Payne Sem./Wilberforce (Ohio) U., 1990—; mem. Black Theology Project, Inc., Nat. Black Presbyn. Caucus. Author: Black Religion and Black Radicalism, 1983, Black and Presbyterian, 1983; editor African Am. Religious Studies, 1990, Jour. Interdenominatinal Theol. Ctr., 1990—. Sgt. inf. AUS, 1943-46, MTO. Recipient Disting. Svc. award Presbyn. Interracial Coun., 1964, Sower's award N.Y. Theol. Sem., 1988. Mem. Soc. for Study Black Religon, Ecumenical Assn. Third World Theologians, Soc. for Study Black Religion (past pres.), NAACP (life), Alpha Phi Alpha. Home: 710 McGill Pl Atlanta GA 30312 Office: Jour of ITC 671 Beckwith St SW Atlanta GA 30314

WILSHIRE, ROBERT VIDAL, priest, theology educator; b. Newcastle, NSW, Australia, Feb. 17, 1937; came to U.S., 1966; s. Alan Gilbert and Hilary Mary Havelock (Vidal) W. B in Econs., U. Queensland, Brisbane, Australia, 1960; Th.L. (with honors), St. Francis Coll., Brisbane, 1962; MDiv, Gen. Theol. Sem., N.Y.C., 1967, STM, 1968. Ordained to ministry Episcopal Ch., 1962. Chaplain The Southport (Queensland) Sch., 1963-66, House of the Redeemer, N.Y.C., 1967-70; rector St. Anne's Episcopal Ch., Sayville, N.Y., 1970-79; prof. theology Mercer Sch. Theology, Garden City, N.Y., 1973—, registrar, 1977—; dean L.I., chief exec. officer Cathedral of the Incarnation, Garden City, 1979—; del. gen. conv. Episcopal Ch., Diocese L.I., 1982, 88. Co-author: Teilard de Chadin: Remythologization, 1979. Bd. dirs., exec. com. Episcopal Health Svcs., Hempstead, N.Y., 1981—. Recipient Disting. Svc. Cross Diocese L.I., 1986. Mem. Cherry Valley Club (Garden City), Rotary (hon. life). Office: Cathedral of the Incarnation 50 Cathedral Ave Garden City NY 11530

WILSON, A. KENNETH, minister; b. Pitts., Sept. 28, 1949; s. Raymond J. and Betty (Jaap) W.; m. Charlotte Lewis, June 17, 1978; 1 child, Kristina Noelle. BA, Temple U., 1971; MA, U. Cin., 1973; commd. lt., Salvation Army Sch., 1978. Corps comdg. officer Salvation Army, Freeport, N.Y., 1978-82; various positions to Capt. Salvation Army, Lancaster, Pa., 1982—. Author: Hard Coal-Soft Hearts, 1990; contbr. articles to Salvation Army publs. Office: The Salvation Army 131 S Queen St Lancaster PA 17603

WILSON, ALFORD M., academic administrator. Head Southeastern Bapt. Coll., Laurel, Miss. Office: Southeastern Bapt Coll 4229 Hwy 15 N Laurel MS 39440*

WILSON, ALLEN RAY, minister; b. Birmingham, Ala., Aug. 7, 1950; s. Charles Ray and Esther Dorothy (Smith) W.; m. Suzanne Baxter, Aug. 20, 1971; children: Joshua Allen, Jonathan David, Jeremiah Raymond-Roy. BS, U. Ala., 1972, LHD (hon.), 1986; M in Ch. Music, So. Sem., Louisville, 1975; DD (hon.), Samford U., 1988. Ordained to ministry Bapt. Ch., 1976. Minister youth/recreation First Bapt. Ch., Memphis, 1980-84; minister recreation First Bapt. Ch., Paducah, Ky., 1984-85; minister with students Shades Mountain Bapt. Ch., Birmingham, Ala., 1985-89; pres. Solid Rock Ministries, Inc., Birmingham, 1989-90; exec. dir. Impact, Inc., Birmingham, 1990—, Re-Entry Ministries Inc., Birmingham, 1990—; bd. mem. Fellowship Christian Athletes, Tuscaloosa, Ala., 1978—; campus ministries bd. Ala. Bapt. Conv., Birmingham, 1985—; mem. Metro Youth Ministers Assn., 1985—; adv. bd. Youth for Christ, 1987—. Author: American Heritage Day Camping, 1984; contbr. articles to profl. jours. Adv. bd. Outstanding High Sch. Students Am., 1987—; adv. Family Ct. Jefferson County, Birmingham, 1989—; mem. Birmingham Task Force on Juvenile Crime, 1990—; mem. Birmingham City Schs. Security Coun., 1991. Mem. Nat. Theatre Assn., Clowns of Am., Christian Magicians Fellowship, Christian Music Assn., U. Ala. Alumni Assn., Pi Tau Chi. Home: 3322 Altaloma Dr Birmingham AL 35216 Office: Impact 510 21st St N Birmingham AL 35203

WILSON, BARRON ORLANDO, minister; b. Jersey City, Jan. 7, 1970; s. Willie Will and Lois Ethel (Crafton) W. Student, Rutgers U., 1988-90. Ordained to ministry Bapt. Ch., 1990. Jr. trustee Mt. Calvery Bapt. Ch., Jersey City, 1987-89, choir dir., 1986-89, min. music, 1988-91, min. youth, 1988—, dir. Christian edn. dept., 1988—; youth counselor St. Paul's Shelter, Jersey City, 1990—. Recipient Martin Luther King award Mt. Calvery Bapt. Ch., 1986. Home: 277 Pacific Ave Jersey City NJ 07304

WILSON, CLIFFORD EARLE, minister; b. Rochester, Pa., Apr. 27, 1928; s. Robert Hill and Flora (Potts) W.; m. Helen K. Lovric, Oct. 10, 1953; 1 child, Francis R. BSL, St. Louis Christian Coll., 1977. Ordained to ministry Christian Ch., 1974. With St. Louis Baby and Mother's Home, 1975-77; missionary Rio Grande Prison Mission, Plano, Tex., 1977-80, Seattle Christian Indian Ch., 1980-81, Cen. Fla. Christian Mission, Orlando, 1981—. With USMC, 1944-53, USAF, 1961-66. Home: CFM Ministry 2005 E Central Blvd Orlando FL 32803-6230

WILSON, DANNY KARL, minister; b. Corinth, Miss., Mar. 24, 1959; s. Troy Leonard Jr. and Shirley Jean (Gann) W. BA, Union U., 1980; MDiv, Southwestern Baptist Theol. Sem., 1984. Ordained to ministry Bapt. Ch., 1985. Minister of youth Germantown (Tenn.) Bapt. Ch., 1980-81; interim minister of youth Handley Bapt. Ch., Ft. Worth, 1982; centrifuge camp dir. ch. recreation dept. Bapt. Sunday Sch. Bd., Nashville, 1982-84; minister of youth First Bapt. Ch., Blytheville, Ark., 1985-88; minister of youth and activities Ea. Hills Bapt. Ch., Montgomery, Ala., 1988—; Mem. adv. bd. Bapt. Student Union Ark. State U., Jonesboro, Ark., 1985-88. Named Outstanding Young Man of Am., 1983-87. Avocations: art, collecting calling cards. Home: 433 Ridgewood Ln Montgomery AL 36109 Office: Ea Hills Bapt Ch 3604 Pleasant Ridge Rd Montgomery AL 36109

WILSON, DAVID JEFFERIES, religious organization administrator; b. Feilding, New Zealand, Dec. 15, 1939; came to U.S., 1971; s. David William and Ngaere (Jefferies) W.; m. Elaine Tomlinson, Feb. 2, 1963; children: Stephen, Mark, James. BA in Bibl. Edn., Columbia (S.C.) Bible Coll., 1970. Lic. airline transport pilot; ordained minister, 1971. Sheep farmer New Zealand, 1958-60; airline pilot New Zealand Nat. Airways Corp., 1961-67; evangelist Open Air Campaigners, 1970—; br. dir. Open Air Campaigners, Balt., 1972-79; overseas ministries dir. Open Air Campaigners, various countries, 1980—; missionary TEAM, Bombay, India, 1979-80. Recipient Award of Merit Mayor of Balt., 1979. Baptist. Office: Open Air Campaigners Inc, 700 Mount Pleasant, Toronto, ON Canada M4S 2N7

WILSON, DAVID PALIR, evangelist; b. N.Y.C., June 13, 1930; s. Norman Hall and Emily (Palir) W.; m. Alma Straatsma, May 5, 1955; children: Victoria Wilson, Hall Mark Wilson. BA, Hope Coll., 1952; MDiv, Western Theol. Sem., Holland, Mich., 1955. Missionary Reformed Ch. in Am., Winnebago, Nebr., 1955-57; min. Reformed Ch. in Am., Lester, Iowa, 1957-59, Presbyn. Ch., Moonachie, N.J., 1960-62; evangelist at large Maywood, N.J., 1962—; pres. Trinity Travel and Tours, Inc., Maywood, 1962—. Author 20 books including The Issue of Bethlehem, The Rape of Innocence, Joy Beyond Belief, Calvary: Where the Cost was Counted...and the Price was Paid!; composer 2,000 hymns, some with music; composer wedding hymn Prince and Princess of Wales, 1981; composer state hymn State of Hawaii, 1983; contbr. poetry to The Chatham Courier. Recipient Israel State medal Govt. Israel, 1965, Poetry award State of N.Y., 1985. Home: 505 Maywood Ave Maywood NJ 07607 Office: Trinity Travel & Tours Inc 505 Maywood Ave Maywood NJ 07607

WILSON, DONALD EDWARD, JR., lawyer; b. New Orleans, Dec. 23, 1951; s. Donald Edward and Nell (Courtney) W.; m. Lynn Susan Whittlesey, Sept. 12, 1981; children: Robert Donald, Thomas Courtney, John Whittlesey. B.A., U. Va., 1973; J.D., Georgetown U., 1976. Bar: La 1976, D.C. 1977. Law clk. U.S. Ct. Appeals (fed. cir.), Washington, 1976-77; assoc. Morgan, Lewis & Bockius, Washington, 1977-81; assoc. counsel to Pres. White House, Washington, 1981-84; gen. counsel, dep. dir. Office Adminstrn., Exec. Office Pres., White House, Washington, 1984-85; spl. asst. to Pres. for adminstrn. White House, Washington, 1984-85; dep. asst. sec. for departmental mgmt. Dept. Treasury, Washington, 1985-86, dep. gen. counsel, 1986-88; ptnr. Prather, Seeger, Doolittle & Farmer, Washington, 1988—. Founder Old Exec. Office Bldg. Hist. Assn., Washington, 1985. Mem. La. State Bar Assn., D.C. Bar Assn., Alban Inst., So. Yacht Club, Met. Club Washington. Republican. Episcopalian. Avocations: sailing; backpacking. Office: Prather Seeger Doolittle & Farmer 1600 M St NW Ste 700 Washington DC 20036

WILSON, EDWARD COX, minister; b. Danville, Va., Sept. 30, 1938; s. James Thomas and Sallie Estelle (Cox) W.; m. Nancy Alva Hudson, Aug. 9, 1960; children: Michael Edward, Suzanne Adams. AB magna cum laude, Elon Coll., 1960; MDiv, Union Sem., 1965. Ordained to ministry Presbyn. Ch. (U.S.A.), 1965. Pastor Meadowbrook Presbyn. Ch., Greenville, N.C., 1965-67, Indian Trail (N.C.) Presbyn. Ch., 1971-86, Locust (N.C.) Presbyn. Ch., 1987—; assoc. pastor Selwyn Ave Presbyn. Ch., Charlotte, N.C., 1968-71; commr. Gen. Assembly, Presbyn. Ch. (U.S.A.), 1973, 79, 86; mem. com. on ministry, nomination com., mem. coun. Presbytery, also moderator, 1976-77. Contbr. articles, sermons, prayers to religious jours. Union Theol. Sem. fellow, 1965. Mem. Alban Inst. Democrat. Home: PO Box 214 Locust NC 28097 Office: Locust Presbyn Ch PO Box 277 Locust NC 28097 *In my life I am discovering that love is the primary law and the basic creed.*

WILSON, EDWARD JOHN, minister, spiritual and mental health counselor; b. Memphis, Mar. 16, 1946; s. Richard Clark Wilson and Helen Jane (Jordan) Burcl; m. Marilyn E. May, May 6, 1978 (div. 1983); 1 child, Elizabeth Claire; m. Kathleen M. Spor, Oct. 20, 1990. BS in Psychology, U. Houston, 1983, M.Ed. in Counseling Psychology, 1985; postgrad. Houston Grad. Sch. Theology; D.D. (hon.), Universal Life Ch., Modesto, Calif., 1981. Ordained to ministry Universal Life Ch., 1980, Congl. Ch. Practical Theology, Springfield, La., 1989. Prin. Wilson Vending Co., Houston, 1968-74; salesman Century 21 Westway Realty, Houston, 1974-75; sales mgr. Century 21 James L. Berry Realty, Houston, 1975-77; v.p. broker svcs. Century 21 of Tex., Inc., Houston, 1977-80; pastor Universal Life Ch., Houston, 1980-90; dir. Congl. Ch. Practical Theology, Houston, 1989—; instr. Houston Bapt. U., 1983-85; exec. dir. Motivational Counseling and Hypnosis Ctr., Houston. Editor, pub. ULC News newsletter, 1984-87; editor, pub., contbg. author The Motivator newsletter, 1988—. Mem. Am. Assn. Counseling and Devel., Tex. Assn. Counseling and Devel., Am. Mental Health Counselors Assn., Tex. Mental Health Counselors Assn., Assn. Religious and Values Issues in Counseling, Nat. Assn. Clergy Hypnotherapists (newsletter editor, pub., contbr. newsletter 1988), Nat. Soc. Hypnotherapists (Nat. chmn. cert. and edn. 1989—), Nat. Assn. Religious Counselors, Assn. Ind. Ministers, Mensa. Republican. Club: Toastmasters (pres. Houston club 1982). Avocations: camping, photography, movies. Home: 14222 Kimberley Ln # 411 Houston TX 77079 Office: Congl Ch of Practical Theology 2715 Bissonnet Ste 409 Houston TX 77005 *At our core we are, above all else, spiritual beings. That is our essence, the truth about who we are. To be "Born Again", born of the spirit, means that one has awakened to this very personal truth about oneself and to the power of the spiritual force within.*

WILSON, ELDON RAY, minister; b. Tieton, Wash., Apr. 16, 1931; s. Frank Madison and Beatrice Jane (Snider) W.; m. LouCelle Charlotte Seward, Aug. 3, 1957; children: Randall Wayne, Gary Ray. BTh, Internat. Bible Coll., San Antonio, 1967; PhD, Sussex Coll., Hayward's Heath, Eng., 1972. Ordained to ministry Emmanuel Ch., 1956. Founder, pastor Emmanuel Tabernacle, Port Arthur, Tex., 1958-63; evangelist U.S., Can., 1963-65; founder, pastor Gospel Tabernacle, Ilion, N.Y., 1965-70; pastor Full Gospel Ch., Halifax, N.S., Can., 1970-72; missionary Europe, Africa, 1972-77; founder, pastor New Covenant Ch., Columbus, Ohio, 1977-84; missionary New Covenant Ministries, Columbus, 1984—; bd. dirs. Good News Mission, Bogota, Colombia, 1985—; trustee Team Missions, Internat., Elkton, Md., 1989—. Author: The New Creation, 1975. Bd. dirs. Kuyahoora Valley Libr., Newport, N.Y., 1985—. With USN, 1951-55; Korea. Republican. Home: 7417 West St Newport NY 13416

WILSON, EVERETT LEROY, minister; b. Omaha, June 11, 1936; s. Leonard Snider and Lillian May (Leggat) W.; m. Donna Ileen Hiatt, Aug. 11, 1959; children: Miriam, Joel, Priscilla, Sarah, Ruth, Jonathan, James. BA, Hastings Coll., 1957; BDiv, North Pk. Theol. Sem., Chgo., 1962; M of Sacred Theology, Luth. Theol. Sem., Saskatoon, Sask., Can., 1987. Ordained to ministry Evang. Covenant Ch., 1964. Pastor Evang. Covenant Ch., Escanaba, Mich., 1962-66, Ceresco, Nebr., 1966-76; pastor Coll. Pk. Covenant Ch., Saskatoon, 1976-88, 1st Covenant Ch., Marinette, Wis., 1988—; pres. Saskatoon Ministerial Assn., 1979-80, Twin County Area Clergy Coun., Marinette, 1990-91; chmn. Evang. Covenant Ch. Can., Prince Albert, Sask., 1983-86; moderator annual meeting Evang. Covenant Ch., Chgo., 1984-85; pres. Ministerium of the Evang. Covenant Ch., 1991—; part-time instr. N.E. Wis. Tech. Coll., Marinette, 1991. Author: The Touch of God, 1975, Jesus and the End-Time, 1977, Christ Died for Me, 1980; contbr. articles to profl. jours. Chmn. Village Planning Commn., Ceresco, 1970, 74-75; sec. Friendship Inn, Saskatoon, 1982; 2d v.p. citizens coun. Pub. Sch. Bd., Saskatoon, 1982; team mem. Child Health Care Team-Human Svcs., Marinette, 1990. Mem. Covenant Ministerium (bd. dirs. 1974—, 76, 77—, 79). Office: 1st Covenant Ch 940 Carney Blvd Marinette WI 54143

WILSON, FREDERIC ROWLAND, educator; b. Council Bluffs, Iowa, Dec. 14, 1947; s. Frederic Clarke and Hazel (Burke) W.; m. Sallie Anjeanette Hall, May 17, 1969; children: Fred, Gregory, Anjeanette, Thomas. BS in Bible/Missions, Phila. Coll. of Bible, 1970; ThM, Dallas Theol. Sem., 1975; PhD in Adult Edn., Kans. State U., 1983. Licensed to ministry, Bapt. Ch. Dir. youth St. Paul's Evang. Ch., Camden, N.J., 1969-70; mem. campus staff InterVarsity Christian Fellowship, Madison, Wis., 1972-75, cons., 1975-88; asst. prof. Christian Edn. Can. Bible Coll./Can. Theol. Sem., Regina, Sask., Can., 1975-80, acad. v.p., dean of faculty, prof. Christian edn., 1990—; asst. prof. youth leadership Sterling (Kans.) Coll., 1980-83; assoc. prof. Christian Edn. Biola U., La Mirada, Calif., 1983-90, dir. D of Edn. program, 1985-90; dir. Christian Edn. Whittier (Calif.) Hills Bapt. Ch., 1984-86; interim pastorate Reformed Presbyn. Ch., Sterling, 1980-82; cons. Can. Sunday Sch. Mission, Sask., 1976-80. Contbr. articles, revs. to jours. Mem. Nat. Assn. Profs. Christian Edn. (bd. dirs. and newsletter editor 1990-94), Conf. on Faith and History, Religious Edn. Assn. (exec. bd. Greater Los Angeles Sunday Sch. conv. 1988-90), Assn. Profs. and Researchers in Religious Edn. Avocations: baseball, basketball, bicycle trips. Home: 86 Motherwell Crescent, Regina, SK Canada S4S 2W7 Office: Can Theol Sem, 4400 4th Ave, Regina, SK Canada S4T OH8

WILSON, GEORGE HARLEY, retired minister; b. Seymour, Ind., May 26, 1904; s. Cyrus L.D. and Elizabeth (Everett) W.; m. Berenice Andrews, Aug. 5, 1930; children: G. Hugh, Paul F., E. Gaye, E. Dee. BD, Butler Sch. Religion, Indpls., 1935. Ordained to ministry Christian Ch. (Disciples of Christ), 1935. Pastor 1st Christian Ch., Benton Harbor, Mich., 1934-42; State dir. religious edn. Mo. Christian Chs., 1942-46; mem. Coun. of Chs., Kansas City, Mo., 1946-50, St. Joseph, Mo., 1950-54; with New Orleans Fedn. Chs., 1954-72; moderator Christian Chs. (statewide), La. Mem. Rotary. Democrat. Home: 1071 S Edgewood Ave Jacksonville FL 32205

WILSON, GEORGE MCCONNELL, religious organization executive; b. Churchs Ferry, N.D., Oct. 19, 1913; s. Clarence McNair and Mary Belle (McConnell) W.; m. Helen Josephine Bjorck, Sept. 3, 1940; children: Jean Elizabeth (Mrs. Ralph Bertram Greener), Judith (Mrs. Larry Grimes), Janet (Mrs. Steve Hanks). Student, N.D. State Sch. of Sci., 1932-33, U. Minn., 1936, Northwestern Coll., 1933-37; Litt. D. (hon.) Houghton Coll., 1962; LL.D. (hon.) Gordon Coll., 1969. Owner, mgr. Wilson Press & NW Book & Bible House, Mpls., 1940-50; asst. to pres., bus. mgr. Northwestern Coll., Mpls., 1947-50; bus. mgr., sec.-treas. Billy Graham Evangelistic Assn., Mpls., 1950—, exec. v.p., 1962-87; pres. World Wide Publs., Mpls., 1970-88; bd. dirs. Billy Graham Evangelistic Assn., Eng., Australia, Can., France, Ger., Hong Kong, U.S.; pres., founder Evang. Coun. for Fin. Accountability, Washington; Sec. Christian Broadcasting Assn., Honolulu, Global Concern, Montrose, Calif.; treas. Blue Ridge Broadcasting Corp., Black Mountain, N.C.; asst. treas. World Wide Pictures, Burbank, Calif.; v.p., bd. dirs. Bank of Mpls. and Trust Co., chmn. bd., 1985—. Author: 20 Years Under God, 1971. Compiler: Words of Wisdom, 1967. Mng. editor Decision mag. Bd. dirs. Children's Heart Fund, Mpls., pres., 1980-83; chmn. bd. Prison Fellowship, Washington; bd. dirs. Mail Users Coun., chmn. 1969; bd. dirs. Laubach Literacy Found., 1963-67, Youth for Christ U.S.A., Wheaton, Ill., Northwestern Coll., Roseville, Minn., Community Coll. Mpls.; founder, dir. Mpls. Youth for Christ; v.p., chmn. exec. com. Tyndale Theol. Sem.; pres. Tom Tipton Ministries. Named Layman of Yr., Nat. Assn. Evangelicals, Tyndale Theol. Sem., World Opportunities Internat., Mgr. of the Yr., Christian Ministries Mgmt. Assn., 1988; apptd. Pres.'s Com. on Mental Retardation, 1988; recipient Managerial Achievement award Adminstrv. Mgmt. Soc., Award of Distinction, Direct Mail Advertising Assn., 1980, William W. Holes Direct Mail award, 1973, Disting. Service award Greater Mpls. C. of C., 1972, Disting. Service award City of Mpls., 1977, Exec. of Yr. award Mpls. Gopher Chpt. Nat. Secs. Assn., 1979, Good Neighbor award Sta. WCCO, Mpls., 1983, 87, Appreciation award Downtown Coun. of Mpls.; George Wilson Day proclaimed in Minnesota by Gov., and Mpls. by Mayor. Mem. Mpls. Press Club, Direct Mail Mktg. Assn., Adminstrv. Mgmt. Soc., Nat. Religious Broadcasters (named Outstanding Christian Mgmt. 1988), Bus. and Profl. award Religious Heritage of Am., 1990, Religious Pub. Relations Coun., Nat. Soc. Fund Raisers, Presdl. Roundtable, Rep. Congrl. Leadership Coun., Rep. Sen. Inner Circle, U.S. Sen. Bus. Adv. Bd., Loring-Nicollet Community Council, Citizens League Mpls., Independent-Republicans of Minn. Elephant Club. Baptist. Clubs: Decathlon, Mpls. Athletic, Six O'clock. Lodge: Kiwanis (bd. dirs. Kiwanis Found., Disting. Svc. to the Community award Downton club 1989). Home: 1425 W 28th St Ste 621 Minneapolis MN 55408 Office: Billy Graham Evangelistic Assn 1300 Harmon Pl Minneapolis MN 55403

WILSON, GUY HARRIS, JR., minister; b. Waycross, Ga., June 13, 1943; s. Guy Harris and Virginia (Pace) W.; m. Bette Lynn Boothe, June 17, 1966; 1 child, Guy Harris III. BA in Religion, Samford U., 1966; M in Ch. Music, So. Bapt. Theol. Sem., Louisville, 1970. Ordained to ministry So. Bapt. Conv., 1978. Min. music and youth 1st Bapt. Ch., Lithonia, Ga., 1970-72; min. music, youth and recreation 1st Bapt. Ch., Opelika, Ala., 1972-76; min. music and youth North Denedin (Fla.) Bapt. Ch., 1976-80; assoc. pastor, min. music 1st Bapt. Ch., Lithia Springs, Ga., 1980-88, Covington, Ga., 1988—. Dir. music Concord Assn., Lithia Springs, 1981-88, coord. women's softball, 1983-87. Home: 5 Deerfield Rd Covington GA 30209 Office: 1st Bapt Ch 1135 Floyd St Covington GA 30209

WILSON, HARRELL THOMAS, minister; b. Athens, Ga., Dec. 12, 1944; s. John Carlton and Noie (Daniels) W.; m. Rebecca Kay Jenkins, July 29, 1945; children: Eugene Thomas, Tamara Kay, Jennifer Renee, Wilson Konkle, Russell Elbert. Student, Pentecostal Bible Inst., Tupelo, Miss., 1964-65; BA in Theology, Ind. Bible Coll., Seymour, 1987. Ordained to ministry, United Pentecostal Ch., 1960. Pastor United Pentecostal Ch., Tipton, Ind., 1965-70, Wabash, Ind., 1972-73, Rockville, Ind., 1973-74, Niles, Mich., 1974-79, Sheridan, Ind., 1980—; presbyter United Pentecostal Ch., Ind. Sect., 3d Dist., 1987—. Home: 602 S California St Sheridan IN 46069-1206 Office: Bible Ch 1478 W State Rd 38 Sheridan IN 46069-1206

WILSON, HARRY COCHRANE, clergyman; b. St. John, N.B., Can., May 31, 1945; s. Harry Shepherd and Gertrude (Cochrane) W.; m. Gloria Lea Trites, Oct. 8, 1965; children: Troy Spurgeon, Kristi Lea. BA, Bethany Bible Coll., 1972, DD (hon.), 1988; DD (hon.), Cen. Wesleyan Coll., S.C., 1989. Br. exec. Can. Permanent Trust Co., Monton, N.B., 1965-70; pastor Wesleyan Ch., Blacks Harbor, N.B., 1971-74, Dartmouth, N.S., Can., 1974-80; dist. supt. Delta dist. Wesleyan Ch., Jackson, Miss., 1981-88; bd. adminstr. Wesleyan Ch., Indpls., 1984—; dir. Sunday schs. Wesleyan Ch. World Hdqrs., Marion, Ind., 1980-81; gen. supt. Wesleyan Ch. Internat. Ctr., Indpls., 1988—. Author: The Wesleyan Adv. Recipient Pastor's award Atlantic Dist., 1975, 77. Mem. Nat. Assn. Evangs., World Meth. Coun. Office: Internat Ctr Wesleyan Ch 6060 Castleway W Dr Indianapolis IN 46250

WILSON, JACQUELINE ETHERIDGE, religious organization executive; b. Washington, Dec. 16, 1937; d. Robert B. and Bessie Lee (Dixon) Etheridge; m. John H. Wilson, Jr., Mar. 2, 1957; children—Margaret Cecelia, John H., Susan Elizabeth, Jacqueline Marie. A.B. in Elem. Edn., Cath. U. Am., 1966; M.Ed. in Adminstrn. and Supervision, Howard U., 1980. Typist law office, 1954-56; clk.-typist U.S. Army Corr. Unit, Pentagon, Washington, 1955; elem. sch. tchr. D.C. Pub. Schs., 1966-79; exec. dir. Office of Black Catholics, archbishop's sec. for black Caths., Archdiocese of Washington, 1979—; math. resource tchr. Benning Sch., 1966-69; mem. textbook evaluation com. D.C. Pub. Schs., 1971-73, cons. career devel. ctr., 1977-78; lectr. Jospehine Sem., Washington, 1981, Washington Theol. Union, 1983, Trinity Coll., 1983—; cons. Black Cath. History Research Project, 1983—; mem. adv. bd. Zest, Inc., 1989—. Catechist, St. Gabriel Ch., 1963-81, charter mem., pres. parish council, 1971-77; master catechist, cons. Cath. edn. and other issues, 1979—; charter mem., pres., bd. dirs. Secretariat for Black Catholics, 1974-78; team mem. IMPAC Teen Retreats, 1976-79; mem. com. Africa and diaspora St. Augustine Ch., Washington, 1981—; mem. planning com. March on Washington, 1983; supporter Mt. Carmel Shelter for Homeless Women, 1982—; founder, dir. Rejoice! Conf. on Black Cath. Liturgy, 1984—; mem. children's programming adv. com. Sta. WDCA, 1984-89; mem. Ctr. for Life; trustee Nat. Black Cath. Congress, regional coord., 1985—; trustee Providence Hosp. Author, editor: Combating Racism; editor Black Cath. News, 1979—. Recipient grants and awards D.C. Pub. Schs., D.C. Community Humanities Council, Archdiocese of Washington, Am. Bd. Cath. Missions, Cath. U. Am. Mem. NAACP, ASCD, Nat. Black Child Devel. Inst., Nat. Urban League, Nat. Assn. Black Cath. Adminstrs.

WILSON, JAMES RICKER, physicist, consultant; b. Berkeley, Calif., Oct. 21, 1922; s. Leslie Ramsey and Ethel Frances (Banker) W.; m. Demetra George Corombos, Feb. 25, 1949; children: Leslie, Marika, George, Tasia, Peter. BS in Chemistry, U. Calif., Berkeley, 1943, PhD in Physics, 1952. Physicist Sandia Corp., Berkeley, 1952-53; physicist Lawrence Livermore (Calif.) Nat. Lab., 1953-88, lab. assoc., 1991—; cons. Lawrence Livermore Nat. Lab., 1988-90. Author: Numerical Modeling in Physics, 1991. With U.S. Army, 1944-46. Fellow Am. Phys. Soc., Murdock Found.; mem. Am. Astron. Soc., Internat. Astronomy Union. Democrat. Achievements include establishment of neutrino heating mechanism for supernova explosions. Home: 737 South M Livermore CA 94550 Office: Lawrence Livermore Nat Lab 7000 East Ave PO Box 808 L-35 Livermore CA 94550

WILSON, JAMES RONALD, minister; b. Mobile, Ala., Apr. 1, 1954; s. Acy William and Annie Louise (Wheat) W.; m. Jody Sue Clanton, Aug. 6, 1977; 1 child, James Matthew. BA, Samford U., 1976; MDiv, Southwestern Bapt. Theol. Sem., Ft. Worth, 1980; postgrad., Baylor U., 1981-82; ThM, Columbia Theol. Sem., Decatur, Ga., 1987. Ordained to ministry So. Bapt. Conv., 1979. Pastor Gholson Bapt. Ch., Waco, Tex., 1981-82, Greenville (Ga.) Bapt. Ch., 1982-85, Center Hill Bapt. Ch., Monroe, Ga., 1985-88, 1st Bapt. Ch., Hartselle, Ala., 1989—. Columnist local weekly newspaper, 1983-85. Chaplain Hartselle High Sch. Varsity Football Team, 1989—; mem. Bread for the World, Washington, 1990-91; bd. dirs. United Way, Morgan County, Ala., 1991—. Mem. Lions, Rotary (v.p. Hartselle club 1991), Masons (sec. Greenville club 1984-85). Office: 1st Bapt Ch 300 Woodland St Hartselle AL 35640

WILSON, JONATHAN REFORD, religious educator; b. Okla. City, Aug. 10, 1951; s. Jesse Reford and Mildred Gene (Lane) W.; m. Martha Ethel Crosby, June 23, 1979; 1 child, Leah. BA, Free Will Bapt. Coll., Nashville, 1975; M in Christian Studies, Regent Coll., Vancouver, British Columbia, 1980, MDiv, 1985; PhD, Duke U., 1989. Lay chaplain G.F. Strong Rehab. Ctr., Vancouver, 1977-80; sr. pastor Edmonds Bapt. Ch., Burnaby, British Columbia, 1980-86; asst. prof. religious studies Westmont Coll., Santa Barbara, Calif., 1989—. Contbr. articles to profl. jours. Mem. Am. Acad. Religion, Soc. Christian Ethics, Soc. Bibl. Lit. Office: Westmont Coll 955 La Paz Rd Santa Barbara CA 93108

WILSON, LOIS M., minister; b. Winnipeg, Man., Can., Apr. 8, 1927; d. Edwin Gardiner Dunn and Ada Minnie (Davis) Freeman; m. Roy F. Wilson, June 9, 1950; children: Ruth, Jean, Neil, Bruce. BA, United Coll., Winnipeg, 1947, BDiv, 1969; Diploma in TV prodn., Ryerson Tech. Inst., 1974; DDiv (hon.), Victoria U., Toronto, 1978, United Theol. Coll., Montreal, 1978, Wycliff Coll., 1983, Queens U., Kingston, 1984, U. Winnipeg, 1986, Mt. Allison U., 1988; LLD (hon.), Trent U., Peterborough, 1984, Dalhousie U., 1989, Dalhousie U., 1989; DCL (hon.), Acadia U., 1984; DHuml (hon.), Mt. St. Vincent, Halifax, 1984. Ordained to ministry United Church of Can., 1965. Minister Thunder Bay, 1965-69, Hamilton, 1969-78, Kingston, 1978-80; moderator United Church of Can., Kingston, 1980-82; McGeachy sr. scholar United Church of Can., 1989-91; pres. Can. Council of Chs., Toronto, Ont., 1976-79; co-dir. Ecumenical Forum Can., Toronto, Ont., 1983-89; pres. World Council of Chs., Geneva, 1983-91; chancellor Lakehead U., Thurder Bay, Ont., 1990—; mem. adv. coun. internat. devel. studies U. Toronto, 1987—; spokesperson Project Ploughshares, 1st and 2d UN Conf. on Disarmament, N.Y.C., 1978-82; lectr. Vancouver Sch. Theology, 1980, Queens Theol. Coll., 1982-83; officer Human Rights Commn., Ont., 1973; bd. regents Victoria U., 1990—. Author: Like a Mighty River, 1981, Turning the World Upside Down, 1989; contbr. articles to profl. publs. Pres. Social Planning Coun., Thunder Bay, 1967-68, Can. Com. for Scientists and Scholars, Toronto, 1982; bd. dirs. Elizabeth Fry Soc., Hamilton, 1976-79, Amnesty Internat., 1978—, Can. Inst. for Internat. Peace and Security, 1984-88, Energy Probe, 1981-86; active Refugee Status Adv. Com., 1985-89; bd. dirs. Can. Univ. Svc. Overseas, 1983-85; chmn. Urban Rural Mission, Can., 1990—; mem. Environ. Assessment Panel Govt. Can., Nuclear Fuel Waste Mgmt. and Disposal Concept, 1989—; trustee Nelson Mandela Fund, 1990—. Decorated Order of Can., 1984, Order of Ont., 1991; recipient Queens Jubilee medal; named hon. pres. Student Christian Movement of Can., Toronto, 1976; recipient World Federalist peace award, 1985; Pearson peace medal UN Assn. of Can., 1985. Mem. Can. Assn. Adult Edn. (bd. dirs. 1986-90), CAW (pub. rev. bd. 1986—), Friends Can. Broadcasting (bd. dirs. 1986—), Civil Liberties Assn. (bd. dirs. 1986—, v.p.). Avocations: skiing; canoeing; camping; reading. Office: World Coun Chs, 150 rue de Ferney, POB 2100, 1211 Geneva 20, Switzerland

WILSON, LONNIE ALEXANDER, minister; b. Statesville, N.C., Jan. 3, 1932. Ordained to ministry Ind. Fundamental Chs. Am. Pastor Temple Bapt Ch, Statesville. With USN, 1951-54. Home: 545 N Oakland Ave Statesville NC 28677 Office: Temple Bapt Ch Museum Rd Statesville NC 28677

WILSON, LYNN JONATHAN, clergyman; b. Roslyn, S.D., Jan. 6, 1958; s. Woodrow Warrenn and Dora (Starkenberg) W. AA, York (Nebr.) Jr. Coll., 1979; BA, U. Nebr., 1981; GTh, Assn Free Luth. Sem., Mpls., 1989. Ordained to ministry Assn. Free Luth. Congregations, 1989. Tchr. mentally retarded Martin Luther Home, York, 1983-85; pastor Finlayson, Minn., 1987—, Valley City, N.D., 1987, Roslyn, 1989—. Lt. U.S. Army Res., 1981-84, 87—. Lt. USAR, 1981-84, 87—. Republican. Home: PO Box 135 Roslyn SD 57261

WILSON, MASON, JR., priest; b. Kansas City, Mo., Aug. 31, 1924; s. Mason and Eula Jane (Bullock) W.; m. Barbara Prue Sherrill, Jan. 2, 1960; children: Mason, Henry Knox Sherrill. BA, U. Tex., 1948; MDiv, Episcopal Theol. Sch., 1951. Ordained priest Episcopal Ch., 1951. Rector Ch. of Messiah, Woods Hole, Mass., 1951-61, St. Andrew's Ch., Framingham, Mass., 1961—; chmn. ecumenical commn. Episcopal Diocese of Mass., Boston, 1980—, mem. standing com., 1982—; mem. Mass. Com. on Christian Unity, 1976—. Commr. Human Rels. Commn., City of Framingham, 1970-82. Named Disting. Citizen, Jaycees, 1977; Norman Nash fellow, 1977. Mem. Mass. Episcopal Clergy Assn. Home: 72 Main St Framingham MA 01701 Office: St Andrew's Episcopal Ch Buckminster Sq Framingham MA 01701

WILSON, NATHANIEL J., minister; b. Visalia, Calif., Dec. 6, 1945; s. Paul R. and Vera D. (Anderson) W.; m. Mary Ruth McDonald, Dec. 17, 1965; children: Rebecca Elaine, Sheila Ruth. BTh., Christian Life Coll., 1965; M in Religion, So. Calif. Coll., Costa Mesa, 1991. Ordained min. Pentecostal Ch. Pastor South Flint (Mich.) Tabernacle, 1973-80; dir., speaker Harvestime Internat. Radio Ministry, St. Louis, 1980-81; founder, pres. Reach Worldwide, Inc., Sacramento, 1981—, Reach Satellite Network, Sacramento, 1981—; pastor The Rock Ch., Sacramento, 1981—. Author: (book) The Man of God and His Work, 1981, The Men of Human History, 1990, (coll. curriculum) The P.A.S.T.O.R.S. Course, 1986; host: (radio program) Word Talk, Sacramento, 1989—. Mem. Progress, Strength, Renewal, Inc. (bd. dirs. 1983—).

WILSON, NEAL CLAYTON, clergyman; b. Lodi, Calif., July 5, 1920; s. Nathaniel Carter and Hannah Myrtle (Wallin) W.; m. Elinor Esther Neumann, July 19, 1942; children—Norman C., Shirley Wilson Anderson. B.A. in Theology and History, Pacific Union Coll., 1942; postgrad., Theol. Sem., Andrews U., 1934-44, D.D. (hon.), 1976. Ordained to ministry Seventh-day Adventist Ch., 1944. Acct. So. Asia div. Seventh-day Adventist Ch., Poona, India, 1939-40; acting treas. Oriental Watchman Press, Poona, India, 1940; asst. to cashier St. Helena Sanitarium, Deer Park, Calif., 1941-42; pastor, evangelist Wyo., 1942; evangelist Gen. Conf. Seventh-day Adventist Ch., 1952-55; pastor, evangelist Middle East div. Seventh-day Adventist Ch., Cairo, 1944-45; pres. Egyptian mission Middle East div. Seventh-day Adventist Ch., 1945-50, pres. Nile Union, 1950-58; sec. Central Calif. Conf. Seventh-day Adventist Ch., 1959-60; sec., then pres. Columbia Union conf. Seventh-day Adventist Ch., Takoma Park, Md., 1960-66; v.p. Gen. Conf. Seventh-day Adventist Ch., Washington, 1966-78, pres. Gen. Conf. Seventh-Day Adventist, 1979—; dir. Pacific Press, Loma Linda Foods, Harris Pine Mills, Internat. Ins. Co., Takoma Park. Contbr. articles to profl. jours. Bd. dirs. Loma Linda, U. Calif., Andrews U., Christian Record Braille Found., Oakwood Coll., Rev. and Herald Pub. Assn. Office: Gen Conf Seventh-day Adventist Ch 6840 Eastern Ave NW Washington DC 20012 also: 12501 Old Columbia Pike Silver Spring MD 20904

WILSON, REAGON WAYNE, JR., minister; b. Ft. Worth, Tex., Feb. 29, 1952; s. Reagon Wayne and Joanne (Goulden) W.; m. Rachel Anne Bender, Dec. 19, 1971; children: Jason Mark, Jeremy Wayne, Jared Dean, Joshua Randal. BS in Bible, BA in History, Okla. Christian U., 1979; MDiv, N.Y. Theol. Sem., N.Y.C., 1982, STM, 1984, DMin, 1986. Ordained to ministry, Chs. of Christ, 1974. Pastor Worcester (Mass.) Ch. of Christ, 1971-72, Methuen (Mass.) Ch. of Christ, 1974-80; assoc. pastor Cen. Ch. of Christ, Topeka, Kans., 1980; pastor Monmouth Ch. of Christ, Tinton Falls, N.J., 1980—; chaplain Riverview Med. Ctr., Red Bank, N.J., 1981-89; v.p. Red Bank Area Ministerium, 1984-89, pres., 1989—; adv. bd. Aslan Youth Ministries, Red Bank, 1984—; dir. Symposium on World Evangelism, 1977-79; trainer for staff John Guest Evangelistic Crusade, 1988; ethics cons. Unilever Rsch., Inc., Edgewater, N.J., 1986—. Author: Scattered Servants, 1986; editor Famity, A Family Resource Newsletter, 1981—. Mem. supt.'s adv. com. on multi-cultural edn. Monmouth Regional High Sch., Tinton Falls, 1991—. Recipient Community Service award, Aslan Youth Ministries, 1989, Outstanding Expository Preacher, Sunset Sch. Preaching, 1973. Home:

28 Riverdale Ave E Tinton Falls NJ 07724 Office: Monmouth Ch of Christ 312 Hance Ave Tinton Falls NJ 07724

WILSON, ROBERT ALLEN, religion educator; b. Geff, Ill., Oct. 7, 1936; s. Perry Arthur and Eva Mae (Dye) W.; m. Patsy Ann Jarrett, June 1, 1957; children: Elizabeth Ann, Angela Dawn, Christine Joy. AB, Lincoln (Ill.) Christian Coll., 1958, Hanover Coll., 1961; MRE, So. Bapt. Seminary, 1965, EdD, 1972. Ordained to ministry Ch. of Christ, 1958. Minister Fowler (Ind.) Christian Ch., 1955-59, Zoah Christian Ch., Scottsburg, Ind., 1959-64; minister of edn. and youth Shively Christian Ch., Louisville, 1964-69; prof. Christian edn. and family life Lincoln (Ill.) Christian Seminary, 1969—; pres. Christian Marriage and Family Enrichment Services, Lincoln, 1980—. Contbr. articles to profl. jours. Mem. Nat. Assn. Profs. Christian Edn. (editor newsletter 1975-79, pres. 1979-80), Religious Edn. Assn. Lodge: Rotary (bd. dirs. Lincoln chpt. 1988—). Home: 330 Campus View Dr Lincoln IL 62656 Office: Lincoln Christian Coll and Seminary 100 Campus View Dr Box 178 Lincoln IL 62656

WILSON, RONALD AMOS, music minister; b. Montgomery, Ala., Dec. 17, 1946; s. Amos Henry Jr. and Verna Lorraine (Watts) W.; m. Mary Antrim Bell, Aug. 3, 1968; children: Tamara Leigh, Amy Elizabeth. B Music Edn., Samford U., 1970; M Ch. Music, Southwestern Bapt. Theol. Sem., 1973; postgrad., U. Ala., 1980-81. Ordained to ministry So. Bapt. Conv., 1968. Min. music/youth 2d Bapt. Ch., Bessemer, Ala., 1966-70; asst. min. music Travis Ave Bapt. Ch., Ft. Worth, 1971-73; min. music/youth Normandale Bapt. Ch., Montgomery, Ala., 1973-75; min. music 1st Bapt. Ch., Tuscaloosa, Ala., 1976—. Mem. Theatre Tuscaloosa, Tuscaloosa Civic Chorus, 1978-90; bd. dirs. Tuscaloosa Summer Show, 1980-83, Community Soup Bowl, Tuscaloosa, 1981—. Mem. Ala. Bapt. Singing Men, Ala. Bapt. Edn. Music Assn. (pres. 1987-88), So. Bapt. Ch. Music Conf. Republican. Avocations: civic theater, TV commls., golf, fishing, racquet ball. Office: 1st Bapt Ch 721 Greensboro Ave Tuscaloosa AL 35401

WILSON, RONALD LEE, minister, printing company owner; b. Warren, Ohio, Apr. 28, 1967; s. Ronald Glenn Wilson and Beulah Imogene (Baker) Meeks; m. Shirley Anne Cutlip, May 21, 1988. AA, Ohio Valley Coll., 1987, BA, 1989; postgrad., Ref. Theol. Sem., Orlando, Fla., 1990—. Cert. police officer. Preacher Ch. of Christ, Ohio Valley area, W.Va., 1985-89; min. Sorrento (Fla.) Ch. of Christ, 1989-91; video sales rep. Video Biz, Mt. Dora, Fla., 1990—; owner Penguin Printing, Eustis, Fla., 1991; tchr. World Bible Sch., Mt. Dora, 1990-91; chaplain Lake County Vo-Tech Police Acad., Eustis, 1990-91. Mem. Young Dems., Moundsville, W.Va., 1985. Mem. Didasko Bible Ministries (pres. 1989—), Fla. Peace Officers Assn., Gideons Internat. Democrat. Home and Office: 36329 Clear Lake Dr Eustis FL 32726

WILSON, STANTON RODGER, minister; b. Hammond, N.Y., Sept. 21, 1923; s. Earl Stanton and Alice Nancy (Rodger) W.; m. Marion Agnes Stout, July 26, 1949; children: John Wallace, James Stout, Nancy Catherine, Scott James. AB, Cornell U., 1943; BD, Princeton Theol. Sem., 1949, ThM, 1958; postgrad., San Francisco Sem., San Anselmo, Calif., 1964, 66, 68; DD, Bloomfield Coll., 1969. Ordained to ministry Presbyn. Ch. (U.S.A.), 1949. Pastor 1st Presbyn. Ch., New Gretna, N.J., 1949-51; missionary United Presbyn. Ch., Andong, Republic of Korea, 1951-64; mission exec. United Presbyn. Ch., Seoul, 1964-80; assoc. pastor Grosse Pointe (Mich.) Meml. Ch., 1980-90; parish assoc. Presbyn. Parish of Valleys, Stephens City, Va., 1990—; Korea rep. Ch. World Svc., Seoul, 1967-78; vice chmn. bd. dirs. Presbyn. Theol. Sem., Seoul, 1970-75; auditor Yonsei U., Seoul, 1974-78; vis. fellow Princeton (N.J.) Theol. Sem., 1978-80; mem. Presbytery of Shenandoah, 1991—. Author: Report from the ROK, 1969, Korea and Korean Church, 1969, The Writings of Dr. John A. Mackay, 1979; conbr.: The Ecumenical Era in Church and Society, 1959; assoc. editor Presbyn. Outlook, 1974. Chmn. bd. dirs. Keimyung U., Taegu, Republic of Korea, 1967-73, Seoul Fgn. Sch., 1974-77; founder Korea Foreigners Counseling Svc., Seoul, 1973. With U.S. Army, 1943-46; capt. USAR, 1978. Decorated Welfare medal (Republic of Korea); scholar State of N.Y., 1940-43. Mem. Econ. Club (Detroit), Detroit Country Club. Home: 4579 Stanley Dr Stephens City VA 22655

WILSON, THOMAS RAIFORD, JR., clergyman, counselor; b. Memphis, Aug. 11, 1930; s. Thomas Raiford Sr. and Evelyn (Harris) W.; m. Mary Louise Simpson, Sept. 8, 1952; children: Susan Wilson Mann, Daniel Raiford Wilson. BS, Memphis State Coll., 1951; MDiv, Vanderbilt U., 1973; MS, Memphis State U., 1984; D in Ministry, St. Paul Sch. Theol., 1987. Minister Dresden (Tenn.) Cir. Meth. Ch., 1951-53, Oakfield-Mt. Carmel Meth. Ch., Jackson, Tenn., 1953-55; assoc. minister St. Lukes Meth. Ch., Memphis, 1955-58; sr. minister Grace Meth. Ch., Memphis, 1958-69, Mullins United Meth. Ch., Memphis, 1969-77, First United Meth. Ch., Memphis, 1977—; founder, chief exec. officer Hospice of Memphis, Inc., 1980-85. Author: The In Between Generation, 1987. Pres. Whitehaven Ministers Assn., Memphis, 1962, Downtown Chs. Assn., Memphis, 1987. Fed. Govt. grantee, 1980, 82; recipient Frank K. Houston award Vanderbilt U., 1954. Diplomate Am. Assn. Family Counselors; mem. Am. Mental Health Counselors Assn., Am. Assn. for Counseling and Devel., Guild of Clergy Counselors, Am. Assn. Christian Counselors. Home: 6804 Stout Rd Memphis TN 38119 Office: First United Meth Ch 204 N Second St Memphis TN 38105

WILSON, WILLIAM ARTHUR, educator; b. St. Louis, Aug. 22, 1949; s. James Walter and Paula Elda (Bender) W.; m. Lynn Joyce Jolly, June 18, 1977; children: John William, Luke William. BSEd in Math., Concordia Coll., 1972; MAR in Biblical Theology, Concordia Sem., 1976; EdD in Higher Edn., Coll. William and Mary, 1985. Assoc. dir. Am. Assn. Bible Colls., Fayetteville, Ark., 1987—. Author, editor: Am. Assn. Bible Colls. Manual, 1991. Office: Am Assn Bible Colls 130 F North College Ave Fayetteville AR 72701

WILSON, WILLIAM MARION, minister, church organization administrator; b. Owensboro, Ky., Oct. 4, 1958; s. Marion Alva and Joyce Marie (Collins) W.; m. Lisa Carole Miller, June 2, 1978; children: William Ashley, Sara Elisabeth. BS, Western Ky. U., 1979; cert., Bible Tng. Inst., Cleveland, Tenn., 1983. Ordained to ministry Ch. of God of Prophecy, 1979. State evangelist Ch. of God of Prophecy, Elizabethtown, Ky., 1979-80, state youth sec., 1980-83; pastor, state youth sec. Ch. of God of Prophecy, Willard, Ohio, 1983; gen. youth sec. Ch. of God of Prophecy, Cleveland, 1983—; mem. CCI, Wheaton, Ill., 1983—, RCMA, Cleveland, 1988—. Editor Victory mag. Trustee Tomlinson Coll., Cleveland, 1987—. Office: Ch of God of Prophecy Keith St NW Box 2910 Cleveland TN 37311

WIMAN, RICHARD PAYNE, minister; b. Brandon, Miss., July 31, 1950; s. James Puryear and Mary Frances (Williams) W.; m. Dorothy Helen Caulfield, June 8, 1974; children: Lydia Ruth, Joy Elizabeth, Lindsay Caroline. BA in History, U. So. Miss., 1972; MDiv., Reformed Sem., 1976. Ordained to ministry Presbyn. Ch., 1976. Dir. youth Brandon (Miss.) Presbyn. Ch., 1974; pastor Calvary Presbyn. Ch., Mize, Miss., 1976-81, First Presbyn. Ch., Belzoni, 1982—; chaplain Boy Scouts Am. Jamboree, Fort A.P. Hill, Va., 1985, Humphreys Acad., Belzoni, 1989—, Humphreys County Meml. Hosp., Belzoni, 1990—. Author: (book) Tired Tubes and Ten-Speed Turkeys, 1991; newspaper columnist Belzoni Banner, 1982—; contbr. articles to profl. jours. Scoutmaster Troop 91 Boy Scouts Am., Belzoni, 1986—, Troop 201, Clarksdale, Miss., 1989; vice chmn. Humphrey's County Rep. Party, Belzoni, 1987—. Recipient Scouter's Key Boy Scouts Am., Clarksdale, 1985, Woodbadge Tng. award, 1987, Vigil Honor Order of the Arrow, 1988, Dist. award of merit, Greenville, Miss., 1988, Silver Beaver award Boy Scouts Am., 1991. Mem. Humphreys County C. of C. (bd. dirs. 1986), Rotary (pres. Belzoni club 1990-91). Home: 503 Holmes St Belzoni MS 39038 Office: 1st Presbyn Ch 201 Pecan St Belzoni MS 39038

WIMBERLY, JOHN WILLIAM, JR., minister; b. Jackson, Mich., Apr. 21, 1947; s. John William and Dorothy (Graf) W.; m. Phyllis Birch. BA, U. Wis., 1972; MDiv, McCormick Theol. Sem., Chgo., 1975; PhD, Cath. U., Washington, 1991. Ordained to ministry Presbyn. Ch. (USA), 1974. Asst. pastor St. John's United Presbyn. Ch., Houston, 1974-76; assoc. pastor Bradley Hills Presbyn. Ch., Bethesda, Md., 1976-83; pastor Western Presbyn. Ch., Washington, 1983—; moderator Synod of the Piedmont, 1985-86, Nat. Capital Presbytery, Washington, 1990; trustee Barber Scotia Coll., Concord, N.C., 1988—. Co-founder Miriam's Kitchen for the Homeless, Washington, 1983—. Recipient award for Outstanding Community Svc., Potomac Power & Elec. Co., 1989, Centro Communal Unidad, 1988. Home: 6243 29th St NW Washington DC 20015 Office: Western Presbyn Ch 1906 H St NW Washington DC 20006

WIMER, BARNEY DALE, religious educator, librarian; b. Roseburg, Oreg., Aug. 12, 1939; s. Everett Guy and Troas (Church) W.; m. Mary Ellen Anderson, Aug. 1, 1964; 1 child, Wendy Leigh. B.A., N.W. Christian Coll., Eugene, Oreg., 1962; M.Div., Emmanuel Sch. Religion, Johnson City, Tenn., 1969; M.L.S., U. Wash., 1976, Ph.D., 1985; Prof., librarian Puget Sound Christian Coll., Edmonds, Wash., 1969-86; ind. research and ednl. cons., 1986—. Home: 6343 NE 158th St Bothell WA 98011 Office: Puget Sound Christian Coll 410 4th Ave N Edmonds WA 98020

WIMMER, JOHN RICHARD, minister; b. Rushville, Ind., Nov. 8, 1956; s. John Howard and Dorothy (Brown) W.; m. Jan S. Blaising, June 17, 1978. BA, U. Indpls., 1979; MDiv, Duke U., 1982; PhD, U. Chgo., 1991. Ordained to ministry United Meth. Ch., 1984. Pastor 1st United Meth. Ch., West Lafayette, Ind., 1982-86, Lafayette, Ind., 1987—; adj. faculty U. Indpls., 1991—. Author: Torrents of Grace, 1990, No Pain, No Gain: Hope for Those Who Struggle, 1985 (main selection Guideposts Book Club, 1987). John Wesley fellow Found. for Theol. Edn., 1986. Mem. Am. Acad. of Religion, Am. Hist. Assn., Soc. Bibl. Lit., Soc. John Wesley Scholars.

WINBERY, CARLTON LOYD, religion educator; b. Urania, La., Feb. 15, 1937; s. Tillman L. and Elma (Foshee) W.; m. Sarah Ann Hatten, May 24, 1957; children: Stephen L., Jerry L., Cuong D., Shannon. BA in Religion, La. Coll., 1959; ThM, New Orleans Bapt. Sem., 1968, ThD, 1973; post-doctorate student, Oxford (Eng.) U., 1983-84. Instr. New Testament New Orleans Bapt. Sem., 1969-72; asst. prof. Bapt. Coll. at Charleston (S.C.), 1973-76; from assoc. prof. to prof. New Testament and Greek New Orleans Bapt. Sem., 1976-89; Foggleman prof. religion, chmn. religion dept. La. Coll., Pineville, 1989—; Staley Christian scholar lectr. Bapt. Coll. at Charleston, 1977. Co-author: Syntax of New Testament Greek, 1978; contbr. articles to profl. jours. Recipient Am. Legion award Olla (La.) post Am. Legion, 1955. Mem. Bapt. Assn. Profs. Religion, Soc. Bibl. Lit., Novum Testamentum, Kiwanis. Democrat. Home: 114 Beall St Pineville LA 71360 Office: La Coll College Station 1008 Pineville LA 71359

WINBUSH, ROY L. H., bishop. Bishop of Western La. Ch. of God in Christ, Lafayette. Office: Ch of God in Christ 317 12th St Lafayette LA 70501*

WINCHELL, CHARMAINE LOUISE, minister; b. Greymouth, New Zealand, Aug. 31, 1947; came to U.S., 1968; d. Walter and Ivy R. Doherty; children: Hilary Annette, Paul Gavin. BA, So. Oreg. State Coll., 1972, MA, 1983; MDiv, Fuller Theol. Sem., 1989. Ordained to ministry Am. Bapt. Chs. in U.S.A., 1989. Coord. Christian edn. Eastwood Bapt. Ch., Medford, Oreg., 1979-84; min. Christian edn. 1st Bapt. Ch., Riverside, Calif., 1984-91, Am. Bapt. Chs. of West, Oakland, Calif., 1991—; moderator Women in Ministry, Am. Bapt. Ch. S.W., 1987-89, sec.-treas. Min.'s Coun., 1988-91, designer tng., 1988-90. Mem. Min.'s Coun. Pacific S.W. (newsletter editor 1990-91). Democrat. Office: Am Bapt Chs of the West 268 Grand Ave Oakland CA 94610

WINCHELL, RICHARD MARION, minister; b. Columbus, Ohio, Nov. 2, 1928; s. Harold Brooks and Marion (Shattuck) W; m. Marjorie Alice Lundquist, Dec. 26, 1949; children: Peter, Martha, Leigh, Barry. AB in Theology, Gordon Coll., Beverly Farms, Mass., 1950; DD, Biola U., 1985. Ordained to ministry, 1950. Missionary Evang. Alliance Mission (TEAM), Republic of South Africa, 1950-68; founder, dir. Word of Life Publs. TEAM, Republic of South Africa, 1957, assoc. gen. dir., 1968-75, gen. dir., 1975—. Mem. Interdnom. Fgn. Missions Assn. (bd. dirs. 1971—, pres. 1983-86, 1990—). Home: 1720 N Washington St Wheaton IL 60187 Office: PO Box 969 Wheaton IL 60187 *A great heritage of our great nation is its moral foundations rooted in the Bible. In our places of influence we are privileged to remind others of this unchanging source as they consider their own value systems. Our grown children, successful in life, exemplary in character and devoted to God, are the crown of life for us. Daily teaching of the Bible in their younger years has, by their own testimony, produced the results seen now in their adult years. We accept it humbly as another evidence of the Grace of God.*

WIND, JAMES PRESLYN, minister, foundation executive; b. St. Louis, June 7, 1948; s. Preslyn August and Roberta Catherine (Dierker) W.; m. Kathleen Marie Buuck, June 19, 1971; children: Joshua James, Rachel Kathleen. BA, Concordia Sr. Coll., Ft. Wayne, 1970; MDiv, Luth. Sch. Theology, Chgo., 1974, STM, 1981; PhD, U. Chgo., 1983. Ordained to ministry Evang. Luth. Ch. Am., 1978. Asst. pastor Grace Luth. Ch., River Forest, Ill., 1978-81; rsch. assoc. Inst. for Advanced Study Religion, U. Chgo., 1981-83; dir. rsch. and publs. Park Ridge Ctr. for Study Health, Faith and Ethics, Chgo., 1984-90, sr. fellow, 1990—; program dir., religion div. Lilly Endowment, Inc., Indpls., 1990—. Author: The Bible and The University: The Messianic Vision of William Rainey Harper, 1988, Places of Worship, 1990; also numerous articles; editor: (book series) Health, Medicine and Faith Traditions, 1985-90; editor Second Opinion jour., 1986-90. Mem. Am. Acad. Religion, Am. Soc. Ch. History. Home: 10645 Courageous Dr Indianapolis IN 46236 Office: Lilly Endowment Inc 2801 N Meridian Indianapolis IN 46208 *The greatest challenge for me is to discern everything that is going on in each of life's daily occasions.*

WINDFUHR, GERNOT LUDWIG, Iranian studies educator; b. Essen, Ruhr, Germany, Aug. 2, 1938; came to U.S., 1966; s. Helmut and Lisbeth (Krueger) W.; m. Gudrun Martha E. Spindler, Aug. 20, 1965; children: Holger Gernot, Kirsten Lisbeth. Student, U. Cologne, U. Tehran; Ph.D. in Iranian Studies, U. Hamburg, 1965. Mem. faculty U. Kiel, Fed. Republic of Germany, 1964-66; asst. prof. Iranian studies U. Mich., Ann Arbor, 1966-73, prof., 1973—, chmn. dept. Near Eastern studies, 1977-87; cons. in field. Author: (with Cheragh Ali Azami) A Dictionary of Sangesari, With a Grammatical Outline, 1972, (with Hassan Tehranisa) Modern Persian, Elementary Level, 1979, Persian Grammar, History and State of Research, 1979, (with Shapoor Bostanbakhsh) Modern Persian, Intermediate Level I, rev. edit, 1980, Modern Persian, Intermediate Level II, 1982; also articles, chpts. and monographs on Iranian linguistics, lit. and Zoroastrianism. Served with German Army, 1958. Grantee, fellow Horace Rackham Sch. Grad. Studies U. Mich., 1967, 73-74, 75-76; fellow Ctr. Near Eastern and North African Studies, 1968-74; Guggenheim fellow, 1974-75; Social Sci. Research Council grantee, 1974-75, 76-77; U.S. Office Edn. grantee, 1977-81; NEH grantee, 1985-88. Mem. Am. Oriental Soc., Mid. East Studies Assn. N.Am., Linguistic Soc. Am., Soc. Linguistica Europaea (a founder), Am. Assn. Tchrs. of Persian (pres. 1989—), Am. Acad. Religion. Office: 3072 Frieze Bldg U Mich Ann Arbor MI 48103

WINDLE, JOSEPH RAYMOND, bishop; b. Ashdad, Ont., Can., Aug. 28, 1917; s. James David and Bridget (Scollard) W. Student, St. Alexander's Coll., Limbour, Que., 1936-39; D.D., Grand Sem., Montreal, 1943; D.C.L., Lateran U., Rome, 1953. Ordained priest Roman Catholic Ch., 1943; asst. priest, later parish priest and vice-chancellor Pembroke Diocese, 1943-61; titular bishop of Ugita and aux. bishop of Ottawa, 1961-69; coadjutor bishop of Pembroke, 1969-71; bishop, 1971—. Club: K.C. Office: Chancery Office, Box 7 188 Renfrew St, PO Box 7, Pembroke, ON Canada K8A 6X1

WINDSOR, MAURA KATHLEEN, religious organization administrator; b. Youngstown, Ohio, Feb. 8, 1937; d. Harold Cecil and Isabel Dorothy (Donahue) Cowher; m. Charles Robert Windsor, Jan. 23, 1960; children: Terri, Charles Jr., Donald C., David S. BS in nursing, Youngstown State U., 1960; M in Religious Studies, Ursuline Coll., 1982; RN, Youngstown Hosp., 1958; student, Youngstown State U., 1983. RN, Ohio. RN Western Reserve Care System, Youngstown, Ohio, 1958-70, Assumption Nursing Home, Youngstown, Ohio, 1976-82; spl. programs coordinator Mahoning County Alcoholism Services, Youngstown, Ohio, 1987—. Dir. Respect Life Cath. Charities Diocese of Youngstown, 1982—; prin. C.C.D. Holy Family Parish, Poland, Ohio, 1982-83; catechist Holy Family Parish, Poland, 1967—; chmn. bd. dirs. state diocesan Pro-life Convocation Ohio Cath. Conf., Columbus, Ohio, 1985—, asst. dir. exec. com., 1988—; mem. adv. com. to Pro Life com. Nat. Conf. Cath. Bishops, Washington, 1986; co-chmn. Mahoning County Alcohol Services, Youngstown, 1986, Teen Action Day, Youngstown, Just Say No Week, Youngstown; chmn. Mahoning County Crop Walk, Youngstown, 1985; mem. Task Force on Capital Punishment, Columbus, 1986, 87; pres. Poland Baseball Mom's Club, 1976, 77, Poland Football Mom's Club, 1977, 79; mem. Mahoning County Task Force on Drinking/Driving, Ohio Coalition Against Death Penalty, Columbus. Recipient Distinguished Service award Boy Scouts of Am., 1985. Mem. Ohio Nurses Assn., Nat. Assn. Cath. Charities. Avocations: camping, painting, gardening, crafts, swimming. Home: 7435 Forest Hill Poland OH 44514 Office: Diocese Youngstown Cath Charities 225 Elm St Youngstown OH 44503

WINE, DAVID JOHN, minister; b. Portland, Ind., June 29, 1950; s. John Carl and Ruth Emma (Watson) W.; m. Donna Ruth Peck, Nov. 24, 1972; children: Jeffrey David, Janelle Deanne. BA, Olivet Nazarene Coll., 1972; MA, Ohio State U., 1977. Ordained minister Ch. of the Nazarene, 1985. Music/youth minister First Ch. of the Nazarene, Lima, Ohio, 1972-73; Christian edn./youth First Ch. of the Nazarene, Mt. Vernon, Ohio, 1973-80, Canton, Ohio, 1980-85; assoc. prof. Malone Coll., Canton, 1981-85; minister of edn. Coll. Ch. of the Nazarene, Bourbonnais, Ill., 1985—; dist. pres. Nazarene Youth Internat., north cen. Ohio, 1977-80, regional rep., 1980-85, gen. sec., Kansas City, Mo., 1985-89. Contbg. author: Footprints: Following Jesus for Junior Highers, 1979. Mem. Nat. Fedn. of the Blind, Bourbonnais, 1988-90. Named one of Outstanding Young Men of Am. Avocations: golf, video photography. Office: Coll Ch of the Nazarene 200 University Ave Bourbonnais IL 60914

WINE, SHERWIN THEODORE, rabbi; b. Detroit, Jan. 25, 1928; s. William Harry and Tillie (Israel) W. B.A., U. Mich., 1950, A.M., 1952; B.H.L., Hebrew Union Coll., Cin., M.H.L., 1956, rabbi, 1956. Rabbi Temple Beth El, Detroit, 1956-60, Windsor, Ont., Can., 1960-64; Rabbi Birmingham (Mich.) Temple, 1964—; cons. editor Humanistic Judaism, 1966—. Author: A Philosophy of Humanistic Judaism, 1965, Meditation Services for Humanistic Judaism, 1977, Humanistic Judaism-What Is It?, 1977, Humanist Haggadah, 1980, High Holidays for Humanists, 1980, Judaism Beyond God, 1985, Celebration, 1988. Bd. dirs. Center for New Thinking, Birmingham, 1977—; founder Soc. Humanistic Judaism, 1969; pres. N.Am. Com. for Humanism, 1982—. Served as chaplain AUS, 1956-58. Mem. Conf. Liberal Religion (chmn. 1985—), Leadership Conf. Secular and Humanistic Jews (chmn. 1983—), Internat. Inst. Secular Humanistic Judaism (co-chmn. 1985—), Internat. Assn. Humanist Educators, Counselors and Leaders (pres. 1988—). Home: 555 S Woodward Birmingham MI 48011 Office: 28611 W Twelve Mile Rd Farmington Hills MI 48018

WINEMAN, ARYEH, rabbi; b. Toledo, May 27, 1932; s. Charles and Sarah (Seligman) W.; m. Dorothy Rhea Colodner, Aug. 14, 1977; children: Immanuel, Temima, Ayala. BA, Washington U., 1954; M. Hebrew Letters, Jewish Theol. Sem., 1959, DD (hon.), 1984; grad. studies, Hebrew U., 1967-73; PhD, UCLA, 1977. Ordained rabbi, 1959. Asst. dir. B'nai Brith Hillel Found., Ohio State U., 1960-62; mem. staff Nitzanim Youth Village, Israel, 1963-73; rabbi Temple Beth El, Troy, N.Y., 1985—. Author: (in Hebrew) Aggadah and Art - Studies in Works of Agnon, 1982, Beyond Appearances - Stories From the Kabbalistic Ethical Writings, 1988; contbr. articles to scholarly publs. NEH rsch. grantee, 1983, 89. Mem. Rabbinical Assembly, Assn. for Jewish Studies. Home: 407 Hoosick St Troy NY 12180 Office: Temple Beth El 411 Hoosick St Troy NY 12180

WING, MICHAEL RUSSELL, minister; b. Medford, Oreg., June 29, 1957; s. Herbert G. and Janet Elizabeth (Russell) W.; m. Kathleen Lynne Hansen, Aug. 26, 1978; children: David, Jonathan, Matthew. B of Music Edn., U. Oreg., 1980; MA in Ministries, Pacific Christian Coll., 1985. Ordained to ministry Christian Ch., 1984. Prin. Roseburg (Oreg.) Christian Sch., 1980-83; assoc. minister Griffith Park Christian Ch., L.A., 1983-84, Tujunga, Calif., 1984-86, Westside Christian Ch., Roseburg, 1986—; music chmn. Clyde Dupin Crusade, Roseburg, 1987. Author, editor: 20-20 Vision, 1989; contbr. articles to local newspaper. Mem. Vintage Singers, Roseburg, 1988-90; bd. dirs. Douglas County Crisis Pregnancy Ctr., Roseburg, 1988-89; pres. Douglas County Christian Minister Assn., 1989-90. Recipient Max Reisinger award U. Oreg., 1979. Mem. Christian Ministries Mgmt. Assn. Republican. Home: 1884 NW Calkins Roseburg OR 97470 Office: Westside Christian Ch 2712 W Harvard Roseburg OR 97470

WINGENBACH, GREGORY CHARLES, minister, religious-ecumenical agency director; b. Washington, Feb. 1, 1938; s. Charles Edward and Pearl Adeline (Stanton) W.; m. MaryAnn Pearce, Sept. 16, 1961; children: Mary-Adele, Karl Eduard, John Clair, Evgenia Kisa Maria. Student, Georgetown U., 1958-62; BA, Goddard Coll., 1972; postgrad., U. Thessalonike, Greece, 1973-74; MDiv, Louisville Presbyn. Theol. Sem., 1976, D of Ministry in Pastoral and Ecumenical Theology, 1982. Ordained to ministry Greek Orthodox Archdiocese North and South Am. as deacon, 1971, assoc. priest, 1973. Rsch. and legis. asst. U.S. Senator Clair Engle, Calif., 1962-63; mgr. community rels. programs U.S. Exec. Office Econ. Opportunity, Washington, 1965-69; regional program devel. officer AEC-Oak Ridge (Tenn.) Assn. Univs., 1970-73; assoc. St. George's Ch., Knoxville, Tenn., 1971-73; chaplain St. John Chrysostomos Ch. and Vlatadon Monastery, Thessalonike, 1973-74; named steward, preacher Met. Archdiocese of Thessalonike, 1974; pastor Assumption of Virgin Mary Ch., Louisville, 1974-79, Holy Trinity Ch., Nashville, 1979-82; named father confessor Greek Orthodox Archdiocese North and South Am., 1980; pastor St. Spyridon's Ch., Monessen, Pa., 1983-86; nat. dir. family life/pastoral ministries Greek Orthodox Archdiocese North and South Am., N.Y.C. and Brookline (Mass.), 1986-90; exec. dir. Kentuckiana Interfaith Community, Louisville, 1990—; Orthodox del. Louisville Area Interchurch Coun. and Ecumedia Com., 1974-79; pres., exec. adminstr. LAIOS-Kentuckiana Interfaith Coun., 1977-79; diocesan rep. Archdiocese Nat. Presbyters Coun., 1982-85; archdiocese del. Nat. Coun. Chs., Orthodox/Luth. Dialogues Consultation, Orthodox Nat. Missions Bd., 1981—. Author: The Peace Corps, 1961, Guide to the Peace Corps, 1965, Broken...Yet Never Sundered: The Ecumenical Tradition, 1987; editorial researcher: Richard Nixon, 1959, Duel at the Brink, 1960, The Floating Revolution, 1962. Mem. Fellowship St. Alban and St. Sergius, Orthodox Theol. Soc. Am. (exec. bd.), N.Am. Acad. Ecumenists (exec. bd.). Office: Kentuckiana Interfaith Community 1115 S 4th St Louisville KY 40203

WINGER, WALTER ORVAL, minister; b. Kindersley, Saskat., Can., July 14, 1929; came to U.S., 1967; s. Marshal A. and Mary Ethel (Bitner) W.; m. Lois Pauline, Aug. 21, 1951; children: Larry Aldon, Marshal Lee, Wayne Scott. BTh, Ont. Bible Coll., 1960; MS, Temple U., 1972; D of Ministry, Eastern Bapt. Theol. Seminary, Phila., 1976. Ordained to ministry Brethren in Christ Ch., 1960. Sr. pastor Port Colborne (Ont.) Brethren in Christ Ch., 1955-67, Carlisle (Pa.) Brethren in Christ Ch., 1967-79; pres. Niagra Christian Coll., Fort Erie, Ont., Can., 1979-83; sr. pastor Browncroft Community Ch., Rochester, N.Y., 1983-89, Upland (Calif.) Brethren in Christ Ch., 1989—; adj. lectr. Messiah Coll., Grantham, Pa., 1973-79, Roberts Wesleyan Coll., Rochester, 1983-84, Azusa (Calif.) Pacific U., 1990—. Fellow Profl. Soc. Doctors of Ministry; mem. Kiwanis (bd. dirs. Carlisle chpt. 1970-79, com. chmn. Upland chpt. 1990—). Home: 857 W Arrow Hwy Upland CA 91786 Office: Upland Brethren Christ Ch 845 West Arrow Hwy Upland CA 91786 *For the Christian there are only four important questions—Who is Jesus Christ? What did He do? What is He now doing? What is He going to do? Answering these questions gives focus to a life.*

WINGFIELD, STEPHEN RAY, evangelist; b. Lynchburg, Va., June 1, 1947; s. Floyd Jackson and Annie (Lawrence) W.; m. Barbara Ann Beam, June 8, 1974; children: Michelle Lee, David Stephen. BS, Ea. Mennonite Coll., 1974; MS, Trinity Evang. Div. Sch., Deerfield, Ill., 1983. Ordained to ministry Wesleyan Ch., 1975. Pastor 1st Wesleyan Ch., Roanoke, Va., 1974-80; evangelist Steve Wingfield Ministries, Harrisburg, Va., 1980—. Office: Steve Wingfield Ministries PO Box 1464 Harrisburg VA 22801

WINJUM, JAMES MARLOW, chaplain; b. Detroit Lakes, Minn., Jan. 28, 1950; s. Gordon A. and Ruth (Moe) W.; m. Joan Elizabeth Pauling, June 12, 1976; children: Benjamin John, David Andrew. BA, U. Minn., 1972; MDiv, Luther Sem., St. Paul, 1976; MS in Edn., U. Ky., 1984. Ordained to ministry Luth. Ch., 1976; cert. supr. clin. pastoral edn. Parish pastor Luverne (N.D.) Hofva Luth. Ch., 1976-81; resident chaplain U. Ky. Med.

Ctr., Lexington, 1981-84; chaplain, dir. pastoral edn. Luth. Social Svcs., Gettysburg, Pa., 1984—; educator pastoral care with elderly Luth. Social Svcs. and Luth. Sem., Gettysburg, 1984—. Contbr. articles on pastoral care and edn. to profl. jours. and newspapers. Supr. pastoral care Hospice, Gettysburg, 1987—. Fellow Coll. Chaplains. Home: 955 Barlow Dr Gettysburg PA 17325 Office: Luth Social Svcs 1075 Old Harrisburg Rd Gettysburg PA 17325

WINK, WALTER PHILIP, theologian, educator; b. Dallas, May 21, 1935; s. N. Edwin and Florence (Gidinghagen) W.; m. June Keener, Feb. 10, 1979; children from previous marriage: Stephen, Christopher, Rebecca. BA magna cum laude, So. Meth. U., 1956; BD, Union Theol. Sem., 1959, PhD, 1963. Ordained to ministry United Meth. Ch., 1961. Youth worker E. Harlem Protestant Parish and Broadway Temple Meth. Ch., N.Y.C., 1956-59; pastor 1st Meth. ch., Hitchcock, Tex., 1962-67; chaplain, dir. Meth. Ministry U. Tex. Med. Br., 1967; asst. prof. N.T. Union Theol. Sem., N.Y.C., 1967-70, assoc. prof., 1970-76; prof. bibl. interpretation Auburn Theol. Sem., N.Y.C., 1976—; staff assoc. Hartford (Conn.) Sem., 1976-80; vis. lectr. Sch. Theology, Drew U., spring 1969, Columbia U., spring 1970, 73, Hartford Sem., 1975-76, N.Y. Theol. Sem., 1974, 82, 86. Author: John the Baptist in the Gospel Tradition, 1968, The Bible in Human Transformation, 1973, German transl., 1976, Transforming Bible Study, 1980, German tranls. 1982, Naming the Powers, 1984, Unmasking the Powers, 1986, Violence and Nonviolence in South Africa, 1987, German transl., 1988, Jesus' Third Way: The Relevance of Nonviolence in South Africa, 1988; med. editorial bd. Forum, Jour. Violence and Religion, Jour. of Guild for Psychol. Studies; contbr. articles to jours. in field. Mem. Sandisfield Town Solid Waste Com. Mem. Studiorum Novi Testamenti Societas, Soc. Bibl. Lit., Am. Acad. Religion, Clergy and Laity Concerned (former mem. steering and program coms.), Fellowship of Reconciliation. Home: HC 66 Box 23 Sandisfield MA 01255 Office: Auburn Theol Sem 3041 Broadway New York NY 10027 *Not just information, transformation.*

WINKELMANN, JOHN PAUL, pharmacist; b. St. Louis, Sept. 14, 1933; s. Clarence Henry and Alyce Marie (Pierce) W.; m. Margaret (Peggy) Ann Grandy, June 16, 1967; children: John Damian and James Paul (twins), Joseph Peter, Christopher Louis, Sean Martin. BS, St. Louis U., 1955; BS in Pharmacy, St. Louis Coll. Pharmacy, 1960; ScD, London Coll. Applied Sci., 1972; EdD, Internat. Inst. for Advanced Studies, 1987. Registered pharmacist, Mo.; notary pub.; cert. profl. mgr. Pres., chief pharmacist Winkelmann Apothecary, Ltd., Clayton, Mo., 1960-76; exec. dir Nat. Catholic Pharmacists Guild of U.S., St. Louis, 1970—; distbr. pharms. and medicines to missions worldwide. Author: History of the St. Louis College of Pharmacy, 1964, Catholic Pharmacy, 1966; founding editor The Cath. Pharmacist Jour., 1967—; contbr. articles to profl. publs. Unit commr. Greater St. Louis coun. Boy Scouts Am.; charter mem. Mo. Statewide Profl. Svcs. Rev. Orgn., 1976-78, Rep. Presdl. Task Force, Washington, 1982—; trustee St. Louis Coll. Pharmacy, 1961-84, chmn. audit com., 1968-83; worker St. Louis Archdiocesan Devel. Appeal, 1969-88; trustee Missionary Sisters St. Peter Claver Adv. Bd., 1974-77; retreat capt. for parish ch., 1976-83. Capt. USAFR, ret. Decorated Knight of Malta by Pope Paul VI, Knight, Knight Comdr. with Star of the Order of the Holy Sepulchre of Jerusalem by Pope John Paul II, Papal Knight Assn. Pontifical Knights, Knight, Knight Officer (Denmark), Knight Officer of Constantinian Order St. George, Knigh, Knight Comdr. of Patriarchila Equestrian Oder of Holy Cross Jerusalm, Knight of Order of White Eagle, Knight Grand Cordon of Order of St. Stanislas, Knight Grand Cordon of Order Polonia Restituta, Grant of Arms (Spain), Certification of Arms (Rep. Ireland), over 50 others; recipient Pharm. Scholarship award Meyer Bros., 1959, Lunsford Richardson Nat. Pharmacy award, 1959-60, 1st prize Roerig Nat. Pharm. Econs. Essay Contest, 1960, Medallion Cir. award Nat. Assn. Holy Name Soc., 1984, citations Govs. Mo., Ky., mayor of Paducah, Ky., County Exec. Pulaski County, Ky, mayor Louisville; named Cath. Pharmacist of Yr., Nat. Cath. Pharmacists Guild U.S., 1970, hon. citizen Ala., Ariz., Kans., Ind., Okla., Nebr., Tenn., Wyo., Tex., City of New Orleans, Indpls., Lexington, Ky., , hon. dep. marshal Dodge City, Kans., Ark. traveler and amb., hon. mountaineer W.Va. Fellow Royal Soc. Health, Nat. Cath. Pharmacists Guild, Am. Coll. Apothecaries, Am. Coll. Pharmacists, Soc. Apothecaries of London Faculty of History of Medicine and Pharmacy; mem. Am. Bd. Diplomates in Pharmacy (charter), Am. Inst. History Pharmacy (coun. 1977-80, state rep. 1980—, Commendation award 1966), Inst. Cert. Profl. Mgrs. (cert.), Am. Pharm. Assn. Acad. Pharm. Practice (charter 1967), St. Louis Vet. Druggists Assn., Assn. Mil. Surgeons U.S., Nat. Assn. Holy Name Soc. (v.p.), St. Louis Archdiocesan Union Holy Name Soc. (pres. 1982-84), AMVETS, Am. Legion, Army and Navy Union, Mil. Order of World Wars, Anchor and Caduceus Soc.of USPHS, Rho Chi. Home and Office: 1012 Surrey Hills Dr Saint Louis MO 63117-1438

WINKLER, TONY, minister; b. Aug. 16, 1946; s. Robert F. Winkler and Flora (Kinser) Purkey; m. Kathryn Ann, June 25, 1965; children: Linda, David, Kelly, Mindy. Grad. high sch., Genoa, Ill. Pastor Ch. of God, Bulls Gap, Tenn., 1982-90; evangelist Ch. of God, Russellville, Tenn., 1990—; broker Power Prodns., Bulls Gap, Tenn., 1982—. Home and Office: St Clair Ch of God Rte 1 Bulls Gap TN 37711

WINNIG, PAULA JAYNE, rabbi; b. Wausau, Wis., Oct. 8, 1959; d. Sidney and Marion (Marko) W.; m. Robert L. Knight; children: Karmi Knight-Winnig, Shai Knight Winnig. BA with honors, U. Wis., 1980; MA in Hebrew Letters, Hebrew Union Coll., 1983, postgrad., 1984-85. Ordained rabbi, 1986. Student rabbi Vista Del Mar, L.A., 1981-83, Temple Shalom, Auckland, N.Z., 1983-84; asst. rabbi Temple Sinai, Roslyn, N.Y., 1986-88; rabbi Temple Sholom, Floral Park, N.Y., 1988—; Jewish support chmn. Cen. Am. refugee ctr. Carecen, Hempstead, N.Y., 1988—. Mem. L.I. Bd. Rabbis (sec. 1989-90), L.I. Assn. Reform Rabbis (treas. 1989-91, v.p. 1991—), N.Y. Assn. Reform Rabbis (lit. com. 1991—), Cen. Conf. Am. Rabbis, Women's Rabbinical Network, L.I. Temple Educators, Conf. for Alternatives in Jewish Edn., Sigma Epsilon Sigma. Office: Temple Sholom 263-10 Union Turnpike Floral Park NY 11004

WINOKUR, HARVEY JAY, rabbi; b. Bklyn., Aug. 16, 1950; s. Douglas Louis and Miriam (Weinberg) W.; m. Beverly F. Beren, May 31, 1976. BA in Sociology, SUNY, Buffalo, 1971; MA, Hebrew Union Coll., 1974. Ordained rabbi, 1976. Rabbi The Temple, Atlanta, 1976-79, Temple Sinai, Atlanta, 1979-80, Balt. Hebrew Congregation, 1980-82, Temple Kehillat Chaim, Roswell, Ga., 1982—. Co-author: Lehava, 1979. Co-chair Ann. City-wide Appeal to Address Homelessness; trustee Girl Scouts of N.W. Ga., Atlanta, 1983-86; officer Nat. Coalition Against Death Penalty, N.Y.C., 1982-86; mem. Atlanta/Fulton County Commn. on Children and Youth, Leadership Atlanta Class of 1992. Mem. Cen. Conf. of Am. Rabbis (social action commn. 1987-89), N.Am. Bd. World Union for Progressive Judaism, Atlanta Rabbinical Assn. (pres. 1988-90), Am. Jewish Com. (bd. dirs. Atlanta chpt. 1991-92), Atlanta Jewish Fedn. (bd. dirs. 1988-91), Leadership Atlanta. Avocations: travel, nature photography, computers, music. Office: Temple Kehillat Chaim 10200 Woodstock Rd. Roswell GA 30075

WINQUIST, CHARLES E., religion educator, clergyman; b. Toledo, June 11, 1944; s. Donald Edwin and Gladys June (Bryant) W.; m. Anna Lois Davis, Nov. 8, 1963; children: Diane, Heidi. BA in Philosophy, U. Toledo, 1965; AM in Theology, U. Chgo., 1968, PhD in Philos. Theology, 1970. Ordained to ministry, 1973. Instr. Cen. YMCA Community Coll., 1965-68; asst. prof. Union Coll., 1968-69; prof. Calif. State U., Chico, 1969-86; Thomas J. Watson prof. Syracuse (N.Y.) U., 1986—. Author: The Transcendental Imagination, 1972, The Communion of Possibility, 1975, Homecoming, 1975, Practical Hermeneutics, 1980, The Archaeology of the Imagination, 1981, Epiphanies of Darkness, 1986; assoc. editor Sem. jour., 1980-86. Mem. Am. Acad. Religion (assoc. editor jour. 1978—). Home: 126 Jamesville Ave # H5 Syracuse NY 13210 Office: Syracuse U Dept Religion 501 Hall of Languages Syracuse NY 13244-1170*

WINSKIE, RICHARD CLAY, youth and music minister; b. Warrenton, Va., Sept. 19, 1962; s. Mark Walton and Norma Jean (Jolley) W.; m. Laynette Elaine Lykins, May 18, 1985; 1 child, Crystal Brooke. AS, Jacksonville Coll., 1983; postgrad., Stephen F. Austin U., 1983, U. Tex., 1984-85, Bapt. Sem., 1984-85. Minister of music Shady Grove Bapt. Ch., Purdon, Tex., 1979-81; guitarist, songwriter Calvary Boys Quartet, Teneha, Tex., 1984-89; music mgr. Better Books Christian Ctr., Tyler, Tex., 1984-89; minister of music Enterprise Bapt. Ch., Jacksonville, Tex., 1984-89; minister of music and youth 1st Bapt. Ch., Waldo, Ark., 1989—. Author: (song) Appointment with the Lord, 1984; contbr. articles to religion jours; program dir., engr. syndicated gospel radio show Southern Sunshine, 1986-87. Mem. Columbia County Right to Life, Magnolia, Ark., 1990—, Vol. Fire Dept., Waldo, Ark., 1989—, Moral Majority, Lynchburg, Va., 1983. Named to The Nat. Dean's List, 1983. Mem. Bapt. Music Fellowship Am., Circle K Club, Bapt. Missionary Assn. (del. 1985, 89, 90), Assn. Bapt. Students (trustee 1988-89). Home and Office: 205A S Olive PO Box 220 Waldo AR 71770 *I am constantly amazed at the number of people who insist on separating life into "spiritual" and "secular". The Bible's instruction, "Do all to the glory of God," reminds me even the "secular" things are to be done with a purpose and are "spiritual" because of God's constance presence with me.*

WINSLOW, DAVID ALLEN, chaplain, naval officer; b. Dexter, Iowa, July 12, 1944; s. Franklin E. and Inez Maude (McPherson) W.; m. Frances Lavinia Edwards, June 6, 1970; children: Frances, David. BA, Bethany Nazarene Coll., 1968; MDiv, Drew U., 1971, STM, 1974. Ordained to ministry United Meth. Ch., 1969. Assoc. minister All Sts. Episcopal. Ch., Millington, N.J., 1969-70; asst. minister Marble Collegiate Ch., N.Y.C., 1970-71; min. No. N.J. Conf., 1971-75; joined chaplain corps USN, 1974, advanced through grades to lt. comdr., 1980. Contbr. articles to profl. jours. Bd. dirs. disaster svcs. and family svcs. ARC, Santa Ana, Calif., 1988-91, Child Abuse Prevention Ctr., Orange, Calif., 1990-91. Mem. AACD, Internat. Soc. for Traumatic Stree Studies, Am. Mental Health Counsellors Assn., Greater Irvine Rep. Assembly, Rep. Assocs. Orange County, USN League (hon.), 69th Assembly Club, Sunrise Exch. Club (chaplain 1989-91), Dick Richards Breakfast Club (chaplain 1988—), Masons, Shriners. Avocations: golf, skiing, sailing. Home: 19 Soaring Hawk Irvine CA 92714

WINSLOW, GERALD RAY, Christian ethics educator; b. Salem, Oreg., Mar. 12, 1945; s. Arthur W. and Elsie (Haeder) W.; m. Betty Jean Wehtje, Aug. 21, 1966; children: Lisa, Angela. BA, Walla Walla Coll., 1967; MA, Andrews U., 1968; PhD, Grad. Theol. Union, 1979. Assoc. dean of men Walla Walla Coll., College Place, Wash., 1968-71, from instr. to prof. religion, 1971-87; prof. ethics Loma Linda (Calif.) U., 1987-89, Pacific Union Coll., Angwin, Calif., 1989—; sr. rsch. scholar ethics ctr. Loma Linda (Calif.) U., 1989—; mem. ethics and aging project NEH, Loma Linda, 1990. Author: Triage and Justice, 1982; mem. editorial bd. Second Opinion, 1986—. Mem. adv. bd. Wash. Health Choices, 1985-87, Oreg. Health Decisions, 1984-89. NEH fellow, 1983. Mem. Mem. Soc. Christian Ethics, Am. Philos. Assn., Soc. Bioethics Cons., Hastings Ctr. Office: Pacific Union Coll Angwin CA 94508

WINSTANLEY, ALAN LESLIE, bishop; b. Leigh, Eng., May 7, 1949; arrived in Latin Am., 1981; s. John Leslie and Eva (Smith) W.; m. Vivien Mary Parkinson, Aug. 5, 1972; children: Christopher, Kathryn, Andrew. A.L.C.D., St. John's Coll., Nottingham, Eng., 1972; BTh, U. Nottingham, 1972. Ordained to ministry Ch. of Eng. as deacon, 1972, as priest, 1973; bishop Anglican Ch. of South Am., 1988. Asst. curate St. Andrew's Ch., Blackburn, U.K., 1972-75, St. Mary's Ch., Great Sankey, U.K., 1975-77; rector St. Paul's Ch., Penketh, U.K., 1977-81; missionary Lima, Arequipa, Peru, 1981-88; bishop of Peru and Bolivia, 1988—. Office: Iglesia Cristiana Episcopal, Apdo 18-1032, Lima 18, Peru

WINSTEAD, SANDRA CHESHIRE, church music director, tax professional; b. Rocky Mount, N.C., June 19, 1944; d. Thomas Sidney and Helen (Bullard) Cheshire; m. Robert D. Winstead, Nov. 29, 1963; children: David, Matthew, Valerie. Student, Hardbarger Jr. Coll., 1962-63, U. N.C., 1973, Southeastern Sem., 1988—. Dir. music Arlington Bapt. Ch., Rocky Mount, 1969—; tax asst. Hardee's Food Systems, Inc., Rocky Mount, 1981—. Mem. United Daus. Confederacy. Democrat. Home: 1234 Rosewood Ave Rocky Mount NC 27801-6054 *I strive in my ministry to not only bring people to the word (of the Cross) but to the blood (of the Savior) also. Too often we are guilty of seeing the first and missing the latter.*

WINTER, NATHAN HAROLD, religion educator; b. N.Y.C., Mar. 20, 1926; s. Sol Winter and Fannie Sacks; m. Magda Markowitz, Feb. 5, 1949; children: Steven, Elaine, Jonathan. BA, NYU, 1949, MA, 1955, PhD, 1955; B. Religious Edn., Jewish Theol. Sem., N.Y.C., 1951; JD, Bklyn. Law Sch., 1954; D Pedagogy (hon.), Jewish Theol. Sem., 1977. Prof. dept. Hebrew and Judaic studies NYU, N.Y.C., 1968—, Ethel and Irvin prof. of Hebrew and Judaic studies, 1980—; edn. cons. United Synagogue of Am., N.J., 1954-80; dir. tng. for communal edn. Am. Assn. for Jewish Edn., N.Y.C., 1976-84; lectr. in edn. Rabbinical Sch., Jewish Theol. Sem., N.Y.C., 1972-76. Author: Jewish Education in a Pluralist Society, 1960, Jewish Education in America, The Jewish Experience, 1977, The Bible World, 1980. Sgt. U.S. Army, 1943-46. Mem. Jewish Educators Assembly (hon. pres. 1978—), Assn. for Jewish Studies, World Coun. of Jewish Studies, Coun. of Jewish Edn. (v.p. 1978-84), Nat. Assn. Profs. of Hebrew (mem. editorial bd. 1970-82). Home: 46 Burroughs Way Maplewood NJ 07040 Office: NYU Dept Hebrew and Judaic Studies 51 Washington Sq S New York NY 10003

WINTER, ROBERT ALLAN, priest; b. Grand Rapids, Mich., Oct. 22, 1935; s. Garrett Egbert and Wilhelmina Therese (Sprick) W.; m. Catherine Esther Boyd, Sept. 17, 1960 (div. 1970); children: Christopher Martin, Jeffrey Michael; m. Penney Ann Morse, Aug. 4, 1972; children: Andrew Robert, Paul Garrett. AB, Hope Coll., 1957; student, Bowling Green State, 1957-59, U. Mich., 1958-59; MDiv cum laude, Episcopal Theol., 1962. Ordained to ministry Episcopal Ch. as deacon, 1962, as priest, 1963. Marquis fellow Christ Ch. Cranbrook, Bloomfield Hills, Mich., 1962-63; asst. rector St. Mark's Episcopal Ch., Riverside, R.I., 1963-65; rector St. Mark's Episcopal Ch., Warren, R.I., 1965-68, Grace Episcopal Ch., Holland, Mich., 1968-71, St. Thomas of Canterbury, Greendale, Wis., 1972-83, St. Thomas Episcopal, Berea, Ohio, 1983—; chaplain Warren (R.I.) Fire Dept., 1967-68, Berea Fire Dept., 1991—; spiritual dir. Ohio Episcopal Cursillo, Cleve., 1988-90; bd. examining chaplains Diocese of Ohio, Cleve., 1987—. Contbr. articles to profl. jours. review commn. City of Berea, 1990. Named Priest of Yr. Diocese of Milw., 1982. Democrat. Home: 533 Race St Berea OH 44017-2220 Office: St Thomas Episcopal Church 50 E Bagley Rd Berea OH 44017-2009

WINTERS, BRENT ALLAN, headmaster, writer, geologist; b. Terre Haute, Ind., Oct. 14, 1954; s. Fredrick Douglas and Wanda Mae (Hudson) W.; m. Susan Kay Armstrong, Oct. 14, 1977; children: Caleb Allan, Jeremiah Brent, Cacey Ariana, Jennifer Beth, Christy Autumn. BS, Ea. Ill. U., 1981; MDiv., Biola U., 1984, ThM, 1987; postgrad., U. Mo., 1988—. Ordained to ministry Christian Ch., 1988. Pastor New Life Bible Fellowship, Terre Haute, Ind., 1988-90; headmaster C.M. Hudson Acad., Martinsville, Ill., 1985—; geologist Sunburst Gold Mining Project, Weaver, Ariz., 1990—, also bd. dirs. Author: Book by Book, 1990, Educate for Freedom, 1991. Speech writer Rep. congl. primary, Ill., 1987. With USN, 1975-85. Office: C M Hudson Acad PO Box 41 R1 Martinsville IL 62442-9709

WINTERS, GEORGE EUGENE, minister; b. Ashland, Ohio, May 19, 1952; s. George Bell and Evelyn Virginia (Glenn) W.; m. Linda Meredith, May 11, 1985; 1 child, Glenn Richard. BA cum laude, Ashland Coll., 1974; MDiv, So. Bapt. Theol. Sem., Louisville, 1977, DMin, 1990. Ordained to ministry Am. Bapt. Chs. in U.S.A., 1977. Pastor Newman Bapt. Ch., Massillon, Ohio, 1977-80; minister of Christian edn. and youth 1st Bapt. Ch., Newark, Ohio, 1980-83; assoc. pastor 1st Bapt. Ch., Lima, Ohio, 1983-90; pastor East Bapt. Ch., Columbus, Ohio, 1990—; pres. campus ministry coun. Ohio State U., Lima, 1984-86; trustee Ohio Bapt. Conv., Granville, 1988-90, Ohio Bapt. Edn. Soc., Granville, 1989—, Columbus Bapt. Assn., 1990—. Bd. dirs. Westside Neighborhood Assn., Lima, 1986-90. Mem. Am. Bapt. Ministers Coun. Office: East Bapt Ch 4295 E Broad St Columbus OH 43213 *To encounter God authentically in the midst of my life I find I must constantly summon the courage to be both curious and accepting.*

WINTERS, SISTER MARY ANN, religious organization administrator; b. Paterson, N.J., Nov. 15, 1937; d. Russell Lewis and Nellie Marie (Cramer) W. BA, Seton Hill Coll., 1967; PhD, U. Pitts., 1972. Tchr. various cath. schs., Pa., Ariz., 1957-67; from instr. to chmn. chemistry dept. Seton Hill Coll., Greensburg, Pa., 1967-68, 72-81; councilor Sisters of Charity Seton Hill, Greensburg, Pa., 1981-85, major superior, 1985—; mem. task force Leadership Conf. Women Religious, Silver Springs, Md. 1986-88; retreat dir. Sisters of Charity Seton Hill, Greensburg, Pa., 1977-81. Trustee Seton Hill Coll., Greensburg, Pa., Jeannette Dist. Meml. Hosp., Jeannette, Pa., DePaul Inst., Pitts.; mem. Ethics Task Force Forbes Regional, Pitts. Named Teacher of Yr., Seton Hill Coll., Greensburg, Pa., 1981. Mem. Am. Chem. Soc., Tri-Diocesan Sisters' Leadership Coun. (pres. 1988—), Elizabeth Seton Fedn. (exec. com. 1989—). Avocations: walking, handwork, listening to music, cooking. Office: Sisters Charity Seton Hill De Paul Ctr Mt Thor Rd Greensburg PA 15601

WINTERS, MATTHEW LITTLETON, minister; b. Chare, Mich., Sept. 23, 1926; s. Matthew Littleton and Bertha Alexsandra (Ruthven) W.; m. Elizabeth Wiegand, Oct. 16, 1954; children: Deborah Anne, Matthew IV. BA, Wittenberg U., 1950; MDiv, Hamma Divinity Sch., 1954; DD (hon.), Gettysburg Coll., 1972. Ordained to ministry Evang. Luth. Ch. in Am., 1954. Assoc. pastor Holy Trinity Luth. Ch., Buffalo, 1954-60; sr. pastor Trinity Luth. Ch., Camp Hill, Pa., 1960-75, Holy Trinity Luth. Ch., Buffalo, 1975—; pres. Luth. Co-ordinated Ministry Buffalo, 1984-89; bd. dirs. Concerned Ecumenical Ministry, Buffalo. Pres. Lothlorien Therapeutic Riding Ctr., E. Aurora, N.Y., 1989—. Mem. Rotary. Republican. Avocations: baseball, reading, traveling, giving book revs. Home: 16 Huntington Ct Williamsville NY 14221 Office: Holy Trinity Luth Ch 1080 Main St Buffalo NY 14209

WINTERS, ORLANDO KARL, minister; b. Canton, Ohio, Sept. 18, 1959; s. Henry Richard and Loretta Frances (Morrow) W.; m. Patricia Ann Jones, Oct. 29, 1983; children: Yolanda, Orlando II. BA in Christian Ministries, Malone Coll., Canton, Ohio, 1981; MA in Theology, Ashland Theol. Sem., Ohio, 1987, MA in N.T Studies, 1988. Ordained to ministry Bapt. Ch., 1982. Counselor, coord. Young Life Ministries, Inc., Canton, 1977-81; part-time prof. Malone Coll., Canton, 1989-90; pastor Mt. Pleasant Bapt. Ch., Canton, 1984—; lectr. Progressive Nat. Bapt. Conv., 1990—, dean Congress, Ohio conv., 1990—; program chmn., sec. United Pastors, Inc. of Canton, 1983-86; advisor Black United Students for Christ, Malone Coll., 1985-86. Bd. trustees Malone Coll. Alumni Bd., 1989—, Begin-A-New Job Tng., Massillon, Ohio, 1988—, Family Svcs. Inc. of Stark County, 1991—. Mem. Akron & Vicinity Bapt. Ministers Conf. Home: 4817 Cranberry Ave NW Canton OH 44709 Office: Mt Pleasant Bapt Ch 830 Mahoning Rd NE Canton OH 44705

WINTERS, STEPHEN MARK See **WINZENBURG, STEPHEN MARK**

WINTLE, THOMAS D., religious organization administrator. Pres. Unitarian Universalist Christian Fellowship, Boston, Mass. Office: PO Box 66 Lancaster MA 01523*

WINZENBURG, STEPHEN MARK (STEPHEN MARK WINTERS), radio station executive; b. Mankato, Minn., Dec. 18, 1954; s. Frank Edward and Kathryn Helen (Trier) W.; m. Patricia Ann Liffrig, Dec. 20, 1981; children—Kathryn Frances, Mary Collette. B.A., U. S.D.; M.A. in Journalism, U. Minn. News dir. Sta. WCIE, Lakeland, Fla., 1977-80; prof. Fla. So. Coll., Lakeland, 1982-84, Marycrest Coll., Davenport, Iowa, 1984; dir. syndication Second Thoughts, Belleville, Ill., 1984-85; gen. mgr. Sta. KNDR, Bismarck, N.D., 1985, Sta. WRFW, River Falls, Wis., 1985—; asst. prof. journalism U. Wis., River Falls, 1985—; corr. Internat. Media Service, Washington, 1977-80. Author: The Happy Homemaker Cookbook, 1978. Recipient Commendation award Am. Women in Radio and TV, 1985, Fla. News award AP, 1980, Enterprise award Enterprise Radio Network, 1978; named Citizen of Yr., Women for Responsible Legislation, 1980. Republican. Lodges: Kiwanis, Rotary. Office: U Wis 310 N Hall River Falls WI 54022

WIRBEL, JUDITH LYNNE, lay church worker; b. Kenton, Ohio, Jan. 25, 1958; d. Marion Ernest and Shirley Jean (Renfrew) W. AS in Social Svc., U. Toledo, 1978. Camp coord. Epworth United Meth. Ch., Kenton, 1983-85, chmn. edn., 1985-90, sec. bd., 1990—, chmn. evangelism, 1991—, lay speaker, 1991—; mgr. James Floor & Interiors, Kenton, 1985—. Author: (plays) Mary's Story, 1987, Grandma's Story, 1988, Miracle of Wishing, 1989. Mem. United Meth. Women. Republican. Home: 822 E Summit St Kenton OH 43326

WIRE, ANTOINETTE CLARK, religion educator; b. Kuling, Jiangxi, China, Sept. 4, 1934; d. William Harold and Antoinette (Black) C.; m. Hugh Brinley Wire, June 13, 1959; children: Antoinette Margaret, Joseph Marshall. BA, Pomona Coll., 1956; BD, Yale Divinity Sch., 1959; PhD, Claremont Grad. Sch., 1974. From asst. prof. to prof. San Francisco Theol. Sem., San Anselmo, Calif., 1974—; mem. brief statement of faith com. Presbyn. Ch. USA, 1985—. Author: The Corinthian Women Prophets: A Reconstruction Through Paul's Rhetoric, 1990, The Parable is a Mirror, 1983; mem. editorial bd. Jour. Bibl. Lit., 1984—; contbr. articles to profl. jours. Layne Archeol. fellow. Mem. Soc. Bibl. Lit., Am. Acad. Religion. Home: 2617 Le Conte Berkeley CA 94709

WIRZ, GEORGE O., bishop; b. Monroe, Wis., Jan. 17, 1929. Student, St. Francis Sem., Milw., Marquette U., Milw., Cath. U. Ordained priest Roman Cath. Ch., 1952. Appointed titular bishop of Municipa Roman Cath. Ch., Madison, Wis., 1978—; aux. bishop Roman Cath. Ch., Madison, 1978—. Office: St Patrick Ch 404 E Main St Madison WI 53703 also: 15 E Wilson St Box 111 Madison WI 53701

WISCHMANN, DEE, charitable organization administrator. Exec. dir. Cath. Charities, Santa Clara, Calif. Office: Cath Charities 100 N Winchester Blvd Ste 262 Santa Clara CA 95050*

WISE, JAY ALLAN, minister, real estate consultant; b. Mpls., Sept. 26, 1946; s. Howard Van and Shirley (Pomerantz) W.; m. Mary Louise Defrance, June 11, 1988; children from previous marriage: Myriam, Rachael. BA, U. Minn., 1968; MA, U. Madrid, Spain, 1972; DDiv, Cen. Sem., Mpls., 1981. Ordained to ministry Ind. Pentecostal Ch. Am., 1968. Pres. Allstate, Inc., Mpls., 1982—; minister Cen. Ch., Mpls., 1983—; bd. dirs. Service Investments, Inc., Mpls. Pub. (jour.) Luth. Courier, 1985. Mem. bd. Human Rights Commn., Robbinsdale, Minn., 1975-77. Mem. Am. Soc. Religious Freedom, Assn. Real Estate Cons., Minn. Real Estate Assn. (v.p.), Christian-Jewish Assn. (chmn. Mpls. 1984—). Avocations: pilot, race car driver, golf, tennis. Office: care WISE 6336 Boone N # 303 Minneapolis MN 55428

WISE, PAUL ALLEN, clergyman; b. Anaheim, Calif., Dec. 13, 1959; s. Charles Leroy Wise and Ruby (Gene) Howard; m. Suzanne Marie Darrow, July 16, 1983; children: Corey, Jaime, Jodi. Assoc., Southwestern Coll., 1979, BS, 1981. Ordained to ministry Pentecostal Ch., 1980. Evangelist Pentecostal Ch. of God, El Reno, Okla., 1981-83; pastor Pentecostal Ch. of God, Oil City, Mich., 1983-84; state youth dir. Pentecostal Ch. of God, St. John's, Mich., 1984—; state dir. Pentecostal Young Peoples Assn., St. Johns, 1983—, asst. gen., Joplin, Mo., 1987—. Home: 1932 Mead Rd St Johns MI 48879 Office: Pentecostal Young Peoples 680 N Lansing Saint Johns MI 48879

WISE, PHILIP DOUGLAS, minister; b. Andalusia, Ala., Jan. 3, 1949; s. Harold L. and Doris M. (Jones) W.; m. Cynthia Adams, June 22, 1968; children: Myra D., Philip D., Fisher E. BA with honors, Samford U., 1970; ThM with honors, New Orleans Bapt. Theol. Sem., 1973, ThD, 1980; postgrad., Mansfield Coll., U. Oxford, Eng., 1973-76. Ordained to ministry, Bapt. Ch., 1970. Lectr. Culham Coll., Abingdon, Eng., 1974-76, New Orleans Bapt. Theol. Sem., 1977-78; pastor Fairview Bapt. Ch., Selma, Ala., 1978-82, Morningview Bapt. Ch., Montgomery, Ala., 1982-89, 1st Bapt. Ch., Dothan, Ala., 1889—; pres. U. Oxford Grad. Reps. Conf., 1975. Co-author: Dictionary of Theological Terms, 1983. Mem. Montgomery Race Rels. Com., 1984; chmn. Ala. Bapt. Christian Life Comm., 1985-89; pres. Wiregrass Habitat for Humanity, 1990; chmn. Dothan-Houston County Substance Abuse Bd. Democrat. Home: 116 Pine Tree Dr Dothan AL 36303 Office: 1st Bapt Ch 300 W Main St Dothan AL 36301 *It takes more faith to live with ambiguity than with certainty.*

WISEHART, MARY RUTH, educator; b. Myrtle, Mo., Nov. 2, 1932; d. William Henry and Ora (Harbison) W. BA, Free Will Baptist Bible Coll.,

1955; BA, George Peabody Coll. Tchrs., 1959, MA, 1960, PhD, 1976. Tchr. Free Will Bapt. Bible Coll., Nashville, 1956-60, chmn. English dept., 1961-85; exec. sec.-treas. Free Will Bapt. Woman's Nat. Aux. Conv., 1985—. Author: Sparks Into Flame, 1985; contbr. poetry to jours. Mem. Nat. Council Tchrs. English, Christian Mgmt. Assn., Religious Conf. Mgmt. Assn., Scxribbler's Club. Avocations: photography, music, drama. Office: Woman's Nat Aux Conv Free Will Bapt PO Box 1088 Nashville TN 37202

WISMAR, GREGORY JUST, minister; b. Jersey City, Jan. 9, 1946; s. Adolph Harold and Norma Adela (Just) W.; m. Priscilla Emily Ames, June 7, 1969; children: Eric Andrew, Sarah Emily, Elizabeth Victoria, Jessica Eve. BA, Concordia Sr. Coll., Ft. Wayne, Ind., 1967; MDiv, Concordia Sem., St. Louis, 1971; MS, So. Conn. State U., 1977; D of Ministry, Hartford Sem., 1990. Ordained to ministry Luth. Ch.-Mo. Synod, 1971. Asst. pastor Immanuel Luth. Ch., Danbury, Conn., 1971-72; pastor St. Paul's Luth. Ch., Naugatuck, Conn., 1972-78, Redeemer Luth. Ch., Cape Elizabeth, Maine, 1978-83, Messiah Luth. Ch., Lynnfield, Mass., 1983-87, Christ the King Luth. Ch., Newtown, Conn., 1987—; v.p. New Eng. dist. Luth. Ch.—Mo. Synod, Springfield, Ill., 1979-83, mem. nominations com., St. Louis, 1985-86, archivist New Eng. dist., 1989—, mem. commn. on worship, St. Louis, 1990—; rsch. fellow Yale Inst. Sacred Music, Liturgy and Arts, 1991. Author: A Parish Portrait, 1990. Mem. CT-5 Congl. Adv. Bd., Waterbury, Conn., 1975-78, Ft. Williams Com., Cape Elizabeth, 1981-83, Newtown Family Life Ctr., 1988-90; guest chaplain U.S. Ho. of Reps., Washington, 1977, U.S. Senate, Washington, 1982; chmn. Lynnfield Arts Commn., 1985-87. Recipient Svc. award NED Youth Commn., 1987, award Kodak Internat., 1988. Mem. New Eng. Luth. Hist. Soc. Home: 81 Mount Pleasant Rd Newtown CT 06470 Office: Christ the King Luth Ch 85 Mt Pleasant Rd Newtown CT 06470 *There are many opportunities for enjoyment in our lives and days—enjoyment of God and of the people in our circles of relationship. Celebrations stemming from our perceptions of faith and life strengthen the self, build family bonds and enrich the communities of which we are part.*

WISSEMANN, ANDREW FREDERICK, bishop; b. N.Y.C., June 9, 1928; s. Frederick Conrad and Helen Anna (Gauhs) W.; m. Nancy Whittemore, July 16, 1953; children: Michael, Anne, Mary, Martha. BA in German Lit., Wesleyan U., Middletown, Conn., 1950; student, Union Theol. Seminary, 1950-51, The Gen. Theol. Seminary, 1953; DD, The Gen. Theol. Seminary, 1984. Ordained priest Episc. Ch., 1953. Curate Christ Ch., Greenwich, Conn., 1953-56; vicar St. John's Chapel, Byram, Conn., 1953-56; rector Christ Ch., Unionville, Conn., 1956-60, St. James' Ch., Greenfield, Mass., 1960-68; priest-in-charge St. Andrew's Ch., Turners Falls, Mass., 1964-68; priest-in-charge, coordinator Cen. Berkshire (Mass.) Area Ministry, 1968-83; rector St. Stephen's, Pittsfield, Mass., 1968-84; bishop Diocese Western Mass., Springfield, 1984—; Mem. diocesan council Diocese Western Mass., 1962-68, dept. adminstrn. and fin., 1968-74, mem. standing com., 1974-82, sec. 1979-80, pres. 1980-82, mem. commn. on ministry, 1979-84, dean of N. Berkshire, 1976-79, dep. to gen. conv., 1976, 79, 82; supr. New Eng. Parish Tng. Program, 1965-78. Contbr. articles to profl. jours. Chaplain Greenfield Fire Dept., 1960-68; bd. dirs. Greenfield YMCA and Pittsfield YMCA. Mem. Cen. Berkshire Clergy Assn. (pres. 1977-79), Alumni of Gen. Theol. Seminary (exec. com. 1975-80), Phi Beta Kappa. Avocations: flower and vegetable gardening, music. Office: Diocese Western Mass 37 Chestnut Springfield MA 01103

WITCHER, ROBERT CAMPBELL, bishop; b. New Orleans, Oct. 5, 1926; s. Charles Swanson and Lily Sebastian (Campbell) W.; m. Elisabeth Alice Cole, June 4, 1957; 2 children. BA, Tulane U., 1949; MDiv, Seabury-Western Theol. Sem., 1952, DD, 1974; MA, La. State U., 1960, PhD, 1968; DCL (hon.), Nashotah House, 1989. Ordained priest Episcopal Ch., 1953; consecrated bishop, 1975; priest-in-charge St. Andrew Ch., Linton, La. and St. Patrick Ch., Zachary, La., 1953-56; priest-in-charge St. Augustine Ch., Baton Rouge, La., 1953-54; rector St. Augustine Ch., 1954-61; canon pastor Christ Ch. Cathedral, New Orleans, 1961-62; rector St. James Ch., Baton Rouge, 1962-75; coadjutor bishop L.I., 1975-77; bishop, 1977-91; also prof. ch. history Mercer Sch. Theology; interim bishop of Armed Forces, 1989-90; dean Christ Ch. Cathedral, New Orleans, 1991—; pres. Mercer Scholarship Fund; trustee Ch. Pension Fund; pres. bd. trustees estate belonging to Diocese of L.I.; pres. Anglican Soc. N.Am., 1980-83; sec. pastoral com. House of Bishops; chmn. Com. To Revise Title III; chmn. Com. on Developing Guidelines for Theol. Edn. Author: The Episcopal Church in Louisiana, 1801-1861. Trustee U. of South, 1963-69, Seabury-Western Theol. Sem., 1963-82, Gen. Theol. Sem., 1979-88, Ch. Pension Fund, 1985—; pres. Episcopal Health Svcs.; bd. dirs. Nat. Coun. Alcoholism, L.I. Coun. Alcoholism, St. Mary's Hosp. for Children. Capt. USNR, ret. Mem. N.Y. State Council Chs., L.I. Council Chs. (com. social justice). Address: 1934 Steele Blvd Baton Rouge LA 70808

WITHERSPOON, LAVERN, pastor; b. Kingstree, S.C., Oct. 14, 1954; s. James and Harold Phordom (Cooper) W.; m. Audrey Dianne Goodwin, Nov. 1983; children: Jacintha Dyan, André LaVern. BA, Bapt. Coll. Charleston, 1976; MDiv, Interdenominational Theol. Ctr., 1983. Pastor Shady Grove-St. Peter AME Ch., Abbeville, S.C., 1977-78, Shiloh-Springfield AME ch., McCormick, S.C., 1978-82, Oldfield Bethel & Mt. Sinai AME Ch., Bradley, S.C., 1982-85, Weston Chapel AME Ch., Greenwood, S.C., 1985—; chaplain Greenwood Correctional Ctr., 1986—. Prevention coord. Laurens (S.C.) Alcohol and Drug Abuse Commn.; pastoral care com. S.C. Commn. on Alcohol and Drug Abuse, 1989; bd. dirs. One-Ch. One-Child Adoption Bd., 1989. 1st lt. U.S. Army N.G., 1989—. Mem. NAACP, Greenwood County Mental Health Assn. (bd. dirs.), Masons, Order of Eastern Star, Alpha Phi Alpha (pres. Greenwood chpt. 1982—, state sec. 1985—, Man of Yr. 1985). Democrat. Avocations: cooking, baking, fishing. Home: 131 Valley Rd Greenwood SC 29646 Office: 805 E Cambridge Greenwood SC 80322-9680

WITHERSPOON, WILLIAM, investment economist; b. St. Louis, Nov. 21, 1909; s. William Conner and Mary Louise (Houston) W.; student Washington U. Evening Sch., 1928-47; m. Margaret Telford Johanson, June 25, 1938; children: James Tomlin, Jane Telford, Elizabeth Witherspoon Vodra. Rsch. dept. A. G. Edwards & Sons, 1928-31; pres. Witherspoon Investment Co., 1931-34; head rsch. dept. Newhard Cook & Co., 1934-43; chief price analysis St. Louis Ordnance Dist., 1943-45; head rsch. dept. Newhard Cook & Co., 1945-53; owner Witherspoon Investment Counsel, 1953-64; ltd. ptnr. Newhard Cook & Co., economist, investment analyst, 1965-68; v.p. rsch. Stifel, Nicolaus & Co., 1968-81; lectr. on investments Washington U., 1948-67. Mem. Clayton Bd. of Edn., 1955-68, treas., 1956-68, pres., 1966-67; mem. Clayton Park and Recreation Commn., 1959-60; trustee Ednl. TV, KETC, 1963-64; mem. investment com. Gen. Assembly Mission Bd. Presbyn. Ch. (USA), Atlanta, 1976-79, mem. permanent com. ordination exams, 1979-85. Served as civilian Ordnance Dept., AUS, 1943-45. Chartered fin. analyst. Mem. St. Louis Soc. Fin. Analysts (pres. 1949-50). Club: Mo. Athletic (St. Louis). Home: 6401 Ellenwood Clayton MO 63105-2228 *Many of the current social and ethical problems of today might be resolved if theology would be influenced by the 4th dimension of space-time plus the 5th dimension of the mind, the 6th dimension of the spirit and the 7th dimension of God the Father.*

WITHERUP, RONALD D., religion educator, seminary dean; b. Franklin, Pa., May 18, 1950; s. David Earl and Rose (Malene) W. BA in Philosophy, St. Bonaventure Coll., 1972; S.T.M. in Scripture, St. Mary's Sem. and U., 1976; ThM in Spirituality, Grad. Theol. Union, 1979; PhD in Bibl. Studies, Union Theol. Sem., Richmond, Va., 1985. High sch. tchr. Kennedy Christian High Sch., Sharon, Pa., 1976-78; instr. St. Mary's Sem. and U., Balt., 1979-81; teaching fellow Union Theol. Sem., Richmond, 1981-85; counseling assoc. Cath. U. Am., Washington, 1985-86; assoc. prof. St. Patrick's Sem., Menlo Park, Calif., 1986—, acad. dean, 1987—; adj. faculty St. Mary's Sem. and U., Balt., 1979-81, Inst. Continuing Edn./Ecumenical Inst., 1985-86; retreat dir. various dioceses, 1979—; dir. scriptural and counseling workshops, 1981—. Author: (with others) The New Jerome Biblical Commentary; contbr. articles and revs. to profl. jours. Mem. Soc. Bibl. Lit., Cath. Bibl. Assn. (task force lit. study of Matthew's Gospel 1985-87, co-chair task force narrative study of the New Testament 1988—). Roman Catholic. Home and Office: 320 Middlefield Rd Menlo Park CA 94025

WITKOWIAK, STANLEY BENEDICT, priest; b. Dortmund, Germany, May 18, 1909; came to U.S., 1909, naturalized, 1930; s. Stanley Paul and Helen Barbara (Groblena) W. BA, St. Francis (Wis.) Sem., 1931, MA, 1935; PhD, Cath. U. Am., 1942. Ordained priest Roman Cath. Ch., 1935. Asst. pastor, athletic dir. St. Stanislaus Parish and High Sch., Milw., 1935-39; prin. St. Catherine's High Sch., Racine, Wis., 1942-72, prin. emeritus, 1972-74; pastor St. Stanislaus Parish and Grade Sch., Racine, 1974—. Bd. dirs. Racine Libr., 1973-76, Racine Jr. Achievement, 1963-76. Recipient Citizen of Yr. award City of Racine, 1967, Jr. Achievement award Racine, 1975. Mem. Priests Forum, Racine Clergy Assn. Home and Office: 1754 Grand Ave Racine WI 53403

WITKOWSKI, SISTER MARY JULIA, nun, educator; b. North Tonawanda, N.Y., July 11, 1917; d. Anthony and Frances (Blachud) W. Student music, Nazareth Coll., Rochester, N.Y., 1940; BE, Medaille Coll., 1945; postgrad., Bonaventure U., 1959, U. Buffalo, 1970-72; MA in Sacred Scis., Queen's U., Kingston, Ont., 1974. Joined Congregation of Felician Sisters, Roman Cath. Ch., 1936. Coun. mem. Congregation of Felician Sisters, Buffalo, 1976-82, dir. formation, 1978-82, provincial superior, 1982-89; LCWR mem. Diocese Buffalo, 1976-89; del. Gen. Chpt. Felician Congregation, Rome, 1988; coord. religious curriculum for secondary schs., Mississauga, Ont., 1974; dir. music dept. Villa Maria Coll., Buffalo, 1976-78, mem. exec. com., trustee, 1976-83, inst. adv. com., 1983—; catechist Diocese Buffalo; prin. accreditation of Mary Immaculate Sch., Sao Paulo, Brasil, So. Assn. Schs. and Colls., 1971. Co-author: Fundamentals of Formation for Felician Sisters, 1981. Bd. dirs. Cantalician Ctr. for Learning. Recipient Community Svc. award Cheektowago (N.Y.) C. of C., 1989, Pres.'s medal Villa Maria Coll., 1989; ednl. grantee Cornell U., 1968, Clark U., 1966, W. Carolina U., 1971. Address: 2003 Halley Rd North Collins NY 14111 *As we approach the turn of the 21st century, it behooves us to remember that God reveals in his dealings with his chosen people that it is not for us to glory in the Golden Age of accomplishments but rather to dedicate our lives to his messianic message, embracing each day with new life.*

WITROD, SISTER MARY ROSALITA, nursing home administrator; b. Chgo., Oct. 17, 1920; d. Anthony and Agatha (Kolodziejczyk) W. Grad., Holy Family Hosp. Sch. Nursing, 1945; BS, Marquette U., 1960, M in Nursing Edn., 1961. Joined Congregation of Sisters of St. Francis, Roman Cath. Ch., 1939; lic. nursing home adminstr. Dir. nursing St. Mary's Hosp., Centralia, Ill., 1947-51; staff nurse Community Hosp., Bastrop, La., 1951-54; ICU instr. St. Mary Sch. Nursing, Chgo., 1977-81; quality assurance coord. St. Frances Hosp., Milw., 1981-84; long term care adminstr. St. Andrew Home, Niles, Ill., 1984—. Mem. Am. Coll. Nursing Home Adminstrs., Ill. Assn. Nursing Home Adminstrs. Home: 3800 W Peterson Ave Chicago IL 60659

WITT, JAMES BRADLEY, clergyman; b. Dallas, Mar. 30, 1954; s. Bradley Monroe and Nancy Corinne (Gibson) W.; m. Alyson Diane Essa, Oct. 27, 1990. BA in Psychology, Baylor U., 1976; MA in Clin. Psychology, Northwestern U., 1980; MDiv, Southwestern Bapt. Theol. Sem., 1984. Ordained to ministry Bapt. Ch. Chaplain intern Shannon West Tex. Meml. Hosp., San Angelo, 1985-86; minister single adults Sagamore Hill Bapt. Ch., Ft. Worth, 1986-87; minister single adults and missions First Bapt. Ch., Alexandria, Va., 1987—; mem. adv. group So. Bapt. Assn. Ministers Single Adults, Nashville, 1991—. Home: 4801 Kenmore Ave Alexandria VA 22304 Office: First Bapt Ch 2932 King St Alexandria VA 22302

WITTENBRINK, BONIFACE LEO, priest; b. Evansville, Ill., June 30, 1914; s. Max C. and Catherine Rose (Pautler) W. PhL, Gregorian U., Rome, 1939; STL, Ottawa (Can.) U., 1943; MA, Cath. U. Am., 1947. Ordained priest Oblates of Mary Immaculate, Roman Cath. Ch., 1941. Instr. Latin, logic, history and religion St. Henry's Coll., Belleville, Ill., 1943-48; instr., registrar, prin. high sch. dept. Coll. of Our Lady of the Ozarks, Carthage, Mo., 1948-52; founding dir. King's House of Retreats, Buffalo, Minn., 1952-53; mission procurator Roman Cath. Ch., St. Paul, 1955-56, 59-62; prin. Alemany High Sch. for Boys, Oblate Western Province, San Fernando, Calif., 1956-59; permanent sec. Conf. Maj. Superiors of Men, Washington, 1963-69; exec. dir., sec. Found. for Community Creativity, Washington, 1970-71; founder, dir., then dir. devel. Radio Info. Svc. for Blind and Handicapped, Belleville, 1972-84; pres., then local dir. Friends of Eye Rsch., Boston, 1983-87; exec. v.p. Citizens for Eye Rsch., Belleville, 1987—; pres. Oblate Ednl. Assn., St. Paul, 1961-62; sci. adv. bd. Nat. Acad. Child Devel., 1984-86; mem. com. Eye Experience St. Louis, 1984; adv. bd. Welfare of the Blind, Inc., 1984—; adv. coun. svcs. for print-handicapped Nat. Pub. Radio, 1976-77; active Internat. Christian Leadership, 1968-72; bd. dirs. LOGOS Translators. Bd. dirs. Technoserve, 1968-72, Internat. Book Svc., 1969-72; vol. Ill. Literacy Project, 1989-90; founding charter mem., bd. dirs. Washington Workshops Found. Mem. Madison County Assn. Blind, Mo. Coun. Blind, Am. Coun. of Blind (ednl. radio com. 1974-76), Am. Found. for Blind (radio talking book com. 1973-76), Inst. for Study of Econ. Systems (bd. dirs. 1971-72), Ednl. Communications Assn., Coun. for Dept. of Peace, Wycliffe Bible Translators Assn., Vols. for Internat. Tech. Assistance, Ill. Radio Info. Svc., Soc. Internat. Devel., UN Assn., Rotary Internat., Belleville Econ. Progress, Eagles, KC, Press Club St. Louis, Am. Assn. Ret. Persons. Avocations: reading, walking, travel. Home: 9500 Illinois Rte # 15W Belleville IL 62223-1017 Office: Citizens for Eye Rsch 5901 W Main St Belleville IL 62223

WITTHUHN, NORMAN EDWARD, minister; b. Wheeling, W.Va., Oct. 12, 1946; s. Louis Albright and Elizabeth Josephine (Krauskopf) W.; m. Mary Joan Tidd, Dec. 30, 1967; children: Elizabeth Ann, Jennifer Ann. AB, Bethany Coll., 1968; D in Ministry, Lexington Theol. Sem., 1975. Ordained to ministry Christian Ch. (Disciples of Christ), 1974. Prin. chaplain Commonwealth of Ky. Treatment Ctr., Crittenden, 1972-80; assoc. min. Cen. Christian Ch., Huntington, Ind., 1980-82; min. Ch. of Christ Uniting, Lexington, Ill., 1982-86, First Christian Ch., Russellville, Ky., 1986-89, Calvary Christian Ch., Covington, Va., 1989—; rep. regional bd., pres. local dist. Christian Ch. in Va., Lynchburg, 1991—; treas. COPE Inc., Covington, 1990—. Actor locally produced plays including The Wizard of Oz, 1986, The King and I, 1987; singer musical arts coun. Logan Rev., 1987. Mem. Kiwanis (sec. Russellville, Ky. club 1988-89, bd. dirs. Lexington club 1985-86). *I have held to the premise that happiness is always found by making the best of what one already has, as one strives to improve.*

WITTKAMPER, THOMAS JOHN, Christian school administrator; b. Gary, Ind., Mar. 25, 1943; s. Verne R. and Gladys E. (Fagner) W.; m. Cathy E. Hubbard, Aug. 26, 1968; children: Tammy S., Kimberly J. BS, John Brown U., 1965; MS in Edn. Adminstrn., Purdue U., 1972. Tchr. pub. schs. Ind., 1965-69, Dayton Christian High Sch., Dayton, Ohio, 1969-70; youth pastor Faith Bapt. Ch., Lafayette, Ind., 1970-71; high sch. prin. Indpls. Bapt. Schs. Inc., 1971-75; supr. Heritage Christian Sch. Inc., Milw., 1975—; exec. bd. mem. Assn. Christian Schs. Internat., Lahabra, Calif., 1978—, mid-Am. region dist. rep., 1978-87, chmn. exec. bd., 1984-85. Republican. Office: Heritage Christian Schs Inc 1300 S 109th St Milwaukee WI 53214

WITTSCHEN, NORMAN RILEY, minister; b. Charleston, S.C., Oct. 9, 1935; s. Norman Riley Wittschen and Grace Minerva (Motley) Forbes; m. Bette Barbara French, July 25, 1960; children: Norman Riley III, R. Lee. BS, Capital U., 1978; MDiv, Trinity Luth. Sem., 1980. Ordained to ministry Evang. Luth. Ch. Am., 1980. Pastor Calvary Luth. Ch., Irene, S.D., 1980-86; pastor, pres., chief exec. officer Faith Mission, Inc., Columbus, Ohio, 1986—; lay dir. Luth Cursillo Movement, Miami, Fla., 1971-76; spiritual dir. Ohio Via de Cristo Retreats, Columbus, 1987-89. Councilman City of Irene, 1981-86. Mayor's award for community svc. City of Columbus, 1980; Dir.'s award S.E. Community Mental Health Ctr., 1986. Mem. Sertoma (dir. Downtown club 1990—, Gem award 1986, Centurion award 1990), Univ. Club. Home: 3914 Barley Circle Columbus OH 43207-4603 Office: Faith Mission Inc 181 Long St Columbus OH 43215 *The degree to which the poor and needy, especially our homeless brothers and sisters, can be helped by understanding, compassion and guidance cannot be overestimated.*

WIZMAN, RAPHAEL, rabbi; b. Casablanca, Morocco, July 25, 1943; came to U.S., 1956; s. Haim and Mazal (Levy) W.; m. Bella Gruber, June 27, 1965; children: Eliezer, Chaim-Tova. MA in Theology, New Brunswick Theol. Sem., 1972; pastoral degree, N.Y. Bd. Rabbis, 1974; EdD, Rutgers U., 1976. Ordained rabbi, 1965. Rabbi Congregation Etz Ahaim, Highland Park, N.J., 1966-70, Sephardic Congregation, Forest Hills, N.Y., 1970-72, Young Israel of Commack, N.Y., 1972—. Bd. dirs. Rainbow Spl. Edn. Sch., Commack, 1983—. Mem. N.Y. Bd. Rabbis, Suffolk. Bd. Rabbis. Home and Office: Young Israel of Commack 40 Kings Park Rd Commack NY 11725 *Love of mankind is equal to love of God. For, "Men were created in the image of God."*

WODRIG, OSCAR SAMUEL, minister; b. Williamsport, Pa., July 4, 1938; s. Oscar Samuel Sr. and Helen Elizabeth (Cowden) W.; m. Barbara Lenora Stum, Jan. 10, 1959; children: Nora Lee, Daniel Lee, Michael Lee. BA in Psychology, Lycoming Coll., 1982; MDiv, United Theol. Sem., Dayton, Ohio, 1985, MRE, 1986. Ordained as elder United Meth. Ch., 1988. Pastor Eagle-Mill Creek United Meth. Charge, Williamsport, 1980-82, Ebenezer United Meth. Ch., Middletown, Pa., 1986-89, Grace United Meth. Ch., Philipsburg, Pa., 1989—; chaplain Pa. Coun. of Chs., Promised Land State Pk., 1984-85, coord. worship, Black Moshannon State Pk., 1990—; coord. chaplains Poly Clinic Hosp., Harrisburg, Pa., 1987-89; sec., treas. Philipsburg Area Ministerium, 1991—. Pres. West Decatur (Pa.) Sr. Citizens Group, 1990-91; regional rep. Centre County Community action Agy., Philipsburg, 1991—. With U.S. Army, 1956-67. Democrat. Home: 910 E Pine St Philipsburg PA 16866-1365 Office: Grace United Meth Ch 912 E Pine St Philipsburg PA 16866-1365

WOELLER, IDA MAY, lay worker; b. Florence, N.J., Dec. 14, 1964; d. Harold Oliver and Ida May (Denning) W. AS in Acctg., Burlington County Coll., Pemberton, N.J., 1986. Treas. Sunday Sch. 1st Wesleyan Ch., Florence, 1984-88, ch. treas., mem. bd. administrn., 1988—; acctg. clk. Super Fresh Food Markets, Florence, 1988—; mem. fin. com., nominating com., edn. com. 1st Wesleyan Ch., Florence, 1989—. Home: 38 E Second St Florence NJ 08518 *Every person in his/her life has at least one great challenge to take. Every challenge in life should be met with courage, faith, hope, knowledge and the support of family and friends. These qualities not only help a person when he or she is met with a challenge but in a person's everyday life. Life in general is tough, but those qualities alone have the greatest strength for overcoming every challenge that any person may encounter. You have these qualities within you, so all you have to do is put them to work for you. As a result, you may discover that your life has become a little easier than you had anticipated.*

WOERNER, AUGUST JOHN, retired minister; b. Newark, Sept. 27, 1925; s. August J. and Augusta (Marbach) W.; m. Beatrice Hilda Berg, Aug. 13, 1955; children: Susan Constance, Sharon Christine. BA, U. Bridgeport, 1951; MDiv, Andover Newton Theol. Sch., 1956. Ordained to ministry United Ch. of Christ, 1956. Min. Christian edn. State St. Ch., Portland, Maine, 1955-58, 1st Congl. Ch., Melrose, Mass., 1958-61, 2d Congl. Ch., Greenwich, Conn., 1961-63, Hope Ch., Springfield, Mass., 1963-66, South Congl. Ch., New Britain, Conn., 1966-77, Short Hills (N.J.) Community Ch., 1977-79, Haddonfield (N.J.) United Meth. Ch., 1979-84, Barrington (R.I.) Congl. Ch., 1984-91. With USNR, 1943-46. Mem. Assn. United Ch. Educators, Clergy Assn. of R.I. United Ch. of Christ, Clergy Assn. Westerly, R.I. Democrat. Home: 53 Apache Dr Westerly RI 02891-2045 Office: Barrington Congl Ch 461 County Rd Barrington RI 02806

WOERZ, CHRISTIAN HAYWARD, priest; b. L.A., Mar. 27, 1944; s. Christian Helmuth and Ruth Elizabeth (Rountree) W. AA, E. L.A. Coll., 1972; MDiv, St. Albert's Coll., Oakland Calif., 1975; MST, Jesuit Sch. Theol., Berkeley, Calif., 1976; D of Ministry, St. Mary's U., Balt., 1986. Ordained priest Roman Cath. Ch., 1976. Tchr. Don Bosco Tech. Inst., Rosemead, Calif., 1963-69, dept. chmn., 1969-72; vocat. dir. Salesians of Don Bosco, Bellflower, Calif., 1976-83, dir. formation, 1990—; retreat dir. St. Joseph's Youth Renewal Ctr., Rosemead, 1983-90; bd. dirs. Nat. Cath. Vocation Coun., Washington, 1978-82; chair. Western Vocation Dirs. Assn., Rosemead, 1978-82; pres. Nat. Conf. Religious Vocation Dirs., Chgo., 1981-82. Author, ventriloquist TV series, EWTN-TV, Birmingham, Ala., 1979, video program The Kingdom Kids, 1980. Recipient John Paul II award, Nat. Conf. Religious Vocation Dirs., 1982. Mem. Am. Camping Assn. Home and Office: Salesian of Don Bosco 9720 Foster Rd Bellflower CA 90706

WOFFORD, CLINTON FRIE, clergyman; b. Senath, Mo., May 15, 1933; s. Charles Clinton and Ella Eulalie (Frie) W.; m. Carolyn Lowell Christian, June 11, 1955; children—David Clinton, Cheryl Lynn, Susan Carol. B.S., U. Mo., 1955, Ph.D., 1962; M.Div., St. Paul Sch. Theology, 1972. Ordained to ministry United Methodist Ch., 1970, elder, 1973. Research chemist Phillips Petroleum Co., Bartlesville, Okla., 1961-67, group leader, 1967-69; pastor South Prospect United Meth. Ch., Kansas City, Mo., 1970-72, New Arlington United Meth. Ch., Kansas City, 1972; assoc. minister Trinity United Meth. Ch., Kansas City, 1973-74; interim pastor, 1974; pastor College Heights United Meth. Ch., Kansas City, 1974-78; dir. ch. relations Central Meth. Coll., Fayette, Mo., 1978-79; pastor Wayland (Mo.) Circuit, United Meth. Ch., 1979-83; pastor United Meth. Ch., Centralia, Mo., 1983-84, East Prairie (Mo.)-Bridges Charge, United Meth. Ch., 1984—; dir. Nowlin Hall, Kansas City, 1974-78; mem. East Central Bd., Kansas City, 1975-79; mem. Met. Interchurch Agy. Quality Edn. Task Force, Kansas City, 1976-79. Community rep. to Head Start Policy Council N.E. Mo., 1982-83. Served with USNR, 1955-57. McNeil fellow, 1959. Fellow Am. Inst. Chemists; mem. Mo. East Ann. Conf. United Meth. Ch., Sigma Xi. Clubs: Masons, Rotary. Patentee polymer chemistry. Home: 485 Miles Ave Centralia MO 65240 Office: PO Box 108 Centralia MO 65240

WOFFORD, MILTON GENE, religion and philosophy educator; b. Wichita Falls, Tex., Sept. 23, 1930; s. Joe Lee and Mary Easter (Fulcher) W.; m. Dorothy Jean Brod, June 13, 1953; children: Sharon Diane Wofford Callaway, Gary Gene. BA, Hardin-Simmons U., 1952; ThD, Southwestern Bapt. Theol. Sem., Ft. Worth, 1961. Ordained to ministry So. Bapt. Conv., 1949. Pastor Long Lake Bapt. Ch., Palestine, Tex., 1953-57, 1st Bapt. Ch., Houston, 1957-64, 1st Bapt. Ch. of Nederland, Tex., 1964-67, East Grand Bapt. Ch., Dallas, 1967-75; prof. Houston Bapt. U., 1975—. Home: 8803 Sterlingame Houston TX 77031 Office: Houston Bapt U Dept Christianity 7502 Fondren Rd Houston TX 77074

WOGAMAN, JOHN PHILIP, minister, educator; b. Toledo, Mar. 18, 1932; s. Donald Ford and Ella Louise (Kilbury) W.; m. Carolyn Jane Gattis, Aug. 4, 1956; children—Stephen Neil, Donald George, Paul Joseph, Jean Ann. B.A., U. Pacific, 1954; S.T.B., Boston U., 1957, Ph.D., 1960. Ordained to ministry United Methodist Ch., 1957. Pastor First Meth. Ch., Marlborough, Mass., 1956-58; staff asst., div. world missions United Meth. Ch., 1960-61; asst. prof., then assoc. prof. U. Pacific, 1961-66; prof. Christian social ethics Wesley Theol. Sem., Washington, 1966—, dean, 1972-83; mem. com. religious and civil liberties Nat. Council Chs., 1966-68, mem. com. internat. affairs, 1967-69; chairperson United Meth. Infant Formula Task Force, 1980-84, World Meth. Council, 1986—. Author: Methodism's Challenge in Race Relations, 1960; Protestant Faith and Religious Liberty, 1967; Guaranteed Annual Income: The Moral Issues, 1968; A Christian Method of Moral Judgement, 1976; Christians and the Great Economic Debate, 1977; Faith and Fragmentation, 1985; Economics and Ethics, 1986; Christian Perspectives on Politics, 1988. Editor: The Population Crisis and Moral Responsibility, 1973. Pres. Stockton (Calif.) Fair Housing Com., 1963-64, Suburban Md. Fiar Housing, 1970; mem. Calif. Democratic Central Com., 1964-66. Lilly fellow, 1959-60; recipient Research award Assn. Theol. Schs., 1975. Mem. Am. Soc. Christian Ethics (pres. 1976-77), Am. Theol. Soc. Home: 4620 45th St NW Washington DC 20016 Office: 4400 Massachusetts Ave NW Washington DC 20016

WOHL, AMIEL, rabbi; b. Cin., June 29, 1930; s. Samuel and Belle (Myers) W.; m. Ivy Lowenthal, Aug. 12, 1981; children: Susan, Elliot Dewey. BA, U. Cin., 1953; MHL, Hebrew Union Coll.-Jewish Inst. Religion, 1957, DD (hon.), 1983. Sr. rabbi Temple Israel of New Rochelle, N.Y., 1973—; pres. Interreligious Coun. New Rochelle, 1981-82, Westchester Jewish Conf., 1978-79, Westchester Bd. Rabbis, 1977-78, No. Pacific region Zionist Orgn. Am., 1969-72; mem. exec. bd. CCAR, 1980-82; chaplain Calif. State Senate, 1972; rabbinic overseer Hebrew Union Coll.-Jewish Inst. Religion; with radio broadcast svc. in N.Y., N.J. and Conn. areas. Contbr. numerous articles to profl. jours. Founder Black-Jewish dialogue group Coalition for Mut. Respect. Recipient Disting. Citizen award B'nai B'rith Internat., Champion of Freedom award Am. Forum for Christian-Jewish Cooperation, Wolfe Duberstein award Anti-Defamation League. Home: 3 Brookwood New Rochelle NY 10804 Office: Temple Israel 1000 Pinebrook Blvd New Rochelle NY 10804

WOHLWEND, GINA, minister; b. Knoxville, Tenn., Feb. 4, 1960; d. Vernon and Ople Christine (Monday) W. BS, U. Tenn., 1981; MA in Christian Edn., So. Bapt. Theol. Seminary, Louisville, 1986. Bible study leader Centrifuge Bapt. Sunday Sch. Bd., Glorieta, N.Mex., summers 1983-85; campus ministry intern Columbus and LaGrange Colls., Ga., 1986-87; summer youth min. First Bapt. Ch., Columbus, Ga., 1987; group leader Ga. Bapt. Children's Home, Meansville, 1988-89; min. of youth/edn. 1st Bapt. Ch., Gatlinburg, Tenn., 1989—; mem. Gatlinburg Ministerial Assn., 1989—; youth com. Columbus Bapt. Assn., 1986-87. Home: 420 Stuart Lane Apt 204 Gatlinburg TN 37738 Office: First Baptist Church PO Box 347 Gatlinburg TN 37738

WOITA, STEVEN RAY, minister; b. Neenah, Wis., June 7, 1949. BA, St. Olaf Coll., 1971; MDiv, Luther Northwestern Sem., 1976; MS, No. Ill. U., 1988; postgrad., Spertus Coll. Ordained to ministry Luth. Ch., 1976. Youth dir. N. Heights Ch., St. Paul, 1971-74; pastor Bethlehem Ch., Morris, Ill., 1976-78, 1st Ch., Lee, Ill., 1979-85, Luth. Campus Ministry, DeKalb, Ill., 1986, St. John's Ch., Creston, Ill., 1990—; dir. Luth. Social Svcs., DeKalb, 1986-91; chmn. bd. dirs. Luth. Campus Ministry, 1987-90. Mem. Am. Assn. Marriage and Family Therapy. Office: St Johns Ch Prairie and South Sts Creston IL 60113

WOJTYLA, KAROL JOZEF See JOHN PAUL II, HIS HOLINESS POPE

WOLBERG, RICHARD ALLEN, cantor; b. Hartford, Conn., June 27, 1941; s. Philip Sidney and Gertrude (Cohn) W. MusB, U. Hartford, 1964. Cantor Temple Beth El, Norwalk, Conn., 1964-69, Fall River, Mass., 1976—; music dir. Greater Fall River Religious Sch., 1976—; crisis intervention counselor Marble Collegiate Ch., N.Y.C., 1970-74. Advisor Bristol County Juvenile Ct., Fall River, 1978-81; vol. United Jewish Appeal, Fall River, 1976—. Cantor Richard Wolberg Day proclaimed in his honor Commonwealth of Mass., 1980. Mem. Cantor's Assembly Am. (exec. coun. 1987-90, 91—, commd. Hazzan-Minister of Jewish Faith 1980). Office: Temple Beth El 385 High St Fall River MA 02720 *Although it seems quite gloomy when it is raining, it would be an unending gloom were it not to rain at all. I have also discovered that the ultimate cost of failure is infinitely higher than the initial investment for success.*

WOLBRECHT, THOMAS PAUL, principal, educator; b. Missoula, Mont., Dec. 2, 1944; s. Walter F. and Marie H. (Suedekum) W.; m. Cheryl K. Milam, July 1, 1967; children: Christina, Eric, Bethany. BA, Concordia Sr. Coll., 1966; MDiv, Concordia Theol. Sem., 1970; MS in Edn. and Counseling, Portland (Oreg.) State U., 1974, EdD, 1990. Ordained to ministry Luth. Ch., 1970. Dean of students Luth. High Sch., Portland, 1970-77; dean of students Concordia Coll., Portland, 1978-84, prof. religion and psychology, 1984-88; assoc. exec. dir. Portland Luth. Sch., 1988-90, prin., 1990—; pastoral supr. N.IE. Luth. Mission, Portland, 1980-85. Vice pres. Oreg. Access-Handicapped, Portland, 1981. 1st lt. USAR, 1968-72. Mem. Am. Assn. Pastoral Counselors (affiliate), Assn. Luth. Devel. Execs., Oreg. Counselors Assn., Kappa Delta Pi. Democrat. Office: Portland Luth Sch 740 SE 182d Ave Portland OR 97233

WOLCSON, GERALD J., minister; b. N.Y.C., Aug. 25, 1947; s. John Joseph and Mary Veronica (Kiernan) W.; m. Teresa Ann Martin, Nov. 3, 1978. BS, Southwestern Coll., Waxahache, Tex., 1981. Ordained to ministry Ch. of the Rock, N.Am., 1982. Sr. high youth dir. Lakewood Assemblies of God Ch., Dallas, 1978-79; sr. pastor Ch. of the Rock, Tulsa, 1982-84; founder, pres. JWM Inc., Gladewater, Tex., 1984-89; U.S. dir. The Redeemed Evang. Mission, Lagos, Nigeria, 1985-89; sr. pastor Faith Christian Ch., West Haven, Conn., 1990-91, Ch. on the Rock, New Haven, 1991—; bd. dirs. Internat. Students USA, Yale U., 1990—; chaplain Cops for Christ, New Haven, 1990—; dean emeritus Gods Army Bible Coll., Lagos, 1986—. Author/editor numerous videos for overseas leadership tng., children's TV broadcasts for Nigeria, Bible Coll. video courses. With U.S. Army, 1968-69. Republican. Office: Ch on the Rock 1 Long Wharf Dr New Haven CT 06511

WOLD, ANTHONY JOHN, youth pastor; b. San Bernardino, Calif., Nov. 17, 1964; s. James Thomas and Frances (Banuellos) W.; m. Jodene Robinette Hieb, Oct. 6, 1990. AS in Electronic Engring. Tech., Heald Coll., 1984; BA in Religion, Azusa Pacific U., 1989. High sch. recreation dir. Forest Home Christian Conf. Camp, Forest Falls, Calif., 1986; high sch. youth intern Pkwy. Community Ch., Fairfield, Calif., 1987-88; mens dean Hume (Calif.) Lake Christian Camps, 1989; youth pastor Crosswinds Ch., Pleasonton, Calif., 1989—; high sch. substitute tchr. Pleasanton Unified Sch. Dist., 1990—. Coach football Amador Valley High Sch., Pleasanton, 1990. Home: 9085 Alcosta Blvd # 401 San Ramon CA 94583 Office: Cross Winds Ch 7116 Johnson Dr Pleasanton CA 94588

WOLD, DAVID C., bishop. Sishop of Southwestern Wash. Evang. Luth. Ch. in Am., Tacoma. Office: Synod of Southwestern Washington 420 121st St S Tacoma WA 98444*

WOLD, MARGARET BARTH, religion educator; b. Chgo., Mar. 6, 1919; d. Frank Philip and Esther Sophie (Pedersen) Barth; m. Erling Henry Wold, Oct. 4, 1942; children: John, Michael, Kristi Wold de Merlier, Stephen Ganzkow-Wold, Erling Jr. BA, Luther Coll., 1941; MA, Luther Sch. Theology, Chgo., 1950; DD (hon.), Luther Coll., 1986; LittD (hon.), Calif. Luth. U., 1973; DD (hon.), Wartburg Sem., 1985. Exec. bd. Am. Luth. Ch. Women, Mpls., 1966-73, exec. dir., 1973-74; dir. for ministry in changing communities So. Pacific dist., Am. Luth. Ch., 1977-84; assoc. prof. N.T. Calif. Luth. U., Thousand Oaks, 1985-89, coord. sr. mentor program, 1986—; cons. Pub. Welfare Bd., Bismarck, N.D., 1967-68; v.p. So. Calif. West Synod, Evang. Luth. Ch. in Am., 1987-90; keynote speaker Luth. World Fedn. Assembly, Budapest, Hungary, 1984; C.C. Hein Meml. lectr., 1985. Author: The Shalom Woman, 1975, The Critical Moment, 1978, Women of Faith and Spirit, 1987, The Power of Ordinary Christians, 1988; also 5 books co-authored with Erling H. Wold. Bd. dirs. Grand Forks (N.D.) Unified Sch. Dist., 1968-70; bd. dirs. Pacific Luth. Theol. Sem., Berkeley, Calif., 1974-86, pres. bd. dirs., 1978-84. Recipient Martin Luther 450th Anniversary award Luth. Brotherhood, 1967, Disting. Svc. award Luther Coll., 1968, 125th Anniversary award Augustana Coll., S.D., 1968. Mem. Am. Acad. Religion, Soc. for Bibl. Lit. Democrat. Office: Calif Luth U 60 Olsen Rd Thousand Oaks CA 91360 *To live and survive with joy in today's kind of world demands the giving and receiving of hope, humor and hugs. As we bring these gifts into our daily contacts, they come back to enrich our individual lives and move out to increase the collective positive energies of the human spirit.*

WOLF, ALFRED, rabbi; b. Eberbach, Germany, Oct. 7, 1915; came to U.S., 1935, naturalized, 1941; s. Hermann and Regina (Levy) W.; m. Miriam Jean Office, June 16, 1940; children: David B., Judith C. (dec.), Dan L. BA, U. Cin., 1937; MHL, Hebrew Union Coll., 1941; DD, 1966; PhD, U. So. Calif., 1961; DHL, U. Judaism, 1987, Loyola Marymount U., 1990. Ordained rabbi, 1941. Rabbi Temple Emanuel, Dothan, Ala., 1941-46; S.E. regional dir. Union Am. Hebrew Congregations, 1944-46; Western regional dir. Union Am. Hebrew Congregations, Los Angeles, 1946-49; rabbi Wilshire Blvd. Temple Los Angeles, 1949-85, rabbi emeritus, 1985—; dir. Skirball Inst. on Am. Values of Am. Jewish Com., 1985—; lectr. U. So. Calif., 1955-69, Hebrew Union Coll., Jewish Inst. Religion, Calif., 1963-65, 74; lectr. religion Seven Seas div. Chapman Coll., 1967; adj. prof. theology Loyola U. Los Angeles, 1967-74; lectr. sociology Calif. State U., Los Angeles, 1977. Author: (with Joseph Gaer) Our Jewish Heritage, 1957, (with Monsignor Royale M. Vadakin) Journey Of Discovery - A Resource Manual for Catholic-Jewish Dialogue, 1989,. Mem. camp commn. adminstv. com. Camp. Hess Kramer, 1951—; mem. Los Angeles Com. on Human Relations, 1956-72, mem. exec. bd., 1960—, chmn., 1964-66, hon. mem., 1972—; pres. Anytown U.S.A., 1964-66; mem. United Way Planning Council Bd., chmn., 1974—; mem. youth adv. com. NCCJ, 1968—, exec. bd., 1972—; founding pres. Interreligious Council So. Calif., 1970-72; chmn. clergy adv. com. Los Angeles Sch. Dist., 1971-81; chmn. Nat. Workshop on Christian-Jewish Relations, 1978; bd. govs. Hebrew Union Coll., bd. alumni overseers, 1972—; mem. Los Angeles 2000 Com., 1986-89, The 2000 Partnership, 1989—, Berlin Sister City Com., Los Angeles, 1987-89; bd. dirs. Jewish Fedn. Council, 1978-85, bd. govs., 1985—; bd. dirs. Jewish Family Service Los Angeles, sec., 1978-80. Recipient Samuel Kaminker award as Jewish educator of year Western Assn. Temple Educators, 1965, John Anson Ford Human Relations award County Commn. on Human Relations, 1972, 90, Harry Hollzer Meml. award Los Angeles Jewish Fedn. Council, 1978, Volpert Community Service award, 1986, Community Service award United Way of Los Angeles, 1980, Leadership award Los Angeles Bd. Edn., 1981, Service to Edn. award Associated Adminstrs. Los Angeles, 1983, Pub. Service award Jewish Chautauqua Soc., 1986, N.Am. Interfaith Leadership award Nat. Workshop for Christian-Jewish Rels., 1990. Mem. Bd. Rabbis So. Calif. (pres.), Am. Jewish Com. (exec. com. Los Angeles chpt., Max Bay Meml. award 1986), Central Conf. Am. Rabbis (exec. bd., mem. commn. on Jewish edn. 1970-72, treas. 1975-79, chmn. interreligious activities com. 1975-79, hon. mem. 1991—), Pacific Assn. Reform Rabbis (pres.), So. Calif. Assn. Liberal Rabbis (pres.), Synagogue Council Am. (mem. com. interreligious affairs), Alumni Assn. Hebrew Union Coll.-Jewish Inst. Religion, Town Hall, Los Angeles World Affairs Council, U. So. Calif. Alumni Assn. Home: 3389 Ley Dr Los Angeles CA 90027 Office: Skirball Inst on Am Values 635 S Harvard Blvd Los Angeles CA 90005-2511

WOLF, ARNOLD JACOB, rabbi, educator; b. Chgo., Mar. 19, 1924; s. Max A. and Nettie (Schanfarber) W.; m. Margery Steiner, Nov. 1, 1948 (div. Mar. 1960); m. Lois Blumberg, Dec. 26, 1963; children: Jonathan, Benjamin, Sara. AA, U. Chgo., 1942; BA, U. Cin., 1945; M of Hebrew Lit., Hebrew Union Coll., Cin., 1948; DD (hon.), Hebrew Union Coll., N.Y.C., 1973. Rabbi Congregation Solel, Highland Park, Ill., 1957-72; chaplain and instr. Yale U., New Haven, 1972-80; rabbi KAM-Isaiah Israel, Chgo., 1980—; chmn. Breira, N.Y.C., 1976-79; dir. Jewish Coun. Urban Affairs, Chgo., 1981—; lectr. U. Chgo., 1980—. Author: Challenge to Confirmands, 1963; editor: What is Man?, 1968; Rediscovering Judaism, 1965; Sh'ma, 1970—. Mem. ethics com. City of Chgo., 1983—; Jewish rep. World Coun. Chs., Nairobi, Kenya, 1985. Lt. (j.g.) USNR, 1951-53. Mem. Cen. Conf. Am. Rabbis. Office: KAM-Isaiah Israel Congregat 1000 E Hyde Park Blvd Chicago IL 60615

WOLF, SISTER MARY WILMA, nun, home economics educator; b. Little Cedar, Iowa, Apr. 2, 1918; d. William Michael and Sophia Emma (Miller) W. B.A., State U. Iowa, 1943, M.A., 1944. Joined Sisters of Mercy, Roman Catholic Ch., 1936. Tchr. St. Berchman's Sch., Marion, Iowa, 1937-38, Immaculate Conception Sch., Charles City, Iowa, 1939-40, St. John's Sch., Waterloo, Iowa, 1940-41; asst. prof. home econs. Mount Mercy Coll., Cedar Rapids, Iowa, 1945—. Demonstrator, Gazette Cook-Off, Cedar Rapids, 1984, 85; speaker Mount Mercy Speaker's Bur., 1960-76. Avocations: cooking; sewing; crafts. Home and Office: Mount Mercy Coll 1330 Elmhurst Dr NE Cedar Rapids IA 52402

WOLFE, FRED HARTWELL, pastor; b. Rock Hill, S.C., Dec. 5, 1937; s. Fred Walters and Margaret Wolfe; m. Patricia Anne Heath; children: Mark, Jeffrey. BA, U. S.C., 1960; MDiv, Southwestern Bapt. Theol. Sem., 1967; DD (hon.), Mobile Coll., 1982. Ordained to ministry So. Bapt. Conv. Pastor Monaghan Bapt. Ch., Greenville, S.C., 1967-69, Woodlawn Bapt. Ch., Decatur, Ga., 1969-72, Cottage Hill Bapt. Ch., Mobile, Ala., 1972-79, 80—, 1st Bapt. Ch., Lubbock, Tex., 1979-80; pres. Pastors Conf., So. Bapt. Conv., 1983, chmn. com. on order, 1984-85, 87-88, sec. exec. com., 1990, vice chmn. exec. com., 1991—. Author: The Divine Pattern, 1982. Avocations: golf, fishing, hunting. Office: Cottage Hill Bapt Ch PO Box 9129 Mobile AL 36691

WOLFE, L. DANIEL, clergyman; b. Detroit, Jan. 5, 1937; s. Louis Martin and Mildred (Harbaugh) W.; m. Janice Jean Blauser, Aug. 22, 195k9; children: Daniel Martin, Matthew Brian, Allison Elizabeth. BA summa cum laude, Huntington (Ind.) Coll., 1959; MDiv, Asbury Sem., Wilmore, Ky., 1962, postgrad., 1988—. Ordained to ministry Fellowship of Covenant Mins. and Chs. Sr. pastor United Brethren in Christ, Harrison, Mich., 1962-67; lectr. theology Sierra Leone (Africa) Bible Coll., 1967-70, prin., 1968-69; sr. pastor United Brethren in Christ, Kalamazoo, 1970-73, Agape' Christian Fellowship, Kalamazoo, 1973-87, New Covenant Christian Ch., Reston, Va., 1987—; president elder S.W. Mich. Presbytery, Kalamazoo, 1980-87; pres. Karis Found., Reston, 1989—. Pres. Citizens for Decency Through Law, Kalamazoo, 1985-87. Office: New Covenant Christian Ch 626 C Grant St Herndon VA 22070

WOLFE, LINDA KAY, church administration worker; b. Phila., Jan. 2, 1949; d. Elmer Wilson Wolfe and Mildred Mae (Heffner) Maberry. BA, Houghton Coll., 1970. Cert. elem. edn. tchr., Fla. Staff mem. Teen Missions Internat., Merritt Island, Fla., 1975-82; youth dir. Cornerstone Ch., Merritt Island, 1982-84, pastor's sec., 1984-89; mgr. Cornerstone Media, Inc., Merritt Island, 1989—. Home: 555 Aster Ct # 7 Merritt Island FL 32953 Office: Cornerstone Media Inc 3500 N Courtney Pkwy Merritt Island FL 32953

WOLFE, MARK JAMES, minister; b. Eaton Rapids, Mich., Aug. 16, 1962; s. Lonnie James and Grace Maureen (Miller) W.; m. Janet Ann Howe, Aug. 16, 1980; children: Jonathan James, Heather Joy. BA, Hungtington Coll., 1984, M in Christian Ministry, 1986. Ordained to ministry Ch. of the United Brethren in Christ, 1986. Pastor Plum Tree United Ch. of Christ, Warren, Ind., 1983-85, Claytonville United Brethren in Christ Ch., Shippensburg, Pa., 1985-86; pastor youth Colwood United Brethren in Christ Ch., Caro, Mich., 1986-90; pastor youth and Christian edn. West Windsor United Brethren in Christ Ch., Diamondale, Mich., 1990-91; pastor Chicora United Brethren in Christ Ch., Allegan, Mich., 1991—; v.p. Warren Area Ministerial Assn., 1984-85; sec. Rock River United Brethren in Christ Camp Bd., Adeline, Ill., 1985-86; mem. youth task force Ch. of United Brethren in Christ, Huntington, Ind., 1989—. Home and Office: 4399 108th Ave Allegan MI 49010 *I have a plaque on my office wall that has my life's goal written on it. It says, "I want to know Christ and the power of His resurrection and the fellowship of sharing in His sufferings, becoming like Him in His death." (Philippians 3:10) Just below this verse is a question: "Is what I am now doing getting me closer to my goal? I am continually brought back to this question when new activities come my way. I then evaluate whether or not I should become involved with them. Many times I have to say no to things which I would like to do but which would not help me to reach my life's goal.*

WOLFE, PAUL DAVID, minister; b. Evanston, Ill., Aug. 14, 1950; s. Richard Schuyler and Elizabeth (Schmidt) W.; children: Michael, Andrew. BA, U. Cen. Fla., 1974; MDiv, Nashotah (Wis.) House, 1978. Ordained deacon, Episcopal Ch., 1978, ordained priest, 1979. Asst. St. Andrew's Episcopal Ch., Ft. Pierce, Fla., 1978-81; rector Holy Cross Episcopal Ch., Winter Haven, Fla., 1981—; bd. dirs. The Diocese of Cen. Fla., Orlando, 1989—; bd. dirs. The Inst. for Christian Studies, Orlando, Anchor House Home for Boys, Auburndale, Fla., 1988-90. Editor ch. curriculum; contbr. articles to profl. jours. Guardian ad Litem Polk County Juv. Ct., Fla., 1989—; mem. sex edn. com., Polk County Schs., 1988. Recipient Svc. award The Diocese of Cen. Fla., 1988. Mem. The Alban Inst. Office: Holy Cross Episcopal Ch 201 Kipling Lane Winter Haven FL 33884

WOLFE, WILLIAM EUGENE, religious broadcaster, educator; b. Bristol, Tenn., June 16, 1937; s. William Eugene and Evelyn (Preston) W.; m. Martha Campbell, June 17, 1961; children: Janita Wolfe Thomas, Maria Neal Wolfe-Jones, Christina Jean. BA, King Coll., 1959; M in Christian Edn., Presbyn. Sch. Christian Edn., 1961. Cert. Presbyn. Christian educator. Pres. Relay Prodns., Inc., 1968—; dir. sr. high edn. United Meth. Bd. Discipleship, Nashville, Tenn., 1971-89; exec. dir. Presbyn. Appalachian Broadcasting Coun., Nashville, Tenn., 1989—; dir. programs East Brentwood (Tenn.) Presbyn. Ch., 1989—; dir. Christian edn. Hillsboro Presbyn. Ch., Nashville, 1990—; team leader Yokefellow Fellowship at Deberry Correctional Inst., Nashville, 1985—. Author: The Basic Encyclopedia for Youth Ministry, 1981, Leader's Guide for the Yearbook: Untold Stories, 1983, The Yearbook: Untold Stories, 1983, Inviting Youth, 1988; exec. producer: (films) Harry Chapin on World Hunger, 1980, One Can Help, 1983; producer: (videotapes) Active Learning for Youth, 1984, Servants Not Stars, 1986, Being a Gifted Teacher, 1986. Mem. Assn. Presbyn. Christian Educators, World Assn. Christian Communicators. Home: 607 Shenandoah Dr Brentwood TN 37027 Office: PO Box 40472 Nashville TN 37204 *There are two sources of my hope: God is still in charge of the world, and people can change.*

WOLFF, RAPHAEL GUSTAVE, English educator; b. Riverside, Calif., Oct. 17, 1958; s. Raphael Gustave and Melody (Morgan) W.; m. Ellen Louise Redinger, Sept. 20, 1988. BA in English, Cedarville (Ohio) Coll., 1980; MDiv, Grace Sem., Winona Lake, Ind., 1988; postgrad., U. N.D., 1988—. Tchr. high sch. English Warsaw (Ind.) High Sch., 1988—. Mem. Kappa Delta Pi. Republican. Baptist. Home: 3458 W John Rd Warsaw IN 46580

WOLFGRAM, CRAIG ARVIN, minister; b. Appleton, Wis., Apr. 29, 1960; s. Arvin T. and Betty (Malueg) W.; m. Kathryn L. Snyder, Sept. 8, 1984. BA, Carthage Coll., 1982; MDiv., Luther-Northwestern Theol. Sem, 1986. Ordained to ministry Evangelical Ch. in America. Pastor Faith and Bethany Luth. Chs., Rock and Perkins, Mich., 1986—; com. rep. congl. life and mission com. No. Great Lakes Synod, 1988—. Trustee, Mid Peninsula Sch. Bd., Rock, 1988—. Mem. Lions. Avocations: photography, skiing, travel. Office: Faith Luth Ch 14326 Hwy M-35 Rock MI 49880

WOLFMAN, DAVID S., rabbi; b. N.Y.C., June 21, 1960; s. Richard S. and Marsha M. (Katz) W.; m. Jane L. Liebeskind, Aug. 21, 1982; children: Jennifer Shira, Rachel Shoshana. BA cum laude, Boston U., 1982; MAHL, Hebrew Union Coll., Cin., 1986. Ordained rabbi, 1987. Assoc. rabbi Temple Isaiah, Lexington, Mass., 1987—; youth commr. N.E. Coun., Union Am. Hebrew Congregations-Cen. Conf. Am. Rabbis Reg. Youth Commn., 1990—, exec. bd., 1989-91, mem. outreach com., 1989—. Editor, originator book/study project: Our Jewish Lives, 1989. Office: Temple Isaiah 55 Lincoln St Lexington MA 02173

WOLFROM, WAYNE DENNIS, minister, principal; b. Warren, Mich., May 21, 1940; s. Clarence Henry and Viola Loretta (Baze) W.; m. Paula Jean Kirschner, July 18, 1970 (dec. 1982); children: Jeremiah, Lisa. BA, Mich. State U., 1961; MA, Concordia U., River Forest, Ill., 1973. Ordained to ministry Luth. Ch.-Mo. Synod, 1963. Tchr., youth dir. St. Paul Luth. Ch., Melrose Park, Ill., 1963-73; prin., tchr. Timothy Luth. Ch., Chgo., 1973-77; prin. Holy Cross Luth. Ch., Detroit, 1977-84, Greenfield Peace Luth. Ch., Detroit, 1984-85, East Bethlehem Luth. Ch., Detroit, 1985—; bd. dirs. no. Ill. dist., Chgo., 1976-77. Home: 11341 Chicago Rd Warren MI 48093 Office: East Bethlehem Luth Ch 3510 E Outer Dr Detroit MI 48234 *Leading and teaching children to serve others with all of their heart, soul and mind is the challenge given us that this generation might have the mind of Jesus and pass it to the next.*

WOLFRUM, WILLIAM HARVEY, bishop; b. Warrensburg, Mo., Jan. 16, 1926; s. Oscar William and Lucille Bales (Insley) W.; m. Beverly Ann Gunn, Nov. 30, 1947; 3 children. BS, Cen. Mo. State Coll., 1949; MS, Cornell U., 1953; BD, Episcopal. Theol. Sem. of S.W., 1959, DD, 1981. Ordained deacon, Episcopal. Ch., 1959, priest, 1960. Deacon-in-charge St. Paul Ch., Artesia, N.Mex., 1959-60, rector, 1960-62; rector Trinity-on-the-Hill Ch., Los Alamos, N.Mex., 1962-68; chaplain, chmn. dept. religious studies St. Stephen's Sch., Austin, 1968-71; rector St. Alban's Ch., Worland, Wyo., 1971-81; suffragan bishop Diocese of Colo., Denver, 1981—. Address: Box 18-M Capitol Hill Sta 1300 Washington Denver CO 80218

WOLLAN, THOMAS CARL, clergyman; b. Libertyville, Ill., Oct. 22, 1960; s. Telford Clifford and Joanne May (Brunsvold) W.; m. Barbara Jean Stobb, Oct. 13, 1984; 1 child, Kathryn Jean. BS, N.D. State U., 1982; MDiv, Luther Northwestern Theol. Sem., 1987. Ordained to ministry Evang. Luth. Ch. in Am., 1987. Pastor Calvary Luth. Ch., Buffalo, Iowa, 1987-90; assoc. pastor Grace Luth. Ch., Davenport, Iowa, 1990—; coun. mem. Illowa Luth. Coalition, Moline, Ill., 1988-90, v.p., 1990—. Mem. Scott County Recycling Com., Davenport, Iowa, 1989-90. Home: 2427 LeClaire Ave Davenport IA 52803 Office: Grace Luth Ch Davenport IA 52803

WOLLERSHEIM, GARY MATTHEW, clergyman; b. Chgo., Feb. 25, 1951; s. Irving Matthew and Evelyn Ovedia (Gunderson) W.; m. Paulette Ann Swanson, Aug. 25, 1972; children: Ruth, Matthew, Rachel. BA, Augsburg Coll., 1973; MDiv, Luther-Northwestern Sem., 1977. Ordained to ministry Evang. Luth. Ch. in Am. 1977. Pastor Gethsemane Luth. Ch., Cicero, Ill., 1977-80; pastor, developer Luth. Ch. in Am., St. Charles, Ill., 1980-81, dist. dean Ill. Synod, 1978-80, evangelism leader, 1981-90; asst. to bishop No. Ill., mem. staff for new ministries devel. and evangelism Evang. Luth. Ch. in Am., St. Charles, 1990—; pastor Hosanna! Luth. Ch., St. Charles, 1981-90. Home: 1819 Indiana St Saint Charles IL 60174 Office: Evang Luth Ch in Am No Ill Synod PO Box 1189 Saint Charles IL 60174

WOLSONOVICH, NICHOLAS, school system administrator. Supt. schs. Diocese of Youngstown, Ohio. Office: Office Supt Schs 144 W Wood St Youngstown OH 44503*

WOMACK, EDWIN BAXTER, minister; b. Flagstaff, Ariz., Mar. 9, 1931; s. Baxter G. and Alta Mae (Osborn) W.; m. Norma Jean Bruner, June 14, 1952; children: Kenneth, Paul, Sharon Womack Tolliver, Janet Womack Neilson. AA with honors, Phoenix Coll., 1951; BA with honors, Coll. of Pacific, 1953; MDiv, Garrett Bibl. Inst., Evanston, Ill., 1957. Ordained to ministry Meth. Ch. as deacon, 1955, as elder, 1957. Pastor Claypool (Ariz.) Meth. Ch., 1957-59, Avondale (Ariz.) Community Ch., 1959-64, Wahiawa (Hawaii) Community Meth. Ch., 1964-73, Epworth United Meth. Ch., Phoenix, 1973-77, First United Meth. Ch., Lompoc, Calif., 1977-85, Trinity United Meth. Ch., Los Osos, Calif., 1985—. Author: Come, Follow Me, 1982. Mem. State Bd. Edn., Honolulu, 1971-72; pres. Lompoc (Calif.) Valley Community Project, 1984-85. Mem. Hawaiian Malacological Soc., Santa Barbara Malacological Soc. (pres. 1989—), Conchologists Am. Home: 2111 Pine Ave Los Osos CA 93402 Office: Trinity United Meth Ch 490 Los Osos Valley Rd Los Osos CA 93402 *The world belongs to God, not to us. God created us to love and wants all people to have life. Love holds life together, and unlove tears it apart. Abundant living comes from knowing we belong to God and being grateful for God's love.*

WOMACK, ERIC, minister; b. Newark, Feb. 26, 1959; s. Donald and Joan (Nash) W. D of Naturopathy, Clayton Sch. Natural History, 1979; DD, Internat. Bible Sem. Inst., 1986, Internat. Bible Inst., 1987; ThD, Trinity Bible Coll., 1988. Min. music Faith Temple Victory, 1973-81; deacon Faith Temple Victory, Newark, 1977-78; pres. Black Covenant Ministries World Outreach Assn., Bloomfield, N.J., 1990—; pastor Christian Bible Ctr., Bloomfield, 1991—; cons. nutrition Living Well Clinic, Bloomfield, 1988—. Author: Come Back Home Daddy Ain't Mad With You, 1978, God's Advisious Are Pleasant, 1985, You Are a New Person, 1984, The Black Man According to God, 1987; song writer, God Has a Season for You, 1988. campaing mgr., Cen. Ward Councilman, Newark, 1978. Mem. Am. Assn. Nutritional Cons. Address: PO Box 258 Orange NJ 07050 Office: Christian Bible Ctr 430 Franklin St Bloomfield NJ 07003

WOMACK, MORRIS M., minister, educator; b. Daylight, Tenn., Dec. 12, 1927; s. Oscar Black Womack and Ida Le (Green) Deadmon; m. Ada E. Womack, May 9, 1948; children: Richard Henry, Leanne Marie, James Morris (dec.). BA, Butler U., 1954, BD, 1958; PhD, Wayne State U., 1967. Instr. Mich. Christian Coll., Rochester, 1959-66; prof. communications Pepperdine U., L.A., 1967—; min. various Chs. of Christ, 1945—; cons. various police depts., Calif., 1968—, Pacific Bell Telephone, San Francisco, 1983. Author: J.P. Sanders, 1988, (with others) Communications: A Unique Significance for Law Enforcement, 1984, Speech for Foreign Students, 1990. Mem. Speech Communications Assn., Optimists (bd. dirs. Agoura chpt. 1987). Republican. Mem. Ch. of Christ. Avocations: Playing golf, writing, wood carving. Home: 155 N Kanan Rd Agoura CA 91301 Office: Pepperdine U Dept Communications Malibu CA 90263

WOMER, JAN LINWOOD, minister; b. Beaver Falls, Pa., Dec. 13, 1939; s. L. Arthur and Emma (Mortensen) W.; m. Sharyn Elizabeth Edelblute, Sept. 6, 1967; children: Justin A.L., Colin C.E. BA, U. Calif.-Riverside, 1961; MDiv, Pacific Luth. Theol. Sem., 1965; MA, PhD, U. Oxford. Ordained to ministry Lutheran Ch., 1968. Prof. theology Nommensen U., Sumatra, Indonesia, 1971-75; pastor Mt. Calvary Luth. Ch., Cypress, Calif., 1975-80; asst. to bishop Pacific S.W. Synod, Luth. Ch. Am., Los Angeles, 1980-83; lectr. theology and fellow Mansfield Coll., U. Oxford, Eng., 1983—, acting prin., 1985-86, prin., 1986-88; dir. worship, music, arts Evang. Luth. Ch. in Am., 1988-91; sr. pastor St. Paul's Luth. Ch., Fullerton, Calif., 1991—; mem. co-opted staff Assembly Luth. World Fedn., Budapest, Hungary, 1984; del. nat. conv. Luth. Ch. Am., Seattle, 1980, Toronto, 1984, ecumenical officer Pacific S.W. Synod, Los Angeles, 1981-83, mem. cons. com. worship, Phila., 1978-82; lectr. Luth. Confs. Worship and Music, 1978-83; cons. Internat. Anglican-Luth. Dialogues, 1986—. Author: Morality and Ethics in Early Christianity, 1987; Author and editor: Ecclesia-Leiturgia-Ministerium, 1977. Contbr. articles to profl. jours. Recipient Disting. Alumni award Pacific Luth. Theol. Sem., 1991. Pres. youth adv. bd. City of Concord, Calif., 1979-81. Mem. N.Am. Acad. Liturgy, Soc. Study Theology, Soc. Study Christian Ethics (U.K.), Soc. Christian Ethics (U.S.), Convocation Oxford U., Luth. Council Great Britain, Societas Liturgica, United Oxford and Cambridge U. Club, Oxford Soc., Oxford Union Club, Rotary. Home: 111 W Las Palmas Dr Fullerton CA 92635

WONG, CORINNE HONG SLING, minister; b. Hong Kong, China, Nov. 24, 1930; came to U.S., 1940; d. William Hong Sling and Clara Grace (Low) Shen; m. Howard Marn Yung Wong, Sept. 16, 1953; children: Alison Marie Wong Noto, Mark David, Martin John. BS, Houghton Coll., 1951; MRE, N.Y. Theol. Sem., 1954; MDiv, Princeton Theol. Sem., 1986. ordained Am. Bapt. Chs., 1992. Asst. to pastor 1st Presbyn. Ch., Honolulu, 1986-87; min. Christian edn. Wahiawa (Hawaii) Korean Christian Ch., 1988-89; interim lay pastor St. Elizabeth's Episcopal Ch., Honolulu, 1989-90; min. adult ministries 1st Bapt. Ch. Honolulu, 1991—. Author: Studies in the Gospel of Mark, 1979, Studies in Colossians, 1984. Recipient grants for religious study Chinese Christian Assn., Honolulu, 1984-86, C.K. Ai Found., Honolulu, 1984-86, Presbyn. Ch. (U.S.A.), 1985-86. Office: First Bapt Ch Honolulu 1313 Pensacola St Honolulu HI 96814 *The greatest need we human beings have is to know we are accepted and loved unconditionally by God and by significant people in our lives and to be able to love others with this same kind of love.*

WONNEBERGER, REINHARD, theology educator, computer scientist; b. Forchheim, Germany, Sept. 30, 1946; s. Arthur and Elfriede (Blasig) W.; m. Brigitte Goecke, Apr. 25, 1980; children: Sigrun, Henrike. I. Theol.Exam., Bayrische Landeskirche, Munich, Fed. Republic Germany, 1970; II. Theol. Exam., Badische Landeskirche, Karlsruhe, Fed. Republic Germany, 1975; Dr. theol., U. Heidelberg, Fed. Republic Germany, 1975; Habilitation, U. Mainz, Fed. Republic Germany, 1991. Asst. prof. theology and EDP, U. Heidelberg, 1972-76, U. Hamburg, Fed. Republic Germany, 1977-86; computer scientist Electronic Data Systems (Deutschland) GmbH, Rüsselsheim, 1986—; privatdozent U. Mainz, 1991—. Author: Syntax und Exegese, 1979; Understanding BHS (Biblica Hebraica Stuttgartensia), 1990; German, 1986, Japanese, 1990; Verheissung und Versprechen, 1986; Kompaktführer LaTeX, 1988; Redaktion, 1992; also numerous articles; expert in linguistics, on ethics of EDP. Lutheran. Office: EDS, Eisenstrasse 56 (N15), 6090 Rüsselsheim Federal Republic of Germany

WOOD, CHARLES MONROE, theology educator; b. Salida, Colo., Nov. 22, 1944; s. Roy Milton and Ruth (Avery) W.; m. Jean Ann Fesler, Sept. 4, 1966; 1 child, Leslie Anne. BA, U. Denver, 1966; ThM, Boston U., 1969; M. Philosophy, Yale U., 1971, PhD, 1972. Ordained to ministry United Meth. Ch. as deacon, 1967, as elder, 1973. Pastor Rocky Mountain Conf., United Meth. Ch., 1972-76; asst. prof. theology Perkins Sch. Theology, So. Meth. U., Dallas, 1976-82, assoc. prof. theology, 1982-88, prof. theology, 1988—, assoc. dean for acad. affairs, 1990—; mem. Rocky Mountain Conf., United Meth. Ch. Author: Theory and Religious Understanding, 1975, Formation of Christian Understanding, 1981, Vision and Discernment, 1985; contbr. articles to profl. jours. Mem. Am. Acad. Religion, Am. Theol. Soc., AAUP, Phi Beta Kappa, Omicron Delta Kappa. Office: So Meth U Perkins Sch of Theology Dallas TX 75275-0133

WOOD, CHESTER ELVIN, religion educator; b. Indpls., Feb. 2, 1941; s. Clarence E. and Sarah M. (Tyler) W.; m. Dolores Garippa, Aug. 8, 1964; children: Elisabeth, Rebekah, Ruth, Deborah. BA, Columbia (S.C.) Bible Coll., 1963; BD, Trinity Evang. Div. Sch., Deerfield, Ill., 1966; ThM, Trinity Evang. Div. Sch., 1968; PhD, St. Andrews (Scotland) U., 1976. Asst. prof. John Brown U., Siloam Springs, Ark., 1967-70; vis. prof. Columbia Grad. Sch. of Bible/Mission, 1970-71; prof. N.T. Asian Theol. Sem., Manila, 1976-81; assoc. prof. Bethel Coll., St. Paul, 1982—; adj. prof. Nairobi Evang. Grad. Sch. Theology, 1984—; exec. dir. Light of the World Ministries, Inc., Indpls., 1986—. Recipient Alumnus of Yr. award Trinity Evang. Div. Sch., 1983, Disting. Faculty Svc. award Bethel Coll., 1989-90. Mem. Soc. Bibl. Lit. Office: Bethel Coll 3900 Bethel Dr Saint Paul MN 55112

WOOD, DANIEL WARREN, minister; b. Durham, N.C., Sept. 24, 1955; s. Warren Clemons and Helen Viola (Holmes) W.; m. Deborah Lynn Langdon, June 17, 1978; children: Lauren, Kevin. BA, U. N.C., 1977; MDiv, Southwestern Bapt. Theol. Sem., Ft. Worth, 1981; D Ministry, Southeastern Theol. Sem., 1987. Ordained to ministry So. Bapt. Conv., 1981. Pastor 1st Bapt. Ch., Franklinville, N.C., 1981—; del. Bapt. State Conv. N.C., Cary, 1981—, spl. youth worker, 1983—; instr. adult edn. Randolph Tech. Coll., Asheboro, N.C., 1984—; adj. prof. N.T., Gardner-Webb Coll., Boiling Springs, N.C. Mem. Randolph Bapt. Pastors' Conf. (pres. 1984), Randolph Bapt. Assn. (del. 1981—, mem. AssisTeam 1982—), Bapt. Men Club, Lions (chaplain Franklinville club 1983). Home: 208 Park St Franklinville NC 27248 Office: 1st Bapt Ch PO Box 111 Franklinville NC 27248

WOOD, DAVID LEE, minister; b. Alma, Mich., Nov. 2, 1951; s. Raymond Leon and Bety Lon (Packer) W.; m. Mona Marie Pitts, Dec. 4, 1970; children: Jonathan, Joel, Janna, Joy. Student, Great Lakes Bible Coll., Lansing, Mich., 1969-74; BS, Cen. Mich. U., 1982. Ordained to ministry Christian Ch./Ch. of Christ, 1976. Assoc. minister Ch. of Christ, Henderson, Mich., 1970-72, Deerfield Ch. of Christ, Lapeer, Mich., 1972-74; minister St. John Ch. of Christ, St. Johns, Mich., 1974-77; tchr. First Christian Ch. Sch, Clermont, Fla., 1983-88; minister First Christian Ch., Clermont, Fla., 1988—. Republican. Office: First Christian Ch 796 Hook St Clermont FL 34711

WOOD, DEBORAH SWIFT, minister; b. Oneonta, N.Y., Jan. 31, 1954; d. Frederic Fay and Norma (Wood) Swift. BA, Hartwick Coll., 1975; MS, SUNY, Oneonta, 1980; MDiv, Colgate Rochester Div. Sch., 1990. Ordained to ministry Presbyn. Ch. (U.S.A.), 1990; cert. tchr., N.Y. Dir. youth music 1st Presbyn. Ch., Oneonta, 1974-78; tchr. music pub. sch. Sidney, N.Y., 1975-83; faculty of music, dir. music admissions Wilkes Coll., Wilkes-Barre, Pa., 1984-86; worship coord. Colgate Rochester (N.Y.) Div. Sch., 1988-89; interim pastor United Presbyn. Ch., East Bethany, N.Y., 1990—; mem. Genesee Valley Presbytry, Rochester, 1990—, chmn. worship com., 1991—; mem. preparation for women in ministry com. Colgate Rochester Div. Sch., 1988-89. Co-author: The Story of Popular Music in America, 1977, What Everyone Should Know about Music, 1985; composer over 350 choral and solo vocal works. Camp dir. N.Y. State Music Camp, Oneonta, 1974-83; founder, dir. Encore Music Camp Pa., Wilkes-Barre, 1984-86. John Christopher Hartwick scholar Hartwick Coll., 1974; Gene Bartlet scholar Colgate Rochester Div. Sch., 1989. Mem. Presbyn. Interim Pastor's Network, Sigma Alpha Iota. Home: 452 Linden St Rochester NY 14620

WOOD, GARY WAYNE, minister; b. Silsbee, Tex., Jan. 2, 1951; s. Alexander John and Frances Maxine (Sparks) W.; m. Carolyn Kaye Owens, Dec. 18, 1971; children: Randall Scott, Jared Ryan. BS in Edn., Stephen F. Austin U., 1975. Music evangelist Randy Smith, Evangelist, Dallas, 1970-72; minister of music, youth First Bapt. Ch., Hemphill, Tex., 1972-73, Huntington (Tex.) Bapt. Ch., 1973-75, Harlandale Bapt. Ch., San Antonio, 1975-77, First Bapt. Ch., Alvin, Tex., 1977-85; minister of music North Side Bapt. Ch., Weatherford, Tex., 1985—. Recs. made 1979, 85. coach Alvin Soccer Assn., 1983-85; speaker career day Alvin Jr. High Sch., 1982-85, Fellowship of Christian Athletes, Weatherford, 1986. Mem. Gulf Coast Bapt. Assn. (dir. youth camp 1980, assoc. minister of youth 1980-81, asst. associational music dir. 1982-84), Parker Bapt. Assn. (music dir. 1986—), Singing Men of North Tex., Singing Men of SE Tex. Democrat. Avocations: golf, hunting, fishing. Home: 202 Camelot Dr Weatherford TX 76086 Office: North Side Bapt Ch 910 N Main Drawer A Weatherford TX 76086

WOOD, GERALD DAVID, religious organization administrator; b. Narrows, Va., Oct. 16, 1947; s. Curtis Edmond and Myrtle Isabella (Jernigan) W.; m. Sandra Fay Harris, Aug. 24, 1968; children: Angela Dawn, Anthony David, Jonathan David, Beth Lynette. Student, Kjesaters, Vingaker, Sweden, 1966-67, Washington and Lee U., 1967-68, U. Va., 1968-69, Emmanuel Coll., 1973-81. Ordained to ministry Internat. Pentecostal Holiness Ch., 1968. Pastor Charlottesville (Va.) Pentecostal Holiness Ch., 1968-72, St. Paul Pentecostal Holiness Ch., Max Meadows, Va., 1972-82; sec.-treas. Va. Conf. Sunday Sch. Bd., Dublin, 1974-80; treas. Va. Conf. Christian Edn. Bd., 1980-86; pastor New Covenant Pentecostal Holiness Ch., Princeton, W.Va., 1982-86; dir. Christian edn. Va. conf. Pentecostal Holiness Ch., Dublin, 1986—; mem. gen. Christian edn. bd., Internat. Pentecostal Holiness Ch., Oklahoma City, 1987—; dir. radio ministry, Wythe County Ministerial Assn., Wytheville, Va., 1978-80; pres. W.Va. Camp Meeting Assn., Princeton, 1982-84; bd. dirs., Mountaineer Food Bank, Gassaway, W.Va., 1986, Maranatha Inst., Dublin, 1986—, treas., 1989—. Pres. Dublin Elem. Sch. PTA, 1988-90, Pulaski County Advocates for Talented and Gifted, 1989—; sec. New River Dist. PTA, 1990—. Mem. Coun. for Exceptional Children, Internat. Platform Assn., Am. Inst. Profl. Bookkeepers, Pentecostal Fellowship N.Am. (v.p. Princeton chpt. 1982-83). Republican. Avocation: amateur radio. Office: Va Conf Office PO Box 1086 Dublin VA 24084 *My father taught me: "Always be honest with God, with others and with yourself. Love others the way God loves you. Serve God with everything you are." I have chosen to live in this way.*

WOOD, GREGG DOUGLAS, minister, educator; b. Stoneham, Mass., Feb. 1, 1941; s. Harry Lee Jr. and Edna Alice (Bennett) W.; m. Jane Bertha Strunsky, Oct. 15, 1977; children from previous marriage: Lisa, Paula. AB, Harvard U., 1962; postgrad., Harvard Div. Sch., 1962-64; MDiv, Episcopal Div. Sch., Cambridge, Mass., 1967; postgrad., Blanton-Peale Grad. Inst., 1977-79. Ordained o ministry Episcopal Ch. as deacon, 1967, as priest, 1968. Various positions N.Y., Mass., 1967-70; rector Ch. of Epiphany and St. Simon, Bklyn., 1970-77; chaplain Bklyn. Devel. Ctr., 1973-79; dir. pastoral care St. John's Episcopal Hosp., Smithtown, N.Y., 1979—; prof. pastoral counseling George Mercer Sch. Theology, Garden City, N.Y., 1983—. Contbr. articles to profl. jours. Robbins fellow Episcopal Div. Sch., 1978. Fellow Coll. Chaplains (state rep. 1987—); mem. Am. Assn. Pastoral Counselors. Office: St John's Episcopal Hosp Rte 25-A Smithtown NY 11787

WOOD, IRA WAYNE, minister, church administrator; b. Waxahachie, Tex., May 4, 1930; s. Ira Isaac and Mamie Estell (Pilant) W.; m. Clara Ann Cooper, July 7, 1961; children: Camye Ann, Timothy Wayne. BA, Baylor U., 1957; MRE, Southwestern Bapt. Theol. Sem., 1961; postgrad., East Tex. State U., 1969. Ordained to ministry So. Bapt. Conv. Min. Plymouth Pk. Bapt. Ch., Irving, Tex., 1956-67, Pioneer Dr. Bapt. Ch., Abilene, Tex., 1967-68, Northlake Bapt. Ch., Dallas, 1968-69, N.W. Bapt. Ch., Oklahoma City, 1969-72, Calvary Bapt. Ch., Garland, Tex., 1972-74; pastor Woodhaven Bapt. Ch., Garland, 1974-83; interim min. 1st Bapt. Ch., Irving, 1985-87, Cedar Heights Bapt. Ch., Cedar Hill, Tex., 1987-88, Trinity Bapt. Ch., Irving, 1989-90, Calvary Bapt. Ch., Joplin, Mo., 1990—; founder, dir. Religious Edn. Action Program, Garland, 1967—; pres. Religious Edn. Music Conf., Dallas Bapt. Assn.; pres. Oklahoma City chpt. Bapt. Religious Edn. Assn., 1970-71, mem. various coms. Contbr. articles to profl. jours. Builder chs. in Brazil with vols., in 1980s. Cpl. U.S. Army, 1948-49, USAR, 1956. Home: 2113 Michael Garland TX 75040

WOOD, JAMES E., JR., religion educator, author; b. Portsmouth, Va., July 29, 1922; s. James E. and Elsie Elizabeth (Bryant) W.; m. Alma Leacy McKenzie, Aug. 12, 1943; 1 son, James Edward III. BA, Carson-Newman Coll., 1943; MA, Columbia U., 1949; BD, So. Bapt. Theol. Sem., 1947, ThM, 1948; PhD, So. Baptist Theol. Sem., 1957; postgrad., U. Tenn., 1943-44; cert. in Chinese, Yale U., 1949-50; Japanese diploma, Naganuma Sch. Japanese Studies, Tokyo, 1950-51, Oxford U., Eng., 1983; LLD hon., Seinan Gakuin U., Japan, 1983. Ordained to ministry So. Bapt. Ch., 1942. Pastor So. Bapt. chs., Tenn. and Ky., 1942-48; Bapt. missionary to Japan, 1950-55; prof. religion and lit. Seinan Gakuin U., Japan, 1951-55; prof. history of religions Baylor U., Waco, Tex., 1955-73, dir. honors program, 1959-64; dir. J.M. Dawson Inst. Ch.-State Studies Baylor U., 1957-73, 80—, chmn. interdeptl. grad. degree program in ch.-state studies, 1962-73, 80—, Simon and Ethel Bunn prof. ch.-state studies, 1980—, chmn. faculty-student Far Eastern exchange program, 1970-72; exec. dir. Bapt. Joint Com. on Public Affairs, Washington, 1972-80; mem. central panel Bapt. World Alliance Commn. on Religious Liberty and Human Rights, 1965-75, Commn. on Freedom, Justice and Peace, 1976-80, Commn. Human Rights, 1981—; chmn. Bapt. Com. on Bicentennial, 1973-76; mem. So. Bapt. Inter-Agy. Council, 1972-80, vice chmn., 1975-76, sec., 1976-77; vis. prof. So. Bapt. Theol. Sem., Louisville, 1974, Okla. Bapt. U., Shawnee, 1977, N.Am. Bapt. Sem., Sioux Falls, S.D., 1974, 79, Naval Coll. of Chaplains, Providence, 1988—; vis. lectr. Ashland (Ohio) Theol. Sem., 1971, ecumenical consultation on edn. Nat. Coun. Chs., 1974 ; Vernon Richardson lectr. Univ. Bapt. Ch., Balt., 1975; lectr. First World Congress on Religious Liberty, Amsterdam, 1977, 2d congress, Rome, 1984; lectr. Stetson U., 1976, Wake Forest U., 1976, Notre Dame U., 1980; Carver-Barnes lectr. Southeastern Bapt. Theol. Sem., 1981; Asian Found. lectr. Seinan Gakuin U., Japan, 1983, Univ. Faculty of Law, Warsaw, Poland, Inst. Religion Chinese Acad. Social Scis., Beijing, ; lectr. Campbell U., 1985, Brigham Young U., 1986, U. Kans., 1987, Union Theol. Sem. Va., 1989, Faculty of Law U. Oviedo, Spain, 1989; vice chmn. Nat. Com. for Amish Religious Freedom, 1960-68; mem. Nat. Com. for Restoration Blue Lake Lands to Taos Indians, 1963-70; cons. asst. secretariat on religious liberty World Coun. Chs., 1963-65. Author: A History of American Literature: An Anthology, 1952, (co-author) Church and State in Scripture, History and Constitutional Law, 1958, The Problem of Nationalism, 1969, Nationhood and the Kingdom, 1977, Secular Humanism and the Public Schools, 1986; editor: Markham Press Fund, Baylor U. Press, 1970-72; founding editor: Jour. Ch. and State, 1959-73, 80—, mem. editorial council, 1973-80; mem. editorial bd. Religion and Pub. Edn., Religious Freedom Reporter; editor, contbr.: Church and State, 1960, Jewish-Christian Relations in Today's World, 1971, Baptists and the American Experience, 1977, Religion and Politics, 1983, Religion, the State, and Education, 1984, Religion and the State, 1985, Report from the Capital, 1975-80, Ecumenical Perspectives on Church and State: Protestant, Catholic and Jewish, 1988, Readings on Church and State, 1989, The First Freedom: Religion and the Bill of Rights, 1990, The Role of Religion in the Making of Public Policy, 1991; area editor, contbr. to Ency. So. Bapts., 1982; contbr. We Hold These Truths, 1964, The Teacher's Yoke, 1964, The Best of Church and State, 1948-75, Issues in Church and State, 1977, Taxation and the Free Exercise of Religion, 1978, First World Congress on Religious Liberty, 1978, The Church, The State and Human Rights, 1980, The Minister's Manual: 1982-83, Freedom of Religion in America, 1982, Government Intervention in Religious Affairs 1982, Dictionary of Theology, 1982, Religion, Education and the First Amendment, 1986, Taking Sides: Clashing Views on Controversial Political Issues, 1986, Church and State in American History, 1987, Global Outreach: Global Congress of the World's Religions, 1987, Dictionary of Christianity in America, 1988; contbr. over 200 articles to profl. jours. Sponsor Ams. for Public Schs., 1963-68; bd. dirs. Waco (Tex.) Planned Parenthood, 1966-72, pres., 1971-72; sponsor Christians Concerned for Israel, 1968—, Tex. Conf. Chs. Consultation on Religion and Public Edn., 1971, Nat. Christian Leadership Conf. for Israel, 1978—; pres. Waco area ACLU, bd. dirs. Tex. unit, 1968-72; pres. Nat. Council Religion and Public Edn., 1979-83, exec. com., 1975—, bd. dirs., 1972—; chmn. exec. com. Council Washington Reps. on UN, 1977-80, mem. council exec. com., 1973-80; exec. com. Nat. Coalition on Public Edn. and Religious Liberty, 1973—; mem. religious liberty com. Nat. Council Chs. U.S.A., 1972—, also mem. com. internat. concerns on human rights; Am. rep. Chs. Montreux Colloquium on Helsinki Final Act, 1977; v.p. Waco Conf. Christians and Jews, pres., 1990—; v.p. Internat. Acad. for Freedom of Religion and Belief, 1985-90, pres., 1990—; trustee Internat. Devel. Conf., 1974-80; nat. coun. Am.-Israel Friendship League, 1977—; founder, chmn. Waco Human Rights Week, 1981—; mem. ch. rels. com., U.S. Holocaust Meml. Coun., 1990—. Recipient Disting. Alumnus award Carson-Newman Coll., 1974, Religious Liberty award Alliance for Preservation of Religious Liberty, 1980, Henrietta Szold award Tex. region Hadassah, 1981, Human Rights award Waco Conf. Christians and Jews, 1986; hon. Tex. col., 1969. Mem. Am. Soc. Ch. History, Am. Acad. Religion, Am. Soc. Internat. Law, Am. Soc. Sci. Study of Religion, N. Am. Soc. Ecumenists, NCCJ (ad. com. on ch. state and taxation 1979-85), ACLU, Phi Eta Sigma, Pi Kappa Delta, Alpha Psi Omega. Home: 3306 Lake Heights Dr Waco TX 76708 Office: Baylor U Box 97308 Waco TX 76798-7308

WOOD, JAN SMITH, religion educator; b. L.A., June 13, 1954; d. Tom Earl and Leona Dolores (Tregenza) Smith; m. Philip Sullivan Wood, June 30, 1979; children: Charlotte Elizabeth, Ardith Emily. BA, Univ. Calif., Santa Barbara, 1976; MDiv with distinction, Ch. Divinity Sch. of the, Pacific, Berkeley, Calif., 1986. Dir. religious edn. Christ Ch., Winnetka, Ill., 1986-90; minister youth/edn. Diocese of El Camino Real, Monterey, Calif., 1990—; del. Provincial Youth Coun., western U.S.; convenor Diocesan Commn. on Edn., Chgo., 1988-90. Mem. Network Lay Profls. Office: Diocese of El Camino Real PO Box 1903 Monterey CA 93942

WOOD, JEFFREY CHARLES, religious organization administrator; b. N.Y.C., Feb. 7, 1940; s. Charles Arthur and Marion Josephine (Miller) W.; m. Margaret Ann Lloyd, Dec. 31, 1967; children: Rebecca Marie, Adam Matthew. AB, Dickinson Coll., Carlisle, Pa., 1961; MDiv, Princeton Theol. Seminary, 1964; fellow, Fund for Theol. Edn., Princeton, N.J., 1971-72; DMin, N,.Y. Theol. Seminary, 1981. Ordained minister, 1964. Asst. pastor 1st Presby. Ch., Greenlawn, N.Y., 1964-67; pastor Bay Ridge United Presby. Ch., Bklyn., 1967-73; exec. assoc. Presby. Ch. USA Program Agy., N.Y.C., 1973-83; sr. pastor Morningside Presby. Ch., Fullerton, Calif., 1983-88; exec. dir. Joint Strategy and Action Com., Inc., N.Y.C., 1988-90; pastor First Presbyn. Ch., Passaic, N.J., 1990—; pres. Presby. Staff Assn., N.Y.C., 1975-83; ecumenical resource com. World Coun. Chs., Geneva, Switzerland, 1988—; chmn. worship 89 Synod of So. Calif. and Hawaii and San Francisco Seminary, L.A., 1987-89; guest lectr. Princeton Seminary, 1979—, N.Y. Theol. Seminary, 1988; adj. faculty Drew U., Madison, N.J., 1983-85; organizer Nat. Coun. Chs. Conf. on Rich and Poor, Dominican Republic, 1982; dir. Spl. Ministries to Japanese, N.Y.C., 1980-83. Author: Evangelism Resource Catalog, 1984; editor: I Pledge Allegiance, 1975; producer: (film) Faith Sharing, 1982. Founding dir. Pacific Peace Prize, Fullerton, Calif., 1987; active Nat. Interreligious Task Force on Criminal Justice, N.Y.C., 1988. Mem. Palisades Presbytery. Democrat. Avocations: horseback riding, gourmet cooking, house restoration, writing. Home: 119 Rock Rd Glen Rock NJ 07452

WOOD, JOHN RALPH, minister; b. Chgo., Dec. 19, 1927; s. John Walter and Lydia Neonta (DuKate) W.; m. Anna Jean Mitchell, Oct. 1, 1949; 1 child, Ronald Mark. Student, Moody Bible Inst., 1947-49. Ordained to ministry Bapt. Ch., 1953. Pastor Lapaz (Ind.) Union Ch., 1952-54; pastor Calvary Bapt. Ch., Ecorse, Mich., 1955-62, Bellefontaine, Ohio, 1962-73; state rep., editor Mich. Assn. Regular Bapt. Chs., 1973-82; pastor First Bapt. Ch., Cass City, Mich., 1983—; trustee Skyview Ranch Youth Camp, Millersburg, Ohio, 1971-73; coun. mem. Ohio Assn. Regular Bapts., 1972-73; exec. bd. dirs. Grand Rapids (Mich.) Bapt. Coll., 1975—; bd. dirs. Continental Bapt. Missions, Grand Rapids, 1987—. Editor: Baptist Testimony, 1974-83; contbr. articles to religious jours. Home: 4644 Oak St Cass City MI 48726 Office: First Bapt Ch 6420 Houghton St Cass City MI 48726

WOOD, MILTON LEGRAND, retired bishop; b. Selma, Ala., Aug. 21, 1922; s. Milton LeGrand and Roberta Owen (Hawkins) W.; m. Ann Scott, May 3, 1949; children: Leigh Wood Pate, Ann Wood Benedict, Milton LeGrand IV, Roberta Wood Conroy. BA, U. of South, 1943, MDiv, 1945, DD (hon.), 1967. Ordained to ministry Episcopal Ch., 1946, as bishop, 1967. Rector St. Paul's Ch., Mobile, Ala., 1946-52, All Saints Ch., Atlanta, 1952-60; archdeacon, dir. Appleton Home, Macon, Ga., 1960-63; canon to ordinary, Atlanta, 1963-67; suffragan bishop Episcopal Diocese of Atlanta, 1967-74; v.p., dep. for adminstrn. for presiding bishop Nat. Episcopal Ch., N.Y.C., 1974-84; ret., 1984. Bd. dirs. Egleston Hosp., Atlanta. Mem. Ga. Interch. Assn. (pres.). Home: PO Box 420 Elberta AL 36530

WOOD, R. A., bishop. Bishop of Saskatoon The Anglican Ch. of Can., Sask. Office: Anglican Ch Can, Box 1965, Saskatoon, SK Canada S7K 3S5*

WOOD, RICHARD WALTER, minister; b. Dayton, Oh., May 12, 1961; s. Rufus Walter and Helen Marie (Johnson) W.; m. Jacqueline Ann Blossfeld, Aug. 29, 1987; child: Meagan Marie. BA in music edn., Evangel Coll., 1984. Ordained to ministry Ga. dist. Assemblies of God, 1986. Min. music Trinity Temple Assembly of God, Columbus, Ga., 1987-89, Escatawpa Assembly of God, Escatawpa, Miss., 1989—. Composer numerous religious music. Assembly of God. Home: 7520 Frank Griffin Rd Escatawpa MS 39552 Office: Escatawpa Assembly of God 7405 Hwy 613 Escatawpa MS 39552

WOOD, STEPHEN WRAY, minister, religion educator, state legislator; b. Winston Salem, N.C., Oct. 6, 1948; s. D.W. and Annie Lee (Harris) W.; m. Starr Smith, June 18, 1978; children: Allyson, Joshua. BTh., John Wesley Coll., 1970; BA, Asbury Coll., 1973; MA, U. N.C., 1979; DMin, Luther Rice Sem., Fla., 1980; MDiv, Houston Grad. Sch. Theology, 1990. Ordained to ministry Soc. of Friends, 1980. Asst. dean, asst. prof. Wesley Coll., High Point, N.C., 1975-81; assoc. pastor Glenwood Friends Ch., Greensboro, N.C., 1979-81; pastor Deep River Friends Ch., High Point, 1981-84, Battle Forest Friends, Greensboro, 1986—; pres. Triad Christian Counseling, Greensboro, 1979. Contbr. articles to religious jours., Dictionary of N.C. Biography; composer, singer religious music. Trustee John Wesley Coll., High Point, 1981—; bd. dirs. Friends Ctr.-Guilford Coll., Greensboro, 1982-89; vice chmn. Guilford County Rep. Party, N.C., 1981-85; rep. N.C. State Ho. of Reps., 1985-86, 89-90, 90-91; chaplain High Point Jaycees. Wth U.S. Army, 1970-71; capt. N.C. State Militia. Mem. Broadcast Music Inc. (affiliate songwriter 1978—). Avocations: golf, book collecting, fishing, tennis. Office: PO Box 5172 High Point NC 27262 *I often reflect upon the maternal advice proffered me as a child, "Steve, if at first you don't succeed, try, try again." We may be down but not out. There is no such thing as the good old days because the future is just as bright as the promises of God. We conquer by continuing.*

WOOD, STEVEN DOYLE, minister; b. Atlanta, Feb. 2, 1958; s. James Doyle and Margaret (Weatherford) W.; m. LeAnne Knowles Wood, June 14, 1986; 1 child, Lauren Elizabeth. BBA, U. Ga., 1980; MDiv, Asbury Theol. Sem., 1986. Ordained to ministry Meth. Ch. Chaplain VA Hosp., Lexington, Ky., 1985-86; assoc. pastor First United Meth. Ch., Georgetown, Ky., 1986; pastor Red Oak United Meth. Ch., College Park, Ga., 1986-89; sr. pastor New Covenant United Meth. Ch., Douglasville, Ga., 1989—; dist. youth coord. United Meth. Ch., Atlanta, 1986-88, chmn. dist. enrichment sch., 1989; sec., trustee com. on ch. devel. N. Ga. Conf. United Meth. Ch., Atlanta, 1990—. Author: Our Methodist Heritage, 1990. Dist. rep. United Way, Atlanta, 1976; mem. Young Reps., Atlanta, 1990—. Office: New Covenant United Meth Ch 7156 Highway 5 Douglasville GA 30135

WOOD, STEVEN DUANE, minister; b. Flint, Mich., June 21, 1962; s. James Quinton and Audrey Lou (Harty) W.; m. Melanie Francene Whitten, Dec. 22, 1984; 1 child, Mallory Kristene. Student, Oakland City (Ind.) Coll., 1981-84. Youth dir. Fentown Lawn Gen. Bapt. Ch., Flint, Mich., 1981; children's ch. dir. Main Str. Bapt. Ch., Boonville, Ind., 1981-82; youth min. First Gen. Bapt. Ch., Mt. Carmel, Ill., 1982-84; min. youth and Christian edn. First Gen. Bapt. Ch., Flint, 1984-91; min. Christian edn. Twelfth Ave. Gen. Bapt. Ch., Evansville, Ind., 1991—; youth camp dir. Mich. Assn. Gen. Bapts., 1985-90, youth coun. dir., 1987-91; teen choir dir. Flint Area Gen. Bapts., 1987-89; bd. Christian edn. Gen. Bapts., Poplar Bluff, Mo., 1989—. Author: (manual) Teen Discipleship Training, 1991, (musical/comedy script) A Bridge For The Crossing, 1989. Speaker Carman-Ainsworth Community Schs., Flint, 1990; coach Greater Flint Baseball Commn., 1984-87. Office: Twelfth Ave Baptist Ch PO Box 6473 Evansville IN 47719

WOOD, WILLIAM PAPE, minister; b. Atlanta, July 14, 1943; s. Francis Lloyd Ferguson and Mary (Pape) W.; m. Lucile McKown White, July 5, 1969; children: Grace, William, Lucy. AB in History, Davidson Coll., 1965; BD, ThM, Union Theol. Sem., 1968, 69, PhD in Old Testament, 1974; DD, Tusculum, 1982. Ordained min. Presbyn. Ch., 1970. Assoc. min. First Presbyn. Ch., San Antonio, 1972-76; sr. min. First Presbyn. Ch., Kingsport, Tenn., 1976-83, Charlotte, N.C., 1983—; trustee Davidson (N.C.) Coll., 1985—, Union Theol. Sem., Richmond, Va., 1989—. Democrat. Home:

1820 Sterling Rd Charlotte NC 28209 Office: First Presbyn Ch 200 W Trade St Charlotte NC 28202

WOODARD, EARL NATHAN, minister; b. Balt., Feb. 23, 1961; s. Lorenza and Virginia (Ross) W. BA, Howard U., 1983; MDiv, Princeton Sem., 1986; D of Ministry, Drew U., 1990. Ordained to ministry Bapt. Ch., 1978. Assoc. minister David Meml. Bapt. Ch., Balt., 1976-78, interim pastor, 1978-79, pastor, 1979—; prof. Va. Sem. & Coll., Lynchburg, Va., 1989; exec. bd. Balt. Bapt. Assn., 1989—. Recipient Citizen Citation, Mayor of Balt., 1990, Congl. Achievement award Rep. Kwesi M. Fume, 1990, Pres. Cert. of Merit, City Coun. Pres., 1990, City Coun. Resolution, City Coun. Balt., 1990. Democrat. Office: David Meml Bapt Ch 1401 N Milton Ave Baltimore MD 21213

WOODARD, EDWARD JOSEPH, JR., banker, lay church worker; b. Portsmouth, Va., Mar. 9, 1943; s. Edward Joseph Sr. and Catherine (Gay) W.; m. Sharon Ann Williamson, Oct. 14, 1967; 1 child, Troy Brandon. Student, Frederick Coll., Portsmouth, 1961-64, Old Dominion U., 1967-72, Am. Inst. Banking, 1967-72. Chmn., pres., chief exec. officer Bank of Commonwealth, Norfolk, Va., 1973—, chmn. adv. bd., 1983—; pres., chief exec. officer, chmn. bd. Commonwealth Bankshares, Inc., 1988—, also bd. dirs.; credit mgr. Am. Fin. Systems, Norfolk, 1964-67; asst. v.p., br. mgr. 1st Va. Bank of Tidewater, Norfolk, 1967-72; mem. exec. com. Urban Bus. Devel. Corp., 1982, pres., chmn. loan rev. com., 1983—, also bd. dirs.; pres., bd. dirs. Boush Bank Bldg. Corp., 1984—; ltd. ptnr. Boush Bank Bldg. Assocs., 1984—. Mem. calvary class Talbot Park Bapt. Ch., 1972—, mem. fin. com., chmn. pers. com. 1981—, mem. budget planning com., budget promotion com., 1983—, ch. coun., 1984—, tchr. adult class, 1985—, bd. dirs. median adult div., 1990—, chmn. endowment com., 1990—, vice chmn. fin. com., 1991—; mem. ann. scouting show com. Tidewater coun. Boy Scouts Am., 1984—; mem. adv. coun. Jr. Achievement, 1986—; bd. dirs., sec. Photography Alliance of Chrysler Mus., 1987—; capt. United Way of South Hampton Rds., 1989-90, chmn. local unit, 1991—; bd. dirs., mem. downtown revitalization com. Greater Norfolk Corp., 1991—. With Va. N.G., 1964-71. Mem. Am. Inst. Banking (adv. bd. Tidewater chpt. 1973—), Am. Bankers Assn., Va. Bankers Assn. (advisor 1983—, mem. human resources com. 1985—, task force 1990—, capt. congl. team 1989—), NCCJ (dinner com. 1979—), Am. Heart Assn. (Meritorious Svc. award Va. chpt. 1985, Disting. Svc. and Leadership award 1986), Navy League U.S., Norfolk Yacht and Country Club, Phi Beta Kappa. Office: Bank of Commonwealth 403 Boush St Norfolk VA 23510

WOODARD, MARSHA BROWN, minister, consultant; b. St. Louis, Mar. 22, 1949; d. Portia and Laura (Daniels) Brown; m. Melvin Woodard, Oct. 5, 1971 (dec. Nov. 1973). BA, Ottawa U., 1971; MDiv, Eden Theol. Sem., 1980. Ordained to ministry Am. Bapt. Assn., 1980. Min. Christian edn. Antioch Bapt. Ch., St. Louis, 1977-83; program assoc. Bd. Ednl. Ministries, Am. Bapt. Chs., Valley Forge, Pa., 1983-87; assoc. pastor Sts. Meml. Bapt. Ch., Brywn Mawr, Pa., 1987—; asst. to exec. min. Am. Bapt. Chs. South, Laurel, Md., 1987-90; program assoc. Phila. Bapt. Assn., 1989—; founder, pres. Diversity Is-Uniquely Designed Cons. Svcs., Bryn Mawr, 1988—; mem. conf. planning team Nat. Conf. Chs., Racial-Ethnic Women in Ministry Conf., N.Y.C., 1988-89, planning and design team Am. Bapt. Women in Ministry, N.Y.C., 1989-90; clergy rep. Ea. Coll. Multi-cultural Adv. Bd., St. Davids, Pa., 1990—. Author: Poverty in Our Midst, 1988; editor: Making Sense of Your Faith, 1987; contbr. articles to profl. jours. Bd. dirs. Montgomery County Opportunities Indsl. Ctr., Norristown, Pa., 1986-89; sec.-treas. Bldg. Better Families Found., Phila., 1988—. Recipient Community Svc. award Elks, 1982, appreciation Am. Bapt. Chs. of South, 1988. Mem. NAACP (mem. exec. bd. Main Line br. 1989—), Am. Bapt. Mins. Coun., Main Line Interdenomination Clergy Alliance (sec. 1990—), Main Line Black Bus. Assn. (v.p., then pres. Bryn Mawr chpt. 1988—). Democrat. Office: Sts Meml Bapt Ch 47 Warner Ave Bryn Mawr PA 19010

WOODARD, ROBERT E., bishop. Bishop, Ch. of God in Christ, S.E. Tex., Houston. Office: Ch of God in Christ 2614 Wichita Houston TX 77004

WOODBURY, PAUL D., JR., retired minister; b. Glenridge, N.J., July 25, 1924; s. Paul Dodge Sr. and Lillian May (Law) W.; m. Minnie L. Highsmith (dec. 1977); m. Florence P. Beauregard (div. 1985); m. Gail Doris Maglon, May 16, 1986. Ordained to ministry United Meth. Ch.; cert. mental health chaplain. Ret. United Meth. Ch., 1990. Contbg. author: Roots and Branches, 1989. With USN, 1943-46, PTO. Mem. Coll. Chaplains, Mental Health Chaplain's Assn., Assn. Pastoral Care, Assn. Clin. Pastoral Edn., N.E. Meth. Hist. Soc. (pres.).

WOODCOCK, RUTH MILLER, religious organization executive; b. Harrisburg, Pa., Sept. 1, 1927; d. Evan Jones and Ruth (Wills) Miller; 1 dau., Deborah. B.A., Wells Coll., 1949; M.A., Fletcher Sch. Law and Diplomacy, 1950. Assoc. exec. dir. Community Action Agy., Harisburg, Pa., 1964-69, YWCA of City N.Y., 1969-75, Ch. Women United in U.S.A., N.Y.C., 1975-80, McBurney YWCA, N.Y.C., 1980-81; exec. dir. YWCA Retirement Fund, Inc., N.Y.C., 1981-86; assoc. gen. sec. for adminstrn. and fin. Nat. Council Chs. of Christ, 1986—. Vol. Tri-County Welfare Council, Harrisburg, 1960s, Susquehanna council Girl Scouts U.S.A., 1960s, YMCA and YWCA Day Care Corp., N.Y.C., 1970s; nat. bd. dirs. Am. Friends Service Com., Phila., 1980s, Women in Community Service, Washington, 1980s. Rotary Found. fellow, Geneva, 1950-51. Quaker. Office: Nat Council Chs of Christ 475 Riverside Dr New York NY 10015

WOODEN, WELDON FREDERICK, clergyman; b. Takoma Park, Md., Feb. 4, 1953; s. Donald Gminder and Vivian Lavaun (Beam) W.; m. Wendy Webster Ricker, Oct. 13, 1976; 1 child, Aaron Ricker. AB, Washington U., St. Louis, 1974; AM, U. Chgo., 1977; DMin, Meadville Theol. Sch., Chgo., 1979. Ordained minister, 1980. Minister 1st Congl. Parish, Unitarian, Petersham, Mass., 1980-85, 1st Parish Ch. Groton (Mass.), Unitarian, 1985-90, First Unitarian Ch., Austin, 1990—; columnist Fitchburg (Mass.) Sentinel, 1985—, Leominster (Mass.) Enterprise, 1985—; hymnbook editor Unitarian Universalist Assn., Boston, 1986—. Mem. Unitarian Universalist Minister's Assn., ACLU, Amnesty Internat. Democrat. Avocations: exercise, gardening, language study. Office: 1st Parish Ch Groton PO Box 457 Groton MA 01450

WOODHALL, WILLIAM FULTON, minister, religious organization administrator; b. Peoria, Ill., Jan. 27, 1944; s. William Rozell and Elsie Lucille (Fulton) W.; m. Gayle Marie Phillips, May 11, 1964; children: Heather Suzanne Dominguez, Matthew Charles, Blake Jarrod. BA, Sacramento Bapt. Coll., 1972; ThB, Sacramento Bapt. Theol. Sem., 1973, MA, 1973, MDiv, 1977, ThM, 1979; BA, Bapt. Christian Coll., 1984; PhD, Bapt. Christian U., 1981, ThD, 1983; DD (hon.), Calif. Christian Coll., 1973; LLD (hon.), John Wesley Coll., 1980. Lic. minister, 1968; ordained to ministry, 1970. Pastor E. Belmont Community Bible Ch., Fresno, Calif., 1970-71, Sierra Hills Bapt. Ch., Auberry, Calif., 1972-74; sr. pastor Fountain Ave. Bapt. Ch., Hollywood, Calif., 1975-76, Mountain View Presbyn., Grand Terrace, Calif., 1976-85; pvt. practice as ch. cons. Eugene, Oreg., 1986; pres. Bible Analysis Cons., Inc., Grand Terrace, 1987—; vis. lectr. Calif. Christian Coll., Fresno, 1973-74; prof. Bible Thomas Road Bible Inst., Fresno, 1973-74; chaplain, reserve officer Los Angeles Police Dept. Hollywood div., 1975-76; prof. hermeneutics San Bernardino (Calif.) Bible Coll., 1979. Mem. Pacific Presbytery-Presbyn. Ch. Am. (stated clk. 1977-82), Fellowship Christian Peace Officers (assoc.), Christian Edn. Fellowship (hon.), Christian Legal Soc. Ctr. Law and Religious Studies (assoc.). Republican. Avocations: collecting oak antiques, Steiffs, dolls. Home: 5745 Via Dos Caminos Riverside CA 92504 Office: Bible Analysis Cons Inc 22797 Barton Rd Ste 171 Grand Terrace CA 92324-5207

WOODING, DANIEL TANSWELL, religious organization administrator, journalist, broadcaster; b. Vom, Plateau, Nigeria, Dec. 19, 1940; came to U.S., 1982; s. Alfred and Anne (Blake) W.; m. Norma Alice Knight, June 16, 1959; children: Andrew Daniel, Peter David. Chief reporter The Christian Newspaper, London, 1969-70, Middlesex County Times, London, 1979-75; sr. reporter Sunday People, London, 1975-78, Sunday Mirror, London, 1978; media cons. London, 1978-82; chief reporter, founder Open Doors News Svc. (now News Network Internat.), Santa Ana, Calif., 1982-88; founder, internat. dir., U.S. pres. Aid to Spl. Saints in Strategic Times, Bellflower, Calif., 1988—; commentator UPI Radio Network, Washington, 1988—; syndicated columnist newspapers and mags., U.S., Can., U.K., Australia, New Zealand, The Philippines, 1988—. Author 23 books, latest being: Twenty-Six Lead Soldiers, 1988, Singing in the Dark, 1990, Lost for Words, 1990. Recipient reporting awards Evang. Press Assn., 1983, Bronze Halo award So. Calif. Motion Picture Coun., 1984, Silver Angel award Religion in Media, 1988. Mem. Nat. Union Journalists, Assoc. Ch. Press, Arts Ctr. Group (London). Office: ASSIST PO Box 2166 Garden Grove CA 92642

WOOD PARRISH, VICTORIA ANN, minister; b. Norwood, Mass., June 21, 1950; d. Ernest O. and Martha Lou (Foreman) Wood; m. W. Keith Parrish, Aug. 15, 1982; children: Heather, Kathleen, W. James. B in Music Edn., DePauw U., 1972; MDiv, Princeton Theol. Sem., 1976. Asst. pastor Arlington Ave. Presbyn. Ch., East Orange, N.J., 1973-74; chaplain Memphis City Hosp., 1974-75; asst. pastor Pearson Meml. United Meth. Ch., Trenton, N.J., 1975-76; assoc. pastor First United Meth. Ch., Franklin, Pa., 1977-79, Erie, Pa., 1979-85; pastor 10th St. United Meth. Ch., Erie, 1985—; clergy team mem. Erie Hospice, 1983-90. Mem. Coll. of Chaplains (profl. affiliate), Am. Assn. Pastoral Counselors, Assn. for Clin. Pastoral Edn., AAUW. Republican. United Methodist. Avocations: reading, music, skiing, quilting. Home: 5525 Cherry St Erie PA 16503 Office: 10th St United Meth Ch 538 E 10th St Erie PA 16503

WOODRING, DEWAYNE STANLEY, religion association executive; b. Gary, Ind., Nov. 10, 1931; s. J. Stanley and Vera Luella (Brown) W.; m. Donna Jean Wishart, June 15, 1957; children: Judith Lynn (Mrs. Richard Bigelow), Beth Ellen (Mrs. Michael Maheffey). B.S. in Speech with distinction, Northwestern U., 1954, postgrad. studies in radio and TV broadcasting, 1954-57; M.Div., Garrett Theol. Sem., 1957; L.H.D., Mt. Union Coll., Alliance, Ohio, 1967; D.D., Salem (W.Va.) Coll., 1970. Asso. youth dir. Gary YMCA, 1950-55; ordained to ministry United Methodist Ch., 1955; minister of edn. Griffith (Ind.) Meth. Ch., 1955-57; minister adminstrn. and program 1st Meth. Ch., Eugene, Oreg., 1957-59; dir. pub. relations Dakotas area Meth. Ch., 1959-60, dir. pub. relations Ohio area, 1960-64; adminstrv. exec. to bishop Ohio East area United Meth. Ch., Canton, 1964-77; asst. gen. sec. Gen. Council on Fin. and Adminstrn., United Meth. Ch., Evanston, Ill., 1977-79; assoc. gen. sec. Gen. Council on Fin. and Adminstrn., 1979-84; exec. dir., chief exec. officer Religious Conf. Mgmt. Assn., 1982—; mem. staff, dept. radio services 2d assembly World Council Chs., Evanston, 1954;vice chmn. commn. on entertainment and program North Central Jurisdictional Conf., 1968-72, chmn., 1972-76; mem. commn. on gen. conf. United Meth. Ch., 1972—, bus. mgr., exec. dir., 1976—, mem. div. interpretation, 1969-72; chmn. communications commn. Ohio Coun. Chs., 1961-65; mem. exec. com. Nat. Assn. United Meth. Founds., 1968-72; del. World Meth. Conf., London, Eng., 1966, Dublin, Ireland, 1976, Honolulu, 1981, Nairobi, 1986, Singapore, 1991, exec. com. World Meth. Council, 1986—; bd. dirs. Ohio East Area United Meth. Found., 1967-78, v.p., 1967-76; chmn. bd. mgrs. United Meth. Bldg., Evanston, 1977-84; lectr., cons. on fgn. travel. Creator: nationally distbd. radio series The Word and Music; producer, dir.: TV series Parables in Miniature, 1957-59. Adviser East Ohio Conf. Communications Commn., 1968-76; pres. Guild Assocs., 1971—; trustee, 1st v.p. Copeland Oaks Retirement Ctr., Sebring, Ohio, 1969-76; bd. dirs. First Internat. Summit on Edn., 1989. Recipient Cert. Meeting Profl. award, 1985, Cert. Expt. Mgr. award, 1988; named to Ky. Cols., 1989. Mem. Am. Soc. Assn. Execs., Ind. Soc. Assn. Execs. (Meeting Planner of Yr. award 1990), Meeting Planners Internat., Conv. Liaison Coun. (bd. dirs., officer), Def. Orientation Conf. Assn. (dir.), Cert. Meeting Profls. (bd. dirs.), Nat. Assn. Exposition Mgrs., Found. for Internat. Meetings (bd. dirs.). Home: 7224 Chablis Ct Indianapolis IN 46278 Office: One Hoosier Dome Ste 120 Indianapolis IN 46225

WOODROFFE, GERALDINE M., lay worker, accountant; b. Phila., Oct. 17, 1939; d. John Wesley and Maris Jean (Mertz) W. BBA, U. Pa., 1976; BS in Health Records Adminstrn., Temple U., 1987. Acct. bd. pensions Evang. and Ref. Ch., Phila., 1960-65, acct. div. publs., 1965-68; med. records coding supr. St. Christopher's Hosp. for Children, Phila., 1988—; deacon Old 1st Ref. Ch., Phila., 1982-89, treas., 1985—, elder, 1990—. Mem. Am. Soc. Women Accts., Am. Med. Records Assn. Office: Old First Reformed Ch 4th and Race Philadelphia PA 19106

WOODRUFF, BOYKIN MAXWELL, JR., minister, advertising sales counselor; b. Mobile, Ala., Nov. 26, 1946; s. Boykin Maxwell Sr. and Evelyn (Findley) W.; m. Sophie Garrett I, Nov. 5, 1971; children: Sophie Garrett II, Boykin Maxwell III. BA, Berry Coll., 1968; MA, U. Ga., 1975; postgrad., New Orleans Bapt. Theol. Sem., 1982-86. Cert. secondary tchr., Ala. Min. Oakmont Christian Ch., Disciples of Christ, Mobile, 1975-89; interim min. 1st Christian Ch., So. Bapt. Conv., Mobile, 1991; sales counselor Woodruff Spltys., Inc., Mobile, 1976—; mem. regional com. on resolutions Christian Ch. in Ala. and N.W. Fla., Birmingham, 1977-80, regional Christian bd. and nominating com., 1984-88, regional capitol campaign com., 1985-88; dir. 3d grade Sunday sch., Spring Hill Bapt. Ch., Mobile, 1989-91, tchr. ungraded adult, 1991, mem. sanctuary choir, 1989-90, chamber choir, 1991—. Editor Ramification mag., Berry Coll., 1966-68, bus. mgr. South Winds mag., 1966-67. mem. John Will PTA, Mobile, 1982-91, Phillips Prep. PTA, 1989-91. Recipient awards Nat. Evang. Assn., 1978-87; Faculty scholar U. Mil. Sch., Mobile, 1969-73. Mem. Sigma Tau Delta, Kappa Alpha. Home: 904 Memory Ln Mobile AL 36608 Office: 2450 Old Shell Rd Mobile AL 36608

WOODRUFF, C(HARLES) ROY, professional association executive; b. Anniston, Ala., Sept. 27, 1938; m. Kay Carolyn Jernigan, June 26, 1962; children: Charles R. Jr., Earl David. BA, U. Ala., 1960; BD, So. Bapt. Theol. Sem., 1963, PhD in Psychology of Religion and Pastoral Care, 1966. Lic. profl. counselor, Va. Asst. pastor Ft. Mitchell Bapt. Ch., South Ft. Mitchell, Ky., 1960-63; Protestant chaplain Silvercrest Hosp., New Albany, Ind., 1963-66; dir. dept. pastoral care and edn. Bryce State Hosp., Tuscaloosa, Ala., 1966-71; assoc. prof., chaplain supr. dept. patient counseling Med. Coll. Va., Richmond, 1971-76; assoc. prof., chmn. dept. psychology of religion and pastoral care Midwestern Bapt. Theol. Sem., Kansas City, Mo., 1976-78; exec. dir. Peninsula Pastoral Counseling Ctr., Newport News, Va., 1978-88, Am. Assn. Pastoral Counselors, Washington, 1988—; lecturing fellow Interpreter's House, Lake Junaluska, N.C., 1968-78; pastoral counselor, clin. supr. Psychol. Clinic, U. Ala., Tuscaloosa, 1969-71; adj. staff mem. The Counseling Inst., Kansas City, 1976-78. Author: Alcoholism and Christian Experience, 1968; (with others) Alcohol, In and Out of the Church, 1968, Work Adjustment: The Goal of Rehabilitation, 1973, Pastoral Theology and Ministry, Key Resources, 1983, The Dictionary of Pastoral Care and Counseling, 1990; also articles. Apptd. by Gov. of Va. to Bd. Profl. Counselors, Commonwealth of Va., 1987—; mem. Nat. Mental Health Leadership Forum, 1990—. United Meth. Ch. Gen. Bd. Christian Social Concerns grantee, 1965; So. Bapt. Theol. Sem. teaching fellow, 1965-66. Fellow Coll. Chaplains of Am. Protestant Hosp. Assn.; mem. Assn. for Clin. Pastoral Edn. (cert. supr.), Assn. Couples for Marriage Enrichment (cert.). Home: 10827 Burr Oak Way Burke VA 22015 Office: Am Assn Pastoral Counselors 9504A Lee Hwy Fairfax VA 22031

WOODRUFF, RICHARD D., broadcasting executive; b. Mt. Clemens, Mich., Aug. 17, 1954; s. Kenneth Oliver and Dorothy (Lenzini); m. Margaret Guerra, Nov. 7, 1981; children: Mallorie, Megan. BS, So. Ill. U., 1976. Ops. mgr. Interstate Broadcasting, Sta. KRDS, Phoenix, 1984—. Republican. Office: Sta KRDS Radio 8611 N Black Canyon Hwy Ste 206 Phoenix AZ 85021

WOODRUFF, WILLIAM JENNINGS, theology educator; b. Vassar, Kans., Sept. 30, 1925; s. Kenneth Arthur and Carrie (Brecheisen) W.; m. Wanda Lea Shuck, Aug. 18, 1962; children: Teresa Kaye, Bruce Alan, Neal Wayne. BA, Ottawa U., 1954; MDiv, Fuller Theol. Sem., Pasadena, Calif., 1958; MRE, Asbury Theol. Sem., Wilmore, Ky., 1963, ThM, 1964. Youth dir. Hyde Park EUB Ch., Wichita, 1958-59; tchr. Lenora (Kans.) Rural High Sch., 1959-60; pastor Attica (Kans.) EUB Ch., 1960-62, Jersey City EUB Ch., 1964-65, Phila. EUB Ch., 1965-68; with Olivet Nazarene U., Kankakee, Ill., 1968—, prof. Contbr. to Religious and Theol. Abstracts, 3 jours., 1968-90; contbr. articles to profl. jours. Cpl. U.S. Army, 1951-53, Republic of Korea. Mem. Evang. Theol. Soc., Evang. Tchrs. Tng. Assn., Wesleyan Theol. Soc., Near East Archaeol. Soc., Phi Delta Lambda, Theta Pi, Kappa Delta Pi. Avocations: photography, travel, camping. Home: 482 E Grand Dr Bourbonnais IL 60914 Office: Olivet Nazarene Univ Kankakee IL 60901

WOODRUFF, WILLIAM MATTHEW, religion education administrator; b. Providence, Oct. 11, 1951; s. William Love and Rita (McCoombs) W. BA, R.I. Coll., 1974; MA, Providence Coll., 1991. Assoc. Presentation of Blessed Virgin Mary Ch., North Providence, R.I., 1973-78; dir. St. Peter's Ch., Warwick, R.I., 1978-79, Presentation of Blessed Virgin Mary Ch., North Providence, 1986—; lector, eucharistic minister Presentation of Blessed Virgin Mary Ch., North Providence, 1981—. Mem. Profl. Religious Educators Providence, Nat. CAth. Edn. Assn. Home: 141 Urban Ave North Providence RI 02904-4930 Office: Presentation of Blessed Virgin Mary Ch 1081 Mineral Spring Ave North Providence RI 02904-4199

WOODS, DANIEL CHRISTIAN, lay worker; b. Green Bay, Wis., Sept. 28, 1956; s. George Daniel and Ardis Amelia (Wellnitz) W.; m. Gina Lynn Wooten, Oct. 28, 1984; 1 child, Kayla Lynn. BS in Mech. Engring., U. South Fla., 1980, MS in Mech. Engring., 1983. Sabbath sch. supt. 7th Day Adventist Ch., Melbourne, Fla., 1983-86, deacon, 1983-86; deacon 7th Day Adventist Ch., Florence, S.C., 1987-89, dir. personal ministries, 1988—, elder, 1990—; mech. engr. med. systems div. Gen. Electric, Florence, 1986—. Patentee power operated contact apparatus for superconductive circuit. Chmn. sch. bd. Florence Adventist Ch. Sch., 1988—. Republican. Home: 838 Wood Duck Ln Florence SC 29505 Office: GE Med Systems 3001 W Radio Dr Florence SC 29501 *As we consider how the Lord led the Israelites to the Promised Land, we are reminded that we should fear nothing for the future except that we should forgot how the Lord has led us in the past.*

WOODS, DAVID DONALD, minister; b. Ardmore, Okla., Jan. 8, 1950; s. Joe Donald and Edna (Baurell) W.;m. Retta Jean Revel, Jan. 3, 1975; children: David Nathanael, Joseph Dylan. BSL, Ozark Christian, Joplin, Mo., 1977. Ordained to ministry Christian Ch., 1977. Minister 1st Christian, Hurst, ill., 1977-85, Pershing Ave. Christian Ch., Liberal, Kans., 1985—; pres. Minister Alliance, Liberal, 1990-91, Hurst, 1977-84, sec., Liberal, 1987-90; chaplin Good Samaritan Home. Sec., bd. dirs. Liberal B.J. Baseball, Liberal, 1988-90; chmn. Internat. Pancake Day, Liberal, 1990-91. Mem. Lions Club (sec. Liberal chpt. 1987, Lion of Yr. 1989-90). Home: 404 N Tulane Liberal KS 67901 Office: Pershing Ave Christian Ch 919 N Pershing Ave Liberal KS 67901

WOODS, DEBBY LYNNE, religious organization administrator; b. Anniston, Ala., Nov. 23, 1952; d. Herbert and Lucille W. BS in Physical Edn., Jacksonville State U., 1975; MS in Adult Edn., U. So. Miss., 1977; postgrad., U. Ala., 1977. Supr. adult edn. Birmingham, Ala., 1979-85; pres., founder Racerunners, Inc., Birmingham, 1985—. Author: Racerunners, It's Just Like a Weenie Roast, 1985, Deeper Into the Heart of God, 1988, Journey Into the Heart of God, 1989.

WOODS, JERRY DWAIN, minister; b. Dyer, Tenn., Nov. 11; s. J.H. and Geneva Louise (Garrett) W.; m. Glenda Diane White, Dec. 19, 1969; 1 child, Jeremy Scott. BS in BA, U. Tenn., 1973; student, Southwestern Bapt. Sem., Ft. Worth, Tex., 1975-79. Pastor Harmony Bapt. Ch., Newbern, Tenn., 1972-74; Bible instr. Elliston Bapt. Acad., Memphis, 1974-75; pastor Antioch Bapt. Ch., Bells, Tex., 1977-79, First Bapt. Ch., Trenton, Tex., 1979-82, Second Bapt. Ch., Vernon, Tex., 1982-84, Southside Bapt. Ch., Wichita Falls, Tex., 1984—. Vice pres. Lake Lavon Encampment exec. bd., 1981; treas. Chaparral Encampment, Wichita Falls, 1985; pres. Wichita-Archer-Clay Ministers Conf., 1987-88. Mem. Wichita-Archer-Clay Assn. Repubican. Baptist. Avocations: travel, fish, genealogy. Office: Southside Baptist Ch 2210 Holliday Wichita Falls TX 76301

WOODS, JOHN THOMAS, JR., broadcast station manager; b. Durham, N.C., Feb. 1, 1947; s. John Thomas Sr. and Eleanor Maye (Whitt); m. Henri Jean Gibson, Oct 28, 1970, (div. May 1980); m. Jessie Lynn Rich, June 8, 1980; children: John Thomas III, Joseph Michael. Grad. high sch., Durham, 1967. Lic. broadcaster. With Sta. WSSB, Durham, N.C., 1966; air personality Sta. WTMA, Charleston, S.C., 1967, Sta. WKIX, Raleigh, N.C., 1968, Sta. WWOK, Miami, Fla., 1969, Sta. KWIZ, L.A., 1970; dir. prodn. Sta. KLOK, San Jose, Calif., 1971-79; announcer, producer Sta. KNTV-TV, San Jose, 1971-75, Sta. KICU-TV, San Jose, 1976-82; pres. J.Thomas Woods Advt., San Jose, Lake Tahoe, 1981-85; adminstrv. asst. Sta. KVIP, Redding, Calif., 1985-88, mgr., 1989—; cons. Community Access TV, Redding, 1988—; sr. cons. 1st. dist. Calif. State Assembly, 1991. Author curriculum on TV producing, 1988. Govt. chair Shasta County Grand Jury, Calif., 1988—; mem., del. Atty. Gen.'s Commn. on Drugs, Shasta County, 1986; mem. mayor's adv. bd. City of San Jose, 1976; mem. Pres.' Congl. Task Force, 1990, 91; bd. mem. Shasta Bible Coll., Redding, 1989. With U.S. Army, 1967-68. Mem. Nat. Assn. Broadcasters, Nat. Religious Broadcasters. Republican. Avocations: skiing, golf, landscaping. Home: 1288 Dusty Ln Redding CA 96002 Office: Pacific Cascade Communicaitons 1139 Hartnell Ave Redding CA 96049-2727

WOODS, MARGIE MCDANIEL, pastor; b. Stoddard County, Mo., Dec. 29, 1941; d. Chester Forrest McDaniel and Iva Day (James) Phelps; m. Robert Gail Woods, Dec. 20, 1960. Assoc. degree, Hannibal-LaGrange, 1961; BS in Edn., NE Mo. State U., 1963; MDiv, St. Paul Sch. Theology, 1986. Ordained to ministry Meth. Ch., 1988. Pastor Callao (Mo.) Cir. United Meth. Chs., 1985-86; assoc. pastor Concord Trinity United Meth. Ch., St. Louis, 1986-89; pastor Clayton United Meth. Ch., St. Louis, 1989-91, Maplewood United Meth. Ch., St. Louis, 1991—; bd. dirs. Kingdom House, St. Louis, 1988—, program chair, 1989—; vice-chairperson bd. of ch. and soc. Mo. East Annual Conf., United Meth. Ch., 1988—. Bd. dirs. Epworth Children's Home, St. Louis, 1987—. Democrat. Home: 4507 Canoe Dr Saint Louis MO 63123 Office: Maplewood United Meth Ch 7409 Flora Saint Louis MO 63143 *Deep within the very center of my being I have become convinced that God's will for each of us is that we might be made completely whole and, in turn, seek to help others reach this same goal.*

WOODS, NORMAN JAMES, academic administrator; b. Springfield, Mo., Mar. 5, 1934; s. Norman O. and Doris Ena (Noblitt) W.; m. Phyllis Darlene Foster, Aug. 16, 1959; children: Michael J., Julie L. Woods Scott. BA, Union Coll., Lincoln, Nebr., 1960; MEd, Cen. Wash. U., 1966; PhD, U. Oreg., 1969. Tchr., asst. dean men Auburn (Wash.) Acad., 1960-61; Tchr., asst. dean men Auburn Acad., Wash., 1960-61; asst., then assoc. and dean men Walla Walla Coll., College Place, Wash., 1961-66; dean students Loma Linda U., Calif., 1966-67, asst. then assoc. dean admissions and student affairs, 1969-74, v.p. acad. adminstrn., 1974-84, pres., 1984—. With U.S. Army, 1956-58. Mem. Am. Assn. Pres. Ind. Colls. and Univs. (bd. dirs. 1985—). Seventh-day Adventist. Avocations: golf, tennis. Office: Loma Linda U Office of Pres Loma Linda CA 92350

WOODS, RICHARD JOHN FRANCIS, priest, writer, educator; b. Albuquerque, July 30, 1941; s. James Everett and Margaret Louise (Corcoran) W. BA in Philosophy, Aquinas Inst., River Forest, Ill., 1964, MA in Philosophy, 1966; MA in Theology, Aquinas Inst., Dubuque, Iowa, 1970; PhD, Loyola U., Chgo., 1978. Joined Dominican order, 1962; ordained priest Roman Cath. Ch., 1969. Ordained priest Dominican Order, 1969—; adj. prof. Stritch Sch. Medicine Loyola U., Chgo., 1981—; pres. Ctr. for Religion and Soc., Chgo., 1985—, also bd. dirs.; assoc. prof. Inst. Pastoral Studies Loyola U., Chgo., 1989—; lectr. Loyola U., 1971—; vis. prof. Grad. Theol. Union, Berkeley, Calif., 1977-78; therapist Sexual Dysfunction Clinic, Loyola U., 1981—. Author: Mysterion, 1980; Eckhart's Way, 1986; Christian Spirituality, 1988; Another Kind of Love, 3d edit., 1988; columnist National Catholic Reporter; also articles; exec. editor Spirituality Today, 1986-90. Richard John F. Woods endowed chair Coll. of St. Thomas, St. Paul, 1984-85. Mem. Am. Cath. Philos. Assn., Am. Acad. Religion, Cath. Theol. Soc. Am., Authors Guild, Am. Soc. for Psychical Research, C.G. Jung Soc. Avocations: music, harp making, photography. Home: 6418 N Lakewood Ave Chicago IL 60626 Office: Inst Pastoral Studies 6525 N Sheridan Rd Chicago IL 60626

WOODS, ROBERT GAIL, minister; b. Columbia, Mo., Oct. 17, 1939; s. Robert Luther and Stella Elizabeth (Edwards) W.; m. Margie Sue McDaniel, Dec. 20, 1960. AA, Hannibal-LaGrange Coll., 1961; BA, Northeast Mo. State Tchrs. Coll., 1963; BD, So. Bapt. Theol. Sem., 1967, ThM, 1968, PhD, 1971. Ordained to ministry Bapt. Ch., 1961, United Meth. Ch., 1976, as elder, 1976. Pastor Farber (Mo.) Bapt. Ch., 1960-63, Ten Mile Bapt. Ch., Canton, Mo., 1961-63, Patriot (Ind.) Bapt. Ch., 1964-67; interim pastor Mt. Moriah Advent Christian Ch., Henryville, Ind., 1969-70; pastor North Park

Bapt. Ch., Moberly, Mo., 1972-73; pastor Centenary and Wesley Chapel United Meth. Chs., Louisiana, Mo., 1973-77; pastor Taylor Ave. and Elvins. United Meth. Chs., Flat River and Elvins, Mo., 1977-79, Immanuel United Meth. Ch., Canton, 1979-86, Herculaneum (Mo.) United Meth. Ch., 1986-87, Zion United Meth. Ch., St. Louis, 1987—; pres. Canton Coun. Chs., 1981; sec. commn. on archives and history Mo. East Ann. Conf., 1976-84, vice chmn., 1988—, retirement rels. coord. bd. ordained ministry, 1984—; adj. instr. Cen. Meth. Coll., Fayette, Mo., 1978-79. Contbr. articles to religious jours. Garrett fellow So. Bapt. Theol. Sem., 1970-71. Home: 4507 Canoe Dr Saint Louis MO 63123 Office: Zion United Meth Ch 1603 Union Rd Saint Louis MO 63125 *Like Jesus, who knew "that he had come from God and was going to God" (John 13:3), we find in the Eternal One our own origin and destination. This is our noblest identity.*

WOODS, WILLIAM EDWARD, minister; b. Roanoke, Va., June 26, 1936; s. Marlin Denny and Virginia Elizabeth (Hypes) W.; m. Barbara Ann Pearson, Mar. 21, 1959; children: Deborah Lyn, Cynthia Ann, Stephen Edward. BA in Ministry, Bethany Bible Coll., Dothan, Ala., 1991. Ordained to ministry Ch. of God, 1976. Assoc. pastor Skyway Ch. of God., Renton, Wash., 1970-73; pastor First Ch. of God, Port Angeles, Wash., 1973-77; pastoral adminstrn. asst. Community Ch. of God, Capitola, Calif., 1977-80; assoc. pastor First Ch. of God, Fresno, Calif., 1980-82; pastor First Ch. of God, Hastings, Nebr., 1982—; pres. Adams County-Hastings Ministerial Assn., Hastings, Nebr., 1987-88, sec./treas., 1989-90, pres. 1990-91. Bd. dirs. Youth for Christ, Hastings, 1988-89; ministerial rep. Multi-Agy. Enforcement Task Force Community Action Group, Hastings, 1991. Home: 1914 W 8th St Hastings NE 68901 Office: First Ch of God 503 N Lincoln Ave Hastings NE 68901

WOODS, WILLIAM RAY, minister, evangelist, educator; b. Berea, Ky., Feb. 10, 1947; s. Jack and Marie (Newman) W.; m. Peggy Ann Conner, Aug. 26, 1967; children: William Matthew, Mark Anthony. BS, Ea. Ky. U., 1969; postgrad., No. Ky. U., 1990. Ordained to ministry So. Bapt. Conf. Evangelist So. Bapt. Ministry, Ky., 1963-77; min. Peytontown Bapt. Ch., Richmond, Ky., 1977-82, Calvary Bapt. Ch., Berea, 1982-89, Middletown Bapt. Ch., Berea, 1989—; lectr. Social Ministries, Inc., Berea, 1963—; instr. social work Ky. Dept. for Social Ins., Lexington, 1971—; chmn. ch. and pastor rels. Tates Creek Assn. Bapt. Chs., Richmond, 1985-90, chmn. student ministries, 1990-91. Mem. Am. Pub. Welfare Assn., Ky. Human Svcs. Assn. Home: 1277 Blue Lick Rd Berea KY 40403 Office: Dept for Social Ins 627 W 4th St Lexington KY 40508

WOODSON, TIMOTHY PAUL, minister; b. Whittier, Calif., Apr. 4, 1957; s. Charles Cleo and June Vera (Cottage) W.; m. Donna Virginia Dodd, June 3, 1977; children: Amy Lynn, Lori Deona, Jonathan Marc. Student, Groveton (Tex.) High Sch. Pres. Inner Seed Ministries, Memphis, 1975—. Avocations: woodworking, musical instruments. Office: Inner Seed Ministries PO Box 341774 Memphis TN 38184

WOODWARD, JOSEPH WAYNE, minister; b. Savannah, Ga., Nov. 18, 1967; s. Donald Willis and Rebecca (Mobley) W. Ordained to ministry So. Bapt. Conv., 1989. Missionary Home Missions Bd.; assoc. pastor Musella (Ga.) Bapt. Ch., 1988—. 2d lt. USAR, 1990—. Republican.

WOODWARD, WAYNE WILLIAM, librarian, minister; b. Greenburg, Ind., May 4, 1930; s. Arthur Coy and Hazel Prue (Ayres) W.; m. H. Corinne Vaughn, Jan. 17, 1956; children: Gail, Karen. AB, Taylor U., 1952; BDiv, Asbury Theol. Sem., 1955; MA, Appalachian State U. (formerly Appalachian Coll.), Boone, N.C., 1960; MLS, U. Ky., 1967. Pastor United Meth. Ch., N.C., 1955-59, 61-64; asst. to the libr. Asbury Theol. Sem., Wilmore, Ky., 1965-67; libr. Asbury Coll., Wilmore, 1967-77, reference libr., 1977-78; dir. libr. svc. Wesley Bibl. Sem., Jackson, Miss., 1978—. Office: Wesley Bibl Sem Box 9938 Jackson MS 39286-0938

WOODWORTH, HAROLD G., minister; b. Milw., Apr. 28, 1933; s. Harold G. and Nettie A. (Megow) W.; m. Bernice M. Livangood, June 9, 1956; children: Mark, David, Karen, Kathryn. BTh, Concordia Sem., Springfield, Ill., 1958, MDiv, 1973; MA, Sangamon State U., 1973; D Ministry, Wartburg Theol. Sem., 1976. Ordained to ministry Luth. Ch.-Mo. Synod, 1958. Pastor Prince of Peace Luth. Ch., New Orleans, 1958-63, Concordia Luth. Ch., Birmingham, Ala., 1963-64, Zion Luth. Ch., Colby, Wis., 1964-65, Salem Luth. Ch., Jacksonville, Ill., 1968-76, Our Redeemer Luth. Ch., Jacksonville, 1976—; chmn. bd. Heartland Sch. Bus., Jacksonville; cir. counselor Luth. Ch.-Mo. Synod, New Orleans, 1960-63, sec. mission bd., 1960-64; bd. dirs. Concordia Tract Mission, St. Louis, 1980—. Contbr. articles to profl. jours. Bd. dirs. Sherwood Eddy YMCA, Jacksonville, 1970-76; pres. Morgan County ARC, 1972-74; dist. chmn. Student Aid Com., Springfield, 1982—; v.p. Community Svcs. Block Grant Bd., Morgan County, 1983-85. Served to capt. U.S. Army, 1965-68, Vietnam. Recipient Servus Ecclesiae Christi award Concordia Sem., 1979. Mem. Ill. Sociol. Assn., Midwest Sociol. Assn., SAR (pres. Ill. soc.), Soc. of Mayflower Descendents (lt. gov. Lincolnland colony), Kiwanis (pres., lt. gov.), Phi Delta Kappa. Home: 47 Westfair Dr Jacksonville IL 62650 Office: Our Redeemer Luth Ch 405 Massey Ln Jacksonville IL 62650 *God has given us the opportunity and challenge of life so that we could be a good and productive neighbor in a neighborhood as wide as Christ's loving heart.*

WOODWORTH, MARGO DEANE, religious organization administrator; b. Tacoma, Sept. 28, 1941; d. Owen Reeves and Margaret (Lewis) Smith; m. James W. Woodworth, Jan. 27, 1965; children: Sherri, Shannon. BA, Tex. Christian U., 1963. Dir. parents' tng. Advance-Zales Found. Project, Dallas, 1975-76; dir. children's activities and membership devel. Casa View Christian Ch., Dallas, 1976-78; dir. adminstrn., treas. Nat. Evangelistic Assn. of Christian Ch., Lubbock, Tex., 1979—; meeting planner cons. for religious conf. Nat. Evangelistic Assn. and Workshop, Lubbock, 1979—. Chmn. publicity Dudley Strain Lectureship Contact, Lubbock, 1986-87. Named to hon. order Ky. Cols., 1987. Mem. Nat. Assn. of Ch. Bus. Adminstrn., Religious Conf. Mgmt. Assn., Christian Ministries Mgmt. Assn., Am. Soc. Assn. Execs. Democrat. Avocation: travel. Office: Nat Evangelistic Assn 5001 Ave N Lubbock TX 79412

WOODYARD, MARCIA WEEKS, clergywoman; b. Columbus, Ga., Oct. 12, 1961; d. Archie Daniel and Wenda Joyce (Pritchett) Weeks; m. Christopher David Woodyard, Jan. 19, 1991; 1 stepchild, Matthew David. BA, Ky. Wesley Coll., 1983; MDiv., Asbury Theol. Sem., 1986; postgrad., U. Ky., 1987-89. Ordained to ministry Meth. Ch. as deacon, 1989, as elder, 1991. Youth worker Wesley Heights United Meth. Ch., Owensboro, Ky., 1982; dir. religious activities Meth. Home of Ky., Versailles, 1986-89; assoc. pastor Trinity Hill United Meth. Ch., Lexington, Ky., 1989—; dist. dir. Ky. Conf. Com. on Ch. and Soc., 1989—; mem. Ky. Conf. Singles Task Force, 1989—. Mem. Charter Ridge's Community Adv. Bd., Lexington, 1991. Mem. NASW, Christian Educator's Fellowship, Kappa Delta Alumni. Republican. Office: Trinity Hill United Meth Ch 3600 Tates Creek Rd Lexington KY 40517

WOOLBRIGHT, THURMAN ALFRED, retired minister; b. Abbeville, S.C., Jan. 9, 1922; s. Elijah Prophet and Edith Mae (Brown) W.; m. Lila Laura Mae Sutherland, Feb. 28, 1944; children: Wallace Alfred, Michael Eugene. BA, Furman U., 1949; BD, New Orleans Bapt. Theol. Sem., 1952, MDiv, 1975. Lic. to ministry So. Bapt. Conv., 1946, ordained, 1948. Pastor New Zion Bapt. Ch., Kentwood, La., 1948-54, Friendship Bapt. Ch., Lyman, S.C., 1952-59, Calvary Bapt. Ch., Gaffney, S.C., 1959-76, First Bapt. Ch., Norris, Cross Hill, Iva and Westminster, S.C., 1966-73; assoc. pastor Woodfields Bapt. Ch., Greenwood S.C., 1976-79, Second Bapt. Ch., Belton, S.C., 1979-82; assoc. pastor Durham Meml. Bapt. Ch., Charlotte, N.C., 1982-85, ret., 1985; pastor Sunset Forest Bapt. Ch., Gastonia, N.C., 1986-88; instr. Union Bapt. Theol. Sem., New Orleans, 1949-52; pres. Greer (S.C.) Bapt. Ministers, 1965-66; missions chmn. Greer Bapt. Assn., 1964-65, Beaverdam Bapt. Assn., Westminster, S.C., 1967-69; registrar, instr. sem. extension So. Bapt. Conv., Westminster, 1967-73; mission tour Israel-Europe, 1969; preaching mission Jamaica, 1970; mem. Examining Coun. Mecklinburg Bapt. Assn., Charlotte, N.C., 1983-85; coun. Dr. Crain's Ministry, S.C., 1952-73; preacher ann. message Greer Bapt. Assn., 1965, Broad River Bapt. Assn., 1976; spl. participation/leader Sunday Confs., N.C. State Bapt. Conv., 1986-87. Author ch. news column Westminster Witness, 1966-73, spl. papers and columns. Bd. dirs. ARC, Iva, 1955; founder S.O.C.K.S., Springfield Crisis Ministry, Gastonia, N.C., 1986-88; bd. assocs. North Greenville Coll., 1966-73; mem. nominating com. S.C. State Bapt. Conv., 1968, mem. program, Myrtle Beach, 1981, rep. rural ch. conf., Atlantic City, 1965. With USN, 1942-44, World War II. Recipient Anderson Daily Mail Salutes award, 1957, Spl. Recognition award Sunday Sch. Bd. So. Bapt. Conv., 1983; named Man of Yr., Iva., S.C., 1956. Home: 1401 N Main St Mount Holly NC 28120-2415 *As I have come to retirement years of the Christian Ministry, looking back I could wish I were able to begin again. Having the experience of these years, I would like to have accomplished a great deal more. The call, challenge and contribution is of tremendous need for today and man's hope for tomorrow.*

WOOLRIDGE, JAMES ROBERT, SR., pastor; b. Monticello, Ill., Apr. 4, 1948; s. Raymond Ira and Nadine Elizabeth (Shonkwiler) W.; m. Darla Jean Hendrickson, Aug. 6, 1971; children: James Robert II, Bobbi Jean. Grad. high sch., Bement, Ill. Ordained to ministry So. Bapt. Conv., 1989. Pastor Cen. Bapt. Ch., Burna, Ky., 1989—; machinist TekService, Inc., Paducah, Ky., 1988—; trustee Mid-Continent Bapt. Bible Coll., Mayfield, Ky., 1991—. With USNR, 1965-71. Democrat. Home: Rte 9 Box 484 Benton KY 42025 Office: Cen Bapt Ch Rte 9 Box 484 Benton KY 42065

WOOLUMS, JAMES, JR., minister; b. Versailles, Ky., July 20, 1959; s. Jesse James and Nora (Shepard) W.; m. Pegge Karen McCain, June 20, 1981; children: Jessica, Jacqueline. BA, Asbury Coll., 1981; MA, Asbury Theol. Sem., 1985; EdD, So. Bapt. Theol. Sem., 1988. Ordained to ministry So. Bapt. Conv., 1986. Min. of youth Midway (Ky.) United Meth. Ch., 1977-79; pastor West Bend United Meth. Ch., Clay City, Ky., 1979-82; min. edn. and evangelism Christ United Meth. Ch., Lexington, Ky., 1983-86; dir. edn. Elkhorn Bapt. Assn., Lexington, 1986-88; pastor Lexington's First Bapt. Ch., 1988—; bd. dirs. Resource Office for Social Ministry, Lexington, 1989—; chaplain Emerson Ctr., Lexington, 1986-88. Bd. dirs. Teen Challenge Inc., Lexington, 1984-86; trustee, treas. Acad. Christian Sch. Inc., Lexington, 1984-86; mem. Lexington Mayor's Task Force on Homeless, 1990—. Mem. Lexington Alliance of Religious Leaders, Greater Lexington Ministerial Alliance, Assn. of Mins. and Coords. of Discipleship, Internat. Christian Edn. Assn. Democrat. Office: First Bapt Ch 548 W Short St Lexington KY 40507 *My father did not have a great deal of formal schooling yet had a God-given common sense. His best advice to me was, "Wherever you go love people and you'll be successful."*

WOOTEN, LOREN WESLEY, minister; b. Flippin, Ark., May 24, 1919; s. Elmer and Margaret (Casandra) W.; m. Bernice Irene Jackson, Nov. 19, 1939; children: Bernice Jeanene, Judith Ann. Diploma, Cen. Bible Inst., Springfield, Mo., 1939. Ordained to ministry Assemblies of God, 1942. Pastor, evangelist Assemblies of God, Springfield, 1939-85; dist. youth dir. Assemblies of God, Springfield, 1942-45, dist. ednl. dir., 1950-55, nat. evangelist field rep., 1973-76, 80-85. Author bible study notes used in evangelism crusades. Mem. New Life Christian Fellowship (founder, pres. 1990—), Men Aflame Fellowship (pres., founder 1980—). Home: PO Box 67 Sullivan MO 63080-0067 Office: PO Box 69 Leasburg MO 65535

WOOTERS, BRIAN ALLAN, minister; b. E. St. Louis, Ill., Aug. 9, 1954; s. Alfred Elbert Wooters and Marjorie Loucile Steele McClain; m. Susan Marie Franklin, June 22, 1974; 1 child, Christina Marie. BA, Union U., Jackson, Tenn., 1984; MDiv, So. Bapt. Sem., 1987. Ordained to ministry, So. Bapt. Conv., 1978. Pastor Tumbling Creek Bapt. Ch., Gleason, Tenn., 1978-84, Meadows Bapt. Mission, Clarksville, Ind., 1985-86, Plattsmouth (Nebr.) Bapt. Ch., 1987—; instr. Sem. Extension of So. Bapt. Conv., Nashville, 1989. Reviewer book series: Search, 1990-91; author sermon series: Proclaim: Jour. for Preaching, 1991; contbr. Dorian's Minister's Manual, 1992. Coun. mem. Domestic Abuse Adv. Coun., Cass County, Nebr., 1989—, recipient Svc. award 1990. Presdl. Preaching scholar, 1984, Am. Bible Soc. awardee, Union U., 1984. Mem. Plattsmouth Area Ministerial Assn. (pres. 1989—), Alpha Chi. Republican. Home: 1009 Pleasant Dr Plattsmouth NE 68048 *The goal of life may be defined in various ways by different people. Terms like "satisfaction," "oneness," "wholeness," or "having it all together" can be used. All such ideas find their telos in one Biblical word: peace.*

WORDEN, BARBARA STANDLEY, religion educator, English educator; b. Cleve., June 22, 1942; d. George Prince and Louise Francis (Clark) Standley; m. Ronald Dean Worden, June 22, 1968; 1 child, Mark Standley. AB, Mt. Holyoke Coll., South Hadley, Mass., 1964; MA, Case-Western Res. U., 1965; PhD, Boston U., 1974. Asst. prof. George Fox Coll., Newburg, Oreg., 1971-83; prof. Friends Bible Coll., Haviland, Kans., 1974-83, Houston Grad. Sch. Theology, 1983—; instr. English Houston Community Coll., 1988—; overseer Friendswood (Tex.) Friends Ch., 1985-87; del. Internat. Conf. Friends, Guatemala, 1987, Internat. Friends Women Theologists, Woodbrook, U.K., 1990; mem. interpretation bd., U.S. sect. Friends World Com. for Consultation, Evang. Friends Ch. NEH grantee Rice U., 1977, NYU, 1982; recipient Founder's award Houston Grad. Sch. Alumni Assn., 1989. Mem. MLA, Am. Acad. Religion (regional sec. 1981-82), Conf. Christianity and Lit. Democrat. Home: 9423 Kings Valley Houston TX 77075 *Power from God, the quiet gentle power that drive a wild flower through a crack in cement, can drive a person through the hardest circumstances.*

WORDEN, RONALD DEAN, religion educator, academic educator; b. Grainfield, Kans., Apr. 10, 1938; s. Otis Dean and Helen June (Dillon) W.; m. Barbara Louise Standley, June 22, 1968; 1 child, Mark. AB, George Fox Coll., 1960; BD, Asbury Theol. Seminary, 1965; ThM, Harvard Divinity Sch., 1967; PhD, Princeton Theol. Seminary, 1973. Recorded min., Soc. of Friends, 1968. Pastor Fairview Friends Ch., Carthage, Mo., 1960-62; assoc. prof. George Fox Coll., Newberg, Oreg., 1970-73; pastor United Meth. Ch., Dufur and Tygh Valley, Oreg., 1973-74; prof. Friends Bible Coll., Haviland, Kans., 1974-83; acad. dean Houston (Tex.) Grad. Sch. of Theology, 1983—, v.p. for acad. affairs, 1991—; chmn. Com. on Recording Friendswood (Tex.) Friends Ch., 1985—. Contbr. articles to profl. jours. Mem. Soc. Bibl. Lit., Am. Schs. Oriental Rsch., Coun. S.W. Theol. Schs. (sec. 1988-90, pres. 1990—). Office: Houston Grad Sch Theology 1129 Wilkins Ste 202 Houston TX 77030

WORDEN, WILLIAM PATRICK, deacon; b. Chgo., July 23, 1933; s. Shannon Gerard and Florence Marie (Chouinard) W.; m. Shirley Ann Poerio, Apr. 1, 1956; children: Mary Patricia Maloney, Judith Ann Laverdiere, Ellen Jean. BEE, Ill. Inst. Tech., 1955; MA in Pastoral Studies, Loyola U., Chgo., 1986; D Ministry, Grad. Theol. Found., Bristol, Ind., 1991. Deacon St. Peter and Paul Parish, Naperville, Ill., 1980-85, St. Thomas the Apostle Parish, Naperville, 1985—; chaplain DuPage County Jail, Wheaton, Ill., 1991—; mem. reactor safety rev. com. Argonne Nat. Lab., Darien, Ill., 1989—; del. Region VII Deaconal Orgn., 1981-84. Author: (with others) Decontamination and Decommissioning of Nuclear Facilities, 1980; contbr. articles to jours. in field. Bd. dirs. Interfaith Counseling Svc., Naperville, 1980-85, Just of DuPage Jail Ministry, Wheaton, 1986-90. Office: St Thomas the Apostle Ch 1500 Brookdale Naperville IL 60540

WORGUL, GEORGE S., JR., religion educator; b. N.Y.C., Nov. 9, 1947. BA, Niagara U., 1968, MA, 1972; PhD, U. Louvain, Belgium, 1974, STD, 1975. Lectr. Our Lady of Angels Sem., 1971-72, Siena Coll., 1975-78; asst. prof. systematic theology Duquesne U., Pitts., 1978-81, assoc. prof., 1981-85, prof., 1985—, acting chmn. dept., 1989-91, chair dept., 1991—; lectr. in theology St. Anthony on the Hudson Sem., 1977; vis. prof. U. Notre Dame, 1981, W.Va. U., 1987. Author: From Magic To Metaphor: A Validation of Christian Sacraments, 1980; mem. editorial bd. Bibl. Theology Bull., 1976-87. Blondel Archives grantee, 1983-84. Mem. Cath. Theol. Soc. Am., Coll. Theology Soc., Am. Acad. Religion. Roman Catholic. Office: Duquesne U Theology Dept 414 Canevin Hall Pittsburgh PA 15282

WORKMAN, CLAIR BLAINE, religious organization administrator; b. Salt Lake City, Apr. 11, 1951; s. Clair McKee and Donna (Thompson) W.; m. Marian Schlange, Aug. 7, 1980; children: Lily Ann, Kathryn Marie, Ellen Jane. BS, Brigham Young U., 1975; MBA, U. Utah, 1984. Auditor Peat, Marwick and Mitchell, Los Angeles, 1975-77; controller Deseret Industries, Los Angeles, 1977-80, Salt Lake Deseret Industries, Salt Lake City, 1980-81; fin. analyst Latter-day Saints Welfare Services, Salt Lake City, 1981-85; area fin. mgr. Latter-day Saints Welfare Services, Seattle, 1985—. Missionary Jesus Christ Latter-day Saints, French Polynesia, 1970-72; treas. So. Calif. Mormon Choir, Los Angeles, 1978-80; mem. Salt Lake Symphonic Choir, 1981-85. John Einer Anderson scholar Brigham Young U., Provo, Utah, 1974, Dean's scholar Brigham Young U., 1969-70, Acad. scholar Brigham Young U., 1972-73. Mem. Phi Kappa Phi. Republican. Avocations: music, skiing, swimming. Office: Latter-day Saints Welfare Services 220 S 3d Pl Renton WA 98055

WORLEY, DAVID WAYNE, pastor, religion educator; b. Herrin, Ill., July 3, 1950; s. Paul Elmin and Phyllis Dean (Overturf) W.; m. Bonita Jean McGraw, Nov. 4, 1972. B of Religious Edn., BTh., Trinity Coll. of Bible, 1981; MDiv., Trinity Theol. Sem., 1983; BA, Western Ill. U., 1991. Assoc. pastor Pentecostal Assembly, Bangor, Maine, 1971-73, The First Pentecostal Ch., Murphysboro, Ill., 1973—; prin. Murphysboro (Ill.) Christian Acad., 1976—; dir. Bethel Ministerial Acad., Evansville, Ind., 1989—; v.p. Murphysboro (Ill.) Ministerial Alliance, 1991—; seminar tchr. New Life Ctrs., Guatemala, 1991. Mem. Bethel Ministerial Assn., Global Christian Ministries. Office: 1st Pentecostal Ch 16th and Poplar Sts Murphysboro IL 62966 *To have information is to possess knowledge. To have inspiration is to possess motivation. To have illumination is to possess wisdom. Success demands all three.*

WORLEY, GARY ALBERT, minister; b. Albertville, Ala., Aug. 24, 1957; s. Albert Russell and Wilma Kay (Edmonson) W.; m. Shelia Diane Samples, Aug. 27, 1976; 1 child, Rachel Amanda. Student, Internat. Bible Sch., 1985, Faulkner U., 1985-86, Freed-Hardeman U., 1985. Ordained to ministry Ch. of Christ, 1985. Assoc. min. Geraldine (Ala.) Ch. of Christ, 1984-86, Blessing Ch. of Christ, Albertville, 1984-86, N. Broad St. Ch. of Christ, Albertville, 1984-86; deacon Antioch Ch. of Christ, Snead, Ala., 1987-90; min. Hackleburg (Ala.) Ch. of Christ, 1990—; tchr. World Bible (Corr.) Sch.; presenter Truth in Love radio Bible broadcast, 1986-87; missionary Campaigns for Christ, Jamaica, W.I.,1986, 88, 89, 90; lectr. gospel meetings, PTA meetings, youth rallys. Home and Office: 530 Diane Ave Albertville AL 35950

WORLEY, L. DARYLE, JR., minister; b. Toccoa, Ga., Feb. 1, 1961; s. L. Daryle and Lois C. (Cox) W.; m. Jean M. Lawhead, June 10, 1983; children: Natalie Jean, Nicole Marie. Diploma in Theology and Greek, Moody Bible Inst., 1983; BA in Religion and Philosophy, Judson Coll., 1984; MA in Christian Thought, Trinity Evang. Div. Sch., 1986. Ordained to ministry, 1988. Pastor single adults The Moody Ch., Chgo., 1987—. Contbg. author: Single to Single, 1991; author 7 children's books. Mem. Nat. Assn. Single Adult Leaders (bd. dirs. 1991—). Office: The Moody Ch 1609 N LaSalle Dr Chicago IL 60614

WORLEY, MICHAEL GENE, youth pastor; b. San Jose, Calif., Apr. 4, 1960; s. Donald Gene and Marilynn Allen (Peterson) W.; m. Leesa Ann Worley, July 24, 1982; children, Michael, Katie, Jeremy. AA, West Valley Coll., Saratoga, Calif., 1981; BRE, Multnomah Sch. of the Bible, Portland, Oreg., 1984. Youth pastor Los Gatos (Calif.) Christian Ch., 1984—. Author: Brand Name Christians, 1988; devotional editor Hume Lake Camps, 1986—; contbr. articles to profl. jours.; speaker for camps, retreats, 1986—. Bd. dirs., advisor Project Hope Inner City, San Jose, 1989—, Crisis Pregnancy Ctr., San Jose; svc. ministry dir. Impact Youth Ministries, Los Gatos, 1986—; baseball chaplain San Jose Giants, 1990—. Mem. Nat. Network of Youth Mins., San Jose Reps. Home: 770 Regent Park Dr San Jose CA 95123 Office: Los Gatos Christian Ch 16845 Hicks Rd Los Gatos CA 95032

WORSLEY, RICHARD, JR., pastor; b. Bethel, N.C., Sept. 6, 1942; s. James Richard and Ethel (Knight) W.; m. Annie Doris Williams, Jan. 12, 1964; children: Richard L., Steven L., Kimberly Ann, Darlene. BTh, Internat. Sem., 1988; AA in Social Scis., Brookdale Community Coll., 1989. Ordained to ministry Ch. of God Internat., 1975; cert. master tng. Youth dir. Ch. of God, Freehold, N.J., 1971-82, mem. state coun., 1982—; pastor Long Br. (N.J.) Ch. of God, 1971—; mem. ministerial examining bd. Ch. of God, N.J., 1984-90; mem. exec. bd. Chs. of God in the N.E., 1986-90; call min. Riverview Hosp., Red Bank, N.J., 1986—, Monmouth Med. Ctr., Long Branch, 1980—; educator Ch. of God, Long Branch, 1971—. Del. Bd. Edn., Long Branch, 1991—. Recipient citation U.S Ho. Reps., Washington, 1989, 90, Community Svc. award City of Long Branch, 1987, 89, citation State Senate of N.J., 1985, 86, 87.

WORST, SUSAN GAIL, lay worker; b. Chgo., Mar. 29, 1964; d. Raymond John and Karen Ann (Wolff) W.; m. Laurence Cohen, May 26, 1991. BA, Washington U., 1986; postgrad., Harvard U., 1986-87. Deacon U. Luth. Ch., Cambridge, Mass., 1988—; edit. asst. to dir. Beacon Press, Boston, 1988—; mem. bd. worship, U. Luth. Ch., 1990—, mem. Ch. coun., 1991. Mem. Women Scholary Publishing (publicist 1990-91), Phi Beta Kappa.

WORTH, DAVID ALBERT, minister; b. Mt. Holly, N.J., Sept. 7, 1943; s. Albert Fred and Muriel (Amison) W.; m. Nancy Rebmen, June 4, 1966; children: Douglas, James. BA, Wheaton Coll., 1966; MDiv, McCormick Seminary, Chgo., 1970; D of Ministry, Fuller Theol. Seminary, Pasadena, Calif., 1982. Ordained to ministry Presbyn. Ch., 1970. Asst. pastor First Presbyn. Ch., River Forest, Ill., 1966-72; assoc. pastor Solana Beach (Calif.) Presbyn. Ch., 1972-76; sr. pastor Malibu (Calif.) Presbyn. Ch., 1976—. Crest Adv. Bd., Pepperdine U., Malibu, 1987—. Mem. Optomist. Office: Malibu Presbyn Ch 3324 Malibu Canyon Rd Malibu CA 90265

WORTHING, CAROL MARIE, minister; b. Duluth, Minn., Dec. 27, 1934; d. Truman James and Helga Maria (Bolander) W.; children: Gregory Alan Beatty, Graydon Ernest Beatty. BS, U. Minn., 1965; Master of Divinity, Northwestern Theol. Seminary, 1982; D of Ministry, Grad. Theol. Found., Notre Dame, Ind., 1988. Secondary educator Ind. (Minn.) Sch. Dist., 1965-78; teaching fellow U. Minn., 1968-70; contract counselor Luth. Social Svc., Duluth, 1976-78; media cons. Luth. Media Svcs., St. Paul, 1978-80; asst. pastor Messiah Luth. Ch., Fargo, N.D., 1982-83; vice pastor Messiah Luth. Ch., Fargo, 1983-84; assoc. editor Luth. Ch. Am. Ptnrs., Phila., 1982-84; editorial assoc. Luth. Ptnrs. Evang. Luth. Ch. Am., Phila. and Mpls., 1984—; parish pastor Resurrection Luth. Ch., Pierre, S.D., 1984-89; assoc. pastor Bethlehem Luth. Ch., Cedar Falls, Iowa, 1989-90; gen. sec., chief exec. officer Ill. Conf. Chs., Springfield, 1990—; mem. pub. rels. and interpretation com. Red River Valley Synod, Fargo, 1984-86, mem. ch. devel., Pierre, 1986-87; mem. mgmt. com. Luth. Ch. in Am., N.Y.C., Phila., 1984-88; mem. mission ptnrs. S.D. Synod, 1998, chmn. assembly resolutions com., 1988; mem. pre-assembly planning com., ecumenics com., chmn. resolutions com. N.E. Iowa Synod, 1989-90; mem. ch. and society com. Cen. and So. Ill. Synod, 1990—; cons. Am. Film Inst., Washington, 1967-70; chaplain state legis. bodies, Pierre, 1984-89. Author: Cinematics and English, 1967, Peer Counseling, 1977, Tischrede Lexegete, 1986, 88, 90, Way of the Cross, Way of Justice Walk, 1987. Co-facilitator Parents of Retarded Children, 1985; bd. dirs. Countryside Hospice, 1985; cons. to adminstrv. bd. Mo. Shores Women's Ctr., 1986; chair resolutions com. N.E. Iowa Synod, 1989-90; mem. ch. and soc. com. Cen./So. Ill. Synod, 1990—. Mem. Nat. Assn. Ecumenical Staff, Pierre-Ft. Pierre Ministerium (v.p. 1986-87, pres. 1987-88), NAFE. Democrat. Avocations: writing prose and poetry, concerts, theater, art, photography. Home: 1520 Seven Pines Rd Apt J Springfield IL 62704 Office: Ill Conf Churches 615 S Fifth St Springfield IL 62703 *Ecumenism is, I believe, about convergence, not consensus. The Spirit of God calls the church to come together for a compassionate purpose: to respond to all who suffer, so that the world might be transformed into God's own vision of peace, justice, and love.*

WORTHINGTON, DON ROY, lay worker; b. Columbus, Ohio, July 19, 1946; s. Emma Lou (Cheadle) W.; m. Becky Jean Hutzelman, Apr. 19, 1969; children: Kristin, Quincy. BA, Denison U., 1968; postgrad., U. Cin., 1976-78, Gannon U., 1978-80. Vice moderator Lake Erie Presbytery, Erie, Pa., 1990—; v.p. sales Flex-Y-Plan, Fairview, Pa., 1978—; elder Wayside Presbyn. Ch., Erie, 1989—. Lt. comdr. USN, 1968-88. Mem. Rotary (pres. Elk Valley chpt. 1986-87). Home: 7290 Tulip Dr Fairview PA 16415

WORTHINGTON, MELVIN LEROY, minister, writer; b. Greenville, N.C., June 17, 1937; s. Wilbur Leroy and Alma Lee (Braxton) W.; m. Anne Katherine Wilson, Sept. 12, 1959; children: Daniel Edward, Lydia Anne. Diploma, Imperial Detective Acad., Cin., 1965; B.Bibl.Edn., Columbia

Bible Coll., S.C., 1959; B.Th., Luther Rice Sem., Jacksonville, Fla., 1967, B.Div., 1969, M.Th., 1970, D.Th., 1974; M.Ed., Ga. State U.-Atlanta, 1979. Ordained to ministry, Central Conf. Free Will Baptists, 1957. Pastor Union Chapel Free Will Bapt. Ch., Chocowinity, N.C., 1959-62, Palmetto Free Will Bapt. Ch., Vanceboro, N.C., 1959-62, First Free Will Bapt. Ch., Darlington, S.C., 1962-66, Wesconnett Free Will Bapt. Ch., Jacksonville, Fla., 1967; pastor First Free Will Bapt. Ch., Amory, Miss., 1967-72, Albany, Ga., 1972-79; exec. sec. Nat. Assn. Free Will Bapt., Inc., Nashville, 1979—, chmn. Sunday Sch. bd., 1975-77, asst. moderator, 1977-79, chmn. grad. study com., 1976-77; clk. S.C. State Assn. Free Will Bapt., Florence, 1966-67; asst. moderator Ga. State Assn. Free Will Bapt., Moultrie, 1973-74, moderator, 1975-79; pres. Ga. Bible Inst., Albany, 1978. Editor in chief: Contact mag., 1979—, author editorial, 1980—; contbr. articles to profl. jours. Adv. bd. Nat. Fedn. Decency, 1985; nat. bd. dirs. Christian Leaders for Responsible TV, 1986. Mem. Evang. Press Assn., Religious Conf. Mgmt. Assn. (dir. 1983, v.p. 1986, pres. 1989), Nashville C. of C., Future Farmers Am. (N.C. Farmer degree 1955, Am. Farmer degree 1957). Democrat. Home: 3308 Timber Tr Antioch TN 37103 Office: Nat Assn Free Will Bapt Inc PO Box 1088 5002-5233 Mt View Rd Antioch TN 37013-2306 *The basic principle which has guided, governed and guarded my life has been a burning desire to find, follow and finish the will of God.*

WORTHLEY, HAROLD FIELD, minister, educator; b. Brewer, Maine, Nov. 3, 1928; s. Herbert Morrison and Aline May (Field) W.; m. Barbara Louise Bent, June 25, 1955; children—Susan Louise Rieksts, Laura May, David Bruce. A.B., Boston U., 1950, M.A., 1951; S.T.B., Harvard Div. Sch., 1954, S.T.M., 1956, Th.D., 1970. Ordained to ministry United Ch. of Christ, 1954. Minister Congl. chs., Maine, N.H., Mass., 1951-62; assoc. prof. religion and chaplain Wheaton Coll., Norton, Mass., 1963-77; exec. sec., archivist Congl. Christian Hist. Soc., Boston, 1971—; librarian Congl. Library, Boston, 1977—; editor Bull. of Congl. Library, 1976—, Hist. Intelligencer, 1980-86. Author: Inventory of the Records of the Particular Churches of Massachusetts, 1620-1805, 1970; contbr. articles to profl. jours. Fellow Pilgrim Soc., Congl. Christian Hist. Soc.; mem. United Ch. of Christ Hist. Council. Home: 14 Mansfield Ave Norton MA 02766 Office: The Congregational Library 14 Beacon St Boston MA 02108

WORTINGER, JOHN KEITH, minister; b. Mishawaka, Ind., Oct. 9, 1946; s. Kenneth Melvin and Norma Marie (Merchant) W.; m. Linda Lou Reichard, Aug. 26, 1967; children: Melinda, Mark. BA, U. Indpls., 1968; MDiv, United Theol. Sem., 1971. Ordained to ministry United Meth. Ch. as deacon, 1970, as elder, 1972. Pastor Rochester (Ind.) Larger Parish, 1971-74, Star City (Ind.) United Meth. Ch., 1974-79, Butler (Ind.) United Meth. Ch., 1979-84, Salem United Meth. Ch., Bremen, Ind., 1984-87; sr. pastor First United Meth. Ch., Lowell, Ind., 1987—; vice chmn. Calumet Dist. Missionary Soc., Merrillville, Ind., 1989. Author: Wortingers of America, 1984. Mem. Butler Ministerial Assn. (pres. 1981-84), Bremen Ministerial Assn. (pres. 1985-87), Lowell Ministerial Assn. (pres. 1989-90), U.S. Chess Fedn. (class A), Forest Lodge. Office: First United Meth Ch 520 E Commercial Ave Lowell IN 46356 *Life is to be lived in relationship. Live is in relationship to God and our fellow man.*

WORTMAN, ALLEN L., music educator; b. Le Claire, Iowa, Jan. 7, 1935; s. Verne Victor and Lenore M. (Coulter) W.; m. Bette Arlene Outland, June 17, 1961; children: Joel Allen, Michelle Marie. BA, Cen. Coll., Pella, iowa, 1957; MA, U. No. Colo., 1962, EdD, 1967. Prof. music Mankato (Minn.) State U., 1966—; dir. music, lay leader 1st Presbyn. Ch., Mankato, 1966—; prof. music Mankato State U., 1966—; mem. ministerial relations com. Mankaty Presbytery, 1968-70. Commr. Presbyn. Gen. Assembly, Phoenix, 1984; mem. vocations com. Presbytery of Minn. Valleys, Willmor, 1984—. Mem. Am. Guild English Handbell Ringers (chmn. area VII 1984-86, nat. chmn. ednl. resource 1987-89), Music Educators Nat. Conf., Am. Choral Dirs. Assn. Democrat. Lodges: Kiwanis (bd. dirs. Mankato club 1984-86). Avocations: tennis, golfing, photography. Home: 24 Southview Dr Mankato MN 56001 Office: Mankato State U Music Dept Manakto MN 56001

WOSH, PETER JOSEPH, archivist, librarian; b. Perth Amboy, N.J., Nov. 15, 1954; s. Frank J. and Josephine (Lojewski) W.; m. Patricia L. Schall, May 31,1986. BA in History, Rutgers U., 1976; MA, NYU, 1978, PhD, 1988. Archivist Seton Hall U., Roman Cath. Archdiocese of Newark, South Orange, N.J., 1978-84; archivist Am. Bible Soc., N.Y.C., 1984-89, dir. archives and libr. svcs., 1989—. Author: Episcopal Journal of Michael Augustine Corrigan, Bishop of Newark, 1987; editor: Guide to Northern N.J. Catholic Parish and Institutional Records, 1984. NEH grantee, 1982, Nat. Hist. Pub. Records Commn. grantee, 1987, Inst. for Study Am. Evangelism grantee, 1989, N.Y. State Dept. Edn. grantee, 1990. Mem. Soc. Am. Archivists (chmn. religious archives 1987-89), Mid Atlantic Regional Archives Conf. (N.J. rep. 1985-87), Orgn. Am. Historians, Am. Hist. Assn., Am. Theol. Libr. Assn. Home: 157 Sandford Ave North Plainfield NJ 07060 Office: Am Bible Soc 1865 Broadway New York NY 10023

WOTISKA, SISTER DORITA, school system administrator. Supt. schs. Diocese of Lansing, Mich. Office: Office Supt Schs 300 W Ottawa St Lansing MI 48933*

WOUDENBERG, PAUL RICHARD, chaplain; b. Highland Park, Ill., Sept. 1, 1927; s. John Anton and Rosina Wilhelmina (Maechtle) W.; m. Emily Wiltse, June 5, 1967; children: Mary C., Elizabeth L. BA, Occidental Coll., 1949; MDiv, Boston U., 1952, PhD, 1959. Ordained to ministry Meth. Ch., 1952. Minister Echo Park United Meth. Ch., L.A., 1954-61, Calif. Heights United Meth. Ch., Long Beach, Calif., 1961-67, 1st United Meth. Ch., Santa Monica, Calif., 1968-76, Ch. of the Wayfarer, Carmel, Calif., 1975-86; chaplain Robert Louis Stevenson Sch., Pebble Beach, Calif., 1986--. Author: Ford in the Thirties, 1976, Lincoln--The Postwar Years, 1980, Buyer's Guide to Rolls Royce, 1984, Buyer's Guide to Fords, 1987, Buyer's Guide to Lincolns, 1990. Served with USN, 1945-46. Republican. Avocation: automobile collecting. Home: PO Box 1583 Pebble Beach CA 93953

WOUK, HERMAN, writer; b. N.Y.C., May 27, 1915; s. Abraham Isaac and Esther (Levine) W.; m. Betty Sarah Brown, Dec. 9, 1945; children: Abraham Isaac (dec.), Nathaniel, Joseph. AB with gen. honors, Columbia U., 1934; LHD (hon.), Yeshiva U., 1954; LLD (hon.), Clark U., 1960; LittD (hon.), Am. Internat. Coll., 1979; PhD (hon.), Bar-Ilan U., 1990. Writer radio programs for various comedians N.Y.C., 1935; asst. writer weekly radio scripts comedian Fred Allen, 1936-41; Presdl. cons. to U.S. Treasury, 1941; vis. prof. English Yeshiva U., 1952-57; scholar-in-residence Aspen Inst. Humanistic Studies, 1973-74. Author (novels) Aurora Dawn, 1947, The City Boy, 1948, Slattery's Hurricane, 1949, The Caine Mutiny, 1951 (Pulitzer Prize award for fiction 1952), Marjorie Morningstar, 1955, Youngblood Hawke, 1962, Don't Stop the Carnival, 1965, The Winds of War, 1971, War and Remembrance, 1978, Inside, Outside, 1985 (Washingtonian Book award 1986), (dramas) The Traitor, 1949, The Caine Mutiny Court-Martial, 1953, (comedy) Nature's Way, 1957, (non-fiction) This is My God, 1959, (screenplays for TV serials) The Winds of War, 1983, War and Remembrance, 1986. Trustee Coll. of V.I., 1961-69; bd. dirs. Washington Nat. Symphony, 1969-71, Kennedy Ctr. Prodns., 1974-75. Exec. officer U.S.S. Southard USNR, 1942-46, PTO. Recipient Richard H. Fox prize, 1934, Columbia U. medal for Excellence, 1952, Alexander Hamilton medal, 1980, U. Calif.-Berkeley medal, 1984, Golden Plate award Am. Acad. Achievement, 1986, USN Meml. Found. 'Lone Sailor' award, 1987, Yad Vashem KaZetnik award, 1990. Mem. Naval Res. Assn., Dramatists Guild, Authors Guild, Internat. Platform Assn. (Ralph Waldo Emerson award 1981), PEN. Jewish. Clubs: Bohemian (San Francisco); Cosmos, Metropolitan (Washington); Century Assn. (N.Y.C.). Office: care BSW Literary Agy 3255 N St NW Washington DC 20007

WOZENCRAFT, SHARON ANNE, minister; b. Lubbock, Tex., Apr. 19, 1945; d. W. T. and Frances Geraldine (Ball) W.; m. Gary Lynn Ries, July 4, 1963 (div. Apr. 1974); children: Krista Lynn Buster, Tanya Michele Bouwman; m. George Nelson Thompson, Nov. 19, 1989. AA in Design, Chgo. Sch. of Design, 1968; MTh, Rhema Bible Tng. Ctr., 1984; BA in Sociology summa cum laude, Northwestern State U., Taalequah, Okla., 1986; MDiv, Boston U., 1989. Ordained to ministry, Christian Ch., 1984, Meth. Ch., 1985; lic. minister, 1982. News reporter Reporter-Telegraph & Avalanche Jour., Lubbock and Midland, Tex., 1962-65; adminstr. Heritage Acad., Midland, 1965-67; news dir. Sta. KKKK, Midland, 1967-68; owner, designer Total Interiors of Tex., Lubbock, 1969-75; dir. Manasseh Mission, Lubbock, 1972-79; assoc. pastor Our Lord's Bible Ch., Oklahoma City, 1979-82; pastor Maranatha Fellowship, Broken Arrow, Okla., 1982-84, United Meth. Ch., Porter, Okay and Hulbert, Okla., 1984-86, East Natick United Meth. Ch., Natick, Mass., 1987—; prof. Trinity Bible Inst., Lubbock, 1976-80, Faith Bible Inst., Oklahoma City, 1981-82; ministerial mem. Natick Alcohol & Drug Adv. Coun., 1990—; trustee Bright Beginning Day Care, Natick, 1990—. Author: The Way of Truth, 1970, God's Grace & Human Will, 1989; contbr. articles to profl. jours. Active Citizens' Com. on Housing, Midland, 1975, Task Force on Flood Relief, Okay, Okla., 1986, Alliance for the Mentally Ill, Mass., 1987-89; bd. dirs. Arthritis Found., Midland, 1969-79. Okla. State Regents scholar Tulsa State Coll., 1984, Northeastern State U., 1985-87, Wesley scholar Boston U., 1987-90, Warren Found. scholar, 1989-90. Mem. AAUW, Natick Clergy Assn. (chair 1990—, co-host TV show 1988—), AAUW, Am. Assn. Ret. Persons, Evang. Women's Caucus, Alpha Chi. Democrat. Home: 2 Keane Rd Natick MA 01760 Office: East Natick United Meth Ch 28 Wellesley Rd Natick MA 01760 *That any of us should suppose that what we know is applicable to all other persons is preposterous presumption. What I know is of far less importance than the recognition of my own ignorance and my willingness to learn. There is no shame in ignorance, only in the arrogance which refuses to acknowledge it and is unwilling to remedy the lack. Life is ongoing change; learning is one form of that change, and that which refuses change ceases to live, choosing instead extinction.*

WREGE, HANS-THEO, religious education educator; b. Bad Gandersheim, Germany, Nov. 16, 1934; s. Hans and Marie (Elger) W.; m. Ilse Dithmar, Aug. 30, 1962; children—Hans-Ulrich, Wolf-Reinhard, Antje. Abitur Kamen, Westfalen, Germany, 1954; I Theol. Examen, U. Göttingen, Germany, 1959, Promotion, 1964; II Theol. Examen, Landeskirchenamt, Wolfenbüttel, Germany, 1961; Habilitation, U. Kiel, Germany, 1976. Pastor Lutheran Ch. Germany, 1959-82, clergyman and adult edn. leader, 1970-80; tchr. Schleswig-Holstein, Germany, 1981-82; prof. Pädagogische Hochschule Kiel, 1982—. Author, editor: Exegesis of New Testament/Religious Education; Ü berlieferungsgeschichte der Bergpredigt, 1968; Gestalt des Evangeliums, 1978; Wirkungsgeschichte des Evangeliums, 1982; Das Sondergut des Matthäusevangeliums, 1991. Cons. Hermann-Ehlers Akademie Kiel, 1982. Home: Dachsbau 13,, D-2380 Schleswig Federal Republic of Germany Office: Pädagogische Hochschule Kiel,, Olshausenstr 75,, 2300 Kiel Federal Republic of Germany

WREN, JOE RICHARD, minister; b. Gaffney, S.C., Apr. 12, 1944; s. John Everette and Mary B. Lanche (Petty) W.; m. Kaye Diane Patterson, Aug. 14, 1965; children: Beth, Joey, Clary. BA, Winthrop Coll., 1970; MDiv, Southeastern Bapt. Sem., 1973; DD, So. Bapt. Sem., 1979. Pastor Pine Grove Bapt. Ch., Clover, S.C., 1966-71; pastor Union View Bapt. Ch., Franklinton, N.C., 1971-74, Belmont Bapt. Ch., Columbia, S.C., 1974-77, Broadway Bapt. Ch., Maryville, Tenn., 1977-82, 1st Bapt. Ch., Sevierville, Tenn., 1982-90, Summerville (S.C.) Bapt. Ch., 1990—; moderator Sevier County Bapt. Assn., Sevierville, Tenn., 1986-88. Mem. Child Abuse Rev. Team, Sevierville, 1984—, Drop-out Task Force, Sevier County, Tenn., 1986—; bd. dirs. Tenn. Adult Homes, 1982-83. Mem. Personnel Com. for Baptist (chmn. 1984—), Tenn. Bapt. Conv. (exec. bd. 1983—), Rotary. Avocations: golf, walking.

WREN, JOHN E., minister; b. Gaffney, S.C., Nov. 19, 1939; s. John E. and Mary Blanch (Petty) W.; Joyce Cash, Sept. 4, 1960; children: Jeff, Joel, Joy. AA, Gardner-Webb Coll., 1960; BA, Limestone Coll., 1962; BD, Luther Rice Theol. Sem., 1968, ThD, 1972. Ordained to ministry So. Bapt. Conv. Min. Rose Hill Bapt. Ch., Texarkana, Tex., 1968-72, Calvary Bapt. ch., Tulsa, 1972-76, 1st Bapt. Ch., Maryville, Tenn., 1976-82, Forest Park Bapt. Ch., Joplin, Mo., 1982—; chmn. Four States Youth Congress, Texarkana; mem. exec. bd. Tex. Bapt. Conv., 1989—; mem. budget com. Chilhowee Bapt. Assn., Maryville, Tenn., Youth and Bapt. student Union; evangelism chmn. Spring River Bapt. Assn., Joplin; chmn. com. on Conv. Coms., Mo. Bapt. Conv. Author: Echoes from the Pulpit: Psalms 23, 1977, How to Get to Heaven, 1984. Mem. pastor's adv. com. E. Tex. Bapt. Coll.; bd. dirs. Lake LaVon Encampment. Mem. Grapevine (Tex.) Ministerial Alliance, Mount Vernon (Tex.) Ministerial Alliance, Blount County Ministerial Alliance, Rehoboth (Tex.) Bapt. Assn. (moderator), Mo. Bapt. Pastors' Conf. (sec.-treas. 1988). Avocations: jogging, hunting, travel, golf, reading. Home: 3406 Silver Creek Rd Joplin MO 64804

WREN, PETER, minister; b. Mulga, Ala., June 3, 1949; s. David and Gertrude (Densmore) W.; m. Carol Louise Luter, June 28, 1969; children: Kathy, Lenora Peter Jr., Christopher, Sharon. AA, Jeffersosn State Jr. Coll., Pinson, Ala., 1974; BS, U. Ala., 1977, MA, 1981. Ordained to ministry Ch. of God in Christ, 1972; cert. elem. and spl. edn. tchr., Ala. Youth motivator Freewill Ch. of God in Christ, Hueytown, Ala., 1962-72; co-pastor Besemer (Ala.) No. 1 Ch. of God in Christ, 1972-78; sr. pastor East Birmingham (Ala.) Ch. of God in Christ, 1978—, pres. bd. govs., 1990—; chmn. fin., treas. 2d Jurisdiction, Ch. of Christ in God, Ala., 1980—. Author: Things Believers Must Know, 1985. With USAF, 1967-71. Recipient cert. of recognition The Ala. Ch. News, 1987, Outstanding Leadership award Ch. of God in Christ Ministerial Staff, 1990. Mem. Nat. Elder's Coun. Home: 1310 32d St N Birmingham AL 35234 Office: East Birmingham Ch of God in Christ 900 39th St N Birmingham AL 35222

WRENN, WILLIAM JAMES, JR., minister; b. Hillsborough, N.C., Feb. 5, 1932; s. William James Sr. and Eugenia Lee (Burroughs) W.; m. Rayma Rebecca Hedgecock, Aug. 2, 1970. BA, U. N.C., 1955; MDiv, Union Theol. Sem., 1958, D in Ministry, 1974. Ordained to ministry Presbyn. Ch., 1958. Minister Trinity Presbyn. Ch., Chester, S.C., 1958-61, Griers-Pleasant Presbyn. Ch., Leasburg and Yanceyville, N.C., 1961-66, Milton-Red House Presbyn. Ch., Milton and Semora, N.C., 1966-69, Brentwood Presbyn. Ch., High Point, N.C., 1969—. Vol. Hospice of Piedmont, High Point, 1984—; chaplain assoc. High Point Regional Hosp., 1978—; scoutmaster Boy Scouts Am., Milton, 1967; blood program dir. ARC, Chester, 1960-61; bd. dirs. High Point Drug Action Coun., 1974-77. Mem. Salem Presbytery, Lions (bd. dirs. 1975-78, tailtwister 1978, chaplain 1969-78). Democrat. Avocations: fishing, hunting, walking, painting. Home: 2031 Wesley Dr High Point NC 27260 Office: Brentwood Presbyn Ch 1710 E Green Dr High Point NC 27260

WRIGHT, ARDIS RUTH, minister; b. Dell Rapids, S.D., Jan. 10, 1939; d. A. Edwin and Leonora (Staven) Thoreson; m. Donald Wright, May 4, 1963; children: Daniel, David, Sarah. BS, Augustana Coll., Sioux Falls, S.D., 1961; MDiv, Luther Northwestern Sem., St. Paul, 1983. Ordained to ministry, Am. Luth. Ch. Interim pastor Luth. Ch. Peace, Maplewood, Minn., 1985; chaplain Lynblomsten Nursing Care Ctr., St. Paul, 1985-86; interim pastor various chs., 1986—; sales mgr. Interactive Computer Tech., Lake Elmo, Minn., 1988—; bd. dirs. S.E. Asian Ministries, St. Paul, 1984-87. Author: Classics and Possibilities, 1990. Mem. Interim Ministry Network, Zonta (bd. dirs. 1989-90). Home: 2069 Lake Elmo Ave Lake Elmo MN 55042

WRIGHT, CHARLES EDWARD, minister; b. Clintwood, Va., Feb. 15, 1953; s. James Garfield and Mamie (Mullens) W.; m. Deborah Long, June 13, 1975; children: Aaron, Jordan. BA in Bus., Clinch Valley Coll., 1975; MDiv, Anderson U., 1980. Pastor South River Park Ch. of God, Fairhope, Ala., 1980-83, First Ch. of God, Knoxville, Tenn., 1983-87, The Grace Gathering, Knoxville, 1987—. Pres. Nat. Fedn. for Decency, Knoxville, 1984-86.

WRIGHT, CLOYD, clergyman; b. Glenwood, Ark., July 14, 1922; s. Joel S. and Retter (Grant) W.; m. Mildred Marie Short, Dec. 1941; 1 child, Patsy Ann Podbevsek. Ordained to ministry American Baptist Association, 1949. Pastor chs., Ark., N.Mex., 1955-58; evangelistic work Ark., N.Mex., Okla., Tex., 1956-58; missionary, Carlsbad, N.Mex., 1955-58; founder 1st Missionary Bapt. Ch., Carlsbad, 1956; pastor Mt. Moriah Missionary Bapt. Ch., Bonnerdale, Ark., 1980—; chmn. local assn. of 20 Missionary Bapt. chs. in west central Ark. Sec.-treas. Mt. Tabor Cemetery Assn., Montgomery County, 1970—.

WRIGHT, DONALD KENNETH, clergyman; b. Woodruff, S.C., June 29, 1951; s. James Melvin and Margaret Rebecca (Goodwin) W.; m. Shirley Mae Biggerstaff, Aug. 13, 1972; children: Jonathan Matthew, David Benjamin, Melanie Elizabeth. BA, Limestone Coll., 1974; M.R.E., So. Bapt. Theol. Sem., 1976. Ordained to ministry So. Baptist Ch., 1979. Minister mus. Cherokee Ave. Bapt. Mission, Gaffney, S.C., 1971-74; children's dir. Deer Park Bapt. Ch., Louisville, 1975-76; minister edn., youth Florence Bapt. Ch., Forest City, N.C., 1976-79; minister edn. First Baptist Ch., Rockingham, N.C., 1979-81; minister edn. to youth and coll. Wieuca Rd. Bapt. Ch., Atlanta, 1981-86; Christian edn. cons. Atlanta Bapt. Assn., Atlanta, 1986-87; dir. devel. Habersham Christian Learning Ctr., Cornelia, Ga., 1987—. Editor Jour. for Weekday Religious Edn., 1989—. Tchr. Student Assn., 1988-90; scoutmaster troop 24 Boy Scouts of Am.. 1988—. Mem. Habersham County Community Coord. Com., Nat. Assn. Released Time Christian Edn. (nat. dir.), Ga. Assn. Released Time Christian Edn. (sec. 1989—), Am. Assn. Counseling and Devel., Nat. Career Devel. Assn., Assn. for Supervision and Curriculum Devel, Am. Assn. Family Counselors, Internat. Soc. Pres.' Non-Profit Orgns., Am. Assn. Christian Counselors, Assn. Religious and Value Issues in Counseling, Am. Assn. Counseling and Devel., NE Ga. Peace Council, Inst. Motivational Living (cert. behavioral analysis, 1987). Avocations: reading, painting, coin collecting, music, weight training. Home: 111 Jones St Cornelia GA 30531

WRIGHT, FAYE See DAYA MATA, SRI

WRIGHT, JAMES EDWARD, religion educator; b. Astoria, Oreg., Jan. 29, 1956; s. James Edward and Virginia Lucille (Doyle) W.; m. Keeley Jan Williams, Sept. 25, 1976; 1 child, Angela Jan. MA, Western Sem., 1982, Brandeis U., 1987; PhD, Brandeis U., 1991. Youth minister Gresham (Oreg.) Community Ch., 1977-81; prof. Western Sem., Portland, Oreg., 1987-90, U. Ariz., Tucson, 1990—. Author: (with others) Pseudo-Ezekiel, 1991. J.H. Thayer fellowship Am. Schs. of Oriental Rsch., 1986-87, Meml. Found. for Jewish Culture fellowship Hebrew U., 1985-86, Hirshfield fellowship, Brandeis U., 1982-89. Mem. Soc. Bibl. Lit., Am. Acad. Religion, Assn. for Jewish Studies, Nat. Assn. Profs. Hebrew. Office: U Ariz Dept Near Eastern Studies Tucson AZ 85721

WRIGHT, JAMES HOUSTON, evangelist, marriage and family counselor; b. Oak Ridge, Tenn., Oct. 10, 1954; s. Olney Houston and Nora Ann (Waters) W.; m. Deborah Gail Foote, Dec. 29, 1973; children: Daniel, Elizabeth, Richard. BA, David Lipscomb Coll., Nashville, 1976; MA, Middle Tenn. State U., Murfreesboro, 1981. Intern minister Mayfair Ch. of Christ, Huntsville, Ala., 1974, Ch. of Christ, Williston, S.D., 1975; evangelist Sycamore Chapel Ch. of Christ, Ashland City, Tenn., 1975-81; pvt. practice marriage and family counseling Ashland City, Tenn., 1981, Indpls., 1982—; evangelist N. Cen. Ch. of Christ, Indpls., 1982-88; sr. evangelist Woodstock (Ga.) Ch. of Christ, 1988—; psychol. cons. Cheatham County Bd. Edn., Ashland City, 1979-81; dir. Wabashi Valley Youth Camp, Terre Haute, Ind., 1982—; co-dir. Mid-Am. Evang. Workshop, Indpls., 1984, dir., 1985. Chaplain Ashland City Civitan, 1980, pres. 1981. Recipient Best Sermon award Cheatham Soil Conservation Dist., 1976; named one of Outstanding Young Men of Am., U.S. Jaycees, 1980, 83, 85. Mem. Ch. of Christ. Lodge: Lions (chaplain Indpls. club 1983-84). Avocations: reading, woodworking, writing, camping. Home: 128 Creekview Dr Woodstock GA 30188 Office: Woodstock Ch Christ PO Box 507 Woodstock GA 30188

WRIGHT, JEREMIAH ALVESTA, JR., minister; b. Phila., Sept. 22, 1941; s. Jeremiah A. and Mary Elizabeth (Henderson) W.; m. Ramah E. Bratton, Oct. 22, 1989; 1 child, Jamila; children from previous marriage: Janet Marie Wright Hall, Jeri Lynn Wright Haynes, Nikol Reed, Nathan Reed. AB, Howard U., 1968, MA, 1969; MA in Religion, U. Chgo., 1974; D Ministry, United Theol. Sem., Dayton, Ohio, 1990. Ordained to ministry Am. Bapt. Ch., 1967. Asst. pastor Mt. Calvary Bapt. Ch., Rockville, Md., 1967-69; interim pastor Zion Bapt. Ch., Hagerstown, Md., 1969; asst. pastor Beth Eden Bapt. Ch., Chgo., 1969-71; pastor Trinity United Ch. of Christ, Chgo., 1972—; rsch. asst. Am. Assn. Theol. Schs., Chgo., 1970-72; exec. dir. Chgo. Ctr. for Black Religious Studies, 1974-75; adj. prof. Chgo. Theol. Sem., 1974-75, Cath. Theol. Union, 1975; lectr. Chgo. Cluster of Theol. Schs., 1975—; mem. com. for racial justice United Ch. of Christ, 1976-80, ecumenical strategy com. Ill. Conf., 1975-76, resolutions com., 1973-74, urban mins. com. task force, 1975-76. Author: God Will Answer Prayer, 1974, (songs) Jesus Is His Name, 1975; contbr. articles to profl. jours. Dir. Creative Writing Workshop, Chgo., 1969-70; proposal writer, editor Dropout Prevention Program Chgo. Bd. Edn., 1971-72; bd. dirs. Malcolm X Sch. Nursing, 1974-84, Office of Ch. in Soc., United Ch. Christ, 1974-76. Recipient commendations Pres. of U.S., 1965-66; Howard U. grad. fellow, 1968-69, Rockefeller fellow, 1970-72. Mem. Ch. Fedn. Greater Chgo., Emergency Sch. Aid Act, Urban Ministerial Alliance, Ill. Conf. Chs., Mins. for Racial and Social Justice, United Black Christians, Omega Psi Phi, Alpha Kappa Mu. Home: 9167 S Pleasant St Chicago IL 60620 Office: Trinity United Ch of Christ 400 W 95th St Chicago IL 60628 *If there is one thing in this world that God's children need to learn, it is that being different does not mean that one is deficient!.*

WRIGHT, JOHN CHARLES, minister; b. Highland Park, Mich., May 12, 1941; s. John Hershey and Dorothy (Grisby) W.; m. Patricia Ann Beery, Aug. 15, 1964; children: James Patrick, Rebecca Sue, Andrew Stephen. BSEE, Lawrence Tech. U., 1970; A of Religious Edn., Gt. Lakes Bible Sch., 1981; postgrad., Great Lakes Bible Sch., 1981. Ordained to ministry Chs. of Christ, 1980. Interim min. Eastmoreland Ch. of Christ, Oreg., 1981; min. Sanktown Christian Ch., Mill Creek, Ind., 1981-86, First Christian Ch., Knox, Ind., 1986—; min. Sumit Prison Farm, Sauk Town Christian Ch., La Porte, Ind., 1981-86; asst. chaplain, La Porte Hosp., 1982-86. Bd. dirs. Community Guidance for Youth, Knox, 1991. Mem. Kiwanis. Home: 106 N McGill Knox IN 46534 Office: First Christian Ch 301 S Pearl Knox IN 46534

WRIGHT, JOHN MURRAY, minister; b. New Orleans, La., Nov. 22, 1951; s. Perry J. and Edna (Blansett) W.; m. Susan Gayle Bougere, Aug. 7, 1971; children: Adam David, Aaron Jacob, Amanda Jean. A in Div., New Orleans Bapt. Theol. Sem., 1987; BS, Liberty U., 1990; postgrad., Covington Theol. Sem., 1991—. Ordained to ministry So. Bapt. Conv., 1986. Pastor Trinity Bapt. Ch., Hammond, La., 1986-87, Punta Gorda, Fla., 1988--; dir. of evangelism Peace River Bapt. Assn., Punta Gorda, Fla. 1989--; arrangements chmn. Charlotte County Evang. Min. Assn., Port Charlotte, Fla. 1989--. Republican. Southern Baptist. Home: 5331 Grovewood Circle Punta Gorda FL 33982 Office: Trinity Baptist Church 11234 Royal Rd Punta Gorda FL 33955 *Today, people need an anchor that will hold steadfast in the treacherous winds and turbulent currents of this ever changing age. The Bible is the Word of God and says of itself that it will abide forever. It is my purpose not only to study the Bible as an academic exercise, but to apply it's truths, it's principles, and it's precepts to the lives of men. The study and application of this word is worthy of my life's devotion, for the apostle Paul wrote: "And that from a child thou hast known the holy scriptures, which are able to make thee wise unto salvation throuth faith which is in Christ Jesus." (II Timothy 3:15 KJV).*

WRIGHT, LATHAM EPHRAIM, JR., minister; b. Curitiba, Parana, Brazil, Oct. 16, 1925; came to U.S. 1945; s. Latham E. and Maggie Belle (Miller) W.; m. Roberta Adeline Shaw, July 23, 1949; children: Kathleen Wright Banner, Elizabeth Wright Schoenfeld, Chicke Wright Fitzgerald. BA, U. Ozarks, Clarksville, Ark., 1947; MDiv, McCormick Theol. Sem., Chgo., 1950; CPE, St. Luke's Hosp., Milw., 1974. Ordained to ministry Presbyn. Ch. (U.S.A.), 1950. Prof. Presbyn. Thel. Sem., Lisbon, Portugal, 1950-55; pastor Harrison County Parish, Elizabeth, Ind., 1956-58; pastor First Presbyn. Ch., Rushville, Ind., 1958-65, Greenfield, Ind., 1965-70; pastor Cleveland Ave. Presbyn. Ch., West Allis, Wis., 1970-73; ret.; chaplain St. Luke's Hosp., Milw., 1973-74. Chmn. bd. Westminster Community Ctr., New Castle, Ind., 1960-65, ARC, Greenfield, Ind., 1966-69; mem. com. Coop. West Side Assn., Milw., 1976-88. Mem. Lions. Home: 50 Whitcomb Cir # 1 Madison WI 53711 *Faithfulness in striving to accomplish a dream of building a world community where God's justice and compassion prevail, is better than being caught in the performance trap which is success oriented. We are inspired by the vision we hope to see fulfilled.*

WRIGHT, MARJORIE ANN, minister; b. Olean, N.Y., Dec. 16, 1940; d. Clyde Henry and Pauline Ruth (Skinner) Day; m. Eugene Allen Wright, May 24, 1969; children: Sherrie Elizabeth, Pamelyn Sue. Diploma, Jamestown (N.Y.) Sch. Nursing, 1961; BRE, Toronto (Ont., Can.) Bible Coll., 1970; cert. in respiratory therapy, Boston Coll. Extension, Lynn, Mass., 1972; MDiv, San Francisco Theol. Sem., San Anselmo, Calif., 1980. Ordained to ministry Presbyn. Ch.; cert. evang. tchr., N.Y. Interim min. St. Stephen's Presbyn. Ch., North Highland, Calif., 1979-80; assoc. min. Carmichael (Calif.) Presbyn. Ch., 1980-86; youth min. 1st United Meth. Ch., Indio, Calif., 1988—; Mem., min. Sierra Mission Presbytery, Sacramento, 1980—. Author: Programmmed to Die, 1991; pub.: Struggle to Live. Mem. team Marine Med. Mission, B.C., Can., 1965. Home: 511-780 Ave Villa La Quinta CA 92253 Office: 1st United Meth Ch 45-501 Deglet Noor St Indio CA 92201

WRIGHT, ROBERT BRADLEY, religion educator; b. Jersey City, Apr. 6, 1934; s. Leonard and Marion (Macdonald) W.; m. Mary Lynette Halterman, Dec. 27, 1956; children: Kevin, Karen. BD, Drake U., 1960; STM, Hartford Sem. Found., 1964, PhD, 1966. Ordained to ministry United Ch. of Christ. Lectr. Boston U., 1966-67; asst. prof. Gettysburg (Pa.) Coll., 1967-69; adj. prof. Wilson Coll., Chambersburg, Pa., 1969-72; assoc. prof. dept. religion Temple U., Phila., 1972—, assoc. dean for grad. affairs, 1984-86, chmn. dept., 1986-90; mem. archaeol. staff Gezer excavations Harvard U. and Hebrew Union Coll., 1966-71. Maps and photography editor Westminster Dictionary of the Bible, 1969; editor, The Psalms of Solomon. Mem. Moorestown Twp. (N.J.) Sch. Bd., 1975-80. Mem. Soc. Bibl. Lit., Cath. Bibl. Assn., Am. Acad. Religion (exec. assoc. 1969-72). Office: Temple U Dept Religion Box CD10 Philadelphia PA 19122

WRIGHT, RONALD EDWARD, clergyman, educator; b. Port Elizabeth, S. Africa, Aug. 27, 1930; s. Cecil Valentine and Isabel Jacoba (Barnard) W.; came to U.S., 1970; diploma S. Africa Bible Coll., 1956; B.A., Central Bible Coll., Springfield, Mo., 1960; M.R.E., Central Bapt. Sem., 1963; M.Div., N.W. Bapt. Theol. Coll., 1967; m. Barbara Joy Kolo Colling, Feb. 4, 1956; 1 dau., Catherine Joy. Evangel. and pastoral ministry, S. Africa, 1946-58, England, 1958, U.S., 1958-60; ordained to ministry Assemblies of God, 1962; assoc. pastor, minister edn., Toronto, Ont., Can., 1960-63; dir. summer children's camps, Apsley, Ont., 1960-63; prof. religion, dean, v.p. Western Pentecostal Bible Coll., North Vancouver, B.C., Can., 1963-70; prof. N.T. lang. and lit. Central Bible Coll., Springfield, 1970-75; prof. religion So. Calif. Coll., Costa Mesa, 1975—; adj. faculty Melodyland Sch. Theology, Anaheim, Calif., 1976-82; sr. adj. in N.T., Am. Christian Theol. Sem., Anaheim, Calif., 1982—. Mem. Soc. Pentecostal Studies, Evang. Theol. Soc. Office: So Calif Coll 55 Fair Dr Costa Mesa CA 92626

WRIGHT, RONALD TODD, minister; b. Gadsden, Ala., June 8, 1964; s. Alfred William and Villa Dean (Clark) W.; m. Lisa Joy Wood, June 12, 1982; 1 child, Hannah Elizabeth. Student, Liberty U. Cert. Evangelism Explosion III, 1987. Assoc. pastor Riverside Bapt. Ch., Tallapoosa, Ga., 1984, One Way Bapt. Ch., Augusta, Ga., 1984-86; assoc. pastor Mt. Zion Bapt. Ch., Jonesboro, Ga., 1986-88, sr. pastor, 1988—; pres. Mt. Zion Christian Acad., Jonesboro, 1988—. Mem. Community Adv. Com., Mt. Zion High Sch., Morrow, Ga., 1989—. Recipient Appreciation award Ga. Bapt. Conv., 1987, Costa Rican Bapt. Assn., San Jose, Costa Rica, 1990, Baptisms award Ga. Bapt. Conv., Mt. Zion Bapt. Ch., 1989. Mem. So. Bapt. Conv., Ga. Bapt. Conv., South Metro Assn. (adminstrv. bd. 1988—). Office: Mt Zion Baptist Church 7102 Mt Zion Blvd Jonesboro GA 30236

WRIGHT, STEVEN RANDALL, minister; b. Griffin, Ga., Aug. 9, 1947; s. Garnett A. and Ellis (Boyt) W.; m. Patricia Anne Wright, Jan. 21, 1967; children: Christopher, Kevin. BA, Cen. Wesleyan Coll., 1969; postgrad., No. Bapt. Theol. Sem., 1976-78. Ordained to ministry Wesleyan Ch., 1969. Min. youth and music 1st Wesleyan Ch., Westminster, S.C., 1965-66, Pickens View Wesleyan Ch., Pickens, S.C., 1966-67; pastor Wesley Chapel, Greensboro, Ga., 1967-70; sr. pastor 1st Wesleyan Ch., Savannah, Ga., 1970-73, Farnham St. Wesleyan Ch., Galesburg, Ill., 1973-76, Wesleyan Community Ch., Oak Lawn, Ill., 1976—; dist. pres. Wesleyan Youth, Ga., 1969-71; treas. So. area Wesleyan Youth, 1970-73; mem. bd. ministerial standing, Ga. and Ill., 1970-88; sec., mem. adminstrn. bd. Ga. dist. Wesleyan Ch., Inc., 1969-73, adminstrn. bd. Ill. dist., 1976-80, 88; chmn. Ill. dist. bd. Evangelism and Ch. Growth, 1988—, sec., 1988—; chmn. bds. mission and evangelism Bd. Christian Edn., Ga. dist., 1970-72. Contbr. articles to profl. jours. Pres. local Young Reps., S.C., 1968; founder New Life, 1974—, Men Alive Prayer Breakfast, 1976—, Orland Park Community Ch., 1980, HOPES, 1977—. Mem. Nat. Assn. Evangls., So. Mins. Alliance, Kiwanis (various spiritual aims coms. Oak Lawn club 1977-84, Outstanding Achievement award 1979). Home: 10340 S Kolin Ave Oak Lawn IL 60453 Office: Wesleyan Community Ch 8844 S Austin Ave Oak Lawn IL 60453 *The real sanctuary for ministry is our life, not a structure made from mortar, wood and glass. Worshipping and serving our living Lord daily causes effective ministry.*

WROTENBERY, CARL RICHARD, library director, minister; b. Mt. Pleasant, Tex., Dec. 14, 1929; s. P.H. and Gertrude E. (Cates) W.; m. Julia M. Winn, July 27, 1952; children: Richard Alan (dec.), Martha Ellen. BA, Baylor U., 1951; MDiv, Southwestern Bapt. Theol. Sem., 1954, ThD, 1964; MLS, U. Tex., 1969. Ordained to ministry So. Bapt. Conv., 1954. Pastor various Bapt. chs. Tex. and Kans., 1954-60; libr., prof. religion U. Corpus Christi, 1962-68, dean faculty, 1968-72; libr. Corpus Christi State U., 1972-80; dir. libr. Houston Bapt. U., 1980-84; dir. librs. Southwestern Bapt. Theol. Sem., Ft. Worth, 1984—. Contbr., presenter articles, workshops in field. Mem. So. Bapt. Librs. Assn. (pres. 1991—), Tex. Bapt. Hist. Soc. (instl. sponsor 1984—). Home: 6908 Trail Lake Dr Fort Worth TX 76133 Office: Southwestern Bapt Theol Sem Roberts-Bowld Librs PO Box 22000 Fort Worth TX 76122-0490

WUCHTER, MICHAEL DAVID, pastor; b. Atlantic City, Feb. 16, 1946; s. Robert Zimmerman and Eleanor Joyce (Freed) W.; m. Shirley Ann Dyer, Aug. 16, 1969; children: Andrew, J. Kirsten. BA, Wittenberg U., 1968; M of Div., The Luth. Theol. Sem., 1972; D of Ministry, Princeton Theol. Sem., 1983. Ordained to ministry Luth. Ch., 1972. Pastor Resurrection Luth. Ch., Hamilton Sq., N.J., 1972-79; pastor to the univ. Wittenberg U., Springfield, Ohio, 1979—; pres. Trenton (N.J.) Campus Ministry, 1974-79; chaplain Lakeside (Ohio) Luth. Conf., 1980; chaplain to 75th anniversary conf. Luth. Ednl. Conf. N.Am., Washington, 1985; participant summer seminar Fulbright-Hays Faculty Devel., New Delhi, 1984; bd. dirs. Clrk Co. Children's Trust Fund. Author: (study guide) Disarmament in a Nuclear Age, 1983, (contbg.) In Praise of Preaching, 1984, Religions of India and Human Values, 1985; author numerous book revs. Pres., co-founder The Nottingham Recreation Ctr. for the Physically Ltd., Mercer County, N.J., 1979; bd. dirs. Springfield Pastoral Counseling Ctr., 1983, Specialized Ministries Council, Springfield, 1985, Springfield Peace Sch., 1988; bd. dirs. community adv. bd. Teen Suicide Prevention Project, Springfield, 1985, chmn., 1988. Fulbright-Hay Faculty Devel. Program grantee, 1984. Mem. Am. Acad. Religion, Nat. Assn. Coll. and Univ. Chaplains, Luth. Coll. Chaplains Assn. Democrat. Home: 710 Riverside Dr Springfield OH 45504 Office: Wittenberg U Springfield OH 45501

WUELLNER, WILHELM HERMANN, religion educator; b. Bochum, Fed. Republic of Germany, Feb. 21, 1927; came to U.S., 1954; s. Wilhelm Georg and Emma Henriette (Beckmann) W.; m. Flora May Slosson, May 28, 1954; children: Christine Collins, Virginia Henriette, Lucy Elizabeth. PhD, U. Chgo., 1958. Asst. prof. Mission House Theol. Seminary, Sheboygan, Wis., 1957-58, Grinnell (Iowa) Coll., 1958-60; assoc. prof. Hartford (Conn.) Seminary Found., 1960-65; prof. New Testament Pacific Sch. Religion and Grad. Theol. Union, Berkeley, Calif., 1965—; mission developer Luth. Bd. Home Mission, Amana Colony, Iowa, 1958-60; coll. chaplain Grinnell Coll., 1958-60. Author: Meaning of Fishers of Men, 1967, (with R. Leslie) The Surprising Gospel, 1984, (with H. Perelmuter) Paul the Jew, 1990; editor: Colloquies of Center for Hermenentical Studies, 1970-83. Am. Assn. Theol. Schs. fellow, 1970-71, NEH fellow, 1977-78, Luth. Brotherhood fellow, 1984-85. Mem. Soc. Bibl. Lit. (pres. Pacific Coast sect. 1968-69), Cath. Bibl. Assn., Studiorum Novi Testamenti Societas, Dolger Inst. für Antike und Christentum, Internat. Soc. for History Rhetoric. Office: Pacific Sch Religion 1798 Scenic Berkeley CA 94709

WUERCH, HARRY, bishop. Gen. sec. Ind. Assemblies of God Can., London, Ont. Office: Independent Assemblies God, 1211 Lancaster St, London, ON Canada N5V 2L4*

WUERL, DONALD W., bishop; b. Pittsburgh, Nov. 12, 1940. Educated, Catholic U. of America, N. Am. Coll., Angelicum, Rome. Ord. priest, Roman Cath. Ch., Dec. 17, 1966, Rome. Ord. aux. bishop of Seattle, titular bishop of Rosmarkaeum, 1986, bishop of Pittsburgh, 1988—. Office: Diocese of Pittsburgh 111 Blvd of Allies Pittsburgh PA 15222

WULFEKUEHLER, EDWARD GEORGE, JR., interim minister; b. St. Louis, Apr. 28, 1928; s. Edward George and Mildred Hazel (Kanne) W.; m. Marilyn Lewis, Sept. 21, 1957 (div. Dec. 1981); children: Deborah Susan Wulfekuehler King, David Edward, Christopher Arden; m. Shirley Jean Heyne, Jan. 3, 1982. BA, Drury Coll., 1950; MDiv, Pacific Sch. Religion, 1953, D Ministry, 1977. Ordained to ministry United Ch. Christ, 1953; cert. interim minister, 1989. Min. Congl. Ch., Medford, Oreg., 1965-69; sr. min. 1st Congl. Ch., Bakersfield, Calif., 1969-80; res. chaplain advisor to chief of army chaplains Washington, 1980-84; min. Evang. United Ch. Christ, Boonville, Mo., 1984-89; interim min. United Ch. Christ, 1989—; pres., v.p. Greater Bakersfield Ministerial Assn. 1972-74, Greater Bakersfield Coun. Chs., 1973-75. Col. U.S. Army, 1976-88. Decorated Legion of Merit; recipient Disting. Svc. award, Jr. C. of C., 1962. Mem. Mil. Chaplains Assn., Res. Officers Assn., Interim Ministry Network, Order of DeMolay (Legion of Honor 1962), Shriners (chaplain 1960-89). Home: 7308 North Shore Dr Hartsburg MO 65039

WURZBURGER, WALTER SAMUEL, rabbi, philosophy educator; b. Munich, Germany, Mar. 29, 1920; s. Adolf W. and Hedwig (Tannenwald) W.; m. Naomi C. Rabinovitz, Aug. 19, 1947; children—Benjamin W., Myron I., Joshua J. BA, Yeshiva U., 1944, DD (hon.), 1987; MA, Harvard U., 1946, PhD, 1951. Ordained rabbi, 1944. Rabbi Congregation Chai Odom, Boston, 1944-53, Shaarei Shomayim Congregation, Toronto, Ont., Can., 1953-67, Shaaray Tefila Congregation, Lawrence, N.Y., 1967—; editor Tradition, N.Y.C., 1961-87; columnist Toronto Telegram, 1957-67; adj. assoc. prof. philosophy Yeshiva U., 1967-80, adj. prof., 1980—; bd. dirs. Union Orthodox Jewish Congregations Am. Editor: A Treasury of Tradition, 1967; contbg. editor Sh'ma; contbr. articles to profl. jours., chpts. to books, Ency. Judaica, Ency. of Religion, Ency of Bioethics. Mem. exec. com. United Jewish Welfare Funds of Toronto, 1965-67; past chmn. commn. on adoptions, synagogue commn., trustee Fedn. Jewish Philanthropies N.Y.; bd. dirs. Union Orthodox Jewish Congregations Am.; chmn. com. on interreligious affairs Synagogue Coun. Am., 1973-75, 83-87, pres., 1981-83, hon. pres., 1983-85; mem. interfaith com. United Community Funds of Toronto, 1960-67; v.p. synagogue commn. Fedn. Philanthropies, 1973-75; mem. nat. adv. com. United Jewish Appeal Am., 1971-78. Recipient Nat. Rabbinic Leadership award Union Orth. Jewish Congregations Am., 1983. Mem. Rabbinical Coun. Am. (past pres.), Rabbinical Coun. Can. (past pres.). Home: 138 Hards Ln Lawrence NY 11559 Office: Congregation Shaaray Tefila 25 Central Ave Lawrence NY 11559

WYATT, JOHN MARIE, principal; b. N.Y.C., Mar. 16, 1949; d. Thomas Oliver and Kornyce Lillian (Campbell) W. AA, Assumption Coll. of Sisters, Mendham, N.J., 1972; BS, Richmond Coll., 1975; MA, Villanova U., 1983. Joined Roman Catholic Ch. Tchr., vice prin., grades 6-8 St. Joseph Hill Acad., Staten Island, N.Y., 1972-79; tchr., vice prin., grades 6-8 St. Stephen of Hungary, grades 6-8, N.Y.C., 1979-81, prin., 1981-85; tchr., grades 6-8 St. Thomas the Apostle, Old Bridge, N.J., 1985-88, Cardinal Hayes High Sch., Bronx, N.Y., 1988-89; prin. St. Thomas the Apostle, Old Bridge, 1989—; del. Provincial chpt. FDC, Staten Island, 1977, 80, 83, del., liturgy coord., 1989, del., liturgy coord., steering com., Ossining, N.Y., 1986. Mem. Nat. Cath. Edn. Assn. Office: St Thomas the Apostle 333 Highway 18 Old Bridge NJ 08857

WYATT, STEPHEN THOMAS, minister; b. Gallipolis, Ohio, July 26, 1955; s. Thomas H. and Eleanor (Smith) W.; m. Vanessa Dale Ferguson, May 21, 1976; children: Andrea Dale, Jessica Leigh, Joshua David. BA, Ky. Christian Coll., 1977, M of Ministry, 1985. Evangelist Ky. Christian Coll., Garyson, Ky., 1974-75; youth minister Cen. Ch. of Christ, Portsmouth, Ohio, 1975-77; minister Northwest Ave Ch. of Christ, Tallmadge, Ohio, 1977-81, Cullen Ave. Christian Ch., Evansville, Ind., 1981—. Author: (tng. manuals) Leadership, 1985, Celebration of Marriage, 1986, Lay Evangelism, 1988; composer: Worship Music; contbr. articles to profl. jours; columnist: Evansville (Ind.) Reporter, 1988-89; speaker on WCBF, Evansville and at orgn. meetings, 1982—. Mem. N. Am. Christian Conv. (bd. dirs. 1983-85, outstanding young Am. minister, 1989), Round Lake Christian Assembly (bd. dirs. 1980-81). Office: Cullen Ave Christian Ch 621 Cullen Ave Evansville IN 47715

WYCKOFF, JOHN WESLEY, religion educator; b. Mooreland, Okla., Mar. 8, 1944; s. John Wayne and Loretta Jane (Kelso) W.; m. Myrna Loene Green, June 7, 1969; children: Ryan Keith, Bethany Dawn. BS, Southwestern State U., Weatherford, Okla., 1966, Southwestern Assemblies of God, Waxhachie, Tex., 1970; MA, So. Nazarene U., 1972; PhD in Religion, Baylor U., 1990. Ordained to ministry Assemblies of God, 1972. Pastor Assemblies of God, Humboldt, Kans., 1972-76; prof. Southwestern Assemblies of God Coll., 1976—, chmn. ch. ministries div., 1983—, dir. Christian svc., 1976-80; local ch. leader Univ. Assemblies of God, Waxahachie, 1976—. Mem. Am. Assn. Bible Colls. (hon.), Soc. for Pentecostal Studies, Delta Epsilon Chi (hon.). Office: Southwestern Assemblies of God Coll 1200 Sycamore St Waxahachie TX 75165 *Strength and courage for life come as we give of ourselves to strengthen and encourage others.*

WYLE, EWART HERBERT, clergyman; b. London, Sept. 12, 1904; s. Edwin and Alice Louise (Durman) W.; B.A., U. Louisville, 1930; B.D., Lexington Theol. Sem., 1933; postgrad. Louisville Presbyn. Theol. Sem., Temple U., 1933-35; D.D., Tex. Christian U., 1953; m. Prudence Harper, June 12, 1959; 1 son, Ewart Herbert. Ordained to ministry Christian Ch., 1935; pastor First Ch., Palestine, Tex., 1935-37, First Ch., Birmingham, Ala., 1937-41, First Ch., Tyler, Tex., 1944-54, Country Club Ch., Kansas City, Mo., 1954-59; minister Torrey Pines Ch., La Jolla, Calif., 1959-79, minister emeritus, 1979—. Bd. dirs. Scripps Meml. Hosp., pres., 1980-81. Served as chaplain, maj., AUS, 1941-44. Mem. Mil. Order World Wars, Am. Legion, Tau Kappa Epsilon, Pi Kappa Delta. Clubs: Masons (32 deg.), Shriners, Rotary, LaJolla Beach and Tennis. Home: 8850 LaJolla Scenic Dr N La Jolla CA 92037

WYLIE, SANFORD WILLIE, pastor; b. Poteau, Okla., Apr. 9, 1944; s. Sanford W. and Gladys Virginia (Deering) W.; m. Diana Susan Scaggs, June 2, 1973; children: Benjamin, Micah. BA, U. Tulsa, 1966; BD, Yale Divinity Sch., 1970; DMin, Vanderbilt Divinity Sch., 1984. Ordained to ministry Meth. Ch., 1971. Pastor St. Stephen's United Meth. Ch., Broken Arrow, Okla., 1970-75, Aldersgate United Meth. Ch., Del City, Okla., 1975-76; assoc. pastor Grace United Meth. Ch., Oklahoma City, 1976-79; pastor Highland Park United Meth. Ch., Stillwater, Okla., 1979-81, St. Paul's United Meth. Ch., Lawton, Okla., 1982-87, Univ. United Meth. Ch., Tulsa, 1987—; worker Iona Community, Ch. of Scotland, 1968-69; pres. Kendall-Whittier Ministry, Tulsa, 1989—. Major, chaplain Okla. Army Nat. Guard, 1976-87. Recipient Mersick Preaching prize Yale U., 1970, 1st place Kristallnacht Sermon Contest, Okla. Conf. Chs., 1988. Mem. Jaycees (treas. Broken Arrow chpt. 1972-73). Democrat. Home: 4652 S Jamestown Tulsa OK 74135-1933 Office: Univ United Meth Ch 2915 E 5th Tulsa OK 74104-3105

WYLIE, SCOTT ELWOOD, pastor; b. Carbondale, Ill., May 27, 1951; s. Elwood Kinzer and Emma Jean (Managan) W.; m. Nancy Elizbeth Witman, Dec. 17, 1977; children: Rachael Elizabeth, Sarah Spencer Witman Wylie. BS in Econs., U. Ill., 1973; M in Mgmt., Northwestern U., 1979; MDiv, Pacific Sch. of Religion, 1986. Ordained to ministry, Meth. Ch. Leadership cons. Delta Upsilon Internat. Fraternity, Indpls., 1973-74; sales engr. Honeywell Comml. Div., Lincolnwood, Ill., 1974-77; fin. analyst Datapoint Corp., San Antonio, 1979-82; assoc. pastor Ch. of the Wayfarer, Carmel, Calif., 1986-88; pastor First United Meth. Ch., DeLano, Calif., 1988—. Mem. San Antonio Symphony Opera, 1980-81; mem. chorus San Antonio Master Chorale, 1981-82, Carmel Bach Festival, 1987. Avocations: soloist, jogging, tennis, softball, photography. Office: First United Meth Ch 1002 11th Ave Delano CA 93215

WYMAN, WALTER EDWARD, JR., religion educator; b. Bangor, Maine, June 15, 1946; s. Walter E. and Barbara (Gove) W.; m. Sara C. Wyman, Sept. 7, 1968; children: Walter III, Christian, Rachel. BA, Oberlin (Ohio) Coll., 1968; MTh, U. Chgo., 1970, MA, 1973, PhD, 1980. Assoc. prof. dept. religion Whitman Coll., Walla Walla, Wash., 1982—; asst. prof. St. Olaf Coll., Northfield, Minn., 1981-82, Carleton Coll., Northfield, 1979-81; instr. Coll. Wooster (Ohio), 1978-79. Author: The Concept of Glaubenslehre, 1983. Mem. Am. Acad. Religion, Ernst Troeltsch Gesellschaft. Office: Whitman Coll Walla Walla WA 99362

WYMER, MARY ANN, youth minister; b. Dayton, Ohio, Nov. 7, 1946; d. Paul Jerome and Kathleen Mae (Zugelder) McCarthy; m. Oct. 30, 1965 (div. Sept. 1976); children: Patricia Lynn, Douglas Allen. B in Gen. Studies, U. Dayton, 1983; M in Pastoral Studies, Loyola U., New Orleans, 1988. Assoc. dir. youth ministry Archdiocese of Cin., 1980-84; youth coord. St. Catherine's Cath. Ch., Orange Park, Fla., 1984—; youth cons. Marywood Ctr. for Spirituality, Switzerland, Fla., 1990—; speaker Youth Specialties Speakers Bur., Loveland, Colo., 1989-90. Author: Peer to Peer Renew for Teens, 1986, Here I Am, 1990, The Die-Mond Bequest, 1990. Mem. Nat. Pastoral Life Ctr., Cath. Women in the Workplace, Mensa. Office: St Catherines Parish 1649 Kingsley Ave Orange Park FL 32073

WYNN, DANIEL ARTHUR, religious organization administrator; b. Edinburg, Tex., Apr. 5, 1948; s. Connie A. and Bessie L. (Jinks) W.; m. Bobbye F. Winstead, Aug. 18, 1970; children: Ashley, Joy. AA, So. Bapt. Coll., 1968; BS, Union U., 1970; MRE, Southwestern Bapt. Theol. Sem., 1974. Ordained to ministry So. Bapt. Conv., 1969. Min. music Holly Grove Bapt. Ch., Bells, Tenn., 1968-70; min. music and youth First Bapt. Ch., Lakeside, Tex., 1970-71; min. music, youth, edn. Pearson Bapt. Ch., Pearl, Miss., 1971-73; minstrn. edn. Oak Forest Bapt. Ch., Jackson, Miss., 1974-80; min. edn., adminstrn. First Bapt. Ch., Natchez, Miss., 1980—; moderator Adams Bapt. Assn., Natchez, 1990—, Sunday sch. dir., 1981—; area coord. Royal Ambs., Miss., 1975—. Mem. home mission bd. Christian Svc. Corps, Atlanta, 1981. Mem. Nat. Assn. Ch. Bus. Adminstrn., So. Bapt. Religious Edn. Assn., So. Bapt. Ch. Bus. Adminstrn. Assn., So. Bapt. Computer Users Assn., Southwestern Bapt. Religious Edn. Assn., Southwestern Bapt. Theol. Sem. Alumni Assn. (pres. 1987), Natchez Garden Club. Office: 1st Bapt Ch 150 D'Evereaux Dr Natchez MS 39120

WYNN, LARRY W., minister; b. Fitzgerald, Ga., June 6, 1953; m. Ethel Button, Mar. 3, 1973; children: Amanda Leigh, Dana Renee, Adam W. Student, Abraham Baldwin Coll., 1972; BA, Mercer U., 1977; postgrad., New Orleans Sem., Luther Rice Sem., 1990—. Ordained to ministry So. Bapt. Conv., 1974. Assoc. pastor Children's Ministry Hebron Bapt. Ch., Dacula, Ga., 1975-76; pastor Met. Bapt. Ch., Norcross, Ga., 1976-78; sr. pastor Hebron Bapt. Ch., Dacula, 1978—; v.p. Pastor's Conf. So. Bapt. Conv. Chmn. ch. emphasis Am. Cancer So., Gwinnett County, 1978-82; chaplain Gwinnett County Fire Dept., 1983—. Named Outstanding Vol. Gwinnett County Fire Dept., 1984, 90, Vol. Svc. award Gwinnett C. of C., 1989. Mem. Ga. Bapt. Conv. (trustee Sun. sch. bd. 1989-94, v.p. 1989-90). Home: PO Box 118 Dacula GA 30211 Office: PO Box 279 202 Hebron Ch Rd Dacula GA 30211

WYNN, RICHARD ROLAND, national youth organization administrator; b. North Branch, Mich., Sept. 16, 1939; s. Alexander Arnett and Esther Ora (Abbott) W.; m. Janet Gail Moore, June 30, 1962; children: Ronda WynnChapin, Jeffrey Wynn. BS, Owosso Coll., 1962; postgrad., Mich. State U., 1962-63, Western Mich. U., 1968-69, Schuler Leadership SCh., Garden Grove, Calif., 1983. Club dir. Pontiac (Mich.) Youth for Christ, 1962-64, Delta-Thumb Youth for Christ, Marlette, Mich., 1964-68; exec. dir. Battle Creek (Mich.) Youth for Christ, 1968-73, Grand Rapids (Mich.) Youth for Christ, 1973-77; regional dir. Ea. Great Lakes Reiong/Youth for Christ, Grand Rapids, 1974-81; nat. field dir. Youth for Christ USA, Wheaton, Ill., 1981-86; pres. Youth for Christ USA, Denver, 1986—. Trustee Houghton (N.Y.) Coll., 1986—, Teen Ranch, Marlette, Mich., 1966—, Youth for Christ Internat., Singapore, 1987—, Evang. Coun. for Fin. Accountability, Washington, 1990—. Named Alumnus of Yr., Owosso Coll., 1980. Office: Youth for Christ USA PO Box 228822 Denver CO 80222

WYNN, THOMAS ROBERT, lay worker; b. Wilkes-Barre, Pa., Oct. 20, 1943; s. Thomas Watkin and Matilda (Pugh) W.; m. Janice Rita Tluzcek, Feb. 6, 1970; children: Charles, Daniel, Michale, Christine, Michele. Grad. high sch., Wilkes-Barre. Mgr. P&G Paper Products; trustee Christian and Missionary Alliance, West Pittston, Pa., 1984—, treas., 1985—, v.p. Alliance Men, 1987-88, elder, 1989—; del. Eastern Dist. Christian and Missionary Alliance Prayer Conf., West Pittston, 1989, prayer ptnr., 1988—. Sgt. USMC, 1963-67, Vietnam. Republican. Home: 68 Theodore St RD 1 Harding PA 18643

WYRICK, STEPHEN VON, religion educator, minister; b. Dallas, Mar. 1, 1952; s. Floyd A. and Maxine (Clark) W.; m. Janet Lynn Matthews, Aug. 2, 1974; children: Bradley, Paul. BA, Dallas Bapt. U., 1973; MDiv, Southwestern Bapt. Theol. Sem., Fort Worth, 1976; PhD, Southwestern Bapt. Theol. Sem., 1981. Ordained to ministry So. Bapt. Ch., 1976. Pastor Northrich Bapt. Ch., Richardson, Tex., 1982-86; chmn. div. of religion, assoc. prof. Calif. Bapt. Coll., Riverside, 1986—; adjunct prof. Golden Gate Bapt. Theol. Sem., Brea, Calif., 1987—. Recipient NEH grants, 1988, '89. Mem. Soc. Bibl. Lit., Am. Schs. of Oriental Rsch., Israel Exploration Soc., Glaser Archaeol. Found. (bd. dirs.). Office: Calif Bapt Coll 8432 Magnolia Riverside CA 92504

WYSS, LEON F., minister; b. Jefferson City, Mo., Aug. 5, 1934; s. Charles F. and Frieda L. (Peters) W.; m. Elizabeth Anne Findlay, Aug. 28, 1955; 1 child, Brent F. BA, So. Nazarene U., 1956. Ordained to ministry Ch. of Nazarene. Pastor Northside Ch. Nazarene, St. Joseph, Mo., 1956-58, Richmond (Mo.) Ch. Nazarene, 1958-60, Glen Park Ch. Nazarene, Ft. Worth, 1960-63; evangelist Ch. Nazarene, 1963-68; pastor Norwalk Ch. Nazarene, Calif., 1968-71, Mission Valley Ch. Nazarene, San Diego, 1971-78; asst. to pres. Pt. Loma Nazarene Coll., San Diego, 1978-80; dist. supt. N.Mex. Dist. Ch. Nazarene, 1980-89, Colo. Dist. Ch. Nazarene, Littleton, 1989—. Trustee Pt. Loma Coll., San Diego, 1974-78, 81-89, Nazarene Indian Bible Coll., Albuquerque, 1981-89, Nazarene Bible Coll., Colorado Springs, Colo., 1990—; regent N.W. Nazarene Coll., Nampa, Idaho, 1989—. Named Hon. Alumnus Nazarene Indian Bible Coll., 1986. Mem. Kiwanis (pres. East San Diego chpt., 1978-79). Republican. Avocations: golf, travel, computer, fishing. Office: Colo Dist Ch Nazarene PO Box 2300 Littleton CO 80161

XIONG, TOUSU SAYDANGNMV, minister; b. Xieng Khouang, Laos, June 23, 1966; came to U.S., 1976; s. Nhialue Saydang and May (Vang) X. BA in Bibl. Studies, Simpson Coll., San Francisco, 1989; ThM, Mennonite Brethren Bibl. Sem., Fresno, Calif., 1991. Ordained to ministry Christian and Missionary Alliance, 1991. Assoc. min. Hmong San Raphael (Calif.) Bapt. Ch., 1986-88; youth min. Hmong Alliance Ch. of Santa Barbara, Goleta, Calif., 1984-85, Hmong Alliance Ch. of Fresno, 1989—. Scoutmaster Boy Scouts Am., 1984-85. Home: 87 W Beechwood Ave Pinedale CA 93650 Office: Hmong Alliance Ch Fresno 8234 E Belmont Ave Fresno CA 93727 *In my life as I have experienced both the world of the Hmong Animistic Religion in the East and the Christian faith from the West, I have come to realized that Jesus Christ is superior, for Jesus is the way, the truth and the life pointing us towards the Supreme and Creator Being.*

XUEREB, PUBLIUS MARIO, priest; b. Malta, Sept. 8, 1947; came to U.S. 1969; s. Francis and Nicolina (Axisa) X. MA, U. Dallas, Irving, Tex., 1971. Ordained priest Roman Cath. Ch., 1968. Dir. St. Joseph's Orphanage, Malta, 1968-69; assoc. pastor Ft. Worth, Tex., 1970-78; pastor St. Peter the Apostle Ch., Ft. Worth, 1978—; chaplain Nat. Coun. of Cath. Women, Ft. Worth, 1985—. Author: History of the Knights of Malta, 1985. Knight of Malta, 1975. Home and Office: St Peter the Apostle Ch 1201 S Cherry Ln Fort Worth TX 76108-3256 *When you are assigned a job or face a challenge, give it your very best. Your face will forever be reflected in your words and actions; in your failures and successes. Remember there is only one of you on earth.*

YAEGER, JACOB CHARLES, minister; b. Jamestown, N.D., June 23, 1957; s. Jacob Duane and Lois Ann (Dewitt) Y.; m. Denise Lynn Quin, Aug. 11, 1979; children: Rachel Joy, Bethany Ann. BA in Bible, Bapt. Bible Co.,

Springfield, Mo., 1981, ThG, 1980. Ordained to ministry, Ind. Bapt. Ch., 1985. Ch. planter Bible Bapt. Ch., Hartville, Mo., 1980-81; assoc. pastor Bible Bapt. Ch., Xenia, Ohio, 1981-83; sec. edn. tchr. Xenia (Ohio) Christian Acad., 1981-83; ch. planter/pastor Bible Bapt. Ch., Tiffin, Ohio, 1983—. Mem. Bapt. Bible Fellowship. Republican. Home: 68 E Davis St Tiffin OH 44883 Office: Bible Bapt Ch 130 Brace Ave Tiffin OH 44883

YAGO, BERNARD CARDINAL, archbishop; b. Pass, Ivory Coast, July 1916. Ordained priest Roman Cath. Ch., 1947. Archbishop of Abidjan (Ivory Coast), 1960—; elevated to Sared Coll. of Cardinals, 1983; pres. Ivory Coast Episcopal Conf. Mem. Secretariat Christian Unity. First native mem. of ch. hierarchy from Ivory Coast. Address: Archeveche, Ave Jean Paul, II, 01 BP 1287, Abidjan 01, Ivory Coast

YAMAOKA, SEIGEN HARUO, bishop; b. Fresno, Calif., Aug. 21, 1934; s. Haruichi and Rika (Ogawa) Y.; m. Shigeko Masuyama, Apr. 3, 1966; children—Jennifer Sae, Stacy Emi. B.A., Calif. State U.-Fresno, 1956; M.A., Ryukoku U., Kyoto, Japan, 1961; M.R.E., Pacific Sch. Religion, Berkeley, Calif., 1969, D.Min., 1979. Ordained to ministry Buddhist Chs. Am., 1961. Minister Oakland Buddhist Ch., Calif., 1964-71; registrar Inst. Buddhist Studies, Berkeley, 1969-71, lectr., mem. Curriculum com., 1969-81, pres., 1981—; minister Stockton Buddhist Temple, Calif., 1971-81; treas. No. Calif. Radio Ministry, 1975-76; cons. ethnic studies Stockton Unififed Sch. Dist., 1974-76; chmn. Buddhist Chs. Am. Ministers Assn., 1979-81; bishop Buddhist Chs. Am., San Francisco, 1981—, research com., 1970-79; English sec. Ministerial Assn., 1972-75; assoc. in doctrinal studies Hokyo, Kyoto, 1974; mem. Bd. Buddhist Edn., 1975; vice chmn. No. Calif. Ministers Assn., 1976; trustee Numata Ctr. for Buddhist Translation and Research, Buddhist Dharma Kyokai Soc. of Am. Author: Compassion in Encounter, 1970, Teaching and Practice Jodo Shinshu, 1974, Jodo Shinshu: Religion of Human Experience, 1976, Meditation-Gut-Enlightenment... Way of Hara, 1976, Awakening of Gratitude in Dying, 1978; editor, advisor, writer: Dharma School Teachers Guide, 1979. Mem. Japan Karate Fedn., Shinshu Acad. Soc., San Francisco-Japanese Am. Citizens League, Calif. State U.-Fresno Alumni Assn., Pacific Sch. Religion Alumni Assn., Internat. Assn. Shin Buddhist Studies, Internat. Translation Ctr. Kyoto, Hongwanji Bishops Council Kyoto. Home: 37 Waterloo Ct Belmont CA 94002 Office: Buddhist Chs of Am 1710 Octavia St San Francisco CA 94109

YANCEY, JOHN FRANKLIN, minister; b. Kansas City, Mo., Apr. 22, 1968; s. Daniel H. and Ruth A. (Powell) Y.; m. K. Kathleen Aston, Aug. 25, 1989. BA, N.W. Nazarene Coll., Nampa, Idaho, 1990. Lic. to ministry, Ch. of the Nazarene. Local lic. min. Ch. of the Nazarene-Karcher, Nampa, 1984-87; dist. lic. minister Ch. of the Nazarene, Nampa, 1987-90, Salem, 1990—; assoc. pastor Ch. of the Nazarene, Tillamook, Oreg., 1990—; teaching asst. religion and Spanish N.W. Nazarene Coll., Nampa, 1987-90, peer tutor religion, 1989-90; del. Dist. Assembly, Nazarene Ch., Nampa, 1987-90, Nazarene Youth Internat., Portland, Oreg., 1990—, Salem, 1990—, Dist. Assembly, Portland, 1991—. Recipient Award for Outstanding Acad. Achievement, Cunningham Found., 1986-90. Mem. Tillamook County Ministerial Assn., Phi Delta Lambda. Office: Ch of the Nazarene 2611 3d St Tillamook OR 97141 *Life without riches may breed simplicity; life without health may breed patience; life without freedom may breed endurance; life without friendship may invent strength, but life without Christ can breed nothing but piercing loneliness.*

YANDO, EMMANUEL, minister, religious organization administrator. Pastor, pres. Eglise Protestante Méthodiste, Abidjan, Ivory Coast. Office: Protestant Meth Ch, 01 BP, 1282, 41 Blvd Republique, Abidjan 01, Ivory Coast*

YANG, C. S., religious organization executive. Gen. sec. Presbyn. Ch. in Taiwan, Taipei. Office: Tai-oan Ki-tok Tiu-Lo Kau-hoe, 3 Ln 269, Roosevelt Rd, #3, Taipei 10763, Republic of China*

YANG, LONG NHA, clergyman; b. Nong-Phi, Laos, Nov. 9, 1962; came to U.S., 1976; s. Wang Toua and Ka (Xiong) Y.; m. May Kao Lee, July 26, 1986; children: Kong Mong, Rachel. BA in Ministry, Iowa Christian Coll., 1985; MDiv in Theology and Philosophy, Lincoln Christian Sem., 1989; D Ministry in Theology, Covington Theol. Sem., 1991. Ordained to ministry Christian and Missionary Alliance, 1989. Pastor Hmong Alliance Ch., Des Moines, 1982-85; missionary Christian and Missionary Alliance, France, 1986-87; pastor Denver Hmong Alliance Ch., Westminster, Colo., 1989—; mem. exec. com. Mnong dist. Christian and Missionary Alliance, Brighton, Colo., 1990—, mem. hymn com., 1982—. Contbr. articles to religious jours. Recipient Ch. Growth award Nat. Ch. Growth Ctr., Washington, 1985, Hmong Educator award Hmong Ednl. Coun., Fresno, Calif., 1990. Home: 8195 Orchard Dr Denver CO 80221 Office: Denver Hmong Alliance Ch 8135 N Knox Ct Westminster CO 80030 *Courage isn't having the strength to go on, it's going on when you don't have the strength. Do all the good you can, in all the ways you can, for all the people you can, while you can.*

YANOWITZ, BENNETT, lawyer, religious organization administrator; b. Cleve., Feb. 25, 1923; s. Jacob and Mollie (Berkowitz) Y.; m. Donna Yanowitz, May 6, 1951; children: Gerald H., Joel H., Alan H. AB, U. Mich., 1947; LLB, Western Res. U., 1949. Bar: Ohio 1949. Prin. Kahn, Kleinman, Yanowitz & Arnson, Cleve., 1964—; pres. Akiva High Sch. Vice pres., trustee Jewish Community Fedn., Cleve.; trustee Coun. Jewish Fedns., Menorah Park Jewish Home for Aged; chmn. Nat. Jewish Community Rels. Adv. Coun., N.Y.C.; immediate past pres. Jewish Edn. Svc. N.Am. Capt. U.S. Army, 1943-46. Mem. Ohio Bar Assn., Cleve. Bar Assn. *Involvement in organizational life has permitted, indeed required, combining continued learning and study of both current issues and traditional texts with their practical application in working with others seeking to build a better world.*

YANSANGWARA, SOMDEJ PHRA, religious leader. Supreme Patriarch of Thailand Buddhism. Office: Supreme Patriarch, Bangkok Thailand*

YAP, MOODY BOON-WAN, minister; b. Kulangsu, Fukien, China, Feb. 23, 1930; came to U.S., 1964; s. Chong Ho and Ai Yeh (Young) Y.; m. Jean Chua, 1955; children: Daniel, Esther, Ruth. BA, U. Baguio, 1964; MDiv, Western Theol. Sem., 1967; D of Ministry, N.Am. Bapt. Sem., 1977. Ordained to ministry Ref. Ch. in Am., 1967. Pastor Chinese Bible Ch., Detroit, 1967-70; minister of evangelism Classis of Lake Erie Reformed Ch., 1971-77; founding pastor Christ Community Ch., Farmington Hills, Mich., 1978-80, Christ Ch. of the Bay Area, San Mateo, Calif., 1981—; moderator, commn. on nomination Reformed Ch. in Am., 1986-88; founding pres. Coun. for Pacific and Asian Ministry Reformed Ch. in Am., 1980-86; vice-moderator World Mission Div., Reformed Ch. in Am., 1988—; pres. Classis of Cen. Calif. Reformed Ch. in Am., 1990—. Home: 6 Antique Forest Belmont CA 94002 Office: Christ Ch of the Bay Area 234 Ninth Ave San Mateo CA 94401

YARBROUGH, JESSE THOMAS, minister; b. Roxboro, N.C., May 24, 1951; s. Hubert Long and Ruby Lee (Painter) Y.; m. Belinda Ann Thompson, Dec. 19, 1971; children: Shelley Marie, Amanda Carol. BA, Gardner-Webb Coll., 1973; MDiv, Southeastern Bapt. Theol. Sem., 1976, D Ministry, 1983. Ordained to ministry So. Bapt. Conv., 1974. Pastor Spring Garden Bapt. Ch., New Bern, N.C., 1973-77, Cold Water Bapt. Ch., Concord, N.C., 1977-84, Caroleen (N.C.) Bapt. Ch., 1984—; pres. Sandy Run Mins. Conf., Forest City, N.C., 1985-86, 90-91; mem. Resolutions Com., N.C. Bapt. State Conv., 1991—. Organizer, pres. Citizens Against Drug Abuse, Caroleen, 1990; mem. Drug Free Schs. and Communities Adv. Coun., Forest City, Rutherford County, 1991. Recipient Cert. Appreciation Rutherford County Bd. Edn., 1985. Mem. Neuro-Linguistic Programming of Gastonia. Home: PO Box 215 Caroleen NC 28019 Office: Caroleen Bapt Ch PO Box 489 Caroleen NC 28019 *To live successfully, I must know God's ways of dealing in life and the world. To know God's ways, I must know God's word. To live successfully I must know myself in reflection of God's word and love others with undying compassion.*

YARBROUGH, LEROY, religious music director, organist, educator; b. Rome, Ga.; m. Edwyna McGee: children: Melody Ruth Macaulay, Regina Beth Howell. MusB, Baylor U., MusM; PhD, La. State U.; postgrad., U. Tex., Loyola U., Tenn. Temple Coll., San Antonio Coll., U. New Orleans. Exec. editor, dir. music pub., rec. divs. Crescendo Publs., Dallas; min. music 1st Bapt. Ch., Altus, Okla., Faith Bapt. Ch., Kaiserslautern, Fed. Republic Germany, Trinity Bapt. Ch., San Antonio; chmn. div. ch. music ministries New Orleans Bapt. Sem., prof. choral conducting and music theory; music dir. Bapt. World Alliance Congress, Seoul, Republic of Korea, 1990; dir. La. Bapt. Singing Mins.; music dir. or organist Tex. Bapt. Conv., Bapt. Evang. Confs., Tex., Calif., European Bapt. Conv., Ridgecrest and Glorieta Bapt. Conf. Ctrs.; dir. music Bapt. World Alliance Youth Conf., Glasgow, Scotland; former dir. Singing Churchmen Miss. Producer, arranger, orchestrator, condr. over 50 recs., U.S., Tokyo, Mexico City, London; composer, arranger choral music for 7 pub. cos.; condr. choral and orchestral works: St. Paul, Mendelssohn, Lobegesang (Symphony No. 2), Mendelssohn, Messiah, Handel, Israel in Egypt, Handel, Christ lag in Todesbanden (Cantata No. 4), J.S. Bach, Ein fest Burg (Cantata No. 80, J.S. Bach, Gloria, Poulenc, Gloria, Vivaldi, Testament of Freedom, Thompson, King David, Honneger, Rhapsody for Alto and Men's Chorus, Brahms, A German Requiem, Brahms, Symphony No. 5, Mendelssohn, Christ on the Mount of Olives, Beethoven, The Creation, Haydn, Amahl and the Night Visitors, Menotti, Passion (Seven Last Words), Haydn, God's Trombones, Ringwald, Seven Last Words of Christ, Dubois, Uns ist ein Kind geboren (Cantata No. 142), J.S. Bach, Elijah, Mendelssohn, Symphony No. 3, Ives, Symphony of Psalms, Stravinsky, Chichester Psalms, Bernstein, additional cantatas, musicals, anthems. Mem. ASCAP, Am. Guild Organists, So. Bapt. Ch. Music Conf., Am. Choral Dirs. Assn. Home: 4325 Seminary Pl New Orleans LA 70126 Office: New Orleans Bapt Theol Sem 3939 Gentilly Blvd New Orleans LA 70126-4858

YATES, WILLIAM TYLER, minister; b. Long Beach, Calif., Apr. 11, 1956; s. Raymond A. and H. Lorraine (Buros) Y.; m. Deborah Jean Schmidt, Aug. 6, 1978; children: Rachael, Kristen, James. BA, Valparaiso (Ind.) U., 1978; MDiv, Concordia Theol. Sem., 1982; STM, Yale U , 1983; diploma, USAF Air U., 1989. Assoc. pastor St. Paul Luth. Ch. & Sch., Grafton, Wis., 1983-87; pastor Immanuel Luth. Ch. & Sch., Manchester, N.H., 1987-90, Calvary Luth. Ch. & Sch., Indpls., 1990—; guest prof. Concordia Sem., St. Louis, 1985—; adj. prof. Concordia U., Mequon, Wis., 1985-87; regional counselor New Eng. Dist. Luth. Ch.-Mo. Synod., 1988-90; air command staff advisor Maine Air N.G., Bangor, 1987-90; installation staff chaplain 181st Tac Fighter Group, Ind. Air. N.G. Coord. disaster relief svcs. Manchester Fedn. of Chs./ARC, 1988-90; mem. adv. coun. Luth. Counseling and Family Svcs., Wis., 1984-87; bd. dirs. Ozaukee County (Wis.) COPE Svcs., Cedarburg, 1985-87. With USAFR, 1985—. Recipient Disting. Svc. award State of Maine, 1990. Mem. Assn. for Clin. Pastoral Edn., Air Force Assn., Res. Officers Assn., Nat. Guard Assn., Mil. Chaplains Assn. Office: Calvary Luth Ch 6111 Shelby St Indianapolis IN 46227 *The genious of Christianity is that it is not a this-world religion or an other-world religion, it is both. And the substance of it is found in this: by faith we ascend beyond ourselves into God; by love we descend beneath ourselves into our neighbor.*

YEAGER, IVER FRANKLIN, religion and philosophy educator; b. Yoder, Wyo., Apr. 24, 1922; s. Charles Franklin Yeager and Elise Marie (Thingelstad) Afdahl; m. Natalee Ruth Carlander, Mar. 1, 1946; children: Larry, Kenneth, Ruth. BA, Macalester Coll., 1944; MA, Chgo. Theol. Sem., 1948; PhD, U. Chgo., 1957. Ordained to ministry United Ch. of Christ, 1951. Instr. religion Coll. of Wooster (Ohio), 1952-56; assoc. prof. religion and philosophy Missouri Valley Coll., Marshall, Mo., 1956-58; acad. dean, prof. religion Ill. Coll., Jacksonville, 1958-70, prof. religion and philosophy, dept. chair, 1970-88, Dunbaugh Disting. prof., 1977-88, prof. emeritus, 1988—. Author: Church and College, Illinois Frontier, 1980 (Pres.'s award Congregational Christian Hist. Soc. 1981); author, editor booklet Congregational Ch., Jacksonville, 1983; editor: Sesquicentennial Papers, 1982; editor, contbr. Illinois College: 160th Anniversary Papers, 1990. Pres. Rotary Club, Jacksonville, 1970-71. Lt. (j.g.) USNR, 1944-46, PTO. Paul Harris fellow Rotary Club, Jacksonville, 1982. Mem. AAUP, Soc. for Sci. Study of Religion.

YEAGER, NORMAN ALBERT, minister; b. Toledo, Aug. 19, 1944; s. George Fredrick Yeager and Elsa (Fredia) Ley; m. Joyce Faye Swett, June 4, 1967; children: Jeffrey Norman, Brian James. BA, Andrews U., 1967, MDiv, 1970, D of Ministry, 1988. Ordained to ministry Seventh-day Adventist, 1974. Min. Mich. Conf. Seventh-day Adventists, Lansing, Mich., 1970-88, Tex. Conf. Seventh-day Adventists, Alvarado, Tex., 1988—; contract prof. Southwestern Adventist Coll., Keene, Tex., 1990-91. Mem. Adventist Theol. Soc., Grand Prairie Ministerial Assn. Home: 1318 Cedar Run Dr Duncanville TX 75137 Office: Seventh-day Adventist Ch 418 E Tarrant Rd Grand Prairie TX 75050

YEAKEL, JOSEPH HUGHES, clergyman; b. Mahanoy City, Pa., Mar. 12, 1928; s. Claude Harrison and Florence Mae (Hughes) Y.; m. Lois Josephine Shank, Mar. 26, 1948; children—Claudia Jo, Joseph Douglas, Joanna Irene, Mary Jo, Jody Lucile. A.B., Lebanon Valley Coll., 1949, D.D. (hon.), 1968; M.Div., United Theol. Sem., 1952; LL.D. (hon.), Otterbein Coll.; S.T.D. (hon.), Keuka Coll. Ordained to ministry United Methodist Ch., 1952; student asst. pastor Euclid Ave. Evang. United Brethren Ch., Dayton, Ohio, 1949-52; asst. pastor Otterbein Evang. United Brethren Ch., Hagerstown, Md., 1952-55; pastor Messiah Evang. United Brethren Ch., York, Pa., 1955-61, Meml. Evang. United Brethren Ch., Silver Spring, Md., 1961-63; asst. sec. Gen. Bd. Evangelism, Evang. United Brethren Ch., 1963-65, exec. sec., 1965-68; gen. sec. Gen. Bd. Evangelism United Meth. Ch., Nashville, 1968-72; bishop N.Y. West area United Meth. Ch., 1972-84, bishop Washington area, 1984—. Served with USNR, Seabees, 1945-46, PTO. Home: 8684 Doves Fly Way Laurel MD 20707 Office: 9226 Colesville Rd Silver Spring MD 20910

YEARLEY, LEE HOWARD, religion educator; b. Chgo., Apr. 30, 1940; s. Bernard Cain and Mary (Howard) Y.; m. Sally Gressens, May 20, 1983; children: Jennifer H., John C. BA, Haverford Coll., 1962; MA, U. Chgo., 1966, PhD, 1969. Prof., chair religious studies Stanford (Calif.) U., 1969—; Luce prof. Amherst Coll., 1987-88. Author: The Ideas of Newman Christianity and Human Religiosity, 1978, Mencius and Aquinas Theories of Virtue and Conceptions of Courage, 1990. Nat. Humanities Inst. fellow, 1978-79, NEH sr. fellow, 1984-85, Henry Luce fellow Inst. for Advanced Study of Religion, 1991—. Home: 97 Peter Coutts Stanford CA 94305 Office: Stanford U Dept Religious Studies Stanford CA 94305

YEARSLEY, PAMELA J., minister; b. Kansas City, Mo., May 23, 1946; d. Harold Nolen and Sue Emily (Liston) McGregor; m. Francis Stephen Yearsley, Nov. 28, 1964; (div. June, 1979); children: Nichole (Yearsley) Wells, Jason M. Student, Coll. of Divine Metaphysics, 1990. Ordained Unity minister, 1990. Editor Unity Sch. of Christianity, Unity Village, Mo., 1976-90; minister asst. Unity Ch. of Christianity, Pensacola, Fla., 1990—. Editor: 23 books, Unity Mag.; contbr. articles to religious mags. Bd. dirs. Hope House, Independence, Mo., 1986-87. Mem. Mid Am. Publishers Group (bd. dirs. 1988-90), Soc. for Scholarly Publishing. Avocations: music, literature, study of human psychology. Office: Unity Ch of Christianity 716 N 9th Ave Pensacola FL 32504

YEE, GALE A., religion educator; b. Cin., Apr. 9, 1949; s. John and Mary Kay (Luke) Y. BA, Loyola U., Chgo., 1973, MA, 1975; PhD, U. St. Michael's Coll., Toronto, 1985. Assoc. prof. U. St. Thomas, St. Paul, 1984—. Author: Composition and Tradition in Book of Hosea, 1987, Jewish Feasts and the Gospel of John, 1989; contbr. articles to profl. jours. NCCJ fellow, 1986; recognized for excellence in teaching and rsch. Burling No. Found., 1987. Mem. Soc. Bibl. Lit., Cath. Bibl. Assn. (Young Scholars fellow 1990). Democrat. Roman Catholic. Office: Coll Saint Thomas 2115 Summit Ave Mail #4362 Saint Paul MN 55105

YELEK, SISTER ANTOINETTE, health facility administrator; b. Selden, Kans., Sept. 25, 1924. Diploma nursing, Marquette U., 1947, B, 1954, M, 1962. Various positions, 1947-59; dir. nursing svc. St. Joseph Hosp. Rehab. Ctr., Wichita, Kans., 1959-61, 62-63; with adminstr. St. Rose Hosp., Hayward, Calif., 1963-71; gen. supr. Srs. of St. Joseph, Wichita, 1972-80; exec. v.p. health svcs. Srs. of St. Joseph Coordinated Svcs., Wichita, 1980-82; pres. CSJ Health System, Wichita, 1982—. Mem. ANA, NLN, AWH. Office: CSJ Health System 3720 E Bayley Wichita KS 67218

YEPES, ELIAS HERNANDO, religion educator; b. Granada, Colombia, Jan. 27, 1945; s. Antonio and Teresa (Giraldo) Y.; m. Olga Iris Hernandez, Mar. 24, 1972; children: Laura Theresa, Diana Maria. Dipl. in Philosophy, Major Sem. Manizalez, Colombia, 1965. Coord. religious edn. Our Lady of Sorrows Ch., Corona, N.Y., 1989—; permanent deacon St. Michael's Ch., Flushing, N.Y., 1988—; coord. natural family planning Apostolate for Hispanics, Diocese of Bklyn., 1982—; adv. mem. Permanent Diaconate Prog., Bklyn. Diocese, 1990—, prison chaplain, 1989-90; adv. mem. Hispanic Family Life Ministry, Bklyn., 1985—, mem. clergy panel 2nd Chance Queens Dist. Atty.'s Office, 1991—; bd. dirs. Pastoral Inst., Bklyn. Diocese, 1991—; coord. and founder Encuentros-Faith Sharing Group, St. Michael's Ch., Flushing, 1987—. Mem. St. Michael's Hispanic Assn., 1980—, coord. ESL Program, 1991. Recipient Cert. of Appreciation, Immigration and Refugee Apostolate of Diocese of Bklyn., 1989. Mem. Nat. Cath. Edn. Assn., Religious Edn. Adminstrs., Nat. Hispanic Deacons Assn. Home: 43-10 Kissena Blvd Flushing NY 11355 Office: Our Lady of Sorrows Ch 104-11 37th Ave Corona NY 11368 *Only when faith and trust in God became my central innermost value, did my life acquire its true meaning and fulfillment. Prior to that, it had been scattered and egoistic. Jesus' words: "Without me you can do nothing" now mean everything to me. With Him I've done what before seemed almost impossible.*

YERES, MOSHE JOSEPH, rabbi; b. N.Y.C., Feb. 13, 1954; s. Irvin and Shirley (Gall) Y.; m. Esty Frankel, June 20, 1978; children: Haviva, Israel, Batsheva, Sara, Aaron. BA, Yeshiva U., 1975, MA, 1977, PhD, 1987. Ordained rabbi, 1978. Rabbi Congregaton Beth David, Brantford, Ont., Can., 1978-82, B'nai Shalom Synagogue, Waterbury, Conn., 1982-87, Congregation Or Torah, Skokie, Ill., 1987-90, Congregation Ohav Zedek, Wilkes-Barre, Pa., 1990—; bd. dirs. Jewish Fedn. Greater Wilkes-Barre, 1990—; hon. bd. dirs. Jewish Home of Ea. Pa., Scranton, 1990—; exec. bd. United Hebrew Inst., Kingston, Pa., 1990—; chmn. Vaad Hakashrut of Luzerne County, Wilkes-Barre, Pa., 1990—. Contbr. articles to profl. jours. Recipient Rabbinical Centennial award, Yeshiva U., 1986, Rabbinical award, Coun. Jewish Fedns., 1984. Mem. Rabbinical Coun. Am. (nat. exec. bd.), Chgo. Rabbinical Coun. (sec. 1988-90), Rabbinic Alumni Yeshiva U. (exec. com. 1985-88). Home: 290 S Franklin St Wilkes-Barre PA 18702 Office: Congregation Ohav Zedek 242 S Franklin Wilkes-Barre PA 18702

YEUN, PAUL LORENZO, minister; b. Hong Kong, Apr. 14, 1944; came to U.S., 1960; s. Kaki Yeun and Carmen (Flores) Pio; m. Elisabeth Wendy Chan, June 19, 1971; children: Evangeline, Abigail. BA, Azusa Pacific U., 1968; MDiv, Asbury Sem., 1971, MA, 1974; DMin, Lexington Sem., 1977. Ordained to ministry Meth. Ch., 1973; cert. marriage and family therapist; lic. profl. counselor; cert. profl. mental health clergy. Parish pastor Aberdeen (Ohio) United Meth. Ch., 1971-72, Morrow (Ohio) United Meth. Ch., 1972-76, Albany (Ohio) United Meth. Ch., 1976-78, Oakland Park United Meth. Ch., Columbus, Ohio, 1978-81; group chaplain USAF, Rickenbacker AFB, Ohio, 1980-81; protestant chaplain USAF, George Air Force Base, Calif., 1981-84; installation chaplain USAF, Clark Air Base, Philippines, 1984-87; sr. protestant chaplain USAF, Davis Monthan AFB, Tucson, 1987—; counselor Pastoral Counseling Ctr., Columbus, 1979-81; advisor Asian Pacific Fellowship, Tucson, 1987—; chair ch. and soc. South Dist. United Meth. Ch., Tucson, 1989-90; bd. dirs. Ariz. Marriage and Family Therapy, Tucson Met. Ministries. Author: Dealing with the Psychological needs of Aged, 1985, Meaning of our Membership Vows, 1987. Mem. Task Force in Credentialing, State of Ariz., 1989—. Major USAF, 1980—. Decorated Air Force Commendation medal; recipient award Air Force Best Sermons, 1985, Man of Achievement award; named to Ky. Cols. Mem. Am. Assn. Marriage and Family Therapy (clin.), Internt. Acad. Behavior, Medicine and Psychotherapy (diplomate), Asian Pacific Fellowship, Tucson Chaplain Assn. (steering com. 1987-90), Lions. Democrat. Home: 8921 E Rosewood St Tucson AZ 85710 Office: 836 CSG/HC Davis Monthan AFB Tucson AZ 85707 *Authentic preaching is telling the stories of Jesus and His love the best we can with the expectation that those who heard may enter a loving relationship with God.*

YINGLING, REBECCA MARIE, Religious counseling organization administrator; b. Alton, Ill., June 1, 1951; d. John Louis and Ruby Marie (Parker) Wardle; m. Winston Lyle Yingling, Mar. 22, 1974; children: Larry, Whitney. BA, Valdosta State Coll., 1986, MS, 1988. Counselor Life Skills Programs, Valdosta, Ga., 1989; dir./counselor New Day Christian Counseling, Valdosta, 1989—. Bd. dirs. Woman's Missionary Union of Valdosta Bapt. Assn., 1988—. Mem. Pi Gamma Mu. Avocations: music, reading. Office: New Day Christian Couns 1115 Slater St Valdosta GA 31601

YOCHAM, DAVID LEN, minister; b. Phoenix, Mar. 11, 1959; s. Virgil Almous and Joy Faye (Hogue) Y.; m. Johnna Anne Long, Jan. 9, 1986; children: Joshua David, James Len. Student, Lubbock Christian U., 1977-80, Sunset Sch. Preaching, 1986-89. Ordained to ministry Ch. of Christ, 1989. Min. Broadway Ch. of Christ, Pueblo, Colo., 1989—; Speaker in field. Home: 2881 Azalea Pueblo CO 81005 Office: Broadway Ch of Christ 611 Broadway Pueblo CO 81004

YOCUM, GLENN EARL, religion educator; b. Hershey, Pa., July 14, 1943; s. Earl and Orpha (Fausnacht) Y.; m. Emelie Ann Olson, Aug. 29, 1979; children—Stuart, Shanta. B.A., Franklin and Marshall Coll., 1965; diploma theology Oxford U., 1967; M.Div., Union Theol. Sem., 1969; Ph.D., U. Pa., 1976. Instr., asst. prof. religion Whittier Coll. (Calif.), 1973-77; asst. prof. religion Williams Coll., Williamstown, Mass., 1977-78; asst. prof., assoc. prof. Whittier Coll., 1978-83, Connick prof., 1983—, chmn. dept. philosophy and religion, 1983-85; social sci. cons. Whittier Union High Sch. Dist., 1987-88 . Editor for Asian religions Religious Studies Rev., 1980-85, jour. editor, 1986—; reader Ind. U. Press, 1985, Princeton U. Press, 1985-86, 90, SUNY Press, 1986; evaluator NEH, 1986; author: Hymns to the Dancing Siva, 1982; editor: Religious Festivals in South India and Sri Lanka, 1982, Structural Approaches to South Indian Studies, 1974; contbr. articles to profl. jours. Recipient Graves award in humanities Pomona Coll., 1983; Penfield fellow U. Pa., 1973, Am. Inst. Indian Studies sr. rsch. fellow, 1981-82, 89-90, Fulbright-Hays Faculty Rsch. Abroad fellow, Turkey, 1989-90. Mem. Am. Acad. Religion, Assn. Asian Studies, Am. Oriental Soc., Mid. East Studies Assn., Turkish Studies Assn., Soc. South India Studies (newsletter editor 1975-78), Conf. Religion in South India, Phi Beta Kappa. Home: PO Box 2861 Wrightwood CA 92397 Office: Whittier Coll Dept Religious Studies Whittier CA 90608

YODER, ALLAN HENRY, religious organization administrator, minister; b. Sellarsville, Pa., May 1, 1952; s. Henry Paul and Mildred (Clemens) Y.; m. Rebeca Jimenez, July 7, 1975; children: A. Mauricio, H. Andres, Joshua D. AA, Hesston Coll., 1972; student, Seminario Bibl. Latinoamericano, 1975, Fuller Theol. Sem., 1976-77, 83-84, 88-89, Goshen Bibl. Sem., 1985; BA, Goshen Coll., 1976. Ordained to ministry Mennonite Ch., 1980. Vol. Rosedale Mennonite Bd. Missions, Costa Rica, 1972-74; founding pastor Iglesia Menonita Emanuel, Surprise, Ariz., 1977-84; min. for Calif. S.W. Mennonite Conf., L.A., 1985-91; dir. evangelism and ch. devel. Mennonite Bd. Missions, Elkhart, Ind., 1991—; dir. extension and evangelism S.W. Mennonite Conf., L.A., 1980-91;, asst. moderator, Phoenix, 1980-84; mem. divisional com. Home Ministries Mennonite Bd. Missions, Elkhart, 1980-87; bd. dirs. Mennonite Bd. Congl. Ministries, Elkhart, 1987-91; founding pres. Coun. Anabapts. in L.A., 1985—. Councilman City of Surprise, 1980-82. Democrat. Home: 206 Constitution Goshen IN 46526 Office: Mennonite Bd Missions PO Box 370 Elkhart IN 46515

YODER, DONALD EUGENE, minister; b. Middlebury, Ind., Dec. 16, 1930; s. Quinton J. and Edith Elizabeth Yoder; m. Bonnie Lou Miller, Sept. 25, 1955; children: LuAnne Beth Yoder Hershberger, Ross Arlin. BA, Goshen Coll., 1953; Th.B., Goshen Bibl. Sem., 1954. Ordained to ministry Mennonite Ch., 1953. Pastor Forks Mennonite Ch., Middlebury, Ind., 1953-64, Trinity Mennonite Ch., Glendale, Ariz., 1964-76, Koinonia Mennonite Ch., Chandler, Ariz., 1976-82; sec. evangelism Gen. Conf. Mennonite Ch., Newton, Kans., 1979-89; pastor Koinonia Mennonite Ch., Chandler, 1989—; mem. devel. disabilities com. Mennonite Cen. Com., Reedley, Calif., 1988—. Contbr. articles to religious publs. Bd. overseers Hesston (Kans.) Coll., 1982-90. Democrat. Office: Koinonia Mennonite Ch 2505 N Dobson Rd Chandler AZ 85224

YODER, ELIZABETH ANN, lay worker; b. Meyersdale, Pa., Dec. 5, 1966; d. POerry Lynn and Alice Ann (Klink) Y. BS summa cum laude, Frostburg State U., 1989. Cert. secondary sch. tchr., Pa. Vacation Bible Sch. tchr., asst. Summit Mills Grace Brethren Ch., Meyersdale, 1979-84, 90, pianist, 1983-91, youth competition advisor, coach, judge, 1986-90, Women's Group Bible Study leader, 190—; pianist Community Grace Brethren Ch., Warsaw, Ind., 1983—; camp counselor Camp Albryoca, Meyersdale, 1984-85, 87, 89-90; participant Brethren Nat. Youth Conf., Cullowhee, N.C., 1990, Dist. Cong. Allegheny Dist. of the Fellowship of Grace Brethren Chs., Uniontown, Pa., 1990; continuing edn. instr. Frostburg State U., 1988—; substitute tchr. Somerset County, Pa. Pub. Schs., 1990—; accompaniest voice lessons Grace Coll., 1991—. Clerical worker Summit Twp Election Bd., 1990. Mem. Psi Chi, Sigma Tau Delta, Phi Eta Sigma. Republican. Home: Rte 1 Box 227 Meyersdale PA 15552-9625

YODER, HARRY WALTER, minister; b. Otsego, Mich., Feb. 1, 1922; s. Harry Alwin and Maud Emma (Howe) Y.; m. Mary Elizabeth Kelly (div. 1976); children: Colleen, Nancy, John, Teresa. BA, Kalamazoo Coll., 1944; BD, U. Chgo., 1946. Ordained to ministry Congl. Ch., 1946. Pastor St. Paul Congl. Ch., Chgo., 1945-49, First Congl. Ch., Rockford, Mich., 1946-57, Northland Congl. Ch., Rockford, 1957-58, New Ch. the Holy Spirit (formerly Religious Counseling Ctr.), Grand Rapids, Mich., 1958—; owner Yoder Distbrs., Grand Rapids, 1964—; advisor Pilgrim Fellowship, Chgo., 1948-49; mem. adv. bd. Grand Rapids Assn. Congl. Ch., Rockford, 1955; del. Congl. Christian Coun., New Haven, 1956. Mem. editorial bd. Sexology Mag., 1961-65; contbr. articles to profl. jours. Recipient Man of Month award Pastoral Psychology jour., 1958. Home: 1422 Wealthy SE Grand Rapids MI 49506 *The necessary focus of attention on the ecology of our planet will provide new guiding metaphors for our human relations and understanding of God's action.*

YODER, JOHN HOWARD, theology educator; b. Smithville, Ohio, Dec. 29, 1927; s. Howard C. and Ethel (Good) Y.; m. Anne Marie, July 14, 1952; children: Rebecca, Marthe, Daniel, Elisabeth, Esther, John-David. Dr. Theol., U. Basel, 1957. Prof. Goshen Bibl. Sem., Elkhart, Ind., 1965-84, U. Notre Dame (Ind.), 1977—. Author: Politics of Jesus, 1972, Priestly Kingdom, 1985. Mem. Soc. of Christian Ethics (pres. 1987-88). Office: U Notre Dame Dept of Theology Notre Dame IN 46556

YODER, KEITH EDWARD, minister; b. Belleville, Pa., Nov. 15, 1944; s. Jonas Jonathon and Estella Pearl (Harshbarger) Y.; m. Marian Elaine Ressler, Sept. 12, 1970. BS in Elem. Edn., Millersville U., 1966; MS in Libe. Sci., Drexel U., 1968; EdD in Ednl. Leadership, U. Pa., 1985. Ordained to ministry The Worship Ctr., 1982; cert. permanent tchr., specialist in ednl. media. Dean Living World Sch. Ministry, Leola, Pa., 1981-82, Living World Tng. Ctr., Mt. Joy, Pa., 1982-87; dir. Teaching the World Ministries, Leola, 1987—; v.p. bd. dirs., Loving and Caring Inc., Lancaster, Pa., 1989—. Author: Spiritual Warfare: Battle of Words, 1985, Amen: The Spirit of Prayer, 1986; contbr. articles to profl. jours. Home: 50 Holly Dr Leola PA 17540

YODER, LAWRENCE MCCULLOH, religion educator, minister; b. Mt. Joy, Pa., Apr. 14, 1943; s. Leroy G. and Vida (McCulloh) Y.; m. Shirlee Kohler, June 18, 1966; children: Christopher Jonathan, Gregory Matthew, Bradley David. BA, Messiah Coll., 1966; MDiv, Mennonite Bibl. Sem., 1969; ThM, Fuller Theol. Sem., 1981, PhD, 1987. Lic. to ministry Brethren in Christ Ch., 1969. Tchr. Akademi Kristen Wiyata Wacana Sem., Pati, Indonesia, 1970-79; rep. Mennonite Cen. Com., Pati, 1973-77; prof. missiology, dir. Ctr. for Evang. and Ch. Planting, Ea. Mennonite Sem., Harrisonburg, Va., 1983—. Author: Sejarah Gereja Kristen Muria Indonesia, 1985; contbr. articles to profl. jours. Mem. Am. Soc. Missiology, Soc. for Sci. Study Religion. Democrat. Home: 1301 Mt Clinton Pike Harrisonburg VA 22801 Office: Ea Mennonite Sem Harrisonburg VA 22801 *I have learned that much more can happen through ministry in the name of Jesus and following his example than my post-enlightenment materialistic—but also Christian—mindset would for much of my life allow.*

YOHN, RICHARD VAN, clergyman; b. Lancaster, Pa., Apr. 16, 1937; s. Henry Martin and Ada (Dommel) Y.; m. Linda Harriet Anderson, June 18, 1960; children—Richard Van, Steven Eric. Student Franklin and Marshall Coll., 1956; B.S., Phila. Coll. Bible, 1960; Th.M., Dallas Theol. Sem., 1964; D.Min., Talbot Theol. Sem., 1980. Ordained to ministry Evangelical Free Ch., 1971; dir. Christian edn. Oliver Presbyn. Ch., Mpls., 1964-67; pastor Windsor Park Evang. Free Ch., Winnipeg, Man., Can. 1967-71, Evang. Free Ch. Fresno, Calif., 1971-84, Grace Ch., Edina, Minn., 1984-87, Evang. Free Ch., Orange, Calif., 1987—; originator radio program Living Word, 1980; pres. Contact Ministries Inc., 1980—; mem. faculty Winnipeg Bible Coll., 1969-70. Recipient Mark of Excellence award Campus Life Mag., 1975. Mem. Nat. Assn. Evangelicals. Author: Discover Your Spiritual Gift and Use It, 1974; Now That I'm A Disciple, 1976; What Every Christian Should Know About God, 1976; God's Answers to Life's Problems, 1976; God's Holy Spirit for Christian Living, 1977; Getting Control of Your Life, 1978; God's Answer to Financial Problems, 1978; Getting Control of Your Inner Self, 1981; What Every Christian Should Know About Bible Prophecy, 1982; Explore the Bible Yourself, 1982; Finding Time, 1984; Overcoming, 1985; Living Securely in an Unstable World, 1985. Office: 5300 France Ave S Edina MN 55410

YONCHEV, ELIA (BISHOP KYRILL OF PITTSBURGH), bishop. Bishop of Pitts. Orthodox Ch. Am., Wexford, Pa. Office: Orthodox Ch Am PO Box R Wexford PA 15090

YONKER, NICHOLAS J(UNIOR), religious studies educator, administrator; b. Muskegon, Mich., May 28, 1927; s. John Cornelius and Grace (Langeland) Y.; m. Thea Johanna Grunsfelder, May 28, 1960; children—Nicholas, Robert, Mark. B.A. in Philosophy, Hope Coll., 1950; M.A. in Religion, Columbia U., 1956, Ph.D. in Religion, 1961. Prof. religious studies Oreg. State U., Corvallis, 1962-92, chmn. dept., 1982-88. Author: God, Man and the Planetary Age, 1978. Mem. Am. Acad. Religion, Ctr. for Process Studies, AAUP. Home: 333 NW 33rd Corvallis OR 97330 Office: Oreg State U Dept Religious Studies Corvallis OR 97331

YONTECK, ELIZABETH BARBARA, minister, health care consultant; b. Miami, Fla., Oct. 20, 1931; d. Frederick and Mary (Enyedy) Y. BS, U. Miami, 1953; MDiv, Columbia Theol. Sem., Decatur, Ga., 1971, D of Ministry, 1988. Ordained to ministry Presbyn. Ch. (U.S.A.), 1971. Ednl. missionary Presbyn. Ch. (U.S.A.), Japan, 1959-70; pastor various chs. W.Va. Presbytery, Presbyn. Ch. (U.S.A.), 1971-84; cons. surveys Cen. Pk. Lodges Inc., Sarasota, Fla., 1989—; coord. children's ministry 1st Presbyn. Ch., Sarasota, 1990—; mem. Mission Gd. Gen. Assembly, Presbyn. Ch. (U.S.A.), Atlanta, 1974-78, chair standing com. Gen. Assembly, 1976; presenter women's issues and health care workshops, 1989—. Contbr. articles to profl. jours. Chair evaluation Planned Approach to Community Health, Sarasota County, 1987—; v.p. Adv. Commn. on Status of Women, Sarasota County, 1988-89. Mem. Acad. Parish Clergy (bd. dirs. 1986—), Assn. for Clin. Pastoral Edn., Nat. Coun. for Family Rels. (cert. family life educator), Bay Area Consortium for Women (sec. region 1988—). Office: 1st Presbyn Ch 501 Bowman Ct Sarasota FL 34237

YONTS, JACK E., religious organization administrator. Gen. dir. home mission United Pentecostal Ch. Internat., Hazelwood, Mo. Office: United Pentacostal Ch 8855 Dunn Rd Hazelwood MO 63042*

YONTS, MARTIN L., bishop. Bishop of Southeastern Tex.-So. La. Evang. Luth. Ch. in Am., Houston. Office: Evang Luth Ch in Am 350 350 Glenborough Dr Ste 310 Houston TX 77067*

YORK, MICHAEL RAY, minister; b. Pineville, Ky., Dec. 3, 1954; s. James Robert York and Lola May (King) Wynn; m. Carolyn Jane Mowdy, Aug. 3, 1979; children: Jonathan, Jennifer, Michael C. BTh., Clear Creek Bible Coll., Pineville, Ky., 1982; MDiv, New Orleans Bapt. Theol. Sem., 1988. Ordained to ministry, 1981. Pastor First Bapt. Ch., Ewing, Va., 1981-82; chaplain Santa Barbara (Calif.) Rescue Mission, 1982-83; pastor Fairfield Bapt. Ch., Moselle, Miss., 1984-85; missionary Eastview Mission, New Orleans, 1986-88; pastor Madison Heights (Mich.) Fellowship Ch., 1988—; exec. bd. mem. Bapt. State Conv. of Mich., 1990-93. Home: 1221 Beaupre Madison Heights MI 48071 Office: Madison Heights Fellowship 215 W Eleven Mile Rd Madison Heights MI 48071

YORK, THURNACE, minister, evangelist; b. Ada, Okla., Apr. 10, 1926; s. Walter Daniel and Eliza Jane (Jennings) Y.; m. Virginia Ethelyn Sutton, Dec. 3, 1955; children: Christopher Thurnace, Robin Lyn. BTh., Holmes Theol. Sem., Gardenville, S.C., 1948; BA, East Cen. State U., Ada, 1950; MS, NYU, Buffalo, 1968; EdD, Nova U., 1986; DD (hon.), Pioneer Theol. Sem., Rockford, Ill., 1954. Ordained to ministry Assemblies of God. Adminstr., educator Visalia (Calif.) Unified Sch. Dist., 1960-65; administr., curriculum specialist Buffalo Bd. Edn., 1966-68; supr. dept. of exceptional edn. Niagara Falls (N.Y.) Bd. Edn., 1968-71; adminstr., educator Fresno (Calif.) Bd. Edn. Adolescent Day Care Ctr., 1971-73; internat. lectr. Better Life Seminars, Fresno, 1974—; provost Heritage U. P.T.L., Charlotte, N.C., 1977-79; C.P.E. assoc. dir. Oral Roberts U. City of Faith, Tulsa, 1981-85; adminstr. Casa de Oro (HUD), Corpus Christi, Tex., 1985-88; gen. mgr. Sta. TV50/TV7, Corpus Christi, 1987-91; artist Western Chalk Artist Sch., Calif.,1960-65; lectr. on mental retardation NYU Study Coun., 1967-71. Writer, artist Advocate Press, 1946-50. Counselor YMCA Juvenile Dept., 1950-59; pres. Siskeyaut County, Calif. Tchrs. Assn., 1960; amb.-at-large region 6 U.S. Dept. Transp., Washington, 1983-85; mem. NEA, Washington, 1958, Coun. Adminstrs. Spl. Edn., Buffalo, 1967, Com. on Drugs and Crime Prevention, Granite City, Ill., 1981. Fellow Royal Geog. Soc. (London); mem. Nat. Christian Counselors Assn. Avocations: music, art, travel. Office: Better Life Found 6805 Crosstimbers Dr Corpus Christi TX 78413

YORKS, MELVIN JOSEPH (MEL YORKS), minister; b. Monroe, La., May 11, 1956; s. Roger Irwin and Alice Lorraine (Warlick) Y.; m. Dixie Ann Harrison, Dec. 30, 1978; 1 child, Sarah Dianne. B in Music Edn., Northeast La. U., 1978; MRE, New Orleans Bapt. Theol. Sem., 1989, M in Ch. Music, 1990. Tchr. choral and instrumental music East Ascension High Sch., Gonzales, La., 1978-88; min. music/youth and sr. adults 1st Bapt. Ch., Logansport, La., 1989—; associational music dir. Ascension Bapt. Assn., Ascension Parish, La., 1979-88; cons. La. Bapt. Conv., Alexandria, 1978-89; family ministry dir. DeSoto Parish Bapt. Assn., 1989—. Dir. Community Band, Logansport, 1989—. Mem. So. Bapt. Conv. Music Conf., Am. Choral Dirs. Assn., So. Bapt. Conv. Religious Educators' Assn. Avocations: golf, gardening, coin collecting. Home: PO Box 789 Logansport LA 71049 Office: 1st Bapt Ch PO Box 380 Logansport LA 71049

YOST, HEDLEY EMANUEL, organist, choirmaster; b. York County, Pa., Aug. 3, 1935; s. Emanuel Jacob and Helen Alverta (Beck) Yost. MusB, Westminster Choir Coll., 1957, MusM, 1959. Acting univ. organist Stanford U., Palo Alto, Calif., 1959-60; organist, choirmaster The Presbyn. Ch.-on-the-Green, Morristown, N.J., 1962-70; assoc. organist St. George's Episcopal Ch., N.Y.C., 1970-72; organist, choirmaster St. Mark's Episcopal Ch., New Canaan, Conn., 1972—; lectr. in music Resources Unlimited, New Canaan, 1975—. With U.S. Army, 1960-62. Mem. Stamford Chpt. Am. Guild Organists, Assn. Anglican Musicians, St. Wilfrid Club. Home: 50 Glenbrook Rd #2C Stamford CT 06902 Office: Saint Mark's Ch 111 Oenoke Ridge New Canaan CT 06840

YOST, LARRY ALLEN, minister, retail associate; b. Tazewell, Va., July 15, 1951; s. Thomas George Jr. and Mary Louise (Lester) Y.; m. Barbara Sue Blystone, Oct. 20, 1984; children: Bruce Allen, Beth Elaine. Student, Piedmont Bible Coll., Winston-Salem, N.C., 1970-75; BRE, Tri-State Bible Coll., South Point, Ohio, 1980; M Ministry in Christian Counseling, Bethany Bible Coll. and Theol. Sem., Dothan, Ala., 1990. Lic. to ministry Ind. Fundamental Ch. Am., 1982. Min. music Broadway Hills Bapt. Ch., Winston-Salem, N.C., 1973-75; youth dir. Walnut Hills Bapt. Ch., Huntington, W.Va., 1979-80, deacon, music dir., 1982—; chmn. Child Evangelism Fellowship, Huntington, 1986—; retail assoc. J.C. Penney, Huntington, 1981—. V.p. Cabell County Rescue, Huntington, 1982-84; instr. ARC, Huntington, 1979-84, Am. Heart Assn., Huntington, 1981-84. Mem. Nat. Christian Counselor Assn. (lic. pastoral counselor, field officer 1989—), Am. Assn. Christian Counselors (rep. 1990—), Inst. for Christian Living (facilitator 1990—, behavior and career cons.), Am. Assn. Family Counselors. Home: 4621 Auburn Rd Huntington WV 25704 Office: Walnut Hills Bapt Ch Oney Ave and Davis St Huntington WV 25705 *The greatest challenge in life is living it to the fullest for the Lord Jesus Christ, because what is done for Him will last and be pleasing to Him.*

YOST, PATRICIA ANN, music minister; b. Kansas City, Mo., Dec. 6, 1937; d. Walter Blair and Margaret Ann Pelz Goree; m. Joseph Allen Yost, Aug. 20, 1963; children: Margaret, Ann David, Joseph, Robert, Joseph Dean, Marjorie. BS in Edn., Ga. Southwestern Coll., 1974; MusM, Ga. State U., 1983. Music dir. Thundering Springs (Ga.) Bapt. Ch., 1975-76; music and youth dir. First Bapt. Ch., Putney, Ga., 1977-78; youth dir. Westview Bapt. Ch., Albany, Ga., 1979-82; children's choir coord. First Bapt. Ch., Albany, Ga., 1983-90; choir dir. Protestant Chapel, M.C.L.B., Albany, Ga., 1983—; cantor, choir dir. Cath. Chapel M.C.L.B., Albany, Ga., 1988—; dir. Sr. Ctr., Albany, 1990—. Editor Friends of the Library newsletter, 1990; writer History of Albany Community Chorus, 1983. Bd. dirs. Friends of the Dougherty County Libr., 1991; historian Albany Community Chorus, 1984—. Mem. Hymn Soc. N. Am. and Can., Nat. Assn. Pastoral Musicians. Home: 500 Vintage Rd Albany GA 31705 Office: Senior Ctr 311 Pine Ave Albany GA 31701

YOU, SANGUINE, public administration educator, university chancellor; b. Puyo, Korea, Feb. 20, 1922; s. Won Joon and Won Ja (Yoon) Y.; children by previous marriage—Young Ku, Benjamin, Ben Woo, Byung Joo; m. Myong Ja Lee, 1970; children—Hyung Suck, Ji Hong. Student U. Pitts., 1957, U. Minn., 1958; M.P.A., Seoul Nat. U., 1962; LL.D., Korea U., Seoul, 1967; Ph.D. (hon.), Los Angeles Bible Coll. and Sem., 1982. Prof. pub. adminstrn. Myong Ji U., Seoul, 1961-69, pres., 1969-75, chancellor, 1977—; vice minister Nat. Unification Bd., Republic of Korea, 1975, cabinet minister, 1975-76. Author: Historical Study on Bureaucracy in Korea, 1968; Public Administration, 1969; Guide to Christianity, 1982; College Education and Liberal Arts Education, 19 booklets, 1983. Founder, chmn. Myong Ji Ednl. Found., Seoul, 1956—; pres. Korea-Pakistani Friendship Assn., Seoul, 1965—; mem. exec. com. People to People Internat., Kansas City, 1973—; bd. dirs. Korean-Am. Friendship Assn., 1979—; elder Myong Ji Univ. Ch., Seoul, 1979—; pres. Korean Christian Council of Missions, Seoul, 1977—; v.p. Christian Businessmen's Com. of Korea, 1977—; internat. dir. Internat. Christian Businessmen's Com., 1983—; chmn. Asian Christian Businessmen's Com., 1983—; chmn. Central Council of New Community Movement for Bus. (Sae Maul Undong), Korea, 1982—. Decorated Verleihungurkinde in Anerkennung (Fed. Republic Germany), Order Green Stripes (Republic of Korea). Mem. Korea Internat. Law Assn., Korea Pub. Adminstrn. Assn. (v.p. 1973-74). Home: 392-8 Hongeun-Dong, Sudaemun-ku, Seoul 120, Republic of Korea Office: Myong Ji U Found, 58-17 Suhsomun-Dong, Chung-ku Seoul 100, Republic of Korea

YOUAKIM, SABA, archbishop. Archbishop of Petra, Phila. and all Transjordan Melkite Rite, Roman Cath. Ch., Jabal, Amman, Jordan. Office: Archeveche Grec-Melkite, Catholique, POB 2435, Jabal Amman Jordan*

YOUDOVIN, IRA S., rabbi; b. N.Y.C., Apr. 10, 1941; s. Julius M. and Ann (Goldberg) Y.; m. Susan Schaalman, Aug. 21, 1983; children: Julie Naomi, Joshua Aaron. BA, Columbia U., 1962; MA in Hebrew Letters., Hebrew Union Coll., 1968. Ordained rabbi, 1968. Asst. rabbi Temple Emanuel, Worcester, Mass., 1970-73; N.Am. dir. World Union for Progressive Judaism, N.Y.C., 1973-77; exec. dir. Assn. Reform Zionists Am., N.Y.C., 1977-84; rabbi Temple Beth-El, St. Petersburg, Fla., 1984-91; sr. rabbi Stephen Wise Free Synagogue, N.Y.C., 1991—; Pres. Jewish Fedn., Pinellas County, Fla., 1987-88; mem. rabbinical adv. coun. United Jewish Appeal, N.Y.C., 1980—; v.p. Clergy Assn. Greater St. Petersburg, 1990-91; mem. World Zionist Exec., N.Y.C., 1978-79. Contbr. articles to profl. publs. Trustee Pinellas County Mental Health Assn., St. Petersburg, 1985-87. Capt. USAF, 1985-87. Mem. Cen. Conf. Am. Rabbis. Office: Stephen Wise Free Synagogue 30 W 68th St New York NY 10023

YOUMANS, PAUL CARR, minister; b. Atlanta, June 19, 1965; s. Harold Carr and Christine Elaine (Shelnutt) Y.; m. Cathy Annette Beeson, July 18, 1987; 1 child, Micah Paul. BTh, Piedmont Bible Coll., 1988. Lic. to ministry Bapt. Ch., 1989. Youth pastor Emmanuel Bapt. Ch., Hartsville, S.C., 1988—. Republican. Home: 212 Sunnyside Dr Hartsville SC 29550 *From the midst of the uncertain and ever-changing events of this world, the immutable Word of God quietly reminds us that through faith in Jesus Christ one "might have life, and might have it more abundantly."*

YOUNCE, DALE RICHARD, minister; b. Foley, Ala., July 3, 1937; s. Dallas Campbell and Nettie Mae (Dukes) Y.; m. Theresa Overstreet, June 10, 1963 (div. 1974); children: Dale Richard Jr., Dallas Webster; m. Alice Barron, Oct. 10, 1980; children: William Robert, Margaret Mae. BA, Miss. Coll., Clinton, 1959; ThM, Dallas Theol. Sem., 1963, ThD, 1969. Minister Grace Ch., Wichita Falls, Tex., 1963-68, Faith Covenant Ch., Borger, Tex., 1969-73; instr. Frank Phillips Coll., Borger, 1969-73; prin. Satsuma (Ala.) Christian Sch., 1974; asst. pastor First Bapt. Ch., Chickasaw, Ala., 1975-80; minister to single adults Dauphin Way Bapt. Ch., Mobile, Ala., 1980-82; pastor, tchr. King's Way Bapt. Ch., Mobile, 1982-90; instr. Dallas Bible Coll., 1964, Mobile Coll., 1977-78; pres. Tri-Cities Pastors Assn., Borger, Tex., 1970; writer Bapt. Sunday Sch. Bd., Nashville, 1975-80; Latin tchr. UMS Prep. Sch., Mobile, 1985-86. Columnist religious articles Borger News-Herald, 1970-73, Union Gospel Press, Cleve., 1970-80. Mgr. Dal C. Younce Campaign for Ala. Legis., Mobile, 1977. Named one of Outstanding Young Men of Am. U.S. Jaycees, 1972; recipient Community Service award Altrusa Internat., 1973. Mem. Mobile Bapt. Assn. (exec. com. 1975—, dir Sunday Sch. 1975-80). Republican. Avocations: camping, jogging. Home: 6001 Burnt Oak Ct Mobile AL 36609

YOUNG, CHARLES WILLIAM, minister; b. Salem, Ind., Aug. 9, 1952; s. Roy Russell and Andra Beatrice (Burton) Y.; m. Brenda Grace Mason, June 15, 1974; children: Rachel Maria, Zachary Mason, Jacob Lincoln. BA, Circleville Bible Coll., 1974; MDiv, Asbury Theol. Sem., 1977. Ordained to ministry Free Meth. Ch. Assoc. pastor Cypress Ave Wesleyan Ch., Columbus, Ohio, 1971; student pastor Free Meth. Ch., New Lexington, Ohio, 1973-74, Cin., 1974-78; sr. pastor Cornerstone Free Meth. Ch., Akron, Ohio, 1978—; del. gen. conf. Free Meth. Ch., Indpls., 1985, 89; chmn. Ohio Bd. Social Action, 1983-85; bd. dirs. Chapel Hill Christian Schs., Akron, 1989—. Author: Belonging: Membership Training Course, 1990, Seeds for Life: A Guide for New Believers, 1991. Mem. Circleville Bible Coll. Alumni Assn. (pres. 1985-91). Home: 2865 Bender Ave Akron OH 44319 Office: Cornerstone Ch 578 Killian Rd Akron OH 44319

YOUNG, CORRINE ORELIA, retired religion educator; b. Hendersonville, N.C., Oct. 14, 1924; d. Elzie Charran and Amanda Eleanor (Schuster) Graham; m. Alvis Thomas Young, Sept. 20, 1951 (dec. 1991); 1 child, Alva Jean. BS, So. Missionary Coll., 1964; MEd, Ga. State U., 1972. Bible instr. Ga. Cumberland Conf., Calhoun, 1948-53; tchr. Savannah, Columbus, Albany and Calhoun, Ga., 1953-68, Carolina Conf., Asheville-Pisqah and Candler, N.C., 1972-75, Ky.-Tenn. Conf., Memphis, 1975-84, Threshold Montessori, Memphis, 1984-86; ret., 1989. Home: 6911 7th Rd Bartlett TN 38134 *As a teacher it has been my aim to prepare every youth under my care to be a blessing to the world.*

YOUNG, DANIEL MERRITT, minister; b. Flint, Mich., Jan. 17, 1953; s. George Mardlin and Madeline C. (Merritt) Y.; m. Dianne Kay Rosenberger, Aug. 11, 1973; children: Daniel Laurence, Rachael Kathleen. BS in Psychology magna cum laude, Cen. Mich. U., 1975, postgrad., 1975-77, 84-87; MDiv cum laude, Boston U. Sch. Theology, 1980, D of Ministry, 1981. Ordained to ministry United Meth. Ch. as deacon, 1978, elder, 1983. Youth min. Carson City (Mich.) United Meth. Ch., 1973-75; dir. Christian Edn. Alma (Mich.) 1st United Meth. Ch., 1975-77; intern pastor St. Matthews United Meth. Ch., Acton, Mass., 1978-81; assoc. pastor Cen. Meth. Ch., Detroit, 1981-84; pastor Ortonville (Mich.) United Meth. Ch., 1984-91, Escanaba (Mich.) Cen. United Meth. Ch., 1991—; trustee Detroit Ann. Conf., United Meth. Ch., 1987—; video specialist, media communications technician, Boston U. Sch. Theology, 1978-81; mem. Mercy Corps internat. study trip, Israel and Jordan, 1990. Mem. adv. bd. Planned Parenthood of Mich., 1982-86; dean Detroit Conf. Youth Leadership Camp, summers 1981-84; mem. Conf. Coun. on Youth Ministries, 1981-84. Fellow The Acad. for Preaching (1st class 1990), Acad. for Preaching (study tour Holy Land 1989); mem. Detroit East Dist. Clergy Assn. (v.p. 1982-84), Local Ch. Ministries Div. Leadership Devel. (bd. dirs. 1982-86), Ortonville Pastors' Assn. (v.p. 1985-87), Flint Dist. United Meth. Ch. Clergy and Spouses' Assn. (v.p. 1985-86, pres. 1986-89, Genesee Astron. Soc., Rotary (v.p.-elect 1991-92, scholarship chmn. 1986-91). Avocations: astronomy, photography, physical fitness, camping. Office: Cen United Meth Ch PO Box 815 322 S Lincoln Rd Escanaba MI 49829 *I believe that life is a gift of God—even when there is pain or trouble. Then we know the grace of God as we find God with us in the midst of events.*

YOUNG, DAVID SAMUEL, minister; b. Mechanicsburg, Pa., Nov. 3, 1944; s. Grace Wolf Young; m. Joan Elizabeth Reznar, Nov. 26, 1966; children: Jonathan, Andrew. BS magna cum laude, Elizabethtown (Pa.) Coll., 1966; MDiv cum laude, Bethany Theol. Sem., Oak Brook, Ill., 1970, DMin, 1976. Ordained to ministry Ch. of the Brethren, 1970. Pastor Bush Creek Ch. of Brethren, Monrovia, Md., 1970-78, Everett (Pa.) Ch. of Brethren, 1978-80, Goshen (Ind.) City Ch. of Brethren, 1980-82, Mingo Ch. of the Brethren, Royersford, Pa., 1983-86; hospice pastor Crozer Chester Med. Ctr., Upland, Pa., 1987—; adj. prof. ch. renewal Ea. Bapt. Theol. Sem., Phila., 1986—; bd. dirs. Bethany Theol. Sem., Oak Brook, 1978-83; chmn. nurture Mid-Atlantic Dist., Md., 1977-78; dean Ctr. for Bibl. Studies, Frederick, Md., 1977-78. Editor: Study War No More, 1981, James: Practical Faith and Active Love, 1992; contbr. articles to profl. jurs. NSF fellow, 1966, 66, 67. Mem. Ministers Assn., Assn. Brethren Caregivers. Home: 107 Valley Dr West Chester PA 19382 Office: Crozer Chester Med Ctr One Med Ctr Blvd Upland PA 19013 *Awakened to God's living presence, the life of faith is one of gratitude, strength, and obedience. In an era of spiritual renewal, our life of continual prayer is joyously turned into faithful action.*

YOUNG, DENNIS JAMES, minister; b. St. Louis, June 5, 1949; s. James A. and Betty J. (Elz) Y.; m. Vivian F. Moynihan, June 4, 1988. BS in Edn., Concordia Coll., Seward, Nebr., 1971; MDiv, Concordia Sem. in Exile, St. Louis, 1975; postgrad. studies, Luth. Sch. of Theol., 1988—. Ordained to ministry Assn. Evang. Luth. Chs., 1980. Assoc. dir. Ecunemical Inst., Jerusalem, Israel, 1976-78, Internship Program Christ Sem., St. Louis, 1978-81; dir. field edn. Christ Sem., St. Louis, 1977-81; pastor Resurrection Luth. Ch., Godfrey, Ill., 1985—; dean West Cen. Conf., Springfield Ill., 1987-90; mem. Synod Coun. Cen. So. Ill. Synod Evangel. Luth. Ch., Springfield, 1987-90, Bishops Mutual Ministry Com., 1987-90; co-chmn. Appointments Commn., Springfield, 1987-90. Author (book of poetry) Reflections from the Rooftops, 1971; editor (newsletter) The Resurrectionist, 1985—. Mem. Family and Svcs. Alton, Ill., 1989—, Racism Task Force, Alton, 1989—, River Bend in the 90's, 1989—. Mem. Soc. of Bibl. Lit. Office: Resurrection Luth Ch 1020 W Delmar Godfrey IL 62035

YOUNG, EARL LAVAUGHN, minister; b. Kingstree, S.C., May 1, 1938; s. Hubert Eugene and Orie Fanny (Bingham) Y.; m. Sarah Magdalene Powell, July 23, 1960; 1 child, Joyce Ann. BS in Sacred Lit., Holmes Coll. of Bible, 1957, BS in Theology, 1972; BS in Sociology, Francis Marion Coll., 1973; MA in Counseling, Liberty U., 1991. Ordained to ministry Christian Ch., 1960; cert. tchr., profl. counseling. Pastor Life Christian Assembly, Charleston, S.C., 1989—; field promoter, Internat. Christian Ch., Daytona Beach, Fla., 1983-89, seminar tchr., Internat. Life Christ Ministries, Daytona Beach, 1983-89, v.p. Rep. princint promoter. Rockingham, N.C., 1976-78, Sumter, S.C., 1986-88. Mem. Nat. Christian Counselors Assn. (counselor). Home: 8165 Windsor Hill Blvd Charleston SC 29420 Office: Life Christian Assembly 8137 Windsor Hill Blvd Charleston SC 29420

YOUNG, GERALD LEWIS, minister, teacher; b. St. Louis, Oct. 15, 1944; s. Herbert Lewis and Ruth Ellen (Piper) Y.; m. Gerry Sue Trantham, June 20, 1964; children: Stephen Paul, Karen Sue, John Robert. BA, Ouachita Bapt. U., 1966; MDiv, Midwestern Bapt. Theol. Sem., 1970, D Ministry, 1977. Ordained to ministry Bapt. Ch., 1968. Pastor Antioch Bapt. Ch., Sweet Springs, Mo., 1967-68; assoc. pastor 1st Bapt. Ch. of St. John's, St. Louis, 1970-77; pastor Northside Bapt. Ch., Florissant, Mo., 1977-84, Savannah Ave. Bapt. Ch., St. Joseph, Mo., 1985-89, Blvd. Bapt. Ch., Falls Church, Va., 1989—; mem. adj. faculty Midwestern Bapt. Theol. Sem., Kansas City, 1981—. Author: (with others) Youth Apprenticeship Guide. Mem. Mo.

Bapt. Conv. (exec. bd. Jefferson City, Mo. chpt. 1978-85), Midwestern Bapt. Sem. (mem. bd. of trustees Kansas City chpt. 1977-87), St. Joseph Bapt. Assn. (pres. 1987-89). Avocations: golf, reading, traveling, photograph, sports. Office: Blvd Bapt Ch 7000 Arlington Blvd Falls Church VA 22042

YOUNG, GLENN RAYMOND, minister; b. Winslow, Ariz., May 30, 1944; s. Glenn Ellis and Corky (Whittington) Y.; m. Penny Kay Chernosky, July 27, 1968; 1 child, Matthew Ragan. BA, Calif. Bapt. Coll., 1966; M in Ch. Music, Southwestern Bapt. Theol. Sem., 1970; D in Ministry, Calif. Grad. Sch. of Theol., 1987. Ordained to ministry Bapt. Ch., 1974. Min. of music and edn. Elmhurst Bapt. Ch., Hayward, Calif., 1973-75, First So. Bapt. Ch., Orange, Calif., 1975-80; min. of music and youth Twin Lakes Bapt. Ch., Las Vegas, Nev., 1982-87; pastor Harvard Terrace Bapt. Ch., Fresno, Calif., 1987—; missionary journeyman Fgn. Mission Bd., Philippines, 1966-68; music dir. Orange County Bapt. Assn., 1976-80; cons. youth Vacation Bible Sch., Nev. Bapt. Conv., 1984-87; dir. pastoral ministries Mid-Valley Bapt. Assn., Fresno, 1989—; mem. Mid-Valley Assn. Mins. Fellowship, 1987—, Calif. So. Bapt. Mins. Conf., 1970—. Named one of Outstanding Young Men in Am., U.S. Jaycees, 1973, 76, 78. Republican.

YOUNG, GORDON JAMES, clergyman; b. Havre, Mont., July 13, 1950; s. James Gordon and Juanita Avon (Hoehner) Y.; m. Dayle Marie Bergquist, Apr. 11, 1980; children: Kathryn Ruth, Elizabeth Marie. AA, Concordia Coll., St. Paul, 1970; BA, Concordia Sr. Coll., Ft. Wayne, Ind., 1972; MDiv, Seminex, St. Louis, 1976. Ordained to ministry Evang. Luth Ch. in Am., 1978. Asst. pastor Salem Luth Ch., Mt. Vernon, Wash., 1978-79; pastor St. John Luth. Ch., Chehalis, Wash., 1979-87, Luth. Ch. of Good Shepherd, Pocatello, Idaho, 1987—; protestant chief of chaplains St. Helen Hosp., Chehalis, 1983-87. Bd. advisors Family Living Program, Chehalis, 1985. Mem. Pocatello Interfaith Fellowship, Rotary. Democrat. Home: 169 Filmore Ave Pocatello ID 83201 Office: Luth Ch of Good Shepherd PO Box 4191 18th and E Clark Sts Pocatello ID 83201

YOUNG, H. RICHARD, clergyman; b. Springfield, Ohio, July 21, 1939; s. David Wilson and Ruth Irene (Brown) Y.; m. Charlotte Delores Ashley, June 20, 1959; children: Beverly Jo Young Pulaski, Sherrie Lynn Young Carpenter. Grad., Apostolic Bible Inst., 1966. Ordained to ministry United Pentecostal Ch., 1967. Pastor United Pentecostal Ch., Mankato, Minn., 1966-68, New Lexington, Ohio, 1968—; Sunday sch. sec. Ohio Dist., 1973-81, Sunday sch. dir., 1981—. Home and Office: PO Box 400 New Lexington OH 43764 *In a world so full of change and uncertainty, it is so wonderful to have the secure, unchanging word of God. We need a return to full obedience to its doctrines and principles both as a people and as individuals.*

YOUNG, HOWARD LEE, minister; b. Mena, Ark., Mar. 9, 1949; s. Alex Adolph and Mildred Agnus (Belknap) Y.; m. Barbara Kay Dorris, Oct. 5, 1970; children: Michele Marie, Melinda Kay. BTh, Trinity Bible Coll., 1978; MDiv, Western Evang. Sem., 1983, MA in Edn., 1984; B in Pastoral Sci., North Cen. Bible Coll., 1988. Ordained to ministry Assemblies of God, 1972. Pastor Assembly of God, Seward, Alaska, 1975-78; co-pastor Assembly of God, Anchorage, 1978-79; pastor Assembly of God, Woodburn, Oreg., 1980-85; assoc. prof. North Cen. Bible Coll., Mpls., 1985-89; sr. pastor Cen. Assembly of God, Green Bay, Wis., 1990—; Christian sch. adminstr. Muldoon Community Assembly, Anchorage, Alaska, 1978-79, Faith Christian Schs., Woodburn, Oreg., 1980-85; asst. dist. youth dir. Alaska dist. Assemblies of God, 1975, 76, asst. sectional presbyter, Wis., 1991—. Author: The Craft of Preaching, 1987, Intervention for Marriage, 1991; contbr. articles to profl. jours. Sch. bd. mem. Seward Pub. Schs., 1978-79. Office: Cen Assembly of God 831 Schoen Green Bay WI 54311

YOUNG, J. A., bishop. Bishop of N.W. Okla. Ch. of God in Christ, Lawton. Office: Ch of God in Christ PO Box 844 Lawton OK 73501*

YOUNG, JERRY WAYNE, minister, science educator; b. Memphis, Oct. 2, 1946; s. Elmer Louis and Hazel Marie (Shell) Y.; m. Sandra Lee Henning, Mar. 6, 1971; children—Tara, Tasha, Tory. B.S., Memphis State U., 1969; M.Ed., Drury Coll., 1974; D.Min., Luther Rice Sem., 1979. Ordained to ministry, 1975. Cert. tchr. Chmn. sci. dept. Gainesville High Sch., Mo., 1969-79; prin. Temple Christian Sch., Dallas, 1979-81; prof., dean of students Bapt. Bible Coll., Springfield, Mo., 1981—; pastor Calvary Bapt. Ch., Gainesville, 1974-79; minister of edn. Pleasant Grove Bapt. Ch., Dallas, 1979-81; evangelist Cherry St. Bapt. Ch., Springfield, 1984—. Author: Creation and Evolution: A Serious Analysis, 1979. Contbr. articles to profl. jours. Republican. Avocations: fishing; gardening; art. Office: Bapt Bible Coll 628 E Kearney Springfield MO 65803

YOUNG, JOHN TERRY, religion educator; b. Houston, Sept. 22, 1929; s. Gene E. and Mildred A. (Thiel) Y.; m. Dorothy L. Smith, Aug. 20, 1954; children: Elizbeth Sue, Cheryl Diane (Young) White. BA, Baylor U., 1951; BDiv, Southwestern Bapt. Theol. Sem., 1955, ThD, 1962. Ordained to ministry Bapt. Ch., 1951. Pastor Algoa (Tex.) Bapt. Ch., 1951-53, First So. Bapt. Ch., Chula Vista, Calif., 1957-62, Village Bapt. Ch., San Lorenzo, Calif., 1962-63; editor The Calif. So. Bapt., Fresno, Calif.; prof. theology New Orleans Bapt. Theol. Sem., 1971—. Author: (books) The Spirit Within You, 1977, The Church--Alive and Growing, 1978, Compelled by the Cross, 1980; co-author (with others) Disciples Study Bible, 1988. Mem. Am. Acad. Religion, Soc. Bibl. Lit. Democrat. Office: New Orleans Bapt Theol Sem 3939 Gentilly Blvd New Orleans LA 70126

YOUNG, M(ARVIN) JOE, minister, educator; b. DeWitt, Ark., Nov. 24, 1949; s. Marvin and Donna (Rawls) Y.; m. Joanne Carter Adams, June 11, 1976; children: Donna Jodell, Marvin Joe Jr., Joel Thomas. BA, Henderson State Coll., Arkadelphia, Ark., 1971; MDiv, Midwestern Sem., Kansas City, Mo., 1974; postgrad., Delta State U., Cleveland, Miss., 1978-79, 83-84. Ordained to ministry So. Bapt. Conv., 1973. Student missionary Almirante, Panama, 1969; staff min. 2d Bapt. Ch., Arkadelphia, 1970-71, 1st Bapt. Ch., Independence, Mo., 1971-72; pastor 1st Bapt. Ch., Winston, Mo., 1972-73, Cascilla (Miss.) Bapt. Ch., 1973-77, Paul Bapt. Ch., Scobey, Miss., 1978-85, Parks Bapt. Ch., Drew, Miss., 1985—; trustee Bapt. Student Union, NW Community Coll., Senatobia, Miss., 1980—, instr., 1982—; founding pastor Calvary Chapel, Miss. State Penitentiary, Parchman, 1990; tchr. Spanish, East Tallahatchie Pub. Schs., Charleston, Miss., 1987—; mem. alumni adv. bd. Midwestern Sem., 1979-81; chmn. Lakeside Bapt. Assembly, Scobey, 1983-89. Contbr. articles to denominational pubs. Mem. Rosebloom Vol. Fire Dept., Charleston, 1978-85; chmn. Tallahatchie County Christmas Parade, Charleston, 1986-89, East Tallahatchie County Lit. Coun., 1988-89, PTA, 1974—. Mem. Tallahatchie Pastors' Conf., Miss. Profl. Educators, Midwestern Sem. Alumni Assn. (pres. 1979-81). Office: Parks/Calvary Bapt Ch Rte 1 Box 227 Drew MS 38737

YOUNG, SAM K(AYE), minister; b. Lebanon, Ind., Jan. 31, 1942; s. Charles William and Helen Lucile (Pickering) Y.; m. Judith C. Rush, Dec. 24, 1961; children: Cheryl, Lynn, Eric, Damon. BA, U. Indpls., 1964; MDiv, Christian Theol. Seminary, Indpls., 1967, D of Ministry, 1971; MA, Butler U., 1975. Ordained to ministry Disciples of Christ Ch., 1966. Youth dir. Evangel. United Brethren Ch., Lebanon, 1964-66; sr. minister Providence Christian Ch., Bargersville, Ind., 1966-74, Ninth St. Christian Ch., Logansport, Ind., 1974-89, East Lynn Christian Ch., Anderson, Ind., 1989—; instr. Bible and religion Anderson (Ind.) U., 1991—; chmn. Bicentennial Com. Cass County, Logansport, Ind., 1976, chmn. radio ministry, 1978; chmn. pastoral care dept. Meml. Hosp., Logansport, 1977-78; bd. dirs., pres. Pastoral Counseling Ctr., Logansport, 1980-82. Contbr. articles/essays to religious jours. Recipient Philosophy award U. Indpls., 1964, award for Acad. Excellence, Christian Bd. Publ., St. Louis, 1967; named Outstanding Young Religious Leader, Logansport, 1977. Mem. Madison County Ministerial Assn., Theta Phi. Republican. Home: 3908 Eastern Dr Anderson IN 46012

YOUNG, W. DON, clergyman; b. Ouawah, Tex., Jan. 1, 1938; s. Jack Edwin and M. Dovie (Reeves) Y.; married, July 3, 1955; children: Don Brent, Scott Burton. ThG, Bapt. Bible Coll., 1960. Ordained to ministry Bapt. Ch., 1960. Pastor Bible Bapt. Ch., Paducah, Ky., 1960—; pres. TV ministry program Young at Heart, Paducah, 1971—. Pres. Bellemeade Neighborhood, Paducah, 1988—. Mem. Ind. Ministries Internat. (pres. 1988—). Office: Bible Bapt Ch 1915 N 10th St Paducah KY 42002-0150

YOUNG, WILLIAM DAVID, minister; b. Beeville, Tex., May 31, 1937; s. Justin Richard and Ruth Clair (Ferris) Y.; m. Joycelyn Leuschner; children: Ann Michelle, James David. BA, Harding U., 1964; MEd, U. Rochester, N.Y., 1976; postgrad., Gordon Conwell Theol. Sem., 1987—. Minister Cen. Ch. of Christ, Birmingham, Okla., 1964-65; missions minister Meml. Ch. of Christ, Houston, 1965-67; minister Southside Ch. of Christ, Rochester, 1967-69; exec. dir. Drug and Alcohol Council, Rochester, 1969-70; asst. dir. Monroe County Dept. Mental Health, Rochester, 1970-72; dep. dir. Monroe County Dept. Mental Health, 1974-77; exec. dir. adolescent crisis ctr. dept. pediatrics U. Roch. Med. Sch., 1972-74; minister Cornerstone Christian Fellowship, Rochester, 1977—; cons. New Jerusalem Community Ch., Rochester, 1980-86, Gospel Tabernacle, Oneonta, N.Y., 1981—; cons. Monroe County Probation Dept., Rochester, 1972-74; trainer in counselling U. Roch. Threshold, 1973-75. Served with USN, 1956-69. Republican. Avocations: fishing, hunting, gardening. Home: 21 Shepard St Rochester NY 14620 Office: Conerstone Christian Fellowship 820 S Clinton Ave Rochester NY 14620

YOUNG, WILLIAM EDGAR, religious organization official; b. Whitesburg, Ga., July 28, 1930; s. Edgar Woodfin and Maude Alva (Duke) Y.; student Warren Wilson Coll., 1951, 54; AB, Mercer U., 1956; M.R.E., Southwestern Bapt. Theol. Sem., 1958; postgrad. George Peabody Coll. Tchrs., U. Tenn., Nashville, So. Meth. U., U. San Francisco, Lesley Coll.; m. Mary Todd Watts, Mar. 9, 1963; children: William Jefferson, Todd Woodfin. Minister of edn. and music 1st Bapt. Ch., Swainsboro, Ga., 1958-59, Sherman, Tex., 1960-64; tchr. North Cobb High Sch., Marietta, Ga., 1959-60; ch. bus. adminstrn. cons., 1964-65; dir. ch. adminstrn. field svcs. Bapt. Sunday Sch. Bd., Nashville, 1965-70, mgr. presch. children's sect. discipleship devel. dept., 1970—; adj. prof. Sch. Religious Edn., So. Bapt. Theol. Sem., Louisville; adj. prof. childhood edn. Golden Gate Bapt. Theol. Sem., Mill Valley, Calif., 1980, Sch. Religious Edn., Southwestern Bapt. Theol. Sem., Ft. Worth, 1984; guest lectr. creative writing East Tex. State U., Texarkana. Chmn. Dist. II citizens adv. coun. Metro Schs., 1975-76; pres. Stanford PTA, 1974-75, Grassland PTA, 1977-78; lectr. European Bapt. Conv.; pres. Franklin High Community Assn.; parent rep. Williamson County curriculum assessment group Middle Sch. Task Force, 1979; mem. adv. council edn. dept. Belmont Coll.; bd. dirs. Tenn. Parents Anonymous. Served with USAF, Korea, 1951-54. Recipient Disting. Service award Metro Assn. Religious Edn. Dirs., 1980; Founders award Ga. Ch. Secs. Assn., 1981. Mem. So. Bapt. Religious Edn. Assn. (pres. 1977-78, sec.-treas., bd. dirs. 1984, 85, 86), Assn. Supervision and Curriculum Devel., Assn. Childhood Edn. Internat. (pub. affairs com., early adolescent com.), Nat. Assn. Edn. of Young Children, Am. Soc. Tng. and Devel. Author: Moses, God's Helper, 1976; Jesus, Lord and Savior, 1984, How To Plan and Conduct A Conference, 1987; compiler, writer: Developing Your Children's Church Training Program, 1977; contbg. author: The Ministry of Childhood Education, 1985; contbr. chpts. in books; curriculum writer religious publs. Home: 605 Williamsburg Dr Franklin TN 37064 Office: Bapt Sunday Sch Bd 127 9th Ave N Nashville TN 37234

YOUNG, WILLIAM LAWRENCE, JR., priest; b. Trenton, N.J., Apr. 11, 1944; s. William Lawrence Sr. and Jane (Price) Y. BA, U. St. Thomas, 1966, ThM, 1969. Ordained priest Roman Cath. Ch., 1970. Asst. pastor St. Augustine Ch., Houston, 1970-73, St. Ambrose Ch., Houston, 1973-76, St. Thomas More Ch., 1976-79; dir. office Radio - TV Diocese of Galveston-Houston, 1976-81; tchr., campus min. Marian Christian High Sch., Houston, 1981-86; prin. Mount Carmel High Sch., Houston, 1986—; local and nat. rep. Worldwide Marriage Encounter, Houston, 1976-86, Nat. Cath. Broadcasters, Tex. and Okla., 1980-81. Author (radio and tv scripts) Sounds of Faith. V.p., coach Southwest Houston Softball Assn., 1980-83. Mem. ASCD, Nat. Cath. Edn. Assn., Tex. Assn. Secondary Sch. Prins. Home: 5560 Laurel Creek Houston TX 77087 Office: Mount Carmel High Sch 6700 Mount Carmel Dr Houston TX 77087-6699 *We have no power over the storm, earthquake, or the evils of others, but we always have the freedom to respond with love and gentleness. No one has the power to take that freedom save the self, the worst of all who would enslave.*

YOUNGBLOOD, JOE THOMAS, JR., minister; b. Columbia, S.C., Aug. 7, 1954; s. Joe Thomas Sr. and Milwee (Medlin) Y.; m. Connie Richardson, Sept. 5, 1975; children: Sara Lynn, Joe Thomas III. BS, Midland Tech. Coll., 1974; BA, Charleston So. U., 1983; postgrad, Luther Rice Sem. Ordained to ministry So. Bapt. Conv. Pastor Zion Bapt. Ch., Walterboro, S.C., 1981-85, 1st Bapt. Ch., Gloverville, S.C., 1985—. Mem. Aiken County Quality of Life Com., 1988—; organizer and pres. Com. to Save Gloverville and Warrenville Schs.,1989. Named Nat. Quality in the Pastorial Role, So. Sem., Louisville, 1990. MEM. Aiken County Pastors Conf., Colleton Bapt. Assn. (v.p. pastor's conf. 1983-84, pres. Sunday sch. growth com. 1982-83), Aiken Bapt. Assn. (pres. pastor's conf. 1990-91). Republican. Home: PO Box 603 Gloverville SC 29828-0603 Office: Gloverville 1st Bapt Ch PO Box 157 Gloverville SC 29828-0157

YOUNGBLOOD, REBECCA CAROL, minister; b. Macon, Ga., Dec. 6, 1951; d. John Wesley and Nora Louise (Havard) Y.; m. James Richard Robbins, Jan. 14, 1984. BA in Sociology, Millsaps Coll., 1973; MDiv, Emory U., 1979. Ordained to ministry United Meth. Ch., 1978. Assoc. pastor St. John's United Meth. Ch., Greenwood, Miss., 1979-83; pastor Mt. Pleasant (Miss.) United Meth. Ch., 1983-85, Taylor & Pine Flat United Meth. Ch., Oxford, Miss., 1985-86; co-pastor (with husband) 1st United Meth. Ch., Cleveland, Miss., 1986—, Merigold (Miss.) United Meth. Ch., 1986—. Bd. dirs. Bolivar County Habitat for Humanity, Miss., 1987—. Mem. AAUW, Gen. Bd. Higher Edn. and Ministry (chairperson div. ordained ministry 1988—). Avocations: reading, gardening. Office: 1st United Meth Ch 318 S Court St Cleveland MS 38732-0130

YOUNGBLOOD, RONALD FRED, religious educator; b. Chgo., Aug. 10, 1931; s. William C. and Ethel V. (Arenz) Y.; m. Carolyn J. Johnson, Aug. 16, 1952; children: Glenn, Wendy. BA, Valparaiso U., 1952; BD, Fuller Seminary, Pasadena, Calif., 1955; PhD, Dropsie Coll., Phila., 1961; postgrad., NYU, 1966. Prof. Old Testament Bethel Theol. Seminary, St. Paul, 1961-78; dean, prof. Old Testament Wheaton (Ill.) Coll., 1978-81; prof. Old Testament Trinity Evang. Divinity Sch., Deerfield, Ill., 1981-82, Bethel Seminary West, San Diego, 1982—. Author: Heart of the Old Testament, 1971, Themes From Isaiah, 1983, Exodus, 1983, Book of Genesis: An Introductory Commentary, 1991; editor: The Genesis Debate, 1986, NIV Study Bible, 1985. Owen D. Young fellow Gen. Electric Found., 1959-61, Hebrew Union Coll. fellow, 1967-68. Mem. Evang. Theol. Soc. (editor 1976—), Soc. Bibl. Lit., Near East Archaeol. Soc. (sec. 1978—), Inst. for Bibl. Rsch., Internat. Bible Soc. (bd. dirs. 1989—). Office: Bethel Seminary West 6116 Arosa St San Diego CA 92115

YOUNGER, DORIS ANNE, church association executive; b. Allentown, PA, June 30, 1924; d. W. Chester and Esther M. (Peters) Hill; m. George Dana Younger, June 4, 1949; children—Judith Anne Younger Laspesa, Dana Reed, Stephen Peters, Samuel Hill. B.S. in Edn., U. Pa., Phila., 1946; diploma, Phila. Sch. Occupational Therapy, 1947; M.Div., Yale U., 1950; D.Min., N.Y. Theol. Sem., 1978. Mem. faculty Coll. for Human Services, N.Y.C., 1967-71; mem. faculty Kennedy King Coll., Chgo., 1972-76; exec. dir. Am. Baptist Women, Valley Forge, Pa, 1976-83; gen. dir. Ch. Women United, N.Y.C., 1983-89; ret., 1989; interim dir. Am. Bapt. Commn. on the Ministry, Valley Forge, Pa., 1990-91. Mem. Yale U. Council, New Haven, 1984-89. Democrat. Baptist. Home: 50 Warren Ct South Orange NJ 07079

YOUNGER, GEORGE DANA, minister; b. Mt. Kisco, N.Y., July 24, 1926; s. G. Dana and Dorothy Isabelle (Diggdon) Y.; m. Doris Anne Hill, June 4, 1949; children: Judith Anne, Dana Reed, Stephen Peters, Samuel Hill. BA, Yale Coll., 1947; MDiv., Yale Divinity Sch., 1950; DMin., N.Y. Theol. Sem., 1978. Ordained to ministry Am. Bapt. Ch. in U.S.A., 1950. Pastor First Bapt. Ch., Rochester, Pa., 1951-55, Mariners Temple Bapt. Ch., N.Y.C., 1955-66; program assoc., div. of evangelism Am. Bapt. Ch./USA, Valley Forge, Pa., 1966-68; acting dir. Met. Urban Svc. Tng., N.Y.C., 1968-72; co-dir. Urban Tng. Ctr. for Christian Mission, Chgo., 1972-75; exec. min. Am. Bapt. Chs. of N.J., East Orange, N.J., 1976—; bd. dirs. Navesink House, Red Bank, N.J., Am. Bapt. Found., Valley Forge; exec. com. N.J. Coun. of Chs., East Orange, 1976-91; pres. Coalition of Religious Leaders, N.J., 1979-80. Author: The Bible Calls for Action, 1958, The Church and Urban Power Structure, 1963, The Church and Urban Renewal, 1966, From New Creation to Urban Crisis, 1987; editor: Foundations, 1958-68, Two Bridges News, 1957-68. Chmn. Local Sch. Bd. 3, N.Y.C., 1962-64, 66-70; mem. adv. com. on recycling, N.J., 1984-86. With U.S. Army, 1945-46. Mem. Soc. for Christian Ethics, Soc. for the Scientific Study of Religion, Religious Rsch. Assn. (assoc. editor 1987—), Assn. for Sociology Religion, Am. Evaluation Assn., Nat. Assn. Bapt. Profs. Religion, Yale Glee Club Assocs. Democrat. Office: Am Bapt Chs of NJ 161 Freeway Dr E East Orange NJ 07018

YOUNGER, KENNETH LAWSON, JR., biblical studies educator; b. Richmond, Va., Nov. 29, 1953; s. Kenneth Lawson and Doris (Hastings) Y.; m. Patti Catchings, Aug. 5, 1978; children: Kenneth Lawson III, William Andrew, Rebecca Rachel. BA, ThB, Fla. Bible Coll., Kissimmee, 1976, 78; ThM, Dallas Theol. Sem., Dallas, 1982; postgrad., The Hebrew U., Jerusalem, 1982-83; PhD, Sheffield (Eng.) U., 1988. Teaching asst. Sheffield U., 1985-86; asst. prof. LeTourneau U., Longview, Tex., 1988—. Author: Ancient Conquest Accounts, 1990. Rotary Found. scholar The Hebrew U., 1982-83, overseas rsch. scholar British Govt. grantee, Sheffield U., 1984-86, Tyndale Fellowship grantee, Cambridge U., 1986-87, NEH summer seminar grantee, Yale U., 1990. Mem. Soc. Bibl. Lit., Am. Schs. Oriental Rsch. Office: LeTourneau U PO Box 7001 Longview TX 75607-7001

YOUNGQUIST, GERALD LEE, minister; b. Gowrie, Iowa, Aug. 29, 1930; s. G. Alvin and Ruby (Jacobson) Y.; m. Rozella June Youngquist, Apr. 22, 1953; children: Grant, Andrew, Karl. BA, Gustavus Adolphus Coll., 1958; MDiv, Augustan Theol. Sem., 1962; postgrad., Inst. Advanced Pastoral Study, Detroit, 1983—. Ordained to ministry Evang. Luth. Ch. in Am., 1962. Pastor lst Luth. Ch., Kirkland, Ill., 1962-71; sr. pastor lst Luth. Ch., Monmouth, Ill., 1971—; del. Luth. Ch. in Am. Conv., Chgo., 1978, Toronto, Ont., Can., 1984. Bd. dirs. Augustana Coll., 1972-82. With U.S. Army, 1951-53. Mem. Rotary (pres.). Democrat. Home: 122 S 4th St Monmouth IL 61462 Office: lst Luth Ch 116 South B St Monmouth IL 61462

YOUNGREN, PETER JONAS, evangelist; b. Sweden, Oct. 6, 1954; s. Jonas and Irene Ljunggren; m. Evangeline Price (div.); children: Peter, Rachel; m. Roxanne Rutkay; children: Marcus, Stephanie. Founder, pres. World Impact Ministries, Niagara Falls, Ont., Can., 1974—, Peter Youngren Ministries, Niagara Falls, 1980—, World Impact Bible Inst., St. Catharines, Ont., 1988—. Author: God the Healer, The Coming Canadian Awakening; producer Peter Youngren Presents telecast, 1989—. Office: World Impact Ministries, PO Box 823, Niagara Falls, ON Canada L2E 6V6

YOUNT, ROYALL AUSTIN, bishop; b. Hickory, N.C., May 19, 1922; s. Floyd Stephen and Lottie May (Austin) Y.; m. Martha Lee Townsend, June 14, 1945; children: Royal Austin, John Timothy. AB, Lenoir Rhyne Coll., Hickory, 1942; MDiv, Luth. Theol. So. Sem., Columbia, S.C., 1945; DD hon., Newberry Coll., S.C., 1956. Ordained to ministry Lutheran Ch. in Am., 1945, bishop 1980. Pastor St. Paul Luth. Ch., Tampa, Fla., 1945-52; pres. Fla. synod. United Luth. Ch. Am., 1950-62; pres., bishop Fla. synod. Luth. Ch. in Am., Tampa, 1962—; dir. bd. pensions Luth. Ch. in Am., 1978—, com. mem. div. svc. to mil. personnel, 1976—. Mem. Tampa Selective Service Vd., 1983; trustee Newberry Coll., 1950—. Luth. Theol. So. Sem., 1950—. Democrat.

YOUNT, WILLIAM MCKINLEY, minister, librarian, educator; b. Cin., Feb. 3, 1945; s. James Niles and Daisy Norma (Kammerer) Y.; m. Helen Charlene Glover, June 24, 1966; children: William Barton, Jennifer Leigh, Amy Joy, Katherine Lorene. BA, Asbury Coll., 1967; MA, MDiv, Trinity Evang. Div. Sch., Deerfield, Ill., 1971; ThM, Princeton Theol. Sem., 1974; MLS, U. So. Miss., 1982; EdD, No. Ill. U., 1986. Ordained to ministry Presbyn. Ch. in Am., 1973. Min. 1st Presbyn. Ch., Trussville, Ala., 1973-75, Green Cove Springs, Fla., 1975-79; instr. Whitworth Coll., Brookhaven, Miss., 1979-81; libr. Trinity Evang. Div. Sch., Deerfield, 1982-86, Reformed Theol. Sem., Jackson, Miss., 1986-91; min. Ackerman (Miss.) Presbyn. Ch., 1991—; asst. prof. history and philosophy Jackson (Miss.) State U., 1991—; min., mem. Presbytery of No. Ill., 1982—. Mem. Miss. Libr. Assn. (pres. spl. librs. com. 1990-91), Rotary (bd. dirs. Clinton club 1986—). Office: Jackson State U Dept History and Philosophy 1200 J R Lynch St Jackson MS 39217

YOVCHEV, GEORGI IVANOY, church administrator. Apostolic adminstr. Diocese of Sofia and Plovdiv, Latin Rite, Roman Cath. Ch., Bulgaria. Office: Diocese of Sofia and Plovdiv, Lilyana Dimitrova St 3, 4000 Plovdiv Bulgaria*

YRIGOYEN, CHARLES, JR., church denomination executive; b. Phila., Dec. 9, 1937; s. Charles and Erma Mae (Suters) Y.; m. Jeanette Alice Brittingham, Dec. 13, 1958; children: Debra Jean, Charles III. BS in Econs., U. Pa., 1959; BD, Lancaster (Pa.) Theol. Sem., 1962; ThM, Ea. Bapt. Theol. Sem., Phila., 1964; PhD, Temple U., 1973; DD (hon.), Albright Coll., 1987. Ordained to ministry United Meth. Ch., 1960. Pastor various chs. Meth. Ch., Pa., 1958-66; campus min. Meth. Ch., Phila., 1966-68; chaplain, prof. religion Albright Coll., Reading, Pa., 1968-82; gen. sec. Gen. Com. on Archives and History, United Meth. Ch., Madison, N.J., 1982—; vis. scholar Union Theol. Sem., N.Y.C., 1980, lectr., 1982—; adj. prof. ch. history Drew U., Madison, 1982—; mem. exec. com. World Meth. Coun., 1986—. Author: Acts for Our Time, 1987; editor: Reformed and Catholic, 1978, Catholic and Reformed, 1979; Meth. History jour., 1982—. Trustee Pennington (N.J.) Sch., 1987—. Masland fellow Union Theol. Sem., 1975, 80. Mem. World Meth. Hist. Soc. (gen. sec. 1987—), Wesley Hist. Soc., Wesleyan Theol. Soc., Am. Soc. Ch. History, Charles Wesley Soc. Republican. Home: 2 Hemlock Ln Morristown NJ 07960 Office: Gen Com on Archives and History PO Box 127 Madison NJ 07940

YU, DAVID CHIEN-SENG, religion educator; b. Fuzhou, Republic of China, July 13, 1918; came to U.S. 1947; s. Nan-heng and Ming-chien (Hu) Yu; divorced 1984; children: David Nathan, Nancy Ellen. BD, Nanjing Theol. Sem., Republic of China, 1944; ThM, Cen. Bapt. Theol. Sem., 1950; MA, U. Mo., Kansas City, 1950; PhD, U. Chgo., 1959. Asst prof. Religion Bluefield (W.Va.) State Coll., 1959-61, U. Va., Charlottesville, 1961-67; prof. Religion Colo. Women's Coll., Denver, 1967-81, Maryville (Tenn.) Coll., 1983-88. Author: Guide to Chinese Religion, 1985; co-author: Religions of the World, 1969; contbr. articles to profl. jours. Buddhist Studies Fellow Assn. of Midwest Colls., 1968. Mem. Am. Acad. Religion, Soc. for the Study of Chinese Religions, Assn. for Asian Studies, Internat. Soc. for Chinese Philosophy. Democrat. Baptist. Home: 2761 East Court Richmond CA 94806

YU, JOSEPH TIENTU, minister; b. Chengtu, China, July 25, 1926; came to U.S. 1959; s. Chi Sung and Su Lan (Chou) Y.; m. Yoshico Wang, Mar. 29, 1958; children: Matthew, Mark, Luke, John. MDiv, Taiwan Bapt. Sem., 1968, Midwestern Bapt. Sem., Kansas City, Mo., 1978. Ordained to ministry So. Bapt. Conv., 1973. Pastor Shihmen Bapt. Ch., Tao Yuan, Taiwan, 1968-75; lang. missionary So. Bapt. Conv., Atlanta, 1979—; pastor St. Louis Chinese Bapt. Ch., St. Louis, 1979—. Author: Amos, 1967. Lt. col. Chinese Army, 1945-64. Mem. Ministers Conf. of St. Louis. Home: 1766 Craig Rd Saint Louis MO 63146 Office: St Louis Chinese Bapt Ch 2831 Ashby Rd Saint Louis MO 63114

YUDEWTIZ, BRUCE J., social service administrator; b. Bklyn., Apr. 19, 1951; s. Norman and Selma (Weinman) Y.; m. Sharon Danis, Oct. 8, 1972; children: Uriel, Elisha, Efraim, Gila. BA in History and Social Studies, Boston U., 1973; MA in Contemporary Jewish Studies, Brandeis U., 1976. Dir. community rels. Springfield (Mass.) Jewish Fedn., 1976-78; asst. exec. v.p. Jewish Fedn. of Greater Dayton (Ohio), 1978-84; campaign dir. Jewish Fedn. of Ft. Lauderdale (Fla.), 1984-86; exec. dir. Jewish Fedn. of North Shore, Marblehead, Mass., 1986—; program chair Intermediate Cities Execs. Inst., 1991; mem. com. on collective responsibility Coun. Jewish Fedns., 1991; bd. dirs. B'nai B'rith Hillel Found., Boston U., 1990—. Ch.-chair North Shore Ad Hoc Task Force Against Discrimination, Marblehead, 1989—. Fedn. Exec. Recruitment Edn. Program scholar, 1973, 74. Mem. Assn. Jewish Community Orgn. Profls. (bd. dirs. 1983-86), Hornstein Alumni Assn. (v.p. 1986-90), Conf. of Jewish Communal Svc. Office: Jewish Fedn of North Shore 4 Community Rd Marblehead MA 01945

YUDKIN, MARJORIE SUE, rabbi; b. St. Paul, May 21, 1956; d. Gerald Simeon and Elaine Audrey (Aronson) Y.; m. John Randolph Tiffany, Dec.

23, 1979; children: Shira, Talia. BA, Yale U., 1978; MA in Hebrew Lit., Hebrew Union Coll., 1981. Ordained rabbi, 1983. Asst. rabbi Congregation Emanu-El, Rye, N.Y., 1983-85; asst. dir. Hillel Found., Princeton (N.J.) U., 1985-86; rabbi Temple Covenant of Peace, Easton, Pa., 1986—; adj. faculty Hebrew Union Coll.-Jewish Inst. Religion, N.Y.C., 1985-91. Exec. com. Project of Easton, 1986—. Mem. Cen. Conf. Am. Rabbis, Women's Rabbinic Network (treas. 1989—), Religious Edn. Assn. (v.p. 1990—). Office: Temple Covenant of Peace 1451 Northampton St Easton PA 18042

YUGUSUK, BENJAMINA W., archbishop. Archbishop in Sudan The Anglican Communion, Nairobi. Office: care PO Box 44838, Nairobi Kenya*

YUHAUS, CASSIAN J., priest, educator, researcher, consultant; b. Hazleton, Pa., July 12, 1923; s. Adam Anthony and Elizabeth Anne (Alasko) Y. MA in Theology, St. Paul Sem., Union City, N.J., 1951; ThD, Gregorian U., Rome, 1962. Ordained priest Roman Cath. Ch. Dir. sem. Scranton, Pa., Hartford, Conn., 1962-65; prof. theology Cath. sems., Boston and Hartford, 1962-74; exec. dir. Ministry for Religions, Pitts., 1985—. Author: 4 books; contbr. numerous articles to profl. jours. Address: St Paul Monastery 148 Monastery Ave Pittsburgh PA 15203

YUKEI, HASEBE YOSHIKAZU, religious studies educator; b. Tokyo, July 7, 1929; s. Yoichi Koyu and Shii (Watanabe) H.; m. Reiko H. Nobuta, Oct. 28, 1963. B degree, Komazawa U., Tokyo, 1955, MA, 1957, PhD, 1989. Lectr. Zen culture Shogen Jr. Coll., Minokama, Gifu, Japan, 1963-65; asst. prof. Aichigakuin U., Nagoya, Aichi, Japan, 1965-75, prof., 1975—. Author: Introduction to the Studies of Ming and Ching Buddhism, 1979. Mem. Japanese Assn. Indian and Buddhist Studies, Japanese Assn. for Religious Studies, The Nippon Buddhist Rsch. Assn., Tokai Assn. of Indian and Buddhist Studies, The Japan Art History Soc. Office: Aichigakuin U, 12 Araike, Iwasaki, Nishin-cho, Aichi-ken Japan

YUN, SAMUEL, minister, educator; b. Ulsan, Republic of Korea, June 19, 1958; came to U.S., 1984; s. Eungoh and Chanho (Kim) Y.; m. Kyungim Martha Mah, Jan. 10, 1984; children: Miriam, Joseph, Mikyung. BTh, Yonsei U., Seoul, Republic of Korea, 1980, MTh, 1984; MA in Religion, U. Dubuque, 1985; ThM, Harvard U., 1987; postgrad., Boston U., 1991—. Ordained to ministry Korean Presbyn. Ch. in Am., 1987. Preacher Carmel-Peniel Presbyn. Ch., Rewey, Wis., 1984-85; assoc. pastor, dir. edn. Korean Presbyn. Ch. in Boston, Cambridge, Mass., 1985-88; pastor The Peace Ch., Brockton, Mass., 1988-90, Korean Presbyn. Garden Ch., Hackensack, N.J., 1990—; prof., dean acad. affairs Presbyn. Theol. Sem. in Am., Corona, N.Y., 1986—; sec. gen. Coun. Korean Chs. in New Eng., Boston, 1989-90; rec. sec. Coun. Korean Chs. in N.J., 1991—. Author: The Living Word, 1990; translator The Black Gold and Isram, 1985. Mem. Am. Acad. Religion, Soc. Bibl. Lit. Home: 176 14th St Cresskill NJ 07626 Office: The Korean Presbyn Garden Ch 64 Passaic St Hackensack NJ 07601

YUNG, KOK-KWONG, minister; b. Hong Kong, Dec. 2, 1927; s. Ting-Sang and Tam Lok-In Yung; m. Nancy Chung, Nov. 24, 1962; children: Wilma Wai Mun, Wilson Wai Shun, Vincent Wai Sang. BA, BTh, Lingnan U., Canton, People's Republic of China, 1951; MDiv, United Theol. Sem., Dayton, Ohio, 1962. Ordained to ministry Ch. of Christ in China, 1955; registered mgr. secondary and primary schs. Min. Yan Chai Ch., Canton, 1951-57, Hop Yat Ch., Hong Kong, 1957-82; gen. sec. The Ch. of Christ in China, Hong Kong Coun., Hong Kong, 1985—; chief, sem. examiner religious knowledge Hong Kong Cert. Edn. Examination Bd., 1964-75; vice chmn. Hong Kong Christian Coun., 1986—; chmn. Hong Kong Christian Svc., 1987—. Bd. dirs. Nethersole Hosp., 1963—, United Christian Med. Svc., 1986—; trustee, mem. theol. coun. Chung Chi Coll., Chinese U. Hong Kong, 1986—; mem. Appeals Bd. Edn., Hong Kong, 1990. Office: Ch of Christ in China Hong Kong Coun, 191 Prince Edward Rd, Kowloon Hong Kong

YUSKA, WILLIAM W., music ministry director; b. Bklyn., Aug. 27, 1946; s. Walter A. and Angela E. (Valentas) Y.; 1 child, Randy E. Dir. music Our Lady of Loreto Roman Cath. Ch., Bklyn., 1968-70, St. Pius X Roman Cath. Ch., Rosendale, N.Y., 1970-78; dir. music ministry St. Clare's Roman Cath. Ch., Rosendale, 1979-82, Our Lady of Lourdes Roman Cath. Ch., Malverne, N.Y., 1982-85; dir. music ministry, bus. mgr. Sacred Heart Roman Cath. Ch., Bennington, Vt., 1989—. Chmn. St. Clare's Parish Coun., Rosendale, 1980-82. Mem. Nat. Assn. Pastoral Musicians, KC (fin. sec. Fr. Clancy coun. 1989-90). Republican. Home: Box 3980 Coleville Rd Bennington VT 05201 Office: Sacred Heart Parish 307 School St Bennington VT 05201

ZABOROWSKI, ROBERT RONALD JOHN, archbishop; b. Detroit, Mich., Mar. 14, 1946; s. Richard Kuhlman and Bernice J. Zaborowski-Kuhlman. Student, Holy Cross Old Cath. Sem., 1964-68, St. Ignatius B.M. Theol. Sem., 1968-72; PhD, St. Ignatius B.M. Theol. Sem., 1976, STD, 1976. Pastor Holy Cross Old Cath. Ch., Detroit, 1968-71; prime bishop Mariavite Old Cath. Ch., Province of No. Am., Wyandotte, Mich., 1974—. Contbr. articles to profl. publs., newspapers; author various works on Mariavite Old Catholicism. Named Count of the City of Crete, Italy. Mem. St. Iranaeus Inst. of France (hon.), Knights of Malta, Knights Hospitaller, Sovereign Teutonic Order of the Levant, Vilatte Guild (pres.). Home and Office: 2803 10th St Wyandotte MI 48192-4994

ZABRISKIE, STEWART CLARK, bishop; b. White Plains, N.Y., Nov. 7, 1936; s. Cornelius and Florence I. (Caffrey) Z.; m. Sarah Kirby Miller, Sept. 14, 1963; children: Joanna Ellen, Michael Stewart. BA, Yale U., 1958; STB, Gen. Theol. Sem., N.Y.C., 1963, DD (hon.), 1986. Ordained to ministry Episcopal Ch., 1963. Asst. to rector Ch. of Incarnation, N.Y.C., 1963-65; rector St. Mary's, Scarborough, N.Y., 1966-69; asst. to rector St. John's, Pleasantville, N.Y., 1969-73; rector St. Andrew's and Christ Ch., Cloquet and Proctor, Minn., 1973-77, Ch. of the Epiphany, Plymouth, Minn., 1977-86; consecrated bishop Diocese of Nev., Reno, 1986—; trustee Ch. Div. Sch. of Pacific, Berkeley, Calif., 1987—. Mem. adv. com. Sex Edn., Washoe County, Nev., 1987—. Office: Diocese of Nev Box 6357 Reno NV 89513-6357

ZACCARDI, NICHOLAS STEPHEN, minister; b. Boston, Apr. 1, 1957; s. Nicholas and Elizabeth (Cavallaro) Z.; m. Cheryl Ann Fagan, Aug. 2, 1980; children: Elizabeth, Sarah, Nicole. BSEE, U. Lowell, 1980. Ordained to ministry World Evangelistic Assn., 1990. Instr. Logos Bible Coll., Severn, Md., 1983-87; vice prin. Calvary Chapel Christian Acad., Severn, 1984-87; asst. pastor 1st Bapt. Ch. of Watertown, Mass., 1987-88, pastor, 1988—; advisor Women's Aglow Fellowship, Lexington, Mass., 1990—, Joshua Ministries, Glen Burnie, Md., 1990—. Host local cable talk show New Horizons, 1988. County coord. Freedom Coun., Anne Arundel County, Md., 1984; mem. Watertown Reading Adv. Coun., 1990, 91. Mem. World Evangelistic Assn., So. Bapt. Conv. (pastor), Am. Bapt. Conv. (pastor), Watertown Ministerial Assn. (co-pres. 1988-89). Home: 128 Mount Auburn St Watertown MA 02172 Office: 1st Bapt Ch 134 Mt Auburn St Watertown MA 02172

ZACHARIAS, RAVI KUMAR, minister, religious organization administrator; b. Madras, India, Mar. 26, 1946; arrived in Can., 1966; came to U.S., 1968; s. Oscar T. J. and Isabella (Manickam) Z.; m. Margaret Jean Reynolds, May 6, 1972; children: Sarah Elizabeth, Naomi Michal, Nathan John. BTh., Ont. Bible Coll., Toronto, Can., 1972; MDiv, Trinity Div. Sch., 1976; DD, Houghton (N.Y.) Coll., 1980; LLD (hon.), Asbury Coll., 1990. Internat. evangelist Christian & Missionary Alliance, Colorado Springs, Colo., 1977—; chmn. dept. evangelism and contemporary thought Alliance Theol. Sem., Nyack, N.Y., 1981-84; pres. Ravi Zacharias Internat. Ministries, Atlanta, 1984—, also bd. dirs. Mem. Lausanne Com. for World Evangelisation (alt. mem.).

ZACHER, ALLAN NORMAN, JR., clergyman, psychologist, lawyer; b. Decatur, Ill., May 23, 1928; s. Allan Norman and Eleanor (Shaw) Z.; student Washington U. Sch. Bus. and Pub. Adminstrn., St. Louis, 1946, 48-50; J.D., Washington U., 1952, Ph.D., 1971; M.Div., Va. Theol. Sem., 1955; S.T.M., Eden Theol. Sem., 1966; m. Estelle Medalie, July 19, 1952 (dec. Mar. 1982); children—Allan Norman III, Mark, John; m. Deborah Bradley, Dec. 27, 1985. Bar: Mo. 1952; ordained to ministry Episcopal Ch., 1955. Assoc. Fred B. Whalen, St. Louis, 1950-52; asst. rector Truro Episcopal Ch., Fairfax, Va., 1955-58; canon counselor Christ Ch. Cathedral, St. Louis, 1958-64; dir. Pastoral Counseling Inst., St. Louis, 1958—; vicar Grace Episcopal Ch., St. Louis, 1958-63; vis. lectr. Eden Sem., St. Louis U., Washington U.; chmn. dept. Christian social relations Diocese of Mo., 1959-63, mem. council, 1969-63; pvt. practice clin. psychology, St. Louis, 1971—; cons. to family life, assoc. joint family life com. Nat. Council Episcopal Ch., 1962-65; labor arbitrator Fed. Mediation and Conciliation Service, 1959—. Pres. mem. steering com. St. Louis Group Psychotherapy Forum, 1962-65; mem. St. Louis Bd. Edn., 1963-69; pres. Northside Neighborhood Council, St. Louis, 1959-61; treas. Mo. Council Family Relations. Chmn. psychodrama and religion round table, 1st Internat. Congress of Psychodrama, Milan, Italy, 1964, 2d Internat. Congress, Barcelona, Spain, 1966. Bd. dirs. Grace Hill House, St. Louis, chaplain, 1958-63. Served with AUS, 1946-48, Kent fellow, 1968; Community Mental Health Research fellow, 1968; cert. trainer and practitioner in psychodrama and group psychotherapy Am. Bd. Examiners; lic. clin. psychologist, Mo., Ill.; mem. Nat. Register Health Service Providers in Psychology. Fellow Am. Acad. Matrimonial lawyers; mem. St. Louis (family law com.), Am. (family law com. on marriage and family counseling conciliation), Mo. (family law com.), Fed. bar, assns., Am. Soc. Group Psychotherapy and Psychodrama, Episcopal Soc. for Racial Unity (nat. bd.), Am. Assn. Pastoral Counselors (diplomate; mem. funding bd. 1963-65), Am. Assn. Marriage Counselors, Mo. Psychol. Assn., Soc. St. Louis Psychologists (past pres.), Assn. for Clin. Pastoral Edn., Soc. for Religion in Higher Edn. Contbr. articles to religious, psychol. and legal publs. Home: 16 Hortense Pl Saint Louis MO 63108 Office: 8420 Delmar Blvd Saint Louis MO 63124

ZACHER, MARK PAUL, minister; b. Charleroi, Pa., Mar. 15, 1958; s. Charles Hugo Richard and Mildred Lucille (Geist) Z.; m. Jill Ann Aucker, June 14, 1980. BA in Philosophy, Indiana U. Pa., 1980; MDiv, Luth. Sem., 1984; postgrad., Covington Sem., 1987—. Ordained to ministry Luth. Ch., 1984. Pastor Immanuel Evang. Luth. Ch., Williamstown, Pa., 1984—; basketball coach Williams Valley Jr./Sr. High Sch., Tower City, Pa., 1989—; mem. adv. coun. Susquehanna Luth. Village, Millersburg, Pa., 1985-90; pres. Williams Valley Ministerium, Tower City, Pa., 1985-90; exec. bd. Lower Susquehanna Synod, Evang. Luth. Ch. Am., 1991—; lowe sound engr. Face the Issue radio program, Harrisburg, Pa., 1990—; bd. dirs. Telerad, 1991—. Contbr. In Sure and Certain Hope, 1985. Driver Williamstown (Pa.) Ambulance Assn., 1985—; bd. mem. Williams Valley Food Pantry, Tower City, Pa., 1985—; chaplain WV High Sch. Varsity Football, Tower City, 1987—; coord. Williamstown Youth Athletic Assn., 1986; bd. dirs. Susquehanna Housing Inc., Millersburg, 1989-90. Recipient Citation, Pa. Ho. of Reps., Harrisburg, 1989. Republican. Home: 134 East St Williamstown PA 17098 Office: Immanuel Luth Ch East and Vine Sts PO Box 37 Williamstown PA 17098

ZACKRISON, EDWIN HARRY, theology educator; b. Hinsdale, Ill.; s. Harry Albin and Esther Virginia (Thorp) Z.; m. Jolene Ann Martinson, June 11, 1963; children: Jill Rochelle, Mark Edwin. BA, Loma Linda U., 1963; MA, Andrews U., 1964, BDiv, 1966, PhD, 1984. Youth pastor So. Calif. Conf. of Seventh-day Adventists, Glendale, 1966-67, pastor, 1967-72; prof. So. Coll. of Seventh-day Adventists, Collegedale, Tenn., 1972-84; tchr. La Sierra Acad., Riverside, 1984-88; prof. LaSierra U., Riverside, 1988—; artistic dir. La Sierra Acad. Performing Arts Soc., Inc., Riverside; dir. Expressions Drama Co., Riverside, Destination Players Drama Co., Riverside; co-dir., writer Scription Drama Co., 1990—; pres. La Sierra Community Performing Arts Assn., Inc., 1990—; editor La Sierra U. Press, 1988—. Cons. editor, writer: These Times mag., 1978-84. Prin. clarinet So. Coll. Symphony Orch., Collegedale, Calif., 1979-84, LaSierra U. Symphony Orch., Riverside, 1984-89. Recipient Community Svc. award La Sierra Acad. Performing Arts Soc., 1988. Mem. Am. Acad. Religion, Religious Edn. Assn., Ednl. Theatre Assn., Evang. Theol. Assn., Assn. Adventist Forums, La Sierra U. Alumni Assn. (pres. 1989—, editor La Sierra U. press). Republican. Avocations: writing, golf, swimming. Home: 5651 Peacock Ln Riverside CA 92505 Office: LaSierra U Sch Religion Pierce St Riverside CA 92515

ZAGRAY, ALLAN HOWARD, pastor; b. Toledo, Mar. 2, 1934; s. Alfred C. and Lois E. (Hoover) Z.; m. Mardell Janice Boyce, 1955 (div. 1976); m. Roberta Grace Pierson, Feb. 1, 1977. BA, Otterbein Coll., 1954; MDiv, Evang. Theol. Sem., Naperville, Ill., 1957; D of Ministry, Meth. Theol. Sch., Delaware, Ohio, 1980. Ordained to ministry Evang. United Brethren Ch., 1957. Dist. supt. Akron (Ohio) Dist. United Meth. Ch., 1983-89; pastor various congregations, Ohio, 1957-73, Woodlawn United Meth. Ch., Bucyrus, Ohio, 1973-76, New Concord (Ohio) United Meth. Ch., 1976-83, Grace United Meth. Ch., Coshocton, Ohio, 1989—; sec. East Ohio Conf. United Meth. Ch., North Canton, 1964-80; ministerial mem. Gen. Conf. United Meth. Ch., 1966, 68, 76, North Cen. Jurisdictional Conf. United Meth. Ch., 1968, 72, 76, 80, 84, 88; mem. Jurisdictional Ct. Appeals United Meth. Ch., 1988—. Trustee Otterbein Coll., Westerville, Ohio, 1987-91, Healthaven Corp., Akron, 1983-87; pres. Family Svc. Bd., Bucyrus, 1974-75. Mem. Kiwanis. Office: Grace United Meth Ch 422 Walnut St Coshocton OH 43812

ZAIMAN, JOEL HIRSH, rabbi; b. Chgo., Mar. 10, 1938; s. Solomon and Ruth (Levy) Z.; m. Ann Shanok, July 1, 1959; children: Elana Beth, Sarina, Ari Lev. BS, DePaul U., 1957; Master of Hebrew Letters, Jewish Theol. Sem., N.Y.C., 1962. Assoc. rabbi Temple Emanu-El, Providence, 1962-73, sr. rabbi, 1973-80; sr. rabbi Chizuk Amuno Congregation, Balt., Md., 1980—; pres. Balt. Bd. Rabbis, 1985-87; first v.p. Synagogue Council Am., 1988—; bd. dirs. Chancellors Rabbinic Cabinet, Jewish Theol. Seminary Bd., Associated Jewish Charities and Welfare Fund, Levindale Long Range Planning Com. Contbr. articles to profl. jours. Chmn. Solomon Schecter Day Sch. Edn. Com., Balt., 1983; bd. dirs. Levindale Hebrew Geriatric Ctr. and Hosp., Balt., 1984—, Baltimore Bd. Jewish Edn., Md. Commn. on Hereditary and Congential Disorders, Associated Jewish Charities and Welfare Fund, Levindale Long Range Planning Com.; active Assoc. Jewish Charities and Welfare Fund; 1st v.p. Synagogue Coun. Am., 1988, pres. 1989-91; mem. chancellor's rabbinic cabinet Jewish Theol. Sem. Fellow Pearlstone Inst. Jewish Living (program planning com.); mem. Rabbinical Assembly (exec. council, long range planning com.), United Synagogue Commn. Jewish Edn. (chmn.), Md. Jewish Hist. Soc. Home: 7912 Winterset Ave Baltimore MD 21209 Office: Chizuk Amuno Congregation 8100 Stevenson Rd Baltimore MD 21208

ZAMBO, PAUL W., religious organization executive; b. Bethlehem, Pa., Aug. 22, 1944; s. Ladislaus J. and Elizabeth M. (Vehafric) Z.; m. Rosemary Ripper, July 24, 1971; children: David, Beth Ann, Jamie Marie, Mary Elizabeth. BA, St. Charles Sem., Phila., 1967; postgrad., St. Charles Sem., 1967-69; MA in Govt., Lehigh U., Bethlehem, Pa., 1974. Cert. fund raising exec. Adminstrv. asst. Allentown (Pa.) Redevel. Authority, 1969-71, project coordinator, 1971, asst. exec. dir., 1971-74, exec. dir., 1974-85; exec. v.p. Allentown Devel. Corp., 1978-85; dir. devel. Diocese of Allentown, 1985—. Contbr. articles to profl. jours. Bd. dirs. Allentown Econ. Devel. Corp., 1985—. Recipient Mayor's Commendation, Allentown, 1985. Mem. Nat. Soc. Fund Raising Execs. (chpt. bd. dirs. 1989—, v.p. 1991—), Nat. Cath. Stewardship Coun., Nat. Cath. Devel. Conf. Roman Catholic. Home: 1030 N Wahneta St Allentown PA 18103 Office: Diocese of Allentown 2141 Downyflake Ln Box F Allentown PA 18105

ZANDEE, JAN, theology educator; b. Leiden, Zuid-Holland, Sept. 9, 1914; s. Pieter C. and Geertruida (Van Polanen) Z.; m. Elly A. Zwaan, Feb. 21, 1939 (div. Mar. 1987); children—Pieter C., Andries R., Geertruida M., Johanna M. Dr. Theology, U. Leiden, 1948, Dr. Egyptology, 1960. Minister, Nederlands Hervormde Kerk, 's.-Heer Hendrikskindren, 1939-45, Warmond, 1945-57; asst. prof. theology U. Utrecht, 1957-69; prof. Egyptology, U. Amsterdam, 1965-79; prof. theology and Egyptology U. Utrecht, 1969-82; chmn. Teylers Godgeleerd Genootschap, Haarlem, 1981-84. Author: De Hymnen aan Amon, 1948; Death as an Enemy, 1960; An Ancient Egyptian Crossword Puzzle, 1966; The Teachings of Silvanus and Clement of Alexandria, 1977. Mem. Deutsches Archaeologisches Institut, Société Française d'Egyptologie. Address: Turandotdreef 5, 3561 HB Utrecht The Netherlands

ZANETOS, JOHN CONSTANTINE, priest; b. Karavas, Cyprus, Mar. 16, 1920; came to U.S., 1937, naturalized, 1945; s. Coastas and Eugenia (Spanos) Z.; m. Irene Greos, July 1, 1945; children: Dean J., Eugenia Buba. Diploma, Holy Cross Sch. Theology, 1942; BD, Hartford Sem., 1945. Ordained priest Greek Orthodox Ch., 1945. Pastor Assumption Ch., Poughkeepsie, N.Y., 1945-49, St. Bpyridon Ch., N.Y.C., 1949-50, Sts. Constantine and Helen Ch., Bklyn., 1950-56; dean Annunciation Cathedral, Boston, 1956-81; pastor St. Anthony's Ch., Pasadena, Calif., 1982-86. Trustee Hellenic Coll., Brookline, Mass. Mem. Ret. Greek Orthodox Clergy Am. (founder, pres.). Home: 22130 Colony Dr Boca Raton FL 33433 *Live as if this day may be the last day on this earth, but live each day as if you expect to live forever.*

ZANNER, RICHARD FERDINAND, church administrator, clergyman; b. Nurnberg, Germany, Apr. 10, 1934; came to South Africa, 1980; s. Paul and Steffi (Ocskay) Z.; m. Valerie auditore, July 10, 1954; children—Ingrid, Chere, Nicole, Richard. Mining Engr., Govt. Mining Tng. Schs., Johannesburg, South Africa, 1955; grad. in Theology, No. Theol. Coll. Florida (South Africa), 1966; D.Div., Mid-Am. U., Olathe, Kans., 1979. Ordained to ministry Ch. of Nazarene, 1963. Shift boss Rand Leases, Roodepoort, South Africa, 1955-60; pastor Ch. of the Nazarene, Frankfurt, Germany, 1960-69; dist. supt, Middle Europe, 1969-80, regional dir. Africa, Florida, South Africa, 1980—; internat. mem. World Youth Council, Kansas City, Mo., 1968-72; v.p. World Help (internat. aid orgn.), Frankfurt, W.Ger.; vice chmn. Internat. Gen. Bd. of Denomination, Kansas City, Mo., 1976-80. Author: No Other Gospel, 1980; contbr. numerous articles to ch. mags.; editor Perspekiven Des Glaubens, 1970-80; editor-in-chief continental ch. mag. Trans African. Pres. Evang. Alliance, Frankfurt, 1978-80. Office: Regional Office, Ch of the Nazarene Box 1460, Manzini Swaziland

ZANNONI, ARTHUR EDWARD, religion educator; b. Cleve., Oct. 13, 1942; s. Gene Charles and Stella Marie (Scarano) Z.; m. Meribeth Wrzesinski, Aug. 16, 1969 (div. 1981); children: Laura C., Luke A.; m. Kathleen Flannery, Feb. 14, 1987. BA, Athenaeum of Ohio, 1965; MA, U. S.F., 1969; PhD, Marquette U., 1976. Vis. asst. prof. theology U. Notre Dame, West Lafayette, Ind., 1976-84; asst. dir. Ctr. Religious Edn. U. St. Thomas, St. Paul, 1985-86, acting dean grad. programs in pastoral studies, 1986-88, assoc. prof. of Old Testament and ministerial edn., 1988—; bd. dirs. Ctr. for Jewish-Christian Learning, U. St. Thomas. Editor: Procedings of the Center for Jewish-Christian Learning, 1985—. Recipient Excellence In Teaching award Edward A. Uhrig Found., 1973, 75. Democrat. Roman Catholic. Home: 1337 Hartford Ave Saint Paul MN 55116

ZARGES, ROBERT SCOTT, JR., minister; b. Cornwall, N.Y., June 4, 1966; s. Robert Scott Sr. and Marilyn Bradford (Clapp) Z.; m. Susan Lynn Sleigh, Jan. 6, 1990. BS in Bible and Christian Edn., Houghton Coll., 1989; M in Counseling, Gordon-Connell Theol. Seminary, South Hamilton, Mass., 1991. Dir. Camp Sandy Hill, Md., 1988-90; assoc. minister of youth and Christian edn. Cen. Bapt. Ch., Quincy, Mass., 1989—; youth coord. Northeast Bapt. Conf., Worcester, Mass., 1991—, camp com., 1991—. Active Big Bros. of Greater Boston, 1991, youth comm. City of Quincy, 1990, Fellowship Christian Athletes, Quincy, 1990. Home: 21 Newcomb St #1 Quincy MA 02169 Office: Central Baptist Church 65 Washington St Quincy MA 02269

ZARLENGA, STELLA MARIE, nun, lawyer; b. Providence, Mar. 27, 1940; d. Lucius Celeste and Angelina (Zinno) Z. BA, Salve Regina Coll., 1962; MA in Teaching, R.I. Coll., 1972; JD, Suffolk U., 1981; cert., Pastoral Inst. Celem Medellin, Colombia, 1976. Bar: R.I. 1984, U.S. Dist. Ct. R.I. 1985; joined Sisters of Mercy, Roman Cath. Ch. Tchr. Cath. Schs., R.I. and Mass., 1962-67; missionary, tchr., interim prin., pastoral worker Cath. High Schs. Diocese San Pedro Sula Honduras, 1967-80; legal asst. Zarlenga & Assocs., Providence, 1981-84, assoc., 1984—; tchr. ESL Colombo Am. Ctr., Medellin, 1976; bilingual pre-sch. dir. Elmwood Community Ctr., Providence, 1980-81. Nelson Burke scholar Suffolk U. Law Sch., 1982-84. Mem. ABA, R.I. Bar Assn., Women's Bar Assn. R.I., Assn. Trial Lawyers Am. Club: Forecourts II (Cumberland, R.I.). Avocations: swimming, racquetball, motorcycling, bicycling. Home: Mercyknoll Convent Highland View Rd RD #3 Cumberland RI 02864 Office: Zarlenga & Assocs 95 Humboldt Ave Providence RI 02906

ZASPEL, FRED GEORGE, minister; b. Chgo., Jan. 2, 1958; s. James Arthur and Constance Pauline (Hanson) Z.; m. Kimberly Ann Barrows, June 8, 1979; children: Gina Ruth, James Paul. BA, Bob Jones U., Greenville, S.C., 1980, MA, 1981; postgrad., Denver Bapt Theol. Sem., 1981-82, Valley Bapt. Theol. Sem., 1983-85, Bibl. Theol. Sem., Hatfield, Pa., 1988—. Lic. to ministry Bapt. Ch. Assoc. pastor Beth Eden Bapt. Ch., Denver, 1981-82; pastor Faith Bapt. Ch., Anderson, Ind., 1982-83, Word of Life Bapt. Ch., Pottsville, Pa., 1985—. Author: Now Concerning Spiritual Gifts, 1987; editor Words of Life newsletter, 1990—. Republican. Home: 845 Elizabeth Dr Orwigsburg PA 17961 Office: Word of Life Bapt Ch 302 N Centre St Pottsville PA 17901

ZAWISTOWSKI, JOSEPH K., bishop. Bishop of Western Diocese Polish Nat. Cath. Ch. of Am., Chgo. Office: Polish Nat Cath Ch Am 2019 W Charleston St Chicago IL 60647*

ZAYEK, FRANCIS MANSOUR, bishop; b. Manzanillo, Cuba, Oct. 18, 1920; s. Mansour and Mary (Coury) Z. Student, St. Joseph's Catholic U., Beirut, 1938; D.D., U. Propagation of Faith, 1947, Ph.D., 1947; D.C.L., Lateran U., 1951. Ordained priest Roman Catholic Ch., 1946; rector Maronite Cathedral of Holy Family, Cairo, 1951-56; Oriental sec. to Vatican Apostolic Internunciature; mem. Archdiocesan Tribunal, 1951-56; promoter of justice Sacred Roman Rota, 1956-58; prof. Oriental canon law Internat. Coll. St. Anselm, Rome, 1958-60, Lateran U., Rome, 1960-61; aux. bishop to Cardinal James De Barros Camera; archbishop of Rio de Janeiro, 1962; titular bishop of Callinicum, maronite bishop Rio de Janeiro, 1962-64; presided over First Ann. Maronite Conv., Washington, 1964; first maronite exarch of U.S.A., 1966—, first eparch of St. Maron of Detroit, 1972-77, first eparch of St. Maron of Bklyn., 1977—, given title of archbishop, 1982. Decorated knight comdr. Equestrian Order of Holy Sepulchre of Jerusalem; recipient medal of merit Govt. of Republic Italy, 1966. Address: 8070 Harbor View Terr Brooklyn NY 11209

ZEBROWSKI, SISTER MARY THEODORETTE, religious educator, artist; b. South River, N.J., Aug. 30, 1916; d. Charles W. and Emily (Rawa) Z. Tchr. diploma, Cath. U. Am., 1940; BA in Fine Arts, Phila. Coll. Art, 1954; MA in Edn., Seton Hall U., 1974. Joined Bernardine Sisters of St. Francis, 1934. Tchr., missionary, prin. various schs., Pa. and, Brazil, 1937-69; tchr. St. Dominic's Sch., Bricktown, N.J., 1969-70; tchr., prin. Sacred Heart Sch., Manville, N.J., 1970-75; prof. Alvernia Coll., Reading, Pa., 1975—, chmn. dept., 1975-88, freelance sculptor, 1989. Exhibited in group shows in U.S., Europe and S.Am. Recipient svc. award Alvernia Coll., 1985, Prof. (Artist) Emeritus, 1989. Mem. Nat. Conf. Adminstrv. Artists, Archives Am. Art, Nat. Art Adminstrs. Assn., Smithsonian Assocs. Avocations: numismatics, philately. Home: Alvernia Coll Reading PA 19607 Office: Bernardine Sisters OSF 647 Springmill Rd Villanova PA 19085

ZECHMAN, DONALD EUGENE, minister, ecumenical broadcast coordinator; b. Harrisburg, Pa., Dec. 6, 1938; s. Harry William and Vesta Mae (Harner) Z.; m. Faye Elizabeth Gamber, Sept. 26, 1964; children: Scott Alan, Craig Alan. BA, Lebanon Valley Coll., 1960; postgrad., Luth. Theol. Sem., 1960-62; BD, United Theol. Sem., 1964; MA in Speech Communication, U. Mich., 1969. Ordained to ministry Evang. United Brethren Ch., 1964. Asst. pastor Derry St. Evang. United Brethren Ch., Harrisburg, 1964-67; organist, choir dir. St. Matthew's Ch., Livonia, Mich., 1967-70; pastor Bethany United Meth. Ch., Lancaster, Pa., 1970-78; program coord. South Cen. Pa. TV and Radio Ministry, Harrisburg, 1972-89; assoc. pastor Salem United Meth. Ch., Manheim, Pa., 1978-86, sr. pastor, 1986—; coord. Manheim Chem. People, 1983-86. Author Sunday sch. curriculum materials; exec. producer shows The Magic Cocoon, Sta. WGAL-TV, Lancaster, 1971-78, Real-to-Reel, Sta. WHTM-TV, Harrisburg, 1983-89. Mem. planning com. CROP Walk for Hungry, Lancaster County, 1973—; bd. dirs. Lancaster County Coun. of Chs., 1983-87. Mem. Am. Guild Organists, Manheim Area Mins. Assn. (exec. com. 1980-84). Home: 110 N Grant St Manheim PA 17545 Office: Salem United Meth Ch 140 N Penn St Manheim PA 17545

ZEEK, PAUL STEWART, minister; b. Ukiah, Calif., Jan. 5, 1959; s. Donald Horace and Marjorie Jane (Goudge) Z.; m. Terriann Evon Harper, Aug. 15, 1980; children: Taryn, Verity, Victoria. AA, Mendocino Coll.,

1979; BA in Biblical Studies, Fresno Pacific Coll., 1983. Intern 1st Bapt. Ch., Ukiah, 1977-79; campus leader 1st Bapt. Ch., Modesto, Calif., 1979-82, intern, 1982-88, assoc. minister/jr. high ministry, 1988—. Office: First Baptist Church PO Box 4309 Modesto CA 95352-4309

ZEHNDER, GEORGE PHILIP, minister; b. Cleve., Sept. 26, 1949; s. Phillip George and Louise O. (Keske) Z.; m. Kathleen Sue Miller, July 30, 1977; children: Geoffrey, Kevin, Lynn. BBA, Kent (Ohio) State U., 1973; MDiv, Concordia Theol. Sem., 1984; postgrad., Notre Dame U., 1988-90. Sr. pastor Emmaus Luth. Ch., South Bend, Ind., 1983-90; chaplain Meml. Hosp., South Bend, 1983-85; with Youth Bd. of Dist., Ft. Wayne, Ind., 1986-90; minister Urban Ministries Inst., South Bend, 1990—. With U.S. Army, 1973-74. Mem. Luth. Svc. Club of Ind. (pres. 1988—). Home: 1519 Sheffield Ct South Bend IN 46614 Office: Emmaus Ministries 929 E Milton South Bend IN 46613-2898

ZEHR, CLYDE JAMES, church administrator; b. Valley Ctr., Kans., Oct. 4, 1934; s. John Wesley and Anna Mae (Carithers) Z.; m. Leona Mae Zehr, Nov. 23, 1957; children: Karen Elaine, Mark Wesley. BS, U. Kans., 1957; ThM, Western Evang. Sem., Portland, Oreg., 1961; MBA, Seattle U., 1976. Ordained to ministry Evang. Meth. Ch. Structural engr. Boeing Co., Seattle, 1957-59; pastor Rockwood Evang. Meth. Ch., Portland, 1961-63; missionary OMS Internat., Seoul, Republic of Korea, 1964-80; dir. Christian Leadership Seminars, Kent, Wash., 1980-82; supt. N.W. dist. Evang. Meth. Ch., Kent, 1982-86; gen. supt. Evang. Meth. Ch., Wichita, Kans., 1986—. Author: Study Notes on Leadership, 1982. Trustee Western Evang. Sem., Portland, 1982—. Republican. Office: Evang Meth Ch Hdqrs 3000 W Kellogg Wichita KS 67213

ZEHR, DAN, religious organization administrator. Exec. dir. Mennonite Cen. Community Can., Winnipeg, Man. Office: Mennonite Cen Comm, 134 Plaza Dr, Winnipeg, MB Canada R3T 5K9*

ZEIDAN, KIMBERLY DAWN, religious organization administrator; b. Canton, Ohio, Feb. 8, 1961; d. Paul Edward and Delores Ann (Pyle) Adkins; m. Mazen A. Zeidan, Aug. 10, 1982; 1 child, Ramzy Mazen. BA in Polit. Sci., Va. Commonwealth Univ., 1982, M in Spl. Edn., 1991. Dir. Cath. Charities, Richmond, Va., 1988-90; exec. dir. The Grace House, Richmond, 1990—. Author: (newsletter) The Messenger, 1991. Bd. dirs. Richmond Child Care Coun., 1990—, Neighborhood Coalition, 1990—. Home: 4312 Gladewater Rd Richmond VA 23229 Office: The Grace House 116 Floyd Ave Richmond VA 23220

ZEISER, WILLARD ARTHUR, minister; b. St. Louis, Mo., Feb. 21, 1940; s. Raymond Russell and Helen Mae (Hale) Z.; m. Juel Belle Johnson, May 15, 1965; children: JaLyn Kay, Jared Ray. AA, SW Bapt. Coll., 1960; BA, Okla. U., 1962; MA, Southwestern Bapt. Theol. Sem., 1965. Minister of youth First Bapt. Ch., Abilene, Tex., 1965-66, San Angelo, Tex., 1966-69; minister edn. adminstrn. Park Hill Bapt. Ch., No. Litte Rock, Ark., 1969-76; minister edn. Wilshire Bapt. Ch., Dallas, 1976-78; assoc. pastor First Bapt. Ch., Oklahoma City, 1978-82; program coordinator, exec. bd. Mo. Bapt. Conv., Jefferson City, 1982—; various positions local Bapt. Chs., Jefferson City, Mo.; prof various ednl. orgns. Recipient Jaycee Outstanding Young Men award. Mem. Mo. Bapt. Religious Edn. Assn., So. Bapt. Rligious Edn. Assn. Baptist. Avocations: cooking, fishing, funiture refinisher. Office: Mo Bapt Conv 400 E High Jefferson City MO 65101

ZELDEN, DOUGLAS HOWARD, rabbi; b. Chgo., Jan. 12, 1960; s. Stuart F. and Barbara J. (Schmidt) Z. BA, Northeastern Ill. U., Chgo., 1981; postgrad., Spertus Coll., Chgo. Ordained rabbi, 1983. Tchr./rabbi Anshe Emet Sch., Chgo., 1980-83, Bnai Torah Religious Sch., Highland Park, Ill., 1980—, Solomon Schechter Middle Sch., Skokie, Ill., 1983-88, Assoc. Talmud Torahs, Russian Transitional Sch., Chgo., 1988-89; high holiday rabbi Congregation Bnai Jacob, Ft. Wayne, Ind., 1989; rabbi Congregation Ezras Israel Orthodox Svc., Chgo., 1988—; tchr./rabbi Jewish Childrens Bur. Therapeutic Sch., Chgo., 1990—; rabbi/spl. project tchr. Ida Crown Jewish Acad., Chgo., 1988-89; interim rabbi Maine Twp. Jewish Congregation, Des Plaines, Ill., 1987; tchr./rabbi Menorah Sunday Sch., Chgo., 1987—; tchr. Oak Therapeutic Sch., Chgo., 1989-90; rabbi commentator Sta. WLUP AM 1000, Chgo., 1986—; rabbinical Kashruth supr. Chgo. Rabbinical Coun., Chgo., 1976—; substitute chaplain/rabbi Luth. Gen. Hosp., Park Ridge, Ill., 1981-84; chaplain Hampton Pla. Nursing Home, Niles, Ill., 1991—; ritual instr. Congregation KINS, Chgo., 1991—. Commentator articles and letters to the Sentinel Newspaper; contbr. articles to profl. jours. Mem. Fellowship of Traditional Orthodox Rabbis, Chgo. Bd. Rabbis.

ZELIZER, NATHAN, rabbi; b. Stavisk, Poland, Sept. 22, 1905; s. Henry and Rose (Kaddish) Z.; m. Florence Handler, Oct. 31, 1937 (dec. 1981); m. Jeanette Zelizer; children: Gerald Lee, Deborah Zelizer Kaplan. BS, NYU, 1930; MA, Columbia U., 1931; MHL, Jewish Theol. Sem., 1931, DHL, 1966. Ordained rabbi, 1931. Rabbi Tifereth Israel Congregation, Columbus, Ohio, 1931-73; ret. Author: History of Higher Jewish Education, 1930. Capt. U.S. Army, 1943-45. Mem. South County Rabbinical Assembly (pres. 1987-89), B'nai B'rith. Republican. Home: 1200 S Ocean Blvd 14E Boca Raton FL 33432

ZELL, SHAWN BLAIR, rabbi; b. Winnipeg, Man., Can., July 19, 1953; s. Philip and Ida (Greenberg) Z.; m. Shirah Sarah Rosenberg, Aug. 26, 1975; children: Hadassah, Ariel. BA, U. Man., 1974; B. Jewish Lit., Jewish Tchrs. Sem. People's U., 1977; MA, Jewish Theol. Sem., 1977. Ordained rabbi, 1981. Rabbi Congregation Shaare Zion, Sioux City, Iowa, 1981-84, Temple Beth O'r, Clark, N.J., 1984—; tchr. Solomon Schechter Day Sch., Cranford, N.J., 1985—. Home: 117 John St Clark NJ 07066 Office: Temple Beth O'r 111 Valley Rd Clark NJ 07066

ZELLER, BARBARA ANN, nun, health care facility administrator; b. Evansville, Ind., Aug. 18, 1945; d. Wilbert John and Dorothy Elizabeth (Tremor) Z. BA in Edn., St. Mary-of-the-Woods Coll., 1968; MA Studies in Aging, North Tex. State U., 1971. Dir. gerontology Sisters of Providence, St. Mary-of-the-Woods, Ind., 1971-76, 78-81; adminstrv. asst. archdiocesan social ministries Cath. Charities Archdiocese of Indpls., 1976-78; exec. dir. Maryvale, Inc., S. Mary-of-the-Woods, 1978-81; dir. social svcs. Pfister and Co., Inc., Terre Haute, Ind., 1981-82; exec. dir. Providence Retirement Home, Inc., New Albany, Ind., 1982—; cons., Poor Handmaids of Jesus Christ, Donaldson, Ind., Little Company of Mary Sisters, Evergreen Park, Ill., Sisters of St. Francis, Joliet, Ill., numerous other orders and ednl. instns. in Ind., Ill., Ohio and Ky.; presenter courses, seminars and workshops on aging and retirement; speaker in field. Author materials and problem solving kits in field. Recipient George E. Davis award, Interfaith Fellowship on Religion and Aging,1985; named Ky. Col., 1988, Sagamore of the Wabash, Gov. of Ind., 1988, Disting. Hoosier Gov. of Ind., 1988. Mem. Ind. Assn. of Homes for Aging, Internat. Soc. Pre-Retirement Planners. Democrat. Avocations: pet therapy, handcrafts.

ZELLER, SISTER LETA MADENE, pastoral associate; b. Evansville, Ind., Nov. 21, 1949; d. Louis Michael and Lorraine Marian (Marjanski) Z. BA in Ministry Formation, Psychology and Religious Studies summa cum laude, Brescia Coll., 1990. Joined Sister of St. Benedict, 1986; cert. in religious edn., gerontology. Religious edn. tchr. St. Theresa Parish, Evansville, Ind., 1968-77, St. Joseph Parish, Evansville, 1977-81; vol. Ferdinand, Ind., 1981-83; pastoral asst. Holy Redeemer Parish, Evansville, 1983-87; pastoral assoc. St. Francis Xavier, Poseyville, Ind., 1990—; dir. religious edn. vol. St. Stephens Cathedral, Owensboro, Ky., 1987-90; youth bd. Evansville Diocese, 1983-87. Hospice vol. Deaconess Ohio Valley Hospice, Evansville, 1990—, Ohio Valley Hospice, Evansville, 1974-87; crisis line phone counselor Green River Comp Care, Owenboro, Ky., 1987-90; dir. inner city youth program Coun. of Chs., Owensboro, 1987-90. Recipient Outstanding Student Vol. Greenriver Comp Care, 1989, Natural Sci. award, 1988. Mem. Benedictines for Peace, Sister Senate, Nat. Fedn. Cath. Youth Ministry. Home: 1210 Harmony Way Evansville IN 47720-6146 Office: St Francis Xavier Parish 20 St Francis Ave PO Box 578 Poseyville IN 47633

ZELLMER, DAVID BRUCE, minister; b. Mpls., Dec. 21, 1953; s. Bruce Edward and Ila Corrine (Johnson) Z.; m. LaDonna Jean Graves, Mar. 6, 1976; children: Christina, Joshua, Sarah, Michael. BS in Psychology, Southwestern Okla. State U., 1977; MDiv, Luther-Northwestern Theol Sem., 1981. Ordained to ministry Am. Luth. Ch., 1981. Pastor, chaplain Scandinavia/Bethany Luth. Parish and Bethesda Nursing Home, Aberdeen, S.D., 1981-85; pastor Trinity Luth. Ch., Mitchell, S.D., 1085—; chmn. Luth. Outdoors Bd. of the S.D. Synod, Evang. Luth. Ch. Am., 1991—. Home: 1400 E 2nd Mitchell SD 57301

ZELLMER, JOHANNES (ERNST), minister; b. Mieczkowo, Poland, Dec. 22, 1920; arrived in Germany, 1921; s. Wilhelm Friedrich and Emma Emilie (Reek) Z.; m. Helene Kusch, Oct. 3, 1946; children: Christoph, Elisabeth, Matthias. Diploma in theology, Luth. U., Kiel, Germany, 1950. Ordained to ministry Evang.-Luth. Ch., 1950. Vicar Gemeinde, Schwerin, Fed. Republic Germany, 1950-59, pastor, 1952-56; pastor Gemeinde, Cottbus, Fed. Republic Germany, 1956-64; supt. Lausitz/Cottbus Diocese, 1964-74; pastor, pres. Oberkirchenkollegium, Evang.-Luth. Ch., Cottbus, Berlin, 1974—. Home: Muehlen-Strasse 34, 0-7500 Cottbus Brandenburg, Federal Republic of Germany Office: Evang-Luth Kirche, Annenstrasse 53, 0-1020 Berlin Federal Republic of Germany

ZELLNER, ANNIE ROSE, lay worker; b. Macon, Ga., Nov. 15, 1928; d. Joe C. and Annie Mae (Williams) Hill; m. Robert L. Hogan, Oct. 5, 1944 (div. 1948); 1 child, Betty R.; m. William J. Zellner, Dec. 10, 1949; children: Anthony M., Aubrey S. Diploma, Warren's Bible Inst., Cleve., 1973. Friendly vis. St. Vincent Hosp., Cleve., 1972-74; youth dir. Calvary Hill Bapt. Ch., Cleve., 1976-80, Sunday Sch. tchr., 1968-88, Bible tchr., 1984—; family circle tchr. Annie Hill Family Circle, Cleve., 1974-78; div. clk. St. Luke Hosp., Cleve., 1979-91. Home: 19613 Gladstone Rd Warrensville Heights OH 44122

ZELLO, SUZANNA MARIE, religious educator; b. Bridgeport, Conn., May 22, 1951; d. Ralph Louis and Elsie Ernestine(Zeleznik) Z. BA, Sacred Heart U., Fairfield, Conn., 1973; MS, Fairfield U., Fairfield, Conn., 1981. CCD tchr. St. Charles Parish, Bridgeport, Conn., 1970-90, youth minister, 1980-88; youth minister Our Lady of Grace Parish, Stratford, Conn., 1980-84; tchr. Blessed Sacrament/St. Mary Sch., Bridgeport, 1975-89, prin., 1989-91; prin. St. Peter Sch., Bridgeport, 1991—; mem. catechetical adv. bd. Diocese of Bridgeport, 1990—, vicariate coord. for youth ministry, 1991—; adult leader Christian Leadership Inst., Bridgeport, 1987—; coord. Liturgy Commn., Bridgeport, 1989—, coord. lectors, St. Charles, 1985—; del. New Eng. Cath. Youth Ministers, 1989-90. Office: St Peter Sch 659 Beechwood Ave Bridgeport CT 06605

ZEMAN, ANDREW HOWARD, minister; b. Hartford, Conn., May 7, 1946; s. William Saxe and Evelyn (Shimelman) Z.; m. Linda S. Fine, Sept. 21, 1985; 1 child, William. BA, Marietta Coll., 1968; MDiv, Yale U., 1971. Ordained to ministry Episc. Ch. Curate Christ Ch. Cathedral, Hartford, 1971-75; vicar Christ Episcopal Ch., Bethlehem, Conn., 1975-81; rector Christ Episcopal Ch., Easton, Conn., 1981-90, Holy Trinity Episcopal Ch., Onancock, Va., 1990—; chmn. Anglican/Roman Cath. Dialogue, Fairfield County, Conn., 1986-88. Office: Holy Trinity Episcopal Ch PO Box 338 Onancock VA 23417-0338

ZENS, JON HARDESTY, pastor, editor; b. Barstow, Calif., Apr. 25, 1945; s. Paul Henry and Goldie Pearl (Hardesty) Z.; m. Dorothea Faith Martin, June 3, 1968; children: Adam S., Eve J., Hannah C. BA, Covenant Coll., 1969; MDiv, Westminster Theol. Sem., 1972; DMin, Calif. Grad. Sch. Theology, 1983. Pastor Nashville Reformed Bapt. Ch., Nashville, 1976-80, Malin (Oreg.) Bapt. Ch., 1981-83, Word of Life Ch., Dresser, Wis., 1983—; mem. steering com. Bapt. Council on Theology, Plano, Tex., 1980-82. Author: (book) Dispensationalism: An Inquiry Into Its Figures and Features, 1978, Studies in Theology and Ethics, 1981; editor Bapt. Reformation Rev., Nashville, 1978-81, Searching Together, St. Croix Falls, Wis., 1982—. Avocations: jogging, golf, bowling, tennis. Home: 104 Dresser St E Dresser WI 54009 Office: Word of Life Ch PO Box 548 Dresser WI 54009

ZENZ, JOHN PATRICK, priest; b. Monroe, Mich., June 6, 1950; s. John Thomas and Helen Gertrude (Strimbel) Z. BA, Sacred Heart Sem., 1972; Licentiate in Sacred Theology summa cum laude, Gregorian U., Rome, 1977, STD magna cum laude, 1984. Ordained priest Roman Cath. Ch., 1978. Assoc. pastor St. Raphael, Garden City, Mich., 1978-81; prof., dean of students Sacred Heart Sem., Detroit, 1981-82, prof., spiritual dir., 1983-84; dir. religious edn. Archdiocese of Detroit, 1984-86, chancellor, 1986-90, moderator of the cuna, 1990—; chaplain Christ Child Soc., Detroit, 1985—; confessor Carmelite Cloistered Sisters, Detroit, 1985—. Named Monsignor Vatican, 1990. Mem. Cath. Theol. Soc. of Am. Home: 75 E Boston Detroit MI 48202 Office: Archdiocese of Detroit 1234 Washington Blvd Detroit MI 48226

ZERCHER, DAVID LYNN, minister; b. Elkhart, Ind., Oct. 28, 1960; s. John Engle and Alice Grace (Hostetter) Z. BA, Messiah Coll., Grantham, Pa., 1983; MDiv, Eastern Bapt. Sem., Phila., 1987; postgrad., U. N.C., 1991—. Lic. to ministry Brethren in Christ Ch., 1987. Min. pastoral care Grantham Ch., 1986-91. Author: Life with God: Being the Church. Recipient Alumni award Messiah Coll. Alumni Assn., 1983. Home: 209 Conner Dr Apt 8 Chapel Hill NC 27514

ZERIN, EDWARD, rabbi, marriage and family counselor; b. N.Y.C., May 5, 1920; s. Joseph Gabriel and Ida (Mazur); m. Marjory Bernice Fisher, Oct. 27, 1946; children: Jonathan Joseph, Wendy Sue, Jefffrey Michael. BA, U. Del., 1941; BHL, Hebrew Union Coll., 1943, MHL, 1946, DD (hon.), 1971, PhD, 1953. Ordained rabbi. Rabbi various congregations, 1946-74; co-dir. Westlake Ctr. for Marital and Family Counseling, Westlake Village, Calif., 1974—; mem. faculty Drake U., 1955-66, Grinnell Coll., 1964-66, Boston U., 1970-72, UCLA, 1975-76. Author: Living Judaism, Vol. I, 1958, Vol. II, 1959, Vol. III, 1962, Teachers Guide to Justice and Judaism, 1958, Our Jewish Neighbors, 1959, The Birth of the Torah, 1963, What Catholics Should Know About Jews, 1980, The "Q" Model for the Effective Management of Personal Stress, 1985; contbr. articles to profl. jours.; cons. 45 Cath. textbooks, 1966—. Commr. Jewish Edn., CCAR, 1960-64, Gov.'s Human Rights Commn., Iowa, 1965, Mental Health, 1958, UN, 1956; del. to White House Conf. on Children and Youth, 1960. Mem. So. Calif. Assn. Marriage and Family Therapists (pres. 1977-78), Cen. Conf. Am. Rabbis (nat. chmn. Doris Lurie Chesky Inst. for Judaism and Psychotherapy 1990—), Am. Assn. Marriage and Family Therapists (clin.), Internat. Transactional Analysis Assn. (clin.), Phi Kappa Phi. Avocations: photography, travel. Home: Westlake Village CA 91361 Office: 3823 Bowsprit Circle Westlake Village CA 91361

ZESS, RONALD GEORGE, religious organization administrator; b. Milw., Mar. 5, 1938; s. George Paul and Dorothy Elenor (Bragg) Z.; m. Marita Jenz, Aug. 21, 1964; 1 child, Kassandra Renee. BTh, Jackson Coll., 1959; ThM, Evang. Coll., 1980; DMin, Bradford U., 1988. Ordained to ministry Apostolic Luth. Ch. Am., 1959. Pastor, developer Holy Apostles Congregation, Atlanta, 1960-62; evang., tchr. Assn. of Jesus Christ, Mich., 1963-73; dir. ch. edn. St. John's Evang. Ch., Wauwatosa, Wis., 1973-75; pres. Cluster 4 Evang. Luth. Ch. Am., Milw., 1987-90; assoc. dean travel, tourism MBTI Bus. Tng. Inst., Milw., 1985—; dir. Hispanic ministry, Los Companeros de Jesus, Milw., 1989—; cert, instr., Crossways Internat., Mpls., 1989—; mem. Presbytery Apostolic Luth. Ch. Am., 1990—. Author: The Devil Made Me Do It, 1990; contbr. articles to profl. jours. With U.S. Army, 1961-63. Recipient Dept. Tourism award State of Israel, 1968, 89. Mem. Soc. Travel and Tourism Educators, Nat. Assn. Travel Execs., Assn. Evang. Gospel Assemblies. Home: 8213 Rockway Pl Wauwatosa WI 53213 Office: Apostolic Luth Ch Am PO Box 642 Elm Grove WI 53122 *Certainly God's greatest gift after the cross is the ability to understand it.*

Z'GRAGGEN, JOHN ANTON, religious organization director, researcher; b. Schattdorf, Switzerland, June 24, 1932; arrived in Papua New Guinea, 1963.; s. Alois and Josephina (Herger) Z. MA, C.U.A., Washington, 1962; PhD, A.N.U., Canberra, Australia, 1969. Catholic priest Divine Word Missionaries, 1961—; mem. Anthropos Inst., St. Augustin, 1970-85; dir. Divine Word Inst., Madang, 1983—, founder, dir. rsch., 1984-89. Author: numerous pubs. on lang. of Madang Province, 1962—. Research grant Swiss Nat. Funds, Berne, 1971, 80, UNESCO, Paris, 1985. Avocations: photography, reading, swimming. Office: Divine Word Inst, PO Box 483, Madang Papua New Guinea

ZICHEK, MELVIN EDDIE, retired clergyman, educator; b. Lincoln, Nebr., May 5, 1918; s. Eddie and Agnes (Varga) Z.; A.B., Nebr. Central Coll., 1942; M.A., U. Nebr., 1953; D.Litt., McKinley-Roosevelt Ednl. Inst., 1955; m. Dorothy Virginia Patrick, May 28, 1942; 1 dau., Shannon Elaine. Ordained to ministry Christian Ch., 1942; minister Christian chs., Brock, Nebr., 1941, Ulysses, Nebr., 1942-43, Elmwood, Nebr., 1943-47, Central City, Nebr., 1947-83, ret., 1983; rural tchr., Merrick County, Nebr., 1937-40; prin. Alvo (Nebr.) Consol. High Sch., 1943-47; supt. Archer (Nebr.) Pub. Schs., 1948-57; head dept. English and speech Central City (Nebr.) High Sch., 1957-63; supt. Marquette (Nebr.) Consol. Schs., 1963-79. Served as chaplain's asst. AUS, 1942. Mem. Internat. Platform Assn., Disciples of Christ Hist. Soc., Nat. Sch. Adminstrs. Assn. Club: Buffy. Home: 2730 North Rd Grand Island NE 68803

ZICK, LYN, preschool director; b. St. Louis, Oct. 16, 1930; d. Virgil Frederick and Lillian Lizette (ritter) Winchell; m. Arthur Gordon Zick, Jan. 17, 1953; children: Robert, Stewart, Douglas. BS, U. Mo., 1953; postgrad., Meramec Coll., St. Louis, Maryville Coll., St. Louis, Am. U., Paris. Cert. elem. sch. tchr. Dir. Alamance Kindergarten, Greensboro, N.C., 1969-70, Kirk of the Hills Christian Sch., St. Louis, 1978—. Pres. St. Louis Mothers of Twins Club, 1966, picnic chmn., 1965; pres. homemakers club Mo. U., St. Louis. Mem. St. Louis Artists Guild. Republican. Office: Kirk Christian Preschool 12928 Ladue Rd Saint Louis MO 63141 *To accept the young child where he is, to guide, to nurture, to open up the world and introduce him to art, good music, the sharing of a classroom community, to explain the love and joy of Our Lord to him, to hold him in our arms and our hearts—this is teaching.*

ZIECH, WILLIAM ALAN, lay pastoral assistant; b. Joliet, Ill., Mar. 26, 1962; s. William R. and Anna Rose (Helton) Z.; m. Marianne Oliviero, July 12, 1986; 1 child, Jacob William. BA in Psychology, Eastern Ill. U., 1984; MA in Clin. Psychology, Wheaton Coll., 1989, Cert. Advanced Bibl. Studies, 1989. Camp counselor Lutherdale Bible Camp, Elkhorn, Wis., summers 1980/81; youth dir. Messiah Luth. Ch., Joliet, 1986, lay pastoral asst., 1986—; facilitator Peer Teams of Messiah, Joliet, 1990—, tchr. Teleios Ministry, 1987—, counselor, 1989—, tchr. Parenting Teen Classes, 1987—. Named to Outstanding Young Men of Am., 1989; recipient Recognition of Achievement award Youth Ministry Univ./Group Mag., 1990, 91, Marriage Counseling award Emerge Ministries, 1988. Office: Messiah Lutheran Church 19901 S Houbolt Rd Joliet IL 60436

ZIEGENFUS, WILLIAM JOHN, minister; b. Northampton, Pa., May 4, 1942; s. Robert Ernest Jr. and Elizabeth Fiana (Mummey) Z.; m. Mary Christine Auer, June 3, 1967; children: Andrew W., Patrick R., Robert A. BA, Ursinus Coll., 1964; BD, Lancaster Theol. Sem., 1968, MDiv, 1973; DMin., Eden Theol. Sem., 1985. Ordained to ministry United Ch. of Christ, 1968. Pastor Ziegel United Ch. of Christ, Breinigsville, Pa., 1968-75, Union Congregational Ch., Avon Park, Fla., 1975-82, United Ch. of Christ, New Smyrna Beach, Fla., 1982—; chmn. SW Mission Coun., Fla. Conf. United Ch. of Christ, 1982, St. Johns Mission Coun., 1991. Pres. Rotary Club Allentown West, Allentown, Pa., 1980, Kiwanis Club New Smyrna Beach, 1986; bd. dirs. Rotary Club Avon Park, 1982; asst. dist. commr. Halifax Dist. Cen. Fla. Coun., Orlando, 1987—. Mem. New Smyrna Ministerial Assn. (pres. 1986-87), Halifax Urban Ministry (adv. bd., chmn. 1988—).

ZIEGLER, EARL KELLER, minister; b. Sheridan, Pa., Mar. 4, 1929; s. Abraham Hoffman and Rhoda Bucher (Keller) Z.; m. Vivian Zug Snyder, Aug. 12, 1951; children: Karen Louise Zimmerman, Randall Earl, Doreen Kay Creighton, Michael Wayne, Konnae Lee Manatrakoon, Sulien Micodemus. BA, Elizabethtown (Pa.) Coll., 1951; MDiv, Bethany Theol. Sem., Chgo., 1954; DDiv, Lancaster (Pa.) Theol. Sem., 1982. Ordained to ministry Ch. of the Brethren, 1950. Pastor Woodbury (Pa.) Congregation, Pa., 1954-60, Black Rock Ch. of Brethren, Brodbecks, Pa., 1960-70, Mechanic Grove Ch. of Brethren, Quarryville, Pa., 1970-83, Atlantic N.E. Dist. Exec., Harrisburg, Pa., 1983-89, Lampeter (Pa.) Ch. of the Brethren, 1989—; moderator various dists., Pa., 1959—; mem. Gen. Bd., Ch. of Brethren, 1975-80; chmn. Parish Ministerial Commn., 1979-80; dir. Family Life Inst., 1961, 64, mem. Nat. Korean Cons. Com., 1988-91, Denominational Structure Com., 1990-91, others; adj. prof. ch. history Evang. Sem., Myerstown, Pa., 1988—. Author: Divorce Among the Church of the Brethren Clergy, 1981; contbr. articles to profl. jours. Pres. Manheim Elem. PTA, 1964-65; trustee Elizabethtown Coll., 1965-83; dir. Community Choir, Lineboro, Md., 1966-70; dir. Solanco Community Men's Chorus, Quarryville, 1976-83. Recipient Alumni citation, Elizabethtown Coll. Alumni Assn., 1964, award for Outstanding Ch. Planting in Azua Province of Dominican Republic, 1990, Award of Appreciation, Germantown Ch. of Brethren, 1990. Mem. Lampeter Willow St. Ministerium (pres. 1989-91). Republican. Home: 1720 Pioneer Rd Lancaster PA 17602-1516 Office: Lampeter Ch of Brethren 1900 Lampeter Rd Box 38 Lampeter PA 17537-0038 *"You shall have what your faith expects," were the words of Jesus to two blind men. These words challenge the potential within each of us, a faith that conquers, a spirit that soars. Between the possible and the impossible is the attitude and will of the individual and society.*

ZIEGLER, JESSE H., minister, theology and medicine educator; b. Limerick, Pa., Jan. 7, 1913; s. Harry H. and Mary (Hunsberger) Z.; m. Harriet E. Curry, Aug. 22, 1939; 1 dau., Harriet Anne. A.B., Bridgewater (Va.) Coll., 1935, D.D., 1959; M.A., Catholic U. Am., 1937, Ph.D., 1942; B.D., Bethany Theol. Sem., Chgo., 1944; D.D., Presbyn. Theol. Coll., Montreal, 1967. Diplomate: counseling psychology Am. Bd. Examiners Profl. Psychology. Ordained to ministry Ch. of Brethren, 1931; pastor University Park, Md., 1935-41; from asso. prof. to prof. psychology and Christian edn. Bethany Theol. Sem., 1941-59; assoc. dir. Am. Assn. Theol. Schs., 1959-66, exec. dir., 1966-80; prof. community health Wright State U. Sch. Medicine, Dayton, Ohio, 1980—; prof. religion and health United Theol. Sem., Dayton, 1981—; vis. lectr. Garrett Theol. Sem., Oberlin Grad. Sch. Theology, Yale Div. Sch. Sec., Ministry Studies Bd., 1960-64; mem. gen. bd. Ch. of Brethren, 1970-76; sec. bd. York Center Community Housing Coop., Inc., 1944-54. Author: The Broken Cup: A Socio-Psychological Study of a Changing Rural Culture, 1942, Psychology and the Teaching Church, 1962, Focus on Adults, 1966, ATS Through Two Decades, 1984; editor quar.: Theol. Edn., 1964-80. Bd. dirs. Fund Theol. Edn., 1966-80; trustee Suicide Prevention Ctr. Inc., 1985-90. Mem. Am. Psychol. Assn. Democrat. Home: 822 Kenneth Ave Vandalia OH 45377 Office: Wright State U Dept Community Health PO Box 927 Dayton OH 45401

ZIEGLER, JOHN, clergyman; b. Madison, Sask., Can., Dec. 12, 1929; came to U.S., 1950; m. Mildred Lorene Richert, July 30, 1954; children: Kim Marie Schmick, Mark John. BA, Augustana Coll., 1953; BD, NAm. Bapt Sem, 1956; MDiv, United Theol Sem., 1963, STM, 1968. Ordained to ministry Bapt. Ch., 1956. Pastor Community Bapt. Ch., Beavercreek, Ohio, 1960-67, Oak St. Bapt. Ch., Burlington, Iowa, 1967-76; dir. ch. extension N.Am. Bapt., Oakbrook Terrace, Ill., 1976-81; pastor First Bapt. Ch., Colfax, Wash., 1981-87; ea. area minister N.Am. Bapts. Inc., Amherst, N.Y., 1987—; chmn. Ch. Ministries Dept., N.Am. Bapts., Forest Park, Ill., 1964-65, bd. mem. Com. on Higher Edn., 1966-67; bd. mem. Bapt. World Alliance, Washington, 1965-68, Burlington (Iowa) Pub. Schs., 1975. Home and Office: 73 Jeanmoor Dr Amherst NY 14228

ZIEGLER, LEVI JOHN, minister; b. Lebanon County, Pa., May 17, 1931; s. Jesse Hoffman and Mary (Darkes) Z.; m. Helen Ruth Trimmer, Aug. 30, 1953; children: John Levi, Dale Trimmer, Robert Allen. BA, Elizabethtown Coll., 1953; MDiv, Bethany Theol. Sem., 1956. Ordained to ministry Ch. of the Brethren, 1956. Pastor Greenland and Allegheny Chs. of the Brethren, 1956-58, Westernport (Md.) Ch. of the Brethren, 1958-64, Roxbury Ch. of the Brethren, Johnstown, Pa., 1964-68, Community United Ch., Erie, Pa., 1969-78, Conewago Ch. of the Brethren, Hershey, Pa., 1979-86; pastor, chaplain, assoc. Brethren Village Retirement Ctr., Lancaster, Pa., 1986-91, pastor, 1991—; moderator Jennersville Ch. of the Brethren, West Grove, Pa., 1988—; dir. lic. mins. course, Harrisburg, Pa., 1987—.

ZIEL, CATHERINE AGNES, minister; b. Newark, July 22, 1949; d. Walter O. and Catherine A. (Wood) Z. AB, Rutgers U., 1971; MDiv., Luth. Sem.,

1981; PhD, Princeton Sem., 1991. Ordained min. Evang. Luth. Ch., 1981. Sr. pastor Hope Luth. Ch., Cherryville, Pa., 1981-85; instr. Meth. Theol. Sch., Columbus, Ohio, 1988; lectr. Luth. Sem., Phila., 1989; exec. coun. mem. Luth. Ch. in Am., N.Y.C., 1982-87. Bd. mem. Turning Point, Bethlehem, Pa., 1989-91. Mem. Acad. of Homiletics. Home: 265 D So Penn St Allentown PA 18102

ZIELONKA, DAVID M., rabbi; b. Tampa, Fla., Apr. 30, 1935; s. David L. and Carol (Ciener) Z.; m. Martha K. Harris, 1956; 5 children. BA, U. Cin., 1957; MAHL, Hebrew Union Coll., Cin., 1962, postgrad., 1962-64, DD (hon.), 1991. Ordained rabbi, 1962. Rabbi Valley Temple, Wyoming, Ohio, 1964-68, Temple B'nai Israel, Elmira, N.Y., 1968-73, Temple Covenant of Peace, Easton, Pa., 1973-76; weekend rabbi Temple Beth El, Sunbury, Pa., 1976-77; dir. adminstrv. and vol. svcs. and sr. family counselor Valley Youth House, Bethlehem, Pa., 1976-79; rabbi Albany (Ga.) Hebrew Congregation and Temple Beth El, 1979-83, Temple Emanuel, Gastonia, N.C., 1983-91; chaplain Ranch Industries, Gastonia, N.C., 1991—; adj. faculty Gaston Coll., 1984-88, Belmont Abbey Coll., 1985—; lectr. in field. Co-author: The Eager Immigrants, 1972; editor: Manual of American Jewish Archives, 1962; contbr. articles to profl. jours. Active Boy Scouts Am.; Jewish chaplain West Elmira (N.Y.) Vol. Fire Dept.; co-founder Day of Understanding Interfaith Inst., Easton, 1974; chmn. Jewish Com. for Bicentennial, Easton, 1976; pres. Look Up Gaston Found. Bd., 1988. Recipient Gaston County Commrs. award for vol. svc., 1988. Mem. Greater Gastonia Ministerial Felelowship (pres. 1985). Home: 640 Downey Pl Gastonia NC 28054 Office: Ranch Industries Hwy 321 S Gastonia NC 28052

ZIEMAN, JOHN WAYNE, minister; b. Pierre, S.D., Aug. 31, 1958; s. Zane and Doreen (Staley) Z.; m. Debra Ann Oertle, Apr. 17, 1982; children: Abigail Grace, Joshua Christian. AS in Electronics, U. S.D., Springfield, 1981; BA in Music Edn., Huron (S.D.) U., 1982; MDiv, U. Dubuque (Iowa) Theol. Sem., 1989. Ordained to ministry Presbyn. Ch., 1989. Elder Lyndsey Meml. Ch., Martin, S.D., 1976-78, First Presbyn. Ch., Huron, S.D., 1984-86; student pastor Golden Congl. Ch., Ryan, Iowa, 1987-89; pastor Bethlehem Presbyn. Ch., Logansport, Ind., 1989-91, 1st Presbyn. Ch., Rowley, Iowa, 1991—; assoc. pastor 1st Presbyn. Ch., Independence, Iowa, 1991—; counselor Pastoral Counseling Ctr., Logansport. Mem. Cass County Chs. United (bd. dirs. 1990-91), Cass County Ministerial Assn. (treas. 1990-91). Home and Office: 212 Park Ave Box 134 Rowley IA 52329

ZIEMANN, G. PATRICK, bishop; b. Pasadena, Calif., Sept. 13, 1941. Attended, St. John's Coll. and St. John's Sem., Camarillo, Calif., Mt. St. Mary's Coll., L.A. Ordained priest Roman Cath., 1967. Titular bishop Obba; aux. bishop L.A., 1987—. Office: Chancery Office 1531 W 9th St Los Angeles CA 90015

ZIETLOW, HAROLD HOWARD, theology educator; b. Marion, Wis., Oct. 17, 1926; s. Frederick Ludwig Christian and Grace (Handschke) Z.; m. Miriam Lovina Miller, June 25, 1950; children: Paul, Mark, John, Mary, Ruth. AB, Capital U., Columbus, Ohio, 1947; MA, Ohio State U., 1949; BD, Evangelical Luth. Seminary, Columbus, 1951; PhD, U. Chgo., 1961. Ordained minister Luth. Ch., 1954. Pastor St. Paul's Luth. Ch., Gilman, Ill., 1954-60; assoc. prof. systematic theology Luth. Theol. Sem., Columbus, 1960-70, prof. contemporary theology, 1970-78; prof. practical theology and missions Concordia Theol. Sem., Fort Wayne, Ind., 1979—; cons. internat. rels. Bd. Social Actions, Ill., 1958-59. Producer: (movie) Who Sent You, 1976. Sec. Social Action Com., Ill., 1958-59. Lutheran Brotherhood fellow, 1987, scholar, 1951, 74, Am. Assn. Theol. Schs., 1966. Mem. Acad. Profs. Evangelism, Media Profl. Assocs. Republican. Avocations: reading, swimming, jogging, auto mechanics, writing. Home: 2104 Parkland Dr Fort Wayne IN 46825 Office: Concordia Theol Seminary 6600 N Clinton St Fort Wayne IN 46825

ZIEV, JOEL DAVID, religious organization administrator; b. Phila., Feb. 8, 1941; s. Meyer and Bebe (Brown) Z.; m. Patricia Buckheit, May 24, 1981; children: Jonathan, Jennifer, Christi, Jeffrey. BS in Edn., Temple U., 1963, EdM, 1966; EdD, NYU, 1987. Exec. dir. N.Y. Soc. for the Deaf, 1980—; chmn. com. on disabled United Jewish Appeal Fedn., N.Y.C., 1986-91; v.p. N.Y. Commn. on Synagogue Rels., 1987—. Author: Survey of Laws on Interpreting, 1989; contbr. articles to jours. in field. Home: 17 N Plandome Rd Port Washington NY 11050 Office: NY Soc for the Deaf 817 Broadway New York NY 10003

ZIGLAR, WILLIAM LARRY, academic administrator, religion educator; b. Yazoo City, Miss., Aug. 25, 1938; s. W. Hubert and Freida Belle (Waaser) Z.; m. Brenda Joy Helms, June 25, 1960; children: Scott Lawrence, Heidi Lynn. BA, Miss. Coll., 1960, MA, 1961; PhD, U. Maine, 1972. Dir. music, youth dept. Midway Bapt. Ch., Jackson, Miss., 1957-59; mem. faculty Ea. Coll., St. David's, Pa., 1964-89, prof., Kea chair Am. history, dean spl. programs, 1979-89, dean acad. affairs, 1986-89, v.p. for acad. affaris, dean of coll., 1989; provost, v.p. acad. affairs Wingate (N.C.) Coll., 1990-91, interim pres., 1991—; Disting. Christian scholar/lectr. Staley Found., 1983—; scholar-in-residence Radnor Pub. Libr./NEH, Wayne, 1980-81, Wayne Presbyn. Ch., Pa., 1981; ch. sch. tchr. Ch. of the Good Samaritan, Paoli, Pa., 1984—. Author: Roots of American Diversity, 1991; contbr. articles to profl. jours. V.p. Wayne PTA, 1979-80; bd. dirs. Presbyn. Hist. Commn., Phila., 1981-84; historian North Wayne Protective Assn., 1984-85. Recipient Goddard medal Nat. Space Assn., 1979, Lindback Disting. Coll. Tchr. award, 1979, Legion of Honor Chapel of 4 Chaplains, 1983; grantee Shell Found., 1970, NEH, 1979-80; McLemore lectr., 1985, Fulbright scholar, 1989-90. Mem. Am. Studies Assn., Am. Hist. Assn., Am. Assn. for State and Local History, Hist. Soc. Pa., Soc. History of Tech., Am. Soc. Ch. History, Phi Alpha Theta, Pi Kappa Delta, Pi Gamma Mu, Kappa Delta Pi, Omicron Delta Kappa, Delta Mu Delta, Sigma Zeta, Alpha Chi. Home: 408 Oak Ln Wayne PA 19087 Office: Wingate Coll Wingate NC 28174

ZIKMUND, BARBARA BROWN, minister, seminary president, church history educator; b. Ann Arbor, Mich., Oct. 16, 1939; d. Henry Daniels and Helen (Langworthy) Brown; m. Joseph Zikmund II, Aug. 26, 1961; 1 child, Brian Joseph. BA, Beloit Coll., 1961; BDiv, Duke U., 1964, PhD, 1969; D in Div (hon.), Doane Coll., 1984, Chgo. Theol. Sem., 1985, Ursinus Coll., 1989. Ordained to ministry United Ch. of Christ, 1964. Instr. Albright Coll., Reading, Pa., 1964-67, Temple U., Phila., 1967-68, Ursinus Coll., Collegeville, Pa., 1968-69; asst. prof. religion studies Albion Coll., Mich., 1970-75; asst. prof. ch. history, dir. studies Chgo. Theol. Sem., 1975-80; dean and assoc. prof. ch. history Pacific Sch. Religion, Berkeley, Calif., 1981-85, dean and prof. ch. history, 1985-90; pres. Hartford (Conn.) Sem., 1990—; chmn. United Ch. of Christ Hist. Coun., 1983-85, mem. coun. for ecumenism, 1983-89; mem. Nat. Coun. Chs. Commn. on Faith and Order, 1979-87, World Coun. of Chs. Programme Theol. Edn., 1984—. Author: Discovering the Church, 1983. Editor: Hidden Histories in the UCC, 1984, vol. 2, 1987; (with Manschreck) American Religious Experiment, 1976; mem. editorial bd. Jour. Ecumenical Studies, 1987—, Mid-Stream, 1991—; contbr. articles to profl. jours. Mem. City Coun., Albion, Mich., 1972-75. Woodrow Wilson fellow, 1964-66; NEH grantee, 1974-75; vis. scholar Schlesinger Libr. Women's History, Radcliffe Coll., 1988-89. Mem. Assn. Theol. Schs. (v.p. 1984-86, pres. 1986-88, issues implementation grantee 1983-84), Am. Soc. Ch. History (council 1983-85), Internat. Assn. Women Ministers (v.p. 1977-79), AAUW (v.p. 1973-75). Democrat. Office: Hartford Sem 77 Sherman St Hartford CT 06105

ZILZ, MELVIN LEONARD, pastor, ministry educator; b. Detroit, Apr. 15, 1932; s. Charles William and Merle Martha (Yaeger) Z.; m. Carole Jean Brandt, Aug. 17, 1957; children: Karen, Kathryn, Paul. BS, Concordia U., River Forest, Ill., 1953; MS, MA, U. Mich., 1964; PhD, Wayne State U., 1970; colloquy diploma, Concordia Theol. Sem., Ft. Wayne, Ind., 1978. Ordained to ministry Luth. Ch., 1978. Instr. Concordia Luth. Sch., Chgo., 1953-57, Luth. High Sch. East, Detroit, 1957-65; asst. prof. biology Concordia Sr. Coll., Ft. Wayne, 1965-72, assoc. prof., 1972-76, chmn. dept. biology, 1971-72, registrar, 1972-77; assoc. prof. pastoral ministry Concordia Theol. Sem., 1976-78, prof., 1978—, asst. to pres., 1976-78, assoc. acad. dean, 1977-78, dean of adminstrn., 1978-83; pastor Clear Lake Luth. Ch., Fremont, Ind., 1983-84, Bethlehem Luth. Ch., Ossian, Ind., 1987-88, New Hope Luth. Ch., Ossian, 1988, Zion Luth. Ch., Columbia City, Ind., 1988—. Foster parent Luth. Social Svcs., Ft. Wayne. NSF study fellow, 1960-64, 65-67. Avocations: classical music, travel, cooking, photography, fishing. Home: 1704 Frenchman's Crossing Fort Wayne IN 46825-5903 Office: Concordia Theol Sem 6600 N Clinton Fort Wayne IN 46825-4996

ZIMANY, ROLAND DANIEL, theology educator; b. East Orange, N.J., Aug. 5, 1936; s. Daniel and Margaret (Zigo) Z.; m. Barbara Bowen, May 15, 1976. A.B., Princeton U., 1958; M.B.A., NYU, 1965; M.Div., Union Theol. Sem., N.Y.C., 1974; Ph.D., Duke U., 1980; postgrad. U. Tübingen, Fed. Republic Germany, 1976-77, U. Chgo., 1986-87. Mgmt. analyst, pers. rep. Port Authority N.Y. and N.J., N.Y.C., 1958-69; mgmt. cons. Mgmt. Practice, N.Y.C., 1969-70; mgr. mgmt. systems Nat. Urban League, N.Y.C., 1970-72; teaching asst. theology Duke Div. Sch., Durham, N.C., 1975,77; asst. prof. philosophy religion Blackburn Coll., Carlinville, Ill., 1980-87, assoc. prof., 1987-90, prof., 1990—; project dir. directory Ednl. Opportunities in Pub. Admin., 1968. Contbr. articles to profl. jours. Served with U.S. Army, 1958-59. Duke U. grad. scholar, 1975,77; alt. travelling fellow Union Theol. Sem., 1974; recipient Duke U. travel award, 1976. Mem. Am. Acad. Religion. Democrat. Lutheran. Home: 413 Morgan St Carlinville IL 62626 Office: Blackburn Coll Carlinville IL 62626

ZIMMERMAN, CURTIS ROY, priest; b. Santa Monica, Calif., Dec. 22, 1942; s. Thomas Henry and Verna Ruth (Naylor) Z. BMus, U. Redlands, 1966; MDiv, Ch. Div. Sch. of the Pacific, 1974. Ordained to ministry Episcopal Ch. as priest, 1974. Asst. to rector St. Francis Ch., San Jose, Calif., 1971-74; canon St. Andrew's Cathedral, Honolulu, 1974-79; rector Christ Ch., Puyallup, Wash., 1979-91, Tacoma, Wash., 1991—; lectr., advisor Anglican Liturgical Renewal, 1967—; facilitator for parish renewal, 1983—. Contbr. articles to ch. jours. Served as staff sgt. USAF, 1966-70. Recipient Oscar Greene Meml. Preaching Prize, Ch. Div. Sch. of Pacific, 1974. Mem. Acad. Parish Clergy, Clergy Assn. Puyallup (co-founder 1982-85), Order of the Holy Cross (assoc.), Am. Guild Organists, Aircraft Owners and Pilots Assn. Avocations: flying, computer programing, traveling, photography. Home: 3008 N Narrows Dr # D-301 Tacoma WA 98407 Office: Christ Episcopal Ch 210 Fifth St SW Puyallup WA 98371

ZIMMERMAN, DANIEL RAY, religion educator; b. Chgo., Nov. 22, 1948; s. Raymond Zimmerman and Kathleen (Benton) Dickie. AA, Triton Coll., 1968; BS in Edn., No. Ill. U., 1970; PhD, Universal Life U., 1982, DD (hon.), 1978; postgrad., Inst. Advanced Study of Human Sexuality, 1984—. Cert. tchr., Ill., Iowa. Tchr., spl. edn. tchr. Cedar Rapids (Iowa) Schs., 1970-86; minister Universal Life Ch., Cedar Rapids, 1976-86; administr. Universal Life Ch., Modesto, Calif., 1980—, supr., 1982—, at. law witness, 1982—; assoc. prof. religion Universal Life U., Modesto, 1983—, counselor sexual minorities, 1984—; presenter seminars in field; govtl. rep. Kingdom of Aqualandia, 1986—. Author: Universal Life Church Principles and Practices, 1983. Foster parent Linn County Human Services, Cedar Rapids, 1976-83; active Civil Rights Advocates, Washington, 1985. Recipient Tchr. Incentive award Dept. Edn. State of Iowa, 1974. Mem. Am. Humanist Assn., Am. Fedn. Tchrs., NEA. Democrat. Avocations: group presentations, networking and network information. Office: Universal Life Ch 601 3d St Modesto CA 95351

ZIMMERMAN, SHELDON, rabbi; b. Toronto, Ont., Can., Feb. 21, 1942; s. Morris and Helen Z.; m. Judith Elaine Baumgarten, Aug. 9, 1964; children: Brian, Kira, David, Micol. BA, U. Toronto, 1964, MA, 1965; BHL, Hebrew Union Coll., Jewish Inst. Religion, 1969, MAHL, 1970. Ordained rabbi, 1970. Asst. rabbi Cen. Synagogue, N.Y.C., 1970-72, sr. rabbi, 1972-85; rabbi Temple Emanu-El, Dallas, 1985—; adj. prof. religious studies So. Meth. U., Dallas; adj. faculty Auburn Theol. Sem.; lectr. liturgy and rabbinics N.Y. Sch. of Hebrew Union Coll.-Jewish Inst. Religion; lectr. theology Fordham U.; instr. philosophy Hunter Coll. of CUNY; v.p. Cen. Conf. of Am. Rabbis; bd. trustees Union Am. Hebrew Congregations; mem. Nat. Rabbinic Cabinet of United Jewish Appeal; bd. dirs. World Ctr. for Jewish Unity; bd. govs. Synagogue Coun. Am.; lectr. in field. Contbr. articles to profl. jours. Bd. dirs. Vis. Nurses Assn. Tex., Children's Med. Found., Jewish Fedn. Dallas, Solomon Schechter Acad. Dallas, S.W. REgion of Am. Jewish Congress, Community Outreach Coalition.; adv. bd. CONTACT-Dallas Telephone Counseling Ctr., Downtown Dallas Family Shelter, The AIDS-ARMS Adv. Coun. Dallas, Pastoral Care Adv. Com. of Children's Med. Ctr., Women's Ctr. of Dallas, Chaplain's ADv. Bd. of So. Meth. U.; v.p. Jewish Community Rels. Coun. Dallas. Recipient Marshall Hochhauser Meml. Award, Fedn. Jewish Philanthropies, N.Y.C. Office: Temple Emanu-El 8500 Hillcrest Dallas TX 75225 *We are the sanctifiers-in-process, there we and our lives can make the ultimate difference in the journey to the fulfillment of the promise.*

ZINN, ELMER, deacon; b. Pruntytown, W.Va., July 8, 1918; s. L. Glenn and Addie Columbia (Ryan) Z.; m. Rita Katherine Brown, July 31, 1945; children: Michael, Regina, Suzanne, Theresa, Gregory, James, Rita, Stephen, Christina. BS in Secondary Edn., Alderson Broaddus Coll., 1938; grad., Oregon State U., 1943. Ordained deacon Roman Cath. Ch., 1974. Editor Western Mich. Cath., Grand Rapids, 1973-86; staff mem. Cath. Info. Ctr., Grand Rapids, 1988—. With U.S. Army, 1943-45, ETO. Home: 220 Lawndale NE Grand Rapids MI 49503-3736

ZINN, GROVER ALFONSO, JR., religion educator; b. El Dorado, Ark., June 18, 1937; s. Grover Alfonso and Cora Edith (Saucke) Z.; m. Mary Mel Farris, July 28, 1962; children: Jennifer Anne, Andrew Grover. BA, Rice U., 1959; BD, Duke U., 1962, PhD, 1969; spl. student, U. Glasgow, Scotland, 1962-63. Asst. minister The Barony Ch., Glasgow, 1962-63; instr. in religion Oberlin (Ohio) Coll., 1966-68, asst. prof., 1968-74, assoc. prof., 1974-79, prof., 1979—, Danforth prof. religion, 1986—, chmn. dept. religion, 1980-84, 85-86. Translator: Richard of St. Victor: The Twelve Patriarchs, The Mystical Ark, and Book Three of the Trinity, 1979; gen. co-editor Medieval France: An Encyclopedia; mem. editorial bd. Dictionary of Biblical Interpretation; contbr. articles on medieval Christian mysticism and theology. H.H. Powers Travel grantee Oberlin Coll., 1969, 85; Dempster fellow United Meth. Ch., 1965-66, NEH Younger Humanist fellow, 1972-73, Research Status fellow Oberlin Coll., 1972-73, Faculty Devel. fellow Oberlin Coll. 1985, Lilly Endowment fellow U. Pa., 1981-82; recipient ACLS Travel award, 1982. Mem. Medieval Acad. Am. (councillor 1983-86), Am. Soc. Ch. History (coun. class of 1992), Ecclesiastical History Soc. Democrat. Methodist. Avocations: photography, electronics. Home: 249 Oak St Oberlin OH 44074 Office: Oberlin Coll Rice Hall Oberlin OH 44074

ZLOTOWITZ, BERNARD M., rabbi; b. N.Y.C., July 11, 1925; s. Aron and Fannie (Pasternak) Z.; B.A., Bklyn. Coll., 1948; M.A., Columbia U., 1965; B.H.L., Hebrew Union Coll.-Jewish Inst. Religion, N.Y.C., 1953, rabbi, M.H.L., 1955 D.H.L., 1974, DD (hon.), 1980; Editor One People, 1982; book rev. editor Reform Judaism. 1980; m. Shirley Masef, June 12, 1949; children—Debra, Robin, Richard C., Alice R. Rabbi congregations in N.Y., N.C. and N.J., 1955-75; regional dir. N.J. council Union Am. Hebrew Congregations, N.Y.C., 1975-80, N.Y. Fedn., 1980-91; sr. scholar Union Am. Hebrew Congregations, 1992—; lectr. Bible, Hebrew Union Coll.-Jewish Inst. Religion, 1962-72; adj. asst. prof. religion C.W. Post Coll., 1968-72, U. N.C., Charlotte, 1973-74; lectr. Bibl. archaeology Jewish Museum, N.Y.C., 1972, Charlotte Mus., 1973; lectr. Hebrew Union Coll., 1977-89, NYU Sch. Continuing Edn., 1985-89. Bd. dirs. Nyack (N.Y.) Hosp., 1959-61. Mem. World Union Progressive Judaism (bd. dirs. 1985—), Internat. Orgn. Masoretic Studies (treas. 1972—), Central Conf. Am. Rabbis, N.J. Assn. Reform Rabbis, N.Y. Bd. Rabbis (exec. com. 1957-62, 80—), Am. Schs. Oriental Research, Soc. Bib. Lit., N.Y. Acad. Scis., Am. Oriental Soc., AAUP, Asssn. Reform Rabbis N.Y.C. and Vicinity. Clubs: Masons, KP, Rotary. Author: Folkways and Minhagim, 1970; Art in Judaism, 1975; The Septuagint Translation of the Hebrew Terms in Relation to God in the Book of Jeremiah, 1980; co-author: Drugs, Sex and Integrity, 1991, Abraham's Great Discovery, 1991; columnist Reform Judaism Jewish Question and Answer; contbg. editor Keeping Posted; book rev. editor Reform Judaism. Home: 15 Aberdeen Pl Fair Lawn NJ 07410 Office: 838 Fifth Ave New York NY 10021

ZOA, JEAN, archbishop. Archbishop of Yaounde Roman Cath. Ch., Cameroon. Office: Archbishop of Yaounde, BP 207, Yaounde Cameroon*

ZODHIATES, SPIROS GEORGE, association executive; b. Cyprus, Mar. 13, 1922; came to U.S., 1946, naturalized, 1949; s. George and Mary (Toumazou) Z.; m. Joan Carol Wassel, Jan. 10, 1948; children: Priscilla Zodhiates Barnes, Lois Zodhiates Jenks, Philip, Mary. Student, Am. U., Cairo, 1941-45; B.Th., Shelton Coll., 1947; M.A., N.Y. U., 1951; Th.D., Luther Rice Sem., 1978. Ordained to ministry Gen. Assn. Regular Baptist Chs., 1947; gen. sec. Am. Mission to Greeks (name changed to AMG Internat. 1974), Ridgefield, N.J., 1946-65; pres. Am. Mission to Greeks (name changed to AMG Internat. 1974), 1965—. Author: numerous Bible-study books and booklets including Behavior of Belief, 1959, The Pursuit of Happiness, 1966, To Love is to Live, 1967, Getting the Most Out of Life, 1976, Life after Death, 1977, Hebrew Greek Key Study Bible, 1984, Complete Word Study New Testament, 1991; editor in chief: numerous Bible-study books and booklets including Voice of the Gospel, 1946—, Pulpit Helps, 1975—. Served with Brit. Army, 1943-46. Recipient Gold Cross Greek Red Cross, 1951; decorated Order Brit. Empire. Home: 8927 Villa Rica Chattanooga TN 37421 Office: AMG Internat 6815 Shallowford Rd Chattanooga TN 37422

ZOLLER, DARRYL CLAUDE, minister; b. Balt., Oct. 31, 1950; s. Harry Adam and Betty (Giles) Z.; m. Christine Elizabeth Kay Zoller, June 29, 1974; children: Nicholas Clark, Zachary Phillip, Benjamin Jordan. AA, Anne Arundel Community Coll., 1970; BA, U. Md., Balt., 1972; MDiv, Wesley Sem., Washington, 1976. Ordained to ministry United Meth. Ch. as deacon, 1973, as elder, 1977. Pastor Piney Plains Charge, United Meth. Ch., Little Orleans, Md., 1974-76, Carrolls-Gills Charge, Lutherville, Md., 1976-80, Greenmount Charge, Hampstead, Md., 1980-83, Fork (Md.)-Waugh Charge, 1983-88, Darlington (Md.) Charge, 1988—; dist. rep. Conf. Bd. Discipleship, United Meth. Ch., Balt., 1988—. Advisor Darlington Dinosaurs Ben Franklin Stamp Club, 1989—. Mem. Acad. Parish Clergy (sec. 1990-91, pres. Capital chpt. 1991—), Am. Family Assn. (v.p. local chpt. 1988—), Am. Topical Assn., Harford County Stamp Club, Am. Philatelic Soc., Christopher Columbus Philatelic Soc., Lions (chaplain local dist. 1991—). Republican. Office: Darlington Charge 2118 Shuresville Rd Darlington MD 21034

ZOOK, NICHOLAS JAMES, minister; b. Chgo., May 31, 1955; s. Nicholas and Lola (Andersen) Z.; m. Stephanie Marie Daczyszyn, Aug. 29, 1981; children: Alexander, Gregory. BA summa cum laude, DePaul U., 1977; MDiv with honors, Gettysburg Sem., 1981. Ordained to ministry Evangelical Luth. Ch. Pastor Concordia Luth. Ch., Chgo., 1981—; mem. Luth./Roman Cath. Covenant Commn., Chgo., 1987—, co-chair, 1990—. Bd. dirs. L.S.S.I. Day Care Ctr., Chgo., 1986-90, Lakeview Emergency Relief Project, Chgo., 1986-90; bd. dirs. Common Pantry, Chgo., 1986—; pres. Concordia Child Care Ctr., Chgo., 1981—. Home: 3750 N Hoyne Chicago IL 60618 Office: Concordia Luth Ch 3855 N Seeley Chicago IL 60618

ZOOK, VERNON DEAN, pastor; b. Goshen, Ind., Sept. 30, 1959; s. Henry S. and Rosa Ellen (Eash) Z.; m. Laurie E. Helmuth, Feb. 2, 1980; children: Crystal, Shauna, Rochelle. AA, Eastern Mennonite Coll., 1989. Ordained min. Youth leader Ashton Mennonite Ch., Sarasota, Fla., 1983-87; dir. Youth Creations Ministries, Sarasota, 1985-87; youth leader Cornerstone Mennonite Fellowship, Harrisonburg, Va., 1988-89, youth and children's pastor, 1989—; prin. Cornerstone Christian Sch., Broadway, Va., 1990—; dir. Youth Under Constrn. Prodns., Harrisonburg, 1990—; team leader Cornerstone Short-Term Missions, Harrisonburg, 1989—. Mem. Sonlife Strategy.

ZOSCHKE, DAVID N., music minister; b. Parsons, Kans., June 28, 1951; s. Charles Frederic and Ennice Caldonna (Tiffin) Z.; m. Alice June Forbach, Aug. 4, 1987. BA, Calvary Bible Coll., 1973; MA, Bob Jones U., 1978; DMA, U. Mo., Kansas City, 1991. Music dir. Southwest Bible Ch., Prairie Village, Kans., 1973-74; tchr. Markoma Bible Acad., Tahlequah, Okla., 1979-85, Calvary Bible Coll., Kansas City, Mo., 1985-87; music min. 1st Baptist of Shawnee, Shawnee, Kans., 1987--. Mem. Fellowship Am. Bapt. Musicians, Am. Choral Dirs. Assc. Am. Baptist. Office: 1st Baptist of Shawnee 1140 Johnson Dr Shawnee KS 66203

ZOSSO, TERISSE, communications executive; b. Chillicothe, Mo., Feb. 9, 1926; d. Henry Nicholas and Nothburga Mary (Sparber) Z. BA in Theology summa cum laude, Mundelein Coll., 1969; MA in New Testament, Marquette U., 1972, PhD in Theology and Psychology, 1976. Joined Holy Spirit Missionary Sisters, Roman Cath. Ch., 1943. Theology and tchr. trainer various parts of the country, 1947-66; vicar for religious Diocese of Charlotte (N.C.), 1978-80; assoc. prof. theology Divine Word Coll., Epworth, Iowa, 1980-86, Rockhurst Coll., Kansas City, Mo., 1986-87; communications dir. Holy Spirit Missionary Sisters, Techny, Ill., 1987—. Editor: A Century of Mission Service, 1989. Mem. Am. Acad. Religion, Cath. Theol. Soc. Am. Home and Office: Communications Ctr 2600 Waukegan Rd Techny IL 60082

ZOUNGRANA, PAUL CARDINAL, archbishop of Ouagadougou; b. Ouagadougou, Burkina Faso, Sept. 3, 1917. Ordained priest Roman Cath. Ch., 1942; archbishop of Ouagadougou, 1960—; elevated to Sacred Coll. Cardinals, 1965; titular ch. St. Camillus de Lellis. Mem. Congregation Evangelization of Peoples, Congregation Culte divisi et sacrements, Congregation Inst. vie consacrée et sociétés de vie apostolique, Conseil Pontifical Pastorale des Agestes de Santé. Address: 01 BP 1472, Ouagadougou Burkina Faso

ZUCAL, STEVEN JOSEPH, priest; b. Denver, Sept. 3, 1959. BA in Communications, Regis Coll. Ordained priest Western Orthodox Ch. in Am., 1983. Pastor St. Ignatius of Antioch Parish, Englewood, Colo., 1983—; resident dir. Adsum House, Englewood, 1984-86; dir. mktg. Diakonia Credit Union, Denver, 1981-89; regional dir. Servants of the Good Shepherd, 1982—; vol. chaplain Dept. Institutions Div. Youth Services, 1980—; mem. Commn. on Western Orthodox Liturgy, 1983-91, Commn. on Ecumenical Witness and Religious Dialogue, Colo. Coun. Chs., 1989-91, Commn. on Instl. Ministries, Colo. Coun. Chs., 1988—; co-dir. Info. Services Team, Englewood, 1983—. Co-author (calendar) Ecclesiastical Calendar, 1984, 85; editor: The Ch. Manual, 1984-85. Mem. ad hoc com. Juvenile Advocacy, Denver, 1985, bd. dirs. Juvenile Advocacy Group, Golden, Colo., 1985—; advisor Colo. Teen. Inst., Denver, 1984, steering com., 1985; bd. dirs. Youth in Prison, Denver, 1984; mem. K.I.D.S. (Kids In-Transition Developing Spiritually); mem. standing adv. coun. SGS/WOCA. Named Outstanding Vol., Colo. Teen Inst., 1984, Outstanding Bd. Mem., Mile High Coun. on Alcoholism and Drug Abuse, 1990; recipient appreciation St. Luke's Hosp. Addictions Recovery Unit, 1983. Mem. Nat. Chaplains Assn. Youth Rehab., Mile High Council on Alcoholism and Drug Abuse. Home: 2842 S Broadway Englewood CO 80110 Office: St Ignatius of Antioch Parish 2842 S Broadway Englewood CO 80110

ZUCK, LOWELL HUBERT, religious educator; b. Ephrata, Pa., June 24, 1926; s. Abram Willis and Verdie Bollinger (Hibshman) Z.; m. Maya Stauch, Sept. 14, 1950; 1 child, Peter Martin. BA, Elizabethtown Coll., 1947; BD, Bethany Theol. Sem., 1950; MA, Yale U., 1952, PhD, 1955. Ordained to ministry Ch. of the Brethren, 1946, Evang. and Ref. Ch., 1957. Vis. prof. Philosophy and Religion Coll. of Idaho, Caldwell, 1954-55; asst., assoc. prof. Ch. History Eden Theol. Sem., St. Louis, 1955-62, prof. Ch. History, 1962-90, United Ch. Christ prof. Theol. and History, 1990—; vis. prof. Early Modern Hist., Washington U., St. Louis, 1981-82; dir. summer insts. Ctr. for Ref. Rsch., St. Louis, 1967-81; dir. Eden Archives United Ch. Christ, St. Louis, 1967—; v.p. Evang. and Ref. Hist. Soc., Lancaster, Pa., 1959—; mem. Hist. Coun., United Ch. Christ, Cleve., 1964-74, 88—; mem. Ch. Coun. Evang. United Ch. of Christ, 1989—. Author: European Roots of the United Church of Christ, 1976, Socially Responsible Believers, 1986; editor: Christianity and Revolution, 1975, History of the Evangelical and Reformed Church, 1990; editor: 30th anniversary edition Historical Intelligencer, 1987. Recipient D.A.A.D. grants German Acad. Exchange Agy., 1976, 91, Assn. Theol. Schs. U.S., Can. grants, 1964, 75, 87, Am. Philos. Soc. grant, 1980. Fellow Clare Hall, Cambridge U.; vis. rsch. fellow Ch. History Seminar; mem. Am. Hist. Assn. Home: 208 Oakwood Ave Webster Groves MO 63119 Office: Eden Theol Sem 475 E Lockwood Ave Saint Louis MO 63119

ZUCK, NEVIN HAROLD, minister; b. Ephrata, Pa., June 17, 1915; s. Abram W. and Verdie b. (Hibshman) Z.; m. Leah Musser, June 15, 1940; children: Barbara Christensen, Mary Knecht, Nevin II. AB, Elizabethtown Coll., 1936, DD, 1955; MDiv, Ea. Bapt. Sem., 1939; STM, Mt. Airy Luth. Sem., 1941. Ordained to ministry Ch. of the Brethren, 1934. Pastor

Elizabethtown (Pa.) Ch. of the Brethren, 1945-70, City Ch. of Brethren, Goshen, Ind., 1970-81, Brethren Vill., Lancaster, Pa., 1981—. Home and Office: 3001 Lititz Pike PO Box 5093 Lancaster PA 17601

ZUERCHER, SISTER SUZANNE, religious organization administrator; b. Evanston, Ill., July 13, 1931; d. Charles Robert and Clara (Kettenhofen) Z. AB in English, Loyola U., Chgo., 1960, MA in Clin. Psychology, 1967. Joined Benedictine Sisters, Roman Cath. Ch., 1949. Lic. psychologist, Ill. Elem. tchr. Archdiocese of Chgo., 1952-60; tchr. St. Scholastica High Sch., Chgo., 1960-64, psychologist, 1964-72; campus minister Loyola U., 1972-76, mem. staff Inst. for Spiritual Leadership, 1976-87; writing sabbatical, 1987-88; first councilor Benedictine Sisters, Chgo., 1969-71, formation directress, 1974-80, 88—, sec. 1986—; lectr. in field. Author: poetry book I Don't Expect An Answer, 1991, Ennergram Spirituality: From Compulsion to Contemplation, 1991. Mem. Ill. Psychol. Assn. Home: 7416 N Ridge Blvd Chicago IL 60645

ZUMBRUN, MORRIS, bishop. Bishop of Del.-Md. region Evang. Luth. Ch. in Am., Balt. Office: Evang Luth Ch in Am 7604 York Rd Baltimore MD 21204*

ZUMWALT, LARRY DEAN, pastor, social worker; b. Granite City, Ill., Mar. 15, 1947; s. Dean Burdette and Geneva Mae (Howell) Z.; m. Carol Ann Hattery, May 28, 1978; children: Kimberly Ann, Rachel Renee. BA in Sacred Music and Christian Edn., Lincoln (Ill.) Christian Coll., 1971. Youth minister Christian Ch., Williamsport, Ind., 1970; min. youth and music Ch. of Christ, Reidsville, N.C., 1971-73; counselor, trainer His Place Ministries, Joplin, Mo., 1973-75, New Hope Street Ministry, Joplin, 1975-76; tchr. Cen.

Christian Acad., Joplin, 1978-79; music pastor 1st Assembly of God Ch., Peru, Ind., 1981-82; assoc. pastor Faithh Christian Ctr., Peru, 1982-86, New Hope Christian Ctr., Newport, Ky., 1987—; social worker dept. social svcs. Cabinet for Human Resources, Commonwealth of Ky., Covington, 1987—. Mem. Peru Ministerial Assn. (v.p. 1986). Home: 160 Tracy Ln Southgate KY 41071 Office: Cabinet for Human Resources Dept Social Svcs 303 Court St Rm 601 Covington KY 41011

ZUMWALT, MARY ELLEN, religion educator; b. Effingham, Ill., Aug. 31, 1955; d. Earl Emery and Mabel Augusta (Schmohe) Budde; m. Donald Edward Zumwalt, Nov. 28, 1976; children: Elizabeth Suzanne and Catherine Suzanne (twins), David Edward. AA, St. Paul's Coll., Concordia, Mo., 1975; BA, Concordia Tchrs. Coll., River Forest, Ill., 1977. Tchr. elem. grades Luth. schs., Houston, 1977-80; tchr. ABC Child Care, Effingham, Ill., 1980-83; tchr. elem. grades, prin. Bethlehem Luth. Sch., Altamont, Ill., 1983-87; tchr., asst. prin. Altamont Luth. Interparish Sch., 1987—; dir. Effingham Area Spl. Teaching of Ednl. Religion, 1980—. Mem. Bethlehem Luth. Ch. Ladies Aid, Altamont, 1986—, Parent-Tchr. League Altamont Luth. Sch., 1987—. Recipient Citizenship award Effingham County 4-H, 1975. Mem. Luth. Women's Missionary League (internat. youth del. Minn. conv. 1975, pres. Altamont chpt. 1989—, mem. mission svc. com. 1990—), Mothers of Twins club (pres. 1989, v.p. 1990-91). Home: RR 1 Box 148 Altamont IL 62411 Office: Altamont Luth Sch 7 S Edwards Altamont IL 62411

ZUSTIAK, GARY BLAIR, youth minister, educator; b. Cottage Grove, Oreg., Mar. 7, 1952; s. George J. and Janice M. (Garrison) Z.; m. Mary S. Seablom, Nov. 27, 1970; children: Joshua B., Aaron J., Caleb C. BA, Boise

Bible Coll., 1976; MA, MDiv, Lincoln Christian Sem., 1982. Ordained to ministry, Christian Ch., 1976. Youth min. First Christian Ch., Emmett, Idaho, 1973-77, Farmer City, Ill., 1977-78; min. Broadwell (Ill.) Christian Ch., 1978-82; assoc. min. First Christian Ch., Sandpoint, Idaho, 1982-86; prof. Ozark Christian Coll., Joplin, Mo., 1986—. Contbr. articles to profl. jours. Founder Parents Support Group, Sandpoint, 1985-86; mem. Insight Drug Intervention Program, Sandpoint, 1985-86; chmn. Recreation Com. for City, Sandpoint, 1985-86; vol. 4-State Community AIDS project, Joplin, 1989—. Recipient scholarships, Eastern Star, 1978-82. Republican. Avocations: chess, tae kwon do, motor-cross, guitar. Office: Ozark Christian Coll 1111 N Main Joplin MO 64801

ZWEIBACK LEVENSON, AMY JOY, rabbi; b. N.Y.C., July 31, 1958; d. Leslie and Annette (Rothkerch) Zweiback; m. Paul S. Schlecker, June 11, 1978 (div. 1981); m. Edward Richard Zweiback Levenson, Nov. 23, 1983; children: Judah, Aliza, Benjamin. BS in Elem. Edn., Temple U., 1980; MA in Ednl. Adminstrn., Villanova U., 1986; MAHL, Reconstructionist Rabbinical, Wyncote, Pa., 1987. Ordained rabbi, 1987. Rabbi Hemlock FArms Jewish Fellowship, Hawley, Pa., 1983-87; prin. Kerem Torah Sch., Vineland, N.J., 1985-87; Midwest reg. dir. Fedn. of Reconstructionist Congregations, South Bend, Ind., 1988-90; rabbi B'nai Yisrael Reconstructionist Congregation, South Bend, Ind., 1984-89, Temple B'nai Shalom, Benton Harbor, Mich., 1989—; chmn. Interfaith Task Force, South Bend, 1988-89. Mem. Meml. Hosp. Pastoral Adv. Com., South Bend, 1988-89; chmn. Phila. Reg. CAJE Conf., 1986; bd. dirs. Planned Parenthood of S.W. Mich., Benton Harbor, Samaritan Ctr. of S.W. Mich., St. Joseph. Mem. Reconstructionist Rabbinical Assn. (bd. dirs., sec. 1989—), Coalition for Advancement of Jewish Edn. (bd. dirs. 1985-86), NOW, Rotary. Democrat. Office: Temple B'nai Shalom 2050 Broadway Benton Harbor MI 49022